Collins

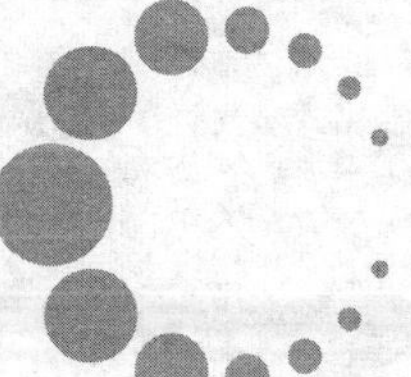

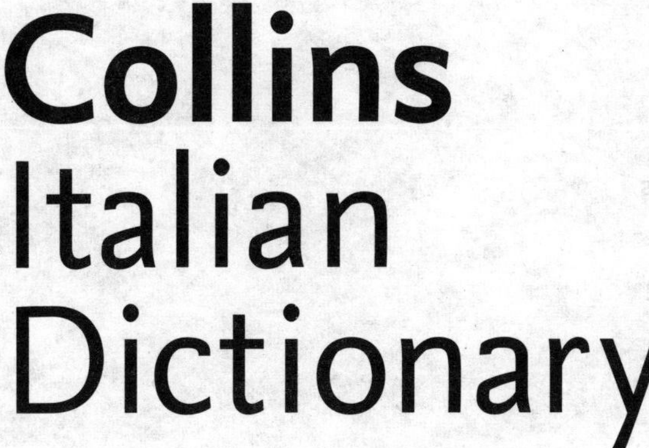
Collins
Italian
Dictionary

William Collins' dream of knowledge for all began with the publication of his first book in 1819. A self-educated mill worker, he not only enriched millions of lives, but also founded a flourising publishing house. Today, staying true to this spirit, Collins books are packed with inspiration, innovation, and practical expertise. They place you at the centre of a world of possibility and give you exactly what you need to explore it.

Language is the key to this exploration, and at the heart of Collins Dictionaries is language as it is really used. New words, phrases, and meanings spring up every day, and all of them are captured and analysed by the Collins Word Web. Constantly updated, and with over 2.5 billion entries, this living language resource is unique to our dictionaries.

Words are tools for life. And a Collins Dictionary makes them work for you.

Collins. Do more.

Collins
Italian Dictionary

HarperCollins Publishers
Westerhill Road
Bishopbriggs
Glasgow
G64 2QT
Great Britain

Second Edition/Seconda Edizione 2005

ISBN-13 978-0-00-718385-2
ISBN-10 0-00-0718385-2

Collins® is a registered trademark of
HarperCollins Publishers Limited

www.collins.co.uk

A catalogue record for this book is available
from the British Library

HarperCollins Publishers, Inc.
10 East 53rd Street, New York, NY 10022

ISBN-13 978-0-06-074908-8
ISBN-10 0-06-074908-3

Library of Congress Cataloging-in-Publication
Data has been applied for

www.harpercollins.com

HarperCollins books may be purchased for
educational, business, or sales promotional use.
For information, please write to:
Special Markets Department, HarperCollins
Publishers Inc., 10 East 53rd Street, New York,
NY 10022

Boroli Editore
Via G. B. Grassi, 15
20157 Milano

www.borolieditore.it

ISBN 88-7493-707-5

Typeset by/Fotocomposizione
RefineCatch Ltd, Wordcraft Glasgow

Printed in Italy by/Stampato in Italia da
Legoprint S.p.A.

Acknowledgements
We would like to thank those authors and
publishers who kindly gave permission for
copyright material to be used in the Collins
Word Web. We would also like to thank Times
Newspapers Ltd for providing valuable data.

FOR THE PUBLISHERS/A CURA DI
Lorna Knight
Michela Clari
Helen Forrest

EDITORS/REDAZIONE
Gabriella Bacchelli, Liz Potter, Loredana Riu,
Helen Hyde, Andrea Cavatorti, Francesca Logi,
Stefano Ondelli, Stefano Longo,
Annamaria Rubino

EDITORIAL STAFF/SEGRETERIA DI REDAZIONE
Susie Beattie, Joyce Littlejohn, Maggie Seaton

WITH/CON
Anne Convery, Sandra Harper, Val McNulty,
Cindy Mitchell, Jill Williams

COMPUTING/ELABORAZIONE AUTOMATICA DEI DATI
Thomas Callan

First Edition/Prima Edizione

FOR THE PUBLISHERS/A CURA DI
Michela Clari, Catherine E. Love, Donald Watt,
Janice McNeillie

EDITORS/REDAZIONE
Gabriella Bacchelli, Daphne Day,
Loredana Riu, Mirella Alessio, Francesca Logi

WITH/CON
Katherine Snell, Timothy Shaw, David Katan,
Martin de Sa'Pinto, Judy Moss, Carol Peters,
Eugenio Picchi

EDITORIAL ASSISTANCE/SEGRETERIA DI REDAZIONE
Carmela Celino, Sandra Harper, Gail Norfolk,
Anne Convery, Angela Jack, Anne-Marie Banks

Our thanks also go to Prof. John M. Dodds of the
Scuola Superiore per Interpreti e Traduttori of
the University of Trieste

Si ringrazia il Prof. John M. Dodds della Scuola
Superiore per Interpreti e Traduttori
dell'Università degli Studi di Trieste

INDICE

CONTENTS

I MARCHI REGISTRATI ®

I termini che a nostro parere costituiscono un marchio registrato sono stati contrassegnati come tali. In ogni caso, né la presenza né l'assenza di tale indicazione implica alcuna valutazione del loro reale stato giuridico.

NOTE ON TRADEMARKS ®

Entered words which we have reason to believe constitute trademarks have been designated as such. However, neither the presence nor the absence of such designation should be regarded as affecting the legal status of any trademark.

INTRODUZIONE

Nato da una moderna concezione lessicografica che privilegia la lingua attuale, i modi di dire colloquiali, il linguaggio dei mass media, senza tuttavia trascurare le espressioni di carattere più formale, il *Dizionario Inglese Collins* è un'opera di consultazione completa, moderna ed affidabile.
L'opera include i neologismi entrati a far parte della lingua inglese e di quella italiana in questi ultimi anni e molti termini tratti da linguaggi settoriali come quello informatico, commerciale e scientifico, oggi sempre più diffusi. La scelta di lemmi, significati e locuzioni di quest'opera, basata su criteri di frequenza d'uso, è stata dettata dalla volontà di presentare all'utente l'inglese e l'italiano attuali. Per la scelta e la verifica di lemmi, locuzioni e traduzioni i lessicografi hanno potuto consultare il Collins Word Web, un database costituito da migliaia e migliaia di libri, giornali, riviste, opuscoli, conversazioni e trasmissioni radiotelevisive. Con oltre 2,5 miliardi di parole, esso rappresenta attualmente la fonte linguistica più esauriente utilizzata per un dizionario bilingue di queste dimensioni.
La modernità dei contenuti, l'affidabiltà delle traduzioni e la ricchezza di esempi ed espressioni idiomatiche fanno di quest'opera uno strumento indispensabile per esprimersi in un inglese corretto e idiomatico.

INTRODUCTION

The *Collins Italian Dictionary* is comprehensive, up-to-date and reliable. It is based on modern principles, with its main focus on present-day language, including colloquial expressions, slang and the language of the mass media. More formal language, however, is by no means neglected.
The dictionary includes many recent additions to the English and Italian languages, and widely-used terms from key fields such as computing, business and science. The criteria governing the selection of material for inclusion in the dictionary were frequency of use, typicality and naturalness. An invaluable resource available to compilers and translators is the Collins Word Web. This database consists of many thousands of texts: books, newspapers, magazines, leaflets, conversations and radio and television broadcasts. It was possible to access this corpus of 2.5 billion words to judge whether particular words or structures merited inclusion because of the frequency of their occurrence, and to establish how they are typically used.
Whether you wish to read, speak or write Italian, you will find the dictionary an indispensable tool, thanks to the range of words treated, the accuracy and clarity of translations and the wealth of examples and illustrative phrases.

COME USARE IL DIZIONARIO

Il dizionario contiene moltissime informazioni, rappresentate in modo sintetico. Alcune parole sono complesse in quanto hanno molti significati e diverse traduzioni, altre possono avere più di una funzione grammaticale, cioè possono essere sia sostantivo sia aggettivo oppure verbo, avverbio e così via, a seconda del contesto. È importante sviluppare una strategia di consultazione per evitare inutili frustrazioni e perdite di tempo nella consultazione, ed è per questo che occorre conoscere le convenzioni usate se si vuole accedere in modo ottimale alle informazioni di cui si ha bisogno. Nel dizionario sono stati usati numeri, simboli e caratteri tipografici diversi (neretto, corsivo, tondo ecc.); è necessario capire come sono stati usati e farvi attenzione.

quadratini grigi

Quando una parola ha più di una funzione grammaticale, il passaggio da una parte del discorso a un'altra è segnalato da un quadratino grigio ■. Se per esempio volete tradurre la parola **fondere** in frasi come "il metallo fonde a temperature elevate", stabilirete innanzitutto quale sia la funzione grammaticale del verbo nel vostro contesto. In questo caso il verbo **fondere** è usato intransitivamente e quindi la traduzione va cercata nella categoria ■ VI. L'elenco delle abbreviazioni usate per indicare le diverse parti del discorso si trova a pagina xxviii.

> **fondere** ['fondere] VB IRREG
> ■VT **1** (*gen*) to melt; (*metallo*) to fuse, melt; (*fig: colori*) to blend, merge; (: *enti, classi, Inform*) to merge
> **2** (*statua, campana*) to cast
> ■VI (*aus* **avere**) to melt; **mi fonde il cervello** (*fig*) I can't think straight any more, my brain has seized up;

numeri

I numeri sono stati usati in due modi:

Numeri in posizione esponenziale

I numeri in posizione esponenziale rispetto al lemma sono stati usati per distinguere gli omografi, ossia parole che presentano la stessa grafia ma che sono completamente diverse dal punto di vista del significato, come in italiano **diritto¹** (retto) e **diritto²** (prerogativa) e in inglese **fine¹** (bello) e **fine²** (multa). Se quello che trovate nella prima voce non è quello di cui avete bisogno, consultate la seconda o eventalmente la terza.

Numeri all'interno della voce

I numeri all'interno della voce differenziano i diversi significati di una parola. Possono farvi risparmiare tempo, specialmente se avete a che fare con una parola come **attaccare**, che ha svariati significati. Se per esempio volete tradurre la frase "mi ha attaccato l'influenza" e cercate **attaccare**, dovete innanzitutto individuare la funzione grammaticale della parola; dato che si tratta di un verbo transitivo, andrete a VT. Dovete quindi stabilire che significato ha la parola nel vostro contesto. **1** (*far aderire*) è la prima possibilità, ma non si adatta al contesto; nemmeno **2** (*Mil, Sport, fig*) e **3** (*cominciare: discorso, lite*) coprono il significato del verbo nella vostra frase; passate quindi a **4** (*contagiare, anche fig*), che vi darà la traduzione appropriata. Quando cercate una parola inglese e trovate una serie di traduzioni diverse, scorrete velocemente le sezioni precedute dai numeri per trovare quella che si adatta al vostro contesto.

> **attaccare** [attak'kare] VT **1** (*far aderire*) to attach; (*incollare: manifesto*) to stick up; (: *francobollo*) to stick (on); (*cucire*) to sew (on); (*legare*) to tie (up); (*appendere: quadro*) to hang (up); **devo attaccare due bottoni** I've got to sew two buttons on; **non so dove attaccare questo poster** I don't know where to stick this poster **2** (*Mil, Sport, fig*) to attack **3** (*cominciare: discorso, lite*) to start, begin; **attaccare discorso con qn** to start a conversation with sb **4** (*contagiare, anche fig*) to affect;

indicazioni in corsivo

Il testo in corsivo aiuta a individuare i significati di una parola: può trattarsi di un sinonimo, un aggettivo o un sostantivo che compaiono spesso assieme alla parola, quando essa ha un certo significato. Per esempio, quando **dare** significa **organizzare**, tra le cose che si possono organizzare ci sono una festa, un banchetto, oppure uno spettacolo: queste parole compaiono in corsivo. Quando si cerca di individuare la traduzione giusta va tenuto conto di queste indicazioni in corsivo, che si differenziano sia dal testo nella lingua di partenza, che appare in grassetto, sia dalle traduzioni, che appaiono in tondo.

dove cercare i lemmi

I lemmi sono elencati in ordine alfabetico. Si noti che vanno ignorati nell'ordinamento alfabetico i trattini all'interno di parola. Il carattere &, usato in parole come **B&B**, **R&R** ecc. viene trattato come "and": l'ordine sarà pertanto come appare nel seguente esempio: **candour, C&W, candy**.

dove cercare i lemmi composti

In inglese sono stati considerati come lemmi a sé stanti anche alcuni composti formati da due o più parole aventi grafia separata, come **fast food** e **state of the art**, che sono elencati quindi in ordine alfabetico. Dovendo tradurre espressioni come **back page** e **back number**, potreste essere incerti su dove cercarle e chiedervi se **back** vada considerato un aggettivo, nel qual caso bisognerebbe guardare nella relativa sezione sotto **back**, oppure sia il primo elemento di una parola composta, che andrebbe cercata al suo posto nell'ordine alfabetico.

Sarà utile ricordare che se la combinazione non compare come lemma a sé stante, bisognerà cercarla sotto il primo elemento che la compone – cioè sotto **back** e non sotto **page** o **number**.

In italiano invece nomi composti come **pesce rosso** o **acqua di rose** non compaiono come parole a sé stanti ma vanno in genere ricercati sotto il primo elemento che li compone.

dove cercare i verbi + avverbio/ preposizione

Nelle frasi "she came into the room" e "she came into a large fortune" compaiono lo stesso verbo e la stessa preposizione ("come" e "into") ma solo nel secondo caso si tratta di un phrasal verb, cioè di una combinazione fissa con un significato particolare (**ereditare**), che compare come voce a sé stante, contrassegnata dal simbolo ▸.

Per tradurre il primo esempio, invece, bisogna guardare sotto il verbo **come**. In caso di dubbio, verificate innanzitutto se si tratta di un phrasal verb. Se la ricerca non vi fornirà le indicazioni di cui avete bisogno, cercate sotto il verbo in questione.

dove cercare le locuzioni

In genere locuzioni ed espressioni idiomatiche si trovano sotto il primo elemento fondamentale della locuzione. Per esempio "filare diritto" si trova sotto **filare** e "to burn one's boats", sotto **burn**. Tuttavia, nel caso di verbi con molti significati, come **fare**, **mettere**, **prendere** o **set**, **do** e **get**, le locuzioni compaiono generalmente sotto un'altra parola che compone l'espressione. Per esempio "to set a trap" è stata posta sotto **trap** per facilitare l'utente, che troverà più rapidamente l'espressione alla voce breve **trap** piuttosto che alla voce **set**, molto più complessa.

LEMMARIO E STRUTTURA DELLE VOCI

L'intento di questa sezione è di fornire un elenco completo degli elementi che costituiscono il dizionario e delle informazioni che è possibile ricavarne. Una conoscenza approfondita di questi elementi insieme a una corretta strategia di consultazione consentiranno all'utente di sfruttare al meglio il dizionario.

lemmario

I lemmi sono elencati naturalmente in ordine alfabetico e sono stampati in neretto. Nel margine superiore di ogni pagina compare una testatina che riporta il primo e l'ultimo lemma di quella pagina: ciò renderà più rapida la consultazione del dizionario.

derivati

Per maggiore facilità di consultazione i derivati, ad esempio **fortunately**, **delivery**, **deliverance** e **installazione**, **utilità**, **utilmente**, compaiono tutti come lemmi principali (in alcuni dizionari essi compaiono sotto la parola da cui derivano).

nomi composti

nailbrush, **backache**, **accendisigari** e **capostazione** sono nomi composti e sono inseriti in ordine alfabetico. Nella parte inglese-italiano anche molti nomi composti formati da due o più parole (es. **news agency**), o ancora da due o più parole unite da un trattino (es. **do-it-yourself**), compaiono come lemmi principali in ordine alfabetico.

Nella parte italiano-inglese, questi compaiono all'interno della voce corrispondente alla prima parola, preceduti dal simbolo ■.

phrasal verbs

I phrasal verbs come **make up** o **put up with** compaiono in forma di sottolemmi in ordine alfabetico, in neretto, dopo il lemma principale.

▶ è il simbolo che precede i phrasal verbs nella parte inglese-italiano.

nomi propri

Nel lemmario sono stati inclusi i principali nomi geografici come **Francia**, **Venezia**, **Alpi**, **Edinburgh**, **Thames** e i nomi dei personaggi biblici e mitologici più importanti, come **Mosè** e **Adone**.

sigle e abbreviazioni

Per maggior facilità di consultazione le abbreviazioni e le sigle come **IVA**, **UNESCO** e **ab.** sono state inserite nel testo e non in tavole a parte.

LA STRUTTURA DELLE VOCI

suddivisione in sillabe

Sulla parte inglese-italiano è stata data indicazione, mediante l'introduzione di puntini, di come possono essere suddivise le parole inglesi, come per esempio **pae·di·at·ric**.

trascrizione fonetica

Tutti i lemmi sono seguiti dalla pronuncia, che si trova tra parentesi quadre. Come in tutti i principali dizionari moderni è stato adottato il sistema noto come "alfabeto fonetico internazionale". A pagina xxvi troverete un elenco completo dei caratteri utilizzati in questo sistema.

Nella parte inglese-italiano, per la pronuncia di nomi composti formati da due o più parole non unite dal trattino, si dovrà cercare la trascrizione di ciascuna parola alla rispettiva posizione alfabetica.

categorie grammaticali

Quando il lemma ha una sola funzione grammaticale la categoria grammaticale di appartenenza compare in maiuscoletto subito dopo la trascrizione fonetica.

lemma	pronuncia	categoria grammaticale	traduzione
rissa	['rissa]	SF	fight, brawl

Se invece ha più di una funzione, ogni categoria grammaticale dopo la prima viene contrassegnata dal simbolo ■.

col·lar ['kɒlə^r] N (*of shirt, blouse, coat*) colletto, collo; (*for dog*) collare *m*; (*Tech*) anello, fascetta; **to grab sb by the collar** afferrare qn per il bavero
■VT (*fam*: *person, object*) beccare

categorie di significato

Quando un lemma ha più di un significato la voce viene suddivisa in categorie di significato, ognuna preceduta da un numero: **1**, **2**, **3**, ecc.

Ciascuna categoria di significato può riportare una o più accezioni seguite da una serie di frasi illustrative in grassetto, seguite dalle relative traduzioni in tondo.

◎al·to·geth·er [ˌɔːltəˈgɛðəʳ] ADV **1** (*in all*) in tutto, complessivamente; (*on the whole*) tutto considerato, tutto sommato, nel complesso, nell'insieme; **you owe me twenty pounds altogether** in tutto mi devi venti sterline; **altogether it was rather unpleasant** tutto sommato *or* in complesso è stato piuttosto spiacevole; **how much is that altogether?** quant'è in tutto?
2 (*entirely*) del tutto, completamente; **I'm not altogether sure** non sono del tutto *or* proprio sicuro

indicatori

Si chiamano "indicatori" le informazioni in corsivo tra parentesi che introducono le diverse accezioni di un lemma. Come già accennato al paragrafo **indicazioni in corsivo**, la funzione degli indicatori è di guidare l'utente nella scelta della traduzione più adatta ad un contesto specifico. A volte gli indicatori appaiono dopo una traduzione per segnalarne il registro o l'ambito d'uso.

Moltissime parole hanno più di un significato o diverse sfumature di significato; altre, pur mantenendo un significato relativamente unitario, si traducono in modo diverso a seconda del contesto in cui si trovano o dei loro collocatori, cioè delle parole assieme alle quali vengono usate più di frequente. Nel dizionario sono stati usati diversi tipi di indicatori:

- indicatori che sostituiscono il lemma
- indicatori contestuali
- indicatori di campo semantico
- indicatori di stile o registro
- indicatori cronologici
- indicatori dell'uso figurato o letterale
- indicatori di uso regionale

Questi indicatori si riferiscono alla lingua di partenza, e sono in italiano nella parte italiano-inglese e in inglese nella parte inglese-italiano; compaiono tra parentesi tonde e in corsivo subito prima della traduzione.

Indicatori che sostituiscono il lemma

Uno degli indicatori che troverete più di frequente consiste in un sinonimo o in una parziale definizione del lemma.

malizia [maˈlittsja] SF (*cattiveria*) malice, spite; (*furbizia*) mischievousness; (*astuzia*) clever trick; **con malizia** maliciously, spitefully; mischievously; cleverly

Indicatori contestuali

Gli indicatori contestuali forniscono i contesti tipici in cui è possibile trovare il lemma. Possono essere di vario tipo: qui di seguito troverete gli indicatori contestuali più comuni.

- soggetto tipico di un verbo intransitivo: **fiorire** ... (*albero*) ... (*fig: sentimento*) ... (*: commercio, arte*) ...
- oggetto tipico di un verbo transitivo: **dissotterrare** ... (*cadavere*) ... (*tesori, rovine*) ... (*fig: sentimento*) ...
- sostantivo che viene usato spesso in combinazione con l'aggettivo in questione: **collerico** ... (*persona*) ... (*parole*) ... (*temperamento*) ...
- sostantivo che viene usato spesso in combinazione con il sostantivo in questione: **groviglio** ... (*di fili, lana*) ... (*fig: di idee*) ...
- aggettivo che viene usato spesso in combinazione con l'avverbio in questione: **tenuamente** ... (*colorato*) ... (*illuminato*) ...
- verbo che viene usato spesso in combinazione con l'avverbio in questione: **involontariamente** ... (*sorridere*) ... (*spingere*) ...

Indicatori di campo semantico

Gli indicatori di campo semantico (cioè *Med, Pol, Bot* ecc.) vengono usati per differenziare i vari significati del lemma secondo una specifica suddivisione in campi semantici. Questi indicatori, sempre tra parentesi e in corsivo, hanno l'iniziale maiuscola e sono spesso abbreviazioni (per l'elenco completo delle abbreviazioni vedere pagina xxviii).

> **nervatura** [nerva'tura] SF (*Anat*) nerves *pl*, nervous system; (*Bot*) veining; (*Archit, Tecn*) rib

Questi indicatori vengono anche usati quando il significato di una parola è chiaro nella lingua d'origine ma può essere ambiguo nella lingua di arrivo. Per esempio il sostantivo **oratorio** in inglese ha solo il significato musicale, mentre in italiano può indicare anche l'edificio annesso alla chiesa in cui si svolgono attività ricreative e spirituali per ragazzi.

Indicatori di stile e di registro

Gli indicatori di stile o registro sono stati usati per tutti i vocaboli che esulano dal linguaggio standard. Alcuni indicatori compaiono sia nella sezione inglese-italiano che in quella italiano-inglese; si tratta di *(frm)* per l'uso formale, *(fam)* per l'uso informale o colloquiale e *(iro)* per l'uso ironico. L'uso letterario è contrassegnato da *(liter)* nella parte inglese e da *(letter)* in quella italiana.
Per quello scherzoso sono stati usati rispettivamente *(hum)* e *(scherz)*, mentre *(euph)* ed *(euf)* evidenziano le espressioni eufemistiche e *(pej)* e *(pegg)* l'uso peggiorativo.

Le espressioni informali e volgari, pur essendo largamente diffuse, sono a nostro parere da usare con estrema cautela. Per aiutare il lettore ad identificarle è stato usato l'indicatore *(fam!)*.

Da evitare anche quelle parole contrassegnate dagli indicatori *(offensive)* ed *(offensivo)*.

Indicatori cronologici

Quando l'uso di una parola o di un'espressione è da considerarsi ormai sorpassato, compare l'indicatore *(old)* in inglese e *(ant)* in italiano.

Indicatori di uso letterale e figurato

Sono *(lit)* per l'uso letterale e *(fig)* per quello figurato.

Indicatori di uso regionale

Tra gli indicatori di uso regionale ricordiamo *(Scot)* per le parole o espressioni scozzesi, *(Ir)* per quelle irlandesi e *(dial)* per segnalare che una parola o espressione è di uso prevalentemente dialettale.

Americanismi

L'abbreviazione *(Am)* segnala le grafie e le pronunce americane e le parole ed espressioni che, sebbene generalmente conosciute sia dai parlanti americani che da quelli inglesi, sono usate con maggiore frequenza negli Stati Uniti.
Quando una parola o un'espressione viene usata prevalentemente nell'inglese britannico, ciò è segnalato dall'indicatore *(Brit)*.

Uso della punteggiatura negli indicatori

Prima di una traduzione troverete spesso due o più indicatori, in corsivo e nella stessa parentesi. Nella voce **marino**, riportata qui di seguito, il fatto che *aria* e *fondali* siano separati tra loro da una virgola indica che la traduzione **sea** funziona sia dovendo tradurre "aria marina" che "fondale marino". Analogamente **seaside** può essere usata sia per tradurre "città marina" che "colonia marina".

> **marino, a** [ma'rino] AGG (*aria, fondali*) sea *attr*; (*fauna*) marine; (*città, colonia*) seaside *attr*

Se invece gli indicatori sono separati da due punti, come ad esempio in **refresh** riportato qui sotto, ciò indica che essi si riferiscono insieme alla traduzione. Se il soggetto di **refresh** è **drink**, la traduzione adatta è **rinfrescare**, mentre se il soggetto del verbo è **sleep** oppure **bath**, la traduzione è **ristorare**. L'indicatore "subj" non viene ripetuto la seconda volta, ma viene richiamato dai due punti. Ogni volta che i due punti compaiono come primo elemento dell'indicatore ci si dovrà riferire all'indicatore precedente.

> **re·fresh** [rɪ'frɛʃ] VT (*subj*: *drink*) rinfrescare; (*: food, sleep, bath*) ristorare; (*fig*: *memory*) rinfrescare; **this will refresh your memory** questo ti rinfrescherà la memoria

traduzioni

Tutte le traduzioni nel dizionario corrispondono il più possibile ai loro equivalenti nella lingua di partenza sia a livello semantico che a livello sintattico e di registro linguistico. Particolare attenzione è stata fatta alle costruzioni tipiche e ai loro equivalenti nella lingua di arrivo.

Spesso, dopo uno stesso indicatore, compaiono più traduzioni separate tra di loro da una virgola, come ad esempio in **ammonimento**.

> **ammonimento** [ammoni'mento] SM (*rimprovero*) reprimand, admonishment; (*lezione*) lesson, warning

Va sottolineato che queste traduzioni sono sempre intercambiabili con riferimento al significato riportato dall'indicatore. Ogni volta che un contesto diverso ha richiesto una traduzione diversa, questo è stato segnalato inserendo un nuovo indicatore.

A volte parte della traduzione è opzionale, e quindi compare tra parentesi. Per esempio alla voce **neo** la traduzione per il senso figurato è (**slight**) **flaw**.

> **neo** ['nɛo] SM (*gen*) mole; (*sul viso*) beauty spot; (*fig: imperfezione*) (slight) flaw; (*: di persona*) slight defect

In alcuni casi all'interno della voce compare un rimando ad un'altra parola (per es. *vedi vt)* seguito da più traduzioni separate tra di loro da punti e virgola. Ciò succede, ad esempio, con alcuni derivati, come per esempio **appianamento**, che deriva da **appianare**. In questo caso le varianti di traduzione vanno riferite al sistema di indicatori della parola indicata dal rimando. Nel caso specifico, **levelling** va referito a *(terreno)*, **settlement** a (*fig: contesa, lite*) e **ironing out** a (*difficoltà*). L'introduzione dei punti e virgola invece delle virgole segnala quindi che le traduzioni non sono intercambiabili.

> **appianamento** [appjana'mento] SM (*vedi vt*) levelling; settlement; ironing out
> **appianare** [appja'nare] VT (*terreno*) to flatten, level; (*fig: contesa, lite*) to settle; (*difficoltà*) to iron out, smooth away
> ▶ **appianarsi** VIP (*divergenze*) to be ironed out

glosse esplicative ed equivalenti culturali

Non sempre è possibile fornire una traduzione corrispondente al lemma di partenza, basti pensare al caso di istituzioni o concetti che esistono nella cultura italiana ma non in quella inglese e viceversa, e quindi non hanno un traducente efficace nell'altra lingua. A volte è stato quindi necessario usare una glossa esplicativa, che compare in corsivo (vedere ad esempio le voci **angel dust** o **ginnasio**), altre volte è stato dato un equivalente approssimativo nell'altra lingua (vedere ad esempio **ACI** o **Speaker** (*Brit Parliament*). ≈ è il simbolo che precede gli equivalenti culturali.

INFORMAZIONI GRAMMATICALI

genere

Sia nel lato italiano-inglese sia in quello inglese-italiano sono state indicate le desinenze femminili degli aggettivi italiani e dei sostantivi riferiti a persona.

plurali

I plurali irregolari e quelli la cui formazione può creare delle difficoltà compaiono dopo il lemma in entrambe le lingue.

verbi irregolari

È stata data indicazione dell'irregolarità dei verbi italiani subito dopo la categoria grammaticale; per i verbi irregolari inglesi sono state introdotte, subito dopo il lemma, le forme irregolari del passato e del participio passato.

verbi ausiliari

È stato indicato l'ausiliare **essere** o **avere** per tutti i verbi intransitivi italiani; per i verbi transitivi non compare alcuna indicazione in quanto i tempi composti di tali verbi si formano sempre con l'ausiliare **avere**.

verbi riflessivi e intransitivi pronominali

I verbi riflessivi come **radersi** e **vestirsi** sono stati distinti dai verbi intransitivi pronominali come **sbagliarsi** e **ricordarsi** mediante la distinzione tra le categorie grammaticali VR (verbo riflessivo) e VIP (verbo intransitivo pronominale). Le forme riflessive reciproche (come "si amano") e le forme riflessive indirette (come "lavarsi le mani") sono state differenziate all'interno della voce principale. Le forme riflessive reciproche compaiono nella categoria grammaticale VR, precedute dall'indicatore *(uso reciproco)*, mentre quelle riflessive indirette sono state inserite come esempi sotto la categoria del transitivo, dato che si tratta di forme pronominali transitive in quanto prendono l'oggetto diretto. In inglese non esiste la forma pronominale del verbo, e quando un verbo viene usato insieme a **oneself** traduce in generale una forma riflessiva vera e propria. Si confrontino, ad esempio, le traduzioni di **ammazzarsi** nel senso di **suicidarsi** e quindi realmente riflessivo (**to kill o.s.**) e **ammazzarsi** nel senso di trovare la morte (**to die**, **be killed**).

phrasal verbs

Verbi come **get off** e **make up**, i cosiddetti phrasal verbs, costituiscono spesso un problema per gli studenti stranieri che incontrano difficoltà nel distinguerli dalle normali costruzioni con avverbi o preposizioni (ad esempio "he came into the room", normale costruzione con preposizione, e il phrasal verb "he came into money"). I phrasal verbs sono suddivisi in base alla funzione grammaticale degli elementi che li costituiscono. Alla voce **get off**, come vediamo qui di seguito, le qualifiche grammaticali sono VT + ADV, VI + PREP e VI + ADV. Alcuni phrasal verbs sono composti da tre elementi, come per esempio **get off with**.

> ▸ **get off**
> ■ VT + ADV
> **1** *(remove: clothes, stain)* levare, togliere
> **2** *(send off)* spedire; **she got the baby off to sleep** ha fatto addormentare il bambino
> **3** *(save from punishment)* far assolvere, tirar fuori
> **4** *(have as holiday: day, time)* prendersi; **we got 2 days off** abbiamo avuto 2 giorni liberi
> ■ VI + PREP *(bus, train, plane, bike)* scendere da; *(fam: escape: chore, lessons)* evitare, sfuggire a
> ...
> ▸ **get off with** VI + ADV + PREP *(fam: start relationship with)* mettersi con

forme irregolari

Per rendere più agevole la ricerca del lettore abbiamo inserito in ordine alfabetico le principali forme irregolari di verbi e sostantivi con un rimando alla voce in cui il lemma viene trattato per esteso. Ad esempio participi passati quali l'inglese **gone** o l'italiano **corso**, e plurali irregolari quali **mice** (topi) e **buoi** compaiono in ordine alfabetico con un rimando alla voce principale.

parole chiave

Alle parole che in qualche modo costituiscono i cardini della lingua, come i verbi ausiliari, le principali preposizioni, congiunzioni e così via, è stato riservato un trattamento particolare, sia dal punto di vista grafico sia da quello linguistico, con una strutturazione più chiara e articolata e una fraseologia molto ricca. Tali voci sono contrassegnate dal titoletto **PAROLA CHIAVE** sul lato italiano-inglese e **KEYWORD** su quello inglese-italiano:

> ◎**a** [eɪ, ə] **KEYWORD**
> INDEF ART (*before vowel or silent h* **an** [æn, ən, n])
> **1** un *m* (uno + *s impure, gn, pn, ps, x, z*), una *f* (un' + *vowel*);
> **he's a friend** è un amico; **a herring** un'aringa; **an apple** una mela; **I haven't got a car** non ho la ...

Nella sezione inglese-italiano, le parole che sono state identificate nel Collins Word Web come termini ad alta frequenza d'uso sono precedute dal simbolo ◎.

note culturali

Ulteriori informazioni relative ad argomenti significativi dal punto di vista culturale quali istituzioni, tradizioni, usanze e festività vengono presentate in una nota esplicativa che segue la voce in questione, per una miglior comprensione della vita e della cultura italiana e di quella dei paesi anglofoni.

> **THANKSGIVING (DAY)**
>
> Negli Stati Uniti il quarto giovedì di novembre ricorre il **Thanksgiving (Day)**, festa nazionale che commemora il primo raccolto in terra americana ottenuto dai Padri Pellegrini, i primi coloni inglesi, nel 1621. È tradizione trascorrere la festa in famiglia (anche affrontando lunghi viaggi) con un pranzo a base di tacchino e tortino di zucca. Vedi anche **PILGRIM FATHERS**

"falsi amici"

Esistono parole molto simili, o addirittura identiche, in italiano e in inglese, che però hanno un significato del tutto diverso. Per aiutare il lettore ad evitare potenziali errori nella traduzione, al termine della voce in questione è stata introdotta una nota dal titoletto LO SAPEVI...? sul lato italiano-inglese e DID YOU KNOW ...? sul lato inglese-taliano:

> **LO SAPEVI...?**
> **fondo** non si traduce mai con la parola inglese *fond*

indirizzi Internet

Nel dizionario molte voci sono corredate da indirizzi Internet d'interesse relativo alla voce sotto cui compaiono.

> ◎**bank·ing** ['bæŋkɪŋ] N attività bancaria; **to study banking** fare studi bancari *or* di tecnica bancaria
> ▷ www.bankofengland.co.uk

Internet offre a chiunque disponga di un computer e di una connessione la possibilità di ottenere informazioni da qualsiasi individuo, organizzazione o istituzione collegati in rete. L'editore ritiene che tali informazioni possano risultare estremamente utili a chi impara una lingua, poiché permettono di scoprire, analizzare e studiare esempi autentici dell'uso della lingua in contesto. Allo stesso tempo, rappresentano anche uno strumento di approfondimento di aspetti e concetti specifici della cultura espressa dalla lingua che si sta studiando.

Esistono tre tipologie d'uso di cui abbiamo tenuto conto al momento della selezione degli indirizzi Internet forniti nel dizionario:

- lo studio di argomenti, istituzioni o settori, dalla *Bank of England* e la *Federal Reserve*, al *tea* e al *Christmas pudding*, in quanto componente fondamentale di un apprendimento strutturato. Pensiamo che questi siti rappresentino una risorsa utile, sia per gli insegnanti che per gli studenti.

• l'attenzione a interessi e a hobby personali, come *astronomy*, *beer*, *chess*, *cinema*.
• informazioni pratiche sulla cultura e sullo stile di vita del paese.

Ogni sito web è stato controllato per garantire che i contenuti fossero pertinenti e sicuri. Per la maggior parte si tratta di siti non commerciali anche se, quando lo si è ritenuto utile, è stato inserito anche qualche sito commerciale.

Oltre a fornire ulteriori informazioni sugli argomenti che vi interessano, i siti web offrono anche utili esempi dell'uso reale della lingua, per una lettura rapida o approfondita. Tuttavia, se pensate di utilizzare un brano tratto da un sito web come modello per l'apprendimento linguistico, è bene assicurarvi che l'autore sia un madrelingua, poiché anche chi ha un'ottima conoscenza di una lingua straniera può scrivere in un modo che non risulta del tutto idiomatico. Considerata l'enorme diffusione dell'inglese come lingua di comunicazione internazionale, consigliamo perciò di controllare che il sito che state consultando abbia sede in un paese anglofono o sia ospitato da un'organizzazione che ha l'inglese tra le lingue ufficiali, in modo da garantire la massima affidabilità linguistica.

La maggior parte degli indirizzi Internet inclusi in questo volume riguarda siti di enti ufficiali di diverso tipo. Potete dunque stare certi che sono stati redatti con grande cura e che difficilmente contengono errori di lingua. Inoltre, le informazioni fornite provengono molto probabilmente da fonti affidabili. Nel caso di siti non ufficiali occorre tenere presente che i contenuti potrebbero essere stati verificati solamente dagli autori stessi o dal responsabile del sito, dunque sono possibili imprecisioni legate alla lingua o ai contenuti.

Bisogna anche tenere conto del registro della lingua utilizzata nel sito web. Se si tratta di un sito ufficiale, è possibile che vengano usati termini tecnici che non sono adatti alla comunicazione orale o scritta. Lo stesso discorso vale anche per il linguaggio informale che può caratterizzare altri siti web. Se intendete usare una parola, una frase o una struttura che avete trovato su Internet, dovreste prima consultare il dizionario, che vi fornirà indicazioni precise per quanto riguarda il regisro.

per uso sicuro di Internet

Internet contiene una quantità immensa di informazioni, in gran parte gratuite, su una vasta gamma di argomenti. La rete non è controllata da nessuno e non appartiene a nessuna organizzazione, nessun governo, nessun paese. Anche se talvolta ci si lamenta dell'anarchia determinata da questa mancanza di controllo centralizzato, l'assenza di una struttura gerarchica offre grande vantaggi per quanto riguarda la disponibilità delle informazioni e l'ineguagliabile potenziale in termini di comunicazione e diffusione delle idee.

Anche se questi vantaggi sono incalcolabili, esiste il rovescio della medaglia. Siccome Internet non è né regolamentato, né centralizzato, non esiste alcun meccanismo di controllo della qualità: l'unico requisito necessario per creare un sito web è rappresentato dalla capacità tecnica. Molti dei contenuti offerti via Internet sono di scarso valore.

Maggiore preoccupazione è destata dai possibili impieghi criminali. La facilità di accesso e il carattere pervasivo di Internet possono fornire nuovi strumenti a chi desidera seminare odio, compiere oscenità o sfruttare chi è più vulnerabile o ingenuo. Poiché ci sono sempre più famiglie con figli in età scolare collegate in rete, è importante che genitori e tutori siano consapevoli dei potenziali rischi, oltre che dei vantaggi.

I siti ufficiali provengono da fonti affidabili e in genere i loro contenuti risultano sicuri ed affidabili. È possibile identificarli tramite il codice relativo alle organizzazioni contenuto nell'indirizzo Internet. Riportiamo qui sotto i codici più comuni delle organizzazioni ufficiali:

.ac:	istituzione accademica in Gran Bretagna
.co:	società privata*
.com:	società commerciale*
.edu:	organizzazione accademica negli USA
.gov:	organizzazione governativa
.org:	organizzazione non a fini di lucro

* sebbene ufficiali, i siti .co e .com appartengono a organizzazioni commerciali e possono comprendere pubblicità e/o collegamenti, spesso relativi ad argomenti non correlati. Il contenuto di questi siti può non sottostare alle stesse regole osservate all'interno del sito che visitiamo.

Molti siti italiani, sia commerciali che culturali, hanno solamente l'estensione .it.

Altri codici, come .net, rappresentano siti non ufficiali i cui contenuti non sono sottoposti ad alcun controllo ufficiale. Anche se ciò non significa automaticamente che questi siti non sono sicuri, scegliendo i siti ufficiali si ottengono maggiori garanzie sulla validità dei contenuti.

Altri elementi che indicano che i siti sono sottoposti a regolamentazione sono i seguenti:

- l'ultima data di aggiornamento, che in genere è riportata in fondo allo schermo
- informazioni relative a come contattare i responsabili
- informazioni sulle fonti – possono trovarsi sulla home page o, seguendo un link, all'interno di una sezione specifica (per es. "Chi siamo")
- nel caso di siti ufficiali, la politica sulla privacy adottata dall'organizzazione.

HOW TO USE THE DICTIONARY

The dictionary contains a great deal of information, in a condensed form. Some words are complicated – they have a large number of senses, or they have several different meanings.

Another problem is that one word may function as a verb, a noun, an adjective, an adverb etc. To avoid time-wasting and frustration, you should develop a strategy for approaching entries, and to do this you need to be aware of the pointers that are provided to guide you to the particular information you want. These pointers are shaded boxes, numbers and typefaces: it is important to understand how they are used and to pay attention to them.

shaded boxes

When a word is not just a noun, or just a verb, (i.e. if it can be more than one part of speech), a shaded box ■ is used along with the part of speech to indicate each additional function it can perform. Thus, if you want to translate "he cleaned his teeth", and you need to look up **clean**, decide first of all what function the word has. Having decided that it is a verb with an object (i.e. a transitive verb) you can then run your eye down the numbered items in the entry until you get to ■ VT (verb, transitive) – which is what you want. Abbreviations used to indicate parts of speech appear on page xxviii.

> **clean** [kli:n] ADJ (*comp* **-er**, *superl* **-est**) (*gen*) pulito(-a); (*sheet of paper*) nuovo(-a); (*smooth, clear: outline, movement, break*) netto(-a); (*fair: fight, game*) leale, corretto(-a); **to wipe sth clean** pulire qc; **to make a clean sweep** fare piazza pulita; **the doctor gave me a clean bill of health** il medico ha garantito che godo di ottima salute; **to make a clean breast of sth** togliersi qc dalla coscienza; **a clean record** (*Police*) una fedina penale pulita; **to have a clean driving licence** (*Am*): **to have a clean record** non aver mai preso contravvenzioni
> ■ ADV: **he clean forgot** si è completamente dimenticato; **he got clean away** se l'è svignata senza lasciare tracce; **the ball went clean through the window** la palla prese in pieno la finestra; **to come clean** (*fam: admit guilt*) confessare; (*: tell unpleasant truth*) dire veramente come stanno le cose; **I'm clean out of cigarettes** non ho neanche mezza sigaretta
> ■ N pulita, ripulitura
> ■ VT (*gen*) pulire; (*blackboard*) cancellare; (*shoes*) lucidare; **to clean one's teeth** (*Brit*) lavarsi i denti; **he never cleans the bath** non pulisce mai la vasca da bagno

numbers

Numbers are used in two ways:

Numbers at the end of a headword

When words are spelt the same, but are actually separate entities – e.g. **fine** in English (which could mean good, or a financial penalty) or **piano** in Italian (flat, a plan or a musical instrument) they are given as separate entries, with the headword followed by a superscript number. If what you find at the first entry is obviously not what you want, go on to look at the following one(s).

Numbers within an entry

These are used to distinguish different senses of a word. Paying attention to them can save a lot of time when you are dealing with a word such as **get** that has all sorts of meanings: if, for example, you wanted to translate "I was starting to get tired" and were looking up **get**, you should first decide on the word's grammatical function (it's a verb without an object, i.e. an intransitive verb) – that will take you to ■ VI. Next you need to decide what meaning the word has in your particular context. **1** (*go*) is the first possibility, but this doesn't fit – so you look next at **2** *(become, be)* – which takes you to the right translation.

When you look up an Italian word and find a number of different translations, scan the numbered sections for the one that fits your context.

Looking first at the numbered categories means you waste no time looking at irrelevant sections.

material appearing in italics

Material appearing in italics helps you pinpoint the sense of a word. It may be another way of saying the same thing, or an adjective, noun etc that often occurs with the word when it has a particular sense – e.g. when **get** means **receive**, letters and presents are typical examples of things you can get, so these appear in italics. When you are trying to track down the right translation, make sure you take note of these italic pointers, which are distinguishable at a glance from the bold type used for the source language, and normal type used for translations.

where to look for headwords

Headwords are listed in alphabetical order. However you should note that hyphens are ignored and the character & which appears in forms like **B&B, R&R** etc. is treated as "and" when deciding alphabetical order. The order is therefore as follows: **candour, C&W, candy**.

where to look for combinations of words

When faced by such combinations as **back number** and **back page** you may be uncertain where to look. Is **back** an adjective, in which case you should look in the appropriate section under **back**, or is it the first element in a compound word, which you should look for in its alphabetical place?

The important things to remember are:

- You should look for such items under their first element – e.g. under **back**, not under **number** or **page**.
- You should bear in mind that the combination may appear as a separate entry, as does **back number**, or under the first element, as does **back page**. If you don't find it at the first option, try the second.

Italian combinations of two words or more such as **pesce rosso** and **acqua di rose** are not treated as separate entries but generally appear under their first element.

where to find verb + adverb/preposition combinations

"She came into the room" and "she came into a large fortune" include the same verb + preposition, (**come** + **into**), but the second combination is a phrasal verb, with a special sense (**inherit**), and is treated in a separate entry, which is marked by the symbol ▸.

To find how to translate the first example you should look under **come**. If you are in doubt in such cases, the quickest thing is to look first for a phrasal verb entry. If that doesn't provide the information you need, look then at the entry for the verb on its own.

where to look for phrases

Idioms and set phrases generally appear under their first important element, thus "filare diritto" appears under **filare** and "to burn one's boats" appears under **burn**. However, in the case of verbs that have a great many meanings, such as **prendere**, **fare**, **mettere**, or **set**, **do** and **get**, phrases appear under another key word in the expression. For exmple, "to set a trap" comes under **trap**. This is to make things easier for the user, who will find the phrase more quickly in the short entry **trap** than in the long and complicated entry **set**.

THE DESIGN OF THE DICTIONARY

The previous section is intended to help solve problems that may be encountered in using the dictionary. However, to exploit fully the information this dictionary offers, users will find it worthwhile to familiarize themselves in more detail with the way the dictionary is organized and how entries are structured.

Headwords are listed in alphabetical order and printed in bold. The running heads at the top of each page show you the first and last headword on each page in order to make it quicker to find the word you are looking for.

Derived words such as **fortunately**, **delivery**, **deliverance**, and **installazione**, **utilità**, **utilmente** appear as headwords. (In some dictionaries such words are treated under the word they derive from.)

Compound words in English may consist of one word (e.g. **housewife**), two or more words (e.g. **news agency**, **state of the art**) or two or more words joined by a hyphen (e.g. **do-it-yourself**). All types can appear as headwords. Compounds consisting of two or more words are set as headwords.

In Italian, compounds proper consist of a single word, e.g. **accendisigari**, **capostazione**, and these appear as headwords. Combinations of two words or more, such as **strisce pedonali** or **acqua minerale** are to be found under their first element (i.e. **striscia** or **acqua**). If the compound shows a new sense of the headword, it is preceded by the symbol ■.

Phrasal verbs, for example **make up** or **put up with**, appear in bold type, under the main verb. They are marked by the symbol ▶.

Proper nouns, for example **Francia**, **Venezia**, **Alpi**, **Edinburgh**, **Thames**, **Adonis**, **Mosè**, are included in the dictionary, as are important place names and well-known Biblical and mythological names.

Acronyms and abbreviations for example **IVA**, **UNESCO**, **ad**, appear in the main body of the dictionary, not in a separate supplement.

THE ORGANIZATION OF ENTRIES

syllable points

On the English-Italian side of the dictionary, syllable points appear in headwords, to show how they may be hyphenated: **pae·di·at·ric.**

phonetic transcription

Headwords are followed by their pronunciation in square brackets, in the International Phonetic Alphabet. You will find a full list of the symbols used in this system in on page xxvi.

parts of speech

If the headword functions only as a noun, verb etc, the relevant part of speech appears in small capitals after the phonetics.

headword	pronunciation	part of speech category	translations
collar	[ˈkɒləʳ]	N	colletto, collo

If it has more than one function, each part of speech after the first is indicated with a ■.

> **col·lar** [ˈkɒləʳ] N (*of shirt, blouse, coat*) colletto, collo; (*for dog*) collare *m*; (*Tech*) anello, fascetta; **to grab sb by the collar** afferrare qn per il bavero
> ■ VT (*fam: person, object*) beccare

meaning categories

When a headword has more than one sense, the entry is divided into sections marked by a number: **1, 2, 3.**

Each meaning category can include a number of related senses. At the end of each category there may be phrases, in bold type, with translations in roman.

> ◎ **al·to·geth·er** [ˌɔːltəˈgɛðəʳ] ADV **1** (*in all*) in tutto, complessivamente; (*on the whole*) tutto considerato, tutto sommato, nel complesso, nell'insieme; **you owe me twenty pounds altogether** in tutto mi devi venti sterline; **altogether it was rather unpleasant** tutto sommato *or* in complesso è stato piuttosto spiacevole; **how much is that altogether?** quant'è in tutto?
> **2** (*entirely*) del tutto, completamente; **I'm not altogether sure** non sono del tutto *or* proprio sicuro

indicators

The section on page xviii on **material appearing in italics** gives a partial explanation of the pointers, or indicators, which are provided to help the user choose the most suitable translation for a particular context.

Clear and effective indicators are of great importance since many words have several meanings or shades of meaning, while others, which seem to have only one meaning in one language, call for different translations, depending on context or the other words (collocates) used with them. The full range of indicators used in the dictionary can be listed as follows:

- substitutes for the headword
- contextual indicators
- subject field indicators
- style and register labels
- chronological labels
- literal/figurative labels
- regional labels

These labels relate to the source language and are in English on the English-Italian side of the dictionary, and in Italian on the Italian-English side. They appear in italics, within round brackets, and immediately precede the translation.

Substitutes for the headword

Synonyms or partial definitions of the headword often appear as indicators.

> **dis·trac·tion** [dɪsˈtrækʃən] N **1** (*interruption*) distrazione *f*; (*entertainment*) distrazione, diversivo; **a distraction from our concerns** una distrazione dalle nostre preoccupazioni **2** (*distress, madness*): **to drive sb to distraction** far impazzire qn

Contextual indicators

These provide typical contexts in which the user may find or wish to use the headword. They are of various types: some of the commonest are listed below:

- typical noun subjects of an intransitive verb: **fluc·tu·ate** ... (*cost*) ... (*person*) ...
- typical noun objects of a transitive verb: **ful·fil** ... (*duty*) ... (*promise*) ...
- typical noun complements of an adjective: **full-length** ... (*portrait*) ... (*dress*) ...
- typical noun complements of another noun: **full·ness** ... (*of detail*) ...
- typical adjective complements of an adverb: **in·tense·ly** ... (*moved*) ...
- typical verb complements of an adverb: **un·fair·ly** ... (*treat, criticize*) ...

Subject field indicators

Subject field indicators (eg *Med, Pol, Bot*) are used to distinguish meanings of the headword according to specific fields of application. They begin with capital letters and are often abbreviated. For the full list, and explanations of what the abbreviations stand for, see page xxviii.

> **at·tack** [əˈtæk] N **1** (*Mil, fig*) attacco; (*on individual*) aggressione *f*; **a savage attack** una feroce aggressione; **surprise attack** attacco a sorpresa; **attack on sb's life** attentato alla vita di qn; **to be under attack (from)** essere attaccato(-a) (da); **to launch an attack (on)** (*Mil, Sport, fig*) sferrare un attacco (a) **2** (*Med*) attacco, accesso

They are also used when the meaning in the source language is clear, but possibly ambiguous in the target language. This is true in the case of **oratorio**, which in English has only a musical sense, while in Italian it can also be an oratory.

Style and register labels

These have been given to words that are not neutral language. On both sides of the dictionary you will find the labels (*frm*) = formal, (*fam*) = informal or colloquial and (*iro*) = ironic. Literary use is marked as (*liter*) on the English side and (*letter*) on the Italian. Humorous use is labelled (*hum*) or (*scherz*) on the Italian side. (*euph*) or (*euf*) indicates euphemistic use and (*pej*) or (*pegg*) pejorative language. The labels (*offensive*) or (*offensivo*) speak for themselves.
In all languages there are colloquial and vulgar expressions which are widely used, but which non-native speakers need to approach with caution. Such words are marked (*fam!*).

Chronological labels

When a word or expression would generally be regarded as old fashioned, we have the label (*old*), or (*ant*) on the Italian side.

Literal/figurative labels

(*lit*) and (*fig*) indicate literal and figurative senses.

Regional labels

These include (*Scot*) = Scottish, (*Ir*) = Irish and (*dial*) = dialect.

American English

(*Am*) is used to mark American spellings and pronunciations, and words and expressions that are more current in the US than in Britain – though they may be familiar to many speakers of British English. (*Brit*) labels words and phrases used mainly in Britain.

The use of punctuation in indicators

You will often find two or more words in italics (indicators) preceding a translation. In the entry for **passenger** (see below), the fact that there are commas between *boat, plane* and *car* shows that the translation "passeggero" works in relation to all three words. Similarly, when used as an adjective with aircraft or liner the word can be translated "di linea" or "passeggeri".

> **pas·sen·ger** ['pæsɪndʒəʳ] N (*in boat, plane, car*) passeggero(-a); (*on train*) viaggiatore(-trice), passeggero(-a)
> ■ ADJ (*aircraft, liner*) di linea, passeggeri *inv*; (*train*) viaggiatori *inv*

If, however, there is a colon between words in italics, as in the entry **refresh** (see below), a different reading is called for. In the case of **refresh**, if the subject of the verb is a drink, the appropriate translation is "rinfrescare", while if the subject is sleep, or a bath, it is "ristorare". (*Subj*) is not repeated a second time – the colon which appears at the beginning of the second set of brackets stands for it. Whenever a colon is the first element inside brackets it refers back to a word that has already appeared as an indicator.

> **re·fresh** [rɪ'frɛʃ] VT (*subj: drink*) rinfrescare; (*: food, sleep, bath*) ristorare; (*fig: memory*) rinfrescare; **this will refresh your memory** questo ti rinfrescherà la memoria

use of "tu" and "lei"

Partly as a consequence of the dictionary's emphasis on colloquial language, and also to avoid confusion between the 2nd and 3rd person use of "lei", the familiar form "tu" (you) occurs in examples somewhat more often that the formal "lei". Numerous examples of the 2nd person use of "lei" are to be found in the LANGUAGE IN USE supplement.

translations

It will often be found that a particular indicator is followed by two or more translations, separated by commas. These translations are interchangeable, each of them serving equally well to translate the sense in question.

When a different sense calls for a different translation a further indicator appears.

Sometimes part of a translation is optional, and therefore appears in brackets, thus at **neo** (mole) the translation for the figurative use is "(slight) flaw".

> **neo** ['nɛo] SM (*gen*) mole; (*sul viso*) beauty spot; (*fig: imperfezione*) (slight) flaw; (*: di persona*) slight defect

In the case of some derived words, such as **absurdity** and **absurdly**, the user is referred to the entry for the root word (*see adj*). At **absurd** two translations are given, to match the different senses indicated. In the entries for **absurdity** and **absurdly** there is the same sense division, and appropriate translations, but the indicators are not repeated. The user chooses the appropriate translation by looking back at **absurd**. Here the translations are not interchangeable and they are therefore separated by semi-colons rather than commas.

> **ab·surd** [əb'sɜ:d] ADJ assurdo(-a); (*appearance, hat*) ridicolo(-a)
> **ab·surd·ity** [əb'sɜ:dɪtɪ] N **1** (*no pl: see adj*) assurdità, assurdo; ridicolaggine *f* **2** (*thing etc*) assurdità *f inv*; **the absurdities of life** le assurdità della vita
> **ab·surd·ly** [əb'sɜ:dlɪ] ADV (*see adj*) assurdamente; in modo ridicolo

explanatory glosses and cultural equivalents

It is not always possible to give a direct translation of words or phrases, given that there are British concepts and institutions that have no equivalents in Italian culture, and vice versa. Sometimes it is necessary to offer instead an explanatory gloss, which appears in italics – see for example **angel dust** or **ginnasio**. In other cases an approximate equivalent is given – see for example **ACI** or **Speaker**. Such equivalents are preceded by the symbol ≈ .

GRAMMATICAL INFORMATION

gender

Both sides of the dictionary give the feminine endings for Italian adjectives, and where appropriate the feminine form of nouns.

plurals

Irregular plurals and those presenting any sort of difficulty appear after the headword.

irregular forms

Irregular plurals of nouns, such as **mice** and **buoi** (oxen) also appear alphabetically in the word list, with a cross reference to the singular. Similarly, irregular verb forms such as **went**, **gone**, **abbia** and **corso** are listed, and cross-referred to their infinitives.

The fact that an Italian verb is irregular is noted immediately after the part of speech number. English irregular verbs are followed immediately by their past tenses and past participles.

auxiliary verbs

Information is given on whether Italian intransitive verbs take the auxiliary **essere** or **avere**. No such information is given for transitive verbs, since they always form compound tenses with **avere**.

italian reflexive and pronominal verbs

Reflexive verbs such as **radersi** and **vestirsi** are distinguished from intransitive pronominal verbs such as **sbagliarsi** and **ricordarsi**. Reflexives are to be found under the part of speech headed VR (verbo riflessivo), pronominal verbs under VIP (verbo intransitivo pronominale). Some verbs can be used both ways: **ammazzarsi**, for example, used reflexively, means "to kill oneself", while used as a pronominal intransitive it means "to die".

ammazzare [ammat'tsare] VT (*uccidere*) to kill; (*fig: affaticare*) to exhaust, wear out; **ammazzare il tempo** to kill time
▶ **ammazzarsi** VR (*uso reciproco*) to kill each other; (*suicidarsi*) to kill o.s, commit suicide; **ammazzarsi di lavoro** to kill o.s. with work, work o.s. to death;
▶ **ammazzarsi** VIP (*rimanere ucciso*) to die, be killed

Reciprocal reflexives are treated under the VR heading: **ammazzarsi** can also translate as "to kill each other".

Indirect reflexives, such as **lavarsi le mani**, which take a direct object, are to be found as examples under the transitive verb category.

keywords

Words that are the nuts and bolts of the language, such as auxiliary and modal verbs, and the main prepositions and conjunctions, are given specially clear and detailed treatment, with a large number of examples. These entries are identified by the term **KEYWORD** on the English-Italian side and **PAROLA CHIAVE** on the Italian-English side:

◉ **a** [eɪ, ə] **KEYWORD**
INDEF ART (*before vowel or silent h* **an** [æn, ən, n])
1 un *m* (uno + *s impure, gn, pn, ps, x, z*), una *f* (un' + *vowel*); **he's a friend** è un amico; **a herring** un'aringa; **an apple** una mela; **I haven't got a car** non ho la ...

On the English-Italian side, words which are identified in the Collins Word Web as high-frequency are preceded by the symbol ◉.

culture notes

Extra information on culturally significant events, institutions, traditions and customs which cannot be given in an ordinary translation or gloss is given in the form of a note following the relevant entry. These notes are intended to help the user gain a greater insight into and understanding of life and culture in Italian- and English-speaking countries.

THANKSGIVING (DAY)

Negli Stati Uniti il quarto giovedì di novembre ricorre il **Thanksgiving (Day)**, festa nazionale che commemora il primo raccolto in terra americana ottenuto dai Padri Pellegrini, i primi coloni inglesi, nel 1621. È tradizione trascorrere la festa in famiglia (anche affrontando lunghi viaggi) con un pranzo a base di tacchino e tortino di zucca. Vedi anche **PILGRIM FATHERS**

false friends

Words which are similar or identical in both languages can be easily confused. In order to help users to avoid these potential translation pitfalls, a note has been given at the end of the dictionary entry where such confusion could occur. These notes are identified by the heading "DID YOU KNOW ...?" on the English-Italian side, and "LO SAPEVI...?" on the Italian-English side.

DID YOU KNOW ...?
gentle is not translated by the Italian word ***gentile***

website addresses

Many entries include helpful or interesting URLs relating to them.

◉ **bank·ing** ['bæŋkɪŋ] N attività bancaria; **to study banking** fare studi bancari *or* di tecnica bancaria

▷ www.bankofengland.co.uk

The Internet offers the opportunity to gather information from any person, institution or organization with Internet access. Collins believe that such information can be of great benefit to language learners, since it allows them to browse, analyze and study authentic examples of language in context. At the same time, it also provides them with a means of delving further into specific concepts and aspects of life in the cultures of the languages being studied.

There are three kinds of research we have kept constantly in mind when selecting the websites given in the dictionary:

- investigating a given topic, institution or subject area, from *Accademia della Crusca* and *Banca d'Italia* to *birra* and *olio d'oliva*, as part of structured learning. We believe these sites will prove an invaluable resource for teachers and students alike.
- pursuing individual interests and hobbies, from *astronomia* to *birra*, and from *scacchi* to *cinema*.
- practical and cultural information about the country and experience of living there.

Every website has been vetted to ensure that its content is relevant and safe. The majority of sites are non-commercial, though a few commercial sites are included where appropriate.

Apart from giving you further information about the subject you are interested in, websites also provide extremely useful examples of natural language, for intensive or extended reading. However, if you are intending to take anything on the website as a model for your own use of language, it is best to use a site written by a mother-tongue speaker, since even people with a very good knowledge of another language may write in a manner which is not completely idiomatic. You can do this by checking that the site you are consulting is either based in an English-speaking country or hosted by an organization where English is an official language, in order to ensure absolutely reliable language.

The majority of URLs included in this book are sites of official bodies of various kinds. You can therefore be confident that the language has been carefully chosen and is unlikely to contain any mistakes. In addition, any facts they give are likely to be from a reliable source. With non-official sites, you should bear in mind that the content may not have been vetted by anyone other than the authors or webmasters of the site, and so there may be linguistic or factual inaccuracies.

You should also bear in mind the register of language used on the website. If a site is official it may use formal terms that would not be appropriate in all kinds of speech and writing. This also applies to the informal language you may find on other websites. If you want to use a word, phrase or structure you find on a website, you should first check in your dictionary, where you will be given clear guidance as to its register.

using the Internet safely

The Internet contains a huge amount of information on a vast range of topics. It does not belong to and is not controlled by any single organization, government, or nation. This lack of a top-down structure provides many benefits in terms of availability of information and the potential for communication and the spread of ideas. There are downsides, however. As the Internet is unregulated and decentralized there is no quality-control mechanism; the only barrier preventing someone from setting up a website is technical ability. There is much of little merit on the Internet.

More worrying is the potential for criminal misuse. The Internet's accessibility and inclusiveness is exploited by those who wish to disseminate hate or obscenity or to take advantage of the vulnerable or gullible. As more and more households with school-age children are online it is important that parents and carers are aware of the potential dangers as well as the benefits.

Official sites come from a reliable source and their content is generally safe and accurate. These may be identified by the organization code in their URL. Common official organization codes are listed below.

.ac:	academic institution in the UK
.co:	private company*
.com:	public company*
.edu:	academic organization in the USA
.gov:	government organization
.org:	non-profit-making organization

* .co and .com sites, while official, are sites of commercial organizations and are likely to include advertisements and / or links, often to unrelated businesses. The content of these sites may not be subject to the same regulation as the site being visited.

Many Italian sites – commercial, cultural etc – only have the indicator .it.

Other indicators, such as .net, represent unofficial sites whose content is unregulated by any official source. While it does not necessarily follow that unofficial sites are unsafe, choosing those which are offers greater security in the validity of the content.

Other indicators of well-regulated sites are:

• date when last updated, generally at the foot of the screen

• contact information

• source information – this may be on the home page or in an "About us" section with a link from the home page

• for official sites, the privacy policy of the organization.

TRASCRIZIONE FONETICA / **PHONETIC TRANSCRIPTION**

Consonanti / Consonants

p, b, t, d, k, g in inglese sono seguiti dall'aspirazione.

p, b, t, d, k, g are not aspirated in Italian.

padre	p	puppy
bambino	b	baby
tutto	t	tent
dado	d	daddy
cane che	k	cork kiss chord
gola ghiro	g	gag guess
sano	s	so rice kiss
svago esame	z	cousin buzz
scena	ʃ	sheep sugar
	ʒ	pleasure beige
pece lanciare	tʃ	church
giro gioco	dʒ	judge general
afa faro	f	farm raffle
vero bravo	v	very rev
	θ	thin maths
	ð	that other
letto ala	l	little ball
gli	ʎ	
rete arco	r	rat brat
ramo madre	m	mummy comb
no fumante	n	no ran
gnomo	ɲ	
	ŋ	singing bank
	h	hat reheat
buio piacere	j	yet
uomo guaio	w	wall bewail
	x	loch

TRASCRIZIONE FONETICA

Vocali

La messa in equivalenza di certi suoni indica solo una rassomiglianza approssimativa.

PHONETIC TRANSCRIPTION

Vowels

The pairing of some vowel sounds only indicates approximate equivalence.

vino idea	iː i	heel bead
	ɪ	hit pity
stella edera	e	set tent
epoca eccetto	ɛ	
mamma amore	æ a	apple bat
	ɑː	after car calm
	ʌ	fun cousin
	ə	over above
	ɛː	urn fern work
rosa occhio	ɒ ɔ	wash pot
	ɔː	born cork
ponte ognuno	o	
utile zuccau	u	full soot
	uː	boon lewd

Dittonghi / Diphthongs

ɪə	beer tier
ɛə	tear fair day
eɪ	date plaice day
aɪ	life buy cry
aʊ	owl foul now
əʊ	low no
ɔɪ	boil boy oily
ʊə	poor tour

Varie / Miscellaneous

ʳ per l'inglese: la 'r' finale viene pronunciata se seguita da una vocale
ˈ primary or strong stress
ˌ secondary or weak stress

ABBREVIATIONS		ABBREVIAZIONI
abbreviazione	***abbr***	abbreviation
aggettivo	***adj***	adjective
amministrazione	***Admin***	administration
avverbio	***adv***	adverb
aeronautica, trasporti aerei	***Aer***	aviation, aeronautics
aggettivo	***agg***	adjective
agricoltura	***Agr***	agriculture
americano	***Am***	American
amministrazione	***Amm***	administration
anatomia	***Anat***	anatomy
antico	***ant***	old
archeologia	***Archeol***	archaeology
architettura	***Archit***	architecture
articolo	***art***	article
astrologia	***Astrol***	astrology
astronomia	***Astron***	astronomy
attributivo	***attr***	attributive
ausiliare	***aus***	auxiliary
automobile, automobilismo	***Aut***	cars and motoring
ausiliare	***aux***	auxiliary
avverbio	***avv***	adverb
biologia	***Bio***	biology
botanica	***Bot***	botany
britannico, Gran Bretagna	***Brit***	British, Great Britain
chimica	***Chem, Chim***	chemistry
cinema	***Cine***	cinema
commercio	***Comm***	commerce
comparativo	***comp***	comparative
informatica, computer	***Comput***	computing
condizionale	***cond***	conditional
congiunzione	***cong***	conjunction
congiuntivo	***congiunt***	subjunctive
congiunzione	***conj***	conjunction
edilizia	***Constr***	building trade
culinaria, cucina	***Culin***	cooking
davanti a	***dav a***	before
determinativo	***def***	definite
dimostrativo	***dem***	demonstrative
determinativo	***det***	definite
dialetto	***dial***	dialect
difettivo	***dif***	defective
dimostrativo	***dimostr***	demonstrative
diritto	***Dir***	law
eccetera	***ecc***	et cetera
economia	***Econ***	economics
edilizia	***Edil***	building trade
elettricità, elettronica	***Elec, Elettr***	electricity, electronics

esclamazione	***escl***	exclamation
specialmente	***esp***	especially
eccetera	***etc***	et cetera
eufemismo	***euph, euf***	euphemistic
esclamazione	***excl***	exclamation
femminile	***f***	feminine
familiare, colloquiale	***fam***	informal, colloquial, familiar
volgare, tabù	***fam!***	vulgar, taboo
ferrovia	**Ferr**	railways
figurato	***fig***	figurative
finanza	**Fin**	finance
fisica	**Fis**	physics
fotografia	**Fot**	photography
formale	***frm***	formal
calcio	**Ftbl**	football
generale, nella maggior parte dei casi	***gen***	generally, in most senses
geografia	**Geog**	geography
geologia	**Geol**	geology
geometria	**Geom**	geometry
grammatica	**Gram, Gramm**	grammar
scherzoso	***hum***	humorous
impersonale	***impers***	impersonal
indefinito	***indef***	indefinite
indeterminativo	***indet***	indefinite
indicativo	***indic***	indicative
indiretto	***indir***	indirect
infinito	***infin***	infinitive
informatica, computer	**Inform**	computing
interrogativo	***interrog***	interrogative
invariabile	***inv***	invariable
irlandese	**Ir**	Irish
ironico	***iro***	ironic
irregolare	***irreg***	irregular
linguistica	**Ling**	linguistics
letterale	***lit***	literal
letterario	***liter***	literary
maschile	***m***	masculine
matematica	**Math, Mat**	mathematics
medicina	**Med**	medicine
meteorologia	**Met, Meteor**	meteorology, weather
maschile o femminile, secondo il sesso	***m/f***	either masculine or feminine depending on sex
militare	**Mil**	military
mitologia	**Mitol**	mythology
musica	**Mus**	music
mitologia	**Myth**	mythology

ABBREVIATIONS		ABBREVIAZIONI
sostantivo	***n***	noun
nautica	***Naut***	nautical, naval
negativo	***neg***	negative
non ha plurale	***no pl***	no plural
oggetto	***obj, ogg***	object
	o.s.	oneself
passivo	***pass***	passive
passato remoto	***pass rem***	past historic
peggiorativo	***pej, pegg***	pejorative
persona, personale	***pers***	person, personal
fotografia	***Phot***	photography
fisica	***Phys***	physics
plurale	***pl***	plural
poetico, letterario	***poet***	poetic, literary
politica	***Pol***	politics
possessivo	***poss***	possessive
participio passato	***pp***	past participle
predicativo	***pred***	predicative
prefisso	***pref***	prefix
preposizione	***prep***	preposition
presente	***pres***	present
pronome	***pron***	pronoun
participio presente	***prp***	present participle
psicologia	***Psych, Psic***	psychology
passato	***pt***	past tense
qualcosa	***qc***	something
qualcuno	***qn***	someone
ferrovia	***Rail***	railways
religione	***Rel***	religion
relativo	***rel***	relative
sostantivo	***s***	noun
qualcuno	***sb***	somebody
scherzoso	***scherz***	humorous
scienza	***Sci***	science
sistema scolastico	***Scol***	school
scozzese	***Scot***	Scottish
singolare	***sg***	singular
sociologia	***Sociol***	sociology
soggetto	***sogg***	subject
specialmente	***spec***	especially
qualcosa	***sth***	something
congiuntivo	***sub***	subjunctive
soggetto	***subj***	subject
suffisso	***suff***	suffix
superlativo	***superl***	superlative
tecnica, tecnologia	***Tech, Tecn***	technology, technical
telecomunicazioni	***Telec***	telecommunications

ABBREVIATIONS		**ABBREVIAZIONI**
tipografia	***Tip***	typography, printing
televisione	***TV***	television
tipografia	***Typ***	typography, printing
università	***Univ***	university
di solito	***usu***	usually
verbo	***vb***	verb
verbo intransitivo	***vi***	intransitive verb
verbo intransitivo pronominale	***vip***	intransitive pronominal verb
verbo riflessivo	***vr***	reflexive verb
verbo transitivo	***vt***	transitive verb
zoologia	***Zool***	zoology
marchio registrato	®	registered trademark
introduce un'equivalenza culturale	≈	introduces a cultural equivalent

INFINITIVE	PAST	PAST PARTICIPLE
ARISE	arose	arisen
AWAKE	awaked, awoke	awaked, awoken
BE (AM, IS, ARE; BEING)	was, were	been
BEAR	bore	borne, born
BEAT	beat	beaten
BECOME	became	become
BEGIN	began	begun
BEHOLD	beheld	beheld
BEND	bent	bent
BESEECH	besought	besought
BESET	beset	beset
BET	bet, betted	bet, betted
BID	bid, bade	bid, bidden
BIND	bound	bound
BITE	bit	bitten
BLEED	bled	bled
BLOW	blew	blown
BREAK	broke	broken
BREED	bred	bred
BRING	brought	brought
BROADCAST	broadcast, broadcasted	broadcast, broadcasted
BUILD	built	built
BURN	burnt, burned	burnt, burned
BURST	burst	burst
BUY	bought	bought
CAN	could	(been able)
CAST	cast	cast

INFINITIVE	PAST	PAST PARTICIPLE
CATCH	caught	caught
CHOOSE	chose	chosen
CLING	clung	clung
COME	came	come
COST	cost	cost
CREEP	crept	crept
CUT	cut	cut
DARE	dared, durst	dared
DEAL	dealt	dealt
DIG	dug	dug
DO (DOES)	did	done
DRAW	drew	drawn
DREAM	dreamed, dreamt	dreamed, dreamt
DRINK	drank	drunk
DRIVE	drove	driven
DWELL	dwelt	dwelt
EAT	ate	eaten
FALL	fell	fallen
FEED	fed	fed
FEEL	felt	felt
FIGHT	fought	fought
FIND	found	found
FLEE	fled	fled
FLING	flung	flung
FLY (FLIES)	flew	flown
FORBID	forbade, forbad	forbidden
FORECAST	forecast, forecasted	forecast, forecasted
FORGET	forgot	forgotten

INFINITIVE	PAST	PAST PARTICIPLE
FORGIVE	forgave	forgiven
FORSAKE	forsook	forsaken
FREEZE	froze	frozen
GET	got	got, (*Am*) gotten
GIVE	gave	given
GNAW	gnawed	gnawed, gnawn
GO (GOES)	went	gone
GRIND	ground	ground
GRIP	gripped	gripped
GROW	grew	grown
HANG	hung, hanged	hung, hanged
HAVE (HAS; HAVING)	had	had
HEAR	heard	heard
HIDE	hid	hidden
HIT	hit	hit
HOLD	held	held
HURT	hurt	hurt
KEEP	kept	kept
KNEEL	knelt, kneeled	knelt, kneeled
KNOW	knew	known
LAY	laid	laid
LEAD	led	led
LEAN	leant, leaned	leant, leaned
LEAP	leapt, leaped	leapt, leaped
LEARN	learnt, learned	learnt, learned

INFINITIVE	PAST	PAST PARTICIPLE
LEAVE	left	left
LEND	lent	lent
LET	let	let
LIE (LYING)	lay	lain
LIGHT	lit, lighted	lit, lighted
LOSE	lost	lost
MAKE	made	made
MAY	might	—
MEAN	meant	meant
MEET	met	met
MISTAKE	mistook	mistaken
MOW	mowed	mown, mowed
MUST	(had to)	(had to)
OVERCOME	overcame	overcome
PAY	paid	paid
PROVE	proved	proved, proven
PUT	put	put
QUIT	quit, quitted	quit, quitted
READ [riːd]	read [rɛd]	read [rɛd]
RID	rid, ridded	rid, ridded
RIDE	rode	ridden
RING	rang	rung
RISE	rose	risen
RUN	ran	run
SAW	sawed	sawn, sawed
SAY	said	said
SEE	saw	seen
SEEK	sought	sought

INFINITIVE	PAST	PAST PARTICIPLE
SELL	sold	sold
SEND	sent	sent
SET	set	set
SEW	sewed	sewn, sewed
SHAKE	shook	shaken
SHALL	should	—
SHEAR	sheared	shorn, sheared
SHED	shed	shed
SHINE	shone	shone
SHOE	shod	shod
SHOOT	shot	shot
SHOW	showed	shown, showed
SHRINK	shrank, shrunk	shrunk, shrunken
SHUT	shut	shut
SING	sang	sung
SINK	sank	sunk, sunken
SIT	sat	sat
SLAY	slew	slain
SLEEP	slept	slept
SLIDE	slid	slid
SLING	slung	slung
SLIT	slit	slit
SMELL	smelt, smelled	smelt, smelled
SOW	sowed	sown, sowed
SPEAK	spoke	spoken
SPEED	sped, speeded	sped, speeded

INFINITIVE	PAST	PAST PARTICIPLE
SPELL	spelt, spelled	spelt, spelled
SPEND	spent	spent
SPILL	spilt, spilled	spilt, spilled
SPIN	spun	spun
SPIT	spat	spat
SPLIT	split	split
SPOIL	spoiled, spoilt	spoiled, spoilt
SPREAD	spread	spread
SPRING	sprang	sprung
STAND	stood	stood
STEAL	stole	stolen
STEP	stepped	stepped
STICK	stuck	stuck
STING	stung	stung
STINK	stank, stunk	stunk
STREW	strewed	strewn, strewed
STRIDE	strode	stridden
STRIKE	struck	struck, stricken
STRING	strung	strung
STRIVE	strove	striven
SWEAR	swore	sworn
SWEEP	swept	swept
SWELL	swelled	swollen, swelled
SWIM	swam	swum
SWING	swung	swung
TAKE	took	taken
TEACH	taught	taught

VERBI INGLESI

INFINITIVE	PAST	PAST PARTICIPLE
TEAR	tore	torn
TELL	told	told
THINK	thought	thought
THROW	threw	thrown
THRUST	thrust	thrust
TREAD	trod	trodden, trod
UNDERSTAND	understood	understood
UPSET	upset	upset
WAKE	woke, waked	woken, waked
WEAR	wore	worn
WEAVE	wove, weaved	woven, weaved
WED	wedded, wed	wedded, wed
WEEP	wept	wept
WIN	won	won
WIND	wound	wound
WITHDRAW	withdrew	withdrawn
WORK	worked	worked
WRING	wrung	wrung
WRITE	wrote	written

	Gerund	Past Participle	Present	Imperfect	Past Historic
PARLARE	parlando	parlato	parlo parli parla parliamo parlate parlano	parlavo parlavi parlava parlavamo parlavate parlavano	parlai parlasti parlò parlammo parlaste parlarono
VENDERE	vendendo	venduto	vendo vendi vende vendiamo vendete vendono	vendevo vendevi vendeva vendevamo vendevate vendevano	vendei *o* vendetti vendesti vendette vendemmo vendeste vendettero
DORMIRE	dormendo	dormito	dormo dormi dorme dormiamo dormite dormono	dormivo dormivi dormiva dormivamo dormivate dormivano	dormii dormisti dormì dormimmo dormiste dormirono
FINIRE	finendo	finito	finisco finisci finisce finiamo finite finiscono	finivo finivi finiva finivamo finivate finivano	finii finisti finì finimmo finiste finirono
AVERE	avendo	avuto	ho hai ha abbiamo avete hanno	avevo avevi aveva avevamo avevate avevano	ebbi avesti ebbe avemmo aveste ebbero
ESSERE	essendo	stato	sono sei è siamo siete sono	ero eri era eravamo eravate erano	fui fosti fu fummo foste furono

Future	Present Conditional	Present Subjunctive	Imperfect Subjunctive	Imperative
parlerò parlerai parlerà parleremo parlerete parleranno	parlerei parleresti parlerebbe parleremmo parlereste parlerebbero	dorma dorma dorma dormiamo dormiate dormano	parlassi parlassi parlasse parlassimo parlaste parlassero	parla! parli! parlate! parlino!
venderò venderai venderà venderemo venderete venderanno	venderei venderesti venderebbe venderemmo vendereste venderebbero	venda venda venda vendiamo vendiate vendano	vendessi vendessi vendesse vendessimo vendeste vendessero	venda! vendi! vendete! vendano!
dormirò dormirai dormirà dormiremo dormirete dormiranno	dormirei dormiresti dormirebbe dormiremmo dormireste dormirebbero	dorma dorma dorma dormiamo dormiate dormano	dormissi dormissi dormisse dormissimo dormiste dormissero	dormi! dorma! dormite! dormano!
finirò finirai finirà finiremo finirete finiranno	finirei finiresti finirebbe finiremmo finireste finirebbero	finisca finisca finisca finiamo finiate finiscano	finissi finissi finisse finissimo finiste finissero	finisci! finisaca! finite! finiscano!
avrò avrai avrà avremo avrete avranno	avrei avresti avrebbe avremmo avreste avrebbero	abbia abbia abbia abbiamo abbiate abbiano	avessi avessi avesse avessimo aveste avessero	abbi! abbia! abbiate! abbiano!
sarò sarai sarà saremo sarete saranno	sarei saresti sarebbe saremmo sareste sarebbero	sia sia sia siamo siate siano	fossi fossi fosse fossimo foste fossero	sii! sia! siate! siano!

ITALIAN VERBS

[1] Gerund [2] Past Participle [3] Present [4] Imperfect [5] Past Historic [6] Future [7] Conditional [8] Present Subjunctive [9] Imperfect Subjunctive [10] Imperative

ACCADERE	*like*	**cadere**
ACCEDERE	*like*	**concedere**
ACCENDERE	[2] acceso [5] accesi, accendesti	
ACCINGERSI	*like*	**cingere**
ACCLUDERE	*like*	**alludere**
ACCOGLIERE	*like*	**cogliere**
ACCONDISCENDERE	*like*	**scendere**
ACCORGERSI	*like*	**scorgere**
ACCORRERE	*like*	**correre**
ACCRESCERE	*like*	**crescere**
ADDIRSI	*like*	**dire**
ADDURRE	*like*	**ridurre**
AFFIGGERE	[2] affisso [5] affissi, affiggesti	
AFFLIGGERE	[2] afflitto [5] afflissi, affliggesti	
AGGIUNGERE	*like*	**giungere**
ALLUDERE	[2] alluso [5] allusi, alludesti	
AMMETTERE	*like*	**mettere**
ANDARE	[3] vado, vai, va, andiamo, andate, vanno [6] andrò *etc* [8] vada [10] va'!, vada!, andate!, vadano!	
ANNETTERE	[2] annesso [5] annettei, annettesti	
ANTEPORRE	*like*	**porre**
APPARIRE	[2] apparso [3] appaio, appari, appare, appaiono [5] apparvi, apparisti, apparve, apparvero [8] appaia	
APPARTENERE	*like*	**tenere**
APPENDERE	[2] appeso [5] appesi, appendesti	
APPORRE	*like*	**porre**
APPRENDERE	*like*	**prendere**
APRIRE	[2] aperto [3] apro [5] aprii *o* apersi, apristi [8] apra	
ARDERE	[2] arso [5] arsi, ardesti	
ARRENDERSI	*like*	**rendere**
ARRIDERE	*like*	**ridere**
ASCENDERE	*like*	**scendere**
ASCRIVERE	*like*	**scrivere**
ASPERGERE	[2] asperso [5] aspersi, aspergesti	
ASSALIRE	*like*	**salire**
ASSISTERE	[2] assistito [5] assistei *o* assistetti, assistesti	
ASSOLVERE	[2] assolto [5] assolvei *o* assolvetti *o* assolsi, assolvesti	
ASSUEFARE	*like*	**fare**
ASSUMERE	[2] assunto [5] assunsi, assumesti	

ASTENERSI	*like*	tenere
ASTRARRE	*like*	trarre
ATTENDERE	*like*	tendere
ATTENERSI	*like*	tenere
ATTINGERE	*like*	tingere
ATTRARRE	*like*	trarre
AVERE	*see pages xxxvi–xxxvii*	
AVVEDERSI	*like*	vedere
AVVENIRE	*like*	venire
AVVINCERE	*like*	vincere
AVVOLGERE	*like*	volgere
BENEDIRE	*like*	dire
BERE	[1] bevendo [2] bevuto [3] bevo *etc* [4] bevevo *etc* [5] bevvi *o* bevetti, bevesti [6] berrò *etc* [8] beva *etc* [9] bevessi *etc*	
CADERE	[5] caddi, cadesti [6] cadrò *etc*	
CAPOVOLGERE	*like*	volgere
CHIEDERE	[2] chiesto [5] chiesi, chiedesti	
CHIUDERE	[2] chiuso [5] chiusi, chiudesti	
CINGERE	[2] cinto [5] cinsi, cingesti	
CIRCONCIDERE	*like*	decidere
COESISTERE	*like*	esistere
COGLIERE	[2] colto [3] colgo, colgono [5] colsi, cogliesti [8] colga	
COINCIDERE	[2] coinciso [5] coincisi, coincidesti	
COINVOLGERE	*like*	volgere
COMMETTERE	*like*	mettere
COMMUOVERE	*like*	muovere
COMPARIRE	*like*	apparire
COMPIACERE	*like*	piacere
COMPIANGERE	*like*	piangere
COMPORRE	*like*	porre
COMPRENDERE	*like*	prendere
COMPRIMERE	[2] compresso [5] compressi, comprimesti	
COMPROMETTERE	*like*	mettere
CONCEDERE	[2] concesso [5] concessi *o* concedei *o* concedetti, concedesti	
CONCLUDERE	*like*	alludere
CONCORRERE	*like*	correre
CONDISCENDERE	*like*	scendere
CONDIVIDERE	*like*	dividere
CONDURRE	*like*	ridurre
CONFONDERE	*like*	fondere
CONGIUNGERE	*like*	giungere

CONNETTERE	*like*	**annettere**
CONOSCERE	[2] conosciuto [5] conobbi, conoscesti	
CONSISTERE	*like*	**assistere**
CONTENDERE	*like*	**tendere**
CONTENERE	*like*	**tenere**
CONTORCERE	*like*	**torcere**
CONTRADDIRE	*like*	**dire**
CONTRADDISTINGUERE	*like*	**distinguere**
CONTRAFFARE	*like*	**fare**
CONTRAPPORRE	*like*	**porre**
CONTRARRE	*like*	**trarre**
CONTRAVVENIRE	*like*	**venire**
CONVENIRE	*like*	**venire**
CONVERGERE	[2] converso [5] conversi, convergesti	
CONVINCERE	*like*	**vincere**
CONVIVERE	*like*	**vivere**
COPRIRE	*like*	**aprire**
CORREGGERE	*like*	**reggere**
CORRERE	[2] corso [5] corsi, corresti	
CORRISPONDERE	*like*	**rispondere**
CORRODERE	*like*	**rodere**
CORROMPERE	*like*	**rompere**
COSPARGERE	*like*	**spargere**
COSTRINGERE	*like*	**stringere**
COSTRUIRE	[2] costruito [5] costruii, costruisti	
CRESCERE	[2] cresciuto [5] crebbi, crescesti	
CROCIFIGGERE	*like*	**affliggere**
CUOCERE	[2] cotto [3] cuocio, cuociamo *o* cociamo, cuocesti *o* cuociono [5] cossi, cocesti	
DARE	[3] do, dai, dà, diamo, date, danno [5] diedi *o* detti, desti, diede *o* dette, demmo, deste, diedero *o* dettero [6] darò *etc* [8] dia *etc* [9] dessi *etc* [10] da'!, dai!, date!, diano!	
DECADERE	*like*	**cadere**
DECIDERE	[2] deciso [5] decisi, decidesti	
DECOMPORRE	*like*	**porre**

DECORRERE	*like*	**correre**
DECRESCERE	*like*	**crescere**
DEDURRE	*like*	**ridurre**
DELUDERE	*like*	**alludere**
DEMORDERE	*like*	**mordere**
DEPORRE	*like*	**porre**
DEPRIMERE	*like*	**comprimere**
DERIDERE	*like*	**ridere**
DESCRIVERE	*like*	**scrivere**
DESISTERE	*like*	**esistere**
DESUMERE	*like*	**assumere**
DETENERE	*like*	**tenere**
DETERGERE	*like*	**tergere**
DETRARRE	*like*	**trarre**
DEVOLVERE	[2] devoluto [5] devolvei *o* devolvetti, devolvesti	
DIFENDERE	[2] difeso [5] difesi, difendesti	
DIFFONDERE	*like*	**fondere**
DIMETTERE	*like*	**mettere**
DIPENDERE	*like*	**appendere**
DIPINGERE	*like*	**tingere**
DIRE	[1] dicendo [2] detto [3] dico, dici, dice, diciamo, dite, dicono [4] dicevo *etc* [5] dissi, dicesti [6] dirò *etc* [8] dica, diciamo, diciate, dicano [9] dicessi *etc* [10] di'!, dica!, dite!, dicano!	
DIRIGERE	[2] diretto [5] diressi, dirigesti	
DISCENDERE	*like*	**scendere**
DISCHIUDERE	*like*	**chiudere**
DISCIOGLIERE	*like*	**sciogliere**
DISCONOSCERE	*like*	**conoscere**
DISCORRERE	*like*	**correre**
DISCUTERE	[2] discusso [5] discussi, discutesti	
DISDIRE	*like*	**dire**
DISFARE	*like*	**fare**
DISGIUNGERE	*like*	**giungere**
DISILLUDERE	*like*	**alludere**

DISPERDERE	*like*	**perdere**
DISPIACERE	*like*	**piacere**
DISPORRE	*like*	**porre**
DISSOLVERE	[2] dissolto *o* dissoluto [5] dissolsi *o* dissolvetti *o* dissolvei, dissolvesti	
DISSUADERE	*like*	**persuadere**
DISTENDERE	*like*	**tendere**
DISTINGUERE	[2] distinto [5] distinsi, distinguesti	
DISTOGLIERE	*like*	**togliere**
DISTORCERE	*like*	**torcere**
DISTRARRE	*like*	**trarre**
DISTRUGGERE	*like*	**struggere**
DIVENIRE	*like*	**venire**
DIVERGERE	*like*	**convergere**
DIVIDERE	[2] diviso [5] divisi, dividesti	
DOLERE	[3] dolgo, duoli, duole, dolgono [5] dolsi, dolesti [6] dorrò *etc* [8] dolga	
DORMIRE	*see pages xxxvi–xxxvii*	
DOVERE	[3] devo *o* debbo, devi, deve, dobbiamo, dovete, devono *o* debbono [6] dovrò *etc* [8] deva *o* debba, dobbiamo, dobbiate, devano *o* debbano	
ECCELLERE	[2] eccelso [5] eccelsi, eccellesti	
ELEGGERE	*like*	**leggere**
ELIDERE	[2] eliso [5] elisi, elidesti	
ELUDERE	*like*	**alludere**
EMERGERE	[2] emerso [5] emersi, emergesti	
EMETTERE	*like*	**mettere**
EQUIVALERE	*like*	**valere**
ERIGERE	*like*	**dirigere**
ERODERE	*like*	**rodere**
EROMPERE	*like*	**rompere**
ESCLUDERE	*like*	**accludere**
ESIGERE	[2] esatto [5] esigei *o* esigetti, esigesti	
ESISTERE	[2] esistito [5] esistei *o* esistetti, esistesti	
ESPANDERE	*like*	**spandere**

ESPELLERE	[2] espulso [5] espulsi, espellesti	
ESPLODERE	[2] esploso [5] esplosi, esplodesti	
ESPORRE	*like*	**porre**
ESPRIMERE	*like*	**comprimere**
ESSERE	*see pages xxxvi–xxxvii*	
ESTENDERE	*like*	**tendere**
ESTINGUERE	*like*	**distinguere**
ESTORCERE	*like*	**torcere**
ESTRARRE	*like*	**trarre**
ESTROMETTERE	*like*	**mettere**
EVADERE	[2] evaso [5] evasi, evadesti	
EVOLVERSI	[2] evoluto [5] evolvetti *o* evolvei *o* evolsi, evolvesti	
FARE	[1] facendo [2] fatto [3] faccio, fai, fa, facciamo, fate, fanno [4] facevo *etc* [5] feci, facesti [6] farò *etc* [8] faccia *etc* [9] facessi *etc* [10] fa'!, faccia!, fate!, facciano!	
FENDERE	[2] fesso	
FINGERE	*like*	**cingere**
FINIRE	*see pages xxxvi–xxxvii*	
FLETTERE	[2] flesso [5] flettei, flettesti	
FONDERE	[2] fuso [5] fusi, fondesti	
FOTOCOMPORRE	*like*	**porre**
FRAINTENDERE	*like*	**tendere**
FRAMMETTERE	*like*	**mettere**
FRAPPORRE	*like*	**porre**
FRIGGERE	[2] fritto [5] frissi, friggesti	
FUNGERE	[5] funsi, fungesti	
GENUFLETTERSI	*like*	**flettere**
GIACERE	[3] giaccio, giaci, giace, giacciamo, giacete, giacciono [5] giacqui, giacesti [8] giaccia *etc* [10] giaci!, giaccia!, giacete!, giacciano!	
GIUNGERE	[2] giunto [5] giunsi, giungesti	
GIUSTAPORRE	*like*	**porre**
GODERE	[6] godrò *etc*	
ILLUDERE	*like*	**alludere**
IMMERGERE	*like*	**emergere**

IMMETTERE	*like*	**mettere**
IMPORRE	*like*	**porre**
IMPRIMERE	*like*	**comprimere**
INCIDERE	*like*	**decidere**
INCLUDERE	*like*	**accludere**
INCORRERE	*like*	**correre**
INCUTERE	*like*	**discutere**
INDIRE	*like*	**dire**
INDISPORRE	*like*	**porre**
INDULGERE	[2] indulto [5] indulsi, indulgesti	
INDURRE	*like*	**ridurre**
INFERIRE[1]	[2] inferto [5] infersi, inferisti	
INFERIRE[2]	[2] inferito [5] inferii, inferisti	
INFIGGERE	*like*	**affiggere**
INFLIGGERE	*like*	**affliggere**
INFRANGERE	[2] infranto [5] infransi, infrangesti	
INFONDERE	*like*	**fondere**
INGIUNGERE	*like*	**giungere**
INSCRIVERE	*like*	**scrivere**
INSISTERE	*like*	**assistere**
INSORGERE	*like*	**sorgere**
INTENDERE	*like*	**tendere**
INTERCORRERE	*like*	**correre**
INTERDIRE	*like*	**dire**
INTERPORRE	*like*	**porre**
INTERROMPERE	*like*	**rompere**
INTERVENIRE	*like*	**venire**
INTINGERE	*like*	**tingere**
INTRAPRENDERE	*like*	**prendere**
INTRATTENERE	*like*	**tenere**
INTRAVEDERE	*like*	**vedere**
INTRODURRE	*like*	**ridurre**
INTROMETTERSI	*like*	**mettere**
INVADERE	*like*	**evadere**

IRROMPERE	*like*	**rompere**
ISCRIVERE	*like*	**scrivere**
ISTRUIRE	*like*	**costruire**
LEDERE	[2] leso [5] lesi, ledesti	
LEGGERE	[2] letto [5] lessi, leggesti	
LIQUEFARE	*like*	**fare**
MALEDIRE	*like*	**dire**
MANOMETTERE	*like*	**mettere**
MANTENERE	*like*	**tenere**
METTERE	[2] messo [5] misi, mettesti	
MISCONOSCERE	*like*	**conoscere**
MORDERE	[2] morso [5] morsi, mordesti	
MORIRE	[2] morto [3] muoio, muori, muore, moriamo, morite, muoiono [6] morirò *o* morrò *etc* [8] muoia	
MUNGERE	[2] munto [5] munsi, mungesti	
MUOVERE	[2] mosso [5] mossi, movesti	
NASCERE	[2] nato [5] nacqui, nascesti	
NASCONDERE	[2] nascosto [5] nascosi, nascondesti	
NUOCERE	[2] nociuto [3] noccia *o* nuoccio, nuoci, nuoce, nociamo *o* nuociamo, nocete *o* nuocete, nocciono *o* nuocciono [4] nocevo *o* nuocevo *etc* [5] nocqui, nocesti [6] nocerò *o* nuocerò *etc* [7] noccia *o* nuoccia	
OCCORRERE	*like*	**correre**
OCCLUDERE	*like*	**accludere**
OFFENDERE	*like*	**difendere**
OFFRIRE	[2] offerto [3] offro [5] offrii *o* offersi, offristi [8] offra	
OMETTERE	*like*	**mettere**
OPPORRE	*like*	**porre**
OPPRIMERE	*like*	**comprimere**
OTTENERE	*like*	**tenere**
OTTUNDERE	[2] ottuso [5] ottusi, ottundesti	
PARERE	[2] parso [3] paio, paiamo, paiono [5] parvi, paresti [6] parrò *etc* [8] paia, paiamo, paiate, paiano	
PARLARE	*see pages xxxvi–xxxvii*	
PERCORRERE	*like*	**correre**

PERCUOTERE	[2] percosso [5] percossi, percuotesti	
PERDERE	[2] perso *o* perduto [5] persi *o* perdei *o* perdetti, perdesti	
PERMANERE	*like*	**rimanere**
PERMETTERE	*like*	**mettere**
PERSISTERE	*like*	**esistere**
PERSUADERE	[2] persuaso [5] persuasi, persuadesti	
PERVADERE	*like*	**invadere**
PERVENIRE	*like*	**venire**
PIACERE	[2] piaciuto [3] piaccio, piacciamo, piacciono [5] piacqui, piacesti [8] piaccia *etc*	
PIANGERE	[2] pianto [5] piansi, piangesti	
PIOVERE	[5] piovve	
PORGERE	[2] porto [5] porsi, porgesti	
PORRE	[1] ponendo [2] posto [3] pongo, poni, pone, poniamo, ponete, pongono [4] ponevo *etc* [5] posi, ponesti [6] porrò *etc* [8] ponga, poniamo, poniate, pongano [9] ponessi *etc*	
POSPORRE	*like*	**porre**
POSSEDERE	*like*	**sedere**
POTERE	[3] posso, puoi, può, possiamo, potete, possono [6] potrò *etc* [8] possa, possiamo, possiate, possano	
PRECLUDERE	*like*	**accludere**
PRECORRERE	*like*	**correre**
PREDILIGERE	[2] prediletto [5] predilessi, prediligesti	
PREDIRE	*like*	**dire**
PREDISPORRE	*like*	**porre**
PREESISTERE	*like*	**esistere**
PREFIGGERSI	*like*	**affiggere**
PRELUDERE	*like*	**alludere**
PREMETTERE	*like*	**mettere**
PRENDERE	[2] preso [5] presi, prendesti	
PREPORRE	*like*	**porre**
PRESCEGLIERE	*like*	**scegliere**
PRESCINDERE	*like*	**scindere**
PRESCRIVERE	*like*	**scrivere**
PRESIEDERE	*like*	**sedere**

PRESUMERE	*like*	**assumere**
PRESUPPORRE	*like*	**porre**
PRETENDERE	*like*	**tendere**
PREVALERE	*like*	**valere**
PREVEDERE	*like*	**vedere**
PREVENIRE	*like*	**venire**
PRODURRE	*like*	**ridurre**
PROFERIRE	*like*	**inferire**[2]
PROFONDERE	*like*	**fondere**
PROMETTERE	*like*	**mettere**
PROMUOVERE	*like*	**muovere**
PROPENDERE	[2] propenso	
PROPORRE	*like*	**porre**
PROROMPERE	*like*	**rompere**
PROSCIOGLIERE	*like*	**sciogliere**
PROSCRIVERE	*like*	**scrivere**
PROTEGGERE	[2] protetto [5] protessi, proteggesti	
PROTENDERE	*like*	**tendere**
PROTRARRE	*like*	**trarre**
PROVENIRE	*like*	**venire**
PROVVEDERE	*like*	**vedere**
PUNGERE	[2] punto [5] punsi, pungesti	
PUTREFARE	*like*	**fare**
RACCHIUDERE	*like*	**chiudere**
RACCOGLIERE	*like*	**cogliere**
RADERE	[2] raso [5] rasi, radesti	
RADIOTRASMETTERE	*like*	**mettere**
RAGGIUNGERE	*like*	**giungere**
RAPPRENDERSI	*like*	**prendere**
RAREFARE	*like*	**fare**
RAVVEDERSI	*like*	**vedere**
RAVVOLGERE	*like*	**volgere**
RECIDERE	*like*	**decidere**
REDIGERE	[2] redatto [5] redassi, redigesti	

REDIMERE	[2] redento [5] redensi, redimesti	
REGGERE	[2] retto [5] ressi, reggesti	
RENDERE	[2] reso [5] resi, rendesti	
REPRIMERE	*like*	**comprimere**
RESCINDERE	*like*	**scindere**
RESISTERE	*like*	**esistere**
RESPINGERE	*like*	**spingere**
RESTRINGERE	*like*	**stringere**
RETROCEDERE	*like*	**concedere**
RIACCENDERE	*like*	**accendere**
RIAMMETTERE	*like*	**mettere**
RIANDARE	*like*	**andare**
RIAPPARIRE	*like*	**apparire**
RIAPPENDERE	*like*	**appendere**
RIAPRIRE	*like*	**aprire**
RIASSUMERE	*like*	**assumere**
RIAVERE	*like*	**avere**
RICADERE	*like*	**cadere**
RICHIEDERE	*like*	**chiedere**
RICHIUDERE	*like*	**chiudere**
RICOMPARIRE	*like*	**apparire**
RICOMPORRE	*like*	**porre**
RICONDURRE	*like*	**ridurre**
RICONGIUNGERE	*like*	**giungere**
RIDERE	[2] riso [5] risi, ridesti	
RIDIRE	*like*	**dire**
RIDISCENDERE	*like*	**scendere**
RIDURRE	[1] riducendo [2] ridotto [3] riduco *etc* [4] riducevo *etc* [5] ridussi, riducesti [6] ridurrò *etc* [8] riduca *etc* [9] riducessi *etc*	
RIELEGGERE	*like*	**leggere**
RIEMERGERE	*like*	**emergere**
RIEMPIRE	[1] riempiendo [3] riempio, riempi, riempie, riempiono	
RIFARE	*like*	**fare**
RIFLETTERE	[2] riflettuto *o* riflesso	

RIFONDERE	*like*	**fondere**
RIFRANGERE	*like*	**infrangere**
RIFULGERE	[2] rifulso [5] rifulsi, rifulgesti	
RILEGGERE	*like*	**leggere**
RIMANERE	[2] rimasto [3] rimango, rimangono [5] rimasi, rimanesti [6] rimarrò *etc* [8] rimanga	
RIMETTERE	*like*	**mettere**
RIMORDERE	*like*	**mordere**
RIMPIANGERE	*like*	**piangere**
RIMUOVERE	*like*	**muovere**
RINASCERE	*like*	**nascere**
RINCHIUDERE	*like*	**chiudere**
RINCORRERE	*like*	**correre**
RINCRESCERE	*like*	**crescere**
RINVENIRE	*like*	**venire**
RIPERCORRERE	*like*	**correre**
RIPERCUOTERSI	*like*	**percuotere**
RIPORRE	*like*	**porre**
RIPRENDERE	*like*	**prendere**
RIPRODURRE	*like*	**ridurre**
RIPROMETTERSI	*like*	**mettere**
RIPROPORRE	*like*	**porre**
RISCOPRIRE	*like*	**aprire**
RISCRIVERE	*like*	**scrivere**
RISCUOTERE	*like*	**scuotere**
RISOLVERE	*like*	**assolvere**
RISORGERE	*like*	**sorgere**
RISPONDERE	[2] risposto [5] risposi, rispondesti	
RITENERE	*like*	**tenere**
RITORCERE	*like*	**torcere**
RITRARRE	*like*	**trarre**
RITRASMETTERE	*like*	**mettere**
RIUSCIRE	*like*	**uscire**
RIVEDERE	*like*	**vedere**

RIVIVERE	*like*	**vivere**
RIVOLGERE	*like*	**volgere**
RODERE	[2] roso [5] rosi, rodesti	
ROMPERE	[2] rotto [5] ruppi, rompesti	
SALIRE	[3] salgo, sali, salgono [6] salga	
SAPERE	[3] so, sai, sa, sappiamo, sapete, sanno [5] seppi, sapesti [6] saprò *etc* [8] sappia *etc* [10] sappi!, sappia!, sappiate!, sappiano!	
SCADERE	*like*	**cadere**
SCEGLIERE	[2] scelto [3] scelgo, scegli, sceglie, scegliamo, scegliete, scelgono [5] scelsi, scegliesti [8] scelga, scegliamo, scegliate, scelgono [10] scegli!, scelga!, scegliamo!, scegliete!, scelgano!	
SCENDERE	[2] sceso [5] scesi, scendesti	
SCHIUDERE	*like*	**chiudere**
SCINDERE	[2] scisso [5] scissi, scindesti	
SCIOGLIERE	[2] sciolto [3] sciolgo, sciogli, scioglie, sciogliamo, sciogliete, sciolgono [5] sciolsi, sciogliesti [8] sciolga, sciogliamo, sciogliate, sciolgano [10] sciogli!, sciolga!, sciogliamo!, scogliete!, sciolgano!	
SCOMMETTERE	*like*	**mettere**
SCOMPARIRE	*like*	**apparire**
SCOMPORRE	*like*	**porre**
SCONFIGGERE	[2] sconfitto [5] sconfissi, sconfiggesti	
SCONVOLGERE	*like*	**volgere**
SCOPRIRE	*like*	**aprire**
SCORGERE	[2] scorto [5] scorsi, scorgesti	
SCORRERE	*like*	**correre**
SCRIVERE	[2] scritto [5] scrissi, scrivesti	
SCUOTERE	[2] scosso [3] scuoto, scuoti, scuote, scotiamo, scotete, scuotono [5] scossi, scotesti [6] scoterò *etc* [8] scuota, scotiamo, scotiate, scuotano [10] scuoti!, scuota!, scotiamo!, scotete!, scuotano!	
SEDERE	[3] siedo, siedi, siede, siedono [8] sieda	
SEDURRE	*like*	**ridurre**
SEPPELLIRE	[2] sepolto	
SFARE	*like*	**fare**
SMETTERE	*like*	**mettere**
SMUOVERE	*like*	**muovere**
SOCCHIUDERE	*like*	**chiudere**

SOCCORRERE	*like*	**correre**
SODDISFARE	*like*	**fare**
SOFFRIGGERE	*like*	**friggere**
SOFFRIRE	[2] sofferto [5] soffrii *o* soffersi, soffristi	
SOGGIACERE	*like*	**giacere**
SOGGIUNGERE	*like*	**giungere**
SOLERE	[2] solito [3] soglio, suoli, suole, sogliamo, solete, sogliono [8] soglia, sogliamo, sogliate, sogliano	
SOMMERGERE	*like*	**emergere**
SOPPRIMERE	*like*	**comprimere**
SOPRAFFARE	*like*	**fare**
SOPRAGGIUNGERE	*like*	**giungere**
SOPRASSEDERE	*like*	**sedere**
SOPRAVVENIRE	*like*	**venire**
SOPRAVVIVERE	*like*	**vivere**
SOPRINTENDERE	*like*	**tendere**
SORGERE	[2] sorto [3] sorsi, sorgesti	
SORPRENDERE	*like*	**prendere**
SORREGGERE	*like*	**reggere**
SORRIDERE	*like*	**ridere**
SOSPENDERE	*like*	**appendere**
SOSPINGERE	*like*	**spingere**
SOSTENERE	*like*	**tenere**
SOTTINTENDERE	*like*	**tendere**
SOTTOESPORRE	*like*	**porre**
SOTTOMETTERE	*like*	**mettere**
SOTTOPORRE	*like*	**porre**
SOTTOSCRIVERE	*like*	**scrivere**
SOTTOSTARE	*like*	**stare**
SOTTRARRE	*like*	**trarre**
sovraesporre	*like*	**porre**
SOVRAPPORRE	*like*	**porre**
SOVRASTARE	*like*	**stare**
SOVVENIRE	*like*	**venire**

SPANDERE	[2] spanto [5] spandei, spandesti	
SPARGERE	[2] sparso [5] sparsi, spargesti	
SPARIRE	[5] sparii, sparisti	
SPEGNERE	[2] spento [3] spengo, spengono [5] spensi, spegnesti [8] spenga	
SPENDERE	[2] speso [5] spesi, spendesti	
SPINGERE	[2] spinto [5] spinsi, spingesti	
SPIOVERE	*like*	**piovere**
SPORGERE	*like*	**porgere**
STARE	[2] stato [3] sto, stai, sta, stiamo, state, stanno [5] stetti, stesti [6] starò *etc* [8] stia *etc* [10] sta'!, stia!, state!, stiano!	
STENDERE	*like*	**tendere**
STINGERE	*like*	**tingere**
STORCERE	*like*	**torcere**
STRACUOCERE	*like*	**cuocere**
STRAFARE	*like*	**fare**
STRAMALEDIRE	*like*	**dire**
STRAVEDERE	*like*	**vedere**
STRAVINCERE	*like*	**vincere**
STRAVOLGERE	*like*	**volgere**
STRINGERE	[2] stretto [5] strinsi, stringesti	
STRUGGERE	[2] strutto [5] strussi, struggesti	
STUPEFARE	*like*	**fare**
SUCCEDERE	*like*	**concedere**
SUDDIVIDERE	*like*	**dividere**
SUPPORRE	*like*	**porre**
SVENIRE	*like*	**venire**
SVOLGERE	*like*	**volgere**
TACERE	[2] taciuto [3] taccio, tacciono [5] tacqui, tacesti [8] taccia	
TELETRASMETTERE	*like*	**mettere**
TENDERE	[2] teso [5] tesi, tendesti *etc*	
TENERE	[3] tengo, tieni, tiene, tengono [5] tenni, tenesti [6] terrò *etc* [8] tenga	
TERGERE	[2] terso [5] tersi, tergesti	
TINGERE	[2] tinto [5] tinsi, tingesti	

TOGLIERE	[2] tolto [3] tolgo, togli, toglie, togliamo, togliete, tolgono [5] tolsi, togliesti [8] tolga, togliamo, togliate, tolgano [10] togli!, tolga!, togliamo!, togliete!, tolgano!	
TORCERE	[2] torto [5] torsi, torcesti	
TORREFARE	*like*	**fare**
TRADURRE	*like*	**ridurre**
TRAFIGGERE	*like*	**sconfiggere**
TRANSIGERE	*like*	**esigere**
TRARRE	[1] traendo [2] tratto [3] traggo, trai, trae, traiamo, traete, traggono [4] traevo *etc* [5] trassi, traesti [6] trarrò *etc* [8] tragga [9] traessi *etc*	
TRASCENDERE	*like*	**scendere**
TRASCORRERE	*like*	**correre**
TRASCRIVERE	*like*	**scrivere**
TRASFONDERE	*like*	**fondere**
TRASMETTERE	*like*	**mettere**
TRASPARIRE	*like*	**apparire**
TRASPORRE	*like*	**porre**
TRATTENERE	*like*	**tenere**
TRAVOLGERE	*like*	**volgere**
TUMEFARE	*like*	**fare**
UCCIDERE	[2] ucciso [5] uccisi, uccidesti	
UDIRE	[3] odo, odi, ode, odono [8] oda	
UNGERE	[2] unto [5] unsi, ungesti	
USCIRE	[3] esco, esci, esce, escono [8] esca	
VALERE	[2] valso [3] valgo, valgono [5] valsi, valesti [6] varrò *etc* [8] valga	
VEDERE	[2] visto *o* veduto[5] vidi, vedesti [6] vedrò *etc*	
VENDERE	*see pages xxxvi–xxxvii*	
VENIRE	[2] venuto [3] vengo, vieni, viene, vengono [5] venni, venisti [6] verrò *etc* [8] venga	
VILIPENDERE	*like*	**appendere**
VINCERE	[2] vinto [5] vinsi, vincesti	
VIVERE	[2] vissuto [5] vissi, vivesti	
VOLERE	[3] voglio, vuoi, vuole, vogliamo, volete, vogliono [5] volli, volesti [6] vorrò *etc* [8] voglia *etc* [10] vogli!, voglia!, vogliate!, vogliano!	
VOLGERE	[2] volto [5] volsi, volgesti	

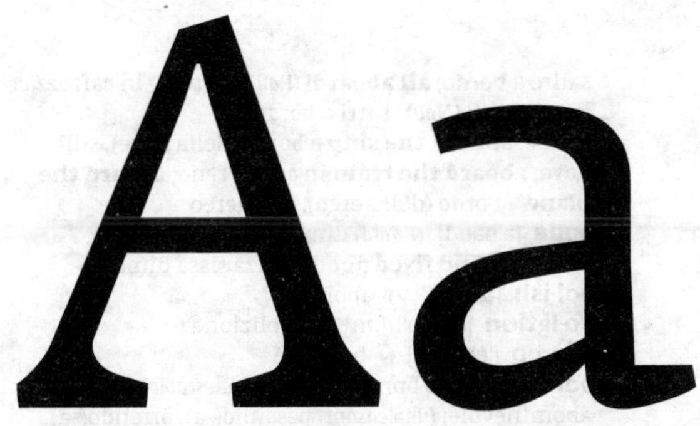

A, a [eɪ] N **1** (*letter*) A, a *f or m inv*; **A for Andrew,** (*Am*) **A for Able** ≈ A come Ancona; **to know sth from A to Z** sapere *or* conoscere qc dall'a alla zeta; **to get from A to B** spostarsi da un punto all'altro **2 A9** (*Brit: road*) ≈ SS 9 (= *strada statale*) **3** (*Mus*) la *m inv*; **it's in A flat** è in la bemolle **4** (*Scol: mark*) ≈ 10, ≈ ottimo; **I got an A for my essay** nel compito ho preso ottimo

◎ **a** [eɪ, ə] **KEYWORD**
INDEF ART (*before vowel or silent h* **an** [æn, ən, n])
1 un *m* (uno + *s impure, gn, pn, ps, x, z*), una *f* (un' + *vowel*); **he's a friend** è un amico; **a herring** un'aringa; **an apple** una mela; **I haven't got a car** non ho la macchina; **a child is full of curiosity** i bambini sono molto curiosi; **he's a doctor** è medico, fa il medico; **a drink would be nice** berrei volentieri qualcosa; **half an hour** mezz'ora; **a hundred pounds** cento sterline; **as a young man** da giovane; **a mirror** uno specchio; **a Mr Smith called to see you** l'ha cercata un certo signor Smith; **what a surprise!** che sorpresa!
2 (*each*) a, per; **2 apples a head** 2 mele a testa *or* (per) ciascuno; **50 kilometres an hour** 50 chilometri all'ora; **3 times a month** 3 volte al mese; **£4 a person** *or* **a head** 4 sterline per *or* a persona; **£4 a pound** 4 sterline alla libbra

A-1 [ˌeɪ'wʌn] ADJ di prim'ordine, eccellente
a. ABBR = **acre**
AA [eɪ'eɪ] N ABBR **1** (*Brit:* = **Automobile Association**) ≈ ACI *m* (= *Automobile Club d'Italia*) **2** (= **Alcoholics Anonymous**) AA *f* (= *Anonima Alcolisti*) **3** (*Am:* = **Associate in Arts**) ≈ laurea in lettere **4** (*Mil*) = **anti-aircraft**
AAA [ˌeɪeɪ'eɪ] N ABBR **1** (= **American Automobile Association**) ≈ ACI *m* (= *Automobile Club d'Italia*) **2** (*Brit*) = *Amateur Athletics Association*
A & E [ˌeɪənd'iː] N ABBR = **accident and emergency**
A & R [ˌeɪənd'ɑː^r] N ABBR (*Mus:* = **Artists & Repertoire**) **A & R man** talent scout *m inv*
aard·vark ['ɑːdˌvɑːk] N oritteropo
AAUP [ˌeɪeɪjuː'piː] N ABBR = *American Association of University Professors*

AB [eɪ'biː] N ABBR (*Am*) = **able-bodied seaman**
■ ABBR (*Canada*) = **Alberta**
aback [ə'bæk] ADV: **to be taken aback** essere colto(-a) *or* preso(-a) alla sprovvista, rimanere sconcertato(-a); **I was taken aback by his reaction** sono rimasto sconcertato dalla sua reazione
aba·cus ['æbəkəs] N (*pl* **abacuses** *or* **abaci** ['æbəsaɪ]) abaco, pallottoliere *m*
aba·lo·ne [ˌæbə'ləʊnɪ] N (*Zool*) orecchia di mare
◎ **aban·don** [ə'bændən] VT **1** (*desert*) abbandonare; **to abandon ship** abbandonare la nave **2** (*give up: plan, hope, game*) abbandonare, rinunciare a; **to abandon o.s. to sth** abbandonarsi a qc, lasciarsi andare a qc
■ N abbandono; **with gay abandon** sfrenatamente, spensieratamente
◎ **aban·doned** [ə'bændənd] ADJ (*unrestrained: manner*) disinvolto(-a), spontaneo(-a)
aban·don·ment [ə'bændənmənt] N abbandono
abase [ə'beɪs] VT (*frm*) umiliare, mortificare; **to abase o.s.** umiliarsi, abbassarsi
abashed [ə'bæʃt] ADJ imbarazzato(-a)
abate [ə'beɪt] VI (*frm: anger, enthusiasm, storm*) placarsi, calmarsi; (*: pain*) calmarsi; (*: fever*) abbassarsi, calare; (*: flood*) abbassarsi; (*: noise*) diminuire, affievolirsi
abate·ment [ə'beɪtmənt] N (*frm: of pollution, noise*) soppressione *f*, eliminazione *f*; **Noise Abatement Society** *associazione contro l'inquinamento acustico*
ab·at·toir ['æbətwɑː^r] N (*Brit*) macello, mattatoio
ab·bess ['æbɪs] N badessa
ab·bey ['æbɪ] N abbazia, badia
ab·bot ['æbət] N abate *m*
ab·bre·vi·ate [ə'briːvɪeɪt] VT abbreviare
ab·bre·via·tion [əˌbriːvɪ'eɪʃən] N abbreviazione *f*
ABC [ˌeɪbiː'siː] N (*Am:* **ABC's** *npl*) abbicci *m inv*, alfabeto; **as easy as ABC** facile come bere un bicchier d'acqua
■ N ABBR (= **American Broadcasting Company**) *rete televisiva americana*
ab·di·cate ['æbdɪkeɪt] VI abdicare
■ VT (*throne*) abdicare a; (*responsibility*) rinunciare a
ab·di·ca·tion [ˌæbdɪ'keɪʃən] N (*of monarch*) abdicazione *f*
ab·do·men ['æbdəmən] N addome *m*

Aa

ab·domi·nal [æb'dɒmɪnl] ADJ addominale
ab·duct [æb'dʌkt] VT rapire
ab·duc·tion [æb'dʌkʃən] N rapimento, sequestro di persona
ab·duc·tor [æb'dʌktəʳ] N rapitore(-trice)
abed [ə'bɛd] ADV (*liter*) a letto
Abel ['eɪbəl] N Abele *m*
Ab·er·do·nian [,æbə'dəʊnɪən] ADJ di Aberdeen
■ N abitante *m/f or* originario(-a) di Aberdeen
ab·er·rant [ə'bɛrənt] ADJ (*Bio, gen*) aberrante
ab·er·ra·tion [,æbə'reɪʃən] N aberrazione *f*; **in a moment of mental aberration** in un momento di aberrazione mentale; **a youthful aberration** una follia *or* un errore giovanile
abet [ə'bɛt] VT (*Law*) *see* **aid**
abey·ance [ə'beɪəns] N (*frm*): **to be in abeyance** (*law, custom*) essere in disuso; (*matter, plan*) essere in sospeso
ab·hor [əb'hɔːʳ] VT aborrire, provare orrore per
ab·hor·rence [əb'hɒrəns] N avversione *f*, orrore *m*; **to have an abhorrence of sth** detestare qc
ab·hor·rent [əb'hɒrənt] ADJ odioso(-a), detestabile, ripugnante; **to be abhorrent to sb** ripugnare a qn
abide [ə'baɪd] (*pt, pp* **abided**) VT (*only neg*) sopportare, soffrire; **I can't abide him** non lo posso soffrire *or* sopportare
▸ **abide by** VI + PREP (*rules*) rispettare, conformarsi a, attenersi a; (*consequences*) accettare; (*promise*) tener fede a, rispettare
abid·ing [ə'baɪdɪŋ] ADJ (*memory etc*) duraturo(-a)
◎ **abil·ity** [ə'bɪlɪtɪ] N capacità *f inv*, abilità *f inv*; **abilities** NPL capacità *fpl*, doti *fpl*; **to the best of my ability** con il massimo impegno; **a person of great abilities** una persona molto dotata; **Ian's got plenty of ability, but he doesn't work hard enough** Ian ha le capacità ma non si applica abbastanza
ab·ject ['æbdʒɛkt] (*frm*) ADJ (*poverty*) abietto(-a); (*apology*) umiliante; (*coward*) indegno(-a), vile
ab·ject·ly ['æbʒɛktlɪ] (*frm*) ADV (*behave, apologize*) bassamente, servilmente; (*lie, act*) indegnamente, vilmente
ab·jure [əb'dʒuəʳ] VT (*frm*) abiurare
ablaze [ə'bleɪz] ADV, ADJ in fiamme; **the house was ablaze with light** (*fig*) la casa era tutta illuminata, la casa risplendeva di luci
◎ **able** ['eɪbl] ADJ (*person*) capace, bravo(-a); (*piece of work*) abile, intelligente; **to be able to do sth** poter fare qc, essere in grado di fare qc; **he's not able to walk** non può *or* non è in grado di *or* non è in condizione di camminare; **those who are able to pay** coloro che sono in condizione *or* che possono permettersi di pagare
able-bodied [,eɪbl'bɒdɪd] ADJ robusto(-a), valido(-a); **able-bodied citizen** cittadino idoneo *or* abile (al servizio militare)
■ N: **the disabled and the able-bodied** i disabili e i non disabili
able-bodied seaman N (*Brit*) marinaio scelto
ab·lutions [ə'bluːʃənz] NPL (*Rel, also hum*) abluzioni *fpl*
ably ['eɪblɪ] ADV abilmente
ABM [,eɪbiː'ɛm] N ABBR (*Mil:* = **antiballistic missile**) ABM *m inv* (= *missile antibalistico*)
ab·nor·mal [æb'nɔːməl] ADJ anormale
ab·nor·mal·ity [,æbnɔː'mælɪtɪ] N (*condition*) anormalità *f inv*; (*instance*) anomalia
ab·nor·mal·ly [æb'nɔːməlɪ] ADV in modo anormale; (*exceptionally*) insolitamente, stranamente
aboard [ə'bɔːd] ADV (*Naut, Aer*) a bordo; **to go aboard** salire a bordo; **all aboard!** (*Rail*) (signori) in carrozza *or* in vettura!; (*Naut*) tutti a bordo!
■ PREP: **aboard the ship** a bordo (della nave), sulla nave; **aboard the train** in *or* sul treno; **aboard the plane** a bordo (dell'aereo); sull'aereo
abode [ə'bəʊd] N (*old*) dimora; (*Law*) domicilio, dimora; **of no fixed abode** senza fissa dimora
abol·ish [ə'bɒlɪʃ] VT abolire
abo·li·tion [æbəʊ'lɪʃən] N abolizione *f*
A-bomb ['eɪ,bɒm] N bomba A
abomi·nable [ə'bɒmɪnəbl] ADJ (*detestable*) abominevole; (*unpleasant*) pessimo(-a), orrendo(-a), orribile
abomi·nably [ə'bɒmɪnəblɪ] ADV disgustosamente; **to be abominably rude to sb** essere terribilmente maleducato(-a) con qn
abomi·nate [ə'bɒmɪneɪt] VT (*frm*) aborrire
abom·ina·tion [ə,bɒmɪ'neɪʃən] N (*feeling*) avversione *f*, disgusto; (*detestable act, thing*) azione *f* (*or* cosa) orrenda; **to hold sth in abomination** detestare qc
Abo·rigi·nal [,æbə'rɪdʒɪnəl] N aborigeno(-a) d'Australia
■ ADJ (*settlement, culture*) aborigeno(-a)
abo·rigi·nal [,æbə'rɪdʒɪnəl] ADJ (*indigenous*) aborigeno(-a), indigeno(-a)
Abo·rigi·ne [,æbə'rɪdʒɪnɪ] N aborigeno(-a) d'Australia
▷ www.cs.williams.edu/~lindsey/myths/myths_13.html
▷ www.pantheon.org/areas/mythology/oceania/aboriginal/
abort [ə'bɔːt] VI (*Med*) abortire; (*fig: plans, space mission*) fallire (prematuramente)
■ VT **1** (*Med*): **to abort a baby** *or* **a pregnancy** interrompere una gravidanza **2** (*fig*) sospendere, rinunciare a portare a termine; (*Comput*) interrompere l'esecuzione di
◎ **abor·tion** [ə'bɔːʃən] N (*Med*) aborto; **to have an abortion** (*termination*) abortire; (*miscarriage*) avere un aborto (spontaneo)
abor·tion·ist [ə'bɔːʃənɪst] N chi esegue aborti clandestini
abor·tive [ə'bɔːtɪv] ADJ (*Med*) abortivo(-a); (*fig: plan*) fallito(-a), mancato(-a); (*: attempt*) vano(-a), infruttuoso(-a)
abound [ə'baʊnd] VI (*frm: exist in great quantity*) abbondare; (*: have in great quantity*): **to abound in** *or* **with** abbondare di, essere ricco(-a) di

◎ **about** [ə'baʊt] KEYWORD
■ ADV
1 (*place: here and there*) qua e là, in giro; **to be about again** (*after illness*) essere di nuovo in piedi; **we were about early** eravamo in piedi presto; **is Paul about?** (*Brit*) hai visto Paul in giro?; **to look about** guardarsi intorno; **they left all their things lying about** hanno lasciato tutta la loro roba in giro; **to run about** (*Brit*) correre qua e là; **there's a lot of measles about** c'è molto morbillo in giro; **to walk about** camminare; **it's the other way about** (*Brit fig*) è il contrario, è viceversa
2 (*approximately*) circa, quasi, pressappoco; **she's about the same age as you** ha pressappoco la tua età; **it's just about finished** è quasi finito; **it takes about 10 hours** ci vogliono circa 10 ore; **(at) about 2 o'clock** verso le due; **it is about 2 o'clock** sono circa le due; **about 50 people** una cinquantina di persone; **that's about right** è più o meno giusto

3 **to be about to do sth** stare per fare qc; **he was about to cry** stava per piangere; **I'm not about to do all that for nothing** non ho intenzione di fare tutto questo per niente; **they were about to fire when ...** erano sul punto di sparare quando..., erano lì lì per sparare quando...

■ PREP

1 (*place*) intorno a; **somewhere about here** qui intorno da qualche parte; **he looked about him** si è guardato intorno; **to do jobs about the house** fare lavori in casa; **her clothes were scattered about the room** i suoi vestiti erano tutti sparsi *or* in giro per la stanza; **to wander about the town** andare in giro per la città

2 (*relating to*) su, a proposito di, riguardo a; **I'm phoning you about tomorrow's meeting** ti chiamo a proposito della riunione di domani; **do something about it!** fai qualcosa!; **how about coming with us?** che ne dici *or* diresti di venire con noi?; **how about a drink?** beviamo qualcosa?, e se bevessimo qualcosa?; **how about going to the cinema?** e se andassimo al cinema?; **there's something about a soldier which ...** c'è qualcosa nei soldati che...; **there's something interesting about her** ha qualcosa di interessante; **we talked about it** ne abbiamo parlato; **a book about travel** un libro sui viaggi; **what is it about?** di che si tratta?; **what about me?** e io?; **what about it?** (*what do you say*) che te ne pare?, cosa ne pensi?; (*what of it*) e allora?

3 (*occupied with*): **while you're about it ...** già che ci sei...

about-face [əˌbaʊt'feɪs], **about-turn** [əˌbaʊt'tɜːn] N (*Mil, fig*) dietro front *m inv*

◎ **above** [ə'bʌv] ADV di sopra, al di sopra; (*in text*) prima, sopra; **mentioned above** summenzionato(-a); **from above** dall'alto; **the flat above** l'appartamento di sopra *or* al piano di sopra; **the clouds above** le nuvole sovrastanti; **children of 7 years or above** ragazzi dai 7 anni in su *or* a partire dai 7 anni; **orders from above** ordini superiori *or* (che vengono) dall'alto; **the address above** l'indirizzo di cui sopra

■ PREP sopra; **above all** soprattutto; **he raised his hands above his head** ha sollevato le mani sopra la testa; **above the clouds** al di sopra delle nuvole; **the Thames above London** il Tamigi a monte di Londra; **2,000 metres above sea level** 2.000 metri sopra il livello del mare; **he is above me in rank** ha un grado superiore al mio; **I couldn't hear above the din** non riuscivo a sentire in mezzo a *or* attraverso tutto quel frastuono; **she's above that sort of thing** è superiore a queste cose; **he's not above a bit of blackmail** non rifuggirebbe dal ricatto; **it's above me** è troppo complicato per me, è al di sopra delle mie possibilità; **to get above o.s.** montarsi la testa; **children above 7 years of age** ragazzi al di sopra dei 7 anni (di età); **costing above £10** più caro di 10 sterline

above·board [əˌbʌv'bɔːd] ADJ leale, onesto(-a); **are you sure this is aboveboard?** sei sicuro che sia una faccenda pulita?

above-mentioned [əˌbʌv'mɛnʃənd] ADJ (*frm*) summenzionato(-a), di cui sopra

above-named [əˌbʌv'neɪmd] ADJ (*frm*) suddetto(-a)

abra·sion [ə'breɪʒən] N abrasione *f*; (*injury*) escoriazione *f*, abrasione *f*

abra·sive [ə'breɪsɪv] ADJ abrasivo(-a); (*fig: person, personality*) caustico(-a); (*: voice*) stridente; (*: manner*) brusco(-a)

■ N abrasivo

abra·sive·ly [ə'breɪsɪvlɪ] ADV (*fig*) aspramente

abreast [ə'brɛst] ADV di fianco, fianco a fianco; **to march 4 abreast** marciare in riga per 4; **to come abreast of** affiancarsi a; **to keep abreast of the news/times** tenersi aggiornato(-a)

abridge [ə'brɪdʒ] VT ridurre

abridged [ə'brɪdʒd] ADJ ridotto(-a)

abridge·ment [ə'brɪdʒmənt] N (*act of abridging*) riduzione *f*; (*shortened version*) edizione *f* ridotta

◎ **abroad** [ə'brɔːd] ADV (*in foreign parts*) all'estero; **to go abroad** andare all'estero; **there is a rumour abroad that ...** (*fig frm*) si sente dire in giro che..., circola la voce che...; **how did the news get abroad?** (*fig frm*) come si è sparsa *or* diffusa la notizia?

ab·ro·gate ['æbrəʊˌgeɪt] VT (*law*) abrogare; (*agreement*) revocare; (*responsibility*) venir meno a

ab·rupt [ə'brʌpt] ADJ (*halt, person*) brusco(-a); (*departure*) improvviso(-a); (*slope*) ripido(-a), erto(-a); (*style*) discontinuo(-a), sconnesso(-a); **his abrupt departure aroused suspicion** Lasua improvvisa partenza ha sollevato dei sospetti; **he was a bt abrupt with me** E' stato un po' brusco con me.; **the film came to an abrupt end** il film terminò bruscamente

ab·rupt·ly [ə'brʌptlɪ] ADV bruscamente

ab·rupt·ness [ə'brʌptnɪs] N (*of person*) rudezza; (*of halt*) repentinità; (*of slope*) ripidezza; (*of style*) discontinuità

ABS [ˌeɪbiː'ɛs] SIGLA M (= **anti-lock braking system**) ABS *mpl*

abs [æbz] NPL (*fam*: = **abdominals**) addominali *mpl*

ab·scess ['æbsɛs] N (*Med*) ascesso

ab·scond [əb'skɒnd] VI fuggire, scappare

ab·seil ['æbseɪl] VI (*Mountaineering*) discendere a corda doppia

ab·seil·ing ['æbseɪlɪŋ] N discesa a corda doppia

◎ **ab·sence** ['æbsəns] N (*of person*) assenza; (*of thing*) mancanza; **in the absence of** (*person*) in assenza di; (*thing*) in mancanza di; **in my absence** in mia assenza; **in the absence of any evidence** non essendoci prove; **absence of mind** distrazione *f*; **absence of proof** mancanza di prove

ab·sent [*adj* 'æbsənt; *vb* æb'sɛnt] ADJ (*person*) assente; (*thing*) assente, mancante; (*fig: also* **absent-minded**) distratto(-a); **to be absent without leave** (*Mil*) essere assente ingiustificato(-a)

■ VT: **to absent o.s. from sth** non presentarsi a qc

ab·sen·tee [ˌæbsən'tiː] N assente *m/f*

ab·sen·tee·ism [ˌæbsən'tiːɪzəm] N assenteismo

ab·sen·tia [ˌæb'sɛntɪə] N (*frm*): **he was sentenced in absentia** fu condannato in contumacia

ab·sent·ly ['æbsəntlɪ] ADV distrattamente

absent-minded [ˌæbsənt'maɪndɪd] ADJ distratto(-a)

absent-mindedly [ˌæbsənt'maɪndɪdlɪ] ADV distrattamente

absent-mindedness [ˌæbsənt'maɪndɪdnɪs] N distrazione *f*

ab·sinthe, **ab·sinth** ['æbsɪnθ] N assenzio

◎ **ab·so·lute** ['æbsəluːt] ADJ (*gen*) assoluto(-a); (*support*) totale, completo(-a), senza riserve; (*proof*) inconfutabile; (*denial*) categorico(-a); (*lie*) bello(-a) e buono(-a); **he's an absolute idiot** è un perfetto idiota; **it's an absolute scandal** è un autentico scandalo

■ N assoluto

◎ **ab·so·lute·ly** ['æbsəluːtlɪ] ADV completamente, assolutamente; **absolutely!** altroché!; **do you think**

Aa

it's a good idea? — absolutely! ti sembra una buona idea? — altroché!; **Jill's absolutely right** Jill ha assolutamente ragione

ab·so·lu·tion [,æbsə'lu:ʃən] N (*Rel*) assoluzione *f*

ab·so·lut·ism ['æbsəlu:,tɪzm] N (*Pol*) assolutismo

ab·solve [əb'zɒlv] VT: **to absolve sb (from** *or* **of)** (*sin etc*) assolvere qn (da); **to absolve sb from** (*oath*) sciogliere qn da; (*obligation etc*) liberare qn da

ab·sorb [əb'sɔ:b] VT (*also fig*) assorbire; (*costs*) ammortizzare; (*information*) assimilare; **she was absorbed in a book** era immersa *or* assorta nella lettura di un libro

ab·sor·ben·cy [ab'sɔ:bənsɪ] N capacità d'assorbimento

ab·sor·bent [əb'sɔ:bənt] ADJ assorbente

absorbent cotton N (*Am*) cotone *m* idrofilo

ab·sorb·ing [əb'sɔ:bɪŋ] ADJ avvincente, molto interessante

> DID YOU KNOW ...?
> **absorbing** is not translated by the Italian word ***assorbente***

ab·sorp·tion [əb'sɔ:pʃən] N **1** (*Physiology*) assorbimento; (*Aut*) ammortizzamento; (*fig: of person into group*) integrazione *f* **2** (*fig*) concentrazione *f*; **his absorption in his work prevented him from noticing ...** era così assorto nel suo lavoro che non ha notato...

ab·stain [əb'steɪn] VI (*in election*): **to abstain (from)** astenersi (da); **to abstain from drinking/smoking** astenersi dal bere/dal fumare; **three MPs abstained** tre deputati si sono astenuti

ab·stain·er [əb'steɪnə[r]] N (*teetotaller*) astemio(-a)

ab·ste·mi·ous [əb'sti:mɪəs] ADJ (*person: in eating, drinking*) moderato(-a)

> DID YOU KNOW ...?
> **abstemious** is not translated by the Italian word ***astemio***

ab·ste·mi·ous·ness [əb'sti:mɪəsnɪs] N sobrietà, temperanza

ab·sten·tion [əb'stɛnʃən] N astensione *f*

ab·sti·nence ['æbstɪnəns] N astinenza

ab·sti·nent ['æbstɪnənt] ADJ astinente

ab·stract [*adj, n* 'æbstrækt; *vb* æb'strækt]
ADJ astratto(-a)
■ N (*summary*) riassunto, sommario; (*picture*) opera astratta; **in the abstract** in teoria, in astratto
■ VT (*remove*) estrarre; (*summarize*) riassumere

ab·stract·ed [æb'stræktɪd] ADJ (*expression, look*) distratto(-a)

ab·strac·tion [æb'strækʃən] N **1** (*absence of mind*) distrazione *f* **2** (*Philosophy etc*) astrazione *f*, concetto astratto

ab·struse [əb'stru:s] ADJ (*theory, concept*) astruso(-a)

ab·surd [əb'sɜ:d] ADJ assurdo(-a); (*appearance, hat*) ridicolo(-a)

ab·surd·ity [əb'sɜ:dɪtɪ] N **1** (*no pl: see adj*) assurdità, assurdo; ridicolaggine *f* **2** (*thing etc*) assurdità *f inv*; **the absurdities of life** le assurdità della vita

ab·surd·ly [əb'sɜ:dlɪ] ADV (*see adj*) assurdamente; in modo ridicolo

ABTA ['æbtə] N ABBR = *Association of British Travel Agents*

Abu Dha·bi [,æbʊ'dɑ:bɪ] N Abu Dhabi *f*

abun·dance [ə'bʌndəns] N abbondanza, gran quantità; **in abundance** in abbondanza, in gran quantità

abun·dant [ə'bʌndənt] ADJ (*crop, supply*) abbondante; (*proof*) ampio(-a)

abun·dant·ly [ə'bʌndəntlɪ] ADV in grande abbondanza; **he made it abundantly clear to me that ...** mi ha fatto chiaramente capire che...

◎ **abuse** [*n* ə'bju:s; *vb* ə'bju:z] N **1** (*insults*) insulti *mpl*, ingiurie *fpl*, improperi *mpl*; **to heap abuse on sb** coprire qn di insulti **2** (*cruel treatment: of children*) abuso; (*: of patients, prisoners*) maltrattamento; **child abuse** violenza sui minori **3** (*misuse: of drugs, solvents*) abuso; **drug abuse** abuso di sostanze stupefacenti; **abuse of power** abuso di potere; **open to abuse** che si presta ad abusi
■ VT **1** (*misuse: position, power*) abusare di; (*: drugs, solvents*) far abuso di **2** (*revile*) insultare **3** (*maltreat: children*) approfittare sessualmente di; (*: patients, prisoners*) maltrattare; **to be abused** subire violenza; **children who have been abused ...** i bambini che hanno subito violenza...

abu·sive [əb'ju:sɪv] ADJ (*person*) offensivo(-a); (*language*) offensivo(-a), ingiurioso(-a)

> DID YOU KNOW ...?
> **abusive** is not translated by the Italian word ***abusivo***

abu·sive·ly [əb'ju:sɪvlɪ] ADV offensivamente

abut [ə'bʌt] VI: **to abut on sth** confinare con qc

abys·mal [ə'bɪzməl] ADJ (*ignorance*) abissale, crasso(-a); (*result, food*) pessimo(-a); (*weather, job*) da cani; **abysmal poverty** la povertà più nera

abys·mal·ly [ə'bɪzməlɪ] ADV in modo atroce; **abysmally ignorant** di un'ignoranza crassa; **to fail abysmally** fallire miseramente; **his work is abysmally bad** il suo lavoro è un disastro

abyss [ə'bɪs] N (*liter*) abisso, baratro

AC [,eɪ'si:] N ABBR **1** (*Elec:* = **alternating current**) c.a. (= *corrente alternata*) **2** (*Am*) = *athletic club*

a/c ABBR (*Banking etc:* = **account, account current**) c

aca·cia [ə'keɪʃə] N (*pl* **acacias** *or* **acacia**) acacia

◎ **aca·dem·ic** [,ækə'dɛmɪk] ADJ **1** (*Scol*) accademico(-a), universitario(-a); (*intellectual*) intellettuale; **academic life** vita universitaria; **academic subjects** materie *fpl* umanistiche e scientifiche; **his academic performance** il suo rendimento scolastico; **I'm not very academic** Non sono molto portato per gli studi **2** (*irrelevant*) puramente formale; **that's rather academic now** ormai è un po' superfluo al lato pratico
■ N (*teaching*) docente *m/f* universitario(-a), universitario(-a); (*doing research*) studioso(-a)

acad·emi·cian [ə,kædɪ'mɪʃən] N accademico

aca·demi·cism [,ækə'dɛmi,sizəm], **aca·dem·ism** [ə'kædə,mɪzəm] N (*Art*) accademismo

academic year N (*Brit*) anno accademico

acad·emy [ə'kædəmɪ] N (*learned body*) accademia; (*school*) scuola privata; **academy of music** (*Brit*) conservatorio; **military/naval academy** accademia militare/navale

ACAS ['eɪkæs] N ABBR (*Brit:* = **Advisory, Conciliation and Arbitration Service**) *comitato per il miglioramento della contrattazione collettiva*

ac·cede [æk'si:d] (*frm*) VI: **to accede to** (*throne*) salire a, ascendere a; (*office, position*) accedere a; (*request*) aderire a, accedere a

ac·cel·er·ate [æk'sɛləreɪt] VT accelerare, affrettare
■ VI (*Aut*) accelerare

ac·cel·era·tion [æk,sɛlə'reɪʃən] N (*Aut, Phys*) accelerazione *f*; **an old car with little acceleration** una vecchia macchina con poca ripresa

ac·cel·era·tor [æk'sɛləreɪtəʳ] N (*Aut, Tech*) acceleratore *m*

accelerator card N (*Comput*) scheda di accelerazione

ac·cent ['æksənt] N (*all senses*) accento; **he hasn't got an accent** non ha alcun accento; **she spoke with a strong Spanish accent** parlava con un forte accento spagnolo

ac·cent·ed ['æksəntɪd] ADJ: **he speaks in heavily accented English** parla inglese con un forte accento straniero

ac·cen·tu·ate [æk'sɛntjuːeɪt] VT (*syllable*) accentuare; (*need, difference etc*) accentuare, mettere in risalto *or* in evidenza

ac·cen·tua·tion [æk,sɛntjuː'eɪʃən] N accentuazione *f*

◎ **ac·cept** [ək'sɛpt] VT (*gen*) accettare; (*acknowledge*) ammettere; **to accept responsibility for something** assumersi la responsabilità di qualcosa; **I can't accept that he's really in financial difficulties** mi rifiuto di credere che abbia davvero delle difficoltà economiche; **he refused to accept defeat** non ha voluto ammettere la sua sconfitta; **I decided to accept the offer** ho deciso di accettare l'offerta

◎ **ac·cept·able** [ək'sɛptəbl] ADJ (*satisfactory*) accettabile; (*welcome: gift, offer*) gradito(-a); **tea is always acceptable** un tè è sempre ben accetto, un tè lo si beve sempre volentieri

ac·cept·ance [ək'sɛptəns] N accettazione *f*; (*of person: by others*) accoglienza (favorevole); (*: for job, membership*) accettazione; (*of proposal*) accoglimento; **I've received two acceptances** ho ricevuto due risposte positive; **to meet with general acceptance** incontrare il favore *or* il consenso generale

◎ **ac·cep·ted** [ək'sɛptɪd] ADJ (*behaviour, pronunciation*) accettato(-a); (*use, ideas*) comunemente accettato(-a); **it's the accepted thing** è un'usanza comunemente accettata

◎ **ac·cess** ['æksɛs] N accesso; **wheelchair access** accesso per disabili; **to have/gain access to sb/sth** avere/ottenere libero accesso presso qn/a qc; **the burglars gained access through a window** i ladri sono penetrati da *or* attraverso una finestra; **we don't have access to a good sports complex** non abbiamo l'opportunità di frequentare un buon centro sportivo; **her ex husband has access to the children** suo marito ha diritto a vedere i bambini
■ VT (*Comput*) accedere a

ac·ces·sibil·ity [æk,sɛsɪ'bɪlɪtɪ] N accessibilità

ac·ces·sible [æk'sɛsəbl] ADJ (*place*) accessibile, che si può raggiungere facilmente; (*person, information*) facilmente reperibile

ac·ces·sion [æk'sɛʃən] N (*addition*) aggiunta; (*to library*) accessione *f*, acquisto; (*of king*) ascesa *or* salita al trono

ac·ces·so·ry [æk'sɛsərɪ] N **1** (*gen pl: Dressmaking, Comm*) accessorio; **fashion accessory** accessorio di moda; **toilet accessories** (*Brit*) articoli *mpl* da toletta **2** (*Law*) complice *m/f*; **accessory to the crime** complice del delitto

access point N (*Comput: to network, Internet*) punto di accesso

access pro·vid·er ['æksɛsprə,vaɪdəʳ] N (*Comput: to Internet*) provider *m inv*

access road N strada d'accesso; (*to motorway*) raccordo di entrata

access time N (*Comput*) tempo di accesso

◎ **ac·ci·dent** ['æksɪdənt] N (*harmful*) incidente *m*, disgrazia; (*unexpected*) (puro) caso; **road accident** incidente stradale; **to meet with** *or* **to have an accident** avere un incidente; **accidents at work** infortuni *mpl* sul lavoro; **by accident** (*by chance*) per caso; (*unintentionally*) senza volere, per sbaglio; **they made the discovery by accident** lo hanno scoperto per caso; **the burglar killed him by accident** il ladro lo ha ucciso per sbaglio; **accidents will happen** sono cose che capitano *or* succedono; **the fog caused several accidents** la nebbia ha provocato diversi incidenti

ac·ci·den·tal [,æksɪ'dɛntl] ADJ (*by chance*) accidentale, fortuito(-a), casuale; (*unintentional*) involontario(-a); **accidental death** morte *f* accidentale

ac·ci·den·tal·ly [,æksɪ'dɛntəlɪ] ADV (*by chance*) per caso; (*unintentionally*) senza volere, inavvertitamente; **accidentally on purpose** (*fam*) di proposito, ma senza darlo a vedere

accident and emergency N (*Brit*) pronto soccorso

accident black spot N luogo famigerato per gli incidenti

accident insurance N assicurazione *f* contro gli infortuni

accident-prone ['æksɪdənt,prəʊn] ADJ predisposto(-a) agli incidenti; **he's very accident-prone** gli succede sempre di tutto

acclaim [ə'kleɪm] VT acclamare
■ N (*approval*) consenso; (*applause*) applauso

ac·cla·ma·tion [,æklə'meɪʃən] N (*approval*) acclamazione *f*; (*applause*) applauso; **by acclamation** per acclamazione

ac·cli·ma·ti·za·tion [ə,klaɪmətaɪ'zeɪʃən], **ac·cli·ma·tion** [,æklaɪ'meɪʃən] (*Am*) N acclimatazione *f*

ac·cli·ma·tize [ə'klaɪmətaɪz], **ac·cli·mate** [,æklɪ,meɪt] (*Am*) VT acclimatare; **to acclimatize o.s. (to)** acclimatarsi (a), adattarsi (a); **to become acclimatized** acclimatarsi

ac·co·lade ['ækəleɪd] N (*frm: praise*) elogio, encomio; (*: award, honour*) onorificenza

ac·com·mo·date [ə'kɒmədeɪt] VT **1** (*lodge, have room for: person*) ospitare, alloggiare; (*: thing*) ospitare, accogliere; **the flat can accommodate five people** ci si può stare in cinque nell'appartamento; **this car accommodates 4 people comfortably** quest'auto può trasportare comodamente 4 persone **2** (*oblige, help*) favorire; (*satisfy*) venire incontro a **3** (*differences*) conciliare **4** (*adjust to: idea, situation*): **accommodate o.s. to** venire incontro a, adattarsi a

> DID YOU KNOW ...?
> **accommodate** is not translated by the Italian word *accomodare*

ac·com·mo·dat·ing [ə'kɒmədeɪtɪŋ] ADJ (*easy to deal with*) accomodante, conciliante; (*willing to help*) gentile, premuroso(-a)

◎ **ac·com·mo·da·tion** [ə,kɒmə'deɪʃən] N **ac·com·mo·da·tions** (*Am*) NPL **1** *place to live*) sistemazione *f*, alloggio; (*space*) posto; **"accommodation to let"** "camere in affitto"; **have you any accommodation (available)?** avete posto?; **seating accommodation** (*Brit*) posti a sedere **2** (*frm: adjustment, adaptation*) adattamento **3** (*Anat*) accomodazione *f*

> DID YOU KNOW ...?
> **accommodation** is not translated by the Italian word *accomodamento*

accommodation address N recapito

accommodation bureau, accommodation agency (*Brit*) N agenzia immobiliare

Aa

ac·com·pa·ni·ment [əˈkʌmpənɪmənt] N (*also Mus*) accompagnamento
ac·com·pa·nist [əˈkʌmpənɪst] N (*Mus*) accompagnatore(-trice)
◎ **ac·com·pa·ny** [əˈkʌmpənɪ] VT (*gen*) accompagnare; (*Mus*): **to accompany (on)** accompagnare (a)
ac·com·plice [əˈkʌmplɪs] N: **accomplice (in)** complice *m/f* (di)
ac·com·plish [əˈkʌmplɪʃ] VT (*task, mission*) compiere, portare a termine; (*one's design*) realizzare; (*purpose*) ottenere; **I don't think much will be accomplished** non credo si otterrà molto
ac·com·plished [əˈkʌmplɪʃt] ADJ (*pianist, cook*) esperto(-a)
ac·com·plish·ment [əˈkʌmplɪʃmənt] N (*completion*) realizzazione *f*, compimento, completamento; (*thing achieved*) risultato, impresa; **accomplishments** NPL (*skills*) doti *fpl*
◎ **ac·cord** [əˈkɔːd] N (*harmony*) accordo; **of his own accord** spontaneamente, di sua iniziativa; **with one accord** all'unanimità, di comune accordo; **to be in accord with** essere d'accordo con
■ VT accordare
■ VI: **to accord (with)** andare d'accordo (con), accordarsi (con)
ac·cord·ance [əˈkɔːdəns] N: **in accordance with** secondo, in conformità di *or* a (or) con
ac·cord·ing [əˈkɔːdɪŋ] PREP: **according to** secondo, stando a; **according to him** secondo lui; **according to what he says** stando a quanto dice; **they will be punished according to the seriousness of their crimes** saranno puniti a seconda della gravità dei loro delitti; **it went according to plan** è andata secondo quanto previsto
ac·cord·ing·ly [əˈkɔːdɪŋlɪ] ADV (*all senses*) di conseguenza
ac·cor·di·on [əˈkɔːdɪən] N (*Mus*) fisarmonica
ac·cor·di·on·ist [əˈkɔːdɪənɪst] N (*Mus*) fisarmonicista *m/f*
ac·cost [əˈkɒst] VT (*confront*) abbordare; (*approach*) avvicinare
◎ **ac·count** [əˈkaunt] N
1 (*report*) resoconto, relazione *f*; **to give an account of sth** fare un resoconto di *or* una relazione su qc; **to keep an account of** tenere nota di; **to bring** *or* **call sb to account for sth/for having done sth** chiedere a qn di render conto di qc/per aver fatto qc; **by** *or* **from all accounts** a detta di tutti, a quanto si dice; **to give a good account of o.s.** farsi onore, dare un'ottima prova di sé
2 (*consideration*) considerazione *f*, conto; (*importance*) importanza, conto; **it's of no account** non importa; **of little account** di poca importanza; **on no account** per nessuna ragione, per nessun motivo, in nessun caso; **on account of** a causa di; **we couldn't go out on account of the bad weather** non siamo potuti uscire a causa del maltempo; **on his account** (*for his benefit*) per lui; **to take account of sth, take sth into account** tener conto di qc, prendere in considerazione qc; **to turn sth to good account** trarre profitto da qc
3 (*at shop, bank, Comm*) conto; **a bank account** un conto in banca; **to open an account (with)** aprire un conto (presso); **"account payee only"** (*Brit: on cheque*) "non trasferibile"; **they have the Pirelli account** la Pirelli è fra i loro clienti; **your account is still outstanding** il suo conto non è ancora stato saldato; **to get £50 on account** ricevere 50 sterline come *or* in *or* di acconto, ricevere un acconto di 50 sterline; **to put £50 down on account** versare un acconto di 50 sterline; **to buy sth on account** comprare qc a credito
4 (*Comm*): **accounts** ■ NPL conti *mpl*; **to keep/do the accounts** tenere la contabilità; **accounts department** ufficio *m* contabilità *inv*
▶ **account for** VI + PREP
1 (*explain*) spiegare, giustificare; (*give reckoning of: actions, expenditure*) render conto di, rispondere di; **that accounts for it** questo spiega tutto; **if she was ill, that would account for her poor results** se fosse malata si spiegherebbero gli scarsi risultati; **all the children were accounted for** nessun ragazzo mancava all'appello; **there's no accounting for tastes** tutti i gusti son gusti
2 (*represent*) rappresentare
3 (*destroy, kill*) uccidere, distruggere
ac·count·abil·ity [əˌkauntəˈbɪlɪtɪ] N responsabilità
ac·count·able [əˈkauntəbl] ADJ: **to be accountable for sth** essere responsabile di qc; **to be accountable to sb** dover rendere conto a qn
ac·count·an·cy [əˈkauntənsɪ] N ragioneria
ac·count·ant [əˈkauntənt] N ragioniere(-a), contabile *m/f*; (*for personal finances*) ≈ commercialista *m/f*
ac·count·ing [əˈkauntɪŋ] N (*auditing*) contabilità; (*subject, field*) ragioneria
▷ www.fasb.org
▷ www.iasb.org.uk/
▷ www.cipfa.org.uk/
accounting period N esercizio finanziario, periodo contabile
account number N numero di conto
account payable N (*Am*) conto passivo
account receivable N (*Am*) conto da esigere
ac·cou·tre·ments [əˈkuːtrəmənts] NPL (*frm, hum*) equipaggiamento *msg*
ac·cred·it·ed [əˈkredɪtɪd] ADJ (*authorized*) accreditato(-a)
ac·cre·tion [əˈkriːʃən] N (*frm, gen, Law*) accrescimento
ac·crue [əˈkruː] VI (*mount up*) aumentare; (*: interest*) maturare; **to accrue to** derivare a; **the notoriety that accrued to him** la notorietà che gliene è derivata
ac·crued [əˈkruːd] ADJ (*interest*) maturato(-a); **accrued charges** ratei *mpl* passivi
ac·cu·mu·late [əˈkjuːmjʊleɪt] VT accumulare; **to accumulate wealth** accumulare ricchezza
■ VI accumularsi; **his debts are accumulating** i suoi debiti si stanno accumulando
ac·cu·mu·la·tion [əˌkjuːmjʊˈleɪʃən] N (*amassing*) accumulo, accumulazione *f*; (*mass, heap*) mucchio, cumulo
ac·cu·mu·la·tor [əˈkjuːmjʊleɪtəʳ] N (*Elec*) accumulatore *m*
ac·cu·ra·cy [ˈækjʊrəsɪ] N (*see adj*) accuratezza; esattezza; precisione *f*; fedeltà
◎ **ac·cu·rate** [ˈækjʊrɪt] ADJ (*description, report, assessment*) accurato(-a), esatto(-a), preciso(-a); (*observation, estimate*) accurato(-a); (*answer*) corretto(-a), esatto(-a); (*shot, instrument, worker*) preciso(-a); (*copy*) fedele
ac·cu·rate·ly [ˈækjʊrɪtlɪ] ADV (*see adj*) accuratamente; con esattezza; correttamente; con precisione; fedelmente
ac·cu·sa·tion [ˌækjʊˈzeɪʃən] N accusa
ac·cu·sa·tive [əˈkjuːzətɪv] ADJ (*Gram*) accusativo(-a)
■ N (*Gram*) accusativo; **in the accusative** all'accusativo
◎ **ac·cuse** [əˈkjuːz] VT: **to accuse sb (of)** accusare qn (di)

ac·cused [ə'kju:zd] N (*Law*): **the accused** l'accusato(-a), l'imputato(-a)
ac·cus·er [ə'kju:zəʳ] N accusatore(-trice)
ac·cus·ing [ə'kju:zɪŋ] ADJ (*look, tone*) accusatore(-trice), d'accusa
ac·cus·ing·ly [ə'kju:zɪŋlɪ] ADV con fare d'accusa
ac·cus·tom [ə'kʌstəm] VT: **to accustom sb to sth/to doing sth** abituare qn a qc/a fare qc; **to accustom o.s. to sth** abituarsi a qc
ac·cus·tomed [ə'kʌstəmd] ADJ (*usual*) abituale; **to be accustomed to sth** essere abituato(-a) a qc; **to get accustomed to sth/to doing sth** abituarsi *or* adattarsi a qc/a fare qc
AC/DC ['eɪsi:'di:si:] N ABBR (= **alternating current/ direct current**) c.a./c.c. (= *corrente alternata/corrente continua*)
■ ADJ ABBR (*fam: bisexual*) bisessuale
ACE [eɪs] N ABBR = *American Council on Education*
ace [eɪs] N (*Cards, fig: sportsman, driver*) asso; **to be within an ace of** (*Brit*) essere a un pelo da; **to keep an ace up one's sleeve** avere un asso nella manica; **to serve an ace** (*Tennis*) effettuare un servizio vincente
■ ADJ (*fam: excellent*) eccezionale; **to be ace at sth** essere bravissimo(-a) in *or* a qc; **sixty of his ace pilots** sessanta dei suoi piloti migliori
acer·bic [ə'sɜ:bɪk] ADJ (*frm: also fig*) acido(-a)
ac·etate ['æsɪteɪt] N acetato
acetic [ə'si:tɪk] ADJ acetico(-a)
acetic acid N acido acetico
ac·etone ['æsɪtəʊn] N acetone *m*
acety·lene [ə'sɛtɪli:n] N acetilene *m*; **acetylene burner** becco ad acetilene; **acetylene welding** saldatura ad acetilene
ache [eɪk] N (*pain*) dolore *m*, male *m*; **aches in your muscles** dolori ai muscoli; **stomach ache** mal *m* di stomaco; **I've got stomach ache** *or* (*Am*) **a stomach ache** ho mal di stomaco; **I'm full of aches and pains** mi fa male dappertutto, sono pieno di dolori
■ VI (*hurt*) far male, dolere; **it makes my head ache** mi fa venire *or* mi dà il mal di testa; **my leg's aching** mi fa male la gamba; **I'm aching all over** sono tutto indolenzito, mi duole dappertutto; **it made her heart ache to see ...** (*fig*) le piangeva il cuore vedere...
■ VT (*yearn*): **to ache to do sth** morire dalla voglia di fare qc
◎ **achieve** [ə'tʃi:v] VT (*aim*) raggiungere; (*success, effect*) ottenere; (*victory*) riportare; (*result*) conseguire; **you won't achieve anything** non otterrai nulla
■ VI (*be successful*) avere successo
◎ **achieve·ment** [ə'tʃi:vmənt] N (*act*) realizzazione *f*, raggiungimento, compimento; (*thing achieved*) risultato, successo; **that's quite an achievement** è una bella impresa, è un bel successo; **it was a fantastic achievement for our team** è stato un risultato fantastico per la nostra squadra
achiev·er [ə'tʃi:vəʳ] N (*Sociol*): **she is a high achiever** ha una personalità vincente
Achilles [ə'kɪli:z] N Achille *m*
Achilles heel N tallone *m* di Achille
Achilles tendon N (*Anat*) tendine *m* di Achille
ach·ing ['eɪkɪŋ] ADJ (*gen*) dolorante; (*sad*) afflitto(-a)
◎ **acid** ['æsɪd] N (*Chem, drug*) acido
■ ADJ (*Chem*) acido(-a); (*sour*) acido(-a), acidulo(-a); (*fig: wit, remark*) caustico(-a); **acid salts** (*Chem*) sali *mpl* acidi; **acid oxides** (*Chem*) ossiacidi *mpl*
acid-base ['æsɪd,beɪs] ADJ (*Chem*): **acid-base reactions** reazioni *fpl* acido-base *inv*
acid·ic [ə'sɪdɪk] ADJ acido(-a)
acidi·fi·ca·tion [ə,sɪdɪfɪ'keɪʃən] N acidificazione *f*
acidi·fy [ə'sɪdɪ,faɪ] VT, VI acidificare
acid·ity [ə'sɪdɪtɪ] N acidità
ac·id·ly ['æsɪdlɪ] ADV acidamente
acid rain N pioggia acida
acid test N prova del fuoco; (*of theory, idea*) prova del nove
◎ **ac·knowl·edge** [ək'nɒlɪdʒ] VT (*mistake*) riconoscere, ammettere; (*truth*) riconoscere; (*claim*) prendere atto di; (*letter: also*, **acknowledge receipt of**) accusare ricevuta di; (*help, present*) manifestare la propria gratitudine per; (*greeting*) rispondere a, ricambiare; **to acknowledge sb as leader** riconoscere qn come capo; **to acknowledge o.s. beaten** ammettere la propria sconfitta; **he won't acknowledge there's a problem** non vuole riconoscere che c'è un problema; **I smiled at him but he didn't even acknowledge me** gli ho sorriso ma lui non ha nemmeno dato segno di accorgersi di me
ac·knowl·edged [ək'nɒlɪdʒd] ADJ (*leader, expert etc*) riconosciuto(-a)
ac·knowl·edge·ment [ək'nɒlɪdʒmənt] N **1** (*admission*) ammissione *f*, riconoscimento; (*of letter*) conferma (di aver ricevuto); **in acknowledgement of a** riconoscimento di **2 acknowledgements** NPL (*in book*) ringraziamenti *mpl*
ACLU [,eɪsi:ɛl'ju:] N ABBR (= **American Civil Liberties Union**) *unione americana per le libertà civili*
acme ['ækmɪ] N (*frm*) culmine *m*, acme *f*
acne ['æknɪ] N acne *f*
aco·lyte ['ækəʊlaɪt] N (*Rel, liter*) accolito
acorn ['eɪkɔ:n] N (*Bot*) ghianda
acous·tic [ə'ku:stɪk] ADJ acustico(-a)
acous·ti·cal·ly [ə'ku:stɪklɪ] ADV acusticamente
acoustic coupler [ə'ku:stɪk'kʌpləʳ] N (*Comput*) accoppiatore *m* acustico
acous·tics [ə'ku:stɪks] NSG (*Phys*) acustica
■ NPL (*of room*) acustica *nsg*
acoustic screen N pannello acustico
ac·quaint [ə'kweɪnt] VT **1** (*inform*): **to acquaint sb with sth** informare qn di qc, far sapere qc a qn, mettere qn al corrente di qc; **he's already acquainted with the facts** è già informato *or* a conoscenza dei fatti; **to acquaint o.s. with sth** familiarizzarsi con qc, impratichirsi su qc **2** (*with person*): **to be acquainted with sb** conoscere (personalmente) qn; **to become acquainted with sb** fare la conoscenza di qn; **we became acquainted in Paris** ci siamo conosciuti a Parigi
ac·quaint·ance [ə'kweɪntəns] N **1** (*with person, subject etc*): **acquaintance (with)** conoscenza (di); **to make sb's acquaintance** fare la conoscenza di qn; **it improves on acquaintance** più lo si conosce e più lo si apprezza **2** (*person*) conoscente *m/f*, conoscenza; **a business acquaintance** una conoscenza di lavoro; **an acquaintance of mine** un mio conoscente
ac·qui·esce [,ækwɪ'ɛs] VI (*frm: agree*): **to acquiesce (to)** acconsentire (a)
ac·qui·es·cence [,ækwɪ'ɛsns] N (*frm*) acquiescenza, consenso
ac·qui·es·cent [,ækwɪ'ɛsnt] ADJ (*frm*) acquiescente
◎ **ac·quire** [ə'kwaɪəʳ] VT (*possessions, territory, knowledge*) acquisire; (*language*) apprendere; (*habit*) contrarre, prendere; (*reputation*) farsi; **to acquire a taste for** prender gusto a
ac·quired [ə'kwaɪəd] ADJ acquisito(-a); **it's an acquired taste** è una cosa che si impara ad apprezzare

Aa

ac·quir·er [ə'kwaɪərə^r] N (*Comm: company*) investitore *m*; **corporate acquirer** investitore istituzionale

◎ **ac·qui·si·tion** [ˌækwɪ'zɪʃən] N acquisto

ac·quisi·tive [ə'kwɪzɪtɪv] ADJ (*person*) a cui piace accumulare; (: *pej*) materialista

ac·quisi·tive·ness [ə'kwɪzɪtɪvnɪs] N tendenza ad accumulare; (*pej*) materialismo

ac·quit [ə'kwɪt] VT **1** (*Law*): **to acquit sb (of)** assolvere qn (da) **2 to acquit o.s. (well/badly)** (*frm*) cavarsela (bene/male)

ac·quit·tal [ə'kwɪtl] N (*Law*) assoluzione *f*

◎ **acre** ['eɪkə^r] N acro (= *4047 m²*)

acre·age ['eɪkərɪdʒ] N superficie *f* in acri

ac·rid ['ækrɪd] ADJ (*smell*) acre, pungente; (*fig*) pungente

Ac·ri·lan® ['ækrɪlæn] N fibra acrilica

ac·ri·mo·ni·ous [ˌækrɪ'məʊnɪəs] ADJ (*frm: remark*) astioso(-a), malevolo(-a); (: *argument*) aspro(-a)

ac·ri·mo·ny ['ækrɪmənɪ] N (*frm*) acrimonia

ac·ro·bat ['ækrəˌbæt] N acrobata *m/f*

ac·ro·bat·ic [ˌækrəʊ'bætɪk] ADJ acrobatico(-a)

ac·ro·bat·ics [ˌækrəʊ'bætɪks] NPL acrobazie *fpl*

ac·ro·nym ['ækrənɪm] N acronimo

Acropo·lis [ə'krɒpəlɪs] N: **the Acropolis** l'Acropoli *f*

◎ **across** [ə'krɒs] PREP **1** (*from one side to other of*) attraverso; **to go across a bridge** attraversare un ponte; **to run across the road** attraversare di corsa la strada; **to take sb across the road** far attraversare la strada a qn; **there was a motif printed across the front of his tee-shirt** c'era un disegno stampato sul davanti della sua maglietta; **a bridge across the river** un ponte sul fiume; **he gave interviews across the country** ha concesso delle interviste in tutto il paese **2** (*on the other side of*) dall'altra parte di, al di là di; **the shop across the road** il negozio sull'altro lato *or* dall'altra parte della strada; **across from** di fronte a; **across the street from our house** di fronte *or* dirimpetto a casa nostra; **he sat down across from her** si è seduto di fronte a lei **3** (*crosswise over*) di traverso a

■ADV **1** (*direction*) dall'altra parte; **to jump across** saltare dall'altra parte, attraversare con un salto; **I helped the old man across** ho aiutato il vecchio ad attraversare; **don't go round, go across** non fare il giro, attraversa *or* passa nel mezzo; **to cut sth across** tagliare qc per *or* di traverso; **3 across** (*in crosswords*) 3 orizzontale; **to get sth across to sb** (*fig*) far capire qc a qn **2** (*measurement*) in larghezza; **the lake is 12 km across** il lago ha una larghezza di 12 km *or* è largo 12 km

across-the-board [ə'krɒsðə'bɔːd] ADJ generale

acryl·ic [ə'krɪlɪk] ADJ acrilico(-a)

■N acrilico

ACT N ABBR (= **American College Test**) *esame di ammissione ai college americani*

◎ **act** [ækt] VI **1** (*take action*) agire; **the police acted quickly** la polizia ha agito prontamente; **he acted to stop it** è intervenuto per fermarlo **2** (*function: thing, person*): **to act as** fungere da, fare da; (: *drug*) agire; **he acts as my assistant** mi fa da assistente; **acting in my capacity as chairman, I ...** in qualità di presidente, io...; **it acts as a deterrent** serve da deterrente; **to act for sb** agire in nome *or* per conto di qn; **who is acting for the defendant?** chi è l'avvocato difensore? **3** (*behave*) comportarsi; **to act like a fool** fare lo(-a) stupido(-a), comportarsi come uno(-a) stupido(-a); **she acted as if she was upset** si era mostrata contrariata **4** (*Theatre, Cine*) recitare; **he's only acting** sta solo facendo finta *or* recitando

■VT (*play*) rappresentare, mettere in scena; (*part*) recitare, interpretare; **to act Hamlet** recitare la parte di Amleto; **to act the fool** (*fig*) fare lo(-a) stupido(-a) *or* il/la cretino(-a)

■N **1** (*deed*) atto; **an act of kindness** un atto di gentilezza; **an act of folly** una pazzia, una follia; **I was in the act of writing to him** stavo (proprio) scrivendo a lui; **to catch sb in the act** cogliere qn in flagrante *or* sul fatto; **I caught him in the act of stealing** l'ho sorpreso a rubare **2** (*also:* **act of Parliament**) legge *f* **3** (*Theatre: of play*) atto; (*in circus, music-hall*) numero; (*fig: pretence*) scena, messinscena; **in the first act** nel primo atto; **it's only an act** è tutta scena, è solo una messinscena

▸ **act on, act upon** VI + PREP (*advice*) seguire, agire in base a; (*order, instructions*) agire in base a, eseguire

▸ **act out** VT (*event*) ricostruire; (*fantasies*) mettere in atto

▸ **act up** VI + ADV (*fam: person*) fare i capricci; (: *injury*) farsi sentire; (: *machine*) fare degli scherzi

act·ing ['æktɪŋ] ADJ che fa le funzioni di; **he is the acting manager** fa le veci del direttore

■N recitazione *f*; **to do some acting** fare del teatro (*or* del cinema); **the acting was marvellous** la recitazione è stata fantastica

◎ **ac·tion** ['ækʃən] N **1** (*doing*) azione *f*; (*deed*) fatto, azione; (*movement: of horse, athlete*) stile *m*; (*effect: of acid, drug etc*) azione, effetto; (*Mil*) azione, combattimento; (*Tech: of clock, machine*) meccanismo; **to take action** passare all'azione, agire; **to take firm action against** prendere misure energiche contro; **to put a plan into action** realizzare un piano; **to be out of action** essere fuori combattimento; (*machine etc*) non funzionare, essere fuori uso; **killed in action** (*Mil*) ucciso(-a) in combattimento; **the film was full of action** nel film c'erano molte scene d'azione **2** (*Law*) azione *f* legale, processo; **to bring an action against sb** (*Law*) intentare causa contro qn

action replay N (*Brit TV*) replay *m inv*

action stations NPL (*Mil*): **action stations!** ai posti di combattimento!

ac·ti·vate ['æktɪveɪt] VT attivare; (*mechanism*) fare funzionare; (*Chem, Phys*) rendere attivo(-a)

ac·ti·va·tion [æktɪ'veɪʃən] N attivazione *f*

activation order N (*Mil*) ordine *m* di attivazione

◎ **ac·tive** ['æktɪv] ADJ (*gen, Gram, volcano*) attivo(-a); **to play an active part in** partecipare attivamente a, prendere parte attiva in; **we are giving it active consideration** lo stiamo considerando attentamente

ac·tive·ly ['æktɪvlɪ] ADV attivamente; **to be actively involved in** prendere parte attiva in

active partner N (*Comm*) socio effettivo *or* accomandatario

active service active duty (*Am*) N (*Mil*): **to be on active service** prestar servizio in zona di operazioni

active voice N (*Gram*) forma attiva

◎ **ac·tiv·ist** ['æktɪvɪst] N attivista *m/f*

◎ **ac·tiv·ity** [æk'tɪvɪtɪ] N (*gen*) attività *f inv*; (*of scene*) animazione *f*, movimento; **outdoor activities** attività all'aria aperta; **social activities** attività ricreative

act of God N calamità *f inv* naturale

Act of Parliament N legge *f*

◎ **ac·tor** ['æktə^r] N attore *m*

◎ **ac·tress** ['æktrɪs] N attrice *f*

Acts of the Apostles N (*Bible*): **the Acts of the Apostles** gli Atti degli Apostoli
ACTT [ˌeɪsiːtiːˈtiː] N ABBR (*Brit:* = **Association of Cinematograph and Television Technicians**) *sindacato dei tecnici cinematografici, televisivi e affini*
◎ **ac·tual** [ˈæktjʊəl] ADJ (*amount, result*) reale, vero(-a), effettivo(-a); (*example*) concreto(-a); **what's the actual amount?** qual è la cifra effettiva?; **these stories are based on actual people, places and events** questi racconti sono basati su personaggi, luoghi e fatti reali; **in actual fact** in realtà; **what were his actual words?** cosa ha detto esattamente?

> DID YOU KNOW ...?
> **actual** is not translated by the Italian word ***attuale***

ac·tu·al·ity [ˌæktʃʊˈælɪtɪ] N: **but in actuality ...** ma in realtà...

> DID YOU KNOW ...?
> **actuality** is not translated by the Italian word ***attualità***

◎ **ac·tu·al·ly** [ˈæktjʊəlɪ] ADV (*really*) veramente, davvero; (*even*) addirittura, perfino; **Fiona's awful, isn't she? — actually, I quite like her** Fiona è odiosa, no? — veramente a me è abbastanza simpatica; **I'm not a student, I'm a doctor, actually** non sono uno studente, sono un medico; **I was so bored I actually fell asleep!** ero così annoiato che mi sono addormentato!; **you only pay for the electricity you actually use** si paga solo per l'elettricità effettivamente consumata; **he actually expected us to put him up for the whole holiday** si aspettava nientemeno che lo ospitassimo per tutta la vacanza!; **that's not true, actually** questo non è affatto vero; **I wasn't actually there** a *or* per dire la verità io non c'ero, veramente io non c'ero

> DID YOU KNOW ...?
> **actually** is not translated by the Italian word ***attualmente***

ac·tu·ary [ˈæktjʊərɪ] N attuario(-a)
ac·tu·ate [ˈæktjʊeɪt] VT (*frm: person*) spingere; (*Tech: machine*) attivare; **actuated by** animato(-a) da
acu·ity [əˈkjuːɪtɪ] N (*frm*) acutezza
acu·men [ˈækjʊmɛn] N acume *m*, perspicacia; **business acumen** fiuto negli affari
acu·punc·ture [ˈækjʊpʌŋktʃəʳ] N agopuntura
acu·punc·tur·ist [ˌækjʊˈpʌŋktʃərɪst] N agopuntore(-trice)
acute [əˈkjuːt] ADJ (*eyesight, accent, angle*) acuto(-a); (*hearing, smell etc*) fine; (*pain, anxiety, joy*) intenso(-a); (*crisis, shortage*) grave; (*person, mind*) perspicace, dotato(-a) di acume
acute·ly [əˈkjuːtlɪ] ADV (*intensely*) intensamente; (*shrewdly*) con perspicacia
AD [ˌeɪˈdiː] ADV ABBR (= **Anno Domini**) d.C.
■ N ABBR (*Am Mil*) = active duty
◎ **ad** [æd] N ABBR (*fam*) = **advertisement**; (*on TV*) spot *m inv* (pubblicitario), pubblicità *f inv*; (*in newspaper*) inserzione *f* pubblicitaria, pubblicità; (: *for jobs etc*) inserzione *f*, annuncio; **to put an ad in the paper** mettere un annuncio sul giornale; **an ad for soap powder** la pubblicità di un detersivo; **during the ads** (*on TV*) durante la pubblicità
ad·age [ˈædɪdʒ] N (*old*) adagio, detto
ada·gio [əˈdɑːdʒɪəʊ] (*Mus*) ADV adagio
■ N (*piece of music*) adagio
Adam [ˈædəm] N Adamo; **I don't know him from Adam** non ho idea di chi sia
ada·mant [ˈædəmənt] ADJ inflessibile, irremovibile
Adam's apple N pomo d'Adamo
a·dapt [əˈdæpt] VT (*machine*) modificare, fare delle modifiche a; (*building*) trasformare; (*text*) adattare; **to adapt o.s. to sth** adattarsi a qc
■ VI: **to adapt (to)** adattarsi (a)
adapt·abil·ity [əˌdæptəˈbɪlɪtɪ] N adattabilità, capacità di adattamento
adapt·able [əˈdæptəbl] ADJ (*person, device*) adattabile, che sa adattarsi; (*device*) adattabile; **he's very adaptable** si adatta facilmente
ad·ap·ta·tion [ˌædæpˈteɪʃən] N adattamento
adapt·er [əˈdæptəʳ], **adap·tor** [əˈdæptəʳ] N **1** (*Elec: for several plugs*) presa multipla; (: *for 2-pin to 3-pin system*) adattatore *m*, riduttore *m* **2** (*of novel*) chi cura un adattamento
ADC [ˌeɪdiːˈsiː] N ABBR **1** (*Mil*) = **aide-de-camp** **2** (*US:* = **Aid to Dependent Children**) *sussidio per figli a carico* **3** (= **analogue-digital converter**) convertitore *m* analogico-digitale
ADD [ˌeɪdiːˈdiː] N ABBR = **attention deficit disorder**
◎ **add** [æd] VT: **to add (to)** aggiungere (a); (*Math*) sommare (a), addizionare (a); **he added that ...** ha aggiunto che...; **added to which ...** e per giunta..., e per di più...; **to add insult to injury** aggiungere al danno le beffe; **add a bit of sugar** aggiungi un po' di zucchero
■ VI (*count*) fare le addizioni *or* le somme, addizionare
▸ **add in** VT + ADV aggiungere, includere
▸ **add on** VT + ADV aggiungere
▸ **add to** VI + PREP aumentare, accrescere
▸ **add up** VT + ADV (*figures*) addizionare, sommare; (*advantages etc*) mettere insieme
■ VI + ADV: **it adds up to 25** la somma è 25; **it doesn't add up** (*fig fam*) non quadra, non ha senso; **it doesn't add up to much** (*fig*) non è un granché; **it's all beginning to add up** (*fig fam*) tutto comincia a diventare chiaro
added value N (*Comm, fig*) valore *m* aggiunto
ad·den·dum [əˈdɛndəm] N (*pl* **addenda** [əˈdɛndə]) aggiunta; **addenda** NPL (*to book, report*) addenda *mpl*
ad·der [ˈædəʳ] N vipera
ad·dict [ˈædɪkt] N tossicomane *m/f*, drogato(-a); (*fig*) fanatico(-a); **drug addict** tossicodipendente *m/f*, tossicomane *m/f*; **heroin addict** eroinomane *m/f*; **television addict** teledipendente *m/f*

> DID YOU KNOW ...?
> **addict** is not translated by the Italian word ***addetto***

ad·dicted [əˈdɪktɪd] ADJ: **addicted (to)** (*drugs etc*) dipendente (da); (*fig*) fanatico(-a) (di), maniaco(-a) (di); **to be addicted to drugs** essere tossicodipendente; **to become addicted to cocaine** diventare cocainomane; **to be addicted to drink** essere dedito(-a) al bere; **to be addicted to chocolate** essere un(-a) cioccolato-dipendente; **she's addicted to soaps** è appassionata di telenovelas
ad·dic·tion [əˈdɪkʃən] N assuefazione *f*; (*Med*) tossicomania; **drug addiction** tossicodipendenza; **to have an addiction to chocolate** essere cioccolato-dipendente

> DID YOU KNOW ...?
> **addiction** is not translated by the Italian word ***addizione***

ad·dic·tive [əˈdɪktɪv] ADJ che dà assuefazione
ad·ding ma·chine [ˈædɪŋməˈʃiːn] N addizionatrice *f*

Aa

Ad·dis Aba·ba ['ædɪs'æbəbə] N Addis Abeba *f*

◎**ad·di·tion** [ə'dɪʃən] N aggiunta; (*Math*) addizione *f*; **if my addition is correct** se ho fatto bene i conti; **there has been an addition to the family** la famiglia si è accresciuta; **in addition to** oltre a, in aggiunta a; **in addition, ...** inoltre,...

◎**ad·di·tion·al** [ə'dɪʃənl] ADJ supplementare

ad·di·tion·al·ly [ə'dɪʃnəlɪ] ADV in più, per di più

ad·di·tive ['ædɪtɪv] N additivo

◎**ad·dress** [ə'drɛs] N **1** (*of house etc*) indirizzo, recapito; (*on envelope, Comput*) indirizzo; **absolute/relative address** (*Comput*) indirizzo assoluto/relativo **2** (*talk*) discorso, allocuzione *f* **3 form of address** (*gen*) formula di cortesia; (*in letters*) formula d'indirizzo *or* di intestazione; **the correct form of address for a bishop** la maniera corretta di rivolgersi ad un vescovo
■VT **1** (*direct: letter*) indirizzare; (*: write name etc on envelope*) mettere *or* scrivere l'indirizzo su; (*remarks etc*) rivolgere; **this letter is wrongly addressed** l'indirizzo su questa lettera è sbagliato; **please address your complaints to the manager** (*frm*) per i reclami si rivolga al direttore; **to address o.s. to sth** (*frm*) indirizzare le proprie energie verso qc **2** (*person*) rivolgersi a; (*meeting*) parlare a, fare un discorso a; **she addressed him as "Your Lordship"** si rivolse a lui chiamandolo "Sua Eccellenza"; **the judge addressed the jury** il giudice si è rivolto alla giuria

address book N rubrica

ad·dressee [,ædrɛ'si:] N destinatario(-a)

ad·duce [ə'dju:s] VT (*frm: fact, reason*) addurre

Aden ['eɪdən] N Aden *f*; **the Gulf of Aden** il golfo di Aden

ad·enoids ['ædɪnɔɪdz] NPL adenoidi *fpl*

adept ['ædɛpt] ADJ: **adept in** *or* **at sth/at doing sth** abile *or* esperto(-a) in qc/nel fare qc
■N: **adept (in, at)** esperto(-a) (in)

ad·equa·cy ['ædɪkwəsɪ] N adeguatezza

◎**ad·equate** ['ædɪkwɪt] ADJ (*amount, supply*): **adequate (for/to do sth)** sufficiente (a/per fare qc); (*reward, description, explanation*): **adequate (for)** adeguato(-a) (a); (*tool*): **adequate (to)** adatto(-a) (a); (*essay, performance*) passabile; (*person*) all'altezza; **to feel adequate to a task** sentirsi all'altezza di un compito

ad·equate·ly ['ædɪkwɪtlɪ] ADV (*heated, paid*) adeguatamente, sufficientemente; (*perform, answer*) convenientemente; **will he do it adequately?** sarà all'altezza?

ADHD [,eɪdi:eɪtʃdi:] N ABBR = **attention deficit hyperactivity disorder**

ad·here [əd'hɪə^r] VI: **to adhere to** (*surface, party, policy*) aderire a; (*belief*) rimanere fedele a; (*promise*) mantenere; (*rule, decision*) attenersi a, seguire

ad·her·ence [əd'hɪərəns] N: **adherence (to)** adesione *f* (a)

ad·her·ent [əd'hɪərənt] N (*person*) aderente *m/f*

ad·he·sion [əd'hi:ʒən] N (*Tech*) aderenza; (*fig: of supporters*) consenso

ad·he·sive [əd'hi:zɪv] ADJ adesivo(-a); **adhesive tape** (*Brit: for parcels etc*) nastro adesivo; (*Am Med*) cerotto adesivo
■N adesivo

ad·he·sive·ness [əd'hi:zɪvnɪs] N adesività

ad hoc [,æd'hɒk] ADJ (*decision*) ad hoc *inv*; (*committee*) apposito(-a)

adieu [ə'dju:] N addio

ad in·fi·ni·tum [,ædɪnfi'naɪtəm] ADV all'infinito

adi·pose ['ædɪ,pəʊs] ADJ adiposo(-a)

ad·ja·cen·cy [ə'dʒeɪsənsɪ] N attiguità

ad·ja·cent [ə'dʒeɪsənt] ADJ: **adjacent (to)** adiacente (a)

ad·jec·ti·val [,ædʒɛk'taɪvəl] ADJ aggettivale

ad·jec·ti·val·ly [,ædʒɛk'taɪvəlɪ] ADV con funzione di aggettivo

ad·jec·tive ['ædʒɛktɪv] N aggettivo

ad·join [ə'dʒɔɪn] VT essere contiguo(-a) a *or* attiguo(-a) a; **the room adjoining mine** la stanza accanto alla mia

ad·join·ing [ə'dʒɔɪnɪŋ] ADJ contiguo(-a), attiguo(-a), adiacente

ad·journ [ə'dʒɜ:n] VT (*suspend*) aggiornare, rimandare, rinviare; **to adjourn a meeting till the following week** aggiornare *or* rinviare un incontro alla settimana seguente; **to adjourn a meeting for a month** rinviare un incontro di un mese
■VI **1** sospendere la seduta; (*Parliament*) sospendere i lavori **2** (*move*) spostarsi; **they adjourned to the pub** (*fam*) si sono trasferiti al pub

ad·journ·ment [ə'dʒɜ:nmənt] N (*of meeting*) rinvio, aggiornamento

Adjt ABBR (*Mil*) = **adjutant**

ad·ju·di·cate [ə'dʒu:dɪkeɪt] VT (*contest*) giudicare; (*claim*) decidere su

ad·ju·di·ca·tion [ə'dʒu:dɪ'keɪʃən] N (*of contest*) giudizio; (*of claim*) decisione *f*

ad·ju·di·ca·tor [ə'dʒu:dɪ,keɪtə^r] N (*of dispute, competition*) arbitro

ad·junct ['ædʒʌŋkt] N (*gen*) aggiunta; (*Gram*) complemento

◎**ad·just** [ə'dʒʌst] VT (*instrument, tool, speed*) regolare; (*wages, prices*) modificare; (*aim, tie, dress*) aggiustare; **you can adjust the height of the seat** si può regolare l'altezza della sedia
■VI: **to adjust (to)** adattarsi (a)

ad·just·able [ə'dʒʌstəbl] ADJ regolabile; **adjustable pliers** pinza *fsg* regolabile; **the volume is adjustable** si può regolare il volume

ad·just·ed [ə'dʒʌstɪd] ADJ (*Psych*) integrato(-a)

ad·just·er [ə'dʒʌstə^r] N = *loss adjuster*

ad·just·ing en·try [ə'dʒʌstɪŋ'ɛntrɪ] N (*Econ*) scrittura di conguaglio

ad·just·ment [ə'dʒʌstmənt] N (*of instrument*) regolazione *f*; (*of wages, prices*) modifica, aggiustamento; (*of person*) adattamento; **to make an adjustment to one's plans** modificare i propri piani

ad·ju·tant ['ædʒətənt] N (*Mil*) aiutante *m/f*

ad-lib [æd'lɪb] VT, VI improvvisare
■N improvvisazione *f*
■ADJ improvvisato(-a), estemporaneo(-a)
■ADV (*speak*) a piacere

ad·man ['ædmæn] N (*fam*) pubblicitario

ad·min ['ædmɪn] N ABBR (*fam:* = **administration**) amministrazione *f*; **her job is mostly admin** il suo lavoro è principalmente amministrativo

ad·min·is·ter [əd'mɪnɪstə^r] VT **1** (*manage: company*) dirigere, gestire; (*: fund*) amministrare **2** (*dispense: medicine*) somministrare; (*: justice, laws*) amministrare; **to administer an oath to sb** far prestare giuramento a qn

◎**ad·min·is·tra·tion** [əd,mɪnɪs'treɪʃən] N **1** (*of company*) direzione *f*, gestione *f*; (*of fund, justice*) amministrazione *f*; (*of medicine*) somministrazione *f* **2** (*Am Pol*) governo

ad·min·is·tra·tive [əd'mɪnɪstrətɪv] ADJ amministrativo(-a)

ad·min·is·tra·tive·ly [əd'mɪnɪstrətɪvlɪ] ADV amministrativamente

ad·min·is·tra·tor [əd'mɪnɪstreɪtəʳ] N amministratore(-trice); (*of will*) curatore(-trice)
ad·mi·rable ['ædmərəbl] ADJ ammirevole
ad·mi·rably ['ædmərəblɪ] ADV ammirevolmente; **he is admirably suited to the job** è perfettamente adatto a quel lavoro
ad·mi·ral ['ædmərəl] N ammiraglio
Ad·mi·ral·ty ['ædmərəltɪ] N (*Brit*): **the Admiralty** l'Ammiragliato
ad·mi·ral·ty ['ædmərəltɪ] N ammiragliato
Admiralty Board N: **the Admiralty Board** (*Brit*) ≈ il Ministero della Marina Militare
ad·mi·ra·tion [,ædmə'reɪʃən] N ammirazione *f*
◎ **ad·mire** [əd'maɪəʳ] VT ammirare; **she was admiring herself in the mirror** si rimirava allo *or* davanti allo specchio
ad·mir·er [əd'maɪərəʳ] N ammiratore(-trice)
ad·mir·ing [əd'maɪərɪŋ] ADJ (*person*) pieno(-a) di ammirazione; (*look*) di ammirazione
ad·mir·ing·ly [əd'maɪərɪŋlɪ] ADV con ammirazione
ad·mis·sible [əd'mɪsəbl] ADJ ammissibile
ad·mis·sion [əd'mɪʃən] N **1** (*entry: to society, school etc*) ammissione *f*; (: *to exhibition, night club, building*) entrata, ingresso; (*price*) prezzo del biglietto (d'ingresso); **"admission free"** *or* **"free admission"** "ingresso gratuito" **2** (*confession*) ammissione *f*, confessione *f*; **it would be an admission of defeat** sarebbe come dichiararsi sconfitto; **by his own admission** per sua ammissione
◎ **ad·mit** [əd'mɪt] VT **1** (*allow to enter*) lasciar entrare, far entrare; (: *air, light*) lasciar passare; **children not admitted** vietato l'ingresso ai bambini; **this ticket admits two** questo biglietto è valido per due persone; **he was admitted to hospital** è stato ricoverato all'ospedale **2** (*acknowledge*) ammettere, riconoscere; (: *crime*) ammettere *or* confessare (di aver compiuto); **it is hard, I admit** è difficile, lo ammetto *or* devo ammetterlo; **I must admit that ...** devo ammettere *or* confessare che...; **he admitted that he'd done it** ha confessato di averlo fatto
▸ **admit of** VI + PREP (*frm*) dare adito a
▸ **admit to** VI + PREP riconoscere
ad·mit·tance [əd'mɪtəns] N ingresso; **they refused me admittance** mi hanno rifiutato il permesso di entrare; **to gain admittance** riuscire a entrare; **"no admittance"** "vietato l'ingresso"
ad·mit·ted·ly [əd'mɪtɪdlɪ] ADV bisogna ammettere *or* riconoscere (che), va detto (che)
ad·mon·ish [əd'mɒnɪʃ] VT (*frm: reprimand*) ammonire; **to admonish sb (for)** riprendere qn (per)
ad·moni·tion [ædmə'nɪʃən] N (*frm*) ammonizione *f*
ad nau·seam [,æd'nɔ:sɪæm] ADV fino alla nausea, a non finire
ado [ə'du:] N: **without (any) more ado** senza più indugi
ado·les·cence [,ædəʊ'lɛsns] N adolescenza
ado·les·cent [,ædəʊ'lɛsnt] ADJ, N adolescente (*m/f*)
Adonis [ə'dəʊnɪs] N Adone *m*
◎ **adopt** [ə'dɒpt] VT (*child, method*) adottare; (*report, suggestion*) approvare; (*Pol: candidate*) scegliere
adopt·ed [ə'dɒptɪd] ADJ adottivo(-a)
adop·tion [ə'dɒpʃən] N (*see vb*) adozione *f*; approvazione *f*; scelta
adop·tive [ə'dɒptɪv] ADJ adottivo(-a)
ador·able [ə'dɔ:rəbl] ADJ adorabile
ador·ably [ə'dɔ:rəblɪ] ADV adorabilmente
ado·ra·tion [,ædə'reɪʃən] N adorazione *f*
adore [ə'dɔ:ʳ] VT adorare
ador·ing [ə'dɔ:rɪŋ] ADJ (*look, glance*) pieno(-a) di adorazione, adorante; **he has adoring parents** i suoi genitori lo adorano
ador·ing·ly [ə'dɔ:rɪŋlɪ] ADV con adorazione, con venerazione
adorn [ə'dɔ:n] VT (*liter*) abbellire, ornare
adorn·ment [ə'dɔ:nmənt] N (*liter*) ornamento, decorazione *f*
ADP [,eɪdi:'pi:] N ABBR = **automatic data processing**
ad·re·nal [ə'dri:nəl] ADJ surrenale; **adrenal (gland)** (ghiandola) surrenale *f*
adrena·lin [ə'drɛnəlɪn] N adrenalina; **it gets the adrenalin going** ti dà una scarica di adrenalina
Adri·at·ic [,eɪdrɪ'ætɪk] ADJ adriatico(-a)
■ N: **the Adriatic (Sea)** l'Adriatico, il mare Adriatico
adrift [ə'drɪft] ADV (*esp Naut*) alla deriva; **to come adrift** (*wire, rope etc*) essersi staccato(-a) *or* sciolto(-a)
adroit [ə'drɔɪt] ADJ abile, destro(-a)
adroit·ly [ə'drɔɪtlɪ] ADV abilmente
adroit·ness [ə'drɔɪtnɪs] N abilità
ADSL [,eɪdi:ɛs'ɛl] N ABBR (= **asynchronous digital subscriber line**) ADSL *m*
ADT [,eɪdi:'ti:] N ABBR (*Am*: = **Atlantic Daylight Time**) *ora estiva nel fuso orario di New York*
adu·late ['ædjʊleɪt] VT (*frm*) adulare
adu·la·tion [,ædjʊ'leɪʃən] N adulazione *f*
◎ **adult** ['ædʌlt] ADJ (*person, animal*) adulto(-a); (*behaviour*) da adulto; (*film, book*) per adulti
■ N adulto(-a); **"adults only"** ≈ "vietato ai minori di 18 anni"
adult education N scuola per adulti
adul·ter·ate [ə'dʌltəreɪt] VT adulterare
adul·tera·tion [ə'dʌltə,reɪʃən] N (*of food, drink*) adulterazione *f*
adul·ter·er [ə'dʌltərəʳ] N adultero
adul·ter·ess [ə'dʌltərɪs] N adultera
adul·ter·ous [ə'dʌltərəs] ADJ (*relationship*) adulterino(-a); (*person*) adultero(-a)
adul·tery [ə'dʌltərɪ] N adulterio
adult·hood [ə'dʌlthʊd] N età adulta
◎ **ad·vance** [əd'vɑ:ns] VT **1** (*move forward: time, date*) anticipare; (*further: plan, knowledge*); (*Mil: troops*) far avanzare; (*promote: interests*) favorire; (: *person: in career*) promuovere **2** (*idea, suggestion, claim*) avanzare **3** (*money*) anticipare; **she wants him to advance her a loan** vuole che lui le faccia un prestito
■ VI (*move forward, also Mil*) avanzare; (*science, technology*) fare progressi, progredire; (*civilization, mankind*) migliorare, fare progressi; **to advance on sb** (*threateningly*) avanzare contro qn; **technology has advanced a great deal** la tecnologia ha fatto grandi progressi
■ N **1** (*Mil*) avanzata; (*fig: progress*) passo (in) avanti, progresso; **the advance of old age** l'avanzare dell'età *or* degli anni; **recent advances in technology** i recenti progressi della tecnica; **to make advances to sb** (*gen*) tentare un approccio con qn; (*amorously*) fare delle avances a qn; **in advance** in anticipo; **to arrive in advance of sb** arrivare in anticipo su qn *or* prima di qn; **to send sth a week in advance** spedire qc con una settimana di anticipo **2** (*loan*): **advance (on)** anticipo (su); (: *from bank*) anticipazione *f* bancaria (su)
■ ADJ (*payment, booking*) anticipato(-a); (*copy of book*) distribuito(-a) in anticipo; **we weren't given any advance warning of his visit** non ci avevano dato nessun preavviso del suo arrivo

Aa

DID YOU KNOW ...?
advance is not translated by the Italian word *avanzo*

◎**ad·vanced** [əd'vɑ:nst] ADJ (*ideas, civilization etc*) progredito(-a), avanzato(-a); (*Scol: studies*) superiore; (*: class*) avanzato(-a); (*: student*) di livello più avanzato; **of advanced years** avanti negli anni

ad·vance·ment [əd'vɑ:nsmənt] N (*improvement*) miglioramento; (*promotion*) promozione *f*, avanzamento; **career advancement** avanzamento di carriera

advance notice N preavviso

advance party N (*Mil*) squadra di perlustrazione; (*of explorers*) gruppo che va in avanscoperta

◎**ad·van·tage** [əd'vɑ:ntɪdʒ] N (*gen, Tennis*) vantaggio; **she has the advantage of youth** ha il vantaggio di essere giovane; **the plan has many advantages** il progetto presenta molti vantaggi; **it's to our advantage** è nel nostro interesse, torna a nostro vantaggio; **to have an advantage over sb** avere un vantaggio su qn; **to take advantage of** (*opportunity*) approfittare di, sfruttare; **to take advantage of sb** (*unfairly, sexually etc*) approfittare *or* approfittarsi di qn

ad·van·taged [əd'vɑ:ntɪdʒd] ADJ (*person, group*) privilegiato(-a)

ad·van·ta·geous [ædvən'teɪdʒəs] ADJ: **advantageous (to)** vantaggioso(-a) (per)

ad·van·ta·geous·ly [ˌædvən'teɪdʒəslɪ] ADV vantaggiosamente

Ad·vent ['ædvənt] N (*Rel*) Avvento

ad·vent ['ædvənt] N (*frm: arrival*) avvento

Advent calendar N calendario dell'Avvento

ad·ven·ti·tious [ˌævɛn'tɪʃəs] ADJ (*frm: event, situation*) fortuito(-a)

ad·ven·ture [əd'vɛntʃə^r] N avventura
■ADJ (*story, film*) di avventure

adventure playground N campo giochi attrezzato

ad·ven·tur·er [əd'vɛntʃərə^r] N avventuriero

ad·ven·tur·ess [əd'vɛntʃərɪs] N avventuriera

ad·ven·tur·ous [əd'vɛntʃərəs] ADJ avventuroso(-a)

ad·ven·tur·ous·ly [əd'vɛntʃərəslɪ] ADV avventurosamente

ad·verb ['ædvɜ:b] N avverbio

ad·ver·bial [æd'vɜ:bɪəl] ADJ avverbiale

ad·ver·bial·ly [æd'vɜ:bɪəlɪ] ADV avverbialmente

ad·ver·sa·rial [ˌædvə'sɛərɪəl] ADJ (*Brit: Law*) basato(-a) sul contraddittorio

ad·ver·sary ['ædvəsərɪ] N avversario(-a), antagonista *m/f*

ad·verse ['ædvɜ:s] ADJ (*criticism, decision, effect*) sfavorevole; (*wind*) contrario(-a); **adverse to** contrario(-a) a; **adverse weather conditions** condizioni atmosferiche avverse; **in adverse circumstances** nelle avversità

ad·verse·ly [æd'vɜ:slɪ] ADV sfavorevolmente

ad·ver·sity [əd'vɜ:sɪtɪ] N avversità *f inv*

ad·vert ['ædvɜ:t] N ABBR (*Brit fam*) = **advertisement** (*on TV*) spot *m inv* (pubblicitario), pubblicità *f inv*; (*in newspaper*) inserzione *f* pubblicitaria, pubblicità; (*: for jobs etc*) inserzione *f*, annuncio; *see also* advertisement

◎**ad·ver·tise** ['ædvətaɪz] VT (*Comm etc*) fare pubblicità *or* réclame a, reclamizzare; **to advertise a flat for sale** mettere un annuncio per vendere un appartamento; **they're advertising the new model** stanno facendo pubblicità per il nuovo modello
■VI fare (della) pubblicità *or* (della) réclame; **to advertise for** (*staff*) cercare tramite annuncio; **they're advertising for editors** cercano redattori; **to advertise on television** fare pubblicità in televisione

ad·ver·tise·ment [əd'vɜ:tɪsmənt] N (*Comm*) réclame *f inv*, pubblicità *f inv*; (*on TV*) spot *m inv*; (*in classified ads*) inserzione *f*, annuncio; **to put an advertisement in the paper** mettere un annuncio sul giornale; **an advertisement for soap** la réclame *or* la pubblicità di un sapone

DID YOU KNOW ...?
advertisement is not translated by the Italian word *avvertimento*

ad·ver·tis·er ['ædvətaɪzə^r] N azienda che reclamizza un prodotto; (*in newspaper*) inserzionista *m/f*

ad·ver·tis·ing ['ædvətaɪzɪŋ] N pubblicità (commerciale); (*advertisements collectively*) pubblicità, réclame *f inv*; **my brother's in advertising** mio fratello lavora nel settore pubblicitario

advertising agency N agenzia pubblicitaria *or* di pubblicità

advertising campaign N campagna pubblicitaria

Advertising Standards Authority N *organismo di controllo della pubblicità nel Regno Unito*

ad·ver·to·rial [ˌædvə'tɔ:rɪəl] N reportage *m inv* pubblicitario

◎**ad·vice** [əd'vaɪs] N consiglio, consigli *mpl*; **a piece of advice** un consiglio; **some advice** dei consigli; **legal advice** consulenza legale; **to ask (sb) for advice** chiedere il consiglio (di qn), chiedere un consiglio (a qn); **to take sb's advice** seguire il consiglio *or* i consigli di qn

DID YOU KNOW ...?
advice is not translated by the Italian word *avviso*

advice column N (*Am*) posta del cuore

advice columnist N (*Am*) *chi tiene la rubrica della posta del cuore*

advice line N servizio di assistenza telefonica

advice note N (*Brit Comm*) avviso di spedizione

ad·vis·able [əd'vaɪzəbl] ADJ consigliabile, raccomandabile; **I do not think it advisable for you to come** non le consiglierei di venire

◎**ad·vise** [əd'vaɪz] VT **1** (*counsel*): **to advise sb (on sth)** consigliare qn (a proposito di qc); **to advise sb to do sth** consigliare a qn di fare qc; **to advise sb against sth** sconsigliare qc a qn; **to advise against doing sth** sconsigliare a qn di fare qc; **he advises the President on foreign affairs** è il consigliere del Presidente in materia di affari esteri; **you would be well/ill advised to go** (*frm*) faresti bene/male ad andare **2** (*frm: inform*): **to advise sb of sth** avvisare qn di qc

ad·vis·ed·ly [əd'vaɪzɪdlɪ] ADV (*deliberately*) deliberatamente

◎**ad·vis·er, ad·vis·or** [əd'vaɪzə^r] N (*in politics*) consigliere(-a); (*in business*) consulente *m/f*

ad·vi·so·ry [əd'vaɪzərɪ] ADJ (*body*) consultivo(-a); **in an advisory capacity** in veste di consulente
■N (*Am*) comunicato ufficiale

ad·vo·ca·cy ['ædvəkəsɪ] N: **the advocacy of** l'appoggio a

◎**ad·vo·cate** [*n* 'ædvəkɪt; *vb* 'ædvəkeɪt] N (*Scot Law*) avvocato (difensore); (*fig*) sostenitore(-trice); **to be an advocate of** essere a favore di
■VT sostenere la validità di, propugnare

advt. ABBR = **advertisement**

AEA [ˌeɪi:'eɪ] N ABBR (*Brit:* = **Atomic Energy Authority**) ≈ ENEA *m*

AEC [ˌeɪiːˈsiː] N ABBR (*Am*: = **Atomic Energy Commission**) ≈ ENEA *m*

Aegean [iːˈdʒiːən] N: **the Aegean (Sea)** il mar *m* Egeo, l'Egeo

aegis [ˈiːdʒɪs] N (*frm*): **under the aegis of** sotto l'egida di

Aeneas [ɪˈniːəs] N Enea *m*

aeo·lian [iːˈəʊlɪən] ADJ (*Geol*) eolico(-a); **aeolian harp** arpa eolia

Aeolus [ˈiːələs] N Eolo

aeon, (*esp Am*) **eon** [ˈiːən] N eternità *f inv*

aer·ate [ˈɛəreɪt] VT (*water*) gassare; (*blood*) ossigenare; (*soil*) aerare

aera·ted [ˈɛəreɪtɪd] ADJ (*Chem*) aerato(-a); **aerated water** acqua gassata

aer·ial [ˈɛərɪəl] ADJ aereo(-a); **aerial photograph** fotografia aerea; **aerial railway** teleferica, funivia
■ N (*Brit*: *Radio, TV*) antenna

aero... [ˈɛərəʊ] PREF aero...

aero·bat·ics [ˈɛərəʊˈbætɪks] NPL (*stunts*) acrobazie *fpl* aeree

aero·bic [ɛəˈrəʊbɪk] ADJ aerobico(-a)

aero·bics [ɛəˈrəʊbɪks] NSG aerobica

aero·drome [ˈɛərəˌdrəʊm] N (*esp Brit*) aerodromo

aero·dy·nam·ic [ˈɛərəʊdaɪˈnæmɪk] ADJ aerodinamico(-a)

aero·dy·nam·ics [ˈɛərəʊdaɪˈnæmɪks] NSG aerodinamica

aero·gramme [ˈɛərəʊˌɡræm] N aerogramma *m*

aero·naut·ical [ˌɛərəˈnɔːtɪkəl] ADJ aeronautico(-a)

aero·naut·ics [ˌɛərəˈnɔːtɪks] NSG aeronautica
▷ www.nasa.gov/
▷ http://aerospace.sae.org/
▷ www.nasa.gov

aero·plane [ˈɛərəˌpleɪn] N (*esp Brit*) aeroplano

aero·sol [ˈɛərəˌsɒl] N (*can*) aerosol *m inv*

aero·space in·dus·try [ˈɛərəʊspeɪsˈɪndəstrɪ] N industria aerospaziale
▷ www.aia-aerospace.org/
▷ www.aero.org/
▷ www.aia-aerospace.org/about/about.cfm

Aeschylus [ˈiːskələs] N Eschilo

Aesop [ˈiːsɒp] N Esopo

aes·thete, (*Am*) **es·thete** [ˈiːsθiːt] N esteta *m/f*

aes·thet·ic, (*Am*) **es·thet·ic** [iːsˈθɛtɪk] ADJ estetico(-a)

aes·theti·cal·ly, (*Am*) **es·theti·cal·ly** [iːsˈθɛtɪkəlɪ] ADV esteticamente

aes·thet·ics, (*Am*) **es·thet·ics** [iːsˈθɛtɪks] NSG estetica

AEU [ˌeɪiːˈjuː] N ABBR (*Brit*: = **Amalgamated Engineering Union**) *sindacato dei metalmeccanici*

afar [əˈfɑːʳ] ADV (*old, liter*) lontano; **from afar** da lontano

AFB [ˌeɪɛfˈbiː] N ABBR (*Am*) = *Air Force Base*

AFDC [ˌeɪɛfdiːˈsiː] N ABBR (*Am*: = **Aid to Families with Dependent Children**) ≈ AF (= *assegni familiari*)

af·fabil·ity [ˌæfəˈbɪlɪtɪ] N affabilità

af·fable [ˈæfəbl] ADJ affabile

af·fably [ˈæfəblɪ] ADV affabilmente

◎ **af·fair** [əˈfɛəʳ] N **1** (*event*) faccenda, affare *m*; (*love affair*) relazione *f* (amorosa); (: *brief*) avventura; **it will be a big affair** sarà un avvenimento; **the Watergate affair** il caso Watergate; **that's my affair** sono affari *or* fatti miei; **it's a bad state of affairs** è una brutta situazione; **the government has mishandled the affair** il governo ha gestito male la faccenda; **she's having an affair with a married man** ha una relazione con un uomo sposato **2 affairs** NPL (*business*) affari; **foreign affairs** affari esteri; **affairs of state** affari di stato

◎ **af·fect** [əˈfɛkt] VT **1** (*have an effect on*) influire su, incidere su; (*concern*) riguardare, concernere; (*harm*: *health etc*) danneggiare; **it did not affect my decision** non ha influenzato la mia decisione, non ha influito sulla mia decisione; **these changes won't affect me** questi cambiamenti non avranno alcun impatto su di me; **millions have been affected by the drought** la siccità ha colpito milioni di persone **2** (*move emotionally*) colpire, toccare; **he seemed much affected** sembrava molto colpito; **the divorce affected him deeply** l'esperienza del divorzio l'ha segnato profondamente **3** (*feign*) fingere

af·fec·ta·tion [ˌæfɛkˈteɪʃən] N affettazione *f*; **affectations** NPL modi *mpl* affettati, leziosaggini *fpl*

af·fect·ed [əˈfɛktɪd] ADJ affettato(-a)

af·fect·ed·ly [əˈfɛktɪdlɪ] ADV affettatamente

af·fect·ing [əˈfɛktɪŋ] ADJ (*liter*: *scene, story*) toccante

af·fec·tion [əˈfɛkʃən] N affetto

af·fec·tion·ate [əˈfɛkʃənɪt] ADJ affettuoso(-a)

af·fec·tion·ate·ly [əˈfɛkʃənɪtlɪ] ADV affettuosamente

af·fi·da·vit [ˌæfɪˈdeɪvɪt] N (*Law*) affidavit *m inv*

af·fili·ate [əˈfɪlɪeɪt] VT: **to affiliate to/with** associare a; **to affiliate o.s. to** associarsi a
■ N affiliata

af·fili·ated [əˈfɪlɪeɪtɪd] ADJ: **affiliated (to** *or* **with)** affiliato(-a) (a), associato(-a) (a); **affiliated company** filiale *f*

af·filia·tion [əˌfɪlɪˈeɪʃən] N affiliazione *f*; **to have affiliations with** essere affiliato(-a) a

af·fine [ˈæfaɪn] ADJ (*Math*) affine

af·fin·ity [əˈfɪnɪtɪ] N (*relationship*) affinità *f inv*; (*liking*) simpatia

affinity card N *carta di credito che prevede il versamento di una percentuale dei pagamenti a una certa istituzione*

af·firm [əˈfɜːm] VT affermare, asserire

af·fir·ma·tion [æfəˈmeɪʃən] N affermazione *f*, asserzione *f*

af·firma·tive [əˈfɜːmətɪv] ADJ affermativo(-a)
■ N: **to answer in the affirmative** rispondere affermativamente *or* di sì

af·firma·tive·ly [əˈfɜːmətɪvlɪ] ADV affermativamente

af·fix[1] [əˈfɪks] VT (*signature etc*) apporre; (*stamp*) attaccare

af·fix[2] [ˈæfɪks] N (*Gram*) affisso

af·flict [əˈflɪkt] VT affliggere

af·flic·tion [əˈflɪkʃən] N (*suffering*) afflizione *f*, sofferenza; (*bodily*) infermità *f inv*

af·flu·ence [ˈæfluəns] N (*wealth*) ricchezza; (*plenty*) abbondanza

> DID YOU KNOW ...?
> **affluence** is not translated by the Italian word ***affluenza***

af·flu·ent [ˈæfluənt] ADJ ricco(-a); **the affluent society** la società del benessere

◎ **af·ford** [əˈfɔːd] VT **1 to afford sth/to do sth** permettersi qc/di fare qc; **can we afford a car?** possiamo permetterci un'automobile?; **I can't afford the time** non ho proprio il tempo, non ho veramente tempo; **I can't afford not to do it** non mi posso permettere di non farlo; **an opportunity you cannot afford to miss** un'occasione che non puoi lasciarti sfuggire **2** (*frm*: *provide*: *opportunity*) offrire, fornire

af·ford·able [əˈfɔːdəbl] ADJ (che ha un prezzo) abbordabile

Aa

af·for·esta·tion [æˌfɒrɪsˈteɪʃən] N imboschimento

af·fray [əˈfreɪ] N (*Law*) rissa

af·front [əˈfrʌnt] N affronto
■ VT fare un affronto a; **to be affronted (by)** offendersi (per)

Af·ghan [ˈæfgæn] N (*person*) afgano(-a); (*language*) afgano; (*dog*: *also*: **Afghan hound**) levriero afgano
■ ADJ afgano(-a)

Af·ghani·stan [æfˈgænɪˌstɑːn] N l'Afganistan *m*

afield [əˈfiːld] ADV: **far afield** lontano, distante

AFL-CIO [ˌeɪɛfˈɛlˌsiːaɪˈəʊ] N ABBR (= **American Federation of Labor and Congress of Industrial Organizations**) *confederazione sindacale*

afloat [əˈfləʊt] ADV, ADJ a galla; **to keep afloat** (*also fig*) rimanere a galla

afoot [əˈfʊt] ADJ, ADV in preparazione, in corso; **there's trouble afoot** ci sono guai in vista; **there is something afoot** si sta preparando qualcosa

afore·men·tioned [əˌfɔːˈmɛnʃənd], **afore·said** [əˈfɔːsɛd] ADJ (*Law*) suddetto(-a), summenzionato(-a)

◎ **afraid** [əˈfreɪd] ADJ impaurito(-a); **to be afraid** aver paura; **to be afraid for sb** temere per qn, preoccuparsi per qn; **to be afraid of sb/sth** aver paura di qn/qc; **I was afraid to ask** avevo paura di *or* non osavo domandare; **I'm afraid of hurting her** temo di *or* ho paura di farle male; **I'm afraid he's out** (*regret*) mi rincresce *or* dispiace, ma è fuori; **I'm afraid I have to go now** mi dispiace, ma adesso devo proprio andare; **I'm afraid so!** ho paura di sì !, temo proprio di sì !; **I'm afraid not** no, mi dispiace, purtroppo no, temo di no; **I am afraid that I'll be late** mi dispiace, ma farò tardi

afresh [əˈfrɛʃ] ADV da capo, di nuovo; **to start afresh** ricominciare (tutto) da capo

Af·ri·ca [ˈæfrɪkə] N Africa

Af·ri·can [ˈæfrɪkən] ADJ, N africano(-a)

African-American [ˌæfrɪkənəˈmɛrɪkən] ADJ, N afroamericano(-a)

African-Caribbean [ˌæfrɪkənkærɪˈbiːən] ADJ, N afrocaraibico(-a)

Af·ri·kaans [ˌæfrɪˈkɑːnz] N afrikaans *m*

Af·ri·kan·er [ˌæfrɪˈkɑːnə^r] N africander *m/f inv*

Afro [ˈæfrəʊ] N (*fam*) pettinatura *f* afro *inv*

Afro-American [ˈæfrəʊəˈmɛrɪkən] ADJ, N afroamericano(-a)

Afro-Caribbean [ˌæfrəʊkærɪˈbiːən] ADJ, N afrocaraibico(-a)

AFT [ˌeɪɛfˈtiː] N ABBR (= **American Federation of Teachers**) *sindacato degli insegnanti*

aft [ɑːft] ADV (*Naut*) a *or* verso poppa; **to go aft** andare a poppa

◎ **af·ter** [ˈɑːftə^r] ADV (*afterwards*) dopo; **the day after** il giorno dopo *or* seguente
■ PREP **1** (*time, order, place*) dopo; **day after day** giorno dopo giorno; **for kilometre after kilometre** per chilometri e chilometri; **you tell me lie after lie** mi stai dicendo una bugia dopo l'altra; **time after time** tantissime volte; **after dinner** dopo cena; **the day after tomorrow** dopodomani; **soon after eating it** poco dopo averlo mangiato; **after all** dopotutto, malgrado tutto; **half after two** (*Am*) le due e mezzo; **one after the other** uno(-a) dopo l'altro(-a); **shut the door after you** chiudi la porta dietro di te; **after you!** prima lei!, dopo di lei! **2** (*in pursuit*) dietro; **he ran after me** mi è corso dietro, mi ha rincorso; **the police are after him** è ricercato dalla polizia; **what/who are you after?** (*fam*) (che) cosa/chi cerca?
■ CONJ dopo che; **after he had eaten he went out** dopo aver mangiato *or* che ebbe mangiato uscì
■ ADJ (*Naut*) poppiero(-a)

after·birth [ˈɑːftəˌbɜːθ] N placenta (e membrane fetali)

after·care [ˈɑːftəˌkɛə^r] N (*Brit*: *of patients*) assistenza medica post-degenza; (: *of prisoners*) servizio di assistenza per ex-detenuti

after-dinner [ˈaːftəˌdɪnə^r] ADJ: **after-dinner drink** digestivo; **after-dinner speaker** *oratore che viene invitato a parlare alla fine di un pranzo o ricevimento*

after-effect [ˈɑːftərɪfekt] N (*of events*) ripercussione *f*, conseguenza; (*of drug*) reazione *f*; (*of illness, experience*) postumi *mpl*

after·life [ˈɑːftəˌlaɪf] N vita dell'al di là

after·market [ˈɑːftəˌmɑːkɪt] N **1** (*for cars*) mercato dei ricambi **2** (*Stock Market*: *for shares and bonds*) mercato secondario

after·math [ˈɑːftəˌmæθ] N conseguenze *fpl*, strascichi *mpl*; **in the aftermath of** nel periodo dopo

◎ **after·noon** [ˈɑːftəˈnuːn] N pomeriggio; **in the afternoon** nel *or* di pomeriggio; **at 3 o'clock in the afternoon** alle 3 del pomeriggio; **good afternoon!** buon giorno!

afternoon performance N matinée *f inv*

afternoon tea N tè *m inv*

af·ters [ˈɑːftəz] N (*Brit fam*: *dessert*) dessert *m inv*; **what's for afters?** cosa c'è per dessert?

after-sales service [ˌɑːftəˈseɪlzˌsɜːvɪs] N servizio assistenza clienti

after-shave (lotion) [ˈɑːftəʃeɪv(ˌləʊʃən)] N (lozione *f*) dopobarba *m inv*

after·shock [ˈɑːftəʃɒk] N scossa di assestamento

after·taste [ˈɑːftəˌteɪst] N retrogusto

after·thought [ˈɑːftəˌθɔːt] N ripensamento; **it was very much an afterthought** è stata una cosa completamente improvvisata; **we added it as an afterthought** l'abbiamo aggiunto solo più tardi

◎ **after·wards** [ˈɑːftəwədz] ADV dopo, più tardi, in seguito; **soon afterwards** poco dopo

after·word [ˈɑːftəwɜːd] N nota conclusiva

Aga® [ˈɑːgə] N *grosso fornello con scaldaacqua, usato anche per riscaldare la casa*

◎ **again** [əˈgɛn] ADV ancora, di nuovo, un'altra volta; **to begin/see again** ricominciare/rivedere; **he opened it again** l'ha aperto di nuovo, l'ha riaperto; **they're friends again** sono di nuovo amici; **come again soon!** torna presto!; **again and again** ripetutamente, tante volte; **I've told him again and again** gliel'ho detto e ripetuto; **never again!** mai più!; **not ...again** non... più; **I won't go there again** lì non ci torno più; **now and again** di tanto in tanto, a volte; **as much again** due volte tanto; **then again** (*on the other hand*) d'altra parte; (*moreover*) inoltre

◎ **against** [əˈgɛnst] PREP **1** (*in contact with*) a, contro; **I was leaning against the desk** ero appoggiato alla scrivania; **he leaned the ladder against the wall** appoggiò la scala al *or* contro il muro **2** (*in opposition to*) contro; **I'm against nuclear testing** sono contro gli esperimenti nucleari; **he was against going** era contrario ad andare; **what have you got against me?** cos'hai contro di me?; **it's against the law** è contrario alla *or* contro la legge; **to run against sb** (*Pol*) contrapporre la propria candidatura a quella di qn **3** (*in contrast to*): **against the light** controluce; **against a blue background** su uno sfondo azzurro **4** (*Brit*: *in comparisons*): **(as) against** in confronto a, contro

Agamemnon [ˈægəˈmɛmnɒn] N Agamennone *m*

agape [ə'geɪp] ADJ (*person: surprised*) a bocca aperta; (*mouth*) spalancato(-a)

agar ['eɪgəʳ], **agar-agar** [ˌeɪgər'eɪgəʳ] N agar-agar *m inv*

◎ **age** [eɪdʒ] N **1** età *f inv*; (*of thing*) anni *mpl*; **old age** vecchiaia; **what's his age?** *or* **what age is he?** quanti anni ha?; **when I was your age** quando avevo la tua età; **he doesn't look his age** non dimostra la sua età *or* i suoi anni; **at the age of** all'età di; **to come of age** diventare maggiorenne, raggiungere la maggiore età **2** (*period*) epoca, era; **the Iron Age** l'età del ferro **3** (*fam: long time*): **we waited (for) ages** abbiamo aspettato per ore; **it's an age** *or* **ages since I saw him** sono secoli che non lo vedo
■ VT fare invecchiare, invecchiare
■ VI invecchiare

◎ **aged** ['eɪdʒɪd; *sense b* eɪdʒd] ADJ **1** (*old*) anziano(-a), attempato(-a) **2** dell'età di; **a boy aged 10** un ragazzo di 10 anni
■ NPL: **the aged** (*elderly*) gli anziani, i vecchi

age group N fascia d'età; **the 40 to 50 age group** le persone fra i 40 e i 50 anni

age·ing ['eɪdʒɪŋ] ADJ che diventa vecchio(-a); **an ageing film star** una diva stagionata

age·less ['eɪdʒlɪs] ADJ (*eternal*) eterno(-a); (*always young*) senza età

age limit N limite *m* di età

◎ **agen·cy** ['eɪdʒənsɪ] N **1** (*office*) agenzia; (*distributorship*) rappresentanza **2** (*instrumentality*): **through** *or* **by the agency of** grazie a, per mezzo *or* per opera di

◎ **agen·da** [ə'dʒɛndə] N ordine *m* del giorno, agenda; **on the agenda** all'ordine del giorno

◎ **agent** ['eɪdʒənt] N **1** (*Comm, Police, Theatre etc*) agente *m/f*; (*representative*) rappresentante *m/f*; **to be sole agent for** avere la rappresentanza esclusiva per; **agent's commission** provvigione *f*; **he is not a free agent** (*fig*) non è padrone di fare quel che vuole; **an estate agent** un agente immobiliare; **a travel agent** un agente di viaggio **2** (*Chem*) agente *m*

agent pro·vo·ca·teur [aʒɑ̃ prɔvɔkatœr] N agente *m* provocatore

age of consent N *see* **consent**

age-old ['eɪdʒˌəʊld] ADJ secolare

ag·glom·er·ate [ə'glɒmərɪt] N (*Geol*) agglomerato

ag·glom·era·tion [əglɒmə'reɪʃən] N agglomerazione *f*

ag·gran·dize·ment, ag·gran·dise·ment [ə'grændɪzmənt] N: **for aggrandizement** per aumentare il proprio prestigio

ag·gra·vate ['ægrəveɪt] VT aggravare, peggiorare; (*annoy*) esasperare, irritare

ag·gra·vat·ed ['ægrəveɪtɪd] ADJ **1** (*Law*): **aggravated assault** aggressione aggravata; **aggravated burglary** furto aggravato; **aggravated robbery** rapina aggravata; **aggravated murder** omicidio aggravato **2** (*annoyed: person*) esasperato

ag·gra·vat·ing ['ægrəveɪtɪŋ] ADJ esasperante, irritante

ag·gra·va·tion [ægrə'veɪʃən] N (*of situation etc*) aggravamento, peggioramento; (*annoyance*) esasperazione *f*, irritazione *f*

ag·gre·gate ['ægrɪgɪt] N **1** (*total*) insieme *m*; **in the aggregate** nel complesso; **on aggregate** (*Sport*) con punteggio complessivo **2** (*Geol*) aggregato; (*Constr*) materiali *mpl* inerti
■ ADJ complessivo(-a)

ag·gres·sion [ə'grɛʃən] N aggressione *f*; (*aggressiveness*) aggressività

◎ **ag·gres·sive** [ə'grɛsɪv] ADJ aggressivo(-a); (*salesman, approach etc*) intraprendente

ag·gres·sive·ly [ə'grɛsɪvlɪ] ADV aggressivamente

ag·gres·sive·ness [ə'grɛsɪvnɪs] N aggressività

ag·gres·sor [ə'grɛsəʳ] N aggressore/aggreditrice

ag·grieved [ə'gri:vd] ADJ: **aggrieved (at, by)** offeso(-a) (da), addolorato(-a) (da)

ag·gro ['ægrəʊ] N ABBR (*Brit fam: aggression*) aggressività; (*: problems*) grane *fpl*

aghast [ə'gɑ:st] ADJ: **aghast (at)** (*shocked*) sbigottito(-a) (a); (*terrified*) inorridito(-a) (a), atterrito(-a) (a); **to be aghast at the idea of doing sth** essere atterrito(-a) all'idea di fare qc

ag·ile ['ædʒaɪl] ADJ agile, svelto(-a)

agil·ity [ə'dʒɪlɪtɪ] N agilità *f inv*

agin [ə'gɪn] PREP (*esp Scot*): **to be agin sth** essere contro qc

agi·tate ['ædʒɪteɪt] VT (*perturb*) turbare, mettere in (uno stato di) agitazione; (*shake*) agitare
■ VI (*Pol*): **to agitate (for/against)** fare un'agitazione (per/contro)

agi·tat·ed ['ædʒɪteɪtɪd] ADJ agitato(-a), inquieto(-a)

agi·ta·tion [ˌædʒɪ'teɪʃən] N agitazione *f*

agi·ta·tor ['ædʒɪteɪtəʳ] N (*Pol: usu pej*) agitatore(-trice)

aglow [ə'gləʊ] ADJ (*liter: sky, mountains*) splendente; (*: fig: person*) raggiante

AGM [ˌeidʒi:'ɛm] N ABBR = **annual general meeting**

ag·nos·tic [æg'nɒstɪk] ADJ, N agnostico(-a)

ag·nos·ti·cism [æg'nɒstɪsɪzəm] N agnosticismo

◎ **ago** [ə'gəʊ] ADV: **a week ago** una settimana fa; **long ago** molto tempo fa; **not long ago** poco tempo fa; **as long ago as 1960** già nel 1960; **how long ago?** quanto tempo fa?; **how long ago was it?** quanto tempo fa è successo?, da quanto tempo è successo?

agog [ə'gɒg] ADJ: **(all) agog (to hear sth)** ansioso(-a) *or* impaziente (di sentire qc); **agog with excitement** emozionato(-a), eccitato(-a)

ago·nize ['ægənaɪz] VI: **to agonize (over)** angosciarsi (per)

ago·nized ['ægəˌnaɪzd] ADJ (*moan, indecision*) angoscioso(-a)

ago·niz·ing ['ægənaɪzɪŋ] ADJ (*cry, decision*) penoso(-a), angoscioso(-a); (*pain, death*) straziante

ago·ny ['ægənɪ] N (*pain*) dolore *m* atroce; (*: mental*) angoscia, tormento; **I was in agony** avevo dei dolori atroci; **it was agony!** è stata una tortura!, soffrivo atrocemente; **to suffer agonies of doubt** avere dei dubbi atroci

> DID YOU KNOW ...?
> **agony** is not translated by the Italian word *agonia*

agony aunt N (*Brit*) *chi tiene la rubrica della posta del cuore*

agony column N posta del cuore

ago·ra·pho·bia [ˌægərə'fəʊbɪə] N (*Psych*) agorafobia

ago·ra·pho·bic [ˌægərə'fəʊbɪk] N (*Psych*) agorafobo(-a)

agrar·ian [ə'grɛərɪən] ADJ agrario(-a)

◎ **agree** [ə'gri:] VI **1** (*be in agreement*): **to agree (with sb/sth)** essere *or* trovarsi d'accordo (con qn/qc); **to agree on/about sth** essere d'accordo su/riguardo a qc; **I quite agree** sono perfettamente d'accordo; **don't you agree?** non sei d'accordo? **2** (*come to terms*): **to agree (on sth)** mettersi d'accordo (su qc), accordarsi (su qc) **3** (*consent*): **to agree to sth** accettare qc, acconsentire a qc **4** (*be in harmony: things*) andare d'accordo, concordare; (*: persons: get on together*) andare d'accordo; (*Gram*) concordare **5** (*food*): **garlic doesn't agree with me** non riesco a digerire l'aglio, l'aglio mi rimane sullo stomaco

Aa

■VT **1** (*come to agreement*): **to agree (that)** essere d'accordo (sul fatto che); (*admit*) ammettere (che); **I agree that it's difficult** ammetto che è difficile; **it was agreed that ...** è stato deciso (di comune accordo) che...; **are we all agreed?** siamo tutti d'accordo?; **is that agreed?** (siamo) d'accordo?; **to agree to differ** rimanere ognuno della propria idea; **to agree a price** pattuire un prezzo **2** (*consent*): **to agree to do sth** accettare di fare qc, acconsentire a fare qc; **he agreed to go and pick her up** ha accettato di andare a prenderla

agree·able [ə'griːəbl] ADJ (*pleasing*) piacevole, gradevole; (*willing*) disposto(-a); **to be agreeable to sth/to doing sth** essere ben disposto(-a) a qc/a fare qc; **if you are agreeable** se sei d'accordo; **are you agreeable to this?** è d'accordo con questo?

agree·ably [ə'griːəblɪ] ADV piacevolmente

agreed [ə'griːd] ADJ (*time, place*) stabilito(-a); **at the agreed time** all'ora stabilita

◎ **agree·ment** [ə'griːmənt] N (*gen*) accordo; (*consent*) consenso; **by mutual agreement** di comune accordo; **to come to an agreement** venire a un accordo, accordarsi; **in agreement** d'accordo; **to be in agreement with sb** essere *or* trovarsi d'accordo con qn

◎ **ag·ri·cul·tur·al** [ˌægrɪ'kʌltʃərəl] ADJ (*gen*) agricolo(-a); (*college, studies*) agrario(-a); **agricultural expert** agronomo(-a)

ag·ri·cul·tur·al·ist [ˌægrɪ'kʌltʃərəlɪst], **ag·ri·cul·tur·ist** [ˌægrɪ'kʌltʃərɪst] N (*agricultural scientist*) agronomo(-a)

◎ **ag·ri·cul·ture** ['ægrɪkʌltʃəʳ] N agricoltura; **commercial agriculture** agricoltura di mercato

▷ www.agnic.org
▷ www.fao.org/ag/

aground [ə'graʊnd] ADV (*Naut*) in secca; **to run aground** arenarsi, incagliarsi

◎ **ah** [ɑː] EXCL ah

◎ **ahead** [ə'hɛd] ADV **1** (*in space*) avanti, davanti; **she looked straight ahead** guardava dritto davanti a sé; **ahead of** davanti a; **they were (right) ahead of us** erano (proprio) davanti a noi; **to go ahead** andare avanti; **go ahead!** avanti!; (*fig*) fai pure!, prego!; **to get ahead of sb** superare qn; **go right** *or* **straight ahead!** vada diritto!; **to be ahead** (*in competition*) essere in vantaggio; **Italy is five points ahead** l'Italia è in vantaggio di cinque punti **2** (*in time: book, plan*) in anticipo; **ahead of time** in anticipo; **Italy is one hour ahead of Britain at the moment** attualmente l'Italia è un'ora avanti *or* avanti di un'ora rispetto all'Inghilterra; **he finished half an hour ahead of the others** ha finito con mezz'ora di anticipo sugli *or* rispetto agli altri, ha finito mezz'ora prima degli altri; **to look ahead** (*fig*) guardare avanti, pensare all'avvenire; **to plan ahead** pianificare; **to be ahead of one's time** precorrere i propri tempi

ahoy [ə'hɔɪ] EXCL ehi!; **ship ahoy!** ehi della nave!

AI [ˌeɪ'aɪ] N ABBR **1** = **Amnesty International** **2** (*Comput*) = **artificial intelligence** **3** = **artificial insemination**

AID [ˌeɪaɪ'diː] N ABBR **1** (= **artificial insemination by donor**) inseminazione *f* artificiale eterologa **2** (*Am*: = **Agency for International Development**) AID *f*

◎ **aid** [eɪd] N aiuto, assistenza; **economic aid** aiuti *mpl* economici, assistenza economica; **humanitarian aid** aiuti umanitari; **with the aid of** con l'aiuto di; **in aid of** a favore di; **in aid of charity** a scopo di beneficenza; **what's all this in aid of?** (*fam*) a cosa serve tutto questo?; **to come to the aid of** venire in aiuto a

■VT (*person*) aiutare; (*progress, recovery*) contribuire a; **to aid sb to do sth** aiutare qn a fare qc; **to aid and abet sb** (*Law*) essere complice di qn

aide [eɪd] N (*person*) aiutante *m/f*; (*Mil*) aiutante *m* di campo, addetto (militare); (*Pol*) consigliere(-a), addetto(-a)

aide-de-camp [ˌeɪddə'kɒŋ] N (*Mil*) aiutante *m* di campo

◎ **AIDS** [eɪdz] N ABBR (= **acquired immune deficiency syndrome**) AIDS *m or f*

AIH [ˌeɪaɪ'eɪtʃ] N ABBR (= **artificial insemination by husband**) inseminazione *f* artificiale omologa

ail [eɪl] VI (*old*) essere sofferente

ailer·on ['eɪlərɒn] N (*Aer*) alettone *m*

ail·ing ['eɪlɪŋ] ADJ infermo(-a), sofferente; (*fig: economy, industry etc*) in difficoltà

ail·ment ['eɪlmənt] N malanno

> DID YOU KNOW ...?
> **ailment** is not translated by the Italian word *alimento*

◎ **aim** [eɪm] N (*of weapon*) mira; (*fig: purpose, object*) scopo; proposito; **his aim is bad** non ha una buona mira; **to take aim** prendere la mira; **to take aim at sth/sb** mirare a qc/qn; **to have no aim in life** non avere un preciso scopo nella vita

■VT: **to aim (at)** (*gun*) puntare (su *or* contro); (*missile*) lanciare (contro); (*blow etc*) tirare (a); (*remark, criticism*) rivolgere (a); (*camera*) dirigere (verso); **he aimed the gun at me** mi ha puntato contro la pistola; **to aim to do sth** aspirare a fare qc; (*less formal*) avere l'intenzione di fare qc

■VI (*also:* **to take aim**) prendere la mira, mirare; **to aim at sth** (*also fig*) mirare a qc; **it's aimed at a young audience** è diretto ad un pubblico giovane; **to aim for the goal** (*Ftbl*) tirare in porta

aim·less ['eɪmlɪs] ADJ senza scopo

aim·less·ly ['eɪmlɪslɪ] ADV senza scopo

ain't [eɪnt] ABBR (*fam!: incorrect use*) = **am not, is not, are not, has not, have not**

◎ **air** [ɛəʳ] N **1** aria; **in the open air** all'aria aperta, all'aperto; **by air** (*travel*) in aereo; (*Post*) per via *or* posta aerea; **to get some fresh air** andare a prendere una boccata d'aria (fresca); **to clear the air** (*fig*) chiarire la situazione; **there's something in the air** (*fig*) c'è qualcosa nell'aria; **our plans are up in the air** (*fig*) i nostri progetti non sono ancora ben definiti **2** (*Radio, TV*): **to be on the air** (*programme*) essere in onda; (*station*) trasmettere; (*person*) parlare alla radio (*or* alla televisione); **we're now going off the air** la trasmissione si conclude qui **3** (*appearance*) aria, aspetto; **with a guilty air** con aria colpevole; **she had an air of mystery about her** aveva una certa aria di mistero; **to give o.s. airs** darsi delle arie

■VT (*room, bed*) arieggiare; (*clothes*) far prendere aria a; (*idea, grievance*) esprimere pubblicamente, manifestare; (*views*) far conoscere

■ADJ (*current, bubble*) d'aria; (*pressure*) atmosferico(-a); (*Mil: base, attack etc*) aereo(-a)

air ambulance N eliambulanza; (*service*) elisoccorso

air bag N airbag *m inv*

air base N base *f* aerea

air bed N (*Brit*) materassino gonfiabile

air·borne ['ɛəˌbɔːn] ADJ (*troops*) aerotrasportato(-a), aviotrasportato(-a); (*plane*) in volo; **as soon as the plane was airborne** appena l'aereo ebbe decollato; **suddenly we were airborne** in un attimo avevamo già preso quota

air brake N (*Aut*) freno pneumatico
air·bus ['ɛə,bʌs] N aerobus *m inv*, airbus *m inv*
air cargo N carico trasportato per via aerea
air cleaner N (*Aut*) filtro dell'aria
air-con ['ɛəkɒn] N (*fam*: = **air conditioning**) condizionamento d'aria; **a car with air-con** una macchina con climatizzatore
air-conditioned ['ɛəkən,dɪʃnd] ADJ con *or* ad aria condizionata
air-conditioner ['ɛə,kən'dɪʃənəʳ] N climatizzatore *m*, condizionatore *m* (d'aria)
air conditioning N aria condizionata, condizionamento d'aria
air-cooled ['ɛə,ku:ld] ADJ raffreddato(-a) ad aria
air corridor N corridoio aereo
◎**air·craft** ['ɛə,krɑ:ft] N INV aeromobile *m*, apparecchio, velivolo; **there were two aircraft on the runway** c'erano due aerei sulla pista
▷ www.aerospaceweb.org/aircraft/index.shtml
▷ www.airliners.net/info/
aircraft carrier N portaerei *f inv*
air·crew ['ɛə,kru:] N equipaggio (*di un aereo*)
air cushion N cuscino gonfiabile; (*Tech*) cuscino d'aria
air·drome ['ɛə,drəʊm] N (*Am*) = **aerodrome**
air·field ['ɛə,fi:ld] N campo d'aviazione
air·flow ['ɛəfləʊ] N flusso d'aria
◎**air force** N aviazione *f* militare
air freight N (*mode of transport*) spedizione *f* merci per via aerea; (*goods*) carico spedito per via aerea
■ ADV (*send*) per via aerea
air guitar N chitarra immaginaria (*che si finge di suonare ascoltando musica*)
air·gun ['ɛə,gʌn] N pistola ad aria compressa
air·head ['ɛəhɛd] N (*fam*) testa vuota
air hostess N hostess *f inv*
airi·ly ['ɛərɪlɪ] ADV con disinvoltura
air·ing ['ɛərɪŋ] N: **to give an airing to** (*linen*) arieggiare, far prendere aria a; (*room*) arieggiare; (*fig*: *ideas etc*) ventilare
airing cupboard N *armadio riscaldato per asciugare panni*
air lane N corridoio aereo
air·less ['ɛəlɪs] ADJ (*room*) senz'aria; (*day*) senza un filo di vento
air letter N aerogramma *m*
air·lift ['ɛə,lɪft] N ponte *m* aereo
◎**air·line** ['ɛə,laɪn] N linea *or* compagnia aerea, aviolinea
▷ http://routesinternational.com/air.htm
▷ www.airliners.net/info
▷ http://airlines.afriqonline.com/airlines/index.html
air·lin·er [ɛə'laɪnəʳ] N aereo di linea
air·lock ['ɛə,lɒk] N (*in pipe*) bolla d'aria; (*in spacecraft etc*) camera d'equilibrio
air·mail ['ɛə,meɪl] N posta aerea; **by airmail** per via *or* posta aerea
air·man ['ɛəmən] N (*pl* **-men**) aviere *m*
air marshal N agente *m/f* armato a bordo (*di aereo*)
air mattress N materassino gonfiabile
Air Miles ® NPL (*Brit*) miglia *fpl* (*punti da collezionare per l'acquisto di biglietti aerei*)
air navigation N navigazione *f* aerea
air·plane ['ɛə,pleɪn] N (*Am*) aeroplano
air pocket N vuoto d'aria
◎**air·port** ['ɛə,pɔ:t] N aeroporto
■ ADJ (*staff*) aeroportuale; (*manager, security etc*) dell'aeroporto
▷ http://routesinternational.com/airports.htm
▷ www.internationalairportguide.com
airport tax N tassa aeroportuale
air pump N pompa per l'aria
air rage N *comportamento aggressivo dei passeggeri di un aereo*
air raid N incursione *f* aerea
air rifle N fucile *m* ad aria compressa
air-sea rescue [,ɛəsi:'rɛskju:] N salvataggio aereo in mare
air·ship ['ɛəʃɪp] N dirigibile *m*, aeronave *f*
▷ http://spot.colorado.edu/~dziadeck/airship.html
air show N (*trade exhibition*) salone *m* dell'aviazione; (*flying display*) manifestazione *f* aerea
air·sick ['ɛə,sɪk] ADJ: **to be airsick** soffrire di mal d'aria *or* d'aereo
air sickness N mal *m* d'aria
air·space ['ɛə,speɪs] N spazio aereo
air·speed ['ɛə,spi:d] N velocità *f inv* di crociera (*Aer*)
air·strike ['ɛə,straɪk] N attacco aereo
air·strip ['ɛə,strɪp] N pista d'atterraggio
air·taxi ['ɛə,tæksɪ] N aereotaxi *m inv*
air terminal N air-terminal *m inv*
air·tight ['ɛə,taɪt] ADJ (*container*) a chiusura ermetica; (*seal, cap*) ermetico(-a)
air time N (*Radio*) spazio radiofonico; (*TV*) spazio televisivo
air-to-air ['ɛətʊ'ɛəʳ] ADJ (*Mil*) aria-aria *inv*
air-to-ground ['ɛətə'graʊnd], **air-to-surface** ['ɛətə'sɜ:fɪs] ADJ (*Mil*) aria-terra *inv*
air traffic control N controllo del traffico aereo
air traffic controller N controllore *m* del traffico aereo
air·waves ['ɛə,weɪvz] NPL onde *fpl* radio *inv*
air·way ['ɛə,weɪ] N **1** (*Aer*) rotta aerea **2 the airways** NPL le vie *fpl* respiratorie
air waybill N (*Comm*) bolletta di trasporto aereo
air·worthi·ness ['ɛə,wɜ:ðɪnɪs] N idoneità al volo
air·worthy ['ɛə,wɜ:ðɪ] ADJ idoneo(-a) al volo, in condizione di poter volare
airy ['ɛərɪ] ADJ (*comp* **-ier**, *superl* **-iest**) (*place*) arieggiato(-a); (*room*) arioso(-a); (*remark etc*) superficiale; (*manner*) spensierato(-a), noncurante
airy-fairy ['ɛərɪ'fɛərɪ] ADJ (*fam*) vago(-a)
aisle [aɪl] N (*of church*: *lateral*) navata laterale: *central, navata centrale*; (*of theatre, train, coach, plane*) corridoio; **an aisle seat** un posto sul corridoio; (*in supermarket*) passaggio; **it had them rolling in the aisles** li ha fatti rotolare (per terra) dalle risate
aitch [eɪtʃ] N acca; **to drop one's aitches** (*Brit*) non pronunciare l'acca (iniziale)
ajar [ə'dʒɑ:ʳ] ADV, ADJ socchiuso(-a)
Ajax ['eɪdʒæks] N Aiace *m*
AK ABBR (*Am Post*) = *Alaska*
aka [,eɪkeɪ'eɪ] ABBR (= **also known as**) alias
akim·bo [ə'kɪmbəʊ] ADV: **with arms akimbo** con le mani sui fianchi
akin [ə'kɪn] ADJ: **akin to** (*similar to*) equivalente a, simile a; (*of same family as*) imparentato(-a) a
AL ABBR (*Am Post*) = *Alabama*
Ala·bama [,ælə'bæmə] N Alabama *m*
▷ www.alabama.gov/
ala·bas·ter ['æləbɑ:stəʳ] N alabastro
à la carte [ɑ:lɑ:'kɑt] ADJ, ADV alla carta
alac·rity [ə'lækrɪtɪ] N: **with alacrity** prontamente
à la mode [ɑ:lɑ:'məʊd] ADJ di moda
■ ADV alla moda
◎**alarm** [ə'lɑ:m] N (*warning, signal*) allarme *m*; **fire alarm** allarme antincendio; **smoke alarm** rivelatore *m* di fumo; **to raise the alarm** dare l'allarme; **there's no**

Aa

need for any alarm non c'è bisogno di allarmarsi
■ VT allarmare, spaventare; **to be alarmed (at)** essere preoccupato(-a) (per) *or* allarmato(-a) (da)
alarm clock N sveglia
alarmed [ə'lɑ:md] ADJ (*person*) allarmato(-a); (*house, car etc*) dotato(-a) di allarme
alarm·ing [ə'lɑ:mɪŋ] ADJ allarmante, preoccupante
alarm·ing·ly [ə'lɑ:mɪŋlɪ] ADV in modo allarmante; **alarmingly close** pericolosamente vicino(-a)
alarm·ist [ə'lɑ:mɪst] N allarmista *m/f*
alas [ə'læs] EXCL (*frm*) ohimè!, ahimè!
Alas·ka [ə'læskə] N l'Alasca
▷ www.state.ak.us/
Al·ba·nia [æl'beɪnɪə] N l'Albania
Al·ba·nian [æl'beɪnɪən] ADJ albanese
■ N (*person*) albanese *m/f*; (*language*) albanese *m*
al·ba·tross ['ælbətrɒs] N albatro
al·be·it [ɔ:l'bi:ɪt] CONJ (*frm*) sebbene + *sub*, benché + *sub*
Al·ber·ta [æl'bɜ:tə] N (*Geog*) Alberta *m*
▷ www.gov.ab.ca
▷ www.travelalberta.com/
al·bi·no [æl'bi:nəʊ] ADJ, N albino(-a)
◎ **al·bum** ['ælbəm] N album *m inv*; (*L.P.*) 33 giri *m inv*, L.P. *m inv*; **photograph album** (*containing photos*) album di *or* delle fotografie; (*new*) album per fotografie
al·bu·men ['ælbjʊmɪn] N albume *m*
al·che·mist ['ælkɪmɪst] N alchimista *m/f*
al·che·my ['ælkɪmɪ] N alchimia
◎ **al·co·hol** ['ælkəhɒl] N alcool *m inv*; **I never touch alcohol** non bevo (mai) alcolici
alcohol-free ['ælkəhɒl'fri:] ADJ analcolico(-a)
al·co·hol·ic [,ælkə'hɒlɪk] ADJ alcolico(-a); **alcoholic drinks** bevande alcoliche
■ N alcolizzato(-a)
al·co·hol·ism ['ælkəhɒlɪzəm] N alcolismo
al·cove ['ælkəʊv] N alcova
Ald. ABBR = **alderman**
al·der ['ɔ:ldə^r] N ontano
alderman ['ɔ:ldəmən] N (*pl* **-men**) consigliere *m* comunale
ale [eɪl] N birra
◎ **alert** [ə'lɜ:t] ADJ (*acute, wide-awake*) sveglio(-a); (*watchful*) vigile; (*mind*) pronto(-a), agile, vivace; (*expression*) intelligente; **to be alert to sth** (*fact, danger*) essere consapevole di qc; **he's a very alert baby** è un bambino molto sveglio; **we must stay alert** dobbiamo stare all'erta
■ N allarme *m*; **to be on the alert** (*person*) stare all'erta; (*troops*) essere in stato di allarme
■ VT: **to alert sb (to sth)** avvisare qn (di qc), avvertire qn (di qc); **to alert sb to the dangers of sth** mettere qn in guardia contro qc
alert·ness [ə'lɜ:tnɪs] N prontezza; **mental alertness** lucidità mentale
Aleu·tian Is·lands [ə'lu:ʃən 'aɪləndz] NPL: **the Aleutian Islands** le isole *fpl* Aleutine
A level ['eɪ,levl] N (*Brit*) *diploma di studi superiori*; **I did French at A level** il francese è una delle materie che ho studiato per la maturità

A LEVELS

Gli **A levels**, esami sostenuti in due, tre o quattro materie al termine della scuola secondaria in Inghilterra, Galles e Irlanda del Nord, sono paragonabili al diploma di maturità. I corsi di preparazione durano in genere due anni e gli studenti sostengono l'esame finale a 18 anni; l'ammissione all'università di solito dipende dai risultati ottenuti negli **A levels.**
In Scozia il diploma equivalente è chiamato "Higher" o "Higher Grade". Al termine del corso di preparazione, che dura un anno, gli studenti portano all'esame da una a cinque materie. *See also* **GCSE; AS level**
▷ www.dfes.gov.uk/qualifications/mainSection.cfm?sID=43
▷ www.jcgq.org.uk/

Al·ex·an·dria [,ælɪg'zændrɪə] N Alessandria (d'Egitto)
al·fal·fa [æl'fælfə] N erba medica
al·fres·co [æl'freskəʊ] ADJ, ADV all'aperto
al·gae ['ældʒi:] NPL alghe *fpl*
al·ge·bra ['ældʒɪbrə] N algebra
al·ge·bra·ic [,ældʒɪ'breɪɪk] ADJ algebrico(-a)
Al·ge·ria [æl'dʒɪərɪə] N Algeria
◎ **Al·ge·rian** [æl'dʒɪərɪən] ADJ, N algerino(-a)
Al·giers [æl'dʒɪəz] N Algeri *fsg*
al·go·rithm ['ælgə,rɪðəm] N (*Comput*) algoritmo
ali·as ['eɪlɪəs] N falso nome *m*, pseudonimo
■ ADV alias, altrimenti detto(-a)
ali·bi ['ælɪbaɪ] N alibi *m inv*
al·ien ['eɪlɪən] ADJ (*very different*): **alien to** estraneo(-a) (a), alieno(-a) (da); (*of foreign country*) straniero(-a), forestiero(-a)
■ N (*foreigner*) straniero(-a), forestiero(-a); (*extra-terrestrial*) extraterrestre *m/f*, alieno(-a)
al·ien·ate ['eɪlɪəneɪt] VT alienare; **her behaviour has alienated her friends** il suo comportamento ha fatto allontanare gli amici
al·iena·tion [,eɪlɪə'neɪʃən] N alienazione *f*
alight[1] [ə'laɪt] ADJ: **to be alight** (*building*) essere in fiamme; (*fire*) essere acceso(-a)
alight[2] [ə'laɪt] VI (*from vehicle*): **to alight (from)** scendere (da); (*bird*): **to alight (on)** posarsi (su)
align [ə'laɪn] VT allineare; **to align o.s. with** allinearsi con, schierarsi dalla parte di
align·ment [ə'laɪnmənt] N (*Tech, Pol*) allineamento; (*Aut*: *also*: **wheel alignment**) assetto; **out of alignment (with)** non allineato(-a) (con); **a new alignment of political forces** un nuovo schieramento delle forze politiche
alike [ə'laɪk] ADJ PRED simile, uguale; **to be alike** *or* **to look alike** assomigliarsi; **the two sisters look alike** le due sorelle si assomigliano; **you're all alike!** siete tutti uguali!
■ ADV allo stesso modo; **winter and summer alike** sia d'estate che d'inverno
ali·men·ta·ry [,ælɪ'mentərɪ] ADJ alimentare
alimentary canal N tubo digerente
ali·mo·ny ['ælɪmənɪ] N (*Law*: *payment*) alimenti *mpl*
◎ **alive** [ə'laɪv] ADJ (*living*) vivo(-a), in vita, vivente; (*fig*: *lively*) vivace, sveglio(-a); (: *active*) attivo(-a); **to stay alive** sopravvivere; **he was buried alive** è stato sepolto vivo; **it's good to be alive** essere vivi è una bella cosa; **he's the best footballer alive** è il miglior calciatore vivente *or* esistente; **to keep a tradition alive** mantener viva *or* in vita una tradizione; **to come alive** (*fig*) risvegliarsi, rianimarsi; **to be alive with** (*insects etc*) brulicare *or* pullulare di; **alive to** (*danger, honour*) conscio(-a) di
al·ka·li ['ælkəlaɪ] N alcali *m inv*
al·ka·line ['ælkəlaɪn] ADJ alcalino(-a)

al·kane ['ælkeɪn] N alcano
al·kene ['ælki:n] N alcheno
al·kyne ['ælkaɪn] N alchino

◎ **all** [ɔ:l] **KEYWORD**
■ ADJ tutto(-a), tutti(-e) *pl*; **all day** tutto il giorno; **all his life** tutta la sua vita; **all men** tutti gli uomini; **it's not as hard/bad as all that** non è mica così duro/cattivo; **all the books** tutti i libri; **all the country** tutto il paese; **all the time** tutto il tempo; **we can't be together all the time** non possiamo stare assieme tutto il tempo; **for all their efforts** nonostante tutti i loro sforzi; **all three** tutti(-e) e tre; **all three books** tutti e tre i libri
■ PRON
1 tutto(-a); **he ate it all** l'ha mangiato tutto; **all is lost** tutto è perduto; **all of it** tutto(-a); **is that all?** non c'è altro?; (*in shop*) basta così ?, altro?; **that's all I can remember** è tutto ciò che ricordo; **if that's all then it's not important** se è tutto lì allora non ha importanza
2 (*plural*) tutti(-e); **all of the girls** tutte le ragazze; **all of them** tutti(-e) (loro); **all of us went** ci siamo andati tutti; **we all sat down** ci sedemmo tutti quanti, noi tutti ci sedemmo
3 (*in phrases*): **above all** soprattutto, più di tutto; **after all** dopotutto; **not at all** (*in answer to question*) niente affatto, per niente; (*in response to thanks*) prego!, s'immagini!, si figuri!; **I'm not at all tired** non sono affatto *or* per niente stanco; **anything at all will do** andrà bene qualsiasi cosa; **for all I know** per quel che ne so io, per quanto ne so; **all in all** tutto sommato; **50 men in all** 50 uomini in tutto; **most of all** (*more than anybody*) più di chiunque altro, soprattutto; (*more than anything*) più di qualsiasi altra cosa, soprattutto
■ ADV tutto; **all alone** tutto(-a) solo(-a); **all but** quasi; **it's all dirty** è tutto sporco; **dressed all in black** vestito(-a) tutto(-a) di nero; **to be/feel all in** (*fam*) essere/sentirsi sfinito(-a) *or* distrutto(-a); **to go all out** mettercela tutta; **she was going all out down the motorway** stava andando a tutto gas sull'autostrada; **things aren't all that good/bad** le cose non vanno poi così bene/male; **the score is two all** il punteggio è di due a due; **all wrong** tutto sbagliato(-a); *see also* **over, right, alone**

Allah ['ælə] N Allah *m*
al·lay [ə'leɪ] VT (*frm: fears*) dissipare
all clear N (*Mil*) cessato allarme *m inv*; (*fig*) okay *m*
all-comers [ɔ:l'kʌməʳs] N tutti(-e); **the competition is open to all-comers** la gara è aperta a tutti
all-day ['ɔ:l'deɪ] ADJ che dura tutto il giorno
◎ **al·le·ga·tion** [ˌælɪ'geɪʃən] N accusa, asserzione *f*
al·lege [ə'lɛdʒ] VT asserire, dichiarare; **he is alleged to have said ...** avrebbe detto che...
◎ **al·leged** [ə'lɛdʒd] ADJ presunto(-a); **the alleged crime** il presunto delitto
al·leg·ed·ly [ə'lɛdʒɪdlɪ] ADV da quel che si dice, secondo quanto si asserisce
al·le·giance [ə'li:dʒəns] N fedeltà, lealtà; **to swear allegiance to** fare giuramento di fedeltà a
al·le·gor·ical [ˌælɪ'gɒrɪkəl], **al·le·gor·ic** [ˌælɪ'gɒrɪk] ADJ allegorico(-a)
al·le·gori·cal·ly [ˌælɪ'gɒrɪklɪ] ADV allegoricamente
al·le·go·ry ['ælɪgərɪ] N allegoria

all-embracing [ˌɔ:lɪm'breɪsɪŋ] ADJ che abbraccia tutto, universale
al·ler·gic [ə'lɜ:dʒɪk] ADJ: **allergic to** allergico(-a) a
al·ler·gy ['ælədʒɪ] N allergia
al·le·vi·ate [ə'li:vɪeɪt] VT alleviare
al·le·via·tion [əli:vɪ'eɪʃən] N alleviamento
al·ley ['ælɪ] N (*between buildings*) vicolo; (*in garden, park*) vialetto; (*Am Tennis*) corridoio; **blind alley** vicolo cieco
alley·way ['ælɪˌweɪ] N vicolo
◎ **al·li·ance** [ə'laɪəns] N (*Pol*) alleanza
◎ **allied** ['ælaɪd] ADJ alleato(-a)
al·li·ga·tor ['ælɪgeɪtəʳ] N alligatore *m*
all-important [ˌɔ:lɪm'pɔ:tənt] ADJ cruciale, fondamentale, importantissimo(-a)
all-in [ˌɔ:l'ɪn] ADJ, ADV (*Brit: price, charge*) tutto compreso *inv*; **I'll let you have them at an all-in price** te li farò avere ad un prezzo forfettario
all-in wrestling N lotta americana
al·lit·era·tion [əˌlɪtə'reɪʃən] N allitterazione *f*
all-night [ˌɔ:l'naɪt] ADJ (*café, garage*) aperto(-a) tutta la notte; (*vigil, party*) che dura (*or* è durato(-a) *etc*) tutta la notte
al·lo·cate ['æləʊkeɪt] VT (*allot*): **to allocate (to)** (*duties, sum, time*) assegnare (a); (: *in budget: money*) stanziare (per); (*distribute*): **to allocate (among)** ripartire (fra), distribuire (fra)
al·lo·ca·tion [æləʊ'keɪʃən] N (*see vb*) assegnazione *f*, stanziamento; distribuzione *f*; **allocation of overheads** imputazione *f* delle spese generali
al·lot [ə'lɒt] VT 1 (*assign: task, share, time*): **to allot (to)** dare (a), assegnare (a) 2 (*share among group*) spartire (tra); **in the allotted time** nel tempo fissato *or* prestabilito
al·lot·ment [ə'lɒtmənt] N (*Brit: land*) piccolo lotto di terreno (*dato in affitto per coltivazioni ad uso familiare*); (*share*) spartizione *f*
al·lo·trope ['æləˌtrəʊp] N allotropo
all-out [ˌɔ:l'aʊt] ADJ (*attack*) con tutti i mezzi a disposizione; (*effort etc*) totale; **to make an all-out effort to do sth** impegnare tutte le proprie energie per fare qc
all-over [ˌɔ:l'əʊvəʳ] ADJ (*gen*) totale; **all-over tan** abbronzatura integrale
◎ **al·low** [ə'laʊ] VT 1 (*permit*): **to allow sb to do sth** permettere a qn di fare qc, autorizzare qn a fare qc; **his mum allowed him to go out** sua madre gli ha permesso di uscire; **smoking is not allowed** è vietato fumare, non è permesso fumare; **to be allowed to do something** avere il permesso di fare qc; **he is allowed to do it** lo può fare; **he's not allowed alcohol** gli hanno proibito l'alcol; **to allow sb in/out** *etc* lasciare entrare/uscire *etc* qn; **allow me!** mi permetta!, se mi permette!, prego! 2 (*make provision for*) tener conto di, calcolare; **we must allow 3 days for the journey** dobbiamo calcolare 3 giorni per il viaggio; **allow two hours for the paint to dry** lasciate asciugare la vernice per due ore; **allow 5 cm for the hem** lasciare 5 cm in più per il bordo 3 (*grant: money, rations*) concedere, accordare; (*Law: claim, appeal*) riconoscere, ammettere; (*Sport: goal*) convalidare; **to allow that** (*frm: concede*) ammettere che
► **allow for** VI + PREP tener conto di, calcolare
al·low·able [ə'laʊəbəl] ADJ 1 (*Fin: expenses, costs*) deducibile 2 (*behaviour*) lecito(-a)
al·low·ance [ə'laʊəns] N (*payment*) assegno; (*for travelling, accommodation*) indennità *f inv*; (*ration*) razione *f*; (*Tax*) detrazione *f* d'imposta; (*discount*) riduzione *f*,

Aa

sconto; **travelling allowance** indennità di trasferta; **monthly clothing allowance** cifra mensile per il vestiario; **baggage allowance** bagaglio consentito; **family allowance** (*old: child benefit*) assegni *mpl* familiari; **to make allowance(s) for** (*person*) scusare; (*allow for: shrinkage etc*) tener conto di

al·loy ['ælɔɪ] N lega; (*fig*) ombra
■ ADJ: **alloy wheels** (*Aut*) cerchi *mpl* in lega

all-party ['ɔ:l'pɑ:tɪ] ADJ (*Pol*) di tutti i partiti

all-powerful ['ɔ:l'paʊəfʊl] ADJ onnipotente

all-purpose ['ɔ:l'pɜ:pəs] ADJ per tutti gli usi

◎ **all right** ADV (*feel, work*) bene; **all right!** va bene!; **everything turned out all right** tutto è andato bene; **to be all right** (*well, safe*) stare bene; (*satisfactory*) andare bene; **I'm all right** sto bene; **is that all right with you?** per te va bene?

all-round ['ɔ:l'raʊnd] ADJ (*athlete etc*) completo(-a), versatile; (*education*) ampio(-a), completo(-a); **an all-round improvement** un miglioramento generale

all-rounder [ˌɔ:l'raʊndə^r] N: **to be a good all-rounder** (*Brit esp Sport*) essere bravo(-a) in tutto

All Saints' Day N Ognissanti *m inv*

all-singing all-dancing [ɔ:lˌsɪŋɪŋɔ:l'dɑ:nsɪŋ] ADJ (*Brit*) ipersofisticato(-a)

All Souls' Day N il Giorno dei Morti

all·spice ['ɔ:lˌspaɪs] N pepe *m* della Giamaica

all-star ['ɔ:l'sta:^r] ADJ (*film, play*) recitato(-a) da attori famosi; **an all-star cast** un cast di attori famosi

all-time ['ɔ:l'taɪm] ADJ (*record*) senza precedenti, assoluto(-a)

al·lude [ə'lu:d] VI: **to allude to** alludere a, fare allusione a

al·lure [ə'ljʊə^r] N fascino
■ VT allettare, affascinare

al·lur·ing [ə'ljʊərɪŋ] ADJ allettante, seducente

al·lu·sion [ə'lu:ʒən] N accenno, allusione *f*; (*Literature*) riferimento

al·lu·sive [ə'lu:sɪv] ADJ allusivo(-a), pieno(-a) di allusioni; (*Literature*) pieno(-a) di riferimenti

al·lu·sive·ly [ə'lu:sɪvlɪ] ADV allusivamente

al·lu·vial [ə'lu:vɪəl] ADJ alluvionale

al·lu·vium [ə'lu:vɪəm] N materiale *m* alluvionale

all-weather [ˌɔ:l'wɛðə^r] ADJ per tutte le stagioni

◎ **ally** [*n* 'ælaɪ; *vb* ə'laɪ] N alleato(-a)
■ VT: **to ally o.s. with** allearsi con

al·ma·nac ['ɔ:lmənæk] N almanacco

al·mighty [ɔ:l'maɪtɪ] ADJ onnipotente; (*fam*) enorme, colossale
■ N: **the Almighty** l'Onnipotente

al·mond ['ɑ:mənd] N (*nut*) mandorla; (*also:* **almond tree**) mandorlo

almond paste N (*Culin*) pasta di mandorle

◎ **al·most** ['ɔ:lməʊst] ADV quasi; **he almost fell** per poco non è caduto

alms [ɑ:mz] NPL (*old*) elemosina *sg*; **to give alms** fare l'elemosina

alms·house ['ɑ:mzˌhaʊs] N ospizio

aloft [ə'lɒft] ADV in alto; (*Naut*) sull'alberatura

◎ **alone** [ə'ləʊn] ADJ, ADV (da) solo(-a); **all alone** tutto(-a) solo(-a); **leave me alone!** lasciami in pace!, lasciami stare!; **to let** *or* **leave sth alone** (*object*) lasciar stare qc; (*business, scheme*) non immischiarsi in qc; **leave my things alone!** lascia stare le mie cose!; **let alone ...** figuriamoci poi..., tanto meno...; **he can't read, let alone write** non sa leggere, figuriamoci scrivere; **you can't do it alone** non puoi farlo da solo; **she lives alone** vive da sola; **am I alone in thinking so?** sono il solo a pensarla così ?; **the flight alone cost £600** il volo da solo costa 600 sterline, solo il volo costa 600 sterline

◎ **along** [ə'lɒŋ] ADV: **to move along** (*person, car*) andare avanti; **he was hopping/limping along** veniva saltellando/zoppicando; **come along with me** vieni con me; **are you coming along?** vieni anche tu?; **move along there!** muovetevi, avanti!; (*said by policeman*) circolare!; **along with the others** con gli altri, insieme agli altri; **take it along** prendilo con te; **I knew all along** sapevo fin dall'inizio
■ PREP lungo; **to walk along the street** camminare lungo la strada; **the trees along the path** gli alberi lungo il sentiero; **along here** per di qua; **somewhere along the way** (*also fig*) da qualche parte lungo la strada

◎ **along·side** [ə'lɒŋ'saɪd] ADV (*Naut*) sottobordo; **we brought our boat alongside** (*of a pier/shore etc*) abbiamo accostato la barca (al molo/alla riva *etc*)
■ PREP (*along*) lungo; (*beside*) accanto a; **the railway runs alongside the beach** la ferrovia costeggia la spiaggia; **to come alongside the quay** accostare al molo; **to work alongside other people** lavorare assieme ad altre persone

aloof [ə'lu:f] ADJ riservato(-a), distaccato(-a)
■ ADV a distanza, in disparte; **to stand aloof (from)** tenersi a distanza (da) *or* in disparte (da)

aloof·ness [ə'lu:fnɪs] N riserbo, distacco

aloud [ə'laʊd] ADV ad alta voce, a voce alta

al·paca [æl'pækə] N (*animal, wool*) alpaca *m inv*

al·pha ['ælfə] N alfa *m or f inv*
■ ADJ (*Phys*): **alpha particle** particella *f* alfa *inv*

al·pha·bet ['ælfəbɛt] N alfabeto
▷ www.omniglot.com/writing/atoz.htm

al·pha·beti·cal [ˌælfə'bɛtɪkəl] ADJ alfabetico(-a); **in alphabetical order** in ordine alfabetico

al·pha·beti·cal·ly [ˌælfə'bɛtɪkəlɪ] ADV alfabeticamente

al·pha·bet·ize ['ælfəbətaɪz] VT mettere in ordine alfabetico

al·pha·nu·mer·ic [ˌælfənju:'mɛrɪk] ADJ alfanumerico(-a)

al·pine ['ælpaɪn] ADJ alpino(-a); (*plant, pasture*) alpestre; **alpine skiing** sci *m* alpino

alpine hut N rifugio alpino

al·pin·ism ['ælpɪnɪzəm] N alpinismo

al·pin·ist ['ælpɪnɪst] N alpinista *m/f*

Alps [ælps] NPL: **the Alps** le Alpi

◎ **al·ready** [ɔ:l'rɛdɪ] ADV già; **Liz had already gone** Liz se n'era già andata

al·right [ɔ:l'raɪt] ADJ = **all right**

Al·sace [æl'sæs] N l'Alsazia

Al·sa·tian [æl'seɪʃən] N **1** (*Brit: dog*) pastore *m* tedesco, (cane *m*) lupo **2** (*person*) alsaziano(-a)
■ ADJ alsaziano(-a)

◎ **also** ['ɔ:lsəʊ] ADV **1** (*too*) anche, pure; **her cousin also came** è venuto anche suo cugino **2** (*moreover*) inoltre, anche; **also, I must explain ...** (e) inoltre devo spiegare..., devo anche spiegare...

also-ran ['ɔ:lsəʊˌræn] N (*Sport*) (cavallo) non piazzato; (*fam: person*) perdente *m/f*

al·tar ['ɒltə^r] N altare *m*; **high altar** altar maggiore

altar boy N chierichetto

altar·piece ['ɒltəpi:s] N (*in church*) pala

◎ **al·ter** ['ɒltə^r] VT (*gen*) modificare, cambiare, alterare; (*opinion: one's own*) cambiare, mutare; (*: sb else's*) far cambiare *or* mutare; (*garment, building*) fare una

modifica (*or* delle modifiche) a
■ VI cambiare
al·tera·tion [ˌɒltəˈreɪʃən] N (*act: see vb*) modifica, cambiamento; (*in appearance*) cambiamento, trasformazione *f*; **alterations** NPL (*to garment, building*) modifiche *fpl*; **timetable subject to alteration** orario soggetto a variazioni; **without any alteration** senza modifiche; **to make alterations in sth** apportare delle modifiche a qc
al·ter·ca·tion [ˌɒltəˈkeɪʃən] N (*frm*) alterco, litigio
al·ter·nate [*adj* ɒlˈtɜːnɪt; *vb* ˈɒltəneɪt] ADJ (*alternating: layers*) alternato(-a); (*every other: days*) alterni(-e) *pl*, uno(-a) sì e uno(-a) no; **on alternate days** ogni due giorni, a giorni alterni; **alternate angles** angoli alterni
■ VI: **to alternate (with/between)** alternarsi (a/fra), avvicendarsi (a/fra)
■ VT (*crops*) alternare, avvicendare
al·ter·nate·ly [ɒlˈtɜːnɪtlɪ] ADV alternatamente
al·ter·nat·ing cur·rent [ˈɒltəneɪtɪŋˈkʌrənt] N corrente *f* alternata
◎ **al·ter·na·tive** [ɒlˈtɜːnətɪv] ADJ (*solutions*) alternativo(-a), altro(-a); (*medicine, energy*) alternativo(-a)
■ N (*choice*) alternativa; **you have no alternative but to go** non hai altra alternativa che andare; **you have no alternative** non hai alternative; **there are several alternatives** ci sono diverse alternative *or* possibilità; **there is no alternative** non c'è altra alternativa *or* scelta
al·ter·na·tive·ly [ɒlˈtɜːnətɪvlɪ] ADV in alternativa, altrimenti; **alternatively, we could just stay at home** altrimenti potremmo semplicemente stare a casa
alternative medicine N medicina alternativa
al·ter·na·tor [ˈɒltəneɪtəʳ] N (*Elec, Aut*) alternatore *m*
◎ **al·though** [ɔːlˈðəʊ] CONJ anche se, benché + *sub*, sebbene + *sub*; **although she was tired, she stayed up late** nonostante fosse stanca è rimasta alzata fino a tardi
al·time·ter [ˈæltɪmiːtəʳ] N altimetro
al·ti·tude [ˈæltɪtjuːd] N altitudine *f*, altezza, quota; (*Geom*) altezza; **at these altitudes** a questa altezza; **to gain/lose altitude** (*Aer*) prendere/perdere quota
alto [ˈæltəʊ] N (*instrument*) contralto; (*male*) contraltino; (*female*) contralto
◎ **al·to·geth·er** [ˌɔːltəˈɡɛðəʳ] ADV **1** (*in all*) in tutto, complessivamente; (*on the whole*) tutto considerato, tutto sommato, nel complesso, nell'insieme; **you owe me twenty pounds altogether** in tutto mi devi venti sterline; **altogether it was rather unpleasant** tutto sommato *or* in complesso è stato piuttosto spiacevole; **how much is that altogether?** quant'è in tutto?
2 (*entirely*) del tutto, completamente; **I'm not altogether sure** non sono del tutto *or* proprio sicuro
al·tru·ism [ˈæltrʊɪzəm] N altruismo
al·tru·is·tic [ˌæltrʊˈɪstɪk] ADJ altruistico(-a)
al·tru·is·ti·cal·ly [ˌæltrʊˈɪstɪklɪ] ADV altruisticamente
alu·min·ium [ˌæljʊˈmɪnɪəm], **alu·mi·num** [əˈluːmɪnəm] (*Am*) N alluminio
alum·na [əˈlʌmnə] N (*Am Univ*) ex allieva
alum·nus [əˈlʌmnəs] N (*Am Univ*) ex allievo
al·veo·lar [ælˈvɪələʳ] ADJ alveolare
al·veo·lus [ælˈvɪələs] N alveolo
◎ **al·ways** [ˈɔːlweɪz] ADV sempre; **as always** come sempre; **he's always moaning** si lamenta sempre; **you can always go by train** puoi sempre prendere il treno

always-on [ˌɔːlweɪzˈɒn] ADJ (*Comput*): **always-on connection** connessione *f* permanente
Alzheimer's [ˈæltshaɪməz] N (*also:* **Alzheimer's disease**) morbo di Alzheimer
AM [ˌeɪˈɛm] ABBR (= **amplitude modulation**) AM
■ N ABBR (= **Assembly Member**) deputato(-a) gallese
am [æm] 1ST PERS SG PRESENT *of* **be**
a.m. [ˌeɪˈɛm] ADV ABBR (= **ante meridiem**) del mattino; **at four a.m.** alle quattro del mattino
AMA [ˌeɪɛmˈeɪ] N ABBR = *American Medical Association*
amalgam [əˈmælɡəm] N amalgama *m*
amal·gam·ate [əˈmælɡəmeɪt] VT (*metals, also fig*) amalgamare; (*Comm*) fondere
■ VI (*metals, also fig*) amalgamarsi; (*Comm*) fondersi
amal·gama·tion [əˌmælɡəˈmeɪʃən] N (*see vb*) amalgamazione *f*; fusione *f*
amanu·en·sis [əˌmænjʊˈɛnsɪs] N (*pl* **amanuenses** [əˌmænjʊˈɛnsiːz]) (*frm*) amanuense *m*
amass [əˈmæs] VT accumulare, ammassare
◎ **ama·teur** [ˈæmətəʳ] N dilettante *m/f*
■ ADJ (*player, painter*) dilettante; (*activity*) dilettantistico(-a), per dilettanti
amateur dramatics N filodrammatica
▷ www.drama.ac.uk
▷ http://vl-theatre.com
▷ www.amdram.co.uk/
▷ www.drama.ac.uk/
ama·teur·ish [ˈæmətərɪʃ] ADJ (*pej*) dilettantesco(-a), da dilettanti
ama·teur·ism [ˈæmətərɪzm] N dilettantismo
amaze [əˈmeɪz] VT stupire, sbalordire; **to be amazed (at)** essere sbalordito(-a) (da)
amaze·ment [əˈmeɪzmənt] N stupore *m*, meraviglia; **to my amazement ...** con mia gran sorpresa...; **he looked at me in amazement** mi guardò stupito
◎ **amaz·ing** [əˈmeɪzɪŋ] ADJ sorprendente, sbalorditivo(-a); (*bargain, offer*) sensazionale; **that's amazing news!** è una notizia incredibile!; **Vivian's an amazing cook** Vivian è una cuoca eccezionale
amaz·ing·ly [əˈmeɪzɪŋlɪ] ADV incredibilmente
Ama·zon [ˈæməzən] N **1 the Amazon** (*river*) il Rio delle Amazzoni **2** (*Myth*) Amazzone *f*
■ ADJ (*basin*) amazzonico(-a); **the Amazon rainforest** la foresta amazzonica
Ama·zo·nian [æməˈzəʊnɪən] ADJ amazzonico(-a)
◎ **am·bas·sa·dor** [æmˈbæsədəʳ] N ambasciatore(-trice)
ambassador-at-large [æmˈbæsədərətˈlɑːdʒ] N (*Am*) ambasciatore(-trice) a disposizione
am·bas·sa·dor·ial [æmˌbæsəˈdɔːrɪəl] ADJ di ambasciatore
am·ber [ˈæmbəʳ] N ambra
■ ADJ (*colour*) ambra *inv*, ambrato(-a); (*Brit: traffic light*) giallo(-a); **the light is amber!** è giallo!
am·ber·gris [ˈæmbəˌɡriːs] N ambra grigia
am·bi·dex·trous [ˌæmbɪˈdɛkstrəs] ADJ ambidestro(-a)
am·bi·ence [ˈæmbɪəns] N (*liter: atmosphere*) ambiente *m*; **the restaurant has a pleasant ambience** il ristorante ha un'atmosfera piacevole
am·bi·ent [ˈæmbɪənt] ADJ ambiente *inv*; **ambient temperature** temperatura ambiente
am·bi·gu·ity [ˌæmbɪˈɡjʊɪtɪ] N ambiguità *f inv*
am·bigu·ous [æmˈbɪɡjʊəs] ADJ ambiguo(-a)
am·bigu·ous·ly [æmˈbɪɡjʊəslɪ] ADV ambiguamente
am·bit [ˈæmbɪt] N (*frm*) ambito
◎ **am·bi·tion** [æmˈbɪʃən] N ambizione *f*, aspirazione *f*; **he has no ambition** non ha nessuna ambizione; **to**

Aa

achieve one's ambition realizzare le proprie aspirazioni *or* ambizioni
am·bi·tious [æm'bɪʃəs] ADJ ambizioso(-a); **to be ambitious for one's children** avere delle ambizioni per i propri figli
am·bi·tious·ly [æm'bɪʃəslɪ] ADV ambiziosamente
am·biva·lence [æm'bɪvələns] N ambivalenza
am·biva·lent [æm'bɪvələnt] ADJ ambivalente
am·ble ['æmbl] VI (*also:* **to amble along** *or* **about:** *person*) camminare tranquillamente *or* senza fretta; **he ambled up to me** mi è venuto incontro senza fretta
■ N (*of horse*) ambio
am·bro·sia [æm'brəʊzɪə] N (*liter*) ambrosia
am·bu·lance ['æmbjʊləns] N ambulanza, autoambulanza
■ ADJ: **ambulance driver** guidatore(-trice) d'ambulanza
am·bush ['æmbʊʃ] N (*attack*) imboscata, agguato; (*place*) agguato; **to lie in ambush** stare in agguato; **to lie in ambush for sb** tendere un'imboscata a qn
■ VT tendere un'imboscata a qn
ame·ba [ə'mi:bə] N (*Am*) = **amoeba**
ame·lio·rate [ə'mi:lɪə,reɪt] VT (*frm*) migliorare
ame·lio·ra·tion [ə,mi:lɪə'reɪʃən] N (*frm*) miglioramento
amen ['ɑ:'mɛn] EXCL così sia, amen
ame·nable [ə'mi:nəbl] ADJ: **amenable to** (*advice*) ben disposto(-a) verso; **amenable to flattery** sensibile alle lusinghe; **amenable to reason** ragionevole
amend [ə'mɛnd] VT (*law etc*) emendare; (*text*) correggere
◎ **amend·ment** [ə'mɛndmənt] N (*see vb*) emendamento; correzione *f*
amends [ə'mɛndz] NPL: **to make amends (to sb) for sth** (*apologize*) farsi perdonare (da qn) per qc; (*compensate*) risarcire *or* indennizzare (qn) per qc
amen·ity [ə'mi:nɪtɪ] N (*facility*) *struttura ricreativa o commerciale*; **a house with all amenities** una casa con tutte le comodità
Amerasian [,(ae]mə'reɪʃn] N *persona che ha un genitore americano e uno asiatico*
Ameri·ca [ə'mɛrɪkə] N America
▷ www.firstgov.gov/
Ameri·can [ə'mɛrɪkən] ADJ americano(-a)
■ N (*person*) americano(-a); (*language: also:* **American English**) americano
Ameri·can·ism [ə'mɛrɪkənɪzəm] N americanismo
Ameri·can·ize [ə'mɛrɪkənaɪz] VT americanizzare
am·ethyst ['æmɪθɪst] N ametista
Amex ['æmɛks] N ABBR **1** (= **American Stock Exchange**) AMEX *f; borsa valori americana*
2 ® = **American Express; Amex® card** carta dell'American Express
Am·har·ic [æm'hærɪk] ADJ amarico(-a)
■ N (*language*) amarico
ami·abil·ity [,eɪmɪə'bɪlɪtɪ] N amabilità, affabilità
ami·able ['eɪmɪəbl] ADJ affabile, amabile
ami·ably ['eɪmɪəblɪ] ADV affabilmente
ami·cable ['æmɪkəbl] ADJ amichevole
ami·cably ['æmɪkəblɪ] ADV amichevolmente; **to part amicably** lasciarsi senza rancori; (*divorcing couple*) separarsi consensualmente
AMICUS ['æmɪkəs] N (*Brit*) sindacato del personale scientifico, tecnico e manageriale
◎ **amid** [ə'mɪd], **amidst** [ə'mɪdst] PREP (*frm, liter*) in mezzo a, fra, tra
amid·ships [ə'mɪdʃɪps] ADV (*Naut*) a mezzanave
ami·no acid [ə'mi:nəʊ'æsɪd] N amminoacido
amiss [ə'mɪs] ADJ, ADV: **there's something amiss** c'è qualcosa che non va; **don't take it amiss** non avertene a male
am·meter ['æm,mi:tə^r] N amperometro
ammo ['æməʊ] N ABBR (*fam:* = **ammunition**) munizioni *fpl*
am·mo·nia [ə'məʊnɪə] N ammoniaca
am·mo·nite ['æmə,naɪt] N ammonite *f*
am·mo·nium [ə'məʊnɪəm] N ammonio
ammonium hydroxide N idrossido di ammonio
ammonium ion N ione *m* ammonio *inv*
am·mu·ni·tion [,æmjʊ'nɪʃən] N munizioni *fpl*; (*fig*) arma
ammunition belt N cartucciera
ammunition dump N deposito di munizioni
am·ne·sia [æm'ni:zɪə] N amnesia
am·nes·ty ['æmnɪstɪ] N amnistia; **to grant an amnesty to** concedere l'amnistia a, amnistiare
Amnesty International N Amnesty International *f*
am·ni·on ['æmnɪən] N (*pl* **amnions** *or* **amnia** ['æmnɪə]) amnio
am·ni·ot·ic [,æmnɪ'ɒtɪk] ADJ amniotico(-a)
amoe·ba, (*Am*) **ame·ba** [ə'mi:bə] N ameba
am·oebia·sis [,æmɪ'baɪəsɪs] N (*pl* **amoebiases** [,æmɪ'baɪə,si:z]) amebiasi *f*
amok [ə'mɒk] ADV = **amuck**
◎ **among** [ə'mʌŋ], **amongst** [ə'mʌŋst] PREP tra, fra, in mezzo a; **among friends** tra amici; **he is among those who ...** fa parte di quelli che..., è uno di quelli che...; **share it among yourselves** dividetevelo tra (di) voi; **among other things** tra l'altro, tra le altre cose
amor·al [eɪ'mɒrəl] ADJ amorale
amo·ral·ity [,eɪmə'rælɪtɪ] N amoralità
amo·rous ['æmərəs] ADJ amoroso(-a); (*stronger*) appassionato(-a)
amor·phous [ə'mɔ:fəs] ADJ amorfo(-a)
amortization [ə,mɔ:taɪ'zeɪʃən] N (*Comm*) ammortamento
◎ **amount** [ə'maʊnt] N (*sum of money*) somma, cifra; (*of invoice, bill etc*) importo; (*quantity*) quantità *f inv*; **in small amounts** poco per volta; **the total amount** (*of money*) l'importo totale; (*of things*) la quantità totale; **a huge amount of rice** una grossa quantità di riso; **a large amount of money** una grossa somma di denaro; **he has any amount of time/money** ha tutto il tempo/tutti i soldi che vuole
▸ **amount to** VI + PREP (*total*) ammontare a; (*fig: be equivalent to*) equivalere a, non essere altro che; **this amounts to a refusal** questo equivale a un rifiuto; **he'll never amount to much** non conterà mai granché
amp [æmp], **am·père** ['æmpɛə^r] N ampere *m inv*; **a 13 amp(ère) plug** una spina con fusibile da 13 ampere
am·per·age ['æmpərɪdʒ] N amperaggio
am·per·sand ['æmpə,sænd] N "e" *f* commerciale
am·pheta·mine [æm'fɛtəmi:n] N anfetamina
am·phib·ian [æm'fɪbɪən] N (*Bio, vehicle*) anfibio
am·phibi·ous [æm'fɪbɪəs] ADJ (*Bio, vehicle*) anfibio(-a)
am·phi·thea·tre, (*Am*) **am·phi·thea·ter** ['æmfɪ,θɪətə^r] N anfiteatro
am·pho·ter·ic [,æmfə'tɛrɪk] ADJ (*Chem*) anfotero(-a)
am·ple ['æmpl] ADJ (*comp* **-er**, *superl* **-est**) **1** (*large: boot of car*) ampio(-a), spazioso(-a); (*: garment*) ampio(-a)
2 (*more than enough: money*) in abbondanza; (*: space, means, resources*) abbondante, ampio(-a); **we have ample reason to believe that ...** abbiamo parecchie

ragioni per credere che...; **we have ample time to finish it** abbiamo tutto il tempo (necessario) per finirlo; **that should be ample** *(time, money etc)* dovrebbe essere più che sufficiente

am·pli·fi·ca·tion [ˌæmplɪfɪˈkeɪʃən] N *(of sound)* sistema *m* di amplificazione; *(of idea, statement)* ampliamento

am·pli·fi·er [ˈæmplɪfaɪəʳ] N amplificatore *m*

am·pli·fy [ˈæmplɪfaɪ] VT *(sound)* amplificare; *(statement etc)* ampliare

am·pli·tude [ˈæmplɪˌtjuːd] N *(Math, Phys)* ampiezza

am·ply [ˈæmplɪ] ADV ampiamente

am·poule, *(Am)* **am·pule** [ˈæmpuːl] N *(Med)* fiala

am·pu·tate [ˈæmpjʊteɪt] VT amputare

am·pu·ta·tion [ˌæmpjʊˈteɪʃən] N amputazione *f*

am·pu·tee [æmpjʊˈtiː] N mutilato(-a) *(chi ha subito un'amputazione)*

Am·ster·dam [ˌæmstəˈdæm] N Amsterdam *f*

amt ABBR = **amount**

amuck [əˈmʌk], **amok** [əˈmɒk] ADV: **to run amuck** *(madman)* essere preso(-a) da follia omicida; *(children, fans)* scatenarsi; *(animals)* correre all'impazzata

amuse [əˈmjuːz] VT *(cause mirth)* divertire, far ridere; *(entertain)* (far) divertire; **to be amused at** essere divertito(-a) da; **he was most amused by the story** la storia lo divertì molto; **he was not amused** non l'ha trovato divertente; **to amuse o.s. with sth/by doing sth** divertirsi con qc/a fare qc; **run along and amuse yourselves** andate a divertirvi

amuse·ment [əˈmjuːzmənt] N **1** divertimento; **much to my amusement** con mio grande spasso; **a look of amusement** un'aria divertita
2 *(entertainment)* divertimento, svago; **they do it for amusement only** lo fanno solo per divertirsi *or* per svago

amusement arcade N sala *f* giochi *inv*

amusement park N luna park *m inv*

amus·ing [əˈmjuːzɪŋ] ADJ divertente

amus·ing·ly [əˈmjuːzɪŋlɪ] ADV in modo divertente

am·yl·ase [ˈæmɪˌleɪz] N amilasi *f*

an [æn, ən, n] INDEF ART *see* **a**

ANA [ˌeɪɛnˈeɪ] N ABBR **1** = *American Newspaper Association* **2** = *American Nurses Association*

anabo·lism [əˈnæbəˈlɪzəm] N anabolismo

anach·ro·nism [əˈnækrənɪzəm] N anacronismo

anach·ro·nis·tic [əˈnækrəˈnɪstɪk] ADJ anacronistico(-a)

ana·con·da [ˌænəˈkɒndə] N anaconda *m inv*

anaemia, *(Am)* **anemia** [əˈniːmɪə] N anemia

anaemic, *(Am)* **anemic** [əˈniːmɪk] ADJ anemico(-a)

an·aer·obe [ænˈɛərəʊb], **an·aero·bium** [ˌ[æ]nɛəˈrəʊbɪəm] N *(pl* **anaerobia** [ˌænɛəˈrəʊbɪə]) anaerobio

an·aero·bic [ˌænɛəˈrəʊbɪk] ADJ anaerobico(-a)

an·aes·the·sia, *(Am)* **an·es·the·sia** [ˌænɪsˈθiːzɪə] N anestesia

an·aes·thet·ic, *(Am)* **an·es·thet·ic** [ˌænɪsˈθɛtɪk] N anestetico; **under (the) anaesthetic** sotto anestesia; **local/general anaesthetic** anestesia locale/totale
■ ADJ anestetico(-a)

anaes·the·tist, *(Am)* **anes·the·tist** [æˈniːsθɪtɪst] N anestetista *m/f*

anaes·the·tize, *(Am)* **anes·the·tize** [æˈniːsθɪtaɪz] VT anestetizzare

ana·gram [ˈænəgræm] N anagramma *m*

anal [ˈeɪnəl] ADJ anale

an·alge·sic [ˌænælˈdʒiːzɪk] ADJ analgesico(-a)
■ N analgesico

analog computer N calcolatore *m* analogico

ana·logi·cal·ly [ˌænəˈlɒdʒɪklɪ] ADV analogicamente

analo·gous [əˈnæləgəs] ADJ: **analogous (to, with)** analogo (a), affine (a)

ana·logue, *(Am)* **ana·log** [ˈænəlɒg] ADJ *(watch)* analogico(-a)
■ N cosa analoga

anal·ogy [əˈnælədʒɪ] N analogia; **to draw an analogy between** fare un'analogia tra

ana·lyse [ˈænəlaɪz] VT *(Brit)* analizzare, fare l'analisi di

◎ **analy·sis** [əˈnæləsɪs] N *(pl* **analyses** [əˈnælɪsiːz]) analisi *f inv*; *(Psych)* (psic)analisi *f inv*; **in the last analysis** in ultima analisi

◎ **ana·lyst** [ˈænəlɪst] N *(political, financial)* analista *m/f*; *(Am: also:* **psychoanalyst**) (psic)analista *m/f*

ana·lyti·cal [ˌænəˈlɪtɪkəl], **ana·lyt·ic** [ˌænəˈlɪtɪk] ADJ analitico(-a)

ana·lyti·cal·ly [ˌænəˈlɪtɪklɪ] ADV analiticamente

ana·lyze [ˈænəlaɪz] VT *(Am)* = **analyse**

an·ar·chic [æˈnɑːkɪk] ADJ anarchico(-a)

an·ar·chi·cal [æˈnɑːkɪkəl], **an·ar·chic** [æˈnɑːkɪk] ADJ anarchico(-a)

an·ar·chism [ˈænəˌkɪzm] N *(Pol)* anarchismo

an·ar·chist [ˈænəkɪst] N, ADJ anarchico(-a); **to be an anarchist** essere anarchico(-a)

an·ar·chy [ˈænəkɪ] N anarchia

anath·ema [əˈnæθɪmə] N *(Rel, fig)* anatema *m*; **it is anathema to him** non ne vuol neanche sentir parlare

ana·tomi·cal [ˌænəˈtɒmɪkəl] ADJ anatomico(-a)

ana·tomi·cal·ly [ˌænəˈtɒmɪklɪ] ADV anatomicamente

anato·mist [əˈnætəmɪst] N anatomista *m/f*

anato·my [əˈnætəmɪ] N anatomia
▷ www.innerbody.com
▷ www.innerbody.com/
▷ www.bartleby.com/107

ANC [ˌeɪɛnˈsiː] N ABBR = *African National Congress*

an·ces·tor [ˈænsɪstəʳ] N antenato(-a), avo(-a)

an·ces·tral [ænˈsɛstrəl] ADJ *(of family)* avito(-a); *(of former times)* ancestrale, atavico(-a); **ancestral home** casa avita

an·ces·try [ˈænsɪstrɪ] N *(origin)* lignaggio, ascendenza, stirpe *f*; *(forebears)* antenati *mpl*

an·chor [ˈæŋkəʳ] N ancora; *(fig)* ancora di salvezza; *(of team, organization)* perno, pilastro; **to be (lying) at anchor** essere alla fonda; **to drop anchor** gettare l'ancora; **to weigh anchor** salpare *or* levare l'ancora
■ VT *(also fig)* ancorare
■ VI ancorarsi

an·chor·age [ˈæŋkərɪdʒ] N ancoraggio

anchor·man [ˈæŋkəmən] N *(pl* **-men**) *(Radio, TV)* anchor man *m inv*

an·cho·vy [ˈæntʃəvɪ] N acciuga, alice *f*

anchovy paste N pasta d'acciughe

◎ **an·cient** [ˈeɪnʃənt] ADJ *(old: classical)* antico(-a); *(fam: person)* decrepito(-a); (: *object)* vecchio(-a) come il cucco, vecchissimo(-a); **ancient monument** monumento storico; **ancient Rome** l'antica Roma; **an ancient record player** un vecchissimo giradischi

> DID YOU KNOW ...?
> **ancient** is not translated by the Italian word *anziano*

an·cil·lary [ænˈsɪlərɪ] ADJ ausiliario(-a)

◎ **and** [ænd, ənd, nd, ən] CONJ e, ed *(often used before vowel)*; **you and me** tu ed io; **one and a half** uno e

Aa

mezzo; **three hundred and ten** trecentodieci; **faster and faster** sempre più veloce; **better and better** sempre meglio; **more and more** sempre di più; **without shoes and socks** senza scarpe né calze; **there are lawyers and lawyers!** ci sono avvocati e avvocati!; **he talked and talked** (e) parlava (e) parlava; **try and do it** prova a farlo; **wait and see** aspetta e vedrai; **come and sit here** vieni a sedere qui; **and so on** e così via

An·des ['ændi:z] NPL: **the Andes** le Ande

An·dor·ra [,æn'dɔ:rə] N Andorra

an·dro·gyne ['ændrə,dʒaɪn] N *(Bio, frm)* androgino

an·drogy·nous [æn'drɒdʒɪnəs] ADJ *(Bio, frm)* androgino(-a)

an·drogy·ny [æn'drɒdʒɪnɪ] N **1** *(Bio)* androginia **2** *(fig: in appearance, behaviour)* androginia

Andromache [æn'drɒməkɪ] N Andromaca

An·drom·eda [æn'drɒmɪdə] N Andromeda

an·ec·do·tal [ænɪk'dəʊtl] ADJ aneddotico(-a)

an·ec·dote ['ænɪkdəʊt] N aneddoto

anemia *etc* [ə'ni:mɪə] = **anaemia** *etc*

an·emom·eter [,ænɪ'mɒmɪtə^r] N anemometro

anemo·ne [ə'nɛmənɪ] N *(Bot)* anemone *m*; *(also:* **sea anemone)** anemone *m* di mare, attinia

an·es·thet·ic *etc* [,ænɪs'θɛtɪk] = **anaesthetic** *etc*

anew [ə'nju:] ADV *(liter)* di nuovo; **to begin anew** ricominciare

an·gel ['eɪndʒəl] N angelo; **be an angel and fetch my gloves** se mi vai a prendere i guanti sei proprio un angelo

angel dust N *sedativo usato a scopo allucinogeno*

an·gel·ic [æn'dʒɛlɪk] ADJ angelico(-a)

an·gel·ica [æn'dʒɛlɪkə] N *(Bot)* angelica

angel shark, angel fish N squadro

An·ge·lus ['ændʒɪləs] N Angelus *m inv*

◎ **an·ger** ['æŋgə^r] N rabbia, collera; **red with anger** rosso(-a) per *or* dalla rabbia; **in anger** nell'impeto della collera

■ VT far arrabbiare; **he is easily angered** si arrabbia facilmente

an·gi·na [æn'dʒaɪnə] N angina

an·gi·na pec·to·ris [æn'dʒaɪnə'pɛktərɪs] N angina pectoris

◎ **an·gle**[1] ['æŋgl] N **1** *(Geom)* angolo; **right angle** angolo retto; **at right angles to** ad angolo retto con, perpendicolare a; **at an angle of 80°** a un angolo di 80°; **at an angle** di sbieco; **to cut sth at an angle** tagliare qc di traverso **2** *(fig: point of view)* punto di vista; **from their angle** dal loro punto di vista; **to look at sth from a different angle** *(fig)* considerare qc da un altro punto di vista *or* sotto un altro aspetto

an·gle[2] ['æŋgl] VI *(fish)* pescare (con l'amo); **to angle for** *(fig)* cercare di avere

an·gler ['æŋglə^r] N pescatore *m* con la lenza

An·gli·can ['æŋglɪkən] ADJ, N anglicano(-a)

▷ www.anglicancommunion.org

An·gli·can·ism ['æŋglɪkənɪzəm] N anglicanesimo

an·gli·cize ['æŋglɪsaɪz] VT anglicizzare

an·gling ['æŋglɪŋ] N pesca con la lenza

Anglo- ['æŋgləʊ] PREF anglo-

Anglo-Italian ['æŋgləʊɪ'tæljən] ADJ, N italo-britannico(-a)

an·glo·phile ['æŋgləʊfaɪl] N anglofilo(-a)

an·glo·phobe ['æŋgləʊfəʊb] N anglofobo(-a)

Anglo-Saxon ['æŋgləʊ'sæksən] ADJ, N anglosassone *m/f*

An·go·la [æŋ'gəʊlə] N Angola

An·go·lan [æŋ'gəʊlən] ADJ, N angolano(-a)

an·go·ra [æŋ'gɔ:rə] ADJ d'angora

■ N angora

an·gri·ly ['æŋgrɪlɪ] ADV con rabbia

◎ **an·gry** ['æŋgrɪ] ADJ *(comp* **-ier**, *superl* **-iest)** *(gen)* arrabbiato(-a), furioso(-a); *(annoyed)* irritato(-a); *(wound)* infiammato(-a); *(sky)* minaccioso(-a); **to be angry with sb/about** *or* **at sth** essere arrabbiato(-a) *or* in collera con qn/per qc; **to get angry** arrabbiarsi; **to make sb angry** far arrabbiare qn; **your father looks very angry** tuo padre ha l'aria molto arrabbiata; **you won't be angry, will you?** non ti arrabbi, vero?; **he was angry at being treated so badly** era arrabbiato perché lo avevano trattato così male

angst [æŋst] N *(liter)* ansietà *f inv*

an·guish ['æŋgwɪʃ] N angoscia; **to be in anguish** essere angosciato(-a)

an·guished ['æŋgwɪʃt] ADJ *(expression, look)* angosciato(-a); *(cry)* angoscioso(-a)

an·gu·lar ['æŋgjʊlə^r] ADJ angoloso(-a), spigoloso(-a); *(measurement etc)* angolare

an·hy·dride [æn'haɪdraɪd] N anidride *f*

an·hy·drous [æn'haɪdrəs] ADJ anidro(-a)

ani·line ['ænɪlɪn] N anilina

◎ **ani·mal** ['ænɪməl] N animale *m*; *(pej: person)* bestia, bruto

■ ADJ animale

animal husbandry [-'hʌzbəndrɪ] N allevamento di animali

animal kingdom N: **the animal kingdom** il regno animale

animal rights NPL diritti *mpl* degli animali

■ ADJ *(organization, activist)* animalista; **animal rights campaign** campagna animalista; **animal rights campaigner** *or* **activist** animalista *m/f*

animal spirits NPL vivacità *f inv*

animal testing N sperimentazione *f* sugli animali

ani·mate [*adj* 'ænɪmɪt; *vb* 'ænɪmeɪt] ADJ *(animal, plants)* vivente; *(capable of movement)* animato(-a)

■ VT animare

ani·mat·ed ['ænɪmeɪtɪd] ADJ animato(-a); **to become animated** animarsi

animated cartoon N cartone *m* animato

ani·mat·ed·ly ['ænɪmeɪtɪdlɪ] ADV animatamente

ani·ma·tion [,ænɪ'meɪʃən] N animazione *f*

ani·ma·tor ['ænɪ,meɪtə^r] N *(Cine)* animatore(-trice)

ani·ma·tron·ics [,ænɪmə'trɒnɪks] N animazione *f* con il computer

ani·mos·ity [,ænɪ'mɒsɪtɪ] N animosità

ani·mus ['ænɪməs] N animosità

an·ion ['æn,aɪən] N anione *m*

ani·seed ['ænɪsi:d] N semi *mpl* di anice

An·ka·ra ['æŋkərə] N Ankara

an·kle ['æŋkl] N caviglia; **I've twisted my ankle** mi sono slogato la caviglia

ankle·bone ['æŋkl,bəʊn] N astragalo

ankle socks NPL calzini *mpl*

an·nals ['ænəlz] NPL annali *mpl*

an·neal [ə'ni:l] VT *(Tech: glass, metal)* ricuocere

an·neal·ing [ə'ni:lɪŋ] N: *of glass, metal* ricottura

an·nelid ['ænəlɪd] N anellide *m*

an·nex [*vb* ə'nɛks; *n* 'ænɛks] VT *(territory)*: **to annex (to)** annettere (a)

■ N *(Brit: annexe)* (edificio) annesso

an·nexa·tion [,ænɛk'seɪʃən] N annessione *f*

an·ni·hi·late [ə'naɪəleɪt] VT annientare, annichilire; *(argument)* demolire

an·ni·hi·la·tion [əˌnaɪəˈleɪʃən] N annientamento
◎ **an·ni·ver·sa·ry** [ˌænɪˈvɜːsərɪ] N anniversario; **it's their wedding anniversary** è il loro anniversario di matrimonio
■ ADJ: **anniversary celebration** celebrazione *f* dell'anniversario; **anniversary dinner** pranzo per l'anniversario, cena commemorativa
Anno Domi·ni [ˈænəʊˈdɒmɪnaɪ] ADV anno Domini
an·no·tate [ˈænəʊteɪt] VT annotare
an·no·ta·tion [ænəʊˈteɪʃən] N annotazione *f*
◎ **an·nounce** [əˈnaʊns] VT (*gen*) annunciare; **to announce the marriage/death of sb** annunciare le nozze/la morte di qn; **he announced that he wasn't going** ha dichiarato che non (ci) sarebbe andato
◎ **an·nounce·ment** [əˈnaʊnsmənt] N (*declaration*) comunicazione *f*, annuncio; (*official: through media*) comunicato; (*private: in newspaper*) annuncio; (*letter, card*) partecipazione *f*; **I'd like to make an announcement** ho una comunicazione da fare; **there's just been an announcement about our flight** c'è stato un annuncio riguardo al nostro volo un attimo fa
an·nounc·er [əˈnaʊnsəʳ] N (*Radio, TV: linking programmes*) annunciatore(-trice); (*: introducing people*) presentatore(-trice)
an·noy [əˈnɔɪ] VT dare fastidio a, infastidire, dare noia a; **to be annoyed about sth** essere seccato(-a) per qc, essere contrariato(-a) *or* irritato(-a) da qc; **to be annoyed (at sth/with sb)** essere seccato(-a) *or* irritato(-a) (per qc/con qn); **he's just trying to annoy you** sta solo cercando di stuzzicarti; **to get annoyed** arrabbiarsi; **don't get so annoyed!** non prendertela tanto!

> DID YOU KNOW ...?
> **annoy** is not translated by the Italian word *annoiare*

an·noy·ance [əˈnɔɪəns] N (*state*) fastidio, irritazione *f*; (*cause of annoyance*) seccatura, noia; **to her annoyance** con suo gran dispetto
an·noy·ing [əˈnɔɪɪŋ] ADJ (*person, habit, noise*) irritante, seccante; **it's annoying to have to wait** è (una cosa) seccante dover aspettare

> DID YOU KNOW ...?
> **annoying** is not translated by the Italian word *annoiato*

an·noy·ing·ly [əˈnɔɪɪŋlɪ] ADV fastidiosamente
◎ **an·nual** [ˈænjʊəl] ADJ (*income*) annuo(-a); (*event, plant*) annuale
■ N (*book*) pubblicazione *f* annuale, annuario; (*children's comic book*) almanacco; (*Bot*) pianta annuale
annual general meeting N (*Brit*) assemblea generale
an·nual·ly [ˈænjʊəlɪ] ADV annualmente, ogni anno
annual report N relazione *f* annuale
an·nu·ity [əˈnjuːɪtɪ] N annualità *f inv*, rendita annuale; (*also:* **life annuity**) vitalizio; **pension annuity** (*policy*) ≈ polizza di pensione integrativa
an·nul [əˈnʌl] VT annullare; (*law*) rescindere
an·nul·ment [əˈnʌlmənt] N annullamento; (*of law*) rescissione *f*
an·nu·lus [ˈænjʊləs] N (*pl* **annulses** *or* **annuli** [ˈænjʊˌlaɪ]) corona circolare
an·num [ˈænəm] N *see* **per annum**
An·nun·cia·tion [əˌnʌnsɪˈeɪʃən] N: **the Annunciation** l'Annunciazione *f*
an·ode [ˈænəʊd] N anodo
ano·dize [ˈænəˌdaɪz] VT anodizzare
ano·dyne [ˈænəʊˌdaɪn] N (*Med*) analgesico, calmante *m*; (*fig liter*) rimedio; **he used to speak of work as "the great anodyne"** soleva definire il lavoro la migliore delle medicine
■ ADJ (*Med*) analgesico(-a), calmante; (*fig: bland, neutral*) anodino
anoint [əˈnɔɪnt] VT (*Rel*) ungere; **to anoint sb king** consacrare qn re
anoma·lous [əˈnɒmələs] ADJ anomalo(-a)
anoma·ly [əˈnɒməlɪ] N anomalia
anon [əˈnɒn] ADV (*old, hum*): **see you anon!** a presto!
anon. [əˈnɒn] ADJ ABBR = **anonymous**
ano·nym·ity [ˌænəˈnɪmɪtɪ] N anonimato
anony·mous [əˈnɒnɪməs] ADJ anonimo(-a); **to remain anonymous** mantenere l'anonimato
anony·mous·ly [əˈnɒnɪməslɪ] ADV anonimamente; **to write anonymously to sb** scrivere una lettera anonima a qn
ano·rak [ˈænəræk] N (*esp Brit*) giacca a vento
ano·rexia [ænəˈrɛksɪə], **ano·rexia ner·vo·sa** [ænəˈrɛksɪə nɜːˈvəʊsə] N anoressia
ano·rex·ic [ænəˈreksɪk] ADJ, N anoressico(-a)
◎ **an·oth·er** [əˈnʌðəʳ] ADJ (*additional*) un altro/un'altra, ancora un(-a); (*different*) un altro/un'altra; (*second*) un altro/un'altra, un(-a) secondo(-a); **another book** (*one more*) un altro libro, ancora un libro; **I've got another T-shirt in my bag** ho un'altra maglietta nella borsa; **another drink?** bevi ancora qualcosa?; **in another 5 years** fra altri 5 anni; **without another word** senza aggiungere una sola *or* nemmeno una parola; **that's quite another matter** è tutt'un'altra cosa; **he's another Shakespeare** è un nuovo *or* altro Shakespeare
■ PRON un altro/un'altra, ancora uno(-a); **from one town to another** da una città all'altra; **they love one another** si vogliono bene; *see also* **one**
ANSI [ˌeɪɛnɛsˈaɪ] N ABBR (= **American National Standards Institute**) *ufficio nazionale americano per la normalizzazione*
◎ **an·swer** [ˈɑːnsəʳ] N **1** (*reply*) risposta; **in answer to your question** in risposta *or* per rispondere alla tua domanda; **to know all the answers** (*fig*) saper tutto, saperla lunga; **we need an answer by Tuesday** abbiamo bisogno di una risposta entro martedì **2** (*solution*) soluzione *f*; (*Math etc*) soluzione, risposta; **the answer to the problem** la soluzione del problema; **there is no easy answer** non è un problema facile da risolvere
■ VT **1** (*reply to*) rispondere a; **our prayers have been answered** le nostre preghiere sono state esaudite; **to answer the door** andare ad aprire (la porta); **to answer the phone** rispondere (al telefono) **2** (*fulfil: needs*) rispondere a, soddisfare; (*: expectations, description*) corrispondere a, rispondere a; (*: purpose*) servire a, rispondere a; (*problem*) risolvere; (*prayer*) esaudire
■ VI rispondere
▸ **answer back** VI + ADV (*fam*): **to answer (sb) back** rispondere (a qn) (con impertinenza)
▸ **answer for** VI + PREP (*action, crime*) rispondere di; (*sb's safety*) essere responsabile di; (*truth of sth*) garantire; **he's got a lot to answer for** ci sono molte cose di cui deve render conto
▸ **answer to** VI + PREP (*description*) corrispondere a; (*name*) rispondere a
an·swer·able [ˈɑːnsərəbl] ADJ **1** (*responsible*) responsabile; **to be answerable (to sb for sth)** dover rispondere *or* render conto (a qn di qc); **I am answerable to no-one** non devo rispondere a nessuno **2** (*question*) (a) cui si può rispondere

Aa

an·swer·ing ma·chine [ˈɑːnsərɪŋməˈʃiːn] N segreteria telefonica
ant [ænt] N formica
ANTA [ˌeɪɛntiːˈeɪ] N ABBR = *American National Theater and Academy*
an·tago·nism [ænˈtægənɪzəm] N antagonismo
an·tago·nist [ænˈtægənɪst] N antagonista *m/f*
an·tago·nis·tic [ænˌtægəˈnɪstɪk] ADJ antagonistico(-a)
an·tago·nize [ænˈtægəˌnaɪz] VT provocare l'ostilità di, inimicarsi; **I don't want to antagonize her** non voglio inimicarmela
Ant·arc·tic [æntˈɑːktɪk] ADJ antartico(-a)
■ N: **the Antarctic** l'Antartico
Ant·arc·ti·ca [æntˈɑːktɪkə] N Antartide *f*
Antarctic Circle N: **the Antarctic Circle** il Circolo polare antartico
Antarctic Ocean N: **the Antarctic Ocean** l'Oceano antartico
ante [ˈæntɪ] N (*fam*): **to up the ante** (*in game, also fig*) alzare la posta
ante... [ˈæntɪ] PREF anti..., ante..., pre...
ant·eater [ˈæntˌiːtə^r] N formichiere *m*
ante·ced·ent [ˌæntɪˈsiːdənt] N antecedente *m*, precedente *m*; **antecedents** NPL (*past history*) antecedenti, precedenti; (*ancestors*) antenati *mpl*
ante·cham·ber [ˈæntɪˌtʃeɪmbə^r] N anticamera
ante·date [ˈæntɪˈdeɪt] VT **1** (*precede*) precedere **2** (*document etc*) retrodatare
ante·di·lu·vian [ˈæntɪdɪˈluːvɪən] ADJ (*liter, hum*) antidiluviano(-a)
ante·lope [ˈæntɪləʊp] N antilope *f*
ante·na·tal [ˈæntɪˈneɪtl] ADJ prenatale
antenatal clinic N assistenza medica preparto
an·ten·na [ænˈtɛnə] N (*pl* **antennae** [ænˈtɛniː]) (*Radio, TV: Zool*) antenna
ante·ri·or [ænˈtɪərɪə^r] ADJ (*frm: position*) anteriore; (*: time*) precedente
ante·room [ˈæntɪˌrʊm] N anticamera
an·them [ˈænθəm] N inno; **national anthem** inno nazionale
an·ther [ˈænθə^r] N antera
ant hill N formicaio
an·tho·logi·cal [ˌænθəˈlɒdʒɪkəl] ADJ antologico(-a)
an·tholo·gist [ænˈθɒlədʒɪst] N antologista *m/f*
an·thol·ogy [ænˈθɒlədʒɪ] N antologia
an·thra·cite [ˈænθrəsaɪt] N antracite *f*
an·thrax [ˈænθræks] N (*Med*) antrace *m*
an·thro·poid [ˈænθrəʊpɔɪd] ADJ, N antropoide (*m*)
an·thro·po·logi·cal [ˌænθrəpəˈlɒdʒɪkəl] ADJ antropologico(-a)
an·thro·polo·gist [ˌænθrəˈpɒlədʒɪst] N antropologo(-a)
an·thro·pol·ogy [ˌænθrəˈpɒlədʒɪ] N antropologia
▷ www.anth.ucsb.edu/glossary/index2.html
▷ www.museum.upenn.edu/
▷ www.cyberpursuits.com/anthro/default.asp
an·thro·po·mor·phic [ˌænθrəpəˈmɔːfɪk] ADJ antropomorfo(-a)
anti... [ˈæntɪ] PREF anti...; **he's anti-everything** è un bastian contrario
anti-aircraft [ˈæntɪˈɛəkrɑːft] ADJ (*gun*) contraereo(-a), antiaereo(-a)
anti-aircraft defence N difesa antiaerea
anti·bal·lis·tic [ˈæntɪbəˈlɪstɪk] ADJ antibalistico(-a)
anti·bi·ot·ic [ˈæntɪbaɪˈɒtɪk] N antibiotico
■ ADJ antibiotico(-a)
anti·body [ˈæntɪˌbɒdɪ] N anticorpo
Anti·christ [ˈæntɪˌkraɪst] N: **the Antichrist** l'Anticristo
an·tici·pate [ænˈtɪsɪpeɪt] VT **1** (*expect: trouble*) prevedere, aspettarsi; (*: pleasure*) pregustare, assaporare in anticipo; **this is worse than I anticipated** è peggio di quel che immaginavo *or* pensavo; **to anticipate that ...** prevedere che...; **I anticipate seeing him tomorrow** presumo *or* mi immagino che lo vedrò domani; **as anticipated** come previsto **2** (*forestall: person*) prevenire, precedere; (*foresee: event*) prevedere; (*: question, objection, wishes*) prevenire
an·tici·pa·tion [ænˌtɪsɪˈpeɪʃən] N: **in anticipation (of)** in previsione *or* attesa (di); **we waited in great anticipation** (*excitement*) abbiamo aspettato con grande impazienza; **in anticipation of an enjoyable week** pregustando una bella settimana; **thanking you in anticipation** vi ringrazio in anticipo; **there is an atmosphere of anticipation** c'è un'atmosfera di grande aspettativa
anti·cleri·cal [ˌæntɪˈklɛrɪkl] ADJ, N anticlericale (*m/f*)
anti·cli·max [ˈæntɪˈklaɪmæks] N delusione *f*; **the game came as an anticlimax** la partita si rivelò una delusione
anti·cline [ˈæntɪˌklaɪn] N anticlinale *f*
anti·clock·wise [ˈæntɪˈklɒkwaɪz] ADV, ADJ in senso antiorario
anti·co·agu·lant [ˌæntɪkəʊˈægjʊlənt] ADJ, N anticoagulante (*m*)
an·tics [ˈæntɪks] NPL (*of clown etc*) lazzi *mpl*, buffonerie *fpl*; (*of child, animal etc*) buffe acrobazie *fpl*; (*pej*) scherzetti *mpl*
anti·cy·clone [ˈæntɪˈsaɪkləʊn] N anticiclone *m*
anti·cy·clon·ic [ˌæntɪsaɪˈklɒnɪk] ADJ anticiclonico(-a)
anti-depressant [ˈæntɪdɪˈprɛsənt] N antidepressivo
■ ADJ antidepressivo(-a)
anti·dote [ˈæntɪdəʊt] N antidoto
anti·fas·cist [ˈæntɪˈfæʃɪst] ADJ, N antifascista (*m/f*)
anti-flu [ˈæntɪˈfluː] ADJ antinfluenzale
anti·freeze [ˈæntɪˈfriːz] N antigelo *inv*, anticongelante *m*
anti·gen [ˈæntɪdʒən] N antigene *m*
anti-globalization [ˌæntɪgləʊbəlaɪˈzeɪʃən] ADJ antiglobalizzazione *inv*
Antigone [ænˈtɪgənɪ] N Antigone *f*
anti·he·ro [ˈæntɪˌhɪərəʊ] N (*pl* **antiheroes**) antieroe *m*
anti·his·ta·mine [ˌæntɪˈhɪstəmɪn] N antistaminico
An·til·les [ænˈtɪliːz] NPL: **the Antilles** le Antille
anti·lock (device) [ˈæntɪˈlɒk] N dispositivo *m* antibloccaggio *inv*
anti·loga·rithm [ˌæntɪˈlɒgəˌrɪðəm] N antilogaritmo
anti·mat·ter [ˈæntɪˌmætə^r] N antimateria
anti·mili·ta·rism [ˌæntɪˈmɪlɪtərɪzəm] N antimilitarismo
anti·mili·ta·ris·tic [ˌantɪˌmɪlɪtəˈrɪstɪk] ADJ antimilitaristico(-a)
anti·mo·ny [ˈæntɪmənɪ] N antimonio
anti·node [ˈæntɪˌnəʊd] N (*Phys*) ventre *m*, antinodo
anti·nu·clear [ˌæntɪˈnjuːklɪə^r] ADJ antinucleare
anti·oxi·dant [ˌæntɪˈɒːksɪdənt] N, ADJ antiossidante (*m*)
an·tipa·thy [ænˈtɪpəθɪ] N antipatia
anti·per·spi·rant [æntɪˈpɜːspɪrənt] N deodorante *m* (ad azione) antitraspirante
anti·phon [ˈæntɪfən] N (*Rel*) antifona
an·tipo·dean [ænˌtɪpəˈdiːən] ADJ degli antipodi

An·tipo·des [æn'tɪpədi:z] NPL: **the Antipodes** gli antipodi

anti·quar·ian [ˌæntɪ'kweərɪən] ADJ: **antiquarian bookshop** libreria antiquaria
■ N antiquario(-a)

anti·quary ['æntɪkwərɪ] N antiquario(-a)

anti·quat·ed ['æntɪkweɪtɪd] ADJ (*pej*) antiquato(-a), sorpassato(-a)

◎ **an·tique** [æn'ti:k] ADJ (*furniture etc*) antico(-a), d'epoca
■ N oggetto antico, pezzo d'antiquariato; **antiques** NPL antichità *f inv*; **he deals in antiques** commercia in antiquariato; **I bought an antique** ho comprato un pezzo d'antiquariato
▷ www.antiqueweb.com
▷ www.pbs.org/wgbh/pages/roadshow/
▷ http://antiquerestorers.com

antique dealer N antiquario(-a)

antique shop N bottega *or* negozio di antiquario, negozio d'antichità

an·tiq·uity [æn'tɪkwɪtɪ] N antichità; **of great antiquity** molto antico(-a)

anti-retroviral [ˌæntɪ'rɛtrəʊ,vaɪərəl] ADJ, N (*Med*) antiretrovirale (*m*)

an·tir·rhi·num [ˌæntɪ'raɪnəm] N antirrino

anti-Semitic ['æntɪsɪ'mɪtɪk] ADJ antisemitico(-a), antisemita

anti-Semitism ['æntɪ'sɛmɪtɪzəm] N antisemitismo

anti·sep·sis [ˌæntɪ'sɛpsɪs] N antisepsi *f*

anti·sep·tic [ˌæntɪ'sɛptɪk] ADJ antisettico(-a)
■ N antisettico

anti·skid [ˌæntɪ'skɪd] ADJ antisdrucciolevole

anti·so·cial ['æntɪ'səʊʃəl] ADJ (*behaviour, tendency: against society*) antisociale; (*unsociable*) scorbutico(-a), asociale

anti·spas·mod·ic [ˌæntɪspæz'mɒdɪk] ADJ antispastico(-a)

anti·stat·ic [ˌæntɪs'tætɪk] ADJ antistatico(-a)

anti·tank [ˌæntɪ'tæŋk] ADJ anticarro *inv*

anti·theft [ˌæntɪ'θɛft] ADJ antifurto *inv*

an·tith·esis [æn'tɪθɪsɪs] N (*pl* **antitheses** [æn'tɪθɪsi:z]) antitesi *f inv*; (*contrast*) carattere *m* antitetico

anti·theti·cal [ˌæntɪθɛtɪkəl] ADJ antitetico(-a)

anti·tox·in [ˌæntɪ'tɒksɪn] N antitossina

anti·trust ['æntɪ'trʌst] ADJ (*Comm*): **anti-trust law/legislation** legge *f*/legislazione *f* antitrust *inv*

anti·vivi·sec·tion·ist ['æntɪ,vɪvɪ'sɛkʃənɪst] N antivivisezionista *m/f*

ant·ler ['æntlə^r] N palco; **antlers** NPL corna *fpl*

an·to·no·ma·sia [ˌæntənə'meɪzɪə] N (*frm*) antonomasia

an·to·nym ['æntənɪm] N (*Gram*) antonimo

Ant·werp ['æntwɜ:p] N Anversa

anus ['eɪnəs] N ano

an·vil ['ænvɪl] N incudine *f*

◎ **anxi·ety** [æŋ'zaɪətɪ] N **1** ansia, ansietà *f inv*; **I have no anxieties about them** non sono in ansia per loro; **it is a great anxiety to me** è una grossa preoccupazione per me **2** (*eagerness*): **anxiety (to do sth)** smania (di fare qc); **in his anxiety to be gone he forgot his case** nella furia *or* fretta di andarsene si è dimenticato la borsa

◎ **anx·ious** ['æŋkʃəs] ADJ **1** (*worried*) preoccupato(-a), ansioso(-a), in ansia, inquieto(-a); **I'm very anxious about you** sono molto preoccupato *or* in pensiero per te; **with an anxious glance** con uno sguardo pieno d'ansia **2** (*causing worry: moment*) angoscioso(-a) **3** (*eager*): **anxious for sth/to do sth** impaziente di qc/di fare qc; **I am anxious that she should do it** ci tengo moltissimo che lo faccia; **he is anxious for success** ha un grande desiderio di successo; **I'm not very anxious to go** ho poca voglia di andarci

anx·ious·ly ['æŋkʃəslɪ] ADV ansiosamente, con ansia

◎ **any** ['ɛnɪ] **KEYWORD**

■ ADJ

1 (*in questions etc: some*) del (dell', dello) *m*, della (dell') *f*, dei (degli) *mpl*, delle *fpl*, qualche; **is there any meat?** c'è (della) carne?; **have you any money?** hai (dei) soldi?, hai qualche soldo?; **are there any others?** ce ne sono (degli) altri?; **if there are any tickets left** se ci sono ancora (dei) biglietti, se c'è ancora qualche biglietto

2 (*with negative*) alcuno(-a), nessuno(-a); **I haven't any bread** non ho pane, sono senza pane; **I don't see any cows** non vedo alcuna *or* nessuna mucca, non vedo mucche; **I haven't any money** non ho soldi, sono senza soldi; **without any difficulty** senza (nessuna *or* alcuna) difficoltà; **I haven't any work** non ho lavoro, sono senza lavoro

3 (*no matter which*) (uno(-a)) qualsiasi, (uno(-a)) qualunque; (*each and every*) ogni *inv*, tutto(-a); **in any case** in ogni caso; **any excuse will do** (una) qualunque *or* qualsiasi scusa andrà bene, una scusa qualunque *or* qualsiasi andrà bene; **any farmer will tell you** qualunque *or* qualsiasi *or* ogni agricoltore te lo dirà; **wear any hat (you like)** mettiti un cappello qualsiasi *or* qualunque; **any time you like** quando vuoi; **at any moment** da un momento all'altro; **at any rate** ad ogni modo; **come (at) any time** vieni a qualsiasi ora

■ PRON

1 (*in negative and interrogative sentences*): **are there any?** ce ne sono?; **are any of them coming?** viene qualcuno di loro?; **there aren't any left** non ce ne sono più; (*emphatic*) non ne è rimasto nemmeno uno; **can any of you sing?** c'è qualcuno che sa cantare?; **have you got any?** ne hai?; **I haven't got any (of them)** non ne ho

2 (*whichever one*) uno(-a) qualsiasi; (*anybody*) chiunque; **few, if any** pochi, sempre che ce ne siano; **take any of those books (you like)** prendi qualsiasi libro

■ ADV (*in negative sentences*) per niente; (*in interrogative sentences*) un po'; **are you feeling any better?** ti senti un po' meglio?; **don't wait any longer** non aspettare più; **I can't hear him any more** non lo sento più; **do you want any more tea?** vuoi ancora un po' di tè?, vuoi ancora del tè?; **she's not any more intelligent than her sister** sua sorella è altrettanto intelligente

◎ **any·body** ['ɛnɪbɒdɪ] PRON **1** (*in interrogative sentences*) qualcuno, nessuno; **has anybody got a pen?** qualcuno ha una penna?; **did you see anybody?** hai visto qualcuno *or* nessuno?; **is anybody in** *or* **home?** c'è nessuno (in casa)? **2** (*in negative sentences*) nessuno; **I can't** *or* **don't see anybody** non vedo nessuno; **without anybody seeing him** senza che nessuno lo vedesse, senza esser visto da nessuno **3** (*no matter who*) chiunque, qualsiasi persona; **anybody will tell you the same** chiunque ti dirà la stessa cosa; **anybody else would have laughed** chiunque altro avrebbe riso; **she's not going to marry just anybody** non sposerà il primo che le capita *or* uno qualunque

any·how ['ɛnɪ,haʊ] ADV **1** (*at any rate*) ad *or* in ogni modo, comunque; **I'm going anyhow** ci vado lo stesso; **he doesn't want to go out and anyhow he's not**

Aa

allowed non vuole uscire e comunque non ha il permesso di farlo; **what business is it of yours, anyhow?** e tu di che t'impicci? **2** (*haphazard*) come capita, in qualsiasi modo; **do it anyhow you like** fallo come ti pare; **I finished it anyhow** in qualche modo l'ho finito; **he leaves things just anyhow** lascia tutto come (gli) capita

◎ **any·one** ['ɛnɪ,wʌn] PRON = **anybody**

any·place ['ɛnɪ,pleɪs] PRON (*Am fam*) = **anywhere**

◎ **any·thing** ['ɛnɪ,θɪŋ] PRON **1** (*in interrogative sentences*) niente, qualcosa; **do you need anything?** hai bisogno di niente?; **are you doing anything tonight?** fai qualcosa stasera?; **anything else?** (*in shop*) basta (così)?, nient'altro?, altro?; **is there anything else you want to tell me?** hai qualcos'altro *or* nient'altro da dirmi?; **can't anything be done?** (non) si può fare qualcosa *or* niente? **2** (*in negative sentences*) non... niente, non... nulla; **it wasn't anything serious** non era niente di serio; **I saw hardly anything** non ho visto quasi niente; **the bridge is anything but safe** il ponte non è affatto sicuro; **it isn't anything like as cold as it was** non è più così freddo come prima **3** (*no matter what*) qualsiasi cosa, qualunque cosa; **anything could happen** potrebbe succedere qualunque cosa; **you can say anything you like** puoi dire quello che vuoi; **anything but that** tutto tranne questo; **they'll eat anything** mangiano qualsiasi cosa *or* di tutto; **it can cost anything between £15 and £20** può costare qualcosa come 15 o 20 sterline; **if anything, I have more to do now** se mai *or* piuttosto adesso ho più da fare

any·time ['ɛnɪ,taɪm] ADV (*happen*) in qualunque momento; (*come*) a qualsiasi ora

◎ **any·way** ['ɛnɪ,weɪ] ADV **1** (*besides*) in ogni caso; **I forgot to buy cough sweets – they don't do much good anyway** ho dimenticato di comprare le caramelle per la tosse – tanto non servono un granché **2** (*just the same*) comunque; **thanks, anyway** grazie, comunque **3** (*at least, at any rate*) almeno; **everything is ok, as far as I know anyway** va tutto bene, per quel che ne so io **4** (*in narrative, conversation: well, then*) bene; **anyway, I've got to go** be', devo andare; **it's a long story – anyway the upshot was that ...** è una lunga storia – a farla breve il risultato fu che...

◎ **any·where** ['ɛnɪ,wɛəʳ] ADV **1** (*in interrogative sentences*) da qualche parte, in qualche posto; **can you see him anywhere?** lo vedi da qualche parte?; **anywhere else?** da qualche *or* nessun'altra parte?, in qualche *or* nessun altro posto? **2** (*in negative sentences*) da nessuna parte, in nessun posto; **I can't see him anywhere** non lo vedo da nessuna parte; **they never go anywhere else** non vanno mai da nessun'altra parte **3** (*no matter where*) da qualsiasi *or* qualunque parte, in qualunque *or* qualsiasi posto, dovunque; **anywhere in the world** dovunque nel mondo; **put the books down anywhere** metti i libri dove ti capita

An·zac ['ænzæk] N ABBR (= **Australia-New Zealand Army Corps**) ANZAC *m*; (*soldier*) soldato dell'ANZAC

Anzac Day N *festa nazionale australiana e neozelandese in commemorazione dello sbarco a Gallipoli del 25 aprile 1915*

ANZAC DAY

L'**Anzac Day** è una festa nazionale australiana e neozelandese che cade il 25 aprile e commemora il famoso sbarco delle forze armate congiunte dei due paesi a Gallipoli nel 1915, durante la prima guerra mondiale.

▷ www.anzacday.org.au/

AOB [,eɪəʊ'bi:] N ABBR (= **any other business**) *varie ed eventuali*

aor·ta [eɪ'ɔ:tə] N aorta

apace [ə'peɪs] ADV (*liter*) rapidamente

◎ **apart** [ə'pɑ:t] ADV **1** (*separated*) a distanza, separatamente; **we live 3 miles apart** abitiamo a 3 miglia di distanza (l'uno dall'altro); **their birthdays are two days apart** i loro compleanni sono a distanza di due giorni l'uno dall'altro; **nothing will keep them apart** niente li terrà lontani l'uno dall'altra; **she stood apart from the others** se ne stava *or* rimase in disparte; **to live apart** vivere separati; **he lives apart from his wife** vive separato da sua moglie; **I can't tell them apart** non li distinguo l'uno dall'altro; **joking apart** scherzi a parte, a parte gli scherzi; **these problems apart** a parte questi problemi; **apart from** a parte, eccetto; **apart from the fact that** a parte il fatto che; **apart from that, everything's fine** a parte quello, va tutto bene; **with one's legs apart** con le gambe divaricate **2** (*in pieces*) a pezzi; **to fall apart** cadere a pezzi, sfasciarsi; **to take sth apart** smontare qc

apart·heid [ə'pɑ:teɪt] N apartheid *m*

◎ **apart·ment** [ə'pɑ:tmənt] N (*esp Am: flat*) appartamento; (*Brit: room in palace*) sala

apartment building N (*Am*) stabile *m*, caseggiato

apa·thet·ic [,æpə'θɛtɪk] ADJ apatico(-a), indifferente

apa·theti·cal·ly [,æpə'θɛtɪklɪ] ADV apaticamente

apa·thy ['æpəθɪ] N apatia, indifferenza

APB [,eɪpi:'bi:] N ABBR (*Am: police expression*: = **all points bulletin**) *espressione della polizia che significa "priorità assoluta: trovate..."*

ape [eɪp] N (*esp anthropoid*) scimmia; **to go ape** (*Am fam*) diventare stupido(-a)

■ VT scimmiottare

DID YOU KNOW ...?
ape is not translated by the Italian word *ape*

Ap·en·nines ['æpə,naɪnz] NPL: **the Apennines** gli Appennini *mpl*

aperi·ent [ə'pɪərɪənt] ADJ lassativo(-a)

■ N lassativo

ape·ri·tif [ə'pɛrɪtɪf] N aperitivo

ap·er·ture ['æpətʃjʊəʳ] N fessura; (*Phot*) apertura

APEX ['eɪpɛks] N ABBR **1** (*Brit*: = **Association of Professional, Executive, Clerical and Computer Staff**) *associazione dei professionisti, dirigenti, impiegati ed informatici* **2** (*Aer*: = **advance purchase excursion**) APEX *m inv*

apex ['eɪpɛks] N (*Geom*) vertice *m*; (*fig*) vertice *m*, apice *m*

apha·sia [ə'feɪzɪə] (*Med*) N afasia

aphid ['eɪfɪd] N afide *m*

apho·rism ['æfərɪzəm] N aforisma *m*

aph·ro·disi·ac [,æfrəʊ'dɪzɪæk] N, ADJ afrodisiaco(-a)

Aphrodite [,æfrə'daɪtɪ] N Afrodite *f*

API [,eɪpi:'aɪ] N ABBR = *American Press Insitute*

api·ary ['eɪpɪərɪ] N apiario

apiece [ə'pi:s] ADV ciascuno(-a); **he gave them £10 apiece** ha dato loro dieci sterline (per) ciascuno; **these pens sell at 90p apiece** queste penne si vendono a 90 pence l'una

aplomb [ə'plɒm] N disinvoltura; **with great aplomb** senza scomporsi, con gran disinvoltura

APO [,eɪpi:'əʊ] N ABBR (*Am*: = **Army Post Office**) *ufficio postale dell'esercito*

apoca·lypse [ə'pɒkəlɪps] N apocalisse *f*
apoca·lyp·tic [ə,pɒkə'lɪptɪk] ADJ apocalittico(-a)
Apoc·ry·pha [ə'pɒkrɪfə] NPL (*Rel*): **the Apocrypha** i libri apocrifi
apoc·ry·phal [ə'pɒkrɪfəl] ADJ apocrifo(-a)
apo·gee ['æpəʊdʒi:] N (*Astron, fig frm*) apogeo
apo·liti·cal [,eɪpə'lɪtɪkəl] ADJ apolitico(-a)
Apollo [ə'pɒləʊ] N Apollo
apolo·get·ic [ə,pɒlə'dʒɛtɪk] ADJ (*look, remark, letter*) di scuse; **he was very apologetic about it/for not coming** si è scusato moltissimo di ciò/per *or* di non essere venuto
apolo·geti·cal·ly [ə,pɒlə'dʒɛtɪkəlɪ] ADV per scusarsi
apolo·gist [ə'pɒlədʒɪst] N apologeta *m/f*
apolo·gize [ə'pɒlədʒaɪz] VI: **to apologize (to sb for sth)** scusarsi (con qn per *or* di qc), chiedere scusa (a qn per *or* di qc); **I apologize!** Chiedo scusa!; **they apologized for being late** si sono scusati per il ritardo; **there's no need to apologize** non c'è bisogno che ti scusi
apol·ogy [ə'pɒlədʒɪ] N scuse *fpl*; **I demand an apology** esigo delle scuse; **I owe you an apology** ti devo delle scuse; **please accept my apologies** la prego di accettare le mie scuse; **an apology for a lunch** (*pej*) un tentativo mal riuscito di pranzo
apo·plec·tic [,æpə'plɛktɪk] ADJ (*Med*) apoplettico(-a); **apoplectic with rage** (*fam*) livido(-a) per la rabbia
apo·plexy ['æpəplɛksɪ] N apoplessia
apos·tate [ə'pɒsteɪt] N (*frm*) apostata *m/f*
apos·tle [ə'pɒsl] N apostolo
Apostles' Creed N: **the Apostles' Creed** il credo apostolico
ap·os·tol·ic [,æpəs'tɒlɪk] ADJ apostolico(-a)
apos·tro·phe [ə'pɒstrəfɪ] N (*Gram: sign*) apostrofo
apoth·ecary [ə'pɒθɪkərɪ] N farmacista *m/f*
apoth·eo·sis [ə,pɒθɪ'əʊsɪs] N **1** **apotheosis of** perfetto esempio di **2** (*Art*) apoteosi *f inv*
ap·pal, (*Am*) **ap·pall** [ə'pɔ:l] VT sconvolgere, atterrire; **to be appalled at** restare sconvolto(-a) davanti a
Ap·pa·la·chian Moun·tains [,æpə'leɪʃən 'maʊntɪnz] NPL: **the Appalachian Mountains** (*also:* **the Appalachians**) i (monti) Appalachi
ap·pal·ling [ə'pɔ:lɪŋ] ADJ (*ignorance, conditions, destruction*) spaventoso(-a), impressionante; (*fam: film, taste*) pessimo(-a), spaventoso(-a); **she's an appalling cook** è un disastro come cuoca
ap·pal·ling·ly [ə'pɔ:lɪŋlɪ] ADV spaventosamente; (*behave*) molto male
ap·pa·rat·us [,æpə'reɪtəs] N (*for heating etc*) impianto; (*for filming, camping, in gym*) attrezzatura; (*in lab*) strumenti *mpl*; (*Anat*) apparato; (*system*) sistema *m*
ap·par·el [ə'pærəl] N (*frm*) abbigliamento, confezioni *fpl*
◎ **ap·par·ent** [ə'pærənt] ADJ (*seeming*) apparente; (*clear*) evidente, ovvio(-a); **for no apparent reason** senza motivo apparente; **to become apparent** manifestarsi, rivelarsi; **it is apparent that** è evidente che; **it was becoming increasingly apparent to me that ...** stava diventando sempre più evidente per me che...
◎ **ap·par·ent·ly** [ə'pærəntlɪ] ADV **1** (*it seems*) evidentemente; **apparently...** a quanto pare...; **did they give him the money? — apparently not** gli hanno dato i soldi? — no, a quanto pare **2** (*seemingly: unaffected, normal*) all'apparenza, apparentemente
ap·pa·ri·tion [,æpə'rɪʃən] N fantasma *m*, apparizione *f*
◎ **ap·peal** [ə'pi:l] VI **1** (*call, beg*): **to appeal (to sb)** implorare (qn), supplicare (qn); **to appeal for** chiedere (con insistenza); **to appeal for funds** lanciare un appello per ottenere dei fondi; **he appealed for silence** ha invitato al silenzio; **he appealed to them for help** si è rivolto a loro per un aiuto; **she appealed to her attacker for mercy** ha supplicato il suo assalitore di avere pietà; **they appealed for help from the international community** hanno chiesto aiuto alla comunità internazionale **2** (*Law*): **to appeal (against sth/to sb)** appellarsi (contro qc/presso qn), ricorrere in appello (contro qc/presso qn) **3** (*attract*) attirare, attrarre; **it doesn't appeal to me** mi dice poco; **Greece doesn't appeal to me** la Grecia non mi attira; **it appeals to the imagination** stimola la fantasia
■ N **1** (*call*) appello; (*request*) richiesta; **an appeal for funds** una richiesta di aiuti economici *or* di fondi; **he made an appeal for calm** ha fatto appello alla calma **2** (*Law*) appello, ricorso (legale); **right of appeal** diritto d'appello **3** (*attraction*) attrattiva, fascino; **a book of general appeal** un libro di interesse generale
Appeal Court N Corte *f* d'Appello
ap·peal·ing [ə'pi:lɪŋ] ADJ (*attractive*) attraente; (*pleading*) supplichevole
ap·peal·ing·ly [ə'pi:lɪŋlɪ] ADV (*attractively*) in modo attraente; (*pleadingly*) in modo supplichevole
◎ **ap·pear** [ə'pɪə^r] VI **1** (*gen*) apparire, comparire; (*ghost*) apparire; **the bus appeared around the corner** l'autobus è apparso all'angolo della strada; **he appeared from nowhere** è saltato fuori all'improvviso **2** (*in public*) esibirsi; (*Theatre*) recitare; (*book etc*) uscire, essere pubblicato(-a); **to appear on TV** apparire in televisione; **to appear in Hamlet** recitare nell'Amleto **3** (*Law*) comparire, presentarsi; **who is appearing for the defendant?** chi è l'avvocato difensore? **4** (*seem*) sembrare, parere; **she appears to want to leave** sembra che voglia andarsene; **she appeared to be asleep** sembrava che dormisse; **the house appears to be empty** la casa sembra vuota; **he appears tired** sembra stanco, ha l'aria stanca; **it appears that ...** a quanto pare..., sembra che...; **it would appear that ...** sembrerebbe che; **so it would appear** pare proprio di sì
◎ **ap·pear·ance** [ə'pɪərəns] N **1** (*act*) apparizione *f*; (*Theatre*) comparsa, apparizione; (*of book etc*) uscita, pubblicazione *f*; **in order of appearance** in ordine di apparizione; **to make one's first appearance** fare il proprio debutto, debuttare; **to put in** *or* **make an appearance** fare atto di presenza **2** (*look, aspect*) aspetto; **she takes great care over her appearance** cura molto il suo aspetto; **in appearance** a vedersi; **he was rather sickly in appearance** aveva un aspetto malaticcio *or* un'aria malaticcia; **appearances can be deceptive** non bisogna fidarsi delle apparenze, le apparenze ingannano; **to all appearances** a giudicar dalle apparenze; **to keep up appearances** salvare le apparenze
ap·pease [ə'pi:z] VT (*pacify*) placare; (*satisfy: curiosity*) appagare; (*: hunger*) calmare, soddisfare
ap·pease·ment [ə'pi:zmənt] N (*Pol*) appeasement *m inv*
ap·peas·er [ə'pi:zə^r] N (*Pol*) pacificatore *m*, appeaser *m*
ap·pel·late court [ə'pɛlɪt ,kɔ:t] N (*Law*) corte *f* d'appello
ap·pend [ə'pɛnd] VT (*frm: add: signature*) apporre: *attach, allegare*; (*Comput*) aggiungere (in coda)

Aa

ap·pend·age [əˈpɛndɪdʒ] N (*frm: adjunct*) appendice *f*; (*Bot, Zool*) peduncolo
ap·pen·dec·to·my [,æpɛnˈdɛktəmɪ] N appendicectomia
ap·pen·di·ci·tis [ə,pɛndɪˈsaɪtɪs] N appendicite *f*
ap·pen·dix [əˈpɛndɪks] N (*pl* **appendices** [əˈpɛndɪsi:z]) **1** (*Anat*) appendice *f*; **to have one's appendix out** operarsi *or* farsi operare di appendicite **2** (*to book etc*) appendice *f*
ap·per·tain [,æpəˈteɪn] VI (*frm*): **to appertain to** essere pertinente a
ap·pe·tite [ˈæpɪtaɪt] N: **appetite (for)** appetito (per); (*fig*) voglia (di), desiderio (di); **to have a good appetite** godere di *or* avere un ottimo appetito; **he has a big appetite** ha molto appetito; **that walk has given me an appetite** la passeggiata mi ha messo *or* fatto venire appetito
ap·pe·tiz·er [ˈæpɪtaɪzəʳ] N (*food*) stuzzichino; (*drink*) aperitivo
ap·pe·tiz·ing [ˈæpɪtaɪzɪŋ] ADJ appetitoso(-a), invitante
ap·plaud [əˈplɔ:d] VT applaudire; (*fig*) lodare, approvare
■ VI applaudire
ap·plause [əˈplɔ:z] N applauso; (*fig*) lode *f*, elogio; **a round of applause** un applauso
◎ **ap·ple** [ˈæpl] N (*fruit*) mela; **the apple of one's eye** (*fam*) la pupilla dei propri occhi; **apple tree** melo
apple blossom N fiore *m* di melo
apple·cart [ˈæpəl,kɑ:t] N: **to upset the applecart** (*fig*) rompere le uova nel paniere
apple core N torsolo (della mela)
apple corer N cavatorsoli *m inv*
apple orchard N meleto
apple pie N *crostata di mele ricoperta di pasta*; **in apple-pie order** in ordine perfetto
apple sauce N salsa di mele
ap·plet [ˈæplɪt] N (*Comput*) applet *m inv*, micro-programma *m*
apple tart N crostata di mele
apple turnover N sfogliatella alle mele
ap·pli·ance [əˈplaɪəns] N apparecchio; **electrical appliances** elettrodomestici *mpl*
ap·plic·abil·ity [,æplɪkəˈbɪlɪtɪ] N applicabilità
ap·pli·cable [əˈplɪkəbl] ADJ applicabile; **the law is applicable from January** la legge entrerà in vigore in gennaio; **to be applicable to** essere valido(-a) per
ap·pli·cant [ˈæplɪkənt] N (*for a post etc*) candidato(-a); (*Admin: for benefit, housing*) chi ha fatto domanda *or* richiesta; **there were a hundred applicants for that job** cento persone hanno fatto domanda per quel posto
◎ **ap·pli·ca·tion** [,æplɪˈkeɪʃən] N **1** (*act of applying*) applicazione *f*; **for external application only** (*Med*) (solo) per uso esterno; **the practical application of the theory** l'applicazione pratica della teoria **2** (*request: for university place, grant etc*) domanda; **a job application** una domanda di lavoro; **application for a job** domanda di assunzione; **on application** su richiesta; **further details may be had on application to X** per informazioni più dettagliate rivolgersi a X **3** (*Comput*) applicazione *f* **4** (*diligence*) applicazione *f*, impegno
application form N modulo di domanda
application program N (*Comput*) programma *m* applicativo
applications package N (*Comput*) software *m inv* applicativo
ap·plied [əˈplaɪd] ADJ applicato(-a); **applied linguistics** linguistica applicata; **applied arts** arti *fpl* applicate
ap·pli·qué [æˈpli:keɪ] N (*Sewing*) applicazione *f*
◎ **ap·ply** [əˈplaɪ] VT: **to apply (to)** (*ointment*) applicare (su), spalmare (su); (*plaster*) mettere (su), applicare (su); (*paint*) dare (a), stendere (su); (*rule, law, theory*) applicare (a); **to apply one's knowledge to sth** servirsi delle proprie nozioni per qc; **to apply one's mind to a problem** concentrarsi su un problema; **to apply o.s. (to one's studies)** applicarsi (nello studio); **to apply the brakes** azionare i freni, frenare
■ VI **1** (*be applicable*): **to apply (to)** applicarsi (a), essere valido(-a) (per); (*be suitable for, relevant to*) riguardare, riferirsi (a); **the law applies to everybody** la legge è valida *or* vale per tutti; **this rule doesn't apply** questa regola non vale; **this rule doesn't apply to us** questa norma non ci riguarda **2** (*request*) fare *or* presentare domanda; **to apply for a job** fare domanda d'impiego; **to apply for a visa** chiedere un visto; **to apply to a university** fare domanda d'ammissione all'università; **to apply to sb for sth** rivolgersi a qn per qc
◎ **ap·point** [əˈpɔɪnt] VT **1** (*nominate*) nominare; **they appointed him chairman** lo hanno nominato presidente; **they appointed a new teacher** hanno assunto un nuovo insegnante **2** (*frm: time, place*) fissare, stabilire; **at the appointed time** all'ora stabilita **3** **a well-appointed house** una casa ben attrezzata

> DID YOU KNOW ...?
> **appoint** is not translated by the Italian word *appuntare*

ap·poin·tee [əpɔɪnˈti:] N incaricato(-a)
◎ **ap·point·ment** [əˈpɔɪntmənt] N **1** (*arrangement to meet*) appuntamento; **by appointment** su *or* per appuntamento; **have you an appointment?** (*to caller*) ha un appuntamento?; **to keep an appointment** non mancare a un appuntamento; **she won't be able to keep the appointment** non potrà venire all'appuntamento; **to make an appointment with sb** prendere un appuntamento con qn; **I've got a dental appointment** ho un appuntamento dal dentista **2** (*to a job*) nomina; (*job*) posto, carica; (: *Press*): **"appointments (vacant)"** "offerte di impiego"
ap·por·tion [əˈpɔ:ʃən] VT (*praise, blame*) attribuire
ap·po·site [ˈæpəzɪt] ADJ (*frm: question, remark*) appropriato(-a), pertinente
ap·po·si·tion [,æpəˈzɪʃən] N (*Gram*) apposizione *f*
ap·prais·al [əˈpreɪzəl] N valutazione *f*, stima; (*fig*) giudizio
ap·praise [əˈpreɪz] VT (*value*) valutare, fare una stima di; (*fig*) dare *or* esprimere un giudizio su: *situation, fare il bilancio di*
ap·pre·ci·able [əˈpri:ʃəbl] ADJ (*increase, effect*) sensibile; (*change*) notevole
ap·pre·ci·ably [əˈpri:ʃəblɪ] ADV (*increase*) sensibilmente; (*change*) notevolmente
◎ **ap·pre·ci·ate** [əˈpri:ʃɪeɪt] VT **1** (*be grateful for*) apprezzare, essere riconoscente di, essere grato(-a) per; **I appreciated your help** ti sono grato per l'aiuto **2** (*value*) apprezzare; **I am not appreciated here** qui nessuno mi apprezza abbastanza **3** (*understand: problem, difference*) rendersi conto di; **yes, I appreciate that** certo, me ne rendo conto

■VI (*Comm: property*) aumentare (di valore)

ap·pre·cia·tion [əˌpriːʃɪ'eɪʃən] N **1** (*understanding*) comprensione *f*; (*praise*) apprezzamento; (*gratitude*) riconoscimento; (*Art: critique*) critica; **he showed no appreciation of my difficulties** non ha dimostrato di rendersi conto delle mie difficoltà; **as a token of my appreciation** in segno della mia gratitudine; **he has no appreciation of good music** non apprezza la buona musica **2** (*Comm: rise in value*) aumento (del valore)

ap·pre·cia·tive [ə'priːʃɪətɪv] ADJ (*look*) di ammirazione; (*comment*) di elogio, elogiativo(-a); (*audience*) caloroso(-a); **he was very appreciative of what I had done** mi era molto grato di *or* ha dimostrato di apprezzare molto quello che avevo fatto

ap·pre·cia·tive·ly [ə'priːʃɪətɪvlɪ] ADV (*look*) con ammirazione; (*applaud*) calorosamente

ap·pre·hend [ˌæprɪ'hɛnd] VT (*frm: arrest*) arrestare; (*: understand*) comprendere

> **DID YOU KNOW ...?**
> **apprehend** is not translated by the Italian word *apprendere*

ap·pre·hen·sion [ˌæprɪ'hɛnʃən] N **1** (*fear*) apprensione *f*, inquietudine *f*; **my chief apprehension is ...** la mia paura più grande è... **2** (*arrest*) arresto

ap·pre·hen·sive [ˌæprɪ'hɛnsɪv] ADJ (*person*) in apprensione; (*expression*) apprensivo(-a)

ap·pre·hen·sive·ly [ˌæprɪ'hɛnsɪvlɪ] ADV apprensivamente

ap·pren·tice [ə'prɛntɪs] N apprendista *m/f*; **a plumber's apprentice** *or* **an apprentice plumber** un apprendista idraulico

■VT: **to apprentice to** mettere come apprendista presso; **to be apprenticed to** lavorare come apprendista presso

ap·pren·tice·ship [ə'prɛntɪsʃɪp] N apprendistato, tirocinio; **to serve one's apprenticeship** fare il proprio apprendistato *or* tirocinio

ap·prise [ə'praɪz] VT (*frm*): **to apprise sb of sth** mettere qn a conoscenza di qc, informare qn di qc

ap·pro [æ'prəʊ] N ABBR (*Brit Comm: fam*) = **approval; on appro** salvo vista e verifica

◎ **ap·proach** [ə'prəʊtʃ] VT **1** (*come near: person*) avvicinarsi a, avvicinare; (*: animal*) avvicinarsi a; (*: place*) stare per arrivare a, avvicinarsi a; (*fig: subject, problem, job*) impostare, affrontare; **he approached the house** si è avvicinato alla casa; **I'm not sure how to approach the problem** non so come affrontare il problema; **I approached it with an open mind** ho considerato la cosa senza pregiudizi; **he's approaching 50** si avvicina ai 50, va per i 50; **no other painter approaches him** (*fig*) nessun altro pittore lo uguaglia **2** (*with request etc*): **to approach sb about sth** rivolgersi a qn per qc

■VI avvicinarsi; **the approaching elections** le imminenti elezioni

■N **1** (*act*) l'avvicinarsi *m*, avvicinamento; **at the approach of night** all'avvicinarsi della notte **2** (*to problem, subject*) modo di affrontare, approccio; **a new approach to maths** un nuovo approccio alla matematica **3** (*access*) accesso; **the northern approaches to the city** le vie d'accesso a nord della città **4** (*proposal, inquiry: about a job, project*) proposta; (*: to committee, department*) presa di contatto; **to make an approach to sb** contattare qn; **to make approaches to sb** (*amorous*) fare degli approcci *or* delle avances a qn

■ADJ di avvicinamento

ap·proach·able [ə'prəʊtʃəbl] ADJ (*person*) avvicinabile, accessibile

approach lights NPL (*Aer*) sentiero luminoso di avvicinamento

approach road N strada d'accesso

approach shot N (*Tennis*) colpo d'approccio

ap·pro·ba·tion [ˌæprə'beɪʃən] N (*frm*) approvazione *f*, benestare *m*

◎ **ap·pro·pri·ate** [*adj* ə'prəʊprɪɪt; *vb* ə'prəʊprɪeɪt] ADJ (*moment, name*) adatto(-a), opportuno(-a); (*remark*) opportuno(-a); (*word*) giusto(-a), adatto(-a); (*authority*) competente; **appropriate for** *or* **to** adatto(-a) a, appropriato(-a) a, adeguato(-a) a; **an outfit appropriate to the job** un abbigliamento adatto al lavoro; **it would not be appropriate for me to comment** non sta a me fare dei commenti; **tick the appropriate box** barrare l'apposita casella; **whichever seems more appropriate** ciò che sembra più adatto; **appropriate behaviour** comportamento corretto; **he is the appropriate person to ask** è lui il competente in materia

■VT **1** (*take for one's own use*) appropriarsi di **2** (*frm: allocate*) destinare, stanziare

ap·pro·pri·ate·ly [ə'prəʊprɪɪtlɪ] ADV in modo adatto *or* appropriato; **he was appropriately insured** era assicurato in modo adeguato *or* convenientemente

ap·pro·pria·tion [əprəʊprɪ'eɪʃən] N (*taking for oneself*) appropriazione *f*; (*allocation*) stanziamento

◎ **ap·prov·al** [ə'pruːvəl] N (*consent*) approvazione *f*, consenso; **on approval** (*Comm*) in prova, in esame; **to meet with sb's approval** essere di gradimento di qn, soddisfare qn

◎ **ap·prove** [ə'pruːv] VT approvare

▸ **approve of** VI + PREP approvare; **I don't approve of his choice** non approvo la sua scelta; **I don't approve of kids going to pubs** non approvo *or* disapprovo che i ragazzi vadano al pub; **she doesn't approve of me** disapprova il mio modo di essere

ap·proved [ə'pruːvd] ADJ **1** (*method, practice*) riconosciuto(-a), approvato(-a); **read and approved** letto e approvato **2** (*authorized*) autorizzato(-a)

approved school [ə'pruːvd'skuːl] N (*Brit: old*) riformatorio

ap·prov·ing [ə'pruːvɪŋ] ADJ d'approvazione

ap·prov·ing·ly [ə'pruːvɪŋlɪ] ADV con approvazione

approx. ABBR = **approximately**

ap·proxi·mate [*adj* ə'prɒksɪmɪt; *vb* ə'prɒksɪmeɪt] ADJ approssimativo(-a), approssimato(-a)

■VI: **to approximate to** essere un'approssimazione di, avvicinarsi a

ap·proxi·mate·ly [ə'prɒksɪmətlɪ] ADV approssimativamente, pressappoco, circa

ap·proxi·ma·tion [əˌprɒksɪ'meɪʃən] N approssimazione *f*

ap·pur·te·nances [ə'pɜːtɪnənsɪz] NPL accessori *mpl*

APR [ˌeɪpiː'ɑːʳ] N ABBR (= **annual percentage rate**) tasso percentuale annuo

Apr. ABBR (= **April**) apr. (= *aprile*)

après-ski [ˌæpreɪ'skiː] N *attività ricreative in una località sciistica*

apri·cot ['eɪprɪˌkɒt] N (*fruit*) albicocca; **apricot tree** albicocco

April ['eɪprəl] N aprile *m*; *for usage see* **July**

April fool N (*victim*) pesce *m* d'aprile

April Fool's Day N il primo d'aprile

Aa

APRIL FOOL'S DAY

April Fool's Day è il primo aprile, il giorno degli scherzi e delle burle. Il nome deriva dal fatto che, se una persona cade nella trappola che gli è stata tesa, fa la figura del fool, cioè dello sciocco. Persino i giornalisti a volte inventano vicende incredibili per burlarsi dei lettori.
▷ www.bbc.co.uk/dna/ww2/A516791

a prio·ri [ɑːprɪ'ɔːrɪ] ADJ (*frm: argument*) a priori; (*: judgment, statement*) aprioristico(-a); **an a priori decision** una decisione presa a priori
apron ['eɪprən] N **1** (*gen, workman's*) grembiule *m*; **tied to his mother's/wife's apron strings** attaccato alle sottane di sua madre/moglie **2** (*Aer*) area di stazionamento
apron stage N (*Theatre*) proscenio
ap·ro·pos [,æprə'pəʊ] PREP (*with regard to*): **apropos (of)** a proposito di
■ ADV (*frm: incidentally*) a proposito
■ ADJ (*frm*) appropriato(-a)
apse [æps] N (*Archit, Geom*) abside *f*
APT [,eɪpiː'tiː] N ABBR (*Brit:* = **advanced passenger train**) treno ad alta velocità
apt [æpt] ADJ (*comp* **-er**, *superl* **-est**) **1** (*suitable: remark*) appropriato(-a), adatto(-a), pertinente; (*: description*) felice, indovinato(-a), giusto(-a) **2** (*liable*): **to be apt to do sth** avere (la) tendenza a fare qc; **I am apt to be out on Mondays** generalmente di lunedì non ci sono; **we are apt to forget that ...** tendiamo a dimenticare che... **3** (*pupil, student: able*) dotato(-a), capace
apt. ABBR = **apartment**
ap·ti·tude ['æptɪtjuːd] N (*ability*) abilità *f inv*
aptitude test N test *m inv* attitudinale
apt·ly ['æptlɪ] ADV appropriatamente, in modo adatto; **she was aptly dressed for the occasion** aveva un vestito adatto all'occasione
apt·ness ['æptnɪs] N opportunità *f inv*
aq ABBR = **aqueous solution**
aqua·lung ['ækwə,lʌŋ] N autorespiratore *m*
aqua·marine [,ækwəmə'riːn] N acquamarina
■ ADJ acquamarina *inv*
aqua·plane ['ækwə,pleɪn] N acquaplano
■ VI **1** (*Sport*) praticare l'acquaplano **2** (*Aut*) andare in aquaplaning
aquar·ium [ə'kwɛərɪəm] N acquario
Aquar·ius [ə'kwɛərɪəs] N Acquario; **to be Aquarius** essere dell'Acquario
aquat·ic [ə'kwætɪk] ADJ acquatico(-a)
aque·duct ['ækwɪ,dʌkt] N acquedotto
aque·ous ['eɪkwɪəs] ADJ acquoso(-a); **aqueous solution** soluzione *f* acquosa
aqui·fer ['ækwɪfə^r] N (*Geol*) acquifero
aqui·line ['ækwɪ,laɪn] ADJ aquilino(-a)
AR ABBR (*Am Post*) = **Arkansas**
ARA [,eɪɑːr'eɪ] N ABBR (*Brit*) = *Associate of the Royal Academy*
Arab ['ærəb] N (*person*) arabo(-a); (*horse*) cavallo arabo; **the Arabs** gli arabi
■ ADJ arabo(-a)
ara·besque [,ærə'besk] N arabesco
Ara·bia [ə'reɪbɪə] N Arabia
Ara·bian [ə'reɪbɪən] ADJ arabo(-a), arabico(-a)
Arabian Desert N: **the Arabian Desert** il Deserto arabico
Arabian Nights N: **the Arabian Nights** le Mille e una Notte
Arabian Sea N: **the Arabian Sea** il mare *m* Arabico
Ara·bic ['ærəbɪk] N (*language*) arabo
■ ADJ arabo(-a), arabico(-a)
Arabic numerals NPL numeri *mpl* arabi, numerazione *fsg* araba
ar·able ['ærəbl] ADJ arabile, arativo(-a); **arable farming** coltura del terreno
Ara·gon ['ærəgən] N Aragona
Ara·ma·ic [,ærə'meɪɪk] N (*language*) aramaico
■ ADJ aramaico(-a)
ar·bi·ter ['ɑːbɪtə^r] N (*frm*) arbitro
ar·bi·trage ['ɑːbɪtrɪdʒ] N (*Fin*) arbitraggio
ar·bi·tra·geur [,ɑːbɪtræ'ʒɜː^r] N (*Fin*) arbitraggista *m/f*
ar·bi·trari·ly ['ɑːbɪtrərəlɪ] ADV arbitrariamente
ar·bi·trary ['ɑːbɪtrərɪ] ADJ arbitrario(-a)
ar·bi·trate ['ɑːbɪtreɪt] VI fare da arbitro, arbitrare
ar·bi·tra·tion [,ɑːbɪ'treɪʃən] N (*Law*) arbitrato; (*Industry*) arbitraggio; **the dispute went to arbitration** la controversia è stata sottoposta ad arbitrato
ar·bi·tra·tor ['ɑːbɪtreɪtə^r] N arbitro
ar·bour, ar·bor ['ɑːbə^r] N pergolato
ARC [,eɪɑː'siː] N ABBR **1** (= **Aids Related Complex**) ARC *m* **2** (= **American Red Cross**) ≈ CRI *f*
arc [ɑːk] N arco
ar·cade [ɑː'keɪd] N (*passage with shops*) galleria; (*series of arches*) portico; (*round public square*) porticato, portici *mpl*; **a shopping arcade** una galleria con negozi
Ar·ca·dia [ɑː'keɪdɪə] N Arcadia
Ar·ca·dian [ɑː'keɪdɪən] ADJ arcadico(-a)
■ N arcade *m/f*
ar·cane [ɑː'keɪn] ADJ (*frm*) arcano(-a)
arch[1] [ɑːtʃ] N **1** (*Archit*) arco, arcata **2** (*of foot*) arco *or* arcata plantare
■ VT (*back, body*) arcuare, inarcare; (*eyebrows*) inarcare
arch[2] [ɑːtʃ] ADJ grande (*before n*), per eccellenza; **an arch villain** un grande criminale; **the arch villain** il cattivo per eccellenza; **his arch rival** il suo rivale per eccellenza
arch[3] [ɑːtʃ] ADJ (*liter: playful: look, smile*) furbesco(-a); (*: tone*) malizioso(-a)
arch- [ɑːtʃ] PREF grande
ar·chaeo·logi·cal [,ɑːkɪə'lɒdʒɪkəl] ADJ archeologico(-a)
ar·chae·olo·gist [,ɑːkɪ'ɒlədʒɪst] N archeologo(-a)
ar·chae·ol·ogy [,ɑːkɪ'ɒlədʒɪ] N archeologia
▷ www.english-heritage.org.uk/
▷ www.english-heritage.org.uk/default.asp
▷ www.archaeologychannel.org/
▷ www.ashmol.ox.ac.uk/
▷ www.oxfordarch.co.uk/
▷ www.cyberpursuits.com/archeo/
ar·cha·ic [ɑː'keɪɪk] ADJ arcaico(-a)
ar·cha·ism ['ɑːkeɪɪzəm] N arcaismo
arch·angel ['ɑːk,eɪndʒəl] N arcangelo
arch·bishop ['ɑːtʃ'bɪʃəp] N arcivescovo
arch·deacon ['ɑːtʃ'diːkən] N arcidiacono
arch·duke ['ɑːtʃ'djuːk] N arciduca *m*
arched [ɑːtʃt] ADJ arcuato(-a), ad arco
arch·en·emy [,ɑːtʃ'ɛnɪmɪ] N **1** (*chief enemy*) nemico per eccellenza **2** (*Rel*): **the Arch-enemy** (*the Devil*) il diavolo
archeology *etc* [,ɑːkɪ'ɒlədʒɪ] (*esp Am*) = **archaeology** *etc*
arch·er ['ɑːtʃə^r] N arciere *m*
ar·chery ['ɑːtʃərɪ] N tiro con l'arco
ar·che·typ·al ['ɑːkɪtaɪpəl] ADJ tipico(-a)

ar·che·type ['ɑ:kɪ,taɪp] N (*original*) archetipo; (*epitome*) prototipo
Archimedes [,ɑ:kɪ'mi:di:z] N Archimede *m*
archi·pela·go [,ɑ:kɪ'pɛlɪgəʊ] N (*pl* **archipelagos** *or* **archipelagoes**) arcipelago
archi·tect ['ɑ:kɪ,tɛkt] N architetto
archi·tec·tur·al [,ɑ:kɪ'tɛktʃərəl] ADJ (*plan, drawing*) architettonico(-a); (*practice, student*) di architettura
arch·itec·tur·al·ly ['ɑ:kɪ,tɛktʃərəlɪ] ADV architettonicamente
archi·tec·ture ['ɑ:kɪ,tɛktʃə^r] N architettura
▷ www.architecture.com
▷ www.architectureweek.com
▷ www.bluffton.edu/~sullivanm/index
archive file ['ɑ:kaɪv] N (*Comput*) file *m inv* di archivio
ar·chives ['ɑ:kaɪvz] NPL archivio *msg*, archivi *mpl*
archi·vist ['ɑ:kɪvɪst] N archivista *m/f*
arch·ly ['ɑ:tʃlɪ] ADV (*speak, smile*) maliziosamente
arch-rival [,ɑ:tʃ'raɪvəl] N rivale *m/f* di sempre
arch·way ['ɑ:tʃweɪ] N (*passage*) (passaggio a) volta; (*arch*) arco, arcata
arc light N lampada ad arco
ARCM [,eɪɑ:si:'ɛm] N ABBR (*Brit*) = *Associate of the Royal College of Music*
arc·tic ['ɑ:ktɪk] ADJ artico(-a); (*fig: very cold*) polare
■ N: **the Arctic** l'Artico
Arctic Circle N: **the Arctic Circle** il Circolo polare artico
arctic fox N volpe *f* polare *or* bianca
Arctic Ocean N: **the Arctic Ocean** l'Oceano artico
arctic skua ['ɑ:ktɪk'skju:ə] N labbo
arc welding N saldatura ad arco
ar·dent ['ɑ:dənt] ADJ (*supporter*) ardente, fervente; (*desire, lover*) ardente
ar·dent·ly ['ɑ:dəntlɪ] ADV ardentemente
ar·dour, (*Am*) **ar·dor** ['ɑ:də^r] N (*frm*) ardore *m*
ar·du·ous ['ɑ:djʊəs] ADJ arduo(-a)
ar·du·ous·ly ['ɑ:djʊəslɪ] ADV a fatica, con difficoltà
ar·du·ous·ness ['ɑ:djʊəsnɪs] N difficoltà *f inv*
are[1] [ɑ:^r, ə^r] 2ND PERS SG, 1ST, 2ND AND 3RD PERS PL PRESENT *of* **be**
are[2] [ɑ:^r] N (*unit of measure*) ara
◎ **area** ['ɛərɪə] N **1** (*surface extent*) area, superficie *f*; (*Geom*) area; **the field has an area of 2000 square metres** il campo ha una superficie di 2000 metri quadrati **2** (*region*) zona; (*district*) zona, settore *m*; **the London area** la zona di Londra; **my favourite area of London is Chelsea** il quartiere londinese che preferisco è Chelsea **3** (*fig: of knowledge*) campo; (: *of responsibility etc*) sfera; **matters outside my area of responsibility** questioni che esulano dalla mia competenza; **in the area of £5,000** sulle *or* intorno alle 5.000 sterline
area code N (*Am Telec*) prefisso
area manager N direttore *m* di zona
arena [ə'ri:nə] N arena
◎ **aren't** [ɑ:nt] = are not
Ar·gen·ti·na [,ɑ:dʒən'ti:nə] N l'Argentina
Ar·gen·tin·ian [,ɑ:dʒən'tɪnɪən] ADJ, N argentino(-a)
argie-bargie ['ɑ:dʒɪ'bɑ:dʒɪ] N = **argy-bargy**
ar·gon ['ɑ:gɒn] N argo
Ar·go·naut ['ɑ:gə,nɔ:t] N argonauta *m*
ar·gu·able ['ɑ:gjʊəbl] ADJ (*rather doubtful*) discutibile; (*capable of being argued for*): **it is arguable that ...** si può sostenere che...; **it is arguable whether ...** è una cosa discutibile se... *+sub*
ar·gu·ably ['ɑ:gjʊəblɪ] ADV: **it is arguably ...** si può sostenere che sia...
◎ **ar·gue** ['ɑ:gju:] VI **1** (*dispute*) litigare; **to argue about sth (with sb)** litigare per *or* a proposito di qc (con qn); **don't argue!** senza tante discussioni!, non discutere!; **they're always arguing** litigano sempre **2** (*reason*) ragionare; **to argue against/for** portare degli argomenti contro/in favore di
■ VT (*debate: case, matter*) dibattere, discutere; (*persuade*): **to argue sb into doing sth** persuadere *or* convincere qn a fare qc; **to argue that ...** (*maintain*) sostenere *or* affermare che...; **it could be argued that little progress has been made since** si può dire che da allora non sono stati fatti molti progressi
◎ **ar·gu·ment** ['ɑ:gjʊmənt] N **1** (*reasons*) argomento, ragione *f*, motivo; **argument for/against** argomento a *or* in favore di/contro; **there are strong arguments against lowering the price** ci sono motivi validi per non abbassare il prezzo; **I don't follow your argument** non ti seguo **2** (*discussion*) discussione *f*, dibattito; (*quarrel*) litigio, lite *f*; **to have an argument** litigare; **to hear both sides of the argument** ascoltare entrambe le versioni
ar·gu·men·ta·tive [,ɑ:gjʊ'mɛntətɪv] ADJ polemico(-a)
argy-bargy ['ɑ:dʒɪ'bɑ:dʒɪ] N (*fam*) discussione *f*, litigio
aria ['ɑ:rɪə] N aria
Ariadne [,ærɪ'ædnɪ] N Ariadne *f*
ARIBA [ə'ri:bə] N ABBR (*Brit*) = *Associate of the Royal Institute of British Architects*
arid ['ærɪd] ADJ arido(-a); (*fig*) piatto(-a)
arid·ity [ə'rɪdɪtɪ] N aridità
ar·id·ly ['ærɪdlɪ] ADV aridamente
Aries ['ɛəri:z] N Ariete *m*; **to be Aries** essere dell'Ariete
aright [ə'raɪt] ADV **1 if I heard aright** se ho sentito bene **2 to set things aright** sistemare le cose
◎ **arise** [ə'raɪz] (*pt* **arose**, *pp* **arisen**) [ə'rɪzn] VI **1** (*occur: opportunity, problem*) presentarsi, offrirsi; (*result*): **to arise (from)** derivare (da); **difficulties have arisen** sono sorte delle difficoltà; **should the need arise** dovesse presentarsi la necessità, in caso di necessità; **a storm arose** si scatenò una tempesta; **the question does not arise** la questione non si pone **2** (*old: get up*) levarsi (*frm*), alzarsi
aris·en [ə'rɪzn] PP *of* **arise**
ar·is·toc·ra·cy [,ærɪs'tɒkrəsɪ] N aristocrazia
aris·to·crat ['ærɪstə,kræt] N nobile *m/f*, aristocratico(-a)
aris·to·crat·ic [,ærɪstə'krætɪk] ADJ aristocratico(-a)
aris·to·crati·cal·ly [,ærɪstə'krætɪklɪ] ADV aristocraticamente
Aristophanes [,ærɪs'tɒfə,ni:z] N Aristofane *m*
Ar·is·to·telian [,ærɪstə'ti:lɪən] ADJ aristotelico(-a)
Aristotle ['ærɪ,stɒtl] N Aristotele *m*
arith·me·tic [*n* ə'rɪθmətɪk; *adj* ,ærɪθ'mɛtɪk] N aritmetica; **mental arithmetic** calcolo mentale
■ ADJ aritmetico(-a); **arithmetic progression** progressione *f* aritmetica
arith·meti·cal [,ærɪθ'mɛtɪkəl] ADJ aritmetico(-a)
Ariz. ABBR (*Am*) = **Arizona**
Ari·zo·na [,ærɪ'zəʊnə] N Arizona
▷ http://az.gov/webapp/portal/
Ark. ABBR (*Am*) = **Arkansas**
ark [ɑ:k] N (*Bible*) arca; **Noah's Ark** l'arca di Noè; **it must have come out of the ark!** (*hum fam*) sembra un reperto archeologico
Ar·kan·sas ['ɑ:kənsɔ:] N Arkansas *m*
▷ www.state.ar.us/

Aa

◎ **arm** [ɑːm] N (*Anat*) braccio; (*of chair*) bracciolo; **arm in arm** a braccetto, sottobraccio; **with open arms** (*fig*) a braccia aperte; **within arm's reach** a portata di mano; **to keep sb at arm's length** (*fig*) tenere qn a distanza; **to put one's arm round sb** mettere un braccio intorno alle spalle di qn; *see also* **arms**
■ VT (*person, ship*) armare; **he armed himself with some good arguments** si è armato di validi argomenti
ar·ma·da [ɑːˈmɑːdə] N armata (navale)
ar·ma·dil·lo [ˌɑːməˈdɪləʊ] N armadillo
ar·ma·ments [ˈɑːməmənts] NPL (*weapons*) armamenti *mpl*
ar·ma·ture [ˈɑːmətjʊəʳ] N (*Elec, Sculpture*) armatura
arm·band [ˈɑːmˌbænd] N bracciale *m*
arm·chair [ˈɑːmˌtʃɛəʳ] N poltrona
◎ **armed** [ɑːmd] ADJ armato(-a); **armed to the teeth** armato(-a) fino ai denti; **she was armed with all the facts** aveva in mano tutti i fatti
◎ **armed forces** NPL forze *fpl* armate
armed robbery N rapina a mano armata
Ar·me·nia [ɑːˈmiːnɪə] N Armenia
Ar·me·nian [ɑːˈmiːnɪən] ADJ armeno(-a)
■ N (*person*) armeno(-a); (*language*) armeno
arm·ful [ˈɑːmfʊl] N bracciata
arm·hole [ˈɑːmˌhəʊl] N giro *m* manica *inv*
ar·mi·stice [ˈɑːmɪstɪs] N armistizio
ar·mour, (*Am*) **ar·mor** [ˈɑːməʳ] N armatura; (*also:* **armour-plating**) corazza, blindatura; (*Mil: tanks*) mezzi *mpl* blindati
ar·moured, ar·mored [ˈɑːməd] (*Am*) ADJ
1 **armoured divisions** divisioni *fpl* corazzate **2** (*Zool*) rivestito(-a) di aculei *or* corazza
armoured car, (*Am*) **armored car** [ˈɑːməd ˈkɑːʳ] N autoblinda *f inv*
armour-plated [ˌɑːməˈpleɪtɪd] ADJ (*tank, warship*) corazzato(-a); (*fig: alibi*) di ferro
ar·moury, (*Am*) **ar·mory** [ˈɑːmərɪ] N arsenale *m*, armeria
arm·pit [ˈɑːmˌpɪt] N ascella
arm·rest [ˈɑːmˌrɛst] N bracciolo
arms [ɑːmz] NPL **1** (*weapons*) armi *fpl*; **to be up in arms** (*fig*) essere sul piede di guerra **2** (*Heraldry: also:* **coat of arms**) stemma *m*
arms control N controllo degli armamenti
arms factory N fabbrica d'armi
arms race N corsa agli armamenti
◎ **army** [ˈɑːmɪ] N (*Mil, fig*) esercito; **to join the army** arruolarsi
army life N vita militare
aro·ma [əˈrəʊmə] N aroma *m*
aroma·thera·py [əˌrəʊməˈθɛrəpɪ] N aromaterapia
aro·mat·ic [ˌærəʊˈmætɪk] ADJ aromatico(-a)
arose [əˈrəʊz] PT *of* **arise**
◎ **around** [əˈraʊnd] ADV **1** (*place*) attorno, intorno; **she ignored the people around her** ha ignorato la gente che aveva intorno; **around here** da queste parti; **is there a chemist's around here?** c'è una farmacia da queste parti?; **for miles around** nel raggio di chilometri; **he must be somewhere around** dev'essere qui in giro *or* nei paraggi; **do you know your way around?** conosci il luogo?, sai come muoverti qui attorno? **2** (*approximately*) all'incirca, circa; **around 10 o'clock** verso le 10; **it costs around 100 pounds** costa circa 100 sterline
■ PREP intorno a; **it's just around the corner** è appena girato l'angolo; **I've travelled around the country** ho girato tutto il paese

arous·al [əˈraʊzəl] N (*sexual*) eccitazione *f*; (*awakening*) risveglio
arouse [əˈraʊz] VT (*awaken: sleeper*) svegliare; (*fig: person*) eccitare, stimolare; (*: feelings*) suscitare
ar·peg·gio [ɑːˈpɛdʒɪəʊ] N (*Mus*) arpeggio
ar·raign [əˈreɪn] VT (*Law*) accusare; **to be arraigned for sth/on charges of sth** venir accusato di qc
ar·raign·ment [əˈreɪnmənt] N (*Law*) lettura dell'atto di accusa
◎ **ar·range** [əˈreɪndʒ] VT **1** (*put into order: books, thoughts, furniture*) sistemare, ordinare; (*hair*) acconciare; (*flowers*) sistemare; **the chairs were arranged in a circle** le sedie erano sistemate in cerchio **2** (*Mus*) adattare, arrangiare **3** (*decide on: meeting*) combinare, organizzare; (*: date*) stabilire, fissare; (*: programme*) stabilire, preparare; **to arrange a time for** stabilire *or* fissare una data per; **everything is arranged** è tutto a posto; **it was arranged that ...** è stato deciso *or* stabilito che...; **she arranged a trip to Scotland** ha organizzato un viaggio in Scozia; **what did you arrange with him?** per *or* su che cosa siete rimasti d'accordo?; **to arrange to do sth** mettersi d'accordo per fare qc; **they arranged to go out together on Friday** si sono messi d'accordo per uscire venerdì
■ VI mettersi d'accordo, combinare; **to arrange for sth/for sb to do sth** organizzare *or* predisporre qc/che qn faccia qc; **we have arranged for a taxi to pick you up** la faremo venire a prendere da un taxi; **I have arranged for you to go** ho dato disposizione in modo che lei vada
◎ **ar·range·ment** [əˈreɪndʒmənt] N **1** (*order, act of ordering*) sistemazione *f*, disposizione *f*; (*Mus*) arrangiamento; **a flower arrangement** una composizione floreale **2** (*agreement*) accordo; **to come to an arrangement (with sb)** venire a un accordo (con qn), mettersi d'accordo *or* accordarsi (con qn); **we have an arrangement** siamo d'accordo; **by arrangement** su richiesta; **by arrangement with the tour operator** secondo gli accordi con l'operatore turistico; **by arrangement with La Scala** con l'autorizzazione del Teatro della Scala **3** (*plan*) piano, programma *m*; **arrangements** NPL (*preparations*) preparativi *mpl*; **I'll make arrangements for you to be met** darò disposizioni *or* istruzioni perché ci sia qualcuno ad incontrarla; **we must make arrangements to help** dobbiamo organizzarci per dare un aiuto; **all the arrangements for the party are made** sono stati ultimati i preparativi per la festa; **Pamela is in charge of the travel arrangements** Pamela si occupa dei preparativi del viaggio
ar·rant [ˈærənt] ADJ: **arrant nonsense** colossali sciocchezze *fpl*
ar·ray [əˈreɪ] N **1** (*of troops, police etc*) schieramento; **in battle array** in ordine di battaglia; **a fine array of hats/cakes** tanti cappelli/tante torte in bella mostra **2** (*Math*) tabella; (*Comput*) array *m inv*, matrice *f*
ar·rears [əˈrɪəz] NPL (*of money*) arretrati *mpl*; **arrears of filing** pratiche *fpl* arretrate da archiviare; **in arrears** in arretrato; **to be in arrears with one's rent** essere in arretrato con l'affitto
◎ **ar·rest** [əˈrɛst] N arresto; **to be under arrest** essere in (stato di) arresto; **to place sb under arrest** arrestare qn, mettere qn in stato di arresto; **you're under arrest!** la dichiaro in arresto!
■ VT (*criminal*) arrestare; (*attention, interest*) fermare, attirare; (*halt: progress, decay etc*) arrestare, bloccare

ar·rest·ing [əˈrɛstɪŋ] ADJ (*fig*) che colpisce
ar·rhyth·mia [əˈrɪðmɪə] N aritmia
◎ **ar·ri·val** [əˈraɪvəl] N (*gen*) arrivo; (*person*) arrivato(-a); **a new arrival** (*newcomer*) un/a nuovo(-a) venuto(-a); (*baby*) un/a neonato(-a); **on arrival** all'arrivo
◎ **ar·rive** [əˈraɪv] VI (*gen*) arrivare; (*day, time*) arrivare, giungere; **we arrived at eight** siamo arrivati alle otto ▸ **arrive at** VI + PREP (*place, price*) arrivare a; (*decision, solution*) arrivare a, giungere a
ar·ro·gance [ˈærəgəns] N arroganza
ar·ro·gant [ˈærəgənt] ADJ arrogante
ar·ro·gant·ly [ˈærəgəntlɪ] ADV in modo arrogante
ar·row [ˈærəʊ] N freccia
arrow·head [ˈærəʊˌhɛd] N **1** punta di freccia **2** (*Bot*) sagittaria
arse [ɑːs] N (*Brit fam!*) culo (*fam!*)
arse·hole [ˈɑːsˌhəʊl] N (*Brit fam!*) **1** (*anus*) buco del culo (*fam!*) **2** coglionazzo(-a) (*fam!*)
ar·senal [ˈɑːsɪnl] N arsenale *m*
ar·senic [ˈɑːsnɪk] N arsenico
ar·son [ˈɑːsn] N incendio doloso
ar·son·ist [ˈɑːsənɪst] N incendiario(-a)
◎ **art** [ɑːt] N **1** arte *f*; (*craft*) mestiere *m*; (*Scol: subject*) disegno e storia dell'arte; **to study art** fare degli studi artistici; **Greek art** l'arte greca; **he's good at art** è bravo nelle materie artistiche; **work of art** opera d'arte; *see also* **arts**
■ ADJ d'arte
art collection N collezione *f* d'arte
ar·te·fact, (*Am*) **ar·ti·fact** [ˈɑːtɪfækt] N manufatto
Artemis [ˈɑːtɪmɪs] N Artemide *f*
ar·te·rial [ɑːˈtɪərɪəl] ADJ (*Anat*) arterioso(-a); (*road etc*) di grande comunicazione; **arterial roads** le (grandi *or* principali) arterie
ar·te·rio·sclero·sis [ɑːˈtɪərɪəʊsklɪˈrəʊsɪs] N arteriosclerosi *f*
ar·tery [ˈɑːtərɪ] N (*Anat, fig*) arteria
ar·te·sian well [ɑːˈtiːzɪən wɛl] N: **artesian well** pozzo artesiano
art·ful [ˈɑːtfʊl] ADJ (*person*) furbo(-a), abile; (*trick*) abile
art·ful·ly [ˈɑːtfəlɪ] ADV astutamente, abilmente
art·ful·ness [ˈɑːtfʊlnɪs] N astuzia, abilità *f inv*
art gallery N (*museum*) museo, galleria d'arte; (*shop*) galleria d'arte
ar·thrit·ic [ɑːˈθrɪtɪk] ADJ, N artritico(-a)
ar·thri·tis [ɑːˈθraɪtɪs] N artrite *f*
arthro·pod [ˈɑːθrəˌpɒd] N artropode *m*
Arthur [ˈɑːθəʳ] N: **King Arthur** re Artù
▹ www.kingarthursknights.com/
▹ www.legends.dm.net/kingarthur/
Ar·thu·rian [ɑːˈθjʊərɪən] ADJ arturiano(-a), di re Artù
ar·ti·choke [ˈɑːtˌɪtʃəʊk] N (*globe artichoke*) carciofo; (*Jerusalem artichoke*) topinambur *m inv*
◎ **ar·ti·cle** [ˈɑːtɪkl] N **1** (*Admin, Law, Comm, Gram*) articolo; (*object*) oggetto; **articles of clothing** articoli *mpl* di vestiario, indumenti *mpl* **2** **articles** NPL (*Brit Law, Admin*) contratto di tirocinio; **to be in articles** fare il tirocinio
ar·ti·cled [ˈɑːtɪkld] ADJ (*Law: clerk*): **to be articled to sb** svolgere la pratica presso qn
article of faith N credo
articles of association NPL (*Comm*) statuto sociale
ar·ticu·late [*adj* ɑːˈtɪkjʊlɪt; *vb* ɑːˈtɪkjʊleɪt] ADJ (*account, diction*) chiaro(-a); (*person*) che si esprime bene
■ VT (*words*) articolare, pronunciare
ar·ticu·lated lor·ry [ɑːˈtɪkjʊleɪtɪdˈlɒrɪ] N (*Brit*) autoarticolato
ar·ticu·late·ly [ɑːˈtɪkjʊlɪtlɪ] ADV chiaramente
ar·ticu·la·tion [ɑːˌtɪkjʊˈleɪʃən] N (*of sounds*) articolazione *f*; (*of speech*) dizione *f*
ar·ti·fact [ˈɑːtɪˌfækt] N (*Am*) = **artefact**
ar·ti·fice [ˈɑːtɪfɪs] N (*frm: cunning*) abilità, destrezza; (*: trick*) artificio
ar·ti·fi·cial [ˌɑːtɪˈfɪʃəl] ADJ (*synthetic*) artificiale; (*fig pej: smile, manner*) studiato(-a), affettato(-a); (*: tears, situation*) falso(-a)
artificial insemination N inseminazione *f or* fecondazione *f* artificiale
artificial intelligence N intelligenza artificiale
ar·ti·fi·ci·al·ity [ˌɑːtɪfɪʃɪˈælɪtɪ] N artificiosità
ar·ti·fi·cial·ly [ˌɑːtɪˈfɪʃəlɪ] ADV (*gen*) artificialmente; (*behave, smile*) artificiosamente
artificial respiration N respirazione *f* artificiale
ar·til·lery [ɑːˈtɪlərɪ] N artiglieria
ar·ti·san [ˈɑːtɪˌzæn] N artigiano(-a)
◎ **art·ist** [ˈɑːtɪst] N artista *m/f*
ar·tiste [ɑːˈtiːst] N (*Cine, Theatre, TV*) artista *m/f*
ar·tis·tic [ɑːˈtɪstɪk] ADJ artistico(-a); **to be artistic** avere una sensibilità artistica
ar·tis·ti·cal·ly [ɑːˈtɪstɪkəlɪ] ADV artisticamente
art·ist·ry [ˈɑːtɪstrɪ] N (*skill*) arte *f*, abilità artistica
art·less [ˈɑːtlɪs] ADJ ingenuo(-a), semplice
art·less·ly [ˈɑːtlɪslɪ] ADV ingenuamente
arts [ɑːts] NPL (*Univ*) lettere *fpl*, studi *mpl* umanistici; **the arts** le belle arti; **arts and crafts** artigianato; **Faculty of Arts** facoltà di Lettere; **You can study arts or science.** Si possono fare studi umanistici o scientifici
art school N scuola d'arte
Arts degree N laurea in lettere
Arts student N studente(-essa) di discipline umanistiche
art student N studente(-essa) di belle arti
art·work [ˈɑːtˌwɜːk] N materiale *m* illustrativo
arty [ˈɑːtɪ] ADJ: **arty types** pseudo artisti *mpl*
arty farty [ˌɑːtɪˈfɑːtɪ] ADJ pretenzioso(-a), con pretese artistiche
ARV [ˌeɪɑːˈviː] N ABBR (= **American Revised Version**) *traduzione americana della Bibbia*
Aryan [ˈɛərɪən] ADJ, N ariano(-a)
AS [ˌeɪˈɛs] N ABBR (*Am Univ:* = **Associate in Sciences**) *laurea in discipline scientifiche*
■ ABBR (*Am Post*) = *American Samoa*

◎ **as** [æz, əz] KEYWORD
■ CONJ
1 (*time*) mentre, quando; **as I get older, I ...** con l'età io...; **as the years went by** col passare degli anni; **he came in as I was leaving** è arrivato nel momento in cui *or* quando stavo per andarmene; **as a child ...** da bambino...; **as** *or* **so long as** finché; **as soon as she arrived I left** me ne sono andato appena lei è arrivata
2 (*because*) visto che, poiché, dal momento che, siccome; **as he had been up since 4 a.m. he was exhausted** era esausto perché si era alzato alle 4; **as it's Sunday, you can have a lie-in** visto che è domenica puoi restare a letto fino a tardi
3 (*although*): **much as I like them, ...** per quanto mi siano simpatici, ...; **try as he might, he couldn't do it** malgrado i suoi sforzi, non ha potuto farlo; **young as he was he understood the situation perfectly** anche se giovane capì perfettamente la situazione
4 (*way, manner: also preposition*) come; **you've got plenty as it is** ne hai già abbastanza; **do as you wish** fa' come

Aa

vuoi; **leave things as they are** lascia tutto così com'è; **as I've said before ...** come ho già detto...
5 (*concerning*): **as for, as regards, as to** per quanto *or* quello che riguarda, quanto a; **as for the children, they were exhausted** quanto ai bambini, erano sfiniti; **as to that I can't say** su quello non ti so dire
6 as if, as though come se + *sub*; **he fought as if his life depended on it** si è battuto come se ne andasse della sua vita; **he got up as if to leave** si alzò come per andarsene; **he looked as if he was ill** aveva l'aria di star male
7 (*providing*): **as** *or* **so long as** purché
■ ADV (*in comparisons*): **as big as** tanto grande quanto; **twice as big as** due volte più grande di; **this car will go as fast as 120 m.p.h.** questa macchina raggiunge le 120 miglia all'ora; **I didn't know it could go as fast as that** non sapevo che fosse così veloce; **as many (as)** tanti(-e) (... quanti(-e)); **you've got as much as she has** ne hai (tanto) quanto ne ha lei; **twice as old** due volte più vecchio(-a); **her coat cost twice as much as mine** il suo cappotto è costato il doppio del mio; **as pale as death** pallido(-a) come un morto; **as quickly as possible** il più rapidamente possibile; **as soon as possible** prima possibile; **as tall as him** alto(-a) come lui; **Peter's as tall as Michael** Peter è alto come Michael
■ PREP
1 (*in the capacity of*) da; **he works as a waiter in the holidays** durante le vacanze lavora come cameriere; **disguised as a nun** travestito(-a) da suora; **he gave it to me as a present** me lo ha regalato; **he succeeded as a politician** come politico ha avuto successo; **as such** come tale
2 (*time*): **as of** *or* **from tomorrow** (a partire *or* a cominciare) da domani; *see* **be, same, such, so, well** *etc*

ASA [ˌeɪɛs'eɪ] N ABBR **1** (*Brit*: = **Advertising Standards Authority**) *ente che verifica a la conformità della pubblicità agli standard dell'industria* **2** (*Brit*) = *Amateur Swimming Association* **3** (*Am*: = **American Standards Association**) *associazione americana per la normalizzazione*
▷ www.asa.org.uk
asap [ˌeɪɛseɪ'pi:] ADV ABBR (= **as soon as possible**) prima possibile
as·bes·tos [æs'bɛstɒs] N amianto, asbesto
as·bes·to·sis [ˌæsbɛs'təʊsɪs] N asbestosi *f*
ASBO ['æzbəʊ] N ABBR (= **anti-social behaviour order**) provvedimento restrittivo per comportamento antisociale
as·cend [ə'sɛnd] VT (*frm*: *stairs*) salire; (*mountain*) scalare; (*throne*) salire a, ascendere a
■ VI salire
as·cend·ancy [ə'sɛndənsɪ] N ascendente *m*
as·cend·ant [ə'sɛndənt] N: **to be in the ascendant** essere in auge
as·cend·ing [ə'sɛndɪŋ] ADJ ascendente
as·cen·sion [ə'sɛnʃən] N (*Rel*): **the Ascension** l'Ascensione *f*
Ascension Island N isola dell'Ascensione
as·cen·sion·ist [ə'sɛnʃənɪst] N (*Mountaineering*) ascensionista *m/f*
as·cent [ə'sɛnt] N (*of mountain*) ascensione *f*, scalata; (*in plane*) salita; **we made a rapid ascent to our cruising altitude** siamo saliti rapidamente fino alla quota di crociera

as·cer·tain [ˌæsə'teɪn] VT (*frm*) accertare; **have you ascertained her real name yet?** ha accertato quale sia il suo vero nome?
as·cet·ic [ə'sɛtɪk] ADJ ascetico(-a)
■ N asceta *m*
as·ceti·cism [ə'sɛtɪsɪzəm] N ascetismo
ASCII ['æskɪ] N ABBR (= **American Standard Code for Information Interchange**) ASCII *m*
ascor·bic acid [əˌskɔ:bɪk'æsɪd] N acido ascorbico
as·cribe [ə'skraɪb] VT: **to ascribe sth to sth/sb** attribuire qc a qc/qn
ASCU [ˌeɪɛssi:'ju:] N ABBR (*Am*) = *Association of State Colleges and Universities*
ASE [ˌeɪɛs'i:] N ABBR = *American Stock Exchange*
asep·tic [eɪ'sɛptɪk] ADJ asettico(-a)
asexu·al [eɪ'sɛksjʊəl] ADJ asessuale
ASH [æʃ] N ABBR (*Brit*: = **Action on Smoking and Health**) *iniziativa contro il fumo*
ash[1] [æʃ] N (*of cigarette*) cenere *f*; **ashes** NPL (*of fire*) cenere *f*; (*of dead*) ceneri *fpl*; **burnt to ashes** carbonizzato(-a)
ash[2] [æʃ] N (*Bot*) frassino
ashamed [ə'ʃeɪmd] ADJ pieno(-a) di vergogna, vergognoso(-a); **to be** *or* **feel ashamed (of o.s.)** vergognarsi; **to be ashamed of sb/sth/to do sth** vergognarsi di qn/qc/di fare qc; **you ought to be ashamed of yourself!** dovresti vergognarti!, vergognati!; **it's nothing to be ashamed of** non è una cosa di cui ci si debba vergognare
A shares NPL (*Brit Stock Exchange*) azioni *fpl* con scarsi diritti di voto
ash blond ash blonde ADJ biondo(-a) cenere *inv*
ash can N (*Am*) bidone *m* per le immondizie
ash·en ['æʃn] ADJ cinereo(-a); (*pale*) livido(-a)
ashore [ə'ʃɔ:ʳ] ADV a terra; **to go ashore** scendere a terra, sbarcare
ash·tray ['æʃˌtreɪ] N portacenere *m inv*, posacenere *m inv*
Ash Wednesday N mercoledì *m inv* delle Ceneri
Asia ['eɪʃə] N Asia
Asia Minor N Asia minore
Asian ['eɪʃn], **Asi·at·ic** [ˌeɪʃɪ'ætɪk] ADJ, N asiatico(-a)
◎ **aside** [ə'saɪd] ADV da parte; **to take sb aside** prendere qn da parte
■ PREP: **aside from** (*as well as*) oltre a, a parte; (*except for*) a parte, salvo, eccetto
■ N (*esp Theatre*) a parte *m inv*
asi·nine ['æsɪnaɪn] ADJ (*liter*) asinesco(-a), asinino(-a)
◎ **ask** [ɑ:sk] VT **1** (*inquire*): **to ask sb sth** domandare qc a qn, chiedere qc a qn; **to ask sb a question** fare una domanda a qn; **to ask sb the time** chiedere l'ora a qn; **don't ask me!** (*fam*) non domandarlo a me!, a me lo chiedi?; **"have you finished?" she asked** "hai finito?" chiese; **she asked him about his father** gli domandò (notizie) di suo padre **2** (*request*): **to ask sb for sth/sb to do sth** chiedere qc a qn/a qn di fare qc; **to ask sb a favour** chiedere un piacere *or* un favore a qn; **how much are they asking for it?** quanto chiedono per quello?; **that's asking a lot!** questo è pretendere un po' troppo! **3** (*invite*): **to ask sb to sth/to do sth** invitare qn a qc/a fare qc; **have you asked Matthew to the party?** hai invitato Matthew alla festa?; **to ask sb to dinner** invitare qn a cena
■ VI (*inquire*) chiedere; (*request*) richiedere; **to ask about sth** informarsi su *or* di qc; **I asked about train times to Leeds** mi sono informato sugli orari dei treni per Leeds; **you should ask at the information desk**

dovresti rivolgerti all'ufficio informazioni; **it's yours for the asking** non hai che da chiederlo
■ N: **it's a big** *or* **tough ask!** (*fam*) è domandare molto!
▸ **ask after** VI + PREP chiedere di, domandare *or* chiedere (notizie) di, informarsi di
▸ **ask for** VI + PREP (*person*) chiedere di, cercare; (*help, information, money*) chiedere, domandare; **he asked for a cup of tea** ha chiesto una tazza di tè; **I asked him for help** gli ho chiesto aiuto *or* di aiutarmi; **it's just asking for trouble** è proprio (come) andarsele a cercare
▸ **ask out** VI + ADV: **to ask sb out** chiedere a qn di uscire; **Peter asked her out** Peter le ha chiesto di uscire con lui

askance [ə'skɑ:ns] ADV: **to look askance at sb/sth** guardare qn/qc storto *or* di traverso

askew [ə'skju:] ADV di traverso, storto

ask·ing price ['ɑ:skɪŋ'praɪs] N prezzo

asleep [ə'sli:p] ADJ addormentato(-a); **to be asleep** dormire; **he's asleep** dorme; **to be fast asleep** dormire profondamente; **to fall asleep** addormentarsi; **I fell asleep in front of the TV** mi sono addormentato davanti alla TV; **my foot's asleep** mi si è addormentato *or* intorpidito il piede

ASLEF ['æzlɛf] N ABBR (*Brit*: = **Associated Society of Locomotive Engineers and Firemen**) *sindacato dei conducenti dei treni e dei fuochisti*

AS level [eɪ'ɛs,lɛvl] N *qualifica intermedia di istruzione secondaria, tra GCSE e A level*
▹ www.dfes.gov.uk/qualifications/mainSection.cfm?sID=43&ssID=124
▹ www.bbc.co.uk/education/asguru/

ASM N ABBR = **assistant stage manager**

asp [æsp] N (*poisonous snake*) aspide *m*; (*Zool*) cobra *m inv* egiziano

as·para·gus [əs'pærəgəs] N (*plant*) asparago; (*food*) asparagi *mpl*

asparagus tips NPL punte *fpl* d'asparagi

ASPCA [,eɪɛspi:si:'eɪ] N ABBR (= **American Society for the Prevention of Cruelty to Animals**) ≈ ENPA *m* (= *Ente Nazionale Protezione Animali*)

◎ **as·pect** ['æspɛkt] N **1** (*of person, situation*) aspetto; **to study all aspects of a question** esaminare una questione sotto tutti gli aspetti **2** (*of building etc*) esposizione *f*; **a house with a northerly aspect** una casa esposta a nord

as·pen ['æspən] N (*Bot*) tremolo

As·per·ger's syndrome ['æspɜ:dʒəs,sɪndrəʊm] N sindrome *f* di Asperger (*tipo di autismo*)

as·per·ity [æ'spɛrɪtɪ] N (*frm*: *of manners, voice*) asprezza

as·per·sion [əs'pɜ:ʃən] N (*frm*) calunnia, maldicenza; **to cast aspersions on sth/sb** (*often hum*) diffamare qc/qn

as·phalt ['æsfælt] N asfalto

as·phyxia [æs'fɪksɪə] N asfissia

as·phyxi·ate [æs'fɪksɪeɪt] VT, VI asfissiare

as·phyxia·tion [æs,fɪksɪ'eɪʃən] N asfissia

as·pic ['æspɪk] N: **chicken in aspic** aspic *m inv* di pollo

as·pi·dis·tra [,æspɪ'dɪstrə] N aspidistra

as·pir·ant ['æspɪrənt] N aspirante *m/f*

as·pi·rate [*adj, n* 'æspərɪt; *vb* 'æspəreɪt] ADJ aspirato(-a)
■ N suono aspirato
■ VT aspirare

as·pi·ra·tion [,æspə'reɪʃən] N aspirazione *f*

as·pi·ra·tion·al [,æspə'reɪʃənəl] ADJ (*person*) che aspira a migliorare la propria posizione sociale; (*product*) per chi aspira a migliorare la propria posizione sociale

as·pire [əs'paɪə^r] VI: **to aspire to** aspirare a, ambire a

as·pi·rin ['æsprɪn] N aspirina

as·pir·ing [əs'paɪərɪŋ] ADJ aspirante

ass[1] [æs] N (*Zool*) asino, somaro; (*fig fam*) scemo(-a); **to make an ass of o.s.** rendersi ridicolo(-a)

ass[2] [æs] N (*Am fam!*) culo (*fam!*)

as·sail [ə'seɪl] VT: **to assail (with)** assalire (di)

as·sail·ant [ə'seɪlənt] N assalitore(-trice)

as·sas·sin [ə'sæsɪn] N assassino(-a)

as·sas·si·nate [ə'sæsɪneɪt] VT assassinare

as·sas·si·na·tion [ə,sæsɪ'neɪʃən] N assassinio

◎ **as·sault** [ə'sɔ:lt] N: **assault (on)** (*Mil*) assalto (a); (*Law*) aggressione *f* (a); **assault and battery** (*Law*) minacce *fpl* e vie *fpl* di fatto
■ VT (*Mil*) assaltare, assalire; (*Law*) aggredire; **to assault sexually** compiere atti di libidine violenta contro

assault course N percorso di guerra

as·sem·ble [ə'sɛmbl] VT (*objects, ideas*) radunare, raccogliere; (*people*) radunare, riunire; (*Tech*) montare, assemblare
■ VI radunarsi, riunirsi

as·sem·bler [ə'sɛmblə^r] N (*Comput*) programma *m* assemblatore

◎ **as·sem·bly** [ə'sɛmblɪ] N (*meeting*) assemblea; (*of machine, furniture*) assemblaggio, montaggio; (*Comput*) assemblaggio; **right of assembly** libertà di riunione; **the Welsh Assembly** *organo legislativo autonomo gallese*; **school assembly** riunione *f* mattutina

assembly industry N industria di assemblaggio

assembly language N (*Comput*) linguaggio assemblativo

assembly line N catena di montaggio

assembly plant N stabilimento di assemblaggio

assembly worker N assemblatore *m*

as·sent [ə'sɛnt] N benestare *m*, assenso, consenso; **by common assent** di comune accordo
■ VI assentire; **to assent (to sth)** approvare (qc)

as·sert [ə'sɜ:t] VT (*declare*) affermare, asserire; (*insist on: rights*) far valere; **to assert o.s.** farsi valere

as·ser·tion [ə'sɜ:ʃən] N affermazione *f*, asserzione *f*

as·ser·tive [ə'sɜ:tɪv] ADJ che sa imporsi

as·ser·tive·ness [ə'sɜ:tɪvnɪs] N decisione *f*

◎ **as·sess** [ə'sɛs] VT (*gen*) valutare; (*property, tax*) accertare l'imponibile di; (*damages*) valutare; (*fig: situation*) giudicare

◎ **as·sess·ment** [ə'sɛsmənt] N (*of value, damages*) valutazione *f*; (*of property, tax*) accertamento; (*judgment*): **assessment (of)** giudizio (su)

as·ses·sor [ə'sɛsə^r] N **1** (*Scol*) *consulente esterno incaricato della valutazione di un curriculum o della preparazione degli studenti* **2** (*of taxes*) ≈ perito dell'ufficio del catasto **3** (*Law*) perito

◎ **as·set** ['æsɛt] N (*useful quality*) bene *m*, qualità *f inv*, vantaggio; (*person*) elemento prezioso; **assets** NPL (*Fin: of individual*) beni *mpl*, disponibilità *fpl*; (: *of company*) attivo *msg*, attività *fpl*; **to be an asset for** essere prezioso per; **the film's chief asset is its cast** il cast è il punto di forza del film

asset-stripping ['æsɛt,strɪpɪŋ] N (*Comm*) *acquisto di una società in fallimento allo scopo di rivenderne le attività*

as·si·du·ity [,æsɪ'djʊɪtɪ] N diligenza, assiduità

as·sidu·ous [ə'sɪdjʊəs] ADJ assiduo(-a)

as·sidu·ous·ly [ə'sɪdjʊəslɪ] ADV diligentemente

as·sign [ə'saɪn] VT: **to assign (to)** (*allot: task, room, resources*) assegnare (a); (*reason, cause, meaning*) dare (a), attribuire (a); (*Law: property*) cedere (a), trasferire (a);

Aa

(*appoint*): **to assign sb to** dare a qn l'incarico di; **to assign a date to sth** fissare la data di qc; **she assigned us homework to be done by Friday** ci ha assegnato i compiti da fare per venerdì

as·sig·na·tion [ˌæsɪɡ'neɪʃən] N (*frm: of lovers*) convegno galante

as·sign·ment [ə'saɪnmənt] N (*task*) incarico; (*Scol*) compito; **we have to do three written assignments** dobbiamo fare tre compiti scritti

as·simi·late [ə'sɪmɪleɪt] VT assimilare

as·simi·la·tion [əˌsɪmɪ'leɪʃən] N assimilazione *f*

◎ **as·sist** [ə'sɪst] VT: **to assist sb (to do** *or* **in doing sth)** aiutare qn (a fare qc), assistere qn (a *or* nel fare qc); **can I assist in any way?** posso aiutare in qualche modo?; **we assisted him to his car** lo abbiamo aiutato a raggiungere la sua macchina

■ VI (*help*): **to assist in sth** aiutare in qc, essere di aiuto in qc

◎ **as·sis·tance** [ə'sɪstəns] N aiuto, assistenza; **can I be of any assistance?** posso esserle utile (in qualcosa)?; (*in shop*) desidera?; **to come to sb's assistance** venire in aiuto a qn

◎ **as·sis·tant** [ə'sɪstənt] N aiutante *m/f*, assistente *m/f*, aiuto; (*Brit*: *also*: **shop assistant**) commesso(-a)

■ ADJ aiuto *inv*

assistant headmaster N vicepreside *m/f*

assistant librarian N aiuto bibliotecario(-a)

assistant manager N vicedirettore(-trice)

assistant referee N assistente *m/f* dell'arbitro, guardalinee *m/f inv*

assistant stage manager N (*Theatre*) assistente *m/f* del direttore di scena

as·sizes [ə'saɪzɪz] NPL assise *fpl*

◎ **as·so·ci·ate** [*vb* ə'səʊʃɪeɪt; *n, adj* ə'səʊʃɪɪt] VT associare, collegare; **to associate o.s. with** associarsi a, unirsi a; **I don't wish to be associated with it** non voglio che si pensi che io abbia a che fare con la cosa

■ VI: **to associate with sb** frequentare qn

■ N (*colleague*) collega *m/f*, socio(-a); (*accomplice*) complice *m/f*; (*member: of club*) socio(-a) aggregato(-a); (*: of learned society*) membro aggregato

■ ADJ (*company*) consociato(-a); (*member*) aggregato(-a), aggiunto(-a)

as·so·ci·at·ed com·pa·ny [ə'səʊsɪeɪtɪd'kʌmpənɪ] N (*Comm*) consociata

associate director N amministratore *m* aggiunto

◎ **as·so·cia·tion** [əˌsəʊsɪ'eɪʃən] N (*most senses*) associazione *f*; **his association with her family** i suoi legami con la famiglia di lei; **in association with** in collaborazione con; **full of historic associations** ricco(-a) di reminiscenze storiche; **the name has unpleasant associations** il nome ha delle connotazioni negative

association football N (*Brit frm*) (gioco del) calcio

as·so·cia·tive [ə'səʊʃɪətɪv] ADJ (*frm, Math*) associativo(-a)

as·sort·ed [ə'sɔ:tɪd] ADJ assortito(-a); **in assorted sizes** in diverse taglie; **ill-/well-assorted** (*matched*) mal/ben assortito(-a)

as·sort·ment [ə'sɔ:tmənt] N (*Comm: mixture*) assortimento; **there was a strange assortment of guests** c'era uno strano miscuglio di invitati

Asst. ABBR = **assistant**

as·suage [ə'sweɪdʒ] VT (*frm: feelings, pain*) attenuare, alleviare; (*: appetite*) placare

◎ **as·sume** [ə'sju:m] VT **1** (*suppose*) supporre, presumere, presupporre; **I assume so** suppongo di sì ; **assuming that ...** supponendo che...; **I assumed he was coming** ho dato per scontato che venisse **2** (*power, control, attitude*) assumere, prendere; **to assume responsibility for** assumersi la responsabilità di

as·sumed name [ə'sju:md'neɪm] N nome *m* falso; **under an assumed name** sotto falso nome

◎ **as·sump·tion** [ə'sʌmpʃən] N **1** (*supposition*) supposizione *f*, ipotesi *f inv*; **on the assumption that** partendo dal presupposto che; **to work on the assumption that** partire dal presupposto che **2 the Assumption** (*Rel*) l'Assunzione *f*

as·sur·ance [ə'ʃʊərəns] N **1** (*guarantee*) assicurazione *f*, garanzia; **I can give you no assurances** non posso assicurarle *or* garantirle niente **2** (*confidence*) sicurezza, convinzione *f*; (*self-confidence*) fiducia in se stesso(-a), sicurezza di sé; **she spoke with assurance** ha parlato con convinzione; **she's got such assurance!** ha una tale sicurezza! **3** (*Brit*): **life assurance** assicurazione *f* sulla vita

as·sure [ə'ʃʊə^r] VT (*reassure*): **to assure sb (of sth)** assicurare qn (di qc); **I assured him of my support** gli ho assicurato il mio appoggio; **he assured me he was coming** mi ha assicurato che sarebbe venuto

◎ **as·sured** [ə'ʃʊəd] ADJ (*confident*) sicuro(-a); (*certain: promotion*) assicurato(-a); **success was assured** il successo era garantito *or* assicurato

as·sur·ed·ly [ə'ʃʊərɪdlɪ] ADV certamente, senza alcun dubbio

AST [ˌeɪes'ti:] ABBR (*Am*: = **Atlantic Standard Time**) *ora invernale nel fuso orario di New York*

as·ter ['æstə^r] N astro della Cina

as·ter·isk ['æstərɪsk] N asterisco

astern [ə'stɜ:n] ADV a poppa

as·ter·oid ['æstərɔɪd] N asteroide *m*

asth·ma ['æsmə] N asma

asth·mat·ic [æs'mætɪk] ADJ, N asmatico(-a)

astig·ma·tism [æs'tɪɡmətɪzəm] N astigmatismo

astir [ə'stɜ:^r] ADJ (*out of bed*) in piedi; (*on the move*) in movimento

ASTMS [ˌeɪesti:ɛm'ɛs] N ABBR (*Brit*: *Association of Scientific, Technical and Managerial Staffs*) *sindacato del personale scientifico, tecnico e manageriale*

aston·ish [ə'stɒnɪʃ] VT stupire, meravigliare; **you astonish me!** ma chi l'avrebbe mai detto!; **I was astonished to learn that ...** fui sorpreso nell'apprendere che...

aston·ish·ing [ə'stɒnɪʃɪŋ] ADJ sorprendente, stupefacente; **I find it astonishing that ...** mi stupisce che...

aston·ish·ing·ly [ə'stɒnɪʃɪŋlɪ] ADV straordinariamente, incredibilmente

aston·ish·ment [ə'stɒnɪʃmənt] N stupore *m*, meraviglia; **in astonishment** in modo attonito; **she gave me a look of astonishment** mi ha lanciato uno sguardo stupito; **to my astonishment** con mia gran meraviglia, con mio grande stupore

astound [ə'staʊnd] VT sbalordire; **he was astounded to hear ...** è rimasto stupefatto *or* allibito nel sentire...

astound·ing [ə'staʊndɪŋ] ADJ (*resemblance*) sorprendente; (*price*) sbalorditivo(-a)

as·tra·khan [ˌæstrə'kæn] ADJ di astrakan

■ N astrakan *m*

astray [ə'streɪ] ADV: **to go astray** perdere la strada, smarrirsi, perdersi; (*morally*) mettersi su una cattiva strada, traviarsi; **to go astray in one's calculations** sbagliare i calcoli; **to lead sb astray** portare qn su una cattiva strada

astride [əˈstraɪd] PREP (*fence*) a cavalcioni di; (*animal*) a cavallo di; (*horse*) in sella a
■ ADV a cavalcioni
as·trin·gent [əsˈtrɪndʒənt] ADJ, N astringente (*m*)
as·trolo·ger [əsˈtrɒlədʒəʳ] N astrologo(-a)
as·tro·logi·cal [ˌæstrəˈlɒdʒɪkəl] ADJ astrologico(-a)
as·trol·ogy [əsˈtrɒlədʒɪ] N astrologia
as·tro·naut [ˈæstrəˌnɔːt] N astronauta *m/f*
as·trono·mer [əsˈtrɒnəməʳ] N astronomo(-a)
as·tro·nomi·cal [ˌæstrəˈnɒmɪkəl] ADJ (*also fig*) astronomico(-a)
as·tro·nomi·cal·ly [ˌæstrəˈnɒmɪkəlɪ] ADV astronomicamente; **the wine is astronomically expensive** il vino ha un prezzo astronomico
as·trono·my [əsˈtrɒnəmɪ] N astronomia
▷ http://hubblesite.org
▷ www.nasa.gov/centers/goddard/home/index.html
▷ www.astronomy.net
▷ www.astronomytoday.com
▷ www.bbc.co.uk/science/space
▷ www.rog.nmm.ac.uk
as·tro·phys·ics [ˈæstrəʊˈfɪzɪks] NSG astrofisica
as·tute [əsˈtjuːt] ADJ (*shrewd*) accorto(-a)
as·tute·ly [əsˈtjuːtlɪ] ADV accortamente
as·tute·ness [əsˈtjuːtnɪs] N accortezza
asun·der [əˈsʌndəʳ] ADV (*liter*): **to tear asunder** strappare
ASV [ˌeɪɛsˈviː] N ABBR (= **American Standard Version**) *traduzione americana della Bibbia*
asy·lum [əˈsaɪləm] N **1** (*refuge*) asilo, rifugio; **to seek political asylum** chiedere asilo politico; **seven per cent of asylum seekers** il sette per cento di chi chiede asilo politico **2** (*also:* **lunatic asylum**) manicomio
asylum seeker N chi chiede asilo politico
asym·met·rical [ˌeɪsɪˈmɛtrɪkəl], **asym·met·ric** [ˌeɪsɪˈmɛtrɪk] ADJ asimmetrico(-a)
asym·met·ri·cal·ly [ˌeɪsɪˈmɛtrɪklɪ] ADV asimmetricamente
asym·me·try [æˈsɪmɪtrɪ] N asimmetria

◎ **at** [æt] KEYWORD
PREP
1 (*position*) a; (*direction*) verso; **to aim at the target** mirare al bersaglio; **at the bottom of the page** a fondo pagina; **at the desk** al banco; **to stand at the door** stare sulla porta; **at home** a casa; **at John's** da John, a casa di John; **at the office** in ufficio; **to look at sth** guardare qc; **at school** a scuola; **at the top** in cima
2 (*time*): **at Christmas** a *or* per Natale; **at night** di notte; **at 4 o'clock** alle quattro; **at a time like this** in un momento come questo; **at times** talvolta
3 (*rate*) a; **at 50p each** a 50 pence l'uno(-a); **two at a time** due alla *or* per volta
4 (*activity*): **to be good at sth** riuscire bene in qc, essere bravo(-a) in qc *or* a fare qc; **while you're at it** (*fam*) già che ci sei; **she's at it again** (*fam*) eccola che ricomincia, ci risiamo; **he's always (on) at me** (*fam*) mi tormenta continuamente; **to play at cowboys** giocare ai cowboy; **to be at work** essere al lavoro, stare lavorando
5 (*manner*): **at 50 km/h** a 50 km/h; **at peace** in pace; **at a run** di corsa, correndo; **at full speed** a tutta velocità
6 (*cause*): **annoyed at** seccato(-a) per; **I was shocked at the news** sono rimasto colpito dalla notizia; **at his suggestion** dietro suo consiglio; **he was surprised at her reaction** lo stupì la sua reazione

ate [ɛt, eɪt] PT *of* **eat**
athe·ism [ˈeɪθɪɪzəm] N ateismo
athe·ist [ˈeɪθɪɪst] N ateo(-a); **to be an atheist** essere ateo(-a)
athe·is·tical [ˌeɪθɪˈɪstɪkəl], **athe·is·tic** [ˌeɪθɪˈɪstɪk] ADJ (*person, philosophy*) ateo(-a); (*views, principles*) ateistico(-a)
Athena [əˈθiːnə], **Athene** [əˈθiːniː] N Atena
Athe·nian [əˈθiːnɪən] ADJ, N ateniese *m/f*
Ath·ens [ˈæθɪnz] N Atene *f*
◎ **ath·lete** [ˈæθliːt] N atleta *m/f*
ath·let·ic [æθˈlɛtɪk] ADJ (*meeting etc*) di atletica, atletico(-a); (*person: muscular*) atletico(-a); (*: sporty*) sportivo(-a)
ath·leti·cal·ly [æθˈlɛtɪklɪ] ADV atleticamente
ath·let·ics [æθˈlɛtɪks] NSG atletica
At·lan·tic [ətˈlæntɪk] ADJ dell'Atlantico, atlantico(-a)
■ N: **the Atlantic (Ocean)** l'(Oceano) Atlantico
Atlas [ˈætləs] N (*Myth*) Atlante *m*
at·las [ˈætləs] N atlante *m*; **road atlas** carta stradale
Atlas Mountains NPL: **the Atlas Mountains** i Monti dell'Atlante
ATM [ˌeɪtiːˈɛm] N ABBR (= **automated teller machine**) sportello automatico, Bancomat *m inv*®
◎ **at·mos·phere** [ˈætməsˌfɪəʳ] N (*Geog, fig*) atmosfera; (*air*) aria
at·mos·pher·ic [ˌætməsˈfɛrɪk] ADJ atmosferico(-a); (*music*) che crea un'atmosfera; (*film*) pieno(-a) di atmosfera
at·mos·pher·ics [ˌætməsˈfɛrɪks] NPL (*Radio*) scariche *fpl* elettriche
at·oll [ˈætɒl] N atollo
atom [ˈætəm] N atomo; (*fig*): **not an atom of truth** nemmeno un pizzico di verità
atom·ic [əˈtɒmɪk] ADJ atomico(-a)
atomic bomb, atom bomb N bomba atomica
ato·mic·ity [ˌætəˈmɪsɪtɪ] N (*Chem*) atomicità
atomic mass N (*Chem*) massa atomica
atomic number N (*Chem*) numero atomico
at·om·ize [ˈætəmaɪz] VT (*all senses*) atomizzare
at·om·iz·er [ˈætəˌmaɪzəʳ] N atomizzatore *m*
atone [əˈtəʊn] VI: **to atone for** (*frm: crime, sins*) espiare; (*: mistake, rudeness*) riparare a
atone·ment [əˈtəʊnmənt] N (*frm*) espiazione *f*; (*Rel*) redenzione *f*; **to make atonement for a mistake** riparare ad un errore
atop [əˈtɒp] PREP (*Am*) sopra; **atop the hill** in cima alla collina
ATP [ˌeɪtiːˈpiː] N ABBR (= **adenosine triphosphate**) ATP *m*
atrium [ˈeɪtrɪəm] N (*Archit, Anat*) atrio
atro·cious [əˈtrəʊʃəs] ADJ atroce, pessimo(-a)
atro·cious·ly [əˈtrəʊʃəslɪ] ADV (*cruelly*) atrocemente; (*appallingly*) terribilmente
atroc·ity [əˈtrɒsɪtɪ] N atrocità *f inv*
at·ro·phy [ˈætrəfɪ] (*Med, fig*) N atrofia
■ VT atrofizzare
■ VI atrofizzarsi
◎ **attach** [əˈtætʃ] VT: **to attach (to) 1** (*fasten, stick*) attaccare (a); (*tie*) legare (a); (*join*) annettere (a), attaccare (a); (*document, letter*) allegare (a); **please find attached ...** allego...; **the attached letter** la lettera acclusa *or* allegata; **they attached a rope to the car** hanno attaccato una corda alla macchina; **he attached himself to us** si è appiccicato a noi **2** (*Comput*) allegare **3** (*attribute: importance, value*) attribuire (a), dare (a) **4** (*assign: troops, employee*)

Aa

assegnare (a) **5** (*Law*: *person*) trarre in arresto; (: *property*) sequestrare
at·ta·ché [əˈtæʃeɪ] N addetto (di ambasciata), attaché *m inv*; **cultural attaché** addetto culturale
attaché case N valigetta *f* portadocumenti *inv*, valigetta (diplomatica)
at·tached [əˈtætʃt] ADJ (*fond*): **to be attached to sb** essere attaccato(-a) *or* affezionato(-a) a qn; (*fam*: *married, engaged*) impegnato(-a)
attachment [əˈtætʃmənt] N **1** (*device*) accessorio **2** (*Comput*) allegato **3** (*affection*): **attachment (to)** attaccamento (a), affetto (per); **his attachment to his mother** il suo attaccamento alla madre
◎**at·tack** [əˈtæk] N **1** (*Mil, fig*) attacco; (*on individual*) aggressione *f*; **a savage attack** una feroce aggressione; **surprise attack** attacco a sorpresa; **attack on sb's life** attentato alla vita di qn; **to be under attack (from)** essere attaccato(-a) (da); **to launch an attack (on)** (*Mil, Sport, fig*) sferrare un attacco (a) **2** (*Med*) attacco, accesso
■ VT (*Mil, Med, fig*) attaccare; (*person*) aggredire, assalire; (*tackle*: *job, problem*) affrontare
at·tack·er [əˈtækəʳ] N aggressore *m*, assalitore(-trice)
at·tack·ing [əˈtækɪŋ] ADJ (*Sport*: *style*) aggressivo; **to play a more attacking style** giocare maggiormente in attacco
at·tain [əˈteɪn] VT (*ambition*) realizzare; (*age, rank, happiness*) raggiungere, arrivare a
at·tain·able [əˈteɪnəbl] ADJ (*see vb*) realizzabile; raggiungibile
at·tain·ment [əˈteɪnmənt] (*frm*) N (*of ambition*) realizzazione *f*; (*of position, happiness*) raggiungimento; (*achievement*) risultato ottenuto; **attainments** (*accomplishments*) cognizioni *fpl* (acquisite); **linguistic attainments** abilità *fpl* linguistiche
◎**at·tempt** [əˈtɛmpt] N (*try*) tentativo; **after several attempts** dopo diversi tentativi; **he made no attempt to help** non ha (neanche) tentato *or* cercato di aiutare; **to make an attempt on sb's life** attentare alla vita di qn
■ VT: **to attempt sth/to do sth** tentare qc/di fare qc; **he attempted the exam** ha tentato l'esame; **I attempted to write a song** ho tentato di scrivere una canzone; **attempted murder** (*Law*) tentato omicidio
◎**at·tend** [əˈtɛnd] VT **1** (*be present at*: *meeting etc*) andare a, assistere a, essere presente a; (*regularly*: *school, church*) frequentare; (: *course, classes*) seguire, frequentare; **the lecture was well attended** c'era molta gente alla conferenza **2** (*subj*: *bridesmaid, lady-in-waiting*) accompagnare; (: *doctor*) avere in cura, curare, assistere
■ VI (*be present*) essere presente, esserci; (*pay attention to*) prestare attenzione, stare attento(-a)
▸ **attend to** VI + PREP (*needs, affairs*) prendersi cura di; (*customer, work*) occuparsi di; **are you being attended to?** (*in shop*) la stanno servendo?
at·tend·ance [əˈtɛndəns] N (*act*): **attendance (at)** presenza (a); (: *regular*) frequenza (a); (*those present*) persone *fpl* presenti; **what was the attendance like at the meeting?** quanti erano i presenti alla riunione?; **there was a doctor in attendance on the queen** c'era un dottore al servizio della regina
attendance officer N *funzionario preposto a controllare la frequenza scolastica*
at·tend·ant [əˈtɛndənt] N (*in car park, museum*) custode *m/f*; (*servant*) attendente *m/f*, persona di servizio
■ ADJ (*frm*) concomitante
◎**at·ten·tion** [əˈtɛnʃən] N **1** attenzione *f*; **to call sb's attention to sth** richiamare qc all'attenzione di qn; **it has come to my attention that ...** sono venuto a conoscenza (del fatto) che...; **to pay attention (to)** stare attento(-a) (a), fare attenzione (a); **for the attention of** (*Admin*) all'attenzione di **2** (*Mil*): **attention!** attenti!; **to come to/stand at attention** mettersi/stare sull'attenti **3** **attentions** NPL (*kindnesses*) attenzioni *fpl*, premure *fpl*
attention deficit disorder N (*Med*) disturbo dell'attenzione
attention deficit hyper·ac·tiv·ity disorder [-ˌhaɪpəræk'tɪvɪtɪ-] N (*Med*) disturbo dell'attenzione con iperattività
attention-seeking [əˈtɛnʃənˌsiːkɪŋ] ADJ *che fa di tutto per attirare l'attenzione altrui*
attention span N capacità *f inv* di concentrazione
at·ten·tive [əˈtɛntɪv] ADJ (*audience*) attento(-a); (*escort*) premuroso(-a), sollecito(-a)
at·ten·tive·ly [əˈtɛntɪvlɪ] ADV attentamente
at·ten·tive·ness [əˈtɛntɪvnɪs] N attenzione *f*; (*consideration*) sollecitudine *f*
at·tenu·ate [əˈtɛnjʊeɪt] (*frm*) VT ridurre, attenuare
■ VI attenuarsi
at·test [əˈtɛst] (*frm*) VT attestare; (*signature*) autenticare
■ VI: **to attest to** testimoniare, attestare
at·tes·ta·tion [ˌætɛsˈteɪʃən] (*frm*) N dichiarazione *f*
At·tic [ˈætɪk] ADJ attico(-a)
at·tic [ˈætɪk] N soffitta, solaio; (*room*) mansarda
At·ti·ca [ˈætɪkə] N Attica
Attila [əˈtɪlə] N Attila *m*
at·tire [əˈtaɪəʳ] (*frm*) N tenuta, abbigliamento
■ VT: **to attire (in)** abbigliare (con)

> DID YOU KNOW ...?
> **attire** is not translated by the Italian word ***attirare***

◎**at·ti·tude** [ˈætɪtjuːd] N (*view*) atteggiamento; (*posture*) posa; (*opinion*): **attitude (towards)** punto di vista (nei confronti di); **attitude of mind** modo di pensare; **if that's your attitude** se la prendi così

> DID YOU KNOW ...?
> **attitude** is not translated by the Italian word ***attitudine***

at·ti·tu·di·nize [ˌætɪˈtjuːdɪnaɪz] VI posare, assumere un'aria affettata
◎**at·tor·ney** [əˈtɜːnɪ] N (*Am*: *lawyer*) avvocato; (*representative*) procuratore *m*; (*having proxy*) mandatario; **power of attorney** procura
Attorney General N (*Brit*) Procuratore *m* Generale; (*Am*) ≈ Ministro della Giustizia
◎**at·tract** [əˈtrækt] VT (*subj*: *magnet*) attirare, attrarre; (*fig*: *interest, attention etc*) attirare, suscitare; **the Lake District attracts lots of tourists** la Regione dei Laghi attira molti turisti
at·trac·tion [əˈtrækʃən] N attrazione *f*, fascino; (*pleasant feature*) attrattiva; **city life has no attraction for me** la vita di città non mi attira affatto; **one of the attractions was a free car** uno dei vantaggi era quello di una macchina gratis
◎**at·trac·tive** [əˈtræktɪv] ADJ (*person, dress, place*) attraente, affascinante; (*idea, offer, price*) allettante, interessante
at·trac·tive·ly [əˈtræktɪvlɪ] ADV in modo attraente
at·trac·tive·ness [əˈtræktɪvnɪs] N (*of proposition, offer*) attrattiva; (*of voice, person*) fascino
at·trib·ut·able [əˈtrɪbjʊtəbl] ADJ attribuibile
at·trib·ute [*n* ˈætrɪbjuːt; *vb* əˈtrɪbjuːt] N attributo
■ VT: **to attribute sth to** attribuire qc a

at·tribu·tion [ˌætrɪ'bjuːʃən] N attribuzione *f*
at·tribu·tive [ə'trɪbjʊtɪv] ADJ (*Gram*) attributivo(-a)
at·tri·tion [ə'trɪʃən] N usura (per attrito); **war of attrition** guerra di logoramento
at·tuned [ə'tjuːnd] ADJ (*person*): **to be attuned to sth** poter apprezzare qc; (*eye, ears*): **attuned to** attento(-a) a
Atty. Gen. ABBR = **Attorney General**
ATV [ˌeɪtiː'viː] N ABBR **1** (*Brit:* = **Associated Television**) *rete televisiva indipendente* **2** (*Mil:* = **all terrain vehicle**) jeep *f inv*
atypi·cal [eɪ'tɪpɪkəl] ADJ atipico(-a)
auber·gine ['əʊbəʒiːn] N (*esp Brit*) melanzana
auburn ['ɔːbən] ADJ (*hair*) ramato(-a), color rame *inv*
Auck·land ['ɔːklənd] N Aukland *m*
▷ www.aucklandcity.govt.nz
▷ www.aucklandnz.com
◎ **auc·tion** ['ɔːkʃən] N (*also:* **sale by auction**) asta
■ VT (*also:* **to sell by auction**) vendere all'asta; (*also:* **to put up for auction**) mettere all'asta
auc·tion·eer [ˌɔːkʃə'nɪəʳ] N banditore(-trice)
auction room N sala dell'asta
auction sale N vendita all'asta
auda·cious [ɔː'deɪʃəs] ADJ (*bold*) audace; (*impudent*) sfrontato(-a)
audac·ity [ɔː'dæsɪtɪ] N (*boldness*) audacia; (*impudence*) sfacciataggine *f*, sfrontatezza
audibil·ity [ˌɔːdɪ'bɪlɪtɪ] N udibilità
audible ['ɔːdɪbl] ADJ udibile, percettibile; **there was an audible sigh** si è chiaramente sentito un sospiro; **he was hardly audible** si riusciva a malapena a sentirlo
audibly ['ɔːdɪblɪ] ADV in modo che si senta, in modo chiaro
◎ **audi·ence** ['ɔːdɪəns] N **1** (*gathering*) pubblico; (*Radio*) ascoltatori *mpl*; (*TV*) telespettatori *mpl*; (*of speaker*) uditorio; **a huge audience** un grandissimo pubblico; **there was a big audience at the theatre** c'erano molti spettatori *or* c'era un gran pubblico al teatro; **the concerts attracted huge audiences** i concerti hanno attirato tantissima gente **2** (*formal interview*) udienza; **an audience with the Queen** un'udienza con la Regina
audience participation N partecipazione *f* del pubblico
audience rating N indice *m* di ascolto
audio ['ɔːdɪˌəʊ] ADJ: **audio equipment** apparecchi *mpl* audiovisivi; **audio tape** audiocassetta
audio-typist ['ɔːdɪəʊˌtaɪpɪst] N dattilografo(-a) che trascrive da nastro
audio·visual [ˌɔːdɪəʊ'vɪzjʊəl] ADJ audiovisivo(-a); **audiovisual aids** sussidi *mpl* audiovisivi
audit ['ɔːdɪt] N revisione *f* dei conti, verifica (ufficiale) dei conti
■ VT (*accounts*) rivedere, verificare

DID YOU KNOW ...?
audit is not translated by the Italian word *udito*

audi·tion [ɔː'dɪʃən] N (*Theatre*) audizione *f*; (*Cine*) provino
■ VT fare un'audizione (*or* un provino) a
■ VI fare un'audizione (*or* un provino)
audi·tor ['ɔːdɪtəʳ] N revisore *m* dei conti
audi·to·rium [ˌɔːdɪ'tɔːrɪəm] N sala, auditorio
audi·tory ['ɔːdɪtərɪ] ADJ uditivo(-a); **auditory canal** condotto uditivo
AUEW [ˌeɪjuːiː'dʌbljuː] N ABBR (*Brit:* = **Amalgamated Union of Engineering Workers**) *sindacato dei metalmeccanici*
Aug. ABBR (= **August**) ago., ag. (= *agosto*)
aug·ment [ɔːg'mɛnt] VT, VI (*frm*) aumentare
aug·menta·tive [ɔːg'mɛntətɪv] ADJ (*frm*) accrescitivo(-a)
augur ['ɔːgəʳ] VI, VT (*frm*): **to augur well/ill** essere di buon/cattivo augurio *or* auspicio
August ['ɔːgəst] N agosto; *see also* **July**
august [ɔː'gʌst] ADJ (*frm*) augusto(-a)
◎ **aunt** [ɑːnt] N zia; **my aunt and uncle** i miei zii, mia zia e mio zio
auntie, **aunty** ['ɑːntɪ] N (*fam*) zietta; **auntie Jane** zia Jane
au pair (girl) ['əʊ'pɛəʳ(ˌgɜːl)] N ragazza *f* alla pari *inv*
aura ['ɔːrə] N aura
auri·cle ['ɔːrɪkəl] N (*of heart*) orecchietta; (*of ear*) padiglione *m* auricolare
auro·ra bo·real·is [ɔː'rɔːrəbɔːrɪ'eɪlɪs] N aurora boreale
aus·pices ['ɔːspɪsɪz] NPL: **under the auspices of** sotto gli auspici di
aus·pi·cious [ɔːs'pɪʃəs] (*frm*) ADJ (*sign*) di buon augurio *or* auspicio; (*occasion*) propizio(-a), favorevole; **to make an auspicious start** iniziare sotto buoni auspici
aus·pi·cious·ly [ɔːs'pɪʃəslɪ] ADV (*frm*) favorevolmente, sotto buoni auspici; **to begin auspiciously** incominciare sotto buoni auspici
Aus·sie ['ɒzɪ] (*fam*) = **Australian**
aus·tere [ɒs'tɪəʳ] ADJ austero(-a)
aus·tere·ly [ɒs'tɪəlɪ] ADV in modo austero, austeramente
aus·ter·ity [ɒs'tɛrɪtɪ] N austerità *f inv*
Aus·tral·asia [ˌɒstrə'leɪzɪə] N l'Australasia
Aus·tralia [ɒs'treɪlɪə] N l'Australia
▷ www.fed.gov.au
▷ www.gov.au
▷ www.tourism.sa.gov.au
▷ www.australia.com/ProcessSplashResults.aust?C=GB&L=en
▷ www.csu.edu.au/australia/tourism.html
Australia Day N *giorno di festa nazionale che celebra l'arrivo dei britannici in Australia nel 1788*
▷ www.australiaday.gov.au
Aus·tral·ian [ɒs'treɪlɪən] ADJ, N australiano(-a)
Australian Rules NSG *gioco australiano simile al rugby*
▷ www.afl.com.au
Aus·tria ['ɒstrɪə] N l'Austria
Aus·trian ['ɒstrɪən] ADJ, N austriaco(-a)
AUT [ˌeɪjuː'tiː] N ABBR (*Brit:* = **Association of University Teachers**) *associazione dei docenti universitari*
authen·tic [ɔː'θɛntɪk] ADJ autentico(-a)
authen·ti·cal·ly [ɔː'θɛntɪklɪ] ADV autenticamente
authen·ti·cate [ɔː'θɛntɪkeɪt] VT (*signature, document*) autenticare; (*statement, information*) verificare, stabilire la veridicità di
au·then·tic·ity [ˌɔːθɛn'tɪsɪtɪ] N autenticità
◎ **author** ['ɔːθəʳ] N autore(-trice)
author·ess ['ɔːθərɪs] N autrice *f*
author·ing ['ɔːθərɪŋ] N (*Comput*) authoring *m*; *creazione di documenti, specialmente in Internet*
authori·tar·ian [ˌɔːθɒrɪ'tɛərɪən] ADJ autoritario(-a)
authori·tar·ianism [ɔːˌθɒrɪ'tɛərɪənɪzm] N (*Pol*) autoritarismo
authori·ta·tive [ɔː'θɒrɪtətɪv] ADJ (*account, judgement*) autorevole; (*manner*) autoritario(-a)
authori·ta·tive·ly [ɔː'θɒrɪtətɪvlɪ] ADV autorevolmente
◎ **author·ity** [ɔː'θɒrɪtɪ] N **1** (*power*) autorità; (*permission*)

Aa

autorizzazione *f*; **those in authority** i dirigenti, i governanti; **to be in authority over** dare gli ordini a; **to have authority to do sth** avere l'autorizzazione a fare *or* il diritto di fare qc **2 the authorities** NPL (*government, council*) le autorità; **the health authorities** l'autorità *sg* sanitaria **3** (*expert*): **he's an authority (on)** è un'autorità (in materia di); **I have it on good authority that ...** so da fonte sicura *or* autorevole che...

authori·za·tion [ˌɔːθəraɪˈzeɪʃən] N autorizzazione *f*

author·ize [ˈɔːθəraɪz] VT: **to authorize sth/sb (to do sth)** autorizzare qc/qn (a fare qc)

author·ized capi·tal [ˈɔːθəˌraɪzdˈkæpɪtl] N (*Fin*) capitale *m* nominale

Author·ized Ver·sion [ˈɔːθəraɪzdˌvɜːʃən] N: **the Authorized Version** *traduzione inglese della Bibbia del 1611*

author·ship [ˈɔːθəʃɪp] N paternità (*letteraria etc*)

autism [ˈɔːtɪzm] N autismo

autis·tic [ɔːˈtɪstɪk] ADJ autistico(-a)

◎ **auto** [ˈɔːtəʊ] N (*Am*) auto *f inv*

auto... [ˈɔːtəʊ] PREF auto...

auto·bio·graph·ic [ˈɔːtəʊˌbaɪəʊˈgræfɪk], **auto·bio·graphi·cal** [ˈɔːtəʊˌbaɪəʊˈgræfɪkəl] ADJ autobiografico(-a)

auto·bi·og·ra·phy [ˌɔːtəʊbaɪˈɒgrəfɪ] N autobiografia

auto·clave [ˈɔːtəˌkleɪv] N autoclave *f*

auto·crat [ˈɔːtəʊˌkræt] N autocrate *m*

auto·crat·ic [ˌɔːtəʊˈkrætɪk] ADJ autocratico(-a)

Auto·cue® [ˈɔːtəʊˌkjuː] N (*Brit TV*) gobbo

auto·graph [ˈɔːtəˌgrɑːf] N autografo
■ VT firmare

autograph album N libro degli autografi

autograph hunter N cacciatore(-trice) di autografi

auto·im·mune [ˌɔːtəʊɪˈmjuːn] ADJ autoimmune

auto·mat [ˈɔːtəˌmæt] N (*vending machine*) distributore *m* automatico; (*Am: room*) *tavola calda fornita esclusivamente di distributori automatici*

automa·ta [ɔːˈtɒmətə] NPL *of* **automaton**

auto·mate [ˈɔːtəˌmeɪt] VT automatizzare

auto·mat·ed [ˈɔːtəˌmeɪtɪd] ADJ automatizzato(-a)

◎ **auto·mat·ic** [ˌɔːtəˈmætɪk] ADJ automatico(-a)
■ N (*pistol*) (pistola) automatica; (*car*) automobile *f* con cambio automatico; (*washing machine*) lavatrice *f* automatica

auto·mati·cal·ly [ˌɔːtəˈmætɪkəlɪ] ADV automaticamente

automatic data processing N elaborazione *f* automatica dei dati

automatic pilot N: **on automatic pilot** (*Aer, fig*) con pilota automatico

automatic telling machine [ˌɔːtəˈmætɪkˈtɛlɪŋməʃiːn] N cassa prelievi automatica

auto·ma·tion [ˌɔːtəˈmeɪʃən] N automazione *f*

automa·ton [ɔːˈtɒmətən] N (*pl* **automatons** *or* **automata** [ɔːˈtɒmətə]) automa *m*

auto·mo·bile [ˈɔːtəməˌbiːl] N (*Am*) automobile *f*

auto·mo·tive [ˌɔːtəˈməʊtɪv] ADJ (*industry, design*) automobilistico(-a)

auto·nom·ic [ˌɔːtəˈnɒmɪk] ADJ (*Med*) involontario(-a)

autonomic nervous system N (*Med*) sistema *m* neurovegetativo

autono·mous [ɔːˈtɒnəməs] ADJ autonomo(-a)

autono·mous·ly [ɔːˈtɒnəməslɪ] ADV autonomamente

autono·my [ɔːˈtɒnəmɪ] N autonomia

auto·pi·lot [ˌɔːtəʊˈpaɪlət] N (*Aer*) = **automatic pilot**

autop·sy [ˈɔːtɒpsɪ] N autopsia

auto·radio·graph [ˌɔːtəʊˈreɪdɪəˌgrɑːf] N autoradiografia

auto·sug·ges·tion [ˈɔːtəʊsəˈdʒɛstʃən] N autosuggestione *f*

auto·troph·ic [ˌɔːtəˈtrɒfɪk] ADJ autotrofo(-a)

◎ **autumn** [ˈɔːtəm] N autunno; **in autumn** in autunno; **last autumn** lo scorso autunno
■ ADJ autunnale

autum·nal [ɔːˈtʌmnəl] ADJ autunnale, d'autunno

aux·ilia·ry [ɔːgˈzɪlɪərɪ] ADJ ausiliario(-a); (*Gram*) ausiliare
■ N (*assistant*) assistente *m/f*, aiuto; (*verb*) ausiliare *m*; **auxiliaries** NPL (*Mil*) truppe *fpl* ausiliarie

aux·in [ˈɔːksɪn] N auxina

AV [ˌeɪˈviː] N ABBR (= **Authorized Version**) *traduzione inglese della Bibbia*
■ ABBR = **audiovisual**

Av. Ave. ABBR = **Avenue**

avail [əˈveɪl] N: **of no avail** inutile; **to no avail** invano, inutilmente
■ VT: **to avail o.s. of** (*opportunity*) servirsi di, approfittare *or* approfittarsi di; (*rights*) (av)valersi di

avail·abil·ity [əveɪləˈbɪlɪtɪ] N disponibilità

◎ **avail·able** [əˈveɪləbl] ADJ disponibile; **the amount of money available** la cifra disponibile; **to make sth available to sb** mettere qc a disposizione di qn; **is the manager available?** è libero il direttore?; **every available means** tutti i mezzi disponibili

ava·lanche [ˈævəlɑːnʃ] N valanga

avalanche warning N avviso di valanghe

avant-garde [ˈævɒŋˈgɑːd] N avanguardia
■ ADJ d'avanguardia

ava·rice [ˈævərɪs] N avarizia

ava·ri·cious [ˌævəˈrɪʃəs] ADJ avaro(-a)

avdp. ABBR *of* **avoirdupois**

Ave. ABBR = **Avenue**

avenge [əˈvɛndʒ] VT vendicare; **to avenge o.s. (on sb)** vendicarsi (di qn)

aveng·er [əˈvɛndʒəʳ] N vendicatore(-trice)

aveng·ing [əˈvɛndʒɪŋ] ADJ vendicatore(-trice)

av·enue [ˈævənjuː] N viale *m*; (*fig*) strada, via

aver [əˈvɜːʳ] VT (*frm*) dichiarare, asserire

◎ **av·er·age** [ˈævərɪdʒ] ADJ medio(-a); (*pej*) qualsiasi *inv*, ordinario(-a); **the average price** il prezzo medio
■ N media; **on average** in media; **above/below (the) average** sopra/sotto la media
■ VT fare una media di
▸ **average out** VT (*set of numbers*) fare *or* calcolare la media fra
▸ **average out at** VI (*reach an average of*) aggirarsi in media su, essere in media di

averse [əˈvɜːs] ADJ: **averse to** (*opposed*) contrario(-a) a; (*disinclined*) restio(-a) a; **to be averse to sth/doing sth** essere contrario(-a) a qc/a fare qc; **I'm not averse to an occasional drink** non mi dispiace bere un bicchierino ogni tanto; **I wouldn't be averse to the idea** non avrei nulla in contrario all'idea

aver·sion [əˈvɜːʃən] N (*dislike*): **aversion (for *or* to)** avversione *f* (per); **spiders are his aversion** ha la fobia dei ragni; **my pet aversion** ciò che detesto di più; **to have an aversion to sb/sth** avere *or* nutrire un'avversione nei confronti di qn/qc

avert [əˈvɜːt] VT (*prevent: accident, danger*) evitare; (*turn away: eyes, thoughts*): **to avert (from)** distogliere (da), allontanare (da)

aviary [ˈeɪvɪərɪ] N voliera, uccelliera

avia·tion [ˌeɪvɪˈeɪʃən] N aviazione *f*
▷ www.icao.int
aviation industry N industria aeronautica
avia·tor [ˈeɪvɪeɪtəʳ] N aviatore *m*
avid [ˈævɪd] ADJ: **avid (for)** desideroso(-a) (di), avido(-a) (di); **an avid reader** una accanito(-a) *or* appassionato(-a) lettore(-trice)
avid·ity [əˈvɪdɪtɪ] N avidità
av·id·ly [ˈævɪdlɪ] ADV avidamente
avo·ca·do [ˌævəˈkɑːdəʊ] N (*Brit: also*: **avocado pear**) avocado *m inv*
◎ **avoid** [əˈvɔɪd] VT (*obstacle*) scansare, schivare, evitare; (*argument etc*) evitare; (*danger*) sfuggire a; **to avoid doing sth** evitare di fare qc; **avoid going out on your own at night** evita di uscire da sola di sera; **try to avoid being seen** cerca di non farti vedere; **are you trying to avoid me?** stai cercando di evitarmi?
avoid·able [əˈvɔɪdəbl] ADJ evitabile
avoid·ance [əˈvɔɪdəns] N: **her avoidance of me has been noticed by everyone** tutti hanno notato che mi evita; **his avoidance of his duty** la sua mancanza al dovere; *see also* **tax**
av·oir·du·pois [ˌævədəˈpɔɪz] N *sistema ponderale usato in Gran Bretagna basato su libbra, oncia e multipli*
avow [əˈvaʊ] VT (*frm: declare*) dichiarare apertamente
avow·al [əˈvaʊəl] N (*of intentions, innocence*) dichiarazione *f*; (*of guilt*) ammissione *f*
avowed [əˈvaʊd] ADJ dichiarato(-a)
avow·ed·ly [əˈvaʊɪdlɪ] ADV apertamente, dichiaratamente; (*professedly*) dichiaratamente
AVP [ˌeɪviːˈpiː] N ABBR (*Am*) = *assistant vice-president*
avun·cu·lar [əˈvʌŋkjʊləʳ] ADJ (*liter: man*) bonario(-a)
AWACS [ˈeɪwæks] N ABBR (= **airborne warning and control system**) *sistema di allarme e controllo in volo*
◎ **await** [əˈweɪt] VT aspettare, attendere; **long awaited** tanto atteso(-a); **awaiting attention** (*Comm: letter*) in attesa di risposta; (*: order*) in attesa di essere evaso(-a)
awake [əˈweɪk] ADJ sveglio(-a); **to be awake** essere sveglio(-a); **to lie awake** rimanere sveglio(-a) a letto; **coffee keeps me awake** il caffè mi fa star sveglio; **to be awake to** (*fig*) essere cosciente *or* conscio(-a) *or* consapevole di
■ VT (*pt* **awoke** *or* **awaked**, *pp* **awoken** *or* **awaked**) svegliare; (*fig: emotions, memories*) risvegliare, ridestare; (*: suspicions*) destare
■ VI svegliarsi; **to awake to sth** (*fig*) rendersi conto di qc, aprire gli occhi su qc
awak·en [əˈweɪkən] VT, VI = **awake** VT, VI
awak·en·ing [əˈweɪknɪŋ] N risveglio
◎ **award** [əˈwɔːd] N (*prize*) premio; (*scholarship*) borsa di studio; (*Law: decision*) sentenza arbitrale, decreto; (*: sum*) ricompensa, risarcimento
■ VT: **to award sb sth** *or* **to award sth to sb** (*prize*) assegnare qc a qn; (*medal*) conferire qc a qn, concedere; **to award sb damages** a qn il risarcimento dei danni
award-winning [əˈwɔːdˌwɪnɪŋ] ADJ premiato(-a)
◎ **aware** [əˈwɛəʳ] ADJ: **to be aware of** (*conscious*) rendersi conto di; (*informed*) essere al corrente di, essere conscio(-a) di; **to become aware of** accorgersi di; **not that I am aware of** non che io sappia; **I am fully aware that** mi rendo perfettamente conto che; **to make sb aware of sth** rendere qn consapevole di qc; **to be politically/socially aware** aver coscienza politica/sociale
aware·ness [əˈwɛənɪs] N (*consciousness*) coscienza; (*knowledge*) consapevolezza; **to develop people's awareness (of)** sensibilizzare la gente (su)
awash [əˈwɒʃ] ADJ: **awash (with)** inondato(-a) (da)
◎ **away** [əˈweɪ] ADV **1** lontano; **away from** lontano da; **far away from home** molto lontano da casa; **the village is 3 miles away** il paese è a 3 miglia di distanza *or* è lontano 3 miglia; **two hours away by car** a due ore di distanza in macchina; **away in the distance** in lontananza; **the holiday was two weeks away** mancavano due settimane alle vacanze **2** (*absent*): **to be away** essere via; **Jason was away on a business trip** Jason era via per lavoro; **he's away in Milan** è (andato) a Milano; **he's away for a week** è andato via per una settimana; **go away!** vai via (di qui)!, via di qui!, vattene!; **to take away** portare via **3** **to turn away** girarsi, voltarsi; **to die away** (*sound*) spegnersi in lontananza; **the snow melted away** la neve si è completamente sciolta; **to play away** (*Sport*) giocare in trasferta *or* fuori casa; **to talk away** parlare in continuazione; **to work away** continuare a lavorare; **he was still working away in the library** stava ancora lavorando in biblioteca
away game, away match N (*Sport*) partita fuori casa *or* in trasferta
away team N (*Sport*) squadra in trasferta
awe [ɔː] N timore *m* reverenziale; **to stand in awe of** aver soggezione di
■ VT intimidire
awe-inspiring [ˈɔːɪnˌspaɪərɪŋ], **awe·some** [ˈɔːsəm] ADJ imponente
awe-struck [ˈɔːˌstrʌk] ADJ sgomento(-a)
◎ **aw·ful** [ˈɔːfəl] ADJ terribile, orribile; **the weather's awful** il tempo è orribile; **I feel awful** mi sento malissimo; **an awful lot of** (*people, cars, dogs*) un numero incredibile di; (*jam, flowers*) una quantità incredibile di; **how awful!** che orrore!
aw·ful·ly [ˈɔːflɪ] ADV (*very*) terribilmente; **thanks awfully** mille grazie; **I'm awfully sorry** sono terribilmente spiacente
awhile [əˈwaɪl] ADV (per) un po'
awk·ward [ˈɔːkwəd] ADJ **1** (*difficult: problem, question, situation, task*) delicato(-a), difficile; (*silence*) imbarazzante; (*Aut: corner*) brutto(-a); (*inconvenient*) scomodo(-a); (*time, moment*) poco opportuno(-a); (*tool*) poco maneggevole, scomodo(-a); (*shape*) difficile; **you've caught me at an awkward time** mi hai pescato in un momento poco opportuno; **Friday is awkward for me** venerdì mi riesce scomodo; **she's being awkward about it** sta rendendo la cosa un po' difficile; **he's an awkward customer** è un tipo difficile **2** (*clumsy: person*) goffo(-a); (*: gesture, movement*) impacciato(-a); (*style, phrasing*) contorto(-a); **the awkward age** l'età difficile
awk·ward·ly [ˈɔːkwədlɪ] ADV (*behave*) goffamente; (*move*) in modo impacciato; (*write*) in modo contorto
awk·ward·ness [ˈɔːkwədnɪs] N (*of situation, problem*) difficoltà, delicatezza; (*of arrangement*) scomodità; (*of silence*) imbarazzo; (*of movement, behaviour*) goffaggine *f*; **the awkwardness of his prose style** lo stile contorto della sua prosa
awl [ɔːl] N punteruolo
awn·ing [ˈɔːnɪŋ] N (*of shop, hotel etc*) tenda, tendone *m*; (*of tent*) veranda
awoke [əˈwəʊk] PT *of* **awake**
awok·en [əˈwəʊkən] PP *of* **awake**
AWOL [ˈeɪwɒl] ADJ ABBR (*Mil*) = **absent without leave**; *see* **absent**
awry [əˈraɪ] ADV di traverso
■ ADJ storto(-a); **to go awry** andare a monte

Aa

axe, (*Am*) **ax** [æks] N ascia, scure *f*; **to have an axe to grind** (*fig*) fare i propri interessi *or* il proprio tornaconto
■VT (*fig*: *expenditure*) ridurre drasticamente; (: *person*) liquidare (*per ragioni economiche*); (: *project etc*) annullare; (: *jobs*) sopprimere
axi·om ['æksɪəm] N assioma *m*
axio·mat·ic [,æksɪəʊ'mætɪk] ADJ assiomatico(-a)
Axis ['æksɪs] N: **the Axis** l'Asse
axis ['æksɪs] N (*pl* **axes** ['æksi:z]) (*Geom*, *of the earth*) asse *m*
axle ['æksl] N (*of wheel*) semiasse *m*; (*also*: **axletree**) asse *m*
axle grease N lubrificante *m* per gli assi
axon ['æksɒn] N, **axone** ['æksəʊn] N assone *m*
aye, **ay** [aɪ] EXCL (*esp Scot*: *yes*) sì
■N voto favorevole
AYH [,eɪwaɪ'eɪtʃ] N ABBR (= **American Youth Hostels**) ≈ A.I.G. *f* (= *Associazione Italiana Alberghi per la Gioventù*)
AZ ABBR (*Am Post*) = **Arizona**
azalea [ə'zeɪlɪə] N azalea
Azer·bai·jan [,æzəbaɪ'dʒɑ:n] N Azerbaigian *m*
Azer·bai·ja·ni [,æzəbaɪ'dʒɑ:nɪ], **Aze·ri** [ə'zɛərɪ] ADJ azerbaigiano(-a)
■N azerbaigiano(-a), azero(-a); (*language*) azerbaigiano
Azores [ə'zɒ:z] NPL: **the Azores** le Azzorre
AZT [,eɪzɛd'ti:] N ABBR (= **azidothymidine**) AZT *m*
Az·tec ['æztɛk] ADJ azteco(-a)
■N (*person*) azteco(-a); (*language*) azteco
az·ure ['eɪʒə^r] ADJ azzurro(-a)
■N azzurro

Bb

B, b [bi:] N **1** *(letter)* B, b *f or m inv* **2** *(Mus)* si *m* **3** *(Scol: mark)* ≈ 8 *(buono)*; **B for Benjamin** *(Am)*: **B for Baker** ≈ B come Bologna

b. ABBR = born

B2B [ˌbi:tu:ˈbi:] ABBR *(Comm* = **business to business***)* commercio elettronico tra aziende

B2C [ˌbi:tu:ˈsi:] ABBR *(Comm* = **business to consumer***)* commercio elettronico dal produttore al consumatore

B4 [bɪˈfɔ:ʳ] ABBR (= **before**) prima; **B4 lunch** prima di pranzo

BA [ˌbi:ˈeɪ] N ABBR (= **Bachelor of Arts**) laurea in discipline umanistiche; **she's got a BA in history** ha una laurea in storia

bab·ble [ˈbæbl] N *(of voices)* mormorio; *(of baby)* balbettio; *(of stream)* gorgoglio; *(foolish)* ciance *fpl*
■ VI *(indistinctly)* farfugliare; *(chatter)* cianciare; *(baby)* balbettare; *(stream)* gorgogliare

bab·bling [ˈbæblɪŋ] ADJ *(stream)* che gorgoglia

babe [beɪb] N *(old)* bimbo(-a), bebè *m inv*; *(esp Am fam: endearment)* piccolo(-a), tesoro; **babe in arms** bimbo(-a) in fasce; *(fig)* ingenuo(-a)

Ba·bel [ˈbeɪbəl] N Babele *f*; **the Tower of Babel** la torre di Babele

ba·boon [bəˈbu:n] N babbuino

◎ **baby** [ˈbeɪbɪ] N *(human)* bambino(-a), bimbo(-a); *(of animal)* piccolo; *(fam: as address: to woman)* piccola, bimba mia; *(: to man)* piccolo, bello; **a baby girl** una bambina piccola; **the baby of the family** il/la piccolino(-a) di casa; **don't be such a baby!** non fare il bambino!; **to throw the baby out with the bathwater** *(fig)* buttar via il bambino con l'acqua sporca; **the new system was his baby** *(fam)* il nuovo sistema era la sua creatura; **I was left holding the baby** *(fam)* mi hanno piantato lì a sbrogliarmela da solo
■ ADJ *(clothes, food)* per la prima infanzia

baby-battering [ˈbeɪbɪˌbætərɪŋ] N maltrattamento dei bambini

baby bird N uccellino

baby boy N maschietto

baby carriage N *(Am)* carrozzina

baby-doll pyjamas [ˌbeɪbɪdɒl-] NPL baby-doll *m inv*

baby face N viso da bambino

baby girl N femminuccia

baby grand N *(also:* **baby grand piano***)* pianoforte *m* a mezza coda

ba·by·hood [ˈbeɪbɪhʊd] N prima infanzia

ba·by·ish [ˈbeɪbɪɪʃ] ADJ puerile, infantile

Baby·lon [ˈbæbɪlən] N Babilonia

Baby·lo·nian [ˌbæbɪˈləʊnɪən] ADJ babilonese
■ N *(person)* babilonese *m/f*; *(language)* babilonese *m*

baby-minder [ˈbeɪbɪˌmaɪndəʳ] N bambinaia *(per madri che lavorano)*

baby rabbit N coniglietto

baby seat N *(Aut)* sedile *m* per bambini

baby-sit [ˈbeɪbɪsɪt] VI: **to baby-sit (for sb)** guardare i bambini (a qn), fare il *(or* la) babysitter (per qn)

baby-sitter [ˈbeɪbɪˌsɪtəʳ] N baby-sitter *m/f inv*

baby-sitting [ˈbeɪbɪˌsɪtɪŋ] N: **to go baby-sitting** fare il *(or* la) baby-sitter; **a baby-sitting service** un servizio di baby-sitting

baby talk N linguaggio infantile

baby-walker [ˈbeɪbɪˌwɔ:kəʳ] N girello

Bacchus [ˈbækəs] N Bacco

bach·elor [ˈbætʃələʳ] N scapolo

bach·elor·hood [ˈbætʃələhʊd] N celibato

Bachelor of Arts N *(Univ: degree)* laurea in discipline umanistiche lettere; *(: person)* laureato(-a) in discipline umanistiche

Bachelor of Science N *(Univ: degree)* ≈ laurea in scienze; *(: person)* ≈ laureato(-a) in scienze

bachelor party N *(Am)* festa di addio al celibato

Bachelor's Degree N *diploma di laurea*

BACHELOR'S DEGREE

Il **Bachelor's Degree** è il riconoscimento che viene conferito a chi ha completato un corso di laurea di tre o quattro anni all'università. I Bachelor's degrees più importanti sono il "BA" (Bachelor of Arts), il "BSc" (Bachelor of Science), il "BEd" (Bachelor of Education) e il "LLB" (Bachelor of Laws). *See also* **Master's degree; doctorate**
▷ www.dfes.gov.uk/hegateway/
▷ http://educationusa.state.gov/undergrad/about/

degrees.htm
▷ www.aucc.ca/can_uni/general_info/overview_e.html
▷ www.internationaleducationmedia.com/newzealand/
▷ www.southafrica.info/ess_info/sa_glance/education/education.htm

ba·cil·lus [bəˈsɪləs] N (*pl* **bacilli** [bəˈsɪlaɪ]) bacillo

◎ **back** [bæk] N

1 (*of person*) schiena; (*of animal*) dorso, schiena; **he fell on his back** è caduto di schiena; **he's got a bad back** ha problemi alla schiena; **with one's back to the light** con la luce alle spalle; **seen from the back** visto(-a) di spalle; **back to back** di spalle (uno(-a) contro l'altro(-a)), schiena contro schiena; **on the horse's back** in groppa al cavallo; **behind sb's back** alle spalle di qn; (*fig*) alle spalle *or* dietro le spalle di qn; **to break one's back** rompersi la schiena; **to break the back of a job** (*Brit*) fare il grosso *or* il peggio di un lavoro; **to put one's back into it** (*fam*) mettercela tutta; **to have one's back to the wall** (*fig*) essere *or* trovarsi con le spalle al muro; **to put sb's back up** (*fam*) far irritare qn; **to get off sb's back** (*fam*) lasciare qn in pace; **I was glad to see the back of him** (*fam*) ero contento che se ne fosse andato

2 (*as opposed to front*) dietro; (*of cheque, envelope, medal, page*) retro, rovescio; (*of head*) nuca; (*of hand*) dorso; (*of hall, room*) fondo; (*of house, car*) parte *f* posteriore, dietro; (*of chair*) spalliera, schienale *m*; (*of train*) coda; **on the back of the cheque** sul retro dell'assegno; **at the back of the class** in fondo alla classe; **at the back of the house** sul retro della casa; **in the back of the car** sul sedile posteriore dell'auto; **back to front** all'incontrario; **at the back of my mind was the thought that ...** sotto sotto pensavo che...; **it's always there at the back of my mind** è sempre lì , non riesco a togliermelo dalla mente; **I know Naples like the back of my hand** conosco Napoli come il palmo della mia mano *or* come le mie tasche; **at the back of beyond** (*fam*) in capo al mondo; **he's at the back of all this** c'è lui dietro a questa storia

3 (*Sport*) terzino; **right/left back** terzino destro/sinistro

■ ADJ ATTR

1 (*rear*) di dietro; (: *wheel, seat*) posteriore; **the back seat** il sedile posteriore; **the back door** la porta sul retro; **back garden/room** giardino/stanza sul retro (della casa); **back cover** retro della copertina; **back kitchen** retrocucina *m*; **back pass** (*Ftbl*) passaggio indietro; **on the back page** in ultima pagina; **to take a back seat** (*fig*) restare in secondo piano; **he's a back seat driver** sta sempre a criticare chi guida; **back street** vicolo; **he grew up in the back streets of Cardiff** è cresciuto nei bassifondi di Cardiff

2 (*overdue*: *rent*) arretrato(-a); **back payments** arretrati *mpl*

■ ADV

1 (*again, returning*) (*often* **ri-** *+verb*) **to give back** ridare; **to be back** essere tornato(-a); **when will you be back?** quando torni?; **he's not back yet** non è ancora tornato; **on the way back** al ritorno; **30 km there and back** 30 km fra andata e ritorno; **put it back on the shelf** rimettilo sullo scaffale; **she hit him back** gli restituì il colpo; **I smiled back** ho ricambiato il sorriso; **throw the ball back** rilancia la palla; **he called back** ha richiamato; **can I have it back?** posso riaverlo?; **he ran back** tornò indietro di corsa; **we went there by bus and walked back** siamo andati in autobus e siamo ritornati a piedi

2 (*in distance*) indietro; **stand back!** indietro!; **back and forth** avanti e indietro; **a house set back from the road** una casa che non si affaccia sulla strada

3 (*in time*): **some months back** mesi fa *or* addietro; **as far back as the 13th century** già nel duecento

■ VT

1 (*car*): **to back the car (into)** entrare (*or* uscire) in retromarcia (in); **he backed the car out of the garage** è uscito in retromarcia dal garage

2 (*support*: *plan, person, candidate*) appoggiare, sostenere, spalleggiare; (: *financially*) finanziare; **the union is backing his claim for compensation** il sindacato appoggia la sua domanda di indennizzo

3 (*bet on*: *horse*) puntare su; **I'm backing Red Rum at Epsom** ho puntato su Red Rum per la corsa di Epsom

■ VI (*move*: *person*) indietreggiare; (: *car*) fare marcia indietro; **he backed into me** ha fatto un passo indietro e mi è venuto addosso; (*in car*) mi è venuto addosso a marcia indietro

► **back away** VI + ADV: **to back away (from)** indietreggiare (davanti a), tirarsi indietro (davanti a)

► **back down** VI + ADV (*fig*) abbandonare, arrendersi, fare marcia indietro

► **back off** VI + ADV tirarsi indietro

► **back on to** VI + ADV + PREP: **the house backs on to the golf course** il retro della casa dà sul campo da golf

► **back out** VI + ADV (*fig*) tirarsi indietro; **to back out of sth** (*undertaking*) sottrarsi a; (*deal*) ritirarsi da; **they promised to help us and then backed out** avevano promesso di aiutarci, ma si sono tirati indietro

► **back up** VT + ADV

1 (*support*: *person*) appoggiare, sostenere; (: *claim, theory*) confermare, avvalorare; **she complained, and her colleagues backed her up** ha fatto reclamo e i suoi colleghi l'hanno appoggiata; **there's no evidence to back up his theory** non ci sono prove a sostegno della sua teoria

2 (*car*): **to back the car up** far marcia indietro

3 (*Comput*) copiare, fare una copia di riserva di

■ VI + ADV

1 (*in car*) fare marcia indietro

2 (*Am*: *traffic*) ingorgarsi

back·ache [ˈbækˌeɪk] N mal *m* di schiena; **I've got an awful backache** ho un terribile mal di schiena

back·bench [ˈbækbentʃ] ADJ: **a backbench MP** un deputato senza incarichi ufficiali; **a backbench revolt** una rivolta dei deputati senza incarichi ufficiali

back·bencher [ˈbækˈbentʃəʳ] N deputato(-a) senza incarichi ufficiali

back benches NPL *scanni dei deputati senza incarichi ufficiali*

BACK BENCHES

Nella "House of Commons", una delle camere del Parlamento britannico, sono chiamati **back benches** gli scanni dove siedono i "backbenchers", parlamentari che non hanno incarichi né al governo né all'opposizione. Nelle file davanti ad essi siedono i "frontbenchers". *See also* **front benches**

▷ www.explore.parliament.uk/
▷ www.parliament.uk/

back·bit·ing ['bæk,baɪtɪŋ] N maldicenze *fpl*
back·bone ['bæk,bəʊn] N (*also fig*) spina dorsale; **the backbone of the organization** l'anima dell'organizzazione; **he's got no backbone** è uno smidollato
back·break·ing ['bæk,breɪkɪŋ] ADJ (*work, task*) massacrante
back·chat ['bæk,tʃæt] N (*Brit fam*) impertinenza
back·cloth ['bæk,klɒθ] N (*Brit: Theatre*) fondale *m*; (: *fig*) sfondo
back·comb ['bæk,kəʊm] VT (*Brit*) cotonare
back·comb·ing ['bæk,kəʊmɪŋ] N cotonatura
back·date [,bæk'deɪt] VT (*arrangement, document*) retrodatare; **backdated pay rise** aumento (di stipendio) retroattivo
back·drop ['bæk,drɒp] N = **backcloth**
back·er ['bækəʳ] N (*supporter*) fautore(-trice), sostenitore(-trice); (*Comm*) finanziatore(-trice)
back·fire ['bæk'faɪəʳ] VI (*Aut*) avere un ritorno di fiamma; (*fig: plan, policy*) avere effetto contrario; **to backfire on sb** ritorcersi contro qn; **the trick backfired on him** lo scherzo gli si è ritorto contro
back·gam·mon [bæk'gæmən] N backgammon *m*, tavola reale
◎ **back·ground** ['bæk,graʊnd] N **1** (*gen*) sfondo; (*fig*) sfondo, scenario; **in the background** sullo sfondo; (*fig*) nell'ombra; **on a red background** su sfondo rosso; **a house in the background** una casa sullo sfondo **2** (*of person*) background *m inv*; (: *basic knowledge*) base *f*; (: *experience*) esperienza; (*of problem, event*) retroscena *m*, background *m inv*; **she comes from a wealthy background** è di famiglia ricca; **family background** ambiente familiare
■ ADJ (*music, noise*) di fondo; (*Comput*) a bassa priorità; **background noise** rumori *mpl* di fondo
background radiation N radiazione *f* di fondo
background reading N letture *fpl* complementari
back·hand ['bæk,hænd] N (*Tennis: backhand stroke*) rovescio
back·hand·ed [,bæk'hændɪd] ADJ (*blow*) con il dorso della mano; (*Tennis: stroke*) di rovescio; **backhanded compliment** complimento ambiguo
back·hand·er ['bæk,hændəʳ] N (*Brit: bribe*) bustarella
◎ **back·ing** ['bækɪŋ] N **1** (*support*) appoggio, sostegno; (*Comm*) finanziamento; **they promised their backing** hanno garantito il loro appoggio **2** (*Mus*) accompagnamento **3** (*protective layer of paper, cloth etc*) rivestimento, strato protettivo
back·lash ['bæk,læʃ] N (*fig*) reazione *f* (violenta)
back·log ['bæk,lɒg] N: **backlog of work** lavoro arretrato; **the strike has resulted in a backlog of orders** a causa dello sciopero si sono accumulate le ordinazioni
back number N (*of magazine*) numero arretrato
back·pack ['bæk,pæk] N zaino
back·packer ['bæk,pækəʳ] N *chi viaggia con zaino e sacco a pelo*
backpack·ing ['bæk,pækɪŋ] N: **to go backpacking** viaggiare con zaino e sacco a pelo
back passage N (*Anat*) retto
back pay N arretrato di stipendio
back-pedal [,bæk'pɛdəl] VI (*on bicycle*) pedalare all'indietro; (*fig*) fare marcia indietro
back·scratch·er ['bæk,skrætʃəʳ] N manina (grattaschiena *inv*)
back scrub·ber ['bæk,skrʌbəʳ] N spazzola da bagno
back-seat driver [,bæksiːt'draɪvəʳ] N *passeggero che dà consigli non richiesti al guidatore*
back·side [,bæk'saɪd] N (*fam*) didietro *m inv*, sedere *m*; **a kick in the backside** un calcio nel sedere
back-slap·ping ['bæk,slæpɪŋ] N (*fam*) scambio di pacche sulle spalle
back·slash ['bæk,slæʃ] N (*Typ*) barra obliqua inversa
back·slid·ing ['bæk,slaɪdɪŋ] N ricaduta (*in vizio, errore*)
back·space ['bæk,speɪs] VI (*in typing*) battere il tasto di ritorno
back·stage [,bæk'steɪdʒ] ADV, ADJ dietro le quinte
back·stairs ['bæk'stɛəz] NPL scala *sg* di servizio
backstairs gossip N pettegolezzi *mpl*, chiacchiere *fpl* di corridoio
back·stay ['bæk,steɪ] N (*Naut*) paterazzo
back·street ['bæk,striːt] N vicolo
■ ADJ (*shop, factory*) situato(-a) in un vicolo; (*fig: shady*) losco(-a); **a backstreet cafe** un bar d'infima categoria; **backstreet abortionist** praticante *m/f* di aborti clandestini
back·stroke ['bæk,strəʊk] N (*Swimming*) dorso
back·swing ['bæk,swɪŋ] N (*Tennis*) movimento di apertura
back-to-back ['bæktə'bæk] ADJ (*Brit*): **back-to-back houses** *tipo di case a schiera con la parete posteriore in comune*
back·track ['bæk,træk] VI (*retrace one's steps*) tornare indietro; (*fig: backpedal*) fare marcia indietro
back·up ['bækʌp] ADJ (*gen, Comput*) di riserva
■ N (*support*) sostegno, appoggio; (*substitute*) sostituto; (*Comput*) backup *m inv*; **a backup file** un file di backup; **they've got a generator as an emergency backup** hanno un generatore di riserva per le emergenze
back·ward ['bækwəd] ADJ **1** (*motion, glance*) all'indietro; **a backward step** un passo indietro **2** (*pupil*) che è indietro, tardivo(-a); (*pej: country*) arretrato(-a) **3** (*reluctant*): **backward (in doing sth)** restio(-a) (a fare qc)
backward-looking ['bækwəd,lʊkɪŋ] ADJ (*pej*) retrogrado(-a)
back·ward·ness ['bækwədnɪs] N (*pej: of country*) arretratezza
back·wards ['bækwədz], **back·ward** (*Am*) ['bækwəd] ADV indietro; **he took a step backwards** ha fatto un passo indietro; **to walk backwards** camminare all'indietro; **to fall backwards** cadere all'indietro; **backwards and forwards** avanti e indietro; **to bend over backwards to do sth** (*fam*) farsi in quattro per fare qc; **to know sth backwards** (*fam*) sapere qc a menadito
back·wash ['bæk,wɒʃ] N (*of waves*) risacca; (*of ship, aircraft*) risucchio; (*fig: repercussions*) strascico, ripercussione *f*
back·water ['bæk,wɔːtəʳ] N acqua stagnante; (*fig pej*) buco, angolo sperduto; **this town is a cultural backwater** questa città è culturalmente arretrata
back·woods ['bækwʊdz] NPL (*Am*) zona *sg* rurale isolata
■ ADJ rurale
back yard N (*Brit: paved area*) cortile *m* sul retro della casa; (*Am: garden*) giardino sul retro della casa
ba·con ['beɪkən] N pancetta; **bacon and eggs** uova *fpl* con pancetta
bac·te·ria [bæk'tɪərɪə] NPL batteri *mpl*
bac·te·rial [bæk'tɪərɪəl] ADJ batterico(-a)
bac·te·rio·logi·cal [bæk,tɪərɪə'lɒdʒɪkəl] ADJ batteriologico(-a)

Bb

bac·te·ri·olo·gist [bæk,tɪərɪ'ɒlədʒɪst] N batteriologo(-a)
bac·te·ri·ol·ogy [bæk,tɪərɪ'ɒlədʒɪ] N batteriologia
Bac·trian cam·el ['bæktrɪən'kæməl] N cammello (asiatico)
◎ **bad** [bæd] ADJ (*comp* **worse**, *superl* **worst**) **1** (*gen*) cattivo(-a); (*child*) cattivello(-a); (*habit*) cattivo(-a); (*news, weather*) brutto(-a); (*habit, news, weather*) brutto(-a), cattivo(-a); (*workmanship, film*) scadente, brutto(-a); (*mistake, illness, cut*) brutto(-a), grave; **bad language** parolacce *fpl*; **you bad boy!** (brutto) cattivo!; **he's in a bad mood** è di cattivo umore; **to be bad at sth** non essere bravo(-a) in qc; **he's bad at keeping appointments** non sa rispettare un impegno; **smoking is bad for you** il fumo fa male alla salute; **not bad** (*quite good*) non male, niente male; (*less enthusiastic*) così così ; **how are you feeling? — not bad** come si sente? — non c'è male; **not bad, eh?** mica male, eh?; **that wouldn't be a bad thing** non sarebbe una cattiva idea; **a bad accident** un grave incidente; **that's too bad** (*sympathetic*) che peccato; **that's just too bad** (*unsympathetic*) tanto peggio per te (*or* lei *etc*); **it's too bad of you** è poco carino da parte tua; **I feel bad about it** mi sento un po' in colpa; **business is bad** gli affari vanno male; **from bad to worse** di male in peggio; **to have a bad time of it** passarsela male; **to be in a bad way** (*in difficulties*) essere nei guai; (*ill*) stare molto male; **bad faith** malafede *f* **2** (*rotten: food*) guasto(-a), andato(-a) a male; (: *smell*) cattivo(-a); (: *tooth*) cariato(-a), guasto(-a); **to go bad** andare a male **3** **to have a bad back/stomach** avere dei problemi alla schiena/allo stomaco; **his bad leg** la sua gamba malata; **to feel bad** (*sick*) sentirsi male; **I feel bad about it** (*guilty*) mi sento un po' in colpa; **there's no need for you to feel bad about it** non è il caso di prendersela
bad cheque N assegno a vuoto
bad debt N credito inesigibile
bad·die ['bædɪ] N (*fam*) cattivo
bade [bæd, beɪd] PT *of* **bid**
badge [bædʒ] N (*of policeman, Scol*) distintivo; (*Mil*) mostrina; (*stick-on*) adesivo
badg·er ['bædʒə[r]] N (*Zool*) tasso
■ VT tormentare
bad hair day N (*fam*) *giornata in cui non ci si sente molto attraenti*; (*fig*) giornataccia
◎ **bad·ly** ['bædlɪ] ADV (*comp* **worse**, *superl* **worst**) **1** (*work, dress*) male; **she behaved badly** si è comportata male; **a badly behaved child** un(a) bambino(-a) maleducato(-a); **things are going badly** le cose vanno male; **to treat sb badly** trattar male qn; **badly paid** mal pagato(-a) **2** (*seriously: wounded*) gravemente; **badly hurt** gravemente ferito(-a) **3** (*very much*): **I need it badly** ne ho assolutamente bisogno; **I want it badly** lo voglio ad ogni costo; **it badly needs painting** ha proprio bisogno di una mano di vernice; **he needs help badly** ha urgente bisogno di aiuto
badly off ADJ povero(-a)
bad-mannered [,bæd'mænəd] ADJ maleducato(-a), sgarbato(-a)
bad·min·ton ['bædmɪntən] N badminton *m*
bad-mouth ['bæd,maʊθ] VT: **to bad-mouth sb** parlare male di qn, sparlare di qn
bad·ness ['bædnɪs] N (*wickedness*) cattiveria
bad-tempered [,bæd'tempəd] ADJ irascibile, irritabile; (*look*) antipatico(-a); **to be bad-tempered** (*always*) avere un brutto carattere; (*at a particular time*) essere di malumore
baf·fle ['bæfl] VT (*puzzle*) lasciare perplesso(-a), confondere; **it baffles me how she does it** non riesco a capire come faccia
baf·fle·ment ['bæflmənt] N perplessità
baf·fling ['bæflɪŋ] ADJ sconcertante
BAFTA ['bæftə] N ABBR (= **British Academy of Film and Television Arts**) *accademia britannica delle arti cinematografiche e televisive che annualmente assegna premi alle migliori produzioni*
◎ **bag** [bæg] N (*gen*) borsa; (*paper bag, carrier*) sacchetto; (*handbag*) borsa, borsetta; (*suitcase*) valigia; (*of hunter*) carniere *m*; (*animals taken by hunter*) carniere, bottino di caccia; **I put it in my bag** l'ho messo in borsa; **to pack one's bags** fare le valigie; **it's in the bag** (*fam*) ce l'ho (*or* ce l'hai *etc*) in tasca, è cosa fatta; **bags under the eyes** borse sotto gli occhi; **bags of** (*fam: lots*) un sacco di
■ VT (*fam: seat, place*) accaparrarsi
▸ **bag up** VT + ADV (*flour*) insaccare
bag·ful ['bægfʊl] N sacco (pieno)
bag·gage ['bægɪdʒ] N bagaglio, bagagli *mpl*; **where is your baggage?** dove sono i tuoi bagagli?; **a piece of baggage** un bagaglio
baggage car N (*Am*) bagagliaio
baggage check N controllo bagagli
baggage handler N addetto ai bagagli
baggage identification tag N tagliando (di) controllo (del) bagaglio
baggage reclaim N ritiro bagagli
bag·gy ['bægɪ] ADJ largo(-a), sformato(-a)
Bagh·dad [bæg'dæd] N Bagdad *f*
bag lady N (*fam*) straccìona, barbona
bag·pipes ['bæg,paɪps] NPL (*in Scotland*) cornamusa *sg*; (*in Italy*) zampogna *sg*
bag-snatcher ['bæg,snætʃə[r]] N (*Brit*) scippatore(-trice)
bag-snatching ['bæg,snætʃɪŋ] N (*Brit*) scippo
Ba·ha·mas [bə'hɑ:məz] NPL: **the Bahamas** le Bahamas
Bah·rain, Bah·rein [bɑ:'reɪn] N il Bahrein *m*
bail¹ [beɪl] N (*Law*) cauzione *f*; **he was granted bail** ha ottenuto la libertà provvisoria su cauzione; **to stand bail for sb** rendersi garante di *or* per qn; **to be released on bail** essere rilasciato(-a) su cauzione
▸ **bail out** VT + ADV (*Law*) mettere in libertà provvisoria su cauzione; (*fig*) tirare fuori dai guai
bail² [beɪl] VT, VI *see* **bale out** VT, VI **1**
bail·iff ['beɪlɪf] N (*Law*) ufficiale *m* giudiziario; (*on estate*) amministratore *m*, fattore *m*
bairn [bɛən] N (*Scot*) bambino(-a)
bait [beɪt] N (*also fig*) esca; **he didn't rise to the bait** (*fig*) non ha abboccato (all'amo)
■ VT (*hook*) innescare; (*trap*) munire di esca; (*torment: person, animal*) stuzzicare, tormentare
baize [beɪz] N panno
◎ **bake** [beɪk] VT (*bread, cake*) cuocere (al forno); (*bricks*) cuocere; **she baked a cake today** ha fatto un dolce oggi; **baked potatoes** patate *fpl* (con la buccia) cotte al forno
■ VI cuocersi al forno
baked beans ['beɪkt'bi:nz] NPL ≈ fagioli *mpl* all'uccelletto
Ba·ke·lite® ['beɪkə,laɪt] N bachelite® *f*
bak·er ['beɪkə[r]] N fornaio(-a), panettiere(-a); **baker's (shop)** panetteria, forno; **at/to the baker's** dal panettiere, dal fornaio
baker's dozen N (*old*) *tredici cose*
bak·ery ['beɪkərɪ] N panetteria, forno

bak·ing [ˈbeɪkɪŋ] N cottura (al forno); **Monday was her day for doing the baking** il lunedì faceva il pane (e/o i dolci)
■ ADJ (*fam: hot*): **it's baking in here** qui dentro è un forno, qui dentro si muore di caldo
baking dish N pirofila
baking powder N lievito (minerale) in polvere
baking sheet, baking tray N placca da forno, teglia
baking soda N bicarbonato di soda
baking tin N stampo, tortiera
bala·cla·va [ˌbæləˈklɑːvə] N (*also:* **balaclava helmet**) passamontagna *m inv*
◎ **bal·ance** [ˈbæləns] N **1** (*equilibrium*) equilibrio; **to lose one's balance** perdere l'equilibrio; **to throw sb off balance** far perdere l'equilibrio a qn; (*fig*) sconcertare qn, far mancare la terra sotto i piedi a qn; **balance of power** equilibrio di potere; **to strike the right balance** trovare il giusto mezzo; **on balance** (*fig*) a conti fatti, tutto sommato; **a nice balance of humour and pathos** una equilibrata combinazione di humour e pathos **2** (*scales*) bilancia; **to hang in the balance** (*fig*) essere incerto(-a) *or* in bilico **3** (*Comm*) bilancio; (: *difference*) saldo; (: *remainder*) resto; **balance brought** *or* **carried forward** saldo riportato, saldo da riportare
■ VT **1** tenere in equilibrio *or* in bilico; (*Aut: wheel*) fare l'equilibratura di; (*fig: compare*) soppesare, valutare; (*make up for*) compensare; **the two things balance each other out** le due cose si compensano; **this must be balanced against that** nel considerare questo fattore bisogna tener presente l'altro **2** (*Comm: account*) saldare; (: *budget*) pareggiare, far quadrare; **to balance the books** fare il bilancio **3** (*Chem, Math: equations*) bilanciare
■ VI **1** tenersi in equilibrio **2** (*accounts*) quadrare, essere in pareggio
bal·anced [ˈbælənst] ADJ (*views*) moderato(-a); (*personality, diet*) equilibrato(-a)
balance of payments N bilancia dei pagamenti
balance of trade N bilancia commerciale
balance sheet N bilancio (di esercizio)
bal·anc·ing [ˈbælənsɪŋ] N **1** messa in equilibrio; (*Aut: of wheels*) equilibratura **2** (*Comm, Fin: of account*) saldo; (: *of budget*) pareggiamento; **balancing of the books** bilancio
balancing act N: **to do a balancing act** (*also fig*) fare dell'equilibrismo
bal·co·ny [ˈbælkənɪ] N balcone *m*; (*Theatre*) prima galleria, balconata
bald [bɔːld] ADJ (*person*) calvo(-a); (*tyre*) liscio(-a); (*statement*) asciutto(-a); (*style*) spoglio(-a); **to go bald** perdere i capelli
bal·der·dash [ˈbɔːldəˌdæʃ] N (*old*) sciocchezze *fpl*, stupidaggini *fpl*
bald-headed [ˌbɔːldˈhɛdɪd] ADJ calvo(-a)
bald·ing [ˈbɔːldɪŋ] ADJ con una calvizie incipiente
bald·ly [ˈbɔːldlɪ] ADV senza tanti complimenti
bald·ness [ˈbɔːldnɪs] N calvizie *fsg*
baldy [ˈbɔːldɪ] N (*fam*) testa pelata
bale¹ [beɪl] N (*of cloth, hay*) balla
bale² [beɪl] VT, VI *see* **bale out** VT, VI **1**
▸ **bale out** VT + ADV (*Naut: water*) vuotare; (: *boat*) sgottare, aggottare
■ VI + ADV **1** (*Naut*) saltare in acqua **2** (*Aer*) gettarsi col paracadute
Bal·ear·ic [ˌbælɪˈærɪk] ADJ: **the Balearic Islands** le (isole) Baleari
bale·ful [ˈbeɪlfʊl] ADJ (*look*) malevolo(-a)
bale·ful·ly [ˈbeɪlfəlɪ] ADV malevolmente
balk, baulk [bɔːk] VI: **to balk (at the idea of)** (*person*) recalcitrare (all'idea di), tirarsi indietro (davanti a); (*horse*) recalcitrare *or* impennarsi (di fronte a)
Bal·kan [ˈbɔːlkən] ADJ balcanico(-a)
Bal·kans [ˈbɔːlkənz] NPL: **the Balkans** i Balcani
◎ **ball¹** [bɔːl] N (*gen*) palla; (*inflated: Ftbl etc*) pallone *m*; (*for golf etc*) pallina; (*of wool, string*) gomitolo; **pass the ball to me!** passami la palla!; **a tennis ball** una pallina da tennis; **a rugby ball** un pallone da rugby; **a glass ball** un globo di vetro; **he rolled the paper into a ball** ha appallottolato la carta; **the ball of the foot** la punta del piede; **the ball of the thumb** il polpastrello del pollice; **to be on the ball** (*fig: competent*) essere in gamba; (: *quick*) essere sveglio(-a); (*alert*) stare all'erta; **to play ball (with sb)** (*fig*) stare al gioco (di qn); **to start the ball rolling** (*fig*) fare la prima mossa; **to keep the ball rolling** (*fig*) mandare avanti le cose; **the ball is in your court** (*fig*) tocca a te
ball² [bɔːl] N (*dance*) ballo; **a fancy dress ball** un ballo in maschera; **to have a ball** (*fig fam*) divertirsi da matti, spassarsela
bal·lad [ˈbæləd] N ballata
bal·last [ˈbæləst] N zavorra
ball bearing N cuscinetto a sfere
ball cock [ˈbɔːlˌkɒk] N galleggiante *m* (*in serbatoio*)
bal·le·ri·na [ˌbæləˈriːnə] N ballerina (classica)
bal·let [ˈbæleɪ] N (*dance*) balletto; (*art*) danza classica; **we went to a ballet** siamo andati a vedere un balletto; **ballet lessons** corso di danza classica
▷ http://info.royaloperahouse.org/ballet/index.cfm?ccs=473&cs=1004
▷ www.australianballet.com.au
▷ www.national.ballet.ca
▷ www.nzballet.org.nz/
ballet dancer N ballerino(-a) (classico(-a))
ball game N (*gen*) gioco con la palla; (*Am*) partita di baseball; **it's a whole new ball game** (*fam*) è un altro paio di maniche
bal·lis·tic [bəˈlɪstɪk] ADJ balistico(-a); **intercontinental ballistic missile** missile *m* a gettata intercontinentale
bal·lis·tics [bəˈlɪstɪks] NSG balistica
ball machine N (*Tennis*) macchina *f* lanciapalle *inv*
bal·loon [bəˈluːn] N (*toy*) palloncino; (*Aer*) pallone *m* aerostatico, mongolfiera; (*in comic strip*) fumetto
■ VI gonfiarsi
bal·loon·ist [bəˈluːnɪst] N aeronauta *m/f*
◎ **bal·lot** [ˈbælət] N votazione *f* (a scrutinio segreto); **on the first ballot** alla prima votazione
■ VT (*members*) consultare tramite votazione
ballot box N urna (elettorale)
ballot paper N scheda (elettorale)
ball·park [ˈbɔːlˌpɑːk] N (*Am*) stadio di baseball
ballpark figure N (*fam*) cifra approssimativa
ball-point [ˈbɔːlˌpɔɪnt], **ball-point pen** [ˈbɔːlˌpɔɪntˈpɛn] N penna a sfera
ball·room [ˈbɔːlˌrʊm] N sala da ballo
ballroom dancing N ballo liscio
balls [bɔːlz] (*fam!*) NPL coglioni *mpl* (*fam!*); (*fig: bullshit*) cazzate *fpl* (*fam!*)
balls-up (*fam!*) VT + ADV incasinare
■ N pasticcio; **you can rely on George to make a balls-up of everything** puoi star sicuro che George incasinerà tutto
ballsy [ˈbɔːlzɪ] ADJ (*fam!: person*) con le palle; (: *music*) grintoso(-a)

Bb

bal·ly·hoo [ˌbælɪˈhuː] N battage *m inv*
balm [bɑːm] N (*also fig*) balsamo
balmy [ˈbɑːmɪ] ADJ **1** (*breeze, air*) balsamico(-a) **2** (*Brit fam*) = **barmy**
ba·lo·ney [bəˈləʊnɪ] N (*Am fam*) sciocchezze *fpl*, stupidaggini *fpl*
BALPA [ˈbælpə] N ABBR = **British Airline Pilots' Association**
bal·sa [ˈbɔːlsə] N (*also:* **balsawood**) (legno di) balsa
bal·sam [ˈbɔːlsəm] N balsamo
Bal·tic [ˈbɔːltɪk] ADJ, N baltico(-a); **the Baltic (Sea)** il (mar) Baltico
bal·us·trade [ˌbæləsˈtreɪd] N balaustrata
bam·boo [bæmˈbuː] N bambù *m inv*
■ ADJ di bambù
bam·boo·zle [bæmˈbuːzl] VT (*fam*) abbindolare, infinocchiare
◎ **ban** [bæn] N divieto, bando; **to put a ban on sth** proibire qc
■ VT (*pt, pp* **banned**) (*alcohol, book, film*) proibire; **to ban sb from sth** proibire qc a qn; **to ban sb from doing sth** proibire a qn di fare qc; **to ban sb from a place** proibire a qn di andare in un posto; **they banned him from the competition** lo hanno escluso dalla gara; **arms sales were banned last year** la vendita di armi è stata vietata l'anno scorso; **he was banned from driving** (*Brit*) gli hanno tolto (*or* ritirato) la patente
ba·nal [bəˈnɑːl] ADJ banale
ba·nal·ity [bəˈnælɪtɪ] N banalità *f inv*
ba·nal·ly [bəˈnɑːlɪ] ADV banalmente
ba·na·na [bəˈnɑːnə] N (*fruit*) banana; (*tree*) banano
banana boat N bananiera
banana republic N (*fam pej*) repubblica delle banane
banana skin N (*also fig*) buccia di banana
banana split N banana split *f inv*
band[1] [bænd] N (*gen*) banda, striscia; (*of hat, cigar*) nastro
◎ **band**[2] [bænd] N **1** (*Mus*) banda (musicale); (*jazz band, pop group*) complesso (musicale); (*Mil*) fanfara; **the procession was led by a band** la processione era preceduta da una banda; **he plays the guitar in a band** suona la chitarra in un gruppo **2** (*group of people*) banda
▸ **band together** VI + ADV mettersi in gruppo
band·age [ˈbændɪdʒ] N fascia, benda
■ VT fasciare, bendare
Band-Aid® [ˈbændˌeɪd] N (*Am*) cerotto
ban·dana, **ban·dan·na** [bænˈdænə] N fazzolettone *m*
B & B, **b. and b.** [ˌbiːəndˈbiː] N ABBR = **bed and breakfast**
ban·dit [ˈbændɪt] N bandito, brigante *m*
ban·dit·ry [ˈbændɪtrɪ] N banditismo
band saw N segatrice *f* a nastro
bands·man [ˈbændzmən] N (*pl* **-men**) suonatore di banda
band·stand [ˈbændˌstænd] N palco coperto dell'orchestra (*in parco pubblico*)
band·wagon [ˈbændˌwægən] N: **to jump on the bandwagon** (*fig*) seguire la corrente
band·width [ˈbændwɪdθ] N (*Comput*) larghezza di banda
ban·dy [ˈbændɪ] VT (*jokes, insults*) scambiarsi
▸ **bandy about** VT + ADV (*word, phrase*) ripetere con insistenza; **to bandy sb's name about** parlare con insistenza di qn
bandy-legged [ˈbændɪˈlɛgɪd] ADJ dalle *or* con le gambe storte

bane [beɪn] N: **it** (*or* **he** *etc*) **is the bane of my life** è la mia rovina
bane·ful [ˈbeɪnfʊl] ADJ dannoso(-a), nocivo(-a)
bang[1] [bæŋ] N (*noise: of explosion, gun*) scoppio, colpo; (: *of sth falling*) tonfo; (*blow*) botta, colpo; **I heard a loud bang** ho sentito un forte scoppio; **he closed the door with a bang** ha sbattuto la porta; **a bang on the head** un colpo sulla testa; **it went with a bang** (*fam*) è stato una bomba
■ ADV: **to go bang** esplodere, fare bang; **to be bang on time** (*Brit fam*) spaccare il secondo; **bang went £10** mi (*or* gli *etc*) sono volate 10 sterline
■ VT (*thump*) battere, picchiare; (*hit, knock, slam*) sbattere, battere (violentemente); **he banged the receiver down** ha sbattuto giù il telefono; **I banged my head** ho sbattuto la testa; **to bang one's head against a wall** (*fig*) battere *or* picchiare la testa contro il muro
■ VI (*explode*) scoppiare, esplodere; (*slam: door*) sbattere; **to bang at/on sth** picchiare a/su qc; **to bang at** *or* **on the door** picchiare alla porta; **to bang into sth** sbattere contro qc
▸ **bang about** (*fam*) VT + ADV sbatacchiare
■ VI far rumore
bang[2] [bæŋ] N (*fringe*) frangetta
bang·er [ˈbæŋəʳ] N (*Brit fam*) **1** (*sausage*) salsiccia; **bangers and mash** salsicce e purè di patate **2** (*firework*) mortaretto **3** (*old car*) macinino
Bang·kok [bæŋˈkɒk] N Bangkok *f*
Bang·la·desh [bæŋgləˈdɛʃ] N il Bangladesh *m*
Bang·la·deshi [ˌbɑːŋgləˈdɛʃɪ] ADJ del Bangladesh
■ N abitante *m/f* del Bangladesh
ban·gle [ˈbæŋgl] N braccialetto
ban·ish [ˈbænɪʃ] VT: **to banish (from)** (*person*) bandire (da), esiliare (da); (*thought, fear*) bandire (da)
ban·ish·ment [ˈbænɪʃmənt] N esilio, bando
ban·is·ters [ˈbænɪstəz] NPL ringhiera *sg*
ban·jo [ˈbændʒəʊ] N banjo *m inv*
◎ **bank** [bæŋk] N **1** (*Fin, Med*) banca; (*Gambling*) banco; **the bank is closed** la banca è chiusa **2** (*of river*) sponda, riva; (: *embankment*) argine *m*; (*of road, racetrack*) terrapieno; **we walked along the river bank** abbiamo camminato lungo la riva del fiume **3** (*heap: of earth, mud*) mucchio; (: *of snow*) cumulo; (: *of clouds, sand*) banco **4** (*Aer*) virata
■ VT (*money*) depositare in banca
■ VI **1** servirsi di una banca; **they bank with Pitt's** (*Comm*) sono clienti di Pitt's; **where do you bank?** qual è la sua banca? **2** (*Aer*) inclinarsi in virata
▸ **bank on** VI + PREP far conto su, contare su; **he was banking on a pay rise** contava su un aumento; **I wouldn't bank on it** non ci conterei
▸ **bank up** VT + ADV (*sand*) ammucchiare
bank account N (*gen*) conto in banca; (*frm*) conto bancario
bank balance N saldo; **a healthy bank balance** un solido conto in banca
bank·book [ˈbæŋkˌbʊk] N libretto di banca, libretto di risparmio
bank card N = **cheque card**
bank charges NPL (*Brit*) spese *fpl* bancarie; (*on currency transaction*) commissioni *fpl* bancarie
bank clerk N impiegato(-a) di banca
bank draft N tratta bancaria
◎ **bank·er** [ˈbæŋkəʳ] N banchiere *m*
banker's card [ˈbæŋkəzˈkɑːd] N (*Brit*) = **cheque card**
banker's draft N (*Fin*) tratta bancaria

banker's order N = standing order
bank giro N bancogiro
bank holiday N (*Brit*) giorno di festa civile; **Monday's a bank holiday** lunedì è festa

BANK HOLIDAY

Una **bank holiday**, in Gran Bretagna, è una giornata in cui le banche e molti negozi sono chiusi. Generalmente le bank holidays cadono di lunedì e molti ne approfittano per fare una breve vacanza fuori città. Di conseguenza, durante questi fine settimana lunghi ("bank holiday weekends") si verifica un notevole aumento del traffico sulle strade, negli aeroporti e nelle stazioni e molte località turistiche registrano il tutto esaurito.
▷ www.adviceguide.org.uk/index/life/employment/bank_and_public_holidays/

◎**bank·ing** ['bæŋkɪŋ] N attività bancaria; **to study banking** fare studi bancari *or* di tecnica bancaria
▷ www.eib.org/
▷ www.ecb.int/home/html/index.en.html
▷ www.bankofengland.co.uk
▷ www.rba.gov.au
▷ www.rbnz.govt.nz
▷ www.resbank.co.za
▷ www.bankofcanada.ca/en/
▷ www.worldbank.org
banking hours NPL orario di sportello
banking house N istituto bancario *or* di credito
bank loan N prestito bancario
bank manager N direttore(-trice) di banca
bank·note ['bæŋk,nəʊt] N banconota
bank rate N tasso ufficiale di sconto
bank·roll ['bæŋk,rəʊl], (*Am*) VT finanziare
■N finanziamento
bank·rupt ['bæŋkrʌpt] ADJ fallito(-a); (*fam: penniless*) senza una lira; **to go bankrupt** fallire, fare fallimento *or* bancarotta
■N fallito(-a)
■VT portare al fallimento
bank·rupt·cy ['bæŋkrəptsɪ] N fallimento, bancarotta; **bankruptcy proceedings** procedura fallimentare
bank statement N estratto *m* conto *inv*
banned substance [,bænd'sʌbstəns] N (*Sport*) sostanza al bando
ban·ner ['bænəʳ] N stendardo, bandiera; (*with slogan*) striscione *m*
banner ad N (*on website*) striscione *m* pubblicitario
banner headline N titolo a tutta pagina
ban·nis·ters ['bænɪstəz] NPL = **banisters**
banns [bænz] NPL pubblicazioni *fpl* (di matrimonio); **to read** *or* **publish the banns** esporre le pubblicazioni
ban·quet ['bæŋkwɪt] N banchetto
ban·tam ['bæntəm] N gallo "bantam"
bantam·weight ['bæntəm,weɪt] N (*Boxing*) peso gallo
ban·ter ['bæntəʳ] N scherzi *mpl* bonari
BAOR [,biːeɪəʊ'ɑːʳ] N ABBR = **British Army of the Rhine**
bap·tism ['bæptɪzəm] N battesimo
bap·tis·mal [bæp'tɪzməl] ADJ (*font, ceremony*) battesimale; (*robes*) da battesimo
Bap·tist ['bæptɪst] ADJ, N (*Rel*) battista (*m/f*); **St John the Baptist** San Giovanni Battista
▷ www.baptist.org/
bap·tize [bæp'taɪz] VT battezzare
◎**bar¹** [bɑːʳ] N **1** (*pub*) bar *m inv*; (*counter: in pub*) banco **2** (*piece: of wood, metal etc*) sbarra, barra; (*of chocolate*) tavoletta; (*of electric fire*) elemento; **it's the most popular bar in town** è il locale più frequentato della città; **please order meals at the bar** si prega di ordinare le consumazioni al banco; **a bar of chocolate** una tavoletta di cioccolata; **bar of soap** saponetta **3** (*of window, cage*) sbarra; (*on door*) spranga; **bar (to)** (*fig: obstacle*) barriera (a), ostacolo (a); **behind bars** (*prisoner*) dietro le sbarre **4** (*Law: professional group*): **the Bar** l'ordine *m* degli avvocati; **the prisoner at the bar** (*area in court*) l'imputato(-a); **to be called to** *or* (*Am*) **admitted to the Bar** essere ammesso(-a) all'ordine degli avvocati **5** (*Mus*) battuta
■VT (*obstruct: way*) sbarrare; (*fasten: door, window*) sbarrare, sprangare; (*ban: person*) escludere; (*: activity, thing*) proibire, interdire
bar² [bɑːʳ] PREP ad esclusione di, tranne; **the fastest sprinter bar none** il velocista più veloce in assoluto
barb [bɑːb] N (*of hook, arrow*) punta
Bar·ba·dos [bɑː'beɪdɒs] N Barbados *fsg*
bar·bar·ian [bɑː'bɛərɪən] N barbaro(-a)
bar·bar·ic [bɑː'bærɪk], **bar·ba·rous** ['bɑːbərəs] ADJ (*cruelty, behaviour*) barbaro(-a); (*splendour*) barbarico(-a)
bar·ba·rism ['bɑːbə,rɪzəm] N (*of society*) barbarie *f inv*, barbarismo
bar·bar·ity [bɑː'bærɪtɪ] N barbarie *f inv*; **the barbarities of modern warfare** le atrocità della guerra moderna
bar·becue ['bɑːbɪkjuː] N (*grill*) barbecue *m inv*; (*party*) grigliata all'aperto
■VT cuocere alla brace
barbecue sauce N salsa piccante per barbecue
barbed ['bɑːbd] ADJ (*hook, arrow*) con barbigli; (*fig: wit, comment*) pungente, tagliente
barbed wire ['bɑːbd,waɪəʳ] N filo spinato
bar·ber ['bɑːbəʳ] N barbiere *m*; **to go to the barber's (shop)** andare dal barbiere
barber·shop ['bɑːbəʃɒːp] N (*music*) barbershop *m*; *tipo di musica melodica cantata senza strumenti d'accompagnamento*; (*Am: shop*) barbiere *m*
▷ www.barbershop.org.uk/
▷ www.spebsqsa.org/
bar·bi·tu·rate [bɑː'bɪtjʊrɪt] N barbiturico
Bar·ce·lo·na [bɑːsɪ'ləʊnə] N Barcellona
bar chart N diagramma *m* a colonna
bar code N codice *m* a barre
bard [bɑːd] N bardo
◎**bare** [bɛəʳ] ADJ **1** (*gen*) nudo(-a); (*arms, legs*) nudo(-a), scoperto(-a); (*head*) scoperto(-a); (*landscape*) spoglio(-a), brullo(-a); (*ground, tree, room*) nudo(-a), spoglio(-a); (*cupboard*) vuoto(-a); (*Elec: wire*) scoperto(-a); **there's a bare patch on the carpet** c'è un pezzo spelacchiato nella moquette; **with his bare hands** a mani nude; **the bare facts** i fatti nudi e crudi; **to lay bare** (*fig*) mettere a nudo, svelare **2** (*meagre: majority*) risicato(-a); **to strip sth down to the bare essentials** (*structure, narrative*) ridurre qc all'essenziale; **the bare necessities** lo stretto necessario; **to earn a bare living** guadagnare appena da vivere
■VT scoprire, denudare; (*teeth*) mostrare; **to bare one's heart** (*fig*) mettere a nudo il proprio animo
bare·back ['bɛə,bæk] ADV senza sella
bare·faced ['bɛə,feɪst] ADJ sfacciato(-a), spudorato(-a)
bare·foot ['bɛə,fʊt], **bare·footed** [,bɛə'fʊtɪd] ADJ, ADV scalzo(-a), a piedi nudi; **the children go around barefoot** i bambini vanno in giro scalzi

Bb

bare·headed [ˌbɛəˈhɛdɪd] ADJ, ADV a capo scoperto
bare·legged [ˌbɛəˈlɛgd] ADJ a gambe scoperte
◎ **bare·ly** [ˈbɛəlɪ] ADV appena; **they had barely enough money** avevano appena denaro a sufficienza; **he was so drunk he could barely stand** era così ubriaco che riusciva a malapena a stare in piedi; **I could barely hear what she was saying** sentivo a malapena quello che diceva
bare·ness [ˈbɛənɪs] N nudità
Bar·ents Sea [ˈbærənts'si:] N: **the Barents Sea** il mar di Barents
◎ **bar·gain** [ˈbɑ:gɪn] N **1** (*transaction*) affare *m*; **to make a bargain with sb** fare un patto con qn; (*business*) concludere un affare con qn; **it's a bargain!** affare fatto!; **you drive a hard bargain** lei mi pone delle condizioni difficili; **into the bargain** (*fig*) per giunta, per di più **2** (*cheap thing*) affare *m*, occasione *f*; (*in sales*) occasione; **to get a bargain** fare un affare; **it's a (real) bargain** è un affarone, è un'occasione
■ VI (*negotiate*) contrattare; (*haggle*) tirare sul prezzo
► **bargain for** VI + PREP (*fam*): **to bargain for sth** aspettarsi qc; **he got more than he bargained for** non si aspettava quello che è successo
bargain basement N reparto occasioni
bargain hunter N *chi va in giro per i negozi a caccia di occasioni*
bar·gain·ing [ˈbɑ:gɪnɪŋ] ADJ: **bargaining position** posizione *f* di negoziato; **to be in a weak/strong bargaining position** non avere/avere potere contrattuale; (*fig*) non essere/essere nella posizione di poter trattare; **bargaining power** potere *m* contrattuale; **bargaining process** processo di negoziato
■ N contrattazione *f*
bargain offer N affare *m*, occasione *f*
bargain price N prezzo d'occasione
bargain sale N svendita, liquidazione *f*
barge [bɑ:dʒ] N chiatta, barcone *m*; (*ceremonial*) lancia
► **barge in** VI + ADV (*fam pej: enter*) precipitarsi dentro, piombare dentro; (*: interrupt*) intromettersi
► **barge into** VI + PREP (*fam: knock*) andare a sbattere contro, urtare contro; (*: enter*) piombare in; (*: interrupt*) intromettersi in
bar·gee [bɑ:ˈdʒi:] N, **barge·man** (*Am*) [ˈbɑ:dʒmən]
■ N barcaiolo
barge pole N: **I wouldn't touch it with a barge pole** (*fam: revolting*) non lo toccherei nemmeno con un dito; (*: risky*) girerei alla larga
bari·tone [ˈbærɪtəʊn] N baritono
bar·ium [ˈbɛərɪəm] N bario
barium meal N (pasto di) bario
bark[1] [bɑ:k] N (*of tree*) corteccia
bark[2] [bɑ:k] N (*of dog*) latrato, abbaiare *m*; **his bark is worse than his bite** abbaia ma non morde
■ VI: **to bark (at)** abbaiare a; **to be barking up the wrong tree** essere sulla strada sbagliata, sbagliarsi di grosso
► **bark out** VT + ADV (*order*) urlare, abbaiare
bar·keeper [ˈbɑ:ˌki:pəʳ] N (*Am*) barista *m/f*
bark·ing [ˈbɑ:kɪŋ] N abbaiare *m*
bar·ley [ˈbɑ:lɪ] N orzo
barley sugar N zucchero d'orzo
barley water N orzata
bar·maid [ˈbɑ:ˌmeɪd] N barista *f*
bar·man [ˈbɑ:mən] N (*pl* **barmen**) barista *m*
bar·my [ˈbɑ:mɪ] ADJ (*Brit fam*) tocco(-a), toccato(-a), suonato(-a)

barn [bɑ:n] N fienile *m*, granaio; (*for animals*) stalla
bar·na·cle [ˈbɑ:nəkl] N cirripede *m*
barnacle goose N oca dalle guance bianche
barn dance N danza campestre
barn owl N barbagianni *m inv* nostrano
barn·yard [ˈbɑ:nˌjɑ:d] N aia
ba·rom·eter [bəˈrɒmɪtəʳ] N barometro
baro·met·ric [ˌbærəˈmɛtrɪk] ADJ (*pressure, chart*) barometrico(-a); (*reading*) del barometro
bar·on [ˈbærən] N barone *m*; (*fig*) magnate *m*; **the press barons** i baroni della stampa; **the oil barons** i magnati del petrolio
bar·on·ess [ˈbærənɪs] N baronessa
bar·on·et [ˈbærənɪt] N baronetto
ba·roque [bəˈrɒk] ADJ barocco(-a)
bar·rack [ˈbærək] VT (*Brit*): **to barrack sb** subissare qn di grida e fischi
bar·rack·ing [ˈbærəkɪŋ] N (*Brit*): **to give sb a barracking** subissare qn di grida e fischi
barrack-room [ˈbærəkˈrʊm] ADJ: **to be a barrack-room lawyer** (*fig*) *dare pareri (non richiesti) legali senza avere alcuna competenza*
bar·racks [ˈbærəks] NPL caserma *sg*; **confined to barracks** consegnato(-a) in caserma

> **DID YOU KNOW ...?**
> **barracks** is not translated by the Italian word *baracche*

bar·ra·cu·da [ˌbærəˈkju:də] N barracuda *m inv*
bar·rage [ˈbærɑ:ʒ] N (*dam*) (opera di) sbarramento; (*Mil*) sbarramento; **a barrage of questions** una raffica di *or* un fuoco di fila di domande
barrage balloon N pallone *m* di sbarramento
◎ **bar·rel** [ˈbærəl] N barile *m*; (*of gun*) canna; **a barrel of beer** un barile di birra
barrel organ N organetto
bar·ren [ˈbærən] ADJ (*land*) arido(-a), povero(-a); (*tree*) infruttuoso(-a); (*animal*) sterile
bar·ren·ness [ˈbærənnɪs] N (*of land*) sterilità
bar·ri·cade [ˌbærɪˈkeɪd] N barricata
■ VT barricare
◎ **bar·ri·er** [ˈbærɪəʳ] N barriera; (*Brit also:* **crash barrier**) guardrail *m inv*; (*Rail: in station*) cancello; (*fig*) barriera, ostacolo
barrier cream N (*Brit*) crema protettiva
bar·ring [ˈbɑ:rɪŋ] PREP = **bar** VT
bar·ris·ter [ˈbærɪstəʳ] N (*Brit*) avvocato (*con diritto di parlare davanti a tutte le corti*)

> **DID YOU KNOW ...?**
> **barrister** is not translated by the Italian word *barista*

BARRISTER

Il **barrister** è un membro della più prestigiosa delle due branche della professione legale (l'altra è quella dei "solicitors"); la sua funzione è quella di rappresentare i propri clienti in tutte le corti ("magistrates' court", "crown court" e "Court of Appeal"), generalmente seguendo le istruzioni del caso preparate dai "solicitors". *See also* **solicitor; lawyer**

▷ www.online-law.co.uk/
▷ www.barcouncil.org.uk/

bar·row[1] [ˈbærəʊ] N (*wheelbarrow*) carriola; (*market stall*) carretto, carrettino
bar·row[2] [ˈbærəʊ] N (*Archeol*) tumulo

Bart. ABBR (*Brit*) = **baronet**
bar·tender ['bɑːˌtɛndəʳ] N (*Am*) barista *m/f*
bar·ter ['bɑːtəʳ] VT: **to barter sth (for sth)** barattare qc (con qc)
■ VI: **to barter with sb (for sth)** barattare (qc) con qn
■ N baratto
bas·alt ['bæsɔːlt] N basalto
◎ **base¹** [beɪs] N (*gen, Mil*) base *f*
■ VT (*troops*): **to base at** mettere di stanza a; (*opinion, relationship*): **to base on** basare su, fondare su; **the film is based on a play by Shakespeare** il film è basato su una commedia di Shakespeare; **I'm based in London** sono di base *or* ho base a Londra; **the job is based in London** la sede di lavoro è a Londra; **a Paris-based firm** una ditta con sede centrale a Parigi; **coffee-based** a base di caffè
base² [beɪs] ADJ (*liter: action, motive*) basso(-a); (*: behaviour*) ignobile
◎ **base·ball** ['beɪsˌbɔːl] N baseball *m*; **a baseball cap** un berretto da baseball
▷ www.majorleaguebaseball.com
base·board ['beɪsbɔːd] N (*Am*) battiscopa *m inv*
base camp N campo *m* base *inv*
Ba·sel ['bɑːzəl] N = **Basle**
base·less ['beɪslɪs] ADJ (*gossip etc*) infondato(-a)
base·line ['beɪsˌlaɪn] N (*Tennis*) linea di fondo; (*Baseball*) linea di base
base·ly ['beɪslɪ] ADV (*liter: act, behave*) ignobilmente
base·ment ['beɪsmənt] N (*of house*) seminterrato; (*of shop*) scantinato; **a basement flat** un appartamento nel seminterrato

DID YOU KNOW ...?
basement is not translated by the Italian word *basamento*

base metal N metallo vile
base·ness ['beɪsnɪs] N (*liter: of action, behaviour*) bassezza (morale)
base rate N (*Fin*) tasso base
bases ['beɪsiːz, 'beɪsɪz] **1** NPL *of* **basis** **2** NPL *of* **base**
bash [bæʃ] (*fam*) N **1** (*blow*) botta; **the car has had a bash** la macchina ha preso una botta; **I'll have a bash (at it)** (*Brit fam*) ci proverò **2** (*fam: party*) festa
■ VT (*fam: thing*) sbattere; (*: person*) picchiare, menare
▸ **bash in** VT + ADV (*fam*) sfondare; **to bash sb's head in** spaccare la testa a qn; **bashed in** sfondato(-a)
▸ **bash on** VI: **to bash on with** andare avanti con
▸ **bash up** VT + ADV (*fam: car*) sfasciare; (*: Brit: person*) riempire di botte
bash·ful ['bæʃfʊl] ADJ timido(-a)
bash·ful·ly ['bæʃfʊlɪ] ADV timidamente
bash·ful·ness ['bæʃfʊlnɪs] N timidezza
bash·ing ['bæʃɪŋ] N: **to take a bashing** prendere una batosta; **union-bashing** denigrazione *f* sistematica dei sindacati
BASIC ['beɪsɪk] N ABBR (*Comput:* = **Beginner's All-purpose Symbolic Introduction Code**) BASIC *m*
◎ **ba·sic** ['beɪsɪk] ADJ **1** (*fundamental: reason, problem*) fondamentale, base *inv* (*after n*); (*rudimentary: knowledge*) rudimentale; (*: equipment: essential*) essenziale; (*: poor*) primitivo(-a); (*elementary: principles, precautions, rules*) elementare; (*salary*) base *inv* (*after n*); **it's one of the basic requirements** è uno dei requisiti fondamentali; **it's a basic model** è un modello base; **"Basic Italian"** "Italiano elementare"; **the accommodation is pretty basic** l'alloggio è piuttosto modesto **2** (*Chem: oxide, salt*) basico(-a)
◎ **ba·si·cal·ly** ['beɪsɪklɪ] ADV fondamentalmente, sostanzialmente
basic rate N (*of tax*) aliquota minima
ba·sics ['beɪsɪks] NPL principi fondamentali
bas·il ['bæzl] N basilico
ba·sili·ca [bə'zɪlɪkə] N basilica
ba·sin ['beɪsn] N (*Brit: for food*) terrina; (*washbasin*) lavabo, lavandino; (*Geog*) bacino
◎ **ba·sis** ['beɪsɪs] N (*pl* **bases** ['beɪsiːz]) (*foundation*) base *f*, fondamento; **on the basis of what you've said** in base a quello che hai detto; **on a daily basis** quotidianamente; **on a regular basis** regolarmente
bask [bɑːsk] VI: **to bask in the sun** crogiolarsi al sole; **to bask in sb's favour** godere del favore di qn
basket ['bɑːskɪt] N (*gen: bread basket, wastepaper basket*) cestino; (*large*) cesto, cesta; (*shopping basket*) cestino della spesa; (*at supermarket*) cestello; (*wicker basket*) paniere *m*; (*Basketball*) canestro; (*Fin*) paniere *m*
basket·ball ['bɑːskɪtˌbɔːl] N pallacanestro *f*, basket *m*
▷ www.fiba.com/
▷ www.nba.com
basketball player N cestista *m/f*
bask·ing shark ['bɑːskɪŋ'ʃɑːk] N squalo elefante
Basle [bɑːl] N Basilea
bas·ma·ti rice [bæsˌmɑːtɪ'raɪs] N riso basmati; *varietà di riso usato nella cucina indiana*
Basque [bæsk] ADJ basco(-a)
■ N (*person*) basco(-a); (*language*) basco
◎ **bass¹** [beɪs] (*Mus*) ADJ basso(-a)
■ N (*voice*) voce *f* di basso; (*singer*) basso; (*double bass*) contrabbasso; (*guitar*) basso (elettrico); (*on hi-fi*) basso
bass² [bæs] N (*fish: freshwater*) pesce *m* persico; (*: seawater*) spigola
bass clef [ˌbeɪs'klɛf] N chiave *f* di basso
bas·soon [bə'suːn] N fagotto
bas·tard ['bɑːstəd] N bastardo(-a); (*fam! pej*) figlio di puttana (*fam!*)
■ ADJ (*child*) illegittimo(-a)
baste [beɪst] VT (*Culin*) ungere, inumidire col suo sugo; (*Sewing*) imbastire
bas·ti·on ['bæstɪən] N (*castle wall*) bastione *m*; (*stronghold: fig*) baluardo
BASW [ˌbiːeɪɛs'dʌbljʊ] N ABBR (= **British Association of Social Workers**) ≈ sindacato degli assistenti sociali
◎ **bat¹** [bæt] N (*Cricket, Baseball*) mazza; (*Brit: Table-Tennis*) racchetta; **off one's own bat** (*fam*) di testa propria, di propria iniziativa
■ VI (*Sport*) battere
■ VT: **he didn't bat an eyelid** (*fam*) non ha battuto ciglio
bat² [bæt] N (*Zool*) pipistrello; **to have bats in the belfry** (*fig fam*) essere picchiato(-a) *or* suonato(-a); **like a bat out of hell** come un fulmine
batch [bætʃ] N (*of applicants, letters*) gruppo; (*of work*) sezione *f*; (*of goods*) partita, lotto; (*of recruits*) contingente *m*; (*of bread*) infornata; (*of papers*) cumulo; **the next batch of students** il prossimo gruppo di studenti; **batch of statistics** insieme di dati
batch processing N (*Comput*) elaborazione *f* a blocchi
bat·ed ['beɪtɪd] ADJ: **with bated breath** col fiato sospeso
◎ **bath** [bɑːθ] N (*pl* **baths** [bɑːðz]) **1** (*tub*) vasca (da bagno); (*wash*) bagno; **room with bath** camera con vasca da bagno; **to have a bath** fare *or* farsi un bagno **2** ESP PL: **swimming baths** piscina
■ VI fare *or* farsi un bagno
■ VT fare il bagno a

Bb

bath·cap ['bɑ:θ,kæp] N cuffia per la doccia
Bath chair ['bɑ:θ,tʃɛəʳ] N *(Brit)* poltrona a rotelle
bathe [beɪð] N *(in sea, pool)* bagno
■ VI **1** *(swim)* fare i bagni, bagnarsi; **to go bathing** andare a fare il bagno *or* a nuotare; **it was too cold to bathe** era troppo freddo per fare il bagno **2** *(Am)* = **bath** VI
■ VT **1** *(wound)* lavare **2** *(Am)* = **bath** VT
bath·er ['beɪðəʳ] N bagnante *m/f*
bath·house ['bɑ:θhaʊs] N bagni *mpl* pubblici
bath·ing ['beɪðɪŋ] N bagni *mpl*; **"bathing is forbidden"** "è vietata la balneazione"
bathing cap N cuffia da bagno
bathing costume, bathing suit N costume *m* da bagno
bathing trunks ['beɪðɪŋ,trʌŋks] NPL pantaloncini *mpl or* costume *m* da bagno
bath·mat ['bɑ:θ,mæt] N tappetino da bagno
bath oil N olio da bagno
bath·robe ['bɑ:θ,rəʊb] N *(towelling)* accappatoio; *(Am)* = **dressing gown**
◎ **bath·room** ['bɑ:θrʊm] N (stanza da) bagno; *(Am)* bagno, toilette *f inv*
bathroom cabinet N armadietto (da bagno)
bathroom scales NPL bilancia pesapersone
baths [bɑ:ðz] NPL bagni *mpl* pubblici
bath towel N asciugamano da bagno
bath·tub ['bɑ:θ,tʌb] N *(old)* vasca da bagno
bath·water ['bɑ:θ,wɔ:təʳ] N acqua del bagno
bathy·scaph ['bæθɪ,skæf] N batiscafo
bat·man ['bæt,mæn] N *(pl* **batmen***)* *(Brit Mil)* attendente *m*
baton ['bætən] N *(Mus)* bacchetta; *(Mil)* bastone *m* di comando; *(of policeman)* sfollagente *m inv*, manganello; *(in race)* testimone *m*
baton charge N carica con lo sfollagente
bats·man ['bætsmən] N *(pl* **-men***)* **1** *(Cricket)* battitore *m* **2** *(Aer)* segnalatore *m*
bat·tal·ion [bə'tælɪən] N battaglione *m*
bat·ten ['bætən] N listello di legno; *(Carpentry)* assicella, correntino; *(for flooring)* tavola; *(Naut)* serretta; *(: on sail)* stecca
▸ **batten down** VT + ADV *(Naut)*: **to batten down the hatches** chiudere i boccaporti; *(fig)* prepararsi per un'emergenza
bat·ter¹ ['bætəʳ] N *(Culin)* pastella
bat·ter² ['bætəʳ] VT *(person)* ridurre in cattivo stato; *(wife, baby)* maltrattare; *(subj: wind, waves)* colpire violentemente
▸ **batter down** VT + ADV abbattere, buttare giù
bat·tered ['bætəd] ADJ *(car, building)* malridotto(-a); *(baby, wife)* maltrattato(-a), vittima *inv* di maltrattamenti; *(hat)* sformato(-a); *(pan)* ammaccato(-a)
bat·ter·ing ram ['bætərɪŋ,ræm] N ariete *m*
bat·tery ['bætərɪ] N *(Elec)* pila; *(Aut, Mil)* batteria; *(large number: of lights, tests)* batteria; *(: of questions)* pioggia, raffica
battery charger N caricabatterie *m inv*
battery farming N allevamento in batteria
battery lead connection ['bætərɪ'li:dkə'nɛkʃən] N *(Aut)* morsetto della batteria
◎ **bat·tle** ['bætl] N *(Mil)* battaglia, combattimento; *(fig)* lotta, battaglia; **killed in battle** ucciso in combattimento; **I had quite a battle to get permission** ho dovuto lottare per ottenere il permesso; **a battle of wits** una gara d'ingegno; **that's half the battle** *(fam)* è già una mezza vittoria; **to fight a losing battle** *(fig)* battersi per una causa persa
■ VI *(fig)*: **to battle (for)** lottare (per), combattere (per); **he battled to retain his self-control** dovette fare uno sforzo per controllarsi; **to battle against the wind** lottare con *or* contro il vento
battle-axe ['bætəl,æks] N *(pej)*: **she was a terrible old battle-axe** era proprio un carabiniere
battle cruiser N incrociatore *m* da battaglia
battle cry N grido di battaglia
battle dress N uniforme *f* da combattimento
battle·field ['bætl,fi:ld], **battle·ground** ['bætl,graʊnd] N campo di battaglia
battle formation N schieramento di battaglia
bat·tle·ments ['bætlmənts] NPL bastioni *mpl*
battle royal N *(fig: quarrel)* violenta discussione *f*
battle-scarred ['bætəl,skɑ:d] ADJ *(person)* con cicatrici di guerra; *(town)* che mostra i segni della guerra
battle·ship ['bætlʃɪp] N nave *f* da guerra
battle zone N zona del conflitto
bat·ty ['bætɪ] ADJ *(comp* **-ier**, *superl* **-iest***)* *(fam: person)* svitato(-a), strambo(-a); *(: behaviour, idea)* strampalato(-a); **I must be going batty!** sto proprio rimbambendo!
bau·ble ['bɔ:bl] N ninnolo
baud [bɔ:d] N *(Comput)* baud *m inv*
baulk [bɔ:lk] VI = **balk**
baux·ite ['bɔ:ksaɪt] N bauxite *f*
Ba·varia [bə'vɛərɪə] N Baviera
Ba·var·ian [bə'vɛərɪən] ADJ, N bavarese *(m/f)*
bawdy ['bɔ:dɪ] ADJ piccante, spinto(-a), salace; **bawdy song** canzonaccia
bawl [bɔ:l] VI *(cry)* strillare; *(shout)* urlare, sbraitare
▸ **bawl out** VT + ADV **1** urlare (a squarciagola) **2** *(fam)*: **to bawl sb out** fare una sfuriata *or* una lavata di testa a qn
◎ **bay¹** [beɪ] N *(Geog)* baia; **the Bay of Biscay** il golfo di Biscaglia
bay² [beɪ] N **1** *(Archit)* campata **2** *(Brit: for parking)* piazzola di sosta; *(for loading)* piazzale *m* di (sosta e) carico
bay³ [beɪ] VI *(hound)* abbaiare, latrare
■ N *(bark)* latrato; **to keep sb/sth at bay** *(fig)* tenere a bada qn/qc
bay⁴ [beɪ] ADJ *(horse)* baio(-a)
bay⁵ [beɪ] N *(also:* **bay tree***)* alloro
bay bar N *(Geog)* barra
bay leaf ['beɪ,li:f] N foglia d'alloro
bayo·net ['beɪənɪt] N baionetta
■ VT infilzare con la baionetta
bayonet charge N carica alla baionetta
bay window² N bovindo
ba·zaar [bə'zɑ:'] N *(sale of work)* vendita di beneficenza; *(Oriental market)* bazar *m inv*
ba·zoo·ka [bə'zu:kə] N bazooka *m inv*
BB [,bi:'bi:] N ABBR *(Brit:* = **Boys' Brigade***)* *organizzazione giovanile a fine educativo*
BBB [,bi:bi:'bi:] N ABBR *(Am:* = **Better Business Bureau***)* *organismo per la difesa dei consumatori*
BBC [,bi:bi:'si:] N ABBR (= **British Broadcasting Corporation**) BBC *f*

BBC

La **BBC** è l'azienda statale che fornisce il servizio radiofonico e televisivo in Gran Bretagna. Pur dovendo rispondere al Parlamento del proprio operato, la BBC non è soggetta al controllo dello stato per scelte e programmi, anche perché si autofinanzia con il ricavato dei canoni d'abbonamento. La BBC ha diversi canali televisivi e radiofonici sia a livello nazionale che locale, alcuni dei quali sono anche digitali. Fornisce inoltre un servizio di informazione internazionale, il "BBC World Service", trasmesso in tutto il mondo.

▷ www.bbc.co.uk

BBQ ABBR = **barbecue**

BC [ˌbiːˈsiː] ADV ABBR (= **before Christ**) a.C.
■ ABBR = **British Columbia**

BCG [ˌbiːsiːˈdʒiː] N ABBR (= **Bacillus Calmette-Guérin**) vaccino antitubercolare

BD [ˌbiːˈdiː] N ABBR (= **Bachelor of Divinity**) laurea in teologia

B/D ABBR = **bank draft**

BDS [ˌbiːdiːˈɛs] N ABBR (= **Bachelor of Dental Surgery**) laurea in odontoiatria e protesi dentaria

B/E ABBR = **bill of exchange**

◎ **be** [biː]; KEYWORD
(*present* **am, is, are**, *pt* **was, were**) (*pp* **been**)
■ VI
1 (*exist*) essere, esistere; **leave it as it is** lascialo così ; **the best singer that ever was** il miglior cantante mai esistito; **how much was it?** quanto è costato?, quant'era?; **let me be!** lasciami in pace!; **so be it** sia pure, e sia; **be that as it may** sia come sia, comunque sia; **his wife to be** la sua futura moglie; **to be or not to be** essere o non essere
2 (*in place*) essere, trovarsi; **she won't be here tomorrow** non ci sarà domani; **we've been here for ages** sono secoli che siamo qui; **Edinburgh is in Scotland** Edimburgo è *or* si trova in Scozia; **it's on the table** è *or* sta sul tavolo
3 **there is** c'è; **there are** ci sono; **there were 3 of us** eravamo in 3; **there will be dancing** si ballerà; **there was once a house here** qua una volta c'era una casa; **let there be light** sia la luce
4 (*presenting, pointing out*): **here is** *or* **here are** ecco; **there is** *or* **there are** (*over there*) ecco; **here you are (take it)** ecco qua (prendi); **there's the church** ecco la chiesa
5 (*come, go: esp in perfect tense*): **I've been to China** sono stato in Cina; **where have you been?** dove sei stato?
■ COPULATIVE VB
1 essere; **2 and 2 are 4** 2 più 2 fa 4; **he's a pianist** è (un) pianista; **they're English** sono inglesi; **be good!** sii buono!; **I'm hot** ho caldo; **the book is in French** il libro è in francese; **I'm not Sue, I'm Mary** non sono Sue, sono Mary; **he's tall** è alto
2 (*health*) stare; **I'm better now** ora sto meglio; **how are you?** come stai (*or* sta)?
3 (*age*): **how old is she? — she's 9** quanti anni ha? — ne ha 9 *or* ha 9 anni
■ IMPERS VB
1 **it is said that ...** si dice che... + *sub*; **it is possible that ...** può darsi *or* essere che... + *sub*
2 (*time*) essere; **it's the 3rd of May** è il 3 (di) maggio; **it's 8 o'clock** sono le 8
3 (*measurement*): **it's 5 km to the village** da qui al paese sono 5 km
4 (*weather*) fare; **it's too hot** fa troppo caldo
5 (*emphatic*): **it's only me** sono solo io
■ AUX VB
1 (*with present participle: forming continuous tenses*): **they're coming tomorrow** vengono domani; **what are you doing?** che fai?, che stai facendo?; **he's always grumbling** brontola sempre, non fa che brontolare; **I'll be seeing you** ci vediamo; **I've been waiting for her for 2 hours** l'aspetto da 2 ore
2 (*with past participle: forming passives*) essere; **what's to be done?** che fare?; **he is nowhere to be found** non lo si trova da nessuna parte; **to be killed** essere *or* venire ucciso(-a); **the box had been opened** la scatola era stata aperta
3 (*in tag questions*): **he's back again, is he?** così è tornato, eh?; **he's handsome, isn't he?** è un bell'uomo, vero?; **it was fun, wasn't it?** è stato bello, no?
4 (+ *to* + *infinitive*): **he's to be congratulated on his work** dobbiamo fargli i complimenti per il suo lavoro; **you're to do as I tell you** devi fare come ti dico; **he was to have come yesterday** sarebbe dovuto venire ieri; **he's not to open it** non deve aprirlo; **the car is to be sold** abbiamo (*or* hanno *etc*) intenzione di vendere la macchina; **am I to understand that ...?** devo dedurre che...?
5 (*modal: supposition*): **if it was** *or* **were to snow ...** (se) dovesse nevicare...; **if I were you ...** se fossi in te...
▶ **be in for** VI + ADV + PREP: **you'll only be in for a disappointment** non puoi che restare deluso; **we may be in for some trouble here** mi sa che qui potremmo avere delle grane
▶ **be on to** VI + ADV + PREP: **to be on to something** essere sulla pista giusta; **I think they're on to us** penso che abbiano dei sospetti su di noi

Bb

◎ **beach** [biːtʃ] N spiaggia; **on the beach** in spiaggia
■ VT tirare in secco

beach ball N pallone *m* da mare *or* da spiaggia

beach buggy N dune buggy *f inv*

beach·comber [ˈbiːtʃˌkəuməʳ] N *persona che si aggira sulle spiagge alla ricerca di soldi, oggetti ecc*

beach·head [ˈbiːtʃˌhɛd] N testa di sbarco

beach·wear [ˈbiːtʃˌwɛəʳ] N abbigliamento da spiaggia

bea·con [ˈbiːkən] N (*fire*) fuoco di segnalazione; (*lighthouse*) faro, fanale *m*; (*radio beacon*) radiofaro; (*marker*) segnale *m*

bead [biːd] N perlina; (*of rosary*) grano; (*of dew, sweat*) goccia

beads ■ NPL (*necklace*) collana; (*also:* **rosary beads**) corona (del rosario), rosario

beady [ˈbiːdɪ] ADJ: **beady eyes** occhi *mpl* piccoli e penetranti

beady-eyed [ˈbiːdɪˈaɪd] ADJ dagli occhi piccoli e penetranti

bea·gle [ˈbiːgl] N bracchetto

beak [biːk] N becco

beak·er [ˈbiːkəʳ] N coppa; (*Chem*) becher *m inv*

be-all and end-all [ˌbiːɔːlənd'ɛndɔːl] N: **the be-all and end-all (of sth)** il fine ultimo (di qc)

beam [biːm] N 1 (*Archit*) trave *f* 2 (*Naut*) baglio 3 (*of light, sunlight*) raggio; (*of torch*) fascio (di luce); (*Radio*) fascio (d'onde); **to drive with headlights on full** *or* (*Am*) **high beam** guidare con gli abbaglianti accesi
4 (*smile*) sorriso raggiante
■ VT (*Radio*) trasmettere con antenna direzionale
■ VI (*smile*) sorridere radiosamente; **to beam at sb** fare un largo sorriso a qn

beam·ing ['bi:mɪŋ] ADJ (*sun*) splendente; (*face, smile*) raggiante

◎**bean** [bi:n] N fagiolo; (*broad bean*) fava; (*runner bean*) fagiolino; (*of coffee*) grano, chicco; **green beans** fagiolini; **full of beans** (*fam: child*) che ha l'argento vivo addosso; (*: adult*) in gran forma

bean curd N tofu *m inv*

bean·pole ['bi:n,pəʊl] N (*fam*) spilungone(-a)

bean·sprouts ['bi:n,spraʊts], **bean·shoots** ['bi:n,ʃu:ts] NPL germogli *mpl* di soia

◎**bear**[1] [bɛə^r] (*vb: pt* **bore**, *pp* **borne**) VT
1 (*carry: burden, signature, date, name*) portare; (*: news, message*) recare; (*: traces, signs*) mostrare; **to bear some resemblance to** somigliare a; **he bore himself like a soldier** (*of posture*) aveva un portamento militare; (*of behaviour*) si comportò da soldato; **the love he bore her** l'amore che le portava; **to bear sb ill will** portare *or* serbare rancore a qn
2 (*support: weight*) reggere, sostenere; (*: cost*) sostenere; (*: responsibility*) assumere; (*: comparison*) reggere a; **the roof couldn't bear the weight of the snow** il tetto non ha retto il *or* al peso della neve
3 (*endure: pain*) sopportare; (*stand up to: inspection, examination*) reggere a; **he bore his sufferings bravely** ha sopportato con coraggio la sofferenza; **I can't bear it!** non lo sopporto!; **I can't bear him** non lo posso soffrire *or* sopportare; **I can't bear to look** non ho il coraggio di guardare; **it doesn't bear thinking about** non ci si può neanche pensare; **it won't bear close examination** non bisogna guardarlo troppo da vicino
4 (*produce: fruit*) produrre, dare; (*: young*) partorire; (*: child*) generare, dare alla luce; (*Fin: interest*) fruttare
■VI
1 (*move*): **to bear right/left** andare a destra/sinistra, piegare a destra/sinistra; **to bear away** (*Naut*) poggiare
2 **to bring sth to bear (on)** (*influence, powers of persuasion*) esercitare qc (su); **to bring pressure to bear on sb** fare pressione su qn; **to bring one's mind to bear on sth** concentrarsi su qc
▶ **bear down** VI + ADV: **to bear down (on)** (*ship*) venire dritto (contro); (*person*) stare per piombare addosso (a)
▶ **bear on** VI + PREP (*frm*) essere in relazione con
▶ **bear out** VT + ADV (*theory, suspicion*) confermare, convalidare; (*person*) dare il proprio appoggio a
▶ **bear up** VI + ADV farsi coraggio; **he bore up well under the strain** ha sopportato bene lo stress
▶ **bear with** VI + PREP (*sb's moods, temper*) sopportare (con pazienza); **bear with me a minute** solo un attimo, prego; **if you'll bear with me ...** se ha la cortesia di aspettare (un attimo)...

bear[2] [bɛə^r] N orso(-a); (*Stock Exchange*) ribassista *m/f*; **the Great Bear** (*Astron*) l'Orsa Maggiore; **to be like a bear with a sore head** (*hum*) avere la luna di traverso

bear·able ['bɛərəbl] ADJ sopportabile

bear cub N cucciolo di orso

beard [bɪəd] N barba
■VT: **to beard the lion in his den** (*hum*) affrontare il nemico in casa sua

beard·ed ['bɪədɪd] ADJ barbuto(-a)

bear·er ['bɛərə^r] N (*of news, cheque*) portatore *m*; (*of passport*) titolare *m/f*

bearer bond N obbligazione *f* al portatore

bear garden N (*fig*) manicomio

◎**bear·ing** ['bɛərɪŋ] N 1 (*of person*) portamento 2 (*relevance*): **bearing (on)** attinenza (con) 3 (*Tech*): **ball bearings**
■NPL cuscinetti *mpl* a sfere 4 (*position*): **to take a compass bearing** effettuare un rilevamento con la bussola; **to take a ship's bearings** fare il punto nave; **to get** *or* **find one's bearings** (*fig*) orientarsi; **to lose one's bearings** (*fig*) perdere l'orientamento

bear·ish ['bɛərɪʃ] ADJ (*Comm: market*): **in a bearish mood** in ribasso; (*: trader*) pessimista

bear market N (*Comm*) mercato in ribasso

bear pit N gabbia degli orsi

bear·skin ['bɛə,skɪn] N pelle *f* d'orso; (*hat*) colbacco

beast [bi:st] N (*animal, fam: disagreeable person*) bestia, animale *m*; (*cruel person*) bruto; **beast of burden** bestia da soma; **it's a beast of a job** (*fam*) è un lavoraccio

beast·ly ['bi:stlɪ] ADJ (*fam: person, behaviour*) insopportabile; (*: food*) orrendo(-a); (*: weather*) da cani

◎**beat** [bi:t] (*vb: pt* **beat**, *pp* **beaten**) N 1 colpo; (*of drum: single beat*) colpo; (*: repeated beating*) rullo; (*of heart*) battito; (*Mus: rhythm*) ritmo; (*: quaver, crotchet*) battuta; **to give the beat** dare il tempo 2 (*of policeman*) giro d'ispezione (a piedi), ronda; **on the beat** in giro d'ispezione, di ronda 3 (*Phys*) battimento
■VT 1 (*hit*) battere, picchiare; (*person: as punishment*) picchiare; (*: with stick*) bastonare; (*carpet*) battere, sbattere; (*drum*) suonare; **the bird beat its wings** l'uccello batteva le ali; **to beat time** (*Mus*) battere il tempo; **beat it!** (*fam*) fila!, aria! 2 (*defeat: team, army*) battere, sconfiggere; (*record*) battere; **we beat them three-nil** li abbiamo battuti tre a zero; **we were beaten** siamo stati battuti; **I beat him to it** (*fam*) ci sono arrivato prima di lui; **nothing beats a good cup of coffee** (*fam*) non c'è niente di meglio di un bel caffè; **that beats everything!** (*fam*) questo è il colmo!; **it beats me how they found out about it** (*fam*) non riesco a spiegarmi come l'abbiano scoperto; **it's got me beat(en)** (*fam*) devo arrendermi 3 (*Culin*) sbattere, battere
■VI (*heart*) battere, palpitare; (*drums*) rullare; **to beat on a door** picchiare a una porta; **the rain was beating against the windows** la pioggia batteva contro le finestre; **don't beat about the bush** non menare il can per l'aia
■ADJ 1 (*pred: fam: tired*) sfinito(-a) 2 (*usu attr: group, music*) beat *inv*
▶ **beat back** VT + ADV respingere
▶ **beat out** VT + ADV (*flames*) spegnere (battendo); (*dent*) ribattere, martellare; (*rhythm*) battere
▶ **beat down** VT + ADV (*door*) abbattere, buttare giù; (*price*) far abbassare; (*seller*) far scendere
■VI + ADV (*rain*) scrosciare; (*sun*) picchiare
▶ **beat off** VT + ADV respingere
▶ **beat up** VT + ADV (*person*) picchiare, pestare; (*egg whites*) montare; **they beat him up** l'hanno picchiato

◎**beat·en** ['bi:tn] PP *of* **beat** ■ADJ (*metal*) battuto(-a); **off the beaten track** fuori mano

beaten-up [,bi:tən'ʌp] ADJ (*car etc*) malconcio(-a)

beat·er ['bi:tə^r] N (*Culin*) frullino; (*carpet beater*) battipanni *m inv*

bea·tif·ic [,bi:ə'tɪfɪk] ADJ (*liter: smile, expression*) beato(-a)

be·ati·fi·ca·tion [bɪ,ætɪfɪ'keɪʃən] N (*Rel*) beatificazione *f*

be·ati·fy [bi:'ætɪfaɪ] VT (*Rel*) beatificare

◎**beat·ing** ['bi:tɪŋ] N 1 (*punishment*) botte *fpl*; **to give sb a beating** riempire qn di botte 2 (*defeat*) sconfitta, batosta; **to take a beating** prendere una (bella) batosta

beating up N (*pl* **beatings up**) **to give sb a beating up** pestare qn

beat·nik ['bi:tnɪk] N beatnik *m/f inv*

beat-up [,bi:t'ʌp] ADJ (*fam*) scassato(-a)

beau·ti·cian [bju:'tɪʃən] N estetista *m/f*

◎ **beau·ti·ful** ['bju:tɪfʊl] ADJ bello(-a), splendido(-a); **thank you for the beautiful present** grazie del bel regalo; **a beautiful old watch** un bell'orologio antico; **a beautiful sapphire** un bello zaffiro; **thanks for the beautiful flowers** grazie dei bei fiori; **he's got beautiful eyes** ha begli occhi; **the weather was really beautiful** ha fatto bellissimo tempo; **his sisters are beautiful** le sue sorelle sono belle

beau·ti·ful·ly ['bju:tɪflɪ] ADV splendidamente, magnificamente

beau·ti·fy ['bju:tɪfaɪ] VT abbellire

◎ **beau·ty** ['bju:tɪ] N (*concept*) bello; (*of person, thing*) bellezza; **beauty is in the eye of the beholder** non è bello ciò che è bello, è bello ciò che piace; **the beauty of it is that ...** il bello è che...; **his car's a beauty!** (*fam*) ha una macchina che è una meraviglia *or* una bellezza!

■ ADJ (*consultant, counter*) di bellezza

beauty contest N concorso di bellezza

beauty pageant N (*Am*) concorso di bellezza

beauty parlour N istituto di bellezza

beauty queen N miss *f inv*, reginetta di bellezza

beauty salon N istituto di bellezza

beauty sleep N: **to get one's beauty sleep** (*hum*) farsi un sonno ristoratore

beauty spot N (*in country*) luogo di particolare bellezza; (*on face*) neo

beauty treatment N trattamento di bellezza

bea·ver ['bi:vəʳ] N castoro

▸ **beaver away** VI + ADV lavorare di buona lena

be·calmed [bɪ'kɑ:md] ADJ: **to be becalmed** essere fermo(-a) per mancanza di vento

be·came [bɪ'keɪm] PT *of* **become**

◎ **be·cause** [bɪ'kɒz] CONJ (*gen*) perché; **I ate it because I was hungry** l'ho mangiato perché ero affamato; **all the more surprising because** ancora più sorprendente dal momento che *or* poiché; **because of** a causa di

beck [bɛk] N: **to be at sb's beck and call** dover essere a completa disposizione di qn

beck·on ['bɛkən] VT, VI: **to beckon to sb** chiamare qn con un cenno; **he beckoned a waitress** ha chiamato una cameriera con un cenno; **he beckoned me in/over** mi ha fatto cenno di entrare/di avvicinarmi

◎ **be·come** [bɪ'kʌm] (*vb: pt* **became**, *pp* **become**)

VI diventare, divenire; **to become famous** diventare famoso(-a); **to become fat/thin** ingrassare/dimagrire; **to become angry** arrabbiarsi; **to become accustomed to sth** abituarsi a qc; **to become a doctor** diventare medico; **it became increasingly difficult to cover costs** è diventato sempre più difficile far fronte ai costi; **it became known that** si è venuto a sapere che

■ IMPERS VB: **what has become of him?** che ne è stato di lui?; **whatever can have become of that book?** dove sarà mai finito quel libro?

■ VT: **it does not become her** (*dress etc*) non le sta bene; (*behaviour*) non le si addice

be·com·ing [bɪ'kʌmɪŋ] ADJ (*frm: clothes*) grazioso(-a), che dona; (*: behaviour, language*) adatto(-a), che si addice alla situazione

BECTU ['bɛktu:] N ABBR (*Brit*) = **Broadcasting Entertainment Cinematographic and Theatre Union**

BEd [,bi:'ɛd] N ABBR (= **Bachelor of Education**) *laurea con abilitazione all'insegnamento alla scuola primaria*

◎ **bed** [bɛd] N **1** letto; **a single bed** un letto singolo; **a double bed** un letto matrimoniale; **to go to bed** andare a letto; **to go to bed with sb** andare a letto con qn; **to get out of bed** alzarsi dal letto; **to get out of bed on the wrong side** alzarsi col piede sbagliato; **to make the bed** (ri)fare il letto; **to put sb to bed** mettere qn a letto; **I was in bed** ero a letto; **could you give me a bed for the night?** puoi tenermi a dormire per stanotte?; **his life's not a bed of roses** la sua vita non è tutta rose e fiori **2** (*of sea, lake*) fondo; (*of river*) letto; **the river bed** il letto del fiume; **the sea bed** il fondo marino **3** (*flower bed*) aiuola; **oyster bed** banco di ostriche; **vegetable bed** orticello **4** (*layer: of coal, ore, clay*) strato; (*: in roadbuilding*) massicciata

▸ **bed out** VT + ADV (*plants*) piantare a intervalli regolari

▸ **bed down** VI + ADV sistemarsi (per dormire)

bed and breakfast N ≈ bed and breakfast *m inv*; **to book in for bed and breakfast** prenotare una camera con prima colazione

BED AND BREAKFAST (B & B)

I **bed and breakfasts**, anche **B & Bs**, sono piccole pensioni a conduzione familiare, in case private o fattorie, dove si affittano camere e viene servita al mattino la tradizionale colazione all'inglese. Queste pensioni offrono un servizio di camera con prima colazione, appunto "bed and breakfast", a prezzi più contenuti rispetto agli alberghi.

Bb

bed·bath ['bɛd,bɑ:θ] N: **to give sb a bedbath** lavare qn a letto

bed blocker N (*Brit*) *persona anziana che continua a occupare un letto in ospedale perché non è in grado di rientrare a casa propria e badare a se stessa*

bed·bug ['bɛd,bʌg] N cimice *f* (dei letti)

bed·clothes ['bɛd,kləʊðz] NPL coperte e lenzuola *fpl*; **the bedclothes** la biancheria da letto

bed·cov·er ['bɛd,kʌvəʳ] N copriletto

bed·ding ['bɛdɪŋ] N coperte e lenzuola *fpl*; (*for animal*) lettiera; **the bedding** la biancheria da letto

bedding plane N (*Geol*) piano di stratificazione

bedding plant N piantina da mettere a dimora

be·deck [bɪ'dɛk] VT ornare, decorare

be·dev·il [bɪ'dɛvl] VT (*person*) affliggere, tormentare; (*enterprise*) intralciare, ostacolare continuamente

bed·fellow ['bɛd,fɛləʊ] N: **they are strange bedfellows** (*fig*) fanno una coppia ben strana

bed·head ['bɛd,hɛd] N testata (del letto)

bed jacket N liseuse *f inv*

bed·lam ['bɛdləm] N baraonda

bed linen N biancheria da letto

Bedou·in ['bɛdʊɪn] N, ADJ beduino(-a)

bed·pan ['bɛd,pæn] N padella

bed·post ['bɛd,pəʊst] N colonnina del letto

be·drag·gled [bɪ'drægld] ADJ (*person, clothes*) sbrindellato(-a); (*hair*) scompigliato(-a); (*wet*) bagnato(-a) fradicio(-a)

bed·rid·den ['bɛd,rɪdən] ADJ costretto(-a) *or* inchiodato(-a) a letto

bed·rock ['bɛd,rɒk] N (*Geol*) basamento; (*fig*) fondamento, base *f*; **the moral bedrock of the nation** il fondamento morale della nazione

bed·roll ['bɛd,rəʊl] N sacco a pelo
◎ **bed·room** ['bɛd,rʊm] N camera (da letto), stanza da letto; **a three-bedroom house** una casa con tre camere da letto
bedroom farce N (*Theatre*) pochade *f inv*
bedroom slipper N pantofola
bedroom suite N camera da letto (*mobili*)
Beds [bɛdz] N ABBR (*Brit*) = **Bedfordshire**
bed settee N divano *m* letto *inv*
bed·side ['bɛd,saɪd] N: **at his bedside** al suo capezzale
■ ADJ: **to have a good bedside manner** (*doctor*) saper trattare i pazienti
bedside lamp N lampada da comodino, abat-jour *m inv*
bedside rug N scendiletto
bedside table N comodino
bed-sit ['bɛd,sɪt], **bed-sitter** ['bɛd,sɪtəʳ], **bed-sitting room** [,bɛd'sɪtɪŋrʊm] N monolocale *m*
bed·socks ['bɛd,sɒks] NPL calze *fpl* da notte
bed·sore ['bɛd,sɔ:ʳ] N piaga da decubito
bed·spread ['bɛd,sprɛd] N copriletto
bed·stead ['bɛd,stɛd] N fusto del letto
bed·straw ['bɛd,strɔ:] N: **lady's bedstraw** (*Bot*) erba zolfina
bed·time ['bɛd,taɪm] N: **it's bedtime** è ora di andare a letto; **bedtime!** a nanna!; **ten o'clock is my usual bedtime** generalmente vado a letto alle dieci; **it's past your bedtime** a quest'ora dovresti già essere a letto
■ ADJ: **will you tell me a bedtime story?** mi racconti una storia prima di dormire?
bed-wetting ['bɛd,wɛtɪŋ] N incontinenza notturna
bee¹ [bi:] N (*Zool*) ape *f*; **to have a bee in one's bonnet (about sth)** avere la fissazione (di qc)
bee² [bi:] N (*esp Am*): **spelling bee** gara di ortografia; **to have a sewing bee** riunirsi per cucire
beech [bi:tʃ] N faggio
beech·nut ['bi:tʃ,nʌt] N faggina
beef [bi:f] N (*Culin*) manzo; **roast beef** roast beef *m inv*, arrosto di manzo
▶ **beef up** VT + ADV (*fam*) rinforzare
beef breed N razza da macello *or* da carne
beef·bur·ger ['bi:f,bɜ:gəʳ] N hamburger *m inv*
beef cattle NPL bovini *mpl* da macello
beef·eater ['bi:f,i:təʳ] N *guardia della Torre di Londra*
beef olive N (*Culin*) involtino di manzo
beef·steak ['bi:f,steɪk] N bistecca di manzo
beef tea N brodo di manzo, consommé *m inv*
beefy [,bi:fɪ] ADJ (*fam*) muscoloso(-a); **a big beefy fellow** un tipo grande e grosso
bee·hive ['bi:,haɪv] N alveare *m*
bee·keeper ['bi:,ki:pəʳ] N apicoltore *m*
bee·keep·ing ['bi:,ki:pɪŋ] N apicoltura
bee·line ['bi:,laɪn] N: **to make a beeline for sb/sth** (*fam*) andare diretto(-a) verso qn/qc
been [bi:n] PP *of* **be**
beep [bi:p] N (*of horn*) colpo di clacson; (*of phone etc*) segnale *m* (acustico), bip *m inv*
■ VI (*horn*) suonare; (*computer, pager*) fare bip
beep·er ['bi:pəʳ] N cicalino; (*of doctor etc*) cercapersone *m inv*
◎ **beer** [bɪəʳ] N birra
▷ www.camra.org.uk
▷ www.history-of-beer.com
beer belly N (*fam*) stomaco da bevitore
beer can N lattina di birra
beer glass N boccale *m*, bicchiere *m* da birra
bees·wax ['bi:z,wæks] N cera d'api
beet [bi:t] N barbabietola
bee·tle ['bi:tl] N (*Zool*) coleottero; (*: scarab*) scarabeo; (*: black beetle*) scarafaggio
■ VI (*fam*): **to beetle in/out** entrare/uscire di corsa; **to beetle off** correre via
beetle-browed ['bi:tl,braʊd] ADJ dalle folte sopracciglia
beet·root ['bi:t,ru:t] N (*Brit*) barbabietola
be·fall [bɪ'fɔ:l] (*pt* **befell** [bɪ'fɛl], *pp* **befallen** [bɪ'fɔ:lən]) VT accadere a
be·fit [bɪ'fɪt] IMPERS VB (*frm*): **to befit sb** addirsi a qn, confarsi a qn; **it ill befits you to speak in this way** non ti si addice *or* non ti si confàparlare così
be·fit·ting [bɪ'fɪtɪŋ] ADJ adatto(-a); **in the manner befitting his status** come si conviene alla sua posizione
◎ **be·fore** [bɪ'fɔ:ʳ] PREP **1** (*in time*) prima di; **before 7 o'clock** prima delle 7; **before Tuesday** prima di martedì ; **the day before last** *or* **yesterday** due giorni fa, l'altro ieri, ieri l'altro; **before Christ** avanti Cristo; **before long** fra poco, fra non molto **2** (*in place, rank, in the presence of*) davanti a; **a new life lay before him** una nuova vita si apriva davanti a lui; **to appear before a judge** comparire davanti *or* dinanzi a un giudice; **the question before us** la questione di cui ci dobbiamo occupare; **before my very eyes** proprio sotto i miei occhi; **ladies before gentlemen** prima le signore, la precedenza alle signore; **to put friendship before money** anteporre l'amicizia all'interesse
■ ADV prima; **the day before** il giorno prima *or* precedente; **I've seen this film before** questo film l'ho già visto; **I've never seen it before** è la prima volta che lo vedo; **the week before** la settimana prima; **I knew long before that ...** sapevo da molto tempo che...
■ CONJ (*time*) prima di + *infin*, prima che + *sub*; (*rather than*) piuttosto che; **before doing it you ...** *or* **before you do it, you ...** prima di farlo, tu..., prima che tu lo faccia, tu...; **he will die before he betrays his friends** morirebbe piuttosto che tradire gli amici
before·hand [bɪ'fɔ:,hænd] ADV prima, in anticipo; **let me know your plans beforehand** fammi sapere i tuoi piani in anticipo
be·friend [bɪ'frɛnd] VT mostrare amicizia a
be·fud·dled [bɪ'fʌdld] ADJ confuso(-a)
beg [bɛg] VT **1** (*entreat*) supplicare, pregare; (*favour*) chiedere; (*subj: beggar: food, money*) mendicare; **he begged me for mercy** mi supplicava di aver pietà; **he begged me to help him** mi ha supplicato *or* pregato di aiutarlo; **to beg forgiveness** implorare perdono; **I beg your pardon** (*apologising*) mi scusi; (*not hearing*) scusi?; **I beg to differ** mi permetto di non essere d'accordo **2 this begs the question** questo dà per scontato ciò che dev'essere ancora dimostrato
■ VI (*entreat*): **to beg for** implorare; (*beggar*) chiedere l'elemosina *or* la carità; **there were a lot of people begging** c'era molta gente che chiedeva l'elemosina; **it's going begging** (*fam*) non lo vuole proprio nessuno
▶ **beg off** VI + ADV disdire
be·gan [bɪ'gæn] PT *of* **begin**
be·get [bɪ'gɛt] VT (*pt* **begot**, *pp* **begotten**) originare; (*child*) generare
beg·gar ['bɛgəʳ] N mendicante *m/f*; **lucky beggar!** (*fam*) che fortuna sfacciata!; **poor beggar!** (*fam*) povero diavolo!; **beggars can't be choosers** o mangiar questa minestra o saltar dalla finestra

■ VT (*ruin*) ridurre sul lastrico *or* in miseria; **it beggars description** è indescrivibile

beg·gar·ly [ˈbɛgəlɪ] ADJ (*amount*) misero(-a), irrisorio(-a); (*existence*) miserabile; (*salary*) da fame

◎ **be·gin** [bɪˈgɪn] (*vb: pt* **began**, *pp* **begun**) VT (*gen*) cominciare, incominciare, iniziare; (*originate: fashion*) lanciare; (: *custom*) inaugurare; (: *war*) scatenare; **to begin doing sth** *or* **to begin to do sth** incominciare *or* iniziare a fare qc; **it began to rain** ha cominciato *or* si è messo a piovere; **this skirt began life as an evening dress** questa gonna in origine era un abito da sera; **it doesn't begin to compare with ...** non c'è nemmeno da paragonarlo con...; **I can't begin to thank you** non so proprio come ringraziarti

■ VI incominciare, cominciare; (*fashion, custom*) nascere; (*rumour*) spargersi; **to begin with sth/by doing sth** cominciare con qc/col fare qc; **to begin on sth** cominciare qc; **it began to rain** ha iniziato a piovere; **the match began at 10 a.m** la partita è iniziata alle dieci del mattino; **the film has just begun** il film è appena iniziato; **let me begin by saying ...** permettetemi di cominciare col dire...; **to begin with, I'd like to know ...** tanto per cominciare vorrei sapere...; **to begin with there were only two of us** all'inizio eravamo solo in due; **beginning on Monday** a partire da lunedì ; **the service began at 9 a.m.** la funzione ha avuto inizio alle 9

be·gin·ner [bɪˈgɪnəʳ] N principiante *m/f*; **it's just beginner's luck** è la solita fortuna del principiante

◎ **be·gin·ning** [bɪˈgɪnɪŋ] N inizio, principio; **in the beginning** all'inizio; **at the beginning of the century** all'inizio *or* al principio del secolo; **right from the beginning** fin dal primo momento, fin dall'inizio; **start at the beginning and tell me all about it** raccontami tutto (cominciando *or* a partire) dall'inizio; **the beginning of the end** il principio della fine; **to make a beginning** cominciare; **the beginning of the world** le origini del mondo; **Buddhism had its beginnings ...** il buddismo nacque *or* ebbe origine...

be·gonia [bɪˈgəʊnɪə] N begonia

be·grudge [bɪˈgrʌdʒ] VT = **grudge**

be·guile [bɪˈgaɪl] VT (*enchant*) incantare

be·guil·ing [bɪˈgaɪlɪŋ] ADJ seducente; (*charming*) allettante

be·gun [bɪˈgʌn] PP *of* **begin**

◎ **be·half** [bɪˈhɑːf] N: **on behalf of** *or* (*Am*) **in behalf of** (*prep*) per conto di; (*thank, accept*) a nome di; **he spoke on my behalf** ha parlato a nome mio

◎ **be·have** [bɪˈheɪv] VI (*also:* **behave o.s.**: *conduct o.s.*) comportarsi; (: *conduct o.s. well*) comportarsi bene; **he behaved like an idiot** si è comportato da stupido; **you behaved very wisely** hai agito saggiamente; **to behave well towards sb** comportarsi bene nei confronti di qn; **did the children behave themselves?** si sono comportati bene i bambini?; **behave (yourself)!** comportati bene!

◎ **be·hav·iour,** (*Am*) **be·hav·ior** [bɪˈheɪvjəʳ] N comportamento; **to be on one's best behaviour** sforzarsi di comportarsi bene

be·hav·iour·al, (*Am*) **be·hav·ior·al** [bɪˈheɪvjərəl] ADJ comportamentale

be·hav·iour·ism, (*Am*) **be·hav·ior·ism** [bɪˈheɪvjərɪzəm] N comportamentismo

be·hav·iour·ist, (*Am*) **be·hav·ior·ist** [bɪˈheɪvjərɪst] N comportamentista *m/f*

be·head [bɪˈhɛd] VT decapitare

be·held [bɪˈhɛld] PT, PP *of* **behold**

be·hest [bɪˈhɛst] N: **at his behest** su suo ordine

◎ **be·hind** [bɪˈhaɪnd] PREP dietro; (*time*) in ritardo con; **behind the sofa** dietro il divano; **look behind you!** guarda dietro di te!; **what's behind all this?** (*fig*) cosa c'è sotto?; **we're behind them in technology** (*fig*) siamo più indietro *or* più arretrati di loro nella tecnica; **his family is behind him** (*fig*) ha l'appoggio della famiglia; **behind the scenes** dietro le quinte

■ ADV dietro; **to stay behind (to do sth)** fermarsi (a fare qc); **to leave sth behind** dimenticare di prendere qc; **to be behind with sth** essere indietro con qc; (*payments*) essere in arretrato con qc; **I'm behind with my work** sono indietro con il lavoro

■ N (*fam*) didietro *m inv*

behind·hand [bɪˈhaɪnd,hænd] ADV indietro

be·hold [bɪˈhəʊld] (*pt, pp* **beheld**) VT (*old, liter*) scorgere, vedere

be·hold·en [bɪˈhəʊldən] ADJ (*frm*): **to be beholden to sb for sth** sentirsi obbligato(-a) verso qn per qc

be·hove [bɪˈhəʊv], (*Am*) **be·hoove** [bɪˈhuːv] IMPERS VT (*old, frm*): **to behove sb to do sth** stare a qn (il) fare qc

beige [beɪʒ] ADJ, N beige (*m*) *inv*

Bei·jing [ˈbeɪˈdʒɪŋ] N Pechino *f*

◎ **be·ing** [ˈbiːɪŋ] N **1** (*existence*) essere *m*, esistenza; **to come into being** nascere, essere creato(-a); **to bring sth into being** creare qc **2** (*creature*) essere *m*

Bei·rut [beɪˈruːt] N Beirut *f*

be·jew·elled [bɪˈdʒuːəld] ADJ ingioiellato(-a)

be·la·bour, (*Am*) **be·la·bor** [bɪˈleɪbəʳ] VT (*beat*) bastonare; **to belabour with** (*fig: questions*) tartassare di; (: *insults*) bombardare di

be·lat·ed [bɪˈleɪtɪd] ADJ in ritardo; **his belated arrival** il suo ritardo

be·lay [bɪˈleɪ] VT, VI (*Mountaineering*) assicurare

belch [bɛltʃ] N rutto

■ VI ruttare

■ VT (*also:* **belch out**: *smoke*) sputare (fuori); (*flames*) eruttare, vomitare

be·lea·guered [bɪˈliːgəd] ADJ (*city*) assediato(-a); (*person*) assillato(-a); (*army*) accerchiato(-a); (*project, organization*) pieno(-a) di problemi

Bel·fast [ˈbɛlfɑːst] N Belfast *f*
▷ www.belfastcity.gov.uk/

bel·fry [ˈbɛlfrɪ] N campanile *m*

Bel·gian [ˈbɛldʒən] ADJ, N belga (*m/f*)

Bel·gium [ˈbɛldʒəm] N Belgio

Bel·grade [bɛlˈgreɪd] N Belgrado *f*

be·lie [bɪˈlaɪ] VT (*prove false*) smentire; (*give false impression of*) nascondere

◎ **be·lief** [bɪˈliːf] N (*faith*) fede *f*; (*trust*) fiducia; (*tenet, doctrine, opinion*) convinzione *f*, opinione *f*; (*acceptance as true*) credenza; **belief in God** fede in Dio; **it's a belief held by all Christians** è credenza comune a tutti i cristiani; **it's beyond belief** è incredibile; **rich beyond belief** incredibilmente ricco(-a); **a man of strong beliefs** un uomo dalle ferme convinzioni; **it is my belief that** sono convinto che; **in the belief that** nella convinzione che

be·liev·able [bɪˈliːvəbəl] ADJ credibile

◎ **be·lieve** [bɪˈliːv] VT (*story, person*) credere a; **to believe (that)** (*be of the opinion that*) credere (che); **I don't believe he'll come** non credo che verrà *or* che venga; **don't you believe it!** non crederci!; **I don't believe a word of it!** non credo a una parola di tutto questo!; **he is believed to be abroad** si pensa (che) sia all'estero

Bb

■ VI credere; **to believe in** (*God*) credere in; (*ghosts*) credere a; (*method*) avere fiducia in; **do you believe in ghosts?** credi ai fantasmi?; **I don't believe in corporal punishment** sono contrario alle punizioni corporali

be·liev·er [bɪˈliːvəʳ] N (*Rel*) credente *m/f*; **to be a believer in** (*in idea, activity*) essere a favore di; **a great believer in** una grana sostenitore(-trice) di

Belisha bea·con [bəˈliːʃəˈbiːkən] N *segnale luminoso arancione che indica un attraversamento pedonale*

be·lit·tle [bɪˈlɪtl] VT sminuire

Be·lize [bɛˈliːz] N Belize *m*

◎ **bell** [bɛl] N (*small, on door, electric*) campanello; (*church bell*) campana; (*on cats, harness*) sonaglio; (*on cow*) campanaccio; (*of telephone*) soneria; **I rang the bell, but nobody came** ho suonato il campanello, ma non è arrivato nessuno; **the church bell** la campana della chiesa; **the bell goes at half past three** la campanella suona alle tre e mezza; **that rings a bell** (*fig*) mi ricorda qualcosa

bel·la·don·na [ˈbɛləˈdɒnə] N (*Bot, Med*) belladonna

bell-bottoms [ˈbel,bɒtəmz] NPL pantaloni *mpl* a zampa d'elefante

bell·boy [ˈbɛl,bɔɪ], **bell·hop** (*Am*) [ˈbɛl,hɒp] N ragazzo d'albergo, fattorino d'albergo

belle [bɛl] N: **the belle of the ball** la regina della festa

bell heather N erica campanulata di Scozia

bel·li·cose [ˈbɛlɪkəʊs] ADJ bellicoso(-a)

bel·lig·er·ence [bɪˈlɪdʒərəns] N (*see adj*) belligeranza; bellicosità

bel·lig·er·ent [bɪˈlɪdʒərənt] ADJ (*at war*) belligerante; (*fig*) bellicoso(-a)

bel·lig·er·ent·ly [bɪˈlɪdʒərəntlɪ] ADV bellicosamente

bell jar N campana di vetro

bel·low [ˈbɛləʊ] N (*of bull etc*) muggito; (*of person*) urlo

■ VI (*see n*) muggire; urlare (a squarciagola)

■ VT (*also:* **bellow out**: *order, song*) urlare (a squarciagola)

bel·lows [ˈbɛləʊz] NPL (*of forge, organ*) mantice *m*; (*for fire*) soffietto

bell pepper N (*Am*) peperone *m*

bell push N bottone *m or* pulsante *m* del campanello

bell-ringer [ˈbɛl,rɪŋəʳ] N campanaro

bell-shaped [ˈbɛl,ʃeɪpt] ADJ a campana

bell tent N tenda conica

bell tower N torre *f* campanaria

bel·ly [ˈbɛlɪ] N pancia

belly·ache [ˈbɛlɪ,eɪk] (*fam*) N mal *m* di pancia

■ VI (*fam*) mugugnare

belly·button [ˈbɛl,bʌtn] N (*fam*) ombelico

belly dance N danza del ventre

belly dancer N *ballerina che esegue la danza del ventre*

belly flop N (*Swimming*) spanciata

bel·ly·ful [ˈbɛlɪ,fʊl] N (*fam*): **to have had a bellyful of sb/sth** aver fatto un'indigestione di qn/qc

belly landing N (*Aer*) atterraggio sul ventre

belly laugh N grassa risata

◎ **be·long** [bɪˈlɒŋ] VI **1** **to belong to sb/sth** (*be the property of*) appartenere a qn/qc; **this ring belonged to my grandmother** quest'anello era di mia nonna; **who does this belong to?** questo di chi è?; **that belongs to me** è mio; **to belong to a club** essere socio(-a) di un club **2** (*have rightful place*): **put it back where it belongs** rimettilo al suo posto; **where does this belong?** dove va questo?; **it belongs on the shelf** va sullo scaffale; **I felt I didn't belong** mi sentivo un estraneo

be·long·ings [bɪˈlɒŋɪŋz] NPL ciò che si possiede, cose *fpl* (*fam*); **he lost all his belongings** ha perso tutto ciò che possedeva; **I collected my belongings and left** ho raccolto le mie cose e me ne sono andato; **personal belongings** effetti *mpl* personali

Be·lo·rus·sia [,bɛləʊˈrʌʃə] N = **Byelorussia**

Be·lo·rus·sian [,bɛləʊˈrʌʃən] ADJ, N = **Byelorussian**

be·lov·ed [bɪˈlʌvɪd] ADJ, N adorato(-a)

◎ **be·low** [bɪˈləʊ] PREP sotto, al di sotto di; **ten degrees below freezing** dieci gradi sotto zero; **temperatures below normal** temperature al di sotto del normale; **on the floor below** al piano di sotto; **they live in the flat below us** abitano nell'appartamento sotto al nostro

■ ADV sotto, di sotto; **the mountains below** le montagne sottostanti; **the flat below** l'appartamento al piano di sotto; **see below** (*on page*) vedi sotto *or* oltre

below stairs ADV (*also fig*) nei piani bassi

◎ **belt** [bɛlt] N (*gen*) cintura; (*of trousers*) cintura, cinghia; (*Tech*) cinghia; (*Geog: zone*) zona, regione *f*; **industrial belt** zona industriale; **the cotton belt** la zona di coltivazione del cotone; **to tighten one's belt** (*fig*) tirare la cinghia; **that was below the belt** (*fig*) è stato un colpo basso

■ VT (*fam: thrash*) usare la cinghia con, picchiare; **he belted me one** mi ha mollato un pugno

■ VI (*fam: rush*): **to belt in/out** *etc* entrare/uscire *etc* di gran carriera; **he was belting up the motorway at 100 mph** filava sull'autostrada a 100 miglia all'ora

▸ **belt out** VT + ADV (*song*) cantare a squarciagola

▸ **belt up** VI + ADV (*fam: be quiet*) chiudere la boccaccia; **belt up!** chiudi quella boccaccia!

belt rack N portacinture *m inv*

belt·way [ˈbɛlt,weɪ] N (*Am Aut*) circonvallazione *f*; (*motorway*) raccordo anulare; **inside/outside the Beltway** (*Am*) all'interno/all'esterno di Washington DC

be·moan [bɪˈməʊn] VT lamentare

be·mused [bɪˈmjuːzd] ADJ perplesso(-a), stupito(-a)

bench [bɛntʃ] N (*seat: with back*) panchina; (*: without back*) panca; (*in parliament, workbench*) banco; **to be on the Bench** (*Law*) essere giudice

bench·mark [ˈbentʃmɑːk] N (*Econ*) benchmark *m inv*; indice *m* di riferimento

■ VT rapportare ad un indice di riferimento

bench·mark·ing [ˈbɛntʃ,mɑːkɪŋ] (*Comm*) N benchmarking *m inv*

◎ **bend** [bɛnd] (*vb: pt, pp* **bent**) N (*in road*) curva; (*in river*) ansa, gomito; (*in arm, knee*) piega; (*in pipe*) gomito; **he drives me round the bend!** (*fam*) mi fa diventare matto!

■ VT (*wire etc*) curvare, piegare; (*knee*) flettere, piegare; (*arm*) piegare; (*head*) piegare, chinare; **I can't bend my arm** non riesco a piegare il braccio

■ VI piegarsi, curvarsi; (*road*) fare una curva; (*river*) fare un gomito; (*person*) chinarsi; **it bends easily** si piega facilmente

▸ **bend down** VI + ADV chinarsi; **she bent down to pick a flower** si è chinata a raccogliere un fiore

▸ **bend over** VI + ADV chinarsi, piegarsi; **to bend over backwards** (*fig*) farsi in quattro

bend·er [ˈbɛndəʳ] N (*fam*) sbronza; **to go on a bender** prendersi una sbronza

bends [bɛndz] NPL (*Med*): **the bends** un'embolia

bendy [ˈbɛndɪ] ADJ (*comp* **-ier**, *superl* **-iest**) (*flexible*) flessibile; (*road*) tortuoso(-a)

◎ **be·neath** [bɪˈniːθ] PREP sotto, al di sotto di; (*unworthy of*) indegno(-a) di; **it is beneath my notice** non è degno della mia attenzione; **it is beneath him to do**

such a thing non si degnerebbe mai di fare una cosa del genere; **he thinks it's beneath him** si ritiene superiore
■ADV sotto, di sotto; **the flat beneath** l'appartamento al piano di sotto
Ben·edic·tine [ˌbɛnɪˈdɪktɪn] ADJ, N benedettino(-a)
ben·edic·tion [ˌbɛnɪˈdɪkʃən] N benedizione *f*
ben·efac·tor [ˈbɛnɪfæktəʳ] N benefattore *m*
ben·efac·tress [ˈbɛnɪˌfæktrɪs] N benefattrice *f*
ben·efice [ˈbɛnɪfɪs] N (*Rel*) beneficio ecclesiastico
be·nefi·cence [bɪˈnɛfɪsəns] N (*frm: quality*) beneficenza; (*: act*) opera di carità
be·nefi·cent [bɪˈnɛfɪsənt] ADJ (*frm*) benefico(-a)
ben·efi·cial [ˌbɛnɪˈfɪʃəl] ADJ benefico(-a); **beneficial to** che giova a, che fa bene a; **vitamin A is beneficial to one's health** la vitamina A fa bene alla salute
ben·efi·cial·ly [ˌbɛnɪˈfɪʃəlɪ] ADV beneficamente
bene·fi·ciary [ˌbɛnɪˈfɪʃərɪ] N (*Law*) beneficiario(-a)
◎**benefit** [ˈbɛnɪfɪt] N **1** vantaggio, beneficio; **the benefits of a good education** i vantaggi di una buona educazione; **the benefits of this treatment** i benefici di questa terapia; **it might be of some benefit to you** potrebbe giovarti; **for the benefit of one's health** per la propria salute; **to give sb the benefit of the doubt** concedere a qn il beneficio del dubbio **2** (*allowance*) indennità *f inv*, sussidio; **unemployment benefit** indennità di disoccupazione; **state benefits** sussidio dello Stato; **to live on benefit** vivere col sussidio dello Stato **3** manifestazione *f* di beneficenza; **a benefit concert** un concerto di beneficenza
■VI trarre vantaggio *or* profitto da; **he'll benefit from it** ne trarrà beneficio *or* profitto; **he'll benefit from the change** il cambiamento gli farà bene
■VT giovare a, far bene a; **a service which will benefit rich and poor** un servizio che gioverà sia ai ricchi che ai poveri; **the scheme benefits children** il programma si rivolge ai bambini
benefit association N (*Am*) società di mutuo soccorso
benefits package N *pacchetto di agevolazioni e vantaggi concessi a un dipendente*
Bene·lux [ˈbɛnɪlʌks] ADJ: **the Benelux countries** i paesi del Benelux
■N il Benelux *m*
be·nevo·lence [bɪˈnɛvələns] N benevolenza
be·nevo·lent [bɪˈnɛvələnt] ADJ benevolo(-a)
benevolent fund N ≈ società *f inv* di mutuo soccorso
be·nevo·lent·ly [bɪˈnɛvələntlɪ] ADV con benevolenza
BEng [ˌbiːˈɛndʒ] N ABBR (= **Bachelor of Engineering**) laurea in ingegneria
Ben·ga·li [bɛnˈgɔːlɪ] ADJ bengalese
■N **1** (*person*) bengalese *m/f inv* **2** (*language*) bengalese *m*
be·nign [bɪˈnaɪn] ADJ benevolo(-a); (*Med*) benigno(-a); **the tumour was benign** il tumore era benigno
be·nign·ly [bɪˈnaɪnlɪ] ADV con benevolenza
bent[1] [bɛnt] PT, PP *of* **bend**
■ADJ **1** (*wire, pipe*) piegato(-a), storto(-a); (*fam: dishonest*) losco(-a); (*offensive: homosexual*) invertito(-a) **2** (*fig: determined*): **to be bent on sth/on doing sth** essere deciso(-a) a qc/a fare qc; **to be bent on a quarrel** voler proprio litigare
■N (*aptitude*) inclinazione *f*, disposizione *f*; **to follow one's bent** seguire la propria inclinazione
bent[2] [bɛnt] N (*Bot*): **common bent** agrostide *f* bianca
bent·wood [ˈbɛntˌwʊd] ADJ di legno ricurvo
Ben·ze·drine® [ˈbɛnzɪˌdriːn] N benzedrina®
ben·zene [ˈbɛnziːn] N benzene *m*
be·queath [bɪˈkwiːð] VT: **to bequeath sth to sb** lasciare qc in eredità a qn
be·quest [bɪˈkwɛst] N lascito
be·rate [bɪˈreɪt] VT rimproverare, redarguire
be·reaved [bɪˈriːvd] ADJ in lutto; **the bereaved**
■NPL i familiari in lutto
be·reave·ment [bɪˈriːvmənt] N lutto
be·reft [bɪˈrɛft] ADJ (*frm*): **to be bereft of sth** essere privo(-a) di qc
be·ret [ˈbɛreɪ] N berretto
berg·schrund [ˈbɛrkʃrʊnt] N crepaccio terminale
Bering Sea [ˈbɛərɪŋˈsiː] N: **the Bering Sea** il mare di Bering
Bering Strait [ˈbɛərɪŋˈstreɪt] N: **the Bering Strait** lo stretto di Bering
berk [bɜːk] N (*Brit fam!*) povero(-a) scemo(-a)
Berks [bɑːks] N ABBR (*Brit*) = **Berkshire**
Ber·lin [bɜːˈlɪn] N Berlino *f*; **East/West Berlin** Berlino est/ovest
Ber·lin·er [bɜːˈlɪnəʳ] N berlinese *m/f*
Ber·mu·da [bɜːˈmjuːdə] N: **the Bermudas** le Bermude
Bermuda shorts NPL bermuda *mpl*
Bern [bɜːn] N Berna *f*
ber·ry [ˈbɛrɪ] N bacca; **poisonous berries** bacche velenose; **brown as a berry** abbronzatissimo(-a)
ber·serk [bəˈsɜːk] ADJ: **to go berserk** dare in escandescenze; (*with anger*) andare *or* montare su tutte le furie, andare in bestia
berth [bɜːθ] N (*on ship, train*) cuccetta; (*Naut: place at wharf*) ormeggio; **to give sb a wide berth** (*fig*) tenersi alla larga da qn
■VI ormeggiare; (*in harbour*) entrare in porto
ber·yl [ˈbɛrɪl] N berillo
be·ryl·lium [bɛˈrɪlɪəm] N berillio
be·seech [bɪˈsiːtʃ] (*pt, pp* **besought**) VT (*liter*) implorare
be·seech·ing [bɪˈsiːtʃɪŋ] ADJ implorante
be·seech·ing·ly [bɪˈsiːtʃɪŋlɪ] ADV in modo implorante
be·set [bɪˈsɛt] (*pt, pp* **beset**) VT (*afflict*) assillare; (*attack*) assalire; **a policy beset with dangers** una politica irta *or* piena di pericoli
be·set·ting [bɪˈsɛtɪŋ] ADJ: **his besetting sin** il suo più grande difetto
◎**be·side** [bɪˈsaɪd] PREP (*at the side of*) accanto a, vicino a; (*compared with*) rispetto a, in confronto a; **beside the television** accanto al televisore; **to be beside o.s. (with)** (*anger, joy etc*) essere fuori di sé (da); **that's beside the point** questo non c'entra niente
◎**be·sides** [bɪˈsaɪdz] PREP (*in addition to*) oltre a; (*apart from*) all'infuori di, a parte; **besides, it's too expensive** e inoltre è troppo caro; **besides which ...** per di più...
■ADV (*in addition*) inoltre; (*anyway*) poi, del resto, per di più; **and more besides** e altro ancora
be·siege [bɪˈsiːdʒ] VT (*Mil, fig*) assediare, assalire; **we were besieged with inquiries** siamo stati tempestati di domande
be·sieg·er [bɪˈsiːdʒəʳ] N assediante *m/f*
be·smirch [bɪˈsmɜːtʃ] VT (*liter*) screditare
be·som [ˈbiːzəm] N ramazza
be·sot·ted [bɪˈsɒtɪd] ADJ: **besotted with sb** infatuato(-a) di qn
be·sought [bɪˈsɔːt] PT, PP *of* **beseech**
be·spat·tered [bɪˈspætəd] ADJ: **bespattered with** schizzato(-a) di
be·spec·ta·cled [bɪˈspɛktɪkld] ADJ occhialuto(-a)

Bb

be·spoke [bɪˈspəʊk] ADJ (*Brit: garment*) su misura; **bespoke tailor** sarto (*che lavora su ordinazione*)

◎ **best** [bɛst] ADJ (*superl of* **good**) migliore; **to be best** essere il/la migliore; **he's the best player in the team** è il migliore giocatore della squadra; **the best pupil in the class** il/la primo(-a) della classe; **in her best dress** vestita del suo abito migliore; **my best friend** il/la mio(-a) migliore amico(-a); **the best thing about her is ...** la cosa più bella di lei è...; **the best thing to do is ...** la cosa migliore da fare *or* farsi è...; **for the best part of the year** per la maggior parte dell'anno; **may the best man win!** vinca il migliore!
■ ADV (*superl of* **well**) meglio; **Emma sings best** Emma canta meglio di tutti; **the best liked** il/la più amato(-a); **the best dressed** il/la più elegante; **as best I could** meglio che ho potuto; **you know best** tu sai meglio di chiunque; **John came off best** John ha avuto la meglio; **you had best leave now** faresti meglio ad andartene ora; **best before ...** da consumarsi preferibilmente prima del...
■ N il/la migliore; **she's the best at drawing** disegna meglio di tutti; **he deserves the best** si merita quanto c'è di meglio; **at best** nella migliore delle ipotesi, tutt'al più; **he wasn't at his best** non era in vena *or* in piena forma; **he's not exactly patient at the best of times** non è mai molto paziente; **I acted for the best** ho agito per il meglio; **let's hope for the best** speriamo che tutto vada per il meglio; **to the best of my knowledge** per quel che ne so io; **I did it to the best of my ability** l'ho fatto come meglio ho potuto; **to do one's best** fare del proprio meglio; **it's not perfect, but I did my best** non è perfetto, ma ho fatto del mio meglio; **she looks her best in casual clothes** l'abbigliamento casual le dona molto; **to look its best** (*house, flat*) esser bello(-a) ed ordinato(-a); **to make the best of it** accontentarsi; **we'll have to make the best of it** dovremo accontentarci; **to make the best of a bad job** far buon viso a cattivo gioco; **all the best!** saluti!; **she can dance with the best of them** è una ballerina di prima classe

bes·tial [ˈbɛstɪəl] ADJ bestiale

bes·ti·al·ity [bɛstɪˈælɪtɪ] N bestialità

be·stir [bɪˈstɜːʳ] VT: **to bestir o.s.** muoversi

best man N testimone *m* dello sposo

be·stow [bɪˈstəʊ] VT: **to bestow sth on sb** (*title*) conferire qc a qn; (*honour, affections*) accordare qc a qn

best·sell·er [ˌbɛstˈsɛləʳ] N bestseller *m inv*

◎ **bet** [bɛt] (*vb: pt, pp* **bet** *or* **betted**) N scommessa; **to put a bet on** fare una scommessa su; **it's a safe bet** (*fig*) è molto probabile
■ VI: **to bet (on)** scommettere (su); **to bet on a horse** scommettere *or* puntare su un cavallo; **are you going? — you bet!** (*fam*) ci vai? — ci puoi giurare!; **I'm not a betting man** non sono uno scommettitore
■ VT scommettere; **he bet £5 on the favourite** ha giocato *or* puntato 5 sterline sul favorito; **I bet you a pound that ...** scommettiamo una sterlina che...; **I bet you he won't come** (*fam*) scommetti che non viene?; **you can bet your life that ...** (*fam*) puoi scommetterci la testa che...

Beth·le·hem [ˈbɛθlɪˌhɛm] N Betlemme *f*

be·to·ken [bɪˈtəʊkən] VT (*liter*) denotare

beto·ny [ˈbɛtənɪ] N erba betonica

be·tray [bɪˈtreɪ] VT (*also fig*) tradire; **he betrayed her trust** ha tradito la sua fiducia; **to betray sb to the enemy** consegnare qn nelle mani del nemico; **his face betrayed his surprise** il suo viso tradiva la sorpresa

be·tray·al [bɪˈtreɪəl] N tradimento

be·troth·al [bɪˈtrəʊðəl] N fidanzamento

be·troth·ed [bɪˈtrəʊðd] (*liter*) ADJ promesso(-a); **the betrothed couple** i promessi sposi
■ N sposo(-a) promesso(-a)

◎ **bet·ter**[1] [ˈbɛtəʳ] ADJ (*comp of* **good**) migliore; **this one's better than that one** questo è migliore di quello; **I'm better at German than French** riesco meglio in tedesco che in francese; **he's better than his brother at mending cars** è più bravo di suo fratello ad aggiustare le macchine; **are you better now?** (*in health*) stai meglio adesso?; **are you feeling better now?** ti senti meglio ora?; **to get better** migliorare; (*Med*) star meglio, rimettersi; **that's better!** così va meglio!; **it couldn't be better** non potrebbe andar meglio (di così); **it would be better to go now** sarebbe meglio andare adesso; **he's no better than a thief** non è né più né meno che un ladro; **it lasted the better part of a year** è durato quasi un anno
■ ADV (*comp of* **well**) meglio; **he speaks French better than Italian/his brother** parla il francese meglio dell'italiano/di suo fratello; **better known** meglio *or* più conosciuto(-a); **so much the better** *or* **all the better** tanto meglio, meglio così ; **he was all the better for it** ci ha guadagnato, gli ha fatto molto bene; **better still** meglio ancora; **you'd be better off staying where you are** faresti meglio a restare dove sei; **I had better go** dovrei andare; **hadn't you better ask him?** non sarebbe meglio se lo chiedessi a lui?; **to think better of it** cambiare idea
■ N: **a change for the better** un cambiamento in meglio; **for better or worse** nella buona o nella cattiva sorte; **to get the better of sb** avere la meglio su qn; **one's betters** i propri superiori
■ VT migliorare; **to better o.s.** migliorare la propria condizione

bet·ter[2] [ˈbɛtəʳ] N scommettitore *m*

bet·ter·ment [ˈbɛtəmənt] N miglioramento

better-off [ˌbɛtəʳˈɒf] ADJ: **to be better-off** (*gen*) stare meglio; (*financially*) avere più soldi

bet·ting [bɛtɪŋ] N scommesse *fpl*; **what's the betting he'll be late?** (*fig*) quanto scommettiamo che arriverà in ritardo?

betting shop N (*Brit*) ufficio dell'allibratore *m*

betting slip N talloncino per scommesse

bet·tor [ˈbɛtəʳ] N (*Am*) = **better**[2]

◎ **be·tween** [bɪˈtwiːn] PREP (*gen*) tra, fra; **the road between here and London** la strada da qui a Londra; **a village between Florence and Pisa** un paese tra Firenze e Pisa; **between fifteen and twenty minutes** tra i quindici e i venti minuti; **between now and next week we must ...** da qui alla settimana prossima dobbiamo...; **I sat (in) between John and Sue** ero seduto (in mezzo) tra John e Sue; **it's between 5 and 6 metres long** è lungo fra i 5 e i 6 metri; **we shared it between us** ce lo siamo diviso tra di noi; **just between you and me** *or* **ourselves ...** (sia detto) tra me e te..., sia detto tra noi (due)...; **we only had £5 between us** fra tutti e due avevamo solo 5 sterline
■ ADV (*also:* **in between**: *of place*) in mezzo; (*of time*) nel frattempo; **few and far between** rarissimi

be·twixt [bɪˈtwɪkst] ADV: **to be betwixt and between** essere una via di mezzo

bev·el [ˈbɛvəl] N (*surface*) superficie *f* obliqua; (*bevel edge*) spigolo smussato
■ VT smussare

bevel square N squadra falsa *or* zoppa

bevel wheel N ruota conica dentata
bev·er·age ['bɛvərɪdʒ] N bevanda
bevy ['bɛvɪ] N banda; **a bevy of** una banda di
be·wail [bɪ'weɪl] VT lamentare
be·ware [bɪ'wɛəʳ] VI: **beware!** attento!; **to beware of sb/sth** stare attento(-a) a qn/qc, guardarsi da qn/qc; **you must beware of falling** devi stare attento a non cadere; **beware of the dog!** attenti al cane!
be·wil·der [bɪ'wɪldəʳ] VT sconcertare, disorientare
be·wil·dered [bɪ'wɪldəd] ADJ sconcertato(-a), disorientato(-a)
be·wil·der·ing [bɪ'wɪldərɪŋ] ADJ sconcertante, sbalorditivo(-a)
be·wil·der·ing·ly [bɪ'wɪldərɪŋlɪ] ADV in modo sconcertante, in modo sbalorditivo
be·wil·der·ment [bɪ'wɪldəmənt] N perplessità, sbalordimento
be·witch [bɪ'wɪtʃ] VT stregare; (*fig*) affascinare, ammaliare
be·witch·ing [bɪ'wɪtʃɪŋ] ADJ (*fig: person*) affascinante, seducente; (*: smile, look*) ammaliatore(-trice)
be·witch·ing·ly [bɪ'wɪtʃɪŋlɪ] ADV (*fig*) in modo affascinante; **bewitchingly beautiful** bello(-a) da impazzire
◎ **be·yond** [bɪ'jɒnd] PREP (*in place, time*) al di là di; (*: further than*) più in là di; (*exceeding*) al di là di, al di sopra di; (*apart from*) oltre a; **I heard footsteps beyond the door** ho sentito dei passi oltre la porta; **the wheat fields and the mountains beyond ...** i campi di grano e le montagne più in là...; **beyond my reach** fuori della mia portata; **it would be unwise to delay it beyond 2008** sarebbe poco saggio rimandarlo oltre il 2008; **it's (almost) beyond belief** è incredibile; **that job is beyond him** quel lavoro è al di sopra delle sue capacità; **it's beyond me why ...** non arriverò mai a capire perché...; **that's beyond a joke** questo non è più uno scherzo; **beyond doubt** senza dubbio; **beyond repair** irreparabile
■ ADV più oltre, più in là, più avanti
be·zique [bɪ'zi:k] N bazzica
b/f ABBR = **brought forward**
BFPO [ˌbi:efpi:'əʊ] N ABBR (= **British Forces Post Office**) *recapito delle truppe britanniche all'estero*
bha·ji ['bɑ:dʒɪ] N (*Culin*) verdure *fpl* piccanti in pastella (*piatto indiano*)
bhan·gra ['bæŋgrə] N musica bhangra (*di origine indiana*)
bhp [ˌbi:eɪtʃ'pi:] N ABBR (*Aut:* = **brake horsepower**) ≈ CV (*potenza del freno*)
bi... [baɪ] PREF bi...
bi·an·nual [baɪ'ænjuəl] ADJ semestrale
bias ['baɪəs] N **1** (*inclination*): **bias (towards** *or* **in favour of)** preferenza (per); **bias (against)** (*prejudice*) pregiudizio (contro); **her bias towards life in the city** la sua preferenza per la vita in città; **a right-wing bias** una tendenza di destra **2** (*of material*) sbieco; **to cut sth on the bias** tagliare qc in sbieco
■ VT: **to bias sb towards** influenzare qn a favore di; **to bias sb against** prevenire qn contro
bias binding N (*Sewing*) fettuccia in sbieco
bi·ased, **bi·assed** ['baɪəst] ADJ parziale; **to be biased against** essere prevenuto(-a) contro
bi·ath·lon [baɪ'æθlən] N biathlon *m inv*
bib [bɪb] N (*for child*) bavaglino; (*on dungarees*) pettorina; **in one's best bib and tucker** (*fam*) in ghingheri
◎ **Bi·ble** ['baɪbl] N: **the Bible** la Bibbia
▷ http://unbound.biola.edu/
▷ www.bible-history.com/
Bible-thumper ['baɪbl'θʌmpəʳ], **Bible-basher** ['baɪbl'bæʃəʳ] N (*fam*) *accanito sostenitore della Bibbia*
bib·li·cal ['bɪblɪkəl] ADJ biblico(-a)
bib·li·og·ra·pher [ˌbɪblɪ'ɒgrəfəʳ] N bibliografo(-a)
bib·lio·graph·ic [ˌbɪblɪəʊ'græfɪk], **bib·lio·graph·ical** [ˌbɪblɪəʊ'græfɪkəl] ADJ bibliografico(-a)
bib·li·og·ra·phy [ˌbɪblɪ'ɒgrəfɪ] N bibliografia
bibu·lous ['bɪbjʊləs] ADJ (*hum*) avvinazzato(-a)
bi·car·bo·nate of soda [baɪ'kɑ:bənɪtəv'səʊdə] N bicarbonato (di sodio)
bi·cen·tenary [ˌbaɪsɛn'ti:nərɪ], **bi·cen·ten·nial** (*Am*) [baɪsɛn'tɛnɪəl] N, ADJ bicentenario
bi·ceps ['baɪsɛps] NSG bicipite *m*
bick·er ['bɪkəʳ] VI bisticciare
bick·er·ing ['bɪkərɪŋ] N bisticci *mpl*
bi·cy·cle ['baɪsɪkl] N bicicletta; **to ride a bicycle** andare in bicicletta; **bicycle parts** ricambi *mpl* per bicicletta
▷ www.sustrans.org.uk
bicycle pump N pompa della bicicletta
bicycle race N gara ciclistica
bicycle rack N rastrelliera per biciclette; (*on car*) portabiciclette *m inv*
bicycle shed N rimessa per biciclette
bicycle track N sentiero ciclabile
◎ **bid** [bɪd] N offerta; (*Comm: tender*) offerta (di appalto); (*attempt*) tentativo; (*Cards*) dichiarazione *f*; **the highest bid** l'offerta più alta; **a rescue bid** un tentativo di salvataggio; **a suicide bid** un tentativo di suicidio; **to make a bid for freedom/power** fare un tentativo per ottenere la libertà/per impadronirsi del potere
■ VT **1** (*pt, pp* **bid**) offrire; **to bid £100 for** offrire 100 sterline per; **they bid 3 million pounds** hanno fatto un'offerta di 3 milioni di sterline **2** (*pt* **bade**, *pp* **bidden**) (*frm: order*): **to bid sb do sth** ingiungere a qn di fare qc **3** (*pt* **bade**, *pp* **bidden**) **to bid sb good morning/farewell** dare il buon giorno/l'addio a qn, dire buon giorno/addio a qn; **he bade me goodnight** mi ha augurato la buonanotte
■ VI **1** (*pt, pp* **bid**) (*gen*): **to bid (for)** fare un'offerta (per); (*Cards*) dichiarare; **to bid against sb** gareggiare contro qn **2** (*pt* **bade**, *pp* **bidden**) **to bid fair to be/do sth** promettere di essere/fare qc
bid·den ['bɪdn] PP *of* **bid**
bid·der ['bɪdəʳ] N offerente *m/f*; (*Cards*) chi fa la dichiarazione; **the highest bidder** il/la miglior offerente
bid·ding ['bɪdɪŋ] N **1** (*at auction*) offerte *fpl*; (*Cards*) dichiarazioni *fpl*; **the bidding opened at £50** le offerte sono partite da 50 sterline **2** **I did his bidding** ho fatto ciò che voleva
bide [baɪd] VT: **to bide one's time** aspettare il momento giusto
bi·det ['bi:deɪ] N bidè *m inv*
bi·di·rec·tion·al [ˌbaɪdɪ'rɛkʃənəl] ADJ bidirezionale
bid price N (*Comm*) prezzo d'acquisto
bi·en·nial [baɪ'ɛnɪəl] ADJ biennale
■ N (*plant*) biennale *f*
bier [bɪəʳ] N (*for coffin*) catafalco; (*for corpse*) feretro, bara
biff [bɪf] N (*Brit fam*) botta
bi·fo·cals [baɪ'fəʊkəlz] NPL occhiali *mpl* bifocali
bi·fur·cate ['baɪfɜ:keɪt] VI (*frm*) biforcarsi
◎ **big** [bɪg] ADJ (*comp* **-ger**, *superl* **-gest**) **1** (*in height, age: building, tree, person*) grande; (*in bulk, amount: parcel, lie, increase*) grosso(-a); (*important*) grande, importante; **a**

Bb

big house una casa grande; **Taiwan's biggest companies** le più grosse aziende di Taiwan; **my big brother** mio fratello maggiore **2** **to make the big time** sfondare; **to earn big money** guadagnare forte; **to have big ideas** avere delle grandi idee; **to do things in a big way** fare le cose in grande; **he's too big for his boots** (*fam*) ha delle belle pretese; **why don't you keep your big mouth shut!** (*fam*) ma perché non tieni chiusa quella boccaccia?; **that's big of you!** (*iro*) che generosità!; **big deal!** (*iro*) capirai!; **it's no big deal** fa niente
■ADV (*fam*): **to talk big** dirne tante; **to think big** avere delle grandi idee

biga·mist [ˈbɪgəmɪst] N bigamo(-a)

biga·mous [ˈbɪgəməs] ADJ bigamo(-a)

biga·my [ˈbɪgəmɪ] N bigamia

Big Bang N: **the Big Bang** (*Astron*) il Big Bang; (*Fin*) l'informatizzazione della Borsa di Londra; **Big-Bang theory** la teoria del Big Bang

big beast N (*fig*) pezzo grosso

big-boned [ˌbɪgˈbəʊnd] ADJ che ha ossa grosse

big brother N Grande Fratello

big business N (*large organizations*) la grande industria; (*profitable activity*) un'attività redditizia; **pop music is big business** la musica pop è un grosso affare

big deal N (*fam*): **to be a big deal (for sb)** essere importante (per qn); **it's no big deal** non è niente di tale; **to make a big deal about sth** fare un sacco di storie per qc; **so she's going out with Ryan, big deal!** esce con Ryan, e allora?

big dipper N montagne *fpl* russe

big end N (*Aut*) testa di biella

big game hunting N caccia grossa

big·gie [ˈbɪgɪ] N (*fam: person*) grande *m/f*; (*: film, song*) successo

big·gish [ˈbɪgɪʃ] ADJ (*see* **big**) piuttosto grande; piuttosto grosso(-a)

big gun N (*fam: person*) pezzo grosso; **the big guns of English football** le più importanti squadre inglesi

big·head [ˈbɪgˌhɛd] N (*fam*) montato(-a)

big·headed [bɪgˈhɛdɪd] ADJ (*fam*): **to be bigheaded** darsi un sacco di arie

big-hearted [ˌbɪgˈhɑːtɪd] ADJ generoso(-a), di buon cuore

big hitter [-ˈhɪtəʳ] N (*Sport*) battitore *m*; (*fig*) persona influente

Big Issue N *rivista venduta per strada da senzatetto che trattengono parte del prezzo di copertina*

big·mouth [ˈbɪgˌmaʊθ] N (*fam*) chiacchierone(-a)

big noise, big shot N (*fam*) pezzo grosso

big·ot [ˈbɪgət] N (*pej*) fazioso(-a)

big·ot·ed [ˈbɪgətɪd] ADJ (*pej*) fazioso(-a)

big·ot·ry [ˈbɪgətrɪ] N (*pej*) faziosità

big shot N = big noise

big time N: **"big time" politics** politica con la 'p' maiuscola

big toe N alluce *m*

big top N (*circus*) circo; (*main tent*) tendone *m* del circo

big wheel N (*at fair*) ruota (panoramica); (*Am*) = **big noise**

big·wig [ˈbɪgwɪg] N (*fam*) pezzo grosso

◎**bike** [baɪk] N (*fam*) bici *f inv*; (*motorbike*) moto *f inv*; **can you ride a bike?** sai andare in bici?

bike lane N (*Brit*) pista ciclabile

bike·way [ˈbaɪkweɪ] N (*Am*) pista ciclabile

bi·ki·ni [bɪˈkiːnɪ] N bikini *m inv*

bikini briefs NPL slip *m inv*

bikini line N linea *f* bikini *inv*

bi·lat·er·al [baɪˈlætərəl] ADJ bilaterale

bi·lat·er·al·ly [baɪˈlætərəlɪ] ADV bilateralmente

bil·berry [ˈbɪlbərɪ] N mirtillo

bile [baɪl] N (*Med, fig*) bile *f*

bilge [bɪldʒ] N **1** (*Naut*) sentina; (*also:* **bilge water**) acqua di sentina **2** (*fam: nonsense*) idiozie *fpl*, cretinate *fpl*

bilge pump N pompa di sentina

bi·lin·gual [baɪˈlɪŋgwəl] ADJ bilingue

bili·ous [ˈbɪlɪəs] ADJ (*Med*) biliare; (*fig: irritable*) collerico(-a); **bilious attack** attacco di bile

◎**bill**[1] [bɪl] N **1** (*account*) fattura; (*: in hotel, restaurant*) conto; (*: for gas, electricity*) bolletta; **could I have the bill please?** il conto, per piacere; **the gas bill** la bolletta del gas **2** (*Parliament*) progetto di legge **3** (*Am: banknote*) banconota, biglietto; **a five-dollar bill** una banconota da cinque dollari **4** (*notice*) avviso; **"post no bills"** "divieto di affissione"; **that fits the bill** (*fig*) quello fa proprio al caso mio (*or tuo etc*) **5** (*Theatre*) cartellone *m*, manifesto; (*: smaller*) locandina; **to top the bill** essere in cima al cartellone; **on the bill** in cartellone **6** (*Comm, Fin*) cambiale *f*
■VT **1** (*customer*): **to bill sb for sth** mandare la fattura di qc a qn **2** (*Theatre*) mettere in cartellone

bill[2] [bɪl] N (*of bird*) becco
■VI: **to bill and coo** tubare

bill·board [ˈbɪlˌbɔːd] N tabellone *m* pubblicitario

bil·let [ˈbɪlɪt] N acquartieramento
■VT: **to billet sb (on sb)** acquartierare qn (presso qn)

bill·fold [ˈbɪlˌfəʊld] N (*Am*) portafoglio

bill·hook [ˈbɪlˌhʊk] N falcetto

billiard ball [ˈbɪljəd-] N palla da biliardo

billiard cue N stecca da biliardo

bil·liards [ˈbɪljədz] NSG biliardo

billiard table N tavolo da biliardo

bill·ing [ˈbɪlɪŋ] N **1** (*performer*): **to get top** *or* **star billing** essere l'attrazione principale **2** (*sending bills*) fatturazione *f*

◎**bil·lion** [ˈbɪljən] N miliardo; (*Brit old*) mille miliardi

bill of exchange N cambiale *f*, tratta

bill of fare N lista delle vivande

bill of health N *see* **clean**

bill of lad·ing [ˌbɪləvˈleɪdɪŋ] N polizza di carico

bill of rights N dichiarazione *f* dei diritti

BILL OF RIGHTS

Si chiamano **Bill of Rights** i primi dieci emendamenti alla costituzione americana, in vigore dal 1791. Nei paragrafi numerati del documento sono elencati i diritti garantiti a ogni cittadino americano e vengono definiti i vari poteri dello stato e del governo federale. Tra i diritti riconosciuti dal **Bill** vi sono la libertà di religione, di associazione e di stampa (First Amendment), il diritto a portare armi (Second Amendment) e il diritto a un processo equo (Sixth Amendment). Tra gli emendamenti apportati alla costituzione dopo il 1791 ricordiamo il diritto all'eguaglianza di fronte alla legge (Fourteenth Amendment) e il diritto di voto (Fifteenth Amendment).

▷ http://memory.loc.gov/ammem/help/constRedir.html

bill of sale N atto di vendita
bil·low ['bɪləʊ] N (*of smoke*) nuvola; (*of sail*) rigonfiamento
■ VI (*smoke*) alzarsi in volute; (*sail*) gonfiarsi
bill·poster ['bɪl,pəʊstəʳ] N, **bill·sticker** (*Am*) ['bɪl,stɪkəʳ]
■ N attacchino
bills payable ['bɪlz'peɪəbl] NPL effetti *mpl* passivi
bills receivable ['bɪlzrɪ'si:vəbl] NPL effetti *mpl* attivi
bil·ly·can ['bɪlɪ,kæn] N pentolino
bil·ly goat ['bɪlɪ,gəʊt] N caprone *m*, becco
bill·yo, billy·oh ['bɪlɪ,əʊ] N (*Brit fam*): **they were fighting like billyo(h)** si riempivano di botte; **it was raining like billyo(h)** pioveva a dirotto
bim·bo ['bɪmbəʊ] N (*pej*) pollastrella, svampitella
bi·me·tal·lic [,baɪmɪ'tælɪk] ADJ bimetallico(-a)
bi·month·ly [baɪ'mʌnθlɪ] ADJ bimestrale
■ ADV bimestralmente
bin [bɪn] N (*for coal, rubbish*) bidone *m*; (*for bread*) cassetta; (*Brit: dustbin*) pattumiera; (*litterbin*) cestino
bi·na·ry ['baɪnərɪ] ADJ binario(-a); **binary system** (*Math*) sistema *m* binario
binary code N (*Comput*) codice *m* binario
binary fission N (*Bio*) scissione *f* binaria
binary star N (*Astron*) stella binaria
bind [baɪnd] (*vb: pt, pp* **bound**) VT **1** (*tie together, make fast*) legare; (*: fig*) legare, unire; (*Culin*) legare; (*Sewing: seam*) orlare; (*book*) rilegare; **bound hand and foot** legato(-a) mani e piedi **2** (*encircle*) avvolgere; (*: wound, arm*) fasciare, bendare **3** (*oblige*): **to bind sb to sth/to do sth** obbligare qn a qc/a fare qc; **to be bound to** essere obbligato(-a) a; **the authorities are legally bound to take action** le autorità sono obbligate per legge ad intervenire
■ N (*fam: nuisance*) scocciatura
▸ **bind together** VT + ADV (*sticks etc*) legare (insieme); (*fig*) unire
▸ **bind over** VT + ADV (*Law*) dare la condizionale a
▸ **bind up** VT + ADV (*wound*) fasciare, bendare; **to be bound up in** (*work, research etc*) essere completamente assorbito(-a) da; **to be bound up with** (*person*) dedicarsi completamente a
bind·er ['baɪndəʳ] N **1** (*file*) classificatore *m* **2** (*Agr*) mietilegatrice *f*
bind·ing ['baɪndɪŋ] N (*of book*) rilegatura, legatura; (*Sewing*) fettuccia, bordo; (*on skis*) attacco
■ ADJ (*agreement, contract*) vincolante; **to be binding on sb** essere vincolante per qn
bind·weed ['baɪnd,wi:d] N convolvolo
binge [bɪndʒ] (*fam*) N: **to have a binge** far baldoria; **to go on a (shopping) binge** darsi alle spese folli; **to go on a (drinking) binge** prendersi una solenne sbronza
■ VI (*eat excessively*) mangiare in modo eccessivo; **to binge on chocolate** abbuffarsi di cioccolato
binge drinker N forte bevitore(-trice)
binge drinking N il bere troppo
bin·go ['bɪŋgəʊ] N ≈ tombola (*giocata in stabilimenti pubblici*)
bin-liner ['bɪn,laɪnəʳ] N (*Brit*) sacchetto per l'immondizia
bin·ocu·lar [bɪ'nɒkjʊləʳ] ADJ binoculare
bin·ocu·lars [bɪ'nɒkjʊləz] NPL binocolo *sg*; **a pair of binoculars** un binocolo
bi·no·mial [baɪ'nəʊmɪəl] (*Math*) ADJ binomio(-a)
■ N binomiale *f*
bio·chemi·cal [,baɪəʊ'kɛmɪkəl] ADJ biochimico(-a)
bio·chem·ist ['baɪəʊ'kɛmɪst] N biochimico(-a)
bio·chem·is·try ['baɪəʊ'kɛmɪstrɪ] N biochimica
bio·deg·ra·da·bil·ity [,baɪəʊdɪgreɪdə'bɪlɪtɪ] N biodegradabilità
bio·degrad·able ['baɪəʊdɪ'greɪdəbl] ADJ biodegradabile
bio·di·ver·sity [,baɪəʊdaɪ'vɜ:sɪtɪ] N biodiversità
▹ www.eti.uva.nl
▹ www.biodiv.org
bio·dy·nam·ics [,baɪəʊdaɪ'næmɪks] N biodinamica
bio·en·gi·neer·ing, bio-engineering [,baɪəʊɛndʒɪ'nɪərɪŋ] N **1** (*genetic engineering*) bioingegneria **2** (*Med*) bioingegneria
bio·eth·ics [,baɪəʊ'eθɪks] N bioetica
bio·fuel ['baɪəʊfjʊəl] N carburante *m* biologico
bio·gen·esis ['baɪəʊ'dZenIsIs] N biogenesi *f*
bio·genet·ic [,baɪəʊdʒɪ'netɪk] ADJ biogenetico(-a)
bi·og·raph·er [baɪ'ɒgrəfəʳ] N biografo(-a)
bio·graphi·cal [,baɪəʊ'græfɪkəl] ADJ biografico(-a)
bi·og·ra·phy [baɪ'ɒgrəfɪ] N biografia
bio·haz·ard ['baɪəʊhæzəd] N materiale *m* pericoloso di origine biologica
bio·logi·cal [,baɪə'lɒdʒɪkəl] ADJ biologico(-a)
biological clock N orologio biologico
biological warfare N guerra biologica
biological washing powder N detersivo non ecologico
biological weapon N arma biologica
bi·olo·gist [baɪ'ɒlədʒɪst] N biologo(-a)
bi·ol·ogy [baɪ'ɒlədʒɪ] N biologia
▹ http://biology-online.org/
▹ http://cellbiol.com/
bio·medi·cal [,baɪəʊ'medɪkəl] ADJ biomedico(-a)
bio·medi·cine [,baɪəʊ'medsɪn] N biomedicina
bio·met·ric [,baɪə'metrɪk] ADJ biometrico(-a)
bio·met·rics [baɪə'metrɪks] N, **biometry** [baɪ'ɒmɪtrɪ] N biometria
bi·on·ic [baɪ'ɒnɪk] ADJ bionico(-a)
bi·on·ics [baɪ'ɒnɪks] NSG bionica
bio·physi·cal [,baɪəʊ'fɪzɪkəl] ADJ biofisico(-a)
bio·physi·cist [,baɪəʊ'fɪzɪsɪst] N biofisico(-a)
bio·phys·ics [,baɪəʊ'fɪzɪks] NSG biofisica
bio·pic ['baɪəʊpɪk] N film-biografia *m inv*
bi·op·sy ['baɪɒpsɪ] N biopsia
biorhythm ['baɪəʊ,rɪðəm] N bioritmo
bio·sphere ['baɪə,sfɪəʳ] N: **the biosphere** la biosfera
bio·syn·the·sis [,baɪəʊ'sɪnθɪsɪs] N biosintesi *f*
bio·tech ['baɪəʊtɛk] N biotecnologia
bio·tech·nol·ogy [,baɪəʊtɛk'nɒlədʒɪ] N biotecnologia
▹ www.cato.com/biotech
▹ www.academicinfo.net/biotechmeta.html
bio·ter·ror·ism [,baɪəʊ'terərɪzm] N bioterrorismo
bio·ter·ror·ist [,baɪəʊ'terərɪst] N bioterrorista *m/f*
bi·par·ti·san [,baɪpɑ:tɪ'zæn] ADJ bipartitico(-a)
bi·ped ['baɪpɛd] N bipede *m*
bi·plane ['baɪ,pleɪn] N biplano
bi·po·lar disorder [,baɪpəʊlədɪs'ɔ:dəʳ] N (*Psych*) sindrome *f* bipolare
birch [bɜ:tʃ] N (*tree, wood*) betulla; (*for whipping*) frusta (di betulla)
birch·ing ['bɜ:tʃɪŋ] N fustigazione *f*
◎ **bird** [bɜ:d] N uccello; (*Brit fam: girl*) tipa, bambola; **have you put the bird in the oven?** hai messo il pollo (*or* il tacchino *etc*) nel forno?; **a little bird told me** (*hum*) me l'ha detto l'uccellino; **the early bird catches the worm** (*Proverb*) chi dorme non piglia pesci; **a bird in the hand is worth two in the bush** (*Proverb*) meglio un uovo oggi che una gallina domani; **birds of a feather flock together** (*Proverb*) chi si assomiglia si

Bb

piglia; **to kill two birds with one stone** prendere due piccioni con una fava

bird·bath ['bɜːdˌbɑːθ] N vasca per gli uccelli

bird cage N gabbia per uccelli

bird flu N influenza aviaria

birdie ['bɜːdɪ] N (*Golf*): **to get a birdie** fare birdie
■ VT (*Golf*): **to birdie a hole** realizzare un birdie a una buca

bird of prey N (uccello) rapace *m*

bird sanctuary N riserva per uccelli

bird·seed ['bɜːdˌsiːd] N becchime *m*

bird's-eye view ['bɜːdzaɪ'vjuː] N vista a volo d'uccello

bird-watcher ['bɜːd'wɒtʃəʳ] N bird watcher *m/f inv*

bird-watching ['bɜːdˌwɒtʃɪŋ] N bird-watching *m*
▷ www.birder.com
▷ www.birdwatching.com

Biro® ['baɪərəʊ] N biro® *f inv*

◎**birth** [bɜːθ] N (*also fig*) nascita; (*childbirth*) parto; **it was a difficult birth** è stato un parto difficile; **at birth** alla nascita; **Italian by birth** italiano di nascita; **date of birth** data di nascita; **place of birth** luogo di nascita; **to give birth to** partorire, dare alla luce; (*fig*) dare inizio a

birth certificate N certificato *or* atto di nascita

birth control N controllo delle nascite, contraccezione *f*

◎**birth·day** ['bɜːθˌdeɪ] N compleanno
■ ADJ (*present, party, cake*) del *or* di compleanno; **a birthday card** un biglietto d'auguri; **in my/his** *etc* **birthday suit** (*fam*) come mamma m'ha/l'ha *etc* fatto

birth·mark ['bɜːθˌmɑːk] N voglia (*sulla pelle*)

birth·place ['bɜːθˌpleɪs] N luogo di nascita; (*town*) città natale

birth rate N (indice *m or* tasso di) natalità

birth·right ['bɜːθˌraɪt] N (*fig*) diritto di nascita

bi·rya·ni, biriani [ˌbɪrɪ'ɑːni] N (*Culin*) *piatto indiano a base di riso, con carne o pesce condito con una salsa*

Biscay ['bɪskeɪ] N: **the Bay of Biscay** il golfo di Biscaglia

bis·cuit ['bɪskɪt] N (*Brit*) biscotto; (*Am*) panino al latte; **to take the biscuit** (*fam*) essere assolutamente incredibile

bi·sect [baɪ'sɛkt] VT tagliare in due (parti); (*Math*) bisecare

bi·sex·ual [baɪ'sɛksjʊəl] ADJ, N bisessuale (*m/f*), bisex (*m/f*) *inv*

bi·sexu·al·ity [baɪˌsɛksjʊ'ælɪtɪ] N bisessualità

bish·op ['bɪʃəp] N vescovo; (*Chess*) alfiere *m*

bish·op·ric ['bɪʃəprɪk] N vescovado

bis·muth ['bɪzməθ] N bismuto

bi·son ['baɪsn] N bisonte *m*

bis·tro ['biːstrəʊ] N bistrot *m inv*

◎**bit**[1] [bɪt] N **1** (*piece*) pezzo; (*smaller*) pezzetto; **a bit of** (*paper, wood, cake*) un pezzo di; (*wine, sunshine, peace*) un po' di; **a bit of cake** un pezzo di torta; **would you like another bit?** ne vuoi un altro pezzo?; **a bit of music** un po' di musica; **a bit too much** un po' troppo; **a bit bigger/smaller** un po' più grande/più piccolo(-a); **a little bit dearer** un pochino più caro(-a); **a good bit cheaper** molto più economico(-a), molto più a buon mercato; **a bit of news** (*fam*) una notizia; **a bit of advice** un (piccolo) consiglio; **a bit of luck** una fortuna; **a bit mad/dangerous** un po' matto(-a)/ pericoloso(-a); **bit by bit** a poco a poco; **they have a bit of money** hanno un po' di soldi; **it was a bit of a shock** è stato un po' un colpo; **it's a bit of a nuisance** è un po' una scocciatura; **that's not a bit of help** questo non aiuta affatto; **to take sth to bits** smontare qc; **to come to bits** (*break*) andare a pezzi; (*be dismantled*) essere smontabile; **in bits (and pieces)** (*broken*) a pezzi; (*dismantled*) smontato(-a); **to fall to bits** cadere a pezzi; **bring all your bits and pieces** porta tutte le tue cose; **to do one's bit** fare la propria parte **2** (*short time*): **a bit** un momento, un attimo; **wait a bit!** aspetta un attimo! **3** (*considerable sum*): **a good bit** *or* **quite a bit** un bel po' **4** (*Am: coin*) ottavo di dollaro

bit[2] [bɪt] N (*tool*) punta; (*of horse*) morso

bit[3] [bɪt] PT *of* **bite**

bit[4] [bɪt] N (*Comput*) bit *m inv*

bitch [bɪtʃ] N **1** (*of canines*) femmina; (*of dog*) cagna; **a terrier bitch** un terrier femmina **2** (*offensive: woman*) stronza, puttana (*fam!*)
■ VI (*fam: complain*) mugugnare

bitchy ['bɪtʃɪ] ADJ (*comp* **-ier**, *superl* **-iest**) maligno(-a); **a bitchy remark** una cattiveria

◎**bite** [baɪt] (*vb: pt* **bit**, *pp* **bitten**) N **1** (*act, wound: of dog, snake*) morso; (*of insect*) puntura; **to take a bite at** dare un morso a, addentare; **a dog bite** il morso di un cane; **lots of mosquito bites** molte punture di zanzara **2** (*of food*) boccone *m*; **there's not a bite to eat** non c'è niente da mettere sotto i denti; **do you fancy a bite (to eat)?** ti va di mangiare qualcosa? **3** (*Fishing*): **he didn't get a single bite** non ha abboccato neanche un pesce
■ VT (*gen*) mordere; (*subj: dog*) morsicare, mordere; (*: insect*) pungere; **the dog bit him** il cane lo ha morso; **my dog's never bitten anyone** il mio cane non ha mai morso nessuno; **I got bitten by mosquitoes** mi hanno punto le zanzare; **to bite one's nails** mangiarsi le unghie; **once bitten twice shy** una volta scottati...; **to bite the hand that feeds you** (*fig*) sputare nel piatto in cui si mangia; **to bite the dust** (*die*) lasciarci la pelle
■ VI **1** (*dog etc*) mordere; (*insect*) pungere **2** (*fish*) abboccare **3** (*fig: policy, action*) farsi sentire
▸ **bite back** VT + ADV trattenersi dal dire
▸ **bite into** VI + PREP (*subj: person*) addentare, dare un morso a; (*: acid*) intaccare
▸ **bite off** VT + ADV staccare con un morso; **to bite off more than one can chew** (*fig*) fare il passo più lungo della gamba; **to bite sb's head off** (*fig*) aggredire (*verbalmente*) qn
▸ **bite through** VT + ADV tagliare con i denti

bit·ing ['baɪtɪŋ] ADJ (*cold, wind*) pungente; (*criticism, sarcasm*) pungente, mordace; (*remark*) caustico(-a)

bit·ing·ly ['baɪtɪŋlɪ] ADV (*speak*) in modo pungente, in modo caustico; **a bitingly cold wind** un vento freddo e pungente

bit·map ['bɪtmæp] N (*Comput*) bitmap *f inv; tipo di file grafico*

bit part N (*in film, play*) particina, parte *f* secondaria

bit·ten ['bɪtn] PP *of* **bite**

◎**bit·ter** ['bɪtəʳ] ADJ **1** (*taste: gen*) amaro(-a); (*: of fruit*) aspro(-a); **it tastes bitter** ha un sapore amaro; **a bitter pill to swallow** (*fig*) un boccone amaro da ingoiare **2** (*icy: weather*) gelido(-a); (*wind*) pungente; **it's bitter today** oggi si gela **3** (*enemy, hatred*) acerrimo(-a); (*quarrel*) aspro(-a); (*disappointment*) amaro(-a); (*person*) risentito(-a); **to the bitter end** fino all'ultimo, a oltranza
■ N (*Brit: beer*) birra amara

bitter lemon N (*drink*) limonata amara

bit·ter·ly ['bɪtəlɪ] ADV (*disappoint, complain, weep*) amaramente; (*oppose, criticise*) aspramente; (*jealous*)

profondamente; **it's bitterly cold** fa un freddo gelido
bit·tern ['bɪtɜ:n] N tarabuso
bit·ter·ness ['bɪtənɪs] N *(gen)* amarezza; *(of fruit, fig: of quarrel)* asprezza
bitter·sweet ['bɪtə,swi:t] ADJ *(taste)* agrodolce; *(love affair)* dolceamaro(-a)
bit·ty ['bɪtɪ] ADJ *(Brit fam)* frammentario(-a)
bi·tu·men ['bɪtjʊmɪn] N bitume *m*
bi·tu·mi·nous [bɪ'tju:mɪnəs] ADJ bituminoso(-a)
bivou·ac ['bɪvʊæk] *(vb: pt, pp* **bivouacked***)* N bivacco
■VI bivaccare
bi·zarre [bɪ'zɑ:ʳ] ADJ bizzarro(-a)
bk ABBR **1** = **bank** **2** = **book**
BL [,bi:'ɛl] N ABBR **1** (= **Bachelor of Law**) laurea in legge **2** (= **Bachelor of Letters, (***Am*) Bachelor of Literature) laurea in lettere
B/L b/l, b.l. [,bi:'ɛl] N ABBR = **bill of lading**
blab [blæb] *(fam)* VT *(also:* **blab out***)* spifferare
■VI *(chatter)* cianciare; *(to police)* vuotare il sacco
blab·ber ['blæbəʳ] VI *(fam)* parlare a vanvera
◎**black** [blæk] ADJ **1** nero(-a); *(in darkness)* buio(-a); *(fig: gloomy: prospects)* poco allegro(-a); *(: despair)* nero(-a), cupo(-a); *(: future)* poco promettente; *(: wicked: thought, deed)* malvagio(-a); **things look pretty black** *(fig)* c'è poco da star allegri; **she looked as black as thunder** *(fig)* aveva un'aria furiosa; **black coffee** caffè *m inv* nero lungo **2** *(person)* nero(-a)
■N **1** *(colour)* nero; **dressed in black** vestito(-a) di *or* in nero; **in the black** *(Fin)* in attivo; **to swear that black is white** *(obstinate person)* negare l'evidenza; *(liar)* mentire spudoratamente **2** *(person)* nero(-a); **she's black** è nera
■VT *(Brit Industry: goods, firm)* boicottare
▸ **black out** VT + ADV **1** *(obliterate)* cancellare **2** *(in wartime)* oscurare; *(subj: power cut)* far piombare nell'oscurità
■VI + ADV *(faint)* svenire
black and blue ADJ pieno(-a) di lividi, tutto(-a) pesto(-a); **to beat sb black and blue** riempire qn di lividi
black and white ADJ *(photograph, film, TV)* in bianco e nero; **there it is in black and white** *(fig)* eccolo nero su bianco; **he sees things in black and white terms** per lui non ci sono vie di mezzo
black·ball ['blæk,bɔ:l] VT: **to blackball sb** votare a sfavore di qn
black belt N *(Sport)* cintura nera; *(Am)*: **the black belt** *zona abitata principalmente da afro-americani*
black·berry ['blækbərɪ] N mora (di rovo); **blackberry bush** cespuglio di more
black·bird ['blæk,bɜ:d] N merlo
black·board ['blæk,bɔ:d] N lavagna
black box N *(Aer)* scatola nera
Black Country N *(Brit)*: **the Black Country** zona industriale dell'Inghilterra centrale
black·cur·rant [,blæk'kʌrənt] N ribes *m inv* nero; **blackcurrant jam** marmellata di ribes nero
black economy N *(Brit)* economia sommersa
black·en ['blækən] VI annerirsi; *(sky)* oscurarsi
■VT annerire; *(fig: reputation)* macchiare
black eye N occhio nero; **to give sb a black eye** fare un occhio nero a qn
Black Forest N: **the Black Forest** la Foresta Nera
black·guard ['blægɑ:d] N *(old pej)* canaglia
black·head ['blæk,hɛd] N punto nero, comedone *m*
black hole N *(Astron)* buco nero
black humour N umorismo nero
black ice N strato invisibile di ghiaccio *(su strada)*
black·ing ['blækɪŋ] N *(for shoes, metal)* nero
black·ish ['blækɪʃ] ADJ nerastro(-a)
black·jack ['blæk,dʒæk] N *(Cards)* ventuno; *(at casino)* blackjack *m inv*; *(Am: truncheon)* manganello
black·leg ['blæk,lɛg] N *(Brit)* crumiro(-a)
black·list ['blæk,lɪst] N lista nera
■VT mettere sulla lista nera
black magic N magia nera
black·mail ['blækmeɪl] N ricatto
■VT ricattare; **to blackmail sb into doing sth** ricattare qn affinché faccia qc
■ADJ *(letter, phone call)* ricattatorio(-a); *(attempt)* di ricatto
black·mail·er ['blæk,meɪləʳ] N ricattatore(-trice)
Black Maria [-məraɪə] N (furgone *m*) cellulare
black mark N *(fig)* nota di demerito
black market N mercato nero; *(in wartime)* borsa nera; **on the black market** al mercato nero; alla borsa nera
black marketeer [blæk,mɑ:kə'tɪəʳ] N borsanerista *m/f*
black·ness ['blæknɪs] N colore *m* nero; *(darkness)* buio, oscurità
black·out ['blæk,aʊt] N **1** *(of lights, TV)* black-out *m inv*; *(during war)* oscuramento **2** *(Med)* svenimento; **to have a blackout** perdere conoscenza
black pepper N pepe *m* nero
Black Power N Black Power *m*, Potere *m* Nero
black pudding N sanguinaccio
Black Sea N: **the Black Sea** il mar Nero
black sheep N *(fig)* pecora nera
Black·shirt ['blæk,ʃɜ:t] N *(Pol)* Camicia nera
black·smith ['blæk,smɪθ] N fabbro ferraio
black spot N *(Aut)* = **accident black spot**
black·thorn ['blæk,θɔ:n] N prugnolo, pruno selvatico
black tie N: **"black tie"** *(on invitations)* "abito scuro"
blad·der ['blædəʳ] N *(Anat)* vescica (urinaria)
blade [bleɪd] N *(cutting edge)* lama; *(: of safety razor)* lametta; *(of propeller)* pala; **blade of grass** filo d'erba
blah blah ['blɑ: 'blɑ:] N *(fam)* blablà *m*
blam·able ['bleɪməbəl] ADJ biasimevole
◎**blame** [bleɪm] N *(responsibility)* colpa, responsabilità; *(censure)* biasimo; **to lay the blame for sth on sb** attribuire la responsabilità di qc a qn, dare la colpa di qc a qn
■VT **1** *(hold responsible)*: **to blame sb for sth** dare la colpa a qn di qc, ritenere qn responsabile di qc; **to be to blame for** essere responsabile di; **don't blame me!** non dare la colpa a me!; **he's not to blame** non è colpa sua; **blame it on the weather** dai la colpa al tempo; **you have only yourself to blame** puoi ringraziare solo te stesso **2** *(reproach)* criticare, biasimare; **and I don't blame him** e non gli dò torto
blame·less ['bleɪmlɪs] ADJ irreprensibile
blame·less·ly ['bleɪmlɪslɪ] ADV in modo irreprensibile
blame·worthy ['bleɪm,wɜ:ðɪ] ADJ biasimevole
blanch [blɑ:ntʃ] VI *(person)* sbiancare in viso
■VT *(Culin)* scottare
blanc·mange [blə'mɒnʒ] N biancomangiare *m*
bland [blænd] ADJ *(smile)* blando(-a); *(character)* insulso(-a); *(food)* insipido(-a); **a bland reply** una risposta evasiva; **it tastes a bit bland** è un po' insipido, ha poco sapore
blan·dish·ments ['blændɪʃmənts] NPL *(frm)* lusinghe *fpl*
blank [blæŋk] ADJ *(paper, space)* bianco(-a); *(wall)* cieco(-a); *(empty: expression)* vacuo(-a); *(look)* distratto(-a);

Bb

a **blank sheet of paper** un foglio di carta bianca; **a blank cassette** una cassetta vergine; **a look of blank amazement** uno sguardo allibito; **my mind went blank** ho avuto un vuoto
■ N *(void)* vuoto; *(in form)* spazio in bianco; *(blank cartridge)* cartuccia a salve; **his mind was a blank** si sentiva la testa vuota; **fill in the blanks** riempi gli spazi in bianco; **to draw a blank** *(fig)* non aver nessun risultato

blank cheque N, **blank check** *(Am)* N assegno in bianco; **to give sb a blank cheque to do sth** *(fig)* dare carta bianca a qn per fare qc

blan·ket ['blæŋkɪt] N coperta; *(fig: of snow, fog)* coltre *f*; *(: of smoke)* cappa

blanket cover N: **to give blanket cover** *(subj: insurance policy)* coprire tutti i rischi

blank·ly ['blæŋklɪ] ADV *(say)* senza espressione; *(stare)* con aria assente

blank verse N versi *mpl* sciolti

blare [blɛəʳ] N *(of trumpet, car horn)* strombettio; *(of siren)* urlo; *(of radio)* frastuono
■ VT *(also: **blare out**)* far risuonare
■ VI *(see n)* strombettare; urlare; suonare a tutto volume

blar·ney ['blɑːnɪ] N *(fam)* moine *fpl*, lusinghe *fpl*

blasé ['blɑːzeɪ] ADJ blasé *inv*

blas·pheme [blæs'fiːm] VI bestemmiare

blas·phem·er [blæs'fiːməʳ] N bestemmiatore(-trice)

blas·phe·mous ['blæsfɪməs] ADJ blasfemo(-a)

blas·phe·mous·ly ['blæsfɪməslɪ] ADV in modo blasfemo

blas·phe·my ['blæsfɪmɪ] N bestemmia

◎ **blast** [blɑːst] N **1** *(of air, steam)* getto; *(of wind)* raffica; **(at) full blast** *(also fig)* a tutta forza **2** *(sound: of trumpet)* squillo; *(: of car horn, siren)* colpo; **(at) full blast** *(radio)* a tutto volume **3** *(of explosion)* spostamento d'aria; *(noise)* esplosione *f*; **a bomb blast** un'esplosione
■ VT *(strike: with explosives)* far saltare; *(: by lightning)* bruciare; *(fig: hopes, future)* distruggere
■ EXCL *(Brit fam)* mannaggia!; **blast him!** mannaggia a lui!
▸ **blast away** VI + ADV **1** *(gun)* sparare a raffica **2** *(band)* suonare a tutto volume
▸ **blast off** VI + ADV *(Space)* essere lanciato(-a)

blast·ed ['blɑːstɪd] ADJ *(fam)* maledetto(-a)

blast furnace N altoforno

blast·ing ['blɑːstɪŋ] N *(Tech)* brillamento; **"blasting in progress"** "attenzione: esplosione mine"

blast·off ['blɑːst,ɒf] N *(of rockets)* lancio

bla·tant ['bleɪtənt] ADJ sfacciato(-a); **a blatant lie** una bugia palese

bla·tant·ly ['bleɪtəntlɪ] ADV sfacciatamente; **it's blatantly obvious** è lampante

blath·er ['blæðəʳ] VI blaterare

blaze¹ [bleɪz] N *(fire: of buildings)* incendio; *(glow: of fire, sun)* bagliore *m*; *(of gems, beauty)* splendore *m*; **a blaze of colour** un'esplosione di colori; **a blaze of anger** un impeto d'ira; **in a blaze of publicity** circondato(-a) da grande pubblicità; **go to blazes!** *(fam)* va' al diavolo!; **like the blazes** *(fam)* come un matto
■ VI *(fire)* ardere, fiammeggiare; *(conflagration)* divampare; *(building)* essere in fiamme; *(sun)* sfolgorare; *(light)* risplendere; **to blaze with anger** *(eyes)* fiammeggiare dalla rabbia; **to blaze with passion** ardere di passione
▸ **blaze away** VI + ADV: **to blaze away (at)** continuare a far fuoco (su)
▸ **blaze up** VI + ADV fare una fiammata; *(fig: feelings)* accendersi

blaze² [bleɪz] N *(mark: on horse)* stella; *(: on tree)* segno
■ VT *(tree)* segnare; **to blaze a trail** *(also fig)* aprire una nuova via

blaz·er ['bleɪzəʳ] N blazer *m inv*

blaz·ing ['bleɪzɪŋ] ADJ *(building)* in fiamme; *(fire)* ardente; *(sun)* infuocato(-a); *(light)* sfolgorante; *(jewel)* sfavillante; *(eyes)* fiammeggiante; *(colour, quarrel, anger)* acceso(-a)

bleach [bliːtʃ] N decolorante *m*; **liquid bleach** acqua ossigenata; **household bleach** candeggina, varechina
■ VT *(material)* candeggiare; *(bones)* sbiancare; *(hair)* ossigenare

bleached [bliːtʃt] ADJ decolorato(-a); **bleached hair** capelli ossigenati

bleach·ers ['bliːtʃəz] NPL *(Am)* posti *mpl* di gradinata

bleach·ing ['bliːtʃɪŋ] N decolorazione *f*; *(of hair)* ossigenazione *f*

bleak [bliːk] ADJ *(landscape)* desolato(-a); *(weather)* gelido(-a); *(smile)* pallido(-a); *(prospect, future)* tetro(-a), deprimente; **a bleak area** un'area desolata; **the future looks bleak** il futuro sembra tetro; **the prospects of your getting a job here are bleak** le probabilità che tu trovi un lavoro qui sono molto scarse

bleak·ly ['bliːklɪ] ADV in modo tetro, tetramente

bleak·ness ['bliːknɪs] N *(of landscape, future)* desolazione *f*; *(of room, furnishings)* austerità; *(of weather)* rigidità; *(of smile)* tristezza

blea·ri·ly ['blɪərɪlɪ] ADV: **he looked up blearily at Tom** fissò Tom con occhi appannati

bleary ['blɪərɪ] ADJ *(eyes)* appannato(-a)

bleary-eyed ['blɪərɪ'aɪd] ADJ: **to be bleary-eyed** avere gli occhi appannati

bleat [bliːt] N belato
■ VI belare; *(fig fam)* piagnucolare

bled [blɛd] PT, PP *of* **bleed**

bleed [bliːd] *(vb: pt, pp* **bled** [blɛd]*)* VI sanguinare; **his nose is bleeding** gli sanguina il naso, gli esce il sangue dal naso; **to bleed to death** morire dissanguato(-a); **my heart bleeds for him** *(iro)* mi fa proprio compassione, poverino!
■ VT **1** salassare, dissanguare **2** *(brakes, radiator)* spurgare

bleed·ing ['bliːdɪŋ] ADJ **1** *(wound, person)* sanguinante; **bleeding gums** le gengive che sanguinano **2** *(Brit fam)* dannato(-a), maledetto(-a); **you bleeding idiot!** pezzo di cretino!
■ N perdita di sangue; *(serious)* emorragia

bleep [bliːp] N breve segnale *m* acustico, bip *m inv*
■ VI suonare
■ VT *(doctor)* chiamare con il cercapersone

bleep·er ['bliːpəʳ] N *(of doctor etc)* cercapersone *m inv*

blem·ish ['blɛmɪʃ] N imperfezione *f*; *(on fruit)* ammaccatura; *(on reputation)* macchia
■ VT deturpare

blench [blɛntʃ] VI *(flinch)* sussultare; *(turn pale)* impallidire

blend [blɛnd] N *(gen)* mescolanza, miscuglio; *(of tea, whisky)* miscela; *(of tobacco)* mistura
■ VT *(teas)* mischiare; *(colours)* mescolare, mischiare; *(Culin)* amalgamare
■ VI *(harmonize)*: **to blend (with)** *(gen)* mescolarsi (a); *(sounds, perfumes)* confondersi (con); *(styles)* essere in armonia (con); *(opinions, races, colours)* fondersi (con)

blend·er ['blɛndəʳ] N (*Culin*) frullatore *m*

bless [blɛs] VT benedire; **the priest blessed the children** il prete ha benedetto i bambini; **God bless the queen!** Dio benedica la regina!; **bless you!** sei un angelo!; (*after sneezing*) salute!; **I'm blessed if I know!** (*fam*) non ne so un accidente!; **bless my soul!** santo cielo!; **to be blessed with** godere di

bless·ed ['blɛsɪd] ADJ **1** (*Rel: holy*) benedetto(-a); (*: happy*) beato(-a); **Blessed Margaret Sinclair** Beata Margaret Sinclair **2** (*fam*) benedetto(-a); **every blessed day** tutti i santi giorni; **where's that blessed book?** dov'è quel benedetto libro?

Blessed Sacrament N: **the Blessed Sacrament** il Santissimo Sacramento

Blessed Virgin N: **the Blessed Virgin** la Santa Vergine

bless·ing ['blɛsɪŋ] N **1** (*Rel*) benedizione *f* **2** (*advantage*) vantaggio, fortuna; **losing my job was a blessing, really** perdere il lavoro è stata in realtà una benedizione; **to count one's blessings** ritenersi fortunato(-a); **what a blessing that ...** meno male che...; **it was a blessing in disguise** in fondo è stato un bene

blest [blɛst] (*poet*) PP *of* **bless**

bleth·er ['blɛðəʳ] VI = **blather**

blew [blu:] PT *of* **blow**

blight [blaɪt] N (*Bot*) *malattia che fa avvizzire le piante*; (*fig*) piaga
■ VT (*plants etc*) far avvizzire; (*fig: future, hopes*) rovinare, distruggere

blight·er ['blaɪtəʳ] N (*fam*) disgraziato(-a); **you lucky blighter!** beato te!

bli·mey ['blaɪmɪ] EXCL (*Brit fam*) accidenti!

◎ **blind** [blaɪnd] ADJ (*person, obedience, anger*) cieco(-a); **blind in one eye** cieco da un occhio, orbo; **blind as a bat** (*fam*) cieco come una talpa; **to go blind** diventare cieco; **he was blind to her faults** non vedeva i suoi difetti; **to turn a blind eye to** chiudere un occhio su; **it's not a blind bit of use** (*fam*) non serve a un bel niente; **he doesn't take a blind bit of notice of ...** (*fam*) non bada minimamente a...
■ N **1 the blind**
■ NPL i ciechi; **it's a case of the blind leading the blind** è come mettere insieme uno storpio e uno sciancato **2** (*shade*) tenda avvolgibile; **Venetian blind** veneziana
■ ADV (*fly, land*) alla cieca; **blind drunk** (*fam*) ubriaco(-a) fradicio(-a)
■ VT accecare; **he was blinded in the war** ha perso la vista in guerra; **her love blinded her to his faults** il suo amore la rendeva cieca ai suoi difetti

blind alley N vicolo cieco

blind corner N (*Brit*) svolta cieca

blind date N *appuntamento galante con qualcuno che non si conosce*

blind·ers ['blaɪndəz] NPL (*Am*) = **blinkers**

blind·fold ['blaɪnd,fəʊld] ADV con gli occhi bendati; **I could do it blindfold** potrei farlo a occhi chiusi
■ N benda (per occhi)
■ VT bendare (gli occhi a)

blind·ing ['blaɪndɪŋ] ADJ (*flash, light*) accecante; (*pain*) atroce

blind·ly ['blaɪndlɪ] ADV ciecamente

blind man's buff N moscacieca

blind·ness ['blaɪndnɪs] N cecità; **blindness to the realities of life** rifiuto di guardare in faccia la realtà

blind spot N (*Anat*) punto cieco; (*Aut*) angolo in cui manca la visibilità; (*fig*) punto debole

blind trust N (*Comm*) blind trust *m inv*; *accordo finanziario in base al quale il fiduciario non rende conto delle modalità di amministrazione di un bene o un patrimonio*

bling(-bling) [blɪŋ('blɪŋ)] (*fam!*) ADJ vistoso(-a)
■ N stile *m* vistoso

blink [blɪŋk] N battito di ciglia; **to be on the blink** (*fam: car, machine*) essere scassato(-a)
■ VT: **to blink one's eyes** sbattere le palpebre
■ VI sbattere le palpebre; (*light*) lampeggiare

blink·ered ['blɪŋkəd] ADJ (*fig: person*) che ha i paraocchi; **to have a blinkered view of reality** vedere la realtà con i paraocchi

blink·ers ['blɪŋkəz] NPL (*Brit*) paraocchi *mpl*

blink·ing ['blɪŋkɪŋ] ADJ (*Brit fam*) dannato(-a), maledetto(-a); **this blinking ...** questo maledetto...

blip [blɪp] N (*on radar etc*) segnale *m* intermittente; (*on graph*) piccola variazione; (*fig*) momentanea battuta d'arresto

bliss [blɪs] N (*Rel*) beatitudine *f*; (*happy state*) (immensa) felicità; **ignorance is bliss** (*Proverb*) beata ignoranza; **it's bliss!** (*fam*) è meraviglioso!

bliss·ful ['blɪsfʊl] ADJ (*event, day*) stupendo(-a), meraviglioso(-a); (*smile*) beato(-a); **in blissful ignorance** nella (più) beata ignoranza

bliss·ful·ly ['blɪsfəlɪ] ADV (*sigh, smile*) beatamente; **blissfully happy** magnificamente felice

blis·ter ['blɪstəʳ] N (*on skin*) vescica; (*of paint*) bolla
■ VT (*skin*) far venire le vesciche a; (*paint*) produrre delle bolle in
■ VI (*skin*) coprirsi di bollicine; (*paint*) formare delle bolle

blis·ter·ing ['blɪstərɪŋ] ADJ (*sun*) che spacca le pietre; (*fig: attack*) sferzante

blister pack N (*Comm*) blister *m inv*

blithe [blaɪð] ADJ (*thoughtless*) spensierato(-a); (*old: happy*) gioioso(-a), allegro(-a)

blithe·ly ['blaɪðlɪ] ADV (*unthinkingly*) spensieratamente; (*happily*) allegramente

blith·er·ing ['blɪðərɪŋ] ADJ (*fam*): **this blithering idiot** questo pezzo d'idiota

BLitt [,bi:'lɪt] N ABBR (= **Bachelor of Letters**) laurea in lettere

Blitz [blɪts] N: **the Blitz** *il bombardamento aereo della Gran Bretagna*

blitz [blɪts] N (*Mil*) blitz *m inv*; **to have a blitz on sth** (*fig*) prendere d'assalto qc
■ VT bombardare

blitz·krieg ['blɪts,kri:g] N guerra *f* lampo *inv*

bliz·zard ['blɪzəd] N bufera di neve

bloat·ed ['bləʊtɪd] ADJ (*also fig*): **bloated (with)** gonfio(-a) (di)

bloat·er ['bləʊtəʳ] N (*herring*) aringa affumicata; (*mackerel*) sgombro affumicato

blob [blɒb] N (*drop*) goccia; (*stain, spot*) macchia; (*lump: of mud*) pallina; **a blob of glue** una goccia di colla

bloc [blɒk] N (*Pol*) blocco

◎ **block** [blɒk] N **1** (*of stone, ice*) blocco; (*toy*) cubo (per fare le costruzioni); (*butcher's, executioner's*) ceppo; **to knock sb's block off** (*fam*) rompere la zucca a qn **2** (*building*) palazzo; (*esp Am: group of buildings*) isolato; **he lives in our block** abita nel nostro palazzo; **block of flats** caseggiato; **to walk around the block** fare il giro dell'isolato; **3 blocks from here** a 3 isolati di distanza da qui **3** (*section: of tickets*) blocchetto; (*: of shares*) pacchetto; (*Comput*) blocco **4** (*blockage: in pipe*) ingorgo; (*Med*) blocco; **mental block** blocco mentale
■ VT (*gen, Comput*) bloccare; (*pipe*) ingorgare, bloccare;

Bb

(*Ftbl*) stoppare; **to block sb's way** sbarrare la strada a qn; **to block sb's view** coprire la vista a qn

▸ **block in** VT + ADV **1** **to block sb in** (*with car*) chiudere qn (con l'auto) **2** (*fill with paint*) colorare

▸ **block off** VT + ADV bloccare

▸ **block out** VT + ADV (*obscure*: *light*) escludere; (*obliterate*: *picture*) cancellare

▸ **block up** VT + ADV (*obstruct*: *passage*) bloccare; (: *pipe*) ingorgare, intasare; (*fill in*: *gap*) tappare; (: *window, entrance*) murare; **my nose is blocked up** ho il naso chiuso

block·ade [blɒ'keɪd] N (*Mil*) blocco
■ VT bloccare

block·age ['blɒkɪdʒ] N (*obstruction*) ingorgo; (*Med*) blocco

block and tackle N (*Tech*) paranco

block booking N prenotazione *f* in blocco

block·bust·er ['blɒk,bʌstə^r] N (*fam*: *film, TV series*) successone *m*

block·head ['blɒk,hɛd] N (*fam*) testa di legno

block letters, block capitals NPL stampatello

block release N (*Brit*) *periodo pagato concesso al tirocinante per effettuare studi superiori*

block vote N (*Brit*) voto per delega

blog [blɒg] N (*Comput*) blog *m inv*; *diario in Internet*

blog·ger ['blɒgə^r] N (*Comput*) blogger *m/f inv*, redattore(-trice) di blog
▷ www.blogger.com

bloke [bləʊk] N (*Brit fam*) tipo, tizio; **he's a really nice bloke** è un tipo veramente simpatico

blokey ['bləʊkɪ] ADJ, **blokeish** ['bləʊkɪʃ]
■ ADJ (*fam*: *activity, gestures*) da maschio; **a blokeish sense of humour** un senso dell'umorismo tipicamente maschile

blond [blɒnd] N (*man*) biondo
■ ADJ biondo(-a)

blonde [blɒnd] N (*woman*) bionda
■ ADJ biondo(-a)

◎ **blood** [blʌd] N sangue *m*; **to give blood** donare sangue; **of royal blood** di sangue reale; **there's bad blood between them** corre cattivo sangue fra di loro; **new blood** (*fig*) nuova linfa; **it's like trying to get blood out of a stone** è come voler cavare sangue dalle pietre; **in cold blood** a sangue freddo; **blood is thicker than water** (*Proverb*) il sangue non è acqua; **it's in the blood** ce l'ho (*or* l'hai *etc*) nel sangue; **he's after my blood** (*hum*) se mi prende m'ammazza; **my blood ran cold** mi son sentito gelare il sangue

blood-and-thunder [,blʌdən'θʌndə^r] ADJ (*novel, play, film*) a sensazione

blood bank N banca del sangue

blood bath N bagno di sangue

blood brother N fratello di sangue

blood cell N globulo

blood count N esame *m* emocromocitometrico

blood·curdling ['blʌd,kɜ:dlɪŋ] ADJ raccapricciante, da far gelare il sangue

blood donor N donatore(-trice) di sangue

blood group N gruppo sanguigno

blood heat N temperatura corporea

blood·hound ['blʌd,haʊnd] N segugio

blood·less ['blʌdlɪs] ADJ (*pale*) smorto(-a), esangue; (*coup*) senza spargimento di sangue

blood-letting ['blʌd,lɛtɪŋ] N (*fig*) spargimento di sangue; (*Med*) salasso

blood lust N sete *f* di sangue

blood money N denaro sporco (*somma pagata ad un killer o per una delazione*)

blood orange N arancia sanguigna

blood poisoning N setticemia

blood pressure N pressione *f* del sangue *or* sanguigna; **to have high/low blood pressure** avere la pressione alta/bassa

blood red ADJ rosso sangue *inv*

blood relation N consanguineo(-a)

blood·shed ['blʌd,ʃɛd] N spargimento di sangue

blood·shot ['blʌd,ʃɒt] ADJ: **bloodshot eyes** occhi iniettati di sangue

blood sports NPL sport cruenti

blood·stain ['blʌd,steɪn] N macchia di sangue

blood·stained ['blʌd,steɪnd] ADJ insanguinato(-a), macchiato(-a) di sangue

blood·stock ['blʌd,stɒk] N purosangue *inv*

blood·stone ['blʌd,stəʊn] N eliotropio

blood·stream ['blʌd,stri:m] N (circolazione *f* del) sangue *m*

blood·sucker ['blʌd,sʌkə^r] N (*also fig*) sanguisuga

blood test N analisi *fpl* del sangue

blood·thirsty ['blʌd,θɜ:stɪ] ADJ sanguinario(-a), assetato(-a) di sangue

blood transfusion N trasfusione *f* di sangue

blood type N gruppo sanguigno

blood vessel N vaso sanguigno

◎ **bloody** ['blʌdɪ] ADJ **1** (*bleeding*) sanguinante, che sanguina; (*bloodstained*) insanguinato(-a); (*cruel*: *battle, feud*) sanguinoso(-a); **a bloody war** una guerra sanguinosa **2** (*Brit fam*) maledetto(-a), dannato(-a); **this bloody ...** questo maledetto...; **bloody good** maledettamente buono(-a); **a bloody awful day** una giornata di merda; **it's bloody hard** è un casino difficile; **bloody hell!** porca miseria!; **I'm a bloody genius!** madonna, che genio che sono!
■ ADV (*Brit fam*): **that's no bloody good!** questo non serve a un cavolo!; **she runs bloody fast!** cavolo, se corre veloce!

bloody-minded [,blʌdɪ'maɪndɪd] ADJ (*Brit fam*) indisponente

bloody-mindedness [,blʌdɪ'maɪndɪdnɪs] N (*Brit fam*) ostinazione *f*

bloom [blu:m] N (*flower*) fiore *m*; (*on fruit*) lanugine *f*; (*on complexion*) colorito roseo; **in bloom** (*flower*) sbocciato(-a); (*tree*) in fiore; **in full bloom** in piena fioritura; **in the full bloom of youth** nel fiore della giovinezza
■ VI (*flower*) aprirsi; (*tree*) sfiorire

bloom·ers ['blu:məz] NPL mutandoni *mpl* a sbuffo

bloom·ing ['blu:mɪŋ] ADJ (*fam*) dannato(-a), maledetto(-a); **this blooming ...** questo dannato ...

blos·som ['blɒsəm] N (*with pl sense*) fiori *mpl*; (*single flower*) fiore *m*; **apple blossom** fiori di melo
■ VI fiorire; **to blossom into** (*fig*) diventare

blot [blɒt] N macchia; **to be a blot on the landscape** rovinare il paesaggio
■ VT **1** (*spot with ink*) macchiare d'inchiostro; **to blot one's copy book** (*fig*) farla grossa **2** (*dry*: *ink, writing*) asciugare

▸ **blot out** VT + ADV (*memories, words*) cancellare; (*view, sun*) nascondere, offuscare; (*nation, city*) annientare; **she blotted out all memory of the incident** ha cancellato qualsiasi ricordo dell'incidente; **clouds blotted out the sun** le nuvole nascondevano il sole

blotch [blɒtʃ] N (*of ink, colour*) macchia, chiazza; (*on skin*) chiazza

blotched [blɒtʃt] ADJ chiazzato(-a), macchiato(-a)
blotchy ['blɒtʃɪ] ADJ pieno(-a) *or* coperto(-a) di macchie
blot·ter ['blɒtə^r] N tampone *m* (di carta assorbente)
blot·ting pa·per ['blɒtɪŋ,peɪpə^r] N carta assorbente, carta asciugante
blot·to ['blɒtəʊ] ADJ (*Brit fam*) sbronzo(-a); **to get blotto** sbronzarsi
blouse [blaʊz] N camicetta
blou·son ['blu:zɒn] N blouson *m inv*
blow[1] [bləʊ] N (*gen*) colpo; (*with fist*) pugno; **a blow with a hammer** un colpo di martello; **at one blow** in un colpo (solo); **to come to blows** venire alle mani; **the news came as a great blow to her** la notizia fu un duro colpo per lei
◎ **blow**[2] [bləʊ] (*vb: pt* **blew**, *pp* **blown**) VT
1 (*subj: wind: ship*) spingere; (*: hair*) far svolazzare; **a gale blew the ship off course** una bufera ha fatto uscire di rotta la nave
2 (*trumpet, horn*) suonare; **to blow a whistle** fischiare; **the referee blew his whistle** l'arbitro fischiò; **to blow one's own trumpet** cantare le proprie lodi
3 (*bubbles*) fare; (*glass*) soffiare; (*kiss*) mandare; **to blow one's nose** soffiarsi il naso
4 (*fuse, safe*) far saltare; **to blow money on sth** (*fam*) buttare via dei soldi per qc; **to blow a secret** spifferare un segreto; **to blow sb's cover** scoprire il gioco di qn; **to blow one's top** (*fam*) esplodere, andare su tutte le furie; **blow the expense!** crepi l'avarizia!; **well, blow me!** *or* **well, I'll be blowed!** (*old: expressing surprise*) accidenti!; **I'll be blowed if ...** (*expressing indignation*) che mi venga un accidente se...
■ VI **1** (*wind, person*) soffiare; (*leaves*) svolazzare; (*flag*) sventolare; **a cold wind was blowing** soffiava un vento freddo; **to blow on one's fingers** scaldarsi le mani soffiando; **to blow on one's soup** soffiare sulla minestra; **to see which way the wind blows** (*fig*) vedere che aria tira; **his hat blew out of the window** il suo cappello è volato fuori dalla finestra; **the door blew open/shut** un colpo di vento ha spalancato/chiuso la porta
2 (*make sound: trumpet*) suonare; **they were one-all when the whistle blew** erano uno a uno quando l'arbitro ha fischiato la fine
3 (*fuse*) saltare; (*tyre*) scoppiare
▸ **blow away** VI + ADV volare via
■ VT + ADV (*papers, leaves*) far volare via; (*hat*) portare via
▸ **blow down** VI + ADV essere abbattuto(-a) dal vento
■ VT + ADV abbattere
▸ **blow in** VI + ADV (*window*) sfasciarsi; (*enter: leaves, dust*) volar dentro; **look who's just blown in!** (*fam*) ma guarda chi è arrivato!
▸ **blow off** VI + ADV (*hat*) volar via
■ VT + ADV (*hat*) portare via; **to blow off steam** (*fig fam*) sfogarsi
▸ **blow out** VT + ADV (*candle*) spegnere; (*swell out: cheeks*) gonfiare; **he has blown out the candles** ha spento le candeline
■ VI + ADV scoppiare
▸ **blow over** VT + ADV (*tree*) abbattere
■ VI + ADV (*tree*) rovesciarsi; (*storm*) passare, calmarsi; (*fig: dispute*) calmarsi
▸ **blow up** VT + ADV (*bridge*) far saltare; (*tyre, balloon*) gonfiare; (*photo*) ingrandire; (*event*) esagerare; **they blew up a plane** hanno fatto saltare un aereo; **we've blown up the balloons** abbiamo gonfiato i palloncini
■ VI + ADV (*bomb, fig: person*) esplodere; (*row*) scoppiare; (*storm: gather*) arrivare; **the house blew up** la casa è saltata in aria
blow-by-blow ['bləʊbaɪ,bləʊ] ADJ (*account*) minuto per minuto
blow-dry ['bləʊ,draɪ] N (*hairstyle*) messa in piega a phon
■ VT asciugare con il phon
blow·er ['bləʊə^r] N (*fam*) telefono
blow·fly ['bləʊ,flaɪ] N moscone *m* della carne
blow·hole ['bləʊ,həʊl] N (*Geol*) sfiatatoio
blow·lamp ['bləʊ,læmp] N (*Brit*) cannello per saldare/ sverniciare
blown [bləʊn] PP *of* **blow** VI
blow·out ['bləʊ,aʊt] N (*fam: big meal*) abbuffata; (*of tyre*) scoppio; (*of fuse*) corto circuito
blow·pipe ['bləʊ,paɪp] N (*weapon*) cerbottana
blowsy ['blaʊzɪ] ADJ = **blowzy**
blow·torch ['bləʊ,tɔ:tʃ] N (*Am*) = **blowlamp**
blow-up ['bləʊ,ʌp] N (*Phot*) ingrandimento, esplosione *f*; (*fam: quarrel*) litigio, baruffa
blowy ['bləʊɪ] ADJ ventoso(-a)
blowzy, **blowsy** ['blaʊzɪ] ADJ (*woman*) sciatto(-a), trasandato(-a)
BLT N ABBR = **bacon, lettuce and tomato a BLT** *un tramezzino con bacon, lattuga e pomodoro*
blub·ber ['blʌbə^r] N (*of whales*) grasso di balena
■ VI (*weep*) frignare
bludg·eon ['blʌdʒən] VT prendere a randellate; **to bludgeon sb to death** ammazzare qn a randellate; **to bludgeon sb into doing sth** (*fig*) costringere qn a fare qc
◎ **blue** [blu:] ADJ **1** (*light blue*) azzurro(-a), celeste; (*darker*) blu *inv*; **bright blue** bluette *inv*; **navy blue** blu; **blue with cold** livido(-a) dal freddo; **once in a blue moon** a ogni morte di papa; **you can talk till you're blue in the face** puoi parlare fino a domani; **to be in a blue funk** (*old*) avere una fifa nera **2** (*obscene: film, book*) porno *inv*; (*: joke*) sporco(-a), sconcio(-a); **a blue movie** un film porno **3** (*fam: sad*): **to feel blue** sentirsi giù
■ N (*colour: see adj*) azzurro, celeste *m*; blu *m inv*; **the blue** (*sky*) l'azzurro; **out of the blue** (*fig*) all'improvviso
blue baby N neonato(-a) cianotico(-a)
blue·bell ['blu:,bɛl] N giacinto dei boschi
blue·berry ['blu:bərɪ] N (*Am*) mirtillo
blue·bird ['blu:,bɜ:d] N uccello azzurro
blue blood·ed [blu:'blʌdɪd] ADJ (*fig*) di sangue blu
blue·bottle ['blu:,bɒtl] N moscone *m*
blue cheese N ≈ gorgonzola
blue-chip investment ['blu:'tʃɪpɪn'vɛstmənt] N investimento sicuro
blue-collar worker ['blu:,kɒlə^r'wɜ:kə^r] N operaio(-a), tuta *f* blu *inv*
blue-eyed ['blu:'aɪd] ADJ dagli occhi azzurri; **blue-eyed boy** (*fig*) favorito
blue gum N (*Bot*) blu gum *m inv* della Tasmania
blue jeans NPL (blue-)jeans *mpl*
blue·print ['blu:,prɪnt] N cianografia; **blueprint (for)** (*fig*) formula (di)
blues [blu:z] NPL (*Mus*): **the blues** il blues; **to have the blues** (*fam: depression*) essere giù
▷ www.bbc.co.uk/radio2/soldonsong/genres/blues.shtml
blue·tit ['blu:,tɪt] N cinciarella
bluff[1] [blʌf] ADJ (*person*) senza peli sulla lingua, brusco(-a)
bluff[2] [blʌf] N (*cliff*) scogliera a picco
bluff[3] [blʌf] N bluff *m inv*; **to call sb's bluff** far mettere le carte in tavola a qn

Bb

■VT: **to bluff it out** cavarsela bluffando
■VI bluffare
bluff·er ['blʌfəʳ] N bluffatore(-trice)
blun·der ['blʌndəʳ] N (*serious mistake*) abbaglio; **to make a blunder** prendere un abbaglio
■VI **1** (*see n*) prendere un abbaglio **2** (*move clumsily*): **to blunder about** andare *or* muoversi a tentoni; **to blunder into sb/sth** andare a sbattere contro qn/qc
blun·der·er ['blʌndərəʳ] N imbranato(-a)
blun·der·ing ['blʌndərɪŋ] ADJ imbranato(-a); **you blundering idiot!** razza d'imbranato!
blunt [blʌnt] ADJ **1** (*not sharp*: *edge*) non tagliente, smussato(-a); (: *knife*) che non taglia; (: *point*) spuntato(-a); **the knife was blunt** il coltello era spuntato; **this pencil is blunt** questa matita non ha più la punta; **blunt instrument** (*Law*) corpo contundente **2** (*outspoken*) brutale; (*manners*) brusco(-a); **he was blunt with me** è stato brusco con me
■VT (*knife*) smussare; (*point*) spuntare; (*fig*: *nerves, feelings*) rendere insensibile
blunt·ly ['blʌntlɪ] ADV (*speak*) senza mezzi termini
blunt·ness ['blʌntnɪs] N (*fig*: *of person*) brutale franchezza
blur [blɜːʳ] N (*shape*) massa indistinta *or* confusa; **my mind was a blur** avevo la mente annebbiata
■VT (*writing*) rendere (quasi) illeggibile; (*outline, sight, memory, judgment*) offuscare
■VI (*see vt*) diventare (quasi) illeggibile; offuscarsi; **her eyes blurred with tears** gli occhi le si velarono di lacrime
blurb [blɜːb] N (*publicity material*) trafiletto pubblicitario; (*on book jacket*) note *fpl* di copertina
blurred [blɜːd] ADJ (*TV*) sfocato(-a); (*photo*) mosso(-a)
blur·ry ['blɜːrɪ] ADJ (*comp* **-ier**, *superl* **-iest**) confuso(-a), indistinto(-a)
blurt [blɜːt] VT (*also*: **blurt out**) spifferare
blush [blʌʃ] N rossore *m*; **with a blush** arrossendo; **without a blush** senza neppure arrossire; **to spare sb's blushes** evitare di mettere in imbarazzo qn
■VI: **to blush (with)** arrossire (per *or* da)
blush·er ['blʌʃəʳ] N **1** (*Cosmetics*) fard *m inv* **2** (*mushroom*) tignosa vinata
blush·ing ['blʌʃɪŋ] ADJ: **the blushing bride** (*hum*) la dolce sposina
blus·ter ['blʌstəʳ] N bravate *fpl*, spacconate *fpl*; (*threats*) vuote minacce *fpl*
■VI (*wind*) infuriare; (*person*: *boast*) fare lo/la spaccone(-a); (: *rage*) dare in escandescenze
blus·ter·ing ['blʌstərɪŋ] ADJ (*tone, manner*) da spaccone
blus·tery ['blʌstərɪ] ADJ (*wind*) a raffiche; (*day*) ventoso(-a); (*weather*) burrascoso(-a)
Blvd ABBR = **Boulevard**
BM [ˌbiː'ɛm] N ABBR **1** = **British Museum** **2** (*Univ*: = **Bachelor of Medicine**) laurea in medicina
BMA [ˌbiːɛm'eɪ] N ABBR = **British Medical Association**
BMI [ˌbiːɛm'aɪ] N ABBR (*Med*: = **body mass index**) indice *m* di massa corporea
BMJ [ˌbiːɛm'dʒeɪ] N ABBR = **British Medical Journal**
B movie N film *m inv* di serie B
BMus ABBR (= **Bachelor of Music**) laurea in discipline musicali
BMX [ˌbiːɛm'ɛks] N ABBR (= **bicycle motocross**) ciclocross *m inv*; **BMX bike** mountain bike *f inv* per cross, BMX *f inv*
bn ABBR (= **billion**) mld; **2 bn dollars** 2 mld di dollari
BO [ˌbiː'əʊ] N ABBR **1** (= **body odour**) odori *mpl* sgradevoli (del corpo) **2** = **box office** botteghino
boa ['bəʊə] N (*snake*: *boa constrictor*) (serpente *m*) boa *inv*; (*of feathers*) boa *m inv*
boar [bɔːʳ] N (*male pig*) verro; (*wild boar*) cinghiale *m*
◎ **board** [bɔːd] N **1** (*of wood*) asse *f*, tavola; (*for chess*) scacchiera; (*blackboard*) lavagna; (*on wall*) tabellone *m*; **a chopping board** un tagliere; **there were six pawns on the board** c'erano sei pedoni sulla scacchiera; **write it on the board** scrivilo sulla lavagna; **there's a notice on the board** c'è un avviso in bacheca; **across the board** (*fig*: *adv*) per tutte le categorie; (: *adj*) generale; **to go by the board** (*fig*) andare a monte, venir messo(-a) da parte; **above board** (*fig*) regolare; **to take on board** recepire **2** (*provision of meals*) vitto; **half board** (*Brit*) mezza pensione *f*; **full board** (*Brit*) pensione *f* completa **3** (*Naut, Aer*): **on board** a bordo; **to go on board** salire a bordo **4** (*group of officials*) commissione *f*; **board of examiners** commissione esaminatrice *or* d'esame **5** (*institution*) ente *m*
■VT (*ship, plane*) imbarcarsi su, salire a bordo di; (*enemy ship*) andare all'abbordaggio di; (*bus, train*) salire su *or* in
■VI: **to board with sb** essere a pensione da qn
▶ **board out** VT + ADV mettere a pensione presso
▶ **board up** VT + ADV (*door*) chiudere con assi
board and lodging N vitto e alloggio
board·er ['bɔːdəʳ] N pensionante *m/f*; (*Scol*) collegiale *m/f*, convittore(-trice)
board game N gioco da tavolo
board·ing ['bɔːdɪŋ] N **1** (*floor*) impiantito (di legno); (*fence*) recinzione *f* di legno **2** (*of ship, plane*) imbarco
boarding card, boarding pass N (*Aer, Naut*) carta d'imbarco
boarding house N pensione *f*
boarding party N (*to take control*) *gruppo che assume il controllo di una nave come forma di protesta*; (*for inspection*) squadra di ispezione (*del carico di una nave*)
boarding school N collegio, convitto
board meeting N riunione *f* di consiglio
board of directors N (*Comm*) consiglio di amministrazione
Board of Trade N (*Brit*: *Admin*) Ministero del commercio
board room N sala del consiglio
board·walk ['bɔːdˌwɔːk] N (*Am*) passeggiata a mare
boast [bəʊst] N vanteria; **it is his boast that he's never lost a match** si fa vanto di non aver mai perso un incontro
■VT (*possession, achievement*) vantare; **the country boasts many tourist attractions** il paese vanta numerosi luoghi d'interesse turistico; **the village boasted only one small store** nel paese c'era solo un negozietto
■VI: **to boast (about** *or* **of)** vantarsi (di)
boast·er ['bəʊstəʳ] N spaccone(-a)
boast·ful ['bəʊstfʊl] ADJ pieno(-a) di sé, che si vanta sempre
boast·ful·ly ['bəʊstfəlɪ] ADV vantandosi
boast·ful·ness ['bəʊstfəlnɪs] N vanagloria
boast·ing ['bəʊstɪŋ] N vanterie *fpl*
◎ **boat** [bəʊt] N (*gen*) barca; (*ship*) nave *f*; **to go by boat** andare in barca *or* in nave; **a rowing boat** una barca a remi; **we're all in the same boat** (*fig fam*) siamo tutti nella stessa barca
boat·builder ['bəʊtˌbɪldəʳ] N costruttore *m* di barche
boat·building ['bəʊtˌbɪldɪŋ] N costruzione *f* di barche

boat·er ['bəʊtəʳ] N (*hat*) paglietta
boat hook N mezzo marinaio
boat·house ['bəʊt,haʊs] N rimessa per barche
boat·ing ['bəʊtɪŋ] N nautica da diporto
boat neck N (*of sweater, dress*) scollo a barchetta
boat people N boat people *mpl*
boat race N gara di canottaggio
boat·swain ['bəʊsn] N nostromo
boat train N *treno in coincidenza con il traghetto*
boat·yard ['bəʊt,jɑːd] N cantiere *m* (*per costruzione e riparazione di barche*)
bob[1] [bɒb] N (*curtsy*) riverenza, inchino
■ VI (*also:* **bob up and down**) andare su e giù
▸ **bob up** VI + ADV spuntare, saltare fuori
bob[2] [bɒb] N caschetto
bob[3] [bɒb] N, PL INV (*old: Brit fam*) scellino
bob·bin ['bɒbɪn] N spoletta, bobina; (*of sewing machine*) rocchetto
bob·ble ['bɒbl] N (*on hat*) pompon *m inv*
bob·by ['bɒbɪ] N (*Brit fam*) poliziotto
bob·cat ['bɒb,kæt] N (*Am*) lince *f*
bob·sleigh ['bɒb,sleɪ] N bob *m inv*
bod [bɒd] N (*Brit fam*) tipo; **he's an odd bod** è un tipo strano
bode [bəʊd] VI: **to bode well** promettere bene; **to bode ill** non promettere nulla di buono
bodge [bɒdʒ] (*Brit*) VT raffazzonare
■ N lavoro raffazzonato
bod·ice ['bɒdɪs] N (*of dress*) corpino, corpetto
bodice ripper ['bɒdɪs'rɪpəʳ] N (*fam*) romanzo rosa a sfondo storico
bodi·ly ['bɒdɪlɪ] ADJ (*comfort, needs*) materiale; (*functions*) corporale
■ ADV (*carry*) in braccio; (*lift*) di peso
◎ **body** ['bɒdɪ] N **1** (*of person, animal*) corpo; (*dead body*) corpo, cadavere *m*; **the human body** il corpo umano; **they've found the body** hanno trovato il cadavere; **to keep body and soul together** tirare avanti; **over my dead body!** neanche se mi ammazzi! **2** (*main part: of structure*) corpo; (*: of car*) carrozzeria; (*: of plane*) fusoliera; (*: of ship*) scafo, corpo; (*: of speech, document*) parte *f* principale **3** (*mass, collection: of facts*) massa, quantità *f inv*; (*: of laws*) raccolta; (*: of people, water*) massa; (*: of troops*) grosso; **the student body** gli studenti; **in a body** in massa **4** (*organization*) associazione *f*, organizzazione *f*, ente *m*; **a public body** un ente pubblico; **legislative body** organo legislativo; **ruling body** direttivo **5** (*of wine, hair*) corpo; **a wine with body** un vino corposo **6** (*also:* **body stocking**) body *m inv*
body bag N sacco mortuario; (*fig*) morto
body blow N (*fig*) duro colpo
body·board ['bɒdɪbɔːd] N (*Sport*) surf *m inv* (*su cui ci si stende*)
body·board·ing ['bɒdɪbɔːdɪŋ] N (*Sport*) surf *m* (*stendendosi sulla tavola*)
body builder N culturista *m/f*
body building N culturismo
body double N (*actor*) doppio
body·guard ['bɒdɪ,gɑːd] N (*person, group*) guardia del corpo
body image N (*Psych*) immagine *f* del proprio corpo
body language N linguaggio del corpo
body mass index N indice *m* di massa corporea
body mike N microfono a clip; (*hidden*) microfono nascosto
body odour N odore *m* di sudore
body politic N (*frm*): **the body politic** lo Stato
body repairs NPL (*Aut*) lavori *mpl* di carrozzeria
body search N perquisizione *f* personale; **to carry out a body search on sb** effettuare una perquisizione personale su qn; **to submit to** *or* **undergo a body search** essere sottoposto(-a) a perquisizione personale
body stocking N body *m inv*
body·suit ['bɒdɪsuːt] N body *m inv*
body-surf ['bɒdɪsɜːf] VI *cavalcare le onde senza surf*; (*fam*) gettarsi a corpo morto sopra la folla
body-surfer ['bɒdɪsɜːfəʳ] N *chi cavalca le onde senza surf*
body-surfing ['bɒdɪsɜːfəʳ] N *il cavalcare le onde senza surf*
body warmer [-,wɔːməʳ] N giubbotto imbottito senza maniche
body·work ['bɒdɪ,wɜːk] N (*Aut*) carrozzeria
body wrap N trattamento di bellezza con bendaggi
Boer ['bʊəʳ] N, ADJ boero(-a)
bof·fin ['bɒfɪn] N (*Brit fam*) scienziato(-a)
bog [bɒg] N palude *f*; (*Brit fam: toilet*) cesso
▸ **bog down** VT + ADV: **to get bogged down (in)** impantanarsi (in)
bo·gey ['bəʊgɪ] N (*worry*) spauracchio
bogey·man ['bəʊgɪ,mæn] N babau *m inv*
bog·gle ['bɒgl] VI (*fam*): **the mind boggles!** è incredibile!; **his eyes boggled at the sight** ha fatto tanto d'occhi davanti a quella scena
bog·gy ['bɒgɪ] ADJ paludoso(-a)
BOGOF ABBR (= **buy one get one free**) paghi uno prendi due
Bo·go·tá [,bəʊgə'tɑː] N Bogotà *f*
bog-standard ['bɒg'stændəd] ADJ (*fam*) ordinario(-a)
bo·gus ['bəʊgəs] ADJ (*jewels, claim*) falso(-a), fasullo(-a); (*person, attitude*) finto(-a)
Bo·he·mia [bəʊ'hiːmɪə] N Boemia
Bo·he·mian [bəʊ'hiːmɪən] ADJ (*Geog*) boemo(-a); (*artist, life*) bohémien
■ N (*Geog*) boemo(-a); (*artist, writer*) bohémien *m inv*
boil[1] [bɔɪl] N (*Med*) foruncolo
◎ **boil[2]** [bɔɪl] N: **to bring to the boil** (*Am*): **to bring to a boil** portare a ebollizione; **to come to the boil** (*Am*): **to come to a boil** raggiungere l'ebollizione; **on the boil** che bolle; **it's off the boil** ha smesso di bollire
■ VT (far) bollire; (*potatoes, meat*) (far) bollire, (far) lessare; **boil some water** fai bollire dell'acqua; **boiled egg** uovo alla coque; **boiled ham** prosciutto cotto; **boiled potatoes** patate *fpl* bollite *or* lesse
■ VI (*water etc*) bollire; **the kettle is boiling** l'acqua bolle; **to let a saucepan boil dry** lasciar evaporare tutta l'acqua da una pentola; **to boil with rage** (*fig*) bollire di rabbia
▸ **boil away** VI + ADV (*liquid*) evaporare; (*fig*) sfumare
▸ **boil down** VI + ADV (*fig*): **to boil down to** ridursi a
▸ **boil over** VI + ADV traboccare (bollendo); (*fig: anger*) esplodere
▸ **boil up** VT + ADV far bollire
boil·er ['bɔɪləʳ] N (*gen*) caldaia; (*for domestic hot water*) scaldabagno, scaldaacqua *m inv*
boiler·maker ['bɔɪlə,meɪkəʳ] N operaio metallurgico
boiler suit N (*Brit*) tuta (da lavoro)
boil·ing ['bɔɪlɪŋ] ADJ (*also fig*) bollente; **a boiling hot day** un giorno torrido; **I'm boiling (hot)** (*fam*) sto morendo di caldo; **it's boiling in here!** qui dentro si soffoca!
boiling point N punto di ebollizione
boil-in-the-bag [,bɔɪlɪnðə'bæg] ADJ (*rice etc*) da bollire nel sacchetto

Bb

bois·ter·ous ['bɔɪstərəs] ADJ *(meeting)* turbolento(-a); *(person)* chiassoso(-a); *(party)* animato(-a)

bold [bəʊld] ADJ **1** *(brave: person, attempt)* audace; *(fig: plan, move)* ardito(-a); **he was bold enough to ask her a question** fu abbastanza coraggioso da farle una domanda; **bold economic reforms** coraggiose riforme economiche **2** *(forward: child, remark)* sfacciato(-a), sfrontato(-a) **3** *(striking: line, pattern)* vistoso(-a), che salta all'occhio; *(colour)* deciso(-a)

bold·ly ['bəʊldlɪ] ADV *(see adj)* audacemente; arditamente; sfacciatamente; vistosamente

bold·ness ['bəʊldnɪs] N *(of person, plan)* audacia; *(impudence)* sfacciataggine *f*, impudenza

bold type N *(Typ)* neretto, grassetto

bo·lero [bə'lɛərəʊ] N bolero

Bo·livia [bə'lɪvɪə] N Bolivia

Bo·liv·ian [bə'lɪvɪən] ADJ, N boliviano(-a)

bol·lard ['bɒləd] N *(on quay)* bitta; *(Brit: to bar way)* pilastrino di chiusura al traffico; *(at junction)* colonnina luminosa

bol·locks ['bɒləks] NPL *(fam!)*: **to talk a load of bollocks** dire stronzate *or* cazzate *(fam!)*

Bol·ly·wood ['bɒlɪwʌd] N cinema *m* indiano

Bol·she·vik ['bɒlʃəvɪk] ADJ, N bolscevico(-a)

Bol·she·vism ['bɒlʃəvɪzəm] N bolscevismo

bol·shy ['bɒlʃɪ] ADJ *(comp* **-ier**, *superl* **-iest***)* *(Brit fam)* piantagrane, ribelle; **to be in a bolshy mood** essere in vena di piantar grane

bol·ster ['bəʊlstə^r] N capezzale *m*
■VT *(also:* **bolster up***)* sostenere; **to bolster sb's courage** incoraggiare qn

bolt [bəʊlt] N **1** *(on door)* chiavistello, catenaccio; *(of lock)* catenaccio; *(Tech)* bullone *m*; *(of crossbow)* dardo; *(of cloth)* pezza; **there was a heavy bolt on the door** c'era un pesante catenaccio alla porta; **nuts and bolts** dadi e bulloni; **he's shot his bolt** *(fig)* ha giocato la sua ultima carta **2** *(dash)*: **to make a bolt for the door** fare un balzo *or* schizzare verso la porta; **to make a bolt for it** darsela a gambe **3** *(lightning)* fulmine *m*; **a bolt of lightning** un fulmine; **a bolt from the blue** *(fig)* un fulmine a ciel sereno
■ADV: **bolt upright** diritto(-a) come un fuso
■VT **1** *(door)* chiudere con il catenaccio *or* il chiavistello, serrare; *(Tech: bolt together)* imbullonare **2** *(food: bolt down)* ingollare
■VI *(run away: person)* darsela a gambe; *(: horse)* imbizzarrirsi; *(rush)* scappare via

bolt hole N *(Brit)* rifugio

◎ **bomb** [bɒm] N bomba; **it went like a bomb** *(fam: party)* è andato a meraviglia; **it goes like a bomb** *(fam: car)* va come un razzo
■VT *(target)* bombardare
▸ **bomb out** VT + ADV *(building)* distruggere; **they were bombed out** hanno dovuto abbandonare la casa bombardata

bom·bard [bɒm'bɑːd] VT *(Mil)*: **to bombard (with)** bombardare (con); **I was bombarded with questions** sono stato bombardato di domande

bom·bard·ment [bɒm'bɑːdmənt] N bombardamento

bom·bast ['bɒmbæst] N magniloquenza

bom·bas·tic [bɒm'bæstɪk] ADJ magniloquente, ampolloso(-a)

bomb disposal expert N artificiere *m*

bomb disposal unit N corpo degli artificieri

bomb·er ['bɒmə^r] N *(aircraft)* bombardiere *m*; *(terrorist)* dinamitardo(-a), bombarolo(-a)

bomber jacket N bomber *m inv*

bomb·ing ['bɒmɪŋ] N bombardamento
■ADJ *(expedition)* di bombardamento

bomb·proof ['bɒm,pruːf] ADJ a prova di bomba

bomb scare N sospetta presenza di un ordigno esplosivo; **there was a bomb scare at Harrods** Harrods era in stato d'allarme per paura di una bomba

bomb·shell ['bɒmʃɛl] N *(fig: news)* bomba; **a blonde bombshell** una bionda esplosiva

bomb site N luogo bombardato

bona fide ['bəʊnə'faɪdɪ] ADJ *(antique, excuse)* autentico(-a); *(offer)* serio(-a), onesto(-a)

bo·nan·za [bə'nænzə] N periodo di boom

◎ **bond** [bɒnd] N **1** *(link)* legame *m*, vincolo
bonds ■NPL *(chains etc)* catene *fpl*; **there is a special bond between them** c'è un legame particolare tra loro **2** *(agreement)* impegno, accordo; **to enter into a bond (to do sth)** impegnarsi (a fare qc); **his word is his bond** ci si può fidare completamente della sua parola **3** *(Fin)* obbligazione *f* **4** *(Comm)*: **in bond** in attesa di sdoganamento **5** *(adhesion)* aderenza **6** *(Chem)* legame *m* **7** *(also:* **bond paper***)* carta fine
■VT *(bricks)* cementare; *(subj: glue)* far aderire, incollare
■VI *(people)* stabilire un legame affettivo; *(objects)* incollarsi

bond·age ['bɒndɪdʒ] N servitù, schiavitù

bond·ed ware·house ['bɒndɪd 'wɛəhaʊs] N magazzino doganale

bonds·man ['bɒndzmən] N *(pl* **-men***)* servo, schiavo

◎ **bone** [bəʊn] N *(gen)* osso; *(of fish)* lisca, spina; **a broken bone** un osso rotto; **I feel it in my bones** me lo sento, qualcosa me lo dice; **I have a bone to pick with you** *(fam)* devo regolare un conto con te; **she made no bones about saying what she thought** ci ha detto quello che pensava senza fare tante cerimonie
■VT *(meat)* disossare; *(fish)* diliscare, spinare
■ADJ *(buttons)* d'osso

bone china N porcellana fine

boned [bəʊnd] ADJ **1** *(meat)* disossato(-a); *(fish)* spinato(-a) **2** *(corset)* fornito(-a) di stecche

bone density N *(Med)* densità *f* ossea

bone-dry ['bəʊn'draɪ] ADJ *(fam)* asciuttissimo(-a)

bone idle ADJ: **to be bone idle** essere un(-a) fannullone(-a)

bone marrow N midollo osseo

bone meal N *(fertilizer)* farina d'ossa

bone of contention N pomo della discordia

bon·er ['bəʊnə^r] N *(Am)* gaffe *f inv*; *(fam!)*: **to have a boner** avere il cazzo duro *(fam!)*

bone·shaker ['bəʊnʃeɪkə^r] N *(hum: bicycle, car)* catorcio

bon·fire ['bɒn,faɪə^r] N falò *m inv*

bonfire night N *notte del 5 novembre, anniversario dell'attentato al Parlamento del 1609 che viene celebrato con fuochi d'artificio e falò*
▷ www.guy-fawkes.com
▷ www.bonefire.org/guy/

bong [bɒŋ] N pipa ad acqua *(per cannabis)*

bon·go ['bɒŋgəʊ] N bongos *mpl*

bon·ing ['bəʊnɪŋ] N *(see vb)* disossamento; diliscamento

boning knife N coltello per disossare

bonk [bɒŋk] VT, VI *(Brit hum, fam)* scopare *(fam!)*

bonk·bust·er ['bɒŋkbʌstə^r] N *(Brit fam) romanzo di successo, con molte scene di sesso*

bonk·ers ['bɒŋkəz] ADJ *(Brit fam)*: **to be bonkers** essere suonato(-a); **to go bonkers** diventare matto(-a)

Bonn [bɒn] N Bonn *f*

bon·net ['bɒnɪt] N **1** *(Brit Aut)* cofano **2** *(woman's,*

baby's) cuffia; (*esp Scot: man's*) berretto
bon·ny ['bɒnɪ] ADJ (*esp Scot*) bello(-a), carino(-a)
bon·sai ['bɒnsaɪ] N bonsai *m inv*
bo·nus ['bəʊnəs] N (*on wages*) gratifica; (*insurance etc*) dividendo; (*fig*) sovrappiù *m*; **Christmas bonus** ≈ tredicesima
bony ['bəʊnɪ] ADJ (*comp* **-ier**, *superl* **-iest**) (*thin: person*) angoloso(-a), ossuto(-a); (*made of bone: frame*) osseo(-a); (*: fish*) pieno(-a) di lische; (*: meat*) con parecchio osso; (*like bone*) simile a osso; **a bony face** un viso ossuto
boo [bu:] EXCL bu!; **she wouldn't say boo to a goose** (*fam*) ha paura della sua ombra
■N: **boos** NPL fischi *mpl*
■VT fischiare; **he was booed off the stage** l'hanno cacciato di scena a suon di fischi
boob [bu:b] N (*Brit fam: mistake*) gaffe *f inv*; (*: breast*) tetta
boo·by prize ['bu:bɪ,praɪz] N premio per il peggior contendente
boo·by trap ['bu:bɪ,træp] N trabocchetto; (*Mil*) congegno che esplode al contatto
booby-trapped ['bu:bɪ,træpt] ADJ: **a booby-trapped car** una macchina carica di esplosivo
boo·gie ['bu:gɪ] VI (*fam*) ballare
◎ **book** [bʊk] N libro; (*notebook*) quaderno; (*of matches*) bustina; (*of tickets*) blocchetto; **I read it in a book** l'ho letto in un libro; **he wrote it down in his book** l'ha scritto nel quaderno; **the books** (*Comm*) i libri contabili; **to keep** *or* **do the books** tenere la contabilità; **to be in sb's bad books** essere nel libro nero di qn; **to bring sb to book (for sth)** costringere qn a render conto (di qc); **to throw the book at sb** (*in accusing*) imputare a qn tutte le accuse possibili; (*in punishing*) condannare qn al massimo della pena; **by the book** secondo le regole; **in my book** a mio avviso, a parer mio
■VT **1** (*reserve: seat, room, table*) prenotare, fissare, riservare; (*ticket*) prendere, comprare **2** (*Police: driver*) fare una contravvenzione a, multare; (*Ftbl*) ammonire
■VI (*see vt 1*) prenotare; (*ticket*) prendere il biglietto
▸ **book in** VI + ADV (*at hotel*) prendere una camera
■VT + ADV (*person*) prenotare (una camera) per
▸ **book up** VT + ADV riservare, prenotare; **the hotel is booked up** l'albergo è al completo; **tonight's performance is booked up** la rappresentazione di stasera è esaurita; **I'm booked up** (*fam*) sono occupatissimo
book·able ['bʊkəbl] ADJ (*seat etc*) prenotabile, riservabile; **seats are bookable** si possono prenotare i posti
book·binder ['bʊk,baɪndəʳ] N rilegatore(-trice)
book·binding ['bʊk,baɪndɪŋ] N rilegatura
book·case ['bʊk,keɪs] N libreria, scaffale *m*
book club N club *m inv* del libro
book ends NPL reggilibri *mpl*
bookie ['bʊkɪ] N (*fam*) = **bookmaker**
book·ing ['bʊkɪŋ] N (*Brit: in hotel*) prenotazione *f*; (*: Sport*) ammonizione *f*
booking clerk N impiegato(-a) della biglietteria
booking office N (*Rail*) biglietteria, ufficio *m* prenotazioni *inv*; (*Theatre*) botteghino
book·ish ['bʊkɪʃ] ADJ (*person*) (troppo) studioso(-a); (*phrase*) libresco(-a)
book-keeper ['bʊk,ki:pəʳ] N contabile *m/f*
book-keeping ['bʊk,ki:pɪŋ] N contabilità
book·let ['bʊklɪt] N opuscolo, libretto
book·maker ['bʊk,meɪkəʳ] N bookmaker *m inv*, allibratore *m*
book·mark ['bʊkmɑ:k] N (*also Comput*) segnalibro
■VT (*Comput*) mettere un segnalibro a; (*Internet Explorer*) aggiungere a "Preferiti"
book·mobile ['bʊkmə,bi:l] N (*Am*) biblioteca ambulante
book·plate ['bʊk,pleɪt] N ex libris *m inv*
book·seller ['bʊk,seləʳ] N libraio
book·shelf ['bʊk,ʃɛlf] N mensola per libri; **bookshelves** ■NPL (*bookcase*) libreria
book·shop ['bʊk,ʃɒp], **book·store** (*Am*) ['bʊk,stɔ:ʳ] N libreria
book·stall ['bʊk,stɔ:l] N (*in station*) edicola, chiosco (dei giornali); (*secondhand books*) bancarella (dei libri)
book token N buono *m* libro *inv*
book value N valore *m* contabile
book·worm ['bʊk,wɜ:m] N (*fig*) topo di biblioteca
◎ **boom¹** [bu:m] N (*in prices, shares*) forte incremento; (*of product*) boom *m inv*, improvvisa popolarità; (*of sales*) esplosione *f*; (*period of growth*) boom (economico); **a boom in popularity** un aumento improvviso della popolarità
■VI (*trade*) andare a gonfie vele; (*sales*) aumentare vertiginosamente; (*industry, town*) essere in forte espansione, svilupparsi enormemente
boom² [bu:m] N (*of guns, thunder*) rombo, rimbombo; (*deeper*) boato
■VI (*voice, radio, sea: boom out*) rimbombare; (*gun*) tuonare
■VT (*also:* **boom out**) urlare con voce tonante
boom³ [bu:m] N (*Naut*) boma; (*of crane*) braccio; (*across harbour*) sbarramento; (*of microphone*) giraffa
boom·er·ang ['bu:məræŋ] N boomerang *m inv*
■VI (*fig*) avere effetto contrario; **to boomerang on sb** ritorcersi contro qn
boom·ing¹ ['bu:mɪŋ] ADJ (*sales*) in rapida ascesa; (*trade, business*) che va a gonfie vele
boom·ing² ['bu:mɪŋ] ADJ (*guns, voice*) tonante
boom town N ≈ città *f inv* in rapidissima espansione
boon [bu:n] N (*blessing*) benedizione *f*
boon·dog·gle ['bu:ndɒgl] N (*Am fam*) buco nero; **the new runway is a billion-dollar boondoggle** la nuova pista è un buco nero che inghiotte miliardi di dollari
boor [bʊəʳ] N bifolco, zotico
boor·ish ['bʊərɪʃ] ADJ (*manners*) da zoticone, da bifolco
boor·ish·ly ['bʊərɪʃlɪ] ADV maleducatamente, da bifolco
boor·ish·ness ['bʊərɪʃnɪs] N maleducazione *f*
◎ **boost** [bu:st] N **1** (*encouragement*) spinta, sprone *m*; **to give a boost to** (*morale*) tirar su; **it gave a boost to his confidence** è stata per lui un'iniezione di fiducia **2** (*upward thrust: to person*) spinta (in su); (*: to rocket*) spinta propulsiva
■VT (*increase: sales, production*) incentivare; (*fig: hopes*) rinforzare; (*promote: product*) promuovere (sul mercato); (*Elec: voltage*) aumentare; (*radio signal*) amplificare; (*Space*) lanciare; **they're trying to boost the economy** stanno cercando di dare una spinta all'economia; **the win boosted the team's morale** la vittoria ha sollevato il morale della squadra
boost·er ['bu:stəʳ] N (*TV*) amplificatore *m* di segnale; (*Elec*) amplificatore; (*booster rocket*) razzo vettore; (*Med: injection*) (iniezione *f* di) richiamo
booster seat N , **booster cushion** ■N seggiolino
◎ **boot¹** [bu:t] N **1** (*gen*) stivale *m*; (*ankle boot*) stivaletto; (*of soldier, skier, workman*) scarpone *m*; (*for hiking*) scarpone da montagna; **football boots** scarpe *fpl* da calcio; **to give sb the boot** (*fam*) mettere qn alla porta **2** (*Brit*

Bb

Aut) portabagagli *m inv*, bagagliaio
■ VT **1** (*fam: kick*) dare un calcio a; **to boot sb out** buttar fuori *or* cacciar via qn (a pedate) **2** (*Comput*) inizializzare
boot² [bu:t] N (*old liter*): **to boot** (*in addition*) in (*or* per di) più, per giunta, come se non bastasse
bootee [bu:'ti:] N (*baby's*) scarpetta; (*woman's*) stivaletto (da donna)
booth [bu:ð] N (*at fair*) bancarella, baraccone *m*; (*Telec, voting booth*) cabina
boot·jack ['bu:t,dʒæk] N cavastivali *m inv*
boot·lace ['bu:t,leɪs] N laccio, stringa
boot·leg ['bu:t,lɛg] ADJ di contrabbando; **bootleg recording** registrazione *f* pirata *inv*
boot·leg·ger ['bu:t,lɛgəʳ] N contrabbandiere *m* di alcolici
boot-polish ['bu:t,pɒlɪʃ] N lucido (da scarpe)
boot·strap ['bu:t,stræp] N (*Comput*) programma di innesco; **to pull o.s. up by one's bootstraps** (*fig*) tirarsi su con le proprie forze
boo·ty ['bu:tɪ] N bottino, refurtiva
booze [bu:z] (*fam*) N alcolici *mpl*; **bring your own booze** portatevi da bere
■ VI sbevazzare, alzare il gomito
booz·er ['bu:zəʳ] (*fam*) N (*person*) beone *m*; (*Brit: pub*) osteria
booze-up ['bu:zʌp] N (*fam*) bevuta
boozy ['bu:zɪ] ADJ (*fam: person*) che alza spesso il gomito
bo·ra·cic [bə'ræsɪk] ADJ boracico(-a)
bor·age ['bɒrɪdʒ] N borragine *f*
bo·rax ['bɔ:ræks] N borace *m*
◎ **bor·der** ['bɔ:dəʳ] N **1** (*frontier*) confine *m*; **the Borders** NPL (*Brit*) *zona al confine tra la Scozia e l'Inghilterra*; **we crossed the Hungarian border** abbiamo passato il confine con l'Ungheria **2** (*edge: as decoration*) bordo, orlatura, orlo; (: *as boundary*) margine *m*, limite *m* **3** (*in garden*) aiuola (laterale)
■ VT (*line, adjoin*) fiancheggiare, costeggiare
▸ **border on, border upon** VI + PREP confinare con; (*fig: come close to being*) sfiorare, rasentare
border incident N incidente *m* di frontiera
border·line ['bɔ:də,laɪn] ADJ (*candidate*) su cui è difficile decidere; **borderline case** caso limite; **he was a borderline failure** è stato bocciato per poco
■ N (*fig*) linea di demarcazione
border raid N incursione *f*
border town N città *f inv* di confine
◎ **bore¹** [bɔ:ʳ] N (*person*) noioso(-a), seccatore(-trice), noia; (*event*) noia, barba; **what a bore!** che noia!; **the party/office bore** l'attaccabottoni *m/f inv* (di una festa/un ufficio)
■ VT (*person*) annoiare
bore² [bɔ:ʳ] N (*also:* **bore hole**) foro di sonda; (*diameter*) diametro interno; (: *of gun*) calibro; **a 12-bore shotgun** un fucile calibro 12
■ VT (*hole*) praticare; (*tunnel*) scavare
■ VI: **to bore for** perforare *or* trivellare alla ricerca di
bore³ [bɔ:ʳ] PT *of* **bear** VI
bored ['bɔ:d] ADJ annoiato(-a); **to get bored** annoiarsi; **he's bored to tears** *or* **bored to death** *or* **bored stiff** è annoiato a morte, si annoia da morire
bore·dom ['bɔ:dəm] N noia
bore·hole ['bɔ:,həʊl] N foro di trivellazione
bor·ing ['bɔ:rɪŋ] ADJ (*tedious*) noioso(-a)
◎ **born** [bɔ:n] ADJ nato(-a); **to be born** (*also fig*) nascere; **I was born in 1955** sono nato nel 1955; **born blind** cieco(-a) dalla nascita; **a Roman born and bred** un romano di Roma, un romano doc; **the revolution was born of the workers' discontent** la rivoluzione scaturì dallo scontento degli operai; **to be born again** rinascere; **I wasn't born yesterday!** (*fam*) non sono nato ieri!; **in all my born days** (*fam*) in tutta la mia vita; **a born actor/musician** un attore/musicista nato; **a born liar** un*a* bugiardo(-a) matricolato(-a); **a born fool** un*a* perfetto(-a) cretino(-a)
born-again [,bɔ:nə'geɪn] ADJ: **born-again Christian** convertito(-a) alla chiesa evangelica
borne [bɔ:n] PP *of* **bear** VI
Bor·neo ['bɔ:nɪ,əʊ] N Borneo
bo·ron ['bɔ:rɒn] N boro
bo·ro·sili·cate [,bɔ:rəʊ'sɪlɪkɪt] N borosilicato
borosilicate glass N vetro al borosilicato
bor·ough ['bʌrə] N comune *m*, circoscrizione *f* amministrativa; (*in London*) distretto
◎ **bor·row** ['bɒrəʊ] VT: **to borrow (from)** prendere in prestito (da), farsi prestare (da); (*idea, word*) prendere (da); **to borrow sth from sb** farsi prestare qc da qn; **could I borrow your car?** puoi prestarmi la macchina?
bor·row·er ['bɒrəʊəʳ] N (*gen*) chi prende in prestito; (*Econ*) mutuatario(-a)
bor·row·ing ['bɒrəʊɪŋ] N prestito
bor·stal ['bɔ:stl] N (*Brit*) riformatorio
Bos·nia ['bɒznɪə] N Bosnia
Bosnia-Herzegovina [,bɒznɪəhɜ:tsəgəʊ'vi:nə], **Bosnia-Hercegovina** [,bɒznɪəhɜ:tsə'gɒvɪnə] N Bosnia-Erzegovina
Bos·nian ['bɒznɪən] ADJ, N bosniaco(-a)
bos·om ['bʊzəm] N (*of woman, fig*) seno; **in the bosom of the family** in seno alla famiglia
bosom friend N amico(-a) del cuore
◎ **boss** [bɒs] N (*employer, owner*) capo, padrone *m*, principale *m*; (*manager, of organization*) capo; (*of criminal organization*) boss *m inv*
■ VT (*also:* **boss about** *or* **around**: *pej*) comandare a bacchetta; **stop bossing everyone about!** smettila di dare ordini a tutti!
bossy ['bɒsɪ] ADJ (*person*) autoritario(-a); **don't you get bossy with me!** non cominciare a darmi ordini!
bo·sun ['bəʊsən] N = **boatswain**
bot [bɒt] N (*Comput*) bot *m inv*; *programma per il reperimento di informazioni in Internet*
bo·tan·ical [bə'tænɪkəl], **bo·tan·ic** [bə'tænɪk] ADJ botanico(-a)
botanic gardens [bə'tænɪk-] NPL orto botanico
bota·nist ['bɒtənɪst] N botanico(-a)
bota·ny ['bɒtənɪ] N botanica
▷ www.ou.edu/cas/botany-micro/www-vl
▷ www.academicinfo.net/bot.html
botch [bɒtʃ] N (*of job*) pasticcio, macello
■ VT (*job*) raffazzonare; (*attempt*) fallire
▸ **botch up** VT (*job*) raffazzonare
◎ **both** [bəʊθ] ADJ tutti(-e) *pl* e due, entrambi(-e) *pl*, ambedue *inv*; **both books/boys** tutti e due *or* entrambi *or* ambedue i libri/ragazzi
■ PRON tutti(-e) *pl* e due, entrambi(-e) *pl*, ambedue *inv*; **they were both there** *or* **both of them were there** c'erano tutti e due; **both of us went** *or* **we both went** ci siamo andati tutt'e due; **both are to blame** la colpa è di tutti e due; **both of us agree** siamo d'accordo tutti e due; **come in both of you** entrate tutti e due; **she has 2 daughters: both are blonde** ha 2 figlie, bionde entrambe
■ ADV: **both... and** sia... che, sia... sia; **John and I both**

went ci siamo andati sia John che io; **both you and I saw it** l'abbiamo visto sia tu che io; **both this and that** sia questo che quello; **she was both laughing and crying** piangeva e rideva a un tempo *or* allo stesso tempo; **he both plays and sings** oltre a suonare canta; **they sell both meat and poultry** vendono sia carne che pollame

◎ **both·er** ['bɒðəʳ] N (*nuisance*) seccatura, noia; (*trouble*) fastidio, disturbo; **it is a bother to have to go** è una seccatura dover andare; **(it's) no bother, I'll see to it** non c'è problema, ci penso io; **the children were no bother at all** i bambini non hanno dato nessun fastidio; **it wasn't any bother** (*don't mention it*) si figuri!, s'immagini!; **he had a spot of bother with the police** ha avuto delle noie con la polizia
■ VT (*worry*) preoccupare; (*annoy*) seccare, infastidire, dar fastidio a; **to bother doing** *or* **to do sth** darsi la pena di fare qc; **what's bothering you?** cosa c'è che ti preoccupa?; **I'm sorry to bother you** scusa se ti disturbo; **I'm sorry to bother you with my problems** mi spiace importunarti con i miei problemi; **does the noise bother you?** ti dà fastidio il rumore?; **don't bother me!** lasciami in pace!; **I can't be bothered going out** *or* **to go out** proprio non mi va di uscire; **his leg bothers him** gli fa un po' male la gamba; **he didn't even bother to write** non si è nemmeno sprecato a scrivere due righe; **I'm not bothered** per me fa lo stesso
■ VI: **to bother (about)** preoccuparsi (di *or* per); **please don't bother** non si scomodi, lasci perdere
■ EXCL uffa!, accidenti!

Bot·swa·na [ˌbɒts'wɑːnə] N Botswana *m*

◎ **bot·tle** ['bɒtl] N bottiglia; (*of perfume, shampoo*) flacone *m*; (*baby's*) biberon *m inv*, poppatoio; **bottle of wine/milk** bottiglia di vino/latte; **wine/milk bottle** bottiglia da vino/del latte
■ VT (*wine*) imbottigliare; (*fruit*) conservare (in vasetti)
▸ **bottle out** VI + ADV (*Brit*): **to bottle out (of sth)** tirarsi indietro (da qc)
▸ **bottle up** VT + ADV (*emotion*) soffocare, reprimere

bottle bank N contenitore *m* per la raccolta del vetro

bottle-fed ['bɒtl,fɛd] ADJ allattato(-a) artificialmente

bottle·neck ['bɒtl,nɛk] N (*road*) strozzatura; (*traffic*) ingorgo

bottle-nosed whale ['bɒtlnəʊzd'weɪl] N iperdonte *m*

bottle-opener ['bɒtl,əʊpnəʳ] N apribottiglie *m inv*

bottle party N *festa a cui gli invitati portano da bere*

◎ **bot·tom** ['bɒtəm] N (*gen*) fondo; (*of mountain, tree*) piedi *mpl*; (*of shoe*) suola; (*of chair*) sedile *m*; (*of ship*) opera viva; (*of person*) sedere *m*; **at the bottom of** (*hill, ladder*) ai piedi di; (*road, list*) in fondo a; **at the bottom of the page** in fondo alla pagina, a piè di pagina; **to be bottom of the class** essere l'ultimo(-a) della classe; **on the bottom (of)** (*shoe etc*) sotto; (*sea, lake etc*) sul fondo (di); **the boat floated bottom up** la barca galleggiava capovolta; **do these trousers make my bottom look big?** questi pantaloni mi fanno il sedere grosso?; **I fell flat on my bottom** sono caduto battendo il sedere; **at bottom** in fondo; **from the bottom of my heart** con tutto il cuore, dal profondo del cuore; **to get to the bottom of sth** (*fig*) andare al fondo di *or* in fondo a qc; **he's at the bottom of it** (*fig*) qui ci dev'essere il suo zampino; **bottoms up!** (*fam*) cin-cin!; **bikini bottom** slip *mpl* del bikini
■ ADJ (*lowest: shelf, step*) più basso(-a), inferiore; (*corner, part*) inferiore; **the bottom shelf** il ripiano inferiore
▸ **bottom out** VI + ADV assestarsi al livello più basso

bottom drawer N (*fig*) dote *f*

bottom gear N (*Aut*) prima

bottom half N (*of box*) parte *f* inferiore; (*of list, class*) seconda metà

bot·tom·less ['bɒtəmlɪs] ADJ (*pit*) senza fondo; (*funds, supply*) inesauribile

bottom line N: **the bottom line** (*Fin*) il risultato finanziario; (*essential point*) l'essenziale *m*; (*result*) il risultato

bot·tom·most ['bɒtəm,məʊst] ADJ ultimo(-a) (in basso), più basso(-a)

botu·lism ['bɒtjʊ,lɪzəm] N botulismo

bou·clé ['buːkleɪ] N lana (*or* tessuto) bouclé
■ ADJ bouclé *inv*

bou·gain·vil·lea, bou·gain·vil·laea [ˌbuːgən'vɪlɪə] N buganvillea

bough [baʊ] N ramo

bought [bɔːt] PT, PP *of* **buy**

boul·der ['bəʊldəʳ] N masso, macigno

boule·vard ['buːləvɑːʳ] N viale *m*

bounce [baʊns] N (*of ball*) rimbalzo; (*springiness: of hair, mattress*) elasticità; **he's got plenty of bounce** (*fig*) è molto esuberante
■ VT (*ball*) far rimbalzare
■ VI (*ball*) rimbalzare; (*child*) saltare, balzare; (*fam: cheque*) essere scoperto(-a) *or* a vuoto; **the ball bounced** la palla è rimbalzata; **the cheque he gave me bounced** (*fam*) l'assegno che mi ha dato era scoperto (*or* a vuoto); **to bounce in** entrare di slancio *or* con foga
▸ **bounce back** VI + ADV (*person*) riprendersi

bounc·er ['baʊnsəʳ] N (*fam*) buttafuori *m inv*

bounc·ing ['baʊnsɪŋ] ADJ: **bouncing baby** bambino(-a) pieno(-a) di salute

bouncy ['baʊnsɪ] ADJ (*comp* **-ier**, *superl* **-iest**) (*ball*) che rimbalza bene; (*hair*) vaporoso(-a); (*mattress*) (ben) molleggiato(-a); (*person*) dinamico(-a), esuberante

bouncy castle ® N *grande castello gonfiabile per giocare*

◎ **bound**[1] [baʊnd] PT, PP *of* **bind** ■ ADJ **1** (*prisoner*) legato(-a); **bound hand and foot** legato(-a) mani e piedi **2** (*book*) rilegato(-a) **3** (*certain*): **he's bound to say yes** vedrai che dirà di sì ; **he's bound to fail** sicuramente fallirà; **there are bound to be price rises** ci sarà sicuramente un aumento dei prezzi; **it was bound to happen** doveva succedere, era da prevedersi **4** (*obliged*): **to be bound to do sth** essere obbligato(-a) a *or* tenuto(-a) a fare qc; **I'm bound to say that ...** devo dire che...

bound[2] [baʊnd] ADJ (*destined*): **bound for** (*person, train, ship*) diretto(-a) a, in viaggio per; (*parcel*) indirizzato(-a) a, diretto(-a) a; **where are you bound (for)?** dove sei diretto?; **California bound** diretto(-a) in California; **westbound traffic** traffico diretto verso ovest

bound[3] [baʊnd] N (*jump*) salto, balzo
■ VI (*person, animal*) saltare, balzare; **he bounded out of bed** è saltato fuori *or* è balzato giù dal letto; **his heart bounded with joy** il cuore gli balzò in petto dalla gioia

bound[4] [baʊnd] VT: **bounded by** limitato(-a) da

bounda·ry ['baʊndərɪ] N confine *m*

bound·er ['baʊndəʳ] N maleducato(-a), cafone(-a)

bound·less ['baʊndlɪs] ADJ (*also fig*) illimitato(-a), sconfinato(-a)

bounds [baʊndz] NPL limiti *mpl*; **out of bounds** vietato *or* proibito l'accesso; **within the bounds of modesty** nei limiti della decenza; **his ambition knows no bounds** la sua ambizione è senza limiti *or* non conosce limiti

Bb

boun·ti·ful [ˈbaʊntɪfʊl] ADJ (*person*) munifico(-a); (*God*) misericordioso(-a); (*supply*) abbondante
boun·ty [ˈbaʊntɪ] N (*generosity*) liberalità, munificenza; (*reward*) taglia
bounty hunter N cacciatore *m* di taglie
bou·quet [ˈbʊkeɪ] N (*of flowers, wine*) bouquet *m inv*
Bourbon [ˈbʊəbən] ADJ, N borbonico(-a)
bour·bon [ˈbʊəbən] N (*Am also*: **bourbon whiskey**) bourbon *m inv*
bour·geois [ˈbʊəʒwɑː] ADJ, N borghese (*m/f*)
bour·geoi·sie [ˌbʊəʒwɑːˈziː] N borghesia
bout [baʊt] N **1** (*of illness, malaria*) attacco, accesso; **a severe bout of flu** una brutta influenza; **a drinking bout** una sbronza; **he's had several bouts of illness** è stato ammalato diverse volte; **a bout of hard work** un periodo di intenso lavoro **2** (*boxing match*) incontro
bou·tique [buːˈtiːk] N boutique *f inv*
bo·vine [ˈbəʊvaɪn] ADJ (*also fig: pej*) bovino(-a)
bow[1] [bəʊ] N arco; (*Mus*) archetto; (*knot*) fiocco, nodo
bow[2] [baʊ] N inchino; **to take a bow** inchinarsi al pubblico *or* all'applauso del pubblico
■VT (*lower: head*) chinare; (*bend: back*) curvare, piegare; **bowed down by cares** schiacciato(-a) dalle preoccupazioni
■VI: **to bow (to)** inchinarsi (a), fare un inchino (a); (*fig: yield*) inchinarsi (di fronte a); **to bow to the inevitable** rassegnarsi all'inevitabile
▸ **bow down** VI + ADV: **to bow down (to)** prostrarsi (davanti a)
▸ **bow out** VI + ADV (*fig*) uscire di scena
bow[3] [bau] N (*Naut: bows*) prua; **on the port/starboard bow** di prua a sinistra/a destra
bowd·ler·ize [ˈbaʊdləˌraɪz] VT espurgare
bow·el [ˈbaʊəl] N (*gen pl*) intestino, intestini *mpl*; **cancer of the bowel** cancro all'intestino; **bowels of the earth** viscere *fpl* della terra
bow·ing [ˈbəʊɪŋ] N (*Mus*) archeggio
◎ **bowl[1]** [bəʊl] N **1** (*for soup*) scodella; (*for cereal, fruit*) coppetta; (*mixing bowl*) terrina; (*for salad*) insalatiera; (*for washing up*) bacinella, catino; **bowl of cornflakes** ciotola di cornflakes; **bowl of soup** piatto di minestra **2** (*hollow: of lavatory*) tazza; (: *of spoon*) incavo, cavo; (: *of pipe*) fornello **3** (*Am: stadium*) stadio
▸ **bowl over** VT + ADV rovesciare (a terra); (*fig*) lasciare strabiliato(-a)
bowl[2] [bəʊl] VT (*ball*) lanciare
■VI (*Cricket*) servire; (*Bowls*) tirare
bow-legged [ˌbəʊˈlɛgɪd] ADJ (*person*) con le gambe arcuate
bowl·er [ˈbəʊləʳ] N **1** (*Cricket*) lanciatore(-trice); (*Bowls*) giocatore(-trice) di bocce **2** (*Brit: bowler hat*) bombetta
bow·line [ˈbəʊlɪn] N (*Naut: bowline knot*) gassa d'amante
bowl·ing [ˈbəʊlɪŋ] N (*indoor*) bowling *m inv*; (*on grass*) gioco delle bocce; **to go bowling** andare a giocare a bowling
bowling alley N (pista da) bowling *m inv*
bowling green N campo da bocce (*su erba*)
bowls [bəʊlz] NSG gioco delle bocce; **he plays bowls** gioca a bocce
bow·man [ˈbaʊmən] N (*pl* **-men**) (*Naut*) prodiere *m*
bow·sprit [ˈbəʊˌsprɪt] N (*Naut*) bompresso
bow tie [ˌbəʊˈtaɪ] N (cravatta a) farfalla
bow window [ˌbəʊˈwɪndəʊ] N bow-window *m inv*
bow-wow [ˈbaʊˌwaʊ] N (*dog, noise*) bau bau *m inv*
◎ **box[1]** [bɒks] N **1** scatola; (*crate, also for money*) cassetta; (*for jewels*) cofanetto; (*on page*) casella; **a box of matches** una scatola di fiammiferi; **the box** (*fam: TV*) la tele; **to watch the box** guardare la tele **2** (*Theatre*) palco; (*Law: for witness, press etc*) banco
▸ **box in** VT + ADV (*bath*) incassare; (*car*) incastrare; **to feel boxed in** sentirsi imprigionato(-a)

DID YOU KNOW ...?
box is not translated by the Italian word *box*

box[2] [bɒks] N: **a box on the ear** uno scapaccione
■VT: **to box sb's ears** prendere qn a scapaccioni
■VI (*Sport*) fare il pugile; (: *fight*) combattere
box[3] [bɒks] N (*Bot*) bosso
box·car [ˈbɒkskɑːʳ] N (*Am*) carro merci *inv*
box·er [ˈbɒksəʳ] N (*Sport*) pugile *m*, boxeur *m inv*; (*dog*) boxer *m inv*
box file N scatola di archivio
box·ing [ˈbɒksɪŋ] N (*Sport*) pugilato, boxe *f*
Boxing Day N (*Brit*) ≈ Santo Stefano

BOXING DAY

Il **Boxing Day**, è il primo giorno infrasettimanale dopo Natale e cade generalmente il 26 di dicembre. Prende il nome dall'usanza di donare pacchi regalo natalizi, un tempo chiamati "Christmas boxes", a fornitori e dipendenti.
▹ www.pch.gc.ca/progs/cpsc-ccsp/jfa-ha/boxing_e.cfm

boxing gloves NPL guantoni *mpl* (da pugile *or* da boxe)
boxing match N incontro di pugilato
boxing ring N ring *m inv*
box junction N (*Brit Aut*) area d'incrocio
box number N (*for advertisements*) casella
box office N botteghino
box·room [ˈbɒksˌrʊm] N (*Brit*) ripostiglio, stanzino
◎ **boy** [bɔɪ] N ragazzo; (*small*) bambino; (*son*) figlio; (*servant*) servo; **a boy of fifteen** un ragazzo di quindici anni; **a boy of seven** un bambino di sette anni; **she has two boys and a girl** ha due maschi e una femmina; **she had a boy** ha avuto un maschio; **a baby boy** un maschietto; **school for boys** scuola maschile; **when I was a boy** quand'ero piccolo; **boys will be boys** che vuoi, sono maschi; **he's out with the boys** è fuori con gli amici; **old boy** vecchio mio; **my dear boy** mio caro; **oh boy!** mamma mia!
boy band N boy band *f inv*; *gruppo pop di soli ragazzi creato per far presa su un pubblico giovane*
boy·cott [ˈbɔɪkɒt] N boicottaggio
■VT boicottare
◎ **boy·friend** [ˈbɔɪˌfrɛnd] N ragazzo; **he's not her boyfriend, they're just friends** non è il suo ragazzo, sono solo amici
boy·hood [ˈbɔɪhʊd] N infanzia; (*as teenager*) adolescenza
boy·ish [ˈbɔɪɪʃ] ADJ (*appearance, manner*) da ragazzo
Bp ABBR = **bishop**
bps [ˌbiːpiːˈes] N ABBR (*Comput* = **bits per second**) bps *m inv*
BR [ˌbiːˈɑːʳ] N ABBR = **British Rail**
bra [brɑː] N reggiseno
brace [breɪs] N **1** (*Constr*) rinforzo, sostegno; (*dental*) apparecchio (ortodontico), macchinetta (per i denti); (*Typ*) graffa **2** (*pl inv: pair: of game birds*) coppia, paio
■VT (*strengthen*) rinforzare; **to brace o.s.** (*also fig*) tenersi forte

DID YOU KNOW ...?
brace is not translated by the Italian word *brace*

brace and bit N trapano a manubrio
brace·let ['breɪslɪt] N braccialetto
braces ['breɪsɪz] NPL (*Brit*) bretelle *fpl*
brac·ing ['breɪsɪŋ] ADJ (*air*) tonificante, vivificante
brack·en ['brækən] N (*plant*) felce *f*; (*area of bracken*) felci *pl*
brack·et ['brækɪt] N **1** (*support*) sostegno; (*shelf*) mensola **2** (*Typ: usu pl*) parentesi *f inv*; **round/square brackets** parentesi tonde/quadre; **in brackets** tra parentesi **3** (*group*) categoria, gruppo; **income bracket** fascia di reddito; **age brackets** fascia d'età
■VT (*Typ*) mettere tra parentesi; (*fig: bracket together*) mettere insieme
brack·ish ['brækɪʃ] ADJ (*water*) salmastro(-a)
brad·awl ['bræd,ɔ:l] N punteruolo
brag [bræg] VT, VI: **to brag (about/that)** vantarsi (di)
brag·gart ['brægət] N (*old*) spaccone *m*
brag·ging ['brægɪŋ] N vanterie *fpl*
■ADJ (*tone*) da spaccone(-a)
Brah·min, Brah·man ['brɑ:mən] N brahmano, bramino
braid [breɪd] N (*on dress*) spighetta; (*Mil, on dressing gown*) cordoncino; (*trimming*) passamano; (*of hair*) treccia
■VT (*hair*) intrecciare
Braille [breɪl] N braille *m*
◎**brain** [breɪn] N **1** (*Anat*) cervello; (*Culin*): **brains** NPL cervella *sg*; **to blow one's brains out** farsi saltare le cervella; **he's got cars on the brain** ha il chiodo fisso delle macchine **2** (*fig fam: intelligence*): **brains** NPL testa; **he's got brains** ha (del) cervello, è intelligente; **he's the brains of the family** è il cervellone di casa
■VT (*fam*) spaccare la testa a
brain·child ['breɪn,tʃaɪld] N creatura, creazione *f*
brain damage N danno cerebrale
brain damaged [-,dæmɪdʒd] ADJ cerebroleso(-a)
brain·dead ['breɪn,dɛd] ADJ (*Med*) che ha subito morte cerebrale; (*fam*) decerebrato(-a), deficiente
brain death N morte *f* clinica
brain drain N fuga di cervelli
brain haemorrhage N emorragia cerebrale
brain·less ['breɪnlɪs] ADJ deficiente, stupido(-a)
brain·storm ['breɪn,stɔ:m] N (*Brit fig*) attacco di pazzia; (*Am*) = **brainwave**
brain·storming ['breɪn,stɔ:mɪŋ] N brain-storming *m inv*
brains trust N trust *m inv* dei cervelli
brain tumour N tumore *m* al cervello
brain·wash ['breɪn,wɒʃ] VT: **to brainwash sb (into doing sth)** fare il lavaggio del cervello a qn (per convincerlo a fare qc)
brain·wash·ing ['breɪn,wɒʃɪŋ] N lavaggio del cervello
brain·wave ['breɪn,weɪv] N (*fam*) idea brillante, lampo di genio
brainy ['breɪnɪ] ADJ (*comp* **-ier**, *superl* **-iest**) (*fam*) geniale
braise [breɪz] VT (*Culin*) brasare
brake [breɪk] N (*on vehicle*) freno; **to put on** *or* **apply the brakes** (*Aut*) azionare i freni; **to put the brakes on sth** (*fig*) mettere un freno a qc
■VI frenare
brake drum N tamburo del freno
brake fluid N olio dei freni
brake light N (fanalino dello) stop *m inv*
brake lining N guarnizione *f* del freno, ferodo®
brake pedal N pedale *m* del freno
brake shoe N ganascia
brak·ing ['breɪkɪŋ] N frenatura
■ADJ (*distance, power*) di frenatura
bram·ble ['bræmbl] N rovo; (*fruit*) mora
bran [bræn] N crusca
◎**branch** [brɑ:ntʃ] N (*also fig*) ramo; (*in road, railway, pipe*) diramazione *f*; (*Comm: of company, bank*) filiale *f*, succursale *f*
■VI (*road*) diramarsi, ramificarsi
▸ **branch off** VI + ADV (*road, path*) diramarsi; (*speaker*) divagare
▸ **branch out** VI + ADV: **to branch out into** (*business*) estendere la propria attività nel ramo di; (*person*) mettersi nel ramo di; **he's branched out on his own** si è messo in proprio
branch line N (*Rail*) linea secondaria
branch manager N direttore *m* di filiale
branch office N filiale *f*, succursale *f*
◎**brand** [brænd] N **1** (*Comm*) marca **2** (*on cattle, prisoner*) marchio; **a famous brand** una marca famosa; **brand loyalty** fedeltà a un marchio
■VT (*cattle, fig: person*) marchiare; **his name is branded on my memory** il suo nome è impresso indelebilmente nella mia memoria; **he was branded (as) a traitor** (*fig pej*) fu tacciato di tradimento
brand·ed ['brændɪd] ADJ di marca
branding-iron ['brændɪŋ,aɪən] N (ferro da) marchio
bran·dish ['brændɪʃ] VT brandire
brand leader N (*Comm*) marca più comune
brand name N marca
brand-new ['brænd'nju:] ADJ nuovo(-a) di zecca, nuovo(-a) fiammante
bran·dy ['brændɪ] N brandy *m inv*
brandy snap N *cialda allo zenzero*
bran mash N pastone *m*
brash [bræʃ] ADJ (*impudent*) sfrontato(-a), sfacciato(-a)
Bra·silia [brə'zɪljə] N Brasilia
brass [brɑ:s] N **1** ottone *m*; **the brass** (*Mus*) gli ottoni **2** (*fam*): **to have the brass (neck) to do sth** avere la faccia tosta di fare qc; **the top brass** (*Mil*) i pezzi grossi dell'esercito
■ADJ (*ornament etc*) d'ottone
brass band N fanfara
brassed off ['brɑ:st-] ADJ (*Brit*): **to be brassed off (with sth)** essere stufo(-a) (di qc)
bras·siere ['bræsɪəʳ] N reggiseno
brass rub·bing ['brɑ:s,rʌbɪŋ] N *ricalco di figure e iscrizioni tombali*
brass tacks NPL: **to get down to brass tacks** (*fam*) venire al sodo
brass·ware ['brɑ:s,wɛəʳ] N ottoni *mpl*
brassy ['brɑ:sɪ] ADJ (*comp* **-ier**, *superl* **-iest**) (*voice, sound*) squillante; (*colour*) chiassoso(-a); (*pej: tone*) insolente; (*: woman*) appariscente
brat [bræt] N (*fam pej*) moccioso(-a); **he's a spoiled brat** è un moccioso viziato
bra·va·do [brə'vɑ:dəʊ] N spavalderia
◎**brave** [breɪv] ADJ coraggioso(-a); **be brave** coraggio!, sii forte!
■N (*Native American*) guerriero *m* pellerossa *inv*
■VT (*weather, danger*) sfidare; **to brave it out** affrontare la situazione
brave·ly ['breɪvlɪ] ADV coraggiosamente
brav·ery ['breɪvərɪ] N coraggio
bra·vo ['brɑ:'vəʊ] EXCL bravo!, bene!

Bb

brawl [brɔ:l] N rissa
■VI azzuffarsi
brawn [brɔ:n] N muscoli *mpl*; (*Culin*) ≈ soppressata
brawny ['brɔ:nɪ] ADJ muscoloso(-a)
bray [breɪ] N raglio
■VI ragliare
bra·zen ['breɪzn] ADJ (*shameless*) sfacciato(-a)
■VT: **to brazen it out** continuare con la massima faccia tosta
bra·zen·ly ['breɪzənlɪ] ADV sfacciatamente
bra·zi·er ['breɪzɪəʳ] N braciere *m*
Bra·zil [brə'zɪl] N Brasile *m*
Bra·zil·ian [brə'zɪlɪən] ADJ, N brasiliano(-a)
Brazilian bikini wax, brazilian N depilazione *f* completa del pube
Brazil nut N noce *f* del Brasile
breach [bri:tʃ] N **1** (*violation: of law*) violazione *f*; (*: of rules*) infrazione *f*; (*: of duty*) abuso **2** (*gap: in wall*) apertura, varco; (*Mil*) breccia; (*estrangement*) rottura
■VT (*defences*) far breccia in
breach of contract N inadempienza di contratto
breach of the peace N violazione *f* dell'ordine pubblico
breach of trust N abuso di fiducia
◎**bread** [brɛd] N pane *m*; (*fam: money*) grana; **brown bread** pane integrale; **sliced white bread** pancarrè *m*; **to earn one's daily bread** guadagnarsi il pane; **to know which side one's bread is buttered on** saper da che parte conviene stare
▷ http://breadnet.net/
bread and butter N: **it's his bread and butter** (*livelihood*) è il suo pane
bread·basket ['brɛd,bɑ:skɪt] N cestino per il pane
bread·bin ['brɛd,bɪn] N (*Brit*) cassetta *f* portapane *inv*
bread·board ['brɛd,bɔ:d] N tagliere *m* (*per il pane*); (*Comput*) pannello per esperimenti
bread·box ['brɛd,bɒks] N (*Am*) cassetta *f* portapane *inv*
bread·crumb ['brɛd,krʌm] N mollica
bread·crumbs ['brɛd,krʌmz] NPL briciole *fpl*; (*Culin*) pangrattato; **fried in breadcrumbs** panato(-a) e fritto(-a)
bread·fruit ['brɛd,fru:t] N frutto dell'albero del pane
bread·knife ['brɛd,naɪf] N (*pl* **-knives** ['brɛd,naɪvz]) coltello per il pane *or* da pane
bread·line ['brɛd,laɪn] N: **to be on the breadline** sbarcare a malapena il lunario
breadth [brɛtθ] N (*also fig*) larghezza; **to be 2 metres in breadth** misurare 2 metri di larghezza, essere largo(-a) 2 metri
breadth·ways ['brɛtθ,weɪz], **breadth·wise** ['brɛtθ,waɪz] ADV nel senso della larghezza
bread·winner ['brɛd,wɪnəʳ] N chi mantiene la famiglia, chi porta i soldi a casa (*fam*); **to be the breadwinner** guadagnare il pane per tutta la famiglia
◎**break** [breɪk] (*vb: pt* **broke**, *pp* **broken**) N
1 (*gen*) rottura; (*fracture*) fenditura; (*: in bone*) frattura; (*in wall, fence*) apertura; (*gap*) breccia; (*in line, row, electric circuit*) interruzione *f*; **with a break in her voice** con voce rotta *or* incrinata dall'emozione; **a break in the clouds** una schiarita; **a break in the weather** un cambiamento di tempo; **at break of day** allo spuntare del giorno, sul far del giorno; **to make a break for it** darsela a gambe
2 (*in conversation*) pausa, interruzione *f*; (*rest: in journey*) sosta; (*tea break*) intervallo; (*Scol*) ricreazione *f*, intervallo; (*holiday*) vacanza; **the Christmas break** le vacanze di Natale; **to have** *or* **take a break** (*few minutes*) fare una pausa; (*rest, holiday*) prendere un po' di riposo; **without a break** senza una pausa
3 (*fam: chance*) possibilità *f inv*; **a lucky break** un colpo di fortuna; **give me a break!** dammi questa possibilità!; (*leave me alone*) lasciami respirare!; (*be reasonable*) ma per carità!
■VT **1** (*gen*) rompere; (*bone*) rompere, fratturare; (*skin*) lacerare; (*surpass: record*) battere; **I've broken a glass** ho rotto un bicchiere; **to break one's back/leg** rompersi la schiena/gamba; **he broke the world record** ha battuto il record mondiale; **to break the surface** (*submarine, diver*) affiorare (alla superficie); **to break a code** decifrare un codice; **to break sb's heart** (*fig*) spezzare il cuore a *or* di qn; **to break the ice** (*fig*) rompere il ghiaccio
2 (*law, rule*) violare; (*promise*) mancare a; (*vow*) rompere; (*appointment*) disdire, mandare all'aria; **to break the law** infrangere la legge
3 (*resistance, spirits*) fiaccare, annientare; (*health*) rovinare; (*strike*) domare, stroncare; **I can't break the habit** non riesco a perdere il vizio; **to break sb** (*financially*) mandare in rovina qn
4 (*silence, spell*) rompere; (*journey*) spezzare, interrompere; (*electrical circuit*) interrompere
5 (*soften: force*) smorzare; (*: fall, blow*) attutire
6 (*bad news*): **to break the news to sb** comunicare per primo la notizia a qn; **try to break it to her gently** cerca di dirglielo con tatto
■VI **1** (*gen*) rompersi; (*wave*) frangersi, infrangersi; (*fig: heart*) spezzarsi; **careful, it'll break!** stai attento che si rompe!; **to break into tiny pieces** andare in frantumi *or* in mille pezzi; **the stick broke in two** il bastone si è spezzato in due; **let's break for lunch** facciamo una sosta per pranzo; **to break with sb** (*fig*) rompere con qn; **to break free** *or* **loose** liberarsi
2 (*dawn, day*) spuntare; (*storm*) scoppiare; (*news*) saltare fuori
3 (*health, spirits*) cedere; (*weather*) cambiare; (*heatwave*) finire; (*voice: boy's*) cambiare; (*: in emotion*) rompersi
▶ **break away** VI + ADV: **to break away (from)** staccarsi (da); (*Ftbl etc*) scattare via (da)
▶ **break down** VT + ADV
1 (*door*) buttare giù, abbattere; (*resistance*) stroncare
2 (*analyse: figures*) analizzare; (*: substance*) scomporre
■VI + ADV (*machine*) rompersi, guastarsi; (*Aut*) restare in panne, avere un guasto, rompersi; (*person: under pressure*) crollare; (*: from emotion*) scoppiare in lacrime; (*: mentally*) avere un esaurimento (nervoso); (*health*) cedere; (*talks*) arenarsi; **she broke down and wept** è crollata e si è messa a piangere
▶ **break even** VI (*in business*) coprire le spese; (*in gambling*) finire pari
▶ **break in** VT + ADV
1 (*door*) sfondare
2 (*train: horse*) domare; (*: new recruit*) addestrare
■VI **1** (*burglar*) fare irruzione; **the thief had broken in through a window** il ladro era entrato forzando una finestra
2 (*interrupt*): **to break in (on sb/sth)** interrompere (qn/qc)
▶ **break into** VI + PREP
1 (*house*) fare irruzione in; (*safe*) scassinare, forzare; (*savings*) intaccare; **thieves broke into the house** dei ladri sono entrati in casa
2 (*begin suddenly*): **to break into song/a trot** mettersi a cantare/trottare

▸ **break off** VT + ADV (*piece*) staccare, spezzare; (*talks, engagement*) rompere
■ VI + ADV
1 (*twig*) staccarsi
2 (*speaker*) interrompersi; (*stop*): **to break off (from doing sth)** smettere (di fare qc); **to break off from work** interrompere il lavoro
▸ **break open** VT (*door*) sfondare
▸ **break out** VI + ADV
1 (*prisoners*): **to break out (of)** evadere (da)
2 (*war, fire, argument*) scoppiare; (*violence*) esplodere; **to break out in spots** coprirsi di macchie
▸ **break through** VI + ADV (*Mil*) aprirsi un varco, sfondare; **the sun broke through** il sole ha fatto capolino tra le nuvole
■ VI + PREP (*defences, barrier*) penetrare in, sfondare; (*crowd*) aprirsi un varco in *or* tra, aprirsi un passaggio in *or* tra
▸ **break up** VT + ADV (*rocks etc*) fare a pezzi, spaccare; (*marriage*) finire; (*crowd, clouds*) disperdere; (*fight etc*) interrompere, far cessare; **police broke up the demonstration** la polizia ha disperso i dimostranti
■ VI + ADV (*ship*) andare in *or* a pezzi, sfondarsi; (*ice*) spaccarsi, disintegrarsi; (*partnership, meeting*) sciogliersi; (*couple*) separarsi; (*marriage*) andare in pezzi, finire; (*crowd, clouds*) disperdersi; (*school*) chiudere; **Richard and Marie have broken up** Richard e Marie si sono lasciati; **the schools break up tomorrow** le scuole chiudono domani; **we break up next Wednesday** mercoledì cominciano le vacanze

break·able ['breɪkəbl] ADJ fragile
break·ables ['breɪkəblz] NPL oggetti *mpl* fragili
break·age ['breɪkɪdʒ] N danni *mpl*; **to pay for breakages** pagare i danni
break·away ['breɪkə,weɪ] ADJ (*group*) scissionista, dissidente
break-dancing ['breɪk,dɑ:nsɪŋ] N breakdance *f*
break·down ['breɪkdaʊn] N **1** (*of machine*) guasto, rottura; (*in system, communications*) interruzione *f*, sospensione *f* di servizio; (*Aut*) guasto, panne *f inv*; (*of talks, in relations*) rottura; (*Med*) collasso; (: *mental*) esaurimento nervoso; **accidents and breakdowns** incidenti e guasti; **we had a breakdown near Leeds** siamo rimasti in panne vicino a Leeds; **the breakdown of their marriage** la fine del loro matrimonio **2** (*of figures*) resoconto analitico; (*Chem*) scomposizione *f*; **a breakdown of the costs** un'analisi dei costi
breakdown service N servizio di soccorso stradale
breakdown van N carro *m* attrezzi *inv*
break·er ['breɪkə^r] N (*wave*) frangente *m*
break·even chart ['breɪki:vən'tʃɑ:t] N grafico del punto di pareggio
break·even point ['breɪk,i:vən'pɔɪnt] N punto di rottura *or* pareggio
◎ **break·fast** ['brɛkfəst] N (prima) colazione *f*; **to have breakfast** fare colazione
■ VI: **to breakfast (on)** fare colazione (con)
breakfast cereal N fiocchi *mpl* d'avena (*or* di mais *etc*)
breakfast television N programmi *mpl* televisivi del mattino
breakfast time N ora di colazione
break-in ['breɪk,ɪn] N irruzione *f*
break·ing and en·ter·ing ['breɪkɪŋənd'ɛntərɪŋ] N (*Law*) violazione *f* di domicilio con scasso
breaking news ['breɪkɪŋ,nju:z] N (*TV*) ultima ora
break·ing point ['breɪkɪŋ,pɔɪnt] N punto di rottura; (*fig: of person*) limite *m* di sopportazione
break·neck ['breɪk,nɛk] ADJ: **at breakneck speed** a rotta di collo
break-out ['breɪk,aʊt] N evasione *f*
break·through ['breɪk,θru:] N (*in research*) scoperta decisiva; (*Mil*) breccia; **they have made a breakthrough in the search for the cause of the disease** hanno fatto una scoperta decisiva nella ricerca sulle cause della malattia
break-up ['breɪk,ʌp] N (*of partnership, marriage*) rottura
break-up value N (*Comm*) valore *m* di realizzo
break·water ['breɪk,wɔ:tə^r] N frangiflutti *m inv*
bream [bri:m] N abramide *m* comune
◎ **breast** [brɛst] N (*Anat, Culin*) petto; (*of woman*) seno, mammella; **chicken breast** petto di pollo; **to make a clean breast of it** (*fig*) vuotare il sacco
■ VT (*finishing tape*) toccare
breast·bone ['brɛst,bəʊn] N sterno
breast-fed ['brɛst,fɛd] ADJ allattato(-a) al seno
breast-feed ['brɛst,fi:d] (*pt, pp* **breast-fed**) VT, VI allattare (al seno)
breast-feeding ['brɛst,fi:dɪŋ] N allattamento al seno
breast pocket N taschino
breast·stroke ['brɛst,strəʊk] N (nuoto a) rana; **to swim** *or* **do the breaststroke** nuotare a rana
◎ **breath** [brɛθ] N fiato, alito; (*act of breathing*) respiro; **she drew a deep breath** fece un respiro profondo; **bad breath** alito cattivo; **in the same breath** nello stesso istante; **out of breath** senza fiato; **under one's breath** sotto voce; **to go out for a breath of air** uscire a prendere una boccata d'aria; **to hold one's breath** trattenere il fiato *or* il respiro; **to get one's breath back** riprendere fiato; **it took my breath away** mi ha lasciato senza fiato, mi ha mozzato il respiro
breatha·lyse, (*Am*) **breatha·lyze** ['brɛθə,laɪz] VT sottoporre ad alcoltest *or* alla prova del palloncino (*fam*)
Breatha·lyz·er, **Breatha·lys·er**® ['brɛθə,laɪzə^r] N (*Brit*) alcoltest *m inv*
◎ **breathe** [bri:ð] VT (*air*) respirare; (*sigh*) tirare; **he breathed garlic all over me** mi ha soffiato addosso il suo alito puzzolente d'aglio; **I won't breathe a word about it** non fiaterò; **to breathe new life into sb/sth** (*fig*) ridar vita a qn/qc
■ VI respirare; **to breathe heavily** ansimare, avere il fiato grosso; **now we can breathe again** (*fig*) adesso possiamo riprendere fiato
▸ **breathe in** VI + ADV inspirare
■ VT + ADV respirare
▸ **breathe out** VT + ADV, VI + ADV espirare
breath·er ['bri:ðə^r] N (*fam*) attimo di respiro
breath·ing ['bri:ðɪŋ] N respiro, respirazione *f*; **heavy breathing** (*on phone*) respiro ansimante (*di maniaco*)
breathing apparatus N (*of diver*) autorespiratore *m*
breathing rate N frequenza respiratoria
breathing space N (*fig*) attimo di respiro
breath·less ['brɛθlɪs] ADJ (*exhausted*) senza fiato; (*with excitement*) con il fiato sospeso; (*silence*) religioso(-a); (*anticipation, anxiety*) vivissimo(-a); **his asthma makes him breathless** l'asma gli fa mancare il fiato
breath·less·ly ['brɛθlɪslɪ] ADV senza fiato
breath·taking ['brɛθ,teɪkɪŋ] ADJ (*sight*) mozzafiato *inv*
breath test N ≈ prova del palloncino
bred [brɛd] PT, PP *of* **breed**
-bred [brɛd] SUFF: **to be well/ill-bred** essere beneducato(-a)/maleducato(-a)

Bb

breech [bri:tʃ] N (*of gun*) culatta
breech birth N parto podalico
breeches ['brɪtʃɪz] NPL (*knee breeches*) calzoni *mpl* alla zuava; (*riding breeches*) pantaloni *mpl* da cavallo
◎ **breed** [bri:d] (*vb: pt, pp* **bred**) N razza, varietà *f inv*; (*fig*) tipo, specie *f inv*
■ VT allevare; (*fig: hate, suspicion*) generare, provocare; **to breed dogs** allevare cani
■ VI (*animals*) riprodursi; **they rarely breed in captivity** in cattività si riproducono raramente
breed·er ['bri:dəʳ] N **1** (*person*) allevatore(-trice) **2** (*Phys: breeder reactor*) reattore *m* autofertilizzante
breed·ing ['bri:dɪŋ] N (*of stock*) allevamento; (*reproduction*) riproduzione *f*; (*of person: good breeding*) (buona) educazione *f*
breeding ground N (*of animal*) zona di riproduzione; (*fig*) terreno fertile (*fig*)
breeze [bri:z] N brezza, venticello; **land/sea breeze** brezza di terra/di mare
■ VI: **to breeze in/out** (*jauntily*) entrare/andarsene *etc* allegramente come se niente fosse; (*briskly*) entrare/andarsene *etc* in fretta
breeze block N (*Brit*) *mattone composto di scorie di coke*
breezy ['bri:zɪ] ADJ (*day, weather*) ventoso(-a); (*spot*) ventilato(-a), ventoso(-a); (*optimism*) superficiale; (*person's manner*) brioso(-a), gioviale
breth·ren ['brɛðrɪn] (*Rel*) NPL *of* **brother**
Bret·on ['brɛtən] ADJ bretone
■ N (*person*) bretone *m/f*; (*language*) bretone *m*
brev·ity ['brɛvɪtɪ] N brevità
brew [bru:] N (*of beer*) fermentazione *f*; (*of tea, herbs*) infuso; **a strong brew** (*of beer*) una qualità forte; (*of tea*) un tè forte
■ VT (*beer*) produrre; (*tea, coffee*) fare; (*herbs*) fare un infuso di; (*fig: scheme, mischief*) macchinare, tramare
■ VI (*beer*) fermentare; (*tea*) farsi; (*fig: storm, crisis*) prepararsi; (*: plot*) ordirsi; **there's trouble brewing** c'è aria di burrasca; **something's brewing** qualcosa bolle in pentola
▸ **brew up** VI + ADV (*Brit*) **1** (*make tea*) preparare il tè; **I'll be brewing up about ten** preparerò il tè verso le dieci **2** (*storm, dispute*) prepararsi; **a big storm was brewing up** si preparava un grosso temporale
brew·er ['bru:əʳ] N birraio
brew·ery ['bru:ərɪ] N fabbrica di birra
brew·ing ['bru:ɪŋ] N fabbricazione *f* della birra
brew-up ['bru:,ʌp] N (*fam*): **to have a brew-up** farsi un tè
bri·ar ['braɪəʳ] N (*bramble*) rovo; (*wild rose*) rosa selvatica; (*pipe*) pipa in radica
briar·root ['braɪə,ru:t], **briar·wood** ['braɪə,wʊd] N radica
bribe [braɪb] N bustarella
■ VT corrompere; **to bribe sb to do sth** pagare qn sottobanco perché faccia qc
brib·ery ['braɪbərɪ] N corruzione *f*
bric-a-brac ['brɪkə,bræk] N, NO PL bric-à-brac *m inv*
brick [brɪk] N (*single*) mattone *m*; (*material*) mattoni *mpl*; (*toy*) cubo; **building bricks** (gioco delle) costruzioni *fpl*; **he came down on me like a ton of bricks** (*fig*) ancora un po' e mi mangiava; **to drop a brick** (*fig fam*) fare una gaffe; **to meet** *or* **come up against a brick wall** (*fig*) trovarsi davanti un ostacolo insormontabile; **I felt I was banging my head against a brick wall** mi sembrava di parlare al muro; **you can't make bricks without straw** (*Proverb*) non si può far niente senza l'occorrente
▸ **brick in, brick up** VT + ADV murare
brick·bat ['brɪk,bæt] N pezzo di mattone; (*fig*) critica
brick-built ['brɪk,bɪlt] ADJ di mattoni
brick·layer ['brɪk,leɪəʳ] N muratore *m*
brick·work ['brɪk,wɜ:k] N muratura in mattoni
brick·works ['brɪk,wɜ:ks] N fabbrica di mattoni
brid·al ['braɪdl] ADJ (*veil, gown*) da sposa, nuziale; (*feast, procession*) nuziale; **bridal party** corteo nuziale
bride [braɪd] N sposa; **the bride and groom** gli sposi, gli sposini
bride·groom ['braɪd,gru:m] N sposo
brides·maid ['braɪdz,meɪd] N damigella d'onore
◎ **bridge¹** [brɪdʒ] N (*gen, Dentistry*) ponte *m*; (*Naut*) ponte di comando, plancia; **bridge of the nose** setto nasale
■ VT gettare un ponte su; **to bridge a gap** (*fig: in knowledge*) colmare una lacuna; (*: in budget*) colmare un disavanzo
bridge² [brɪdʒ] N (*Cards*) bridge *m inv*
▷ www.worldbridge.org
▷ www.pagat.com//boston/bridge.html
bridge·head ['brɪdʒ,hɛd] N (*Mil*) testa di ponte
bridg·ing loan ['brɪdʒɪŋ'ləʊn] N (*Brit*) prefinanziamento
bri·dle ['braɪdl] N briglia
■ VT mettere le briglie a, imbrigliare
■ VI (*with indignation*) adombrarsi, adontarsi
bridle path N sentiero (per cavalli)
◎ **brief** [bri:f] ADJ (*visit, period, moment, speech*) breve; (*glimpse*) veloce, breve; **for a brief moment I thought ...** per un attimo ho creduto...; **I caught a brief glimpse of the queen** ho intravisto per un attimo la regina; **in brief ...** in breve..., a farla breve...
■ N **1** (*Law*) dossier *m inv* **2** (*Mil, gen*) istruzioni *fpl*; **that's outside my brief** non è di mia competenza
■ VT (*Mil*) dare istruzioni a; **to brief sb (about sth)** (*person*) mettere qn al corrente (di qc); (*Law*) affidare una causa a
brief·case ['bri:f,keɪs] N cartella, ventiquattr'ore *f inv*
brief·ing ['bri:fɪŋ] N briefing *m inv*, istruzioni *fpl*
brief·ly ['bri:flɪ] ADV (*speak, visit*) brevemente; (*glimpse*) di sfuggita
brief·ness ['bri:fnɪs] N brevità
briefs [bri:fs] NPL (*man's*) slip *m inv*, mutande *fpl*; (*woman's*) slip *m inv*, mutandine *fpl*; **a pair of briefs** un paio di slip
bri·er ['braɪəʳ] N = **briar**
Brig. ABBR = **brigadier**
bri·gade [brɪ'geɪd] N (*Mil, also hum*) brigata
briga·dier [,brɪgə'dɪəʳ] N generale *m* di brigata
brig·and ['brɪgənd] N bandito, brigante *m*
◎ **bright** [braɪt] ADJ **1** (*day, weather*) sereno(-a); (*room*) luminoso(-a); (*eyes, star, gem, surface*) lucente, brillante; (*sunshine*) splendente; (*light, lamp*) forte; (*fire, flame*) vivo(-a); (*colour*) vivace; **bright intervals** (*Met*) schiarite *fpl*; **bright red** rosso acceso **2** (*cheerful: person*) vispo(-a), allegro(-a); (*: expression*) radioso(-a), animato(-a); (*: future*) brillante, radioso(-a); **bright and early** di buon'ora, di buon mattino; **to look on the bright side** vedere il lato positivo delle cose **3** (*clever: person*) intelligente, dotato(-a); (*: idea, move*) brillante, geniale; **he's not very bright** non è molto sveglio
bright·en ['braɪtn] VT (*also:* **brighten up**: *colour*) ravvivare; (*television picture*) alzare la luminosità di; (*house, room*) rallegrare; (*situation*) migliorare; **a child will brighten up your life** un figlio allieterà la tua vita

■ VI (*also:* **brighten up**: *person*) rianimarsi, rallegrarsi; (*eyes, expression*) illuminarsi; (*weather*) schiarirsi

bright lights NPL: **the bright lights of the big city** (*fig*) l'eccitante vita della metropoli

bright·ly ['braɪtlɪ] ADV (*smile*) radiosamente; (*behave, talk*) con animazione; (*shine*) vivamente, intensamente

bright·ness ['braɪtnɪs] N (*of room*) luminosità; (*of eyes, star*) lucentezza; (*of sunshine*) splendore *m*; (*of flame, colour*) vivacità

bright spark N genio

brill [brɪl] EXCL (*Brit fam*) stupendo!, fantastico!

bril·liance ['brɪljəns] N (*of light*) intensità; (*of colour*) vivacità; (*fig: of person*) genialità

◎ **bril·liant** ['brɪljənt] ADJ (*sunshine*) sfolgorante; (*light, idea, person, success*) brillante; **it's a brilliant idea!** è un'idea fantastica!; **we had a brilliant time!** ci siamo divertiti moltissimo!; **a brilliant scientist** uno scienziato geniale

brim [brɪm] N (*of cup*) orlo; (*of hat*) tesa, falda
■ VI: **to brim (over) with** traboccare di; **eyes brimming with tears** occhi colmi di lacrime

brim·ful ['brɪm'fʊl] ADJ: **brimful (of)** pieno(-a) fino all'orlo (di), traboccante (di); (*fig: confidence, enthusiasm*) pieno(-a) (di); **brimful of happiness** traboccante di felicità

brine [braɪn] N (*Culin*) salamoia; (*liter: sea water*) mare *m*; **tuna in brine** tonno al naturale

◎ **bring** [brɪŋ] (*pt, pp* **brought**) VT (*gen*) portare; (*dissatisfaction, storm*) provocare; (*consequences*) avere; **bring warm clothes** porta vestiti pesanti; **can I bring a friend?** posso portare un amico?; **I've brought you a present** ti ho portato un regalo; **to bring relief** dare sollievo; **to bring luck** portare fortuna; **to bring tears to sb's eyes** fare venire a qn le lacrime agli occhi; **to bring sth to an end** mettere fine a qc; **to bring sth on o.s.** (*fig*) tirarsi qc addosso; **he was brought to justice** fu consegnato alla giustizia; **I couldn't bring myself to say no** non ce l'ho fatta a dirgli di no

▸ **bring along** VT + ADV portare con sé

▸ **bring about** VT + ADV
1 (*change, crisis*) causare, provocare
2 (*turn*): **to bring a boat about** far virare di bordo un'imbarcazione

▸ **bring back** VT + ADV (*person, object*) riportare; (*souvenir*) portarsi a casa; (*memories*) risvegliare; (*old method*) reintrodurre; **he's taken your drill — he'll bring it back tomorrow** ha preso il trapano — lo riporterà domani; **she brought a friend back for dinner** ha portato un'amica a casa per cena; **that song brings back memories** quella canzone mi fa tornare in mente tanti ricordi

▸ **bring down** VT (*lower: prices, temperature*) far scendere; (*opponent: also Ftbl, Rugby*) atterrare; (*enemy plane*) abbattere; (*government*) far cadere

▸ **bring forth** VT + ADV
1 (*protests, criticism*) suscitare
2 (*child*) mettere al mondo

▸ **bring forward** VT + ADV
1 (*person*) far venire avanti; (*chair*) spostare in avanti; (*witness, proof*) produrre
2 (*advance time of: meeting*) anticipare; **the date was brought forward** la data è stata anticipata
3 (*Book-keeping*) riportare

▸ **bring in** VT + ADV
1 (*person*) fare entrare; (*object*) portare dentro; (*Parliament: bill*) presentare; (*: legislation*) introdurre; (*Law: verdict*) emettere
2 (*produce: income*) rendere

▸ **bring off** VT + ADV
1 (*plan, enterprise*) far riuscire, realizzare; (*deal*) concludere; **he didn't bring it off** (*fam*) (il colpo) non gli è riuscito
2 (*people from wreck*) portare in salvo

▸ **bring on** VT + ADV
1 (*illness*) provocare; (*crops, flowers*) far spuntare
2 (*Theatre: performer*) fare entrare; (*: object*) portare in scena; (*Sport: player*) mandare in sostituzione, far scendere in campo

▸ **bring out** VT + ADV (*meaning*) mettere in luce; (*colour, weaknesses*) far risaltare; (*qualities*) valorizzare, mettere in luce; (*new product*) lanciare; (*book*) pubblicare, fare uscire

▸ **bring round** VT + ADV
1 (*persuade*): **to bring sb round (to the idea of sth)** persuadere qn (a fare qc)
2 (*steer: conversation*): **to bring round to** portare su, far cadere su
3 (*unconscious person*) far rinvenire, rianimare

▸ **bring to** VT (*unconscious person*) far rinvenire

▸ **bring together** VT + ADV (*people: introduce*) far incontrare; (*: reconcile*) riconciliare

▸ **bring up** VT + ADV (*person*) far salire; (*rear: child*) allevare; (*mention: question*) sollevare; (*: fact, problem*) far presente; (*vomit*) rimettere, rigurgitare; **she brought up five children on her own** ha allevato cinque figli da sola

bring-and-buy sale [ˌbrɪŋənd'baɪseɪl] N ≈ vendita di beneficenza

brink [brɪŋk] N orlo; **on the brink of doing sth** sul punto di fare qc; **she was on the brink of tears** era lì lì per piangere; **on the brink of collapse** sull'orlo di un collasso

brink·man·ship ['brɪŋkmənʃɪp] N strategia del rischio calcolato

brisk [brɪsk] ADJ (*person, tone*) spiccio(-a), sbrigativo(-a); (*: abrupt*) brusco(-a); (*walk*) svelto(-a); (*wind*) fresco(-a); (*trade*) vivace, attivo(-a); **she was brisk and efficient** era svelta ed efficiente; **business is brisk** gli affari vanno bene; **at a brisk pace** di buon passo; **to go for a brisk walk** fare una camminata di buon passo

bris·ket ['brɪskɪt] N punta di petto

brisk·ly ['brɪsklɪ] ADV (*move, speak*) bruscamente; (*walk*) di buon passo; (*act*) senza indugi; **the wind was blowing briskly** soffiava un vento fresco

brisk·ness ['brɪsknɪs] N (*of person, tone*) sbrigatività; (*of walk*) rapidità; (*of trade*) vivacità; (*of wind*) freschezza

bris·tle ['brɪsl] N (*of beard, animal*) pelo; (*of boar, brush*) setola; **pure bristle brush** spazzola di pura setola; **brush with nylon bristles** spazzola di nylon
■ VI (*also:* **bristle up**) rizzarsi; **to bristle with** (*fig: pins, difficulties*) essere irto(-a) di; (*policemen, guards*) brulicare di; **he bristled with anger** fremeva di rabbia

bris·tly ['brɪslɪ] ADJ (*chin*) ispido(-a); (*beard, hair*) irsuto(-a), ispido(-a)

Brit [brɪt] N ABBR (*fam*) (= **Briton**) inglese *m/f*

Brit·ain ['brɪtən] N (*also:* **Great Britain**) la Gran Bretagna

BRITAIN

Chiamare "Inghilterra" la Gran Bretagna non solo è scorretto ma può anche risultare offensivo per gli scozzesi e i gallesi. È consigliabile usare Gran

Bb

Bretagna, **Britain** o **Great Britain**, Regno Unito, **the United Kingdom** (of Great Britain and Northern Ireland) o **UK**, Isole Britanniche, **the British Isles**.

La Gran Bretagna è la maggiore isola dell'arcipelago britannico e consta di tre regioni: Inghilterra, Scozia e Galles.

Le Isole Britanniche comprendono la Gran Bretagna, l'Irlanda, le Ebridi, le Orcadi, le Shetland, l'isola di Man, l'isola di Anglesey, l'isola di Wight e altre isole minori. Politicamente si distinguono il Regno Unito di Gran Bretagna e Irlanda del Nord e la Repubblica d'Irlanda o Eire.

Il Regno Unito è lo stato costituito da Gran Bretagna e Irlanda del Nord. È una monarchia parlamentare e fa parte dell'Unione Europea.

▷ www.ordnancesurvey.co.uk/oswebsite/freefun/geofacts/
▷ www.statistics.gov.uk/

Bri·tan·nia [brɪ'tænɪə] N la Britannia

Brit·ish ['brɪtɪʃ] ADJ *(economy, team)* britannico(-a), inglese; *(ambassador)* della Gran Bretagna, inglese
■ NPL: **the British** gli inglesi

Brit·ish Co·lum·bia ['brɪtɪʃkə'lʌmbɪə] N Columbia britannica
▷ www.gov.bc.ca
▷ www.bc-tourism.com

British Commonwealth N: **the British Commonwealth** il Commonwealth britannico

British Isles NPL: **the British Isles** le Isole britanniche

British Museum N British Museum *m*

British Rail N ≈ Ferrovie *fpl* dello Stato

British Standards Institution N: **the British Standards Institution** ≈ Ente *m* Nazionale Italiano di Unificazione

British Summer Time N ora legale *(in Gran Bretagna)*

Brit·on ['brɪtən] N inglese *m/f*, britannico(-a)

Brit·pop ['brɪtpɒp] N Britpop *m; musica pop britannica di metà anni '90*

Brit·ta·ny ['brɪtənɪ] N Bretagna

brit·tle ['brɪtl] ADJ fragile

bro. ABBR = brother

broach [brəʊtʃ] VT *(subject)* affrontare; *(bottle of wine)* stappare

B-road ['bi:,rəʊd] N *(Brit Aut)* ≈ strada secondaria

◎ **broad** [brɔ:d] ADJ *(street, smile)* largo(-a); *(mind, view)* aperto(-a); *(hint)* chiaro(-a), esplicito(-a); *(accent)* marcato(-a), spiccato(-a); *(distinction)* generale; **he's got broad shoulders** ha le spalle larghe; **3 metres broad** largo 3 metri; **with a broad smile** con un gran sorriso; **the broad outlines** le grandi linee; **in broad daylight** in pieno giorno; **in the broadest sense** nel senso più ampio
■ N *(Am fam offensive)* femmina

broad·band ['brɔ:dbænd] *(Comput)* N banda larga
■ ADJ a banda larga

broad bean N fava

◎ **broad·cast** ['brɔ:d,kɑ:st] *(vb: pt, pp* **broadcast***)* N *(TV, Radio)* trasmissione *f*
■ VT *(TV)* (tele)trasmettere, mandare in onda; *(Radio)* (radio)trasmettere, mandare in onda; *(fig: news, rumour)* diffondere; **don't broadcast it!** non spargerlo ai quattro venti!
■ VI *(station)* trasmettere; *(person)* fare una trasmissione; **to broadcast live** trasmettere in diretta

broad·cast·er ['brɔ:d,kɑ:stə^r] N giornalista *m/f* radiotelevisivo(-a)

◎ **broad·cast·ing** ['brɔ:d,kɑ:stɪŋ] N *(TV)* televisione *f*; *(Radio)* radiodiffusione *f*; *(broadcasts)* trasmissioni *fpl*

broadcasting station N stazione *f* trasmittente

broad·en ['brɔ:dn] VT *(scope, outlook)* allargare; **the party needs to broaden its appeal** il partito deve far presa su un maggior numero di persone; **to broaden one's mind** allargare i propri orizzonti
■ VI *(also:* **broaden out***)* allargarsi

broad·ly ['brɔ:dlɪ] ADV: **broadly speaking** grosso modo, in linea di massima; **smiling broadly** con un gran sorriso

broadly-based [,brɔ:dlɪ'beɪst] ADJ con ampia base; **he wants it to be a broadly-based movement** vuole che sia un movimento con un'ampia base

broad-minded [,brɔ:d'maɪndɪd] ADJ *(person)* di mente aperta, di larghe vedute; *(attitude)* aperto(-a)

broad-mindedness ['brɔ:d'maɪndɪdnɪs] N larghezza di vedute

broad·ness ['brɔ:dnɪs] N *(see adj)* larghezza; apertura; chiarezza; **the broadness of his accent** il suo accento marcato

broad·sheet ['brɔ:d,ʃi:t] N *(Brit: newspaper)* quotidiano di grande formato

broad-shouldered [,brɔ:d'ʃəʊldəd] ADJ largo(-a) di spalle

broad·side ['brɔ:dsaɪd] N *(Naut)* bordata; *(fig)* attacco

bro·cade [brəʊ'keɪd] N broccato

broc·co·li ['brɒkəlɪ] N *(Bot)* broccolo; *(Culin)* broccoli *mpl*

bro·chure ['brəʊʃjʊə^r] N opuscolo, dépliant *m inv*

brogue¹ [brəʊg] N *(shoe)* scarpone *m*

brogue² [brəʊg] N *(accent)* accento irlandese

broil [brɔɪl] VT *(Am Culin)* fare alla griglia

broil·er ['brɔɪlə^r] N **1** *(chicken)* galletto **2** *(pan)* griglia

broke [brəʊk] PT *of* **break** ■ ADJ: **to be broke** *(fam)* essere al verde, essere spiantato(-a); **to go broke** andare in fallimento

bro·ken ['brəʊkən] PP *of* **break** ■ ADJ **1** *(gen)* rotto(-a); *(stick)* spezzato(-a); *(fig: marriage)* fallito(-a); *(: promise, vow)* infranto(-a), non rispettato(-a); *(: appointment)* mancato(-a); *(: health)* rovinato(-a); *(: spirit)* a pezzi; *(: heart)* infranto(-a); **a broken glass** un vetro rotto; **he comes from a broken home** i suoi sono divisi; **he's a broken old man** è un vecchio finito **2** *(uneven: surface, coastline)* irregolare; *(: ground)* accidentato(-a); *(interrupted: line)* spezzato(-a); *(: sleep)* agitato(-a); **to have a broken night** non riuscire dormire una notte di filato; **he speaks broken English** parla un inglese stentato

broken-down ['brəʊkən'daʊn] ADJ *(car)* in panne, rotto(-a); *(machine)* guasto(-a), fuori uso; *(house)* abbandonato(-a), in rovina

broken-hearted [,brəʊkən'hɑ:tɪd] ADJ affranto(-a) dal dolore, col cuore spezzato; **to be broken-hearted** avere il cuore spezzato

bro·ken·ly ['brəʊkənlɪ] ADV *(say)* con voce rotta; *(sob)* convulsamente

◎ **bro·ker** ['brəʊkə^r] N *(Comm)* mediatore(-trice); *(stock broker)* agente *m/f* di cambio

bro·ker·age ['brəʊkərɪdʒ] N *(Comm)* commissione *f* di intermediazione

brol·ly ['brɒlɪ] N *(Brit fam)* ombrello

bro·mide ['brəʊmaɪd] N *(Chem)* bromuro

bro·mine ['brəʊmi:n] N bromo

bron·chial ['brɒŋkɪəl] ADJ bronchiale

bronchial tubes NPL bronchi *mpl*
bron·chi·tis [brɒŋˈkaɪtɪs] N bronchite *f*
bron·chus [ˈbrɒŋkəs] N (*pl* **bronchi** [ˈbrɒŋkaɪ]) bronco
bron·to·sau·rus [ˌbrɒntəˈsɔːrəs] N brontosauro
bronze [brɒnz] N bronzo
■ADJ (*made of bronze*) di bronzo; (*colour*) bronzeo(-a), color del bronzo *inv*; **the bronze medal** la medaglia di bronzo
■VI abbronzarsi
■VT (*skin*) abbronzare; (*metal*) bronzare
Bronze Age N: **the Bronze Age** l'età del bronzo
bronzed [brɒnzd] ADJ (*person*) abbronzato(-a)
bronz·ing [ˈbrɒnzɪŋ] N (*of metal*) bronzatura
brooch [brəʊtʃ] N spilla, fermaglio
brood [bruːd] N (*of chicks*) covata; (*of birds*) nidiata; (*hum: of children*) prole *f*
■VI (*bird*) covare; (*fig: person*) rimuginare, stare a pensare; **there's no point brooding about the past** non c'è motivo di rimuginare sul passato
▸ **brood on** VI + PREP rimuginare su, stare a pensare a
brood mare N fattrice *f*
broody [ˈbruːdɪ] ADJ (*fig*) cupo(-a) e taciturno(-a)
brook[1] [brʊk] N ruscello
brook[2] [brʊk] VT (*frm: tolerate*) tollerare, ammettere
broom [brʊm] N (*brush*) scopa; (*Bot*) ginestra
broom·stick [ˈbrʊmˌstɪk] N manico di scopa
Bros. ABBR (*Comm:* = **brothers**) F.lli
broth [brɒθ] N minestra (in brodo), brodo
broth·el [ˈbrɒθl] N bordello
◎ **broth·er** [ˈbrʌðəʳ] N (*gen, Rel*) fratello; (*Trade Union etc*) compagno; **do you know her brother?** conosci suo fratello?
brother·hood [ˈbrʌðəˌhʊd] N fratellanza, fraternità; (*group*) confraternita
brother-in-law [ˈbrʌðərɪnˌlɔː] N cognato
broth·er·ly [ˈbrʌðəlɪ] ADJ fraterno(-a)
brother officers NPL compagni *mpl* d'armi
brother workers NPL compagni lavoratori
brought [brɔːt] PT, PP *of* **bring**
brought forward ADJ (*Comm*) riportato(-a)
brow [braʊ] N (*forehead*) fronte *f*; (*old: eyebrow*) sopracciglio; (*of hill*) cima; (*: on road*) dosso; **he wiped his brow** si è asciugato la fronte; **the brow of the hill** la cima della collina
brow·beat [ˈbraʊˌbiːt] (*pt* **browbeat**, *pp* **browbeaten**) VT intimidire; **to browbeat sb into doing sth** costringere qn a fare qc con la prepotenza
◎ **brown** [braʊn] ADJ (*gen*) marrone, bruno(-a); (*hair*) castano(-a); (*bronzed: skin*) scuro(-a), abbronzato(-a); **to go brown** (*person*) abbronzarsi; (*leaves*) ingiallire
■N marrone *m*
■VT (*Culin: meat*) rosolare; (*: onion*) dorare
■VI (*Culin*) rosolarsi
brown ale N birra scura
brown bear N orso bruno
brown bread N pane *m* integrale, pane nero
browned off [ˌbraʊndˈɒf] ADJ: **to be browned off (with sth)** (*fam*) essere stufo(-a) (di qc)
brown·field [ˈbraʊnfiːld] ADJ: **brownfield site** sito edificabile, già adibito in passato a uso industriale o residenziale
brown goods NPL (*Brit: Comm*) TV, stereo, hifi *ecc*, bruno *sg*
Brownie [ˈbraʊnɪ] N coccinella (*scout*), giovane esploratrice *f*
brown·ish [ˈbraʊnɪʃ] ADJ (*stain, mark*) marroncino(-a); (*colour, eyes*) sul marrone
brown paper N carta da pacchi *or* da imballaggio
brown rice N riso integrale
brown sugar N zucchero greggio
browse [braʊz] 1 VI (*in bookshop*) curiosare (*leggicchiando qua e là*); (*in other shop*) guardare in giro, curiosare; (*animal*) brucare; **to browse through a book** sfogliare un libro; **I'm just browsing!** sto solo curiosando! 2 (*Comput*) navigare
■VT: **to browse the Web** navigare in Internet
■N: **to have a browse (around)** dare un'occhiata (in giro)
brows·er [ˈbraʊzəʳ] N (*Comput*) browser *m inv*
bruise [bruːz] N (*on person*) livido; (*on fruit*) ammaccatura
■VT (*leg etc*) farsi un livido a; (*fruit*) ammaccare; (*fig: feelings*) urtare
■VI (*fruit*) ammaccarsi; **I bruise easily** mi vengono facilmente i lividi sulla pelle
bruis·er [ˈbruːzəʳ] N (*fam*) bullo
bruis·ing [ˈbruːzɪŋ] N ecchimosi *f inv*
■ADJ (*encounter, experience*) brutto(-a); (*criticism, defeat*) pesante
Brum [brʌm], **Brum·ma·gem** [ˈbrʌmədʒəm] N (*fam*) = Birmingham
Brum·mie [ˈbrʌmɪ] N (*fam: resident*) abitante *m/f* di Birmingham; (*: native*) originario(-a) di Birmingham
brunch [ˈbrʌntʃ] N (*fam*) *ricca colazione consumata a tarda mattina che sostituisce il pranzo*
bru·nette [bruːˈnɛt] N ragazza (*or* donna) bruna
brunt [brʌnt] N: **to bear the brunt of sth** (*of attack, criticism*) sostenere l'urto di qc; (*of work, cost*) sostenere il peso di qc
◎ **brush** [brʌʃ] N 1 (*gen*) spazzola; (*broom*) scopa; (*hearth brush*) scopettino, scopino; (*scrubbing brush*) spazzola per pavimenti; (*paint brush*) pennello; **hair/shoe brush** spazzola per capelli/da scarpe 2 (*act of brushing*) spazzolata, colpo di spazzola 3 (*quarrel*) schermaglia; **to have a brush with sb** (*verbally*) avere uno scontro con qn; (*physically*) venire alle mani con qn; **to have a brush with the police** avere delle noie con la polizia 4 (*light touch*) lieve tocco; **he felt the brush of her hair against his face** sentiva i capelli di lei che gli sfioravano il viso 5 (*undergrowth*) boscaglia, sottobosco
■VT 1 (*clean: floor*) scopare; (*: clothes, hair*) spazzolare; (*: shoes*) lucidare, spazzolare; (*: teeth*) lavarsi; **to brush one's teeth** lavarsi i denti 2 (*touch lightly*) sfiorare
▸ **brush against** VI + PREP sfiorare
▸ **brush aside** VT + ADV (*fig: protest, objection*) ignorare, rifiutarsi di ascoltare; (*: idea, feeling*) ignorare
▸ **brush away** VT + ADV (*dirt: on clothes*) togliere (con la spazzola); (*: on floor*) scopar via; (*tears*) asciugarsi; (*insects*) cacciare (via)
▸ **brush down** VT + ADV dare una spazzolata a
▸ **brush off** VT + ADV (*mud*) levare con la spazzola; (*fig: suggestion*) scartare; (*: criticism, attentions*) ignorare
▸ **brush past** VI + PREP sfiorare (passando)
▸ **brush up** VT + ADV 1 (*crumbs*) raccogliere (con la spazzola) 2 (*also:* **brush up on**: *revise*) dare una rinfrescata *or* una ripassata a; **to brush up one's English** rispolverare il proprio inglese
brushed [brʌʃt] ADJ 1 (*Tech: steel, chrome*) sabbiato(-a) 2 (*nylon, denim*) pettinato(-a)
brush-off [ˈbrʌʃˌɒf] N (*fam*): **to give sb the brush-off** mandare qn a quel paese
brush-up [ˈbrʌʃˌʌp] N ripulita

Bb

brush·wood ['brʌʃ,wʊd] N (*undergrowth*) sottobosco; (*cuttings*) rami *mpl* tagliati
brush·work ['brʌʃ,wɜ:k] N (*Art*) tocco
brusque [bru:sk] ADJ (*person, manner*) brusco(-a); (*tone*) secco(-a)
brusque·ly ['bru:sklɪ] ADV (*behave, speak*) bruscamente
brusque·ness ['bru:sknɪs] N modi *mpl* bruschi, asprezza
Brus·sels ['brʌslz] N Bruxelles *f*
Brussels sprout N cavoletto di Bruxelles
bru·tal ['bru:tl] ADJ brutale
bru·tal·ity [bru:'tælɪtɪ] N brutalità
bru·tal·ize ['bru:təlaɪz] VT (*harden*) abbrutire; (*ill-treat*) brutalizzare
bru·tal·ly ['bru:təlɪ] ADV brutalmente
brute [bru:t] N (*animal*) bestia; (*person*) bruto; **you brute!** mostro!
■ADJ (*force, strength*) bruto(-a); **by brute force** a viva forza, con la forza
brut·ish ['bru:tɪʃ] ADJ da bruto
Brutus ['bru:təs] N Bruto
BS [bi:'ɛs] N ABBR **1** (= **British Standard**) *numero di standardizzazione assegnato a un certo prodotto dal BSI* **2** (*Am: Univ:* = **Bachelor of Science**) laurea in Scienze **3** (*Am: fam!*) (= **bullshit**) stronzate *fpl* (*fam!*)
bs ABBR = **bill of sale**
BSA [,bi:ɛs'eɪ] N ABBR (*Am*) = **Boy Scouts of America**
BSc [,bi:ɛs'si:] N ABBR (= **Bachelor of Science**) laurea in scienze
BSE [,bi:ɛs'i:] N ABBR (= **bovine spongiform encephalopathy**) encefalite *f* bovina spongiforme
BSI [,bi:ɛs'aɪ] N ABBR = **British Standards Institution**
BST [,bi:ɛs'ti:] N ABBR (= **British Summer Time**) ora legale in Gran Bretagna
Bt ABBR (*Brit*) = **baronet**
btu [,bi:ti:'ju:] N ABBR (= **British thermal unit**) Btu *f* (= *unità termica britannica*)
BTW [,bi:ti:'dʌbljʊ] ABBR (= **by the way**) a proposito
bubble ['bʌbl] N **1** bolla; (*smaller*) bollicina; **soap bubble** bolla di sapone **2** (*Comm: speculative bubble*) bolla speculativa **3** (*of cartoon: speech bubble*) fumetto
■VI ribollire, fare bollicine; (*champagne*) spumeggiare
▸ **bubble over** VI + ADV traboccare; **to bubble over (with)** (*fig*) scoppiare (di *or* da), traboccare (di)
bubble bath N bagnoschiuma *m*
bubble gum N chewing-gum *m inv*
bubblejet printer [,bʌbldʒɛt'prɪntəʳ] N stampante *f* a getto d'inchiostro
bub·bly ['bʌblɪ] ADJ (*liquid*) effervescente; (*fig: personality*) spumeggiante
■N (*fam*) champagne *m inv*
bu·bon·ic plague [bju:'bɒnɪk'pleɪg] ADJ peste *f* bubbonica
buc·ca·neer [,bʌkə'nɪəʳ] N bucaniere *m*
Bu·cha·rest [,bu:kə'rest] N Bucarest *f*
buck [bʌk] N **1** (*Am fam: dollar*) dollaro; **this means big bucks for sb** vuol dire un sacco di soldi per qn **2** (*Zool*) maschio **3** (*of horse*) sgroppata; **to give a buck** dare una sgroppata **4 to pass the buck** (*fam*) scaricare le proprie responsabilità (*or* colpe *etc*) sugli altri
■VI (*horse*) sgroppare
▸ **buck up** (*fam*) VI + ADV (*cheer up*) tirarsi su; (*hurry up*) sbrigarsi, muoversi
■VT + ADV **1** (*make cheerful*) tirar su (il morale di) **2 to buck one's ideas up** (*fam*) darsi una mossa
buck·et ['bʌkɪt] N secchio; (*large*) secchia; **to kick the bucket** (*fam*) tirare le cuoia
■VI (*Brit fam*): **it's bucketing (down) (with rain)** piove a catinelle
bucket seat N sedile *m* anatomico
bucket shop N (*Brit*) *agenzia di viaggi che vende biglietti a prezzi scontati*
Buck·ing·ham Pal·ace [,bʌkɪŋəm'pælɪs] N Buckingham Palace *m*

BUCKINGHAM PALACE

Buckingham Palace è la residenza ufficiale a Londra del sovrano britannico. Costruita nel 1703 per il duca di Buckingham, fu acquistata nel 1762 dal re Giorgio III e ricostruita tra il 1821 e il 1838 sotto la guida dell'architetto John Nash. All'inizio del Novecento alcune sue parti sono state ulteriormente modificate. Attualmente è aperta al pubblico durante l'estate.
▷ www.royal.gov.uk/

buck·le ['bʌkl] N fibbia, fermaglio
■VT **1** (*shoe, belt*) allacciare **2** (*wheel, girder*) distorcere, piegare; (*warp*) deformare
■VI (*see vt*) allacciarsi, chiudersi con una fibbia; distorcersi, piegarsi
▸ **buckle down** VI + ADV: **to buckle down to a job** mettersi a lavorare d'impegno *or* di buzzo buono, mettersi sotto
buck·ram ['bʌkrəm] N tela rigida
Bucks [bʌks] N ABBR (*Brit*) = **Buckinghamshire**
buck·shee [,bʌk'ʃi:] ADJ, ADV (*fam: free*) gratis (*inv*)
buck·shot ['bʌk,ʃɒt] N pallettoni *mpl*
buck·skin ['bʌk,skɪn] N pelle *f* di daino
buck teeth NPL denti *mpl* da coniglio
buck-toothed [,bʌk'tu:θt] ADJ che ha i denti sporgenti
buck·wheat ['bʌk,wi:t] N grano saraceno
bu·col·ic [bju:'kɒlɪk] ADJ (*liter*) bucolico(-a), pastorale
bu·coli·cal·ly [bju:'kɒlɪklɪ] ADV (*liter*) bucolicamente
bud [bʌd] N (*of flower*) bocciolo, boccio; (*on tree, plant*) gemma, germoglio; **to be in bud** (*flower*) essere in boccio; (*tree*) germogliare
■VI (*plant, tree*) germogliare, mettere le gemme; (*flower*) sbocciare
Bu·da·pest [,bju:də'pɛst] N Budapest *f*
Buddha ['bʊdə] N Budda *m inv*
Bud·dhism ['bʊdɪzəm] N buddismo
▷ www.buddhanet.net/
Bud·dhist ['bʊdɪst] ADJ, N buddista (*m/f*)
bud·ding ['bʌdɪŋ] ADJ (*fig: talent*) in erba; (*flower*) in boccio
■N (*Bot*) gemmazione *f*
bud·dy ['bʌdɪ] N (*esp Am*) amico, compagno; **they've been buddies for years** sono amiconi da anni
budge [bʌdʒ] VT (*move*) spostare, smuovere; **I couldn't budge him an inch** (*fig*) non sono riuscito a smuoverlo di un dito
■VI muoversi, spostarsi; (*fig*) smuoversi; **she refused to budge from London** si è rifiutata di spostarsi da Londra; **they'll not budge on this point** non cambieranno opinione su questo punto
▸ **budge up** VI: **budge up, will you** fatti un po' più in là
budg·eri·gar ['bʌdʒərɪgɑ:ʳ] N pappagallino
Budget ['bʌdʒɪt] N (*Brit*): **the Budget** il bilancio (preventivo) dello Stato

◎ **budget** ['bʌdʒɪt] N bilancio (preventivo), budget *m inv*; **to be on a tight budget** avere un budget limitato; **I'm on a tight budget** ho i soldi contati; **she works out her budget every month** fa il preventivo delle spese ogni mese; **the defence budget** il budget per la Difesa; **budget price** prezzo ridotto
■ ADJ (*airline, flight*) a basso costo; (*prices, travel, holiday*) economico(-a)
■ VI fare un preventivo; (*household*) fare i propri conti; **I'm learning how to budget** sto imparando a gestire le mie finanze
▸ **budget for** VI + PREP mettere in conto *or* in preventivo, preventivare

budg·et·ary ['bʌdʒɪtərɪ] ADJ budgetario(-a); **the budgetary year** l'anno finanziario

budgie ['bʌdʒɪ] N ABBR = **budgerigar**

Bue·nos Aires ['bweɪnɒs'aɪrɪz] N Buenos Aires *f*

buff[1] [bʌf] **1** ADJ (*colour*) color paglierino *inv or* camoscio *inv* **2** (*fam*) in forma, tonico(-a)
■ VT (*also:* **buff up**) lucidare, lustrare
■ N: **in the buff** (*fam*) nudo(-a) come un verme

buff[2] [bʌf] N (*fam: enthusiast*) patito(-a), appassionato(-a); **a film buff** un espèrto di cinema

buf·fa·lo ['bʌfələʊ] N (*pl* **buffaloes**) (*wild ox*) bufalo(-a); (*esp Am: bison*) bisonte *m*

buff·er ['bʌfə^r] N **1** (*for railway engine*) respingente *m*; (*fig*) cuscinetto **2** (*Comput*) buffer *m inv*

buff·er·ing ['bʌfərɪŋ] N (*Comput*) bufferizzazione *f*, memorizzazione *f* transitoria

buffer state N stato *m* cuscinetto *inv*

buffer zone N zona *f* cuscinetto *inv*

buf·fet[1] ['bʊfeɪ] N (*for refreshments*) buffet *m inv*, bar *m inv*; (*meal*) buffet, rinfresco; **a cold buffet** un buffet freddo; **a buffet lunch** un buffet

buf·fet[2] ['bʌfɪt] N (*blow*) schiaffo; **the buffets of fate** (*fig*) le avversità della sorte
■ VT (*ship, car etc*) sballottare; (*house*) sferzare; (*fig: person*) travolgere

buffet car ['bufeɪˌkɑː^r] N (*Brit Rail*) ≈ servizio ristoro

buf·fet·ing ['bʌfɪtɪŋ] N (*of wind, waves*) violenza; **the ship took a buffeting in the storm** la nave fu sballottata violentemente durante la tempesta
■ ADJ (*wind*) violento(-a)

buffet lunch [ˌbufeɪ'lʌntʃ] N pranzo in piedi

buffet supper [ˌbufeɪ'sʌpə^r] N cena fredda

buf·foon [bə'fuːn] N buffone(-a); **to play the buffoon** fare il/la buffone(-a)

buf·foon·ery [bə'fuːnərɪ] N buffoneria

bug [bʌg] (*fam*) N **1** (*insect*) insetto; (*germ*) infezione *f*, virus *m inv*; (*fig: obsession*) mania, pallino; **there's a bug going round** c'è in giro un virus; **a stomach bug** una gastroenterite; **I've got the travel bug** (*fig*) mi è presa la mania dei viaggi **2** (*bugging device*) microspia, cimice *f* **3** (*Comput: in program*) errore *m* (nel programma), bug *m inv*
■ VT **1** (*telephone*) mettere sotto controllo; (*room*) installare microspie in **2** (*fam: annoy*) scocciare; **it really bugs me** mi rompe da morire

bug·bear ['bʌgˌbɛə^r] N spauracchio

bug·ger ['bʌgə^r] N **1** (*Law*) sodomita *m* **2** (*fam!*) stronzo (*fam!*); **you stupid bugger!** stronzo!; **poor little bugger!** (*child*) povera bestia!
■ EXCL (*fam!*): **bugger (it)!** merda! (*fam!*)
■ ADV (*fam!*): **bugger all** un cazzo (*fam!*); **I know bugger all about it** non ne so un cazzo
■ VT (*fam!: bugger up*) mandare a puttane *or* in vacca (*fam!*)
▸ **bugger about, bugger around** VI + ADV (*Brit fam!*) non fare un cazzo (*fam!*)
■ VT: **to bugger sb about** *or* **around** rompere le palle a qn (*fam!*)
▸ **bugger off** VI + ADV (*Brit fam!*) togliersi dalle palle (*fam!*); **why don't you bugger off and leave me in peace?** perché non ti togli dalle palle e mi lasci in pace?

bug·gery ['bʌgərɪ] N sodomia

bug·ging ['bʌgɪŋ] N utilizzazione *f* di microfoni nascosti

bugging device N microfono nascosto

bug·gy ['bʌgɪ] N (*also:* **baby buggy**) passeggino; (*cart: two-wheeled*) calesse *m*; (*: four-wheeled*) baghero

bu·gle ['bjuːgl] N (*Mus*) tromba

bu·gler ['bjuːglə^r] N trombettiere *m*

◎ **build** [bɪld] (*vb: pt, pp* **built**) N (*of person*) corporatura, fisico
■ VT (*house*) costruire, fabbricare; (*ship, town, machine*) costruire; (*nest*) fare; (*fig: relationship, career, empire*) costruire; **they're going to build houses here** qui costruiranno delle case; **a new bridge is being built** è in costruzione un nuovo ponte
▸ **build on** VT + ADV aggiungere
■ VT + PREP (*fig*) fondare su, basare su
▸ **build up** VT + ADV (*develop: business*) consolidare; (*: reputation*) fare, consolidare; (*increase: production*) allargare, incrementare; (*stocks etc*) accumulare; (*collection*) mettere insieme; (*spirits, morale*) tirar su; (*hopes*) far crescere; **he has built up a huge collection of stamps** ha messo insieme una vasta collezione di francobolli; **don't build your hopes up too soon** non sperarci troppo; **to build up one's strength** rimettersi in forze
■ VI + ADV (*pressure*) salire; (*Fin: interest*) accumularsi; **the music built up to a crescendo** la musica aumentava in un crescendo continuo; **debts are building up** si stanno accumulando i debiti

build·er ['bɪldə^r] N (*contractor*) costruttore *m*, imprenditore *m* (edile); (*workman*) muratore *m*; (*fig*) creatore(-trice)

◎ **build·ing** ['bɪldɪŋ] N **1** (*place*) costruzione *f*, edificio; (*block*) palazzo **2** (*no pl: activity*) costruzione *f*

building block N componente *m*

building contractor N costruttore *m*, imprenditore *m* (edile)

building industry, building trade N industria edilizia

building site N cantiere *m* di costruzione

building society N (*Brit*) ≈ istituto di credito immobiliare

BUILDING SOCIETY

Le **building societies** sono società immobiliari e finanziarie che forniscono anche numerosi servizi bancari ai clienti che vi investono i risparmi. Chi ha bisogno di un prestito per l'acquisto di una casa si rivolge in genere a una building society.

▷ http://news.bbc.co.uk/1/hi/business/2965412.stm

build-up ['bɪldʌp] N **1** (*of pressure, gas*) aumento, accumulo; (*Mil: of troops*) ammassamento; (*of traffic*) aumento di volume, intensificarsi *m*; (*fig: of tension*) aumento **2** (*publicity*) campagna pubblicitaria; **to give sb/sth a good build-up** fare buona pubblicità a qn/qc

built [bɪlt] PT, PP *of* **build**

Bb

built-in ['bɪlt,ɪn] ADJ (*cupboard*) a muro; (*device, feature*) incorporato(-a); **built-in wardrobe** armadio a muro
built-up ['bɪlt,ʌp] ADJ: **built-up area** abitato
bulb [bʌlb] N (*Bot, of thermometer*) bulbo; (*Elec*) lampadina; **a 100-watt bulb** una lampadina da 100 watt
bulb·ous ['bʌlbəs] ADJ a forma di bulbo, bulboso(-a)
Bul·garia [bʌl'gɛərɪə] N Bulgaria
Bul·gar·ian [bʌl'gɛərɪən] ADJ bulgaro(-a)
■N **1** (*person*) bulgaro(-a) **2** (*language*) bulgaro
bulge [bʌldʒ] N **1** (*in surface*) rigonfiamento; (*in plaster, metal*) bolla; (*curve: of thighs, hips*) curva **2** (*in birth rate, sales*) punta, rapido aumento; **the postwar bulge** l'esplosione demografica del dopoguerra
■VI (*stomach, muscles*) sporgere; (*pocket*): **to bulge (with)** essere gonfio(-a) (di); **the muscles in his neck bulged** gli sporgono i muscoli dal collo
bulg·ing ['bʌldʒɪŋ] ADJ (*see vi*) sporgente, gonfio(-a); **to be bulging with** essere pieno(-a) *or* zeppo(-a) di
bu·limia [bə'lɪmɪə] N bulimia
bulk [bʌlk] N (*of thing*) volume *m*, massa; (*of person*) corporatura massiccia; **the bulk of** la maggior parte di; **the bulk of the work** il grosso del lavoro; **to buy in bulk** comprare in grande quantità
bulk buy·ing ['bʌlk'baɪɪŋ] N *acquisto di merce in grande quantità*
bulk carrier N grossa nave *f* da carico
bulk·head ['bʌlk,hɛd] N (*Naut*) paratia
bulki·ness ['bʌlkɪnɪs] N (*of person*) corporatura massiccia; (*of thing*) voluminosità
bulky ['bʌlkɪ] ADJ grosso(-a), voluminoso(-a); **Mick's bulky figure** la figura massiccia di Mick
bull[1] [bʊl] N **1** toro; (*male of elephant, seal*) maschio; **like a bull in a china shop** come un elefante; **to take the bull by the horns** (*fig*) prendere il toro per le corna **2** (*Stock Exchange*) rialzista *m/f*

> DID YOU KNOW ...?
> **bull** is not translated by the Italian word *bullo*

bull[2] [bʊl] N (*Rel*) bolla (papale)
bull bar N (*Auto*) barre *fpl* di rinforzo anteriori
bull·dog ['bʊl,dɒg] N bulldog *m inv*
bull·doze ['bʊl,dəʊz] VT aprire *or* spianare col bulldozer; **I was bulldozed into doing it** (*fig*) mi ci hanno costretto con la prepotenza
bull·doz·er ['bʊldəʊzəʳ] N bulldozer *m inv*, apripista *m inv*
bul·let ['bʊlɪt] N proiettile *m*, pallottola
bullet hole N foro di proiettile
bul·letin ['bʊlɪtɪn] N (*statement*) comunicato (ufficiale); (*journal*) bollettino; **a bulletin was released at 3 o'clock** fu trasmesso un bollettino alle 3; **a news bulletin** un notiziario
bulletin board N (*Comput*) bulletin board *m inv*, bacheca elettronica
bullet point N punto; **bullet points** elenco *sg* puntato
bullet·proof ['bʊlɪt,pru:f] ADJ a prova di proiettile; **bulletproof vest** giubbotto *m* antiproiettile *inv*
bull·fight ['bʊl,faɪt] N corrida
bull·fighter ['bʊl,faɪtəʳ] N torero
bull·fighting ['bʊl,faɪtɪŋ] N tauromachia
bull·finch ['bʊl,fɪntʃ] N ciuffolotto
bull·frog ['bʊl,frɒg] N rana toro
bul·lion ['bʊljən] N oro (*or* argento) in lingotti
bull·ish ['bʊlɪʃ] ADJ (*Comm: market*) in rialzo; (*trader, person*) ottimista
bull market N (*Comm*) mercato in rialzo
bull-necked ['bʊl,nɛkt] ADJ dal collo taurino
bull·ock ['bʊlək] N manzo
bull·ring ['bʊl,rɪŋ] N arena (*per corride*)
bull's-eye ['bʊlz,aɪ] N (*of target*) centro (del bersaglio); **to hit the bull's-eye** (*fig*) far centro, colpire nel segno
bull·shit ['bʊl,ʃɪt] (*fam!*) N stronzate *fpl* (*fam!*)
■VI, VT raccontare stronzate (a) (*fam!*)
bull terrier N bull terrier *m inv*
bul·ly[1] ['bʊlɪ] N bullo, prepotente *m/f*; **he's a big bully** è un grande prepotente
■VT (*also:* **bully around**) fare il/la prepotente con; (*subj: children*) fare le prepotenze a; **to be bullied by** essere oggetto di prepotenze da parte di; **to bully sb into doing sth** far fare qc a qn con la prepotenza
bul·ly[2] ['bʊlɪ] N (*also:* **bully beef**) carne *f* di manzo in scatola
bul·ly·ing ['bʊlɪɪŋ] N prepotenze *fpl*
■ADJ (*person, tone, behaviour*) prepotente
bul·rush ['bʊl,rʌʃ] N stiancia
bul·wark ['bʊlwək] N (*Mil, fig*) baluardo, bastione *m*; (*Naut*) parapetto
bum[1] [bʌm] N (*Brit fam: bottom*) culo
bum[2] [bʌm] (*fam*) N (*esp Am: idler*) fannullone(-a); (*tramp*) barbone(-a), vagabondo(-a)
■ADJ scadente; **bum advice** consiglio di merda (*fam!*)
■VT (*money, food*) scroccare
▶ **bum around** VI + ADV (*fam*) vagabondare
bum-bag ['bʌm,bæg] N (*fam*) marsupio
bum·ble ['bʌmbl] VI **1** (*speak*) borbottare; **what on earth are you bumbling about?** che diavolo stai borbottando? **2** (*move*) muoversi goffamente
bumble·bee ['bʌmbl,bi:] N (*Zool*) bombo
bumf [bʌmf] N (*fam: documents, forms*) scartoffie *fpl*
bummed [bʌmd] ADJ (*Am fam*) stufo(-a)
bum·mer ['bʌməʳ] N (*fam*) rottura
bump [bʌmp] N **1** (*blow*) botta, colpo; (*noise*) botto; (*jolt of vehicle*) botta, scossa **2** (*lump*) bernoccolo, bozzo, gonfiore *m*; (: *on skin*) gonfiore; (: *on road*) cunetta, bozzo; **we felt a sudden bump** abbiamo sentito una scossa improvvisa; **I've got a bump on my forehead** ho un bernoccolo sulla fronte
■VT (*car*) urtare, sbattere; **to bump one's head** sbattere la testa
▶ **bump along** VI procedere sobbalzando
▶ **bump into** VI + PREP **1** (*vehicle*) andare a sbattere contro **2** (*fam: meet*) imbattersi in, incontrare per caso; **I bumped into Paul yesterday** ho incontrato per caso Paul, ieri; **fancy bumping into you!** ma guarda chi si vede!
▶ **bump off** VT + ADV (*fam*) far fuori
▶ **bump up** VT + ADV (*fam: increase: prices*) far salire, far aumentare; (: *sales*) incrementare
bump·er[1] ['bʌmpəʳ] N (*Brit Aut*) paraurti *m inv*
bump·er[2] ['bʌmpəʳ] ADJ: **bumper harvest** raccolto eccezionale
bumper cars NPL autoscontro
bumph [bʌmf] N = **bumf**
bump·tious ['bʌmpʃəs] ADJ arrogante, presuntuoso(-a)
bumpy ['bʌmpɪ] ADJ (*surface, road*) accidentato(-a), dissestato(-a), irregolare; (*journey, flight*) movimentato(-a); **we had a bumpy flight** abbiamo ballato *or* si ballava in volo
bun [bʌn] N (*Culin*) panino dolce; (*of hair*) chignon *m inv*, crocchia; **to wear one's hair in a bun** portare lo chignon

◎**bunch** [bʌntʃ] N *(of flowers, keys)* mazzo; *(posy)* mazzetto, mazzolino; *(of bananas)* casco; *(of grapes)* grappolo; *(set of people)* gruppo; **to wear one's hair in bunches** portare le codine; **the best of a bad bunch** il *(or* la *etc)* meno peggio
▸ **bunch together** VT + ADV *(objects)* ammucchiare
■ VI + ADV *(people)* ammucchiarsi

bun·dle ['bʌndl] N *(of clothes, rags)* fagotto, involto; *(of sticks)* fascina; *(of papers)* mucchio; *(of newspapers)* fascio; **to be a bundle of nerves** essere tesissimo(-a); essere un fascio di nervi
■ VT **1** *(also:* **bundle up**: *clothes)* fare un fagotto di, raccogliere in un mucchio; (: *papers)* fare un fascio di **2** *(put hastily)* riporre in fretta; (: *person)* spingere, caricare in gran fretta; **he was bundled into a car** è stato spinto in fretta su una macchina; **it's cheaper to buy software bundled with a PC** costa meno comprare il software assieme al PC
▸ **bundle off** VT + ADV *(person)* mandare via in gran fretta; **he was bundled off to Australia** l'hanno spedito in fretta e furia in Australia
▸ **bundle out** VT + ADV far uscire (senza tante cerimonie)

bun fight N *(Brit fam)* tè *m inv (ricevimento)*

bung [bʌŋ] N tappo, turacciolo
■ VT *(Brit fam: throw)* buttare
▸ **bung up** VT + ADV *(pipe, hole)* tappare, otturare; **my nose is bunged up** *(fam)* ho il naso otturato

bun·ga·low ['bʌŋgə,ləʊ] N bungalow *m inv*, villetta a un piano

bun·gee jump·ing ['bʌndʒɪ,dʒʌmpɪŋ] N *salto nel vuoto da ponti, grattacieli ecc, con un cavo fissato alla caviglia*

bun·gle ['bʌŋgl] *(fam)* VT fare un pasticcio di
■ VI fare pasticci

bun·gled ['bʌŋgld] ADJ: **it is a bungled job** è un lavoro raffazzonato

bun·gler ['bʌŋgləʳ] N pasticcione(-a)

bun·gling ['bʌŋglɪŋ] ADJ imbranato(-a)
■ N incompetenza

bunion ['bʌnjən] N callo (al piede)

bunk[1] [bʌŋk] N *(Naut, Rail)* cuccetta

bunk[2] [bʌŋk] N *(Brit fam)*: **to do a bunk** tagliare la corda
▸ **bunk off** VT, VI *(Brit fam)*: **to bunk off (school)** marinare la scuola

bunk beds NPL letti *mpl* a castello

bun·ker [bʌŋkəʳ] N *(coal bunker)* carbonaia; *(Mil, Golf)* bunker *m inv*

bun·kum ['bʌŋkəm] N *(fam)* scempiaggini *fpl*

bun·ny ['bʌnɪ] N *(also:* **bunny rabbit**) coniglietto

bunny girl N coniglietta

bunny hill N *(Am Skiing)* pista per principianti

Bun·sen ['bʌnsn] N: **Bunsen burner** becco Bunsen

bunt·ing ['bʌntɪŋ] N *(Naut)* gran pavese *m*; *(in street)* bandierine *fpl*

buoy [bɔɪ] N boa, gavitello
▸ **buoy up** VT + ADV *(person, boat)* tenere a galla; *(fig: spirits)* tener su; (: *hopes)* alimentare

buoy·an·cy ['bɔɪənsɪ] N *(Phys)* galleggiamento; *(of ship, object)* galleggiabilità; *(fig: of person)* ottimismo

buoy·ant [bɔɪənt] ADJ *(ship, log)* che galleggia (bene), galleggiante; *(fig: person)* di ottimo umore, su di corda; (: *nature)* ottimista; *(Fin: market)* sostenuto(-a); *(prices, currency)* stabile; **a buoyant economy** un'economia fiorente

bur·ble ['bɜːbl] VI **1** gorgogliare **2** *(pej)* borbottare; **what's he burbling (on) about?** che cosa sta borbottando?

◎**bur·den** ['bɜːdn] N *(load)* carico, peso; *(fig: of years, responsibility)* peso; *(of taxes, payment)* onere *m*; **the burden of proof lies with him** spetta a lui l'onere della prova; **to be a burden to sb** essere di peso a qn
■ VT: **to burden (with)** *(cares etc)* opprimere (con); **burdened with debts** oberato(-a) di debiti

bur·den·some ['bɜːdnsəm] ADJ *(load, task)* pesante; *(taxes, payment)* gravoso(-a), oneroso(-a)

bu·reau ['bjʊərəʊ] N **1** *(office)* ufficio, agenzia; *(government department)* dipartimento, sezione *f* **2** *(Brit: desk)* secrétaire *m inv*, scrittoio; *(Am: chest of drawers)* cassettone *m*

bu·reau·cra·cy [bjʊə'rɒkrəsɪ] N burocrazia

bu·reau·crat ['bjʊərəʊ,kræt] N burocrate *m/f*

bu·reau·crat·ic [,bjʊərəʊ'krætɪk] ADJ burocratico(-a)

bu·reau·crati·cal·ly [,bjʊərəʊ'krætɪkəlɪ] ADV burocraticamente

bu·reaux ['bjʊərəʊz] NPL *of* **bureau**

bu·rette [bjʊə'rɛt] N buretta

bur·geon ['bɜːdʒən] VI *(liter)* svilupparsi rapidamente

burg·er ['bɜːgəʳ] N hamburger *m inv*

burgh·er ['bɜːgəʳ] N cittadino(-a)

bur·glar ['bɜːgləʳ] N ladro(-a), scassinatore(-trice)

burglar alarm N antifurto *m inv*

bur·glar·ize ['bɜːglə,raɪz] VT *(Am)* svaligiare

burglar-proof ['bɜːglə,pruːf] ADJ antiscasso *inv*

bur·gla·ry ['bɜːglərɪ] N furto (con scasso)

bur·gle ['bɜːgl] VT *(house, shop)* svaligiare; **I've been burgled** mi hanno svaligiato la casa *(or* il negozio *etc)*

Bur·gun·dy ['bɜːgəndɪ] N Borgogna

bur·ial ['bɛrɪəl] N sepoltura, seppellimento

burial ground N cimitero

bur·lesque [bɜː'lɛsk] N parodia

bur·ly ['bɜːlɪ] ADJ ben piantato(-a), robusto(-a)

Bur·ma ['bɜːmə] N Birmania

Bur·mese ['bɜː'miːz] ADJ birmano(-a)
■ N *(person, cat)* birmano(-a); *(language)* birmano

◎**burn** [bɜːn] *(vb: pt, pp* **burned** *or* **burnt**) N *(gen)* bruciatura; *(superficial)* scottatura; *(Med)* ustione *f*
■ VT **1** *(gen)* bruciare; *(set fire to)* incendiare; *(person, skin: also of sun)* bruciare, scottare; *(toast, meat etc)* (far) bruciare; **to burn wood/coal** *(use as fuel: boiler etc)* andare a legna/carbone; **I burned the cake** ho bruciato la torta; **I've burned my hand** mi sono bruciato la mano; **badly burnt** ustionato(-a); **the cigarette burnt a hole in her dress** si è fatta un buco nel vestito con la sigaretta; **to be burnt to death** morire tra le fiamme, morire bruciato(-a) *or* carbonizzato(-a); *(at stake)* essere bruciato(-a) vivo(-a); **I've burnt myself!** mi sono bruciato!; **to burn one's boats** *or* **bridges** **2** *(Comput)* masterizzare; **to burn a CD** masterizzare un CD **3** *(fig)* bruciarsi i ponti alle spalle; **he's been burning the candle at both ends for too long** *(fig)* è da troppo tempo che abusa delle proprie energie
■ VI *(gen)* bruciare; *(fire)* ardere; *(skin, person)* bruciarsi, scottarsi; *(meat, pastry etc)* bruciarsi; *(light, gas)* essere *or* rimanere acceso(-a); **to burn with anger** *(fig)* fremere di rabbia; **to burn with fever** scottare per la febbre; **to burn to do sth** morire dalla voglia di fare qc
▸ **burn down** VT + ADV *(building)* bruciare, dare alle fiamme
■ VI + ADV *(house)* essere distrutto(-a) dal fuoco, bruciarsi; *(candle, fire)* consumarsi, abbassarsi; **the**

Bb

factory burned down la fabbrica è andata distrutta in un incendio
▸ **burn off** VT + ADV (*paint*) togliere col fuoco
▸ **burn out** VT + ADV (*subj: writer*): **to burn o.s. out** esaurirsi; (: *talent*): **to burn itself out** esaurirsi; (: *enthusiasm*) spegnersi
■ VI (*fuse*) saltare; (*candle, lamp*) spegnersi; (*fire*) estinguersi
▸ **burn up** VI (*fire*) ravvivarsi, divampare
■ VT + ADV (*rubbish*) bruciare

burn·er ['bɜ:nəʳ] N (*on cooker*) fornello; (*Tech*) bruciatore *m*, becco (a gas)

burn·ing ['bɜ:nɪŋ] N bruciato; **I can smell burning** sento odore di bruciato
■ ADJ (*building, forest*) in fiamme; (*coals*) acceso(-a); (*flame*) vivo(-a), ardente; (*fig: thirst, fever, desire*) bruciante, divorante; (*tears*) cocente; (*question, topic, issue*) scottante

bur·nish ['bɜ:nɪʃ] VT brunire

bur·nish·ing ['bɜ:nɪʃɪŋ] N brunitura

Burns Night ['bɜ:nz-] N *festa di commemorazione di Robert Burns*

BURNS NIGHT

Burns Night è la festa celebrata il 25 gennaio per commemorare il poeta scozzese Robert Burns (1759-1796). Gli scozzesi festeggiano questa data con una cena a base de "haggis" e whisky, spesso al suono di una cornamusa; durante la cena vengono recitate le poesie di Robert Burns e vengono letti discorsi alla sua memoria.
▷ www.bbc.co.uk/scotland/history/burnsnight/
▷ www.rabbie-burns.com/burnssupper/

burnt [bɜ:nt] PT, PP *of* **burn**

burnt sugar N (*Brit*) caramello

burp [bɜ:p] (*fam*) N rutto; (*of baby*) ruttino
■ VI ruttare, fare un rutto
■ VT (*baby*) far fare il ruttino a

burr, bur [bɜ:ʳ] N **1** (*Bot*) lappa, bardana **2** (*Ling*): **to speak with a burr** arrotare la erre **3** (*sound*) ronzio
■ VI (*plane*) ronzare; (*telephone*) suonare

bur·row ['bʌrəʊ] N (*of rabbit*) tana, cunicolo
■ VT (*hole*) scavare; **to burrow one's way (under/through** *etc*) scavarsi un tunnel (sotto/attraverso *etc*)
■ VI (*rabbits*) scavare gallerie; **he burrowed under the bedclothes** si è rintanato sotto le coperte

bur·sar ['bɜ:səʳ] N (*Univ*) economo(-a)

bur·sa·ry ['bɜ:sərɪ] N (*grant*) borsa di studio

◎ **burst** [bɜ:st] (*vb: pt, pp* **burst**) N (*of shell etc*) scoppio, esplosione *f*; (*in pipe*) rottura; (*of shots*) raffica, scarica; **a burst of applause** uno scroscio d'applausi; **a burst of laughter/activity** uno scoppio di risa/attività; **a burst of speed** uno scatto (di velocità)
■ VT (*gen*) far scoppiare *or* esplodere; (*bag*) sfondare, spaccare; **the river has burst its banks** il fiume ha rotto gli argini *or* ha straripato
■ VI **1** (*gen*) scoppiare; (*tyre: blow out*) scoppiare; (: *puncture*) bucarsi; (*shell, firework*) scoppiare, esplodere; (*bag*) sfondarsi, spaccarsi; (*dam*) cedere; (*blood vessel*) rompersi; **the balloon burst** il palloncino è scoppiato; **the door burst open** la porta si è spalancata di colpo; **filled to bursting point** pieno(-a) da scoppiare; **to be bursting with** (*health, energy*) scoppiare di; **to be bursting with pride** sprizzare soddisfazione da tutti i pori; **to be bursting at the seams (with)** essere pieno(-a) zeppo(-a) (di), traboccare (di); **the room was bursting at the seams** la stanza rigurgitava di persone; **I was bursting to tell you** (*fam*) morivo dalla voglia di dirtelo **2** (*go suddenly*): **to burst out of the room** scappare precipitosamente dalla stanza; **the sun burst through the clouds** è sbucato il sole
▸ **burst into** VI + PREP (*room*) irrompere in; **to burst into flames** prendere fuoco, andare in fiamme; **to burst into tears** scoppiare a piangere
▸ **burst out** VI + ADV **1** (*exclaim*) esclamare **2** (*start*): **to burst out laughing** scoppiare a ridere; **to burst out singing** mettersi (improvvisamente) a cantare

◎ **bury** ['berɪ] VT (*body, treasure*) seppellire; (*plunge: claws, knife*): **to bury (in)** affondare (in); **he buried his face in his hands** si coprì il volto con le mani; **buried by an avalanche** travolto(-a) da una valanga; **to bury the hatchet** (*fig*) seppellire l'ascia di guerra; **to bury one's head in the sand** (*fig*) fare (la politica del)lo struzzo

◎ **bus** [bʌs] N (*pl* **buses** *or* (*Am*) **busses**) autobus *m inv*; **to go by bus** andare in autobus; **I came by bus** sono venuto con l'autobus; **the school bus** il pulmino della scuola
■ ADJ (*driver, service, ticket*) d'autobus

bus boy N (*Am*) aiuto cameriere *m*

bush [bʊʃ] N **1** cespuglio **2** (*in Africa, Australia*): **the bush** la boscaglia

bush·baby ['bʊʃ,beɪbɪ] N galagone *m*

bushed [bʊʃt] ADJ (*fam: exhausted*) distrutto(-a)

bush·el ['bʊʃl] N staio

bush·fire ['bʊʃ,faɪəʳ] N grande incendio in aperta campagna

bushy ['bʊʃɪ] ADJ (*plant, tail, beard*) folto(-a); (*eyebrows*) irsuto(-a)

busi·ly ['bɪzɪlɪ] ADV con impegno, alacremente

◎ **busi·ness** ['bɪznɪs] N **1** (*commerce, trading*) affari *mpl*; **selling books is her business** di mestiere vende libri; **he's in the insurance business** lavora nel campo delle assicurazioni; **he's in the wool business** è nel commercio della lana; **I'm here on business** sono qui per affari; **to be away on business** essere via per affari; **to do business with sb** fare affari con qn; **let's get down to business** (*fam*) bando alle chiacchiere; **business is business** gli affari sono affari; **now we're in business!** ci siamo!; **she means business** fa sul serio, non scherza **2** (*firm*) impresa, azienda; **to set up a business** metter su un'impresa; **it's a family business** è un'impresa familiare; **he's got his own business** ha un'impresa in proprio **3** (*task, duty, concern, matter*) affare *m*; **to make it one's business to do sth** incaricarsi di fare qc; **that's none of your business** non sono affari tuoi, non ti riguarda; **that's my business** (è) affar mio, (sono) affari miei; **it's his business to see that ...** spetta a lui accertarsi che...; **you had no business to do that** non stava a te farlo; **mind your own business** bada ai fatti tuoi, non t'impicciare **4** (*fam: affair, matter*) storia, faccenda; **what an awful business it was!** che orrore che è stato!; **it's a nasty business** è una brutta faccenda, è un brutto affare
■ ADJ (*deal, quarter, relationship*) d'affari; (*studies*) commerciale
▷ www.bized.ac.uk/

business address N indirizzo sul lavoro

business card N biglietto da visita della ditta

business college N istituto commerciale

business expenses NPL spese *fpl*

business·like ['bɪznɪs,laɪk] ADJ *(approach, transaction)* efficiente; *(firm, company)* serio(-a); *(person, manner)* pratico(-a), efficiente

◎ **business·man** ['bɪznɪsmən] N *(pl* **-men***)* uomo d'affari, imprenditore

business plan N piano gestionale dell'impresa

business school N istituto universitario con corsi di gestione aziendale
▷ www.bized.ac.uk/

business sense N senso degli affari

business trip N viaggio d'affari

business·woman ['bɪznɪs,wʊmən] N *(pl* **-women***)* imprenditrice

busk [bʌsk] VI suonare *(or* cantare) per le strade

busk·er ['bʌskə^r] N *(Brit)* suonatore(-trice) ambulante

bus lane N *(Brit)* corsia preferenziale (per autobus)

bus pass N tessera dell'autobus

bus route N percorso dell'autobus

bus shelter N pensilina, fermata coperta

bus station N stazione *f* delle corriere, autostazione *f*

bus stop N fermata d'autobus

bust¹ [bʌst] N *(bosom)* petto, seno; *(Art)* busto
▸ **bust up** VT + ADV *(fam)* sfasciare

bust² [bʌst] *(fam)* ADJ *(broken)* rotto(-a), scassato(-a); **to go bust** *(bankrupt)* fallire, fare fallimento
■ VT **1** = **burst** VT **2** *(Police: arrest)* pizzicare, beccare; (: *raid*) fare irruzione in **3** *(break)* scassare

bust·er ['bʌstə^r] N: **come here, buster!** ehi tu, vieni qui!

bus·tle ['bʌsl] N trambusto
■ VI *(person: bustle about)* darsi da fare, affaccendarsi; *(place)* essere animatissimo(-a)

bus·tling ['bʌslɪŋ] ADJ *(person)* affaccendato(-a), indaffarato(-a); *(place, town)* animatissimo(-a)

bust measurement N giro *m* petto *inv*

bust-up ['bʌst,ʌp] N *(fam: argument)* lite *f*; **they had a bust-up** hanno rotto

busty ['bʌstɪ] ADJ *(woman)* dal seno prosperoso

◎ **busy** ['bɪzɪ] ADJ **1** *(occupied: person)* occupato(-a); **she's busy** *(at the moment)* è occupata; **she's a busy woman** è una donna molto impegnata *or* indaffarata; **he's busy studying/cooking** sta studiando/cucinando; **he's busy at his work** sta lavorando, è molto preso dal lavoro; **let's get busy** *(fam)* diamoci da fare **2** *(active: day, time)* movimentato(-a), intenso(-a); (: *place, town*) animato(-a); **I'd had a busy day and was tired** avevo avuto una giornata intensa ed ero stanco; **Christmas is a busy time of year** a Natale ci sono sempre mille cose da fare; **the Strand is one of London's busiest streets** lo Strand è una delle vie più animate di Londra; **the roads are busy** c'è molto traffico sulle strade **3** *(esp Am: telephone, line)* occupato(-a)
■ VT: **to busy o.s. (doing sth/with sth)** darsi da fare (a fare qc/con qc)

busy·body ['bɪzɪ,bɒdɪ] N ficcanaso *m/f*, impiccione(-a)

busy signal N *(Am)* segnale *m* di occupato

but [bʌt] KEYWORD
■ CONJ *(gen)* ma; **never a week passes but she's ill** mai una settimana che non stia male; **it's small but comfortable** *(car)* è piccola ma comoda
■ ADV solo, soltanto; **she's but a child** è solo una bambina, non è che una bambina; **had I but known** se solo l'avessi saputo; **I cannot help but think that ...** non posso fare a meno di pensare che...; **you can but try** tentar non nuoce
■ PREP eccetto, tranne, meno; **all but finished** quasi finito(-a); **anything but that** tutto ma non questo; **anything but finished** tutt'altro che finito(-a); **but for you** *(Brit)* se non fosse per te; **the last but one** il/la penultimo(-a); **I live in the next street but one** abito due strade più in su *(or* giù); **no one but him** solo lui; **no one but him can do it** è l'unico che lo sappia fare; **nothing but** null'altro che; **he was nothing but trouble** non dava altro che guai
■ N: **no buts about it!** non c'è ma che tenga!

bu·tane ['bju:teɪn] N *(also:* **butane gas***)* butano

butch [bʊtʃ] ADJ *(woman: pej)* mascolina; *(man)* macho *inv*

butch·er ['bʊtʃə^r] N *(also fig)* macellaio; **butcher's knife** coltello da macellaio; *(Culin)* coltello per carne (cruda); **butcher's (shop)** macelleria; **at the butcher's** dal macellaio
■ VT macellare

butcher meat N carne *f* macellata

butch·ery ['bʊtʃərɪ] N **1** *(massacre)* massacro **2** *(work of a butcher)* macellazione *f*, macelleria

but·ler ['bʌtlə^r] N maggiordomo

butt¹ [bʌt] N *(end)* estremità più grossa; *(of gun)* calcio; *(of cigar, cigarette)* mozzicone *m*; *(Am fam)* sedere *m*; **the butt of the rifle** il calcio del fucile; **a cigarette butt** un mozzicone di sigaretta; **she pinched him on the butt** gli ha pizzicato il sedere
▸ **butt in** VI + ADV *(interrupt)* interrompere; *(meddle)* immischiarsi

butt² [bʌt] N *(Shooting, Archery)*: **the butts** il campo *or* poligono di tiro; *(Brit fig)* bersaglio, zimbello; **she's the butt of his jokes** è il bersaglio dei suoi scherzi, è il suo zimbello

butt³ [bʌt] N *(push with head)* testata; *(of goat)* cornata
■ VT dare una testata *(or* una cornata) a

butt⁴ [bʌt] N botte *f*

◎ **but·ter** ['bʌtə^r] N burro; **he looks as if butter wouldn't melt in his mouth** ha una faccia d'angelo
■ VT *(bread)* imburrare, spalmare di burro
▸ **butter up** VT + ADV: **to butter sb up** ruffianarsi con qn

butter bean N fagiolo bianco

butter·cup ['bʌtə,kʌp] N ranuncolo

butter curler N arricciaburro *m inv*

butter dish N burriera

butter·fingers ['bʌtə,fɪŋgəz] N *(fam)* mani *fpl* di ricotta

butter·fly ['bʌtə,flaɪ] N **1** farfalla; **I've got butterflies (in my stomach)** ho il batticuore **2** *(Swimming: butterfly stroke)* (nuoto a) farfalla

butter knife N coltellino da burro

butter·milk ['bʌtə,mɪlk] N latticello

butter·scotch ['bʌtə,skɒtʃ] N *caramella dura a base di burro e zucchero di canna*

but·tock ['bʌtək] N natica

◎ **but·ton** ['bʌtn] N *(on garment)* bottone *m*; *(on doorbell, machine)* pulsante *m*, bottone
■ VT *(also:* **button up***)* abbottonare
■ VI abbottonarsi

button·hole ['bʌtn,həʊl] N asola, occhiello; **to wear a buttonhole** portare un fiore all'occhiello
■ VT *(person)* attaccar bottone a *or* con

button lift N skilift *m inv* (a piattello)

but·tress ['bʌtrɪs] N contrafforte *m*, sperone *m*
■ VT armare di contrafforti, rafforzare (con speroni); *(fig)* tener su, tenere in piedi; (: *argument*) avvalorare

Bb

bux·om ['bʌksəm] ADJ formoso(-a)

◎ **buy** [baɪ] *(vb: pt, pp* **bought***)* N: **a good/bad buy** un buon/cattivo acquisto *or* affare *m*

■ VT comprare, acquistare; *(tickets, petrol)* fare, prendere; *(Comm: company)* acquistare; *(fig: time)* guadagnare; **to buy sb sth/sth from sb** comprare qc per qn/qc da qn; **I've bought my mother some flowers** ho comprato dei fiori per mia madre; **the victory was dearly bought** la vittoria è stata pagata a caro prezzo; **to buy sb a drink** offrire da bere a qn; **he won't buy that explanation** *(fam)* quella scusa non se la beve

▸ **buy back** VT + ADV riprendersi, prendersi indietro

▸ **buy in** VT + ADV *(Brit: goods)* far provvista di

▸ **buy into** VI + PREP *(Brit Comm)* acquistare delle azioni di

▸ **buy off** VT + ADV *(fam: bribe)* comprare

▸ **buy out** VT + ADV *(business)* rilevare

▸ **buy up** VT + ADV *(property etc)* accaparrarsi

buy-back ['baɪbæk] N *(Comm)* opzione *f* di riacquisto

◎ **buy·er** ['baɪəʳ] N acquirente *m/f*

buyer's market ['baɪəz'mɑːkɪt] N mercato favorevole ai compratori

buyout ['baɪaʊt] N *(Comm) acquisto di una società da parte dei suoi dipendenti*

buzz [bʌz] N ronzio; *(of conversation)* brusio; **the buzz of an insect** il ronzio di un insetto; **to give sb a buzz** *(fam: telephone call)* dare un colpo di telefono a qn

■ VT *(call on intercom)* chiamare al citofono; *(: with buzzer)* chiamare col cicalino; *(Aer: plane, building)* passare rasente; **Julie buzzed me** Julie mi ha dato uno squillo; **to get a buzz out of sth** *(fam)* farsi prendere da qc; **it gives me a buzz** *(fam)* mi esalta; **it has a buzz about** *or* **to it** è proprio eccitante

■ VI *(insect, ears)* ronzare; **my head is buzzing** mi gira la testa

▸ **buzz off** VI + ADV *(Brit fam)* filare, levarsi di torno

buz·zard ['bʌzəd] N poiana

buzz·er ['bʌzəʳ] N cicalino; *(in factory)* sirena

buzz·ing ['bʌzɪŋ] N ronzio

buzz saw N sega circolare

buzz word N *(fam)* termine *m* in voga

by [baɪ] KEYWORD

■ ADV (lì) vicino; **by and by** *(in past)* poco dopo; *(in future)* fra breve; **by and large** nel complesso, nell'insieme; **close by** vicinissimo, molto vicino; **to go by** passare; **hard by** vicinissimo, molto vicino; **to lay sth by** mettere qc da parte; **to pass by** passare; **to put sth by** mettere qc da parte; **to rush by** passare correndo

■ PREP

1 *(close to)* vicino a, accanto a, presso; **I've got it by me** ce l'ho a portata di mano *or* sottomano; **the house by the river** la casa sul fiume; **a holiday by the sea** una vacanza al mare

2 *(via, through)* per; **we came by Dover** siamo venuti via Dover

3 *(past)* davanti a; **I go by the post office every day** passo davanti alla posta ogni giorno; **she walked by me** mi è passata accanto

4 *(during)*: **by day** di giorno; **by night** di notte

5 *(not later than)* per; **by then it was too late** ormai era troppo tardi; **by this time tomorrow I'll be in Spain** domani a quest'ora sarò in Spagna; **by the time I got there it was too late** quando sono arrivato era ormai troppo tardi; **by that time I knew** ormai lo sapevo; **it must be finished by 4 o'clock** dev'essere terminato entro le 4

6 *(amount)* a; **by degrees** gradualmente; **by the hour** a ore; **to increase by the hour** aumentare di ora in ora; **by the kilo** a chili; **little by little** a poco a poco; **by the metre** a metri; **one by one** uno(-a) per uno(-a)

7 *(agent, cause)* da; **killed by lightning** ucciso(-a) da un fulmine; **a painting by Picasso** un quadro di Picasso; **surrounded by enemies** circondato(-a) da nemici

8 *(method, manner, means)* per; **by bus** in autobus, con l'autobus; **by car** in macchina, con la macchina; **to pay by cheque** pagare con (un) assegno; **by force** con la forza; **made by hand** fatto(-a) a mano; **to lead sb by the hand** portare qn per mano; **by land and by sea** per terra e per mare; **by moonlight** al chiaro di luna; **(all) by oneself** tutto(-a) solo(-a); **by rail** *or* **train** con il treno, in treno; **by saving hard, he ...** risparmiando molto, lui...

9 *(according to)* per; **to play by the rules** attenersi alle regole; **it's all right by me** per me va bene

10 *(measuring difference)* di; **it missed me by inches** non mi ha preso *or* mi ha mancato per un millimetro; **it's wider by a metre** è un metro più largo

11 *(Math: measure)* per; **to divide/multiply by** dividere/moltiplicare per; **a room 3 metres by 4** una stanza di 3 metri per 4

12 *(points of compass)*: **north by north-east** nord-nordest

13 *(in oaths)*: **I swear by Almighty God** giuro dinanzi a Dio *or* nel nome di Dio

14 **by the way** *or* **by the by(e)** a proposito; **this wasn't my idea by the way** tra l'altro l'idea non era mia

◎ **bye** [baɪ] EXCL *(fam: bye-bye)* ciao!, arrivederci

by-election, bye-election ['baɪɪ,lɛkʃən] N *(Brit)* elezione *f* straordinaria

BY-ELECTION

Una **by-election** in Gran Bretagna e in alcuni paesi del Commonwealth è un'elezione che si tiene per coprire un posto in Parlamento resosi vacante, a governo ancora in carica. È importante in quanto serve a misurare il consenso degli elettori in vista delle successive elezioni politiche.

▹ www.direct.gov.uk/Homepage/fs/en

▹ www.electoralcommission.gov.uk/

Bye·lo·rus·sia [,bjɛləʊ'rʌʃə] N Bielorussia

Bye·lo·rus·sian [,bjɛləʊ'rʌʃən] ADJ bielorusso(-a)

■ N *(person)* bielorusso(-a); *(language)* bielorusso

by·gone ['baɪ,gɒn] ADJ passato(-a); **in bygone days** una volta

■ N: **let bygones be bygones** mettiamoci una pietra sopra

by·lane ['baɪ,leɪn] N stradina

by-law, bye-law ['baɪ,lɔ] N ordinanza locale

by·pass ['baɪ,pɑːs] N *(road)* circonvallazione *f*; *(Med)* by-pass *m inv*

■ VT *(town)* (fare una deviazione per) evitare; *(fig: person)* scavalcare; *(difficulty)* aggirare

by-product ['baɪ,prɒdʌkt] N *(Chem etc)* sottoprodotto; *(fig)* conseguenza; **it's a by-product of petrol refining** è un sottoprodotto della raffinazione del petrolio

byre [baɪəʳ] N *(Brit)* vaccheria, stalla

by·road ['baɪrəʊd], **by·way** ['baɪ,weɪ] N strada secondaria
by·stander ['baɪ,stændəʳ] N astante *m/f*, spettatore(-trice)
byte [baɪt] N (*Comput*) byte *m inv*

by·word ['baɪ,wɜːd] N: **his name is a byword for success** il suo nome è sinonimo di successo
by-your-leave ['baɪjʊə'liːv] N: **without so much as a by-your-leave** senza nemmeno chiedere il permesso

Bb

C, c [siː] N **1** (*letter*) C, c *f or m inv*; **C for Charlie** ≈ C come Como **2** (*Mus*) do *m inv* **3** (*Scol: mark*) ≈ 6 (*sufficiente*)

C ABBR = **Celsius** (= **centigrade**) C

c. ABBR **1** (= **century**) sec **2** (= **circa**) ca **3** (*Am etc*) = **cent(s)**

CA ABBR **1** = **Central America** **2** (*Am Post*) = **California**
■ N ABBR (*Brit*) = **chartered accountant**

C/A ABBR **1** = **capital account** **2** = **credit account** **3**- = **current account**

ca. ABBR (= **circa**) ca

CAA [ˌsiːeɪˈeɪ] N ABBR (*Brit*) = **Civil Aviation Authority**; (*Am*: = **Civil Aeronautics Authority**) *organismo di controllo e di sviluppo dell'aviazione civile*
▷ www.caa.co.uk/

CAB [ˌsiːeɪˈbi] N ABBR (*Brit*: = **Citizens' Advice Bureau**) *organizzazione di volontari che offre gratuitamente assistenza in materie legali e finanziarie*

cab [kæb] N **1** (*taxi*) taxi *m inv*; **by cab** in taxi **2** (*of train, truck, lorry*) cabina **3** (*horsedrawn*) carrozza

ca·bal [kəˈbæl] N (*intrigue*) intrigo; (*group*) cricca

caba·ret [ˈkæbəreɪ] N cabaret *m inv*

cab·bage [ˈkæbɪdʒ] N cavolo

cab·by [ˈkæbɪ] N (*fam*) tassista *m/f*

cab driver N tassista *m/f*

cab·in [ˈkæbɪn] N (*hut*) capanna; (*Naut, Aer*) cabina

cabin baggage N bagaglio a mano

cabin boy N mozzo

cabin crew N personale *m* di bordo

cabin cruiser N cabinato

◎ **cabi·net** [ˈkæbɪnɪt] N **1** (*cupboard*) armadietto; (*glass-fronted*) vetrina; **bathroom cabinet** armadietto del bagno **2** (*Pol: Cabinet*) Consiglio dei Ministri

CABINET

In Gran Bretagna il Consiglio dei ministri, **Cabinet**, è formato da circa 20 ministri nominati dal capo del governo ("Prime Minister"). Prepara e presenta proposte di legge al Parlamento ed è responsabile della politica governativa.

Negli Stati Uniti il **Cabinet** è un organo con funzioni puramente consultive, e come tale non ha potere legislativo né esecutivo. È formato dai vertici dei dipartimenti governativi, non necessariamente uomini politici, scelti dal Presidente e nominati dietro approvazione del Senato.*See also* **Shadow Cabinet**
▷ www.number-10.gov.uk/output/page19.asp
▷ www.cabinetoffice.gov.uk/
▷ www.whitehouse.gov/government/cabinet.html

cabinet-maker [ˈkæbɪnɪtˌmeɪkə^r] N ebanista *m*

cabinet-making [ˈkæbɪnɪtˌmeɪkɪŋ] N ebanisteria

cabinet minister N ministro (*membro del Consiglio*)

cabin trunk N baule *m*

◎ **ca·ble** [ˈkeɪbl] N (*rope*) cavo, fune *f*; (*Elec*) cavo; (*cablegram*) cablogramma *m*
■ VT (*information*) trasmettere per cablogramma, cablare; (*person*) mandare un cablogramma a, telegrafare a

cable car [ˈkeɪblˌkɑː^r] N funivia; (*on rail*) funicolare *f*

ca·ble·gram [ˈkeɪblˌgræm] N cablogramma *m*

cable railway N funicolare *f*

cable stitch N punto treccia

cable television N televisione *f* via cavo

cable·way [ˈkeɪblˌweɪ] N teleferica

cab·man [ˈkæbmən] N (*pl* **-men**) tassista *m/f*

ca·boo·dle [kəˈbuːdl] N (*fam*): **the whole caboodle** baracca e burattini

cache [kæʃ] N (*of arms, food*) deposito segreto

cache memory N (*Comput*) memoria cache

ca·chet [ˈkæʃeɪ] N **1** (*seal*) sigillo; (*mark, stamp*) marchio; (*fig: prestige*) prestigio **2** (*capsule*) cachet *m inv*

cack·le [ˈkækl] N (*of hen*) coccodè *m*; (*laugh*) risolino (stridulo); (*chatter*) chiacchierio
■ VI (*hen*) fare coccodè; (*person: laugh*) ridacchiare

ca·copho·nous [kəˈkɒfənəs] ADJ (*frm*) cacofonico(-a)

ca·copho·ny [kəˈkɒfənɪ] N (*frm*) cacofonia

cac·tus [ˈkæktəs] N (*pl* **cactuses** *or* **cacti** [ˈkæktaɪ]) cactus *m inv*

CAD [kæd] N ABBR (= **computer-aided design**) progettazione *f* assistita dall'elaboratore

cad [kæd] N (*old*) (*pej*) mascalzone *m*

ca·dav·er [kə'deɪvəʳ] N (*Med*) cadavere *m*
ca·dav·er·ous [kə'dævərəs] ADJ (*frm*) cadaverico(-a)
cad·die, cad·dy¹ ['kædɪ] N (*in golf*) caddie *m inv*
cad·dy² ['kædɪ] N (*tea caddy*) barattolo del tè
ca·dence ['keɪdəns] N cadenza
ca·den·za [kə'dɛnzə] N (*Mus*) cadenza
ca·det [kə'dɛt] N (*Mil etc*) cadetto; **cadet officer** allievo ufficiale; **police cadet** allievo poliziotto
cadge [kædʒ] VT (*fam: money, cigarette etc*): **to cadge (from)** scroccare a; **to cadge a lift from sb** scroccare un passaggio a qn; **to cadge a meal (off sb)** scroccare un pranzo (a qn)
cadg·er ['kædʒəʳ] N (*fam*) scroccone(-a)
ca·dre ['kædrɪ] N (*Pol: group*) gruppo scelto
cae·cum ['si:kəm] N (*Anat*) intestino cieco
Caesar ['si:zəʳ] N Cesare *m*
Cae·sar·ean, (*Am*) **Ce·sar·ean** [sɪ:'zɛərɪən] N (*also:* **Caesarean section**) (taglio) cesareo
CAF [ˌsi:eɪ'ɛf] ABBR (*Brit:* = **cost and freight**) Caf *m*
café ['kæfeɪ] N caffè *m inv*, bar *m inv* (*senza licenza per alcolici*)
caf·eteria [ˌkæfɪ'tɪərɪə] N self-service *m inv*; (*in factory etc*) mensa
cafe·tière [ˌkæfə'tjɛəʳ] N (*Brit*) caffettiera a pistone
caf·feine, caf·fein ['kæfi:n] N caffeina
caf·tan, kaf·tan ['kæftæn] N caffettano
cage [keɪdʒ] N (*gen, in mine*) gabbia
■VT mettere in gabbia
▶ **cage in** VT + ADV ingabbiare
cag·ey ['keɪdʒɪ] ADJ (*fam*) evasivo(-a); **to give a cagey answer** dare una risposta evasiva; **to be cagey about doing sth** esitare a fare qc
cag·i·ly ['keɪdʒɪlɪ] ADV prudentemente
ca·goule [kə'gu:l] N K-way® *m inv*
ca·hoots [kə'hu:ts] NPL (*fam*): **to be in cahoots (with sb)** essere in combutta (con qn)
CAI [ˌsi:eɪ'aɪ] N ABBR (= **computer-aided instruction**) istruzione *f* assistita dall'elaboratore
Cain [keɪn] N Caino
cairn [kɛən] N tumulo (di pietre)
cairn·gorm ['kɛənˌgɔ:m] N quarzo affumicato
Cai·ro ['kaɪərəʊ] N il Cairo *f*
ca·jole [kə'dʒəʊl] VT (*coax*) convincere con le buone; (*: deceitfully*) convincere con lusinghe; **to cajole sb into doing sth** convincere qn a fare qc
ca·jol·ery [kə'dʒəʊlərɪ] N (*see vb*) opera di convincimento; lusinghe *fpl*
◎**cake** [keɪk] N **1** (*large*) torta; (*small*) pasticcino; **chocolate cake** torta al cioccolato; **a coffee and a cake** un caffè e una pasta; **piece of cake** fetta di torta; **it's a piece of cake** (*fam*) è una cosa facile *or* da nulla; **driving is a piece of cake** non ci vuole niente a guidare; **to sell like hot cakes** (*fam*) andare a ruba; **he wants to have his cake and eat it** (*fig*) vuole la botte piena e la moglie ubriaca **2** (*of wax*) tavoletta; **cake of soap** saponetta
■VT: **to cake (with)** incrostare (di)
■VI (*blood*) raggrumarsi; (*mud*) incrostarsi
cake mix N preparato per torta
cake rack N griglia per torte
cake shop N pasticceria
cake slice N paletta (da dolce)
cala·mine ['kæləˌmaɪn] N (*also:* **calamine lotion**) *lozione calmante a base di calamina*
ca·lami·tous [kə'læmɪtəs] ADJ disastroso(-a)
ca·lam·ity [kə'læmɪtɪ] N calamità *f inv*
cal·ci·fi·ca·tion [ˌkælsɪfɪ'keɪʃən] N calcificazione *f*
cal·ci·fy ['kælsɪfaɪ] VT calcificare
■VI calcificarsi
cal·cium ['kælsɪəm] N (*Chem*) calcio
cal·cu·late ['kælkjʊˌleɪt] VT (*cost, distance etc*) calcolare; (*estimate: chances, effect*) valutare; **they are calculating the likely cost** stanno calcolando quanto possa costare; **to be calculated to do sth** essere fatto(-a) *or* studiato(-a) per fare qc
■VI (*Math*) fare (i) conti
▶ **calculate on** VI + PREP: **to calculate on sth/on doing sth** contare su qc/di fare qc, tenere conto di qc/di fare qc; **he hadn't calculated on the arrival of the night watchman** non aveva fatto i conti con l'arrivo del guardiano notturno
cal·cu·lat·ed ['kælkjʊˌleɪtɪd] ADJ (*insult, action*) calcolato(-a), intenzionale; **a calculated risk** un rischio calcolato
cal·cu·lat·ing ['kælkjʊˌleɪtɪŋ] ADJ (*scheming*) calcolatore(-trice)
calculating machine N (macchina) calcolatrice *f*
cal·cu·la·tion [ˌkælkjʊ'leɪʃən] N calcolo
cal·cu·la·tor ['kælkjʊˌleɪtəʳ] N calcolatrice *f*
cal·cu·lus ['kælkjʊləs] N calcolo; **differential/integral calculus** calcolo differenziale/integrale
cal·de·ra [kæl'dɛərə] N (*Geol*) caldera
cal·en·dar ['kælɪndəʳ] N calendario; **the Church calendar** il calendario ecclesiastico
calendar month N mese *m* civile
calendar year N anno civile
calender ['kælɪndəʳ] N (*Tech*) calandra
calf¹ [kɑ:f] N (*pl* **calves** [kɑ:vs]) **1** (*young cow*) vitello; **a cow and her calf** una mucca e il suo vitello; **seal/elephant calf** piccolo di foca/elefante **2** = **calfskin**
calf² [kɑ:f] N (*pl* **calves** [kɑ:vs]) (*Anat*) polpaccio
calf·skin ['kɑ:fˌskɪn] N (pelle *f* di) vitello
cali·brate ['kælɪbreɪt] VT (*gun etc*) calibrare; (*scale of measuring instrument*) tarare
cali·bra·tion [ˌkælɪ'breɪʃən] N (*see vb*) calibratura; taratura
cali·bre, (*Am*) **cali·ber** ['kælɪbəʳ] N (*also fig*) calibro
cali·co ['kælɪˌkəʊ] N (tela di) cotone *m* grezzo; (*Am*) cotonina stampata
Cali·for·nia [ˌkælɪ'fɔ:nɪə] N California
▷ www.state.ca.us/
Caligula [kə'lɪgjʊlə] N Caligola *m*
cali·pers ['kælɪpəz] NPL (*Am*) = **callipers**
ca·liph ['keɪlɪf] N califfo
◎**call** [kɔ:l] N
1 (*shout*) richiamo, urlo, grido; (*of bird*) canto; **to give a call** lanciare un grido; **within call** a portata di voce; **please give me a call at 7** per piacere mi chiami alle 7; **whose call is it?** (*Cards*) a chi tocca (giocare)?
2 a 911/999 call *numero telefonico d'emergenza negli Stati Uniti/nel Regno Unito*; una chiamata al 911/999
3 (*Telec: also* **phone call**) telefonata, chiamata; **long-distance call** chiamata interurbana; **to make a call** telefonare, fare una telefonata; **thanks for your call** grazie per la chiamata
4 (*summons: for flight etc*) chiamata; (*fig: lure*) richiamo; **to be on call** essere a disposizione; (*doctor*) essere reperibile; **the call of the sea** il richiamo del mare; **to answer the call of duty** fare il proprio dovere
5 (*short visit: also Med*) visita; **port of call** (porto di) scalo; **to pay a call on sb** fare (una) visita a qn
6 (*need*): **there's not much call for these items** non c'è molta richiesta di questi articoli; **you had no call to say that** non c'era alcun bisogno che tu lo dicessi;

Cc

there is no call for alarm non ci sono motivi di allarme
7 (*claim*): **there are many calls on my time** sono molto preso, ho molti impegni
■ VT
1 chiamare; (*Telec*) chiamare, telefonare a; **to call 911/999** chiamare il 911/99
2 (*announce*: *flight*) annunciare; (*meeting, strike*) indire, proclamare; (*waken*) svegliare, chiamare; **we called the police** abbiamo chiamato la polizia
3 (*name*) chiamare; (*describe as*) considerare; **can I call you by your first name?** posso chiamarti per nome?; **to be called** chiamarsi; **what are you called?** come ti chiami?; **she's called Jane** si chiama Jane; **would you call Italian a difficult language?** diresti che l'italiano è una lingua difficile?; **I call it an insult** questo lo chiamo un insulto, lo considero un insulto; **are you calling me a liar?** mi stai dando del bugiardo?; **let's call it £50** facciamo 50 sterline; **let's call it a day** (*fam*) smettiamo, basta per oggi
■ VI
1 (*shout*: *person*) chiamare; (*bird*) lanciare un richiamo; **to call to sb** gridare a qn
2 (*Telec*): **who's calling?** chi parla?; **I'll tell him you called** gli dirò che hai telefonato; **London calling** (*Radio*) qui Londra
3 (*also:* **call in, call round**: *visit*) passare; **I'll call in at the office later** passerò più tardi in ufficio
▸ **call aside** VT + ADV chiamare da parte *or* in disparte
▸ **call at** VI + PREP (*subj*: *ship*) fare scalo a
▸ **call away** VT + ADV: **to be called away on business** dovere andare via per lavoro
▸ **call back** VT + ADV (*Telec*) ritelefonare a, richiamare; **can I call you back?** ti posso richiamare?
■ VI + ADV (*Telec*) ritelefonare, richiamare; (*return*) ritornare; **I'll call back later** (*on the phone*) richiamo più tardi; (*in person*) ripasso più tardi
▸ **call down** VT + PREP: **to call down sth (on sb)** (*curses*) invocare qc (su qn)
▸ **call for** VI + PREP (*summon*: *wine, the bill*) chiedere; (*demand*: *courage, action*) richiedere; (*collect*: *person*) passare a prendere; (: *goods*) ritirare; **this job calls for strong nerves** questo lavoro richiede nervi saldi; **shall I call for you at seven thirty?** passo a prenderti alle sette e mezzo?; **this calls for a drink!** qui ci vuole un brindisi!
▸ **call forth** VT + ADV (*frm*: *protest, emotion*) suscitare
▸ **call in** VT + ADV
1 (*doctor, expert, police*) chiamare, far venire
2 (*Comm etc*: *faulty goods*) riprendere; (: *currency*) mettere fuori corso
■ VI + ADV = **call** VI
▸ **call off** VT + ADV
1 (*meeting, race*) disdire, revocare; (*deal*) cancellare; **the strike was called off** lo sciopero è stato revocato; **the match was called off** la partita è stata rinviata
2 (*dog*) richiamare
▸ **call on** VI + PREP
1 (*visit*) far visita a, andare a trovare, passare da
2 (*invite*): **to call on sb to do sth** invitare qn a fare qc; (*request*) chiedere a qn di fare qc; **I now call on Mr Brown to speak** ora invito il signor Brown a parlare
▸ **call out** VT + ADV (*doctor, police, troops*) chiamare; **to call workers out on strike** invitare gli operai a fare sciopero
■ VI + ADV (*in pain*) urlare; (*to person*) chiamare; **to call out for help** invocare *or* chiamare aiuto
▸ **call round** VI + ADV passare; **to call round to see sb** passare da qn
▸ **call up** VT + ADV
1 (*Mil*) richiamare, mobilitare
2 (*Telec*) chiamare, telefonare a
3 (*fig*: *memories*) richiamare, evocare
▸ **call upon** VI + PREP = **call on 2**
Cal·lane·tics® [ˌkæləˈnɛtɪks] NSG *tipo di ginnastica basata sulla ripetizione di piccoli movimenti*
call·box [ˈkɔːlˌbɒks] N (*Brit*) cabina telefonica
call centre N call centre *m inv*
call diversion N trasferimento di chiamata
cal·ler [ˈkɔːləʳ] N (*visitor*) visitatore(-trice); (*Telec*) persona che chiama; **hold the line, caller!** rimanga in linea, signore (*or* signora)!
call girl N ragazza *f* squillo *inv*
cal·lig·ra·phy [kəˈlɪgrəfɪ] N calligrafia
▹ www.asia-art.net/chinese_tech_brush.html
▹ www.sakkal.com/ArtArabicCalligraphy.html
▹ www.japan-guide.com/e/e2095.html
call-in [ˈkɔːlˌɪn] N (*Am*) = **phone-in**
call·ing [ˈkɔːlɪŋ] N vocazione *f*
calling card N (*Am*) biglietto da visita
Cal·lio·pe [kəˈlaɪəpɪ] N Calliope *f*
cal·li·pers [ˈkælɪpəz] NPL (*Am*) = **calipers**
cal·lis·then·ics [ˌkælɪsˈθɛnɪks] NSG ginnastica svedese
cal·lous [ˈkæləs] ADJ (*person*) insensibile; (*remark*) crudele
cal·loused [ˈkæləst] ADJ calloso(-a)
cal·lous·ly [ˈkæləslɪ] ADV (*behave*) in modo insensibile; (*speak*) con durezza; (*decide*) cinicamente
cal·lous·ness [ˈkæləsnɪs] N (*of person*) insensibilità; (*of remark*) durezza
cal·low [ˈkæləʊ] ADJ immaturo(-a)
call sign N segnale *m* di chiamata
call-up [ˈkɔːlˌʌp] (*Mil*) N chiamata (alle armi)
call-up papers NPL cartolina precetto
call waiting N avviso di chiamata
◎ **calm** [kɑːm] ADJ (*gen*) calmo(-a); (*weather*) sereno(-a); **calm and collected** padrone(-a) di sé; **keep calm!** sta' calmo!
■ N calma, pace *f*; **the calm before the storm** la quiete che precede la tempesta
■ VT (*also:* **calm down**: *person*) calmare; **he calmed her down** l'ha calmata
▸ **calm down** VT + ADV = **calm** VT
■ VI + ADV calmarsi; **calm down!** calmati!
calm·ly [ˈkɑːmlɪ] ADV tranquillamente, con calma
calm·ness [ˈkɑːmnɪs] N calma, tranquillità
Cal·or Gas® [ˈkæləˌgæs] N (*Brit*) liquigas® *m*
calo·rie [ˈkælərɪ] N caloria; **low-calorie product** prodotto a basso contenuto calorico
calo·rif·ic [ˌkæləˈrɪfɪk] ADJ: **calorific value** (*Phys*) valore *m* calorico
cal·um·ny [ˈkæləmnɪ] N (*frm*) calunnia
calve [kɑːv] VI figliare
calves [kɑːvz] NPL *of* **calf**
calv·ing [ˈkɑːvɪŋ] N parto (*di bovini*)
CAM [kæm] N ABBR (= **computer-aided manufacturing**) fabbricazione *f* assistita dall'elaboratore
cam [kæm] N (*Tech*) camma, eccentrico
ca·ma·ra·derie [ˌkæməˈrædərɪ] N cameratismo
cam·ber [ˈkæmbəʳ] N (*of road*) curvatura, bombatura
cam·bium [ˈkæmbɪəm] N (*pl* **cambiums** *or* **cambia** [ˈkæmbɪə]) (*Bot*) cambio
Cam·bo·dia [kæmˈbəʊdɪə] N Cambogia

Cam·bo·dian [kæm'bəʊdɪən] ADJ, N cambogiano(-a)
Cambs ABBR (*Brit*) = *Cambridgeshire*
cam·cord·er ['kæmkɔːdəʳ] N camcorder *f inv*
came [keɪm] PT *of* **come**
cam·el ['kæməl] N cammello
■ ADJ (*colour*) color cammello *inv*
camel coat N cappotto di cammello
camel hair ['kæməl,hɛəʳ] N (pelo di) cammello
ca·mel·lia [kə'miːlɪə] N camelia
cameo ['kæmɪəʊ] N cammeo
■ ADJ (*ring, brooch*) con cammeo; (*Cine, Theatre*: *role, part*) breve apparizione *f* (*di un attore o un'attrice famoso/a*)
◎ **cam·era** ['kæmərə] N **1** macchina fotografica; (*movie camera*) cinepresa; (*Cine, TV*) telecamera **2** (*Law*): **in camera** a porte chiuse

DID YOU KNOW ...?
camera is not translated by the Italian word *camera*

camera·man ['kæmərə,mæn] N (*pl* **-men**) cameraman *m inv*
camera phone N telefonino con fotocamera integrata
camera-ready copy ['kæmərə,rɛdɪ'kɒpɪ] N (*Typ*) testo pronto per la fotocomposizione
camera-shy ['kæmərəʃaɪ] ADJ che non ama essere fotografato
camera·work ['kæmərə,wɜːk] N riprese *fpl*
Cam·eroon [,kæmə'ruːn] N il Camerun *m*
camo·mile ['kæməʊmaɪl] N camomilla
camouflage ['kæməflɑːʒ] N camuffamento; (*Mil*) mimetizzazione *f*
■ VT camuffare; (*Mil*) mimetizzare; **they were well camouflaged, and invisible from the air** erano ben mimetizzati ed invisibili dall'alto
◎ **camp¹** [kæmp] N (*gen*) accampamento, campo; (*holiday camp*) campeggio; (*Pol etc*) campo, schieramento; **summer camp** campeggio estivo; **refugee camp** campo *m* profughi *inv*
■ VI campeggiare, accamparsi; **to go camping** andare in campeggio; **we went camping in Cornwall** siamo andati in campeggio in Cornovaglia
▸ **camp out** VI + ADV accamparsi, attendarsi, campeggiare
camp² [kæmp] ADJ (*fam*: *theatrical*) melodrammatico(-a); (*: homosexual*) ostentatamente effeminato(-a)
◎ **cam·paign** [kæm'peɪn] N (*Mil, Pol etc*) campagna; **advertising campaign** campagna pubblicitaria
■ VI (*Mil, also fig*): **to campaign (for/against)** fare una campagna (per/contro); **they are campaigning for a change in the law** stanno facendo una campagna per cambiare la legge
cam·paign·er [kæm'peɪnəʳ] N (*Mil*): **old campaigner** veterano, vecchio combattente *m*; **campaigner for** fautore(-trice) di; **campaigner against** oppositore(-trice) di
camp bed N (*Brit*) brandina
camp·er ['kæmpəʳ] N (*person*) campeggiatore(-trice); (*vehicle*) camper *m inv*
camp follower N (*fig*) simpatizzante *m/f*
cam·phor ['kæmfəʳ] N canfora
cam·pho·rat·ed ['kæmfə,reɪtɪd] ADJ canforato(-a)
camp·ing ['kæmpɪŋ] N campeggio; **I like camping** mi piace il campeggio

DID YOU KNOW ...?
camping is not translated by the Italian word *camping*

cam·pi·on ['kæmpɪən] N: **white/red campion** licnide *f* bianca/rossa
camp site, camping site N (zona di) campeggio
cam·pus ['kæmpəs] N campus *m inv*
cam·shaft ['kæmʃæft] N albero a camme; **single camshaft** monoalbero
◎ **can¹** [kæn] KEYWORD
(*neg* **cannot, can't**, *cond and pt* **could**) MODAL AUX VB
1 (*be able to*) potere; **I'll tell you all I can** ti dirò tutto quello che posso; **she was as happy as could be** più felice di così non poteva essere; **she can be very annoying** lei a volte è molto fastidiosa, lei riesce ad essere molto fastidiosa; **he can do it if he tries hard** è capace di farlo se si sforza; **they couldn't help it** non potevano farci niente; **I can't** *or* **cannot go any further** non posso andare oltre
2 (*know how to*) essere capace di, sapere; **I can speak French** so parlare francese; **can you speak Italian?** parli italiano?; **I can swim/drive** so nuotare/guidare; **he can't swim/drive** non sa nuotare/guidare
3 (*may*) potere; **can't I come too?** non posso venire anch'io?; **could I have a word with you?** potrei parlarti un attimo?; **can I use your telephone?** posso usare il tuo telefono?
4 (*expressing disbelief, puzzlement*): **how could you lie to me!** come hai potuto dirmi una bugia!; **she can't possibly marry that creep!** (*fam*) non è possibile che sposi quell'essere!; **you can't be serious!** scherzi?; **this can't be true!** non può essere vero!; **what CAN he want?** cosa può mai volere?; **they can't have left already!** non è possibile che siano già partiti!
5 (*expressing possibility, suggestion etc*): **they could have forgotten** potrebbero essersene dimenticati; **he could be in the library** può darsi che sia in biblioteca, potrebbe essere in biblioteca; **I could have cried/screamed!** mi sarei messo a piangere/urlare!
6 (*not translated*): **can you hear me?** mi senti?; **I can't see you** non ti vedo
can² [kæn] N (*container*: *for foodstuffs*) scatola; (*: for oil, water*) latta; (*esp Am*: *garbage can*) bidone *m*; **a can of peas** una scatola di piselli; **a can of beer** una lattina di birra; **to carry the can** (*Brit fam*) prendere la colpa
■ VT (*food*) inscatolare

Cana·da ['kænədə] N Canada *m*
▷ http://canada.gc.ca
▷ www.travelcanada.ca/
Canada Day N *anniversario del giorno in cui il Canada, che precedentemente era una colonia britannica, divenne uno stato federale*
▷ www.pch.gc.ca/progs/cpsc-ccsp/jfa-ha/canada_e.cfm
Ca·na·dian [kə'neɪdɪən] ADJ, N canadese (*m/f*)
Canadian football N *gioco canadese simile al rugby*
▷ www.cfl.ca
ca·nal [kə'næl] N canale *m*
canal harbour N porto canale *m inv*
cana·li·za·tion [,kænəlaɪ'zeɪʃən] N canalizzazione *f*
cana·lize ['kænə,laɪz] VT (*frm*) canalizzare, convogliare
Ca·naries [kə'nɛərɪz] NPL: **the Canaries** le Canarie
ca·nary [kə'nɛərɪ] N canarino
Canary Islands NPL: **the Canary Islands** le isole *fpl* Canarie
canary yellow ADJ, N giallo canarino *inv*
ca·nas·ta [kə'næstə] N canasta

Cc

Can·ber·ra ['kænbərə] N Canberra
▷ www.act.gov.au
▷ www.nationalcapital.gov.au

◎**can·cel** ['kænsəl] VT **1** (*call off: holiday, booking*) cancellare, annullare, disdire; (*meeting, event*) cancellare, sospendere; (*train*) sopprimere; (*annul: order, contract*) annullare; **they cancelled their booking at the last moment** hanno annullato la prenotazione all'ultimo momento; **I had to cancel my appointment** ho dovuto disdire l'appuntamento; **our flight was cancelled** il nostro volo è stato cancellato; **the train has been cancelled** il treno è stato soppresso **2** (*obliterate: name*) cancellare, radiare; (: *stamp*) timbrare, annullare; (: *cheque*) annullare **3** (*Math: figures*) semplificare
▸ **cancel out** VT + ADV (*Math*) semplificare; (*fig*) annullare; **they cancel each other out** (*also fig*) si annullano a vicenda
■ VI + ADV (*Math*) semplificarsi

can·cel·la·tion [ˌkænsə'leɪʃən] N (*see vt 1, 3*) cancellazione *f*, annullamento, disdetta; sospensione *f*; soppressione *f*; annullamento; semplificazione *f*

Can·cer ['kænsəʳ] N (*Astron, Geog*) Cancro; **to be Cancer** (*Astrol*) essere del Cancro

◎**can·cer** ['kænsəʳ] N (*Med*) cancro; **he's got cancer** ha il cancro

can·cer·ous ['kænsərəs] ADJ canceroso(-a)

cancer patient N malato(-a) di cancro

cancer research N ricerca sul cancro

cancer specialist N cancerologo(-a)

can·de·la·bra [ˌkændɪ'lɑ:brə] N candelabro

C and F [ˌsi:ənd'ɛf] ABBR (*Brit:* = **cost and freight**) Caf *m*

can·did ['kændɪd] ADJ franco(-a), onesto(-a)

can·di·da·cy ['kændɪdəsɪ], **can·di·da·ture** (*Brit*) ['kændɪdətʃəʳ] N candidatura

◎**can·di·date** ['kændɪˌdeɪt] N candidato(-a)

can·did·ly ['kændɪdlɪ] ADV francamente, onestamente

can·died ['kændɪd] ADJ candito(-a); **candied peel** scorzette *fpl* di frutta candita; **candied apple** (*Am*) mela caramellata

can·dle ['kændl] N candela; (*in church*) cero; **he lit a candle** ha acceso una candela; **a cake with fifteen candles** una torta con quindici candeline

candle grease N sego

candle·light ['kændl,laɪt] N lume *m* di candela; **by candlelight** a lume di candela

Candle·mas ['kændəlməs] N Candelora

candle·stick ['kændl,stɪk], **candle·holder** ['kændl,həʊldəʳ] N bugia, portacandele *m inv*; (*large, ornate*) candeliere *m*

candle·wick ['kændl,wɪk] N ciniglia (di cotone)

can·dour, (*Am*) **can·dor** ['kændəʳ] N candore *m*, franchezza, sincerità

C & W ['si:ən'dʌbljʊ] N ABBR = **country and western (music)**

can·dy ['kændɪ] N (*Am: sweet*) caramella; (: *sweets, confectionery*) dolciumi *mpl*; **do you want a candy?** vuoi una caramella?; **I don't eat candy** non mangio dolciumi
■ VT (*fruit*) candire

candy·floss ['kændɪ,flɒs] N (*Brit*) zucchero filato

candy store N (*Am*) ≈ pasticceria

candy-striped ADJ (*fabric*) a righine bianche e rosa

cane [keɪn] N (*Bot*) canna; (*for baskets, chairs*) bambù *m*; (*wicker*) vimini *m*; (*stick: for walking*) bastone *m* (da passeggio); (: *for punishment*) bacchetta; **he leaned on a cane** si appoggiava ad un bastone; **to get the cane** (*Scol*) prenderle con la bacchetta
■ VT (*Brit Scol: pupil*) picchiare con la bacchetta

> DID YOU KNOW ...?
> **cane** is not translated by the Italian word *cane*

cane chair N sedia di vimini *or* di bambù

cane furniture N mobili *mpl* di vimini *or* di bambù

cane sugar N zucchero di canna

can·ine ['keɪnaɪn] ADJ canino(-a)
■ N (*canine tooth*) (dente *m*) canino

ca·ning ['keɪnɪŋ] N: **to give sb a caning** dare bacchettate a qn (*per punizione*)

can·is·ter ['kænɪstəʳ] N (*for tea, coffee*) barattolo (*metallico*); (*for gas*) candelotto

can·ker ['kæŋkəʳ] N **1** (*frm: evil*) cancro **2** (*Med*) afta, stomatite *f* **3** (*Bot*) cancro

can·na·bis ['kænəbɪs] N canapa indiana

canned [kænd] PT, PP *of* **can²**
■ ADJ (*food*) in scatola; (*fam: recorded: music*) registrato(-a); (*Brit fam: drunk*) sbronzo(-a); (*Am fam: worker*) licenziato(-a)

can·nery ['kænərɪ] N conservificio

can·ni·bal ['kænɪbəl] N cannibale *m/f*

can·ni·bal·ism ['kænɪbəlɪzəm] N cannibalismo

can·ni·bal·is·tic [ˌkænɪbə'lɪstɪk] ADJ cannibalesco(-a)

can·ni·bal·ize ['kænɪbəlaɪz] VT (*car etc*) smontare (*per riutilizzare alcuni singoli pezzi*)

can·ning ['kænɪŋ] N conservazione *f* dei cibi in scatola

can·non ['kænən] N (*pl* **cannon** *or* **cannons**) (*gun*) cannone *m*
■ VI: **to cannon into** *or* **against** sbattere violentemente contro

cannon·ball ['kænən,bɔ:l] N palla di cannone

cannon fodder N carne *f* da cannone

can·not ['kænɒt] = **can not**

can·ny ['kænɪ] ADJ (*comp* **-ier**, *superl* **-iest**) furbo(-a)

ca·noe [kə'nu:] N canoa
■ VI andare in canoa; **on holiday we canoed and swam** in vacanza siamo andati in canoa e abbiamo nuotato

ca·noe·ing [kə'nu:ɪŋ] N (*sport*) canottaggio; **I like canoeing** mi piace il canottaggio; **we went canoeing** abbiamo fatto canottaggio

ca·noe·ist [kə'nu:ɪst] N canoista *m/f*, canottiere *m*

can·on ['kænən] N **1** (*clergyman*) canonico **2** (*principle*) canone *m*

can·oni·za·tion [ˌkænənaɪ'zeɪʃən] N canonizzazione *f*

can·on·ize ['kænə,naɪz] VT canonizzare

canon law N (*Rel*) diritto canonico

ca·noo·dle [kə'nu:dl] VI (*fam*) sbaciucchiarsi

can opener N apriscatole *m inv*

cano·py ['kænəpɪ] N (*above bed, throne*) baldacchino; (*Naut*) tendalino

can't [kɑ:nt] = **can not**

cant¹ [kænt] N (*hypocritical talk*) discorsi *mpl* ipocriti; (*jargon*) gergo

cant² [kænt] VI (*tilt*) inclinarsi
■ VT inclinare; (*overturn*) rovesciare

Cantab. ABBR (*Brit:* = **cantabrigiensis**) (dell')Università di Cambridge

can·tan·ker·ous [kæn'tæŋkərəs] ADJ irascibile, stizzoso(-a)

can·teen [kæn'ti:n] N **1** (*restaurant*) mensa; **I don't eat in the canteen** non mangio in mensa **2** (*Brit*): **a canteen of cutlery** un servizio di posate

DID YOU KNOW ...?
canteen is not translated by the Italian word *cantina*

can·ter ['kæntə[r]] N piccolo galoppo; **counter canter** galoppo rovescio
■VI andare a piccolo galoppo

can·ti·lever ['kæntɪ,li:və[r]] N trave *f* a sbalzo

cantilever bridge N ponte *m* a mensola

can·ton ['kæntɒn] N cantone *m*

can·vas ['kænvəs] N tela; **under canvas** (*in a tent*) in tenda; (*Naut*) a vele spiegate

can·vass ['kænvəs] VT (*Pol: district*) fare un giro elettorale di; (*: person*) fare propaganda elettorale a; (*Comm: district*) battere (*per raccogliere ordinazioni*); (*: citizens, opinions*) fare un sondaggio di; **they canvassed the views of local people** hanno fatto un sondaggio d'opinione tra la gente del posto
■VI (*Pol*) raccogliere voti; (*Comm*) battere la zona per raccogliere ordinazioni; **she canvassed for the Labour Party in the last election** ha fatto propaganda per il partito laburista alle ultime elezioni

can·vass·er ['kænvəsə[r]] N (*Pol*) propagandista *m/f* (elettorale); (*Comm*) piazzista *m*

can·vass·ing ['kænvəsɪŋ] N sollecitazione *f*

can·yon ['kænjən] N canyon *m inv*

CAP [,si:eɪ'pi:] N ABBR (= **Common Agricultural Policy**) PAC *f*, Politica Agricola Comune

◎ **cap** [kæp] N **1** (*hat, also Sport*) berretto; (*for swimming*) cuffia; (*riding cap*) cap *m inv*; **cap in hand** (*fig*) umilmente; **if the cap fits wear it** chi ha orecchie per intendere intenda; **he's got his cap for England** (*Sport*) è stato scelto per la nazionale inglese **2** (*of bottle, radiator etc*) tappo; (*of pen*) cappuccio; (*Brit: contraceptive: also:* **Dutch cap**) diaframma *m*; **please put the cap back on the toothpaste** rimetti il tappo al dentifricio, per favore
■VT **1** (*bottle*) tappare; (*tooth*) ricoprire **2** (*surpass: story, joke*) superare, essere meglio di; **and to cap it all, he ...** e per completare l'opera, lui... **3** **he's been capped 15 times for England** (*Brit Sport*) ha rappresentato l'Inghilterra 15 volte; **this is his second cap for Scotland** è la seconda volta che veste la maglia della nazionale scozzese

ca·pa·bil·ity [,keɪpə'bɪlətɪ] N (*no pl: competence*) capacità, competenza, abilità; (*potential ability*) possibilità *f inv*

◎ **ca·pable** ['keɪpəbl] ADJ **1** (*competent*) capace, abile **2** (*able to*): **capable of (doing) sth** in grado di fare qc, capace di fare qc; **your son's capable of doing better at school** suo figlio potrebbe riuscire meglio a scuola; **I think she's capable of achieving much more** penso che sia capace di ottenere molto di più; **they realized he was capable of murder** capirono che era capace di uccidere; **she's quite capable of letting someone else take the blame** sarebbe capace di dar la colpa a un altro

ca·pably ['keɪpəblɪ] ADV con abilità

ca·pa·cious [kə'peɪʃəs] ADJ capace

ca·paci·tor [kə'pæsɪtə[r]] N (*Phys*) condensatore *m*

◎ **ca·pac·ity** [kə'pæsɪtɪ] N **1** (*Elec, Phys, of container etc*) capacità; (*of lift etc*) capienza; **the tank has a 40-litre capacity** il serbatoio ha una capacità di 40 litri; **seating capacity** capienza; **filled to capacity** pieno(-a) zeppo(-a); **the auditorium was filled to capacity** la sala era al completo; **to work at full capacity** (*factory etc*) lavorare a pieno ritmo **2** (*position*) posizione *f*, funzione *f*; **in my capacity as chairman** nella mia veste di presidente, in qualità di presidente; **in an advisory capacity** a titolo consultativo; **in his official capacity** nell'esercizio delle sue funzioni **3** (*ability*) capacità; **to have a capacity for hard work** essere un gran lavoratore(-trice); **this work is beyond my capacity** questo lavoro è al di là delle mie possibilità

capacity audience N sala piena

cape[1] [keɪp] N (*Geog*) capo

cape[2] [keɪp] N (*garment*) cappa, mantello; (*of policeman, cyclist*) mantella

Cape Horn N Capo Horn

Cape of Good Hope N Capo di Buona Speranza

ca·per[1] ['keɪpə[r]] N (*Culin*) cappero

ca·per[2] ['keɪpə[r]] N (*escapade*) scherzetto, birichinata; (*leap*) saltello
■VI (*child*) saltellare

cap·er·cail·lie [,kæpə'keɪljɪ] N gallo cedrone, urogallo

Cape Town N Città del Capo
▷ www.capetown.gov.za/default.asp
▷ www.sa-venues.com/general_info_nationwide.htm

cap·ful ['kæpfʊl] N (*measure of liquid*): **3 capfuls to 4 litres of water** 3 tappi ogni 4 litri d'acqua

ca·pil·lar·ity [,kæpɪ'lærɪtɪ] N (*Phys*) capillarità

ca·pil·lary [kə'pɪlərɪ] ADJ, N capillare (*m*)

capi·ta ['kæpɪtə] *see* **per capita**

◎ **capi·tal** ['kæpɪtl] N **1** (*also:* **capital letter**) (lettera) maiuscola; **in capitals** in stampatello **2** (*also:* **capital city**) capitale *f*; **Cardiff is the capital of Wales** Cardiff è la capitale del Galles **3** (*Fin*) capitale *m*; **to make capital out of sth** (*fig*) sfruttare qc
■ADJ **1** (*letter*) maiuscolo(-a); **with a capital C** con la C maiuscola **2** (*Law*): **capital offence** delitto passibile di pena capitale **3** (*old: idea*) meraviglioso(-a), splendido(-a)

capital account N conto capitale

capital allowance N ammortamento fiscale

capital assets NPL capitale *msg* fisso

capital expenditure N spese *fpl* in capitale

capital gains tax N imposta sulla plusvalenza

capital goods N beni *mpl* d'investimento, beni capitali

capital-intensive ['kæpɪtlɪn'tensɪv] ADJ ad alta intensità di capitale

capi·tal·ism ['kæpɪtəlɪzəm] N capitalismo

capi·tal·ist ['kæpɪtəlɪst] ADJ, N capitalista (*m/f*)

capi·tal·ist·ic [,kæpɪtə'lɪstɪk] ADJ (*pej*) capitalistico(-a)

capi·tali·za·tion [,kæpɪtəlaɪ'zeɪʃən] N (*Fin*) capitalizzazione *f*; (*total sum of capital*) capitale *m* complessivo

capi·tal·ize ['kæpɪtə,laɪz] VT **1** (*Fin: provide with capital*) capitalizzare **2** (*word*) scrivere (in) maiuscolo
▶ **capitalize on** VI + PREP (*fig*) trarre vantaggio da

capital punishment N pena capitale

capital reserves NPL riserve *fpl* (di capitale)

capital transfer tax N (*Brit*) imposta sui trasferimenti di capitali

Capi·tol ['kæpɪtəl] N: **the Capitol** il Campidoglio

CAPITOL

Il **Capitol** è l'edificio che ospita le riunioni del Congresso degli Stati Uniti. È situato sull'omonimo colle, "Capitol Hill", a Washington DC. In molti stati americani il termine **Capitol** viene usato per indicare l'edificio dove si riuniscono i rappresentanti dello stato.
▷ www.aoc.gov/

Cc

ca·pitu·late [kəˈpɪtjʊleɪt] VI capitolare
ca·pitu·la·tion [kəˌpɪtjʊˈleɪʃən] N capitolazione *f*
ca·pon [ˈkeɪpən] N cappone *m*
ca·price [kəˈpriːs] N capriccio
ca·pri·cious [kəˈprɪʃəs] ADJ capriccioso(-a)
ca·pri·cious·ly [kəˈprɪʃəslɪ] ADV capricciosamente
Cap·ri·corn [ˈkæprɪˌkɔːn] N Capricorno; **to be Capricorn** (*Astrol*) essere del Capricorno
cap rock N (*Geol*) roccia di copertura
caps [kæps] NPL, ABBR *of* **capital letters**; *see* **capital**
cap·si·cum [ˈkæpsɪkəm] N (*Bot*) capsico; (*Culin*) peperone *m*
cap·size [kæpˈsaɪz] VT ribaltare, capovolgere
■ VI ribaltarsi, capovolgersi; (*boat*) ribaltarsi, scuffiare; **the boat capsized** la barca si è capovolta
cap·stan [ˈkæpstən] N (*Naut*) argano
cap·sule [ˈkæpsjuːl] N capsula
Capt. ABBR (= **captain**) Cap.
◎ **cap·tain** [ˈkæptɪn] N capitano, comandante *m*; **captain of industry** capitano d'industria
■ VT (*team*) essere capitano di, capitanare; (*ship*) comandare
cap·tain·cy [ˈkæptɪnsɪ] N ruolo di capitano
◎ **cap·tion** [ˈkæpʃən] N (*heading*) intestazione *f*; (*to cartoon*) fumetto; (*for illustration, table*) didascalia
cap·tious [ˈkæpʃəs] ADJ (*frm*) ipercritico(-a)
cap·ti·vate [ˈkæptɪˌveɪt] VT affascinare, incantare, avvincere
cap·tive [ˈkæptɪv] ADJ (*person*) prigioniero(-a); (*animal*) in cattività; **he had a captive audience** i presenti hanno dovuto ascoltarlo per forza
■ N prigioniero(-a); **to hold sb captive** tenere prigioniero qn
cap·tiv·ity [kæpˈtɪvɪtɪ] N prigionia; (*of animal*) cattività; **in captivity** (*animal*) in cattività
cap·tor [ˈkæptəʳ] N (*lawful*) chi ha catturato; (*unlawful*) rapitore(-trice); **he managed to escape from his captors** riuscì a sfuggire a quelli che l'avevano catturato
◎ **cap·ture** [ˈkæptʃəʳ] N (*of animal, soldier, escapee*) cattura; (*of city etc*) presa; (*thing caught*) preda; (*data capture*) registrazione *f or* rilevazione *f* di dati
■ VT (*animal*) catturare, prendere; (*escapee, soldier*) catturare, far prigioniero; (*city etc*) prendere; (*fig: attention*) attirare, cattivare; (*Art: atmosphere etc*) cogliere, rendere
◎ **car** [kɑːʳ] N **1** (*Aut*) macchina, automobile *f*, auto *f inv*; **by car** in macchina; **we went by car** siamo andati in macchina **2** (*esp Am: in train*) vagone; (: *in tram*) vettura; **dining car** vagone ristorante
ca·rafe [kəˈræf] N caraffa
carafe wine N (*in restaurant*) ≈ vino sfuso
car alarm N allarme *m*
car allowance N: **do you get a car allowance?** ti pagano le spese della macchina?
cara·mel [ˈkærəməl] N caramello; (*sweet*) caramella
■ ADJ (*custard, flavouring*) al caramello
car·at [ˈkærət] N carato; **18 carat gold** oro a 18 carati
cara·van [ˈkærəˌvæn] N **1** (*gipsies'*) carrozzone *m*; (*Brit*) (*Aut*) roulotte *f inv* **2** (*in desert*) carovana
■ VI viaggiare con la roulotte
cara·van·ette [ˌkærəvəˈnɛt] N camper *m inv*
cara·van·se·rai [ˌkærəˈvænsəˌraɪ] N caravanserraglio
caravan site N (*Brit*) campeggio per roulotte
cara·way [ˈkærəˌweɪ] N (*Bot*) cumino (dei prati); **caraway seed** seme *m* di cumino
car·bine [ˈkɑːbaɪn] N carabina
car·bo·hy·drate [ˌkɑːbəʊˈhaɪdreɪt] N (*Chem, starchy food*) carboidrato
car·bo·lic acid [kɑːˈbɒlɪkˈæsɪd] N acido fenico, fenolo
car bomb N autobomba *inv*
◎ **car·bon** [ˈkɑːbən] N (*Chem*) carbonio; (*also:* **carbon paper**) carta carbone
car·bon·ate [ˈkɑːbənɪt] N carbonato
car·bon·at·ed [ˈkɑːbəˌneɪtɪd] ADJ (*drink*) gassato(-a)
carbon copy N (*Typing*) copia (in carta carbone); (*fig*) copia *f* carbone *inv*; **he's a carbon copy of his father** è tutto suo padre, è la copia carbone di suo padre, è identico a suo padre
carbon credit N carbon credit *m inv*, credito sull'emissione di anidride carbonica
carbon cycle N (*Chem*) ciclo del carbonio
carbon dating [-ˈdeɪtɪŋ] N *datazione effettuata per mezzo del carbonio 14*
carbon dioxide N anidride *f* carbonica, biossido di carbonio
car·bon·ic [kɑːˈbɒnɪk] ADJ carbonico(-a)
car·bon·if·er·ous [ˌkɑːbəˈnɪfərəs] ADJ carbonifero(-a)
car·boni·za·tion [ˌkɑːbənaɪˈzeɪʃən] N carbonizzazione *f*
car·bon·ize [ˈkɑːbənaɪz] VT carbonizzare
carbon monoxide N monossido di carbonio
carbon paper N carta carbone
carbon ribbon N nastro carbonato
carbon sink N *serbatoio in grado di assorbire anidride carbonica*
carbon steel N acciaio al carbonio
carbon tax N carbon tax *f inv*, tassa sull'emissione di anidride carbonica
car-boot sale [kɑːʳbuːtseɪl] N (*Brit*) *vendita di oggetti usati*

CAR-BOOT SALE, GARAGE SALE

In Gran Bretagna i **car-boot sales** sono dei particolari mercatini dell'usato in cui la mercanzia viene messa in vendita nel bagagliaio della propria auto. Di solito si tengono in ampi spazi all'aperto che spesso hanno piazzuole di sosta a pagamento. Negli Stati Uniti la vendita di oggetti usati o di cui ci si vuol disfare, detta **garage sale** o "yard sale", avviene davanti al garage di casa.

▷ www.bbc.co.uk/antiques/buying_and_selling/carbootselling.shtml

Car·bo·run·dum® [ˌkɑːbəˈrʌndəm] N carborundum *m*
car·bun·cle [ˈkɑːˌbʌŋkl] N (*Med*) foruncolo
car·bu·ret·tor, (*Am*) **carburetor** [ˌkɑːbjʊˈrɛtəʳ] N carburatore *m*
car·cass, **car·case** [ˈkɑːkəs] N (*of animal*) carcassa
car·cino·gen [kɑːˈsɪnədʒən] N (*Med*) cancerogeno
car·cino·gen·ic [ˌkɑːsɪnəˈdʒɛnɪk] ADJ (*Med*) cancerogeno(-a)
car·ci·no·ma [ˌkɑːsɪˈnəʊmə] N (*Med*) carcinoma *m*
car crash N incidente *f* stradale
◎ **card** [kɑːd] N (*greetings card, visiting card*) biglietto; (*membership card*) tessera; (*index card*) scheda; (*playing card*) carta (da gioco); (*thin cardboard*) cartoncino; **I'd like to send him a card for his birthday** vorrei spedirgli un biglietto per il suo compleanno; **I sent all my friends cards from New York** ho mandato una cartolina da New York a tutti i miei amici; **here is my card** ecco il mio biglietto da visita; **to play cards** giocare a carte; **I like playing cards** mi piace giocare a carte; **it's on the**

cards (*fig*) è probabile; **to lay one's cards on the table** (*also fig*) mettere le carte in tavola; **to play one's cards right** (*fig*) giocare bene le proprie carte
■ VT (*Golf*) totalizzare; (*Ftbl*): **to be red-/yellow-carded** essere ammonito(-a) con il cartellino rosso/giallo

car·da·mom ['kɑːdəməm], **car·da·mon** ['kɑːdəmən] N cardamomo

card·board ['kɑːdˌbɔːd] N cartone *m*

cardboard box N (scatola di) cartone *m*

cardboard city N *luogo dove dormono (in scatole di cartone) emarginati senza tetto*

card-carrying ['kɑːdˌkærɪɪŋ] ADJ tesserato(-a); (*fig*) convinto(-a)

card game N gioco di carte

car·di·ac ['kɑːdɪæk] ADJ (*Med*) cardiaco(-a)

cardiac arrest N (*Med*) arresto cardiaco

Car·diff ['kɑːdɪf] N Cardiff *f*
▷ www.visitcardiff.info/

car·di·gan ['kɑːdɪgən] N cardigan *m inv*

car·di·nal ['kɑːdɪnl] ADJ, N cardinale (*m*)

card index N schedario

car·di·oid ['kɑːdɪˌɔɪd] N (*Math*) cardioide *f*

car·dio·logi·cal [ˌkɑːdɪə'lɒdʒɪkəl] ADJ (*Med*) cardiologico(-a)

car·di·olo·gist [ˌkɑːdɪ'ɒlɪdʒɪst] N (*Med*) cardiologo(-a)

car·di·ol·ogy [ˌkɑːdɪ'ɒlədʒɪ] N (*Med*) cardiologia

card·phone ['kɑːdfəʊn] N telefono a scheda (magnetica)

card player N giocatore(-trice) (di carte)

card·sharp ['kɑːdˌʃɑːp] N baro

card table N tavolo da gioco

card vote N (*Brit*) voto (palese) per delega

CARE [kɛəʳ] N ABBR (= **Cooperative for American Relief Everywhere**) *confederazione americana di enti no-profit*

◎ **care** [kɛəʳ] N
1 (*worry*) preoccupazione *f*; **without a care in the world** senza alcuna preoccupazione; **he hasn't a care in the world** non ha preoccupazioni di sorta; **the cares of State** i problemi di Stato
2 (*carefulness*) attenzione *f*, cura; (*charge*) cura, custodia; **"with care"** "fragile", "con cura"; **to take care to do sth** fare attenzione a *or* badare a fare qc; **take care!** (*as warning*) (stai) attento!; (*as good wishes*) stammi bene!; **to take care of** (*details, arrangements*) occuparsi di, curarsi di; **to take care of sb** (*child*) badare a qn; (*sick person*) curare qn; **I take care of the children on Saturdays** io mi occupo dei bambini di sabato; **I'll take care of him!** (*fam*) lo sistemo io!; **she can take care of herself** sa badare a se stessa; **take care not to drop it!** stai attento a non farlo cadere!; **care of** (*on letter*) presso; **I'll leave it/him in your care** te lo affido; **the child has been taken into care** il bambino è stato affidato ad un ente assistenziale
■ VI (*be concerned*): **to care (about)** interessarsi (di), preoccuparsi (di); **of course I care about him** certo che m'importa di lui; **I don't care** non m'importa, non me ne importa; **I couldn't care less** non me ne importa un bel niente; **to care deeply about** tenere molto a; **for all I care** per quello che mi interessa; **who cares?** chi se ne frega? (*fam!*), chi se ne importa?
■ VT
1 (*be concerned*): **I don't care what you think** non mi interessa quello che pensi; **I couldn't care less what people say** me ne infischio di quel che dice la gente
2 (*frm: like*) volere, desiderare; **would you care to come this way?** le dispiacerebbe venire da questa parte?; **I wouldn't care to do it** non lo vorrei fare; **I shouldn't care to meet him** preferirei non incontrarlo
▸ **care for** VI + PREP
1 (*look after*) curare, aver cura di; **they'll employ a nurse to care for her** assumeranno un'infermiera che si prenderà cura di lei
2 (*be fond of: person*) voler bene a; **I still care a lot for you** ti voglio ancora tanto bene; **she no longer cares for him** non le importa più niente di lui; **it's the most expensive model, but I don't care much for it** è il modello più costoso, ma non mi piace granché; **I don't care for coffee** non amo particolarmente il caffè; **would you care for a drink?** gradiresti qualcosa da bere?

ca·reen [kə'riːn] VI (*ship*) sbandare
■ VT carenare

◎ **ca·reer** [kə'rɪəʳ] N (*occupation*) professione *f*; (*working life*) carriera; **she had a successful career in journalism** ha fatto una brillante carriera come giornalista
■ VI (*also:* **career along**) sfrecciare, andare di gran carriera
■ ADJ (*diplomat, soldier etc*) di carriera

career break N (*Brit*) congedo temporaneo non retribuito (*dopo il quale non è automatica la riassunzione*)

career guidance N orientamento professionale

ca·reer·ist [kə'rɪərɪst] N carrierista *m/f*

careers officer N consulente *m/f* d'orientamento professionale

career woman N donna in carriera

care·free ['kɛəˌfriː] ADJ spensierato(-a), libero(-a) da preoccupazioni; **a carefree childhood** un'infanzia spensierata

◎ **care·ful** ['kɛəfʊl] ADJ 1 (*taking care, cautious*) attento(-a), cauto(-a); **(be) careful!** (stai) attento!, attenzione!; **to be careful with sth** fare attenzione a qc; **he's very careful with his money** sta molto attento a quanto spende; **be careful what you say to him** stai attento a come gli parli; **he was careful not to offend her** badava a non offenderla 2 (*painstaking: work*) accurato(-a); (: *writer, worker etc*) attento(-a), diligente, zelante

care·ful·ly ['kɛəfəlɪ] ADV (*cautiously*) attentamente, con attenzione, cautamente; (*painstakingly*) con cura, accuratamente; **think carefully!** pensaci attentamente!; **drive carefully!** guida con prudenza!; **she carefully avoided talking about it** ha evitato accuratamente di parlarne

care·ful·ness ['kɛəfʊlnɪs] N (*see adj*) attenzione *f*; accuratezza

care home N (*for elderly people*) casa di riposo; (*for children in care*) casa *f* famiglia *inv*

care·less ['kɛəlɪs] ADJ (*worker, driver, driving*) distratto(-a), disattento(-a), negligente; (*work*) fatto(-a) con poco impegno; (*thoughtless: remark*) senza tatto, privo(-a) di tatto; **she's very careless** è molto sbadata; **careless mistake** errore *m* di distrazione; **careless driver** guidatore(-trice) distratto(-a)

care·less·ly ['kɛəlɪslɪ] ADV (*act, drive*) con disattenzione, distrattamente; (*work*) con poco impegno, negligentemente; (*speak*) senza tatto

care·less·ness ['kɛəlɪsnɪs] N (*see adj*) disattenzione *f*; mancanza d'impegno, negligenza; mancanza di tatto

car·er ['kɛərəʳ] N *familiare che bada a persone anziane o handicappate*

ca·ress [kə'rɛs] N carezza
■ VT carezzare, accarezzare

Cc

care·taker ['kɛə,teɪkəʳ] N custode *m/f*; (*of school*) bidello(-a)
caretaker government N (*Brit*) governo *m* ponte *inv or* provvisorio
care worker N assistente *m/f*; per anziani o bambini con problemi
care·worn ['kɛə,wɔːn] ADJ sciupato(-a) (*dalle preoccupazioni*)
car-ferry ['kɑː,fɛrɪ] N traghetto, nave *f* traghetto *inv*
car·go ['kɑːgəʊ] N carico
cargo boat N cargo
cargo plane N aereo da carico
car hire N (*Brit*) autonoleggio
Car·ib·bean [kærɪ'biːən] ADJ caraibico(-a)
■ N: **the Caribbean** i Caraibi; **we're going to the Caribbean** andremo ai Caraibi; **the Caribbean (Sea)** il Mar dei Caraibi
cari·ca·ture ['kærɪkə,tjʊəʳ] N caricatura
■ VT fare una caricatura di
cari·ca·tur·ist [,kærɪkə'tjʊərɪst] N caricaturista *m/f*
cari·es ['kɛəriːz] N (*Dentistry*) carie *f*
ca·ril·lon [kə'rɪljən] N carillon *m inv*
◎ **car·ing** ['kɛərɪŋ] ADJ (*parent, person*) affettuoso(-a), premuroso(-a); (*society, organization*) umanitario(-a); **the caring professions** professioni in campo medico o sociale; **ours is not a caring society** viviamo in una società ben poco altruista
car mat N tappetino
Car·mel·ite ['kɑːmə,laɪt] N carmelitano(-a)
car·mine ['kɑːmaɪn] ADJ, N carminio *inv*
car·nage ['kɑːnɪdʒ] N carneficina
car·nal ['kɑːnl] ADJ carnale
car·na·tion [kɑː'neɪʃən] N garofano
car·nel·ian [kɑː'niːljən] N cornalina
car·ni·val ['kɑːnɪvəl] N (*public celebration*) carnevale *m*; (*Am: funfair*) luna park *m inv*
car·ni·vore ['kɑːnɪvɔːʳ] N carnivoro
car·nivo·rous [kɑː'nɪvərəs] ADJ carnivoro(-a)
car·ob ['kærəb] N carrubo
car·ol ['kærəl] N: **(Christmas) carol** canto di Natale; canto natalizio
ca·rot·id ar·tery [kə,rɒtɪd'ɑːtərɪ] N carotide *f*
ca·rous·al [kə'raʊzəl] N bevuta
ca·rouse [kə'raʊz] VI far baldoria
carou·sel [,kærʊː'sɛl] N (*Am: merry-go-round*) giostra; (*: at airport: conveyor belt*) nastro trasportatore
carp¹ [kɑːp] N (*fish*) carpa
carp² [kɑːp] VI (*complain*): **to carp at** avere *or* trovare da ridire su
car park N parcheggio
car·pel ['kɑːpəl] N (*Bot*) carpello
car·pen·ter ['kɑːpɪntəʳ] N carpentiere *m*
car·pen·try ['kɑːpɪntrɪ] N carpenteria
car·pet ['kɑːpɪt] N tappeto; (*fitted carpet*) moquette *f inv*; **Persian carpet** tappeto persiano
■ VT (*floor, house*) coprire con tappeto; (*: with fitted carpet*) rivestire di moquette, mettere la moquette a
carpet·bag·ger ['kɑːpɪt,bægəʳ] N (*Pol*) profittatore(-trice) (politico(-a))
carpet bombing N bombardamento a tappeto
car·pet·ing ['kɑːpɪtɪŋ] N moquette *f*
carpet slippers NPL pantofole *fpl*
carpet sweeper N battitappeto
car phone N telefonino per auto
carp·ing ['kɑːpɪŋ] ADJ (*critic*) che trova sempre qualcosa da ridire
■ N lamentele *fpl*

car pool N car pooling *m inv*; (*Comm*) vetture *fpl* di servizio (*di società*)
■ VI fare car pooling; *usare a turno una sola automobile per condividere un tragitto comune*
car·port ['kɑː,pɔːt] N tettoia (per automobile)
car radio N autoradio
car rental N (*Am*) autonoleggio
car·riage ['kærɪdʒ] N **1** (*Brit*)) (*Rail*) carrozza, vagone *m*, vettura; (*horse-drawn*) carrozza; (*of typewriter*) carrello **2** (*of person: bearing*) portamento **3** (*Comm: of goods*) trasporto; (*cost of carriage*) (spese *fpl* di) trasporto; **carriage free** franco di porto; **carriage paid** porto pagato; **carriage forward** porto assegnato
carriage return N (*on typewriter*) leva (*or* tasto) del ritorno a capo
carriage·way ['kærɪdʒ,weɪ] N (*Brit: Aut*) carreggiata
◎ **car·ri·er** ['kærɪəʳ] N **1** (*of goods: person*) corriere *m*; (*: company*) impresa di trasporti, vettore *m*; **by carrier** per corriere **2** (*Med: of disease*) portatore(-trice); **typhoid carrier** portatore(-trice) di tifo **3** (*aircraft carrier*) portaerei *f inv*
carrier bag N (*Brit*) sacchetto, borsa (di plastica)
carrier pigeon N piccione *m* viaggiatore
car·ri·on ['kærɪən] N carogna
carrion crow N cornacchia nera
car·rot ['kærət] N carota
car·roty ['kærətɪ] ADJ: **to have carroty hair** essere un pel di carota
◎ **car·ry** ['kærɪ] VT
1 (*gen*) portare; (*have on one's person: money, documents*) portare *or* avere con sé; (*transport: goods*) trasportare; (*: passengers*) portare; (*message, news*) recare, portare; (*subj: pillar*) sostenere; (*involve: responsibilities etc*) comportare; **I'll carry your bag** porto io la tua borsa; **to carry sth about with one** portarsi dietro qc; **a plane carrying 100 passengers crashed last week** la scorsa settimana è caduto un aereo che trasportava 100 passeggeri; **the wind carried the sound to him** il vento trasportò il suono verso di lui; **the offence carries a £50 fine** il reato prevede una multa di 50 sterline; **both papers carried the story** entrambi i giornali riportarono la storia; **he carries his drink well** regge bene l'alcool; **you're carrying things too far!** stai esagerando!
2 (*Comm: stock*) tenere
3 (*Math: figure*) riportare; (*Fin: interest*) avere; **this loan carries 10% interest** questo prestito ha un interesse del 10%
4 (*approve: motion, bill*) approvare, far passare; (*win: election, point*) vincere; **to carry the day** avere successo
5 he carries himself like a soldier ha il portamento di un militare; **she carries herself well** ha un bel portamento
■ VI (*sound*) trasmettersi, farsi sentire, diffondersi
► **carry away** VT + ADV portare via; **to be carried away** (*fig*) farsi trascinare; **to get carried away by sth** (*fig*) farsi *or* lasciarsi prendere da qc
► **carry back** VT + ADV (*also fig: remind*) riportare
► **carry forward** VT + ADV (*Math, Fin*) riportare
► **carry off** VT + ADV (*seize, take away*) portare via; (*kidnap*) sequestrare, rapire; (*win: prize, medal*) vincere; **he carried it off very well** se l'è cavata molto bene
► **carry on** VT + ADV (*continue: tradition etc*) portare avanti, continuare; (*: business, trade*) mandare avanti; **to carry on a conversation** conversare, parlare
■ VI + ADV

1 **to carry on with sth/doing sth** continuare qc/a fare qc; **she carried on talking** continuò a parlare; **carry on!** va avanti!; **am I boring you? – no, carry on!** ti annoio? – no, va' avanti!
2 (*fam: make a fuss*) fare storie; **how you do carry on!** quante storie fai!
3 (*fam: have an affair*): **to carry on (with)** intendersela (con), filare (con)
▸ **carry out** VT + ADV (*accomplish: plan*) realizzare; (*perform, implement: idea, threat*) mettere in pratica; (*: orders*) eseguire; (*: experiment, search, repairs*) effettuare; (*: investigation*) svolgere; **make sure that he carries out my orders** assicurati che esegua i miei ordini; **I don't believe he'll carry out his threat** non penso che metterà in pratica la sua minaccia
▸ **carry over** VT + ADV riportare
▸ **carry through** VT + ADV (*accomplish: task*) portare a termine, realizzare; (*sustain: person*) sostenere
carry·cot ['kærɪ,kɒt] N (*Brit*) porte-enfant *m inv*, culla portatile
carry-on [,kærɪ'ɒn] N (*fam: fuss*) casino, confusione *f*; (*: fuss*): **what a carry-on!** che casino!
car·sick ['kɑː,sɪk] ADJ: **to be carsick** soffrire il mal d'auto
car·sick·ness ['kɑː,sɪknɪs] N mal *m* d'auto
cart [kɑːt] N carretto; **a horse and cart** un carro trainato da un cavallo; **to put the cart before the horse** (*fig*) mettere il carro davanti ai buoi
■ VT (*fam*) trascinare
carte blanche ['kɑːt'blɑːntʃ] N: **to give sb carte blanche** dare carta bianca a qn
car·tel [kɑː'tɛl] N (*Comm*) cartello
cart·er ['kɑːtəʳ] N carrettiere *m*
Car·tesian [kɑː'tiːzɪən] (*Philosophy*) ADJ cartesiano(-a)
■ N seguace *m/f* di Cartesio
cart·ful ['kɑːt,fʊl] N carrettata
Car·thage ['kɑːθɪdʒ] N Cartagine *f*
Car·tha·gin·ian [,kɑːθə'dʒɪnɪən] ADJ, N cartaginese (*m/f*)
cart·horse ['kɑːt,hɔːs] N cavallo da tiro
car·ti·lage ['kɑːtɪlɪdʒ] N cartilagine *f*
cart·load ['kɑːt,ləʊd] N carrettata
car·tog·ra·pher [kɑː'tɒgrəfəʳ] N cartografo(-a)
car·tog·ra·phy [kɑː'tɒgrəfɪ] N cartografia
car·ton ['kɑːtən] N (*of milk, yogurt*) cartone *m*; (*of ice cream*) vaschetta; (*of cigarettes*) stecca; (*box*) scatola di cartone
car·toon [kɑː'tuːn] N (*in newspaper etc*) vignetta; (*Cine, TV*) cartone *m* animato; (*Art*) cartone; **strip cartoon** fumetto
car·toon·ist [,kɑː'tuːnɪst] N (*in newspaper*) vignettista *m/f*; (*Cine, TV*) disegnatore(-trice) di cartoni animati
cartoon strip N striscia, fumetto
car·tridge ['kɑːtrɪdʒ] N (*for gun, pen*) cartuccia; (*for camera*) caricatore *m*; (*music tape*) cassetta; (*of record player*) testina
cartridge paper N carta da disegno (ruvida)
cart·wheel ['kɑːt,wiːl] N: **to turn a cartwheel** (*Sport etc*) fare la ruota
carve [kɑːv] VT (*Culin: meat*) tagliare; (*stone, wood*) scolpire, intagliare; (*name on tree*) incidere; **dad carved the roast** il papà ha tagliato l'arrosto; **a carved oak chair** una sedia di quercia intagliata; **to carve out a career for o.s** farsi una carriera
■ VI (*Culin*) tagliare la carne
▸ **carve up** VT + ADV (*meat*) tagliare; (*fig: country, money, profits*) suddividere
car·very ['kɑːvərɪ] N *ristorante dove si servono arrosti, tagliati su richiesta del cliente*
carv·ing ['kɑːvɪŋ] N (*Art: in wood, stone*) scultura
carving fork N forchettone *m*
carving knife, carv·er ['kɑːvəʳ] N trinciante *m*
car wash N lavaggio auto; **automatic car wash** autolavaggio automatico
car worker N operaio(-a) dell'industria automobilistica
cas·cade [kæs'keɪd] N cascata
■ VI scendere a cascata; **her hair cascaded over her shoulders** i capelli le ricadevano sulle spalle
◎ **case**[1] [keɪs] N **1** (*gen, Med, Gram*) caso; **the doctor has a lot of cases to see today** il dottore oggi deve vedere molti pazienti; **in any case** in ogni caso, comunque; **in that case** in quel *or* questo caso; **(just) in case** non si sa mai, per precauzione, per sicurezza; **take some money, just in case** prendi un po' di soldi per sicurezza; **I think she knows you're coming, but just in case, you'd better phone her** penso che sappia del tuo arrivo, ma per sicurezza faresti meglio a telefonarle; **in case it rains** caso mai dovesse piovere; **in case he changes his mind** caso mai lui cambiasse idea; **in case of emergency** in caso di emergenza; **a case in point** un esempio tipico; **it's a clear case of murder** è un chiaro caso di omicidio; **in some cases** in alcuni casi; **in most cases** nella maggior parte dei casi, in genere; **it's generally the case that people are selfish** di solito succede che la gente sia egoista; **as this was the case, we decided not to go** stando così le cose, decidemmo di non andare; **if this** *or* **that is the case** quand'è così , se così è; **as the case may be** a seconda del caso **2** (*Law*) caso, processo, causa; (*argument*) motivo, ragione *f*; **the case for the defence/prosecution** le ragioni *or* argomentazioni della difesa/dell'accusa; **the police are investigating the case** la polizia sta indagando sul caso; **to state one's case** esporre le proprie ragioni; (*fig*) perorare la propria causa; **to have a good case** avere pretese legittime; **there's a strong case for reform** ci sono validi argomenti a favore della riforma
case[2] [keɪs] N **1** (*suitcase*) valigia; (*briefcase*) valigetta, cartella; (*packing case*) cassa; (*for camera*) custodia; (*for jewellery*) scatolina, astuccio; (*for spectacles*) custodia, astuccio; (*display case*) vetrinetta; (*of watch*) cassa; **I've packed my case** ho fatto la valigia; **a case of wine** una cassa di vini **2** (*Typ*): **lower/upper case** (carattere *m*) minuscolo/maiuscolo
case file N (*Law, Med*) dossier *m inv*
case-hardened ['keɪs'hɑːdnd] ADJ (*Tech*) cementato(-a); (*fig*) indurito(-a) dall'esperienza
case history N (*Med*) cartella clinica
ca·sein ['keɪsiːɪn] N (*Chem*) caseina
case law N (*Law*) *giurisprudenza basata su sentenze precedenti*
case·ment ['keɪsmənt] N (*window*) finestra
case-sensitive ['keɪs,sensɪtɪv] ADJ (*Comput*) sensibile alle maiuscole o minuscole
case study [keɪs 'stʌdɪ] N casistica
case·work ['keɪs,wɜːk] N (*Sociol*) assistenza sociale
◎ **cash** [kæʃ] N **1** (*coins, notes*) soldi *mpl*, denaro; **in cash** in contanti; **£200 in cash** 200 sterline in contanti; **to pay (in) cash** pagare in contanti; **ready cash** (*fam*) (denaro) contante *m*; **cash in hand** fondo di cassa **2** (*immediate payment*): **to pay cash down** pagare in contanti; **cash with order/on delivery** (*Comm*) pagamento all'ordinazione/alla consegna **3** (*fam: money*) quattrini *mpl*; **he's got plenty of cash** ha un

Cc

sacco di quattrini; **to be short of cash** essere a corto di soldi; **I'm a bit short of cash** sono un po' a corto di soldi
■VT *(cheque)* riscuotere, incassare
▸ **cash in** VT + ADV *(insurance policy)* riscuotere, riconvertire
▸ **cash in on** VI + ADV + PREP sfruttare
cash account N conto *m* cassa *inv*
cash-and-carry ['kæʃənd'kærɪ] N cash and carry *m inv*
cash-book ['kæʃ,bʊk] N libro *or* giornale *m* di cassa
cash box N cassetta *f* portavalori *inv*
cash card N carta per prelievi automatici, carta *f* bancomat *inv*
cash crop N *prodotto agricolo coltivato su larga scala per la vendita*
cash desk N *(Brit)* cassa
cash discount N sconto contanti
cash dispenser N sportello automatico, bancomat *m*
cash·ew [kæ'ʃuː] N *(also:* **cashew nut***)* anacardio
cash flow N liquidità, cash-flow *m inv*
cash·ier[1] [kæ'ʃɪəʳ] N cassiere(-a)
cash·ier[2] [kæ'ʃɪəʳ] VT *(esp Mil: officer)* destituire
cash machine N sportello automatico
cash·mere [kæʃ'mɪəʳ] N cachemire *m inv*, cashmere *m inv*
■ADJ di cachemire; **cashmere jumper** maglione *m* di cachemire
cash on delivery N *(Comm)* pagamento alla consegna
cash payment N pagamento in contanti
cash point N sportello automatico; ≈ Bancomat® *m inv*
cash price N prezzo per contanti
cash prize N premio in denaro
cash register N registratore *m* di cassa
cash sale N vendita per contanti
cas·ing ['keɪsɪŋ] N *(Tech)* rivestimento; *(of tyre)* copertone *m*
ca·si·no [kə'siːnəʊ] N casinò *m inv*
cask [kɑːsk] N barile *m*, botte *f*
cas·ket ['kɑːskɪt] N *(for jewels)* scrigno, cofanetto; *(Am: coffin)* bara
Cas·pian ['kæspɪən] N: **the Caspian Sea** il mar Caspio
Cassandra [kə'sændrə] N *(Myth, fig)* Cassandra
cas·se·role ['kæsə,rəʊl] N *(utensil)* casseruola (a due manici); *(food)*: **chicken/veal casserole** pollo/vitello in casseruola; **to make a casserole** fare uno spezzatino; **casserole dish** casseruola
cas·sette [kæ'sɛt] N cassetta
cassette deck N piastra di registrazione
cassette player N riproduttore *m* a cassetta
cassette recorder N registratore *m* a cassetta
cas·sia ['kæsɪə] N *(Bot)* cassia
Cassius ['kæsɪəs] N Cassio
cas·sock ['kæsək] N tonaca
◎**cast** [kɑːst] *(vb: pt, pp* **cast***)* N **1** *(Fishing)* lancio **2** *(mould)* stampo, forma; *(Med: plaster cast)* gesso, ingessatura; **cast of mind** mentalità *f inv* **3** *(Theatre)* cast *m inv*; **after the play we met the cast** dopo la commedia abbiamo incontrato il cast **4** *(Med: squint)* strabismo; **he has a cast in his right eye** ha l'occhio destro strabico
■VT **1** *(also fig: throw)* gettare; *(fishing line)* lanciare; *(shadow, light)* gettare, proiettare; **to cast doubt on sth** far sorgere dubbi su qc; **to cast one's vote (for)** votare (per); **to cast one's eyes over sth** dare un'occhiata a qc **2** *(shed)* spogliarsi di; *(horseshoe)* perdere; **the snake cast its skin** il serpente ha cambiato la pelle **3** *(metal)* colare, fondere; *(plaster)* gettare; *(bronze etc statue)* fondere, gettare **4** *(Theatre, Cine: part)* affidare; (: *actor)* scritturare, ingaggiare; **to cast sb as Hamlet** scegliere qn per la parte di Amleto
▸ **cast about for** VI + ADV + PREP cercare di trovare
▸ **cast aside** VT + ADV *(reject)* mettere da parte
▸ **cast away** VT + ADV *(Naut)*: **to be cast away** naufragare
▸ **cast down** VT + ADV: **to be cast down** essere giù (di corda), essere depresso(-a)
▸ **cast off** VT + ADV *(Knitting)* diminuire, calare
■VI + ADV *(Naut)* levare gli ormeggi, salpare; *(Knitting)* diminuire, calare
▸ **cast on** *(Knitting)* VT + ADV avviare
■VI + ADV avviare (le maglie)
▸ **cast out** VT + ADV *(liter)* abbandonare
▸ **cast up** VT + ADV: **to cast sth up (at sb)** rinfacciare qc (a qn)
cas·ta·nets [,kæstə'nɛts] NPL castagnette *fpl*, nacchere *fpl*
cast·away ['kæstəweɪ] N naufrago(-a)
caste [kɑːst] N casta
■ADJ di casta
cast·er, cas·tor ['kɑːstəʳ] N *(wheel)* rotella
cas·ter sug·ar ['kɑːstər,ʃʊgəʳ] N zucchero semolato
cas·ti·gate ['kæstɪgeɪt] VT *(frm)* castigare, punire
Cas·tile [kæ'stiːl] N Castiglia
Cas·til·ian [kæs'tɪlɪən] ADJ castigliano(-a)
■N *(person)* castigliano(-a); *(language)* castigliano
cast·ing ['kɑːstɪŋ] N *(object)* pezzo di fusione
cast·ing vote ['kɑːstɪŋ'vəʊt] N *(Brit)* voto decisivo
cast-iron ['kɑːst'aɪən] ADJ di ghisa; *(fig: will, alibi)* di ferro; **the police had a cast-iron case against the drug smuggler** la polizia aveva prove schiaccianti contro il trafficante di droga
cast iron N ghisa
◎**cas·tle** ['kɑːsl] N castello; *(fortified)* rocca; *(Chess)* torre *f*; **castles in the air** *(fig)* castelli in aria
cast·off ['kɑːstɒf] N *(garment)* indumento *or* vestito smesso
cast-off ['kɑːst,ɒf] ADJ *(clothing)* smesso(-a)
Castor ['kɑːstəʳ] N *(Myth, Astron)* Castore *m*
cas·tor ['kɑːstəʳ] N = **caster**
castor oil N olio di ricino
cas·trate [kæs'treɪt] VT castrare
cas·tra·tion [kæs'treɪʃən] N castrazione *f*
cas·ual ['kæʒjʊəl] ADJ **1** *(by chance: meeting)* fortuito(-a), casuale; (: *walk, stroll)* senza meta precisa; (: *glance)* di sfuggita; (: *remark)* fatto(-a) di sfuggita; **a casual remark** un'osservazione buttata là; **we're just casual acquaintances** ci conosciamo appena; **before meeting him she'd had one or two casual affairs** prima di incontrarlo aveva avuto un paio di storie poco importanti; **to have casual sex** avere avventure **2** *(unconcerned: attitude, person)* noncurante, indifferente, disinvolto(-a); **he was very casual about it** si è mostrato indifferente **3** *(informal: discussion, tone etc)* informale; (: *clothing)* sportivo(-a), casual *inv*; **casual wear** casual *m*; **I prefer casual clothes** preferisco i vestiti sportivi **4** *(irregular: work)* saltuario(-a); (: *worker)* saltuario(-a), avventizio(-a); **it's just a casual job** è solo un lavoro saltuario
■NPL **casuals** *(shoes)* calzature *fpl* sportive
cas·ual·ize ['kæzjʊlaɪz] VT *(Brit: Comm)* rendere precario(-a); **a casualized workforce** manodopera precaria
casual labour N manodopera avventizia
casu·al·ly ['kæʒjʊlɪ] ADV *(see adj 1, 2, 3)* casualmente;

senza meta precisa; di sfuggita; con noncuranza, con disinvoltura; in modo informale; in modo sportivo *or* informale; **to dress casually** vestirsi sportivo

◎ **casu·al·ty** ['kæʒjʊltɪ] N (*Mil: dead*) vittima, morto, caduto; (*: wounded*) ferito; (*in accident: dead*) vittima; (*: injured*) ferito; **heavy casualties** grosse perdite *fpl*; **there are no reports of casualties** non è stato segnalato nessun ferito; **the casualties include a young boy killed by shellfire** tra le vittime c'è un ragazzo ucciso in un bombardamento

> **DID YOU KNOW ...?**
> **casualty** is not translated by the Italian word *casualità*

casualty department N (*Brit*) pronto soccorso

CAT [kæt] N ABBR (= **computerized axial tomography**) TAC *f inv* (= *tomografia assiale computerizzata*), **CAT scanner** TAC *f inv*

◎ **cat** [kæt] N gatto(-a); (*species*) felino(-a); **big cats such as lions ...** grossi felini come leoni...; **Siamese cat** gatto siamese; **that's put the cat among the pigeons!** ha suscitato un vespaio!; **that's let the cat out of the bag** questo non è più un segreto; **like a cat on hot bricks** sulle spine, sui carboni ardenti, come un'anima in pena; **to fight like cat and dog** essere come cane e gatto; **when the cat's away the mice will play** quando il gatto non c'è i topi ballano

cata·clysm ['kætə,klɪzəm] N cataclisma *m*

cata·clys·mic [,kætə'klɪzmɪk] ADJ (*liter*) catastrofico(-a)

cata·combs ['kætə,ku:mz] NPL catacombe *fpl*

Cata·lan ['kætə,læn] ADJ catalano(-a)
■ N (*person*) catalano(-a); (*language*) catalano

cata·logue, (*Am*) **cata·log** ['kætə,lɒg] N catalogo
■ VT catalogare

Cata·lo·nia [,kætə'ləʊnɪə] N Catalogna

ca·taly·sis [kə'tæləsɪs] N (*Chem*) catalisi *f*

cata·lyst ['kætəlɪst] N (*all senses*) catalizzatore *m*

cata·lyt·ic [,kætə'lɪtɪk] ADJ 1 (*Chem, property*) catalitico
2 (*fig*): **to have a catalytic effect** fungere da catalizzatore *m*

cata·lyt·ic con·vert·er [,kætə'lɪtɪk,kən'vɜ:tə^r] N (*Aut*) marmitta catalitica, catalizzatore *m*

cata·ma·ran [,kætəmə'ræn] N catamarano

cat-and-mouse ['kæt,ənd'maus] ADJ: **to play a cat-and-mouse game with sb** giocare al gatto e al topo con qn

cata·pult ['kætə,pʌlt] N (*slingshot*) fionda; (*Mil, Aer*) catapulta
■ VT catapultare

cata·ract ['kætə,rækt] N (*Geog, Med*) cateratta

ca·tarrh [kə'tɑ:^r] N catarro

ca·tarrh·al [kə'tɑ:rəl] ADJ catarrale

ca·tas·tro·phe [kə'tæstrəfɪ] N catastrofe *f*

cata·stroph·ic [,kætə'strɒfɪk] ADJ catastrofico(-a)

cata·stroph·ical·ly [,kætə'strɒfɪklɪ] ADV catastroficamente

cat·call ['kæt,kɔ:l] N (*at meeting etc*) fischio
■ VI fischiare

◎ **catch** [kætʃ] (*vb: pt, pp* **caught**)
■ N
1 (*of ball*) presa; (*fish caught*) pescato; **a brilliant catch** un'ottima presa; **he spent all day fishing without a single catch** passò tutta la giornata a pescare senza prendere niente; **he's a good catch** (*fig*) è un buon partito
2 (*fastener: on suitcase, door*) gancio, fermo
3 (*trick, snag*) tranello, inganno, trabocchetto; **what's/where's the catch?** dove sta l'inganno?
4 **with a catch in one's voice** con la voce spezzata *or* rotta
■ VT
1 (*ball*) afferrare, prendere; (*fish*) prendere, pescare; (*thief*) prendere, acchiappare, acciuffare; (*bus, train*) prendere; (*entangle*) impigliare; **I caught my fingers in the door** mi son chiuso le dita nella porta; **I caught my coat on that nail** mi si è impigliato il cappotto in quel chiodo; **to catch sb's attention/eye** attirare l'attenzione/lo sguardo di qn; **to catch sight of** scorgere
2 (*take by surprise: person*) cogliere, sorprendere; **to catch sb doing sth** sorprendere qn a fare qc; **you won't catch me doing ...** non mi vedrai mai fare...; **caught in the act** colto(-a) sul fatto; **caught in the rain** sorpreso(-a) dalla pioggia
3 (*hear, understand: remark*) afferrare, cogliere; (*portray: atmosphere, likeness*) cogliere
4 (*disease*) prendere, contrarre; (*hit*) colpire; **to catch cold** prendere freddo; **to catch fire** prendere fuoco; **the punch caught him on the chin** è stato colpito al mento con un pugno; **to catch one's breath** (*from shock etc*) restare senza fiato; (*after effort*) riprendere fiato; **you'll catch it!** (*fam*) vedrai!
■ VI
1 (*get entangled*) impigliarsi, restare impigliato(-a)
2 (*fire, wood*) prendere

▸ **catch at** VI + PREP (*object*) afferrare; (*opportunity*) cogliere

▸ **catch on** VI + ADV
1 (*understand*): **to catch on (to sth)** capire (qc)
2 (*become popular*) affermarsi, far presa

▸ **catch out** VT + ADV (*Brit fig: with trick question*) cogliere in fallo, prendere in castagna; **to catch sb out in a lie** scoprire qn a dire una bugia

▸ **catch up** VT + ADV (*snatch up*) afferrare; **to catch sb up** (*walking, working etc*) raggiungere qn; **she caught me up** mi ha raggiunto
■ VI + ADV: **to catch up with sb** raggiungere qn; **to catch up on one's work** mettersi in pari col lavoro; **I've got to catch up on my work** devo rimettermi in pari col lavoro; **to catch up with the news** aggiornarsi

catch-22 ['kætʃ,twentɪ'tu:] N: **it's a catch-22 situation** non c'è via d'uscita

catch-as-catch-can ['kætʃəz,kætʃ'kæn] N (*Wrestling*) catch *m inv*

catch·ing ['kætʃɪŋ] ADJ (*Med, fig*) contagioso(-a); **don't worry, it's not catching!** non preoccuparti, non è contagioso!

catch·ment ['kætʃmənt] N (*Geog*) bacino

catchment area N (*Brit: of school, hospital*) bacino di utenza; (*Geog*) bacino imbrifero

catch phrase N slogan *m inv*, tormentone *m*

catch question N domanda *f* trabocchetto *inv*

catch-up ['kætʃəp] N: **to play catch-up** recuperare

catch·word ['kætʃ,wɜ:d] N slogan *m inv*

catchy ['kætʃɪ] ADJ (*tune*) orecchiabile

cat·echism ['kætɪ,kɪzəm] N catechismo

cat·echize ['kætɪ,kaɪz] VT catechizzare

cat·egori·cal [,kætɪ'gɒrɪkəl], **cat·egor·ic** [,kætɪ'gɒrɪk] ADJ categorico(-a)

cat·egori·cal·ly [,kætɪ'gɒrɪkəlɪ] ADV categoricamente

cat·ego·ri·za·tion [,kætɪgəraɪ'zeɪʃən] N catalogazione *f*, classificazione *f*

Cc

cat·ego·rize ['kætɪgə,raɪz] VT catalogare, classificare, dividere per categorie

◎ **cat·ego·ry** ['kætɪgərɪ] N categoria

ca·tena·ry [kə'ti:nərɪ] N (*Phys*) catenaria

ca·ter ['keɪtə^r] VI (*provide food*) provvedere alla ristorazione

■ VT (*esp Am: wedding, party*) provvedere ai rinfreschi per

▸ **cater for** VI + PREP (*Brit: wedding, party*) provvedere ai rinfreschi per; (*: needs*) provvedere a; (*: readers, consumers*) incontrare i gusti di

▸ **cater to** VI + PREP (*Brit: whims, demands*) soddisfare

ca·ter·er ['keɪtərə^r] N chi si occupa di catering *or* ristorazione

ca·ter·ing ['keɪtərɪŋ] N catering *m inv*, ristorazione *f* (collettiva)

catering trade N settore *m* (della) ristorazione

cat·er·pil·lar ['kætə,pɪlə^r] N (*Zool*) bruco; (*vehicle*) cingolato

caterpillar track N cingolo

cat·er·waul ['kætə,wɔ:l] VI (*person, cat*) miagolare

cat·er·waul·ing ['kætə,wɔ:lɪŋ] N miagolio

cat·fight ['kætfaɪt] N baruffa tra donne

cat flap N gattaiola

ca·thedral [kə'θi:drəl] N cattedrale *f*, duomo

cathedral city N sede *f* vescovile

Cath·erine wheel ['kæθərɪn,wi:l] N girandola

cath·eter ['kæθɪtə^r] N (*Med*) catetere *m*

cath·ode ['kæθəʊd] N (*Elec*) catodo

cathode-ray tube ['kæθəʊd,reɪ'tju:b] N (*Elec*) tubo a raggi catodici

◎ **Catho·lic** ['kæθəlɪk] (*Rel*) ADJ (*Roman Catholic*) cattolico(-a); **the Catholic Church** la Chiesa Cattolica

■ N cattolico(-a); **I'm a Catholic** sono cattolico(-a)

catho·lic ['kæθəlɪk] ADJ (*wide-ranging: taste, interests*) ampio(-a), vasto(-a), eclettico(-a)

Ca·tholi·cism [kə'θɒlɪsɪzəm] N Cattolicesimo

Catiline ['kætɪ,laɪn] N Catilina *m*

cati·on ['kætaɪən] N (*Chem*) catione *m*

cat·kin ['kætkɪn] N (*Bot*) amento, gattino

cat·like ['kæt,laɪk] ADJ felino(-a)

cat·mint ['kæt,mɪnt] N gattaia, nepeta

cat·nap ['kæt,næp] N pisolino; **to take a catnap** fare un pisolino

Cato ['keɪtəʊ] N Catone *m*

cat-o'-nine-tails ['kætənaɪn'teɪlz] N gatto a nove code

CAT scanner ['kæt,skænə^r] N (*Med*) apparecchiatura per la TAC *f inv*

cat's cradle N (*game*) ripiglino

cat's-eye ['kæts,aɪ] N (*Brit*) (*Aut*) catarifrangente *m*

cat·suit ['kætsu:t] N tutina-pantalone elasticizzata

cat·sup ['kætsəp] N (*Am*) ketchup *m inv*

cat·ti·ness ['kætɪnɪs] N malignità

cat·tle ['kætl] NPL bestiame *m*

cattle breeder N allevatore *m* di bestiame

cattle grid N *griglia, attraverso strada o sentiero, che impedisce il passaggio del bestiame*

cattle·man ['kætlmən] N (*pl* **-men**) bovaro

cattle shed N stalla

cattle show N mostra di bestiame

cattle truck N carro *m* bestiame *inv*

cat·ty ['kætɪ] ADJ (*comp* **-ier**, *superl* **-iest**) (*fam*) maligno(-a), dispettoso(-a)

Catullus [kə'tʌləs] N Catullo

cat·walk ['kæt,wɔ:k] N passerella (*in sfilata di moda*)

Cau·ca·sian [kɔ:'keɪzɪən] ADJ, N caucasico(-a)

Caucasus ['kɔ:kəsəs] N Caucaso

cau·cus ['kɔ:kəs] N (*Am*) (*Pol*) (riunione *f* del) comitato elettorale; (*Brit Pol: group*) comitato di dirigenti

CAUCUS

Caucus è il termine usato, specialmente negli Stati Uniti, per indicare una riunione informale dei rappresentanti di spicco di un partito politico che precede una riunione ufficiale. Con uso estensivo, la parola indica il nucleo direttivo di un partito politico.

▹ http://fpc.state.gov/fpc/c9810.htm
▹ http://dems.house.gov/
▹ www.gop.gov/defaulthb.asp

caught [kɔ:t] PT, PP *of* **catch**

caul·dron ['kɔ:ldrən] N calderone *m*

cau·li·flow·er ['kɒlɪ,flauə^r] N cavolfiore *m*

cauliflower cheese N (*Culin*) cavolfiori *mpl* gratinati

caus·al ['kɔ:zəl] ADJ causale

cau·sal·ity [kɔ:'zælɪtɪ] N causalità

causa·tive ['kɔ:zətɪv] ADJ causativo(-a)

◎ **cause** [kɔ:z] N **1** causa; (*reason*) motivo, ragione *f*; **cause and effect** causa ed effetto; **with good cause** a ragione; **to be the cause of** essere (la) causa di; **there's no cause for alarm** non c'è motivo di allarme; **there is no cause for concern** non c'è ragione di preoccuparsi; **he had no cause for complaint** non aveva motivo di lamentarsi **2** (*purpose*) causa; **in the cause of justice** per la (causa della) giustizia; **to make common cause with** far causa comune con; **it's all in a good cause** (*fam*) è tutto a fin di bene

■ VT causare; **to cause sth to be done** far fare qc; **to cause sb to do sth** far fare qc a qn

cause·way ['kɔ:z,weɪ] N strada rialzata

caus·tic ['kɔ:stɪk] ADJ (*Chem, fig*) caustico(-a)

caus·ti·cal·ly ['kɔ:stɪklɪ] ADV causticamente

caustic soda N soda caustica

cau·ter·ize ['kɔ:tə,raɪz] VT cauterizzare

cau·tion ['kɔ:ʃən] N (*care*) attenzione *f*, prudenza; (*warning*) avvertimento, ammonizione *f*; (*: from police*) diffida; **a note of caution** una nota di avvertimento; **it should be handled with the utmost caution** dev'essere maneggiato con la massima cautela

■ VT: **to caution sb** (*subj: official*) ammonire qn; (*: policeman*) diffidare qn; **to caution sb against doing sth** diffidare qn dal fare qc

cau·tion·ary ['kɔ:ʃənərɪ] ADJ: **cautionary tale** storiella ammonitrice

◎ **cau·tious** ['kɔ:ʃəs] ADJ cauto(-a), prudente

cau·tious·ly ['kɔ:ʃəslɪ] ADV cautamente, prudentemente

cau·tious·ness ['kɔ:ʃəsnɪs] N prudenza, cautela

cav·al·cade [,kævəl'keɪd] N (*of horses, cars*) sfilata

cava·lier [,kævə'lɪə^r] N (*knight*) cavaliere *m*

■ ADJ (*pej: offhand: person*) brusco(-a); (*: attitude*) non curante

cav·al·ry ['kævəlrɪ] N cavalleria

◎ **cave** [keɪv] N grotta, caverna

■ VI: **to go caving** fare speleologia

▸ **cave in** VI + ADV (*ceiling, roof*) sfondarsi, crollare; (*ground*) franare, cedere

DID YOU KNOW ...?
cave is not translated by the Italian word *cava*

ca·veat ['kævɪ,æt] N ammonimento, avvertimento

cave-in ['keɪv,ɪn] N crollo

cave·man ['keɪv,mæn] N (*pl* **-men**) cavernicolo, uomo delle caverne

cave painting N pittura rupestre

cav·er ['keɪvəʳ] N speleologo(-a)

cav·ern ['kævən] N caverna

cav·ern·ous ['kævənəs] ADJ (*eyes, cheeks*) incavato(-a), infossato(-a); (*pit*) ampio(-a) e profondo(-a); (*darkness*) fitto(-a)

cavi·ar, **cavi·are** ['kævɪ,ɑːʳ] N caviale *m*

cav·il ['kævɪl] VI (*pt, pp* **cavilled,** *Am* **caviled**) **to cavil (at)** cavillare (su)

cav·ity ['kævɪtɪ] N cavità

cavity-wall in·su·la·tion ['kævɪtɪ,wɔːlɪnsjʊ'leɪʃən] N isolamento per pareti a intercapedine

ca·vort [kə'vɔːt] VI saltellare, far capriole

caw [kɔː] N gracchio
■ VI gracchiare

cay·enne [ˈkeɪɛn] N: **cayenne (pepper)** pepe *m* di Caienna

cay·man ['keɪmən] N caimano

CB [,siː'biː] N ABBR **1** (*Brit:* = **Companion (of the Order) of the Bath**) *titolo onorifico* **2** (= **Citizens' Band (Radio)**) CB *m*; **CB radio (set)** baracchino

CBC [,siːbiː'siː] N ABBR = *Canadian Broadcasting Corporation*

CBE [,siːbiː'iː] N ABBR (*Brit:* = **Commander (of the Order) of the British Empire**) *titolo onorifico*

CBI [,siːbiː'aɪ] N ABBR (= **Confederation of British Industry**) ≈ CONFINDUSTRIA (= *Confederazione generale dell'industria italiana*)
▹ www.cbi.org.uk

CBS [,siːbiː'ɛs] N ABBR (*Am*) = *Columbia Broadcasting System*

CC [,siː'siː] ABBR (*Brit*) = **county council**

cc [,siː'siː] ABBR **1** (= **cubic centimetres**) CC **2** (*on email*) Cc

CCA [,siːsiː'eɪ] N ABBR (*Am:* = **Circuit Court of Appeals**) corte *f* d'appello itinerante

CCTV [,siːsiːtiː'viː] N (= **closed-circuit television**) televisione *f* a circuito chiuso

CCU [,siːsiː'juː] N ABBR (*Am:* = **coronary care unit**) unità coronarica

CD [,siː'diː] N ABBR **1** (= **compact disc**) CD *m inv* **2** (*Mil: Brit*) = *Civil Defence (Corps)* (: *Am*) = *Civil Defense*
■ ABBR (*Brit:* = **Corps Diplomatique**) CD

CD burner N, **CD writer** N masterizzatore *m*

CDC [,siːdiː'siː] N ABBR (*Am*) = *center for disease control*

CD-I® [,siːdiː'aɪ] N ABBR (= **compact disc interactive**) CDI *m inv*

CD player N lettore *m* CD *inv*

CD-R ABBR (= **compact disc recordable**) CD-R *m inv*

Cdr. ABBR (= **commander**) Com.

CD-ROM [,siːdiː'rɒm] N ABBR (= **compact disc read-only memory**) CD-rom *m inv*

CD-ROM drive N lettore *m* CD-ROM

CD-RW [,siːdiːɑː'dʌbljʊ] ABBR (= **compact disc rewritable**) CD-RW *m inv*, CD *m inv* riscrivibile

CDT [,siːdiː'tiː] ABBR **1** (*Am:* = **Central Daylight Time**) *ora estiva nel fuso orario degli Stati Uniti centrali* **2** (*Brit: Scol:* = **Craft, Design and Technology**) educazione *f* tecnica

CD writer N = **CD burner**

◎ **cease** [siːs] VT, VI cessare, smettere

◎ **cease-fire** [,siːs'faɪəʳ] N cessate il fuoco *m inv*

cease·less ['siːslɪs] ADJ incessante, continuo(-a), senza sosta

cease·less·ly ['siːslɪslɪ] ADV continuamente, senza sosta

CED [,siːiː'diː] N ABBR (*Am*) = *Committee for Economic Development*

ce·dar ['siːdəʳ] N cedro
■ ADJ di cedro

cedar of Lebanon N cedro del Libano

cede [siːd] VT (*territory*) cedere; (*argument*) cedere su

ce·dil·la [sɪ'dɪlə] N cediglia

CEEB [,siːiːiː'biː] N ABBR (*Am:* = **College Entrance Examination Board**) *commissione per l'esame di ammissione al college*

cei·lidh ['keɪlɪ] N *festa con musiche e danze popolari scozzesi o irlandesi*
▹ http://website.lineone.net/~trotternish/ceilidh2.html
▹ www.scottishdance.net/ceilidh/dances.html

ceil·ing ['siːlɪŋ] N (*of room etc*) soffitto; (*of boat*) pagliolato; (*fig: upper limit*) tetto, limite *m* massimo

cel·an·dine ['sɛlən,daɪn] N (*Bot*) celidonia

ce·leb [sə'leb] N (*fam*) celebrità *f inv*

◎ **cel·ebrate** ['sɛlɪ,breɪt] VT (*event, festival, birthday*) celebrare, festeggiare; (*mass*) celebrare; **I celebrated my birthday last week** ho festeggiato il mio compleanno la settimana scorsa
■ VI far festa

cel·ebrat·ed ['sɛlɪ,breɪtɪd] ADJ celebre

◎ **cel·ebra·tion** [,sɛlɪ'breɪʃən] N (*act*) celebrazione *f*; (*festivity*) celebrazione, festa

cel·ebra·tory [,sɛlɪ'breɪtrɪ] ADJ (*frm*) per celebrare

ce·leb·rity [sɪ'lebrɪtɪ] N celebrità *f inv*

ce·leri·ac [sə'lɛrɪ,æk] N sedano *m* rapa *inv*

cel·ery ['sɛlərɪ] N sedano; **head/stick of celery** testa/gambo di sedano

ce·les·tial [sɪ'lɛstɪəl] ADJ (*also fig*) celestiale, celeste

celi·ba·cy ['sɛlɪbəsɪ] N celibato

celi·bate ['sɛlɪbɪt] ADJ, N (*man*) celibe (*m*); (*woman*) nubile (*f*)

◎ **cell** [sɛl] N (*in prison, monastery*) cella; (*Bio*) cellula; (*Elec*) elemento (di batteria); **prisoners spend many hours in their cells** i prigionieri trascorrono molte ore in cella; **dry cell** (*Chem*) cella a secco

cel·lar ['sɛləʳ] N cantina; **in the cellar** in cantina

cell differentiation N (*Bio*) differenziazione *f* cellulare

cell division N (*Bio*) divisione *f* cellulare

cel·list ['tʃɛlɪst] N violoncellista *m/f*

cel·lo ['tʃɛləʊ] N violoncello

cel·lo·phane® ['sɛlə,feɪn] N cellophane® *m*

cell·phone ['sɛl,fəʊn] N cellulare *m*

cel·lu·lar ['sɛljʊləʳ] ADJ (*Bio*) cellulare; **cellular blanket** coperta a tessitura rada

cel·lu·loid ['sɛljʊlɔɪd] N celluloide *f*

cel·lu·lose ['sɛljʊləʊs] N cellulosa

cell wall N (*Bio*) parete *f* cellulare

Celsius ['sɛlsɪəs] ADJ Celsius *inv*; **Celsius scale of temperature** scala Celsius

Celt [kɛlt, sɛlt] N celta *m/f*
▹ www.ibiblio.org/gaelic/celts.html
▹ http://celt.net/

Celt·ic ['kɛltɪk] ADJ celtico(-a)
■ N (*language*) celtico

ce·ment [sə'mɛnt] N cemento; (*glue*) adesivo; **cement floor** pavimento di cemento
■ VT cementare

cement mixer N betoniera

cem·etery ['semɪtrɪ] N cimitero, camposanto

ceno·taph ['sɛnə,tɑːf] N cenotafio

cen·sor ['sɛnsəʳ] N censore *m*

Cc

■VT censurare, sottoporre a censura
cen·so·ri·ous [ˌsɛnˈsɔːrɪəs] ADJ critico(-a)
cen·sor·ship [ˈsɛnsəʃɪp] N censura
cen·sure [ˈsɛnʃəʳ] N biasimo, censura
■VT biasimare, censurare
cen·sus [ˈsɛnsəs] N censimento
▷ www.census.gov/ipc/www/idbnew.html
▷ www.statistics.gov.uk/census2001/cb_1.asp
▷ http://www12.statcan.ca/english/census01/home/index.cfm
▷ www.abs.gov.au/
▷ www.stats.govt.nz/census/default.htm
▷ www.statssa.gov.za/census01/html/default.asp
cent [sɛnt] N (*coin: of dollar, euro*) centesimo; **I haven't a cent** non ho una lira *or* un centesimo; *see also* **per cent**
cen·taur [ˈsɛntɔːʳ] N centauro
cen·te·nar·ian [ˌsɛntɪˈnɛərɪən] N centenario(-a)
cen·te·nary [sɛnˈtiːnərɪ] N centenario
cen·ten·nial [sɛnˈtɛnɪəl] ADJ centennale, centenario
■N (*Am*) = **centenary**
cen·ter [ˈsɛntəʳ] (*Am*) = **centre**
cen·ti·grade [ˈsɛntɪˌgreɪd] ADJ centigrado(-a); **30 degrees centigrade** 30 gradi centigradi
cen·ti·li·tre, (*Am*) **cen·ti·li·ter** [ˈsɛntɪˌliːtəʳ] N centilitro
cen·ti·me·tre, (*Am*) **cen·ti·me·ter** [ˈsɛntɪˌmiːtəʳ] N centimetro
cen·ti·pede [ˈsɛntɪˌpiːd] N millepiedi *m inv*, centopiedi *m inv*
◎**cen·tral** [ˈsɛntrəl] ADJ centrale
Central African Republic N la Repubblica Centrafricana
Central America N l'America centrale
Central Europe N l'Europa centrale
central government N il governo
central heating N riscaldamento autonomo
cen·tral·ism [ˈsɛntrəlɪzm] N (*Pol*) centralismo
cen·tral·ity [ˌsɛnˈtrælɪtɪ] N (*frm*) centralità *f inv*
cen·tral·ize [ˈsɛntrəˌlaɪz] VT centralizzare, accentrare
cen·tral·ly [ˈsɛntrəlɪ] ADV: **centrally heated** che ha il riscaldamento autonomo
central nervous system N sistema *m* nervoso centrale
central processing unit N (*Comput*) unità *f inv* centrale di elaborazione
central reservation N (*Brit Aut*) banchina *f* spartitraffico *inv*
◎**cen·tre**, (*Am*) **cen·ter** [ˈsɛntəʳ] N centro; **the city centre** il centro della città; **sports centre** centro sportivo; **she is the centre of attention** è al centro dell'attenzione
■VT **1** centrare, mettere al centro **2** (*concentrate*): **to centre (on)** concentrare (su); **their demands centred round pay** gran parte delle loro richieste riguardavano il salario; **her plans centre on her child** i suoi progetti ruotano attorno al bambino
■VI centrare
centre·board [ˈsɛntəˌbɔːd] N (*Naut*) deriva
centre·fold, (*Am*) **centerfold** [ˈsɛntəˌfəʊld] N (*of magazine*) paginone *m* centrale
centre forward [ˌsɛntəˈfɔːwəd] N (*Sport*) centravanti *m inv*
centre half [ˌsɛntəˈhɑːf] N (*Sport*) centromediano
centre mark N (*Tennis*) linea centrale di servizio
centre of gravity N baricentro, centro di gravità
centre parties NPL (*Pol*) partiti di centro
centre·piece, (*Am*) **centerpiece** [ˈsɛntəˌpiːs] N centrotavola *m*; (*fig*) pezzo forte, punta di diamante
centre service line N (*Tennis*) linea di divisione centrale
centre spread N (*Brit*) pubblicità *f inv* a doppia pagina
centre-stage [ˌsɛntəˈsteɪdʒ] N: **to take centre-stage** porsi al centro dell'attenzione
cen·trifu·gal [sɛnˈtrɪfjʊgəl] ADJ (*Phys*) centrifugo(-a)
cen·tri·fuge [ˈsɛntrɪˌfjuːʒ] N centrifuga
cen·trip·etal [sɛnˈtrɪpɪtl] ADJ (*Phys*) centripeto(-a)
cen·trist [ˈsɛntrɪst] ADJ, N (*Pol*) centrista *(m/f)*
cen·tu·ri·on [sɛnˈtjʊərɪən] N centurione *m*
◎**cen·tu·ry** [ˈsɛntjʊrɪ] N secolo; (*in cricket*) cento punti; **in the twenty first century** nel ventunesimo secolo
CEO [ˌsiːiːˈəʊ] N ABBR = **chief executive officer**
cep [sɛp] N (*mushroom*) porcino
ce·ram·ic [sɪˈræmɪk] ADJ in *or* di ceramica; (*arts*) ceramico(-a)
■**ceramics** NPL ceramica
▷ www.acers.org
▷ www.ceramicstoday.com
Cerberus [ˈsɜːbərəs] N Cerbero
ce·real [ˈsɪərɪəl] N (*crop*) cereale *m*; (*breakfast cereal*) cereali *mpl*; **I have cereal for breakfast** mangio cereali per colazione
cer·ebel·lum [ˌsɛrɪˈbɛləm] N (*Anat*) cervelletto
cere·bral [ˈsɛrɪbrəl] ADJ (*frm*) cerebrale
cerebral palsy [ˌsɛrɪbrəlˈpɔːlzɪ] N paralisi *f inv* cerebrale
cer·ebrum [ˈsɛrɪbrəm] N (*Anat*) cervello
cer·emo·nial [ˌsɛrɪˈməʊnɪəl] ADJ (*rite*) formale, solenne; (*dress*) da cerimonia; **on ceremonial occasions** in occasione di cerimonie ufficiali
■N cerimoniale *m*; (*rite*) rito
cer·emo·ni·al·ly [ˌsɛrɪˈməʊnɪəlɪ] ADV secondo il rituale
cer·emo·ni·ous [ˌsɛrɪˈməʊnɪəs] ADJ formale; (*pej*) cerimonioso(-a)
cer·emo·ni·ous·ly [ˌsɛrɪˈməʊnɪəslɪ] ADV (*see adj*) in modo formale; in modo cerimonioso
◎**cer·emo·ny** [ˈsɛrɪmənɪ] N (*event*) cerimonia; (*no pl: formality*) cerimonie *fpl*; **to stand on ceremony** attenersi all'etichetta, fare complimenti
Ceres [ˈsɪəriːz] N Cerere *f*
cert [sɜːt] N (*Brit fam*): **it's a dead cert** non c'è alcun dubbio
◎**cer·tain** [ˈsɜːtən] ADJ **1** (*sure*) certo(-a), sicuro(-a); (*inevitable: death, success*) sicuro(-a); (*cure*) infallibile, garantito(-a); **he's certain to leave his job** è certo che lui lascerà il lavoro; **it is certain that ...** è certo che...; **I am certain he's not coming** sono certo che non verrà; **I am certain of it** ne sono certo; **he is certain to be there** lui ci sarà certamente; **for certain** per certo, di sicuro; **I can't say for certain that ...** non posso dire con certezza che...; **be certain to tell her** ricordati *or* non dimenticarti di dirglielo; **to make certain of sth** accertarsi di qc **2** (*before n: particular*) certo(-a); **a certain person** una certa persona; **a certain gentleman called** ha telefonato un certo signore
◎**cer·tain·ly** [ˈsɜːtənlɪ] ADV certamente, certo; **certainly!** (ma) certo!; **certainly not!** no di certo!; **I shall certainly be there** ci sarò sicuramente, ci sarò certamente
cer·tain·ty [ˈsɜːtəntɪ] N certezza; **faced with the certainty of disaster** di fronte al sicuro disastro; **we**

know for a certainty that ... sappiamo per certo che...
cer·ti·fi·able [ˌsɜːtɪˈfaɪəbl] ADJ (*fact, claim*) dimostrabile; (*fam: mad*) pazzo(-a) da legare
cer·tifi·cate [səˈtɪfɪkɪt] N (*gen*) certificato; (*academic*) diploma *m*; **birth certificate** certificato di nascita
cer·tifi·cat·ed [səˈtɪfɪˌkeɪtɪd] ADJ (*gen*) diplomato(-a); (*doctor, teacher*) abilitato(-a)
cer·ti·fi·ca·tion [ˌsɜːtɪfɪˈkeɪʃən] N (*act*) certificazione *f*; (*document*) certificato
cer·ti·fied [ˈsɜːtɪfaɪd] ADJ (*cheque*) autenticato(-a); (*translation*) giurato(-a), autenticato(-a); (*person: declared insane*) malato(-a) di mente
certified letter N (*Am*) lettera raccomandata
certified public accountant N (*Am*) ≈ commercialista *m/f*
cer·ti·fy [ˈsɜːtɪfaɪ] VT **1** certificare, attestare; **the will has been certified** il testamento è stato autenticato **2** (*Med*): **to certify sb** dichiarare malato(-a) di mente qn
cer·ti·tude [ˈsɜːtɪˌtjuːd] N (*frm*) certezza, sicurezza
cer·vi·cal [ˈsɜːvɪkəl] ADJ (*Anat*): **cervical cancer** cancro al collo dell'utero *or* alla cervice uterina
cervical smear N pap-test *m inv*, striscio (*fam*)
cer·vix [ˈsɜːvɪks] N (*pl* **cervices** [səˈvaɪsiːz]) (*Anat*) collo dell'utero, cervice *f* uterina
Ce·sar·ean [siːˈzɛərɪən] N, ADJ (*Am*) = **Caesarean**
ces·sa·tion [sɛˈseɪʃən] N (*frm*) cessazione *f*, arresto
cess·pit [ˈsɛsˌpɪt], **cess·pool** [ˈsɛsˌpuːl] N pozzo nero
CET [ˌsiːiːˈtiː] ABBR (= **Central European Time**) *fuso orario dell'Europa Centrale*
Ceylon [sɪˈlɒn] N Ceylon *f*
cf. ABBR (= **compare**) Cfr.
c/f ABBR (*Comm*) = **carried forward**
CFC [ˌsiːɛfˈsiː] N ABBR = *chlorofluorocarbon*
■ NPL **CFCs** CFC *m*
CG [siːˈdʒiː] ABBR (*Am*) = **coastguard**
cg ABBR (= **centigram**) cg
CH ABBR (*Brit: Companion of Honour*) *titolo onorifico*
ch. ABBR (= **chapter**) cap.
c.h. ABBR (*Brit*) = **central heating**
Chad [tʃæd] N Ciad *m*
cha·dor [ˈtʃʌdəʳ] N chador *m*, velo
chafe [tʃeɪf] VT (*irritate: skin*) sfregare contro, irritare; (*rub to warm*) frizionare
■ VI **1** (*become sore*) irritarsi **2** (*fig*): **to chafe (at)** irritarsi (per); **to chafe against** scontrarsi con
chaff [tʃɑːf] N (*husks*) pula, loppa; (*animal food*) foraggio
chaf·finch [ˈtʃæfɪntʃ] N fringuello
cha·grin [ˈʃægrɪn] N (*frm*) disappunto, dispiacere *m*
◎ **chain** [tʃeɪn] N (*gen*) catena; **gold chain** catenina d'oro; **the gate was fastened with a chain** il cancello era chiuso con una catena; **a chain of events** una serie di avvenimenti
■ VT (*also:* **chain up**) incatenare
▸ **chain up** VT + ADV (*prisoner*) incatenare; (*dog*) mettere alla catena
chain mail N cotta di maglia
chain reaction N reazione *f* a catena
chain saw N motosega
chain-smoke [ˈtʃeɪnˌsməʊk] VI fumare una sigaretta dopo l'altra
chain smoker N fumatore(-trice) accanito(-a)
chain store N *grande magazzino o supermercato che fa parte di una catena*
◎ **chair** [tʃɛəʳ] N sedia, seggiola; (*armchair*) poltrona; (*seat*) posto (a sedere); (*Univ*) cattedra; (*Am: electric chair*): **the chair** la sedia elettrica; **a table and four chairs** un tavolo e quattro sedie; **a sofa and two chairs** un divano e due poltrone; **dentist's chair** poltrona del dentista; **to take the chair** (*at meeting*) assumere la presidenza
■ VT (*meeting*) presiedere
chair lift N seggiovia
◎ **chair·man** [ˈtʃɛəmən] N (*pl* **-men**) presidente *m*
chair·man·ship [ˈtʃɛəmənʃɪp] N presidenza
chair·person [ˈtʃɛəˌpɜːsn] N presidente(-essa)
chair·woman [ˈtʃɛəˌwʊmən] N (*pl* **-women**) presidentessa
chal·cedo·ny [kælˈsɛdənɪ] N calcedonio
cha·let [ˈʃæleɪ] N (*in mountains*) chalet *m inv*; (*in holiday camp etc*) bungalow *m inv*
chal·ice [ˈtʃælɪs] N calice *m*
chalk [tʃɔːk] N gesso; **a (piece of) chalk** un gesso; (*child's*) un gessetto; **not by a long chalk** (*fam*) proprio per niente *or* nulla, niente affatto; **they are as different as chalk and cheese** sono diversi come il giorno e la notte
■ VT (*message*) scrivere col gesso; (*luggage*) segnare col gesso
▸ **chalk up** VT + ADV scrivere col gesso; (*fig: success*) ottenere; (*: victory*) riportare
chalk·board [ˈtʃɔːkbɔːd] N (*Am: blackboard*) lavagna
chalk·pit [ˈtʃɔːkˌpɪt] N cava di gesso
chalky [ˈtʃɔːkɪ] ADJ (*water, soil*) calcareo(-a); (*complexion*) biancastro(-a)
◎ **chal·lenge** [ˈtʃælɪndʒ] N sfida; (*of sentry*) intimazione *f*; **to issue a challenge** lanciare una sfida; **to take up the challenge** accettare *or* raccogliere la sfida; **this task is a great challenge** questo compito è una grande sfida
■ VT (*to contest*) sfidare; (*subj: sentry*) intimare l'alt *etc* a; (*dispute: fact, point, statement, right*) mettere in dubbio, contestare; **to challenge sb to a fight/game** sfidare qn a battersi/ad una partita; **she challenged me to a race** mi ha sfidato ad una gara; **to challenge sb to do sth** sfidare qn a fare qc; **to challenge sb to a duel** sfidare qn a duello
chal·leng·er [ˈtʃælɪndʒəʳ] N (*Sport*) sfidante *m/f*
chal·leng·ing [ˈtʃælɪndʒɪŋ] ADJ (*situation, work*) impegnativo(-a); (*remark, look*) provocatorio(-a); (*book*) stimolante; **a challenging job** un lavoro impegnativo
◎ **cham·ber** [ˈtʃeɪmbəʳ] N (*of parliament*) camera; (*old: room*) stanza; **chambers** NPL (*of judge, lawyer*) studio
cham·ber·lain [ˈtʃeɪmbəlɪn] N ciambellano
chamber·maid [ˈtʃeɪmbəˌmeɪd] N cameriera al piano
chamber music N musica da camera
chamber of commerce N camera di commercio
▹ www.iccwbo.org
▹ www.chamberonline.co.uk
▹ www.acci.asn.au
▹ www.sacob.co.za/
▹ www.nzchamber.co.nz/
chamber·pot [ˈtʃeɪmbəˌpɒt] N vaso da notte
cha·me·le·on [kəˈmiːlɪən] N camaleonte *m*
cham·ois [ˈʃæmwɑː] N (*Zool*) camoscio
chamois leather N (pelle *f* di) camoscio
champ[1] [tʃæmp] VI masticare rumorosamente; **to champ at the bit** mordere il freno
■ VT (*gum*) masticare rumorosamente
champ[2] [tʃæmp] N (*fam*) (= **champion**) campione(-essa)
cham·pagne [ʃæmˈpeɪn] N champagne *m inv*
cham·pers [ˈʃæmpəz] NSG (*Brit fam*) sciampagnino

Cc

◎**cham·pi·on** ['tʃæmpjən] N (*Sport*) campione(-essa); (*of cause*) difensore *m*; **boxing champion** campione di boxe
■VT difendere, lottare per

◎**cham·pi·on·ship** ['tʃæmpjənʃɪp] N (*contest*) campionato

◎**chance** [tʃɑːns] N **1** (*possibility*) probabilità *f inv*; **the chances are that ...** probabilmente..., è probabile che... + *sub*; **the team's chances of winning** le possibilità di vittoria della squadra; **he doesn't stand** *or* **he hasn't a chance of winning** non ha nessuna possibilità di vittoria; **there is little chance of his coming** è molto improbabile che venga; **no chance!** impossibile! **2** (*opportunity*) possibilità *f inv*, occasione *f*; **it's the chance of a lifetime** è un'occasione unica; **he never had a chance in life** non ha mai avuto nessuna possibilità nella vita; **to give sb a chance to do sth** dare a qn la possibilità (di fare qc); **to have an eye to the main chance** (*pej*) essere sempre pronto(-a) ad approfittare, non perdere occasioni; **I'll write when I get the chance** scriverò quando ne avrò l'opportunità **3** (*risk*) rischio; **an element of chance** una parte di fortuna; **to take a chance** rischiare; **I'm taking no chances** non voglio lasciar niente al caso, non intendo rischiare! **4** (*luck*) caso; **game of chance** gioco d'azzardo; **by chance** per caso; **do you by any chance know each other?** per caso vi conoscete?; **to leave nothing to chance** non lasciare nulla al caso
■VT (*happen*): **to chance to do sth** (*frm*) fare per caso qc; **I'll chance it** (*risk*) ci provo, rischio
■ADJ (*meeting, remark, error*) casuale, fortuito(-a); **a chance meeting** un incontro casuale
▸ **chance on, chance upon** VI + PREP (*person*) incontrare per caso, imbattersi in; (*thing*) trovare per caso

chan·cel ['tʃɑːnsəl] N coro

◎**chan·cel·lor** ['tʃɑːnsələʳ] N cancelliere *m*; (*of university*) rettore *m* (onorario)

Chancellor of the Exchequer N (*Brit*) Cancelliere dello Scacchiere; ≈ Ministro del Tesoro

chancy, chancey ['tʃɑːnsɪ] ADJ (*comp* **-ier**, *superl* **-iest**) rischioso(-a)

chan·de·lier [ʃændə'lɪəʳ] N lampadario

DID YOU KNOW ...?
chandelier is not translated by the Italian word *candeliere*

◎**change** [tʃeɪndʒ] N
1 cambiamento; **a change for the better/worse** un miglioramento/peggioramento, un mutamento per il meglio/peggio; **just for a change** tanto per cambiare; **he likes a change** gli piace cambiare; **change of address** cambiamento di indirizzo; **a change of clothes** un cambio (di vestiti); **to have a change of heart** cambiare idea; **to have a change of scene** cambiare aria; **there's been a change in the weather** il tempo è cambiato; **there's been a change of plan** c'è stato un cambiamento di programma
2 (*small coins*) moneta, spiccioli *mpl*; (*money returned*) resto; **small** *or* **loose change** spiccioli *mpl*; **can you give me change for £1?** mi può cambiare una sterlina?; **I haven't got any change** non ho spiccioli; **here's your change** ecco il resto; **keep the change** tenga il resto; **you don't get much change out of £20** non avanza molto da 20 sterline
■VT
1 (*by substitution*) cambiare; **to change hands** cambiare padrone, passare di mano; **a sum of money changed hands** c'è stato un movimento di denaro; **to change gear** (*Aut*) cambiare (marcia); **to change places** (*two people*) scambiarsi di posto; **I changed places with him** ho scambiato il mio posto con il suo, ci siamo scambiati di posto; **to change trains/buses (at)** cambiare treno/autobus (a); **to change the rein** (*Horse-riding*) cambiare di mano; **to change sides** (*Pol etc*) cambiare bandiera; **let's change the subject** cambiamo argomento; **he wants to change his job** vuole cambiare lavoro
2 (*exchange: in shop*) cambiare; **to change ends** (*Tennis, Ftbl*) effettuare il cambio di campo
3 (*alter: person, idea*) cambiare; (*transform: person*) trasformare; (*: thing*) tramutare; **to change one's mind** cambiare idea; **I've changed my mind** ho cambiato idea
4 (*money*) cambiare; **I'd like to change £50** vorrei cambiare 50 sterline
■VI
1 (*alter*) cambiare, mutare; **you've changed!** come sei cambiato!; **the town has changed a lot** la città è molto cambiata
2 (*change clothes*) cambiarsi; **to get changed** cambiarsi; **I've got to get changed** devo cambiarmi
3 (*Rail*) cambiare; **all change!** si cambia!
▸ **change down** VI + ADV (*Aut*) scalare (la marcia)
▸ **change into** VI + PREP
1 (*become*) trasformarsi in
2 (*different clothes*): **she changed into an old skirt** si è cambiata e ha messo una vecchia gonna
■VT + PREP: **to change sb/sth into** trasformare qn/qc in
▸ **change over** VI + ADV (*make complete change*): **to change over from sth to sth** passare da qc a qc; (*players etc*) scambiarsi (*di posto o di campo*)
▸ **change up** VI + ADV (*Aut*) cambiare, mettere una marcia superiore

change·abil·ity [,tʃeɪndʒə'bɪlɪtɪ] N (*see adj*) mutevolezza; variabilità

change·able ['tʃeɪndʒəbl] ADJ (*person*) mutevole; (*weather*) mutevole, variabile; **the weather's very changeable in autumn** il tempo è molto variabile in autunno

change·less ['tʃeɪndʒlɪs] ADJ (*frm*) immutabile

change machine N distributore *m* automatico di monete

change management N (*Comm*) gestione *f* del cambiamento

change of life N menopausa

change·over ['tʃeɪndʒ,əʊvəʳ] N cambiamento, passaggio

chang·ing ['tʃeɪndʒɪŋ] ADJ (*face, expression*) mutevole; (*colours*) cangiante

Changing of the Guard N: **the Changing of the Guard** il cambio della guardia

changing room ['tʃeɪndʒɪŋ,rʊm] N (*Brit: in shop*) camerino; (*: Sport*) spogliatoio; **three garments only allowed in the changing room** si possono portare solo tre articoli nel camerino

Chan·nel ['tʃænl] N: **the (English) Channel** il Canale della Manica, la Manica

◎**chan·nel** ['tʃænl] N (*Geog, TV*) (*also fig*) canale *m*; (*of river, sea*) alveo; **to go through the usual channels** seguire la normale procedura; **green/red channel** (*Customs*) uscita "niente da dichiarare"/"merci da dichiarare"
■VT (*hollow out: course*) scavare; (*direct: river*) far scorrere, convogliare; (*fig: interest, energies*): **to channel into**

concentrare su, indirizzare verso, canalizzare

Channel Islands NPL: **the Channel Islands** le Isole Normanne *or* del Canale (della Manica)

Channel Tunnel N: **the Channel Tunnel** il tunnel sotto la Manica

chant [tʃɑ:nt] N (*of crowd*) slogan *m inv*; (*Rel, Mus*) canto, salmodia
■ VT (*Rel, Mus*) cantare; (*subj: crowd*): **the demonstrators chanted their disapproval** i dimostranti lanciavano slogan di protesta
■ VI (*see vt*) cantare, salmodiare; lanciare slogan

◎ **cha·os** ['keɪɒs] N caos *m*; **to be in chaos** essere nel caos

chaos theory N teoria del caos

cha·ot·ic [keɪ'ɒtɪk] ADJ caotico(-a), confuso(-a)

cha·oti·cal·ly [keɪ'ɒtɪklɪ] ADV caoticamente

chap[1] [tʃæp] N (*Brit fam: man*) tipo, tizio; **he's a nice chap** è un tipo simpatico; **he's the sort of chap everyone likes** è il tipo di persona che piace a tutti; **old chap** vecchio mio; **poor little chap** povero piccolo

chap[2] [tʃæp] N (*on lip*) screpolatura
■ VT (*skin*) screpolare

chap·el ['tʃæpəl] N (*of church, school*) cappella; (*small church*) cappella, chiesetta

chap·er·one, **chap·er·on** ['ʃæpəˌrəʊn] N accompagnatore(-trice)
■ VT fare da accompagnatore(-trice), accompagnare

chap·lain ['tʃæplɪn] N cappellano

chapped ['tʃæpt] ADJ (*skin*) screpolato(-a)

◎ **chap·ter** ['tʃæptə^r] N capitolo; **to quote chapter and verse** (*fig*) dare dei riferimenti precisi; **a chapter of accidents** una serie di imprevisti

char[1] [tʃɑ:^r] VT (*burn black*) carbonizzare

char[2] [tʃɑ:^r], (*Brit*) N (*charwoman*) donna a ore
■ VI lavorare come donna a ore

chara·banc ['ʃærəˌbæŋ] N *pullman per il trasporto di turisti*

◎ **char·ac·ter** ['kærɪktə^r] N (*gen, Comput*) carattere *m*; (*in novel, play, film*) personaggio; (*eccentric*) originale *m*; **a man of character** un uomo di polso; **a person of good character** una persona a modo; **can you give me some idea of his character?** puoi descrivermi un po' il suo carattere?; **it's quite in/out of character for him to be rude** è/non è nella sua natura essere maleducato; **he's quite a character** è un tipo originale; **character reference** referenza; **Gothic characters** caratteri gotici

character actor N caratterista *m*

character actress N caratterista *f*

character code N (*Comput*) codice *m* di carattere

◎ **char·ac·ter·is·tic** [ˌkærɪktə'rɪstɪk] ADJ caratteristico(-a), tipico(-a); **characteristic of** tipico(-a) di; **with (his) characteristic enthusiasm** con l'entusiasmo che lo caratterizza
■ N caratteristica

char·ac·ter·is·ti·cal·ly [ˌkærɪktə'rɪstɪkəlɪ] ADV tipicamente; **characteristically, she decided at the last moment** com'è tipico suo, ha deciso all'ultimo momento

char·ac·teri·za·tion [ˌkærɪktəraɪ'zeɪʃən] N (*in novel*) caratterizzazione *f*

char·ac·ter·ize ['kærɪktəˌraɪz] VT 1 (*be characteristic of*) caratterizzare 2 (*describe*): **to characterize (as)** descrivere (come)

char·ac·ter·less ['kærəktəlɪs] ADJ ordinario(-a)

character recognition ADJ (*Comput: software*) riconoscimento dei caratteri

cha·rade [ʃə'rɑ:d] N 1 (*pretence*) farsa 2 **charades** NPL (*game*) sciarada *fsg*

char·coal ['tʃɑ:kəʊl] N carbone *m* di legna; (*for sketching*) carboncino; **dark charcoal** color antracite scuro

◎ **charge** [tʃɑ:dʒ] N 1 (*cost*) tariffa, prezzo; **is there a charge?** c'è da pagare?; **is there a charge for delivery?** c'è qualcosa da pagare per la spedizione?; **free of charge** gratis, gratuito(-a); (*adv*) gratuitamente; **extra charge** supplemento; **monthly charge** tariffa mensile; **labour charges** costi *mpl* del lavoro; **I'd like to reverse the charges** vorrei fare una chiamata a carico del destinatario 2 (*Law*) accusa, imputazione *f*; **to bring a charge against sb** accusare qn, imputare qn; **to be on a charge of** essere accusato di; **he's on a charge of robbery** è accusato di furto; **he was arrested on a charge of murder** fu arrestato sotto accusa di omicidio 3 (*control, responsibility*): **the person in charge** il/la responsabile; **to be in charge** essere responsabile; **who is in charge here?** chi è il responsabile qui?; **to be in charge of** essere responsabile di *or* per; **she was in charge of the group** era responsabile per il gruppo; **to take charge (of)** (*firm, situation*) assumere il controllo (di); (*project*) incaricarsi (di); **can you take charge here?** se ne occupa lei?; **to have charge of sb** aver cura di qn; **these children are my charges** questi bambini sono affidati a me 4 (*Mil: attack*) carica 5 (*Phys, Elec*) carica
■ VT 1 (*price*) chiedere, far pagare; (*customer*) far pagare a; **what did they charge you for it?** quanto te l'hanno fatto pagare?; **to charge an expense to sb** addebitare una spesa a qn; **charge it to my account** lo metta *or* addebiti sul mio conto 2 (*Law*): **to charge sb (with)** accusare qn (di); **the police have charged him with murder** la polizia lo ha accusato di omicidio 3 (*gun, battery*) caricare 4 (*Mil: attack*) caricare
■ VI (*Mil etc*) caricare; (*fam: rush*) precipitarsi, lanciarsi; **to charge in/out** precipitarsi dentro/fuori; **to charge up/down the stairs** lanciarsi su/giù per le scale

charge account N (*Am*) conto

charge card N carta di credito commerciale

charged [tʃɑ:ʒd] ADJ (*battery*) carico(-a); (*fig*): **charged with emotion** carico(-a) di; **there was a highly charged atmosphere** c'era molta elettricità nell'aria

char·gé d'af·faires ['ʃɑ:ʒeɪdæ'fɛə^r] N incaricato d'affari

charge hand N (*Brit*) caposquadra *m/f*

charg·er ['tʃɑ:dʒə^r] N (*Elec: also:* **battery charger**) caricabatterie *m inv*; (*old: warhorse*) destriero

charg·ing ['tʃɑ:dʒɪŋ] N (*Phys*) elettrizzazione *f*

chari·ot ['tʃærɪət] N cocchio, carro

chari·ot·eer [ˌtʃærɪə'tɪə^r] N auriga *m*

cha·ris·ma [kə'rɪzmə] N carisma *m*

char·is·mat·ic [ˌkærɪz'mætɪk] ADJ carismatico(-a)

chari·table ['tʃærɪtəbl] ADJ (*organization, society*) filantropico(-a), di beneficenza; (*person*) caritatevole; (*deed*) buono(-a), di carità, caritatevole; (*remark, view*) indulgente, caritatevole

chari·tably ['tʃærɪtəblɪ] ADV in modo caritatevole

◎ **char·ity** ['tʃærɪtɪ] N 1 (*virtue*) carità; **out of charity** per carità *or* misericordia; **to live on charity** vivere di elemosine; **charity begins at home** (*Proverb*) il primo prossimo è la tua famiglia 2 (*organization*) opera pia, associazione *f* benefica; **to collect for charity** raccogliere denaro per beneficenza; **she gave all her money to charity** lasciò tutto il suo denaro in beneficenza; **a cancer charity** un'associazione per la raccolta di fondi contro il cancro

char·lady ['tʃɑ:ˌleɪdɪ] N (*Brit*) = **charwoman**

Cc

char·la·tan [ˈʃɑːlətən] N ciarlatano
Charlemagne [ˈʃɑːlə,meɪn] N Carlo Magno
char·lotte [ˈʃɑːlət] N (*Culin*) charlotte *f inv*
charm [tʃɑːm] N (*of person*) fascino; (*of object*) incanto; (*also fig: magic spell*) incanto, incantesimo; (*on bracelet*) ciondolo; **the charm of this region lies in its beautiful scenery** il fascino di questa regione sta nei suoi paesaggi stupendi; **it worked like a charm** (*fig*) ha funzionato perfettamente; **lucky charm** amuleto
■VT affascinare, incantare; **to lead a charmed life** essere nato(-a) con la camicia
charm bracelet N braccialetto con ciondoli
charm·er [ˈtʃɑːməʳ] N persona affascinante
charm·ing [ˈtʃɑːmɪŋ] ADJ delizioso(-a), incantevole; **she's a charming girl** è una ragazza deliziosa; **Prince Charming** il Principe azzurro
charm·ing·ly [ˈtʃɑːmɪŋlɪ] ADV deliziosamente
Charon [ˈkeərən] N Caronte *m*
◎ **chart** [tʃɑːt] N (*table*) tabella, tavola; (*graph, Med*) grafico; (*Met: weather chart*) carta del tempo; (*Naut: map*) carta (nautica); **the chart shows the rise of unemployment** il grafico mostra l'aumento della disoccupazione; **the charts** la Hit Parade; **to be in the charts** (*record, pop group*) essere nella Hit Parade, essere in classifica; **his record has been in the charts for ten weeks** il suo disco è nella Hit Parade da dieci settimane
■VT (*plot: course*) tracciare; (*: sales, progress*) tracciare il grafico di; (*Naut*) fare la carta nautica di
◎ **char·ter** [ˈtʃɑːtəʳ] N **1** (*document*) carta; (*of city, organization*) statuto **2** (*Naut, Aer etc: hire*) noleggio; **on charter** a nolo
■VT (*plane etc*) noleggiare
char·tered ac·count·ant [ˈtʃɑːtədəˈkaʊntənt] N (*Brit*) ≈ commercialista *m/f*
charter flight N volo *m* charter *inv*
charter party N (*contract*) contratto di noleggio
charter plane N charter *m inv*
char·woman [ˈtʃɑː,wʊmən] N (*pl* **-women**) donna delle pulizie, donna a ore
chary [ˈtʃɛərɪ] ADJ cauto(-a), attento(-a); **to be chary of doing sth** andare con i piedi di piombo prima di fare qc
Cha·ryb·dis [kəˈrɪbdɪs] N Cariddi *f*
◎ **chase** [tʃeɪs] N inseguimento, caccia; **the chase** (*Hunting*) la caccia; **to give chase** dare la caccia, mettersi all'inseguimento; **a car chase** un inseguimento in macchina
■VT inseguire; **the policeman chased the thief** il poliziotto ha inseguito il ladro; **he's always chasing the girls** corre sempre dietro alle ragazze
■VI: **to chase after sb** correre dietro a qn
▸ **chase away, chase off** VT + ADV cacciare via
▸ **chase up** VT + ADV
▸ **chase down** (*Am*) VT + ADV (*information*) scoprire, raccogliere; (*person*) scovare
chas·er [ˈtʃeɪsəʳ] N **1** (*drink*) *bibita poco alcolica bevuta dopo un superalcolico* **2** (*person*) inseguitore(-trice), cacciatore(-trice)
chasm [ˈkæzəm] N voragine *f*, abisso
chas·sis [ˈʃæsɪ] N (*Aut*) telaio
chaste [tʃeɪst] ADJ casto(-a)
chaste·ly [ˈtʃeɪstlɪ] ADV castamente
chas·tened [ˈtʃeɪsnd] ADJ abbattuto(-a), provato(-a)
chas·ten·ing [ˈtʃeɪsnɪŋ] ADJ che fa riflettere
chas·tise [tʃæsˈtaɪz] VT (*frm: punish*) punire, castigare
chas·tise·ment [ˈtʃæstɪzmənt] N (*frm*) punizione *f*, castigo
chas·tity [ˈtʃæstɪtɪ] N castità
chasu·ble [ˈtʃæzjʊbəl] N casula
◎ **chat** [tʃæt] N chiacchierata; **to have a chat** fare quattro chiacchiere, fare una chiacchierata
■VI: **to chat (with** *or* **to)** chiacchierare (con); **I was chatting to my neighbour** stavo chiacchierando con il mio vicino
▸ **chat up** VT + ADV (*Brit fam: girl*) agganciare, abbordare; **he's not very good at chatting up girls** non è molto bravo ad abbordare le ragazze
chat group N (*Comput*) gruppo di discussione in Internet
chat·line [ˈtʃæt,laɪn] N (*Tel*) *servizio telefonico che consente a più utenti di conversare insieme*
chat room N (*Comput*) chat line *f inv*
chat show N (*Brit*) talk show *m inv*
chat·tel [ˈtʃætl] N *see* **goods**
chat·ter [ˈtʃætəʳ] N (*talk*) parlottio, chiacchiere *fpl*, ciarle *fpl*
■VI (*person*) chiacchierare, ciarlare; (*birds*) cinguettare; **her teeth were chattering** batteva i denti
chatter·box [ˈtʃætə,bɒks] N (*fam*) chiacchierone(-a)
chat·ter·ing classes [ˈtʃætərɪŋˈklɑːsɪs] NPL: **the chattering classes** (*fam pej*) gli intellettualoidi
chat·ty [ˈtʃætɪ] ADJ (*person*) ciarliero(-a); (*style*) familiare; **a chatty letter** una lettera scritta in tono cordiale e informale
chauf·feur [ˈʃəʊfəʳ] N autista *m/f*
chau·vin·ism [ˈʃəʊvɪ,nɪzəm] N (*male chauvinism*) maschilismo; (*nationalism*) sciovinismo
chau·vin·ist [ˈʃəʊvɪnɪst] N (*male chauvinist*) maschilista *m*; (*nationalist*) sciovinista *m/f*; **(male) chauvinist pig** (*fam pej*) sporco maschilista
chau·vin·is·tic [,ʃəʊvɪˈnɪstɪk] ADJ (*jingoistic*) sciovinistico(-a); (*sexist*) maschilista
ChE ABBR = *chemical engineer*
◎ **cheap** [tʃiːp] ADJ (*comp* **-er**, *superl* **-est**) (*low cost: goods*) a buon mercato, a basso *or* buon prezzo, economico(-a); (*reduced: ticket*) a prezzo ridotto; (*: fare*) ridotto(-a); (*poor quality*) scadente, di cattiva qualità; (*vulgar, mean: joke, behaviour, trick*) volgare, grossolano(-a), dozzinale; **cheap flight** volo economico; **it was cheap at the price** sono stati soldi ben spesi; **this stuff is cheap and nasty** questa roba è veramente scadente; **she bought a dress made of a cheap material** ha comprato un vestito di stoffa scadente; **cheaper** meno caro(-a), più economico(-a); **the bus is cheaper** l'autobus è più economico; **the cheapest seats are £5** i posti più economici vengono cinque sterline; **cheap money** (*Fin*) denaro a basso tasso di interesse; **to feel cheap (about)** provare vergogna *or* vergognarsi (di *or* per)
■ADV a buon prezzo *or* mercato
■N: **on the cheap** (*fam*) a risparmio
cheap·en [ˈtʃiːpən] VT: **to cheapen o.s.** svendersi, screditarsi; (*woman: sexually*) degradarsi
cheap·ly [ˈtʃiːplɪ] ADV a buon prezzo, a buon mercato
cheap·ness [ˈtʃiːpnɪs] N (*of goods etc*) basso prezzo; (*fig: of joke, behaviour*) bassezza
cheap·skate [ˈtʃiːp,skeɪt] N (*fam*) taccagno(-a)
cheat [tʃiːt] N (*deception*) imbroglio, truffa; (*person*) imbroglione(-a), truffatore(-trice)
■VT imbrogliare, truffare; (*rob*) soffiare, fregare; **to cheat sb out of sth** fregare qc a qn; **I was cheated out of the job** mi è stato soffiato il lavoro

■VI (*at games*) barare, imbrogliare; (*in exam*) copiare; **you're cheating!** stai imbrogliando!; **he's been cheating on his wife** ha tradito sua moglie

cheat·ing ['tʃi:tɪŋ] N truffe *fpl*, imbrogli *mpl*

◎**check** [tʃɛk] N **1** (*inspection*) controllo, verifica; **a thorough check** un controllo accurato; **to keep a check on sb/sth** controllare qn/qc, fare attenzione a qn/qc **2** (*control, restraint*) limitazione *f*; **to hold** *or* **keep sb/sth in check** tenere qn/qc sotto controllo; **to act as a check on sth** fare da freno a qc **3** (*Chess*): **in check** in scacco; **check!** scacco (al re)! **4** (*Am: bill*) conto; (: *receipt*) scontrino **5** (*Am*) = **cheque 6 checks** (*pattern*) quadretti *mpl*, quadri *mpl*, scacchi *mpl*

■VT **1** (*examine: facts, figures*) verificare; (: *passport, ticket, tyres, oil*) controllare; **could you check the oil, please?** può controllare l'olio, per favore? **2** (*stop, halt*) bloccare, fermare, arrestare; (*restrain*) contenere, frenare, controllare; **to check o.s.** frenarsi, controllarsi, contenersi **3** (*Am: tick*) spuntare

■VI controllare; **to check with sb** chiedere a qn; **I'll check with the driver what time the bus leaves** chiederò al conducente quando parte l'autobus; (*official etc*) informarsi presso qn

■ADJ (*also:* **checked**: *pattern, cloth*) a scacchi, a quadretti, a quadri

▸ **check in** VI + ADV (*at airport*) fare il check-in; (*at hotel: arrive*) arrivare; (: *register*) firmare il registro

■VT + ADV (*luggage*) registrare, fare il check-in di

▸ **check off** VT + ADV controllare, spuntare

▸ **check on** VI + PREP (*facts, dates*) controllare, verificare; (*fam: person*) informarsi su

▸ **check out** VI + ADV (*from hotel*) lasciare la camera e saldare il conto

■VT + ADV **1** (*luggage*) ritirare **2** (*investigate: story*) controllare, verificare; (: *fam: person*) prendere informazioni su; **check it out** vedi di che si tratta

▸ **check up** VI + ADV controllare

▸ **check up on** VI + ADV + PREP (*story*) controllare, verificare; (*person*) controllare; **to check up (on sth)** investigare (qc)

check·book ['tʃɛk,bʊk] N (*Am*) = **chequebook**

checked [tʃɛkt] ADJ (*material*) a quadretti, a quadri, a scacchi

check·er ['tʃɛkəʳ] N (*person*) controllore *m*, verificatore *m*

checker·board ['tʃɛkə,bɔ:d] N (*Am*) scacchiera

check·ered ['tʃɛkəd] ADJ (*Am*) = **chequered**

check·ers ['tʃɛkəz] NPL (*Am*) dama

check guarantee card N (*Am*) carta *f* assegni *inv*

check-in ['tʃɛk,ɪn] N (*also:* **check-in desk**: *at airport*) check-in *m inv*, accettazione *f* bagagli *inv*

check·ing ac·count ['tʃɛkɪŋə'kaʊnt] N (*Am*) conto corrente

check·list ['tʃɛk,lɪst] N lista di controllo

check·mate ['tʃɛk,meɪt] N (*in chess, fig*) scacco matto, scaccomatto

■VT dare scacco matto a; (*fig*) bloccare

check·out ['tʃɛk,aʊt] N (*in supermarket*) cassa

check·point ['tʃɛk,pɔɪnt] N posto di blocco

check·room ['tʃɛk,rʊm] N (*Am: for coats*) guardaroba *m inv*; (*for luggage*) deposito *m* bagagli *inv*

check·up ['tʃɛk,ʌp] N (*Med*) check-up *m inv*, controllo medico globale; **to have a checkup** fare una visita di controllo

ched·dar ['tʃɛdəʳ] N (*also:* **cheddar cheese**) *tipo di formaggio*

cheek [tʃi:k] N **1** guancia; (*fam: buttock*) natica; **to dance cheek to cheek** ballare guancia a guancia; **a kiss on the cheek** un bacio sulla guancia; **cheek by jowl** gomito a gomito **2** (*fam: impudence*) faccia tosta, sfacciataggine *f*; **what a cheek!** che faccia tosta!

■VT essere sfacciato(-a) con

cheek·bone ['tʃi:k,bəʊn] N zigomo

cheeki·ly ['tʃi:kɪlɪ] ADV sfacciatamente, impudentemente

cheeki·ness ['tʃi:kɪnɪs] N sfacciataggine *f*, impudenza

cheeky ['tʃi:kɪ] ADJ sfacciato(-a), impudente; **don't be cheeky!** non essere sfacciato(-a)!

cheep [tʃi:p] N (*of bird*) pigolio

■VI pigolare

◎**cheer** [tʃɪəʳ] N (*shout*) evviva *m inv*; (*applause*) applauso; **three cheers for the winner!** tre urrà per il vincitore!

■VT **1** (*applaud: winner etc*) applaudire **2** (*gladden*) rallegrare

■VI applaudire

▸ **cheer on** VT + ADV (*person*) incitare

▸ **cheer up** VI + ADV rallegrarsi, farsi animo; **cheer up!** coraggio!, su con la vita!

■VT + ADV rallegrare, tirar su di morale; **to cheer sb up** tirare qn su di morale; **I was trying to cheer him up** cercavo di tirarlo su di morale

cheer·ful ['tʃɪəfʊl] ADJ allegro(-a)

cheer·ful·ly ['tʃɪəfəlɪ] ADV (*gen*) allegramente; (*willingly*) volentieri

cheer·ful·ness ['tʃɪəfʊlnɪs] N allegria

cheeri·ly ['tʃɪərɪlɪ] ADV allegramente

cheeri·ness ['tʃɪərɪnɪs] N allegria

cheer·ing ['tʃɪərɪŋ] ADJ (*news, sight*) confortante

■N (*of crowd etc*) acclamazioni *fpl*

cheerio [,tʃɪərɪ'əʊ] EXCL (*Brit fam*) ciao!

cheer·leader ['tʃɪə,li:dəʳ] N cheerleader *f inv*

cheer·less ['tʃɪəlɪs] ADJ (*atmosphere*) triste; (*room, place*) desolato(-a)

cheers [tʃɪəz] EXCL (*toast*) (alla) salute!, cin cin!; (*Brit fam: thank you*) grazie!; (: *goodbye*) ciao!

cheery ['tʃɪərɪ] ADJ allegro(-a)

◎**cheese** [tʃi:z] N formaggio; **say cheese!** (*Phot*) sorridi!

▷ www.cheeseboard.co.uk

cheese·board ['tʃi:z,bɔ:d] N piatto portaformaggio

cheese·burg·er ['tʃi:z,bɜ:gəʳ] N cheeseburger *m inv*, hamburger *m inv* al formaggio

cheese·cake ['tʃi:z,keɪk] N *torta al formaggio, a volte con frutta*

cheese·cloth ['tʃi:z,klɒθ] N tela indiana, garza

cheesed off ['tʃi:zd'ɒf] ADJ (*Brit fam*) stufo(-a)

cheese knife N coltello per formaggio

cheese·paring ['tʃi:z,pɛərɪŋ] ADJ (*person*) taccagno(-a), spilorcio(-a); (*attitude, habits*) meschino(-a)

■N (*see adj*) taccagneria, spilorceria; meschinità

cheesy ['tʃi:zɪ] ADJ (*flavour, smell*) di formaggio; (*consistency*) del formaggio

chee·tah ['tʃi:tə] N ghepardo

chef [ʃɛf] N chef *m inv*, capocuoco

◎**chemi·cal** ['kɛmɪkəl] ADJ chimico(-a)

■N prodotto chimico

chemical engineering N ingegneria chimica

▷ www.che.ufl.edu/www-che

chemi·cal·ly ['kɛmɪkəlɪ] ADV chimicamente

chem·ist ['kɛmɪst] N (*Brit: pharmacist*) farmacista *m/f*; (*scientist*) chimico(-a); **chemist's (shop)** (*Brit*) farmacia; **you get it from the chemist** si compra in farmacia

chem·is·try ['kɛmɪstrɪ] N chimica; **chemistry lab** laboratorio di chimica

▷ www.chemweb.com
▷ www.psigate.ac.uk/newsite
chemo ['ki:məʊ] N (*fam*) chemio *f inv*
chemo·thera·py [ˌkeməʊ'θerəpɪ] N chemioterapia
chemo·tro·pism [ˌkɛməʊ'trəʊpɪzəm] N chemiotropismo
cheque, (*Am*) **check** [tʃɛk] N assegno; **a cheque for £20** un assegno di 20 sterline; **he wrote a cheque** ha fatto un assegno; **to pay by cheque** pagare per assegno *or* con un assegno; **can I pay by cheque?** posso pagare con un assegno?
cheque·book, (*Am*) **check·book** ['tʃɛkˌbʊk] N libretto degli assegni
cheque card N (*Brit*) carta *f* assegni *inv*
cheq·uered, (*Am*) **check·ered** ['tʃɛkəd] ADJ a scacchi, a quadretti, a quadri; (*fig*) movimentato(-a); **a chequered career** una carriera movimentata
chequered flag N (*Motor Racing*) bandiera a scacchi
cher·ish ['tʃɛrɪʃ] VT (*person*) avere caro(-a); (*hope etc*) nutrire; **I cherish the memory of it** ne conservo un caro ricordo
cher·ished ['tʃɛrɪʃt] ADJ (*memory*) caro(-a); (*hope, wish, ambition*) grande; **my most cherished possessions** le mie cose più preziose
che·root [ʃə'ru:t] N sigaro spuntato
cher·ry ['tʃɛrɪ] N (*fruit*) ciliegia; (*cherry tree*) ciliegio
■ ADJ (*pie, jam*) di ciliegie
cherry brandy N cherry brandy *m inv*
cherry orchard N ciliegeto
cherry-pick ['tʃerɪpɪk] VT fare una cernita tra
cherry picker N (*fam*) autocestello
cherry plum N susino asiatico
cherry red ADJ rosso ciliegia *inv*
cherry tree N ciliegio
cher·ub ['tʃɛrəb] N **1** (*pl* **cherubs**) (*child*) angioletto **2** (*pl* **cherubim** ['tʃɛrəbɪm]) (*Rel*) cherubino
che·ru·bic [tʃɛ'ru:bɪk] ADJ da cherubino
cher·vil ['tʃɜ:vɪl] N cerfoglio
Ches ABBR (*Brit*) = *Cheshire*
chess [tʃɛs] N scacchi *mpl*; **he likes playing chess** gli piace giocare a scacchi
▷ www.fide.com
chess·board ['tʃɛsˌbɔ:d] N scacchiera
chess·man ['tʃɛsˌmæn] N (*pl* **-men**) pezzo (degli scacchi)
chess·player ['tʃɛsˌpleɪə^r] N scacchista *m/f*
◎ **chest** [tʃɛst] N **1** (*Anat*) petto, torace *m*; **I've got a pain in my chest** ho un dolore al petto; **to get sth off one's chest** (*fam*) togliersi un peso (dallo stomaco), alleggerirsi *or* scaricarsi la coscienza **2** (*box*) baule *m*, cassa, cassapanca
chest cold N: **to catch a chest cold** prendere una bronchite
chest measurement N giro *m* torace *inv*
chest·nut ['tʃɛsˌnʌt] N (*fruit*) castagna; (*chestnut tree*) castagno; **sweet chestnut** (*tree*) castagno comune *or* dolce
■ ADJ (*hair*) castano(-a); (*horse*) sauro(-a)
chest of drawers N comò *m inv*, cassettone *m*
chest specialist N specialista *m/f* in malattie polmonari
chesty ['tʃɛstɪ] ADJ (*comp* **-ier**, *superl* **-iest**) (*cough*) bronchitico(-a); (*Brit fam: person*) che soffre di bronchite
chew [tʃu:] VT masticare; **to chew the cud** ruminare
► **chew over** VT + ADV rimuginare su
► **chew up** VT + ADV mangiucchiare
chew·ing gum ['tʃu:ɪŋˌgʌm] N chewing-gum *m inv*, gomma (americana *or* da masticare)
chewy ['tʃu:ɪ] ADJ (*fam*) gommoso(-a)
chic [ʃi:k] ADJ chic *inv*, elegante
chi·can·ery [ʃɪ'keɪnərɪ] N (*frm*) cavillo
chick [tʃɪk] N (*baby bird*) piccolo (*di volatile*), uccellino; (*baby hen*) pulcino; (*fam*) pollastrella
◎ **chick·en** ['tʃɪkɪn] N pollo; (*fam: coward*) coniglio; **don't count your chickens before they're hatched** (*Proverb*) non dire quattro finché non l'hai nel sacco
■ ADJ (*stock, breast, liver*) di pollo; (*farmer, farming*) di polli; **chicken leg** coscia di pollo
► **chicken out** VI + ADV (*fam*) avere fifa; **to chicken out of sth** tirarsi indietro da qc per fifa *or* paura
chicken feed N (*fig*): **he earns chicken feed** guadagna una miseria
chicken·pox ['tʃɪkɪnˌpɒks] N varicella
chicken wire N rete *f* metallica (a maglie esagonali)
chick flick N (*fam*) filmetto rosa
chick lit N (*fam*) romanzetti *mpl* rosa
chick·pea ['tʃɪkˌpi:] N cece *m*
chick·weed ['tʃɪkˌwi:d] N (*Bot*) centonchio
chico·ry ['tʃɪkərɪ] N cicoria
chide [tʃaɪd] VT riprendere, rimproverare
◎ **chief** [tʃi:f] ADJ (*principal: reason etc*) principale; (*in rank*) capo *inv*; **his chief reason for resigning was the low pay** la ragione principale per cui si è licenziato è lo stipendio basso; **chief steward** (*Aer*) commissario di bordo
■ N capo; **chief of security** capo della sicurezza
Chief Constable N (*Brit*) ≈ questore *m*
chief executive, **chief executive officer** N direttore *m* generale
Chief Justice N ≈ presidente *m* di Corte di Cassazione
chief·ly ['tʃi:flɪ] ADV principalmente, per lo più
Chief of Staff N (*Mil*) Capo di Stato Maggiore
chief·tain ['tʃi:ftən] N capo tribù
chif·fon ['ʃɪfɒn] N chiffon *m inv*
■ ADJ di chiffon
chi·gnon ['ʃi:njɒn] N chignon *m inv*
chi·hua·hua [ˌtʃɪ'wɑ:wɑ:] N chihuahua *m inv*
chil·blain ['tʃɪlˌbleɪn] N gelone *m*
◎ **child** [tʃaɪld] N (*pl* **children**) (*gen*) bambino(-a); (*son/daughter*) figlio(-a), bambino(-a); **a child of six** un bambino di sei anni; **I like children** mi piacciono i bambini; **Susan is our eldest child** Susan è la nostra figlia maggiore; **they've got three children** hanno tre figli
child abuser ['tʃaɪldə'bju:zə^r] N molestatore(-trice) di bambini
child-bearing ['tʃaɪldˌbɛərɪŋ] ADJ: **of child-bearing age** in età feconda
■ N gravidanza, maternità; **constant child-bearing** gravidanze *fpl* ripetute
child benefit N (*Brit*) ≈ assegni *mpl* familiari
child·birth ['tʃaɪldˌbɜ:θ] N parto; **to die in childbirth** morire di parto
child guidance N consulenza psicopedagogica
◎ **child·hood** ['tʃaɪldhʊd] N infanzia; **from childhood** fin dall'infanzia, fin da piccolo(-a)
child·ish ['tʃaɪldɪʃ] ADJ (*pej*) infantile, puerile
child·ish·ly ['tʃaɪldɪʃlɪ] ADV (*pej*) puerilmente, in modo infantile
child·ish·ness ['tʃaɪldɪʃnɪs] N (*pej*) puerilità
child labour N lavoro minorile
child·less ['tʃaɪldlɪs] ADJ senza figli
child·like ['tʃaɪldˌlaɪk] ADJ ingenuo(-a), innocente

child minder [ˈtʃaɪld,maɪndəʳ] N (*Brit*) bambinaia (*che sorveglia i bambini a casa propria*)
child prodigy N bambino(-a) prodigio *inv*
child-proof [ˈtʃaɪld,pru:f] ADJ: **child-proof (door) lock** (*Aut*) sicura (della portiera) a prova di bambino
chil·dren [ˈtʃɪldrən] NPL *of* **child**
children's home N istituto per l'infanzia (*abbandonata o maltrattata*)
child's play [ˈtʃaɪldz,pleɪ] N: **it's child's play** è un gioco da ragazzi, è una cosa da nulla
Child Support Agency N *ente governativo incaricato di valutare e riscuotere da genitori separati i contributi per il mantenimento dei figli*
Chile [ˈtʃɪlɪ] N Cile *m*
Chil·ean [ˈtʃɪlɪən] ADJ, N cileno(-a)
Chile pine N araucaria
chili [ˈtʃɪlɪ] N (*Am*) = chilli
chill [tʃɪl] ADJ (*wind*) freddo(-a), gelido(-a)
■ N freddo; (*Med*) infreddatura, colpo di freddo; **there's a chill in the air** l'aria è fredda; **to take the chill off (a room)** riscaldare un po' (una stanza); **to catch a chill** (*Med*) prendere un colpo di freddo
■ VT (*food, drink*) mettere in fresco; **"serve chilled"** "servire fresco"; **to chill sb's blood** (*fig*) far gelare il sangue a qn; **to be chilled to the bone** essere gelato(-a) fino alle ossa
▸ **chill out** VI (*esp Am fam*) darsi una calmata
chilli, (*Am*) **chili** [ˈtʃɪlɪ] N peperoncino; **chilli con carne** piatto di carne macinata e fagioli con il peperoncino
▹ www.iisr.org/spices/chilli.htm
chill·ing [ˈtʃɪlɪŋ] ADJ (*story, thought*) agghiacciante; (*wind*) gelido(-a)
chill·ness, **chilli·ness** [ˈtʃɪl(ɪ)nɪs] N (*cold*) freddo; (*coolness*) fresco; (*fig*) freddezza
chil·ly [ˈtʃɪlɪ] ADJ (*weather, room*) fresco(-a), freddo(-a); (*fig: person, look, reception*) freddo(-a), gelido(-a); (*sensitive to cold*) freddoloso(-a); **I feel chilly** ho *or* sento freddo, sono *or* mi sento infreddolito
chime [tʃaɪm] N rintocco
■ VT, VI suonare
▸ **chime in** VI + ADV (*fam: interrupt, join in*) intervenire; (: *echo*) fare eco, far coro
chim·ney [ˈtʃɪmnɪ] N (*of house*) camino; (*of factory*) ciminiera
chimney breast N bocca del camino
chimney pot N comignolo
chimney stack N canna fumaria
chimney sweep N spazzacamino
chimp [tʃɪmp] N (*fam*) scimpanzé *m inv*
chim·pan·zee [,tʃɪmpænˈzi:] N scimpanzé *m inv*
chin [tʃɪn] N mento; **(keep your) chin up!** (*fam*) coraggio!, testa alta!
Chi·na [ˈtʃaɪnə] N Cina; **People's Republic of China** Repubblica Popolare Cinese
chi·na [ˈtʃaɪnə] N (*porcelain*) porcellana; (*dishes*) porcellane *fpl*
■ ADJ di porcellana; **a china plate** un piatto di porcellana
China tea N tè *m* cinese
chin·chil·la [tʃɪnˈtʃɪlə] N cincillà *m inv*
Chi·nese [ˈtʃaɪˈni:z] ADJ cinese
■ N (*person: pl inv*) cinese *m/f*; (*language*) cinese *m*; **the Chinese** i cinesi
chink¹ [tʃɪŋk] N (*opening*) fessura; **a chink in the curtains** una fessura tra le tende; **a chink in his armour** (*fig*) il suo punto debole
chink² [tʃɪŋk] N (*noise*) tintinnio; **the chink of glasses** il tintinnio dei bicchieri
■ VT far tintinnare
■ VI tintinnare
chintz [tʃɪnts] N chintz *m inv*
chin·wag [ˈtʃɪn,wæg] N (*Brit fam*): **to have a chinwag** fare una chiacchierata
◎ **chip** [tʃɪp] N **1** (*piece*) frammento; (: *of glass, wood, stone*) scheggia; **he's a chip off the old block** (*fig*) è della stessa razza del padre; **he's got a chip on his shoulder because ...** gli è rimasto sullo stomaco il fatto che... **2** (*gen pl*: *Culin*: *Brit*: *French fry*) patatina fritta; (: *Am*: *crisp*) patatina; **potato chips** (*Am*) patatine *fpl* **3** (*in crockery, furniture*) scheggiatura; **there's a chip in this cup** questa tazza è scheggiata **4** (*in gambling*) fiche *f inv*; **when the chips are down** (*fig*) nei momenti critici, nel momento della verità, alla resa dei conti; **to have had one's chips** (*fig fam*) aver giocato l'ultima carta **5** (*Comput*: *microchip*) chip *m inv*
■ VT (*cup, plate*) scheggiare; **chipped potatoes** (*Culin*) patatine *fpl* fritte
■ VI scheggiarsi
▸ **chip in** VI + ADV (*fam*: *contribute*) contribuire; (: *interrupt*) intromettersi
▸ **chip off** VI + ADV (*paint*) scrostarsi
■ VT + ADV (*paint*) scrostare
Chip and PIN N sistema *m* di pagamento tramite Bancomat
chip·board [ˈtʃɪp,bɔ:d] N truciolato, agglomerato
chip·munk [ˈtʃɪp,mʌŋk] N tamia *m* striato
chip·pings [ˈtʃɪpɪŋz] NPL: **loose chippings** brecciame *msg*
chip shop N (*also*: **fish-and-chip shop**) *friggitoria*

CHIP SHOP

I **chip shops**, anche chiamati "fish-and-chip shops", sono friggitorie che vendono principalmente filetti di pesce impanati e patatine fritte che un tempo venivano serviti ai clienti avvolti in carta di giornale.
▹ www.niagara.co.uk/fish_and_chips.htm

chi·ropo·dist [kɪˈrɒpədɪst] N (*Brit*) callista *m/f*, podiatra *m/f*
chi·ropo·dy [kɪˈrɒpədɪ] N (*Brit*) chiropodia, podiatria, mestiere *m* di callista
chi·ro·prac·tic [,kaɪrəˈpræktɪk] N chiroterapia
chi·ro·prac·tor [ˈkaɪrə,præktəʳ] N chiropratico(-a)
chirp [tʃɜ:p], **chir·rup** [ˈtʃɪrəp] N (*of birds*) cinguettio; (*of crickets*) cri cri *m*
■ VI (*see n*) cinguettare; fare cri cri
chirpy [ˈtʃɜ:pɪ] ADJ (*fam*) pimpante, frizzante
chis·el [ˈtʃɪzl] N scalpello; (*smaller*) cesello; (*for engraving*) bulino
■ VT (*pt, pp* **chiselled**, *Am* **chiseled**) (*also*: **chisel out**) scolpire; cesellare; incidere con il bulino
chit¹ [tʃɪt] N nota *f* spese *inv*
chit² [tʃɪt] N (*old*): **a chit of a girl** una ragazzina
chit·chat [ˈtʃɪt,tʃæt] N (*fam*) chiacchiere *fpl*
chiv·al·rous [ˈʃɪvəlrəs] ADJ cavalleresco(-a)
chiv·al·rous·ly [ˈʃɪvəlrəslɪ] ADV cavallerescamente; (*gallantly*) con cavalleria
chiv·al·ry [ˈʃɪvəlrɪ] N cavalleria
chives [ˈtʃaɪvz] NPL erba cipollina
chiv·vy, (*Am*) **chivy** [ˈtʃɪvɪ] VT (*fam*) tormentare; **to**

Cc

chivvy sb into doing sth tormentare qn perché faccia qc
chlo·rate ['klɔ:reɪt] N (*Chem*) clorato
chlo·ride ['klɔ:raɪd] N (*Chem*) cloruro
chlo·rin·ate ['klɒrɪneɪt] VT clorare
chlo·rine ['klɔ:ri:n] N cloro
chlo·ro·form ['klɒrəfɔ:m] N cloroformio
■ VT cloroformizzare
chlo·ro·phyll ['klɒrəfɪl] N (*Bot*) clorofilla
chlo·ro·plast ['klɔ:rəʊˌplæst] N (*Bot*) cloroplasto
chlo·ro·sis [klɔ:'rəʊsɪs] N (*Med, Bot*) clorosi *f*
choc-ice ['tʃɒkˌaɪs] N *barretta di gelato ricoperto di cioccolato*
chock [tʃɒk] N zeppa
chock-a-block ['tʃɒkə'blɒk] ADJ: **chock-a-block (with)** pieno(-a) zeppo(-a) (di)
chock-full ['tʃɒk'fʊl] ADJ: **chock-full (of)** pieno(-a) zeppo(-a) (di)
◎ **choco·late** ['tʃɒklɪt] N (*substance*) cioccolato, cioccolata; (*individual sweet*) cioccolatino; (*drink*) cioccolata; **hot** *or* **drinking chocolate** cioccolata (calda); **a box of chocolates** una scatola di cioccolatini
■ ADJ (*biscuit, cake*) al cioccolato; (*egg*) di cioccolato; (*colour*) (color) cioccolato *inv*; **chocolate cake** torta al cioccolato
▷ www.bbc.co.uk/science/hottopics/chocolate/
◎ **choice** [tʃɔɪs] N scelta; **he's not really my choice** non è proprio quello che sceglierei io; **I did it by** *or* **from choice** l'ho fatto di mia volontà *or* per mia scelta; **a wide choice** un'ampia scelta; **I had no choice** non avevo scelta; **she had no choice but to go** non aveva altra scelta che andare; **take your choice!** scegli pure!; **the treatment/weapon of choice** la cura/l'arma preferita
■ ADJ (*fruit, wine*) di prima scelta; (*hum: example, remark*) bello(-a); **his language was really choice!** il suo tono non era esattamente garbato!
choir ['kwaɪə^r] N coro
choir·boy ['kwaɪəˌbɔɪ] N corista *m* (*ragazzo*)
choir·mas·ter ['kwaɪəˌmɑ:stə^r] N maestro(-a) del coro; (*in church*) maestro di cappella
choir·stall ['kwaɪəˌstɔ:l] N stallo del coro
choke [tʃəʊk] N (*Aut*) (valvola dell')aria
■ VT (*person*) soffocare; (*: strangle*) strangolare; (*also: choke up: pipe*) intasare
■ VI **1** soffocare; **help him, he's choking!** aiutatelo, sta soffocando! **2** (*fam: lose confidence*) farsi prendere dalla sfiducia
► **choke back** VT + ADV soffocare
chok·er ['tʃəʊkə^r] N collana giracollo
chol·era ['kɒlərə] N colera *m*
cho·les·ter·ol [kə'lɛstərɒl] N colesterolo
chomp [tʃɒmp] VI, VT (*fam*) masticare rumorosamente
◎ **choose** [tʃu:z] (*vb: pt* **chose**, *pp* **chosen**) VT scegliere; **she chose a pale pink skirt** ha scelto una gonna rosa pallido; **to choose to do sth** scegliere *or* decidere di fare qc
■ VI scegliere; **to choose between** scegliere tra; **there is nothing to choose between them** uno vale l'altro; **I don't know which to choose** non so quale scegliere; **have you already chosen?** hai già scelto?; **to choose from** scegliere da *or* tra; **there were several to choose from** vi era parecchia scelta; **as/when I choose** come/quando voglio *or* decido io
choosy ['tʃu:zɪ] ADJ (*comp* **-ier**, *superl* **-iest**) (*fam*): **to be choosy** fare lo/la schizzinoso(-a) *or* difficile
◎ **chop¹** [tʃɒp] N **1** (*blow*) colpo secco, colpo netto; **to get the chop** (*Brit fam: project*) essere bocciato(-a); (*: person: be sacked*) essere licenziato(-a) **2** (*Culin*) costoletta; **pork chop** cotoletta di maiale
■ VT (*wood*) tagliare, spaccare; (*meat, vegetables*) tagliare (a pezzetti)
► **chop down** VT + ADV (*tree*) abbattere
► **chop off** VT + ADV tagliare (via)
► **chop up** VT + ADV (*wood*) spaccare; (*vegetables, meat*) tagliare (a pezzetti)
chop² [tʃɒp] VI: **to chop and change** cambiare continuamente parere
chop·per ['tʃɒpə^r] N (*of butcher*) mannaia; (*Aer: fam*) elicottero
chop·ping ['tʃɒpɪŋ] ADJ: **chopping board** tagliere *m*; **chopping knife** coltello (per tritare)
chord [kɔ:d] N (*Mus*) accordo; (*Geom*) corda; **to touch the right chord** (*fig*) toccare il tasto giusto
chore [tʃɔ:^r] N faccenda; (*pej*) rottura; **household chores** faccende *fpl* (domestiche); **to do the chores** sbrigare *or* fare le faccende; **doing your homework is a bit of a chore** fare i compiti è un po' una scocciatura
cho·reo·graph ['kɒrɪəˌgræf] VI, VT (*ballet*) fare la coreografia (di)
cho·reog·ra·pher [ˌkɒrɪ'ɒgrəfə^r] N coreografo(-a)
cho·reo·graph·ic [ˌkɒrɪəʊ'græfɪk] ADJ coreografico(-a)
cho·reo·graphi·cal·ly [ˌkɒrɪə'græfɪklɪ] ADV coreograficamente
cho·reog·ra·phy [ˌkɒrɪ'ɒgrəfɪ] N coreografia
chor·is·ter ['kɒrɪstə^r] N (*Rel*) corista *m/f*
cho·roid ['kɔ:rɔɪd] N (*Anat*) coroide *f*
chor·tle ['tʃɔ:tl] VI ridacchiare, fare risolini
cho·rus ['kɔ:rəs] N **1** (*musical work, people*) coro; **in chorus** in coro **2** (*refrain: also fig*) ritornello; **everyone joined in the chorus** tutti cantarono insieme il ritornello
■ VT (*answer*) rispondere in coro
chorus girl N girl *f inv*, ragazza che canta e balla
chose [tʃəʊz] PT *of* **choose**
cho·sen ['tʃəʊzn] PP *of* **choose** ■ ADJ: **the chosen (people)** gli eletti
choux pas·try ['ʃu:'peɪstrɪ] N pasta per bignè
chow [tʃaʊ] N (*also:* **chow-chow**) (*dog*) chow chow *m inv*
chow·der ['tʃaʊdə^r] N (*esp Am Culin*) zuppa di pesce
Christ [kraɪst] N Cristo
chris·ten ['krɪsn] VT battezzare
Chris·ten·dom ['krɪsndəm] N cristianità
chris·ten·ing ['krɪsnɪŋ] N battesimo
◎ **Chris·tian** ['krɪstɪən] ADJ cristiano(-a); (*also:* **christian**, *fig*) caritatevole
■ N cristiano(-a)
Chris·ti·an·ity [ˌkrɪstɪ'ænɪtɪ] N cristianesimo
Christian name N nome *m* (di battesimo)
Christ·mas ['krɪsməs] N Natale *m*; **at Christmas** a Natale; **Happy** *or* **Merry Christmas!** Buon Natale!
■ ADJ (*tree, cake, present, party*) di Natale
Christmas card N biglietto di auguri natalizi
Christmas Day N il giorno di Natale
Christmas Eve N la vigilia di Natale
Christmas Island N Isola Christmas
Christmas pudding ['krɪsməs'pʊdɪŋ] N *dolce con frutta secca e spezie cotto a vapore e servito tradizionalmente al termine del pranzo di Natale*
▷ www.christmas.com/worldview/
▷ www.primary-networks.com/wickham/celebrations/xmas/pudding.html
Christmas stocking N ≈ calza della Befana

Christ·mas·time [ˈkrɪsməsˌtaɪm] N periodo natalizio *or* di Natale
Christmas tree N albero di Natale
chro·mat·ic [krəˈmætɪk] ADJ (*Mus*) cromatico(-a)
chro·mati·cism [krəˈmætɪsɪzəm] N (*Mus*) cromatismo
chromatic scale N (*Mus*) scala cromatica
chro·ma·tog·ra·phy [ˌkrəʊməˈtɒgrəfɪ] N (*Chem*) cromatografia
chro·mium [ˈkrəʊmɪəm], **chrome** [krəʊm] N cromo; (*also:* **chromium plating**) cromatura
chromium-plated [ˈkrəʊmɪəmˈpleɪtɪd] ADJ cromato(-a)
chro·mo·some [ˈkrəʊməsəʊm] N cromosoma *m*
chron·ic [ˈkrɒnɪk] ADJ (*invalid, disease*) cronico(-a); (*fig: liar, drunkard*) incallito(-a); (*fam: weather, actor etc*) allucinante; **chronic back pain** mal di schiena cronico; **a chronic problem** un grave problema
chroni·cal·ly [ˈkrɒnɪklɪ] ADV in modo cronico, cronicamente; **he is chronically sick** è un malato cronico; **a hospital that is chronically short of finance** un ospedale affetto da una cronica mancanza di fondi
chronic fatigue syndrome [ˈkrɒnɪkfəˈtiːgˈsɪndrəʊm] N (*Med*) sindrome *f* da affaticamento cronico
chroni·cle [ˈkrɒnɪkl] N cronaca
chrono·logi·cal [ˌkrɒnəˈlɒdʒɪkəl] ADJ cronologico(-a); **in chronological order** in ordine cronologico
chrono·logi·cal·ly [ˌkrɒnəˈlɒdʒɪkəlɪ] ADV cronologicamente
chro·nol·ogy [krəˈnɒlədʒɪ] N cronologia
chro·nom·eter [krəˈnɒmɪtə^r] N cronometro
chrysa·lis [ˈkrɪsəlɪs] N (*pl* **-es**) crisalide *f*
chry·san·themum [krɪˈsænθəməm] N crisantemo
chub [tʃʌb] N cavedano
chub·by [ˈtʃʌbɪ] ADJ paffuto(-a), grassoccio(-a)
chuck¹ [tʃʌk] VT (*fam*) **1** (*throw*) gettare **2** (*also:* **chuck away**) buttare, gettare; **I chucked the letter in the bin** ho gettato la lettera nella spazzatura **3** (*also:* **chuck up, chuck in**: *job*) piantare **4** (*boyfriend, girlfriend*) piantare
▸ **chuck out** VT + ADV (*fam: useless article*) buttare via; (: *person*) sbattere *or* buttare fuori; **you should chuck that stuff out** dovresti buttar via quella roba
chuck² [tʃʌk] N (*also:* **chuck steak**) spalla
chuck³ [tʃʌk] N (*Tech*) mandrino
chuck·le [ˈtʃʌkl] N risolino
■ VI ridacchiare; **to chuckle at** *or* **over** ridere *or* ridacchiare per
chuffed [tʃʌft] ADJ (*Brit fam*): **to be chuffed about sth** essere arcicontento(-a) di qc
chug [tʃʌg] VI **1** (*boat*) sbuffare; (*motor*) scoppiettare **2** (*also:* **chug along**: *boat*) muoversi sbuffando
chum [tʃʌm] N (*fam*) compagno(-a), amicone(-a)
▸ **chum up** VI (*fam*): **to chum up (with sb)** fare amicizia (con qn)
chum·my [ˈtʃʌmɪ] ADJ (*fam*): **to be chummy (with)** essere grande amico(-a) (di)
chump [tʃʌmp] N (*fam*) zuccone(-a)
chunk [tʃʌŋk] N (bel) pezzo; (*of bread*) tocco; **cut the meat into chunks** taglia la carne a grossi pezzi
chunky [ˈtʃʌŋkɪ] ADJ (*comp* **-ier**, *superl* **-iest**) (*furniture etc*) basso(-a) e largo(-a); (*person*) ben piantato(-a); (*knitwear*) di lana grossa
Chun·nel [ˈtʃʌnəl] N (*fam*) = **Channel Tunnel**
◎ **church** [tʃɜːtʃ] N chiesa; **to go to church** andare in chiesa; **after church** dopo la funzione; (*for Catholics*) dopo la messa; **to enter the Church** prendere gli ordini
church·goer [ˈtʃɜːtʃˌgəʊə^r] N fedele *m/f*; **his parents are regular churchgoers** i suoi genitori vanno regolarmente in chiesa
Church of England N: **the Church of England** la Chiesa anglicana
church·warden [ˌtʃɜːtʃˈwɔːdən] N *aiutante del vicario nell'amministrazione della parrocchia*
church·yard [ˈtʃɜːtʃˌjɑːd] N cimitero (*annesso a una chiesa*)
churl·ish [ˈtʃɜːlɪʃ] ADJ rozzo(-a), sgarbato(-a)
churl·ish·ly [ˈtʃɜːlɪʃlɪ] ADV rozzamente, sgarbatamente
churl·ish·ness [ˈtʃɜːlɪʃnɪs] N rozzezza, sgarbataggine *f*
churn [tʃɜːn] N (*for butter*) zangola; (*Brit: for milk*) bidone *m* per il latte
■ VT (*butter*) fare (nella zangola); (*fig: also:* **churn up**: *water*) agitare
■ VI (*water*) agitarsi; (*stomach*) torcersi; **his stomach was churning** aveva il voltastomaco
▸ **churn out** VT + ADV (*often pej*) sfornare in gran quantità
chute [ʃuːt] N (*for parcels, coal, in swimming pool*) scivolo; (*also:* **rubbish chute**) canale *m* di scarico; (*fam*) = **parachute**
chut·ney [ˈtʃʌtnɪ] N salsa piccante (di frutta, zucchero e spezie)
CIA [ˌsiːaɪˈeɪ] N ABBR (*Am:* = **Central Intelligence Agency**) CIA *f*
▹ www.cia.gov/
ci·ca·da [sɪˈkɑːdə] N cicala
Cicero [ˈsɪsəˌrəʊ] N Cicerone *m*
CID [ˌsiːaɪˈdiː] N ABBR (*Brit*) = **Criminal Investigation Department**
ci·der [ˈsaɪdə^r] N sidro
CIF [ˌsiːaɪˈɛf] ABBR (= **cost, insurance and freight**) CIF *m*, costo assicurazione e nolo
ci·gar [sɪˈgɑː^r] N sigaro
cigar case N portasigari *m inv*
◎ **ciga·rette** [ˌsɪgəˈrɛt] N sigaretta; **he's smoking a cigarette** sta fumando una sigaretta
cigarette case N portasigarette *m inv*
cigarette end N mozzicone *m* (di sigaretta), cicca
cigarette holder N bocchino
cigarette lighter N accendino
cigarette paper N cartina
cigar lighter N accendisigari *m inv*
cil·ia [ˈsɪlɪə] NPL (*Anat*) ciglia *fpl*
cili·ary [ˈsɪlɪərɪ] ADJ (*Anat*) ciliare
C-in-C ABBR = **commander in chief**
cinch [sɪntʃ] N (*fam*): **it's a cinch** (*easy thing*) è una cretinata *or* una sciocchezza, è presto fatto; (*sure thing*) è una cosa sicura
Cincinnatus [ˌsɪnsɪˈnɑːtəs] N Cincinnato
cin·der [ˈsɪndə^r] N cenere *f*, brace *f*; **burned to a cinder** (*fig: food*) carbonizzato(-a)
Cinderella [ˌsɪndəˈrɛlə] N Cenerentola
cinder track N (*Sport*) pista di cenere
cine camera [ˈsɪnɪˈkæmərə] N (*Brit*) cinepresa
cine film [ˈsɪnɪfɪlm] N (*Brit*) film *m inv*
◎ **cin·ema** [ˈsɪnəmə] N cinema *m inv*
▹ www.cinema.com
▹ www.learner.org/exhibits/cinema
▹ www.bfi.org.uk
▹ http://imdb.com
▹ www.bafta.org/
▹ www.senseofcinema.com
▹ www.oscars.org/academyawards

Cc

Cin·ema·scope® [ˈsɪnɪmə,skeʊp] N cinemascope® *m*
cin·emat·ic [ˌsɪnɪˈmætɪk] ADJ cinematografico(-a)
cin·emato·graphi·cal·ly [ˌsɪnɪ,mætəˈgræfɪklɪ] ADV cinematograficamente
cin·ema·tog·ra·phy [ˌsɪnɪməˈtɒgrəfɪ] N cinematografia
cine projector [ˈsɪnɪprəˈdʒɛktəʳ] N (*Brit*) proiettore *m*
cin·na·mon [ˈsɪnəmən] N cannella
ci·pher [ˈsaɪfəʳ] N (*code*) codice *m* (cifrato); (*Math*) zero; (*fig: faceless employee etc*) persona di nessun conto, nullità *f inv*; **in cipher** in codice
circa [ˈsɜːkə] PREP circa
Circe [ˈsɜːsɪ] N Circe *f*
◎**cir·cle** [ˈsɜːkl] N (*gen*) cerchio; (*of friends etc*) circolo; (*in theatre, cinema*): **the circle** la galleria; **great/small circle** (*Geom*) cerchio massimo/minore; **to stand in a circle** mettersi in cerchio; **we stood in a circle** ci siamo messi in cerchio; **in some circles** in certi ambienti; **she moves in wealthy circles** frequenta l'alta società; **the family circle** la cerchia familiare; **to come full circle** (*fig*) ritornare al punto di partenza; **to go round in circles** (*fam*) girare sempre attorno allo stesso punto
■ VT (*surround*) accerchiare, circondare; (*move round*) girare attorno *or* intorno a; (*draw round*) segnare con un cerchio, cerchiare
■ VI girare in circolo
◎**cir·cuit** [ˈsɜːkɪt] N (*journey around*) giro; (*Sport, Elec*) circuito; (*of judge*) distretto giudiziario; (*Cine*) rete *f* di distribuzione
circuit board N (*Elec*) piastra; (*Comput*) tavola dei circuiti
circuit breaker N salvavita *m*
cir·cui·tous [sɜːˈkjʊɪtəs] ADJ: **to go by a circuitous route** prendere la strada più lunga
cir·cui·tous·ly [sɜːˈkjʊɪtəslɪ] ADV facendo un lungo giro; (*fig*) indirettamente
cir·cuit·ry [ˈsɜːkɪtrɪ] N circuiteria, circuiti *mpl*
cir·cu·lar [ˈsɜːkjʊləʳ] ADJ circolare
■ N (*letter*) circolare *f*; (*as advertisement*) volantino pubblicitario
cir·cu·lar·ize [ˈsɜːkjʊlə,raɪz] VT inviare circolari a
circular saw N segatrice *f* a disco
cir·cu·late [ˈsɜːkjʊ,leɪt] VI (*gen*) circolare; (*person: socially*) girare e andare un po' da tutti
■ VT far circolare; **they are circulating a petition** stanno facendo circolare una petizione
cir·cu·lat·ing capi·tal [ˈsɜːkjʊ,leɪtɪŋˈkæpɪtl] N (*Comm*) capitale *m* d'esercizio
cir·cu·la·tion [ˌsɜːkjʊˈleɪʃən] N (*gen*) circolazione *f*; (*of news*) diffusione *f*; (*of newspaper etc*) tiratura; **she has poor circulation** (*Med*) ha una cattiva circolazione; **to withdraw sth from circulation** togliere *or* ritirare qc dalla circolazione; **the newspaper has a circulation of around 8000** il giornale ha una tiratura di circa ottomila copie; **he's back in circulation** (*fam*) è tornato in circolazione
cir·cu·la·tory [ˌsɜːkjʊˈleɪtərɪ] ADJ (*Med*) circolatorio(-a)
circulatory system N (*Med*) apparato circolatorio
cir·cum·cise [ˈsɜːkəm,saɪz] VT circoncidere
cir·cum·ci·sion [ˌsɜːkəmˈsɪʒən] N circoncisione *f*
cir·cum·fer·ence [səˈkʌmfərəns] N circonferenza
cir·cum·flex [ˈsɜːkəm,flɛks] N (*also:* **circumflex accent**) accento circonflesso
cir·cum·lo·cu·tion [ˌsɜːkəmləˈkjuːʃən] N (*frm*) circonlocuzione *f*
cir·cum·navi·gate [ˌsɜːkəmˈnævɪgeɪt] VT circumnavigare
cir·cum·navi·ga·tion [ˈsɜːkəm,nævɪˈgeɪʃən] N circumnavigazione *f*
cir·cum·scribe [ˈsɜːkəm,skraɪb] VT (*limit*) limitare; (*Math*) circoscrivere
cir·cum·spect [ˈsɜːkəm,spɛkt] ADJ circospetto(-a)
cir·cum·spec·tion [ˌsɜːkəmˈspɛkʃən] N circospezione *f*
cir·cum·spect·ly [ˈsɜːkəmspɛktlɪ] ADV con circospezione
cir·cum·stances [ˈsɜːkəmstənsɪz] NPL **1** (*conditions*) circostanze *fpl*; **in the circumstances** date le circostanze; **under no circumstances** in nessun caso **2** (*financial state*) condizioni *fpl* finanziarie; **to be in easy/poor circumstances** trovarsi in buone/cattive condizioni finanziarie
cir·cum·stan·tial [ˌsɜːkəmˈstænʃəl] ADJ (*report, statement*) circostanziato(-a), dettagliato(-a)
circumstantial evidence N prova indiziaria
cir·cum·vent [ˌsɜːkəmˈvɛnt] VT (*frm: rule etc*) aggirare
cir·cus [ˈsɜːkəs] N (*entertainment*) circo; (*usu* **Circus:** *street name*) piazza (*di forma circolare*)
▷ www.circusweb.com
▷ www.artmedia.com.au/playspac.htm
cir·rho·sis [sɪˈrəʊsɪs] N (*also:* **cirrhosis of the liver**) cirrosi *f inv* (epatica)
cir·rus [ˈsɪrəs] N (*pl* **cirri** [ˈsɪraɪ]) (*Met*) cirro
CIS [ˌsiːaɪˈɛs] N ABBR (= **Commonwealth of Independent States**) CSI *f*
cis·sy [ˈsɪsɪ] N (*fam*) femminuccia
Cis·ter·cian [sɪˈstɜːʃən] ADJ, N cistercense (*m*)
cis·tern [ˈsɪstən] N serbatoio, cisterna; (*in toilet*) serbatoio d'acqua
cita·del [ˈsɪtədl] N cittadella
ci·ta·tion [saɪˈteɪʃən] N citazione *f*
◎**cite** [saɪt] VT citare; **he was cited to appear in court** (*Law*) fu citato in tribunale; **to cite as an example** portare come esempio
◎**citi·zen** [ˈsɪtɪzn] N (*of state*) cittadino(-a); (*of city*) abitante *m/f*; **the citizens of this town** gli abitanti di questa città
Citizens' Advice Bureau N (*Brit*) *organizzazione di volontari che offre gratuitamente assistenza in materia legale e finanziaria*
▷ www.citizensadvice.org.uk/
Citizens' Band N banda cittadina
citi·zen·ship [ˈsɪtɪzn,ʃɪp] N cittadinanza
cit·ric acid [ˌsɪtrɪkˈæsɪd] N acido citrico
cit·rus fruit [ˈsɪtrəs,fruːt] N agrume *m*
City [ˈsɪtɪ] N: **the City** (*Fin*) la City di Londra
◎**city** [ˈsɪtɪ] N (grande) città *f inv*
■ ADJ (*centre*) della città; (*life*) di città
City and Guilds Institute N (*Brit*) *istituto in cui è possibile conseguire vari diplomi a livello universitario in materie tecniche passando il relativo esame*
▷ www.city-and-guilds.co.uk
city break N (*Tourism*) city break *m inv* (*breve soggiorno specie nelle gradi città darte*)
city centre N (*Brit*) centro (città)
city dweller N chi abita in città
city fathers NPL: **the city fathers** i notabili della città
City Hall N (*Am*) ≈ Comune *m*
city page N (*in newspaper*) pagina finanziaria
city planner N (*Am*) = **town planner**
city slicker [ˈsɪtɪˈslɪkəʳ] N (*pej fam*) cittadino(-a) sofisticato(-a)

city technology college N (*Brit*) istituto tecnico superiore (*finanziato dall'industria*)
▹ www.teachernet.gov.uk/management/atoz/c/citytechnologycolleges/
▹ www.specialistschools.org.uk/

civ·et ['sɪvɪt] N zibetto

civ·ic ['sɪvɪk] ADJ civico(-a)

civic centre N (*Brit*) centro civico

civ·ics ['sɪvɪks] NSG educazione *f* civica

◎ **civ·il** ['sɪvl] ADJ **1** (*war, law, marriage*) civile **2** (*polite*) educato(-a), gentile

Civil Aviation Authority N *organismo di controllo dell'aviazione civile*

civil defence N protezione *f* civile

civil disobedience N resistenza passiva

civil engineer N ingegnere *m* civile

civil engineering N ingegneria civile
▹ www.ce.gatech.edu/WWW-CE/

◎ **ci·vil·ian** [sɪ'vɪlɪən] ADJ (*clothes, government*) civile, borghese; (*life*) da civile, da borghese
■ N civile *m/f*, borghese *m/f*

ci·vil·ity [sɪ'vɪlɪtɪ] N gentilezza

civi·li·za·tion [ˌsɪvɪlaɪ'zeɪʃən] N civiltà *f inv*

civi·lize ['sɪvɪˌlaɪz] VT civilizzare

civi·lized ['sɪvɪˌlaɪzd] ADJ (*country, society*) civilizzato(-a), progredito(-a); (*behaviour, manner*) civile, cortese; **in civilized countries** nei paesi civilizzati

civil law N codice *m* civile; (*study*) diritto civile

civil liberties NPL libertà *fpl* civili

civ·il·ly ['sɪvɪlɪ] ADV civilmente, educatamente, gentilmente

civil rights NPL diritti *mpl* civili

civil rights movement N movimento per i diritti civili

civil servant N impiegato(-a) statale

civil service N: **the Civil Service** l'amministrazione *f* pubblica

◎ **civil war** N guerra civile
▹ http://americancivilwar.com
▹ www.civilwar.com
▹ www.open2.net/civilwar
▹ http://easyweb.easynet.co.uk/~crossby/ECW

civ·vies ['sɪvɪz] NPL (*fam*): **in civvies** in borghese

civ·vy street ['sɪvɪˌstri:t] N (*Brit fam*) vita da civile

CJD [ˌsi:dʒeɪ'di:] N (*Med:* = **Creutzfeldt-Jacob Disease**) malattia di Creutzfeldt-Jacob

cl ABBR (= **centilitre**) cl

clad [klæd] ADJ (*old, liter*) vestito(-a); **clad in** vestito(-a) di

clad·ding ['klædɪŋ] N (*of roof*) rivestimento

◎ **claim** [kleɪm] N **1** (*demand: to title, right*) pretesa, diritto; (*: for expenses, damages, increased pay*) richiesta; (*insurance claim*) domanda d'indennizzo; **the poor have a claim to our sympathy** i poveri hanno diritto alla nostra comprensione; **there are many claims on my time** sono molto preso; **to lay claim to sth** avanzare pretese su qc; **to put in a claim for sth** fare una richiesta di qc; **to put in a claim for a pay rise** chiedere un aumento di stipendio; **to put in a claim for petrol expenses** chiedere il rimborso delle spese per la benzina; **we sent in a claim to our insurance company** abbiamo mandato una richiesta di risarcimento alla nostra assicurazione **2** (*assertion*) affermazione *f*, pretesa; **the manufacturer's claims are obviously untrue** le affermazioni del fabbricante sono ovviamente false; **I make no claim to be infallible** non pretendo di essere infallibile
■ VT **1** (*rights, territory*) pretendere, rivendicare; (*expenses, damages*) (ri)chiedere; (*lost property*) reclamare; **he's claiming compensation from the company** chiede un risarcimento da parte della società; **she's claiming unemployment benefit** riceve il sussidio di disoccupazione; **the explosion claimed five victims** l'esplosione ha fatto cinque vittime; **something else claimed her attention** qualcosa distolse la sua attenzione **2** (*assert*) dichiarare, sostenere; **the new system can claim many advantages over the old one** si può dire che il nuovo sistema offre molti vantaggi rispetto a quello vecchio; **to claim that/to be ...** affermare *or* sostenere che/di essere...; **he claims he found the money** sostiene di aver trovato il denaro; **he claims to have seen her** sostiene di averla vista
■ VI (*for insurance*) fare una domanda d'indennizzo

claim·ant ['kleɪmənt] N (*to social benefit*) richiedente *m/f*; (*in court*) citante *m/f*; (*to throne etc*) pretendente *m/f*

claim form N (*gen*) modulo per ricorsi; (*for expenses*) modulo di rimborso spese

clair·voy·ance [klɛə'vɔɪəns] N chiaroveggenza

clair·voy·ant [klɛə'vɔɪənt] ADJ, N chiaroveggente (*m/f*)

clam [klæm] N vongola
► **clam up** VI + ADV (*fam*) zittirsi

clam·ber ['klæmbəʳ] VI arrampicarsi

clam·my ['klæmɪ] ADJ (*comp* **-ier**, *superl* **-iest**) (*hands*) sudaticcio(-a), viscido(-a); (*weather*) appiccicoso(-a), caldo(-a) e umido(-a)

clam·or·ous ['klæmərəs] ADJ (*crowd, mob*) chiassoso(-a); (*demands*) insistente

DID YOU KNOW ...?
clamorous is not translated by the Italian word *clamoroso*

clam·our, (*Am*) **clam·or** ['klæməʳ] N (*noise*) clamore *m*; (*protest*) protesta
■ VI: **to clamour for sth** chiedere a gran voce qc

clamp [klæmp] N morsetto, morsa
■ VT (*hold in a vice*) stringere con un morsetto; (*immobilize: car*) applicare i ceppi bloccaruote a
► **clamp down** VI + ADV (*fig*): **to clamp down (on)** dare un giro di vite a

clamp·down ['klæmpˌdaʊn] N stretta; **a clampdown on sth/sb** un giro di vite a qc/qn

clan [klæn] N clan *m inv*

clan·des·tine [klæn'dɛstɪn] ADJ clandestino(-a)

clan·des·tine·ly [klæn'dɛstɪnlɪ] ADV clandestinamente

clang [klæŋ] N suono metallico
■ VI emettere un suono metallico; **the gate clanged shut** il cancello si chiuse con fragore

clang·er ['klæŋəʳ] N (*Brit fam*) gaffe *f inv*; **to drop a clanger** fare una gaffe

clank ['klæŋk] N suono metallico
■ VI emettere un suono metallico

clan·nish ['klænɪʃ] (*pej*) ADJ (*group*) chiuso(-a); (*person*) selettivo(-a)

clans·man ['klænzmən] N membro di un clan

clap [klæp] N (*on shoulder*) pacca; (*of the hands*) battimano; (*applause*) applauso; **a clap of thunder** un tuono
■ VT (*applaud*) applaudire; **to clap one's hands** battere le mani; **clap your hands** batti le mani; **to clap a hand over sb's mouth** chiudere la bocca (con la mano) a qn; **they clapped him in prison** (*fam*) lo sbatterono dentro

■ VI (*applaud*) applaudire; **everybody clapped** tutti applaudirono
clap·board ['klæp,bɔ:d] N (*Am*): **a clapboard house** una casa rivestita di assicelle di legno
clapped-out ['klæpt,aʊt] ADJ (*fam*) malridotto(-a)
clapper·board ['klæpə,bɔ:d] N ciac *m*, ciak *m*
clap·ping ['klæpɪŋ] N applausi *mpl*
clap·trap ['klæp,træp] N (*pej fam*) chiacchiere *fpl*, sciocchezze *fpl*
clar·et ['klærət] N chiaretto (originario della regione di Bordeaux)
clari·fi·ca·tion [,klærɪfɪ'keɪʃən] N chiarificazione *f*, chiarimento
clari·fy ['klærɪfaɪ] VT (*statement etc*) chiarire, chiarificare
clari·net [,klærɪ'nɛt] N clarinetto
clari·net·tist [,klærɪ'nɛtɪst] N clarinettista *m/f*
clarion call ['klærɪən-] N (*liter*) appello
clar·ity ['klærɪtɪ] N chiarezza
◎ **clash** [klæʃ] N **1** (*noise*) fragore *m*, frastuono **2** (*Mil, of personalities, interests*) scontro, conflitto; (*of dates, programmes*) conflitto; (*of colours*) contrasto, disarmonia; **a clash with the police** uno scontro con la polizia; **a clash of wills** uno scontro di idee
■ VT (*cymbals*) far risuonare; (*swords*) far cozzare
■ VI: **to clash (with)** (*fig: have an argument*) scontrarsi (con); (*personalities, interests*) scontrarsi (con), essere in conflitto (con); (*colours*) stridere (con), stonare (con); (*dates, events*) coincidere (con); **red clashes with orange** il rosso stona con l'arancio; **the date of the party clashes with the meeting** la data della festa coincide con quella della riunione
clasp [klɑ:sp] N fibbia, fermaglio
■ VT afferrare; **to clasp one's hands (together)** stringere le mani; **to clasp sb in one's arms** stringere qn tra le braccia
clasp knife N coltello a serramanico
◎ **class** [klɑ:s] N (*social class, Bio, Scol, Univ*) classe *f*; (*group, category*) tipo, categoria; (*lesson*) lezione *f*; **we're in the same class** siamo in classe insieme; **I go to dancing classes** vado a lezione di ballo; **to have class** (*fam*) avere classe; **to be in a class of one's own** essere impareggiabile
■ VT: **to class sb as sth** definire qn qc
class action N (*Law*) azione legale collettiva
class-conscious ['klɑ:s,kɒnʃəs] ADJ che ha coscienza di classe
class consciousness N coscienza di classe
class distinction N (*Sociol*) distinzione *f* di classe
◎ **clas·sic** ['klæsɪk] ADJ classico(-a); **a classic example** un esempio classico
■ N classico; **this song is a classic** questa canzone è un classico; *see also* **classics**
◎ **clas·si·cal** ['klæsɪkəl] ADJ classico(-a); **classical scholar** studioso(-a) di lettere antiche; **classical music** musica classica
▷ www.classical.net
clas·si·cal·ly ['klæsɪklɪ] ADV classicamente
clas·si·cism ['klæ,sɪsɪzəm] N classicismo
clas·sics ['klæsɪks] NPL (*Scol, Univ*) studi *mpl* umanistici
clas·si·fi·able ['klæsɪ,faɪəbl] ADJ classificabile
clas·si·fi·ca·tion [,klæsɪfɪ'keɪʃən] N classificazione *f*
clas·si·fied ['klæsɪ,faɪd] ADJ (*information*) segreto(-a), riservato(-a); **classified advertisements** *or* **ads** (*in newspaper*) piccola pubblicità
clas·si·fy ['klæsɪ,faɪ] VT classificare
class interval N (*Math*) intervallo di classe
class·less ['klɑ:slɪs] ADJ (*society*) aclassista, senza distinzioni di classe
class·mate ['klɑ:s,meɪt] N compagno(-a) di classe
class·room ['klɑ:s,rʊm] N classe *f*, aula
classroom assistant N (*Brit*) assistente *m/f* in classe dell'insegnante
class war, class warfare N (*Sociol*) lotta di classe
classy ['klɑ:sɪ] ADJ (*comp* **-ier**, *superl* **-iest**) (*fam*) di classe, chic *inv*
clat·ter ['klætəʳ] N (*of plates*) acciottolìo; (*of hooves*) scalpitìo
■ VI (*metal object etc*) sferragliare; (*hooves*) scalpitare; **the gate clattered behind her** il cancello sbattè con fragore dietro di lei; **to clatter in/out** correre rumorosamente dentro/fuori
■ VT (*plates*) acciottolare
clause [klɔ:z] N (*Gram*) proposizione *f*; (*in contract, law, will*) clausola; **main clause** proposizione *f* principale
claus·tro·pho·bia [,klɔ:strə'fəʊbɪə] N claustrofobia
claus·tro·pho·bic [,klɔ:strə'fəʊbɪk] ADJ (*person*) claustrofobico(-a); (*atmosphere*) claustrofobico(-a), da claustrofobia
clavi·cle ['klævɪkl] N (*Anat*) clavicola
claw [klɔ:] N (*of cat, small bird*) unghia; (*of lion, eagle, bird of prey*) artiglio; (*of lobster*) chela, tenaglia
■ VT graffiare; **to claw sth to shreds** dilaniare qc
■ VI: **to claw at** graffiare; (*prey*) ghermire
▸ **claw back** VT + ADV (*tax, duty etc*) recuperare
claw·back ['klɔ:,bæk] N (*of tax, duty etc*) recupero
claw hammer N martello a granchio
clay [kleɪ] N (*gen*) argilla; (*for pottery*) creta, argilla
clay court N (*Tennis*) campo in terra battuta
clay pigeon shooting N tiro al piattello
clay pipe N pipa di terracotta
◎ **clean** [kli:n] ADJ (*comp* **-er**, *superl* **-est**) (*gen*) pulito(-a); (*sheet of paper*) nuovo(-a); (*smooth, clear: outline, movement, break*) netto(-a); (*fair: fight, game*) leale, corretto(-a); **to wipe sth clean** pulire qc; **to make a clean sweep** fare piazza pulita; **the doctor gave me a clean bill of health** il medico ha garantito che godo di ottima salute; **to make a clean breast of sth** togliersi qc dalla coscienza; **a clean record** (*Police*) una fedina penale pulita; **to have a clean driving licence** (*Am*): **to have a clean record** non aver mai preso contravvenzioni
■ ADV: **he clean forgot** si è completamente dimenticato; **he got clean away** se l'è svignata senza lasciare tracce; **the ball went clean through the window** la palla prese in pieno la finestra; **to come clean** (*fam: admit guilt*) confessare; (*: tell unpleasant truth*) dire veramente come stanno le cose; **I'm clean out of cigarettes** non ho neanche mezza sigaretta
■ N pulita, ripulitura
■ VT (*gen*) pulire; (*blackboard*) cancellare; (*shoes*) lucidare; **to clean one's teeth** (*Brit*) lavarsi i denti; **he never cleans the bath** non pulisce mai la vasca da bagno
▸ **clean off** VT + ADV (*mark*) togliere; (*chalk*) cancellare
▸ **clean out** VT + ADV (*also fig*) ripulire
▸ **clean up** VT + ADV (*room, mess*) pulire, ripulire; (*fig: city, area*) fare un po' di pulizia in; **to clean o.s. up** darsi una ripulita
■ VI + ADV ripulire, far pulizia; (*fig: make profit*) fare una barca di soldi
▸ **clean up after** VT + ADV + PREP: **to clean up after sb** pulire lo sporco lasciato da qn
clean-cut ['kli:n'kʌt] ADJ (*line, shape*) netto(-a),

nitido(-a); (*man*) curato(-a); (*situation etc*) ben definito(-a), chiaro(-a)

clean·er ['kli:nəʳ] N (*person*) addetto(-a) alle pulizie; (*product*) detersivo, detergente *m*; (*also:* **dry cleaner**) tintoria, lavanderia; **he took his coat to the cleaner's** ha portato il cappotto in lavanderia *or* tintoria

clean·ing ['kli:nɪŋ] N pulizia; **to do the cleaning** fare le pulizie

cleaning fluid N (*stain remover*) smacchiatore *m*

cleaning lady N donna delle pulizie

clean-limbed ['kli:n'lɪmd] ADJ proporzionato(-a), ben fatto(-a)

clean·li·ness ['klɛnlɪnɪs] N pulizia

clean-living ['kli:n'lɪvɪŋ] ADJ onesto(-a)

clean·ly ['kli:nlɪ] ADV in modo netto

clean·ness ['kli:nnɪs] N pulizia

cleanse [klɛnz] VT pulire; (*fig: soul etc*) purificare

cleans·er ['klɛnzəʳ] N (*detergent*) detersivo; (*cosmetic*) detergente *m* (*latte, gel, emulsione*)

clean-shaven ['kli:n'ʃeɪvn] ADJ senza barba né baffi, sbarbato(-a)

cleans·ing ['klɛnzɪŋ] N (*see vb*) pulitura; purificazione *f*

cleansing cream N crema detergente

cleansing department N (*Brit*) nettezza urbana

cleansing milk N latte *m* detergente

clean sweep N (*Sport*): **to make a clean sweep of sth** far piazza pulita di qc

clean·up ['kli:n,ʌp] N (*of house*) pulita, ripulita; **this room could do with a good cleanup** questa stanza avrebbe bisogno di una bella ripulita

◎ **clear** [klɪəʳ] ADJ (*comp* **-er**, *superl* **-est**)

1 (*water*) chiaro(-a), limpido(-a); (*glass, plastic*) trasparente; (*air, sky, weather*) sereno(-a); (*complexion*) senza brufoli o macchie; (*photograph, outline*) nitido(-a); (*conscience*) pulito(-a); **a clear plastic bottle** una bottiglia di plastica trasparente; **on a clear day** in una giornata limpida

2 (*sound*) chiaro(-a), distinto(-a); (*impression, meaning, explanation*) chiaro(-a); (*motive, consequence*) ovvio(-a); (*understanding, proof*) certo(-a), sicuro(-a); (*profit, majority*) netto(-a); **a clear case of murder** un chiaro caso di omicidio; **to make o.s. clear** spiegarsi bene; **have I made myself clear?** mi sono spiegato?, sono stato chiaro?; **to make it clear to sb that …** far capire a qn che…; **it is clear to me that …** per me è evidente che…; **as clear as day** chiaro come il sole; **three clear days** tre giorni interi; **to win by a clear head** (*horse*) vincere di un'incollatura

3 (*free: road, way, space*) libero(-a), sgombro(-a); **wait till the road is clear** aspetta finché la strada sarà libera; **I have a clear day tomorrow** (*Brit*) non ho impegni domani; **we had a clear view** avevamo una buona visuale; **the ship was clear of the rocks** la nave aveva superato il pericolo delle rocce; **we're clear of the police now** ora siamo sufficientemente lontani dalla polizia; **all clear!** cessato pericolo!

■ ADV

1 *see* **loud**

2 **clear of** distante da; **to keep clear of sb/sth** tenersi lontano da qn/qc, stare alla larga da qn/qc; **to stand clear of sth** stare lontano da qc

3 (*completely*) completamente; **to get clear away** svignarsela senza lasciar tracce

■ N: **to be in the clear** (*out of debt*) essere in attivo; (*out of suspicion*) essere a posto; (*out of danger*) essere fuori pericolo

■ VT

1 (*place, surface, road, railway track*) liberare, sgombrare; (*site, woodland*) spianare; (*pipe*) sbloccare; (*Med: blood*) purificare; **to clear a space for sth/sb** fare posto *or* spazio per qc/qn; **they are clearing the road** stanno liberando la strada; **he cleared the path of leaves** ha sgombrato le foglie dal viale; **to clear the table** sparecchiare (la tavola); **to clear one's throat** schiarirsi la gola; **to clear the air** (*fig*) chiarire le cose; **to clear one's conscience** togliersi un peso dalla coscienza

2 (*get over: fence etc*) scavalcare; (*get past: rocks*) evitare; **to clear 2 metres** (*athlete, horse*) superare i 2 metri

3 (*declare innocent*) discolpare; **to clear sth (with sb)** (*get permission for*) ottenere il permesso (di qn) per qc; **to be cleared of …** essere scagionato dall'accusa di…; **he was cleared of murder** fu scagionato dall'accusa di omicidio; **to clear o.s.** provare la propria innocenza; **he'll have to be cleared by the security department** dovrà superare il controllo del dipartimento di sicurezza

4 (*debt*) liquidare, saldare; (*stock*) svendere, liquidare; (*cheque*) fare la compensazione di; **to clear a profit** avere un profitto netto

■ VI (*weather, sky*) schiarirsi, rasserenarsi; (*smoke, fog*) dissolversi, andarsene

► **clear away** VI + ADV (*mist, fog*) dissiparsi; (*clear the table*) sparecchiare

■ VT + ADV togliere

► **clear off** VT + ADV (*debt*) saldare, liquidare

■ VI + ADV (*fam: go away*) tagliare la corda, squagliarsela; **clear off and leave me alone!** vattene e lasciami in pace!

► **clear out** VT + ADV (*cupboard*) liberare, sgombrare; (*rubbish*) gettare via

■ VI + ADV = **clear off** VT + ADV

► **clear up** VT + ADV

1 (*matter, mystery*) chiarire, risolvere; **I'm sure we can clear up this problem right away** sono sicuro che possiamo chiarire subito il problema

2 (*tidy: room etc*) mettere in ordine, rassettare; **who's going to clear all this up?** chi metterà tutto in ordine?

■ VI + ADV

1 (*weather*) schiarirsi, rasserenarsi; **I think it's going to clear up** penso che schiarirà

2 (*tidy up*) fare ordine

clear·ance ['klɪərəns] N **1** (*of road, room, surface*) sgombero; (*of woodland*) spianamento; (*of site, slum*) demolizione *f*; (*of rubbish, litter*) rimozione *f*; **clearance of mines** rimozione delle mine **2** (*for boat, car*) spazio libero **3** (*authorization*) autorizzazione *f*, permesso; (*by customs*) sdoganamento; **clearance for take-off** (*Aer*) permesso di decollo **4** (*Ftbl*) rinvio

clearance sale N svendita, (vendita di) liquidazione *f*

clear-cut ['klɪə,kʌt] ADJ ben definito(-a) *or* delineato(-a), distinto(-a)

clear-headed ['klɪə'hɛdɪd] ADJ lucido(-a)

clear·ing ['klɪərɪŋ] N (*in wood*) radura; (*Brit Banking*) clearing *m*

clearing bank N (*Brit Fin*) *banca che fa uso della camera di compensazione*

clearing house N (*Fin*) camera di compensazione

clear·ly ['klɪəlɪ] ADV chiaramente; **clearly this project will cost money** chiaramente il progetto avrà un costo; **to speak clearly** parlare chiaro

clear·ness ['klɪənɪs] N (*of air, water, glass*) trasparenza;

Cc

(*of sky*) serenità; (*of photograph, outline*) nitidezza; (*of sound, impression, thoughts*) chiarezza
clear-sighted ['klɪə'saɪtɪd] ADJ (*fig*) perspicace
clear·way ['klɪə,weɪ] N (*Brit: Aut*) *strada in cui è vietata la sosta*
cleat [kli:t] N (*Naut*) galloccia
cleav·age ['kli:vɪdʒ] N décolleté *m inv*
cleave [kli:v] (*pt* **cleave** *or* **cleft** *or* **clove**, *pp* **cleaved** *or* **cleft** *or* **cloven**) VT (*liter*) spaccare
▸ **cleave to** VI + PREP (*stick to*) aderire a; (*fig*) restare abbarbicato(-a)
cleav·er ['kli:vəʳ] N mannaia; **meat cleaver** (*Culin*) marrancio
cleav·ers ['kli:vəz] NSG (*Bot*) attaccamani *m inv*, attaccavesti *m inv*
clef [klɛf] N (*Mus*) chiave *f*
cleft [klɛft] PT, PP *of* **cleave**
■ N (*in rock*) crepa, fenditura
cleft palate N (*Med*) palatoschisi *f*
cleft stick N: **in a cleft stick** (*fam*) in un vicolo cieco
clema·tis ['klɛmətɪs] N clematide *f*
clem·en·cy ['klɛmənsɪ] N (*frm*) clemenza
clem·ent ['klɛmənt] (*frm*) ADJ (*person*) clemente; (*weather*) mite, clemente
clem·en·tine ['klɛmən,taɪn] N clementina, mandarancio
clench [klɛntʃ] VT stringere; **to clench sth in one's hand** stringere in pugno qc; **she clenched her fists** strinse i pugni
Cleopatra [,kli:ə'pætrə] N Cleopatra
cler·gy ['klɜ:dʒɪ] N clero
clergy·man ['klɜ:dʒɪmən] N (*pl* **-men**) ecclesiastico
cler·ic ['klɛrɪk] N ecclesiastico
cleri·cal ['klɛrɪkəl] ADJ **1** (*Comm: job*) d'ufficio, da impiegato(-a); **clerical worker** impiegato(-a); **clerical error** svista **2** (*Rel*) clericale
clerk [klɑ:k, *Am* klɜ:k] N (*in office, bank*) impiegato(-a); (*Am: shop assistant*) commesso(-a); (*: in hotel*) impiegato(-a) della reception; **Clerk of the Court** (*Law*) cancelliere *m*
clerk of the works N sovrintendente *m/f* ai lavori
◎ **clev·er** ['klɛvəʳ] ADJ (*comp* **-er**, *superl* **-est**) (*gen*) intelligente; (*deft, skilful*) abile; (*ingenious: idea, person, device*) geniale; **she's very clever** è molto intelligente; **to be clever at sth** essere abile in qc; **he is very clever with his hands** è molto abile *or* bravo nei lavori manuali; **he was too clever for us** era più furbo di noi; **a clever system** un sistema ingegnoso; **what a clever idea!** che idea geniale!
clever Dick ['klɛvə,dɪk] N (*fam*) saputo(-a)
clev·er·ly ['klɛvəlɪ] ADV abilmente
clev·er·ness ['klɛvənɪs] N (*intelligence*) intelligenza; (*deftness*) abilità; (*ingenuity*) genialità
clew [klu:] N (*Am*) = **clue**
cli·ché ['kli:ʃeɪ] N cliché *m inv*
click [klɪk] N (*of camera etc*) scatto; (*of high heels*) tacchettio; (*of soldiers' boots*) battito; (*of tongue*) schiocco
■ VT (*heels*) battere; (*tongue*) far schioccare
■ VI (*camera etc*) scattare; (*heels*) ticchettare; **the door clicked shut** la porta si chiuse con uno scatto; **suddenly it all clicked (into place)** (*fig fam*) di colpo tutto è diventato chiaro, improvvisamente ho capito; **we immediately clicked** ci siamo subito piaciuti; **to click on** cliccare su
click·able ['klɪkəbl] (*Comput*) ADJ cliccabile
click·ing ['klɪkɪŋ] N (*of keyboard*) ticchettio; (*of heels*) tacchettio
◎ **cli·ent** ['klaɪənt] N cliente *m/f*
client base N clientela
cli·en·tele [,kli:ɑ̃:n'tɛl] N clientela
client state N (*Pol*) stato *m* satellite *inv*
cliff [klɪf] N scogliera, rupe *f*
cliff·hanger ['klɪf,hæŋəʳ] N (*TV, fig*) *episodio o situazione ecc. ricco di suspense*
cli·mac·tic [klaɪ'mæktɪk] ADJ culminante
◎ **cli·mate** ['klaɪmɪt] N clima *m*; **the climate of popular opinion** l'opinione pubblica
cli·mat·ic [klaɪ'mætɪk] ADJ climatico(-a)
cli·ma·tol·ogy [,klaɪmə'tɒlədʒɪ] N climatologia
cli·max ['klaɪmæks] N culmine *m*; (*of play etc*) momento più emozionante, climax *m inv*; (*sexual climax*) orgasmo; **the climax of her career** l'apice della sua carriera
◎ **climb** [klaɪm] N (*gen*) ascesa, salita; (*of mountain*) scalata, arrampicata; (*Aer*) ascesa
■ VT (*also:* **climb up**: *tree, ladder etc*) salire su, arrampicarsi su; (*: staircase*) salire; (*: mountain, wall*) scalare; **to climb a rope** arrampicarsi su una corda; **they climbed a tree** sono saliti su un albero; **her ambition is to climb Mount Everest** la sua ambizione è quella di scalare l'Everest; **we had to climb three flights of stairs to get there** abbiamo dovuto salire tre rampe di scale per arrivarci
■ VI (*road, person*) salire; (*plane*) prendere quota; (*plant*) arrampicarsi; **the pilot climbed into the cockpit** il pilota si è infilato nella cabina di pilotaggio; **to climb over a wall** scavalcare un muro
▸ **climb down** VI + PREP scendere da
■ VI + ADV scendere; (*fig: abandon one's position*) tornare sui suoi (*or* miei *etc*) passi
climb-down ['klaɪm,daʊn] N ritirata
climb·er ['klaɪməʳ] N (*rock climber*) alpinista *m/f*, scalatore(-trice); (*Bot*) rampicante *m*
climb·ing ['klaɪmɪŋ] N (*rock climbing*) arrampicata; **to go climbing** fare arrampicata
climbing frame N *struttura su cui i bambini possono arrampicarsi*
climbing wall N (*Sport*) parete *f* artificiale (*per arrampicata*)
clinch [klɪntʃ] N: **in a clinch** (*fam: embrace*) abbracciati(-e) stretti(-e)
■ VT (*settle: deal*) concludere; (*: argument*) chiudere; **that clinches it** è fatta
clinch·er ['klɪntʃəʳ] N (*fam*): **the clincher** il fattore decisivo
cling [klɪŋ] VI (*pt, pp* **clung**) **1** **to cling to** (*support, also fig*) aggrapparsi a; tenersi stretto a; **he clung to the wreckage** era aggrappato al relitto; **to cling to one another** stringersi l'uno(-a) all'altro(-a) **2** **to cling (to)** (*subj: clothes*) aderire strettamente (a); (*: smell*) impregnare; **the smell clung to her clothes** l'odore aveva impregnato i suoi abiti
cling·film ['klɪŋ,fɪlm], **clingwrap** ['klɪŋ,ræp] N pellicola trasparente (*per alimenti*)
◎ **clin·ic** ['klɪnɪk] N (*hospital, dental clinic etc*) clinica; (*for guidance etc*) centro; (*session*) seduta
clinical ['klɪnɪkəl] ADJ clinico(-a); (*fig*) freddo(-a), distaccato(-a); **his approach was too clinical** il suo approccio era troppo distaccato; **clinical trials** sperimentazione *fsg* clinica
clini·cal·ly ['klɪnɪklɪ] ADV clinicamente; (*fig*) in modo impersonale
clink [klɪŋk] N tintinnio

■VT: **to clink glasses with sb** brindare *or* fare cin cin con qn
■VI tintinnare
clip[1] [klɪp] N (*Cine*) sequenza; **some clips from her latest film** alcune sequenze del suo ultimo film
■VT (*cut: gen*) tagliare; (*sheep, dog*) tosare; (*hedge*) potare, tagliare; (*ticket*) forare; (*article from newspaper*) ritagliare; **to clip sb's wings** (*fig*) tarpare le ali a qn
clip[2] [klɪp] N (*paperclip*) graffetta; (*Brit: bulldog clip*) fermafogli *m inv*; (*hair clip*) molletta; (*brooch*) spilla, fermaglio; (*holding hose etc*) anello d'attacco
■VT (*also:* **clip together**: *papers*) attaccare (con una graffetta)
▸ **clip on** VT + ADV (*brooch*) agganciare; (*document: with paper clip etc*) attaccare
▸ **clip together** VT + ADV attaccare (con una graffetta)
clip art N (*Comput*) clip art *f inv*
clip·board ['klɪp,bɔːd] N fermablocco *m inv*; (*Comput*) appunti *mpl*
clipped [klɪpt] ADJ: **in a clipped voice** scandendo bene le sillabe
clip·per ['klɪpəʳ] N (*Naut*) clipper *m inv*
clip·pers ['klɪpəz] NPL (*for nails*) tagliaunghie *m inv*; (*for hair*) macchinetta per capelli; (*for hedge*) tosasiepi *m inv*, cesoie *fpl*
clip·ping ['klɪpɪŋ] N (*from newspaper*) ritaglio
clique [kliːk] N cricca
cli·quish ['kliːkɪʃ], **cli·quey** ['kliːkɪ] ADJ (*pej*) che tende ad unirsi in gruppi chiusi
clito·ris ['klɪtərɪs] N clitoride *m or f*
cloak [kləʊk] N cappa, mantello; **under the cloak of darkness** (*fig*) sotto il manto delle tenebre
■VT avvolgere
cloak-and-dagger [,kləʊkən'dægəʳ] ADJ (*film etc*) del mistero; (*activities*) misterioso(-a)
cloak·room ['kləʊk,rʊm] N (*for coats*) guardaroba *m inv*; (*Brit euph*) toilette *f inv*
cloakroom attendant N guardarobiere(-a)
cloakroom ticket N scontrino del guardaroba
clob·ber ['klɒbəʳ] (*fam*) N **1** (*belongings*) roba
■VT **1** (*hit*) pestare **2** (*defeat*) dare una batosta a, battere
◎**clock** [klɒk] N (*gen*) orologio; (*of taxi*) tassametro; **30,000 on the clock** (*Brit Aut*) 30.000 sul contachilometri; **around the clock** ventiquattr'ore su ventiquattro; **to sleep round the clock** *or* **the clock round** dormire un giorno intero; **to work against the clock** lavorare in gara col tempo; **alarm clock** sveglia
■VT (*time*) registrare; (*: of runner*) cronometrare
▸ **clock in, clock on** VI + ADV (*Brit*) timbrare il cartellino (all'entrata)
▸ **clock off, clock out** VI + ADV (*Brit*) timbrare il cartellino (all'uscita)
▸ **clock up** VT + ADV (*Aut*) registrare, fare; (*miles, hours etc*) fare
clock·maker ['klɒk,meɪkəʳ] N orologiaio
clock radio N radiosveglia
clock-watcher ['klɒk,wɒtʃəʳ] N: **to be a clock-watcher** controllare con impazienza l'ora *or* l'orologio (*detto di lavoratore*)
clock·wise ['klɒk,waɪz] ADV in senso orario
clock·work ['klɒk,wɜːk] N: **to go like clockwork** (*fig*) funzionare alla perfezione
■ADJ (*toy, train*) a molla
clod [klɒd] N zolla
clog [klɒg] N zoccolo
■VT (*also:* **clog up**: *pipe, drain*) ostruire, intasare; (*: machine, mechanism*) bloccare
■VI (*also:* **clog up**) intasarsi, bloccarsi
clois·ter ['klɔɪstəʳ] N chiostro
clois·tered ['klɔɪstəd] ADJ (*life*) da recluso(-a)
clone [kləʊn] N clone *m*
■VT clonare
clonk [klɒŋk] (*fam*) N tonfo
■VT colpire
◎**close**[1] [kləʊs] ADV vicino, dappresso; **close by** *or* **close at hand** qui *or* lì vicino; **to hold sb close** tenere stretto(-a) qn; **close together** vicino; **stay close to me** stammi vicino; **to follow close behind** seguire da vicino; **come closer** avvicinati
■ADJ **1** (*near*) vicino(-a); (*: relative, connection, resemblance*) stretto(-a); (*: friend*) intimo(-a); (*almost equal: result*) quasi pari; (*: fight, contest, election, race*) combattuto(-a); **the shops are very close** i negozi sono molto vicini; **the house is close to the shops** la casa è vicina ai negozi; **they're very close** (*in age*) sono molto vicini come età; (*emotionally*) sono molto uniti; **I'm very close to my sister** io e mia sorella siamo molto unite; **we're just inviting close relations** invitiamo solo i parenti stretti; **she's a close friend of mine** è una mia amica intima; **she was close to tears** stava per piangere; **at close quarters** da vicino; **close combat** combattimento corpo a corpo; **that was a close shave** (*fig fam*) l'ho (*or* l'hai *etc*) scampata per un pelo; **it was a very close contest** è stata una gara molto combattuta **2** (*exact, detailed: examination, study*) accurato(-a), attento(-a); (*: investigation, questioning*) approfondito(-a); (*: surveillance, control, watch*) stretto(-a); **to pay close attention to sb/sth** stare ben attento(-a) a qn/qc; **to keep a close watch on sb** guardare qn a vista **3** (*handwriting, texture, weave*) fitto(-a) **4** (*stuffy: atmosphere, room*) soffocante; (*weather*) afoso(-a); **it's rather close in here** qui c'è aria viziata; **it's close this afternoon** c'è afa questo pomeriggio
close[2] [kləʊz] N (*end*) fine *f*, chiusura; **to bring sth to a close** terminare qc; **to draw to a close** avvicinarsi alla fine
■VI (*shut: shop etc*) chiudere; (*: lid, door etc*) chiudersi; (*end*) chiudersi, concludersi, finire; **the shops close at five thirty** i negozi chiudono alle cinque e mezza; **the doors close automatically** le porte si chiudono automaticamente
■VT **1** (*shut: door, road, shop etc*) chiudere; **please close the door** chiudi la porta, per favore; **to close the gap between two things** (*fig*) colmare il divario tra due cose; **to close one's eyes to sth** (*fig*) ignorare qc **2** (*end: discussion, meeting*) chiudere, concludere; (*: bank account*) chiudere, estinguere; (*: bargain, deal*) concludere
▸ **close down** VI + ADV (*business*) chiudersi, chiudere; (*TV, Radio*) terminare le trasmissioni
■VT + ADV chiudere (definitivamente)
▸ **close in** VI + ADV (*hunters*) stringersi attorno; (*evening, night, fog*) calare; **the days are closing in** le giornate si accorciano; **to close in on sb** accerchiare qn
▸ **close off** VT + ADV (*area*) chiudere
▸ **close round** VI + PREP stringersi attorno a
▸ **close up** VI + ADV (*people in queue*) stringersi; (*wound*) rimarginarsi
■VT + ADV (*shop, house, opening*) chiudere; (*wound*) chiudere, suturare
close-cropped [,kləʊs'krɒpt] ADJ (*hair*) corti corti *pl*

Cc

closed [kləʊzd] ADJ chiuso(-a); **sociology is a closed book to me** per me la sociologia è un mistero
closed-circuit tele·vi·sion ['kləʊzd,sɜ:kɪt'tɛlɪ,vɪʒən] N televisione *f* a circuito chiuso
close-down ['kləʊz,daʊn] N (*of shop, factory*) chiusura; (*TV, Radio*) fine *f* delle trasmissioni
closed shop N (*Industry*) *fabbrica, ditta* {*or*} *negozio che assume solo lavoratori iscritti al sindacato*
close-fisted [,kləʊs'fɪstɪd] ADJ avaro(-a), taccagno(-a)
close-fitting [,kləʊs'fɪtɪŋ] ADJ aderente, attillato(-a)
close-hauled [,kləʊs'hɔ:ld] ADJ (*Naut*) di bolina
close-knit [,kləʊs'nɪt] ADJ (*community, group, family*) molto unito(-a)
close-lipped [,kləʊs'lɪpt], **close-mouthed** [,kləʊs'maʊðd] ADJ riservato(-a); **the government is remaining very close-lipped about the matter** il governo non sta lasciando trapelare nulla sulla faccenda
close·ly ['kləʊslɪ] ADV (*guard*) strettamente, attentamente; (*examine, study, watch, follow*) da vicino, attentamente; (*listen*) attentamente; (*resemble*) molto; (*connected*) strettamente; **a closely guarded secret** un segreto gelosamente custodito; **a closely fought race** una gara molto combattuta; **we are closely related** siamo parenti stretti
close·ness ['kləʊsnɪs] N (*nearness*) vicinanza; (*of friendship*) profondità; (*of room*) mancanza d'aria; **the closeness of the weather** il tempo afoso; **the closeness of the resemblance** la stretta somiglianza
close-run [,kləʊs'rʌn] ADJ: **a close-run match** un incontro molto combattuto
close season ['kləʊs,si:sən] N (*Hunting*) stagione *f* di chiusura (*di caccia, pesca etc*)
close-set [,kləʊs'sɛt] ADJ (*eyes*) ravvicinato(-a)
close-shaven [,kləʊs'ʃeɪvn] ADJ ben rasato(-a)
clos·et ['klɒzɪt] N (*Am: cupboard*) armadio; **to come out of the closet** (*fam*) uscire allo scoperto
■ VT: **to be closeted with sb** essersi appartato(-a) con qn
close-up ['kləʊs,ʌp] N primo piano; **in close-up** in primo piano
clos·ing ['kləʊzɪŋ] ADJ (*stages, remarks*) conclusivo(-a), finale; **closing speech** discorso di chiusura; **closing price** (*Stock Exchange*) prezzo di chiusura
closing price N (*Stock Exchange*) prezzo di chiusura
closing time N (*of pub, shop*) orario di chiusura; **when is closing time?** a che ora chiude?
closure ['kləʊʒə^r] N chiusura; (*Psych*) il mettersi alle spalle un fatto negativo
clot [klɒt] N (*Med: also:* **blood clot**) coagulo, grumo; (*fam: idiot*) scemo(-a), zuccone(-a); **to have a clot on the brain/in the leg** avere un grumo (di sangue) nel cervello/in una gamba
■ VI coagularsi
cloth [klɒθ] N (*material*) tessuto, stoffa; (*for cleaning*) panno, straccio; (*Brit: also:* **teacloth**) telo per i piatti; (*also:* **tablecloth**) tovaglia; **5 metres of cloth** cinque metri di stoffa; **wipe it with a damp cloth** puliscilo con uno straccio umido; **a man of the cloth** (*Rel*) un religioso, un ecclesiastico
cloth cap N berretto
clothe [kləʊð] VT vestire
cloth-eared [,klɒθ'ɪəd] ADJ (*fam*) sordo(-a)
◎ **clothes** [kləʊðz] NPL vestiti *mpl*, abiti *mpl*; **to put one's clothes on** vestirsi; **to take one's clothes off** togliersi i vestiti, svestirsi, spogliarsi; **smart clothes** vestiti eleganti
clothes basket N cesto *m* portabiancheria *inv*
clothes brush N spazzola per abiti
clothes hanger N gruccia, portabiti *m inv*
clothes horse N stendibiancheria *m inv*
clothes line N corda del bucato
clothes peg, **clothes pin** (*Am*) N molletta (da bucato)
clothes shop N negozio di abbigliamento
◎ **cloth·ing** ['kləʊðɪŋ] N abbigliamento; **article of clothing** capo di vestiario *or* di abbigliamento
clothing allowance N indennità *f inv* per gli abiti da lavoro
clot·ted cream [,klɒtɪd'kri:m] N (*Brit*) panna rappresa (*ottenuta per riscaldamento*)
◎ **cloud** [klaʊd] N (*Met*) nuvola, nube *f*; (*of dust, smoke, gas*) nube; (*of insects*) nugolo; **to be under a cloud** essere malvisto(-a); **he has his head in the clouds** ha la testa tra le nuvole; **to be on cloud nine** essere al settimo cielo; **every cloud has a silver lining** (*Proverb*) non tutto il male vien per nuocere
■ VT (*liquid*) intorbidire; (*mirror*) appannare; (*fig: judgement*) confondere; (*: mind*) turbare; **a clouded sky** un cielo nuvoloso; **to cloud the issue** imbrogliare la questione
▸ **cloud over** VI + ADV (*also fig*) rannuvolarsi, offuscarsi
cloud·burst ['klaʊd,bɜ:st] N acquazzone *m*
cloud chamber N (*Phys*) camera a nube
cloud-cuckoo-land [,klaʊd'kʊku:,lænd] N mondo dei sogni
cloudi·ness ['klaʊdɪnɪs] N (*see adj*) nuvolosità; torbidezza
cloud·less ['klaʊdlɪs] ADJ sereno(-a), senza nubi
cloudy ['klaʊdɪ] ADJ (*sky*) nuvoloso(-a), coperto(-a); (*liquid*) torbido(-a)
clout [klaʊt] N (*blow*) ceffone *m*; (*fig: power, influence*) influenza; **he gave her a clout** le ha dato un ceffone; **someone with clout** qn con una certa influenza
■ VT colpire
clove[1] [kləʊv] PT *of* **cleave**
■ N chiodo di garofano; **clove of garlic** spicchio d'aglio
clove[2] [kləʊv] ADJ (*Naut*): **clove hitch** (nodo) parlato
clo·ven ['kləʊvən] PP *of* **cleave**
cloven hoof N zoccolo fesso
clo·ver ['kləʊvə^r] N trifoglio; **a four-leaved clover** un quadrifoglio; **red clover** trifoglio pratense *or* rosso; **white clover** trifoglio bianco; **to be in clover** (*fam*) nuotare nell'abbondanza
clover·leaf ['kləʊvə,li:f] N (*Bot*) foglia di trifoglio; (*Aut*) raccordo (a quadrifoglio)
clown [klaʊn] N (*in circus*) pagliaccio, clown *m inv*; (*fam*) buffone *m*
■ VI (*also:* **clown about** *or* **around**) fare il buffone *or* il pagliaccio
clown·ing ['klaʊnɪŋ] N pagliacciate *fpl*, buffonate *fpl*
clown·ish ['klaʊnɪʃ] ADJ claunesco(-a)
cloy [klɔɪ] VI essere nauseante
cloy·ing ['klɔɪɪŋ] ADJ (*taste, smell*) stucchevole
◎ **club** [klʌb] N **1** (*society*) circolo, club *m inv*; **tennis club** circolo di tennis; **youth club** circolo giovanile; **join the club!** (*fig*) non sei il solo! **2** (*stick*) randello; (*of caveman*) clava; **golf club** mazza da golf **3** (*nightclub*) locale notturno; **we had dinner and went on to a club** abbiamo cenato e poi siamo andati in un locale notturno **4 clubs** (*Cards*) fiori *mpl*; **he played a club** ha giocato (una carta di) fiori

■VT (*person*) bastonare; **clubbed to death with sticks** ucciso(-a) a colpi di bastone
■VI: **to club together (to buy)** mettersi insieme (per comprare); **we clubbed together to buy her a present** abbiamo fatto colletta per comprarle un regalo
club·bing ['klʌbɪŋ] N: **to go clubbing** andare in discoteca
club car N (*Am Rail*) carrozza *or* vagone *m* ristorante
club class N (*Aer*) classe *f* club *inv*
club foot N (*Med*) piede *m* affetto da talismo
club·house ['klʌb,haʊs] N circolo
club member N socio(-a) di un club
club sandwich N tramezzino *m*
club soda N (*Am*) soda
cluck [klʌk] VI chiocciare
clue [klu:] N indicazione *f*; (*in a crime etc*) indizio; (*in crosswords*) definizione *f*; **an important clue** un indizio importante; **I'll give you a clue** ti metto sulla strada giusta; **I haven't a clue** (*fam*) non (ne) ho la minima idea
clued-up [klu:d'ʌp], **clued-in** [klu:d'ɪn] ADJ (*fam*) (ben) informato(-a)
clue·less ['klu:lɪs] ADJ (*fam*): **to be clueless** essere un(-a) incapace
clump[1] [klʌmp] N (*of trees*) gruppo; (*flowers*) macchia; (*of grass*) ciuffo
clump[2] [klʌmp] N rumore *m* sordo, tonfo
■VI: **to clump (about)** camminare con passo pesante
clum·si·ly ['klʌmzɪlɪ] ADV goffamente, maldestramente; (*tactlessly*) senza (alcun) tatto; **a clumsily executed forgery** un falso mal eseguito; **a clumsily designed tool** un utensile poco pratico
clum·si·ness ['klʌmzɪnɪs] N (*of person, action, apology*) goffaggine *f*; (*of remark*) mancanza di tatto; (*of painting, forgery*) cattiva esecuzione *f*; (*of tool*) scarsa praticità
clum·sy ['klʌmzɪ] ADJ (*person, action, gesture*) goffo(-a), maldestro(-a); (*painting, forgery*) malfatto(-a); (*object*) mal costruito(-a); (*tool*) poco pratico(-a); (*remark*) maldestro(-a); (*apology*) goffo(-a)
clung [klʌŋ] PT, PP *of* **cling**
clus·ter ['klʌstəʳ] N (*of houses, people, trees*) gruppo; (*of grapes*) grappolo; (*of stars*) ammasso
■VI (*people, things*): **to cluster (round sb/sth)** raggrupparsi (intorno a qn/qc)
clutch[1] [klʌtʃ] N **1** (*Aut*) frizione *f*; (*pedal*) (pedale *m* della) frizione **2** (*grip, grasp*) presa, stretta; **to fall into sb's clutches** cadere nelle grinfie di qn
■VT (*catch hold of*) afferrare; (*hold tightly*) tenere stretto(-a), stringere forte; **she clutched my arm and begged me not to go** mi ha afferrato il braccio e mi ha pregato di non andarmene
■VI: **to clutch at** cercare di afferrare; **to clutch at straws** (*fig*) crearsi delle illusioni
clutch[2] [klʌtʃ] N (*of eggs, chickens*) covata
clutch bag N pochette *f inv*
clutch pedal N (*Aut*) pedale *m* della frizione
clutch plate N (*Aut*) disco della frizione
clut·ter ['klʌtəʳ] N confusione *f*, disordine *m*; **there's so much clutter in here** c'è un gran disordine qua dentro; **in a clutter** in disordine
■VT (*also:* **clutter up**) ingombrare; **to be cluttered up with sth** essere pieno(-a) zeppo(-a) *or* ingombro(-a) di qc
cm ABBR (= **centimetre**) cm
CND [,si:ɛn'di:] N ABBR (*Brit*) = *Campaign for Nuclear Disarmament*
CO N ABBR **1** (= **commanding officer**) Com. **2** (*Brit*) = *Commonwealth Office*
■ABBR (*Am Post*) = **Colorado**
Co. ABBR **1** (= **company**) C.ia **2** = **county** **3**: **and Co.** (*fam*) e company; **Joe and Co.** Joe e company
co- [kəʊ] PREF co...
c/o ABBR (= **care of**) c/o
◎**coach** [kəʊtʃ] N **1** (*bus*) corriera, pullman *m inv*; (: *for excursions*) pullman *m inv*; (*Brit: of train*) carrozza, vettura; (*horse drawn*) carrozza; (: *stage coach*) diligenza; **by coach** in corriera; **coach station** stazione *f* delle corriere **2** (*Sport*) allenatore(-trice); (*tutor*) chi dà ripetizioni
■VT (*team*) allenare; (*student*) dare ripetizioni a
coach·load ['kəʊtʃ,ləʊd] N: **a coachload of football fans** un pullman di tifosi di calcio
coach party N gruppo di gitanti (che viaggia in pullman)
coach trip N escursione *f or* viaggio in pullman
co·agu·lant [kəʊ'ægjʊlənt] N coagulante *m*
co·agu·late [kəʊ'ægjʊleɪt] VT coagulare
■VI coagularsi
co·agu·la·tion [kəʊ,ægjʊ'leɪʃən] N coagulazione *f*
◎**coal** [kəʊl] N carbone *m*; **to carry coals to Newcastle** (*fig*) portare acqua al mare
■ADJ (*fire*) di carbone; (*industry*) del carbone; (*stove*) a carbone
coal-black ['kəʊl'blæk] ADJ nero(-a) come il carbone
coal cellar, coal shed N carbonaia
coal dust N polvere *f* di carbone
coa·lesce [,kəʊə'lɛs] VI (*frm*) fondersi, unirsi
coal·face ['kəʊl,feɪs] N fronte *f* di abbattimento (*di filone carbonifero*)
coal·field ['kəʊl,fi:ld] N bacino carbonifero
coal gas N gas *m inv* illuminante
◎**coa·li·tion** [,kəʊə'lɪʃən] N (*Pol*) coalizione *f*
coal·man ['kəʊl,mæn] N (*pl* **-men**) carbonaio
coal merchant N negoziante *m* di carbone
coal mine N miniera di carbone
coal miner N minatore *m*
coal mining N estrazione *f* del carbone
coal scuttle N secchio del carbone
coal shed N = **coal cellar**
coal tar N catrame *m* minerale
coal tit N (*Zool*) cincia mora
coarse [kɔ:s] ADJ (*comp* **-er**, *superl* **-est**) (*texture, skin, material*) ruvido(-a); (*salt, sand*) grosso(-a); (*sandpaper*) a grana grossa; (*vulgar: character, laugh, remark*) volgare; **the bag was made of coarse black cloth** la borsa era fatta di una stoffa nera ruvida; **the sand is very coarse on that beach** la sabbia di quella spiaggia è molto grossa
coarse-grained [,kɔ:s'greɪnd] ADJ (*sandpaper*) a grana grossa; (*person*) grossolano(-a)
coarse·ly ['kɔ:slɪ] ADV (*ground, woven*) grossolanamente; (*laugh, say*) volgarmente
coars·en ['kɔ:sn] VI (*skin*) irruvidirsi; (*person, manners*) diventare grossolano(-a)
■VT (*see vi*) irruvidire; rendere grossolano(-a)
coarse·ness ['kɔ:snɪs] N (*of material*) ruvidezza; (*of salt, sand*) grossezza; (*of laugh, remark*) volgarità *f inv*
◎**coast** [kəʊst] N costa; (*also:* **coastline**) litorale *m*; **on the coast** sulla costa; **the coast is clear** (*fig*) la via è libera
■VI (*Aut*) andare in folle; (*Cycling*) andare a ruota libera
coast·al ['kəʊstəl] ADJ costiero(-a)
coast·er ['kəʊstəʳ] N **1** (*Naut*) nave *f* da cabotaggio **2** (*for glass*) sottobicchiere *m*

Cc

coast·guard ['kəʊst,gɑ:d] N (*person*) guardacoste *m inv*; (*organization*) guardia costiera
coastguard vessel N guardacoste *m inv* (*nave*)
coast·line ['kəʊst,laɪn] N litorale *m*, linea costiera
◎ **coat** [kəʊt] N **1** (*garment*) cappotto, soprabito; **a nice warm coat** un bel cappotto caldo **2** (*of animal*) pelo, mantello **3** (*layer*) strato; (*of paint*) mano *f*; **a coat of paint** una mano di pittura **4 coat of arms** stemma *m*, blasone *m*
■VT: **to coat sth with** ricoprire qc con uno strato di; (*paint*) dare a qc una mano di
coat hanger ['kəʊt,hæŋəʳ] N gruccia, stampella
coat·ing ['kəʊtɪŋ] N (*film, layer*) mano, strato; (*for protection*) rivestimento (esterno)
coat of mail N cotta di maglia, giaco
coat·stand ['kəʊt,stænd] N attaccapanni *m inv*
coat-tails ['kəʊt,teɪlz] NPL falde *fpl* del frac
co·author ['kəʊ,ɔ:θəʳ] N coautore(-trice)
coax [kəʊks] VT: **to coax sth out of sb** ottenere qc da qn (con le buone); **to coax sb into/out of doing sth** convincere *or* indurre (con moine) qn a fare/non fare qc
coax·ing ['kəʊksɪŋ] N moine *fpl*
coax·ing·ly ['kəʊksɪŋlɪ] ADV con fare dolce, con fare accattivante
cob [kɒb] N *see* **corn**
co·balt ['kəʊbɒlt] N cobalto
cob·ble ['kɒbl] N (*also:* **cobblestone**) ciottolo
cob·bled ['kɒbld] ADJ: **cobbled street** strada pavimentata con ciottoli
cob·bler ['kɒbləʳ] N calzolaio
cobble·stones ['kɒbl,stəʊnz] NPL ciottoli *mpl*
cob·nut ['kɒb,nʌt] N nocciola
COBOL ['kəʊbɔ:l] N ABBR (*Comput:* = **common business orientated language**) COBOL *m*
co·bra ['kəʊbrə] N cobra *m inv*
cob·web ['kɒb,wɛb] N ragnatela
Coca-Cola® [,kəʊkə'kəʊlə] N coca-cola® *f inv*
co·caine [kə'keɪn] N cocaina
coc·cyx ['kɒksɪks] N (*Anat*) coccige *m*
coch·lea ['kɒklɪə] N (*pl* **cochleae** ['kɒklɪ,i:]) (*Anat*) coclea
cock [kɒk] N **1** (*rooster*) gallo; (*male bird*) maschio **2** (*fam!: penis*) cazzo (*fam!*)
■VT (*gun*) armare; **to cock (up) one's ears** (*also fig*) drizzare le orecchie; **to cock a snook at** (*make rude gesture*) fare marameo a; (*fig*) burlarsi di
▸ **cock up** VT + ADV (*Brit fam*) incasinare; *see also* cock-up
cock·ade [kɒ'keɪd] N coccarda
cock-a-doodle-doo [,kɒkə,du:dəl'du:] N chicchirichì *m inv*
cock-a-hoop [,kɒkə'hu:p] ADJ esultante, euforico(-a)
cock-and-bull [,kɒkənd'bʊl] ADJ: **cock-and-bull story** frottola
cocka·too [,kɒkə'tu:] N cacatoa *m inv*
cock·chafer ['kɒk,tʃeɪfəʳ] N maggiolino
cock·crow ['kɒk,krəʊ] N: **at cockcrow** al primo canto del gallo, all'alba
cock·er ['kɒkeʳ] N (*also:* **cocker spaniel**) cocker (spaniel) *m inv*
cock·er·el ['kɒkərəl] N galletto
cock·eyed ['kɒk,aɪd] ADJ (*crooked*) storto(-a); (*absurd*) assurdo(-a), strampalato(-a)
cock·fight ['kɒk,faɪt] N combattimento di galli
cocki·ness ['kɒkɪnɪs] N (*fam pej*) impertinenza
cock·le ['kɒkl] N (*shellfish*) cardio; **it warmed the cockles of my heart** mi riempì il cuore di gioia
cock·ney ['kɒknɪ] N (*person*) cockney *m/f inv; abitante dei quartieri dell'East End di Londra*; (*dialect*) cockney *m*; **he's got a cockney accent** ha un accento cockney
cock·pit ['kɒk,pɪt] N (*Aer*) cabina di pilotaggio, abitacolo
cock·roach ['kɒk,rəʊtʃ] N scarafaggio, blatta
cock·sure [,kɒk'ʃʊəʳ] ADJ troppo sicuro(-a) di sé, baldanzoso(-a)
cock·tail ['kɒk,teɪl] N (*drink*) cocktail *m inv*; **fruit cocktail** macedonia di frutta; **prawn cocktail** (*Am*): **shrimp cocktail** cocktail *m inv* di gamberetti
▹ www.cocktail.com
cocktail bar N bar *m inv* (*di un albergo*)
cocktail cabinet N mobile *m* bar *inv*
cocktail party N cocktail *m inv*
cock·tail shak·er ['kɒt,teɪl'ʃeɪkəʳ] N shaker *m inv*
cock-up N (*Brit fam*) casino
cocky ['kɒkɪ] ADJ (*comp* **-ier**, *superl* **-iest**) (*pej*) troppo sicuro(-a) di sé
co·coa ['kəʊkəʊ] N cacao; (*drink*) cioccolata calda
coco·nut ['kəʊkə,nʌt] N (*fruit*) noce *f* di cocco; (*tree: also:* **coconut palm**) palma di cocco; (*substance*) cocco
coco·nut matting ['kəʊkənʌt'mætɪŋ] N stuoia (di fibra) di cocco
coconut shy N *gioco di tiro al bersaglio in cui si devono abbattere noci di cocco*
co·coon [kə'ku:n] N bozzolo
co·cooned [kə'ku:nd] ADJ chiuso(-a) nel proprio bozzolo
COD [,si:əʊ'di:] ABBR = **cash on delivery**, *Am* **collect on delivery**; *see* **collect**
cod [kɒd] N merluzzo
cod·dle ['kɒdl] VT (*Culin: esp eggs*) cuocere a fuoco lento; (*also:* **mollycoddle**) coccolare
◎ **code** [kəʊd] N codice *m*; (*Telec*) prefisso; **in code** in codice; **it's written in code** è scritto in codice; **what's the code for London?** qual è il prefisso di Londra?; **code of behaviour** regole *fpl* di condotta
■VT cifrare
cod·ed ['kəʊdɪd] ADJ **1** (*lit, in code: message, warning*) in codice **2** (*fig, indirect: language, remarks, message*) velato **3** (*Elec: signal, information*) criptato
co·deine ['kəʊdi:n] N codeina
code name N nome *m* in codice
code number N (numero di) codice *m*
code of practice N codice *m* deontologico
codg·er ['kɒdʒəʳ] N: **an old codger** (*Brit fam*) un nonnetto
codi·cil ['kɒdɪsɪl] N (*Law*) codicillo
codi·fy ['kəʊdɪfaɪ] VT codificare (*leggi*)
cod·ing ['kəʊdɪŋ] N codificazione *f*
cod-liver oil ['kɒdlɪvər'ɔɪl] N olio di fegato di merluzzo
co-driver ['kəʊdraɪvəʳ] N (*in race*) copilota *m/f*; (*of lorry*) secondo autista *m*
cods·wallop ['kɒdz,wɒləp] N (*Brit fam*) stupidaggini *fpl*, sciocchezze *fpl*
co-ed ['kəʊ'ɛd] (*fam*) ADJ misto(-a)
■N (*Am: female student*) studentessa di un'università mista; (*Brit: school*) scuola mista
co·edu·ca·tion ['kəʊ,ɛdjʊ'keɪʃən] N (istruzione *f* in) scuole *fpl* miste
co·edu·ca·tion·al [,kəʊɛdjʊ'keɪʃənl] ADJ misto(-a)
co·ef·fi·cient [,kəʊɪ'fɪʃənt] N coefficiente *m*
co·erce [kəʊ'ɜ:s] VT: **to coerce sb (into doing sth)** costringere qn (a fare qc)
co·er·cion [kəʊ'ɜ:ʃən] N forza; (*Law*) coercizione *f*

co·er·cive [kəʊˈɜːsɪv] ADJ coercitivo(-a)
co·ex·ist [ˈkəʊɪgˈzɪst] VI coesistere
co·ex·ist·ence [ˈkəʊɪgˈzɪstəns] N coesistenza
C. of C. [ˌsiːəvˈsiː] N ABBR = **chamber of commerce**
C of E [ˌsiːəvˈiː] N ABBR = **Church of England**
◎ **cof·fee** [ˈkɒfɪ] N caffè *m inv*; **cup of coffee** tazza di caffè; **black coffee** caffè nero; **white coffee** (*Am*): **coffee with cream** caffè con latte; **two white coffees, please** due caffè con latte, per favore
▷ www.ncausa.org
coffee bar N (*Brit*) caffè *m inv*
coffee bean N grano *or* chicco di caffè *m inv*
coffee break N pausa per il caffè
coffee cake [ˈkɒfɪˌkeɪk] N (*Am*) panino dolce all'uva
coffee cup N tazzina da caffè
coffee mill N macinacaffè *m*, macinino da caffè
coffee morning N *incontro a scopo benefico tenuto al mattino, con caffè e pasticcini*
coffee percolator N caffettiera a pressione
coffee·pot [ˈkɒfɪˌpɒt] N caffettiera
coffee shop N **1** (*bar*) caffè *m inv* **2** (*shop*) torrefazione *f*
coffee spoon N cucchiaino da caffè
coffee table N tavolino
coffee-table book [ˈkɒfɪteɪbl-] N (*pej*) *libro da mettere in mostra*
cof·fer [ˈkɒfəʳ] N (*chest*) forziere *m*
cof·fin [ˈkɒfɪn] N bara
cog [kɒg] N dente *m*; **a cog in the wheel** (*fig*) una rotella in un grande ingranaggio
co·gen·cy [ˈkəʊdʒənsɪ] N (*frm*) forza (di persuasione)
co·gent [ˈkəʊdʒənt] ADJ (*frm*) convincente
co·gent·ly [ˈkəʊdʒəntlɪ] ADV (*frm*) in modo convincente
cogi·tate [ˈkɒdʒɪˌteɪt] VI (*frm*) meditare
cogi·ta·tion [ˌkɒdʒɪˈteɪʃən] N (*frm*) meditazione *f*
cog·nac [ˈkɒnjæk] N cognac *m inv*
cog·ni·tion [ˌkɒgˈnɪʃn] N (*frm*) apprendimento
cog·ni·tive [ˈkɒgnɪtɪv] ADJ (*frm*) cognitivo(-a)
cog·ni·tiv·ism [ˈkɒgnɪtɪˌvɪzəm] N (*Philosophy*) cognitivismo
cog·ni·zance, cog·ni·sance [ˈkɒgnɪzəns] N (*frm*) conoscenza; **to take cognisance of sth** tener conto di qc
cog·ni·zant, cog·ni·sant [ˈkɒgnɪzənt] ADJ: **to be cognizant of** (*frm*) rendersi conto di
co·gno·scen·ti [ˌkɒnjəʊˈʃɛntɪ] NPL: **the cognoscenti** (*frm*) gli esperti
cog·wheel [ˈkɒgˌwiːl] N ruota dentata
co·hab·it [kəʊˈhæbɪt] VI (*frm*): **to cohabit (with sb)** coabitare (con qn)
co·her·ence [kəʊˈhɪərəns] N coerenza
co·her·ent [kəʊˈhɪərənt] ADJ coerente
co·her·ent·ly [kəʊˈhɪərəntlɪ] ADV coerentemente
co·he·sion [kəʊˈhiːʒən] N coesione *f*
co·he·sive [kəʊˈhiːsɪv] ADJ (*fig*) unificante, coesivo(-a)
co·hort [ˈkəʊhɔːt] N (*Mil*) coorte *f*
COI [ˌsiːəʊˈaɪ] N ABBR (*Brit*) = *Central Office of Information*
coil [kɔɪl] N **1** (*roll*) rotolo; (*single loop*) anello, giro; (*of hair*) ciocca; (*of snake*) spira; (*of smoke*) filo; **a coil of rope** un rotolo di spago **2** (*Aut, Elec*) bobina **3 the coil** (*contraceptive*) la spirale
■ VT avvolgere; **to coil sth up** avvolgere qc (in un rotolo)
■ VI attorcigliarsi
coin [kɔɪn] N moneta; **a 5p coin** una moneta da 5 pence
■ VT (*fam: money*) fare soldi a palate; (*fig: word etc*) coniare; **to coin a phrase** (*hum*) per così dire
coin·age [ˈkɔɪnɪdʒ] N **1** (*money, system*) moneta, sistema *m* monetario **2** (*coining*) coniazione *f*, invenzione *f*
coin box N (*Brit*) telefono pubblico a monete
co·in·cide [ˌkəʊɪnˈsaɪd] VI: **to coincide (with)** coincidere (con)
co·in·ci·dence [kəʊˈɪnsɪdəns] N (*chance*) coincidenza, combinazione *f*
co·in·ci·dent·al [kəʊˌɪnsɪˈdɛntl] ADJ: **it's entirely coincidental** è (una) pura combinazione
co·in·ci·dent·al·ly [kəʊˌɪnsɪˈdɛntəlɪ] ADV per (pura) coincidenza
coin·ing [ˈkɔɪnɪŋ] N (*of money*) coniazione *f*; (*of word*) invenzione *f*, coniazione *f*
coin-op [ˈkɔɪnˌɒp] N (*fam*) lavanderia a gettone *or* automatica
coin-operated [ˌkɔɪnˈɒpəreɪtɪd] ADJ (*machine*) (che funziona) a monete
coin·phone [ˈkɔɪnfəʊn] N telefono a monete
Coke® [kəʊk] N (*Coca-Cola*) coca® *f*
coke [kəʊk] N **1** (*fuel*) carbone *m* coke **2** (*fam: cocaine*) coca
Col. ABBR = **colonel**
col·an·der [ˈkʌləndəʳ] N colapasta *m inv*
◎ **cold** [kəʊld] ADJ (*comp* **-er**, *superl* **-est**) (*also fig*) freddo(-a); **it's cold** fa freddo; **it's a cold day** fa freddo oggi; **I'm cold** ho freddo; **are you cold?** hai freddo?; **my feet are cold** ho freddo ai piedi, ho i piedi freddi; **to catch cold** prendere freddo; **to get cold** (*person*) infreddolirsi; (*food etc*) freddarsi, diventare freddo(-a); **it's getting cold** (*weather*) comincia a far freddo; **the room's getting cold** comincia a far freddo in questa stanza; **I can't stand the cold** non sopporto il freddo; **to be out cold** (*fam: unconscious*) essere privo(-a) di sensi; **to knock sb (out) cold** mettere qn fuori combattimento; **in cold blood** a sangue freddo; **it leaves me cold** (*fam*) non mi fa né caldo, né freddo; **to get cold feet** (*fig*) avere fifa; **it's cold comfort** è una magra consolazione; **to put sth into cold storage** (*food*) mettere qc in cella frigorifera; (*fig: project*) accantonare qc
■ N **1** (*Met*) freddo; **to feel the cold** sentire il freddo; **to be left out in the cold** (*fig*) essere lasciato(-a) in disparte **2** (*Med: also:* **common cold**) raffreddore *m*; **to catch a cold** prendere un raffreddore; **to have a cold** avere il raffreddore

DID YOU KNOW ...?
cold is not translated by the Italian word *caldo*

cold-blooded [ˌkəʊldˈblʌdɪd] ADJ a sangue freddo; (*fig*) spietato(-a)
cold-bloodedly [ˌkəʊldˈblʌdɪdlɪ] ADV (*fig*) spietatamente
cold call N (*Comm: on phone*) vendita telefonica; (*: visit*) vendita porta a porta
■ VT vendere per telefono; (*visit*) vendere porta a porta
cold calling N (*Comm: on phone*) vendita telefonica; (*: visit*) vendita porta a porta
cold cream N crema emolliente
cold frame N *cassetta di legno, coperta da un vetro per proteggere le piantine dal freddo*
cold-hearted [ˌkəʊldˈhɑːtɪd] ADJ insensibile
cold·ly [ˈkəʊldlɪ] ADV (*fig*) freddamente
cold·ness [ˈkəʊldnɪs] N (*of weather, room*) freddo; (*of person*) freddezza

Cc

cold-shoulder [ˌkəʊldˈʃəʊldəʳ] VT trattare con freddezza
■ N: **to give sb the cold shoulder** trattare qn con freddezza
cold snap N: **a sudden cold snap** un'improvvisa ondata di freddo
cold sore N (*Med*) febbre *f* (sulle labbra), herpes simplex *m inv*
cold start N, **cold starting** (*Am*) N (*Comput*) partenza a freddo
cold sweat N: **to be in a cold sweat (about sth)** sudare freddo (per qc)
cold turkey N (*fam*): **to go cold turkey** avere la scimmia
cold war N: **the Cold War** la guerra fredda
⊳ www.coldwar.org
⊳ www.learningcurve.gov.uk/coldwar/
cole·slaw [ˈkəʊlˌslɔː] N, NO PL insalata di cavolo bianco, carote e altre verdure con maionese
col·ic [ˈkɒlɪk] N colica
col·icky [ˈkɒlɪkɪ] ADJ che soffre di coliche
co·li·tis [kɒˈlaɪtɪs] N (*Med*) colite *f*
col·labo·rate [kəˈlæbəˌreɪt] VI: **to collaborate (with sb in** *or* **on sth)** collaborare (con qn a *or* in qc)
col·labo·ra·tion [kəˌlæbəˈreɪʃən] N collaborazione *f*
col·labo·ra·tive [kəˈlæbərətɪv] ADJ (*work*) fatto(-a) in collaborazione, di gruppo
col·labo·ra·tor [kəˈlæbəˌreɪtəʳ] N (*on project*) collaboratore(-trice); (*pej: with enemy*) collaborazionista *m/f*
col·lage [kɒˈlɑːʒ] N (*Art*) collage *m inv*
col·la·gen [ˈkɒlədʒən] N collageno
◎ **col·lapse** [kəˈlæps] N (*gen*) crollo; (*of government*) caduta; (*of plans, scheme, business*) fallimento; (*of health*) collasso
■ VI (*see n*) crollare, cadere; fallire; avere un collasso; (*fam: with laughter*) piegarsi in due dalle risate; **the bridge collapsed during the storm** il ponte è crollato durante la tempesta; **he collapsed while playing tennis** ha avuto un collasso mentre giocava a tennis
col·laps·ible [kəˈlæpsəbl] ADJ pieghevole
col·lar [ˈkɒləʳ] N (*of shirt, blouse, coat*) colletto, collo; (*for dog*) collare *m*; (*Tech*) anello, fascetta; **to grab sb by the collar** afferrare qn per il bavero
■ VT (*fam: person, object*) beccare
collar·bone [ˈkɒləˌbəʊn] N clavicola
collar stud N bottone *m* del colletto
col·late [kɒˈleɪt] VT collazionare
col·lat·er·al [kɒˈlætərəl] N (*Fin*) garanzia
col·la·tion [kəˈleɪʃən] N **1** (*of information*) collazione *f* **2** (*frm: light meal*) pasto leggero
◎ **col·league** [ˈkɒliːg] N collega *m/f*
◎ **col·lect** [kəˈlɛkt] VT **1** (*gen*) raccogliere; (*as hobby: stamps, valuables*) fare collezione di, collezionare; **the teacher collected the exercise books** l'insegnante ha raccolto i quaderni; **he collects stamps** fa collezione di francobolli; **to collect o.s.** riprendersi; **to collect one's thoughts** raccogliere le idee **2** (*Brit: call for, pick up: person*) andare *or* passare a prendere; (*: post, ticket*) ritirare; (*: pension, rent, taxes*) riscuotere; (*: donations, subscriptions*) fare una colletta di; (*: rubbish*) portare via, raccogliere; (*: dust*) accumulare; **their mother collects them from school** la mamma li va a prendere a scuola; **I'm collecting for UNICEF** faccio una colletta per l'UNICEF
■ VI (*people*) riunirsi, adunarsi, radunarsi; (*water, dust*) accumularsi; (*rubbish etc*) ammucchiarsi, accumularsi; **to collect for charity** fare una raccolta di beneficenza; **collect on delivery** (*Am Comm*) pagamento alla consegna
■ ADV (*Am*): **to call collect** (*Telec*) fare una chiamata a carico del destinatario
▶ **collect up** VT + ADV raccogliere
col·lect·ed [kəˈlɛktɪd] ADJ **1** (*works, poems*) raccolto(-a); **the collected works of Shakespeare** l'opera completa di Shakespeare **2** (*frm: person: composed*) padrone(-a) di sé
◎ **col·lec·tion** [kəˈlɛkʃən] N (*of information etc*) raccolta; (*of taxes*) riscossione *f*; (*of refuse*) rimozione *f*; (*of stamps*) collezione *f*, raccolta; (*of miscellaneous objects, people*) miscuglio; (*Rel*) questua; (*for charity*) colletta, raccolta; (*Post*) levata; **my CD collection** la mia collezione di CD; **a collection for charity** una colletta per beneficenza
◎ **col·lec·tive** [kəˈlɛktɪv] N collettivo
■ ADJ collettivo(-a)
collective bargaining N trattative *fpl* (sindacali) collettive
col·lec·tive·ly [kəˈlɛktɪvlɪ] ADV collettivamente
collective noun N (*Gram*) sostantivo collettivo
col·lec·tiv·ism [kəˈlɛktɪvɪzəm] N collettivismo
col·lec·tor [kəˈlɛktəʳ] N (*of stamps etc*) collezionista *m/f*; (*of taxes*) esattore *m*; **collector's item** *or* **piece** pezzo da collezionista
◎ **col·lege** [ˈkɒlɪdʒ] N **1** (*of technology, agriculture etc*) istituto superiore; (*Brit, Am Univ*) college *m inv*; **college of art** scuola d'arte; **college of music** conservatorio; **to go to college** (*university*) andare all'università; (*other institution*) andare a un istituto di specializzazione; **college students** studenti *mpl* universitari **2** (*body*) collegio
college of education N ≈ facoltà *f inv* di Magistero
col·lide [kəˈlaɪd] VI: **to collide (with)** scontrarsi (con)
col·lie [ˈkɒlɪ] N (*dog*) collie *m inv*
col·li·er [ˈkɒlɪəʳ] N minatore *m* (di carbone)
col·liery [ˈkɒlɪərɪ] N (*Brit*) miniera di carbone
col·li·ma·tion [ˌkɒlɪˈmeɪʃən] N collimazione *f*
col·li·ma·tor [ˈkɒlɪˌmeɪtəʳ] N collimatore *m*
col·lin·ear [kɒˈlɪnɪəʳ] ADJ (*Math: points*) collineare
col·li·sion [kəˈlɪʒən] N scontro, collisione *f*; **to be on a collision course** (*also fig*) essere in rotta di collisione; **collision damage waiver** (*Insurance*) *clausola che esclude la copertura per danni della vettura assicurata*
col·lo·cate [*n* ˈkɒləkət; *vb* ˈkɒləkeɪt] (*Ling*) N collocazione *f*
■ VI accordarsi
col·loi·dal [kɒˈlɔɪdəl] ADJ colloidale
col·lo·quial [kəˈləʊkwɪəl] ADJ (*word, phrase*) familiare; (*style*) colloquiale
col·lo·qui·al·ism [kəˈləʊkwɪəlɪzəm] N colloquialismo
col·lo·qui·al·ly [kəˈləʊkwɪəlɪ] ADV colloquialmente
col·lude [kɒˈluːd] VI: **to collude with** (*frm*) mettersi d'accordo con
col·lu·sion [kəˈluːʒən] N collusione *f*; **in collusion with** in accordo segreto con
col·ly·wob·bles [ˈkɒlɪˌwɒblz] NPL (*fam*): **to have the collywobbles** (*have stomach trouble*) avere mal di pancia; (*be scared*) avere la tremarella
Co·logne [kəˈləʊn] N (*Geog*) Colonia
co·logne [kəˈləʊn] N (*also:* **eau de cologne**) acqua di colonia
Co·lom·bia [kəˈlɒmbɪə] N Colombia
Co·lom·bian [kəˈlɒmbɪən] ADJ, N colombiano(-a)
co·lon [ˈkəʊlən] N **1** (*punctuation*) due punti *mpl* **2** (*Anat*) colon *m inv*
◎ **colo·nel** [ˈkɜːnl] N colonnello

co·lo·nial [kəˈləʊnɪəl] ADJ coloniale; (*architecture*) di stile coloniale
co·lo·ni·al·ism [kəˈləʊnɪəlɪzəm] N colonialismo
co·lo·ni·al·ist [kəˈləʊnɪəlɪst] ADJ colonialistico(-a)
■ N colonialista *m/f*
colo·nist [ˈkɒlənɪst] N colonizzatore(-trice)
colo·ni·za·tion [ˌkɒlənaɪˈzeɪʃən] N colonizzazione *f*
colo·nize [ˈkɒləˌnaɪz] VT colonizzare
col·on·nade [ˌkɒləˈneɪd] N colonnato
colo·ny [ˈkɒlənɪ] N colonia
col·or *etc* [ˈkʌləʳ] (*Am*) = **colour** *etc*
Colo·ra·do [ˌkɒləˈrɑːdəʊ] N Colorado
▷ www.colorado.gov/
Colorado beetle N dorifora
col·ora·tion [ˌkʌləˈreɪʃən] N colorazione *f*
co·los·sal [kəˈlɒsl] ADJ colossale
co·los·sus [kəˈlɒsəs] N colosso
co·los·to·my [kəˈlɒstəmɪ] N (*Med*) colostomia
◎ **col·our**, (*Am*) **col·or** [ˈkʌləʳ] N **1** (*gen*) colore *m*; **what colour is it?** di che colore è?; **I want to see the colour of his money** voglio vederlo con i soldi in mano; **to change colour** cambiare colore **2** (*complexion*) colore *m*, colorito; **it shouldn't matter what colour you are** non dovrebbe importare il colore della pelle; **to get one's colour back** riprendere colore; **the colour drained from his face** impallidì **3 colours** NPL (*Mil, Naut*) colori *mpl*; (*of party, club*) emblemi *mpl*; **to salute the colours** salutare la bandiera; **to see sth in its true colours** (*fig*: *usu pej*) vedere qc come veramente è; **to show one's true colours** (*fig*: *usu pej*) rivelare la propria vera personalità; **to come through (sth) with flying colours** (*fig*) passare (qc) a pieni voti
■ VT (*gen*) colorare; (*tint, dye*) tingere; (*fig*: *affect*) influenzare; **to colour sth green** tingere *or* colorare qc di verde
■ VI (*blush*: *also*: **colour up**) arrossire
■ ADJ (*film, slide, photograph, television*) a colori; **colour TV** televisore *m* a colori
▸ **colour in** VT + ADV colorare
colour bar, (*Am*) **color bar** N discriminazione *f* razziale (*in locali etc*)
colour-blind, (*Am*) **color-blind** [ˈkʌləˌblaɪnd] ADJ daltonico(-a)
colour blindness, (*Am*) **color-blindness** [ˌkʌləˈblaɪndnɪs] N daltonismo, discromatopsia
◎ **coloured**, (*Am*) **colored** [ˈkʌləd] ADJ colorato(-a); (*person, race*) di colore; **a straw-coloured hat** un cappello color paglia; **highly-coloured** (*tale, account*) molto colorito(-a)
col·our·ful, (*Am*) **col·or·ful** [ˈkʌləfʊl] ADJ (*dress*) dai colori vivaci; (*picture*) ricco(-a) di colore; (*personality*) originale, vivace; (*story*) avvincente
col·our·ful·ly, (*Am*) **col·or·ful·ly** [ˈkʌləfəlɪ] ADV (*gen*) con colori vivaci; (*describe*) in modo pittoresco
col·our·ing, (*Am*) **col·or·ing** [ˈkʌlərɪŋ] N colorazione *f*; (*substance*) colorante *m*; (*complexion*) colorito
colouring book, (*Am*) **coloring book** N album *m inv* da colorare
col·our·less, (*Am*) **col·or·less** [ˈkʌləlɪs] ADJ incolore; (*fig*: *dull*) scialbo(-a)
colour scheme, (*Am*) **color scheme** N combinazione *f* di colori
colour supplement N (*Brit Press*) supplemento a colori
colt [kəʊlt] N puledro
colts·foot [ˈkəʊltsˌfʊt] N (*Bot*) farfara
col·um·bine [ˈkɒləmˌbaɪn] N aquilegia
Co·lum·bus [kəˈlʌmbəs] N: **Christopher Columbus** Cristoforo Colombo
◎ **col·umn** [ˈkɒləm] N (*gen*) colonna; (*in newspaper*) colonna; (: *fashion column, sports column etc*) rubrica; **the editorial column** l'articolo di fondo; **the advertising columns** gli annunci economici; **columns of figures** colonne di cifre
col·umn·ist [ˈkɒləmnɪst] N giornalista *m/f* (*che cura una rubrica*), articolista *m/f*
coma [ˈkəʊmə] N (*Med*) coma *m inv*; **to go into a coma** entrare in coma
co·ma·tose [ˈkəʊməˌtəʊs] ADJ comatoso(-a)
comb [kəʊm] N pettine *m*; **to run a comb through one's hair** darsi una pettinata
■ VT **1** (*hair*) pettinare; **to comb one's hair** pettinarsi; **you haven't combed your hair** non ti sei pettinato **2** (*search*: *area, countryside etc*) rastrellare, setacciare, battere a tappeto
◎ **com·bat** [ˈkɒmbæt] N lotta, combattimento; (*Mil*) combattimento
■ VT (*fig*) combattere, lottare contro
com·bat·ant [ˈkɒmbətənt] N combattente *m/f*
com·bat·ive [ˈkɒmbətɪv] ADJ aggressivo(-a)
combat trousers, combats NPL pantaloni *mpl* larghi con molte tasche; **military-style combats** pantaloni mimetici
◎ **com·bi·na·tion** [ˌkɒmbɪˈneɪʃən] N combinazione *f*
combination lock N serratura a combinazione
◎ **com·bine** [*vb* kəmˈbaɪn; *n* ˈkɒmbaɪn] VT: **to combine (with)** (*projects, proposals*) combinare (con); (*qualities*) unire a; **our combined incomes** i nostri stipendi messi insieme; **to combine business with pleasure** unire l'utile al dilettevole; **it's difficult to combine a career with a family** è difficile conciliare la carriera con la famiglia; **the film combines humour with suspense** il film unisce umorismo e suspense; **to combine forces with sb** unire le proprie forze con qn; **a combined effort** uno sforzo collettivo; **a combined operation** (*Mil*) operazione *f* combinata
■ VI **1** unirsi, mettersi insieme; **to combine with** unirsi a; **to combine against sth/sb** unirsi contro qc/qn **2** (*Chem*): **to combine (with)** combinarsi (con); **combining power** valenza
■ N lega; (*Comm, Fin*) trust *m inv*, associazione *f*; (*Agr*: *also*: **combine harvester**) mietitrebbia *f inv*
com·bo [ˈkɒmbəʊ] N (*Jazz*) gruppo
com·bus·tible [kəmˈbʌstɪbl] ADJ combustibile
com·bus·tion [kəmˈbʌstʃən] N combustione *f*
combustion chamber N camera di combustione
◎ **come** [kʌm] VI (*pt* **came**, *pp* **come**)
1 (*gen*) venire; (*arrive*) venire, arrivare; (*have its place*) venire, trovarsi; **come with me** vieni con me; **Helen came with me** Helen è venuta con me; **can I come too?** posso venire anch'io?; **they came late** sono arrivati tardi; **the letter came this morning** la lettera è arrivata stamattina; **come home** vieni a casa; **come and see us soon** vieni a trovarci presto; **we have come to help you** siamo venuti ad aiutarti; **she has come from London** è venuta da Londra; **we've just come from Paris** siamo appena arrivati da Parigi; **this necklace comes from Spain** questa collana viene dalla Spagna; **they have come a long way** vengono da lontano; (*fig*) hanno fatto molta strada; **people were coming and going all day** c'era gente che andava e veniva tutto il giorno; **to come running** venire di corsa; **to come for sb/sth** venire a prendere qn/qc; **we'll come after you** ti seguiamo; **coming!** vengo!,

Cc

arrivo!; **we came to a village** siamo arrivati a un paese; **to come to a decision** arrivare *or* giungere a una decisione; **the water only came to her waist** l'acqua le arrivava solo alla vita; **it came to me that** (*idea: occur*) mi è venuto in mente che; **it may come as a surprise to you ...** può sorprenderti...; **it came as a shock to her** è stato un colpo per lei; **when it comes to choosing** dovendo scegliere; **when it comes to mathematics** quanto alla matematica; **the time will come when ...** verrà il giorno in cui...; **the new ruling comes into force next year** il nuovo regolamento entrerà in vigore l'anno prossimo; **A comes before B** A viene prima di B; **he came 3rd in the race** è arrivato 3° nella gara
2 (*happen*) accadere, succedere; **come what may** qualunque cosa succeda; **no good will come of it** andrà a finire male; **nothing came of it** non ne è saltato fuori niente, non ha portato a niente; **that's what comes of being careless** ecco cosa succede a non far attenzione; **how does this chair come to be broken?** come mai questa sedia è rotta?; **how come?** (*fam*) come mai?
3 (*be, become*) diventare; **my dreams came true** i miei sogni si sono avverati; **to come undone/loose** slacciarsi/allentarsi; **my shoelaces have come undone** i lacci (delle scarpe) si sono sciolti; **your zip has come undone** ti si è aperta la chiusura lampo; **it comes naturally to him** gli viene spontaneo; **it'll all come right in the end** tutto si accomoderà alla fine; **those shoes come in two colours** quelle scarpe sono disponibili in due colori; **I have come to like her** ho finito col trovarla simpatica; **now I come to think of it** ora che ci penso
4 (*phrases*): **in (the) years to come** negli anni futuri *or* a venire; **if it comes to it** in tal caso; **if it comes to that ...** se è per questo...; **come again?** (*fam*) come?; **he had it coming to him** ha avuto quello che si meritava; **I could see it coming** me lo aspettavo; **he's as daft as they come** è scemo come ce ne sono pochi; **to come between two people** mettersi fra due persone
5 (*fam: have an orgasm*) venire
▸ **come about** VI + ADV accadere, succedere
▸ **come across** VI + ADV
1 (*gen*) attraversare
2 (*fig*): **to come across well/badly** fare una buona/cattiva impressione; **to come across as** dare l'impressione di essere; **she came across as a very nice person** ha dato l'impressione di essere una persona molto simpatica
■ VI + PREP (*find*) trovare (per caso); **I came across a dress that I hadn't worn for years** ho trovato per caso un vestito che non mettevo da anni
▸ **come along** VI + ADV
1 **come along!** sbrigati!, avanti!, andiamo!, forza!
2 (*accompany*) venire
3 (*progress*) far progressi, procedere, migliorare; (*pupil, work*) fare progressi; **how's your arm coming along?** come va il tuo braccio?
▸ **come apart** VI + ADV (*break*) andare in pezzi; (*become detached: sleeve, jacket*) staccarsi (scucendosi); **my jacket is coming apart** la mia giacca si sta scucendo
▸ **come at** VI + PREP
1 (*attack*) avventarsi su; **he came at me with a knife** si è avventato su di me con un coltello
2 (*reach*) arrivare; **to come at the truth** arrivare alla verità
▸ **come away** VI + ADV (*leave*) venir via; (*become detached*) staccarsi; **come away from there!** levati di lì!, vieni via da lì!
▸ **come back** VI + ADV
1 (*return*) tornare; **he came back an hour later** è tornato un'ora dopo; **to come back to what we were discussing ...** per tornare all'argomento di prima...
2 (*reply: fam*): **can I come back to you on that one?** possiamo riparlarne più tardi?
3 (*return to mind*): **it's all coming back to me** mi sta tornando in mente
▸ **come by** VI + PREP: **to come by sth** procurarsi qc
▸ **come down** VI + PREP scendere
■ VI + ADV (*person*): **to come down (from/to)** scendere (da/a); (*building*) essere demolito(-a); (*prices, temperature*) diminuire, calare; **to come down in the world** ridursi male; **she came down on him like a ton of bricks** gli ha fatto una sfuriata; **to come down with a cold** prendersi un raffreddore
▸ **come down to** VI + ADV + PREP: **it all comes down to ...** è tutta questione di...
▸ **come for** VI + PREP
1 (*attack*) avventarsi su
2 (*collect*) passare a prendere; **I'll come for you at seven** passo a prenderti alle sette
▸ **come forward** VI + ADV farsi avanti, presentarsi
▸ **come from** VI + PREP venire *or* provenire da
▸ **come in** VI + ADV (*person*) entrare; (*train*) arrivare; (*tide*) salire; (*in race*) arrivare; (*in election*) salire al potere; **they came in together** entrarono insieme; **come in!** avanti!; **where do I come in?** dove entro in ballo io?; **they have no money coming in** non hanno entrate
▸ **come in for** VI + ADV + PREP (*criticism, blame*) essere oggetto di
▸ **come into** VI + PREP (*inherit*) ereditare; **where do I come into it?** (*be involved*) come vi entro io?; **money doesn't come into it** i soldi non c'entrano
▸ **come off** VI + ADV
1 (*button etc*) staccarsi; (*stain*) andare via; **I don't think this stain will come off** non penso che la macchia andrà via
2 (*event*) avere luogo; (*plans*) attuarsi; (*attempt, experiment*) riuscire
3 (*acquit o.s.*): **to come off best/worst** avere la meglio/la peggio
■ VI + PREP: **a button came off my jacket** mi si è staccato un bottone dalla giacca; **she came off her bike** è caduta dalla bicicletta; **come off it!** (*fam*) piantala!, ma va'!
▸ **come on** VI + ADV
1 (*progress*) = **come along 3**
2 (*exhortation*): **come on!** avanti!, andiamo!, forza!
3 (*protest*): **come on!** ma dai!
4 (*start*) cominciare; **I feel a cold coming on** mi sta venendo un raffreddore; **winter is coming on now** l'inverno si avvicina
5 (*lights, electricity*) accendersi
6 (*Theatre*) entrare in scena
▸ **come on to** VI + ADV + PREP (*turn to*) passare a; (*sexually*) fare delle avance di natura sessuale a
▸ **come out** VI + ADV (*person, object*) uscire; (*flower*) sbocciare; (*sun, stars*) apparire; (*news: esp scandal*) essere divulgato(-a); (*truth*) saltare fuori; (*book, film, magazine*) uscire, essere pubblicato(-a); (*qualities: show*) rivelarsi, mostrarsi; (*stain*) andare via; (*strike*) entrare in sciopero; **to come out of sth** uscire da qc; **we came out of the cinema at 10** siamo usciti dal cinema alle dieci; **her book comes out in May** il suo libro esce a maggio;

none of my photos came out non è venuta nessuna delle mie foto; **it's bound to come out in the newspapers** apparirà senz'altro sui giornali; **he came out in a rash** gli è venuto uno sfogo; **the dye has come out of your jumper** il tuo maglione è scolorito; **to come out on strike** entrare in sciopero, fare sciopero; **to come out against sth** dichiararsi decisamente contrario(-a) a qc; **you never know what he is going to come out with next!** (*fam*) non si sa mai con cosa verrà fuori la prossima volta!

▸ **come over** VI + ADV venire; **they came over to England for a holiday** sono venuti in Inghilterra per una vacanza; **you'll soon come over to my way of thinking** presto sarai anche tu della mia idea; **I came over all dizzy** mi è venuto un giramento di testa; **her speech came over very well** il suo discorso ha fatto una buona impressione, il suo discorso è riuscito bene ■ VI + PREP: **I don't know what's come over him!** non so cosa gli sia preso!; **a feeling of weariness came over her** un forte senso di stanchezza la assalì

▸ **come round** VI + ADV
1 passare, venire; **he is coming round to see us** passa da noi, viene a trovarci
2 (*occur regularly*) ricorrere, venire; **Christmas seems to come round earlier every year** ogni anno sembra che il Natale venga prima
3 (*make detour*): **to come round (by)** passare (per); **we came round by the longer route** abbiamo fatto la strada più lunga
4 (*change one's mind*) cambiare idea; **she'll soon come round to your way of thinking** presto la penserà come te
5 (*throw off bad mood*): **leave him alone, he'll soon come round** lascialo in pace *or* perdere, presto gli passerà
6 (*regain consciousness*) riprendere conoscenza, rinvenire; **he came round after about ten minutes** ha ripreso conoscenza dopo circa dieci minuti

▸ **come through** VI + ADV
1 (*survive*) sopravvivere, farcela
2 (*telephone call*): **the call came through** abbiamo ricevuto la telefonata
■ VI + PREP (*survive: war, danger*) superare, uscire indenne da; **they came through a difficult time in their marriage** hanno superato un periodo difficile del loro matrimonio

▸ **come to** VI + PREP (*add up to: amount*): **how much does it come to?** quanto costa?, quanto viene?
■ VI + ADV (*regain consciousness*) riprendere conoscenza, rinvenire; **she came to in a hospital bed** ha ripreso conoscenza in un letto d'ospedale

▸ **come together** VI + ADV (*assemble*) riunirsi; (*meet*) incontrarsi

▸ **come under** VI + PREP (*heading*) trovarsi sotto; (*influence*) cadere sotto, subire

▸ **come up** VI + ADV
1 salire; **he came up to us with a smile** ci si avvicinò sorridendo
2 (*matters for discussion*) essere sollevato(-a); **to come up (before)** (*accused*) comparire (davanti a); (*lawsuit*) essere ascoltato(-a) (da)
■ VI + PREP venire su, salire; **something has come up so I'll be late home** è saltato fuori un problema, per cui tornerò a casa tardi

▸ **come up against** VI + ADV + PREP (*resistance, difficulties*) urtare contro; **she came up against complete opposition to her proposals** le sue proposte hanno incontrato la più completa opposizione

▸ **come up to** VI + ADV + PREP arrivare (fino) a; **the film didn't come up to our expectations** il film ci ha deluso

▸ **come up with** VI + ADV + PREP (*suggest: idea, plan*) suggerire, proporre; (*offer: money, suggestion*) offrire; **he came up with an idea** venne fuori con un'idea

▸ **come upon** VI + PREP (*object, person*) trovare per caso

come·back ['kʌm,bæk] N **1** (*Theatre, Cine*) rentrée *f*, ritorno; **to make a comeback** (*attore, politico*) tornare sulle scene; (*abiti ecc*) tornare di moda **2** (*reaction*) reazione *f*; (*response*) risultato, risposta

COMECON ['kɒmɪ,kɒn] N ABBR (= **Council for Mutual Economic Aid**) COMECON *m*

co·median [kə'mi:dɪən] N attore comico

co·medi·enne [kə,mi:dɪ'en] N attrice *f* comica

come·down ['kʌm,daʊn] N, NO PL passo indietro

◎ **com·edy** ['kɒmɪdɪ] N (*gen*) commedia brillante; (*humour*) lato comico
▹ www.bbc.co.uk/comedy

come-hither [,kʌm'hɪðə^r] ADJ (*fam*): **a come-hither look** uno sguardo invitante

come·ly ['kʌmlɪ] ADJ (*liter*) avvenente

com·er ['kʌmə^r] N: **open to all comers** aperto(-a) a tutti; **the first comer** il/la primo(-a) venuto(-a)

com·et ['kɒmɪt] N cometa

come·up·pance [,kʌm'ʌpəns] N: **she got her comeuppance** ha avuto quello che si meritava

◎ **com·fort** ['kʌmfət] N **1** (*physical comfort*) comodità *f inv*, benessere *m*; **in the comfort of your own home** nella comodità della propria casa; **to live in comfort** vivere nell'agiatezza; **that car was a bit too close for comfort** quella macchina è passata troppo vicino per i miei gusti **2** (*solace*) consolazione *f*, conforto; **you're a great comfort to me** mi sei di gran conforto
■ VT confortare, consolare

◎ **com·fort·able** ['kʌmfətəbl] ADJ (*house*) confortevole; (*chair, shoes, life*) comodo(-a); (*income, majority*) più che sufficiente; (*temperature*) piacevole; **their house is small but comfortable** la loro casa è piccola ma confortevole; **to make o.s. comfortable** mettersi a proprio agio; **make yourself comfortable** si metta a suo agio; **are you comfortable, sitting there?** sta comodo, seduto lì ?; **I don't feel very comfortable about it** non mi sento molto tranquillo

com·fort·ably ['kʌmfətəblɪ] ADV (*sit etc*) comodamente; (*live*) bene; **to be comfortably off** vivere agiatamente; **to win comfortably** vincere agevolmente

com·fort·er ['kʌmfətə^r] N (*person*) consolatore(-trice); (*scarf*) sciarpa di lana; (*baby's dummy*) ciuccio, succhiotto; (*Am: quilt*) trapunta

com·fort·ing ['kʌmfətɪŋ] ADJ confortante

com·fort·less ['kʌmfətlɪs] ADJ senza comodità, scomodo(-a)

comfort station N (*Am*) (*euph*) toilette *f inv*

comfort zone N (*fig*) situazione *f* di tutta sicurezza

com·fy ['kʌmfɪ] ADJ (*fam*) comodo(-a)

com·ic ['kɒmɪk] ADJ comico(-a)
■ N (*person*) comico/attrice comica; (*magazine*) giornalino (a fumetti)

comi·cal ['kɒmɪkəl] ADJ divertente, buffo(-a), comico(-a)

comi·cal·ly ['kɒmɪkəlɪ] ADV comicamente, in modo buffo

Cc

comic book N (*Am*) fumetti *mpl*; **he reads a lot of comic books** legge un sacco di fumetti
comic opera N opera buffa
comic relief N parentesi *f* comica
comic strip N fumetto
comic verse N poesia umoristica
◎**com·ing** ['kʌmɪŋ] ADJ (*next*) prossimo(-a); (*future*) futuro(-a); **in the coming weeks/election** nelle prossime settimane/elezioni
■N avvento, arrivo
coming and going N, **comings and goings** NPL andirivieni *m inv*, viavai *m inv*; **there have been a lot of comings and goings** c'è stato un continuo andirivieni
Com·in·tern ['kɒmɪn,tɜːn] N KOMINTERN *m*
com·ma ['kɒmə] N virgola
◎**com·mand** [kə'mɑːnd] N (*esp Mil*: *order*) ordine *m*, comando; (: *control*) comando; (*mastery*) padronanza; (*Comput*) comando; **by** *or* **at the command of** per ordine di; **under the command of** sotto il comando di; **to be in command (of)** essere al comando (di); **to have/take command of** avere/prendere il comando di; **to have at one's command** (*money, resources etc*) avere a propria disposizione; **to have a good command of English** avere una buona padronanza dell'inglese
■VT (*order*): **to command sb to do sth** ordinare *or* comandare a qn di fare qc; (*lead*: *men, ship*) essere al comando di; (*have at one's disposal*: *resources*) disporre di, avere a propria disposizione; (*respect*) incutere; **that picture will command a high price** quel quadro sarà venduto ad un prezzo elevato
com·man·dant [,kɒmən'dænt] N comandante *m*
command economy N = **planned economy**
com·man·deer [,kɒmən'dɪəʳ] VT requisire
◎**com·mand·er** [kə'mɑːndəʳ] N capo; (*Mil*) comandante *m*
commander in chief N (*Mil*) comandante *m* in capo
com·mand·ing [kə'mɑːndɪŋ] ADJ (*appearance*) imponente; (*voice, tone*) autorevole; (*lead, position*) dominante
commanding officer N comandante *m*
com·mand·ment [kə'mɑːndmənt] N (*Bible*) comandamento
command module N (*Space*) modulo di comando
com·man·do [kə'mɑːndəʊ] N (*group*) commando *m inv*; (*soldier*) soldato appartenente ad un commando
command performance N *serata di gala su richiesta del capo di Stato o sovrano*
command post N (*Mil*) posto di comando
com·memo·rate [kə'mɛməreɪt] VT commemorare
com·memo·ra·tion [kə,mɛmə'reɪʃən] N commemorazione *f*; **in commemoration of** in memoria di
com·memo·ra·tive [kə'mɛmərətɪv] ADJ commemorativo(-a)
com·mence [kə'mɛns] VT cominciare; **to commence doing sth** cominciare a fare qc
■VI cominciare
com·mence·ment [kə'mɛnsmənt] N (*frm*) inizio
com·mend [kə'mɛnd] VT **1** (*praise*) lodare **2** (*recommend*) raccomandare; **the proposal has little to commend it** la proposta dà poco affidamento **3** (*entrust*): **to commend (to)** affidare a
com·mend·able [kə'mɛndəbl] ADJ lodevole
com·mend·ably [kə'mɛndəblɪ] ADV lodevolmente
com·men·da·tion [,kɒmɛn'deɪʃən] N (*for bravery etc*) encomio, lode *f*; (*recommendation*) raccomandazione *f*
com·men·su·rate [kə'mɛnʃərɪt] ADJ: **commensurate with** proporzionato(-a) a, commisurato(-a) a
◎**com·ment** ['kɒmɛnt] N (*remark*: *written or spoken*) commento, osservazione *f*; (: *critical*) critica; **he made no comment** non fece commenti; **"no comment"** "(non ho) niente da dire"; **to cause comment** provocare critiche
■VI: **to comment (on)** fare commenti *or* dichiarazioni (su); **the police have not commented on these rumours** la polizia non ha fatto commenti sulle voci
■VT: **to comment that** osservare che
com·men·tary ['kɒməntərɪ] N **1** (*Radio*) radiocronaca; (*TV*) telecronaca **2** (*on text*) commento
com·men·tate ['kɒmɛnteɪt] VI commentare
◎**com·men·ta·tor** ['kɒmɛnteɪtəʳ] N (*Radio*) radiocronista *m/f*; (*TV*) telecronista *m/f*
◎**com·merce** ['kɒmɜːs] N commercio; **commerce between the two countries** scambi commerciali fra i due paesi
◎**com·mer·cial** [kə'mɜːʃəl] ADJ commerciale; **the commercial world** il mondo del commercio
■N (*TV*: *also*: **commercial break**) pubblicità *f inv*, spot *m inv* (pubblicitario)
commercial bank N banca commerciale
commercial college N ≈ istituto commerciale
com·mer·cial·ism [kə'mɜːʃə,lɪzəm] N (*pej*) affarismo
com·mer·ciali·za·tion [kə,mɜːʃəlaɪ'zeɪʃən] N (*pej*) commercializzazione *f*
com·mer·cial·ize [kə'mɜːʃə,laɪz] VT (*pej*) commercializzare
com·mer·cial·ly [kə'mɜːʃəlɪ] ADV commercialmente
commercial radio N radio *f inv* privata
commercial television N televisione *f* privata
commercial traveller, (*Am*) **commercial traveler** N viaggiatore *m or* rappresentante di commercio, commesso viaggiatore
commercial vehicle N veicolo per il trasporto di merci, veicolo commerciale
com·mis·er·ate [kə'mɪzəreɪt] VI: **to commiserate with** esprimere il proprio rincrescimento a
com·mis·era·tion [kə,mɪzə'reɪʃən] N commiserazione *f*
com·mis·sar ['kɒmɪsɑːʳ] N commissario
com·mis·sari·at [,kɒmɪ'sɛərɪət] N (*in former Soviet Union*) commissariato; (*Mil*) commissariato militare
◎**com·mis·sion** [kə'mɪʃən] N **1** (*order for work*: *esp of artist*) incarico **2** (*for salesman*) commissione *f*, provvigione *f*; **to work/sell on commission** lavorare/vendere a provvigione; **I get 10% commission** ricevo il 10% sulle vendite; **he gets commission on top of his basic salary** oltre allo stipendio base prende una provvigione; **the bank charges one per cent commission** la banca fa pagare una commissione dell'uno per cento **3** (*committee*) commissione *f*; **commission of inquiry** (*Brit*) commissione *f* d'inchiesta; **a commission has been set up to investigate the tragedy** è stata nominata una commissione per indagare sulla tragedia **4** (*Mil*): **to get one's commission** ricevere la nomina ad ufficiale **5 out of commission** (*machine*) fuori uso; (*Naut*) in disarmo
■VT **1** (*expert, consultant, artist*): **to commission sb to do sth** incaricare qc di fare qc; **to commission sth from sb** (*work of art*) commissionare qc a qn **2** (*Mil*) nominare ufficiale

com·mis·sion·aire [kəˌmɪʃəˈnɛəʳ] N (*Brit: at shop, cinema etc*) portiere *m* in livrea

com·mis·sioned of·fic·er [kəˌmɪʃəndˈɒfɪsəʳ] N (*Mil*) ufficiale *m*

◎ **com·mis·sion·er** [kəˈmɪʃənəʳ] N membro di una commissione; (*Police*) questore *m*; **commissioner of police** ≈ questore *m*

◎ **com·mit** [kəˈmɪt] VT **1** (*crime, act*) commettere; **to commit a crime** commettere un delitto; **to commit suicide** suicidarsi **2 to commit o.s. (to sth/to doing sth)** impegnarsi (in qc/nel fare qc); **I don't want to commit myself** non voglio impegnarmi **3** (*consign*): **to commit sth to sb's care** affidare qc a qn; **to commit to memory** imparare a memoria; **to commit to writing** mettere per iscritto; **to commit sb for trial** rinviare qn a giudizio

◎ **com·mit·ment** [kəˈmɪtmənt] N (*responsibility*) impegno; (*devotion*) dedizione *f*; **he refused to make any commitment** ha rifiutato d'impegnarsi in alcun modo

com·mit·tal [kəˈmɪtl] N (*to prison*) imprigionamento, carcerazione *f*; (*to mental hospital*) ricovero

com·mit·ted [kəˈmɪtɪd] ADJ (*Christian*) convinto(-a); (*writer*) impegnato(-a)

◎ **com·mit·tee** [kəˈmɪtɪ] N, TAKES SG OR PL VB comitato, commissione *f*; (*Parliament*) commissione; **committee of inquiry** commissione d'inchiesta; **to be on a committee** far parte di un comitato *or* di una commissione

committee meeting N riunione *f* di comitato *or* di commissione

com·mo·di·ous [kəˈməʊdɪəs] ADJ spazioso(-a)

com·mod·ity [kəˈmɒdɪtɪ] N prodotto, articolo; (*food*) derrata; **basic commodities** beni *mpl* di prima necessità

DID YOU KNOW ...?
commodity is not translated by the Italian word *comodità*

commodity exchange N borsa *f* merci *inv*
▷ www.euronext.com
▷ www.londonstockexchange.com
▷ www.nyse.com

com·mo·dore [ˈkɒmədɔːʳ] N commodoro

◎ **com·mon** [ˈkɒmən] ADJ **1** comune; (*usual*) normale; **it's a common name** è un nome comune; **it's a common belief that ...** si tende a credere che...; **it's a common occurrence** succede di frequente; **it's common knowledge that ...** è risaputo *or* notorio che..., è di dominio pubblico che...; **it's common courtesy** è una questione di semplice cortesia; **in common use** di uso comune; **common or garden** ordinario(-a); **the common man** l'uomo della strada; **in common parlance** nel linguaggio corrente; **the common people** il popolo; **for the common good** nell'interesse generale, per il bene comune **2** (*pej: vulgar*) volgare, grossolano(-a)
■ N **1** (*land*) parco comunale; **a walk on the common** una passeggiata nel parco comunale **2 in common** in comune; **we have** *or* **we've got a lot in common** abbiamo molto in comune

common cold N: **the common cold** il raffreddore

common denominator N denominatore *m* comune

com·mon·er [ˈkɒmənəʳ] N cittadino(-a) (non nobile)

common ground N (*fig*) punto *mpl* d'incontro *or* d'intesa, terreno comune

common land N terreno di uso pubblico

common-law [ˈkɒmənˌlɔː] ADJ: **common-law wife** convivente *f* more uxorio

common law N diritto consuetudinario

com·mon·ly [ˈkɒmənlɪ] ADV (*see adj*) comunemente, usualmente; in modo volgare

Common Market N: **the Common Market** il Mercato Comune

com·mon·ness [ˈkɒmənnɪs] N (*of method, belief*) diffusione *f*; (*of occurrence*) frequenza; (*of person, accent*) grossolanità, volgarità

common·place [ˈkɒmənˌpleɪs] ADJ comune; (*pej*) banale, ordinario(-a)
■ N (*statement*) luogo comune

common room N (*Scol: staff room*) sala dei professori; (: *for students*) sala di ritrovo

Com·mons [ˈkɒmənz] NPL (*Brit*) (*Pol*): **the (House of) Commons** la Camera dei Comuni

common sense N buon senso

common-sense [ˈkɒmənˌsɛns] ADJ sensato(-a)

Common·wealth [ˈkɒmənˌwɛlθ] N: **the Commonwealth** il Commonwealth

COMMONWEALTH

Il **Commonwealth** è un'associazione di stati sovrani indipendenti e di alcuni territori annessi che facevano parte dell'antico Impero britannico, e che nel 1931 assunsero il nome di **Commonwealth** of Nations, denominazione successivamente semplificata in **Commonwealth**. Ancora oggi molti stati del **Commonwealth** riconoscono simbolicamente il sovrano britannico come capo di stato e i loro rappresentanti si riuniscono per discutere questioni di comune interesse.
▷ www.thecommonwealth.org

com·mo·tion [kəˈməʊʃən] N confusione *f*, tumulto, trambusto; **to make** *or* **cause a commotion** causare confusione

com·mu·nal [ˈkɒmjuːnl] ADJ (*facilities*) in comune; (*for common use*) pubblico(-a); (*life*) di comunità

com·mu·nal·ly [ˈkɒmjuːnəlɪ] ADV (*see adj*) in comune; in una comunità

com·mune [*n* ˈkɒmjuːn; *vb* kəˈmjuːn] N (*group*) comune *f*
■ VI: **to commune with nature** comunicare con la natura

com·mu·ni·cabil·ity [kəˌmjuːnɪkəˈbɪlɪtɪ] N comunicabilità

com·mu·ni·cant [kəˈmjuːnɪkənt] N (*Rel*) comunicante *m/f*

◎ **com·mu·ni·cate** [kəˈmjuːnɪˌkeɪt] VT: **to communicate sth (to sb)** (*thoughts, information*) comunicare qc (a qn); (*frm: disease*) trasmettere qc (a qn)
■ VI (*speak etc*): **to communicate (with)** comunicare (con), mettersi in contatto (con); **communicating rooms** stanze *fpl* comunicanti

◎ **com·mu·ni·ca·tion** [kəˌmjuːnɪˈkeɪʃən] N comunicazione *f*; **to be in communication with** (*frm*) essere in contatto con

communication cord N (*Brit Rail*) segnale *m* d'allarme

communications network N rete *f* delle comunicazioni

communications satellite N satellite *m* per telecomunicazioni

com·mu·ni·ca·tive [kəˈmjuːnɪkətɪv] ADJ (*gen*) loquace; **communicative skills** (*Scol*) capacità *f inv* espressive

Cc

com·mu·ni·ca·tive·ness [kə'mju:nɪkətɪvnɪs] N loquacità

com·mun·ion [kə'mju:nɪən] N (*also Rel*) comunione *f*; **to take communion** ricevere la comunione

communiqué [kə'mju:nɪˌkeɪ] N comunicato, bollettino

com·mun·ism ['kɒmjʊnɪzəm] N comunismo

◎**com·mun·ist** ['kɒmjʊnɪst] ADJ, N comunista (*m/f*)

◎**com·mu·nity** [kə'mju:nɪtɪ] N (*gen*) comunità *f inv*; (*of goods, interests*) comunanza; **the black community** la comunità nera; **the Italian community in Glasgow** la comunità italiana a Glasgow; **the student community** gli studenti; **mental patients now live in the community** i malati di mente ora sono integrati all'interno della società

community centre N circolo ricreativo, centro sociale

community chest N (*Am*) fondo di beneficenza

community health centre N centro socio-sanitario (di quartiere)

community home N (*Brit*) riformatorio

community service N (*Brit*) servizio civile (volontario o in sostituzione della pena per reati minori)

community singing N canto corale

community spirit N (*responsibility*) spirito civico; (*solidarity*) spirito di solidarietà

com·mu·ta·tion tick·et [ˌkɒmjʊ'teɪʃən'tɪkɪt] N (*Am*) biglietto di abbonamento

com·mu·ta·tive [kə'mju:tətɪv] ADJ commutativo(-a)

com·mute [kə'mju:t] VI fare il/la pendolare; **she commutes between Oxford and London** fa la pendolare tra Oxford e Londra
■VT (*payment*): **to commute for** *or* **into** commutare in; (*Law*: *sentence*): **to commute (to)** commutare (a)

com·mut·er [kə'mju:tə^r] N pendolare *m/f*; **the commuter belt** (*Brit*) la periferia abitata dai pendolari; **commuter aircraft** aereo interregionale

com·pact[1] [kəm'pækt] ADJ compatto(-a); **this house is very compact** questa casa è piccola ma funzionale

com·pact[2] ['kɒmpækt] N **1** (*agreement*) patto, contratto **2** (*also:* **powder compact**) portacipria *m inv*

compact disc N compact disc *m inv*

compact disc player N lettore *m* di compact disc

com·pact·ly [kəm'pæktlɪ] ADV senza spreco di spazio

com·pact·ness [kəm'pæktnɪs] N compattezza

com·pan·ion [kəm'pænjən] N compagno(-a); (*lady's*) dama di compagnia; (*book*) manuale *m*, guida

com·pan·ion·able [kəm'pænjənəbl] ADJ (*person*) socievole, di compagnia; **we sat in companionable silence** sedevamo tranquillamente in silenzio

com·pan·ion·ship [kəm'pænjənʃɪp] N compagnia

companion volume N volume *m* complementare

com·pan·ion·way [kəm'pænjənˌweɪ] N (*Naut*) scala

◎**com·pa·ny** ['kʌmpənɪ] N (*gen, also Mil, Theatre*) compagnia; (*Comm, Fin*) società *f inv*, compagnia; **ship's company** equipaggio; **insurance company** compagnia di assicurazione; **theatre company** compagnia teatrale; **he works for a big company** lavora per una grossa società; **Smith and Company** Smith e soci; **he's good/poor company** è di buona/cattiva compagnia; **to keep sb company** tenere *or* fare compagnia a qn; **I'll keep you company** ti farò compagnia; **to get into bad company** farsi cattive amicizie; **to keep bad company** frequentare cattive compagnie; **to part company with sb** dividersi *or* separarsi da qn; **we have company this evening** abbiamo ospiti stasera

company car N macchina (di proprietà) della ditta

company director N amministratore *m*, consigliere *m* di amministrazione

company secretary N (*Brit Comm*) segretario(-a) generale

com·pa·rable ['kɒmpərəbl] ADJ simile; **comparable to** *or* **with** paragonabile a

com·para·tive [kəm'pærətɪv] ADJ (*freedom, luxury, cost*) relativo(-a); (*adjective, adverb*) comparativo(-a); (*study, literature*) comparato(-a); **she's a comparative stranger** la conosco relativamente poco; **the comparative safety of Britain** la relativa sicurezza della Gran Bretagna
■N (*Gram*) comparativo

com·para·tive·ly [kəm'pærətɪvlɪ] ADV (*see adj*) relativamente; comparativamente; **a comparatively easy exercise** un esercizio relativamente facile

◎**com·pare** [kəm'pɛə^r] VT: **to compare sth/sb with/to** paragonare qc/qn a, mettere a confronto *or* confrontare qc/qn con; **compare the two illustrations** mettete a confronto le due illustrazioni; **people always compare him with his brother** tutti lo paragonano sempre a suo fratello; **they compared his work to that of Joyce** hanno paragonato la sua opera a quella di Joyce; **compared with** *or* **to** a paragone di, rispetto a; **Oxford is small compared with London** Oxford è piccola rispetto a Londra; **to compare notes with sb** (*fig*) scambiare le proprie impressioni con qn
■VI: **to compare (with)** essere paragonabile (a), reggere il confronto (con); **how do they compare for speed?** che velocità fanno rispettivamente?; **how do the prices compare?** che differenza di prezzo c'è?; **it doesn't compare with yours** non è paragonabile al tuo
■N: **beyond compare** (*liter*: *adj*) senza confronto *or* paragone; (: *adv*) incomparabilmente

◎**com·pari·son** [kəm'pærɪsn] N paragone *m*, confronto; **in comparison with** *or* **by comparison with** rispetto a, in confronto a/di; **by comparison** a confronto

com·part·ment [kəm'pɑ:tmənt] N comparto, scomparto; (*Brit Rail*) scompartimento; **a first class compartment** uno scompartimento di prima classe

com·part·men·tal·ize [ˌkɒmpɑ:t'mɛntəˌlaɪz] VT dividere in compartimenti

com·pass ['kʌmpəs] N **1** (*Naut etc*) bussola **2** (*Math*): **(a pair of) compasses** un compasso **3** (*fig: range*) portata; **within the compass of** entro i limiti di

com·pas·sion [kəm'pæʃən] N compassione *f*

com·pas·sion·ate [kəm'pæʃənɪt] ADJ (*person*) compassionevole; **on compassionate grounds** per motivi personali

compassionate leave N congedo straordinario (*per gravi motivi di famiglia*)

com·pas·sion·ate·ly [kəm'pæʃənɪtlɪ] ADV pietosamente, in modo compassionevole

com·pat·ibil·ity [kəmˌpætə'bɪlɪtɪ] N compatibilità

com·pat·ible [kəm'pætɪbl] ADJ: **compatible (with)** compatibile (con)

com·pat·ri·ot [kəm'pætrɪət] N compatriota *m/f*

com·pel [kəm'pɛl] VT **1** (*force*): **to compel sb (to do sth)** forzare qn (a fare qc), costringere *or* obbligare qn (a fare qc) **2** (*demand: obedience*) esigere; (: *respect*) incutere

com·pel·ling [kəm'pɛlɪŋ] ADJ (*argument, reason: powerful*) convincente; (*poem*) avvincente; (*painting*) affascinante; **he put forward a compelling argument against the death penalty** ha sollevato un argomento convincente contro la pena di morte; **it's a violent yet compelling film** è un film violento ma avvincente

com·pen·dium [kəm'pɛndɪəm] N (*summary*) compendio, sommario; **compendium of games** (*Brit*) scatola di giochi vari

com·pen·sate ['kɒmpən,seɪt] VT: **to compensate sb (for sth)** compensare qn (per qc); (*financially*) indennizzare *or* risarcire qn (per qc); **workers made redundant will be compensated** i lavoratori in esubero riceveranno un indennizzo
■ VI: **to compensate for** compensare

◎ **com·pen·sa·tion** [,kɒmpən'seɪʃən] N (*see vb*) compensazione *f*; indennità, risarcimento; **in compensation (for)** come compenso (per), come indennizzo (per)

com·pen·sa·tory [kəm'pɛnsətərɪ] ADJ compensativo(-a)

com·pere ['kɒmpɛə^r] N presentatore(-trice)
■ VT presentare

com·père ['kɒmpɛə^r] N presentatore(-trice)
■ VT (*show*) presentare

◎ **com·pete** [kəm'pi:t] VI (*Comm*): **to compete (with)** essere in concorrenza (con), fare concorrenza (a); (*vie*) essere in competizione (con); **to compete in** partecipare a; **I'm competing in the marathon** partecipo alla maratona; **to compete for sth** contendersi qc; (*take part*) concorrere in qc, concorrere per qc; **there are fifty students competing for six places** ci sono cinquanta studenti che concorrono per sei posti; **to compete with one another** farsi concorrenza

com·pe·tence ['kɒmpɪtəns], **com·pe·ten·cy** ['kɒmpɪtənsɪ] N competenza

com·pe·tent ['kɒmpɪtənt] ADJ competente; **this court is not competent to deal with that** questa corte non è competente in materia

com·pe·tent·ly ['kɒmpɪtəntlɪ] ADV con competenza

com·pet·ing [,kɒm'pi:tɪŋ] ADJ (*theories, ideas*) opposto(-a); (*companies*) in concorrenza; (*explanations*) in contrasto tra di loro

◎ **com·pe·ti·tion** [,kɒmpɪ'tɪʃən] N **1** (*Comm*) concorrenza; **in competition with** in concorrenza con; **competition in the computer sector is fierce** c'è una grossa concorrenza nel settore informatico **2** (*gen, Sport*) gara, competizione *f*, concorso; **singing competition** gara di canto; **to go in for** *or* **enter a competition** partecipare ad una gara *or* un concorso; **she won £5000 in a newspaper competition** ha vinto 5000 sterline in un concorso organizzato da un quotidiano

◎ **com·peti·tive** [kəm'pɛtɪtɪv] ADJ **1** (*sports*) agonistico(-a); (*person*) che ha spirito di competizione; (: *in sport*) che ha spirito agonistico, che ha spirito di competizione; **I'm a very competitive person** sono molto competitivo(-a); **competitive examination** concorso **2** (*Comm: price*) concorrenziale, competitivo(-a); (: *goods*) a prezzo concorrenziale *or* competitivo; **to have a competitive advantage in sth** essere avvantaggiato(-a) sulla concorrenza in qc

com·peti·tive·ly [kəm'pɛtɪtɪvlɪ] ADV (*see adj*) agonisticamente; competitivamente; in modo concorrenziale

com·peti·tive·ness [kəm'pɛtɪtɪvnɪs] N competitività, spirito di competizione; (*in sport*) spirito agonistico

◎ **com·peti·tor** [kəm'pɛtɪtə^r] N concorrente *m/f*

com·pi·la·tion [,kɒmpɪ'leɪʃən] N compilazione *f*

com·pile [kəm'paɪl] VT compilare

com·pil·er [kəm'paɪlə^r] N compilatore(-trice)

com·pla·cen·cy [kəm'pleɪsnsɪ] N autocompiacimento, eccessivo compiacimento

com·pla·cent [kəm'pleɪsənt] ADJ compiaciuto(-a), soddisfatto(-a) di sé; **to be complacent** adagiarsi

◎ **com·plain** [kəm'pleɪn] VI: **to complain (to sb about sth)** lamentarsi (con qn di qc), lagnarsi (con qn di qc); (*make a formal complaint*) fare un reclamo (a qn per qc), reclamare (con qn per qc); **we're going to complain to the manager** presenteremo un reclamo al direttore; **she's always complaining about her husband** si lamenta in continuazione di suo marito
▸ **complain of** VI + PREP lamentarsi di; (*Med*) accusare

com·plain·ant [kəm'pleɪnənt] N (*Law*) attore *m*

◎ **com·plaint** [kəm'pleɪnt] N lamentela; (*to manager of shop etc*) reclamo; (*Med: illness*) disturbo, malattia

com·ple·ment [*n* 'kɒmplɪmənt; *vb* 'kɒmplɪ,mɛnt] N **1** (*gen, Gram, Math*) complemento **2** (*staff, crew*) effettivo
■ VT (*enhance*) accompagnarsi bene a, completare

com·ple·men·ta·rity [,kɒmplɪmɛn'tærɪtɪ] N complementarità

com·ple·men·tary [,kɒmplɪ'mɛntərɪ] ADJ complementare; **the food and wine were complementary** il cibo e il vino erano ben assortiti

com·ple·men·ta·tion [,kɒmplɪmɛn'teɪʃən] (*Gram*) N complementazione *f*

◎ **com·plete** [kəm'pli:t] ADJ (*whole*) completo(-a); (*finished*) completo(-a), finito(-a); **complete with** completo(-a) di; **it's a complete disaster** è un vero disastro
■ VT (*set, collection*) completare; (*piece of work*) finire, completare; (*fill in: form*) riempire; **and to complete my misfortunes** e per colmo di sfortuna

com·plete·ly [kəm'pli:tlɪ] ADV completamente

com·plete·ness [kəm'pli:tnɪs] N completezza

com·ple·tion [kəm'pli:ʃən] N completamento; **to be nearing completion** essere in fase di completamento; **on completion of contract** alla firma del contratto

◎ **com·plex** ['kɒmplɛks] ADJ (*all senses*) complesso(-a)
■ N **1** (*Psych*) complesso; **he's got a complex about his weight** ha il complesso del peso, è complessato per il peso **2** (*of buildings*) complesso; **sports/housing complex** complesso sportivo/edilizio

com·plex·ion [kəm'plɛkʃən] N (*of face*) carnagione *f*; (*fig: aspect, appearance*) aspetto; **that puts a different complexion on it** (*fig*) ciò fa apparire la cosa sotto tutta un'altra luce *or* tutto un altro aspetto

com·plex·ity [kəm'plɛksɪtɪ] N complessità *f inv*

com·pli·ance [kəm'plaɪəns] N **1** (*with rules, orders, wishes*): **in compliance with** in conformità con **2** (*submissiveness*) arrendevolezza, acquiescenza

com·pli·ant [kəm'plaɪənt] ADJ (*submissive*) arrendevole, acquiescente

com·pli·ant·ly [kəm'plaɪəntlɪ] ADV arrendevolmente

com·pli·cate ['kɒmplɪ,keɪt] VT complicare

◎ **com·pli·cat·ed** ['kɒmplɪ,keɪtɪd] ADJ complicato(-a), complesso(-a)

com·pli·ca·tion [,kɒmplɪ'keɪʃən] N complicazione *f*

com·plic·ity [,kəmp'lɪsɪtɪ] N (*frm*) complicità *f inv*

com·pli·ment [*n* 'kɒmplɪ,mənt; *vb* 'kɒmplɪmɛnt] N **1** complimento; **to pay sb a compliment (on sth)** fare un complimento a qn (per qc); **he's always paying her compliments** le fa sempre complimenti; **thanks for the compliment** grazie del complimento **2 compliments** NPL (*frm: greetings*) rispetti *mpl*,

Cc

ossequi *mpl*; **compliments of the season** auguri per le festività; **with our compliments** con i nostri omaggi; **with the compliments of Mr X** con gli omaggi del Signor X
■ VT: **to compliment sb (on sth/on doing sth)** congratularsi *or* complimentarsi con qn (per qc/per aver fatto qc); **they complimented me on my Italian** si sono complimentati con me per il mio italiano
com·pli·men·tary [ˌkɒmplɪˈmɛntərɪ] ADJ (*remark etc*) lusinghiero(-a), elogiativo(-a); (*free: ticket*) (in) omaggio *inv*
compliments slip N (*Comm*) cartoncino della società
com·ply [kəmˈplaɪ] VI: **to comply with** (*rules etc*) attenersi a, conformarsi a, osservare; (*wishes, request*) assecondare
◎ **com·po·nent** [kəmˈpəʊnənt] ADJ, N componente (*m*)
com·pose [kəmˈpəʊz] VT **1** (*music, poetry*) comporre; (*letter*) mettere insieme; **to be composed of** essere composto(-a) di **2** (*calm: thoughts*) riordinare; **to compose o.s.** ricomporsi
com·posed [kəmˈpəʊzd] ADJ (*person*) calmo(-a), composto(-a)
com·pos·ed·ly [kəmˈpəʊzɪdlɪ] ADV con calma, tranquillamente
com·pos·er [kəmˈpəʊzəʳ] N (*Mus*) compositore(-trice)
com·po·site [ˈkɒmpəzɪt] ADJ (*gen, Math*) composto(-a); (*Archit*) composito(-a)
com·po·si·tion [ˌkɒmpəˈzɪʃən] N composizione *f*
com·posi·tor [kəmˈpɒzɪtəʳ] N (*Typ*) compositore *m*
com·pos men·tis [ˈkɒmpɒsˈmɛntɪs] ADJ sano(-a) di mente
com·post [ˈkɒmpɒst] N concime *m*
com·po·sure [kəmˈpəʊʒəʳ] N calma, padronanza di sé
com·pote [ˈkɒmpəʊt] N (*Culin*) composta, conserva di frutta
com·pound [*n* ˈkɒmpaʊnd; *adj* kəmˈpaʊnd] N **1** (*enclosed area*) recinto **2** (*Chem*) composto; (*Ling*) parola composta, composto
■ ADJ composto(-a); **compound substance** composto
■ VT (*fig: problem, difficulty*) peggiorare
compound fracture N frattura esposta
compound interest N interesse *m* composto
com·pre·hend [ˌkɒmprɪˈhɛnd] VT capire, comprendere
com·pre·hen·sible [ˌkɒmprɪˈhɛnsəbl] ADJ comprensibile
com·pre·hen·sibly [ˌkɒmprɪˈhɛnsəblɪ] ADV in modo comprensibile
com·pre·hen·sion [ˌkɒmprɪˈhɛnʃən] N (*understanding*) comprensione *f*; (*Scol*) esercizio di comprensione
◎ **com·pre·hen·sive** [ˌkɒmprɪˈhɛnsɪv] ADJ (*study*) esauriente; (*knowledge*) esteso(-a); (*description*) dettagliato(-a); (*report, review*) completo(-a), esauriente; (*measures*) di vasta portata; **a comprehensive guide to New Zealand** una guida completa della Nuova Zelanda; **comprehensive insurance policy** (*Aut*) polizza *f* casco *inv*, polizza *f* multi-rischio *inv*
■ N (*Brit: comprehensive school*) *scuola secondaria dagli 11 ai 18 anni, aperta a tutti*

DID YOU KNOW ...?
comprehensive is not translated by the Italian word *comprensivo*

COMPREHENSIVE SCHOOL

In Gran Bretagna le **comprehensive schools** sono scuole secondarie introdotte negli anni '60 per sostituire il sistema selettivo in base al quale gli alunni più dotati venivano indirizzati verso le "grammar schools" e i meno brillanti verso le "secondary modern schools". Alcune "grammar schools" esistono ancora, ma la stragrande maggioranza dei ragazzi frequenta le **comprehensive schools.**
▷ www.parentscentre.gov.uk/choosingaschool/typesofschool/

com·pre·hen·sive·ly [ˌkɒmprɪˈhɛnsɪvlɪ] ADV (*study, review*) in modo esauriente; (*describe*) dettagliatamente
com·press [*vb* kəmˈprɛs; *n* ˈkɒmprɛs] VT (*substance*) comprimere; (*text etc*) condensare
■ N (*Med*) compressa
com·pres·sion [kəmˈprɛʃən] N compressione *f*
com·pres·sor [kəmˈprɛsəʳ] N compressore *m*
com·prise [kəmˈpraɪz] VT (*also:* **be comprised of**: *be made up of*) comprendere; (*make up*) costituire
◎ **com·pro·mise** [ˈkɒmprəˌmaɪz] N compromesso
■ VI: **to compromise (with sb over sth)** venire a un compromesso (con qn su qc)
■ VT compromettere
■ ADJ (*decision, solution*) di compromesso
com·pro·mis·ing [ˈkɒmprəmaɪzɪŋ] ADJ compromettente
com·pul·sion [kəmˈpʌlʃən] N **1** costrizione *f*, pressione *f*; **under compulsion** sotto costrizione, dietro *or* sotto pressione; **he is under no compulsion (to do it)** nessuno lo costringe (a farlo) **2** desiderio incontrollabile; **a compulsion to tell lies** un impulso incontrollabile a mentire
com·pul·sive [kəmˈpʌlsɪv] ADJ **1** (*Psych: desire, behaviour*) incontrollabile; (*: liar*) patologico(-a); **he's a compulsive drinker/smoker/gambler** ha il vizio del fumo/del bere/del gioco **2** (*novel, film*) avvincente
com·pul·sive·ly [kəmˈpʌlsɪvlɪ] ADV **1** (*Psych: eat*) in modo incontrollato; (*: lie*) in modo patologico; **he gambles/drinks compulsively** ha il vizio del gioco/del bere **2** **compulsively readable** che si legge d'un fiato
com·pul·so·ri·ly [kəmˈpʌlsərɪlɪ] ADV per forza; (*Law*) coattivamente
com·pul·so·ry [kəmˈpʌlsərɪ] ADJ obbligatorio(-a)
compulsory purchase N espropriazione *f*
compulsory retirement N pensionamento obbligatorio
com·punc·tion [kəmˈpʌŋkʃən] N scrupolo; **to have no compunction about doing sth** non farsi scrupoli a fare qc
com·pu·ta·tion [ˌkɒmpjʊˈteɪʃən] N calcolo
com·pute [kəmˈpjuːt] VT calcolare, computare
◎ **com·put·er** [kəmˈpjuːtəʳ] N computer *m inv*, elaboratore *m* elettronico
■ ADJ (*printout*) del computer; (*software*) per computer
computer game N computer game *m inv*, videogioco per computer
com·put·eri·za·tion [kəmˌpjuːtəraɪˈzeɪʃən] N computerizzazione *f*
com·put·er·ize [kəmˈpjuːtəˌraɪz] VT computerizzare
com·put·er·ized [kəmˈpjuːtəˌraɪzd] ADJ computerizzato(-a); **computerized axial tomography** tomografia assiale computerizzata
computer language N linguaggio *m* macchina *inv*
computer-literate [kəmˈpjuːtəˈlɪtətɪt] ADJ: **to be computer-literate** avere dimestichezza coi computer
computer operator N terminalista *m/f*

computer peripheral N unità *f inv* periferica
computer program N programma *m* di computer
computer programmer N programmatore(-trice) di computer
computer programming N programmazione *f* di computer
computer science N informatica
▷ http://foldoc.doc.ic.ac.uk/foldoc/index.html
▷ http://carbon.cudenver.edu/~hgreenbe/glossary/index.php
▷ www.eevl.ac.uk/computing/index.htm
computer scientist N informatico(-a)
com·put·ing [kəm'pju:tɪŋ] N informatica
com·rade ['kɒmrɪd] N compagno(-a)
comrade-in-arms ['kɒmrɪd,ɪn'ɑ:mz] N compagno d'armi
com·rade·ly ['kɒmreɪdlɪ] ADJ (*chat, spirit*) amichevole
com·rade·ship ['kɒmrɪdʃɪp] N cameratismo
Com·sat ['kɒmsæt] N ABBR ® = **communications satellite**
con¹ [kɒn] (*fam*) VT truffare; **to con sb into doing sth** indurre qn a fare qc con raggiri, indurre qn a fare qc raggirandolo; **I've been conned!** mi hanno fregato!
■ N truffa
con² [kɒn] N (*disadvantage*) *see* **pro**
con artist N truffatore(-trice)
con·cat·ena·tion [kɒn,kætɪ'neɪʃən] N (*frm: of events, ideas*) concatenazione *f*
con·cave ['kɒn'keɪv] ADJ concavo(-a)
con·ceal [kən'si:l] VT: **to conceal (sth from sb)** nascondere (qc a qn); (*news*) tenere nascosto(-a) (qc a qn); **concealed lighting** illuminazione *f* indiretta
con·ceal·ment [kən'si:lmənt] N il nascondere; (*of facts*) occultazione *f*; (*of feelings*) dissimulazione *f*
◎ **con·cede** [kən'si:d] VT (*admit: point, defeat*) ammettere; (*: argument*) riconoscere la validità di; (*territory*) cedere; **he finally conceded that Nancy was right** alla fine ammise che Nancy aveva ragione; **to concede victory** darla vinta
■ VI cedere
con·ceit [kən'si:t] N vanità *f inv*, presunzione *f*
con·ceit·ed [kən'si:tɪd] ADJ pieno(-a) di sé, presuntuoso(-a), vanitoso(-a)
con·ceit·ed·ly [kən'si:tɪdlɪ] ADV vanitosamente
con·ceiv·able [kən'si:vəbl] ADJ concepibile; **it is conceivable that ...** può anche darsi che...
con·ceiv·ably [kən'si:vəblɪ] ADV: **he may conceivably be right** può anche darsi che abbia ragione
con·ceive [kən'si:v] VT (*child, idea*) concepire
■ VI: **to conceive of sth/of doing sth** immaginare qc/di fare qc
con·cel·ebrate [kən'sɛlɪ,breɪt] VT (*Rel*) concelebrare
con·cel·ebra·tion [kən'sɛlɪ'breɪʃən] N (*Rel*) concelebrazione *f*
◎ **con·cen·trate** ['kɒnsən,treɪt] VT concentrare; **to concentrate one's thoughts on sth** concentrarsi su qc
■ VI **1** (*pay attention*): **to concentrate (on)** concentrarsi (in *or* su); **I couldn't concentrate** non riuscivo a concentrarmi; **concentrate on getting well** pensa soprattutto a guarire **2** (*group closely*) concentrarsi
■ N (*Chem*) concentrato
con·cen·trat·ed ['kɒnsən,treɪtɪd] ADJ (*juice, attack*) concentrato(-a)
◎ **con·cen·tra·tion** [,kɒnsən'treɪʃən] N (*of mind, also Tech*) concentrazione *f*; (*of people, troops*) concentramento
concentration camp N campo di concentramento

con·cen·tric [kən'sɛntrɪk] ADJ concentrico(-a)
con·cen·tric·ity [,kɒnsən'trɪsɪtɪ] N concentricità
◎ **con·cept** ['kɒnsɛpt] N concetto
con·cep·tion [kən'sɛpʃən] N **1** (*idea*) concetto, concezione *f* **2** (*of child*) concepimento
con·cep·tual [kən'sɛptjʊəl] ADJ concettuale
con·cep·tu·al·ize [kən'sɛptjʊə,laɪz] VT (*frm*) concettualizzare
◎ **con·cern** [kən'sɜ:n] N **1** **what concern is it of yours?** non vedo come ti possa riguardare; **it's of no concern to me** *or* **it's no concern of mine** non mi riguarda **2** (*anxiety*) ansietà *f inv*, preoccupazione *f*; **it is a matter for concern that ...** è preoccupante che...; **they expressed concern about the situation** hanno espresso la loro preoccupazione per la situazione **3** (*firm*) impresa, azienda, ditta; **a going concern** un'azienda in attivo
■ VT riguardare, interessare; **this shouldn't concern you** (*affect*) questo non dovrebbe cambiarti nulla; **this matter does not concern you** questa faccenda non ti riguarda; **their safety is what most concerns me** ciò che mi preoccupa maggiormente è la loro sicurezza; **"to whom it may concern"** "a tutti gli interessati"; **as far as I am concerned** per quanto mi riguarda; **as far as I'm concerned, you can come any time you like** per quanto mi riguarda, puoi venire quando vuoi; **the department concerned** (*under discussion*) l'ufficio in questione; (*relevant*) l'ufficio competente; **it was tragic for everyone concerned** è stato tragico per tutti; **to be concerned with** occuparsi di; **to be concerned in** interessarsi a; **to concern o.s. with** occuparsi di; **they are more concerned to save money than to save lives** ciò che li preoccupa maggiormente è risparmiare denaro e non salvare vite umane
◎ **con·cerned** [kən'sɜ:nd] ADJ **1** (*affected*) interessato(-a) **2** (*worried*) preoccupato(-a), ansioso(-a); **to be concerned at** *or* **by** *or* **about sth/for** *or* **about sb** preoccuparsi per *or* di qc/per qn, essere preoccupato(-a) per qc/per qn; **his mother is concerned about him** sua madre è preoccupata per lui
con·cern·ing [kən'sɜ:nɪŋ] PREP riguardo a, circa; **for further information concerning the job, contact Mr Ross** per maggiori informazioni riguardo al lavoto, contatti il signor Ross
◎ **con·cert** ['kɒnsət] N (*Mus*) concerto; **in concert** in concerto; (*fig*) di concerto
■ ADJ concertistico(-a)
con·cert·ed [kən'sɜ:tɪd] ADJ (*effort, attack*) concertato(-a), collettivo(-a)
concert·goer ['kɒnsət,gəʊəʳ] N frequentatore(-trice) di concerti
concert hall N sala da concerti
con·cer·ti·na [,kɒnsə'ti:nə] N piccola fisarmonica
■ VI accartocciarsi, piegarsi come una fisarmonica
con·cer·to [kən'tʃɛətəʊ] N concerto
concert pianist N concertista *m/f* (*pianista*)
concert tour N serie *f inv* di concerti
◎ **con·ces·sion** [kən'sɛʃən] N concessione *f*
con·ces·sion·aire [kən,sɛʃə'nɛəʳ] N (*Comm*) concessionario
con·ces·sion·ary [kən'sɛʃənərɪ] ADJ (*ticket, fare*) a prezzo ridotto
con·ces·sive [kən'sɛsɪv] ADJ: **concessive clause** (*Gram*) (proposizione *f*) concessiva
conch [kɒntʃ] N (*Zool*) (conchiglia di) strombo

Cc

con·cili·ate [kən'sɪlɪeɪt] VT *(person)* rabbonire, calmare; *(opposing view)* conciliare
con·cili·ation [kən,sɪlɪ'eɪʃən] N conciliazione *f*
con·cilia·tory [kən'sɪlɪətərɪ] ADJ conciliante, conciliatorio(-a), conciliativo(-a)
con·cise [kən'saɪs] ADJ conciso(-a)
con·cise·ly [kən'saɪslɪ] ADV concisamente, brevemente
con·cise·ness [kən'saɪsnɪs], **con·ci·sion** [kən'sɪʒən] N concisione *f*
con·clave ['kɒnkleɪv] N *(meeting)* riunione *f* segreta; *(Rel)* conclave *m*
◎ **con·clude** [kən'klu:d] VT *(all senses)* concludere
■ VI: **to conclude (with)** *(events)* concludersi (con); *(speaker)* concludere
con·clud·ing [kən'klu:dɪŋ] ADJ *(remarks etc)* conclusivo(-a), finale
◎ **con·clu·sion** [kən'klu:ʒən] N *(all senses)* conclusione *f*; **in conclusion** in conclusione; **to come to the conclusion that ...** concludere che..., arrivare alla conclusione che...
con·clu·sive [kən'klu:sɪv] ADJ conclusivo(-a)
con·coct [kən'kɒkt] VT *(food, drink)* mettere insieme; *(lie, story, excuse)* inventare; *(scheme)* architettare
con·coc·tion [kən'kɒkʃən] N *(food, drink)* miscuglio
con·comi·tant [kən'kɒmɪtənt] *(frm)* ADJ concomitante
■ N fatto concomitante
con·cord ['kɒŋkɔ:d] N *(harmony)* armonia, concordia; *(treaty)* accordo
con·cord·ant [kən'kɔ:dənt] ADJ *(frm)* concordante
con·course ['kɒŋkɔ:s] N *(of people)* folla; *(place)* luogo di assembramento; *(in station)* atrio
◎ **con·crete** ['kɒnkri:t] ADJ **1** *(object, advantage)* concreto(-a) **2** *(Constr)* di calcestruzzo
■ N *(Constr)* calcestruzzo
■ VT *(path)* rivestire di calcestruzzo
con·crete·ly ['kɒnkri:tlɪ] ADV concretamente
concrete mixer N betoniera
con·cur [kən'kɜ:ʳ] VI *(frm)* **1** *(agree)*: **to concur (with)** *(opinions etc)* coincidere (con), concordare (con); *(person)* essere d'accordo (con) **2** *(happen at the same time)* coincidere
con·cur·rent [kən'kʌrənt] ADJ simultaneo(-a); **to be concurrent with** coincidere con
con·cur·rent·ly [kən'kʌrəntlɪ] ADV: **concurrently (with)** simultaneamente (a)
con·cussed [kən'kʌst] ADJ: **to be concussed** *(Med)* avere una commozione cerebrale
con·cus·sion [kən'kʌʃən] N *(Med)* commozione *f* cerebrale

> DID YOU KNOW ...?
> **concussion** is not translated by the Italian word *concussione*

◎ **con·demn** [kən'dɛm] VT *(person)* condannare; *(declare unfit: building)* dichiarare inagibile; *(: food)* dichiarare immangiabile; **to condemn sb to death** condannare qn a morte; **the government has condemned the EU's decision** il governo ha condannato la decisione dell'Unione europea
con·dem·na·tion [,kɒndɛm'neɪʃən] N condanna
con·demned [kən'dɛmd] ADJ **1** *(awaiting execution: man, woman)* condannato **2** *(Constr: in a poor state of repair: building)* pericolante
condemned cell N braccio della morte
con·den·sa·tion [,kɒndɛn'seɪʃən] N condensazione *f*
con·dense [kən'dɛns] VT condensare
■ VI condensarsi
con·densed milk [kən'dɛnst'mɪlk] N latte *m* condensato
con·dens·er [kən'dɛnsəʳ] N condensatore *m*
con·de·scend [,kɒndɪ'sɛnd] VI: **to condescend to sb** trattare qn con sussiego; **to condescend to do sth** degnarsi di fare qc, abbassarsi a fare qc
con·de·scend·ing [,kɒndɪ'sɛndɪŋ] ADJ sussiegoso(-a)
con·de·scend·ing·ly [,kɒndɪ'sɛndɪŋlɪ] ADV con aria di sufficienza
con·de·scen·sion [,kɒndɪ'sɛnʃən] N sussiego, aria di superiorità
con·di·ment ['kɒndɪmənt] N condimento
◎ **con·di·tion** [kən'dɪʃən] N **1** condizione *f*; **on condition that** a condizione di, a condizione che *+ sub*; **I'll do it, on one condition...** lo farò, ma ad una condizione...; **under** *or* **in the present conditions** nelle attuali condizioni *or* circostanze; **in good/poor condition** in buone/cattive condizioni; **to be in no condition to do sth** non essere in condizione di fare qc; **to be out of condition** *(person)* essere fuori forma; **physical condition** *(of person)* condizioni fisiche; **physical conditions** condizioni ambientali; **weather conditions** condizioni meteorologiche; **conditions of sale** condizioni di vendita **2** *(disease)* malattia; **to have a heart condition** soffrire di (mal di) cuore
■ VT condizionare, regolare
con·di·tion·al [kən'dɪʃənl] ADJ condizionale; **to be conditional upon** dipendere da
conditional discharge *(Brit: Law)* N sospensione *f* condizionale della pena
con·di·tion·er [kən'dɪʃənəʳ] N *(for hair)* balsamo; *(for clothes)* ammorbidente *m*
conditioning [kən'dɪʃənɪŋ] N condizionamento
con·do ['kɒndəʊ] N ABBR *(Am fam:* = **condominium)** condominio
con·dole [kən'dəʊl] VI *(frm)*: **to condole with sb** porgere le proprie condoglianze a qn
con·do·lences [kən'dəʊlənsɪz] NPL condoglianze *fpl*
con·dom ['kɒndəm] N preservativo
con·do·min·ium [,kɒndə'mɪnɪəm] N *(Am)* condominio
con·done [kən'dəʊn] VT *(forgive)* perdonare, scusare; *(overlook)* passare sopra a; **I do not condone violence** non giustifico la violenza
con·du·cive [kən'dju:sɪv] ADJ: **to be conducive to** favorire, essere favorevole a
◎ **con·duct** [*n* 'kɒndʌkt; *vb* kən'dʌkt] N condotta; **civilized conduct** comportamento civile
■ VT *(gen, Phys)* condurre; *(guide)* accompagnare; *(Law)* presentare; *(Mus)* dirigere; *(manage)* dirigere, amministrare; **to conduct o.s.** comportarsi
con·duct·ed tour [kən'dʌktɪd'tʊəʳ] N giro guidato, visita guidata
con·duc·tion [kən'dʌkʃən] N *(Elec, Phys)* conduzione *f*
con·duc·tiv·ity [,kɒndʌk'tɪvɪtɪ] N *(Elec, Phys)* conduttività
con·duc·tor [kən'dʌktəʳ] N *(of orchestra)* direttore *m* d'orchestra; *(on bus)* bigliettaio; *(Am Rail)* controllore *m*; *(Phys: of heat, electricity)* conduttore *m*
con·duc·tress [kən'dʌktrɪs] N *(on bus)* bigliettaia
con·duit ['kɒndɪt] N *(pipe)* conduttura, condotto, tubo
cone [kəʊn] N *(gen, of ice cream)* cono; *(Aut)* birillo; *(Bot)* pigna; **ice-cream cone** cono di gelato
▶ **cone off** VT + ADV chiudere al traffico *(un'area o un tratto stradale, delimitandolo con birilli)*
con·fab ['kɒnfæb] N *(fam)*: **to have a confab** fare una chiacchieratina

con·fec·tion·er [kən'fɛkʃənəʳ] N pasticciere *m*; **confectioner's (shop)** ≈ pasticceria
con·fec·tion·ery [kən'fɛkʃənərɪ] N (*sweets*) dolciumi *mpl*
con·fed·era·cy [kən'fɛdərəsɪ] N confederazione *f*; **the Confederacy** (*Am*) gli Stati della Confederazione
con·fed·er·ate [kən'fɛdərɪt] ADJ confederato(-a)
■ N (*pej*) complice *m/f*; (*Am History*) confederato
con·fed·era·tion [kən,fɛdə'reɪʃən] N confederazione *f*
con·fer [kən'fɜːʳ] VT: **to confer sth on sb** conferire qc a qn
■ VI: **to confer (with sb about sth)** consultarsi (con qn su qc)
◎ **con·fer·ence** ['kɒnfərəns] N (*convention, meeting*) conferenza, convegno, congresso; (*participants*) partecipanti *mpl* alla conferenza *or* al convegno *etc*; **to be in conference** essere in riunione
con·fess [kən'fɛs] VT confessare, ammettere; **to confess o.s. guilty of** (*sin, crime*) confessare di essere colpevole di, dichiararsi colpevole di
■ VI (*make one's confession*) confessarsi; (*admit*): **to confess (to sth/to doing sth)** confessare (qc/di aver fatto qc); **he confessed to the murder** ha confessato di aver commesso l'omicidio
con·fes·sion [kən'fɛʃən] N confessione *f*; **to go to confession** andare a confessarsi; **to make one's confession** confessarsi; **to hear sb's confession** ascoltare la confessione di qn
con·fes·sion·al [kən'fɛʃənl] N confessionale *m*
con·fes·sor [kən'fɛsəʳ] N confessore *m*
con·fet·ti [kən'fɛtiː] N coriandoli *mpl*
con·fi·dant [,kɒnfɪ'dænt] N confidente *m*
con·fi·dante [,kɒnfɪ'dænt] N confidente *f*
con·fide [kən'faɪd] VT confidare
■ VI: **to confide in sb (about sth)** confidarsi con qn (su qc)
◎ **con·fi·dence** ['kɒnfɪdəns] N **1** (*trust*) fiducia; **to have (every) confidence in sb** avere (piena) fiducia in qn; **I've got a lot of confidence in him** ho molta fiducia in lui; **to have (every) confidence that** essere (assolutamente) certo(-a) che; **motion of no confidence** (*Parliament*) mozione *f* di sfiducia **2** (*also:* **self-confidence**) sicurezza di sé, fiducia in se stesso(-a); **to gain confidence** acquistare sicurezza; **she lacks confidence** non ha fiducia in se stessa **3** (*secret*) confidenza; **in confidence** in via confidenziale; **I'm telling you this in strict confidence** te lo dico in via strettamente confidenziale; **to take sb into one's confidence** confidarsi con qn; **to write in confidence to sb** scrivere a qn con la massima riservatezza
confidence trick N truffa
confidence trickster N truffatore(-trice)
◎ **confident** ['kɒnfɪdənt] ADJ sicuro(-a), fiducioso(-a); (*also:* **self-confident**) sicuro(-a) (di sé); **she seems very confident** sembra molto sicura di sé; **to be confident of doing sth/that** essere sicuro di fare qc/che; **I'm confident everything will be okay** sono sicuro(-a) che tutto andrà bene
con·fi·den·tial [,kɒnfɪ'dɛnʃəl] ADJ (*letter, report, remark*) confidenziale, riservato(-a); (*secretary*) particolare
con·fi·den·ti·al·ity [,kɒnfɪ,dɛnʃɪ'ælɪtɪ] N riservatezza, carattere *m* confidenziale
con·fi·den·tial·ly [,kɒnfɪ'dɛnʃəlɪ] ADV in confidenza
con·fi·dent·ly ['kɒnfɪdəntlɪ] ADV con sicurezza
con·fid·ing [kən'faɪdɪŋ] ADJ fiducioso(-a)
con·figu·ra·tion [kən,fɪgjʊ'reɪʃən] N (*Comput*) configurazione *f*
con·fig·ure [kɒn'fɪgə] VT (*Comput*) configurare
con·fine [kən'faɪn] VT **1** (*imprison, shut up*) rinchiudere; **confined to barracks** consegnato(-a) (in caserma); **confined to bed** costretto(-a) a letto **2** (*limit*) limitare; **to confine o.s. to doing sth** limitarsi a fare qc; *see also* **confines**
con·fined [kən'faɪnd] ADJ (*space*) ristretto(-a); **a confined space** uno spazio ristretto
con·fine·ment [kən'faɪnmənt] N **1** (*imprisonment*) reclusione *f*, detenzione *f*; (*Mil*) consegna; **solitary confinement** cella di isolamento **2** (*Med*) parto
con·fines ['kɒnfaɪnz] NPL (*bounds*) confini *mpl*
◎ **con·firm** [kən'fɜːm] VT (*gen*) confermare; (*strengthen: belief*) rafforzare; (*Rel*) cresimare
con·fir·ma·tion [,kɒnfə'meɪʃən] N conferma; (*Rel*) cresima; **a confirmation of their suspicions** una conferma dei loro sospetti
con·firmed [kən'fɜːmd] ADJ (*smoker, habit etc*) incallito(-a), inveterato(-a); (*bachelor*) impenitente; (*admirer*) fervente
con·fis·cate ['kɒnfɪs,keɪt] VT: **to confiscate sth (from sb)** confiscare qc (a qn)
con·fis·ca·tion [,kɒnfɪs'keɪʃən] N confisca
con·fla·gra·tion [,kɒnflə'greɪʃən] N (*frm*) conflagrazione *f*
◎ **con·flict** [*n* 'kɒnflɪkt; *vb* kən'flɪkt] N conflitto
■ VI: **to conflict (with)** essere in conflitto (con)
con·flict·ing [kən'flɪktɪŋ] ADJ (*reports, evidence, opinions*) contraddittorio(-a); (*opinions*) contrastante
con·flu·ence ['kɒnfluəns] N (*frm*) **1** (*of rivers*) confluenza **2** (*of interests, ideas*) convergenza **3** (*crowd*) folla
con·form [kən'fɔːm] VI: **to conform (to)** conformarsi (a)
con·form·ist [kən'fɔːmɪst] ADJ conformistico(-a)
■ N conformista *m/f*
con·form·ity [kən'fɔːmɪtɪ] N: **in conformity with** in conformità a
con·found [kən'faʊnd] VT (*confuse*) confondere; (*amaze*) sconcertare; (*defeat*) sconfiggere; **confound it!** al diavolo!
con·found·ed [kən'faʊndɪd] ADJ maledetto(-a)
◎ **con·front** [kən'frʌnt] VT (*enemy, danger*) affrontare; (*defiantly*) fronteggiare; **to confront sb with sth** mettere qn a confronto con qc; **I decided to confront him** decisi di affrontarlo; **the problems which confront us** i problemi da affrontare; **the task now confronting them** il compito che ora devono affrontare

DID YOU KNOW ...?
confront is not translated by the Italian word ***confrontare***

◎ **con·fron·ta·tion** [,kɒnfrən'teɪʃən] N scontro
con·fron·ta·tion·al [,kɒnfrən'teɪʃənəl] ADJ polemico(-a), aggressivo(-a)
con·fuse [kən'fjuːz] VT confondere
con·fused [kən'fjuːzd] ADJ confuso(-a); **in a confused state** (*person*) in stato confusionale; (*room, papers*) in disordine; **to get confused** confondersi
con·fus·ed·ly [kən'fjuːzɪdlɪ] ADV confusamente
con·fus·ing [kən'fjuːzɪŋ] ADJ (*signals*) ambiguo(-a); (*plot, layout*) confuso(-a); **it's all very confusing** è tutto molto confuso
con·fu·sion [kən'fjuːʒən] N confusione *f*

Cc

con·geal [kən'dʒiːl] VI rapprendersi; (*blood*) coagularsi, rapprendersi

DID YOU KNOW ...?
congeal is not translated by the Italian word *congelare*

con·gen·ial [kən'dʒiːnɪəl] ADJ (*place, work, company*) piacevole; (*person*) simpatico(-a)
con·geni·tal [kən'dʒɛnɪtl] ADJ (*Med*) congenito(-a)
con·ger ['kɒŋgəʳ] N (*also:* **conger eel**) grongo
con·gest·ed [kən'dʒɛstɪd] ADJ (*gen, Med*) congestionato(-a); (*telephone lines*) sovraccarico(-a)
con·ges·tion [kən'dʒɛstʃən] N (*with traffic, Med*) congestione *f*; (*with people*) sovraffollamento
congestion charge N *pedaggio da pagare per poter circolare in automobile nel centro di alcune città*
congestion charging N *imposizione di un pedaggio da pagare per poter circolare in automobile nel centro di alcune città*
con·ges·tive [kən'dʒɛstɪv] ADJ (*Med: heart failure, condition*) congestizio
con·glom·er·ate [kən'glɒmərɪt] N (*Comm, Geol*) conglomerato
con·glom·era·tion [kən,glɒmə'reɪʃən] N conglomerazione *f*
Con·go ['kɒŋgəʊ] N: **the Congo** (*country, river*) il Congo
con·gratu·late [kən'grætjʊ,leɪt] VT: **to congratulate sb (on sth/on doing sth)** congratularsi con qn (per qc/per aver fatto qc); **my friends congratulated me on passing my test** i miei amici si sono congratulati con me per aver passato l'esame di guida
con·gratu·la·tions [kən,grætjʊ'leɪʃənz] NPL: **congratulations (on)** congratulazioni *fpl* (per); **to give sb one's congratulations** fare le (proprie) congratulazioni a qn; **congratulations!** congratulazioni!, rallegramenti!; **congratulations on your new job!** congratulazioni per il tuo nuovo lavoro!
con·gratu·la·tory [kən'grætjʊlətərɪ] ADJ (*telegram, speech*) di congratulazioni
con·gre·gate ['kɒŋgrɪ,geɪt] VI radunarsi, congregarsi, riunirsi
con·gre·ga·tion [,kɒŋgrɪ'geɪʃən] N (*worshippers*) assemblea (dei fedeli); (*parishioners*) parrocchiani *mpl*, congregazione *f*
Con·gre·ga·tion·al·ism [,kɒŋgrɪ'geɪʃənə,lɪzəm] N congregazionalismo
◎**Con·gress** ['kɒŋgrɛs] N (*Am*) il Congresso

CONGRESS
Il **Congress** è l'assemblea statunitense che si riunisce a Washington D.C. nel "Capitol" per elaborare e discutere le leggi federali. È costituita dalla "House of Representatives" (435 membri, eletti nei vari stati in base al numero degli abitanti) e dal "Senate" (100 senatori, due per ogni stato). Sia i membri della "House of Representatives" che quelli del "Senate" sono eletti direttamente dal popolo.

con·gress ['kɒŋgrɛs] N congresso
◎**con·gres·sion·al** [kɒŋ'grɛʃənl] ADJ (*Am*) del Congresso
congress·man ['kɒŋgrɛsmən] N (*pl* **-men**) (*Am*) membro del Congresso
congress·woman ['kɒŋgrɛs,wʊmən] N (*pl* **-women**) (*Am*) (donna) membro del Congresso
con·gru·ent ['kɒŋgrʊənt] ADJ (*Geom: plane, solid*) congruente
con·ic ['kɒnɪk] N (*also:* **conic section**, *Geog*) (sezione *f*) conica
coni·cal ['kɒnɪkəl] ADJ conico(-a); **conical hat** cappello a cono
co·ni·fer ['kɒnɪfəʳ] N conifera
co·nif·er·ous [kə'nɪfərəs] ADJ (*forest*) di conifere; (*tree*) conifero(-a)
con·jec·tur·al [kən'dʒɛktʃərəl] ADJ congetturale
con·jec·ture [kən'dʒɛktʃəʳ] N congettura
■VT, VI (*frm*) congetturare
con·joined twin [kən,[dz]ɔɪnd'twɪn] N fratello (*or* sorella) siamese
con·ju·gal ['kɒndʒʊgəl] ADJ (*frm*) coniugale
con·ju·gate ['kɒndʒʊ,geɪt] VT coniugare
■VI coniugarsi
■ADJ (*Geom*) coniugato(-a)
con·ju·ga·tion [,kɒndʒʊ'geɪʃən] N (*Gram*) coniugazione *f*
con·junc·tion [kən'dʒʌŋkʃən] N **1** (*Gram*) congiunzione *f* **2 in conjunction with** in accordo con, insieme con *or* a
con·junc·ti·vi·tis [kən,dʒʌŋktɪ'vaɪtɪs] N (*Med*) congiuntivite *f*
con·junc·ture [kən'dʒʌŋktʃəʳ] N (*frm*) congiuntura
con·jure ['kʌndʒəʳ] VI fare giochi di prestigio; **a name to conjure with** un nome prestigioso *or* molto importante
▶ **conjure up** VT + ADV (*memories*) evocare, rievocare; (*ghost, spirit*) evocare; (*meal*) inventare, improvvisare

DID YOU KNOW ...?
conjure is not translated by the Italian word *congiurare*

con·jur·er, con·jur·or ['kʌndʒərəʳ] N prestigiatore(-trice), illusionista *m/f*
con·jur·ing ['kʌndʒərɪŋ] N giochi *mpl* di prestigio, prestidigitazione *f*
■ADJ: **conjuring trick** gioco di prestigio
conk·er ['kɒŋkəʳ] N (*Brit fam*) castagna (d'ippocastano)
conk out [,kɒŋk'aʊt] VI + ADV (*fam: break down*) rompersi
con man N truffatore *m*
con·nect [kə'nɛkt] VT **1** (*gen*) collegare, connettere; (*install: cooker, telephone*) installare, allacciare; **now connect the wires** ora collega i fili; **to connect (with)** (*Telec: caller*) mettere in comunicazione (con); **to connect (to)** (*pipes, drains*) collegare (con); **I am trying to connect you** (*Telec*) sto cercando di darle la linea; **to connect sth (up) to the mains** (*Elec*) collegare qc alla rete; **to connect to the Internet** collegarsi a Internet **2** (*associate*): **to connect sb/sth (with)** associare qn/qc (con), collegare qn/qc (con); **the evidence clearly connected him with the crime** le prove dimostravano chiaramente che era implicato nel delitto; **I wouldn't have connected the two facts** non avrei collegato i due fatti
■VI collegarsi; (*train, planes*): **to connect with** essere in coincidenza con
con·nect·ed [kə'nɛktɪd] ADJ (*languages, species*) connesso(-a); (*events*) collegato(-a); **to be connected (to/with)** (*language, family, species*) essere imparentato(-a) (con); (*event*) essere collegato(-a) (a/con); **these two things are in no way connected** non c'è alcun legame tra le due cose
Connecticut [kə'nɛtɪkət] N Connecticut *m*
▷ www.ct.gov/
◎**con·nec·tion con·nex·ion** [kə'nɛkʃən] N **1** (*Tech, Elec, Telec*) collegamento, connessione *f*; (*train, bus, plane*) coincidenza; (*connecting point*) giuntura; **to miss/make a connection** perdere/prendere la coincidenza; **we missed our connection** abbiamo perso la

coincidenza; **Internet connection** collegamento a Internet; **loose connection** filo staccato **2** *(relationship)* rapporto, relazione *f*, legame *m*; **connection between/with** rapporto tra/con; **what is the connection between them?** in che modo sono legati?; **there's no connection between the two events** non c'è rapporto tra i due fatti; **in connection with** con riferimento a, a proposito di; **in this connection** riguardo a questo; **family connection** legame *m* di parentela; *(person)* parente *m/f*; **she has many business connections** ha molti rapporti d'affari; **she's got the right connections** conosce le persone giuste

con·nec·tive [kə'nɛktɪv] ADJ connettivo(-a)

connective tissue N *(Anat)* tessuto connettivo

con·nec·tiv·ity [ˌkɒnek'tɪvɪtɪ] N *(Comput)* connettività

con·ning tow·er ['kɒnɪŋˌtaʊə[r]] N *(of submarine)* torretta di comando

con·niv·ance [kə'naɪvəns] N *(pej)* connivenza

con·nive [kə'naɪv] VI: **to connive at** *(pej: pretend not to notice)* chiudere un occhio su; (: *aid and abet*) essere connivente in

con·niv·ing [kə'naɪvɪŋ] ADJ: **he's a conniving bastard** è un trafficone

con·nois·seur [ˌkɒnə'sɜː[r]] N conoscitore(-trice), intenditore(-trice)

con·no·ta·tion [ˌkɒnəʊ'teɪʃən] N connotazione *f*

con·no·ta·tive ['kɒnəˌteɪtɪv] ADJ connotativo(-a)

con·note [kɒ'nəʊt] VT connotare

con·nu·bial [kə'njuːbɪəl] ADJ *(frm)* coniugale

con·quer ['kɒŋkə[r]] VT *(territory, nation, castle)* conquistare; *(enemy)* vincere, battere, sconfiggere; *(habit, feelings)* vincere, superare

con·quer·ing ['kɒŋkərɪŋ] ADJ vincitore(-trice)

con·quer·or ['kɒŋkərə[r]] N conquistatore *m*

con·quest ['kɒŋkwɛst] N conquista

cons [kɒnz] NPL *see* **pro, convenience**

con·science ['kɒnʃəns] N coscienza; **with a clear conscience** con la coscienza pulita *or* a posto; **to have a clear/guilty conscience** avere la coscienza pulita/sporca; **to have sth on one's conscience** avere qc sulla coscienza; **in all conscience** onestamente, in coscienza

conscience-stricken ['kɒnʃənsˌstrɪkən] ADJ: **to be conscience-stricken** avere dei rimorsi (di coscienza)

con·sci·en·tious [ˌkɒnʃɪ'ɛnʃəs] ADJ coscienzioso(-a)

con·sci·en·tious·ly [ˌkɒnʃɪ'ɛnʃəslɪ] ADV coscienziosamente

con·sci·en·tious·ness [ˌkɒnʃɪ'ɛnʃəsnɪs] N coscienziosità

conscientious objector N *(Mil)* obiettore *m* di coscienza

◎ **con·scious** ['kɒnʃəs] ADJ **1** *(aware)*: **conscious (of sth/of doing)** consapevole (di qc/di fare), conscio(-a) (di qc/di fare); **she was conscious of it** ne era consapevole; **to become conscious of sth/that** rendersi conto di qc/che **2** *(deliberate: insult, error)* intenzionale, voluto(-a); **he made a conscious decision to tell nobody** ha deciso deliberatamente di non dirlo a nessuno **3** *(Med)* cosciente; **to become conscious** riprendere coscienza; **he was still conscious when the doctor arrived** era ancora in sé quando è arrivato il dottore

con·scious·ly ['kɒnʃəslɪ] ADV consciamente, consapevolmente

◎ **con·scious·ness** ['kɒnʃəsnɪs] N **1** *(awareness)*: **consciousness (of)** consapevolezza *or* coscienza (di) **2** *(Med)* conoscenza; **to lose/regain consciousness** perdere/riprendere conoscenza *or* i sensi; **I lost consciousness** ho perso conoscenza

con·script [*n* 'kɒnskrɪpt; *vb* kən'skrɪpt] N coscritto
■ VT arruolare, chiamare alle armi

con·scrip·tion [kən'skrɪpʃən] N arruolamento (obbligatorio), coscrizione *f*

con·se·crate ['kɒnsɪˌkreɪt] VT consacrare

con·se·cra·tion [ˌkɒnsɪ'kreɪʃən] N consacrazione *f*

con·secu·tive [kən'sɛkjʊtɪv] ADJ consecutivo(-a); **consecutive clause** *(Gram)* proposizione *f* consecutiva; **on three consecutive occasions** tre volte di fila, tre volte consecutive

con·sen·sual [kən'sɛnsjʊəl] ADJ **1** *(approach, view, decision)* basato sul consenso **2** *(Law: sex)* consensuale

con·sen·sus [kən'sɛnsəs] N consenso; **the consensus of opinion** l'opinione *f* unanime *or* comune

con·sent [kən'sɛnt] N consenso, benestare *m*; **by mutual consent** per mutuo consenso; **by common consent** di comune accordo; **age of consent** età legale per avere rapporti sessuali
■ VI: **to consent (to sth/to do sth)** acconsentire (a qc/a fare qc)

consenting adults [kən'sɛntɪŋ'ædʌlts] NPL adulti *mpl* consenzienti

◎ **con·se·quence** ['kɒnsɪkwəns] N **1** *(result)* conseguenza, risultato; **in consequence** di conseguenza **2** *(importance)* importanza; **of consequence** importante; **it is of no consequence** non ha nessuna importanza

con·se·quent ['kɒnsɪkwənt] ADJ conseguente

con·se·quen·tial [ˌkɒnsɪ'kwɛnʃəl] ADJ *(frm)* **1** *(important)* importante **2** *(consequent)* conseguente

con·se·quent·ly ['kɒnsɪkwəntlɪ] ADV di conseguenza, dunque, quindi

con·ser·va·tion [ˌkɒnsə'veɪʃən] N conservazione *f*, tutela; *(of nature)* tutela dell'ambiente; **it's a report on the conservation of rain forests** è una relazione sulla tutela delle foreste pluviali; **people are conscious of the need for conservation** la gente è conscia di quanto sia importante la tutela dell'ambiente; **conservation project** progetto di salvaguardia ambientale; **energy conservation** risparmio energetico

con·ser·va·tion·ist [ˌkɒnsə'veɪʃənɪst] N ambientalista *m/f*

con·serva·tism [kən'sɜːvətɪzəm] N conservatorismo

Con·serva·tive [kən'sɜːvətɪv] ADJ, N *(Brit Pol)* conservatore(-trice); **he votes Conservative** vota per i conservatori

◎ **con·serva·tive** [kən'sɜːvətɪv] ADJ *(Pol, person, style)* conservatore(-trice); *(estimate, guess)* prudente
■ N conservatore(-trice)

Conservative Party N *(Brit)*: **the Conservative Party** il partito conservatore

con·serva·tory [kən'sɜːvətrɪ] N *(greenhouse)* serra; *(Mus)* conservatorio

con·serve [kən'sɜːv] VT conservare; **to conserve one's strength** risparmiare le forze
■ N conserva di frutta

◎ **con·sid·er** [kən'sɪdə[r]] VT **1** *(think about: problem, possibility)* considerare, prendere in considerazione; *(question, matter, subject)* valutare, studiare; **to consider doing sth** considerare la possibilità di fare qc; **all things considered** tutto sommato *or* considerato; **it is my considered opinion that ...** sono fermamente convinto che...; **I'm considering the idea** sto

Cc

prendendo in considerazione l'idea **2** (*take into account*) considerare, tener conto di **3** (*be of the opinion*) ritenere, considerare; **he considers it a waste of time** la ritiene una perdita di tempo; **his teacher considers him too lazy to pass the exams** il suo insegnante lo considera *or* lo ritiene troppo pigro per superare gli esami; **consider yourself lucky** puoi dirti fortunato

◎**con·sid·er·able** [kən'sɪdərəbl] ADJ considerevole, notevole; **to a considerable extent** in gran parte, in misura notevole

con·sid·er·ably [kən'sɪdərəblɪ] ADV notevolmente, decisamente

con·sid·er·ate [kən'sɪdərɪt] ADJ riguardoso(-a), premuroso(-a)

con·sid·er·ate·ly [kən'sɪdərɪtlɪ] ADV premurosamente

◎**con·sid·era·tion** [kən,sɪdə'reɪʃən] N **1** NO PL (*thought, reflection*) considerazione *f*; **to be under consideration** essere in esame; **after due consideration** dopo un attento esame; **to take sth into consideration** considerare qc, prendere qc in considerazione; **taking everything into consideration** tutto considerato *or* sommato **2** NO PL (*thoughtfulness*) attenzione *f*, premura; **out of consideration for** per riguardo a; **to show consideration for sb's feelings** avere riguardo per qn **3** (*factor*) elemento; **my first consideration is my family** il mio primo pensiero è per la mia famiglia; **his age is an important consideration** la sua età è un fattore importante; **it's of no consideration** non ha nessuna importanza **4** (*payment*) rimunerazione *f*, ricompensa; **for a consideration** dietro compenso

con·sid·ered [kən'sɪdəd] ADJ: **it is my considered opinion that ...** dopo lunga riflessione il mio parere è che...

◎**con·sid·er·ing** [kən'sɪdərɪŋ] PREP considerando, considerato(-a)

■ CONJ: **considering (that)** se si considera *or* tiene conto (che); **considering we were there for a month ...** dato che ci siamo rimasti per un mese...

■ ADV: **he did very well, considering** è stato molto bravo, tutto sommato

con·sign [kən'saɪn] VT **1 to consign sb/sth (to)** (*frm: banish*) relegare qn/qc (in); (*commit, entrust*) affidare qn/qc (a) **2** (*Comm: send*) consegnare, spedire

con·signee [,kɒnsaɪ'ni:] N consegnatario(-a), destinatario(-a)

con·sign·ment [kən'saɪnmənt] N (*of goods*) partita, consegna, spedizione *f*

consignment note N (*Comm*) nota di spedizione

con·sign·or [kən'saɪnəʳ] N mittente *m/f*

◎**con·sist** [kən'sɪst] VI: **to consist of** essere composto(-a) di, constare di; consistere di; **to consist in sth/in doing sth** consistere in qc/nel fare qc

con·sist·en·cy [kən'sɪstənsɪ] N **1** (*of person, action*) coerenza **2** (*density*) consistenza

◎**con·sist·ent** [kən'sɪstənt] ADJ **1** (*constant: results, action*) costante; (*: person*) costante **2** (*coherent: argument*) coerente, logico(-a); **to be consistent with** essere coerente con; **it is consistent with his views** è coerente con il suo modo di pensare; **consistent player** giocatore(-trice) dal rendimento costante

> DID YOU KNOW ...?
> **consistent** is not translated by the Italian word *consistente*

con·sist·ent·ly [kən'sɪstəntlɪ] ADV (*argue, behave, happen*) immancabilmente; **consistently high standards** degli standard sempre e comunque elevati

con·so·la·tion [,kɒnsə'leɪʃən] N consolazione *f*

consolation prize N premio di consolazione

con·sole¹ [kən'səʊl] VT: **to console (sb for sth)** consolare (qn per qc)

con·sole² ['kɒnsəʊl] N (*control panel*) console *f inv*, quadro di comando

con·soli·date [kən'sɒlɪ,deɪt] VT **1** (*position, influence*) consolidare **2** (*combine*) unire, fondere

con·soli·da·tion [kən,sɒlɪ'deɪʃən] N (*see vb*) consolidazione *f*; fusione *f*, unione *f*

con·sol·ing [kən'səʊlɪŋ] ADJ confortante, consolante, consolatorio(-a)

con·sol·ing·ly [kən'səʊlɪŋlɪ] ADV (*smile, speak*) in modo confortante

con·sols ['kɒnsɒlz] NPL (*Stock Exchange*) titoli *mpl* del debito consolidato

con·som·mé [kɒn'sɒmeɪ] N (*Culin*) consommé *m inv*, brodo ristretto

con·so·nant ['kɒnsənənt] N consonante *f*

con·so·nan·tal [,kɒnsə'næntl] ADJ consonantico(-a)

con·sort [*n* 'kɒnsɔ:t; *vb* kən'sɔ:t] N consorte *m/f*; **prince consort** principe *m* consorte

■ VI (*often pej*): **to consort with sb** frequentare qn

con·sor·tium [kən'sɔ:tɪəm] N (*pl* **consortia** [kən'sɔ:tɪə]) consorzio

con·spicu·ous [kən'spɪkjʊəs] ADJ (*person, behaviour*) che si fa notare; (*clothes*) vistoso(-a); (*sign, notice*) ben visibile; (*bravery, difference*) notevole, evidente; **a conspicuous lack of sth** una notevole mancanza di qc; **to make o.s. conspicuous** farsi notare; **I felt very conspicuous** sentivo tutti gli sguardi su di me; **to be conspicuous by one's absence** brillare per la propria assenza

con·spicu·ous·ly [kən'spɪkjʊəslɪ] ADV (*behave*) in modo da farsi notare; (*successful*) notevolmente; (*dressed*) vistosamente; **conspicuously absent** palesemente assente

con·spira·cy [kən'spɪrəsɪ] N cospirazione *f*, congiura

con·spira·tor [kən'spɪrətəʳ] N cospiratore(-trice)

con·spira·to·rial [kən,spɪrə'tɔ:rɪəl] ADJ cospiratorio(-a)

con·spire [kən'spaɪəʳ] VI **1** (*people*): **to conspire (with sb against sb/sth)** congiurare *or* cospirare (con qn contro qn/qc) **2** (*events*): **to conspire to do sth** contribuire a fare qc; **everything had conspired to make him happy** tutto aveva contribuito a renderlo felice

con·sta·ble ['kʌnstəbl] N (*Brit*: *also*: **police constable**) agente *m/f* (di polizia)

con·stabu·lary [kən'stæbjʊlərɪ] N polizia

con·stan·cy ['kɒnstənsɪ] N (*of friend, affection*) costanza

◎**con·stant** ['kɒnstənt] ADJ (*interruptions*) continuo(-a), incessante; (*use*) continuo(-a), costante; (*speed, temperature, rhythm*) costante; (*affection*) costante, stabile; (*friend, love*) fedele; **meat must be kept at a constant temperature** la carne deve essere tenuta a temperatura costante

■ N (*Math, Phys*) costante *f*

con·stant·ly ['kɒnstəntlɪ] ADV continuamente, costantemente

con·stel·la·tion [,kɒnstə'leɪʃən] N costellazione *f*

con·ster·na·tion [,kɒnstə'neɪʃən] N costernazione *f*, sgomento; **filled with consternation (at)** costernato(-a) (per)

con·sti·pate ['kɒnstɪ,peɪt] VT (*Med*) causare stitichezza a

con·sti·pat·ed ['kɒnstɪ,peɪtɪd] ADJ (*Med*) stitico(-a)

con·sti·pa·tion [ˌkɒnstɪ'peɪʃən] N (*Med*) stitichezza
con·stitu·en·cy [kən'stɪtjʊənsɪ] N (*district*) collegio elettorale; (*people*) elettori *mpl* (del collegio)

CONSTITUENCY

Con il termine **constituency** viene indicato sia il collegio elettorale che i suoi elettori. In Gran Bretagna ogni collegio elegge un rappresentante che i cittadini possono in seguito incontrare regolarmente in riunioni chiamate "surgeries" per sottoporgli problemi e questioni di interesse locale.

constituency party N sezione *f* locale (del partito)
con·stitu·ent [kən'stɪtjʊənt] N (*Pol: voter*) elettore(-trice); (*part*) ingrediente *m*, componente *m*
■ ADJ costitutivo(-a)
con·sti·tute ['kɒnstɪˌtju:t] VT costituire
◎ **con·sti·tu·tion** [ˌkɒnstɪ'tju:ʃən] N costituzione *f*

CONSTITUTION

A differenza di quella italiana e di quella statunitense la costituzione britannica non è contenuta in un unico atto scritto, ufficiale e solenne, ma è una costituzione non scritta, composta di varie carte (come la Magna Carta del 1215) e di una serie successiva di leggi, sentenze e consuetudini che formano il corpus costituzionale.

▷ www.psa.ac.uk/www/constitutions.htm

◎ **con·sti·tu·tion·al** [ˌkɒnstɪ'tju:ʃənl] ADJ costituzionale
con·sti·tu·tion·al·ity [ˌkɒnstɪˌtju:ʃə'nælɪtɪ] N costituzionalità
con·sti·tu·tion·al·ly [ˌkɒnstɪ'tju:ʃənəlɪ] ADV (*Pol*) costituzionalmente; (*by nature, inherently*) per natura
constitutional monarchy N monarchia costituzionale
con·strain [kən'streɪn] VT costringere
con·strained [kən'streɪnd] ADJ (*awkward*) forzato(-a); **to feel/be constrained to do sth** sentirsi/essere costretto(-a) a fare qc
con·straint [kən'streɪnt] N, NO PL (*compulsion*) costrizione *f*; (*restraint*) limitazione *f*; (*embarrassment*) imbarazzo, soggezione *f*
con·strict [kən'strɪkt] VT (*throat, waist, blood vessels*) stringere; (*movements*) impedire; (*freedom*) limitare
con·strict·ed [kən'strɪktɪd] ADJ (*movements*) limitato(-a); (*point of view*) ristretto(-a)
con·stric·tion [kən'strɪkʃən] N costrizione *f*; (*feeling*) oppressione *f*
con·struct [kən'strʌkt] VT costruire
◎ **con·struc·tion** [kən'strʌkʃən] N (*gen*) costruzione *f*; (*fig: interpretation*) interpretazione *f*; **under construction** in costruzione
construction industry N edilizia, industria edile
con·struc·tive [kən'strʌktɪv] ADJ costruttivo(-a)
constructive dismissal N (*Brit*) dimissioni *fpl* forzate; **to claim constructive dismissal** sostenere di essere stato(-a) costretto(-a) a licenziarsi
con·struc·tive·ly [kən'strʌktɪvlɪ] ADV costruttivamente
con·strue [kən'stru:] VT (*interpret*) interpretare

DID YOU KNOW ...?
construe is not translated by the Italian word *costruire*

con·sul ['kɒnsəl] N console *m*; **consul general** console generale
con·su·lar ['kɒnsjʊləʳ] ADJ consolare
con·su·late ['kɒnsjʊlɪt] N consolato
◎ **con·sult** [kən'sʌlt] VT: **to consult sb (about sth)** consultare qn (su *or* riguardo a qc)
■ VI: **to consult each other** consultarsi
con·sul·tan·cy [kən'sʌltənsɪ] N consulenza
■ ADJ (*fees, business*) di consulenza
consultancy agreement N contratto di consulenza
consultancy fee N onorario di consulenza
◎ **con·sult·ant** [kən'sʌltənt] N consulente *m/f*; (*Brit*) (*Med*) specialista *m/f*; **consultant engineer** ingegnere *m* consulente; **consultant paediatrician** specialista in pediatria; **legal/management consultant** consulente legale/gestionale; **consultant to the government** consulente del governo
con·sul·ta·tion [ˌkɒnsəl'teɪʃən] N consultazione *f*; (*Med, Law*) consulto; **in consultation with** consultandosi con
con·sul·ta·tive [kən'sʌltətɪv] ADJ (*document*) di consulenza; **in a consultative capacity** in veste di consulente
con·sult·ing [kən'sʌltɪŋ] ADJ consulente
consulting hours NPL (*Med*) orario *msg* di visita
consulting room N (*Brit Med*) ambulatorio, studio medico
con·sume [kən'sju:m] VT (*gen*) consumare; **to be consumed with** (*envy*) essere roso(-a) da; (*grief*) consumarsi di
◎ **con·sum·er** [kən'sju:məʳ] N consumatore(-trice); (*of electricity, gas etc*) utente *m/f*
consumer credit N credito al consumatore
consumer durables NPL beni *mpl* durevoli
consumer goods NPL beni *mpl* di consumo
con·sum·er·ism [kən'sju:məˌrɪzəm] N (*consumer protection*) tutela del consumatore; (*Econ*) consumismo; **they have embraced Western consumerism** hanno abbracciato il consumismo occidentale
consumer organization N organizzazione di consumatori
consumer protection N tutela dei consumatori
consumer society N società consumista *or* dei consumi
consumer watchdog N comitato di difesa dei consumatori
con·sum·ing [kən'sju:mɪŋ] ADJ (*passion, desire*) struggente
con·sum·mate [*adj* kən'sʌmɪt; *vb* 'kɒnsəˌmeɪt] ADJ consumato(-a), abile; **with consummate ease** con estrema facilità
■ VT (*marriage*) consumare
con·sum·ma·tion [ˌkɒnsə'meɪʃən] N (*of marriage*) consumazione *f*
con·sump·tion [kən'sʌmpʃən] N **1** (*of food, fuel*) consumo; **not fit for human consumption** non commestibile; **fuel consumption** consumo di carburante **2** (*old: tuberculosis*) consunzione *f*
con·sump·tive [kən'sʌmptɪv] ADJ, N (*old*) tisico(-a)
cont., cont'd ABBR (= **continued**) segue
◎ **con·tact** ['kɒntækt] N (*gen*) contatto; (*person*) conoscenza, contatto; **to be in contact with sb/sth** essere in contatto con qn/qc; **I'm in contact with her** sono in contatto con lei; **to make contact with sb** mettersi in contatto con qn; **to lose contact (with sb)** perdere i contatti (con qn), perdere di vista qn;

Cc

business contacts contatti *mpl* d'affari
■ VT mettersi in contatto con, contattare

contact adhesive N adesivo istantaneo

contact breaker N (*Elec*) ruttore *m*

contact lens N (*pl* **-es**) lente *f* a contatto

con·ta·gion [kən'teɪdʒən] N (*Med, frm*) contagio

con·ta·gious [kən'teɪdʒəs] ADJ contagioso(-a), infettivo(-a)

con·ta·gious·ly [kən'teɪdʒəslɪ] ADV contagiosamente

◎ **con·tain** [kən'teɪn] VT contenere; (*fire, disease*) arginare; **to contain o.s.** contenersi

con·tain·er [kən'teɪnəʳ] N (*box, jug*) contenitore *m*, recipiente *m*; (*Comm: for transport, shipping*) container *m inv*
■ ADJ (*train, lorry, ship*) da container; (*dock, depot, transport*) per container

con·tain·eri·za·tion [kən,teɪnəraɪ'zeɪʃən] N containerizzazione *f*

con·tain·er·ize [kən'teɪnə,raɪz] VT mettere in container

con·tain·ment [kən'teɪnmənt] N contenimento

con·tami·nate [kən'tæmɪ,neɪt] VT contaminare

con·tami·na·tion [kən,tæmɪ'neɪʃən] N contaminazione *f*

cont'd ABBR = **cont.**

con·tem·plate ['kɒntɛm,pleɪt] VT (*gaze at, reflect upon*) contemplare; **to contemplate sth/doing sth** (*consider*) pensare a qc/di fare qc

con·tem·pla·tion [,kɒntɛm'pleɪʃən] N contemplazione *f*

con·tem·pla·tive [kən'tɛmplətɪv] ADJ contemplativo(-a)

con·tem·po·ra·neous [kən'tɛmpə'reɪnɪəs] ADJ (*frm*): **contemporaneous (with)** contemporaneo(-a) (a)

◎ **con·tem·po·rary** [kən'tɛmpərərɪ] ADJ contemporaneo(-a); (*design*) moderno(-a)
■ N contemporaneo(-a)

con·tempt [kən'tɛmpt] N disprezzo, disdegno; **to hold sth/sb in contempt** disprezzare qc/qn; **contempt of court** (*Law*) oltraggio alla Corte; **it's beneath contempt** è oltremodo vergognoso

con·tempt·ible [kən'tɛmptəbl] ADJ vergognoso(-a), spregevole

con·temp·tu·ous [kən'tɛmptjʊəs] ADJ (*person*): **contemptuous (of)** sprezzante (di); (*manner, gesture*) sprezzante, altezzoso(-a), sdegnoso(-a)

con·temp·tu·ous·ly [kən'tɛmptjʊəslɪ] ADV con disprezzo, sprezzantemente

con·tend [kən'tɛnd] VT: **to contend that** (*frm*) sostenere che, asserire che
■ VI (*fig*): **to contend (with sb) for sth** contendersi qc (con qn); **we have many problems to contend with** dobbiamo lottare contro molti problemi; **you'll have me to contend with** dovrai vedertela con me; **he has a lot to contend with** ha un sacco di guai

con·tend·er [kən'tɛndəʳ] N contendente *m/f*, concorrente *m/f*

◎ **con·tent¹** ['kɒntɛnt] N contenuto; **contents** NPL (*of box, case*) contenuto; **(table of) contents** (*of book*) indice *m*

con·tent² [kən'tɛnt] ADJ: **content (with)** contento(-a) *or* soddisfatto(-a) (di); **to be content to do sth** essere contento(-a) di fare qc
■ N contentezza; **to one's heart's content** quanto si ha voglia; **to eat and drink to one's heart content** mangiare e bere a sazietà
■ VT fare contento(-a), soddisfare, contentare; **to content o.s. with sth/with doing sth** accontentarsi di qc/di fare qc

con·tent·ed [kən'tɛntɪd] ADJ: **contented (with)** contento(-a) (di), soddisfatto(-a) (di)

con·tent·ed·ly [kən'tɛntɪdlɪ] ADV con soddisfazione

con·ten·tion [kən'tɛnʃən] N (*strife*) contesa, disputa; (*frm: assertion*) tesi *f inv*; **to be in contention** essere in lizza; **bone of contention** pomo della discordia

con·ten·tious [kən'tɛnʃəs] ADJ polemico(-a)

con·tent·ment [kən'tɛntmənt] N contentezza, soddisfazione *f*

content provider N (*Comput*) content provider *m inv*; *fornitore in Internet di testi, musica, immagini ecc.*

◎ **con·test** [*n* 'kɒntɛst; *vb* kən'tɛst] N (*struggle*) gara, lotta; (*Boxing, Wrestling*) incontro; (*competition*) gara, concorso; **beauty contest** concorso di bellezza; **fishing contest** gara di pesca; **he won the leadership contest by a large margin** ha vinto la lotta per la leadership con un largo margine
■ VT (*dispute: argument*) contestare; (*: right*) contestare, disputare; (*Law*) impugnare; (*compete for*) contendersi, disputare; (*: election, seat*) essere in lizza per

> DID YOU KNOW ...?
> **contest** is not translated by the Italian word *contesto*

con·test·ant [kən'tɛstənt] N (*in competition*) concorrente *m/f*; (*Sport*) contendente *m/f*, avversario(-a); **contestant for a title** aspirante *m/f* a un titolo

◎ **con·text** ['kɒntɛkst] N contesto; **in/out of context** nel/fuori dal contesto

con·tex·tual [kən'tɛkstjʊəl] ADJ contestuale

con·ti·nence ['kɒntɪnəns] N (*frm*) continenza

◎ **con·ti·nent** ['kɒntɪnənt] N **1** continente *m* **2** (*Brit*): **the Continent** l'Europa continentale; **on the Continent** in Europa

con·ti·nen·tal [,kɒntɪ'nɛntl] ADJ continentale; (*Brit: European*) europeo(-a), dell'Europa continentale
■ N (*Brit*) abitante *m/f* dell'Europa continentale

continental breakfast N colazione *f* (*senza cibi caldi*)

continental drift N deriva dei continenti

continental quilt N (*Brit*) piumino

con·tin·gen·cy [kən'tɪndʒənsɪ] N contingenza, evenienza, eventualità *f inv*; **in certain contingencies** in certi frangenti

contingency funds NPL fondi *mpl* di previdenza

contingency plan N misura *or* piano d'emergenza

con·tin·gent [kən'tɪndʒənt] (*frm*) ADJ: **to be contingent upon** dipendere da
■ N (*Mil*) contingente *m*; (*group*) gruppo

con·tin·ual [kən'tɪnjʊəl] ADJ continuo(-a)

con·tinu·al·ly [kən'tɪnjʊəlɪ] ADV continuamente, senza tregua, di continuo

con·tinu·ance [kən'tɪnjʊəns] N (*continuation*) continuazione *f*; (*duration*) durata

con·tinu·ation [kən,tɪnjʊ'eɪʃən] N continuazione *f*; (*resumption*) ripresa; (*of serial story*) seguito

◎ **con·tinue** [kən'tɪnju:] VT (*gen*): **to continue (doing** *or* **to do sth)** continuare (a fare qc); **she continued talking to her friend** ha continuato a parlare alla sua amica; (*start again*) riprendere, continuare; **we continued working after lunch** abbiamo ripreso a lavorare dopo pranzo; (*serial story*): **to be continued** continua; **continued on page 10** segue *or* continua a pagina 10
■ VI (*gen*) continuare; (*resume*) riprendere, continuare;

(*extend*) estendersi, proseguire; **to continue on one's way** continuare per la propria strada

con·tinu·ing edu·ca·tion [kən'tɪnju:ɪŋɛdjʊ'keɪʃən] N formazione *f* continua; (*Am*) corsi *mpl* di aggiornamento

con·ti·nu·ity [ˌkɒntɪ'nju:ɪtɪ] N continuità; (*Cine*) (ordine *m* della) sceneggiatura

continuity girl N (*Cine*) segretaria di produzione

continuity man N (*Cine*) segretario di produzione

con·tinu·ous [kən'tɪnjʊəs] ADJ continuo(-a), ininterrotto(-a); **continuous performance** (*Cine*) spettacolo continuato; **continuous stationery** (*Comput*) modulo continuo

con·tinu·ous·ly [kən'tɪnjʊəslɪ] ADV (*unceasingly*) in continuazione; (*uninterruptedly*) ininterrottamente

continuous performance N (*Cine*) spettacolo continuato

continuous stationery (*Comput*) N carta continua

con·tin·uum [kən'tɪnjʊəm] N (*frm*) continuum *m inv*

con·tort [kən'tɔ:t] VT contorcere

con·tor·tion [kən'tɔ:ʃən] N (*of acrobat*) contorsione *f*, contorcimento

con·tor·tion·ist [kən'tɔ:ʃənɪst] N contorsionista *m/f*

con·tour ['kɒntʊə'] N contorno, profilo; (*also:* **contour line**) curva di livello, isoipsa

contour map N carta a curve di livello

contour ploughing N aratura a girapoggio

contra·band ['kɒntrəˌbænd] N contrabbando
■ ADJ di contrabbando

contra·cep·tion [ˌkɒntrə'sɛpʃən] N contraccezione *f*

contra·cep·tive [ˌkɒntrə'sɛptɪv] ADJ contraccettivo(-a), anticoncezionale
■ N contraccettivo, anticoncezionale *m*

contraceptive pill N pillola anticoncezionale

◎ **con·tract** [*n, adj* 'kɒntrækt; *vb* kən'trækt] N contratto; **contract of employment** contratto di lavoro; **to enter into a contract with sb to do sth/for sth** stipulare un contratto con qn per fare qc/per qc; **to be under contract to do sth** aver stipulato un contratto per fare qc; **to put work out to contract** dare del lavoro in appalto, appaltare un lavoro; **by contract** per contratto; **there's a contract out for him** (*fig fam*) c'è una taglia su di lui
■ VT (*all senses*) contrarre; **to contract with sb to do sth** stipulare un contratto con qn per fare qc
■ VI (*muscles, lips*) contrarsi; (*metal*) restringersi; (*economy*) essere in fase di contrazione
■ ADJ (*date*) del contratto; (*price*) secondo contratto; (*work*) a contratto, in appalto
▸ **contract in** VI + ADV impegnarsi (con un contratto); (*Brit: into pension scheme*) *scegliere di pagare i contributi per una pensione*
▸ **contract out** VI + ADV: **to contract out (of)** ritirarsi (da); **to contract out of a pension scheme** (*Brit Admin*) cessare di pagare i contributi per una pensione

contract bridge N (*Cards*) bridge *m* contratto

con·trac·tile [kən'træktaɪl] ADJ contrattile

con·trac·tion [kən'trækʃən] N contrazione *f*; (*of metal*) restringimento

contract labour N manodopera a tempo determinato

con·trac·tor [kən'træktə'] N (*Constr*) appaltatore *m*, imprenditore *m*; (*Law*) contraente *m*

con·trac·tual [kən'træktʃʊəl] ADJ contrattuale

con·trac·tu·al·ly [kən'træktʃʊəlɪ] ADV contrattualmente

contra·dict [ˌkɒntrə'dɪkt] VT contraddire

contra·dic·tion [ˌkɒntrə'dɪkʃən] N contraddizione *f*; **to be in contradiction with** discordare con; **contradiction in terms** contraddizione (in termini)

contra·dic·tory [ˌkɒntrə'dɪktərɪ] ADJ contraddittorio(-a); **to be contradictory to** contraddire

contra·flow ['kɒntrəˌfləʊ] N *restringimento de carreggiata con veicoli provenienti in senso contrario*

contra·in·di·ca·tion [ˌkɒntrəˌɪndɪ'keɪʃən] N (*Med*) controindicazione *f*

con·tral·to [kən'træltəʊ] N contralto

con·trap·tion [kən'træpʃən] N (*fam pej*) aggeggio

con·tra·ri·ness [kən'trɛərɪnɪs] N testardaggine *f*, cocciutaggine *f*

con·tra·ri·wise [kən'trɛərɪˌwaɪz] ADV (*on the other hand*) d'altro canto, d'altra parte; (*in the opposite direction*) nella direzione opposta, nel senso opposto

con·tra·ry ['kɒntrərɪ; *adj b* kən'trɛərɪ] ADJ **1 contrary (to)** contrario(-a) (a), opposto(-a) (a); **contrary to nature** contro natura; **contrary to** contrariamente a; **contrary to what you may have heard, I am not resigning** contrariamente a quello che potete aver sentito, non mi dimetto; **contrary to what we thought** contrariamente a quanto pensavamo
2 (*self-willed*) difficile, cocciuto(-a), bisbetico(-a)
■ N contrario; **on the contrary** al contrario; **unless you hear to the contrary** salvo contrordine

◎ **con·trast** [*n* 'kɒntrɑ:st; *vb* kən'trɑ:st] N contrasto; **in contrast to** *or* **with** a differenza di, contrariamente a
■ VT: **to contrast (with)** mettere a confronto (con), opporre (a)
■ VI: **to contrast (with)** contrastare (con)

con·trast·ing [kən'trɑ:stɪŋ] ADJ contrastante, di contrasto; **a contrasting colour** un colore contrastante

con·tras·tive [kən'trɑ:stɪv] ADJ contrastivo(-a)

contra·vene [ˌkɒntrə'vi:n] VT (*frm*) contravvenire a

contra·ven·tion [ˌkɒntrə'vɛnʃən] N: **contravention (of)** (*frm*) contravvenzione *f* (a), infrazione *f* (di)

con·tre·temps ['kɒntrəˌtɒŋ] N contrattempo

◎ **con·trib·ute** [kən'trɪbju:t] VT (*sum of money*) offrire, donare, contribuire con; (*help*) offrire; **to contribute an article to a newspaper** contribuire ad un giornale con un articolo
■ VI: **to contribute to** (*charity, collection, success*) contribuire a; (*discussion*) partecipare a; (*newspaper*) collaborare a *or* con, scrivere per; (*Admin*) pagare i contributi per; **everyone contributed to the success of the play** tutti hanno contribuito al successo della commedia; **she contributed £10 to the collection** ha contribuito alla colletta con dieci sterline; **he didn't contribute to the discussion** non ha partecipato alla discussione

◎ **con·tri·bu·tion** [ˌkɒntrɪ'bju:ʃən] N (*money, goods*) contributo, offerta, donazione *f*; (*help, assistance*) contributo, contribuzione *f*; (*Brit: payment*) contributi *mpl*; (*article, story*) contributo, collaborazione; (*in discussion*) intervento

con·tribu·tor [kən'trɪbjʊtə'] N (*of money*) donatore(-trice); (*to journal, newspaper*) collaboratore(-trice)

con·tribu·tory [kən'trɪbjʊtərɪ] ADJ (*cause*) che contribuisce; **it was a contributory factor in ...** quello ha contribuito a...

contributory negligence N (*Law*) concorso di colpa

contributory pension scheme N (*Brit*) *pensionamento finanziato da lavoratore e datore di lavoro*

Cc

con·trite ['kɒntraɪt] ADJ mortificato(-a); (*Rel*) contrito(-a)
con·trite·ly [kən'traɪtlɪ] ADV compuntamente
con·tri·tion [kən'trɪʃən] N (*see adj*) mortificazione *f*; contrizione *f*
con·triv·ance [kən'traɪvəns] N (*machine, device*) congegno; (*scheme*) espediente *m*, stratagemma *m*
con·trive [kən'traɪv] VT (*plan, scheme*) inventare, escogitare; **to contrive a means of doing sth** escogitare un sistema per fare qc; **to contrive to do sth** trovare un modo per fare qc
con·trived [kən'traɪvd] ADJ innaturale, forzato(-a)
◎ **con·trol** [kən'trəʊl] N **1** NO PL (*gen*) controllo; (*of traffic*) regolamentazione *f*; (*of pests*) eliminazione *f*; **the control of cancer** la lotta contro il cancro; **they have no control over their son** non hanno alcuna autorità sul figlio; **to keep sth/sb under control** tenere qc/qn sotto controllo; **to lose control of sth** perdere il controllo di qc; **to lose control of o.s.** perdere il controllo di sé; **he always seems to be in control** non perde mai il controllo della situazione; **to be in** *or* **keep control of** tenere sotto controllo; **she can't keep control of the class** non riesce a tenere la classe sotto controllo; **to take control of** assumere il controllo di; **to bring a fire under control** arginare *or* circoscrivere un incendio; **everything is under control** tutto è sotto controllo; **the car went out of control** la macchina non rispondeva più ai comandi; **to be out of control** essere scatenato(-a); **the class was quite out of control** la classe era in subbuglio; **due to circumstances beyond our control** per circostanze indipendenti dalla nostra volontà; **who is in control?** chi è il responsabile? **2** (*Tech, TV, Radio*): **the controls** i comandi; **to take over the controls** prendere i comandi **3 wage/price controls** NPL (*restrictions*) limitazione *f* dei salari/prezzi **4** (*in experiment*) gruppo di controllo
■ VT (*check*) controllare; (*traffic*) dirigere, regolare; (*operation etc*) dirigere; (*company*) avere controllo di; (*crowd*) tenere sotto controllo; (*disease, fire*) arginare, limitare; (*emotions*) controllare, frenare, dominare; **to control o.s.** controllarsi; **please control yourself, everyone's looking at us** per favore, controllati, tutti ci guardano; **he can't control the class** non riesce a tenere la classe sotto controllo
control freak N (*fam*): **to be control freak** voler avere sempre tutto sotto controllo
control group N (*Med, Psych etc*) gruppo di controllo
control key N (*Comput*) tasto di controllo
con·trolled [kən'trəʊld] ADJ **1** (*emotion*) contenuto(-a); **she was very controlled** era padrona di sé **2** (*Econ*): **controlled economy** economia controllata
con·trol·ler [kən'trəʊlə^r] N controllore *m*
con·trol·ling [kən'trəʊlɪŋ] ADJ (*factor*) dominante
controlling interest N (*Comm*) maggioranza delle azioni
control panel N (*on aircraft, ship, TV*) quadro dei comandi
control point N punto di controllo
control room N (*Naut, Mil*) sala di comando; (*Radio, TV*) sala di regia
control tower N (*Aer*) torre *f* di controllo
control unit N (*Comput*) unità *f inv* di controllo
◎ **con·tro·ver·sial** [ˌkɒntrə'vɜːʃəl] ADJ (*subject, speech, decision, book*) controverso(-a), discusso(-a), che suscita polemiche; (*person*) discusso(-a), polemico(-a); **euthanasia is a controversial subject** l'eutanasia è un argomento controverso
◎ **con·tro·ver·sy** [kən'trɒvəsɪ] N controversia, polemica; **it has caused a lot of controversy** ha causato molte polemiche
con·tu·sion [kən'tjuːʒən] N (*Med*) contusione *f*
co·nun·drum [kə'nʌndrəm] N indovinello
con·ur·ba·tion [ˌkɒnɜː'beɪʃən] N conurbazione *f*
con·va·lesce [ˌkɒnvə'lɛs] VI fare la convalescenza, rimettersi
con·va·les·cence [ˌkɒnvə'lɛsəns] N convalescenza
con·va·les·cent [ˌkɒnvə'lɛsənt] ADJ, N convalescente (*m/f*); **convalescent home** convalescenziario
con·vec·tion [kən'vɛkʃən] N convezione *f*
convection currents NPL correnti *fpl* convettive
con·vec·tor [kən'vɛktə^r] N (*also:* **convector heater, convection heater**) convettore *m*
con·vene [kən'viːn] VT (*people*) convocare; (*meeting*) indire, convocare
■ VI riunirsi, adunarsi, convenire
con·ven·er [kən'viːnə^r] N (*esp Brit*) presidente *m* (*di commissione etc*)
con·veni·ence [kən'viːnɪəns] N **1** (*of house, plan, person*) comodità; **at your earliest convenience** (*Comm*) appena possibile; **at your convenience** a suo comodo **2 conveniences** NPL (*amenities: of house*) comodità *fpl*; **all modern conveniences** (*Brit*): **all mod cons** tutte le comodità moderne **3** (*frm: toilet*) gabinetto
convenience foods NPL cibi *mpl* precotti
convenience store N *negozio di generi alimentari e di consumo che rimane aperto fino a tarda ora*
con·veni·ent [kən'viːnɪənt] ADJ (*tool, size, place etc*) comodo(-a); (*event, time, occasion*) adatto(-a), opportuno(-a); **the house is convenient for the shops** la casa è vicina ai *or* comoda per i negozi; **it is more convenient to eat in the kitchen** è più comodo mangiare in cucina; **if it is convenient to you** se per lei va bene, se non la incomoda; **would tomorrow be convenient?** andrebbe bene domani?; **is it convenient to call tomorrow?** potrei passare domani?; **it's not a convenient time for me** non sono libero a quell'ora
con·veni·ent·ly [kən'viːnɪəntlɪ] ADV (*happen*) a proposito; (*situated*) in una posizione comoda; **very conveniently he arrived late** (*luckily*) è stata una fortuna che sia arrivato in ritardo
con·vent ['kɒnvənt] N convento (di suore)
◎ **con·ven·tion** [kən'vɛnʃən] N (*custom, agreement*) convenzione *f*; (*meeting*) congresso, convegno; **the journalists' annual convention** il convegno annuale dei giornalisti; **a social convention** una convenzione sociale
◎ **con·ven·tion·al** [kən'vɛnʃənl] ADJ (*person, style, weapons*) convenzionale; (*methods*) tradizionale; **conventional weapons** armi *fpl* convenzionali; **my parents are very conventional** i miei genitori sono molto tradizionalisti
con·ven·tion·al·ly [kən'vɛnʃənlɪ] ADV (*dress, behave*) convenzionalmente
convent school N scuola retta da suore
con·verge [kən'vɜːdʒ] VI: **to converge (on)** convergere (su)
con·ver·gence [kən'vɜːdʒəns] N convergenza
con·ver·gent [kən'vɜːdʒənt], **con·ver·ging** [kən'vɜːdʒɪŋ] ADJ convergente
con·ver·sant [kən'vɜːsənt] ADJ: **to be conversant**

with (*car engines, machinery*) essere pratico(-a) di; (*facts*) essere al corrente di; (*language, subject*) avere una buona conoscenza di

◎ **con·ver·sa·tion** [ˌkɒnvəˈseɪʃən] N conversazione *f*; **in conversation with** a colloquio con; **to have a conversation with sb** conversare con qn, parlare con qn; **we had a long conversation** abbiamo fatto una lunga conversazione; **what was your conversation about?** di che cosa parlavate?

con·ver·sa·tion·al [ˌkɒnvəˈseɪʃənl] ADJ (*style, tone*) colloquiale; (*Comput*) conversazionale

con·ver·sa·tion·al·ist [ˌkɒnvəˈseɪʃnəlɪst] N conversatore(-trice)

con·ver·sa·tion·al·ly [ˌkɒnvəˈseɪʃnəlɪ] ADV: **"lovely day", he said conversationally** "bella giornata", ha detto per fare conversazione

conversation mode N (*Comput*) modo conversazionale

conversation piece N (*antique, curiosity*) oggetto di conversazione

conversation stopper N: **that was a conversation stopper** (*fam*) quello ha lasciato tutti a bocca aperta

con·verse[1] [kənˈvɜːs] VI: **to converse (with sb about sth)** (*frm*) conversare (con qn su *or* di qc)

con·verse[2] [ˈkɒnvɜːs] N inverso, contrario, opposto; (*Math*) opposto
■ ADJ opposto(-a), contrario(-a)

con·verse·ly [kɒnˈvɜːslɪ] ADV al contrario, per contro

con·ver·sion [kənˈvɜːʃən] N (*gen, Rel*) conversione *f*; (*Brit: of house*) trasformazione *f*, rimodernamento; (*Rugby, Am Ftbl*) trasformazione

conversion table N tavola *or* tabella di conversione

◎ **con·vert** [*n* ˈkɒnvɜːt; *vb* kənˈvɜːt] N convertito(-a)
■ VT **1** (*Rel*): **to convert (to)** convertire a **2** **to convert (to, into)** (*gen*) convertire (in); (*house*) trasformare (in), convertire (in); **we've converted the loft into a bedroom** abbiamo trasformato la soffitta in una camera da letto **3** (*Rugby, Am Ftbl*) trasformare

con·ver·ter [kənˈvɜːtəʳ] N (*Elec*) convertitore *m*

con·vert·ibil·ity [kənˌvɜːtəˈbɪlɪtɪ] N convertibilità

con·vert·ible [kənˈvɜːtəbl] ADJ (*currency*) convertibile; **convertible settee** divano letto
■ N (*car*) (auto *f inv*) decappottabile *f*

con·vex [ˈkɒnˈvɛks] ADJ convesso(-a)

con·vey [kənˈveɪ] VT (*goods, passengers*) trasportare; (*subj: pipeline*) convogliare; (*thanks, congratulations, sound, order*) trasmettere; (*meaning, ideas*) comunicare, esprimere; **to convey to sb that** comunicare a qn che; **he did not convey the information to his parents** non ha riferito il messaggio ai suoi genitori; **words cannot convey ...** le parole non possono esprimere...; **the name conveys nothing to me** il nome non mi dice niente; **the picture conveys a feeling of tranquillity** il quadro trasmette un senso di tranquillità

con·vey·ance [kənˈveɪəns] N (*of goods*) trasporto; (*vehicle*) mezzo di trasporto

con·vey·anc·ing [kənˈveɪənsɪŋ] N (*Law*) redazione *f* di transazioni di proprietà

con·vey·or [kənˈveɪəʳ] N (*Law*) concedente *m/f*

conveyor belt N (*Industry*) nastro trasportatore

◎ **con·vict** [*n* ˈkɒnvɪkt; *vb* kənˈvɪkt] N carcerato(-a)
■ VT: **to convict (of)** riconoscere colpevole (di), dichiarare colpevole (di); **convicted murderer** persona riconosciuta colpevole di omicidio; **he was convicted of the murder** è stato dichiarato colpevole di omicidio

◎ **con·vic·tion** [kənˈvɪkʃən] N **1** (*belief*) convinzione *f*; **it is my conviction that** sono convinto che; **to carry conviction** essere convincente; **she spoke with great conviction** ha parlato con grande convinzione **2** (*Law*) condanna; **he has three previous convictions for robbery** ha tre precedenti condanne per furto

◎ **con·vince** [kənˈvɪns] VT: **to convince sb (of sth/that)** convincere qn (di qc/che), persuadere qn (di qc/che)

con·vinc·ing [kənˈvɪnsɪŋ] ADJ (*gen*) convincente; (*win*) netto(-a)

con·vinc·ing·ly [kənˈvɪnsɪŋlɪ] ADV (*see adj*) in modo convincente; nettamente

con·viv·ial [kənˈvɪvɪəl] ADJ allegro(-a), gioviale

con·vivi·al·ly [kənˈvɪvɪəlɪ] ADV allegramente, giovialmente

con·vo·ca·tion [ˌkɒnvəˈkeɪʃən] N (*frm: summoning*) convocazione *f*; (*: assembly*) assemblea

con·vo·lut·ed [ˈkɒnvəluːtɪd] (*frm*) ADJ (*shape*) attorcigliato(-a), avvolto(-a); (*argument*) involuto(-a)

con·vo·lu·tion [ˌkɒnvəˈluːʃən] N (*frm, curve*) circonvoluzione *f*; (*Art*) voluta; (*fig: of argument*) involuzione *f*

con·vol·vu·lus [kənˈvɒlvjʊləs] N (*Bot*) convolvolo

con·voy [ˈkɒnvɔɪ] N convoglio; (*escort*) scorta; **in convoy** in convoglio; **under convoy** sotto scorta

con·vulse [kənˈvʌls] VT sconvolgere; **to be convulsed with pain/laughter** contorcersi dal dolore/dalle risa

con·vul·sion [kənˈvʌlʃən] N (*fit, seizure*) convulsione *f*; **in convulsions** (*fam: laughter*) piegato(-a) in due (dalle risate)

con·vul·sive [kənˈvʌlsɪv] ADJ (*movement, laughter*) convulso(-a); (*Med*) convulsivo(-a)

con·vul·sive·ly [kənˈvʌlsɪvlɪ] ADV convulsamente

coo [kuː] VI (*dove*) tubare
■ VT sussurrare dolcemente; **to coo over a baby** fare versetti a un bimbo

◎ **cook** [kʊk] N cuoco(-a); **head cook and bottlewasher** (*fig hum*) tuttofare *m/f*
■ VT **1** cuocere, cucinare; (*meal*) preparare; **she's cooking lunch** sta preparando il pranzo; **shall I cook you an omelette?** ti cucino *or* ti faccio un'omelette?; **the chicken isn't cooked** il pollo non è cotto; **to cook sb's goose** (*fig fam*) rompere le uova nel paniere a qn; **to cook one's own goose** (*fig fam*) darsi la zappa sui piedi **2** (*fam: falsify: accounts*) falsificare, alterare; **to cook the books** falsificare i libri contabili
■ VI (*food*) cuocere; (*person*) cucinare; **I can't cook** non so cucinare; **what's cooking?** (*fig fam*) cosa bolle in pentola?
▸ **cook up** VT + ADV (*fam: excuse, story*) inventare

cook·book [ˈkʊkˌbʊk] N (*Am*) = **cookery book**

cook·er [ˈkʊkəʳ] N (*stove*) cucina (*elettrodomestico*); (*cooking apple*) mela da cuocere; **gas cooker** cucina a gas

cooker hood N cappa aspirante

cook·ery [ˈkʊkərɪ] N cucina (*attività*)
▷ www.cookeryonline.com
▷ www.foodreference.com

cook·ery book N, (*Brit*) libro di ricette

cook·house [ˈkʊkˌhaʊs] N (*esp Am*) cucina (da campo)

cookie [ˈkʊkɪ] N **1** (*Am: biscuit*) biscotto; **that's the way the cookie crumbles** purtroppo è così , così va il mondo **2** (*Comput*) cookie *m inv*

cookie cutter N (*Am*) stampo per biscotti
■ ADJ (*fig: person, house etc*) fatto(-a) con lo stampino

◎ **cook·ing** [ˈkʊkɪŋ] N cucina (*attività e cibo*); **boys are just as keen on cooking as girls are** anche ai ragazzi piace cucinare; **she loves your cooking** adora quello

Cc

che cucini tu; **French cooking** la cucina francese
■ ADJ (*apples, chocolate*) da cuocere; (*utensils, salt, foil*) da cucina

cook·out ['kʊk,aʊt] N (*Am*) pranzo cucinato all'aperto

◎ **cool** [ku:l] ADJ (*comp* **-er**, *superl* **-est**) (*gen*) fresco(-a); (*drink*) freddo(-a); (*dress*) fresco(-a), leggero(-a); (*calm*) calmo(-a); (*unenthusiastic, unfriendly*) freddo(-a); (*impertinent*) sfacciato(-a); **it's cool** (*weather*) fa fresco; **a cool top** una maglietta leggera; **to keep sth cool** *or* **in a cool place** tenere qc in fresco *or* al fresco; **to be cool towards sb** essere freddo(-a) con qn; **to keep cool** mantenersi fresco(-a); (*fig*) conservare la calma; **keep cool!** calma!; **play it cool!** fa' finta di niente!; **they think it's cool to do drugs** pensano che sia figo drogarsi; **to be as cool as a cucumber** (*fig*) essere imperturbabile, conservare il sangue freddo; **he's a pretty cool customer** (*fam*) ha un gran sangue freddo; (*pej*) ha una bella faccia tosta; **that was very cool of you!** (*fam*) che sangue freddo!; **we paid a cool £290,000 for that house** (*fam*) abbiamo pagato la bellezza di 290.000 sterline per quella casa
■ N: **in the cool of the evening** nella frescura serale; **to keep sth in the cool** tenere qc al fresco; **to keep one's cool** (*fam*) conservare la calma; **keep your cool!** calma!; **to lose one's cool** (*fam*) perdere la calma *or* le staffe
■ VT (*air*) rinfrescare, raffreddare; (*food*) raffreddare; (*engine*) far raffreddare; **cool it!** (*fam*) calmati!; **to cool one's heels** (*fam*) aspettare (a lungo)
■ VI (*air, liquid*) raffreddarsi
▸ **cool down** VI + ADV raffreddarsi; (*fig: person, situation*) calmarsi
■ VT + ADV far raffreddare; (*fig*) calmare
▸ **cool off** VI + ADV (*become less angry*) calmarsi; (*lose enthusiasm, become less affectionate*) diventare più freddo(-a)

cool·ant ['ku:lənt] N (*Tech*) (liquido) refrigerante *m*

cool box N borsa termica

cool·er ['ku:lə^r] N (*for food*) ghiacciaia; **to send sb to the cooler** (*fam: prison*) mettere qn al fresco

cool·ing ['ku:lɪŋ] ADJ rinfrescante; **cooling fan** (*Aut*) ventilatore *m* di raffreddamento

cooling-off period [,ku:lɪŋ'ɒf,pɪərɪəd] N (*Industry*) periodo di tregua sindacale

cooling system N (*Aut*) impianto di raffreddamento

cooling tower N torre *f* di raffreddamento *or* refrigerazione

cool·ly ['ku:lɪ] ADV (*calmly*) con padronanza di sé; (*audaciously*) come se niente fosse; (*unenthusiastically*) freddamente

cool·ness ['ku:lnɪs] N (*of air, weather*) frescura, fresco; (*of drink*) freschezza; (*calmness*) calma, controllo, sangue *m* freddo; (*of welcome*) freddezza; (*impudence*) sfacciataggine

coop [ku:p] N stia
▸ **coop up** VT + ADV (*fig*) rinchiudere

co-op ['kəʊ'ɒp] N ABBR (= **cooperative (society)**) coop *f inv*

◎ **co·oper·ate** [kəʊ'ɒpə,reɪt] VI: **to cooperate (with sb in *or* on sth/to do sth)** cooperare (con qn in qc/per fare qc), collaborare (con qn in qc/per fare qc); **will he cooperate?** sarà disposto a collaborare?

co·opera·tion [kəʊ,ɒpə'reɪʃən] N cooperazione *f*, collaborazione *f*

co·opera·tive [kəʊ'ɒpərətɪv] ADJ **1** (*person*) disposto(-a) a collaborare; **you're not very cooperative!** non sei di grande aiuto! **2** (*farm etc*) cooperativo(-a)
■ N cooperativa

co·opera·tive·ly [kəʊ'ɒpərətɪvlɪ] ADV (*jointly*) in cooperazione; (*obligingly*) con spirito di cooperazione

co-operative society N cooperativa

co·opt [kəʊ'ɒpt] VT: **to coopt sb onto/into sth** cooptare qn per qc

co·or·di·nate [*n* kəʊ'ɔ:dnɪt; *vb* kəʊ'ɔ:dɪ,neɪt] N (*Math*) coordinata; **coordinates** NPL (*clothes*) coordinati *mpl*
■ VT coordinare

co·or·di·na·tion [kəʊ,ɔ:dɪ'neɪʃən] N coordinazione *f*

co·or·di·na·tor [kəʊ'ɔ:dɪ,neɪtə^r] N coordinatore(-trice)

coot [ku:t] N (*Zool*) folaga

co-ownership [,kəʊ'əʊnəʃɪp] N comproprietà *f inv*

cop [kɒp] (*fam*) N **1** (*policeman*) poliziotto(-a); **to play at cops and robbers** giocare a guardie e ladri **2 it's not much cop** (*Brit*) non è un granché
■ VT **1 to cop it** buscarle **2** (*something unexpected, unpleasant*) beccare, beccarsi
▸ **cop out** VI + ADV (*fam*) piantare tutto; **to cop out of sth** tirarsi indietro da qc

◎ **cope** [kəʊp] VI farcela; **to cope with** (*task, child*) farcela con; (*situation, difficulties, problems: tackle*) affrontare, far fronte a; (*: solve*) risolvere; **she's got a lot of problems to cope with** ha molti problemi da affrontare; **he's coping pretty well** se la cava abbastanza bene; **it was hard, but we coped** è stato difficile ma ce l'abbiamo fatta; **leave it to me, I'll cope** lascia stare, ci penso io

Co·pen·ha·gen [,kəʊpn'heɪgən] N Copenhagen *f*

Co·per·ni·cus [kə'pɜ:nɪkəs] N Copernico

copi·er ['kɒpɪə^r] N (*also:* **photocopier**) (foto)copiatrice *f*

co-pilot ['kəʊ'paɪlət] N secondo pilota *m/f*, copilota *m/f*

co·pi·ous ['kəʊpɪəs] ADJ (*tears*) copioso(-a); (*harvest*) abbondante, copioso(-a); (*notes, supply*) abbondante

co·pi·ous·ly ['kəʊpɪəslɪ] ADV (*all senses*) abbondantemente, copiosamente

co·pla·nar [kəʊ'pleɪnə] ADJ (*Geom: points, lines*) complanare

cop·per ['kɒpə^r] N **1** rame *m*; (*coin*) monetina; **coppers** NPL spiccioli *mpl* **2** (*Brit fam: police*) poliziotto(-a); **our friendly neighbourhood copper** il nostro cordiale poliziotto di quartiere
■ ADJ (*wire, kettle*) di rame; (*colour*) (color) rame *inv*, ramato(-a); **copper bracelet** braccialetto di rame

copper beech N faggio rosso

copper chloride N cloruro rameico

copper-coloured ['kɒpə,kʌləd], **cop·pery** ['kɒpərɪ] ADJ (color) rame *inv*, ramato(-a)

copper·plate ['kɒpə,pleɪt] N (*for engraving*) lastra di rame per incisione; (*also:* **copperplate handwriting**) calligrafia chiara e regolare

cop·pice ['kɒpɪs], **copse** [kɒps] N bosco ceduo

cop·ra ['kɒprə] N copra

copu·late ['kɒpjʊleɪt] VI accoppiarsi

copu·la·tion [,kɒpjʊ'leɪʃən] N copula, accoppiamento

copu·la·tive ['kɒpjʊlətɪv] ADJ copulativo(-a)

◎ **copy** ['kɒpɪ] N **1** (*gen*) copia; (*book etc*) esemplare *m*; (*of painting*) copia, riproduzione *f*; **rough/fair copy** brutta/bella (copia) **2** (*material: for printing*) materiale *m*, testo; **to make good copy** (*story, scandal*) fare notizia
■ VT (*imitate*) imitare; (*make copy of, cheat*) copiare; **he copied in the exam** all'esame ha copiato
▸ **copy out** VT + ADV ricopiare, trascrivere

copy·book ['kɒpɪ,bʊk] N quaderno; **to blot one's copybook** (*fig*) rovinarsi la reputazione

copy·cat [ˈkɒpɪˌkæt] N (*pej*) copione(-a)
copy·ing [ˈkɒpɪɪŋ] ADJ: **copying ink** inchiostro copiativo
copy·right [ˈkɒpɪˌraɪt] N diritti *mpl* d'autore, copyright *m inv*; **copyright reserved** tutti i diritti riservati
copy typist N dattilografa
copy·writer [ˈkɒpɪˌraɪtəʳ] N copywriter *m/f inv*, autore(-trice) di testi pubblicitari
co·quet·ry [ˈkəʊkɪtrɪ] N (*frm*) civetteria
co·quette [kəʊˈkɛt] N civetta; fig
co·quet·tish [kəʊˈkɛtɪʃ] ADJ (*smile, girl*) civettuolo(-a)
cor [kɔːʳ] EXCL (*Brit*: *also*: **cor blimey!**) perbacco!
cor·al [ˈkɒrəl] N corallo
■ ADJ (*island*) corallino(-a); **coral necklace** collana di corallo
coral reef N barriera corallina
Coral Sea N: **the Coral Sea** il mar dei Coralli
cor anglais [ˈkɔːrˈɑːŋleɪ] N (*Brit*) corno inglese
cord [kɔːd] N **1** (*gen*) corda; (*for pyjamas*) cintura; (*round parcel etc*) corda, spago; (*Elec*) filo **2** (*fabric*) velluto a coste; **cords** NPL (*trousers*) calzoni *mpl* di velluto a coste
cor·dial [ˈkɔːdɪəl] ADJ cordiale
■ N cordiale *m*
cor·di·al·ity [ˌkɔːdɪˈælɪtɪ] N cordialità
cor·di·al·ly [ˈkɔːdɪəlɪ] ADV cordialmente
cord·less [ˈkɔːdlɪs] ADJ (*iron*) senza filo; (*telephone*) cordless *inv*
cor·don [ˈkɔːdn] N cordone *m*
▸ **cordon off** VT + ADV fare cordone intorno a
cor·du·roy [ˈkɔːdəˌrɔɪ] N velluto a coste
CORE [kɔːʳ] N ABBR (*Am*) = *Congress of Racial Equality*
◎ **core** [kɔːʳ] N (*of fruit*) torsolo; (*of cable*) centro; (*of earth, nuclear reactor*) nucleo; (*Mineralogy: sample*) carota; (*of problem*) cuore *m*, nocciolo; **a hard core of resistance** uno zoccolo duro di resistenza; **rotten to the core** marcio(-a) fino al midollo; **English to the core** inglese in tutto e per tutto
■ VT (*fruit*) togliere il torsolo a
cor·er [ˈkɔːrəʳ] N cavatorsoli *m inv*
co-respondent [ˈkəʊrɪsˈpɒndənt] N (*Law*) correo(-a) (*di adulterio*)
Cor·fu [kɔːˈfuː] N Corfù *f*
co·ri·an·der [ˌkɒrɪˈændəʳ] N coriandolo (*pianta*)
Co·rin·thian [kəˈrɪnθɪən] ADJ corinzio(-a); **Corinthian order/capital** (*Archit*) ordine *m*/capitello corinzio
■ N corinzio(-a)
cork [kɔːk] N (*substance*) sughero; (*of bottle*) tappo (di sughero), turacciolo; **to pull the cork out of a bottle** stappare una bottiglia
■ VT (*bottle*: *also*: **cork up**) tappare
■ ADJ di sughero
cork·age [ˈkɔːkɪdʒ] N *somma che il cliente di un ristorante paga per farsi stappare bottiglie (di vino) comprate altrove*
corked [kɔːkt], **corky** [ˈkɔːkɪ] (*Am*) ADJ (*wine*) che sa di tappo
cork oak N quercia da sughero, sughera
cork·screw [ˈkɔːkˌskruː] N cavatappi *m inv*
corm [kɔːm] N (*Bot*) cormo
cor·mo·rant [ˈkɔːmərənt] N cormorano
corn¹ [kɔːn] N (*Brit*: *wheat*) grano, frumento; (*Am*: *maize*) granturco, mais *m*; **fields of corn** campi *mpl* di grano

> DID YOU KNOW ...?
> **corn** is not translated by the Italian word *corno*

corn² [kɔːn] N (*on foot*) callo
cor·nea [ˈkɔːnɪə] N (*Anat*) cornea
corned beef [ˈkɔːndˈbiːf] N carne *f* di manzo in scatola
◎ **cor·ner** [ˈkɔːnəʳ] N **1** angolo; (*of table*) spigolo, angolo; **it's just around the corner** (*also fig*) è proprio dietro l'angolo; (*: in time*) è molto vicino; **the shop on the corner** il negozio all'angolo; **to turn the corner** (*fig*) superare una crisi; **in odd corners** nei posti più strani *or* impensati; **the four corners of the world** i quattro angoli del mondo; **out of the corner of one's eye** con la coda dell'occhio; **to drive sb into a corner** (*fig*) mettere qn con le spalle al muro; **to be in a (tight) corner** (*fig*) essere nei pasticci *or* guai; **to cut a corner** (*Aut*) tagliare una curva; **to cut corners** (*fig*) prendere una scorciatoia **2** (*Ftbl*: *also*: **corner kick**) calcio d'angolo, corner *m inv*
■ VT **1** (*animal*) intrappolare; (*fugitive*) mettere in trappola; (*fig: person: catch to speak to*) bloccare **2** (*Comm: market*) monopolizzare; (*: goods*) accaparrare
■ VI (*Aut*) curvare, prendere una curva
■ ADJ (*seat, table*) d'angolo
corner cupboard N angoliera
corner flag N (*Ftbl*) bandierina d'angolo
corner kick N (*Ftbl*) calcio d'angolo, corner *m inv*
corner shop N ≈ negozio sotto casa
corner·stone [ˈkɔːnəˌstəʊn] N (*also fig*) pietra angolare
cor·net [ˈkɔːnɪt] N **1** (*Mus*) cornetta **2** (*Brit*: *ice cream*) cornetto, cono
cornet player N cornettista *m/f*
corn·field [ˈkɔːnˌfiːld] N (*Brit*) campo di grano; (*Am*) campo di granturco
corn·flakes [ˈkɔːnˌfleɪks] NPL fiocchi *mpl* di granturco, cornflakes *mpl*
corn·flour [ˈkɔːnˌflaʊəʳ] N (*Brit*) ≈ fecola di patate
corn·flower [ˈkɔːnˌflaʊəʳ] N fiordaliso
cor·nice [ˈkɔːnɪs] N (*Archit*) cornicione *m*; (*: interior*) cornice *f*
Cor·nish [ˈkɔːnɪʃ] ADJ della Cornovaglia
Cornish pasty N *sfoglia salata ripiena di carne e verdura*
corn oil N olio di mais
corn on the cob N pannocchia cotta
corn plaster N callifugo (*cerotto*)
corn·starch [ˈkɔːnˌstɑːtʃ] N (*Am*) = **cornflour**
cor·nu·co·pia [ˌkɔːnjʊˈkəʊpɪə] N (*frm*) grande abbondanza
Corn·wall [ˈkɔːnwəl] N Cornovaglia
corny [ˈkɔːnɪ] ADJ (*comp* **-ier**, *superl* **-iest**) (*fam: unoriginal*) banale; (*: sentimental*) sdolcinato(-a)
cor·ol·lary [kəˈrɒlərɪ] N corollario
coro·nary [ˈkɒrənərɪ] ADJ (*artery*) coronario(-a); (*disease*) coronarico(-a)
■ N (*heart attack*) infarto
coronary thrombosis N (*Med*) trombosi *f* coronarica
coro·na·tion [ˌkɒrəˈneɪʃən] N incoronazione *f*
coro·ner [ˈkɒrənəʳ] N coroner *m inv* (*pubblico ufficiale che indaga casi di morte sospetta*)
coro·net [ˈkɒrənɪt] N diadema *m*; (*of peer*) corona nobiliare
Corp. ABBR = **corporation**
cor·po·ral [ˈkɔːpərəl] N (*Mil*) caporalmaggiore *m*
corporal punishment N punizione *f* corporale
◎ **cor·po·rate** [ˈkɔːpərɪt] ADJ (*joint: action, effort*) congiunto(-a), unitario(-a); (*ownership, responsibility*) comune; (*Comm*) corporativo(-a), costituito(-a) (in corporazione); **corporate body** ente unico avente personalità giuridica
corporate hospitality N omaggi *mpl* aziendali (*consistenti in biglietti per spettacoli, cene ecc*)

Cc

corporate identity, corporate image N (*of organization*) immagine *f* dell'azienda
corporate raider N (*Fin*) scalatore(-trice)
◎**cor·po·ra·tion** [ˌkɔːpəˈreɪʃən] N (*Comm*) società *f inv*; (: *Am*) società di capitali; (*of town*) consiglio comunale
corporation tax N ≈ imposta sul reddito di persone giuridiche
cor·po·ra·tism [ˈkɔːpərətɪzəm] N corporativismo
cor·po·real [kɔːˈpɔːrɪəl] ADJ (*frm*) corporeo(-a)
corps [kɔːʳ] N (*pl* **corps** [kɔːz]) corpo; **press corps** ufficio *m* stampa *inv*
corps de bal·let [ˈkɔːdəˈbæleɪ] N corpo di ballo
corpse [kɔːps] N cadavere *m*
cor·pu·lence [ˈkɔːpjʊləns] N corpulenza
cor·pu·lent [ˈkɔːpjʊlənt] ADJ corpulento(-a)
cor·pus [ˈkɔːpəs] N (*pl* **corpora** [ˈkɔːpərə]) corpus *m*
Cor·pus Chris·ti [ˈkɔːpəsˈkrɪstɪ] N (*feast*) Corpus Domini *m*
cor·pus·cle [ˈkɔːpʌsl] N corpuscolo; (*of blood*) globulo (*sia rosso che bianco*)
cor·ral [kɒˈrɑːl] N recinto
◎**cor·rect** [kəˈrɛkt] ADJ (*answer*) corretto(-a), esatto(-a), giusto(-a); (*temperature, time, amount, forecast*) esatto(-a), giusto(-a); (*behaviour*) corretto(-a); (*dress*) adatto(-a); (*procedure*) giusto(-a), corretto(-a); **the correct answer** la risposta esatta; **that's correct** è giusto; **to be correct** avere ragione; **you're absolutely correct** ha proprio ragione
■VT (*mistake, work, proofs*) correggere; **I stand corrected** (ametto che) ho torto
correcting fluid [kəˌrektɪŋ-], **correction fluid** [kəˈrekʃən-] N bianchetto
cor·rec·tion [kəˈrɛkʃən] N correzione *f*
cor·rec·tive [kəˈrɛktɪv] ADJ (*surgery*) correttivo(-a)
■N correttivo
cor·rect·ly [kəˈrɛktlɪ] ADV (*accurately*) correttamente; (*properly*) correttamente, in modo adatto
cor·rect·ness [kəˈrɛktnɪs] N correttezza
cor·re·late [ˈkɒrɪˌleɪt] VT correlare, mettere in relazione *or* correlazione
■VI essere in correlazione; **to correlate with** essere in rapporto con
cor·re·la·tion [ˌkɒrɪˈleɪʃən] N correlazione *f*
cor·re·spond [ˌkɒrɪsˈpɒnd] VI **1** (*be in accordance*): **to correspond (with)** corrispondere a; **to correspond (to)** (*be equivalent*) corrispondere a, equivalere (a) **2** (*by letter*): **to correspond (with sb)** corrispondere (con qn), essere in corrispondenza (con qn); **they correspond** si scrivono
cor·re·spond·ence [ˌkɒrɪsˈpɒndəns] N **1** (*agreement*): **correspondence (between)** accordo (tra) **2** (*letters*) corrispondenza; (*collection of letters*) carteggio **3** (*Math*) corrispondenza
correspondence column N (*Press*) rubrica delle lettere (al direttore)
correspondence course N corso per corrispondenza
◎**cor·re·spond·ent** [ˌkɒrɪsˈpɒndənt] N corrispondente *m/f*; **foreign correspondent** (*Press*) corrispondente dall'estero
cor·re·spond·ing [ˌkɒrɪsˈpɒndɪŋ] ADJ corrispondente
cor·ri·dor [ˈkɒrɪdɔːʳ] N corridoio
cor·rie [ˈkɒrɪ] N (*Geol*) circo
cor·robo·rate [kəˈrɒbəˌreɪt] VT corroborare, confermare
cor·robo·ra·tion [kəˌrɒbəˈreɪʃən] N corroborazione *f*
cor·robo·ra·tive [kəˈrɒbərətɪv] ADJ comprovante
cor·rode [kəˈrəʊd] VT corrodere
■VI corrodersi
cor·ro·sion [kəˈrəʊʒən] N corrosione *f*
cor·ro·sive [kəˈrəʊzɪv] ADJ corrosivo(-a)
cor·ro·sive·ly [kəˈrəʊzɪvlɪ] ADV in modo distruttivo
cor·ro·sive·ness [kəˈrəʊsɪvnɪs] N corrosività
cor·ru·gat·ed [ˈkɒrəˌgeɪtɪd] ADJ ondulato(-a), increspato(-a)
corrugated iron N lamiera di ferro ondulata
cor·rupt [kəˈrʌpt] ADJ corrotto(-a); **corrupt practices** (*dishonesty, bribery*) pratiche *fpl* illecite; **corrupt officials** funzionari *mpl* corrotti
■VT corrompere
◎**cor·rup·tion** [kəˈrʌpʃən] N corruzione *f*
cor·rupt·ly [kəˈrʌptlɪ] ADV corrottamente
cor·set [ˈkɔːsɪt] N (*undergarment*) corsetto, busto; (*Med*) busto (ortopedico)
Cor·si·ca [ˈkɔːsɪkə] N Corsica
Cor·si·can [ˈkɔːsɪkən] ADJ, N corso(-a)
cor·tège [kɔːˈteɪʒ] N corteo
cor·tex [ˈkɔːtɛks] N (*pl* **cortices** [ˈkɔːtɪsiːz]) (*Anat, Bot*) corteccia
cor·ti·sone [ˈkɔːtɪˌzəʊn] N cortisone *m*
co·rus·cat·ing [ˌkɒrəˈskeɪtɪŋ] ADJ (*frm*) scintillante
c.o.s. ABBR (= **cash on shipment**) pagamento alla spedizione
co·secant [kəʊˈsiːkənt] N (*Math*) cosecante *f*
cosh [kɒʃ] (*Brit*) N manganello, randello
■VT (*fam*) pestare, manganellare
co·sig·na·tory [kəʊˈsɪgnətərɪ] N cofirmatario(-a)
co·si·ly [ˈkəʊzɪlɪ] ADV (*furnished*) in modo accogliente; **she was cosily wrapped up in her shawl** era avvolta in uno scialle bello caldo
co·sine [ˈkəʊsaɪn] N (*Math*) coseno
co·si·ness [ˈkəʊzɪnɪs] N (*of room*) comodità; (*of atmosphere*) intimità, calore *m*
cos lettuce [ˈkɒsˈlɛtɪs] N lattuga romana
cos·met·ic [kɒzˈmɛtɪk] ADJ (*preparation*) cosmetico(-a); (*surgery*) estetico(-a); (*fig: reforms*) solo apparente
■N cosmetico, prodotto di bellezza
cos·mic [ˈkɒzmɪk] ADJ cosmico(-a)
cos·mog·ra·pher [kɒzˈmɒgrəfəʳ] N cosmografo
cos·mog·ra·phy [kɒzˈmɒgrəfɪ] N cosmografia
cos·mol·ogy [kɒzˈmɒlədʒɪ] N cosmologia
cos·mo·naut [ˈkɒzməˌnɔːt] N cosmonauta *m/f*
cos·mo·poli·tan [ˌkɒzməˈpɒlɪtən] ADJ, N cosmopolita (*m/f*)
cos·mos [ˈkɒzmɒs] N cosmo
cos·set [ˈkɒsɪt] VT coccolare, vezzeggiare
◎**cost** [kɒst] N costo; (*Law*): **costs** spese *fpl*; **to be ordered to pay costs** (*Law*) essere condannato(-a) a pagare le spese; **cost, insurance and freight** (*Comm*) costo, assicurazione e nolo; **to bear the cost of** sostenere la spesa di; **at great cost** a caro prezzo; **at cost (price)** a prezzo di costo; **at any cost** *or* **at all costs** (*fig*) a tutti i costi, a ogni costo; **whatever the cost** (*fig*) costi quel che costi; **to my cost** (*fig*) a mie spese; **at the cost of his life/health** rimettendoci la vita/la salute
■VT **1** (*pt, pp* **cost**) costare; **how much does it cost?** quanto costa?, quanto viene?; **what will it cost to have it repaired?** quanto costerà farlo riparare?; **it cost him a lot of money** gli è costato un sacco di soldi; **it costs the earth** (*fam*) costa un occhio della testa; **it cost him his life/job** gli è costato la vita/il lavoro; **it cost me a great deal of time/effort** mi è costato molto tempo/molta fatica; **it costs nothing to be polite** essere educati non costa nulla; **whatever it**

costs (*fig*) costi quel che costi; **it costs £5/too much** costa 5 sterline/troppo **2** (*pt, pp* **costed**) (*Comm*) stabilire il prezzo di

cost accountant N analizzatore *m* dei costi

cost analysis N analisi *f inv* dei costi

co-star ['kəʊstɑː[r]] N co-protagonista *m/f*

Cos·ta Rica ['kɒstə'riːkə] N Costa Rica

Cos·ta Ri·can ['kɒstə'riːkən] ADJ, N costaricano(-a)

cost centre N (*also:* **costing centre**) centro di costo

cost control N controllo dei costi

cost-effective [ˌkɒstɪ'fɛktɪv] ADJ (*Comm*) redditizio(-a), efficiente; (*gen*) conveniente, economico(-a)

cost-effectiveness [ˌkɒstɪ'fɛktɪvnɪs] N convenienza

cos·ter·mon·ger ['kɒstəˌmʌŋgə[r]] N (*Brit*) (*old*) venditore(-trice) ambulante di frutta e verdura

cost·ing ['kɒstɪŋ] N (determinazione *f* dei) costi *mpl*

cost·li·ness ['kɒstlɪnɪs] N alto costo

cost·ly ['kɒstlɪ] ADJ costoso(-a), caro(-a)

cost of living N costo della vita

cost-of-living [ˌkɒstəv'lɪvɪŋ] ADJ: **cost-of-living allowance** indennità *f inv* di contingenza; **cost-of-living index** indice *m* del costo della vita

cost price N (*Brit*) prezzo all'ingrosso

cos·tume ['kɒstjuːm] N (*gen*) costume *m*; (*Brit: also*: **swimming costume**) costume da bagno

costume ball N ballo in maschera *or* in costume

costume drama N dramma *m* storico

costume jewellery N bigiotteria

cosy, (*Am*) **cozy** ['kəʊzɪ] ADJ (*comp* **-ier**, *superl* **-iest**) (*room, atmosphere*) accogliente, intimo(-a); (*clothes*) bello(-a) caldo(-a); **I'm very cosy here** sto proprio bene qui; **we had a cosy chat** abbiamo fatto due chiacchiere in confidenza

■ N (*tea cosy*) copriteiera *m inv*; (*egg cosy*) copriuovo

cot [kɒt] N (*Brit: child's*) lettino; (*Am: folding bed*) brandina

co·tan·gent [kəʊ'tændʒənt] N (*Math*) cotangente *f*

cot death N (*Brit*) *improvvisa e inspiegabile morte nel sonno di un neonato*

co·terie ['kəʊtərɪ] N (*frm*) gruppo ristretto

Cots·wolds ['kɒtsˌwəʊldz] NPL: **the Cotswolds** *zona collinare del Gloucestershire*

◎ **cot·tage** ['kɒtɪdʒ] N villetta, cottage *m inv*

cottage cheese N fiocchi *mpl* di latte

cottage hospital N ospedale *m* di campagna

cottage industry N *industria artigianale basata sul lavoro a cottimo*

cottage pie N *pasticcio di carne macinata e patate*

cot·ter ['kɒtə[r]] N (*Tech*): **cotter pin** copiglia

◎ **cot·ton** ['kɒtn] N (*cloth, plant*) cotone *m*; (*thread*) (filo di) cotone

■ ADJ (*shirt, dress*) di cotone

▶ **cotton on** VI + ADV (*fam*): **to cotton on (to sth)** afferrare (qc)

cotton buds NPL cotton fioc® *m inv*

cotton candy N (*Am*) zucchero filato

cotton grass N (*Bot*) erioforo

cotton industry N industria cotoniera

cotton mill N cotonificio

cotton wool N (*Brit*) cotone *m* idrofilo

coty·ledon [ˌkɒtɪ'liːdən] N (*Bot*) cotiledone *m*

couch [kaʊtʃ] N (*gen*) divano, sofà *m inv*; (*in doctor's surgery*) lettino; **he was sitting on the couch** era seduto sul divano

■ VT (*statement, request*) esprimere

cou·chette [kuː'ʃɛt] N cuccetta

couch potato N (*fam*) pigrone(-a) teledipendente

cou·gar ['kuːgə[r]] N coguaro

◎ **cough** [kɒf] N (*single instance*) colpo di tosse; (*illness*) tosse *f*; **I've got a cough** ho la tosse

■ VI tossire

▶ **cough up** VT + ADV (*blood, phlegm*) sputare; (*fig fam: money*) tirare fuori

■ VI + ADV (*fig fam*) cacciare i soldi

cough drop, cough sweet N pasticca per la tosse

cough mixture, cough syrup N sciroppo per la tosse

◎ **could** [kʊd] PT, COND *of* **can**

couldn't ['kʊdnt] PT, COND = **could not**

cou·loir ['kuːlwɑː] N canalone (di montagna) *m inv*

◎ **coun·cil** ['kaʊnsl] N consiglio; **council of war** consiglio di guerra; **city** *or* **town council** consiglio comunale; **he's on the council** fa parte del consiglio comunale; **the Security Council of the United Nations** il Consiglio di Sicurezza delle Nazioni Unite; **Council of Europe** Consiglio d'Europa

council estate N (*Brit*) complesso di case popolari

council flat N (*Brit*) casa popolare

council house N (*Brit*) casa popolare

council housing N (*Brit*) alloggi *mpl* popolari

council housing estate N (*Brit*) complesso di alloggi popolari

coun·cil·lor ['kaʊnsɪlə[r]] N consigliere *m*; **local councillor** consigliere *m/f* comunale

council meeting N seduta del consiglio

council tax N (*Brit*) imposta comunale sugli immobili

◎ **coun·sel** ['kaʊnsəl] N **1** (*advice*) consiglio, consultazione *f*; **to keep one's own counsel** tenere le proprie opinioni per sé **2** PL INV (*Law*) avvocato(-essa); **counsel for the defence/the prosecution** avvocato difensore/di parte civile; **Queen's (or King's) Counsel** avvocato della Corona

■ VT: **to counsel sth/sb to do sth** consigliare qc/a qn di fare qc; (*caution*) raccomandare qc/a qn di fare qc

coun·sel·ling, coun·sel·ing (*Am*) ['kaʊnsəlɪŋ] N terapia; **marriage counselling** terapia di coppia

coun·sel·lor, (*Am*) **coun·se·lor** ['kaʊnslə[r]] N (*adviser*) consulente *m/f*; (*Psych*) assistente *m/f* socio-psicologico(-a); (*Am: lawyer*) avvocato(-essa)

◎ **count**[1] [kaʊnt] N **1** conteggio; (*of votes at election*) spoglio; **to be out for the count** (*Boxing*) essere fuori combattimento; (*fam*) essere K.O.; **to keep count of sth** tenere il conto di qc; **you made me lose count** mi hai fatto perdere il conto **2** (*Law*): **he was found guilty on all counts** è stato giudicato colpevole di tutti i capi di accusa

■ VT **1** (*gen*) contare; (*one's change etc*) controllare; **don't count your chickens before they're hatched** non vendere la pelle dell'orso prima di averlo ucciso, non dir quattro se non l'hai nel sacco; **to count sheep** (*fig*) contare le pecore; **to count the cost of** calcolare il costo di; (*fig*) valutare il prezzo di; **without counting the cost** (*also fig*) senza badare al prezzo; **count your blessings** considera la tua fortuna **2** (*include*) contare; (*consider*): **to count sb among** annoverare qn tra; **not counting the children** senza contare i bambini; **ten counting him** dieci compreso lui; **count yourself lucky** considerati fortunato; **will you count it against me?** te la prenderai con me?; **I count it an honour (to do/that)** mi ritengo onorato (a fare/che + sub)

■ VI **1** contare; **to count (up) to 10** contare fino a 10; **counting from today** a partire da oggi, oggi compreso **2** (*be considered, be valid*) valere, contare; **two children count as one adult** due bambini valgono come un

Cc

adulto; **that doesn't count** quello non conta; **it will count against him** deporrà a suo sfavore; **it counts for very little** non conta molto, non ha molta importanza

▶ **count in** VT + ADV comprendere nel conto; **count me in!** (*fam*) ci sto anch'io!

▶ **count on, count upon** VI + PREP contare su; **you can count on me** puoi contare su di me; **to count on doing sth** contare di fare qc

▶ **count out** VT + ADV **1** (*Boxing*): **to be counted out** essere dichiarato(-a) K.O. **2** (*money, small objects*) contare **3** (*fam*): **count me out!** non ci sto!

▶ **count towards** VI + PREP (*subj*: *payment*) andare a incrementare

▶ **count up** VT + ADV contare; (*column of figures*) sommare, addizionare

count² [kaʊnt] N (*nobleman*) conte *m*

count·able ['kaʊntəbl] ADJ computabile; **a countable noun** (*Gram*) un sostantivo numerabile

count·down ['kaʊnt,daʊn] N conto alla rovescia

coun·te·nance ['kaʊntɪnəns] (*frm*) N (*face*) (espressione *f* del) volto; **to keep one's countenance** restare impassibile

■ VT (*permit*): **to countenance sth/sb doing sth** ammettere qc/che qn faccia qc

counter... ['kaʊntəʳ] PREF contro...

◎ **count·er¹** ['kaʊntəʳ] N **1** (*of shop, canteen*) banco, bancone *m*; (*position: in post office, bank*) sportello; **to buy under the counter** (*fig*) comperare sottobanco **2** (*in game*) gettone *m* **3** (*Tech*) contatore *m*

coun·ter² ['kaʊntəʳ] ADV: **counter to** contrariamente a; **to run counter to** andare contro a

■ VT: **to counter sth with sth/by doing sth** rispondere a qc con qc/facendo qc; **to counter an attack** rispondere ad un attacco

■ VI: **to counter with** rispondere con; (*words*) ribattere con

counter·act [,kaʊntər'ækt] VT (*counterbalance*) controbilanciare, agire in opposizione a; (*neutralize*) neutralizzare, annullare gli effetti di; **pills to counteract high blood pressure** pillole per combattere l'alta pressione

counter·at·tack ['kaʊntərə,tæk] N contrattacco

■ VT, VI contrattaccare

counter·bal·ance ['kaʊntə,bæləns] N contrappeso

■ VT controbilanciare, fare da contrappeso a

counter·clockwise [,kaʊntə'klɒk,waɪz] ADV (*Am*) in senso antiorario

counter·es·pio·nage [,kaʊntər'ɛspɪə,nɑːʒ] N controspionaggio

counter·feit ['kaʊntəfɪt] ADJ contraffatto(-a), falsificato(-a), falso(-a); (*money*) falso(-a)

■ N falso, contraffazione *f*; (*coin*) moneta falsa

■ VT contraffare, falsificare

counter·feit·er ['kaʊntə,fɪtəʳ] N contraffattore(-trice)

counter·foil ['kaʊntə,fɔɪl] N matrice *f*

counter·in·tel·li·gence [,kaʊntərɪn'tɛlɪdʒəns] N = counterespionage

counter·mand ['kaʊntə,mɑːnd] VT annullare

countermeasure ['kaʊntə,mɛʒəʳ] N contromisura

counteroffensive ['kaʊntərə,fɛnsɪv] N controffensiva

counter·pane ['kaʊntə,peɪn] N copriletto *m inv*

◎ **counter·part** ['kaʊntə,pɑːt] N (*of person*) omologo(-a); (*of document etc*) copia, duplicato; **the minister and his French counterpart** il ministro e la sua controparte francese

counter·pro·duc·tive [,kaʊntəprə'dʌktɪv] ADJ controproducente

counter·pro·pos·al ['kaʊntəprə,pəʊzəl] N controproposta

Counter-Reformation [,kaʊntə,rɛfə'meɪʃən] N Controriforma

▷ www.lepg.org/religion.htm

counter-revolution [,kaʊntə,rɛvə'luːʃən] N controrivoluzione *f*

counter-revolutionary [,kaʊntə,rɛvə'luːʃənrɪ] N, ADJ controrivoluzionario(-a)

counter·sign ['kaʊntə,saɪn] VT controfirmare

counter·sink ['kaʊntə,sɪŋk] VT (*pt* **countersank**, *pp* **countersunk**) (*hole*) svasare; (*screw*) accecare

counter·ten·or [,kaʊntə'tɛnəʳ] N tenore *m* leggero

counter-turn ['kaʊntə,tɜːn] N (*Skiing*) controcurva

coun·tess ['kaʊntɪs] N contessa

count·less ['kaʊntlɪs] ADJ: **on countless occasions** in mille occasioni, in innumerevoli occasioni; **countless numbers of** un'infinità di

coun·tri·fied ['kʌntrɪ,faɪd] ADJ rustico(-a), campagnolo(-a)

◎ **coun·try** ['kʌntrɪ] N **1** (*gen*) paese *m*; (*native land*) patria; **to go to the country** (*Pol*) indire le elezioni; **to die for one's country** morire per la patria; **the border between the two countries** il confine tra i due paesi **2** (*as opposed to town*) campagna; (*terrain, land*) territorio; (*region*) regione *f*; **in the country** in campagna; **I live in the country** abito in campagna; **there is some lovely country further south** ci sono delle campagne bellissime più a sud; **mountainous country** territorio montagnoso; **unknown country** (*also fig*) terra sconosciuta

■ ADJ (*life, road*) di campagna

country and western, country and western music N musica country e western, country *m inv*

▷ www.ucwdc.com/

▷ www.bbc.co.uk/radio2/soldonsong/genres/country.shtml

coun·try bumpkin ['kʌntrɪ'bʌmpkɪn] N (*pej*) burino(-a)

country club N *circolo sportivo e ricreativo in campagna*

country cottage N villetta di campagna

country cousin N (*fig*) provinciale *m/f*

country dancing N (*Brit*) danza popolare

▷ www.cdss.org

▷ www.cam.ac.uk/societies/round/dances/elements.htm

▷ www.rscds.org/

country dweller N campagnolo(-a)

country house N villa di campagna

country·man ['kʌntrɪmən] N (*pl* **-men**) (*compatriot*) compatriota *m*, connazionale *m*; (*country dweller*) campagnolo

country seat N residenza di campagna

◎ **country·side** ['kʌntrɪ,saɪd] N campagna

country-wide ['kʌntrɪ,waɪd] ADJ (su scala) nazionale, diffuso(-a) in tutto il paese

■ ADV in tutto il paese, su scala nazionale

country·woman ['kʌntrɪ,wʊmən] N (*pl* **-women**) (*compatriot*) compatriota *f*, connazionale *f*; (*country dweller*) campagnola

◎ **coun·ty** ['kaʊntɪ] N contea

■ ADJ (*boundary, court*) di contea

county council N (*Brit*) consiglio di contea

county court N (*Brit: Law*) tribunale *m* locale

county town N (*Brit*) capoluogo (di contea)

◎**coup** [ku:] N (*Pol*: *also*: **coup d'état**) colpo di stato, golpe *m inv*; (*triumph*) bel colpo; **getting her to take the part was a real coup** convincerla ad accettare la parte è stato veramente un bel colpo

coup de grace [ˌku:də'grɑ:s] N (*frm*) colpo di grazia

cou·pé ['ku:peɪ] N (*Aut*) coupé *m inv*

◎**cou·ple** ['kʌpl] N (*of animals, people*) coppia; **a couple of times/hours/books** (*two or three*) un paio di volte/ore/libri; **the couple who live next door** la coppia che vive qui accanto
■VT **1** (*idea, name*): **to couple with** associare con **2** (*railway carriages*): **to couple (on** *or* **up)** agganciare

cou·plet ['kʌplɪt] N distico

cou·pling ['kʌplɪŋ] N (*Rail*) agganciamento

cou·pon ['ku:pɒn] N (*voucher*) buono; (*Comm*) coupon *m inv*; (*football pools coupon*) schedina

◎**cour·age** ['kʌrɪdʒ] N coraggio; **I haven't the courage to refuse** non ho il coraggio di rifiutare; **to have the courage of one's convictions** avere il coraggio delle proprie opinioni *or* convinzioni; **to take one's courage in both hands** prendere il coraggio a due mani

cou·ra·geous [kə'reɪdʒəs] ADJ coraggioso(-a)

cou·ra·geous·ly [kə'reɪdʒəslɪ] ADV coraggiosamente

cour·gette [ˌkʊə'ʒɛt] N (*Brit*) zucchina, zucchino

cou·ri·er ['kʊrɪə[r]] N (*messenger*) corriere *m*; (*for tourists*) accompagnatore(-trice) turistico(-a), tour leader *m/f inv*; **they sent it by courier** l'hanno spedito con il corriere
■VT: **to courier sth to sb** mandare con il corriere qc a qn

◎**course** [kɔ:s] N **1 of course** naturalmente, ovviamente; senz'altro, certo; **yes, of course!** sì, certo!; **(no) of course not!** certo che no!, no di certo!; **do you love me? – of course I do!** mi ami? – ma certo!; **of course you can** certo che puoi; **of course I won't do it** certo che non lo farò **2** (*Scol, Univ*) corso; **a French course** un corso di francese; **to take a course in French** seguire un corso di francese; **a course of lectures on a subject** una serie di conferenze *or* lezioni su un argomento; **a course of treatment** (*Med*) una cura **3** (*part of meal*) piatto, portata; **a three-course meal** un pasto di tre portate; **first course** primo piatto; **main course** portata principale **4** (*route: of ship*) rotta; (*: of river*) corso; (*: of planet*) orbita; **to set course for** (*Naut*) far rotta per; **to change course** (*Naut, fig*) cambiare rotta; **to go off course** deviare dalla rotta; **to hold one's course** seguire *or* mantenere la rotta; **to take/follow a course of action** (*fig*) imboccare/seguire una politica; **we have no other course but to ...** non possiamo far altro che...; **there are two courses open to us** abbiamo due possibilità; **the best course would be to ...** la cosa migliore sarebbe...; **to let things/events take** *or* **run their course** lasciare che le cose/gli eventi seguano il loro corso; **as a matter of course** come una cosa scontata **5** (*duration*): **in the course of** (*life, disease, events*) nel corso di; **in due course** a tempo debito; **in the course of time** col passare del tempo; **in the normal** *or* **ordinary course of events** normalmente; **in (the) course of construction** in (via di) costruzione; **in the course of the next few days** nel corso dei prossimi giorni **6** (*Sport: golf course*) campo (di golf); (*: race course*) pista
■VI (*water, tears*) scorrere; **it sent the blood coursing through his veins** gli ha rimescolato il sangue nelle vene

◎**court** [kɔ:t] N **1** (*Law*) corte *f*; (*: room*) aula; **to take sb to court (over sth)** citare in tribunale qn (per qc); **to settle a case out of court** conciliare una causa in via amichevole; **to rule out of court** dichiarare inammissibile; **he was brought before the court on a charge of theft** fu processato sotto accusa di furto **2** (*also*: **tennis court**) campo da tennis **3** (*royal*) corte *f*
■VT (*woo*) corteggiare, fare la corte a; (*fig: favour, popularity*) cercare di conquistare; (*: death, disaster*) sfiorare, rasentare
■VI (*old: Culin*) corteggiarsi

COURT

In Inghilterra, Galles e Irlanda del Nord i processi penali per i reati più gravi si svolgono nella "Crown **Court**", davanti a un giudice e a una giuria popolare formata da 12 giurati. I reati minori sono invece di competenza delle "magistrates' **courts**", di fronte a un magistrato ma senza giuria. Le "local **courts**" si occupano della maggior parte dei processi civili di minore entità, mentre quelli più complessi vengono giudicati dalla "High **Court**". In appello, sia i processi penali che quelli civili si svolgono in primo grado di fronte alla "**Court** of Appeal" e in ultima istanza di fronte alla Camera dei Lord.
Nel sistema giudiziario scozzese la **High Court of Justiciary** si occupa dei processi penali per i reati più gravi e le **sheriff courts** di quelli per i reati minori. La **Court of Session** rappresenta il tribunale civile di grado superiore. *See also* **federal court**
▷ www.hmcourts-service.gov.uk/
▷ www.dca.gov.uk/
▷ www.scotcourts.gov.uk/

court-bouillon [ˌkɔ:t'bu:jɒn] N court-bouillon *m*

court card N (*Cards*) figura

cour·teous ['kɜ:tɪəs] ADJ cortese

cour·teous·ly ['kɜ:tɪəslɪ] ADV cortesemente

cour·tesan [ˌkɔ:tɪ'zæn] N cortigiana

cour·tesy ['kɜ:tɪsɪ] N (*politeness*) cortesia, gentilezza; (*polite act*) cortesia, piacere *m*; **by courtesy of** per gentile concessione di; **with the utmost courtesy** con la massima cortesia; **you might have had the courtesy to tell me** avresti potuto farmi la cortesia di dirmelo; **to exchange courtesies** scambiarsi convenevoli

courtesy coach N autobus *m inv* gratuito (*di hotel, aeroporto*)

courtesy light N (*Aut*) luce *f* interna

courtesy visit N visita di cortesia

court·house ['kɔ:thaʊs] N (*Am*) tribunale *m*, palazzo di giustizia

cour·ti·er ['kɔ:tɪə[r]] N cortigiano(-a)

court·ing ['kɔ:tɪŋ] ADJ: **courting couple** coppietta, coppia di innamorati

court·ly ['kɔ:tlɪ] ADJ (*comp* **-ier**, *superl* **-iest**) cortese, raffinato(-a)

court martial ['kɔ:t'mɑ:ʃəl] N (*pl* **court martials** *or* **courts martial**) corte *f* marziale

court-martial ['kɔ:t'mɑ:ʃəl] VT processare in corte *f* marziale

court of appeal N corte d'appello

court of inquiry N commissione *f* d'inchiesta

court·room ['kɔ:tˌru:m] N aula (di tribunale)

court·ship ['kɔ:tʃɪp] N corteggiamento

court shoe N scarpa *f* décolleté *inv*

Cc

court·yard [ˈkɔːtˌjɑːd] N cortile *m*
cous·cous [ˈkuːskuːs] N (*Culin*) cuscus *m inv*
◎ **cous·in** [ˈkʌzn] N cugino(-a)
cou·ture [kuːˈtʊəʳ] N couture *f inv*
cou·tu·ri·er [kuːˈtʊərɪeɪ] N couturier *m inv*
co·va·lent [kəʊˈveɪlənt] ADJ: **covalent bond** (*Chem*) legame *m* covalente
cove [kəʊv] N piccola baia, cala
cov·enant [ˈkʌvɪnənt] N accordo (scritto)
■ VT: **to covenant to do sth** impegnarsi (per iscritto) a fare qc; **to covenant £200 per year to a charity** impegnarsi a versare 200 sterline all'anno a un'organizzazione benefica
Cov·en·try [ˈkɒvəntrɪ] N: **to send sb to Coventry** (*fig*) dare l'ostracismo a qn
◎ **cov·er** [ˈkʌvəʳ] N
1 (*gen*) copertura; (*of dish, bowl, saucepan*) coperchio; (*of furniture, typewriter*) fodera; (*for merchandise, on vehicle*) telo, telone *m*; (*bedspread*) copriletto; (*often pl: blanket*) coperta; (*of book, magazine*) copertina; **under separate cover** (*Comm*) a parte, in plico separato; **to read a book from cover to cover** leggere un libro dalla prima all'ultima pagina
2 (*shelter*) riparo; (*covering fire*) copertura; **to take cover** (*hide*) nascondersi; (*Mil: shelter*) ripararsi; **to break cover** uscire allo scoperto; **under cover** al coperto, al riparo; (*hiding*) nascosto(-a); **under cover of darkness** con il favore delle tenebre, protetto(-a) dall'oscurità
3 (*Fin, Comm, Insurance, in espionage etc*) copertura; **without cover** (*Fin*) senza copertura; **fire cover** copertura contro i rischi d'incendio
4 (*frm: at table*) coperto
5 (*Mus: also:* **cover version**) cover *f inv*, riedizione *f* di canzone di successo
■ VT
1 (*gen*): **to cover (with)** coprire (con *or* di); **covered with confusion** (*fig*) tutto(-a) confuso(-a); **covered with shame** pieno(-a) di vergogna; **to cover o.s. with glory/disgrace** coprirsi di gloria/infamia; **he covered his face** si coprì il viso
2 (*hide: facts, mistakes*) nascondere; (*: feeling*) nascondere, dissimulare; (*: noise*) coprire
3 (*protect: Mil, Sport, Insurance*) coprire; **he only said that to cover himself** lo disse solo per coprirsi le spalle; **I've got you covered!** ti copro io!
4 (*be sufficient for, include*) coprire; **£100 will cover everything** 100 sterline saranno sufficienti; **we must cover all possibilities** dobbiamo prevedere tutte le possibilità
5 (*distance*) coprire, percorrere; **to cover a lot of ground** (*also fig*) fare molta strada
6 (*Press: report on*) fare un servizio su
7 (*Mus*) fare una cover *or* una riedizione di
■ VI: **to cover for sb** (*at work etc*) sostituire qn
▸ **cover over** VT + ADV (ri)coprire
▸ **cover up** VT + ADV (*child, object*): **to cover up (with)** coprire (con *or* di); (*fig: hide: truth, facts*) nascondere; **the government tried to cover up the details of the accident** il governo ha cercato di tenere nascosti i particolari dell'incidente; **to cover up one's tracks** (*also fig*) cancellare le tracce
■ VI + ADV (*warmly*) coprirsi; **to cover up for sb** (*fig*) coprire qn
◎ **cov·er·age** [ˈkʌvərɪdʒ] N (*Press, TV, Radio*): **to give full coverage to an event** fare un ampio servizio su un avvenimento, dare grande spazio *or* risonanza a un avvenimento; **the visit got nationwide coverage** (*Radio, TV*) la visita fu trasmessa su tutta la rete nazionale
cover·alls [ˈkʌvərˌɔːlz] NPL (*Am*) tuta
cover charge N (*in restaurant*) coperto (*quota*)
cover girl N cover girl *f inv*, ragazza-copertina
cov·er·ing [ˈkʌvərɪŋ] N copertura; (*of snow, dust etc*) strato
covering letter, **cover letter** (*Am*) N nota esplicativa, lettera d'accompagnamento
cov·er·let [ˈkʌvəlɪt] N copriletto
cover·mount [ˈkʌvəmaʊnt] N regalo allegato a una rivista
cover·mounted [ˈkʌvəmaʊntɪd] ADJ allegato(-a) a una rivista
cover note N (*Insurance*) polizza (di assicurazione) provvisoria
cover price N prezzo di copertina
cov·ert [ˈkʌvət] ADJ (*gen*) nascosto(-a); (*glance*) di sottecchi, furtivo(-a)
cov·ert·ly [ˈkʌvətlɪ] ADV (*glance, act*) di nascosto, furtivamente
cover-up [ˈkʌvərˌʌp] N occultamento (di informazioni)
cover version N = **cover N5**
cov·et [ˈkʌvɪt] VT concupire, bramare
cov·et·ous [ˈkʌvɪtəs] ADJ avido(-a), bramoso(-a)
cov·et·ous·ly [ˈkʌvɪtəslɪ] ADV avidamente, bramosamente
cov·et·ous·ness [ˈkʌvɪtəsnɪs] N avidità, brama
◎ **cow** [kaʊ] N (*bovine*) mucca, vacca; (*female elephant*) elefantessa; (*female seal*) (foca) femmina; (*fam!: woman*) stronza (*fam!*); **you can cry till the cows come home, but you're not having it** puoi piangere quanto ti pare, tanto non te lo do
■ VT (*person*) intimidire; **a cowed look** un'aria da cane bastonato
■ ADJ femmina
cow·ard [ˈkaʊəd] N vigliacco(-a)
cow·ard·ice [ˈkaʊədɪs], **cow·ard·li·ness** [ˈkaʊədlɪnɪs] N vigliaccheria
cow·ard·ly [ˈkaʊədlɪ] ADJ vigliacco(-a)
cow·boy [ˈkaʊˌbɔɪ] N cowboy *m inv*; **to play cowboys and Indians** giocare agli indiani (e ai cowboys)
cow·er [ˈkaʊəʳ] VI acquattarsi (per paura)
cow·herd [ˈkaʊˌhɜːd] N vaccaro
cow·hide [ˈkaʊˌhaɪd] N vacchetta
cowl [kaʊl] N (*hood*) cappuccio
cow·man [ˈkaʊmən] N (*pl* **-men**) vaccaro
co-worker [ˈkəʊˈwɜːkəʳ] N collega *m/f*
cow parsley N (*Bot*) cerfoglio selvatico
cow·pox [ˈkaʊˌpɒks] N vaiolo bovino
cow·rie, **cow·ry** [ˈkaʊrɪ] N ciprea
cow·shed [ˈkaʊʃed] N stalla
cow·slip [ˈkaʊˌslɪp] N (*Bot*) primula odorosa
cox [kɒks] N (*Rowing*) timoniere *m*
■ VT essere al timone di
■ VI fare da timoniere
cox·swain [ˈkɒksən] N nocchiere *m*
coy [kɔɪ] ADJ (*comp* **-er**, *superl* **-est**) (*affectedly shy: person*) che fa il/la vergognoso(-a); (*: smile*) falsamente timido(-a); (*evasive*) evasivo(-a); (*coquettish*) civettuolo(-a)
coy·ly [ˈkɔɪlɪ] ADV (*smile*) con falsa timidezza; (*answer*) evasivamente; (*coquettishly*) con civetteria
coy·ness [ˈkɔɪnɪs] N (*affected shyness*) falsa timidezza; (*evasiveness*) evasività; (*coquetry*) civetteria
coy·ote [kɔɪˈəʊtɪ] N coyote *m inv*

coy·pu ['kɔɪpu:] N (*pl* **coypu** *or* **coypus**) (*Zool*) nutria, castorino

cozy ['kəʊzɪ] ADJ (*Am*) = cosy

cp. ABBR (= **compare**) cfr.

c/p ABBR (*Brit*) *see* **carriage paid**

CPI [,si:pi:'aɪ] N ABBR (*Am*: = **Consumer Price Index**) *indice dei prezzi al consumo*

Cpl. ABBR = **corporal**

CP/M [,si:pi:'ɛm] N ABBR (= **Control Program for Microcomputers**) CP/M *m*

cps [,si:pi:'ɛs] ABBR (= **characters per second**) cps

CPSA [,si:pi:ɛs'eɪ] N ABBR (*Brit*: = **Civil and Public Services Association**) *sindacato dei servizi pubblici*

CPU [,si:pi:'ju:] N ABBR = **central processing unit**

cr. ABBR **1** = **credit** **2** = **creditor**

crab¹ [kræb] N granchio

crab² [kræb] N (*Mountaineering*) moschettone *m*

crab apple N (*fruit*) mela selvatica; (*tree*) melo selvatico

crab·by ['kræbɪ], **crab·bed** ['kræbɪd] ADJ (*fam*) acido(-a), scontroso(-a)

crab louse N piattola

crab meat N polpa di granchio

◎**crack** [kræk] N **1** (*split, slit: in glass, pottery*) incrinatura, scheggiatura; (: *in wall, plaster, ground, paint*) crepa, spaccatura; (: *in skin*) screpolatura; **to open the door a crack** aprire la porta lasciandola accostata; **through the crack in the door** (*slight opening*) dalla fessura della porta; **at the crack of dawn** alle prime luci dell'alba **2** (*noise: of twigs*) scricchiolio, crepitio; (: *of whip*) schiocco; (: *of rifle, of gun*) colpo; (: *of thunder*) boato **3** (*blow*): **a crack on the head** una botta in testa **4** (*fam: attempt*): **to have a crack at sth** tentare qc; **I'll have a crack at it** ci proverò **5** (*fam: joke, insult*) battuta **6** (*Drugs*) crack *m inv*

■ VT **1** (*break: glass, pottery*) incrinare; (: *wood*) schiantare; (: *nut*) schiacciare; (: *egg*) rompere; (*fig fam: safe*) scassinare; (: *bottle*) stappare, aprire; **to crack one's skull** spaccarsi la testa; **he cracked his head on the pavement** ha sbattuto la testa sul marciapiedi; **to crack sb over the head** dare un colpo in testa a qn **2** (*cause to sound: whip, finger joints*) (far) schioccare; **to crack jokes** (*fam*) dire battute, scherzare **3** (*case, mystery: solve*) risolvere; (*code*) decifrare; **I think we've cracked it!** penso che ci siamo!

■ VI **1** (*break: pottery, glass*) incrinarsi: *ground, wall, creparsi;* (*dry wood*) schiantarsi; (*skin*) screpolarsi; **to crack under the strain** (*person*) non reggere alla tensione **2** (*whip*) schioccare; (*dry wood*) scricchiolare; **to get cracking** (*fam*) darsi una mossa

■ ADJ (*team, regiment*) scelto(-a); (*athlete*) di prim'ordine; **a crack shot** un tiratore infallibile

▸ **crack down** VI + ADV: **to crack down (on)** prendere serie misure contro, porre freno a; **the police are cracking down on motorists who drive too fast** la polizia sta prendendo serie misure contro gli automobilisti che vanno troppo veloci

▸ **crack up** (*fam*) VI + ADV crollare; **I must be cracking up!** (*hum*) sto dando i numeri!

■ VT + ADV: **he's not all he's cracked up to be** non è così meraviglioso come dicono

crack·down ['kræk,daʊn] N repressione *f*

cracked [krækt] ADJ (*fam: mad*) tocco(-a), matto(-a)

crack·er ['krækəʳ] N **1** (*biscuit*) cracker *m inv* **2** (*firework*) petardo; (*Christmas cracker*) *specie di mortaretto natalizio con sorpresa* **3** (*Brit fam: girl, dress, car*) schianto; **a cracker of a ...** una ...formidabile

crack·ers ['krækəz] ADJ (*Brit fam*) pazzo(-a), tocco(-a); **he's crackers** è un po' tocco

crack·ing ['krækɪŋ] ADJ: **at a cracking pace** di buon passo

■ N **1** (*Chem*) cracking *m* **2** (*of paint, varnish*) crepe *fpl*

crack·le ['krækl] VI (*twigs burning*) crepitare, scoppiettare; (*sth frying*) sfrigolare

■ N (*see vb*) crepitio, scoppiettio; sfrigolio; (*on telephone*) disturbo

crack·ling ['kræklɪŋ] N **1** (*sound*) crepitio; (*on radio, telephone*) disturbo; (*of frying food*) sfrigolio **2** (*of pork*) cotenna (di maiale) arrostita

crack·pot ['kræk,pɒt] (*fam*) N imbecille *m/f* con idee assurde

■ ADJ (*idea*) assurdo(-a)

crack-up ['kræk,ʌp] N (*fam*) crollo

cra·dle ['kreɪdl] N culla; (*of telephone*) forcella; (*Constr*) gabbia

■ VT (*child*) tenere tra le braccia; (*object*) reggere tra le braccia

cradle snatch·er ['kreɪdl'snætʃəʳ] N (*pej*) chi se la fa con quelli(-e) più giovani

cradle·song ['kreɪdl,sɒŋ] N ninnananna

◎**craft** [krɑ:ft] N **1** (*handicraft*) artigianato; (*art*) arte *f*, mestiere *m*; (*profession*) mestiere; (*fig: skill*) abilità, maestria **2** (*cunning: pej*) furbizia, astuzia **3** (*boat: pl inv*) barca, imbarcazione *f*

crafti·ly ['krɑ:ftɪlɪ] ADV (*see adj*) furbamente, astutamente; abilmente

crafti·ness ['krɑ:ftɪnɪs] N (*see adj*) furbizia, astuzia; abilità

craft shop N negozio di prodotti d'artigianato

crafts·man ['krɑ:ftsmən] N (*pl* **-men**) artigiano

crafts·man·ship ['krɑ:ftsmənʃɪp] N (*skill*) arte *f*, abilità, maestria; **a piece of craftsmanship** un pezzo di artigianato

crafty ['krɑ:ftɪ] ADJ (*comp* **-ier**, *superl* **-iest**) (*person*) furbo(-a), astuto(-a); (*action*) abile

crag [kræg] N rupe *f*

crag·gy ['krægɪ] ADJ (*comp* **-ier**, *superl* **-iest**) (*rock*) scosceso(-a), dirupato(-a); (*features*) marcato(-a); (*face*) dai tratti marcati

cram [kræm] VT (*stuff: books, papers*): **to cram into** infilare in, stipare in, pigiare in; (: *people, passengers*) ammassare in; (*fill*): **to cram sth with** riempire qc di; **we crammed our stuff into the boot** abbiamo stipato la nostra roba nel bagagliaio; **she crammed her bag with books** ha riempito la borsa di libri; **to cram in** far stare, trovare posto per; **his head is crammed with strange ideas** ha la testa piena di idee strane; **the room was crammed with furniture/people** la stanza era stipata di mobili/affollata di gente; **she crammed her hat down over her eyes** si calcò il cappello sugli occhi; **to cram o.s. with food** abbuffarsi, rimpinzarsi

■ VI **1** (*people*): **to cram (into)** affollarsi (in), accalcarsi (in), stiparsi (in) **2** (*pupil: for exam*) fare una sgobbata finale

cram·mer ['kræməʳ] N (*school*) istituto che prepara agli esami; (*tutor*) insegnante *m/f* che cura la preparazione agli esami

cramp [kræmp] N (*Med*): **cramp (in)** crampo (a)

■ VT (*hinder: person*) impacciare, inibire; (: *progress*) ostacolare, frenare; **you're cramping my style** mi inibisci

cramped [kræmpt] ADJ (*room etc*) angusto(-a); (*writing*) fitto(-a); (*position*) rannicchiato(-a)

Cc

cram·pon ['kræmpən] N (*Mountaineering*) rampone *m*
cran·berry ['krænbərɪ] N mirtillo
cranberry sauce N salsa di mirtilli
crane [kreɪn] N (*Zool, Tech*) gru *f inv*
■VT, VI: **to crane forward, to crane one's neck** allungare il collo
crane driver N gruista *m*
cra·nial ['kreɪnɪəl] ADJ (*Anat*) cranico(-a)
cra·nium ['kreɪnɪəm] N (*pl* **cranium**) (*Anat*) cranio
crank [kræŋk] N **1** (*Tech*) manovella **2** (*person*) eccentrico(-a), persona stramba
■VT (*also:* **crank up**) avviare a manovella
crank·case ['kræŋk,keɪs] N (*Aut*) basamento (del motore)
crank·pin ['kræŋk,pɪn] N (*Aut*) perno di biella
crank·shaft ['kræŋkʃɑ:ft] N (*Aut*) albero motore, albero a gomiti
cranky ['kræŋkɪ] ADJ (*comp* **-ier**, *superl* **-iest**) (*strange: ideas, people*) eccentrico(-a), strambo(-a); **to be cranky** (*bad-tempered*) avere i nervi
cran·ny ['krænɪ] N *see* **nook**
crap [kræp] (*fam!*) N merda (*fam!*); (*nonsense*) cazzate *fpl* (*fam!*); **to have a crap** cacare (*fam!*)
crape [kreɪp] N = **crêpe**
crap·py ['kræpɪ] ADJ (*comp* **-ier**, *superl* **-iest**) (*fam!*) di merda (*fam!*)
◎**crash** [kræʃ] N **1** (*accident*) incidente *m*; **there has been a plane crash** un aereo è precipitato **2** (*noise*) fragore *m*, fracasso; (*of thunder*) fragore **3** (*of business*) fallimento; (*Stock Exchange*) crollo
■VT (*smash: car*) avere un incidente con, fracassare, sfasciare; **he crashed the car into a wall** andò a sbattere contro un muro con la macchina; **the pilot crashed the plane** il pilota ha fatto precipitare l'aereo
■VI **1** (*car*) avere un incidente; (*plane*) cadere, precipitare; (*collide: two vehicles*) scontrarsi; **to crash into sth** scontrarsi con qc, andare a sbattere contro qc, schiantarsi contro qc; **the plane crashed** l'aereo è precipitato; **the two cars crashed** le due macchine si sono scontrate; **the plates came crashing down** i piatti sono andati in frantumi **2** (*business*) fallire, andare in rovina; (*stock market*) crollare **3** (*computer*) impiantarsi; **I'd nearly finished when my computer crashed** avevo quasi finito quando il computer si è impiantato
■ADJ (*diet, course*) intensivo(-a), rapido(-a)
crash barrier N (*Brit Aut*) guardrail *m inv*
crash course N corso intensivo
crash helmet N casco (di protezione)
crash·ing ['kræʃɪŋ] ADJ (*fam* (*old*): **it's/he's a crashing bore** è tremendamente noioso, è di una noia mortale
crash landing N atterraggio forzato, atterraggio di fortuna
crass [kræs] ADJ crasso(-a)
crass·ly ['kræslɪ] ADV (*stupidly*) grossolanamente
crass·ness ['kræsnɪs] N (*of error*) grossolanità
crate [kreɪt] N cassa, cassetta
cra·ter ['kreɪtə[r]] N cratere *m*
crater lake N lago vulcanico
cra·vat [krə'væt] N (*for men*) foulard *m inv* da collo
crave [kreɪv] VT **1** (*desire*) desiderare disperatamente **2** (*frm: pardon, permission*) implorare
■VI: **to crave for** = VT **1**
cra·ven ['kreɪvən] ADJ (*frm pej*) vigliacco(-a)
crav·ing ['kreɪvɪŋ] N: **craving (for)** (*for food, cigarettes etc*) (gran) voglia (di); (*in pregnancy*) voglia; (*for affection, attention*) desiderio estremo
craw·fish ['krɔ:,fɪʃ] N = **crayfish**
crawl [krɔ:l] N **1** (*slow pace*) passo lento; **the traffic went at a crawl** il traffico procedeva a passo d'uomo **2** (*Swimming*) stile *m* libero, crawl *m*; **to do the crawl** nuotare a stile libero, nuotare a crawl
■VI **1** (*drag o.s.*) trascinarsi, strisciare; (*child*) andare gattoni *or* carponi; (*traffic*) avanzare lentamente, procedere a passo d'uomo; (*time*) non passare mai; **to crawl in/out** *etc* trascinarsi carponi dentro/fuori *etc*; **to be crawling with ants** brulicare di formiche **2** (*fam: suck up*): **to crawl to sb** arruffianarsi qn
crawl·er ['krɔ:lə[r]] N leccapiedi *m/f inv*; (*Comput*) programma *m* di indicizzazione siti
crawler lane N (*Brit Aut*) corsia riservata al traffico lento
cray·fish ['kreɪ,fɪʃ] N gambero (d'acqua dolce)
cray·on ['kreɪən] N (*wax*) pastello a cera; (*chalk*) gessetto; (*coloured pencil*) matita colorata
craze [kreɪz] N mania
■VT **1** far diventare pazzo(-a) **2** (*pottery, glaze*) incrinare
■VI (*pottery, glaze, windscreen*) incrinarsi
crazed [kreɪzd] ADJ (*look, person*) folle, pazzo(-a); (*pottery, glaze*) incrinato(-a)
cra·zi·ly ['kreɪzɪlɪ] ADV pazzamente, follemente
◎**cra·zy** ['kreɪzɪ] ADJ (*comp* **-ier**, *superl* **-iest**) **1** (*mad*) pazzo(-a), matto(-a), folle; **to go crazy** uscir di senno, impazzire; **crazy with jealousy** pazzo(-a) di gelosia; **it was a crazy idea** era un'idea folle; **you were crazy to do it** sei stato un pazzo a farlo **2** (*fam: keen*): **to be crazy about sb** essere pazzo(-a) di qn; **she's crazy about him** è pazza di lui; **to be crazy about sth** andare matto(-a) per qc; **Paul is crazy about football** Paul va matto per il calcio **3** (*angle, slope*) pericolante
crazy paving N (*Brit*) lastricato a mosaico irregolare
creak [kri:k] VI (*wood, shoe etc*) scricchiolare; (*hinge etc*) cigolare; **the floorboards creaked** le assi del pavimento scricchiolavano
■N (*see vb*) scricchiolio; cigolio
creaky ['kri:kɪ] ADJ (*shoes, floorboards*) scricchiolante; (*hinge, joint*) cigolante, stridente
◎**cream** [kri:m] N **1** (*Culin*) panna; **single/double cream** panna da cucina liquida/densa; **whipped cream** panna montata; **a chocolate cream** (*a sweet*) un cremino al cioccolato; **cream of tomato soup** crema di pomodoro; **strawberries and cream** fragole con panna; **the cream of society** (*fig*) la crème della società **2** (*lotion: for face, shoes etc*) crema; **sun cream** crema solare
■ADJ (*colour*) (color) crema *inv*, (color) panna *inv*; (*Culin: made with cream*) alla panna; **a cream silk blouse** una camicetta di seta color crema
■VT (*mix: also:* **cream together**) amalgamare; **creamed potatoes** puré *m* di patate
▸ **cream off** VT + PREP (*best talents, part of profits*) portarsi via
cream cake N torta alla panna
cream cheese N formaggio fresco spalmabile; formaggio cremoso
cream cracker N *cracker da mangiare con i formaggi*
cream·ery ['kri:mərɪ] N (*factory*) caseificio; (*shop*) latteria
cream jug N bricco per la panna
cream tea N *tè servito con "scones", "clotted cream" e marmellata*; *see* **scone, clotted cream**
creamy ['kri:mɪ] ADJ (*comp* **-ier**, *superl* **-iest**) (*taste,*

texture) cremoso(-a); (*colour*) crema *inv*, panna *inv*

crease [kri:s] N (*fold: in trousers*) piega; (*wrinkle: in cloth*) grinza; (*: in face*) ruga, grinza
■VT sgualcire, spiegazzare; **his face was creased with laughter** aveva il volto contratto dalle risate
■VI sgualcirsi

crease-resistant ['kri:sɪ,zɪstənt] ADJ ingualcibile

◎**cre·ate** [kri:'eɪt] VT (*gen*) creare; (*impression, fuss, noise*) fare; **to create a sensation** destare *or* fare scalpore; **he was created a peer by the Queen** fu nominato pari dalla Regina
■VI (*fam*) fare un sacco di storie

crea·tion [kri:'eɪʃən] N creazione *f*

crea·tion·ism [kri:'eɪʃənIzəm] N creazionismo

crea·tion·ist [kri:'eɪʃənIst] N creazionista *m/f*

◎**crea·tive** [kri:'eɪtɪv] ADJ creativo(-a)
■N creativo(-a)

crea·tive·ly [kri:'eɪtɪvlɪ] ADV creativamente

creative writing N scrittura creativa

crea·tiv·ity [,kri:eɪ'tɪvɪtɪ] N creatività

crea·tor [krɪ'eɪtə^r] N creatore(-trice)

crea·ture ['kri:tʃə^r] N (*gen*) creatura; **the creatures of the deep** (*liter*) le creature degli abissi; **a creature from outer space** un extraterrestre; **the poor creature had no home** il poverino era senza casa; **a creature of habit** una persona abitudinaria

creature comforts NPL comodità *fpl*

crèche [kreɪʃ] N asilo *m* nido *inv*

cre·dence ['kri:dəns] N credenza, fede *f*

cre·den·tials [krɪ'dɛnʃəlz] NPL (*qualifications*) titoli *mpl*; (*identifying papers, of diplomat*) credenziali *fpl*; (*letters of reference*) referenze *fpl*

cred·ibil·ity [,krɛdə'bɪlɪtɪ] N (*see adj*) credibilità; attendibilità

cred·ible ['krɛdɪbl] ADJ (*gen*) credibile; (*witness, source*) attendibile

◎**cred·it** ['krɛdɪt] N **1** (*Fin*) credito; **to give sb credit** fare credito a qn; **you have £100 to your credit** lei ha 100 sterline a suo credito; **on credit** a credito; **is his credit good?** gli si può dare credito?; **in credit** in attivo; **to be in credit** (*person*) essere creditore(-trice); (*bank account*) essere coperto(-a) **2** (*honour*) onore *m*; **to one's credit** a proprio onore; **it is to his credit that ...** bisogna riconoscergli che...; **he's a credit to his family** fa onore alla sua famiglia; **to give sb credit for (doing) sth** riconoscere a qn il merito di (aver fatto) qc; **I gave you credit for more sense** ti reputavo più sensato; **it does you credit** ti fa onore; **to take credit for (doing) sth** attribuirsi il merito di (aver fatto) qc **3** (*Univ: esp Am*) *certificato di compimento di una parte di un corso universitario; see also* **credits**
■VT **1** (*believe: also:* **give credit to**) credere, prestar fede a **2** (*attribute*) attribuire il credito a; **to credit sb with sth** attribuire qc a qn; **I credited him with more sense** credevo che avesse più cervello; **he credited them with the victory** attribuì a loro il merito della vittoria **3** (*Comm*): **to credit £50 to sb, to credit sb with £50** accreditare 50 sterline a qn
■ADJ (*limit, agency etc*) di credito; **on the credit side** (*fig*) a suo favore

cred·it·able ['krɛdɪtəbl] ADJ che fa onore, lodevole, degno(-a) di lode

cred·it·ably ['krɛdɪtəblɪ] ADV lodevolmente

credit account N (*in shop etc*) conto (di credito), conto (aperto)

credit agency, credit bureau (*Am*) N agenzia di analisi di credito

credit balance N saldo attivo

credit card N carta di credito

credit control N controllo dei crediti

credit entry N (*Comm*) scrittura di accredito

credit facilities NPL agevolazioni *fpl* creditizie

credit limit N limite *m* di credito

credit note N (*Brit*) nota di credito

credi·tor ['krɛdɪtə^r] N creditore(-trice)

credit rating N affidabilità *f inv* di credito

cred·its ['krɛdɪts] NPL (*Cine, TV: opening*) titoli *mpl* di testa; (*: closing*) titoli *mpl* di coda

credit squeeze N limitazione *f* dei crediti, stretta creditizia

credit terms NPL condizioni *fpl* di credito

credit transfer N bancogiro, postagiro

credit·worthy ['krɛdɪt,wɜ:ðɪ] ADJ autorizzabile al credito

cre·du·lity [krɪ'dju:lɪtɪ] N credulità

credu·lous ['krɛdjʊləs] ADJ credulo(-a)

credu·lous·ly ['krɛdjʊləslɪ] ADV con credulità

creed [kri:d] N credo, dottrina

creek [kri:k] N (*inlet*) insenatura; (*Am*) piccolo fiume *m*

creel [kri:l] N cestino per il pesce; (*also:* **lobster creel**) nassa

creep [kri:p] (*vb: pt, pp* **crept**) VI (*animal*) strisciare; (*plant*) arrampicarsi; (*person: stealthily*) avanzare furtivamente; (*: slowly*) avanzare lentamente; **to creep in/out** entrare/uscire quatto(-a) quatto(-a); **to creep up on sb** avvicinarsi quatto(-a) quatto(-a) a qn; (*fig: old age etc*) cogliere qn alla sprovvista; **a feeling of peace crept over him** lo avvolse un senso di pace; **it made my flesh creep** mi fece accapponare la pelle; **an error has crept in** ci è scappato un errore
■N (*fam*): **it gives me the creeps** mi fa venire la pelle d'oca; **he's a creep** è un tipo viscido

Cc

creep·er ['kri:pə^r] N (*Bot*) rampicante *m*

creep·ing ['kri:pɪŋ] ADJ (*plant*) rampicante; **creeping paralysis** paralisi *f* progressiva

creepy ['kri:pɪ] ADJ (*comp* **-ier**, *superl* **-iest**) (*frightening*) che fa accapponare la pelle; **it was a really creepy place** era un posto che dava proprio i brividi

creepy-crawly ['kri:pɪ,krɔ:lɪ] N (*fam*) bestiolina, insetto

cre·mate [krɪ'meɪt] VT cremare

cre·ma·tion [krɪ'meɪʃən] N cremazione *f*

crema·to·rium [,krɛmə'tɔ:rɪəm] N (*pl* **crematoria** [,krɛmə'tɔ:rɪə]) (forno) crematorio

cren·el·lat·ed ['krɛnɪ,leɪtɪd] ADJ merlato(-a)

cre·ole ['kri:əʊl] ADJ, N creolo(-a)

creo·sote ['krɪə,səʊt] N creosoto
■VT dare il creosoto a

crêpe [kreɪp] N **1** (*fabric*) crespo **2** (*also:* **crêpe rubber**) para **3** (*pancake*) crêpe *f inv*, crespella

crêpe bandage N (*Brit*) fascia elastica

crêpe paper N carta crespata

crêpe sole N (*on shoes*) suola di para

crept [krɛpt] PT, PP *of* **creep**

cre·scen·do [krɪ'ʃɛndəʊ] N (*Mus, fig*) crescendo

cres·cent ['krɛsnt] ADJ (*moon*) crescente; (*shape*) a mezzaluna
■N (*shape*) mezzaluna; (*street*) via (*a semicerchio*)

cress [krɛs] N crescione *m*

crest [krɛst] N (*of bird, wave, mountain*) cresta; (*on helmet*) pennacchio; (*Heraldry*) cimiero; **to be on the crest of the wave** (*fig*) essere sulla cresta dell'onda

crest·fallen ['krɛst,fɔ:lən] ADJ abbattuto(-a),

mortificato(-a); **to look crestfallen** avere un'aria mogia

Cre·tan ['kri:tən] ADJ, N cretese *(m/f)*

Crete [kri:t] N Creta

cret·in ['krɛtɪn] N *(fam pej)* cretino(-a)

cret·in·ous ['krɛtɪnəs] ADJ *(fam pej)* da cretino(-a)

cre·vasse [krɪ'væs] N crepaccio

crev·ice ['krɛvɪs] N crepa, fessura

◎ **crew[1]** [kru:] N *(Naut, Aer)* equipaggio; *(Rowing etc: team)* squadra; *(gang)* banda, compagnia; **film crew** troupe *f inv* cinematografica
■VI *(Sailing)*: **to crew for sb** far parte dell'equipaggio di qn

crew[2] [kru:] PT *of* **crow**

crew cut N: **to have a crew cut** avere i capelli a spazzola

crew-neck ['kru:ˌnɛk] ADJ: **crew-neck sweater** maglione *m* a girocollo

crib [krɪb] N **1** *(small cot)* culla; *(Rel)* presepio; *(manger)* mangiatoia **2** *(plagiarism)* plagio; *(Scol: answer book)* traduttore *m*, bigino *(fam)*
■VT *(Scol)* copiare

crib·bage ['krɪbɪdʒ] N *tipo di gioco di carte*

crib death N *(Am)* = **cot death**

crick [krɪk] N: **crick in the neck** torcicollo; **crick in the back** dolore *m* alla schiena
■VT: **to crick one's neck** prendere il torcicollo; **to crick one's back** farsi male alla schiena

◎ **crick·et[1]** ['krɪkɪt] N *(sport)* cricket *m*; **I play cricket** gioco a cricket; **that's not cricket** *(fig)* questo non è leale
▷ www.ecb.co.uk/

crick·et[2] ['krɪkɪt] N *(insect)* grillo

cricket ball N palla da cricket

crick·et·er ['krɪkɪtə^r] N giocatore(-trice) di cricket

cricket match N partita di cricket

cri·key ['kraɪkɪ] EXCL *(Brit fam)* cribbio

◎ **crime** [kraɪm] N *(in general)* criminalità; *(instance)* crimine *m*, delitto; **crime is rising** la criminalità è in aumento; **he committed a crime** ha commesso un crimine; **the scene of the crime** la scena del delitto; **it's a crime** *(fig)* è una vergogna

crime prevention N prevenzione della criminalità

crime wave N ondata di criminalità

◎ **crimi·nal** ['krɪmɪnl] N criminale *m/f*; **a dangerous criminal** un pericoloso criminale
■ADJ criminale; *(fig)* vergognoso(-a); **criminal lawyer** (avvocato) penalista *m/f*; **criminal offence** reato; **to study criminal law** fare studi penalistici; **to have a criminal record** avere precedenti penali; **to take criminal proceedings against sb** istruire una causa penale contro qn

Criminal Investigation Department N ≈ polizia giudiziaria

crimi·nal·ity [ˌkrɪmɪ'nælɪtɪ] N criminalità *f inv*

crimi·nal·ly ['krɪmɪnəlɪ] ADV criminosamente

crimi·nolo·gist [ˌkrɪmɪ'nɒlədʒɪst] N criminologo

crimi·nol·ogy [ˌkrɪmɪ'nɒlədʒɪ] N criminologia

crimp [krɪmp] VT *(hair)* arricciare; *(material)* pieghettare

crim·son ['krɪmzn] ADJ, N cremisi *(m) inv*

cringe [krɪndʒ] VI *(in terror)*: **to cringe (from)** ritrarsi impaurito(-a) (da); **to cringe (before)** *(in servility)* strisciare (davanti a); **the very thought of it makes me cringe** *(fam: in embarrassment)* solo a pensarci mi sento sprofondare

crin·kle ['krɪŋkl] VT spiegazzare, sgualcire

crin·kly ['krɪŋklɪ] ADJ *(comp* **-ier**, *superl* **-iest**) *(hair)* crespo(-a); *(paper etc)* crespato(-a)

crino·line ['krɪnəli:n] N crinolina

crip·ple ['krɪpl] N *(lame)* zoppo(-a); *(disabled)* invalido(-a); *(maimed)* mutilato(-a)
■VT **1** rendere invalido(-a); **crippled with arthritis** invalido(-a) per l'artrite **2** *(production, exports)* paralizzare

crip·pled ['krɪpld] ADJ *(handicapped)* invalido(-a); *(production, exports)* paralizzato(-a); *(frm: seriously damaged)* seriamente danneggiato(-a); **to be crippled in an accident** rimanere invalido(-a) in seguito ad un incidente; **to be crippled with arthritis** soffrire di una grave forma di artrite

crip·pling ['krɪplɪŋ] ADJ *(disease)* che provoca invalidità; *(taxes, debts)* esorbitante

◎ **cri·sis** ['kraɪsɪs] N *(pl* **crises** ['kraɪsi:z]) crisi *f inv*; **to come to a crisis** entrare in crisi; **we have a crisis on our hands** ci troviamo di fronte a una crisi

crisis management N: **crisis management team** unità *f inv* di crisi

crisp [krɪsp] ADJ *(comp* **-er**, *superl* **-est**) *(bacon, biscuit, lettuce)* croccante; *(snow)* fresco(-a); *(bank note)* nuovo(-a) di zecca; *(linen)* inamidato(-a); *(air)* fresco(-a), frizzante; *(manner, tone, reply)* secco(-a), brusco(-a); *(style)* conciso(-a) e vivace

crisp·bread ['krɪspˌbrɛd] N cracottes® *fpl*

crisp·ly ['krɪsplɪ] ADV *(speak)* con tono secco; *(write)* in modo vivace

crisp·ness ['krɪspnɪs] N *(of bacon, biscuit, snow)* friabilità; *(of linen)* freschezza; *(of apple)* sodezza; *(of style)* vivacità; **I like the crispness of new banknotes** mi piace toccare le banconote nuove di zecca

crisps [krɪsps] NPL *(Brit)* patatine *fpl*; **a bag of crisps** un sacchetto di patatine

crispy ['krɪspɪ] ADJ *(comp* **-ier**, *superl* **-iest**) croccante

criss-cross ['krɪsˌkrɒs] ADJ *(lines)* incrociato(-a), intrecciato(-a); *(pattern)* a linee incrociate
■VT incrociare

cri·teri·on [kraɪ'tɪərɪən] N *(pl* **criteria** [kraɪ'tɪərɪə]) criterio; **I don't understand what their criteria were** non riesco a capire i criteri che hanno seguito; **only one candidate met all the criteria** un solo candidato soddisfaceva tutti i requisiti

◎ **crit·ic** ['krɪtɪk] N critico(-a)

◎ **criti·cal** ['krɪtɪkəl] ADJ *(all senses)* critico(-a); **to be critical of sb/sth** criticare qn/qc, essere critico(-a) verso qn/qc; **at a critical moment** in un momento critico; **a critical success** *(book, play)* un successo di critica

criti·cal·ly ['krɪtɪkəlɪ] ADV criticamente; **to be critically ill** versare in gravi condizioni, versare in condizioni critiche, essere gravemente malato(-a); **critically important** di importanza vitale

critical mass N **1** *(Phys)* massa critica **2** *(fig)* massa critica; **to reach critical mass** raggiungere la massa critica

◎ **criti·cism** ['krɪtɪsɪzəm] N critica

◎ **criti·cize** ['krɪtɪsaɪz] VT criticare

cri·tique [krɪ'ti:k] N critica, saggio critico

croak [krəʊk] N *(of raven)* gracchio; *(of frog)* gracidio, gracidare *m*
■VI *(raven)* gracchiare; *(frog)* gracidare; *(person)* dire con voce rauca

Cro·at ['krəʊæt] N croato(-a)

Croa·tia [krəʊ'eɪʃə] N Croazia

Croa·tian [krəʊ'eɪʃən] ADJ croato(-a)

■ N (*person*) croato(-a); (*language*) croato
cro·chet ['krəʊʃeɪ] N lavoro all'uncinetto
■ VT, VI lavorare all'uncinetto
▷ www.crochet.org
crochet hook N uncinetto
crock [krɒk] N coccio; (*fam*: *person*: *also*: **old crock**) rottame *m*; (: *car, bicycle*) rottame *m*, macinino
crock·ery ['krɒkərɪ] N (*earthenware*) vasellame *m* (di terracotta); (*plates, cups*) stoviglie *fpl*
croco·dile ['krɒkədaɪl] N coccodrillo; **to walk in a crocodile** (*Brit fam*) camminare in fila per due
crocodile tears NPL lacrime *fpl* di coccodrillo
cro·cus ['krəʊkəs] N croco
Croesus ['kri:səs] N Creso
croft [krɒft] N (*Scot*) piccola fattoria
croft·er ['krɒftə^r] N (*Scot*) fattore *m* (*di piccola fattoria*)
crois·sant ['krwæsɒŋ] N croissant *m inv*, cornetto
crone [krəʊn] N vecchiarda
cro·ny ['krəʊnɪ] N (*fam*) amicone(-a)
crook [krʊk] N **1** (*fam*: *thief*) ladro(-a), truffatore(-trice); **he's a crook** è un imbroglione; **a petty crook** un piccolo delinquente **2 the crook of one's arm** l'incavo del braccio **3** (*shepherd's*) bastone *m* (da pastore); (*bishop's*) pastorale *m*
■ VT (*arm, finger*) piegare
crook·ed ['krʊkɪd] ADJ (*stick, person*) curvo(-a), storto(-a); (*picture*) storto(-a); (*path*) tortuoso(-a); (*smile*) forzato(-a); (*dishonest*: *deal, means, person*) disonesto(-a); **a crooked line** una linea storta; **a crooked policeman** un poliziotto disonesto
crook·ed·ly ['krʊkɪdlɪ] ADV (*hang etc*) di traverso; (*smile*) forzatamente
crook·ed·ness ['krʊkɪdnɪs] N (*deformity*) deformità *f inv*; (*dishonesty*) disonestà
croon [kru:n] VT, VI (*sing quietly*) canticchiare; (*professionally*) cantare
croon·er ['kru:nə^r] N cantante *m/f* melodico
◎ **crop** [krɒp] N **1** (*produce*) coltivazione *f*; (*amount produced*: *of fruit, vegetables*) raccolto; (: *of cereals*) raccolto, messe *f*; (*fig*: *of problems, applicants*) serie *f inv*; **the crops** il raccolto **2** (*of bird*) gozzo, ingluvie *f* **3** (*of whip*) manico; (*riding crop*) frustino
■ VT (*cut*: *hair*) tagliare, rapare; (*subj*: *animals*: *grass*) brucare
▶ **crop up** VI + ADV (*fig*: *arise*) sorgere, presentarsi; **something must have cropped up** dev'essere capitato *or* successo qualcosa
crop·per ['krɒpə^r] N (*fam*): **to come a cropper** (*fall badly*) fare un capitombolo; (*fail completely*) fare fiasco
crop rotation N rotazione *f* delle colture
crop spraying [-spreɪɪŋ] N spruzzatura di antiparassitari
crop top N top *m inv* corto
cro·quet ['krəʊkeɪ] N croquet *m*
cro·quette [krəʊ'kɛt] N (*Culin*) crocchetta
◎ **cross** [krɒs] N **1** (*mark, symbol*) croce *f*; (*on questionnaire*) crocetta, croce; **Greek/Latin cross** croce greca/latina; **to mark with a cross** segnare con una crocetta; **we each have our cross to bear** (*fig*) ognuno ha la propria croce (da portare) **2** (*Zool, Bio*) incrocio, ibrido; **it's a cross between geography and sociology** è un misto di geografia e sociologia **3** (*bias*): **cut on the cross** tagliato(-a) in sbieco
■ ADJ (*comp* **-er**, *superl* **-est**) (*angry*) arrabbiato(-a), seccato(-a); **to be/get cross with sb (about sth)** essere arrabbiato(-a)/arrabbiarsi con qn (per qc); **it makes me cross when ...** mi fa arrabbiare quando...; **he was cross about something** era arrabbiato per qualcosa
■ VT **1** (*gen*) attraversare; (*threshold*) varcare; **this road crosses the motorway** questa strada incrocia *or* interseca l'autostrada; **it crossed my mind that ...** mi è venuto in mente che...; **we'll cross that bridge when we come to it** (*fig*) ogni cosa a tempo debito **2** (*cheque, letter t*) sbarrare; **to cross o.s.** farsi il segno della croce, segnarsi; **cross my heart!** giuro (sulla mia vita)! **3** (*arms*) incrociare; (*legs*) accavallare, incrociare; **to keep one's fingers crossed** (*fig*) fare gli scongiuri; **to cross swords with sb** (*fig*) scontrarsi con qn; **we've got a crossed line** (*Brit*: *on telephone*) c'è un'interferenza; **they've got their lines crossed** (*fig*) si sono fraintesi **4** (*thwart*: *person, plan*) contrastare, ostacolare **5** (*animals, plants*) incrociare
■ VI **1** (*also*: **cross over**): **the boat crosses from Dieppe to Newhaven** il traghetto fa la traversata da Dieppe a Newhaven **2** (*roads*) intersecarsi; (*letters, people*) incrociarsi
▶ **cross off, cross out** VT + ADV cancellare (tirandoci una riga sopra)
▶ **cross over** VI attraversare
cross·bar ['krɒs,ba:^r] N (*of bicycle*) canna; (*of goal post*) traversa
cross·bill ['krɒs,bɪl] N (*Zool*) crociere *m*
cross·bow ['krɒs,bəʊ] N balestra
cross·breed ['krɒs,bri:d] N incrocio, ibrido
cross-Channel fer·ry [krɒs,tʃænəl'fɛrɪ] N traghetto che attraversa la Manica
cross-check [,krɒs'tʃɛk] N controprova
■ VT fare una controprova di
■ VI fare una controprova
cross-country [,krɒs'kʌntrɪ] ADJ (*race*) campestre, cross-country *inv*; **cross-country skiing** sci *m* di fondo; **a cross-country race** una corsa campestre
■ ADV (*walk, travel*) attraverso i campi
■ N (corsa) campestre, cross-country *m inv*
cross·court ['krɒs,kɔ:t] ADJ (*Tennis*): **crosscourt shot** diagonale *m*
cross-cultural ['krɒs,kʌltʃərəl] ADJ transculturale
cross-dressing [,krɒs'drɛsɪŋ] N travestitismo
crossed [krɒst] ADJ (*cheque*) sbarrato(-a)
cross-examination ['krɒsɪg,zæmɪ'neɪʃən] N (*Law*) interrogatorio in contraddittorio, controinterrogatorio
cross-examine [,krɒsɪg'zæmɪn] VT (*Law*) interrogare in contraddittorio, controinterrogare
cross-eyed ['krɒsaɪd] ADJ strabico(-a)
cross·fire ['krɒs,faɪə^r] N fuoco incrociato
cross·ing ['krɒsɪŋ] N (*sea-passage*) traversata; (*of equator*) attraversamento; (*road junction*) incrocio, crocicchio; (*also*: **pedestrian crossing**) strisce *fpl* pedonali, passaggio pedonale; (*level crossing*) passaggio a livello; **a ten-hour crossing** una traversata di dieci ore; **cross at the crossing** attraversa sulle strisce
crossing point N valico di frontiera
cross-legged [,krɒs'lɛgɪd] ADV a gambe incrociate
cross·ly ['krɒslɪ] ADV in tono arrabbiato, con rabbia
cross-multiply [,krɒs'mʌltɪplaɪ] VT (*Math*) fare una moltiplicazione incrociata di
cross·patch ['krɒs,pætʃ] N (*fam*) permaloso(-a), musone(-a)
cross-purposes [,krɒs'pɜ:pəsɪz] NPL: **to be at cross-purposes with sb** (*disagree*) essere in contrasto con qn; (*misunderstand*) fraintendere qn; **to talk at cross-purposes** fraintendersi

Cc

cross-question ['krɒs,kwɛstʃən] VT (*witness*) sottoporre a controinterrogatorio; (*fig*) interrogare
cross-refer ['krɒsrɪ'fɜːʳ] VT rimandare
cross-reference [,krɒs'rɛfərəns] N rinvio, rimando
cross·roads ['krɒs,rəʊdz] NSG incrocio, crocicchio
cross section N (*Bio etc*) sezione *f* trasversale; (*of population*) rappresentativo *m*; (*Topography*) profilo trasversale
cross·tree ['krɒs,triː] N (*Naut*) crocetta
cross·walk ['krɒs,wɔːk] N (*Am*) strisce *fpl* pedonali, passaggio pedonale
cross·wind ['krɒs,wɪnd] N vento di traverso
cross·wise ['krɒs,waɪz] ADV (*in the form of a cross*) a forma di croce; (*across*) di traverso
cross·word ['krɒs,wɜːd] N: **crossword (puzzle)** parole *fpl* crociate, cruciverba *m inv*
▷ www.crossword-puzzles.co.uk
crotch [krɒtʃ] N **1** (*also*: **crutch**: *Anat*) inforcatura **2** (*of garment*) cavallo
crotch·et ['krɒtʃɪt] N (*Brit*: *Mus*) semiminima
crotch·ety ['krɒtʃɪtɪ] ADJ (*fam*: *person*) burbero(-a), irritabile, stizzoso(-a)
cro·ton ['krəʊtən] N (*Bot*) croton *m inv*
crouch [kraʊtʃ] VI (*also*: **crouch down**: *person, animal*) accucciarsi, accovacciarsi, acquattarsi
croup [kruːp] N (*Med*) crup *m*
crou·pi·er ['kruːpɪeɪ] N croupier *m inv*
crou·ton ['kruːtɒn] N (*Culin*) crostino
crow [krəʊ] N **1** (*bird*) cornacchia; **hooded crow** cornacchia grigia; **as the crow flies** in linea d'aria **2** (*noise*: *of cock*) canto del gallo, chicchirichì *m inv*; (: *of baby, person*) gridolino
■VI **1** (*pt* **crowed** *or* **crew**, *pp* **crowed**) (*cock*) cantare, fare chicchirichì **2** (*pt, pp* **crowed**) (*child*) lanciare gridolini; (*fig*): **to crow over** *or* **about sth** vantarsi di qc; **to crow with delight** lanciare gridolini di piacere
crow·bar ['krəʊbɑːʳ] N piede *m* di porco
◎**crowd** [kraʊd] N folla; **crowds of people** un sacco di gente; **the crowd** (*common humanity*) la massa; **to follow the crowd** (*fig*) seguire la massa; **I don't like that crowd at all** non mi piace affatto quella gente; **she is part of the university crowd** appartiene alla cricca dell'università
■VT (*place*) affollare, gremire; **to crowd sth into** (*things*) ammassare qc in, stipare qc in
■VI affollarsi, ammassarsi; **to crowd in** entrare in massa; **to crowd round sb/sth** affollarsi attorno a qn/qc, accalcarsi intorno a qn/qc; **the children crowded round the model** i bambini si sono affollati attorno al modellino
▸ **crowd out** VT + ADV (*not let in*) escludere (dal proprio gruppo); **the bar was crowded out** il bar era così pieno(-a) che non si poteva entrare
crowd·ed ['kraʊdɪd] ADJ (*meeting, event, place etc*) affollato(-a), gremito(-a); (*town*) molto popolato(-a); (*day*) pieno(-a); (*profession*) inflazionato(-a); **crowded with** pieno(-a) di, gremito(-a) di, stipato(-a) di
crowd scene N (*Cine, Theatre*) scena di massa
◎**crown** [kraʊn] N **1** corona; **the Crown** (*Law*) ≈ il Pubblico Ministero **2** (*top*: *of hat, head*) cocuzzolo; (: *of hill*) cima, vetta, cocuzzolo; (: *of road*: *raised centre*) centro; (: *of tooth*) corona; (: *artificial*) capsula
■VT **1** (*king etc, fig*) incoronare; (*tooth*) incapsulare; **and to crown it all ...** (*fig*) e per giunta..., e come se non bastasse... **2** (*fam*: *hit*) dare una botta in testa a; **I'll crown you if you do that again!** se lo fai ancora ti do una botta in testa!
crown court N (*Brit Law*) ≈ corte *f* d'assise
crown·ing ['kraʊnɪŋ] ADJ (*achievement, glory*) supremo(-a)
crown jewels NPL gioielli *mpl* della Corona
crown prince N principe *m* ereditario
Crown Prosecution Service N (*Law*) organismo inglese e gallese che decide quali casi devono essere giudicati da un tribunale
crown prosecutor N (*Law*) ≈ Procuratore della Repubblica
crow's-feet ['krəʊz'fiːt] NPL zampe *fpl* di gallina
crow's-nest ['krəʊz,nɛst] N (*Naut*) coffa
◎**cru·cial** ['kruːʃəl] ADJ cruciale, decisivo(-a); **crucial to** essenziale per; **his approval is crucial to the success of the project** la sua approvazione è essenziale per il successo del progetto
cru·cial·ly ['kruːʃəlɪ] ADV: **it is crucially important that ...** è di vitale importanza che...
cru·ci·ble ['kruːsɪbl] N crogiolo
cru·ci·fix ['kruːsɪfɪks] N crocifisso
cru·ci·fix·ion [,kruːsɪ'fɪkʃən] N crocifissione *f*
cru·ci·fy ['kruːsɪ,faɪ] VT crocifiggere; (*fig*: *punish*) mettere in croce, fare a pezzi; (: *criticize*: *performance, actor*) stroncare; **if he catches us he'll crucify us** se ci pesca ci ammazza
crude [kruːd] ADJ (*comp* **-r**, *superl* **-st**) **1** (*pej*: *clumsy, unsophisticated*: *method, idea*) rozzo(-a); (*light, colour*) violento(-a) **2** (*simple*: *device, tool*) rudimentale; (: *drawing*) (appena) abbozzato(-a); **to make a crude attempt at doing sth** fare un rozzo tentativo di fare qc **3** (*vulgar*) volgare, grossolano(-a); **crude language** linguaggio volgare **4** (*unprocessed*: *materials*) grezzo(-a); (: *oil*) greggio(-a)
■N (*also*: **crude oil**) (petrolio) greggio

DID YOU KNOW ...?
crude is not translated by the Italian word *crudo*

crude·ly ['kruːdlɪ] ADV (*paint, make*) rozzamente; (*say, express*) brutalmente
crude·ness ['kruːdnɪs], **crud·ity** ['kruːdɪtɪ] N (*of method, idea*) rozzezza; (*of device, drawing*) rudimentalità; (*of expression, language*) volgarità
cru·el ['krʊəl] ADJ (*comp* **-ler**, *superl* **-lest**) **cruel (to** *or* **towards)** crudele (con *or* nei confronti di)
cru·el·ly ['krʊəlɪ] ADV crudelmente
cru·el·ty ['krʊəltɪ] N crudeltà *f inv*; **mental cruelty** crudeltà mentale
cru·et ['kruːɪt] N saliera e pepiera
◎**cruise** [kruːz] N crociera; **to go on a cruise** fare una crociera
■VI (*ship, plane*) viaggiare a velocità di crociera; (*holidaymakers*) fare una crociera; (*taxi, patrol car*) circolare; **the car cruises at 100 kph** (*Aut*) la velocità di crociera dell'auto è di 100 km/h
cruise missile N missile *m* cruise *inv*
cruis·er ['kruːzəʳ] N (*Naut*) incrociatore *m*
cruis·ing speed ['kruːzɪŋspiːd] N velocità *f inv* di crociera
crumb [krʌm] N (*of bread, cake etc*) briciola; (*inner part of bread*) mollica; **a crumb of comfort** (*fig*) un briciolo di conforto; **crumbs of information** ben poche informazioni; **crumbs!** (*fam*) accidenti!
crum·ble ['krʌmbl] VT sbriciolare
■VI (*bread*) sbriciolarsi; (*earth, land*) sbriciolarsi, franare; (*building etc*) andare in rovina; (*plaster, bricks*) sgretolarsi; (*fig*: *hopes, power*) crollare
crum·bly ['krʌmblɪ] ADJ friabile

crum·my ['krʌmɪ] ADJ (*fam: flat*) scadente; (: *idea*) stupido(-a); **a crummy town** un postaccio

crum·pet ['krʌmpɪt] N **1** (*Culin*) *specie di crespella piuttosto spessa da tostare e mangiare calda con burro, marmellata ecc.* **2 a piece of crumpet** (*fam!*) un bel tocco di ragazza

crum·ple ['krʌmpl] VT (*also:* **crumple up**: *paper*) accartocciare; (: *clothes*) stropicciare, sgualcire, spiegazzare
■VI (*see vt*) accartocciarsi; stropicciarsi, sgualcirsi, spiegazzarsi; **the man crumpled to the ground** l'uomo si è accasciato al suolo; **her face crumpled** il suo viso ha assunto un'espressione addolorata

crunch [krʌntʃ] N (*of broken glass, gravel*) scricchiolio; **if** *or* **when it comes to the crunch** (*fig*) al momento cruciale
■VT (*with teeth*) sgranocchiare
■VI (*gravel*) scricchiolare

crunchy ['krʌntʃɪ] ADJ (*comp* **-ier**, *superl* **-iest**) croccante

cru·sade [kruː'seɪd] N crociata
■VI (*fig*): **to crusade for/against** fare una crociata per/contro
▷ www.medievalcrusades.com
▷ www.the-orb.net/encyclop/religion/crusades/crusade.html

cru·sad·er [kruː'seɪdə^r] N (*History*) crociato; (*fig*): **crusader (for)** sostenitore(-trice) (di)

crush [krʌʃ] N **1** (*crowd*) ressa, calca, folla **2** (*fam: infatuation*) cotta; **to have a crush on sb** avere una cotta per qn; **she's had a crush on him for months** ha una cotta per lui da mesi **3** (*drink*): **orange/lemon crush** spremuta di arancia/limone
■VT (*squash: also fig*) schiacciare; (*crumple: clothes, paper*) sgualcire; (: *garlic*) tritare, schiacciare; (: *ice*) tritare; (: *grapes*) pigiare; (: *scrap metal*) pressare; (: *stones*) frantumare; **to be crushed to a pulp** essere ridotto(-a) in poltiglia; **crush two cloves of garlic** tritate due spicchi d'aglio
■VI (*clothes*) sgualcirsi, spiegazzarsi

crush barrier N (*Brit*) transenna

crush·ing ['krʌʃɪŋ] ADJ (*defeat, blow*) schiacciante; (*reply*) mordace

crush-resistant ['krʌʃrɪˌzɪstənt] ADJ ingualcibile

crust [krʌst] N crosta; (*layer*) strato; **the Earth's crust** la crosta terrestre

crus·ta·cean [krʌs'teɪʃən] N (*Zool*) crostaceo

crusty ['krʌstɪ] ADJ (*comp* **-ier**, *superl* **-iest**) (*bread*) croccante; (*fam: person*) brontolone(-a); (: *remark*) brusco(-a)

crutch [krʌtʃ] N **1** (*Med*) stampella, gruccia; (*support*) sostegno **2** = **crotch 2**

crux [krʌks] N **1 the crux of the matter** il nocciolo della questione **2** (*Mountaineering*) passaggio chiave

◎ **cry** [kraɪ] N **1** (*call, shout*) grido, urlo; (*of animal*) verso; **to give a cry** emettere un grido; **a cry for help** un grido di aiuto; **it's a far cry from ...** (*fig*) è tutt'un'altra cosa da...; **with a cry, she rushed forward** con un grido si lanciò in avanti; **"jobs, not bombs" was their cry** "lavoro non bombe" era il loro slogan **2** (*weep*): **she had a good cry** si è fatta un bel pianto
■VI **1** (*also:* **cry out**: *call out, shout*) gridare, urlare; **he cried (out) with pain** urlò di dolore; **to cry for help** gridare aiuto; **to cry for mercy** invocare pietà; **"you're wrong," he cried** "hai torto," gridò **2** (*weep*) piangere; **what are you crying about?** perché piangi?; **the child was crying for his mother** il bambino piangeva perché voleva la mamma; **I laughed till I cried** risi fino alle lacrime; **I'll give him something to cry about!** (*fam*) glielo darò io un motivo per piangere!; **it's no good crying over spilt milk** (*fig*) è inutile piangere sul latte versato
■VT **1** gridare, urlare **2 to cry o.s. to sleep** piangere fino ad addormentarsi
▸ **cry off** VI + ADV (*fam*) ritirarsi
▸ **cry out** VI + ADV (*shout*) urlare, gridare; **this car is crying out to be resprayed** (*fam*) questa macchina ha un gran bisogno di essere riverniciata
■VT + ADV **1** (*call*) gridare, urlare **2 to cry one's eyes** *or* **heart out** piangere tutte le proprie lacrime
▸ **cry out against** VI + ADV + PREP protestare vigorosamente contro

cry·baby ['kraɪˌbeɪbɪ] N (*fam*) piagnone(-a)

cry·ing ['kraɪɪŋ] ADJ (*child*) in lacrime, piangente; (*fam: need*) disperato(-a), urgente; (*injustice*) palese; **it's a crying shame** è una vera vergogna
■N (*weeping*) pianto

cryo·lite ['kraɪəˌlaɪt] N criolite *f*

cryo·sur·gery [ˌkraɪəʊ'sɜːdʒərɪ] N criochirurgia

crypt [krɪpt] N cripta

cryp·tic ['krɪptɪk] ADJ (*mysterious*) oscuro(-a); (*puzzling*) enigmatico(-a); **cryptic crossword** cruciverba *m* a crittogramma

cryp·ti·cal·ly ['krɪptɪkəlɪ] ADV (*see adj*) in modo oscuro; in modo enigmatico

cryp·to·gram ['krɪptəʊˌgræm] N crittogramma *m*

cryp·to·graph ['krɪptəʊˌgrɑːf] N crittografia

◎ **crys·tal** ['krɪstl] N (*gen*) cristallo; (*watch glass*) vetro
■ADJ (*glass, vase*) di cristallo; (*clear: water, lake*) cristallino(-a)

crystal ball N sfera di cristallo

crystal-clear [ˌkrɪstl'klɪə^r] ADJ (*water, wine*) cristallino(-a); (*fig*) chiaro(-a) (come il sole)

crystal-gazing ['krɪstlˌgeɪzɪŋ] N predizione *f* del futuro

crys·tal·line ['krɪstəˌlaɪn] ADJ cristallino(-a)

crys·tal·li·za·tion [ˌkrɪstəlaɪ'zeɪʃən] N cristallizzazione *f*

crys·tal·lize ['krɪstəˌlaɪz] VT (*Chem*) cristallizzare; (*fig*) concretizzare, concretare; **crystallized fruits** (*Brit*) frutta candita
■VI (*see vt*) cristallizzarsi; concretizzarsi, concretarsi

CSA [ˌsiːɛs'eɪ] N ABBR (*Brit:* = **Child Support Agency**) *ente governativo incaricato di valutare e riscuotere da genitori separati i contributi per il mantenimento dei figli*

CSE [ˌsiːɛs'iː] N ABBR (*Brit:* = **Certificate of Secondary Education**) *diploma di istruzione secondaria, nel vecchio sistema scolastico indicava il diploma di istruzione secondaria; accorpato al GCE, è stato sostituito dal GCSE*

CSEU [ˌsiːɛsiː'juː] N ABBR (*Brit:* = **Confederation of Shipbuilding and Engineering Unions**) *confederazione dei sindacati della costruzione navale e meccanica*

CS gas [ˌsiːɛs'gæs] N (*Brit*) *tipo di gas lacrimogeno*

CSM [ˌsiːɛs'ɛm] N ABBR (*Brit:* = **Committee for the Safety of Medicines**) *comitato governativo per la vigilanza sui farmaci*

CST [ˌsiːɛs'tiː] N ABBR (*Am:* = **central standard time**) *ora invernale nel fuso orario degli Stati Uniti centrali*

CSU [ˌsiːɛs'juː] N ABBR (*Brit:* = **Civil Service Union**) *sindacato dei dipendenti statali*

CT ABBR (*Am Post*) = **Connecticut**

ct ABBR = **carat**

CTC [ˌsiːtiː'siː], (*Brit*) N ABBR = **city technology college**

cu. ABBR = **cubic**

Cc

cub [kʌb] N **1** cucciolo; **lion cub** leoncino; **wolf cub** lupetto **2** (*also*: **cub scout**) lupetto
Cuba ['kju:bə] N Cuba
Cu·ban ['kju:bən] ADJ, N cubano(-a)
cubby·hole ['kʌbɪˌhəʊl] N angolo, cantuccio
cube [kju:b] N cubo; (*of sugar*) cubetto, zolletta; **to cut into cubes** tagliare a cubetti
■VT (*Math*) elevare al cubo *or* alla terza potenza
cube root N radice *f* cubica
cu·bic ['kju:bɪk] ADJ (*shape, volume*) cubico(-a); (*metre, foot*) cubo(-a); **cubic capacity** (*Aut*) cilindrata; **cubic function** (*Math*) funzione *f* cubica; **cubic metre** metro cubo
cu·bi·cle ['kju:bɪkəl] N cabina; **shower cubicle** box *m inv* doccia
cub·ism ['kju:bɪzəm] N cubismo
cub·ist ['kju:bɪst] ADJ, N cubista (*m/f*)
cu·boid ['kju:bɔɪd] ADJ cuboide
■N parallelepipedo rettangolo
cuck·old ['kʌkəld] (*old*) N (*man*) becco, cornuto
■VT fare becco
cuckoo ['kʊku:] N cuculo, cucù *m inv*
■ADJ (*fam*) tocco(-a), matto(-a)
cuckoo clock N orologio a cucù
cu·cum·ber ['kju:kʌmbə^r] N cetriolo; **tomatoes and cucumbers** pomodori e cetrioli; **to be as cool as a cucumber** essere imperturbabile
cud [kʌd] N: **to chew the cud** (*cows*) ruminare; (*fig*) rimuginare
cud·dle ['kʌdl] N abbraccio, coccole *fpl*; **come and give me a cuddle** vieni ad abbracciarmi; **kisses and cuddles** baci e carezze
■VT abbracciare, coccolare
■VI: **to cuddle down** accoccolarsi; **to cuddle up to sb** accoccolarsi contro qn
cud·dly ['kʌdlɪ] ADJ (*comp* **-ier**, *superl* **-iest**) (*child, animal*) coccolone(-a); (*toy*) morbido(-a), da tenere stretto(-a); **cuddly toy** animale *m* di peluche
cudg·el ['kʌdʒəl] N (*weapon*) manganello, randello; **to take up the cudgels for sb/sth** (*fig*) mettersi a lottare per qn/qc
■VT: **to cudgel one's brains** scervellarsi, spremersi le meningi
◎**cue** [kju:] N **1** (*Theatre: verbal, by signal*) segnale *m*, imbeccata; (*Mus: by signal*) segnale; **to give sb his cue** suggerire a qn la battuta, dare l'imbeccata a qn; **to take one's cue from sb** (*fig*) prendere esempio da qn **2** **right on cue** esattamente al momento giusto; (*Billiards*) stecca
▸**cue in** VT + ADV (*Theatre*) chiamare in scena; (*Radio, TV*) dare il segnale a
cuff¹ [kʌf] N (*blow*) schiaffo
■VT dare uno schiaffo a
cuff² [kʌf] N (*of shirt, coat*) polsino; (*Am: of trousers*) risvolto; **off the cuff** (*fig*) improvvisando
cuff link N gemello
cu. ft. ABBR = cubic feet
cu. in. ABBR = cubic inches
cui·sine [kwɪ'zi:n] N cucina; **French cuisine** la cucina francese
cul-de-sac ['kʌldə'sæk] N vicolo cieco
culi·nary ['kʌlɪnərɪ] ADJ culinario(-a)
cull [kʌl] VT (*select: fruit*) scegliere; (*kill selectively: animals*) selezionare e abbattere
■N selezione *f*; **seal cull** abbattimento selettivo delle foche
cull·ing ['kʌlɪŋ] N eliminazione *f* selettiva
cul·mi·nate ['kʌlmɪˌneɪt] VI: **to culminate in** culminare con *or* in
cul·mi·na·tion [ˌkʌlmɪ'neɪʃən] N culmine *m*; (*Astron*) culminazione *f*
cu·lottes [kju:'lɒts] NPL gonna *f* pantalone *inv*
cul·pable ['kʌlpəbl] ADJ colpevole
culpable homicide N (*Law*) omicidio colposo
cul·prit ['kʌlprɪt] N colpevole *m/f*
cult [kʌlt] N (*Rel, fig*) culto; **to make a cult of sth** avere un culto per qc
cult figure N idolo
cul·ti·vable ['kʌltɪvəbl] ADJ coltivabile
cul·ti·vate ['kʌltɪˌveɪt] VT (*also fig*) coltivare
cul·ti·vat·ed ['kʌltɪˌveɪtɪd] ADJ (*land*) coltivato(-a); (*refined: person, manner*) raffinato(-a); (*cultured*) colto(-a)
cul·ti·va·tion [ˌkʌltɪ'veɪʃən] N (*Agr*) coltivazione *f*, coltura
cul·ti·va·tor ['kʌltɪˌveɪtə^r] N **1** (*machine*) coltivatore *m* **2** (*person*) coltivatore(-trice)
◎**cul·tur·al** ['kʌltʃərəl] ADJ culturale
cul·tur·al·ly ['kʌltʃərəlɪ] ADV culturalmente
◎**cul·ture** ['kʌltʃə^r] N **1** cultura; (*civilization*) civiltà **2** (*Bio, Agr*) coltura; **people from different cultures** persone *fpl* di culture diverse
cul·tured ['kʌltʃəd] ADJ (*person, mind*) colto(-a); (*voice*) da persona colta; (*manners*) raffinato(-a); (*pearl*) coltivato(-a)
culture shock N: **to experience culture shock** essere scioccato(-a) dall'impatto con una cultura diversa
cum·ber·some ['kʌmbəsəm] ADJ ingombrante
cum·in ['kʌmɪn] N (*spice*) cumino
cum·mer·bund ['kʌməˌbʌnd] N fascia dello smoking
cu·mu·la·tive ['kju:mjʊlətɪv] ADJ cumulativo(-a); **cumulative frequency** (*Statistics*) frequenza cumulata
cu·mu·lo·nim·bus [ˌkju:mjʊləʊ'nɪmbəs] N (*Met*) cumulonembo
cu·mu·lus ['kju:mjələs] N cumulo
cu·nei·form ['kju:nɪˌfɔ:m] ADJ, N cuneiforme (*m*)
cun·ning ['kʌnɪŋ] ADJ (*pej: crafty*) furbo(-a), astuto(-a); (*clever: device, idea*) ingegnoso(-a); **a cunning plan** un piano ingegnoso
■N furbizia, astuzia
cun·ning·ly ['kʌnɪŋlɪ] ADV (*see adj*) ingegnosamente; astutamente
cunt [kʌnt] N (*fam!*) figa (*fam!*); (*insult*) pezzo di merda (*fam!*)
◎**cup** [kʌp] N (*for tea*) tazza; (*as prize, of brassière*) coppa; **a cup of tea/coffee** una tazza di tè/caffè; **tea cup** tazza da tè; **it's not everyone's cup of tea** (*fam*) non è una cosa che piace a tutti; **that's just not my cup of tea** (*fam*) non è proprio il mio genere
■VT (*hands*) riunire (a coppa); **to cup one's hands round sth** prendere qc fra le mani
cup·board ['kʌbəd] N armadio
cupboard love N (*Brit*) amore *m* interessato
cup final N (*Brit: Ftbl*) finale *f* di coppa
cup·ful ['kʌpfʊl] N tazza (*contenuto*)
Cupid ['kju:pɪd] N (*Myth*) Cupido; **Cupid's bow** (*lip shape*) labbro arcuato
cupid ['kju:pɪd] N (*cherub*) cupido, amoretto
cu·pid·ity [kju:'pɪdɪtɪ] N cupidigia
cu·po·la ['kju:pələ] N cupola
cup·pa ['kʌpə] N (*Brit fam*) tazza di tè
cup tie N (*Brit*) (*Ftbl*) partita eliminatoria
cur [kɜ:^r] N **1** (*pej: dog*) cagnaccio **2** (*pej: man*) disgraziato
cur·able ['kjʊərəbl] ADJ guaribile, curabile

cu·rate ['kjʊərɪt] N curato, cappellano
cu·ra·tive ['kjʊərətɪv] ADJ curativo(-a)
■N cura, rimedio
cu·ra·tor [kjʊə'reɪtə^r] N direttore(-trice) (di museo *etc*)
curb[1] [kɜ:b] N freno
■VT (*fig: temper, impatience etc*) frenare, tenere a freno; (*: expenditure*) limitare
curb[2] [kɜ:b] N (*Am*) = **kerb**
curd [kɜ:d] N, USU PL **curds**
■NPL latte *m* cagliato
curd cheese N cagliata
cur·dle ['kɜ:dl] VT (*gen*) far cagliare; (*mayonnaise*) far impazzire
■VI (*see vt*) cagliarsi, cagliare; impazzire; **it made my blood curdle** mi ha gelato il sangue nelle vene
◎**cure** [kjʊə^r] N (*remedy*) cura; (*recovery*) guarigione *f*; **to take a cure** fare una cura
■VT **1** (*Med: disease, patient*) guarire; (*fig: poverty, injustice, evil*) eliminare; **to be cured of sth** essere guarito(-a) da qc; **to cure sb of a habit** far perdere a qn un'abitudine **2** (*preserve: in salt*) salare; (*: by smoking*) affumicare; (*: by drying*) seccare, essiccare; (*: animal hide*) conciare, trattare
cure-all ['kjʊər,ɔ:l] N (*also fig*) panacea, toccasana *m inv*
cur·few ['kɜ:fju:] N coprifuoco
cu·rio ['kjʊərɪəʊ] N curiosità *f inv*, oggetto insolito
cu·ri·os·ity [,kjʊərɪ'ɒsɪtɪ] N curiosità *f inv*; **curiosity killed the cat** la curiosità si paga cara
◎**cu·ri·ous** ['kjʊərɪəs] ADJ **1** (*inquisitive*) curioso(-a); **I'm curious about him** m'incuriosisce; **I'd be curious to know** sarei curioso di sapere **2** (*strange*) strano(-a), curioso(-a)
cu·ri·ous·ly ['kjʊərɪəslɪ] ADV (*see adj*) con curiosità; stranamente; **curiously enough, ...** per quanto possa sembrare strano,...
curl [kɜ:l] N (*of hair*) ricciolo, riccio; (*of smoke*) anello
■VT (*hair*) ondulare; (*tightly*) arricciare; **she curled her lip in scorn** arricciò sprezzantemente le labbra
■VI (*hair*) arricciarsi; **it's enough to make your hair curl** (*fam*) è una cosa da far drizzare i capelli
▸ **curl up** VI + ADV (*leaves, paper*) accartocciarsi; (*cat*) acciambellarsi; (*person, dog*) accoccolarsi, rannicchiarsi; (*fam: with shame*) sprofondare (dalla vergogna); (*with laughter*) piegarsi in due (dalle risate)
curl·er ['kɜ:lə^r] N **1** (*for hair*) bigodino **2** (*Sport*) giocatore(-trice) di curling
cur·lew ['kɜ:lu:] N chiurlo
curl·ing ['kɜ:lɪŋ] N (*Sport*) curling *m*
▷ www.curling.ca/index.asp?lang=e
▷ www.worldcurlingfederation.org/
▷ www.usacurl.org/
curling tongs, **curling irons** (*Am*) NPL (*for hair*) arricciacapelli *m inv*
curly ['kɜ:lɪ] ADJ (*comp* **-ier**, *superl* **-iest**) (*gen*) riccio(-a), ricciuto(-a); (*eyelashes*) ricurvo(-a); **curly hair** capelli ricci
curly-haired [,kɜ:lɪ'hɛəd], **curly-headed** [,kɜ:lɪ'hɛdɪd] ADJ ricciuto(-a)
cur·rant ['kʌrənt] N (*dried grape*) uva passa; (*bush, fruit*) ribes *m inv*
currant bun N panino con l'uva passa
◎**cur·ren·cy** ['kʌrənsɪ] N **1** moneta; **foreign currency** valuta estera; **hard currency** moneta forte; **paper currency** banconote *fpl* **2** (*fig: of ideas*): **to gain currency** acquistare larga diffusione, acquistare credito; **to have wide currency** essere molto diffuso(-a)
currency note N banconota
currency rate N tasso di cambio
◎**cur·rent** ['kʌrənt] ADJ (*fashion, opinion, year*) corrente; (*tendency, price, event*) attuale; (*phrase*) di uso corrente; **in current use** in uso corrente, d'uso comune; **the current financial year** l'anno finanziario corrente; **the current issue of a magazine** l'ultimo numero di una rivista; **her current boyfriend** il suo attuale ragazzo; **the current situation is quite unacceptable** la situazione attuale è del tutto inaccettabile
■N (*of air, water, Elec, fig*) corrente *f*; **direct/alternating current** (*Elec*) corrente continua/alternata; **to go against the current** (*fig*) andare controcorrente
current account N (*Brit: Bank*) conto corrente
current affairs ['kʌrəntə'fɛəz] NPL attualità *f inv*; **she presents a current affairs programme on Monday evenings** presenta un programma d'attualità il lunedì sera
current assets ['kʌrənt'æsɛts] NPL (*Fin*) attivo realizzabile e disponibile
current liabilities ['kʌrənt,laɪə'bɪlɪtɪz] NPL (*Fin*) passività *fpl* correnti
cur·rent·ly ['kʌrəntlɪ] ADV attualmente, al momento
current ratio N (*Econ*) rapporto di liquidità
cur·ricu·lum [kə'rɪkjʊləm] N (*pl* **curricula** *or* **curriculums** [kə'rɪkjʊlə]) (*Scol, Univ*) programma *m*
cur·ricu·lum vi·tae [kə,rɪkjʊləm'vi:taɪ] N curriculum vitae *m inv*
cur·ried ['kʌrɪd] ADJ al curry
cur·ry[1] ['kʌrɪ] N (*dish*) pietanza al curry; (*spice*) curry *m inv*; **chicken curry** pollo al curry; **beef/vegetable curry** manzo/verdure al curry; **a spoonful of curry** un cucchiaio di curry; **to go out for a curry** andare al ristorante indiano
■VT cucinare al curry
cur·ry[2] ['kʌrɪ] VT: **to curry favour with sb** cercare di accattivarsi (il favore di) qn
curry powder N curry *m*
curse [kɜ:s] N **1** maledizione *f*; **curses!** NPL (*fam*) maledizione!; **to put a curse on sb** maledire qn; **there seems to be a curse on my family** sembra esserci una maledizione sulla mia famiglia **2** (*bane*) rovina, flagello; **the curse of it is that ...** il guaio è che...
3 (*swearword*) imprecazione *f*; (*blasphemous*) bestemmia
4 (*fam: menstruation*): **she's got the curse** ha le sue cose
■VT maledire
■VI bestemmiare
curs·ed ['kɜ:sɪd] ADJ (*under a curse*) dannato(-a); **to be cursed with** (*fig*) essere tormentato(-a) da
cur·sor ['kɜ:sə^r] N (*Comput*) cursore *m*
cur·so·ri·ly ['kɜ:sərɪlɪ] ADV (*glance*) di sfuggita, in fretta; (*read through*) rapidamente, in fretta
cur·sory ['kɜ:sərɪ] ADJ (*glance*) di sfuggita, superficiale; **a cursory reading** una rapida scorsa, una lettura veloce
curt [kɜ:t] ADJ brusco(-a), secco(-a); **with a curt nod** con un breve cenno del capo

DID YOU KNOW ...?
curt is not translated by the Italian word *corto*

cur·tail [kɜ:'teɪl] VT (*visit etc*) accorciare; (*wages, expenditure*) ridurre, decurtare, tagliare
cur·tail·ment [kɜ:'teɪlmənt] N (*of holiday*) interruzione *f*; (*of wages, financial support*) riduzione *f*

Cc

◎**cur·tain** ['kɜ:tn] N tenda; (*Theatre*) sipario; **to draw the curtains** (*together*) chiudere *or* tirare le tende; (*apart*) aprire le tende; **it'll be curtains for you!** (*fam*) per te sarà la fine!
▸ **curtain off** VT + ADV separare con una tenda
curtain call N (*Theatre*) chiamata alla ribalta
curtain hook N gancio della tenda
curtain ring N anello della tenda
curtain rod N asta *or* bastone *m* della tenda
curt·ly ['kɜ:tlɪ] ADV bruscamente, seccamente
curt·ness ['kɜ:tnɪs] N bruschezza
curt·sy, **curt·sey** ['kɜ:tsɪ] N inchino, riverenza
■ VI fare un inchino *or* una riverenza
cur·va·ceous [kɜ:'veɪʃəs] ADJ (*fam: woman*) formoso(-a)
cur·va·ture ['kɜ:vətʃəʳ] N curvatura; **curvature of the spine** (*Med*) deviazione *f* della colonna vertebrale
curve [kɜ:v] N (*gen*) curva; (*of river*) ansa; **simple closed curve** (*Math*) curva chiusa semplice; **throw sb a curve (ball)** (*Am*) prendere qn di sorpresa
■ VT curvare
■ VI (*road, river*) fare una curva; (*line, surface, arch*) curvarsi
curved [kɜ:vd] ADJ curvo(-a)
cush·ion ['kʊʃən] N cuscino; (*of billiard table*) sponda (elastica)
■ VT (*blow, fall, shock*) attutire, fare da cuscinetto a; **to cushion sb against sth** proteggere qn da qc
cushy ['kʊʃɪ] ADJ (*comp* **-ier**, *superl* **-iest**) (*fam*): **a cushy job** un lavoro di tutto riposo
cusp [kʌsp] N cuspide *f*
cuss [kʌs] (*fam*) N **1** (*oath*) bestemmia **2** (*person*) tipo(-a) palloso(-a)
■ VI bestemmiare
cuss·ed ['kʌsɪd] ADJ (*fam*) ostinato(-a), testardo(-a)
cuss·ed·ness ['kʌsɪdnɪs] N (*fam*) ripicca, spirito di contraddizione
cus·tard ['kʌstəd] N (*pouring*) crema (pasticcera); (*set*) ≈ budino
custard cream N (*biscuit*) biscotto farcito alla crema
custard pie N *tartina alla crema*
custard powder N (*Brit*) preparato in polvere per crema
custard tart N crostata alla crema
cus·to·dial sen·tence [kʌs,təʊdɪəl'sɛntəns] N condanna ad una pena detentiva
cus·to·dian [kʌs'təʊdɪən] N (*gen*) custode *m/f*; (*of museum etc*) soprintendente *m/f*
cus·to·dy ['kʌstədɪ] N (*Law: of child*) custodia; (*for offenders*) arresto; (*police custody*) detenzione *f* (preventiva); **to be in custody** essere in stato di detenzione; **to take sb into custody** mettere qn in detenzione preventiva; **in safe custody** al sicuro; **in the custody of** alla custodia di
cus·tom ['kʌstəm] N **1** costume *m*, usanza, consuetudine *f*; (*Law*) consuetudine; **social customs** convenzioni *fpl* sociali; **it is her custom to go for a walk each evening** è sua consuetudine fare una passeggiata ogni sera **2** (*Comm*): **to get sb's custom** ottenere qn per cliente; **the shop has lost a lot of custom** il negozio ha perso molti clienti; *see also* customs
cus·tom·ary ['kʌstəmərɪ] ADJ consueto(-a); **it is customary to wear black** è consuetudine vestire di nero
custom-built ['kʌstəm,bɪlt] ADJ *see* **custom-made**
◎**cus·tom·er** ['kʌstəməʳ] N cliente *m/f*; **he's an awkward customer** (*fam*) è un tipo incontentabile; **ugly customer** (*fam*) brutto tipo
customer base N clientela
customer profile N profilo del cliente
cus·tom·ize ['kʌstəmaɪz] VT personalizzare; **customized software** software *m inv* personalizzato
cus·tom·ized ['kʌstə,maɪzd] ADJ personalizzato(-a); (*car*) fuoriserie *inv*
custom-made ['kʌstəm'meɪd] ADJ (*clothes*) fatto(-a) su misura; (*other goods: also:* **custom-built**) fatto(-a) su ordinazione
cus·toms ['kʌstəmz] NPL (*also:* **Customs**) dogana; **to go through (the) customs** passare la dogana
Customs and Excise N (*Brit*) Ufficio Dazi e Dogana
customs control N controllo doganale
customs duty N dazio doganale
customs house, customs post N casotto *or* ufficio della dogana
customs officer N doganiere *m*
◎**cut** [kʌt] (*vb: pt, pp* **cut**) N
1 (*gen*) taglio; (*Med*) taglio, incisione *f*; (*Cards*) alzata; **the cut and thrust of politics** i vivaci contrasti della politica; **he's a cut above the others** è di gran lunga migliore degli altri
2 (*reduction: in salary, spending*) riduzione *f*, taglio; (*deletion: in film, text*) taglio; **power cut** interruzione di corrente elettrica; **to take a cut in salary** avere una riduzione dello stipendio
3 (*of clothes, hair*) taglio
4 (*of meat: piece*) taglio, pezzo, parte *f*; (*fam: share*) parte; **cold cuts** (*Am*) affettati *mpl*
■ ADJ (*flowers*) reciso(-a); (*glass*) intagliato(-a)
■ VT
1 (*gen*) tagliare; (*Cards*) alzare; **to cut o.s.** tagliarsi; **to cut one's finger** tagliarsi un dito; **to cut a tooth** mettere un dente; **to cut sth in half/in two** tagliare qc a metà/in due; **he is cutting his own throat** (*fig*) si sta dando la zappa sui piedi; **to cut to pieces** (*army, fig*) fare a pezzi, distruggere; **to cut sth to size** tagliare qc su misura; **to cut open** aprire con un coltello (*or* con le forbici *etc*); **he cut his head open** si è spaccato la testa; **to cut sb free** liberare qn (*tagliando qc*); **it cut me to the quick** *or* **the heart** (*fig*) mi ha ferito profondamente
2 (*shape: gen, jewel*) tagliare; (*steps, channel*) scavare; (*key*) fare una copia di, riprodurre; (*glass*) lavorare; (*figure, statue*) scolpire; (*engrave*) incidere, intagliare; (*record*) incidere; **to cut one's way through** aprirsi la strada attraverso; **to cut one's coat according to one's cloth** (*fig*) non fare il passo più lungo della gamba
3 (*clip, trim: hair, nails, hedge etc*) tagliare; **to get one's hair cut** farsi tagliare i capelli
4 (*reduce: wages, prices, production etc*) ridurre; (*expenses*) ridurre, limitare, tagliare; (*speech*) abbreviare; (*text, film*) tagliare; (*interrupt*) interrompere; **to cut sb/sth short** interrompere qn/qc; **to cut 30 seconds off a record** (*Sport*) abbassare un record di 30 secondi
5 (*intersect*) intersecare, tagliare
6 (*fam: avoid: class, lecture, appointment*) saltare; **to cut sb dead** ignorare qn completamente
■ VI
1 (*person, knife*) tagliare; **she cut into the melon** ha affondato il coltello nel melone; **it cuts both ways** (*fig*) è un'arma a doppio taglio; **to cut and run** (*fam*) tagliare la corda; **to cut loose (from sth)** (*fig*) staccarsi (da qc)
2 (*hurry*): **to cut across country/through the lane** tagliare per la campagna/per il sentiero; **I must cut**

along now ora devo avviarmi
3 (*Cine*): **the film cut from the bedroom to the garden** la scena del film si è spostata dalla stanza da letto al giardino; **cut!** stop!
4 (*Cards*) tagliare il mazzo
▸ **cut away** VT + ADV tagliare via
▸ **cut across** VI + PREP (*fig*: *barriers, boundaries*) trascendere
▸ **cut back** VI + ADV (*on costs etc*) limitare *or* tagliare le spese; (*on staff*) ridurre il personale
■ VT + ADV (*plants*) potare; (*production, expenditure, staff*) ridurre
▸ **cut down** VT + ADV
1 (*tree*) abbattere; (*enemy*) falciare
2 (*reduce*: *consumption, expenses*) ridurre, tagliare; **to cut sb down to size** (*fig*) sgonfiare *or* ridimensionare qn
▸ **cut down on** VI + ADV + PREP ridurre, diminuire; **I'm cutting down on coffee and cigarettes** sto riducendo il caffè e le sigarette
▸ **cut in** VI + ADV: **to cut in (on)** (*interrupt*: *conversation*) intromettersi (in); (*Aut*) tagliare la strada (a)
▸ **cut off** VT + ADV
1 (*gen*) tagliare; **to cut off one's nose to spite one's face** (*fam*) farsi dispetto
2 (*disconnect*: *telephone, gas, electricity*) tagliare; (*engine*) spegnere; **the electricity has been cut off** l'elettricità è stata tagliata; **we've been cut off** (*Telec*) è caduta la linea
3 (*isolate*) isolare; **they feel very cut off** si sentono tagliati fuori dal mondo *or* isolati; **to cut o.s. off from sth/sb** allontanarsi *or* isolarsi da qc/qn; **to cut off the enemy's retreat** tagliare la ritirata al nemico; **to cut sb off without a penny** diseredare qn
▸ **cut out** VI + ADV (*engine*) spegnersi; **the engine cut out at the traffic lights** il motore si è spento al semaforo
■ VT + ADV
1 (*article, picture*) ritagliare; (*statue, figure*) scolpire; (*dress etc*) tagliare; **I'll cut the article out of the paper** ritaglierò l'articolo dal giornale; **to be cut out for sth/to do sth** (*fig*) essere tagliato(-a) per qc/per fare qc; **you'll have your work cut out for you** avrai un bel daffare
2 (*delete*) eliminare, togliere
3 (*stop, give up*) eliminare; **cut it out!** (*fam*) dacci un taglio!
▸ **cut up** VT + ADV
1 (*gen*) tagliare; (*chop*: *food*) sminuzzare
2 (*fam*): **to be cut up about sth** (*hurt*) rimanere sconvolto(-a) per qc; (*annoyed*) essere arrabbiato(-a) per qc
■ VI + ADV: **to cut up rough** (*fam*) perdere le staffe
cut-and-dried [ˌkʌtənˈdraɪd] ADJ (*also*: **cut-and-dry**: *fig*) assodato(-a)
cut and paste (*Comput*) VT: **"cut and paste"** "taglia e incolla"
■ N funzione *f* taglia e incolla
cut·away [ˈkʌtəˌweɪ] ADJ, N: **cutaway (drawing)** spaccato
cut·back [ˈkʌtˌbæk] N 1 (*in expenditure, staff, production*) taglio, riduzione *f*; **over the past year there have been many cutbacks in public services** nell'ultimo anno ci sono stati molti tagli nei servizi pubblici
2 (*Cine*: *flashback*) flashback *m inv*
cute [kjuːt] ADJ (*esp Am*: *sweet*) carino(-a), grazioso(-a); (*clever*) furbo(-a), astuto(-a)
cut glass N cristallo
cu·ti·cle [ˈkjuːtɪkl] N (*of fingernails*) cuticola, pellicina; (*Bot, Zool*) cuticola
cuticle remover N (*tool*) scalzapelli *m inv*; (*cream*) *crema per le pellicine*
cut·lass [ˈkʌtləs] N (*History*) sciabola
cut·ler [ˈkʌtləʳ] N coltellinaio
cut·lery [ˈkʌtlərɪ] N posate *fpl*
cutlery drainer N scolaposate *m inv*
cutlery tray N portaposate *m inv*
cut·let [ˈkʌtlɪt] N cotoletta, costoletta
cut·off [ˈkʌtˌɒf] N (*also*: **cutoff point**) limite *m*
cutoff switch N interruttore *m*
cut·out [ˈkʌtˌaʊt] N (*paper, cardboard figure*) ritaglio; (*switch*) interruttore *m*
cut-price [ˈkʌtˌpraɪs], **cut-rate** [ˈkʌtˌreɪt], (*Am*) ADJ (*goods*) scontato(-a), a prezzo ridotto; (*shop*) che fa prezzi bassi
cut·ter [ˈkʌtəʳ] N 1 (*person*) tagliatore(-trice); (*tool*) taglierina 2 (*sailing ship*) cutter *m inv*; (*ship's boat*) lancia
cut·throat [ˈkʌtˌθrəʊt] N assassino(-a)
■ ADJ (*razor*) da barbiere; (*business*) spietato(-a); **cutthroat competition** concorrenza spietata
◎ **cut·ting** [ˈkʌtɪŋ] N 1 (*of plant*) talea 2 (*Brit*: *from newspaper*) ritaglio; (*Cine*) montaggio 3 (*Brit*: *for road, railway*) scavo
■ ADJ (*cold*: *wind etc*) pungente; (*fig*: *remark*) tagliente, mordace
cutting edge N 1 (*of knife*) taglio, filo 2 (*fig*): **on** *or* **at the cutting edge of sth** all'avanguardia di qc
cutting room N (*Cine*) sala di montaggio
cuttle·bone [ˈkʌtlˌbəʊn] N osso di seppia
cuttle·fish [ˈkʌtlˌfɪʃ] N seppia
cut-up [ˈkʌtˌʌp] ADJ sconvolto(-a)
CV [ˌsiːˈviː] N ABBR CV *m inv*, curriculum vitae *m inv*
cwo ABBR = **cash with order**; *see* **cash**
cwt. ABBR *of* **hundredweight**
CWU [ˌsiːdʌbljʊˈjuː] N ABBR (*Brit*) = **Communications Workers Union**
CYA [ˈsiːjə] ABBR (= **see you**) C ved (= *ci vediamo*)
cya·nide [ˈsaɪəˌnaɪd] N cianuro
cya·not·ic [ˌsaɪəˈnɒtɪk] ADJ cianotico(-a)
cy·ber·café [ˈsaɪbəˌkæfeɪ] N cibercaffè *m*
cy·ber·net·ics [ˌsaɪbəˈnɛtɪks] NSG cibernetica
cy·ber·sex [ˈsaɪbəseks] N sesso virtuale
cy·ber·space [ˈsaɪbəspeɪs] N ciberspazio
cy·ber·squat·ting [ˈsaɪbəskwɒtɪŋ] N (*Comput*) *acquisto di un dominio per poi rivenderlo ad un prezzo più alto*
cy·ber·ter·ror·ism [ˌsaɪbəˈtɛrərɪzəm] N ciberterrorismo
cyc·la·men [ˈsɪkləmən] N ciclamino
◎ **cy·cle** [ˈsaɪkl] N 1 (*bicycle*) bicicletta 2 (*of seasons, poems*) ciclo
■ VI andare in bicicletta; **I cycle to school** vado a scuola in bicicletta
cycle path N pista ciclabile
cycle race N gara *or* corsa ciclistica
cycle rack N portabiciclette *m inv*
cycle ride N giro in bicicletta
cycle shed N riparo per le biciclette
cy·clic [ˈsaɪklɪk] ADJ ciclico(-a)
cy·cli·cal [ˈsaɪklɪkəl] ADJ ciclico(-a)
cy·cling [ˈsaɪklɪŋ] N ciclismo; **the roads round here are ideal for cycling** le strade qua attorno sono l'ideale per andare in bicicletta
cycling holiday N vacanza in bicicletta; **to go on a cycling holiday** (*Brit*) fare una vacanza in bicicletta

Cc

cy·clist ['saɪklɪst] N ciclista *m/f*
cy·cloid ['saɪklɔɪd] N (*Geom*) cicloide *f*
cy·clone ['saɪkləʊn] N ciclone *m*
Cy·clops ['saɪ'klɒps] N (*pl* **Cyclopes** [saɪ'klɒʊpi:z] *or* **Cyclopses**) ciclope *m*
cy·clo·style ['saɪklə,staɪl] VT ciclostilare
cy·clo·tron ['saɪklə,trɒn] N ciclotrone *m*
cyg·net ['sɪgnɪt] N cigno giovane
cyl·in·der ['sɪlɪndə^r] N cilindro; **a 6-cylinder engine** un motore a 6 cilindri; **to fire on all four cylinders** avere tutti e quattro i cilindri in azione; (*fig*) andare a tutto gas
cylinder block N monoblocco
cylinder head N testata
cylinder head gasket N guarnizione *f* della testata del cilindro
cy·lin·dri·cal [sɪ'lɪndrɪkəl] ADJ cilindrico(-a)
cym·bal ['sɪmbəl] N piatto (*Mus*)
cyn·ic ['sɪnɪk] N cinico(-a)
cyni·cal ['sɪnɪkəl] ADJ cinico(-a)
cyni·cal·ly ['sɪnɪklɪ] ADV cinicamente
cyni·cism ['sɪnɪsɪzəm] N cinismo
CYO [,si:waɪ'əʊ] N ABBR (*Am*) = *Catholic Youth Organization*
cy·press ['saɪprɪs] N cipresso; **Lawson's cypress** cedro bianco
Cyp·ri·ot ['sɪprɪət] ADJ, N cipriota (*m/f*)
Cy·prus ['saɪprəs] N Cipro; **in Cyprus** a Cipro
Cy·re·ne [saɪ'ri:nɪ] N: **Simon of Cyrene** il Cireneo
Cy·ril·lic [sɪ'rɪlɪk] ADJ cirillico(-a)
■ N alfabeto cirillico
cyst [sɪst] N cisti *f inv*
cys·ti·tis [sɪs'taɪtɪs] N (*Med*) cistite *f*
cy·to·plasm ['saɪtəʊ,plæzəm] N citoplasma *m*
czar [zɑ:^{r}] N zar *m inv*
cza·ri·na [zɑ:'ri:nə] N zarina
czar·ist ['zɑ:rɪst] ADJ, N zarista (*m/f*)
Czech [tʃɛk] ADJ ceco(-a)
■ N (*person*) ceco(-a); (*language*) ceco; **the Czechs** i cechi
Czecho·slo·vak [,tʃɛkəʊ'sləʊvæk], **Czecho·slo·vakian** ['tʃɛkəʊslə'vækɪən] ADJ cecoslovacco(-a)
■ N (*person*) cecoslovacco(-a); (*language*) cecoslovacco
Czecho·slo·va·kia ['tʃɛkəʊslə'vækɪə] N Cecoslovacchia
Czech Republic ADJ: **the Czech Republic** la repubblica Ceca

D, d [di:] N **1** (*letter*) D, d *f or m inv*; **D for David** (*Am*): **D for Dog** ≈ D come Domodossola **2** (*Mus*) re *m inv*
D. ABBR (*Am Pol*) = **Democrat(ic)**
d [di:] ABBR (*Brit old*) = **penny**
d. ABBR (= **died**) *see* **die**
DA [di:'eɪ] N ABBR (*Am*) = **district attorney**
DAB [ˌdi:eɪ'bi:] N ABBR (= **digital audio broadcasting**) DAB *m*
▷ www.worlddab.org
dab¹ [dæb] N (*light stroke*) colpetto, tocco; (: *of paint*) pennellata; (*small amount*) pochino, punta; (: *of glue*) goccio; **a dab of paint** un colpetto di vernice
■ ADJ: **to be a dab hand at sth/at doing sth** (*fam*) essere in gambissima in qc/a fare qc
■ VT (*touch lightly*: *also*: *dab at*) picchiettare lievemente; (*eyes, wound*) tamponare; (*apply*: *paint, cream*): **to dab sth on sth** applicare qc con colpetti leggeri su qc
dab² [dæb] N (*fish*) limanda
dab·ble ['dæbl] VT: **to dabble one's hands/feet in the water** sguazzare con le mani/i piedi nell'acqua
■ VI (*fig*): **to dabble in sth** occuparsi di qc a tempo perso, dilettarsi di qc; **to dabble in politics** dilettarsi di politica
dab·bler ['dæbləʳ] N (*pej*) dilettante *m/f*
Dac·ca ['dækə] N Dacca
da·cha ['dætʃə] N dacia
dachs·hund ['dækshʊnd] N bassotto
Da·cron® ['dækrɒn] N Dacron® *m inv*
◎ **dad** [dæd], **dad·dy** ['dædɪ] N (*fam*) papà *m inv*, babbo; **I'll ask Dad** lo chiederò al papà
daddy-long-legs [ˌdædɪ'lɒŋlegz] N, PL INV zanzarone *m*, tipula (*Zool*)
dado ['deɪdəʊ] N (*of wall*) zoccolo decorato; (*Archit*) dado
Daedalus ['di:dələs] N (*Myth*) Dedalo
daf·fo·dil ['dæfədɪl] N trombone *m*, giunchiglia
daffodil yellow N giallo *m* brillante *inv*
■ ADJ giallo brillante *inv*
daft [dɑ:ft] ADJ (*comp* **-er**, *superl* **-est**) (*fam*) sciocco(-a); **to be daft about sb** aver perso la testa per qn; **to be daft about sth** andare pazzo(-a) per qc
dag·ger ['dægəʳ] N pugnale *m*, stiletto; (*Typ*) croce *f*; **to be at daggers drawn (with sb)** essere ai ferri corti (con qn); **to look daggers at sb** fare gli occhiacci a qn
dago ['deɪgəʊ] N (*offensive*) ≈ marocchino (*fam!*)
da·guerreo·type [də'gerəʊˌtaɪp] N dagherrotipo
dahl [dɑ:l] N = **dal**
dahl·ia ['deɪlɪə] N dalia
◎ **dai·ly** ['deɪlɪ] ADJ (*routine, task*) quotidiano(-a), giornaliero(-a); (*wage, output, consumption*) giornaliero(-a); **he takes a daily walk** fa una passeggiata ogni giorno; **our daily bread** il nostro pane quotidiano; **the daily grind** il tran-tran quotidiano
■ ADV quotidianamente, ogni giorno, tutti i giorni; **twice daily** due volte al giorno; **the pool is open daily from nine until six** la piscina è aperta ogni giorno dalle nove alle diciotto
■ N **1** (*also*: **daily paper**) quotidiano **2** (*Brit*) (*old*: *cleaner*) donna di servizio
dain·ti·ly ['deɪntɪlɪ] ADV (*eat, hold*) delicatamente; (*move, walk*) con grazia
dain·ti·ness ['deɪntɪnɪs] N (*of food, person*) delicatezza; (*of gestures, manners*) grazia
dain·ty ['deɪntɪ] ADJ (*comp* **-ier**, *superl* **-iest**) (*person, figure*) minuto(-a); (*child, manners*) aggraziato(-a); (*flowers, gesture*) delicato(-a), grazioso(-a); (*dishes, food*) delicato(-a); (*dress, shoes*) grazioso(-a)
dairy ['dɛərɪ] N (*shop*) latteria; (*organization, on farm*) caseificio
■ ADJ caseario(-a); (*breed, cow*) da latte; **dairy farm** caseificio; **dairy farming** industria casearia; **dairy ice cream** gelato gusto crema; **dairy produce** latticini *mpl*
dairy·ing ['dɛərɪɪŋ] N industria casearia
dairy·maid ['dɛərɪˌmeɪd] N operaia di caseificio
dairy·man ['dɛərɪmən] N (*pl* **-men**) operaio di caseificio
dais ['deɪɪs] N pedana, palco
dai·sy ['deɪzɪ] N (*wild*) pratolina, margheritina; (*cultivated*) margherita
daisy chain N ghirlanda di margherite
daisy wheel N (*on printer*) margherita
daisy-wheel printer ['deɪzɪˌwi:l'prɪntəʳ] N stampante *f* a margherita
Da·kar ['dækəʳ] N Dakar *f*

Dd

dal, **dahl** [dɑːl] N (*Culin*) *piatto indiano a base di legumi*
dale [deɪl] N (*in North of England, also liter*) valle *f*
dal·ly ['dælɪ] VI (*delay*) dilungarsi; **to dally about** perdere tempo; **to dally over sth** perdere tempo con qc
dal·ma·tian [dæl'meɪʃən] N (*dog*) dalmata *m*
dam [dæm] N (*wall*) diga, sbarramento; (*reservoir*) bacino artificiale
■ VT (*also:* **dam up**: *river*) sbarrare con una diga; (: *lake*) costruire una diga su; (: *fig*) arginare, frenare
◎ **dam·age** ['dæmɪdʒ] N **1** (*also fig*) danno, danni *mpl*; **damage to property** danni materiali; **to suffer damage** riportare *or* subire danni; **the fire did a lot of damage** l'incendio ha provocato danni ingenti; **to do damage to a relationship** pregiudicare un rapporto; **what's the damage?** (*fam*: *cost*) quanto ci tocca sborsare? **2 damages** NPL (*Law*) danni *mpl*; **liable for damages** tenuto(-a) al risarcimento dei danni; **to pay £5000 in damages** pagare 5000 sterline di indennizzo
■ VT (*furniture, crops, machine*) danneggiare; (*health, eyesight*) rovinare; (*hopes, reputation*) compromettere; (*relationship*) guastare; (*cause*) compromettere, recar danno a
damage limitation, (*Am*) **damage control** N contenimento del danno
dam·ag·ing ['dæmɪdʒɪŋ] ADJ: **damaging (to)** nocivo(-a) (a)
Da·mas·cus [də'mɑːskəs] N Damasco *f*
dam·ask ['dæməsk] N damasco
■ ADJ damascato(-a)
dame [deɪm] N (*title, also Am fam*) donna, madama; (*in pantomime*) *personaggio comico di donna attempata recitato da un uomo*
dam·mit ['dæmɪt] EXCL (*fam*) maledizione!
damn [dæm] VT (*Rel*) dannare; (*curse*) maledire; (*condemn*: *film, book*) stroncare; **damn it!** (*fam*) accidenti!; **damn him/you!** (*fam*) accidenti a lui/a te!; **well I'll be damned!** (*fam*) che mi venga un accidente!; **I'll be damned if I will!** (*fam*) (non lo faccio) manco morto!
■ N (*fam*): **I don't give a damn** me ne infischio, non me ne importa un fico; **it's not worth a damn** non vale un fico secco
■ ADJ (*fam*: *damned*) maledetto(-a); **this damn machine won't work** questa maledetta macchina non funziona; **it's a damn nuisance!** che gran seccatura!
■ ADV (*fam*: *damned*): **it's damn hot** fa un caldo del diavolo; **he knew damn well** lo sapeva benissimo; **damn all** un bel niente, un accidente
dam·nable ['dæmnəbl] ADJ (*old*: *behaviour*) vergognoso(-a); (: *weather*) orribile
dam·na·tion [dæm'neɪʃən] N (*Rel*) dannazione *f*
■ EXCL (*old*) dannazione!, diavolo!
damned·est ['dæmdɪst] N (*fam*): **to do one's damnedest (to do sth)** fare l'impossibile (per fare qc)
damn-fool ['dæmfuːl] ADJ cretino(-a); **another one of his damn-fool ideas!** un'altra delle sue cretinate!
damn·ing ['dæmɪŋ] ADJ (*implications*) fortemente negativo(-a); **damning evidence** prove *fpl* schiaccianti; **damning criticism** stroncatura
damp [dæmp] ADJ (*comp* **-er**, *superl* **-est**) umido(-a); **damp with perspiration** madido(-a) di sudore; **that was a damp squib** (*fam*) è stato un vero fiasco
■ N (*dampness*) umidità, umido
■ VT = **dampen**
▸ **damp down** VT (*fire*) coprire
damp·course ['dæmp,kɔːs] N strato *m* isolante antiumido *inv*
damp·en ['dæmpən] VT (*cloth, rag*) inumidire; (*fig*: *enthusiasm*) raffreddare; (: *hopes*) diminuire; **to dampen sb's courage** scoraggiare qn; **to dampen sb's spirits** buttar giù qn
▸ **dampen down** = **damp down**
damp·er ['dæmpəʳ] N (*Mus*) sordina; (*of fire*) valvola di tiraggio; **to put a damper on sth** (*fig*: *atmosphere*) gelare; (: *enthusiasm*) raffreddare
damp·ness ['dæmpnɪs] N umidità, umido
damp-proof ['dæmp,pruːf] ADJ impermeabile
damp-proof course N = **dampcourse**
dam·sel ['dæmzəl] N (*old*) damigella
dam·son ['dæmzən] N (*fruit*) susina *or* prugna selvatica; (*tree*) damaschino, susino selvatico
◎ **dance** [dɑːns] N (*activity*) ballo, danza; (*traditional, in ballet*) danza; (*event*) ballo, serata danzante; **the last dance was a waltz** l'ultimo ballo era un valzer; **it's a Scottish dance** è una danza scozzese; **to lead sb a dance** (*fig*) far girare qn come una trottola
■ VT (*waltz, tango*) ballare; **to dance attendance on sb** girare intorno a qn
■ VI ballare, danzare; (*fig*: *flowers, boat on waves*) danzare; **will you dance with me?** vuoi ballare (con me)?; **to go dancing** andare a ballare; **to dance about** saltellare; **to dance for joy** ballare dalla gioia *or* dalla contentezza
▹ www.culturekiosque.com/dance
▹ www.streetswing.com/histmain/z3modrn1.htm
▹ www.artindia.net/modern.html
▹ www.irelandseye.com/dance.html
▹ www.dosado.com/articles/hist-maca.html
dance band N orchestra da ballo
dance floor N pista da ballo
dance hall N dancing *m inv*, sala da ballo
dance music N musica da ballo
danc·er ['dɑːnsəʳ] N ballerino(-a)
◎ **danc·ing** ['dɑːnsɪŋ] N ballo
▹ www.dancesport.uk.com
D and C N ABBR (*Med*: = **dilation and curettage**) raschiamento
dan·de·lion ['dændɪlaɪən] N dente *m* di leone
dan·druff ['dændrəf] N forfora
dan·dy ['dændɪ] N dandy *m inv*, elegantone *m*
■ ADJ (*comp* **-ier**, *superl* **-iest**) (*Am fam*) fantastico(-a)
Dane [deɪn] N danese *m/f*
◎ **dan·ger** ['deɪndʒəʳ] N pericolo; **in danger** in pericolo; **out of danger** fuori pericolo; **to put sb's life in danger** mettere in pericolo la vita di qn; **to be in danger of falling** rischiare di cadere; **there was no danger that he would be caught** non c'era pericolo che lo prendessero; **there is a danger of fire** c'è pericolo di incendio; **"danger! men at work"** "attenzione! lavori in corso"; **"danger! keep out"** "pericolo! vietato l'accesso"
■ ADJ (*zone, sign*) di pericolo
danger list N (*Med*): **on the danger list** in prognosi riservata
danger money N indennità di rischio
◎ **dan·ger·ous** ['deɪndʒrəs] ADJ (*gen*) pericoloso(-a); (*illness*) grave, pericoloso(-a)
dan·ger·ous·ly ['deɪndʒrəslɪ] ADV (*gen*) pericolosamente; (*wounded*) gravemente; **dangerously ill** in pericolo di vita, gravemente malato(-a)
dan·gle ['dæŋgl] VT (*arm, leg*) (far) dondolare; (*object on*

string) far oscillare; (*fig: tempting offer*): **to dangle sth in front of sb** allettare qn con qc
■ VI pendere, penzolare; **with one's legs dangling** con le gambe penzoloni

Daniel ['dænjəl] N Daniele *m*

Dan·ish ['deɪnɪʃ] ADJ danese
■ N (*language*) danese *m*

Danish blue N (*also:* **Danish blue cheese**) *formaggio tipo gorgonzola*

Danish pastry N *dolce di pasta sfoglia*

dank [dæŋk] ADJ (*comp* **-er**, *superl* **-est**) freddo(-a) e umido(-a)

Dan·ube ['dænju:b] N: **the Danube** il Danubio

dap·per ['dæpəʳ] ADJ (*man*) azzimato(-a)

dap·pled ['dæpld] ADJ screziato(-a); (*horse*) pomellato(-a)

Dar·da·nelles [ˌdɑ:də'nɛlz] NPL: **the Dardanelles** i Dardanelli

◎ **dare** [dɛəʳ] VT **1** osare; **to dare (to) do sth** osare fare qc; **I don't dare tell him** (*Brit*): **I daren't tell him** non oso dirglielo; **how dare you!** come si permette!, come osa! **2 I dare say** immagino; **I dare say he'll turn up** immagino che spunterà **3** (*challenge*): **to dare (sb to do sth)** sfidare (qn a fare qc); **I dare you!** ti sfido a farlo!; **to dare death/sb's anger** sfidare la morte/l'ira di qn
■ N sfida; **I did it for a dare** l'ho fatto per scommessa

DID YOU KNOW ...?
dare is not translated by the Italian word *dare*

dare·devil ['dɛəˌdɛvl] N scavezzacollo *m/f*

Dar es Sa·laam ['dɑ:rɛssə'lɑ:m] N Dar-es-Salaam *f*

dar·ing ['dɛərɪŋ] ADJ audace, ardito(-a)
■ N audacia

dar·ing·ly ['dɛərɪŋlɪ] ADV audacemente

◎ **dark** [dɑ:k] ADJ (*comp* **-er**, *superl* **-est**) **1** (*lacking light: room, night*) scuro(-a), buio(-a); **it is/is getting dark** è/si sta facendo buio; **the dark side of the moon** l'altra faccia della luna **2** (*in colour*) scuro(-a); (*complexion, hair, colour*) scuro(-a), bruno(-a); **dark blue/red** blu/rosso scuro *inv*; **a dark green sweater** un maglione verde scuro; **dark brown hair** capelli castano scuro; **he's tall, dark and handsome** è alto, bruno e bello; **dark chocolate** cioccolata amara **3** (*fig: sad, gloomy*) nero(-a), tetro(-a), cupo(-a); (*: sinister: secret, plan, threat*) oscuro(-a); **to keep sth dark** non far parola di qc
■ N: **the dark** il buio, l'oscurità; **in the dark** al buio; **before dark** prima che faccia (*or* facesse) buio; **after dark** col buio, a notte fatta; **until dark** fino a sera; **to be in the dark about sth** (*fig*) essere all'oscuro di qc

Dark Ages NPL: **the Dark Ages** l'alto medioevo
▷ http://cfcc.net/dutch/DarkAges.htm
▷ www.fernweb.pwp.blueyonder.co.uk/mf

dark·en ['dɑ:kən] VT (*room*) oscurare; (*colour, photo*) scurire
■ VI (*room, sky*) oscurarsi; (*colour*) scurirsi

dark-eyed ['dɑ:k'aɪd] ADJ dagli occhi scuri

dark glasses NPL occhiali *mpl* scuri

dark-haired [ˌdɑ:k'hɛəd] ADJ bruno(-a), dai capelli scuri

dark horse N (*fig*): **to be a dark horse** essere un'incognita

dar·kie, dar·ky ['dɑ:kɪ] N (*fam: offensive*) negro(-a)

dark·ly ['dɑ:klɪ] ADV (*sinisterly*) minacciosamente; (*gloomily*) cupamente, con aria cupa

dark matter N (*Astron*) materia nera

dark·ness ['dɑ:knɪs] N oscurità, buio; (*of hair*) colore *m* scuro; **the house was in darkness** la casa era immersa nel buio *or* nell'oscurità

dark·room ['dɑ:krum] N camera oscura

dark-skinned [ˌdɑ:k'skɪnd] ADJ di pelle *or* carnagione scura

dar·ling ['dɑ:lɪŋ] N **1** tesoro; **he's a little darling** è un amore; **be a darling ...** (*fam*) sii un angelo *or* un tesoro...; **come here darling** vieni qui tesoro **2** (*in shops*): **what can I do for you, darling?** desidera, cara?
■ ADJ (*daughter, husband*) caro(-a); (*dress, house*) adorabile, delizioso(-a)

darn¹ [dɑ:n] VT (*socks, clothes*) rammendare
■ N rammendo

darn² [dɑ:n] VT (*fam euph*) = **damn**

darn·ing ['dɑ:nɪŋ] N (*action*) rammendo; (*items to be darned*) roba da rammendare
■ ADJ (*needle, wool*) da rammendo

dart [dɑ:t] N **1** dardo, freccia; (*Sport*) freccetta; **to play darts** giocare a freccette **2** (*Sewing*) pince *f inv*, ripresa **3 to make a dart towards** precipitarsi verso
■ VT (*look*) lanciare
■ VI: **to dart in/out** *etc* entrare/uscire *etc* come una freccia; **to dart away** sfrecciar via; **to dart at sth** lanciarsi verso qc; **to dart towards** precipitarsi verso; **to dart along** passare come un razzo

dart·board ['dɑ:tˌbɔ:d] N bersaglio per freccette

darts [dɑ:ts] NSG tiro al bersaglio con freccette; **to play darts** giocare a freccette

dash¹ [dæʃ] N **1** (*rush*): **to make a dash (at, towards)** lanciarsi (verso), scattare (verso); **he had to make a dash for it** ha dovuto fare una corsa; **a dash to the hospital** una corsa all'ospedale; **the 100-metre dash** (*Am*) i 100 metri piani **2** (*small quantity: of liquid*) goccio, goccino; (*: of seasoning*) pizzico; (*: of colour*) tocco; **a dash of vinegar** un goccio d'aceto **3** (*punctuation mark*) lineetta, trattino; (*Morse*) linea
■ VT **1** (*throw*) scaraventare, gettare con violenza; **to dash sth to pieces** mandare qc in frantumi; **to dash one's head against sth** battere la testa contro qc **2** (*fig: spirits*) abbattere; (*: hopes*) infrangere; **all his hopes were dashed** tutte le sue speranze naufragarono
■ VI **1** (*smash: object, waves*): **to dash against** infrangersi su *or* contro **2** (*rush*) precipitarsi; **everyone dashed to the window** tutti si sono precipitati alla finestra; **I must dash** (*fam*) devo scappare; **to dash away** scappare via; **to dash in/out** entrare/uscire di corsa; **to dash towards** precipitarsi verso
▸ **dash off** VT + ADV (*letter, drawing*) buttar giù

Dd

dash² [dæʃ] VT (*fam euph*) = **damn**

dash·board ['dæʃˌbɔ:d] N (*Aut*) cruscotto

dash·ing ['dæʃɪŋ] ADJ brillante, affascinante

das·tard·ly ['dæstədlɪ] ADJ (*old*) vile

DAT [ˌdi:eɪ'ti:] N ABBR (= **digital audio tape**) Dat *f inv*

◎ **data** ['deɪtə] NSG OR PL dati *mpl*

data bank N banca *f* dati *inv*

data·base ['deɪtəˌbeɪs] N database *m inv*

data capture N registrazione *f* di dati

data mining N (*Comput*) data mining *m*; *ricerca di informazioni da un database*

data processing N elaborazione *f* (elettronica) dei dati

data protection N (*Brit: Comput*) tutela dei dati sensibili

data set N (*Comput*) set *m inv* di dati

data transmission N trasmissione *f* di dati

◎ **date¹** [deɪt] N **1** data; **what's the date today?** quanti ne abbiamo oggi?; **date of birth** data di nascita; **closing date** scadenza, termine *m*; **to date** fino a oggi; **to be up to date** (*person, document, information*) essere aggiornato(-a); (*person: fashionable*) essere alla moda; (*: with one's work*) essere nei termini; (*building*) essere moderno(-a); **to bring up to date** (*correspondence, information*) aggiornare; (*method*) modernizzare; (*person*) mettere al corrente, aggiornare; **to be out of date** (*information*) non essere aggiornato(-a); (*document*) essere scaduto(-a); (*person, style*) essere fuori moda; (*technology*) superato(-a) **2** (*fam: appointment*) appuntamento; (*: boyfriend*) ragazzo; (*: girlfriend*) ragazza; **to make a date with sb** fissare un appuntamento con qn; **I have a date with Mark** ho un appuntamento con Mark; **he asked her for a date** le ha chiesto di uscire con lui

■ VT **1** (*letter*) datare; (*ruin, manuscript*) attribuire una data a, datare; **dated the 13th** datato il 13; **thank you for your letter dated 5th July** *or* **July 5th** la ringrazio per la sua lettera in data 5 luglio; **his style of dress dates him** il suo abbigliamento tradisce la sua età **2** (*fam: esp Am: girl, boy*) uscire con

■ VI **1 to date (back) from** risalire a **2** (*become old-fashioned*) passare di moda

date² [deɪt] N (*fruit*) dattero; (*also:* **date palm**) palma da dattero

dat·ed ['deɪtɪd] ADJ (*style*) antiquato(-a), fuori moda, passato(-a) di moda; (*film*) datato(-a)

date·less [ˌdeɪtlɪs] ADJ sempre attuale

date·line ['deɪtˌlaɪn] N linea del cambiamento di data

date rape N *stupro perpetrato durante un appuntamento galante*

date stamp N (*on library book*) timbro datario; (*on fresh food*) scadenza; (*postmark*) timbro

dating agency N agenzia per cuori solitari

da·tive ['deɪtɪv] ADJ dativo(-a)

■ N dativo; **in the dative** al dativo

daub [dɔːb] VT: **to daub (with)** imbrattare (di)

◎ **daugh·ter** ['dɔːtəʳ] N figlia

daughter-in-law ['dɔːtərɪnlɔː] N nuora

daunt [dɔːnt] VT scoraggiare, intimidire; **nothing daunted ...** per nulla scoraggiato...

daunt·ing ['dɔːntɪŋ] ADJ (*prospect*) non allettante

daunt·less ['dɔːntlɪs] ADJ (*liter*) impavido(-a), intrepido(-a)

daunt·less·ly ['dɔːntlɪslɪ] ADV (*liter*) impavidamente

David ['deɪvɪd] N Davide *m*

daw·dle ['dɔːdl] VI (*in walking*) ciondolare, bighellonare; **to dawdle over one's work** gingillarsi con il lavoro

daw·dler ['dɔːdləʳ] N bighellone(-a), fannullone(-a)

daw·dling ['dɔːdlɪŋ] ADJ (*person, crowd*) ozioso(-a)

■ N: **no dawdling in the corridors, please** non attardatevi nei corridoi, per favore

dawn [dɔːn] N **1** alba; **at dawn** all'alba; **from dawn to dusk** dall'alba al tramonto **2** (*fig: dawning: of civilization*) albori *mpl*; **the dawn of a new age** l'inizio di una nuova era

■ VI (*day*) spuntare

▶ **dawn on, dawn upon** VI + PREP: **the truth gradually dawned on us** poco a poco cominciammo a vederci chiaro; **the idea dawned upon me that ...** mi è balenata nella mente l'idea che...; **it suddenly dawned on him that ...** improvvisamente gli è venuto in mente che...

dawn chorus N (*Brit*) coro mattutino degli uccelli

dawn·ing ['dɔːnɪŋ] ADJ (*day, hope*) appena nato(-a)

■ N = dawn N 2

dawn raid N (*of police etc*) irruzione *f* di primo mattino

◎ **day** [deɪ] N

1 (*24 hours*) giorno; **what day is it today?** che giorno è oggi?; **2 days ago** 2 giorni fa; **one day** un giorno; **(on) the day that ...** il giorno che *or* in cui...; **(on) that day** quel giorno; **the day before** il giorno avanti *or* prima; **the day before yesterday** l'altro ieri; **the day before his birthday** la vigilia del suo compleanno; **the day after** il giorno dopo; **the following day** il giorno seguente; **the day after tomorrow** dopodomani; **her mother died 3 years ago to the day** oggi sono 3 anni che è morta sua madre; **he works 8 hours a day** lavora 8 ore al giorno; **any day now** da un giorno all'altro; **every day** ogni giorno; **every other day** un giorno sì e uno no, ogni due giorni; **twice a day** due volte al giorno; **one of these days** uno di questi giorni, un giorno o l'altro; **the other day** l'altro giorno; **from one day to the next** da un giorno all'altro; **day after day** giorno dopo giorno; **day in day out** un giorno dopo l'altro, tutti i santi giorni; **for days on end** per giorni e giorni; **day by day** giorno per giorno; **to live from day to day** *or* **from one day to the next** vivere alla giornata; **it made my day to see him smile** (*fam*) mi ha fatto veramente felice vederlo sorridere; **he's fifty if he's a day!** (*fam*) cinquant'anni li ha di sicuro!; **that'll be the day, when he offers to pay!** (*fam*) figuriamoci se offre di pagare!

2 (*daylight hours*) giorno, giornata; (*working hours*) giornata; **by day** di giorno; **to travel by day** *or* **during the day** viaggiare di giorno *or* durante il giorno; **to work all day** lavorare tutto il giorno; **to work day and night** lavorare giorno e notte; **it's a fine day** è una bella giornata; **to arrive on a fine/wet day** arrivare col bel tempo/con la pioggia; **one summer's day** un giorno d'estate; **a day off** un giorno libero; **to work an 8-hour day** avere una giornata lavorativa di 8 ore; **it's all in a day's work** fa parte del mestiere; **paid by the day** pagato(-a) a giornata; **to work days** fare il turno di giorno

3 (*period of time, age*) tempo, tempi *mpl*, epoca; **in this day and age** ai nostri tempi; **these days** di questi tempi, oggigiorno; **to this day ...** ancor oggi...; **in days to come** in futuro; **in those days** a quei tempi, a quell'epoca; **in the days when ...** all'epoca in cui...; **in Queen Victoria's day** ai tempi della regina Vittoria; **he was famous in his day** ai suoi tempi era famoso; **in his younger days** quand'era (più) giovane; **in the good old days** ai bei tempi; **the happiest days of one's life** il periodo più felice della propria vita; **during the early days of the strike** nelle prime fasi dello sciopero; **it's had its day** ha fatto il suo tempo

day bed N divano *m* letto *inv*

day·book ['deɪˌbʊk] N (*Brit Book-keeping*) brogliaccio

day·boy ['deɪbɔɪ] N (*esp Brit Scol*) alunno esterno

day·break ['deɪbreɪk] N: **at daybreak** allo spuntar del giorno, all'alba

day-care centre ['deɪˌkeəʳsɛntəʳ] N (*Am*) scuola materna

day·dream ['deɪˌdriːm] N sogno a occhi aperti

■ VI sognare a occhi aperti

day girl N (*esp Brit Scol*) alunna esterna

day·light ['deɪˌlaɪt] N luce *f* (del giorno); **at daylight** (*dawn*) alle prime luci, all'alba; **in the daylight** *or* **by daylight** alla luce del giorno; **it is still daylight** è ancora giorno; **I am beginning to see daylight** (*fig:*

understand) ora comincio a vederci chiaro; (: *near the end of a job*) comincio a vedere uno spiraglio di luce; **daylight attack** attacco di giorno
daylight hours NPL ore *fpl* diurne *or* del giorno
daylight robbery N (*Brit fam*): **it's daylight robbery!** è un vero furto!
daylight-saving time ['deılaıt'seıvıŋtaım] N (*Am*) ora legale
day·long ['deılɒŋ] ADJ che dura tutta la giornata; **we had a daylong meeting** la nostra riunione si è protratta per tutta la giornata
day nursery N scuola materna
day of reckoning N: **the day of reckoning** il giorno del giudizio
day release N: **to be on day release** *avere un congedo settimanale per formazione professionale*
day release course N *corso di formazione professionale esterno per dipendenti*
day return N (*Brit*: also: *day return ticket*)
■ N biglietto giornaliero di andata e ritorno
day school N scuola privata (*che non prevede pernottamento*)
day shift N turno di giorno; **to be on day shift** fare il turno di giorno
day·time ['deıtaım] N giorno; **in the daytime** di giorno
■ ADJ di giorno; **daytime TV** televisione *f* del mattino e del pomeriggio
day-to-day ['deıtəˌdeı] ADJ (*routine*) quotidiano(-a); (*expenses*) giornaliero(-a); **on a day-to-day basis** a giornata
day trader N (*Fin*) day dealer *m/f inv*; *operatore che compra e vende titoli nel corso della stessa giornata*
day trip N gita (di un giorno)
day tripper N gitante *m/f*
daze [deız] N: **in a daze** stordito(-a), inebetito(-a)
■ VT (*subj: drug*) inebetire; (: *blow*) stordire
daz·zle ['dæzl] VT abbagliare
daz·zling ['dæzlıŋ] ADJ (*light*) abbagliante; (*colour*) violento(-a); (*smile*) smagliante
daz·zling·ly ['dæzlıŋlı] ADV (*bright*) in modo abbagliante; (*beautiful*) in modo smagliante
dB db N ABBR = **decibel**
DBS [ˌdi:bi:'ɛs] N ABBR (= **digital broadcasting by satellite**) DBS *m*
DC [ˌdi:'si:] N ABBR (*Elec:* = **direct current**) c.c.
■ ABBR (*Am Post:* = **District of Columbia**) distretto della Columbia; **Washington DC** Washington DC *f*
DCC® [ˌdi:si:'si:] N ABBR (= **digital compact cassette**) DCC *m inv*
DCMS [ˌdi:si:ɛm'ɛs] N ABBR (*Brit*) = *Department for Culture, Media and Sport*
DD [ˌdi:'di:] ABBR **1** (= **Doctor of Divinity**) *titolare di un dottorato in teologia* **2** = **direct debit**
dd ABBR (*Comm*) = *delivered*
D-day ['di:ˌdeı] N D-day *m*; *giorno dello sbarco alleato in Normandia*
▷ www.dday.co.uk
DDS [ˌdi:di:'ɛs] N ABBR (*Am:* = **Doctor of Dental Surgery**) *titolare di un dottorato in odontoiatria*
DDT [ˌdi:di:'ti:] N ABBR (= **dichlorodiphenyl trichloroethane**) DDT *m*
DE [ˌdi:'i:] ABBR (*Am Post*) = **Delaware**
DEA [ˌdi:i:'eı] N ABBR (*Am:* = **Drug Enforcement Administration**) ≈ squadra *f* narcotici *inv*
dea·con ['di:kən] N diacono
dea·con·ess ['di:kənɛs] N diaconessa

de·ac·tiv·ate [di:'æktıˌveıt] VT disattivare
◎ **dead** [dɛd] ADJ **1** (*person, animal, plant*) morto(-a); (*matter*) inanimato(-a); (*fingers, leg*): **to go dead** intorpidirsi; **to fall** *or* **drop (down) dead** morire; **he was dead** era morto; **he was shot dead** fu colpito a morte; **he's been dead for 2 years** è morto da due anni; **dead and buried** (*also fig*) morto(-a) e sepolto(-a); **dead or alive** vivo(-a) o morto(-a); **over my dead body!** (*fam*) manco morto!; **I feel absolutely dead!** (*fig fam*) sono (stanco) morto!; **to be a dead duck** (*fam*) essere spacciato(-a) **2** (*volcano, cigarette*) spento(-a); (*battery*) scarico(-a); (*telephone line*) caduto(-a); (*language, town, party*) morto(-a); (*custom*) scomparso(-a), estinto(-a); **the line has gone dead** (*Telec*) è caduta la linea; **he was dead to the world** (*fig*) era proprio partito (*fig*) **3** (*complete: silence, calm*) assoluto(-a), totale; **to hit sth dead centre** centrare qc in pieno; **to come to a dead stop** fermarsi (del tutto); **to fall into a dead faint** cadere in svenimento
■ ADV (*completely*): **dead certain** assolutamente certo(-a), sicurissimo(-a); **to stop dead** fermarsi di colpo; **you're dead right!** hai assolutamente ragione!; **dead ahead** sempre dritto; **it's dead ahead of us** è proprio davanti a noi; **dead on time** in perfetto orario; **to land dead on target** fare centro; **dead slow** (*Aut*) a passo d'uomo; (*Naut*) avanti piano; **to be dead set on doing sth** volere fare qc a tutti i costi; **to be dead set against sth** (*fam*) essere assolutamente contrario(-a) a qc; **dead broke** (*fam*) senza il becco di un quattrino; **dead drunk** (*fam*) ubriaco(-a) fradicio(-a); **dead tired** (*fam*) stanco(-a) morto(-a)
■ N **1 the dead** NPL i morti; **2 at dead of night** nel cuore della notte; **in the dead of winter** nel cuore dell'inverno
dead ball line N (*Rugby*) linea di pallone morto
dead beat ADJ (*fam*) stanco(-a) morto(-a)
dead·en ['dɛdn] VT (*noise, pain, blow, sound*) attutire; (*nerve*) rendere insensibile
dead-end [dɛd'ɛnd] ADJ: **a dead-end job** un lavoro senza sbocchi
dead end N (*also fig*) vicolo cieco
dead·en·ing ['dɛdnıŋ] ADJ (*boredom*) mortale; (*job, task*) alienante
dead heat N (*Sport*): **it was a dead heat** è stata una vittoria a pari merito; **to finish in a dead heat** finire alla pari
dead-letter office [ˌdɛdlɛtə'ɒfıs] N ufficio della posta in giacenza
◎ **dead·line** ['dɛdˌlaın] N termine *m* (di consegna), scadenza; **to work to a deadline** avere una scadenza da rispettare; **we'll never meet the deadline** ci sarà impossibile rispettare la scadenza
dead·lock ['dɛdˌlɒk] N punto morto, impasse *f inv*
dead·locked ['dɛdˌlɒkt] ADJ: **to be deadlocked** (*talks, negotiations*) essere in una fase di stallo
dead loss N (*fam*): **to be a dead loss** (*person, thing*) non valere niente
dead·ly ['dɛdlı] ADJ (*comp* **-ier**, *superl* **-iest**) (*gen*) mortale; (*weapon, poison, aim*) micidiale; (*disease*) letale; **they are deadly enemies** sono acerrimi nemici; **the seven deadly sins** i sette peccati capitali; **he is in deadly earnest** fa (*or* parla) sul serio, non scherza; **this book is deadly** (*fam: very boring*) questo libro è un mattone; **she finds these parties deadly** trova terribili queste feste
■ ADV: **deadly dull** di una noia mortale; **deadly pale** pallido(-a) come un cadavere

Dd

dead-nettle ['dɛd,nɛtl] N ortica bianca, lamio
dead·pan ['dɛd,pæn] ADJ (*face*) impassibile; (*humour*) all'inglese
■ ADV (*with a straight face*) senza fare una piega
Dead Sea N: **the Dead Sea** il mar Morto
dead season N (*Tourism*): **the dead season** la stagione morta
dead weight N peso morto
dead·wood ['dɛd,wʊd] N (*also fig*) rami *mpl* secchi
deaf [dɛf] ADJ (*comp* **-er**, *superl* **-est**) sordo(-a); **deaf in one ear** sordo(-a) da un orecchio; **to be deaf to sth** (*fig*) restare sordo(-a) a qc; **to turn a deaf ear to sth** fare orecchi da mercante a qc; **as deaf as a (door)post** sordo(-a) come una campana
■ NPL: **the deaf** i sordi
deaf-aid ['dɛf,eɪd] N (*Brit fam*) apparecchio acustico
deaf-and-dumb ['dɛfən'dʌm] ADJ (*person*) sordomuto(-a); (*language*) dei sordomuti
deaf·en ['dɛfn] VT assordare
deaf·en·ing ['dɛfnɪŋ] ADJ assordante, fragoroso(-a)
deaf·en·ing·ly ['dɛfnɪŋlɪ] ADV in modo assordante
deaf-mute ['dɛf,mju:t] N sordomuto(-a)
deaf·ness ['dɛfnɪs] N sordità
◎ **deal**[1] [di:l] (*vb: pt, pp* **dealt**) N
1 (*agreement*) accordo; (*also:* **business deal**) affare *m*; **to do** *or* **strike a deal with sb** fare un affare con qn; **perhaps we can do a deal?** forse ci si può aggiustare fra di noi?; **he made a deal with the kidnappers** ha fatto un accordo con i rapitori; **it's a deal!** (*fam*) affare fatto!; **a new deal** (*Pol, Econ, Sociol*) un piano di riforme; **to get a good/bad deal** (*Comm*) fare/non fare un buon affare; **he got a good deal from them** l'hanno trattato bene; **a fair deal for working mothers** un trattamento equo per le madri che lavorano; **to get a rough/raw deal** venir trattato(-a) ingiustamente
2 (*Cards*) turno (*nel dare le carte*); **it's my deal** adesso tocca a me dare le carte
3 (*in expressions of quantity*): **a good** *or* **great deal** molto, parecchio; **to have a great deal to do** avere molto da fare; **there's a good deal of truth in what he says** c'è molto di vero in quel che dice; **she spends a great deal of her time alone** passa buona parte del suo tempo da sola; **he thinks a great deal of his father** ha una grande stima di suo padre; **that's saying a good deal** non è dire poco; **it means a great deal to me** vuol dire molto per me; **a great deal cleverer** di gran lunga più intelligente
■ VT
1 **to deal sb a blow** assestare un colpo a qn
2 (*Cards: also:* **deal out**) distribuire, dare
▶ **deal in** VI + PREP (*Comm*) occuparsi di; (*drugs*) spacciare; **they deal in antiques** trattano oggetti d'antiquariato
▶ **deal out** VT + ADV (*cards, money*) distribuire; **to deal out justice** far giustizia
▶ **deal with** VI + PREP
1 (*handle: person, task, application*) occuparsi di; (*: problem*) affrontare; (*: Comm: order*) sbrigare; **he promised to deal with it immediately** ha promesso di occuparsene immediatamente; **I don't know who dealt with the booking** non so chi si è occupato della prenotazione; **I'll deal with you later!** con te facciamo i conti più tardi!; **to know how to deal with sb** sapere come prendere qn; **he's not easy to deal with** è un tipo difficile
2 (*subj: book, film: be about*) trattare di; **the part of the book which deals with the subject** la parte del libro che tratta dell'argomento
3 (*Comm: company, organization, person*) trattare con
deal[2] [di:l] N legno di pino (*or* di abete)
■ ADJ di pino (*or* di abete)
◎ **deal·er** ['di:ləʳ] N **1** (*Comm*): **dealer (in)** commerciante *m/f* (di); **an antique dealer** un*a* antiquario(-a) **2** (*also:* **drug dealer**) spacciatore(-trice) **3** (*Cards*) chi fa *or* dà le carte
deal·er·ship ['di:ləʃɪp] N (*Comm*) concessione *f*
dealing room N (*Fin*) sala delle transazioni
deal·ings ['di:lɪŋz] NPL **1** (*relationship*) rapporti *mpl*; **to have dealings with sb** avere a che fare con qn
2 (*Comm, Stock Exchange: in goods, shares*) transazioni *fpl*
dealt [dɛlt] PT, PP *of* **deal**
dean [di:n] N (*of college, university*) preside *m/f*; (*Rel*) decano
dean·ery ['di:nərɪ] N (*Rel*) decanato
◎ **dear** [dɪəʳ] ADJ (*comp* **-er**, *superl* **-est**) **1** (*loved, lovable*) caro(-a); **I hold it very dear** mi è molto caro; **my dearest wish** il mio più ardente desiderio; **what a dear little boy!** che amore di bambino!; **a dear little cottage** una casetta deliziosa **2** (*in letter writing*): **Dear Daddy/Peter** Caro papà/Peter; **Dearest Paul** Carissimo Paul; **Dear Mr/Mrs Smith** Gentile Signor/Signora Smith; **Dear Mr and Mrs Smith** Gentili Signori Smith; **Dear Sir/Madam** Egregio Signore/Gentile Signora **3** (*expensive*) caro(-a); **dear money** (*Comm*) denaro ad alto interesse
■ EXCL: **oh dear!** oh Dio!, mamma mia!; **dear me!** Dio mio!
■ N caro(-a); **my dear** caro(-a) mio(-a); **my dearest** amore mio; **(you) poor dear!** poverino!; **he's a dear!** (*fam*) è un tesoro!; **post this letter for me, there's a dear** (*fam*) sii gentile, imbucami questa lettera
■ ADV caro; **to pay dear for sth** pagare caro qc; **he bought his freedom dear** la sua libertà gli è costata cara
dear·est ['dɪərɪst] N, ADJ *see* **dear**
dear·ly ['dɪəlɪ] ADV: **to love sb/sth dearly** amare qn/qc moltissimo; **I should dearly love to go there** mi piacerebbe moltissimo andarci; **to pay dearly for sth** (*esp fig*) pagar qc caro *or* a caro prezzo
dearth [dɜ:θ] N (*of food, resources, ideas, money*) penuria, mancanza
◎ **death** [dɛθ] N morte *f*; (*Med, Admin, Law*) decesso; (*of plans, hopes*) fine *f*; **to be burnt to death** morire carbonizzato(-a); **to drink o.s. to death** uccidersi a forza di bere; **to sentence sb to death** condannare a morte qn; **to put sb to death** mettere a morte qn, giustiziare qn; **a fight to the death** un duello all'ultimo sangue; **to be at death's door** essere in punto di morte; **it will be the death of him** sarà la sua rovina; **you'll be the death of me** (*fam: fig*) mi farai morire; **you look like death warmed up** (*fam*) sembri un morto che cammina; **bored to death** (*fam*) annoiato(-a) a morte; **I'm sick** *or* **tired to death of it** (*fam*) ne ho fin sopra i capelli
death·bed N letto di morte; **on one's deathbed** in punto di morte
■ ADJ (*confession*) in punto di morte
death·blow ['dɛθ,bləʊ] N colpo di grazia
death camp N campo di sterminio
death certificate N (*Admin*) certificato di morte
death duty N, GEN PL (*Brit*) tassa di successione
death·ly ['dɛθlɪ] ADJ (*comp* **-ier**, *superl* **-iest**) (*pallor*) mortale; (*appearance*) cadaverico(-a); (*silence*) di tomba
■ ADV: **deathly pale** pallido(-a) come un cadavere

death march N (*Mus*) marcia funebre
death mask N maschera mortuaria
death penalty N pena di morte
death rate N (tasso di) mortalità
death rattle N rantolo
death row N (*Am*): **to be on death row** essere nel braccio della morte
death sentence N condanna a morte, pena di morte
death's-head ['dɛθs,hɛd] N teschio
death squad N squadra della morte
death throes NPL (*also fig*) ultimi spasimi *mpl*; **in one's death throes** agonizzante
death toll N numero delle vittime
death·trap ['dɛθ,træp] N trappola mortale
death warrant N sentenza di morte
death wish N desiderio di morte
deb [dɛb] N ABBR (*Brit fam*) (= **debutante**) *ragazza di buona famiglia che debutta in società*
de·ba·cle [deɪ'bɑ:kl] N disastro; (*defeat*) disfatta; (*collapse*) sfacelo
de·bar [dɪ'bɑ:ʳ] VT (*frm*): **to debar sb from sth** escludere qn da qc; **to debar sb from doing sth** vietare a qn di fare qc
de·base [dɪ'beɪs] VT (*person, relationship, word*) degradare, svilire; (*coinage*) svilire, adulterare
de·base·ment [dɪ'beɪsmənt] N (*of person, relationship, word*) degradazione *f*, svilimento
de·bat·able [dɪ'beɪtəbl] ADJ discutibile; **that's debatable** questo è discutibile; **it is debatable whether ...** è in dubbio se...
◎ **de·bate** [dɪ'beɪt] VT (*discuss*) discutere, dibattere; (*consider*): **he debated the advisability of leaving** si chiedeva se fosse saggio partire; **we debated whether to go or not** discutemmo se andare o meno
■ VI: **to debate (with sb about sth)** discutere (con qn di qc); **to debate with o.s. (about, (up)on sth)** essere in dubbio (su qc)
■ N dibattito, discussione *f*; **after much debate** dopo lunga discussione
de·ba·ting so·ci·ety [dɪ'beɪtɪŋ sə'saɪətɪ] N (*Scol, Univ*) *circolo che organizza dibattiti con votazione finale*
de·bauch [dɪ'bɔ:tʃ] VT (*old*) (*frm*) corrompere
de·bauched [dɪ'bɔ:tʃt] ADJ (*old: person*) debosciato(-a); (*: taste, morals*) dissoluto(-a), vizioso(-a)
de·bauch·ery [dɪ'bɔ:tʃərɪ] N dissolutezza
de·ben·ture [dɪ'bɛntʃəʳ] N (*Fin*) obbligazione *f*
de·bili·tate [dɪ'bɪlɪ,teɪt] VT (*frm*) debilitare
de·bil·ity [dɪ'bɪlɪtɪ] N (*frm*) debilitazione *f*
deb·it ['dɛbɪt] (*Fin*) N addebito
■ VT addebitare; **to debit sb/sb's account with a sum** *or* **to debit a sum to sb** *or* **to sb's account** addebitare una somma a qn/sul conto di qc
debit balance N saldo passivo *or* debitore
debit card N carta di addebito
debit note N nota di addebito
debit side N colonna del dare; (*fig*): **on the debit side is the fact that ...** il lato negativo è che...
debo·nair [,dɛbə'nɛəʳ] ADJ (*young man*) gioviale e disinvolto(-a)
de·brief [,di:'bri:f] VT (*Mil*) chiamare a rapporto (a operazione ultimata)
de·brief·ing [,di:'bri:fɪŋ] N rapporto *or* resoconto (a operazione ultimata)
de·bris ['dɛbri:] N detriti *mpl*
◎ **debt** [dɛt] N debito; **debts of £5000** debiti per 5000 sterline; **he's still paying off his debts** sta ancora pagando i debiti; **a debt of honour/gratitude** un debito d'onore/di gratitudine *or* di riconoscenza; **to be in debt (to sb)** essere indebitato(-a) (con qn), avere debiti (con qn); **I am £500 in debt** sono in debito di 500 sterline; **to be in sb's debt** (*fig*) essere in debito verso qn; **to get into debt** far debiti, indebitarsi; **to be out of debt** essere libero(-a) da debiti; **debt burden** indebitamento; **debt forgiveness** cancellazione *f* del debito; **debt relief** riduzione *f* del debito
debt collector N agente *m* di recupero crediti
debt·or ['dɛtəʳ] N debitore(-trice)
debt-ridden ['dɛt,rɪdn] ADJ oberato(-a) dai debiti
de·bug [di:'bʌg] VT (*Comput: program*) localizzare e rimuovere errori da; (*room*) togliere i microfoni da
de·bunk [,di:'bʌŋk] VT (*theory*) demistificare; (*claim*) smentire; (*person, institution*) screditare
◎ **de·but** ['deɪbju:] N debutto; **to make one's debut** debuttare, fare il proprio debutto; **to make one's stage/film debut** debuttare sulle scene/sullo schermo
debu·tante ['dɛbju:tɑ:nt] N debuttante *f*
Dec. ABBR (= **December**) dic. (= *dicembre*)
◎ **dec·ade** ['dɛkeɪd] N decennio
deca·dence ['dɛkədəns] N decadenza
deca·dent ['dɛkədənt] ADJ decadente
de·caf [di:'kæf] ADJ ABBR (*fam*) decaffeinato(-a)
■ N ABBR decaffeinato
de·caf·fein·at·ed [di:'kæfɪ,neɪtɪd] ADJ decaffeinato(-a)
de·cal [dɪ'kæl] N (*Am: transfer*) decalcomania
de·camp [dɪ'kæmp] VI filarsela
de·cant [dɪ'kænt] VT (*wine*) decantare
de·cant·er [dɪ'kæntəʳ] N bottiglia di cristallo (*per liquori o vini*)
de·capi·tate [dɪ'kæpɪteɪt] VT (*frm*) decapitare
de·cath·lon [dɪ'kæθlən] N decathlon *m inv*
de·cay [dɪ'keɪ] VI (*teeth*) cariarsi; (*vegetation, flesh*) decomporsi; (*Phys: radioactive nucleus*) disintegrarsi; (*building, urban area*) andare in rovina; (*fig: civilization*) decadere; (*: one's faculties*) deteriorarsi
■ N (*of teeth*) carie *f*; (*of vegetation, body*) decomposizione *f*; (*of radioactivity*) disintegrazione *f*; (*of building, urban area*) stato di abbandono, decadimento; (*of civilization*) rovina; (*of faculties*) deterioramento; **urban decay** degrado urbano
de·cay·ing [dɪ'keɪɪŋ] ADJ (*vegetation, flesh*) in decomposizione; (*teeth*) cariato(-a); (*building, urban area*) in rovina; (*civilization*) in declino
de·cease [dɪ'si:s] (*Law*) N decesso
■ VI decedere
de·ceased [dɪ'si:st] (*Law, also frm*) ADJ deceduto(-a)
■ N: **the deceased** il/la defunto(-a)
de·ceit [dɪ'si:t] N (*quality*) disonestà; (*action*) inganno, truffa
de·ceit·ful [dɪ'si:tfʊl] ADJ (*person*) falso(-a), disonesto(-a); (*words, behaviour*) menzognero(-a), ingannatore(-trice)
de·ceit·ful·ly [dɪ'si:tfəlɪ] ADV in modo falso, disonestamente
de·ceit·ful·ness [dɪ'si:tfʊlnɪs] N falsità *f inv*, disonestà
de·ceive [dɪ'si:v] VT ingannare; **she deceived me into thinking that ...** mi ha ingannato facendomi credere che...; **unless my eyes deceive me** se gli occhi non m'ingannano; **don't be deceived by appearances** non ti fare ingannare dalle apparenze; **to deceive o.s.** ingannarsi, illudersi
de·ceiv·er [dɪ'si:vəʳ] N ingannatore(-trice)
de·cel·er·ate [di:'sɛləreɪt] VT, VI decelerare
de·cel·era·tion ['di:,sɛlə'reɪʃən] N decelerazione *f*

Dd

De·cem·ber [dɪˈsɛmbəʳ] N dicembre *m*; *for usage see* **July**

de·cen·cy [ˈdiːsənsɪ] N *(moral sense)* rispetto per i valori umani; *(propriety)* decenza, decoro; **he has no sense of decency** non ha un minimo di rispetto; **to have the decency to do sth** avere la decenza di fare qc; **out of common decency** per gentilezza, se non altro

de·cent [ˈdiːsənt] ADJ **1** *(respectable: person, house)* perbene *inv*, ammodo *inv*; *(proper: clothes, behaviour, language)* decente **2** *(kind)* gentile, bravo(-a); **he was very decent to me** si è comportato molto bene con me; **to do the decent thing** fare quello che è giusto; **they were very decent about it** sono stati molto corretti in merito **3** *(satisfactory: meal, house)* decente, discreto(-a)

de·cent·ly [ˈdiːsəntlɪ] ADV *(respectably)* decentemente, convenientemente; *(kindly)* gentilmente

de·cen·trali·za·tion [diːˌsɛntrəlaɪˈzeɪʃən] N *(Admin, Pol)* decentramento

de·cen·tral·ize [diːˈsɛntrəˌlaɪz] VT *(Admin, Pol)* decentrare

de·cep·tion [dɪˈsɛpʃən] N inganno; **to practise deception on sb** raggirare qn

de·cep·tive [dɪˈsɛptɪv] ADJ *(likely to deceive)* ingannevole; *(meant to deceive)* ingannatore(-trice)

de·cep·tive·ly [dɪˈsɛptɪvlɪ] ADV: **deceptively simple** (solo) apparentemente facile

de·cep·tive·ness [dɪˈsɛptɪvnɪs] N carattere *m* ingannevole; *(deliberate)* carattere infido

deci·bel [ˈdɛsɪbɛl] N decibel *m inv*

◎ **de·cide** [dɪˈsaɪd] VT *(question, argument)* decidere, risolvere; **to decide to do sth** decidere di fare qc, decidersi a fare qc; **to decide that** decidere che; **the goal that decided the match** il gol decisivo per la partita; **I decided to write to her** ho deciso di scriverle; **he decided not to go** ha deciso di non andare; **to decide sb** far decidere qn; **what decided him ...** ciò che l'ha fatto decidere...

■ VI decidere, decidersi; **to decide for** *or* **in favour of sb** decidere a favore di qn; **to decide on/against sth** optare per/contro qc; **to decide on doing sth** scegliere *or* decidere di fare qc; **to decide against doing sth** decidere di non fare qc; **I can't decide** non so decidermi

de·cid·ed [dɪˈsaɪdɪd] ADJ *(tone, improvement)* deciso(-a); *(risk)* certo(-a); *(opinions, views)* chiaro(-a), preciso(-a)

de·cid·ed·ly [dɪˈsaɪdɪdlɪ] ADV *(extremely)* decisamente; *(emphatically)* in modo deciso

de·cid·er [dɪˈsaɪdəʳ] N *(Sport)* spareggio

de·cid·ing [dɪˈsaɪdɪŋ] ADJ decisivo(-a); **the deciding factor** il fattore decisivo

de·cidu·ous [dɪˈsɪdjʊəs] ADJ deciduo(-a)

deci·mal [ˈdɛsɪməl] ADJ decimale; **the decimal system** il sistema decimale; **to 3 decimal places** al terzo decimale

■ N (numero) decimale *m*

deci·mali·za·tion [ˌdɛsɪməlaɪˈzeɪʃən] N *(Brit)* conversione *f* al sistema metrico decimale

deci·mal·ize [ˈdɛsɪməˌlaɪz] VT *(Brit)* convertire al sistema metrico decimale

decimal point N ≈ virgola *(in numero decimale)*

deci·mate [ˈdɛsɪˌmeɪt] VT decimare

de·ci·pher [dɪˈsaɪfəʳ] VT decifrare

de·ci·pher·able [dɪˈsaɪfərəbl] ADJ decifrabile

◎ **de·ci·sion** [dɪˈsɪʒən] N decisione *f*; **to make a decision** prendere una decisione

decision-making [dɪˈsɪʒənˌmeɪkɪŋ] N: **to be good at decision-making** saper prendere decisioni

de·ci·sive [dɪˈsaɪsɪv] ADJ *(victory, factor)* decisivo(-a); *(influence)* determinante; *(manner, person)* risoluto(-a), deciso(-a); *(reply)* deciso(-a), categorico(-a)

de·ci·sive·ly [dɪˈsaɪsɪvlɪ] ADV *(act)* con decisione

de·ci·sive·ness [dɪˈsaɪsɪvnɪs] N *(of manner, person)* risolutezza, decisione *f*

◎ **deck** [dɛk] N **1** *(Naut)* (ponte *m* di) coperta; **to go up on deck** salire in coperta; **below deck** sotto coperta; **to clear the decks** *(fig)* sgombrare il campo; **to hit the deck** *(fam)* cascare a terra (bocconi) **2** *(of bus)*: **top** *or* **upper deck** piano di sopra; **bottom** *or* **lower deck** piano di sotto **3** *(of cards)* mazzo **4** *(of record player)* piatto; **record deck** piatto (giradischi); **cassette deck** piastra (di registrazione) **5** piattaforma di legno *(in giardino)*

■ VT **1** *(also:* **deck out***)*: **to deck (with)** decorare (con) **2** *(fam)* stendere

deck·chair [ˈdɛktʃɛəʳ] N sedia *f* sdraio *inv*

deck hand N mozzo

deck·ing [ˈdɛkɪŋ] N *see* **deck** N **5**

deck shoe N scarpa bassa con la suola di gomma

de·claim [dɪˈkleɪm] VI declamare

dec·la·ma·tion [ˌdɛkləˈmeɪʃən] N declamazione *f*

de·clama·tory [dɪˈklæmətərɪ] ADJ *(speech, tone)* declamatorio(-a)

◎ **dec·la·ra·tion** [ˌdɛkləˈreɪʃən] N dichiarazione *f*

◎ **de·clare** [dɪˈklɛəʳ] VT *(gen)* dichiarare; *(Fin, Pol: results)* annunciare; **have you anything to declare?** *(Customs)* ha qualcosa da dichiarare?, dichiara?; **to declare that** dichiarare che; **he declared that he was innocent** ha dichiarato di essere innocente, si è dichiarato innocente; **to declare war (on** *or* **against sb)** dichiarare guerra (a qn); **to declare for** pronunciarsi a favore di

de·clas·si·fy [diːˈklæsɪˌfaɪ] VT *(documents, records)* declassificare

de·clen·sion [dɪˈklɛnʃən] N *(Gram)* declinazione *f*

◎ **de·cline** [dɪˈklaɪn] N: **decline (in)** *(decrease)* calo (di); *(deterioration)* declino (di); **decline in living standards** abbassamento del tenore di vita; **to be on the decline** *(gen)* essere in diminuzione; *(prices)* essere in ribasso

■ VT **1** *(frm: refuse: invitation)* declinare, rifiutare; **to decline to do sth** rifiutare *or* rifiutarsi di fare qc; **he declined the offer** ha rifiutato l'offerta **2** *(Gram)* declinare

■ VI **1** *(power, influence)* diminuire, declinare; *(empire)* decadere; *(health)* deteriorare; **the birth rate is declining** il tasso di natalità sta calando; **in his declining years** negli ultimi anni della sua vita; *(of public figure)* negli anni del suo declino; **to decline in importance** diminuire d'importanza **2** *(Gram)* declinarsi

de·clutch [ˈdiːˈklʌtʃ] VI *(Aut)* premere la frizione

de·code [ˈdiːˈkəʊd] VT *(message)* decifrare; *(Comput, Ling)* decodificare

de·cod·er [diːˈkəʊdəʳ] N *(Comput, TV)* decodificatore *m*

de·coke [*vb* diːˈkəʊk; *n* ˈdiːkəʊk] *(Aut)* VT decarburare

■ N decarburazione *f*

de·colo·niza·tion [diːˌkɒlənaɪˈzeɪʃən] N decolonizzazione *f*

de·colo·nize [diːˈkɒləˌnaɪz] VT decolonizzare

de·com·pose [ˌdiːkəmˈpəʊz] VI decomporsi

■ VT decomporre

de·com·po·si·tion [ˌdiːkɒmpəˈzɪʃən] N decomposizione *f*

de·com·press [ˌdiːkəmˈprɛs] VT fare la decompressione di
de·com·pres·sion [ˌdiːkəmˈprɛʃən] N decompressione *f*
decompression chamber N camera di decompressione
de·con·gest·ant [ˌdiːkənˈdʒɛstənt] N decongestionante *m*
de·con·secrat·ed [ˌdiːˈkɒnsɪˌkreɪtɪd] ADJ sconsacrato(-a)
de·con·tami·nate [ˌdiːkənˈtæmɪˌneɪt] VT decontaminare
de·con·tam·in·ation [ˌdiːkənˌtæmɪˈneɪʃən] N decontaminazione *f*
de·con·trol [ˌdiːkənˈtrəʊl] VT (*trade*) liberalizzare; (*prices*) togliere il controllo governativo a
dé·cor [ˈdeɪkɔːʳ] N arredamento, decorazione *f*
◎**deco·rate** [ˈdɛkəˌreɪt] VT **1** **to decorate (with)** (*adorn*) decorare (con) **2** (*paint and wallpaper: room*) pitturare e tappezzare **3** (*honour: soldier*) decorare
deco·rat·ing [ˈdɛkəˌreɪtɪŋ] N: **to do some decorating** mettere la carta da parati (e pitturare)
deco·ra·tion [ˌdɛkəˈreɪʃən] N decorazione *f*; **Christmas decorations** decorazioni natalizie
deco·ra·tive [ˈdɛkərətɪv] ADJ decorativo(-a)
deco·ra·tor [ˈdɛkəreɪtəʳ] N decoratore(-trice)
deco·rous [ˈdɛkərəs] ADJ decoroso(-a)
deco·rous·ly [ˈdɛkərəslɪ] ADV decorosamente
de·co·rum [dɪˈkɔːrəm] N decoro; **out of a sense of decorum** per rispetto delle convenienze; **a breach of decorum** una sconvenienza
de·coy [ˈdiːkɔɪ] N (*bird*) (uccello da) richiamo; (*fig: bait: thing*) tranello; (*: person*) esca; **police decoy** poliziotto in borghese (*usato come esca*)
de·crease [*n* ˈdiːkriːs; *vb* diːˈkriːs] N: **decrease (in)** (*amount, numbers, population, power*) diminuzione *f* (di); (*birth rate, value, production, enthusiasm*) calo (di); (*prices*) ribasso (di); (*strength, dose*) riduzione *f* (di); **to be on the decrease** essere in diminuzione; **there has been a decrease in the number of people out of work** c'è stata una diminuzione del numero dei disoccupati
■VT (*see n*) diminuire; far calare; ribassare; ridurre; **after three weeks I decreased the dose** dopo tre settimane ho diminuito la dose
■VI (*amount, numbers etc*) diminuire; (*prices, birthrate etc*) calare; (*Knitting*) calare (le maglie); **to decrease by 10%** diminuire del 10%; **the number has decreased** il numero è diminuito
de·creas·ing [diːˈkriːsɪŋ] ADJ in diminuzione
de·cree [dɪˈkriː] N (*Law, Pol*) decreto; (*municipal*) ordinanza; (*divorce*): **decree absolute** sentenza di divorzio definitiva; **decree nisi** sentenza provvisoria di divorzio
■VT: **to decree (that)** decretare (che) + *sub*
de·crep·it [dɪˈkrɛpɪt] ADJ (*building*) cadente; (*person*) decrepito(-a)
de·crepi·tude [dɪˈkrɛpɪtjuːd] N (*frm*) decrepitezza
de·cry [dɪˈkraɪ] VT (*frm*) condannare, deplorare
dedi·cate [ˈdɛdɪˌkeɪt] VT dedicare, consacrare; (*book etc*) dedicare; **to dedicate one's life** *or* **o.s. to sth/to doing sth** dedicare la propria esistenza a qc/a fare qc
dedi·cat·ed [ˈdɛdɪˌkeɪtɪd] ADJ coscienzioso(-a); (*Comput*) dedicato(-a); **a very dedicated teacher** un insegnante che ama molto il suo lavoro
dedi·ca·tion [ˌdɛdɪˈkeɪʃən] N (*in book*) dedica; (*devotion*) dedizione *f*
de·duce [dɪˈdjuːs] VT: **to deduce sth from sth** dedurre qc da qc; **to deduce that** dedurre che
de·duct [dɪˈdʌkt] VT: **to deduct (from)** (*gen*) dedurre (da); (*from wages*) trattenere (su); (*from price*) fare una riduzione (su); (*Scol: marks*) togliere (da)
de·duct·ible [dɪˈdʌktəbl] ADJ deducibile
de·duc·tion [dɪˈdʌkʃən] N **1** (*inference*) deduzione *f* **2** (*subtraction*) detrazione *f*; (*from wages*) trattenuta
de·duc·tive [dɪˌdʌktɪv] ADJ deduttivo(-a)
de·duc·tive·ly [dɪˈdʌktɪvlɪ] ADV deduttivamente
deed [diːd] N **1** azione *f*, atto; **brave deed** impresa; **good deed** buona azione; **in deed** di fatto **2** (*Law*) atto (notarile); **deed of covenant** atto di donazione
deed poll N: **by deed poll** con atto unilaterale
deem [diːm] VT (*frm*) giudicare, ritenere; **she deemed it wise to go** ha ritenuto prudente andarsene
◎**deep** [diːp] ADJ (*comp* **-er**, *superl* **-est**) **1** (*water, hole, wound*) profondo(-a); (*snow*) alto(-a); **the lake was 16 metres deep** il lago era profondo 16 metri; **how deep is the water?** quanto è profonda l'acqua?; **knee-deep in water** in acqua fino alle ginocchia; **we were ankle-deep in mud** il fango ci arrivava alle caviglie; **to be in deep water** (*fig*) navigare in cattive acque; **the deep end** (*of swimming pool*) la parte più profonda; **to be thrown in (at) the deep end** (*fig fam*) avere il battesimo del fuoco; **to go off (at) the deep end** (*fig fam: angry*) partire per la tangente **2** (*shelf, cupboard*) profondo(-a); (*border, hem*) lungo(-a); **these kitchen units are 30 cm deep** questi mobili da cucina hanno una profondità di 30 cm **3** (*voice, sigh*) profondo(-a); **deep breathing exercises** esercizi *mpl* respiratori; **he took a deep breath** fece un respiro profondo **4** (*feeling, sleep, writer, insight*) profondo(-a); (*colour*) intenso(-a), cupo(-a); (*relief*) immenso(-a); (*interest, concern*) vivo(-a); **to be deep in thought/in a book** essere immerso(-a) nei propri pensieri/nella lettura
■ADV: **deep in her heart** in fondo al cuore; **the spectators were standing 6 deep** c'erano 6 file di spettatori in piedi; **don't go in too deep if you can't swim** non andare nell'acqua alta se non sai nuotare; **to dig deep** scavare in profondità; **deep in the forest** nel cuore della foresta; **deep into the night** fino a tarda notte; **to be deep in debt** essere nei debiti fino al collo; **buried deep in snow** coperto(-a) da uno spesso strato di neve
■N: **the deep** (*liter*) il mare
deep·en [ˈdiːpən] VT (*hole, knowledge, understanding*) approfondire; (*sound, friendship, love*) rendere più profondo(-a); (*colour*) scurire; (*interest*) ravvivare; (*sorrow*) aggravare
■VI (*gen*) diventare più profondo(-a), approfondirsi; (*colour*) diventare più intenso(-a); (*mystery*) infittirsi; (*darkness*) farsi più intenso(-a)
deep·freeze [ˌdiːpˈfriːz] N congelatore *m*
deep-freeze [diːpˈfriːz] (*vb: pt* **deep-froze**, *pp* **deep-frozen**) VT surgelare
deep-fry [ˌdiːpˈfraɪ] VT friggere in olio abbondante
deep·ly [ˈdiːplɪ] ADV (*breathe*) profondamente; (*dig*) in profondità; (*drink*) a gran sorsi; (*interested, concerned*) vivamente; (*moving*) estremamente; (*grateful, offended*) profondamente; **to regret sth deeply** rammaricarsi profondamente di qc; **to go deeply into sth** approfondire qc; **deeply depressed** estremamente depresso
deep-rooted [ˌdiːpˈruːtɪd] ADJ (*prejudice*) profondamente radicato(-a); (*affection*) profondo(-a); (*habit*) inveterato(-a)

Dd

deep-sea [ˌdiːpˈsiː] ADJ (*creatures, plants*) pelagico(-a), abissale; (*fisherman, fishing*) d'alto mare; **deep-sea diver** palombaro; **deep-sea diving** immersione *f* a grande profondità
deep-seated [ˌdiːpˈsiːtɪd] ADJ (*beliefs*) radicato(-a)
deep-set [ˈdiːpˌsɛt] ADJ: **deep-set eyes** occhi *mpl* infossati
Deep South N: **the Deep South** il profondo sud (*in America*)
deep vein thrombosis N (*Med*) trombosi *f inv* venosa profonda
deer [dɪəʳ] N, PL INV cervo(-a); **the deer family** la famiglia dei cervidi
deer·skin [ˈdɪəˌskɪn] N pelle *f* di daino
deer·stalker [ˈdɪəˌstɔːkəʳ] N (*hat*) berretto da cacciatore
deer·stalking [ˈdɪəˌstɔːkɪŋ] N caccia al cervo a piedi
de-escalate [diːˈɛskəˌleɪt] VT (*crisis*) ridimensionare; (*tension*) portare ad un rilassamento di
de·face [dɪˈfeɪs] VT (*wall, monument*) deturpare; (*work of art*) sfregiare; (*statue*) mutilare; (*poster*) imbrattare
de facto [deɪˈfæktəʊ] ADJ, ADV (*frm*) de facto *inv*
defa·ma·tion [ˌdɛfəˈmeɪʃən] N (*frm*) diffamazione *f*
de·fama·tory [dɪˈfæmətərɪ] ADJ (*frm*) diffamatorio(-a)
de·fame [dɪˈfeɪm] VT (*frm*) diffamare
de·fault [dɪˈfɔːlt] N **1 by default** per esclusione; **he got the job by default** ha ottenuto il lavoro in assenza di altri candidati; **judgement by default** (*Law*) sentenza in contumacia; **to win by default** vincere per abbandono dell'avversario; **in default of** in mancanza di **2** (*Comput: also*: **default value**) default *m inv*
■ VI (*gen*) essere inadempiente; (*Law: not appear*) non presentarsi in giudizio, essere contumace; (*: not pay*) risultare inadempiente; **to default on a debt** non onorare un debito
de·fault·er [dɪˈfɔːltəʳ] N (*on debt*) inadempiente *m/f*, debitore(-trice) moroso(-a); (*Law: at trial*) contumace *m/f*
de·fault·ing [dɪˈfɔːltɪŋ] ADJ (*debtor, borrower*) inadempiente, moroso(-a); (*witness*) contumace
default option N (*Comput*) opzione *f* di default
◎ **de·feat** [dɪˈfiːt] N (*of army, team*) sconfitta; (*: more serious*) disfatta; (*of ambition, plan*) fallimento, insuccesso
■ VT (*army, team, opponent*) sconfiggere, battere; (*plan, ambition, efforts*) frustrare; (*Pol: party*) sconfiggere; (*: bill, amendment*) respingere; **she refused to let these problems defeat her** non ha voluto che i problemi prendessero il sopravvento su di lei; **to defeat one's own ends** far fallire i propri obiettivi
de·feat·ism [dɪˈfiːtɪzəm] N disfattismo
de·feat·ist [dɪˈfiːtɪst] N, ADJ disfattista (*m/f*)
def·ecate [ˈdɛfəkeɪt] VI (*frm*) defecare
de·fect [*n* ˈdiːfɛkt; *vb* dɪˈfɛkt] N (*gen*) difetto; **physical defect** difetto fisico; **mental defect** anomalia mentale; **moral defect** difetto
■ VI (*from country*) scappare; (*from political party*) defezionare; **to defect to the enemy/the West** passare al nemico/all'Ovest
de·fec·tion [dɪˈfɛkʃən] N (*from country*) fuga; (*from political party*) defezione *f*
de·fec·tive [dɪˈfɛktɪv] ADJ (*machine, workmanship, eyesight*) difettoso(-a); (*system, reasoning*) cattivo(-a); (*Gram*) difettivo(-a); **to be defective in sth** mancare di qc
de·fec·tor [dɪˈfɛktəʳ] N fuor(i)uscito(-a); (*political*) rifugiato(-a) politico(-a)
◎ **de·fence,** (*Am*) **de·fense** [dɪˈfɛns] N difesa; **in defence of** in difesa di; **in his defence** in sua difesa; **the Ministry of Defence** (*Brit*): **the Department of Defense** (*Am*) il Ministero della Difesa; **the case for the defence** la difesa; **witness for the defence** teste *m/f* a difesa; **the body's defences against disease** le difese naturali dell'organismo contro la malattia; **as a defence against** per ripararsi da, come difesa contro
■ ADJ (*policy, strategy*) di difesa; **defence spending** *spese per la difesa*
de·fence·less, (*Am*) **de·fense·less** [dɪˈfɛnslɪs] ADJ inerme, indifeso(-a), senza difesa
defence mechanism N (*Psych*) meccanismo di difesa
◎ **de·fend** [dɪˈfɛnd] VT (*gen*) difendere; (*decision, action*) giustificare; (*opinion*) sostenere; **to defend o.s. (against)** difendersi (da)
de·fend·ant [dɪˈfɛndənt] N (*Law*) imputato(-a)
de·fend·er [dɪˈfɛndəʳ] N (*Sport*) difensore/difenditrice; (*: of title*) detentore(-trice); **Defender of the Faith** (*Brit: title of monarch*) difensore *m* della fede
de·fend·ing [dɪˈfɛndɪŋ] ADJ: **defending champion** (*Sport*) campione(-essa) in carica; **defending counsel** (*Law*) avvocato difensore
de·fense [dɪˈfɛns] N (*Am*) = **defence**
de·fen·sible [dɪˈfɛnsɪbl] ADJ giustificabile
de·fen·sive [dɪˈfɛnsɪv] ADJ difensivo(-a); (*person*) sulla difensiva
■ N: **on the defensive** sulla difensiva
de·fer [dɪˈfɜːʳ] VT (*postpone*) rimandare, rinviare; (*Law: case*) aggiornare
■ VI (*submit*): **to defer to sb/sth** rimettersi a qn/qc; **to defer to sb's (greater) knowledge** rimettersi alla scienza di qn
def·er·ence [ˈdɛfərəns] N deferenza, riguardo; **out of** *or* **in deference to** per riguardo a
def·er·en·tial [ˌdɛfəˈrɛnʃəl] ADJ deferente
de·fer·ment [dɪˈfɜːmənt], **de·fer·ral** [dɪˈfɜːrəl] N rinvio, differimento
de·fi·ance [dɪˈfaɪəns] N (atteggiamento di) sfida; **in defiance of** a dispetto di; **in defiance of orders/the law** sfidando gli ordini/la legge; **his courageous defiance of the government** la sua coraggiosa sfida al governo
de·fi·ant [dɪˈfaɪənt] ADJ (*person*) ribelle; (*tone, attitude*) di sfida; (*reply*) insolente
de·fi·ant·ly [dɪˈfaɪəntlɪ] ADV con aria (*or* tono) di sfida
de·fib·ril·la·tor [dɪˈfɪbrɪleɪtəʳ] N (*Med*) defibrillatore *m*
de·fi·cien·cy [dɪˈfɪʃənsɪ] N **1** (*of goods*) mancanza, insufficienza; (*of vitamins, minerals, protein*) carenza **2** (*in system, plan*) carenza
deficiency disease N malattia da carenza
de·fi·cient [dɪˈfɪʃənt] ADJ deficiente, insufficiente; **to be deficient in sth** mancare di qc
◎ **defi·cit** [ˈdɛfɪsɪt] N (*Fin*) deficit *m inv*, disavanzo; **to be in deficit** essere in deficit
de·file[1] [dɪˈfaɪl] VT (*frm: pollute*) deturpare
de·file[2] [ˈdiːfaɪl] N (*liter: passage*) gola
■ VI (*march*) sfilare
de·file·ment [dɪˈfaɪlmənt] N (*frm*) deturpazione *f*
de·fin·able [dɪˈfaɪnəbl] ADJ definibile, precisabile
◎ **de·fine** [dɪˈfaɪn] VT (*all senses*) precisare, definire; **the skyscraper was clearly defined against the sky** il grattacielo si stagliava nettamente contro il cielo; **to define a block of text** (*Comput*) definire un blocco di testo
defi·nite [ˈdɛfɪnɪt] ADJ **1** (*exact, clear: date, plan, intention*) preciso(-a); (*: answer, agreement*) definitivo(-a); (*positive, decided: sale, order*) sicuro(-a); (*: tone, manner*)

deciso(-a); **I haven't got any definite plans** non ho un programma preciso; **is it definite that ...?** è sicuro che...?; **maybe we'll go to Spain, but it's not definite** forse andremo in Spagna, ma non è sicuro; **it's too soon to give a definite answer** è troppo presto per dare una risposta definitiva; **he was definite about it** (*certain*) ne era sicuro; (*unequivocal*) è stato chiaro al proposito **2** (*clearly noticeable*) netto(-a); **it's a definite improvement** è un netto miglioramento **3** (*Gram*): **past definite tense** passato remoto

definite article N (*Gram*) articolo determinativo

◎ **def·i·nite·ly** ['dɛfɪnɪtlɪ] ADV (*certainly*) di sicuro, certamente; (*emphatically: state*) categoricamente; (*appreciably: better, worse*) decisamente; **he's definitely the best player** è decisamente il miglior giocatore; **yes, definitely!** sicuramente!; **definitely not!** no di certo!

◎ **defi·ni·tion** [ˌdɛfɪ'nɪʃən] N (*Ling, Phot, TV*) definizione *f*

de·fini·tive [dɪ'fɪnɪtɪv] ADJ definitivo(-a)

de·flate [di:'fleɪt] VT **1** (*tyre*) sgonfiare; (*fig: person*) fare abbassare la cresta a **2** (*Econ*) deflazionare

de·fla·tion [di:'fleɪʃən] N (*Econ*) deflazione *f*

de·fla·tion·ary [di:'fleɪʃənərɪ] ADJ (*Econ*) deflazionistico(-a)

de·flect [dɪ'flɛkt] VT (*ball, bullet, attention, criticism*) (far) deviare; (*person*): **to deflect (from)** distogliere (da)

de·flow·er [di:'flaʊə^r] VT (*liter*) deflorare

de·fog [di:'fɒg] VT (*Am Aut*) sbrinare

de·fog·ger [di:'fɒgə^r] N (*Am Aut*) sbrinatore *m*

de·fo·li·ant [di:'fəʊlɪənt] N defogliante *m*

de·fo·li·ate [di:'fəʊlɪeɪt] VT distruggere con il defogliante

de·for·esta·tion [di:ˌfɒrɪs'teɪʃən] N deforestazione *f*

de·form [dɪ'fɔ:m] VT deformare

de·formed [dɪ'fɔ:md] ADJ (*person, limb, body*) deforme; (*structure*) deformato(-a)

de·form·ity [dɪ'fɔ:mɪtɪ] N (*of body*) deformità *f inv*

Defra ['dɛfrə] N ABBR (*Brit:* = **Department for Environment, Food and Rural Affairs**) Ministero per l'ambiente e le politiche agricole

de·frag·ment [ˌdi:fræg'mɛnt] VT (*Comput*) deframmentare

de·fraud [dɪ'frɔ:d] VT: **to defraud (of)** defraudare (di)

de·fray [dɪ'freɪ] VT (*frm: expenses*) sostenere

de·frock [di:'frɒk] VT costringere a lasciare l'abito talare; **a defrocked priest** un prete spretato

de·frost [di:'frɒst] VT (*refrigerator*) sbrinare; (*frozen food*) scongelare

deft [dɛft] ADJ (*comp* **-er**, *superl* **-est**) abile, destro(-a)

deft·ly ['dɛftlɪ] ADV abilmente

deft·ness ['dɛftnɪs] N abilità *f inv*, destrezza

de·funct [dɪ'fʌŋkt] ADJ (*company*) scomparso(-a); (*scheme*) morto(-a) e sepolto(-a)

de·fuse [di:'fju:z] VT (*bomb*) disinnescare; **to defuse the situation** fare in modo che la situazione non degeneri; **to defuse tensions** allentare la tensione

defy [dɪ'faɪ] VT **1** (*person*) rifiutare di obbedire a; (*authority, death, danger*) sfidare; (*resist: efforts*) resistere a; **thousands defied the ban** migliaia di persone si sono rifiutate di obbedire al divieto; **it defies description** supera ogni descrizione **2** (*challenge*): **to defy sb (to do sth)** sfidare qn (a fare qc); **I defy you to find a single advantage in the scheme** ti sfido a trovare anche un solo vantaggio nel programma

de·gen·era·cy [dɪ'dʒɛnərəsɪ] N degenerazione *f*

de·gen·er·ate [*vb* dɪ'dʒɛnəˌreɪt; *adj, n* dɪ'dʒɛnərɪt] VI: **to degenerate (into)** degenerare (in)

■ ADJ (*person*) degenere; (*morals, art*) degenerato(-a)

■ N degenerato(-a)

de·gen·era·tion [dɪˌdʒɛnə'reɪʃən] N degenerazione *f*

de·gen·era·tive [dɪ'dʒɛnərɪtɪv] ADJ degenerativo(-a)

deg·ra·da·tion [ˌdɛgrə'deɪʃən] N degradazione *f*

de·grade [dɪ'greɪd] VT degradare

de·grad·ing [dɪ'greɪdɪŋ] ADJ degradante, umiliante

◎ **de·gree** [dɪ'gri:] N **1** (*gen, Math, Geog*) grado; **10 degrees below freezing** 10 gradi sotto zero; **a temperature of thirty degrees** una temperatura di trenta gradi **2** (*amount*): **a high degree of uncertainty** un largo margine d'incertezza; **a considerable degree of risk** una grossa percentuale di rischio **3** (*step in scale*): **by degrees** a poco a poco, gradualmente; **to some degree** *or* **to a certain degree** in certa misura, fino a un certo punto **4** (*Univ*) ≈ laurea; **first degree** ≈ laurea; **honorary degree** ≈ laurea ad honorem; **to get one's degree** ≈ prendere la laurea, laurearsi; **I'm doing a degree in languages** sono iscritto a lingue; **a (first) degree in maths** ≈ una laurea in matematica

de·hu·man·ize [di:'hju:məˌnaɪz] VT disumanizzare

de·hu·midi·fi·er [ˌdi:hju:'mɪdɪfaɪə^r] N deumidificatore *m*

de·hy·drate [ˌdi:'haɪdreɪt] VT disidratare; **dehydrating agent** disidratante *m*

de·hy·dra·ted [di:haɪ'dreɪtɪd] ADJ (*person, vegetables*) disidratato(-a); (*milk, eggs*) in polvere

de·hy·dra·tion [ˌdi:haɪ'dreɪʃən] N disidratazione *f*

de-ice ['di:'aɪs] VT (*car windows*) sbrinare; (*roads*) liberare dal ghiaccio

de-icer ['di:'aɪsə^r] N (*thermal*) sbrinatore *m*; (*chemical*) scongelante *m*

de-icing ['di:'aɪsɪŋ] N rimozione *f* del ghiaccio; **de-icing spray** (*Aut*) spray *m inv* sghiacciante

dei·fy ['di:ɪfaɪ] VT (*frm*) divinizzare

deign [deɪn] VT: **to deign to do sth** degnarsi di fare qc

de·ity ['di:ɪtɪ] N divinità *f inv*, dio/dea; **the Deity** la Divinità, Dio

déjà vu [ˌdeɪʒɑ:'vu:] N déjà vu *m inv*; **a feeling** *or* **sense of déjà vu** una sensazione di déjà vu

de·ject·ed [dɪ'dʒɛktɪd] ADJ abbattuto(-a), avvilito(-a); **to become dejected** abbattersi

de·ject·ed·ly [dɪ'dʒɛktɪdlɪ] ADV (*say, talk*) con tono abbattuto; (*move, act*) con aria abbattuta

de·jec·tion [dɪ'dʒɛkʃən] N abbattimento, avvilimento

de jure [ˌdeɪ'dʒʊərɪ] (*Law*) ADJ legittimo

■ ADV de jure, in teoria

dek·ko ['dɛkəʊ] N (*Brit: fam*): **to have a dekko at sth** dare un'occhiata a qc

del. ABBR = **delete**

Dela·ware ['dɛləwɛə^r] N Delaware *m*

▷ www.delaware.gov/

◎ **de·lay** [dɪ'leɪ] N ritardo; **a delay of twenty minutes** un ritardo di venti minuti; **without delay** immediatamente; **without further delay** senza ulteriore indugio; **delays to traffic** rallentamenti *mpl* al traffico

■ VT (*postpone: journey*) rimandare, rinviare; (*: payment*) differire; (*hold up: person*) trattenere; (*: traffic*) far rallentare; (*: action, event*) ritardare; **we decided to delay our departure** decidemmo di rimandare la partenza; **his train must have been delayed** il suo treno avrà fatto ritardo; **our flight was delayed** il nostro volo ha subito un ritardo

Dd

■VI: **to delay (doing sth)** ritardare (a fare qc); **don't delay!** non perdere tempo!
delayed-action [dɪleɪd'ækʃən] ADJ (*Phot: shutter*) ad azione ritardata; **delayed-action bomb** ordigno a scoppio ritardato
de·lay·ing [dɪ'leɪɪŋ] ADJ: **delaying tactics** tattiche *fpl* per prendere tempo
de·lec·table [dɪ'lɛktəbl] ADJ delizioso(-a)
de·lec·tably [dɪ'lɛktəblɪ] ADV deliziosamente
de·lec·ta·tion [ˌdi:lɛk'teɪʃən] N (*frm*) diletto
◎**del·egate** [*n* 'dɛlɪˌgɪt; *vb* 'dɛlɪgeɪt] N: **delegate (to)** delegato(-a) (a)
■VT (*duties, responsiblities, power*) delegare; **to delegate sth to sb** delegare qc a qn; **to delegate sb to do sth** delegare qn a fare qc
◎**del·ega·tion** [ˌdɛlɪ'geɪʃən] N **1** (*of work, power*) delega **2** (*group*) delegazione *f*
de·lete [dɪ'li:t] VT (*gen, Comput*) cancellare; **to delete (from)** (*item: from list, catalogue*) togliere (da); (*mistake, line*) cancellare (da)
del·eteri·ous [ˌdɛlɪ'tɪərɪəs] ADJ (*frm*): **deleterious (to)** deleterio(-a) (per)
de·letion [dɪ'li:ʃən] N soppressione *f*, eliminazione *f*
Del·hi ['dɛlɪ] N Delhi *f*
deli ['dɛlɪ] N ABBR (*fam: shop:* = **delicatessen**) gastronomia
◎**de·lib·er·ate** [*adj* dɪ'lɪbərɪt; *vb* dɪ'lɪbəˌreɪt] ADJ **1** (*intentional: insult, action*) intenzionale, voluto(-a); (*: mistake*) voluto(-a); (*: lie*) calcolato(-a) **2** (*cautious, thoughtful*) ponderato(-a); (*unhurried: manner, voice*) posato(-a); (*pace*) misurato(-a)
■VT (*think about*) considerare, riflettere su; (*discuss*) discutere
■VI: **to deliberate (on)** deliberare (su)
de·lib·er·ate·ly [dɪ'lɪbərɪtlɪ] ADV (*intentionally*) deliberatamente, volutamente; (*cautiously, slowly*) posatamente
de·lib·era·tion [dɪˌlɪbə'reɪʃən] N **1** (*consideration*) riflessione *f*; (*discussion*) discussione *f*, deliberazione *f*; **after due deliberation** dopo matura riflessione **2** (*slowness*) ponderatezza, posatezza
de·lib·era·tive [dɪ'lɪbərətɪv] ADJ (*assembly*) con potere deliberante
deli·ca·cy ['dɛlɪkəsɪ] N **1** (*of person, thing*) delicatezza; (*of workmanship*) finezza **2** (*special food*) specialità *f inv*, ghiottoneria; **local delicacies** specialità locali; **it's a delicacy for Chinese people** è una prelibatezza per i cinesi
deli·cate ['dɛlɪkɪt] ADJ (*gen*) delicato(-a); (*workmanship, design*) fine
deli·cate·ly ['dɛlɪkɪtlɪ] ADV (*gen*) delicatamente; (*act, express*) con delicatezza
deli·ca·tes·sen [ˌdɛlɪkə'tɛsn] N ≈ salumeria
de·li·cious [dɪ'lɪʃəs] ADJ delizioso(-a), squisito(-a)
◎**de·light** [dɪ'laɪt] N (*feeling of joy*) piacere *m*, gioia; (*pleasurable thing*) delizia, (gran) piacere *m*; **the delights of good food** i piaceri della buona tavola; **to my delight** con mia grande gioia; **it is a delight to the eye** è un piacere guardarlo; **to take delight in sth** dilettarsi di qc; **to take delight in doing sth** divertirsi a fare qc; **to be the delight of** essere la gioia di
■VT riempire di gioia
▸**delight in** VI + PREP: **to delight in sth/in doing sth** dilettarsi di qc/nel fare qc
◎**de·light·ed** [dɪ'laɪtɪd] ADJ: **delighted (with sb/sth)** contentissimo(-a) (di qn/qc), felice (di qn/qc); **delighted at sth** contentissimo(-a) di qc, felice di qc; **to be delighted to do sth/that** essere felice di fare qc/che + *sub*; **he'll be delighted to see you** sarà contentissimo di vederti; **I'd be delighted** con grande piacere
de·light·ful [dɪ'laɪtfʊl] ADJ (*person, place, meal*) delizioso(-a); (*manner, smile*) incantevole; **Lucy is a delightful child** Lucy è una bambina deliziosa; **thank you for a delightful evening** grazie per l'incantevole serata
de·light·ful·ly [dɪ'laɪtfəlɪ] ADV deliziosamente; **the hotel is delightfully situated** l'albergo è situato in una posizione incantevole
de·lim·it [di:'lɪmɪt] VT (*frm*) delimitare
de·lin·eate [dɪ'lɪnɪˌeɪt] VT (*frm*) delineare
de·lin·ea·tion [dɪˌlɪnɪ'eɪʃən] N (*frm*) delineamento
de·lin·quen·cy [dɪ'lɪŋkwənsɪ] N delinquenza
de·lin·quent [dɪ'lɪŋkwənt] ADJ (*behaviour*) delinquenziale, da delinquente; **a delinquent youth** un giovane delinquente
■N delinquente *m/f*
de·liri·ous [dɪ'lɪrɪəs] ADJ (*Med, fig*) delirante, in delirio; **to be delirious** delirare; (*fig*) farneticare; **delirious with joy** pazzo(-a) di gioia
de·liri·ous·ly [dɪ'lɪrɪəslɪ] ADV: **deliriously happy** fuori di sé dalla gioia
de·lir·ium [dɪ'lɪrɪəm] N (*Med*) delirio; **delirium tremens** delirium *m inv* tremens *inv*
◎**de·liv·er** [dɪ'lɪvə[r]] VT **1** (*goods*) consegnare; (*letter, parcel*) recapitare, consegnare; **they delivered the parcel this morning** mi hanno consegnato il pacco stamattina; **he delivered me home safely** mi ha portato a casa sano e salvo; **to deliver a message** dare un messaggio; **he delivered the goods** (*fig fam*) ha fatto quel che doveva fare **2** (*speech, sermon, verdict*) pronunciare; (*lecture*) tenere, fare; (*ultimatum*) dare; (*blow, punch*) tirare **3** (*subj: doctor, midwife: baby*) far nascere **4** (*old: rescue*): **to deliver (from)** liberare (da)
de·liv·er·ance [dɪ'lɪvərəns] N (*old*) liberazione *f*
de·liv·er·er [dɪ'lɪvərə[r]] N (*old*) salvatore(-trice)
◎**de·liv·ery** [dɪ'lɪvərɪ] N **1** (*of goods, parcels*) consegna; (*of mail*) recapito; **allow 28 days for delivery** calcola 28 giorni per la consegna; **there is no delivery on Sundays** (*Post*) non c'è posta la domenica; **to take delivery of** prendere in consegna **2** (*of speaker*) dizione *f* **3** (*Med*) parto
delivery boy N fattorino
delivery note N bolla di consegna
delivery room N (*Med*) sala *f* parto *inv*
delivery van, (*Am*) **delivery truck** N furgoncino (per le consegne)
dell [dɛl] N (*liter*) valletta
de·louse [di:'laʊs] VT spidocchiare
del·ta ['dɛltə] N delta *m inv*
delta wing N ala a delta
de·lude [dɪ'lu:d] VT illudere, ingannare; **to delude sb into thinking that ...** indurre qn a credere che...; **to delude o.s** illudersi, farsi (delle) illusioni

> **DID YOU KNOW ...?**
> **delude** is not translated by the Italian word ***deludere***

de·lud·ed [dɪ'lu:dɪd] ADJ illuso(-a)
del·uge ['dɛlju:dʒ] N diluvio; **a deluge of protests** un diluvio di proteste
■VT (*fig*): **to deluge (with)** subissare (di), inondare (di)
de·lu·sion [dɪ'lu:ʒən] N illusione *f*; (*Psych*) fissazione *f*

> **DID YOU KNOW ...?**
> **delusion** is not translated by the Italian word *delusione*

de luxe [dɪ'lʌks] ADJ di lusso

delve [dɛlv] VI: **to delve into** *(pocket, bag)* frugare in; *(subject)* far ricerche in

Dem. *(Am Pol)* N ABBR = Democrat ■ ADJ = Democratic

dema·gogue ['dɛməgɒg] N *(pej)* demagogo

◎ **de·mand** [dɪ'mɑ:nd] N **1** *(request)*: **demand (for)** *(help, money)* richiesta (di); *(better pay)* richiesta (di), rivendicazione *f* (di); **by popular demand** a richiesta generale; **on demand** su richiesta; **I have many demands on my time** sono impegnatissimo **2** *(Comm)*: **demand (for)** domanda (di); **to be in demand** essere richiesto(-a)
■ VT *(ask for)*: **to demand sth (from *or* of sb)** pretendere qc (da qn), esigere qc (da qn); *(need)* richiedere; **to demand that** richiedere che + *sub*; **I demand an explanation** pretendo una spiegazione; **I demand to see the manager** esigo di vedere il direttore; **international crises demanding their attention** crisi internazionali che richiedono la loro attenzione

> **DID YOU KNOW ...?**
> **demand** is not translated by the Italian word *domandare*

demand draft N *(Comm)* tratta a vista

de·mand·ing [dɪ'mɑ:ndɪŋ] ADJ *(person)* esigente; *(work: physically)* stancante; *(: mentally)* impegnativo(-a); **a demanding child** un bambino esigente; **it's a very demanding job** è un lavoro molto impegnativo

de·mar·ca·tion [ˌdi:mɑ:'keɪʃən] N *(frm)* demarcazione *f*; **demarcation dispute** controversia settoriale *or* di categoria; **demarcation line** linea di demarcazione

de·ma·teri·al·ize [dɪmə'tɪərɪəˌlaɪz] VI smaterializzarsi

de·mean [dɪ'mi:n] VT svilire; **to demean o.s** abbassarsi

de·mean·ing [dɪ'mi:nɪŋ] ADJ degradante

de·mean·our, *(Am)* **de·mean·or** [dɪ'mi:nə^r] N *(frm)* contegno

de·ment·ed [dɪ'mɛntɪd] ADJ folle, demente

de·ment·ed·ly [dɪ'mɛntɪdlɪ] ADV come un(a) folle

de·men·tia [dɪ'mɛnʃɪə] N *(Med)* demenza

dem·erara [ˌdɛmə'rɛərə] N *(also: **demerara sugar**)* zucchero grezzo di canna

de·mer·it [di:'mɛrɪt] N *(frm)* difetto

demi... ['dɛmɪ] PREF semi...

demi·god ['dɛmɪˌgɒd] N semidio

demi·john ['dɛmɪˌdʒɒn] N damigiana

de·mili·ta·ri·za·tion ['di:ˌmɪlɪtəraɪ'zeɪʃən] N smilitarizzazione *f*

de·mili·ta·rize [di:'mɪlɪtəˌraɪz] VT smilitarizzare

de·mili·ta·rized zone [di:'mɪlɪtəˌraɪzd'zəʊn] N zona smilitarizzata

de·mise [dɪ'maɪz] N *(frm)* decesso

de·mist [di:'mɪst] VT *(Brit Aut)* sbrinare

de·mist·er [di:'mɪstə^r] N *(Brit Aut)* sbrinatore *m*

demo ['dɛməʊ] N ABBR *(fam)* **1** *(Brit:* = **demonstration***)* manifestazione *f* **2** *(of music)* demo *f inv* **3** *(Comput: software)* demo *f inv*

de·mo·bi·li·za·tion ['di:ˌməʊbɪlaɪ'zeɪʃən] N smobilitazione *f*

de·mo·bi·lize [di:'məʊbɪlaɪz] VT smobilitare

◎ **de·moc·ra·cy** [dɪ'mɒkrəsɪ] N democrazia

◎ **demo·crat** ['dɛməˌkræt] N **1** democratico(-a) **2 Democrat** *(Am: Pol)* democratico(-a)

◎ **demo·crat·ic** [ˌdɛmə'krætɪk] ADJ **1** democratico(-a) **2 Democratic** *(Am: Pol)* democratico(-a)

demo·crati·cal·ly [ˌdɛmə'krætɪkəlɪ] ADV democraticamente

Democratic Party N *(Am)*: **the Democratic Party** il partito democratico

de·moc·ra·tize [dɪ'mɒkrəˌtaɪz] VT democratizzare

de·mog·ra·pher [dɪ'mɒgrəfə^r] N demografo(-a)

de·mo·graph·ic [ˌdɛmə'græfɪk] ADJ demografico(-a)

de·mog·ra·phy [dɪ'mɒgrəfɪ] N demografia

de·mol·ish [dɪ'mɒlɪʃ] VT *(gen)* demolire; *(hum: cake, food)* far fuori

demo·li·tion [ˌdɛmə'lɪʃən] N demolizione *f*; **demolition squad** squadra di demolizione; **demolition zone** area *or* zona di demolizione

de·mon ['di:mən] N *(also fig)* demonio; **he's a demon for work** *(fam)* è uno stacanovista
■ ADJ: **a demon squash player** un mago dello squash; **a demon driver** un asso del volante

de·mo·ni·ac [dɪ'məʊnɪæk], **de·mo·nia·cal** [ˌdi:məʊ'naɪəkəl] ADJ demoniaco(-a), diabolico(-a)

de·mon·strable ['dɛmənstrəbl] ADJ dimostrabile

de·mon·strably ['dɛmənstrəblɪ] ADV palesemente

◎ **dem·on·strate** ['dɛmənˌstreɪt] VT **1** *(truth, ability)* dimostrare; *(emotion)* manifestare; **you have to demonstrate that you are reliable** devi dimostrare di essere affidabile **2** *(appliance)* fare una dimostrazione di; **she demonstrated the technique** ha fatto una dimostrazione della tecnica
■ VI *(Pol)*: **to demonstrate (for/against)** manifestare (per/contro); **they demonstrated outside the court** hanno manifestato fuori dal tribunale

◎ **dem·on·stra·tion** [ˌdɛmən'streɪʃən] N dimostrazione *f*; *(Pol)* manifestazione *f*; **to hold a demonstration** *(Pol)* tenere una manifestazione

de·mon·stra·tive [dɪ'mɒnstrətɪv] ADJ *(person)* espansivo(-a); *(Gram)* dimostrativo(-a)

◎ **de·mon·stra·tor** ['dɛmənstreɪtə^r] N *(Pol)* dimostrante *m/f*; *(Comm: sales person)* dimostratore(-trice); *(: Am: car, computer)* modello per dimostrazione

de·mor·ali·za·tion [dɪˌmɒrəlaɪ'zeɪʃən] N demoralizzazione *f*

de·mor·al·ize [dɪ'mɒrəˌlaɪz] VT demoralizzare

de·mor·al·ized [dɪ'mɒrəˌlaɪzd] ADJ demoralizzato(-a)

de·mor·al·iz·ing [dɪ'mɒrəlaɪzɪŋ] ADJ demoralizzante

de·mote [dɪ'məʊt] VT degradare

de·mo·tion [dɪ'məʊʃən] N degradazione *f*

de·mur [dɪ'mɜ:^r] VI *(frm)*: **to demur (at)** sollevare obiezioni (a *or* su)
■ N: **without demur** senza obiezioni

de·mure [dɪ'mjʊə^r] ADJ *(girl)* pieno(-a) di contegno; *(smile)* contegnoso(-a)

de·mure·ly [dɪ'mjʊəlɪ] ADV contegnosamente

de·mure·ness [dɪ'mjʊənɪs] N contegno

de·mur·rage [dɪ'mʌrɪdʒ] N *(Comm)* controstallia

de·mu·tu·al·ise [di:'mju:tjʊəlaɪz] VI *(Brit: Fin) convertirsi in una società a responsabilità limitata*

de·mys·ti·fy [di:'mɪstɪˌfaɪ] VT demistificare

den [dɛn] N *(of wild animal)* tana, covo; *(room)* stanzetta; **a lion's den** la tana di un leone; **he's up in his den reading** è su in camera sua a leggere; **a den of iniquity** un luogo di perdizione; **a den of thieves** un covo di ladri

de·na·tion·ali·za·tion ['di:ˌnæʃnəlaɪ'zeɪʃən] N snazionalizzazione *f*, denazionalizzazione *f*

de·na·tion·al·ize [di:'næʃnəˌlaɪz] VT snazionalizzare, denazionalizzare

de·ni·able [dɪ'naɪəbəl] ADJ negabile

de·ni·al [dɪ'naɪəl] N **1** *(of accusation, guilt)* diniego,

Dd

rifiuto; **the government issued an official denial** il governo ha rilasciato una smentita ufficiale; **to be in denial** non accettare la realtà **2** (*refusal: of request*) rifiuto; (*: of rights*) mancato riconoscimento

den·ier [ˈdɛnɪə^r] N denaro (*di filati, calze*)

deni·grate [ˈdɛnɪˌgreɪt] VT denigrare

deni·gra·tory [ˈdɛnɪˌgreɪtərɪ] ADJ denigratorio(-a)

den·im [ˈdɛnɪm] N tessuto jeans; **denims** NPL (*clothes*) blue jeans *mpl*

■ ADJ (*jacket, skirt*) di jeans; **a denim jacket** una giacca di jeans

deni·zen [ˈdɛnɪzn] N (*liter: inhabitant*) abitante *m/f*

Den·mark [ˈdɛnmɑːk] N Danimarca

de·nomi·na·tion [dɪˌnɒmɪˈneɪʃən] N (*Rel*) confessione *f*; (*of coin*) valore *m*; **bank notes in small denominations** banconote di piccolo taglio

de·nomi·na·tor [dɪˈnɒmɪˌneɪtə^r] N (*Math*) denominatore *m*

de·note [dɪˈnəʊt] VT (*indicate*) denotare, indicare; (*subj: word*) significare

de·noue·ment, dénouement [deɪˈnuːmɒn] N epilogo

de·nounce [dɪˈnaʊns] VT (*accuse publicly*) accusare; (*to police*) denunciare; **to denounce sb as a liar** accusare pubblicamente qn di essere un bugiardo

dense [dɛns] ADJ (*comp* **-r**, *superl* **-st**) (*fog*) denso(-a), fitto(-a); (*forest, crowd*) fitto(-a); (*fur*) folto(-a); (*fam: person: stupid*) tonto(-a), ottuso(-a); **dense smoke prevented firemen from entering the building** un fumo denso impediva ai pompieri di entrare; **he's so dense!** è così ottuso!

dense·ly [ˈdɛnslɪ] ADV: **densely populated** densamente popolato(-a); **densely wooded** coperto(-a) di fitti boschi

den·sity [ˈdɛnsɪtɪ] N densità *f inv*; **single-/double-density disk** (*Comput*) disco a singola/doppia densità

dent [dɛnt] N (*in metal*) ammaccatura, bozzo; (*in wood*) tacca, intaccatura; **to make a dent in** (*fig*) intaccare; **the holiday left a dent in our savings** la vacanza ha intaccato i nostri risparmi

■ VT (*car, hat*) ammaccare; (*fig*) intaccare

> DID YOU KNOW ...?
> **dent** is not translated by the Italian word *dente*

den·tal [ˈdɛntl] ADJ (*surgery, care*) dentistico(-a), odontoiatrico(-a); (*appointment*) dal dentista; **dental treatment** cure dentistiche; **dental orthopaedics** ortodonzia; **dental technician** odontotecnico

dental floss N filo interdentale

dental surgeon N medico dentista *m/f*, odontoiatra *m/f*

den·ti·frice [ˈdɛntɪfrɪs] N dentifricio

den·tist [ˈdɛntɪst] N dentista *m/f*; **dentist's chair** poltrona del dentista; **dentist's surgery** (*Brit*) studio dentistico

den·tis·try [ˈdɛntɪstrɪ] N odontoiatria
▷ www.dental--health.com

den·ti·tion [dɛnˈtɪʃən] N (*teeth*) dentatura; (*teething*) dentizione *f*

den·tures [ˈdɛntʃəz] NPL (*false teeth*) dentiera

de·nude [dɪˈnjuːd] VT (*frm*): **to denude (of)** spogliare (di), denudare (di)

de·nun·cia·tion [dɪˌnʌnsɪˈeɪʃən] N denuncia; (*in public*) pubblica accusa

◎ **deny** [dɪˈnaɪ] VT **1** (*possibility, truth of statement, charge*) negare; (*report*) smentire; **there's no denying it** è innegabile; **he denies having said it** nega di averlo detto **2** (*refuse*): **to deny sb sth** negare qc a qn, rifiutare qc a qn; **to deny o.s. sth** negarsi qc, privarsi di qc

de·odor·ant [diːˈəʊdərənt] N deodorante *m*

de·odor·ize [diːˈəʊdəˌraɪz] VT deodorare

de·part [dɪˈpɑːt] VI: **to depart (from)** (*train*) partire (da); (*person*) andar via (da), allontanarsi (da); **to depart from tradition/the truth** scostarsi dalla tradizione/dalla verità

de·part·ed [dɪˈpɑːtɪd] ADJ (*bygone: glory*) trascorso(-a), passato(-a); (*dead*) scomparso(-a)

■ N: **the dear departed** il/la caro(-a) estinto(-a)

◎ **de·part·ment** [dɪˈpɑːtmənt] N (*Admin*) sezione *f*, reparto; (*in shop*) reparto; (*in government*) ministero; (*Univ*) istituto, dipartimento; **the English Department** (*in school*) i professori di inglese; (*in university*) l'istituto di inglese; **the toy department** il reparto giocattoli; **that's not my department** (*fig*) questo non è di mia competenza; **Department of State** (*Am*) Dipartimento di Stato; **Department of Trade and Industry** (*Brit*) Ministero del Commercio e dell'Industria

de·part·men·tal [ˌdiːpɑːtˈmɛntl] ADJ (*meeting*) di sezione; **departmental manager** caporeparto *m/f*

department store N grande magazzino

◎ **de·par·ture** [dɪˈpɑːtʃə^r] N (*gen*) partenza; (*fig: from custom, principle*): **departure from** deviazione *f* da, abbandono di; **after his departure** dopo la sua partenza; **a new departure** (*fig*) una svolta (decisiva); **departure board** (*Aer*) tabellone *m* (delle partenze); **departure lounge** (*Aer*) sala d'attesa

◎ **de·pend** [dɪˈpɛnd] VI **1** **to depend (up)on** (*rely*) contare su, dipendere da; (*be dependent on*) dipendere (economicamente) da, essere a carico di; **you can depend on it** sta pur certo **2** **to depend (on)** (*be influenced by*) dipendere (da); **it (all) depends on the weather** (tutto) dipende dal tempo; **it (all) depends what you mean** dipende da che cosa vuoi dire; **that depends** *or* **it depends** dipende; **depending on a** seconda di; **depending on the result ...** a seconda del risultato...

de·pend·abil·ity [dɪˌpɛndəˈbɪlɪtɪ] N affidabilità

de·pend·able [dɪˈpɛndəbl] ADJ (*person*) fidato(-a), serio(-a); (*machine, car*) affidabile

de·pend·ant [dɪˈpɛndənt] N persona a carico

de·pend·ence [dɪˈpɛndəns] N: **dependence (on)** dipendenza (da)

de·pend·en·cy [dɪˈpɛndənsɪ] N (*country*) possedimento

de·pend·ent [dɪˈpɛndənt] ADJ: **to be dependent (on)** (*gen*) dipendere (da); (*child, relative*) essere a carico (di); **psychologically he's dependent on her** psicologicamente dipende da lei

■ N = **dependant**

de·per·son·ali·za·tion [dɪˌpɜːsnəlaɪˈzeɪʃən] N (*frm*) spersonalizzazione *f*

de·per·son·al·ize [diːˈpɜːsənəˌlaɪz] VT (*frm*) spersonalizzare

de·pict [dɪˈpɪkt] VT (*in picture*) rappresentare; (*in words*) descrivere, dipingere; **a picture depicting a sunset** un quadro che raffigura un tramonto; **he was depicted as a lonely old man** era descritto come un vecchio solitario

de·pic·tion [dɪˈpɪkʃən] N (*in picture*) rappresentazione *f*; (*in words*) descrizione *f*

de·pila·tory [dɪˈpɪlətərɪ] N (*also:* **depilatory cream**) crema depilatoria

de·plete [dɪˈpliːt] VT ridurre

de·plet·ed [dɪˈpliːtɪd] ADJ diminuito(-a); **depleted uranium** uranio impoverito

de·ple·tion [dɪˈpliːʃən] N riduzione *f*, impoverimento

de·plor·able [dɪˈplɔːrəbl] ADJ (*frm*) deplorevole, lamentevole; **this deplorable incident** questo deplorevole incidente

de·plor·ably [dɪˈplɔːrəblɪ] ADV (*frm*) deplorevolmente

de·plore [dɪˈplɔːʳ] VT (*frm*) deplorare

de·ploy [dɪˈplɔɪ] VT (*Mil: soldiers, forces*) schierare, spiegare; (*fig: resources*) impiegare, far uso di

de·ploy·ment [dɪˈplɔɪmənt] N (*Mil*) schieramento, spiegamento; (*fig*) impiego

de·popu·late [ˌdiːˈpɒpjʊleɪt] VT spopolare

de·popu·la·tion [ˈdiːˌpɒpjʊˈleɪʃən] N spopolamento

de·port [dɪˈpɔːt] VT deportare

de·por·ta·tion [ˌdiːpɔːˈteɪʃən] N deportazione *f*; **deportation order** ≈ foglio di via obbligatorio

de·por·tee [diːpɔːˈtiː] N deportato(-a)

de·port·ment [dɪˈpɔːtmənt] N (*old: bearing*) portamento; (*: behaviour*) comportamento

de·pose [dɪˈpəʊz] VT (*monarch, leader*) deporre

◎ **de·pos·it** [dɪˈpɒzɪt] N **1** (*in bank*) deposito; (*Comm: part payment*) acconto; (*: returnable security*) cauzione *f*; **to put down a deposit of £50** versare un acconto di 50 sterline; **you get the deposit back when you return the bike** quando riporti la bici ti ridanno la cauzione **2** (*Chem, Geol*) deposito, sedimento; (*of ore, oil*) giacimento
■ VT **1** (*put down*) posare; (*leave: luggage*) mettere *or* lasciare in deposito, depositare **2** (*money: in bank*) depositare

deposit account N ≈ libretto di risparmio

de·posi·tary [dɪˈpɒzɪtərɪ] N = **depository 2**

depo·si·tion [ˌdiːpəˈzɪʃən] N (*Geol, Law, also of monarch*) deposizione *f*

de·posi·tor [dɪˈpɒzɪtəʳ] N depositante *m/f*

de·posi·tory [dɪˈpɒzɪtərɪ] N **1** (*place*) deposito **2** (*person*) depositario(-a)

de·pot [ˈdɛpəʊ, *Am* ˈdiːpəʊ] N **1** (*storehouse*) magazzino, deposito *m* merci *inv*; (*Brit: bus garage*) deposito; (*Am: railway station*) stazione *f* ferroviaria; (*: bus station*) stazione *f* degli autobus; **an arms depot** un deposito di armi

de·praved [dɪˈpreɪvd] ADJ (*frm*) depravato(-a)

de·prav·ity [dɪˈprævɪtɪ] N (*frm*) depravazione *f*

dep·re·cate [ˈdɛprɪˌkeɪt] VT (*frm*) deprecare

dep·re·cat·ing [ˈdɛprɪˌkeɪtɪŋ], **dep·re·ca·tory** [ˈdɛprɪkətərɪ] ADJ (*disapproving*) di biasimo, di disapprovazione; (*apologetic*): **a deprecating smile** un sorriso di scusa

dep·re·cat·ing·ly [ˈdɛprɪkeɪtɪŋlɪ] ADV (*disapprovingly*) con (aria di) disapprovazione; (*apologetically*) con aria di scusa

de·pre·ci·ate [dɪˈpriːʃɪeɪt] VI deprezzarsi, svalutarsi
■ VT deprezzare, svalutare

de·pre·cia·tion [dɪˌpriːʃɪˈeɪʃən] N deprezzamento, svalutazione *f*

dep·re·da·tions [ˌdɛprɪˈdeɪʃənz] NPL (*old*) saccheggi *mpl*

de·press [dɪˈprɛs] VT **1** (*person*) deprimere; (*spirits*) buttar giù **2** (*trade*) ridurre; (*prices*) far scendere, abbassare **3** (*frm: press down: lever*) abbassare

de·pres·sant [dɪˈprɛsnt] N (*Med*) sedativo

de·pressed [dɪˈprɛst] ADJ **1** (*person*) depresso(-a); **to feel depressed** sentirsi depresso(-a); **to get depressed** deprimersi **2** (*area*) depresso(-a); (*industry*) in crisi; (*Fin: market, trade*) stagnante, in ribasso

de·press·ing [dɪˈprɛsɪŋ] ADJ deprimente, demoralizzante

de·press·ing·ly [dɪˈprɛsɪŋlɪ] ADV in modo deprimente

◎ **de·pres·sion** [dɪˈprɛʃən] N (*gen, Med, Econ, Met*) depressione *f*; **the economy is in a state of depression** è in atto una crisi economica; **the Depression** la Grande depressione

de·pres·sive [dɪˈprɛsɪv] ADJ depressivo(-a)
■ N (*Psych*) depresso(-a)

dep·ri·va·tion [ˌdɛprɪˈveɪʃən] N (*act*) privazione *f*; (*state*) indigenza

de·prive [dɪˈpraɪv] VT: **to deprive sb of sth** privare qn di qc; **to deprive o.s. of sth** privarsi di qc

de·prived [dɪˈpraɪvd] ADJ bisognoso(-a)

dept. ABBR = **department**

◎ **depth** [dɛpθ] N (*gen, of knowledge, thought*) profondità *f inv*; (*of snow*) altezza, spessore *m*; (*of shelf*) profondità, larghezza; (*of colour, feeling*) intensità *f inv*; **at a depth of 3 metres** a 3 metri di profondità, a una profondità di 3 metri; **the depths of the sea** gli abissi del mare; **to be out of one's depth** (*swimmer*) non toccare; (*fig*) non sentirsi all'altezza della situazione; **in the depths of the forest** nel cuore della foresta; **in the depths of winter** in pieno inverno, nel cuore dell'inverno; **in the depths of despair** in preda alla disperazione; **to study sth in depth** studiare qc in profondità

depth charge N (*Mil*) bomba di profondità

depth gauge N profondimetro

depu·ta·tion [ˌdɛpjʊˈteɪʃən] N deputazione *f*, delegazione *f*

de·pute [dɪˈpjuːt] VT (*frm*): **to depute sth to sb** delegare qc a qn; **to depute sb to do sth** deputare *or* delegare qn a fare qc

depu·tize [ˈdɛpjʊˌtaɪz] VI: **to deputize (for sb)** fare le veci (di qn), sostituire (qn)

◎ **depu·ty** [ˈdɛpjʊtɪ] N (*second-in-command*) vice *m/f*; (*replacement*) sostituto(-a), supplente *m/f*
■ ADJ: **deputy chairman** vicepresidente *m*; **deputy head** (*Scol*) vicepreside *m/f*; **deputy leader** (*Brit Pol*) sottosegretario; **deputy secretary** vicesegretario

de·rail [dɪˈreɪl] VT far deragliare; **to be derailed** deragliare

de·rail·leur [dəˈreɪljəʳ] N, **de·rail·leur gears** NPL (*Cycling*) deragliatore *m*

de·rail·ment [dɪˈreɪlmənt] N deragliamento

de·ranged [dɪˈreɪndʒd] ADJ (*mind*) sconvolto(-a); (*person*) squilibrato(-a); **to be (mentally) deranged** essere uno(-a) squilibrato(-a)

der·by [ˈdɑːbɪ] N **1** (*sporting event*) derby *m inv* **2** (*Am: hat*) bombetta

de·regu·late [dɪˈrɛgjʊˌleɪt] VT deregolamentare

de·regu·la·tion [dɪˌrɛgjʊˈleɪʃən] N deregolamentazione *f*

der·elict [ˈdɛrɪlɪkt] ADJ (*ruined*) cadente, fatiscente; (*abandoned*) abbandonato(-a)
■ N (*frm: person*) derelitto(-a)

der·elic·tion [dɛrɪˈlɪkʃən] N: **dereliction of duty** (*frm*) negligenza del dovere

de·ride [dɪˈraɪd] VT deridere

de rigueur [də rigœr] ADJ di rigore

de·ri·sion [dɪˈrɪʒən] N derisione *f*

de·ri·sive [dɪˈraɪsɪv] ADJ (*laughter*) di scherno, di derisione; (*smile*) beffardo(-a)

de·ri·sive·ly [dɪˈraɪsɪvlɪ] ADV (*smile, laugh, gesture*) beffardamente

de·ri·sory [dɪˈraɪsərɪ] ADJ **1** (*amount*) irrisorio(-a) **2** = **derisive**

Dd

deri·va·tion [ˌdɛrɪ'veɪʃən] N derivazione *f*
de·riva·tive [dɪ'rɪvətɪv] ADJ (*pej: literary work, style*) poco originale
■ N (*Chem, Ling*) derivato; (*Math*) derivata
de·rive [dɪ'raɪv] VT: **to derive (from)** (*profit, comfort, pleasure*) ricavare (da), trarre (da); (*name*) derivare (da); (*origins*) trarre (da)
■ VI: **to derive from** (*subj: word, language*) derivare da; (*: power, fortune*) provenire da
der·ma·ti·tis [ˌdɜːmə'taɪtɪs] N dermatite *f*
der·ma·tolo·gist [ˌdɜːmə'tɒlədʒɪst] N dermatologo(-a)
der·ma·tol·ogy [ˌdɜːmə'tɒlədʒɪ] N dermatologia
de·roga·tory [dɪ'rɒgətərɪ] ADJ (*remark*) denigratorio(-a); (*term*) spregiativo(-a)
der·rick ['dɛrɪk] N (*in port*) albero di carico, gru *f inv*; (*over oil well*) derrick *m inv*
derv [dɜːv] N (*Brit*) gasolio
der·vish ['dɜːvɪʃ] N (*Rel*) derviscio
de·sali·nate [diː'sælɪˌneɪt] VT dissalare
de·sali·na·tion [diːˌsælɪ'neɪʃən] N desalinizzazione *f*, dissalazione *f*
des·cale [diː'skeɪl] VT disincrostare
des·cant ['dɛskænt] N (*Mus*) discanto
de·scend [dɪ'sɛnd] VT **1** (*frm: stairs*) scendere **2 to be descended from sb** (*Genealogy*) discendere da qn
■ VI **1** (*go down*): **to descend (from)** (di)scendere (da); (*road*) scendere (da); **we descended to the cellar** scendemmo in cantina; **in descending order of importance** in ordine decrescente d'importanza
2 (*property, customs*): **to descend from ...to** passare da... a; **to descend from generation to generation** tramandarsi di generazione in generazione
▸ **descend on, descend upon** VI + PREP (*subj: enemy, large group, angry person*) assalire, piombare su; invadere; (*liter: gloom, silence*) scendere su; **hordes of tourists descend on the village every summer** il paese è invaso ogni estate da orde di turisti; **visitors descended on us** ci sono capitati ospiti inaspettati
▸ **descend to** VI + PREP (*lower o.s. to*): **to descend to sth** abbassarsi a qc; **to descend to doing sth** abbassarsi a fare qc
de·scend·ant [dɪ'sɛndənt] N discendente *m/f*
de·scent [dɪ'sɛnt] N (*going down*) discesa; (*ancestry*): **descent (from)** discendenza (da); origine *f* (da); **of African descent** di origine africana
◎ **de·scribe** [dɪs'kraɪb] VT descrivere; **describe him for us** descrivicelo; **she describes herself as a teacher** dice di essere insegnante
◎ **de·scrip·tion** [dɪs'krɪpʃən] N **1** (*of person, scene, object*) descrizione *f*; (*of event*) racconto; (*of suspect*) connotati *mpl*, descrizione; **beyond description** oltre ogni dire **2** (*sort*) genere *m*, specie *f*; **he carried a gun of some description** aveva una pistola di qualche tipo; **of every description** di ogni genere e specie
de·scrip·tive [dɪs'krɪptɪv] ADJ descrittivo(-a)
des·ecrate ['dɛsɪˌkreɪt] VT profanare
des·ecra·tion [ˌdɛsɪ'kreɪʃən] N profanazione *f*
de·seg·re·gate [diː'sɛgrɪˌgeɪt] VT abolire la segregazione in; **desegregated schools** *scuole in cui non vige la segregazione razziale*
de·seg·re·ga·tion ['diːˌsɛgrɪ'geɪʃən] N abolizione *f* della segregazione razziale
de·sen·si·tize [diː'sɛnsɪˌtaɪz] VT desensibilizzare
◎ **des·ert**[1] ['dɛzət] N deserto
■ ADJ (*climate, region*) desertico(-a)
de·sert[2] [dɪ'zɜːt] VT abbandonare, lasciare; **his courage deserted him** il coraggio l'ha abbandonato; **her husband deserted her** suo marito l'ha abbandonata
■ VI (*Mil*): **to desert (from)** disertare (da); **to desert (to)** passare (a)
desert boot [ˌdɛzət 'buːt] N scarponcino
de·sert·ed [dɪ'zɜːtɪd] ADJ (*streets*) deserto(-a); (*wife*) abbandonato(-a)
de·sert·er [dɪ'zɜːtə^r] N (*Mil*) disertore *m*
des·er·ti·fi·ca·tion [dɪˌzɜːtɪfɪ'keɪʃən] N desertificazione *f*
de·ser·tion [dɪ'zɜːʃən] N (*Mil*) diserzione *f*; (*of spouse*) abbandono del tetto coniugale
desert island [ˌdɛzət'aɪlənd] N isola deserta
de·serts [dɪ'zɜːts] NPL: **to get one's just deserts** avere ciò che ci si merita
◎ **de·serve** [dɪ'zɜːv] VT meritare; **he deserves to win** merita di vincere; **he got what he deserved** ha avuto quel che si meritava
de·serv·ed·ly [dɪ'zɜːvɪdlɪ] ADV meritatamente, giustamente
de·serv·ing [dɪ'zɜːvɪŋ] ADJ (*person, case, cause*) che merita aiuto; (*praiseworthy*) meritevole; **deserving of** degno(-a) di; **an idea deserving of consideration** un'idea degna di considerazione; **a crime deserving of severe punishment** un delitto che merita una severa punizione
des·ic·ca·ted ['dɛsɪˌkeɪtɪd] ADJ essiccato(-a); **desiccated coconut** noce *f* di cocco essiccata
◎ **de·sign** [dɪ'zaɪn] N **1** (*plan, drawing: of building*) progetto, disegno; (*: of dress, car*) modello; (*: of machine*) progettazione *f*; (*style*) linea, design *m inv*; (*pattern*) disegno, fantasia, motivo; (*art of design*) design *m*; **a new design of lawnmower** un nuovo modello di tagliaerba; **the design of the plane makes it safer** il design rende più sicuro l'aereo; **a design fault** un difetto di progettazione; **dress with a floral design** vestito a fiori; **a geometric design** un disegno geometrico; **industrial design** disegno industriale
2 (*intention*) intenzione *f*; **by design** intenzionalmente, di proposito; **to have designs on sb/sth** avere delle mire su qn/qc
■ VT **1** (*building etc*) disegnare; (*Industry*) progettare; (*perfect crime, scheme*) concepire, elaborare; **she designed the dress herself** ha disegnato lei stessa il vestito; **we will design an exercise plan specially for you** elaboreremo un programma di esercizi apposta per te **2** (*intend*): **to be designed for sb/sth** essere fatto(-a) espressamente per qn/qc; **a well designed house** una casa progettata bene
des·ig·nate [*vb* 'dɛzɪgˌneɪt; *adj* 'dɛzɪgnɪt] VT: **to designate sb/sth (as)** designare qn/qc (come); **to designate sb to do sth** designare qn a fare qc
■ ADJ (*after n*) designato(-a)
designated driver N *persona che si impegna a non bere per poter guidare e riportare a casa altre persone*
des·ig·na·tion [ˌdɛzɪg'neɪʃən] N (*title*) titolo, designazione *f*
◎ **de·sign·er** [dɪ'zaɪnə^r] N (*fashion designer*) stilista *m/f*, disegnatore(-trice) di moda; (*of machines etc*) disegnatore(-trice), progettista *m/f*; (*of furniture*) designer *m/f inv*; (*of theatre sets*) scenografo(-a); **designer clothes** abiti firmati; **a furniture designer** un designer di mobili
designer baby N bambino su ordinazione
de·sign·ing [dɪ'zaɪnɪŋ] ADJ (*scheming*) astuto(-a), intrigante

de·sir·abil·ity [dɪˌzaɪərəˈbɪlɪtɪ] N (*allure*) desiderabilità; (*value*) vantaggio

de·sir·able [dɪˈzaɪərəbl] ADJ (*woman, man*) desiderabile; (*house, job*) attraente; (*offer*) vantaggioso(-a); **it is desirable that** è opportuno che + *sub*; **desirable qualities** qualità auspicabili

◎ **de·sire** [dɪˈzaɪəʳ] N desiderio, voglia; (*sexual*) desiderio; **desire (for/to do sth)** desiderio (di/di fare qc); **I have no desire to see him** non ho nessuna voglia di vederlo ■ VT (*person*) desiderare; **to desire sth/to do sth/that** desiderare qc/di fare qc/che + *sub*; **it leaves much to be desired** lascia molto a desiderare

de·sir·ous [dɪˈzaɪərəs] ADJ (*frm*): **desirous (of)** desideroso(-a) (di)

de·sist [dɪˈzɪst] VI (*frm*): **to desist (from)** desistere (da)

◎ **desk** [dɛsk] N (*in office*) scrivania; (*Scol, in hotel, at airport*) banco; (*Brit: in shop, restaurant*) cassa; **desk diary** agenda da tavolo; **desk job** lavoro d'ufficio; **desk lamp** lampada da tavolo

desk clerk N (*Am*) receptionist *m/f inv*

de·skill [ˌdiːˈskɪl] VT dequalificare

de·skill·ing [ˌdiːˈskɪlɪŋ] N dequalificazione *f*

desk·top, desk-top [ˈdɛsktɒp] N (*Comput: icons*) desktop *m inv*

desk·top com·put·er [ˈdɛskˌtɒp kəmˈpjuːtəʳ] N (computer) desk top *m inv*

desk·top pub·lish·ing [ˈdɛskˌtɒp ˈpʌblɪʃɪŋ] N desktop publishing *m inv*

deso·late [ˈdɛsəlɪt] ADJ (*place*) desolato(-a), deserto(-a); (*building*) abbandonato(-a); (*outlook, future*) nero(-a); (*person: grief-stricken*) affranto(-a) (dal dolore), desolato(-a); (*: friendless*) abbandonato(-a) da tutti

deso·lat·ed [ˈdɛsəleɪtɪd] ADJ (*saddened*) desolato(-a); (*deserted: house*) abbandonato(-a)

deso·late·ly [ˈdɛsəlɪtlɪ] ADV (*weep, sigh*) con aria affranta

deso·la·tion [ˌdɛsəˈleɪʃən] N (*bleakness, grief*) desolazione *f*; (*liter: devastation*) devastazione *f*

des·pair [dɪsˈpɛəʳ] N disperazione *f*; **in despair** disperato(-a); **to drive sb to despair** far disperare qn ■ VI: **to despair (of)** disperare (di); **don't despair!** non disperare!

des·pair·ing [dɪsˈpɛərɪŋ] ADJ disperato(-a)

des·pair·ing·ly [dɪsˈpɛərɪŋlɪ] ADV disperatamente

des·patch [dɪsˈpætʃ] N, VT = **dispatch**

des·pe·ra·do [ˌdɛspəˈrɑːdəʊ] N (*old*) bandito

◎ **des·per·ate** [ˈdɛspərɪt] ADJ (*gen*) disperato(-a); (*criminal*) capace di tutto; (*measures*) estremo(-a); **a desperate situation** una situazione disperata; **we are getting desperate** siamo sull'orlo della disperazione; **to be desperate to do sth** volere disperatamente fare qc; **I'm desperate for money** (*fam*) ho un disperato bisogno di soldi

des·per·ate·ly [ˈdɛspərɪtlɪ] ADV (*say, look*) con disperazione; (*fight*) disperatamente; (*extremely*) terribilmente, estremamente; **he was desperately trying to persuade her** stava tentando disperatamente di convincerla; **we're desperately worried** siamo estremamente preoccupati; **desperately ill** gravemente malato(-a), tra la vita e la morte; **desperately in love** perdutamente innamorato(-a)

des·pera·tion [ˌdɛspəˈreɪʃən] N disperazione *f*; **an act of desperation** un gesto disperato; **in (sheer) desperation** per (pura) disperazione

des·pic·able [dɪsˈpɪkəbl] ADJ spregevole; (*behaviour*) vergognoso(-a); (*person*) ignobile

des·pi·cably [dɪsˈpɪkəblɪ] ADV (*behave*) ignobilmente

des·pise [dɪsˈpaɪz] VT (*person*) disprezzare, sdegnare; (*sb's attentions, offer*) disdegnare

◎ **de·spite** [dɪsˈpaɪt] PREP malgrado, a dispetto di, nonostante

de·spond·en·cy [dɪsˈpɒndənsɪ] N (*frm*) abbattimento, avvilimento

de·spond·ent [dɪsˈpɒndənt] ADJ (*frm*): **despondent (about)** avvilito(-a) (per), abbattuto(-a) (per); **he is despondent about his future** quanto al suo futuro è molto demoralizzato

de·spond·ent·ly [dɪsˈpɒndəntlɪ] ADV con aria avvilita *or* abbattuta

des·pot [ˈdɛspɒt] N despota *m*

des·pot·ic [dɛsˈpɒtɪk] ADJ dispotico(-a)

des·poti·cal·ly [dɛsˈpɒtɪkəlɪ] ADV dispoticamente

des·pot·ism [ˈdɛspətɪzəm] N dispotismo

des·sert [dɪˈzɜːt] N dessert *m inv*, dolce *m*; **dessert plate** piatto da dessert; **dessert wine** vino da dessert

▷ http://thefoody.com/pudding/

dessert·spoon [dɪˈzɜːtˌspuːn] N cucchiaio da dessert

de·sta·bi·lize [diːˈsteɪbɪˌlaɪz] VT (*regime*) destabilizzare

des·ti·na·tion [ˌdɛstɪˈneɪʃən] N destinazione *f*

des·tine [ˈdɛstɪn] VT (*frm*) destinare

des·tined [ˈdɛstɪnd] ADJ PRED **1** **destined for sth/sb/to do sth** (*by fate*) destinato(-a) a qc/qn/a fare qc; **we were destined to meet** eravamo destinati a incontrarci **2** (*bound for*): **destined for London** con destinazione Londra, diretto(-a) a Londra

des·ti·ny [ˈdɛstɪnɪ] N destino, sorte *f*

des·ti·tute [ˈdɛstɪˌtjuːt] ADJ (*frm*) indigente; **utterly destitute** ridotto(-a) in miseria; **destitute of** privo(-a) di

> DID YOU KNOW ...?
> **destitute** is not translated by the Italian word *destituito*

des·ti·tu·tion [ˌdɛstɪˈtjuːʃən] N (*frm*) indigenza

> DID YOU KNOW ...?
> **destitution** is not translated by the Italian word *destituzione*

◎ **de·stroy** [dɪsˈtrɔɪ] VT (*gen*) distruggere; (*kill: dangerous or diseased animal*) abbattere; (*: pet*) sopprimere; (*: vermin*) eliminare; (*mood, appetite*) rovinare

de·stroy·er [dɪsˈtrɔɪəʳ] N (*Naut*) cacciatorpediniere *m*

de·struct [dɪsˈtrʌkt] (*Mil*) VT (*missile*) distruggere ■ VI (*also:* **self-destruct**) autodistruggersi

de·struct·ible [dɪsˈtrʌktəbl] ADJ distruttibile

◎ **de·struc·tion** [dɪsˈtrʌkʃən] N (*gen*) distruzione *f*; (*caused by war, fire*) danni *mpl*

de·struc·tive [dɪsˈtrʌktɪv] ADJ (*person*) distruttore(-trice); (*policy*) rovinoso(-a); (*action, power, criticism*) distruttivo(-a)

de·struc·tive·ly [dɪsˈtrʌktɪvlɪ] ADV (*act, criticise*) in modo distruttivo

de·struc·tive·ness [dɪsˈtrʌktɪvnɪs] N (*gen*) carattere *m* distruttivo; (*of child*) tendenza a distruggere

de·struc·tor [dɪsˈtrʌktəʳ] N (*for refuse*) inceneritore *m*

des·ul·tory [ˈdɛsəltərɪ] (*frm*) ADJ (*conversation*) sconnesso(-a); (*reading*) disordinato(-a); (*contact*) saltuario(-a), irregolare

de·tach [dɪˈtætʃ] VT staccare, distaccare

de·tach·able [dɪˈtætʃəbl] ADJ staccabile, smontabile

de·tached [dɪˈtætʃt] ADJ **1** staccato(-a), separato(-a) **2** (*impartial: opinion*) imparziale, obiettivo(-a); (*unemotional: manner, attitude*) distaccato(-a), distante

detached house N villetta unifamiliare; villa

Dd

de·tach·ment [dɪ'tætʃmənt] N **1** (*aloofness*) distacco **2** (*Mil*) distaccamento

◎ **de·tail** ['di:teɪl] N **1** (*gen*) particolare *m*, dettaglio; (*part of painting*) particolare; **I can't remember the details** non ricordo i dettagli; **his attention to detail** la sua minuziosità; **in detail** nei particolari; **to go into detail(s)** entrare nei dettagli **2** (*Mil*) piccolo distaccamento
■ VT **1** (*list: items, facts*) elencare dettagliatamente **2** (*Mil*) distaccare; **to detail sb (for)** assegnare qn (a)

◎ **de·tailed** ['di:teɪld] ADJ dettagliato(-a), particolareggiato(-a)

de·tain [dɪ'teɪn] VT (*delay*) trattenere; (*in custody*) detenere

de·tainee [ˌdi:teɪ'ni:] N detenuto(-a)

de·tect [dɪ'tɛkt] VT (*signs, traces, drug, motive*) scoprire; (*feeling*) avvertire; (*Radar*) individuare; (*gas, smoke*) avvertire la presenza di

de·tect·able [dɪ'tɛktəbl] ADJ (*see vb*) scopribile; avvertibile; individuabile; (*perceptible*) percettibile

de·tec·tion [dɪ'tɛkʃən] N scoperta, individuazione *f*; **crime detection** indagini *fpl* criminali; **to escape detection** (*mistake*) passare inosservato(-a); (*criminal*) eludere le ricerche

◎ **de·tec·tive** [dɪ'tɛktɪv] N investigatore(-trice); (*private detective*) investigatore(-trice) privato(-a)

detective story N romanzo poliziesco, (romanzo) giallo

de·tec·tor [dɪ'tɛktəʳ] N rivelatore *m*, detector *m inv*; **radiation detector** indicatore *m* di radiazioni

de·tente, dé·tente [deɪ'tɑ:nt] N (*frm*) distensione *f*

de·ten·tion [dɪ'tɛnʃən] N (*of criminal, spy*) detenzione *f*; (*of schoolchild*) punizione *f* (*trattenendo l'alunno alla fine delle lezioni*); **to get a detention** essere trattenuto a scuola

de·ter [dɪ'tɜ:ʳ] VT: **to deter sb (from doing sth)** dissuadere qn (dal fare qc)

de·ter·gent [dɪ'tɜ:dʒənt] N detersivo, detergente *m*

de·terio·rate [dɪ'tɪərɪəˌreɪt] VI deteriorarsi

de·terio·ra·tion [dɪˌtɪərɪə'reɪʃən] N deterioramento

de·ter·min·able [dɪ'tɜ:mɪnəbl] ADJ determinabile

de·ter·mi·nant [dɪ'tɜ:mɪnənt] ADJ, N determinante (*m*)

de·ter·mi·na·tion [dɪˌtɜ:mɪ'neɪʃən] N **1** (*of person*): **determination (to do)** determinazione *f* (di fare) **2** (*of cause, position*) determinazione *f*, individuazione *f*

de·ter·mi·na·tive [dɪ'tɜ:mɪnətɪv] ADJ (*determining*) determinante; (*Gram*) determinativo(-a)
■ N (*Gram*) = **determiner**

◎ **de·ter·mine** [dɪ'tɜ:mɪn] VT **1** (*decide*) determinare; (*: outcome, situation*) decidere **2** (*ascertain: cause, meaning*) determinare, stabilire **3** (*resolve*): **to determine to do sth** decidere di fare qc; **to determine sb to do sth** far decidere a qn di fare qc
▸ **determine on** VI + PREP decidersi per

◎ **de·ter·mined** [dɪ'tɜ:mɪnd] ADJ (*person*) risoluto(-a), deciso(-a); **she's a very determined woman** è una donna molto determinata; **a determined effort** uno sforzo di volontà; **to be determined to do sth** essere determinato(-a) *or* deciso(-a) a fare qc; **she's determined to succeed** è determinata a riuscire

de·ter·mined·ly [dɪ'tɜ:mɪndlɪ] ADV grintosamente

de·ter·min·er [dɪ'tɜ:mɪnəʳ] N (*Gram*) determinante *m*

de·ter·min·ing [dɪ'tɜ:mɪnɪŋ] ADJ determinante

de·ter·min·ism [dɪ'tɜ:mɪˌnɪzəm] N determinismo

de·ter·rence [dɪ'tɛrəns] N deterrenza

de·ter·rent [dɪ'tɛrənt] N deterrente *m*; **to act as a deterrent** funzionare *or* fungere da deterrente

de·test [dɪ'tɛst] VT detestare

de·test·able [dɪ'tɛstəbl] ADJ detestabile

de·test·ably [dɪ'tɛstəblɪ] ADV in modo detestabile

de·tes·ta·tion [ˌdi:tes'teɪʃən] N odio, avversione *f*

de·throne [di:'θrəʊn] VT detronizzare

deto·nate ['dɛtəˌneɪt] VT far detonare
■ VI detonare

deto·na·tion [ˌdɛtə'neɪʃən] N detonazione *f*

deto·na·tor ['dɛtəˌneɪtəʳ] N detonatore *m*

de·tour ['di:ˌtʊəʳ] N giro più lungo, deviazione *f*; **to make a detour (through)** fare una deviazione (passando per)

de·tract [dɪ'trækt] VI: **to detract from** (*value*) sminuire; (*reputation*) intaccare; (*pleasure*) attenuare

de·trac·tor [dɪ'træktəʳ] N detrattore(-trice)

det·ri·ment ['dɛtrɪmənt] N detrimento, danno; **to the detriment of** a *or* con detrimento di, a danno di; **without detriment to** senza danno a

det·ri·men·tal [ˌdɛtrɪ'mɛntl] ADJ: **detrimental (to)** dannoso(-a) (a), nocivo(-a) (a); **to be detrimental to sth** pregiudicare qc

de·tri·tus [dɪ'traɪtəs] N **1** (*rubbish*) rifiuti *mpl*; (*fig*): **the detritus of society** i rifiuti della società **2** (*Geol*) rocce *fpl* detritiche

de trop [də tro] ADJ (*frm*) di troppo

deuce [dju:s] N (*Tennis*) deuce *m inv*, quaranta pari *m inv*

Deu·ter·ono·my [ˌdju:tə'rɒnəmɪ] N Deuteronomio

de·valua·tion [ˌdɪvæljʊ'eɪʃən] N (*Fin*) svalutazione *f*

de·value ['di:'vælju:] VT (*Fin*) svalutare

dev·as·tate ['dɛvəˌsteɪt] VT (*place*) devastare; (*opponent, opposition*) sbaragliare, annientare; (*upset greatly*) sconvolgere; **he was devastated by the news** la notizia l'aveva sconvolto

dev·as·tat·ing ['dɛvəˌsteɪtɪŋ] ADJ (*flood, storm*) devastatore(-trice); (*news, effect*) micidiale; (*beauty*) travolgente; **she received some devastating news** ha ricevuto notizie sconvolgenti; **unemployment has a devastating effect on people** la disoccupazione ha un effetto devastante sulle persone

dev·as·tat·ing·ly ['dɛvəˌsteɪtɪŋlɪ] ADV (*beautiful, funny*) da morire, irresistibilmente; (*critical, scornful*) terribilmente

dev·as·ta·tion [ˌdɛvə'steɪʃən] N devastazione *f*

◎ **de·vel·op** [dɪ'vɛləp] VT **1** (*skill, ability, also Phot*) sviluppare; (*mind*) allargare; **I'll get the film developed** farò sviluppare la pellicola **2** (*acquire: habit*) prendere (a poco a poco *or* gradualmente); **to develop a taste for sth** imparare a gustare qc; **she has developed an interest in politics** è sorto in lei un interesse per la politica **3** (*resources*) sviluppare, valorizzare; (*region*) valorizzare, promuovere lo sviluppo di; **to develop land** costruire su un terreno; **this land is to be developed** qui costruiranno
■ VI **1** (*gen*) svilupparsi; (*person: mentally, emotionally*) maturare; (*baby*) crescere; (*plot, illness*) progredire; **girls develop faster than boys** le ragazze si sviluppano prima rispetto ai ragazzi; **the area has developed industrially** la zona si è sviluppata sotto il profilo industriale; **to develop into** diventare, trasformarsi in; **the argument developed into a fight** la discussione si trasformò in una lite **2** (*come into being: symptoms, feelings*) comparire, manifestarsi; (*come about: crisis, situation*) verificarsi, prodursi

de·vel·op·er [dɪ'vɛləpəʳ] N **1** (*also:* **property developer**) costruttore *m* (edile) **2** (*Phot*) sviluppatore *m*

de·vel·op·ing [dɪˈvɛləpɪŋ] ADJ (*industry*) in via di sviluppo; (*crisis, storm*) che sta per scoppiare, imminente
■N (*Phot*) sviluppo
developing country N paese *m* in via di sviluppo
◎**de·vel·op·ment** [dɪˈvɛləpmənt] N (*gen*) sviluppo; **to await developments** attendere ulteriori sviluppi; **the latest developments** gli ultimi sviluppi (della situazione); **development process** processo di sviluppo; **development grant** *finanziamento per un programma di sviluppo*
development area N (*Brit*) area di sviluppo industriale
de·vi·ance [ˈdi:vɪəns] N devianza
de·vi·ant [ˈdi:vɪənt] ADJ (*behaviour*) deviante; (*development*) anormale; (*sexually*) pervertito(-a)
■N deviante *m/f*; (*also*: **sexual deviant**) pervertito(-a)
de·vi·ate [ˈdi:vɪ,eɪt] VI: **to deviate (from)** deviare (da); discostarsi da
de·via·tion [,di:vɪˈeɪʃən] N: **deviation (from)** deviazione *f* (da); **standard deviation** (*Math*) scarto quadratico medio
◎**de·vice** [dɪˈvaɪs] N **1** (*gadget*) congegno, dispositivo **2** (*scheme*) stratagemma *m*; **leave him to his own devices** lascia che si arrangi da solo **3** (*also*: **explosive device**) ordigno esplosivo
dev·il [ˈdɛvl] N **1** (*evil spirit*) diavolo; **the Devil** il Diavolo, il Demonio **2** (*fam: person*) diavolo; **poor devil** povero diavolo!; **be a devil!** fai uno strappo!; **you little devil!** monellaccio!; **she is a devil to work for** lavorare per lei è un inferno **3** (*fam: as intensifier*): **it's the devil of a job** è un lavoraccio; **he had the devil of a job to find it** ha sudato sette camicie per trovarlo; **I'm in the devil of a mess** sono in un pasticcio del diavolo; **to work/run like the devil** lavorare/correre come un dannato; **how/what/who the devil ...?** come/che/chi diavolo...?; **there will be the devil to pay** saranno guai **4** (*phrases*): **between the devil and the deep blue sea** tra Scilla e Cariddi; **go to the devil!** (*fam*) vai al diavolo!; **speak** *or* **talk of the devil!** (*fam*) lupus in fabula!, si parla del diavolo...; **(to) give the devil his due ...** bisogna riconoscerglielo..., siamo giusti...
dev·il·ish [ˈdɛvlɪʃ] ADJ (*wicked*) diabolico(-a); (*mischievous: child*) indiavolato(-a); (: *mood*) infernale
■ADV (*old*) terribilmente
dev·il·ish·ly [ˈdɛvlɪʃlɪ] ADV (*laugh etc*) in modo diabolico; (*old: extremely*) terribilmente
devil-may-care [ˈdɛvlmeɪˈkɛəʳ] ADJ (*attitude*) sprezzante
dev·il·ment [ˈdɛvlmənt] (*old*) N (*mischief*) birichinate *fpl*; (*wickedness*) cattiveria
dev·il·ry [ˈdɛvlrɪ] N (*old*) = **devilment**
devil's advocate [ˈdɛvəlzˈædvə,kɪt] N: **to play (the) devil's advocate** fare l'avvocato del diavolo
de·vi·ous [ˈdi:vɪəs] ADJ (*person, means, methods, mind*) subdolo(-a); (*path, argument*) tortuoso(-a)
de·vi·ous·ly [ˈdi:vɪəslɪ] ADV (*act*) subdolamente
de·vi·ous·ness [ˈdi:vɪəsnɪs] N (*of scheme, behaviour*) disonestà, doppiezza; (*of person*) modi subdoli
de·vise [dɪˈvaɪz] VT escogitare, concepire, ideare
de·vi·tal·ize [di:ˈvaɪtə,laɪz] VT devitalizzare
de·void [dɪˈvɔɪd] ADJ: **devoid of** privo(-a) di, senza
de·vo·lu·tion [,di:vəˈlu:ʃən] N (*Pol*) decentramento
de·volve [dɪˈvɒlv] VT (*power, responsibility*) devolvere
■VI: **to devolve (up)on** ricadere su; **it devolved on me to tell him** è stato compito mio dirglielo
de·vote [dɪˈvəʊt] VT: **to devote (to)** dedicare (a); **to devote o.s. to** dedicarsi a; (*to a cause*) consacrarsi a, dedicarsi a
de·vot·ed [dɪˈvəʊtɪd] ADJ (*friend, admirer*) devoto(-a); (*father, aunt*) amoroso(-a); **to be devoted to sb** essere molto attaccato(-a) a qn; **he's completely devoted to her** le è estremamente attaccato
de·vot·ed·ly [dɪˈvəʊtɪdlɪ] ADV devotamente, con devozione
devo·tee [,dɛvəʊˈti:] N **1 devotee (of)** (*enthusiast*) appassionato(-a) di **2** (*Rel*) devoto(-a)
de·vo·tion [dɪˈvəʊʃən] N: **devotion (to)** (*studies etc*) devozione *f* (a), dedizione *f* (a); (*friend, family*) attaccamento (a), fedeltà (a); **devotions** NPL (*Rel*) devozioni *fpl*
de·vo·tion·al [dɪˈvəʊʃənl] ADJ (*Rel*) devozionale
de·vour [dɪˈvaʊəʳ] VT (*food*) divorare; **devoured by jealousy** divorato(-a) dalla gelosia
de·vour·ing [dɪˈvaʊərɪŋ] ADJ (*flames, jealousy*) divoratore(-trice)
de·vout [dɪˈvaʊt] ADJ (*person*) devoto(-a), pio(-a); (*prayer, hope*) devoto(-a), fervido(-a)
de·vout·ly [dɪˈvaʊtlɪ] ADV (*frm: wish, hope*) fervidamente; (*live, pray*) devotamente
dew [dju:] N rugiada
dew·drop [ˈdju:,drɒp] N goccia di rugiada; (*fig: on end of nose*) goccia
dewy [ˈdju:ɪ] ADJ bagnato(-a) di rugiada, rugiadoso(-a)
dewy-eyed [ˈdju:ɪˈaɪd] ADJ (*innocent*) innocente
dex·ter·ity [dɛksˈtɛrɪtɪ] N: **dexterity (in doing sth)** (*of hands*) destrezza (a fare qc); (*of mind*) abilità (nel fare qc)
dex·terous, **dex·trous** [ˈdɛkstrəs] ADJ (*skilful*) destro(-a), abile; (*movement*) agile
dex·ter·ous·ly, **dex·trous·ly** [ˈdɛkstrəslɪ] ADV (*with physical skill*) con destrezza; (*with mental skill*) sagacemente
DfES [,di:i:ˈɛs] N ABBR (*Brit*: = **Department for Education and Skills**) ≈ ministero istruzione, università e ricerca
▷ www.dfes.gov.uk
dg [,di:ˈdʒi:] ABBR (= **decigram**) dg
DHSS [,di:eɪtʃɛsˈɛs] N ABBR (*Brit*: *also*: **Department of Health and Social Security**) *nome dell'attuale DWP, ancora usato nel linguaggio parlato*
dia·be·tes [,daɪəˈbi:ti:z] N diabete *m*
dia·bet·ic [,daɪəˈbɛtɪk] N diabetico(-a)
■ADJ (*gen*) diabetico(-a); (*chocolate, jam*) per diabetici
dia·boli·cal [,daɪəˈbɒlɪkəl] ADJ (*fam: dreadful*) infernale, atroce; (: *incredible*) incredibile; (*satanic*) diabolico(-a)
dia·boli·cal·ly [,daɪəˈbɒlɪkəlɪ] ADV (*see adj*) (*behave*) in modo diabolico; (*hot, dangerous*) terribilmente
dia·crit·ic [,daɪəˈkrɪtɪk] N segno diacritico
dia·dem [ˈdaɪə,dɛm] N diadema *m*
di·aer·esis, **di·er·esis** [daɪˈɛrɪsɪs] N (*pl* **diaereses**, **diereses** [daɪˈɛrɪsi:z]) dieresi *f inv*
di·ag·nose [ˈdaɪəgnəʊz] VT diagnosticare; **it was diagnosed as bronchitis** hanno diagnosticato una bronchite
di·ag·no·sis [,daɪəgˈnəʊsɪs] N (*pl* **diagnoses** [,daɪəgˈnəʊsi:z]) diagnosi *f inv*
di·ag·nos·tic [,daɪəgˈnɒstɪk] ADJ (*gen*) diagnostico(-a); (*probe, X-ray*) a scopo diagnostico
di·ag·nos·ti·cian [,daɪəgnɒsˈtɪʃən] N diagnostico(-a), diagnosta *m/f*
di·ago·nal [daɪˈægənl] ADJ, N diagonale (*f*)
di·ago·nal·ly [daɪˈægənəlɪ] ADV (*cut, fold*) in diagonale, diagonalmente; **to go diagonally across** attraversare

Dd

in senso *or* in direzione diagonale; **diagonally opposite** dall'altra parte in diagonale

dia·gram ['daɪəˌgræm] N diagramma *m*, schema *m*; (*Math*) diagramma, grafico

dia·gram·mat·ic [ˌdaɪəgrə'mætɪk] ADJ schematico(-a)

dial ['daɪəl] N (*of clock, instrument*) quadrante *m*; (*of radio*) scala; (*of telephone*) disco (combinatore)
■ VT (*Telec: number*) fare; (*more formal*) comporre; **to dial a wrong number** sbagliare numero; **can I dial London direct?** si può chiamare Londra in teleselezione?; **to dial 999** ≈ chiamare il 113

dial. ABBR = dialect

dia·lect ['daɪəˌlɛkt] N dialetto; **the local dialect** il dialetto del luogo; **dialect word** termine *m* dialettale

dia·lec·tic [ˌdaɪə'lɛktɪk] N (*Philosophy*) dialettica

dia·lec·ti·cal [ˌdaɪə'lɛktɪkəl] ADJ dialettico(-a)

dial·ling code ['daɪəlɪŋˌkəʊd], (*Am*) **dial code** N (*Telec*) prefisso

dial·ling tone ['daɪəlɪŋˌtəʊn], (*Am*) **dial tone** N (*Telec*) segnale *m* di libero

dia·log box ['daɪəlɒg-] N (*Comput*) finestra di dialogo

◎ **dia·logue** ['daɪəlɒg] N dialogo

dial-up ['daɪəlöp] ADJ (*Comput: connection*) tramite linea telefonica; **dial-up modem** modem *m inv* DSL

di·aly·sis [daɪ'æləsɪs] N (*Med*) dialisi *f*

di·am·eter [daɪ'æmɪtəʳ] N diametro; **it is one metre in diameter** misura un metro di diametro

dia·met·ric, [ˌdaɪə'mɛtrɪk], **dia·met·ri·cal** [ˌdaɪə'mɛtrɪkəl] ADJ diametrale

dia·met·ri·cal·ly [ˌdaɪə'mɛtrɪkəlɪ] ADV: **diametrically opposed (to)** diametralmente opposto(-a) (a)

dia·mond ['daɪəmənd] N **1** (*stone*) diamante *m*, brillante *m*; (*shape*) rombo, losanga **2** (*Cards*): **diamonds** NPL quadri *mpl*; **the Queen of diamonds** la donna di quadri
■ ADJ (*necklace*) di diamanti *or* brillanti; **diamond ring** anello di brillanti; (*with single diamond*) anello con brillante; **diamond-shaped** a forma di losanga

diamond jubilee N sessantesimo anniversario

diamond wedding N nozze *fpl* di diamante

dia·per ['daɪəpəʳ] N (*Am*) pannolino

di·apha·nous [daɪ'æfənəs] ADJ diafano(-a)

dia·phragm ['daɪəfræm] N diaframma *m*

di·ar·rhoea, (*Am*) **di·ar·rhea** [ˌdaɪə'ri:ə] N diarrea

◎ **dia·ry** ['daɪərɪ] N (*daily record*) diario; (*for engagements*) agenda; **I've got her phone number in my diary** ho il suo numero di telefono nella mia agenda; **to keep a diary** tenere un diario; **her diaries are being published** i suoi diari saranno pubblicati

Di·as·po·ra [daɪ'æspərə] N Diaspora

di·as·po·ra [daɪ'æspərə] N (*frm*) diaspora

di·as·to·le [daɪ'æstəlɪ] N (*Med*) diastole *f*

dia·tribe ['daɪəˌtraɪb] N (*frm*): **diatribe (against)** diatriba (contro)

di·ba·sic [ˌdaɪ'beɪsɪk] ADJ (*Chem*) dibasico(-a)

dice [daɪs] N, PL INV dado; **throw the dice** getta i dadi; **to play dice** giocare a dadi
■ VT (*Culin*) tagliare a dadini
■ VI: **to dice with death** scherzare con la morte

dicey ['daɪsɪ] ADJ (*fam*): **it's a bit dicey** è un po' un rischio

di·choto·my [dɪ'kɒtəmɪ] N (*frm*) dicotomia

dick [dɪk] N (*fam!: penis*) cazzo (*fam!*)

dick·ens ['dɪkɪnz] N (*fam*) = **devil 3**

Dick·en·sian [dɪ'kɛnzɪən] ADJ dickensiano(-a)

dick·head ['dɪkˌhɛd] N (*fam!*) testa *m or f* di cazzo (*fam!*)

dicky ['dɪkɪ] N (*of shirt*) pettino
■ ADJ (*comp* **-ier**, *superl* **-iest**) (*Brit: fam: heart*) malandato(-a)

di·coty·ledon [daɪˌkɒtɪ'li:dən] N (*Bot*) dicotiledone *m*

Dic·ta·phone® ['dɪktəˌfəʊn] N dittafono®

dic·tate [*vb* dɪk'teɪt; *n* 'dɪkteɪt] VT, VI (*all senses*) dettare; **he decided to act as circumstances dictated** decise di agire come gli dettavano le circostanze
■ NPL **dictates** (*of heart, fashion*) dettami *mpl*
▸ **dictate to** VI + PREP (*person*) dare ordini a, dettar legge a; **he cannot be allowed to dictate to us** non dovrebbe poterci dare ordini; **I won't be dictated to** non ricevo ordini

dic·ta·tion [dɪk'teɪʃən] N (*to secretary*) dettatura; (*Scol*) dettato; **at dictation speed** a velocità di dettatura

dic·ta·tor [dɪk'teɪtəʳ] N dittatore(-trice)

dic·ta·tor·ial [ˌdɪktə'tɔ:rɪəl] ADJ dittatoriale, da dittatore

dic·ta·to·ri·al·ly [ˌdɪktə'tɔ:rɪəlɪ] ADV in modo dittatoriale, da dittatore

dic·ta·tor·ship [dɪk'teɪtəʃɪp] N dittatura

dic·tion ['dɪkʃən] N dizione *f*

dic·tion·ary ['dɪkʃənrɪ] N vocabolario, dizionario
▹ www.collins.co.uk/wordexchange/

dic·tum ['dɪktəm] N (*pl* **dictums** *or* **dicta**) **1** (*pronouncement*) affermazione *f* **2** (*maxim*) massima

did [dɪd] PT *of* **do**

di·dac·tic [dɪ'dæktɪk] ADJ (*frm: educational*) didattico(-a); (*pej: person*) pedante

di·dac·ti·cal·ly [dɪ'dæktɪklɪ] ADV didatticamente

did·dle ['dɪdl] VT (*fam*) infinocchiare; **to diddle sb out of sth** fregare qc a qn

didn't ['dɪdənt] = **did not**

Dido ['daɪdəʊ] N (*Myth*) Didone *f*

◎ **die**[1] [daɪ] (*prp* **dying**) VI (*person, animal, plant*): **to die (of** *or* **from)** morire (di); (*engine*) spegnersi, fermarsi; (*fig: friendship*) finire; (*: interest, enthusiasm*) spegnersi; **he died last year** è morto l'anno scorso; **I'm dying of boredom** muoio di noia; **to be dying** star morendo; **to be dying for sth/to do sth** morire dalla voglia di qc/di fare qc; **to die a natural/violent death** morire di morte naturale/violenta; **he died a hero** è morto da eroe; **the daylight was dying fast** si stava facendo buio in fretta; **never say die** (*fig fam*) non bisogna disperare; **I nearly died** (*laughing*) per poco non morivo (dal ridere); (*with embarrassment*) avrei voluto sprofondare; **old habits die hard** il lupo perde il pelo ma non il vizio
▸ **die away** VI + ADV affievolirsi
▸ **die back** VI + ADV (*plant*) seccarsi
▸ **die down** VI + ADV (*fire*) spegnersi; (*flames*) abbassarsi, languire; (*storm, wind, emotion*) calmarsi; **the wind died down** il vento si calmò
▸ **die off** VI + ADV (*plants, animals, people*) morire uno(-a) dopo l'altro(-a)
▸ **die out** VI + ADV estinguersi, scomparire

die[2] [daɪ] N **1** (*pl* **dice**) **the die is cast** il dado è tratto **2** (*in minting*) conio; (*Tech*) matrice *f*; (*in press forging*) stampo

die·hard ['daɪˌhɑ:d] N conservatore(-trice)
■ ADJ (*supporter, opponent*) convinto(-a)

di·er·esis [daɪ'ɛrɪsɪs] N = **diaeresis**

die·sel ['di:zəl] N (*car*) diesel *m inv*; (*fuel*) gasolio; **our car is a diesel** la nostra macchina è un diesel

diesel engine N motore *m* diesel *inv*

diesel fuel, diesel oil N gasolio (per motori diesel)

diesel train N (treno con) locomotiva diesel

◎**diet** [ˈdaɪət] N **1** *(customary food)* alimentazione *f*, regime *m* alimentare; **a healthy diet** un'alimentazione sana; **to live on a diet of** nutrirsi di **2** *(restricted food)* dieta; **to be/go on a diet** essere/mettersi a dieta; **I'm on a diet** sono in dieta
■ VI seguire una dieta; **I've been dieting for two months** sto seguendo una dieta da due mesi
■ ADJ *(food, drink)* dietetico(-a); **diet drinks** bibite dietetiche; **diet yoghurt** yoghurt *m inv* magro

di·etary [ˈdaɪətərɪ] ADJ dietetico(-a)

di·etet·ic [ˌdaɪəˈtɛtɪk] ADJ dietetico(-a)

di·etet·ics [ˌdaɪəˈtɛtɪks] NSG dietetica

di·eti·cian [ˌdaɪəˈtɪʃən] N dietista *m/f*

dif·fer [ˈdɪfəʳ] VI **1** *(be unlike)*: **to differ from sth** differire da qc, essere diverso(-a) da qc; **this version differs from the original in several ways** questa versione differisce da quella originale in molti modi **2** *(disagree)*: **to differ (with sb on** *or* **over** *or* **about sth)** dissentire (da qn su qc), discordare (da qn su qc); **we differed over the matter** ci siamo trovati in disaccordo sulla questione

◎**dif·fer·ence** [ˈdɪfrəns] N **1 difference (in/between)** differenza (di/tra); **there's not much difference in age between us** non c'è molta differenza d'età tra noi; **the new system has made a big difference** il nuovo sistema ha apportato un grosso miglioramento; **that makes all the difference** questo cambia tutto; **it makes no difference to me** per me è lo stesso; **a car with a difference** una macchina diversa dalle altre; **the difference in her is amazing** è incredibile com'è cambiata; **I'll make up the difference later** *(of money)* ti do il resto dopo; **common difference** *(Math)* ragione *f* **2** *(quarrel)*: **a difference of opinion** una divergenza di opinioni; **they could not settle their differences** non sono riusciti a mettersi d'accordo

◎**dif·fer·ent** [ˈdɪfrənt] ADJ **1** *(not alike)*: **different (from** *or* **to)** diverso(-a) (da), differente (da); *(changed)* altro(-a), diverso(-a); **London is different from Rome** Londra è diversa da Roma; **that's quite a different matter** è tutt'altra cosa, è una faccenda completamente diversa; **I feel a different person** mi sento un altro **2** *(various)* diverso(-a), vario(-a); **it comes in several different colours** è disponibile in diversi *or* vari colori

dif·fer·en·tial [ˌdɪfəˈrɛnʃəl] N *(Econ)* scarto salariale; *(Math, Aut)* differenziale *m*
■ ADJ differenziale; **differential calculus** *(Math)* calcolo differenziale; **differential erosion** erosione *f* selettiva; **differential gear** *(Aut)* differenziale *m*; **differential housing** scatola del differenziale

dif·fer·en·ti·ate [ˌdɪfəˈrɛnʃɪˌeɪt] VT: **to differentiate (from)** *(distinguish)* distinguere (fra); *(make different)* differenziare (da)
■ VI: **to differentiate (between)** *(perceive a difference)* distinguere (tra), differenziare (tra)

dif·fer·en·tia·tion [ˌdɪfəˌrɛnʃɪˈeɪʃən] N *(see vb)* distinzione *f*; differenziazione *f*

dif·fer·ent·ly [ˈdɪfrəntlɪ] ADV in modo diverso *or* differente; **she thinks quite differently now** la pensa diversamente adesso

◎**dif·fi·cult** [ˈdɪfɪkəlt] ADJ difficile; **difficult to understand** difficile da capire; **she is difficult to get on with** ha un carattere difficile; **I find it difficult to believe (that ...)** mi pare difficile da credere (che...); **getting started is the difficult thing** il difficile sta nel cominciare

◎**dif·fi·cul·ty** [ˈdɪfɪkəltɪ] N difficoltà *f inv*; **he has difficulty in walking/breathing** ha difficoltà a camminare/di respirazione; **to have difficulties with** *(police, landlord)* avere noie con; **to get o.s. into difficulty** mettersi nei guai; **to be in difficulty** *or* **difficulties** essere *or* trovarsi in difficoltà; **to be in (financial) difficulties** avere delle difficoltà economiche

dif·fi·dence [ˈdɪfɪdəns] N riservatezza

> DID YOU KNOW ...?
> **diffidence** is not translated by the Italian word ***diffidenza***

dif·fi·dent [ˈdɪfɪdənt] ADJ *(person)* poco sicuro(-a) di sé; *(smile)* timido(-a), imbarazzato(-a); **to be diffident about doing sth** esitare a fare qc

> DID YOU KNOW ...?
> **diffident** is not translated by the Italian word ***diffidente***

dif·fi·dent·ly [ˈdɪfɪdəntlɪ] ADV *(smile, answer, behave)* con esitazione

dif·frac·tion [dɪˈfrækʃən] N *(Phys)* diffrazione *f*

dif·fuse [*vb* dɪˈfjuːz; *adj* dɪˈfjuːs] VT *(light, heat, gas, information)* diffondere; *(heat, perfume)* emanare
■ VI diffondersi
■ ADJ *(light)* diffuso(-a); *(style, writing)* prolisso(-a); *(organization)* ramificato(-a)

dif·fu·sion [dɪˈfjuːʒən] N *(of ideas, information)* diffusione *f*; *(of light, heat, substances)* spargimento

◎**dig** [dɪg] *(vb: pt, pp* **dug***)* N **1** *(with elbow)* gomitata; **to give sb a dig in the ribs** dare una gomitata (nel fianco) a qn **2** *(fam: taunt)* frecciata, insinuazione *f*; **to have a dig at sb/sth** lanciare una frecciata a qn/qc **3** *(Archeol)* scavo, scavi *mpl*
■ VT **1** *(ground, hole)* scavare; *(garden)* zappare, vangare; **they're digging a hole in the road** stanno scavando un buco nella strada; **Dad's out digging the garden** il papà è fuori a zappare il giardino **2** *(poke, thrust)*: **to dig sth into sth** conficcare qc in qc; **to dig one's nails into** conficcare le unghie in **3** *(old fam)*: **dig that beat, man!** senti che forza quel ritmo!; **I don't dig that kind of scene** *(old fam)* quell'ambiente non mi va a genio; **he really digs jazz** *(old fam)* va pazzo per il jazz
■ VI *(gen, Tech)* scavare; *(Archeol)* fare degli scavi; **to dig for minerals** scavare alla ricerca di minerali; **to dig into one's pockets for sth** frugarsi le tasche cercando qc
▸ **dig in** VI + ADV **1** *(fam: eat)* attaccare a mangiare; **dig in!** dateci sotto! **2** *(also:* **dig o.s. in***)* *(Mil)* trincerarsi; (: *fig)* insediarsi, installarsi
■ VT + ADV *(compost)* interrare; *(knife, claw)* affondare; **she dug her nails into his back** gli ha conficcato le unghie nella schiena; **to dig in one's heels** *(fig)* impuntarsi
▸ **dig out** VT + ADV *(survivors, car from snow)* tirar fuori (scavando), estrarre (scavando); *(fig)* scovare
▸ **dig up** VT + ADV *(potatoes, treasure, body)* dissotterrare; *(tree etc)* sradicare; *(weeds)* estirpare; *(fig fam: fact, information)* pescare; **the cat's dug up my plants** il gatto ha sradicato le mie piante; **they're trying to dig up evidence against him** stanno cercando di tirar fuori delle prove contro di lui

di·gest [*vb* daɪˈdʒɛst; *n* ˈdaɪdʒɛst] VT digerire; *(information)* assimilare; **it is easily digested** *(food)* è facilmente digeribile
■ VI digerirsi
■ N *(summary)* compendio

di·gest·ible [dɪˈdʒɛstəbl] ADJ digeribile

Dd

di·ges·tion [dɪ'dʒɛstʃən] N digestione *f*
di·ges·tive [dɪ'dʒɛstɪv] ADJ digestivo(-a); **digestive system** apparato digerente; **digestive (biscuit)** *biscotto tipo frollino di farina integrale*
dig·ger ['dɪgər] N (*machine*) escavatore *m*
dig·gings ['dɪgɪŋz] NPL (*Archeol*) scavi *mpl*
digi·cam ['dɪdʒɪkæm] N fotocamera digitale
dig·it ['dɪdʒɪt] N (*Math*) cifra; (*frm: finger, thumb, toe*) dito
◎ **digi·tal** ['dɪdʒɪtəl] ADJ (*clock, computer*) digitale
digital camera N fotocamera digitale, macchina fotografica digitale
digital compact cassette N lettore-registratore *m* digitale
digital radio N radio digitale
▹ www.drm.org
digital signature N (*Comput*) firma digitale
digital television, digital TV N televisione *f* digitale
▹ www.digitaltelevision.gov.uk
dig·ni·fied ['dɪgnɪˌfaɪd] ADJ dignitoso(-a), pieno(-a) di dignità
dig·ni·fy ['dɪgnɪˌfaɪ] VT **1** (*make impressive: building*) nobilitare **2** (*make respectable*) dare dignità a; **I wouldn't dignify that question with an answer** è una domanda che non merita risposta
dig·ni·tary ['dɪgnɪtərɪ] N dignitario
dig·nity ['dɪgnɪtɪ] N dignità; **it would be beneath his dignity to do it** non si abbasserebbe mai a farlo
di·gress [daɪ'grɛs] VI: **to digress (from)** divagare (da), fare digressioni (da)
di·gres·sion [daɪ'grɛʃən] N digressione *f*
digs [dɪgz] NPL (*Brit fam*): **to be in digs** affittare una camera (*presso privati*)
dike [daɪk] N = **dyke**
di·lapi·da·ted [dɪ'læpɪˌdeɪtɪd] ADJ (*building*) in pessime condizioni, cadente; (*vehicle*) sgangherato(-a), scassato(-a)
di·lapi·da·tion [dɪˌlæpɪ'deɪʃən] N (*of building*) sfacelo, disfacimento
di·late [daɪ'leɪt] VI (*pupils, eyes, cervix*) dilatarsi
■ VT dilatare
di·la·tion [daɪ'leɪʃən] N dilatazione *f*
dila·to·ri·ness ['dɪlətərɪnɪs] N (*frm: of person*) lentezza
di·la·tory ['dɪlətərɪ] ADJ (*frm: person*) lento(-a); (*action, policy*) dilatorio(-a)
di·lem·ma [daɪ'lɛmə] N dilemma *m*; **to be in a dilemma** essere di fronte a un dilemma
dil·et·tante [ˌdɪlɪ'tɑːntɪ] N dilettante *m/f*
dili·gence ['dɪlɪdʒəns] N diligenza
dili·gent ['dɪlɪdʒənt] ADJ (*person*) diligente, attento(-a); (*work, search*) accurato(-a), diligente
dili·gent·ly ['dɪlɪdʒəntlɪ] ADV diligentemente
dill [dɪl] N aneto
dilly-dally ['dɪlɪˌdælɪ] VI (*fam*) gingillarsi
di·lute [daɪ'luːt] VT (*concentrated liquid*) diluire, allungare; (*wine*) annacquare; (*fig: statement, concept*) diluire; **"dilute to taste"** "aggiungere acqua a piacere"
■ ADJ diluito(-a)
di·lu·tion [daɪ'luːʃən] N diluizione *f*
dim [dɪm] ADJ (*comp* **-mer**, *superl* **-mest**) (*light*) debole, fioco(-a); (*sight*) debole; (*forest*) oscuro(-a); (*room*) in penombra; (*shape, outline, memory, sound*) indistinto(-a), vago(-a); (*fam: person*) tonto(-a), ottuso(-a); **a dim light** una luce debole; **the prospects are dim** le prospettive sono scarse; **to grow dim** (*light*) affievolirsi; (*eyesight*) indebolirsi; **to take a dim view of sth** (*fam*) non vedere qc di buon occhio
■ VT (*light*) abbassare; (*Am: headlights*) abbassare; (*sound, memory, colour*) affievolire; (*shape, outline, beauty, glory*) offuscare; (*sight, senses*) annebbiare; (*metal*) annerire
■ VI (*light, sight, memory*) affievolirsi; (*outline*) divenire indistinto(-a)
dime [daɪm] N (*USA and Canada*) *monetina da 10 cent*; **they're a dime a dozen** (*fam*) ce n'è un sacco
di·men·sion [daɪ'mɛnʃən] N (*size*) dimensione *f*, proporzione *f*; (*Math, fig*) dimensione; **to add a new dimension to** (*fig*) dare una dimensione nuova a
-dimensional [daɪ'mɛnʃənl] ADJ SUFF: **two-dimensional** bidimensionale; **three-dimensional** tridimensionale
di·min·ish [dɪ'mɪnɪʃ] VT (*effect, enthusiasm, authority, speed*) diminuire, ridurre; (*value, person*) sminuire
■ VI diminuire, ridursi; (*value*) scendere; **the threat of nuclear war has diminished** la paura di una guerra nucleare è diminuita
di·min·ished [dɪ'mɪnɪʃt] ADJ (*value, importance*) ridotto(-a)
diminished responsibility N (*Law*) incapacità d'intendere e di volere
dimi·nu·tion [ˌdɪmɪ'njuːʃən] N (*of value, power*) diminuzione *f*; (*of strength, enthusiasm*) affievolimento
di·minu·tive [dɪ'mɪnjʊtɪv] ADJ (*frm*) minuto(-a), minuscolo(-a)
■ N (*Gram*) diminutivo
dim·ly ['dɪmlɪ] ADV (*hear, remember*) vagamente; (*shine*) debolmente; **she dimly recalled the circumstances** si ricordava vagamente delle circostanze; **dimly lit** illuminato debolmente
dim·mer ['dɪmər] N (*also:* **dimmer switch**) dimmer *m inv*, interruttore *m* a reostato
dim·mers ['dɪməz] NPL (*Am Aut: dipped headlights*) anabbaglianti *mpl*; (: *parking lights*) luci *fpl* di posizione
dim·ness ['dɪmnɪs] N (*of light, sight*) debolezza; (*of place*) oscurità; (*of outline*) vaghezza; (*of sound*) carattere *m* indistinto; (*fam: of person*) stupidità
dim·ple ['dɪmpl] N (*in cheek, chin etc*) fossetta
dim·wit ['dɪmˌwɪt] N (*fam*) cretino(-a)
dim-witted [dɪm'wɪtɪd] ADJ (*fam*) sciocco(-a), stupido(-a)
din [dɪn] N (*from people, in classroom*) chiasso, fracasso, baccano; (*from machine, factory, traffic*) rumore *m* infernale
■ VT: **to din sth into sb** (*fam*) ficcare qc in testa a qn; **he tried to din it into her that ...** ha cercato di ficcarle in testa che...
di·nar ['diːnɑːr] N dinaro
dine [daɪn] VI (*frm*) cenare; **to dine (on)** pasteggiare (a *or* con); **to dine out** cenare fuori
din·er ['daɪnər] N (*person: in restaurant*) cliente *m/f*; (*Rail*) carrozza *or* vagone *m* ristorante *inv*; (*Am: eating place*) tavola calda
ding-dong ['dɪŋdɒŋ] N **1** (*of bells*) dindon *m inv* **2** (*Brit: fam*) rissa
■ ADJ (*Brit: fam*): **a ding-dong argument** un battibecco
din·ghy ['dɪŋgɪ] N (*rubber boat*) gommone *m*; (*sailing dinghy*) dinghy *m inv*
din·gi·ness ['dɪndʒɪnɪs] N squallore *m*
din·go ['dɪŋgəʊ] N (*Zool*) dingo
din·gy ['dɪn(d)ʒɪ] ADJ (*shabby*) squallido(-a); (*dark*) scuro(-a), tetro(-a)
din·ing area ['daɪnɪŋˌɛərɪə] N zona *f* pranzo *inv*
din·ing car ['daɪnɪŋˌkɑːr] N carrozza *or* vagone *m* ristorante *inv*
din·ing hall ['daɪnɪŋˌhɔːl] N refettorio

din·ing room [ˈdaɪnɪŋˌrʊm] N sala da pranzo
din·ing ta·ble [ˈdaɪnɪŋˌteɪbl] N tavola *or* tavolo da pranzo
◎ **din·ner** [ˈdɪnəʳ] N *(evening meal)* cena; *(lunch)* pranzo; *(banquet)* banchetto; **dinner is at seven o'clock** la cena è alle sette; **to have dinner** cenare; **we're having people to dinner this evening** abbiamo gente a cena stasera; **to go out to dinner in a restaurant/at friends** andare a cena fuori/da amici; **they have dinner at school** pranzano a scuola; **the dinner hour** l'intervallo del pranzo; **it's half past twelve – nearly dinner time!** è mezzogiorno e mezza, è quasi ora di pranzo!; **dinner's ready!** a tavola!; **school dinners** refezione *f* scolastica
dinner jacket N *(Brit)* smoking *m inv*
dinner party N cena (con amici)
dinner plate N piatto piano
dinner service N servizio da tavola
dinner time N ora di pranzo (*or* cena)
di·no·saur [ˈdaɪnəsɔːʳ] N dinosauro
dint [dɪnt] N: **by dint of (doing) sth** a forza di (fare) qc
di·oc·esan [daɪˈɒsɪsən] ADJ diocesano(-a)
dio·cese [ˈdaɪəsɪs] N diocesi *f inv*
diode [ˈdaɪəʊd] N *(Elec)* diodo
di·ox·ide [daɪˈɒksaɪd] N *(Chem)* biossido; **carbon dioxide** anidride *f* carbonica
Dip. ABBR *(Brit)* = **diploma**
dip [dɪp] N **1** *(swim)* nuotatina; **to go for a dip** andare a fare una nuotatina **2** *(hollow)* cunetta; *(slope)* pendenza, discesa **3** *(Culin)* salsetta **4** *(for sheep)* bagno
■ VT **1** *(into liquid)* immergere, bagnare; *(hand: into bag)* infilare; *(sheep)* immergere nel disinfestante; **he dipped his hand in the water** ha immerso la mano nell'acqua; **to dip one's pen in ink** intingere la penna nell'inchiostro; **he dipped a biscuit into his tea** ha inzuppato un biscotto nel tè **2 to dip one's headlights** *(Brit Aut)* abbassare i fari
■ VI *(slope down: road)* essere in pendenza, andare in discesa; *(move down: bird, plane)* abbassarsi; *(temperature, sun)* calare; **the boat dipped slightly under his weight** la barca si è abbassata leggermente sotto il suo peso; **the sun dipped below the horizon** il sole è sceso sotto l'orizzonte; **to dip into one's pocket/savings** *(fig)* attingere al portafoglio/ai propri risparmi; **to dip into a book** scorrere un libro; **to dip into an author** leggere brani di un autore
Dip Ed ABBR *(Brit)* = *Diploma in Education*
diph·theria [dɪfˈθɪərɪə] N difterite *f*
diph·thong [ˈdɪfθɒŋ] N dittongo
dip·loid [ˈdɪplɔɪd] N *(Bio)* diploide *f*
di·plo·ma [dɪˈpləʊmə] N diploma *m*; **to have a diploma in** avere un diploma in, essere diplomato(-a) in
di·plo·ma·cy [dɪˈpləʊməsɪ] N *(Pol, fig)* diplomazia
◎ **dip·lo·mat** [ˈdɪpləˌmæt] N diplomatico
◎ **dip·lo·mat·ic** [ˌdɪpləˈmætɪk] ADJ *(also fig)* diplomatico(-a); **diplomatic bag** *(Am)*: **diplomatic pouch** valigia diplomatica; **diplomatic service** diplomazia; **to break off diplomatic relations** rompere le relazioni diplomatiche
dip·lo·mati·cal·ly [ˌdɪpləˈmætɪkəlɪ] ADV diplomaticamente
diplomatic corps N corpo diplomatico
diplomatic immunity N immunità diplomatica
di·pole [ˈdaɪˌpəʊl] *(Elec)* N dipolo; **dipole aerial** antenna a dipolo
dip·per [ˈdɪpəʳ] N *(ladle)* mestolo; *(Zool)* merlo acquaiolo
dip·ping [ˈdɪpɪŋ] N *(of sheep)* bagno
dip·so·ma·nia [ˌdɪpsəʊˈmeɪnɪə] N dipsomania
dip·so·ma·ni·ac [ˌdɪpsəʊˈmeɪnɪæk] N dipsomane *m/f*
dip·stick [ˈdɪpˌstɪk] N *(Aut)* astina dell'olio
dip·switch [ˈdɪpˌswɪtʃ] N *(Aut)* levetta dei fari
dire [ˈdaɪəʳ] ADJ *(warning)* minaccioso(-a); *(consequences)* disastroso(-a); *(event)* terribile; *(poverty)* nero(-a); **a dire warning** un terribile avvertimento; **dire necessity** dura necessità; **in dire straits** nei guai
◎ **di·rect** [daɪˈrɛkt] ADJ *(gen)* diretto(-a); *(answer)* chiaro(-a); *(refusal)* esplicito(-a); *(manner, person)* franco(-a), diretto(-a); **direct object** *(Gram)* complemento oggetto; **the most direct route** la strada più diretta; **to be a direct descendant of** discendere in linea diretta da; **the direct opposite** l'esatto opposto; **the direct opposite of** esattamente il contrario di; **to make a direct hit** colpire in pieno
■ ADV *(go)* direttamente; *(fly)* senza scalo; *(dial)* in teleselezione; **you can go direct, without changing at Crewe** si può andarci direttamente senza cambiare a Crewe
■ VT **1** *(aim: remark, gaze, attention)*: **to direct at/to** dirigere a, rivolgere a; *(address: letter)*: **to direct sth to** indirizzare qc a; **is that remark directed at me?** è diretta a me questa osservazione?; **can you direct me to the station?** può indicarmi la strada per la stazione? **2** *(control: traffic, business, actors)* dirigere; *(play, film, programme)* curare la regia di, dirigere **3** *(frm: instruct)*: **to direct sb to do sth** dare direttive a qn di fare qc
direct cost N *(Comm)* costo diretto
direct current N *(Elec)* corrente *f* continua
direct debit N mandato di pagamento permanente
direct dialling [daɪˌrɛkt ˈdaɪəlɪŋ] N *(Telec)* ≈ teleselezione *f*
di·rect·ed [dɪˈrɛktɪd] ADJ *(Math)*: **directed numbers** numeri *mpl* ordinati
direct hit N *(Mil)* colpo diretto
◎ **di·rec·tion** [dɪˈrɛkʃən] N **1** *(way)* direzione *f*; *(fig)* scopo, direzione; **in the direction of** in direzione di; **we're going in the wrong direction** stiamo andando nella direzione sbagliata; **sense of direction** senso dell'orientamento **2** *(management: of business)* direzione *f*, amministrazione *f*; *(of play, film, programme)* regia NPL **3 directions** *(instructions: to a place)* indicazioni *fpl*; *(: for use)* istruzioni *fpl*; *(advice)* chiarimenti *mpl*; **to ask for directions** chiedere la strada; **stage directions** didascalie *fpl*
di·rec·tion·al [dɪˈrɛkʃənl] ADJ direzionale
di·rec·tion find·er [dɪˌrɛkʃənˈfaɪndəʳ] N radiogoniometro
di·rec·tive [dɪˈrɛktɪv] N direttiva, ordine *m*; **a government directive** una disposizione governativa
direct labour N manodopera diretta
di·rect·ly [dɪˈrɛktlɪ] ADV *(gen)* direttamente; *(at once)* subito; *(descended)* in linea diretta; *(frankly: speak)* con franchezza, senza peli sulla lingua; *(completely: opposite)* proprio; **the ball went directly to the goalkeeper** la palla è arrivata direttamente al portiere; **directly below me** proprio sotto di me; **directly after the meeting** subito dopo l'incontro
■ CONJ (non) appena; **he'll come directly he's ready** verrà non appena sarà pronto
direct mail N mailing *m*

Dd

direct mailshot N (*Brit*) materiale *m* pubblicitario ad approccio diretto

direct marketing N (*Comm*) vendita diretta ▷ www.the-dma.org

di·rect·ness [daɪ'rɛktnɪs] N (*of person, speech*) franchezza

◎ **di·rec·tor** [dɪ'rɛktəʳ] N (*Comm*) dirigente *m/f*, direttore(-trice) (d'azienda); (*of play, film, TV programme*) regista *m/f*; **the artistic director** il direttore artistico

Director of Public Prosecutions N (*Brit*) ≈ Procuratore *m* della Repubblica

di·rec·tor·ship [dɪ'rɛktəʃɪp] N direzione *f*; (*post*) carica di direttore

di·rec·tory [dɪ'rɛktərɪ] N (*telephone directory*) elenco (telefonico); (*street directory*) stradario; (*trade directory*) repertorio del commercio; (*Comput*) directory *m inv*

directory enquiries, (*Am*) **directory assistance** N (*Telec*) servizio informazioni, informazioni *fpl* elenco abbonati

direct selling N (*Comm*) vendita diretta

direct tax N imposta diretta

dirge [dɜːdʒ] N lamento funebre

dirt [dɜːt] N (*on face, clothes etc*) sporco, sporcizia; (*earth*) terra; (*mud*) fango; **I started to scrub off the dirt** ho cominciato a grattare via la sporcizia; **dog dirt** bisogni *mpl* di un cane; **to treat sb like dirt** (*fam*) trattare qn come uno straccio; **to dig up dirt about sb** (*fam*) pescare nel torbido a proposito di qn; **to spread the dirt about sb** (*fam*) sparlare di qn; **have you heard the latest dirt on ...?** (*fam*) hai sentito l'ultimo scandalo riguardo a...?

dirt bike N enduro *m inv*

dirt-cheap ['dɜːt'tʃiːp] ADJ (*fam*) regalato(-a)

dirti·ly ['dɜːtɪlɪ] ADV sudiciamente

dirti·ness ['dɜːtɪnɪs] N sporcizia, sudiciume *m*

dirt-poor [ˌdɜːt'pʊəʳ] ADJ poverissimo(-a)

dirt road N strada non asfaltata

dirt track N stradina sterrata

◎ **dirty** ['dɜːtɪ] ADJ (*comp* **-ier**, *superl* **-iest**) (*gen*) sporco(-a); (*cut, wound*) infetto(-a); (*indecent: novel, story, joke*) sporco(-a), spinto(-a); **dirty socks** calzini sporchi; **to get dirty** sporcarsi; **dirty trick** brutto scherzo; **to play a dirty trick on sb** farla sporca a qn, giocare un brutto scherzo a qn; **to give sb a dirty look** (*fam*) lanciare un'occhiataccia a qn; **to have a dirty mind** pensare solo a quello; **a dirty old man** un vecchio sporcaccione; **dirty word** parolaccia; **it's a dirty word these days** oggigiorno è un argomento tabù; **do your own dirty work!** non passare a me le tue gatte da pelare!
■ VT sporcare, insudiciare

dirty bomb N bomba convenzionale contenente materiale radioattivo

dis·abil·ity [ˌdɪsə'bɪlɪtɪ] N (*injury etc*) menomazione *f*, infermità *f inv*; (*state*) invalidità *f inv*, handicap *m inv*; (*Law, fig*) incapacità *f inv*; **people with disabilities** persone con invalidità; **disability allowance** ≈ pensione *f* d'invalidità

dis·able [dɪs'eɪbl] VT (*subj: illness, accident*) rendere invalido(-a); (*tank, gun*) mettere fuori uso; (*Law: disqualify*) rendere inabile

dis·abled [dɪs'eɪbld] ADJ handicappato(-a), invalido(-a); (*maimed*) mutilato(-a); (*through illness, old age*) inabile; **disabled ex-serviceman** invalido di guerra; **the disabled** NPL i disabili; gli invalidi

dis·able·ment [dɪs'eɪblmənt] N (*injury*) menomazione *f*; (*condition*) invalidità; **disablement pension** ≈ pensione di invalidità

dis·abuse [ˌdɪsə'bjuːz] VT: **to disabuse sb (of sth)** (*frm*) disingannare qn (su qc)

dis·ad·vant·age [ˌdɪsəd'vɑːntɪdʒ] N svantaggio; **to be to sb's disadvantage** tornare a svantaggio *or* sfavore di qn; **to be at a disadvantage** essere svantaggiato(-a)

dis·ad·van·taged [ˌdɪsəd'vɑːntɪdʒd] ADJ (*person*) svantaggiato(-a)

dis·ad·van·ta·geous [ˌdɪsædvɑːn'teɪdʒəs] ADJ svantaggioso(-a), sfavorevole

dis·af·fect·ed [ˌdɪsə'fɛktɪd] ADJ (*voters, supporters*) deluso(-a); (*young people*) ribelle

dis·af·fec·tion [ˌdɪsə'fɛkʃən] N malcontento, insoddisfazione *f*

dis·agree [ˌdɪsə'griː] VI **1 to disagree (with sb on** *or* **about sth)** essere in disaccordo (con qn su qc), dissentire (da qn su qc); (*quarrel*) litigare; (*stories, accounts, figures: conflict*) essere discordante; **I disagree with you** non sono d'accordo con te; **we always disagree** non siamo mai d'accordo **2 to disagree with sth** (*oppose*) non essere d'accordo su qc **3 to disagree with** (*subj: climate, food*) non fare bene a; **a hot climate disagrees with me** il clima caldo non mi si confà; **onions disagree with me** non digerisco la cipolla

dis·agree·able [ˌdɪsə'griːəbl] ADJ (*gen*) spiacevole; (*weather*) brutto(-a); (*person*) antipatico(-a); (*tone of voice*) sgradevole

dis·agree·able·ness [ˌdɪsə'griːəblnɪs] N (*gen*) spiacevolezza; (*of person, tone of voice*) sgradevolezza

dis·agree·ably [ˌdɪsə'griːəblɪ] ADV (*surprised*) sgradevolmente, in modo sgradevole; (*behave*) in modo spiacevole, in modo antipatico

dis·agree·ment [ˌdɪsə'griːmənt] N (*with opinion*) disaccordo; (*quarrel*) dissapore *m*, litigio; (*between stories, accounts, figures*) discrepanza, discordanza; **to have a disagreement with sb** litigare con qn

dis·al·low ['dɪsə'laʊ] VT respingere; (*Ftbl: goal*) annullare

◎ **dis·ap·pear** [ˌdɪsə'pɪəʳ] VI scomparire, sparire; **he disappeared from sight** è scomparso alla vista; **to make sth disappear** far sparire qc

dis·ap·pear·ance [ˌdɪsə'pɪərəns] N scomparsa, sparizione *f*; **the disappearance of the money** la scomparsa del denaro

dis·ap·point [ˌdɪsə'pɔɪnt] VT deludere

◎ **dis·ap·point·ed** [ˌdɪsə'pɔɪntɪd] ADJ deluso(-a)

dis·ap·point·ing [ˌdɪsə'pɔɪntɪŋ] ADJ deludente

dis·ap·point·ing·ly [ˌdɪsə'pɔɪntɪŋlɪ] ADV in modo deludente

dis·ap·point·ment [ˌdɪsə'pɔɪntmənt] N (*cause of dejection*) delusione *f*; (*dejection*) disappunto

dis·ap·prov·al [dɪsə'pruːvəl] N disapprovazione *f*

dis·ap·prove [ˌdɪsə'pruːv] VI: **to disapprove (of sb/sth)** disapprovare (qn/qc)

dis·ap·prov·ing [ˌdɪsə'pruːvɪŋ] ADJ di disapprovazione

dis·ap·prov·ing·ly [ˌdɪsə'pruːvɪŋlɪ] ADV con aria (*or* tono) di disapprovazione

dis·arm [dɪs'ɑːm] VT disarmare
■ VI (*Mil*) disarmarsi

dis·arma·ment [dɪs'ɑːməmənt] N disarmo; **disarmament talks** conferenza sul disarmo

dis·arm·ing [dɪs'ɑːmɪŋ] ADJ (*smile*) disarmante

dis·arm·ing·ly [dɪs'ɑːmɪŋlɪ] ADV in modo disarmante

dis·ar·range [ˌdɪsə'reɪndʒ] VT (*things*) buttare all'aria; (*hair*) scompigliare

dis·ar·ray [ˌdɪsəˈreɪ] N: **in disarray** (*troops*) in rotta; (*thoughts*) confuso(-a); (*clothes*) in disordine; **to throw into disarray** (*things, plans*) buttare all'aria; (*people*) portare lo scompiglio in

◎ **dis·as·ter** [dɪˈzɑːstəʳ] N (*also fig*) disastro; **disaster area** zona disastrata; **disaster fund** *raccolta di fondi a favore delle vittime di un disastro*

dis·as·trous [dɪˈzɑːstrəs] ADJ disastroso(-a)

dis·as·trous·ly [dɪˈzɑːstrəslɪ] ADV disastrosamente

dis·avow [ˌdɪsəˈvaʊ] VT (*frm: one's opinions*) sconfessare; (*: one's words*) ritrattare; (*: one's faith*) rinnegare

dis·band [dɪsˈbænd] VT (*army*) congedare, smobilitare; (*organization*) sciogliere
■ VI sciogliersi; **the party disbanded** il partito si sciolse

dis·be·lief [ˈdɪsbəˈliːf] N incredulità; **in disbelief** incredulo(-a)

dis·be·lieve [ˈdɪsbəˈliːv] VT (*person, story*) non credere a, mettere in dubbio; **I don't disbelieve you** non è che non ti creda

dis·be·liev·ing [ˌdɪsbəˈliːvɪŋ] ADJ (*smile, look*) incredulo(-a)

dis·be·liev·ing·ly [ˌdɪsbəˈliːvɪŋlɪ] ADV in modo incredulo, con incredulità

dis·burse [dɪsˈbɜːs] VT (*frm*) sborsare

dis·burse·ment [dɪsˈbɜːsmənt] N (*frm*) esborso

disc [dɪsk] N **1** (*gen, record, Anat*) disco; (*identity disc: of dog*) targhetta di riconoscimento; (*: of soldier*) piastrina di riconoscimento **2** (*Comput*) = **disk**

dis·card [dɪsˈkɑːd] VT (*clothes*) smettere; (*unwanted things*) sbarazzarsi di; (*idea, plan, playing card*) scartare; (*people*) abbandonare

disc brakes NPL (*Aut*) freni *mpl* a disco

dis·cern [dɪˈsɜːn] VT (*frm*) distinguere, discernere

dis·cern·ible [dɪˈsɜːnəbl] ADJ (*frm*) percepibile

dis·cern·ing [dɪˈsɜːnɪŋ] ADJ (*buyer, reader, collector*) esperto(-a), perspicace; (*eye*) da intenditore(-trice); (*taste*) raffinato(-a), sicuro(-a)

dis·cern·ment [dɪˈsɜːnmənt] N discernimento

dis·charge [*n* ˈdɪstʃɑːdʒ; *vb* dɪsˈtʃɑːdʒ] N **1** (*of cargo*) operazione *f* di scarico; (*of gun*) scarica **2** (*of patient*) dimissione *f*; (*of worker*) licenziamento; (*of soldier*) congedo; (*of prisoner*) rilascio; (*of duty*) adempimento; (*of debt*) estinzione *f* **3** (*Elec*) scarica; (*of gas, chemicals*) emissione *f*; (*of water, waste*) scarico; (*Med: from wound*) secrezione *f*; (*: vaginal discharge*) perdite *fpl* (bianche)
■ VT **1** (*ship, load*) scaricare; (*waste*) scaricare; (*shot*) far partire; (*liquid*) versare; (*Med: pus etc*) spurgare, emettere; **to discharge one's gun** fare fuoco **2** (*dismiss: employee*) licenziare: *soldier, congedare: patient, dimettere: prisoner, rilasciare: defendant, prosciogliere;* **discharged bankrupt** *fallito cui il tribunale ha concesso la riabilitazione* **3** (*settle: debt*) pagare, estinguere; (*complete: task*) assolvere, adempiere a; (*duties*) compiere
■ VI (*wound, sore*) spurgare; (*Elec*) scaricarsi

dis·ci·ple [dɪˈsaɪpl] N (*also fig*) discepolo(-a)

dis·ci·pli·nar·ian [ˌdɪsɪplɪˈnɛərɪən] N chi impone la disciplina; **to be a strict disciplinarian** far osservare rigorosamente la disciplina

dis·ci·pli·nary [ˈdɪsɪplɪnərɪ] ADJ disciplinare; **to take disciplinary action against sb** prendere un provvedimento disciplinare contro qn

◎ **dis·ci·pline** [ˈdɪsɪplɪn] N disciplina; (*punishment*) punizione *f*, castigo; **to keep/maintain discipline** tenere/mantenere la disciplina
■ VT (*punish*) punire, castigare; **to discipline o.s. to do sth** imporsi di fare qc; **to discipline o.s** darsi una regola

disc jockey N disc jockey *m inv*

dis·claim [dɪsˈkleɪm] VT (*frm*) negare, smentire; **to disclaim all knowledge of sth** negare di essere a conoscenza di qc

dis·claim·er [dɪsˈkleɪməʳ] N (*frm*) smentita; **to issue a disclaimer** pubblicare una smentita

dis·close [dɪsˈkləʊz] VT (*all senses*) rivelare, svelare

dis·clo·sure [dɪsˈkləʊʒəʳ] N rivelazione *f*

dis·co [ˈdɪskəʊ] N (*fam: place*) discoteca; (*: event*) festa (con disc jockey)

dis·col·our, (*Am*) **dis·col·or** [dɪsˈkʌləʳ] VT scolorire, sbiadire; (*whites*) ingiallire
■ VI scolorirsi, sbiadire; (*whites*) ingiallire

dis·col·oura·tion, (*Am*) **dis·col·ora·tion** [dɪsˌkʌləˈreɪʃən] N (*see adj*) scolorimento; ingiallimento

dis·col·oured, (*Am*) **dis·col·ored** [dɪsˈkʌləd] ADJ scolorito(-a), sbiadito(-a); (*whites*) ingiallito(-a)

dis·com·fit [dɪsˈkʌmfɪt] VT (*liter*) sconcertare

dis·com·fi·ture [dɪsˈkʌmfɪtʃəʳ] N (*liter*) disagio, imbarazzo

dis·com·fort [dɪsˈkʌmfət] N (*lack of comfort*) scomodità *f inv*; (*uneasiness*) disagio, imbarazzo; **his wound gave him some discomfort** la ferita gli procurava un certo disagio

dis·con·cert [ˌdɪskənˈsɜːt] VT sconcertare

dis·con·cert·ed [ˌdɪskənˈsɜːtɪd] ADJ sconcertato(-a)

dis·con·cert·ing [ˌdɪskənˈsɜːtɪŋ] ADJ sconcertante

dis·con·cert·ing·ly [ˌdɪskənˈsɜːtɪŋlɪ] ADV sorprendentemente, in modo sconcertante

dis·con·nect [ˈdɪskəˈnɛkt] VT (*pipe, television*) staccare; (*electricity, gas, water*) sospendere (l'erogazione di); **I've been disconnected** (*Telec: for non-payment*) mi hanno staccato il telefono; (*: in mid-conversation*) è caduta la linea, si è interrotta la comunicazione

dis·con·nec·ted [ˌdɪskəˈnɛktɪd] ADJ (*speech, thoughts, facts*) sconnesso(-a)

dis·con·so·late [dɪsˈkɒnsəlɪt] ADJ sconsolato(-a)

dis·con·so·late·ly [dɪsˈkɒnsəlɪtlɪ] ADV sconsolatamente

dis·con·tent [ˈdɪskənˈtɛnt] N scontentezza, dispiacere *m*; (*Pol*) malcontento, scontento

dis·con·tent·ed [ˈdɪskənˈtɛntɪd] ADJ: **discontented (with/about)** scontento(-a) (di), insoddisfatto(-a) (di)

dis·con·tent·ed·ly [ˌdɪskənˈtɛntɪdlɪ] ADV con insoddisfazione

dis·con·tinue [ˈdɪskənˈtɪnjuː] VT interrompere, cessare; (*Comm*): **discontinued line** articolo fuori produzione; **to be discontinued** (*product*) uscire di produzione

dis·con·ti·nu·ity [dɪsˌkɒntɪˈnjuːɪtɪ] (*frm*) N (*quality*) discontinuità *f inv*; (*gap*) interruzione *f*

dis·con·tinu·ous [ˌdɪskənˈtɪnjʊəs] ADJ (*process*) discontinuo(-a); (*speech*) incoerente

dis·cord [ˈdɪskɔːd] N disaccordo, discordia; (*Mus*) dissonanza

dis·cord·ant [dɪsˈkɔːdənt] ADJ (*gen*) discordante; (*sound*) dissonante, stonato(-a)

dis·co·theque [ˈdɪskəʊtɛk] N discoteca

◎ **dis·count** [*n* ˈdɪskaʊnt; *vb* dɪsˈkaʊnt] N (*reduction*) sconto, riduzione *f*; **a discount for students** una riduzione per studenti; **a twenty per cent discount** uno sconto del venti per cento; **to be at a discount** (*Comm*) essere scontato(-a); (*fig: little valued*) essere svalutato(-a); **to buy at a discount** comprare a prezzo

Dd

scontato; **to give sb a discount on sth** fare uno sconto a qn su qc; **discount for cash** sconto cassa *inv*; **discount rate** tasso di sconto
■VT (*Comm*) scontare; (*fig: report, idea, theory*) non badare a

dis·count·er [ˈdɪskaʊntəʳ] N discount *m inv*

discount house N **1** (*Brit Fin*) istituto di sconto, discount house *f inv* **2** (*Am*) = **discount store**

discount store N negozio di vendita diretta, discount *m inv*

dis·cour·age [dɪsˈkʌrɪdʒ] VT **1** (*dishearten*) scoraggiare; **I don't want to discourage you, but ...** non vorrei scoraggiarti, ma...; **to get discouraged** scoraggiarsi **2** (*dissuade, deter*) tentare di dissuadere; **to discourage sb from doing sth** tentare di dissuadere qn dal fare qc

dis·cour·age·ment [dɪsˈkʌrɪdʒmənt] N (*dissuasion*) disapprovazione *f*; (*depression*) scoraggiamento; **to act as a discouragement to** scoraggiare

dis·cour·ag·ing [dɪsˈkʌrɪdʒɪŋ] ADJ scoraggiante, avvilente

dis·course [ˈdɪskɔːs] N **1** (*disquisition*) dissertazione *f* **2** (*conversation*) conversazione *f*; (*written*) dissertazione *f*
■VI: **to discourse on/upon** dissertare su

discourse analysis N (*Ling*) analisi *f inv* del discorso

dis·cour·teous [dɪsˈkɜːtɪəs] ADJ scortese

dis·cour·teous·ly [dɪsˈkɜːtɪəslɪ] ADV scortesemente

dis·cour·tesy [dɪsˈkɜːtɪsɪ] N scortesia

◎**dis·cov·er** [dɪsˈkʌvəʳ] VT (*gen*) scoprire; (*after search*) scovare, trovare; (*notice: loss, mistake*) scoprire, accorgersi di

dis·cov·er·er [dɪsˈkʌvərəʳ] N scopritore(-trice)

◎**dis·cov·ery** [dɪsˈkʌvərɪ] N scoperta

dis·cred·it [dɪsˈkrɛdɪt] (*frm*) N discredito; **to bring discredit on sb/sth** far cadere qn/qc in discredito
■VT screditare

dis·cred·it·able [dɪsˈkrɛdɪtəbl] ADJ (*frm*) disonorevole

dis·creet [dɪsˈkriːt] ADJ discreto(-a)

dis·creet·ly [dɪsˈkriːtlɪ] ADV discretamente, con discrezione

dis·crep·an·cy [dɪsˈkrɛpənsɪ] N discrepanza

dis·crete [dɪsˈkriːt] ADJ (*separate, distinct*) separato(-a), distinto(-a); (*Statistics*) discreto(-a)

dis·cre·tion [dɪsˈkrɛʃən] N discrezione *f*; **at your/his** *etc* **discretion** a tua/sua *etc* discrezione; **use your own discretion** giudica tu

dis·cre·tion·ary [dɪsˈkrɛʃənərɪ] ADJ (*powers, payment*) discrezionale

dis·crimi·nate [dɪsˈkrɪmɪˌneɪt] VI: **to discriminate (between)** (*gen*) distinguere (tra); **to discriminate against/in favour of** fare discriminazioni ai danni di/a favore di; **to discriminate against women** fare discriminazioni contro le donne

dis·crimi·nat·ing [dɪsˈkrɪmɪˌneɪtɪŋ] ADJ (*person*) esigente; (*judgment*) acuto(-a); (*ear*) fine

dis·crimi·na·tion [dɪsˌkrɪmɪˈneɪʃən] N **1** (*prejudice*): **discrimination (against/in favour of)** discriminazione *f* (ai danni di/a favore di); **racial/sexual discrimination** discriminazione razziale/sessuale **2** (*good judgment*) discernimento

dis·crimi·na·tory [diˈskrɪmɪnətərɪ] ADJ discriminatorio(-a)

dis·cus [ˈdɪskəs] N disco; **discus thrower** lanciatore(-trice) di disco

◎**dis·cuss** [dɪsˈkʌs] VT (*general topic*) discutere di; (*problem, plan*) discutere; (*debate*) dibattere; **we discussed the topic all evening** abbiamo discusso tutta la sera dell'argomento; **to discuss sth at length** dibattere qc a lungo

◎**dis·cus·sion** [dɪsˈkʌʃən] N discussione *f*; (*meeting*) colloquio, dibattito; **it's still under discussion** (*plan, policy*) non è ancora definitivo

discussion group N gruppo di discussione

dis·dain [dɪsˈdeɪn] N disdegno
■VT sdegnare; **to disdain to do sth** disdegnare di fare qc

dis·dain·ful [dɪsˈdeɪnful] ADJ (*person, tone*) sdegnoso(-a); (*look, laugh*) sprezzante

dis·dain·ful·ly [dɪsˈdeɪnfəlɪ] ADV (*act, speak*) sdegnosamente; (*look, laugh*) in modo sprezzante

◎**dis·ease** [dɪˈziːz] N malattia

dis·eased [dɪˈziːzd] ADJ malato(-a)

dis·em·bark [ˌdɪsɪmˈbɑːk] VI, VT sbarcare

dis·em·bar·ka·tion [ˌdɪsɛmbɑːˈkeɪʃən] N sbarco

dis·em·bod·ied [ˈdɪsɪmˈbɒdɪd] ADJ incorporeo(-a); (*voice*) etereo(-a); (*soul, spirit*) disincarnato(-a)

dis·em·bow·el [dɪsɪmˈbaʊəl] VT sbudellare, sventrare

dis·em·pow·er [ˌdɪsɪmˈpaʊəʳ] VT privare della propria autonomia

dis·en·chant·ed [ˌdɪsɪnˈtʃɑːntɪd] ADJ disincantato(-a); **disenchanted (with)** deluso(-a) (da)

dis·en·chant·ment [ˌdɪsɪnˈtʃɑːntmənt] N disincanto

dis·en·fran·chise [ˈdɪsɪnˈfræntʃaɪz] VT privare del diritto di voto; (*Comm*) togliere il privilegio commerciale a

dis·en·gage [ˌdɪsɪnˈgeɪdʒ] VT (*object, hand*) liberare; (*Aut: clutch*) disinnestare; (*Mil: forces*) disimpegnare
■VI (*see vt*): **to disengage (from)** disinnestarsi (da); disimpegnarsi (da)

dis·en·gage·ment [ˌdɪsɪnˈgeɪdʒmənt] N (*of clutch*) disinnesto; (*Pol*) disimpegno

dis·en·tan·gle [ˈdɪsɪnˈtæŋgl] VT (*string, wool*) sbrogliare; **to disentangle o.s. from** (*fig*) districarsi da, sbrogliarsi da

dis·fa·vour, (*Am*) **dis·fa·vor** [dɪsˈfeɪvəʳ] N (*frm*) disapprovazione *f*; **to fall into disfavour** cadere in disgrazia; **to be in disfavour with sb** avere la disapprovazione di qn; **to look with disfavour on** disapprovare

dis·fig·ure [dɪsˈfɪgəʳ] VT (*person*) sfigurare; (*landscape*) deturpare

dis·fig·ure·ment [dɪsˈfɪgəmənt] N: **to have a hideous disfigurement** essere orribilmente sfigurato(-a); **his disfigurement was caused by an accident** rimase sfigurato in un incidente

dis·gorge [dɪsˈgɔːdʒ] VT (*contents*) scaricare; (*subj: vehicle, building*) scaricare

dis·grace [dɪsˈgreɪs] N (*state of shame*) disonore *m*, vergogna; (*shameful thing*) vergogna; (*disfavour*) disgrazia; **he's a disgrace to the school/family** è il disonore della scuola/della famiglia; **he's brought disgrace upon himself** si è ricoperto di vergogna; **he resigned in disgrace** caduto in disgrazia, si è dimesso; **to be in disgrace** essere in disgrazia; (*child, dog*) essere in castigo; **it's a disgrace!** è una vergogna!
■VT (*family, country*) disonorare, far cadere in disgrazia; **he disgraced himself** ha fatto una pessima figura; **he was publicly disgraced** fu svergognato pubblicamente

dis·grace·ful [dɪsˈgreɪsful] ADJ vergognoso(-a), scandaloso(-a)

dis·grace·ful·ly [dɪsˈgreɪsfəlɪ] ADV vergognosamente, scandalosamente

dis·grun·tled [dɪsˈgrʌntld] ADJ (*person*) di malumore, di cattivo umore; (*look*) seccato(-a)
dis·guise [dɪsˈgaɪz] N travestimento; **in disguise** travestito(-a)
■ VT (*gen*) travestire; (*voice*) contraffare; (*feelings*) mascherare; **to disguise o.s.** mascherarsi; **to disguise o.s. as** travestirsi da; **there's no disguising the fact that ...** non si può nascondere (il fatto) che...
dis·gust [dɪsˈgʌst] N disgusto; **much to my disgust** con mio profondo disgusto; **she left in disgust** se n'è andata disgustata
■ VT disgustare, far schifo a
dis·gust·ed [dɪsˈgʌstɪd] ADJ: **to be disgusted (at)** essere disgustato(-a) (di fronte a)
dis·gust·ed·ly [dɪsˈgʌstɪdlɪ] ADV con disgusto
dis·gust·ing [dɪsˈgʌstɪŋ] ADJ schifoso(-a), disgustoso(-a)
dis·gust·ing·ly [dɪsˈgʌstɪŋlɪ] ADV disgustosamente
◎ **dish** [dɪʃ] N piatto; (*food*) piatto, pietanza; **a vegetarian dish** un piatto vegetariano; **put the peas in a serving dish** metti i piselli in un piatto da portata; **to wash** *or* **do the dishes** lavare *or* fare i piatti
▶ **dish out** VT + ADV (*food*) servire; (*advice*) dispensare; (*money*) sganciare; (*exam papers*) distribuire
▶ **dish up** VT + ADV (*food*) servire; (*facts, statistics*) presentare
dis·ha·bille [ˌdɪsæˈbiːl] N déshabillé *m inv*; **in dishabille** in déshabillé
dis·har·mo·ny [dɪsˈhɑːmənɪ] N (*frm*) disaccordo
dish·cloth [ˈdɪʃˌklɒθ] N strofinaccio dei piatti
dis·heart·en [dɪsˈhɑːtn] VT scoraggiare
dis·heart·en·ed [dɪsˈhɑːtənd] ADJ scoraggiato(-a), avvilito(-a)
dis·heart·en·ing [dɪsˈhɑːtnɪŋ] ADJ scoraggiante, deprimente
di·shev·elled, (*Am*) **di·shev·eled** [dɪˈʃɛvəld] ADJ (*hair*) arruffato(-a); (*clothes*) tutto(-a) in disordine
dish·mop [ˈdɪʃˌmɒp] N strofinaccio per i piatti
dis·hon·est [dɪsˈɒnɪst] ADJ (*person, action*) disonesto(-a); (*means*) sleale
dis·hon·est·ly [dɪsˈɒnɪstlɪ] ADV disonestamente, in modo disonesto
dis·hon·es·ty [dɪsˈɒnɪstɪ] N (*see adj*) disonestà *f inv*; slealtà *f inv*
dis·hon·our, (*Am*) **dis·hon·or** [dɪsˈɒnə^r] N (*frm*) disonore *m*; **to bring dishonour on** gettare il disonore su, far disonore a
■ VT (*family, woman*) disonorare; (*cheque*) non onorare
dis·hon·our·able, (*Am*) **dis·hon·or·able** [dɪsˈɒnərəbl] ADJ disonorevole
dis·hon·our·ably, (*Am*) **dis·hon·or·ably** [dɪsˈɒnərəblɪ] ADV disonorevolmente
dish·rack [ˈdɪʃˌræk] N scolapiatti *m inv*
dish·towel [ˈdɪʃˌtaʊəl] N strofinaccio dei piatti
dish·washer [ˈdɪʃˌwɒʃə^r] N (*machine*) lavastoviglie *f inv*; (*person: in restaurant*) lavapiatti *m/f inv*
dish·water [ˈdɪʃˌwɔːtə^r] N sciacquatura dei piatti
dishy [ˈdɪʃɪ] ADJ (*comp* **-ier**, *superl* **-iest**) (*Brit fam: esp man*) figo(-a)
dis·il·lu·sion [ˌdɪsɪˈluːʒən] VT disilludere, disingannare; **to become disillusioned (with)** perdere le illusioni (su)
■ N = **disillusionment**
dis·il·lu·sion·ment [ˌdɪsɪˈluːʒənmənt] N disillusione *f*, disinganno
dis·in·cen·tive [ˌdɪsɪnˈsɛntɪv] N (*frm*): **to act as a disincentive (to)** agire da freno (su); **to be a disincentive to** scoraggiare
dis·in·cli·na·tion [ˌdɪsɪnklɪˈneɪʃən] N (*frm*): **disinclination (for/to do)** riluttanza (a/a fare)
dis·in·clined [ˈdɪsɪnˈklaɪnd] ADJ: **to be disinclined to do sth** essere poco propenso(-a) a fare qc
dis·in·fect [ˌdɪsɪnˈfɛkt] VT disinfettare
dis·in·fect·ant [ˌdɪsɪnˈfɛktənt] N disinfettante *m*
dis·in·fec·tion [ˌdɪsɪnˈfɛkʃən] N disinfezione *f*
dis·in·fla·tion [ˌdɪsɪnˈfleɪʃən] N (*Econ*) disinflazione *f*
dis·in·for·ma·tion [ˌdɪsɪnfəˈmeɪʃən] N disinformazione *f*
dis·in·genu·ous [ˌdɪsɪnˈdʒɛnjʊəs] ADJ insincero(-a)
dis·in·her·it [ˈdɪsɪnˈhɛrɪt] VT diseredare
dis·in·te·grate [dɪsˈɪntɪgreɪt] VI disintegrarsi; (*fig: society, theory*) disgregarsi
dis·in·te·gra·tion [dɪsˌɪntɪˈgreɪʃən] N (*see vb*) disintegrazione *f*; disgregamento
dis·in·ter·est·ed [dɪsˈɪntrɪstɪd] ADJ (*impartial*) disinteressato(-a); (*strictly incorrect: uninterested*) non interessato(-a), indifferente
dis·in·ter·est·ed·ness [dɪsˈɪntrɪstɪdnɪs] N (*impartiality*) disinteresse *m*, imparzialità *f inv*; (*incorrect use: lack of interest*) disinteresse *m*
dis·joint·ed [dɪsˈdʒɔɪntɪd] ADJ sconnesso(-a), slegato(-a)
dis·joint·ed·ly [dɪsˈdʒɔɪntɪdlɪ] ADV in modo sconnesso, in modo slegato
disk [dɪsk] N **1** = **disc**
2 (*Comput*) disco; **the hard disk** il disco rigido
disk drive N (*Comput*) unità disco
disk·ette [dɪsˈkɛt] N (*Comput*) dischetto, floppy disk *m inv*
disk operating system N (*Comput*) sistema *m* operativo a disco
disk pack N (*Comput*) pila di dischi
disk space N (*Comput*) spazio (su) disco
disk storage N (*Comput*) memoria (su) disco
dis·like [dɪsˈlaɪk] N: **dislike (of)** antipatia (per), avversione *f* (per); **to take a dislike to sb/sth** prendere in antipatia qn/qc; **my likes and dislikes** ciò che mi piace e ciò che non mi piace
■ VT (*thing, person*): **I dislike it** non mi piace; **I dislike the idea** l'idea non mi va; **I dislike her intensely** mi è fortemente antipatica, mi è antipaticissima
dis·lo·cate [ˈdɪsləʊkeɪt] VT (*Med*) slogare, lussare; (*fig: plans*) scombussolare; **he dislocated his shoulder** si è lussato una spalla
dis·lo·ca·tion [ˌdɪsləʊˈkeɪʃən] N (*Med*) slogatura, lussazione *f*
dis·lodge [dɪsˈlɒdʒ] VT (*gen*) rimuovere; (*enemy*) far sgomberare
dis·loy·al [ˈdɪsˈlɔɪəl] ADJ: **disloyal (to)** sleale (verso)
dis·loy·al·ly [ˈdɪsˈlɔɪəlɪ] ADV slealmente
dis·loy·al·ty [ˈdɪsˈlɔɪəltɪ] N slealtà
dis·mal [ˈdɪzməl] ADJ (*gloomy*) tetro(-a), cupo(-a); (*weather*) grigio(-a); **it was a dismal failure** è stato un misero fallimento
dis·mal·ly [ˈdɪzməlɪ] ADV tetramente, cupamente; **to fail dismally** fallire miseramente
dis·man·tle [dɪsˈmæntl] VT (*machine etc*) smontare; (*service, system*) smantellare; (*fort, warship*) disarmare
dis·may [dɪsˈmeɪ] N sgomento, costernazione *f*; **in dismay** costernato(-a); **much to my dismay** con mio gran sgomento
■ VT costernare, sgomentare
dis·mem·ber [dɪsˈmɛmbə^r] VT (*frm*) smembrare

Dd

◎**dis·miss** [dɪs'mɪs] VT **1** (*worker*) licenziare; (*official*) destituire; (*assembly*) sciogliere **2** (*gen*) congedare; (*charge, accusation*) respingere; (*problem, possibility, idea*) scartare; **she dismissed the suggestion immediately** ha scartato subito il suggerimento; **the judge dismissed the case** (*Law*) il giudice ha dichiarato il non luogo a procedere; **class dismissed!** (*Scol*) potete andare!
■VI (*Mil*) rompere i ranghi

dis·mis·sal [dɪs'mɪsəl] N congedo; (*of worker*) licenziamento; (*of official*) destituzione *f*; (*of assembly*) scioglimento; **the dismissal of public opinion** l'ignorare l'opinione pubblica; **the dismissal of a case** (*Law*) il non luogo a procedere

dis·miss·ive [dɪs'mɪsɪv] ADJ: **dismissive (of)** sprezzante (nei confronti di)

dis·mount [dɪs'maʊnt] VI: **to dismount (from)** smontare (da), scendere (da)
■VT **1** (*gun*) smontare **2** (*rider*) disarcionare

Dis·ney·land ['dɪznɪˌlænd] N Disneyland *f*

dis·obedi·ence [ˌdɪsə'bi:dɪəns] N disubbidienza

dis·obedi·ent [ˌdɪsə'bi:dɪənt] ADJ disubbidiente

dis·obey ['dɪsə'beɪ] VT (*person, order*) disubbidire a; (*rule*) trasgredire; **he disobeyed instructions** ha disobbedito alle istruzioni

dis·oblig·ing ['dɪsə'blaɪdʒɪŋ] ADJ (*frm*) poco disponibile

dis·or·der [dɪs'ɔ:dəʳ] N **1** (*confusion*) confusione *f*, caos *m*; (*untidiness*) disordine *m*; **in disorder** in disordine **2** (*Pol: rioting*) disordini *mpl*, tumulto; **civil disorder** disordini *mpl* (interni) **3** (*Med*) disturbi *mpl*

dis·or·dered [dɪs'ɔ:dəd] ADJ (*room*) disordinato(-a), in disordine; (*thoughts*) disordinato(-a), confuso(-a); (*Psych: mind*) turbato(-a)

dis·or·der·ly [dɪs'ɔ:dəlɪ] ADJ (*room*) disordinato(-a); (*behaviour, crowd*) turbolento(-a); (*meeting*) tumultuoso(-a), burrascoso(-a)

disorderly conduct N (*Law*) *comportamento atto a turbare l'ordine pubblico*

dis·or·gani·za·tion [dɪsˌɔ:gənaɪ'zeɪʃən] N disorganizzazione *f*

dis·or·gan·ize [dɪs'ɔ:gəˌnaɪz] VT disorganizzare

dis·or·gan·ized [dɪs'ɔ:gəˌnaɪzd] ADJ (*person, life*) disorganizzato(-a); (*system, meeting*) male organizzato(-a)

dis·ori·ent [dɪs'ɔ:rɪənt] VT disorientare

dis·ori·en·tate [dɪs'ɔ:rɪənˌteɪt] VT disorientare

dis·own [dɪs'əʊn] VT rinnegare, ripudiare

dis·par·age [dɪs'pærɪdʒ] VT (*frm: person, achievements*) denigrare

dis·par·age·ment [dɪs'pærɪdʒmənt] N (*frm*) denigrazione *f*, diffamazione *f*

dis·par·ag·ing [dɪs'pærɪdʒɪŋ] ADJ (*comment, remark*) denigratorio(-a); **to be disparaging about sb/sth** denigrare qn/qc

dis·par·ag·ing·ly [dɪs'pærɪdʒɪŋlɪ] ADV con tono denigratorio

dis·par·ate ['dɪspərɪt] ADJ (*frm*) disparato(-a)

dis·par·ity [dɪs'pærɪtɪ] N disparità *f inv*

dis·pas·sion·ate [dɪs'pæʃənɪt] ADJ (*unbiased*) spassionato(-a), imparziale; (*unemotional*) calmo(-a)

dis·pas·sion·ate·ly [dɪs'pæʃənɪtlɪ] ADV (*without bias*) spassionatamente, in modo imparziale; (*unemotionally*) con calma

dis·patch, **des·patch** [dɪs'pætʃ] N **1** (*sending: of goods*) spedizione *f*, invio; (*: of person*) invio; **dispatch department** reparto spedizioni **2** (*Mil, Press: report*) dispaccio; **mentioned in dispatches** (*Mil*) citato(-a) all'ordine del giorno **3** (*promptness*) prontezza, rapidità
■VT **1** (*send: letter, goods*) spedire, inviare; (*: messenger, troops*) inviare **2** (*deal with: business*) sbrigare **3** (*old: kill*) uccidere, ammazzare; (*hum*) mandare all'altro mondo

dispatch rider N (*Mil*) corriere *m*, portaordini *m inv*

dis·pel [dɪs'pɛl] VT (*doubts, fears*) dissipare, scacciare

dis·pen·sable [dɪs'pɛnsəbl] ADJ di cui si può fare a meno

dis·pen·sa·ry [dɪs'pɛnsərɪ] N farmacia; (*clinic*) dispensario, ambulatorio

dis·pen·sa·tion [ˌdɪspɛn'seɪʃən] N (*Law, Rel*) dispensa

dis·pense [dɪs'pɛns] VT (*food, money*) dispensare, distribuire; (*justice*) amministrare; (*medicine*) preparare e dare; **to dispense prescriptions** preparare e dare medicine su ricetta
▸ **dispense with** VT + PREP (*do without*) fare a meno di

dis·pens·er [dɪs'pɛnsəʳ] N (*container*) distributore *m*

dis·pens·ing chem·ist [dɪ'spɛnsɪŋ'kɛmɪst] N (*Brit: shop*) farmacia; (*: person*) farmacista *m/f*

dis·per·sal [dɪs'pɜ:səl] N (*gen*) dispersione *f*; (*Bot*) disseminazione *f*

dis·perse [dɪs'pɜ:s] VT (*crowd, demonstrators, oil slick*) disperdere
■VI (*crowd*) disperdersi; (*mist*) dissiparsi

dis·per·sion [dɪs'pɜ:ʃən] N = **dispersal**

dis·pir·it·ed [dɪs'pɪrɪtɪd] ADJ abbattuto(-a), scoraggiato(-a); (*sigh*) di avvilimento

dis·pir·it·ed·ly [dɪs'pɪrɪtɪdlɪ] ADV con aria abbattuta, con aria scoraggiata; (*speak*) con tono avvilito

dis·pir·it·ing [dɪs'pɪrɪtɪŋ] ADJ deprimente

dis·place [dɪs'pleɪs] VT (*move*) spostare; (*replace*) rimpiazzare, soppiantare; (*remove from office*) destituire; (*water: Naut*) dislocare; (*: Phys*) spostare

dis·placed per·son [dɪs'pleɪsd'pɜ:sn] N (*Pol*) profugo(-a)

dis·place·ment [dɪs'pleɪsmənt] N (*see vb*) spostamento; rimpiazzo; destituzione *f*; dislocamento

◎**dis·play** [dɪs'pleɪ] N **1** (*of goods for sale, paintings*) mostra, esposizione *f*; (*also:* **window display**) vetrina; (*of emotion*) manifestazione *f*; (*of strength, authority, force, interest*) dimostrazione *f*; (*pej: ostentation*) sfoggio, ostentazione *f*; **on display** (*gen*) in mostra; (*goods*) in vetrina; (*results, art*) esposto(-a); **a firework display** uno spettacolo di fuochi d'artificio; **display window** vetrina; **the assistant took the watch out of the display** il commesso ha preso l'orologio dalla vetrina **2** (*military display*) parata (militare) **3** (*computer display*) display *m inv*
■VT (*gen*) esporre; (*ostentatiously*) ostentare, far sfoggio di; (*emotion, ignorance*) mostrare, manifestare; (*notice, results*) affiggere; (*departure/arrival times*) indicare; **the watches displayed in the shop window** gli orologi esposti in vetrina; **she proudly displayed her medal** ha mostrato con orgoglio la sua medaglia

display advertisement N (*Press*) locandina

display advertising N (*Press*) pubblicità tabellare

dis·please [dɪs'pli:z] VT dispiacere a, scontentare; **displeased with** scontento(-a) di

dis·pleas·ing [dɪs'pli:zɪŋ] ADJ: **displeasing (to)** sgradevole (a)

dis·pleas·ure [dɪs'plɛʒəʳ] N: **displeasure (at)** dispiacere *m* (per)

dis·pos·able [dɪs'pəʊzəbl] ADJ (*not reusable: razor, camera*) usa e getta *inv*; **disposable income** reddito netto; **disposable nappy** (*Brit*) pannolino

dis·pos·al [dɪsˈpəʊzəl] N (*of rubbish*) eliminazione *f*, smaltimento; (*of property etc: by selling*) vendita; (*: by giving away*) cessione *f*; **to put sth at sb's disposal** mettere qc a disposizione di qn; **to have at one's disposal** avere a propria disposizione

dis·pose [dɪsˈpəʊz] VT (*frm: arrange: furniture*) disporre; (*: troops*) disporre, schierare
▶ **dispose of** VI + PREP **1** (*get rid of: unwanted goods, evidence, rubbish*) sbarazzarsi di, disfarsi di; (*Comm: sell*) vendere **2** (*deal with: matter, problem*) sistemare

dis·posed [dɪsˈpəʊzd] ADJ: **to be disposed to do sth** essere disposto(-a) a fare qc; **to be well disposed towards sb/sth** essere ben disposto(-a) verso qn/qc

dis·po·si·tion [ˌdɪspəˈzɪʃən] N (*frm*) **1** (*temperament*) indole *f*, temperamento; (*tendency*): **disposition to sth/to do sth** tendenza a qc/a fare qc, inclinazione *f*; **he was always of a nervous disposition** è sempre stato ansioso di carattere **2** (*arrangement*) disposizione *f*

dis·pos·sess [ˈdɪspəˈzɛs] VT: **to be dispossessed (of sth)** (*property*) essere spossessato(-a) (di qc)

dis·pro·por·tion [ˌdɪsprəˈpɔːʃən] N sproporzione *f*

dis·pro·por·tion·ate [ˌdɪsprəˈpɔːʃnɪt] ADJ: **disproportionate (to)** sproporzionato(-a) (a *or* rispetto a)

dis·pro·por·tion·ate·ly [ˌdɪsprəˈpɔːʃnɪtlɪ] ADV in modo sproporzionato; **disproportionately large** di una grandezza sproporzionata

dis·prove [dɪsˈpruːv] VT confutare

dis·put·able [dɪsˈpjuːtəbl] ADJ discutibile, contestabile

◎ **dis·pute** [dɪsˈpjuːt] N (*quarrel*) disputa; (*controversy*) discussione *f*, controversia; (*legal*) lite *f*; **a dispute between neighbours** una lite tra vicini; **industrial dispute** controversia sindacale; **beyond dispute** fuori discussione; **the company is in dispute with the government** la società è in disaccordo con il governo; **to be in dispute** (*matter*) essere in discussione; (*territory*) essere oggetto di contesa
■ VT **1** (*question: statement, claim*) contestare; **I don't dispute the fact** non contesto questo fatto **2** (*debate: matter, question*) discutere **3** (*compete for: possession, victory*) disputarsi
■ VI (*argue*): **to dispute (about** *or* **over)** discutere (su)

dis·put·ed [dɪsˈpjuːtɪd] ADJ (*territory*) contestato(-a)

dis·quali·fi·ca·tion [dɪsˌkwɒlɪfɪˈkeɪʃən] N (*from competition*) squalifica; (*of member*) espulsione *f*; (*Brit: from driving*) ritiro della patente

dis·quali·fy [dɪsˈkwɒlɪˌfaɪ] VT: **to disqualify sb (from)** (*from competition*) squalificare qn (da); **to disqualify sb from doing sth** vietare a qn di fare qc; **to disqualify sb from driving** (*Brit*) ritirare la patente a qn; **it disqualified him for the job** lo ha reso non adatto al lavoro

dis·qui·et [dɪsˈkwaɪət] N (*frm*) inquietudine *f*

dis·qui·et·ing [dɪsˈkwaɪətɪŋ] ADJ (*frm*) inquietante, allarmante

dis·re·gard [ˈdɪsrɪˈgɑːd] N (*indifference*): **disregard (for)** (*feelings*) insensibilità, indifferenza (verso); (*danger*) sprezzo (di); (*money*) disprezzo (di); (*non-observance*): **disregard (of)** (*law, rules*) inosservanza (di)
■ VT (*remark, feelings, fact*) ignorare, non tenere conto di; (*duty*) trascurare; (*authority*) non curarsi di

dis·re·pair [ˈdɪsrɪˈpɛəʳ] N cattivo stato; **to fall into disrepair** (*building*) andare in rovina; (*road*) deteriorarsi

dis·repu·table [dɪsˈrɛpjʊtəbl] ADJ (*person*) poco raccomandabile; (*clothing, behaviour*) indecente; (*area*) malfamato(-a), poco raccomandabile

dis·repu·tably [dɪsˈrɛpjʊtəblɪ] ADV (*behave, dress*) indecentemente

dis·re·pute [ˈdɪsrɪˈpjuːt] N: **to bring into disrepute** rovinare la reputazione di; **to fall into disrepute** rovinarsi la reputazione

dis·re·spect [ˈdɪsrɪsˈpɛkt] N mancanza di rispetto

dis·re·spect·ful [ˌdɪsrɪsˈpɛktfʊl] ADJ (*person*) poco rispettoso(-a); (*comment*) irriverente; **to be disrespectful to** *or* **towards** mancare di rispetto a *or* verso

dis·re·spect·ful·ly [ˌdɪsrɪsˈpɛktfəlɪ] ADV (*behave*) in modo irrispettoso; (*speak*) in modo irriverente

dis·rupt [dɪsˈrʌpt] VT (*meeting, lesson*) disturbare, interrompere; (*public transport*) creare il caos in; (*plans*) scombussolare

dis·rup·tion [dɪsˈrʌpʃən] N (*see vb*) interruzione *f*; caos *m*; scombussolamento; **the disruption of rail services** il caos dei servizi ferroviari

dis·rup·tive [dɪsˈrʌptɪv] ADJ (*pupil*) indisciplinato(-a); (*influence*) negativo(-a), deleterio(-a); (*strike action*) paralizzante

diss [dɪs] VT (*fam*) sputtanare

dis·sat·is·fac·tion [ˈdɪsˌsætɪsˈfækʃən] N scontentezza; **dissatisfaction (with)** insoddisfazione *f* (per), scontento (per *or* a causa di)

dis·sat·is·fied [ˈdɪsˈsætɪsfaɪd] ADJ: **dissatisfied (with)** insoddisfatto(-a) (di), scontento(-a) (di); **a dissatisfied customer** un cliente insoddisfatto; **we were dissatisfied with the service** non eravamo soddisfatti del servizio

dis·sect [dɪˈsɛkt] VT (*animal, body, specimen*) sezionare; (*fig*) sviscerare

dis·sec·tion [dɪˈsɛkʃən] N (*see vb*) dissezione *f*; sviscerамento

dis·sem·ble [dɪˈsɛmbl] VT, VI (*liter*) dissimulare

dis·semi·nate [dɪˈsɛmɪˌneɪt] VT (*information*) diffondere

dis·semi·na·tion [dɪˌsɛmɪˈneɪʃən] N diffusione *f*

dis·sen·sion [dɪˈsɛnʃən] N (*frm*) dissenso

dis·sent [dɪˈsɛnt] N dissenso
■ VI (*gen*): **to dissent (from)** dissentire (da)

dis·sent·er [dɪˈsɛntəʳ] N (*Rel, Pol*) dissidente *m/f*

dis·sent·ing [dɪˈsɛntɪŋ] ADJ dissenziente

dis·ser·ta·tion [ˌdɪsəˈteɪʃən] N (*Univ*) tesi *f inv*, dissertazione *f*

dis·ser·vice [ˈdɪsˈsɜːvɪs] N: **to do sb a disservice** rendere un cattivo servizio a qn

dis·si·dence [ˈdɪsɪdəns] N dissidenza

dis·si·dent [ˈdɪsɪdənt] (*Pol*) N dissidente *m/f*
■ ADJ (*speech, voice*) di dissenso; (*group*) dissidente

dis·simi·lar [ˈdɪˈsɪmɪləʳ] ADJ: **dissimilar (to)** dissimile (da), diverso(-a) (da); **two very dissimilar cases** due casi molto diversi tra loro

dis·simi·lar·ity [ˌdɪsɪmɪˈlærɪtɪ] N: **dissimilarity (between)** dissomiglianza (tra)

dis·simu·late [dɪˈsɪmjʊˌleɪt] VI (*frm*) dissimulare

dis·simu·la·tion [dɪˌsɪmjʊˈleɪʃən] N (*frm*) dissimulazione *f*

dis·si·pate [ˈdɪsɪˌpeɪt] VT (*frm*) dissipare

dis·si·pat·ed [ˈdɪsɪˌpeɪtɪd] ADJ (*person, life*) dissipato(-a); (*behaviour*) dissoluto(-a)

dis·si·pa·tion [ˌdɪsɪˈpeɪʃən] N (*frm: of fears*) dissolvimento; (*: of money, fortune, effort*) dissipazione *f*; (*debauchery*) dissolutezza

dis·so·ci·ate [dɪˈsəʊʃɪˌeɪt] VT: **to disassociate (from)** dissociare (da), separare (da); **to disassociate o.s. from** dichiarare di non avere niente a che fare con; (*from political line*) dissociarsi da

Dd

dis·so·cia·tion [dɪˌsəʊsɪˈeɪʃən] N dissociazione *f*
dis·so·lute [ˈdɪsəˌluːt] ADJ dissoluto(-a)
dis·so·lute·ly [ˈdɪsəˌluːtlɪ] ADV dissolutamente
dis·so·lu·tion [ˌdɪsəˈluːʃən] N (*of partnership, Pol*) scioglimento; (*decay*) dissoluzione *f*
dis·solve [dɪˈzɒlv] VT (*gen*) dissolvere, sciogliere; (*partnership, business, marriage, Pol*) sciogliere
■ VI dissolversi, sciogliersi; (*Pol*) sciogliersi; **it dissolves in water** si scioglie in acqua; **she dissolved into tears** si è sciolta in lacrime; **to dissolve into thin air** svanire nel nulla
dis·so·nance [ˈdɪsənəns] N (*frm*) dissonanza
dis·so·nant [ˈdɪsənənt] ADJ **1** (*Mus: chord, harmony*) dissonante **2** (*clashing: voices*) discordante; (*images*) discrepante
dis·suade [dɪˈsweɪd] VT: **to dissuade sb (from doing)** dissuadere qn (dal fare), distogliere qn (dall'idea di fare)
dis·sua·sion [dɪˈsweɪʒən] N (*liter*) dissuasione *f*
dis·sua·sive [dɪˈsweɪsɪv] (*liter*) ADJ (*person*) che cerca di dissuadere; (*powers*) di dissuasione
distaff side [ˈdɪstɑːfˌsaɪd] N: **on the distaff side** per parte di madre
◎ **dis·tance** [ˈdɪstəns] N (*between two things*) distanza; **the distance between the houses** la distanza *or* lo spazio tra le case; **it's a good distance** dista un bel po', è parecchio lontano; **it's within walking distance** ci si arriva a piedi; **a distance of forty kilometres** una distanza di quaranta chilometri; **at a distance of 2 metres** a 2 metri di distanza; **in the distance** in lontananza; **from a distance** da lontano; **distance race** gara di fondo; **distance runner** fondista *m/f*; **distance ratio** rapporto di distanza; **at this distance in time** a distanza di tanto tempo; **to keep sb at a distance** tenere qn a distanza; **to keep one's distance** tenersi a distanza
■ VT (*fig*) allontanare; **to distance o.s from** allontanarsi da, staccarsi da
dis·tant [ˈdɪstənt] ADJ (*gen*) lontano(-a); (*country*) distante, lontano(-a); (*likeness*) vago(-a), lontano(-a); (*fig: aloof: manner, person*) distaccato(-a); **in the distant past/future** nel lontano passato/futuro
dis·tant·ly [ˈdɪstəntlɪ] ADV (*smile, say*) con distacco; (*resemble*) vagamente; **we are distantly related** siamo lontani parenti
dis·taste [ˈdɪsˈteɪst] N: **distaste (for)** ripugnanza (per)
dis·taste·ful [dɪsˈteɪstfʊl] ADJ sgradevole, ripugnante; **the very idea is distasteful to me** la sola idea mi ripugna
Dist. Atty. ABBR (*Am*) = district attorney
dis·tem·per[1] [dɪsˈtɛmpəʳ] N (*paint*) tempera
dis·tem·per[2] [dɪsˈtɛmpəʳ] N (*disease*) cimurro
dis·tend [dɪsˈtɛnd] VT dilatare
■ VI dilatarsi
dis·tend·ed [dɪsˈtɛndɪd] ADJ (*stomach*) dilatato(-a)
dis·til, (*Am*) **dis·till** [dɪsˈtɪl] VT distillare; **distilled water** acqua distillata
dis·til·la·tion [ˌdɪstɪˈleɪʃən] N distillazione *f*
dis·till·er [dɪsˈtɪləʳ] N (*person*) distillatore(-trice); (*company*) distilleria
dis·till·ery [dɪsˈtɪlərɪ] N distilleria
dis·tinct [dɪsˈtɪŋkt] ADJ **1** (*different: species, type*): **distinct (from)** diverso(-a) (da), distinto(-a) (da); **the book is divided into two distinct parts** il libro si divide in due parti distinte; **as distinct from** a differenza di **2** (*clear*) (: *sound, shape*) chiaro(-a), distinto(-a); (*unmistakable: increase, change*) palese, netto(-a); (*definite: preference, progress, feeling*) definito(-a)
dis·tinc·tion [dɪsˈtɪŋkʃən] N (*difference*) distinzione *f*, differenza; (*mark of honour*) onorificenza; **a writer of distinction** un eminente scrittore; **to make** *or* **draw a distinction between** fare (una) distinzione tra; **she got a distinction in English** (*Scol*) ha avuto il massimo dei voti in inglese; (*Univ*) ≈ ha ottenuto la lode
dis·tinc·tive [dɪsˈtɪŋktɪv] ADJ tutto(-a) particolare
dis·tinc·tive·ly [dɪsˈtɪŋktɪvlɪ] ADV in modo tutto particolare
dis·tinct·ly [dɪsˈtɪŋktlɪ] ADV (*see, hear*) distintamente; (*promise, remember*) chiaramente; (*prefer*) nettamente; (*better, odd*) decisamente
dis·tin·guish [dɪsˈtɪŋgwɪʃ] VT distinguere, discernere; **he could just distinguish the form of a man** riusciva a malapena a distinguere la sagoma di un uomo; **he can't distinguish red from green** non distingue il rosso dal verde; **to distinguish o.s. (as)** distinguersi (come)
■ VI: **to distinguish (between)** distinguere (tra)
dis·tin·guish·able [dɪsˈtɪŋgwɪʃəbl] ADJ (*discernible*) distinguibile; **they were barely distinguishable from each other** si riusciva a distinguerli a malapena
dis·tin·guished [dɪsˈtɪŋgwɪʃt] ADJ (*eminent: pianist, writer*) eminente, noto(-a); (: *scholar*) insigne; (: *career*) brillante; (*refined*) distinto(-a), signorile
dis·tin·guish·ing [dɪsˈtɪŋgwɪʃɪŋ] ADJ (*marks, characteristics, features*) distintivo(-a), caratteristico(-a)
dis·tort [dɪsˈtɔːt] VT (*also fig*) distorcere; (*face, also Tech*) deformare; (*account, news*) falsare; **the media distort reality** i mass media distorcono la realtà; **a distorted impression** una falsa impressione
dis·tor·tion [dɪsˈtɔːʃən] N (*gen*) distorsione *f*; (*of truth*) alterazione *f*; (*of facts*) travisamento; (*Tech*) deformazione *f*
dis·tract [dɪsˈtrækt] VT (*person*): **to distract sb (from sth)** distrarre qn (da qc); **to distract sb's attention (from sth)** distrarre *or* sviare l'attenzione di qn (da qc)
dis·tract·ed [dɪsˈtræktɪd] ADJ (*confused*) confuso(-a); (*inattentive*) distratto(-a); **to drive sb distracted** far impazzire qn
dis·tract·ed·ly [dɪsˈtræktɪdlɪ] ADV distrattamente
dis·tract·ing [dɪsˈtræktɪŋ] ADJ: **to be distracting** deconcentrare, distrarre; **I find the noise very distracting** il rumore mi disturba molto
dis·trac·tion [dɪsˈtrækʃən] N **1** (*interruption*) distrazione *f*; (*entertainment*) distrazione, diversivo; **a distraction from our concerns** una distrazione dalle nostre preoccupazioni **2** (*distress, madness*): **to drive sb to distraction** far impazzire qn
dis·traint [dɪsˈtreɪnt] N (*Law*) pignoramento
dis·traught [dɪsˈtrɔːt] ADJ stravolto(-a), sconvolto(-a)
dis·tress [dɪsˈtrɛs] N **1** (*mental anguish*) angoscia, pena; (*pain*) dolore *m*; **to be in great distress** essere sconvolto(-a) *or* affranto(-a) dal dolore; **to cause someone distress** arrecare sofferenza a qualcuno **2** (*poverty*) bisogno **3** (*danger*) pericolo; **in distress** (*Brit: ship*) in difficoltà, in pericolo
■ VT addolorare, affliggere
dis·tressed [dɪsˈtrɛst] ADJ (*upset*) addolorato(-a); (*poor*) bisognoso(-a); **distressed area** zona sinistrata
dis·tress·ing [dɪsˈtrɛsɪŋ] ADJ penoso(-a), doloroso(-a)
distress signal N segnale *m* di richiesta di soccorso
dis·trib·ute [dɪsˈtrɪˌbjuːt] VT (*leaflets, prizes, load*) distribuire; (*tasks*) ripartire

◎**dis·tri·bu·tion** [dɪstrɪˈbjuːʃən] N distribuzione *f*; **distribution costs** costi *mpl* di distribuzione

dis·tribu·tive [dɪsˈtrɪbjʊtɪv] ADJ (*Comm, Gram*) distributivo(-a); **distributive law** (*Math*) legge *f* di distribuzione

dis·tribu·tor [dɪsˈtrɪbjʊtəʳ] N **1** (*Comm*) concessionario; (*Cine*) distributore *m* **2** (*Aut, Tech*) distributore *m*; **distributor cap** calotta dello spinterogeno

◎**dis·trict** [ˈdɪstrɪkt] N (*of country*) regione *f*; (*of town*) quartiere *m*; (*administrative area*) distretto; **the shopping district** la zona dei negozi; **district manager** responsabile *m* di zona

district attorney N (*Am*) ≈ Procuratore *m* della Repubblica

district council N (*Brit*) *organo amministrativo locale*

DISTRICT COUNCIL

In Inghilterra e in Galles, il **district council** è l'organo responsabile dell'amministrazione dei paesi più piccoli e dei distretti di campagna. È finanziato tramite una tassa locale e riceve un contributo da parte del governo. I **district councils** vengono eletti a livello locale ogni quattro anni. L'organo amministratico delle città è invece il "city council".

▷ www.lga.gov.uk/

district nurse N (*Brit*) infermiere(-a) (*che fa visite a domicilio*)

District of Co·lum·bia [-kəˈlʌmbɪə] N distretto della Columbia

DISTRICT OF COLUMBIA

Il distretto di Columbia, **District of Columbia**, è la sede del governo statunitense. È un distretto federale autonomo negli Stati Uniti orientali, vasto circa 180 kmq, che consiste esclusivamente nella capitale federale, Washington. Il nome è spesso abbreviato in **DC** e posposto al nome della capitale: Washington, **DC**.

▷ www.dc.gov/

dis·trust [dɪsˈtrʌst] N: **distrust (of)** diffidenza (verso), sfiducia (nei confronti di)
■VT diffidare di, non fidarsi di

dis·trust·ful [dɪsˈtrʌstfʊl] ADJ diffidente

dis·trust·ful·ly [dɪsˈtrʌstfəlɪ] ADV con diffidenza

dis·turb [dɪsˈtɜːb] VT **1** (*bother*) disturbare, importunare; (*inconvenience*) scomodare; **sorry to disturb you** scusi se la disturbo; **"please do not disturb"** "non disturbare" **2** (*worry: person*) turbare; (*disrupt: sleep, order, meeting*) turbare, disturbare; (*ruffle: water*) turbare **3** (*disarrange: papers*) scompigliare; (*move*) spostare

dis·turb·ance [dɪsˈtɜːbəns] N **1** (*uneasiness, upset*) turbamento; (*interruption*) interruzione *f*; **sleep disturbance** disturbi del sonno **2** (*social, political*) disordini *mpl*, tumulto; (*affray*) tafferuglio

disturbance of the peace N (*Law*) disturbo alla quiete pubblica

dis·turbed [dɪsˈtɜːbd] ADJ turbato(-a); **he was disturbed to hear that ...** lo ha preoccupato la notizia che...; **to be emotionally disturbed** (*Psych*) avere problemi emotivi; **to be mentally disturbed** (*Psych*) essere malato(-a) di mente

dis·turb·ing [dɪsˈtɜːbɪŋ] ADJ inquietante

dis·turb·ing·ly [dɪsˈtɜːbɪŋlɪ] ADV in modo inquietante

dis·unite [ˌdɪsjʊˈnaɪt] VT (*frm: government, political party*) creare divisioni all'interno di

dis·unity [dɪsˈjuːnɪtɪ] N (*frm*): **disunity (in** *or* **within/among)** disunione *f* (in *or* all'interno di/fra)

dis·use [ˈdɪsˈjuːs] N: **to fall into disuse** cadere in disuso

dis·used [ˈdɪsˈjuːzd] ADJ abbandonato(-a), in disuso

ditch [dɪtʃ] N fosso; (*irrigation channel*) fosso *or* canale *m* d'irrigazione
■VT (*fam: get rid of: car*) abbandonare, mollare; (*: person*) piantare, mollare; **she's just ditched her boyfriend** ha appena mollato il suo ragazzo

ditch·water [ˈdɪtʃˌwɔːtəʳ] N: **(as) dull as ditchwater** (*fam*) noioso(-a) da morire

dith·er [ˈdɪðəʳ] (*fam*) N: **to be in a dither** essere in agitazione
■VI titubare; **to dither over a decision** tentennare di fronte a una decisione

dit·to [ˈdɪtəʊ] N (*in lists*) idem come sopra; **ditto marks** virgolette *fpl*; **a coffee, please — ditto (for me)** (*fam*) per me caffè — per me idem
■ADV (*likewise*): **I'm really fed up — ditto!** sono proprio stufa — anch'io!

dit·ty [ˈdɪtɪ] N canzoncina

dit·zy, ditsy [ˈdɪtsɪ] ADJ (*fam*) svampito(-a)

di·uret·ic [ˌdaɪjʊˈrɛtɪk] ADJ diuretico(-a)
■N diuretico

di·van [dɪˈvæn] N divano; **divan bed** divano *m* letto *inv*

dive [daɪv] N **1** (*of swimmer, goalkeeper*) tuffo; (*of submarine*) immersione *f*; (*Aer*) picchiata **2** (*pej fam: club etc*) bettola, buco
■VI **1** (*swimmer*): **to dive (into)** tuffarsi (in); (*submarine*) immergersi; (*Aer*) scendere in picchiata; (*Ftbl*) tuffarsi **2** (*fam: move quickly*): **to dive into** (*doorway, hole*) buttarsi dentro; (*car, taxi*) saltare su; **he dived into the crowd** si tuffò *or* si lanciò tra la folla; **he dived for cover** si è buttato al riparo; **he dived for the exit** si è lanciato *or* precipitato verso l'uscita

dive-bomb [ˈdaɪvˌbɒm] VT (*town etc*) bombardare in picchiata; **dive-bombing** bombardamento in picchiata

div·er [ˈdaɪvəʳ] N **1** (*swimmer*) tuffatore(-trice); (*deep-sea diver*) palombaro; **diver's buoy** segnasub *m inv* **2** (*Zool*) strolaga

di·verge [daɪˈvɜːdʒ] VI divergere

di·ver·gence [daɪˈvɜːdʒəns] N divergenza

di·ver·gent [daɪˈvɜːdʒənt] ADJ divergente

di·verse [daɪˈvɜːs] ADJ svariato(-a), vario(-a)

di·ver·si·fi·ca·tion [ˈdaɪˌvɜːsɪfɪˈkeɪʃən] N diversificazione *f*

di·ver·si·fy [daɪˈvɜːsɪfaɪ] VT rendere vario(-a); (*Comm*) diversificare
■VI (*Comm*) diversificarsi

di·ver·sion [daɪˈvɜːʃən] N (*Brit Aut*) deviazione *f*; (*of river*) diversione; (*distraction*) divertimento; (*old: pastime*) diversivo, distrazione *f*; **to create a diversion** creare un'azione diversiva

di·ver·sion·ary tac·tics [daɪˈvɜːʃnərɪˈtæktɪks] NPL tattica *fsg* diversiva

di·ver·sity [daɪˈvɜːsɪtɪ] N varietà *f inv*, diversità *f inv*

di·vert [daɪˈvɜːt] VT **1** (*traffic, river*) deviare; (*conversation, attention, person*) sviare; (*train, plane*) dirottare **2** (*old: amuse*) distrarre, divertire

Dd

di·vest [daɪ'vɛst] VT (*frm*): **to divest of** spogliare di
◎ **di·vide** [dɪ'vaɪd] VT: **to divide (from/into)** dividere (da/in); **divide the pastry in half** dividete la pasta a metà; **to divide (between** *or* **among)** dividere (tra), ripartire (tra); **to divide 6 into 36** *or* **36 by 6** dividere 36 per 6; **40 divided by 5** 40 diviso 5
■ VI (*road, river*) dividersi, biforcarsi; (*Math*) essere divisibile; **we divided into two groups** ci siamo divisi in due gruppi
▸ **divide off** VI + ADV (*road*) separarsi
■ VT + ADV (*area*) separare
▸ **divide out** VT + ADV: **to divide out (between** *or* **among)** (*sweets, proceeds*) distribuire (tra); (*tasks*) distribuire *or* ripartire (tra)
▸ **divide up** VT + ADV dividere
di·vid·ed [dɪ'vaɪdɪd] ADJ (*country, couple*) diviso(-a); **divided opinions** opinioni *fpl* discordi; **to be divided in one's mind about sth** essere indeciso(-a) su qc
divided highway N (*Am*) strada a doppia carreggiata
divided skirt N gonna *f* pantalone *inv*
◎ **divi·dend** ['dɪvɪˌdɛnd] N (*Fin*) dividendo
di·vid·ers [dɪ'vaɪdəz] NPL (*Math*) compasso a punte fisse
di·vid·ing [dɪ'vaɪdɪŋ] ADJ (*fence, wall, line*) divisorio(-a)
di·vine [dɪ'vaɪn] ADJ (*Rel, fig*) (*old*) divino(-a); **what divine weather!** che tempo favoloso!
■ VT (*future*) divinare, predire; (*truth*) indovinare; (*water*) individuare (*tramite rabdomanzia*)
di·vine·ly [dɪ'vaɪnlɪ] ADV divinamente
di·vin·er [dɪ'vaɪnə[r]] N (*water diviner*) rabdomante *m/f*
divine right N (*fam*) diritto divino
div·ing ['daɪvɪŋ] N tuffi *mpl*
diving bell N campana da palombaro
diving board N trampolino
diving suit N scafandro
di·vin·ing rod [dɪ'vaɪnɪŋˌrɒd] N bacchetta
di·vin·ity [dɪ'vɪnɪtɪ] N divinità *f inv*; (*as study*) teologia
di·vi·sible [dɪ'vɪzəbl] ADJ: **divisible (by)** divisibile (per)
◎ **di·vi·sion** [dɪ'vɪʒən] N (*gen*) divisione *f*; (*Brit Ftbl*) serie *f inv*; **the division into two states** la divisione in due stati; **the sales division** il reparto vendite; **First Division** serie A; **to call a division** (*Parliament*) procedere alla votazione, passare ai voti
di·vi·sion·al [dɪ'vɪʒənl] ADJ di divisione
division of labour N divisione *f* del lavoro
division sign N (*Math*) segno di divisione
di·vi·sive [dɪ'vaɪsɪv] ADJ che causa discordia
di·vi·sor [dɪ'vaɪzə[r]] N (*Math*) divisore *m*
◎ **di·vorce** [dɪ'vɔ:s] N divorzio; **divorce proceedings** pratiche *fpl* per il divorzio
■ VI divorziare
■ VT divorziare da; (*fig*) separare; **she divorced him last year** ha divorziato da lui l'anno scorso
divorcé [dɪ'vɔ:seɪ] N divorziato
di·vorced [dɪ'vɔ:st] ADJ divorziato(-a)
di·vor·cee [dɪˌvɔ:'si:] N divorziata
div·ot ['dɪvɪt] N (*Golf*) zolla di terra (*sollevata accidentalmente*)
di·vulge [daɪ'vʌldʒ] VT divulgare, rivelare; (*evidence, information*) rendere pubblico(-a)
DIY [ˌdi:aɪ'waɪ] (*Brit*: = **do-it-yourself**) N ABBR fai da te *m*
■ ADJ ABBR di fai da te
diz·zi·ly ['dɪzɪlɪ] ADV (*spin, rise, fall*) vertiginosamente; (*walk*) con un senso di vertigine
diz·zi·ness ['dɪzɪnɪs] N capogiro, vertigini *fpl*; **an attack of dizziness** un capogiro
diz·zy ['dɪzɪ] ADJ (*height*) vertiginoso(-a); **I am** *or* **feel dizzy** ho il capogiro, mi gira la testa; **to make sb dizzy** far girare la testa a qn; **the height made me dizzy** la grande altezza mi ha dato le vertigini
DJ [di:'dʒeɪ] N ABBR (= **disc jockey**) DJ *m/f inv*, disc jockey *m/f inv*
dj [di:'dʒeɪ] N ABBR = **dinner jacket**
Dja·kar·ta [dʒə'kɑ:tə] N Giacarta
DJIA ['di:dʒeɪaɪ'eɪ] N ABBR (*Am Stock Exchange*: = **Dow-Jones Industrial Average**) indice *m* Dow-Jones
dl ABBR (= **decilitre**) dl
DLitt, **DLit** [di:'lɪt] N ABBR = *Doctor of Literature, Doctor of Letters*
DLO [di:ɛl'əʊ] N ABBR = **dead-letter office**
dm ABBR (= **decimetre**) dm
DMus ABBR = *Doctor of Music*
DMZ [di:ɛm'zɛd] N ABBR = **demilitarized zone**
DNA [di:ɛn'eɪ] N ABBR (= **deoxyribonucleic acid**) DNA *m inv*
DNA test N test *m inv* del DNA

◎ **do**[1] [du:] KEYWORD
(*3rd pers sg present* **does**, *pt* **did**) (*pp* **done**)
■ AUX VB
1 **do you speak English?** parla inglese?; **do you understand?** capisci?; **I don't understand** non capisco; **do you want some?** ne vuoi?; **didn't you ask?** non (l')hai chiesto?; **didn't you know?** non lo sapevi?; **he didn't laugh** non ha riso
2 (*for emphasis*): **DO come!** dai, vieni!; **so you DO know him!** dunque è vero che lo conosci!; **but I DO like it!** sì che mi piace!; **DO shut up!** ma sta' zitto!; **DO sit down** (*polite*) si accomodi la prego, prego si sieda; (*annoyed*) insomma siediti; **DO tell me!** su, dimmelo!; **I DO wish I could ...** magari potessi...
3 (*used to avoid repeating verb*): **neither do we** nemmeno noi; **he doesn't like it and neither do we** a lui non piace e a noi nemmeno; **so does he** anche lui; **you speak better than I do** parli meglio di me
4 (*in question tags*): **he lives here, doesn't he?** abita qui, vero?, abita qui, no?; **I don't know him, do I?** non lo conosco, vero?
5 (*in answers, replacing verb*): **do you speak English?** — **yes, I do/no, I don't** parli inglese? — sì /no; **do you agree?** — **I do** è d'accordo? — sì ; **may I come in?** — **please do!** posso entrare? — certo!; **who made this mess?** — **I did** chi ha fatto questo disordine? — io!, sono stato io!; **do you really?** davvero?, ah sì ?
■ VT
1 (*gen*) fare; **I'll do all I can** farò tutto il possibile; **I've got nothing to do** non ho niente da fare; **I shall do nothing of the sort** non farò niente del genere; **that's done it!** (*fam*) sono fregato! (*or* siamo fregati! *etc*); **have you done the washing?** hai fatto il bucato?; **I'm going to do the washing up** adesso faccio i piatti; **well done!** bravo!, benissimo!; **what are you doing tonight?** che fai stasera?; **what does he do for a living?** cosa fa per vivere?; **what am I to do with you?** dimmi tu come devo fare con te!; **what can I do for you?** (*in shop*) desidera?; **what's to be done?** che fare?; **what's done cannot be undone** quello che è fatto è fatto; **it will have to be done again** è tutto da rifare
2 **I'll do the flowers** i fiori li sistemo io; **who does your hair?** chi ti fa i capelli?; **to do Italian** fare italiano; **to do one's nails** farsi le unghie; **she does her guests proud** i suoi ospiti li tratta da principi; **this room needs doing** questa stanza è ancora da fare; **to do Shakespeare** (*Scol*) fare Shakespeare; **to do**

one's teeth pulirsi i denti
3 (*only as past tense, past participle: finish*): **the job's done** il lavoro è fatto; **I haven't done telling you** (*fam*) non ho ancora finito la storia
4 (*visit: city, museum*) fare, visitare
5 (*Aut*) fare; **the car was doing 100 (mph)** ≈ la macchina faceva i 160 (km/h); **we've done 200 km already** abbiamo già fatto 200 km
6 (*fam: be sufficient*) bastare; (*: be suitable*) andar bene; **that won't do him** questo non gli basta; **that'll do me nicely** per me va benissimo
7 (*play role of*) fare (la parte di); (*mimic*) imitare
8 (*fam: cheat*) imbrogliare, farla a; (*: rob*) ripulire; **to do sb out of sth** fregare qc a qn; **he did her out of a job** le ha fregato *or* soffiato il posto; **I've been done!** mi hanno fregato!
9 (*Culin*) fare; **to do the cooking** cucinare; **how do you like your steak done?** come preferisci la bistecca?; **the meat's done** la carne è pronta; **done to a turn** (*meat*) cotto(-a) a puntino; **well done** ben cotto(-a)
■ VI
1 (*act*) fare, agire; **do as I do** fai come me, fai come faccio io; **he did well to take your advice** ha fatto bene a seguire il tuo consiglio
2 (*get on, fare*) andare; **he's doing badly at school** va male a scuola; **how are you doing?** (*fam*) come va?; **how do you do?** (*in introductions*) piacere; **she did well at university** era molto brava all'università; **his business is doing well** gli affari gli vanno bene
3 (*finish: in past tenses only*): **I've done** ho fatto, ho finito; **have you done?** hai fatto?, hai finito?; **hasn't he done with that book yet?** ancora non ha finito con quel libro?
4 (*suit*) andare bene; **this coat will do as a cover** questo cappotto potrà fare da coperta; **to make do (with)** arrangiarsi (con); **you'll have to make do with £10** dovrai arrangiarti con 10 sterline; **this room will do** questa stanza va bene; **will it do?** andrà bene?; **that will never do!** non se ne parla nemmeno!; **will it do if I come back at 8?** va bene se torno alle 8?; **it doesn't do to upset her** è meglio non agitarla
5 (*be sufficient*) bastare; **will £5 do?** bastano *or* vanno bene 5 sterline?;; **that'll do** basta così ; **that'll do!** (*in annoyance*) ora basta!
■ N (*fam*)
1 (*party*) festa; (*formal gathering*) ricevimento; **it was rather a grand do** è stato un ricevimento piuttosto imponente; **we're having a little do on Saturday** facciamo una festicciola sabato
2 (*in phrases*): **the dos and don'ts** le regole del gioco; **fair dos!** (*be fair*) quel che è giusto è giusto!; **it's a poor do** è brutto segno
▸ **do away with** VT + PREP (*abolish*) abolire; (*kill*) far fuori
▸ **do by** VI + PREP: **to do well/badly by sb** comportarsi bene/male con qn; **to be hard done by** essere *or* venire trattato(-a) male
▸ **do down** VT + ADV (*fam*) screditare; **don't do yourself down!** non sminuirti!
▸ **do for** VI + PREP
1 (*finish off: project*) mandare all'aria; (*: person*) spacciare; **he's done for!** è spacciato!
2 (*Brit old: clean for*) fare i servizi per
▸ **do in** VT + ADV (*fam: kill*) far fuori
▸ **do out** VT + ADV (*room*) fare
▸ **do over** VT + ADV (*fam*)
1 (*Am: do again: work, essay*) rifare; (*: redecorate: house*) rimettere a posto (*pitturare, tapezzare etc*)
2 (*Brit: rob: house*) ripulire
3 (*Brit: hurt*) pestare
▸ **do up** VT + ADV
1 (*dress,shoes*) allacciare; (*zip*) tirar su; (*buttons*) abbottonare; **books done up in paper** libri impacchettati
2 (*renovate: house,room*) rimettere a nuovo, rifare; **to do o.s. up** farsi bello(-a)
▸ **do with** VT + PREP
1 (*with could: need*) avere bisogno di; **I could do with some help** mi servirebbe una mano; **I could do with a drink** un bicchierino non guasterebbe; **it could do with a wash** una lavata non gli farebbe male
2 **what has that got to do with it?** che c'entra?; **it has to do with ...** ha a che vedere *or* fare con...; **money has a lot to do with it** è una questione di soldi; **that has nothing to do with you!** non sono affari tuoi!, non ti riguarda!; **I won't have anything to do with it** non voglio aver niente a che farci
3 **what have you done with my slippers?** cosa hai fatto delle mie pantofole?; **what did he do with the cat?** che ne ha fatto del gatto?; **what's he done with his hair?** che si è fatto ai capelli?
▸ **do without**
■ VI + PREP fare a meno di
■ VI + ADV fare senza

do² [dəʊ] N (*Mus*) do *m inv*
do. ABBR = **ditto**
DOA [ˌdiːəʊ'eɪ] ABBR (= **dead on arrival**) morto(-a) durante il trasporto
do·able ['duːəbl] ADJ (*fam*) fattibile
d.o.b. ABBR = **date of birth**; *see* **date**
Do·ber·man ['dəʊbəmən] N (*also:* **Doberman pinscher**) dobermann *m inv*
doc [dɒk] N (*fam*) dottore(-essa)
doc·ile ['dəʊsaɪl] ADJ docile
do·cil·ity [dəʊ'sɪlɪtɪ] N docilità
dock¹ [dɒk] N (*Naut*) bacino; (*: wharf*) molo; (*: for repairs*) darsena; **docks** dock *m inv*, porto; **dock dues** diritti *mpl* di banchina
■ VT mettere in bacino
■ VI entrare in bacino
dock² [dɒk] N (*in court*) banco degli imputati
dock³ [dɒk] VT 1 (*tail*) mozzare 2 (*pay*) decurtare
dock⁴ [dɒk] N (*Bot*) romice *m*
dock·er ['dɒkəʳ] N scaricatore *m* (di porto), portuale *m*
dock·et ['dɒkɪt] N (*on parcel etc*) etichetta, cartellino
dock·ing ['dɒkɪŋ] N 1 (*of animals*) taglio della coda 2 (*of space vehicle*) aggancio
docking station N (*Comput*) docking station *f inv*
dock·land ['dɒkˌlænd] N, **dock·lands** ['dɒkˌlændz] NPL zona portuale
dock·side ['dɒkˌsaɪd] N: **the dockside** i docks *mpl*
dock·yard ['dɒkˌjɑːd] N cantiere *m* (navale)
◎ **doc·tor** ['dɒktəʳ] N 1 (*Med*) dottore(-essa), medico; **Doctor Brown** il Dottor Brown; **doctor's office** (*Am*) studio medico, ambulatorio 2 (*Univ: Ph.D.*) dottore(-essa); **Doctor of Philosophy** (*degree*) ≈ dottorato di ricerca (*person*) ≈ titolare *m/f* di un dottorato di ricerca
■ VT 1 (*interfere with: food, drink*) adulterare; (*: text, document*) alterare, manipolare 2 (*treat: cold*) curare 3 (*fam: castrate: cat*) castrare
doc·tor·ate ['dɒktərɪt] N ≈ dottorato di ricerca

Dd

DOCTORATE

Il **doctorate** è il riconoscimento accademico più prestigioso in tutti i campi del sapere e viene conferito in seguito alla presentazione di una tesi originale di fronte ad una commissione di esperti. Generalmente tale tesi è un compendio del lavoro svolto durante più anni di studi. *See also* **Bachelor's degree; Master's degree**

▷ www.dfes.gov.uk/hegateway/
▷ http://educationusa.state.gov/graduate/about.htm
▷ www.aucc.ca/can_uni/general_info/degrees_e.html
▷ www.internationaleducationmedia.com/newzealand/
▷ www.southafrica.info/ess_info/sa_glance/education/education.htm

doc·tri·naire [ˌdɒktrɪˈnɛəʳ] ADJ (*pej*) dottrinario(-a)

doc·tri·nal [dɒkˈtraɪnl] ADJ dottrinale

doc·trine [ˈdɒktrɪn] N dottrina

docu·dra·ma [dɒkjʊˈdrɑːmə] N (*TV*) ricostruzione *f* filmata

◎ **docu·ment** [*n* ˈdɒkjʊmənt; *vb* ˈdɒkjʊmɛnt] N documento; **document case** cartella, borsa portadocumenti; **document wallet** cartelletta
■ VT documentare

docu·men·tary [ˌdɒkjʊˈmɛntərɪ] ADJ documentario(-a); (*evidence*) documentato(-a); **documentary letter of credit** lettera di credito contro documenti
■ N (*Cine, TV*) documentario

docu·men·ta·tion [ˌdɒkjʊmɛnˈteɪʃən] N documentazione *f*

docu·soap [ˈdɒkjʊˌsəʊp] N (*Brit: TV*) *documentario sulla vita quotidiana di un gruppo di persone*

DOD [ˌdiːəʊˈdiː] N ABBR (*Am*) = *Department of Defense*; *see* **defense**

dod·der [ˈdɒdəʳ] VI camminare con passo malfermo

dod·der·er [ˈdɒdərəʳ] N (*fam*) vecchio(-a) decrepito(-a), rudere *m*

dod·der·ing [ˈdɒdərɪŋ], **dod·dery** [ˈdɒdərɪ] ADJ malfermo(-a) sulle gambe

dod·dle [ˈdɒdəl] N (*Brit fam*): **it's a doddle** è un gioco da ragazzi

Do·deca·nese [ˌdəʊdɪkəˈniːz] NPL: **the Dodecanese** il Dodecanneso; **the Dodecanese Islands** le isole del Dodecanneso

dodge [dɒdʒ] N (*fam: trick*) espediente *m*, trucco; **a tax dodge** un trucchetto per evadere le tasse
■ VT (*blow, missile*) schivare; (*pursuer, question, difficulty*) eludere; (*tax*) evadere; (*work, duty*) sottrarsi a; **to dodge the issue** girare intorno all'argomento
■ VI scansarsi; (*Sport*) fare una schivata; **to dodge out of the way** scansarsi; **to dodge through the traffic** destreggiarsi nel traffico; **to dodge behind a tree** nascondersi dietro un albero

dodg·ems [ˈdɒdʒəmz] NPL (*also:* **dodgem cars**) autoscontro *msg*

dodgy [ˈdɒdʒɪ] ADJ (*comp* **-ier**, *superl* **-iest**) (*fam: plan*) azzardato(-a), rischioso(-a); (*: deal*) sospetto(-a), poco chiaro(-a); (*: person*) losco(-a); **a dodgy character** un tipo losco; **we're in a dodgy situation** navighiamo in cattive acque

dodo [ˈdəʊdəʊ] N **1** (*Zool*) dodo; **as dead as a dodo** morto(-a) e sepolto(-a) **2** (*fam: fool*) scemo(-a)

DOE [ˌdiːəʊˈiː] N ABBR (*Am*) = *Department of Energy*; *see* **energy**

doe [dəʊ] N (*deer*) femmina di daino; (*rabbit*) coniglia

doer [ˈduːəʳ] N tipo dinamico

does [dʌz] 3RD PERS SG PRESENT *of* **do**

◎ **doesn't** [ˈdʌznt] = **does not**

doff [dɒf] VT (*old: hat, coat*) togliere; **to doff one's hat to sb** levarsi il cappello davanti a qn

◎ **dog** [dɒg] N (*male*) cane *m*; (*female*) cagna; (*male fox, wolf*) maschio; **he's a lucky dog** (*fam*) è nato con la camicia; **every dog has its day** ognuno ha il suo momento di gloria; **he's a dog in the manger** *non lascia che gli altri si godano ciò che lui non può godersi*; **to go to the dogs** (*person*) lasciarsi andare, ridursi male; (*nation*) andare in malora; **it's a dog's life!** che vita da cani!; **he hasn't a dog's chance** non ha la benché minima probabilità (di successo)
■ VT (*follow closely*) pedinare; (*fig: subj: problems, injuries*) perseguitare; **dogged by ill luck** perseguitato(-a) dalla scalogna; **he dogs my footsteps** mi sta alle costole, mi sta alle calcagna
■ ADJ (*breed, show*) canino(-a); (*fox, wolf*) maschio; **dog biscuits** biscotti *mpl* per cani; **dog food** cibo per cani

dog collar N (*fam: clergyman's*) collarino; (*dog's*) collare *m*

dog-eared [ˈdɒgˌɪəd] ADJ (*book*) con orecchie

dog·fight [ˈdɒgˌfaɪt] N **1** (*planes*) combattimento ravvicinato fra aerei da caccia **2** (*dogs*) combattimento fra cani

dog-fish [ˈdɒgˌfɪʃ] N (*also:* **lesser spotted dog-fish**) gattuccio

dog·ged [ˈdɒgɪd] ADJ tenace, accanito(-a)

dog·ged·ly [ˈdɒgɪdlɪ] ADV tenacemente, accanitamente

dog·ger·el [ˈdɒgərəl] N poesia di scarso valore

dog·go [ˈdɒgəʊ] ADV (*fam*): **to lie doggo** fare il morto

dog·gone [ˈdɒgɒn] ADJ (*Am: fam*) dannato(-a)

dog·gy, **dog·gie** [ˈdɒgɪ] N (*fam*) cane *m*, cagnolino

doggy bag N sacchetto per gli avanzi da portare a casa

doggy paddle, **doggie paddle** N: **to do the doggy paddle** (*fam*) nuotare a cagnolino

dog·house [ˈdɒgˌhaʊs] N: **he's in the doghouse** (*fam*) è caduto in disgrazia

dog·leg [ˈdɒgˌlɛg] N (*in road*) curva a gomito

dog·ma [ˈdɒgmə] N dogma *m*

dog·mat·ic [dɒgˈmætɪk] ADJ (*person, attitude*) dogmatico(-a); (*tone*) autoritario(-a)

dog·mati·cal·ly [dɒgˈmætɪkəlɪ] ADV (*see adj*) dogmaticamente; con tono autoritario

do-gooder [ˈduːˈgʊdəʳ] N (*fam: pej*): **to be a do-gooder** fare il filantropo

dog paddle N = **doggy paddle**

dogs·body [ˈdɒgzˌbɒdɪ] N (*Brit fam*) tirapiedi *m/f inv*

dog-tired [ˌdɒgˈtaɪəd] ADJ (*fam*) stanco(-a) morto(-a)

dog·wood [ˈdɒgwʊd] N (*Bot*) corniolo

DoH [ˌdiːəʊˈeɪtʃ] N ABBR (*Brit*) = *Department of Health*; *see* **health**

doh [dəʊ] N (*Mus*) = **do²**

doi·ly, **doy·ley**, **doy·ly** [ˈdɔɪlɪ] N centrino di carta sottopiatto

do·ing [ˈduːɪŋ] N: **this is your doing** è opera tua!, sei stato tu!; **that takes some doing** non è una cosa facile

do·ings [ˈduːɪŋz] NPL **1** (*exploits*) imprese *fpl* **2** (*Brit fam: thing*): **that doings over there** quel coso là

do-it-yourself [ˈduːɪtjəˈsɛlf] N fai da te *m inv*, bricolage *m inv*; **do-it-yourself magazine** rivista di bricolage; **do-it-yourself store** negozio di bricolage

dol·drums [ˈdɒldrəmz] NPL (*fig*): **to be in the doldrums** (*person*) essere giù (di corda); (*business*) attraversare un momento difficile

dole [dəʊl] N (*Brit fam*) sussidio di disoccupazione; **to be on the dole** ricevere un sussidio di disoccupazione; **to go on the dole** fare domanda per il sussidio di disoccupazione
▶ **dole out** VT + ADV distribuire

dole·ful ['dəʊlfʊl] ADJ (*expression*) afflitto(-a); (*song, prospect*) triste

dole·ful·ly ['dəʊlfəlɪ] ADV (*see adj*) con aria afflitta; tristemente

doll [dɒl] N bambola; **doll's house** casa delle bambole
▶ **doll up** VT + ADV: **to doll o.s. up** (*fam*) farsi bello(-a); **to get (all) dolled up** mettersi in ghingheri

◎ **dol·lar** ['dɒlə^r] N dollaro; **dollar area** area del dollaro; **dollar bill** biglietto da un dollaro

dollar diplomacy N politica di penetrazione economica

dol·lop ['dɒləp] N (*of jam etc*) cucchiaiata

dol·ly ['dɒlɪ] N (*fam*) bambola

dol·men ['dɒlmɛn] N dolmen *m inv*

dol·phin ['dɒlfɪn] N (*Zool*) delfino

dolt [dəʊlt] N imbecille *m/f*

dolt·ish ['dəʊltɪʃ] ADJ (*person*) imbecille, stupido(-a); (*behaviour*) stupido(-a)

do·main [dəʊ'meɪn] N (*lands*) domini *mpl*; (*fig*) campo, sfera; (*Math*) dominio; **in the domain of art** nel campo dell'arte; **in the public domain** di dominio pubblico

domain name N (*Comput*) nome *m* di dominio

dome [dəʊm] N cupola

domed [dəʊmd] ADJ (*roof*) a cupola; (*forehead*) bombato(-a)

Domes·day Book ['du:mzdeɪˌbʊk] N (*Brit*) *libro del Catasto fatto compilare da Guglielmo il Conquistatore*
▷ www.historylearningsite.co.uk/domesday.htm
▷ www.nationalarchives.gov.uk/museum/item.asp?item_id=1

◎ **do·mes·tic** [də'mɛstɪk] ADJ **1** (*industry, flight*) nazionale; (*affairs, policy*) interno(-a); (*news*) dall'interno **2** (*chores, duties, animal*) domestico(-a); **domestic bliss** le gioie della famiglia; **domestic peace** pace in famiglia; **to be in domestic service** essere a servizio; **domestic servant** domestico(-a)
■ N (*cleaner*) inserviente *m/f*

do·mes·ti·cate [də'mɛstɪˌkeɪt] VT (*animal*) addomesticare

do·mes·ti·cat·ed [də'mɛstɪˌkeɪtɪd] ADJ (*animal*) addomesticato(-a); (*person*) casalingo(-a)

do·mes·ti·city [ˌdəʊmɛs'tɪsɪtɪ] N vita di famiglia

domestic science N economia domestica

domestic violence N violenza tre le mura domestiche

domi·cile ['dɒmɪˌsaɪl] N (*frm*) domicilio

domi·ciled ['dɒmɪˌsaɪld] ADJ (*frm*) domiciliato(-a)

domi·nance ['dɒmɪnəns] N (*influence*) influenza; (*pre-eminence*) predominio

domi·nant ['dɒmɪnənt] ADJ (*gen, Mus*) dominante; (*influence*) predominante

◎ **domi·nate** ['dɒmɪˌneɪt] VT, VI dominare

domi·na·tion [ˌdɒmɪ'neɪʃən] N dominazione *f*

domi·neer [ˌdɒmɪ'nɪə^r] VI: **to domineer (over)** fare il tiranno (con)

domi·neer·ing [ˌdɒmɪ'nɪərɪŋ] ADJ dispotico(-a), autoritario(-a)

Do·mini·can¹ [də'mɪnɪkən] ADJ, N (*Rel*) domenicano(-a)

Do·mini·can² [də'mɪnɪkən] ADJ, N (*Geog*) dominicano(-a)

Dominican Republic N Repubblica Dominicana

do·min·ion [də'mɪnɪən] N (*rule*) dominio, sovranità; (*territory*) dominio, possedimenti *mpl*; (*Brit Pol*) dominion *m inv*

domi·no ['dɒmɪnəʊ] N tessera del domino; **dominoes** NPL (*game*) domino *msg*

don¹ [dɒn] N (*Brit*) (*Univ*) docente *m/f* universitario(-a)

don² [dɒn] VT (*old: garment*) indossare

do·nate [dəʊ'neɪt] VT elargire; **he donated his collection to the museum** ha donato la sua collezione al museo

do·na·tion [dəʊ'neɪʃən] N elargizione *f*

◎ **done** [dʌn] PP *of* **do**

don·gle ['dɒŋgl] N (*Comput*) chiave *f* di protezione da copie illegali

don·key ['dɒŋkɪ] N asino(-a); **I've known him for donkey's years** (*fam*) lo conosco da secoli

donkey jacket N giaccone *m* pesante

donkey-work ['dɒŋkɪwɜ:k] N (*Brit fam*) *la parte meno interessante di un lavoro*

do·nor ['dəʊnə^r] N (*gen, Med*) donatore(-trice)

donor card N tessera di donatore di organi; ≈ tessera dell'A.I.D.O.

don't [dəʊnt] = **do not**

do·nut ['dəʊnʌt] N (*Am*) = **doughnut**

doo·dah ['du:dɑ:] (*Am*) **doo·dads** ['du:dæd], N (*fam*) coso

doo·dle ['du:dl] N scarabocchio
■ VI scarabocchiare

doom [du:m] N (*ruin*) rovina; (*fate*) destino; **impending doom** disastro incombente; **it's not all doom and gloom** non è tutto nero come sembra
■ VT (*destine*): **to doom (to)** condannare (a); **doomed to failure** destinato(-a) al fallimento

dooms·day ['du:mzˌdeɪ] N: **till doomsday** (*fig*) fino al giorno del giudizio

doomsday cult N setta apocalittica

◎ **door** [dɔ:^r] N (*gen*) porta; (*of vehicle*) sportello, portiera; (*of aircraft*) portello; **the first door on the right** la prima porta a destra; **at the door** alla porta; **"pay at the door"** "pagare all'entrata"; **front/back door** porta principale/di servizio; **3 doors down the street** 3 case più giù; **from door to door** di porta in porta

door·bell ['dɔ:ˌbɛl] N campanello

do-or-die ['du:ɔ:'daɪ] ADJ disperato(-a)

door-handle ['dɔ:ˌhændl] N maniglia della porta

door·keeper ['dɔ:ˌki:pə^r] N portiere *m*

door·knob ['dɔ:ˌnɒb] N pomello

door·man ['dɔ:ˌmæn] N (*pl* **-men**) (*in hotel*) portiere *m* (in livrea); (*in block of flats*) portinaio

door·mat ['dɔ:ˌmæt] N stoino, zerbino; (*fam: downtrodden person*) pezza da piedi

door·nail ['dɔ:ˌneɪl] N: **as dead as a doornail** morto(-a) stecchito(-a)

door·step ['dɔ:ˌstɛp] N gradino della porta, soglia; **on our doorstep** (*close by*) a un passo
■ VT: **to doorstep sb** recarsi a casa di qn per intervistarlo (*spesso contro la sua volontà*)

door-to-door ['dɔ:tə'dɔ:^r] ADJ (*selling*) porta a porta; (*salesman*) a domicilio

door·way ['dɔ:ˌweɪ] N porta; **in the doorway** nel vano della porta

dope [dəʊp] N **1** (*fam: drugs*) roba (*fam*); (*Sport*) droga; **he takes dope** si droga; **dope test** (controllo) anti-doping *m inv* **2** (*fam: information*) informazioni *fpl*; **to give sb the dope (on sth)** fare una soffiata a qn (su qc) **3** (*fam: stupid person*) tonto(-a)

Dd

■VT (*horse, person, drink*) drogare

dopey ['dəʊpɪ] (*fam*) ADJ (*comp* **-ier**, *superl* **-iest**) (*drugged*) inebetito(-a); (*stupid*) stupidotto(-a); (*sleepy*) addormentato(-a)

dop·ing ['dəʊpɪŋ] (*Sport*) N doping
■ADJ (*offence, allegation, charge*) di doping; (*scandal, test*) doping

Doppler effect ['dɒplərɪ,fɛkt] N (*Phys*) effetto Doppler

dor·mant ['dɔ:mənt] ADJ (*Bot, volcano*) quiescente; (*energy*) latente; **to lie dormant** (*fig*) rimanere latente

dor·mer ['dɔ:mə[r]] N (*also:* **dormer window**) abbaino

dor·mi·tory ['dɔ:mɪtrɪ] N, ADJ dormitorio; (*Am: hall of residence*) casa dello studente; **the boys' dormitory** il dormitorio dei ragazzi; **dormitory town** città *f inv* dormitorio *inv*

dor·mouse ['dɔ:,maʊs] N (*pl* **dormice** ['dɔ:,maɪs]) ghiro

dor·sal ['dɔ:sl] ADJ dorsale; **dorsal fin** pinna dorsale

DOS [dɒs] N ABBR (*Comput:* = **disk operating system**) DOS *m*

dos·age ['dəʊsɪdʒ] N (*on medicine bottle*) posologia

dose [dəʊs] N (*of medicine*) dose *f*; (*Brit: of fever etc*) attacco; **to get a dose of flu** prendersi l'influenza; **in small doses** (*fig*) a piccole dosi
■VT: **to dose sb with sth** somministrare qc a qn

dosh [dɒʃ] N (*Brit fam*) grana

doss [dɒs] VI: **to doss (down)** (*fam*) sistemarsi (per la notte)

dos·ser ['dɒsə[r]] N (*Brit: fam*) barbone(-a)

doss·house ['dɒs,haʊs] N (*Brit: fam*) ≈ dormitorio pubblico

dos·si·er ['dɒsɪeɪ] N: **dossier (on)** dossier *m inv* (su)

DOT [,di:əʊ'ti:] N ABBR (*Am*) = *Department of Transportation; see* **transportation**

dot [dɒt] N (*gen*) punto; (*on material*) pois *m inv*; (*stain*) macchiolina; (*in punctuation*): **dots** puntini *mpl* di sospensione; (*morse*): **dots and dashes** punti *mpl* e linee *fpl*; **polka dots** pois; **on the dot** (*fig*) in punto
■VT (*fig*): **to dot one's i's and cross one's t's** mettere i puntini sulle i; **a field dotted with flowers** un campo punteggiato di fiori; **they are dotted about the country** sono disseminati per il paese

dot·age ['dəʊtɪdʒ] N: **to be in one's dotage** essere rimbambito(-a)

dot·com [dɒt'kɒm] N (*Comput*) azienda che opera in Internet

dot command N (*Comput*) commando punto

dote on ['dəʊt,ɒn] VI + PREP stravedere per

dot·ing ['dəʊtɪŋ] ADJ: **doting mother** madre *f* che stravede per i figli; **doting husband** marito che stravede per la moglie

dot-matrix printer [,dɒt'meɪtrɪks'prɪntə[r]] N stampante *f* ad aghi

dot·ted line ['dɒtɪd'laɪn] N linea punteggiata; **to sign on the dotted line** firmare (nell'apposito spazio); (*fig*) accettare; **to tear along the dotted line** strappare lungo la linea tratteggiata

dot·ty ['dɒtɪ] ADJ (*Brit fam: mad*) tocco(-a), strambo(-a); **to be dotty about sth** andare pazzo(-a) per qc; **he's dotty about her** ha completamente perso la testa per lei

◉**dou·ble** ['dʌbl] ADJ **1** (*gen*) doppio(-a); **a double helping** una porzione doppia; **a double whisky** un doppio whisky; **double spacing** (*Typ*) interlinea doppia **2** (*dual*) duplice; **with a double meaning** a doppio senso; **to lead a double life** avere una doppia vita; **to play a double game** fare il doppio gioco **3** (*Brit: repeated*): **double five two six (5526)** (*Telec*) cinque cinque due sei; **spelt with a double "l"** scritto con due elle *or* con doppia elle
■ADV (*bend*) in due; (*see*) doppio; **double the amount (of sth)** il doppio (di qc); **to cost double** costare il doppio
■N **1** (*amount*) doppio; (*person*) sosia *m inv*; (*Cine*) controfigura; **at the double** *or* **on the double** (*running*) a passo di corsa **2** (*bet*) accoppiata
■VT **1** (*increase twofold: money, quantity etc*) raddoppiare **2** (*fold: also:* **double over**) piegare in due
■VI **1** (*quantity etc*) raddoppiare **2** **to double as** (*have two uses*) funzionare *or* servire anche da; (*Theatre, Cine*) fare anche la parte di
▸ **double back** VI + ADV (*person*) tornare sui propri passi
▸ **double up** VI + ADV **1** (*bend over*) piegarsi in due; **he doubled up with laughter** si sbellicava dal ridere **2** (*share bedroom*) dividere la stanza

double agent N agente *m* segreto che fa il doppio gioco

double-barrelled [,dʌbl'bærəld] ADJ (*gun*) a doppia canna; (*Brit: surname*) cognome *m* doppio

double bass [,dʌbl'beɪs] N contrabbasso

double bed N letto matrimoniale, letto a due piazze

double bend N (*Brit*) doppia curva

double-blind [,dʌbl'blaɪnd] ADJ a doppio cieco

double bluff N: **it's a double bluff on his part** vuol farci credere che mente

double-breasted [,dʌbl'brɛstɪd] ADJ (*jacket*) doppiopetto *inv*

double-check [,dʌbl'tʃɛk] VT, VI ricontrollare

double chin N doppio mento

double-click ['dʌbl,klɪk] VI (*Comput*): **to double click (on)** fare doppio click (su)

double-clutch ['dʌbl'klʌtʃ] VI (*Am*) (*Aut* = **double-declutch**)

double cream N (*Brit*) panna da cucina

double-cross [,dʌbl'krɒs] VT (*fam*) fare il doppio gioco con

double-dealer ['dʌbəl 'di:lə[r]] N doppio-giochista *m/f*

double-dealing [,dʌbl'di:lɪŋ] N doppio gioco

double-decker [,dʌbl'dɛkə[r]] N (*also:* **double-decker bus**) autobus *m inv* a due piani; (*also:* **double-decker sandwich**) doppio tramezzino

double-declutch ['dʌbl,di:'klʌtʃ] (*Am*) **double-clutch** ['dʌbl'klʌtʃ] VI (*Aut*) fare la doppietta

double-density [,dʌbl'dɛnsɪtɪ] ADJ (*Comput*) a doppia densità

double-density disk [,dʌbl,dɛnsɪtɪ'dɪsk] N (*Comput*) disco a doppia densità

double-digit [,dʌbl'dɪdʒɪt] ADJ a due cifre

double digits NPL doppia cifra

double-Dutch [,dʌbl'dʌtʃ] N (*Brit fam*): **it was double-Dutch to me** per me era come se parlasse turco *or* arabo

double-edged [,dʌbl'ɛdʒd] ADJ (*remark*) a doppio taglio

dou·ble en·ten·dre ['dʌblɑ:n'tɑ:ndrə] N doppio senso

double exposure N (*Phot*) sovrimpressione *f*

double fault N doppio fallo

double glazing [,dʌbl'gleɪzɪŋ] N (*Brit*) doppiovetro; **to put in double glazing** mettere i doppivetri

double helix N (*Biochemistry*) doppia elica

double-jointed [,dʌbl'dʒɔɪntɪd] ADJ snodato(-a)

double negative N (*Ling*) doppia negazione *f*

double-page ['dʌbl,peɪdʒ] ADJ: **double-page spread** pubblicità a doppia pagina

double-park [ˌdʌblˈpɑːk] VI parcheggiare in doppia fila; **double-parking** parcheggio in doppia fila
double-quick [ˌdʌblˈkwɪk] ADV di corsa
double room N camera per due, (camera) doppia, (camera) matrimoniale *f*
dou·bles [ˈdʌblz] NPL (*Tennis*) doppio; **a game of mixed/ladies' doubles** un doppio misto/femminile
double standard N: **to have double standards** avere due pesi e due misure
dou·blet [ˈdʌblɪt] N (*History: jacket*) farsetto
double take N: **to do a double take** (*fig*) reagire a scoppio ritardato
double talk [ˈdʌbl,tɔːk] N discorsi *mpl* ambigui
double time N *tariffa doppia per lavoro straordinario*
dou·ble wham·my [ˌdʌblˈwæmɪ] N (*fam*) doppia mazzata (*fig*)
dou·bly [ˈdʌblɪ] ADV doppiamente; **to be doubly careful** stare doppiamente attento(-a)
◎ **doubt** [daʊt] N dubbio; **to be in doubt** essere in dubbio; **without (a) doubt** senza dubbio; **beyond doubt** fuor di dubbio; **if in doubt** nell'incertezza, in caso di dubbio; **no doubt** sicuramente; **as you no doubt know ...** come saprai sicuramente...; **no doubt he will come** è probabile che venga; **there is no doubt of that** su questo non c'è dubbio; **I have my doubts about whether he'll come** ho i miei dubbi che venga
■ VT **1** (*truth of statement*) dubitare di; **I don't doubt her honesty** non dubito della sua onestà; **to doubt one's own eyes** non credere ai propri occhi; **I doubt it very much** ne dubito proprio; **you're a real doubting Thomas** sei proprio come San Tommaso **2** (*be uncertain*): **to doubt whether** *or* **if** *or* **that** dubitare che + *sub*; **I don't doubt that he will come** non dubito *or* non ho dubbi che verrà
doubt·er [ˈdaʊtəʳ] N scettico(-a)
doubt·ful [ˈdaʊtfʊl] ADJ (*uncertain: person*) poco convinto(-a); (*: look*) dubbioso(-a); (*: result, success, future*) dubbio(-a), incerto(-a); (*debatable: question*) discutibile; (*questionable: taste, reputation*) dubbio(-a); **she sounds doubtful** sembra poco convinta; **to be doubtful about sth** non essere convinto(-a) di qc, avere dei dubbi su qc; **I'm doubtful about going by myself** sono incerto se andare da solo; **I'm a bit doubtful** non sono tanto sicuro; **it's doubtful whether ...** non è sicuro che... + *sub*
doubt·ful·ly [ˈdaʊtfəlɪ] ADV (*unconvincedly*) con aria dubbiosa, senza convinzione
doubt·ful·ness [ˈdaʊtfʊlnɪs] N (*hesitation*) esitazione *f*, indecisione *f*; (*uncertainty*) incertezza
doubt·less [ˈdaʊtlɪs] ADV senza dubbio, indubbiamente
douche [duːʃ] N (*shower*) doccia; (*Med: internal*) irrigazione *f*
dough [dəʊ] N **1** impasto, pasta **2** (*fam: money*) grana
dough·nut, (*Am*) **do·nut** [ˈdəʊnʌt] N krapfen *m inv*, bombolone *m*; **a jam doughnut** un krapfen con la marmellata
dough·ty [ˈdaʊtɪ] ADJ (*comp* **-tier**, *superl* **-tiest**) (*old*) valoroso(-a)
doughy [ˈdəʊɪ] ADJ (*bread*) molliccio(-a); (*fig: complexion*) pallidino(-a)
dour [ˈdʊəʳ] ADJ (*grim*) arcigno(-a)
douse [daʊs] VT (*with water*) infradiciare; (*flames*) spegnere
dove [dʌv] N colombo(-a); (*fig*) ((*Pol*) colomba; **collared dove** colombo(-a) dal collare
dove·cote [ˈdʌv,kəʊt] N colombaia
dove·tail [ˈdʌv,teɪl] N (*also:* **dovetail joint**) incastro a coda di rondine
■ VT (*fig*): **to dovetail with/into** connettere a/con
■ VI (*fig*) combaciare, collimare
dowa·ger [ˈdaʊədʒəʳ] N vedova titolata
dow·di·ly [ˈdaʊdɪlɪ] ADV (*dressed*) in modo scialbo
dow·di·ness [ˈdaʊdɪnɪs] N aspetto scialbo
dowdy [ˈdaʊdɪ] ADJ (*comp* **-ier**, *superl* **-iest**) scialbo(-a)
Dow-Jones average [ˈdaʊˈdʒəʊnzˈævərɪdʒ] N (*Am*): **the Dow-Jones average** l'indice *m* Dow-Jones
◎ **down**[1] [daʊn] ADV
1 (*movement*) giù; (*to the ground*) giù, a terra; (*to a dog*): **down!** a cuccia!; **get down!** scendi!; **to fall down** cadere; **to run down** correre giù; **he threw down his racket** ha gettato a terra la racchetta; **he came down from Glasgow** è venuto giù da Glasgow; **from the year 1600 down to the present day** dal 1600 fino ai giorni nostri; **from the biggest down to the smallest** dal più grande al più piccolo; **down with traitors!** abbasso i traditori!
2 (*position*) giù; **down there** là in fondo, laggiù; **down here** quaggiù; **the blinds are down** le tapparelle sono tirate giù *or* abbassate; **to kick a man when he's down** (*fig*) uccidere un uomo morto; **his office is down on the first floor** il suo ufficio è giù al primo piano; **I'll be down in a minute** scendo tra un minuto; **I've been down with flu** sono stato a letto con l'influenza; **he lives down south** abita nel sud; **the tyres are down** le gomme sono sgonfie *or* a terra; **his temperature is down** la febbre gli è scesa; **England is two goals down** l'Inghilterra sta perdendo per due goal; **the price of meat is down** il prezzo della carne è sceso; **write this down** scrivi; **I've got it down in my diary** ce l'ho sulla mia agenda; **you're down for the next race** sei iscritto alla prossima gara
3 (*as deposit*): **to pay £20 down** dare 20 sterline in acconto *or* di anticipo
■ PREP (*indicating movement*) giù per; (*at a lower point on*) più giù; **he ran his finger down the list** percorse la lista col dito; **he went down the hill** discese la collina; **he's down the hill** è in fondo alla collina; **he lives down the street** abita un po' più giù; **looking down this road, you can see ...** guardando fino in fondo alla strada, vedrai...; **down the ages** nel corso della storia; **he's gone down the pub/down town** (*fam*) è andato al pub/in città
■ ADJ (*train, line*) che parte da una grande città; **I'm feeling a bit down** (*fam*) mi sento un po' giù; **to be down** (*computer*) non funzionare
■ VT (*opponent*) atterrare; (*fam: drink*) scolarsi; **he downed a pint of beer** si è scolato una pinta di birra; **to down tools** (*fig*) incrociare le braccia (*fig*)
■ N: **to have a down on sb** (*fam*) avercela con qn
down[2] [daʊn] N (*on bird, in quilts*) piumino *m inv*; (*on person, fruit*) peluria, lanugine *f*
down[3] [daʊn] N (*hill*) collina, colle *m*
down-and-out [ˈdaʊnəndˈaʊt] ADJ (*destitute*) sul lastrico
■ N (*tramp*) barbone *m*
down-at-heel [ˌdaʊnætˈhiːl] ADJ scalcagnato(-a); (*fig*) trasandato(-a)
down·beat [ˈdaʊn,biːt] N (*Mus*) tempo in battere
■ ADJ (*fam: gloomy*) pessimistico(-a); (*: relaxed*) distaccato(-a)
down·cast [ˈdaʊn,kɑːst] ADJ (*sad*) abbattuto(-a), avvilito(-a); (*eyes*) basso(-a)

Dd

down·er ['daʊnəʳ] N (*fam: drug*) sedativo; **to be on a downer** (*depressed*) essere giù
down·fall ['daʊn,fɔ:l] N rovina, caduta
down·grade ['daʊn,greɪd] VT (*job, hotel*) declassare; (*person*) degradare
down·hearted [,daʊn'hɑ:tɪd] ADJ scoraggiato(-a), demoralizzato(-a); **don't be downhearted!** non scoraggiarti!
down·hill [,daʊn'hɪl] ADV: **to go downhill** (*road*) andare in discesa; (*car*) andare giù per la discesa; (*fig: person*) lasciarsi andare; (*: business*) andare sempre peggio; andare a rotoli; **downhill race** (*Skiing*) gara di discesa (libera); **downhill racer** discesista *m/f*; **downhill ski** sci *m inv* a valle
Downing Street ['daʊnɪŋ,stri:t] N (*Brit*): **10 Downing Street** *residenza del primo ministro inglese*

DOWNING STREET

Downing Street è la via di Westminster che porta da Whitehall al parco di St James dove, al numero 10, si trova la residenza del primo ministro inglese. Nella stessa via, al numero 11, si trova la residenza del Cancelliere dello Scacchiere. Spesso si usa **Downing Street** per indicare il governo britannico.
▷ www.number-10.gov.uk

down-in-the-mouth ['daʊnɪnðə'maʊθ] ADJ: **to look down-in-the-mouth** avere un'aria abbattuta
down·load [*vb* 'daʊn,ləʊd; *n* 'daʊnləʊd] VT (*Comput*) scaricare
■ N (*Comput*) download *m inv*, scaricamento
down·load·able [,daʊn'ləʊdəbl] ADJ scaricabile
down-market ['daʊn,mɑ:kɪt] ADJ rivolto(-a) ad una fascia di mercato inferiore; (*product*) dozzinale
■ ADV: **to go down-market** rivolgersi ad una fascia inferiore di pubblico
down payment N acconto
down·play ['daʊn,pleɪ] VT (*Am*) minimizzare
down·pour ['daʊn,pɔ:ʳ] N acquazzone *m*
down·right ['daʊn,raɪt] ADJ (*person, manner*) franco(-a); (*lie, liar*) bell'e buono(-a); (*refusal*) categorico(-a), assoluto(-a); **downright bad manners** vera e propria maleducazione
■ ADV (*rude, disgusting*) davvero; **downright dangerous** davvero pericoloso
Downs [daʊnz] NPL (*Brit*): **the Downs** *colline di gesso nel sud-est dell'Inghilterra*
down·shift ['daʊnʃɪft] VI (*Brit*) accettare un lavoro meno pagato ma anche meno stressante; (*Am: Aut*) scalare (la marcia)
down·side ['daʊnsaɪd] N inconveniente *m*
down·size ['daʊn,saɪz] VT (*workforce*) ridurre
Down's syndrome ['daʊnz,sɪndrəʊm] N sindrome *f* di Down; **a Down's syndrome baby** un(*a*) bambino(-a) Down
down·stairs ['daʊn'stɛəz] ADJ (*on the ground floor*) al pianterreno, al pianterra; (*on the floor underneath*) al piano di sotto; **the downstairs bathroom** il bagno al piano terra
■ ADV di sotto, giù; **to come** *or* **go downstairs** scendere (al piano di sotto); **she lives downstairs** abita al piano di sotto; **the people downstairs** le persone che abitano al piano di sotto
down·stream ['daʊn'stri:m] ADV: **downstream (from)** a valle (di)
down·swing ['daʊn,swɪŋ], **down·turn** ['daʊn,tɜ:n] N (*Statistics*) calo; **an economic downswing** un rallentamento economico
down·time ['daʊn'taɪm] N (*Comm*) tempi *mpl* morti
down-to-earth ['daʊntʊ'ɜ:θ] ADJ (*person*) coi piedi per terra, pratico(-a); (*advice, approach*) pratico(-a)
down·town ['daʊn'taʊn] ADV (*Am*) in città, in centro; **he works downtown** lavora in centro
■ ADJ: **downtown San Francisco** il centro di San Francisco
■ N centro (città)
down·trod·den ['daʊn,trɒdn] ADJ oppresso(-a)
down·turn ['daʊn,tɜ:n] N = **downswing**
down under (*fam*) N gli antipodi
■ ADV agli antipodi
down·ward ['daʊnwəd] ADJ (*curve, movement etc*) in giù, verso il basso; (*slope*) in discesa; **a downward trend** una diminuzione progressiva; **a downward trend in prices** una tendenza al ribasso dei prezzi
down·ward(s) ['daʊnwəd(z)] ADV (*go*) in giù, in discesa; (*look*) verso il basso; **face downwards** (*person*) bocconi; (*object*) a faccia in giù; **from the President downwards** dal Presidente in giù
down·wind ['daʊn'wɪnd] ADV: **downwind (of** *or* **from)** sottovento (rispetto a)
downy ['daʊnɪ] ADJ (*skin, peach*) ricoperto(-a) di peluria, lanuginoso(-a)
dow·ry ['daʊrɪ] N dote *f*
dowse [daʊz] VI praticare la rabdomanzia
doy·en ['dɔɪən] N: **the doyen of** (*frm*) il decano di
doy·enne [dɔɪ'ɛn] N: **the doyenne of** (*frm*) la decana di
doz. ABBR = **dozen**
doze [dəʊz] N sonnellino, pisolino
■ VI sonnecchiare
▸ **doze off** VI + ADV appisolarsi
◎ **doz·en** ['dʌzn] N dozzina; **80p a dozen** 80 pence la dozzina; **a dozen eggs** una dozzina d'uova; **two dozen** due dozzine; **dozens of times** centinaia *or* migliaia di volte; **dozens of people** decine *fpl* di persone
dozy ['dəʊzɪ] ADJ (*comp* **-ier**, *superl* **-iest**) (*sleepy*) assonnato(-a); (*fam: stupid*) addormentato(-a)
DPhil [,di:'fɪl], **DPh** N ABBR (= **Doctor of Philosophy**) ≈ dottorato di ricerca
DPP [,di:pi:'pi:] N ABBR (*Brit*) = **Director of Public Prosecutions**
DPW [di:pi:'dʌblju:] N ABBR (*Am*) = *Department of Public Works*
Dr. ABBR (= **doctor**) Dott./Dott.ssa; (*in street names*) = **Drive**
dr ABBR (*Comm*) = **debtor**
drab [dræb] ADJ (*comp* **-ber**, *superl* **-best**) (*colour*) cupo(-a); (*clothes*) triste; (*life*) grigio(-a), tetro(-a)
drab·ness ['dræbnɪs] N (*of colour*) cupezza; (*of clothes*) aspetto triste; (*of life*) grigiore *m*
drach·ma ['drækmə] N (*pl* **drachmas** *or* **drachmae** ['drækmi:]) (*coin*) dracma
dra·co·nian [drə'kəʊnɪən] ADJ draconiano(-a)
◎ **draft** [drɑ:ft] N **1** (*outline*) abbozzo, brutta (copia); (*of contract, document*) minuta; **draft letter** prima stesura (di una lettera); **a draft law** un progetto di legge **2** (*Mil: detachment*) distaccamento; **the draft** (*Am Mil: conscription*) la leva **3** (*Comm: also:* **banker's** *or* **bank draft**) tratta; assegno circolare **4** (*Am*) = **draught**
■ VT **1** (*also:* **draft out**) abbozzare; (*: plan*) tracciare; (*: document, report*) stendere (in versione preliminare) **2** (*Mil: for specific duty*) distaccare; (*Am Mil: conscript*) arruolare

draft dodg·er ['drɑ:ft,dɒdʒəʳ] N (*Am Mil*) renitente *m* alla leva
drafts·man ['drɑ:ftsmən] N (*Am*) = **draughtsman**
drafts·man·ship ['drɑ:ftsmən,ʃɪp] N (*Am*) = **draughtsmanship**
drafty ['drɑ:ftɪ] N (*Am*) = **draughty**
◎ **drag** [dræg] N **1** (*Aer, Naut: resistance*) resistenza (aerodinamica) **2** (*fam: boring thing, task, person*) noia, strazio; **what a drag!** che scocciatura! **3** (*on cigarette*) tirata **4** (*women's clothing worn by men*): **in drag** travestito (da donna)
■ VT **1** (*object*) trascinare, tirare; (*person*) trascinare; **to drag one's feet over sth** (*fig*) farla lunga con qc, trascinare qc **2** (*sea bed, river*) dragare
■ VI **1** (*anchor*) arare **2** (*go very slowly: evening, conversation etc*) trascinarsi, non finire mai
▶ **drag along** VT + ADV (*person*) trascinare (controvoglia); (*object*) tirare
▶ **drag away** VT + ADV: **to drag away (from)** tirare via (da)
▶ **drag down** VT + ADV trascinare giù, trascinare in basso; **to drag sb down to one's own level** (*fig*) far abbassare qn al proprio livello
▶ **drag in** VT + ADV (*subject, topic*) tirare in ballo
▶ **drag into** VT + PREP: **to drag sb/sth into** (*introduce unnecessarily*) trascinare qn/qc in
▶ **drag on** VI + ADV (*meeting, conversation*) trascinarsi, passare lentamente
▶ **drag up** VT + ADV (*mention unnecessarily*) ritirare in ballo, tirar fuori di nuovo
drag-and-drop [,drægən'drɒp] VT (*Comput*) trascinare; **to drag-and-drop a file** trascinare un file
drag coefficient, drag factor N (*Aut*) coefficiente *m* di resistenza
drag lift N (*Skiing*) skilift *m inv*
drag·net ['dræg,nɛt] N rete *f* a strascico; (*fig*) rastrellamento
drag·on ['drægən] N drago
dragon·fly ['drægən,flaɪ] N libellula
dra·goon [drə'gu:n] N (*Mil: cavalryman*) dragone *m*
■ VT: **to dragoon sb into doing sth** (*Brit*) costringere qn a fare qc
drag racing N *corsa automobilistica con macchine truccate*
◎ **drain** [dreɪn] N **1** (*outlet*) scarico, canale *m* di scolo; (*: pipe*) tubatura di scarico; (*drain cover*) tombino; **to throw one's money down the drain** (*fig*) buttare i soldi dalla finestra **2 the drains** NPL (*sewage system*) le fognature; **the drains are blocked** gli scarichi sono ostruiti **3** (*fig: source of loss*): **a drain on** (*energies, resources*) un salasso per; **it has been a great drain on her** l'ha veramente spossata
■ VT (*land, lake*) prosciugare; (*marshes*) bonificare, drenare; (*vegetables, pasta*) scolare; (*glass, bottle of wine*) svuotare; (*radiator*) (far) svuotare; (*Med: wound*) drenare; **to feel drained (of energy)** (*fig*) sentirsi svuotato(-a) (di energie), sentirsi sfinito(-a)
■ VI (*washed dishes, vegetables*) scolare; (*liquid, stream*): **to drain (into)** defluire (in)
▶ **drain away** VT + ADV (*liquid*) far scolare
■ VI + ADV (*liquid*) scolare; (*strength*) esaurirsi
▶ **drain off** VT + ADV (*liquid*) far scolare
drain·age ['dreɪnɪdʒ] N (*of land: natural*) scolo; (*: artificial*) drenaggio; (*of lake*) prosciugamento; (*system of drains*) fognature *fpl*
drain·er ['dreɪnəʳ] N scolapiatti *m inv*
drain·ing board ['dreɪnɪŋ,bɔ:d] (*Am*) **drain·board** ['dreɪnbɔ:d] N piano del lavello
drain·pipe ['dreɪn,paɪp] N **1** tubo di scarico **2 drainpipes** (*trousers*) pantaloni *mpl* a tubo
drake [dreɪk] N maschio dell'anatra
dram [dræm] N bicchierino (di whisky *etc*)
◎ **dra·ma** ['drɑ:mə] N (*gen*) dramma *m*, teatro; (*play*) commedia; (*event*) dramma; **a TV drama** un dramma televisivo; **drama critic** critico teatrale; **drama school** scuola d'arte drammatica; **drama student** studente(-essa) di arte drammatica; **drama is my favourite subject** la recitazione è la mia materia preferita
▷ www.ncdt.co.uk/
◎ **dra·mat·ic** [drə'mætɪk] ADJ (*change*) spettacolare; (*event, improvement, effect*) straordinario(-a); (*entrance*) teatrale; (*art*) drammatico(-a); **dramatic news** notizie sensazionali; **the dramatic arts** le arti drammatiche
dra·mati·cal·ly [drə'mætɪkəlɪ] ADV (*improve, change*) in modo straordinario, moltissimo; (*enter, pause*) in modo teatrale
dra·mat·ics [drə'mætɪks] NPL **1 amateur dramatics** filodrammatica **2** (*histrionics*) modi *mpl* teatrali
dra·ma·tis per·so·nae ['dræmətɪspɜ:'səʊnaɪ] N personaggi *mpl*
drama·tist ['dræmətɪst] N drammaturgo(-a)
drama·ti·za·tion [,dræmətaɪ'zeɪʃən] N (*adaptation of novel: for cinema*) riduzione *f* cinematografica; (*: for TV*) riduzione televisiva
drama·tize ['dræmətaɪz] VT (*events, situation*) drammatizzare; (*novel: for TV*) ridurre *or* adattare per la televisione; (*: for cinema*) ridurre *or* adattare per il grande schermo
drank [dræŋk] PT *of* **drink**
drape [dreɪp] N *see* **drapes**
■ VT: **to drape (with)** (*altar*) drappeggiare (con); (*shoulders*) avvolgere (in); **to drape (over)** (*cloth, clothing*) avvolgere (intorno a)
drap·er ['dreɪpəʳ] N (*Brit old*) negoziante *m/f* di stoffe
dra·pery ['dreɪpərɪ] N (*hanging folds*) drappeggio; (*shop*) negozio di tessuti; **draperies** NPL (*rich and heavy*) drappi *mpl*
drapes [dreɪps] NPL (*Am*) tende *fpl*
dras·tic ['dræstɪk] ADJ drastico(-a); **to take drastic action** agire in modo drastico
dras·ti·cal·ly ['dræstɪkəlɪ] ADV drasticamente
drat [dræt] EXCL (*old fam*): **drat it!** accidenti!
draught, (*Am*) **draft** [drɑ:ft] N **1** (*of air*) corrente *f* (d'aria), spiffero; (*for fire*) tiraggio; (*Naut*) pescaggio **2** (*drink*): **he took a long draught of beer** ha bevuto una lunga sorsata di birra; **on draught** alla spina
draught beer N birra alla spina
draught·board ['drɑ:ft,bɔ:d] N scacchiera
draughts ['drɑ:fts] N (*Brit*) (gioco della) dama
draughts·man, (*Am*) **draftsman** ['drɑ:ftsmən] N (*pl* **-men**) (*in drawing office*) disegnatore(-trice)
draughts·man·ship, (*Am*) **drafts·man·ship** ['drɑ:ftsmənʃɪp] N (*skill*) arte *f* del disegno
draughty, (*Am*) **drafty** ['drɑ:ftɪ] ADJ (*comp* **-ier**, *superl* **-iest**) (*room*) pieno(-a) di spifferi; (*street corner*) ventoso(-a)
◎ **draw** [drɔ:] (*vb: pt* **drew**, *pp* **drawn**) N
1 (*lottery*) lotteria, riffa; (*picking of tickets*) estrazione *f*, sorteggio; (*for sporting events*) sorteggio
2 (*Sport: equal score*) pareggio; **the match ended in a draw** la partita è finita con un pareggio
3 (*attraction*) attrazione *f*
4 to be quick on the draw essere veloce con la pistola; (*fig*) avere i riflessi pronti

Dd

■ VT
1 (*pull: bolt, curtains*) tirare; (*: caravan, trailer*) trainare, rimorchiare; (*: bow*) tendere la corda di; **he drew his finger along the table** ha passato il dito sul tavolo; **he drew his hat over his eyes** si è calato il cappello sugli occhi; **she drew him to one side** lo tirò da una parte; **he drew her towards him** la tirò verso di sé; **she's drawn the curtains** ha tirato le tende
2 (*extract: from pocket, bag*) tirar fuori; (*: from well, tap*) attingere; (*: sword*) sguainare; (*: teeth*) estrarre; (*: cork*) cavare; (*salary, money from bank*) ritirare; (*cheque*) cambiare, riscuotere; (*Culin: fowl*) pulire; **to draw a bath** preparare un bagno; **to draw blood** fare uscir il sangue; (*fig*) colpire nel vivo; **to draw a card** estrarre una carta (dal mazzo); **to draw a breath** tirare un respiro; **to draw breath** (ri)prendere fiato; **to draw comfort from sth** trovare conforto in qc; **to draw a smile from sb** strappare un sorriso a qn
3 (*attract: attention, crowd, customer*) attrarre, attirare; **to feel drawn to sb** sentirsi attratto(-a) verso qn, provare attrazione per qn
4 (*sketch: picture, portrait*) fare; (*: object, person*) disegnare; (*: plan, line, circle*) tracciare; (*: map*) disegnare, fare; (*fig: situation*) fare un quadro di; (*: character*) disegnare; **to draw a picture** fare un disegno; **to draw a picture of sb** fare il ritratto a qn; **he drew a line** ha tracciato una linea; **I draw the line at (doing) that** (*fig*) mi rifiuto (di farlo)
5 (*formulate: conclusion*): **to draw (from)** trarre (da), ricavare (da); (*: comparison, distinction*): **to draw (between)** fare (tra)
6 (*Ftbl etc*): **to draw a match** pareggiare
■ VI
1 (*move*): **to draw (towards)** avvicinarsi (a), avanzare (verso); **he drew to one side** si è tirato da parte *or* in disparte; **the train drew into the station** il treno è entrato in stazione; **the car drew over to the kerb** la macchina si è accostata al marciapiede; **he drew ahead of the other runners** ha staccato gli altri corridori; **to draw level** affiancarsi; **to draw near** avvicinarsi; **to draw to an end** *or* **to a close** volgere alla fine, avvicinarsi alla conclusione
2 (*in cards*): **to draw for trumps** scegliere il seme *or* la briscola
3 (*chimney*) tirare
4 (*Sport: be equal: two teams*) pareggiare; **we drew two-all** abbiamo pareggiato due a due; **the teams drew for second place** le due squadre sono arrivate seconde a pari merito
5 (*sketch*) disegnare; **I can't draw** non so disegnare
▸ **draw aside** VI + ADV (*person*) scostarsi
■ VT + ADV (*person*) tirare in disparte; (*object*) spostare (da un lato)
▸ **draw away** VI + ADV: **to draw away (from)** (*go away*) allontanarsi (da); (*move ahead: athlete*) portarsi in vantaggio (su)
■ VT + ADV (*person*) allontanare, portare via; (*object*) togliere
▸ **draw back** VT + ADV (*object, hand*) tirare indietro, ritirare; (*curtains*) tirare
■ VI + ADV (*move back*): **to draw back (from)** indietreggiare (di fronte a), tirarsi indietro (di fronte a)
▸ **draw down** VT + ADV (*gen*) abbassare; (*blame*): **to draw down (on)** tirare addosso a
▸ **draw in** VI + ADV
1 (*Brit: car*) accostarsi; (*: train*) entrare in stazione
2 **the days are drawing in** le giornate si accorciano
■ VT + ADV (*breath*) tirare; (*air*) aspirare; (*pull back in: claws*) ritirare; (*attract: crowds*) richiamare
▸ **draw off** VT + ADV (*siphon off*) spillare
▸ **draw on** VI + ADV (*time*) avanzare
■ VT + ADV (*gloves, stockings*) infilare lentamente
■ VI + PREP (*resources*) attingere a; (*imagination, person*) far ricorso a; **he drew on his own experience to write the book** ha fatto ricorso alla propria esperienza per scrivere il libro
▸ **draw out** VI + ADV (*lengthen*) allungarsi
■ VT + ADV
1 (*take out: handkerchief*) tirar fuori; (*money from bank*) ritirare; **to draw sb out (of his shell)** (*fig*) tirare qn fuori dal suo guscio
2 (*prolong: meeting*) tirare per le lunghe
▸ **draw up** VT + ADV
1 (*formulate: will*) redigere; (*: contract*) stendere; (*: plans*) formulare; (*: document*) compilare; **she drew up a list of priorities** compilò un elenco di priorità
2 (*chair*) avvicinare; (*troops*) schierare; **to draw o.s. up (to one's full height)** raddrizzarsi (con tutta la persona)
■ VI + ADV (*stop*) arrestarsi, fermarsi; **to draw up (beside sth/sb)** accostarsi (a qc/qn)

draw·back ['drɔːˌbæk] N inconveniente *m*, svantaggio
draw·bridge ['drɔːˌbrɪdʒ] N ponte *m* levatoio
drawee [drɔː'iː] N (*Fin*) trassato, trattario
draw·er [drɔː'] N **1** (*furniture*) cassetto **2** (*of cheque*) traente *m/f*
draw·ing ['drɔːɪŋ] N (*picture*) disegno; **I'm no good at drawing** non so disegnare; **drawing pen** (*Art*) tiralinee *m inv*
drawing board N tavolo da disegno; **back to the drawing board!** (*fig*) ricominciamo da capo!
drawing pin N (*Brit*) puntina da disegno
drawing room N salotto
drawl [drɔːl] N cadenza strascicata
■ VT strascicare
■ VI strascicare le parole
drawn [drɔːn] PP *of* **draw**
■ ADJ (*haggard: with tiredness*) tirato(-a); (*: with pain*) contratto(-a) (dal dolore)
drawn-out [drɔːn'aʊt] ADJ prolungato(-a)
draw·string ['drɔːˌstrɪŋ] N cordone *m*, cordoncino
dread [drɛd] N terrore *m*
■ VT avere il terrore di, tremare all'idea di
dread·ful ['drɛdfʊl] ADJ (*crime, sight, suffering*) terribile, spaventoso(-a), orribile; (*weather*) tremendo(-a); **a dreadful mistake** un terribile errore; **you look dreadful** hai un aspetto orribile; **I feel dreadful!** (*ill*) mi sento uno straccio!; (*ashamed*) vorrei scomparire (dalla vergogna)!
dread·fully ['drɛdfəlɪ] ADV terribilmente; **I'm dreadfully sorry** sono terribilmente spiacente
dread·locked ['drɛdlɒkt] ADJ con le treccine rasta
dread·locks ['drɛdlɒks] NPL treccine *fpl* rasta
◎ **dream** [driːm] (*vb: pt, pp* **dreamed** *or* **dreamt**) N sogno; **to have a dream about sb/sth** sognare di qn/qc; **I had a bad dream** ho fatto un brutto sogno; **sweet dreams!** sogni d'oro!; **that museum is an archaeologist's dream** quel museo è un paradiso per gli archeologi; **it worked like a dream** ha funzionato a meraviglia; **she goes about in a dream** ha sempre la testa tra le nuvole; **rich beyond his wildest dreams** ricco come non si era mai sognato in vita sua; **isn't he a dream?** non è un sogno *or* un amore?; **it's my dream house** è

la casa dei miei sogni; **dream world** mondo immaginario
■VT sognare; (*imagine*) sognarsi, credersi; **I didn't dream that ...** non mi sarei mai sognato che... + *sub*; **who could have dreamt such a thing would happen?** chi avrebbe potuto immaginare un disastro come questo?
■VI sognare; (*imagine*) sognarsi; **to dream (of** *or* **about sb/sth)** sognare ((di) qn/qc); **she dreamed about her son** ha sognato di suo figlio; **there were more than I'd ever dreamed of** ce n'erano di più di quanto avessi mai immaginato; **I wouldn't dream of it!** non me lo sognerei neanche!; **I'm sorry, I was dreaming** mi scusi, stavo fantasticando
▸ **dream up** VT + ADV (*reason, excuse*) inventare; (*plan, idea*) escogitare

dream·er ['dri:mə^r] N sognatore(-trice)
dream·ily ['dri:mılı] ADV con aria sognante
dream·land ['dri:m,lænd] N paese *m* dei sogni
dream·less ['dri:mlıs] ADJ senza sogni
dream·like ['dri:mlaık] ADJ irreale
dreamt [drɛmt] PT, PP *of* **dream**
dream team N squadra dei sogni
dream ticket N (*Pol: ideal combination of candidates*) accoppiata ideale
dreamy ['dri:mı] ADJ (*comp* **-ier**, *superl* **-iest**) (*person*) distratto(-a), sognatore(-trice); (*look, voice*) sognante; (*music, quality*) di sogno
dreari·ly ['drıərılı] ADV (*dressed*) in modo deprimente; (*speak*) in modo noioso
dreari·ness ['drıərınıs] N (*of landscape, weather*) tetraggine *f*; (*of life*) squallore *m*; (*of book, speech*) monotonia
dreary ['drıərı] ADJ (*comp* **-ier**, *superl* **-iest**) (*landscape*) tetro(-a); (*weather*) deprimente; (*life*) squallido(-a); (*work, book, speech*) noioso(-a), monotono(-a)
dredge[1] [drɛdʒ] VT (*river*) dragare
▸ **dredge up** VT + ADV tirare alla superficie; (*fig: unpleasant facts*) rivangare
dredge[2] [drɛdʒ] VT (*Culin*): **to dredge with** (*sugar, flour*) spolverizzare di
dredg·er[1] ['drɛdʒə^r], **dredge** [drɛdʒ] N (*ship*) draga
dredg·er[2] ['drɛdʒə^r] N (*also:* **sugar dredger**) spargizucchero *m inv*
dredg·ing ['drɛdʒıŋ] N dragaggio
dregs [drɛgz] NPL (*also fig*) feccia *fsg*
drench [drɛntʃ] VT inzuppare, infradiciare; **to get drenched** bagnarsi fino all'osso; **drenched to the skin** bagnato(-a) fradicio(-a), bagnato(-a) fino all'osso
drench·ing ['drɛntʃıŋ] ADJ (*rain*) torrenziale
■N: **to get a drenching** inzupparsi fino all'osso
Dres·den ['drɛzdən] N Dresda
Dresden china N porcellana di Meissen
◎ **dress** [drɛs] N (*frock*) vestito, abito; (*no pl: clothing*) abbigliamento; **in summer dress** in abiti estivi
■VT **1** vestire; **to dress o.s.** *or* **to get dressed** vestirsi; **dressed in green** vestito(-a) di verde **2** (*Culin: salad*) condire; (*: chicken, crab*) preparare **3** (*Med: wound*) medicare, fasciare **4** (*decorate: shop window*) allestire
■VI vestirsi; **I got up, dressed, and went downstairs** mi alzai, mi vestii e scesi dabbasso; **she dresses very well** veste molto bene
▸ **dress down** VI + ADV **1** (*Brit: casually*) mettersi qualcosa di meno elegante (del solito) **2** (*scold*): **to dress sb down** fare una lavata di capo a qn; *see also* **dressing-down**
▸ **dress up** VI + ADV (*in smart clothes*) vestirsi bene; (*in fancy dress*) vestirsi in costume, mascherarsi
■VT + ADV (*improve appearance of: facts*) presentare sotto una veste migliore

dres·sage ['drɛsɑ:ʒ] N (*Horse-riding*) dressage *m*
dress circle N prima galleria
dress code N regole *fpl* sull'abbigliamento; **to have a dress code** seguire una rigida politica sull'abbigliamento
dress designer N stilista *m/f*
dress-down Friday [,drɛsdaʊn'fraıdı] N *giorno in cui il personale può vestirsi in modo meno formale*
dress·er ['drɛsə^r] N **1** (*in kitchen*) credenza; (*Am: dressing table*) toilette *f inv* **2** (*Theatre*) assistente *m/f* di camerino
dress·ing ['drɛsıŋ] N **1** (*act*) il vestirsi; (*style*) (modo di) vestire **2** (*Med: bandage*) fasciatura, benda **3** (*Culin: salad dressing*) condimento
dressing-down [,drɛsıŋ'daʊn] N lavata di capo
dressing gown N (*Brit*) vestaglia, veste *f* da camera
dressing room N (*in theatre*) camerino; (*Sport*) spogliatoio
dressing table N toilette *f inv*
dress·maker ['drɛs,meıkə^r] N sarto(-a)
dress·making ['drɛs,meıkıŋ] N sartoria; (*school subject*) taglio e cucito
dress rehearsal N prova generale
dress sense N gusto nel vestire
dress shirt N camicia da sera
dressy ['drɛsı] ADJ (*comp* **-ier**, *superl* **-iest**) (*fam*) elegante
drew [dru:] PT *of* **draw**
drib·ble ['drıbl] N (*of saliva*) bava, filo di saliva; (*Ftbl*) dribbling *m*
■VT (*liquid*) sbrodolare
■VI (*baby*) sbavare; (*liquid*) sgocciolare; (*Ftbl*) dribblare, fare un dribbling; (*people*): **to dribble in/out** entrare/uscire alla spicciolata
dribs and drabs ['drıbzən'dræbz] NPL: **in dribs and drabs** (*pay, send etc*) un po' alla volta; (*arrive*) alla spicciolata
dried [draıd] ADJ (*fruit, beans, flowers, herbs*) secco(-a); (*milk,eggs*) in polvere; (*soup*) liofilizzato(-a)
dri·er ['draıə^r] N = **dryer**
◎ **drift** [drıft] N **1** (*direction: of current*) direzione *f*; (*: of events*) corso; (*: of conversation, opinion*) tendenza **2** (*meaning: of questions*) senso; **the drift of the speech** il senso generale del discorso; **to catch sb's drift** capire dove qn vuole arrivare **3** (*loss of direction*) deriva **4** (*mass of snow, sand*) cumulo, mucchio; **a snow drift** un cumulo di neve
■VI (*in wind, current*) andare alla deriva; (*clouds*) essere sospinto(-a) dal vento; (*boat*) essere trasportato(-a) dalla corrente; (*sand, snow*) accumularsi, ammucchiarsi; (*person*) vagare; (*events*): **to drift (towards)** scivolare (verso); **to drift downstream** venir portato(-a) a valle dalla corrente; **he drifted into marriage** ha finito con lo sposarsi; **to drift into crime** scivolare nell'illegalità; **to let things drift** lasciare che le cose vadano come vogliono; **to drift apart** (*friends*) perdersi di vista; (*lovers*) allontanarsi l'uno dall'altro
▸ **drift off** VI + ADV (*fall asleep*) scivolare nel sonno

drift·er ['drıftə^r] N *persona che ha una vita instabile*
drift·wood ['drıftwʊd] N legno portato dalla corrente
drill[1] [drıl] N (*for wood, metal, dentist's drill*) trapano; (*in mine, quarry*) perforatrice *f*; (*in oilfield*) trivella; (*pneumatic drill*) martello pneumatico

Dd

■ VT (*wood etc*) forare, trapanare; (*tooth*) trapanare; (*oil well*) trivellare, scavare; **to drill a hole** fare un buco con il trapano
■ VI: **to drill (for)** fare trivellazioni (alla ricerca di)

drill² [drɪl] N (*Scol: exercises*) esercizi *mpl*; (*Mil*) esercitazione *f*; **a grammar drill** un esercizio orale di grammatica
■ VT (*soldiers*) esercitare, addestrare; (*pupils: in grammar*) fare esercitare, far fare esercizi a; **to drill sb** far esercitare qn; **to drill good manners into a child** fare entrare la buona educazione in testa a un bambino
■ VI (*Mil*) fare esercitazioni

drill³ [drɪl] N (*fabric*) *spesso tessuto di cotone*

drill·ing ['drɪlɪŋ] N (*of metal, wood*) perforazione *f*; (*for oil*) trivellazione *f*; (*by dentist*) trapanazione *f*; **drilling ship** nave *f* per la trivellazione

drilling rig N (*on land*) torre *f* di perforazione; (*at sea*) piattaforma (per trivellazioni subacquee)

dri·ly ['draɪlɪ] ADV = **dryly**

◎ **drink** [drɪŋk] (*vb: pt* **drank**, *pp* **drunk**) N **1** (*liquid to drink*) bevanda, bibita; **a cold drink** una bibita fresca; **a hot drink** una bevanda calda; **there's food and drink in the kitchen** c'è da mangiare e da bere in cucina; **would you like a drink?** vuoi qualcosa da bere?; **could I have a drink?** posso avere qualcosa da bere?; **can I have a drink of water, please?** mi dai un po' d'acqua?; **to give sb a drink** dare qualcosa da bere a qn
2 (*glass of alcohol*): **a drink** un bicchierino; **we had drinks before lunch** abbiamo preso l'aperitivo; **let's have a drink** beviamo qualcosa; **to go out for a drink** andare fuori a bere qualcosa; **I need a drink** ho bisogno di bere qualcosa di forte; **to invite sb for drinks** invitare qn a bere qualcosa **3** (*alcoholic liquor*) alcolici *mpl*; **he has a drink problem** è uno che beve, ha il vizio del bere; **to take to drink** darsi al bere; **to smell of drink** puzzare d'alcool; **his worries drove him to drink** le preoccupazioni lo hanno spinto al bere
■ VT (*gen*) bere; (*soup*) mangiare; **she drank her tea** ha bevuto il suo tè; **would you like something to drink?** vuole qualcosa da bere?; **what would you like to drink?** cosa vuoi da bere?; **to drink sb under the table** far finire qn sotto il tavolo (completamente ubriaco(-a))
■ VI (*gen*) bere; **he doesn't drink** non beve (alcolici); **"don't drink and drive"** "non bevete se dovete guidare"; **he drinks like a fish** beve come una spugna; **to drink to sth/sb** bere a qc/alla salute di qn
▸ **drink in** VT + ADV (*subj: person: fresh air*) aspirare; (*: story*) ascoltare avidamente; (*: sight*) ammirare, bersi con gli occhi
▸ **drink up** VT + ADV bere tutto
■ VI + ADV finire di bere; **drink up!** (*to child*) su, finiscilo!; (*in pub*) finisci il bicchiere!

drink·able ['drɪŋkəbl] ADJ (*not polluted: water*) potabile; (*palatable*) bevibile

drink driver N (*Brit*) guidatore(-trice) in stato di ebbrezza

drink-driving ['drɪŋk'draɪvɪŋ] N guida in stato di ebbrezza

drink-driving campaign N campagna sociale contro la guida in stato di ebbrezza

drink-driving offence N reato di guida in stato di ebbrezza

drink·er ['drɪŋkə^r] N bevitore(-trice); **a heavy drinker** un forte bevitore

drink·ing ['drɪŋkɪŋ] N (*of alcohol*) il bere; **drinking song** ≈ canzone *f* goliardica; **an all-night drinking bout** una notte passata a ubriacarsi

drinking fountain N fontanella

drinking water N acqua potabile

drip [drɪp] N **1** (*droplet*) goccia; (*: of blood, dew*) stilla; (*sound: of water*) sgocciolio **2** (*fam: spineless person*) lavativo(-a) **3** (*Med*) fleboclisi *f inv*; **he's on a drip** gli stanno facendo la flebo
■ VT (*liquid*) sbrodolare; **you're dripping paint everywhere!** stai schizzando vernice dappertutto!
■ VI (*tap*) perdere, gocciolare; (*washing*) sgocciolare; (*wall*) trasudare; **to be dripping with sweat/blood** grondare sudore/sangue

drip-dry ['drɪp'draɪ] ADJ (*shirt*) che non si stira

drip-feed ['drɪp,fi:d] VT alimentare mediante fleboclisi

drip·ping ['drɪpɪŋ] N (*Culin*) grasso (dell'arrosto)
■ ADJ (*tap*) che gocciola; (*washing, coat*) tutto(-a) bagnato(-a)
■ ADV: **dripping wet** (*fam*) bagnato(-a) fradicio(-a)

◎ **drive** [draɪv] (*vb: pt* **drove**, *pp* **driven**) N
1 (*outing*) giro; (*journey*) tragitto; **to go for a drive** andare a fare un giro in macchina; **it's a long drive** è un lungo viaggio; **it's 3 hours' drive from London** è a 3 ore di macchina da Londra
2 (*leading to house*) vialetto (d'accesso); **he parked his car in the drive** ha parcheggiato la macchina nel vialetto
3 (*Tennis*) diritto; (*Golf*) drive *m inv*
4 (*energy*) grinta, energia; (*motivation*) spinta, stimolo; (*Psych*) impulso; (*effort*) sforzo eccezionale; **sex drive** libido *f inv*; **to have drive** avere grinta
5 (*Comm, Pol*) campagna; **sales drive** campagna di vendita; **a national recruitment drive** una campagna di reclutamento a livello nazionale
6 (*Tech*) trasmissione *f*; (*Aut*): **front-/rear-wheel drive** trazione *f* anteriore/posteriore; **left-/right-hand drive** guida a sinistra/destra; **four-wheel drive** a quattro ruote motrici
7 (*Comput: also*: **disk drive**) disk drive *m inv*, unità *f inv* a dischi magnetici VT
1 (*cause to move: people, animals*) condurre; (*: clouds, leaves*) sospingere; **the gale drove the ship off course** la tempesta ha spinto la nave fuori rotta; **to drive sb hard** (*fig*) far sgobbare qn; **to drive sb to (do) sth** spingere qn a (fare) qc; **I was driven to it** sono stato costretto a farlo; **he is driven by greed/ambition** è spinto dall'avidità/dall'ambizione; **to drive sb mad** far impazzire qn; **he drives her mad** la fa diventare matta; **to drive sb to despair** ridurre qn alla disperazione
2 (*vehicle*) guidare; (*passenger*) portare (in macchina *etc*); **he drives a taxi** fa il tassista; **he drives a Mercedes** ha una Mercedes; **I'll drive you home** ti porto a casa (in macchina)
3 (*operate: machine*) azionare; **steam-driven train** treno a vapore; **machine driven by electricity** macchina che funziona a elettricità
4 (*nail, stake*): **to drive (into)** conficcare (in), piantare (in); **to drive this point home, she pointed out that ...** per farsi capire bene, ha sottolineato che...
■ VI (*drive a car*) guidare; (*travel by car*) andare in macchina; **to drive away/back** partire/ritornare in macchina; **he drove from London to Edinburgh** ha guidato da Londra ad Edimburgo; **we never drive into the town centre** non andiamo mai in macchina in

centro; **can you drive?** sai guidare?; **to drive at 50 km an hour** guidare *or* andare a 50 km all'ora; **to drive on the left** guidare a sinistra

▸ **drive at** VI + PREP (*fig*: *intend, mean*) mirare a, voler dire

▸ **drive back** VT + ADV (*person, army*) respingere, ributtare indietro

▸ **drive off** VT + ADV (*enemy*) cacciare

▸ **drive on** VI + ADV proseguire, andare (più) avanti

■ VT + ADV (*incite, encourage*) sospingere, spingere

▸ **drive out** VT + ADV cacciare; (*fig*) fare allontanare

▸ **drive up** VI + ADV (*car*) sopraggiungere, arrivare; (*person*) arrivare (in macchina)

drive-by ['draɪv,baɪ] N (*also*: **drive-by shooting**) sparatoria dalla macchina; **he was killed in a drive-by shooting** lo hanno ammazzato sparandogli da una macchina in corsa

drive-in ['draɪv,ɪn] N (*esp Am*) drive-in *m inv*

■ ADJ: **drive-in cinema/restaurant/bank** cinema/ fastfood/banca drive-in; **drive-in window** sportello di drive-in

driv·el ['drɪvl] N (*fam*: *nonsense*) stupidaggini *fpl*, sciocchezze *fpl*

▸ **drivel on** VI + ADV (*fam*): **to drivel on (about)** non smettere di cianciare (di)

driv·en ['drɪvn] PT *of* **drive**

◎ **driver** ['draɪvə^r] N **1** (*of car*) guidatore(-trice); (*professional*: *of car, lorry*) autista *m/f*; (: *of bus*) conducente *m/f*, autista *m/f*; (*of taxi*) tassista *m/f*; **to be in the driver's seat** essere seduto(-a) nel posto del conducente; (*fig*) essere al timone; **he's a good driver** guida bene; **he's a terrible driver** è un pessimo guidatore **2** (*Comput*) driver *m inv*

driver's license, N (*Am*) = **driving licence**

drive-through ['draɪvθru:] ADJ, N drive-in (*m*) *inv*

drive·way ['draɪv,weɪ] N vialetto d'accesso

driv·ing ['draɪvɪŋ] N (*Aut*) guida; **his driving is awful** guida veramente male

■ ADJ **1** (*Aut*) di guida; **driving instructor** istruttore(-trice) di (scuola) guida; **driving lesson** lezione *f* di guida; **driving mirror** specchietto retrovisore; **driving school** scuola guida *inv*; **driving test** esame *m* di guida; **to pass/fail one's driving test** superare/non superare l'esame di guida **2** (*necessity*) impellente; (*force*) trainante; (*rain, sleet*) battente, sferzante

driving licence, (*Am*) **driver's license** N patente *f* (di guida)

driving range N (*Golf*) driving range *m inv*

driz·zle ['drɪzl] N pioggerella, acquerugiola

■ VI piovigginare

driz·zly ['drɪzlɪ] ADJ piovigginoso(-a)

droll [drəʊl] ADJ (*old*: *humour*) ameno(-a); (: *expression*) buffo(-a), strambo(-a)

drom·edary ['drɒmɪdərɪ] N dromedario

drone [drəʊn] N **1** (*male bee*) fuco, pecchione *m*
2 (*noise*: *of bees, aircraft*) ronzio; (: *of voices*) brusio

■ VI (*bee, engine, aircraft*) ronzare; (*person*: *also*: **drone on**) continuare a parlare (in modo monotono); (*voice*) continuare a ronzare

drool [dru:l] VI (*baby*) sbavare; **to drool over sb/sth** (*fig*) andare in estasi per qn/qc

droop [dru:p] VI (*head*) chinarsi; (: *with sleep*) cadere; (*shoulders*) piegarsi; (*flower, plant*) afflosciarsi; (*person*) abbattersi; **she was drooping with tiredness** cascava di stanchezza; **his spirits drooped** si è molto abbattuto, si è avvilito

droopy ['dru:pɪ] ADJ (*comp* **-ier**, *superl* **-iest**) (*moustache*) cascante

◎ **drop** [drɒp] N

1 (*gen*) goccia; (*of wine, tea*) goccio, goccino; **would you like some milk? – just a drop** vuoi del latte? – solo una goccia; **drop by drop** goccia a goccia; **a drop in the ocean** (*fig*) una goccia nel mare; **he's had a drop too much** (*fam*) ha bevuto un bicchiere di troppo; **drops** NPL (*Med*) gocce *fpl*; **lemon drops** (*sweets*) caramelle *fpl* al limone

2 (*fall*: *in price*) calo, ribasso; (: *in temperature*) abbassamento; (: *in salary*) riduzione *f*, taglio; **a drop of 10%** un calo del 10%; **a drop in temperature** un calo della temperatura; **at the drop of a hat** in quattro e quattr'otto

3 (*downward slope*) salto, dislivello; (*fall*) salto; **a drop of 10 metres** un salto di 10 metri

4 (*unloading by parachute*: *of supplies, arms*) lancio

■ VT

1 (*let fall*) far *or* lasciar cadere; (: *bomb*) lanciare, sganciare; (: *liquid*) gocciolare; (: *stitch*) lasciar cadere; (*lower*: *hemline*) allungare; (: *price, eyes, voice*) abbassare; (*set down from car*: *object, person*) lasciare; (*from boat*: *cargo, passengers*) sbarcare; **could you drop me at the station?** puoi lasciarmi alla stazione?; **to drop anchor** gettare l'ancora

2 (*utter casually*: *remark, name, clue*) lasciar cadere; **to drop a word in sb's ear** dire una parolina nell'orecchio a qn; **to drop (sb) a hint about sth** far capire qc (a qn)

3 (*postcard, note*) mandare, scrivere; **to drop sb a line** mandare due righe a qn

4 (*omit*: *word, letter*) dimenticare; (: *aitches*) omettere, non pronunciare; (: *intentionally*: *person*) escludere; (: *thing*) omettere

5 (*abandon*: *work*) lasciare; (: *topic*) lasciar cadere; (: *idea*) abbandonare; (: *candidate*) escludere; (: *boyfriend, girlfriend*) piantare, mollare; **let's drop the subject** lasciamo perdere; **I'm going to drop chemistry** ho intenzione di non fare più chimica; **drop it!** (*fam*: *subject*) piantala!; (: *gun*) buttalo!

6 (*lose*: *money, game*) perdere

■ VI

1 (*fall*: *object*) cadere, cascare; **the book dropped onto the floor** il libro è caduto sul pavimento; **she was about to drop** (*fam*) stava per crollare; **I'm ready to drop** (*fam*) sto morendo; **drop dead!** (*fam*) va' al diavolo!

2 (*decrease*: *wind, temperature, price*) calare; (: *numbers, attendance*) diminuire; (: *voice*) abbassare; **the temperature will drop tonight** la temperatura diminuirà stanotte

▸ **drop back** VI + ADV (rallentare per) restare indietro; **he dropped back on purpose** ha rallentato apposta per restare indietro

▸ **drop behind** VI + ADV restare indietro

▸ **drop down** VI + ADV cadere, cascare

▸ **drop in** VI + ADV (*fam*: *visit*): **to drop in (on)** fare un salto (da), passare (da)

▸ **drop off** VI + ADV

1 (*fall asleep*) addormentarsi

2 (*decline*: *sales, interest*) calare, diminuire; (: *craze*) passare

■ VT + ADV: **to drop sb off** (*from car*) far scendere qn; **to drop sth off** lasciare qc

▸ **drop out** VI + ADV (*contents*) cascar fuori; (*fig*: *from*

Dd

contest) ritirarsi; (: *student*) smettere di studiare; **to drop out of society/university** abbandonare la società/gli studi universitari

drop-dead ['drɒpded] ADV: **drop-dead gorgeous** (*fam*) fighissimo(-a)

drop-down menu [ˌdrɒpdaʊn'mɛnjuː] N (*Comput*) menu *m inv* a tendina

drop goal N (*Rugby*) drop *m inv*

drop-in ['drɒpɪn] ADJ: **drop-in centre** centro di assistenza (*per persone con vari problemi, dove non è necessario prendere appuntamento*)

drop kick N (*Rugby*) calcio di drop

drop-leaf table ['drɒp,liːf'teɪbl] N tavolo con piano ribaltabile

drop·let ['drɒplɪt] N gocciolina

drop-off ['drɒp,ɒf] N: **drop-off (in)** (*sales, demand*) calo (di)

drop·out ['drɒpaʊt] N **1** (*from school, university*) chi ha abbandonato gli studi; (*from society*) chi si mette ai margini della società; **the school/college dropout rate** la percentuale di abbandono della scuola/università **2** (*Rugby*) calcio di rinvio

drop·per ['drɒpəʳ] N (*Med*) contagocce *m inv*

drop·pings ['drɒpɪŋz] NPL (*of bird, animal*) escrementi *mpl*, sterco *msg*

drop shot N (*Tennis*) smorzata; **drop volley** volée *f inv* smorzata

dross [drɒs] N (*Metallurgy*) scoria; (*fig: rubbish*) spazzatura

drought [draʊt] N siccità

drove [drəʊv] PT *of* **drive**

■N (*of cattle*) mandria; **droves of people** centinaia *fpl* di persone; **they came in droves** sono arrivati a frotte

drown [draʊn] VT (*people, animals*) affogare, annegare; (*land*) allagare; (*also:* **drown out**: *sound*) coprire; **you look like a drowned rat** (*fam*) sei tutto fradicio!

■VI (*also:* **to be drowned**) annegare, affogare

drown·ing ['draʊnɪŋ] ADJ che sta annegando *or* affogando

■N annegamento

drowse [draʊz] VI sonnecchiare, essere mezzo assopito(-a)

drowsi·ly ['draʊzɪlɪ] ADV con aria assonnata; **she answered drowsily** rispose con voce assonnata

drowsi·ness ['draʊzɪnɪs] N sonnolenza

drowsy ['draʊzɪ] ADJ (*comp* **-ier**, *superl* **-iest**) (*sleepy: person, smile, look*) assonnato(-a); (*soporific: afternoon, atmosphere*) sonnolento(-a); **to feel drowsy** sentirsi insonnolito(-a)

drub·bing ['drʌbɪŋ] N (*fam*) batosta

drudge [drʌdʒ] N (*person*) uomo/donna di fatica

drudg·ery ['drʌdʒərɪ] N fatica; **housework is sheer drudgery** sbrigare le faccende domestiche è un lavoro pesante e ingrato

◎**drug** [drʌg] N (*Med*) medicina, medicinale *m*, farmaco; (*addictive substance*) droga, stupefacente *m*; **hard drugs** droghe pesanti; **soft drugs** droghe leggere; **to take drugs** drogarsi; **he's on drugs** si droga; (*Med*) è in cura; **the drugs squad** la squadra narcotici

■ADJ di droga; **drug dealer** spacciatore(-trice) di droga; **drug runner** trafficante *m/f* di droga; **drug running** = drug traffic; **drug traffic** traffico di droga

■VT (*person, wine, food*) drogare; **to be in a drugged sleep** dormire sotto l'effetto di narcotici

drug abuser [-ə'bjuːzəʳ] N chi fa abuso di droghe

drug addict N tossicodipendente *m/f*, tossicomane *m/f*

drug addiction N tossicodipendenza

drug·gist ['drʌgɪst] N (*Am*) farmacista *m/f*

drug·store ['drʌg,stɔːʳ] N (*Am*) *negozio di generi vari con un bar*

drug-taker ['drʌg,teɪkəʳ] N chi fa uso di droga *or* di stupefacenti

drug-taking ['drʌg,teɪkɪŋ] N uso di droga

dru·id ['druːɪd] N druido; (*today*) persona che crede nella new age

▹ www.crystalinks.com/druids.html

▹ http://celt.net/Celtic/History/d_overview.html

◎**drum** [drʌm] N **1** (*Mus*) tamburo; **a drum kit** una batteria; **the drums** la batteria; **to play the drums** suonare la batteria; **big drum** grancassa; **drum roll** rullio di tamburi **2** (*container: for oil, petrol*) bidone *m*, fusto; (*Tech: cylinder, machine part*) tamburo

■VT: **to drum one's fingers on the table** tamburellare con le dita sul tavolo; **to drum sth into sb** (*fig*) ficcare qc in testa a qn

■VI (*Mus*) battere *or* suonare il tamburo; (*tap: with fingers*) tamburellare; **the noise was drumming in my ears** il rumore mi martellava nel cervello

▸ **drum up** VT + ADV (*enthusiasm, support*) conquistarsi

drum·beat ['drʌm,biːt] N colpo di tamburo

drum brake N (*Aut*) freno a tamburo

drum·lin ['drʌmlɪn] N collina morenica

drum major N tamburo maggiore

drum majorette [-ˌmeɪdʒə'ret] N majorette *f inv*

drum·mer ['drʌməʳ] N (*in military band*) tamburo; (*in jazz band, pop group*) batterista *m/f*

drum·stick ['drʌm,stɪk] N **1** (*Mus*) bacchetta **2** (*chicken leg*) coscia di pollo

drunk [drʌŋk] PP *of* **drink**

■ADJ ubriaco(-a); (*fig*) ebbro(-a), ubriaco(-a); **to get drunk** ubriacarsi; **to arrest sb for being drunk and disorderly** arrestare qn per ubriachezza molesta

■N ubriaco(-a)

drunk·ard ['drʌŋkəd] N beone(-a), ubriacone(-a)

drunk driver N (*Am*) guidatore(-trice) in stato di ebbrezza

drunk driving N (*Am*) guida in stato di ebbrezza

drunk·en ['drʌŋkən] ADJ (*intoxicated*) ubriaco(-a); (: *habitually*) alcolizzato(-a); (*brawl, orgy*) di ubriachi; (*rage*) provocato(-a) dall'alcol; (*voice*) da ubriaco; **drunken hooligans** hooligans ubriachi; **drunken driving** guida in stato di ebbrezza

drunk·en·ness ['drʌŋkənnɪs] N (*state*) ubriachezza, ebbrezza; (*habit, problem*) abuso di alcolici

drunk·om·eter [drʌŋ'kɒmɪtəʳ] N (*Am*) alcoltest *m inv*

◎**dry** [draɪ] ADJ (*comp* **-ier**, *superl* **-iest**) **1** (*gen*) secco(-a); (*clothes*) asciutto(-a); (*day*) senza pioggia; (*battery*) a secco; **it's been exceptionally dry this spring** il clima è stato insolitamente secco in primavera; **a long dry period** un lungo periodo senza pioggia; **on dry land** sulla terraferma; **as dry as a bone** completamente asciutto(-a); **to be dry** (*thirsty*) avere la gola secca; **the reservoir ran dry** il lago artificiale si è prosciugato **2** (*humour*): **a dry sense of humour** un senso dell'umorismo all'inglese; (*uninteresting: lecture, subject*) poco avvincente

■VT (*subj: person: hair, hands, clothes, child*) asciugare; (: *herbs, figs, flowers*) far seccare; (*subj: sun, wind*) seccare; **to dry one's hands/hair/eyes** asciugarsi le mani/i capelli/gli occhi; **she was drying a customer's hair** stava asciugando i capelli ad una cliente; **there's nowhere to dry clothes here** qui non c'è posto per far

asciugare i vestiti; **to dry the dishes** asciugare i piatti; **to dry o.s** asciugarsi
■ VI asciugarsi
▸ **dry off** VI + ADV (*clothes etc*) asciugarsi
■ VT + ADV asciugare
▸ **dry out** VI + ADV seccarsi; (*alcoholic*) disintossicarsi
■ VT + ADV asciugare
▸ **dry up** VI + ADV **1** (*river, well*) seccarsi; (*moisture*) asciugarsi; (*source of supply*) esaurirsi; (*fig: imagination*) inaridirsi **2** (*dry the dishes*) asciugare (i piatti) **3** (*fall silent: speaker*) azzittirsi; **dry up!** (*fam*) chiudi il becco!

dry-clean [ˌdraɪˈkliːn] VT pulire *or* lavare a secco; **"dry-clean only"** (*on label*) "pulire a secco"
dry-cleaner's [ˌdraɪˈkliːnəz] N lavasecco *m inv*, tintoria
dry-cleaning [ˌdraɪˈkliːnɪŋ] N lavaggio a secco; **shall I pick up your dry-cleaning for you?** vado a prenderti la roba in tintoria?
dry dock N (*Naut*) bacino di carenaggio
dry·er, dri·er [ˈdraɪə^r] N (*for hair*) föhn *m inv*, asciugacapelli *m inv*; (*at hairdresser's*) casco *m* asciugacapelli *inv*; (*for clothes*) asciugabiancheria *m inv*; **tumble dryer** asciugabiancheria; **hair dryer** asciugacapelli
dry-eyed [ˌdraɪˈaɪd] ADJ: **she remained dry-eyed throughout the funeral** non ha pianto per tutto il funerale
dry goods NPL (*Am Comm*) tessuti *mpl* e mercerie *fpl*; **dry goods store** negozio di stoffe
dry ice N ghiaccio secco
dry·ing [ˈdraɪɪŋ] N (*of clothes*) asciugatura; (*of herbs, flowers*) essiccazione *f*; **drying cupboard** ambiente *m* riscaldato per asciugare i panni
drying-up [ˌdraɪɪŋˈʌp] N: **to do the drying-up** asciugare i piatti
dry iron N ferro da stiro (a secco)
dry·ly, dri·ly [ˈdraɪlɪ] ADV (*coldly*) con fare distaccato; (*with dry humour*) con una punta d'ironia
dry·ness [ˈdraɪnɪs] N (*gen*) secchezza; (*of ground*) aridità; **she remarked with some dryness that ...** osservò con una punta d'ironia che...
dry rot N fungo del legno
dry run N (*fig*) prova
dry ski slope N pista artificiale
dry-stone wall [ˈdraɪsteʊnˈwɔːl] N muro a secco
DSc N ABBR = *Doctor of Science*
DST [ˌdiːɛsˈtiː] ABBR (*Am*) = **daylight-saving time**
DTI [ˌdiːtiːˈaɪ] N ABBR (*Brit*) = **Department of Trade and Industry**; *see* **department**
▹ www.dti.gov.uk
DTP [ˌdiːtiːˈpiː] N ABBR (= **desktop publishing**) DTP
DT's [ˌdiːˈtiːz] NPL ABBR (= **delirium tremens** (*fam*)): **the DT's** delirium *m inv* tremens *inv*
dual [ˈdjʊəl] ADJ doppio(-a), duplice; **dual controls** doppi comandi *mpl*; **dual nationality** doppia nazionalità
■ N (*Gram*) duale *m*; (*Geom*) duale *f*
dual carriageway N (*Brit*) strada a doppia carreggiata
dual·ism [ˈdjuːəlɪzəm] N dualismo
dual·ist [ˈdjuːəlɪst] N dualista *m/f*
dual-purpose [ˈdjʊəlˈpɜːpəs] ADJ a doppio uso
dub [dʌb] VT **1** (*Cine*) doppiare **2** (*nickname*) ribattezzare, soprannominare; **they dubbed him "Shorty"** l'hanno ribattezzato *or* soprannominato "Shorty"
dubbed [dʌbd] ADJ (*film*) doppiato(-a)
dub·bing [ˈdʌbɪŋ] N (*Cine*) doppiaggio

du·bi·ety [djuːˈbaɪətɪ] N (*frm*) incertezza
du·bi·ous [ˈdjuːbɪəs] ADJ (*gen*) dubbio(-a); (*look, smile*) dubbioso(-a); (*character, manner*) ambiguo(-a), equivoco(-a); **to feel dubious about** *or* **as to what to do next** essere incerto(-a) sul da farsi; **I'm very dubious about it** ho i miei dubbi in proposito
du·bi·ous·ly [ˈdjuːbɪəslɪ] ADV con esitazione
du·bi·ous·ness [ˈdjuːbɪəsnɪs] N (*uncertainty*) incertezza
Dub·lin [ˈdʌblɪn] N Dublino *f*
▹ www.visitdublin.com
Dublin Bay prawn N gamberone *m*
Dub·lin·er [ˈdʌblɪnə^r] N dublinese *m/f*
duch·ess [ˈdʌtʃɪs] N duchessa
duchy [ˈdʌtʃɪ] N ducato
duck [dʌk] N anatra; **wild duck** anatra selvatica; **she's taken to her new school like a duck to water** si è trovata subito benissimo nella nuova scuola; **to play (at) ducks and drakes** tirare i sassi a fior d'acqua
■ VT (*plunge in water: person, head*) spingere sotto (acqua); **to duck one's head** abbassare la testa
■ VI (*also:* **duck down**) accucciarsi; (*in fight*) fare una schivata; (*under water*) tuffarsi sott'acqua
▸ **duck out of** VI + PREP (*fam*): **to duck out of doing sth** svignarsela per evitare di fare qc
duck·board [ˈdʌkˌbɔːd] N passerella
duck-egg blue [ˈdʌkɛgˌbluː] ADJ, N verdazzurro(-a) chiaro(-a)
duck·ing [ˈdʌkɪŋ] N: **to give sb a ducking** spingere qn sott'acqua (*per gioco*)
duck·ling [ˈdʌklɪŋ] N anatroccolo
duct [dʌkt] N (*Tech, Anat*) condotto, canale *m*
duc·tile [ˈdʌktaɪl] ADJ (*metal*) duttile
dud [dʌd] (*fam*) ADJ (*shell, bomb*) inesploso(-a); (*not working: machine*) inservibile; (*false: coin, note*) fasullo(-a); (*: cheque*) a vuoto
■ N: **to be a dud** (*object, tool*) non servire a un bel niente, non funzionare; (*person*) essere una nullità; (*shell*) fare cilecca
dudg·eon [ˈdʌdʒən] N: **in high dudgeon** profondamente indignato(-a)
◎ **due** [djuː] ADJ **1** (*owing: sum, money*) dovuto(-a); **due date** (*Comm*) data di scadenza; **the rent's due on the 30th** l'affitto scade il 30; **our thanks are due to him** gli è dovuto un grazie; **I am due 6 days' leave** mi spettano 6 giorni di ferie **2** (*proper: care, respect, attention*) dovuto(-a), giusto(-a); **with all due respect** con rispetto parlando; **after due consideration** dopo un attento esame; **in due course** a tempo debito **3** (*expected*) atteso(-a); **the train is due at 8** il treno è atteso per le 8; **she is due back tomorrow** dovrebbe essere di ritorno domani; **he's due to arrive tomorrow** lo attendiamo per domani; **it is due to be demolished** è destinato alla demolizione; **when's the baby due?** quando deve nascere il bambino? **4 due to** (*caused by*) dovuto(-a) a; (*because of*) a causa di; (*thanks to*) grazie a; **the trip was cancelled due to bad weather** il viaggio è stato annullato a causa del maltempo
■ ADV: **due west of** direttamente a ovest di; **to go due north** andare dritto verso nord; **to face due south** guardare dritto verso sud
■ N: **to give him his due, he did try hard** per essere onesti (nei suoi confronti), bisogna riconoscere che ce l'ha messa tutta; *see also* **dues**
duel [ˈdjʊəl] N duello
■ VI battersi in duello

Dd

dues [dju:z] NPL (*club, union fees*) quota; **harbour dues** diritti *mpl* di porto

duet [dju:'ɛt] N duetto; **to sing/play a duet** cantare/suonare un duetto; **a violin/piano duet** (*performance*) un duetto al violino/al piano; (*composition*) un duetto per violino/per piano

duff [dʌf] ADJ (*Brit fam: effort, attempt*) balordo(-a)
▶ **duff up** VT + ADV (*Brit: fam*) tempestare di pugni

duf·fel, **duf·fle** ['dʌfəl] N montgomery *m inv*

duffel bag N sacca da viaggio di tela

duffel coat N ≈ duffel

duf·fer ['dʌfə^r] N (*fam*) schiappa

dug [dʌg] PT, PP *of* **dig**

dug·out ['dʌg,aʊt] N **1** (*Mil*) trincea coperta; (*Sport*) panchina **2** (*canoe*) *canoa ricavata da un tronco d'albero*

duke [dju:k] N duca *m*

dul·cet ['dʌlsɪt] ADJ (*liter, hum*) soave; **I thought I heard your dulcet tones** (*hum*) mi pareva di aver sentito la tua dolce voce

dull [dʌl] ADJ (*comp* **-er**, *superl* **-est**) **1** (*boring: book, evening*) noioso(-a); (*: person, style*) insulso(-a); **he's nice, but a bit dull** è simpatico, ma un po' noioso; **as dull as ditchwater** una vera pizza **2** (*dim: colour, eyes*) spento(-a); (*metal*) opaco(-a); (*overcast: weather, day, sky*) cupo(-a), scuro(-a), fosco(-a); (*muffled: sound, pain, thud*) sordo(-a); (*Comm: trade, business*) stagnante; (*lacking spirit: person, mood*) svogliato(-a); (*blade*) smussato(-a); **a dull day** una giornata nuvolosa **3** (*sight, hearing*) debole; (*slow-witted: person, mind*) ottuso(-a); (*: pupil*) lento(-a)
■VT (*mind, senses*) ottundere, annebbiare; (*blade*) smussare; (*impression, memory*) offuscare; (*pleasure, pain, grief*) attenuare, attutire; (*sound, colour*) smorzare; (*metal*) rendere opaco(-a)

dull·ard ['dʌləd] N (*old*) tonto(-a)

dull·ness ['dʌlnɪs] N **1** (*of life, evening*) tedio; (*of person: uninteresting character*) l'essere noioso(-a); (*: slow-wittedness*) ottusità; (*: lack of vitality*) inerzia; (*of books, ideas, approach*) mancanza di originalità **2** (*of colour, metal*) opacità; (*of sound*) tono sordo

dul·ly ['dʌllɪ] ADV (*listen*) con aria imbambolata; (*act*) senza mostrare interesse; (*talk, write*) in modo monotono, in modo insipido

duly ['dju:lɪ] ADV (*properly*) come si deve, debitamente; (*as expected*) come previsto, secondo le previsioni; (*on time*) a tempo debito; **he duly arrived at 3** è arrivato alle 3 come previsto; **everybody was duly shocked** tutti sono rimasti debitamente scioccati

dumb [dʌm] ADJ (*comp* **-er**, *superl* **-est**) **1** (*Med*) muto(-a); (*with surprise*) senza parole, ammutolito(-a); **a dumb person** un*a* muto(-a); **deaf and dumb** sordomuto; **dumb animals** gli animali; **to be struck dumb** (*fig*) restare senza parole, ammutolire **2** (*fam: stupid*) stupido(-a); **I was so dumb!** che stupido sono stato!; **that was a really dumb thing I did!** ho fatto proprio una stupidaggine!; **to act dumb** fare lo gnorri; **a dumb blonde** una bionda svampita

dumb·bell ['dʌm,bɛl] N (*Sport*) manubrio, peso

dumb·found [dʌm'faʊnd] VT sbigottire

dumb·found·ed [,dʌm'faʊndɪd] ADJ: **to be dumbfounded** rimanere sbigottito(-a)

dumb·ness ['dʌmnɪs] N **1** (*Med*) mutismo **2** (*fam: stupidity*) idiozia, stupidità

dumbo ['dʌmbəʊ] N (*fam*) scemo(-a)

dumb·struck ['dʌm,strʌk] ADJ: **to be dumbstruck** restare senza parole

dumb·waiter ['dʌm,weɪtə^r] N montavivande *m*

dum·my ['dʌmɪ] N **1** (*Comm: imitation*) cosa finta, riproduzione *f*; (*tailor's model*) manichino; (*ventriloquist's dummy*) pupazzo; (*Sport*) finta; (*Bridge*) morto **2** (*Brit: for baby*) tettarella, succhiotto **3** (*fam: idiot*) tonto(-a)
■ADJ (*not real*) finto(-a), falso(-a); **dummy weapons** armi giocattolo

dummy run N giro di prova

◎**dump** [dʌmp] N **1** (*pile of rubbish*) mucchio di immondizie *or* di rifiuti; (*place for refuse*) discarica pubblica; **to be (down) in the dumps** (*fam*) essere giù di corda **2** (*Mil*) deposito **3** (*pej fam: town, hotel etc*) buco; (*: house*) catapecchia; **it's a real dump!** è proprio un postaccio! **4** (*Comput*) stampa della memoria, dump *m inv*
■VT **1** (*get rid of: rubbish etc*) buttare; (*: Comm: goods*) svendere; (*fam: person*) piantare, scaricare **2** (*put down: load*) scaricare; (*: fam: parcel, passenger, coat*) mollare; **we dumped our bags at the hotel and went to the beach** abbiamo mollato i bagagli all'albergo e siamo andati in **3** (*Comput*) riversare

dump·ing ['dʌmpɪŋ] N **1** (*of rubbish*) scarico; **"no dumping"** (*of waste, rubbish*) "vietato lo scarico" **2** (*Econ*) dumping *m inv*

dump·ling ['dʌmplɪŋ] N (*Culin*) gnocco di pasta

dump truck N (*also:* **dumper truck**) autocarro con cassone ribaltabile

dumpy ['dʌmpɪ] ADJ tracagnotto(-a)

dun [dʌn] ADJ bigio(-a), grigiastro(-a)

dunce [dʌns] N (*Scol*) asino(-a), somaro(-a)

dune [dju:n] N duna

dung [dʌŋ] N (*of horse, cow*) sterco; (*as manure*) letame *m*, concime *m*

dun·ga·rees [,dʌŋgə'ri:z] NPL (*child's*) tutina; (*adult's*) salopette *f inv*; (*of workmen*) tuta

dun·geon ['dʌndʒən] N segreta, prigione *f* sotterranea

dung·hill ['dʌŋ,hɪl] N letamaio

dunk [dʌŋk] VT intingere, inzuppare; **to dunk one's bread in one's soup** inzuppare il pane nella minestra

duo ['dju:əʊ] N (*gen, Mus*) duo *m inv*

duo·deci·mal [,dju:əʊ'dɛsɪməl] ADJ duodecimale

duo·de·nal [,dju:əʊ'di:nl] ADJ (*ulcer*) duodenale

duo·denum [,dju:əʊ'di:nəm] N duodeno

dupe [dju:p] N zimbello(-a); **to be sb's dupe** lasciarsi ingannare da qn
ingannare, gabbare; **to dupe sb into doing sth** ingannare qn per fargli fare qc

du·plex ['dju:plɛks] N (*Am: also:* **duplex apartment**) appartamento su due piani

du·pli·cate [*vb* 'dju:plɪ,keɪt; *n, adj* 'dju:plɪkɪt] VT (*document*) fare una doppia copia di; (*on machine*) riprodurre, duplicare; (*repeat: action*) ripetere, riprodurre
■N (*document*) duplicato; **in duplicate** in duplice copia, in doppia copia; **duplicate key** doppione *m* della chiave
■ADJ (*copy*) conforme, esattamente uguale; **duplicate key** doppione; **duplicate receipt pad** bollettario

du·pli·cat·ing ma·chine ['dju:plɪ,keɪtɪŋməʃi:n], **du·pli·ca·tor** ['dju:plɪkeɪtə^r] N duplicatore *m*

du·pli·ca·tion [,dju:plɪ'keɪʃən] N (*gen*) ripetizione *f*; **we want to avoid duplication of work/effort** vogliamo evitare un doppio lavoro/sforzo

duplicitous [dju:'plɪsɪtəs] ADJ (*frm*) subdolo(-a)

du·plic·ity [dju:'plɪsɪtɪ] N (*frm*) doppiezza, duplicità

du·rabil·ity [,djʊərə'bɪlɪtɪ] N (*of materials*) resistenza; (*of relationship*) durevolezza

du·rable ['djʊərəbl] ADJ (*material, clothes*) resistente;

(*Comm*) durevole; (*friendship*) duraturo(-a); **durable goods** beni durevoli

du·ra·tion [djʊəˈreɪʃən] N durata; **of 6 years' duration** della durata di 6 anni

du·ress [djʊəˈrɛs] N: **under duress** sotto costrizione, con la coercizione

Durex® [ˈdjʊərɛks] N, PL INV (*Brit*) preservativo

◎**dur·ing** [ˈdjʊərɪŋ] PREP durante

dur·mast [ˈdɜːmɑːst] N (*Bot: also*: **durmast oak**) eschia

dusk [dʌsk] N (*twilight*) crepuscolo; (*gloom*) (semi)oscurità; **at dusk** sul far della sera, al crepuscolo; **in the dusk** (*liter*) nella semioscurità

dusky [ˈdʌskɪ] ADJ (*complexion, room, light*) scuro(-a); **dusky pink** rosa antico *inv*

◎**dust** [dʌst] N (*on furniture etc*) polvere *f*
■ VT, VI (*furniture*) spolverare; **she dusted the cake with sugar** ha spolverato il dolce di zucchero
▸ **dust off** VT + ADV rispolverare

dust·bin [ˈdʌstˌbɪn] N bidone *m* della spazzatura

dust bowl N (*Geog*) *regione semi-arida soggetta a tempeste di polvere*

dust·cart [ˈdʌstˌkɑːt] N camion *m inv* della nettezza urbana *or* delle immondizie

dust·er [ˈdʌstəʳ] N (*cloth*) straccio per la polvere; (*for blackboard*) cancellino, cimosa

dust·ing [ˈdʌstɪŋ] N: **to do the dusting** spolverare; **to give sth a dusting** dare una spolverata a qc
■ ADJ: **dusting powder** borotalco

dust jacket, dust cover N (*of book*) sopraccoperta, copertina

dust·man [ˈdʌstmən] N (*pl* **-men**) (*Brit*) netturbino

dust·pan [ˈdʌstˌpæn] N paletta

dust sheet N (*Brit*) telo di protezione

dust storm N tempesta di sabbia

dust-up [ˈdʌstˌʌp] N (*fam*) zuffa

dusty [ˈdʌstɪ] ADJ (*comp* **-ier**, *superl* **-iest**) polveroso(-a); **to get dusty** impolverarsi

Dutch [dʌtʃ] ADJ olandese; **Dutch elm disease** fungo parassita dell'olmo
■ N **1 the Dutch** NPL (*people*) gli olandesi
2 (*language*) olandese *m*
■ ADV: **to go Dutch** *or* **dutch** (*fam*) fare alla romana

Dutch auction N asta all'olandese

Dutch cap N diaframma *m*

Dutch courage N: **to give o.s. Dutch courage** farsi coraggio con un bicchierino

Dutch·man [ˈdʌtʃmən] N (*pl* **-men**) olandese *m*

Dutch·woman [ˈdʌtʃˌwʊmən] N (*pl* **-women**) olandese *f*

du·ti·able [ˈdjuːtɪəbl] ADJ soggetto(-a) a dazio

du·ti·ful [ˈdjuːtɪfʊl] ADJ (*child*) rispettoso(-a); (*husband*) premuroso(-a); (*employee*) coscienzioso(-a)

du·ti·ful·ly [ˈdjuːtɪfəlɪ] ADV (*obey, act*) con il dovuto rispetto; (*work*) coscienziosamente

◎**duty** [ˈdjuːtɪ] N **1** (*moral, legal*) dovere *m*; **it was his duty to tell the police** era suo dovere dirlo alla polizia; **I carried out my duties** ho svolto i miei compiti; **to do one's duty (by sb)** fare il proprio dovere (verso qn); **to make it one's duty to do sth** assumersi l'obbligo di fare qc **2** (*often pl: task, responsibility*) mansione *f*, funzione *f*; **on duty** (*Med: in hospital*) di guardia; (*Mil*) di servizio; (*Admin, Scol*) di turno; **off duty** (*gen*) fuori servizio; (*Mil*) in libera uscita; **duty rota** piano dei turni di lavoro **3** (*tax*) tassa; (: *at customs*) dazio; **to pay duty on sth** pagare il dazio su qc; **import duties** tassi d'importazione

duty-bound [ˈdjuːtɪˌbaʊnd] ADJ (*frm*): **to be duty-bound to do sth** avere il dovere morale di fare qc

duty-free [ˌdjuːtɪˈfriː] ADJ (*goods*) esente da dogana *or* dazio; (*at airport*) duty-free *inv*

duty-free shop N duty free *m inv*

duty officer N (*Mil*) ufficiale *m* di servizio

du·vet [ˈduːveɪ] N (*Brit*) piumone® *m*

DV [ˌdiːˈviː] ADV ABBR = *Deo volente*

DVD [ˌdiːviːˈdiː] N (= **digital video** *or* **versatile disk**) DVD *m inv*

DVD player N lettore *m* DVD *inv*

DVD-R [ˌdiːviːdiːˈɑːə] N (= **digital video** *or* **versatile disk recordable**) DVD-R *m inv*

DVD-RW [ˌdiːviːdiːɑːˈdʌbljʊ] N (= **digital video** *or* **versatile disk rewritable**) DVD-RW *m inv*, DVD *m inv* riscrivibile

DVLA [ˌdiːviːɛlˈeɪ] N ABBR (= **Driver and Vehicle Licensing Authority**) ≈ IMCTC *m* (= *Ispettorato generale della Motorizzazione Civile e dei Trasporti in Concessione*)

DVLC [ˌdiːviːɛlˈsiː] N ABBR (*Brit*) = *Driver and Vehicle Licensing Centre*

DVM [ˌdiːviːˈɛm] N ABBR (*Am*) = *Doctor of Veterinary Medicine*

DVT [ˌdiːviːˈtiː] N ABBR *see* **deep vein thrombosis**

dwarf [dwɔːf] ADJ, N nano(-a)
■ VT (*subj: building, person*) fare sembrare piccolissimo(-a), far scomparire; (*achievement*) eclissare

dwarf·ism [ˈdwɔːfɪzəm] N (*Med*) nanismo

dwell [dwɛl] (*pt, pp* **dwelt**) VI (*poet*) dimorare
▸ **dwell (up)on** VI + PREP (*think about*) rimuginare; (*talk about*) soffermarsi su, indugiare su; (*subj: conversation*) aggirarsi su; **don't let's dwell upon it** non insistiamo su questo punto; **he has never dwelt on the past** non ha mai rimuginato sul passato

dwell·er [ˈdwɛləʳ] N abitante *m/f*; **city dweller** cittadino(-a)

dwell·ing [ˈdwɛlɪŋ] N (*frm, liter*) dimora; **dwelling house** (*Law*) abitazione *f*

dwelt [dwɛlt] PT, PP *of* **dwell**

dwin·dle [ˈdwɪndl] VI (*numbers, supplies*) assottigliarsi, diminuire, decrescere; (*interest*) affievolirsi; **to dwindle to** ridursi a

dwin·dling [ˈdwɪndlɪŋ] ADJ (*strength, interest*) che si affievolisce; (*resources, supplies*) in diminuzione

DWP [ˌdiːdʌbljuːˈpiː] N ABBR (*Brit*: = **Department for Work and Pensions**) ≈ Ministero del lavoro e politiche sociali

dye [daɪ] N colore *m*; (*chemical*) colorante *m*, tintura; **hair dye** tinta per capelli, tintura per capelli; **the dye has run** si è stinto
■ VT (*fabric*) tingere; **to dye sth red** tingere qc di *or* in rosso; **to dye one's hair blond** farsi biondo(-a); **dyed hair** capelli *mpl* tinti

dyed-in-the-wool [ˈdaɪdnðəˈwʊl] ADJ (*fig*) inveterato(-a)

dye·ing [ˈdaɪɪŋ] N tintura

dyer [ˈdaɪəʳ] N tintore(-a)

dye·stuffs [ˈdaɪˌstʌfs] NPL sostanze *fpl* coloranti (per tintura)

dye·works [ˈdaɪˌwɜːks] NSG tintoria

dy·ing [ˈdaɪɪŋ] N (*death*) morte *f*; **the dying** NPL i morenti
■ ADJ (*person, plant*) morente; (*custom, race*) in via di estinzione; **his dying words were ...** le sue ultime parole furono...; **to my dying day** finché vivrò

dyke [daɪk] N **1** (*barrier*) diga, argine *m*; (*channel*)

canale *m* di scolo; (*causeway*) sentiero rialzato
2 (*offensive: lesbian*) lesbica
dy·nam·ic [daɪˈnæmɪk] ADJ dinamico(-a)
dy·nam·ics [daɪˈnæmɪks] NSG dinamica
dy·na·mism [ˈdaɪnəmɪzəm] N dinamismo
dy·na·mite [ˈdaɪnə,maɪt] N **1** dinamite *f* **2** (*fig*) (*fam*): **he's dynamite!** è una bomba!; **the story is dynamite** è una storia esplosiva
■VT far saltare con la dinamite
dy·na·mo [ˈdaɪnəməʊ] N dinamo *f inv*
dy·nas·tic [daɪˈnæstɪk] ADJ dinastico(-a)
dyn·as·ty [ˈdɪnəstɪ, *Am* ˈdaɪnəstɪ] N dinastia
d'you [dju:] = do you
dys·en·tery [ˈdɪsɪntrɪ] N dissenteria
dys·lexia [dɪsˈlɛksɪə] N dislessia
dys·lex·ic [dɪsˈlɛksɪk] ADJ, N dislessico(-a)
dys·pep·sia [dɪsˈpɛpsɪə] N dispepsia
dys·pep·tic [dɪsˈpɛptɪk] ADJ (*Med*) dispeptico(-a)
dys·to·pia [dɪsˈtəʊpɪə] N distopia
dys·to·pian [dɪsˈtəʊpɪən] ADJ distopico(-a)
dys·tro·phy [ˈdɪstrəfɪ] N distrofia; **muscular dystrophy** distrofia muscolare

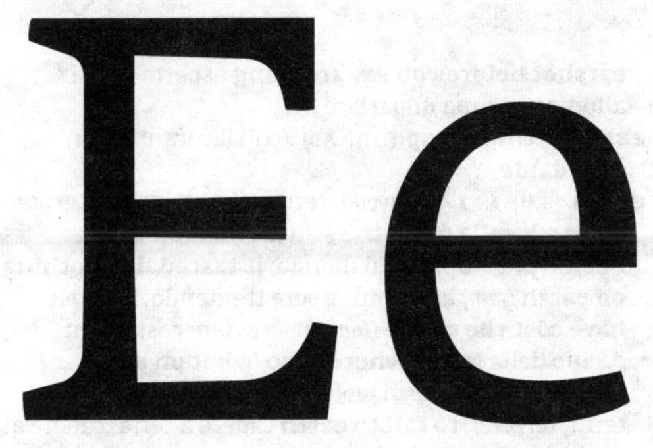

E, **e** [iː] N **1** (*letter*) E, e *f or m inv*; **E for Edward** (*Am*): **E for Easy** ≈ E come Empoli **2** (*Mus*) mi *m inv*

E ABBR (= **east**) E

■ N ABBR (*fam*) = **ecstasy**

e- [iː] PREF (*Comput*) e-

E111 [ˌiːwʌnɪˈlɛvn] N ABBR (*also:* **form E111**) modulo E111 (*per rimborso spese mediche all'estero*)

ea. ABBR = **each**

◎ **each** [iːtʃ] ADJ ogni *inv*, ciascuno(-a); **in each hand** in ciascuna mano; **each day** ogni giorno; **each one** ognuno(-a); **each one of them** ciascuno(-a) *or* ognuno(-a) di loro

■ PRON **1** ognuno(-a), ciascuno(-a); **each of us** ciascuno(-a) *or* ognuno(-a) di noi; **a little of each please** un po' di tutto, per favore **2 each other** l'un(-a) l'altro(-a), si (*or* ci *etc*); **they love each other** si amano; **we hate each other** ci odiamo; **you know each other** vi conoscete; **we write to each other** ci scriviamo; **people must help each other** ci si deve aiutare a vicenda *or* l'un l'altro; **separated from each other** separati l'uno dall'altro; **next to each other** uno accanto all'altro; **you are jealous of each other** siete gelosi l'uno dell'altro

■ ADV l'uno(-a), per uno(-a), ciascuno(-a); **they have ten points each** hanno dieci punti ciascuno; **we gave them an apple each** abbiamo dato una mela a ciascuno; **they cost £5 each** costano 5 sterline l'uno; **they have 2 books each** hanno 2 libri ciascuno

each way (*Brit*) ADJ: **each way bet** scommessa su un piazzato

■ ADV: **to bet on a horse each way** scommettere su un (cavallo) piazzato

◎ **eager** [ˈiːɡəʳ] ADJ (*keen: pupil*) appassionato(-a), attento(-a); (*: search, desire*) appassionato(-a); **to be eager to do sth** (*impatient*) essere impaziente *or* ansioso(-a) di fare qc, non veder l'ora di fare qc; **he was eager to tell us about his experiences** era impaziente di raccontarci le sue esperienze; **to be eager for** (*knowledge, power*) essere avido(-a) di; (*affection*) essere desideroso(-a) di; (*happiness*) desiderare ardentemente; **he gave me an eager look** mi ha guardato speranzoso

eager beaver N (*fam: worker*) stacanovista *m/f*; (*: student*) secchione(-a)

eager·ly [ˈiːɡəlɪ] ADV (*listen, watch*) attentamente; (*speak, work*) con entusiasmo; (*wait*) ansiosamente

eager·ness [ˈiːɡənɪs] N (*see adj*) passione *f*; impazienza, ansia; (*for happiness, affection*) desiderio; (*for knowledge, power*) sete *f*

eagle [ˈiːɡl] N aquila

eagle-eyed [ˈiːɡlˈaɪd] ADJ (*person*) dagli occhi di lince

E & OE [ˌiːəndˈəʊiː] ABBR (= **errors and omissions excepted**) S.E.eO. (= *salvo errori e omissioni*)

◎ **ear¹** [ɪəʳ] N orecchio, orecchia; **to keep one's ears open** tenere le orecchie aperte; **to be all ears** essere tutt'orecchi; **he could not believe his ears** non credeva alle proprie orecchie; **your ears must have been burning** non ti fischiavano le orecchie?; **it goes in one ear and out the other** mi (*or* ti *etc*) entra da un orecchio ed esce dall'altro; **to be up to one's ears in debt** essere nei debiti fino al collo; **to be up to one's ears in work** avere una mole enorme di lavoro; **to have a good ear for music** avere molto orecchio; **to have a good ear for languages** avere molto orecchio per le lingue; **to play sth by ear** (*tune*) suonare qc a orecchio; **I'll play it by ear** (*fig*) vedrò come si mettono le cose

ear² [ɪəʳ] N (*of wheat, barley*) spiga; (*of corn*) pannocchia

ear·ache [ˈɪərˌeɪk] N mal *m* d'orecchi; **to have earache** avere mal d'orecchi

ear·drum [ˈɪəˌdrʌm] N timpano

ear·ful [ˈɪəfʊl] N: **to give sb an earful** fare una ramanzina a qn

earl [ɜːl] N conte *m*

◎ **ear·ly** [ˈɜːlɪ] (*comp* **-ier**, *superl* **-iest**) ADV presto; (*ahead of time*) in anticipo; **I came home early** sono tornato a casa presto; **as early as possible** il più presto possibile; **early in the morning/afternoon** nelle prime ore del mattino/del pomeriggio; **early in the spring/19th century** all'inizio della primavera/dell'Ottocento; **he was 10 minutes early** è arrivato con 10 minuti di anticipo; **to book early** prenotare in anticipo; **I can't come any earlier** non posso venire

prima; **I saw him earlier** l'ho visto prima; **earlier on** poco tempo prima
■ ADJ (*man*) primitivo(-a); (*Christians, settlers*) primo(-a); (*fruit, plant*) precoce; (*death*) prematuro(-a); (*reply*) pronto(-a); **it's still early** è ancora presto; **an early general election** elezioni *fpl* generali anticipate; **at an early date** prossimamente; **an early edition of the book** una precedente edizione del libro; **you're early!** sei in anticipo!; **to be an early riser** *or* **an early bird** essere mattiniero(-a); **at an early hour** presto; **in the early morning** al mattino presto; **in the early 19th century** ai primi dell'Ottocento; **she's in her early forties** ha appena passato la quarantina; **from an early age** fin dall'infanzia; **his early youth** la sua prima giovinezza; **Shakespeare's early work** le prime opere di Shakespeare; **an early Victorian table** un tavolo del primo periodo vittoriano; **to have an early night** andare a letto presto; **to make an early start** iniziare presto; **at your earliest convenience** (*Comm*) non appena possibile

early adopter N: **an early adopter** uno(-a) dei/delle primi(-e) utilizzatori(-trici) (*di prodotto all'avanguardia, specie tecnologico*)

early closing N (*Brit Comm*) chiusura pomeridiana settimanale; **early closing day** giorno di chiusura pomeridiana settimanale

early music N musica medievale e rinascimentale
▷ www.medieval.org/emfaq/
▷ www.s-hamilton.k12.ia.us/antiqua/instrumt.html

early retirement N pensionamento anticipato, prepensionamento

early warning system N sistema *m* di preallarme

ear·mark ['ɪəˌmɑːk] VT: **to earmark (for)** (*money*) mettere da parte (per); (*person, job*) destinare (a)

◎ **earn** [ɜːn] VT (*money, salary*) guadagnare; (*Fin: interest*) maturare; (*praise, reward, rest*) meritare, meritarsi; **she earns five pounds an hour** guadagna cinque sterline all'ora; **to earn one's living** guadagnarsi da vivere; **this earned him much praise** *or* **he earned much praise for this** si è attirato grandi lodi per questo

earned income ['ɜːnd'ɪnkʌm] N (*Brit Fin*) reddito derivante da lavoro

earn·er ['ɜːnə^r] N: **to be the sole earner** essere l'unico in famiglia ad avere un reddito; **families with a sole earner** famiglie *fpl* monoreddito *inv*; **it is a nice little earner** è una buona fonte di guadagno

ear·nest ['ɜːnɪst] ADJ (*person, character, request*) serio(-a); (*wish*) sincero(-a)
■ N 1 **in earnest** (*with determination*) con serietà, con coscienza; (*seriously*) sul serio 2 (*Law*: *also*: **earnest money**) caparra

ear·nest·ly ['ɜːnɪstlɪ] ADV (*speak*) con serietà; (*work*) con coscienza; (*pray*) con fervore

ear·nest·ness ['ɜːnɪstnɪs] N serietà

◎ **earn·ings** ['ɜːnɪŋz] NPL (*of individual*) guadagni *mpl*; (*salary*) stipendio *sg*; (*of company*) proventi *mpl*; **average earnings rose two percent last year** l'anno scorso lo stipendio medio è aumentato del due percento

ear nose and throat specialist N otorinolaringoiatra *m/f*

ear·phones ['ɪəˌfəʊnz] NPL (*Telec*) cuffia *sg*

ear·piece ['ɪəˌpiːs] N 1 auricolare *m* 2 (*of glasses*) stanghetta

ear·plug ['ɪəˌplʌg] N tappo per le orecchie

ear·ring ['ɪərɪŋ] N orecchino

ear·shot ['ɪəʃɒt] N: **out of/within earshot** fuori portata/a portata d'orecchio; **wait till he's out of earshot before you say anything** aspetta che si allontani prima di parlare

ear-splitting ['ɪəˌsplɪtɪŋ] ADJ (*yell*) lacerante; (*din*) assordante

◎ **earth** [ɜːθ] N 1 (*the world*) terra; **(the) Earth** la Terra; **on earth** sulla terra; **the silliest man on earth** l'uomo più stupido del mondo; **it tasted like nothing on earth** (*fam*) aveva un sapore tremendo; **it must have cost the earth!** (*fam*) deve essere costato un occhio della testa!; **where/who/what on earth ...?** (*fam*) dove/chi/che diavolo...? 2 (*ground*) terra; (*soil*) terra, terreno; **to fall to earth** cadere a terra, cadere al suolo 3 (*of fox, badger*) tana; **to run to earth** (*animal*) inseguire fino alla tana; (*person*) scovare, stanare 4 (*Brit Elec*) terra, massa
■ VT (*Brit Elec: apparatus*) mettere *or* collegare a terra

earthed [ɜːθt] ADJ (*Elec: plug, appliance*) con la presa a terra

earth·en ['ɜːθən] ADJ (*of earth*) di terra; (*of baked clay*) di terracotta

earthen·ware ['ɜːθənwɛə^r] N terraglie *fpl*, terracotta
■ ADJ di terracotta

earth·ling ['ɜːθlɪŋ] N (*Science Fiction: human*) terrestre

earth·ly ['ɜːθlɪ] ADJ terreno(-a); **earthly paradise** paradiso terrestre; **there is no earthly reason to think ...** non vi è nessunissima ragione di pensare...; **it's of no earthly use** non serve assolutamente a nulla

earth·quake ['ɜːθˌkweɪk] N terremoto

earth·shaking ['ɜːθʃeɪkɪŋ] ADJ (*fig*) sconvolgente

earth-shattering ['ɜːθʃætərɪŋ] ADJ stupefacente; (*momentous*) molto importante

earth tremor N scossa sismica

earth·ward(s) ['ɜːθwəd(z)] ADV verso terra

earth wire (*Elec*) N terra

earth·work ['ɜːθˌwɜːk] N (*Mil*) terrapieno

earthworks ['ɜːθˌwɜːks] NPL lavori *mpl* di sterro

earth·worm ['ɜːθˌwɜːm] N lombrico

earthy ['ɜːθɪ] ADJ 1 (*taste, smell*) di terra 2 (*person*) terra terra *inv*; (*humour*) grossolano(-a)

ear·wax ['ɪəˌwæks] N cerume *m*

ear·wig ['ɪəˌwɪg] N (*insect*) forbicina

◎ **ease** [iːz] N 1 disinvoltura, scioltezza; **the camera's ease of use** la facilità d'impiego della macchina fotografica; **with ease** senza difficoltà 2 (*freedom from worry*) tranquillità, agio; **a life of ease** una vita comoda; **to feel at ease/ill at ease** sentirsi a proprio agio/a disagio; **to put sb at his** *or* **her ease** mettere qn a suo agio; **(stand) at ease!** (*Mil*) riposo!
■ VT (*task*) facilitare; (*pain*) alleviare, calmare; (*rope, strap, pressure*) allentare; (*collar*) slacciare; **to ease the pain ...** per calmare il dolore...; **to ease sb's mind** tranquillizzare *or* rassicurare qn; **to ease sth out/in** facilitare l'uscita/l'entrata di qc; **to ease in the clutch** (*Aut*) rilasciare la frizione dolcemente
■ VI (*situation*) distendersi; **the pressure has eased** la pressione è diminuita
▸ **ease off** VI + ADV (*slow down*) rallentare; (*work, business*) diminuire; (*pressure, tension*) allentarsi; (*pain*) calmarsi; (*relax*) rilassarsi
▸ **ease up** VI + ADV (*person*) calmarsi; (*situation*) distendersi; **ease up a bit!** prenditela calma!; **the pressure had eased up** la pressione era diminuita; **we can't ease up yet** non possiamo mollare ancora

easel ['iːzl] N cavalletto

◎ **easi·ly** ['iːzɪlɪ] ADV (*without effort: win, climb*) facilmente, agevolmente; **this can easily be done** questo si può fare facilmente; **he may easily change his mind** potrebbe benissimo cambiare idea; **it's easily the best** è senza dubbio il migliore, è di gran lunga il migliore; **there were easily 500 at the meeting** c'erano almeno 500 persone alla riunione; **it could easily be another year before he's back** è facile che passi un altro anno prima che ritorni

easi·ness [ˈi:zɪnɪs] N **1** facilità, semplicità **2** (*of manners*) disinvoltura

◎ **east** [i:st] N est *m*, oriente *m*; **the mysterious East** l'Oriente misterioso; **the East** (*Geog*) l'Oriente; (*Pol: formerly*) i Paesi dell'Est; **in the east** ad est; **the wind is in the east** *or* **from the east** il vento viene da est; **to the east of** a est di; **in the east of** nella parte orientale di

■ ADJ (*side, coast*) orientale; (*wind*) dell'est, di levante; **the East End** il quartiere est di Londra; **East Africa** l'Africa orientale

■ ADV (*travel*) a est, verso est, a oriente; **east of the border** a est della frontiera

east·bound [ˈi:stˌbaʊnd] ADJ (*traffic*) diretto(-a) a est; (*carriageway*) che porta a est

East·er [ˈi:stəʳ] N Pasqua; **at Easter** a Pasqua

■ ADJ (*holidays*) pasquale, di Pasqua week di Pasqua

▷ www.bbc.co.uk/religion/religions/christianity/holydays/easter.shtml

Easter egg N uovo di Pasqua

Easter Island N Isola di Pasqua

east·er·ly [ˈi:stəlɪ] ADJ (*point, aspect*) orientale; (*wind*) da est, di levante, dell'est; **in an easterly direction** in direzione est

Easter Monday N Pasquetta

◎ **east·ern** [ˈi:stən] ADJ orientale, d'oriente; **France's eastern border** il confine orientale della Francia; **Eastern Europe** l'Europa orientale, l'Europa dell'est; **the Eastern bloc** (*Pol: formerly*) i Paesi *mpl* dell'Est; **Eastern Standard Time** (*Am*) *ora invernale nel fuso orario della costa orientale degli Stati Uniti*

Eastern Cape N Capo orientale

▷ www.ecprov.gov.za

▷ www.ectourism.co.za

east·ern·er [ˈi:stənəʳ] N originario(-a) della parte orientale del paese

east·ern·most [ˈi:stənˌməʊst] ADJ più a est

Easter Sunday N domenica di Pasqua

East Germany N la Germania dell'Est

east·ward [ˈi:stwəd] ADJ (*direction*) est *inv*

east·ward(s) [ˈi:stwəd(z)] ADV a est, verso est, verso levante

◎ **easy** [ˈi:zɪ] (*comp* **-ier**, *superl* **-iest**) ADJ **1** (*not difficult*) facile; **it's easy to understand** è facile da capire; **it is easy to see that ...** è facile comprendere che...; **he's easy to get on with** ha un buon carattere; **he came in an easy first** ha vinto di larga misura; **easier said than done** si fa presto a dirlo; **easy money** facili guadagni *mpl* **2** (*carefree: life*) agiato(-a), tranquillo(-a); (*: relationship*) cordiale; (*relaxed: manners, style*) disinvolto(-a); **to feel easy in one's mind** sentirsi tranquillo(-a); **payment on easy terms** (*Comm*) facilitazioni *fpl* di pagamento; **I'm easy** (*fam*) non ho problemi

■ ADV: **easy does it!** piano!; **to take it** *or* **things easy** prendersela con calma; **take it easy!** (*don't worry*) non prendertela!; (*don't rush*) calma!; **go easy with the sugar** vacci piano con lo zucchero; **go easy on him** non essere troppo duro con lui; **stand easy!** (*Mil*) riposo!

easy chair N poltrona

easy-going [ˌi:zɪˈgəʊɪŋ] ADJ (*person*) accomodante; (*attitude*) tollerante; **to be easy-going** avere un buon carattere

easy listening [-ˈlɪsnɪŋ] N musica leggera americana, easy listening *m*

▷ www.bbc.co.uk/radio2/soldonsong/genres/analysis/easy.shtml

easy touch N (*fam*): **to be an easy touch** lasciarsi spillare denaro facilmente

◎ **eat** [i:t] (*vb: pt* **ate**, *pp* **eaten**) VT (*food*) mangiare; **would you like sth to eat?** vuoi mangiare qc?; **we slowly ate our sandwiches** abbiamo mangiato lentamente i nostri panini; **to eat one's fill** mangiare a sazietà; **he's eating us out of house and home** (*fam*) è un mangiapane a tradimento; **he won't eat you** (*fam*) non ti mangia mica; **what's eating you?** (*fam*) che cosa ti rode?; **to eat one's words** (*fig*) rimangiarsi quello che si è detto

■ VI mangiare; **he eats like a horse** mangia come un lupo; **I've got him eating out of my hand** pende dalle mie labbra, fa tutto quello che voglio io

▸ **eat away** VT + ADV (*subj: sea*) erodere; (*: acid*) corrodere; (*: mice*) rosicchiare

▸ **eat away at** VI + PREP rodere

▸ **eat in** VI + ADV mangiare a casa

▸ **eat into** VI + PREP rodere; (*subj: acid*) corrodere; (*savings*) intaccare

▸ **eat out** VI + ADV mangiare fuori

■ VT + ADV: **to eat one's heart out** mangiarsi *or* rodersi il fegato

▸ **eat up** VT + ADV (*meal*) finire di mangiare; **it eats up electricity** consuma un sacco di corrente; **this car eats up the miles** questa macchina macina i chilometri

■ VI + ADV: **eat up!** finisci di mangiare!

eat·able [ˈi:təbl] ADJ (*fit to eat*) mangiabile; (*safe to eat*) commestibile

eat·en [ˈi:tn] PP *of* eat

eat·er [ˈi:təʳ] N: **a big eater** un(-a) gran mangiatore(-trice), una buona forchetta

eat·ery [ˈi:tərɪ] N (*fam*) posto per mangiare

eat·ing [ˈi:tɪŋ] ADJ (*apple*) da mangiare

eating hall N (*Am*) mensa

eau de Co·logne [ˈəʊdəkəˈləʊn] N acqua di colonia

eaves [ˈi:vz] NPL gronda *sg*

eaves·drop [ˈi:vzdrɒp] VI: **to eavesdrop (on a conversation)** origliare (una conversazione)

eaves·drop·per [ˈi:vzˌdrɒpəʳ] N chi origlia

ebb [ɛb] N (*of tide*) riflusso; **ebb and flow** flusso e riflusso; **to be at a low ebb** (*fig: person, spirits*) avere il morale a terra; (*: business*) andar male; diminuire

■ VI rifluire; (*fig: also:* **ebb away**): **to ebb and flow** (*tide*) fluire e rifluire; **his strength was ebbing fast** le forze gli venivano meno rapidamente

ebb tide N marea discendente

eb·ony [ˈɛbənɪ] N ebano

e-book [ˈi:bʊk] N (*Comput*) libro elettronico, e-book *m inv*

ebul·lience [ɪˈbʌlɪəns] N esuberanza

ebul·lient [ɪˈbʌlɪənt] ADJ esuberante

ebul·lient·ly [ɪˈbʌlɪəntlɪ] ADV con esuberanza

e-business [ˈi:ˌbɪznɪs] N (*business*) azienda che opera in Internet; (*activity*) commercio elettronico, e-business *m inv*

EC [ˌi:ˈsi:] N ABBR (= **European Community**) CE *f* (= *Comunità Europea*)

Ee

ECB [ˌiːsiːˈbiː] N ABBR (= **European Central Bank**) BCE *f* (= *Banca Centrale Europea*)
ec·cen·tric [ɪkˈsɛntrɪk] ADJ, N eccentrico(-a)
ec·cen·tri·cal·ly [ɪkˈsɛntrɪkəlɪ] ADV eccentricamente
ec·cen·tri·city [ˌɛksənˈtrɪsɪtɪ] N eccentricità *f inv*
Ec·cle·si·as·tes [ɪˌkliːzɪˈæstiːz] N Ecclesiaste *m*
ec·cle·si·as·tic [ɪˌkliːzɪˈæstɪk] N, ADJ ecclesiastico(-a)
ec·cle·si·as·ti·cal [ɪˌkliːzɪˈæstɪkəl] ADJ ecclesiastico(-a)
ECG [ˌiːsiːˈdʒiː] N ABBR (= **electrocardiogram**) ECG *m inv*
ECGD [ˌiːsiːdʒiːˈdiː] N ABBR (= **Export Credits Guarantee Department**) *servizio di garanzia finanziaria per l'esportazione*
eche·lon [ˈɛʃəˌlɒn] N **1** grado **2** (*Mil*) scaglione *m*
echi·no·derm [ɪˈkiːnəˌdɜːm] N echinoderma *m*
◎**echo** [ˈɛkəʊ] N (*pl* **echoes**) eco *m or f*
■ VI (*sound*) echeggiare, riecheggiare; **the room echoed with their laughter** la stanza riecheggiava delle loro risate
■ VT fare eco a, ripetere
echo chamber N camera sonora
echo·graph [ˌɛkəʊˈgrɑːf] N ecografo
echo·graph·ic [ˌɛkəʊˈgræfɪk] ADJ ecografico(-a)
echo sounder N ecoscandaglio
éclair [ˈeɪklɛəʳ] N ≈ bigné *m inv*
ec·lec·tic [ɪˈklɛktɪk] ADJ eclettico(-a)
ec·lec·ti·cism [ɪˈklɛktɪsɪzəm] N eclettismo
eclipse [ɪˈklɪps] N eclissi *f inv*
■ VT eclissare
ECM [ˌiːsiːˈɛm] N ABBR (*Am*: = **European Common Market**) MEC *m*
eco... [ˈiːkəʊ] PREF eco...
eco-friendly [ˈiːkəʊˈfrɛndlɪ] ADJ ecologico(-a), che rispetta l'ambiente
eco·logi·cal [ˌiːkəʊˈlɒdʒɪkəl] ADJ ecologico(-a)
eco·logi·cal·ly [ˌiːkəˈlɒdʒɪkəlɪ] ADV ecologicamente
ecolo·gist [ɪˈkɒlədʒɪst] N (*scientist*) ecologo(-a); (*conservationist*) ecologista *m/f*
ecol·ogy [ɪˈkɒlədʒɪ] N ecologia
e-commerce [ˈiːˌkɒmɜːs] N commercio elettronico, e-commerce *m inv*
◎**eco·nom·ic** [ˌiːkəˈnɒmɪk] ADJ **1** (*problems, development, geography*) economico(-a) **2** (*profitable*: *price*) vantaggioso(-a); (: *business*) redditizio(-a)
eco·nomi·cal [ˌiːkəˈnɒmɪkəl] ADJ (*method, appliance, car*) economico(-a); (*person*) parsimonioso(-a), economo(-a); **economical with the truth** non del tutto sincero
eco·nomi·cal·ly [ˌiːkəˈnɒmɪkəlɪ] ADV **1** con economia **2** (*regarding economics*) dal punto di vista economico; **economically strong** forte dal punto di vista economico
economic migrant N migrante *m/f* economico(-a); *chi emigra da un paese povero ad un paese ricco in cerca di fortuna*
economic migration N migrazione *f* economica; *emigrazione da un paese povero ad un paese ricco in cerca di fortuna*
◎**eco·nom·ics** [ˌiːkəˈnɒmɪks] NSG (*science*) economia; **he's doing economics at university** fa economia all'università
■ NPL (*financial aspects*) aspetto *or* lato economico
▷ www.economist.com
economies of scale [ɪˈkɒnəmɪzəvˈskeɪl] NPL (*Econ*) economie *fpl* di scala
◎**econo·mist** [ɪˈkɒnəmɪst] N economista *m/f*
econo·mize [ɪˈkɒnəˌmaɪz] VI: **to economize (on)** fare economia (di), risparmiare (su)
◎**econo·my** [ɪˈkɒnəmɪ] N (*all senses*) economia; **the economy is doing well** l'economia sta andando bene; **economy size** confezione economica; **we must make economies** dobbiamo fare economia
economy class N (*Aer*) classe *f* turistica
economy drive N: **to have an economy drive** adottare una politica del risparmio
economy size N confezione *f* economica
eco·sys·tem [ˈiːkəʊˌsɪstəm] N ecosistema *m*
eco-tourism [ˌiːkəʊˈtʊərɪzəm] N turismo ecologico
eco-tourist [ˈiːkəʊˌtʊərɪst] N turista *m/f* ecologico(-a)
eco-warrior [ˈiːkəʊˌwɒrɪəʳ] N militante *m/f* ecologista
ECSC [ˌiːsiːɛsˈsiː] N ABBR (= **European Coal & Steel Community**) CECA *f* (= *Comunità Europea del Carbone e dell'Acciaio*)
ec·sta·sy [ˈɛkstəsɪ] N **1** (*Rel, fig*) estasi *f inv*; **to go into ecstasies over** andare in estasi per **2** (*drug*) ecstasy *f*
ec·stat·ic [ɛksˈtætɪk] ADJ estatico(-a), in estasi
ec·stati·cal·ly [ɛkˈstætɪkəlɪ] ADV estaticamente
ECT [ˌiːsiːˈtiː] N ABBR = **electroconvulsive therapy**
ec·top·ic [ɛkˈtɒpɪk] ADJ (*Med*): **ectopic pregnancy** gravidanza extrauterina
ECU [ˈeɪkjuː] N ABBR (= **European Currency Unit**) ECU *m or f inv*, ecu *m or f inv*
Ecua·dor [ˈɛkwəˌdɔːʳ] N Ecuador *m*
ecu·meni·cal [ˌiːkjʊˈmɛnɪkəl] ADJ ecumenico(-a)
ecu·meni·cism [ˌiːkjʊˈmɛnɪsɪzəm], **ecu·meni·cal·ism** [ˌiːkjʊˈmɛnɪkəlɪzəm] N ecumenismo
ec·ze·ma [ˈɛksɪmə] N eczema *m*
eddy [ˈɛdɪ] VI (*water*) far mulinelli; (*wind, air*) turbinare
■ N (*of water*) mulinello, gorgo; (*of wind, air*) turbine *m*
eddy current N (*Phys*) corrente *f* di Foucault
◎**edge** [ɛdʒ] N (*of table, plate, cup*) orlo, bordo; (*of cube, brick*) spigolo; (*of page*) margine *m*; (*of lake*) sponda; (*of road*) ciglio; (*of forest*) limitare *m*; (*of knife, razor*) taglio, filo; (*of ski*) lamina; **the water's edge** il bagnasciuga; **on the edge of the town** ai margini della città; **the trees at the edge of the road** gli alberi lungo il ciglio della strada; **a book with gilt edges** un libro con i bordi dorati; **to be on edge** (*fig*) essere nervoso(-a), avere i nervi a fior di pelle; **it sets my teeth on edge** (*voice, accent*) mi dà sui nervi; **to be on the edge of disaster** essere sull'orlo del disastro; **to be on the edge of extinction** stare per estinguersi; **that took the edge off my appetite** mi ha calmato i morsi della fame; **to have the edge over sb/sth** essere in vantaggio su qn/qc
■ VT **1** **to edge (with)** (*garment, garden*) bordare (di) **2** (*move carefully*) spostare piano piano
■ VI **1** **to edge past** passar rasente; **to edge forward** avanzare a poco a poco; **to edge away from sb/sth** allontanarsi piano piano da qn/qc **2** (*Skiing*) spigolare
edge·ways [ˈɛdʒˌweɪz] ADV di fianco; **I couldn't get a word in edgeways** (*fam*) non sono riuscito a infilare neppure una parola
edgi·ness [ˈɛdʒɪnɪs] N irritabilità
edg·ing [ˈɛdʒɪŋ] N bordo
edging shears NPL cesoie *fpl*
edgy [ˈɛdʒɪ] ADJ nervoso(-a), teso(-a)
ed·ibil·ity [ˌɛdɪˈbɪlɪtɪ] N commestibilità
ed·ible [ˈɛdɪbl] ADJ (*fit to eat*) mangiabile; (*produce, mushrooms*) commestibile
edict [ˈiːdɪkt] N editto
edi·fi·ca·tion [ˌɛdɪfɪˈkeɪʃən] N (*often iro*) cultura, educazione *f*
edi·fice [ˈɛdɪfɪs] N costruzione *f*, edificio
edi·fy [ˈɛdɪˌfaɪ] VT edificare
edi·fy·ing [ˈɛdɪˌfaɪɪŋ] ADJ edificante

Ed·in·burgh [ˈɛdɪnbərə] N Edimburgo *f*
▹ www.edinburgh.org/
▹ www.eif.co.uk/
▹ www.edfringe.com/

◎ **edit** [ˈɛdɪt] VT (*newspaper, magazine*) dirigere; (*book, series*) curare; (*article, speech, text*) fare la revisione di; (*tape, film*, TV: *programme*) montare; (*Comput*) editare, correggere e modificare
▸ **edit out** VT + ADV tagliare

edit·ing [ˈɛdɪtɪŋ] N **1** (*one's own article, manuscript*) revisione *f*; (*text written by sb else*) redazione *f* **2** (*film, programme*) montaggio
■ ADJ (*Comput: package, software, tools*) per l'editing

editing room N (*Cine, TV*) cabina di montaggio

◎ **edi·tion** [ɪˈdɪʃən] N edizione *f*

◎ **edi·tor** [ˈɛdɪtəʳ] N (*of newspaper, magazine: managing director*) direttore(-trice); (*: editorial director*) redattore(-trice) capo; (*of section of newspaper, magazine*) redattore(-trice); (*publisher's editor: of series*) editore(-trice); (*: of text*) redattore(-trice); (*: of author's work*) curatore(-trice); (*film editor*) responsabile *m/f* del montaggio; **the political editor** il redattore della pagina politica

◎ **edi·to·rial** [ˌɛdɪˈtɔːrɪəl] ADJ redazionale, editoriale; **editorial assistant** assistente *m/f* di redazione; **editorial staff** redazione *f*
■ N (*in newspaper*) editoriale *m*, articolo di fondo

edi·to·ri·al·ize [ˌɛdɪˈtɔːrɪəlaɪz] VI (*Press: in article*) esprimere delle opinioni (*invece di limitarsi ad esporre i fatti*)

edi·tor·ship [ˈɛdɪtəʃɪp] N direzione *f* (*di pubblicazione*)

EDP [ˌiːdiːˈpiː] N ABBR = **electronic data processing**

EDT [ˌiːdiːˈtiː] N ABBR (*Am*: = **Eastern Daylight Time**) *ora estiva nel fuso orario di New York*

edu·cable [ˈɛdjʊkəbl] ADJ educabile

edu·cate [ˈɛdjʊkeɪt] VT (*pupil*) istruire; (*the public, the mind*) educare; (*tastes*) affinare; **I was educated abroad** ho fatto i miei studi all'estero; **to be educated at a private school** frequentare una scuola privata

edu·cat·ed [ˈɛdjʊˌkeɪtɪd] ADJ (*person*) istruito(-a), colto(-a)

> DID YOU KNOW ...?
> **educated** is not translated by the Italian word *educato*

educated guess N supposizione *f inv* ben fondata

◎ **edu·ca·tion** [ˌɛdjʊˈkeɪʃən] N (*schooling*) istruzione *f*; (*teaching*) insegnamento; (*knowledge, culture*) cultura; (*studies*) studi *mpl*; (*training*) formazione *f*; (*Univ: subject etc*) pedagogia; **she wants to complete her education** vuole completare la sua istruzione; **there should be more investment in education** si dovrebbero fare più investimenti nella scuola; **Ministry of Education** Ministero della Pubblica Istruzione; **primary education**, (*Am*): **elementary education** scuola elementare *or* primaria; **secondary education** scuola secondaria; **physical education** educazione *f* fisica
▹ www.dfes.gov.uk/index.htm
▹ www.siliconglen.com/Scotland/17_1.html
▹ www.sosig.ac.uk/education
▹ http://canada.gc.ca/azind/eindex_e.html
▹ www.education.gov.au/goved/go
▹ www.minedu.govt.nz
▹ http://education.pwv.gov.za/

◎ **edu·ca·tion·al** [ˌɛdjʊˈkeɪʃənl] ADJ (*establishment, institution*) scolastico(-a); (*methods*) didattico(-a), d'insegnamento; (*system*) pedagogico(-a); (*film, visit, role*) educativo(-a); (*experience, event*) istruttivo(-a); **educational technology** tecnologie *fpl* applicate alla didattica

edu·ca·tion·al·ist [ˌɛdjʊˈkeɪʃnəlɪst], **edu·ca·tion·ist** [ˌɛdjʊˈkeɪʃnɪst] N (*theorist*) pedagogista *m/f*; (*teacher*) pedagogo(-a)

edu·ca·tion·al·ly [ˌɛdjʊˈkeɪʃnəlɪ] ADV dal punto di vista dell'istruzione; **the educationally deprived** le persone culturalmente svantaggiate

educational psychology N psicopedagogia

edu·ca·tive [ˈɛdjʊkətɪv] ADJ (*experience, event*) istruttivo(-a); (*film, visit, role*) educativo(-a); (*method*) didattico(-a)

edu·ca·tor [ˈɛdjʊkeɪtəʳ] N educatore(-trice), docente

Ed·ward·ian [ɛdˈwɔːdɪən] ADJ edoardiano(-a)

EEC [ˌiːiːˈsiː] N ABBR (= **European Economic Community**) CEE *f* (= *Comunità Economica Europea*)

EEG [ˌiːiːˈdʒiː] N ABBR (= **electroencephalogram**) EEG *m inv*

eel [iːl] N anguilla

EEOC [ˌiːiːəʊˈsiː] N ABBR (*Am*) = **Equal Employment Opportunity Commission**

eerie [ˈɪərɪ] ADJ sinistro(-a), che fa accapponare la pelle

EET [ˌiːiːˈtiː] N ABBR (= **Eastern European Time**) *fuso orario dell'Europa orientale*

ef·face [ɪˈfeɪs] VT (*frm*) cancellare

◎ **ef·fect** [ɪˈfɛkt] N **1** (*result*) effetto; **to have an effect on sb/sth** avere *or* produrre un effetto su qn/qc; **to have no effect** non avere *or* produrre alcun effetto; **to no effect** invano; **to such good effect that** con risultati così buoni che; **to recover from the effects of an illness** rimettersi dai postumi di una malattia; **to put into effect** (*rule*) rendere operativo; (*plan*) attuare; **to take effect** (*drug*) fare effetto; **to come into** *or* **take effect** (*Law*) entrare in vigore; **in effect** in realtà, effettivamente, in effetti; **his letter is to the effect that ...** (*frm*) il tenore della sua lettera è che...; **or words to that effect** o qualcosa di simile
2 (*impression*) effetto, impressione *f*; **to create an effect** fare effetto; **he said it for effect** l'ha detto per far colpo; *see also* **effects**
■ VT (*bring about*) effettuare; (*: saving, transformation, reunion*) operare

◎ **ef·fec·tive** [ɪˈfɛktɪv] ADJ **1** (*efficient*) efficace; **to become effective** (*Law*) entrare in vigore **2** (*striking: display, outfit*) che fa colpo **3** (*actual*) effettivo(-a); **effective date** data d'entrata in vigore

ef·fec·tive·ly [ɪˈfɛktɪvlɪ] ADV (*efficiently*) efficacemente; (*in effect*) in effetti; (*strikingly*) ad effetto; (*in reality*) di fatto

> DID YOU KNOW ...?
> **effectively** is not translated by the Italian word *effettivamente*

ef·fec·tive·ness [ɪˈfɛktɪvnɪs] N efficacia

ef·fects [ɪˈfɛkts] NPL **1** (*Cine, Theatre: visual*) effetti *mpl* scenici; (*: sound*) effetti *mpl* sonori **2** (*property*) effetti *mpl*

ef·fec·tual [ɪˈfɛktjʊəl] ADJ (*frm*) efficace

ef·fec·tu·al·ly [ɪˈfɛktjʊəlɪ] ADV (*frm*) efficacemente

ef·femi·na·cy [ɪˈfɛmɪnəsɪ] N effeminatezza

ef·femi·nate [ɪˈfɛmɪnɪt] ADJ effeminato(-a)

ef·fer·vesce [ˌɛfəˈvɛs] VI (*also fig*) essere in effervescenza; **she effervesced with excitement** sprizzava felicità da tutti i pori

ef·fer·ves·cence [ˌɛfəˈvɛsns] N effervescenza

ef·fer·ves·cent [ˌɛfəˈvɛsnt] ADJ effervescente

ef·fete [ɪˈfiːt] ADJ (*pej*) decadente

ef·fi·ca·cious [ˌɛfɪˈkeɪʃəs] ADJ (*frm*) efficace

Ee

ef·fi·ca·cy ['ɛfɪkəsɪ] N *(frm)* efficacia

ef·fi·cien·cy [ɪ'fɪʃənsɪ] N *(see adj)* efficienza; efficacia; rendimento

efficiency apartment N *(Am)* miniappartamento

◎ **ef·fi·cient** [ɪ'fɪʃənt] ADJ *(person)* efficiente; *(remedy, product, system)* efficace; *(machine, car)* che ha un buon rendimento; **his secretary is very efficient** la sua segretaria è molto efficiente; **it's a very efficient system** è un sistema molto efficace

ef·fi·cient·ly [ɪ'fɪʃəntlɪ] ADV *(see adj)* efficientemente; efficacemente; **the new machine works efficiently** il nuovo macchinario ha un buon rendimento

ef·fi·gy ['ɛfɪdʒɪ] N effigie *f*

ef·flo·res·cence [ˌɛflɔː'rɛsns] N *(Chem, Med)* efflorescenza

ef·flu·ent ['ɛflʊənt] N effluente *m*

◎ **ef·fort** ['ɛfət] N sforzo; **to make an effort to do sth** sforzarsi di fare qc; **to make every effort to do sth** fare il possible per fare qc; **he made no effort to be polite** non si è sforzato minimamente di essere gentile; **he won a prize for effort** gli è stato dato un premio per l'impegno dimostrato; **it's not worth the effort** non vale la pena; **that's a good effort** *(fam)* non è niente male; **his latest effort** *(fam pej)* la sua ultima fatica

ef·fort·less ['ɛfətlɪs] ADJ *(success)* facile; *(movement)* disinvolto(-a)

ef·fort·less·ly ['ɛfətlɪslɪ] ADV senza sforzo

ef·fron·tery [ɪ'frʌntərɪ] N sfrontatezza, sfacciataggine *f*

ef·fu·sion [ɪ'fjuːʒən] N effusione *f*

ef·fu·sive [ɪ'fjuːsɪv] ADJ *(person)* espansivo(-a); *(welcome, letter)* caloroso(-a); *(thanks, apologies)* interminabile

ef·fu·sive·ly [ɪ'fjuːsɪvlɪ] ADV calorosamente; **he apologised effusively** si è profuso in scuse interminabili

e-fit ['iːfɪt] N identikit *m inv* ricostruito al computer

EFL [ˌiːɛf'ɛl] N ABBR *(Scol)* = *English as a Foreign Language*

EFTA ['ɛftə] N ABBR (= **European Free Trade Association**) EFTA *f*
▷ www.efta.int

e.g., eg [ˌiː'dʒiː] ADV ABBR (= **exempli gratia:** *for example*) ad es.

egali·tar·ian [ɪˌgælɪ'tɛərɪən] ADJ egualitario(-a)

egali·tari·an·ism [ɪˌgælɪ'tɛərɪənɪzəm] N egualitarismo

◎ **egg** [ɛg] N uovo; *(Bio: seed)* ovulo; **a hard-boiled egg** un uovo sodo; **scrambled eggs** uova strapazzate; **egg custard** ≈ crema pasticciera; **don't put all your eggs in one basket** *(fig)* non puntare tutto su una sola carta; **to get egg on one's face** *(fig)* fare una brutta figura
▶ **egg on** VT + ADV: **to egg sb on (to do sth)** incitare *or* spingere qn (a fare qc)

egg·beater ['ɛgˌbiːtəʳ] N = **egg whisk**

egg cup N portauovo *m inv*

egg·head ['ɛgˌhɛd] N *(pej fam)* intellettualoide *m/f*

egg·nog [ˌɛg'nɒg], **egg flip** ['ɛgˌflɪp] N ≈ zabaione *m*

egg·plant ['ɛgplɑːnt] N *(esp Am)* melanzana

egg-shaped ['ɛgʃeɪpt] ADJ ovoidale

egg·shell ['ɛgʃɛl] N guscio d'uovo
■ ADJ *(paint finish)* a guscio d'uovo; *(colour)* color guscio d'uovo *inv*

egg-timer ['ɛg'taɪməʳ] N clessidra *(per misurare il tempo di cottura delle uova)*

egg whisk N frusta *(da cucina)*

egg white N albume *m*, bianco d'uovo

egg yolk N tuorlo, rosso (d'uovo)

ego ['iːgəʊ] N *(Psych)* ego, io; *(pride)* amor *m* proprio

ego·cen·tric [ˌɛgəʊ'sɛntrɪk], **ego·cen·tric** [ˌɛgəʊ'sɛntrɪk] ADJ egocentrico(-a)

ego·ism ['ɛgəʊɪzəm] N egoismo

ego·ist ['ɛgəʊɪst] N egoista *m/f*

ego·is·tic [ˌɛgəʊ'ɪstɪk], **ego·is·tical** [ˌɛgəʊ'ɪstɪkəl] ADJ egoista, egoistico(-a)

ego·ma·nia [ˌɛgəʊ'meɪnɪə] N egocentrismo

ego·ma·ni·ac [ˌiːgəʊ'meɪnɪæk] N egocentrico(-a)

ego·tism ['ɛgəʊˌtɪzəm] N egotismo

ego·tist ['ɛgəʊtɪst] N egotista *m/f*

ego·tis·tical [ˌɛgəʊ'tɪstɪkəl], **ego·tis·tic** [ˌɛgəʊ'tɪstɪk] ADJ egotistico(-a)

ego trip N *(fam)*: **to be on an ego trip** gasarsi

Egypt ['iːdʒɪpt] N Egitto

Egyp·tian [ɪ'dʒɪpʃən] ADJ egiziano(-a), egizio(-a)
■ N *(person)* egiziano(-a); *(: ancient)* egizio(-a); *(language)* egiziano

eider ['aɪdəʳ] N *(also:* **eider duck***)* edredone *m*

eider·down ['aɪdəˌdaʊn] N *(quilt)* trapunta di piuma

◎ **eight** [eɪt] ADJ otto *inv*
■ N otto *m inv*; **he's had one over the eight** *(fam)* ha alzato troppo il gomito; *for usage see* **five**

◎ **eight·een** ['eɪ'tiːn] ADJ diciotto *inv*
■ N diciotto *m inv*; *for usage see* **five**

◎ **eight·eenth** ['eɪ'tiːnθ] ADJ diciottesimo(-a)
■ N *(in series)* diciottesimo(-a); *(fraction)* diciottesimo; *for usage see* **fifth**

◎ **eighth** [eɪtθ] ADJ ottavo(-a)
■ N *(in series)* ottavo(-a); *(fraction)* ottavo; *for usage see* **fifth**

◎ **eighti·eth** ['eɪtɪɪθ] ADJ ottantesimo(-a)
■ N *(in series)* ottantesimo(-a); *(fraction)* ottantesimo; *for usage see* **fifth**

◎ **eighty** ['eɪtɪ] ADJ ottanta *inv*
■ N ottanta *m inv*; *for usage see* **five**

Eire ['ɛərə] N Repubblica d'Irlanda

◎ **either** ['aɪðəʳ] ADJ **1** *(one or other)* l'uno(-a) o l'altro(-a); **either day would suit me** mi va bene sia un giorno che l'altro **2** *(each)* entrambi(-e), ciascuno(-a); **on either side** su entrambi i lati; **in either hand** in ciascuna mano
■ PRON: **either (of them)** (o) l'uno(-a) o l'altro(-a); **I don't want either of them** non voglio né l'uno né l'altro; **give it to either of them** dallo a uno dei due; **take either of them** prendi quello che vuoi; **do either of you smoke?** uno di voi due fuma?; **which bus will you take? — either** che autobus prendi? — uno qualsiasi dei due; **I don't like either** non mi piace né l'uno né l'altro
■ CONJ: **either ...or** o... o; *(after neg)* né... né; **either today or tomorrow** oggi o domani; **either come in or stay out** o entri o stai fuori; **I have never been to either Paris or Rome** non sono mai stato né a Parigi né a Roma; **I haven't seen either one or the other** non ho visto né l'uno né l'altro
■ ADV neanche, nemmeno, neppure; **he can't sing either** non sa neppure cantare; **I don't like milk, and I don't like eggs either** non mi piace il latte e neanche le uova; **no, I don't/haven't either** no, neanch'io, no, nemmeno io

ejacu·late [ɪ'dʒækjʊˌleɪt] VI, VT **1** *(semen)* eiaculare **2** *(liter: cry out)* esclamare

ejacu·la·tion [ɪˌdʒækjʊ'leɪʃən] N *(see vb)* eiaculazione *f*; esclamazione *f*

eject [ɪ'dʒɛkt] VT *(Tech)* sganciare, eiettare; *(flames)*

emettere; (*cartridge*) espellere; (*troublemaker*) espellere, allontanare
■VI (*pilot*) catapultarsi; **the pilot ejected** il pilota si è lanciato dall'aereo

ejec·tion [ɪ'dʒɛkʃən] N (*gen*) espulsione *f*; (*of bomb*) sganciamento, lancio

ejec·tor seat [ɪ'dʒɛktəʳˌsi:t] N (*in plane*) seggiolino eiettabile

eke [i:k] VT: **to eke out** (*food, supplies, money*) far bastare, far durare; (*income*) arrotondare; **to eke out a living** sbarcare il lunario

EKG [ˌi:keɪ'dʒi:] N ABBR (*Am*: = **electrocardiogram**) ECG *m inv*

el [ɛl] N ABBR (*Am fam*) = **elevated railroad**

elabo·rate [*adj* ɪ'læbərɪt; *vb* ɪ'læbəˌreɪt] ADJ (*gen*) elaborato(-a); (*design, pattern*) complicato(-a); (*plan*) minuzioso(-a), particolareggiato(-a); (*hairstyle*) elaborato(-a); (*style of writing*) elaborato(-a), ricercato(-a); (*meal*) raffinato(-a); **an elaborate system** un sistema elaborato
■VT (*work out*) elaborare; (*describe*) illustrare
■VI entrare in dettagli; **to elaborate on sth** approfondire qc

elabo·rate·ly [ɪ'læbərɪtlɪ] ADV (*done, prepared, planned*) minuziosamente; (*written, dressed, styled etc*) con ricercatezza

elapse [ɪ'læps] VI (*time*) trascorrere, passare

elas·tic [ɪ'læstɪk] ADJ elastico(-a)
■N elastico

elastic band N (*Brit*) elastico

elas·tici·ty [ˌi:læs'tɪsɪtɪ] N elasticità

elastic stockings NPL calze *fpl* elastiche

Elas·to·plast® [ɪ'læstəˌplɑ:st] N garza autoadesiva

elate [ɪ'leɪt] VT esaltare, rendere euforico(-a)

elat·ed [ɪ'leɪtɪd] ADJ esultante, euforico(-a)

ela·tion [ɪ'leɪʃən] N esultanza, euforia

el·bow ['ɛlbəʊ] N (*Anat*) gomito; **at his elbow** al suo fianco, accanto
■VT: **to elbow sb aside** scostare qn a gomitate; **to elbow one's way through the crowd** farsi largo tra la folla a gomitate

elbow grease N (*fam*) olio di gomito

elbow·room ['ɛlbəʊˌrʊm] N spazio; **give me some elbowroom** fammi spazio

el·der[1] ['ɛldəʳ] ADJ (*brother, sister*) maggiore, più vecchio(-a); **my elder sister** la mia sorella maggiore
■N **1 he is your elder** è più anziano di te; **one's elders** i più anziani; **you should respect your elders** devi rispettare chi è più anziano di te **2 elders** NPL (*of tribe*) anziani *mpl*

el·der[2] ['ɛldəʳ] N (*Bot*) sambuco

elder·berry ['ɛldəˌbɛrɪ] N (*fruit*) bacca di sambuco; (*tree*) = elder

elderberry wine N vino di sambuco

◎**el·der·ly** ['ɛldəlɪ] ADJ anziano(-a)
■NPL: **the elderly** gli anziani

elder statesman N (*Pol*) uomo politico di grande esperienza e prestigio

eld·est ['ɛldɪst] ADJ maggiore; **my eldest brother** il maggiore dei miei fratelli; **the eldest (child)** il/la maggiore (dei bambini)

◎**elect** [ɪ'lɛkt] VT **1** (*Pol etc*): **to elect (to)** eleggere (a); **he was elected chairman** è stato eletto presidente **2 to elect to do** (*decide*) decidere *or* scegliere di fare; **he elected to remain** ha deciso di restare
■ADJ futuro(-a); **the president elect** il presidente designato

◎**elec·tion** [ɪ'lɛkʃən] N elezione *f*; (*of Government*) elezioni *fpl*; **to hold an election** indire un'elezione; **the election will be held next week** l'elezione avrà luogo la settimana prossima
▷ www.electionworld.org/unitedkingdom.htm

election campaign N campagna elettorale

election day N giorno delle elezioni

elec·tion·eer [ɪˌlɛkʃə'nɪəʳ] VI fare propaganda elettorale

elec·tion·eer·ing [ɪˌlɛkʃə'nɪərɪŋ] N propaganda elettorale

elec·tive [ɪ'lɛktɪv] ADJ elettivo(-a)

elec·tor [ɪ'lɛktəʳ] N elettore(-trice)

◎**elec·tor·al** [ɪ'lɛktərəl] ADJ elettorale

electoral college N collegio elettorale

ELECTORAL COLLEGE

I cittadini americani non eleggono direttamente il presidente e il vicepresidente degli Stati Uniti ma votano per degli "elettori" che a loro volta voteranno per i candidati presidenziali. Nel loro complesso questi elettori costituiscono il collegio elettorale, **electoral college**, come previsto dalla costituzione.
▷ www.fec.gov/pages/ecmenu2.htm

electoral roll, electoral register N (*Brit*) liste *fpl* elettorali

elec·tor·ate [ɪ'lɛktərɪt] N elettorato

Electra [ɪ'lɛktrə] N Elettra

◎**elec·tric** [ɪ'lɛktrɪk] ADJ elettrico(-a); **the atmosphere was electric** (*fig*) l'atmosfera era elettrica

elec·tri·cal [ɪ'lɛktrɪkəl] ADJ elettrico(-a)

electrical engineer N elettrotecnico

electrical engineering N elettrotecnica
▷ www.eeel.nist.gov/

electrical failure N guasto all'impianto elettrico

elec·tri·cal·ly [ɪ'lɛktrɪkəlɪ] ADV elettricamente

electric blanket N coperta elettrica, termocoperta

electric-blue [ɪ'lɛktrɪkblu:] ADJ blu *inv* elettrico
■N blu *m inv* elettrico

electric chair N sedia elettrica

electric cooker N cucina elettrica

electric current N corrente *f* elettrica

electric fire N (*Brit*) stufa elettrica

elec·tri·cian [ɪlɛk'trɪʃən] N elettricista *m*

◎**elec·tric·ity** [ɪlɛk'trɪsɪtɪ] N elettricità; **to switch on/off the electricity** attaccare/staccare la corrente

electricity board N (*Brit*) ente *m* regionale per l'energia elettrica

electric light N luce *f* elettrica

electric shock N scossa (elettrica)

electric storm N tempesta elettromagnetica

elec·tri·fi·ca·tion [ɪ'lɛktrɪfɪ'keɪʃən] N (*of railway*) elettrificazione *f*; (*of audience*) elettrizzazione *f*

elec·tri·fy [ɪ'lɛktrɪˌfaɪ] VT (*railway system, fence*) elettrificare; (*audience*) elettrizzare

elec·tri·fy·ing [ɪ'lɛktrɪfaɪɪŋ] ADJ elettrizzante

electro... [ɪ'lɛktrəʊ] PREF elettro...

elec·tro·car·dio·gram [ɪˌlɛktrəʊ'kɑ:dɪəˌɡræm] N elettrocardiogramma *m*

elec·tro·car·dio·graph [ɪˌlɛktrəʊ'kɑ:dɪəˌɡræf] N elettrocardiografo

elec·tro·chemi·cal [ɪˌlɛktrəʊ'kɛmɪkəl] ADJ elettrochimico(-a)

elec·tro·chem·istry [ɪˌlɛktrəʊ'kɛmɪstrɪ] N elettrochimica

Ee

elec·tro·con·vul·sive therap·y [ɪˌlɛktrəʊkən'vʌlsɪv'θɛrəpɪ], **elec·tro·shock thera·py** [ɪ'lɛtrəʊʃɒk'θɛrəpɪ] N elettroshockterapia
elec·tro·cute [ɪ'lɛktrəˌkju:t] VT (*see n*) folgorare (*con la corrente elettrica*); giustiziare sulla sedia elettrica
elec·tro·cu·tion [ɪˌlɛktrə'kju:ʃən] N (*electric shock*) folgorazione *f*; (*Am: execution*) elettroesecuzione *f*, elettrocuzione *f*
elec·trode [ɪ'lɛktrəʊd] N elettrodo
elec·tro·dy·nam·ics [ɪˌlɛktrəʊdaɪ'næmɪks] NSG elettrodinamica
elec·tro·en·cepha·lo·gram [ɪˌlɛktrəʊen'sɛfələˌgræm] N elettroencefalogramma *m*
elec·tro·en·cepha·lo·graph [ɪ'lɛktrəʊen'sɛfələˌgræf] N elettroencefalografo
elec·troly·sis [ɪlɛk'trɒlɪsɪs] N elettrolisi *f*
elec·tro·lyte [ɪ'lɛktrəʊˌlaɪt] N elettrolita *m*
elec·tro·mag·net [ɪ'lɛktrəʊ'mægnɪt] N elettromagnete *m*
elec·tro·mag·net·ic [ɪ'lɛktrəʊmæg'nɛtɪk] ADJ elettromagnetico(-a)
elec·tro·mo·tive [ɪˌlɛktrəʊ'məʊtɪv] ADJ elettromotore(-trice)
electromotive force N (*Phys*) forza elettromotrice
elec·tron [ɪ'lɛktrɒn] N elettrone *m*
elec·tro·nega·tiv·ity [ɪˌlɛktrəʊˌnɛgə'tɪvɪtɪ] N elettronegatività
electron gun N proiettore *m* elettronico
◎ **elec·tron·ic** [ɪlɛk'trɒnɪk] ADJ elettronico(-a); **electronic configuration** (*Chem*) configurazione *f* degli elettroni
elec·troni·cal·ly [ɪlɛk'trɒnɪkəlɪ] ADV elettronicamente
electronic data processing N elaborazione *f* elettronica di dati
electronic mail N posta elettronica
electronic monitoring [-'mɒnɪtərɪŋ] N (*Am*) monitoraggio tramite bracciale elettronico
electronic publishing N editoria elettronica
elec·tron·ics [ɪlɛk'trɒnɪks] NSG elettronica
▹ www.eskimo.com/~billb/amateur/elehob.html
▹ www.eetuk.com
electronic tagging [-tægɪŋ] N (*Brit*) monitoraggio tramite bracciale elettronico
electron microscope N microscopio elettronico
elec·tro·plat·ed [ɪ'lɛktrəʊˌpleɪtɪd] ADJ galvanizzato(-a), placcato(-a) (mediante galvanostegia)
elec·tro·scope [ɪ'lɛktrəʊˌskəʊp] N elettroscopio
elec·tro·shock treat·ment [ɪ'lɛktrəʊʃɒkˌtri:tmənt] N = electroconvulsive therapy
elec·tro·thera·py [ɪˌlɛktrəʊ'θɛrəpɪ] N elettroterapia
elec·tro·va·lent [ɪˌlɛktrəʊ'veɪlənt] ADJ elettrovalente
el·egance ['ɛlɪgəns] N eleganza
◎ **el·egant** ['ɛlɪgənt] ADJ elegante
el·egant·ly ['ɛlɪgəntlɪ] ADV in modo elegante, con eleganza
el·egi·ac [ˌɛlɪ'dʒaɪək] ADJ (*liter*) elegiaco(-a)
el·egy ['ɛlɪdʒɪ] N elegia
◎ **el·ement** ['ɛlɪmənt] N (*gen*) elemento; (*of surprise, luck*) fattore *m*, componente *f*; (*of heater, kettle*) resistenza; **the elements** (*weather*) gli elementi; **the elements of mathematics** i fondamenti della matematica; **to be in one's element** essere nel proprio elemento *or* ambiente naturale
el·ement·al [ˌɛlɪ'mɛntl] ADJ (*basic*) fondamentale; (*Chem, Phys*) elementare; (*forces*) della natura
el·emen·ta·ry [ˌɛlɪ'mɛntərɪ] ADJ elementare; **elementary physics** i primi rudimenti di fisica
elementary school N ≈ scuola primaria

ELEMENTARY SCHOOL

Negli Stati Uniti e in Canada i bambini frequentano la **elementary school** per almeno sei anni, a volte anche per otto. Negli Stati Uniti la scuola primaria si chiama anche "grade school" o "grammar school".

el·ephant ['ɛlɪfənt] N elefante(-essa)
el·ephan·tine [ˌɛlɪ'fæntaɪn] ADJ (*fig*) mastodontico(-a), elefantesco(-a)
el·evate ['ɛlɪˌveɪt] VT **1** (*raise in rank, importance*): **to elevate (to)** elevare (a) **2** (*fig: mind*) elevare
el·evat·ed ['ɛlɪˌveɪtɪd] ADJ (*gen*) elevato(-a); (*railway*) soprelevato(-a); (*thoughts*) nobile
elevated railroad N (*Am*) (ferrovia) soprelevata
el·evat·ing ['ɛlɪˌveɪtɪŋ] ADJ (*fig*) esaltante
el·eva·tion [ˌɛlɪ'veɪʃən] N (*gen*) elevazione *f*; (*Archit*) prospetto; (*of style, thought*) alto livello; (*altitude*) altitudine *f*, altezza
el·eva·tor ['ɛlɪˌveɪtə^r] N (*Am: lift*) ascensore *m*; (*hoist*) montacarichi *m inv*
◎ **elev·en** [ɪ'lɛvn] ADJ undici *inv*
■ N undici *m inv*; **the first eleven** (*Sport*) la prima squadra; *for usage see* **five**
elev·en·ses [ɪ'lɛvnzɪz] NPL (*Brit fam*) ≈ pausa per il caffè a metà mattina
◎ **elev·enth** [ɪ'lɛvnθ] ADJ undicesimo(-a); **at the eleventh hour** (*fig*) all'ultimo minuto
■ N (*in series*) undicesimo(-a); (*fraction*) undicesimo; *for usage see* **fifth**
elf [ɛlf] N (*pl* **elves**) elfo
elf·in ['ɛlfɪn] ADJ da elfo; (*belonging to elves*) degli elfi
elic·it [ɪ'lɪsɪt] VT: **to elicit sth (from sb)** (*truth, secret*) strappare qc (a qn); (*admission, reply*) ottenere qc (da qn)
elide [ɪ'laɪd] VT (*Ling*) elidere
eli·gibil·ity [ˌɛlɪdʒə'bɪlɪtɪ] N (*see adj*) idoneità; eleggibilità
eli·gible ['ɛlɪdʒəbl] ADJ (*suitable*): **eligible (for)** idoneo(-a) (a); (*for membership, grant*) che ha i requisiti richiesti (per); (*public office*) eleggibile a; **to be eligible for a pension** essere pensionabile; **to be eligible to vote** avere diritto di voto; **he's a very eligible young man** è un buon partito
◎ **elimi·nate** [ɪ'lɪmɪˌneɪt] VT (*gen*) eliminare; (*suspect, possibility*) scartare
elimi·na·tion [ɪˌlɪmɪ'neɪʃən] N eliminazione *f*; **by process of elimination** per eliminazione
eli·sion [ɪ'lɪʒən] N elisione *f*
élite [eɪ'li:t] N élite *f inv*
élit·ism [eɪ'li:tɪzəm] N elitarismo
élit·ist [eɪ'li:tɪst] ADJ elitario(-a)
elix·ir [ɪ'lɪksə^r] N elisir *m inv*
Eliza·bethan [ɪˌlɪzə'bi:θən] ADJ, N elisabettiano(-a)
elk [ɛlk] N alce *m*
el·lipse [ɪ'lɪps] N ellisse *f*
el·lip·sis [ɪ'lɪpsɪs] N (*pl* **ellipses** [ɪ'lɪpsi:z]) N (*Gram*) ellissi *f inv*
el·lip·tical [ɪ'lɪptɪkəl], **el·lip·tic** [ɪ'lɪptɪk] ADJ ellittico(-a)
elm [ɛlm] N olmo; **English elm** olmo inglese
elo·cu·tion [ˌɛlə'kju:ʃən] N dizione *f*, elocuzione *f*
elon·gate ['i:lɒnˌgeɪt] VT allungare
elon·gat·ed ['i:lɒŋˌgeɪtɪd] ADJ allungato(-a)

elon·ga·tion [ˌiːlɒŋˈgeɪʃən] N allungamento
elope [ɪˈləʊp] VI (*lovers*) fuggire insieme (*per sposarsi*)
elope·ment [ɪˈləʊpmənt] N fuga romantica
elo·quence [ˈɛləkwəns] N eloquenza
elo·quent [ˈɛləkwənt] ADJ eloquente
elo·quent·ly [ˈɛləkwəntlɪ] ADV eloquentemente
El Sal·va·dor [ɛlˈsælvəˌdɔːʳ] N El Salvador *m*
◎ **else** [ɛls] ADV **1** (*other*) altro; **anybody else would have done it** chiunque altro l'avrebbe fatto; **is it anybody else's?** è di qualcun altro?; **I'd prefer anything else rather than ...** preferirei qualsiasi altra cosa piuttosto che...; **is there anything else I can do?** posso fare qualcos'altro?; **anything else, sir?** (*shop assistant*) desidera altro, signore?; **I'd go anywhere else but there** andrei ovunque fuorché lì ; **have you tried anywhere else?** hai provato da qualche altra parte?; **everyone else** tutti gli altri; **everything else** tutto il resto; **everywhere else** in qualsiasi altro luogo; **nobody else** nessun altro/ nessun'altra; **nothing else** nient'altro; **nothing else, thank you** (*in shop*) è tutto, grazie; **nowhere else** nessun altro posto; **I went nowhere else** non sono andato in nessun altro posto; **somebody else** qualcun altro/qualcun'altra; **something else** qualcos'altro; **it's something else!** (*fam*) è qualcosa di speciale!; **somewhere else** da qualche altra parte, altrove; **who/ what/where/how else?** chi/che/dove/come altro?; **where else?** in quale altro luogo?; **little else** poco altro; **there is little else to be done** rimane ben poco da fare; **he said that, and much else** ha detto questo e altro ancora **2** (*otherwise*): **or else** altrimenti; **keep quiet or else go away** stai zitto, altrimenti vai via; **do as I say, or else!** (*fam*) fai come ti dico, se no vedi!
◎ **else·where** [ˈɛlsˈwɛəʳ] ADV altrove; **these flowers cannot be found elsewhere** questi fiori non si trovano da nessun'altra parte
ELT [ˌiːɛlˈtiː] N ABBR (*Scol*) = *English Language Teaching*
▷ www.arels.org.uk
▷ www.iatefl.org/
elu·ci·date [ɪˈluːsɪˌdeɪt] VT delucidare
elu·ci·da·tion [ɪˌluːsɪˈdeɪʃən] N delucidazione *f*
elude [ɪˈluːd] VT (*arrest, pursuit, enemy, observation*) sfuggire a; (*question*) eludere; **success has eluded him** il successo non gli ha arriso
elu·sive [ɪˈluːsɪv] ADJ (*prey, enemy*) inafferrabile; (*thoughts, word, success etc*) che sfugge; (*glance*) sfuggevole; **he is very elusive** è proprio inafferrabile; **it is an extremely elusive concept** è un concetto del tutto inafferrabile
elves [ɛlvz] NPL *of* **elf**
ema·ci·at·ed [ɪˈmeɪsɪˌeɪtɪd] ADJ emaciato(-a)
ema·cia·tion [ɪˌmeɪsɪˈeɪʃən] N deperimento, dimagrimento
e·mail, e-mail [ˈiːmeɪl] N ABBR (= **electronic mail**) (*sistema*) e-mail *f*, posta elettronica; (*messaggio*) e-mail, mail *f inv*; **email account** account *m inv* di posta elettronica; **email address** indirizzo di posta elettronica, indirizzo e-mail
■ VT: **to email sb** inviare un'e-mail a qn
ema·nate [ˈɛməˌneɪt] VI: **to emanate from** (*frm*) provenire da, emanare da
ema·na·tion [ˌɛməˈneɪʃən] N (*frm*) emanazione *f*
eman·ci·pate [ɪˈmænsɪˌpeɪt] VT (*women, slaves*) emancipare; (*fig*) liberare
eman·ci·pa·tion [ɪˌmænsɪˈpeɪʃən] N emancipazione *f*
emas·cu·late [ɪˈmæskjʊˌleɪt] VT (*fig*) rendere impotente
emas·cu·la·tion [ɪˈmæskjʊˌleɪʃən] N indebolimento
em·balm [ɪmˈbɑːm] VT imbalsamare
em·balm·er [ɪmˈbɑːməʳ] N imbalsamatore(-trice)
em·bank·ment [ɪmˈbæŋkmənt] N (*of path*) terrapieno; (*of road, railway*) massicciata; (*of canal, river*) argine *m*; (*dyke*) diga
em·bar·go [ɪmˈbɑːgəʊ] N (*pl* **-es**) (*Comm, Naut*) embargo; **to put an embargo on sth** mettere l'embargo su qc
■ VT mettere l'embargo su
em·bark [ɪmˈbɑːk] (*Naut, Aer*) VI imbarcarsi
■ VT imbarcare
▸ **embark on** VI + PREP (*journey*) intraprendere; (*business venture, explanation, discussion*) imbarcarsi in
em·bar·ka·tion [ˌɛmbɑːˈkeɪʃən] N imbarco
embarkation card N carta d'imbarco
em·bar·rass [ɪmˈbærəs] VT mettere in imbarazzo, imbarazzare; **to be embarrassed** essere imbarazzato(-a); **I was embarrassed by the question** la domanda mi ha messo in imbarazzo; **to be financially embarrassed** avere difficoltà economiche
em·bar·rass·ing [ɪmˈbærəsɪŋ] ADJ imbarazzante
em·bar·rass·ment [ɪmˈbærəsmənt] N imbarazzo; **to be an embarrassment to sb** essere fonte d'imbarazzo per qn; **financial embarrassments** difficoltà *fpl* economiche
◎ **em·bas·sy** [ˈɛmbəsɪ] N ambasciata; **the Italian Embassy** l'ambasciata italiana
em·bat·tled [ɪmˈbætld] ADJ **1** (*castle*) assediato(-a) **2** (*person, government*) in difficoltà
em·bed [ɪmˈbɛd] VT (*in wood, cement, rock*) incastrare; (*weapon, teeth*) conficcare; (*jewel*) incastonare; **it is embedded in my memory** è impresso nella mia memoria
em·bel·lish [ɪmˈbɛlɪʃ] VT: **to embellish (with)** (*decorate*) abbellire (con); (*fig: story, truth*) infiorettare (con)
em·bel·lish·ment [ɪmˈbɛlɪʃmənt] N (*see vb*) abbellimento; infiorettatura
em·bers [ˈɛmbəz] NPL braci *fpl*
em·bez·zle [ɪmˈbɛzl] VT appropriarsi indebitamente di
em·bez·zle·ment [ɪmˈbɛzlmənt] N appropriazione *f* indebita, malversazione *f*
em·bez·zler [ɪmˈbɛzləʳ] N malversatore(-trice)
em·bit·ter [ɪmˈbɪtəʳ] VT amareggiare, inasprire; **embittered by constant failure** amareggiato(-a) dai continui fallimenti
em·bla·zon [ɪmˈbleɪzən] VT: **to emblazon with** decorare con
em·blem [ˈɛmbləm] N emblema *m*
em·blem·at·ic [ˌɛmbləˈmætɪk] ADJ emblematico(-a)
em·bodi·ment [ɪmˈbɒdɪmənt] N incarnazione *f*, personificazione *f*
em·body [ɪmˈbɒdɪ] VT **1** (*spirit, quality*) incarnare; (*thought, theory, ideas*): **to embody (in)** esprimere (in) **2** (*include: features*) comprendere, racchiudere
em·bold·en [ɪmˈbəʊldən] VT incitare, incoraggiare
em·bo·lism [ˈɛmbəlɪzəm] N (*Med*) embolia
em·boss [ɪmˈbɒs] VT (*metal*) lavorare a sbalzo; (*leather, paper*) imprimere in rilievo, goffrare
em·bossed [ɪmˈbɒst] ADJ (*see vb*) a sbalzo; impresso(-a) in rilievo, goffrato(-a); **embossed with ...** con in rilievo...
em·brace [ɪmˈbreɪs] VT **1** (*person, religion, cause*) abbracciare **2** (*include*) comprendere
■ VI abbracciarsi
■ N abbraccio

Ee

em·bro·ca·tion [ˌɛmbrəʊ'keɪʃən] N (*lotion*) linimento
em·broi·der [ɪm'brɔɪdəʳ] VT ricamare; (*fig: truth, facts, story*) ricamare su, abbellire
em·broi·dery [ɪm'brɔɪdərɪ] N ricamo; **embroidery thread** filo da ricamo
▷ www.embroiderersguild.org.uk
em·broil [ɪm'brɔɪl] VT: **to embroil sb in sth** coinvolgere qn in qc; **to become embroiled (in sth)** restare invischiato(-a) (in qc)
em·bryo ['ɛmbrɪˌəʊ] N (*also fig*) embrione *m*; **in embryo** in embrione
em·bry·ol·ogy [ˌɛmbrɪ'ɒlədʒɪ] N embriologia
em·bry·on·ic [ˌɛmbrɪ'ɒnɪk] ADJ (*also fig*) embrionale
embryo sac ['ɛmbrɪəʊ'sæk] N sacco embrionale
em·cee [ˌɛm'siː] N ABBR = **master of ceremonies**
emend [ɪ'mɛnd] VT (*text*) correggere, emendare
emen·da·tion [ˌiːmɛn'deɪʃən] N correzione *f*, emendamento
em·er·ald ['ɛmərəld] N (*stone*) smeraldo; (*colour*) verde *m* smeraldo
■ ADJ (*necklace, bracelet etc*) di smeraldi; (*colour: also:* **emerald green**) verde smeraldo *inv*
Emerald Isle N: **The Emerald Isle** (*liter*) l'Isola di Smeraldo (*Irlanda*)
◎ **emerge** [ɪ'mɜːdʒ] VI: **to emerge (from)** spuntare (da); (*from water, fig: truth, facts, theory*) emergere (da); (: *problems, new nation*) sorgere (da); **it later emerged that …** più tardi emerse che…
emer·gence [ɪ'mɜːdʒəns] N (*of new ideas, theory*) apparizione *f*; (*of submarine*) emersione *f*; (*of nation*) nascita

DID YOU KNOW …?
emergence is not translated by the Italian word *emergenza*

◎ **emer·gen·cy** [ɪ'mɜːdʒənsɪ] N emergenza; **this is an emergency!** questa è un'emergenza!; **in an emergency** in caso di emergenza; **prepared for any emergency** pronto(-a) ad ogni emergenza; **to declare a state of emergency** dichiarare lo stato di emergenza
■ ADJ (*measures, powers*) di sicurezza; (*repairs*) di fortuna; (*Med: operation*) d'urgenza; (*rations, fund*) di riserva

EMERGENCY

In Gran Bretagna e negli Stati Uniti esiste un numero unico per le emergenze. In Gran Bretagna quando si vuole chiamare la polizia, l'ambulanza o i vigili del fuoco si compone il 999, negli Stati Uniti il 911.

emergency case N caso urgente
emergency exit N uscita di sicurezza
emergency landing N atterraggio di fortuna
emergency lane N (*Am Aut*) corsia d'emergenza
emergency road service N (*Am*) servizio di soccorso stradale
emergency room N (*Am*) pronto soccorso
emergency service N servizio di pronto intervento
emergency stop N (*Aut Brit*) frenata d'emergenza
emergency ward N reparto di pronto soccorso
emer·gent [ɪ'mɜːdʒənt] ADJ emergente; **emergent nation** paese *m* in via di sviluppo
em·ery ['ɛmərɪ] N smeriglio
emery board N limetta (di carta smerigliata) per unghie
emery paper N carta vetrata, carta smerigliata
emet·ic [ɪ'mɛtɪk] N emetico
emi·grant ['ɛmɪɡrənt] N emigrante *m/f*
emi·grate ['ɛmɪˌɡreɪt] VI emigrare
emi·gra·tion [ˌɛmɪ'ɡreɪʃən] N emigrazione *f*
émi·gré ['ɛmɪˌɡreɪ] N (*frm*) esule *m*
emi·nence ['ɛmɪnəns] N **1** (*fame*) eminenza, reputazione *f*; **to gain** *or* **win eminence** farsi un nome *or* una reputazione **2** (*Rel*): **His Eminence** Sua Eminenza **3** (*frm: hill*) altura
emi·nent ['ɛmɪnənt] ADJ (*person*) eminente, insigne; (*quality*) eccellente
emi·nent·ly ['ɛmɪnəntlɪ] ADV assolutamente, perfettamente
emir [ɛ'mɪəʳ] N emiro
emir·ate [ɛ'mɪərɪt] N emirato
em·is·sary ['ɛmɪsərɪ] N emissario
emis·sion [ɪ'mɪʃən] N (*of fumes, gas*) esalazione *f*
emit [ɪ'mɪt] VT (*radiation*) emettere; (*fumes*) esalare
emolu·ment [ɪ'mɒljʊmənt] N (*often pl: frm*) emolumento
emo·ti·con [ɪ'məʊtɪkən] N (*Comput*) faccina, emoticon *m inv*
◎ **emo·tion** [ɪ'məʊʃən] N emozione *f*; (*love, jealousy etc*) sentimento; **his voice trembled with emotion** gli tremava la voce dall'emozione; **reason and emotion** ragione e sentimento
◎ **emo·tion·al** [ɪ'məʊʃənl] ADJ (*person, nature*) emotivo(-a); (*moment, experience, story, scene*) commovente; (*tone, speech*) carico(-a) d'emozione; **she's very emotional** è molto emotiva; **he got very emotional at the farewell party** si è molto commosso alla festa d'addio; **emotional state** condizione *f* mentale; **to be in a very emotional state** essere in uno stato di estrema confusione mentale; **some films have a strong emotional appeal** certi film fanno presa sui sentimenti dello spettatore *or* coinvolgono emotivamente lo spettatore; **euthanasia is a very emotional issue** l'eutanasia è una questione molto sentita
emo·tion·al·ism [ɪ'məʊʃnəlɪzəm] N (*pej*) sentimentalismo
emo·tion·al·ly [ɪ'məʊʃnəlɪ] ADV (*behave, be involved*) sentimentalmente; (*speak*) con emozione; **to be emotionally deprived** soffrire di carenze affettive; **to be emotionally disturbed** avere turbe emotive
emo·tive [ɪ'məʊtɪv] ADJ che fa presa sui sentimenti; **emotive power** capacità di commuovere; **it's an emotive issue** è una questione che ha un grosso impatto emotivo
em·pa·thize ['ɛmpəˌθaɪz] VI simpatizzare
em·pa·thy ['ɛmpəθɪ] N immedesimazione *f*; **to feel empathy with sb** immedesimarsi nei sentimenti di qn
Empedocles [ɛm'pɛdəˌkliːz] N Empedocle *m*
em·per·or ['ɛmpərəʳ] N imperatore *m*
◎ **em·pha·sis** ['ɛmfəsɪs] N (*pl* **emphases** ['ɛmfəsiːz]) enfasi *f inv*; (*in word, phrase*) accento; **to speak with emphasis** parlare con enfasi; **with great emphasis** con grande enfasi; **to lay** *or* **place emphasis on sth** (*fig*) mettere in risalto *or* in evidenza qc, dare importanza a; **the emphasis is on sport** si dà molta importanza allo sport
◎ **em·pha·size** ['ɛmfəˌsaɪz] VT (*word, fact, point, feature*) sottolineare; (*subj: garment etc*) mettere in evidenza; **he emphasized the importance of the point** ha sottolineato l'importanza della questione; **I must emphasize that …** devo sottolineare il fatto che…

em·phat·ic [ɪm'fætɪk] ADJ *(tone, manner, person)* energico(-a), vigoroso(-a); *(speech)* enfatico(-a); *(condemnation, denial)* categorico(-a), netto(-a); **they were emphatic that they had seen nobody** hanno detto chiaramente di non aver visto nessuno

em·phati·cal·ly [ɪm'fætɪkəlɪ] ADV *(speak)* con enfasi; *(deny, refuse)* categoricamente

em·phy·sema [ɛmfɪ'siːmə] N *(Med)* enfisema *m*

◎ **em·pire** ['ɛmpaɪə^r] N impero

empire builder N *(fam pej)* accentratore(-trice) di potere (economico)

empire building N *(fam pej)* accentramento di potere (economico)

Empire State Building N Empire State Building *m*
▷ www.esbnyc.com/index2.cfm

em·piri·cal [ɛm'pɪrɪkəl] ADJ empirico(-a)

em·piri·cal·ly [ɛm'pɪrɪkəlɪ] ADV empiricamente

em·piri·cism [ɛm'pɪrɪ,sɪzəm] N empirismo

em·piri·cist [ɛm'pɪrɪsɪst] N, ADJ empirista *(m/f)*

◎ **em·ploy** [ɪm'plɔɪ] VT *(give job to)* dare lavoro a, impiegare; *(appoint)* assumere; *(make use of: thing, method, person)* servirsi di, impiegare; *(: time)* impiegare; **the factory employs six hundred people** la fabbrica dà lavoro a seicento persone; **to be employed** lavorare; **he's employed in a bank** lavora in banca; **we employed a painter to decorate the house** ci siamo serviti di un imbianchino per pitturare la casa
■ N *(frm)*: **in the employ of sb** alle dipendenze di qn

◎ **em·ployee** [,ɛmplɔɪ'iː] N dipendente *m/f*

◎ **em·ploy·er** [ɪm'plɔɪə^r] N datore(-trice) di lavoro; **employer's contribution** *(to National Insurance)* contributi *mpl (versati dal datore di lavoro)*

◎ **em·ploy·ment** [ɪm'plɔɪmənt] N occupazione *f*, impiego; *(a job)* lavoro; **to take up employment** prendere servizio; **to find employment** trovare impiego *or* lavoro; **without employment** disoccupato(-a); **full employment** piena occupazione; **place of employment** *(frm)* sede dell'attività lavorativa

employment agency N agenzia di collocamento

employment exchange N *(old)* ufficio *m* di collocamento

employment office N *(Brit)* ufficio *m* di collocamento

em·po·rium [ɛm'pɔːrɪəm] N *(old)* emporio

em·pow·er [ɪm'paʊə^r] VT *(give control over)* dare maggior potere a; **to empower sb to do sth** *(authorize)* concedere l'autorità a qn di fare qc

em·pow·er·ment [ɪm'paʊəmənt] N: **the empowerment of** la concessione *f* dell'autorizzazione a; *(control)* la concessione di maggior potere a

em·press ['ɛmprɪs] N imperatrice *f*

emp·ties ['ɛmptɪz] NPL *(bottles)* vuoti *mpl*

emp·ti·ness ['ɛmptɪnɪs] N vuoto

◎ **emp·ty** ['ɛmptɪ] *(comp* **-ier**, *superl* **-iest**) ADJ *(gen)* vuoto(-a); *(street, area)* deserto(-a); *(post)* vacante; *(fig: threat, promise)* vano(-a); *(words)* vacuo(-a), privo(-a) di significato; **on an empty stomach** a stomaco vuoto
■ VT *(contents, container)* vuotare; *(liquid)* versare; **to empty (out) one's pockets** vuotarsi le tasche; **to empty a liquid from** *or* **out of sth into sth** travasare un liquido da qc in qc; **she emptied everything out of her bag onto the bed** ha rovesciato sul letto il contenuto della borsa
■ VI *(room, container)* vuotarsi; *(liquid)* scaricarsi; *(river)*: **to empty into** gettarsi in

empty-handed [,ɛmptɪ'hændɪd] ADJ a mani vuote; **to arrive/leave empty-handed** arrivare/andarsene a mani vuote

empty-headed [,ɛmptɪ'hɛdɪd] ADJ sciocco(-a)

EMS [,iːɛm'ɛs] N ABBR (= **European Monetary System**) SME *m* (= *Sistema Monetario Europeo*)

EMU [,iːɛm'juː] N ABBR (= **European Monetary Union**) UME *f*

emu ['iːmjuː] N emù *m inv*

emu·late ['ɛmjʊ,leɪt] VT emulare

emul·si·fy [ɪ'mʌlsɪ,faɪ] VT emulsionare
■ VI emulsionarsi

emul·sion [ɪ'mʌlʃən] N *(liquid)* emulsione *f*; *(also:* **emulsion paint**) pittura (murale)

◎ **en·able** [ɪ'neɪbl] VT: **to enable sb to do sth** consentire *or* permettere a qn di fare qc

-enabled [ɪ'neɪbld] SUFFIX *(Comput)*: **web-enabled** con connessione *f* Internet; **Java-enabled** compatibile con Java

en·act [ɪn'ækt] VT **1** *(law)* emanare **2** *(play, scene)* rappresentare

en·act·ment [ɪ'næktmənt] N **1** emanazione *f* **2** *(in play)* rappresentazione *f*

enam·el [ɪ'næməl] N smalto
■ VT smaltare
■ ADJ smaltato(-a)

enamel paint N vernice *f* a smalto

enam·el·ware [ɪ'næməl,wɛə^r] N stoviglie *fpl* smaltate

en·am·oured, *(Am)* **en·am·ored** [ɪ'næməd] ADJ: **enamoured of** innamorato(-a) di

enc. ABBR = **encl.**

en·camp [ɪn'kæmp] VI *(frm)* accamparsi

en·camp·ment [ɪn'kæmpmənt] N accampamento

en·cap·su·late [ɪn'kæpsjʊ,leɪt] VT *(fig)* racchiudere

en·case [ɪn'keɪs] VT: **to encase in** *(contain)* racchiudere in; *(cover)* rivestire di

encash [ɪn'kæʃ] VT *(Brit frm)* incassare

en·cepha·li·tis [,ɛnsɛfə'laɪtɪs] N encefalite *f*

en·chant [ɪn'tʃɑːnt] VT incantare; *(subj: magic spell)* stregare

en·chant·er [ɪn'tʃɑːntə^r] N incantatore *m*

en·chant·ing [ɪn'tʃɑːntɪŋ] ADJ incantevole, affascinante

en·chant·ing·ly [ɪn'tʃɑːntɪŋlɪ] ADV incantevolmente

en·chant·ment [ɪn'tʃɑːntmənt] N *(charm, spell)* incantesimo; *(delight)*: **to fill with enchantment** incantare

en·chant·ress [ɪn'tʃɑːntrɪs] N incantatrice *f*

en·chi·la·da [,ɛntʃɪ'lɑːdə] N *(Culin)* tortilla ripiena di carne o verdure; **the big enchilada** *(Am fam)* il/la più importante; **the whole enchilada** *(Am fam)* tutto

en·cir·cle [ɪn'sɜːkl] VT circondare; *(Mil)* accerchiare; *(waist, shoulders)* stringere

encl., enc. ABBR *(on letters:* = **enclosed, enclosure**) all., alleg.

en·clave ['ɛnkleɪv] N enclave *f inv*

en·clit·ic [ɪn'klɪtɪk] ADJ enclitico(-a)

en·close [ɪn'kləʊz] VT **1** *(land, garden)* recintare, recingere, circondare **2** *(with letter)*: **to enclose (with)** allegare (a); **please find enclosed a copy of ...** si allega copia di...; **please find enclosed ...** in allegato...

en·closed [ɪn'kləʊzd] ADJ *(garden, field)* recintato(-a); *(space)* chiuso(-a); *(in letter)* allegato(-a)

en·clo·sure [ɪn'kləʊʒə^r] N *(act)* recinzione *f*; *(place)* recinto; *(at racecourse)* tondino; *(in letter)* allegato

en·code [ɪn'kəʊd] VT codificare

en·cod·er [ɪn'kəʊdə^r] N *(Comput)* codificatore *m*

Ee

en·com·pass [ɪn'kʌmpəs] VT comprendere
en·core [ɒŋ'kɔːʳ] EXCL bis
■ N bis *m inv*; **to give an encore** concedere un bis
◎ **en·coun·ter** [ɪn'kaʊntəʳ] VT (*person*) incontrare; (*difficulty, danger, enemy*) imbattersi in
■ N incontro
encounter group N (*Psych*) gruppo d'incontro
◎ **en·cour·age** [ɪn'kʌrɪdʒ] VT (*person*) incoraggiare; (*industry, growth etc*) favorire; **to encourage sb (to do sth)** incoraggiare qn (a fare qc)
en·cour·age·ment [ɪn'kʌrɪdʒmənt] N incoraggiamento
en·cour·ag·ing [ɪn'kʌrɪdʒɪŋ] ADJ incoraggiante
en·cour·ag·ing·ly [ɪn'kʌrɪdʒɪŋlɪ] ADV in modo incoraggiante
en·croach [ɪn'krəʊtʃ] VI: **to encroach (up)on** (*rights*) usurpare; (*land*: *of neighbour*) sconfinare in; (*subj*: *sea*: *land*) avanzare sopra; (*time*) abusare di
en·croach·ment [ɪn'krəʊtʃmənt] N violazione *f*
en·crust·ed [ɪn'krʌstɪd] ADJ: **encrusted with** (*diamonds*) tempestato(-a) di; (*rust*) incrostato(-a) di
en·crypt [ɪn'krɪpt] VT (*also Comput*) criptare
en·cum·ber [ɪn'kʌmbəʳ] VT: **to encumber (with)** (*person*: *with luggage*) caricare (di); (: *with debts*) gravare (di); (*room*) ingombrare (di)
en·cum·bered [ɪn'kʌmbəd] ADJ: **to be encumbered (with)** essere carico(-a) di
en·cum·brance [ɪn'kʌmbrəns] N peso; **to be an encumbrance to sb** essere di peso *or* di impaccio a qn
en·cyc·li·cal [ɪn'sɪklɪkəl] N enciclica
en·cy·clo·pedia, en·cy·clo·paedia [ɪnˌsaɪkləʊ'piːdɪə] N enciclopedia
en·cy·clo·pedic, en·cy·clo·paedic [ɪnˌsaɪkləʊ'piːdɪk] ADJ enciclopedico(-a)
◎ **end** [ɛnd] N
1 (*of line, table, rope*) estremità *f inv*; (*of pointed object*) punta; (*of town*) parte *f*; **3rd from the end** il 3° a partire dalla fine; **at the end of the street** in fondo alla strada; **to place end to end** mettere un'estremità contro l'altra; **from end to end** da un'estremità all'altra; **to stand sth on end** mettere qc in piedi *or* ritto(-a); **his hair stood on end** gli si sono rizzati i capelli; **to change ends** (*Sport*) cambiare campo; **it's the end of the road** *or* **line for us** (*fig*) non abbiamo futuro; **to make ends meet** (*fig*) far quadrare il bilancio, sbarcare il lunario; **to keep one's end up** (*fam*) difendersi abbastanza bene; **to get hold of the wrong end of the stick** (*fig*) prendere fischi per fiaschi
2 (*conclusion*) fine *f*; **the end of the film** la fine del film; **at the end of the day** (*Brit fig*) in fin dei conti; **it's not the end of the world** (*fam*) non è poi la fine del mondo; **we'll never hear the end of it** (*fam*) non avremo più pace; **there's no end to it** (*fam*) non finisce mai; **that was the end of that!** e quella fu la fine!; **to the bitter end** fino all'ultimo sangue; **to come to a bad end** finire male; **in the end** alla fine, da ultimo; **to be at an end** essere finito(-a), arrivare alla fine; **to get to the end of** (*book, supplies, work etc*) finire; **to be at the end of** (*strength, patience*) essere al limite di; **to bring to an end** (*work, speech*) concludere; **to draw to an end** stare per finire; **to come to an end** finire; **to put an end to** (*argument, relationship, sb's tricks*) porre fine a; **for hours on end** per ore e ore; **for 5 hours on end** per 5 ore di fila; **no end of trouble** (*fam*) problemi a non finire; **it upset me no end** (*adv*: *fam*) mi ha turbato enormemente; **without end** a non finire; **that's the end!** (*fam*) è il colmo!; **he's the end!** (*fam*) è impossibile!
3 (*remnant*: *of loaf, meat*) avanzo; (: *of candle*) moccolo; **cigarette end** mozzicone *m* di sigaretta
4 (*aim*) fine *m*, scopo; **to achieve one's end** raggiungere i propri scopi; **it's an end in itself** è fine a se stesso; **to no end** invano; **to this end, with this end in view** a questo fine; **the end justifies the means** il fine giustifica i mezzi
■ VI finire, terminare; (*road, period of time*) terminare; **what time does the film end?** a che ora finisce il film?; **to end by saying** concludere dicendo; **to end in** (*dispute, conflict*) sfociare in; (*subj*: *word*) finire per *or* in
■ VT (*gen*) porre fine a; (*speech, writing, broadcast*): **to end (with)** concludere (con); **to end one's life** mettere fine ai propri giorni; **to end it all** (*fam*) farla finita; **that was the meal to end all meals!** (*fam*) quel pranzo era imbattibile!
▸ **end up** VI + ADV (*finish*) finire, terminare; **to end up in prison** finire in prigione
en·dan·ger [ɪn'deɪndʒəʳ] VT mettere in pericolo; **he endangered patients' lives** ha messo in pericolo la vita dei pazienti; **to endanger one's life** mettere a repentaglio la propria vita; **an endangered species** (*of animal*) una specie in via di estinzione
en·dear [ɪn'dɪəʳ] VT: **to endear sb to** rendere qn caro(-a) (a); **to endear o.s. to sb** accattivarsi le simpatie di qn
en·dear·ing [ɪn'dɪərɪŋ] ADJ (*smile*) accattivante; (*characteristic, personality*) simpatico(-a)
en·dear·ing·ly [ɪn'dɪərɪŋlɪ] ADV (*see adj*) in modo accattivante; simpaticamente
en·dear·ment [ɪn'dɪəmənt] N: **to whisper endearments** sussurrare tenerezze; **term of endearment** vezzeggiativo, appellativo affettuoso
en·deav·our, (*Am*) **en·deav·or** [ɪn'dɛvəʳ] (*frm*) VT: **to endeavour to do sth** cercare *or* sforzarsi di fare qc
■ N (*attempt*) sforzo, tentativo; **to make every endeavour to do sth** fare ogni sforzo per fare qc
en·dem·ic [ɛn'dɛmɪk] ADJ endemico(-a)
end·game ['ɛndgeɪm] N (*of game, situation*) fasi *fpl* finali
end·ing ['ɛndɪŋ] N fine *f*, conclusione *f*; (*Gram*) desinenza; **I didn't like the ending** non mi è piaciuto il finale; **a film with a happy ending** un film a lieto fine
en·dive ['ɛndaɪv] N (*curly*) indivia (riccia); (*smooth, flat*) indivia belga
end·less ['ɛndlɪs] ADJ (*gen*) senza fine; (*road, speech*) interminabile, senza fine; (*attempts*) innumerevole; (*arguments*) continuo(-a); (*patience*) infinito(-a); (*possibilities*) illimitato(-a); (*resources*) inesauribile
end·less·ly ['ɛndlɪslɪ] ADV senza fine
endo·crine ['ɛndəʊˌkraɪn] ADJ endocrino(-a); **endocrine (ductless) gland** ghiandola endocrina a secrezione interna
en·dorse [ɪn'dɔːs] VT (*approve*: *opinion, claim, plan*) approvare, appoggiare; (*Brit*: *driving licence*) annotare un'infrazione su; (*sign*: *cheque*) girare
en·dor·see [ˌɪndɔː'siː] N giratario(-a)
en·dorse·ment [ɪn'dɔːsmənt] N (*approval*) approvazione *f*; (*Brit*: *on driving licence*) infrazione *f* annotata; (*signature*) girata, firma
en·dor·ser [ɪn'dɔːsəʳ] N girante *m/f*
endo·skel·eton [ˌɛndəʊ'skɛlɪtən] N endoscheletro
endo·ther·mic [ˌɛndəʊ'θɜːmɪk] ADJ endotermico(-a)
en·dow [ɪn'daʊ] VT **1** (*equip*): **to endow with** fornire

di, dotare di; **to be endowed with** (*fig*) essere dotato(-a) di **2** (*prize*) istituire; (*hospital*) fondare; (*provide with money: institution*) devolvere denaro a; **to endow sth with sth** devolvere qc a favore di qc
en·dow·ment [ɪn'daʊmənt] N **1** (*gift of money*) donazione *f* **2** (*see vt b*) istituzione *f*; fondazione *f*; donazione **3** (*frm: talent*) talento
endowment assurance, endowment insurance N assicurazione *f* mista
endowment mortgage N *mutuo garantito da un'assicurazione sulla vita*
endowment policy N assicurazione *f* sulla vita a polizza mista
end·papers ['ɛnd,peɪpəz] NPL (*of book*) risguardi *mpl*
end product N (*Industry*) prodotto finale *or* finito; (*fig*) risultato
end result N risultato finale
en·dur·able [ɪn'djʊərəbl] ADJ sopportabile
en·dur·ance [ɪn'djʊərəns] N resistenza; **to come to the end of one's endurance** arrivare al limite della propria sopportazione; **past or beyond endurance** al di là di ogni sopportazione; **tried beyond endurance** messo(-a) a dura prova
endurance test N prova di resistenza
en·dure [ɪn'djʊəʳ] VT sopportare; **I can't endure being teased** non sopporto di essere preso in giro
■ VI (*friendship, memory, peace*) durare; (*book, building*) resistere
en·dur·ing [ɪn'djʊərɪŋ] ADJ duraturo(-a)
end user N (*Econ*) consumatore(-trice) finale; (*Comput*) utente *m/f* finale
end·ways ['ɛnd,weɪz] (*Am*) **end·wise** ['ɛnd,waɪz], ADV (*endways on*) longitudinalmente; (*end to end*) l'uno(-a) contro l'altro(-a) (longitudinalmente)
end zone N (*in American football*) zona di meta
en·ema ['ɛnɪmə] N (*Med*) clistere *m*
◎ **en·emy** ['ɛnəmɪ] N (*person*) nemico(-a); (*Mil*) nemico; **to make an enemy of sb** inimicarsi qn; **he is his own worst enemy** è il peggior nemico di se stesso
■ ADJ (*territory, forces, aircraft*) nemico(-a); (*morale, strategy*) del nemico
enemy-occupied ['ɛnəmɪ, ɒkjʊpaɪd] ADJ occupato(-a) dal nemico
en·er·get·ic [,ɛnə'dʒɛtɪk] ADJ (*person, protest etc*) energico(-a); (*day*) attivo(-a); **she's very energetic** è molto attiva; **do you feel energetic enough to go for a walk?** sei abbastanza in forze per fare una passeggiata?
en·er·geti·cal·ly [,ɛnə'dʒɛtɪkəlɪ] ADV energicamente
en·er·gize ['ɛnədʒaɪz] VT (*invigorate*) stimolare; (*Elec*) alimentare (a corrente)
◎ **en·er·gy** ['ɛnədʒɪ] N energia; **I haven't the energy** non ho la forza; **to put all one's energy into sth** dedicare tutte le proprie energie *or* forze a qc; **Department of Energy** Ministero delle risorse energetiche
energy crisis N crisi *f* energetica
energy-giving ['ɛnədʒɪ,gɪvɪŋ] ADJ energetico(-a)
energy-saving ['ɛnədʒɪ,seɪvɪŋ] ADJ (*policy*) di risparmio energetico; (*device*) che risparmia energia
■ N risparmio energetico
en·er·vate ['ɛnə,veɪt] VT snervare
en·er·va·ting ['ɛnə,veɪtɪŋ] ADJ snervante
en·fee·bled [ɪn'fi:bld] ADJ indebolito(-a)
en·fold [ɪn'fəʊld] VT (*frm: hug*) abbracciare; (*: wrap*) avvolgere
en·force [ɪn'fɔ:s] VT (*decision, policy*) attuare; (*law, regulation*) far osservare, far rispettare; (*obedience*) imporre; (*argument*) rafforzare
en·forc·ed [ɪn'fɔ:st] ADJ imposto(-a), forzato(-a)
en·force·ment [ɪn'fɔ:smənt] N (*of discipline*) imposizione *f*
en·fran·chise [ɪn'fræntʃaɪz] VT (*frm: give vote to*) concedere il diritto di voto a; (*: set free*) affrancare
en·fran·chise·ment [ɪn'fræntʃɪzmənt] N (*frm: see vb*): **enfranchisement (of)** concessione *f* del diritto di voto a; affrancamento (di)
◎ **en·gage** [ɪn'geɪdʒ] VT (*occupy: attention, interest*) assorbire; (*attract: attention*) attrarre; (*hire: servant, worker*) assumere; (*: actor*) ingaggiare; (*: lawyer*) incaricare; (*reserve: room*) prenotare; (*Mil: enemy*) attaccare; **to engage to do sth** impegnarsi a fare qc; **to engage sb in conversation** attaccare conversazione con qn; **to engage gear/the clutch** (*Tech*) innestare la marcia/la frizione
■ VI (*Tech*) innestarsi, ingranare; **to engage in** (*discussion, politics*) impegnarsi in
en·gaged [ɪn'geɪdʒd] ADJ **1** (*to be married*) fidanzato(-a); **to get engaged** fidanzarsi; **she's engaged to Brian** è fidanzata con Brian **2** (*occupied*): **to be engaged in doing sth** essere impegnato(-a) a fare qc; **she is engaged in research/a survey** si occupa di ricerca/di un'inchiesta; **to be engaged on sth** occuparsi di qc **3** (*Brit: phone number, lavatory*) occupato(-a)
engaged tone N (*Brit Telec*) segnale *m* di occupato
en·gage·ment [ɪn'geɪdʒmənt] N **1** (*appointment, undertaking*) impegno; **I have a previous engagement** ho già un impegno **2** (*of worker, servant*) assunzione *f*; (*of actor, speaker*) ingaggio; (*of lawyer*) nomina **3** (*to marry*) fidanzamento; **to break off one's engagement** rompere il fidanzamento **4** (*Mil: battle*) scontro, combattimento
engagement ring N anello di fidanzamento
en·gag·ing [ɪn'geɪdʒɪŋ] ADJ attraente
en·gag·ing·ly [ɪn'geɪdʒɪŋlɪ] ADV in modo attraente
en·gen·der [ɪn'dʒɛndəʳ] VT produrre, causare
◎ **en·gine** ['ɛndʒɪn] N (*motor: in car, ship, plane*) motore *m*; (*Rail*) locomotiva; **facing/with your back to the engine** nel senso della/in senso contrario alla marcia; **front-to-back engine** (*Aut*) motore longitudinale
engine block N (*Aut*) blocco motore
engine driver N (*Brit: of train*) macchinista *m*
◎ **en·gi·neer** [,ɛndʒɪ'nɪəʳ] N (*gen*) ingegnere *m*; (*mechanic*) meccanico; (*Brit: for electrical appliances*) tecnico; (*Naut, Am Rail*) macchinista *m*; **civil/mechanical engineer** ingegnere civile/meccanico; **the Engineers** (*Mil*) il Genio
■ VT (*contrive*) architettare, organizzare
◎ **en·gi·neer·ing** [,ɛndʒɪ'nɪərɪŋ] N ingegneria
■ ADJ (*works, factory, worker*) metalmeccanico(-a)
▷ www.er-online.co.uk/others.htm
▷ www.eevl.ac.uk
engine failure N guasto al motore
engine pod N (*Aer*) gondola del motore
engine room N (*Naut*) sala *f* macchine *inv*
engine trouble N panne *f inv*
Eng·land ['ɪŋglənd] N Inghilterra
▷ www.ordnancesurvey.co.uk/oswebsite/freefun/geo-facts/
▷ www.statistics.gov.uk/
Eng·lish ['ɪŋglɪʃ] ADJ inglese; **English people** gli inglesi
■ N **1 the English** (*people*) gli inglesi **2** (*language*)

Ee

inglese *m*; **do you speak English?** parli inglese?; **in plain English** in parole povere; **the King's** *or* **Queen's English** l'inglese corretto; **English students** chi studia l'inglese; **the English teacher** l'insegnante di inglese

English breakfast N colazione *f* all'inglese

English Channel N: **the English Channel** il Canale della Manica

English·man ['ɪŋglɪʃmən] (*pl* **-men**) N inglese *m*

English-speaker ['ɪŋglɪʃˌspiːkəʳ] N anglofono(-a)

English-speaking ['ɪŋglɪʃˌspiːkɪŋ] ADJ di lingua inglese

English·woman ['ɪŋglɪʃˌwʊmən] (*pl* **-women**) N inglese *f*

en·grave [ɪn'greɪv] VT (*Art, Typ etc*) incidere; (*: wood*) intagliare; (*fig*) imprimere

en·grav·er [ɪn'greɪvəʳ] N incisore *m*

en·grav·ing [ɪn'greɪvɪŋ] N (*picture*) incisione *f*

en·grossed [ɪn'grəʊst] ADJ: **engrossed in** assorto(-a) in, immerso(-a) in, preso(-a) da

en·gross·ing [ɪn'grəʊsɪŋ] ADJ (*study, game*) appassionante; (*book*) avvincente

en·gulf, **in·gulf** [ɪn'gʌlf] VT (*also fig*) inghiottire

◎ **en·hance** [ɪn'hɑːns] VT (*beauty, attraction*) valorizzare; (*position, reputation*) migliorare; (*chances, value*) aumentare, accrescere; **it can enhance the quality of your life** può migliorare la qualità della vita; **this qualification will enhance your chances of employment** questa qualifica aumenterà le tue probabilità di trovare un impiego

en·hance·ment [ɪn'hɑːnsmənt] N **1** (*improvement: quality, appearance, condition*) miglioramento; **image enhancement** (*by computer*) miglioramento dell'immagine *f*; **digital enhancement** miglioramento digitale; **breast enhancement** ingrandimento del seno **2** (*Fin: to pension, salary*) aumento

enig·ma [ɪ'nɪgmə] N enigma *m*

en·ig·mat·ic [ˌɛnɪg'mætɪk] ADJ enigmatico(-a)

en·ig·mati·cal·ly [ˌɛnɪg'mætɪkəlɪ] ADV enigmaticamente

en·join [ɪn'dʒɔɪn] VT (*frm: obedience, silence, discretion*): **to enjoin (on)** imporre (a); **to enjoin sb to do sth** ingiungere a qn di fare qc

◎ **en·joy** [ɪn'dʒɔɪ] VT **1** (*take delight in*): **did you enjoy the film/wine/book?** ti è piaciuto il film/vino/libro?; **I enjoy reading** mi piace leggere; **he enjoys (going for) long walks** gli piace fare lunghe passeggiate; **to enjoy life** godersi la vita; **to enjoy o.s** divertirsi; **enjoy yourself!** divertiti! **2** (*have: success, fortune*) avere; (*have benefit of: health, respect*) godere (di); (*: income, advantage*) fruire di

en·joy·able [ɪn'dʒɔɪəbl] ADJ piacevole

en·joy·ment [ɪn'dʒɔɪmənt] N piacere *m*; **to find enjoyment in sth/in doing sth** provare piacere in qc/nel fare qc

en·large [ɪn'lɑːdʒ] VT (*Phot*) ingrandire; (*house, circle of friends*) ampliare

▸ **enlarge on**, **enlarge upon** VI + ADV (*subject*) dilungarsi su

en·larged [ɪn'lɑːdʒd] ADJ (*edition*) ampliato(-a); (*Med: organ, gland*) ingrossato(-a); (*: pores*) dilatato(-a)

en·large·ment [ɪn'lɑːdʒmənt] N (*gen*) ampliamento; (*Med*) ingrossamento; (*Phot*) ingrandimento

en·larg·er [ɪn'lɑːdʒəʳ] N (*Phot*) ingranditore *m*

en·light·en [ɪn'laɪtn] VT (*inform*): **to enlighten sb (about** *or* **on sth)** illuminare qn (su qc)

en·light·ened [ɪn'laɪtnd] ADJ illuminato(-a)

en·light·en·ing [ɪn'laɪtnɪŋ] ADJ istruttivo(-a)

en·light·en·ment [ɪn'laɪtnmənt] N (*explanations*) chiarimenti *mpl*; **the (Age of) Enlightenment** (*History*) l'Illuminismo

en·list [ɪn'lɪst] VT **1** (*Mil: men*) arruolare **2** (*support*) assicurarsi, procurarsi; **to enlist sb's help** assicurarsi l'aiuto di qn

■ VI (*Mil*): **to enlist (in)** arruolarsi (in); **enlisted man** (*Am Mil*) soldato semplice

en·list·ment [ɪn'lɪstmənt] N arruolamento

en·liv·en [ɪn'laɪvn] VT (*people*) rallegrare; (*events*) ravvivare

en·mesh [ɪn'mɛʃ] VT impigliare; **to become** *or* **be enmeshed in** rimanere impigliato(-a) in; (*fig*) rimanere coinvolto(-a) in

en·mity ['ɛnmɪtɪ] N inimicizia

en·no·ble [ɪ'nəʊbl] VT nobilitare; (*with title*) conferire un titolo nobiliare a

enor·mity [ɪ'nɔːmɪtɪ] N (*of crime, action*) atrocità *f inv*; (*of problem*) gravità

◎ **enor·mous** [ɪ'nɔːməs] ADJ (*gen*) enorme; (*patience*) infinito(-a); (*strength*) prodigioso(-a); (*risk*) immenso(-a); **an enormous number of** (*people, things*) una moltitudine di

enor·mous·ly [ɪ'nɔːməslɪ] ADV enormemente

◎ **enough** [ɪ'nʌf] ADJ, N (*sufficient*) abbastanza; **enough people/money/time** abbastanza gente/soldi/tempo; **more than enough money** denaro più che sufficiente; **have you had enough to eat?** hai mangiato abbastanza?; **have you got enough?** ne hai abbastanza *or* a sufficienza?; **we earn enough to live on** guadagniamo quel tanto che basta per vivere; **will £5 be enough?** bastano 5 sterline?; **that's enough** basta così ; **that's enough, thank you** basta, grazie; **there's more than enough for everyone** ce n'è più che a sufficienza per tutti; **enough!** basta!; **enough's enough!** (*fam*) adesso basta!; **I've had enough!** (*protest*) non ne posso più!; **I've had enough of (doing) this** ne ho avuto abbastanza di (fare) questo; **I've had enough of his lies!** ne ho abbastanza delle sue bugie!; **it's enough to drive you mad** (*fam*) è sufficiente a farti diventare matto; **you can never have enough of this scenery** non ci si stancherebbe mai di questo paesaggio; **it was enough to prove his innocence** è stato sufficiente a dimostrare la sua innocenza

■ ADV abbastanza; **big enough** abbastanza grande; **it's hot enough (as it is!)** fa già abbastanza caldo (così)!; **he's old enough to go alone** è abbastanza grande da poterci andare da solo; **she was fool enough** *or* **enough of a fool to listen to him** è stata così stupida da dargli retta; **he was kind enough to lend me the money** è stato così gentile da prestarmi i soldi; **you know well enough that ...** sai molto bene che...; **he has not worked enough** non ha lavorato abbastanza; **oddly enough, ...** stranamente...; **sure enough** come volevasi dimostrare; **fair enough!** (*fam*) d'accordo!

en·quire *etc* [ɪn'kwaɪəʳ] VT, VI = **inquire** *etc*

en·rage [ɪn'reɪdʒ] VT fare arrabbiare

en·rap·ture [ɪn'ræptʃəʳ] VT estasiare, rapire

en·rich [ɪn'rɪtʃ] VT arricchire

en·rich·ment [ɪn'rɪtʃmənt] N arricchimento

en·rol, (*Am*) **en·roll** [ɪn'rəʊl] VT (*gen*) iscrivere; (*Univ*) immatricolare

■ VI: **to enrol (in)** iscriversi a

en·rol·ment, (*Am*) **en·roll·ment** [ɪn'rəʊlmənt] N (*see vb*) iscrizione *f*; immatricolazione *f*

enrol(l)ment fee N tasse *fpl* d'iscrizione; (*Univ*) tasse d'immatricolazione

en route [ɒnʳru:t] ADV: **en route for/from/to** in viaggio per/da/a; **it was stolen en route** è stato rubato durante il viaggio

en·sconce [ɪn'skɒns] VT: **to ensconce o.s.** sistemarsi bene

en·sem·ble [ɑ̃:n'sɑ̃:mbl] N **1** (*gen*) insieme *m* **2** (*Mus*) ensemble *m inv* **3** (*outfit*) completo

en·shrine, **in·shrine** [ɪn'ʃraɪn] VT custodire

en·sign [*1, 2* 'ɛnsən, *3* 'ɛnsaɪn] N **1** (*flag*) insegna, bandiera **2** (*Mil*) portabandiera *m inv* **3** (*Am Naut*) guardiamarina *m inv*

en·slave [ɪn'sleɪv] VT rendere schiavo(-a), schiavizzare

en·slave·ment [ɪn'sleɪvmənt] N asservimento

en·snare [ɪn'snɛəʳ] VT prendere in trappola; (*fig*) intrappolare

en·sue [ɪn'sju:] VI (*follow*) seguire; **to ensue (from)** (*result*) risultare (da)

en·su·ing [ɪn'sju:ɪŋ] ADJ (*chaos, event*) che segue

en suite [ɑ̃ sɥit] ADJ: **en suite bedroom** stanza con bagno; **en suite facilities** servizi *mpl*
■ ADV (*in hotel*): **with bathroom en suite** con stanza da bagno annessa

◎ **en·sure** [ɪn'ʃʊəʳ] VT garantire, assicurare; **to ensure that ...** assicurarsi che...

ENT [ˌiɛn'ti:] N ABBR (= **Ear, Nose & Throat**) ORL (= *Otorinolaringoiatria*)

en·tail [ɪn'teɪl] VT comportare; **it entailed buying a new car** comportava l'acquisto di una nuova macchina

en·tan·gle [ɪn'tæŋgl] VT (*thread*) impigliare; **to become entangled in sth** (*fig*) rimanere impegolato(-a) in qc

en·tan·gle·ment [ɪn'tæŋglmənt] N (*fig: gen*) coinvolgimento; (*: romantic*) relazione *f* sentimentale

◎ **en·ter** ['ɛntəʳ] VT **1** (*go into: house, vehicle*) entrare in; (*road*) prendere; (*navy, army*) arruolarsi in; (*profession*) intraprendere; (*college, school*) iscriversi a; (*club*) associarsi a; (*debate, discussion, contest, competition*) partecipare a; **there was a sudden silence when she entered the room** ci fu un improvviso silenzio quando entrò nella stanza; **the thought never entered my head** non mi è mai passato per la testa *or* l'anticamera del cervello; **he entered the Church** si è fatto prete **2** (*write down: name, amount, order*) registrare; (*Comput: data*) immettere, inserire, introdurre; **they entered the name into the computer** hanno immesso il nome nel computer; **to enter sb/sth for sth** (*enrol: pupil, candidate, racehorse*) iscrivere qn/qc a qc
■ VI entrare; **enter Othello** (*Theatre*) entra Otello; **to enter for** (*competition, race*) iscriversi a
▸ **enter into** VI + PREP **1** (*participate in*) entrare in; (*negotiations, argument, debate*) prendere parte a, partecipare a; (*explanation*) lanciarsi in; (*agreement*) concludere; **to enter into conversation with sb** intavolare una conversazione con qn **2** (*sb's plans, calculations*) rientrare in; **that doesn't enter into it** questo non c'entra **3 to enter into the spirit of things** entrare nello spirito delle cose
▸ **enter upon** VI + PREP cominciare

en·teri·tis [ˌɛntə'raɪtɪs] N enterite *f*

◎ **en·ter·prise** ['ɛntəˌpraɪz] N **1** (*firm, undertaking, company*) impresa **2** (*initiative*) iniziativa

en·ter·pris·ing ['ɛntəˌpraɪzɪŋ] ADJ (*person*) intraprendente; (*venture*) audace

en·ter·pris·ing·ly ['ɛntəpraɪzɪŋlɪ] ADV con intraprendenza

◎ **en·ter·tain** [ˌɛntə'teɪn] VT **1** (*audience*) divertire; (*guest*) intrattenere, ricevere; **he entertained us with his stories** ci ha divertito con le sue storie; **to entertain sb to dinner** invitare qn a cena **2** (*consider: idea, proposal, plan*) prendere in considerazione; (*hopes, doubts*) nutrire
■ VI (*have visitors*) avere ospiti

en·ter·tain·er [ˌɛntə'teɪnəʳ] N artista *m/f* (di cabaret, radio, TV)

en·ter·tain·ing [ˌɛntə'teɪnɪŋ] ADJ divertente
■ N: **to do a lot of entertaining** ricevere molti ospiti

◎ **en·ter·tain·ment** [ˌɛntə'teɪnmənt] N **1** (*amusement*) divertimento; (*of guests*) trattenimento; **the most popular form of entertainment** la forma di intrattenimento più popolare **2** (*show*) spettacolo; **Las Vegas is the capital of entertainment** Las Vegas è la capitale del divertimento

entertainment allowance N spese *fpl* di rappresentanza

entertainment world N: **the entertainment world** il mondo dello spettacolo

en·thral, (*Am*) **en·thrall** [ɪn'θrɔ:l] VT affascinare, avvincere

en·thral·ling [ɪn'θrɔ:lɪŋ] ADJ affascinante, avvincente

en·throne [ɛn'θrəʊn] VT (*frm: king, queen*) intronizzare, collocare sul trono

en·thuse [ɪn'θu:z] VI: **to enthuse (over** *or* **about)** entusiasmarsi (per)

◎ **en·thu·si·asm** [ɪn'θu:zɪˌæzəm] N entusiasmo; **it failed to arouse my enthusiasm** non mi ha entusiasmato

en·thu·si·ast [ɪn'θu:zɪˌæst] N appassionato(-a); **a jazz** *etc* **enthusiast** un(a) appassionato(-a) di jazz *etc*

en·thu·si·as·tic [ɪnˌθu:zɪ'æstɪk] ADJ (*response*) entusiastico(-a); (*person*) entusiasta; **to be enthusiastic about sth/sb** essere entusiasta di qc/qn; **to become enthusiastic about sth** entusiasmarsi per qc

en·thu·si·as·ti·cal·ly [ɪnˌθju:zɪ'æstɪkəlɪ] ADV entusiasticamente, con entusiasmo

en·tice [ɪn'taɪs] VT allettare, attirare; **to entice sb away from sb/sth** persuadere qn a lasciare qn/qc; **to entice sb into doing sth** indurre qn a fare qc; **to entice sb with food/an offer** *etc* allettare qn col cibo/con un'offerta *etc*

en·tice·ment [ɪn'taɪsmənt] N (*act*) allettamento; (*attraction*) attrattiva

en·tic·ing [ɪn'taɪsɪŋ] ADJ allettante, attraente

en·tic·ing·ly [ɪn'taɪsɪŋlɪ] ADV in modo allettante

◎ **en·tire** [ɪn'taɪəʳ] ADJ (*whole*) intero(-a), tutto(-a); (*complete*) completo(-a), intero(-a); (*unreserved*) assoluto(-a), pieno(-a); **the entire world** il mondo intero

◎ **en·tire·ly** [ɪn'taɪəlɪ] ADV completamente, interamente; (*agree*) assolutamente, pienamente; **an entirely new approach** un approccio completamente nuovo; **I agree entirely** sono pienamente d'accordo

en·tirety [ɪn'taɪərətɪ] N: **in its entirety** nel suo complesso

◎ **en·ti·tle** [ɪn'taɪtl] VT **1** (*book, poem*) intitolare **2 to entitle sb to ...** dare diritto a qn di...; **this entitles him to a free ticket/to do it** questo gli dà diritto ad un biglietto gratis/a farlo; **to be entitled to sth/to do sth** avere diritto a qc/a fare qc; **you are quite entitled to do as you wish** sei libero di fare come credi

Ee

en·ti·tled [ɪn'taɪtld] ADJ (*book*) che si intitola, dal titolo
en·ti·tle·ment [ɪn'taɪtəlmənt] N: **entitlement (to sth)** diritto (a qc)
en·tity ['ɛntɪtɪ] N entità *f inv*
ento·mo·logi·cal ['ɛntəmə'lɒdʒɪkəl] ADJ entomologico(-a)
ento·molo·gist [,ɛntə'mɒlədʒɪst] N entomologo(-a)
ento·mol·ogy [,ɛntə'mɒlədʒɪ] N entomologia
en·tou·rage [,ɒntʊ'rɑ:ʒ] N entourage *m inv*
entrails ['ɛntreɪlz] NPL interiora *fpl*
◎**en·trance**[1] ['ɛntrəns] N **1** (*way in, of person*) entrata, ingresso; (*right to enter*) ammissione *f*, ingresso; **to gain entrance to** (*university etc*) essere ammesso(-a) a; **to make one's entrance** (*Theatre*) fare il proprio ingresso
en·trance[2] [ɪn'trɑ:ns] VT estasiare, incantare
entrance examination N (*to school*) esame *m* di ammissione
entrance fee N (*for club etc*) quota di ammissione, tassa d'iscrizione; (*to museum etc*) biglietto d'ingresso
en·tranc·ing [ɪn'trɑ:nsɪŋ] ADJ incantevole
en·tranc·ing·ly [ɪn'trɑ:nsɪŋlɪ] ADV incantevolmente
en·trant ['ɛntrənt] N (*in race, competition*) concorrente *m/f*, partecipante *m/f*; (*Brit: in exam*) candidato(-a); **he's a new entrant to teaching** è nuovo all'insegnamento
en·trap [ɪn'træp] VT (*frm*) intrappolare
en·treat [ɪn'tri:t] VT: **to entreat sb (to do sth)** implorare *or* supplicare qn (di fare qc)
en·treaty [ɪn'tri:tɪ] N supplica; **a look of entreaty** uno sguardo supplichevole; **at his earnest entreaty** dietro sua viva supplica
en·trée ['ɒntreɪ] N (*Culin*) entrée *f inv*
en·trenched [ɪn'trɛntʃt] ADJ (*Mil*) trincerato(-a); (*fig*) radicato(-a)
en·trench·ment [ɪn'trɛntʃmənt] N trincea
en·tre·pre·neur [,ɒntrəprə'nɜ:ʳ] N imprenditore(-trice)
en·tre·pre·neur·ial [,ɒntrəprə'nɜ:rɪəl] ADJ imprenditoriale
en·tro·py ['ɛntrəpɪ] N entropia
en·trust [ɪn'trʌst] VT: **to entrust sth to sb** *or* **to entrust sb with sth** affidare qc a qn
◎**en·try** ['ɛntrɪ] N **1** (*way in*) ingresso, entrata **2** (*act*) ingresso; **"no entry"** "vietato l'ingresso", "ingresso vietato"; (*Aut*) "divieto d'accesso" **3** (*Sport etc: total*) numero degli iscritti; (: *thing, person entered in competition*) iscrizione *f* **4** (*in reference book*) voce *f*; (*in diary, ship's log*) annotazione *f*; (*in account book, ledger, list*) registrazione *f*; **single/double entry book-keeping** partita semplice/doppia
entry form N modulo d'iscrizione
en·try·ism ['ɛntrɪɪzm] N entrismo
entry-level ['ɛntrɪ,lɛvl] ADJ (*product*) di base; **entry-level job** impiego per cui non sono richieste precedenti esperienze lavorative
entry permit N visto d'ingresso
entry phone N (*Brit*) citofono
en·twine [ɪn'twaɪn] VT intrecciare
E-number ['i:,nʌmbəʳ] N additivo (alimentare)
enu·mer·ate [ɪ'nju:məreɪt] VT enumerare
enu·mera·tion [ɪ,nju:mə'reɪʃən] N enumerazione *f*
enun·ci·ate [ɪ'nʌnsɪeɪt] VT (*words*) articolare, pronunciare; (*sound*) articolare; (*theory, idea*) enunciare, esporre
enun·cia·tion [ɪ,nʌnsɪ'eɪʃən] N (*see vt*) articolazione *f*; enunciazione
enu·resis [,ɛnjʊ'ri:sɪs] N enuresi *f*
enu·ret·ic [,ɛnjə'rɛtɪk] ADJ enuretico(-a)

en·vel·op [ɪn'vɛləp] VT: **to envelop (in)** avvolgere (in), avviluppare (in)
en·velope ['ɛnvələʊp] N busta; **in a sealed envelope** in busta sigillata *or* chiusa; **on the back of an envelope** sulla carta del droghiere; **to push the envelope** superare i limiti
en·vi·able ['ɛnvɪəbl] ADJ invidiabile
en·vi·ably ['ɛnvɪəblɪ] ADV invidiabilmente
en·vi·ous ['ɛnvɪəs] ADJ: **envious (of sb/sth)** invidioso(-a) (di qn/qc)
en·vi·ous·ly ['ɛnvɪəslɪ] ADV con invidia
◎**en·vi·ron·ment** [ɪn'vaɪərənmənt] N ambiente *m*; **Department of the Environment** (*Brit*) ≈ Ministero dell'Ambiente
▷ www.conservation.org
◎**en·vi·ron·men·tal** [ɪn,vaɪərən'mɛntl] ADJ ambientale; **environmental studies** *or* **science** (*in school*) ecologia
en·vi·ron·men·tal·ist [ɪn,vaɪərən'mɛntəlɪst] N ambientalista *m/f*
en·vi·ron·men·tal·ly [ɪn,vaɪərən'mɛntəlɪ] ADV: **environmentally friendly** che rispetta l'ambiente
Environmental Protection Agency N (*Am*) ≈ Agenzia nazionale di protezione ambientale
en·vi·rons [ɪn'vaɪrənz] NPL dintorni *mpl*
en·vis·age [ɪn'vɪzɪdʒ] (*Am*) **en·vi·sion** [ɪn'vɪʒən], VT (*expect*) prevedere; (*imagine*) prefigurare
en·voy ['ɛnvɔɪ] N (*gen*) inviato(-a); (*diplomat*) ministro plenipotenziario
envy ['ɛnvɪ] N invidia; **her new car was the envy of all the neighbours** la sua macchina nuova era l'invidia di tutto il vicinato
■ VT: **to envy (sb sth)** invidiare (qn per qc)
en·zyme ['ɛnzaɪm] N enzima *m*
eon ['i:ɒn] N = **aeon**
ephem·er·al [ɪ'fɛmərəl] ADJ effimero(-a)
epic ['ɛpɪk] ADJ epico(-a)
■ N poema *m* epico, epopea; (*film*) epopea
epi·cen·tre, (*Am*) **epi·cen·ter** ['ɛpɪ,sɛntəʳ] N epicentro
epi·cure ['ɛpɪkjʊəʳ] N buongustaio(-a)
epi·cu·rean [,ɛpɪkjʊə'ri:ən] ADJ, N epicureo(-a)
Epicurus [,ɛpɪ'kjʊərəs] N Epicuro
epi·dem·ic [,ɛpɪ'dɛmɪk] ADJ epidemico(-a)
■ N epidemia
epi·der·mis [ɛpɪ'dɜ:mɪs] N (*Anat, Bot, Zool*) epidermide *f*
epi·dur·al [,ɛpɪ'djʊərəl] ADJ epidurale
■ N anestesia epidurale
epi·glot·tis [,ɛpɪ'glɒtɪs] N epiglottide *f*
epi·gram ['ɛpɪ,græm] N epigramma *m*
epi·gram·mat·ical [,ɛpɪgrə'mætɪkəl], **epi·gram·mat·ic** [,ɛpɪgrə'mætɪk] ADJ epigrammatico(-a)
epi·graph ['ɛpɪ,grɑ:f] N epigrafe *f*
epi·lep·sy ['ɛpɪ,lɛpsɪ] N epilessia
epi·lep·tic [,ɛpɪ'lɛptɪk] ADJ, N epilettico(-a)
epi·logue ['ɛpɪ,lɒg] N epilogo
Epipha·ny [ɪ'pɪfənɪ] N Epifania
epis·co·pal [ɪ'pɪskəpəl] ADJ episcopale
Epis·co·pa·lian [ɪ,pɪskə'peɪlɪən] ADJ, N episcopaliano(-a)
epi·sode ['ɛpɪsəʊd] N episodio
epi·sod·ic [,ɛpɪ'sɒdɪk] ADJ episodico(-a)
epi·sodi·cal·ly [,ɛpɪ'sɒdɪkəlɪ] ADV episodicamente
epis·temol·ogy [ɪ,pɪstə'mɒlədʒɪ] N epistemologia
epis·tle [ɪ'pɪsl] N epistola
epi·taph ['ɛpɪtɑ:f] N epitaffio
epi·thelium [,ɛpɪ'θi:lɪəm] N epitelio
epi·thet ['ɛpɪθɛt] N epiteto

epito·me [ɪ'pɪtəmɪ] N (*frm*): **the epitome of kindness** la personificazione della gentilezza
epito·mize [ɪ'pɪtəmaɪz] VT (*frm*) incarnare
epoch ['iːpɒk] N (*period*) epoca, era
epoch-making ['iːpɒk,meɪkɪŋ] ADJ che fa epoca
epony·mous [ɪ'pɒnɪməs] ADJ (*liter*) eponimo
epoxy resin [ɪ,pɒksɪ'rezɪn] N resina epossidica
eq·uable ['ɛkwəbl] ADJ (*character*) tranquillo(-a); (*climate*) costante
eq·uably ['ɛkwəblɪ] ADV tranquillamente
◎ **equal** ['iːkwəl] ADJ: **equal (to)** uguale (a); **divide the mixture into three equal parts** dividi l'impasto in tre parti uguali; **equal numbers of men and women** un numero uguale di uomini e donne; **an equal amount of time** lo stesso tempo; **to be equal in strength** avere la stessa forza; **women demand equal rights at work** le donne chiedono di avere pari diritti sul lavoro; **all things being equal** se tutto va bene; **with equal ease/indifference** con la stessa facilità/indifferenza; **on equal terms** su un piano di parità; **to be/feel equal to** (*task*) essere/sentirsi all'altezza di
■ N (*person, thing*) pari *m/f inv*, simile *m/f*, uguale *m/f*; **without equal** senza pari
■ VT (*Math*) fare; (*record, rival*) uguagliare; **eight and twelve equals twenty** otto più dodici è uguale a venti; **this score has never been equalled** questo punteggio non è stato mai eguagliato; **there is nothing to equal it** non ha rivali
Equal Employment Opportunity Commission N (*Am*) Commissione *f* per le pari opportunità
equali·ty [ɪ'kwɒlɪtɪ] N uguaglianza; (*parity*) parità
equal·ize ['iːkwə,laɪz] VT (*society*) livellare; (*wealth, possessions*) distribuire uniformemente; (*salaries*) equiparare; (*pressure, temperature*) rendere uniforme
■ VI (*Sport*) pareggiare
equal·iz·er ['iːkwə,laɪzəʳ] N **1** (*Sport*) pareggio **2** (*Tech*) equalizzatore *m*
◎ **equal·ly** ['iːkwəlɪ] ADV ugualmente; (*share*) in parti uguali; **they are equally clever** sono intelligenti allo stesso modo; **she is equally clever** è altrettanto intelligente; **equally, you must remember ...** allo stesso modo, ti devi ricordare...
equal opportunities NPL pari opportunità *fpl*
Equal Opportunities Commission N Commissione *f* per le pari opportunità
equal(s) sign N (*Math*) segno d'uguale *or* d'uguaglianza
equa·nim·ity [,ɛkwə'nɪmɪtɪ] N equanimità, serenità d'animo
equate [ɪ'kweɪt] VT **1 to equate (with)** identificare (con), considerare uguale a; (*compare*) paragonare (a); **I don't equate money and happiness** non identifico il denaro con la felicità **2** (*Math: make equal*) uguagliare; **to equate A to B** mettere in equazione A e B
equa·tion [ɪ'kweɪʒən] N (*Math*) equazione *f*; **equations of motion** (*Phys*) equazioni del moto
equa·tor [ɪ'kweɪtəʳ] N: **the equator** l'equatore *m*
equa·to·rial [,ɛkwə'tɔːrɪəl] ADJ equatoriale
Equatorial Guinea N Guinea Equatoriale
eques·trian [ɪ'kwɛstrɪən] ADJ equestre
■ N (*man*) cavaliere *m*; (*woman*) amazzone *f*
equi·dis·tant ['iːkwɪ'dɪstənt] ADJ equidistante
equi·lat·eral [,iːkwɪ'lætərəl] ADJ equilatero; **equilateral triangle** triangolo equilatero
equi·lib·rium [,iːkwɪ'lɪbrɪəm] N equilibrio
equine ['ɛkwaɪn] ADJ equino(-a)
equi·nox ['iːkwɪnɒks] N equinozio
equip [ɪ'kwɪp] VT: **to equip (with)** (*room etc*) equipaggiare (con), attrezzare (con); (*person*) preparare a; **vocational courses equip you for a particular job** i corsi di formazione professionale preparano per un lavoro specifico; **equipped with** (*machinery etc*) dotato(-a) di; (*supplies etc*) fornito(-a) di; **he is well equipped for the job** ha i requisiti necessari per quel lavoro; **ill/poorly equipped** (*hospital, expedition*) male equipaggiato(-a)/attrezzato(-a)
◎ **equip·ment** [ɪ'kwɪpmənt] N, NO PL attrezzatura; (*Tech, Elec*) apparecchiatura; **skiing equipment** attrezzatura da sci
equi·table ['ɛkwɪtəbl] ADJ equo(-a)
equi·tably ['ɛkwɪtəblɪ] ADV equamente
equi·ties ['ɛkwɪtɪz] NPL (*Brit: shares*) azioni *fpl* ordinarie
◎ **equi·ty** ['ɛkwɪtɪ] N equità
equity capital N capitale *m* azionario
equiva·lence [ɪ'kwɪvələns] N equivalenza
◎ **equiva·lent** [ɪ'kwɪvələnt] ADJ equivalente; **to be equivalent to** equivalere a
■ N equivalente *m*
equivo·cal [ɪ'kwɪvəkəl] ADJ equivoco(-a); (*open to suspicion*) dubbio(-a)
equivo·cal·ly [ɪ'kwɪvəkəlɪ] ADV in modo equivoco
equivo·cate [ɪ'kwɪvə,keɪt] VI esprimersi in modo equivoco
equivo·ca·tion [ɪ,kwɪvə'keɪʃən] N parole *fpl* equivoche
ER ABBR **1** (*Brit*) = *Elizabeth Regina* **2** (*Am*) = **emergency room**
ERA [,iːɑːr'eɪ] N ABBR (*Am Pol:* = **Equal Rights Amendment**) *proposta di emendamento per le pari opportunità nella Costituzione statunitense*
◎ **era** ['ɪərə] N era
eradi·cate [ɪ'rædɪ,keɪt] VT sradicare
eradi·ca·tion [ɪ,rædɪ'keɪʃən] N sradicamento
eras·able [ɪ'reɪzəbl] ADJ cancellabile
erase [ɪ'reɪz] VT cancellare
eras·er [ɪ'reɪzəʳ] N (*frm, Am: rubber*) gomma (da cancellare)
eras·ure [ɪ'reɪʒəʳ] N (*frm*) cancellatura
erect [ɪ'rɛkt] (*frm*) VT (*statue, monument, temple*) erigere; (*flats, factory*) costruire; (*barricade, mast*) innalzare; (*machinery, tent*) montare; (*theory, system*) edificare; (*obstacles*) creare
■ ADJ eretto(-a), dritto(-a); **with head erect** a testa alta
erec·tion [ɪ'rɛkʃən] N **1** (*act: gen*) erezione *f*; (*of building*) costruzione *f*; (*of machinery*) montaggio **2** (*Anat*) erezione *f*
er·ga·tive ['ɜːgətɪv] ADJ (*Gram*): **ergative verb** *verbo con il quale uno stesso sostantivo può essere soggetto o complemento oggetto*
ergo ['ɜːgəʊ] ADV ergo
er·go·nom·ics [,ɜːgə'nɒmɪks] NSG ergonomia
Eri·trea [,ɛrɪ'treɪə] N Eritrea
ERM [,iːɑːr'ɛm] N ABBR = **Exchange Rate Mechanism**
er·mine ['ɜːmɪn] N ermellino
ERNIE ['ɜːnɪ] N ABBR (*Brit:* = **Electronic Random Number Indicator Equipment**) *sistema che seleziona i numeri vincenti di buoni del Tesoro*
erode [ɪ'rəʊd] VT (*Geol*) erodere; (*metal, fig*) corrodere
erog·enous [ɪ'rɒdʒɪnəs] ADJ: **erogenous zone** zona erogena
Eros ['iːrɒs] N Eros *m*
ero·sion [ɪ'rəʊʒən] N (*see vb*) erosione *f*; corrosione *f*
ero·sive [ɪ'rəʊzɪv] ADJ (*see vb*) erosivo(-a); corrosivo(-a)
erot·ic [ɪ'rɒtɪk] ADJ erotico(-a)

Ee

eroti·ca [ɪ'rɒtɪkə] N (*art*) arte *f* erotica; (*literature*) letteratura erotica
eroti·cal·ly [ɪ'rɒtɪkəlɪ] ADV eroticamente
eroti·cism [ɪ'rɒtɪ,sɪzəm] N erotismo
err [ɜːʳ] VI (*be mistaken*) sbagliare, errare; (*sin*) peccare; **it is better to err on the side of caution** la prudenza non è mai troppa
er·rand ['ɛrənd] N commissione *f*; **to run errands** fare commissioni; **errand of mercy** atto di carità
errand boy N fattorino
er·rant ['ɛrənt] ADJ (*frm: wrong*) in errore; (: *unfaithful*) infedele
er·ra·ta [ɪ'rɑːtə] N (*Typ*) errore *m* di stampa
er·rat·ic [ɪ'rætɪk] ADJ (*person, conduct, opinions, mood*) incostante, imprevedibile; (*results etc*) irregolare, discontinuo(-a); (*driving*) irregolare; (*Geol*) erratico(-a)
■ N (*Geol*) masso erratico
er·rati·cal·ly [ɪ'rætɪkəlɪ] ADV in modo erratico
er·ro·neous [ɪ'rəʊnɪəs] ADJ erroneo(-a)
◎ **er·ror** ['ɛrəʳ] N errore *m*; **typing/spelling error** errore di battitura/di ortografia; **in error** per errore; **to see the error of one's ways** riconoscere i propri errori
error message N (*Comput*) messaggio di errore
er·satz ['ɛəzæts] ADJ surrogato(-a); **ersatz coffee** caffè surrogato
erst·while ['ɜːst,waɪl] (*old*) ADJ di un tempo
■ ADV un tempo, tempo addietro
eru·dite ['ɛrʊ,daɪt] ADJ erudito(-a)
eru·dite·ly ['ɛrʊ,daɪtlɪ] ADV eruditamente
eru·di·tion [,ɛrʊ'dɪʃən] N erudizione *f*
erupt [ɪ'rʌpt] VI (*volcano*) entrare in eruzione *or* in attività; (*spots*) spuntare; (*anger*) esplodere; (*fighting, quarrel*) scoppiare; **he erupted into the room** ha fatto irruzione nella stanza
erup·tion [ɪ'rʌpʃən] N (*of volcano, spots*) eruzione *f*; (*of anger, violence*) esplosione *f*
eryth·ro·cyte [ɪ'rɪθrəʊ,saɪt] N eritrocita *m*
ESA [,iːɛs'eɪ] N ABBR (= **European Space Agency**) ESA *f* (= *Agenzia spaziale europea*)
es·ca·late ['ɛskə,leɪt] VI **1** (*violence, fighting, bombing*) intensificarsi; **the dispute could escalate** la controversia può inasprirsi **2** (*costs*) salire
■ VT intensificare
es·ca·la·tion [,ɛskə'leɪʃən] N escalation *f inv*; (*of prices*) aumento
es·ca·la·tor ['ɛskə,leɪtəʳ] N scala mobile
escalator clause N clausola di indicizzazione *or* di revisione
es·ca·lope ['ɛskə,lɒp] N scaloppina
es·ca·pade [,ɛskə'peɪd] N (*adventure*) avventura; (*misdeed*) scappatella
◎ **es·cape** [ɪs'keɪp] N (*gen*) fuga; (*of prisoner*) fuga, evasione *f*; (*of gas*) fuga, fuoriuscita; **to have a lucky escape** scamparla bella; **to make one's escape** evadere
■ VT (*capture, pursuers, punishment*) sfuggire a; (*death*) scampare; (*danger*) scampare a; (*consequences*) sottrarsi a; **he narrowly escaped being killed** per poco non è rimasto ucciso; **his name escapes me** il suo nome mi sfugge; **to escape notice** passare inosservato(-a); **it had escaped his notice** era sfuggito alla sua attenzione; **nothing escapes her (attention)** non le sfugge nulla
■ VI (*gen*) scappare; (*prisoner*) evadere; (*liquid, gas: fuoriuscire: Comput*) uscire; **a lion has escaped** è scappato un leone; **to escape from** (*person*) sfuggire a; (*prison*) evadere da; **to escape to** (*another place*) fuggire in; (*freedom, safety*) fuggire verso; **he escaped with a few bruises** (*fig*) se l'è cavata con qualche livido; **to escape unhurt** (*fig*) rimanere illeso(-a); **an escaped prisoner** un*a* evaso(-a)
escape artist N = **escapologist**
escape clause N (*in agreement*) clausola liberatoria
es·capee [ɪskeɪ'piː] N evaso(-a)
escape hatch N (*in submarine, space rocket*) portello di sicurezza
escape key N (*Comput*) tasto di escape
escape plan N piano di fuga
escape route N percorso di fuga
escape velocity N (*Astron*) velocità di fuga
es·cap·ism [ɪs'keɪpɪzəm] N escapismo, evasione *f* (dalla realtà)
es·cap·ist [ɪs'keɪpɪst] ADJ d'evasione
■ N persona che cerca di evadere dalla realtà
es·ca·polo·gist [,ɛskə'pɒlədʒɪst] N (*Brit*) *illusionista specializzato nel liberarsi da funi, catene ecc.*
es·carp·ment [ɪs'kɑːpmənt] N scarpata
eschew [ɪs'tʃuː] VT (*frm*) evitare
es·cort [*n* 'ɛskɔːt; *vb* ɪs'kɔːt] N (*Mil, Naut*) scorta; (*male companion*) cavaliere *m*, accompagnatore *m*; (*female companion*) accompagnatrice *f*; **a police escort** una scorta di polizia
■ VT accompagnare; (*Mil, Naut*) scortare
escort agency N agenzia di accompagnatrici
escort duty N servizio di scorta
escort vessel N battello di scorta
es·crow ['ɛskrəʊ] N (*Law*) deposito fiduciario; **escrow account** conto vincolato
e-signature ['iː,sɪgnʳtʃəʳ] N (*Comput*) firma elettronica
Es·ki·mo ['ɛskɪ,məʊ] (*pl* **Eskimos** *or* **Eskimo**) ADJ eschimese
■ N (*person*) eschimese *m/f*; (*language*) eschimese *m*
ESL [,iːɛs'ɛl] N ABBR (*Scol*) = *English as a Second Language*
esopha·gus [ɪ'sɒfəgəs] N (*Am*) = **oesophagus**
eso·ter·ic [,ɛsəʊ'tɛrɪk] ADJ esoterico(-a)
ESP [iːɛs'piː] N ABBR **1** = **extrasensory perception** **2** (*Scol*) = *English for Specific or Special Purposes*
esp. ABBR (= **especially**) spec.
es·pa·drilles [,ɛspə'drɪlz] NPL espadrilles *fpl*
es·pe·cial [ɪs'pɛʃəl] ADJ particolare
◎ **es·pe·cial·ly** [ɪs'pɛʃəlɪ] ADV (*particularly*) particolarmente; (*above all*) soprattutto, specialmente; (*expressly*) appositamente, espressamente; **it is especially difficult** è particolarmente difficile; **it's very hot there, especially in the summer** fa molto caldo lì , soprattutto d'estate; **especially when it rains** soprattutto quando piove; **why me, especially?** perché proprio io?
Es·pe·ran·tist [,ɛspə'ræntɪst] N esperantista *m/f*
Es·pe·ran·to [,ɛspə'ræntəʊ] N esperanto
■ ADJ in esperanto
es·pio·nage [,ɛspɪə'nɑːʒ] N spionaggio
es·pla·nade [,ɛsplə'neɪd] N lungomare *m*
es·pous·al [ɪs'paʊzl] N: **espousal of** (*frm*) appoggio a
es·pouse [ɪs'paʊz] VT (*fig frm*) abbracciare
espy [ɪ'spaɪ] VT (*old*) notare
Esq. ABBR (*Brit frm: on an envelope*) = **Esquire**
es·quire [ɪs'kwaɪəʳ] N: **Colin Smith Esquire** Egregio Signor Colin Smith
es·say ['ɛseɪ] N (*Literature*) saggio; (*Scol*) tema *m*, composizione *f*; **a history essay** un tema di storia
es·say·ist ['ɛseɪɪst] N saggista *m/f*
es·sence ['ɛsəns] N (*gen, Culin*) essenza; **this is the**

essence of the problem questa è l'essenza del problema; **in essence** in sostanza; **speed is of the essence** la velocità è di estrema importanza

◎**es·sen·tial** [ɪ'sɛnʃəl] ADJ (*gen*) essenziale; (*basic*) fondamentale; (*important*) indispensabile; **it is essential that** è essenziale che + *sub*
■ N, OFTEN PL elemento essenziale

◎**es·sen·tial·ly** [ɪ'sɛnʃəlɪ] ADV essenzialmente, fondamentalmente

EST [ˌiːɛs'tiː] N ABBR (*Am*; = **Eastern Standard Time**) *see* **eastern**

est. ABBR **1** = **established**; **est. 1900** dal 1900 **2** = **estimate(d)**

◎**es·tab·lish** [ɪs'tæblɪʃ] VT **1** (*set up: company*) costituire; (*: business*) avviare; (*: state*) creare; (*: committee*) istituire; (*: custom, precedent, relations*) stabilire; (*: power, authority, reputation*) affermare; (*: peace, order*) ristabilire; **they finally established contact** alla fine hanno stabilito un contatto; **he established his reputation as an architect** si è affermato come architetto **2** (*prove: fact, identity, sb's innocence*) dimostrare; **tests have established she is not their child** alcuni test hanno accertato che non è figlia loro

es·tab·lished [ɪs'tæblɪʃt] ADJ (*person*) affermato(-a); (*business*) avviato(-a); (*custom*) radicato(-a); (*fact*) stabilito(-a); **the Established Church** la religione di Stato; **a well-established business** un'attività ben avviata

◎**es·tab·lish·ment** [ɪs'tæblɪʃmənt] N **1** (*of company*) costituzione *f*; (*of state*) creazione *f*; (*of committee*) istituzione *f*; (*of law*) instaurazione *f*; (*of reputation*) affermazione *f* **2** (*business*) azienda; (*Admin, Mil, Naut: personnel*) effettivo; **commercial establishments** aziende; **a teaching establishment** un istituto d'istruzione; **the Establishment** la classe dirigente, l'establishment *m inv*; **the values of the Establishment** i valori tradizionali; **the cultural Establishment** l'establishment culturale

◎**es·tate** [ɪs'teɪt] N **1** (*land*) proprietà *f inv*, tenuta; (*Brit: also:* **housing estate**) complesso edilizio; **I live on a new estate** vivo in un nuovo complesso edilizio; **country estate** tenuta in campagna **2** (*Law: on death*) patrimonio, beni *mpl*; **his estate is valued at $150,000** il suo patrimonio è valutato 150.000 dollari

> DID YOU KNOW ...?
> **estate** is not translated by the Italian word *estate*

estate agency N (*Brit*) agenzia immobiliare

estate agent N (*Brit*) agente *m/f* immobiliare

estate car N (*Brit*) auto modello familiare, station wagon *f inv*

estate duty N tassa di successione

es·teem [ɪs'tiːm] (*frm*) N stima; **I hold him in high esteem** gode della mia più alta stima
■ VT (*think highly of*) stimare; (*consider*) considerare; **I would esteem it an honour** sarebbe un onore per me

es·ter ['ɛstəʳ] N estere *m*

es·thet·ic [iːs'θɛtɪk] ADJ (*Am*) = **aesthetic** *etc*

Es·thon·ia [ɛ'stəʊnɪə] N = **Estonia**

Es·tho·nian [ɛ'stəʊnɪən] ADJ, N = **Estonian**

es·ti·mable ['ɛstɪməbl] ADJ stimabile

◎**es·ti·mate** [*n* 'ɛstɪmɪt; *vb* 'ɛstɪˌmeɪt] N (*judgment*) valutazione *f*, stima; (*Comm: for work to be done*) preventivo; **to give sb an estimate of** fare a qn un preventivo (*or* una stima) di; **at a rough estimate** ad un calcolo approssimativo
■ VT valutare, stimare; (*Comm*) preventivare; **we estimate the cost to be £150** preventiviamo un costo di circa 150 sterline; **they estimated it would take three weeks** hanno calcolato che ci sarebbero volute tre settimane
■ VI (*Comm*): **to estimate for** fare il preventivo per

es·ti·ma·tion [ˌɛstɪ'meɪʃən] N **1** (*judgment*) giudizio; **in my estimation** a mio giudizio, a mio avviso **2** (*esteem*) stima, opinione *f*; **she has gone up in my estimation** ho maggiore stima di lei

es·ti·ma·tor ['ɛstɪmeɪtəʳ] N estimatore(-trice)

Es·ton·ia, Es·thon·ia [ɛ'stəʊnɪə] N Estonia

Es·to·nian, Es·thon·ian [ɛ'stəʊnɪən] ADJ estone
■ N (*person*) estone *m/f*; (*language*) estone *m*

es·tranged [ɪ'streɪndʒd] ADJ separato(-a); **to become estranged** allontanarsi, disaffezionarsi

es·trange·ment [ɪs'treɪndʒmənt] N allontanamento

es·tro·gen ['iːstrədʒən] N (*Am*) = **oestrogen**

es·tu·ary ['ɛstjʊərɪ] N estuario

ET [ˌiː'tiː] ABBR (*Am*: = **Eastern Time**) *fuso orario della costa orientale*

ETA [ˌiːtiː'eɪ] N ABBR **1** (= **estimated time of arrival**) ora di arrivo prevista **2** (= **Euzkadi ta Askatsuna**) ETA *f Basque separatist organization*

e-tailer ['iːteɪləʳ] N venditore(-trice) in Internet

e-tailing ['iːteɪlɪŋ] N commercio in Internet

et al. [ɛt'æl] ABBR (= **et alii**: *and others*) ed altri

etc ABBR (= **et cetera**) ecc., etc.

etch [ɛtʃ] VT incidere all'acquaforte

etch·ing ['ɛtʃɪŋ] N (*process*) incisione *f* all'acquaforte; (*print made from plate*) acquaforte *f*

ETD [ˌiːtiː'diː] N ABBR (= **estimated time of departure**) ora di partenza prevista

eter·nal [ɪ'tɜːnl] ADJ eterno(-a); (*pej: complaints etc*) continuo(-a); **the eternal triangle** il classico triangolo

eter·nal·ly [ɪ'tɜːnəlɪ] ADV eternamente

eter·nity [ɪ'tɜːnɪtɪ] N eternità

ethane ['iːθeɪn] N etano

etha·nol ['ɛθəˌnɒl] N alcol *m* etilico

eth·ene ['ɛθiːn] N = **ethylene**

ether ['iːθəʳ] N etere *m*

ethe·real [ɪ'θɪərɪəl] ADJ etereo(-a)

eth·ic ['ɛθɪk] N etica; **the work ethic** l'etica del lavoro, la deontologia professionale

ethi·cal ['ɛθɪkəl] ADJ etico(-a), morale; **ethical bank/investment** banca/investimento etico

ethi·cal·ly ['ɛθɪkəlɪ] ADV eticamente

eth·ics ['ɛθɪks] N (*sg: study*) etica; (*pl: principles, system*) morale *f*
▷ www.bbc.co.uk/religion/
▷ www.ethics.org/

Ethio·pia [ˌiːθɪ'əʊpɪə] N Etiopia

Ethio·pian [ˌiːθɪ'əʊpɪən] ADJ etiopico(-a), etiope
■ N (*person*) etiope *m/f*; (*language*) etiope *m*

◎**eth·nic** ['ɛθnɪk] ADJ etnico(-a); **an ethnic minority** una minoranza etnica

eth·ni·cal·ly ['ɛθnɪkəlɪ] ADV etnicamente

ethnic cleansing N pulizia etnica

eth·nog·ra·phy [ɛθ'nɒgrəfɪ] N etnografia

eth·no·logi·cal [ˌɛθnəʊ'lɒdʒɪkəl] ADJ etnologico(-a)

eth·nolo·gist [ɛθ'nɒlədʒɪst] N etnologo(-a)

eth·nol·ogy [ɛθ'nɒlədʒɪ] N etnologia

ethos ['iːθɒs] N (*of culture, group*) ethos *m*, norma di vita

ethyl ['iːθaɪl] N etile *m*

ethyl acetate N acetato di etile

eth·yl·ene ['ɛθɪliːn] N etilene *m*

ethyne ['iːθaɪn] N acetilene *m*

Ee

e-ticket [ˈiːˌtɪkɪt] N biglietto acquistato in Internet
eti·quette [ˈɛtɪˌkɛt] N etichetta; **court etiquette** (*royal*) cerimoniale di corte; **medical etiquette** prassi *f* medica
Etrus·can [ɪˈtrʌskən] ADJ etrusco(-a)
ETU [ˌiːtiːˈjuː] N ABBR (*Brit*: = **Electrical Trades Union**) *sindacato dei lavoratori dell'industria elettrica*
ETV [ˌiːtiːˈviː] N ABBR (*Am*) = *Educational Television*
ety·mo·logi·cal [ˌɛtɪməˈlɒdʒɪkəl] ADJ etimologico(-a)
ety·mo·logi·cal·ly [ˌɛtɪməˈlɒdʒɪkəlɪ] ADV etimologicamente
ety·mol·ogy [ˌɛtɪˈmɒlədʒɪ] N etimologia
EU [ˌiːˈjuː] N ABBR (= **European Union**) UE *f*
▷ www.europa.eu.int/index_en.htm
▷ www.eia.org.uk/websites.htm
euca·lyp·tus [juːkəˈlɪptəs] N eucalipto
Eucha·rist [ˈjuːkərɪst] N Eucaristia
Euclid [ˈjuːklɪd] N Euclide *m*
Euclid·ean [juːˈklɪdɪən] ADJ euclideo(-a)
eugen·ics [juːˈdʒɛnɪks] NSG eugenica
eulo·gize [ˈjuːləˌdʒaɪz] VT elogiare, encomiare
eulogy [ˈjuːlədʒɪ] N elogio, encomio
eunuch [ˈjuːnək] N eunuco
eu·phe·mism [ˈjuːfəˌmɪzəm] N eufemismo
euphemis·tic [ˌjuːfəˈmɪstɪk] ADJ eufemistico(-a)
euphemis·ti·cal·ly [ˌjuːfɪˈmɪstɪkəlɪ] ADV eufemisticamente
euphon·ic [juːˈfɒnɪk] ADJ eufonico(-a)
eupho·ria [juːˈfɔːrɪə] N euforia
euphor·ic [juːˈfɒrɪk] ADJ euforico(-a)
euphor·ical·ly [juːˈfɒrɪkəlɪ] ADV euforicamente
Eura·sia [jʊəˈreɪʃə] N Eurasia
Eura·sian [jʊəˈreɪʃn] ADJ eurasiatico(-a)
■ N eurasiano(-a)
Euratom [jʊəˈrætəm] N ABBR (= **European Atomic Energy Community**) EURATOM *f*
Euripides [jʊˈrɪpɪˌdiːz] N Euripide *m*
Euro- [jʊərəʊ] PREF euro-
euro [ˈjʊərəʊ] N euro *m inv*
Euro·bond [ˈjʊərəʊbɒnd] N (*Econ*) obbligazione *f* in euro, eurobond *m inv*
Euro·cheque [ˈjʊərəʊˌtʃɛk] N eurochèque *m inv*
Euro·crat [ˈjʊərəʊˌkræt] N eurocrate *m/f*
Euro·dol·lar [ˈjʊərəʊˌdɒləʳ] N eurodollaro
euro·land, **Euroland** [ˈjʊərəʊlænd] N Eurolandia
Europa [jʊˈrəʊpə] N (*Myth*) Europa
Europe [ˈjʊərəp] N Europa; **to go into** *or* **join Europe** (*Pol*) entrare nella Comunità Europea
Euro·pean [ˌjʊərəˈpiːən] ADJ europeo(-a); **European plan** (*Am: in hotel*) solo pernottamento (pasti esclusi)
■ N europeo(-a)
European Court of Justice N Tribunale *m* della Comunità Europea
European Economic Community N Comunità Economica Europea
Euro·pol [ˈjʊərəʊpɒl] N Europol *f*
Euro-sceptic [ˈjʊərəʊˌskɛptɪk] N euroscettico(-a)
Euro·vis·ion [ˈjʊərəʊˌvɪʒən] N (*TV*) eurovisione *f*
Euro·zone [ˈjʊərəʊzəʊn] N zona euro
Eurydice [jʊˈrɪdɪsɪ] N Euridice *f*
Eusta·chian tube [juːˈsteɪʃənˈtjuːb] N tromba di Eustachio
eutha·na·sia [ˌjuːθəˈneɪzɪə] N eutanasia
evacu·ate [ɪˈvækjʊˌeɪt] VT (*people*) sfollare; (*building, area, Med*) evacuare
evacu·ation [ɪˌvækjʊˈeɪʃən] N (*see vb*) sfollamento; evacuazione *f*
evac·uee [ɪˌvækjʊˈiː] N sfollato(-a)
evade [ɪˈveɪd] VT (*capture, pursuers*) sfuggire a; (*punishment, blow*) schivare; (*question*) eludere; (*issue, truth, sb's gaze*) evitare; (*responsibility, duties, obligation, military service*) sottrarsi a; (*tax, customs duty*) evadere
evalu·ate [ɪˈvæljʊˌeɪt] VT valutare
evalu·ation [ɪˌvæljʊˈeɪʃən] N valutazione *f*
eva·nesce [ˌɛvəˈnɛs] VI (*liter*) svanire
evan·geli·cal [ˌiːvænˈdʒɛlɪkəl] ADJ evangelico(-a)
evan·gelism [ɪˈvændʒəˌlɪzm] N evangelizzazione *f*
evan·gelist [ɪˈvændʒəlɪst] N (*writer: also*: **Evangelist**) evangelista *m*; (*preacher*) predicatore *m* evangelista
evan·gelize [ɪˈvændʒɪˌlaɪz] VT evangelizzare
■ VI predicare il vangelo
evapo·rate [ɪˈvæpəreɪt] VT (*liquid*) far evaporare
■ VI (*liquid*) evaporare; (*fig: hopes, fears, anger*) svanire
evapo·rat·ed milk [ɪˈvæpəˌreɪtɪdˈmɪlk] N latte *m* condensato
evapo·ra·tion [ɪˌvæpəˈreɪʃən] N evaporazione *f*
eva·sion [ɪˈveɪʒən] N evasione *f*
eva·sive [ɪˈveɪsɪv] ADJ (*answer*) evasivo(-a); (*person*) sfuggente; **to take evasive action** defilarsi
eva·sive·ly [ɪˈveɪsɪvlɪ] ADV evasivamente
Eve [iːv] N Eva
eve [iːv] N vigilia; **on the eve of** alla vigilia di; **Christmas Eve** la vigilia di Natale; **New Year's Eve** la vigilia di Capodanno, la notte di San Silvestro
◎ **even** [ˈiːvən] ADV **1** perfino, anche; **even on Sundays** perfino di domenica; **and she even sings** e sa anche *or* addirittura cantare; **not even ...** nemmeno *or* neppure *or* neanche...; **he didn't even say hello** non ha neanche salutato; **even though** *or* **even if** anche se; **even as** proprio nel momento in cui; **even now he can't do it** non lo sa fare nemmeno ora; **without even reading it** senza neppure leggerlo; **he can't even read** non sa nemmeno leggere; **even so** ciò nonostante; **not even if/when** nemmeno *or* neppure se/quando
2 (*+ comp adj or adv*) ancora; **even faster** ancora più veloce; **even more** ancora di più; **you'll have even more fun tomorrow** domani vi divertirete ancora di più
■ ADJ **1** (*smooth*) liscio(-a); (*level*): **even (with)** allo stesso livello (di); **to make even** livellare; **an even surface** una superficie liscia **2** (*uniform: speed, breathing*) regolare; (*temperature*) costante; (*temper*) calmo(-a); (*tone, voice, colour*) uniforme **3** (*equal: quantities*) uguale; (*: score*) di parità, pari *inv*; **the scores are even** sono a pari punteggio; **to have an even chance (of doing sth)** avere una buona probabilità (di fare qc); **to get even with sb** vendicarsi di qn; **to break even** (*Fin*) chiudere in pareggio; **that makes us even** (*in game, fig*) siamo pari; **they are an even match** sono allo stesso livello **4** (*number*) pari *inv*
▶ **even out** VT + ADV (*smooth: also fig*) appianare; (*number, score*) pareggiare
■ VI + ADV pareggiarsi
▶ **even up** VT + ADV livellare; (*fig*) appianare
even-handed [ˌiːvənˈhændɪd] ADJ imparziale, equo(-a)
◎ **eve·ning** [ˈiːvnɪŋ] N sera; (*as duration, event*) serata; **in the evening** di sera, la sera; **this evening** stasera, questa sera; **tomorrow/yesterday evening** domani/ieri sera; **on Sunday evening** domenica sera; **on the evening of the 30th** la sera del 30; **all evening** tutta la sera; **she spends her evenings knitting** trascorre le sue serate a fare la maglia; **we had a lovely evening** è stata una bella serata; **good evening!** buona sera!
■ ADJ (*paper, prayers, service*) della sera; (*performance*) serale

evening class N corso serale
evening dress N (*woman's*) abito da sera; **in evening dress** (*man*) in abito scuro; (*woman*) in abito lungo
evening primrose N enotera
evening star N stella della sera
even·ly [ˈiːvənlɪ] ADV (*distribute, space, spread*) uniformemente; (*divide*) in parti uguali; (*breathe*) in modo regolare
even·song [ˈiːvən,sɒŋ] N ≈ vespro
◎ **event** [ɪˈvɛnt] N avvenimento; (*Sport: in a programme*) gara; **it was one of the most important events in his life** è stato uno degli avvenimenti più importanti della sua vita; **she took part in two events at the last Olympic Games** ha preso parte a due gare alle ultime Olimpiadi; **a sporting event** una manifestazione sportiva; **"Events"** "Spettacoli e manifestazioni"; **social events for the students** iniziative per gli studenti; **at all events** *or* **in any event** in ogni caso; **in either event** in entrambi i casi; **in the event of/that ...** in caso di/che + *sub*...; **in the event** in realtà, di fatto; **in that event** in quel caso; **in the normal course of events** secondo le regole, nel corso naturale delle cose; **in the course of events** nel corso degli eventi
even-tempered [,iːvənˈtɛmpəd] ADJ equilibrato(-a)
event·ful [ɪˈvɛntfʊl] ADJ (*life*) ricco(-a) di avvenimenti; (*match, day*) movimentato(-a), denso(-a) di eventi
event·ing [ɪˈvɛntɪŋ] N (*Sport*) concorso ippico
even·tual [ɪˈvɛntʃʊəl] ADJ finale; **the eventual outcome** il risultato finale; **it resulted in the eventual loss of many lives** ha avuto come risultato finale la perdita di molte vite umane

DID YOU KNOW ...?
eventual is not translated by the Italian word ***eventuale***

even·tu·al·ity [ɪ,vɛntʃʊˈælɪtɪ] N eventualità *f inv*, possibilità *f inv*; **to be ready for any eventuality** essere pronto(-a) a ogni evenienza
◎ **even·tu·al·ly** [ɪˈvɛntʃʊəlɪ] ADV (*at last*) alla fine, finalmente; **eventually the species will become extinct** (*given time*) la specie finirà per estinguersi

DID YOU KNOW ...?
eventually is not translated by the Italian word ***eventualmente***

◎ **ever** [ˈɛvəʳ] ADV **1** (*always*) sempre; **ever ready** sempre pronto(-a); **ever since (then) they have been very careful** da allora in poi sono stati molto prudenti; **ever since I met him** da quando l'ho incontrato; **ever since I've known him** sin da quando lo conosco; **it will become ever more complex** diventerà sempre più complicato; **with ever increasing frequency** con sempre maggior frequenza; **they lived happily ever after** e vissero per sempre felici e contenti; **as ever** come sempre; **for ever** per sempre; **they are for ever fighting** litigano di continuo; **yours ever** (*Brit: in letters*) sempre tuo(-a) **2** (*at any time*) mai; **hardly ever** quasi mai; **nothing ever happens** non succede mai nulla; **if you ever go there** se ti capita di andarci; **did you ever meet him?** l'hai mai incontrato?; **have you ever been there?** ci sei mai stato?; **we haven't ever tried it** non l'abbiamo mai provato; **more handsome than ever** più bello che mai; **now if ever is the time** *or* **moment to ...** ora o mai più è il momento di...; **for the first time ever** per la prima volta in assoluto; **the best ever** il/la migliore che ci sia mai stato(-a); **the best film ever** il miglior film che si sia mai visto; **he's a liar if ever there was one** se c'è un bugiardo al mondo quello è lui **3** (*emphasizing*): **as soon as ever you can** al più presto possibile; **why ever did you do it?** perché mai l'hai fatto?; **why ever not?** ma perché no?; **never ever** mai e poi mai; **ever so pretty** così bello(-a); **he's ever so strong** è fortissimo; **ever so slightly drunk** leggermente sbronzo; **we're ever so grateful** siamo estremamente grati; **thank you ever so much** grazie mille; **as if I ever would!** non sia mai detto!
Ev·er·est [ˈɛvərɪst] N (*also:* **Mount Everest**) l'Everest *m*, il monte *m* Everest
ever·green [ˈɛvə,griːn] ADJ, N sempreverde (*m or f*)
ever·lasting [,ɛvəˈlɑːstɪŋ] ADJ eterno(-a); (*pej*) continuo(-a)
ever·lasting·ly [,ɛvəˈlɑːstɪŋlɪ] ADV (*see adj*) eternamente, in eterno; continuamente, incessantemente
ever·more [,ɛvəˈmɔːʳ] ADV sempre; **for evermore** per sempre
◎ **every** [ˈɛvrɪ] ADJ (*each*) ogni *inv*; (*all*) tutti(-e) *pl*; **every pupil** ogni scolaro; **every one of them** ognuno(-a) di loro; **every one of** tutti; **every one of the components was faulty** tutti i componenti erano difettosi; **I gave you every assistance** ti ho dato tutta l'assistenza; **I have every confidence in him** ho piena fiducia in lui; **we wish you every success** ti auguriamo ogni successo; **every day** ogni giorno, tutti i giorni; **every other day** un giorno sì e uno no; **every other car** una macchina su due; **every second month** ogni due mesi; **every three days** *or* **every third day** ogni tre giorni; **every few days** ogni due o tre giorni; **every so often** *or* **every now and then** *or* **every now and again** di tanto in tanto, di quando in quando, ogni tanto; **every time that** ogni volta che; **every single time** proprio tutte le volte; **her every wish** ogni suo desiderio; **I enjoyed every minute of the party** mi sono divertito moltissimo alla festa; **every bit of the carpet** proprio tutto il tappeto; **every bit as clever as** tanto intelligente quanto; **in every way** sotto tutti i profili; **every man for himself** ognuno per sé
◎ **every·body** [ˈɛvrɪ,bɒdɪ] PRON ognuno, ciascuno; (*all*) tutti(-e) *pl*; **everybody knows about it** lo sanno tutti; **everybody makes mistakes** tutti fanno errori; **everybody has their** *or* (*frm*) **his own view** ognuno *or* ciascuno la pensa come crede; **everybody else** tutti gli altri
every·day [ˈɛvrɪ,deɪ] ADJ quotidiano(-a), di ogni giorno; (*expression*) di uso corrente; (*use, occurrence, experience*) comune; (*shoes, clothes*) di tutti i giorni; **in everyday life** nella vita quotidiana; **it is not an everyday event** non capita tutti i giorni
◎ **every·one** [ˈɛvrɪ,wʌn] PRON = **everybody**
every·place [ˈɛvrɪ,pleɪs] ADV (*Am*) = **everywhere**
◎ **every·thing** [ˈɛvrɪ,θɪŋ] PRON tutto, ogni cosa; **you've thought of everything!** hai pensato a tutto!; **everything is ready** è tutto pronto; **everything you say is true** tutto ciò che dici è vero; **this shop sells everything** questo negozio vende di tutto; **he did everything possible** ha fatto tutto il possibile
◎ **every·where** [ˈɛvrɪ,wɛəʳ] ADV dappertutto, in ogni luogo; (*wherever*) ovunque; **I looked everywhere, but I couldn't find it** ho cercato dappertutto, ma non l'ho trovato; **everywhere you go you meet ...** ovunque tu vada trovi...
evict [ɪˈvɪkt] VT sfrattare
evic·tion [ɪˈvɪkʃən] N sfratto
eviction notice N avviso di sfratto

Ee

◎ **evi·dence** [ˈɛvɪdəns] N INV *(proof)* prova; *(testimony)* testimonianza; *(sign)* indizio, traccia; **there is no evidence to support this theory** non c'è prova a sostegno di questa teoria; **to show evidence of** mostrare segni di; dare segni di; **evidence of a break-in** tracce di scasso; **to give evidence** testimoniare, deporre; **his cousin gave evidence against him** suo cugino ha deposto contro di lui; **to turn King's** *or* **Queen's** *or (Am)* **State's evidence** testimoniare contro i propri complici; **to be in evidence** essere visibile *or* in vista; **she was nowhere in evidence** non la si vedeva da nessuna parte

evi·dent [ˈɛvɪdənt] ADJ evidente, chiaro(-a); **it is evident from his speech that ...** risulta chiaro *or* evidente dal suo discorso che...

evi·dent·ly [ˈɛvɪdəntlɪ] ADV *(clearly)* chiaramente; *(apparently)* evidentemente; **evidently he cannot come** evidentemente non può venire

◎ **evil** [ˈiːvl] N male *m*; **the lesser of two evils** il minore tra due mali; **a necessary evil** un male necessario
■ ADJ *(person, deed)* malvagio(-a), cattivo(-a); *(reputation, influence)* pessimo(-a); *(spirit, spell, influence)* malvagio(-a); *(unhappy: hour, times)* infausto(-a)

evil·doer [ˈiːvlˌduːəʳ] N persona malvagia

evil eye N: **to put the evil eye on sb** gettare il malocchio su qn

evil·ly [ˈiːvɪllɪ] ADV malvagiamente

evil-minded [ˌiːvlˈmaɪndɪd] ADJ malvagio(-a)

evince [ɪˈvɪns] VT *(frm)* manifestare

evo·ca·tion [ˌɛvəˈkeɪʃən] N evocazione *f*

evoca·tive [ɪˈvɒkətɪv] ADJ: **evocative (of)** evocativo(-a) (di)

evoca·tive·ly [ɪˈvɒkətɪvlɪ] ADV in modo evocativo

evoke [ɪˈvəʊk] VT *(memories)* evocare; *(admiration)* suscitare

evo·lu·tion [ˌiːvəˈluːʃən] N *(development)* sviluppo; *(Bio)* evoluzione *f*

evo·lu·tion·ary [ˌiːvəˈluːʃənrɪ] ADJ evolutivo(-a)

evo·lu·tion·ist [ˌiːvəˈluːʃənɪst] ADJ evoluzionistico(-a)
■ N evoluzionista *m/f*

evolve [ɪˈvɒlv] VT *(system, theory, plan)* elaborare, sviluppare
■ VI *(species)* evolversi; *(system, plan, science)* svilupparsi

ewe [juː] N pecora

ewer [ˈjuːəʳ] N *(old)* brocca

ex [ɛks] N *(ex-husband, ex-wife)* ex *m/f inv*; **he's one of my exes** è uno dei miei ex
■ PREP *(out of)*: **the price ex works** il prezzo franco fabbrica

ex- [ɛks] PREF *(former: husband, president)* ex-

ex·ac·er·bate [ɪɡˈzæsəˌbeɪt] *(frm)* VT *(pain)* aggravare; *(relations, situation)* esacerbare, inasprire

ex·ac·er·ba·tion [ɪɡˌzæsəˈbeɪʃən] N *(see vb)* aggravamento; esacerbazione *f*, inasprimento

◎ **ex·act** [ɪɡˈzækt] ADJ *(number, value, meaning, time)* esatto(-a); *(instructions, description)* preciso(-a); **it's an exact copy of the original** è una copia perfetta dell'originale; **her exact words were ...** le sue precise parole sono state...; **to be exact, there were three of us** per essere precisi eravamo in tre; **the exact opposite (of)** l'esatto contrario (di)
■ VT: **to exact sth (from)** *(frm)* esigere qc (da)

ex·act·ing [ɪɡˈzæktɪŋ] ADJ *(task, profession, work)* impegnativo(-a); *(person)* esigente; **exacting standards** standard molto alti

ex·acti·tude [ɪɡˈzæktɪtjuːd] N precisione *f*, esattezza

◎ **ex·act·ly** [ɪɡˈzæktlɪ] ADV *(describe, know, resemble)* esattamente; *(of time)* in punto; **exactly the same** esattamente uguale; **exactly!** esatto!; **that's exactly what I thought** è proprio quello che pensavo; **it's exactly 5 o'clock** sono le 5 in punto

ex·act·ness [ɪɡˈzæktnɪs] N esattezza, precisione *f*

ex·ag·ger·ate [ɪɡˈzædʒəˌreɪt] VT *(overstate)* esagerare; *(emphasize)* accentuare
■ VI esagerare

ex·ag·ger·at·ed [ɪɡˈzædʒəˌreɪtɪd] ADJ esagerato(-a); **to have an exaggerated opinion of o.s.** stimarsi troppo

ex·ag·gera·tion [ɪɡˌzædʒəˈreɪʃən] N esagerazione *f*

ex·alt [ɪɡˈzɔːlt] VT *(frm)* **1** *(in rank)* promuovere **2** *(praise)* esaltare, magnificare

ex·al·ta·tion [ˌɛɡzɔːlˈteɪʃən] *(frm)* N esaltazione *f*

ex·alt·ed [ɪɡˈzɔːltɪd] ADJ *(frm: high: rank, position, person)* elevato(-a); *(: elated)* esaltato(-a)

exam [ɪɡˈzæm] N ABBR *(Scol: =* **examination***)* esame *m*; **a French exam** un esame di francese; **the exam results** i risultati degli esami; **to take an exam** fare un esame

◎ **ex·ami·na·tion** [ɪɡˌzæmɪˈneɪʃən] N *(Scol)* esame *m*; *(inspection: of machine, premises)* ispezione *f*; *(: of accounts, passport, at Customs)* controllo; *(of witness, suspect)* interrogatorio; *(Med)* visita; **to take** *or* **sit an examination** sostenere *or* dare un esame; **on examination** in seguito all'esame; **the matter is under examination** la questione è all'esame; **a medical examination** una visita medica

◎ **ex·am·ine** [ɪɡˈzæmɪn] VT *(inspect: machine, wreckage)* ispezionare; *(: luggage, passport)* controllare; *(Med)* visitare, esaminare; *(witness, suspect)* interrogare; *(test: pupil, candidate)*: **to examine sb in** esaminare qn in; *(orally)* interrogare qn in; **experts are examining the wreckage of the plane** gli esperti stanno esaminando il relitto dell'aereo; **he examined her passport** le ha controllato il passaporto; **the doctor examined him** il dottore l'ha visitato

ex·am·in·er [ɪɡˈzæmɪnəʳ] N esaminatore(-trice)

◎ **ex·am·ple** [ɪɡˈzɑːmpl] N *(gen)* esempio; *(person)* esempio, modello; *(copy)* esemplare *m*; **for example** ad *or* per esempio; **to quote sth/sb as an example** portare qc/qn come esempio; **to set a good/bad example** dare il buon/cattivo esempio; **to make an example of sb** dare l'esempio (punendo qn); **to punish sb as an example** punire qn per dare l'esempio

ex·as·per·ate [ɪɡˈzɑːspəˌreɪt] VT esasperare; **exasperated by** *or* **at** *or* **with** esasperato(-a) da; **to become exasperated** esasperarsi

ex·as·per·at·ing [ɪɡˈzɑːspəˌreɪtɪŋ] ADJ esasperante

ex·as·per·at·ing·ly [ɪɡˈzɑːspəˌreɪtɪŋlɪ] ADV in modo esasperante

ex·as·pera·tion [ɪɡˌzɑːspəˈreɪʃən] N esasperazione *f*

ex·ca·vate [ˈɛkskəˌveɪt] VT *(ground)* scavare; *(Archeol)* effettuare gli scavi di

ex·ca·va·tion [ˌɛkskəˈveɪʃən] N scavo; *(Archeol)* scavi *mpl*

ex·ca·va·tor [ˈɛkskəˌveɪtəʳ] N *(machine)* escavatrice *f*, escavatore *m*

ex·ceed [ɪkˈsiːd] VT *(gen, speed limit)*: **to exceed (by)** superare (di); *(limit, bounds)* oltrepassare; *(powers, instructions, duty)* eccedere; *(time limit)* superare

ex·ceed·ing·ly [ɪkˈsiːdɪŋlɪ] ADV estremamente

ex·cel [ɪkˈsɛl] VT superare; **to excel o.s.** superare se stesso
■ VI: **to excel at** *or* **in** eccellere in; **to excel as** primeggiare come

ex·cel·lence [ˈɛksələns] N superiorità

Ex·cel·len·cy ['ɛksələnsɪ] N: **His Excellency** Sua Eccellenza

◎**ex·cel·lent** ['ɛksələnt] ADJ eccellente, ottimo(-a); **her results were excellent** i suoi risultati erano eccellenti

ex·cel·lent·ly ['ɛksələntlɪ] ADV eccellentemente, ottimamente

◎**ex·cept** [ɪk'sɛpt] PREP (*also:* **except for, excepting**) eccetto, salvo, tranne; **everyone except me** tutti tranne me; **except that/if/when** salvo che/se/quando; **there is nothing we can do except wait** non c'è nulla che possiamo fare se non aspettare; **except for** ad eccezione di; **except for one old lady** ad eccezione di *or* tranne una vecchia signora
■VT: **to except (from)** escludere (da); **present company excepted** esclusi i presenti; **always excepting the possibility ...** sempre se si esclude la possibilità...; **not excepting ...** senza esclusione di...

◎**ex·cep·tion** [ɪk'sɛpʃən] N eccezione *f*; **with the exception of** ad eccezione di, fatta eccezione per; **without exception** senza eccezioni; **to make an exception** fare un'eccezione; **the exception proves the rule** l'eccezione conferma la regola; **to take exception to** fare obiezione a, trovare da ridire su

ex·cep·tion·al [ɪk'sɛpʃənl] ADJ eccezionale; (*unusual*) insolito(-a)

ex·cep·tion·al·ly [ɪk'sɛpʃənəlɪ] ADV eccezionalmente

◎**ex·cerpt** ['ɛksɜːpt] N (*from film*) spezzone *m*; (*from TV play*) estratto; (*from book, Mus*) brano

◎**ex·cess** [ɪk'sɛs] N eccesso; **the excess of losses over profits** l'eccedenza delle perdite sui guadagni; **in excess of** al di sopra di; **sums in excess of £10,000** somme superiori alle 10.000 sterline; **to excess** all'eccesso; **to carry sth to excess** spingere qc all'eccesso
■ADJ (*profit, weight*) in eccesso; **excess fat** grasso in eccesso

excess baggage, excess luggage N bagaglio in eccedenza

excess fare N supplemento di prezzo *or* di tariffa

ex·ces·sive [ɪk'sɛsɪv] ADJ (*drinking, spending, interest*) smodato(-a); (*charges, rates*) eccessivo(-a); (*fear*) esagerato(-a)

ex·ces·sive·ly [ɪk'sɛsɪvlɪ] ADV (*see adj*) smodatamente; eccessivamente; esageratamente

excess luggage N = **excess baggage**

excess supply N eccesso di offerta

◎**ex·change** [ɪks'tʃeɪndʒ] N **1** scambio; **in exchange (for)** in cambio (di); **what will you give me in exchange?** cosa mi darai in cambio?; **I'd like to do an exchange with an Italian student** vorrei fare uno scambio con uno studente italiano; **an exchange of gunfire** uno scontro a fuoco **2** (*Comm*): **foreign exchange** cambio **3** (*also:* **telephone exchange**) centralino
■VT: **to exchange sth for sth/with sb** scambiare qc con qc/con qn; (*prisoners, stamps, greetings*) scambiarsi; **to exchange blows** venire alle mani

ex·change·able [ɪks'tʃeɪndʒəbl] ADJ cambiabile

exchange control N (*Fin*) controllo dei cambi

exchange market N mercato dei cambi

◎**exchange rate** N tasso di cambio

Exchange Rate Mechanism N meccanismo dei tassi di cambi

Ex·cheq·uer [ɪks'tʃɛkə^r] N: **the Exchequer** (*Brit*) ≈ il ministero delle Finanze

ex·cis·able [ɪk'saɪzəbl] ADJ soggetto(-a) a dazio

ex·cise [*n* 'ɛksaɪz; *vb* ɪk'saɪz] N (*also:* **excise tax**) dazio
■VT (*frm*) asportare

excise duties ['ɛksaɪz'djuːtɪz] NPL dazi *mpl*

ex·cit·abil·ity [ɪk,saɪtə'bɪlɪtɪ] N eccitabilità

ex·cit·able [ɪk'saɪtəbl] ADJ eccitabile

ex·cite [ɪk'saɪt] VT **1** (*person*) far agitare; (*: pleasantly*) riempire di gioia (*or* interesse *etc*); (*: sexually*) eccitare; **to excite sb to anger** far arrabbiare qn **2** (*anger*) provocare; (*interest, enthusiasm*) suscitare

ex·cit·ed [ɪk'saɪtɪd] ADJ: **excited (about)** eccitato(-a) (per); **to get excited (about sth)** agitarsi (per qc); **it's nothing to get excited about** (*fig*) non è niente di particolare

ex·cit·ed·ly [ɪk'saɪtɪdlɪ] ADV con eccitazione

ex·cite·ment [ɪk'saɪtmənt] N eccitazione *f*, agitazione *f*; **in the excitement of the departure/preparations** nell'eccitazione *or* agitazione della partenza/dei preparativi; **the book caused great excitement** il libro ha fatto sensazione; **she enjoys excitement** le piacciono le emozioni

◎**ex·cit·ing** [ɪk'saɪtɪŋ] ADJ (*gen*) emozionante; (*idea, fashion, person*) entusiasmante; (*film, book*) appassionante; **an exciting match** una partita entusiasmante; **an exciting story** una storia appassionante; **an exciting adventure** un'avventura eccitante

excl. ABBR **1** = **excluding 2** = **exclusive (of)**

ex·claim [ɪks'kleɪm] VT esclamare
■VI: **to exclaim at sth** (*indignantly*) indignarsi per qc; (*admiringly*) esprimere meraviglia davanti a qc

ex·cla·ma·tion [,ɛksklə'meɪʃən] N esclamazione *f*

exclamation mark, (*Am*) **exclamation point** N (*Gram*) punto esclamativo

ex·clude [ɪks'kluːd] VT (*gen*) escludere; (*possibility*) scartare; **I'm excluded from taking part** non ho il diritto di partecipare

ex·clud·ing [ɪks'kluːdɪŋ] PREP: **excluding VAT** IVA esclusa; **excluding the cleaners** escluse le donne delle pulizie

ex·clu·sion [ɪks'kluːʒən] N esclusione *f*; **women's exclusion from political power** l'esclusione delle donne dal potere politico; **to the exclusion of** escludendo; **exclusion from school** espulsione dalla scuola

exclusion clause N clausola di esclusione di rischi

exclusion zone N area interdetta

ex·clu·sive [ɪks'kluːsɪv] ADJ **1** (*gen, club*) esclusivo(-a); (*district*) snob *inv*; (*interest, attention*) totale; **you will have exclusive use of the pool** avrete uso esclusivo della piscina; **exclusive agency agreement** (*Comm*) accordo di esclusiva; **exclusive rights** diritti *mpl* esclusivi; **an interview exclusive to ...** un'intervista in esclusiva a... **2** (*not including*): **exclusive of postage** spese postali escluse; **exclusive of service** servizio escluso; **exclusive of VAT** IVA esclusa

ex·clu·sive·ly [ɪks'kluːsɪvlɪ] ADV esclusivamente

ex·com·muni·cate [,ɛkskə'mjuːnɪ,keɪt] VT scomunicare

ex·com·mu·ni·ca·tion ['ɛkskə,mjuːnɪ'keɪʃən] N scomunica

ex·cre·ment ['ɛkskrɪmənt] N (*frm*) escremento

ex·cres·cence [ɪks'krɛsns] N (*frm*) escrescenza

ex·cre·ta [ɪks'kriːtə] NPL (*frm*) escrementi *mpl*, escrezioni *fpl*

ex·crete [ɪks'kriːt] VT (*frm*) espellere

ex·cre·tion [ɪks'kriːʃən] N (*frm*) escrezione *f*

ex·cru·ci·at·ing [ɪks'kruːʃɪ,eɪtɪŋ] ADJ (*pain, suffering, fam: film*) atroce; (*noise*) insopportabile

Ee

ex·cru·ci·at·ing·ly [ɪks'kru:ʃɪˌeɪtɪŋlɪ] ADV *(see adj)* atrocemente; insopportabilmente; **my leg is excruciatingly painful** ho un dolore atroce alla gamba

ex·cul·pate ['ɛkskʌlˌpeɪt] VT *(frm)*: **to exculpate (from)** scagionare (da), discolpare (da)

ex·cur·sion [ɪks'kɜ:ʃən] N *(journey)* escursione *f*, gita; *(fig)* digressione *f*

excursion ticket N biglietto a tariffa turistica

excursion train N treno speciale (per escursioni)

ex·cus·able [ɪks'kju:zəbl] ADJ scusabile, perdonabile

◎ **ex·cuse** [*n* ɪks'kju:s; *vb* ɪks'kju:z] N scusa; **there's no excuse for this** non ci sono scuse *or* scusanti per questo; **on the excuse that ...** con la scusa *or* il pretesto che...; **to make excuses for sb** trovare giustificazioni per qn

■ VT **1** *(forgive)* scusare; **excuse me!** *(to attract attention, apologize)* scusi!; *(when you want to get past)* permesso!; **now, if you will excuse me ...** ora mi scusi ma...; **excuse me?** *(Am)* come (dice), scusi? **2** *(justify)* giustificare; **to excuse o.s. (for (doing) sth)** giustificarsi (per (aver fatto) qc) **3** *(exempt)*: **to excuse sb (from sth/from doing sth)** esonerare *or* dispensare qn (da qc/dal fare qc); **to excuse o.s. (from sth/from doing sth)** farsi esonerare *or* dispensare (da qc/dal fare qc); **to ask to be excused** chiedere di essere scusato(-a)

ex-directory [ˌɛksdɪ'rɛktərɪ] ADJ *(Brit)* fuori elenco; **to go ex-directory** non avere il numero di telefono sull'elenco; **ex-directory (phone) number** numero (telefonico) fuori elenco

exec [ɪg'zɛk] N *(fam)* dirigente *m/f*, executive *m/f inv*

ex·ecrable ['ɛksɪkrəbl] ADJ *(frm: gen)* pessimo(-a); (: *manners*) esecrabile

ex·ecrably ['ɛksɪkrəblɪ] *(frm)* ADV *(see adj)* pessimamente; in modo esecrabile

ex·ecrate ['ɛksɪˌkreɪt] VT *(frm)* esecrare, aborrire

ex·ecra·tion [ˌɛksɪ'kreɪʃən] N *(frm)* esecrazione *f*

ex·ecut·able ['ɛksɪkju:təbl] ADJ *(Comput)* eseguibile

◎ **ex·ecute** ['ɛksɪkju:t] VT **1** *(put to death: prisoner)* giustiziare **2** *(carry out: plan, movement)* eseguire; (: *scheme*) attuare; *(work of art)* realizzare; *(Law: will)* rendere esecutivo(-a)

ex·ecu·tion [ˌɛksɪ'kju:ʃən] N *(see vb)* esecuzione *f*; attuazione *f*; realizzazione *f*; **in the execution of one's duty** nell'adempimento del proprio dovere

ex·ecu·tion·er [ˌɛksɪ'kju:ʃnə^r] N boia *m inv*

◎ **ex·ecu·tive** [ɪg'zɛkjʊtɪv] ADJ *(powers, committee)* esecutivo(-a); *(position, job, duties)* direttivo(-a); *(secretary)* di direzione; *(offices, suite)* della direzione; *(car, plane)* dirigenziale

■ N *(Admin, Industry)* dirigente *m/f*, manager *m/f*; **the executive** *(Pol)* l'esecutivo

executive director N amministratore(-trice)

ex·ecu·tor [ɪg'zɛkjʊtə^r] N *(of will)* esecutore(-trice) testamentario(-a)

ex·egesis [ˌɛksɪ'dʒi:sɪs] N *(frm)* esegesi *f*

ex·em·plar [ɪg'zɛmplə^r] *(frm)* N *(example)* esempio; *(model)* modello

ex·em·pla·ry [ɪg'zɛmplərɪ] ADJ esemplare

ex·em·pli·fi·ca·tion [ɪgˌzɛmplɪfɪ'keɪʃən] N esemplificazione *f*

ex·em·pli·fy [ɪg'zɛmplɪˌfaɪ] VT *(illustrate)* spiegare con esempi, esemplificare; *(be an example of)* essere un esempio di

ex·empt [ɪg'zɛmpt] ADJ: **exempt (from)** *(person: from tax)* esentato(-a) (da); (: *from military service etc*) esonerato(-a) (da); *(goods)* esente (da); **tax exempt** esentasse

■ VT: **to exempt (from)** *(see adj)* esentare (da); esonerare (da)

ex·emp·tion [ɪg'zɛmpʃən] N *(see adj)* esenzione *f*; esonero

◎ **ex·er·cise** ['ɛksəˌsaɪz] N *(gen)* esercizio; *(physical activity)* esercizio fisico; *(Mil)* esercitazione *f*; **page 10, exercise 3** pagina 10, esercizio numero 3; **in the exercise of one's duties** nell'esercizio delle proprie funzioni; **to take** *or* **do exercise** fare del movimento *or* moto, fare ginnastica

■ VT **1** *(use: authority, right, influence)* esercitare; (: *patience, restraint, tact*) usare **2** *(mind, muscle, limb)* tenere in esercizio; *(dog)* fare passeggiare, portar fuori

■ VI fare del movimento *or* moto

exercise bike, exercise cycle N cyclette® *f inv*

exercise book N quaderno

ex·ert [ɪg'zɜ:t] VT *(force)* impiegare; *(influence, authority)* esercitare; **to exert o.s** *(physically)* fare uno sforzo; **don't exert yourself!** *(hum)* non sforzarti troppo!

ex·er·tion [ɪg'zɜ:ʃən] N sforzo

ex·eunt ['ɛksɪˌʌnt] VI *(Theatre)* escono

ex·fo·li·ate [ɛks'fəʊlɪeɪt] VI fare il peeling

■ VT fare il peeling a

ex·fo·lia·tion [ɛksˌfəʊlɪ'eɪʃən] N esfoliazione *f*

ex gra·tia [ˌɛks'greɪʃə] ADJ: **ex gratia payment** gratifica

ex·hale [ɛks'heɪl] VT, VI espirare

◎ **ex·haust** [ɪg'zɔ:st] N *(also:* **exhaust pipe***)* tubo di scappamento

■ VT *(gen)* esaurire; *(tire out: person)* stremare; **an exhausting journey/day** un viaggio/una giornata estenuante; **to exhaust o.s** sfiancarsi

ex·haust·ed [ɪg'zɔ:stɪd] ADJ *(tired)* esausto(-a), sfinito(-a); *(used up: supplies)* esaurito(-a)

exhaust fumes NPL gas *m inv* di scarico

ex·haust·ing [ɪg'zɔ:stɪŋ] ADJ estenuante, sfibrante

ex·haus·tion [ɪg'zɔ:stʃən] N esaurimento; **nervous exhaustion** sovraffaticamento mentale, surmenage *m*

ex·haus·tive [ɪg'zɔ:stɪv] ADJ *(research, inquiry, inspection)* approfondito(-a), minuzioso(-a); *(account, description)* esauriente; *(list)* completo(-a)

ex·haust·ive·ly [ɪg'zɔ:stɪvlɪ] ADV *(see adj)* minuziosamente, in modo approfondito; in modo esauriente

exhaust system N scappamento

ex·hib·it [ɪg'zɪbɪt] VT *(painting)* esporre; *(signs of emotion)* mostrare; *(courage)* dar prova di; *(skill, ingenuity)* dimostrare

■ VI *(painter)* esporre

■ N *(object on show)* oggetto esposto; *(Law)* reperto

◎ **ex·hi·bi·tion** [ˌɛksɪ'bɪʃən] N *(act)* esposizione *f*, dimostrazione *f*; *(of rudeness)* dimostrazione; *(a public show)* mostra; **to be on exhibition** essere esposto(-a); **to make an exhibition of o.s** dare spettacolo di sé

ex·hi·bi·tion·ism [ˌɛksɪ'bɪʃəˌnɪzəm] N *(also Psych)* esibizionismo

ex·hi·bi·tion·ist [ˌɛksɪ'bɪʃənɪst] N esibizionista *m/f*

ex·hibi·tor [ɪg'zɪbɪtə^r] N espositore(-trice)

ex·hila·rate [ɪg'zɪləˌreɪt] VT *(subj: sea, air)* tonificare; (: *good company, wine*) rallegrare

exhilarating [ɪg'zɪləreɪtɪŋ] ADJ *(see vb)* tonificante; che rallegra

ex·hila·ra·tion [ɪgˌzɪlə'reɪʃən] N allegria

ex·hort [ɪg'zɔ:t] VT *(frm)*: **to exhort sb (to sth/to do sth)** esortare qn (a qc/a fare qc)

ex·hor·ta·tion [ˌɛgzɔːˈteɪʃən] N (*frm*): **exhortation (to)** esortazione *f* (a)
ex·hu·ma·tion [ˌɛkshjʊˈmeɪʃən] N (*frm*) esumazione *f*
ex·hume [ɛksˈhjuːm] VT (*frm*) esumare
exi·gen·cy [ˈɛksɪdʒənsɪ] N (*frm*) esigenza
◎ **ex·ile** [ˈɛksaɪl] N (*state*) esilio; (*person*) esule *m/f*; **in(to) exile** in esilio
■ VT esiliare
◎ **ex·ist** [ɪgˈzɪst] VI **1** (*live*) vivere; **to exist on sth** vivere di qc **2** (*be in existence*) esistere; (: *doubt*) sussistere; (*occur*) trovarsi
◎ **ex·ist·ence** [ɪgˈzɪstəns] N esistenza; **to be in existence** esistere; **to come into existence** essere creato(-a); **the only one in existence** l'unico esistente
ex·ist·ent [ɪgˈzɪstənt] ADJ (*frm*) esistente
ex·is·ten·tial [ˌɛgzɪsˈtɛnʃəl] ADJ (*frm*) esistenziale
ex·is·ten·tial·ism [ˌɛgzɪsˈtɛnʃəˌlɪzəm] N esistenzialismo
ex·is·ten·tial·ist [ˌɛgzɪsˈtɛnʃəlɪst] ADJ, N esistenzialista (*m/f*)
◎ **ex·ist·ing** [ɪgˈzɪstɪŋ] ADJ (*law, state of affairs*) attuale
exit [ˈɛksɪt] N uscita; **to make one's exit** uscire
■ VI (*Theatre, Comput*) uscire
exit poll N exit poll *m inv*
exit ramp N (*Am Aut*) rampa di uscita
exit runway N (*Aer*) bretella
exit visa N visto d'uscita
exo·dus [ˈɛksədəs] N (*gen, Rel*) esodo
ex of·fi·cio [ˌɛksəˈfɪʃɪəʊ] (*frm*) ADV (*act*) d'ufficio
■ ADJ (*member*) di diritto
ex·on·er·ate [ɪgˈzɒnəˌreɪt] VT (*frm*): **to exonerate sb (from sth)** discolpare qn (da qc)
ex·or·bi·tance [ɪgˈzɔːbɪtəns] N eccessività
ex·or·bi·tant [ɪgˈzɔːbɪtənt] ADJ (*price*) esorbitante; (*demands*) spropositato(-a)
ex·or·bi·tant·ly [ɪgˈzɔːbɪtəntlɪ] ADV eccessivamente
ex·or·cise, ex·or·cize [ˈɛksɔːsaɪz] VT esorcizzare
ex·or·cism [ˈɛksɔːsɪzəm] N esorcismo
ex·or·cist [ˈɛksɔːsɪst] N esorcista *m*
exo·skel·eton [ˌɛksəʊˈskɛlɪtən] N esoscheletro
exo·ther·mic [ˌɛksəʊˈθɜːmɪk] ADJ esotermico(-a)
ex·ot·ic [ɪgˈzɒtɪk] ADJ esotico(-a)
ex·oti·cal·ly [ɪgˈzɒtɪkəlɪ] ADV esoticamente
ex·oti·cism [ɪgˈzɒtɪˌsɪzəm] N esotismo
◎ **ex·pand** [ɪksˈpænd] VT (*chest, muscles, economy*) sviluppare; (*market, operations*) espandere; (*statement, notes*) ampliare; (*knowledge*) approfondire; (*horizons*) allargare; (*influence*) estendere; **we want to expand our business** vogliamo espandere l'attività
■ VI (*see vt*) svilupparsi; espandersi; (*gas*) espandersi; (*metal, lungs*) dilatarsi; **the ceramic industry expanded at the end of the century** l'industria della ceramica si è sviluppata alla fine del secolo; **the economy is expanding** l'economia è in espansione; **to expand on** (*notes, story etc*) ampliare, approfondire; **he didn't expand on his previous remarks** non ha approfondito ciò che aveva detto prima
ex·pand·ing [ɪksˈpændɪŋ] ADJ (*universe, industry*) in espansione; **after six months her expanding waistline became impossible to hide** dopo sei mesi le riuscì impossibile nascondere il pancione
ex·panse [ɪksˈpæns] N distesa, estensione *f*
◎ **ex·pan·sion** [ɪksˈpænʃən] N (*gen*) espansione *f*; (*of town, economy, idea*) sviluppo; (*of production*) aumento; (*of knowledge*) approfondimento; (*of influence*) estendersi *m*; (*of gas*) espansione, dilatazione *f*; (*of metal*) dilatazione
expansion bolt N vite *f* a espansione
expansion card N (*Comput*) scheda di espansione
ex·pan·sion·ism [ɪksˈpænʃənɪzəm] N espansionismo
ex·pan·sion·ist [ɪksˈpænʃənɪst] ADJ espansionistico(-a)
expansion slot N (*Comput*) slot *m inv* di espansione
ex·pan·sive [ɪksˈpænsɪv] ADJ (*fig: sociable*) espansivo(-a); (*frm: extensive*) considerevole
ex·pan·sive·ly [ɪksˈpænsɪvlɪ] ADV (*fig*) in modo espansivo
ex·pat [ɛksˈpæt] N, ADJ (*fam*) espatriato(-a); **expat lifestyle** vita da espatriato
ex·pa·ti·ate [ɪksˈpeɪʃɪˌeɪt] VI (*frm*): **to expatiate on** *or* **upon** dilungarsi (su)
ex·pat·ri·ate [ɛksˈpætrɪˌeɪt] N espatriato
■ ADJ espatriato(-a)
■ VT espatriare
◎ **ex·pect** [ɪksˈpɛkt] VT **1** (*anticipate*) aspettarsi, prevedere; (*count on*) contare su; (*hope for*) sperare in; (*wait for: letter, guests, baby*) aspettare; **I didn't expect that from him** non me l'aspettavo da lui; **I didn't expect him to agree** non mi aspettavo che fosse d'accordo; **it's easier than I expected** è più facile del previsto; **as expected** come previsto; **to expect to do sth** pensare *or* contare di fare qc; **I expected as much** me l'aspettavo; **that was (only) to be expected** non potevamo che aspettarcelo; **I did not know what to expect** non sapevo che cosa aspettarmi; **we'll expect you for supper** ti aspettiamo per cena; **she's expecting a baby** sta aspettando un bambino; **I'll expect you when I see you** (*fam*) ci vediamo quando ci vediamo **2** (*suppose*) pensare, supporre; **I expect he'll be late** immagino che arriverà tardi; **I expect so** credo di sì , immagino di sì ; **yes, I expect it is** sì , non ne dubito **3** (*require*): **to expect sth (from sb)** esigere qc (da qn); **to expect sb to do sth** pretendere *or* esigere che qn faccia qc; **I expect you to be punctual** esigo che tu sia puntuale; **you can't expect too much from him** non puoi pretendere troppo da lui; **what do you expect me to do about it?** cosa vuoi che ci faccia?
■ VI: **to be expecting** (*a baby*) essere incinta *or* in stato interessante
ex·pec·tan·cy [ɪksˈpɛktənsɪ] N attesa; **life expectancy** speranza (media) di vita
ex·pec·tant [ɪksˈpɛktənt] ADJ (*person, crowd*) in attesa; (*look*) di attesa
ex·pect·ant·ly [ɪksˈpɛktəntlɪ] ADV (*look, listen*) con un'aria d'attesa; **the crowds waited expectantly** c'era un'aria di attesa tra la folla
expectant mother N gestante *f*
◎ **ex·pec·ta·tion** [ˌɛkspɛkˈteɪʃən] N attesa, aspettativa; **there is little expectation of sunshine today** ci sono poche speranze che venga fuori il sole oggi; **in expectation of** in previsione di; **against** *or* **contrary to all expectation(s)** contro ogni aspettativa; **to come** *or* **live up to sb's expectations** rispondere alle aspettative di qn; **beyond (all) expectation** al di là di ogni aspettativa; **the results exceeded expectations** i risultati furono superiori alle aspettative
ex·pec·to·rant [ɪkˈspɛktərənt] N (*Med*) espettorante *m*
ex·pedi·ence [ɪksˈpiːdɪˌəns], **ex·pedi·en·cy** [ɪkˈpiːdɪənsɪ] N (*advisability*) convenienza, opportunità *f inv*; (*pej*) interesse personale; **for the sake of expedience** per una questione di convenienza
ex·pedi·ent [ɪksˈpiːdɪənt] N espediente *m*
■ ADJ (*convenient, politic*) conveniente, opportuno(-a)
ex·pedite [ˈɛkspɪdaɪt] VT (*frm: speed up*) accelerare;

Ee

(: *official matter, legal matter*) sollecitare; (: *task*) affrettare

> DID YOU KNOW ...?
> **expedite** is not translated by the Italian word *spedire*

ex·pedi·tion [ˌɛkspɪˈdɪʃən] N spedizione *f*
ex·pedi·tion·ary force [ˌɛkspɪˈdɪʃənərɪˈfɔːs] N (*Mil*) corpo di spedizione
ex·pedi·tious [ˌɛkspɪˈdɪʃəs] ADJ (*frm*) spedito(-a), sollecito(-a)
ex·pedi·tious·ly [ˌɛkspɪˈdɪʃəslɪ] ADV (*frm*) speditamente, sollecitamente
ex·pel [ɪksˈpɛl] VT espellere; **to get expelled** essere espulso(-a)
ex·pend [ɪksˈpɛnd] VT (*frm: money*) spendere; (: *time, effort, energy*) consacrare; (: *use up*) consumare
ex·pend·able [ɪksˈpɛndəbl] ADJ sacrificabile
ex·pendi·ture [ɪksˈpɛndɪtʃəʳ] N (*of money etc*) spesa; (*of time, effort*) dispendio; **an item of expenditure** una spesa; **expenditure on health** la spesa per la sanità
◎ **ex·pense** [ɪksˈpɛns] N (*cost*) spesa; **an unnecessary expense** una spesa inutile; **expenses** spese; **can you claim this on expenses?** puoi metterlo tra le spese?; **at the expense of** (*fig*) a spese di; **at the expense of his life** a prezzo della vita; **at great expense** con grande impiego di mezzi; **at their own expense** a proprie spese; **at my expense** a mie spese; (*fig*) alle mie spalle; **to go to the expense (of)** sobbarcarsi la spesa (di); **regardless of expense** senza badare a spese; **to put sb to the expense of** fare affrontare a qn la spesa di; **to meet the expense of** affrontare la spesa di
expense account N conto *m* spese *inv*
ex·penses [ɪksˈpɛnsɪs] NPL (*Comm*) spese *fpl*; **all expenses paid** spesato(-a) di tutto; **it's on expenses** paga la ditta
◎ **ex·pen·sive** [ɪksˈpɛnsɪv] ADJ (*dear*) caro(-a); (*costly*) costoso(-a); (*fig: victory*) a caro prezzo; **she has expensive tastes** le piacciono le cose costose
ex·pen·sive·ly [ɪksˈpɛnsɪvlɪ] ADV (*dress*) in modo costoso
ex·pen·sive·ness [ɪksˈpɛnsɪvnɪs] N dispendiosità
◎ **ex·peri·ence** [ɪksˈpɪərɪəns] N (*all senses*) esperienza; **to learn by experience** imparare per esperienza; **I know from bitter experience** ho imparato a mie spese; **he has no experience of grief/being out of work** non sa che cosa voglia dire il dolore/restare senza lavoro; **she has plenty of experience** ha moltissima esperienza; **have you any previous experience?** ha esperienza in questo campo?; **practical/teaching experience** esperienza pratica/d'insegnamento; **to have a pleasant/frightening experience** avere un'esperienza piacevole/terrificante; **it was quite an experience** (*also iro*) è stata una bella esperienza
■ VT (*feel: emotions, sensations, pleasure*) provare; (*suffer: defeat, losses, hardship etc*) subire; **he experienced fear and pain** ha provato paura e dolore; **they're experiencing some problems** stanno avendo qualche problema; **she experiences some difficulty in walking** ha qualche difficoltà a camminare
ex·peri·enced [ɪksˈpɪərɪənst] ADJ (*teacher, lawyer*) che ha esperienza; (*driver, politician*) consumato(-a); **experienced (in)** esperto(-a) (di)
◎ **ex·peri·ment** [*n* ɪksˈpɛrɪˌmənt; *vb* ɪksˈpɛrɪmɛnt] N esperimento; **to perform** *or* **carry out an experiment** fare un esperimento; **as an experiment** a titolo di esperimento
■ VI fare un esperimento, sperimentare; **to experiment with a new vaccine** sperimentare un nuovo vaccino
ex·peri·men·tal [ɪksˌpɛrɪˈmɛntl] ADJ sperimentale; **the process is still at the experimental stage** il procedimento è ancora allo stadio sperimentale
ex·peri·men·tal·ly [ɪksˌpɛrɪˈmɛntəlɪ] ADV sperimentalmente
ex·peri·men·ta·tion [ɪksˌpɛrɪmɛnˈteɪʃən] N sperimentazione *f*
ex·peri·ment·er [ɪkˈspɛrɪməntəʳ] N sperimentatore(-trice)
◎ **ex·pert** [ˈɛkspɜːt] ADJ (*gen*) esperto(-a); (*advice, help*) da esperto; **expert in** *or* **at doing sth** esperto(-a) nel fare qc
■ N esperto(-a); **an expert on sth/in** *or* **at doing sth** un*a* esperto(-a) di qc/nel fare qc
expert evidence N (*Law*) testimonianza di perito
ex·per·tise [ˌɛkspəˈtiːz] N (*frm*) competenza
ex·pert·ly [ˈɛkspɜːtlɪ] ADV abilmente, con perizia
expert opinion N (*Law*) perizia
expert system N (*Comput*) sistema *m* esperto
expert witness N (*Law*) perito
ex·pi·ate [ˈɛkspɪˌeɪt] VT (*fam*) espiare
ex·pi·ra·tion [ˌɛkspɪˈreɪʃən] N **1** (*frm: end*) scadenza; **after the expiration of a year** allo scadere di un anno **2** (*Med*) espirazione *f*
ex·pire [ɪksˈpaɪəʳ] VI (*document, time limit*) scadere; (*die*) spirare
ex·pi·ry [ɪksˈpaɪərɪ] N scadenza
◎ **ex·plain** [ɪksˈpleɪn] VT (*gen*) spiegare; (*mystery*) chiarire; **to explain o.s.** spiegarsi
► **explain away** VT cercare di dare una motivazione a
ex·plain·able [ɪksˈpleɪnəbl] ADJ spiegabile
◎ **ex·pla·na·tion** [ˌɛkspləˈneɪʃən] N spiegazione *f*; **to find an explanation for sth** trovare una spiegazione per qc; **what have you to say in explanation?** qual è la sua giustificazione?
ex·plana·tory [ɪksˈplænətərɪ] ADJ (*words*) di spiegazione; (*notes*) esplicativo(-a)
ex·pletive [ɪksˈpliːtɪv] N (*frm: swear word*) imprecazione *f*
ex·pli·cable [ɛksˈplɪkəbəl] ADJ (*frm*) spiegabile; **for no explicable reason** senza un motivo plausibile
ex·plic·it [ɪksˈplɪsɪt] ADJ (*definite*) netto(-a); (*instructions, intention, denial*) esplicito(-a); (*details*) chiaro(-a)
ex·plic·it·ly [ɪkˈsplɪsɪtlɪ] ADV (*see adj*) nettamente; esplicitamente; chiaramente
◎ **ex·plode** [ɪksˈpləʊd] VI esplodere; **to explode with laughter** scoppiare dalle risa
■ VT far esplodere; (*fig: theory*) demolire; **to explode a myth** distruggere un mito; **exploded drawing** disegno esploso
◎ **ex·ploit** [*vb* ɪksˈplɔɪt; *n* ˈɛksplɔɪt] VT sfruttare
■ N impresa
ex·ploit·able [ɛksˈplɔɪtəbəl] ADJ sfruttabile
ex·ploi·ta·tion [ˌɛksplɔɪˈteɪʃən] N sfruttamento
ex·ploita·tive [ɛksˈplɔɪtətɪv] ADJ (*frm*) profittatore(-trice)
ex·ploit·er [ɛksˈplɔɪtəʳ] N sfruttatore(-trice); **they were the first exploiters of Lebanon timber** furono i primi a sfruttare il legname del Libano
ex·plo·ra·tion [ˌɛksplɔːˈreɪʃən] N esplorazione *f*
ex·plora·tory [ɪksˈplɒrətərɪ] ADJ (*talks*) esplorativo(-a);

(*expedition*) d'esplorazione; (*step, discussion*) preliminare; **exploratory operation** (*Med*) intervento esplorativo

◎ **ex·plore** [ɪks'plɔːʳ] VT (*gen, Med*) esplorare; (*fig: problems, subject, possibilities*) esaminare; **to explore every avenue** sondare tutte le possibilità

ex·plor·er [ɪks'plɔːrəʳ] N esploratore(-trice)

◎ **ex·plo·sion** [ɪks'pləʊʒən] N (*also fig*) esplosione *f*

ex·plo·sive [ɪks'pləʊzɪv] ADJ (*also fig*) esplosivo(-a)
■ N esplosivo

expo ['ɛkspəʊ] N esposizione *f* universale, expo *f inv*

ex·po·nent [ɪks'pəʊnənt] N **1** (*person*) esponente *m/f* **2** (*Math*) esponente *m*

ex·po·nen·tial [ˌɛkspəʊ'nɛnʃəl] ADJ (*Math also fig*) esponenziale

◎ **ex·port** [*n* 'ɛkspɔːt; *vb* ɪks'pɔːt] N esportazione *f*; (*item*) merce *f* d'esportazione; **a drive to promote exports** una campagna di promozione delle esportazioni
■ VT esportare
■ ADJ (*goods, permit, duty*) d'esportazione

ex·por·ta·tion [ˌɛkspɔː'teɪʃən] N esportazione *f*

export drive N campagna a favore dell'esportazione

ex·port·er [ɪks'pɔːtəʳ] N esportatore(-trice)

export licence N licenza d'esportazione

export manager N dirigente *m/f* responsabile dei rapporti con i mercati esteri

export trade N esportazioni *fpl*

◎ **ex·pose** [ɪks'pəʊz] VT (*gen, also Phot*) esporre; (*uncover*) scoprire; (*sexual parts*) esibire; (*fig: reveal: plot*) rivelare; (*: criminal*) smascherare; (*one's ignorance*) mettere a nudo; **they were exposed to high levels of radiation** erano esposti ad alti livelli di radiazioni; **after the scandal was exposed, ...** dopo che emerse lo scandalo,...; **he was exposed as a liar** è risultato essere un bugiardo; **to be exposed to view** offrirsi alla vista; **to expose sb/o.s. to ridicule** esporre qn/esporsi al ridicolo; **to expose o.s.** (*indecently*) fare l'esibizionista

ex·posed [ɪks'pəʊzd] ADJ (*land, house, town*) esposto(-a); (*Elec: wire; Mil: terrain, country*) scoperto(-a); (*pipe, beam*) a vista; **as a politician, he is in a very exposed position** come politico, è in una posizione molto vulnerabile

ex·po·si·tion [ˌɛkspə'zɪʃən] N (*frm*) esposizione *f*

ex·pos·tu·late [ɪks'pɒstjʊˌleɪt] VI (*frm*): **to expostulate with sb about sth** fare le proprie rimostranze a qn per qc

ex·pos·tu·la·tion [ɪksˌpɒstjʊ'leɪʃən] N (*frm*) rimostranza

◎ **ex·po·sure** [ɪks'pəʊʒəʳ] N (*gen*) esposizione *f*; (*of plot*) smascheramento; (*Phot*) esposizione; (*: photo*) posa; (*Med*) assideramento; **exposure to lead** esposizione al piombo; **exposure on television** pubblicità per televisione; **a 24 exposure film** un rullino a 24 pose; **to die of exposure** morire assiderato(-a); **to threaten sb with exposure** minacciare di denunciare qn

exposure meter N (*Phot*) esposimetro

ex·pound [ɪks'paʊnd] VT (*theory, text*) spiegare; (*one's views*) esporre

◎ **ex·press** [ɪks'prɛs] ADJ (*all senses*) espresso(-a); **express letter** espresso
■ ADV: **to send sth express** spedire qc per espresso
■ N (*also:* **express train**) espresso
■ VT esprimere; **to express o.s.** esprimersi

◎ **ex·pres·sion** [ɪks'prɛʃən] N (*all senses*) espressione *f*; **set expression** modo di dire

ex·pres·sion·ism [ɪks'prɛʃənɪzəm] N espressionismo

ex·pres·sion·ist [ɪk'sprɛʃənɪst] ADJ, N espressionista (*m/f*)

ex·pres·sion·less [ɪk'sprɛʃənlɪs] ADJ (*pej: face*) impassibile; (*: of artistic performance*) senza sentimento; **an expressionless voice** una voce che non tradisce (*or* tradiva) emozioni

ex·pres·sive [ɪks'prɛsɪv] ADJ (*look, face, language*) espressivo(-a); (*gesture*) eloquente

ex·pres·sive·ly [ɪks'prɛsɪvlɪ] ADV (*see adj*) in modo espressivo; in modo eloquente

ex·press·ly [ɪks'prɛslɪ] ADV espressamente

ex·press·way [ɪks'prɛsˌweɪ] N (*esp Am*) autostrada urbana

ex·pro·pri·ate [ɛks'prəʊprɪˌeɪt] VT espropriare

ex·pul·sion [ɪks'pʌlʃən] N espulsione *f*

expulsion order N ordine *m* di espulsione

ex·punge [ɪk'spʌndʒ] VT (*frm*) espungere

ex·pur·gate ['ɛkspəˌgeɪt] VT (*frm*) espurgare

ex·quis·ite [ɪks'kwɪzɪt] ADJ (*gen*) squisito(-a); (*manners, sensibility, charm*) raffinato(-a); (*sense of humour*) sottile; (*pain*) acuto(-a); (*joy, pleasure*) vivo(-a)

ex·quis·ite·ly [ɪks'kwɪzɪtlɪ] ADV **1** (*paint, embroider*) squisitamente; (*dress*) in modo raffinato **2** (*extremely*) estremamente

ex-serviceman [ˌɛks'sɜːvɪsmən] N (*Brit*) ex combattente *m*

ext. ABBR (*Telec:* = **extension**) int. (= *interno*)

ex·tant [ɛks'tænt] ADJ (*frm*) esistente

ex·tem·po·re [ɪks'tɛmpərɪ] (*frm*) ADV senza preparazione
■ ADJ estemporaneo(-a)

ex·tem·po·rize, ex·tem·po·rise [ɪks'tɛmpəˌraɪz] VI (*frm*) improvvisare

◎ **ex·tend** [ɪks'tɛnd] VT **1** (*frm: stretch out: hand, arm*) tendere; (*: offer: friendship, help, hospitality*) offrire; (*: thanks, condolences, welcome*) porgere; (*: invitation*) estendere; (*Fin: credit*) accordare **2** (*prolong: road, line, deadline*) prolungare; (*: visit*) protrarre; (*enlarge*) (*: building, business, vocabulary*) ampliare; (*knowledge, research*) approfondire; (*powers*) estendere; (*frontiers*) allargare; **they decided to extend their visit** hanno deciso di protrarre la visita; **perhaps the deadline could be extended** forse si potrebbe prorogare la scadenza; **the building has recently been extended** l'edificio è stato ampliato di recente; **extended walk/trot** (*Horse-riding*) passo/trotto allungato
■ VI (*land, wall*): **to extend to** *or* **as far as** estendersi fino a; **the caves extend for 18 km** le grotte si estendono per 18 chilometri; **to extend to/for** (*term, meeting*) protrarsi fino a/per; **the contract extends to/for ...** il contratto è valido fino a/per...

ex·tend·able [ɪk'stɛndəbəl] ADJ (*ladder, tentacles*) allungabile; (*tenancy*) prorogabile

ex·ten·sion [ɪks'tɛnʃən] N (*for table, electric flex*) prolunga; (*of road, term*) prolungamento; (*of contract, deadline*) proroga; (*building*) annesso; (*telephone: in private house*) derivazione *f*: *in office*, interno; **he's been given a six month extension** gli hanno dato una proroga di sei mesi; **to have an extension built onto one's house** far ingrandire la casa; **extension 3718** interno 3718

extension cable, (*Brit***) extension lead,** (*Am*) **extension cord** N (*Elec*) prolunga

extension ladder N scala allungabile

◎ **ex·ten·sive** [ɪks'tɛnsɪv] ADJ (*grounds, forest, damage*) vasto(-a), esteso(-a); (*knowledge, research*) approfondito(-a); (*inquiries, reforms, investments*) su vasta

Ee

scala; (*use*) largo(-a); (*alterations*) radicale; **the hotel is set in extensive grounds** l'albergo sorge su un vasto terreno; **extensive research** ricerche approfondite; **to get extensive coverage** essere trattato ampiamente; **extensive damage** danni ingenti; **extensive farming** agricoltura estensiva

ex·ten·sive·ly [ɪks'tɛnsɪvlɪ] ADV (*altered, damaged etc*) radicalmente; (*study, investigate*) a fondo; (*use, travel*) molto; **he's travelled extensively** ha viaggiato molto

◎ **ex·tent** [ɪks'tɛnt] N (*of land*) estensione *f*; (*of road*) lunghezza; (*of knowledge, activities, power*) portata; (*degree: of damage, loss*) proporzioni *fpl*; **the extent of the damage is not yet known** non è ancora nota l'entità dei danni; **to what extent** in che misura, fino a che punto; **to some extent** in una certa misura; **to a certain/large extent** in certa/larga misura; **to such an extent that** a tal punto che; **to the extent of** fino al punto di; **to some extent** fino a un certo punto

ex·tenu·at·ing [ɪks'tɛnjʊˌeɪtɪŋ] ADJ (*frm*): **extenuating circumstances** (circostanze) attenuanti *fpl*

ex·tenu·ation [ɪkˌstɛnjʊ'eɪʃən] N attenuante *f*

ex·te·ri·or [ɪks'tɪərɪəʳ] ADJ esterno(-a), esteriore
■ N (*of house, box*) esterno; (*of person*) aspetto esteriore; **on the exterior** all'esterno; (*fig*) in apparenza

ex·ter·mi·nate [ɪks'tɜːmɪˌneɪt] VT sterminare

ex·ter·mi·na·tion [ɪksˌtɜːmɪ'neɪʃən] N sterminio

ex·ter·mi·na·tor [ɪk'stɜːmɪˌneɪtəʳ] N addetto(-a) alla disinfestazione

ex·ter·nal [ɛks'tɜːnl] ADJ (*walls etc*) esterno(-a); (*appearance*) esteriore; **external affairs** (*Pol*) affari *mpl* esteri; **for external use only** (*Med*) solo per uso esterno; **external examiner** esaminatore(-trice) esterno(-a); **external processes** (*Geol*) fenomeni *mpl* esogeni
■ N: **the externals** le apparenze

ex·ter·nal·ize [ɪk'stɜːnəˌlaɪz] VT (*frm*) esternare

ex·ter·nal·ly [ɛks'tɜːnəlɪ] ADV dall'esterno, esternamente

ex·tinct [ɪks'tɪŋkt] ADJ (*volcano*) spento(-a), inattivo(-a); (*animal, race*) estinto(-a); **dinosaurs are extinct** i dinosauri sono estinti; **to become extinct** estinguersi

ex·tinc·tion [ɪks'tɪŋkʃən] N (*of fire*) estinzione *f*, spegnimento; (*of race*) estinzione *f*

ex·tin·guish [ɪks'tɪŋgwɪʃ] VT (*frm: fire*) estinguere, spegnere; (*: cigarette*) spegnere; (*fig*) annientare

ex·tin·guish·er [ɪks'tɪŋgwɪʃəʳ] N estintore *m*

ex·tol, (*Am*) **ex·toll** [ɪks'təʊl] VT (*frm: merits, virtues*) magnificare; (*person*) celebrare

ex·tort [ɪks'tɔːt] VT: **to extort (from)** (*money, confession*) estorcere a; (*promise*) strappare a

ex·tor·tion [ɪks'tɔːʃən] N estorsione *f*

ex·tor·tion·ate [ɪks'tɔːʃənɪt] ADJ esorbitante

◎ **ex·tra** ['ɛkstrə] ADJ in più; **an extra blanket** una coperta in più; **she needs extra help** ha bisogno di maggior aiuto; **an extra charge** un supplemento; **wine is extra** il vino è escluso; **breakfast is extra** la colazione è a parte; **take extra care!** stai molto attento!; **for extra safety** per maggior sicurezza; **extra transport** corse *fpl* supplementari *or* straordinarie; **they won after extra time** hanno vinto dopo i tempi supplementari
■ ADV (*specially*) eccezionalmente; (*in addition: pay, charge*) di più; **extra fine** extra sottile; **extra large sizes** taglie *fpl* forti; **be extra careful!** stai attentissimo!
■ N extra *m inv*; (*Cine, Theatre: actor*) comparsa

extra... PREF extra...

ex·tract [*n* 'ɛkstrækt; *vb* ɪks'trækt] N (*from book*) brano; (*from film*) spezzone *m*; (*Culin, Chem*) estratto
■ VT: **to extract (from)** (*take out*) estrarre (da); (*obtain: promise, confession, money*) estorcere a, strappare a; (*select: from book etc*) stralciare (da)

ex·trac·tion [ɪks'trækʃən] N estrazione *f*; (*descent*) origine *f*; **of German extraction** di origine tedesca

ex·trac·tor fan [ɪk'stræktəˌfæn] N aspiratore *m*

extra·cur·ricu·lar ['ɛkstrəkə'rɪkjʊləʳ] ADJ (*Scol*) parascolastico

extra·dite ['ɛkstrəˌdaɪt] VT: **to extradite sb (from/to)** estradare qn (da/in)

extra·di·tion [ˌɛkstrə'dɪʃən] N estradizione *f*

extra·mari·tal ['ɛkstrə'mærɪtl] ADJ extraconiugale

extra·mu·ral ['ɛkstrə'mjʊərəl] ADJ (*Univ*): **extramural course** *corso libero tenuto da docenti accreditati presso l'università*

extra·neous [ɪks'treɪnɪəs] ADJ (*frm*): **extraneous (to)** estraneo(-a) (a)

extraor·di·nari·ly [ɪks'trɔːdnrɪlɪ] ADV straordinariamente

◎ **extraor·di·nary** [ɪks'trɔːdnrɪ] ADJ (*gen*) straordinario(-a); (*very strange*) strano(-a); **the extraordinary thing is that ...** la cosa strana è che...

extraordinary general meeting N assemblea generale straordinaria

ex·trapo·late [ɛks'træpəˌleɪt] VT estrapolare

ex·trapo·la·tion [ˌɪkstræpəʊ'leɪʃən] N estrapolazione *f*

extra·sen·so·ry per·cep·tion ['ɛkstrə'sɛnsərɪ pə'sɛpʃən] N percezione *f* extrasensoriale

extra·ter·res·trial [ˌɛkstrətɪ'rɛstrɪəl] ADJ extraterrestre

extra time N (*Ftbl*) tempo supplementare

ex·trava·gance [ɪks'trævəgəns] N (*excessive spending*) sperpero; (*wastefulness*) spreco; (*thing bought*) stravaganza; **her only extravagance was ...** l'unico lusso che si concedeva era ...

ex·trava·gant [ɪks'trævəgənt] ADJ stravagante; (*spending, claim, opinion*) eccessivo(-a); (*lavish: person*) prodigo(-a); (*: tastes*) dispendioso(-a); (*exaggerated: praise*) esagerato(-a); (*: prices*) esorbitante; **I'm not extravagant, but I do like nice clothes** non sono sprecone, ma mi piacciono i vestiti eleganti; **don't be extravagant with the butter** non esagerare con il burro

ex·trava·gant·ly [ɪks'trævəgəntlɪ] ADV (*lavishly*) in modo dispendioso; (*exaggeratedly*) esageratamente

ex·trava·gan·za [ɪkˌstrævə'gænzə] N rappresentazione *f* spettacolare

◎ **ex·treme** [ɪks'triːm] ADJ estremo(-a); (*sorrow, anger*) profondo(-a); **the extreme left/right** (*Pol*) l'estrema sinistra/destra; **the extreme end of sth** l'estremità di qc; **there's no need to be so extreme** non c'è bisogno di essere così drastico
■ N estremo; **extremes of temperature** gli estremi *mpl* della scala termica; **dangerous in the extreme** estremamente pericoloso(-a); **to go/be driven to extremes** arrivare/essere spinto(-a) agli estremi

◎ **ex·treme·ly** [ɪks'triːmlɪ] ADV estremamente

extreme sport N sport *m inv* estremo

ex·trem·ism [ɪks'triːmɪzəm] N estremismo

ex·trem·ist [ɪks'triːmɪst] ADJ, N estremista (*m/f*)

ex·trem·ity [ɪks'trɛmɪtɪ] N (*gen*) estremità *f inv*; (*fig: of despair etc*) culmine

ex·tri·cate ['ɛkstrɪˌkeɪt] VT (*object*) liberare; **to extricate sth (from)** districare qc (da); **to extricate**

sb/o.s. from a difficult situation togliere qn/ togliersi d'impaccio
extro·vert ['ɛkstrəʊvɜ:t] ADJ, N estroverso(-a)
exu·ber·ance [ɪg'zu:bərəns] N esuberanza
exu·ber·ant [ɪg'zu:bərənt] ADJ esuberante
exu·ber·ant·ly [ɪg'zu:bərəntlɪ] ADV in modo esuberante
ex·ude [ɪg'zju:d] VT, VI trasudare, stillare; (*fig*) emanare
ex·ult [ɪg'zʌlt] VI (*frm*): **to exult in** *or* **over** *or* **at** esultare per
ex·ult·ant [ɪg'zʌltənt] ADJ (*frm: person, smile*) esultante; (*: shout, expression*) di giubilo
ex·ul·ta·tion [ˌɛgzʌl'teɪʃən] N giubilo; **in exultation** per la gioia
◎**eye** [aɪ] N occhio; (*of needle*) cruna; (*for hook*) occhiello; **I've got green eyes** ho gli occhi verdi; **he gave him a black eye** gli ha fatto un occhio nero; **eyes right/left!** (*Mil*) attenti a destra/sinistra!; **as far as the eye can see** a perdita d'occhio; **it happened before my very eyes** mi è successo proprio sotto gli occhi; **I saw it with my own eyes** l'ho visto con i miei occhi; **keep your eyes on the road ahead!** guarda la strada!; **I could hardly keep my eyes open** non riuscivo a tenere gli occhi aperti; **he didn't take his eyes off her** non le toglieva gli occhi di dosso; **to catch sb's eye** attirare l'attenzione di qn; **to look sb (straight) in the eye** guardare qn (dritto) negli occhi; **to be in the public eye** essere in vista; **in the eyes of** agli occhi di; **under the (watchful) eye of** sotto lo sguardo (vigile) di; **to keep an eye on sb/sth** tenere d'occhio qn/qc; **to keep an eye on things** (*fam*) tenere d'occhio la situazione; **to keep an eye out for sth/sb** *or* **one's eyes open for sth/sb** tenere gli occhi aperti per trovare qc/qn; **to look at sth with the eye of an expert** guardare qc con l'occhio dell'esperto; **with an eye to sth** in vista di qc; **with an eye to doing sth** (*Brit*) con l'idea di fare qc; **with one's eyes (wide) open** (*fig*) perfettamente conscio(-a) di ciò che si fa; **to shut one's eyes to sth** (*fig: to the truth, dangers, evidence*) chiudere gli occhi di fronte a qc; (*: to sb's shortcomings*) chiudere un occhio su qc; **to be up to one's eyes in work** essere pieno(-a) di lavoro fin sopra i capelli; **to have an eye for sth** avere occhio per qc; **there's more to this than meets the eye** non è così semplice come sembra; **I don't see eye to eye with him** non condivido il suo punto di vista; **it's five years since I last set** *or* **laid eyes on him** sono cinque anni che non lo vedo; **use your eyes!** (*fam*) guarda un po' meglio!; **to cry one's eyes out** piangere a calde lacrime; **that's one in the eye for him** (*fig fam*) gli sta bene; **to make eyes at sb** (*fam*) fare gli occhi dolci a qn; **she was all eyes** era tutt'occhi; **an eye for an eye and a tooth for a tooth** occhio per occhio dente per dente
■ VT (*look at carefully*) scrutare; (*ogle*) adocchiare; **the children eyed the parcel with interest** i bambini scrutavano il pacco con interesse
► **eye up** VT + ADV (*fam*) occhieggiare; **he's been eyeing me up all evening** non mi ha staccato gli occhi di dosso per tutta la sera
eye·ball ['aɪˌbɔ:l] N bulbo oculare; **eyeball to eyeball** (*fig*) faccia a faccia
eye·bath ['aɪˌbɑ:θ], (*Am*) **eye cup** N occhino
eye·brow ['aɪˌbraʊ] N sopracciglio; **to raise one's eyebrows** inarcare le sopracciglia
eyebrow pencil N matita per le sopracciglia
eyebrow tweezers NPL pinzette *fpl* per le sopracciglia
eye-catching ['aɪˌkætʃɪŋ] ADJ che attira l'attenzione
eye clinic N studio oculistico
eye cup N = eyebath
eye·drops ['aɪˌdrɒps] N collirio
eye·ful ['aɪful] N (*fam*): **to get an eyeful (of)** avere l'occasione di dare una bella sbirciata
eye·glass ['aɪˌglɑs] N monocolo; **eyeglasses** NPL occhiali *mpl*
eye·lash ['aɪˌlæʃ] N ciglio
eye·let ['aɪlɪt] N occhiello
eye·lev·el ['aɪˌlɛvl] ADJ all'altezza degli occhi
eye·lid ['aɪˌlɪd] N palpebra
eye·liner ['aɪˌlaɪnə^r] N eye-liner *m inv*
eye-opener ['aɪˌəʊpnə^r] N rivelazione *f*
eye·shade ['aɪˌʃeɪd] N visiera
eye·shadow ['aɪˌʃædəʊ] N ombretto
eye·sight ['aɪˌsaɪt] N vista
eye·sore ['aɪˌsɔ:^r] N pugno in un occhio
eye·strain ['aɪˌstreɪn] N: **to get eyestrain** stancarsi gli occhi
eye-tooth [ˌaɪ'tu:θ] N (*pl* **-teeth**) canino superiore; **to give one's eye-teeth for sth/to do sth** (*fam fig*) dare non so che cosa per qc/per fare qc
eye·wash ['aɪˌwɒʃ] N (*liquid*) collirio; (*fam: nonsense*) balle *fpl*
eye·wear ['aɪwɛə^r] N occhiali *mpl*
eye·witness ['aɪˌwɪtnɪs] N testimone *m/f* oculare
ey·rie ['ɪərɪ] N nido d'aquila
e-zine ['i:zi:n] N rivista elettronica, e-zine *f inv*

Ee

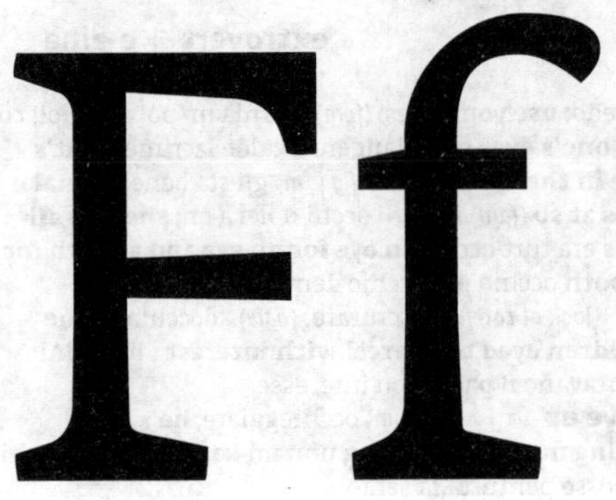

F, f [ɛf] N **1** (*letter*) F, f *f or m inv*; **F for Frederick** (*Am*): **F for fox** ≈ F come Firenze **2** (*Mus*): **F** fa *m inv*

F ABBR (= **Fahrenheit**) F

FA [ɛf'eɪ] N ABBR (*Brit*) = *Football Association*

fa [fɑː] N (*Mus*) fa *m*

FAA [ˌɛfeɪ'eɪ] N ABBR (*Am*) = *Federal Aviation Administration*

▷ www.faa.gov/

fa·ble ['feɪbl] N favola

fa·bled ['feɪbld] ADJ favoloso(-a), leggendario(-a)

◎ **fab·ric** ['fæbrɪk] N **1** (*cloth*) stoffa, tessuto **2** (*Archit*) struttura; **the fabric of society** (*fig*) la struttura della società

DID YOU KNOW ...?
fabric is not translated by the Italian word *fabbrica*

fab·ri·cate ['fæbrɪkeɪt] VT fabbricare

fab·ri·ca·tion [ˌfæbrɪ'keɪʃən] N fabbricazione *f*

fabric ribbon N (*Typ*) nastro dattilografico

fabu·lous ['fæbjʊləs] ADJ (*mythical*) favoloso(-a); (*fam: wonderful*) meraviglioso(-a), fantastico(-a)

fabu·lous·ly ['fæbjʊləslɪ] ADV favolosamente

fa·çade, fa·cade [fə'sɑːd] N (*Archit*) facciata; (*fig*) facciata, apparenza

◎ **face** [feɪs] N (*gen*) faccia; (*Anat*) faccia, volto, viso; (*expression*) faccia, espressione *f*; (*grimace*) smorfia; (*of dial, watch, clock*) quadrante *m*; (*surface: of the earth*) superficie *f*, faccia; (*of building*) facciata; (*of mountain, cliff*) parete *f*; **face down(wards)** (*person*) a faccia in giù, bocconi; (*object*) a faccia in giù; (*card*) coperto(-a); **face up(wards)** (*person, object*) a faccia in su; (*card*) scoperto(-a); **the north face of the mountain** la parete nord della montagna; **in the face of** (*difficulties etc*) di fronte a; **to laugh in sb's face** ridere in faccia a qn; **to look sb in the face** guardare qn in faccia; **to say sth to sb's face** dire qc in faccia a qn; **I told him to his face** gliel'ho detto in faccia; **you can shout till you're black** *or* **blue in the face ...** puoi urlare fino a sgolarti...; **he was red in the face** era rosso in faccia; **don't show your face here again!** non farti più vedere qui!; **it's vanished off the face of the earth** è sparito(-a) dalla faccia della terra; **to have a good memory for faces** essere una buona fisionomista; **to pull a long face** fare la faccia lunga, fare il muso; **to keep a straight face** rimanere serio(-a); **to pull a face** fare una smorfia; **to make** *or* **pull faces (at sb)** fare le boccacce (a qn); **his face fell** (*fig*) ha fatto una faccia!; **on the face of it** a prima vista; **they put a brave face on it** hanno fatto buon viso a cattivo gioco; **to lose/save face** perdere/salvare la faccia; **to take sth at face value** giudicare qc dalle apparenze

■ VT
1 (*be facing, be opposite*) essere di fronte a; (*overlook: road*) dare su; (*: sea*) guardare verso; **face the wall!** girati verso il muro!; **to sit facing the engine** (*on train*) sedersi nella direzione della marcia; **the picture facing page 20** la figura a fianco di pagina 20; **they faced each other** erano uno di fronte all'altro; **the difficulties facing us** i problemi che ci aspettano
2 (*confront: attacker, danger*) affrontare, fronteggiare; **I can't face him** (*ashamed*) non ho il coraggio di guardarlo in faccia; (*reluctant*) non ho nessuna voglia di vederlo; **I can't face doing it** non ho nessuna voglia di farlo; **to face the music** (*fig*) far fronte alla tempesta; **to face facts** affrontare la realtà; **to face the fact that ...** riconoscere *or* ammettere che...; **we are faced with serious problems** ci troviamo di fronte a gravi problemi; **let's face it!** (*fam*) diciamocelo chiaramente!
3 (*Tech*) rivestire, ricoprire; **a wall faced with concrete** un muro rivestito di cemento

■ VI (*person*): **to face this way** girarsi da questa parte; **it faces east/towards the east** è esposto(-a) a/guarda verso est

► **face down** VT + ADV (*Am fig*): **to face sb down** sfidare qn

► **face out** VT + ADV (*Brit*) affrontare

► **face up to** VI + ADV + PREP (*difficulty etc*) affrontare, far fronte a; **to face up to the fact that ...** accettare che...; **he refuses to face up to his responsibilities** rifiuta di accettare le proprie responsabilità

face card N (*Am*) figura

face cloth N (*Brit*) ≈ guanto di spugna

face cream N crema per il viso

face flannel N (*Brit*) ≈ guanto di spugna
face·less ['feɪslɪs] ADJ anonimo(-a)
face lift N lifting *m inv*; (*of façade, building*) ripulita, restauro
face pack N maschera di bellezza
face powder N cipria
face-saver [feɪsseɪvəʳ] N: **it was clearly a face-saver on their part** l'hanno ovviamente fatto per salvarsi la faccia
face-saving ['feɪs,seɪvɪŋ] ADJ che salva la faccia
fac·et ['fæsɪt] N (*of gem*) sfaccettatura, faccetta; (*fig*) sfaccettatura, aspetto, lato
fa·cetious [fə'siːʃəs] ADJ faceto(-a); **don't be facetious** non fare lo spiritoso
fa·cetious·ly [fə'siːʃəslɪ] ADV spiritosamente
face-to-face [,feɪstə'feɪs] ADV, ADJ faccia a faccia, a quattr'occhi
face value N (*of coin*) valore *m* facciale *or* nominale; **to take sth at face value** (*fig*) giudicare qc dalle apparenze
fa·cia ['feɪʃɪə] N = **fascia**
fa·cial ['feɪʃəl] ADJ del viso, facciale
■ N trattamento di bellezza per il viso
fa·cial·ly ['feɪʃəlɪ] ADV di faccia
fac·ile ['fæsaɪl] ADJ (*gen pej: remark, answer*) superficiale; (: *victory*) facile
fa·cili·tate [fə'sɪlɪ,teɪt] VT facilitare, agevolare
◎ **fa·cil·ity** [fə'sɪlɪtɪ] N **1** (*easiness*) facilità; (*skill*) abilità; (*with languages*) predisposizione *f* **2** **facilities** NPL (*gen*) servizi *mpl*; (*educational, leisure*) attrezzature *fpl*; (*transport*) mezzi *mpl*; **credit facilities** facilitazioni *fpl* di credito
fac·ing ['feɪsɪŋ] N (*Constr: of wall etc*) rivestimento; (*Sewing*) passafino
fac·simi·le [fæk'sɪmɪlɪ] N facsimile *m inv*
facsimile machine N facsimile *m inv*, telecopiatrice *f*
facsimile publication N pubblicazione *f* in facsimile
◎ **fact** [fækt] N fatto; **it's a fact that ...** è un dato di fatto che...; **to know for a fact that ...** sapere per certo che...; **the facts of life** (*sex*) i fatti riguardanti la vita sessuale; (*realities*) le realtà della vita; **facts and figures** fatti *mpl* e cifre *fpl*; **fact and fiction** realtà e fantasia; **story founded on fact** storia basata sui fatti; **it has no basis in fact** non si basa su fatti realmente accaduti; **as a matter of fact** *or* **in point of fact** per la verità; **the fact (of the matter) is that ...** la verità è che...; **in fact** in realtà, in effetti; **he finally accepted the fact that she didn't love him any more** alla fine ha accettato il fatto che lei non lo amasse più
fact-finding ['fækt,faɪndɪŋ] ADJ: **a fact-finding tour/mission** un viaggio/una missione d'inchiesta
◎ **fac·tion** ['fækʃən] N fazione *f*
fac·tion·al ['fækʃənəl] ADJ (*fighting*) tra fazioni
fac·ti·tious [fæk'tɪʃəs] ADJ (*frm*) artificiale
◎ **fac·tor** ['fæktəʳ] N **1** (*fact*) fattore *m*, elemento; **the human factor** il fattore umano; **safety factor** coefficiente *m* di sicurezza **2** (*Math*) fattore *m* **3** (*Comm: company*) società *f inv* di factoring; (: *agent*) factor *m inv*
■ VI (*Comm*) esercitare il factoring
fac·torial [fæk'tɔːrɪəl] ADJ (*Math*) fattoriale
◎ **fac·to·ry** ['fæktərɪ] N fabbrica, stabilimento; **a car factory** una fabbrica di automobili
■ ADJ (*inspector, work*) di fabbrica

> **DID YOU KNOW ...?**
> **factory** is not translated by the Italian word ***fattoria***

factory farming N (*Brit*) allevamento su scala industriale
factory floor N: **the factory floor** (*workers*) gli operai; (*area*) il reparto produzione; **on the factory floor** nel reparto produzione
factory outlet N outlet *m inv*; *negozio che vende articoli di marca a prezzi scontati*
factory ship N nave *f* fattoria *inv*
fac·to·tum [fæk'təʊtəm] N factotum *m/f inv*
fac·tual ['fæktjʊəl] ADJ (*report, description*) che si limita ai fatti; (*error*) che riguarda i fatti
fac·tu·al·ly ['fæktjʊəlɪ] ADV riguardo ai fatti
fac·ul·ty ['fækəltɪ] N facoltà *f inv*; (*Am: teaching staff*) corpo insegnante; **faculty of Engineering** facoltà di ingegneria
fad [fæd] N (*fashion*) moda, mania; (*personal*) capriccio, mania, fisima
fad·dy ['fædɪ] ADJ capriccioso(-a); **to be a faddy eater** essere schizzinoso(-a)
◎ **fade** [feɪd] VI **1** (*flower*) appassire; (*colour, fabric*) scolorire *or* scolorirsi, sbiadire *or* sbiadirsi; **my jeans have faded** i miei jeans si sono scoloriti **2** (*also:* **fade away**: *light*) affievolirsi, attenuarsi; (: *eyesight, hearing, memory*) indebolirsi; (: *hopes, smile*) svanire; (: *sounds*) affievolirsi, attutirsi; (: *person*) deperire; (*object*): **to fade from sight** scomparire alla vista; **hopes of a peaceful solution are fading** sta svanendo ogni speranza di trovare una soluzione
▸ **fade in** VT + ADV (*TV, Cine*) aprire in dissolvenza; (*Radio: sound*) aumentare gradualmente d'intensità
■ VI + ADV (*TV, Cine*) aprirsi in dissolvenza; (*Radio*) aumentare gradualmente d'intensità
▸ **fade out** VT + ADV (*TV, Cine*) chiudere in dissolvenza; (*Radio*) diminuire gradualmente l'intensità di
■ VI + ADV (*TV, Cine*) chiudere in dissolvenza; (*Radio*) diminuire gradualmente d'intensità
fad·ed ['feɪdɪd] ADJ (*material*) scolorito(-a); (*flower, beauty*) sfiorito(-a)
fade-in ['feɪd,ɪn] N (*Cine*) dissolvenza in apertura; (*Radio*) aumento graduale del suono
fade-out ['feɪd,aʊt] N (*Cine*) dissolvenza in chiusura; (*Radio*) diminuzione *f* graduale del suono
fae·ces, (*Am*) **fe·ces** ['fiːsiːz] NPL feci *fpl*
fag[1] [fæg] N **1** (*Brit fam: effort, job, chore*) faticata, sfacchinata **2** (*Brit: Scol*) *studente che fa piccoli servizi ad uno più anziano*
■ VT (*fam: also:* **fag out**) stancare, affaticare
fag[2] [fæg] N (*Brit fam: cigarette*) sigaretta, cicca
fag[3] [fæg] N (*Am offensivo*) = **faggot[1]**
fag end N fine *f*, sgoccioli *mpl*; (*Brit fam: of cigarette*) mozzicone *m*, cicca
fagged [fægd] ADJ (*Brit fam: also:* **fagged out**) stanco(-a) morto(-a)
fag·got[1] ['fægət] N (*Am offensive*) frocio (*fam!*)
fag·got[2] ['fægət] N **1** (*wood*) fascina **2** (*Brit: Culin*): **faggots** NPL *polpette a base di fegato di maiale*
fah [fɑː] N (*Mus*) fa *m inv*
Fahr·en·heit ['færənhaɪt] ADJ Fahrenheit *inv*; **Fahrenheit scale** scala Fahrenheit
◎ **fail** [feɪl] VI **1** (*gen*) fallire; (*in exam: candidate*) essere respinto(-a) *or* bocciato(-a); (*show, play*) essere un fiasco; **to fail in one's duty** mancare al proprio dovere; **to fail to do sth** non riuscire a fare qc; **they failed to reach the quarter-finals** non sono riusciti a raggiungere i quarti di finale; **a quarter of the students failed** un

Ff

quarto degli studenti sono stati bocciati **2** (*power, light, supplies*) mancare; (*crops*) andare perduto(-a); (*sight, light*) indebolirsi; (*strength, health*) venire a mancare; (*plan*) fallire; (*engine*) fermarsi; (*brakes*) non funzionare; **the lorry's brakes failed** i freni del camion non hanno funzionato; **the plan failed** il piano è fallito
■ VT **1** (*exam, subject*) non superare, essere bocciato(-a) in; (*candidate*) respingere, bocciare, rimandare; **he failed his driving test** non ha superato l'esame di guida **2** (*subj: person, memory, nerve*) abbandonare, mancare a; **don't fail me!** non deludermi!; **his courage failed him** gli è mancato il coraggio; **words fail me!** mi mancano le parole! **3** **to fail to do sth** (*neglect*) non fare qc, mancare di fare qc; (*be unable*) non riuscire a fare qc; **I fail to see why/what** *etc* non vedo perché/che cosa *ecc*
■ N: **without fail** senza fallo, senz'altro; **D is a pass, E is a fail** con D si passa, con E si viene bocciati

failed [feɪld] ADJ fallito(-a)

fail·ing ['feɪlɪŋ] PREP in mancanza di; **failing that** se questo non è possibile
■ N difetto

fail·safe ['feɪl,seɪf] ADJ (*device etc*) di sicurezza

◎ **fail·ure** ['feɪljəʳ] N (*gen*) fallimento; (*in exam*) bocciatura; (*of crops*) perdita; (*breakdown*) guasto, avaria; (*person*) fallito(-a); (*omission*): **his failure to come/answer** il fatto che non sia venuto/abbia risposto; **to end in failure** fallire; **the attempt was a complete failure** il tentativo è stato un fallimento completo; **I feel a failure** mi sento un fallito; **failure rate** (*gen*) numero di insuccessi; (*Scol*) numero di respinti; **heart failure** insufficienza cardiaca

faint [feɪnt] ADJ (*comp* **-er**, *superl* **-est**) (*smell, breeze, trace*) leggero(-a); (*outline, mark*) indistinto(-a); (*sound, voice*) fievole, debole; (*hope*) debole; (*idea, recollection, resemblance*) vago(-a); **to feel faint** sentirsi svenire; **I haven't the faintest (idea)** (*fam*) non ne ho la più pallida idea; **faint with hunger** debole per la fame; **his voice was very faint** la sua voce era molto debole
■ N svenimento
■ VI: **to faint (from)** svenire (da)

faint-hearted [,feɪnt'hɑːtɪd] ADJ pusillanime
■ NPL: **the faint-hearted** tipi impressionabili

faint·ly ['feɪntlɪ] ADV (*call, say, shine, smile*) debolmente; (*write, mark*) leggermente; **faintly reminiscent of** che ricorda vagamente

faint·ness ['feɪntnɪs] N (*of voice, sound etc*) debolezza

◎ **fair¹** [fɛəʳ] ADJ (*comp* **-er**, *superl* **-est**) **1** (*person, decision etc*) giusto(-a), equo(-a); (*hearing*) imparziale; (*sample*) rappresentativo(-a); (*fight, competition, match*) leale; **it's/that's not fair!** non è giusto!; **to be fair (to her) ...** per essere giusti (nei suoi confronti)...; **it's only fair that ...** è più che giusto che...; **it's fair to say that ...** bisogna riconoscere che...; **fair enough!** d'accordo!, va bene!; **by fair means** *or* **foul** con ogni mezzo; **his fair share of** la sua buona parte di **2** (*reasonable, average: work, result*) discreto(-a); **he has a fair chance** *or* **hope of success** ha buone probabilità di riuscire; **I have a fair chance of winning** ho discrete probabilità di vincere **3** (*quite large: sum*) discreto(-a), bello(-a), considerevole; (*: speed, pace*) buono(-a); **a fair amount of** un bel po' di; **that's a fair distance** è una bella distanza **4** (*light-coloured: hair, person*) biondo(-a); (*: complexion, skin*) chiaro(-a); **people with fair skin** le persone con la pelle chiara **5** (*fine: weather*) bello(-a)
■ ADV: **to play fair** giocare correttamente; **to act/win fair and square** agire/vincere onestamente; **the ball hit me fair and square in the face** la palla mi ha colpito in piena faccia

fair² [fɛəʳ] N (*market*) fiera, mercato; (*trade fair*) fiera campionaria; (*Brit: funfair*) luna park *m inv*, parco dei divertimenti; **I won a furry dog at the fair** ho vinto un cane di peluche al parco dei divertimenti

fair copy N bella copia

fair game N: **to be fair game** (*person*) essere bersaglio legittimo

fair·ground ['fɛə,graʊnd] N luna park *m inv*

fair-haired [,fɛə'hɛəd] ADJ (*person*) biondo(-a)

◎ **fair·ly** ['fɛəlɪ] ADV **1** (*justly*) in modo imparziale *or* equo, equamente; (*according to the rules*) lealmente, correttamente; **the money was divided fairly** il denaro è stato diviso equamente **2** (*quite*) abbastanza, piuttosto; **I'm fairly sure** sono abbastanza sicuro; **fairly good** discreto(-a); **my car is fairly new** la mia macchina è abbastanza nuova **3** (*fam: utterly*) completamente; **she was fairly raging** era completamente fuori di sé

fair-minded [,fɛə'maɪndɪd] ADJ equo(-a), imparziale

fair·ness ['fɛənɪs] N **1** onestà, equità, giustizia; (*of decision*) imparzialità; **in all fairness** per essere giusti, a dire il vero; **in (all) fairness to him** per essere giusti nei suoi confronti **2** (*of hair, skin*) chiarezza

fair play N correttezza

fair sex N (*old, hum*): **the fair sex** il gentil sesso

fair-sized ['fɛə'saɪzd] ADJ (*crowd, audience*) numeroso(-a); (*piece*) bello(-a)

fair-skinned [,fɛə'skɪnd] ADJ di carnagione chiara

fair trade N commercio equo e solidale
■ ADJ (*product*) del commercio equo e solidale

fair·way ['fɛə,weɪ] N: **the fairway** (*Golf*) il fairway *m inv*

fairy ['fɛərɪ] N **1** fata; **fairy queen** regina delle fate **2** (*offensive: homosexual*) finocchio

fairy godmother N fata buona

fairy·land ['fɛərɪ,lænd] N paese *m* delle fate

fairy lights NPL (*Brit*) lanternine *fpl* colorate

fairy tale N fiaba; (*lie*) frottola

fait ac·com·pli [,fɛtəkɒm'pliː] N fatto compiuto

◎ **faith** [feɪθ] N **1** (*trust*) fiducia; **to have faith in sb/sth** avere fiducia in qn/qc; **to put one's faith in sb/sth** fidarsi di qn/qc; **to keep/break faith with sb** mantenere la parola/mancare di parola con qn; **to lose faith in sb/sth** perdere fiducia in qn/qc; **people have lost faith in the government** la gente ha perso fiducia nel governo; **in (all) good faith** in buona fede; **in bad faith** in malafede **2** (*Rel: belief*) fede *f*, religione *f*; **Faith, Hope and Charity** Fede, Speranza e Carità

faith·ful ['feɪθfʊl] ADJ: **faithful (to)** fedele (a)
■ NPL: **the faithful** (*Rel*) i fedeli

faith·ful·ly ['feɪθfəlɪ] ADV fedelmente; **he promised faithfully to come** ci ha dato la sua parola che sarebbe venuto; **yours faithfully** (*Brit: in letters*) distinti saluti

faith·ful·ness ['feɪθfʊlnɪs] N: **faithfulness (to)** fedeltà (a)

faith healer N guaritore(-trice)

faith healing N guarigione *f* mistica

faith·less ['feɪθlɪs] ADJ infedele

faith·less·ness ['feɪθlɪsnɪs] N: **faithlessness (to)** infedeltà *f inv* (a)

fake [feɪk] N (*picture*) falso; (*thing*) imitazione *f*; (*person*) impostore(-a); **his illness is a fake** fa finta di essere malato; **the painting was a fake** il quadro era un falso
■ ADJ falso(-a), fasullo(-a); **a fake banknote** una

banconota falsa; **a fake fur coat** una pelliccia sintetica
■ VT (*accounts*) falsificare; (*illness*) fingere; (*painting*) contraffare
■ VI fingere

fal·con ['fɔ:lkən] N falco, falcone *m*

fal·con·ry ['fɔ:lkənrɪ] N (*skill*) falconeria

Falk·land Is·lands ['fɔ:lklənd,aɪləndz], **Falk·lands** ['fɔ:lkləndz] NPL: **the Falkland Islands** *or* **Falklands** le isole *fpl* Falkland, le isole Malvine

◎ **fall** [fɔ:l] (*vb: pt* **fell**, *pp* **fallen**) N
1 (*gen*) caduta; (*decrease*) diminuzione *f*, calo; (*: in prices*) ribasso; (*: in temperature*) abbassamento; **he had a bad fall** ha fatto una brutta caduta; **a fall of earth** uno smottamento; **a fall of snow** (*Brit*) una nevicata; **a heavy/light fall of rain** una pioggia forte/leggera
2 (*Am: autumn*) autunno; **in the fall** in autunno; *see also* **falls**
■ VI
1 (*gen*) cadere; (*building*) crollare; (*decrease: temperature, price*) abbassarsi, diminuire; **he tripped and fell** è inciampato e caduto; **she's fallen** è caduta; **prices are falling** i prezzi stanno calando; **night is falling** scende la notte; **darkness is falling** si fa buio; **to fall to** *or* **on one's knees** cadere in ginocchio; **to fall on one's feet** cadere in piedi; **to let sth fall** lasciar cadere qc; **to let fall that ...** lasciar capire che...; **to fall into bad habits** *or* **bad ways** prendere delle cattive abitudini; **to fall into conversation with sb** mettersi a parlare con qn; **his poems fall into three categories** le sue poesie si dividono in tre categorie; **to fall from grace** (*Rel*) perdere la grazia di Dio; (*fig*) cadere in disgrazia; **he fell in my estimation** ha perso ai miei occhi; **it all began to fall into place** (*fig*) ha cominciato a prendere forma; **the responsibility falls on you** la responsabilità ricade su di te; **my birthday falls on a Saturday** il mio compleanno cade di sabato; **he fell to wondering if ...** si mise a pensare se...; **it falls to me to say ...** (*frm*) tocca a me *or* è mio compito dire...; **to fall short of** (*sb's expectations*) non corrispondere a; (*perfection*) non raggiungere; **the dart fell short of the board** la freccetta è caduta poco prima del bersaglio; **to fall flat** (*on one's face*) cadere bocconi; (*subj*) (*: joke, party*) essere un fiasco; (*: plan*) fallire, fare cilecca; **to fall foul of** scontrarsi con
2 (*become*): **to fall asleep** addormentarsi; **to fall into arrears** accumulare degli arretrati; **to fall due** scadere; **to fall ill** ammalarsi; **to fall in love (with sb/sth)** innamorarsi (di qn/qc); **to fall silent** farsi silenzioso(-a)
▸ **fall about** VI + ADV (*fig fam*) torcersi dalle risa
▸ **fall apart** VI + ADV cadere a pezzi; (*fig*) crollare
▸ **fall away** VI + ADV (*slope steeply: ground*) scendere; (*crumble: plaster*) scrostarsi, sgretolarsi; (*fig: diminish*) diminuire
▸ **fall back** VI + ADV (*retreat*) indietreggiare; (*Mil*) ritirarsi
▸ **fall back on** VI + ADV + PREP (*also fig*): **to have sth to fall back on** avere qc di riserva
▸ **fall behind** VI + ADV (*in race etc*) rimanere indietro; (*fig: with payments*) essere in arretrato; (*: with work*) essere indietro
▸ **fall down** VI + ADV (*person*) cadere; (*building, hopes*) crollare; **but it falls down in one aspect** (*fig*) ma ha un punto debole; **to fall down on the job** (*fig*) non essere all'altezza del lavoro
▸ **fall for** VI + PREP
1 (*fam: person*) prendere una cotta per, innamorarsi di; **Anne fell for him immediately** Anne si è subito presa una cotta per lui
2 (*fam: be deceived by*): **to fall for a trick** (*or* **a story** *etc*) cascarci; **they fell for it!** ci sono cascati!
▸ **fall in** VI + ADV
1 (*person*) cadere dentro; (*roof, walls*) crollare
2 (*Mil*) mettersi in riga, allinearsi
■ VI + PREP: **to fall in(to)** cadere in
▸ **fall in with** VI + ADV + PREP: **to fall in with sb** (*meet*) trovare qn; **to fall in with sb's plans** (*person*) trovarsi d'accordo con i progetti di qn; (*event*) coincidere con i progetti di qn
▸ **fall off** VI + ADV (*person, leaf*) cadere; (*part*) staccarsi; (*diminish: demand, numbers, interest*) diminuire, abbassarsi; (*: quality*) scadere; **the exhaust fell off** è caduto il tubo di scarico; **unemployment has fallen off** la disoccupazione è diminuita
■ VI + PREP cadere da
▸ **fall on, fall upon** VI + PREP (*attack*) scagliarsi su; (*responsibility*) ricadere su
▸ **fall out** VI + ADV
1 (*person, object*): **to fall out (of)** cadere (da)
2 (*Mil*) rompere le righe
3 (*fig: quarrel*): **to fall out (with sb over sth)** litigare (con qn per qc); **Sarah's fallen out with her boyfriend** Sarah ha litigato col suo ragazzo
4 (*happen*): **it fell out that ...** è andata a finire che...; **events fell out (just) as we had hoped** andò a finire proprio come avevamo sperato
▸ **fall over** VI + ADV cadere
■ VI + PREP: **he fell over the table** è inciampato nel tavolino ed è caduto; **he was falling over himself** *or* **over backwards to be polite** (*fam*) si faceva in quattro per essere gentile; **they were falling over each other to get it** (*fam*) si accapigliavano per averlo
▸ **fall through** VI + ADV (*plan, project*) fallire
▸ **fall upon** VI + PREP = **fall on**

fal·la·cious [fə'leɪʃəs] ADJ (*frm*) fallace

fal·la·cy ['fæləsɪ] N errore *m*

fall·back ['fɔ:l,bæk] ADJ: **fallback position** posizione *f* di ripiego

fall·en ['fɔ:lən] PP *of* **fall**
■ ADJ caduto(-a); (*morally: woman, angel*) perduto(-a)
■ NPL: **the fallen** (*Mil*) i caduti

fallen arches N piedi *mpl* piatti; **to have fallen arches** (*Med*) avere i piedi piatti

fal·libil·ity [,fælɪ'bɪlɪtɪ] N fallibilità *f inv*

fal·lible ['fæləbl] ADJ (*frm*) fallibile

fall·ing ['fɔ:lɪŋ] ADJ: **falling market** (*Fin*) mercato in ribasso

falling-off ['fɔ:lɪŋ'ɒf] N calo

falling star N stella cadente

fall line N (*Skiing*) linea di massima pendenza

Fal·lo·pian tube [fə,ləʊpɪən'tju:b] N (*Anat*) tuba di Fallopio

fall·out ['fɔ:l,aʊt] N pioggia radioattiva; (*fig: repercussions*) ripercussione *f*; **fallout shelter** rifugio antiatomico

fal·low ['fæləʊ] ADJ incolto(-a), a maggese; **to lie fallow** rimanere a maggese

fallow deer N, PL INV daino(-a)

falls [fɔ:lz] NPL (*waterfall*) cascate *fpl*; **the Niagara Falls** le cascate del Niagara

◎ **false** [fɔ:ls] ADJ (*gen*) falso(-a); **false ceiling** controsoffitto; **a false step** un passo falso; **under**

Ff

false pretences con l'inganno; **with a false bottom** con doppio fondo
false alarm N falso allarme *m*
false friend N (*Ling*) falso amico
false·hood ['fɔ:ls,hʊd] N (*frm: lie*) menzogna; **truth and falsehood** il vero e il falso
false·ly ['fɔ:lslɪ] ADV (*accuse*) a torto; (*state*) falsamente
false move N passo falso
false·ness ['fɔ:lsnɪs] N falsità
false start N falsa partenza
false teeth NPL (*Brit*) denti *mpl* finti, dentiera
fal·set·to [fɔ:l'sɛtəʊ] N falsetto
■ ADJ di falsetto
fal·si·fi·ca·tion [,fɔ:lsɪfɪ'keɪʃən] N falsificazione *f*
fal·si·fy ['fɔ:lsɪ,faɪ] VT falsificare; (*figures*) alterare
fal·sity ['fɔ:lsɪtɪ] N = **falseness**
fal·ter ['fɔ:ltə^r] VI (*voice, speaker*) esitare; (*interest*) scemare; (*engine*) perder colpi; **his voice faltered with emotion** la sua voce era rotta dall'emozione; **his steps faltered** ha vacillato
fal·ter·ing ['fɔ:ltərɪŋ] ADJ incerto(-a)
fame [feɪm] N fama, celebrità; **his fame as a musician** la sua fama di musicista
famed [feɪmd] ADJ famoso(-a), celebre
fa·mil·ial [fə'mɪlɪəl] ADJ (*frm*) familiare
◎ **fa·mili·ar** [fə'mɪljə^r] ADJ **1** (*well-known: face, person, place*) conosciuto(-a), familiare; (*common: experience, complaint, event*) comune; **her face looks familiar** la sua faccia non mi è nuova; **the name sounded familiar to me** il nome mi suonava familiare; **to be on familiar ground** (*fig*) trovarsi sul proprio terreno **2** (*well-acquainted*): **to be familiar (with sb/sth)** conoscere bene (qn/qc); **I'm familiar with his work** conosco bene i suoi lavori; **to make o.s. familiar with** familiarizzarsi con, acquistare dimestichezza con **3** (*language*) familiare; (*intimate: tone of voice*) di eccessiva confidenza; **to be on familiar terms with** essere in confidenza con; **to get too familiar with sb** (*pej*) prendersi troppa confidenza con qn
fa·mili·ar·ity [fə,mɪlɪ'ærɪtɪ] N (*knowledge*): **familiarity (with)** conoscenza (di), dimestichezza (con); (*of tone etc*) confidenza, familiarità, intimità; **familiarity breeds contempt** dar troppa confidenza fa perdere il rispetto
fa·mil·iar·ize [fə'mɪlɪə,raɪz] VT: **to familiarize o.s. with** familiarizzarsi con; **to familiarize sb with sth** far conoscere qc a qn
fa·mili·ar·ly [fə'mɪljəlɪ] ADV con molta confidenza
◎ **fami·ly** ['fæmɪlɪ] N (*gen*) famiglia; **the Cooke family** la famiglia Cooke; **it runs in the family** è di famiglia; **she's quite one of the family** è come se facesse parte della famiglia
■ ADJ (*jewels, life, business*) di famiglia, familiare
family allowance N (*Brit: old*) assegni *mpl* familiari
family butcher N macellaio di quartiere
family credit N (*Brit*) ≈ assegni *mpl* familiari
family doctor N (*Brit*) medico di famiglia
family man N uomo amante della famiglia, padre *m* di famiglia
family name N = **surname**
family planning N pianificazione *f* familiare
family planning clinic N consultorio familiare
family tree N albero genealogico
fam·ine ['fæmɪn] N carestia
fam·ished ['fæmɪʃt] ADJ affamato(-a); **I'm famished!** (*fam*) ho una fame da lupi!
◎ **fa·mous** ['feɪməs] ADJ famoso(-a), celebre; **famous last words!** (*fam hum*) le ultime parole famose!
fa·mous·ly ['feɪməslɪ] ADV (*get on*) a meraviglia
◎ **fan**[1] [fæn] N ventaglio; (*machine*) ventilatore *m*; **a silk fan** un ventaglio di seta
■ VT (*face, person*) fare aria a, fare vento a; (*fire*) alimentare; **to fan the flames** (*fig*) soffiare sul fuoco
▸ **fan out** VI + ADV spargersi (a ventaglio)
fan[2] [fæn] N (*gen*) fan *m/f inv*, ammiratore(-trice); (*Sport*) tifoso(-a), fan *m/f inv*; **I'm one of his greatest fans** sono uno dei suoi più grandi ammiratori; **the England fans** i tifosi inglesi; **she's a jazz fan** è una patita di jazz
fa·nat·ic [fə'nætɪk] N fanatico(-a)
fa·nati·c(al) [fə'nætɪk(əl)] ADJ fanatico(-a)
fa·nati·cal·ly [fə'nætɪkəlɪ] ADV fanaticamente
fa·nati·cism [fə'nætɪ,sɪzəm] N fanatismo
fan belt N (*Aut*) cinghia della ventola
fan·cied ['fænsɪd] ADJ **1** (*imaginary*) immaginario(-a) **2** (*horse, candidate*) favorito(-a)
fan·ci·ful ['fænsɪfʊl] ADJ (*explanation*) fantastico(-a); (*person, idea, drawing*) fantasioso(-a); (*object*) di fantasia
fan·ci·ful·ly ['fænsɪfəlɪ] ADV (*see adj*) fantasticamente; in modo fantasioso
fan club N fan club *m inv*
◎ **fan·cy** ['fænsɪ] N **1** (*whim*) voglia, capriccio; **a passing fancy (for sth)** una voglia passeggera (di qc); **when the fancy takes him** quando ne ha voglia; **to take a fancy to** (*person, thing*) affezionarsi a, incapricciarsi di; **to catch or take sb's fancy** entusiasmare qn; **it took** *or* **caught my fancy** mi è piaciuto **2** (*imagination*) fantasia, immaginazione *f*; **in the realm of fancy** nel regno della fantasia; **I have a fancy that he'll be late** (*vague idea*) ho la vaga impressione che arriverà tardi; **is it just my fancy, or did I hear a knock at the door?** mi sbaglio o hanno bussato alla porta?
■ ADJ (*comp* **-ier**, *superl* **-iest**) **1** (*ornamental*) elaborato(-a); **a fancy design** un disegno fantasia; **nothing fancy** niente di speciale; **fancy cakes** pasticcini *mpl* **2** (*pej: price*) esorbitante; (: *idea*) stravagante
■ VT **1** (*imagine*) immaginare, credere; **to fancy that** immaginare che; **I rather fancy he's gone out** credo proprio che sia uscito; **fancy that!** (*fam*) pensa un po'!, ma guarda!; **fancy meeting you here!** (*fam*) che combinazione incontrarti qui! **2** (*feel like, want*) avere voglia di; **do you fancy (going for) a stroll?** hai voglia o ti va di fare una passeggiatina?; **I don't fancy the idea** l'idea non mi attira; **he fancies himself** (*fam*) ha un'alta opinione di sé; **he fancies himself as a footballer** (*fam*) crede di essere un gran calciatore; **she fancies him** (*fam*) lui le piace (*sessualmente*) **3** (*predict success for: team, horse*) dare per vincente; **I don't fancy his chances of winning** non credo che vincerà
fancy dress N costume *m*, maschera; **fancy-dress ball** ballo in maschera; **fancy-dress party** festa mascherata
fancy goods NPL articoli *mpl* da regalo
fancy man N (*old pej*) amico
fancy woman N (*old pej*) amica
fan·dan·go [fæn'dæŋgəʊ] N fandango
fan·fare ['fænfɛə] N fanfara
fang [fæŋ] N zanna; (*of snake*) dente *m*
fan heater N (*Brit*) termoventilatore *m*
fan·light ['fæn,laɪt] N lunetta (a ventaglio)
fan mail N lettere *fpl* degli ammiratori
fan·ny ['fænɪ] N (*Brit fam!*) figa (*fam!*); (*Am fam*) culo
fan·ta·sia [fæn'teɪzɪə] N (*Mus*) fantasia
fan·ta·size ['fæntə,saɪz] VI fantasticare, sognare

fan·tas·tic [fæn'tæstɪk] ADJ *(gen)* fantastico(-a); *(idea)* assurdo(-a)

fan·tas·ti·cal·ly [fæn'tæstɪkəlɪ] ADV in modo fantastico, fantasticamente; **he is fantastically rich** è incredibilmente *or* favolosamente ricco

◎**fan·ta·sy** ['fæntəsɪ] N *(imagination)* fantasia, immaginazione *f*; *(fanciful idea, wish)* sogno, idea fantastica, chimera; **in a world of fantasy** in un mondo fantastico; **fantasies of romance** fantasie romantiche

fantasy football N calcio virtuale

fan·zine ['fæn,zi:n] N fanzine *f inv*

FAO [,ɛfeɪ'əʊ] N ABBR (= **Food and Agriculture Organization**) FAO *f*

FAQ [,ɛfeɪ'kju:] NPL ABBR *(Comput:* = **frequently asked questions**) FAQ *fpl*, domande *fpl* frequenti
■ABBR (= **free alongside quay**) FAQ, franco lungo banchina

◎**far** [fɑ:ʳ]) ADV *(comp* **farther** *or* **further**, *superl* **farthest** *or* **furthest**
1 lontano; **is it far (away)?** è lontano?; **is it far to London?** è lontana Londra?; **how far is it?** quanto dista?; **how far is it to the river?** quanto è lontano il fiume?; **it's not far (from here)** non è lontano (da qui); **it's not far from London** non è lontano da Londra; **as far as** fino a; **as far as the eye can see** a perdita d'occhio; **to go as far as Milan** andare fino a Milano; **to come from as far away as Milan** venire addirittura da Milano; **she swam as far as the others** ha nuotato tanto lontano quanto gli altri; **as far back as I can remember** per quanto *or* per quello che posso ricordare; **as far back as 1945** già nel 1945; **as** *or* **so far as I know** per quel che ne so, per quanto ne sappia; **as** *or* **so far as I am concerned** per quanto mi riguarda; **as far as possible** nei limiti del possibile; **I would go as** *or* **so far as to say that ...** arriverei al punto di dire...; **from far and near** da ogni parte; **to come from far and wide** venire da ogni parte; **to travel far and wide** viaggiare in lungo e in largo; **far away** *or* **off** lontano, distante; **far away** *or* **off in the distance** in lontananza; **not far away** *or* **off** non lontano; **far away from one's family** lontano dalla famiglia; **Christmas is not far off** Natale non è lontano, non manca molto a Natale; **far beyond** molto al di là di; **far from** *(place)* lontano da; **far from (doing sth)** invece di (fare qc); **we are far from having finished** siamo ben lungi dall'aver finito; **far from it!** al contrario!; **he is far from well** non sta affatto *or* per niente bene; **far be it from me to interfere, but ...** non ho la minima intenzione di immischiarmi, ma...; **far from easy** tutt'altro che facile; **far into the night** fino a notte inoltrata; **far out at sea** in alto mare; **our calculations weren't far out** i nostri calcoli non erano poi così sbagliati; **to go far** *(person)* andare lontano; **he'll go far** farà molta strada; **it won't go far** *(money, food)* non basterà; **how far are you going?** fin dove vai?; **how far have you got with your work?** dove sei arrivato con il tuo lavoro?; **he's gone too far this time** questa volta ha esagerato *or* oltrepassato i limiti; **he's gone too far to back out now** si è spinto troppo oltre per tirarsi indietro adesso; **the plans are too far advanced** i piani sono a uno stadio troppo avanzato; **he was far gone** *(fam: ill)* era molto malato; (: *drunk)* era ubriaco fradicio; **this far** *(in distance)* fin qui; **so far** *(in time)* finora, fino ad ora; **so far so good** fin qui tutto a posto; **so** *or* **thus far and no further** fin qui e non oltre
2 *(with comp: very much)* di gran lunga; **far better** assai migliore; **it's far and away the best** *or* **it's by far the best** è di gran lunga il migliore; **this car is far faster (than)** questa macchina è molto più veloce (di); **she's the prettiest by far** è di gran lunga la più carina; **it is far better not to go** è molto meglio non andare
■ADJ: **the Far North** l'estremo Nord; **the far east** *etc* **of the country** la zona orientale *ecc* del paese; **on the far side of** dall'altra parte di; **at the far end of** in fondo a, all'altro capo di; **the far left/right** *(Pol)* l'estrema sinistra/destra

far·away ['fɑ:rə,weɪ] ADJ *(distant)* lontano(-a); *(voice, look)* assente

farce [fɑ:s] N *(Theatre, fig)* farsa

far·ci·cal ['fɑ:sɪkl] ADJ farsesco(-a), ridicolo(-a); **the trial was farcical** il processo fu una farsa

far-distant [,fɑ:'dɪstənt] ADJ lontano(-a)

◎**fare** [fɛəʳ] N **1** *(cost: on trains, buses)* tariffa; (: *in taxi)* prezzo della corsa; **full fare** la tariffa intera; **"fares please!"** *(conductor on bus)* "biglietti?"; **railway fares are very high in Britain** le tariffe ferroviarie sono molto alte in Gran Bretagna **2** *(passenger in taxi)* passeggero(-a), cliente *m/f* **3** *(frm: food)* cibo, vitto; **bill of fare** *(menu)* lista delle vivande
■VI: **how did you fare?** com'è andata?; **I think they will fare badly if ...** penso che le cose si metteranno male per loro se...

Far East N: **the Far East** l'Estremo Oriente *m*

fare stage N *(for bus)* tronco

fare·well [,fɛə'wɛl] N, EXCL addio; **to bid farewell (to sb)** salutare (qn), dire addio (a qn)
■ADJ *(party)* d'addio; (: *dinner, speech)* d'addio, di commiato

far-fetched [,fɑ:'fɛtʃt] ADJ *(explanation)* stiracchiato(-a), forzato(-a); *(idea, scheme, story)* inverosimile

far-flung [,fɑ:'flʌŋ] ADJ *(remote)* remoto(-a); *(widely distributed: empire, operations)* esteso(-a)

◎**farm** [fɑ:m] N fattoria, podere *m*; **farm produce** prodotti *mpl* agricoli
■VT coltivare
■VI *(as profession)* fare l'agricoltore
▸ **farm out** VT + ADV *(work)*: **farm out (to sb)** dare in consegna (a qn); *(children)*: **to farm out (on)** affidare (a)

◎**farm·er** ['fɑ:məʳ] N agricoltore *m*, contadino(-a), coltivatore(-trice); *(owner of farm)* proprietario(-a) terriero(-a)

farm·hand ['fɑ:m,hænd], **farm labourer**, *(Am)* farm laborer N bracciante *m/f*

farm·house ['fɑ:m,haʊs] N casa colonica, fattoria

farm·ing ['fɑ:mɪŋ] N agricoltura; **organic farming** agricoltura biologica; **sheep farming** allevamento di pecore; **farming community** comunità *f inv* agricola; **farming methods** metodi *mpl* di coltivazione

farm·land ['fɑ:m,lænd] N terreno coltivo

farm·stead ['fɑ:m,stɛd] N fattoria

farm worker N = **farmhand**

farm·yard ['fɑ:m,jɑ:d] N aia

Faroe Is·lands ['fɛərəʊ'aɪləndz], **Faroes** ['fɛərəʊz] NPL: **the Faroe Islands** le isole *fpl* Faeroer

far-off ['fɑ:,rɒf] ADJ lontano(-a), distante

far-reaching [,fɑ:'ri:tʃɪŋ] ADJ *(effect)* di larga *or* vasta portata

far·ri·er ['færɪəʳ] N maniscalco

far·row ['færəʊ] VI *(Zool)* figliare *(di scrofa)*

far-sighted [,fɑ:'saɪtɪd] ADJ **1** *(person)* previdente, lungimirante; *(plan, decision, measure)* lungimirante **2** *(Am: long-sighted)* presbite

Ff

fart [fɑːt] (*fam!*) N scoreggia, peto (*fam!*)
■ VI scoreggiare, fare un peto (*fam!*)

far·ther ['fɑːðəʳ] COMP *of* **far**
■ ADV *see* **further** ADV 1
■ ADJ più lontano(-a); **on the farther side of the street** dall'altra parte della strada

far·thest ['fɑːðɪst] ADJ, ADV, SUPERL *of* **far**; *see* **furthest**

far·thing ['fɑːðɪŋ] N (*coin*) *moneta da un quarto di penny, non più in circolazione*; **it does not matter a brass farthing if ...** (*old fam*) non me ne importa un fico secco se...

FAS ABBR (*Brit*: = **free alongside ship**) FAS, franco banchina nave

fas·cia, fa·cia ['feɪʃɪə] N **1** (*Aut*) cruscotto **2** (*of mobile phone*) mascherina

fas·ci·nate ['fæsɪˌneɪt] VT affascinare; **it fascinates me how/why ...** sono affascinato da come/ perché...

fas·ci·nat·ing ['fæsɪˌneɪtɪŋ] ADJ affascinante

fas·ci·nat·ingly ['fæsɪˌneɪtɪŋlɪ] ADV affascinante

fas·ci·na·tion ['fæsɪˌneɪʃən] N fascino

fas·cism ['fæʃɪzəm] N fascismo

fas·cist ['fæʃɪst] ADJ, N fascista (*m/f*)

◎**fash·ion** ['fæʃən] N **1** (*manner*) modo, maniera; **after a fashion** (*finish, manage etc*) così così ; **in his usual fashion** nel solito modo; **in similar fashion** in maniera simile; **in the Greek fashion** alla greca **2** (*vogue: in clothing, speech etc*) moda; **to set a fashion for sth** lanciare la moda di qc; **to be in fashion** essere di/alla moda; **to be out of fashion** essere fuori moda, essere passato(-a) di moda; **to come into/go out of fashion** diventare/passare di moda; **the latest fashion** l'ultima moda; **the new Spring fashions** i nuovi modelli per la primavera; **it's no longer the fashion** non va più di moda; **women's/men's fashions** moda femminile/maschile
■ VT (*gen*) fabbricare; (*in clay*) modellare
■ ADJ (*editor, house, show*) di moda

fash·ion·able ['fæʃnəbl] ADJ alla moda, di moda; (*writer*) di grido; **it is fashionable to do ...** è/va di moda fare...

fash·ion·ably ['fæʃnəblɪ] ADV: **to be fashionably dressed** essere vestito(-a) alla moda

fashion designer N stilista *m/f*, disegnatore(-trice) di moda

fashion model N indossatore(-trice), modello(-a)

fashion victim N (*pej*) schiavo(-a) della moda

◎**fast¹** [fɑːst] (*comp* **-er**, *superl* **-est**) ADJ **1** (*speedy*) veloce, svelto(-a), rapido(-a); (*film*) ad alta sensibilità; **fast train** rapido; **a fast car** una macchina veloce; **he's a fast worker** (*fig*) non perde certo tempo; **to pull a fast one on sb** (*fam*) giocare un brutto tiro a qn **2** (*clock*): **to be fast** andare avanti; **my watch is 5 minutes fast** il mio orologio va avanti di 5 minuti **3** (*dissipated: woman*) dissoluto(-a); (*: life*) dissipato(-a), dissoluto(-a) **4** (*firm: friend*) devoto(-a), fedele; (*: colour, dye*) resistente, che non stinge; **to make a boat fast** (*Brit*) ormeggiare una barca
■ ADV **1** (*quickly*) in fretta, velocemente, rapidamente; **to drive too fast** correre troppo; **as fast as I can** più in fretta possibile; **he ran off as fast as his legs would carry him** è corso via come il vento *or* più veloce che poteva; **how fast can you type?** a che velocità scrivi a macchina?; **not so fast!** piano!; **the rain was falling fast** pioveva forte *or* a dirotto **2** (*firmly: stuck, held*) saldamente, bene; **tie it fast** legalo bene; **it's stuck fast** (*door*) è saldamente bloccato; (*nail, screw*) è completamente incastrato; **fast asleep** profondamente addormentato(-a)

fast² [fɑːst] N digiuno
■ VI digiunare

fast bowler N (*Cricket*) lanciatore *m* svelto

fas·ten ['fɑːsn] VT (*with rope, string etc*) legare; (*with nail*) inchiodare; (*secure: belt, dress, seat belt*) allacciare; (*: door, box, window*) chiudere; (*attach*) attaccare, fissare; **fasten your seat belt** allacciatevi le cinture di sicurezza; **to fasten the blame/responsibility (for sth) on sb** (*fig*) dare la colpa/addossare la responsabilità (di qc) a qn
■ VI (*door etc*) chiudersi; (*dress*) allacciarsi, abbottonarsi
▸ **fasten down** VT + ADV fissare bene
▸ **fasten on** VT + ADV fissare
▸ **fasten up** VT + ADV (*clothing, coat*) allacciare, abbottonare
▸ **fasten (up)on** VI + PREP (*idea*) cogliere al volo; (*excuse*) ricorrere a

fas·ten·er ['fɑːsnəʳ], **fas·ten·ing** ['fɑːsnɪŋ] N chiusura, fermaglio; (*zip*) chiusura *f* lampo *inv*

fast food N fast food *m inv*

fas·tidi·ous [fæ'stɪdɪəs] ADJ (*person: about cleanliness*) pignolo(-a); (*: in taste*) difficile, esigente

> DID YOU KNOW ...?
> **fastidious** is not translated by the Italian word *fastidioso*

fas·tidi·ous·ly [fæs'tɪdɪəslɪ] ADV (*examine, check, clean*) meticolosamente, scrupolosamente

fas·tidi·ous·ness [fæ'stɪdɪəsnɪs] N pignoleria; (*excessive cleanliness*) mania della pulizia

fast·ing [fɑːstɪŋ] N digiuno

fast lane N (*Aut*) ≈ corsia di sorpasso; **in the fast lane** nella corsia di sorpasso

fast·ness ['fɑːstnɪs] N (*liter*) roccaforte *f*

fast track N modo più rapido; **the fast track to sth** il modo più rapido per ottenere qc
■ VT (*application, case*) mandare avanti rapidamente; (*in career*) far avanzare rapidamente nella carriera

◎**fat** [fæt] (*comp* **-ter**, *superl* **-test**) ADJ (*person, meat*) grasso(-a); (*face, cheeks*) paffuto(-a); (*arm, leg*) grassoccio(-a); (*book*) grosso(-a); (*wallet*) gonfio(-a); (*wage packet*) cospicuo(-a); **to get fat** ingrassare, diventare grasso(-a); **she thinks she's too fat** pensa di essere troppo grassa; **he grew fat on the proceeds/ profits** (*fig*) si è arricchito con i guadagni/gli incassi; **a fat lot he knows about it!** (*fam iro*) che vuoi che ne sappia lui!; **a fat lot of good that is!** (*fam iro*) bella roba!
■ N grasso; (*Anat*) adipe *m*; **to fry in deep fat** friggere in molto olio; **it's very high in fat** contiene molti grassi; **to live off the fat of the land** vivere nel lusso, avere ogni ben di Dio; **the fat's in the fire** (*fig*) adesso son guai

fa·tal ['feɪtl] ADJ (*injury, disease, accident*) fatale, mortale; (*mistake*) fatale; (*consequences, result*) disastroso(-a); (*influence*) nefasto(-a); (*fateful: words, decision*) fatidico(-a); **it was fatal to mention that** è stato un grave errore parlarne

fa·tal·ism ['feɪtəˌlɪzəm] N fatalismo

fa·tal·ist ['feɪtəlɪst] N fatalista *m/f*

fa·tal·is·tic [ˌfeɪtə'lɪstɪk] ADJ fatalistico(-a)

fa·tal·ity [fə'tælɪtɪ] N (*death*) incidente *m* mortale; (*person killed*) morto(-a), vittima

fa·tal·ly ['feɪtəlɪ] ADV (*wounded, injured*) mortalmente, a morte; (*damaged, flawed*) irrimediabilmente; (*exposed, incriminated*) in modo disastroso; **fatally ill** condannato(-a)

◎**fate** [feɪt] N **1** (*force*) destino, sorte *f*, fato; **the Fates**

(*Myth*) le Parche; **what has fate in store for us?** cosa ci riserva il destino? **2** (*person's lot*) sorte *f*, destino; **to leave sb to his fate** abbandonare qn alla propria sorte *or* al proprio destino; **a terrible fate** un terribile destino; **to meet one's fate** (*death*) trovare la morte

fat·ed ['feɪtɪd] ADJ (*governed by fate*) destinato(-a); (*person, project, friendship etc*) destinato(-a) a finire male; **it was fated that ...** era destino che...

fate·ful ['feɪtfʊl] ADJ (*momentous: day, event*) fatale; (*prophetic: words*) fatidico(-a)

fat-free ['fæt'fri:] ADJ senza grassi

fat·head ['fæt,hɛd] N (*fam*) scemo(-a), babbeo(-a)

◎ **fa·ther** ['fɑ:ðəʳ] N (*gen*) padre *m*; **my father** mio padre; **Our Father** (*Rel*) Padre Nostro; **from father to son** di padre in figlio; **like father like son** tale padre tale figlio; **Old Father Time** il Tempo

Father Christmas N Babbo Natale

father confessor N (*Rel*) padre confessore; (*fig*) refugium peccatorum *m inv*

father-figure ['fɑ:ðə,fɪgəʳ] N figura paterna

father·hood ['fɑ:ðə,hʊd] N paternità

father-in-law ['fɑ:ðəɪn,lɔ:] N suocero

father·land ['fɑ:ðə,lænd] N patria

fa·ther·less ['fɑ:ðəlɪs] ADJ orfano(-a) di padre

fa·ther·ly ['fɑ:ðəlɪ] ADJ paterno(-a)

fath·om ['fæðəm] N (*Naut*) braccio (=*1,83m*)
■ VT (*fig: also:* **fathom out**) capire; (*mystery*) penetrare, sondare; **I can't fathom why** non riesco a capire perché; **I can't fathom it out** non ci capisco assolutamente niente; **I couldn't fathom what he meant** non sono riuscito a comprendere cosa intendeva

fath·om·less ['fæðəmlɪs] ADJ insondabile, inesplorabile; (*fig*) incomprensibile

fa·tigue [fə'ti:g] N stanchezza, fatica; **to be on fatigue** (*Mil*) essere di corvé
■ VT (*frm*) affaticare, stancare

fa·tigued [fə'ti:gd] ADJ (*person*) affaticato(-a)

fat·less ['fætlɪs] ADJ senza grassi

fat·ness ['fætnɪs] N grassezza

fat·ted ['fætɪd] ADJ: **to kill the fatted calf** (*old*) uccidere il vitello grasso

fat·ten ['fætn] VT, VI (*also:* **fatten up**) ingrassare

fat·ten·ing ['fætnɪŋ] ADJ ingrassante; **to be fattening** far ingrassare; **chocolate is fattening** la cioccolata fa ingrassare; **some foods are not fattening** alcuni cibi non fanno ingrassare

fat·ty ['fætɪ] ADJ (*foods*) grasso(-a); (*Anat: tissue*) grasso(-a), adiposo(-a)
■ N (*fam*) ciccione(-a)

fa·tu·ity [fə'tju:ɪtɪ], **fatu·ous·ness** ['fætjʊəsnɪs] N fatuità

fatu·ous ['fætjʊəs] ADJ fatuo(-a)

fatu·ous·ly ['fætjʊəslɪ] ADV stupidamente

fat·wa(h) ['fætwɑ:] N fatwa

fau·cet ['fɔ:sɪt] N (*Am*) rubinetto

◎ **fault** [fɔ:lt] N **1** (*defect*) difetto; (*mistake*) errore *m*; (*Tennis*) fault *m inv*, fallo; (*Geol*) faglia; **he has his faults, but I still like him** ha i suoi difetti, ma mi piace lo stesso; **a technical fault** un guasto tecnico; **generous to a fault** eccessivamente generoso(-a); **to find fault with sb/sth** trovare da ridire su qn/qc; **to be at fault** avere torto; **your memory is at fault** non ricordi bene **2** (*responsibility*) colpa; **it's all your fault** è tutta colpa tua; **it wasn't my fault** non è stata colpa mia; **whose fault is it (if ...)?** di chi è la colpa (se...)?
■ VT trovare da ridire su, criticare

fault-finding ['fɔ:lt,faɪndɪŋ] ADJ ipercritico(-a)
■ N critica pedante

fault·less ['fɔ:ltlɪs] ADJ (*person, behaviour*) irreprensibile; (*work, English*) impeccabile, perfetto(-a)

fault·less·ly ['fɔ:ltlɪslɪ] ADV (*gen*) perfettamente; (*dress*) in modo impeccabile

fault line N (*Geol*) linea di faglia; (*fig*) punto di contrasto

faulty ['fɔ:ltɪ] ADJ (*comp* **-ier**, *superl* **-iest**) difettoso(-a)

fau·na ['fɔ:nə] N fauna

faux pas [fəʊ'pɑ:] N gaffe *f inv*

fave [feɪv] ADJ, N (*Brit fam*) favorito(-a), preferito(-a)

fa·vor *etc* ['feɪvəʳ] (*Am*) = **favour** *etc*

◎ **fa·vour**, (*Am*) **fa·vor** ['feɪvəʳ] N **1** (*kindness*) favore *m*; **to do sb a favour** fare un favore *or* una cortesia a qn; **to ask a favour of sb** chiedere un favore a qn; **as a favour to me** per farmi un favore; **could you do me a favour?** potresti farmi un favore?; **do me a favour and close the window** fammi un favore, chiudi la finestra **2** (*approval*) favore *m*; **to be in favour (with sb)** (*person*) essere nelle grazie di qn; (*idea*) essere ben visto(-a) (da qn); **to be out of favour** (*person*) essere in disgrazia; (*idea, practice*) essere mal visto(-a); **to find favour with sb** (*subj: person*) entrare nelle buone grazie di qn; (*: suggestion*) avere l'approvazione di qn; **to gain sb's favour** *or* **gain favour with sb** guadagnarsi la stima di qn **3** (*support, advantage*) favore *m*; **to be in favour of sth** essere favorevole a qc, essere a favore di qc; **to be in favour of doing sth** essere favorevole a fare qc; **that's a point in his favour** è un punto a suo favore; **to decide in favour of sb/sth** decidere in favore di qn/qc; **to decide in favour of doing sth** decidere di fare qc; **to show favour to sb** mostrarsi parziale verso qn, favorire qn
■ VT (*approve: idea, scheme, approach*) essere a favore di; (*prefer: person, party, proposition*) preferire, essere favorevole a; (*: pupil*) favorire; (*: team*) essere per; **he eventually favoured us with a visit** finalmente ci ha fatto l'onore di una visita

fa·vour·able, (*Am*) **fa·vor·able** ['feɪvərəbl] ADJ: **favourable (to sb/sth, for doing sth)** favorevole (a qn/qc, a fare qc)

fa·vour·ably, (*Am*) **fa·vor·ably** ['feɪvərəblɪ] ADV favorevolmente

fa·voured, (*Am*) **fa·vored** ['feɪvəd] ADJ favorito(-a); **the favoured few** i pochi privilegiati

◎ **fa·vour·ite**, (*Am*) **fa·vor·ite** ['feɪvərɪt] ADJ favorito(-a), preferito(-a)
■ N favorito(-a), preferito(-a); (*Horse-racing*) favorito(-a); **it's my favourite** è il mio preferito; **it's a favourite of mine** è uno dei miei preferiti, è tra i miei favoriti; **he sang some old favourites** ha cantato dei vecchi successi

fa·vour·it·ism, (*Am*) **fa·vor·it·ism** ['feɪvərɪ,tɪzəm] N favoritismo

fawn[1] [fɔ:n] N **1** (*Zool*) cerbiatto **2** (*colour*) marroncino
■ ADJ (*also:* **fawn-coloured**) marroncino(-a)

fawn[2] [fɔ:n] VI: **to fawn (up)on sb** (*subj: dog*) fare le feste a qn; (*: person: fig*) adulare servilmente qn

fawn·ing ['fɔ:nɪŋ] ADJ (*person*) servile, untuoso(-a); (*dog*) espansivo(-a), affettuoso(-a)

fax [fæks] N (*document, machine*) facsimile *m inv*, fax *m inv*
■ VT spedire via fax, teletrasmettere; **to fax sb sth** spedire via fax qc a qn; **I'll fax you the document** ti spedirò via fax il documento

Ff

FBI [ˌɛfbiːˈaɪ] N ABBR (*Am*: = **Federal Bureau of Investigation**) FBI *f*

FCC [ˌɛfsiːsiː] N ABBR (*Am*) = *Federal Communications Commission*

FCO [ˌɛfsiːˈəʊ] N ABBR (*Brit*: = **Foreign and Commonwealth Office**) ≈ Ministero Affari Esteri

FD [ˌɛfˈdiː] N ABBR (*Am*) = **fire department**

FDA [ˌɛfdiːˈeɪ] N ABBR (*Am*: = **Food and Drug Administration**) *organismo federale statunitense per il controllo di alimenti e farmaci*

FE [ˌɛfˈiː] N ABBR (*Brit*) = **further education**

fe·al·ty [ˈfiːəltɪ] N fedeltà

◎**fear** [fɪəʳ] N paura, timore *m*; **there are fears that ...** si teme che...; **grave fears have arisen for ...** si nutrono seri timori per...; **for fear of sb/of doing sth** per paura di qn/di fare qc; **for fear that** per paura di (*or* che + *sub*); **to live in fear of sb/sth/doing sth** vivere con la paura di qn/qc/fare qc; **to go in fear of one's life/of being discovered** temere per la propria vita/di essere scoperto(-a); **fear of heights** vertigini *fpl*; **fear of enclosed spaces** claustrofobia; **have no fear!** non temere!; **in fear and trembling** tremante di paura; **to put the fear of God into sb** (*fam*) far venire una paura del diavolo a qn; **without fear nor favour** imparzialmente; **no fear!** (*fam*) neanche per sogno!; **there's no fear of that!** neanche per sogno!; **there's not much fear of his coming** non c'è pericolo che venga
■ VT (*person, God*) temere, avere paura di; **to fear the worst** temere il peggio; **to fear that** temere di (*or* che +*sub*), avere paura di (*or* che +*sub*); **I fear I/he may be late** temo di essere in ritardo/che sia in ritardo; **I fear so/not** temo di sì /di no, ho paura di sì /di no
■ VI: **to fear for** temere per, essere in ansia per

fear·ful [ˈfɪəfʊl] ADJ **1** (*frightened*): **to be fearful of** temere, avere paura di; **to be fearful that ...** temere *or* avere paura che... **2** (*frightening*: *accident*) pauroso(-a), spaventoso(-a); (: *sight, noise*) terrificante, spaventoso(-a), terribile; **there may be fearful consequences** ci potrebbero essere terribili conseguenze

fear·ful·ly [ˈfɪəfəlɪ] ADV **1** (*timidly*) timorosamente **2** (*fam*: *very*) terribilmente, spaventosamente

fear·ful·ness [ˈfɪəfʊlnɪs] N paura, timore *m*

fear·less [ˈfɪəlɪs] ADJ intrepido(-a), senza paura; **to be fearless of** non aver paura di

fear·less·ly [ˈfɪəlɪslɪ] ADV intrepidamente, senza paura

fear·less·ness [ˈfɪəlɪsnɪs] N coraggio

fear·some [ˈfɪəsəm] ADJ (*opponent*) formidabile, terribile; (*sight*) terrificante

fea·sibil·ity [ˌfiːzəˈbɪlɪtɪ] N fattibilità, attuabilità

feasibility study N studio di fattibilità, studio delle possibilità di realizzazione

fea·sible [ˈfiːzəbl] ADJ **1** (*practicable*: *plan, suggestion*) realizzabile, fattibile, attuabile **2** (*likely*: *theory, explanation*) verosimile, credibile

feast [fiːst] N (*meal*) pranzo, banchetto; (*Rel, fig*) festa; **feast day** festa, festività *f inv*
■ VT: **to feast one's eyes on sth/sb** deliziarsi alla vista di qc/qn
■ VI banchettare; **to feast on sth** banchettare a qc, gustare qc; **they feasted on exotic dishes** hanno gustato piatti esotici

feast·ing [ˈfiːstɪŋ] N banchetto

feat [fiːt] N impresa, prodezza; **a feat of engineering** un trionfo dell'ingegneria; **that was quite a feat** è stata un'impresa non da poco, non è stata un'impresa da poco

feath·er [ˈfɛðəʳ] N penna, piuma; **as light as a feather** leggero(-a) come una piuma; **that is a feather in his cap** è un fiore all'occhiello per lui; **you could have knocked me down with a feather** (*fam*) avresti potuto farmi cadere con un soffio
■ VT: **to feather one's nest** (*fig*) arricchirsi
■ ADJ (*mattress, bed, pillow*) di piuma

feather boa N boa *m inv* (di piume)

feather·brained [ˈfɛðəˌbreɪnd] ADJ sciocco(-a), sventato(-a)

feather duster N piumino

feath·ered [ˈfɛðəd] ADJ piumato(-a); **our feathered friends** i nostri amici pennuti

feather·weight [ˈfɛðəˌweɪt] (*Boxing*) ADJ dei pesi piuma
■ N peso *m* piuma *inv*

◎**fea·ture** [ˈfiːtʃəʳ] N **1** (*gen, Comm, Tech*) caratteristica **2** (*of face*): **features** NPL lineamenti *mpl*, fisionomia *fsg*, fattezze *fpl* **3** (*also*: **feature film**) film *m inv* (principale), lungometraggio **4** (*Press*) articolo, servizio speciale; **a regular feature in** (*newspapers*) un articolo che appare regolarmente in; **a (special) feature on sth/sb** un servizio speciale su qc/qn
■ VT (*person*) avere come protagonista; (*event, news*) presentare, dare risalto a
■ VI (*Cine*) apparire, essere protagonista, figurare; **it featured prominently in ...** (*gen*) ha avuto un posto di primo piano in...

fea·ture·less [ˈfiːtʃəlɪs] ADJ privo(-a) di carattere, anonimo(-a)

Feb. ABBR (= **February**) feb. (= *febbraio*)

Feb·ru·ary [ˈfɛbrʊərɪ] N febbraio; **in February** in febbraio; *for usage see* **July**

feces [ˈfiːsiːz] NPL (*Am*) = **faeces**

feck·less [ˈfɛklɪs] ADJ irresponsabile, incosciente

fe·cund [ˈfiːkənd] ADJ (*liter*) fecondo(-a)

fe·cun·dity [fɪˈkʌndɪtɪ] N fecondità

Fed [fɛd] ABBR (*Am*) **1** = **federal** **2** = **federation**

Fed. N ABBR (*Am fam*) = **Federal Reserve Board**

fed [fɛd] PT, PP *of* **feed**

◎**fed·er·al** [ˈfɛdərəl] ADJ federale

fed·eral court N *tribunale*

FEDERAL COURT

Negli Stati Uniti esistono le **federal courts** in cui si svolgono i processi per le violazioni alle leggi federali e quelli in cui il reato vede coinvolto più di uno stato, e le "state courts" per i reati contro le leggi statali. Così come ha un proprio sistema giudiziario, ogni stato ha infatti il potere di legiferare (sempre nel rispetto della Costituzione e delle leggi federali). Negli Stati Uniti non esiste la distinzione fra tribunale penale e civile.
La maggior parte delle controversie federali viene giudicata nelle "district courts", mentre 12 "Courts of Appeal" giudicano in appello le cause provenienti dalle "federal courts" di grado inferiore. Il tribunale superiore, sia a livello federale che statale, è la "Supreme Court". Nel sistema giudiziario statale esistono le "Appellate Courts" (cioè "courts of appeal"), le "county courts" e le "city courts" che hanno giurisdizione su una vasta gamma di controversie. *See also* **court**

▷ www.uscourts.gov/

Federal Republic of Germany N Repubblica Federale Tedesca

Federal Reserve Board N (*Am*) *organo di controllo del sistema bancario statunitense*
▹ www.federalreserve.gov

Federal Trade Commission N (*Am*) *organismo di tutela contro pratiche commerciali abusive*

federate [*vb* ˈfɛdəˌreɪt; *adj* ˈfɛdərɪt] VI federarsi
■ ADJ federato(-a)

◎ **fed·era·tion** [ˌfɛdəˈreɪʃən] N federazione *f*

fed up ADJ (*fam*): **to be fed up (with** *or* **of)** essere stufo(-a) (di); **to be fed up doing sth** essere stufo(-a) di fare qc

◎ **fee** [fiː] N pagamento; (*of doctor, lawyer*) onorario, parcella; (*entrance fee, membership fee*) quota d'iscrizione; **course** *or* **tuition fees** (*Univ*) tasse *fpl* universitarie; **school fees** tasse *fpl* scolastiche; (*for examination*) tassa d'esame; **for a small fee** per una somma modesta

fee·ble [ˈfiːbl] ADJ (*comp* **-er**, *superl* **-est**) (*gen*) debole; (*joke*) pietoso(-a); (*fam: person*) rammollito(-a)

feeble-minded [ˌfiːblˈmaɪndɪd] ADJ deficiente, sciocco(-a)

feeble-mindedness [ˌfiːblˈmaɪndɪdnɪs] N debolezza mentale

fee·ble·ness [ˈfiːblnɪs] N debolezza

fee·bly [ˈfiːblɪ] ADV (*move, smile*) a fatica; (*say, explain*) in modo poco convincente

◎ **feed** [fiːd] (*vb: pt, pp* **fed**) N (*baby's*) pappa; (*fodder*) mangime *m*, foraggio; (*amount, portion*) razione *f*; (*fam: meal*): **to have a good feed** fare una bella mangiata
■ VT **1** (*gen*) nutrire; (*family, horse etc*) dare da mangiare a; **have you fed the cat?** hai dato da mangiare al gatto?; **to feed sth to sb** *or* **sb sth** dare qc da mangiare a qn; **he worked hard to feed his family** lavorava sodo per mantenere la famiglia **2** (*fire, machine*) alimentare; (*information*) fornire; **to feed sth into a machine** introdurre qc in una macchina; **to feed material into sth** introdurre materiale in qc; **to feed information into a computer** introdurre dati in un computer
■ VI (*baby, animal*) mangiare; (*at breast/on bottle*) poppare; **to feed on sth** nutrirsi di qc
► **feed back** VT + ADV (*results*) riferire
► **feed in** VT + ADV (*wire, tape*) introdurre
► **feed on** VI + PREP nutrirsi di
► **feed up** VT + ADV (*person, animal*) ingrassare

feed·back [ˈfiːdˌbæk] N (*from person*) reazioni *fpl*; **to get feedback on one's work** avere un riscontro del lavoro svolto; **the feedback from customers has been positive** i clienti hanno risposto positivamente; (*from computer*) feed-back *m*

feed·er [ˈfiːdəʳ] N **1** (*baby, animal*) mangiatore(-trice); **a heavy feeder** un(-a) mangione(-a) **2** (*road, rail*) secondario(-a)

feed·ing [ˈfiːdɪŋ] N alimentazione *f*

feeding bottle N (*Brit*) biberon *m inv*, poppatoio

feeding ground N pascolo; (*for birds*) zona dove si trova da mangiare

◎ **feel** [fiːl] (*vb: pt, pp* **felt**) N (*sense of touch*) tatto; (*sensation*) sensazione *f*; (*of substance*) consistenza; **to be rough to the feel** essere ruvido(-a) al tatto; **to know sth by the feel of it** riconoscere qc al tatto; **let me have a feel!** fammi toccare!; **to get the feel of sth** (*fig*) abituarsi a qc
■ VT
1 (*touch*) tastare, sentire, toccare; **to feel sb's pulse** sentire *or* tastare il polso a qn; **to feel one's way (towards)** avanzare a tastoni (verso); **I'm still feeling my way** (*fig*) sto ancora tastando il terreno
2 (*be aware of*) sentire; (*experience: pain, pity, anger*) provare, sentire; **he doesn't feel the cold** non sente il freddo; **I didn't feel much pain** non sentivo molto dolore; **she felt a hand on her shoulder** sentì una mano sulla spalla; **I felt something move** ho sentito qualcosa che si muoveva; **we are beginning to feel the effects** cominciamo a sentire gli effetti; **I felt a great sense of relief** ho sentito un grande sollievo; **he feels the loss of his father very deeply** sta risentendo molto della morte del padre
3 (*think, believe*): **to feel (that)** credere (che), pensare (che); **I feel that you ought to do it** penso che dovresti farlo; **he felt it necessary to point out that ...** ritenne necessario far notare che...; **since you feel so strongly about it ...** visto che ci tieni tanto...; **I feel it in my bones that ...** me lo sento nelle ossa che...; **what do you feel about it?** cosa ne pensi?
■ VI
1 (*physically, mentally*) sentirsi; **to feel cold/hungry/sleepy** avere freddo/fame/sonno; **to feel ill** sentirsi male; **I don't feel well** non mi sento bene; **I feel much better** mi sento molto meglio; **to feel lonely** sentirsi solo(-a); **I felt lonely** mi sentivo solo; **she's not feeling quite herself** non si sente molto bene; **I felt (as if I was going to) faint** mi sono sentito svenire; **to feel ashamed** avere vergogna; **I feel sure that ...** sono sicuro che...; **to feel sorry for sb** dispiacersi per qn; **I feel very cross/sorry** *etc* sono molto arrabbiato/triste *ecc*; **he feels bad about leaving his wife alone** gli dispiace lasciare sola la moglie; **I feel as if there is nothing we can do** ho la sensazione che non ci possiamo fare niente; **how do you feel about him/about the idea?** che ne pensi di lui/dell'idea?; **to feel like sth/doing sth** avere voglia di qc/di fare qc; **I don't feel like going out tonight** non ho voglia di uscire stasera; **do you feel like an ice cream?** hai voglia di un gelato?; **what does it feel like to do that?** che effetto ti fa fare ciò?; **I don't feel up to (doing) it** non me la sento (di farlo); **I felt (like) a fool** mi sono sentito uno stupido; **I feel for you!** (*sympathize*) come ti capisco!
2 (*objects*): **to feel hard/cold/damp (to the touch)** essere duro(-a)/freddo(-a)/umido(-a) al tatto; **it feels soft** è morbido al tatto; **the house feels damp** la casa sembra umida; **it feels like silk** sembra seta al tatto; **it feels colder out here** sembra più freddo qui fuori; **it feels like (it might) rain** sembra che voglia piovere; **it felt like being drunk** *or* **as if I was drunk** mi sentivo come se fossi ubriaco
3 (*grope*) cercare a tastoni; **to feel about** *or* **around for** cercare a tastoni; **to feel about** *or* **around for sth in the dark** cercare a tastoni qc al buio; **to feel (about** *or* **around) in one's pocket for** frugarsi in tasca per cercare

feel·er [ˈfiːləʳ] N (*of insect, snail*) antenna; (*of octopus*) tentacolo; **to put out feelers** (*fig*) tastare il terreno

feeler gauge N spessimetro

feel·good [ˈfiːlgʊd] ADJ (*film, song*) dei buoni sentimenti

◎ **feel·ing** [ˈfiːlɪŋ] N **1** (*physical*) senso, sensazione *f*; **a cold feeling** una sensazione di freddo; **a burning feeling** una sensazione di bruciore; **to have no** *or* **to have lost all feeling in one's arm** aver perso completamente la sensibilità in un braccio
2 (*emotion*) sentimento, emozione *f*; (*sensitivity*)

Ff

sensibilità; **bad** *or* **ill feeling** ostilità, rancore *m*; **to speak/sing with feeling** parlare/cantare con sentimento; **he shows no feeling for her** non mostra nessuna simpatia per lei; **a woman of great feeling** una donna molto sensibile; **what are your feelings about the matter?** che cosa ne pensi?; **you can imagine my feelings** puoi immaginare quello che sento/ho sentito; **to hurt sb's feelings** urtare i sentimenti di qn, ferire qn; **he was afraid of hurting my feelings** aveva paura di urtare i miei sentimenti; **feelings ran high about it** la cosa aveva provocato grande eccitazione; **no hard feelings!** senza rancore! **3** *(impression)* senso, impressione *f*; **a feeling of security/isolation** un senso di sicurezza/di isolamento; **my feeling is that ...** ho l'impressione che...; **I have a (funny) feeling that ...** ho la (strana) sensazione che...; **I got the feeling that ...** ho avuto l'impressione che...; **there was a general feeling that ...** il sentimento generale era che...

feel·ing·ly ['fi:lɪŋlɪ] ADV *(speak)* infervoratamente

fee-paying ['fi:ˌpeɪɪŋ] ADJ *(pupil)* che paga; **fee-paying school** scuola privata

feet [fi:t] NPL *of* **foot**

feign [feɪn] VT *(liter)* fingere, simulare

feint [feɪnt] N finta
■ VI fare una finta

fe·lici·tous [fɪ'lɪsɪtəs] ADJ *(frm)* felice

fe·lic·ity [fɪ'lɪsɪtɪ] N *(frm)* felicità

fe·line ['fi:laɪn] ADJ felino(-a)

fell¹ [fɛl] PT *of* **fall**

fell² [fɛl] VT *(with a blow: person)* atterrare; *(: tree)* abbattere

fell³ [fɛl] ADJ: **with one fell blow** con un colpo terribile; **at one fell swoop** in un colpo solo

fell⁴ [fɛl] N *(Brit: mountain)* monte *m*; NPL *(: uplands)*: **the fells** *versante montuoso con scarsa vegetazione*; **fell-walking** passeggiate *fpl* in montagna

◎ **fel·low** ['fɛləʊ] N **1** *(fam: man, boy)* uomo, individuo, tipo; *(: boyfriend)* ragazzo; **poor fellow!** povero diavolo!; **my dear fellow** mio caro, caro mio **2** *(comrade)* compagno; *(equal)* pari *m inv* **3** *(of association, society etc)* membro; *(Univ)* ≈ docente *m/f*
■ ADJ: **fellow citizen** concittadino(-a); **fellow countryman/woman** compatriota *m/f*; **one's fellow creatures** i/le proprie simili; **fellow doctor** collega *m/f* (medico); **their fellow prisoners/students/workers** i loro compagni di prigione/studio/lavoro; **fellow men** simili *mpl*

fellow feeling N simpatia

fel·low·ship ['fɛləʊʃɪp] N *(companionship)* compagnia; *(club, society)* associazione *f*; *(Univ)*: **a research fellowship** un posto di ricercatore(-trice) all'università

fellow traveller N compagno(-a) di viaggio; *(Pol: with communists)* compagno(-a) di strada

fel·on ['fɛlən] N *(Law)* criminale *m/f*

fe·lo·ni·ous [fɪ'ləʊnɪəs] ADJ *(Law)* criminale

felo·ny ['fɛlənɪ] N *(Law)* reato, crimine *m*

felt¹ [fɛlt] PT, PP *of* **feel**

felt² [fɛlt] N feltro
■ ADJ di feltro; **felt hat** cappello di feltro

felt-tip pen ['fɛltˌtɪp'pɛn] N *(also:* **felt-tip***)*
■ N pennarello

◎ **fe·male** ['fi:meɪl] ADJ *(animal, plant, Elec)* femmina *inv*; *(subject, member, worker)* di sesso femminile; *(company, vote)* di donne; *(sex, quality, character)* femminile; **two of the puppies were female** due dei cuccioli erano femmine; **female labour** manodopera femminile; **female student/worker** studentessa/operaia; **male and female students** studenti e studentesse; **female MPs** le parlamentari
■ N *(animal, woman: pej)* femmina

female impersonator N *(Theatre) attore comico che fa parti da donna*

femi·nine ['fɛmɪnɪn] ADJ femminile; **the feminine form** *(Gram)* il femminile
■ N *(Gram)* femminile *m*; **in the feminine** al femminile

femi·nin·ity [ˌfɛmɪ'nɪnɪtɪ] N femminilità

femi·nism ['fɛmɪˌnɪzəm] N femminismo

femi·nist ['fɛmɪnɪst] ADJ, N femminista *(m/f)*

femme fatale [ˈfɛmfəˈtæl] N donna fatale

fe·mur ['fi:mə^r] N *(Anat)* femore *m*

fen [fɛn] N *(often pl: Brit)* zona paludosa; *see also* **Fens**

◎ **fence** [fɛns] N **1** recinto, steccato; *(Racing)* ostacolo; **to sit on the fence** *(fig)* rimanere neutrale **2** *(fam: receiver of stolen goods)* ricettatore(-trice)
■ VT recintare
■ VI *(Sport)* tirare di scherma
▸ **fence in** VT + ADV **1** *(field)* recintare, recingere **2** *(fig)*: **to feel fenced in** sentirsi imprigionato(-a)
▸ **fence off** VT + ADV separare con un recinto

fenced [fɛnst] ADJ recintato(-a)

fence post N palo della staccionata

fenc·er ['fɛnsə^r] N schermidore(-trice)

fenc·ing ['fɛnsɪŋ] N **1** *(Sport)* scherma; **fencing match** incontro di scherma **2** *(material)* materiale *m* per recintare

fend [fɛnd] VI: **to fend for o.s.** arrangiarsi, badare a se stesso(-a)
▸ **fend off** VT + ADV *(attack, attacker)* respingere, difendersi da; *(blow)* parare; *(awkward question)* eludere

fend·er ['fɛndə^r] N *(round fire)* paracenere *m*, parafuoco; *(Am Aut: wing)* parafango; *(Am Rail)* paraurti *m inv*; *(Naut)* parabordo

feng shui [ˌfʌŋ'ʃweɪ] N feng-shui *m inv*

fen·nel ['fɛnl] N finocchio

Fens [fɛnz] NPL *(Brit)*: **the Fens** la regione delle Fens *(regione paludosa dell'Inghilterra orientale)*

fer·ment [*n* 'fɜ:mɛnt; *vb* fə'mɛnt] N *(excitement)* eccitazione *f*, agitazione *f*, fermento; **to be in a state of ferment** essere in fermento *or* in uno stato di agitazione
■ VT far fermentare; *(fig)* fomentare
■ VI fermentare

fer·men·ta·tion [ˌfɜ:mɛn'teɪʃən] N fermentazione *f*

fer·ment·ed [ˌfə'mɛntɪd] ADJ fermentato(-a)

fern [fɜ:n] N felce *f*

fe·ro·cious [fə'rəʊʃəs] ADJ feroce

fe·ro·cious·ly [fə'rəʊʃəslɪ] ADV ferocemente, con ferocia

fe·roc·ity [fə'rɒsɪtɪ] N ferocia

fer·ret ['fɛrɪt] N furetto
■ VI cacciare con il furetto
▸ **ferret about, ferret around** VI + ADV *(fam)* frugare
▸ **ferret out** VT + ADV *(fam: secret, truth)* scoprire; *(: person)* scovare, scoprire

ferris wheel N *(Am)* ruota panoramica

fer·ro·con·crete ['fɛrəʊ'kɒŋkri:t] N cemento armato

fer·rous ['fɛrəs] ADJ ferroso(-a)

fer·rule ['fɛru:l] N puntale *m*

fer·ry ['fɛrɪ] N *(also:* **ferryboat***: small)* traghetto; *(: large: for cars etc)* nave *f inv* traghetto
■ VT: **to ferry sth/sb across** *or* **over** traghettare qc/qn

da una parte all'altra; **to ferry sb to and fro** portare qn avanti e indietro

ferry·man ['fɛrɪmən] N (*pl* **ferrymen**) traghettatore *m*

fer·tile ['fɜ:taɪl] ADJ (*gen*) fertile; (*creature, plant*) fecondo(-a); **fertile period** periodo di fecondità

fer·til·ity [fə'tɪlɪtɪ] N (*see adj*) fertilità; fecondità

fertility drug N farmaco contro la sterilità

fer·ti·li·za·tion [,fɜ:tɪlaɪ'zeɪʃən] N (*see vb*) fecondazione *f*; fertilizzazione *f*

fer·ti·lize ['fɜ:tɪ,laɪz] VT (*egg*) fecondare; (*Agr: land, soil*) fertilizzare

fer·ti·lized ['fɜ:tɪ,laɪzd] ADJ fecondato(-a)

fer·ti·liz·er ['fɜ:tɪ,laɪzə^r] N fertilizzante *m*

fer·vent ['fɜ:vənt], **fer·vid** ['fɜ:vɪd] ADJ (*believer, supporter*) fervente; (*desire*) ardente, fervido(-a); **a fervent admirer of her work** un grandissimo ammiratore del suo lavoro; **in the fervent hope that ...** sperando ardentemente che...

fer·vent·ly ['fɜ:vəntlɪ], **fer·vid·ly** ['fɜ:vɪdlɪ] ADV (*believe, support*) con passione, appassionatamente; (*desire*) intensamente, ardentemente

fer·vour, (*Am*) **fer·vor** ['fɜ:və^r] N (*frm*) fervore *m*, ardore *m*

fes·ter ['fɛstə^r] VI (*Med*) suppurare; (*anger, resentment*) covare

◎ **fes·ti·val** ['fɛstɪval] N (*Rel etc*) festa; (*Art, Mus*) festival *m inv*; **a jazz festival** un festival di musica jazz

fes·tive ['fɛstɪv] ADJ di festa; **the festive season** (*Brit: Christmas*) il periodo delle feste natalizie; **in a festive mood** di umore allegro; **a festive atmosphere** un'atmosfera di festa

fes·tiv·ity [fɛs'tɪvɪtɪ] N **1** (*festival*) festa **2** (*celebrations*): **festivities** NPL festeggiamenti *mpl*

fes·toon [fɛs'tu:n] VT: **to festoon with** ornare di, decorare con

fe·tal ['fi:tl] (*Am*) ADJ = **foetal**

fetch [fɛtʃ] VT **1** (*bring*) portare; (*go and get*) andare a prendere; (: *doctor*) andare a chiamare; **fetch the bucket** vai a prendere il secchio; **fetch it!** (*to dog*) prendi! **2** (*sell for*) essere venduto(-a) per; **how much did it fetch?** a *or* per quanto lo hai venduto?; **his painting fetched five thousand pounds** il suo quadro è stato venduto per cinquemila sterline

► **fetch in** VT + ADV (*object*) portare dentro; (*person*) far venire

► **fetch out** VT + ADV (*person*) far uscire; (*object*) tirare fuori

► **fetch up** VI + ADV (*Brit*) andare a finire

fetch·ing ['fɛtʃɪŋ] ADJ attraente

fetch·ing·ly ['fɛtʃɪŋlɪ] ADV (*dressed*) graziosamente

fête [feɪt] N festa all'aperto (*spesso a scopo di beneficenza*)
■ VT festeggiare

fet·id ['fɛtɪd], **foet·id** ['fi:tɪd] ADJ (*frm*) fetido(-a)

fet·ish ['fɛtɪʃ] N (*obsession*) fissazione *f*, mania; (*object of cult*) feticcio

fet·ish·ism ['fɛtɪʃɪzəm] N feticismo

fet·ish·ist ['fɛtɪʃɪst] N feticista *m/f*

fet·lock ['fɛt,lɒk] N (*joint*) nocca; (*hair*) barbetta

fet·ter ['fɛtə^r] VT (*person*) incatenare; (*fig*) ostacolare

fet·ters ['fɛtəz] NPL catene *fpl*; (*fig*) restrizioni *fpl*

fet·tle ['fɛtl] N (*Brit*): **in fine fettle** in gran forma

fe·tus ['fi:təs] (*Am*) N = **foetus**

feud [fju:d] N faida, contesa, lotta; **a family feud** una faida familiare
■ VI: **to feud (with sb)** essere in lotta (con qn)

feu·dal ['fju:dl] ADJ feudale

feu·dal·ism ['fju:də,lɪzəm] N feudalesimo

fe·ver ['fi:və^r] N **1** (*high temperature*) febbre *f*; **he has a fever** ha la febbre; **a bout of fever** un accesso di febbre; **a high/slight fever** una febbre alta/leggera **2** (*excitement*) eccitazione *f*; **gambling fever** (*fig*) la febbre del gioco; **in a fever of excitement** in uno stato di eccitazione febbrile; **fever pitch** il colmo; **excitement has reached fever pitch** l'eccitazione ha raggiunto il colmo

fe·vered ['fi:vəd] ADJ febbrile; (*person*) febbricitante

fe·ver·ish ['fi:vərɪʃ] ADJ (*also fig*) febbrile; (*person*) febbricitante; **the little girl was feverish** la bambina era febbricitante; **feverish preparations** preparativi *mpl* febbrili

fe·ver·ish·ly ['fi:vərɪʃlɪ] ADV (*fig*) febbrilmente

◎ **few** [fju:] ADJ (*comp* **-er**, *superl* **-est**)
■ PRON **1** (*not many*) pochi(-e); **few books** pochi libri; **he has few friends** ha pochi amici; **few of them** pochi di loro; **few (people) managed to do it** pochi riuscirono a farlo; **few succeed** pochi ci riescono; **she is one of the few (people) who ...** è una delle poche persone che...; **the few who ...** i pochi che...; **in** *or* **over the past few days** in questi ultimi giorni, negli ultimi giorni; **in** *or* **over the next few days** nei prossimi giorni; **every few days/months** ogni due o tre giorni/ mesi; **with few exceptions** con *or* salvo poche eccezioni; **every few weeks** a intervalli di qualche settimana; **they are few and far between** sono rari; **there are very few of us** *or* **we are very few** siamo pochi; **the last** *or* **remaining few minutes** i pochi minuti che rimangono; **as few as three of them** solo tre di loro; **too few** troppo pochi; **there were three too few** ne mancavano tre **2** (*some, several*): **a few** alcuni(-e), qualche; **a few books** alcuni libri, qualche libro; **I invited a few old friends** ho invitato alcuni vecchi amici; **I know a few** ne conosco alcuni; **a few of them** alcuni di loro; **a few more days** qualche altro giorno; **in a few more days** fra qualche giorno; **a good few** *or* **quite a few** parecchi; **a good few** *or* **quite a few books** parecchi libri, un bel po' di libri; **quite a few people** un bel po' di gente; **a good few** *or* **quite a few (people) came** è venuta un bel po' di gente

few·er ['fju:ə^r] ADJ, PRON, COMP *of* **few** meno *inv*, meno numerosi(-e); **fewer than 10** meno di 10; **fewer than you** meno di te; **no fewer than ...** non meno di...; **there are fewer of them now** adesso ce ne sono di meno; **there were fewer people than yesterday** c'era meno gente di ieri

few·est ['fju:ɪst] ADJ, PRON, SUPERL *of* **few** il minor numero di; **we were fewest in number** eravamo i meno numerosi

fez [fɛz] N (*pl* **fezzes**) fez *m inv*

FFA [,ɛfɛf'eɪ] N ABBR = *Future Farmers of America*

FH ABBR (*Brit*) = **fire hydrant**

FHA [,ɛfeɪtʃ'eɪ] N ABBR (*Am*) = *Federal Housing Administration*

fi·an·cé [fi:ɑ̃ŋseɪ] N fidanzato

fi·an·cée [fi:ɑ̃ŋseɪ] N fidanzata

fi·as·co [fɪ'æskəʊ] N fiasco

fiat ['faɪət] N (*frm*) ordine *m*

fib [fɪb] (*fam*) N bugia, frottola; **to tell a fib** dire una bugia
■ VI dire bugie, raccontare storie

fib·ber ['fɪbə^r] N (*fam*) bugiardo(-a)

fi·bre, (*Am*) **fi·ber** ['faɪbə^r] N fibra

fibre·board, (*Am*) **fiber·board** ['faɪbə,bɔ:d] N pannello di fibre

Ff

fibre·glass, (*Am*) **fiber·glass** [ˈfaɪbəˌglɑːs] N fibra di vetro
■ ADJ di fibra di vetro
fibre optics NSG ottica a fibre
fi·bril·la·tion [ˌfaɪbrɪˈleɪʃən] N fibrillazione *f*
fi·broid [ˈfaɪbrɔɪd] N fibroma *m*
fi·bro·ma [faɪˈbrəʊmə] N fibroma *m*
fi·bro·sis [faɪˈbrəʊsɪs] N fibrosi *f*
fi·bro·si·tis [ˌfaɪbrəˈsaɪtɪs] N fibrosite *f*, cellulite *f*
fi·brous [ˈfaɪbrəs] ADJ fibroso(-a)
fi·brous·ness [ˈfaɪbrəsnɪs] N fibrosità
fibu·la [ˈfɪbjʊlə] N (*Anat*) fibula, perone *m*
fick·le [ˈfɪkl] ADJ incostante, volubile
fick·le·ness [ˈfɪklnɪs] N incostanza, volubilità
fic·tion [ˈfɪkʃən] N **1** (*Literature*) narrativa; **a work of fiction** un'opera di narrativa; **light fiction** narrativa leggera **2** (*sth made up*) finzione *f*

DID YOU KNOW ...?
fiction is not translated by the Italian word ***fiction***

fic·tion·al [ˈfɪkʃənl] ADJ immaginario(-a)
fictionalize [ˈfɪkʃənəˌlaɪz] VT romanzare
fic·tion·al·ized [ˈfɪkʃənəˌlaɪzd] ADJ romanzato(-a)
fic·ti·tious [fɪkˈtɪʃəs] ADJ **1** = **fictional** **2** (*false*) falso(-a), fittizio(-a)
fic·ti·tious·ly [fɪkˈtɪʃəslɪ] ADV in modo fittizio
fid·dle [ˈfɪdl] N **1** (*violin*) violino; **to play second fiddle to sb** (*fig*) avere un ruolo di secondo piano rispetto a qn **2** (*fam: cheating*) imbroglio, truffa; **it's a fiddle** è un imbroglio; **tax fiddle** frode *f* fiscale; **an insurance fiddle** una truffa assicurativa; **to work a fiddle** fare un imbroglio; **to be on the fiddle** imbrogliare
■ VI (*fidget*) giocherellare, gingillarsi; **do stop fiddling!** stai fermo!; **to fiddle (about) with sth** giocherellare/gingillarsi con qc
■ VT (*Brit fam: accounts, results etc*) falsificare, alterare
▸ **fiddle about, fiddle around** VT + ADV gingillarsi, giocherellare
fid·dler [ˈfɪdləʳ] N **1** (*Mus*) violinista *m/f* **2** (*fam: cheat*) imbroglione(-a)
fiddle·sticks [ˈfɪdlˌstɪks] EXCL (*old*): **fiddlesticks!** sciocchezze!
fid·dling [ˈfɪdlɪŋ] ADJ insignificante; **fiddling little job** lavoretto
■ N (*fam: cheating*) imbrogli *mpl*
fid·dly [ˈfɪdlɪ] ADJ (*comp* **-ier**, *superl* **-iest**) (*task*) da certosino; (*object*) complesso(-a)
fi·del·ity [fɪˈdelɪtɪ] N (*in relationships*) fedeltà; (*accuracy*) esattezza, accuratezza
fidg·et [ˈfɪdʒɪt] N (*person*) persona irrequieta; **to have the fidgets** essere irrequieto(-a) *or* agitato(-a)
■ VI (*also:* **fidget about** *or* **around**) agitarsi; **to fidget with sth** giocherellare con qc
fidg·ety [ˈfɪdʒɪtɪ] ADJ agitato(-a), irrequieto(-a)
fi·du·ci·ary [fɪˈduːʃɪərɪ] ADJ, N (*Law*) fiduciario(-a)
fief [fiːf] N feudo
◎ **field** [fiːld] N (*gen, Comput*) campo; (*Geol*) giacimento; (*sphere of activity*) campo, settore *m*; **a field of wheat** un campo di grano; **to give sth a year's trial in the field** (*fig*) sperimentare qc sul campo per un anno; **to study sth in the field** osservare *or* studiare qc sul campo; **to die in the field** (*Mil*) cadere sul campo di battaglia; **to take the field** (*Sport*) scendere in campo; **to lead the field** (*Sport, Comm*) essere in testa, essere al primo posto; **my particular field** la mia specialità, il mio campo *or* settore; **field of vision** campo visivo
■ VT (*team*) far giocare, far scendere in campo; (*Cricket: catch: ball*) prendere
field day N (*Mil*) giorno di grandi manovre; **to have a field day** (*fig*) divertirsi, spassarsela
field·er [ˈfiːldəʳ] N (*Cricket*) *giocatore che deve afferrare e rilanciare la palla*
field events NPL (*Athletics*) atletica leggera
field·fare [ˈfiːldˈfɛəʳ] N (*Zool*) viscarda
field glasses NPL (*binoculars*) binocolo
field hockey N (*Am*) hockey *m inv* (su prato)
field hospital N ospedale *m* da campo
field marshal N feldmaresciallo
field mushroom N prataiolo
field sports NPL caccia e pesca
field-test [ˈfiːldˌtɛst] N prova pratica
■ VT testare sul campo
field·work [ˈfiːldˌwɜːk] N (*Sociol etc*) ricerche *fpl* esterne; (*Archeol, Geog, Geol*) lavoro sul campo
fiend [fiːnd] N demonio; **you little fiend!** (*fam*) piccolo delinquente!; **a tennis fiend** un fanatico *or* patito del tennis
fiend·ish [ˈfiːndɪʃ] ADJ (*cruelty, smile, plot*) diabolico(-a); (*fam: difficult and unpleasant*) tremendo(-a); **I had a fiendish time trying to ...** è stato un lavoraccio tentare di...
fiend·ish·ly [ˈfiːndɪʃlɪ] ADV (*see adj*) diabolicamente; tremendamente
◎ **fierce** [fɪəs] ADJ (*comp* **-er**, *superl* **-est**) (*gen*) feroce; (*opponent*) accanito(-a); (*enemy*) acerrimo(-a); (*look, fighting*) fiero(-a); (*wind, storm*) furioso(-a); (*heat*) intenso(-a); **a fierce Alsatian** un feroce cane lupo; **there's fierce competition between companies** c'è una concorrenza spietata tra società; **a fierce attack** un violento attacco
fierce·ly [ˈfɪəslɪ] ADV (*extremely*) intensamente; (*fight*) con accanimento; (*rage*) furiosamente
fierce·ness [ˈfɪəsnɪs] N (*also fig*) ferocia; (*of heat*) intensità
fiery [ˈfaɪərɪ] ADJ (*comp* **-ier**, *superl* **-iest**) (*gen*) infocato(-a), ardente; (*red*) di fuoco; (*temperament, temper, person*) focoso(-a); (*liquor*) che brucia la gola
fi·es·ta [fɪˈɛstə] N fiesta *f inv*
FIFA [ˈfiːfə] N ABBR (= **Fédération Internationale de Football Association**) FIFA *f*
◎ **fif·teen** [fɪfˈtiːn] ADJ quindici *inv*; **about fifteen people** una quindicina di persone
■ N quindici *m inv*; (*Rugby*) squadra; *for usage see* **five**
◎ **fif·teenth** [fɪfˈtiːnθ] ADJ quindicesimo(-a)
■ N (*in series*) quindicesimo(-a); (*fraction*) quindicesimo; *for usage see* **fifth**
◎ **fifth** [fɪfθ] ADJ quinto(-a); **the fifth floor** il quinto piano; **I was (the) fifth to arrive** sono stato il quinto ad arrivare; **he came fifth in the competition** è arrivato quinto al concorso, si è piazzato al quinto posto; **Henry the Fifth** Enrico Quinto; **the fifth of July, July the fifth** il cinque luglio; **I wrote to him on the fifth** gli ho scritto il cinque; **fifth form** (*Brit Scol*) ≈ terzo anno di scuola superiore
■ N (*in series*) quinto(-a); (*fraction*) quinto; (*Mus*) quinta
fifth column N (*Pol*) quinta colonna
fifth columnist N appartenente *m/f* alla quinta colonna
◎ **fif·ti·eth** [ˈfɪftɪɪθ] ADJ cinquantesimo(-a)
■ N (*in series*) cinquantesimo(-a); (*fraction*) cinquantesimo; *for usage see* **fifth**
◎ **fif·ty** [ˈfɪftɪ] ADJ cinquanta *inv*; **about fifty people/cars** una cinquantina di persone/di macchine; **he'll**

be fifty (years old) next birthday al prossimo compleanno avrà/compirà cinquant'anni; **he's about fifty** è sulla cinquantina

■ N cinquanta *m inv*; **the fifties** (*1950s*) gli anni cinquanta; **to be in one's fifties** avere passato la cinquantina; **the temperature was in the fifties** la temperatura era al di sopra dei cinquanta gradi (Fahrenheit); **to do fifty** (*Aut*) andare a 50 (all'ora)

fifty-fifty ['fɪftɪ'fɪftɪ] ADJ, ADV: **to go fifty-fifty with sb** fare a metà con qn; **they split the prize money fifty-fifty** hanno diviso a metà i soldi del premio; **we have a fifty-fifty chance of success** abbiamo una probabilità su due di successo

fig [fɪg] N fico

◎ **fight** [faɪt] (*vb: pt, pp* **fought**) N (*Mil*) combattimento, lotta; (*Boxing*) incontro; (*between 2 persons*) lite *f*; (*brawl*) zuffa, rissa; (*fighting spirit*) combattività; (*struggle, campaign*): **fight (for/against)** lotta (a favore di/ contro); (*argument*): **fight (over)** disputa (su); **Muhammad Ali's last fight** l'ultimo incontro di Muhammad Ali; **there was a fight in the pub** c'è stata una rissa al pub; **to have a fight with sb** (*quarrel, struggle*) avere una lite con qn, litigare con qn; **she had a fight with her best friend** ha litigato con la sua migliore amica; **to put up a good fight** battersi *or* difendersi bene; **there was no fight left in him** aveva perduto la sua combattività; **the fight against cancer** la lotta contro il cancro

■ VT (*Mil: enemy, battle*) combattere; (*fire, disease, proposals*) lottare contro, combattere; (*Law: case*) difendere; **she has fought racism all her life** ha lottato per tutta la vita contro il razzismo; **to fight a duel** battersi in duello; **to fight one's way through a crowd/across a room** farsi strada a fatica tra la folla/ attraverso una stanza

■ VI (*person*) azzuffarsi; (*animal*) battersi; (*troops, countries*): **to fight (against)** combattere (contro); (*quarrel*): **to fight (with sb)** litigare (con qn); (*fig*): **to fight (for/against)** lottare (per/contro); **the fans started fighting** i tifosi hanno cominciato ad azzuffarsi; **the demonstrators fought with the police** i dimostranti si sono scontrati con la polizia; **to fight for one's life** lottare per la (propria) vita; **let us fight for peace** lottiamo per la pace; **they fight sometimes, but they're good friends** a volte litigano ma sono buoni amici

▶ **fight back** VI + ADV difendersi; (*Sport, after illness*) riprendersi; **the attackers ran away when the man fought back** gli assalitori sono scappati quando l'uomo ha reagito

■ VT + ADV (*tears*) trattenere; (*anger*) reprimere; (*despair, doubts*) scacciare

▶ **fight down** VT + ADV (*anger, anxiety*) vincere; (*urge*) reprimere

▶ **fight off** VT + ADV (*attack, attacker*) respingere; (*disease, sleep, urge*) lottare contro

▶ **fight on** VI + ADV continuare a combattere

▶ **fight out** VT + ADV: **to fight it out** risolvere la questione a pugni

◎ **fight·er** ['faɪtə^r] N combattente *m/f*; (*plane*) caccia *m inv*; **he's a fighter for the cause of ...** lotta per la causa di...

fighter-bomber ['faɪtə'bɒmə^r] N cacciabombardiere *m*

fighter pilot N pilota *m* di caccia

fight·ing ['faɪtɪŋ] N (*Mil*) combattimento; (*in streets*) scontri *mpl*; (*in pub etc*) risse *fpl*, zuffe *fpl*; **fighting broke out outside the pub** è scoppiata una rissa fuori dal pub

■ ADJ (*forces, strength, troops*) da combattimento; **fighting spirit** spirito combattivo; **a fighting chance** una buona probabilità

fig leaf N foglia di fico

fig·ment ['fɪgmənt] N: **it's a figment of the imagination** è frutto dell'immaginazione, è un parto della fantasia

fig·ura·tive ['fɪgərətɪv] ADJ (*meaning*) figurato(-a); (*Art*) figurativo(-a)

fig·ura·tive·ly ['fɪgərətɪvlɪ] ADV in modo figurato

◎ **fig·ure** ['fɪgə^r] N **1** (*number*) cifra; **to be good at figures** essere bravo(-a) a fare i conti; **a mistake in the figures** un errore nei calcoli, un errore di calcolo; **can you give me the exact figures?** puoi darmi le cifre esatte?; **to reach double/three figures** raggiungere le due/tre cifre **2** (*body, outline*) figura, forma; **he's a fine figure of a man** è un bell'uomo; **he cuts a fine figure** ha molta classe; **she's got a good figure** ha una bella figura; **to lose one's figure** perdere la linea; **I have to watch my figure** devo stare attenta alla linea **3** (*person*) figura, personaggio; **public figure** personaggio pubblico; **she's an important political figure** è un importante personaggio politico **4** (*drawing, Geom*) figura; (*diagram*) illustrazione *f*

■ VI **1** (*appear*) figurare **2** (*esp Am: make sense*) essere logico(-a), spiegarsi; **that figures!** (*fam*) è logico!

■ VT (*esp Am: think, calculate*) pensare, immaginare

▶ **figure on** VI + PREP (*Am*) contare su; **I figured on him arriving by 6 o'clock** contavo sul fatto che sarebbe arrivato alle 6

▶ **figure out** VT + ADV (*understand*) riuscire a capire; (*calculate: sum*) calcolare; **I just can't figure it out!** non ci arrivo!

figure·head ['fɪgəˌhɛd] N (*Naut*) polena; (*fig*) figura rappresentativa; (*pej*) prestanome *m/f inv*; **he's little more than a figurehead** è poco più che un prestanome

figure-hugging ['fɪgəˌhʌgɪŋ] ADJ (*dress*) fasciante

figure of eight N un otto

figure of speech N figura retorica; **it's just a figure of speech** (*fig*) è solo un modo di dire

figure skating N pattinaggio artistico

figu·rine [ˌfɪgə'riːn] N figurina, statuetta

Fiji ['fiːdʒiː] N: **the Fiji Islands** le isole *fpl* Figi

fila·ment ['fɪləmənt] N filamento

filch [fɪltʃ] VT (*fam: steal*) grattare

◎ **file¹** [faɪl] N (*folder*) cartella, cartellina; (*ring binder*) raccoglitore *m*; (*dossier*) pratica, incartamento; (*in cabinet*) scheda; (*Comput*) file *m inv*; **there was stuff in that file that was private** c'erano delle cose riservate in quella pratica; **the police have a file on him** è schedato dalla polizia; **she put the photocopy into her file** ha messo la fotocopia nella sua cartella

■ VT **1** (*also:* **file away**: *notes, information, papers*) raccogliere; (: *under heading*) archiviare **2** (*Law: claim, application, complaint*) presentare; **to file a suit against sb** (*Law*) intentare causa contro qn

file² [faɪl] N (*tool*) lima; (*for nails*) lima, limetta

■ VT (*metal, wood*) limare; **to file one's nails** limarsi le unghie; **she was filing her nails** si stava limando le unghie

file³ [faɪl] N (*row*) fila; **in single file** in fila indiana

■ VI: **to file in/out** entrare/uscire in fila; **to file past**

Ff

(**sth/sb**) sfilare (davanti a qc/qn), marciare in fila (davanti a qc/qn)

file clerk N = filing clerk

file extension N (*Comput*) estensione *f* del file

file manager N (*Comput*) programma *m* di gestione file

file name N (*Comput*) nome (del) file

file server N (*Comput*) server *m inv*

file-sharing ['faɪlˌʃɛərɪŋ] N (*Comput*) file-sharing *mpl*, condivisione *f* di informazioni in Internet

fil·ial ['fɪljəl] ADJ filiale

fili·bus·ter ['fɪlɪˌbʌstəʳ] (*esp Am Pol*) N ostruzionismo

■ VI fare ostruzionismo

fili·bus·ter·er ['fɪlɪˌbʌstərəʳ] N (*esp Am Pol*) ostruzionista *m/f*

fili·gree ['fɪlɪgri:] N filigrana

■ ADJ a filigrana

fil·ing ['faɪlɪŋ] N archiviazione *f*; *see also* **filings**

filing cabinet N schedario, casellario

filing clerk, (*Am*) **file clerk** N archivista *m/f*

fil·ings ['faɪlɪŋz] NPL limatura

Fili·pi·no [ˌfɪlɪ'pi:nəʊ] ADJ filippino(-a)

■ N **1** (*person*) filippino(-a) **2** (*language*) tagal *m*

◎ **fill** [fɪl] VT (*gen*) riempire; (*tooth*) otturare; (*position*) coprire; (*subj: wind: sails*) gonfiare; (*supply: order, requirements, need*) soddisfare; **to fill with** riempire di *or* con; **she filled the glass with water** ha riempito il bicchiere d'acqua; **we've already filled that vacancy** abbiamo già assunto qualcuno per quel posto; **they asked her to fill the vacancy** le hanno offerto il posto; **the position is already filled** il posto è già preso; **filled with admiration (for)** pieno(-a) di ammirazione (per); **filled with remorse/despair** in preda al rimorso/alla disperazione; **that fills the bill** è quello che ci vuole

■ VI: **to fill (with)** riempirsi (di *or* con)

■ N: **to eat/drink one's fill** mangiare/bere a sazietà; **to have one's fill of sth** (*fig*) averne le tasche piene di qc

▸ **fill in** VT + ADV **1** (*hole, gap, outline*) riempire **2** (*one's name*) mettere; (*form*) riempire, compilare; (*details, report*) completare; **can you fill this form in, please?** può riempire questo modulo, per favore?; **to fill sb in on sth** (*fam*) mettere qn al corrente di qc; **I'll fill you in on what's been happening** ti metterò al corrente su quello che succede

■ VI + ADV: **to fill in for sb** sostituire qn

▸ **fill out** VT + ADV (*form, receipt*) riempire, compilare

■ VI + ADV (*person, face*) ingrassare, ingrassarsi; (*sail*) gonfiarsi

▸ **fill up** VI + ADV **1** (*Aut*) fare il pieno **2** (*room etc*) riempirsi, gremirsi

■ VT + ADV (*container*) riempire; **fill it** *or* **her up, please** (*fam: Aut*) mi faccia il pieno, per piacere

filled [fɪld] ADJ: **filled with** (*room*) completamente occupato(-a) da; **to be filled with resentment** essere colmo(-a) di rancore; **eyes filled with tears** occhi pieni di lacrime

fill·er ['fɪləʳ] N (*for cracks: in wood, plaster*) stucco

fil·let ['fɪlɪt] N filetto

■ VT (*meat*) disossare; (*fish*) tagliare a filetti, sfilettare; **filleted cod** filetti *mpl* di merluzzo

fillet steak N (bistecca di) filetto

fill·ing ['fɪlɪŋ] N (*for tooth*) otturazione *f*; (*Culin*) ripieno

■ ADJ (*food*) sostanzioso(-a)

filling station N stazione *f* di rifornimento

fil·lip ['fɪlɪp] N stimolo, incentivo

fil·ly ['fɪlɪ] N puledra

◎ **film** [fɪlm] N **1** (*at cinema*) film *m inv*; (*Phot*) pellicola; **a 36 exposure film** un rullino da 36 pose *or* foto; **film buff** appassionato(-a) di cinema; **film camera** macchina da presa **2** (*thin layer*) strato sottile, velo; (*wrap*) pellicola

■ VT (*scene*) filmare

film crew N troupe *f inv* cinematografica

film·ing ['fɪlmɪŋ] N: **filming started last week** hanno cominciato a girare (il film) la settimana scorsa

film library N cineteca

film noir [-nwa:] N film noir *m inv*

film rights NPL diritti *mpl* di produzione

film script N copione *m*

film·set ['fɪlmˌsɛt] VT (*Typ*) fotocomporre

film·setting ['fɪlmˌsɛtɪŋ] N (*Typ*) fotocomposizione *f*

film star N divo(-a) del cinema

film·strip ['fɪlmˌstrɪp] N filmina

film studio N studio cinematografico

film theatre N cineteca

filmy ['fɪlmɪ] ADJ trasparente

fi·lo ['fi:ləʊ] N (*Culin: also:* **filo pastry**) sottile pasta sfoglia (*usata nella cucina greca*)

Filo·fax® ['faɪləʊˌfæks] N filofax *f inv*; *agenda ad anelli*

fil·ter ['fɪltəʳ] N filtro

■ VT filtrare

■ VI: **to filter to the left** (*Aut*) immettersi nella corsia di svincolo

▸ **filter in**, **filter out**, **filter through** VI + ADV (*news*) trapelare; **the news started to filter out** le notizie hanno cominciato a trapelare

filter coffee N caffè *m* da passare al filtro

filter feeding N (*Bio*) filtrazione *f*

filter lane N (*Brit Aut*) corsia di svincolo

filter light N (*Brit Aut*) freccia di svolta continua (*nei semafori*)

filter paper N carta da filtro *or* filtrante

filter tip N filtro

filter-tipped ['fɪltəˌtɪpt] ADJ con filtro

filth [fɪlθ] N sudiciume *m*, sporcizia; (*fig*) oscenità; **mess and filth** disordine e sporcizia; **it's just sheer filth** non è altro che una porcheria; **the film is full of filth** il film è pieno di oscenità

filthi·ness ['fɪlθɪnɪs] N (*of room, person*) sporcizia; (*of language*) sudiceria

filthy ['fɪlθɪ] ADJ (*comp* **-ier**, *superl* **-iest**) sudicio(-a), sozzo(-a); (*language*) volgare, osceno(-a); **a filthy joke** una barzelletta sporca; **what filthy weather!** che tempaccio!; **he's got a filthy mind** è uno sporcaccione

fin [fɪn] N (*of fish*) pinna; (*of plane, bomb*) impennaggio verticale

◎ **fi·nal** ['faɪnl] ADJ (*last*) ultimo(-a); (*conclusive*) finale, definitivo(-a); (*victory*) conclusivo(-a); (*exam*) finale; **a final attempt** un ultimo tentativo; **a final decision** una decisione definitiva; **final demand** (*Comm*) ingiunzione *f* (di pagamento); **the judge's decision is final** la decisione del giudice è inappellabile; **... and that's final!** ...e basta!; **I'm not going and that's final!** non ci vado e basta!

■ N (*Sport*) finale *f*; *see also* **finals** **Federer is in the final** Federer è in finale

fi·na·le [fɪ'nɑ:lɪ] N finale *m*; **the grand finale** (*also fig*) il gran finale

fi·nal·ist ['faɪnəlɪst] N (*Sport*) finalista *m/f*

fi·nal·ity [faɪ'nælɪtɪ] N irrevocabilità; **with an air of finality** con risolutezza

fi·na·li·za·tion [,faɪnəlaɪ'zeɪʃən] N (*see vb*) messa a punto; definizione *f*; stesura definitiva

fi·nal·ize ['faɪnə,laɪz] VT (*preparations, arrangements, plans*) mettere a punto; (*agreement, decision, contract*) definire; (*report, text*) dare una stesura definitiva a; (*date*) fissare

◎**fi·nal·ly** ['faɪnəlɪ] ADV (*lastly*) alla fine; (*in conclusion*) infine; (*eventually*) finalmente; (*once and for all*) definitivamente; **finally, I would like to say ...** vorrei dire, infine...; **they finally decided to leave on Saturday** alla fine hanno deciso di partire sabato; **the food finally arrived** finalmente arrivò da mangiare; **and finally...** e per concludere...

fi·nals ['faɪnlz] NPL (*Univ*) esami *mpl* dell'ultimo anno

◎**fi·nance** [faɪ'næns] N **1** (*money management*) finanza; (*funds*) fondi *mpl*, capitale *m*; **Minister of Finance** Ministro delle Finanze; **small businesses have difficulty getting finance** le piccole imprese hanno difficoltà a reperire fondi; **finance is usually the main problem for students** i soldi sono in genere il problema principale degli studenti **2** (*resources*): **finances** NPL finanze *fpl*
■VT finanziare
■ADJ (*page, section, company*) finanziario(-a)

finance company N (società *f inv*) finanziaria

◎**fi·nan·cial** [faɪ'nænʃəl] ADJ finanziario(-a); **financial management** gestione *f* finanziaria; **financial statement** estratto conto finanziario

financial adviser N consulente *m/f* finanziario(-a)

fi·nan·cial·ly [faɪ'nænʃəlɪ] ADV finanziariamente

financial services NPL società *f inv* di servizi finanziari

financial year N anno finanziario, esercizio finanziario

fi·nan·ci·er [fɪ'nænsɪə^r] N finanziatore(-trice)

finch [fɪntʃ] N fringillide *m*

◎**find** [faɪnd] (*vb: pt, pp* **found**) VT
1 (*gen*) trovare; (*sth lost*) trovare, ritrovare; (*learn*) scoprire; **I can't find the exit** non riesco a trovare l'uscita; **I've found it** l'ho trovato; **the book is nowhere to be found** il libro non si trova da nessuna parte; **this plant is found all over Europe** questa pianta si trova in tutta Europa; **it has been found that ...** è stato *or* si è scoperto che...; **if you can find the time** se riesci a trovare il tempo; **no cure has been found** non è stata trovata nessuna cura; **I found it impossible to tell the difference** non riuscivo a distinguerli; **he finds it easy/difficult to do ...** non trova/trova difficoltà a *or* nel fare...; **to find (some) difficulty in doing sth** trovare delle difficoltà nel fare qc; **I find him very pleasant** lo trovo molto simpatico; **we found him in bed/reading** l'abbiamo trovato a letto/che stava leggendo; **I found myself at a loss** non sapevo cosa dire, non riuscivo a trovare le parole; **can you find your (own) way to the station?** sai come andare alla stazione?; **this found its way into my drawer** questo è andato a finire nel mio cassetto; **leave everything as you find it** lascia tutto come trovi; **to find fault with sb/sth** trovare da ridire sul conto di qn/su qc; **to find sb guilty** (*Law*) giudicare qn colpevole; **he was found innocent** (*Law*) fu dichiarato innocente; **to find one's feet** (*fig*) ambientarsi
2 (*obtain*) trovare; **go and find me a pencil** vai a cercarmi una matita; **there are no more to be found** non ce ne sono più; **wages all found** stipendio più vitto e alloggio
■VI (*Law*): **to find for/against sb** emettere un verdetto a favore di/contro qn
■N scoperta, trovata
▸ **find out** VT + ADV informarsi di; (*truth, secret, answer*) scoprire; **to find out that ...** scoprire che...; **to find sb out** smascherare qn
■VI + ADV: **to find out about** scoprire; (*by investigation*) informarsi su; **we found out about his death** abbiamo scoperto che era morto; **we found out all about ...** abbiamo scoperto tutto su...; **she'll be furious when she finds out about it** sarà furiosa quando lo scoprirà; **find out as much as possible about the town** informati il più possibile sulla città

find·ings ['faɪndɪŋz] NPL (*of report, of inquiry*) conclusioni *fpl*; (*Law*) verdetto

◎**fine**[1] [faɪn] ADJ (*comp* **-r**, *superl* **-st**) **1** (*small, delicate, narrow*) fine; (*rain*) leggero(-a); (*fig: distinction*) sottile; **not to put too fine a point on it** per dirlo con schiettezza; **he's got it down to a fine art** lo fa alla perfezione **2** (*not coarse: metal*) fino(-a); (*: sense*) sottile; (*: taste*) raffinato(-a); (*: feelings*) elevato(-a); **she's got very fine hair** ha i capelli molto sottili; **fine workmanship** lavorazione *f* raffinata **3** (*good*) ottimo(-a); (*beautiful, imposing*) bello(-a); (*clothes*) elegante; **if the weather is fine** se il tempo è bello; **it's a fine day today** è una bella giornata oggi; **he's a fine man** è un'ottima persona; **it'll be ready tomorrow. – that's fine, thanks** sarà pronto domani. – va bene, grazie; **he's fine** sta bene; **how are you? – fine, thanks!** come stai? – bene, grazie!; **I feel fine** mi sento bene; **a fine friend you are!** bell'amico sei!; **you're a fine one to talk!** senti chi parla!; **a fine thing!** bella roba!; **one fine day** un bel giorno
■ADV **1** (*well*) molto bene; **you're doing fine** te la cavi benissimo **2** (*finely*) finemente; **to cut it fine** (*of time, money*) farcela per un pelo
▸ **fine down** VT + ADV affinare

fine[2] [faɪn] N multa; **to get a fine for sth/doing sth** ricevere una multa per qc/per aver fatto qc
■VT: **to fine sb (for sth/for doing sth)** multare qn *or* fare una multa a qn (per qc/per aver fatto qc)

fine arts NPL: **the fine arts** (le) belle arti *fpl*

fine·ly ['faɪnlɪ] ADV **1** (*written, sewn*) con raffinatezza **2** (*chop*) finemente; (*adjust*) con precisione

fine·ness ['faɪnnɪs] N (*of silk*) finezza, sottigliezza

fine print N: **the fine print** i caratteri minuti

fin·ery ['faɪnərɪ] N abiti *mpl* eleganti; **to be dressed in all one's finery** essere tutto(-a) in ghingheri

fi·nesse [fɪ'nɛs] N finezza; (*Cards*) impasse *f*

fine-tooth comb ['faɪn,tu:θ'kəʊm] N: **to go through sth with a fine-tooth comb** (*fig*) passare qc al setaccio

◎**fin·ger** ['fɪŋgə^r] N dito; **a ring on every finger** un anello su ogni dito; **my little finger** il mignolo; **his fingers are all thumbs** *or* **he is all fingers and thumbs** è molto maldestro; **keep your fingers crossed** fai gli scongiuri; **they never laid a finger on her** non l'hanno mai nemmeno toccata; **he didn't lift a finger to help** non ha mosso un dito per aiutare; **I can't quite put my finger on what's wrong** non riesco a vedere cosa c'è di sbagliato; **to twist sb round one's little finger** fare quello che si vuole di qn; **to have a finger in every pie** avere le mani in pasta dappertutto; **to pull one's finger out** (*fig fam*) darsi una mossa
■VT toccare, tastare; (*keyboard*) far scorrere le dita su

Ff

finger board N manico
finger bowl N sciacquadita *m inv*
fin·ger·ing ['fɪŋgərɪŋ] N (*Mus*) diteggiatura
finger·mark ['fɪŋgə,mɑːk] N ditata
finger·nail ['fɪŋgə,neɪl] N unghia
finger painting N dipingere con le mani; **to do finger painting** dipingere con le mani
finger·print ['fɪŋgə,prɪnt] N impronta digitale
■VT (*person*) prendere le impronte digitali di *or* a
finger·stall ['fɪŋgə,stɔːl] N ditale *m*
finger·tip ['fɪŋgə,tɪp] N punta del dito; **to have sth at one's fingertips** (*fig*) avere qc sulla punta delle dita; **fingertip hold** (*Mountaineering*) gratton *m inv*
fin·icky ['fɪnɪkɪ] ADJ **1** (*person*): **finicky (about)** pignolo(-a) (su), difficile (per) **2** (*job*) minuzioso(-a)
fin·is ['fɪnɪs] N fine *f*
◎**fin·ish** ['fɪnɪʃ] N **1** (*end: esp Sport*) fine *f*; (*Sport: line*) traguardo; (*Mountaineering*) uscita; **from start to finish** dall'inizio alla fine; **to be in at the finish** essere presente alla fine; **a fight to the finish** un combattimento all'ultimo sangue **2** (*appearance*) finitura
■VT (*gen*) finire, terminare; (*use up*) esaurire; **to finish doing sth** finire di fare qc; **that last mile nearly finished me** (*fam*) quell'ultimo miglio mi ha quasi distrutto
■VI (*session*) finire, terminare; (*book, game*) finire, concludersi; (*contract*) scadere; (*Mountaineering*) uscire; **I've finished!** ho finito!; **have you finished eating?** hai finito di mangiare?; **the party was finishing** la festa stava per finire; **she finished by saying that ...** ha concluso dicendo che...; **to finish first/second** (*Sport*) arrivare primo(-a)/secondo(-a); **I've finished with the paper** ho finito col giornale; **he's finished with politics** ha chiuso con la politica; **she's finished with her boyfriend** (*broken relationship*) ha chiuso con il suo ragazzo
▸ **finish off** VT + ADV finire; (*kill*) uccidere
▸ **finish up** VI + ADV finire; **he finished up in Paris** è finito a Parigi; **it finished up as ...** ha finito col diventare...
■VT + ADV (*food etc*) finire
fin·ished ['fɪnɪʃt] ADJ **1** (*product*) finito(-a); (*performance*) perfetto(-a) **2** (*fam: tired*) sfinito(-a); (*: done for*) finito(-a)
fin·ish·ing line ['fɪnɪʃɪŋ,laɪn] N (*Sport*) traguardo, linea d'arrivo
fin·ish·ing ma·chine ['fɪnɪʃɪŋmə'ʃiːn] N (*Tech*) finitrice *f*
fin·ish·ing school ['fɪnɪʃɪŋ,skuːl] N scuola privata di perfezionamento (*per signorine*)
fin·ish·ing touches [,fɪnɪʃɪŋ'tʌtʃɪz] NPL ultimi ritocchi *mpl*; **to put the finishing touches to sth** dare gli ultimi ritocchi a qc
fi·nite ['faɪnaɪt] ADJ **1** (*limited*) limitato(-a); **finite resources** risorse limitate **2** (*Gram: verb*) finito(-a)
fink [fɪŋk] N (*Am*) informatore(-trice)
Fin·land ['fɪnlənd] N la Finlandia
Finn [fɪn] N finlandese *m/f*
Finn·ish ['fɪnɪʃ] ADJ finlandese
■N (*language*) finlandese *m*
fiord [fjɔːd] N = **fjord**
fir [fɜːʳ] N (*also:* **fir tree**) abete *m*
fir cone N pigna
◎**fire** ['faɪəʳ] N **1** (*gen*) fuoco; (*house fire etc*) incendio; **electric/gas fire** stufa elettrica/a gas; **forest fire** incendio boschivo; **to set fire to sth** *or* **set sth on fire** dar fuoco a qc, incendiare qc; **to catch fire** prendere fuoco; **to be on fire** essere in fiamme; **he made a fire to warm himself up** ha acceso un fuoco per scaldarsi; **the house was destroyed by a fire** la casa è stata distrutta da un incendio; **insured against fire** assicurato(-a) contro gli incendi; **to play with fire** (*fig*) scherzare col fuoco **2** (*Mil*) fuoco; **to open fire (on sb)** aprire il fuoco (contro *or* su qn); **to hold one's fire** cessare il fuoco; **to be/come under fire (from)** essere/finire sotto il fuoco *or* il tiro (di); **the government has come under fire from the opposition** il governo è finito sotto il tiro dell'opposizione
■VT **1** (*gun, shot, salute*) sparare; (*rocket etc*) lanciare; **to fire a gun at sb** fare fuoco contro qn; **to fire questions at sb** bombardare qn di domande **2** (*pottery: in kiln*) cuocere; (*fig: imagination*) accendere, infiammare **3** (*fam: dismiss*) licenziare; **you're fired!** sei licenziato!; **he was fired from his job** è stato licenziato
■VI **1** (*Mil etc*): **to fire (at)** sparare (a), far fuoco (contro); **she fired at him** gli ha sparato; **fire away** *or* **ahead!** (*fig fam*) spara! **2** (*Aut: subj: engine*) accendersi
fire alarm N allarme *m* antincendio *inv*
fire·arm ['faɪər,ɑːm] N arma da fuoco
fire·ball ['faɪə,bɔːl] N (*Astron*) bolide *m*; (*nuclear*) palla di fuoco; (*lightning*) fulmine *m* globulare
fire·bomb ['faɪəbɒm] N bomba incendiaria
■VT attaccare con una bomba incendiaria
fire·brand ['faɪə,brænd] N (*person*) agitatore(-trice), sobillatore(-trice)
fire·break ['faɪə,breɪk] N tagliafuoco
fire·brick ['faɪə,brɪk] N mattone *m* refrattario
fire brigade, (*Am*) **fire department** N (corpo dei) pompieri *mpl or* vigili *mpl* del fuoco
fire·bug ['faɪə,bʌg] N (*fam*) incendiario(-a)
fire chief N (*Am*) comandante *m* dei vigili del fuoco
fire·cracker ['faɪə,krækəʳ] N petardo
fire department N (*Am*) = **fire brigade**
fire·dogs ['faɪə,dɒgz] NPL alari *mpl*
fire door N porta *f* tagliafuoco *inv*
fire drill, fire practice N esercitazione *f* antincendio *inv*
fire-eater ['faɪəʳiːtəʳ] N (*performer*) mangiatore *m* di fuoco; (*fig*) attaccabrighe *m/f*
fire engine N autopompa
fire escape N scala di sicurezza
fire exit N uscita di sicurezza
fire extinguisher N estintore *m*
fire-fighting ['faɪəʳ,faɪtɪŋ] N: **attempts at fire-fighting** tentativi di spegnere l'incendio; **fire-fighting equipment** attrezzatura antincendio *f inv*
fire·fly ['faɪə,flaɪ] N (*pl* **-flies**) lucciola
fire·guard ['faɪə,gɑːd] N (*Brit*) parafuoco
fire hazard N: **that's a fire hazard** può provocare un incendio
fire hydrant N idrante *m*
fire insurance N assicurazione *f* contro gli incendi
fire-irons ['faɪəʳ,aɪəns] N molle *fpl*
fire·light ['faɪə,laɪt] N bagliore *m* del fuoco; **by firelight** alla luce del fuoco
fire lighter N esca (*per accendere il fuoco*)
fire·man ['faɪəmən] N (*pl* **-men**) vigile *m* del fuoco, pompiere *m*
fire·place ['faɪə,pleɪs] N caminetto, focolare *m*
fire·plug ['faɪə,plʌg] N (*Am*) = **fire hydrant**
fire practice N = **fire drill**

fire prevention N prevenzione *f* antincendio
fire·proof ['faɪə,pru:f] ADJ (*material*) resistente al fuoco; (*dish*) resistente al calore
fire rais·er ['faɪə,reɪzəʳ] N incendiario(-a)
fire-raising ['faɪəʳ,reɪzɪŋ] N piromania
fire regulations NPL norme *fpl* antincendio
fire risk N rischio d'incendio
fire sale N *svendita di prodotti danneggiati da un incendio*; **we got them at fire-sale prices** li abbiamo comprati a prezzi stracciati
fire screen N = **fireguard**
fire·side ['faɪə,saɪd] N angolo del focolare; **by the fireside** intorno al focolare
fire station N caserma dei pompieri
fire trap N: **it's a fire trap** in caso di incendio si trasformerà in una trappola
fire truck N (*Am*) autopompa
fire·wall ['faɪəwɔ:l] N (*Comput*) firewall *m inv*
fire·wood ['faɪə,wʊd] N legna da ardere
fire·work ['faɪə,wɜ:k] N fuoco d'artificio
fire·works ['faɪə,wɜ:ks] NPL (*show*) fuochi *mpl* d'artificio; (*fig: temper*) parole *fpl* grosse; (: *virtuosity*) virtuosismi *mpl*
fir·ing ['faɪərɪŋ] N (*Mil*) spari *mpl*, tiro
firing line N linea del fuoco; **to be in the firing line** (*fig: liable to be criticized*) essere sulla linea del fuoco
firing squad N plotone *m* d'esecuzione
◎ **firm¹** [fɜ:m] ADJ (*comp* **-er**, *superl* **-est**) (*gen*) solido(-a); (*steady*) saldo(-a); (*belief*) fermo(-a); (*measures*) severo(-a); (*look, voice*) risoluto(-a); (*prices*) stabile; (*offer, decision*) definitivo(-a); **firm tomatoes** pomodori non troppo maturi; **a firm mattress** un materasso rigido; **a firm grip** una presa salda; **a firm refusal** un netto rifiuto; **as firm as a rock** solido(-a) come una roccia; **to be a firm believer in sth** credere fermamente in qc; **to be firm with sb** essere deciso(-a) con qn; **they are firm friends** sono molto amici; **to keep a firm hold on** tenere saldamente; **to be on firm ground** (*fig*) andare sul sicuro; **to stand firm** *or* **take a firm stand over sth** (*fig*) tener duro per quanto riguarda qc

> DID YOU KNOW ...?
> **firm** is not translated by the Italian word *firma*

firm² [fɜ:m] N azienda, ditta, impresa
firm·ly ['fɜ:mlɪ] ADV (*fixed*) saldamente, solidamente; (*speak*) con fermezza; (*believe*) fermamente
firm·ness ['fɜ:mnɪs] N (*of voice, decision etc*) fermezza; (*of object*) solidità
firm·ware ['fɜ:mwɛəʳ] N (*Comput*) firmware *m inv*; *insieme di istruzioni presenti nella memoria centrale del computer*
◎ **first** [fɜ:st] ADJ primo(-a); **the first of January** il primo (di) gennaio; **the first time** la prima volta; **Charles the First** Carlo Primo; **to win first place** arrivare primo; **in the first place** per prima cosa, innanzitutto; **in the first instance** in primo luogo, prima di tutto; **first thing in the morning** la mattina presto; **I'll do it first thing tomorrow** lo farò per prima cosa domani; **first things first!** prima le cose più importanti!; **I don't know the first thing about it** (*fam*) non ne so un bel niente
■ ADV **1** (*firstly*) prima; (*before other things*) per primo(-a); (*when listing reasons etc*) per prima cosa; **first one, then another** prima uno, poi un altro; **first of all** prima di tutto, innanzitutto; **first and foremost** prima di tutto, innanzitutto; **first and last** (*above all*) prima di tutto; **ladies first!** prima le signore!; **we arrived first** siamo arrivati per primi; **she came first in the race** è arrivata prima nella gara; **at first** sulle prime, all'inizio, dapprima; **it was difficult at first** all'inizio è stato difficile; **finish this work first** finisci questo lavoro prima; **I want to get a job, but first I have to pass my exams** voglio trovare un lavoro, ma prima devo passare gli esami; **head first** a capofitto **2** (*for the first time*) per la prima volta; **I first met him in Paris** l'ho incontrato per la prima volta a Parigi **3** (*rather*) piuttosto; **I'd die first!** piuttosto morirei!
■ N (*person: in race*) primo(-a); **the first to arrive** il/la primo(-a) ad arrivare; **first come, first served** chi tardi arriva, male alloggia; **from the (very) first** fin dall'inizio, fin dal primo momento; **from first to last** dall'inizio alla fine; **in first (gear)** (*Aut*) in prima (marcia); **he gained a first in French** (*Brit Univ: class of degree*) si è laureato in francese col massimo dei voti
first-aid ['fɜ:st'eɪd] ADJ: **first-aid classes** corso di pronto soccorso; **first-aid kit** *or* **box** cassetta di pronto soccorso; **first-aid post** posto di pronto soccorso
first aid N pronto soccorso
first-class ['fɜ:st'klɑ:s] ADJ **1** di prima classe; **first-class ticket** (*Rail etc*) biglietto di prima classe; **first-class compartment** (*Rail*) scompartimento di prima classe; **first-class honours degree** (*Univ*) ≈ laurea con centodieci e lode **2** (*very good*) di prima qualità; **a first-class meal** un pranzo eccellente **3 a first-class stamp** un francobollo per posta prioritaria
■ ADV: **to travel first-class** viaggiare in prima classe; **to send a letter first-class** ≈ spedire una lettera per espresso
first-class mail N ≈ espresso
first cousin N cugino di primo grado
first-day cover [fɜ:stdeɪ'kʌvəʳ] N busta con francobolli del primo giorno di emissione
first-degree ['fɜ:stdɪ'gri:] ADJ (*burn*) di primo grado
first degree N (*Univ*) laurea breve
first edition N prima edizione *f*
first-ever [fɜ:st'evəʳ] ADJ primo(-a) in assoluto
first floor N: **the first floor** (*Brit*) il primo piano; (*Am*) il pianoterreno; **on the first floor** (*Brit*) al primo piano
first form, first year N (*Scol*) ≈ prima media
first fruits N: **the first fruits** i primi risultati
first-generation ['fɜ:st,dʒenə'reɪʃən] ADJ (*immigrant*) di prima generazione; (*computer*) della prima generazione
first-hand ['fɜ:st'hænd] ADJ diretto(-a), di prima mano
■ ADV direttamente
First Lady N (*Am*) moglie *f* del presidente
first language N prima lingua
first·ly ['fɜ:stlɪ] ADV prima, innanzitutto, in primo luogo
First Minister N (*Pol*) *leader m/f inv* del partito di maggioranza (*nel parlamento scozzese o irlandese*)
first name N nome *m* (di battesimo)
first night N (*Theatre*) prima
first offender N (*Law*) incensurato(-a)
first person N: **a novel in the first person** un romanzo in prima persona
first person plural N (*Gram*): **the first person plural** la prima persona plurale
first-rate ['fɜ:st'reɪt] ADJ di prim'ordine, ottimo(-a)
first school N ≈ scuola elementare
First Secretary N (*Pol*) leader *m/f inv* del partito di maggioranza; nel parlamento gallese

Ff

first-time buyer ['fɜ:st'taɪm'baɪəʳ] N acquirente *m/f* di prima casa

First World N: **the First World** i paesi industrializzati

First World War N: **the First World War** la prima guerra mondiale

first year N = first form

◎**fis·cal** ['fɪskəl] ADJ fiscale

fiscal year N (*Am*) anno fiscale

◎**fish** [fɪʃ] N (*pl* **fish** *or* **fishes**) pesce *m*; **I caught three fish** ho pescato tre pesci; **I don't like fish** non mi piace il pesce; **fish and chips** pesce impanato e patatine; **to be like a fish out of water** sentirsi come un pesce fuor d'acqua; **I've got other fish to fry** (*fam*) ho altro da fare

■VI pescare; **to go fishing** andare a pesca; **to go salmon fishing** andare a pesca di salmoni; **to fish for trout** pescare (le) trote; **to fish for compliments/for information** (*fig*) andare a caccia di complimenti/di informazioni; **to fish (around) in one's pockets for sth** frugarsi le tasche in cerca di qc

■VT (*river, pond*) pescare in; (*trout, salmon*) pescare

▶ **fish out** VT + ADV (*from water*) ripescare; (*from box etc*) tirare fuori

fish-and-chip shop ['fɪʃənd'tʃɪp'ʃɒp] N (*Brit*) *see* **chip shop**

fish·bone ['fɪʃˌbəʊn] N lisca, spina

fish·bowl ['fɪʃˌbəʊl] N vaschetta per pesci

fish·cake ['fɪʃˌkeɪk] N crocchetta di pesce

fisher·man ['fɪʃəmən] N (*pl* **-men**) pescatore *m*

fish·ery ['fɪʃərɪ] N zona di pesca

fish farm N vivaio

fish farming N piscicoltura

fish fingers NPL (*Brit*) bastoncini *mpl* di pesce (surgelati)

fish-hook ['fɪʃˌhʊk] N amo

◎**fish·ing** ['fɪʃɪŋ] N pesca

fishing boat N peschereccio

fishing fleet N flotta di pescherecci

fishing grounds NPL zona di pesca

fishing industry N industria della pesca

fishing line N lenza

fishing net N rete *f* da pesca

fishing port N porto di pesca

fishing rod N canna da pesca

fishing tackle N attrezzatura da pesca

fish kettle N pesciera

fish knife N coltello da pesce

fish market N mercato del pesce

fish·monger ['fɪʃˌmʌŋgəʳ] N (*Brit*) pescivendolo; **fishmonger's (shop)** pescheria

fish·pond ['fɪʃˌpɒnd] N (*in garden*) vasca per i pesci

fish shop N pescheria

fish slice N (*Brit*) paletta forata *or* per fritti

fish sticks ['fɪʃˌstɪks] NPL (*Am*) = **fish fingers**

fish tank N acquario

fish·wife ['fɪʃˌwaɪf] N (*pej*) pescivendola

fishy ['fɪʃɪ] ADJ (*comp* **-ier**, *superl* **-iest**) **1** (*smell, taste: usu pej*) di pesce **2** (*fam: suspicious*) losco(-a), sospetto(-a)

fis·sion ['fɪʃən] N fissione *f*; **atomic/nuclear fission** fissione atomica/nucleare

fis·sure ['fɪʃəʳ] N fessura, fenditura

fist [fɪst] N pugno; **to shake one's fist (at sb)** minacciare (qn) con il pugno

fist·fight ['fɪstˌfaɪt] N scazzottata

fist·ful ['fɪstfʊl] N pugno, manciata

fisti·cuffs ['fɪstɪˌkʌfs] NPL scazzottata

fis·tu·la ['fɪstjʊlə] N fistola

◎**fit**[1] [fɪt] ADJ (*comp* **-ter**, *superl* **-test**)

1 (*suitable*) adatto(-a); (*proper*) appropriato(-a), conveniente; **fit for** adatto(-a) a; **to be fit for sth** andare bene per qc; **only two of the bikes were fit for the road** solo due bici erano utilizzabili; **to be fit for nothing** non essere buono(-a) a niente; **a meal fit for a king** un pranzo da re; **he's not fit for the job** non è la persona adatta per questo lavoro; **fit for habitation** abitabile; **he is not fit company for my daughter** non è la compagnia adatta per mia figlia; **to be fit to play** essere in condizione di giocare; **they're not fit to govern** non sono in grado di governare; **he's not fit to teach** non è adatto all'insegnamento; **he's not fit to drive** non è in condizione di guidare; **you're not fit to be seen** non sei presentabile; **it's not fit to eat** *or* **to be eaten** non è mangiabile *or* commestibile; **the water wasn't fit to drink** l'acqua non era potabile; **I'm fit to drop** (*fam*) sto per crollare; **do as you think** *or* **see fit** fai come meglio credi

2 (*in health*) in forma; (*Sport*) in buone condizioni fisiche, in forma; **to keep fit** tenersi in forma; **to be fit for work** (*after illness*) essere in grado di riprendere il lavoro; **to be (as) fit as a fiddle** essere sano(-a) come un pesce; **he felt relaxed and fit after his holiday** si sentiva rilassato e in forma dopo la vacanza

■N: **to be a good fit** (*shoes*) calzare bene; (*clothes*) andare *or* stare bene; **it's a rather tight fit** mi sta un po' stretto

■VT

1 (*subj: clothes*) andare/stare bene a; (*: key etc*) adattarsi a; **it fits you well** ti sta bene; **it fits me like a glove** mi sta a pennello

2 (*match: facts etc*) concordare con; (*: description*) corrispondere a; **the punishment should fit the crime** la punizione dovrebbe essere adeguata al reato

3 (*put in place*) mettere, fissare; **to fit a key in the lock** mettere una chiave nella serratura; **to have a carpet fitted** far mettere la moquette; **to fit sth into place** sistemare qc; **to fit sth on sth** mettere qc a *or* su qc; **it doesn't cost much to fit an alarm** non costa molto installare un allarme

4 (*equip*) fornire, dotare, equipaggiare; **a car fitted with a radio** una macchina fornita di radio; **she has been fitted with a new hearing aid** le hanno messo un nuovo apparecchio acustico

5 (*make fit*) rendere adatto(-a); (*adjust*) aggiustare; **to fit a dress (on sb)** provare un vestito (a qn); **her experience fits her for the job** la sua esperienza la rende adatta a questo lavoro

■VI

1 (*clothes*) andare *or* stare bene; (*part*) adattarsi; (*key, object*) andare, entrare; **does it fit?** ti va bene?

2 (*match: facts*) quadrare; (*: story*) reggere; (*: description*) calzare; **it all fits now!** tutto è chiaro adesso!

▶ **fit in** VI + ADV (*person*) adattarsi; **to fit in (with)** (*fact, statement*) corrispondere (a), concordare (con); **that story doesn't fit in with what he told us** la storia non corrisponde a quanto ci ha detto; **to fit in with sb's plans** adattarsi ai progetti di qn; **he left because he didn't fit in** se ne è andato perché non riusciva ad integrarsi; **she fitted in well at her new school** si è ambientata bene nella nuova scuola

■VT + ADV (*object*) far entrare; (*fig: appointment, visitor*) trovare il tempo per; (*plan, activity*): **to fit in (with)** conciliare (con); **the doctor can't fit you in today** il dottore non ha tempo di vederla oggi

▸ **fit out** VT + ADV (*Brit: ship*) allestire, equipaggiare; (*: person*) fornire, equipaggiare
▸ **fit up** VT + ADV
1 (*provide*): **to fit sb up with sth** fornire qc a qn
2 (*arrange: room etc*) attrezzare
3 (*fam: incriminate*) incastrare

DID YOU KNOW ...?
fit is not translated by the Italian word *fitto*

fit² [fɪt] N **1** (*Med*) attacco; **to have** *or* **suffer a fit** avere un attacco di convulsioni; **to have an epileptic fit** avere un attacco epilettico; **fit of coughing** attacco di tosse **2** (*outburst*) accesso; **fit of anger/enthusiasm** accesso d'ira/d'entusiasmo; **to have a fit of crying** scoppiare in un pianto dirotto; **to get a fit of the giggles** avere un attacco di ridarella; **to have** *or* **throw a fit** (*fam*) andare su tutte le furie; **to be in fits (of laughter)** scoppiare dalle risa; **by** *or* **in fits and starts** a sbalzi

fit·ful ['fɪtfʊl] ADJ saltuario(-a); (*breeze, showers*) intermittente; (*wind*) a raffiche; (*sleep*) agitato(-a)

fit·ful·ly ['fɪtfəlɪ] ADV (*work*) in modo discontinuo; **to sleep fitfully** avere il sonno agitato

fit·ment ['fɪtmənt] N **1** (*accessory: of machine*) accessorio **2** = **fitting** N

fit·ness ['fɪtnɪs] N **1** (*suitability: for post etc*): **fitness (for)** idoneità (a); (*: of remark*) appropriatezza **2** (*health*) forma fisica

fit·ted ['fɪtɪd] ADJ (*garment*) modellato(-a); **fitted carpet** moquette *f inv*; **fitted cupboards** armadi *mpl* a muro; **fitted kitchen** (*Brit*) cucina componibile; **fitted sheet** lenzuolo con gli angoli

fit·ter ['fɪtəʳ] N (*Tech*) installatore(-trice); (*of garment*) sarto(-a)

fit·ting ['fɪtɪŋ] ADJ (*suitable*) adatto(-a), appropriato(-a); **it is fitting that** (*frm*) è opportuno che
■ N (*of dress*) prova; (*of piece of equipment*) installazione *f*; *see also* **fittings**

fit·ting·ly ['fɪtɪŋlɪ] ADV opportunamente

fitting room N (*in shop*) camerino

fittings ['fɪtɪŋz] NPL (*of house*) accessori *mpl*, attrezzature *fpl*; **bathroom fittings** accessori per il bagno

◎**five** [faɪv] ADJ cinque *inv*; **she is five (years old)** ha cinque anni; **they live at number five/at five Green Street** vivono al numero cinque/al numero cinque di Green Street; **there are five of us** siamo in cinque; **all five of them came** sono venuti tutti e cinque; **it costs five pounds** costa cinque sterline; **five and a quarter/half** cinque e un quarto/e mezzo; **it's five (o'clock)** sono le cinque
■ N cinque *m inv*; **to divide sth into five** dividere qc in cinque parti; **they are sold in fives** sono venduti in gruppi di cinque

five-day week ['faɪv'deɪ'wi:k] N settimana di cinque giorni (lavorativi)

five·fold ['faɪv,fəʊld] ADJ quintuplo(-a)
■ ADV cinque volte tanto

five o'clock shadow N (*hum*): **you've got a five o'clock shadow** dovresti farti la barba

fiv·er ['faɪvəʳ] N (*fam: Brit*) biglietto da cinque sterline; (*: Am*) biglietto da cinque dollari

five-star ['faɪv,stɑ:ʳ] ADJ (*hotel*) a cinque stelle; (*restaurant*) ≈ di lusso

five-year ['faɪv'jɪəʳ] ADJ quinquennale; **five-year plan** piano quinquennale

◎**fix** [fɪks] N **1** (*fam: predicament*) pasticcio, guaio; **to be in a fix** essere in un pasticcio, essere nei guai; **to get o.s. into a fix** cacciarsi nei guai **2** (*fam: of drug*) pera **3 the fight was a fix** (*fam*) l'incontro è stato truccato **4** (*Aer, Naut*) posizione *f*; **to take a fix on** fare il punto su
■ VT **1** (*gen, Phot, fig*) fissare; (*with string etc*) legare, fissare; **she fixed the picture to the wall** ha fissato il quadro al muro; **to fix one's gaze on** fermare lo sguardo su; **to fix the blame on sb/sth** dare *or* attribuire la colpa a qn/qc; **to fix sth in one's mind** imprimersi qc nella mente **2** (*date, price*) fissare, stabilire; (*fight, race*) truccare; **let's fix a date for the party** fissiamo una data per la festa; **I'll fix everything** ci penso io, sistemo tutto io; **I'll fix him!** (*fam*) lo sistemo io!, lo metto a posto io! **3** (*repair*) riparare, aggiustare; **can you fix my bike?** puoi aggiustarmi la bici? **4** (*Am: make ready: meal, drink*) preparare; **can I fix you a drink?** cosa posso offrirti da bere?; **I'm fixing lunch** sto preparando da mangiare; **to fix one's hair** darsi una pettinata
▸ **fix on** VT + ADV (*badge, lid*) fissare, attaccare
■ VI + PREP (*decide on*) fissare
▸ **fix up** VT + ADV **1** (*arrange: date, meeting*) fissare, stabilire; **to fix sb up with sth** procurare qc a qn; **I fixed up an appointment to see her** ho fissato un appuntamento per vederla **2** (*clean, repair*) sistemare; **I've fixed up Paul's old room** ho sistemato la vecchia camera di Paul

-fixated [fɪk'seɪtɪd] SUFFIX (*Psych*): **mother-fixated** morbosamente attaccato alla madre; **a pop-fixated journalist** un giornalista con la fissazione del pop

fixa·tion [fɪk'seɪʃən] N (*Psych, fig*) fissazione *f*, ossessione *f*; **to have a fixation on sth** avere la mania di qc

fixa·tive ['fɪksətɪv] N fissativo

◎**fixed** [fɪkst] ADJ **1** (*gen*) fisso(-a); **at a fixed time** ad un'ora stabilita; **fixed price** prezzo fisso; **there's a fixed charge** c'è una quota fissa **2 how are you fixed for money?** (*fam*) a soldi come stai?; **how are you fixed for this evening?** cosa fai stasera?

fixed assets NPL beni *mpl* patrimoniali

fixed costs NPL (*Econ*) costi *mpl* fissi

fix·ed·ly ['fɪksɪdlɪ] ADV fissamente

fixed penalty (fine) N multa di importo fisso

fix·ings ['fɪksɪŋz] NPL (*Am*) (*Culin*) guarnizioni *fpl*

fix·ture ['fɪkstʃəʳ] N **1** (*of house etc*): **fixtures** NPL impianti *mpl* **2** (*Sport*) incontro; **their next fixture** il loro prossimo incontro

fizz [fɪz] N effervescenza
■ VI frizzare
▸ **fizz up** VI + ADV spumeggiare

fiz·zle ['fɪzl] VI (*sputter*) sibilare
▸ **fizzle out** VI + ADV (*fire, firework*) finire per spegnersi; (*enthusiasm, interest*) smorzarsi, svanire; (*plan*) fallire

fizzy ['fɪzɪ] ADJ (*comp* **-ier**, *superl* **-iest**) (*drink*) gassato(-a), frizzante, effervescente

fjord, fiord [fjɔ:d] N fiordo

FL ABBR (*Am Post*) = **Florida**

flab [flæb] N ciccia

flab·ber·gast·ed ['flæbə,gɑ:stɪd] ADJ sbalordito(-a)

flab·bi·ness ['flæbɪnɪs] N (*of flesh*) flaccidezza

flab·by ['flæbɪ] ADJ (*comp* **-ier**, *superl* **-iest**) flaccido(-a), floscio(-a)

◎**flag¹** [flæg] N (*gen*) bandiera; (*for charity etc*) bandierina; **flag of convenience** bandiera di convenienza
▸ **flag down** VT + ADV (*taxi, motorist*) fare cenno (di fermarsi) a

Ff

flag² [flæg] VI (*strength*) indebolirsi; (*person*) stancarsi; (*enthusiasm etc*) affievolirsi; (*conversation*) languire

flag³ [flæg] N (*also:* **flag stone**) pietra per lastricare

flag day N ≈ giornata in cui si vendono bandierine per beneficenza

flag·el·late [ˈflædʒɪˌleɪt] VT (*frm*) fustigare; **to flagellate o.s.** flagellarsi, fustigarsi

flag·el·la·tion [ˌflædʒəˈleɪʃən] N flagellazione *f*

flagged [flægd] ADJ lastricato(-a)

flag·ging [ˈflægɪŋ] ADJ (*interest, enthusiasm*) affievolito(-a)

flag·on [ˈflægən] N bottiglione *m*

flag·pole [ˈflægˌpəʊl] N pennone *m*

fla·grant [ˈfleɪgrənt] ADJ flagrante

fla·grant·ly [ˈfleɪgrəntlɪ] ADV palesemente; **it is flagrantly unjust** è una flagrante ingiustizia

flag·ship [ˈflægˌʃɪp] N nave *f* ammiraglia; (*fig*) fiore all'occhiello

flag stop N (*Am: for bus*) fermata a richiesta, fermata facoltativa

flail [fleɪl] VI (*arms, legs*) agitare

flair [flɛəʳ] N (*for business etc*) fiuto; (*for languages etc*) predisposizione *f*; **to have a flair (for)** essere portato(-a) per; **he's got a flair for business** ha fiuto per gli affari; **she's got a flair for languages** ha predisposizione per le lingue

flak [flæk] N **1** (*Mil*) fuoco d'artiglieria **2** (*fam: criticism*) critiche *fpl*

flake [fleɪk] N **1** (*of paint, rust*) scaglia; (*of skin*) squama; (*of snow, cereal*) fiocco **2** (*Am fam*) strambo(-a)
■VI (*also:* **flake off**: *paint*) scrostarsi; (: *skin*) squamarsi; (*stone*) sfaldarsi
▸ **flake out** VI + ADV (*fam: collapse*) svenire; (*fall asleep*) crollare

flaked [fleɪkt] ADJ: **flaked almonds** scaglie *fpl* di mandorle

flaky [ˈfleɪkɪ] ADJ (*comp* **-ier**, *superl* **-iest**) (*paintwork*) scrostato(-a); (*skin*) squamoso(-a); (*person, thing: Am fam*) strambo(-a)

flaky pastry N (*Culin*) pasta sfoglia

flam·bé [ˈflɒmbeɪ] VT cucinare alla fiamma

flam·boy·ance [flæmˈbɔɪəns] N (*of person, style*) stravaganza

flam·boy·ant [flæmˈbɔɪənt] ADJ (*character, speech*) stravagante; (*dress etc*) sgargiante, vistoso(-a); (*style*) fiorito(-a), ornato(-a)

flam·boy·ant·ly [flæmˈbɔɪəntlɪ] ADV (*dress*) vistosamente, in modo sgargiante; (*behave*) teatralmente

flame [fleɪm] N fiamma; **to burst into flames** divampare; (*Comput*) violento attacco via e-mail
■VI (*also:* **flame up**) divampare; **her cheeks flamed with embarrassment** arrossì per l'imbarazzo
■VT attaccare violentemente via e-mail

fla·men·co [fləˈmɛŋkəʊ] N flamenco

flame·proof [ˈfleɪmˌpruːf] ADJ resistente al calore

flame test N (*Chem*) test *m inv* alla fiamma

flame-thrower [ˈfleɪmˌθrəʊəʳ] N lanciafiamme *m inv*

flam·ing [ˈfleɪmɪŋ] ADJ **1** (*red, orange*) acceso(-a) **2** (*Brit fam: furious*) furibondo(-a), furioso(-a) **3** (*Brit fam: damn*) maledetto(-a)

fla·min·go [fləˈmɪŋgəʊ] N fenicottero

flam·mabil·ity [ˌflæməˈbɪlɪtɪ] N infiammabilità

flam·mable [ˈflæməbl] ADJ infiammabile

flan [flæn] N (*Brit Culin: sweet*) flan *m inv*, torta; (: *savoury*) flan *m inv*, tortino; **a raspberry flan** una torta di lamponi; **a cheese and onion flan** un tortino di formaggio e cipolla

Flan·ders [ˈflɑːndəz] NSG le Fiandre *fpl*

flange [flændʒ] N (*Tech: on wheel*) flangia

flank [flæŋk] N (*gen, Mil*) fianco
■VT fiancheggiare

flan·nel [ˈflænl] N (*fabric*) flanella; (*Brit*) (: *also:* **face flannel**) guanto di spugna; *see also* **flannels**
■ADJ di flanella

flan·nel·ette [ˌflænəˈlɛt] N flanella di cotone

flan·nels [ˈflænlz] NPL pantaloni *mpl* di flanella

flap [flæp] N **1** (*of pocket*) patta, battente *m*; (*of envelope*) linguetta; (*of table*) ribalta; (*Aer*) flap *m inv* **2** (*movement*): **to give sth a flap** sbattere qc; **they could hear the flap of the sails** (*sound*) sentivano sbattere le vele; **to be in a flap** (*fam*) essere in agitazione; **to get into a flap** (*fam*) farsi prendere dal panico
■VT (*subj: bird: wings*) sbattere, battere; (*shake: sheets, newspaper*) agitare, sbattere
■VI **1** (*wings, sails, flag*) sbattere **2** (*fam: panic*) farsi prendere dal panico

flap·jack [ˈflæpˌdʒæk] N (*Brit: biscuit*) biscotto di avena; (*Am: pancake*) frittella

flare [flɛəʳ] N **1** (*blaze*) chiarore *m*; (*signal*) segnale *m* luminoso; (*Mil: for target*) razzo illuminante **2** (*in skirt*) svasatura **3** (*trousers*): **flares** NPL pantaloni *mpl* a zampa d'elefante
■VI (*match, torch*) accendersi con una fiammata
▸ **flare up** VI + ADV (*fire*) divampare; (*fig: person*) infiammarsi di rabbia, saltar su; (: *revolt, situation etc*) scoppiare

flared [ˈflɛəd] ADJ (*skirt, trousers*) svasato(-a)

flare-up [ˈflɛərˌʌp] N (*of fire*) fiammata; (*of quarrel, fighting*) recrudescenza; (*outburst of rage*) scoppio d'ira; (*sudden dispute*) battibecco

◎**flash** [flæʃ] N **1** (*of light*) sprazzo, lampo; (*Am: torch*) torcia elettrica, lampadina tascabile; **flash of lightning** lampo; **flash of inspiration** lampo di genio; **a flash in the pan** (*fig*) un fuoco di paglia; **in a flash** in un baleno, in un lampo **2** (*also:* **news flash**) flash *m inv*, notizia *f* lampo *inv* **3** (*Phot*) flash *m inv*
■VT (*light, torch*) far lampeggiare; (*look*) lanciare; (*send: message*) trasmettere; **to flash one's headlights** (*Aut*) lampeggiare; **a lorry driver flashed him** un camionista gli ha lampeggiato coi fari; **to flash sth about** (*fig fam: flaunt*) ostentare qc; **stop flashing your money about!** smettila di ostentare i tuoi soldi!
■VI **1** (*light, eyes*) lampeggiare; (*lightning*) guizzare, balenare; (*jewels*) brillare, scintillare; **a light was flashing** una luce stava lampeggiando **2** (*move quickly: person, vehicle*): **to flash by** *or* **past** passare come un lampo; **he flashed by** *or* **past us** sfrecciò davanti a noi

flash·back [ˈflæʃˌbæk] N (*Cine*) flashback *m inv*

flash·bulb [ˈflæʃˌbʌlb] N flash *m inv*

flash burn N ustione *f* causata da un'esplosione

flash card N (*Scol*) scheda didattica

flash·cube [ˈflæʃˌkjuːb] N (*Phot*) cubo-flash *m inv*

flash·er [ˈflæʃəʳ] N **1** (*Aut*) lampeggiatore *m* **2** (*Brit fam: man*) esibizionista *m*

flash flood N inondazione *f*

flash·gun [ˈflæʃˌgʌn] N (*Phot*) lampeggiatore *m*

flashi·ly [ˈflæʃɪlɪ] ADV in modo vistoso

flash·ing [ˈflæʃɪŋ] N scossalina

flash·light [ˈflæʃˌlaɪt] N (*Am: torch*) torcia elettrica, lampadina tascabile

flash mob N flash mob *m inv*, gruppo di persone che si incontrano in un certo posto dopo essere state contattate in Internet e poi si disperdono

flash mobbing [-mɔbɪ] N flash mobbing *m*, *incontro lampo di un gruppo di persone organizzato tramite Internet*

flash·point ['flæʃ,pɔɪnt] N punto di infiammabilità; (*fig*) livello critico

flashy ['flæʃɪ] ADJ (*comp* **-ier**, *superl* **-est**) (*pej: car, clothes*) vistoso(-a); (*person*) appariscente

flask [flɑːsk] N (*for brandy etc*) fiaschetta; (*also:* **vacuum flask**) thermos® *m inv*; (*Chem*) pallone *m*, beuta; **a flask of coffee** un thermos di caffè; **a flask of brandy** una fiaschetta di brandy

◎ **flat**[1] [flæt] ADJ (*comp* **-ter**, *superl* **-test**) **1** (*gen*) piatto(-a); (*smooth*) liscio(-a), piano(-a); (*tyre*) sgonfio(-a), a terra; **a flat surface** una superficie piatta; **I've got a flat tyre** ho una gomma a terra; **as flat as a pancake** (*fam*) completamente piatto(-a); (*: Aut: tyre*) completamente sgonfio(-a) *or* a terra; **to fall flat on one's face** cadere a terra lungo(-a) disteso(-a), finire faccia a terra; **flat race** corsa piana; **flat shoes** scarpe basse **2** (*final: refusal, denial*) categorico(-a), netto(-a); **I'm not going, and that's flat!** (*fam*) non ci vado e basta! **3** (*Mus: key*) bemolle *inv*; (*: voice*) stonato(-a); (*: instrument*) scordato(-a); **C flat** do *m inv* bemolle **4** (*dull, lifeless: taste, style*) piatto(-a); (*: joke*) che non fa ridere; (*drink*) che ha perso l'effervescenza, sgassato(-a); (*battery*) scarico(-a); (*colour*) scialbo(-a); **to be feeling rather flat** sentirsi giù di corda *or* di morale **5** (*fixed*): **flat rate of pay** tariffa unica di pagamento; **at a flat rate** a una tariffa unica

■ ADV **1** (*absolutely: refuse, tell etc*) seccamente, recisamente; **flat broke** (*fam*) al verde, in bolletta; **in ten minutes flat** in dieci minuti spaccati; **(to work) flat out** (lavorare) a più non posso **2** **to spread a map out flat on the floor** stendere una cartina sul pavimento; **to be flat out** (*lying*) essere disteso(-a) *or* sdraiato(-a); (*asleep*) dormire della grossa **3** (*Mus: sing, play*) in modo stonato

■ N (*of hand*) palmo; (*of sword*) parte *f* piatta; (*Mus*) bemolle *m inv*; (*Aut*) gomma a terra

flat[2] [flæt] N (*Brit*) appartamento; **to go flat-hunting** cercare un appartamento

flat·bed ['flætbɛd] N (*also:* **flatbed truck**) autocarro a cassone aperto senza sponde

flat-bottomed ['flæt'bɒtəmd] ADJ (*boat etc*) a fondo piatto

flat cap N berretto

flat-chested ['flæt'tʃɛstɪd] ADJ piatta, che ha poco seno

flat·fish ['flætfɪʃ] N pesce *m* piatto

flat-footed ['flæt'fʊtɪd] ADJ: **to be flat-footed** avere i piedi piatti

flat·iron ['flæt,aɪən] (*old*) N ferro da stiro

flat·let ['flætlɪt] N (*Brit*) appartamentino

flat·ly ['flætlɪ] ADV (*refuse etc*) categoricamente, nettamente

flat·mate ['flæt,meɪt] N: **he's my flatmate** (*Brit*) divide l'appartamento con me

flat·ness ['flætnɪs] N (*gen*) piattezza; (*dullness*) piattezza, monotonia; (*of land*) assenza di rilievi

flat-pack ['flætpæk] ADJ: **flat-pack furniture** mobili *mpl* in kit

■ N kit *m inv*

flat racing N (*Horse-racing*) corse *fpl* piane *or* in piano

flat-screen ['flæt'skriːn] ADJ a schermo piatto

flat season N (*Horse Racing*) stagione *f* delle corse piane

flat·ten ['flætn] VT (*road, field*) spianare, appiattire; (*house, city*) abbattere, radere al suolo; (*map*) spiegare, aprire; **the town was flattened in the war** la città fu rasa al suolo durante la guerra; **to flatten o.s. against sth** appiattirsi contro qc; **he flattened himself against the wall** si è appiattito contro il muro

▸ **flatten out** VI + ADV (*road, countryside*) appiattirsi

■ VT + ADV (*path, paper*) spianare

flat·tened ['flætənd] ADJ appiattito(-a)

flat·ter ['flætə[r]] VT (*praise*) adulare, lusingare; (*show to advantage*) donare a; **she was just flattering me** mi stava solo adulando; **clothes that flatter you** vestiti che ti donano; **this photo flatters you** in questa foto sei venuto molto bene; **to flatter o.s. that one is ...** illudersi di essere...

flat·tered ['flætəd] ADJ lusingato(-a)

flat·ter·er ['flætərə[r]] N adulatore(-trice)

flat·ter·ing ['flætərɪŋ] ADJ (*person, remark*) lusinghiero(-a); (*clothes etc*) che dona, che abbellisce; **this photo of you is not very flattering** questa foto non ti fa onore

flat·ter·ing·ly ['flætərɪŋlɪ] ADV in modo lusinghiero

flat·tery ['flætərɪ] N adulazione *f*, lusinghe *fpl*

flat·ties ['flætɪz] NPL (*fam*) scarpe *fpl* basse

flatu·lence ['flætjʊləns] N flatulenza

flat·worm ['flæt,wɜːm] N verme *m* piatto, platelminta *m*

flaunt [flɔːnt] VT (*pej*) sfoggiare, ostentare

flau·tist ['flɔːtɪst] N flautista *m/f*

◎ **fla·vour**, (*Am*) **fla·vor** ['fleɪvə[r]] N sapore *m*, gusto; (*of ice-cream etc*) gusto; (*flavouring*) aroma *m*; (*fig*) atmosfera; **a very strong flavour** un sapore molto forte; **which flavour ice cream would you like?** che gusto di gelato vuoi?

■ VT: **to flavour (with)** (*Culin: cake etc*) aromatizzare (con); (*: savoury dish*) condire (con), insaporire (con); **vanilla-flavoured** al gusto di vaniglia

fla·vour·ing, (*Am*) **fla·vor·ing** ['fleɪvərɪŋ] N (*for cake etc*) aroma *m*, essenza (artificiale); (*for savoury dish*) condimento; **vanilla flavouring** aroma di vaniglia

fla·vour·some ['fleɪvəsəm] ADJ (*tomatoes, oranges etc*) saporito(-a), gustoso(-a); (*wine, coffee*) dal sapore pieno

flaw [flɔː] N (*gen*) difetto; (*crack: in china*) incrinatura

flawed [flɔːd] ADJ (*complexion*) imperfetto(-a); (*china etc*) difettoso(-a); (*argument*) debole; (*character*) pieno(-a) di difetti

flaw·less ['flɔːlɪs] ADJ perfetto(-a), senza difetti

flaw·less·ly ['flɔːlɪslɪ] ADV perfettamente

flax [flæks] N lino

flax·en ['flæksən] ADJ biondo(-a)

flaxen-haired ['flæksən'hɛəd] ADJ dai capelli biondi

flay [fleɪ] VT (*skin*) scorticare; (*criticize*) criticare aspramente, stroncare

flea [fliː] N pulce *f*; **to send sb off with a flea in his ear** (*fam*) mandare qn a quel paese

flea·bite ['fliː,baɪt] N morso di pulce; (*fig*) piccola seccatura

flea-bitten ['fliː,bɪtn] ADJ pulcioso(-a); (*fig*) pidocchioso(-a)

flea market N mercato delle pulci

flea·pit ['fliː'pɪt] N (*fam*) teatrucolo

fleck [flɛk] N (*of mud, paint, colour*) macchiolina; (*of dust*) granello

■ VT (*with blood, mud etc*) macchiettare; **brown flecked with white** marrone screziato di bianco

fled [flɛd] PT, PP *of* **flee**

fledg·ling, **fledge·ling** ['flɛdʒlɪŋ] N uccellino

◎ **flee** [fliː] (*pt, pp* **fled**) VT (*town, country*) fuggire da, scappare da; (*danger, enemy*) sfuggire a

■ VI: **to flee (from)** fuggire (da *or* davanti a); **to flee to**

Ff

sb/sth correre da qn/verso qc; **to flee to safety** mettersi in salvo

fleece [fli:s] N vello
■VT (*fig fam: rob*) pelare

fleecy ['fli:si] ADJ (*comp* **-ier**, *superl* **-iest**) (*blanket*) soffice; (*cloud*) come ovatta

◎**fleet[1]** [fli:t] N flotta; (*of cars*) parco; (*of lorries etc*) convoglio; **the British fleet** la flotta britannica; **they were followed by a fleet of cars** erano seguiti da un corteo di macchine

fleet[2] [fli:t] ADJ (*poet: also:* **fleet-footed**) svelto(-a)

fleet·ing ['fli:tɪŋ] ADJ (*glimpse*) fuggevole; (*moment, beauty*) fugace, passeggero(-a), effimero(-a); (*visit*) volante, veloce

fleet·ing·ly ['fli:tɪŋlɪ] ADV fugacemente

Flem·ing ['flɛmɪŋ] N fiammingo(-a)

Flem·ish ['flɛmɪʃ] ADJ fiammingo(-a)
■N **1** (*language*) fiammingo **2** (*people*): **the Flemish** NPL i Fiamminghi

flesh [flɛʃ] N (*gen*) carne *f*; (*of fruit*) polpa; **in the flesh** in carne ed ossa; **my own flesh and blood** la mia famiglia; **it's more than flesh and blood can stand** è più di quanto un essere umano possa sopportare; **to demand one's pound of flesh** (*fig*) esigere tutto il dovuto

flesh·ly ['flɛʃlɪ] ADJ sensuale

flesh·pot ['flɛʃ,pɒt] N locale *m* porno

flesh wound N ferita superficiale

fleshy ['flɛʃɪ] ADJ (*comp* **-ier**, *superl* **-iest**) carnoso(-a); (*Bot: fruit*) polposo(-a)

flew [flu:] PT *of* **fly**

flex [flɛks] N (*of lamp, telephone*) filo (flessibile)
■VT (*body, knees*) piegare, flettere; (*muscles*) contrarre

flexi·bil·ity [,flɛksɪ'bɪlɪtɪ] N flessibilità, elasticità

◎**flex·ible** ['flɛksɪbl] ADJ flessibile; **flexible working hours** orario di lavoro flessibile

flex·ibly ['flɛksɪblɪ] ADV in modo flessibile

flexi·time ['flɛksɪ,taɪm] N orario flessibile

flick [flɪk] N **1** (*gen*) colpetto; *see also* **flicks**
■VT dare un colpetto a; **he flicked the horse with his whip** ha dato un colpetto al cavallo con la frusta; **she flicked her hair out of her eyes** buttò i capelli da una parte
■VI: **the snake's tongue flicked in and out** la lingua del serpente guizzava
▸ **flick off** VT + ADV (*dust, ash*) mandar via con un colpetto; **he flicked a mosquito off his leg** ha cacciato via la zanzara dalla gamba con un colpetto
▸ **flick through** VI + PREP (*book, pages*) sfogliare, scartabellare

flick·er ['flɪkə^r] N (*of light, flame*) tremolio; (*of eyelid*) battito; (*of hope*) barlume *m*; **a flicker of light** un breve bagliore
■VI (*light*) tremolare; (*flame*) guizzare

flick·er·ing ['flɪkərɪŋ] ADJ (*flame, eyelids*) tremolante

flick knife N (*Brit*) coltello a serramanico

flicks [flɪks] NPL: **the flicks** (*Brit fam*) il cine

fli·er ['flaɪə^r] N aviatore(-trice)

flies [flaɪz] NPL *of* **fly**

◎**flight[1]** [flaɪt] N **1** (*Aer, gen*) volo; (*of bullet*) traiettoria; **in flight** in volo; **how long does the flight take?** quanto dura il volo?; **what time is the flight to Paris?** a che ora è il volo per Parigi?; **"flight closing"** (*Aer*) "volo in chiusura"; **flights of fancy** (*fig*) voli di fantasia; **in the top flight** (*fig*) fra i migliori **2** **flight (of stairs)** rampa (di scale); **he lives two flights up** abita due piani sopra

flight[2] [flaɪt] N (*act of fleeing*) fuga; **to put to flight** mettere in fuga; **to take flight** darsi alla fuga; **they took flight** si sono dati alla fuga

flight attendant N (*Am*) steward *m*, hostess *f inv*

flight coupon N tagliando di volo

flight crew N equipaggio

flight deck N (*on aircraft carrier*) ponte *m* di volo; (*of aeroplane*) cabina di pilotaggio

flight path N (*of aircraft*) aerovia; (*of rocket, projectile*) traiettoria

flight plan N piano di volo

flight recorder N registratore *m* di volo

flight simulator N simulatore *m* di volo

flighty ['flaɪtɪ] ADJ (*comp* **-ier**, *superl* **-iest**) capriccioso(-a), frivolo(-a)

flim·si·ly ['flɪmzɪlɪ] ADV (*dressed*) leggero; **flimsily built** costruito(-a) poco solidamente

flim·si·ness ['flɪmzɪnɪs] N (*of dress*) leggerezza; (*of structure, argument*) scarsa solidità

flim·sy ['flɪmzɪ] ADJ (*comp* **-ier**, *superl* **-iest**) (*thin: dress*) leggero(-a); (*weak: construction*) poco solido(-a); (*: excuse*) debole; (*: argument*) che non sta in piedi, inconsistente; **a flimsy excuse** una debole scusa; **a flimsy nightgown** una camicia da notte leggera

flinch [flɪntʃ] VI trasalire; **without flinching** senza batter ciglio; **to flinch from sth** tirarsi indietro di fronte a qc

fling [flɪŋ] (*vb: pt, pp* **flung**) N (*love affair*) avventura; **to have a last fling** fare un'ultima follia; **to have one's fling** godersela; **to have a fling at doing sth** cercare *or* tentare di fare qc
■VT (*stone etc*) lanciare, gettare, scagliare; **he flung the dictionary onto the floor** ha gettato il dizionario sul pavimento; **to fling one's arms round sb** gettare le braccia al collo di qn; **the door was flung open** la porta fu spalancata; **to fling o.s. into a chair** buttarsi su una poltrona; **to fling o.s. into a job** gettarsi a capofitto in un lavoro; **to fling on one's clothes** vestirsi in fretta e furia
▸ **fling away** VT + ADV (*waste*) gettare via, sperperare
▸ **fling off** VT + ADV togliersi in fretta e furia
▸ **fling on** VT + ADV (*clothes*) mettersi in fretta e furia
▸ **fling out** VT + ADV (*unwanted object*) buttare via; (*person*) buttar fuori
▸ **fling up** VT + ADV lanciare in aria; **to fling up one's arms** alzare le braccia al cielo; **she flung up her head** ha buttato la testa all'indietro

flint [flɪnt] N (*Geol*) selce *f*; (*for lighter*) pietrina; **a flint axe** un'ascia di selce

flint·lock ['flɪnt,lɒk] N fucile *m* ad acciarino

flip [flɪp] N colpetto
■VT (*switch*) dare un colpetto a; (*Am: pancake*) rivoltare (*dando un colpo alla padella*); **to flip a coin** lanciare una moneta in aria, fare a testa e croce; **he flipped the book open** ha aperto il libro con un rapido gesto della mano
■VI **1** (*fam: lose temper*) uscire dai gangheri **2** **to flip for sth** (*Am*) fare a testa e croce per qc
■ADJ (*fam: remark*) poco serio(-a)
▸ **flip through** VI + PREP (*book, records*) dare una scorsa a

flip chart N blocco di fogli per lavagna

flip-flops ['flɪp,flɒps] NPL (*sandals*) infradito *mpl*

flip·pan·cy ['flɪpənsɪ] N frivolezza

flip·pant ['flɪpənt] ADJ (*remark, tone*) poco serio(-a); (*attitude*) frivolo(-a)

flip·pant·ly ['flɪpəntlɪ] ADV (*speak*) in modo poco serio

flip·per ['flɪpə^r] N pinna
flip·ping ['flɪpɪŋ] ADJ (*fam*) maledetto(-a)
flip side N (*of record*) retro
flirt [flɜːt] N (*woman*) civetta; (*man*): **he's a terrible flirt** è un gran donnaiolo
■ VI: **to flirt (with)** flirtare (con); (*woman only*) civettare (con); **to flirt with an idea** trastullarsi con un'idea
flir·ta·tion [flɜː'teɪʃən] N flirt *m inv*
flir·ta·tious [flɜː'teɪʃəs] ADJ civettuolo(-a)
flit [flɪt] VI (*bats, butterflies*) svolazzare; **to flit in/out** (*person*) entrare/uscire svolazzando
■ N (*Brit*): **to do a (moonlight) flit** squagliarsela (*per non pagare l'affitto, il conto in albergo ecc*)
◎**float** [fləʊt] N galleggiante *m*; (*cork*) sughero; (*vehicle in parade*) carro; (*cash*) soldi *mpl* in cassa (*per dare il resto*)
■ VT (*boat, logs*) far galleggiare; (*refloat*) riportare a galla; (*launch: project, plan*) lanciare; (*Fin: company*) lanciare (*emettendo azioni*); (*: currency*) far fluttuare; **to float an idea** ventilare un'idea
■ VI (*gen*) galleggiare; (*ship*) stare a galla; (*bather*) fare il morto; (*Fin: currency*) fluttuare; **to float downstream** essere trascinato(-a) dalla corrente
▸ **float away, float off** VI + ADV (*in water*) andare alla deriva; (*in air*) volare via
float·ing ['fləʊtɪŋ] ADJ a galla
floating voter N elettore *m* indeciso
flock [flɒk] N (*of sheep, also Rel*) gregge *m*; (*of birds*) stormo; (*of people*) stuolo, folla
■ VI (*crowd*) affollarsi, ammassarsi; **to flock around sb** affollarsi intorno a qn
floe [fləʊ] N (*also:* **ice floe**) banchisa
flog [flɒg] VT frustare, flagellare; **to flog a dead horse** (*fig fam*) perdere il proprio tempo; **to flog o.s. to death** (*fig fam*) ammazzarsi di fatica
flog·ging ['flɒgɪŋ] N fustigazione *f*
◎**flood** [flʌd] N inondazione *f*, alluvione *f*; (*of words, tears*) diluvio; **the rain has caused serious floods** la pioggia ha causato gravi inondazioni; **the river is in flood** il fiume è in piena; **the Flood** (*Rel*) il diluvio universale; **he received a flood of letters** ha ricevuto una marea di lettere; **she was in floods of tears** era in un mare di lacrime
■ VT (*town, fields: fig*) inondare, allagare; (*Aut: carburettor*) ingolfare; **the river has flooded the village** il fiume ha allagato il paese; **to flood the market** (*Comm*) inondare il mercato
■ VI (*river*) straripare; **the crowd flooded into the streets** la folla si riversò nelle strade
▸ **flood in** VI + ADV entrare in grande quantità; **the light flooded in through the window** una gran luce entrava dalla finestra
▸ **flood out** VT + ADV (*house*) inondare; **they were flooded out** l'inondazione li ha costretti ad abbandonare le loro case
flood·gates ['flʌd,geɪts] NPL: **to open the floodgates to** aprire le porte a
flood·ing ['flʌdɪŋ] N inondazione *f*
flood·light ['flʌd,laɪt] (*vb: pt, pp* **floodlighted** *or* **floodlit**) N riflettore *m*; **to play a match under floodlights** giocare una partita in notturna
■ VT illuminare a giorno
flood·lit ['flʌd,lɪt] PT, PP *of* **floodlight**
■ ADJ illuminato(-a) a giorno
flood plain N (*Geog*) zona soggetta a inondazioni
flood tide N alta marea, marea crescente
flood·water ['flʌd,wɔːtə^r] N acque *fpl* (*di inondazione*)
◎**floor** [flɔː] N **1** (*gen*) suolo; (*of room*) pavimento; (*of sea, valley*) fondo; (*dance floor*) pista; (*fig: at meeting*): **the floor** il pubblico; **a tiled floor** un pavimento a piastrelle; **on the floor** per terra, sul pavimento; **to take the floor** (*dancer*) mettersi a ballare; **to have the floor** (*speaker*) prendere la parola **2** (*storey*) piano; **ground floor** (*Brit*) pianterreno, piano terra; **on the first floor** (*Brit*) al primo piano; (*Am*) al pianterreno; **top floor** ultimo piano
■ VT **1** (*room*): **to floor (with)** pavimentare (con) **2** (*fam: knock down: opponent*) atterrare; (*: baffle*) confondere
floor·board ['flɔː,bɔːd] N asse *f* di pavimento
floor cleaner N detersivo per pavimenti
floor·cloth ['flɔː,klɒθ] N straccio per il pavimento
floor covering N rivestimento (di pavimento)
floored [flɔːd] ADJ: **room floored with oak** stanza con il pavimento di quercia
floor·ing ['flɔːrɪŋ] N (*floor*) pavimento; (*material*) materiale *m* per pavimentazioni
floor lamp N (*Am*) lampada a stelo
floor polish N cera per pavimenti
floor pol·ish·er ['flɔː,pɒlɪʃə^r] N lucidatrice *f*
floor show N spettacolo di varietà
floor·walker ['flɔː,wɔːkə^r] N (*esp Am*) caporeparto *m/f* (*in grande magazzino*)
floo·zy ['fluːzɪ] N (*fam*) puttanella
flop [flɒp] N (*fam: failure*) fiasco; **the film was a flop** il film è stato un fiasco
■ VI **1** (*person*): **to flop (into/on)** lasciarsi cadere (in/su) **2** (*fam: play*) far fiasco; (*: scheme*) fallire
flop·py ['flɒpɪ] ADJ (*comp* **-ier**, *superl* **-iest**) floscio(-a), molle; **floppy hat** cappello floscio
■ N = **floppy disk**
floppy disk N floppy disk *m inv*
flo·ra [flɔːrə] N flora
flo·ral ['flɔːrəl] ADJ (*arrangement*) floreale; (*fabric, dress*) a fiori; **floral tribute** omaggio floreale
Flor·ence ['flɒrəns] N Firenze *f*
Flor·en·tine ['flɒrən,taɪn] ADJ, N fiorentino(-a)
flo·ret ['flɔːrɪt] N (*Bot*) flosculo
flor·id ['flɔːrɪd] ADJ (*complexion*) florido(-a); (*style*) fiorito(-a)
Flori·da ['flɒrɪdə] N Florida
▷ www.myflorida.com/
flo·rist ['flɒrɪst] N fioraio(-a); **at the florist's (shop)** dal fioraio
floss [flɒs] N filamenti *mpl*; (*thread*) seta da ricamo; **dental floss** filo interdentale
■ VT (*teeth*) pulire col filo interdentale
flo·ta·tion [fləʊ'teɪʃən] N (*Fin*) lancio
flot·sam ['flɒtsəm] N: **flotsam and jetsam** rifiuti *mpl* portati dal mare; (*people*) relitti *mpl*
flounce[1] [flaʊns] VI: **to flounce in/out** entrare/uscire stizzito(-a)
■ N balzo
flounce[2] [flaʊns] N (*frill*) balza
floun·der[1] ['flaʊndə^r] VI (*also:* **flounder about**: *in water, mud*) dibattersi, annaspare; (*: in speech etc*) impappinarsi, esitare
floun·der[2] [flaʊndə^r] N (*fish*) passera di mare
flour ['flaʊə^r] N farina
floured ['flaʊəd] ADJ infarinato(-a)
flour·ish ['flʌrɪʃ] N abbellimento; (*movement*) gran gesto; (*under signature*) svolazzo; (*Mus: fanfare*) fanfara; **to do sth with a flourish** fare qc con ostentazione
■ VI (*gen*) fiorire; (*person*) essere in piena forma; (*writer, artist*) avere successo; (*business etc*) prosperare; **the**

Ff

business flourished la ditta prosperava
■ VT (*weapon, stick*) brandire

flour·ish·ing ['flʌrɪʃɪŋ] ADJ (*plant*) rigoglioso(-a); (*person*) florido(-a), in gran forma; (*business*) fiorente, prospero(-a)

floury ['flaʊərɪ] ADJ (*hands*) infarinato(-a); (*potato*) farinoso(-a)

flout [flaʊt] VT (*order*) contravvenire a; (*advice*) ignorare deliberatamente; (*conventions, society*) sfidare; **they persist in flouting the law** continuano a contravvenire alla legge; **he dared to flout convention** ha osato sfidare le convenzioni

◎ **flow** [fləʊ] N (*of river, also Elec*) corrente *f*; (*of tide*) flusso; (*of blood: from wound*) uscita; (*: in veins*) circolazione *f*; (*of words*) fiume *m*; (*of insults, orders*) caterva, sfilza; **the flow of traffic** la circolazione
■ VI (*gen*) fluire; (*tide*) salire; (*blood in veins, traffic*) circolare; (*hair*) ricadere (morbidamente), scendere; **money flowed in** (*fig*) i soldi sono arrivati in grande quantità; **the river flows into the sea** il fiume sfocia nel mare; **to keep the conversation flowing** mantenere viva la conversazione

flow chart N schema *m* di flusso

flow diagram N diagramma *m* di flusso, organigramma *m*

◎ **flow·er** ['flaʊə^r] N fiore *m*; **a bunch of flowers** un mazzo di fiori; **in flower** in fiore
■ VI fiorire

flower arrangement N composizione *f* floreale

flower·bed ['flaʊə,bɛd] N aiuola

flow·ered ['flaʊəd] ADJ a fiori

flower girl N (*in street*) fioraia; (*at wedding*) damigella

flow·er·ing ['flaʊərɪŋ] N fioritura
■ ADJ (*in flower*) in fiore; (*which flowers*) fiorifero(-a), da fiore

flower·pot ['flaʊə,pɒt] N vaso da fiori

flower shop N negozio di fiori, fioraio

flower show N mostra di fiori

flow·ery ['flaʊərɪ] ADJ (*meadow*) fiorito(-a), in fiore; (*dress, material*) a fiori; (*style, speech*) fiorito(-a)

flow·ing ['fləʊɪŋ] ADJ (*style*) scorrevole, fluido(-a); (*movement*) sciolto(-a); (*dress*) di linea morbida; (*hair*) fluente; **flowing robes** abiti *mpl* dalle linee fluide

flown [fləʊn] PP *of* **fly**

fl. oz. N ABBR = **fluid ounce**

flu [flu:] N (*fam*) influenza

fluc·tu·ate ['flʌktjʊ,eɪt] VI (*cost, rate, speed*) fluttuare, oscillare; (*person*): **he fluctuated between fear and excitement** passava da uno stato di paura a uno stato di eccitazione

fluc·tu·at·ing ['flʌktjʊ,eɪtɪŋ] ADJ oscillante

fluc·tua·tion [,flʌktjʊ'eɪʃən] N fluttuazione *f*, oscillazione *f*

flue [flu:] N canna fumaria

flu·en·cy ['flu:ənsɪ] N facilità, scioltezza; **his fluency in English** la sua scioltezza nel parlare l'inglese

flu·ent ['flu:ənt] ADJ (*style*) fluido(-a), scorrevole; (*speaker*) dalla parola facile; (*speech*) facile, sciolto(-a); (*French*) corrente; **he's a fluent speaker/reader** si esprime/legge senza difficoltà; **he speaks fluent Italian** *or* **he's fluent in Italian** parla l'italiano correntemente

flu·ent·ly ['flu:əntlɪ] ADV (*speak a language*) correntemente; (*speak, write*) con scioltezza, con facilità

fluff [flʌf] N (*from blankets etc*) pelucchi *mpl*; (*of chicks, kittens*) lanugine *f*
■ VT **1** (*also:* **fluff out**) rendere soffice *or* vaporoso(-a); (*feathers*) arruffare; **to fluff up the pillows** sprimacciare i cuscini **2** (*fam: make mistake in*) impaperarsi nel recitare

fluffi·ness ['flʌfɪnɪs] N morbidezza

fluffy ['flʌfɪ] ADJ (*toy*) di peluche; (*kitten, chick*) coperto(-a) di lanugine; (*pullover*) morbido(-a) e peloso(-a); **fluffy towels** asciugamani morbidi

flu·id ['flu:ɪd] ADJ (*substance, movement*) fluido(-a); (*plan, arrangements*) flessibile, elastico(-a)
■ N fluido, liquido; (*in diet*) liquido

flu·id·ity [flu:'ɪdɪtɪ] N (*of substance*) fluidità; (*of movement*) scioltezza; (*of arrangements*) elasticità

fluid ounce N *unità di misura di capacità pari a 0.028 l (Brit) o 0.030 l (Am)*

fluke [flu:k] N (*fam*) colpo di fortuna; **by a fluke** per puro caso

flum·mox ['flʌməks] VT (*fam*) sconcertare, rendere perplesso(-a)

flung [flʌŋ] PT, PP *of* **fling**

flunk [flʌŋk] VT (*esp Am fam: course, exam*) essere bocciato(-a) *or* respinto(-a) in *or* a

flunky ['flʌŋkɪ] N tirapiedi *m/f inv*

fluo·res·cence [,fluə'rɛsəns] N fluorescenza

fluo·res·cent [,fluə'rɛsənt] ADJ (*lighting, tube*) fluorescente

fluori·da·tion [,fluərɪ'deɪʃən] N fluorizzazione *f*

fluo·ride ['fluə,raɪd] N fluoruro

fluoride toothpaste N dentifricio al fluoro

fluo·rine ['fluəri:n] N fluoro

flur·ried ['flʌrɪd] ADJ agitato(-a)

flur·ry ['flʌrɪ] N (*of snow*) turbine *m*; (*of wind*) folata; **a flurry of activity/excitement** un'intensa attività/un'improvvisa agitazione; **in a flurry** in uno stato di agitazione *or* eccitazione

flush [flʌʃ] N **1** (*lavatory flush*) sciacquone *m*; **he heard the flush of a toilet** ha sentito il rumore di uno sciacquone **2** (*blush*) rossore *m*; **there was a slight flush on his cheeks** c'era un leggero rossore sulle sue guance **3** (*of beauty, health, youth*) rigoglio, pieno vigore *m*; (*fig: exhilaration*) ebbrezza; **in the first flush of victory** nell'ebbrezza della vittoria; **in a flush of excitement** in uno stato di eccitazione **4** (*in poker*) colore *m*; *see also* **hot flush**
■ ADJ **1** (*level*): **flush (with)** a livello (di *or* con); **a door flush with the wall** una porta a livello con la parete **2** (*fam*): **to be flush (with money)** essere pieno(-a) di soldi
■ VI (*person, face*): **to flush (with)** arrossire (di); **Irene flushed with embarrassment** Irene è arrossita per l'imbarazzo; **flushed with success** eccitato(-a) dal successo
■ VT **1** pulire con un getto d'acqua; **to flush the lavatory** *or* **the toilet** tirare l'acqua **2** (*also:* **flush out**: *game, birds*) far alzare in volo; (*: fig: criminal*) stanare
▸ **flush away** VT + ADV (*down lavatory*) buttare nel gabinetto (e tirare l'acqua)

flushed [flʌʃt] ADJ tutto(-a) rosso(-a)

flus·ter ['flʌstə^r] N agitazione *f*
■ VT (*confuse, upset*) mettere in agitazione, innervosire; **to get flustered** agitarsi

flus·tered ['flʌstəd] ADJ sconvolto(-a), in uno stato di confusione

flute [flu:t] N flauto

flut·ist ['flu:tɪst] N (*Am*) = **flautist**

flut·ter ['flʌtə^r] N agitazione *f*; (*of eyelashes*) battito; (*of wings*) battito, frullio; **to be in a flutter** (*fig*) essere in uno stato di agitazione; **to have a flutter** (*fam: gamble*)

fare una scommessa
■ VT (*wings*) battere; **to flutter one's eyelashes at sb** fare gli occhi dolci a qn
■ VI svolazzare; (*bird etc*) battere le ali; (*flag*) sventolare; (*heart*) palpitare

flux [flʌks] N **1** **to be in a state of flux** essere in continuo mutamento **2** (*Med, Phys*) flusso; (*Metallurgy*) fondente *m*

◎ **fly¹** [flaɪ] N (*insect*) mosca; **he wouldn't hurt a fly** non farebbe male a una mosca; **they were dropping like flies** morivano come mosche; **the fly in the ointment** (*fig*) la piccola pecca che sciupa tutto; **there are no flies on him** (*fig*) non è nato ieri, non si fa prendere per il naso

fly² [flaɪ] (*vb: pp* **flew**, *pt* **flown**) VI **1** (*gen*) volare; (*passengers*) andare in aereo; (*flag*) sventolare; **the plane flew over London** l'aereo ha sorvolato Londra; **he flew from London to Glasgow** è andato in aereo da Londra a Glasgow; **he's never flown** non è mai andato in aereo **2** (*move quickly: time*) volare, passare in fretta; **to fly past sb** (*subj: car, person*) sfrecciare davanti a qn; **the door flew open** la porta si è spalancata all'improvviso; **to knock** *or* **send sth/sb flying** far volare qc/qn; **I must fly!** devo scappare!; **to let fly at sb** scagliarsi contro qn; **to fly into a rage** infuriarsi; **to fly off the handle** perdere le staffe **3** (*flee*) fuggire, scappare; **to fly for one's life** salvare la pelle scappando
■ VT (*aircraft*) pilotare; (*passenger, cargo*) trasportare (in aereo); (*distances*) percorrere; (*flag*) battere; **to fly the Atlantic** sorvolare l'Atlantico; **to fly a kite** far volare un aquilone
■ N (*on trousers: also:* **flies**) patta
▸ **fly away** VI + ADV volar via
▸ **fly in** VI + ADV (*plane*) arrivare; (*person*) arrivare in aereo; **he flew in from Rome** è venuto da Roma in aereo
■ VT + ADV (*supplies, troops*) trasportare in aereo
▸ **fly off** VI + ADV volare via
▸ **fly out** VI + ADV (*plane*) partire; (*person*) partire in aereo

fly·blown ['flaɪˌbləʊn] ADJ (*meat*) infestato(-a) di uova di mosca

fly·by ['flaɪˌbaɪ] N (*Am*) parata aerea

fly-drive ['flaɪdraɪv] ADJ fly-and-drive *inv*

fly-fishing ['flaɪˌfɪʃɪŋ] N pesca con la mosca

fly·ing ['flaɪɪŋ] ADJ (*gen*) volante; **to pass an exam with flying colours** superare un esame con risultati brillanti; **to take a flying leap** *or* **jump** fare un gran balzo
■ N (*action*) volo; (*activity*) aviazione *f*; **he doesn't like flying** non gli piace viaggiare in aereo

flying ambulance N aereo ambulanza

flying boat N idrovolante *m*

flying buttress N (*Archit*) arco rampante

flying doctor N medico volante

flying fish N pesce *m* volante

flying fox N pteropo

flying picket N picchetto (*proveniente da fabbriche ecc non direttamente coinvolte nello sciopero*)

flying saucer N disco volante

flying squad N (*Police*) (squadra) volante *f*

flying start N partenza lanciata; **to get off to a flying start** (*fig*) partire come un razzo, avere un inizio brillante

flying time N (*of flight*) durata del volo

flying visit N (*of official*) visita-lampo; (*of friends*) breve visita

fly·leaf ['flaɪˌli:f] N (*pl* **-leaves**) risguardo

fly·over ['flaɪˌəʊvəʳ] N (*Brit: bridge*) cavalcavia *m inv*

fly·paper ['flaɪˌpeɪpəʳ] N carta moschicida

fly·past ['flaɪpɑːst] N parata aerea

fly·sheet [flaɪˌʃi:t] N (*for tent*) soprattetto

fly spray N (spray *m inv*) moschicida *m*

fly swat, fly swatter N acchiappamosche *m inv*

fly·weight ['flaɪˌweɪt] (*Boxing*) N peso *m* mosca *inv*
■ ADJ (*contest*) di pesi mosca

fly·wheel ['flaɪˌwi:l] N (*Tech*) volano

FM [ˌɛf'ɛm] N ABBR (*Radio:* = **frequency modulation**) FM; (*Brit Mil*) = **field marshal**

FMB [ˌɛfɛm'bi:] N ABBR (*Am*) = *Federal Maritime Board*

FMCS [ˌɛfɛmsi:'ɛs] N ABBR (*Am:* = *Federal Mediation and Conciliation Service*) *organismo di conciliazione in caso di conflitti sul lavoro*

FO [ˌɛf'əʊ] N ABBR (*Brit*) = **Foreign Office**

foal [fəʊl] N puledro

foam [fəʊm] N (*gen*) schiuma
■ VI (*sea*) spumeggiare; **to foam at the mouth** avere la schiuma alla bocca

foam-backed ['fəʊmˌbækt] ADJ (*carpet*) con il rovescio in gomma

foam bath N bagnoschiuma *m inv*

foam rubber N gommapiuma®

foamy ['fəʊmɪ] ADJ (*comp* **-ier**, *superl* **-iest**) spumeggiante

FOB, f.o.b. ABBR (= **free on board**) FOB, franco a bordo

fob [fɒb] VT: **to fob sb off (with sth)** appioppare *or* rifilare (qc) a qn; **to fob sb off with promises** tenere qn buono(-a) con delle promesse
■ N (*also:* **watch fob**: *chain*) catena per orologio; (: *band of cloth*) nastro per orologio
▸ **fob off on** VT + ADV + PREP rifilare a

FOC ABBR (*Brit*) = **free of charge**; *see* **free**

fo·cal ['fəʊkl] ADJ (*Tech*) focale

focal point N (*fig*) centro; (*of lens, mirror*) punto focale

fo'c'sle ['fəʊksl] N = **forecastle**

◎ **fo·cus** ['fəʊkəs] N (*pl* **focuses** *or* **foci** ['fəʊkaɪ]) (*gen*) fuoco; (*of attention, interest*) centro; **he was the focus of attention** era al centro dell'attenzione; **to be out of focus** (*Phot*) essere sfocato(-a); **in focus** a fuoco
■ VT: **to focus (on)** (*camera, instrument, field glasses*) mettere a fuoco (su); (*attention, eyes*) focalizzare (su); (*light rays*) far convergere (su)
■ VI: **to focus (on)** (*light, heat, rays*) convergere (su); (*person*) fissare lo sguardo (su); **to focus on sth** (*eyes, person*) mettere a fuoco qc; (*subject, problem*) concentrarsi su qc

focus group N (*Pol*) gruppo di discussione, focus group *m inv*

fod·der ['fɒdəʳ] N foraggio

fodder crop N coltura foraggera

FOE [ˌɛfəʊ'i:] N ABBR **1** (= **Friends of the Earth**) Amici della Terra **2** (*Am:* = **Fraternal Order of Eagles**) *organizzazione filantropica*

foe [fəʊ] N (*liter*) nemico(-a)

foe·tal, (*Am*) **fe·tal** ['fi:tl] ADJ fetale

foet·id ['fi:tɪd] ADJ = **fetid**

foe·tus, (*Am*) **fe·tus** ['fi:təs] N feto

fog [fɒg] N nebbia
■ VT (*lens*) far appannare; **to fog the issue** (*fig*) confondere le cose

fog bank N banco di nebbia

fog·bound ['fɒgˌbaʊnd] ADJ fermo(-a) a causa della nebbia

fo·gey, fogy ['fəʊgɪ] N (*fam*): **old fogey** matusa *m inv*

Ff

fog·gi·ness ['fɒgɪnɪs] N nebbiosità

fog·gy ['fɒgɪ] ADJ (*comp* **-ier**, *superl* **-iest**) nebbioso(-a); **it's foggy** c'è nebbia; **a foggy day** una giornata nebbiosa; **I haven't the foggiest (idea)** (*fam*) non ne ho la più pallida idea

fog·horn ['fɒg,hɔ:n] N corno da nebbia; **a voice like a foghorn** una voce tonante

fog light, fog lamp (*Brit*) N (*Aut*) faro *m* antinebbia *inv*

fog signal N (*Rail*) segnale *m* da nebbia

fogy ['fəʊgɪ] N = **fogey**

foi·ble ['fɔɪbl] N debolezza, mania

foil¹ [fɔɪl] N **1** lamina di metallo; (*also:* **tinfoil, kitchen foil**) carta stagnola *or* d'alluminio; **to act as a foil to sb/sth** (*fig*) far risaltare qn/qc **2** (*Fencing*) fioretto

foil² [fɔɪl] VT (*thief*) fermare; (*attempt*) far fallire, sventare

foist [fɔɪst] VT: **to foist sth on sb** rifilare qc a qn

fold¹ [fəʊld] N (*Agr*) ovile *m*; **to come back to the fold** (*fig*) tornare all'ovile

◎ **fold²** [fəʊld] N (*bend, crease, also Geol*) piega

■ VT (*gen*) piegare; (*wings*) ripiegare; **she folded the paper in two** piegò in due la carta; **he folded the newspaper in half** ha piegato a metà il giornale; **to fold one's arms** incrociare le braccia

■ VI (*chair, table*) piegarsi; (*fam: fail: business venture*) crollare; (*: play*) chiudere

▸ **fold away** VI + ADV (*table, bed*) piegarsi, essere pieghevole

■ VT + ADV (*clothes, linen*) piegare, mettere a posto

▸ **fold back** VT + ADV ripiegare

▸ **fold over** VT + ADV ripiegare

▸ **fold up** VI + ADV (*fam: fail: business*) fallire, crollare

■ VT + ADV (*map, paper*) piegare, ripiegare

fold·away ['fəʊldə,weɪ] ADJ (*bed, table*) pieghevole

fold·ed ['fəʊldɪd] ADJ (*paper*) piegato(-a); (*closed*) chiuso(-a)

fold·er ['fəʊldəʳ] N (*file: for papers*) cartella, cartellina; (*binder*) raccoglitore *m*

fold·ing ['fəʊldɪŋ] ADJ (*chair, doors, bed*) pieghevole

folding money N (*Am*) banconote *fpl*

fold mountains NPL montagne *fpl* a pieghe

fo·li·age ['fəʊlɪɪdʒ] N fogliame *m*

fo·lia·tion [,fəʊlɪ'eɪʃən] N fogliazione *f*

fo·lic acid [,fəʊlɪk'æsɪd] N acido folico

fo·lio ['fəʊlɪəʊ] N (*book*) volume *m* in folio; (*sheet*) foglio

◎ **folk** [fəʊk] N **1** (*people*) gente *f*; **country/city folk** gente di campagna/di città; **my folks** (*fam*) la mia famiglia, i miei **2** (*also:* **folk music**) folk *m inv*

folk·lore ['fəʊk,lɔ:ʳ] N folclore *m*

folk music N musica *f* folk *inv*

▹ www.bbc.co.uk/radio2/soldonsong/genres/folk.shtml

folk singer N cantante *m/f* folk *inv*

folk song ['fəʊk,sɒŋ] N canto popolare, canzone *f* folk *inv*

folk·sy ['fəʊksɪ] ADJ (*comp* **-ier**, *superl* **-iest**) (*often pej: person*) senza pretese; (*: art, humour*) popolare

fol·li·cle ['fɒlɪkl] N follicolo

follicle-stimulating hormone ['fɒlɪkl'stɪmjʊ,leɪtɪŋ'hɔ:məʊn] N ormone *m* follicolo-stimolante

◎ **fol·low** ['fɒləʊ] VT (*gen*) seguire; (*football team*) fare il tifo per; **the road follows the coast** la strada segue la costa; **we're being followed** qualcuno ci sta seguendo; **to follow sb's advice** seguire il consiglio di qn; **he followed suit** ha fatto altrettanto; **I don't quite follow you** non sono sicuro di capirti *or* seguirti; **following his resignation ...** in seguito alle sue dimissioni...

■ VI **1** (*gen*) seguire; **as follows** come segue; **you go first and I'll follow** vai tu per primo, io ti seguo; **to follow in sb's footsteps** seguire le orme di qn; **what is there to follow?** che c'è dopo?; **I don't follow** non capisco **2** (*result, deduction etc*) risultare, conseguire; **it follows that ...** ne consegue che...; **it doesn't follow that ...** non vuol dire che...; **that doesn't follow** non necessariamente

▸ **follow about, follow around** VT + ADV seguire dappertutto

▸ **follow on** VI + ADV (*continue*): **to follow on from** seguire

▸ **follow out** VT + ADV (*implement: idea, plan*) eseguire, portare a termine

▸ **follow through** VT + ADV = **follow out**

■ VI + ADV (*Golf*) portare a termine l'azione; (*Tennis*) accompagnare la palla

▸ **follow up** VT + ADV **1** (*investigate: case, clue*) esaminare, seguire; **the police are following up several leads** la polizia sta seguendo diverse piste **2** (*take further action on: offer, suggestion*) seguire **3** (*reinforce: success, victory*) rafforzare, sfruttare; (*letter, offer*) fare seguito a

■ VI + ADV (*Ftbl etc*): **to follow up with another goal** segnare di nuovo

fol·low·er ['fɒləʊəʳ] N (*disciple*) seguace *m/f*, discepolo(-a); (*of team*) tifoso(-a)

◎ **fol·low·ing** ['fɒləʊɪŋ] ADJ seguente, successivo(-a); **following wind** vento in poppa; **the following day** il giorno seguente, l'indomani

■ N **1** (*Pol etc*) seguito, proseliti *mpl*; (*Sport*) tifosi *mpl*; **they have a large following** hanno un grande seguito **2** **he said the following** ha detto quanto segue; **see the following** (*in document etc*) vedi quanto segue; **the following is the text of the statement** riportiamo qui di seguito il testo della dichiarazione

follow-my-leader ['fɒləʊmaɪ'li:dəʳ] N *gioco in cui tutti i bambini ripetono i gesti del capofila*

follow-up ['fɒləʊ,ʌp] N seguito

follow-up letter N lettera (*informativa or di risposta*)

follow-up visit N (*Med*) visita di controllo

fol·ly ['fɒlɪ] N follia, pazzia

fo·ment [fə'ment] VT (*frm: trouble, discord, revolution*) fomentare; (*Med*) applicare impacchi caldi

fond [fɒnd] ADJ (*comp* **-er**, *superl* **-est**) (*loving: memory, look*) affettuoso(-a), tenero(-a); (*doting*) che stravede; (*foolish: hope, desire*) vano(-a); **to be fond of sb** voler bene a qn; **she's fond of swimming** le piace nuotare; **she's fond of dogs** le piacciono i cani

> DID YOU KNOW ...?
> **fond** is not translated by the Italian word *fondo*

fon·dant ['fɒndənt] N fondente *m*

fon·dle ['fɒndl] VT accarezzare

fond·ly ['fɒndlɪ] ADV (*lovingly*) affettuosamente; (*naïvely*) ingenuamente; **he fondly believed that ...** ha avuto l'ingenuità di credere che...

fond·ness ['fɒndnɪs] N: **fondness (for sth)** predilezione *f* (per qc); **fondness (for sb)** affetto (per qn)

fon·due ['fɒndu:] N fonduta, fondue *f inv*

font [fɒnt] N **1** (*in church*) fonte *m* battesimale **2** (*Typ*) carattere *m* (di scrittura)

◎ **food** [fu:d] N cibo; (*for plants*) fertilizzante *m*; **I left**

some food for the cat ho lasciato un po' di cibo per il gatto; **Italian food is very popular** la cucina italiana è molto popolare; **I've no food left in the house** non c'è più niente da mangiare in casa; **the food at the hotel is terrible** si mangia malissimo in albergo; **to be off one's food** (*fam*) aver perso l'appetito; **food for thought** (*fig*) qualcosa su cui riflettere
food chain N catena alimentare
food mixer N frullatore *m*
food parcel N pacco *m* viveri *inv*
food poisoning N intossicazione *f* alimentare
food processor N tritatutto *m inv* elettrico
food rationing N razionamento alimentare
food stamp N (*Am*) *buono alimentare dato agli indigenti*
food·stuff ['fu:d,stʌf] N cibarie *fpl*
food·stuffs ['fu:d,stʌfs] NPL generi *mpl* alimentari
food supplies NPL derrate *fpl* alimentari
◎**fool** [fu:l] N **1** sciocco(-a), stupido(-a), fesso(-a); (*jester*) buffone *m*, giullare *m*; **you fool!** stupido!; **don't be a fool!** non fare lo stupido!; **I was a fool not to go** sono stato stupido a non andarci; **some fool of a civil servant** uno stupido di impiegato statale; **to play the fool** fare lo/la stupido(-a); **to live in a fool's paradise** (*fig*) vivere di illusioni; **he is nobody's fool** non è mica scemo; **to make a fool of sb** far fare a qn la figura dello scemo, prendere in giro qn; **to make a fool of o.s.** rendersi *or* coprirsi di ridicolo(-a); **to go on a fool's errand** fare la strada per niente **2** (*Culin*) frullato
■ADJ (*Am*) sciocco(-a)
■VT (*deceive*) ingannare, far fesso(-a); **you can't fool me** non mi inganni
■VI scherzare; **I was only fooling** stavo solo scherzando
▸ **fool about, fool around** VI + ADV **1** (*waste time*) perdere tempo **2** (*act the fool*) fare lo/la stupido(-a)
fool·ery ['fu:lərɪ] N stupidaggini *fpl*
fool·har·di·ness ['fu:l,hɑ:dɪnɪs] N imprudenza, avventatezza
fool·hardy ['fu:l,hɑ:dɪ] ADJ (*rash*) avventato(-a), imprudente
fool·ish ['fu:lɪʃ] ADJ (*senseless*) sciocco(-a), stupido(-a), insensato(-a); (*ridiculous*) ridicolo(-a), assurdo(-a); (*unwise*) imprudente; **that was very foolish of you** è stato molto sciocco da parte tua
fool·ish·ly ['fu:lɪʃlɪ] ADV stupidamente
fool·ish·ness ['fu:lɪʃnɪs] N stupidità
fool·proof ['fu:l,pru:f] ADJ (*method, plan etc*) infallibile, sicurissimo(-a); (*machine*) facile da usare
fools·cap ['fu:lz,kæp] N carta protocollo
◎**foot** [fʊt] N (*pl* **feet**) **1** (*gen*) piede *m*; (*of animal*) zampa; (*of page, stairs etc*) fondo; **on foot** a piedi; **she's got big feet** ha i piedi grandi; **to be on one's feet** essere in piedi; (*after illness*) essersi rimesso(-a); **to jump/rise to one's feet** balzare/alzarsi in piedi; **it's wet under foot** è bagnato per terra **2** (*fig phrases*): **to fall on one's feet** cadere in piedi; **to find one's feet** ambientarsi; **to get cold feet** avere fifa; **to get under sb's feet** stare tra i piedi a qn; **to have one foot in the grave** avere un piede nella fossa; **to put one's foot down** (*say no*) imporsi; (*Aut*) schiacciare l'acceleratore; **to get a foot in the door** fare il primo passo; **to put one's foot in it** fare una gaffe; **to put one's feet up** (*fam*) riposarsi; **I've never set foot there** non ci ho mai messo piede; **to put one's best foot forward** (*hurry*) sbrigarsi; **to get off on the right/wrong foot** partire col piede giusto/sbagliato; **she didn't put a foot wrong** non ha fatto neanche un errore **3** (*measure*) piede *m* (= *304 mm or 12 inches*); **he's 6 foot** *or* **feet tall** ≈ è alto 1 metro e 80
■VT: **to foot the bill** (*fam*) pagare il conto
foot·age ['fʊtɪdʒ] N (*Cine*) sequenza; (*material*) ≈ metraggio
foot-and-mouth (disease) ['fʊtənd'maʊθ(dɪzi:z)] N afta epizootica
◎**foot·ball** ['fʊt,bɔ:l] N (*ball*) pallone *m*; (*Sport*: *Brit*) calcio; (: *Am*) football *m* americano; **I like playing football** mi piace giocare a calcio; **Paul threw the football over the fence** Paul ha gettato il pallone oltre lo steccato
■ADJ (*team, supporters*) di calcio
▹ www.fifa.com
▹ www.uefa.com
▹ www.premierleague.com/
football coupon N schedina del totocalcio
foot·ball·er ['fʊt,bɔ:ləʳ] N (*Brit*) calciatore(-trice)
football ground N campo di calcio
football league N campionato di calcio
football match N (*Brit*) partita di calcio
football player N (*Brit*) calciatore(-trice); (*Am*) giocatore *m* di football americano
football pools NPL totocalcio; **to do the football pools** giocare la schedina
football special N treno straordinario per tifosi (di calcio)
foot brake N freno a pedale
foot·bridge ['fʊt,brɪdʒ] N passerella
foot·er ['fʊtəʳ] N (*Comput*) piè *m inv* di pagina
foot·fall ['fʊt,fɔ:l] N passo
foot fault N (*Tennis*) fallo di piede
foot·gear ['fʊt,gɪəʳ] N calzatura
foot·hills ['fʊt,hɪlz] NPL contrafforti *fpl*, colline *fpl* pedemontane
foot·hold ['fʊt,həʊld] N punto d'appoggio; **to gain a foothold** (*fig*: *idea, movement*) prendere piede; (: *newcomer*) farsi accettare; **to gain a foothold in a market** (*Comm*) imporsi sul mercato
footie ['fʊtɪ] N = **footy**
foot·ing ['fʊtɪŋ] N (*foothold*) punto d'appoggio; (*fig*: *basis*) posizione *f*; **to lose one's footing** perdere l'equilibrio, mettere un piede in fallo; **on an equal footing** (*fig*) su un piano di parità, in una situazione di parità; **to be on a friendly footing with sb** essere in rapporti d'amicizia con qn
foot·le ['fu:tl] VI: **to footle about** bighellonare
foot·lights ['fʊt,laɪts] NPL (*in theatre*) luci *fpl* della ribalta
foot·ling ['fʊtlɪŋ] ADJ stupido(-a), insignificante
foot·loose ['fʊt,lu:s] ADJ: **footloose and fancy-free** libero(-a) e spensierato(-a)
foot·man ['fʊtmən] N (*pl* **-men**) lacchè *m inv*
foot·mark ['fʊt,mɑ:k] N orma
foot·note ['fʊt,nəʊt] N nota a piè di pagina
foot·path ['fʊt,pɑ:θ] N (*track*) sentiero
foot·plate ['fʊt,pleɪt] N (*Rail*) piattaforma del macchinista
foot·print ['fʊt,prɪnt] N orma, impronta
foot·pump ['fʊt,pʌmp] N pompa a pedale
foot·rest ['fʊt,rest] N poggiapiedi *m inv*
Foot·sie ['fʊtsɪ] N (*fam*: *Fin*) indice *m* FTSE 100
foot·sie ['fʊtsɪ] N (*fam*): **to play footsie with sb** fare piedino a qn
foot soldier N soldato di fanteria, fante *m*
foot·sore ['fʊt,sɔ:ʳ] ADJ: **to be footsore** avere i piedi doloranti, avere mal di piedi

Ff

foot·step ['fʊt,stɛp] N passo
foot·stool ['fʊt,stu:l] N poggiapiedi *m inv*
foot·way ['fʊt,weɪ] N passaggio pedonale
foot·wear ['fʊtwɛəʳ] N calzatura
foot·work ['fʊt,wɜ:k] N (*Sport*) gioco di gambe
footy, footie ['fʊtɪ] N (*fam: Sport*) calcio
fop [fɒp] N gagà *m inv*
FOR [,ɛfəʊ'ɑ:ʳ] ABBR (= free on rail) franco vagone

◎**for** [fɔ:] KEYWORD

■ PREP
1 (*indicating destination, intention*) per; **he left for Rome** è partito per Roma; **here's a letter for you** ecco una lettera per te; **is this for me?** è per me questo?; **for sale** in vendita, vendesi; **he swam for the shore** nuotò verso la riva; **it's time for lunch** è ora di pranzo; **the train for London** il treno per Londra
2 (*indicating purpose*) per; **clothes for children** vestiti per bambini; **a cupboard for toys** un armadio per i giocattoli; **fit for nothing** buono(-a) a niente; **to pray for peace** pregare per la pace; **he went down for the paper** è sceso a prendere il giornale; **what for?** perché?, per cosa?; **what's this button for?** a cosa serve questo bottone?
3 (*representing*) per; **I'll ask him for you** glielo chiederò a nome tuo; **G for George** G come George; **member for Hove** deputato che rappresenta Hove; **I took him for his brother** l'ho scambiato *or* preso per suo fratello
4 (*in exchange for*) per; **to pay 50 pence for a ticket** pagare 50 penny per un biglietto; **I sold it for £50** l'ho venduto per 50 sterline
5 (*with regard to*) per; **anxious for success** avido(-a) di successo; **as for him/that** quanto a lui/ciò; **it's cold for July** è freddo per essere luglio; **for each one who voted yes, 50 voted no** per ogni voto a favore ce n'erano 50 contro; **a gift for languages** un dono per le lingue; **he's mature for his age** è maturo per la sua età; **there's nothing for it but to jump** (*Brit*) non c'è altro da fare che saltare
6 (*in favour of*) per, a favore di; **are you for or against us?** sei con noi o contro di noi?; **I'm all for it** sono completamente a favore; **the campaign for** la campagna a favore di *or* per; **vote for me!** votate per me!
7 (*because of*) per, a causa di; **famous for its cathedral** famoso(-a) per la sua cattedrale; **for fear of being criticised** per paura di essere criticato(-a); **to shout for joy** gridare di gioia; **for this reason** per questa ragione; **do it for my sake** fallo per me; **if it were not for you** se non fosse per te
8 (*in spite of*): **for all that** malgrado ciò; **for all his money** malgrado tutto il suo denaro
9 (*distance*) per; **there were roadworks for 5 km** c'erano lavori in corso per 5 km; **we walked for miles** abbiamo camminato per chilometri
10 (*time*): **can you do it for tomorrow?** lo puoi fare per domani?; **I haven't seen him for a week** non lo vedo da una settimana, è una settimana che non lo vedo; **I'll be away for 3 weeks** starò via (per) 3 settimane; **it has not rained for 3 weeks** non piove da 3 settimane; **he won't be back for a while** non tornerà per un po'; **he was away for 2 years** è stato via per 2 anni; **I have known her for years** la conosco da anni
11 (*with infinitive clauses*): **for this to be possible ...** perché ciò sia possibile...; **it would be best for you to go** sarebbe meglio che te ne andassi; **he brought it for us to see** l'ha portato per farcelo vedere; **it's not for me to decide** non sta a me decidere; **there is still time for you to do it** hai ancora tempo per farlo
12 (*phrases*): **you're for it!** (*fam*) vedrai adesso!; **oh for a cup of tea!** cosa non darei per una tazza di tè!
■ CONJ dal momento che, poiché

for·age ['fɒrɪdʒ] N piante *fpl* foraggere
■ VI: **to forage (for)** andare in cerca (di)
forage cap N bustina
for·ay ['fɒreɪ] N (*esp Mil*) incursione *f*
for·bade, for·bad [fə'bæd] PT *of* **forbid**
for·bear [fɔ:'bɛəʳ] (*pt* **forbore**, *pp* **forborne**) VI: **to forbear from doing, to forbear to do** astenersi dal fare
for·bear·ance [fɔ:'bɛərəns] N pazienza, tolleranza
for·bear·ing [fɔ:'bɛərɪŋ] ADJ paziente, tollerante
for·bid [fə'bɪd] (*pt* **forbad** *or* **forbade**, *pp* **forbidden**) VT proibire, vietare; **to forbid sb sth** proibire qc a qn; **to forbid sb to do sth** proibire a qn di fare qc; **"smoking forbidden"** "vietato fumare"; **God forbid!** Dio non voglia!
forbidden [fə'bɪdn] ADJ vietato(-a)
forbidden fruit N frutto proibito
for·bid·ding [fə'bɪdɪŋ] ADJ arcigno(-a), d'aspetto minaccioso
for·bid·ding·ly [fə'bɪdɪŋlɪ] ADV minacciosamente
for·bore [fɔ:'bɔ:ʳ], **for·borne** [fɔ:'bɔ:n] PT, PP *of* **forbear**

◎**force** [fɔ:s] N **1** (*gen*) forza; **he's against the use of force** è contrario all'uso della forza; **to resort to force** ricorrere alla violenza; **force of gravity** forza di gravità; **a force 5 wind** un vento forza 5; **the forces of evil** (*fig*) le forze del male; **by force** con la forza; **by force of habit** per abitudine; **by sheer force of character, he ...** grazie alla sua forza di carattere, lui...; **to be in force** (*Law*) essere in vigore; **to come into force** (*Law*) entrare in vigore; **to turn out in force** manifestare in gran numero *or* in massa
2 (*body of men*) gruppo; (*Mil*) forza; **the force** (*police force*) la polizia, il corpo di polizia; **UN forces** le forze dell'ONU; **the sales force** (*Comm*) l'effettivo dei rappresentanti **3 the Forces** (*Brit: Mil*) le forze armate
■ VT **1** (*compel: person*) forzare, costringere; **to force sb to do sth** costringere qn a fare qc **2** (*impose*): **to force sth on sb** imporre qc a qn; **to force o.s. on sb** imporsi a qn, imporre la propria presenza a qn **3** (*push, squeeze*) schiacciare; **he forced the clothes into the suitcase** ha fatto entrare a forza i vestiti nella valigia; **to force one's way into** entrare con la forza in; **to force one's way through** (*crowd*) farsi strada tra; (*opening*) penetrare a forza in, passare a forza attraverso
4 (*break open: lock*) forzare; **to force an entry** entrare con la forza; **to force sb's hand** (*fig*) forzare la mano a qn **5** (*produce with effort*): **to force a smile/a reply** sforzarsi di sorridere/rispondere; **don't force the situation** non forzare le cose **6** (*obtain by force: smile, confession*) strappare
▸ **force back** VT + ADV (*crowd, enemy*) respingere; (*urge*) reprimere; (*tears*) ingoiare
▸ **force down** VT + ADV (*food*) sforzarsi di mangiare; (*aircraft*) forzare ad atterrare
▸ **force out** VT + ADV (*person*) costringere ad uscire; (*cork*) far uscire con la forza
forced [fɔ:st] ADJ (*labour, marriage*) forzato(-a)
force-feed ['fɔ:s,fi:d] (*pt, pp* **force-fed**) VT sottoporre ad alimentazione forzata
force field N (*Phys*) campo di forze

force·ful ['fɔːsfʊl] ADJ (*personality*) forte; (*argument*) valido(-a)
force·ful·ly ['fɔːsfəlɪ] ADV (*argue*) efficacemente
force·ful·ness ['fɔːsfʊlnɪs] N forza
force·meat ['fɔːsˌmiːt] N (*Brit Culin*) ripieno
for·ceps ['fɔːsɛps] NPL forcipe *msg*
for·cible ['fɔːsəbl] ADJ (*done by force*) fatto(-a) con la forza; (*effective: argument, style*) convincente, efficace
for·cibly ['fɔːsəblɪ] ADV (*by force: take*) con la forza; (*vigorously: argue*) energicamente, vigorosamente
ford [fɔːd] N guado
■ VT guadare, passare a guado
ford·able ['fɔːdəbl] ADJ guadabile
fore [fɔːʳ] ADJ (*section, part: of animal, ship, aircraft*) anteriore
■ ADV (*Naut*): **fore and aft** da prua a poppa
■ N: **to the fore** in primo piano; **to come to the fore** mettersi in evidenza *or* in luce
fore·arm ['fɔːrˌɑːm] N avambraccio
fore·bear ['fɔːˌbɛəʳ] N antenato(-a)
fore·bod·ing [fɔː'bəʊdɪŋ] N (cattivo) presagio, presentimento; **a sense of foreboding** un brutto presentimento
◎ **fore·cast** ['fɔːˌkɑːst] (*vb: pt, pp* **forecast** *or* **forecasted**) N pronostico, previsione *f*; (*also:* **weather forecast**) previsioni *fpl* del tempo; (*Horse-racing*) accoppiata
■ VT (*also Met*) prevedere
fore·cas·tle, **fo'c's'le** ['fəʊksl] N (*Naut*) castello di prua
fore·close [fɔː'kləʊz] VT (*Law: also:* **foreclose on**) pignorare
fore·clo·sure [fɔː'kləʊʒəʳ] N pignoramento
fore·court ['fɔːˌkɔːt] N (*of garage*) spiazzo; (*of station*) piazzale *m*
fore·deck ['fɔːdɛk] N (*Naut*) ponte *m* anteriore
fore·doomed [fɔː'duːmd] ADJ: **to be foredoomed to failure** essere destinato(-a) a fallire
fore·fathers ['fɔːˌfɑːðəz] NPL progenitori *mpl*, antenati *mpl*, avi *mpl*
fore·finger ['fɔːˌfɪŋgəʳ] N (dito) indice *m*
fore·foot ['fɔːˌfʊt] N (*pl* **-feet**) zampa anteriore
fore·front ['fɔːˌfrʌnt] N: **to be in the forefront of** essere all'avanguardia di
fore·go [fɔː'gəʊ] VT = **forgo**
fore·going [fɔː'gəʊɪŋ] ADJ precedente
fore·gone ['fɔːˌgɒn] PP *of* **forego**
■ ADJ: **it was a foregone conclusion** era un risultato scontato
fore·ground ['fɔːˌgraʊnd] N (*Art*) primo piano; **in the foreground** (*fig*) in una posizione di primo piano
■ ADJ (*Comput*) foreground *inv*, di primo piano
fore·hand ['fɔːˌhænd] N (*Tennis*) diritto
fore·head ['fɔːˌhɛd] N fronte *f*
◎ **for·eign** ['fɒrɪn] ADJ **1** (*language, tourist*) straniero(-a); (*policy, trade*) estero(-a); **foreign countries** paesi stranieri; **foreign investment** investimento all'estero **2** (*not natural*) estraneo(-a); **deceit is foreign to his nature** ingannare non è nel suo carattere
foreign bill N (*Fin*) cambiale *f* pagabile all'estero
foreign body N (*frm*) corpo estraneo
foreign currency N valuta estera
◎ **for·eign·er** ['fɒrɪnəʳ] N straniero(-a)
foreign exchange N cambio di valuta; (*currency*) valuta estera; **foreign exchange market** mercato dei cambi
foreign minister N ministro degli Esteri
Foreign Office N (*Brit*) ministero degli Esteri
foreign secretary N (*Brit*) ministro degli Esteri
fore·leg ['fɔːˌlɛg] N zampa anteriore
fore·man ['fɔːmən] N (*pl* **-men**) (*of workers*) caposquadra *m*; (*Law: of jury*) portavoce *m* della giuria
fore·mast ['fɔːmɑːst] N (*Naut*) (albero di) trinchetto
fore·most ['fɔːˌməʊst] ADJ (*outstanding: writer, politician*) più importante, principale, più in vista; **one of the foremost scholars of Indian culture** uno dei più importanti studiosi di cultura indiana
■ ADV: **first and foremost** innanzitutto
fore·name ['fɔːˌneɪm] N nome *m* di battesimo
fore·noon ['fɔːˌnuːn] N (*frm*) mattina
fo·ren·sic [fə'rɛnsɪk] ADJ (*evidence, laboratory*) medico-legale; **forensic scientist** *or* **expert** esperto(-a) della (polizia) scientifica
forensic medicine N medicina legale
fore·part ['fɔːˌpɑːt] N (*frm*) parte *f* anteriore
fore·play ['fɔːˌpleɪ] N preliminari *mpl* (*nel rapporto sessuale*)
fore·run·ner ['fɔːˌrʌnəʳ] N precursore *m*; (*Skiing*) apripista *m/f inv*
fore·sail ['fɔːˌseɪl] N (*Naut*) (vela di) trinchetto
fore·see [fɔː'siː] (*pt* **foresaw**, *pp* **foreseen**) VT prevedere; **he had foreseen the problem** aveva previsto il problema
fore·see·able [fɔː'siːəbl] ADJ (*opportunity*) prevedibile; **in the foreseeable future** nell'immediato futuro
fore·seen [fɔː'siːn] PP *of* foresee
fore·shad·ow [fɔː'ʃædəʊ] VT (*liter*) presagire, far prevedere
fore·shore ['fɔːˌʃɔːʳ] N battigia
fore·short·en [fɔː'ʃɔːtn] VT (*figure*) rappresentare in scorcio
fore·short·ened [fɔː'ʃɔːtənd] ADJ di scorcio
fore·sight ['fɔːˌsaɪt] N previdenza
fore·skin ['fɔːˌskɪn] N (*Anat*) prepuzio
◎ **for·est** ['fɒrɪst] N foresta
fore·stall [fɔː'stɔːl] VT (*anticipate: event, accident*) prevenire; (*: rival, competitor*) anticipare
fore·stay ['fɔːˌsteɪ] N (*Naut*) strallo di trinchetto
for·est·er ['fɒrɪstəʳ] N guardia forestale
for·est·ry ['fɒrɪstrɪ] N selvicoltura
▷ www.metla.fi/info/vlib/Forestry
▷ www.forestry.gov.uk
Forestry Commission N ≈ Corpo forestale dello Stato
fore·summit ['fɔːˌsʌmɪt] N (*Mountaineering*) antecima
fore·taste ['fɔːˌteɪst] N assaggio
fore·tell [fɔː'tɛl] (*pt, pp* **foretold**) VT predire
fore·thought ['fɔːˌθɔːt] N previdenza; **to act with forethought** essere previdente
fore·told [fɔː'təʊld] PT, PP *of* **foretell**
for·ever [fər'ɛvəʳ] ADV (*eternally*) per sempre, eternamente; (*for good*) per sempre; (*fam: incessantly, repeatedly*) sempre, di continuo; (*: for ages*): **it lasted forever** è durato un'eternità; **it'll take forever** ci vorrà una vita; **yours forever** tuo per sempre; **those days are gone forever** quei giorni non torneranno più; **she's forever complaining** si lamenta sempre
fore·warn [fɔː'wɔːn] VT avvisare in precedenza; **forewarned is forearmed** uomo avvisato è mezzo salvato
forewent [fɔː'wɛnt] PT *of* **forego**
fore·woman ['fɔːˌwʊmən] N (*pl* **-women**) caporeparto *f inv*; (*of jury*) portavoce *f inv* della giuria
fore·word ['fɔːˌwɜːd] N prefazione *f*
for·ex ['fɔːrɛks] N ABBR = **foreign exchange; forex market** mercato dei cambi; **forex dealer** cambista *m/f*

Ff

for·feit ['fɔ:fɪt] N (*penalty*) ammenda; (*in game*) penitenza
■ VT (*esp Law: one's right, status*) perdere; (*one's happiness, health*) giocarsi
for·gave [fə'geɪv] PT *of* **forgive**
forge [fɔ:dʒ] N (*of blacksmith*) fucina
■ VT **1** (*metal, iron*) fucinare, forgiare; (*fig: friendship, plan, unity*) forgiare, formare **2** (*falsify: signature, document*) contraffare, falsificare
▸ **forge ahead** VI + ADV andare avanti (con determinazione)
forged [fɔ:dʒd] ADJ (*document*) falsificato(-a), contraffatto(-a), falso(-a); (*banknote, signature*) falso(-a)
forg·er ['fɔ:dʒə[r]] N falsario(-a), contraffattore(-trice)
for·gery ['fɔ:dʒərɪ] N (*activity*) falsificazione *f*, contraffazione *f*; (*thing*) falso; **the letter was a forgery** la lettera era un falso
◎ **for·get** [fə'gɛt] (*pt* **forgot**, *pp* **forgotten**) VT dimenticare; **I've forgotten his name** ho dimenticato il suo nome; **to forget to do sth** dimenticare di fare qc; **to forget how to do sth** dimenticare come si fa qc; **she never forgets a face** è molto fisionomista; **never to be forgotten** indimenticabile; **forget it!** (*fam*) lascia perdere!; **if that's what you're hoping, you can forget it!** se questo è quello che speri puoi scordartelo!; **to forget o.s.** (*lose self-control*) perdere la testa
■ VI dimenticarsi, scordarsi; **I've forgotten all about it** me ne sono completamente dimenticato; **let's forget about it!** non ne parliamo più!
for·get·ful [fə'gɛtfʊl] ADJ (*absent-minded*) distratto(-a), di poca memoria; **forgetful of** dimentico(-a) di; **it was very forgetful of me not to ...** è stata una grande dimenticanza quella di non...
for·get·ful·ness [fə'gɛtfʊlnɪs] N smemoratezza; (*oblivion*) oblio
forget-me-not [fə'gɛtmɪˌnɒt] N nontiscordardimé *m inv*
for·get·table [fə'gɛtəbl] ADJ non degno(-a) di nota
for·giv·able [fə'gɪvəbl] ADJ perdonabile
for·giv·ably [fə'gɪvəblɪ] ADV comprensibilmente
for·give [fə'gɪv] (*pt* **forgave**, *pp* **forgiven**) VT (*person, fault*) perdonare; **in the end he forgave me** alla fine mi ha perdonato; **to forgive sb for sth/for doing sth** perdonare qc a qn/a qn di aver fatto qc
for·give·ness [fə'gɪvnɪs] N (*pardon*) perdono; (*willingness to forgive*) clemenza, indulgenza
for·giv·ing [fə'gɪvɪŋ] ADJ indulgente
for·go [fɔ:'gəʊ] (*pt* **forwent**, *pp* **forgone**) VT (*do without*) rinunciare a, fare a meno di
for·got [fə'gɒt] PT *of* **forget**
for·got·ten [fə'gɒtn] PP *of* **forget**
fork [fɔ:k] N (*for eating*) forchetta; (*for gardening*) forca, forcone *m*; (*in road*) bivio, biforcazione *f*; **mix it with a fork** mescolalo con una forchetta; **take the left fork** al bivio volta a sinistra
■ VI (*road*) biforcarsi
▸ **fork out** VT + ADV (*fam: money, cash*) sborsare, tirare fuori
■ VI + ADV tirare fuori i soldi, pagare
forked [fɔ:kt] ADJ (*tail, tongue, branch*) biforcuto(-a)
forked lightning N (fulmine *m* a) saetta
fork-lift truck ['fɔ:kˌlɪft'trʌk] N carrello elevatore
for·lorn [fə'lɔ:n] ADJ (*person*) sconsolato(-a); (*deserted: place, house*) abbandonato(-a); (*desperate: attempt*) disperato(-a); **a forlorn hope** una speranza vana; **she looked forlorn** sembrava sconsolata
for·lorn·ly [fə'lɔ:nlɪ] ADV sconsolatamente; (*hope*) vanamente
◎ **form** [fɔ:m] N **1** (*gen*) forma; **in the form of** a forma di, sotto forma di; **I'm against all forms of hunting** sono contrario a qualsiasi forma di caccia; **the same thing in a new form** la stessa cosa presentata in modo diverso; **a form of apology** una specie di scusa; **form and content** forma e contenuto; **to take form** prendere forma; **the correct form of address for a bishop** il corretto modo di rivolgersi a un vescovo **2** (*Sport, fig*): **to be in good form** essere in forma; **in top form** in gran forma; **true to form** come sempre; **he was in great form last night** era in piena forma ieri sera **3** (*document*) modulo; **to fill in a form** riempire un modulo **4** (*old: etiquette*) forma; **it's a matter of form** è una questione di forma; **it's bad form** è maleducato **5** (*bench*) banco **6** (*Brit Scol*) classe *f*; **in the first form** ≈ in prima media; **he's in my form** è in classe con me
■ VT (*gen*) formare; (*plan*) concepire; (*idea, opinion*) formarsi, farsi; (*habit*) prendere; **to form a circle/a queue** fare *or* formare un cerchio/una coda; **he formed it out of a lump of clay** l'ha plasmato *or* modellato su un blocco di creta; **to form a government/group** formare un governo/gruppo; **those who formed the group** quelli che facevano parte del gruppo; **to form part of sth** far parte di qc
■ VI formarsi
◎ **for·mal** ['fɔ:məl] ADJ (*gen*) formale; (*person*) cerimonioso(-a); (*official: visit, offer, acceptance*) ufficiale; **a formal dinner** una cena ufficiale; **formal language** lingua formale; **formal clothes** abiti *mpl* da cerimonia; **there was no formal agreement** non c'era un contratto formale; **formal garden** giardino all'italiana; **formal training** preparazione *f* specifica; **his formal education ended when he was 16** ha smesso di andare a scuola a 16 anni
for·mal·de·hyde [fɔ:'mældɪˌhaɪd] N formaldeide *f*
formal dress N abito da cerimonia; (*evening dress*) abito da sera
for·ma·lin ['fɔ:məlɪn] N formalina
for·mal·ism ['fɔ:məˌlɪzəm] N formalismo
for·mal·ist ['fɔ:mə'lɪst] ADJ, N formalista (*m/f*)
for·mal·is·tic [ˌfɔ:mə'lɪstɪk] ADJ formalistico(-a)
for·mal·ity [fɔ:'mælɪtɪ] N formalità *f inv*; **it's a mere formality** è una semplice formalità
for·mal·ize ['fɔ:məˌlaɪz] VT rendere ufficiale
for·mal·ly ['fɔ:məlɪ] ADV (*see adj*) in modo formale; ufficialmente; **formally dressed** in abito da cerimonia; **to be formally invited** ricevere un invito ufficiale
for·mat ['fɔ:ˌmæt] N formato
■ VT (*Comput*) formattare
for·ma·tion [fɔ:'meɪʃən] N formazione *f*
forma·tive ['fɔ:mətɪv] ADJ formativo(-a); **formative years** anni *mpl* formativi
◎ **for·mer** ['fɔ:mə[r]] ADJ **1** (*earlier, previous*) vecchio(-a) (*before n*), precedente; (*: chairman, wife etc*) ex *inv* (*before n*); **in former days** nei tempi passati, in altri tempi; **a former pupil** un ex alunno; **the former president** l'ex presidente; **the former Yugoslavia/Soviet Union** l'ex Jugoslavia/Unione Sovietica **2** (*of two*) primo(-a)
■ PRON: **the former (...the latter)** il/la primo(-a) (... l'ultimo(-a)), quello(-a)... (questo(-a)); **given the choice, I prefer the former** potendo scegliere, preferisco il primo

for·mer·ly [ˈfɔːməlɪ] ADV in passato, precedentemente
form feed N *(on printer)* alimentazione *f* della carta
For·mi·ca® [fɔːˈmaɪkə] N Fòrmica®
for·mi·dable [ˈfɔːmɪdəbl] ADJ *(task, difficulties)* formidabile, terribile; *(person, appearance)* che incute rispetto
for·mi·dably [ˈfɔːmɪdəblɪ] ADV tremendamente; **a formidably difficult task** un compito tremendamente difficile
form·less [ˈfɔːmlɪs] ADJ *(shape)* informe; *(feelings)* nebuloso(-a)
form master N ≈ coordinatore *m* del Consiglio di classe
form mistress N ≈ coordinatrice *f* del Consiglio di classe
◎**for·mu·la** [ˈfɔːmjʊlə] N *(pl* **formulae** *or* **formulas** [ˈfɔːmjʊˌliː]) *(Math, Chem, fig: plan)* formula; *(Am: baby's feed)* latte *m* in polvere
Formula One N *(Aut)* formula uno
for·mu·late [ˈfɔːmjʊˌleɪt] VT formulare
for·mu·la·tion [ˌfɔːmjʊˈleɪʃən] N formulazione *f*
for·ni·cate [ˈfɔːnɪˌkeɪt] VI fornicare
for·ni·ca·tion [ˌfɔːnɪˈkeɪʃən] N fornicazione *f*
for·sake [fəˈseɪk] *(pt* **forsook**, *pp* **forsaken**) VT *(person)* abbandonare; *(place)* lasciare
for·sythia [fɔːˈsaɪθɪə] N forsizia
fort [fɔːt] N *(Mil)* forte *m*
for·te [ˈfɔːtɪ] N forte *m*
◎**forth** [fɔːθ] ADV *(old)* **1** in avanti; **to go back and forth** andare avanti e indietro; **to set forth** mettersi in cammino; **from this day forth** d'ora in poi **2 and so forth** e così via, e via dicendo
forth·com·ing [ˌfɔːθˈkʌmɪŋ] ADJ *(event, election)* prossimo(-a); *(film)* che sta per uscire, imminente; *(book)* di prossima pubblicazione; *(character)* aperto(-a), comunicativo(-a); **it will be discussed at the forthcoming meeting** verrà discusso nella prossima riunione; **if help is forthcoming** se c'è chi è disposto ad aiutare; **he wasn't very forthcoming about it** non sembrava molto disposto a parlarne
forth·right [ˈfɔːθˌraɪt] ADJ *(person, answer etc)* franco(-a), schietto(-a)
forth·with [ˌfɔːθˈwɪθ] ADV *(frm)* immediatamente, subito
◎**for·ti·eth** [ˈfɔːtɪɪθ] ADJ quarantesimo(-a)
■ N *(in series)* quarantesimo(-a); *(fraction)* quarantesimo; *for usage see* **fifth**
for·ti·fi·ca·tion [ˌfɔːtɪfɪˈkeɪʃən] N fortificazione *f*
for·ti·fied wine [ˈfɔːtɪˌfaɪdˈwaɪn] N vino ad alta gradazione alcolica
for·ti·fy [ˈfɔːtɪˌfaɪ] VT *(Mil)* fortificare; *(fig: person)* rinvigorire, rafforzare; *(enrich: food)* arricchire
for·tis·si·mo [fɔːˈtɪsɪˌməʊ] *(Mus)* ADV fortissimo
■ ADJ fortissimo *inv*
for·ti·tude [ˈfɔːtɪˌtjuːd] N forza d'animo
fort·night [ˈfɔːtˌnaɪt] N *(Brit)* quindici giorni *mpl*, quindicina di giorni, due settimane *fpl*; **to go on a fortnight's holiday** fare due settimane di vacanza; **a fortnight (from) today** oggi a quindici; **it's a fortnight since ...** sono due settimane da quando...; **for a fortnight** per quindici giorni
fort·night·ly [ˈfɔːtˌnaɪtlɪ] *(Brit)* ADJ quindicinale, bimensile
■ ADV ogni quindici giorni
FORTRAN, For·tran [ˈfɔːtræn] N FORTRAN *m*
for·tress [ˈfɔːtrɪs] N fortezza, rocca
for·tui·tous [fɔːˈtjuːɪtəs] ADJ fortuito(-a)
for·tui·tous·ly [fɔːˈtjuːɪtəslɪ] ADV fortuitamente, per caso
for·tu·ity [fɔːˈtjuːɪtɪ] N accidentalità
for·tu·nate [ˈfɔːtʃənɪt] ADJ *(coincidence, event, person)* fortunato(-a); **he is fortunate to have ...** ha la fortuna di avere...; **it is fortunate that** è una fortuna che *+ sub*; **it's fortunate that I remembered the map** è una fortuna che mi sia ricordato della cartina
for·tu·nate·ly [ˈfɔːtʃənɪtlɪ] ADV fortunatamente
◎**for·tune** [ˈfɔːtʃən] N **1** *(chance)* fortuna; **the fortunes of war** le vicende della guerra; **by good fortune** per fortuna; **to tell sb's fortune** predire l'avvenire *or* il futuro a qn **2** *(money)* fortuna; **to come into a fortune** ereditare una fortuna; **to make a fortune** farsi una fortuna *or* un patrimonio; **he made his fortune in Peru** ha fatto fortuna in Perù; **a small fortune** *(fam)* un patrimonio; **it cost a fortune** è costato una fortuna
fortune-hunter [ˈfɔːtʃənˌhʌntəʳ] N cacciatore *m* di dote
fortune-teller [ˈfɔːtʃənˌtɛləʳ] N indovino(-a), chiromante *m/f*
fortune-telling [ˈfɔːtʃənˌtɛlɪŋ] N chiromanzia
◎**for·ty** [ˈfɔːtɪ] N quaranta *m inv*
■ ADJ quaranta *inv*; **to have forty winks** *(fam)* fare *or* schiacciare un pisolino; *for usage see* **fifty**
fo·rum [ˈfɔːrəm] N *(History)* foro; *(fig)* tribuna
◎**for·ward** [ˈfɔːwəd] ADJ **1** *(in movement, position)* in avanti; *(in time)* in anticipo; *(Naut)* prodiero(-a); **forward line** *(Sport)* linea d'attacco; *(Mil)* prima linea; **forward planning** pianificazione *f*; **forward thinking** *(person)* dalle idee innovatrici **2** *(precocious: child)* precoce; *(presumptuous: person, remark)* insolente, sfacciato(-a) **3** *(Comm: delivery, sales, exchange)* a termine
■ N *(Sport)* attaccante *m*, avanti *m inv*
■ VT *(dispatch: parcel, goods)* spedire; *(send on: letter)* inoltrare; *(fig: sb's plans)* promuovere, appoggiare; **"please forward"** "si prega di inoltrare"
for·ward·ing ad·dress [ˈfɔːwədɪŋəˈdrɛs] N: **he didn't leave a forwarding address** non ha lasciato un nuovo recapito
forward-looking [ˈfɔːwədˌlʊkɪŋ] ADJ che guarda al futuro, progressista
for·ward·ness [ˈfɔːwədnɪs] N *(of child)* precocità; *(boldness)* insolenza
forward pass N *(Rugby)* passaggio in avanti
for·ward(s) [ˈfɔːwəd(s)] ADV *(in place)* in avanti; *(in time)* avanti, innanzi; **to step forward** fare un passo avanti; **to push o.s. forward** farsi avanti, mettersi in evidenza; **to come forward** farsi avanti; **to move sth forward** spostare qc in avanti; **from this time forward** d'ora in poi, d'ora innanzi
for·went [fɔːˈwɛnt] PT *of* **forgo**
fos·sil [ˈfɒsl] N, ADJ fossile *(m)*
fossil fuel N combustibile *m* fossile
fos·sili·za·tion [ˌfɒsɪlaɪˈzeɪʃən] N fossilizzazione *f*
fos·sil·ize [ˈfɒsɪˌlaɪz] VI fossilizzarsi
fos·sil·ized [ˈfɒsɪˌlaɪzd] ADJ fossilizzato(-a)
fos·ter [ˈfɒstəʳ] VT *(child)* avere in affidamento; *(hope, ambition)* nutrire, accarezzare; *(encourage)* incoraggiare; **she has fostered more than fifteen children** ha avuto in affidamento più di quindici bambini
■ ADJ *(parent, mother, father)* affidatario(-a); *(child)* preso(-a) in affido; **foster brother** fratellastro, fratello adottivo; **foster sister** sorellastra, sorella adottiva
fos·ter·ing [ˈfɒstərɪŋ] N affidamento
fought [fɔːt] PT, PP *of* **fight**

Ff

foul [faʊl] ADJ (*putrid, disgusting: smell, breath, taste*) disgustoso(-a), rivoltante; (*: water, air*) puzzolente, fetido(-a); (*nasty: weather*) brutto(-a), orribile; (*: mood*) pessimo(-a), nero(-a); (*obscene: language*) volgare, osceno(-a); (*deed*) infame; **the weather was foul** il tempo era orribile; **it smells foul** ha un odore disgustoso; **Brenda is in a foul mood** Brenda è di pessimo umore; **to use foul language** parlare sboccatamente; **to fall foul of sb/the law** entrare in contrasto con qn/con la giustizia
■ N (*Ftbl*) fallo; (*Boxing*) colpo basso
■ VT **1** (*pollute: air*) appestare; **the dog fouled the pavement** il cane ha sporcato il marciapiede **2** (*Sport: opponent*) commettere un fallo su **3** (*entangle: anchor, propeller*) impigliare
▸ **foul up** VT + ADV (*fam: plan, project*) rovinare

foul-mouthed ['faʊl'maʊðd] ADJ sboccato(-a)

foul play N **1** (*murder*) delitto, atto criminale; (*dishonesty*) imbroglio, raggiro; **the police suspect foul play** la polizia sospetta si tratti di un delitto; **a body has been found, but foul play is not suspected** è stato rinvenuto un cadavere, ma si è scartata l'ipotesi di un omicidio **2** (*Sport*) gioco scorretto

foul-smelling ['faʊl'smɛlɪŋ] ADJ puzzolente, fetido(-a)

◎**found**[1] [faʊnd] PT, PP *of* **find**

found[2] [faʊnd] VT (*establish*) fondare; (*opinion, belief*) fondare, basare; **a statement founded on fact** una dichiarazione basata sulla realtà

◎**foun·da·tion** [faʊn'deɪʃən] N **1** (*founding, organization*) fondazione *f* **2** **foundations** NPL (*Archit*) fondamenta *fpl*; **to lay the foundations** gettare le fondamenta; (*fig*) gettare le basi **3** (*basis*) fondamento, base *f*; **the course gives students a good foundation** il corso fornisce agli studenti una buona basev **4** (*justification*): **the story is without foundation** la storia è infondata

foundation course N corso propedeutico

foundation cream N (*also:* **foundation**) fondotinta *m inv*

foundation stone N: **to lay the foundation stone** posare la prima pietra

◎**found·er**[1] ['faʊndəʳ] N fondatore(-trice)

found·er[2] ['faʊndəʳ] VI (*Naut, also fig*) affondare, colare a picco

founder member, founding member N (*Brit*) socio(-a) fondatore(-trice)

found·ing ['faʊndɪŋ] ADJ (*principle, assumption*) di base
■ N fondazione *f*

founding fathers NPL (*esp Am*) padri *mpl* fondatori

found·ling ['faʊndlɪŋ] N trovatello(-a)

found·ry ['faʊndrɪ] N fonderia

fount [faʊnt] N **1** (*liter: source*) fonte *f*, sorgente *f* **2** (*Typ*) carattere *m* (di stampa)

foun·tain ['faʊntɪn] N (*also fig*) fontana; **the fountains in Rome** le fontane di Roma

fountain pen N penna stilografica

◎**four** [fɔː] ADJ quattro *inv*
■ N quattro *m inv*; **on all fours** (a) carponi; *for usage see* **five**

four-door ['fɔː'dɔːʳ] ADJ (*Aut*) a quattro porte

four·fold ['fɔː,fəʊld] ADJ quadruplo(-a)
■ ADV quattro volte tanto

four-footed ['fɔː'fʊtɪd] ADJ quadrupede

four-leaf clover ['fɔː,liːf'kləʊvəʳ], **four-leaved clover** ['fɔː,liːvd'kləʊvəʳ] N quadrifoglio

four-letter word ['fɔː,lɛtə'wɜːd] N parolaccia

four-ply [fɔːplaɪ] ADJ (*wood*) a quattro strati; (*wool*) a quattro capi

four-poster ['fɔː,pəʊstəʳ] N (*also:* **four-poster bed**) letto a baldacchino

four·score ['fɔː'skɔːʳ] ADJ (*old*) ottanta *inv*

four·some ['fɔːsəm] N (*game*) partita a quattro; **we went in a foursome** siamo andati in quattro

four·square [,fɔː'skwɛəʳ] ADJ (*firm*) solido(-a); (*square*) quadrato(-a); (*forthright*) schietto(-a), franco(-a)
■ ADV (*firmly*) solidamente

◎**four·teen** ['fɔː'tiːn] ADJ, N quattordici (*m*) *inv*; *for usage see* **five**

◎**four·teenth** ['fɔː'tiːnθ] ADJ quattordicesimo(-a)
■ N (*in series*) quattordicesimo(-a); (*fraction*) quattordicesimo; *for usage see* **fifth**

◎**fourth** [fɔːθ] ADJ quarto(-a); **fourth finger** anulare *m*
■ N (*in series*) quarto(-a); (*fraction*) quarto; (*Aut: also;* **fourth gear**) quarta; *for usage see* **fifth**

fourth dimension N: **the fourth dimension** la quarta dimensione

fourth·ly ['fɔːθlɪ] ADV in quarto luogo

Fourth of July N: **the Fourth of July** il quattro luglio (*anniversario dell'indipendenza americana*)

FOURTH OF JULY

Il 4 luglio, **Fourth of July** (o "Independence Day"), la principale festa nazionale degli Stati Uniti, celebra la firma della Dichiarazione d'Indipendenza nel 1776. È in pratica il "compleanno" degli Stati Uniti e viene festeggiato all'insegna del patriottismo: molti americani espongono la bandiera a stelle e strisce davanti a casa e ci sono manifestazioni un po' ovunque, con spettacoli pirotecnici, parate e cortei, picnic e grigliate all'aperto.
▹ www.usacitylink.com/usa/

four-wheel drive ['fɔː,wiːl'draɪv] N (*Aut*): **a four-wheel drive** una (macchina a) quattro ruote motrici; **with four-wheel drive** con quattro ruote motrici

fowl [faʊl] N pollame *m*, volatile *m*

fox [fɒks] N volpe *f*; **a sly fox** (*fig*) una volpe, un furbacchione
■ VT (*puzzle*) lasciare perplesso(-a), confondere; (*deceive*) ingannare

fox cub N volpacchiotto

fox fur N (pelliccia di) volpe *f*

fox·glove ['fɒks,glʌv] N (*Bot*) digitale *f*

fox hound N foxhound *m inv*

fox-hunting ['fɒks,hʌntɪŋ] N caccia alla volpe

fox terrier N fox-terrier *m inv*

fox·trot ['fɒks,trɒt] N fox-trot *m inv*

foxy ['fɒksɪ] ADJ astuto(-a), scaltro(-a)

foy·er ['fɔɪeɪ] N (*Theatre*) ridotto, foyer *m inv*

FP [,ɛf'piː] N ABBR **1** (*Brit*) = **former pupil** **2** (*Am*) = **fireplug**

FPA [,ɛfpiː'eɪ] N ABBR (*Brit:* = **Family Planning Association**) ≈ AIED *f* (= *Associazione Italiana Educazione Demografica*)

Fr. ABBR (*Rel*) = **father**

fr. ABBR (= **franc**) fr.

fra·cas ['frækɑː] N rissa, lite *f*

frac·tion ['frækʃən] N (*Math*) frazione *f*; **move it just a fraction** (*fig*) spostalo un pochino

frac·tion·al ['frækʃənl] ADJ (*Math*) frazionario(-a); (*fig*) insignificante

frac·tion·al·ly ['frækʃnəlɪ] ADV un tantino, minimamente

frac·tious ['frækʃəs] ADJ *(person, mood)* irritabile; **to be in a fractious mood** essere irritabile *or* di cattivo umore

frac·ture ['fræktʃəʳ] N frattura
■ VT fratturare; **to fracture one's arm** fratturarsi un braccio
■ VI fratturarsi

frag·ile ['frædʒaɪl] ADJ fragile; **I'm feeling rather fragile this morning** *(hum: esp after drinking)* mi sento piuttosto debole stamattina

fra·gil·ity [frə'dʒɪlɪtɪ] N fragilità

frag·ment [*n* 'frægmənt: *vb* fræg'mɛnt] N frammento; **fragments of conversation** brani *mpl* di conversazione
■ VI frammentarsi

frag·men·tary ['frægməntərɪ] ADJ frammentario(-a)

frag·men·ta·tion [,frægmɛn'teɪʃən] N frammentazione *f*

frag·ment·ed ['frægməntɪd] ADJ frammentario(-a)

fra·grance ['freɪgrəns] N *(of flowers)* fragranza, profumo; *(perfume, of toiletries)* profumo

fra·grant ['freɪgrənt] ADJ fragrante, profumato(-a)

frail [freɪl] ADJ *(comp* **-er**, *superl* **-est***)* *(person, health, structure)* fragile, delicato(-a); *(fig: hope, relationship)* tenue, debole

frail·ty ['freɪltɪ] N *(see adj)* fragilità; *(imperfection)* debolezza

◎**frame** [freɪm] N **1** *(of person)* corpo, ossatura; *(of ship, building, tent)* struttura, armatura; *(of bicycle)* telaio; *(of picture)* cornice *f*; *(of window, door)* telaio, intelaiatura; **a silver frame** una cornice d'argento **2** *(Cine)* immagine *f* **3** *(of spectacles)*: **frames** NPL montatura; **glasses with plastic frames** occhiali con la montatura di plastica
■ VT **1** *(picture)* incorniciare **2** *(formulate: plan)* ideare; *(: question)* formulare; *(: sentence)* costruire **3** **to frame sb** *(fam: incriminate)* incastrare qn

framed [freɪmd] ADJ incorniciato(-a)

frame of mind N stato d'animo, umore *m*; **in a happy frame of mind** di buon umore

frame of reference N *(Sociol)* sistema *m* di riferimento

frame-up ['freɪm,ʌp] N *(fam)* montatura

frame·work ['freɪm,wɜːk] N *(also fig)* struttura

franc [fræŋk] N franco

France [frɑːns] N la Francia

fran·chise ['fræntʃaɪz] N *(Pol)* diritto di voto; *(Comm)* concessione *f*; *(Marine Insurance)* franchigia

fran·chisee ['fræntʃaɪ'ziː] N concessionario(-a)

fran·chis·er ['fræntʃaɪzəʳ] N concedente *m*

Franco-... ['fræŋkəʊ] PREF franco-...; **Franco-British** franco-britannico(-a)

Fran·co·phile ['fræŋkəʊ,faɪl] N francofilo(-a)

Fran·co·phone ['fræŋkəfəʊn] N francofono(-a)

frank¹ [fræŋk] ADJ *(comp* **-er**, *superl* **-est***)* franco(-a), sincero(-a), aperto(-a)

frank² [fræŋk] VT *(letter)* affrancare

Frank·furt ['fræŋkfɜːt] N Francoforte *f*

frank·fur·ter ['fræŋkfɜːtəʳ] N würstel *m inv*

frank·in·cense ['fræŋkɪn,sɛns] N incenso

frank·ing ma·chine ['fræŋkɪŋməʃiːn] N affrancatrice *f*

frank·ly ['fræŋklɪ] ADV francamente, sinceramente

frank·ness ['fræŋknɪs] N franchezza

fran·tic ['fræntɪk] ADJ *(activity, pace)* frenetico(-a); *(desperate: desire)* pazzo(-a), sfrenato(-a: *need*), disperato(-a); *(: search)* affannoso(-a); *(person)* fuori di sé; **frantic with worry** fuori di sé dalla preoccupazione; **frantic with joy** pazzo(-a) di gioia; **to go frantic** perdere la testa; **I was going frantic** stavo perdendo la testa; **there was frantic activity backstage on the opening night** c'era un'attività frenetica dietro le quinte la sera della prima

fran·ti·cal·ly ['fræntɪkəlɪ] ADV *(gen)* freneticamente, affannosamente

fra·ter·nal [frə'tɜːnl] ADJ fraterno(-a)

fra·ter·nal·ly [frə'tɜːnəlɪ] ADV fraternamente

fra·ter·nity [frə'tɜːnɪtɪ] N fraternità; *(club)* associazione *f*; *(spirit)* fratellanza; *(Am Univ) associazione studentesca maschile*

frat·er·ni·za·tion [,frætənaɪ'zeɪʃən] N il fraternizzare

frat·er·nize ['frætə,naɪz] VI: **to fraternize (with)** fraternizzare (con)

◎**fraud** [frɔːd] N *(Law)* frode *f*; *(trickery, trick)* truffa; *(person)* imbroglione(-a), impostore(-a); **he was jailed for fraud** è stato messo in prigione per truffa; **you're a fraud!** sei un impostore!

fraud squad N squadra *f* antifrode *inv*

fraudu·lence ['frɔːdjʊləns] N fraudolenza

fraudu·lent ['frɔːdjʊlənt] ADJ *(behaviour)* disonesto(-a); *(claims)* fraudolento(-a)

fraudu·lent·ly ['frɔːdjʊləntlɪ] ADV con la frode

fraught [frɔːt] ADJ *(tense)* teso(-a); **the situation is rather fraught** la situazione è un po' tesa; **fraught with** pieno(-a) *or* carico(-a) di; **fraught with danger** pieno(-a) di pericoli

fray¹ [freɪ] N *(old: fight)* zuffa, baruffa; **ready for the fray** *(also fig)* pronto(-a) a battersi; **to return to the fray** ributtarsi nella mischia

fray² [freɪ] VT *(cloth, cuff, rope)* consumare, logorare; **tempers were getting frayed** (tutti) cominciavano a innervosirsi, cresceva il nervosismo; **her nerves were frayed** aveva i nervi a pezzi
■ VI consumarsi, logorarsi

frayed [freɪd] ADJ sdrucito(-a), logoro(-a)

fraz·zle ['fræzl] N *(fam)*: **burnt to a frazzle** *(dinner)* completamente carbonizzato(-a); **worn to a frazzle** *(person)* ridotto(-a) a uno straccio

fraz·zled ['fræzəld] ADJ *(fam: person)* logorato(-a); *(bacon)* bruciato(-a)

FRB [,ɛfɑː'biː] N ABBR *(Am)* = **Federal Reserve Board**

FRCM [,ɛfɑːsiː'ɛm] N ABBR *(Brit)* = *Fellow of the Royal College of Music*

FRCO [,ɛfɑːsiː'əʊ] N ABBR *(Brit)* = *Fellow of the Royal College of Organists*

FRCP [,ɛfɑːsiː'piː] N ABBR *(Brit)* = *Fellow of the Royal College of Physicians*

FRCS [,ɛfɑːsiː'ɛs] N ABBR *(Brit)* = *Fellow of the Royal College of Surgeons*

freak [friːk] N *(abnormal: person)* fenomeno da baraccone; *(: animal, plant)* mostro; *(: event)* avvenimento eccezionale; *(fam: enthusiast)* fanatico(-a); **a freak of nature** un capriccio della natura; **the result was a freak** il risultato è stato un caso eccezionale; **health freak** *(fam)* salutista *m/f*; **computer freaks** fanatici del computer; **transexuals were regarded as freaks** i transessuali erano considerati fenomeni da baraccone; **she's a freak** è una tipa strana
■ ADJ *(storm, conditions)* anormale; *(victory)* inatteso(-a)
▶ **freak out** VI + ADV *(fam: get angry)* uscire dai

Ff

gangheri; (: *get excited*) andare su di giri; (: *on drugs*) andare fuori di testa

freak·ish ['fri:kɪʃ] ADJ (*result, appearance*) strano(-a), bizzarro(-a); (*moods*) capriccioso(-a); (*weather*) anormale

freak·ish·ly ['fri:kɪʃlɪ] ADV stranamente

freck·le ['frɛkl] N lentiggine *f*

freck·led ['frɛkld] ADJ lentigginoso(-a)

◎**free** [fri:] ADJ (*comp* **-r**, *superl* **-st**) **1** (*at liberty*): **free (from** *or* **of)** libero(-a) (da); **free from ties/cares** senza legami/preoccupazioni; **to be free of pain** non soffrire; **feel free** fai pure; **to break free (of)** liberarsi (da); **to set free** liberare; **free and easy** rilassato(-a); **he is not free to choose** non è libero di scegliere; **to give free rein to one's anger** *etc* dare libero sfogo alla propria rabbia *ecc*; **to give sb a free hand** dare carta bianca a qn **2** (*not occupied*) libero(-a); **is this seat free?** è libero questo posto?; **are you free tomorrow?** sei libero domani?; **to have one's hands free** avere le mani libere **3** **free (with)** (*generous*) prodigo(-a) (di); **to be free with one's money** spendere con facilità; **he's too free with his remarks** è sempre pronto alla critica **4** (*costing nothing*: *ticket, delivery*) gratuito(-a), gratis *inv*; **a free brochure** un opuscolo gratuito; **a free gift** un omaggio; **free of charge** gratuito(-a); **admission free** entrata libera; **free baggage allowance** (*Aer*) franchigia bagaglio **5** (*improper*: *behaviour*) sfrontato(-a); (*language*) spinto(-a)

■ ADV (*without charge*) gratuitamente, gratis; **I got in free** *or* **for free** (*fam*) sono entrato gratis

■ VT (*gen*) liberare; (*jammed object*) districare; (*untie*: *person, animal*) sciogliere; **to free o.s. from** *or* **of sth** sbarazzarsi di qc

free agent N persona indipendente

free·bie ['fri:bɪ] N (*fam*): **it's a freebie** è in omaggio

free·board ['fri:bɔ:d] N (*Naut*) bordo libero

free climbing N (*Mountaineering*) arrampicata libera

◎**free·dom** ['fri:dəm] N: **freedom (from)** libertà (da); **to give sb the freedom of one's house** mettere la propria casa a disposizione di qn; **the freedom of the press** la libertà di stampa; **to give sb the freedom of the city** dare a qn la cittadinanza onoraria; **freedom of speech** libertà di parola; **freedom of movement** libertà di movimento

freedom fighter N combattente *m/f* per la libertà

free enterprise N liberalismo economico

free fall N (*Parachuting*): **in free fall** in caduta libera

free-floating [fri:'fləʊtɪŋ] ADJ (*currency, exchange rate*) fluttuante

Free·fone® ['fri:ˌfəʊn] N (*Brit*) ≈ numero verde

free-for-all ['fri:fə'rɔ:l] N parapiglia *m* generale

free form ADJ (*poetry*) libero(-a)

free gift N regalo, omaggio

free·hand ['fri:ˌhænd] ADJ, ADV a mano libera

free-handed [fri:'hændɪd] ADJ generoso(-a)

free·hold ['fri:ˌhəʊld] N (*Law*) proprietà assoluta

free kick N (*Ftbl*) calcio di punizione

free·lance ['fri,lɑ:ns] ADJ: **freelance contributor** collaboratore(-trice) esterno(-a); **freelance work** collaborazione *f* esterna; **a freelance photographer** un fotografo freelance

■ N collaboratore(-trice) esterno(-a)

■ VI (*journalist*) essere un(-a) giornalista *m/f* indipendente

free·loader ['fri:ˌləʊdə^r] N (*pej*) scroccone(-a)

free love N libero amore *m*

free·ly ['fri:lɪ] ADV (*confess, speak*) liberamente, francamente; (*generously*) generosamente; **you may come and go freely** puoi andare e venire come vuoi

free·man ['fri:mən] N (*pl* **-men**) **freeman of a city** cittadino(-a) onorario(-a) di una città

free market N (*Econ*) libero mercato

free-market economy ['fri:ˌmɑ:kɪtɪ'kɒnəmɪ] N economia di libero mercato

Free·mason ['fri:ˌmeɪsən] N massone *m*

free·masonry ['fri:ˌmeɪsənrɪ] N massoneria

free pardon N condono

free pass N biglietto gratis

free port N porto franco

Free·post® ['fri:ˌpəʊst] N (*Brit Post*) affrancatura a carico del destinatario

free radical N (*Chem*) radicale *m* libero

free-range ['fri:ˌreɪnʒ] ADJ (*hen*) ruspante; (*eggs*) di gallina ruspante

free sample N campione *m* gratuito

free·sia ['fri:zɪə] N fresia

free speech N libertà di parola

free spirit N spirito indipendente

Free State N Stato Libero
▷ www.fs.gov.za

free·style ['fri:staɪl] N (*in swimming*) stile *m* libero

free·thinker [ˌfri:'θɪŋkə^r] N libero(-a) pensatore(-trice)

free-to-air [ˌfri:tʊ'ɛə^r] ADJ gratuito(-a), non a pagamento

■ ADV non a pagamento

free trade N libero scambio

free verse N verso libero

free·ware ['fri:wɛə^r] N (*Comput*) software *m inv* gratuito, freeware *m inv*

free·way ['fri:ˌweɪ] N (*Am*) superstrada

free·wheel [ˌfri:'wi:l] VI (*coast*: *on bicycle*) andare a ruota libera; (: *in car*) andare in folle

free·wheel·ing [ˌfri:'wi:lɪŋ] ADJ (*fam*: *person*) indipendente

free will N libero arbitrio; **of one's own free will** di spontanea volontà

◎**freeze** [fri:z] (*vb*: *pt* **froze**, *pp* **frozen**) VT (*water*) gelare; (*food*) congelare; (*industrially*) surgelare; (*prices, assets, salaries*) bloccare, congelare

■ VI (*Met*) gelare; (*water, lake*) ghiacciare; (*food*) congelarsi; (*keep still*) bloccarsi; **freezing fog** nebbia gelata; **the lake froze last winter** il lago è gelato lo scorso inverno; **to freeze to death** morire assiderato(-a); **he froze in his tracks** si bloccò; **freeze!** non muoverti!, fermo!

■ N (*Met*) gelata; (*of prices, wages etc*) blocco

▸ **freeze over** VI + ADV (*lake, river*) ghiacciarsi; (*windows, windscreen*) coprirsi di ghiaccio

▸ **freeze up** VI + ADV gelarsi

freeze-dried ['fri:z,draɪd] ADJ liofilizzato(-a)

freeze-dry [ˌfri:z,draɪ] VT liofilizzare

freeze-frame ['fri:z,freɪm] N fotogramma *m*; (*on video*) fermo immagine

freez·er ['fri:zə^r] N (*cabinet*) congelatore *m*; (*also*: **freezer compartment**) freezer *m inv*

freeze-up ['fri:z,ʌp] N (*Met*) gelo, gelata

freez·ing ['fri:zɪŋ] N (*also*: **freezing point**) punto di congelamento; **5 degrees below freezing** 5 gradi sotto zero

■ ADJ (*room, weather*) gelido(-a); **I'm freezing** sono congelato; **it's freezing!** si gela!

freight [freɪt] N (*goods transported*) merce *f*, merci *fpl*; (*charge*) spese *fpl* di trasporto; **freight forward** (*Comm*) spese a carico del destinatario; **freight inward** spese di trasporto sulla merce in entrata

■ VT (*transport: goods*) trasportare
■ ADJ (*yard*) merci *inv*
■ ADV: **to send sth freight** spedire qc per via ordinaria

freight car N (*Am*) carro *m* merci *inv*

freight·er ['freɪtəʳ] N (*Naut*) nave *f* mercantile *or* da carico, mercantile *m*; (*Aer*) aereo da trasporto merci

freight for·ward·er ['freɪt'fɔːwədəʳ] N spedizioniere *m*

freight han·dling ['freɪt'hændlɪŋ] N facchinaggio merci

freight train N (*Am*) treno *m* merci *inv*

French [frɛntʃ] ADJ francese; (*lesson, teacher etc*) di francese
■ N **1** (*language*) francese *m*; **I can speak French** parlo il francese; **the French teacher** l'insegnante di francese **2** (*people*): **the French** NPL i francesi

French bean N fagiolino

French bread N baguette *f inv*

French Canadian ADJ, N franco-canadese (*m/f*)

French chalk N steatite *f*, pietra da sarto

French doors NPL = **French windows**

French dressing N (*Culin*) *condimento per insalata*

French fried potatoes, French fries (*esp Am*) NPL patate *fpl* fritte

French Gui·ana ['frɛntʃgaɪ'ænə] N la Guiana francese

French horn N (*Mus*) corno da caccia

French knickers NPL culottes *fpl*

French leave N: **to take French leave** filarsela all'inglese

French loaf N filoncino

French·man ['frɛntʃmən] N (*pl* **-men**) francese *m*

French polish N vernice *f* all'alcol *or* allo spirito

French Riviera N: **the French Riviera** la Costa Azzurra

French stick, French loaf N filoncino

French windows, (*esp Am*) **French doors** NPL portafinestra

French·woman ['frɛntʃ,wʊmən] N (*pl* **-women**) francese *f*

fre·net·ic [frɪ'nɛtɪk] ADJ frenetico(-a)

fre·neti·cal·ly [frɪ'nɛtɪkəlɪ] ADV freneticamente

fren·zied ['frɛnzɪd] ADJ (*person*) frenetico(-a); (*efforts, shouts*) convulso(-a)

fren·zied·ly ['frɛnzɪdlɪ] ADV (*work*) freneticamente; **his heart was beating frenziedly** il cuore gli batteva all'impazzata

fren·zy ['frɛnzɪ] N frenesia; **he was in a frenzy of anxiety** era quasi impazzito dall'ansia

fre·quen·cy ['friːkwənsɪ] N frequenza; **high/low frequency** alta/bassa frequenza

frequency modulation N modulazione *f* di frequenza

◎ **fre·quent** [*adj* 'friːkwənt; *vb* 'friːkwɛnt] ADJ (*gen*) frequente; (*visitor*) abituale
■ VT frequentare

frequent flier N chi vola spesso; **frequent flier miles** miglia *fpl* (*punti da collezionare per l'acquisto di biglietti aerei*)

fre·quent·ly ['friːkwəntlɪ] ADV frequentemente, spesso

fres·co ['frɛskəʊ] N affresco

◎ **fresh** [frɛʃ] ADJ (*comp* **-er**, *superl* **-est**) **1** (*gen: not stale*) fresco(-a); (*new: sheet of paper, supplies, approach*) nuovo(-a); (*: news*) recente; **is the fish fresh?** il pesce è fresco?; **to put fresh courage into sb** ridare coraggio a qn; **to make a fresh start** ricominciare da capo; **as fresh as a daisy** fresco(-a) come una rosa **2** (*invigorating: breeze*) fresco(-a); **it's a bit fresh** (*Met*) fa un po' freschino **3** (*not salt: water*) dolce **4** (*fam: cheeky*) sfacciato(-a); **to get fresh with sb** prendersi delle libertà con qn
■ ADV (*baked, picked*) appena, da poco; **bread fresh from the oven** pane appena uscito dal forno; **to come fresh from New York** essere arrivato(-a) fresco(-a) fresco(-a) da New York; **a teacher fresh from college** un insegnante appena uscito dall'università

fresh air N aria fresca; **I need some fresh air** ho bisogno di un po' d'aria; **in the fresh air** all'aria aperta

fresh·en ['frɛʃn] VI (*wind, air*) rinfrescare
▸ **freshen up** VI + ADV rinfrescarsi
■ VT + ADV rinfrescare; **to freshen o.s. up** darsi una rinfrescata

fresh·en·er ['frɛʃnəʳ] N (*also:* **skin freshener**) tonico rinfrescante

fresh·er ['frɛʃəʳ] N (*Brit Univ fam*) = **freshman**

fresh·ly ['frɛʃlɪ] ADV di recente, di fresco, appena

fresh·man ['frɛʃmən] N (*pl* **-men**) (*Univ*) matricola *f*

fresh·ness ['frɛʃnɪs] N (*of food, air*) freschezza; (*of approach*) novità; (*impertinence*) impertinenza

fresh·water ['frɛʃ,wɔːtəʳ] ADJ: **freshwater fish** pesce *m* d'acqua dolce

fret [frɛt] VI (*worry*) preoccuparsi, agitarsi, affliggersi; **don't fret** non preoccuparti; **the baby is fretting for its mother** il/la bambino(-a) piange perché vuole la madre

fret·ful ['frɛtfʊl] ADJ (*child*) irritabile

fret·ful·ly ['frɛtfəlɪ] ADV in modo irritato

fret·ful·ness ['frɛtfʊlnɪs] N irritabilità

fret·saw ['frɛt,sɔː] N sega da traforo

fret·ted ['frɛtɪd] ADJ intagliato(-a), traforato(-a)

fret·work ['frɛt,wɜːk] N lavoro di traforo

Freud·ian ['frɔɪdɪən] ADJ freudiano(-a)

Freudian slip N lapsus *m inv* freudiano

FRG [,ɛfɑː'dʒiː] N ABBR (= **Federal Republic of Germany**) RFT *f* (= *Repubblica Federale Tedesca*)

Fri. [a] ABBR (= **Friday**) ven. (= *venerdì*)

fri·abil·ity [,fraɪə'bɪlɪtɪ] N (*frm*) friabilità

fri·able ['fraɪəbəl] ADJ (*frm*) friabile

fri·ar ['fraɪəʳ] N frate *m*

fric·as·see [,frɪkə'siː] N (*Culin*) fricassea

frica·tive ['frɪkətɪv] N (*Ling*) fricativa

fric·tion ['frɪkʃən] N frizione *f*, attrito

friction feed N (*on printer*) trascinamento ad attrito

friction tape N (*Am*) nastro isolante

Fri·day ['fraɪdɪ] N venerdì *m inv*; *for usage see* **Tuesday**

fridge [frɪdʒ] N (*Brit*) frigorifero, frigo

fridge-freezer ['frɪdʒ'friːzəʳ] N frigocongelatore *m*

fried [fraɪd] PT, PP *of* **fry** ■ ADJ (*Culin*) fritto(-a); **fried egg** uovo fritto *or* al tegamino; **fried chicken** pollo fritto

◎ **friend** [frɛnd] N amico(-a); (*at school*) compagno(-a); (*at work*) collega *m/f*; **a friend of mine** una mio(-a) amico(-a); **to make friends with sb** fare amicizia con qn; **let's be friends** facciamo pace; **we're just good friends** siamo solo buoni amici

friend·li·ness ['frɛndlɪnɪs] N cordialità

◎ **friend·ly** ['frɛndlɪ] ADJ (*comp* **-ier**, *superl* **-iest**) cordiale, amichevole; **to be friendly to sb** essere cordiale con qn; **to be friendly with sb** essere amico di qn
■ N (*also:* **friendly match**) (partita) amichevole *f*

friendly fire N (*Mil*) fuoco amico

friendly society N società *f inv* di mutuo soccorso

◎ **friend·ship** ['frɛndʃɪp] N amicizia

frieze [friːz] N (*Archit*) fregio

Ff

frig·ate ['frɪgɪt] N (*Naut*) fregata

frig·ging ['frɪgɪŋ] ADJ (*fam*) dannato(-a)

fright [fraɪt] N paura, spavento; **to get** *or* **have a fright** spaventarsi; **what a fright you gave me!** mi hai fatto paura!; **to take fright (at)** spaventarsi (all'idea di); **she looked a fright** (*fam*) era conciata da far paura

fright·en ['fraɪtn] VT spaventare, far paura a; **horror films frighten him** i film dell'orrore gli fanno paura; **to frighten sb out of their wits** far morire qn dallo spavento; **to be frightened of sth** avere paura di qc; **he was frightened into doing it** l'ha fatto per paura; **I was frightened to death** ero morto di paura

▸ **frighten away**, **frighten off** VT + ADV (*birds, children*) scacciare (facendogli paura)

fright·ened ['fraɪtnd] ADJ: **to be frightened (of)** avere paura (di)

fright·en·ing ['fraɪtnɪŋ] ADJ pauroso(-a), spaventoso(-a)

fright·en·ing·ly ['fraɪtnɪŋlɪ] ADV spaventosamente

fright·ful ['fraɪtfʊl] ADJ terribile, spaventoso(-a), orribile

fright·ful·ly ['fraɪtfəlɪ] ADV (*fam: late, cold*) terribilmente, spaventosamente; **it was frightfully good of her** è stato estremamente gentile da parte sua; **I'm frightfully sorry** mi dispiace moltissimo

fright·ful·ness ['fraɪtfʊlnɪs] N (*of crime*) atrocità *f inv*

frig·id ['frɪdʒɪd] ADJ (*atmosphere, look*) glaciale; (*Psych*) frigido(-a)

fri·gid·ity [frɪ'dʒɪdɪtɪ] N (*of manners, look*) freddezza; (*sexual*) frigidità

frig·id·ly ['frɪdʒɪdlɪ] ADV (*see n*) freddamente; frigidamente

frill [frɪl] N (*on dress*) fronzolo, balza; **without frills** (*fig*) senza fronzoli

frilled [frɪld] ADJ (*blouse*) con la gala, volant; (*curtain, skirt*) a balze

frilly [frɪlɪ] ADJ (*dress*) con pizzi e merletti

fringe [frɪndʒ] N **1** (*on shawl, rug*) frangia; (*Brit: of hair*) frangia, frangetta; **I want my fringe cut** vorrei che mi tagliasse la frangia **2 fringes** NPL (*of forest*) margine *m*; (*of city*) periferia; **on the fringe(s) of society** ai margini della società

■ VT (*shawl*) frangiare; **a road fringed with trees** una strada fiancheggiata da alberi

fringe benefits NPL benefici *mpl* aggiuntivi, fringe benefits *mpl*

fringed [frɪndʒd] ADJ (*lampshade, curtains*) con le frange; **fringed with** (*surrounded by*) contornato(-a) da

fringe theatre N teatro d'avanguardia

frip·pery ['frɪpərɪ] N (*pej*): **fripperies** cianfrusaglie *fpl*

Fris·bee® ['frɪzbi:] N frisbee® *m inv*

frisk [frɪsk] VT (*fam: suspect*) perquisire

■ VI (*frolic*) saltellare allegramente

frisky ['frɪskɪ] ADJ (*comp* **-ier**, *superl* **-iest**) (*person, horse*) vispo(-a), vivace

frit·ter ['frɪtəʳ] N (*Culin*) frittella

▸ **fritter away** VT + ADV sprecare

fri·vol·ity [frɪ'vɒlɪtɪ] N frivolezza

frivo·lous ['frɪvələs] ADJ frivolo(-a)

frivo·lous·ly ['frɪvələslɪ] ADV frivolamente

frizz [frɪz] VT increspare

■ N riccio

frizzed [frɪzd] ADJ crespo(-a)

friz·zle ['frɪzl] VI sfrigolare; **frizzled (up)** troppo croccante

friz·zy ['frɪzɪ] ADJ (*comp* **-ier**, *superl* **-iest**) (*hair*) crespo(-a); **to go frizzy** incresparsi

fro [frəʊ] ADV: **to and fro** avanti e indietro; **to go to and fro between** fare la spola tra

frock [frɒk] N (*woman's*) abito, vestito; (*of monk*) tonaca

frog [frɒg] N rana; **to have a frog in one's throat** avere la voce rauca

frog·ging ['frɒgɪŋ] N alamaro

frog·man ['frɒgmən] N (*pl* **-men**) sommozzatore *m*, uomo *m* rana *inv*

frog·march ['frɒg,mɑ:tʃ] VT (*Brit*): **to frogmarch sb in/out** portar qn dentro/fuori con la forza

frol·ic ['frɒlɪk] (*pt, pp* **frolicked**) VI saltellare allegramente

◎ **from** [frɒm] PREP **KEYWORD**

1 (*indicating starting place*) da; **where has he come from?** da dove arriva?; **to escape from sb/sth** fuggire da qn/qc; **from London to Glasgow** da Londra a Glasgow; **from house to house** di casa in casa; **where is he from?** da dove viene?, di dov'è?

2 (*indicating time*) da; **(as) from Friday** (a partire) da venerdì ; **from January** da gennaio in poi; **from now on** d'ora in poi, d'ora innanzi; **from time to time** ogni tanto, di tanto in tanto; **from one o'clock to** *or* **until** *or* **till two** dall'una alle due

3 (*indicating distance*) da; **the hotel is 1 km from the beach** l'albergo è a 1 km dalla spiaggia; **a long way from home** lontano(-a) da casa

4 (*indicating source, origin*) da; **a telephone call from Mr Smith** una telefonata dal Signor Smith; **to drink from a stream/the bottle** bere a un ruscello/dalla bottiglia; **where did you get that from?** dove l'hai trovato?; **a letter from my sister** una lettera da mia sorella; **painted from life** dipinto(-a) dal vero; **a quotation from Shakespeare** una citazione da Shakespeare; **to steal sth from sb** rubare qc a qn; **take the gun from him!** levagli la pistola!; **tell him from me** diglielo da parte mia

5 (*indicating price, number*) da; **prices range from £10 to £50** i prezzi vanno dalle 10 alle 50 sterline; **there were from 10 to 15 people there** c'erano tra le 10 e le 15 persone; **we have shirts from £18 upwards** abbiamo camicie da 18 sterline in su

6 (*indicating change*): **things went from bad to worse** le cose andarono di male in peggio; **the interest rate increased from 6% to 10%** il tasso d'interesse è aumentato dal 6% al 10%

7 (*indicating difference*): **to be different from sb** essere diverso(-a) da qn; **he can't tell red from green** non sa distinguere il rosso dal verde

8 (*because of, on the basis of*): **to act from conviction** agire per convinzione; **from experience** per esperienza; **to die from exposure** morire assiderato(-a); **weak from hunger** debole per la fame; **from what I can see** a quanto vedo; **from what I understood** da quanto ho capito; **from what he says** a quanto dice

9 (*with preposition*): **from above sth** da sopra qc, dall'alto di qc; **from among the crowd** dalla folla; **from beneath sth** da sotto qc; **from inside the house** dall'interno della casa; **from outside the house** dall'esterno della casa; **from over sth** da sopra qc, dall'alto di qc; **from underneath sth** da sotto qc

fro·mage frais [,frɒmɑ:ʒ'freɪ] N formaggio cremoso

frond [frɒnd] N fronda

◎ **front** [frʌnt] ADJ (*tooth*) davanti *inv*; (*garden*) sul davanti; (*wheel*) anteriore; (*row, page*) primo(-a); (*carriage*) di testa;

(*view*) frontale; **the front seats of the car** i sedili davanti della macchina
■ N **1** (*gen*) davanti *m inv*; (*of house*) facciata, davanti; (*of book*) copertina; (*of train*) testa; (*fig: appearance*) facciata; **in front** davanti; **in front of** davanti a; **Irene sits in front of me in class** Irene è seduta davanti a me in classe; (*opposite*) di fronte a; **at the front of the line** *or* **queue** in cima *or* all'inizio della fila; **at the front of the train** in testa al treno; **to be in front** (*Sport*) essere in testa; **he sat at the front of the class** era seduto nei primi banchi (della classe); **to put on a bold front** (*fig*) mostrare coraggio; **to be a front for sth** (*fam*) servire da copertura per qc **2** (*Mil, Pol, Met*) fronte *m*; **on all fronts** su tutti i fronti; **a united front** un fronte unito **3** (*also:* **sea front**: *promenade*) lungomare *m*
■ VI: **to front onto sth** dare su qc, guardare verso qc

front·age ['frʌntɪdʒ] N facciata

front·al [frʌntl] ADJ frontale

front bench N (*Brit Pol*): **the front bench** (*government ministers*) i ministri *pl*; (*opposition leaders*) *i principali esponenti dell'opposizione*

front·bench·er [ˌfrʌnt'bɛntʃəʳ] N *parlamentare che detiene una carica presso il governo*

front benches [ˌfrʌnt'bɛntʃəz] NPL *posti in Parlamento occupati dai "frontbencher"*

FRONT BENCHES

Nel Parlamento britannico, si chiamano **front benches** gli scanni della "House of Commons" che si trovano alla sinistra e alla destra dello "Speaker" davanti ai "back benches". I front benches sono occupati dai "frontbenchers", parlamentari che ricoprono una carica di governo o che fanno parte dello "shadow cabinet" dell'opposizione. *See also* **back benches**

▷ www.parliament.uk/

front desk N (*Am: in hotel*) reception *f inv*; (*: at doctor's*) accettazione *f*

front door N porta d'ingresso

front end N (*Aut*) avantreno

fron·tier ['frʌntɪəʳ] N frontiera, confine *m*

fron·tiers·man ['frʌntɪəzmən] N pioniere *m*

frontier town N città *f inv* di frontiera

fron·tis·piece ['frʌntɪsˌpiːs] N frontespizio

front line N (*Mil*) prima linea

front man N (*fam: representative*) prestanome *m inv*; (*: presenter*) presentatore *m*

front-page ['frʌntˌpeɪdʒ] ADJ (*news, article*) di prima pagina

front room N (*Brit*) salotto

front runner N (*fig*) favorito(-a)

front seat N (*Aut*) sedile *m* anteriore

front-wheel drive ['frʌntˌwiːl'draɪv] N (*Aut*) trazione *f* anteriore

frost [frɒst] N gelo; (*also:* **hoar frost**) brina; (*on window*) ghiaccio; **a keen frost** un gelo pungente; **there was frost on the ground** c'era brina sulla terra; **an overnight frost** gelata notturna; **4 degrees of frost** 4 gradi sotto zero
■ VT (*esp Am: ice: cakes*) glassare

frost·bite ['frɒstˌbaɪt] N congelamento

frost·bitten ['frɒstˌbɪtn] ADJ congelato(-a)

frost·ed ['frɒstɪd] ADJ (*glass*) smerigliato(-a); (*esp Am: cake*) glassato(-a)

frosti·ly ['frɒstɪlɪ] ADV gelidamente

frostiness ['frɒstɪ-nɪs] N freddezza

frost·ing ['frɒstɪŋ] N (*esp Am: icing*) glassa

frosty ['frɒstɪ] ADJ (*comp* **-ier**, *superl* **-iest**) (*weather, also fig*) gelido(-a); (*surface, window*) coperto(-a) di ghiaccio *or* di brina; **it was frosty last night** ha gelato durante la notte; **one frosty morning** una mattinata gelida; **they gave him a frosty reception** gli hanno riservato un'accoglienza gelida

froth [frɒθ] N schiuma, spuma
■ VI schiumare, spumare; **the dog was frothing at the mouth** il cane aveva la schiuma alla bocca

frothy ['frɒθɪ] ADJ (*beer, mixture*) spumoso(-a), schiumoso(-a); (*lace, nightdress*) vaporoso(-a); (*play, entertainment*) leggero(-a)

frown [fraʊn] N: **he gave me a worried frown** mi ha guardato con aria preoccupata; **he gave me a frown of disapproval** mi ha lanciato un'occhiata di disapprovazione
■ VI aggrottare le sopracciglia; **to frown at sth/sb** guardare qc/qn con cipiglio
▶ **frown upon, frown on** VI + PREP (*fig*) disapprovare

frown·ing ['fraʊnɪŋ] ADJ corrucciato(-a)

frowsy, frowzy ['fraʊzɪ] ADJ (*person, clothes*) trasandato(-a), sciatto(-a); (*room*) che puzza di chiuso

froze [frəʊz] PT *of* **freeze**

fro·zen ['frəʊzn] PP *of* **freeze** ■ ADJ (*food*) congelato(-a); (*industrially deep frozen*) surgelato(-a); (*Econ: assets*) bloccato(-a); **I'm frozen stiff** sono gelato fino alle ossa

FRS [ˌɛfɑːr'ɛs] N ABBR **1** (*Brit*) = *Fellow of the Royal Society* **2** (*Am:* = **Federal Reserve System**) *sistema bancario degli Stati Uniti*

fruc·tose ['frʌktəʊs] N fruttosio

fru·gal ['fruːgəl] ADJ (*person*) economo(-a); (*meal*) frugale

fru·gal·ity [fruː'gælɪtɪ] N frugalità

fru·gal·ly ['fruːgəlɪ] ADV (*live*) frugalmente; (*give out*) con parsimonia

◎ **fruit** [fruːt] N (*collectively*) frutta; (*Bot*) frutto; **would you like some fruit?** vuoi della frutta?; **to bear fruit** dare frutti; (*fig*) dare frutto; **the fruits of one's labour** (*fig*) i frutti del proprio lavoro

fruit·cake ['fruːtˌkeɪk] N plumcake *m inv*; (*fam: person*) picchiatello(-a)

fruit cocktail N macedonia di frutta

fruit dish N fruttiera

fruit·er·er ['fruːtərəʳ] N (*esp Brit*) fruttivendolo(-a); **at the fruiterer's (shop)** dal fruttivendolo

fruit farm N azienda ortofrutticola

fruit fly N mosca della frutta

fruit·ful ['fruːtfʊl] ADJ (*profitable*) fruttuoso(-a); (*soil*) fertile

fruit·ful·ly ['fruːtfəlɪ] ADV (*fig*) fruttuosamente

fruit·ful·ness ['fruːtfʊlnɪs] N (*of discussion etc*) buon esito; (*of soil*) fertilità

frui·tion [fruː'ɪʃən] N: **to come to fruition** (*frm*) realizzarsi

fruit juice N succo di frutta

fruit·less ['fruːtlɪs] ADJ (*fig*) vano(-a), inutile

fruit machine N (*Brit*) slot-machine *f inv*, macchina *f* mangiasoldi *inv*

fruit salad N macedonia

fruit tree N albero da frutto

fruity ['fruːtɪ] ADJ (*comp* **-ier**, *superl* **-iest**) (*taste*) che sa di frutta; (*wine*) fruttato(-a); (*voice*) pastoso(-a)

Ff

frump [frʌmp] N (*woman*) donnetta scialba; **I felt a frump** mi son sentita goffa e scialba

frump·ish ['frʌmpɪʃ], **frumpy** ['frʌmpɪ] ADJ scialbo(-a) e fuori moda

◎**frus·trate** [frʌ'streɪt] VT (*plan, effort, hope*) rendere vano(-a); (*person*) frustrare

frus·trat·ed [frʌ'streɪtɪd] ADJ (*person*) frustrato(-a); (*effort*) reso(-a) vano(-a); **he's a frustrated artist** è un artista mancato; **I got more and more frustrated with it** ci sono impazzito

frus·trat·ing [frʌ'streɪtɪŋ] ADJ (*job*) frustrante; (*day*) disastroso(-a); **how frustrating!** che seccatura!

frus·tra·tion [frʌ'streɪʃən] N (*feeling: of hopes*) frustrazione *f*; (*of plans*) inutilità; (*setback*) scocciatura

◎**fry**[1] [fraɪ] VT, VI friggere

fry[2] [fraɪ] NPL (*Zool*) avannotti *mpl*; *see also* **small fry**

fry·ing pan ['fraɪɪŋ'pæn] N padella; **to jump out of the frying pan into the fire** cadere dalla padella nella brace

fry-up [fraɪʌp] N (*Brit*) ≈ fritto misto

FSA [ˌɛfɛs'eɪ] N ABBR (*Brit*) **1** (= **Food Standards Association**) *organo di controllo degli standard alimentari* **2** (= **Financial Services Authority**) *organo che regolamenta i mercati finanziari di Londra*

FT [ˌɛf'tiː] N ABBR (*Brit*: = **Financial Times**) *giornale finanziario*; **the FT index** l'indice del Financial Times

ft. ABBR = **foot, feet**

FTC [ˌɛftiː'siː] N ABBR (*Am*) = **Federal Trade Commission**

FTP [ˌɛftiː'piː] ABBR (*Comput*: = **file transfer protocol**) FTP *m*

FT-SE 100 Index ['fʊtsɪwʌn,hʌndrəd'ɪndɛks] N ABBR *indice borsistico del Financial Times* ▷ www.ftse.com/

fuch·sia ['fjuːʃə] N (*Bot*) fucsia; (*colour*) fucsia *m*
■ ADJ fucsia *inv*

fuck [fʌk] (*fam!*) VT **1** fottere **2** **fuck you!** va' a farti fottere! (*fam!*)
■ EXCL: **fuck!** cazzo!
▸ **fuck about** (*fam!*) VI + ADV: **to fuck about** *or* **around** cazzeggiare; **he's fucking about all day** non fa un cazzo tutto il giorno; **what is he fucking about with my stereo for?** che cazzo fa con il mio stereo?
■ VT + ADV: **to fuck sb about** *or* **around** prendere qn per il culo
▸ **fuck off** VI + ADV (*fam!*): **fuck off!** vaffanculo! (*fam!*)

fucked [fʌkt] ADJ (*fam!*: *ruined, destroyed*) a puttane (*fam!*)

fucked up ADJ (*fam!*: *person*): **to be fucked up** essersi fottuto(-a) il cervello; (: *thing*) a puttane (*fam!*)

fuck·er ['fʌkəʳ] N (*fam!*) figlio(-a) di puttana (*fam!*)

fuck·ing ['fʌkɪŋ] ADJ (*fam!*) fottuto(-a) (*fam!*), di merda (*fam!*); **you fucking idiot!** stronzo! (*fam!*); coglione! (*fam!*)

fud·dled ['fʌdld] ADJ (*muddled*) confuso(-a); (*tipsy*) brillo(-a)

fuddy-duddy ['fʌdɪ,dʌdɪ] N (*pej*) parruccone *m*

fudge [fʌdʒ] N (*Culin*) *specie di caramella a base di latte, burro e zucchero*
■ VT (*figures, results*) falsificare; (*question, issue*) eludere

◎**fuel** [fjʊəl] N (*gen*) combustibile *m*; (*for engine*) carburante *m*; **the plane ran out of fuel** l'aereo ha finito il carburante; **to add fuel to the flames** (*fig*) soffiare sul fuoco, gettar olio sul fuoco
■ VT (*furnace etc*) alimentare; (*aircraft, ship*) rifornire di carburante
■ VI (*aircraft, ship*) rifornirsi di carburante

fuel cell N cella a combustione

fuel injection N (*Auto*) iniezione *f*; **fuel injection engine** motore *m* a iniezione

fuel oil N olio combustibile, nafta

fuel pump N (*Aut*) pompa del carburante

fuel rod N barra di combustibile nucleare

fuel-saving ['fjʊəl,seɪvɪŋ] ADJ: **fuel-saving device** economizzatore *m*

fuel tank N (*industrial, domestic*) serbatoio del carburante, deposito *m* nafta *inv*; (*on vehicle*) serbatoio (della benzina)

fug [fʌg] N (*Brit*) aria viziata

fu·gi·tive ['fjuːdʒɪtɪv] N fuggitivo(-a), profugo(-a); (*from prison*) evaso(-a)
■ ADJ fuggitivo(-a); (*liter*: *fleeting*) fugace, fuggevole

fugue [fjuːg] N (*Mus*) fuga

ful·crum ['fʊlkrəm] N fulcro

◎**ful·fil**, (*Am*) **ful·fill** [fʊl'fɪl] VT (*duty, function*) compiere; (*promise*) mantenere; (*ambition*) realizzare; (*wish, desire*) soddisfare, appagare; (*order*) eseguire; **to fulfil o.s.** realizzarsi; **he fulfilled his dream to visit China** ha realizzato il suo sogno di fare un viaggio in Cina

ful·filled [fʊl'fɪld] ADJ (*person*) realizzato(-a), soddisfatto(-a)

ful·fil·ling [fʊl'fɪlɪŋ] ADJ (*work*) soddisfacente

ful·fil·ment, (*Am*) **ful·fill·ment** [fʊl'fɪlmənt] N (*see vb*) compimento; mantenimento; realizzazione *f*; soddisfazione *f*, appagamento; esecuzione *f*; **sense of fulfilment** soddisfazione

◎**full** [fʊl] ADJ (*comp* **-er**, *superl* **-est**) **1** (*gen*) pieno(-a); (*vehicle, hotel*) completo(-a); (*timetable*) denso(-a); **the tank's full** il serbatoio è pieno; **to be full of ...** essere pieno(-a) di...; **full of people** gremito(-a) di gente; **to be full of o.s.** essere pieno(-a) di sé; **we are full up for July** siamo al completo per luglio; **he's had a full life** ha avuto una vita piena *or* intensa; **I'm full (up)** (*fam*) sono pieno *or* sazio **2** (*complete*) completo(-a); (: *member*) effettivo(-a); (: *price*) intero(-a); (*details*) ampio(-a); **to pay full fare** pagare la tariffa intera *or* completa; **to fall full length** cadere lungo(-a) disteso(-a); **in full bloom** in piena fioritura; **in full colour** (*illustration*) a colori; **in full dress** in abito da cerimonia; **army at full strength** esercito al gran completo; **to be in full swing** essere in pieno fervore; **in the fullest sense of the word** nel pieno senso della parola; **at full speed** a tutta velocità; **full speed ahead** (*Naut*) avanti tutta; **full price** prezzo intero; **the full particulars** tutti i particolari; **full information** tutte le informazioni; **I waited a full hour** ho aspettato un'ora intera **3** (*rounded*: *face*) pieno(-a); (: *figure*) pienotto(-a); (: *lips*) carnoso(-a); (: *skirt, sleeves*) largo(-a), ampio(-a)
■ ADV: **to know full well that** sapere benissimo che; **it hit him full in the face** l'ha colpito in pieno viso
■ N: **to write sth in full** scrivere qc per intero; **to pay in full** pagare tutto; **to the full** fino in fondo, al massimo

full·back ['fʊl,bæk] N (*Ftbl, Rugby*) terzino

full-blooded [ˌfʊl'blʌdɪd] ADJ (*vigorous*: *attack, support*) vigoroso(-a); (*virile*) virile

full-blown [ˌfʊl'bləʊn] ADJ (*disease, heart attack*) vero(-a) e proprio(-a); (*doctor, architect*) a tutti gli effetti

full board N pensione *f* completa

full-bodied [ˌfʊl'bɒdɪd] ADJ (*wine*) corposo(-a)

full-cream [ˌfʊl'kriːm] ADJ (*Brit*): **full-cream milk** latte *m* intero

full dress N (*Mil*) abito da cerimonia

full employment N (*Econ*) piena occupazione

full-face [ˌfʊl'feɪs] ADJ, ADV di faccia

full-grown [ˌfʊlˈgrəʊn] ADJ maturo(-a)
full house N (*Theatre*) il tutto esaurito
full-length [ˌfʊlˈlɛŋθ] ADJ (*portrait*) in piedi; (*dress*) lungo(-a); (*film*) a lungometraggio
full mon·ty [-ˈmɒntɪ] N (*Brit fam* = **the full monty**) tutto il possibile e l'immaginabile
full moon N luna piena
full name N nome *m* e cognome *m*
full·ness [ˈfʊlnɪs] N (*of detail*) abbondanza; (*of figure, hips*) rotondità; (*of dress*) ampiezza; **in the fullness of time** (*eventually*) col tempo; (*at predestined time*) a tempo debito
full-page [ˌfʊlˈpeɪdʒ] ADJ a tutta pagina
full-scale [ˈfʊlˈskeɪl] ADJ (*search, retreat*) su vasta scala; (*drawing, model*) a grandezza naturale; **a full-scale prototype** un prototipo in grandezza naturale; **a full-scale nuclear war** una guerra nucleare su vasta scala
full-sized [ˌfʊlˈsaɪzd], **full-size** [ˌfʊlˈsaɪz] ADJ (*full-grown*) adulto(-a); (*portrait, model*) a grandezza naturale
full stop N punto
full-throated [ˌfʊlˈθrəʊtɪd] ADJ (*shout*) a piena gola
full-time [ˌfʊlˈtaɪm] ADJ, ADV (*work*) a tempo pieno
full time N (*Sport*) fine *f* partita
◎ **ful·ly** [ˈfʊlɪ] ADV **1** (*completely*) completamente, pienamente, interamente; **fully dressed** completamente vestito(-a) **2** (*at least*) almeno; **fully as big** almeno così grosso(-a)
fully fashioned [ˈfʊlɪˈfæʃənd] ADJ (*sweater*) sciancrato(-a); (*stockings*) modellato(-a)
fully-fledged [ˈfʊlɪˈflɛdʒd] ADJ (*bird*) adulto(-a); (*fig: teacher, member*) a tutti gli effetti
ful·mar [ˈfʊlməʳ] N procellaria dei ghiacci
ful·mi·nate [ˈfʌlmɪˌneɪt] VI: **to fulminate (against)** scagliare fulmini (contro)
ful·mi·na·tion [ˌfʌlmɪˈneɪʃən] N invettiva
ful·some [ˈfʊlsəm] ADJ (*pej: praise*) esagerato(-a), eccessivo(-a); (*: manner*) insincero(-a)
fum·ble [ˈfʌmbl] VI (*also:* **fumble about**): **to fumble (about) in one's pockets** frugare *or* rovistare nelle tasche; **to fumble in the dark** andare a tastoni *or* a tentoni, brancolare; **to fumble with sth** armeggiare con qc
■ VT: **to fumble a catch** mancare una presa; **to fumble a ball** lasciarsi sfuggire di mano una palla
fume [fjuːm] VI (*angry person*) essere furioso(-a); (*car exhaust*) fumare; **to be fuming with rage at** *or* **about sth** fumare di rabbia per qc
fumes [fjuːmz] NPL esalazioni *fpl*, vapori *mpl*; **poisonous fumes** esalazioni velenose; **exhaust fumes** gas di scarico
fu·mi·gate [ˈfjuːmɪˌgeɪt] VT (*room*) suffumicare, fumigare
fu·mi·ga·tion [ˌfjuːmɪˈgeɪʃən] N fumigazione *f*
◎ **fun** [fʌn] N (*enjoyment*) divertimento, spasso; **for** *or* **in fun** per scherzo, per ridere, per divertimento; **it's great fun** è molto divertente; **it's not much fun** non è molto divertente; **don't spoil our fun** non fare il guastafeste; **there'll be fun and games with that** (*fig: iro*) ci sarà da divertirsi; **to do sth for the fun of it** fare qc tanto per ridere; **to have fun** divertirsi; **have fun!** divertiti!; **to make fun of** *or* **poke fun at sb** canzonare *or* prendere in giro qn
◎ **func·tion** [ˈfʌŋkʃən] N **1** (*purpose, Math*) funzione *f* **2** (*reception*) ricevimento; (*official ceremony*) cerimonia, funzione *f*
■ VI (*operate*) funzionare; **the system ceased to function** il sistema ha smesso di funzionare; **to function as** fungere da
func·tion·al [ˈfʌŋkʃənl] ADJ funzionale
func·tion·al·ly [ˈfʌŋkʃənəlɪ] ADV dal punto di vista funzionale
func·tion·ary [ˈfʌŋkʃənərɪ] N funzionario(-a)
function key N (*Comput*) tasto *m* funzione *inv*
◎ **fund** [fʌnd] N **1** (*reserve of money*) fondo, cassa; (*supply*) provvista, riserva; **a pension fund** un fondo pensione; **to be a fund of information** essere una miniera d'informazioni **2** (*cash*): **funds** NPL fondi *mpl*; **to raise funds for** raccogliere fondi per
■ VT (*project*) finanziare
◎ **fun·da·men·tal** [ˌfʌndəˈmɛntl] ADJ fondamentale; **his fundamental honesty** la sua innata onestà
fun·da·men·tal·ism [ˌfʌndəˈmɛntəˌlɪzəm] N fondamentalismo
fun·da·men·tal·ist [ˌfʌndəˈmɛntəlɪst] ADJ, N fondamentalista (*m/f*)
fun·da·men·tal·ly [ˌfʌndəˈmɛntəlɪ] ADV fondamentalmente, essenzialmente
fun·da·men·tals [ˌfʌndəˈmɛntlz] NPL basi *fpl*, fondamenti *mpl*, principi *mpl* fondamentali
◎ **fund·ing** [ˈfʌndɪŋ] N finanziamento, fondi *mpl*
fund-raising [ˈfʌndˌreɪzɪŋ] N raccolta di fondi
■ ADJ (*event*) per la raccolta di fondi
fu·ner·al [ˈfjuːnərəl] N funerale *m*; (*procession*) corteo funebre; (*state funeral*) funerali *mpl*; **that's your funeral!** (*fam*) è affar tuo!
funeral director N impresario di pompe funebri
funeral parlour, (*Am*) **funeral parlor** N impresa di pompe funebri
funeral service N ufficio funebre
fu·ner·ary [ˈfjuːnərərɪ] ADJ (*frm*) funebre
fu·nereal [fjuːˈnɪərɪəl] ADJ funereo(-a), lugubre
fun·fair [ˈfʌnˌfɛəʳ] N (*Brit*) luna park *m inv*
fun·gi [ˈfʌŋgaɪ] NPL *of* **fungus**
fun·gi·cide [ˈfʌndʒɪˌsaɪd] N fungicida *m*; (*for plants*) anticrittogamico
fun·gus [ˈfʌŋgəs] N (*pl* **fungi** [ˈfʌŋgaɪ]) fungo; (*mould*) muffa
fu·nicu·lar [fjuːˈnɪkjʊləʳ] N (*also:* **funicular railway**) funicolare *f*
■ ADJ funicolare
funk [fʌŋk] N **1** (*old*): **to be in a (blue) funk** (*fam*) avere una gran fifa **2** (*Mus*) funk *m*, (musica) funky *m*
■ VT (*old*) evitare (per paura)
funky [ˈfʌŋkɪ] ADJ (*comp* **-ier**, *superl* **-iest**) (*music*) funky *inv*; (*clothes, look etc*) alla moda; (*fam: excellent*) figo(-a)
fun-loving [ˈfʌnˌlʌvɪŋ] ADJ a cui piace divertirsi
fun·nel [ˈfʌnl] N (*for pouring*) imbuto; (*of steam engine, ship*) fumaiolo, ciminiera
fun·ni·ly [ˈfʌnɪlɪ] ADV **1** in modo divertente **2** (*oddly*) stranamente; **funnily enough** strano a dirsi, per una strana coincidenza
◎ **fun·ny** [ˈfʌnɪ] ADJ (*comp* **-ier**, *superl* **-iest**) **1** divertente, buffo(-a); **it was so funny I couldn't stop laughing** era così divertente che non riuscivo a smettere di ridere; **that's not funny** c'è poco da ridere; **to try to be funny** fare lo spiritoso(-a) **2** (*strange*) strano(-a), bizzarro(-a); **this tastes funny** ha uno strano sapore; **a funny feeling came over me** mi sono sentito strano; **the funny thing about it is that ...** la cosa strana è che...; **there's some funny business going on here** (*fam*) qui c'è qualcosa di losco; **there's something funny about him** ha qualcosa di strano
■ N: **the funnies** (*Am fam*) i fumetti
funny bone N (*fam*) osso cubitale

Ff

fun·ny·man ['fʌnɪmæn] N comico
fun run N marcia non competitiva
fur [fɜːʳ] N (*of animal*) pelo, pelame *m*; (*single skin*) pelle *f*; (*as clothing*) pelliccia; (*Brit: in kettle*) incrostazione *f*, calcare *m*; **the cat's fur** il pelo del gatto
fur·bish ['fɜːbɪʃ] VT (*polish*) lucidare; (*renovate, smarten*) ravvivare
fur coat N pelliccia
Furies ['fjʊərɪz] NPL (*Myth*): **the Furies** le Furie
fu·ri·ous ['fjʊərɪəs] ADJ (*person*) furioso(-a), infuriato(-a); (*argument*) violento(-a); (*effort*) grande; **at a furious speed** a velocità folle; **to be furious with sb** essere furioso(-a) con qn; **to be furious at sth/at having done sth** essere furioso(-a) per qc/per aver fatto qc
fu·ri·ous·ly ['fjʊərɪəslɪ] ADV furiosamente, accanitamente
furl [fɜːl] VT (*sail*) piegare
furled [fɜːld] ADJ (*flag, umbrella*) ripiegato(-a)
fur·long ['fɜːˌlɒŋ] N = *201,17 m*
fur·lough ['fɜːləʊ] N (*esp Am*) licenza, permesso, congedo
fur·nace ['fɜːnɪs] N fornace *f*
fur·nish ['fɜːnɪʃ] VT **1** (*room, house*): **to furnish (with)** arredare (con), ammobiliare (con); **furnishing fabric** tessuto da arredamento; **furnished flat** *or* (*Am*) **furnished apartment** appartamento ammobiliato
2 (*frm: supply: excuse, information*) fornire, dare; **to furnish sb with sth** dare qc a qn
fur·nish·ings ['fɜːnɪʃɪŋz] NPL mobili *mpl*, mobilia
◎**fur·ni·ture** ['fɜːnɪtʃəʳ] N mobili *mpl*, mobilia; **a piece of furniture** un mobile; **the furniture is new** i mobili sono nuovi; **to be part of the furniture** (*fig fam*) confondersi con la tappezzeria

> DID YOU KNOW ...?
> **furniture** is not translated by the Italian word ***fornitura***

furniture polish N cera per mobili
furniture removers N (*firm*) impresa di traslochi
furniture shop N negozio di mobili
furniture van N camion *m inv* per *or* dei traslochi
fu·ro·re [fjʊə'rɔːrɪ], (*Am*) **fu·ror** [fjʊə'rɔːʳ] N (*protests*) scalpore *m*; (*enthusiasm*) entusiasmo

> DID YOU KNOW ...?
> **furore** is not translated by the Italian word ***furore***

furred [fɜːd] ADJ (*kettle, pipe*) incrostato(-a); **to have a furred tongue** avere la bocca impastata
fur·ri·er ['fʌrɪəʳ] N pellicciaio(-a)
fur·row ['fʌrəʊ] N (*Agr*) solco; (*on forehead*) solco, ruga
■VT (*forehead, brow*) segnare di rughe, solcare
fur·rowed ['fʌrəʊd] ADJ corrucciato(-a)
fur·ry ['fɜːrɪ] ADJ (*animal*) peloso(-a); (*toy*) di peluche
◎**fur·ther** ['fɜːðəʳ] COMP *of* **far**
■ADV **1** (*in time*) oltre, più avanti; (*in place*) più lontano, oltre, più avanti; **further back** più indietro; **further on** (*also fig*) più avanti; **how much further is it?** quanto manca *or* dista?; **London is further from here than Oxford** Londra è più lontana da qui rispetto a Oxford; **any further** più; **I can't walk any further** non ce la faccio più a camminare; **I got no further with him** (*fig*) non sono riuscito a cavare un ragno dal buco; **nothing is further from my thoughts** non ci penso neanche
2 (*more*) inoltre, di più; **and I further believe that ...** e inoltre *or* per di più credo che...; **further to your letter of ...** (*Comm*) con riferimento alla vostra lettera del...; **further to our conversation ...** facendo seguito alla nostra conversazione...; **he heard nothing further** non c'è stato alcun seguito
■ADJ **1** = **farther**
2 (*additional*) ulteriore, altro(-a), supplementare; **until further notice** fino a nuovo avviso; **after further consideration** dopo un più attento esame; **please write to us if you need any further information** ci scriva se ha bisogno di ulteriori informazioni
■VT (*a cause*) appoggiare, promuovere, favorire; **to further one's interests** fare i propri interessi
fur·ther·ance ['fɜːðərəns] N: **in furtherance of sth** a favore di qc
further education N (*Brit*) ≈ corsi *mpl* di formazione
▷ www.lsda.org.uk/home.asp
further·more ['fɜːðəˌmɔːʳ] ADV inoltre, per di più
further·most ['fɜːðəˌməʊst] ADJ più lontano(-a)
fur·thest ['fɜːðɪst] SUPERL *of* **far**
■ADV: **this is the furthest you can go** non puoi andare più lontano
■ADJ più lontano(-a), più distante
fur·tive ['fɜːtɪv] ADJ (*glance, action*) furtivo(-a); (*person*) circospetto(-a)
fur·tive·ly ['fɜːtɪvlɪ] ADV furtivamente
fury ['fjʊərɪ] N (*of storm, person*) furia, furore *m*; **she flew into a fury** andò su tutte le furie; **like fury** (*fam*) come una furia; **she's a little fury** è una piccola furia; *see also* **Furies**
furze [fɜːz] N ginestrone *m*
fuse, (*Am*) **fuze** [fjuːz] N (*Elec*) fusibile *m*, valvola; (*of bomb*) spoletta, miccia; **to blow a fuse** far saltare una valvola; **a fuse has blown** è saltata una valvola, è saltato un fusibile
■VT **1** (*Elec*): **to fuse the lights** far saltare le valvole
2 (*metals*) fondere
■VI **1** (*Elec*): **the lights have fused** sono saltate le valvole **2** (*metals*) fondersi
fuse box N scatola *or* cassetta dei fusibili
fused [fjuːzd] ADJ con fusibile incorporato
fu·selage ['fjuːzəlɑːʒ] N fusoliera
fuse wire N (filo) fusibile *m*
fu·si·lier [ˌfjuːzɪ'lɪəʳ] N fuciliere *m*
fu·sil·lade [ˌfjuːzɪ'leɪd] N scarica, raffica; (*fig*) raffica
fu·sion ['fjuːʒən] N fusione *f*
fuss [fʌs] N (*complaints, arguments*) storie *fpl*; (*anxious preparations*) agitazione *f*; **to make a fuss about sth** fare storie per qc; **he made a lot of fuss about nothing** ha fatto un sacco di storie per nulla; **don't make such a fuss!** non fare tante storie!; **what's all the fuss about?** cosa sono tutte queste storie?; **to make a fuss of sb** (*Brit*) coprire qn di attenzioni
■VI agitarsi
■VT (*person*) infastidire, scocciare
▸ **fuss about, fuss around** VI + PREP affannarsi
▸ **fuss over** VI + PREP (*person*) circondare di premure
fussi·ly ['fʌsɪlɪ] ADV meticolosamente; **she was fussily dressed** era carica di fronzoli
fussi·ness ['fʌsɪnɪs] N schifiltosità
fuss·pot ['fʌsˌpɒt] N (*Brit fam*) pignolo(-a)
fussy ['fʌsɪ] ADJ (*comp* **-ier**, *superl* **-iest**) (*person: difficult to please*) difficile, esigente; (*: excessively punctilious*) puntiglioso(-a), pignolo(-a); (*clothes*) pieno(-a) di fronzoli; (*style*) elaborato(-a); **I'm not fussy** (*fam*) per me è lo stesso; **she is very fussy about her food** fa la difficile per il cibo
fus·ty ['fʌstɪ] ADJ (*comp* **-ier**, *superl* **-iest**) (*pej: musty*)

(: *smell*) che sa di stantio; (: *old-fashioned*: *ideas, outlook*) stantio(-a)

fu·tile ['fju:taɪl] ADJ futile, vano(-a)

fu·tile·ly ['fju:taɪlɪ] ADV futilmente

fu·til·ity [fju:'tɪlɪtɪ] N futilità

fu·ton [ˌfu:'tɒn] N futon *m inv*, materasso giapponese

◎ **fu·ture** ['fju:tʃəʳ] ADJ futuro(-a); **the future king** il futuro re; **the future tense** il futuro; **at some future date** in futuro

■ N futuro, avvenire *m*; (*Gram*) futuro; **in future** in futuro; **in the near future** in un prossimo futuro; **in the immediate future** nell'immediato futuro; **there's no future in it** non c'è futuro in questo campo

fu·tures ['fju:tʃəz] NPL (*Fin*) futures *mpl*

fu·tur·ism ['fju:tʃəˌrɪzəm] N futurismo

fu·tur·ist ['fju:tʃərɪst] N futurista *m/f*

fu·tur·is·tic [ˌfju:tʃə'rɪstɪk] ADJ futurista, futuristico(-a)

fu·tur·olo·gist [ˌfju:tʃər'ɒlədʒɪst] N futurologo(-a)

fu·tur·ol·ogy [ˌfju:tʃər'ɒlədʒɪ] N futurologia

fuze [fju:z] N, VT, VI (*Am*) = fuse

fuzz [fʌz] N (*frizzy hair*) capelli *mpl* crespi; (*on chin*) peluria; **the fuzz** (*fam*) la polizia

fuzzi·ly ['fʌzɪlɪ] ADV confusamente

fuzzy ['fʌzɪ] ADJ (*comp* **-ier**, *superl* **-iest**) (*hair*) crespo(-a); (*blurred*: *photo*) sfocato(-a), indistinto(-a); (: *memory*) confuso(-a); **a fuzzy image** un'immagine indistinta

fuzzy logic N (*Comput*) logica fuzzy

Ff

G, **g** [dʒiː] N **1** (*letter*) G, g *f or m inv*; **G for George** ≈ G come Genova **2** (*Mus*) sol *m*

G [dʒiː] N ABBR (*Am Cine:* = **General Audiences**) per tutti

g [dʒiː] ABBR **1** (= **gram**) g **2** = **gravity**

G7 [ˈdʒiːˈsɛvn] N ABBR (*Pol:* = **Group of Seven**) G7 *mpl*

G8 [ˈdʒiː ˈeɪt] N ABBR (*Pol:* = **Group of Eight**) G8 *mpl*

GA ABBR (*Am Post*) = **Georgia**

gab [gæb] N (*fam*): **to have the gift of the gab** avere parlantina

gab·ar·dine [ˈgæbəˌdiːn] N = **gaberdine**

gab·ble [ˈgæbl] VT borbottare
■ VI farfugliare; **they were gabbling away in French** chiacchieravano come macchinette in francese

gab·er·dine [ˌgæbəˈdiːn] N (*material*) gabardine *m*; (*coat*) (soprabito di) gabardine

ga·ble [ˈgeɪbl] N frontone *m*

Ga·bon [gəˈbɒn] N Gabon *m*

gad·about [ˈgædəˌbaʊt] N (*fam*) girellone(-a)

gad about [ˈgædəˈbaʊt] VI + ADV (*fam old*) bighellonare, vagabondare

gad·fly [ˈgædˌflaɪ] N tafano

gadg·et [ˈgædʒɪt] N aggeggio, arnese *m*

gadg·et·ry [ˈgædʒɪtrɪ] N aggeggi *mpl*, arnesi *mpl*

Gaea [ˈdʒiːə] N Gaia

Gael·ic [ˈgeɪlɪk] ADJ gaelico(-a)
■ N (*language*) gaelico

Gaelic football N *gioco irlandese simile al rugby*
▷ www.gaa.ie/page/all_about_football.html

gaff [gæf] N **1** (*fam*): **to blow the gaff** spifferare un segreto **2** (*Fishing*) arpione *m*

gaffe [gæf] N gaffe *f inv*

gaf·fer [ˈgæfəʳ] N (*Brit fam*) capo

gag [gæg] N **1** (*over mouth*) bavaglio **2** (*fam: joke*) battuta, gag *f inv*
■ VT (*silence: prisoner etc*) imbavagliare; **he was bound and gagged** è stato legato ed imbavagliato
■ VI (*choke*) soffocare; (*retch*) avere conati di vomito; **the smell made me gag** l'odore mi soffocava

gaga [ˈgɑːgɑː] ADJ (*fam*): **to go gaga** rimbambire; **to go gaga over sb/sth** andare matto(-a) per qn/qc

gage [geɪdʒ] N, VT (*Am*) = **gauge**

gag·gle [ˈgægl] N (*of geese*) branco

gai·ety [ˈgeɪɪtɪ] N allegria, gaiezza

gai·ly [ˈgeɪlɪ] ADV (*sing, chatter*) allegramente, gaiamente; (*painted, decorated*) vivacemente; **gaily coloured** dai colori allegri

◎ **gain** [geɪn] N (*increase*) aumento; (*improvement*) miglioramento; (*advantage*) vantaggio, utile *m*; (*profit*) guadagno, profitto; **gain in weight** aumento di peso; **to do sth for gain** fare qc per lucro; **his loss is our gain** lui ci perde, noi ci guadagniamo; **the Conservatives made several gains** i Conservatori hanno guadagnato parecchi seggi
■ VT (*obtain, acquire: respect, approval*) ottenere; (*: reputation*) farsi; (*: experience, wealth, knowledge, territory*) acquistare; (*reach: summit, shore*) raggiungere, guadagnare; (*: objective*) raggiungere; (*increase: weight*) aumentare di; **to gain 3lbs/kilos (in weight)** aumentare di 3 libbre/chili; **what do I have to gain by staying here?** che ci guadagno restando qui?; **what do you hope to gain by this?** cosa speri di guadagnarci?; **to gain experience** fare esperienza; **I gained valuable experience by working there** ho fatto molta esperienza lavorando lì ; **to gain strength** (*person*) riprendere le forze; (*theory*) avvalorarsi; **to gain possession of** impadronirsi di, impossessarsi di; **to gain ground** guadagnare terreno; **to gain speed** acquistare velocità; **to gain weight** aumentare di peso; **my watch has gained 5 minutes** il mio orologio va avanti di 5 minuti; **to gain an advantage over sb** avvantaggiarsi rispetto a qn
■ VI (*person*) guadagnare; (*watch*) andare avanti; **to gain in/by** aumentare di/con; **to gain in weight** aumentare di peso; **to gain in popularity** acquistare popolarità
▸ **gain upon, gain on** VI + PREP accorciare le distanze da, riprendere

gain·ful [ˈgeɪnfʊl] ADJ (*employment*) remunerativo(-a)

gain·ful·ly [ˈgeɪnfəlɪ] ADV: **to be gainfully employed** avere un lavoro retribuito

gain·say [ˌgeɪnˈseɪ] (*pt, pp* **gainsaid** [ˌgeɪnˈsɛd]) VT (*frm: fact, argument*) contestare, negare; (*: person*) contraddire

gait [geɪt] N (*frm*) passo, andatura

gait·er [ˈgeɪtəʳ] N ghetta

gal. ABBR = gallon
gala ['gɑːlə] N *(festive occasion)* festa; (: *important*) gran galà *m inv*; **a gala evening** una serata di gala; **swimming gala** gare *fpl* di nuoto
ga·lac·tic [gə'læktɪk] ADJ galattico(-a)
Ga·la·pa·gos Is·lands [gə'læpəgəs'aɪləndz] NPL: **the Galapagos Islands** le (isole) Galapagos *fpl*
gala performance N serata di gala
gal·axy ['gæləksɪ] N galassia
gale [geɪl] N *(strong wind)* bufera, vento forte; *(at sea)* burrasca; **gale force 10** vento forza 10
gale force wind N vento di bufera
gale warning N avviso di bufera
gall [gɔːl] N *(Anat)* bile *f*; *(fig: impudence)* fegato, faccia (tosta)
■VT seccare; **it galled him to have to ask permission** gli seccava dover chiedere il permesso
gal·lant ['gælənt] ADJ *(brave)* valoroso(-a), prode; *(towards ladies)* galante; **gallant soldiers** soldati valorosi; **a gallant gentleman** un signore galante; **his gallant fight against cancer** la sua coraggiosa battaglia contro il cancro
gal·lant·ly ['gæləntlɪ] ADV *(see adj)* valorosamente, prodemente; galantemente
gal·lant·ry ['gæləntrɪ] N *(see adj)* valore *m* militare, prodezza; galanteria
gall bladder N cistifellea
gal·leon ['gælɪən] N galeone *m*
◎ **gal·lery** ['gælərɪ] N *(also:* **art gallery**: *state owned)* museo; (: *private*) galleria, loggia; *(for spectators)* tribuna; *(in theatre)* loggione *m*, balconata; **to play to the gallery** parlare *(per accattivarsi il pubblico)*
gal·ley ['gælɪ] N *(ship)* galea; *(ship's kitchen)* cambusa
galley proof N *(Typ)* bozza in colonna
galley slave N galeotto; *(fam: drudge)* schiavo(-a)
Gal·lic ['gælɪk] ADJ *(of Gaul)* gallico(-a); *(French)* francese
gall·ing ['gɔːlɪŋ] ADJ *(irritating)* seccante, irritante; *(humiliating)* umiliante
gal·li·vant ['gælɪˌvænt] VI andare in giro a divertirsi
gal·lon ['gælən] N gallone *m (Brit=4,55 litri; Am=3,79 litri)*
gal·lop ['gæləp] N *(pace)* galoppo; *(ride)* galoppata; **at a gallop** al galoppo
■VI *(horse, rider)* galoppare, andare al galoppo; **to gallop away** galoppare via; *(fig)* andarsene di gran carriera; **he galloped through his homework** *(fig)* ha fatto i compiti di volata
gal·lop·ing ['gæləpɪŋ] ADJ *(horse)* al galoppo; *(fig: inflation, pneumonia)* galoppante
gal·lows ['gæləʊz] NPL forca, patibolo
gallows bird N *(fam)* pendaglio da forca, avanzo di galera
gallows humour N umorismo macabro
gall·stone ['gɑːlˌstəʊn] N calcolo biliare
Gal·lup poll® ['gæləpˌpəʊl] N sondaggio d'opinione; ≈ sondaggio Doxa
ga·lore [gə'lɔːʳ] ADV a iosa, a profusione
ga·loshes [gə'lɒʃɪz] N calosce *fpl*
gal·van·ic [gæl'vænɪk] ADJ *(Elec)* galvanico(-a); *(fig: effect)* galvanizzante
gal·va·ni·za·tion [ˌgælvənaɪ'zeɪʃən] N galvanizzazione *f*
gal·va·nize ['gælvəˌnaɪz] VT galvanizzare; *(fig)* galvanizzare, elettrizzare; **to galvanize sb into action** spronare qn all'azione; **to galvanize sb into action** spronare qn all'azione
gal·va·nized iron ['gælvəˌnaɪzd'aɪən] N ferro zincato
Gam·bia ['gæmbɪə] N: **the Gambia** il Gambia
gam·bit ['gæmbɪt] N *(Chess)* gambetto; *(fig)* mossa; **opening gambit** prima mossa
gam·ble ['gæmbl] N azzardo, rischio; **to take a gamble** rischiare; **the gamble came off** è valsa la pena rischiare; **it's a gamble** è un salto nel buio, è un rischio
■VT *(money)* giocare; **he gambled one hundred pounds at the casino** ha giocato cento sterline al casinò
■VI giocare (d'azzardo); **to gamble on the Stock Exchange** giocare in Borsa; **to gamble on sth** puntare su qc, giocare su qc; **few firms want to gamble on new products** poche ditte vogliono puntare su prodotti nuovi
▶ **gamble away** VT + ADV *(money)* perdere al gioco, giocarsi
gam·bler ['gæmbləʳ] N giocatore(-trice) d'azzardo
gam·bling ['gæmblɪŋ] N gioco (d'azzardo)
gambling debts NPL debiti *mpl* di gioco
gambling den N bisca
gambling house N casinò *m inv*, casa da gioco
gam·bol ['gæmbəl] VI saltellare
◎ **game** [geɪm] N **1** *(gen)* gioco; *(match)* partita; **games** NPL *(Scol)* attività *fpl* sportive; **a game of football** una partita di calcio; **that's three games to you and two to me** siamo tre a due; **to have a game of cards/chess/tennis** fare una partita a carte/scacchi/tennis; **the children were playing a game** i bambini stavano facendo un gioco; **he plays a good game of golf** gioca bene al golf; **game of chance** gioco d'azzardo; **game, set and match** *(Tennis)* game, set e partita; **he was off his game** non era nella sua forma migliore; **to play the game** *(also fig)* rispettare le regole del gioco; **to play sb's game** fare il gioco di qn; **come on lads, play the game** su ragazzi, siate sportivi; **to beat sb at his own game** battere qn con le sue stesse armi; **the game is up** è finita, è la fine; **I wonder what his game is?** mi chiedo a che gioco stia giocando; **two can play at that game** ti *(or* lo *etc)* ripagherò con la stessa moneta; **how long have you been in this game?** *(fam)* da quant'è che fai questo mestiere?; **to be on the game** *(prostitute)* essere nel giro (della prostituzione)
2 *(Culin, Hunting)* selvaggina; **big game** caccia grossa; **there's game on the menu** c'è selvaggina nel menù
■ADJ *(willing)*: **to be game** starci; **to be game (for sth/to do sth)** *(ready)* essere pronto(-a) (a qc/a fare qc); **game for anything** pronto(-a) a tutto
game bird N uccello da cacciagione
game·keeper ['geɪmˌkiːpəʳ] N guardacaccia *m inv*
game·ly ['geɪmlɪ] ADV coraggiosamente
game plan N **1** *(Sport)* tattica **2** *(strategy)* strategia; **a game plan for doing sth** una strategia per fare qc
game·play ['geɪmpleɪ] N *(Comput)* giocabilità
gam·er ['geɪməʳ] N appassionato(-a) di videogiochi
game reserve N riserva di caccia
games console N console *f inv*
game·show ['geɪmˌʃəʊ] N gioco a premi *(televisivo o radiofonico)*
games·man·ship ['geɪmzmənʃɪp] N: **to be a master of gamesmanship** essere una vecchia volpe
games master N insegnante *m* di educazione fisica
games mistress N insegnante *f* di educazione fisica
gam·ete ['gæmiːt] N gamete *m*
game warden N *(on reserve)* guardacaccia *m inv*
gam·ing ['geɪmɪŋ] N **1** *(frm: old)* gioco d'azzardo **2** *(Comput)* videogiochi *mpl*
gam·ma ['gæmə] N gamma *m or f*

Gg

gamma rays NPL raggi *mpl* gamma
gam·mon [ˈgæmən] N *(ham)* ≈ prosciutto; (: *smoked)* ≈ prosciutto affumicato; *(bacon)* ≈ pancetta
gam·my [ˈgæmɪ] ADJ *(fam: leg)* zoppo(-a)
gam·ut [ˈgæmət] N gamma; **to run the (whole) gamut of emotions** provare uno dopo l'altro tutti i sentimenti possibili
gan·der [ˈgændəʳ] N *(Zool)* oca maschio
G & T [ˌdʒiːəndˈtiː] N gin tonic
◎ **gang** [gæŋ] N *(of thieves, youths)* banda; *(of friends)* comitiva; *(of workmen)* squadra
▸ **gang up** VI + ADV: **to gang up (with)** mettersi insieme (a *or* con); **to gang up on** *or* **against sb** far comunella contro qn
Gan·ges [ˈgændʒiːz] N: **the Ganges** il Gange
gang·land [ˈgæŋˌlænd] ADJ della malavita; **gangland killer** sicario
gan·gling [ˈgæŋglɪŋ] ADJ allampanato(-a)
gan·gli·on [ˈgæŋglɪən] N ganglio
gan·gly [ˈgæŋglɪ] ADJ = **gangling**
gang·plank [ˈgæŋˌplæŋk] N passerella
gan·grene [ˈgæŋgriːn] N cancrena
gan·gre·nous [ˈgæŋgrɪnəs] ADJ in cancrena
gang·sta (rap) [ˈgæŋstə(ˈræp)] N *(Mus)* gangsta rap *m*
gang·ster [ˈgæŋstəʳ] N gangster *m inv*
gang·way [ˈgæŋˌweɪ] N *(Naut)* passerella; *(Brit: aisle: in theatre, cinema)* corsia; (: *in train)* corridoio; (: *in bus)* passaggio; **gangway!** largo!
gan·net [ˈgænɪt] N *(Zool)* sula bassana
gan·try [ˈgæntrɪ] N *(for crane, railway signal)* cavalletto; *(for rocket)* torre *f* di lancio
Ganymede [ˈgænɪˌmiːd] N Ganimede *m*
GAO [ˌdʒiːeɪˈəʊ] N ABBR *(Am:* = **General Accounting Office)** ≈ Corte *f* dei Conti
gaol *etc* [dʒeɪl] N, VT *(Brit)* = **jail**
gaol·er [ˈdʒeɪləʳ] N *(Brit)* carceriere *m*
◎ **gap** [gæp] N **1** *(gen)* spazio vuoto; *(in line, traffic)* interruzione *f*; *(in trees, crowd, defences)* vuoto; *(in wall, fence)* apertura, buco; *(mountain pass)* passo, valico; *(between teeth)* spazio; *(between floorboards)* interstizio; *(fig: in knowledge)* lacuna; (: *in conversation)* pausa; *(in time)* intervallo; **there's a gap in the hedge** c'è un buco nella siepe; **a gap of four years** un intervallo di quattro anni; **he left a gap which will be hard to fill** ha lasciato un vuoto difficile da colmare **2** *(difference)*: **gap (between)** divario (tra); **the generation gap** il gap *m inv* generazionale; **the gap between them widened** la distanza tra di loro si fece più grande
gape [geɪp] VI **1** *(mouth, hole)* essere spalancato(-a) **2** *(person)* restare a bocca aperta; **to gape (at sb/sth)** guardare (qn/qc) a bocca aperta
gap·ing [ˈgeɪpɪŋ] ADJ *(wound)* aperto(-a); *(hole)* grosso(-a); **gaping seam** larga scucitura
gap year N *(Brit)* anno di pausa preso prima di iniziare l'università *(per lavorare o viaggiare)*
gar·age [ˈgærɑːʒ] N *(of private house)* garage *m inv*; *(for car repairs)* officina, autofficina; *(filling station)* stazione *f* di servizio
garage mechanic N meccanico
garage proprietor N proprietario dell'officina *or* della stazione di servizio
garb [gɑːb] N abiti *mpl*, vesti *fpl*
gar·bage [ˈgɑːbɪdʒ] N *(esp Am)* immondizie *fpl*, spazzatura, rifiuti *mpl*; *(fig: film, book)* porcheria, robaccia; (: *nonsense)* fesserie *fpl*; **garbage collection** raccolta della spazzatura; **that's garbage** sono fesserie
garbage can N *(Am)* bidone *m* della spazzatura
garbage collector N *(Am)* netturbino(-a)
garbage disposal unit N *(Am)* tritarifiuti *m inv*
garbage truck N *(Am)* camion *m inv* della nettezza urbana
gar·ble [ˈgɑːbl] VT *(story, facts)* ingarbugliare
gar·bled [ˈgɑːbld] ADJ *(speech, account)* ingarbugliato(-a), distorto(-a); *(words)* incomprensibile
◎ **gar·den** [ˈgɑːdn] N giardino; **gardens** NPL *(public)* giardino *sg* (pubblico); *(of stately home)* parco *sg*; giardino; **a lovely garden** un bel giardino; **the Garden of Eden** il Paradiso Terrestre, l'Eden *m*
■ VI fare (lavori di) giardinaggio
garden centre N vivaio
garden city N *(Brit)* città giardino *f inv*
gar·den·er [ˈgɑːdnəʳ] N giardiniere(-a); **he's a gardener** fa il giardiniere
gar·denia [gɑːˈdiːnɪə] N gardenia
gar·den·ing [ˈgɑːdnɪŋ] N giardinaggio
▷ www.rhs.org.uk/
gardening leave N *(Brit) accordo in base al quale chi lascia un lavoro continua a ricevere un salario in cambio dell'impegno a non accettare un altro lavoro*
garden party N festa all'aperto, garden-party *m inv*
garden path N *(fig)*: **to lead sb up the garden path** darla a bere a qn
garden shears NPL tosasiepi *f inv*, cesoie *fpl*
garden shed N capanno
garden tools NPL attrezzi *mpl* da giardinaggio
garden-variety [ˈgɑːdnvəˌraɪətɪ] ADJ *(Am)* ordinario(-a), comune
gar·gan·tuan [gɑːˈgæntjʊən] ADJ *(frm)* gargantuesco(-a)
gar·gle [ˈgɑːgl] N *(act)* gargarismo; *(liquid)* collutorio
■ VI fare gargarismi
gar·goyle [ˈgɑːgɔɪl] N gargolla, gargouille *f inv*
gar·ish [ˈgɛərɪʃ] ADJ sgargiante, vistoso(-a); *(light)* abbagliante
gar·ish·ly [ˈgɛərɪʃlɪ] ADV *(see adj)* in modo sgargiante, in modo vistoso; in modo abbagliante
gar·ish·ness [ˈgɛərɪʃnɪs] N vistosità
gar·land [ˈgɑːlənd] N ghirlanda
gar·lic [ˈgɑːlɪk] N aglio
garlic bread N ≈ bruschetta
gar·licky [ˈgɑːlɪkɪ] ADJ *(sauce, food)* con molto aglio; *(flavour)* di aglio; *(breath)* che puzza di aglio
garlic press N spremiaglio
garlic sausage N salamino all'aglio
gar·ment [ˈgɑːmənt] N *(frm)* articolo di vestiario, indumento
gar·ner [gɑːnəʳ] VT *(frm)* raccogliere
gar·net [ˈgɑːnɪt] N granato
gar·nish [ˈgɑːnɪʃ] N *(Culin)* decorazione *f*
■ VT: **to garnish (with)** guarnire (con)
gar·ret [ˈgærət] N soffitta, mansarda
gar·ri·son [ˈgærɪsən] N guarnigione *f*
■ VT *(town)* piazzare truppe in; (: *subj: troops)* presidiare
garrison town N città *f inv* di guarnigione
gar·rotte [gəˈrɒt] N garrotta
■ VT garrottare
gar·ru·lous [ˈgærʊləs] ADJ loquace, ciarliero(-a)
gar·ru·lous·ness [ˈgærʊləsnɪs] N loquacità
gar·ter [ˈgɑːtəʳ] N giarrettiera; *(Am: suspender)* gancio (di reggicalze)
garter belt N *(Am)* reggicalze *m inv*
garter stitch N (punto) legaccio
◎ **gas** [gæs] N **1** *(gen)* gas *m inv*; *(as anaesthetic)* etere *m*; **Calor gas** ® gas liquido *or* in bombole; **a gas leak** una

fuga di gas **2** (*Am*: *also*: **gasoline**) benzina; **I'll stop soon and get gas** mi fermerò presto a fare benzina; **a tank of gas** un pieno di benzina
■ VT (*person*) asfissiare (col gas); (*Mil*) uccidere col gas asfissiante; **to gas o.s.** asfissiarsi, suicidarsi col gas
■ VI (*fam*: *chatter*) chiacchierare, cianciare
■ ADJ (*industry, pipe*) del gas

gas·bag ['gæs,bæg] N (*fam*) chiacchierone(-a)
gas burner N becco a gas
gas chamber N camera a gas
Gas·co·ny ['gæskənɪ] N Guascogna
gas cooker N (*Brit*) cucina a gas
gas cylinder N bombola del gas
gas·eous ['gæsɪəs] ADJ gassoso(-a)
gas fire N (*Brit*) stufa a gas
gas-fired ['gæs,faɪəd] ADJ (*central heating*) (alimentato(-a)) a gas
gas fitter N gas(s)ista *m*, operaio addetto al gas
gash [gæʃ] N (*in flesh*) taglio profondo, squarcio; (*on face*) sfregio; (*in material*) spacco
■ VT (*arm, head*) fare un brutto taglio in; (*face*) sfregiare; (*seat*) squarciare
gas jet N becco a gas
gas·ket ['gæskɪt] N (*Tech*) guarnizione *f*
gas laws NPL (*Chem*) leggi *fpl* dei gas
gas·light ['gæs,laɪt] N illuminazione *f* a gas
gas lighter N accendisigari *m inv* a gas
gas main N conduttura del gas
gas·man ['gæs,mæn] N (*pl* **-men**) (*fam*): **the gasman** l'uomo del gas
gas mask N maschera *f* antigas *inv*
gas meter N contatore *m* del gas
gaso·line ['gæsəʊli:n] N (*Am*) benzina
gas·om·eter [gæ'sɒmɪtə^r] N gas(s)ometro
gasp [gɑ:sp] N ansito; **she gave a gasp of surprise** la sorpresa le mozzò il fiato; **to be at one's last gasp** star tirando l'ultimo respiro
■ VI ansare, ansimare; (*in surprise*) restare senza fiato; **she was gasping** stava ansimando; **she gasped at the sight of it** è rimasta senza fiato quando lo ha visto; **to gasp for breath** *or* **air** respirare a fatica, boccheggiare
▶ **gasp out** VT + ADV dire affannosamente
gas pipeline N gasdotto
gas ring N fornello a gas
gas station N (*Am*) distributore *m* di benzina
gas stove N cucina a gas
gas·sy ['gæsɪ] ADJ (*usu pej*) troppo gassato(-a)
gas tank N (*Am Aut*) serbatoio (della benzina)
gas tap N (*on pipe*) rubinetto del gas; (*on cooker*) manopola del gas
gas·tric ['gæstrɪk] ADJ gastrico(-a); **gastric flu** influenza *m inv* gastro-intestinale
gastric ulcer N ulcera gastrica
gas·tri·tis [gæs'traɪtɪs] N gastrite *f*
gas·tro·en·teri·tis [,gæstrəʊ,entə'raɪtɪs] N gastroenterite *f*
gas·tro·nome ['gæstrənəʊm] N gastronomo(-a)
gas·tro·nom·ic [,gæstrə'nɒmɪk] ADJ gastronomico(-a)
gas·tro·nomi·cal·ly [,gæstrə'nɒmɪkəlɪ] ADV gastronomicamente
gas·trono·my [gæs'trɒnəmɪ] N gastronomia
gas turbine N turbina a gas
gas worker N lavoratore(-trice) dell'industria del gas
gas·works ['gæs,wɜ:ks] NSG OR NPL impianto di produzione del gas
◎ **gate** [geɪt] N **1** (*in garden, field*) cancello; (*of castle, town, Skiing*) porta; (*at airport*) uscita; (*at level crossing*) barriera **2** (*Sport*: *attendance*) (numero di) spettatori *mpl*, presenze *fpl*; (: *entrance money*) incassi *mpl*
ga·teau ['gætəʊ] N (*pl* **gateaux** ['gætəʊz]) torta
gate-crash ['geɪt,kræʃ] VT (*fam*: *party*) intrufolarsi in, imbucarsi in; (: *enter without paying*) fare il portoghese
gate-crasher ['geɪt,kræʃə^r] N (*fam*: *at party*) intruso(-a), imbucato(-a); (: *at concert etc*) portoghese *m/f*
gated community N *gruppo di case recintate e con entrata sorvegliata*
gate·house ['geɪt,haʊs] N casetta del custode (*all'entrata di un parco*)
gate·post ['geɪt,pəʊst] N pilastrino del cancello; **between you, me and the gatepost** (*fig fam*) che resti tra noi
gate·way ['geɪt,weɪ] N porta; **the gateway to success** la chiave del successo
◎ **gath·er** ['gæðə^r] VT **1** (*also*: **gather together**: *people*) radunare, riunire; (: *objects*) raccogliere, radunare; (*also*: **gather up**: *papers, possessions*) raccogliere; (*also*: **gather in**: *material*) riprendere, increspare; (: *taxes*) riscuotere; **to gather the harvest** fare il raccolto; **to gather dust** raccogliere polvere; **to gather one's thoughts/strength** raccogliere i propri pensieri/le proprie forze; **she gathered her mink around her** si avvolse nel visone **2** (*gain*): **to gather speed** prendere *or* acquistare velocità; **to gather strength** (*wind, waves*) aumentare d'intensità **3** (*understand*): **to gather (from/that)** comprendere (da/che), dedurre (da/che); **I gathered that ...** ne dedussi che...; **I gather (that) you are leaving** ho saputo che parti; **as you will have gathered** come avrai indovinato; **as far as I can gather** da quel che ho potuto capire; **from what he says I gather that ...** da quel che dice mi pare di capire che...
■ VI (*people*: *also*: **gather together**) raccogliersi, radunarsi; (: *crowd*) assembrarsi; (*dust*) accumularsi; (*clouds*) addensarsi
▶ **gather round** VI + ADV radunarsi
gath·er·ing ['gæðərɪŋ] N (*meeting*) raduno, riunione *f*; (*crowd*) gruppo
GATT [gæt] N ABBR (= **General Agreement on Tariffs and Trade**) GATT *m* (= *accordo generale sulle tariffe e sul commercio*)
gauche [gəʊʃ] ADJ goffo(-a)
gauche·ly ['gəʊʃlɪ] ADV goffamente
gauche·ness ['gəʊʃnɪs] N goffaggine *f*
gaudi·ly ['gɔ:dɪlɪ] ADV in modo vistoso, in modo chiassoso
gaudy ['gɔ:dɪ] ADJ (*comp* **-ier**, *superl* **-iest**) vistoso(-a), chiassoso(-a)
gauge [geɪdʒ] N (*standard measure*: *of bullet*) calibro; (: *of pipe, wire*) diametro; (: *of railway track*) scartamento; (*instrument*) indicatore *m* di livello; (*fig*) metro, criterio; **petrol gauge**, (*Am*): **gas gauge** indicatore *m or* spia della benzina; **oil gauge** spia dell'olio; **pressure gauge** manometro
■ VT (*temperature, pressure*) misurare; (*fig*: *sb's capabilities, character*) valutare, stimare; **distance is gauged in kilometres rather than miles** la distanza viene misurata in chilometri piuttosto che in miglia; **he gauged the distance** ha calcolato la distanza; **a survey to gauge consumer reaction** un sondaggio per valutare la reazione dei consumatori; **to gauge the right moment** calcolare *or* valutare il momento giusto
Gaul [gɔ:l] N **1** (*country*) Gallia **2** (*person*) gallo

Gg

gaunt [gɔ:nt] ADJ emaciato(-a); (*face*) smunto(-a), scarno(-a); (*grim, desolate*) desolato(-a)
gaunt·let ['gɔ:ntlɪt] N (*of knight*) guanto d'armatura, manopola; (*of motorcyclist*) (grosso) guanto; **to run the gauntlet of an angry crowd** (*fig*) sottoporsi al fuoco di fila di una folla ostile; **to throw down the gauntlet** gettare il guanto
gaunt·ness ['gɔ:ntnɪs] N (*of person, face*) estrema magrezza
Gauteng [xaʊ'tɛŋ] N Gauteng *m*
▷ www.gpg.gov.za
gauze [gɔ:z] N garza
gave [geɪv] PT *of* **give**
gav·el ['gævl] N martelletto
Gawd [gɔ:d] N (*fam*) = **God**
gawk [gɔ:k] VI (*fam*): **to gawk at** restare a bocca aperta davanti a
gawki·ness ['gɔ:kɪnɪs] N goffaggine *f*
gawky ['gɔ:kɪ] ADJ (*comp* **-ier**, *superl* **-iest**) goffo(-a), sgraziato(-a)
gawp [gɔ:p] VI = **gape 2**
◎**gay** [geɪ] ADJ (*comp* **-er**, *superl* **-est**) **1** (*homosexual*) omosessuale, gay *inv* **2** (*liter: person*) allegro(-a), gaio(-a); (*colour*) vivace, vivo(-a)
■ N (*homosexual*) gay *m*
gay lib [-lɪb], **gay liberation** N movimento per la liberazione dei gay
gaze [geɪz] N sguardo (insistente *or* fisso)
■ VI: **to gaze at** guardare (con insistenza *or* fisso), fissare; **he was gazing at her** la stava fissando; **to gaze in wonderment at sb/sth** guardare rapito(-a) qn/qc; **to gaze into space** guardare nel vuoto
ga·zelle [gə'zɛl] N gazzella
ga·zette [gə'zɛt] N (*newspaper*) gazzetta; (*official publication*) pubblicazione *f* ufficiale
gaz·et·teer [ˌgæzɪ'tɪəʳ] N (*book*) dizionario di nomi geografici; (*section of book*) indice *m* dei nomi geografici
ga·zump [gə'zʌmp] VT (*Brit fam*) *venir meno ad una promessa di vendita di un immobile per accettare un'offerta migliore*; **he was gazumped** non è riuscito a comprare la casa perché qualcun altro ha fatto un'offerta migliore
ga·zump·ing [gə'zʌmpɪŋ] N (*Brit fam*) *il fare un'offerta d'acquisto molto alta per un immobile facendo così annullare un impegno di vendita precedente*
GB [ˌdʒi:'bi:] ABBR (= **Great Britain**) GB
GBH [ˌdʒi:bi:'eɪtʃ] N ABBR (*Brit Law*) = **grievous bodily harm**
GC [ˌdʒi:'si:] N ABBR (*Brit:* = **George Gross**) *decorazione al valore*
GCE [ˌdʒi:si:'i:] N ABBR (*Brit:* = **General Certificate of Education**) *esami sostenuti dagli studenti delle superiori in Inghilterra e Galles verso i 17-18 anni*
GCHQ [ˌdʒi:si:eɪtʃ'kju:] N ABBR (*Brit:* = **Government Communications Headquarters**) *centro per l'intercettazione delle telecomunicazioni straniere*
GCSE [ˌdʒi:si:ɛs'i:] N ABBR (*Brit:* = **General Certificate of Secondary Education**) *serie di esami sostenuti alla fine del quinto anno della scuola secondaria in Inghilterra e Galles; see also* **A levels**

GCSE

In Gran Bretagna il **General Certificate of Secondary Education** o **GCSE** è il diploma che la maggior parte degli studenti consegue a 16 anni al termine della scuola dell'obbligo: si può poi scegliere di non continuare gli studi o di frequentare il biennio preparatorio agli "A levels". La valutazione di merito, espressa in valori da A a G (A è la votazione più alta), comprende sia i risultati ottenuti durante l'anno che l'esito degli esami. In Scozia il diploma equivalente si chiama "Standard Grade". *See also* **A LEVELS**
▷ www.dfes.gov.uk/qualifications/

Gdns ABBR = **gardens**
GDP [ˌdʒi:di:'pi:] N ABBR (= **gross domestic product**) PIL *m* (= *prodotto interno lordo*)
GDR [ˌdʒi:di:'ɑ:ʳ] N ABBR = **German Democratic Republic**
◎**gear** [gɪəʳ] N **1** (*Aut: mechanism*) cambio; (*: speed*) marcia; **in gear** in marcia; **he left the car in gear** ha lasciato la macchina con la marcia inserita; **in first gear** in prima; **the car is in gear** la macchina ha la marcia inserita; **out of gear** in folle; **first** *or* **bottom gear** prima; **low gear** marcia bassa; **top gear**, (*Am*): **high gear** marcia alta; **to put the car into gear** innestare *or* inserire la marcia; **to change gear** cambiare marcia; **she changed into second gear** ha messo *or* inserito la seconda; **to move into top gear** inserire la quinta; **production has moved into high** *or* **top gear** la produzione ha subito una forte accelerazione **2** (*equipment*) attrezzatura, equipaggiamento; (*belongings*) roba, cose *fpl*; (*clothing*) vestiti *mpl*; **camping gear** attrezzatura da campeggio; **sports gear** abbigliamento *or* attrezzatura da ginnastica; **dressed in the latest gear** (*fam*) bardato(-a) all'ultima moda **3** (*Tech*) ruota dentata
■ VT (*fig: adapt*) adattare; **the book is geared to adult students** il libro si rivolge a studenti di età adulta; **our service is geared to meet the needs of the disabled** la nostra organizzazione risponde espressamente alle esigenze degli handicappati
▸ **gear up** VI + ADV: **to gear up (to do)** prepararsi (a fare); **we are geared up (and ready) to do it** siamo tutti pronti a farlo
gear·box ['gɪəˌbɒks] N (*Aut*) scatola del cambio
gear lever, (*Am*) **gear·shift** ['gɪəˌʃɪft] N leva del cambio
gear ratio N (*Cycling*) moltiplica
gear stick N leva del cambio
gear·wheel ['gɪəˌwi:l] N ruota dentata
GED [ˌdʒi:i:'di:] N ABBR (*Am Scol*) = *general educational development*
gee [dʒi:] EXCL (*Am*) cribbio
geese [gi:s] NPL *of* **goose**
gee·zer ['gi:zəʳ] N (*Brit fam*) tizio
Geiger count·er ['gaɪgəˌkaʊntəʳ] N (contatore *m*) geiger *m inv*
gel [dʒɛl] N gel *m inv*; **hair gel** gel per capelli
gela·tine ['dʒɛləˌti:n], **gela·tin** ['dʒɛlətɪn] N gelatina; **in gelatin(e)** in gelatina
geld·ing ['gɛldɪŋ] N castrone *m*
gel·ig·nite ['dʒɛlɪgˌnaɪt] N gelatina esplosiva, gelignite *f*
gem [dʒɛm] N gemma, pietra preziosa; (*fig: person*) gioiello, perla; **I must read you this gem** (*fam*) senti questa perla
Gemi·ni ['dʒɛmɪˌnaɪ] N Gemelli *mpl*; **to be Gemini** essere dei Gemelli; **I'm Gemini** sono dei Gemelli
gem·ol·ogy [dʒɛ'mɒlədʒɪ] N gemmologia
gem·stone ['dʒɛmˌstəʊn] N gemma, pietra preziosa
Gen. ABBR (*Mil:* = **General**) Gen.

gen [dʒɛn] N (*Brit fam*): **to give sb the gen on sth** mettere qn al corrente di qc
gen. ABBR (= **general; generally**) gen.
gen·darme ['ʒɒndɑ:m] N (*French policeman*) gendarme *m inv*
gen·der ['dʒɛndə^r] N (*Gram*) genere *m*; (*frm*: *sex*) sesso; **of the same gender** dello stesso sesso
gender-bender ['[dz]ɛndə,bɛndə^r] N (*fam*) *persona che si veste e si comporta come una persona del sesso opposto*
◎**gene** [dʒi:n] N (*Bio*) gene *m*
ge·nea·logi·cal [,dʒi:nɪə'lɒdʒɪkəl] ADJ genealogico(-a)
ge·nealo·gist [,dʒi:nɪ'ælədʒɪst] N genealogista *m/f*
ge·neal·ogy [,dʒi:nɪ'ælədʒɪ] N genealogia
▷ www.genealogy.org/
▷ www.genealogy.com/index_n.html
◎**gen·er·al** ['dʒɛnərəl] ADJ (*gen*) generale; (*not detailed: plan, view*) generale, complessivo(-a); (: *enquiry*) generico(-a); (*not specialized: trader, store*) di generi vari; **a general improvement** un miglioramento generale; **in general use** d'uso comune *or* corrente; **in general terms** in termini generici, in generale; **as a general rule** di norma, di regola; **the general idea is to ...** l'idea base sarebbe di...
■ ADV: **in general** (*usually*) generalmente; in generale; (*as a whole*) nel complesso
■ N (*Mil*) generale *m*
general anaesthetic N anestesia totale
general delivery N (*Am*) fermo posta *m*
◎**general election** N elezioni *fpl* politiche
general headquarters NPL (*Mil*) quartier *msg* generale
general hospital N ospedale *m* generico, policlinico
gen·er·al·ity [,dʒɛnə'rælɪtɪ] N (*frm*) principio generale; **to talk in generalities** parlare in termini generici
gen·er·ali·za·tion [,dʒɛnərəlaɪ'zeɪʃən] N (*often pej*) generalizzazione *f*
gen·er·al·ize ['dʒɛnərə,laɪz] VI: **to generalize (about)** generalizzare (per quel che riguarda); **to generalize from** generalizzare sulla base di
gen·er·al·ized ['dʒɛnərə,laɪzd] ADJ **1** (*general: discussion*) generalizzato; (*feeling*) diffuso **2** (*Med: problem, condition*) diffuso
general knowledge N cultura generale
◎**gen·er·al·ly** ['dʒɛnərəlɪ] ADV (*usually*) in genere, di solito, generalmente; (*for the most part*) nel complesso; **it's generally true that ...** in genere è vero che...; **he's generally disliked** è antipatico a tutti; **generally speaking** (parlando) in generale
general manager N direttore *m* generale
general practice N: **to go into general practice** fare il medico generico
general practitioner N medico generico; (*personal doctor*) medico di famiglia
general public N: **the general public** il grande pubblico
general-purpose ['dʒɛnərəl'pɜ:pəs] ADJ per tutti gli usi
general secretary N segretario(-a) generale
general staff N (*Mil*) stato maggiore
general strike N sciopero generale
◎**gen·er·ate** ['dʒɛnə,reɪt] VT generare
◎**gen·era·tion** [,dʒɛnə'reɪʃən] N **1** (*age group*) generazione *f*; **the younger/older generation** la nuova/vecchia generazione; **the generation gap** il gap *m inv* generazionale **2** (*of electricity*) produzione *f*
gen·era·tive ['dʒɛnərətɪv] ADJ (*Ling*) generativo(-a)
gen·era·tor ['dʒɛnə,reɪtə^r] N generatore *m*

ge·ner·ic [dʒɪ'nɛrɪk] ADJ generico(-a)
ge·neri·cal·ly [dʒɪ'nɛrɪkəlɪ] ADV genericamente
gen·er·os·ity [,dʒɛnə'rɒsɪtɪ] N generosità
◎**gen·er·ous** ['dʒɛnərəs] ADJ (*gen*) generoso(-a); (*plentiful: supply, quantity*) abbondante, generoso(-a); **to be generous with sth** essere prodigo(-a) di qc; **that's very generous of you** è molto generoso da parte tua
gen·er·ous·ly ['dʒɛnərəslɪ] ADV generosamente
gen·esis ['dʒɛnɪsɪs] N genesi *f*; **Genesis** (*Bible*) la Genesi
ge·net·ic [dʒɪ'nɛtɪk] ADJ genetico(-a)
ge·neti·cal·ly [dʒɪ'nɛtɪkəlɪ] ADV geneticamente
genetically modified ADJ geneticamente modificato(-a), transgenico(-a); **genetically modified organism** organismo geneticamente modificato
genetic code N codice *m* genetico
genetic engineering N ingegneria genetica
ge·net·ic finger·print·ing [dʒɪ'nɛtɪk'fɪŋgə,prɪntɪŋ] N rilevamento delle impronte genetiche
ge·neti·cist [dʒɪ'nɛtɪsɪst] N genetista *m/f*
ge·net·ics [dʒɪ'nɛtɪks] NSG genetica
▷ www.ornl.gov/TechResources/Human_Genome/
▷ http://ghr.nlm.nih.gov
▷ www.hgc.gov.uk
Ge·neva [dʒɪ'ni:və] N Ginevra; **Lake Geneva** il lago di Ginevra
Ge·nevan [dʒɪ'ni:vən] ADJ, N ginevrino(-a)
gen·ial ['dʒi:nɪəl] ADJ (*manner, person*) cordiale, affabile

> DID YOU KNOW ...?
> **genial** is not translated by the Italian word *geniale*

ge·ni·al·ity [,dʒi:nɪ'ælɪtɪ] N cordialità, affabilità

> DID YOU KNOW ...?
> **geniality** is not translated by the Italian word *genialità*

gen·ial·ly ['dʒi:nɪəlɪ] ADV cordialmente, affabilmente
ge·nie ['dʒi:nɪ] N genio
geni·ta·lia [,dʒɛnɪ'teɪlɪə] N (*frm*) genitali *mpl*
geni·tals ['dʒɛnɪtlz] NPL genitali *mpl*
geni·tive ['dʒɛnɪtɪv] ADJ genitivo(-a)
■ N genitivo; **in the genitive** al genitivo
ge·ni·us ['dʒi:nɪəs] N genio; **to have a genius for sth/for doing sth** essere molto bravo(-a) in qc/a fare qc
genned up ['dʒɛnd'ʌp] ADJ (*Brit*) al corrente
Genoa ['dʒɛnəʊə] N Genova
genoa ['dʒɛnəʊə] N (*Naut*) genoa *m inv*
geno·cide ['dʃɛnəʊ,saɪd] N genocidio
Geno·ese ['dʒɛnəʊ'i:z] ADJ, N, PL INV genovese (*m/f*)
geno·type ['dʒɛnəʊ'taɪp] N genotipo
gen·re ['ʒɑ̃:nrə] N (*frm*) genere *m*
gent [dʒɛnt] N ABBR (*Brit fam*: = **gentleman**) signore *m*
gen·teel [dʒɛn'ti:l] ADJ (*affectedly polite*) affettato(-a); (*old: refined*) distinto(-a), raffinato(-a)

> DID YOU KNOW ...?
> **genteel** is not translated by the Italian word *gentile*

Gen·tile ['dʒɛntaɪl] N, ADJ gentile (*m/f*); (*non-Jewish*) non ebreo(-a)
gen·til·ity [dʒɛn'tɪlɪtɪ] N (*see adj*) affettazione *f*; distinzione *f*
◎**gen·tle** ['dʒɛntl] ADJ (*comp* **-r**, *superl* **-st**) (*person, slope, voice*) dolce; (*touch*) delicato(-a); (*hint, reminder*) velato(-a); (*rebuke*) discreto(-a); (*heat, exercise*) moderato(-a); (*breeze, sound*) leggero(-a); **to be gentle with sb** trattare qn con delicatezza; **I gave him a gentle push** gli ho dato una leggera spinta

Gg

DID YOU KNOW ...?
gentle is not translated by the Italian word *gentile*

gentle·man [ˈdʒɛntlmən] N (*pl* **-men**) signore *m*; (*well-mannered, well-bred man*) gentiluomo, signore *m*; **gentlemen!** signori!; **(to be) a perfect gentleman** (dimostrarsi) un vero gentiluomo; **gentleman's agreement** impegno sulla parola, gentleman's agreement *m inv*

gentleman farmer N proprietario terriero

gentle·man·ly [ˈdʒɛntlmənlɪ] ADJ da gentiluomo

gen·tle·ness [ˈdʒɛntlnɪs] N (*see adj*) dolcezza; delicatezza; discrezione *f*; leggerezza

gen·tly [ˈdʒɛntlɪ] ADV (*say, smile*) dolcemente; (*touch*) lievemente, delicatamente; **gently does it!** piano!

gen·tri·fy [ˈdʒɛntrɪfaɪ] VT: **to gentrify an area** *acquistare immobili in una zona non molto ricca rendendola a poco a poco una zona residenziale*

gen·try [ˈdʒɛntrɪ] NPL piccola nobiltà

gents [dʒɛnts] N (*fam: public toilet*) toilette *f inv or* bagno degli uomini; **can you tell me where the gents is, please?** può dirmi dov'è la toilette degli uomini, per favore?; **"gents"** "uomini"

genu·flect [ˈdʒɛnjʊˌflɛkt] VI genuflettersi

genu·ine [ˈdʒɛnjʊɪn] ADJ **1** (*person, belief*) sincero(-a) **2** (*authentic: leather, silver*) vero(-a); (*: painting, antique*) autentico(-a); **these are genuine diamonds** questi sono diamanti veri; **she's a very genuine person** è una persona molto sincera

genu·ine·ly [ˈdʒɛnjʊɪnlɪ] ADV (*believe, welcome*) sinceramente, veramente

ge·nus [ˈdʒɛnəs] N (*pl* **genera** [ˈdʒɛnərə]) genere *m*

geo- [ˈdʒiːəʊ] PREF geo-

ge·og·ra·pher [dʒɪˈɒgrəfə^r] N geografo(-a)

geo·graph·ic [dʒɪəˈgræfɪk], **geo·graph·ical** [dʒɪəˈgræfɪkəl] ADJ geografico(-a)

geo·graphi·cal·ly [ˌdʒɪəˈgræfɪkəlɪ] ADV geograficamente

ge·og·ra·phy [dʒɪˈɒgrəfɪ] N geografia
▹ http://oceanworld.tamu.edu/

geo·logi·cal [dʒɪəʊˈlɒdʒɪkəl] ADJ geologico(-a)

geo·logi·cal·ly [ˌdʒɪəˈlɒdʒɪkəlɪ] ADV geologicamente

ge·olo·gist [dʒɪˈɒlədʒɪst] N geologo(-a)

ge·ol·ogy [dʒɪˈɒlədʒɪ] N geologia
▹ www.earthquakes.bgs.ac.uk
▹ http://nsidc.org/glaciers/information.html
▹ http://pubs.usgs.gov/gip/fossils/

geo·met·rical [dʒɪəʊˈmɛtrɪkəl], **geo·met·ric** [dʒɪəʊˈmɛtrɪk] ADJ geometrico(-a)

geo·met·ri·cal·ly [ˌdʒɪəˈmɛtrɪkəlɪ] ADV geometricamente

geometric mean [dʒɪəˈmetrɪk-] N media geometrica

geometric progression N progressione *f* geometrica

ge·om·etry [dʒɪˈɒmɪtrɪ] N geometria

geo·phys·ics [ˌdʒiːəʊˈfɪzɪks] NSG geofisica

geo·poli·tics [ˌdʒiːəʊˈpɒlɪtɪks] N geopolitica

Geor·die [ˈdʒɔːdɪ] (*fam*) ADJ di Tyneside
■ N abitante *m/f or* originario(-a) del Tyneside

Geor·gia [ˈdʒɔːdʒɪə] N (*in US, Europe*) Georgia
▹ www.georgia.gov/

Geor·gian [ˈdʒɔːdʒɪən] ADJ (*History, Geog*) georgiano(-a)
■ N (*Geog*) georgiano(-a); (*language*) georgiano

geo·syn·cline [ˌdʒiːəʊˈsɪnklaɪn] N geosinclinale *f*

ge·ot·ro·pism [dʒɪˈɒtrəˌpɪzəm] N geotropismo

ge·ra·nium [dʒɪˈreɪnɪəm] N geranio

ger·bil [ˈdʒɜːbɪl] N gerbillo

geri·at·ric [ˌdʒɛrɪˈætrɪk] ADJ geriatrico(-a)

geri·at·rics [ˌdʒɛrɪˈætrɪks] NSG geriatria

germ [dʒɜːm] N (*Med*) microbo; (*Bio, also fig*) germe *m*

Ger·man [ˈdʒɜːmən] ADJ tedesco(-a)
■ N **1** (*person*) tedesco(-a) **2** (*language*) tedesco; **the Germans** i tedeschi; **our German teacher** il nostro insegnante di tedesco

German Democratic Republic N (*formerly*) Repubblica Democratica Tedesca

ger·mane [dʒɜːˈmeɪn] ADJ (*frm*): **to be germane to sth** essere attinente a qc

Ger·man·ic [dʒɜːˈmænɪk] ADJ germanico(-a)

German measles N rosolia

Ger·ma·ny [ˈdʒɜːmənɪ] N Germania; **East/West Germany** Germania dell'Est/dell'Ovest

germ-free [ˈdʒɜːmˌfriː] ADJ asettico(-a)

ger·mi·cid·al [ˌdʒɜːmɪˌsaɪdl] ADJ germicida

ger·mi·cide [ˈdʒɜːmɪˌsaɪd] N germicida *m*

ger·mi·nate [ˈdʒɜːmɪˌneɪt] VI germinare, germogliare

ger·mi·na·tion [dʒɜːmɪˈneɪʃən] N germinazione *f*

germ warfare N guerra batteriologica

ger·on·tolo·gist [ˌdʒɛrɒnˈtɒlədʒɪst] N gerontologo(-a)

ger·on·tol·ogy [ˌdʒɛrɒnˈtɒlədʒɪ] N gerontologia

ger·ry·man·der·ing [ˌdʒɛrɪˈmændərɪŋ] N *alterazione del confine dei distretti elettorali che avvantaggia un solo partito*

ger·und [ˈdʒɛrənd] N gerundio

ge·run·dive [dʒɪˈrʌndɪv] ADJ gerundivo(-a)
■ N gerundivo

ge·stalt [gəˈʃtɑːlt] N gestalt *f inv*

gestalt psychology N gestaltismo

ges·tate [dʒɛsˈteɪt] VI essere in gravidanza

ges·ta·tion [dʒɛsˈteɪʃən] N (*Bio*) gestazione *f*

ges·ticu·late [dʒɛsˈtɪkjʊˌleɪt] VI gesticolare

ges·ture [ˈdʒɛstʃə^r] N gesto; **as a gesture of friendship** in segno d'amicizia; **she made a threatening gesture** ha fatto un gesto minaccioso; **a mere gesture** un gesto simbolico
■ VI: **he gestured towards the door** fece un gesto verso la porta; **to gesture to sb to do sth** far segno a qn di fare qc

get [gɛt] KEYWORD
(*vb: pt, pp* **got**, *pp* (*Am*) **gotten**)
■ VT
1 (*obtain by effort: money, visa*) ottenere, procurarsi; (*: results, permission*) avere, ottenere; (*find: job, flat*) trovare; (*buy*) comprare, prendere; (*fetch: person, doctor*) chiamare; (*: object*) prendere; (*Telec: number*) avere; (*TV, Radio: channel, station*) prendere; **to get breakfast** preparare la colazione; **can I get you a drink?** bevi qualcosa?; **to get sth for sb** prendere *or* procurare qc a qn; **I'll get it for you** vado a prendertelo io; **I've still got one to get** me ne manca ancora uno; **I've been trying to get you (on the phone) all morning** ti ho cercato tutta la mattina al telefono
2 (*receive: present, letter*) ricevere; (*: prize*) ricevere, vincere; (*acquire: reputation*) farsi; **how much did you get for it?** quanto ti hanno dato?; **he got 5 years for robbery** si è beccato 5 anni per rapina; **he gets it from his father** in questo prende da suo padre; **where did you get that idea from?** come ti sei fatta quest'idea?; **I didn't get much from the film** quel film non mi è parso un granché; **get it into your head that ...** mettiti bene in testa che...; **I'll get it!** (*phone*) rispondo io!; (*door*) vado io!; **this room gets very little sun** questa stanza è poco soleggiata; **he's in it for what he can get** lo fa per interesse

3 (*catch*) prendere, acchiappare; (*hit: target*) colpire; **the bullet got him in the leg** il proiettile l'ha colpito alla gamba; **to get sb by the arm/throat** afferrare qn per un braccio/alla gola; **I'll get you for that!** (*fam*) ti faccio vedere io!; **you've got me there!** (*fam*) m'hai preso in castagna!; **got you!** (*fam*) beccato!
4 (*take, move*) portare; **crying won't get you anywhere** piangere non serve a niente; **the discussion got us nowhere** la discussione non è servita a nulla; **to get sth past customs** riuscire a far passare qc alla dogana; **we'll get you there somehow** in un modo o nell'altro ti ci portiamo; **to get sth to sb** far avere qc a qn; **I'll never get this upstairs** non riuscirò mai a portarlo di sopra; **where will that get us?** (*fam*) ma a che pro?
5 (*understand*) afferrare, capire, comprendere; (*hear*) sentire; **I've got it!** ci sono arrivato!, ci sono!; **get it?** (*fam*) capito?; **I don't get it** (*fam*) non capisco, non ci arrivo; **sorry, I didn't get your name** scusi, non ho capito il suo nome
6 (*fam: annoy*) dare ai nervi a
7 (*fam: thrill*) toccare
8 (*have, possess*): **to have got** avere; **how many have you got?** quanti ne hai?
9 **to get sth done** (*do o.s.*) fare qc; (*have done by sb else*) far fare qc; **I wonder how he got his leg broken** mi chiedo come abbia fatto a rompersi la gamba; **to get one's hair cut** farsi tagliare i capelli; **to get one's hands dirty** sporcarsi le mani; **to get the washing/dishes done** fare il bucato/i piatti; **to get sb drunk** (far) ubriacare qn; **to get the car going** *or* **to go** mettere in moto *or* far partire la macchina; **to get sb/sth ready** preparare qn/qc; **to get sb to do sth** far fare qc a qn; **I can't get the lock to turn** non riesco a far scattare la serratura

■ VI

1 (*go*) andare; (*reach*) arrivare; **I've got as far as page 10** sono arrivato (fino) a pagina 10; **he won't get far** non andrà lontano; **to get from** andare da; **how did you get here?** come sei venuto?; **to get home** arrivare *or* tornare a casa; **to get nowhere** (*fig*) non approdare a nulla; **to get somewhere** avere dei risultati; **to get to** andare a; (*reach*) arrivare a
2 (*become, be*) diventare, farsi; **to get (o.s.) dirty** sporcarsi; **to get killed** venire *or* rimanere ucciso(-a); **it's getting late** si sta facendo tardi; **how did it get like that?** (*fam*) come ha fatto a ridursi così ?; **to get married** sposarsi; **to get old** invecchiare; **when do I get paid?** quando mi pagate?; **to get tired** stancarsi; **to get used to sth** abituarsi a qc; **I'm not getting any younger!** il tempo passa anche per me!
3 (*begin*) mettersi a, cominciare a; **let's get going** *or* **started** muoviamoci!; **to get talking to sb** mettersi a parlare con *or* a qn; **to get to know sb** cominciare a conoscere meglio qn; **I'm getting to like him** incomincia a piacermi
4 MODAL AUX VB: **why have I got to do it?** perché devo farlo?; **you've got to tell the police** devi dirlo alla polizia
5 (*be allowed to*): **I never get to go on holiday on my own** non riesco mai ad andare in vacanza da sola

▸ **get about** VI + ADV (*go out: socially, after illness*) uscire, muoversi; (*fig: news, rumour*) spargersi, diffondersi

▸ **get across**

■ VT + ADV far capire; **to get sth across to sb** (*message, meaning*) comunicare qc a qn

■ VI + ADV

1 (*cross road*) attraversare
2 **to get across to** comunicare con

▸ **get after** VT + PREP inseguire

▸ **get ahead** VI + ADV andare avanti, farsi strada; **to get ahead of sb** sorpassare *or* superare qn

▸ **get along** VI + ADV

1 (*leave*) andarsene, scappare; **get along with you!** vattene!
2 (*progress*) procedere; (*manage*) farcela, cavarsela; **how is your son getting along at school?** come va tuo figlio a scuola?
3 (*to be on good terms*) essere in buoni rapporti; **to get along well with sb** andare d'accordo con qn

▸ **get around**

■ VI + ADV

1 = **get about**
2 = **get round** VI + ADV

■ VI + PREP = **get round** VI + PREP

▸ **get at** VI + PREP

1 (*gain access to: object*) arrivare a (prendere); (*: place*) raggiungere, arrivare a; (*ascertain: facts, truth*) accertare, scoprire; **just let me get at him!** (*fam*) lascia che mi capiti fra le mani!
2 **to get at sb** (*fam: criticize, attack*) prendersela con qn
3 (*fam: imply*) avere in mente; **what are you getting at?** dove vuoi arrivare?

▸ **get away** VI + ADV (*depart*) partire; (*go on holiday*) andar via; **to get away (from)** (*work, party*) andarsene (da); (*escape*) liberarsi (da), scappare (da); **to get away from it all** andarsene lontano da tutto e da tutti; **there's no getting away from it** (*fam*) non c'è niente da fare

▸ **get away with** VI + ADV + PREP

1 (*steal*) dileguarsi con
2 (*fam: go unpunished*): **to get away with sth/with doing sth** fare qc e passarla liscia; **he'll never get away with it!** non riuscirà a passarla liscia!; **to get away with murder** essere libero(-a) di fare tutto quello che si vuole

▸ **get back**

■ VT + ADV

1 (*recover: possessions*) recuperare; (*: sth borrowed*) farsi restituire; (*: strength*) riprendere
2 (*return: object, person*) riportare

■ VI + ADV (ri)tornare; **get back!** indietro!; **to get back (home)** ritornare a casa, rincasare; **to get back to** (*start again*) ritornare a; (*contact again*) rimettersi in contatto con; **to get back to sleep** riaddormentarsi

▸ **get back at** VI + ADV + PREP (*fam*): **to get back at sb (for sth)** rendere pan per focaccia a qn (per qc)

▸ **get behind** VI + ADV rimanere indietro

▸ **get by** VI + ADV

1 (*pass*) passare
2 (*manage*) cavarsela; (*be acceptable*) essere passabile; **I can get by in Dutch** mi arrangio in olandese; **don't worry, he'll get by** non preoccuparti, se la caverà

▸ **get down**

■ VT + ADV

1 (*take down*) tirar giù
2 (*swallow*) mandar giù
3 (*note down*) prender nota di
4 (*fam: depress*) buttar giù; **don't let it get you down** non devi abbatterti per questo

■ VI + ADV (*descend*): **to get down (from** *or* **off)** scendere (da); **quick, get down!** giù presto!

Gg

▸ **get down to** VI + ADV + PREP: **to get down to (doing) sth** mettersi a (fare) qc; **to get down to business** venire al dunque

▸ **get in**

■VT + ADV

1 (*bring in*: *harvest*) raccogliere; (*buy, obtain*: *coal, shopping, supplies*) fare provvista di

2 (*plant*: *bulbs, seeds*) piantare

3 (*summon*: *expert*) chiamare, far venire

4 (*insert*: *object*) far entrare, infilare; (: *comment, word*) infilare

■VI + ADV

1 (*enter*) entrare

2 (*arrive*: *train*) arrivare; (*reach home*: *person*) rientrare

3 (*be admitted*: *to club*) entrare; (*be elected*: *party*) salire al potere; (: *MP*) essere eletto(-a); **he got in with a bad crowd** si è messo con una banda di cattivi soggetti

▸ **get in on** VI + ADV + PREP (*fam*) intrufolarsi in

▸ **get into** VI + PREP (*house, clothes*) entrare in; (*vehicle*) salire in, montare in; (*club*) entrare in, essere ammesso(-a) a; **to get into difficulties** trovarsi in difficoltà; **to get into trouble** ficcarsi nei guai; **to get into the habit of doing sth** prendere l'abitudine di fare qc; **to get into bed** mettersi a letto; **to get into a rage** andare su tutte le furie

▸ **get off**

■VT + ADV

1 (*remove*: *clothes, stain*) levare, togliere

2 (*send off*) spedire; **she got the baby off to sleep** ha fatto addormentare il bambino

3 (*save from punishment*) far assolvere, tirar fuori

4 (*have as holiday*: *day, time*) prendersi; **we got 2 days off** abbiamo avuto 2 giorni liberi

■VI + PREP (*bus, train, plane, bike*) scendere da; (*fam*: *escape*: *chore, lessons*) evitare, sfuggire a

■VI + ADV

1 (*from bus, train, plane, bike*) scendere; **to tell sb where to get off** (*fam*) dire a qn di andare a farsi benedire; **to get off to a good start** (*fig*) cominciare bene

2 (*depart*: *person*) andare via

3 (*escape injury, punishment*) cavarsela; **he got off with a fine** se l'è cavata con una multa

4 (*from work*) staccare

▸ **get off with** VI + ADV + PREP (*fam*: *start relationship with*) mettersi con

▸ **get on**

■VI + PREP (*vehicle*): **to get on the bus/train** salire *or* montare in autobus/in treno, salire *or* montare sull'autobus/sul treno; **to get on a horse** montare a cavallo

■VI + ADV

1 (*mount*) montare, salire

2 **to get on (with sth)** (*proceed*) continuare a fare (qc); **get on with it!** su, muoviti!

3 (*progress*) far progressi; (*fare*: *in exam, interview*): **how did you get on?** com'è andata?; **how are you getting on?** come va (la vita)?; **to be getting on** (*person*) essere avanti negli anni; **he's getting on for 70** va per i 70; **time is getting on** si sta facendo tardi

4 (*succeed*) farsi strada

5 (*be on good terms*): **to get on (with sb)** andare d'accordo (con qn)

▸ **get on to** VI + ADV + PREP (*fam*: *contact*: *on phone*) contattare, rintracciare; (*deal with*) occuparsi di

▸ **get out**

■VT + ADV: **to get out (of)** (*take out*) tirare fuori (da); (*money*: *from bank*) ritirare (da); (*stain*) levare (da), togliere (da); (*book*: *from library*) prendere in prestito (da); **get those children out of here!** leva quei bambini di torno!

■VI + ADV (*news*) venirsi a sapere, spargersi; **to get out (of)** (*go out*) uscire (da); (*leave*) andar via (da), uscire (da); (*from vehicle*) scendere (da); (*escape*) scappare (da)

▸ **get out of**

■VT + ADV + PREP (*extract*: *confession, words*) tirare fuori di bocca a; (*gain from*: *pleasure, benefit*) trarre da; **to get sb out of bed** far alzare qn

■VI + ADV + PREP

1 *see also* **get out** VI + ADV; (*difficulty*) togliersi da; (*escape*: *duty, punishment*) sottrarsi a

2 **to get out of the habit of doing sth** perdere l'abitudine di fare qc

▸ **get over**

■VI + ADV (*cross*) attraversare

■VI + PREP

1 (*cross*) attraversare

2 (*recover from*: *illness*) riprendersi da, rimettersi da; (: *disappointment*) superare; (: *surprise, shock*) riaversi da; **I can't get over it!** non riesco a crederci!; **you'll get over it!** ti passerà!

3 (*overcome*: *difficulty*) superare; (: *shyness*) vincere

■VT + ADV

1 (*transport across*) far passare

2 (*have done with*) finire una buona volta; **let's get it over (with)** facciamolo, così ci togliamo il pensiero

3 (*communicate*: *idea*) comunicare, passare

▸ **get round**

■VI + PREP (*difficulty, problem*) aggirare, superare; (*law, regulation*) eludere; (*fig*: *person*) rigirare; **she knows how to get round him** sa come prenderlo

■VI + ADV: **to get round to doing sth** trovare il tempo di fare qc; **I'll get round to it** prima o poi lo farò

▸ **get through**

■VI + PREP

1 (*pass through*: *window*) passare per *or* da; (: *crowd*) passare attraverso, farsi strada attraverso

2 (*finish*: *work*) sbrigare; (: *book*) finire; (*use up*: *food, money*) far fuori, dar fondo a; **we got through a lot of work today** abbiamo sbrigato molto lavoro oggi

3 (*pass*: *exam*) passare

■VT + PREP (*cause to succeed*: *student*) far passare; (: *proposal, bill*) far passare a, far approvare a

■VT + ADV (*succeed in sending*: *message, supplies*) far arrivare *or* pervenire; (*Pol*: *bill*) far passare *or* approvare

■VI + ADV

1 (*pass through*) passare; (*news, supplies*: *arrive*) raggiungere

2 (*pass, be accepted*) passare; **they got through to the semifinal** sono entrati in semifinale

3 (*finish*) finire, terminare

4 (*Telec*) ottenere la comunicazione *or* la linea; **to get through to sb** mettersi in contatto con qn; (*fig*: *communicate with*) comunicare con qn

▸ **get together**

■VT + ADV (*people*) radunare; (*objects, thoughts, ideas*) raccogliere

■VI + ADV (*group, club*) riunirsi; **to get together about sth** vedersi per discutere qc

▸ **get up**

■VI + ADV

1 (*rise*: *from chair, bed*) alzarsi; (*wind*) alzarsi, levarsi

2 (*climb up*) salire

■VT + ADV

1 (*person: from chair, floor*) sollevare, tirar su; (: *wake*) far alzare, svegliare
2 (*gather: strength, speed*) prendere; **to get up enthusiasm for sth** entusiasmarsi per qc
3 (*fam: organize: celebrations*) organizzare
4 (*fam: dress up: person*): **to get o.s. up in** farsi bello(-a) con; **to get o.s. up as** travestirsi da
■ VI + PREP (*tree*) arrampicarsi su; (*ladder*) salire su per
► **get up to** VI + ADV + PREP
1 (*reach*) raggiungere, arrivare a; **I've got up to chapter 4** sono arrivato *or* sono al capitolo 4
2 **to get up to mischief** combinarne di tutti i colori; **what have you been getting up to?** cosa hai combinato?

get-at-able [ˌgɛtˈætəbl] ADJ (*fam*) accessibile
get·away [ˈgɛtəˌweɪ] N: **to make one's getaway** darsi alla fuga; **a quick getaway** una rapida fuga
getaway car N macchina per la fuga
Geth·sema·ne [gɛθˈsɛmənɪ] N Getsemani *m*
get-together [ˈgɛttəˌgɛðəʳ] N (piccola) riunione *f*; (*party*) festicciola
get-up [ˈgɛtˌʌp] N (*fam: outfit*) tenuta
get-well card [gɛtˈwɛlˌkɑːd] N cartolina di auguri di pronta guarigione
gey·ser [ˈgiːzəʳ] N (*Geog*) geyser *m inv*; (*water heater*) scaldabagno
Gha·na [ˈgɑːnə] N Ghana *m*
Gha·na·ian [gɑːˈneɪən] ADJ del Ghana, ganaense
■ N ganaense *m/f*
ghast·ly [ˈgɑːstlɪ] ADJ (*horrible*) atroce, spaventoso(-a), orribile; (*pale*) spettrale; (*fam: very bad: experience*) pauroso(-a); **a ghastly mistake** un terribile errore; **we had a ghastly time last night** è stata una serata orribile ieri sera; **ghastly weather** tempo orribile
ghee [giː] N (*Culin*) *burro chiarificato usato nella cucina indiana*
gher·kin [ˈgɜːkɪn] N cetriolino
ghet·to [ˈgɛtəʊ] N ghetto; **the black ghettos** i ghetti della gente di colore
ghetto blaster [-ˌblɑːstəʳ] N maxistereo portatile
ghost [gəʊst] N fantasma *m*, spettro; **the ghost of a smile** (*fig*) una parvenza di sorriso; **he hasn't the ghost of a chance** (*fig*) non ha la minima possibilità
■ VT (*book*) scrivere per conto di altri
ghost·ly [ˈgəʊstlɪ] ADJ spettrale; **a ghostly apparition** uno spettro
ghost story N storia di fantasmi
ghost town N città *f inv* fantasma *inv*
ghost·writ·er [ˈgəʊstˌraɪtəʳ] N ghost writer *m/f inv*, scrittore(-trice) fantasma *inv*
ghoul [guːl] N *vampiro che si nutre di cadaveri*; **she's a ghoul** (*fig*) ha proprio il gusto del macabro
ghoul·ish [ˈguːlɪʃ] ADJ (*tastes*) macabro(-a)
ghoul·ish·ly [ˌguːlɪʃlɪ] ADV in modo macabro, morbosamente
GHQ [ˌdʒiːeɪtʃˈkjuː] N ABBR (*Mil*: = **general headquarters**) QG (= *quartier generale*)
GI [ˌdʒiːˈaɪ] N ABBR (*Am fam*: = **government issue**) *soldato americano*
◎ **gi·ant** [ˈdʒaɪənt] N gigante(-essa); (*fig*) gigante *m*, colosso
■ ADJ (*fern, panda*) gigante; (*strides*) da gigante; **giant (size) packet** confezione *f* gigante
giant killer N (*Sport*) *atleta o squadra minore che riesce a battere un avversario più forte*
giant slalom N (*Skiing*) slalom *m inv* gigante
gib·ber [ˈdʒɪbəʳ] VI (*monkey*) squittire confusamente; (*idiot*) farfugliare; **to gibber with rage** non connettere più dalla rabbia
gib·ber·ish [ˈdʒɪbərɪʃ] N parole *fpl* senza senso
gib·bet [ˈdʒɪbɪt] N patibolo
gib·bon [ˈgɪbən] N gibbone *m*
gibe [dʒaɪb] N frecciata, malignità *f inv*
■ VI: **to gibe (at)** lanciare frecciate (a)
gib·lets [ˈdʒɪblɪts] NPL rigaglie *fpl*
Gi·bral·tar [dʒɪˈbrɔːltəʳ] N Gibilterra
gid·di·ness [ˈgɪdɪnɪs] N vertigini *fpl*; **I had a bout of giddiness** ho avuto un attacco di vertigini
gid·dy [ˈgɪdɪ] ADJ (*comp* **-ier**, *superl* **-iest**) (*dizzy*): **to be giddy** aver le vertigini; (*causing dizziness: height*) vertiginoso(-a); (: *speed*) folle; **I feel giddy** mi gira la testa
GIF [gɪf] ABBR: (*Comput*: = **Graphic Interchange Format**) GIF *m*
◎ **gift** [gɪft] N 1 (*present*) dono, regalo; (*Comm: also:* **free gift**) omaggio; **a lovely gift** un bel regalo; **as a free gift** in omaggio, in dono; **it's a gift!** (*fam: easy*) è uno scherzo! 2 (*talent*): **to have a gift for sth** essere portato per qc; **Dave's got a gift for painting** Dave è portato per la pittura
Gift Aid (*Brit*) N: **Gift Aid donation** *donazione da portare in detrazione fiscale*
■ VT (*money*) devolvere in modo da poter detrarre fiscalmente
gift·ed [ˈgɪftɪd] ADJ: **gifted (at)** dotato(-a) (per); **one of the most gifted artists** uno degli artisti più dotati; **Janice is a gifted dancer** Janice è una ballerina di talento
gift voucher, gift token N buono (acquisto *inv*)
gift·wrap [ˈgɪftˌræp] VT incartare in confezione regalo
gift·wrap·ping [ˈgɪftˌræpɪŋ] N confezione *f* regalo *inv*
gig [gɪg] N (*fam: of musician*) serata
giga·byte [ˈgaɪgəˌbaɪt] N gigabyte *m inv*
gi·gan·tic [dʒaɪˈgæntɪk] ADJ gigantesco(-a)
gig·gle [ˈgɪgl] N risolino (sciocco); **to get the giggles** farsi prendere dalla ridarella
■ VI ridacchiare (scioccamente), avere la ridarella
gig·gly [ˈgɪglɪ] ADJ ridanciano(-a)
GIGO [ˈgaɪgəʊ] ABBR (*Comput: fam*: = **garbage in, garbage out**) qualità di input = qualità di output
gild [gɪld] VT (*metal, frame*) dorare; (*fig*) indorare; **to gild the lily** (*fig*) aggiungere inutili fronzoli
gild·ed [ˈgɪldɪd] ADJ dorato(-a)
gill[1] [gɪl] N (*of fish*) branchia; **to be green around the gills** (*fig fam*) essere verde per la paura
gill[2] [dʒɪl] N (*measure*) ≈ 0,142 l
gilt [gɪlt] N doratura
■ ADJ dorato(-a)
gilt-edged [ˈgɪltˌɛdʒd] ADJ 1 (*Fin: stocks, securities*) della massima sicurezza 2 (*book*) dal taglio dorato
gim·crack [ˈdʒɪmˌkræk] ADJ (*pej*) dozzinale
gim·let [ˈgɪmlɪt] N (*for wood*) succhiello
gim·me (*fam*) = give me
gim·mick [ˈgɪmɪk] N trovata; **sales gimmick** trovata commerciale
gim·micky [ˈgɪmɪkɪ] ADJ (*fam*): **a gimmicky film** un film pieno di trovate ad effetto
gin [dʒɪn] N (*liquor*) gin *m inv*; **gin and tonic** gin tonic *m inv*
▷ www.ginvodka.org
gin·ger [ˈdʒɪndʒəʳ] N zenzero
■ ADJ (*hair*) rosso(-a); **she's got ginger hair** ha i capelli rossi; **ginger snap** biscotto allo zenzero

Gg

▸ **ginger up** VT + ADV animare
ginger ale N *bibita gassata allo zenzero*
ginger beer N *(Brit) bibita leggermente alcolica allo zenzero*
ginger·bread ['dʒɪndʒə,brɛd] N pan *m* pepato *or* di zenzero
gingerbread man N omino di pan pepato
ginger group N *(Brit: within organization)* gruppo di pressione
ginger-haired [,dʒɪndʒə'hɛəd] ADJ rossiccio(-a)
gin·ger·ly ['dʒɪndʒəlɪ] ADV con circospezione, cautamente
gin·gery ['dʒɪndʒərɪ] ADJ rossiccio(-a)
ging·ham ['gɪŋəm] N *(material)* percalle *m* a righe *(or* quadretti)
gin·seng ['dʒɪnsɛŋ] N ginseng *m inv*
gip·sy ['dʒɪpsɪ] = **gypsy**
gi·raffe [dʒɪ'rɑːf] N giraffa
gird·er ['gɜːdə[r]] N trave *f*
gir·dle ['gɜːdl] N *(corset)* busto, corsetto; *(belt)* cintura
◎ **girl** [gɜːl] N *(child)* bambina, ragazzina; *(young unmarried woman)* signorina, ragazza; *(daughter)* figlia, figliola; *(fam: girlfriend)* ragazza; **a little girl** una bambina; **a five-year-old girl** una bambina di cinque anni; **an English girl** una ragazza inglese; **they've got a girl and two boys** hanno una femmina e due maschi; **factory girl** operaia; **shop girl** commessa; **the old girl next door** *(fam)* la vecchia qui accanto
girl band N girl band *f inv; gruppo pop di sole donne creato per far presa su un pubblico giovane*
girl Friday N impiegata *f* tuttofare *inv*
◎ **girl·friend** ['gɜːl,frɛnd] N *(of boy)* ragazza; *(of girl)* amica; **Paul's girlfriend is called Lee** la ragazza di Paul si chiama Lee; **she often went out with her girlfriends** usciva spesso con le sue amiche
Girl Guide N *(Brit: old)* = **guide** N **2**
girl·hood ['gɜːl,hud] N giovinezza
girlie ['gɜːlɪ] ADJ *(fam: magazine, calendar)* con donnine nude
girl·ish ['gɜːlɪʃ] ADJ da ragazza
Girl Scout N *(Am)* = **guide** N **2**
Giro ['dʒaɪrəʊ] N: **the National Giro** *(Brit)* ≈ la {or} il Bancoposta
giro ['dʒaɪrəʊ] N *(Brit fam: also:* **giro cheque***)* assegno postale *(per indennità di disoccupazione o malattia)*; *(also:* **bank giro***)* bancogiro; *(also:* **post office giro***)* postagiro
girth [gɜːθ] N *(for saddle)* sottopancia *m inv*; *(measure: of tree)* circonferenza; *(: of person's waist)* (giro) vita
gist [dʒɪst] N *(of speech, conversation)* succo, nocciolo; **to get the gist of sth** capire il succo di qc
◎ **give** [gɪv] *(vb: pt* **gave**, *pp* **given***)* VT
1 *(gen)* dare; *(as gift)* regalare, dare (in dono); *(description, promise, surprise)* fare; *(particulars)* dare, fornire; *(decision)* annunciare; *(title, honour)* conferire, dare; *(assign: job)* assegnare, dare; *(dedicate: life, time)* consacrare, dedicare; **to give sb sth** *or* **sth to sb** dare qc a qn; **I gave my sister some money** ho dato dei soldi a mia sorella; **he gave me ten pounds** mi ha dato dieci sterline; **I gave him some money** gli ho dato dei soldi; **to give sb a present** fare un regalo a qn; **they gave their teacher a present** hanno fatto un regalo alla maestra; **one must give and take** bisogna fare delle concessioni; **how much did you give for it?** quanto (l')hai pagato?; **to give sb a kick/push** dare un calcio/una spinta a qn; **to give sb a cold** passare *or* attaccare il raffreddore a qn; **to give sb news of sth** dar notizie di qc a qn; **to give sb something to eat** dare (qualcosa) da mangiare a qn; **12 o'clock, give or take a few minutes** mezzogiorno, minuto più minuto meno; **give or take ten miles** dieci miglia in più o meno; **to give as good as one gets** rendere pan per focaccia; **he gave it everything he'd got** *(fig)* ce l'ha messa tutta; **I'd give a lot/the world/anything to know ...** *(fam)* darei moltissimo/tutto l'oro del mondo/non so che cosa per sapere...; **I can give you 10 minutes** posso darti 10 minuti; **give them my regards** salutali da parte mia; **give yourself an hour to get there** calcola un'ora per arrivare; **that gave me an idea** mi ha fatto venire un'idea; **he's honest, I'll give you that** è onesto, te lo concedo
2 *(produce)* dare, produrre; *(result, help, advice)* dare; **3 times 4 gives 12** 3 per 4 fa 12; **to give the right/wrong answer** dare la risposta giusta/sbagliata
3 *(perform etc: jump, smile)* fare; *(deliver: speech, lecture)* fare, tenere; *(utter: cry)* lanciare; *(: sigh)* tirare, fare; **give us a song** cantaci qualcosa; **he gave a good performance** *(musician)* è stata una buona esecuzione; *(actor)* ha recitato bene
■ VI
1 *(give presents)* dare, donare; **to give to charity** fare della beneficenza
2 *(also:* **give way***: collapse: roof, ground, door)* cedere; *(: knees)* piegarsi; **something's got to give!** *(fam)* non si può andare avanti così !
■ N *(of material)* elasticità; *(of bed)* morbidezza
▸ **give away** VT + ADV
1 *(money, goods)* dar via, donare; *(bride)* condurre all'altare; *(distribute: prizes)* distribuire; **we have six copies to give away** abbiamo sei copie da dare via
2 *(reveal: secret)* rivelare; *(betray: person)* tradire; **her accent gave her away** il suo accento l'ha tradita; **to give the game away** *(fig)* farsi scoprire
▸ **give back** VT + ADV *(return: sb's property)*: **to give back (to)** restituire (a), rendere (a), ridare (a); **I gave the book back to him** gli ho restituito il libro
▸ **give in** VT + ADV *(hand in: form, essay)* consegnare; **to give in one's name** dare il proprio nome
■ VI + ADV *(yield)*: **to give in (to sb)** cedere (a qn); *(in guessing game)*: **I give in!** mi arrendo!; **his Mum gave in and let him go out** sua madre ha ceduto e lo ha lasciato uscire
▸ **give off** VT + ADV *(smell, smoke, heat)* emettere, sprigionare
▸ **give onto** VI + PREP *(subj: door, window)* dare su
▸ **give out** VT + ADV
1 *(distribute)* distribuire; **he gave out leaflets in the street** distribuiva volantini per strada
2 *(make known: news)* annunciare
■ VI + ADV *(be exhausted: supplies)* esaurirsi, venir meno; *(fail: engine)* fermarsi; *(: strength)* mancare; *(: legs)* non reggere più
▸ **give over** VT + ADV
1 *(devote)*: **to give over to** dedicare a
2 *(transfer)*: **to give over to** consegnare a
■ VI + ADV *(fam: stop)* piantarla, smetterla; **give over!** piantala!, smettila!
▸ **give up** VT + ADV
1 *(surrender: place)* cedere; *(hand over: ticket)* consegnare; **to give o.s. up** arrendersi; **he gave himself up** si è arreso; **to give o.s. up to the police** costituirsi alla polizia
2 *(renounce: friend, boyfriend, job)* lasciare; *(abandon: idea)* rinunciare a, abbandonare; *(abandon hope for: patient)* dare per spacciato(-a); *(: expected visitor)* non aspettare più; **I gave it up as a bad job** *(fam)* ci ho rinunciato, ho

abbandonato l'idea; **to give up drinking/smoking** smettere di bere/fumare; **he gave up smoking** ha smesso di fumare
3 (*devote: one's life, time*): **to give up (to)** dedicare (a); **to give up (for)** (*sacrifice: one's life, career*) donare (per), dare (per)
■ VI + ADV (*stop trying*) rinunciare, arrendersi; **I give up!** (*trying to guess*) mi arrendo!; **I couldn't do it, so I gave up** non riuscivo a farlo, così ho lasciato perdere
▶ **give way** VI + ADV
1 *see* give VI 2
2 (*yield*): **to give way (to)** cedere (a); **to give way to despair** lasciarsi andare alla disperazione
3 (*make room for*): **to give way (to)** lasciare il posto (a)
4 (*Brit Aut*) dare la precedenza

give-and-take [ˌgɪvən'teɪk] N (*fam*) elasticità; **there has to be a bit of give-and-take** bisogna venirsi un po' incontro

give·away ['gɪvəˌweɪ] N (*fam*): **her expression was a dead giveaway** le si leggeva tutto in volto; **the exam was a giveaway!** l'esame è stato uno scherzo!
■ ADJ: **giveaway prices** prezzi *mpl* stracciati

◎ **giv·en** ['gɪvn] PP *of* **give** ■ ADJ **1** (*fixed: time, amount*) dato(-a), determinato(-a) **2 to be given to doing sth** essere incline *or* propenso(-a) a fare qc
■ CONJ: **given (that) ...** ammesso che..., supposto che...; **given the circumstances ...** date le circostanze...; **given time, it would be possible** se ci fosse tempo, sarebbe possibile

given name N (*esp Am*) nome *m* di battesimo

giv·er ['gɪvə^r] N donatore(-trice)

GLA [ˌdʒiːɛl'eɪ] N ABBR (*Brit: Greater London Assembly*) *ente locale per l'area londinese istituito nel 2000*

gla·cé ['glæseɪ] ADJ (*fruit*) candito(-a)

gla·cial ['gleɪsɪəl] ADJ glaciale; **glacial advance** espansione *f* glaciale; **glacial retreat** ritiro dei ghiacciai

gla·cia·tion [ˌgleɪsɪ'eɪʃən] N glaciazione *f*

glaci·er ['glæsɪə^r] N ghiacciaio

◎ **glad** [glæd] ADJ (*comp* **-der**, *superl* **-dest**) (*pleased*) contento(-a), compiaciuto(-a); (*news, occasion*) lieto(-a); **to be glad about sth/that** essere contento(-a) *or* lieto(-a) di qc/che + *sub*; **I am glad to hear it** mi fa molto piacere, ne sono felice; **I was glad of his help** gli sono stato grato del suo aiuto; **he was only too glad to do it** non chiedeva di meglio che farlo

glad·den ['glædn] VT rallegrare, allietare

glade [gleɪd] N radura

gladia·tor ['glædɪˌeɪtə^r] N gladiatore *m*

gladio·lus [ˌglædɪ'əʊləs] N gladiolo

glad·ly ['glædlɪ] ADV (*joyfully*) lietamente; (*willingly*) con piacere, volentieri

glad·ness ['glædnɪs] N contentezza, felicità

glad rags ['glædˌrægz] NPL (*fam*) vestito della festa; **she's in her glad rags tonight** è tutta in ghingheri stasera

glam·or·ize ['glæməˌraɪz] VT (*job, event, place*) far apparire (più) prestigioso(-a)

glam·or·ous, **glam·our·ous** ['glæmərəs] ADJ (*gen*) favoloso(-a); (*person*) affascinante; (*occasion*) brillante, elegante

glam·our, (*Am*) **glam·or** ['glæmə^r] N fascino

glamour girl, (*Am*) **glamor girl** N cover girl *f inv*

◎ **glance** [glɑːns] N sguardo, occhiata; **to take** *or* **have a glance at** dare un'occhiata a; **we exchanged glances** ci siamo scambiati un'occhiata; **at a glance** a colpo d'occhio; **at first glance** a prima vista; **without a backward glance** senza voltarsi indietro; (*fig*) senza rimpianti
■ VI (*look*): **to glance at** (*person*) lanciare uno sguardo *or* un'occhiata a; (*headlines*) dare uno sguardo *or* un'occhiata a; **Peter glanced at his watch** Peter ha dato un'occhiata all'orologio; **to glance away** distogliere lo sguardo; **to glance through a report** dare una scorsa a un rapporto
▶ **glance off** VI + PREP (*bullet*): **to glance off sth** rimbalzare di striscio su qc

glanc·ing ['glɑːnsɪŋ] ADJ (*blow*) di striscio

gland [glænd] N (*Anat*) ghiandola

glan·du·lar ['glændjʊlə^r] ADJ ghiandolare

glandular fever N mononucleosi *f inv*

glare [glɛə^r] N **1** (*of light, sun*) luce *f or* bagliore *m* accecante; **the glare of publicity** (*fig*) il chiasso della pubblicità **2** (*look*) occhiata fulminante, sguardo furioso
■ VI **1** (*light*) sfolgorare **2** (*look*): **to glare at** fulminare con lo sguardo

glar·ing ['glɛərɪŋ] ADJ (*dazzling: sun, light*) sfolgorante, accecante; (*: colour*) sgargiante; (*obvious: evidence*) lampante; (*: mistake*) palese

glar·ing·ly ['glɛərɪŋlɪ] ADV: **it is glaringly obvious that ...** è più che evidente che...

glas·nost ['glæsˌnɒst] N glasnost *f inv*

◎ **glass** [glɑːs] N **1** (*material, pane of glass*) vetro; (*glassware*) cristalleria; (*drinking vessel, glassful*) bicchiere *m*; (*barometer*) barometro; (*mirror*) specchio; **a glass of milk** un bicchiere di latte; **a wine glass** un bicchiere da vino, calice *m*; **grown under glass** di serra, coltivato(-a) in serra; *see also* **glasses**
■ ADJ (*bottle, eye*) di vetro; (*industry*) del vetro; **a glass door** una porta di vetro

glass-blowing ['glɑːsˌbləʊɪŋ] N soffiatura del vetro

glass case N teca di vetro

glass ceiling N (*fig*) barriera invisibile

glass cloth N asciugapiatti *m inv* (*per bicchieri*)

glass cutter N (*tool*) rotella tagliavetro

glasses ['glɑːsɪz] NPL (*spectacles*) occhiali *mpl*; **he wears glasses** porta gli occhiali

glass fibre N fibra di vetro

glass·ful ['glɑːsfʊl] N bicchiere *m* (pieno)

glass·house ['glɑːsˌhaʊs] N (*for plants*) serra

glass paper N carta vetrata (fine)

glass·ware ['glɑːsˌwɛə^r] N cristalleria, articoli *mpl* di vetro

glass wool N lana di vetro

glass·works ['glɑːsˌwɜːks] NSG vetreria, fabbrica di vetri

glassy ['glɑːsɪ] ADJ (*comp* **-ier**, *superl* **-iest**) (*sea, lake*) come uno specchio; (*eye, look*) vitreo(-a)

Glas·we·gian [glæz'wiːdʒən] ADJ di Glasgow
■ N abitante *m/f or* originario(-a) di Glasgow

glau·co·ma [glɔː'kəʊmə] N glaucoma *m*

glaze [gleɪz] N (*on pottery*) smalto; (*Culin*) glassa
■ VT **1** (*window, door*) mettere i vetri a, fornire di vetri **2** (*pottery*) invetriare; (*Culin*) glassare
■ VI: **his eyes glazed over** i suoi occhi si fecero vitrei

glazed [gleɪzd] ADJ (*tiles, pottery*) invetriato(-a); (*fig: eye*) vitreo(-a)

gla·zi·er ['gleɪzɪə^r] N vetraio

GLC [ˌdʒiːɛl'siː] N ABBR (*Brit:* = **Greater London Council**) *ex consiglio municipale di Londra e sobborghi abolito nel 1986*

gleam [gliːm] N (*of light*) bagliore *m*; (*of moonlight*) chiarore *m*; (*of metal, water*) luccichio; **with a gleam in one's eye** con gli occhi scintillanti; (*mischievous*) con

Gg

uno sguardo furbesco; **a gleam of hope** un barlume di speranza
■VI (*light, furniture*) brillare; (*metal, water*) luccicare; (*eyes*): **to gleam (with)** brillare (di); **her eyes gleamed with excitement** le brillavano gli occhi dall'eccitazione
gleam·ing ['gli:mɪŋ] ADJ brillante, lucente; **the house was gleaming** la casa era uno specchio
glean [gli:n] VT (*gather: information*) racimolare
glee [gli:] N: **with glee** (*gen*) con gioia; (*laugh*) di gusto
glee·ful ['gli:fʊl] ADJ (*smile, laugh*) gioioso(-a), allegro(-a); (: *malicious*) malizioso(-a)
glee·ful·ly ['gli:fəlɪ] ADV (*see adj*) gioiosamente; maliziosamente
glen [glɛn] N vallone *m*
glib [glɪb] ADJ (*person*) dalla lingua sciolta; (*explanation, excuse*) facile, disinvolto(-a); **glib promises** promesse fatte con leggerezza; **a glib attitude** un atteggiamento facilone; **glib answers** risposte superficiali
glib·ly ['glɪblɪ] ADV con disinvoltura
glide [glaɪd] N (*of dancer etc*) volteggio; (*Aer*) planata; (*Skiing*) scivolata
■VI (*move smoothly*) scivolare silenziosamente; (: *dancer*) volteggiare; (*Aer, birds*) planare; **the boat glided over the water** la barca scivolava sull'acqua; **waiters glided between the tables** i camerieri volteggiavano tra i tavoli; **to glide in** (*person*) entrare silenziosamente
glide path N (*Aer*) sentiero di avvicinamento
glid·er ['glaɪdə^r] N (*Aer*) aliante *m*
glid·ing ['glaɪdɪŋ] N (*Aer*) volo a vela; (*with glider*) volo con l'aliante; **my hobby is gliding** il mio hobby è il volo con l'aliante
glim·mer ['glɪmə^r] N (*of light, also fig*) barlume *m*; (*of water*) luccichio
■VI (*light*) baluginare; (*water*) luccicare
glim·mer·ing ['glɪmərɪŋ] ADJ baluginante
■N barlume *m*
glimpse [glɪmps] N: **to catch a glimpse of** vedere di sfuggita, intravedere
■VT intravedere
glint [glɪnt] N (*of metal etc*) scintillio, luccichio; **he had a glint in his eye** nei suoi occhi brillava una luce strana; **he had an angry glint in his eye** gli occhi gli scintillavano dalla rabbia
■VI brillare, luccicare
glis·ten ['glɪsn] VI (*wet surface, water*) luccicare; (*eyes*): **to glisten (with)** brillare (di)
glit·ter ['glɪtə^r] N (*of gold etc*) scintillio; (*on Christmas cards etc*) polvere *f* d'oro
■VI (*gold etc*) luccicare, scintillare; **all that glitters is not gold** non è tutt'oro quel che luccica
glit·ter·ing ['glɪtərɪŋ] ADJ (*jewels*) scintillante; (*eyes*) lucido(-a); (*career*) brillante; (*prize*) prestigioso(-a)
glitz [glɪts] N (*fam*) vistosità, chiassosità
gloat [gləʊt] VI gongolare; **to gloat over** (*money etc*) covare con gli occhi; (*victory, enemy's misfortune*) gongolare (di gioia) per, esultare per
◎**glob·al** ['gləʊbl] ADJ (*world-wide*) mondiale; (*comprehensive*) globale; **on a global scale** su scala mondiale; **a global view** una visione globale
glob·ali·za·tion [ˌgləʊbəlaɪ'zeɪʃən] N globalizzazione *f*
glo·bal·ize ['gləʊbəlaɪz] VI globalizzarsi
■VT globalizzare
Global Positioning System N sistema *m* GPS, sistema di posizionamento a copertura mondiale
global village N villaggio globale
global warming [-'wɔ:mɪŋ] N riscaldamento dell'atmosfera terrestre
globe [gləʊb] N globo, sfera; (*spherical map*) mappamondo, globo
globe·flower ['gləʊbˌflaʊə^r] N luparia
globe·trotter ['gləʊbˌtrɒtə^r] N giramondo *m/f inv*
globe·trotting ['gləʊb'trɒtɪŋ] N viaggi *mpl* per il mondo
globu·lar ['glɒbjʊlə^r] ADJ (*frm*) globulare
glob·ule ['glɒbju:l] N (*of water etc*) gocciolina; (*Anat*) globulo
globu·lin ['glɒbjʊlɪn] N globulina
glo·meru·lus [glɒ'mɛrʊləs] N glomerulo
gloom [glu:m] N **1** (*darkness*) oscurità, buio; **in the gloom** nell'oscurità, al buio; **she peered into the gloom** aguzzava gli occhi nell'oscurità **2** (*sadness*) tristezza, malinconia; **a feeling of deep gloom** un senso di profonda tristezza
gloomi·ly ['glu:mɪlɪ] ADV cupamente
gloomy ['glu:mɪ] ADJ (*comp* **-ier**, *superl* **-iest**) (*place, character*) cupo(-a), tetro(-a); (*person*) triste; (*atmosphere, weather, day*) deprimente; (*sky*) fosco(-a); (*outlook*) nero(-a); **a huge gloomy church** una chiesa enorme e tetra; **to feel gloomy** sentirsi giù *or* depresso(-a); **she's been feeling very gloomy recently** ultimamente è stata molto depressa; **to feel gloomy about sth** essere pessimista su qc; **to take a gloomy view of things** vedere tutto nero
glo·ri·fi·ca·tion [ˌglɔ:rɪfɪ'keɪʃən] N glorificazione *f*
glo·ri·fy ['glɔ:rɪˌfaɪ] VT (*exalt: God*) glorificare; (: *person*) onorare; (*pej: war, deeds*) magnificare, esaltare; **it was just a glorified ...** non era altro che...
glo·ri·ous ['glɔ:rɪəs] ADJ (*deeds, victory*) glorioso(-a); (*weather, view*) stupendo(-a), magnifico(-a); (*colours*) festoso(-a)
glo·ry ['glɔ:rɪ] N gloria; (*splendour*) splendore *m*, magnificenza; **a moment of glory** un momento di gloria; **one of the glories of the city** uno dei vanti della città; **Rome at the height of its glory** Roma all'apogeo della gloria; **she's in her glory there** (*fam*) ci sguazza in quella situazione; **there she was in all her glory** (*fam*) stava lì in tutto il suo splendore; **glory be!** (*fam*) buon Dio!
■VI: **to glory in sth** (*one's success etc*) gloriarsi di qc; (*another's misfortune*) gustare *or* assaporare qc
glory hole N (*fam*) ripostiglio
Glos ABBR (*Brit*) = *Gloucestershire*
gloss [glɒs] N **1** (*explanation*) glossa, nota esplicativa **2** (*shine*) lucentezza, lustro; (*also:* **gloss paint**) vernice *f* lucida
▸ **gloss over** VT + ADV (*play down*) sorvolare su; (*hide*) coprire, mascherare
glos·sa·ry ['glɒsərɪ] N glossario
gloss finish N: **with a gloss finish** (*paint*) lucido(-a); (*photo*) su carta lucida
glossy ['glɒsɪ] ADJ (*comp* **-ier**, *superl* **-iest**) (*gen*) lucido(-a); **glossy hair** capelli lucidi
glossy magazine N rivista (su carta patinata)
glot·tis ['glɒtɪs] N glottide *f*
glove [glʌv] N guanto; **a pair of gloves** un paio di guanti
glove compartment N (*Aut*) vano portaoggetti
gloved [glʌvd] ADJ inguantato(-a)
glove puppet N burattino (di stoffa)
glow [gləʊ] N (*of lamp, sunset etc*) luce *f* (diffusa); (*of cigarette, fire, city*) bagliore *m*; (*of bright colour*)

luminosità; (*of cheeks*) colorito acceso; (*warm feeling: of pride etc*) vampata
■ VI (*lamp, sunset etc*) ardere; (*fire*) sfavillare; (*colour, face*) essere luminoso(-a); **to glow with health** sprizzare salute (da tutti i pori)

glow·er [ˈglaʊəʳ] VI: **to glower (at sb)** guardare (qn) in cagnesco

glow·er·ing [ˈglaʊərɪŋ] ADJ astioso(-a), torvo(-a)

glow·ing [ˈgləʊɪŋ] ADJ (*light etc*) caldo(-a); (*fire*) ardente; (*complexion*) luminoso(-a); (*cheeks, colour*) acceso(-a); (*person: with health*) florido(-a); (*: with pleasure*) raggiante; (*fig: report, description etc*) entusiasta; **to paint sth in glowing colours** (*fig*) dire meraviglie di qc

glow-worm [ˈgləʊ,wɜːm] N lucciola

glu·cose [ˈgluːkəʊs] N glucosio

glue [gluː] N colla
■ VT: **to glue (to)** incollare (a); **to glue two things together** incollare due cose insieme; **she was glued to the television** (*fig*) stava incollata alla televisione; **he was glued to the spot** (*fig*) rimase di sasso

glue-sniffing [ˈgluː,snɪfɪŋ] N lo sniffare *m* (colla)

gluey [ˈgluːɪ] ADJ appiccicoso(-a)

glum [glʌm] ADJ (*comp* **-mer**, *superl* **-mest**) (*person*) abbattuto(-a); (*mood*) nero(-a); (*expression*) cupo(-a); **to feel glum** sentirsi giù

glut [glʌt] N sovrabbondanza, surplus *m inv*, eccesso
■ VT (*market*) inondare, saturare; (*with food*) saziare

glu·ti·nous [ˈgluːtɪnəs] ADJ colloso(-a), appiccicoso(-a)

glut·ton [ˈglʌtn] N goloso(-a), ghiottone(-a); **a glutton for work** uno(-a) stacanovista, un*a* patito(-a) del lavoro; **a glutton for punishment** un*a* masochista

glut·ton·ous [ˈglʌtənəs] ADJ ghiotto(-a), goloso(-a)

glut·tony [ˈglʌtənɪ] N ghiottoneria, golosità; (*sin*) gola

glyc·er·in [ˈglɪsərɪn], **glyc·er·ine** [,glɪsəˈriːn] N glicerina

gly·co·gen [ˈglaɪkəʊdʒən] N glicogeno

gly·col [ˈglaɪkɒl] N glicol *m*

GM [,dʒiːˈɛm] ADJ ABBR = **genetically modified**

gm (*pl* **gms**) ABBR = **gram(s)**

GMAT [,dʒiːɛmeɪˈtiː] N ABBR (*Am*: = **Graduate Management Admissions Test**) *esame di ammissione all'ultimo biennio di scuola superiore*

GMB [,dʒiːɛmˈbiː] N ABBR (*Brit*) = *General Municipal and Boilermakers (Union)*

GM-free [,dʒiːɛmˈfriː] ADJ senza OGM

GMO [,dʒiːɛmˈəʊ] N ABBR (= **genetically modified organism**) OGM *m inv* (= *organismo geneticamente modificato*)

GMT [,dʒiːɛmˈtiː] ABBR (= **Greenwich Mean Time**) TMG (= *Tempo Medio di Greenwich*)

GMWU [,dʒiːɛmdʌbljʊˈjuː] N ABBR (*Brit*: = **General and Municipal Workers' Union**) *sindacato degli operai non specializzati e comunali*

gnarled [nɑːld] ADJ nodoso(-a)

gnash [næʃ] VT: **to gnash one's teeth** digrignare i denti

gnat [næt] N moscerino

gnaw [nɔː] VT (*chew*) rosicchiare, rodere; (*fig: subj: remorse*) rodere; (*: hunger, pain*) tormentare
■ VI: **to gnaw through** rosicchiare da una parte all'altra; **to gnaw at** rosicchiare; (*fig*) rodere

gnaw·ing [ˈnɔːɪŋ] ADJ (*hunger, pain*) che attanaglia; (*remorse, anxiety*) attanagliante; (*doubt*) assillante

gnome [nəʊm] N gnomo

gno·mic [ˈnəʊmɪk] ADJ (*liter*) gnomico(-a)

GNP [,dʒiːɛnˈpiː] N ABBR (= **gross national product**) PNL *m* (= *prodotto nazionale lordo*)

gnu [nuː] N gnu *m inv*

◎ **go** [gəʊ] (*vb: 3rd pers sg present* **does**, *pt* **went**, *pp* **gone**) VI
1 (*gen*) andare; **to go to London** andare a Londra; **to go by car/on foot** andare in macchina/a piedi; **to go at 50 km/h** andare a 50 km l'ora *or* a 50 all'ora; **to go looking for sb/sth** andare in cerca di qn/qc; **to go swimming/shopping** *etc* andare a nuotare/a fare spese *etc*; **to go for a walk/swim** andare a fare due passi/una nuotata; **to go to a party/to the dentist's** andare a una festa/dal dentista; **to go and see sb** andare a trovare qn; **to go past sth** passare davanti a qc; **the bus goes past the school** l'autobus passa davanti alla scuola; **we went home** siamo andati a casa; **I'm going to the cinema tonight** vado al cinema stasera; **halt, who goes there?** alt, chi va là?; **you go first** (vai) prima tu; **there he goes!** eccolo (là)!; **he went that way** è andato di là; **there you go again!** (*fam*) ci risiamo!
2 (*depart*) andar via, andarsene; (*train etc*) partire; (*disappear: person, object*) sparire; (*: time*) passare; (*: money*): **to go (on)** andarsene (in); (*be sold*): **to go (for)** essere venduto(-a) (per); **where's Judy? – She's gone** dov'è Judy? – È andata via; **I'm going now** io vado; **my voice has gone** m'è andata via la voce; **the cake is all gone** il dolce è finito; **that cupboard will have to go** dobbiamo sbarazzarci di quell'armadio; **go!** (*Sport*) via!; **here goes!** (*fam*) Dio me la mandi buona!; **gone are the days when ...** sono finiti i tempi in cui...; **the day went slowly** la giornata non passava mai; **it's just gone 7** sono appena passate le 7; **only 2 days to go** mancano solo 2 giorni; **going, going, gone!** uno, due, tre, aggiudicato!; **it went for £100** è stato venduto per 100 sterline; **it's going cheap** (*fam*) costa poco
3 (*extend*) arrivare; **the garden goes down to the lake** il giardino arriva fino al lago; **money doesn't go far nowadays** non si fa molto coi soldi oggigiorno; **it's good as far as it goes, but ...** quello che c'è va bene, ma...; **as cooks go, she's quite good** come cuoca non è male; **as hotels in Milan go, it's quite cheap** questo albergo non è molto caro, per essere a Milano
4 (*function: machine etc*) andare; **I couldn't get the car to go at all** non sono riuscito a far partire la macchina; **to keep going** (*person, also fig*) andare avanti; (*machine*) andare; **to make sth go** *or* **to get sth going** far funzionare qc; (*engine, machine*) mettere in moto qc; **let's get going** muoviamoci
5 (*progress, turn out*) andare; **the meeting went well** la riunione è andata bene; **how did it go?** com'è andata?; **how did the exam go?** com'è andato l'esame?; **how's it going?** (*fam*) come va (la vita)?; **we'll see how things go** (*fam*) vediamo come vanno *or* come si mettono le cose; **he has a lot going for him** molte cose giocano a suo favore; **how does that song go?** come fa quella canzone?
6 **to go (with)** (*match*) andare (con); (*coincide, co-occur*) accompagnarsi a; **does this blouse go with that skirt?** questa camicia va con quella gonna?; **the curtains don't go with the carpet** le tende non si intonano col tappeto; **the house goes with the job** la casa è parte integrante del suo contratto di lavoro; **to go with sb** (*also fam*) andare con qn
7 (*become*) diventare, farsi; **to go blind** perdere la vista; **to go hungry** fare la fame; **to go without sth** non avere qc; **to go bad** (*food*) andare a male, guastarsi; **to go mad** impazzire; **to go to sleep** addormentarsi
8 (*fit, be contained*) andare, starci; **it won't go in the**

Gg

case non sta nella valigia; **4 into 3 won't go** il 4 nel 3 non ci sta

9 (*be acceptable*) andare, essere ammesso(-a) *or* ammissibile; **anything goes** (*fam*) tutto è permesso; **that goes for me too** questo vale anche per me; **what he says goes** la sua parola è legge

10 (*break etc: material*) consumarsi, logorarsi; (*: rope*) rompersi, cedere; (*: fuse, button*) saltare; (*: health, eyesight etc*) deteriorarsi; **this jumper has gone at the elbows** questo golf ha i gomiti bucati

11 (*be available*): **there are several jobs going** ci sono diversi posti disponibili; **is there any tea going?** c'è un po' di tè?; **I'll take whatever is going** (*Brit*) prendo quello che mi offrono

12 (*prize, inheritance*): **to go (to)** andare (a), toccare (a); **the money goes to charity** il denaro va in beneficenza; **the money will go towards our holiday** questi soldi li mettiamo da parte per la vacanza; **all his money goes on drink** tutti i suoi soldi se ne vanno in alcolici; **the qualities which go to make him a great writer** le qualità che fanno di lui un grande scrittore

13 (*make: sound, movement*) fare; (*doorbell, phone*) suonare; **go like that (with your right hand)** fai così (con la destra)

14 (*Am*): **...to go** (*food*) ... da portar via, da asporto

■ AUX VB: **I'm going to do it** lo farò; (*intention*) ho intenzione di farlo; **I was going to do it** stavo per farlo; (*intention*) volevo farlo; **I'm going to do it tomorrow** lo farò domani; **it's going to be difficult** sarà difficile; **it's going to rain** sta per piovere; **there's going to be trouble** saranno guai

■ VT (*fam*): **to go it alone** farlo da solo(-a); **to go one better** (*action*) fare di meglio; (*story*) avere di meglio

■ N (*pl* **goes**)

1 (*fam: energy*) dinamismo; **he's always on the go** non si ferma un minuto; **I've got two projects on the go** ho due progetti per le mani; **it's all go** non c'è un attimo di respiro

2 (*success*): **to make a go of sth** riuscire in qc; (*scheme*) mandare in porto qc; **it's no go** (*fam*) (non c'è) niente da fare

3 (*attempt*) tentativo; **to have a go (at doing sth)** provare (a fare qc); **at** *or* **in one go** in un sol colpo; **whose go is it?** a chi tocca?; **it's your go** tocca a te

4 **from the word go** (*fam*) (fin) dal primo momento; **all systems (are) go** tutto a posto

▶ **go about** VI + PREP

1 (*set to work on: task*) affrontare; **how does one go about getting the tickets?** come si fa a procurarsi i biglietti?; **how do I go about this?** qual è la prassi per questo?

2 (*busy o.s. with*) continuare a fare; **to go about one's business** occuparsi delle proprie faccende

■ VI + ADV (*also:* **go around**: *wander about*) aggirarsi; (*circulate: flu etc*) esserci in giro; (*: rumour*) correre, circolare

▶ **go after** VI + PREP (*pursue*) correr dietro a, rincorrere; (*criminal etc*) inseguire; (*job, record etc*) mirare a; (*girl*) star dietro (a), fare il filo (a); **quick, go after them!** veloce, rincorrili!

▶ **go against** VI + PREP (*be unfavourable to: result, events*) essere contro; (*be contrary to: principles, conscience, sb's wishes*) andare contro

▶ **go ahead** VI + ADV (*carry on*) andare *or* tirare avanti; **the show went ahead as planned** lo spettacolo proseguì come previsto; **to go ahead with** mettere in atto; **we'll go ahead with your suggestion** metteremo in atto il tuo suggerimento; **he went ahead with his plan** mise in atto il suo piano; **go (right) ahead!** fai pure!

▶ **go along** VI + ADV (*proceed*) andare avanti, avanzare; **check as you go along** verifica man mano che procedi; **as we went along ...** andando avanti...; **to go along with** (*accompany*) andare con, accompagnare; (*agree with: idea*) sottoscrivere, appoggiare; (*: person*) essere d'accordo con

▶ **go around** VI + ADV *see* **go about** VI + ADV; *see* **go round 1**

▶ **go at** VI + PREP (*fam: attack*) scagliarsi contro; (*tackle: job etc*) buttarsi in; **he really went at it** si è veramente buttato

▶ **go away** VI + ADV (*depart*) andarsene; **go away!** vattene!

▶ **go back** VI + ADV

1 **to go back (to)** (*return, revert*) (ri)tornare (a); **we went back to the same place** siamo ritornati allo stesso posto; **there's no going back now** non si può più tornare indietro

2 (*date back*) risalire; **the controversy goes back to 1929** la controversia risale al 1929

3 (*extend: garden, cave*) estendersi; (*go again*) andare di nuovo

▶ **go back on** VI + ADV + PREP (*word, promise*) rimangiarsi, ritirare; (*decision*) tornare su

▶ **go before** VI + ADV (*happen before*) accadere prima, succedere prima

▶ **go by** VI + PREP

1 (*be guided by: watch, compass*) seguire, basarsi su, attenersi a; **to go by appearances** giudicare dalle apparenze; **going by what he says ...** stando a ciò che dice...

2 **to go by the name of X** farsi chiamare X

■ VI + ADV (*pass by: person, car etc*) passare; (*opportunity*) scappare; (*years, time*) scorrere; **two policemen went by** sono passati due poliziotti; **as time goes by** col passare del tempo

▶ **go down** VI + ADV

1 (*sun*) tramontare, calare; (*person: downstairs*) scendere, andar giù; (*sink: ship*) affondare; (*: person*) andar sotto; (*be defeated*) crollare; **he went down the stairs** ha sceso le scale; **that should go down well with him** dovrebbe incontrare la sua approvazione

2 (*be written down*) venire registrato(-a); **to go down in history/to posterity** passare alla storia/ai posteri

3 (*decrease: price, temperature etc*) scendere, calare; **the price of computers has gone down** il prezzo dei computer è sceso; **he has gone down in my estimation** è sceso nella mia stima

▶ **go down with** VI + ADV + PREP (*fam*): **to go down with flu** beccarsi l'influenza

▶ **go for** VI + PREP

1 (*attack*) lanciarsi contro *or* su, avventarsi su *or* contro; (*fig*) dare addosso a, attaccare; **suddenly the dog went for me** improvvisamente il cane mi ha attaccato

2 (*fam: apply to*): **that goes for me too** questo vale anche per me

3 (*fam: like, fancy*) andar matto(-a) per; **I don't go for his films** i suoi film non mi dicono un granché

▶ **go forward** VI + ADV

1 (*proceed: with plan etc*): **to go forward (with)** procedere con

2 (*be put forward: suggestion*) essere avanzato(-a), venire avanzato(-a)

▸ **go in** VI + ADV
1 (*enter*) entrare; **they all went in** sono entrati tutti
2 **the sun went in** il sole si è oscurato *or* nascosto
3 (*fit*) entrarci, andarci
▸ **go in for** VI + PREP
1 (*enter for: race, competition*) prendere parte a; (*: exam*) presentarsi a
2 (*be interested in: hobby, sport*) interessarsi di, essere appassionato(-a) di; (*take as a career*) scegliere; **she goes in for the latest styles** le piace vestirsi all'ultima moda
▸ **go into** VI + PREP
1 (*investigate, examine*) indagare, esaminare a fondo; (*embark on*) lanciarsi in, imbarcarsi in; **to go into details** entrare nei particolari; **let's not go into all that now** non parliamone per ora
2 (*embark on: career*) darsi a
3 (*trance, coma*) entrare in; **to go into fits of laughter** essere preso(-a) da un convulso di risa
▸ **go off** VI + ADV
1 (*leave*) partire, andarsene; **they went off after lunch** se ne sono andati dopo pranzo; **to go off (to sleep)** addormentarsi
2 (*cease to operate: lights etc*) spegnersi; **all the lights went off** si sono spente tutte le luci
3 (*explode*) esplodere, scoppiare; (*alarm clock*) suonare; **the bomb went off at ten o'clock** la bomba è scoppiata alle 10; **the gun went off by accident** è partito un colpo accidentalmente; **my alarm goes off at seven** la sveglia suona alle sette
4 (*food*) andare a male, guastarsi; **this milk has gone off** il latte è andato a male
5 (*event*) andare; **the party went off well** la festa è riuscita bene
■ VI + PREP (*cease to like: thing*) perdere il gusto di; (*: person*) non poter più vedere; **I've gone off the idea** l'idea non mi piace più; **I've gone off chocolate** la cioccolata non mi piace più
▸ **go off with** VI + ADV + PREP (*boyfriend*) scappare con; (*book*) andarsene con
▸ **go on** VI + PREP (*be guided by: evidence etc*) basarsi su, fondarsi su; **there's nothing to go on** non abbiamo niente su cui basarci
■ VI + ADV
1 (*continue: war, talks*) protrarsi, continuare; (*: on journey*) proseguire; **the concert went on until eleven o'clock** il concerto è durato fino alle undici; **to go on doing** continuare a fare; **he went on reading** ha continuato a leggere; **he went on to say that ...** ha aggiunto che...; **to go on about sth** (*fam*) non finirla più con qc; **go on!** forza!; **go on, tell me what the problem is!** forza, dimmi qual è il problema!; **what a way to go on!** (*pej*) bel modo di comportarsi!
2 (*lights*) accendersi; (*machine*) partire, mettersi in moto
3 (*happen*) succedere, svolgersi; **what's going on here?** che succede *or* che sta succedendo qui?
4 (*pass: time, years*) passare; **as time went on** con l'andar del tempo
▸ **go on at** VI + ADV + PREP (*nag*) assillare
▸ **go on for** VI + ADV + PREP: **it's going on for 3 years now** sono quasi 3 anni ormai; **he's going on for 60** va per la sessantina; **it's going on for 2 o' clock** sono quasi le 2
▸ **go on with** VI + ADV + PREP continuare, proseguire
▸ **go out** VI + ADV
1 (*be extinguished: fire, light*) spegnersi; **suddenly, the lights went out** improvvisamente si sono spente le luci
2 (*leave*) uscire, andar fuori; (*socially*) uscire; (*in cards*) chiudere; (*ebb: tide*) calare; **to go out shopping/for a meal** andare a far spese/a mangiare fuori; **to go out (of fashion)** passare (di moda); **to go out with sb** uscire con qn; **I went out with Steven last night** ieri sera sono uscita con Steven; **to be going out with sb** stare insieme a qn; **I've been going out with him for two months** sono due mesi che stiamo insieme; **they've been going out together for 2 years** sono due anni che stanno insieme, fanno coppia fissa da due anni
▸ **go over** VI + PREP
1 (*examine: report etc*) riguardare, controllare
2 (*rehearse, review: speech, lesson etc*) ripassare; **to go over sth in one's mind** pensare bene a qc
■ VI + ADV
1 **to go over (to)** (*cross over*) andare (a *or* in); (*fig: change habit, size etc*) passare (a)
2 (*be received*) essere accolto(-a); **his speech went over well** il suo discorso è stato accolto bene
▸ **go round** VI + ADV
1 (*revolve*) girare; (*circulate: news, rumour*) circolare; **there is a rumour going round that ...** corre voce che...; **there's a bug going round** c'è un virus in circolazione
2 (*suffice*) bastare (per tutti); **is there enough food to go round?** c'è abbastanza da mangiare per tutti?
3 (*visit*): **to go round (to sb's)** passare (da qn); **let's go round to John's place** facciamo un salto da John
4 (*make a detour*): **to go round (by)** passare (per)
▸ **go through** VI + PREP
1 (*suffer*) passare; **I know what you're going through** so cosa stai passando
2 (*examine: list, book*) leggere da capo a fondo; (*search through*) frugare in; **someone had gone through her things** qn aveva frugato tra le sue cose
3 (*use up: money*) spendere, mangiarsi; (*consume, wear out*) consumare
4 (*perform*) fare; (*: formalities*) sbrigare; **let's go through that scene again** rifacciamo quella scena (da capo)
5 (*town etc*) attraversare
■ VI + ADV (*bill, law*) essere approvato(-a); (*deal*) essere concluso(-a)
▸ **go through with** VI + ADV + PREP (*plan, crime*) mettere in atto, eseguire; **I couldn't go through with it** non sono riuscito ad andare fino in fondo
▸ **go under** VI + ADV (*sink: ship*) affondare, colare a picco; (*: person*) andare sotto; (*fig: business, firm*) fallire
▸ **go up** VI + ADV
1 (*rise: temperature, prices etc*) salire, aumentare; **to go up in price** aumentare (di prezzo); **the price has gone up** il prezzo è salito
2 (*ascend*) andare su
3 (*be built: tower block etc*) venire costruito(-a); (*: new district etc*) sorgere; (*: scaffolding etc*) venire montato(-a)
4 (*explode*) saltare in aria; **to go up in flames** andare in fiamme
■ VI + PREP (*ascend*) salire (su per); **she went up the stairs** ha salito le scale
▸ **go without** VI + PREP fare a meno di

goad [gəʊd] VT: **to goad sb into doing sth** (*fig*) pungolare qn perché faccia qc; **to goad sb on** (*fig*) spronare qn, incitare qn

go-ahead [ˈgəʊəˌhɛd] ADJ (*firm, director*) intraprendente, pieno(-a) d'iniziativa; (*policy, ideas*) avanzato(-a)

Gg

■N: **to give sb/sth the go-ahead** dare l'okay a qn/qc

◎**goal** [gəʊl] N **1** (*Sport: score*) goal *m inv*, gol *m inv*; (*: net etc*) rete *f*, porta; **to win by 4 goals to 2** vincere per 4 reti a 2; **to play in goal** giocare in porta; **he scored the first goal** ha segnato il primo gol **2** (*aim: in life*) scopo, fine *m*, obiettivo; (*: in journey*) meta; **his goal is to become the world champion** il suo obiettivo è quello di diventare campione del mondo

goal area N (*Sport*) area della porta

goal difference N differenza *f* reti *inv*

goalie ['gəʊlɪ] N (*Brit fam*) portiere *m*

goal·keeper ['gəʊl,kiːpəʳ] N portiere *m*

goal kick N (*Ftbl*) rimessa (in gioco) dalla linea di fondo

goal line N linea di porta

goal·mouth ['gəʊl'maʊθ] N: **in the goalmouth** proprio davanti ai pali

goal·post ['gəʊlpəʊst] N palo (della porta)

goat [gəʊt] N capra; **to act the goat** (*fam*) fare lo(-a) stupido(-a); **to get sb's goat** (*fam*) far uscire qn dai gangheri; **goat's cheese** formaggio di capra

goatee ['gəʊtiː] N pizzo

gob·ble ['gɒbl] VT (*also:* **gobble down, gobble up**) trangugiare, ingurgitare

gob·ble·dy·gook, gob·ble·de·gook ['gɒbəldɪ,guːk] N (*fam*) burocratese *m*

go-between ['gəʊbɪ,twiːn] N intermediario(-a)

Gobi De·sert ['gəʊbɪ'dɛzət] N: **the Gobi Desert** il Deserto del Gobi

gob·let ['gɒblɪt] N calice *m*

goblet cell N (*Bio*) cellula caliciforme

gob·lin ['gɒblɪn] N folletto

go-cart ['gəʊ,kɑːt] N go-kart *m inv*

◎**god** [gɒd] N **1 God** Dio; **I believe in God** credo in Dio; **God save the Queen** Dio salvi la Regina; **(my) God!** (*fam*) Dio (mio)!; **for God's sake!** per amor di Dio!; **God forbid!** per carità!; (*stronger*) Dio ce ne scampi e liberi!; **God willing** a Dio piacendo; **God (only) knows** Dio (solo) lo sa **2** (*Myth*) dio **3** (*Brit Theatre*): **the gods** la piccionaia *sg*, il loggione *sg*

god-awful ['gɒd,ɔːfəl] ADJ (*fam*) orrendo(-a)

god·child ['gɒd,tʃaɪld] N (*pl* **-children**) figlioccio(-a)

god·damn(ed) ['gɒd'dæm(d)] (*esp Am fam*) EXCL: **goddamn!** dannazione!, maledizione!

■ADJ dannato(-a)

■ADV dannatamente

god·daughter ['gɒd,dɔːtəʳ] N figlioccia

god·dess ['gɒdɪs] N dea

god·father ['gɒd,fɑːðəʳ] N padrino

god-fearing ['gɒd,fɪərɪŋ] ADJ timorato(-a) di Dio, (molto) pio(-a)

god·forsaken ['gɒdfə,seɪkən] ADJ (*fam: place*) dimenticato(-a) da Dio e dagli uomini, sperduto(-a)

god·head ['gɒd,hɛd] N divinità

god·less ['gɒdlɪs] ADJ empio(-a)

god·like ['gɒd,laɪk] ADJ divino(-a)

god·ly ['gɒdlɪ] ADJ (*comp* **-ier**, *superl* **-iest**) pio(-a)

god·mother ['gɒd,mʌðəʳ] N madrina

god·parents ['gɒd,pɛərənts] NPL: **the godparents** il padrino e la madrina

god·send ['gɒd,sɛnd] N dono del cielo; **it was a godsend to us** è stata una vera manna per noi

god·son ['gɒd,sʌn] N figlioccio

goes [gəʊz] 3RD PERS SG PRESENT *of* **go**

go·fer ['gəʊfəʳ] N (*fam*) galoppino(-a)

go-getter ['gəʊ,gɛtəʳ] N arrivista *m/f*

gog·gle ['gɒgl] VI (*look astonished*) sbarrare gli occhi, sgranare tanto d'occhi; **to goggle (at)** (*stare*) stare con gli occhi incollati *or* appiccicati (a *or* addosso a)

gog·gles ['gɒglz] NPL (*of skin-diver*) maschera; (*of skier*) occhiali *mpl* da sci; (*for workman*) occhiali (di protezione)

◎**go·ing** ['gəʊɪŋ] N **1** (*pace*) andatura, ritmo; **it was slow going** si andava a rilento; **that was good going** è stata una cosa veloce **2** (*state of road surface etc*) percorribilità; (*in horse-racing etc*) terreno; **let's get out while the going is good** è meglio uscirne finché sia possibile; **it's heavy going talking to her** parlare con lei è una faticaccia

■ADJ **1 a going concern** un'azienda avviata **2** (*current: price*) corrente, attuale; **the going rate** la tariffa in vigore; **a going concern** un'azienda avviata

going-over [,gəʊɪŋ'əʊvəʳ] N (*fam*) **1** (*check*) controllata; **they gave the car a thorough going-over** hanno dato una bella controllata alla macchina **2** (*search*): **to give a house a going-over** perquisire una casa **3** (*violent attack*) pestaggio; **to give sb a going-over** pestare qn

goings-on ['gəʊɪŋz'ɒn] NPL (*fam*) fatti *mpl* strani, cose *fpl* strane

goi·tre, (*Am*) **goi·ter** ['gɔɪtəʳ] N gozzo

go-kart ['gəʊ,kɑːt] N = **go-cart**

◎**gold** [gəʊld] N oro; **it's made of gold** è d'oro; **rolled gold** oro laminato

■ADJ (*bracelet, tooth, mine*) d'oro; (*reserves*) aureo(-a); **gold braid** gallone *m* d'oro; **a gold necklace** una collana d'oro

gold card N carta (di credito) oro

gold·crest ['gəʊld,krɛst] N (*Zool*) regolo

gold-digger ['gəʊld,dɪgəʳ] N (*fam pej*): **she's a gold-digger** è un'avventuriera

gold dust N polvere *f* d'oro; **good jobs are like gold dust these days** un buon lavoro è una rarità al giorno d'oggi

◎**gold·en** ['gəʊldən] ADJ (*made of gold*) d'oro, in oro; (*hair etc*) biondo oro *inv*; (*era*) d'oro; (*afternoon*) meraviglioso(-a); (*gold in colour*) dorato(-a); **golden brown** marrone *m* dorato; **her golden hair** i suoi capelli dorati; **a golden opportunity** un'occasione d'oro; **the golden mean** il giusto mezzo; **golden wedding (anniversary)** nozze *fpl* d'oro

golden age N età *f inv* d'oro

golden eagle N aquila reale

golden goal N (*Brit: Sport*) golden gol *m inv*

golden handshake N (*Brit*) gratifica di fine servizio

golden hello N *premio pagato a qualcuno che accetta di lavorare per una certa società*

golden jubilee N cinquantenario; giubileo

golden parachute N gratifica di fine rapporto (*prevista nel contratto di lavoro dei dirigenti*)

golden·rod ['gəʊldən,rɒd] N (*Bot*) verga d'oro

golden rule N regola d'oro

golden syrup N melassa (raffinata)

gold·finch ['gəʊld,fɪntʃ] N cardellino

gold·fish ['gəʊldfɪʃ] N pesce *m* rosso

goldfish bowl N boccia dei pesci rossi

gold leaf N lamina d'oro

gold medal N (*Sport*) medaglia d'oro

gold·mine ['gəʊld,maɪn] N miniera d'oro

gold plate N vasellame *m* d'oro

gold-plated [,gəʊld'pleɪtɪd] ADJ laminato(-a) *or* placcato(-a) d'oro

gold-rimmed [,gəʊld'rɪmd] ADJ bordato(-a) d'oro; **a pair of gold-rimmed glasses** un paio di occhiali con la montatura d'oro; **a gold-rimmed cup** una tazza con bordo d'oro

gold rush N corsa all'oro

gold·smith ['gəʊld,smɪθ] N (*dealer*) orefice *m*; (*artisan*) orafo

gold standard N tallone *m* aureo

◎**golf** [gɒlf] N golf *m*; **to play golf** giocare a golf
■ VI: **to go golfing** giocare a golf

golf ball N palla da golf; (*on typewriter*) pallina

golf club N (*organization*) circolo di golf; (*stick*) bastone *m* or mazza da golf

golf course N campo da golf

golf·er ['gɒlfəʳ] N giocatore(-trice) di golf

golf·ing ['gɒlfɪŋ] N il giocare a golf

Gol·go·tha ['gɒlgəθə] N Golgota *m*

Goliath [gəʊ'laɪəθ] N Golia *m*

gol·li·wog, gol·ly·wog ['gɒlɪ,wɒg] N *bambolotto di pezza con la faccia da negretto*

gol·ly ['gɒlɪ] EXCL **1 golly! have you seen the time!** santo cielo! hai visto che ora è?; **golly, I didn't know he was an expert!** perbacco, non sapevo fosse un esperto! **2** per Giove; **he said he'd do it, and by golly he's succeeded** ha detto che l'avrebbe fatto e, per Giove, ci è riuscito!
■ N = golliwog

gon·ad ['gəʊnæd] N gonade *f*

gon·do·la ['gɒndələ] N gondola

gon·do·lier [,gɒndə'lɪəʳ] N gondoliere *m*

◎**gone** [gɒn] PP *of* go

gon·er ['gɒnəʳ] N (*fam*): **I thought you were a goner** pensavo che ormai fossi spacciato

gong [gɒŋ] N gong *m inv*

gon·na ['gɒnə] VI (*esp Am = going to*): **what are we gonna do?** che facciamo?, cosa faremo?

gon·or·rhoea [,gɒnə'rɪə] N gonorrea

goo [gu:] N (*fam*) sostanza appiccicosa

◎**good** [gʊd] ADJ (*comp* **better**, *superl* **best**)
1 (*gen*) buono(-a); **to lead a good life** condurre una vita virtuosa; **he's a good man** è una brava persona; (*saintly*) è un sant'uomo; **good manners** buona educazione *f*, buone maniere; **he has good judgment** sa giudicare; **be good!** fai il bravo!; **good for you!** bravo!; **she's too good for him** lui non se la merita; **it's just not good enough!** è inaccettabile!; **the job is as good as done** il lavoro è praticamente finito; **as good as new** come nuovo(-a); **she has been as good as gold** è stata un angelo; **(that's) good!** bene!, ottimo!; **that's a good one!** (*iro*) questa sì che è bella!
2 (*pleasant: holiday, day, weather*) bello(-a); (*: news*) buono(-a), bello(-a); **to feel good** sentirsi bene; **have a good journey!** buon viaggio!; **it's good to see you** mi fa piacere vederti
3 (*handsome: looks, features*) bello(-a); **you look good in that dress** quel vestito ti dona *or* ti sta bene; **she has a good figure** ha un bel personale
4 (*beneficial, advantageous, wholesome*) buono(-a); **good to eat** buono(-a) da mangiare; **he's on to a good thing** ha trovato una miniera d'oro; **it's good for you** ti fa bene; **it's a good thing you were there** meno male che c'eri
5 (*child*) bravo(-a); (*competent: teacher, doctor*) bravo(-a), buono(-a); **to be good at** essere bravo(-a) in; **he's good at English/telling jokes** è bravo in inglese/a raccontare barzellette; **she's good with children** ci sa fare coi bambini; **to be good for** andar bene per; **a ticket good for 3 months** un biglietto valido (per) 3 mesi; **he's good for £10** 10 sterline le sgancia; **are you good for another kilometre?** ce la fai a fare un altro chilometro?
6 (*kind*) gentile, buono(-a); **to be good to sb** essere gentile con *or* verso qn; **he's a good sort** (*fam*) è una brava persona; **would you be so good as to sign here?** avrebbe la gentilezza di firmare qui?; **that's very good of you** è molto gentile da parte sua; **good deeds** *or* **works** buone azioni *fpl*, opere *fpl* buone
7 (*considerable, not less than*) buono(-a); **a good many/few people** parecchia/un bel po' di gente; **a good deal of money** un bel po' di soldi; **a good deal of work** parecchio lavoro; **a good 3 hours** 3 ore buone; **it's a good distance from here** dista parecchio *or* un bel po' da qui
8 (*thorough*) bello(-a); **to give sb a good scolding** fare una bella ramanzina a qn; **to have a good cry** farsi un bel pianto; **to take a good look (at sth)** guardare bene (qc)
9 (*in greetings*): **good morning** buongiorno; **good afternoon** buongiorno; **good evening** buonasera; **good night** buonanotte
■ ADV
1 a good strong stick un bel bastone robusto; **good and strong** (*fam*) bello forte; **to hold good (for)** valere (per), reggere (in)
2 (*esp Am fam: well*) bene
■ N
1 (*what is morally right*) bene *m*; **to do good** fare del bene; **good and evil** il bene e il male; **he's up to no good** ne sta combinando qualcuna
2 (*advantage, benefit*) bene *m*, interesse *m*; **it's for your own good** è per il tuo bene; **for the common good** nell'interesse generale, per il bene comune; **to come to no good** andare a finire male; **what's the good of that?** a che pro?, a che serve?; **is this any good?** (*will it do?*) va bene questo?; (*what's it like?*) com'è?; **that's no good to me** non mi va bene, non fa al caso mio; **that's all to the good!** tanto meglio!, tanto di guadagnato!; **it's no good complaining** lamentarsi non serve a niente; **a (fat) lot of good that will do you** (*iro fam*) sai quanto ne ricavi
3 (*people of virtue*): **the good** NPL i buoni
4 (*for ever*): **for good (and all)** per sempre, definitivamente; **the theatre has closed for good** il teatro ha chiuso per sempre; *see also* **goods**

good·bye [,gʊd'baɪ] EXCL arrivederci
■ N saluto, addio; **to say goodbye to** (*person*) salutare; (*fig: holiday, promotion etc*) dire addio a

good faith N buona fede

good-for-nothing ['gʊdfə,nʌθɪŋ] ADJ, N buono(-a) a nulla

Good Friday N Venerdì *m* Santo

good-hearted [,gʊd'ha:tɪd] ADJ buono(-a) (d'animo)

good-humoured [,gʊd'hju:məd] ADJ (*person*) di buon umore; (*remark, joke*) bonario(-a); (*discussion*) cordiale; **to be good-humoured about doing sth** fare qc di buon grado

good-humouredly [,gʊd'hju:mədlɪ] ADV (*see adj*) con buon umore; bonariamente; cordialmente

good-looker [,gʊd'lʊkəʳ] N (*fam: person*) bellezza

good-looking [,gʊd'lʊkɪŋ] ADJ bello(-a), piacente

good·ly ['gʊdlɪ] ADJ (*frm*) consistente

good-natured [,gʊd'neɪtʃəd] ADJ (*person*) affabile; (*discussion*) amichevole, cordiale

good·ness ['gʊdnɪs] N (*virtue, kindness*) bontà (d'animo); (*good quality*) (buona) qualità *f*

■ EXCL (*fam*): **(my) goodness!** *or* **goodness gracious!** santo cielo!, mamma mia!; **for goodness' sake!** per amor del cielo!

◎ **goods** [gʊdz] NPL (*Comm etc*) merci *fpl*, articoli *mpl*; **leather goods** articoli di *or* in pelle; **canned goods** scatolame *m*; **faulty goods** merce *f* difettosa; **all my worldly goods** (*frm*) tutti i miei beni *or* i miei averi; **all his goods and chattels** tutti i suoi beni ed effetti

goods train N (*Brit*) treno *m* merci *inv*

goods yard N (*Brit*) scalo *m* merci *inv*

good-tempered [ˌgʊd'tɛmpəd] ADJ buono(-a)

good-time ['gʊdˌtaɪm] ADJ: **a good-time girl** una ragazza che non pensa ad altro che a divertirsi

good·will [ˌgʊd'wɪl] N buona volontà, buona fede *f*; (*Comm*) (valore *m* d')avviamento; **as a gesture of goodwill** in segno di buona volontà; **to gain sb's goodwill** ingraziarsi qn

goodwill mission N missione *f* di mediazione

goody ['gʊdɪ] EXCL bene!

■ N **1** (*Culin*): **goodies** NPL cose *fpl* buone **2** (*Cine: character*) buono(-a)

goody-goody ['gʊdɪˌgʊdɪ] N (*pej*) santarellino(-a)

goo·ey ['gu:ɪ] (*Brit fam*) ADJ (*comp* **-ier**, *superl* **-iest**) (*mess*) appiccicoso(-a); (*cake, dessert*) molto ricco(-a); (*fig: sentimental*) sdolcinato(-a)

goof [gu:f] (*Am*) VI **1** (*fail*): **they had their chance, and they goofed** hanno avuto un'opportunità e se la sono lasciata sfuggire **2** (*skive*): **to goof off** perdere tempo

■ N **1** (*fool*) gonzo(-a) **2** (*blunder*): **what a goof!** che gaffe!

goofy ['gu:fɪ] ADJ (*comp* **-ier**, *superl* **-iest**) (*Am*) ridicolo(-a)

goo·gle ['gu:gl] VT cercare con Google

goos·an·der [gu:'sændəʳ] N smergo maggiore

goose [gu:s] N (*pl* **geese**) oca; **a flock of geese** (*on the ground*) un branco di oche; (*in the air*) uno stormo di oche; **the goose that lays the golden eggs** la gallina dalle uova d'oro; **don't be such a goose!** (*fam*) non essere così stupido!

goose·berry ['gʊzbərɪ] N uva spina; **to play gooseberry** (*Brit*) tenere *or* reggere la candela

goose·flesh ['gu:sˌflɛʃ] N, **goose·pimples** ['gu:sˌpɪmplz] NPL pelle *f inv* d'oca

goose·grass ['gu:sˌgrɑ:s] N attaccamani *m inv*, attaccavesti *m inv*

goose step N (*Mil*) passo dell'oca

GOP [ˌdʒi:əʊ'pi:] N ABBR (*Am Pol fam*: = **Grand Old Party**) partito repubblicano

go·pher ['gəʊfəʳ] N **1** (*Zool*) geomide *m* **2** (*employee*) = gofer

gore[1] [gɔ:ʳ] N sangue *m*

gore[2] [gɔ:ʳ] VT (*subj: bull etc*) incornare

gore[3] [gɔ:ʳ] N (*of skirt*) godet *m inv*; (*of umbrella*) spicchio

gorge [gɔ:dʒ] N (*Geog, Anat*) gola

■ VT: **to gorge o.s. (with** *or* **on)** rimpinzarsi (di), ingozzarsi (di)

gor·geous ['gɔ:dʒəs] ADJ (*woman, dress, holiday*) stupendo(-a), magnifico(-a); (*meal etc*) fantastico(-a)

Gor·gon ['gɔ:gən] N Gorgone *f*

go·ril·la [gə'rɪlə] N gorilla *m inv*

gorm·less ['gɔ:mlɪs] ADJ (*Brit fam*) tonto(-a); (*: stronger*) deficiente

gorse [gɔ:s] N ginestrone *m*

gory ['gɔ:rɪ] ADJ (*comp* **-ier**, *superl* **-iest**) (*battle, death*) sanguinoso(-a); **the gory details** (*hum*) i dettagli più scabrosi, i particolari più piccanti

gosh [gɒʃ] EXCL (*fam*) cribbio!, perdinci!

gos·hawk ['gɒsˌhɔ:k] N astore *m* nostrano

go-slow [ˌgəʊ'sləʊ] N (*Brit*) ≈ sciopero bianco

gospel ['gɒspəl] N **1** (*Rel*) vangelo; **the Gospel according to St John** il Vangelo secondo (San) Giovanni; **you can take it as gospel** (*fam*) puoi giurarci **2** (*music*) gospel *m inv*

gospel truth N: **it's the gospel truth** è la sacrosanta verità

gos·sa·mer ['gɒsəməʳ] N (*fabric*) garza, mussolina; (*cobweb*) filo di ragnatela

gos·sip ['gɒsɪp] N (*talk*) chiacchiere *fpl*; (*scandal*) pettegolezzi *mpl*; (*person*) pettegolo(-a), chiacchierone(-a); **a piece of gossip** un pettegolezzo; **it's just gossip** sono solo pettegolezzi; **tell me the gossip!** dimmi le ultime!

■ VI (*talk*) chiacchierare; **to gossip (about)** (*talk scandal*) fare pettegolezzi (su), chiacchierare (sul conto di); **they were always gossiping** chiacchieravano in continuazione

gossip column N cronaca mondana

gos·sip·ing ['gɒsɪpɪŋ] ADJ pettegolo(-a)

■ N pettegolezzi *mpl*

gossip writer, gossip columnist N giornalista *m/f* scandalistico(-a)

gos·sipy ['gɒsɪpɪ] ADJ **1** (*pej*) pettegolo(-a); **a gossipy letter** una lettera piena di pettegolezzi **2** (*tone*) frivolo(-a)

◎ **got** [gɒt] PT, PP *of* get

Goth [gɒθ] N Goto

Goth·ic ['gɒθɪk] ADJ gotico(-a)

got·ta ['gɒtə] VI (*esp Am*: = *have got to*): **I gotta get dressed** devo vestirmi; **I've gotta get back** devo tornare

got·ten ['gɒtn] (*Am*) PP *of* **get**

gouge [gaʊdʒ] VT (*also*: **gouge out**: *hole etc*) scavare; (*: initials*) scolpire; (*: sb's eyes*) cavare

gou·lash ['gu:læʃ] N gulasch *m inv*

gourd [gʊəd] N zucca

gour·mand ['gʊəmənd] N buona forchetta, ghiottone(-a)

gour·met ['gʊəmeɪ] N gourmet *m inv*, buongustaio(-a)

gout [gaʊt] N (*Med*) gotta

◎ **gov·ern** ['gʌvən] VT (*rule: country*) governare; (*subj: king*) regnare (in); (*control: business*) dirigere; (*: city*) amministrare; (*: choice, decision*) regolare; (*: person*) guidare; (*: emotions*) dominare; (*Gram*) reggere

gov·er·ness ['gʌvənɪs] N governante *f*, istitutrice *f*

gov·ern·ing ['gʌvənɪŋ] ADJ (*Pol*) al potere, al governo; **governing class** classe *f* dirigente

governing body N consiglio di amministrazione

◎ **gov·ern·ment** ['gʌvənmənt] N governo; **local government** amministrazione *f* locale

▷ www.firstgov.gov/
▷ www.direct.gov.uk/
▷ http://canada.gc.ca/
▷ www.fed.gov.au/
▷ www.wales.gov.uk/
▷ www.irlgov.ie/
▷ www.scotland.gov.uk/
▷ www.gov.za
▷ www.govt.nz/en/aboutnz

gov·ern·men·tal [ˌgʌvən'mɛntl] ADJ governativo(-a)

government department N dipartimento ministeriale

government housing N (*Am*) alloggi *mpl* popolari

government loan N prestito statale

government policy N (*gen*) politica governativa; (*of current government*) politica del governo
government securities NPL (*Fin*) titoli di stato
government stock N titoli *mpl* di stato
◎**gov·er·nor** ['gʌvənəʳ] N **1** (*of colony, state, bank etc*) governatore *m*; (*director: of school, hospital*) membro del consiglio di amministrazione; (*Brit: of prison*) direttore(-trice) **2** (*of engine*) controllo automatico della velocità
Govt ABBR = government
gown [gaʊn] N (*dress*) abito; (*Law, Univ*) toga
GP [ˌdʒiː'piː] N ABBR (= **general practitioner**) medico generico; **who's your GP?** chi è il suo medico di famiglia?
GPMU [ˌdʒiːpiːɛm'juː] N ABBR (*Brit*) = *Graphical, Paper and Media Union*
GPO [ˌdʒiːpiːəʊ] N ABBR (*Am*: = **Government Printing Office**) ≈ Istituto poligrafico dello Stato
GPS [ˌdʒiːpiː'es] ABBR = **Global Positioning System; GPS receiver** GPS *m inv*
gr. ABBR (*Comm*) = gross
◎**grab** [græb] N **1** (*snatch*): **to make a grab at** *or* **for sth** cercare di afferrare qc **2** (*Tech*) benna
■VT (*seize*) afferrare, acchiappare; (: *property, power*) impossessarsi di, impadronirsi di; (*greedily*) agguantare; (*fig: chance etc*) cogliere al volo; **he grabbed my arm** mi ha afferrato il braccio; **to grab sth from sb** strappare qc di mano a qn
■VI: **to grab at** tentare disperatamente di afferrare; (*in falling*) cercare di aggrapparsi a
grace [greɪs] N (*Rel, elegance: of form, movement etc*) grazia; (*graciousness*) garbo, cortesia; **the Graces** (*Myth*) le (tre) Grazie; **the grace of a dancer** la grazia di una ballerina; **he had the grace to apologise** ha avuto il buon gusto di scusarsi, per lo meno si è scusato; **to do sth with good/bad grace** fare qc volentieri/malvolentieri; **his sense of humour is his saving grace** il suo senso dell'umorismo è quello che lo salva; **three days' grace** tre giorni di proroga, una dilazione *f* di tre giorni; **by the grace of God** per grazia di Dio; **to say grace** dire una preghiera; prima del pasto **to be in sb's good graces** essere nelle grazie di qn; **His Grace** (*duke, archbishop*) Sua Eccellenza
■VT (*adorn*) adornare; (*honour: occasion, event*) onorare con la propria presenza; **he graced the meeting with his presence** ci ha fatto l'onore di presenziare alla riunione
grace·ful ['greɪsfʊl] ADJ (*gen*) aggraziato(-a), pieno(-a) di grazia; (*apology*) garbato(-a)
grace·ful·ly ['greɪsfəlɪ] ADV (*see adj*) con grazia; con garbo
grace·ful·ness ['greɪsfʊlnɪs] N grazia
grace·less ['greɪslɪs] ADJ (*dress*) poco elegante; (*rude*) sgarbato(-a)
gra·cious ['greɪʃəs] ADJ (*hostess, permission*) cortese; (*smile*) benevolo(-a); (*mansion*) di raffinata eleganza; (*God*) misericordioso(-a); **gracious living** vita da gran signore
■EXCL: **(good) gracious!** madonna (mia)!
gra·cious·ly ['greɪʃəslɪ] ADV (*see adj*) cortesemente; benevolmente; in modo raffinato ed elegante; misericordiosamente
gra·cious·ness ['greɪʃəsnɪs] N gentilezza, cortesia
gra·date [grə'deɪt] VT graduare
■VI: **the colours/tones gradate** ci sono delle sfumature di colore/di tono
gra·da·tion [grə'deɪʃən] N gradazione *f*
◎**grade** [greɪd] N **1** (*on scale*) categoria, livello; (*in hierarchy, also Mil*) grado; (*Comm*) qualità *f inv*; (*size*) misura, grandezza; **grade A fruit** frutta di prima scelta; **to make the grade** (*fig*) essere all'altezza **2** (*Scol: mark*) voto; (: *Am: class*) classe *f*, anno; **good grades** bei voti **3** (*Am: gradient*) pendenza, gradiente *m*
■VT **1** (*goods, eggs*) classificare; (*level of difficulty*) graduare; **graded profile** (*Geol*) profilo di equilibrio **2** (*Scol: mark*) giudicare, dare un voto a

GRADE

Negli Stati Uniti e nel Canada gli anni scolastici vengono chiamati **grades**, per cui il primo anno di scuola elementare è il "first **grade**" e l'ultimo anno di scuola superiore è il "twelfth **grade**". Negli Stati Uniti gli studenti degli ultimi anni, dal nono al dodicesimo, si chiamano: "freshmen" (ninth **grade**), "sophomores" (tenth **grade**), "juniors" (eleventh **grade**) e "seniors" (twelfth **grade**).
▷ www.ed.gov/index.jhtml
▷ http://educationcanada.cmec.ca/EN/home.php

grade crossing N (*Am Rail*) passaggio a livello
grade school N (*Am*) scuola elementare *or* primaria
gra·di·ent ['greɪdɪənt] N **1** (*of road*) pendenza, gradiente *m*; **a gradient of 1 in 7** una pendenza del 7 per cento **2** (*Math, Phys*) gradiente *m*
grad·ual ['grædjʊəl] ADJ (*change*) graduale; (*slope*) dolce, lieve
◎**gradu·al·ly** ['grædjʊəlɪ] ADV gradualmente, poco alla volta
◎**gradu·ate** [*n* 'grædjʊɪt; *vb* 'grædjʊˌeɪt] N (*Univ*) laureato(-a); (*Am Scol*) diplomato(-a), licenziato(-a); **he's a French graduate** *or* **a graduate in French** è laureato *or* ha la laurea in francese
■VT (*thermometer etc*) graduare
■VI (*Univ*) ≈ laurearsi; (*Am Scol*) diplomarsi; **he graduated from London University last year** si è laureato alla London University l'anno scorso

DID YOU KNOW ...?
graduate is not translated by the Italian word *graduato*

gradu·at·ed pen·sion ['grædjʊˌeɪtɪd'pɛnʃən] N *pensione calcolata sugli ultimi stipendi*
graduate school N (*Am*) scuola di specializzazione
gradua·tion [ˌgrædjʊ'eɪʃən] N (*Univ: ceremony*) consegna delle lauree; (*Am Scol*) consegna dei diplomi; **after graduation he went abroad** dopo la laurea è andato all'estero
graf·fi·ti [grə'fiːtɪ] NPL graffiti *mpl*
graft [grɑːft] N **1** (*Bot, Med*) innesto; **skin graft** innesto di pelle; **kidney graft** trapianto del rene **2** (*fam: corruption*) corruzione *f*; (: *hard work*) duro lavoro
■VT innestare
◎**grain** [greɪn] N **1** (*no pl: cereals*) cereali *mpl*; (*Am: corn*) grano **2** (*single seed: of wheat, rice etc*) chicco, granello; (*particle: of sand, salt, sense*) grano, granello; **there's not a grain of truth in what you say** non c'è un briciolo di verità in quello che dici **3** (*of wood, marble*) venatura; (*of leather, also Phot*) grana; **it goes against the grain** (*fig*) va contro la mia (*or* la sua *etc*) natura
grain elevator N (*Am*) silo per cereali
grain prices NPL prezzo del grano
grainy ['greɪnɪ] ADJ (*comp* **-ier**, *superl* **-iest**) granuloso(-a); (*skin*) butterato(-a)
gram, gramme [græm] N grammo

Gg

gram·mar ['græməʳ] N grammatica; **that's bad grammar** è sgrammaticato; **a grammar book** un libro di grammatica
▷ www.ucl.ac.uk/internet-grammar/home.htm
gram·mar·ian [grə'mɛərɪən] N grammatico(-a)
grammar school N (*Brit*) ≈ liceo
▷ www.ngsa.org.uk/
▷ www.teachernet.gov.uk/teachinginengland/detail.cfm?id=497
gram·mati·cal [grə'mætɪkəl] ADJ (*exercise*) di grammatica; (*structure*) grammaticale; **to be grammatical** (*sentence, language*) essere corretto(-a) grammaticalmente; **grammatical rules** regole grammaticali; **grammatical English** inglese corretto dal punto di vista grammaticale
gram·mati·cal·ly [grə'mætɪkəlɪ] ADV grammaticalmente
gramme [græm] N = gram
gramo·phone ['græmə,fəʊn] N (*Brit*) grammofono
gramophone needle N puntina (del grammofono)
gramophone record N disco
gran [græn] N (*Brit*) nonna
grana·ry ['grænərɪ] N granaio
◎**grand** [grænd] ADJ (*comp* **-er**, *superl* **-est**) (*splendid: occasion, person*) splendido(-a), magnifico(-a); (*person: important*) altolocato(-a); (*style, house*) sontuoso(-a), grandioso(-a); (*fam: very pleasant*) eccezionale, stupendo(-a); **her house is very grand** la sua casa è molto sontuosa; **we had a grand time** ce la siamo proprio spassata
■ N (*fam*) mille dollari *mpl* (*or* sterline *fpl*)

DID YOU KNOW ...?
grand is not translated by the Italian word *grande*

grand·ad, **grand·dad** ['græn,dæd] N (*Brit fam*) = grandpa
Grand Canyon N Grand Canyon *m*
▷ www.nps.gov/grca/
grand·child ['græn,tʃaɪld] N (*pl* **-children**) nipote *m/f*, nipotino(-a) (*di nonno*)
grand·daughter ['græn,dɔːtəʳ] N nipote *f*, nipotina (*di nonno*)
grand duke N granduca *m*
gran·deur ['grændjəʳ] N (*of occasion, scenery etc*) grandiosità *f inv*, maestosità *f inv*; (*of style, house*) splendore *m*; **the grandeur of the scenery** lo splendore del paesaggio; **the grandeur of the occasion** la maestosità della cerimonia
grand·father ['grænd,fɑːðəʳ] N nonno
grandfather clock N orologio a pendolo
grand finale N gran finale *m*
gran·di·ose ['grændɪəʊz] ADJ grandioso(-a); (*pej*) pomposo(-a)
grand jury N (*Am*) giuria (*formata da 12 a 23 membri*)

GRAND JURY

Negli Stati Uniti spetta al **grand jury** stabilire se esistono i presupposti di legge per l'imputazione di un reato e per l'eventuale procedimento giudiziario. La **grand jury** (dalle 12 alle 23 persone) ha il potere di emettere mandati di comparizione e richiedere perizie e deposizioni; le sedute si svolgono di solito a porte chiuse. Nei processi penali la giuria composta da 12 membri si chiama "trial jury" o "petit jury".
▷ www.udayton.edu/~grandjur/fedj/fedj.htm

grand·ma ['græn,mɑː], **grand·mama** ['grænmə,mɑː] N (*fam*) nonna, nonnina
grand·mother ['græn,mʌðəʳ] N nonna
grand opera N opera lirica
grand·pa ['græn,pɑː], **grand·papa** ['grænpə,pɑː] N (*fam*) nonno, nonnino
grand·parent ['græn,pɛərənt] N nonno(-a)
grand piano N pianoforte *m* a coda
Grand Prix [grɒn'priː] N (*Aut*) Gran Premio, Grand Prix *m inv*
grand slam N grande slam *m inv*
grand·son ['græn,sʌn] N nipote *m*, nipotino (*di nonno*)
grand·stand ['græn,stænd] N (*Sport*) tribuna coperta
grand total N somma complessiva
Grand Tour N (*old*) il giro dell'Europa; **we did a** *or* **the Grand Tour of Venice** abbiamo fatto il giro completo di Venezia
gran·ite ['grænɪt] N granito
gran·ny, **gran·nie** ['grænɪ] N (*pl* **grannies**) (*fam*) nonna, nonnina
◎**grant** [grɑːnt] N (*Admin: of money*) sovvenzione *f*, sussidio; (*Brit Univ*) ≈ borsa di studio; **a grant to restore the church** una sovvenzione per il restauro della chiesa; **some students get grants** alcuni studenti ottengono delle borse di studio
■ VT (*allow: extension, favour*) accordare; (*: pension*) assegnare; (*: a request*) accogliere; (*admit*): **to grant (that)** ammettere (che), concedere (che); **granted** *or* **granting that ...** ammesso che...; **I grant him that** glielo concedo; **he grants few interviews** concede poche interviste; **to take sth for granted** dare qc per scontato; **to take sb for granted** non rendersi conto di quanto qn sia importante
grant-aided [,grɑːnt'eɪdɪd] ADJ sovvenzionato(-a)
granu·lar ['grænjʊləʳ] ADJ granulare
granu·lat·ed ['grænjʊleɪtɪd] ADJ: **granulated sugar** zucchero semolato
gran·ule ['grænjuːl] N granello
granu·lo·ma [,grænjʊ'ləʊmə] N granuloma *m*
grape [greɪp] N acino, chicco d'uva; **grapes** NPL uva; **a bunch of grapes** un grappolo d'uva

DID YOU KNOW ...?
grape is not translated by the Italian word *grappa*

grape·fruit ['greɪp,fruːt] N pompelmo
grapefruit knife N coltellino ricurvo
grape harvest N vendemmia
grape juice N succo d'uva
grape·vine ['greɪp,vaɪn] N vite *f*; **I heard it on the grapevine** (*fig*) l'ho sentito dire
graph [grɑːf] N grafico, diagramma *m*
graph·ic ['græfɪk] ADJ (*gen*) grafico(-a); (*vivid: description etc*) di grande efficacia, vivido(-a); **the graphic arts** le arti grafiche
graphi·cal·ly ['græfɪkəlɪ] ADV graficamente
Graphical User Interface ['græfɪkəl-] N (*Comput*) interfaccia grafica
graphic designer N grafico(-a)
graphic equalizer N equalizzatore *m* grafico
graph·ics ['græfɪks] N (*sg: art, process*) grafica; (*pl: drawings*) illustrazioni *fpl*
graph·ite ['græfaɪt] N grafite *f*
graph·olo·gist [græ'fɒlədʒɪst] N grafologo(-a)

graph·ol·ogy [græ'fɒlədʒɪ] N grafologia
graph paper N carta millimetrata
grap·ple ['græpl] VI (*wrestlers etc*): **to grapple (with)** essere alle prese (con), lottare (con); **to grapple with a problem** (*fig*) essere alle prese con un problema
grap·pling iron ['græplɪŋ,aɪən] N (*Naut*) grappino
grasp [grɑːsp] N (*grip*) presa; **to lose one's grasp on reality** (*fig*) perdere contatto con la realtà; **to have sth within one's grasp** avere qc a portata di mano; **it is within everybody's grasp** (*fig*) è alla portata di tutti; **it is beyond my grasp** non ci arrivo; **to have a good grasp of** (*subject*) avere una buona padronanza di; **he has a good grasp of the difficulties** si rende perfettamente conto dei problemi
■VT **1** (*take hold of*) afferrare; (*hold firmly*) stringere; (*fig: chance, opportunity*) cogliere (al volo) **2** (*understand: meaning, hint*) afferrare
► **grasp at** VI + PREP (*rope etc*) afferrarsi a, aggrapparsi a; (*fig: opportunity*) non farsi sfuggire, approfittare di
grasp·ing ['grɑːspɪŋ] ADJ (*fig*) avido(-a)
◎ **grass** [grɑːs] N **1** (*plant*) erba; (*lawn*) prato; (*pasture*) pascolo, prato; **"keep off the grass"** "vietato calpestare l'erba"; **not to let the grass grow under one's feet** (*fig*) non tirarla per le lunghe; **to put out to grass** (*also fig*) mettere a riposo **2** (*slang: marijuana*) erba **3** (*Brit fam: informer*) informatore(-trice); (*: ex-terrorist*) pentito(-a)
■VI (*prison slang*): **to grass (on sb)** fare una soffiata (sul conto di qn)
► **grass over** VT + ADV mettere a prato
grass·hopper ['grɑːs,hɒpəʳ] N cavalletta
grass·land ['grɑːs,lænd] N prateria
grass roots NPL (*fig*) base *f*
grass snake N biscia d'erba
grass widow N vedova bianca
grassy ['grɑːsɪ] ADJ (*comp* **-ier**, *superl* **-iest**) erboso(-a)
grate¹ [greɪt] N (*in fireplace*) grata, griglia
grate² [greɪt] VT **1** (*cheese etc*) grattugiare, grattare **2** (*scrape: metallic object, chalk etc*) far stridere; **to grate one's teeth** digrignare i denti
■VI (*hinge*) cigolare, stridere; **to grate (on** *or* **against)** (*chalk*) stridere (su); **it really grates (on me)** (*fig*) mi dà veramente ai *or* sui nervi
grate·ful ['greɪtfʊl] ADJ: **grateful (for)** grato(-a) (per), riconoscente (per); **I am most grateful to you** le sono enormemente grato
grate·ful·ly ['greɪtfəlɪ] ADV con gratitudine
grat·er ['greɪtəʳ] N grattugia
grati·fi·ca·tion [,grætɪfɪ'keɪʃən] N soddisfazione *f*
grati·fied ['grætɪ,faɪd] ADJ soddisfatto(-a)
grati·fy ['grætɪ,faɪ] VT (*person*) far piacere a, dare soddisfazione a; (*desire, whim etc*) soddisfare, appagare
grati·fy·ing ['grætɪ,faɪɪŋ] ADJ gradito(-a), soddisfacente
grat·in [gra'tɛ̃] N = **au gratin**
grat·ing¹ ['greɪtɪŋ] N (*in wall, pavement*) grata
grat·ing² ['greɪtɪŋ] ADJ (*sound*) stridulo(-a), stridente
gra·tis ['grætɪs] ADV gratis
grati·tude ['grætɪtjuːd] N gratitudine *f*, riconoscenza
gra·tui·tous [grə'tjuːɪtəs] ADJ gratuito(-a)
gra·tui·tous·ly [grə'tjuːɪtəslɪ] ADV **1** (*for no reason*) gratuitamente **2** (*without payment*) gratis
gra·tu·ity [grə'tjuːɪtɪ] N (*Mil*) indennità *f inv* di congedo; (*frm: tip*) mancia

> **DID YOU KNOW ...?**
> **gratuity** is not translated by the Italian word *gratuità*

◎ **grave¹** [greɪv] ADJ (*comp* **-r**, *superl* **-st**) (*gen*) grave, serio(-a); **it had grave consequences for the nation** si ripercosse pesantemente su tutta la nazione
grave² [greɪv] N tomba
grave·dig·ger ['greɪv,dɪgəʳ] N becchino, affossatore *m*
grav·el ['grævəl] N ghiaia
■ADJ (*path, pit*) di ghiaia
grav·el·ly ['grævəlɪ] ADJ (*soil, shore*) ghiaioso(-a); (*voice*) rauco(-a), roco(-a)
grave·ly ['greɪvlɪ] ADV gravemente, solennemente; **gravely ill** in pericolo di vita
grave·ness ['greɪvnɪs] N gravità, serietà
grave robber N ladro(-a) di tombe, tombarolo(-a)
grave·stone ['greɪv,stəʊn] N pietra tombale, lapide *f*
grave·yard ['greɪv,jɑːd] N cimitero
gravi·tate ['grævɪ,teɪt] VI (*fig*): **to gravitate (towards)** gravitare (verso)
gravi·ta·tion [,grævɪ'teɪʃən] N gravitazione *f*
gravi·ta·tion·al [,grævɪ'teɪʃənl] ADJ gravitazionale
grav·ity ['grævɪtɪ] N (*all senses*) gravità; **the law of gravity** la legge di gravità
gravity feed N alimentazione *f* a gravità
gra·vy ['greɪvɪ] N (*Culin*) sugo dell'arrosto, intingolo della carne
gravy boat N salsiera
gravy train N: **to ride the gravy train** (*esp Am fam*) aver trovato la cuccagna
gray [greɪ] ADJ = **grey**
graze¹ [greɪz] VI pascolare, pascere
■VT (*grass, field*) mettere *or* lasciare a pascolo; (*cattle, sheep*) far pascolare; **they graze sheep in the mountains** fanno pascolare le pecore in montagna
graze² [greɪz] N (*injury*) scorticatura, escoriazione *f*
■VT (*touch lightly*) sfiorare, rasentare; (*scrape: skin*) scorticare, escoriare; **to graze one's knees** sbucciarsi *or* escoriarsi le ginocchia; **I grazed my knee** mi sono sbucciato un ginocchio
graz·ing ['greɪzɪŋ] N pascolo
grease [griːs] N (*fat*) grasso, unto; (*lubricant*) grasso, lubrificante *m*
■VT (*baking tin*) ungere; (*Aut etc*) ingrassare, lubrificare; **like greased lightning** (*fam*) come una saetta; **to grease the skids** (*Am fig*) spianare la strada
grease gun N ingrassatore *m*
grease·paint ['griːs,peɪnt] N cerone *m*
grease·proof pa·per ['griːs,pruːf'peɪpəʳ] N (*Brit*) carta oleata
grease-stained ['griːs,steɪnd] ADJ macchiato(-a) di unto
greasi·ness ['griːsɪnɪs] N (*gen*) untuosità; (*of road, surface*) scivolosità
greasy ['griːsɪ] ADJ (*comp* **-ier**, *superl* **-iest**) (*substance etc*) grasso(-a); (*hair*) untuoso(-a), grasso(-a); (*Brit: road, surface*) scivoloso(-a); (*hands, clothes*) unto(-a); (*stains*) d'unto; **he has greasy hair** ha i capelli grassi
◎ **great** [greɪt] ADJ (*comp* **-er**, *superl* **-est**) **1** (*gen*) grande; (*pain, heat*) forte, intenso(-a); (*care etc*) molto(-a); (*age*) venerando(-a); **they're great friends** sono grandi amici; **he was in great pain** soffriva molto; **it's of no great importance** non ha molta importanza; **he took great care to explain clearly** si è impegnato per spiegare in modo chiaro; **he's a great reader** è un lettore accanito; **a great oak tree** una grande quercia; **great big** (*fam*) enorme; **a great many** moltissimi; **Alexander the Great** Alessandro Magno *or* il Grande; **you're a great one for arriving at the wrong moment!** (*fam*) sei speciale per arrivare al momento

Gg

sbagliato!; **the great thing is that ...** il bello è che...; **great Scott!** *(fam)* perbacco! **2** *(fam: excellent)* meraviglioso(-a), magnifico(-a), favoloso(-a); **it was great!** è stato fantastico!; **he's great at football** nel calcio è una cannonata; **he's great on jazz** sa tutto sul jazz; **we had a great time** ci siamo divertiti un mondo; **you look great** hai un aspetto splendido; **you look great in that outfit** quel completo ti sta benissimo

great-aunt [ˌgreɪtˈɑːnt] N prozia

Great Barrier Reef N: **the Great Barrier Reef** la grande barriera corallina

Great Britain N la Gran Bretagna

great·coat [ˈgreɪtˌkəʊt] N cappotto pesante

great·er [ˈgreɪtəʳ] ADJ *(comp of* **great***)* più grande; **Greater London** Londra e sobborghi

great·est [ˈgreɪtɪst] ADJ *(superl of* **great***)* il/la più grande; **he's the greatest!** *(fam)* è grande!

great-grandchild [ˌgreɪtˈgrænˌtʃaɪld] N *(pl* **-children***)* pronipote *m/f (di bisnonno)*

great-granddaughter [ˌgreɪtˈgrænˌdɔːtəʳ] N pronipote *f (di bisnonno)*

great-grandfather [ˌgreɪtˈgrænˌfɑːðəʳ] N bisnonno

great-grandmother [ˌgreɪtˈgrænˌmʌðəʳ] N bisnonna

great-grandparent [ˌgreɪtˈgrænˌpɛərənt] N bisnonno(-a)

great-grand·son [ˌgreɪtˈgrænsʌn] N pronipote *m (di bisnonno)*

great-hearted [ˌgreɪtˈhɑːtɪd] ADJ magnanimo(-a)

Great Lakes NPL: **the Great Lakes** i Grandi Laghi

great·ly [ˈgreɪtlɪ] ADV *(gen)* molto; **greatly superior** di gran lunga superiore; **it is greatly to be regretted that ...** *(frm)* ci rincresce infinitamente che...; **you are greatly mistaken** ti sbagli di grosso

great-nephew [ˌgreɪtˈnɛvjuː] N pronipote *m (di prozio)*

great·ness [ˈgreɪtnɪs] N grandezza

great-niece [ˌgreɪtˈniːs] N pronipote *f (di prozio)*

great northern diver N *(Zool)* tuffatore *m* dei ghiacci

great tit N *(Zool)* cinciallegra

great-uncle [ˌgreɪtˈʌŋkl] N prozio

Great War N: **the Great War** la Grande Guerra

grebe [griːb] N *(Zool)* svasso; **great crested grebe** svasso *m* maggiore

Gre·cian [griːʃən] ADJ greco(-a)

Greece [griːs] N Grecia

greed [griːd] N: **greed (for)** *(for money)* avidità (di), desiderio smodato (di); *(for food: also:* **greediness***)* golosità (per), ingordigia (di); **greed for power** sete *f* di potere; **I ate it out of sheer greed** l'ho mangiato solo per golosità

greedi·ly [ˈgriːdɪlɪ] ADV *(see adj)* avidamente; golosamente, ghiottamente, ingordamente

greedy [ˈgriːdɪ] ADJ *(comp* **-ier**, *superl* **-iest***)* **greedy (for)** *(gen)* avido(-a) (di); *(for food)* goloso(-a) (di), ghiotto(-a) (di), ingordo(-a) (di); **greedy for power** avido di potere; **don't be greedy, leave some cake for Helen** non essere ingordo, lascia un po' di torta per Helen

Greek [griːk] ADJ greco(-a)

■ N **1** *(person)* greco(-a); **the Greeks** i greci **2** *(language)* greco; **ancient/modern Greek** greco antico/moderno; **it's (all) Greek to me** *(fam)* per me è arabo

Greek Orthodox Church N Chiesa Greco-Ortodossa ▷ www.patriarchate.org

◎ **green** [griːn] ADJ *(comp* **-er**, *superl* **-est***)* *(colour, Pol)* verde; *(unripe)* acerbo(-a), verde; *(inexperienced)* alle prime armi, inesperto(-a); *(gullible)* ingenuo(-a); **a green car** una macchina verde; **dark green** verde scuro; **to have green fingers** *(Am)*: **to have a green thumb** *(fig)* avere il pollice verde; **to turn green** *(fig: with nausea)* sbiancare; (: *with envy*) diventare verde; **I'm not as green as I look!** *(fig fam)* non sono mica nato ieri!; **green salad** insalata verde

■ N **1** *(colour)* verde *m*; *(grassy area)* prato, spiazzo erboso; *(bowling green)* campo da bocce; *(of golf course)* green *m inv*; *(also:* **village green***)* ≈ piazza del paese **greens** NPL *(Culin)* verdura *sg* **2** *(Pol)*: **the Greens** i verdi

green·back [ˈgriːnˌbæk] N *(Am fam) biglietto da un dollaro*

green beans NPL fagiolini *mpl*

green belt N *(round town)* cintura di verde

Green Beret N: **Green Berets** *(Mil)* Berretti *mpl* Verdi

green card N *(Brit Aut)* carta verde; *(Am: residence permit)* permesso di soggiorno

green·ery [ˈgriːnərɪ] N verde *m*

green·field [ˈgriːnfiːld] ADJ: **greenfield site** terreno non ancora edificato

green·finch [ˈgriːnˌfɪntʃ] N verdone *m*

green·fly [ˈgriːnˌflaɪ] N afide *m*

green·gage [ˈgriːnˌgeɪdʒ] N susina Regina Claudia

green·grocer [ˈgriːnˌgrəʊsəʳ] N *(Brit)* fruttivendolo(-a); **"greengrocer's"** "frutta e verdura"; **to go to the greengrocer's** andare dal fruttivendolo

green·house [ˈgriːnˌhaʊs] N serra

greenhouse effect N: **the greenhouse effect** l'effetto serra

greenhouse gas N gas *m inv* responsabile dell'effetto serra

green·ish [ˈgriːnɪʃ] ADJ verdognolo(-a), verdastro(-a)

Green·land [ˈgriːnlənd] N Groenlandia

Green·land·er [ˈgriːnləndəʳ] N groenlandese *m/f*

green light N *(of traffic light)* verde *m*; **to give sb/sth the green light** dare il via libera a qn/qc

■ VT *(fam)* dare il via libera a; **to be greenlighted** ottenere il via libera

green·ness [ˈgriːnnɪs] N verde *m*

Green Paper N *(Brit Pol)* ≈ libro bianco

Green Party N: **the Green Party** i Verdi

green pepper N peperone *m* verde

green·room [ˈgriːnˌruːm] N *(Theatre)* camerino

green·stuff [ˈgriːnˌstʌf] N verdura

Green·wich Mean Time [ˈgrɪnɪdʒˈmiːnˌtaɪm], **Green·wich Time** [ˈgrɪnɪdʒˌtaɪm] N tempo medio di Greenwich

greet [griːt] VT accogliere, salutare; **a strange sight greeted his eyes** una strana scena si presentò ai suoi occhi; **the statement was greeted with loud laughter** l'affermazione fu salutata da *or* con grasse risate; **he greeted me with a kiss** mi ha salutata con un bacio

greet·ing [ˈgriːtɪŋ] N saluto; *(welcome)* accoglienza; **greetings** NPL saluti *mpl*; **Season's greetings** Buone Feste; **Christmas/birthday greetings** auguri *mpl* di Natale/di compleanno

greeting card, greetings card N biglietto d'auguri

gre·gari·ous [grɪˈgɛərɪəs] ADJ *(animal)* gregario(-a); *(person)* socievole

grem·lin [ˈgremlɪn] N spiritello

Gre·na·da [greˈneɪdə] N Grenada

gre·nade [grɪˈneɪd] N *(also:* **hand grenade***)* granata, bomba a mano

grew [gruː] PT *of* **grow**

◎ **grey** [greɪ] ADJ *(comp* **-er**, *superl* **-est***)* grigio(-a); *(complexion)* smorto(-a); *(outlook, prospect)* poco roseo(-a);

a grey suit un completo grigio; **to go grey** diventar grigio(-a), ingrigirsi; **to go grey with fear** *(person)* sbiancarsi in viso dalla paura; **grey skies** cielo grigio
■ N *(colour)* grigio
■ VI *(hair)* diventare grigio(-a)

grey area N *(fig)* punto oscuro

grey·beard ['greɪ,bɪəd] N vecchio

grey-haired [,greɪ'hɛəd] ADJ dai capelli grigi

grey·hound ['greɪ,haʊnd] N levriero

grey·lag ['greɪ,læg] N *(also:* **greylag goose***)* oca cenerina

grey matter N *(fig fam)* materia grigia

grid [grɪd] N *(grating)* grata, griglia; *(Elec, Gas: network)* rete *f*; *(on map)* reticolato; *(Am Aut)* area d'incrocio; **the national grid** la rete elettrica nazionale; **a grid of streets** una rete di strade

> DID YOU KNOW ...?
> **grid** is not translated by the Italian word *grido*

grid·dle ['grɪdl] N *(esp Am)* piastra

grid·iron ['grɪd,aɪən] N graticola

grid·lock ['grɪd,lɒk] N *(traffic jam)* paralisi *f inv* del traffico

grid reference N coordinate *fpl* chilometriche

grief [gri:f] N *(sorrow)* dolore *m*; *(cause of sorrow)* dolore, pena; **to come to grief** *(plan)* naufragare; *(person)* finire male; **good grief!** *(fam)* mio Dio!

grief-stricken ['gri:f'strɪkən] ADJ affranto(-a)

griev·ance ['gri:vəns] N *(complaint)* lagnanza, rimostranza; *(cause for complaint)* motivo di risentimento; **their main grievance is low pay** il loro principale motivo di risentimento è la paga bassa; **a sense of grievance** un senso di ingiustizia

grieve [gri:v] VT addolorare; **it grieves me to see ...** mi rattrista vedere...
■ VI addolorarsi, soffrire; **to grieve for** *or* **over sb** compiangere qn; *(dead person)* piangere qn; **she was grieving over the death of her husband** stava piangendo la morte di suo marito; **the family is still grieving** la famiglia è ancora in lutto; **I need time to grieve** ho bisogno di tempo per piangere la sua morte

griev·ous ['gri:vəs] ADJ *(pain)* atroce, intenso(-a); *(injuries, fault, loss)* grave; *(blow)* pesante; *(news)* triste, doloroso(-a); *(crime)* atroce, orrendo(-a)

grievous bodily harm N *(Law)* lesione *f* personale grave

griev·ous·ly ['gri:vəslɪ] ADV *(see adj)* atrocemente; gravemente; pesantemente; tristemente; orribilmente

grif·fin ['grɪfɪn] N *(Myth)* grifone *m*

grif·fon ['grɪfən] N *(Myth, Zool)* grifone *m*

grill [grɪl] N **1** *(Brit: on cooker)* griglia; *(gridiron)* graticola; *(in restaurant: also:* **grillroom***)* grill-room *m inv*; **a mixed grill** una grigliata mista **2** *(also:* **grille***: grating)* griglia; *(: at window)* grata
■ VT **1** *(Culin)* cuocere ai ferri *or* alla griglia; **grilled meat** carne ai ferri *or* alla griglia **2** *(fam: interrogate)* fare il terzo grado a

grille [grɪl] N grata; *(Aut)* griglia

grill·room ['grɪl,rʊm] N grill-room *m inv*

grim [grɪm] ADJ *(comp* **-mer**, *superl* **-mest***)* *(hard, unpleasant: gen)* duro(-a); *(: struggle)* accanito(-a); *(: silence)* sinistro(-a); *(: landscape)* desolato(-a); *(: humour, tale)* macabro(-a); *(determined: face)* risoluto(-a), determinato(-a); *(determination)* feroce; **the outskirts of the city are very grim** la periferia della città è un luogo molto deprimente; **to hold on (to sth) like grim death** attaccarsi (a qc) con le unghie e coi denti; **to feel grim** *(fam: ill)* sentirsi poco bene, sentirsi giù

gri·mace [grɪ'meɪs] N smorfia
■ VI fare smorfie

grime [graɪm] N sporcizia, sudiciume *m*

grim·ly ['grɪmlɪ] ADV *(frown, look)* cupamente; *(continue, hold on)* risolutamente; *(fight)* accanitamente

grimy ['graɪmɪ] ADJ sudicio(-a), sporco(-a)

grin [grɪn] N *(smile)* sorriso smagliante; *(cheeky)* sorrisetto
■ VI: **to grin (at)** fare un gran sorriso (a); **Dave grinned at me** Dave mi fece un gran sorriso; **to grin and bear it** stringere i denti e andare avanti

grind [graɪnd] *(vb: pt, pp* **ground***)* VT *(coffee, corn)* macinare; *(Am: meat)* tritare, macinare; *(car gears)* grattare; *(sharpen: knife)* arrotare; *(polish: gem, lens)* molare; **have you ground the coffee?** hai macinato il caffè?; **to grind one's teeth** digrignare i denti; **to grind sth into the earth** schiacciare qc col piede
■ VI stridere, cigolare; **to grind to a halt** *(vehicle)* rallentare fino a fermarsi; *(fig: talks, scheme)* insabbiarsi; *(: work, production)* cessare del tutto
■ N *(fam: work)* sgobbata; **the daily grind** *(fam)* il trantran *m inv* quotidiano
▶ **grind away** VI + ADV *(fam)* sgobbare
▶ **grind down** VT + ADV *(substance)* levigare; *(fig: oppress)* schiacciare, opprimere
▶ **grind on** VI + ADV continuare; **the years grind on** gli anni avanzano inesorabilmente
▶ **grind up** VT + ADV polverizzare

grind·er ['graɪndə^r] N *(machine: for coffee, pepper)* macinino; *(: for sharpening)* affilacoltelli *m inv*

grind·ing ['graɪndɪŋ] ADJ *(sound)* stridente; *(fig: poverty)* opprimente

grind·stone ['graɪnd,stəʊn] N: **to keep one's nose to the grindstone** darci sotto *or* dentro

◎ **grip** [grɪp] N **1** presa; **to have a firm grip on sb/sth** tenere saldamente qn/qc; **he held her arm in a vice-like grip** le stringeva il braccio come in una morsa; **to take a grip on** afferrare; **to lose one's grip** perdere *or* allentare la presa; *(fig)* perdere la grinta; **in the grip of the recession** *(fig)* nel pieno della recessione; **to get to grips with sb/sth** *(also fig)* venire alle prese con qn/qc; **to come to grips with** affrontare, cercare di risolvere; **to have a good grip of a subject** avere una buona padronanza di una materia; **get a grip on yourself!** *(fam)* controllati! **2** *(of racket, oar)* impugnatura **3** *(holdall)* sacca, borsa da viaggio
■ VT **1** *(hold)* afferrare, stringere; **to grip the road** *(tyres)* far presa sulla strada; *(car)* tenere bene la strada **2** *(fig: enthral)* far presa su; *(: subj: fear)* prendere

gripe [graɪp] N *(fam: complaint)* lagna; **the gripes** *(stomach ache)* colica
■ VI *(fam: complain)*: **to gripe (about)** lagnarsi (di)

grip·ing ['graɪpɪŋ] ADJ *(pain)* lancinante
■ N *(fam: complaining)* lagne *fpl*, lamentele *fpl*

grip·ping ['grɪpɪŋ] ADJ *(story, novel)* avvincente, appassionante

gris·ly ['grɪzlɪ] ADJ *(comp* **-ier**, *superl* **-iest***)* *(murder)* raccapricciante

grist [grɪst] N *(fig)*: **it's (all) grist to the mill** tutto aiuta

gris·tle ['grɪsl] N cartilagine *f*

gris·tly ['grɪslɪ] ADJ *(meat)* tutto(-a) nervi

grit [grɪt] N *(gravel)* ghiaia; *(fig: courage)* fegato; **I've got a piece of grit in my eye** ho un bruscolino nell'occhio; *see also* **grits**

Gg

■VT **1** (*road*) ricoprire di ghiaia **2** **to grit one's teeth** stringere i denti

grits [grɪts] NPL (*Am*) macinato grosso (di granturco)

grit·ty ['grɪtɪ] ADJ (*texture*) granuloso(-a); (*person*) coraggioso(-a)

griz·zle ['grɪzl] VI (*Brit: cry*) piagnucolare

griz·zled ['grɪzld] ADJ (*hair*) brizzolato(-a)

griz·zly ['grɪzlɪ] N (*also:* **grizzly bear**) orso grigio, grizzly *m inv*

groan [grəʊn] N (*of pain*) gemito

■VI gemere; (*tree, floorboard*) scricchiolare; **he groaned with pain** gemette dal dolore

gro·cer ['grəʊsə^r^] N negoziante *m/f* di (generi) alimentari; **grocer's (shop)** negozio di (generi) alimentari

gro·ceries ['grəʊsərɪz] NPL (generi) alimentari *mpl*; **a shop selling groceries** un negozio che vende generi alimentari; **a bag of groceries** una borsa di roba da mangiare; **to go out for some groceries** fare la spesa

gro·cery ['grəʊsərɪ], **grocery store** N (*shop*) negozio di (generi) alimentari

grog [grɒg] N grog *m inv*

grog·gy ['grɒgɪ] ADJ (*comp* **-ier**, *superl* **-iest**) (*dazed*) stordito(-a), intontito(-a); (*shaky*) malfermo(-a), barcollante

groin [grɔɪn] N inguine *m*

groom [gru:m] N (*in stable*) palafreniere *m*; (*also:* **bridegroom**) sposo; **the groom and his best man** lo sposo e il suo testimone

■VT **1** (*horse*) pulire, strigliare **2** (*prepare: person*): **to groom sb for** avviare qn alla carriera di

groom·ing ['gru:mɪŋ] N (*of horse*) strigliatura; **she's known for her immaculate grooming** è famosa per essere sempre curata e perfetta

groove [gru:v] N **1** (*in wood, metal*) solco, scanalatura; (*of record*) solco **2** (*fam: music*) ritmo

groovy ['gru:vɪ] ADJ (*comp* **-ier**, *superl* **-iest**) favoloso(-a)

grope [grəʊp] VI (*also:* **grope around, grope about**) brancolare, andare a tentoni; **to grope for sth** cercare qc a tentoni *or* a tastoni; **he groped for the light switch** cercò a tentoni l'interruttore della luce; (*fig: for words*) cercare (disperatamente)

■VT: **to grope one's way through** farsi strada a tentoni in *or* tra; **to grope one's way towards** andare a tentoni verso; **to grope sb** (*fam: sexually*) mettere le mani addosso a qn

gros·grain ['grəʊ,greɪn] N gros-grain *m*

◎ **gross** [grəʊs] ADJ (*comp* **-er**, *superl* **-est**) **1** (*fat: body*) obeso(-a); (*vegetation*) lussureggiante; (*behaviour, language, error*) grossolano(-a); (*impertinence*) sfacciato(-a); **it was really gross!** è stato veramente disgustoso! **2** (*total: profit, income*) complessivo(-a), totale; (*Comm: weight, income*) lordo(-a); **gross interest** interesse *m* lordo; **£10,000 gross** 10.000 sterline lorde

■N, PL INV (*twelve dozen*) grossa

■VT (*Comm*) incassare, avere un incasso lordo di

> DID YOU KNOW ...?
> **gross** is not translated by the Italian word *grosso*

gross domestic product N prodotto interno lordo

gross·ly ['grəʊslɪ] ADV (*exaggerate*) enormemente; (*overestimate*) di molto; **it's grossly unfair!** è proprio ingiusto!; **we're grossly underpaid** siamo decisamente sottopagati

gross margin N (*Fin*) (percentuale *f* di) utile *m* lordo

gross national product N prodotto nazionale lordo

gross profit N (*Fin*) utile *m* lordo

gro·tesque [grəʊ'tɛsk] ADJ grottesco(-a)

gro·tesque·ly [grəʊ'tɛsklɪ] ADV grottescamente

grot·to ['grɒtəʊ] N grotta

grot·ty ['grɒtɪ] ADJ (*Brit fam*) squallido(-a); **I feel grotty** mi sento a terra

grouch [graʊtʃ] (*fam*) VI brontolare

■N (*person*) brontolone(-a); **she's always got a grouch** (*complaint*) ha sempre da brontolare

grouchy ['graʊtʃɪ] ADJ (*fam*) brontolone(-a)

◎ **ground**[1] [graʊnd] N **1** (*soil*) terra, suolo, terreno; **the ground's wet** la terra è bagnata; **on the ground** per terra **2** (*terrain*) terreno; **high ground** altura; **hilly ground** zona collinosa; **to gain/lose ground** guadagnare/perdere terreno; **to be on dangerous ground** muoversi su un terreno minato; **it suits me down to the ground** mi sta *or* va benissimo; **to cut the ground from under sb's feet** tagliare le gambe a qn **3** (*surface*) terra; (*background*) terreno, sfondo; **on the ground** per terra, a terra; **above ground** in superficie; **below ground** sottoterra; **to fall to the ground** cadere a *or* per terra *or* al suolo; (*fig*) andare in fumo; **to get off the ground** (*aircraft*) decollare; (*plans*) prendere il via; **to stand one's ground** mantenere le proprie posizioni; **he covered a lot of ground in his lecture** ha toccato molti argomenti nel corso della conferenza **4** (*Sport*) campo; (*also:* **football ground**) campo di calcio; **grounds** NPL (*gardens*) giardini *mpl* **5** **grounds** NPL (*of coffee*) fondi *mpl* (di caffè) **6** (*Am Elec: also:* **ground wire**) (presa a) terra **7** (*reason: usu pl*) ragione *f*, motivo; **on medical grounds** per motivi di salute; **we've got grounds for complaint** abbiamo motivo *or* ragione di lamentarci; **on the ground(s) that** per il motivo che

■VT **1** (*plane, pilot*) bloccare a terra; (*ship*) far incagliare **2** (*argument, hope*) basare **3** (*Am Elec*) mettere a terra

■VI (*Naut*) incagliarsi, arenarsi

ground[2] [graʊnd] PT, PP *of* **grind**

■ADJ (*coffee, pepper*) macinato(-a); **ground glass** vetro smerigliato; **ground rice** farina di riso; **ground meat** carne *f* macinata

ground cloth N (*Am*) = **groundsheet**

ground control N (*Aer, Space*) base *f* di controllo

ground floor N pianterreno, pianoterra *m*; **on the ground floor** al pianterreno

ground forces NPL (*Mil*) forze *fpl* di terra

ground frost N brina

ground handling N (*Aer*) assistenza a terra

ground·ing ['graʊndɪŋ] N (*educational*) fondamento, basi *fpl*; **he has a good grounding in French** ha delle buone basi in francese

ground·less ['graʊndlɪs] ADJ infondato(-a)

ground level N (*of house*) pianterreno, pianoterra *m*; **at ground level** al livello del suolo

ground·nut ['graʊnd,nʌt] N arachide *f*

ground plan N pianta

ground rent N (*Brit*) canone *m* di affitto di un terreno

ground rule N: **the ground rules** le regole del gioco

ground rules NPL: **the ground rules** i principi fondamentali

ground·sel ['graʊnsl] N erba calderina

ground·sheet ['graʊnd,ʃi:t] N (*Brit: in tent*) telone *m* impermeabile

grounds·man ['graʊndzmən] N (*pl* **-men**), **grounds·keep·er** (*Am*) ['graʊndz,kipə^r^] N (*Sport*) custode *m* (di campo sportivo)

ground staff N (*Aer*) personale *m* di terra

ground stroke N (*Tennis*) colpo di rimbalzo

grounds·well ['graʊnd,swɛl] N mareggiata; (*fig*) ondata
ground-to-air ['graʊndtu:'ɛəʳ] ADJ terra-aria *inv*
ground-to-ground ['graʊndtə'graʊnd] ADJ terra-terra *inv*; **ground-to-ground missile** missile *m* terra-terra
ground water N acqua freatica
ground wire N (*Am Elec*) filo di massa *or* di terra
ground·work ['graʊnd,wɜ:k] N lavoro preparatorio, preparazione *f*
◎ **group** [gru:p] N (*gen*) gruppo; (*set, clique: of people*) circolo, gruppo; (*Mus: pop group*) complesso, gruppo
■ VT (*also:* **group together**) raggruppare
■ VI (*also:* **group together**) raggrupparsi
■ ADJ (*discussion, photo*) di gruppo, collettivo(-a)
group captain N (*Aer*) comandante *m* di gruppo
groupie ['gru:pɪ] N (*fam*) groupie *m/f*; *fanatico seguace di un gruppo (o un cantante) rock*
group practice N (*Med*) *ambulatorio medico con più dottori*
group therapy N (*Psych*) terapia di gruppo
group·ware ['gru:pwɛəʳ] N (*Comput*) groupware *m inv*; *programma che consente a più utenti di lavorare contemporaneamente sugli stessi dati*
grouse¹ [graʊs] N, PL INV gallo cedrone, urogallo
grouse² [graʊs] (*fam*) N (*complaint*) mugugno
■ VI: **to grouse (about)** brontolare (su)
grout [graʊt] (*Constr*) N gesso
■ VT: **to grout the tiles** mettere il gesso nelle fughe tra le piastrelle
grove [grəʊv] N boschetto
grov·el ['grɒvl] VI (*also fig*): **to grovel to** *or* **before sb** strisciare di fronte a qn
◎ **grow** [grəʊ] (*vb: pt* **grew**, *pp* **grown**) VT (*Agr*) coltivare, far crescere; (*business, economy*) far crescere; **to grow a beard** farsi crescere la barba; **I'm growing a beard** mi sto facendo crescere la barba; **he grew a moustache** si è fatto crescere i baffi; **he grew vegetables in his garden** coltivava ortaggi in giardino; **lettuce was grown by the Ancient Romans** gli antichi romani coltivavano l'insalata
■ VI **1** (*plant, person, hair, business, economy*) crescere; (*increase: in numbers*) aumentare, salire; (*: in membership*) ingrandirsi; (*develop: friendship, love*) rafforzarsi; (*: custom, idea*) affermarsi, diffondersi; **haven't you grown!** come sei cresciuto!; **to grow in stature/popularity** veder aumentare il proprio prestigio/la propria popolarità **2** (*become*) farsi, diventare; **to grow dark** farsi buio; **to grow rich/weak** arricchirsi/indebolirsi; **to grow tired of waiting** stancarsi di aspettare; **to grow to like sb** imparare ad apprezzare qn
▸ **grow apart** VI + ADV (*fig*) estraniarsi
▸ **grow away from** VI + ADV + PREP (*fig*) allontanarsi da, staccarsi da; **we have grown away from each other** i nostri rapporti si sono gradatamente raffreddati
▸ **grow in** VI + ADV (*nail*) incarnarsi
▸ **grow into** VI + PREP **1** (*clothes*): **he'll grow into them** quando crescerà gli andranno bene **2** (*become*) farsi, diventare; **she has grown into a beautiful woman** si è fatta una gran bella donna
▸ **grow on** VI + PREP: **that painting is growing on me** quel quadro più lo guardo più mi piace
▸ **grow out of** VI + ADV + PREP **1** (*clothes*) non entrare più in; (*habit*) perdere (col tempo); **he's grown out of his jacket** non entra più nella giacca; **he'll grow out of it** gli passerà **2** (*arise from*) nascere da, essere la conseguenza di
▸ **grow up** VI + ADV **1** (*become adult*) diventar grande, crescere; **I grew up in the country** sono cresciuto in campagna; **I grew up in Rome** sono cresciuto a Roma; **grow up!** (*fam*) non fare il bambino! **2** (*develop: idea, friendship*) nascere
grow·er ['grəʊəʳ] N (*Agr*) coltivatore(-trice); (*of wine*) viticoltore(-trice)
grow·ing ['grəʊɪŋ] ADJ (*fear, amount*) crescente; **to have a growing desire to do sth** avere un desiderio sempre più forte di fare qc
growing pains NPL problemi *mpl* della crescita; (*fig: of organization*) problemi di avviamento
growl [graʊl] N (*of animal*) ringhio; (*of thunder*) brontolio; **the dog gave a growl** il cane ringhiò
■ VI ringhiare; (*person, thunder*) brontolare
grown [grəʊn] PP *of* **grow** ■ ADJ (*also:* **fully grown**) adulto(-a), grande; **he's a grown man** è un adulto
grown-up [,grəʊn'ʌp] ADJ da grande; **he's very grown-up** è molto maturo
■ N grande *m/f*, adulto(-a)
◎ **growth** [grəʊθ] N **1** (*increase*) crescita, aumento; (*development*) sviluppo; **economic growth** crescita economica; **he has 5 days' growth (of beard)** ha una barba di 5 giorni; **to reach full growth** raggiungere il pieno sviluppo **2** (*Med*) tumore *m*
growth rate N (*Econ*) tasso di crescita
groyne [grɔɪn] N frangiflutti *m inv*
grub [grʌb] N **1** (*larva*) bruco **2** (*fam: food*) roba da mangiare; **grub('s) up!** si mangia!, a tavola!; **get yourself some grub** prenditi qc da mangiare
grub·bi·ness ['grʌbɪnɪs] N sporcizia
grub·by ['grʌbɪ] ADJ (*comp* **-ier**, *superl* **-iest**) sudicio(-a), sporco(-a)
grudge [grʌdʒ] N: **grudge (against)** risentimento (verso), rancore *m* (verso); **to bear a grudge against sb** portare *or* serbare rancore a qn
■ VT: **to grudge sb sth** (*money*) dare qc a qn malvolentieri *or* a malincuore; **it's not the money I grudge, but the time** non me la prendo per i soldi ma per il tempo; **I don't grudge you your success** non t'invidio il tuo successo; **to grudge doing sth** fare qc malvolentieri *or* a malincuore
grudg·ing ['grʌdʒɪŋ] ADJ (*praise, respect*) dato(-a) a malincuore; **she gave him her grudging support** gli ha dato a malincuore il suo appoggio
grudg·ing·ly ['grʌdʒɪŋlɪ] ADV (*accept, support*) malvolentieri, a malincuore
gru·el ['gru:əl] N pappa d'avena
gru·el·ling, (*Am*) **gru·el·ing** ['grʊəlɪŋ] ADJ estenuante
grue·some ['gru:səm] ADJ orrendo(-a), orribile, agghiacciante
gruff [grʌf] ADJ (*comp* **-er**, *superl* **-est**) burbero(-a)
gruff·ly ['grʌflɪ] ADV in modo burbero, burberamente
gruff·ness ['grʌfnɪs] N rudezza, scontrosità
grum·ble ['grʌmbl] N (*complaint*) lamentela; (*noise*) brontolio; (*: of guns*) rombo; **without a grumble** (*agree, accept*) senza lagnarsi
■ VI (*person: complain*): **to grumble (about)** brontolare (su), lagnarsi (di); (*thunder*) rombare
grum·bling ap·pen·dix ['grʌmblɪŋə'pɛndɪks] N appendice *f* infiammata
grumpi·ly ['grʌmpɪlɪ] ADV in modo scorbutico, scorbuticamente
grumpi·ness ['grʌmpɪnɪs] N scontrosità, irritabilità
grumpy ['grʌmpɪ] ADJ (*comp* **-ier**, *superl* **-iest**) scorbutico(-a)
grunge [grʌndʒ] N (*Mus*) grunge *m*; (*style*) moda grunge

grunt [grʌnt] N grugnito; **to give a grunt** emettere un grugnito
■ VI grugnire

GSM [ˌdʒiːɛsˈɛm] N ABBR (*Telec* = **Global System for Mobile communication**) GSM *m*

G-string [ˈdʒiːˌstrɪŋ] N (*garment*) tanga *m inv*

GT [ˌdʒiːˈtiː] N ABBR (*Aut*: = **gran turismo**) GT *f*

GU ABBR (*Am Post*) = *Guam*

gua·no [ˈgwɑːnəʊ] N guano

◎ **guar·an·tee** [ˌgærənˈtiː] N garanzia; (*guarantor*) garante *m/f*, mallevadore *m*; **a year's guarantee** (*on appliances, watch etc*) un anno di garanzia; **it's still under guarantee** è ancora in garanzia; **there's no guarantee that it won't happen again** nessuno ti garantisce che non accadrà di nuovo
■ VT (*gen*) garantire; **I can't guarantee that he did it** non posso garantire che lo abbia fatto; **he can't guarantee (that) he'll come** non può garantire che verrà

guar·an·tor [ˌgærənˈtɔːʳ] N garante *m/f*, mallevadore *m*

◎ **guard** [gɑːd] N **1** (*gen, also Mil, Sport*) guardia; (*security guard*) guardia giurata; (*esp Am*: *prison guard*) secondino; (*Brit Rail*) ≈ capotreno; (*also*: **guard duty**: *watch*) (turno di) guardia; (*fig*: *watchfulness*) vigilanza; **to change guard** (*Mil*) cambiare la guardia; **to be on guard** (*Mil*) essere di guardia; **to be on one's guard** (*fig*) stare in guardia; **to keep sb under guard** tenere qn sotto vigilanza; **to catch sb off his/her guard** cogliere *or* prendere qn alla sprovvista; **to keep guard over sb/sth** (*Mil, fig*) fare la guardia a qn/qc **2** (*safety device*: *on machine*) schermo protettivo; (*protection*) riparo, protezione *f*; (*also*: **fire guard**) parafuoco; (*mud guard*) parafango
■ VT (*prisoner, treasure*) fare la guardia a, stare a guardia di; (*secret*) custodire; (*protect*): **to guard (against** *or* **from)** proteggere (da), salvaguardare (da); **they guarded the palace** facevano la guardia al palazzo
■ ADJ: **guard duty** turno di guardia; **on guard duty** di guardia
▸ **guard against** VI + PREP (*take care to avoid*: *illness*) guardarsi da; (: *suspicion, accidents*) premunirsi contro; **to guard against doing sth** guardarsi dal fare qc

> DID YOU KNOW ...?
> **guard** is not translated by the Italian word *guardare*

guard dog N cane *m* da guardia

guard·ed [ˈgɑːdɪd] ADJ (*reply, tone*) guardingo(-a), cauto(-a), circospetto(-a)

guard·ed·ly [ˈgɑːdɪdlɪ] ADV in modo guardingo, con circospezione

guard·house [ˈgɑːdˌhaʊs] N (*for guards*) corpo di guardia; (*for prisoners*) sala di disciplina

guard·ian [ˈgɑːdɪən] N custode *m/f*; (*of minor*) tutore(-trice); **parent or guardian** genitore o tutore

> DID YOU KNOW ...?
> **guardian** is not translated by the Italian word *guardiano*

guardian angel N angelo custode

guard·rail [ˈgɑːdˌreɪl] N guardrail *m inv*

guard·room [ˈgɑːdˌrʊm] N (*Mil*) corpo di guardia

guards·man [ˈgɑːdzmən] N (*pl* **-men**) (*Brit*) soldato della Guardia Reale; (*Am*) soldato della Guardia Nazionale

guard's van N (*Brit Rail*) vagone *m* di servizio

Gua·te·ma·la [ˌgwɑːtɪˈmɑːlə] N Guatemala *m*

Gua·te·ma·lan [ˌgwɑːtɪˈmɑːlən] ADJ, N guatemalteco(-a)

gudg·eon [ˈgʌdʒən] N (*fish*) gobione *m*

Guern·sey [ˈgɜːnzɪ] N (*island*) (isola di) Guernsey *f*; (*cow*) mucca di Guernsey

◎ **guer·ril·la** [gəˈrɪlə] N guerrigliero(-a); **guerrilla group** gruppo di guerriglieri; **guerrilla tactics** tattica di guerriglia

guerrilla warfare N guerriglia

◎ **guess** [gɛs] N supposizione *f*, congettura; **to take** *or* **make** *or* **have a guess** cercare di indovinare, provare a indovinare; **have a guess!** prova a indovinare!; **at a (rough) guess** a occhio e croce; **my guess is that ...** suppongo che...; **it's anybody's guess** Dio solo (lo) sa; **your guess is as good as mine** ne so quanto te; **it's just a guess** è solo una supposizione
■ VT **1** (*gen*) indovinare; **can you guess what it is?** sai cos'è?; **guess what!** (*fam*) sai l'ultima?; **I guessed as much** me lo immaginavo **2** (*esp Am*: *suppose*) supporre, credere; **I guess so** direi di sì , suppongo di sì ; **I guess you're right** forse hai ragione
■ VI **1** indovinare; **to guess at sth** provare a indovinare qc; **to guess correctly** azzeccarci; **she's just guessing** sta tirando a indovinare; **to keep sb guessing** tenere qn in sospeso *or* sulla corda **2** (*esp Am*: *suppose*) supporre, credere; **he's happy, I guess** è felice, immagino

guess·ti·mate [ˈgɛstɪmɪt] N (*fam*) stima approssimativa

guess·work [ˈgɛsˌwɜːk] N: **I got the answer by guesswork** ho azzeccato la risposta; **it remains a matter of guesswork** resta un mistero; **there is a great deal of guesswork in their calculations** c'è molta approssimazione nei loro calcoli

◎ **guest** [gɛst] N (*in house, on TV programme*) ospite *m/f*; (*at party*) invitato(-a); (*at hotel*) cliente *m/f*; (*in boarding house*) pensionante *m/f*; **we have guests staying with us** abbiamo degli ospiti da noi; **guest of honour** ospite d'onore; **be my guest** (*fam*) fai come ti pare

guest·house [ˈgɛstˌhaʊs] N pensione *f*

guest room N stanza *or* camera degli ospiti

guff [gʌf] N (*fam*) stupidaggini *fpl*, assurdità *fpl*

guf·faw [gʌˈfɔː] N risata fragorosa *or* sonora
■ VI ridere fragorosamente

GUI [ˈguːɪ] N ABBR = **Graphical User Interface**

guid·ance [ˈgaɪdəns] N (*counselling*) consigli *mpl*, guida; (*leadership*) guida, direzione *f*; **for your guidance** a titolo informativo; **help and guidance** aiuto e consigli; **vocational guidance** consulenza per l'avviamento professionale

◎ **guide** [gaɪd] N **1** (*gen*) guida; (*manual*) guida, manuale *m*; (*fig*: *indication, model*) indicazione *f*; **let conscience be your guide** lasciati guidare dalla coscienza; **as a rough guide** approssimativamente **2** **Guide** (*Brit*) Giovane Esploratrice *f*; **the Guides** le Giovani Esploratrici
■ VT guidare; **to be guided by sb/sth** farsi *or* lasciarsi guidare da qn/qc

guide·book [ˈgaɪdˌbʊk] N guida

guid·ed [ˈgaɪdɪd] ADJ (*tour*) guidato(-a)

guided missile N missile *m* teleguidato

guide dog N cane *m* per ciechi

guide·lines [ˈgaɪdlˌaɪnz] NPL (*fig*) direttive *fpl*

guid·ing [ˈgaɪdɪŋ] ADJ (*principle*) informatore(-trice); **he needs a guiding hand** ha bisogno di qualcuno che lo guidi; **guiding light** *or* **star** (*fig*) guida

guild [gɪld] N (*History*) corporazione *f*, arte *f*, gilda; (*club*) associazione *f*

guild·hall ['gɪld,hɔ:l] N (*Brit: town hall*) (palazzo del) municipio

guile [gaɪl] N astuzia

guile·less ['gaɪllɪs] ADJ franco(-a), candido(-a)

guil·le·mot ['gɪlɪ,mɒt] N uria

guil·lo·tine [gɪlə'ti:n] N ghigliottina; (*for paper*) taglierina

guilt [gɪlt] N (*being guilty*) colpevolezza; (*feeling guilty*) colpa, senso di colpa; **feelings of guilt** sensi di colpa; **tormented by guilt** tormentato(-a) dal senso di colpa; **they were convinced of his guilt** erano convinti della sua colpevolezza

guilt complex N (*Psych*) complesso di colpa

guilti·ly ['gɪltɪlɪ] ADV colpevolmente

guilt·less ['gɪltlɪs] ADJ senza colpa, innocente

◎**guilty** ['gɪltɪ] ADJ (*comp* **-ier**, *superl* **-iest**) (*gen, Law*) colpevole; (*conscience*) sporco(-a); **guilty of sth** colpevole di qc; **to have a guilty conscience** avere la coscienza sporca; **the guilty person** *or* **party** il/la responsabile; **to feel guilty (about)** sentirsi in colpa (per); **he felt guilty about lying to her** si sentiva in colpa per averle mentito; **to find sb guilty** riconoscere qn colpevole; **she was found guilty** fu riconosciuta colpevole; **to plead guilty/not guilty** dichiararsi colpevole/innocente

Guinea ['gɪnɪ] N: **Republic of Guinea** la Repubblica di Guinea

guinea ['gɪnɪ] N (*Brit old*) ghinea; ≈ 21 shillings

guinea fowl N faraona

guinea pig N porcellino d'India, cavia; (*fig*) cavia

guise [gaɪz] N maschera, parvenza; **under the guise of** mascherato da

◎**gui·tar** [gɪ'tɑ:ʳ] N chitarra

gui·tar·ist [gɪ'tɑ:rɪst] N chitarrista *m/f*

gulch [gʌltʃ] N (*Am*) burrone *m*

gulf [gʌlf] N (*bay*) golfo; (*chasm, also fig*) abisso; **the (Persian) Gulf** il Golfo Persico; **there's a gulf between rich and poor** c'è un abisso tra ricchi e poveri

Gulf States NPL: **the Gulf States** gli stati del Golfo Persico

Gulf Stream N: **the Gulf Stream** la corrente del Golfo

gull [gʌl] N gabbiano

gul·let ['gʌlɪt] N gargarozzo

gul·li·bil·ity [,gʌlɪ'bɪlɪtɪ] N credulità, semplicioneria

gul·lible ['gʌlɪbl] ADJ credulone(-a), sempliciotto(-a)

gul·ly ['gʌlɪ] N (*ravine*) burrone *m*, gola; (*channel*) canale *m* di scolo

gulp [gʌlp] N (*of liquid*) sorso; (*of food*) boccone *m*; **a gulp of tea** un sorso di te; **in** *or* **at one gulp** in un sorso, (tutto) d'un fiato

■VT (*also:* **gulp down**) trangugiare, tracannare, inghiottire; **I quickly gulped my tea** ho buttato giù in fretta il mio tè

■VI (*while drinking*) deglutire; (*through fear*) sentirsi serrare la gola; (*from emotion*) avere un nodo alla gola

gum[1] [gʌm] N (*Anat*) gengiva; **gums** le gengive; **my gums are bleeding** mi sanguinano le gengive

gum[2] [gʌm] N (*glue*) colla; (*also:* **gum tree**) albero della gomma; (*chewing gum*) gomma americana, chewing gum *m inv*; (*sweet*) caramella gommosa; **I'm chewing gum** sto masticando una gomma

■VT (*stick together*) incollare, ingommare; (*also:* **gum down**: *label*) attaccare, incollare; **gummed label** etichetta adesiva

▶ **gum up** VT + ADV: **to gum up the works** (*fam*) mettere il bastone tra le ruote

gum arabic N gomma arabica

gum·boil ['gʌm,bɔɪl] N ascesso gengivale

gum·boots ['gʌm,bu:ts] NPL (*Brit*) stivali *mpl* di gomma

gump·tion ['gʌmpʃən] N (*fam: initiative*) spirito d'iniziativa; (*: common sense*) buon senso, senso pratico

gum·shield ['gʌm,ʃi:ld] N (*Sport*) paradenti *m inv*

◎**gun** [gʌn] N (*handgun*) pistola, rivoltella; (*rifle*) fucile *m*, carabina; (*shotgun*) fucile da caccia; (*cannon*) cannone *m*; **gun barrel** canna di fucile; **to draw a gun on sb** spianare la pistola contro qn; **to carry a gun** portare la pistola; **the big guns** (*Mil*) l'artiglieria pesante; (*fig fam: people*) i pezzi grossi; **to stick to one's guns** (*fig*) tener duro; **to be going great guns** (*fam*) andare a tutto gas; *see also* **big gun**

■VT (*also:* **gun down**) abbattere a colpi di pistola *or* fucile

▶ **gun for** VI + PREP (*fig*) avercela a morte con

gun·boat ['gʌn,bəʊt] N cannoniera

gun dog N cane *m* da caccia

gun·fight ['gʌn,faɪt] N scontro a fuoco

gun·fire ['gʌn,faɪəʳ] N colpi *mpl* d'arma da fuoco, spari *mpl*

gunge [gʌndʒ] N (*fam*) pappa schifosa

gung-ho ['gʌŋ,həʊ] ADJ (*fam*) fanatico(-a); (*eager to fight in war*) guerrafondaio(-a)

gunk [gʌŋk] N porcherie *fpl*

gun licence N porto d'armi

gun·man ['gʌnmən] N (*pl* **-men**) bandito; (*hired*) sicario

gun·ner ['gʌnəʳ] N artigliere *m*

gun·point ['gʌn,pɔɪnt] N: **at gunpoint** sotto la minaccia delle armi

gun·powder ['gʌn,paʊdəʳ] N polvere *f* da sparo

gun·runner ['gʌn,rʌnəʳ] N trafficante *m/f or* contrabbandiere(-a) di armi

gun·running ['gʌn,rʌnɪŋ] N traffico *or* contrabbando d'armi

gun·shot ['gʌn,ʃɒt] N (*noise*) sparo; **within gunshot** a portata di tiro

gunshot wound N ferita da arma da fuoco

gun·smith ['gʌn,smɪθ] N armaiolo

gun·wale ['gʌnl] N (*Naut*) falchetta

gur·gle ['gɜ:gl] N (*all senses*) gorgoglio

■VI gorgogliare, ciangottare

gur·nard ['gɜ:nəd] N (*Zool*) cappone *m*; **grey gurnard** triglia grigia

guru ['gʊru:] N (*Rel, fig*) guru *m inv*

gush [gʌʃ] N (*of liquid*) getto, fiotto; (*of blood*) fiotto; (*of feeling*) ondata

■VI **1** (*also:* **gush out**: *water, blood*): **to gush (from)** sgorgare (da); **water gushed from the pipe** l'acqua sgorgava dal tubo **2** (*pej: enthuse*): **to gush (about** *or* **over)** abbandonarsi ad effusioni; **he gushed about his love for his wife** parlò con eccessivo entusiasmo del suo amore per la moglie

gush·ing ['gʌʃɪŋ] ADJ (*water*) zampillante; (*pej: person*) svenevole; (*: compliments*) affettato

gus·set ['gʌsɪt] N (*in tights, pants*) rinforzo; (*in skirt*) gherone *m*; (*in glove*) quadrello

gust [gʌst] N (*of wind*) folata; (*: stronger*) raffica; (*of rain*) scroscio; (*of smoke*) sbuffo; (*of laughter*) scoppio

> DID YOU KNOW ...?
> **gust** is not translated by the Italian word *gusto*

gus·to ['gʌstəʊ] N: **with gusto** di *or* con gusto

gusty ['gʌstɪ] ADJ (*comp* **-ier**, *superl* **-iest**) (*wind*) a raffiche; (*day*) tempestoso(-a)

gut [gʌt] N **1** (*Anat*) intestino; (*for violin, racket*) minugia, budello; **the human gut** l'intestino umano **2 guts** NPL (*fam: innards*) budella *fpl*; (*: of animals*) interiora *fpl*; (*fig: courage*) fegato; **it takes guts** ci vuole fegato; **blood and guts** sangue e interiora; **to hate sb's guts** odiare qn a morte
■ VT **1** (*poultry, fish*) levare le interiora a, sventrare **2** (*building*): **the blaze gutted the entire building** le fiamme hanno sventrato completamente l'edificio

gut feeling N sensazione *f* istintiva

gut·less ['gʌtlɪs] ADJ (*fam*) vigliacco(-a), che non ha fegato

gut reaction N reazione *f* istintiva

gutsy ['gʌtsɪ] ADJ (*comp* **-ier**, *superl* **-iest**) (*fam: style*) che ha mordente; (*: plucky*) coraggioso(-a)

gutted ['gʌtɪd] ADJ (*fam: upset*) distrutto(-a)

gut·ter ['gʌtəʳ] N (*in street*) cunetta, (canaletta di) scolo; (*on roof*) grondaia; **to rise from the gutter** (*fig*) venire dai bassifondi *or* dalla strada; **I dropped my keys in the gutter** mi sono cadute le chiavi nella canaletta di scolo

gutter press N: **the gutter press** la stampa scandalistica

gutter·snipe ['gʌtə,snaɪp] N scugnizzo

gut·tur·al ['gʌtərəl] ADJ gutturale

guv [gʌv] N (*fam*) capo

◎ **guy¹** [gaɪ] N (*fam: man*) tizio, tipo; (*effigy*) *fantoccio che si brucia la notte di Guy Fawkes*; **a tough guy** un duro; **he's a nice guy** è simpatico; *see also* **wise guy**; **who's that guy?** chi è quel tipo?

guy² [gaɪ] N (*also:* **guy-rope**: *for tent*) tirante *m*, cavo

Guy·ana [gaɪ'ænə] N Guyana

Guy Fawkes Night [-fɔ:ks] N *festeggiamenti del 5 novembre*

GUY FAWKES NIGHT

La sera del 5 novembre, in occasione della **Guy Fawkes Night**, altrimenti chiamata "Bonfire Night", viene commemorato con falò e fuochi d'artificio il fallimento della Congiura delle Polveri contro Giacomo I nel 1605. La festa prende il nome dal principale congiurato della cospirazione, Guy Fawkes, la cui effigie viene bruciata durante i festeggiamenti.
▷ www.guy-fawkes.com
▷ www.bonefire.org/guy/

guz·zle ['gʌzl] VT (*food*) ingozzare; (*drink*) tracannare; (*hum: petrol*) bere
■ VI gozzovigliare

gybe, jibe [dʒaɪb] VI (*Naut*) strambare

gym [dʒɪm] N (*gymnasium*) palestra; (*gymnastics*) ginnastica; **I go to the gym every day** vado in palestra ogni giorno; **gym classes** corso di ginnastica

gym·kha·na [dʒɪm'kɑ:nə] N gimcana

gym·na·sium [dʒɪm'neɪzɪəm] N palestra

gym·nast ['dʒɪmnæst] N ginnasta *m/f*

gym·nas·tic [dʒɪm'næstɪk] ADJ (*display*) di ginnastica; (*skills*) da ginnasta

gym·nas·tics [dʒɪm'næstɪks] NSG (*art*) ginnastica
■ NPL (*exercises*) ginnastica

gym shoes NPL scarpe *fpl* da ginnastica

gymslip ['dʒɪm,slɪp] N (*Brit*) ≈ grembiule *m* di scuola (*per ragazze*)

gy·nae·co·logi·cal, (*Am*) **gy·ne·co·logi·cal** ['gaɪnɪkə'lɒdʒɪkəl] ADJ (*disorder, examination*) ginecologico(-a); (*specialist*) in ginecologia

gy·nae·co·logi·cal·ly, (*Am*) **gy·ne·co·logi·cal·ly** [,gaɪnɪkə'lɒdʒɪkəlɪ] ADV dal punto di vista ginecologico

gy·nae·colo·gist, (*Am*) **gy·ne·colo·gist** [,gaɪnɪ'kɒlədʒɪst] N ginecologo(-a)

gy·nae·col·ogy, (*Am*) **gy·ne·col·ogy** [,gaɪnɪ'kɒlədʒɪ] N ginecologia
▷ www.obgyn.net

gy·noe·cium, (*Am*) **gy·ne·cium** [dʒaɪ'ni:sɪəm] N (*Bot*) gineceo

gyp·sy, gip·sy ['dʒɪpsɪ] N zingaro(-a)
■ ADJ (*life*) da zingaro, zingaresco(-a); (*caravan*) degli zingari; (*music*) zigano(-a)

gy·rate [,dʒaɪə'reɪt] VI (*spin*) roteare, girare (su se stesso); (*dance*) volteggiare

gy·ra·tion [,dʒaɪə'reɪʃən] N (*spinning*) rotazione *f*; (*when dancing: usu pl*) giravolta

gyro... ['dʒaɪərəʊ] PREF giro...

gy·ro·scope ['dʒaɪərəskəʊp] N giroscopio

Hh

H, h [eɪtʃ] N (*letter*) H, h *f or m inv*; **H for Harry**, (*Am*): **H for How** ≈ H come hotel

ha·beas cor·pus ['heɪbɪəs 'kɔ:pəs] N (*Law*) habeas corpus *m inv*

hab·er·dash·er ['hæbə,dæʃəʳ] N (*Brit*) merciaio(-a); (*Am*) camiciaio(-a)

hab·er·dash·ery [,hæbə'dæʃərɪ] N merceria; (*Am*) camiceria

◎ **hab·it** ['hæbɪt] N **1** (*customary behaviour, individual habit*) abitudine *f*; **a bad habit** una brutta *or* cattiva abitudine; **to be in the habit of doing sth** avere l'abitudine di fare qc; **to fall into bad habits** prendere delle cattive abitudini; **to get out of/into the habit of doing sth** perdere/prendere l'abitudine di fare qc; **to get sb into the habit of doing sth** abituare qn a fare qc; **out of sheer habit** solo per abitudine; **don't make a habit of it!** che non diventi un'abitudine! **2** (*dress: of monk, nun*) tonaca; (*: riding habit*) costume *m* da amazzone **3** (*fam: addiction*) assuefazione

> DID YOU KNOW ...?
> **habit** is not translated by the Italian word *abito*

hab·it·able ['hæbɪtəbl] ADJ abitabile

habi·tat ['hæbɪ,tæt] N habitat *m inv*

habi·ta·tion [,hæbɪ'teɪʃən] N abitazione *f*; **fit for human habitation** abitabile

habit-forming ['hæbɪt,fɔ:mɪŋ] ADJ: **to be habit-forming** causare assuefazione

ha·bitu·al [hə'bɪtjʊəl] ADJ abituale, consueto(-a); (*drunkard, smoker*) incallito(-a); (*liar*) inveterato(-a); **his habitual geniality** la sua consueta genialità; **habitual criminals** delinquenti abituali; **a habitual burglar** un ladro incallito

ha·bitu·al·ly [hə'bɪtjʊəlɪ] ADV abitualmente, d'abitudine

hack¹ [hæk] N (*of sword, axe*) colpo; (*of sabre*) fendente *m*
■ VT **1** (*cut*) tagliare; **to hack one's way through** aprirsi un varco (a colpi d'ascia *etc*) tra; **to hack sth to pieces** tagliare a pezzi qc **2 to hack into** (*Comput: program, system*) inserirsi illegalmente in
▶ **hack about** VT + ADV tagliare; **my book's been hacked about terribly by the editor** il mio libro è stato tagliato senza pietà dal redattore
▶ **hack down** VT + ADV (*tree etc*) abbattere (a colpi d'ascia *etc*)

hack² [hæk] N **1** (*old horse*) ronzino; (*ride*) passeggiata a cavallo **2** (*pej: writer*) scribacchino(-a); **to do hack writing** fare lo scribacchino(-a)
■ VI: **to go hacking** (andare a) fare una passeggiata a cavallo

hack·er ['hækəʳ] N (*Comput*) hacker *m/f inv*

hack·ing ['hækɪŋ] ADJ: **a hacking cough** una brutta tosse

hacking jacket N giacca da equitazione

hack·les ['hæklz] NPL: **to make sb's hackles rise** (*fig*) far arrabbiare qn

hack·ney cab ['hæknɪ,kæb] N carrozza a nolo

hack·ney car·riage ['hæknɪ,kærɪdʒ] N (*frm*) auto pubblica

hack·neyed ['hæknɪd] ADJ (*saying*) trito(-a); **hackneyed expression** luogo comune; **a hackneyed metaphor** una metafora trita e ritrita

hack·saw ['hæk,sɔ:] N seghetto per metalli

hack·work ['hæk,wɜ:k] N *prodotto letterario scadente, scritto su ordinazione*

had [hæd] PT, PP *of* **have**

had·dock ['hædək] N eglefino (*tipo di merluzzo*)

Ha·des ['heɪdi:z] N Ade *m*

hadn't ['hædnt] = had not

haema·tol·ogy, (*Am*) **hema·tol·ogy** [,hi:mə'tɒlədʒɪ] N ematologia

haemo·glo·bin, (*Am*) **hemo·glo·bin** [,hi:məʊ'gləʊbɪn] N emoglobina

hae·moly·sis, (*Am*) **he·moly·sis** [hɪ'mɒlɪsɪs] N emolisi *f*

haemo·philia, (*Am*) **hemo·philia** [,hi:məʊ'fɪlɪə] N emofilia

haemo·phili·ac, (*Am*) **hemo·phili·ac** [,hi:məʊ'fɪlɪæk] N emofiliaco(-a)

haem·or·rhage, (*Am*) **hem·or·rhage** ['hɛmərɪdʒ] N emorragia
■ VI avere un'emorragia

Hh

haem·or·rhoids, (*Am*) **hem·or·rhoids** ['hɛmə,rɔɪdz] NPL emorroidi *fpl*
haemo·stat·ic [,hi:məʊ'stætɪk] ADJ (*action, remedy*) antiemorragico(-a)
hag [hæg] N (*ugly*) befana; (*nasty*) megera; (*witch*) strega
hag·gard ['hægəd] ADJ (*careworn*) tirato(-a); (*gaunt*) smunto(-a)
hag·gis ['hægɪs] N (*Scot Culin*) *insaccato a base di avena e frattaglie di pecora*
hag·gle ['hægl] VI: **to haggle (over)** (*bargain*) contrattare (su); (*argue*) discutere (su); **I didn't haggle over the price** non ho contrattato sul prezzo
hag·gling ['hæglɪŋ] N contrattazione *f*
hag-ridden ['hæg,rɪdn] ADJ tormentato(-a)
Hague [heɪg] N: **the Hague** l'Aia
hail[1] [heɪl] N (*Met*) grandine *f*; (*fig: of bullets*) pioggia; (*: of abuse*) valanga
■ VI grandinare; **it's hailing** grandina
hail[2] [heɪl] N (*greeting, call*) grido di saluto; **within hail** a portata d'orecchio
■ EXCL (*old, liter*): **hail, Caesar!** ave, Cesare!
■ VT (*acclaim*): **to hail (as)** acclamare (come); (*greet*) salutare; (*signal: taxi*) fermare; (*call*) chiamare; **he was hailed in the press as a hero** la stampa lo acclamò come un eroe
■ VI: **where does that ship hail from?** qual è il porto di provenienza di quella nave?; **he hails from Scotland** viene dalla Scozia
hail-fellow-well-met ['heɪl,fɛləʊwɛl'mɛt] ADJ (*pej*) che si prende troppa confidenza
Hail Mary N Ave Maria *f inv*
hail·stone ['heɪl,stəʊn] N chicco di grandine
hail·storm ['heɪl,stɔ:m] N grandinata
◎ **hair** [hɛə^r] N **1** (*collective: of person*) capelli *mpl*; (*: on body*) peli *mpl*; (*: of animal*) pelo; **her hair is lovely** ha dei bellissimi capelli; **to comb one's hair** pettinarsi; **to do one's hair** acconciarsi; **to put one's hair up** raccogliersi i capelli; **to have one's hair done** andare dal parrucchiere; **to get one's hair cut** farsi tagliare i capelli; **to remove unwanted hair** (*from legs, armpits*) depilarsi; **to make sb's hair stand on end** far rizzare i capelli (in testa) a qn; **to let one's hair down** (*fig*) lasciarsi andare; **keep your hair on!** (*fam*) datti una calmata! **2** (*single hair: of head*) capello; (*: of body, animal*) pelo; **he's got hairs on his chest** ha il petto villoso; **to split hairs** (*fig*) spaccare il capello in quattro, cercare il pelo nell'uovo; **he didn't turn a hair** non ha battuto ciglio; **try a hair of the dog (that bit you)** (*fam*) prendi un bicchierino per farti passare la sbornia
hair appointment N appuntamento dal parrucchiere
hair·ball ['hɛə,bɔ:l] N palla di pelo
hair·band ['hɛə,bænd] N (*elastic*) fascia per i capelli; (*rigid*) cerchietto
hair·brained ['hɛə,breɪnd] ADJ = **harebrained**
hair·brush ['hɛə,brʌʃ] N spazzola per capelli
hair·cut ['hɛə,kʌt] N taglio (di capelli); **a nice haircut** un bel taglio; **to have** *or* **get a haircut** farsi tagliare i capelli; **I need a haircut** devo tagliarmi i capelli
hair·do ['hɛə,du:] N (*fam*) pettinatura
hair·dresser ['hɛə,drɛsə^r] N parrucchiere(-a); **at the hairdresser's** dal parrucchiere
hair·dressing ['hɛə,drɛsɪŋ] N mestiere *m* di parrucchiere; **to study hairdressing** seguire un corso per parrucchieri
hair-dryer ['hɛə,draɪə^r] N asciugacapelli *m inv*, föhn *m inv*
-haired [hɛəd] ADJ SUFF: **fair/long-haired** dai capelli biondi/lunghi
hair·grip ['hɛə,grɪp] N molletta (per i capelli)
hair·line ['hɛə,laɪn] N attaccatura dei capelli; **to have a receding hairline** essere stempiato(-a)
hairline crack N incrinatura, sottilissima crepa
hairline fracture N (*Med*) frattura capillare
hair·net ['hɛə,nɛt] N retina (per capelli)
hair oil N brillantina
hair·piece ['hɛə,pi:s] N toupet *m inv*
hair·pin ['hɛə,pɪn] N forcina; **fasten it with hairpins** fissalo con delle forcine
hairpin (bend), (*Am*) **hairpin curve** N tornante *m*
hair-raising ['hɛə,reɪzɪŋ] ADJ (*story, adventure*) da far rizzare i capelli, terrificante
hair remover N crema depilatoria
hair's-breadth ['hɛəz,brɛtθ] N: **by a hair's-breadth** per un pelo
hair slide N fermacapelli *m inv*
hair·splitting ['hɛə,splɪtɪŋ] ADJ pedante, cavilloso(-a)
■ N pedanteria
hair spray N lacca per capelli
hair·style ['hɛə,staɪl] N pettinatura, acconciatura
hairy ['hɛərɪ] ADJ (*comp* **-ier**, *superl* **-iest**) **1** peloso(-a), irsuto(-a) **2** (*fam: frightening*) da far rizzare i capelli
Hai·ti ['heɪtɪ] N Haiti *f*
hake [heɪk] N nasello
hal·al [hə'lɑ:l] ADJ: **halal meat** carne macellata secondo la legge mussulmana
hal·cy·on ['hælsɪən] ADJ sereno(-a)
hale [heɪl] ADJ: **hale and hearty** che scoppia di salute
◎ **half** [hɑ:f] N (*pl* **halves**) **1** (*part*) metà *f inv*, mezzo(-a); **half (of it)** la metà; **half (of)** *or* **half the amount of** la metà di; **half of the cake** metà torta; **one half of the apple** la *or* una metà della mela; **half an orange** mezza arancia; **half a dozen** mezza dozzina; **half a pound** mezza libbra; **half a kilo** mezzo chilo; **two and a half** due e mezzo; **half an hour** mezz'ora; **three and a half hours** tre ore e mezza; **half of my friends** (la) metà dei miei amici; **to cut in half/into halves** tagliare a metà/in due; **I can do the job in half the time** posso fare il lavoro in metà del tempo; **half the time I don't know what he's talking about** spesso non so di che cosa stia parlando; **his (or her) better half** (*fam hum*) la sua (dolce) metà; **she doesn't do things by halves** non fa mai le cose a metà; **to go halves (with sb)** fare a metà (con qn); **bigger by half** una volta e mezzo più grande; **he's too clever by half** (*fam*) è troppo furbo per i miei gusti; **one and two halves, please** un biglietto intero e due ridotti, per favore **2** (*Sport: of match*) tempo; (*: of ground*) metà campo; (*player*) mediano; **left/right half** mediano sinistro/destro **3** (*of beer*) mezza pinta **4** (*child's ticket*) (ridotto per) bambino
■ ADJ (*bottle, quantity, fare, pay*) mezzo(-a), metà *inv*; **a half chicken** mezzo pollo; **half a glass** *or* **a half glass** (un) mezzo bicchiere; **half measures** mezze misure *fpl*
■ ADV **1** (a) metà, (a) mezzo; **half empty/closed** mezzo(-a) vuoto(-a)/chiuso(-a), semivuoto(-a)/ semichiuso(-a); **half asleep** mezzo(-a) addormentato(-a); **she's half French, half Italian** è mezza francese, mezza italiana; **half as big (as)** la metà (di); **half as big again** una volta e mezzo più grande; **I was half afraid that ...** avevo un po' paura che... + *sub*; **not half!** (*fam*) altroché!, eccome!; **it isn't half hot!** (*fam*) scotta! **2** (*time*): **half past 3** le 3 e mezza; **half past 12** le 12 e mezza

half-and-half [ˈhɑːfənˈhɑːf] ADV metà e metà
half·back [ˈhɑːfˌbæk] N (*Sport*) mediano
half-baked [ˌhɑːfˈbeɪkt] ADJ (*fig fam: idea, scheme*) mal combinato(-a), che non sta in piedi
half-breed [ˈhɑːfˌbriːd] N mezzosangue *m*
half-brother [ˈhɑːfˌbrʌðəʳ] N fratellastro
half-caste [ˈhɑːfˌkɑːst] N meticcio(-a)
half-circle [ˌhɑːfˈsɜːkl] N semicerchio
half-crown [ˌhɑːfˈkraʊn] N (*Brit: old coin*) mezza corona
half-dead [ˌhɑːfˈdɛd] ADJ: **half-dead (with)** mezzo(-a) morto(-a) (da *or* per)
half-fill [ˌhɑːfˈfɪl] VT riempire a metà
half-hearted [ˌhɑːfˈhɑːtɪd] ADJ (*effort*) poco convinto(-a), svogliato(-a); **he made a half-hearted attempt** ha fatto un mezzo tentativo
half-heartedly [ˌhɑːfˈhɑːtɪdlɪ] ADV svogliatamente
half holiday N mezza giornata di festa
half-hour [ˌhɑːfˈaʊəʳ] N mezz'ora
half-hourly [ˌhɑːfˈaʊəlɪ] ADJ, ADV ogni mezz'ora
half-life [ˌhɑːfˈlaɪf] N (*Phys*) tempo di dimezzamento
half-light [ˌhɑːfˈlaɪt] N semioscurità
half-mast [ˌhɑːfˈmɑːst] N: **at half-mast** (*flag*) a mezz'asta
half-moon [ˌhɑːfˈmuːn] N mezzaluna; **half-moon spectacles** mezze lunette *fpl*
half-nelson [ˌhɑːfˈnɛlsən] N (*Wrestling*) mezza elson *f inv*
half·penny [ˈheɪpnɪ] N (*pl* **-pennies** *or* **-pence** [ˈheɪpəns]) (*Brit*) mezzo penny *m inv*
half-price [ˌhɑːfˈpraɪs] ADV, ADJ a metà prezzo; **I bought it half-price** l'ho comprato a metà prezzo
half-sister [ˌhɑːfˈsɪstəʳ] N sorellastra
half term N (*Brit Scol*) vacanza a *or* di metà trimestre
half-time [ˌhɑːfˈtaɪm] N (*Sport*) intervallo
■ADJ, ADV all'intervallo; **to work half-time** lavorare mezza giornata
half-truth [ˈhɑːfˈtruːθ] N mezza verità *f inv*
half volley N (*Tennis*) demi-volée *f inv*
half·way [ˈhɑːfˈweɪ] ADV a metà strada; **Reading is halfway between Oxford and London** Reading è a metà strada tra Oxford e Londra; **halfway up (** *or* **down) the stairs** a metà delle scale; **to meet sb halfway** (*fig*) arrivare a un compromesso con qn; **halfway through sth** a metà di qc; **halfway through the film** a metà del film; **we are halfway through the work** abbiamo fatto metà del lavoro
■ADJ (*mark*) di mezzo; **halfway line** (*Sport*) linea mediana
halfway house N (*hostel*) *centro di riadattamento alla vita sociale per ex detenuti*; (*fig*) via di mezzo; **to be a halfway house between** essere una via di mezzo tra
half-wit [ˈhɑːfˌwɪt] N grullo(-a), idiota *m/f*
half-witted [ˌhɑːfˈwɪtɪd] ADJ (*reply, action*) da idiota; **a half-witted person** una idiota
half-yearly [ˌhɑːfˈjɪəlɪ] ADV semestralmente, ogni sei mesi
■ADJ semestrale
hali·but [ˈhælɪbət] N ippoglosso, halibut *m inv*
hali·to·sis [ˌhælɪˈtəʊsɪs] N alitosi *f*
◎**hall** [hɔːl] N **1** (*entrance hall*) ingresso, entrata; (*Am: passage*) corridoio; **he hung his coat in the hall** ha appeso il cappotto nell'ingresso; **her room is down the hall** la sua camera è in fondo al corridoio **2** (*large room*) salone *m*, sala; **church hall** sala dell'oratorio; **a concert hall** una sala concerti; **a sports hall** una palestra; **village hall** sala comunale a disposizione del pubblico **3** (*mansion*) palazzo, maniero, grande villa; (*Brit Univ: also:* **hall of residence**) ≈ casa dello studente
hal·le·lu·jah [ˌhælɪˈluːjə] N, EXCL alleluia *m inv*
hall·mark [ˈhɔːlˌmɑːk] N (*also fig*) marchio
hal·lo [həˈləʊ] EXCL = **hello**
hall of fame N (*of distinguished people*) olimpo; (*Am*) museo
hal·lowed [ˈhæləʊd] ADJ **1** (*respected*) celebrato **2** (*Rel: holy*) sacro; **hallowed be Thy name** sia santificato il tuo nome
Hal·low·een [ˈhæləʊˈiːn] N vigilia d'Ognissanti

HALLOWEEN

Secondo la tradizione anglosassone, durante la notte di **Halloween**, il 31 di ottobre, è possibile vedere le streghe e i fantasmi. I bambini, travestiti da fantasmi, streghe, mostri o simili, vanno di porta in porta e raccolgono dolci e piccoli doni.
▷ www.rampantscotland.com/know/blknow_halloween.htm

hall porter N portiere(-a)
hall stand N attaccapanni *m inv* a stelo
hal·lu·ci·nate [həˈluːsɪˌneɪt] VI avere le allucinazioni
hal·lu·ci·na·tion [həˌluːsɪˈneɪʃən] N allucinazione *f*
hal·lu·ci·no·gen·ic [həˌluːsɪnəʊˈdʒɛnɪk] ADJ allucinogeno(-a)
hall·way [ˈhɔːlˌweɪ] N (*corridor*) corridoio; (*entrance*) ingresso
halo [ˈheɪləʊ] N (*of saint*) aureola; (*Astron*) alone *m*
halo·gen [ˈheɪləʊdʒɪn] N alogeno
halogen light N luce *f* alogena
◎**halt** [hɔːlt] N sosta, fermata; (*train stop*) fermata; **to come to a halt** fermarsi, arrestarsi; **to call a halt (to sth)** (*fig*) mettere *or* porre fine (a qc)
■VT (*vehicle, production*) fermare, arrestare; **the government failed to halt economic decline** il governo non è riuscito ad arrestare il declino economico
■VI fermarsi, arrestarsi; **halt!** alt!
hal·ter [ˈhɔːltəʳ] N (*for horse*) cavezza
halter·neck [ˈhɔːltəˌnɛk] ADJ allacciato(-a) dietro il collo
halt·ing [ˈhɔːltɪŋ] ADJ titubante
halt·ing·ly [ˈhɔːltɪŋlɪ] ADV con titubanza
halt sign N segnale *m* d'arresto
halve [hɑːv] VT (*divide*): **to halve (between)** dividere a metà *or* in due (tra); (*reduce by half*) dimezzare, ridurre della metà; **halve the apples** dividi a metà le mele; **the workforce has been halved** la manodopera è stata dimezzata
halves [hɑːvz] NPL *of* **half**
hal·yard [ˈhæljəd] N (*Naut*) drizza
ham [hæm] N **1** (*Culin*) prosciutto; **a ham sandwich** un panino al prosciutto; **ham and eggs** uova *fpl* al prosciutto **2** (*fam: radio ham*) radioamatore(-trice); (*: ham actor*) gigione(-a)
▸ **ham up** VT + ADV: **to ham it up** (*fam*) fare l'esagerato(-a)
Ham·burg [ˈhæmbɜːg] N Amburgo *f*
ham·burg·er [ˈhæmˌbɜːgəʳ] N hamburger *m inv*
ham-fisted [ˌhæmˈfɪstɪd], (*Am*) **ham-handed** [ˌhæmˈhændɪd] ADJ maldestro(-a)
ham·let [ˈhæmlɪt] N paesetto, paesino
ham·mer [ˈhæməʳ] N (*tool*) martello; (*of gun*) percussore *m*; **to go at it hammer and tongs** (*fam: work*) darci dentro; (*: argue*) azzuffarsi

Hh

■VT martellare; (*fig fam: defeat*) stracciare; (*: thrash*) picchiare; **to hammer nails into wood** piantare chiodi nel legno; **to hammer sth into shape** (*metal*) dare una forma a qc col martello; (*fig: team, plan*) mettere a punto qc; **to hammer a point home to sb** cacciare un'idea in testa a qn

■VI dare colpi di martello; **to hammer on** *or* **at the door** picchiare alla porta

▸ **hammer down** VT + ADV (*lid*) fissare con colpi di martello; (*nail*) piantare (a martellate)

▸ **hammer out** VT + ADV (*metal*) spianare (a martellate); (*fig: solution, agreement*) mettere a punto

hammer and sickle N: **the hammer and sickle** la falce e il martello

hammer drill N martello pneumatico

hammer·head ['hæmə,hɛd] N (*shark*) pesce *m* martello *inv*

ham·mock ['hæmək] N amaca

ham·per[1] ['hæmpəʳ] N (*basket*) cesto, cestino

ham·per[2] ['hæmpəʳ] VT (*hinder*) impedire, ostacolare

ham·ster ['hæmstəʳ] N criceto

ham·string ['hæm,strɪŋ] (*vb: pt, pp* **hamstrung**) N (*Anat*) tendine *m* del ginocchio; (*of horse*) corda del garretto

■VT tagliare i tendini delle gambe a; (*fig*) tagliare le gambe a

◎**hand** [hænd] N

1 (*of person*) mano *f*; (*of clock*) lancetta; **to have in one's hand** (*knife, victory*) avere in mano *or* in pugno; (*book, money*) avere in mano; **to take sb by the hand** prendere per mano qn; **on (one's) hands and knees** carponi, a quattro zampe; **wash your hands!** lavati le mani!; **hands up!** (*during hold-up*) mani in alto!; (*to pupils*) alzate la mano!; **hands off!** (*fam*) giù le mani!; **to be clever** *or* **good with one's hands** avere le mani d'oro; **made/delivered by hand** fatto(-a)/ consegnato(-a) a mano; **to live from hand to mouth** vivere alla giornata; **they gave him a big hand** (*fig*) gli hanno fatto un bell'applauso

2 (*worker: in factory*) operaio(-a), manovale *m*; (*: farm hand*) bracciante *m/f*; (*: deck hand*) marinaio; **all hands on deck!** (*Naut*) tutti in coperta!; **to be an old hand** essere vecchio(-a) del mestiere

3 (*liter: handwriting*) scrittura, mano *f*; **in one's own hand** di proprio pugno, di propria mano

4 (*Cards*) mano *f*; **a hand of bridge/poker** una mano a bridge/poker

5 (*measurement: of horse*) ≈ dieci centimetri

6 (*phrases with verb*): **to be hand in glove with sb** essere in combutta con qn; **to change hands** (*property*) cambiare (di) mano; **to force sb's hand** forzare la mano a qn; **to give** *or* **lend sb a hand** dare una mano a qn; **to keep one's hand in** tenersi in esercizio, non perdere la mano; **she can turn her hand to anything** sa fare un po' di tutto; **he asked for her hand (in marriage)** ha chiesto la sua mano; **to wait on sb hand and foot** essere a totale disposizione di qn; **to have one's hands full (with sb/sth)** essere troppo preso(-a) (con qn/qc); **to win hands down** vincere senza difficoltà; **to be making/losing money hand over fist** fare/perdere un sacco di soldi; **to have a free hand** avere carta bianca; **to have the upper hand** avere la meglio *or* il sopravvento; **to have a hand in sth** essere immischiato(-a) in qc

7 (*phrases with prep before n*): **at hand** a portata di mano; **to be near** *or* **close at hand** essere a due passi; **at first hand** di prima mano; **hand in hand** mano nella mano; **to go hand in hand (with)** (*fig*) andare insieme (a); **to be in sb's hands** essere nelle mani di qn; **in hand** (*work*) in corso; **to have £50 in hand** avere ancora 50 sterline a disposizione; **we have the situation in hand** abbiamo la situazione sotto controllo; **we have the matter in hand** ci stiamo occupando della cosa; **to take sb in hand** controllare qn; **to play into sb's hands** fare il gioco di qn; **to fall into the hands of the enemy** cadere in mano al nemico; **on hand** (*person*) disponibile; (*object*) sottomano, a portata di mano; (*emergency services*) pronto(-a) a intervenire; **on the right/left hand** sulla destra/sinistra; **on the other hand** d'altra parte; **on the one hand ..., on the other hand ...** da un lato..., dall'altro...; **to have sth left on one's hands** ritrovarsi con qc, rimanere con qc; **to take sth off sb's hands** togliere qc di torno a qn; **to condemn sb out of hand** condannare qn a priori; **to get out of hand** sfuggire di mano; **to hand** (*information*) a portata di mano

■VT (*pass*): **to hand sb sth, hand sth to sb** passare qc a qn; **he handed me the book** mi passò il libro; **you've got to hand it to him** (*fam*) questo glielo devi riconoscere; **it was handed to him on a plate** (*fam*) glielo hanno dato su un piatto d'argento

▸ **hand back** VT + ADV restituire

▸ **hand down** VT + ADV (*suitcase*) passare, dare (*con movimento dall'alto al basso*); (*tradition*) tramandare; (*heirloom*) lasciare in eredità; (*Am: sentence, verdict*) emettere

▸ **hand in** VT + ADV (*form*) consegnare; (*resignation*) rassegnare, dare; **Martin handed his exam paper in** Martin consegnò il compito scritto

▸ **hand on** VT + ADV trasmettere, dare, passare

▸ **hand out** VT + ADV (*leaflets*) distribuire; (*advice*) elargire; **the teacher handed out the books** l'insegnante distribuì i libri

▸ **hand over** VT + ADV consegnare; (*powers, property, business*) cedere; **she handed the keys over to me** mi ha consegnato le chiavi

▸ **hand round** VT + ADV (*information, papers*) far circolare; (*distribute: chocolates, cakes*) far girare; (*subj: hostess*) offrire

hand·bag ['hænd,bæg] N borsa, borsetta

hand baggage N bagaglio a mano

hand·ball ['hænd,bɔːl] N pallamano *f*; **we played handball** giocavamo a pallamano

▷ www.ihf.info

hand·basin ['hænd,beɪsn] N lavandino

hand·bell ['hænd,bɛl] N campanello (*strumento musicale*)

hand·bill ['hænd,bɪl] N volantino

hand·book ['hænd,bʊk] N (*manual*) manuale *m*, libretto di istruzioni; (*for tourists*) guida (turistica)

hand·brake ['hænd,breɪk] N freno a mano

handbrake lever N leva del freno a mano

h & c ABBR (*Brit*) = *hot and cold (water)*

hand·clap ['hændklæp] N applauso; **a slow handclap** un applauso lento di disapprovazione

hand controls NPL (*Aut*) comandi *mpl* manuali

hand cream N crema per le mani

hand·cuff ['hænd,kʌf] VT ammanettare

■N: **handcuffs** NPL manette *fpl*

hand·ful ['hændfʊl] N (*quantity*) manciata, pugno; **a handful of sand** una manciata di sabbia; **a handful of people** un gruppetto di persone; **that child's a real handful** (*fam*) quel bambino è proprio un terremoto

hand grenade N bomba a mano

hand-held ['hænd'hɛld] ADJ a mano
■ N portatile *m inv*
handi·cap ['hændɪ,kæp] N (*fig, Sport*) handicap *m inv*
■ VT (*disable*) handicappare, menomare; (*hamper*) ostacolare; **high levels of stress may handicap students** un alto livello di stress può essere d'ostacolo agli studenti; **to be mentally handicapped** essere un handicappato mentale; **to be physically handicapped** essere handicappato
handi·capped ['hændɪ,kæpt] ADJ handicappato(-a), portatore(-trice) di handicap
handi·craft ['hændɪ,krɑːft] N (*art*) lavoro artigianale; **handicrafts** NPL (*products*) prodotti di artigianato
handi·work ['hændɪ,wɜːk] N (*work*) lavoro, opera; (*craft work*) lavorazione *f* a mano; **this looks like his handiwork** (*pej*) qui c'è il suo zampino
hand·ker·chief ['hæŋkətʃɪf] N fazzoletto
hand-knitted [,hænd'nɪtɪd] ADJ (*jumper*) fatto(-a) a mano
◎ **han·dle** ['hændl] N (*gen*) manico; (*of knife*) manico, impugnatura; (*of door, drawer*) maniglia; (*of wheelbarrow*) stanga; (*of pump*) braccio; (*for winding*) manovella; (*of cup*) ansa; **he was too small to reach the door handle** era troppo piccolo per arrivare alla maniglia della porta; **a knife with a plastic handle** un coltello con il manico di plastica; **to fly off the handle** (*fig*) perdere le staffe, uscire dai gangheri
■ VT **1** (*touch*) toccare; **"handle with care"** "fragile"; **the police handled him roughly** è stato malmenato dalla polizia; **to handle the ball** (*Ftbl*) fare un fallo di mano **2** (*deal with: theme*) trattare; (*: situation*) far fronte a; (*: resources*) amministrare; (*cope with: people*) saper come prendere; (*: animals*) occuparsi di; (*Comm: goods*) trattare, occuparsi di; (*ship, car*) manovrare; (*use: gun, machine, money*) maneggiare; **I'll handle this** me ne occupo io, ci penso io; **Kath handled the travel arrangements** Kath si è occupata dell'organizzazione del viaggio; **she knows how to handle her son** sa come prendere suo figlio; **she's good at handling children** sa come trattare i bambini; **it was a difficult situation, but he handled it well** era una situazione difficile, ma l'ha gestita bene; **we handle 2000 travellers a day** abbiamo un traffico di 2000 passeggeri al giorno
■ VI (*ship, plane, car*) rispondere ai comandi
handle·bars ['hændl,bɑːz] NPL, **handle·bar** ['hændl,bɑːʳ] N (*on bicycle*) manubrio
han·dler ['hændləʳ] N (*dog handler*) addestratore(-trice) (di cane)
han·dling ['hændlɪŋ] N **1** (*touching, fingering*) maneggio; **these goods have been damaged through too much handling** questa merce è danneggiata perché è stata maneggiata troppo **2** (*of theme, animals*) trattamento; (*of resources*) amministrazione *f*; (*of car, ship*) controllo; (*of gun*) maneggiamento; **he was criticized for his handling of the situation/the crowd** fu criticato per il suo modo di affrontare *or* trattare la situazione/la folla
handling charges NPL (*for goods*) commissione *f* per la prestazione; (*Banking*) spese *fpl* bancarie
hand-luggage ['hænd,lʌgɪdʒ] N bagaglio a mano
hand·made [,hænd'meɪd] ADJ (*clothes, paper*) fatto(-a) a mano; (*biscuits*) fatto(-a) in casa
hand-me-down ['hændmɪ,daʊn] N vestito smesso
hand·out ['hænd,aʊt] N (*leaflet*) volantino; (*press handout*) comunicato stampa; (*at lecture*) fotocopia; (*fam: money*) elemosina; **a state handout** una sovvenzione statale
hand-picked [,hænd'pɪkt] ADJ (*staff, team*) scelto(-a); (*produce*) scelto(-a), selezionato(-a)
hand·rail ['hænd,reɪl] N (*on staircase*) corrimano
hand·saw ['hænd,sɔː] N sega a mano
hand·set ['hændset] N (*Telec*) ricevitore *m*
hands-free ['hændzfriː] ADJ (*telephone*) con auricolare; (*microphone*) vivavoce *inv*
hand·shake ['hænd,ʃeɪk] N stretta di mano
hand·shaking ['hænd,ʃeɪkɪŋ] N (*Comput*) *procedura di sincronizzazione delle comunicazioni*
hand·some ['hænsəm] ADJ (*comp* **-r**, *superl* **-st**) (*gen*) bello(-a); (*salary*) buono(-a); (*considerable: profit, fortune*) considerevole, grosso(-a); (*reward*) generoso(-a); **my father's very handsome** mio padre è un bell'uomo
hand·some·ly ['hænsəmlɪ] ADV (*generously*) generosamente; (*attractively*) graziosamente
hands-on [,hændz'ɒn] ADJ (*approach*) pragmatico(-a); (*training*) pratico(-a); **hands-on experience** esperienza diretta *or* pratica
hand·spring ['hænd,sprɪŋ] N salto sulle mani
hand·stand ['hænd,stænd] N: **to do a handstand** fare la verticale
hand-to-hand ['hændtə'hænd] ADJ, ADV corpo a corpo
hand-to-mouth [,hændtə'maʊθ] ADJ (*existence*) precario(-a)
hand towel N asciugamani *m inv*
hand·writing ['hænd,raɪtɪŋ] N scrittura, calligrafia
hand·written ['hænd,rɪtn] ADJ (*gen*) scritto(-a) a mano, manoscritto(-a); (*text, musical score*) manoscritto(-a)
handy ['hændɪ] ADJ (*comp* **-ier**, *superl* **-iest**) **1** (*close at hand*) a portata di mano, sottomano **2** (*convenient*) comodo(-a); (*useful: machine, gadget*) pratico(-a), utile; **this knife's very handy** questo coltello è molto pratico; **have you got a pen handy?** hai una penna a portata di mano?; **to come in handy** tornare utile; **that would come in very handy** farebbe proprio molto comodo; **the money came in very handy** il denaro è tornato molto utile **3** (*fam: skilful*) bravo(-a); **he's handy with a paintbrush** è proprio bravo come imbianchino
handy·man ['hændɪ,mæn] N (*pl* **-men**) (*paid*) tuttofare *m inv*; (*amateur*) *uno bravo a fare piccole riparazioni e lavoretti*; **tools for the handyman** arnesi per il fai-da-te; **the hotel's handyman** il tuttofare dell'albergo
◎ **hang** [hæŋ] (*pt, pp* **hung**) VT
1 (*gen*) appendere; (*washing*) stendere; (*door*) montare (sui cardini); (*wallpaper*) mettere, incollare; (*coat, hat*): **to hang (on)** appendere (a); **Mike hung the painting on the wall** Mike ha appeso il quadro al muro; **the walls were hung with tapestries** i muri erano coperti di arazzi; **the Christmas tree was hung with lights** l'albero di Natale era decorato di *or* con luci colorate
2 (*pt, pp* **hanged**) (*criminal*) impiccare; **in the past criminals were hanged** in passato i criminali venivano impiccati; **hang (it)!** (*fam*) accidenti!, porca miseria!
3 **to hang one's head** abbassare la testa (per la vergogna)
■ VI
1 (*rope, dangling object*): **to hang (from)** penzolare (da), pendere (da); (*garment*) cadere; (*hair*) scendere; (*criminal*) essere impiccato(-a); **there was a red bulb hanging from the ceiling** c'era una lampadina rossa che pendeva dal soffitto; **that dress hangs well** quel vestito cade bene

Hh

2 to hang over (*smoke, fog*) sovrastare; (*threat*) incombere su; (*hawk*) essere sospeso(-a) su
■ N: **he couldn't get the hang of the game** (*fam*) non riusciva ad afferrare il senso del gioco; **you'll soon get the hang of this** (*fam*) ti farai presto la mano a questo
▸ **hang about** VI + ADV (*also:* **hang around**: *loiter*) gironzolare, ciondolare; (*: wait*) rimanere ad aspettare; **to keep sb hanging about** far aspettare qn; **they hang around all day playing computer games** non fanno niente tutto il giorno e giocano col computer; **don't hang about, there's work to do** non perder tempo, c'è un sacco di lavoro da fare
■ VI + PREP (*the streets*) aggirarsi per
▸ **hang back** VI + ADV (*hesitate*): **to hang back (from doing)** essere riluttante (a fare)
▸ **hang down** VI + ADV ricadere
■ VT + ADV far ricadere
▸ **hang on** VI + PREP
1 (*depend on: decision*) dipendere da
2 (*listen eagerly*) bersi le parole di; **she hung on his every word** pendeva dalle sue labbra
■ VI + ADV
1 (*keep hold*): **to hang on (to)** aggrapparsi (a), attaccarsi (a); **to hang on to** (*keep*) tenere
2 (*fam: wait*) aspettare; **hang on a minute!** aspetta un momento!; (*polite: on phone*) attenda un attimo!
▸ **hang out** VT + ADV (*washing*) stendere (fuori); (*flags*) metter fuori
■ VI + ADV
1 to hang out of sth penzolare *or* pendere fuori da qc; **his shirt was hanging out** gli usciva la camicia dai pantaloni
2 (*fam: frequent*) frequentare; **he hangs out in the local bars** bazzica nei bar locali
▸ **hang together** VI + ADV (*fam: people*) stare insieme; (*cohere: argument*) stare in piedi
▸ **hang up** VT + ADV (*coat*) appendere; (*picture*) attaccare, appendere
■ VI + ADV (*Telec*) riattaccare, riagganciare; **to hang up on sb** metter giù il ricevitore a qn

hang·ar ['hæŋəʳ] N hangar *m inv*, aviorimessa

hang·dog ['hæŋ,dɒg] ADJ (*guilty: look, expression*) da cane bastonato

hang·er ['hæŋəʳ] N (*for clothes*) ometto, gruccia

hanger-on [,hæŋə'rɒn] N (*pl* **hangers-on**) (*pej*) parassita *m/f*

hang-glider ['hæŋ,glaɪdəʳ] N deltaplano (*velivolo*)

hang-gliding ['hæŋ,glaɪdɪŋ] N (volo col) deltaplano

hang·ing ['hæŋɪŋ] N **1** (*execution*) impiccagione *f* **2** (*curtains*): **hangings** NPL tende *fpl*, tendaggi *mpl*
■ ADJ (*bridge*) sospeso(-a); (*offence, matter*) da punire con l'impiccagione; **hanging lamp** lampadario

hang·man ['hæŋmən] N (*pl* **-men**) boia *m inv*

hang-out ['hæŋ,aʊt] N (*fam*) ritrovo

hang·over ['hæŋ,əʊvəʳ] N **1** (*after drinking*) postumi *mpl* della sbornia; **I woke up with a hangover** mi sono svegliato con un cerchio alla testa **2** (*sth left over*) residuato

hang-up ['hæŋ,ʌp] N (*fam*) complesso, ossessione *f*

hank [hæŋk] N (*of wool*) matassa; (*of hair*) ciocca; (*Naut*) garroccio

hank·er ['hæŋkəʳ] VI: **to hanker after** *or* **for** (*fame, power*) essere assetato(-a) di, bramare; (*sympathy, possessions*) desiderare intensamente

hank·er·ing ['hæŋkərɪŋ] N: **to have a hankering for sth/to do sth** avere una voglia matta di qc/di fare qc

hanky ['hæŋkɪ] N (*fam: handkerchief*) fazzoletto

hanky-panky ['hæŋkɪ'pæŋkɪ] N (*fam*): **there's some hanky-panky going on here** qui c'è del losco; **you can drive me home, but no hanky-panky!** puoi portarmi a casa se tieni le mani a posto!

Hannibal ['hænɪbəl] N Annibale *m*

Hants ABBR (*Brit*) = *Hampshire*

ha'penny ['heɪpnɪ] N = **halfpenny**

hap·haz·ard [,hæp'hæzəd] ADJ (fatto(-a)) a caso *or* a casaccio; (*arrangement*) casuale, fortuito(-a)

hap·haz·ard·ly [,hæp'hæzədlɪ] ADV a caso, a casaccio

hap·less ['hæplɪs] (*liter*) ADJ (*wretched*) disgraziato(-a); (*unfortunate*) sventurato(-a)

hap·loid ['hæplɔɪd] ADJ, N (*Bio*) aploide (*m*)

◎ **hap·pen** ['hæpən] VI **1** succedere, accadere, capitare; **what's happening?** cosa succede?, cosa sta succedendo?; **what happened?** cos'è successo?; **these things will happen** sono cose che capitano *or* succedono; **don't let it happen again** che non si ripeta *or* succeda mai più; **as if nothing had happened** come se niente fosse; **what has happened to him?** (*befallen*) cosa gli è successo?; (*become of*) che fine ha fatto?; **if anything should happen to him ...** se gli dovesse accadere qualcosa... **2** (*chance*): **it happened that ...** si dava il caso che...; **do you happen to know if ...** sai per caso se...; **if anyone should happen to see John** se a qualcuno capita di vedere John; **I happen to know that ...** si dà il caso che io sappia che...; **she happened to be free** per caso era libera; **as it happens** (per) combinazione; **it so happened that ...** guarda caso...
▸ **happen (up)on** VI + PREP imbattersi in

hap·pen·ing ['hæpnɪŋ] N (*event*) avvenimento, evento; (*in theatre*) happening *m inv*

hap·pen·stance ['hæpən,stæns] N (*Am fam*) combinazione *f*

hap·pi·ly ['hæpɪlɪ] ADV (*contentedly: play, work*) tranquillamente; (*cheerfully: say*) con gioia; (*: laugh*) con allegria; (*fortunately*) per fortuna, fortunatamente; **he's happily married** è felicemente sposato; **and they lived happily ever after** e vissero per sempre felici e contenti; **happily, everything went well** fortunatamente tutto è andato bene

hap·pi·ness ['hæpɪnɪs] N felicità, contentezza, gioia

◎ **hap·py** ['hæpɪ] ADJ (*comp* **-ier**, *superl* **-iest**) **1** (*pleased, content*) contento(-a), felice; (*cheerful*) allegro(-a); (*at ease, unworried*) tranquillo(-a); **Janet looks happy** Janet sembra felice; **happy with** (*arrangements*) soddisfatto(-a) di; **we are not entirely happy about the plan** non siamo del tutto contenti del progetto; **we're very happy for you** ci rallegriamo per te, siamo molto felici per te; **yes, I'd be happy to** (certo,) con piacere, (ben) volentieri; **I'm very happy with your work** sono molto soddisfatto del tuo lavoro; **I am happy to tell you that ...** sono felice *or* ho il piacere di informarti che...; **a happy ending** un lieto fine; **to be as happy as a lark** essere felice *or* contento(-a) come una pasqua; **happy birthday!** buon compleanno!; **happy Christmas/New Year!** buon Natale/anno!
2 (*well-chosen: phrase, idea*) felice, indovinato(-a); (*lucky: position*) fortunato(-a), favorevole; **by a happy chance** per fortuna

happy event N (*euph*) lieto evento

happy-go-lucky ['hæpɪgəʊ,lʌkɪ] ADJ spensierato(-a)

happy hour N *orario in cui le consumazioni alcoliche in un bar hanno prezzi ridotti*

happy medium N giusta via di mezzo

Hapsburg ['hæps,bɜ:g] N Asburgo

ha·rangue [hə'ræŋ] N tirata, arringa
■VT arringare
har·ass ['hærəs] VT *(attack persistently)* tormentare; *(trouble)* assillare; **she was sexually harassed** ha subito molestie sessuali
har·assed ['hærəst] ADJ *(under attack)* tormentato(-a); *(troubled)* assillato(-a); *(under pressure)* stressato(-a); **you look harassed** hai una faccia sconvolta
har·ass·ment ['hærəsmənt] N *(action)* persecuzione *f*; *(less severe)* molestia; *(feeling)* insofferenza; **sexual harassment** molestie sessuali
◎**har·bour**, *(Am)* **har·bor** ['hɑ:bər] N porto
■VT *(hold: grudge, resentment)* covare, nutrire; *(shelter: criminal, spy)* dar rifugio a, tener nascosto(-a)
harbour dues, *(Am)* **harbor dues** NPL diritti *mpl* portuali
harbour master, *(Am)* **harbor master** N capitano di porto
◎**hard** [hɑ:d] *(comp* **-er**, *superl* **-est***)* ADJ **1** *(substance)* duro(-a); *(mud)* indurito(-a); **this cheese is very hard** questo formaggio è davvero duro; **to grow hard** indurirsi; **hard cover** *(of book)* copertina cartonata; **a hard nut to crack** *(problem, person)* un osso duro **2** *(severe, tough: gen)* duro(-a); *(: climate, weather, winter)* rigido(-a); *(: frost)* forte; **to take a long hard look at sth** esaminare qc attentamente; **the hard fact is that ...** la verità nuda e cruda è che...; **hard lines!** *or* **hard luck!** *(Brit fam)* peccato!, scalogna!; **a hard luck story** una storia pietosa; **he's as hard as nails** *(physically)* è forte come un toro *or* una quercia; *(in temperament)* è duro di cuore; **to take a hard line over sth** adottare una linea dura in merito a qc; **to be hard on sb** essere severo(-a) con qn; **to be a hard worker** essere una gran/grande lavoratore(-trice) **3** *(difficult: gen)* arduo(-a), difficile; **this exercise is too hard for me** quest'esercizio è troppo difficile per me; **I find it hard to believe that ...** stento *or* faccio fatica a credere che... *+ sub*; **to be hard to please** essere esigente, essere difficile da accontentare
■ADV *(push)* forte; *(work)* sodo; *(think, try)* bene; *(hit)* forte, duramente; **to work hard** lavorare sodo; **to freeze hard** gelare; **it's snowing/raining hard** sta nevicando/piovendo forte; **he was breathing hard** respirava affannosamente; **to be hard hit** *(fig)* essere duramente colpito(-a); **to be hard done by** *(fam)* essere trattato(-a) ingiustamente *or* molto male; **to be hard at it** *(fam)* darci dentro; **to be hard put (to it) to do sth** essere in difficoltà a fare qc; **to try one's hardest to do sth** fare di tutto per fare qc; **to take sth hard** prendere (molto) male qc; **to be hard up for sth** essere a corto di qc; **to look hard at** guardare fissamente, esaminare attentamente; **to drink hard** essere una forte bevitore(-trice)
hard-and-fast [ˌhɑ:dən'fɑ:st] ADJ ferreo(-a)
hard·back ['hɑ:dˌbæk] N *(book)* libro con copertina rigida *or* in edizione rilegata
■ADJ *(edition)* rilegato(-a)
hard-bitten [ˌhɑ:d'bɪtn] ADJ duro(-a)
hard·board ['hɑ:dˌbɔ:d] N faesite *f*
hard-boiled [ˌhɑ:d'bɔɪld] ADJ *(egg)* sodo(-a); *(fig: tough, cynical)* duro(-a)
hard cash N (denaro) contante
hard copy N copia su carta; **on hard copy** su carta; *(Comput)* hard copy *f inv*
hard-core [ˌhɑ:d'kɔ:r] ADJ **1** *(pornography)* hard-core *inv* **2** *(supporters)* irriducibile
■N **1** *(supporters)* zoccolo duro **2** *(for roads, foundations)* massicciata
hard court N *(Tennis)* campo in terra battuta
hard·cover ['hɑ:dˌkʌvər] N *(Am)* libro con copertina rigida *or* in edizione rilegata
hard disk N *(Comput)* hard disk *m inv*, disco rigido
hard drink N l'alcol *m*
hard drug N droga pesante
hard-earned ['hɑ:dˌɜ:nd] ADJ *(money)* sudato(-a), guadagnato(-a) a fatica; *(rest, praise)* meritato(-a)
hard·en ['hɑ:dn] VT *(gen)* indurire; *(steel)* temprare; *(fig: determination)* rafforzare; **to harden one's heart** non lasciarsi commuovere
■VI *(substance)* indurirsi; **the glue soon hardens** la colla si indurisce presto
hard·ened ['hɑ:dnd] ADJ *(criminal)* incallito(-a); **to be hardened to sth** essere (diventato(-a)) insensibile a qc
hard·en·ing ['hɑ:dnɪŋ] N indurimento
hard feeling N rancore *m*; **no hard feelings?** amici come prima?
hard-fought [ˌhɑ:d'fɔ:t] ADJ *(battle, campaign)* accanito(-a)
hard graft N: **by sheer hard graft** lavorando da matti
hard hat N *(for worker)* casco; *(for horse rider)* cap *m inv*
hard-headed [ˌhɑ:d'hɛdɪd] ADJ pratico(-a)
hard-hearted [ˌhɑ:d'hɑ:tɪd] ADJ che non si lascia commuovere, dal cuore duro
hard-hitting [ˌhɑ:d'hɪtɪŋ] ADJ molto duro(-a); **a hard-hitting documentary** un documentario verità *inv*
har·di·ness ['hɑ:dɪnɪs] N robustezza
hard labour N lavori *mpl* forzati
◎**hard·liner** [ˌhɑ:d'laɪnər] N sostenitore(-trice) *or* fautore(-trice) della linea dura
hard-luck story [ˌhɑ:d'lʌkˌstɔ:rɪ] N storia lacrimosa *(per commuovere qn)*
◎**hard·ly** ['hɑ:dlɪ] ADV *(scarcely)* appena, a mala pena; **she can hardly read** riesce a malapena a leggere; **that can hardly be true** non può essere vero; **I hardly know him** lo conosco appena; **it's hardly the case** non è proprio il caso; **I can hardly believe it** stento a crederci; **I need hardly point out that ...** non c'è bisogno che io faccia notare che...; **this is hardly the time** non è di sicuro il momento; **hardly anyone/anything** quasi nessuno/niente; **I've got hardly any money** ho pochissimo denaro; **hardly ever** quasi mai; **hardly anywhere** quasi da nessuna parte; **hardly!** figuriamoci!, neanche per idea!
hard·ness ['hɑ:dnɪs] N *(gen)* durezza
hard-nosed [ˌhɑ:d'nəʊzd] ADJ *(fam: person)* duro(-a); *(: attitude)* da duro
hard of hearing ADJ duro(-a) d'orecchio
hard-pressed [ˌhɑ:d'prɛst] ADJ in difficoltà
hard rock N *(Mus)* hard rock *m inv*, rock duro *m inv*
hard sell N *(Comm)* tecnica aggressiva di vendita; **I don't like his hard sell approach** non mi piace quel suo approccio così aggressivo
hard·ship ['hɑ:dʃɪp] N privazioni *fpl*, avversità *f inv*; *(suffering)* sofferenze *fpl*; **a life of hardship** una vita di sacrifici e privazioni; **economic hardship** difficoltà *fpl* economiche; **the worst hardship is being separated from my family** il sacrificio più grande per me è vivere separato dalla famiglia
hard shoulder N *(Brit Aut)* corsia d'emergenza
hard up ADJ *(fam)*: **to be hard up** essere a corto di soldi
hard·ware ['hɑ:dˌwɛər] N *(for domestic use)* ferramenta *fpl*; *(Mil)* armamenti *mpl*; *(Comput)* hardware *m*

Hh

hardware shop, (*Am*) **hardware store** N (negozio di) ferramenta
hard-wearing [ˌhɑːdˈwɛərɪŋ] ADJ (*gen*) resistente, robusto(-a); (*shoes*) robusto(-a)
hard-wired [ˈhɑːdwaɪəd] ADJ (*Comput*) che fa parte dell'hardware; (*abilities, tendencies etc*) radicato(-a)
hard-won [ˌhɑːdˈwʌn] ADJ sudato(-a)
hard·wood [ˈhɑːdˌwʊd] N legno duro
hard-working [ˌhɑːdˈwɜːkɪŋ] ADJ che lavora sodo
har·dy [ˈhɑːdɪ] ADJ (*comp* **-ier**, *superl* **-iest**) forte, robusto(-a); (*Bot*) resistente al gelo; **hardy people** gente robusta; **hardy plants** piante resistenti al gelo
hare [hɛəʳ] N lepre *f*
hare·bell [ˈhɛəˌbɛl] N campanella scozzese
hare·brained, **hair·brained** [ˈhɛəˌbreɪnd] ADJ scervellato(-a)
hare·lip [ˌhɛəˈlɪp] N labbro leporino
har·em [hɑːˈriːm] N harem *m inv*
hari·cot [ˈhærɪkəʊ] N (*also:* **haricot bean**) fagiolo bianco
hark [hɑːk] VI: **hark!** (*liter*) udite!; **hark at him!** (*fam*) ma sentilo!
▸ **hark back** VI + PREP: **to hark back to** (*former days*) rievocare; (*earlier occasion*) ritornare a *or* su
◎ **harm** [hɑːm] N (*gen*) male *m*; (*damage*) danno; **to do sb harm** far del male a qn; **to do harm to** (*reputation, interests*) danneggiare; **out of harm's way** al sicuro; **to keep out of harm's way** tenersi alla larga; **there's no harm in trying** tentar non nuoce; **it might do more harm than good** potrebbe fare più male che bene; **you will come to no harm** non ti succederà nulla; **he means no harm** non ha nessuna cattiva intenzione; **he meant no harm by what he said** non l'ha detto con cattiveria
■ VT (*person*) far male a; (*reputation, interests, health*) danneggiare, nuocere a; (*object, crops*) danneggiare
harm·ful [ˈhɑːmfʊl] ADJ: **harmful (to)** dannoso(-a) (a), nocivo(-a) (a)
harm·less [ˈhɑːmlɪs] ADJ (*gen*) innocuo(-a), inoffensivo(-a); (*innocent: conversation, joke*) innocente
har·mon·ic [hɑːˈmɒnɪk] ADJ armonico(-a)
har·moni·ca [hɑːˈmɒnɪkə] N armonica a bocca
har·mon·ics [hɑːˈmɒnɪks] NPL (*Mus*) armonia
■ NSG (*Phys*) armonica
har·mo·ni·ous [hɑːˈməʊnɪəs] ADJ armonioso(-a)
har·mo·nium [hɑːˈməʊnɪəm] N armonium *m inv*
har·mo·nize [ˈhɑːməˌnaɪz] VT (*Mus*) armonizzare; (*colours*) intonare, armonizzare
■ VI (*Mus*) armonizzare; **to harmonize (with)** (*colours*) armonizzarsi con, intonarsi (a)
har·mo·ny [ˈhɑːmənɪ] N armonia
har·ness [ˈhɑːnɪs] N (*for horse*) bardatura, finimenti *mpl*; (*for baby*) briglie *fpl*; (*safety harness*) imbracatura; **to get back into harness** (*fig*) tornare al lavoro consueto; **to die in harness** (*fig*) morire sul lavoro *or* sulla breccia
■ VT (*horse*) bardare, mettere i finimenti a; (*: to carriage*) attaccare a; (*resources*) sfruttare; **attempts to harness natural energy** tentativi di sfruttare le fonti energetiche naturali
harp [hɑːp] N arpa
▸ **harp on** VI + ADV (*fam*): **to harp on (about)** continuare a menarla (con)
harp·ist [ˈhɑːpɪst] N arpista *m/f*
har·poon [hɑːˈpuːn] N arpione *m*
■ VT arpionare
harp·si·chord [ˈhɑːpsɪˌkɔːd] N clavicembalo, cembalo
Har·py [ˈhɑːpɪ] N (*Myth, fig*) arpia
har·row [ˈhærəʊ] (*Agr*) N erpice *m*
■ VT erpicare
har·row·ing [ˈhærəʊɪŋ] ADJ (*experience, story*) straziante, sconvolgente
har·ry [ˈhærɪ] VT (*pester*) assillare; (*attack persistently*) attaccare
harsh [hɑːʃ] ADJ (*comp* **-er**, *superl* **-est**) **1** (*punishment, person*) severo(-a), duro(-a); (*words*) duro(-a); (*weather*) rigido(-a); (*taste*) pungente; **a harsh climate** un clima rigido **2** (*discordant: voice*) sgradevole; (*: colour*) chiassoso(-a), squillante; (*light*) troppo forte; (*contrast*) brusco(-a); **she's got a very harsh voice** ha una voce molto sgradevole
harsh·ly [ˈhɑːʃlɪ] ADV (*treat, punish*) duramente; (*speak*) duramente, aspramente
harsh·ness [ˈhɑːʃnɪs] N **1** (*of punishment, person*) durezza; (*of weather*) inclemenza; (*of taste*) asprezza; (*of cloth*) ruvidezza **2** (*of voice*) sgradevolezza; (*of colour*) chiassosità; (*of light*) intensità; (*of contrast*) violenza
har·te·beest [ˈhɑːtɪˌbiːst] N alcelafo
harum-scarum [ˈhɛərəmˈskɛərəm] ADJ sfrenato(-a), scatenato(-a)
■ ADV sfrenatamente, in modo scatenato
har·vest [ˈhɑːvɪst] N (*of crop*) raccolto; (*of grapes*) vendemmia; **a poor harvest** un raccolto scarso
■ VT (*gen*) fare il raccolto di, raccogliere; (*grain*) mietere; (*grapes*) vendemmiare; **they're harvesting the olives** stanno raccogliendo le olive
■ VI (*on farm*) fare il raccolto, mietere; (*in vineyard*) vendemmiare
har·vest·er [ˈhɑːvɪstəʳ] N (*person*) mietitore(-trice); (*machine*) mietitrice *f*; (*combine harvester*) mietitrebbia
harvest festival N festa del raccolto
har·vest·ing [ˈhɑːvɪstɪŋ] N mietitura
harvest moon N plenilunio (*più vicino all'equinozio d'autunno*)
harvest mouse N topolino nano
has [hæz] 3RD PERS SG PRESENT *of* **have**
has-been [ˈhæzˌbiːn] N (*fam: person*): **he's/she's a has-been** ha fatto il suo tempo; (*: thing*) anticaglia
hash [hæʃ] N **1** (*Culin*) *spezzatino fatto con avanzi di carne cotta* **2** (*fam*): **to make a hash of sth** fare un bel pasticcio di qc **3** (*fam: hashish*) erba
hash·ish [ˈhæʃɪʃ] N hascisc *m*
hash key N (*on phone, computer*) cancelletto
hasn't [ˈhæznt] = **has not**
has·sle [ˈhæsl] (*fam*) N seccatura, scocciatura
■ VT seccare, scocciare
has·sock [ˈhæsək] N (*kneeler*) cuscino (*di inginocchiatoio*)
haste [heɪst] N fretta, premura; **to make haste** sbrigarsi, affrettarsi; **more haste less speed** (*Proverb*) presto e bene raro avviene; **in haste** in fretta
has·ten [ˈheɪsn] VT (*growth*) accelerare; (*steps*) affrettare, accelerare; **to hasten sb's departure** affrettare la partenza di qn
■ VI: **to hasten (to do sth)** affrettarsi (a fare qc); **I hasten to add that ...** mi preme aggiungere che...
hasti·ly [ˈheɪstɪlɪ] ADV (*hurriedly*) in (gran) fretta, in fretta e furia; (*without thinking*) senza riflettere, precipitosamente; **he hastily suggested that ...** s'è affrettato a proporre che...; **he left hastily** se n'è andato in gran fretta
has·ty [ˈheɪstɪ] ADJ (*comp* **-ier**, *superl* **-iest**) (*hurried*) frettoloso(-a); (*rash*) affrettato(-a), precipitoso(-a); **a hasty escape** una fuga precipitosa; **a hasty meal** un

pasto frettoloso; **hasty preparations** preparativi *mpl* affrettati

◎ **hat** [hæt] N cappello; **to pass the hat round** (*fig*) fare la colletta; **I take my hat off to him** (*fig*) gli faccio tanto di cappello; **to keep sth under one's hat** (*fig*) tenere qc per sé; **keep it under your hat!** acqua in bocca!; **to talk through one's hat** (*fam*) dire delle stupidaggini; **that's old hat!** (*fam*) sono storie vecchie!

hat·band ['hæt,bænd] N nastro del cappello

hat·box ['hæt,bɒks] N cappelliera

hatch[1] [hætʃ] N (*Naut: hatchway*) boccaporto; (*Brit: service hatch*) sportello passavivande; **down the hatch!** (*fam: when drinking*) salute!

hatch[2] [hætʃ] VT (*chick*) fare nascere; (*eggs*) fare schiudere; (*fig: scheme, plot*) elaborare, mettere a punto
■VI (*chick*) uscire dal *or* rompere il guscio; (*egg*) schiudersi; **the eggs will hatch soon** le uova si schiuderanno presto

hatch·back ['hætʃ,bæk] N (*car*) auto a tre (*or* cinque) porte

hatch cover N (*Naut*) tambucio

hatch·et ['hætʃɪt] N accetta, ascia

hatchet-faced ['hætʃɪt,feɪst] ADJ dal volto affilato

hatchet job N (*fam*) stroncatura

hatchet man N (*fam*) scagnozzo

◎ **hate** [heɪt] N odio
■VT (*person, thing*) odiare; (*weaker*) detestare; **I hate having to do it** detesto doverlo fare; **I hate to trouble you, but ...** mi dispiace disturbarla, ma...; **she hates to be** *or* **she hates being corrected** non sopporta le critiche *or* le osservazioni

hate·ful ['heɪtfʊl] ADJ odioso(-a), detestabile

hate·ful·ly ['heɪtfəlɪ] ADV odiosamente

hat·pin ['hæt,pɪn] N spillone *m*

ha·tred ['heɪtrɪd] N: **hatred (of)** odio (per)

hat stand N attaccapanni *m*

hat·ter ['hætə[r]] N cappellaio; **as mad as a hatter** matto(-a) da legare

hat trick N (*Brit Sport, also fig*) tripletta

haugh·ti·ly ['hɔːtɪlɪ] ADV altezzosamente, in modo altero

haugh·ti·ness ['hɔːtɪnɪs] N altezzosità, alterigia

haugh·ty ['hɔːtɪ] ADJ (*comp* **-ier**, *superl* **-iest**) altezzoso(-a), altero(-a)

haul [hɔːl] N **1** (*distance*) tragitto, viaggio; **it's a long haul** è una lunga tirata **2** (*amount taken: from robbery*) bottino; (: *of fish*) retata, pescata
■VT (*drag: person, heavy object*) tirare, trascinare; **to haul sb over the coals** (*fig*) dare una strigliata a qn
▸ **haul down** VT + ADV (*gen*) tirare giù; (*flag, sail*) ammainare
▸ **haul in** VT + ADV (*subj: police, authorities: suspect*) fare una retata di; (*net, catch, drowning person*) tirare a riva
▸ **haul up** VT + ADV (*flag, sail, load*) issare; (*suspect*) portare

haul·age ['hɔːlɪdʒ] N (*road transport*) trasporto, autotrasporto; (*cost*) costo del trasporto; **a haulage company** una società di trasporti

haulage contractor N (*Brit: firm*) impresa di trasporti; (: *person*) autotrasportatore *m*

haul·ier ['hɔːljə], (*Am*) **haul·er** ['hɔːlə] N autotrasportatore *m*

haunch [hɔːntʃ] N (*of person, animal*) anca; (*Culin*) coscia; **a haunch of venison** una coscia di cervo; **to sit/squat on one's haunches** (*person*) accucciarsi; (*animal*) sedersi (sulle zampe posteriori)

haunt [hɔːnt] N (*of criminals*) covo; **it's one of his favourite haunts** è un dei suoi posticini favoriti
■VT (*subj: ghost*) abitare; (*fig: memory*) perseguitare; (: *fear*) pervadere; **these thoughts haunted her** questi pensieri la tormentavano; **a ghost haunts this house** questa casa è abitata da un fantasma; **he haunts the local bars** frequenta assiduamente i bar della zona; **a ghost haunts this house** questa casa è abitata da un fantasma

haunt·ed ['hɔːntɪd] ADJ (*castle, house*) infestato(-a) dai fantasmi *or* dagli spiriti; (*look*) ossessionato(-a), tormentato(-a)

haunt·ing ['hɔːntɪŋ] ADJ (*sight, music*) che non si riesce a togliere dalla mente, ossessionante

Ha·vana [hə'vænə] N L'Avana

◎ **have** [hæv] KEYWORD
(*3rd pers sg present* **has**, *pt, pp* **had**)
■AUX VB
1 (*gen*) avere; (*with many intransitive verbs*) essere; **to have arrived** essere arrivato(-a); **he has been kind/promoted** è stato gentile/promosso; **to have eaten** aver mangiato; **having finished** *or* **when he had finished, he left** dopo aver finito se n'è andato; **has/hasn't she told you?** te l'ha/non te l'ha detto?
2 (*in tag questions*): **you've done it, haven't you?** l'hai fatto, (non è) vero?; **he hasn't done it, has he?** non l'ha fatto, vero?
3 (*in short answers and questions*): **you've made a mistake — no I haven't/so I have** hai fatto uno sbaglio — ma no, niente affatto/eh sì, è vero; **we haven't paid — yes we have!** non abbiamo pagato — sì che abbiamo pagato!; **I've been there before, have you?** ci sono già stato, e tu?
■MODAL AUX VB (*be obliged*): **to have (got) to do sth** dover fare qc; **I had better leave** è meglio che io vada; **this has got to be a mistake** dev'essere un errore, deve trattarsi di un errore; **she has to do it** lo deve fare; **I have (got) to finish this work** devo finire questo lavoro; **it will have to wait till tomorrow** bisogna rimandarlo a domani; **I don't have to wear glasses** non ho bisogno di portare gli occhiali
■VT
1 (*possess*) avere; **he has (got) blue eyes** ha gli occhi azzurri; **I haven't got blue eyes** *or* **I don't have blue eyes** non ho gli occhi azzurri; **I have (got) an idea** ho un'idea, mi è venuta un'idea; **have you (got)** *or* **do you have a pen?** hai una penna?; **I've got somebody staying next week** ho un ospite la settimana prossima; **I have (got) no Spanish** non so una parola di spagnolo
2 (*meal, shower*) fare; (*drink*) prendere; **to have breakfast** far colazione; **she had a cigarette** fumò una sigaretta; **I'll have a coffee** prendo un caffè; **to have dinner** cenare; **I must have a drink** devo bere qualcosa; **to have lunch** pranzare; **will you have some more?** ne vuoi ancora?; **what will you have?** cosa bevi *or* prendi?
3 (*receive, obtain*) avere, ricevere; **let me have your address** dammi il tuo indirizzo; **there was no bread to be had** non avevano più *or* non c'era più pane; **I must have it by tomorrow** mi occorre per domani; **to have a child** avere un figlio; **you can have it for £5** te lo lascio per 5 sterline; **I have it on good authority that ...** so da fonte sicura che...
4 (*hold*) avere, tenere; **he had him by the throat** lo teneva per la gola; **I have (got) him where I want him**

Hh

ce l'ho in mano *or* in pugno
5 (*maintain, allow*): **she will have it that she is right** sostiene *or* asserisce di aver ragione; **rumour has it (that) ...** si dice *or* corre voce che...; **I won't have it** questo non mi va affatto; **she won't have it said that ...** non permette che si dica che...; **I won't have this nonsense** non tollero queste assurdità
6 (*causative*): **to have sth done** far fare qc; **to have sb do sth** far fare qc a qn; **to have one's luggage brought up** farsi portar su le valigie; **to have one's hair cut** farsi tagliare i capelli; **he had them all dancing** è riuscito a farli ballare tutti; **what would you have me do?** cosa vuoi che faccia?; **I'd have you know that ...** voglio che tu sappia che...; **he had a suit made** si fece fare un abito
7 (*experience, suffer*): **to have an operation** avere *or* subire un'operazione; **she had her bag stolen** le hanno rubato la borsa
8 (*+ noun = verb identical with noun*): **let's have a look** diamo un'occhiata; **to have a swim** fare una nuotata; **let me have a try** fammi *or* lasciami provare; **to have a walk** fare una passeggiata
9 (*phrases*): **to have a pleasant evening** passare una piacevole serata; **you've been had!** (*fam*) ci sei cascato!; **let him have it!** (*fam*) dagliele!, picchialo!; **you've had it!** (*fam*) sei fritto!, sei fregato!; **thank you for having me** grazie dell'ospitalità; **you have me there!** questo proprio non lo so!; **to have a party** dare una festa; **to have a good time** divertirsi

▸ **have in** VT + ADV
1 (*visitor*) avere (in casa); (*candidate*) far passare *or* entrare; (*doctor*) chiamare
2 **to have it in for sb** (*fam*) avercela con qn

▸ **have on**
■ VT + ADV
1 (*garment*) avere addosso
2 (*Brit: be busy with*) avere da fare, avere in programma; **have you anything on tomorrow?** hai qualcosa in programma per domani?
3 (*Brit fam*): **to have sb on** prendere in giro qn
■ VT + PREP (*money*): **I don't have any money on me** non ho soldi con me

▸ **have out** VT + ADV
1 (*tooth, tonsils*) farsi togliere *or* levare
2 **to have sth out with sb** chiarire *or* mettere in chiaro qc con qn

▸ **have up** VT + ADV: **to be had up** (*fam: in court*) essere chiamato(-a) in tribunale

ha·ven [ˈheɪvn] N rifugio, riparo; **a haven of peace** un'oasi di pace
have-nots [ˈhævˌnɒts] NPL *see* **haves**
haven't [ˈhævnt] = **have not**
hav·er·sack [ˈhævəˌsæk] N zaino
haves [hævz] NPL: **the haves and the have-nots** gli abbienti e i non abbienti
hav·oc [ˈhævək] N distruzione *f*, devastazione *f*; **to wreak havoc on** devastare; (*fig*) scombussolare, mettere in subbuglio; **to play havoc with** (*fig*) scombussolare, mettere in subbuglio; **strikes are causing havoc** gli scioperi stanno provocando grande confusione
haw [hɔː] N (*Bot*) bacca di biancospino
Ha·waii [həˈwaɪɪ] N le Hawaii
⊳ www.hawaii.gov/portal/
Ha·wai·ian [həˈwaɪjən] ADJ hawaiano(-a)
■ N 1 (*person*) hawaiano(-a) 2 (*language*) hawaiano

hawk[1] [hɔːk] N (*also fig*) falco
hawk[2] [hɔːk] VT (*goods for sale*) vendere per strada
hawk·er [ˈhɔːkəʳ] N venditore(-trice) ambulante
hawk-eyed [ˈhɔːkˌaɪd] ADJ dagli occhi di falco
hawk·ish [ˈhɔːkɪʃ] ADJ (*politician*) che sostiene la linea dura
haw·thorn [ˈhɔːˌθɔːn] N biancospino
hay [heɪ] N fieno; **to make hay while the sun shines** (*Proverb*) battere il ferro finché è caldo
hay·cock [ˈheɪˌkɒk] N mucchio di fieno
hay fever N raffreddore *m* da fieno
hay·making [ˈheɪˌmeɪkɪŋ] N fienagione *f*
hay·stack [ˈheɪˌstæk] N pagliaio
hay·wire [ˈheɪˌwaɪəʳ] ADJ (*fam*): **to go haywire** (*person*) dare i numeri, perdere la testa; (*machine*) impazzire; (*scheme, system*) andare a catafascio
haz·ard [ˈhæzəd] N (*risk*) rischio; (*more serious*) pericolo; (*chance*) azzardo; **a potential hazard** un potenziale rischio; **occupational hazard** rischio del mestiere; **natural hazard** calamità naturale; **to be a health hazard** essere dannoso(-a) alla salute
■ VT (*one's life*) rischiare, mettere a repentaglio; (*remark*) azzardare; **to hazard a guess** tirare a indovinare; **he refused to hazard people's lives** si rifiutò di mettere a repentaglio la vita delle persone
haz·ard·ous [ˈhæzədəs] ADJ rischioso(-a), pericoloso(-a); **hazardous waste** rifiuti *mpl* pericolosi; **hazardous to health** rischioso per la salute
hazard warning lights NPL (*Aut*) luci *fpl* di emergenza
haze [heɪz] N (*mist*) foschia; (*of smoke*) velo
ha·zel [ˈheɪzl] N (*tree*) nocciolo
■ ADJ (*eyes*) (color) nocciola *inv*
ha·zel·nut [ˈheɪzlˌnʌt] N nocciola
hazy [ˈheɪzɪ] ADJ (*comp* **-ier**, *superl* **-iest**) (*day*) di foschia; (*weather*) caliginoso(-a); (*view*) indistinto(-a); (*photograph*) leggermente sfocato(-a); (*uncertain: person*) confuso(-a); (*unclear: memory, details, idea*) vago(-a); **a hazy notion** una vaga nozione; **hazy sky** cielo fosco
H-bomb [ˈeɪtʃˌbɒm] N bomba H
HDTV [ˌeɪtʃdiːtiːˈviː] N ABBR (= **high definition TV**) televisione *f* ad alta definizione
HE [ˌeɪtʃˈiː] ABBR 1 = **high explosive** 2 (*Diplomacy:* = **His (*or* Her) Excellency**) SE (= *Sua Eccellenza*), (*Rel:* = **His Eminence**) SE (= *Sua Eminenza*)
◎ **he** [hiː] PERS PRON lui, egli; **he has gone out** è uscito; **he loves dogs** lui ama i cani; **there/here he is** eccolo; **"come here," he said** "vieni qui," disse; **it is he who ...** è lui che...; **HE didn't do it** non è stato lui a farlo; **he who hesitates is lost** chi si ferma è perduto
■ N: **it's a he** (*animal, fam: baby*) è un maschio
◎ **head** [hɛd] N
1 (*Anat*) testa, capo; **mind your head!** attenzione alla testa!; **head of hair** capigliatura; **head down** a testa bassa; **head first** a capofitto, di testa; **my head is aching** mi fa male la testa, ho mal di testa; **to fall head over heels in love with sb** innamorarsi perdutamente *or* follemente di qn; **from head to foot** dalla testa ai piedi; **his head's in the clouds** ha la testa fra le nuvole; **to keep one's head above water** (*fig*) mantenersi a galla; **the horse won by a head** il cavallo ha vinto per una testa; **on your head be it** a tuo rischio e pericolo; **I could do it standing on my head** (*fam*) potrei farlo a occhi chiusi; **they went over my head to the manager** mi hanno scavalcato e sono andati direttamente dal direttore; **wine goes to my head** il vino mi dà *or* va alla testa; **success has gone to**

his head il successo gli ha dato alla testa; **to shout one's head off** (*fam*) sgolarsi
2 (*intellect, mind*) cervello, testa; **two heads are better than one** (*Proverb*) due occhi vedono meglio di uno; **it never entered my head** non mi è mai passato per la testa; **to have a head for business** essere tagliato(-a) per gli affari; **to have no head for heights** soffrire di vertigini; **to lose one's head** perdere la testa; **to keep one's head** non perdere la testa, mantenere la calma; **she always manages to keep her head in difficult situations** riesce sempre a mantenere la calma nelle situazioni difficili; **he lost his head and started screaming** ha perso la testa e ha cominciato a gridare; **let's put our heads together** pensiamoci insieme; **it was above** *or* **over their heads** non erano all'altezza di capirlo; **to do a sum in one's head** fare un calcolo a mente; **I couldn't tell you off the top of my head** (*fam*) non te lo saprei dire così su due piedi; **to get sth into one's head** ficcarsi in testa qc; **to be off one's head** (*fam*) essere fuori di testa
3 (*leader: of family, business*) capo; (*: of school*) direttore(-trice), preside *m/f*; **head of state** (*Pol*) capo di Stato
4 (*on coin*) testa; **heads or tails?** testa o croce?; **I couldn't make head nor tail of it** per me non aveva né capo né coda
5 (*no pl: unit*): **20 head of cattle** 20 capi *mpl* di bestiame; **£10 a** *or* **per head** 10 sterline a testa
6 (*of hammer, bed, flower*) testa; (*of nail*) capocchia; (*of arrow*) punta; (*of lettuce*) cespo; (*of river*) sorgente *f*; (*of stairs, page*) cima; (*on beer*) schiuma; (*on tape recorder, computer*) testina; **at the head of** (*organization*) a capo di; (*train, procession*) in testa a, alla testa di; (*queue*) all'inizio di; **to sit at the head of the table** sedersi a capotavola; **to come to a head** (*abscess*) maturare; (*fig: situation*) precipitare
7 (*Naut: of ship*) prua; (*of sail*) penna
■ VT
1 (*parade, poll*) essere in testa a; (*company, group*) essere a capo di; **she headed the list** era in cima all'elenco
2 (*Ftbl*): **to head a ball** colpire di testa una palla
3 (*chapter*) intitolare
■ VI dirigersi; **to head for** dirigersi *or* andare verso; **to head home** andare a casa; **she was heading up the stairs** stava salendo le scale; **he is heading for trouble** sta andando incontro a dei guai
■ ADJ (*clerk, typist*) capo *inv*
▸ **head for** VI + PREP dirigersi verso; **they headed for the church** si sono diretti verso la chiesa
▸ **head off** VT + ADV (*threat, danger*) sventare; (*person, animal*) far cambiare direzione a
▸ **head up** VT + ADV (*Am: team, group*) essere a capo di

head·ache ['hɛd,eɪk] N (*pain*) mal *m* di testa; (*fig*) grattacapo; **to have a headache** avere mal di testa; **I've got a headache** ho mal di testa; **this is a real headache for us** questo è un vero grattacapo per noi

head·band ['hɛd,bænd] N fascia per i capelli

head·board ['hɛd,bɔ:d] N testiera (del letto)

head cold N raffreddore *m* di testa

head collar, (*Am*) **head·stall** ['hɛd,stɔ:l] N cavezza

head·dress ['hɛd,drɛs] N (*made of feathers*) copricapo; (*of bride*) acconciatura

head·ed note·paper [,hɛdɪd'nəʊt,peɪpəʳ] N carta intestata

head·er ['hɛdəʳ] N (*Brit fam: Ftbl*) colpo di testa; (*: fall*) caduta di testa; **he took a header into the water** fece un tuffo di testa nell'acqua

head-first [,hɛd'fɜ:st] ADV a testa in giù, a capofitto; (*fig*) senza pensare

head gardener N capo giardiniere *m*

head·gear ['hɛd,gɪəʳ] N (*hat*) copricapo

head·hunt ['hɛd,hʌnt] VT: **to be headhunted** avere un'offerta di lavoro da un cacciatore di teste

head·hunt·er ['hɛd,hʌntəʳ] N cacciatore *m* di teste

head·ing ['hɛdɪŋ] N (*title*) titolo; (*section*) sezione *f*; (*on letter*) intestazione *f*

head·land ['hɛdlənd] N punta, promontorio

head·light ['hɛd,laɪt], **head·lamp** ['hɛd,læmp] N (*Aut*) faro, fanale *m*

◎ **head·line** ['hɛd,laɪn] N (*in newspaper*) titolo; (*TV, Radio*): **headlines** NPL (*main points*) sommario; **to hit the headlines** fare titolo
■ VT: **to be headlined** (*newspaper etc*) essere titolato(-a); (*show*) avere come attrazione principale

head·long ['hɛd,lɒŋ] ADJ (*fall, dive*) a capofitto, a testa in giù; (*rush*) a tutta velocità
■ ADV (*fall*) a capofitto, a tutta velocità; (*rush*) precipitosamente; **he fell headlong** è caduto a testa in giù; **they rushed headlong to the door** si sono precipitati verso la porta

head·man ['hɛdmən] N (*pl* **-men**) capotribù *m inv*

head·master [,hɛd'mɑ:stəʳ] N (*of primary school*) direttore *m*; (*of secondary school*) preside *m*

head·mistress [,hɛd'mɪstrɪs] N (*of primary school*) direttrice *f*; (*of secondary school*) preside *f*

head office N sede *f* centrale

head-on [,hɛd'ɒn] ADJ (*collision*) frontale; (*confrontation*) diretto(-a), faccia a faccia
■ ADV (*collide*) frontalmente

head·phones ['hɛd,fəʊnz] NPL cuffia *fsg*

◎ **head·quarters** [,hɛd'kwɔ:təz] NPL (*Mil*) quartier *msg* generale; (*of party, organization*) sede *f* centrale; (*Police*) centrale *f*

head·rest ['hɛd,rɛst] N poggiatesta *m inv*

head·room ['hɛd,rʊm] N (*under ceiling*) spazio (per la testa); (*under bridge*) altezza libera di passaggio; (*in car*) altezza dell'abitacolo

head·scarf ['hɛd,skɑ:f], **head·square** ['hɛd,skwɛəʳ] N foulard *m inv*

head·set ['hɛd,sɛt] N cuffia

head·stall ['hɛd,stɔ:l] N = **head collar**

head·stand ['hɛd,stænd] N: **to do a headstand** fare una verticale

head start N (*Sport, fig*): **to have a head start** partire avvantaggiato(-a)

head·stone ['hɛd,stəʊn] N (*on grave*) lapide *f*, pietra tombale

head·strong ['hɛd,strɒŋ] ADJ testardo(-a), cocciuto(-a)

head-to-head [,hɛdtə'hɛd] ADJ, ADV testa a testa *inv*
■ N: **a head-to-head** un testa a testa

head waiter N capocameriere *m*

head·way ['hɛd,weɪ] N (*Naut*) abbrivio; **to make headway** (*fig*) fare progressi *or* passi avanti; (*Naut*) avanzare

head·wind ['hɛd,wɪnd] N vento di prua; **to cycle against a headwind** pedalare controvento

heady ['hɛdɪ] ADJ (*comp* **-ier**, *superl* **-iest**) (*wine, scent, success*) inebriante; (*atmosphere*) euforico(-a)

◎ **heal** [hi:l] VT (*wound*) guarire, cicatrizzare; (*person*) guarire; (*fig: differences*) appianare
■ VI (*also:* **heal up**) cicatrizzarsi

heal·er ['hi:ləʳ] N guaritore(-trice)

heal·ing ['hi:lɪŋ] ADJ (*waters, power*) curativo(-a);

Hh

(*ointment*) curativo(-a), medicamentoso(-a); **to have healing hands** essere una pranoterapeuta *m/f*
■ N guarigione *f*

◎**health** [hɛlθ] N (*gen*) salute *f*; **Ministry of Health** ministero della Sanità; **Health Minister** ministro della Sanità; **Department of Health** ≈ ministero della Sanità; **to be in good/bad health** essere in buona/cattiva salute; **to drink sb's health** bere alla salute di qn; **your health!** (alla tua) salute!
▷ www.food.gov.uk
▷ www.nih.gov/
▷ www.nhsdirect.nhs.uk/

health care N assistenza sanitaria
■ ADJ (*provision*) sanitario(-a); (*worker*) che lavora nella sanità

health centre N (*Brit*) poliambulatorio

health fanatic N salutista *m/f*

health food N cibo macrobiotico

health-giving ['hɛlθ,gɪvɪŋ] ADJ (*food, air, exercise*) sano(-a), salutare

health hazard N pericolo per la salute

healthi·ly ['hɛlθɪlɪ] ADV (*live, eat*) in modo sano

Health Service N: **the Health Service** (*Brit*) ≈ il Servizio Sanitario Nazionale

◎**healthy** ['hɛlθɪ] ADJ (*comp* **-ier**, *superl* **-iest**) (*person*) sano(-a), in buona salute; (*skin, diet, attitude*) sano(-a); (*air, place, climate*) salubre; (*appetite*) robusto(-a); (*exercise, food, fig: respect*) salutare; (*: interest*) vivace; (*: economy*) florido(-a); (*: bank balance*) in attivo

heap [hi:p] N (*pile*) mucchio, cumulo; (*fam: old car*) macinino; (*: lots*): **heaps (of)** un sacco (di), un mucchio (di); **we have heaps of time** abbiamo un mucchio *or* sacco di tempo; **a heap of stones** un mucchio di sassi; **I was struck** *or* **knocked all of a heap** (*fam*) sono rimasto di stucco
■ VT: **to heap sth onto sth** ammucchiare qc su qc; **the waitress heaped potatoes onto my plate** la cameriera mi ha dato una montagna *or* un mucchio di patate; **to heap sth with sth** colmare qc di qc; **to heap favours/praise/gifts on sb** ricolmare qn di favori/lodi/regali; **heaped spoonful** (*Culin*) cucchiaio colmo
▶ **heap up** VT + ADV accumulare, ammucchiare

◎**hear** [hɪə^r] (*pt, pp* **heard** [hɜ:d]) VT (*gen*) sentire; (*be informed of: piece of news*) apprendere, sentire; (*news on radio, TV*) ascoltare; (*lecture*) assistere a; (*Law: case*) esaminare; **I can't hear you** non ti sento; **can you hear me?** mi senti?; **I could hardly make myself heard** facevo fatica a farmi sentire; **I didn't hear anything** non ho sentito niente; **I hear you've lost your watch** ho saputo che hai perso l'orologio; **to hear him speak you'd think ...** a sentirlo parlare si direbbe che...; **have you heard the one about the Irishman who ...** la sai quella dell'irlandese che...
■ VI (*gen*) sentire; (*get news*) aver notizie; **she can't hear very well** non sente molto bene; **to hear about** sentire parlare di; (*have news of*) avere notizie di; **I heard about her from her mother** ho avuto sue notizie tramite sua madre; **did you hear about the move?** hai saputo del trasloco?; **to hear from sb** ricevere notizie da qn; **she was never heard of again** non se ne seppe più nulla; **I've never heard of that book** non ho mai sentito parlare di quel libro; **I've never heard of such a thing** non ho mai sentito una cosa simile; **I won't hear of it** (*allow*) non ne voglio proprio sapere; **I won't hear of you paying for this** non è proprio il caso che tu paghi; **hear! hear!** (*bravo*) bravo!, bene!
▶ **hear out** VT + ADV ascoltare senza interrompere; **hear me out!** fammi finire!

heard [hɜ:d] PT, PP *of* **hear**

hear·er ['hɪərə^r] N uditore(-trice)

◎**hear·ing** ['hɪərɪŋ] N **1** (*sense of hearing*) udito; **she has excellent hearing** ha un udito eccellente; **to be within/out of hearing (distance)** essere/non essere a portata di voce; **in my hearing** in mia presenza
2 (*Law*) udienza; **to give sb a hearing** dare udienza a qn; (*of witnesses*) audizione *f*, escussione *f*; **the hearing was adjourned** l'udienza è stata aggiornata

hearing aid N apparecchio acustico

hear·say ['hɪə,seɪ] N diceria, chiacchiere *fpl*; **by hearsay** per sentito dire

hearse [hɜ:s] N carro funebre

◎**heart** [hɑ:t] N **1** (*also fig*) cuore *m*; **to have a weak heart** avere il cuore debole; **he's a man after my own heart** è proprio il tipo che mi piace; **he's a good boy at heart** in fondo è un bravo ragazzo; **to have sb's interests at heart** avere a cuore gli interessi di qn; **from the (bottom of one's) heart** dal profondo del cuore, con tutto il cuore; **in her heart of hearts** nel suo intimo; **heart and soul** anima e corpo; **his heart was in his boots** (*dejected*) aveva la morte nel cuore; **to wear one's heart on one's sleeve** non fare mistero dei propri sentimenti; **my heart sank** mi sono scoraggiato; **to learn/know/recite by heart** imparare/sapere/ripetere a memoria; **to one's heart's content** quanto si ha voglia; **her heart is in the right place** è di buon cuore; **to cry one's heart out** piangere disperatamente *or* a calde lacrime; **have a heart!** (*fam*) sii buono!; **she has a heart of gold** ha un cuore d'oro; **to take sth to heart** prendersi a cuore qc; **his heart was not in it** gli mancava l'entusiasmo; **to set one's heart on sth/on doing sth** tenere molto a qc/a fare qc; **with all one's heart** con tutto il cuore; **to break sb's heart** spezzare il cuore a qn; **to be in good heart** essere su di morale; **I did not have the heart to tell her** non ho avuto cuore *or* il coraggio di dirglielo; **to have one's heart in one's mouth** avere il cuore in gola; **to lose heart** perdersi di coraggio *or* d'animo, scoraggiarsi; **to take heart** farsi coraggio *or* animo; **in the heart of the country** in mezzo alla campagna; **the heart of the matter** il nocciolo della questione **2** (*Cards*): **hearts** NPL cuori *mpl*; **the ace of hearts** l'asso di cuori
■ ADJ cardiaco(-a); **to have a heart complaint** *or* **to have heart trouble** avere un disturbo cardiaco *or* una cardiopatia; **to have a heart condition** essere cardiopatico(-a)

heart·ache ['hɑ:t,eɪk] N pene *fpl*, dolori *mpl*

heart attack N (*Med*) infarto; **to have a heart attack** avere un infarto

heart·beat ['hɑ:t,bi:t] N (*single*) pulsazione *f*; (*rate*) battiti *mpl* del cuore

heart·break ['hɑ:t,breɪk] N immenso dolore *m*

heart·breaking ['hɑ:t,breɪkɪŋ] ADJ penoso(-a), straziante

heart·broken ['hɑ:t,brəʊkən] ADJ affranto(-a); **to be heartbroken** avere il cuore spezzato *or* infranto

heart·burn ['hɑ:tbɜ:n] N (*Med*) bruciore *m* di stomaco

-hearted ['hɑ:tɪd] SUFF: **a kind-hearted person** una persona di buon cuore

heart·en ['hɑ:tn] VT rincuorare, incoraggiare

heart·en·ing ['hɑ:tnɪŋ] ADJ incoraggiante

heart failure (*Med*) N (*malfunction*) collasso cardiaco; (*arrest*) arresto cardiaco

heart·felt ['hɑːtˌfɛlt] ADJ profondo(-a), sincero(-a)
hearth [hɑːθ] N focolare *m*
hearth rug N tappeto (*che si mette davanti al camino*)
hearti·ly ['hɑːtɪlɪ] ADV (*agree*) in pieno, completamente; (*laugh*) di cuore, di gusto; (*eat*) di buon appetito, di gusto; (*thank, welcome*) calorosamente; **to be heartily sick of** (*Brit*) essere veramente stufo(-a) di, essere arcistufo(-a) di
heart·land ['hɑːtˌlænd] N zona centrale; **Italy's industrial heartland** il cuore dell'industria italiana
heart·less ['hɑːtlɪs] ADJ spietato(-a), crudele, senza cuore, insensibile
heart·less·ly ['hɑːtlɪslɪ] ADV spietatamente, crudelmente
heart·less·ness ['hɑːtlɪsnɪs] N crudeltà
heart·rend·ing ['hɑːtˌrɛndɪŋ] ADJ straziante
heart-searching ['hɑːtˌsɜːtʃɪŋ] N: **after much heart-searching** dopo lunghe meditazioni; **he came to his decision after much heart-searching** la sua fu una decisione lunga e sofferta
hearts·ease ['hɑːtsˌiːz] N (*Bot*) viola del pensiero selvatica
heart·strings ['hɑːtˌstrɪŋz] NPL: **to tug (at) sb's heartstrings** toccare il cuore a qn, toccare qn nel profondo
heart surgeon N cardiochirurgo
heart-throb ['hɑːtˌθrɒb] N: **a teenage heart-throb** un idolo delle ragazzine
heart-to-heart [ˌhɑːttə'hɑːt] ADJ, ADV a cuore aperto
■ N (*conversation*): **to have a heart to heart** parlare a cuore aperto
heart transplant N trapianto di cuore
heart-warming ['hɑːtˌwɔːmɪŋ] ADJ toccante
hearty ['hɑːtɪ] ADJ (*comp* **-ier**, *superl* **-iest**) (*person*) gioviale; (*support*) caloroso(-a); (*dislike*) vivo(-a); (*laugh*) di cuore, di gusto; (*appetite*) robusto(-a); (*meal*) abbondante, sostanzioso(-a); (*welcome, thanks*) cordiale, caloroso(-a); **a hearty eater** una buona forchetta; **a hearty breakfast** una colazione abbondante; **heartiest congratulations!** congratulazioni vivissime!
◎**heat** [hiːt] N **1** (*gen*) calore *m*; (*fig*) ardore *m*; **the heat of the sun** il calore del sole; **I can't stand the heat** non sopporto il caldo; **at low heat** (*Culin: on stove*) a fuoco basso; (*: in oven*) a calore moderato; **take the pan off the heat** togliere la pentola dal fuoco; **in the heat of the moment** (*fig*) nella foga del momento; **in the heat of the battle** nella furia della battaglia; **to put the heat on sb** fare pressione a *or* su qn; **he replied with some heat** rispose piuttosto irritato **2** (*Sport: also*: **qualifying heat**) batteria, prova eliminatoria **3** (*Zool*): **in** *or* **on heat** in calore
■ VT (*far*) scaldare; **heat gently for five minutes** scaldare a fuoco lento per cinque minuti
■ VI scaldarsi
▸ **heat up** VI + ADV (*liquids*) scaldarsi; (*room*) riscaldarsi
■ VT + ADV riscaldare
heat·ed ['hiːtɪd] ADJ riscaldato(-a); (*fig: discussion, argument*) acceso(-a), animato(-a); **a heated swimming pool** una piscina riscaldata; **heated words** parole *fpl* di fuoco; **to grow heated** (*discussion*) accendersi
heat·ed·ly ['hiːtɪdlɪ] ADV (*discuss, argue*) animatamente
heat·er ['hiːtəʳ] N calorifero, termosifone *m*, radiatore *m*; (*stove*) stufa; **I had the heater on and the window open** avevo il riscaldamento acceso e la finestra aperta; **an electric heater** una stufa elettrica; **a water heater** uno scaldaacqua
heath [hiːθ] N (*Brit: moor*) landa, brughiera; (*plant*) erica, brugo
heat haze N foschia dovuta all'afa
hea·then ['hiːðən] ADJ, N pagano(-a)
hea·then·ish ['hiːðənɪʃ] ADJ (*pej: pagan*) pagano(-a); (*: uncivilized*) barbaro(-a)
heath·er ['hɛðəʳ] N erica
heat·ing ['hiːtɪŋ] N riscaldamento
heat loss N perdita di calore
heat rash N (*Med*) eritema *m* (da calore)
heat-resistant ['hiːtrɪˌzɪstənt] ADJ termoresistente
heat-seeking ['hiːtˌsiːkɪŋ] ADJ (*missile*) termoguidato(-a)
heat·stroke ['hiːtˌstrəʊk] N (*Med*) colpo di calore
heat-treatment ['hiːtˌtriːtmənt] N (*Med*) termoterapia; **to have heat-treatment** fare i forni
heat·wave ['hiːtˌweɪv] N ondata di caldo
heave [hiːv] N sforzo; (*of waves*) movimento; (*Geol*) rigetto
■ VT (*pull*) tirare con forza; (*drag*) trascinare a fatica; (*lift*) sollevare a fatica; (*throw*) scagliare; **they heaved the washing machine into the bathroom** hanno trascinato a fatica la lavatrice nel bagno; **to heave a sigh** emettere *or* mandare un sospiro; **to heave a sigh of relief** tirare un sospiro di sollievo; **to heave anchor** (*Naut*) salpare l'ancora
■ VI **1** (*sea, chest, stomach*) alzarsi ed abbassarsi; **to heave at** *or* **to heave on** (*pull*) tirare con forza; **he heaved with all his might** ha tirato con tutta la sua forza **2** (*feel sick*) avere i conati di vomito; **her stomach heaved** le si rivoltò lo stomaco **3** (*liter: pt, pp* **hove**) **to heave in sight** *or* **into view** comparire all'orizzonte
▸ **heave to** (*pt, pp* **hove**) VI + ADV (*Naut*) navigare in cappa
◎**heav·en** ['hɛvn] N **1** (*Rel*) cielo, paradiso; (*fig*) paradiso; **to go to heaven** andare in paradiso; **(good) heavens!** santo cielo!; **thank heaven!** grazie al cielo!; **heaven forbid!** Dio ce ne guardi!; **for heaven's sake!** (*protesting*) santo cielo!, in nome del cielo!; **this is heaven!** (*fam*) che meraviglia!; **to move heaven and earth to do sth** muovere mari e monti *or* farsi in quattro per fare qc; **in seventh heaven** al settimo cielo; **heaven on earth** il paradiso terrestre **2 the heavens** NPL (*liter: sky*) il cielo, la volta celeste; **the heavens opened** si è messo a diluviare
heav·en·ly ['hɛvnlɪ] ADJ (*Rel*) celeste, divino(-a); (*fam: delightful*) divino(-a); **heavenly weather** tempo stupendo; **heavenly kingdom** regno dei cieli
heavenly body N (*Astron*) corpo celeste
heaven-sent ['hɛvnˌsɛnt] ADJ provvidenziale, mandato(-a) dal cielo
heavi·ly ['hɛvɪlɪ] ADV (*move*) con pesantezza; (*tax*) fortemente; (*rain, snow, gamble*) forte; (*breathe*) con difficoltà; (*sigh, sleep*) profondamente; (*rely, drink, smoke, load*) molto; **he drinks heavily** beve molto; **it rained heavily in the night** ha piovuto molto durante la notte; **it weighs heavily on him** questo gli pesa molto; **she sat down heavily on the sofa** si è seduta pesantemente sul divano
heavily-built [ˌhɛvɪlɪ'bɪlt] ADJ di corporatura robusta, massiccio(-a)
heavily-laden [ˌhɛvɪlɪ'leɪdn] ADJ (molto) carico(-a)
heavi·ness ['hɛvɪnɪs] N (*weight*) pesantezza; (*of expense, taxation*) gravosità, onerosità; (*of traffic*) intensità
◎**heavy** ['hɛvɪ] ADJ (*comp* **-ier**, *superl* **-iest**) (*gen, fig*) pesante; (*sigh*) profondo(-a); (*sleep*) profondo(-a),

Hh

pesante; (*blow, rain, taxation*) forte; (*sea*) grosso(-a) (*after n*); (*expense, casualties*) ingente; (*traffic*) intenso(-a); (*atmosphere*) opprimente; (*crop*) abbondante; (*Mil: fighting*) accanito(-a); (*: fire*) nutrito(-a), fitto(-a); (*loss*) grave; (*smoker*) accanito(-a); **this bag's very heavy** questa borsa è molto pesante; **how heavy are you?** quanto pesi?; **to have a heavy cold** avere un forte raffreddore; **it's a heavy burden for her to bear** è un peso troppo grande per lei; **with a heavy heart** col cuore gonfio; **air heavy with scent** aria carica di profumo; **to be a heavy drinker** essere una forte bevitore(-trice); **my car is heavy on petrol** la mia macchina consuma troppo; **to be a heavy sleeper** avere il sonno duro *or* pesante; **it's heavy going** è una gran fatica

heavy cream N (*Am*) panna da montare

heavy-duty [ˌhɛvɪˈdjuːtɪ] ADJ molto resistente

heavy goods vehicle N (*Brit*) autoveicolo pesante da trasporto

heavy-handed [ˌhɛvɪˈhændɪd] ADJ (*clumsy, tactless*) pesante; (*harsh: person*) che ha la mano pesante, severo(-a)

heavy-hearted [ˌhɛvɪˈhɑːtɪd] ADJ: **to be heavy-hearted** avere il cuore gonfio

heavy industry N industria pesante

heavy metal N (*Mus*) heavy metal *m inv*

heavy-set [ˌhɛvɪˈsɛt] ADJ (*esp Am*) tarchiato(-a)

heavy·weight [ˈhɛvɪˌweɪt] N (*Boxing*) (peso) massimo; (*fig: important or influential person*) autorità *f inv*, pezzo *m* grosso

■ ADJ (*issue, subject*) importante

Hebe [ˈhiːbɪ] N Ebe *f*

He·brew [ˈhiːbruː] ADJ (*language*) ebraico(-a); (*person, nation*) ebreo(-a)

■ N (*person*) ebreo(-a); (*language*) ebraico

Heb·ri·des [ˈhɛbrɪˌdiːz] NPL: **the Hebrides** le Ebridi

Heca·te [ˈhɛkətɪ] N Ecate *f*

heck [hɛk] (*fam*) EXCL: **oh heck!** oh cavolo!

■ N: **a heck of a lot of** un casino di

heck·le [ˈhɛkl] VT, VI: **to heckle (sb)** interrompere continuamente (qn) (*un oratore*)

heck·ler [ˈhɛkləʳ] N disturbatore(-trice)

heck·ling [ˈhɛklɪŋ] N interruzioni *fpl*

hec·tare [ˈhɛktɑːʳ] N ettaro

hec·tic [ˈhɛktɪk] ADJ (*busy*) frenetico(-a); (*eventful*) movimentato(-a); **my life's pretty hectic at the moment** attualmente la mia vita è piuttosto movimentata; **a hectic schedule** un orario denso

Hector [ˈhɛktəʳ] N Ettore *m*

hec·tor [ˈhɛktəʳ] VT fare il prepotente con

hec·tor·ing [ˈhɛktərɪŋ] ADJ prepotente

he'd [hiːd] = **he would, he had**

hedge [hɛdʒ] N siepe *f*; (*fig*) difesa; **as a hedge against inflation** per cautelarsi contro l'inflazione

■ VT (*Agr*) recintare con una siepe; **to be hedged about** *or* **around** *or* **in with** (*restricted*) essere limitato(-a) da, essere vincolato(-a) da; **to hedge one's bets** (*fig*) cercare di non compromettersi

■ VI tergiversare, essere elusivo(-a)

hedge·hog [ˈhɛdʒˌhɒg] N riccio

hedge·hop [ˈhɛdʒˌhɒp] VI volare raso terra

hedge·row [ˈhɛdʒrəʊ] N siepe *f*

he·don·ism [ˈhiːdənɪzəm] N (*frm*) edonismo

he·don·ist [ˈhiːdənɪst] N (*frm*) edonista *m/f*

heebie-jeebies [ˈhiːbɪˈdʒiːbɪz] NPL (*fam*): **I had the heebie-jeebies** le gambe mi facevano giacomo giacomo; **it gives me the heebie-jeebies** mi fa venire la tremarella

heed [hiːd] (*frm*) N: **to pay (no) heed to, to take (no) heed of** (non) ascoltare, (non) tener conto di

■ VT fare attenzione a

heed·less [ˈhiːdlɪs] ADJ (*not thinking*) avventato(-a); (*not caring*) noncurante; **to be heedless of** essere insensibile *or* sordo(-a) a

heed·less·ly [ˈhiːdlɪslɪ] ADV (*see adj*) avventatamente; con noncuranza

heel[1] [hiːl] N **1** (*of foot, sock*) tallone *m*, calcagno; (*of shoe*) tacco; **high heels** tacchi alti; **heel, boy!** (*to dog*) qui!; **to bring sb to heel** (*fig*) riportare qn all'ordine; **to be at sb's heels** stare alle calcagna di qn; **to take to one's heels** (*liter*) darsela a gambe; **to turn on one's heel** girare i tacchi **2** (*fam: person*) carogna

■ VT (*shoe*) fare *or* rifare i tacchi a; (*ball*) colpire di tacco

heel[2] [hiːl] VI (*also:* **heel over**: *ship, truck*) inclinarsi (pericolosamente)

heel·ing [ˈhiːlɪŋ] N (*Rugby*) tallonaggio

heel·piece [ˈhiːlˌpiːs] N talloniera

hefty [ˈhɛftɪ] (*fam*) ADJ (*comp* **-ier**, *superl* **-iest**) (*load*) pesante; (*person*) robusto(-a), solido(-a); (*piece, profit*) grosso(-a) (*before n*); (*price*) alto(-a), bello(-a) (*before n*); **a hefty fine** una grossa multa; **a hefty shove** una forte spinta

heif·er [ˈhɛfəʳ] N giovenca

◉ **height** [haɪt] N **1** (*measurement*) altezza; (*of person*) altezza, statura; (*altitude*) altezza, altitudine *f*; (*high ground*) altura; **what height are you?** quanto sei alto?; **of average/medium height** di statura media; **to be 20 metres in height** essere alto(-a) 20 metri; **height above sea level** altitudine sopra il livello del mare; **to be afraid of heights** soffrire di vertigini **2** (*fig: of career, success, glory*) apice *m*; (*: of rudeness, stupidity*) colmo; **at the height of** (*storm, battle*) nel momento culminante di; **it's the height of fashion** è l'ultimo grido della moda; **in the height of summer** nel pieno dell'estate

height·en [ˈhaɪtn] VT (*raise*) alzare; (*increase*) far aumentare; (*enhance: effect*) mettere in risalto, accrescere; (*: experience*) rendere più intenso(-a)

hei·nous [ˈheɪnəs] ADJ (*frm*) nefando(-a), atroce

heir [ɛəʳ] N erede *m/f*

heir apparent N erede *m/f* legittimo(-a)

heir·ess [ˈɛərɛs] N erede *f*; (*rich*) ereditiera

heir·loom [ˈɛəluːm] N: **this picture is a family heirloom** è un quadro di famiglia

heist [haɪst] N (*Am fam: hold-up*) rapina

held [hɛld] PT, PP *of* **hold**

Helen [ˈhɛlɪn] N Elena

heli·cal [ˈhɛlɪkəl] ADJ elicoidale

◉ **heli·cop·ter** [ˈhɛlɪˌkɒptəʳ] N elicottero

▷ www.helicoptermuseum.co.uk/index.htm

heli·port [ˈhɛlɪˌpɔːt] N eliporto

he·lium [ˈhiːlɪəm] N elio

he·lix [ˈhiːlɪks] (*pl* **helices** *or* **helixes** [ˈhɛlɪˌsiːz]) N elica

◉ **hell** [hɛl] N inferno; **in hell** all'inferno; **he'll go to hell** andrà all'inferno; **to go hell for leather** andare *or* correre come un demonio; **all hell broke loose** è successo il *or* un finimondo; **a hell of a noise** (*fam*) un casino infernale, un fracasso del diavolo; **a hell of a lot of** (*fam*) un sacco *or* mucchio *or* casino di; **we had a hell of a time** (*fam: good*) ci siamo divertiti da pazzi; (*: bad*) è stato terribile; **to have a hell of a time doing sth** (*fam*) diventar matto(-a) a fare qc; **to make sb's life hell** (*fam*) rendere la vita un inferno a qn; **to give**

sb hell (*fam: address harshly*) dirne di tutti i colori a qn; **to run like hell** (*fam*) correre come un matto(-a); **what the hell do you want?** (*fam*) che diavolo vuoi?; **just for the hell of it** (*fam*) per il gusto di farlo; **go to hell!** (*fam*) va' all'inferno!, va' al diavolo!; **to hell with it!** (*fam*) al diavolo!; **oh hell!** (*fam*) porca miseria!, accidenti!

he'll [hi:l] = **he will, he shall**

Hel·las ['hɛləs] N Ellade *f*

hell·bent [ˌhɛl'bɛnt] ADJ: **hellbent on doing sth** deciso(-a) a fare qc a tutti i costi

Hel·len·ic [hɛ'lɛnɪk] ADJ ellenico(-a)

hell·ish ['hɛlɪʃ] ADJ (*fam*) infernale, bestiale

hell·ish·ly ['hɛlɪʃlɪ] ADV (*fam*) mostruosamente, atrocemente

◎ **hel·lo** [hə'ləʊ] EXCL (*on meeting sb*) ciao!; (*: more formal*) buon giorno!; (*in surprise*) ma guarda!; (*Telec*) pronto!; (*to attract attention*) ehi!

helm [hɛlm] N (*Naut*) timone *m*; **to be at the helm** (*fig*) essere al comando

hel·met ['hɛlmɪt] N (*of motorcyclist, construction worker*) casco; (*of miner, soldier, policeman*) elmetto; (*of knight*) elmo

helms·man ['hɛlmzmən] N (*pl* **-men**) timoniere *m*

◎ **help** [hɛlp] N **1** (*assistance*) aiuto; **with the help of** con l'aiuto di; **without the help of sb/sth** senza l'aiuto di qn/qc; **to be of help to sb** essere di aiuto *or* essere utile a qn; **to call for help** chiedere *or* gridare aiuto; **he gave me no help** non mi ha dato nessun aiuto; **he is beyond help** è un caso senza speranza; **there's no help for it** non c'è altro *or* nient'altro da fare; **help!** aiuto! **2** (*employee*) aiutante *m/f*; (*domestic*) domestico(-a); (*daily*) donna di servizio

■ VT **1** (*aid, assist*) aiutare; (*scheme, project*) contribuire a; (*progress*) favorire; (*pain*) far passare, alleviare; **can you help me?** mi puoi aiutare?; **to help sb (to) do sth** aiutare qn a far qc; **I'll help you carry it** ti aiuto a portarlo; **to help sb with sth** aiutare qn con qc; **I helped him with his luggage** l'ho aiutato a portare i bagagli; **I got my sister to help me** mi sono fatta aiutare da mia sorella; **that won't help much** non servirà a gran che; **can I help you?** (*in shop*) desidera?; **to help sb on/off with his/her coat** aiutare qn a mettersi/togliersi il cappotto; **to help sb across/up/down** aiutare qn ad attraversare/a salire/a scendere **2** (*at table*): **to help sb to soup** servire la minestra a qn; **to help o.s.** (*to food*) servirsi, prendere; **help yourself!** serviti pure!; (*to other things: steal*) prendersi, arraffare **3** **he can't help coughing** non può fare a meno di tossire; **she can't help being stupid** cosa può farci se è stupida?; **I couldn't help thinking ...** non potevo fare a meno di pensare...; **I couldn't help laughing** non ho potuto fare a meno di ridere; **it can't be helped** non ci si può fare (più) niente, non c'è niente da fare; **he won't do it if I can help it** farò il possibile per impedirglielo; **he can't help himself** non può farne a meno

▸ **help out** VI + ADV aiutare, dare una mano

■ VT + ADV aiutare, dare una mano a

help·er ['hɛlpəʳ] N aiutante *m/f*, assistente *m/f*

help·ful ['hɛlpfʊl] ADJ (*person: willing*) che si rende utile; (*: useful*) di grande aiuto; (*object, advice*) utile; **the staff are always friendly and helpful** il personale è sempre amichevole e disponibile; **he gave me some helpful advice** mi ha dato dei consigli utili

help·ful·ly ['hɛlpfəlɪ] ADV gentilmente

help·ful·ness ['hɛlpfʊlnɪs] N disponibilità

help·ing ['hɛlpɪŋ] N porzione *f*; **you've had two helpings of dessert already** ti sei già servito due volte di dolce

helping hand N aiuto; **to give sb a helping hand** dare una mano a qn

help·less ['hɛlplɪs] ADJ (*rage, person: powerless*) impotente; (*person: vulnerable*) indifeso(-a); (*: physically weak*) debole; **a helpless invalid** un infermo; **a helpless old lady** una povera vecchietta; **helpless with laughter** morto(-a) dalle risate

help·less·ly ['hɛlplɪslɪ] ADV (*struggle, try*) in vano; (*lie, remain*) senza potersi muovere; (*say*) con fare impotente; **he watched helplessly as his parents were shot** guardava impotente mentre i genitori venivano fucilati; **to laugh helplessly** ridere senza potersi fermare

help·less·ness ['hɛlplɪsnɪs] N impotenza

help·line ['hɛlpˌlaɪn] N ≈ telefono amico (*Comm*) servizio *m* informazioni *inv* (*a pagamento*)

Hel·sin·ki ['hɛlsɪŋkɪ] N Helsinki *f*

helter-skelter ['hɛltə'skɛltəʳ] ADV in fretta e furia, in quattro e quattr'otto

■ N (*Brit: in funfair*) scivolo (a spirale)

hem [hɛm] N (*hemline*) orlo; **to let the hem down on a skirt** allungare una gonna

■ VT fare l'orlo a

▸ **hem in** VT + ADV cingere, circondare; **to feel hemmed in** (*fig*) sentirsi soffocare

he-man ['hi:ˌmæn] N (*pl* **-men**) (*fam*) vero maschio

hema·tol·ogy *etc* [ˌhi:mə'tɒlədʒɪ] (*Am*) = **haematology**

hemi·sphere ['hɛmɪsfɪəʳ] N emisfero

hem·lock ['hɛmˌlɒk] N cicuta

hemo·glo·bin [ˌhi:məʊ'gləʊbɪn] N (*Am*) = **haemoglobin**

hemo·philia [ˌhi:məʊ'fɪlɪə] N (*Am*) = **haemophilia**

hem·or·rhage ['hɛmərɪdʒ] N (*Am*) = **haemorrhage**

hem·or·rhoids ['hɛmərɔɪdz] NPL (*Am*) = **haemorrhoids**

hemp [hɛmp] N (*for rope*) canapa; (*drug*) canapa indiana, hascisc *m inv*

hen [hɛn] N (*fowl*) gallina; (*with chicks*) chioccia; (*female bird*) femmina; **hen pheasant** fagiano femmina

hence [hɛns] ADV **1** (*frm: therefore*) per cui, quindi; **the party was divided and hence very weak** il partito era diviso e quindi molto debole **2** (*old: place*) da qui, di qui **3** (*frm: time*): **5 years hence** da qui a 5 anni

hence·forth [ˌhɛns'fɔ:θ] ADV (*frm*) d'ora innanzi *or* in poi

hench·man ['hɛntʃmən] N (*pl* **-men**) (*follower*) accolito; (*pej*) scagnozzo

hen·house ['hɛnˌhaʊs] N pollaio

hen·na ['hɛnə] N henna

hen party N (*fam*) festa di sole donne

hen·pecked ['hɛnˌpɛkt] ADJ (*fam*): **he is henpecked** è succube della moglie

hepa·ti·tis [ˌhɛpə'taɪtɪs] N epatite *f*

◎ **her** [hɜ:ʳ] PERS PRON **1** (*direct: unstressed*) la, l'+ *vowel*; (*: stressed*) lei; **I hear her** la sento; **I heard her** l'ho sentita; **I saw her** l'ho vista; **I've never seen HER** lei, non l'ho mai vista **2** (*indirect*) le; **I gave her the book** le ho dato il libro; **I spoke to her** le ho parlato; **I gave her a book** le ho dato un libro **3** (*after prep, in comparisons*) lei; **without her** senza di lei; **I was thinking of her** pensavo a lei; **she had a case with her** aveva con sé una valigia; **I'm going with her** vado con lei; **look at her!** guardala!; **if I were her** se fossi in lei; **it's her** è lei; **I'm older than her** sono più vecchio di lei

■ POSS ADJ il/la suo(-a), *pl* i/le suoi/sue; **this is her**

Hh

house questa è la sua casa; **her brother** suo fratello; **her address** il suo indirizzo; **her parents** i suoi genitori; **Ann and her two best friends** Ann e le sue due migliori amiche; **Sarah and her father** Sarah e suo padre; **her aunt** sua zia; **she's lost her wallet** ha perduto il portafoglio; **with her hands in her pockets** con le mani in tasca; **she took off her coat** si è tolta il cappotto; **she washed her hair this morning** si è lavata i capelli stamattina

Hera ['hɪərə] N Era

her·ald ['hɛrəld] N araldo; (*fig*) messaggero
■VT annunciare

he·ral·dic [hɛ'rældɪk] ADJ araldico(-a)

her·ald·ry ['hɛrəldrɪ] N araldica
▷ www.college-of-arms.gov.uk
▷ www.heraldica.org

herb [hɜːb] N (*Med*) erba medicinale; **herbs** NPL (*Culin*) erbe *fpl* aromatiche, odori *mpl*
▷ www.culinarycafe.com/Spices_Herbs

her·ba·ceous [hɜː'beɪʃəs] ADJ erbaceo(-a)

herb·al ['hɜːbəl] ADJ di erbe; **herbal tea** tisana

herb·al·ist ['hɜːbəlɪst] N erborista *m/f*

herb garden N orticello di odori

herbi·cide ['hɜːbɪˌsaɪd] N erbicida *m*

her·bi·vore ['hɜːbɪˌvɔː] N erbivoro

her·bivo·rous [hɜː'bɪvərəs] ADJ erbivoro(-a)

Hercules ['hɜːkjʊliːz] N Ercole *m*

herd [hɜːd] N (*of cattle, horses*) mandria; (*of wild animals, swine*) branco; (*of people: pej*): **the (common) herd** il gregge
■VT (*drive, gather: animals*) guidare; (*: people*) radunare
▶ **herd together** VT + ADV radunare
■VI + ADV stringersi uno vicino all'altro

herd instinct N istinto gregale

◎**here** [hɪəʳ] ADV (*place*) qui, qua; (*at this point*) qui, a questo punto; **I live here** vivo qui; **come here!** vieni qui!; **here!** (*at roll call*) presente!; **over here** da questa parte, di qua; **here is** ecco; **here he is!** eccolo qui!; **here I am** eccomi qua; **here are** ecco; **here are the books** ecco (qua) i libri; **here you are!** (*giving sb sth*) ecco qui!; **here she comes** eccola (che viene); **here and there** qua e là; **here, there and everywhere** dappertutto; **winter is here** l'inverno è arrivato; **my friend here will do it** il mio amico qui lo farà; **that's neither here nor there** non ha molta importanza; **here's to John!** alla salute di John!
■EXCL ehi!

here·abouts ['hɪərəˌbaʊts] ADV da queste parti

here·after [ˌhɪər'ɑːftəʳ] ADV (*frm*) d'ora in poi, da qui in avanti, in futuro
■N: **the hereafter** l'aldilà *m*

here·by [ˌhɪə'baɪ] (*frm*) ADV con questo (documento *or* atto *etc*); (*in letter*) con la presente

he·redi·tary [hɪ'rɛdɪtərɪ] ADJ ereditario(-a)

he·red·ity [hɪ'rɛdɪtɪ] N eredità

her·esy ['hɛrəsɪ] N eresia

her·etic ['hɛrətɪk] N eretico(-a)

he·reti·cal [hɪ'rɛtɪkəl] ADJ eretico(-a)

he·reti·cal·ly [hɪ'rɛtɪkəlɪ] ADV ereticamente

here·upon [ˌhɪərə'pɒn] ADV (*frm*) su ciò, su questo

here·with [ˌhɪə'wɪθ] ADV (*Comm*) con la presente

her·it·age ['hɛrɪtɪdʒ] N (*inheritance*) eredità; (*of country, nation*) retaggio; **our national heritage** il nostro patrimonio nazionale; **cultural heritage** il patrimonio culturale

her·met·ic [hɜː'mɛtɪk] ADJ ermetico(-a)

her·meti·cal·ly [hɜː'mɛtɪkəlɪ] ADV ermeticamente; **hermetically sealed** ermeticamente chiuso(-a)

her·mit ['hɜːmɪt] N eremita *m*

hermit crab N paguro, bernardo l'eremita

her·nia ['hɜːnɪə] N ernia

◎**hero** ['hɪərəʊ] N (*pl* **heroes**) eroe *m*

Herod ['hɛrəd] N Erode *m*

Herodotus [hɪ'rɒdətəs] N Erodoto

he·ro·ic [hɪ'rəʊɪk] ADJ eroico(-a)

he·roi·cal·ly [hɪ'rəʊɪkəlɪ] ADV eroicamente

he·ro·ics [hɪ'rəʊɪks] NPL (*pej: words*) parolone *fpl*; (*: actions*) eroismi *mpl* inutili

hero·in ['hɛrəʊɪn] N eroina

heroin addict N eroinomane *m/f*

heroin addiction N eroinomania

hero·ine ['hɛrəʊɪn] N eroina

hero·ism ['hɛrəʊɪzəm] N eroismo

her·on ['hɛrən] N airone *m*

hero worship N culto degli eroi

her·pes ['hɜːpiːz] N herpes *m*

her·ring ['hɛrɪŋ] N aringa

herring·bone ['hɛrɪŋˌbəʊn] N (*pattern*) disegno a spina di pesce
■ADJ spigato(-a), spinato(-a)

herring gull N gabbiano reale

hers [hɜːz] POSS PRON il/la suo(-a), *pl* i/le suoi/sue; **a friend of hers** un suo amico, una sua amica; **hers is red, mine is green** il suo è rosso, il mio è verde; **this is hers** questo è (il) suo; **my dog and hers** il mio cane e il suo; **my parents and hers** i miei genitori e i suoi; **my car is older than hers** la mia macchina è più vecchia della sua; **my friends and hers** le mie amiche e le sue; **whose is this? – it's hers** di chi è questo? – è suo; **is that car hers?** è sua quella macchina?

◎**her·self** [hɜː'sɛlf] PERS PRON (*reflexive*) si; (*emphatic*) lei stessa; (*after preposition*) sé, se stessa; **she did it herself** l'ha fatto lei; **she's not herself today** ha qualcosa che non va oggi; **by herself** da sola; **she doesn't like travelling by herself** non le piace viaggiare da sola; **she did it (all) by herself** l'ha fatto (tutto) da sola; **she's hurt herself** si è fatta male; **she looked at herself in the mirror** si è guardata allo specchio; **she talked mainly about herself** parlava principalmente di sé; *see also* **oneself**

Herts ABBR (*Brit*) = *Hertfordshire*

he's [hiːz] = **he is, he has**

hesi·tan·cy ['hɛzɪtənsɪ] N titubanza

hesi·tant ['hɛzɪtənt] ADJ esitante, indeciso(-a), titubante; **to be hesitant about doing sth** esitare a fare qc

hesi·tant·ly ['hɛzɪtəntlɪ] ADV con esitazione

hesi·tate ['hɛzɪˌteɪt] VI esitare; **to hesitate to do sth** esitare a fare qc; **to hesitate about** *or* **over sth** esitare in qc; **don't hesitate to ask (me)** non aver timore *or* paura di chiedere

hesi·ta·tion [ˌhɛzɪ'teɪʃən] N esitazione *f*; **I have no hesitation in saying (that) ...** non esito a dire che...

Hesperides [hɛ'spɛrɪˌdiːz] NPL Esperidi *fpl*

hes·sian ['hɛsɪən] N tela di canapa

hetero·geneous ['hɛtərəʊ'dʒiːnɪəs] ADJ eterogeneo(-a)

hetero·sex·ual ['hɛtərəʊ'sɛksjʊəl] ADJ, N eterosessuale (*m/f*)

het up [ˌhɛt'ʌp] ADJ (*fam*) agitato(-a); **to get het up** scaldarsi

HEW [ˌeɪtʃiː'dʌbljuː] N ABBR (*Am:* = **Department of Health, Education and Welfare**) *ministero della sanità, della pubblica istruzione e della previdenza sociale*

hew [hju:] (*pt* **hewed**, *pp* **hewed** *or* **hewn**) VT (*wood*) tagliare; (*stone, coal*) scavare; (*statue*) scolpire

hex [hɛks] (*Am*) N stregoneria
■VT stregare

hexa·deci·mal [ˌhɛksəˈdɛsɪməl] N (*Comput: also:* **hexadecimal notation**) notazione *f* esadecimale

hexa·gon [ˈhɛksəgən] N esagono

hex·ago·nal [hɛkˈsægənəl] ADJ esagonale

hey [heɪ] EXCL ehi!

hey·day [ˈheɪˌdeɪ] N età *or* tempi *mpl* d'oro; **in his heyday** quand'era in auge, ai bei tempi; **in the heyday of** ai tempi d'oro di

HF [ˌeɪtʃˈɛf] N ABBR (= **high frequency**) AF (= *alta frequenza*)

HGV [ˌeɪtʃdʒiːˈviː] N ABBR = **heavy goods vehicle**

HI ABBR (*Am Post*) = **Hawaii**

◎**hi** [haɪ] EXCL ciao!, salve!

hia·tus [haɪˈeɪtəs] N (*frm: gap*) vuoto; (*Gram*) iato

hi·ber·nate [ˈhaɪbəˌneɪt] VI andare in letargo, ibernare

hi·ber·na·tion [ˌhaɪbəˈneɪʃən] N letargo, ibernazione *f*

hi·bis·cus [hɪˈbɪskəs] N ibisco

hic·cough, hic·cup [ˈhɪkʌp] N singhiozzo; **to have hiccoughs** avere il singhiozzo
■VI avere il singhiozzo, singhiozzare

hick [hɪk] (*Am fam*) N burino(-a)
■ADJ (*ideas*) da burino(-a); (*town*) provinciale

hid [hɪd] PT *of* **hide**

hid·den [ˈhɪdn] PP *of* **hide**
■ADJ (*gen*) nascosto(-a); (*meaning*) recondito(-a); **there are no hidden extras** è veramente tutto compreso nel prezzo

hidden agenda N programma *m* non dichiarato

◎**hide¹** [haɪd] (*pt* **hid**, *pp* **hidden**) VT (*gen*) nascondere; (*feelings, truth*) dissimulare; **Paula hid the present** Paula ha nascosto il regalo; **the clouds hid the sun** le nuvole hanno nascosto *or* coperto il sole; **to hide sth from sb** nascondere qc a qn
■VI nascondersi; **he hid behind a bush** si è nascosto dietro ad un cespuglio; **he's hiding behind his illness** si trincera dietro la sua malattia; **to hide one's light under a bushel** (*fig*) tenere nascoste le proprie virtù
▸ **hide away** VI + ADV nascondersi, rifugiarsi
■VT + ADV nascondere
▸ **hide out** VI + ADV nascondersi

hide² [haɪd] N (*skin*) pelle *f*; (*leather*) cuoio

hide-and-seek [ˌhaɪdənˈsiːk] N nascondino, rimpiattino; **to play hide-and-seek** giocare a nascondino

hide·away [ˈhaɪdəˌweɪ] N (*hiding place*) nascondiglio; (*secluded spot*) rifugio

hide·bound [ˈhaɪdˌbaʊnd] ADJ limitato(-a), gretto(-a)

hid·eous [ˈhɪdɪəs] ADJ (*sight, person*) orribile, orrendo(-a); (*crime*) atroce

hid·eous·ly [ˈhɪdɪəslɪ] ADV (*deformed, tortured*) orrendamente; (*fig: expensive, disappointed*) estremamente, terribilmente

hide-out [ˈhaɪdˌaʊt] N nascondiglio

hid·ing¹ [ˈhaɪdɪŋ] N: **to be in hiding** tenersi nascosto(-a); **to go into hiding** darsi alla macchia

hid·ing² [ˈhaɪdɪŋ] N botte *fpl*; **to give sb a good hiding** (*fam*) suonarle a qn; **his father will give him a good hiding** suo padre gliele suonerà

hiding place N nascondiglio

hi·er·ar·chy [ˈhaɪəˌrɑːkɪ] N (*frm*) gerarchia

hi·ero·glyph·ic [ˌhaɪərəˈglɪfɪk] ADJ geroglifico(-a)

hieroglyphics [ˌhaɪərəˈglɪfɪks] NPL geroglifici *mpl*

hi-fi [ˈhaɪˈfaɪ] ADJ, N ABBR (= **high fidelity**) hi-fi (*m*) *inv*; **hi-fi system** impianto hi-fi

higgledy-piggledy [ˈhɪgldɪˈpɪgldɪ] ADJ buttato(-a) alla rinfusa
■ADV alla rinfusa

◎**high** [haɪ] ADJ (*comp* **-er**, *superl* **-est**) **1** (*gen*) alto(-a); **the wall's two metres high** il muro è alto due metri; **a building 60 metres high** un palazzo alto 60 metri; **how high is Ben Nevis?** quanto è alto il Ben Nevis?; **since she was so high** (*fam*) fin da quando era grande *or* alta così ; **to leave sb high and dry** (*fig*) piantare in asso qn; **to be on one's high horse** (*fig*) montare *or* salire in cattedra; **to be** *or* **act high and mighty** darsi delle arie **2** (*frequency, pressure, temperature, salary, price*) alto(-a); (*speed, wind*) forte; (*character, ideals*) nobile; (*value, respect, number*) grande; **to pay a high price for sth** pagare (molto) caro(-a) qc; **prices are higher in Germany** i prezzi sono più alti in Germania; **there's high unemployment in Europe** c'è una forte disoccupazione in Europa; **to be high in sth** avere un alto contenuto di qc; **it's very high in fat** ha un altissimo contenuto di grassi; **his colour is very high** è molto rosso in viso; **to have a high old time** (*fam*) spassarsela; **it's high time you were in bed** (*fam*) dovresti essere già a letto da un pezzo **3** (*Mus: note*) alto(-a); (*sound, voice*) acuto(-a); **she's got a very high voice** ha una voce molto acuta **4** (*fam: on drugs*) fatto(-a); (*: on drink*) su di giri **5** (*Brit Culin: meat, game*) frollato(-a); (*: spoilt*) andato(-a) a male
■ADV (*fly, aim, climb*) in alto; **the doves flew high in the sky** le colombe volavano alte nel cielo; **the plane flew high over the mountains** l'aereo volava alto sulle montagne; **high up** molto in alto; **high above the clouds** in alto sopra le nuvole; **higher and higher** sempre più (in) alto; **the bidding went as high as £500** le offerte sono arrivate fino a 500 sterline; **to hunt high and low** cercare per mare e per terra; **feelings were running high** c'era molta tensione
■N **1 on high** (*in heaven*) nell'alto dei cieli; **orders from on high** (*also hum*) ordini dall'alto **2 exports have reached a new high** le esportazioni hanno toccato un nuovo record **3** (*Met*) anticiclone *m*, area di alta pressione

high altar N altare *m* maggiore

high·ball [ˈhaɪˌbɔːl] N (*Am: drink*) *whisky (or brandy) e soda con ghiaccio*

high·boy [ˈhaɪˌbɔɪ] N (*Am*) cassettone *m*

high·brow [ˈhaɪˌbraʊ] N, ADJ intellettualoide (*m/f*)

high·chair [ˈhaɪˌtʃɛəʳ] N seggiolone *m*

high-class [ˈhaɪˌklɑːs] ADJ (*neighbourhood*) elegante; (*hotel*) di prim'ordine; (*person*) di gran classe; (*food*) raffinato(-a)

high command N (*Mil*) stato maggiore

high commissioner N alto commissario

high court N (*Law*) ≈ Corte *f* Suprema

high-density [ˌhaɪˈdɛnsɪtɪ] ADJ (*Comput: disk*) ad alta densità

high-end [ˈhaɪɛnd] ADJ di alta fascia

high·er [ˈhaɪəʳ] ADJ (*form of life, study*) superiore
■ADV più in alto, più in su

◎**higher education** N istruzione *f* superiore *or* universitaria

highest common factor [ˈhaɪɪst-] N: **the highest common factor** il massimo comun divisore

high explosive N esplosivo ad alto potenziale

high·fa·lu·tin [ˌhaɪfəˈluːtɪn] ADJ (*fam*) pomposo(-a)

high fidelity N alta fedeltà

Hh

high finance N alta finanza
high-flier, **high-flyer** [ˌhaɪˈflaɪəʳ] N (*ambitious*) rampante *m/f*, ambizioso(-a); (*gifted*) giovane *m/f* di talento
high-flown [ˌhaɪˈfləʊn] ADJ (*speech*) altisonante(-a); (*language*) ampolloso(-a)
high-flying [ˈhaɪˌflaɪɪŋ] ADJ (*aircraft*) da alta quota; (*fig: person, aim*) ambizioso(-a)
high frequency N alta frequenza
high-handed [ˌhaɪˈhændɪd] ADJ dispotico(-a), autoritario(-a)
high-handedly [ˌhaɪˈhændɪdlɪ] ADV dispoticamente, in modo autoritario
high-handedness [ˌhaɪˈhændɪdnɪs] N dispotismo, autoritarismo
high-heeled [ˌhaɪˈhiːld] ADJ con il tacco alto
high-impact [ˌhaɪˈɪmpækt] ADJ (*aerobics*) ad alto impatto; (*material*) ultraresistente
high·jack [ˈhaɪˌdʒæk] VT, N = **hijack**
high jinks [ˈhaɪˌdʒɪŋks] NPL: **to have high jinks** (*fam*) far baldoria
high jump N (*Sport*) salto in alto; **you'll be for the high jump when Dad finds out** (*fam*) papà ti ammazza quando lo viene a sapere
high jumper N (*Sport: athlete*) saltatore(-trice) in alto
high·lands [ˈhaɪləndz] NPL zona montuosa; **the Highlands** le Highlands scozzesi
high-level [ˈhaɪˌlɛvl] ADJ (*talks, conference*) ad alto livello; (*Comput: language*) di alto livello
high life N: **the high life** la vita dell'alta società *or* del bel mondo
◎ **high·light** [ˈhaɪˌlaɪt] VT (*fig*) mettere in evidenza; (*in painting, drawing*) lumeggiare
■ N (*fig: of evening, trip*) clou *m inv*; (*Art*) luce *f*; **highlights** NPL (*in hair*) colpi *mpl* di sole, riflessi *mpl*; **the highlight of the evening** il clou della serata; **the highlight of the holiday** il momento più bello della vacanza
high·light·er [ˈhaɪˌlaɪtəʳ] N (*pen*) evidenziatore *m*
◎ **high·ly** [ˈhaɪlɪ] ADV estremamente, molto; **highly paid** pagato(-a) molto bene; **highly spiced dishes** piatti molto piccanti; **highly specialized** altamente specializzato(-a); **to think highly of sb** avere molta stima di qn; **to speak highly of** parlare molto bene di
highly-strung [ˌhaɪlɪˈstrʌŋ] ADJ nervoso(-a), teso(-a)
High Mass N messa cantata *or* solenne
high-minded [ˌhaɪˈmaɪndɪd] ADJ (*person*) retto(-a), di alti principi; (*ideals, ambitions*) nobile
high-necked [ˌhaɪˈnɛkt] ADJ (*pullover, blouse*) a collo alto
high·ness [ˈhaɪnɪs] N: **Your Highness** Vostra Altezza
high noon N mezzogiorno
high-octane [ˈhaɪˌɒkteɪn] ADJ (*petrol*) ad alto numero di ottani; (*fig*) eccitante
high-pitched [ˌhaɪˈpɪtʃt] ADJ acuto(-a)
high point N: **the high point** (*of show, evening, holiday*) il clou *m inv*
high-powered [ˌhaɪˈpaʊəd] ADJ (*engine*) molto potente, ad alta potenza; (*fig: person*) di prestigio
high-pressure [ˌhaɪˈprɛʃəʳ] ADJ ad alta pressione; (*fig*) aggressivo(-a)
high pressure N (*Met*) alta pressione
high priest N gran sacerdote *m*
high priestess N **1** (*Rel*) grande sacerdotessa **2** (*fig: expert*): **the high priestess of sth** la grande sacerdotessa di qc
high-ranking [ˌhaɪˈræŋkɪŋ] ADJ di alto rango
high-rise [ˈhaɪˌraɪz] ADJ: **high-rise building** palazzone *m*
high-risk [ˌhaɪˈrɪsk] ADJ **1** (*risky: strategy*) molto rischioso **2** (*at risk: person, group*) ad alto rischio **3** (*Insurance: driver, area*) ad alto rischio **4** (*Fin: bond, security, investment*) ad alto rischio
high·road [ˈhaɪˌrəʊd] N strada principale *or* maestra
high school N (*Brit*) ≈ scuola media inferiore e superiore (*dagli 11 ai 18 anni*), (*Am*) ≈ scuola media superiore

HIGH SCHOOL

Negli Stati Uniti gli studenti dai 15 ai 18 anni(dal "ninth grade" al "twelfth grade") frequentano le **high schools**. Al termine del "twelfth grade", in base ai risultati ottenuti, gli studenti ricevono il loro diploma nel corso di una cerimonia piuttosto formale.
Molti aspetti della vita delle **high schools** americane sono oggetto di programmi televisivi e film, specialmente il ballo dell'ultimo anno scolastico, detto "senior prom", e l'importante ruolo che rivestono sport come il football americano e il basket. I momenti salienti di ogni anno scolastico vengono riportati in una sorta di annuario detto "yearbook", che gli studenti acquistano come ricordo. *Vedi anche* **PROM**
> www.ed.gov/index.jhtml

high seas N: **on the high seas** in altomare
high season N (*Brit*) alta stagione *f*
high society N alta società
high-sounding [ˌhaɪˈsaʊndɪŋ] ADJ (*speech, ideas*) altisonante; (*language*) ampolloso(-a)
high-speed [ˈhaɪˌspiːd] ADJ (*film*) ultrarapido(-a); **high-speed train** treno rapido
high spirits NPL buonumore *msg*; **to be in high spirits** essere euforico(-a)
high spot N clou *m inv*
high street N (*Brit*) strada principale, corso
high summer N piena estate *f*
high table N (*Univ*) tavola dei professori (*nella sala della mensa*)
high tea N (*Brit*) *pasto consumato verso le sei di sera al posto della cena*
high-tech [ˌhaɪˈtek] ADJ high-tech *inv*, ad alto contenuto tecnologico
high tide N alta marea; **at high tide** *or* **water** quando c'è l'alta marea
high treason N alto tradimento
high-up [ˌhaɪˈʌp] N (*person*) pezzo grosso
high·way [ˈhaɪˌweɪ] N strada principale *or* maestra; **public highway** strada pubblica; **he knows all the highways and byways of Tuscany** conosce tutte le strade e stradine della Toscana; **a six-lane highway** una strada a sei corsie
Highway Code N (*Brit*): **the Highway Code** il codice *m* della strada
highway·man [ˈhaɪˌweɪmən] N (*pl* **-men**) ≈ bandito
hi·jab [hɪˈdʒæb] N hijab *m inv*; *copricapo mussulmano*
hi·jack [ˈhaɪˌdʒæk] VT (*aircraft*) dirottare; (*lorry, car*) impadronirsi di
■ N dirottamento
hi·jack·er [ˈhaɪˌdʒækəʳ] N (*of aircraft*) dirottatore(-trice)
hi·jack·ing [ˈhaɪˌdʒækɪŋ] N pirateria aerea; (*incident*) dirottamento

hike [haɪk] N **1** escursione *f* a piedi; **to go on** *or* **for a hike** fare un'escursione *or* una gita a piedi **2** (*fam: in prices*) aumento
■VI fare un'escursione *or* una gita a piedi; **to go hiking** fare escursioni a piedi
■VT (*fam*) aumentare

hik·er ['haɪkəʳ] N escursionista *m/f*

hi·lari·ous [hɪ'lɛərɪəs] ADJ spassosissimo(-a)

hi·lar·ity [hɪ'lærɪtɪ] N ilarità

◎**hill** [hɪl] N collina; (*lower*) colle *m*; (*slope*) pendio, costa; **hills and lakes** colline e laghi; **we pushed the car to the top of the hill** abbiamo spinto la macchina in cima al pendio; **up hill and down dale** per monti e per valli; **to be over the hill** (*fig fam*) essere sul viale del tramonto; **as old as the hills** vecchio(-a) come Matusalemme

hill·bil·ly ['hɪl,bɪlɪ] N (*Am*) montanaro del sud degli Stati Uniti; (*pej*) zotico(-a)

hill farming N ≈ alpeggio

hill·ock ['hɪlək] N collinetta, poggio

hill·side ['hɪl,saɪd] N pendio

hill start N (*Aut*) partenza in salita

hill·top ['hɪl,tɒp] N sommità *f inv* della collina; **on the hilltop** in cima alla collina

hill-walking ['hɪlwɔ:kɪŋ] N: **to go hill-walking** fare passeggiate in collina

hilly ['hɪlɪ] ADJ (*comp* **-ier**, *superl* **-iest**) collinoso(-a), montagnoso(-a); **this road is very hilly** questa strada è un continuo saliscendi

hilt [hɪlt] N (*of sword*) elsa, impugnatura; **to back sb to the hilt** dare il proprio appoggio incondizionato a qn; **to mortgage sth up to the hilt** ipotecare completamente qc

◎**him** [hɪm] PERS PRON **1** (*direct: unstressed*) lo, l'+ *vowel*; (: *stressed*) lui; **I hear him** lo sento; **I heard him** l'ho sentito; **I saw him** l'ho visto; **I've never seen HIM** lui, non l'ho mai visto **2** (*indirect*) gli; **I gave him the book** gli ho dato il libro; **I spoke to him** gli ho parlato **3** (*after prep, in comparatives*) lui; **without him** senza di lui; **I was thinking of him** pensavo a lui; **he had a case with him** aveva con sé una valigia; **I'm going with him** vado con lui; **look at him!** guardalo!; **if I were him** se fossi in lui; **it's him** è lui; **I'm older than him** sono più vecchio di lui

Hima·la·yas [,hɪmə'leɪəz] NPL: **the Himalayas** l'Himalaia *msg*

◎**him·self** [hɪm'sɛlf] PERS PRON (*reflexive*) si; (*emphatic*) lui stesso; (*after preposition*) sé, se stesso; **(all) by himself** (tutto) da solo *or* da sé; **he doesn't like travelling by himself** non gli piace viaggiare da solo; **he's not himself today** ha qualcosa che non va oggi; **he's hurt himself** si è fatto male; **he was looking at himself in the mirror** si guardava allo specchio; **he did it himself** l'ha fatto lui; **he talked mainly about himself** parlava principalmente di sé; *see also* **oneself**

hind¹ [haɪnd] ADJ (*leg*) posteriore; **he would talk the hind leg off a donkey** (*fam*) parla come una macchinetta

hind² [haɪnd] N (*Zool*) cerva

hin·der ['hɪndəʳ] VT (*prevent*): **to hinder sb (from doing sth)** impedire a qn (di fare qc); (*delay*) ritardare; (*obstruct*) ostacolare, intralciare; **I want to help, not hinder you** voglio aiutarti, non intralciarti; **the loss of documents hindered the investigation** la perdita di documenti ha ritardato l'indagine

Hin·di ['hɪndɪ] N (*language*) hindi *m*

hind·quarters ['haɪnd,kwɔ:təz] NPL (*Zool*) posteriore *msg*

hin·drance ['hɪndrəns] N intralcio, impedimento, ostacolo; **to be a hindrance to** intralciare, ostacolare

hind·sight ['haɪnd,saɪt] N senno di poi; **with the benefit of hindsight** con il senno di poi

Hin·du ['hɪn'du:] ADJ, N indù (*m/f*) *inv*

Hin·du·ism ['hɪndu:,ɪzəm] N (*Rel*) induismo
▷ www.hindunet.org/

hinge [hɪndʒ] N (*of door, gate*) cardine *m*; (*of box*) cerniera
■VI: **to hinge on** (*fig*) dipendere da

hinged [hɪndʒd] ADJ (*door*) provvisto(-a) di cardini; (*box, lid*) incernierato(-a)

◎**hint** [hɪnt] N (*suggestion*) allusione *f*, accenno; (*advice*) consiglio; **a hint of garlic** una punta d'aglio; **hints on do-it-yourself** consigli pratici per il fai-da-te; **a gentle hint** una velata allusione; **to give sb a broad hint** far capire chiaramente a qn; **to drop a hint** lasciar capire; **he dropped a hint that he'd like to see her more often** le ha lasciato capire che voleva vederla più spesso; **to take the hint** capire l'antifona; **I told him I was a bit tired, but he didn't take the hint** gli ho detto che ero un po' stanca, ma non ha capito; **with a hint of irony/sadness** con una punta d'ironia/tristezza; **give me a hint** (*clue*) dammi almeno un'idea, dammi un'indicazione
■VT: **to hint (to sb) that ...** lasciar capire (a qn) che...; **he hinted that I had a good chance of getting the job** ha lasciato capire che avevo buone probabilità di ottenere il lavoro
▸ **hint at** VI + PREP accennare a, alludere a, fare allusione a; **just what are you hinting at?** cosa vuoi insinuare?

hinter·land ['hɪntə,lænd] N hinterland *m inv*

◎**hip¹** [hɪp] N (*Anat*) anca; (*side*) fianco; **to put one's hands on one's hips** mettersi le mani sui fianchi; **she put her hands on her hips** si è messa le mani sui fianchi

hip² [hɪp] N (*Bot*) frutto della rosa canina

hip³ [hɪp] ADJ (*fam: trendy*) all'ultima moda, in *inv*

hip bath N semicupio

hip·bone ['hɪp,bəʊn] N ileo, osso iliaco

hip flask N fiaschetta

hip hop N hip-hop *m inv*

hip joint N articolazione *f* dell'anca

hip·pie, **hip·py** ['hɪpɪ] N hippy *m/f inv*

hip·po ['hɪpəʊ] N ippopotamo

hip pocket N tasca posteriore dei calzoni

Hippocrates [hɪ'pɒkrə,ti:z] N Ippocrate *m*

Hippolytus [hɪ'pɒlɪtəs] N Ippolito

hippo·pota·mus [,hɪpə'pɒtəməs] N (*pl* **hippopotamuses** *or* **hippopotami** [,hɪpə'pɒtəmaɪ]) ippopotamo

hippy ['hɪpɪ] N = **hippie**

hip·sters ['hɪpstəz] NPL (*trousers*) pantaloni *mpl* a vita bassa

◎**hire** ['haɪəʳ] N noleggio; (*cost*) nolo; **car hire** noleggio auto; **"for hire"** "noleggiasi"; (*taxi*) "libero"; **on hire** a nolo
■VT (*Brit: car, equipment*) noleggiare; (*employee*) ingaggiare; **we hired a car** abbiamo noleggiato una macchina; **they hired a lawyer** hanno assunto un avvocato; **hired hand** bracciante *m/f*; **hired assassin** sicario prezzolato
▸ **hire out** VT + ADV noleggiare, dare a nolo *or* noleggio, affittare

Hh

hired car [ˌhaɪəd'kɑː], **hire car** N (*Brit*) macchina a nolo

hire-purchase [ˌhaɪə'pɜːtʃɪs] N (*Brit*) acquisto (*or* vendita) a rate; **to buy sth on hire-purchase** comprare qc a rate

◉ **his** [hɪz] POSS ADJ, PRON il/la suo(-a), *pl* i/le suoi/sue; **his address** il suo indirizzo; **his house** la sua casa; **his brother** suo fratello; **his aunt** sua zia; **Joe and his father** Joe e suo padre; **his parents** i suoi genitori; **his opinions** le sue opinioni; **a friend of his** un suo amico; **his is red, mine is green** il suo è rosso, il mio è verde; **this is his** questo è (il) suo; **he took off his coat** si è tolto il cappotto; **he's washing his hair** si sta lavando i capelli; **my dog and his** il mio cane e il suo; **my parents and his** i miei genitori e i suoi; **my car is older than his** la mia macchina è più vecchia della sua; **my shoes and his** le mie scarpe e le sue; **whose is this? – it's his** di chi è questo? – è suo; **is that car his?** è sua quella macchina?

hiss [hɪs] N (*of snake*) sibilo; (*of kettle, protest*) fischio; (*of cat*) soffio; **shouts and hisses** grida e fischi
■ VI (*see n*) sibilare; fischiare; soffiare; **the audience hissed** il pubblico fischiò
■ VT (*speaker*) fischiare; **"get out" she hissed** "sparisci" sibilò

his·to·gram ['hɪstəˌɡræm] N istogramma *m*

his·to·rian [hɪs'tɔːrɪən] N storico(-a)

◉ **his·tor·ic** [hɪs'tɒrɪk] ADJ storico(-a)

◉ **his·tori·cal** [hɪs'tɒrɪkəl] ADJ storico(-a)

his·to·ri·og·ra·pher [hɪˌstɔːrɪ'ɒɡrəfə^r] N storiografo(-a)

◉ **his·to·ry** ['hɪstərɪ] N storia; **a history book** un libro di storia; **to make history** fare storia; **to go down in history** passare alla storia; **there's a long history of that illness in his family** ci sono molti precedenti (della malattia) nella sua famiglia; **a history of drinking problems** un passato da alcolista; **he's history** è finito
▷ www.bbc.co.uk/history/
▷ www.nationalarchives.gov.uk

his·tri·on·ic [ˌhɪstrɪ'ɒnɪk] ADJ (*pej*) istrionesco(-a)

his·tri·on·ics [ˌhɪstrɪ'ɒnɪks] NPL (*pej*) scene *fpl*

◉ **hit** [hɪt] (*vb: pt, pp* **hit**) N
1 (*blow*) colpo; (*Sport*) tiro, colpo; **she made three hits and two misses** ha messo a segno tre colpi e ne ha mancati due; **to score a direct hit** colpire in pieno
2 (*Mus, Theatre, Cine*) successo; **to be a hit** essere un (gran) successo; **the song is a big hit** è una canzone di successo; **the band's latest hit** l'ultimo successo del complesso; **she's a hit with everyone** (*fam*) ha successo con tutti, fa colpo su tutti; **to get a hit/10,000 hits** (*Comput*) trovare una pagina Web/10.000 pagine Web
■ VT
1 (*strike, affect: gen*) colpire; (*thrash: person*) picchiare; (*knock against*) battere; (*collide with: car*) urtare, sbattere contro; **he hit the ball** ha colpito la palla; **Andrew hit him** Andrew l'ha picchiato; **he was hit by a car** è stato investito da una macchina; **to hit the target** colpire il bersaglio; **to hit sb a blow** dare un colpo a qn; **to hit a man when he's down** (*fig*) infierire su chi non può difendersi; **to hit the mark** colpire nel segno, raggiungere lo scopo; **then it hit me** (*realization: fam*) solo allora me ne sono reso conto; **the news hit him hard** la notizia è stata un brutto colpo per lui
2 (*reach: target, musical note*) raggiungere; (*: road*) trovare, raggiungere; (*: speed*) toccare; (*: difficulty, snag*) incontrare, imbattersi in; (*fam: arrive at: town*) arrivare in; **to hit the papers** finire sui giornali; **to hit the headlines** far titolo; **to hit the front page** apparire in prima pagina; **to hit the bottle** (*fam*) darsi al bere; **to hit the ceiling** (*fam*) andare su tutte le furie; **to hit the road** *or* **the trail** (*fam*) levare le tende; **to hit the hay** *or* **the sack** (*fam*) andare a letto
■ ADJ (*song, film*) di successo
▸ **hit against** VI + PREP sbattere contro; **to hit against sth** sbattere contro qc
▸ **hit back** VI + ADV restituire il colpo; **to hit back at sb** (*fig*) reagire contro qn
■ VT + ADV: **to hit sb back** restituire il colpo a qn
▸ **hit off** VT + ADV: **to hit it off with sb** andare d'accordo con qn
▸ **hit on** VI + PREP: **to hit on sb** (*Am fam*) fare avance sessuali a qn
▸ **hit out at** VI + ADV + PREP sferrare (dei) colpi contro; (*fig*) attaccare
▸ **hit (up)on** VI + PREP (*answer*) imbroccare, azzeccare; (*solution*) trovare (per caso)

hit-and-run ['hɪtən'rʌn] ADJ: **hit-and-run driver** pirata *m* della strada; **hit-and-run raid** (*Mil*) attacco *m* lampo *inv*; **hit-and-run tactics** (*Mil*) tattica dell'attacco lampo

hitch [hɪtʃ] N (*impediment, obstacle*) intoppo, contrattempo; (*difficulty*) difficoltà *f inv*; **there's been a slight hitch** c'è stato un piccolo intoppo; **technical hitch** difficoltà tecnica; **without a hitch** senza intoppi, a gonfie vele
■ VT **1** (*fasten*) attaccare; (*: to post*) legare; **to get hitched** (*fam*) sposarsi **2** (*fam*): **to hitch a lift** fare l'autostop
■ VI (*fam*) = **hitchhike**
▸ **hitch up** VT + ADV (*trousers*) tirarsi su; (*horse, cart*) attaccare

hitch·hike ['hɪtʃˌhaɪk] VI fare l'autostop; **we hitchhiked through Europe** abbiamo girato tutta l'Europa in autostop

hitch·hiker ['hɪtʃˌhaɪkə^r] N autostoppista *m/f*

hitch·hiking ['hɪtʃˌhaɪkɪŋ] N autostop *m*

hi-tech ['haɪ'tɛk] ADJ (*Industry*) tecnologicamente avanzato(-a), hi-tech *inv*
■ N (*Industry*) tecnologia avanzata; (*Archit, Design*) hi-tech *m or f inv*

hith·er ['hɪðə^r] ADV (*old*) qui, qua; **hither and thither** (*liter*) qua e là

hither·to ['hɪðə'tuː] ADV (*frm*) finora

hit list N: **to be on a hit list** essere un bersaglio

hit man N (*fam*) sicario, killer *m inv*

hit-or-miss ['hɪtɔː'mɪs] ADJ (*approach*) disinvolto(-a); (*work*) così cosà; **the service in this hotel is very hit-or-miss** il servizio in questo albergo lascia a desiderare

hit parade N hit-parade *f inv*

HI-USA N ABBR (= **Hostelling International USA**) ≈ AIG *f* (= *Associazione italiana alberghi per la gioventù*)

HIV [ˌeɪtʃaɪ'viː] N ABBR (= **human immunodeficiency virus**) HIV *m inv*

hive [haɪv] N alveare *m*; (*bees collectively*) sciame *m*; **the shop was a hive of activity** (*fig*) c'era una grande attività nel negozio
▸ **hive off** VI + ADV: **to hive off (from)** staccarsi (da)
■ VT + ADV staccare; (*privatize*) privatizzare; **waste collection will be hived off to another company** la raccolta dei rifiuti verrà trasferita ad un'altra società

HIV-negative [ˌeɪtʃaɪˌviː'nɛɡətɪv] ADJ sieronegativo(-a)

HIV-positive [ˌeɪtʃaɪˌviːˈpɒzɪtɪv] ADJ sieropositivo(-a)
hl ABBR (= **hectolitre**) hl
HM [ˌeɪtʃˈɛm] N ABBR (= **His (or Her) Majesty**) SM (= *Sua Maestà*)
HMG [ˌeɪtʃɛmˈdʒiː] N ABBR *(Brit)* = *His (or Her) Majesty's Government*
HMI [ˌeɪtʃɛmˈaɪ] N ABBR *(Brit Scol:* = **His (or Her) Majesty's Inspector**) ≈ ispettore(-trice) scolastico(-a)
HMO [ˌeɪtʃɛmˈəʊ] N ABBR *(Am:* = **health maintenance organization**) *organo per la salvaguardia della salute pubblica*
HMS [ˌeɪtʃɛmˈɛs] N ABBR *(Brit)* = *His (or Her) Majesty's Ship*
HMSO [ˌeɪtʃɛmɛsˈəʊ] N ABBR *(Brit:* = **His (or Her) Majesty's Stationery Office**) ≈ Istituto poligrafico dello Stato
HNC [ˌeɪtʃɛnˈsiː] N ABBR *(Brit:* = **Higher National Certificate**) *diploma di istituto tecnico o professionale*
HND [ˌeɪtʃɛnˈdiː] N ABBR *(Brit:* = **Higher National Diploma**) *diploma in materie tecniche equivalente ad una laurea*
hoard [hɔːd] N *(of food)* provviste *fpl*, scorta; *(of money)* gruzzolo
■VT *(also:* **hoard up**: *provisions)* fare incetta *or* provvista di; (: *money*) ammonticchiare; (: *old newspapers*) accumulare
hoard·ing [ˈhɔːdɪŋ] N *(Brit: for advertisements)* tabellone *m or* riquadro per affissioni; *(wooden fence)* staccionata, palizzata
hoar·frost [ˈhɔːˈfrɒst] N brina
hoarse [hɔːs] ADJ *(comp* **-r**, *superl* **-st**) rauco(-a); **they shouted themselves hoarse** si sono sgolati a forza di urlare
hoarse·ly [ˈhɔːslɪ] ADV con voce roca, raucamente
hoarse·ness [ˈhɔːsnɪs] N raucedine *f*
hoary [ˈhɔːrɪ] ADJ *(comp* **-ier**, *superl* **-iest**) *(liter: hair)* bianco(-a); (: *person)* canuto(-a), dai capelli bianchi; *(ancient)* vetusto(-a); **it's a hoary old joke** è una barzelletta vecchia
hoax [həʊks] N scherzo; *(bomb scare)* falso allarme *m*; **it was a hoax** è stato un falso allarme; **the warning call was a hoax** la telefonata minatoria è stata uno scherzo
■VT prendere in giro; **he hoaxed me into believing that ...** mi ha fatto credere che...
hob [hɒb] N piastra (con fornelli)
Ho·bart [ˈhəʊbɑːt] N Hobart *f*
▹ www.hobartcity.com.au/hcc:homepage
▹ www.tased.edu.au/tot/s/hobart.html
hob·ble [ˈhɒbl] VI zoppicare; **to hobble in/out** entrare/uscire zoppicando
hob·by [ˈhɒbɪ] N hobby *m inv*, passatempo (preferito)
hobby-horse [ˈhɒbɪˌhɔːs] N **1** *(fig)* chiodo fisso
2 *(toy) giocattolo di legno raffigurante la testa di un cavallo montata su un bastone*
hob·nail(ed) boots [ˌhɒbneɪl(d)ˈbuːts] NPL scarponi *mpl* chiodati
hob·nob [ˈhɒbˌnɒb] VI *(fam)*: **to hobnob (with)** essere in confidenza (con)
hobo [ˈhəʊbəʊ] N *(Am)* vagabondo
Hobson's choice [ˈhɒbsənzˈtʃɔɪs] N: **it's Hobson's choice** è una questione di prendere o lasciare
hock[1] [hɒk] N *(of animal, Culin)* garretto
hock[2] [hɒk] N *(Brit: wine)* vino bianco del Reno
hock[3] [hɒk] *(fam)* N: **to be in hock** *(debt)* essere indebitato(-a)
■VT *(pawn)* impegnare
hock·ey [ˈhɒkɪ] N hockey *m* (su prato)
▹ www.fihockey.org
hockey stick N bastone *m* da hockey
hocus-pocus [ˈhəʊkəsˈpəʊkəs] N *(trickery)* trucco; *(words: of magician)* abracadabra *m inv*; *(talk)* ciance *fpl*
hod [hɒd] N *(Tech) cassetta per portare i mattoni*
hodge·podge [ˈhɒdʒˌpɒdʒ] N = **hotchpotch**
hoe [həʊ] N zappa
■VT *(ground)* zappare; *(weeds)* sarchiare
hog [hɒg] N porco, maiale *m*; **to go the whole hog** *(fig)* fare le cose fino in fondo
■VT *(fam)* accaparrarsi; **to hog the road** guidare nel mezzo della strada
Hog·man·ay [ˈhɒgməˌneɪ] N *(in Scotland)* ≈ San Silvestro

HOGMANAY

In Scozia il giorno di San Silvestro si chiama **Hogmanay** ed è festeggiato alla grande. È consuetudine organizzare feste e cenoni e, a mezzanotte, brindare e intonare "Auld Lang Syne", un'antica canzone tradizionale scozzeze il cui titolo significa "tempi passati". Si usa poi andare a trovare gli amici per brindare insieme al nuovo anno: il cosiddetto "first footing". La tradizione vuole che sia di buon auspicio per l'anno nuovo se il primo a varcare la soglia dopo la mezzanotte è un uomo dai capelli scuri che porta in dono qualcosa da bere, da mangiare o un pezzetto di carbone.
▹ www.hogmanay.net/hogmanay.htm

hog·wash [ˈhɒgˌwɒʃ] N *(fam)* stupidaggini *fpl*, cretinate *fpl*
hog·weed [ˈhɒgˌwiːd] N panace *m*, sedano dei prati
hoi pol·loi [ˌhɔɪpəˈlɔɪ] N *(pej)*: **the hoi polloi** la plebe
hoist [hɔɪst] VT issare
■N paranco; *(goods lift)* montacarichi *m inv*; *see also* **petard**
hoity-toity [ˌhɔɪtɪˈtɔɪtɪ] ADJ *(fam)* altezzoso(-a)
◎**hold** [həʊld] *(vb: pt, pp* **held**) N
1 presa; **to seize** *or* **grab hold of sth/sb** afferrare qc/qn; **to catch** *or* **get (a) hold of** afferrare, attaccarsi a; **to get hold of sb** *(fig: contact)* mettersi in contatto con qn; **to get hold of sth** procurarsi qc; **where can I get hold of some red paint?** dove posso procurarmi della vernice rossa?; **to get (a) hold of o.s.** *(fig)* trattenersi, controllarsi; **no holds barred** *(fig)* senza esclusione di colpi; **to have a hold over sb** *(fig)* avere un forte ascendente *or* molta influenza su qn
2 *(Naut, Aer)* stiva
3 *(Mountaineering)* appiglio
■VT
1 *(gen)* tenere; *(contain)* contenere; *(fig: audience)* mantenere viva l'attenzione di; (: *attention, interest)* mantenere; (: *belief, opinion)* avere; **he was holding her in his arms** la teneva tra le braccia; **he held the pistol in his right hand** teneva la pistola con la mano destra; **to hold hands** tenersi per mano; **to hold a baby** tenere in braccio un bambino; **she was holding the baby** teneva in braccio il bambino; **it holds ten litres** contiene dieci litri; **the hall holds 500 people** nella sala c'è posto per 500 persone; **the chair won't hold you** la sedia non sopporterà il tuo peso; **to hold o.s. upright/ready** tenersi dritto(-a)/pronto(-a); **to hold one's head high** andare a testa alta; **to hold sb to a promise** far mantenere una promessa a qn; **to hold one's own** sapersi difendere, difendersi bene; **she holds the view that ...** è del parere che...; **to hold**

Hh

the line (*Telec*) rimanere *or* restare in linea; **hold the line!** resti in linea!; **this car holds the road well** questa macchina tiene bene la strada; **what does the future hold?** cosa ci riserva il futuro?
2 (*restrain: person*) trattenere; **to hold sb prisoner** tenere prigioniero qn; **there's no holding him** non lo ferma più nessuno; **to hold one's breath** trattenere il respiro *or* il fiato; **I held my breath in amazement** sono rimasto a bocca aperta per lo stupore; **to hold one's tongue** (*fig*) tacere, star zitto(-a); **hold it!** (*fam*) alt!, fermati!
3 (*position, title, passport*) avere; (*shares: Fin*) possedere, avere; (*record: Sport*) detenere; (*position: Mil*) tenere, mantenere; **to hold office** (*Pol*) essere in carica
4 (*meeting, election*) tenere, indire; (*conversation*) tenere, sostenere; (*Rel: service*) celebrare
5 (*consider*): **to hold (that)** ritenere (che), sostenere (che); **to hold sb in high esteem** avere molta stima di qn; **to hold sth/sb dear** tenere molto a qc/qn; **to hold sb responsible for sth** considerare *or* ritenere qn responsabile di qc
■ VI (*rope, nail*) tenere; (*continue*) mantenersi, durare; (*be valid*) essere valido(-a); **to hold firm** *or* **fast** resistere bene, tenere
▸ **hold against** VT + PREP: **to hold sth against sb** (*fig*) volerne a qn per qc
▸ **hold back** VI + ADV: **to hold back from sth** tirarsi indietro da qc; **to hold back from doing sth** trattenersi dal fare qc; **he always holds back when he meets new people** quando incontra gente nuova è sempre poco espansivo
■ VT + ADV
1 (*restrain: crowd, river*) trattenere, contenere; (*: emotions, tears*) trattenere, frenare; **to hold sb back from doing sth** impedire a qn di fare qc
2 (*information, name*) nascondere, non dare, celare; **he's holding something back** non sta dicendo tutta la verità
▸ **hold down** VT + ADV
1 (*keep low, on ground*) tener giù; (*keep in place*) tener fermo(-a)
2 (*job*) conservare, mantenere
▸ **hold forth** VI + ADV fare *or* tenere una concione
▸ **hold in** VT + ADV (*stomach*) tirare *or* tenere in dentro; **to hold o.s. in** (*fig*) frenarsi, trattenersi
▸ **hold off** VT + ADV (*enemy*) tenere a distanza; (*attack*) sventare; (*visitor*) far aspettare
■ VI + ADV (*rain*): **if the rain holds off** se non si mette a piovere
▸ **hold on** VI + ADV (*endure*) resistere; (*wait*) aspettare; **hold on, I'm coming!** aspettami, arrivo!; **hold on!** (*Telec*) resti in linea!
■ VT + ADV tenere a posto
▸ **hold on to** VI + ADV + PREP (*grasp*) tenersi (attaccato(-a)) a, tenersi (stretto(-a)) a; (*keep*) tenere, conservare; (*fig: retain: hope*) rimanere aggrappato(-a) a
▸ **hold out** VI + ADV
1 (*supplies*) durare
2 (*stand firm*) tener duro; **to hold out for more money** (*fam*) continuare a chiedere più soldi; **to hold out (against)** resistere (a)
■ VT + ADV: **to hold out (sth to sb)** allungare (qc a qn); (*one's arms, hand*) tendere; (*fig: offer*) presentare, offrire; (*: hope*) nutrire
▸ **hold out on** VI + ADV + PREP: **you've been holding out on me!** (*fam*) mi hai tenuto nascosto qualcosa!
▸ **hold over** VT + ADV (*meeting*) rimandare, rinviare
▸ **hold together** VI + ADV (*group*) restare unito(-a)
■ VT + ADV (*factions*) tenere uniti(-e)
▸ **hold up** VT + ADV
1 (*raise*) sollevare, alzare; **hold up your hand** alza la mano; **to hold sth up to the light** alzare qc verso la luce
2 (*support: roof*) sostenere
3 (*delay: person*) trattenere; (*: traffic*) rallentare; (*stop*) bloccare
4 (*rob: bank*) assaltare; (*: person*) assalire
■ VI + ADV (*survive, last*) resistere; **how are your shoes holding up?** in che stato sono le tue scarpe?
▸ **hold with** VI + PREP (*fam*): **she doesn't hold with gambling** è contraria al gioco d'azzardo

hold·all ['həuld,ɔ:l] N (*Brit*) sacca *or* borsa da viaggio, borsone *m*

◎ **hold·er** ['həuldə^r] N **1** (*of ticket*) possessore *m*; (*owner: of property*) proprietario(-a); (*tenant*) affittuario(-a); (*of bonds, shares*) titolare *m/f*, intestatario(-a); (*of title*) chi ha *or* possiede; (*of passport, office, post*) titolare; (*of record*) detentore(-trice) **2** (*container*) contenitore *m*; **pencil holder** portamatite *m inv*

hold·ing ['həuldɪŋ] N (*land*) podere *m*, tenuta; **holdings** terre *fpl*, proprietà *fpl* terriere; **holdings** NPL (*Comm*) azioni *fpl*, titoli *mpl*

holding company N (*Comm*) holding *f inv*

holding pattern N (*Aer*) circuito di attesa

holding position N (*Aer*) area di attesa

hold-up ['həuld,ʌp] N (*robbery*) rapina a mano armata; (*stoppage, delay*) intoppo; (*Brit: of traffic*) ingorgo; **a bank clerk was injured in the hold-up** un impiegato di banca è rimasto ferito nella rapina; **no one explained the reason for the hold-up** nessuno ha spiegato i motivi dell'intoppo; **a hold-up on the motorway** un ingorgo sull'autostrada

◎ **hole** [həul] N **1** (*in ground, road, also Golf*) buca; (*in wall, fence, clothes*) buco; (*in dam, ship*) falla; (*in defences*) breccia; (*of rabbit, fox*) tana; **to wear a hole in sth** usare qc tanto da farci un buco; **to pick holes in** (*fig: argument*) dimostrare che fa acqua; **it made a hole in my savings** ha mangiato gran parte dei miei risparmi
2 (*fig fam: difficulty*): **to be in a hole** essere nei guai; **she got me out of a hole** mi ha tirato fuori dai pasticci *or* dai guai **3** (*fam pej: place*) buco
■ VT bucare; (*Golf: ball*) mandare in buca; **the boat was holed when it hit the rocks** quando la barca ha urtato gli scogli si è aperta una falla nello scafo
▸ **hole out** VI + ADV andare in buca
▸ **hole up** VI + ADV nascondersi, rifugiarsi

hole-and-corner [,həuland'kɔ:nə^r] ADJ (*fam*) furtivo(-a)

hole in one N (*Golf*) hole in one; **to get a hole in one** completare una buca con un colpo solo

hole in the heart N morbo blu

holey ['həulɪ] ADJ pieno(-a) di buchi

◎ **holi·day** ['hɒlədɪ] N (*vacation*) vacanza; (*from work*) ferie *fpl*; (*day off*) giorno di vacanza; **the school holidays** le vacanze scolastiche; **holiday with pay** ferie pagate *or* retribuite; **he took a day's holiday** ha preso un giorno di ferie; **public holiday** festa (nazionale); **next Monday is a holiday** lunedì prossimo è festa; **to be on holiday** essere in vacanza
■ ADJ (*town*) di villeggiatura; **holiday atmosphere** aria di vacanza; **holiday spirit** spirito vacanziero

holiday camp N (*Brit*) ≈ villaggio turistico

holiday home N seconda casa (*per le vacanze*)

holiday job N lavoro estivo (*di studente*)
holiday-maker ['hɒlədɪ,meɪkəʳ] N (*Brit*) villeggiante *m/f*, vacanziere(-a)
holiday pay N: **do you get holiday pay?** hai le ferie pagate?
holiday resort N luogo di villeggiatura
holiday season N stagione *f* delle vacanze
holiday traffic N traffico dell'esodo (*or* del rientro)
Ho·li·ness ['həʊlɪnɪs] N: **his Holiness** Sua Santità
ho·li·ness ['həʊlɪnɪs] N santità
hol·is·tic [həʊ'lɪstɪk] ADJ olistico(-a)
Hol·land ['hɒlənd] N Olanda
hol·ler ['hɒləʳ] VT, VI (*fam*) urlare, gridare
hol·low ['hɒləʊ] ADJ (*comp* **-er**, *superl* **-est**) cavo(-a), vuoto(-a); (*eyes, cheeks*) infossato(-a); (*sound, voice*) cupo(-a); (*sympathy*) falso(-a); (*promises*) vano(-a); **a hollow victory** una vittoria di Pirro; **to give a hollow laugh** ridere a denti stretti
■ ADV: **to beat sb hollow** (*fam*) stracciare qn
■ N (*of back*) incavo; (*of hand*) cavo; (*in ground*) cavità *f inv*, affossamento; (*small valley*) conca; (*in landscape*) valletta, depressione *f*
▸ **hollow out** VT + ADV scavare, incavare
hollow-cheeked [,hɒləʊ'tʃi:kt] ADJ dalle guance incavate
hollow-eyed [,hɒləʊ'aɪd] ADJ dagli occhi infossati
hol·ly ['hɒlɪ] N (*also:* **holly tree**) agrifoglio
hol·ly·hock ['hɒlɪ,hɒk] N malvone *m*
Hol·ly·wood ['hɒlɪ,wʊd] N Hollywood *f*
▷ www.hollywoodsign.org/
holm oak ['həʊm'əʊk] N leccio
holo·caust ['hɒlə,kɔ:st] N olocausto
▷ www.ushmm.org/
▷ www.holocaust-history.org
holo·gram ['hɒlə,græm] N ologramma *m*
ho·lo·gra·phy [hɒ'lɒgrəfɪ] N olografia
holo·phyt·ic [,hɒlə'fɪtɪk] ADJ olofitico(-a)
hols [hɒlz] NPL (*Brit fam*): **the hols** le vacanze *fpl*
hol·ster ['həʊlstəʳ] N fondina
◎ **holy** ['həʊlɪ] ADJ (*comp* **-ier**, *superl* **-iest**) (*gen*) santo(-a); (*ground, bread*) consacrato(-a), benedetto(-a); (*person*) pio(-a); (*vow*) religioso(-a); **the Holy Trinity** la Santissima Trinità; **a holy terror** (*fam*) un demonio
Holy Bible N: **the Holy Bible** la Sacra Bibbia
Holy City N: **the Holy City** (*Jerusalem*) la città santa
Holy Communion N la comunione, l'eucaristia
Holy Father N: **the Holy Father** il Santo Padre
Holy Land N: **the Holy Land** la Terra Santa
holy of holies N sancta sanctorum *m inv*
holy orders NPL ordini *mpl* (sacri)
Holy Spirit, Holy Ghost N: **the Holy Spirit, the Holy Ghost** lo Spirito Santo
Holy Week N la settimana santa
hom·age ['hɒmɪdʒ] N omaggio; **to pay homage to** rendere omaggio a
◎ **home** [həʊm] N
1 (*residence, house*) casa; (*country, area*) patria, paese *m* natale *or* natio; (*Bot: Zool*) habitat *m inv*; **to have a home of one's own** avere una casa propria; **it's near my home** è vicino a casa mia; **it's a home from home** è come essere a casa propria; **there's no place like home** non si sta mai bene come a casa propria; **she comes from a good home** viene da una buona famiglia; **he comes from a broken home** i suoi sono divisi; **to give sb/sth a home** prendersi in casa qn/qc; **he made his home in Italy** si è stabilito in Italia; **Scotland is the home of the haggis** la Scozia è la patria dell'haggis; **at home** a casa; **Celtic is playing at home on Saturday** il Celtic gioca in casa sabato; **make yourself at home** fai come se fossi a casa tua; **to make sb feel at home** mettere qn a proprio agio; **she is at home with the topic** conosce la materia benissimo; **I'm not at home to anyone** (*fig*) non ci sono per nessuno
2 (*institution*) istituto; (*for old people*) casa di riposo; **a children's home** un istituto per l'infanzia
■ ADV
1 a casa; **to go home** andare a casa; **to come home** tornare (a casa); **to stay home** stare a *or* restare in casa; **to get home** arrivare a casa; **I got home at 10 o'clock** sono rientrato alle 10; **I'll be home at five o'clock** sarò a casa alle cinque; **on the way home** sulla via di casa; **can I see you home?** posso accompagnarti a casa?; **it's nothing to write home about** (*fam*) non è gran che, non è niente di speciale; **we're home and dry** (*fig*) siamo salvi
2 (*right in*) a fondo, fino in fondo; **to drive a nail home** conficcare un chiodo; **to bring sth home to sb** (*fig*) aprire gli occhi a qn su qc; **that remark hit home** ciò che ha detto ha colpito nel segno
■ VI (*pigeons*) tornare alla base
■ ADJ (*life*) familiare; (*cooking*) casalingo(-a); (*improvements*) alla casa; (*comforts*) di casa; (*native: village*) natale, natio(-a); (*Econ: trade, market*) nazionale, interno(-a); (*: product, industries*) nazionale; (*news*) dall'interno; (*Sport: team*) di casa; (*: match, win*) in casa
▸ **home in on** VI + ADV + PREP (*missiles*) dirigersi (automaticamente) verso
home address N indirizzo di casa *or* privato
home-baked [,həʊm'beɪkt] ADJ fatto(-a) in casa
home-brew [həʊm'bru:] N birra *or* vino fatto(-a) in casa
home cinema N home theatre *m inv*
home·coming ['həʊm,kʌmɪŋ] N ritorno
home computer N home computer *m inv*
Home Counties NPL: **the Home Counties** le contee intorno a Londra
home economics N economia domestica
home front N fronte *m* interno
home ground N (*fig*): **to be on home ground** essere sul proprio terreno
home-grown [,həʊm'grəʊn] ADJ (*in locality*) nostrano(-a), di produzione locale
home help N (*Brit*) *assistente a domicilio per anziani o disabili stipendiata dai servizi sociali*
home·land ['həʊm,lænd] N patria
home leave N (*Mil*) licenza ordinaria
◎ **home·less** ['həʊmlɪs] ADJ senza tetto; **the homeless** NPL i senzatetto
home loan N mutuo per la casa
home-lover ['həʊm,lʌvəʳ] N persona cui piace stare a casa
home-loving ['həʊm,lʌvɪŋ] ADJ affezionato(-a) alla casa
home·ly ['həʊmlɪ] ADJ (*comp* **-ier**, *superl* **-iest**) (*food, person*) semplice, alla buona; (*atmosphere*) familiare, accogliente; (*advice*) pratico(-a); (*Am: plain: person, features*) insignificante
home-made [,həʊm'meɪd] ADJ fatto(-a) in casa, casalingo(-a)
home·maker ['həʊm,meɪkəʳ] N persona che si occupa della casa; (*woman*) donna di casa
Home Office N (*Brit*): **the Home Office** il Ministero degli Interni

Hh

homeo·path, homoeo·path [ˈhəumɪəupæθ] N omeopatico(-a)
homeo·path·ic, homoeo·path·ic [ˌhəumɪəuˈpæθɪk] ADJ omeopatico(-a)
homeopa·thy, homoeopa·thy [ˌhəumɪˈɒpəθɪ] N omeopatia
homeo·sta·sis [ˌhəumɪəuˈsteɪsɪs] N omeostasi *f*
home page N (*Comput*) home page *f inv*
home port N (*Naut*) porto d'origine
Homer [ˈhəuməʳ] N Omero; **even Homer nods** errare humanum est
hom·er [ˈhəuməʳ] N (*fam*) = **home run**
home rule N autogoverno, autonomia
home run N (*Baseball*) fuoricampo
Home Secretary N (*Brit*) ministro degli Interni
home shopping N shopping *m inv* da casa (*tramite Internet, la TV o un catalogo*)
home·sick [ˈhəumˌsɪk] ADJ: **to be homesick** sentire la mancanza di casa, avere nostalgia di casa
home·sick·ness [ˈhəumˌsɪknɪs] N nostalgia (di casa)
home side N (*Sport*) squadra che gioca in casa
home·spun [ˈhəumˌspʌn] ADJ (*fig*) alla buona; **homespun philosophy** filosofia spicciola
■ N tessuto filato a mano
home·stead [ˈhəumˌsted] N casa colonica
home straight, home stretch N (*Sport*) dirittura d'arrivo; **in the home straight** (*fig*) quasi arrivato(-a)
home team N (*Sport*) squadra che gioca in casa
home town N città *f inv* natale
home truths NPL: **to tell sb a few home truths** dire a qn quello che si merita
home·ward [ˈhəumwəd] ADJ (*journey*) di ritorno
home·ward(s) [ˈhəumwədz] ADV verso casa
home·work [ˈhəumˌwɜːk] N (*Scol*) compiti *mpl* (per casa); **have you done your homework?** hai fatto i compiti?
homi·ci·dal [ˌhɒmɪˈsaɪdl] ADJ omicida
homi·cide [ˈhɒmɪˌsaɪd] N omicidio
homi·ly [ˈhɒmɪlɪ] N (*frm*) omelia
hom·ing [ˈhəumɪŋ] ADJ (*device, missile*) autoguidato(-a)
homing pigeon N piccione *m* viaggiatore
homi·nid [ˈhɒmɪnɪd] N ominide *m*
homoeopa·thy *etc* [ˌhəumɪˈɒpəθɪ] = **homeopathy** *etc*
homo·erot·ic [ˌhəuməuɪˈrɒtɪk] ADJ erotico(-a) per gli omosessuali
homo·genei·ty [ˌhɒməudʒəˈniːɪtɪ] N omogeneità
homo·geneous [ˌhɒməˈdʒiːnɪəs], **homo·genous** [həˈmɒdʒɪnəs] ADJ omogeneo(-a)
ho·mog·enize [həˈmɒdʒəˌnaɪz] VT omogeneizzare
homo·graph·ic [ˌhɒməˈgræfɪk] ADJ omografo(-a)
ho·molo·gous [həuˈmɒləgəs] ADJ omologo(-a)
homo·nym [ˈhɒmənɪm] N omonimo
ho·mony·my [həˈmɒnɪmɪ] N omonimia
homo·pho·bia [ˌhɒməuˈfəubɪə] N omofobia
homo·pho·bic [ˌhɒməuˈfəubɪk] ADJ omofobo(-a)
◎ **homo·sex·ual** [ˈhɒməuˈsɛksjuəl] ADJ, N omosessuale (*m/f*)
homo·sex·ual·ity [ˈhɒməusɛksjuˈælɪtɪ] N omosessualità
homo·zy·gote [ˌhəuməuˈzaɪgəut] N omozigote *m*
Hon. ABBR **1** = **honourable** **2** = **honorary**
hon·cho [ˈhɒntʃəu] N (*fam*): **the head honcho** il gran capo
Hon·du·ras [hɒnˈdjuərəs] N Honduras *m*
hone [həun] VT (*sharpen*) affilare; (*fig*) affinare
◎ **hon·est** [ˈɒnɪst] ADJ (*person, face, actions*) onesto(-a); (*answer*) franco(-a), schietto(-a); (*means, method*) onesto(-a), lecito(-a); (*wages, profit*) decente, ragionevole; (*opinion*) sincero(-a); **an honest man** un uomo onesto; **to be honest ...** onestamente...; **to be quite honest with you ...** se devo dirti la verità...; **please be honest with me** ti prego di essere sincero con me; **tell me your honest opinion** dimmi cosa ne pensi sinceramente
honest broker N mediatore(-trice) esterno(-a)
hon·est·ly [ˈɒnɪstlɪ] ADV onestamente; (*truly*) sinceramente, francamente; **I didn't do it, honestly!** non l'ho fatto, sul serio!; **honestly?** davvero?; **honestly!** (*exasperated*) (ma) veramente!; **did you honestly think we wouldn't notice?** pensavi davvero che non l'avremmo notato?
hon·es·ty [ˈɒnɪstɪ] N **1** onestà; **in all honesty** a voler essere *or* per essere proprio sincero(-a), in tutta onestà **2** (*Bot*) monete *fpl* del Papa
hon·ey [ˈhʌnɪ] N miele *m*; (*Am fam*) tesoro, amore *m*; **a pot of honey** un vaso di miele; **hi honey, I'm here!** ciao cara, sono tornato!
honey·bee [ˈhʌnɪˌbiː] N ape *f*
honey·comb [ˈhʌnɪˌkəum] N favo; (*fig*) disegno *or* struttura a nido d'ape
■ VT (*fig*) sforacchiare, perforare; **honeycombed with tunnels** pieno(-a) di gallerie
honey·dew [ˈhʌnɪˌdjuː] N melata
honeydew melon N *tipo di melone con buccia gialla*
hon·eyed [ˈhʌnɪd] ADJ (*words*) dolce (come il miele)
honey·moon [ˈhʌnɪˌmuːn] N luna di miele, viaggio di nozze
■ VI fare la luna di miele, andare in viaggio di nozze
honeymoon couple N coppia in luna di miele
honey·pot [ˈhʌnɪpɒt] N: **a tourist honeypot** un luogo che attira i turisti
honey·suckle [ˈhʌnɪˌsʌkl] N caprifoglio
Hong Kong [ˈhɒŋˈkɒŋ] N Hong Kong *f*
honk [hɒŋk] VI (*car*) suonare il clacson; (*goose*) schiamazzare
■ N (*of horn*) colpo di clacson
Hono·lu·lu [ˌhɒnəˈluːluː] N Honolulu *f*
hon·or·ary [ˈɒnərərɪ] ADJ (*person*) onorario(-a); (*duty, title*) onorifico(-a); **an honorary degree** una laurea honoris causa *or* ad honorem
honor guard N (*Am*) picchetto d'onore
◎ **hon·our**, (*Am*) **hon·or** [ˈɒnəʳ] N **1** (*gen*) onore *m*; (*esteem, respect*) stima, rispetto; **in honour of** in onore di; **on my honour!** sul mio onore!; **to be on one's honour to do sth** aver dato la propria parola (d'onore) di fare qc; **to do honour to sb** *or* **to do sb honour** (*enhance reputation of*) fare onore a qn; **she did me the honour of attending my exhibition** mi ha fatto l'onore di presenziare alla mostra; **I would consider it an honour** sarebbe un onore per me; **to be an honour to one's profession** fare onore alla propria professione; **it's a great honour to be invited** (*frm*) è un grande onore essere invitati; **I had the honour of meeting him** (*frm*) ho avuto l'onore d'incontrarlo; **(in) honour bound** moralmente obbligato(-a)
2 honours NPL (*distinction, award*) onorificenze *fpl*; (*Univ*): **she got first-class honours in French** ≈ si è laureata in francese con la lode; **to be buried with full honours** essere sepolto(-a) con grandi onori; **to do the honours** (*fam*) fare gli onori di casa **3** (*title*): **Your Honour** (*judge*) Vostro Onore; (*Am: mayor*) signor sindaco
■ VT (*dignify*): **to honour sb (with)** onorare qn (con); **to honour sb with a title** conferire a qn un titolo

hon·our·able, (*Am*) **hon·or·able** [ˈɒnərəbl] ADJ (*gen*) onorevole; (*person*) d'onore

honourable mention, (*Am*) **honorable mention** N menzione *f* onorevole, attestato di merito

hon·our·ably, (*Am*) **hon·or·ably** [ˈɒnərəblɪ] ADV onorevolmente, con onore

honour-bound, (*Am*) **honor-bound** [ˈɒnəˌbaʊnd] ADJ: **to be honour-bound to do** dover fare per una questione di onore

honours degree, (*Am*) **honors degree** N (*Univ*) ≈ laurea

HONOURS DEGREE

In Gran Bretagna esistono titoli universitari di diverso livello. Gli studenti che conseguono ottimi risultati e che approfondiscono una o più materie possono ottenere l'**honours degree**. Questo titolo, abbreviato in Hons, viene posto dopo il titolo ottenuto (ad esempio BA Hons). *Vedi anche* **ordinary degree**

▷ www.dfes.gov.uk/hegateway/
▷ http://educationusa.state.gov/undergrad/about/degrees.htm
▷ www.aucc.ca/can_uni/general_info/overview_e.html
▷ www.internationaleducationmedia.com/newzealand/
▷ www.southafrica.info/ess_info/sa_glance/education/education.htm

honours list N (*Brit*) *elenco ufficiale dei destinati al conferimento di onorificenze*

HONOURS LIST

La **honours list** è un elenco di cittadini britannici e del Commonwealth che si sono distinti in campo imprenditoriale, militare, sportivo ecc., meritando il conferimento di un titolo o di una decorazione da parte del sovrano. Ogni anno vengono redatte dal primo ministro due honours lists, una a Capodanno e una in occasione del compleanno del sovrano.

▷ www.cabinetoffice.gov.uk/ceremonial/honours/index.asp

Hons. ABBR (*Univ*) = **honours degree**

hooch [huːtʃ] N (*Am fam*) liquore *m* (distillato illegalmente)

hood [hʊd] N **1** (*of cloak, raincoat*) cappuccio; (*on pram, Aut*) capote *f inv*; (*Am Aut*) cofano; (*on cooker*) cappa; **a coat with a hood** un cappotto con il cappuccio **2** (*Am fam*) malvivente *m/f*

hood·ed [ˈhʊdɪd] ADJ incappucciato(-a); (*robber*) mascherato(-a)

hood·lum [ˈhuːdləm] N teppista *m/f*

hood·wink [ˈhʊdˌwɪŋk] VT gabbare, imbrogliare, infinocchiare

hoody, hoodie [ˈhʊdɪ] N felpa con cappuccio

hoo·ey [ˈhuːɪ] N (*fam*) fesserie *fpl*

hoof [huːf] N (*pl* **hoofs** *or* **hooves**) zoccolo

hoo-ha [ˈhuːˌhɑː] N (*fam*) casino; **there was a great hoo-ha about it** la cosa ha fatto scalpore

◎**hook** [hʊk] N (*gen, also Boxing*) gancio; (*Fishing*) amo; (*on dress*) gancetto; **hooks and eyes** gancetti; **he hung the painting on the hook** ha appeso il quadro al gancio; **he felt a fish pull at his hook** ha sentito che un pesce abboccava all'amo; **to take the phone off the hook** staccare il ricevitore; **to leave the phone off the hook** lasciare staccato il ricevitore; **by hook or (by) crook** in un modo o nell'altro, di riffa o di raffa; **to get sb off the hook** salvare qn; **he fell for it hook, line and sinker** (*fig*) l'ha bevuta tutta
■VT (*fasten*) agganciare, attaccare; (*Fishing*) prendere all'amo; **to hook one's arms/legs around sth** aggrapparsi a qc con le braccia/le gambe; **she finally hooked him** (*fam*) è finalmente riuscita a incastrarlo; **to be hooked on** (*fam*) essere fanatico(-a) di; **he's hooked on heroin** *or* **cocaine** (*fam*) è un eroinomane *or* cocainomane
■VI (*fasten*) agganciarsi
► **hook on** VI + PREP: **to hook on(to)** agganciarsi (a), attaccarsi (a)
■VT + PREP: **to hook on(to)** agganciare (a)
► **hook up** VT + ADV (*dress*) agganciare; (*Radio, TV*) allacciare, collegare

hook·ah [ˈhʊkə] N narghilè *m inv*

hook·nosed [ˈhʊkˌnəʊzd] ADJ dal naso adunco

hook-up [ˈhʊkˌʌp] N (*TV, Comput, fam*) collegamento

hooky [ˈhʊkɪ] N (*fam*): **to play hooky** marinare la scuola

hoo·li·gan [ˈhuːlɪgən] N teppista *m/f*, hooligan *m/f inv*

hoo·li·gan·ism [ˈhuːlɪgənɪzəm] N teppismo

hoop [huːp] N (*gen*) cerchio; (*for skirt*) guardinfante *m*; (*croquet hoop*) archetto; **to put sb through the hoops** (*fig*) mettere qn sotto il torchio

hoop·la [ˈhuːplɑː] N tiro dei cerchi (*nei luna-park, per vincere premi*)

hoo·poe [ˈhuːpuː] N upupa

hoot [huːt] N (*of owl*) verso; (*of horn*) colpo di clacson; (*of siren*) ululato; **a hoot of derision** una risata di scherno; **I don't give a hoot** (*fam*) non me ne importa un accidente, me ne infischio; **it was a hoot** (*fam*) è stato divertentissimo *or* uno spasso
■VI (*owl*) gufare; (*person: in scorn*) farsi una risata (di scherno); (*Aut: person*) strombazzare, suonare il clacson; (*ship, train, factory hooter*) fischiare; **he stopped outside the house and hooted** si è fermato davanti alla casa e ha suonato il clacson; **to hoot with laughter** farsi una gran risata; **we heard an owl hooting** abbiamo sentito il verso di una civetta

hoot·er [ˈhuːtəʳ] N (*Brit: of ship, factory*) sirena; (*Aut*) clacson *m inv*, tromba (d'automobile); (*Brit fam: nose*) nasone *m*

hoo·ver® [ˈhuːvəʳ] (*Brit*) N aspirapolvere *m inv*
■VT pulire con l'aspirapolvere

hooves [huːvz] NPL *of* **hoof**

hop¹ [hɒp] N (*jump*) saltello; (*dance: fam*) ballo; (*Aer*): **it's a short hop from Paris to London** è un salto da Parigi a Londra in aereo; **to catch sb on the hop** (*fam*) prendere qn alla sprovvista
■VI (*person, bird, animal*) saltellare; **he hopped over the wall** è balzato al di là del muro; **to hop out of bed** saltar giù *or* fuori dal letto; **hop in!** (*car*) salta dentro!, salta su!, monta su!; **hop it!** (*fam*) sparisci!, smamma!

hop² [hɒp] N (*Bot*) luppolo; *see also* **hops**

◎**hope** [həʊp] N speranza; **he is past** *or* **beyond all hope** per lui non c'è più nessuna speranza; **to live in hope** vivere sperando *or* nella speranza; **in the hope of doing sth** nella speranza di fare qc; **in the hope of sth** nella speranza di avere *or* ottenere qc; **there is no hope of that** non c'è da farci nessun conto; **with high hopes** con grandi speranze; **to raise sb's hopes** far nascere delle speranze in qn; **to lose hope** perdere

Hh

ogni speranza *or* tutte le speranze; **to give up hope** abbandonare ogni speranza *or* tutte le speranze; **what a hope!** *or* **some hopes!** *(fam)* figurati!
■ VT: **to hope that/to do** sperare che/di fare
■ VI sperare, augurarsi; **I hope he comes** spero che venga; **to hope for the best** sperare in bene *or* per il meglio; **I hope so/not** spero di sì /no; **let's hope for success** speriamo di riuscire; **to hope against hope** sperare malgrado tutto

hope chest N *(Am)* cassa del corredo

hope·ful ['həʊpfʊl] ADJ *(person)* ottimista *m/f*, pieno(-a) di speranza, fiducioso(-a); *(future, situation)* promettente; *(sign, response)* incoraggiante, buono(-a) *(before n)*; **I'm hopeful that she'll manage to come** ho buone speranze che venga; **the prospects look hopeful** le prospettive sembrano incoraggianti
■ N: **a young hopeful** una giovane *m/f* di belle speranze

hope·ful·ly ['həʊpfəlɪ] ADV **1** *(optimistically: speak)* con ottimismo, con speranza; **to look hopefully at sb** guardare speranzoso(-a) qn **2** *(one hopes: incorrect use)* si spera; **hopefully he will recover** speriamo che si riprenda; **hopefully he'll make it in time** si spera che arrivi in tempo

hope·less ['həʊplɪs] ADJ *(impossible, useless: situation)* impossibile; *(: outlook, case)* disperato(-a), senza speranza; *(drunkard)* incorreggibile, inguaribile; *(bad: work: fam)* disastroso(-a); **I'm hopeless at it** *(fam)* sono completamente negato per questo; **it's hopeless trying to convince her** è perfettamente inutile *or* è fiato sprecato cercare di convincerla; **it is a hopeless task** è un compito impossibile; **many young people feel hopeless about job prospects** molti giovani sentono di non avere prospettive di lavoro; **a hopeless case** un caso disperato

hope·less·ly ['həʊplɪslɪ] ADV *(live)* senza speranza; *(involved, complicated)* spaventosamente; *(late)* disperatamente, irrimediabilmente; **I'm hopelessly confused/lost** sono completamente confuso/perso; **hopelessly in love** perdutamente innamorato(-a)

hop·per ['hɒpəʳ] N *(chute)* tramoggia

hop-picker ['hɒp,pɪkəʳ] N raccoglitore(-trice) di luppolo

hops [hɒps] NPL coni *mpl* di luppolo

hop·scotch ['hɒp,skɒtʃ] N campana *(gioco infantile)*

Horace ['hɒrɪs] N Orazio

horde [hɔ:d] N orda; **hordes of screaming children** un'orda di bambini urlanti

ho·ri·zon [hə'raɪzn] N *(also fig)* orizzonte *m*; **on the horizon** all'orizzonte; **to widen one's horizons** allargare i propri orizzonti

hori·zon·tal [,hɒrɪ'zɒntl] ADJ orizzontale; **the shelf is horizontal to the floor** la mensola è parallela al pavimento
■ N linea *or* piano orizzontale

hori·zon·tal·ly [,hɒrɪ'zɒntəlɪ] ADV orizzontalmente

hor·mo·nal [hɔ:'məʊnəl] ADJ ormonale

hor·mone ['hɔ:məʊn] N ormone *m*

hormone replacement therapy N terapia ormonale *(usata in menopausa)*

horn [hɔ:n] N *(gen, Mus)* corno; *(of snail)* antenna; *(Aut)* clacson *m inv*; **he sounded the horn** ha suonato il clacson; **to draw in one's horns** *(fig: back down)* cedere; *(: spend less)* ridurre le spese

horn·beam ['hɔ:n,bi:m] N *(Bot)* carpino bianco

horned [hɔ:nd] ADJ *(animal)* cornuto(-a)

hor·net ['hɔ:nɪt] N calabrone *m*

horn-rimmed ['hɔ:n'rɪmd] ADJ *(spectacles)* con la montatura di tartaruga

horny ['hɔ:nɪ] ADJ *(comp* **-ier**, *superl* **-iest**) *(like horn)* corneo(-a); *(hands)* incallito(-a), calloso(-a); *(fam: randy)* arrapato(-a), eccitato(-a)

horo·scope ['hɒrə,skəʊp] N oroscopo

hor·ren·dous [hɒ'rɛndəs] N orrendo(-a)

hor·ri·ble ['hɒrɪbl] ADJ *(gen)* orribile, tremendo(-a), orrendo(-a); *(accident)* spaventoso(-a)

hor·ri·bly ['hɒrɪblɪ] ADV *(see adj)* in modo orribile *or* orrendo, tremendamente; spaventosamente

hor·rid ['hɒrɪd] ADJ *(unpleasant: person)* odioso(-a), antipatico(-a); *(: thing, weather)* orribile, orrendo(-a); *(: meal)* schifoso(-a); *(unkind)* cattivo(-a)

hor·rif·ic [hɒ'rɪfɪk] ADJ *(accident)* spaventoso(-a); *(murder)* terrificante

hor·rifi·cal·ly [hɒ'rɪfɪkəlɪ] ADV orrendamente

hor·ri·fy ['hɒrɪ,faɪ] VT lasciare inorridito(-a); **I was horrified by the news** la notizia mi ha lasciato inorridito

hor·ri·fy·ing ['hɒrɪ,faɪɪŋ] ADJ terrificante

◎ **hor·ror** ['hɒrəʳ] N *(terror, dread)* spavento, terrore *m*; *(loathing, hatred)* orrore *m*; *(fam)* peste *f*; **he ran away in horror** è scappato terrorizzato; **to have a horror of** avere il terrore di; **she has a horror of spiders** ha il terrore dei ragni; **that gives me the horrors** *(fam)* quello mi fa venire i brividi; **to my horror I discovered I was locked out** ho scoperto con orrore di essere rimasto chiuso fuori

horror film N film *m inv* dell'orrore

horror-struck ['hɒrə,strʌk], **horror-stricken** ['hɒrə,strɪkən] ADJ inorridito(-a)

hors d'oeuvres [ɔ:'dɜ:vr] NPL *(course)* antipasto; *(individual items)* antipasti *mpl*

◎ **horse** [hɔ:s] N cavallo; **it's straight from the horse's mouth** *(fam)* è di fonte sicura; **never look a gift horse in the mouth** *(Proverb)* a caval donato non si guarda in bocca
▸ **horse about, horse around** VI + ADV *(fam)* fare lo/la sciocco(-a)

horse·back ['hɔ:s,bæk]: **on horseback** ADV a cavallo

horse·box ['hɔ:s,bɒks] N carro *or* furgone *m* per il trasporto dei cavalli

horse brass N ornamento d'ottone per finimenti

horse chestnut N *(tree)* ippocastano; *(nut)* castagna d'India

horse dealer N commerciante *m* di cavalli

horse-drawn ['hɔ:s,drɔ:n] ADJ a cavalli, tirato(-a) da cavalli

horse·flesh ['hɔ:s,flɛʃ] N *(horses)* cavalli *mpl*; *(meat)* carne *f* equina *or* di cavallo

horse·fly ['hɔ:s,flaɪ] N tafano, mosca cavallina

horse·hair ['hɔ:s,hɛəʳ] N crine *m* (di cavallo)

horse laugh N risata cavallina

horse·man ['hɔ:smən] N *(pl* **-men**) cavaliere *m*

horse·man·ship ['hɔ:smən,ʃɪp] N *(riding)* equitazione *f*; *(skill)* abilità di cavaliere

horse mushroom N prataiolo maggiore

horse opera N *(hum)* western *m inv*

horse·play ['hɔ:s,pleɪ] N giochi *mpl* scatenati

horse·power ['hɔ:s,paʊəʳ] N cavallo (vapore)

horse-racing ['hɔ:s,reɪsɪŋ] N *(sport)* ippica; *(events)* corse *fpl* dei cavalli

horse·radish ['hɔ:s,rædɪʃ] N rafano

horse sense N *(fam)* buonsenso

horse·shoe [ˈhɔːʃʃuː] N ferro di cavallo
■ ADJ a ferro di cavallo
horse show N, **horse trials** NPL concorso ippico, gare *fpl* ippiche
horse-trader [ˈhɔːsˌtreɪdəʳ] N commerciante *m/f* di cavalli; (*fig*) vecchia volpe *f*
horse-trading [ˈhɔːsˌtreɪdɪŋ] N mercanteggiamento
horse·whip [ˈhɔːswɪp] VT frustare
horse·woman [ˈhɔːsˌwʊmən] N amazzone *f*
horsey, **horsy** [ˈhɔːsɪ] ADJ (*comp* **-ier**, *superl* **-iest**) (*fam*: *person*) che adora i cavalli; (*appearance*) cavallino(-a), da cavallo
hor·ti·cul·tur·al [ˌhɔːtɪˈkʌltʃərəl] ADJ di orticoltura
hor·ti·cul·ture [ˈhɔːtɪˌkʌltʃəʳ] N orticoltura
▷ www.horticulture.org.uk/IoHLinks.htm
▷ www.rhs.org.uk
hor·ti·cul·tur·ist [ˌhɔːtɪˈkʌltʃərɪst] N orticoltore(-trice)
hose [həʊz] N **1** (*hosepipe*) tubo di gomma; (*also:* **garden hose**) tubo per annaffiare; (*Aut*) manicotto **2** (*pl*: *stockings, socks*) calze *fpl*, calzini *mpl*; (*: old*) calzamaglia
▶ **hose down** VT + ADV lavare con un getto d'acqua
hose·pipe [ˈhəʊzˌpaɪp] N = **hose** N 1
ho·siery [ˈhəʊʒərɪ] N maglieria; (*in shop*) (reparto di) calze *fpl* e calzini *mpl*
hos·pice [ˈhɒspɪs] N *ospedale specializzato nell'assistenza ai malati terminali*
hos·pi·table [hɒsˈpɪtəbl] ADJ ospitale
hos·pi·tably [hɒsˈpɪtəblɪ] ADV in modo ospitale
◎ **hos·pi·tal** [ˈhɒspɪtl] N ospedale *m*; **in hospital** (*Am*): **in the hospital** in ospedale
■ ADJ (*staff, treatment*) ospedaliero(-a); (*bed*) di *or* dell'ospedale
hospital case N caso da ricovero (in ospedale)
hospital facilities NPL attrezzatura ospedaliera
hos·pi·tal·ity [ˌhɒspɪˈtælɪtɪ] N ospitalità
hos·pi·tal·ize [ˈhɒspɪtəˌlaɪz] VT ricoverare (in *or* all'ospedale)
Host [həʊst] N (*Rel*) ostia
◎ **host¹** [həʊst] N ospite *m/f*; (*TV, Radio*) presentatore(-trice); (*Bot, Zool*) ospite *m*; **we thanked our hosts** abbiamo ringraziato i nostri ospiti
■ VT (*TV programme, games*) presentare
host² [həʊst] N (*crowd*) moltitudine *f*; **for a whole host of reasons** per tutta una serie di ragioni; **a host of problems** un mucchio di problemi
◎ **hos·tage** [ˈhɒstɪdʒ] N ostaggio; **to take sb hostage** prendere qn in ostaggio
host country N paese *m* ospite, paese che ospita
hos·tel [ˈhɒstəl] N (*for students, nurses*) pensionato; (*for homeless people*) ospizio, ricovero; (*also:* **youth hostel**) ostello della gioventù
hos·tel·ler [ˈhɒstələʳ] N frequentatore(-trice) di ostelli (della gioventù)
hos·tel·ling [ˈhɒstəlɪŋ] N: **to go (youth) hostelling** passare le vacanze negli ostelli della gioventù
host·ess [ˈhəʊstes] N ospite *f*; (*Aer*) hostess *f inv*; (*in nightclub*) entraîneuse *f inv*; **we thanked our hostess** abbiamo ringraziato la nostra ospite
hos·tile [ˈhɒstaɪl] ADJ: **hostile (to)** ostile (a)
hos·tile·ly [ˈhɒstaɪllɪ] ADV ostilmente
hos·til·ity [hɒsˈtɪlɪtɪ] N ostilità *f inv*
◎ **hot** [hɒt] ADJ (*comp* **-ter**, *superl* **-test**) **1** caldo(-a); **to be hot** (*person*) avere caldo; (*thing*) essere caldo(-a); (*weather*) fare caldo; **a hot bath** un bagno caldo; **I'm hot** ho caldo; **to get hot** (*person*) incominciare ad avere caldo; (*thing*) scaldarsi; (*weather*) incominciare a fare caldo; **this room is hot** fa caldo in questa stanza; **it's hot today** fa caldo oggi; **I don't like hot weather** non sopporto il caldo; **to get hot under the collar** (*fam*) scaldarsi; **to be all hot and bothered** essere tutto accaldato(-a); (*flustered*) essere tutto agitato(-a); **to be/get into hot water** essere/cacciarsi nei guai; **you're getting hot!** (*fig*: *when guessing*) fuochino! **2** (*curry, spice*) piccante; (*news*) fresco(-a); (*temperament*) focoso(-a), ardente; (*conflict, contest*) accanito(-a); **Indian food's too hot for me** il cibo indiano è troppo piccante per me; **she's got a hot temper** è un tipo collerico; **hot favourite** grande favorito(-a); **I've got a hot tip for the Derby** (*fam*) ho un cavallo sicuro per il Derby; **I'll make things hot for you** (*fam*) ti renderò la vita difficile; **to be in hot pursuit of sb** stare alle calcagna di qn; **she's pretty hot at maths** (*fam*) se la cava bene in matematica; **those goods are hot** (*fam*: *stolen*) è roba che scotta
■ ADV: **to be hot on sb's trail** essere sulle tracce di qn; **to be hot on the heels of sb** essere alle calcagna di qn
▶ **hot up** (*fam*) VI + ADV (*situation*) farsi più teso(-a); (*party*) scaldarsi
■ VT + ADV (*pace*) affrettare; (*car engine*) truccare
hot air N (*fam pej*) ciance *fpl*
hot-air balloon [ˌhɒtˌɛəbəˈluːn] N (*Aer*) mongolfiera
hot·bed [ˈhɒtˌbɛd] N (*fig*) focolaio
hot-blooded [ˌhɒtˈblʌdɪd] ADJ dal sangue caldo, appassionato(-a)
hotch·potch [ˈhɒtʃˌpɒtʃ] N (*Brit*) pot-pourri *m*
hot-desking [ˌhɒtˈdɛskɪŋ] N *il condividere la scrivania con altri impiegati dello stesso ufficio*
hot dog N (*Culin*) hot dog *m inv*
hot-dogging [ˌhɒtˈdɒgɪŋ] N (*Am Skiing*) sci *m* acrobatico
◎ **ho·tel** [həʊˈtɛl] N albergo, hotel *m inv*; **hotel room** camera d'albergo; **hotel workers** personale *m* alberghiero
ho·tel·ier [həʊˈtɛlɪəʳ] N albergatore(-trice)
hot flush, (*Am*) **hot flash** N scalmana, caldana
hot·foot [ˈhɒtˌfʊt] ADV di gran carriera
hot·head [ˈhɒtˌhɛd] N (*fig*) testa calda
hot-headed [ˌhɒtˈhɛdɪd] ADJ impetuoso(-a), focoso(-a)
hot-headedness [ˌhɒtˈhɛdɪdnɪs] N impetuosità
hot·house [ˈhɒtˌhaʊs] N serra
hot key N (*Comput*) tasto di scelta rapida
hot line N (*Pol*) telefono rosso
hot link N (*Comput*) collegamento ipertestuale
hot·ly [ˈhɒtlɪ] ADV accanitamente, con accanimento, violentemente; **he was hotly pursued by the policeman** il poliziotto lo rincorreva senza dargli tregua; **a hotly contested decision** una decisione fortemente contestata
hot·plate [ˈhɒtˌpleɪt] N (*on cooker*) piastra (riscaldante); (*for keeping food warm*) scaldavivande *m inv*
hot·pot [ˈhɒtˌpɒt] N (*Brit Culin*) stufato
hot potato N (*fam*) patata bollente; **to drop sb/sth like a hot potato** piantare in asso qn/qc
hot rod N (*Aut*: *fam*) macchina truccata
hot seat N (*fig*): **to be in the hot seat** avere un posto che scotta
hot spot N (*fig*) zona calda
hot spring N sorgente *f* termale
hot stuff N: **to be hot stuff** (*fam*) essere eccezionale
hot-tempered [ˌhɒtˈtɛmpəd] ADJ irascibile
hot-water bottle [ˌhɒtˈwɔːtəˌbɒtl] N borsa dell'acqua calda, boule *f inv*

Hh

hot-wire ['hɒt,waɪəʳ] VT *(fam: car) avviare mettendo in contatto i fili dell'accensione*

hound [haʊnd] N segugio; **the hounds** la muta; **to follow the hounds** *or* **to ride to hounds** fare la caccia alla volpe
■ VT *(fig)* perseguitare
▸ **hound down** VT + ADV riuscire a stanare
▸ **hound out** VT + ADV: **to hound out of** cacciare da

◎ **hour** ['aʊəʳ] N ora; **a quarter of an hour** un quarto d'ora; **two and a half hours** due ore e mezza; **half an hour** mezz'ora; **they work long hours** hanno una giornata lavorativa molto lunga; **at 30 miles an hour** a 30 miglia all'ora; **hour by hour** ora per ora; **on the hour** ad ogni ora precisa; **in the early** *or* **small hours** alle ore piccole; **at all hours (of the day and night)** a tutte le ore (del giorno e della notte); **at this late hour** in questa fase avanzata; **he thought his (last) hour had come** pensò che fosse giunta la sua ora; **in the hour of danger** nel momento del pericolo; **to pay sb by the hour** pagare qn a ore; **to wait (for) hours** aspettare per (delle) ore; **hours and hours** ore e ore; **to keep regular hours** fare una vita regolare; **out of hours** fuori orario; **after hours** *(at office)* dopo le ore d'ufficio; *(at shop, pub)* dopo l'ora di chiusura

hour·glass ['aʊə,glɑːs] N clessidra

hour hand N lancetta delle ore

hour·ly ['aʊəlɪ] ADJ *(intervals)* di un'ora; *(bus service)* (ad) ogni ora; *(rate)* orario(-a); **there are hourly buses** ci sono autobus ogni ora
■ ADV ogni ora; **to be paid hourly** essere pagato all'ora; **hourly paid workers** operai(-e) pagati a ore; **we expected him hourly** lo aspettavamo da un momento all'altro

◎ **house** [*n* haʊs; *vb* haʊz] N (*pl* **houses**) **1** casa; **at (***or* **to) my house** a casa mia; **to keep house** mandare avanti la casa; **to set up house** metter su casa; **house of cards** castello di carte; **to put** *or* **set one's house in order** *(fig)* sistemare i propri affari; **to get on like a house on fire** *(two people: fam)* andare d'amore e d'accordo **2** *(Pol)* camera **3** *(Theatre)* sala; **"house full"** "biglietti esauriti"; **it was a full house** lo spettacolo ha registrato il tutto esaurito; **in the front of the house** tra gli spettatori, in sala; **to bring the house down** *(fig)* scatenare un uragano di applausi; **the second house** il secondo spettacolo **4** *(Comm)* ditta, casa; **it's on the house** *(paid by company)* paga la ditta; *(free)* è offerto dalla casa **5** *(family, line)* casa, casato
■ VT ospitare; **this building houses 6 families** in quest'edificio abitano 6 famiglie

house arrest N arresti *mpl* domiciliari; **to put sb under house arrest** mettere qn agli arresti domiciliari

house·boat ['haʊs,bəʊt] N house boat *f inv*

house·bound ['haʊs,baʊnd] ADJ confinato(-a) in casa

house-break ['haʊs,breɪk] VT *(Am)* = **house-train**

house·break·er ['haʊs,breɪkəʳ] N svaligiatore(-trice), scassinatore(-trice)

house·break·ing ['haʊs,breɪkɪŋ] N furto con scasso

house-broken ['haʊs,brəʊkən] ADJ *(Am: animal)* che non sporca in casa

house·coat ['haʊs,kəʊt] N vestaglia

house doctor N ≈ (medico) interno

house·father ['haʊs,fɑːðəʳ] N responsabile *m* di gruppo *(in un collegio)*

house·fly ['haʊs,flaɪ] N (*pl* **-flies**) mosca (comune)

house·ful ['haʊsfʊl] N: **we had a houseful of children** abbiamo avuto la casa piena di bambini

house guest N ospite *m/f* (della casa)

◎ **house·hold** ['haʊs,həʊld] N casa, famiglia; **many poor households are experiencing real hardship** molte famiglie povere stanno attraversano un periodo di grosse difficoltà; **the head of the household** il capofamiglia
■ ADJ *(accounts, expenses, equipment)* della casa, domestico(-a); **household chores** faccende domestiche

Household Cavalry N *(Mil)* cavalleria della guardia reale

house·holder ['haʊs,həʊldəʳ] N padrone(-a) di casa; *(head of house)* capofamiglia *m/f*

household name, household word N nome *m* che tutti conoscono *or* conosciuto da tutti

house·hunting ['haʊs,hʌntɪŋ] N: **to go househunting** mettersi a cercar casa

house·keeper ['haʊs,kiːpəʳ] N governante *f*

house·keeping ['haʊs,kiːpɪŋ] N *(work)* andamento *or* governo della casa; *(also:* **housekeeping money***)* soldi *mpl* per le spese di casa; *(Comput)* ausilio

house·maid ['haʊs,meɪd] N cameriera, domestica

housemaid's knee N *(Med)* ginocchio della lavandaia

house·man ['haʊsmən] N (*pl* **-men**) *(Brit: in hospital)* ≈ (medico) interno

house·mother ['haʊs,mʌðəʳ] N responsabile *f* di gruppo *(in un collegio)*

house (music) N house music *f*

House of Commons N *(Brit)*: **the House of Commons** la Camera dei Comuni

House of Lords N *(Brit)*: **the House of Lords** la Camera dei Lords

House of Representatives N *(Am)*: **the House of Representatives** la Camera dei Rappresentanti

house-owner ['haʊs,əʊnəʳ] N proprietario(-a) di una casa

house party N riunione *f* di ospiti *(in una casa di campagna)*

house physician N = house doctor

house plant N pianta da appartamento

house-proud ['haʊs,praʊd] ADJ che ha la mania della pulizia

house·room ['haʊs,rʊm] N: **I wouldn't give it houseroom** *(fam)* non lo vorrei avere in casa mia neanche se me lo regalassero

Houses of Parliament *(Brit)* NPL: **the Houses of Parliament** *(building)* il palazzo del Parlamento; *(members)* il Parlamento
▹ www.parliament.uk/index.cfm

house-to-house [,haʊstə'haʊs] ADJ *(search)* casa per casa; *(collection)* porta a porta

house·top ['haʊs,tɒp] N: **to proclaim** *or* **shout sth from the housetops** *(fig)* proclamare qc ai quattro venti

house-train ['haʊs,treɪn] VT *(Brit: pet animal)* addestrare a non sporcare in casa

house-trained ['haʊs,treɪnd] ADJ *(Brit: animal)* che non sporca in casa

house-warming ['haʊs,wɔːmɪŋ] N *(also:* **house-warming party***)* festa per inaugurare la casa nuova

house·wife ['haʊs,waɪf] N (*pl* **-wives**) massaia, casalinga

house·wife·ly ['haʊs,waɪflɪ] ADJ della massaia *or* casalinga

house·work ['haʊs,wɜːk] N faccende *fpl*, lavori *mpl* di casa, lavori domestici; **to do the housework** fare i lavori di casa, sbrigare le faccende

◎**hous·ing** ['haʊzɪŋ] N **1** alloggiamento **2** *(houses)* alloggi *mpl*, case *fpl*

■ADJ *(problem, shortage)* degli alloggi

housing association N cooperativa edilizia

housing benefit N *(Brit) sussidio assegnato ad affituari in difficoltà economiche*

housing conditions NPL condizioni *fpl* di abitazione

housing development N *zona residenziale con case popolari e/o private*

housing estate N *(Brit)* quartiere *m* residenziale

hove [həʊv] PT, PP *of* **heave** VI 3

hov·el ['hɒvəl] N tugurio

hov·er ['hɒvəʳ] VI *(bird)* librarsi; *(helicopter)* volare a punto fisso; **a smile hovered on her lips** un sorriso indugiava sulle sue labbra; **to hover on the brink of disaster** essere sull'orlo del disastro

▶ **hover about, hover around** VI + ADV stare *or* girare intorno; **to hover round sb** aggirarsi intorno a qn

hover·craft ['hɒvə,krɑːft] N hovercraft *m inv*

hover·port ['hɒvə,pɔːt] N porto per hovercraft

◎**how** [haʊ] ADV **1** *(gen)* come; **how did you do it?** come hai fatto?, come l'hai fatto?; **I know how you did it** so come hai fatto; **to know how to do sth** sapere come fare qc; **how are you?** come stai?, come va?; **how's life?** *(fam)* come va (la vita)?; **how is school?** come va la scuola?; **how was the film?** com'era il film?; **how is it that ...?** com'è che...?; **how do you say "apple" in Italian?** come si dice "apple" in italiano?; **how do you do?** molto lieto!, piacere!; **how come?** *(fam)* come mai?; **how come he's leaving?** *(fam)* come mai se ne va?; **how about (going for) a drink?** che ne diresti di (andare a) bere qualcosa?; **and how!** *(fam)* eccome! **2** *(to what degree)* quanto(-a); **how many?** quanti?; **how much?** quanto?; **how much is it?** quanto costa?; **how long have you been here?** da quanto tempo sei qui?; **how old are you?** quanti anni hai?; **how far is it to ...?** quanto è lontano...?; **how far is it to Edinburgh?** quanto dista Edimburgo?; **how long does it take?** quanto tempo ci vuole?; **how many people?** quante persone?; **how much milk?** quanto latte?; **how often do you go?** quanto spesso ci vai?; **how lovely!** che bello!; **how kind of you!** è molto gentile da parte sua! **3** *(that)* che, di come; **she told me how she'd found the money in an old suitcase** mi ha raccontato di come aveva trovato il denaro in una vecchia valigia

how·dy ['haʊdɪ] EXCL *(Am)* salve!

◎**how·ever** [haʊ'ɛvəʳ] CONJ *(still, nevertheless)* però, comunque, tuttavia

■ADV: **however I do it** in qualunque modo lo faccia; **however beautiful ...** per quanto bella sia...; **however cold it is** per quanto freddo faccia; **however much I try** per quanto ci possa provare; **however did you do it?** *(fam)* come diavolo hai fatto?; **however that may be** comunque sia

how·itz·er ['haʊɪtsəʳ] N *(Mil)* obice *m*

howl [haʊl] N *(of animal)* ululato; **a howl of pain** un urlo di dolore; **a howl of protest** un grido di protesta; **howls of laughter** scrosci *mpl* di risate

■VI *(person)* gridare, urlare; *(animal, wind)* ululare; *(weep)* piangere; **the dog howled all night** il cane ha ululato tutta la notte; **to howl with laughter** rotolarsi dalle risate; **he howled with pain** urlava dal dolore

■VT urlare

▶ **howl down** VT + ADV zittire a forza di urla

howl·er ['haʊləʳ] N *(fam)* abbaglio; (: *in homework*) strafalcione *m*

howl·ing ['haʊlɪŋ] ADJ *(wind, gale)* che ulula; **howling success** *(fig)* successo travolgente

HP [,eɪtʃ'piː] N ABBR *(Brit)* = **hire-purchase**

hp [,eɪtʃ'piː] N ABBR *(Aut:* = **horsepower)** CV (= *cavallo vapore)*

HQ [,eɪtʃkjuː] N ABBR (= **headquarters**) QG (= *quartier generale)*

HR [,eɪtʃɑːʳ] N ABBR **1** *(Am)* = **House of Representatives 2** (= **human resources**) risorse *fpl* umane

hr *(pl* **hrs**) ABBR (= **hour**) h (= *ora)*

HRH [,eɪtʃɑːr'eɪtʃ] ABBR (= **His** *or* **Her Royal Highness**) SAR (= *Sua Altezza Reale)*

HRT [,eɪtʃɑː'tiː] N ABBR = **hormone replacement therapy**

HS ABBR *(Am)* = **high school**

HT ABBR (= **high tension**) AT (= *alta tensione)*

HTML [,eɪtʃtiːɛm'ɛl] N ABBR (= **hypertext markup language**) HTML *m*

HTTP [,eɪtʃtiːtiː'piː] N ABBR (= **hypertext transfer protocol**) HTTP *m*

hub [hʌb] N *(of wheel)* mozzo; *(fig)* centro, fulcro; **the financial hub of the country** il cuore finanziario del paese

hub·bub ['hʌbʌb] N baccano

hub·cap ['hʌb,kæp] N *(Aut)* coprimozzo

HUD [hʌd] N ABBR *(Am)* = *Department of Housing and Urban Development*

hud·dle ['hʌdl] N gruppetto, capannello; **to go into a huddle** *(fam)* fare capannello

■VI raggomitolarsi, rannicchiarsi

▶ **huddle down** VI + ADV accucciarsi, rannicchiarsi

▶ **huddle together** VI + ADV stringersi l'uno(-a) vicino all'altro(-a)

▶ **huddle up** VI + ADV rannicchiarsi, raggomitolarsi

hue [hjuː] N *(colour)* colore *m*, tinta

hue and cry N clamorosa protesta

huff [hʌf] N: **in a huff** *(fam)* imbronciato(-a), stizzito(-a)

huffi·ly ['hʌfɪlɪ] ADV *(fam)* con aria imbronciata

huffi·ness ['hʌfɪnɪs] N *(fam)* cattivo umore *m*

huffy ['hʌfɪ] ADJ *(comp* **-ier**, *superl* **-iest**) *(fam)* imbronciato(-a); **to get huffy** fare il broncio

hug [hʌg] N abbraccio, stretta; **to give sb a hug** abbracciare qn

■VT abbracciare, tener stretto(-a) a sé; *(subj: bear)* stringere; *(keep close to: kerb)* tenersi vicino a; **to hug the coast** tenersi sotto costa

◎**huge** [hjuːdʒ] ADJ *(comp* **-r**, *superl* **-st**) *(gen)* enorme; *(appetite, helping)* smisurato(-a); *(success)* strepitoso(-a), immenso(-a)

huge·ly ['hjuːdʒlɪ] ADV enormemente

hulk [hʌlk] N *(abandoned ship)* nave *f* in disarmo; *(building)* costruzione *f* mastodontica; **a great hulk of a man** *(fam)* un colosso

hulk·ing ['hʌlkɪŋ] ADJ *(fam)* mastodontico(-a); **hulking (great)** grosso(-a) e goffo(-a)

hull [hʌl] N *(of ship)* scafo

hul·la·ba·loo [,hʌləbə'luː] N *(fam: noise)* fracasso

hul·lo [hʌ'ləʊ] EXCL = **hello**

hum [hʌm] N *(also Elec)* ronzio; *(of traffic, machines)* rumore *m*; *(of voices)* mormorio, brusio

■VT *(tune)* canticchiare

Hh

■VI (*insect*) ronzare; (*person*) canticchiare a labbra chiuse; (*engine, machine*) rombare; (*wireless*) mandare un brusio; (*fig fam: be busy*) animarsi; **to make things hum** (*fam*) fare procedere le cose speditamente; **to hum with activity** pullulare di attività; **to hum and haw** essere incerto(-a) sul da farsi

◎**hu·man** ['hju:mən] ADJ umano(-a); **she's only human** nessuno è perfetto
■N essere *m* umano

human being N essere *m* umano

hu·mane [hju:'meɪn] ADJ umanitario(-a)

hu·mane·ly [hju:'meɪnlɪ] ADV con umanità

human interest N vita vissuta; **a human interest story** una storia di vita vissuta

hu·man·ism ['hju:məˌnɪzəm] N umanesimo

hu·man·ist ['hju:mənɪst] N umanista *m/f*

hu·mani·tar·ian [hju:ˌmænɪ'tɛərɪən] ADJ umanitario(-a)

hu·man·ity [hju:'mænɪtɪ] N umanità; **the humanities** gli studi letterari *or* umanistici, le lettere; **crimes against humanity** crimini contro l'umanità

hu·man·ly ['hju:mənlɪ] ADV umanamente

human nature N la natura umana; **it's human nature** è nella natura umana, è umano

hu·man·oid ['hju:mənɔɪd] ADJ che sembra umano(-a)
■N umanoide *m/f*

human resources NPL risorse *fpl* umane

◎**human rights** NPL diritti *mpl* dell'uomo

human shield N scudo umano

hum·ble ['hʌmbl] ADJ (*comp* **-r**, *superl* **-st**) umile; (*opinion, occupation*) modesto(-a); **of humble origins** di umili origini; **to eat humble pie** rimangiarsi tutto
■VT umiliare; **to humble o.s.** abbassarsi, umiliarsi

hum·bly ['hʌmblɪ] ADV umilmente, modestamente

hum·bug ['hʌmˌbʌg] N (*person*) impostore *m*; (*nonsense*) frottole *fpl*, falsità; (*Brit: sweet*) caramella alla menta

hum·ding·er ['hʌmˌdɪŋəʳ] N (*fam*): **it's a humdinger!** è una cannonata!; **he's (***or* **she's) a humdinger!** è uno schianto!

hum·drum ['hʌmˌdrʌm] ADJ monotono(-a), banale

hu·mer·us ['hju:mərəs] N omero

hu·mid ['hju:mɪd] ADJ umido(-a)

hu·midi·fi·er [hju:'mɪdɪˌfaɪəʳ] N umidificatore *m*

hu·mid·ity [hju:'mɪdɪtɪ] N umidità

hu·mili·ate [hju:'mɪlɪˌeɪt] VT umiliare

hu·mili·at·ing [hju:'mɪlɪˌeɪtɪŋ] ADJ umiliante

hu·milia·tion [hju:ˌmɪlɪ'eɪʃən] N umiliazione *f*

hu·mil·ity [hju:'mɪlɪtɪ] N umiltà

humming·bird ['hʌmɪŋˌbɜ:d] N colibrì *m inv*

hu·mor·ist ['hju:mərɪst] N umorista *m/f*

hu·mor·ous ['hju:mərəs] ADJ (*person*) spiritoso(-a); (*book, story*) divertente, umoristico(-a); (*tone*) scherzoso(-a); **a humorous magazine** un giornale umoristico

hu·mor·ous·ly ['hju:mərəslɪ] ADV (*see adj*) (*describe*) in modo spiritoso; in modo divertente; (*say*) scherzosamente, con fare scherzoso

◎**hu·mour**, (*Am*) **hu·mor** ['hju:məʳ] N **1** (*comic sense*) umorismo; (*of situation*) lato divertente *or* umoristico; **to have a sense of humour** avere il senso dell'umorismo **2** (*mood*) umore *m*; **to be in a good/bad humour** essere di buon/cattivo umore
■VT (*person*) accontentare, compiacere; (*sb's whims*) assecondare

hu·mour·less, (*Am*) **hu·mor·less** ['hju:məlɪs] ADJ privo(-a) di umorismo

hu·mour·less·ly ['hju:məlɪslɪ] ADV senza umorismo

hump [hʌmp] N (*Anat*) gobba; **it gives me the hump** (*Brit fam*) mi mette di malumore; **we're over the hump** (*fig*) il peggio è passato, il più è fatto
■VT **1** (*arch: back*) inarcare **2** (*fam: carry*) portare

hump·back ['hʌmpˌbæk] N (*also:* **humpback bridge**) ponte *m* a schiena d'asino

hump·backed ['hʌmpˌbækt] ADJ (*offensive: person*) gobbo(-a); (*animal*) con la gobba, gibboso(-a)

hu·mus ['hju:məs] N humus *m*

Hun [hʌn] N (*History*) Unno; (*offensive: German*) crucco(-a)

hunch [hʌntʃ] N **1** (*fam: idea*) impressione *f*; (*premonition*) intuizione *f*; **I have a hunch that ...** ho la vaga impressione che..., ho il vago presentimento che...; **she's acting on a hunch** sta andando a naso; **to follow one's hunch** seguire il proprio fiuto **2** (*hump*) gobba
■VT (*also:* **hunch up**) incurvare
■VI star curvo(-a); **to sit hunched up** star seduto(-a) curvo(-a)

hunch·back ['hʌntʃˌbæk] N (*offensive*) gobbo(-a)

hunch·back·ed ['hʌntʃˌbækt] ADJ (*offensive: person*) gobbo(-a)

hunched ['hʌntʃt] ADJ incurvato(-a)

◎**hun·dred** ['hʌndrɪd] ADJ cento *inv*; **about a hundred people** un centinaio di persone; **three hundred boys and five hundred girls** trecento ragazzi e cinquecento ragazze; **a hundred and one** centouno; **hundred and first** centounesimo(-a); **I'm a hundred per cent sure** sono sicuro(-a) al cento per cento
■N cento *m inv*; **to live to be a hundred** vivere fino all'età di cent'anni; (*less exactly*) diventare centenario(-a); **hundreds of people** centinaia *fpl* di persone; **they came in their hundreds** sono arrivati a centinaia

◎**hun·dredth** ['hʌndrɪdθ] ADJ centesimo(-a)
■N (*in series*) centesimo(-a); (*fraction*) centesimo

hundred·weight ['hʌndrɪdˌweɪt] N (*Brit: 112 lb*) ≈ 50.8 kg, (*Am: 100 lb*) ≈ 45.3 kg

hung [hʌŋ] PT, PP *of* **hang**
■ADJ: **a hung jury** una giuria divisa (sul verdetto)

Hun·gar·ian [hʌŋ'gɛərɪən] ADJ ungherese
■N **1** (*person*) ungherese *m/f* **2** (*language*) ungherese *m*

Hun·ga·ry ['hʌŋgərɪ] N Ungheria

hun·ger ['hʌŋgəʳ] N fame *f*; (*also fig*): **hunger (for)** sete *f* (di)
▸ **hunger after**, **hunger for** VI + PREP desiderare ardentemente, morire dalla voglia di

hunger strike N sciopero della fame

hung over [ˌhʌŋ'əʊvəʳ] ADJ (*fam*): **to be hungover** avere i postumi della sbornia

hun·gri·ly ['hʌŋgrɪlɪ] ADV (*fig*) avidamente; (*eat*) voracemente

hun·gry ['hʌŋgrɪ] ADJ (*comp* **-ier**, *superl* **-iest**) **to be hungry** aver fame, essere affamato(-a); **I'm not hungry** non ho fame; **to make sb hungry** far venire fame a qn; **to go hungry** (*starve*) patire la fame; (*skip a meal*) saltare il pasto; **hungry for** (*fig*) assetato(-a) di; (*lit*) affamato(-a) di

hung up ADJ (*fam*) complessato(-a)

hunk [hʌŋk] N (*of bread, cheese*) bel pezzo; **a gorgeous hunk of a man** (*fam*) un bel fusto

hunky-dory ['hʌŋkɪ'dɔ:rɪ] (*fam*) ADJ (*okay*) soddisfacente; (*fine*) magnifico(-a), meraviglioso(-a); **everything's hunky-dory** va tutto bene

◎**hunt** [hʌnt] N (*gen*) caccia; (*huntsmen*) cacciatori *mpl*;

(*search*): **hunt (for)** ricerca (di); **tiger hunt** caccia alla tigre; **I've had a hunt for the book** ho cercato il libro dappertutto
■ VT (*animal*) andare a caccia di; (*criminal*) dare la caccia a; **they hunt foxes** vanno a caccia di volpi; **detectives have been hunting him for seven months** gli investigatori gli stanno dando la caccia da sette mesi
■ VI (*Sport*) cacciare; (*search*) cercare; **to go hunting** andare a caccia; **to hunt for** (*animal*) cacciare; (*object, information*) cercare dappertutto; **I hunted everywhere for that book** ho cercato quel libro dappertutto; **she hunted in her bag for the keys** ha rovistato nella borsa in cerca delle chiavi
▸ **hunt down** VT + ADV (*criminal, enemy*) dar la caccia a
▸ **hunt out** VT + ADV scovare
▸ **hunt up** VT + ADV scovare

◎ **hunt·er** ['hʌntəʳ] N cacciatore(-trice); (*Brit: horse*) cavallo da caccia

hunter-gatherer [ˌhʌntə'gæθərəʳ] N: **to be a hunter-gatherer** vivere di caccia e della raccolta di bacche ed erbe

hunt·ing ['hʌntɪŋ] N (*Sport*) caccia; **to go hunting** andare a caccia; **fox hunting** caccia alla volpe

hunting lodge N casino di caccia

hunt saboteur N *animalista che partecipa ad azioni contro la caccia*

hunts·man ['hʌntsmən] N (*pl* **-men**) cacciatore *m*

hur·dle ['hɜːdl] N (*for fence*) graticcio; (*fig, Sport*) ostacolo; **the 100 metre hurdles** (*race*) i cento metri a ostacoli

hurdle race N (*Horse-racing*) corsa a ostacoli

hurl [hɜːl] VT (*throw*) scagliare, scaraventare; **to hurl o.s. at sb/sth** scagliarsi su qn/qc; **they were hurled to the ground by the blast** vennero scagliati a terra dall'esplosione; **to hurl abuse** *or* **insults at sb** scagliare *or* lanciare (degli) insulti a qn

hurl·ing ['hɜːlɪŋ] N (*Sport*) hurling *m*
▹ www.gaa.ie/page/all_about_hurling.html

hurly-burly [ˌhɜːlɪ'bɜːlɪ] N chiasso, baccano

hur·rah [hu'rɑː], **hur·ray** [hu'reɪ] EXCL urrà!, evviva!; **hurrah for Mr Jones!** viva Mr Jones!

hur·ri·cane ['hʌrɪkən] N uragano

hurricane lamp N lampada controvento

hur·ried ['hʌrɪd] ADJ (*gen*) affrettato(-a); (*steps*) frettoloso(-a); (*work*) fatto(-a) in fretta; **to eat a hurried meal** buttare giù due bocconi

hur·ried·ly ['hʌrɪdlɪ] ADV in fretta (e furia)

hur·ry ['hʌrɪ] N fretta, premura; **to be in a hurry (to do)** avere una gran fretta (di fare); **to do sth in a hurry** fare qc in fretta; **done in a hurry** fatto(-a) in fretta; **are you in a hurry for this?** ti serve subito?; **what's the hurry?** che fretta c'è?; **there's no hurry** non c'è fretta *or* premura; **he won't do that again in a hurry** (*fam*) non lo rifarà tanto facilmente
■ VT (*person*) far fretta a; (*work*) fare in fretta; **to hurry to do sth** affrettarsi a fare qc; **he won't be hurried** non gli si può far fretta; **she hurried him into the car** l'ha spinto in macchina; **he was hurried to the hospital** è stato portato d'urgenza all'ospedale; **he hurried his lunch** ha mangiato il pranzo alla svelta; **troops were hurried to the spot** le truppe furono spedite in fretta sul posto
■ VI fare in fretta; **to hurry back/home** affrettarsi a tornare indietro/a casa; **Sharon hurried back home** Sharon si affrettò a tornare a casa; **to hurry after sb** precipitarsi dietro a qn; **to hurry in/out** entrare/uscire in fretta
■ VT + ADV far fretta a
▸ **hurry along** VI + ADV camminare in fretta
■ VT + ADV = **hurry up** VT + ADV
▸ **hurry away, hurry off** VI + ADV andarsene in fretta
■ VT + ADV spedire fuori in fretta; **to be hurried off to** essere spedito(-a) in fretta a
▸ **hurry on** VI + ADV: **to hurry on to** passare in fretta a
▸ **hurry up** VI + ADV sbrigarsi, affrettarsi; **hurry up!** sbrigati!
■ VT + ADV (*person*) far fretta a; (*work*) fare in fretta; **hurry him up will you!** digli di fare in fretta!

◎ **hurt** [hɜːt] (*vb: pt, pp* **hurt**) VT **1** (*injure, also fig*) ferire; (*cause pain to, harm*) far male a; **I hurt my arm** mi sono fatto male al braccio; **you're hurting me!** mi fai male!; **to hurt o.s.** farsi male; **have you hurt yourself?** ti sei fatto male?; **where does it hurt you?** dove ti fa male?; **to get hurt** farsi male; **luckily, nobody got hurt** fortunatamente nessuno si è fatto male; (*emotionally*) essere ferito(-a); **to hurt sb's feelings** colpire la suscettibilità di qn; **his criticisms really hurt me** le sue critiche mi hanno proprio ferito
2 (*business, interests*) colpire, danneggiare
■ VI far male; **my arm hurts** mi fa male il braccio; **where does it hurt?** dove ti fa male?; **that hurts!** che male!, fa male!
■ N dolore *m*
■ ADJ (*foot*) ferito(-a); (*feelings, look, tone*) offeso(-a); **is he badly hurt?** è ferito gravemente?

> **DID YOU KNOW ...?**
> **hurt** is not translated by the Italian word ***urtare***

hurt·ful ['hɜːtfʊl] ADJ (*upsetting: remark*) che fa male, che ferisce

hurt·le ['hɜːtl] VI sfrecciare; **to hurtle past/down** passare/scendere a razzo; **she hurtled down the stairs** si è precipitata giù per le scale
■ VT scagliare

◎ **hus·band** ['hʌzbənd] N marito
■ VT dosare; **to husband one's resources** misurare le proprie risorse

hush [hʌʃ] N silenzio, calma, pace *f*; **hush!** silenzio!, zitto(-a)!
■ VT quietare, calmare
▸ **hush up** VT + ADV (*fact*) cercare di far passare sotto silenzio; (*scandal*) mettere a tacere; (*person*) far star zitto(-a), zittire

hushed [hʌʃt] ADJ (*tone, voice*) sommesso(-a); (*silence*) profondo(-a)

hush-hush ['hʌʃ'hʌʃ] ADJ (*fam*) segretissimo(-a)

hush money N: **to pay sb hush money** (*fam*) comprare il silenzio di qn

husk [hʌsk] N (*of wheat, rice, seed*) pula; (*of maize*) cartoccio

huski·ly ['hʌskɪlɪ] ADV con voce roca

huski·ness ['hʌskɪnɪs] N raucedine *f*

husky[1] ['hʌskɪ] ADJ (*comp* **-ier**, *superl* **-iest**) (*voice*) roco(-a); (*tough: person*) ben piantato(-a)

husky[2] ['hʌskɪ] N (*pl* **-ies**) husky *m inv*, cane *m* eschimese

hus·tings ['hʌstɪŋz] NPL (*Brit Pol*) campagna elettorale

hus·tle ['hʌsl] N: **hustle and bustle** trambusto, via vai *m inv*
■ VT (*push: person*) spingere, incalzare; **to hustle in/out**

Hh

spintonare dentro/fuori; **we'll have to hustle things along** dobbiamo fare più in fretta
■VI: **to hustle in/out** entrare/uscire in fretta
hut [hʌt] N (*primitive dwelling*) capanna; (*in mountains*) baita, rifugio; (*Mil*) baracca; (*shed*) capanno
hutch [hʌtʃ] N gabbia (per conigli)
hya·cinth ['haɪəsɪnθ] N giacinto
hy·brid ['haɪbrɪd] N ibrido
■ADJ ibrido(-a)
hy·dran·gea [haɪ'dreɪndʒə] N ortensia
hy·drant ['haɪdrənt] N (*also:* **fire hydrant**) idrante *m*
hy·drate ['haɪdreɪt] N idrato
hy·drau·lic [haɪ'drɒlɪk] ADJ idraulico(-a); **hydraulic ramp** (*Aut*) ponte *m* (sollevatore)
hy·drau·lics [haɪ'drɒlɪks] NSG idraulica
hy·dride ['haɪdraɪd] N idruro
hydro... ['haɪdrəʊ] PREF idro...
hydro·car·bon ['haɪdrəʊ'kɑ:bən] N idrocarburo
hydro·chlo·ric acid [ˌhaɪdrəʊ'klɒrɪk'æsɪd] N acido cloridrico *or* muriatico
hydro·dy·nam·ics ['haɪdrəʊdaɪ'næmɪks] NSG idrodinamica
hydro·elec·tric ['haɪdrəʊɪ'lɛktrɪk] ADJ idroelettrico(-a)
hydro·elec·tric·ity ['haɪdrəʊɪlɛk'trɪsɪtɪ] N idroelettricità
hydro·foil ['haɪdrəˌfɔɪl] N aliscafo
hydro·gen ['haɪdrɪdʒən] N idrogeno
hydrogen bomb N bomba all'idrogeno, bomba H
hydrogen carbonate N carbonato acido, bicarbonato
hydrogen chloride N acido cloridrico
hydrogen ion N ione *m* idrogeno
hydrogen peroxide N acqua ossigenata
hydrogen sulphide N acido solfidrico
hydro·logi·cal [ˌhaɪdrə'lɒdʒɪkəl] ADJ idrologico(-a)
hy·droly·sis [haɪ'drɒlɪsɪs] N idrolisi *f*
hy·drom·eter [haɪ'drɒmɪtə[r]] N idrometro
hydro·phil·ic [ˌhaɪdrəʊ'fɪlɪk] ADJ idrofilo(-a)
hydro·pho·bia [ˌhaɪdrə'fəʊbɪə] N idrofobia
hydro·pho·bic [ˌhaɪdrəʊ'fəʊbɪk] ADJ idrofobo(-a); (*Chem*) idrofugo(-a)
hydro·plane ['haɪdrəʊˌpleɪn] N idrovolante *m*
hydro·pon·ics [ˌhaɪdrə'pɒnɪks] NSG idroponica
hy·drot·ro·pism [haɪ'drɒtrəˌpɪzəm] N idrotropismo
hy·drox·ide [haɪ'drɒksaɪd] N ossidrile *m*
hy·ena [haɪ'i:nə] N iena
hy·giene ['haɪdʒi:n] N igiene *f*
hy·gien·ic [haɪ'dʒi:nɪk] ADJ igienico(-a)
hy·gieni·cal·ly [haɪ'dʒi:nɪkəlɪ] ADV igienicamente
hy·grom·eter [haɪ'grɒmɪtə[r]] N igrometro
hygro·scop·ic [ˌhaɪgrə'skɒpɪk] ADJ igroscopico(-a)
hymn [hɪm] N inno (sacro)
hym·nal ['hɪmnəl] N libro dei canti
hymn book N libro dei canti
hype [haɪp] N (*fam*) battage *m inv*
hyper... ['haɪpə[r]] PREF iper...
hyper·ac·tive [ˌhaɪpər'æktɪv] ADJ iperattivo(-a)
hyper·bo·le [haɪ'pɜ:bəlɪ] N iperbole *f*
hyper·criti·cal [ˌhaɪpə'krɪtɪkəl] ADJ ipercritico(-a)
hyper·link ['haɪpəlɪŋk] N (*Comput*) collegamento ipertestuale
hyper·mar·ket ['haɪpəˌmɑ:kɪt] N (*Brit*) ipermercato
hyper·sen·si·tive [ˌhaɪpə'sɛnsɪtɪv] ADJ (*physically*) ipersensibile; (*easily offended: pej*) permaloso(-a)
hyper·ten·sion [ˌhaɪpə'tɛnʃən] N (*Med*) ipertensione *f*
hyper·text ['haɪpətɛkst] N ipertesto
hyper·ven·ti·la·tion [ˌhaɪpəˌvɛntɪ'leɪʃən] N (*Med*) iperventilazione *f*
hy·phen ['haɪfən] N trattino, lineetta
hy·phen·ate ['haɪfəˌneɪt] VT unire con un trattino
hyp·no·sis [hɪp'nəʊsɪs] N ipnosi *f*
hyp·not·ic [hɪp'nɒtɪk] ADJ ipnotico(-a)
hyp·no·tism ['hɪpnətɪzəm] N ipnotismo
hyp·no·tist ['hɪpnətɪst] N ipnotizzatore(-trice)
hyp·no·tize ['hɪpnəˌtaɪz] VT ipnotizzare; **to hypnotize sb into doing sth** far fare qc a qn sotto ipnosi
hypo·al·ler·gen·ic ['haɪpəʊˌælə'dʒɛnɪk] ADJ anallergico(-a)
hypo·chon·dria [ˌhaɪpəʊ'kɒndrɪə] N ipocondria
hypo·chon·dri·ac [ˌhaɪpəʊ'kɒndrɪæk] N ipocondriaco(-a)
hy·poc·ri·sy [hɪ'pɒkrɪsɪ] N ipocrisia
hypo·crite ['hɪpəkrɪt] N ipocrita *m/f*
hypo·criti·cal [ˌhɪpə'krɪtɪkəl] ADJ ipocrita
hypo·criti·cal·ly [ˌhɪpə'krɪtɪkəlɪ] ADV ipocritamente, in modo ipocrita
hypo·der·mic [ˌhaɪpə'dɜ:mɪk] ADJ ipodermico(-a)
■N (*syringe*) siringa ipodermica
hy·pot·enuse [haɪ'pɒtɪnju:z] N (*Geom*) ipotenusa
hypo·ther·mia [ˌhaɪpəʊ'θɜ:mɪə] N (*Med*) ipotermia
hy·poth·esis [haɪ'pɒθɪsɪs] N (*pl* **hypotheses** [haɪ'pɒθɪsi:z]) ipotesi *f inv*
hy·poth·esize [haɪ'pɒθɪˌsaɪz] VI (*frm*) ipotizzare
hypo·theti·cal [ˌhaɪpəʊ'θɛtɪkəl] ADJ ipotetico(-a)
hypo·theti·cal·ly [ˌhaɪpəʊ'θɛtɪkəlɪ] ADV ipoteticamente, per ipotesi
hys·ter·ec·to·my [ˌhɪstə'rɛktəmɪ] N (*Med*) isterectomia
hys·te·ria [hɪs'tɪərɪə] N (*gen*) isterismo; (*Psych*) isteria
hys·teri·cal [hɪs'tɛrɪkəl] ADJ isterico(-a); **to become hysterical** avere una crisi isterica; **it was hysterical!** era buffissimo!
hys·teri·cal·ly [hɪs'tɛrɪkəlɪ] ADV istericamente; **it was hysterically funny** era buffo da morire
hys·ter·ics [hɪs'tɛrɪks] NPL (*tears*) crisi *f inv* isterica; (*laughter*) attacco di riso; **to be in** *or* **have hysterics** avere una crisi isterica; (*fam: laugh*) crepar dal ridere; **she'll have hysterics** avrà una crisi isterica; **it was so funny, I was in hysterics** era così buffo, mi ha fatto morir dal ridere
Hz ABBR (= hertz) Hz

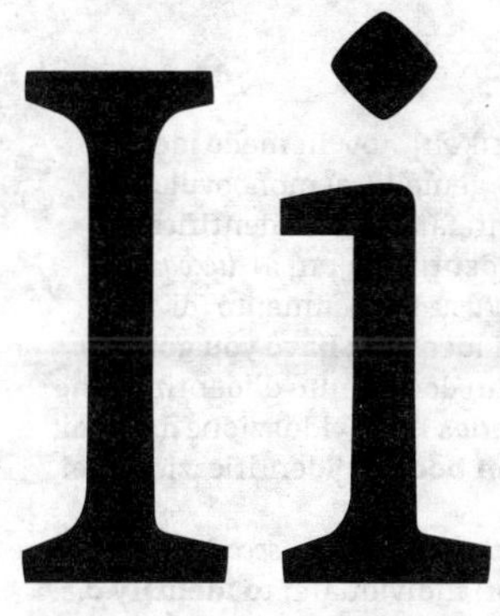

◎**I, i** [aɪ] N *(letter)* I, i *f or m inv*; **I for Isaac** *(Am)*: **I for Item** ≈ I come Imola

I [aɪ] PERS PRON io; **I'll do it** lo faccio io; **he and I were at school together** io e lui eravamo a scuola insieme; **Ann and I** Ann ed io; **I love cats** adoro i gatti

I. ABBR (= **island, isle**) I., Is.

IA ABBR *(Am Post)* = **Iowa**

IAEA [ˌaɪeiː'eɪ] N ABBR (= **International Atomic Energy Agency**) AIEA *f* (= *Agenzia Internazionale per l'Energia Atomica*)

IATA [aɪ'ɑːtə] N ABBR (= **International Air Transport Association**) Associazione internazionale per il trasporto aereo

ib. ABBR = **ibid.**

IBA [ˌaɪbiː'eɪ] N ABBR *(Brit*: = **Independent Broadcasting Authority**) *organo di controllo sulle reti televisive*

Iberian [aɪ'bɪərɪən] ADJ iberico(-a)

Iberian Peninsula N: **the Iberian Peninsula** la penisola iberica

IBEW [ˌaɪbiːiː'dʌbljuː] N ABBR *(Am*: = **International Brotherhood of Electrical Workers**) *associazione internazionale degli elettrotecnici*

ibex ['aɪbeks] N *(Zool)* stambecco

ibid. ['ɪbɪd] ABBR (= **ibidem**: *from the same source*) ibid.

i/c ABBR *(Brit)* = **in charge**; *see* **charge**

Icarus ['ɪkərəs] N Icaro

ICBM [ˌaɪsiːbiː'ɛm] N ABBR (= **intercontinental ballistic missile**) ICBM *m inv*

ICC [ˌaɪsiː'siː] N ABBR **1** (= **International Chamber of Commerce**) CCI *f* (= *Camera di Commercio Internazionale*) **2** *(Am*: = **Interstate Commerce Commission**) *commissione per il commercio tra gli stati degli USA*

◎**ice** [aɪs] N **1** ghiaccio; *(on road)* ghiaccio, strato di ghiaccio; **a sheet of ice** una lastra di ghiaccio; **to be as cold as ice** essere freddo(-a) come il ghiaccio, essere un pezzo di ghiaccio; **to break the ice** *(fig)* rompere il ghiaccio; **it cuts no ice with me** con me non attacca; **to keep sth on ice** *(fig: plan, project)* accantonare qc; **to skate on thin ice** *(fig)* essere sul filo del rasoio **2** *(ice cream)* gelato; **strawberry ice** gelato alla fragola; **a vanilla ice cream** un gelato alla vaniglia

■VT *(cake)* glassare

▸ **ice over, ice up** VI + ADV *(river)* gelarsi, ghiacciarsi; *(windscreen, wings of plane)* incrostarsi di ghiaccio

Ice Age N: **the Ice Age** l'era glaciale

ice axe N piccozza da ghiaccio

ice·berg ['aɪsbɜːg] N iceberg *m inv*; **this is only the tip of the iceberg** *(fig)* questa è solo la punta dell'iceberg

ice·bound ['aɪsˌbaʊnd] ADJ bloccato(-a) dal ghiaccio

ice·box ['aɪsˌbɒks] N *(Am: refrigerator)* frigorifero; *(Brit: freezer compartment)* freezer *m inv*

ice·breaker ['aɪsˌbreɪkə^r] N rompighiaccio *m inv*; *(fig: for group of students) gioco o esercizio fatto per rompere il ghiaccio all'inizio di una lezione*

ice bucket N secchiello del ghiaccio

ice·cap ['aɪsˌkæp] N calotta glaciale; **polar icecap** calotta polare

ice-cold [ˌaɪs'kəʊld] ADJ ghiacciato(-a), gelato(-a)

ice-cool [ˌaɪs'kuːl] ADJ freddo(-a) e impenetrabile

ice cream N gelato

ice-cream soda ['aɪskriːm'səʊdə] N *(Am)* (gelato) affogato al seltz

ice cube N cubetto di ghiaccio

iced [aɪst] ADJ **1** *(drink)* ghiacciato(-a); *(coffee, tea)* freddo(-a) **2** *(cake)* glassato(-a)

ice·fall ['aɪsˌfɔːl] N seraccata

ice floe N banco di ghiaccio, banchisa

ice hammer N martello-piccozza *m inv*

ice hockey N hockey *m* su ghiaccio

▷ www.iihf.com
▷ www.nhl.com

Ice·land ['aɪslənd] N l'Islanda

Ice·land·er ['aɪsləndə^r] N islandese *m/f*

Ice·land·ic [aɪs'lændɪk] ADJ islandese

■N *(language)* islandese *m*

ice lolly N *(Brit)* ghiacciolo

ice pack N impacco di ghiaccio

ice pick N piccone *m* per ghiaccio

ice rink N pista di pattinaggio su ghiaccio

ice sheet N ghiacciaio continentale

ice-skate ['aɪsˌskeɪt] VI pattinare sul ghiaccio

ice skate N pattino da ghiaccio

ice skater N pattinatore(-trice) su ghiaccio

Ii

ice-skating [ˈaɪsˌskeɪtɪŋ] N pattinaggio sul ghiaccio; **to go ice-skating** andare a pattinare sul ghiaccio
ice tray N vaschetta per il ghiaccio
ice water N (*Am*) acqua ghiacciata
ici·cle [ˈaɪsɪkl] N ghiacciolo
ici·ly [ˈaɪsɪlɪ] ADV gelidamente
ic·ing [ˈaɪsɪŋ] N **1** (*on cake*) glassa; **vanilla icing** glassa alla vaniglia **2** (*Aer*) patina di ghiaccio
icing sugar N zucchero a velo
ICJ [ˌaɪsiːˈdʒeɪ] N ABBR = **International Court of Justice**
icky [ˈɪkɪ] (*fam*) ADJ appiccicoso(-a), appiccicaticcio(-a); (*fig: song etc*) sdolcinato(-a)
icon [ˈaɪkɒn] N (*also Comput*) icona
icono·clast [aɪˈkɒnəklæst] N (*frm*) iconoclasta *m/f*
icono·clas·tic [aɪˌkɒnəˈklæstɪk] (*frm*) ADJ (*opinions*) iconoclastico(-a), iconoclasta; (*person*) iconoclasta
ico·nog·ra·phy [ˌaɪkɒˈnɒgrəfɪ] N iconografia
ICR [ˌaɪsiːɑːʳ] N ABBR (*Am*) = **Institute for Cancer Research**
ICRC [ˌaɪsiːɑːsiː] N ABBR (= **International Committee of the Red Cross**) CICR *m*
ICT [ˌaɪsiːˈtiː] N ABBR (*Brit Scol:* = **Information and Communications Technology**) informatica
ic·tus [ˈɪktəs] N ictus *m inv*
ICU [ˌaɪsiːˈjuː] N ABBR = **intensive care unit**; *see* **intensive care**
icy [ˈaɪsɪ] ADJ (*comp* **-ier**, *superl* **-iest**) (*road, hand*) ghiacciato(-a); (*weather, temperature, stare*) gelido(-a); **it's icy cold** si gela; **an icy wind** un vento gelido; **the roads are icy** le strade sono ghiacciate
ID [ˌaɪˈdiː] N ABBR (= **identification**) identità; **have you got some ID?** ha un documento (d'identità)?
■ ABBR (*Am Post*) = **Idaho**
id [ɪd] N (*Psych*) Id *m*, Es *m*
I'd [aɪd] = **I would, I had**
Ida·ho [ˈaɪdəhəʊ] N Idaho
▷ www.accessidaho.org/
ID card N = **identity card**
IDD [ˌaɪdiːˈdiː] N ABBR (*Brit Telec:* = **international direct dialling**) teleselezione *f* internazionale
◎ **idea** [aɪˈdɪə] N idea; **good idea!** buon'idea!; **that was a brilliant idea** è stata un'idea splendida; **she had no idea of the answer** non aveva idea della risposta; **to have an idea that ...** aver l'impressione che...; **I haven't the least** *or* **slightest** *or* **foggiest idea** non ne ho la minima *or* la più pallida idea; **it wouldn't be a bad idea to paint it** non sarebbe una cattiva idea verniciarlo; **to put ideas into sb's head** mettere delle idee in testa a qn; **it wasn't my idea** non è stata un'idea mia, non sono io che ho avuto l'idea; **if that's your idea of a joke ...** se credi di essere spiritoso...; **I've got the general idea** mi sono fatto un'idea; **that's the idea** ecco, proprio così ; **what's the big idea?** (*fam*) cosa credi di fare?; **the idea is to sell it** si tratta di venderlo
◎ **ideal** [aɪˈdɪəl] ADJ, N ideale (*m*)
ideal·ism [aɪˈdɪəˌlɪzəm] N idealismo
ideal·ist [aɪˈdɪəlɪst] N idealista *m/f*
ideal·is·tic [aɪˌdɪəˈlɪstɪk] ADJ (*person*) idealista; (*views*) idealistico(-a)
ideal·ize [aɪˈdɪəˌlaɪz] VT idealizzare
ideal·ly [aɪˈdɪəlɪ] ADV perfettamente; **it is ideally situated** si trova in un posto ideale; **they are an ideally matched couple** sono una coppia ideale; **ideally, I'd like to work abroad** l'ideale per me sarebbe lavorare all'estero
iden·ti·cal [aɪˈdɛntɪˌkəl] ADJ identico(-a)
iden·ti·cal·ly [aɪˈdɛntɪkəlɪ] ADV in modo identico
identical twins NPL gemelli(-e) monoovulari
iden·ti·fi·able [aɪˈdɛntɪˌfaɪəbl] ADJ identificabile
iden·ti·fi·ca·tion [aɪˌdɛntɪfɪˈkeɪʃən] N (*recognition*) identificazione *f*; (*document*) documento (di riconoscimento *or* di identità); **have you got any identification?** ha un documento d'identità?; **the identification of genes** l'individuazione dei geni; **the identification of bodies** l'identificazione dei cadaveri
◎ **iden·ti·fy** [aɪˈdɛntɪfaɪ] VT (*recognize, specify*) identificare, riconoscere; (*point out*) individuare; **to identify o.s. with** identificarsi con; **we managed to identify the problem** siamo riusciti ad individuare il problema; **the police have identified the body** la polizia ha identificato il corpo
■ VI: **to identify with** identificarsi con
Iden·ti·kit® [aɪˈdɛntɪˌkɪt] N: **Identikit (picture)** identikit *m inv*
◎ **iden·tity** [aɪˈdɛntɪtɪ] N identità *f inv*; **a case of mistaken identity** uno scambio di persona
identity card N carta d'identità
identity disc N piastrina di riconoscimento
identity parade N (*Brit*) confronto all'americana
ideo·gram [ˈɪdɪəʊˌgræm], **id·eog·ra·ph** [ˌɪdɪˈɒgrəf] N ideogramma *m*
ideo·logi·cal [ˌaɪdɪəˈlɒdʒɪkəl] ADJ ideologico(-a)
ideol·ogy [ˌaɪdɪˈɒlədʒɪ] N ideologia
idio·cy [ˈɪdɪəsɪ] N idiozia
idi·om [ˈɪdɪəm] N (*phrase*) locuzione *f* idiomatica; (*style of expression*) stile *m*
idio·mat·ic [ˌɪdɪəˈmætɪk] ADJ idiomatico(-a)
idio·mati·cal·ly [ˌɪdɪəˈmætɪkəlɪ] ADV in modo idiomatico
idio·syn·cra·sy [ˌɪdɪəˈsɪŋkrəsɪ] N (*peculiarity, foible*) (piccola) mania; (*characteristic*) particolarità *f inv*
idio·syn·crat·ic [ˌɪdɪəsɪŋˈkrætɪk] ADJ particolare
idi·ot [ˈɪdɪət] N deficiente *m/f*, stupido(-a)
idi·ot·ic [ˌɪdɪˈɒtɪk] ADJ (*person*) idiota; (*price, question*) assurdo(-a)
idi·oti·cal·ly [ˌɪdɪˈɒtɪkəlɪ] ADV (*stare*) con aria da ebete; (*behave*) stupidamente, da idiota
idle [ˈaɪdl] ADJ (*comp* **-r**, *superl* **-st**) **1** (*lazy: student*) pigro(-a), poltrone(-a); (*inactive: machine, factory, workers*) inattivo(-a); (*unemployed: worker*) disoccupato(-a); **the idle rich** i ricchi sfaccendati; **in my idle moments** nei miei momenti liberi; **an idle life** una vita d'ozio; **to stand** *or* **lie idle** (*factory, machine*) rimaner fermo(-a) *or* inattivo(-a) **2** (*fear, speculation*) infondato(-a); (*gossip, pleasures*) futile; (*question*) ozioso(-a); (*threat*) campato(-a) in aria; **it's just idle gossip** sono solo chiacchiere futili; **I asked out of idle curiosity** l'ho chiesto per pura curiosità
■ VI (*person*) oziare; (*engine*) girare al minimo
▶ **idle away** VT + ADV (*time*) sprecare, buttar via
idle·ness [ˈaɪdlnɪs] N pigrizia, ozio
idler [ˈaɪdləʳ] N fannullone(-a), sfaccendato(-a)
idle time N (*esp Comm*) tempi *mpl* morti
idly [ˈaɪdlɪ] ADV pigramente; **he stood idly by, watching the others working** è rimasto lì senza far niente a guardare gli altri che lavoravano
idol [ˈaɪdl] N idolo
idola·trous [aɪˈdɒlətrəs] ADJ (*pej*) idolatra
idola·try [aɪˈdɒlətrɪ] N (*old*) idolatria
idol·ize [ˈaɪdəˌlaɪz] VT idolatrare
id·yll [ˈɪdɪl] N idillio
idyl·lic [ɪˈdɪlɪk] ADJ idilliaco(-a)

i.e. [ˌaɪ'iː] ABBR (= id est: *that is*) cioè

◎**if** [ɪf] CONJ **1** se; **if anyone comes in** se viene *or* venisse qualcuno; **I'll go if you come with me** ci vado se vieni anche tu; **you can have it if you like** puoi prenderlo se vuoi; **I'd be pleased if you could do it** sarei molto contento se potessi farlo; **if necessary** se (è) necessario; **if I were you** se fossi in te, io al tuo posto; **if you ask me ...** secondo me... **2** (*whenever*) tutte le volte *or* ogni volta che, quando; **if we are in Scotland, we always go to see her** quando siamo in Scozia, andiamo sempre a trovarla **3** (*although*): **(even) if** anche se + *sub*; **I am determined to do it, (even) if it takes all week** sono deciso a farlo, dovessi impiegarci tutta la settimana **4** (*whether*) se; **I don't know if he is here** non so se c'è **5** (*in phrases*): **if so** se è così , allora; **are you coming? if so, I'll wait** vieni? allora ti aspetto; **if not** se no, altrimenti; **are you coming? if not, I'll go with Mark** vieni? altrimenti vado con Mark; **if only** se solo *or* soltanto; **if only she were here** se solo fosse qui; **if only I could** se soltanto potessi, magari (potessi); **I would like to see her if only for a few minutes** vorrei vederla magari *or* anche solo per pochi minuti; **if only to show him my gratitude** se non altro per esprimergli la mia gratitudine; **if only I had more money!** se solo avessi più denaro!; **as if** come se; **as if by chance** come per caso; *see also* **as, even** *etc*

■N: **there are a lot of ifs and buts** ci sono molti se e ma; **that's** *or* **it's a big if** è un grosso punto interrogativo

if·fy ['ɪfɪ] ADJ (*comp* **-ier**, *superl* **-iest**) (*fam*) incerto(-a)

ig·loo ['ɪgluː] N igloo *m inv*

ig·ne·ous ['ɪgnɪəs] ADJ (*rock*) eruttivo(-a)

ig·nite [ɪg'naɪt] VT (*fire, match*) accendere; (*wood*) incendiare

■VI accendersi; **the gas ignited at once** il gas si è acceso subito

ig·ni·tion [ɪg'nɪʃən] N (*Aut*) accensione *f*; (*Chem*) ignizione *f*; **to switch on/off the ignition** accendere/spegnere il motore; **the device automatically disconnects the ignition** il dispositivo esclude automaticamente l'accensione

ignition key N (*Aut*) chiave *f* dell'accensione

ignition switch N (*Aut*) interruttore *m* dell'accensione

ig·no·ble [ɪg'nəʊbl] ADJ ignobile

ig·no·mini·ous [ˌɪgnə'mɪnɪəs] ADJ vergognoso(-a), ignominioso(-a)

ig·no·mini·ous·ly [ˌɪgnə'mɪnɪəslɪ] ADV vergognosamente, in modo ignominioso

ig·no·miny ['ɪgnəˌmɪnɪ] N (*frm*) ignominia

ig·no·ra·mus [ˌɪgnə'reɪməs] N ignorante *m/f*

ig·no·rance ['ɪgnərəns] N: **ignorance (of)** ignoranza (di); **to keep sb in ignorance of sth** tenere qn all'oscuro di qc; **to show one's ignorance** dimostrare la propria ignoranza; **it's no use pleading ignorance of the law** la legge non ammette ignoranza

ig·no·rant ['ɪgnərənt] ADJ (*lacking education*) ignorante; **to be ignorant of** (*fact, situation, subject*) ignorare; (*events*) essere all'oscuro di

ig·no·rant·ly ['ɪgnərəntlɪ] ADV per ignoranza

◎**ig·nore** [ɪg'nɔːʳ] VT (*person*) ignorare; (*problem, fact*) trascurare; (*remark*) non far caso a; (*advice, letter*) non tener in nessun conto; (*danger*) non curarsi di; (*sb's behaviour*) chiudere un occhio su

igua·na [ɪ'gwɑːnə] N iguana

ikon ['aɪkɒn] N = **icon**

IL ABBR (*Am Post*) = **Illinois**

ILEA ['ɪlɪə] N ABBR (*Brit*: = **Inner London Education Authority**) *nel passato, provveditorato agli studi della zona centrale di Londra*

il·eum ['ɪlɪəm] N ileo (*intestino*)

ilk [ɪlk] N: **of that ilk** di quel genere

◎**ill** [ɪl] ADJ (*comp* **worse**, *superl* **worst**) **1** (*sick*) ammalato(-a), malato(-a); **to fall** *or* **be taken ill** ammalarsi; **she was taken ill** si è ammalata; **to feel ill (with)** star male (per *or* a causa di); **to be in ill health** essere malaticcio(-a); **he's seriously ill** è gravemente ammalato; **she is seriously ill in hospital** è ricoverata in gravi condizioni all'ospedale **2** (*bad*) cattivo(-a); **ill fortune** *or* **ill luck** sfortuna, scalogna; **ill effects** brutte conseguenze *fpl*; **to be in an ill humour** *or* **temper** essere di cattivo umore; **it's an ill wind that blows nobody any good** (*Proverb*) non tutto il male viene per nuocere

■ADV male; **we can ill afford to lose him/to buy it** non possiamo certo permetterci di perderlo/di comprarlo; **to speak/think ill of sb** parlar/pensar male di qn

■ **ills** NPL (*old frm*) mali *mpl*, malanni *mpl*

I'll [aɪl] = **I will, I shall**

ill-advised [ˌɪləd'vaɪzd] ADJ (*plan, remark, decision, person*) sconsiderato(-a), avventato(-a); *see also* **advise**

ill-assorted [ɪlə'sɔːtɪd] ADJ mal assortito(-a)

ill at ease ADJ a disagio

ill-bred [ˌɪl'brɛd] ADJ maleducato(-a)

ill-conceived [ˌɪlkən'siːvd] ADJ mal congegnato(-a)

ill-considered [ˌɪlkən'sɪdəd] ADJ (*plan*) avventato(-a)

ill-defined [ˌɪldɪ'faɪnd] ADJ mal definito(-a)

ill-disposed [ˌɪldɪs'pəʊzd] ADJ: **to be ill-disposed towards sb/sth** essere maldisposto(-a) verso qn/qc *or* nei riguardi di qn/qc

◎**il·legal** [ɪ'liːgəl] ADJ illegale

il·legal·ity [ˌɪliː'gælɪtɪ] N illegalità

il·legal·ly [ɪ'liːgəlɪ] ADV illegalmente

il·leg·ible [ɪ'lɛdʒəbl] ADJ illeggibile

il·leg·ibly [ɪ'lɛdʒəblɪ] ADV in modo illeggibile

il·legiti·ma·cy [ˌɪlɪ'dʒɪtɪməsɪ] N illegittimità

il·legiti·mate [ˌɪlɪ'dʒɪtɪmɪt] ADJ illegittimo(-a)

il·legiti·mate·ly [ˌɪlɪ'dʒɪtɪmɪtlɪ] ADV illegittimamente

ill-equipped [ɪlɪ'kwɪpt] ADJ (*lacking necessary qualities*) impreparato(-a); (*lacking equipment*) mal equipaggiato(-a); **they were ill-equipped for the part** non avevano i requisiti necessari per la parte

ill-fated [ˌɪl'feɪtɪd] ADJ (*person*) sventurato(-a); (*enterprise*) sfortunato(-a)

ill-favoured, (*Am*) **ill-favored** [ˌɪl'feɪvəd] ADJ (*ugly*) sgraziato(-a), brutto(-a); (*objectionable*) sgradevole

ill feeling N rancore *m*

ill-founded [ɪl'faʊndɪd] ADJ (*gossip*) infondato(-a); (*argument*) senza fondamento

ill-gotten ['ɪlˌgɒtn] ADJ (*frm*): **ill-gotten gains** guadagni *mpl* illeciti

ill health N problemi *mpl* di salute

il·lib·er·al [ɪ'lɪbərəl] ADJ illiberale

il·lic·it [ɪ'lɪsɪt] ADJ illecito(-a)

il·lic·it·ly [ɪ'lɪsɪtlɪ] ADV illecitamente

ill-informed [ˌɪlɪn'fɔːmd] ADJ (*person*) male informato(-a); (*comment, criticism*) che rivela ignoranza

Il·li·nois [ˌɪlɪ'nɔɪ] N Illinois *m*

▷ www.illinois.gov/

il·lit·era·cy [ɪ'lɪtərəsɪ] N analfabetismo

il·lit·er·ate [ɪ'lɪtərɪt] ADJ (*person*) analfabeta, illetterato(-a); (*letter*) sgrammaticato(-a)

■N analfabeta *m/f*, illetterato(-a)

Ii

ill-judged [ˌɪl'dʒʌdʒd] ADJ *(remark)* inopportuno(-a)
ill-mannered [ˌɪl'mænəd] ADJ maleducato(-a), sgarbato(-a)
ill-natured [ˌɪl'neɪtʃəd] ADJ d'indole cattiva
◎**ill·ness** ['ɪlnɪs] N malattia
il·logi·cal [ɪˌlɒdʒɪkəl] ADJ illogico(-a)
il·logi·cal·ity [ɪˌlɒdʒɪ'kælɪtɪ] N illogicità *f inv*
il·logi·cal·ly [ɪ'lɒdʒɪkəlɪ] ADV illogicamente
ill-omened [ɪl'əʊmənd] ADJ nefasto(-a)
ill-starred [ɪl'stɑːd] ADJ *(liter) (person)* nato(-a) sotto una cattiva stella; *(day)* sfortunato(-a)
ill-suited [ˌɪl'suːtɪd] ADJ *(couple)* mal assortito(-a); **he is ill-suited to the job** è inadatto a quel lavoro
ill-timed [ˌɪl'taɪmd] ADJ intempestivo(-a), inopportuno(-a)
ill-treat [ˌɪl'triːt] VT maltrattare
ill-treatment [ˌɪl'triːtmənt] N maltrattamenti *mpl*
il·lu·mi·nate [ɪ'luːmɪˌneɪt] VT *(light up)* illuminare; *(fig: problem, question)* chiarire
il·lu·mi·nat·ed [ɪ'luːmɪˌneɪtɪd] ADJ **1** *(sign, advertising)* luminoso(-a) **2** *(manuscript)* miniato(-a)
il·lu·mi·nat·ing [ɪ'luːmɪˌneɪtɪŋ] ADJ *(comments, remark)* chiarificatore(-trice); *(experience, book)* istruttivo(-a)
il·lu·mi·na·tion [ɪˌluːmɪ'neɪʃən] N **1** *(lighting)* illuminazione *f* **2** *(of manuscript)* miniatura **3 illuminations** NPL *(coloured lights)* luminarie *fpl*
il·lu·sion [ɪ'luːʒən] N illusione *f*; **to be under an illusion** illudersi; **to be under the illusion that** illudersi che; **to have no illusions** non farsi illusioni
il·lu·sive [ɪ'luːsɪv], **il·lu·sory** [ɪ'luːsərɪ] ADJ illusorio(-a)
◎**il·lus·trate** ['ɪləˌstreɪt] VT illustrare
◎**il·lus·tra·tion** [ˌɪləs'treɪʃən] N illustrazione *f*; *(example)* esemplificazione *f*; **by way of illustration** a titolo d'esempio
il·lus·tra·tive ['ɪləstrətɪv] ADJ illustrativo(-a)
il·lus·tra·tor ['ɪləsˌtreɪtə^r] N illustratore(-trice)
il·lus·tri·ous [ɪ'lʌstrɪəs] ADJ illustre
ill will N rancore *m*; **I bear you no ill will** non ti serbo rancore
ILO [ˌaɪel'əʊ] N ABBR (= **International Labour Organization**) OIL *f* (= *Organizzazione Internazionale del Lavoro*)
▷ www.ilo.org/public/english
I'm [aɪm] = **I am**
◎**im·age** ['ɪmɪdʒ] N *(of person, group, organization)* immagine *f*; **to be the very** *or* **the spitting image of sb** essere il ritratto sputato di qn; **she's the image of her mother** è il ritratto di sua madre; **mirror image** immagine speculare; **she has to think of her image** deve pensare alla sua immagine; **the company has changed its image** la società ha cambiato immagine
im·age·ry ['ɪmɪdʒərɪ] N *(Art, Literature)* immagini *fpl*; *(Psych)* immaginario
im·agi·nable [ɪ'mædʒɪnəbl] ADJ immaginabile, che si possa immaginare
im·agi·nary [ɪ'mædʒɪnərɪ] ADJ immaginario(-a)
◎**im·agi·na·tion** [ɪˌmædʒɪ'neɪʃən] N immaginazione *f*; *(inventiveness)* immaginazione, fantasia; **it's all imagination!** sono tutte fantasie!; **it's all in your imagination** è tutto frutto della tua immaginazione; **to have a vivid imagination** avere una fervida fantasia *or* una viva immaginazione; **she lets her imagination run away with her** si lascia trasportare dalla fantasia; **use your imagination!** su, un po' di fantasia!; **she has no imagination** non ha immaginazione
im·agi·na·tive [ɪ'mædʒɪnətɪv] ADJ fantasioso(-a), immaginoso(-a)
im·agi·na·tive·ly [ɪ'mædʒɪnətɪvlɪ] ADV con fantasia *or* immaginazione
◎**im·ag·ine** [ɪ'mædʒɪn] VT **1** *(visualize)* immaginare, immaginarsi; **just imagine!** pensa un po'!; **you can imagine how I felt** puoi immaginare *or* immaginarti come mi sono sentito; **you are just imagining things** che idee!, è tutto frutto della tua immaginazione **2** *(suppose, think)* immaginare, credere; **I never imagined that he would be there** non avrei mai immaginato che lui sarebbe stato lì
im·ag·in·ings [ɪ'mædʒɪnɪŋs] NPL *(liter)* fantasie *fpl*
im·bal·ance [ɪm'bæləns] N squilibrio
im·becile ['ɪmbəsiːl] N ebete *m/f*, imbecille *m/f*
im·becil·ity [ˌɪmbɪ'sɪlɪtɪ] N imbecillità
im·bibe [ɪm'baɪb] VT *(frm also hum: drink)* bere; *(fig: absorb)* assorbire, assimilare
im·bue [ɪm'bjuː] VT *(frm)*: **to imbue sth with** impregnare qc di
IMF [ˌaɪɛm'ɛf] N ABBR = **International Monetary Fund**
▷ www.imf.org
IMHO [ˌaɪɛmeɪtʃ'əʊ] ABBR (= **in my humble opinion**) secondo la mia modesta opinione
imi·tate ['ɪmɪˌteɪt] VT imitare
imi·ta·tion [ˌɪmɪ'teɪʃən] N imitazione *f*; **in imitation of** a imitazione di; **a painting in imitation of the famous work by Picasso** un dipinto che riproduce la famosa opera di Picasso
■ ADJ finto(-a); **imitation leather** finta pelle
imitation jewels NPL gioielli *mpl* falsi
imi·ta·tive ['ɪmɪtətɪv] ADJ imitativo(-a)
imi·ta·tor ['ɪmɪˌteɪtə^r] N imitatore(-trice)
im·macu·late [ɪ'mækjʊlɪt] ADJ *(spotless)* immacolato(-a); *(flawless)* impeccabile
Immaculate Conception N: **the Immaculate Conception** *(Rel)* l'Immacolata Concezione *f*
im·macu·late·ly [ɪ'mækjʊlɪtlɪ] ADV impeccabilmente
im·ma·terial [ˌɪmə'tɪərɪəl] ADJ irrilevante, insignificante; **it is immaterial whether** poco importa se *or* che + *sub*; **it is immaterial whether we like him or not** poco importa se ci piace o no; **that's immaterial!** è indifferente!; **that's quite immaterial to me** questo non ha alcuna importanza per me
im·ma·ture [ˌɪmə'tjʊə^r] ADJ immaturo(-a)
im·ma·tu·rity [ˌɪmə'tjʊərɪtɪ] N immaturità
im·meas·ur·able [ɪ'mɛʒərəbl] ADJ incommensurabile
im·meas·ur·ably [ɪ'mɛʒərəblɪ] ADV incommensurabilmente
im·media·cy [ɪ'miːdɪəsɪ] N immediatezza
◎**im·medi·ate** [ɪ'miːdɪət] ADJ *(decision, answer, reaction)* immediato(-a); *(need, problem)* impellente, immediato(-a); *(neighbour)* della casa accanto; **in the immediate area** nelle immediate vicinanze; **in the immediate future** nell'immediato futuro; **to take immediate action** prendere immediati provvedimenti
◎**im·medi·ate·ly** [ɪ'miːdɪətlɪ] ADV **1** *(at once: reply, come, agree)* immediatamente **2** *(directly: affect, concern)* direttamente; **immediately in front of sb/sth** proprio davanti a qn/qc
■ CONJ (non) appena
im·memo·ri·al [ˌɪmɪ'mɔːrɪəl] ADJ remotissimo(-a); **from time immemorial** da tempo immemorabile
im·mense [ɪ'mɛns] ADJ *(distance)* smisurato(-a); *(size, difference)* enorme; *(enjoyment)* immenso(-a)
im·mense·ly [ɪ'mɛnslɪ] ADV *(differ)* enormemente;

(*difficult, rich*) estremamente; (*like, enjoy*) immensamente
im·men·si·ty [ɪ'mɛnsɪtɪ] N (*of size, difference, problem*) vastità; (*of space*) immensità
im·merse [ɪ'mɜ:s] VT: **to immerse sth in water** immergere qc nell'acqua; **immersed in sth** (*fig*) immerso(-a) *or* assorto(-a) in qc; **to immerse o.s. in sth** (*fig*) buttarsi anima e corpo in qc
im·mer·sion [ɪ'mɜ:ʃən] N immersione *f*
immersion heater N (*Brit*) scaldabagno elettrico
◎**im·mi·grant** ['ɪmɪgrənt] ADJ, N (*newly arrived*) immigrante (*m/f*); (*already established*) immigrato(-a)
im·mi·grate ['ɪmɪˌgreɪt] VI immigrare
◎**im·mi·gra·tion** [ˌɪmɪ'greɪʃən] N immigrazione *f*
immigration authorities NPL ufficio *m* stranieri *inv*
immigration laws NPL leggi *fpl* relative all'immigrazione
im·mi·nence ['ɪmɪnəns] N imminenza
im·mi·nent ['ɪmɪnənt] ADJ imminente
im·mis·cible [ɪ'mɪsɪbəl] ADJ (*frm*) immiscibile
im·mo·bile [ɪ'məʊbaɪl] ADJ immobile
im·mo·bil·ity [ˌɪməʊ'bɪlɪtɪ] N immobilità
im·mo·bi·lize [ɪ'məʊbɪˌlaɪz] VT immobilizzare
im·mo·bi·liz·er [ɪ'məʊbɪlaɪzə[r]] N (*Auto*) immobilizer *m inv*, dispositivo di blocco motore
im·mo·der·ate [ɪ'mɒdərɪt] ADJ (*person*) smodato(-a), sregolato(-a); (*opinion, reaction, demand*) eccessivo(-a)
im·mod·est [ɪ'mɒdɪst] ADJ (*indecent*) indecente; (*boastful*) immodesto(-a)
im·mod·est·ly [ɪ'mɒdɪstlɪ] ADV (*see adj*) indecentemente; immodestamente
im·mod·es·ty [ɪ'mɒdɪstɪ] N (*see adj*) indecenza; immodestia
im·mor·al [ɪ'mɒrəl] ADJ immorale
im·mo·ral·ity [ˌɪmə'rælɪtɪ] N immoralità
im·mor·al·ly [ɪ'mɒrəlɪ] ADV immoralmente
im·mor·tal [ɪ'mɔ:tl] ADJ, N immortale (*m/f*)
im·mor·tal·ity [ˌɪmɔ:'tælɪtɪ] N immortalità
im·mor·tal·ize [ɪ'mɔ:təˌlaɪz] VT immortalare
im·mov·able [ɪ'mu:vəbl] ADJ (*object*) non movibile; (*person*) irremovibile
◎**im·mune** [ɪ'mju:n] ADJ: **immune (to, against)** (*naturally*) immune (da); (*after injection*) immunizzato(-a) (contro); **immune (from)** (*fig*) immune (a)
immune system N sistema *m* immunitario
im·mu·nity [ɪ'mju:nɪtɪ] N (*also fig*) immunità; **diplomatic immunity** immunità diplomatica
im·mu·ni·za·tion [ˌɪmjʊnaɪ'zeɪʃən] N immunizzazione *f*
im·mu·nize ['ɪmjʊˌnaɪz] VT immunizzare
im·mu·no·thera·py [ˌɪmjʊnəʊ'θɛrəpɪ] N immunoterapia
im·mu·table [ɪ'mju:təbl] ADJ (*frm*) immutabile
im·mu·tably [ɪ'mju:təblɪ] ADV (*frm*) immutabilmente
imp [ɪmp] N (*small devil*) folletto; (*child*) diavoletto
◎**im·pact** [*n* 'ɪmpækt; *vb* ɪm'pækt] N (*force of collision*) impatto, (forza d') urto; (*fig: effect*) effetto; **on impact** nell'urto, nell'impatto; **the book made a great impact on me/the public** il libro ha prodotto una forte impressione su di me/sul pubblico
■VT (*drive*) conficcare
■VI (*fig: influence*): **to impact on** influire su
im·pact·ed [ɪm'pæktɪd] ADJ: **an impacted tooth** un dente incluso
im·pair [ɪm'pɛə[r]] VT (*health*) danneggiare, pregiudicare; (*sight, hearing*) deteriorare, menomare; (*visibility*) ridurre; (*relations*) deteriorare
im·paired [ɪm'pɛəd] ADJ (*faculties, hearing*) deteriorato(-a), indebolito(-a); **visually impaired** videoleso(-a)
im·pa·la [ɪm'pɑ:lə] N impala *m inv*
im·pale [ɪm'peɪl] VT impalare
im·part [ɪm'pɑ:t] VT (*frm*) **1** (*make known*) comunicare **2** (*bestow*) impartire
im·par·tial [ɪm'pɑ:ʃəl] ADJ imparziale
im·par·ti·al·ity [ɪmˌpɑ:ʃɪ'ælɪtɪ] N imparzialità
im·par·tial·ly [ɪm'pɑ:ʃəlɪ] ADV con imparzialità
im·pass·able [ɪm'pɑ:səbl] ADJ (*road, mountain pass*) intransitabile, impraticabile; (*barrier*) insuperabile; (*river*) non attraversabile
im·passe [æm'pɑ:s] N impasse *f inv*
im·pas·sioned [ɪm'pæʃnd] ADJ appassionato(-a)
im·pas·sive [ɪm'pæsɪv] ADJ impassibile
im·pa·tience [ɪm'peɪʃəns] N impazienza; **impatience (with sb/to do sth)** impazienza (nei confronti di qn/di fare qc)
im·pa·tient [ɪm'peɪʃənt] ADJ (*eager*) impaziente; (*irascible*) insofferente; **to get** *or* **grow impatient (with sb/over sth)** perdere la pazienza (con qn/per qc); **to get impatient** spazientirsi; **people are getting impatient** la gente si sta spazientendo; **impatient to do sth** impaziente di fare qc; **she was impatient to get back home** era impaziente di tornare a casa
im·pa·tient·ly [ɪm'peɪʃəntlɪ] ADV con impazienza
im·peach [ɪm'pi:tʃ] VT **1** (*esp Am: prosecute: public official*) mettere in stato d'accusa **2** (*challenge: character, motive*) mettere in dubbio
im·peach·ment [ɪm'pi:tʃmənt] N (*Law*) impeachment *m inv*
im·pec·cable [ɪm'pɛkəbl] ADJ impeccabile
im·pec·cably [ɪm'pɛkəblɪ] ADV impeccabilmente
im·pecu·ni·ous [ˌɪmpɪ'kju:nɪəs] ADJ (*frm*) indigente
im·pede [ɪm'pi:d] VT ostacolare
im·pedi·ment [ɪm'pɛdɪmənt] N **1** (*obstacle*) ostacolo **2** (*Law*) impedimento **3** (*Med*) difetto; **speech impediment** difetto di pronuncia
im·pedi·men·ta [ɪmˌpɛdɪ'mɛntə] N (*frm*) impedimenti *mpl*
im·pel [ɪm'pɛl] VT (*force*): **to impel sb (to do sth)** costringere *or* obbligare qn (a fare qc); (*drive*) spingere qn (a fare qc)
im·pend·ing [ɪm'pɛndɪŋ] ADJ (*birth, storm, retirement*) imminente; (*doom, disaster*) incombente
im·pen·etrable [ɪm'pɛnɪtrəbl] ADJ (*jungle*) impenetrabile; (*fortress*) inespugnabile; (*fig*) incomprensibile
im·pen·etrably [ɪm'pɛnɪtrəblɪ] ADV impenetrabilmente
im·peni·tent [ɪm'pɛnɪtənt] ADJ non pentito(-a); **she was quite impenitent about it** non ne era affatto pentita
im·peni·tent·ly [ɪm'pɛnɪtəntlɪ] ADV senza pentirsi
im·pera·tive [ɪm'pɛrətɪv] ADJ **1** (*essential*) essenziale; **it is imperative that he comes** è indispensabile che lui venga; **it's imperative that we act now** è vitale agire adesso **2** (*authoritative: manner, voice*) imperioso(-a); (*Gram*) imperativo(-a)
■N (*Gram*) imperativo; **in the imperative** all'imperativo
im·per·cep·tible [ˌɪmpə'sɛptəbl] ADJ impercettibile
im·per·cep·tibly [ˌɪmpə'sɛptəblɪ] ADV impercettibilmente
im·per·fect [ɪm'pɜ:fɪkt] ADJ **1** (*gen*) difettoso(-a);

Ii

imperfect goods merce *f* difettosa; **it's an imperfect world** il mondo non è perfetto **2** *(Gram)* imperfetto(-a)
■ N *(Gram: imperfect tense)* imperfetto; **in the imperfect** all'imperfetto

im·per·fec·tion [ˌɪmpəˈfɛkʃən] N *(poor quality)* imperfezione *f*; *(flaw)* difetto, imperfezione

im·per·fect·ly [ɪmˈpɜːfɪktlɪ] ADV in modo imperfetto; **an imperfectly produced copy** una copia imperfetta

im·perial [ɪmˈpɪərɪəl] ADJ *(gen)* imperiale; *(imperious)* imperioso(-a); *(Brit: weights, measures) misurato secondo un sistema non metrico*

IMPERIAL SYSTEM

Per quanto il sistema metrico sia entrato in vigore in Gran Bretagna nel 1971, il sistema imperiale, **imperial system**, è a tutt'oggi diffusissimo. A scuola si insegna il sistema metrico, ma i prodotti alimentari si pesano in once e libbre, ("ounces" e "pounds"), la birra si serve in pinte ("pints"), le distanze sono calcolate in miglia ("miles") e il peso corporeo viene espresso in "stones" (14 libbre) e "pounds".
Anche negli Stati Uniti si usa il sistema imperiale, che si differenzia da quello britannico solo per quanto riguarda i liquidi: le misure americane sono leggermente inferiori a quelle britanniche. Negli Stati Uniti il peso corporeo viene espresso di solito in libbre.
▷ www.ex.ac.uk/cimt/dictunit/dictunit.htm

im·peri·al·ism [ɪmˈpɪərɪəˌlɪzəm] N imperialismo

im·peri·al·ist [ɪmˈpɪərɪəlɪst] ADJ, N imperialista *(m/f)*

im·per·il [ɪmˈpɛrɪl] VT *(frm)* mettere in pericolo

im·peri·ous [ɪmˈpɪərɪəs] ADJ imperioso(-a)

im·peri·ous·ly [ɪmˈpɪərɪəslɪ] ADV imperiosamente

im·per·ma·nent [ɪmˈpɜːmənənt] ADJ transitorio(-a)

im·per·meable [ɪmˈpɜːmɪəbl] ADJ *(frm)* impermeabile

im·per·son·al [ɪmˈpɜːsnl] ADJ **1** *(manner, treatment)* impersonale, distaccato(-a) **2** *(Gram)* impersonale

im·per·son·al·ly [ɪmˈpɜːsnəlɪ] ADV impersonalmente

im·per·son·ate [ɪmˈpɜːsəˌneɪt] VT *(person)* fingersi; *(Theatre)* imitare

DID YOU KNOW ...?
impersonate is not translated by the Italian word *impersonare*

im·per·sona·tion [ɪmˌpɜːsəˈneɪʃən] N *(gen: Theatre)* imitazione *f*; *(fraudulent)* usurpazione *f* d'identità

im·per·sona·tor [ɪmˈpɜːsəˌneɪtəʳ] N *(gen: Theatre)* imitatore(-trice)

im·per·ti·nence [ɪmˈpɜːtɪnəns] N impertinenza

im·per·ti·nent [ɪmˈpɜːtɪnənt] ADJ: **impertinent (to)** impertinente (con *or* nei confronti di)

im·per·ti·nent·ly [ɪmˈpɜːtɪnəntlɪ] ADV con impertinenza

im·per·turb·able [ˌɪmpəˈtɜːbəbl] ADJ imperturbabile

im·per·turb·ably [ˌɪmpəˈtɜːbəblɪ] ADV imperturbabilmente

im·per·vi·ous [ɪmˈpɜːvɪəs] ADJ: **impervious (to)** impermeabile (a); *(fig)* indifferente (a), imperturbato(-a) (di fronte a)

DID YOU KNOW ...?
impervious is not translated by the Italian word *impervio*

im·peti·go [ˌɪmpɪˈtaɪgəʊ] N *(Med)* impetigine *f*

im·petu·os·ity [ɪmˌpɛtjʊˈɒsɪtɪ] N impetuosità

im·petu·ous [ɪmˈpɛtjʊəs] ADJ impetuoso(-a)

im·petu·ous·ly [ɪmˈpɛtjʊəslɪ] ADV impetuosamente

im·petus [ˈɪmpɪtəs] N *(force)* spinta, impeto; *(fig)* impulso

im·pi·ety [ɪmˈpaɪətɪ] N *(frm)* empietà

im·pinge [ɪmˈpɪndʒ] VI: **to impinge on** *(person, situation)* influire su; *(freedom, independence)* violare; *(rights)* ledere

im·pi·ous [ˈɪmpɪəs] ADJ *(frm)* empio(-a)

imp·ish [ˈɪmpɪʃ] ADJ malizioso(-a), birichino(-a)

im·plac·able [ɪmˈplækəbl] ADJ implacabile

im·plac·ably [ɪmˈplækəblɪ] ADV implacabilmente

im·plant [*vb* ɪmˈplɑːnt; *n* ˈɪmplɑːnt] VT *(Med)* innestare; *(fig: idea, principle)* inculcare
■ N *(Med)* innesto

im·plan·ta·tion [ˌɪmplɑːnˈteɪʃən] N *(Med)* innesto

im·plau·sible [ɪmˈplɔːzəbl] ADJ poco plausibile

◎ **im·ple·ment** [*vb* ˈɪmplɪˌmɛnt; *n* ˈɪmplɪmənt] VT *(decision, plan, idea)* attuare; *(law)* applicare; **it'll take a few months to implement the plan** ci vorranno alcuni mesi per attuare il piano
■ N *(for cooking)* utensile *m*; *(for garden, farm)* attrezzo

im·pli·cate [ˈɪmplɪˌkeɪt] VT: **to implicate sb in sth** implicare qn in qc

◎ **im·pli·ca·tion** [ˌɪmplɪˈkeɪʃən] N **1** *(hint, suggestion)* insinuazione *f*; **the implication of your remark is that ...** la tua osservazione implica che...; **by implication** implicitamente **2** *(in crime, scandal)* implicazione *f* **3** **implications** NPL *(repercussions)* conseguenze *fpl*, ripercussioni *fpl*; **this event had serious implications for industry** quest'avvenimento ebbe (delle) importanti conseguenze per l'industria; **we must study all the implications** dobbiamo considerare tutte le (possibili) conseguenze

im·plic·it [ɪmˈplɪsɪt] ADJ **1** *(implied: threat)* implicito(-a); *(: agreement)* tacito(-a) **2** *(unquestioning: faith, belief)* assoluto(-a)

im·plic·it·ly [ɪmˈplɪsɪtlɪ] ADV **1** *(agree)* tacitamente; *(condone)* implicitamente **2** *(believe)* senza riserve

im·plore [ɪmˈplɔːʳ] VT: **to implore sb (to do sth)** implorare qn (di fare qc); **to implore sb's forgiveness** implorare il perdono di qn

im·plor·ing [ɪmˈplɔːrɪŋ] ADJ implorante

im·plor·ing·ly [ɪmˈplɔːrɪŋlɪ] ADV in modo implorante

◎ **im·ply** [ɪmˈplaɪ] VT *(hint, suggest)* insinuare; *(indicate)* implicare; **it implies a lot of work** implica un sacco di lavoro; **are you implying I did it on purpose?** stai insinuando che l'ho fatto apposta?

im·po·lite [ˌɪmpəˈlaɪt] ADJ *(person, remark)* maleducato(-a)

im·po·lite·ly [ˌɪmpəˈlaɪtlɪ] ADV maleducatamente

im·po·lite·ness [ˌɪmpəˈlaɪtnɪs] N *(of person, remark)* maleducazione

im·poli·tic [ɪmˈpɒlɪtɪk] ADJ *(frm)* impolitico(-a)

im·pon·der·able [ɪmˈpɒndərəbl] ADJ imponderabile

◎ **im·port** [*n* ˈɪmpɔːt; *vb* ɪmˈpɔːt] N **1** *(Comm: article)* articolo importato; *(: importation)* importazione *f*; **import-export** import-export *m inv* **2** *(frm: significance)* significato
■ VT importare
■ ADJ *(duty, licence)* d'importazione

◎ **im·por·tance** [ɪmˈpɔːtəns] N importanza; **to attach great importance to sth** dare *or* attribuire molta importanza a qc; **to be of great/little importance** essere molto/poco importante

◎ **im·por·tant** [ɪmˈpɔːtənt] ADJ importante; **it's not important** non ha importanza; **it is important that** è importante che + *sub*; **to try to look important** (*pej*) darsi arie d'importanza

im·por·tant·ly [ɪm'pɔːtəntlɪ] ADV significativamente; (*pej*) con (aria d')importanza; **but, more importantly, ...** ma, quel che più conta *or* importa,...

im·por·ta·tion [ˌɪmpɔː'teɪʃən] N importazione *f*

im·port·ed [ɪm'pɔːtɪd] ADJ importato(-a)

im·port·er [ɪm'pɔːtəʳ] N importatore(-trice)

im·por·tu·nate [ɪm'pɔːtjʊnɪt] ADJ (*frm*) importuno(-a)

im·por·tune [ˌɪmpɔː'tjuːn] VT (*frm*) importunare

im·por·tun·ity [ˌɪmpɔː'tjuːnɪtɪ] N (*frm*) insistenze *fpl*

◎**im·pose** [ɪm'pəʊz] VT (*conditions, fine, tax*): **to impose (sth on sb)** imporre (qc a qn)
▸ **impose (up)on** VI + PREP (*person*) approfittare di

im·pos·ing [ɪm'pəʊzɪŋ] ADJ imponente

im·po·si·tion [ˌɪmpə'zɪʃən] N (*of tax, fine, punishment*) imposizione *f*; **it's a bit of an imposition** è pretendere un po' troppo; **to be an imposition on** (*person*) abusare della gentilezza di

im·pos·sibil·ity [ɪmˌpɒsə'bɪlɪtɪ] N: **impossibility (of sth/of doing sth)** impossibilità (di qc/di fare qc)

◎**im·pos·sible** [ɪm'pɒsəbl] ADJ **1** (*task, enterprise, situation*) impossibile; **it is impossible for me to leave now** mi è impossibile andar via adesso; **it is impossible/not impossible for her to do that** le è impossibile/non le è impossibile farlo; **to make it impossible for sb to do sth** mettere qn nell'impossibilità di fare qc; **to do the impossible** fare l'impossibile **2** (*fam: child, person: difficult, intolerable*) impossibile, insopportabile

im·pos·sibly [ɪm'pɒsəblɪ] ADV (*extremely: late, early, difficult*) incredibilmente; (*intolerably: behave, act*) insopportabilmente

im·pos·tor [ɪm'pɒstəʳ] N impostore(-a)

im·pos·ture [ɪm'pɒstʃəʳ] N (*frm*) impostura

im·po·tence ['ɪmpətəns] N (*frm, Med*) impotenza

im·po·tent ['ɪmpətənt] ADJ (*frm, Med*) impotente

im·pound [ɪm'paʊnd] VT (*gen*) sequestrare, confiscare; (*stray animal*) rinchiudere

im·pov·er·ished [ɪm'pɒvərɪʃt] ADJ impoverito(-a)

im·pov·er·ish·ment [ɪm'pɒvərɪʃmənt] N impoverimento

im·prac·ti·cabil·ity [ɪmˌpræktɪkə'bɪlɪtɪ] N inattuabilità

im·prac·ti·cable [ɪm'præktɪkəbl] ADJ inattuabile

im·prac·ti·cal [ɪm'præktɪkəl] ADJ (*person*) privo(-a) di senso pratico; (*plan*) poco realistico(-a), poco pratico(-a)

im·prac·ti·cal·ity [ɪmˌpræktɪ'kælɪtɪ] N (*of person*) mancanza di praticità; (*of plan*) poca praticità

im·pre·ca·tion [ˌɪmprɪ'keɪʃən] N (*frm*) imprecazione *f*

im·pre·cise [ˌɪmprɪ'saɪs] ADJ impreciso(-a)

im·pre·ci·sion [ˌɪmprɪ'sɪʒən] N imprecisione *f*

im·preg·nable [ɪm'prɛgnəbl] ADJ (*fortress, defences*) inespugnabile; (*fig: person, group*) inattaccabile

im·preg·nate ['ɪmprɛgˌneɪt] VT (*fertilize*) fecondare; (*saturate*): **to impregnate (with)** impregnare (di)

im·pre·sa·rio [ˌɪmprɛ'sɑːrɪəʊ] N impresario(-a)

◎**im·press** [ɪm'prɛs] VT **1** (*make good impression on*) fare una buona impressione a *or* su, colpire favorevolmente; **how did she impress you?** che impressione ti ha fatto?; **he impressed me quite favourably** mi ha fatto un'impressione abbastanza buona; **he really impressed me!** mi ha veramente colpito!; **what impressed him most was ...** quello che l'ha colpito di più è stato...; **a group of students trying to impress their teacher** un gruppo di studenti che cercavano di fare bella figura con l'insegnante; **I'm not impressed** non ne sono rimasto colpito **2** (*mark, stamp*) imprimere; **to impress sth on sb** (*fig*) far comprendere qc a qn

◎**im·pres·sion** [ɪm'prɛʃən] N **1** (*most senses*) impressione *f*; **to be under** *or* **have the impression that** avere l'impressione che; **he gives the impression of knowing a lot about it** dà l'impressione di saperne molto; **to make a good/bad impression on sb** fare una buona/cattiva impressione a *or* su qn; **my words made no impression on him** le mie parole non hanno avuto nessun effetto su di lui **2** (*imitation*) imitazione *f*; **to do impressions** fare delle imitazioni

im·pres·sion·able [ɪm'prɛʃnəbl] ADJ (*person*) impressionabile; **to be at an impressionable age** essere nell'età in cui si è facilmente influenzabili

im·pres·sion·ism [ɪm'prɛʃəˌnɪzəm] N (*Art*) impressionismo

im·pres·sion·ist [ɪm'prɛʃənɪst] ADJ, N (*Art*) impressionista (*m/f*); (*mimic*) imitatore(-trice)

im·pres·sion·is·tic [ɪmˌprɛʃə'nɪstɪk] ADJ (*account, story*) approssimativo(-a); (*Art*) impressionista, impressionistico(-a)

◎**im·pres·sive** [ɪm'prɛsɪv] ADJ (*person, achievement*) notevole; (*occasion, event*) di notevole imponenza; (*building*) imponente; **an impressive achievement** un risultato notevole

im·pres·sive·ly [ɪm'prɛsɪvlɪ] ADV (*tall, rich, bright*) straordinariamente; (*displayed, organized*) in modo imponente

im·pri·ma·tur [ɪmprɪ'meɪtəʳ] N (*frm*) imprimatur *m inv*

im·print [*n* 'ɪmprɪnt; *vb* ɪm'prɪnt] N (*Publishing*) sigla editoriale
■ VT imprimere

im·print·ed [ɪm'prɪntɪd] ADJ: **imprinted on** impresso(-a) in

im·pris·on [ɪm'prɪzn] VT incarcerare; **after being imprisoned for three weeks** dopo tre settimane di *or* in carcere

im·pris·on·ment [ɪm'prɪznmənt] N reclusione *f*; **during his imprisonment** mentre era in carcere; **life imprisonment** l'ergastolo

im·prob·abil·ity [ɪmˌprɒbə'bɪlɪtɪ] N (*see adj*) improbabilità; inverosimiglianza

im·prob·able [ɪm'prɒbəbl] ADJ (*event*) improbabile, poco probabile; (*excuse, story*) inverosimile

im·promp·tu [ɪm'prɒmptjuː] ADJ improvvisato(-a), estemporaneo(-a)
■ ADV (*speak*) improvvisando, a braccio

im·prop·er [ɪm'prɒpəʳ] ADJ (*unseemly, indecent*) sconveniente; (*wrong*) scorretto(-a); (*unsuitable*) improprio(-a), inadatto(-a); **he denies doing anything improper** nega di essersi comportato in modo scorretto

improper fraction N (*Math*) frazione *f* impropria

im·prop·er·ly [ɪm'prɒpəlɪ] ADV (*see adj*) sconvenientemente; scorrettamente; impropriamente, in modo inadatto

im·pro·pri·ety [ˌɪmprə'praɪətɪ] N (*frm: of behaviour*) scorrettezza; (*: unseemliness, indecency*) sconvenienza; (*of expression*) improprietà *f inv*

◎**im·prove** [ɪm'pruːv] VT (*gen*) migliorare; (*property, land*) apportare migliorie a; (*production, yield, salary*) aumentare; **to improve one's Italian** perfezionare il proprio italiano; **to improve one's chances of success** aumentare le proprie probabilità di successo; **to improve one's mind** migliorare la propria cultura;

Ii

he's improved his technique ha migliorato la tecnica

■VI (*gen*) migliorare; (*person: in skill*) fare (dei) progressi; **to improve in sth** migliorare *or* fare (dei) progressi in qc; **to improve with age/use** migliorare con gli anni/con l'uso; **this wine improves with age** questo vino migliora con l'invecchiamento; **my Italian improved a lot** il mio italiano è migliorato molto

▸ **improve (up)on** VI + PREP (*offer*) aumentare; (*work*) ottenere dei risultati migliori rispetto a; (*method*) perfezionare; (*quality*) migliorare; **I can't improve on my offer to you** non posso farti un'offerta migliore

◎**im·prove·ment** [ɪm'pru:vmənt] N: **improvement (in)** (*gen*) miglioramento (in); (*in production, salary*) aumento (di *or* in); **it's an improvement on the old one** è meglio di quello vecchio; **there is room for improvement** si può migliorare *or* far meglio; **to make improvements to** migliorare; (*property*) apportare migliorie a; (*method*) perfezionare

improvement grant N *sussidio per la modernizzazione di edifici*

im·provi·dence [ɪm'prɒvɪdəns] N (*frm*) imprevidenza

im·provi·dent [ɪm'prɒvɪdənt] (*frm*) ADJ (*not providing for future*) imprevidente; (*thriftless*) prodigo(-a); (*heedless*) imprudente

im·prov·ing [ɪm'pru:vɪŋ] ADJ (*book*) edificante

im·provi·sa·tion [ˌɪmprəvaɪ'zeɪʃən] N improvvisazione *f*

im·pro·vise ['ɪmprəvaɪz] VT, VI improvvisare

im·pru·dence [ɪm'pru:dəns] N imprudenza

im·pru·dent [ɪm'pru:dənt] ADJ imprudente

im·pru·dent·ly [ɪm'pru:dəntlɪ] ADV imprudentemente

im·pu·dence ['ɪmpjʊdəns] N impudenza

im·pu·dent ['ɪmpjʊdənt] ADJ impertinente, impudente

im·pu·dent·ly ['ɪmpjʊdəntlɪ] ADV impertinentemente, impudentemente

im·pugn [ɪm'pju:n] VT (*frm*) attaccare, contestare

im·pulse ['ɪmpʌls] N impulso; **to act on impulse** agire d'impulso *or* impulsivamente

impulse buy N acquisto fatto d'impulso

im·pul·sion [ɪm'pʌlʃən] N impulso

im·pul·sive [ɪm'pʌlsɪv] ADJ impulsivo(-a)

im·pul·sive·ly [ɪm'pʌlsɪvlɪ] ADV impulsivamente

im·pul·sive·ness [ɪm'pʌlsɪvnɪs] N impulsività

im·pu·nity [ɪm'pju:nɪtɪ] N: **with impunity** impunemente

im·pure [ɪm'pjʊəʳ] ADJ (*Chem, morally*) impuro(-a); (*air*) inquinato(-a)

im·pu·rity [ɪm'pjʊərɪtɪ] N impurità *f inv*

im·pu·ta·tion [ˌɪmpjʊ'teɪʃən] N (*frm*) capo d'imputazione *or* d'accusa

im·pute [ɪm'pju:t] VT (*frm*): **to impute (to)** (*change, development*) attribuire (a); (*crime, blame*) imputare (a)

IN ABBR (*Am Post*) = **Indiana**

◎**in** [ɪn] KEYWORD

■PREP

1 (*place, position*) in; **in the country** in campagna; **in the garden** in giardino; **in my hand** in mano; **in here** qui dentro; **in the house** in casa; **in school** a scuola; **in the school** nella scuola; **in there** lì dentro; **in the town** in città

2 (*with place names: of town*) a; (*: of region, country*) in; **in England** in Inghilterra; **it's in France** è in Francia; **in London** a Londra; **in Sicily** in Sicilia; **it's in the United States** è negli Stati Uniti; **in Yorkshire** nello Yorkshire

3 (*time: during*) in; **in 1994** nel 1994; **at 4 o'clock in the afternoon** alle 4 del pomeriggio; **in autumn** in autunno; **in the 20th century** nel ventesimo secolo; **in those days** a quei tempi, allora; **in the daytime** di *or* durante il giorno, durante la giornata; **in the eighties** negli anni ottanta; **in May** in maggio, a maggio, nel mese di maggio; **in the morning** di *or* alla mattina, la mattina, nella mattinata; **in the mornings** di *or* alla mattina, la mattina; **in the past** nel *or* in passato; **in spring** in primavera; **in (the) summer** in estate, d'estate; **in (the) winter** in inverno, d'inverno; **she has not been here in years** sono anni che non viene qui

4 (*time: in the space of*) in; (*after*) tra, fra; **it will be ready in 2 days** sarà pronto fra due giorni; **I did it in 3 hours** l'ho fatto in 3 ore; **she will return the money in a month** restituirà i soldi tra un mese

5 (*manner, means*): **a statue carved in wood** una statua intagliata nel legno; **to pay in dollars** pagare in dollari; **dressed in green/a skirt/trousers** vestito(-a) di verde/con una gonna/con i calzoni; **in English** in inglese; **in ink** a penna; **in Italian** in italiano; **the man in the hat** l'uomo con il cappello; **in alphabetical order** in ordine alfabetico; **painted in red** dipinto(-a) di rosso; **in part** in parte; **in pencil** a matita; **in person** di persona; **in large/small quantities** in grandi/piccole quantità; **in a loud/soft voice** a voce alta/bassa; **in watercolour** ad acquerello; **in a whisper** sussurrando; **in writing** per iscritto

6 (*circumstance*): **in the dark(ness)** al buio, nell'oscurità; **in (the) daylight** alla *or* con la luce del giorno; **to be 10 metres in height** essere alto(-a) 10 metri; **to be 10 metres in length** essere lungo(-a) 10 metri; **in the moonlight** al chiaro di luna; **a change in policy** un cambiamento di prassi; **a rise in prices** un aumento dei prezzi; **in the rain** sotto la pioggia; **in the shade** all'ombra; **in the sun** al sole; **in all weathers** con qualsiasi tempo, qualsiasi tempo faccia; **to be 10 metres in width** essere largo(-a) 10 metri

7 (*mood, state*): **to act in anger** agire per rabbia; **in good condition** *or* **repair** in buono stato, in buone condizioni; **in despair** disperato(-a); **lame in the left leg** zoppo(-a) dalla gamba sinistra; **to live in luxury** vivere nel lusso; **in private** in privato; **to be in a rage** essere su tutte le furie; **in secret** in segreto; **in tears** in lacrime

8 (*ratio, number*): **in hundreds** a centinaia; **once in a hundred years** una volta ogni cento anni; **one person/car in ten** una persona/macchina su dieci; **20 pence in the pound** 20 pence per sterlina; **in twos** a due a due

9 (*people, works*) in; **this is common in children/cats** questo è comune nei *or* per i bambini/gatti; **she has it in her to succeed** ha in sé la capacità di riuscire; **they have a good leader in him** hanno in lui un ottimo capo; **in (the works of) Shakespeare** in Shakespeare

10 (*in profession*): **to be in the army** essere nell'esercito; **to be in publishing** lavorare nell'editoria; **to be in teaching** fare l'insegnante; insegnare; **to be in the motor trade** lavorare nel settore automobilistico

11 (*after superlative*) di; **the best pupil in the class** il migliore alunno della classe; **the biggest in Europe** il

più grande d'Europa; **the smallest in Europe** il più piccolo d'Europa
12 (*with present participle*): **in saying this** dicendo questo, nel dir questo
13 **in that** dal momento che, visto che; **in all** in tutto
■ ADV: **to be in** (*person*) esserci; (*train, ship, plane*) essere arrivato(-a); (*crops, harvest*) essere raccolto(-a); (*in fashion*) essere di moda; (*fam: in power*) essere al potere; **to ask sb in** invitare qn a entrare; **day in, day out** (*pej*) dalla mattina alla sera; **we're in for a snow storm** si prepara una tormenta; **he is in for trouble** lo aspettano dei guai; **he's in for it** (*fam*) è nei guai, lo aspettano guai seri; **to have it in for sb** (*fam*) avercela con qn; **is he in?** lui c'è?; **to limp in** entrare zoppicando; **my luck is in** la fortuna è dalla mia (parte); **to be in on a plan/secret** essere al corrente di un progetto/segreto; **to be in and out of work** non durare mai molto in un impiego; **to be in and out of hospital/prison** essere sempre dentro e fuori dall'ospedale/di prigione; **their party is in** il loro partito è al potere; **to run in** entrare correndo
■ N: **the ins and outs of the problem** tutti i particolari del problema
■ ADJ (*fam*) in *inv*; **it's an in club** è un club molto 'in'; **it's an in joke** è una cosa nostra; **it's the in thing to do** (*fam*) è la cosa 'in' del momento; **hang-gliding is the in thing to do** fare del deltaplano è 'in'

in. ABBR (*pl* **ins.**) = inch
in·abil·ity [ˌɪnəˈbɪlɪtɪ] N (*physical, mental*) incapacità *f inv*; **inability to do sth** incapacità di fare qc; **his inability to control himself** la sua incapacità di controllarsi; **inability to pay** impossibilità di pagare
in·ac·ces·sibil·ity [ˈɪnækˌsɛsəˈbɪlɪtɪ] N inaccessibilità
in·ac·ces·sible [ˌɪnækˈsɛsəbl] ADJ: **inaccessible (to)** inaccessibile (a)
in·ac·cu·ra·cy [ɪnˈækjʊrəsɪ] N (*see adj*) inaccuratezza; inesattezza; imprecisione *f*; (*usu pl: mistake*) errore *m*
in·ac·cu·rate [ɪnˈækjʊrɪt] ADJ (*statement, report, story*) inaccurato(-a); (*figures*) inesatto(-a); (*translation*) impreciso(-a)
in·ac·cu·rate·ly [ɪnˈækjʊrɪtlɪ] ADV (*state, report, describe*) in modo inaccurato; (*add up, multiply*) in modo inesatto; (*translate*) in modo impreciso
in·ac·tion [ɪnˈækʃən] N inerzia, inazione *f*
in·ac·tive [ɪnˈæktɪv] ADJ inattivo(-a)
in·ac·tiv·ity [ˌɪnækˈtɪvɪtɪ] N inattività
in·ad·equa·cy [ɪnˈædɪkwəsɪ] N inadeguatezza, insufficienza; (*of person*) incapacità *f inv*
in·ad·equate [ɪnˈædɪkwɪt] ADJ (*insufficient*) inadeguato(-a), insufficiente; (*person*) non all'altezza; **to feel inadequate** non sentirsi all'altezza; **he felt quite inadequate** non si sentiva assolutamente all'altezza
in·ad·equate·ly [ɪnˈædɪkwɪtlɪ] ADV inadeguatamente, insufficientemente
in·ad·mis·si·ble [ˌɪnədˈmɪsəbl] ADJ (*evidence*) inammissibile
in·ad·vert·ent [ˌɪnədˈvɜːtənt] ADJ (*unintentional*) involontario(-a); (*unthinking*) inconsapevole
in·ad·vert·ent·ly [ˌɪnədˈvɜːtəntlɪ] ADV (*unintentionally*) inavvertitamente, involontariamente; (*unawares*) inconsapevolmente
in·ad·vis·abil·ity [ˈɪnədˌvaɪzəˈbɪlɪtɪ] N: **the inadvisability (of)** l'inopportunità (di)
in·ad·vis·able [ˌɪnədˈvaɪzəbl] ADJ sconsigliabile
in·al·ien·able [ɪnˈeɪlɪənəbl] ADJ (*frm: right*) inalienabile
in·ane [ɪˈneɪn] ADJ (*remark*) sciocco(-a), stupido(-a)
in·ani·mate [ɪnˈænɪmɪt] ADJ inanimato(-a)
in·an·ity [ɪˈnænɪtɪ] N sciocchezza, stupidità *f inv*
in·ap·pli·cable [ɪnˈæplɪkəbl] ADJ inapplicabile
in·ap·pro·pri·ate [ˌɪnəˈprəʊprɪɪt] ADJ (*action, punishment, treatment*) inadeguato(-a), non appropriato(-a); (*word, phrase, expression*) non appropriato(-a); (*behaviour*) sconveniente; **the scheme is inappropriate to the people's needs** il programma è inadeguato alle necessità della gente; **it would be inappropriate for us to intervene** sarebbe inopportuno da parte nostra intervenire
in·ap·pro·pri·ate·ly [ˌɪnəˈprəʊprɪɪtlɪ] ADV (*punish, treat*) inadeguatamente; (*use: word*) poco appropriatamente; (*behave, act*) sconvenientemente
in·apt [ɪnˈæpt] ADJ (*remark, behaviour*) poco appropriato(-a)
in·ap·ti·tude [ɪnˈæptɪˌtjuːd], **in·apt·ness** [ɪnˈæptnɪs] N (*of remark*) impropriet à
in·ar·ticu·late [ˌɪnɑːˈtɪkjʊlɪt] ADJ (*person*) che non sa esprimersi, che si esprime male; (*speech*) inarticolato(-a), confuso(-a); **he's inarticulate** si esprime male
in·ar·tis·tic [ˌɪnɑːˈtɪstɪk] ADJ (*work*) di scarso valore artistico; (*person*) che manca di senso artistico
in·as·much as [ˌɪnəzˈmʌtʃəz] CONJ (*insofar as*) in quanto, nella misura in cui; (*seeing that*) poiché
in·at·ten·tion [ˌɪnəˈtɛnʃən] N: **inattention (to)** mancanza di attenzione (per *or* nei confronti di), disattenzione *f* (per *or* nei confronti di)
in·at·ten·tive [ˌɪnəˈtɛntɪv] ADJ disattento(-a), distratto(-a)
in·at·ten·tive·ly [ˌɪnəˈtɛntɪvlɪ] ADV distrattamente
in·audible [ɪnˈɔːdəbl] ADJ appena percettibile; **the speech was inaudible** non si riusciva a sentire il discorso
in·audibly [ɪnˈɔːdəblɪ] ADV (*speak*) in modo appena percettibile
in·augu·ral [ɪˈnɔːgjʊrəl] ADJ inaugurale
in·augu·rate [ɪˈnɔːgjʊˌreɪt] VT (*president, official*) insediare; (*start officially: organization, festival*) inaugurare; (*frm: system, idea*) inaugurare, instaurare
in·augu·ra·tion [ɪˌnɔːgjʊˈreɪʃən] N (*of president*) insediamento (in carica); (*opening*) inaugurazione *f*; **the inauguration of a new era** l'inizio di una nuova era
in·aus·pi·cious [ˌɪnɔːsˈpɪʃəs] ADJ poco propizio(-a)
in·aus·pi·cious·ly [ˌɪnɔːsˈpɪʃəslɪ] ADV in modo poco propizio
in-between [ɪnbɪˈtwiːn] ADJ intermedio(-a)
in·board [ˈɪnˌbɔːd] N (*also:* **inboard motor**) entrobordo *m inv*
in·born [ˈɪnˈbɔːn] ADJ (*feeling*) innato(-a); (*defect*) congenito(-a)
in·box [ˈɪnbɒks] N (*Comput*) (cartella della) posta in arrivo
in·bred [ˈɪnˈbrɛd] ADJ (*tendency*) innato(-a); **an inbred family** (*pej*) *una famiglia con un alto indice di unioni fra consanguinei*
in·breed·ing [ˈɪnˈbriːdɪŋ] N (*Zool*) inbreeding *m inv*; (*of people*) unioni *fpl* fra consanguinei
in-built [ˈɪnˈbɪlt] ADJ innato(-a); **in-built limitations** limiti *mpl* intrinseci
Inc. ABBR = **incorporated**
Inca [ɪŋkə] ADJ (*also:* **Incan**) incaico(-a), inca *inv*
■ N inca *m/f inv*
in·cal·cu·lable [ɪnˈkælkjʊləbl] ADJ incalcolabile

Ii

in·can·des·cence [ˌɪnkænˈdɛsns] N (*frm*) incandescenza
in·can·des·cent [ˌɪnkænˈdɛsnt] ADJ (*frm*) incandescente
in·can·ta·tion [ˌɪnkænˈteɪʃən] N incantesimo
in·ca·pabil·ity [ɪnˌkeɪpəˈbɪlɪtɪ] N incapacità
in·ca·pable [ɪnˈkeɪpəbl] ADJ: **incapable (of doing sth)** incapace (di fare qc); **a question incapable of solution** (*frm*) un problema irrisolvibile *or* insolubile
in·ca·paci·tate [ˌɪnkəˈpæsɪˌteɪt] VT (*person*) rendere inabile; (*Law*) inabilitare; **to incapacitate sb from doing sth** rendere qn inabile a fare qc; **a bad fall incapacitated him** una brutta caduta lo ha bloccato
in·ca·paci·tat·ed [ˌɪnkəˈpæsɪˌteɪtɪd] ADJ (*disabled*) inabile; (*Law*) inabilitato(-a); **physically incapacitated** inabile fisicamente
in·ca·pac·ity [ˌɪnkəˈpæsɪtɪ] N incapacità; (*Law*) inabilitazione
incapacity benefit N (*Brit*) sussidio di invalidità
in·car·cer·ate [ɪnˈkɑːsəˌreɪt] VT (*frm*) incarcerare
in·car·nate [*adj* ɪnˈkɑːnɪt; *vb* ɪnˈkɑːneɪt] ADJ (*Rel*) incarnato(-a); **the devil incarnate** il diavolo personificato *or* in persona
■ VT incarnare
in·car·na·tion [ˌɪnkɑːˈneɪʃən] N (*Rel*) incarnazione *f*
in·cau·tious [ɪnˈkɔːʃəs] ADJ incauto(-a)
in·cen·di·ary [ɪnˈsɛndɪərɪ] ADJ incendiario(-a)
■ N (*bomb*) ordigno incendiario
in·cense [*n* ˈɪnsɛns; *vb* ɪnˈsɛns] N incenso
■ VT (*anger*) fare infuriare
incense burner N incensiere *m*
in·censed [ɪnˈsɛnst] ADJ furente, furibondo(-a)
in·cen·tive [ɪnˈsɛntɪv] N incentivo; **there is no incentive to work** non c'è alcun incentivo a lavorare; **it gave me an incentive** mi è servito da incentivo
incentive bonus N premio d'incentivazione
incentive scheme N piano di incentivazione
in·cep·tion [ɪnˈsɛpʃən] N (*frm*) inizio, principio
in·cer·ti·tude [ɪnˈsɜːtɪtjuːd] N (*frm*) incertezza
in·ces·sant [ɪnˈsɛsnt] ADJ incessante
in·ces·sant·ly [ɪnˈsɛsntlɪ] ADV incessantemente
in·cest [ˈɪnsɛst] N incesto
in·ces·tu·ous [ɪnˈsɛstjʊəs] ADJ incestuoso(-a)
◎**inch** [ɪntʃ] N pollice *m* (*cm 2.54; 12 per foot*); **a few inches** ≈ qualche centimetro; **the car missed me by inches** c'è mancato un pelo che la macchina mi investisse; **to lose a few inches** (*fam*) perdere un po' di ciccia; **inch by inch** a poco a poco; **every inch of it was used** è stato utilizzato tutto fino all'ultimo millimetro *or* centimetro; **he's every inch a soldier** è un soldato dalla testa ai piedi; **within an inch of** a un pelo da; **to be within an inch of death/disaster** essere a un passo dalla morte/dalla rovina; **he didn't give** *or* **budge an inch** (*fig*) non ha ceduto di un millimetro
► **inch forward** VI + ADV avanzare pian piano
► **inch up** VI + ADV salire a poco a poco
inch tape N metro a nastro (*da sarto*)
in·ci·dence [ˈɪnsɪdəns] N (*extent, rate: of disease, crime*) incidenza; **the angle of incidence** (*Phys*) l'angolo d'incidenza
◎**in·ci·dent** [ˈɪnsɪdənt] N (*gen*) caso, avvenimento; (*diplomatic, on border*) incidente *m*; (*in book*) episodio; (*in play*) scena; **a minor incident** un piccolo incidente; **without incident** (*uneventful*) senza incidenti (di rilievo); (*without trouble*) senza problemi
in·ci·den·tal [ˌɪnsɪˈdɛntl] ADJ (*secondary*) secondario(-a); (*unplanned*) fortuito(-a); **incidental to** connesso(-a) con; **incidental expenses** spese *fpl* accessorie
■ N (*minor point*) punto di secondaria importanza; **incidentals** NPL (*expenses*) spese *fpl* accessorie
in·ci·den·tal·ly [ˌɪnsɪˈdɛntəlɪ] ADV (*by the way*) fra parentesi, tra l'altro, per inciso; **the system prevents heat loss and incidentally saves you money** il sistema impedisce perdite di calore e tra l'altro fa risparmiare; **incidentally, I saw your sister yesterday** fra parentesi, ho visto tua sorella ieri
incidental music N sottofondo musicale, musica di sottofondo
incident room N (*Police*) centrale *f* operativa
in·cin·er·ate [ɪnˈsɪnəˌreɪt] VT incenerire
in·cin·era·tion [ɪnsɪnəˈreɪʃən] N incenerimento
in·cin·era·tor [ɪnˈsɪnəˌreɪtə^r^] N inceneritore *m*
in·cipi·ent [ɪnˈsɪpɪənt] ADJ (*disease, baldness*) incipiente; (*revolt*) nascente
in·cise [ɪnˈsaɪz] VT (*frm*) incidere
in·ci·sion [ɪnˈsɪʒən] N incisione *f*
in·ci·sive [ɪnˈsaɪsɪv] ADJ (*mind, remark*) acuto(-a); (*criticism*) tagliente; (*speech, style*) incisivo(-a)
in·ci·sive·ly [ɪnˈsaɪsɪvlɪ] ADV (*remark, question, describe*) incisivamente
in·ci·sor [ɪnˈsaɪzə^r^] N (*Anat*) incisivo
in·cite [ɪnˈsaɪt] VT: **to incite sb (to sth/to do sth)** incitare qn (a qc/a fare qc), istigare qn (a qc/a fare qc)
in·cite·ment [ɪnˈsaɪtmənt] N incitamento, istigazione *f*
in·ci·vil·ity [ˌɪnsɪˈvɪlɪtɪ] N inciviltà *f inv*
incl. ABBR = **including, inclusive (of)**
in·clem·ent [ɪnˈklɛmənt] ADJ inclemente
in·cli·na·tion [ˌɪnklɪˈneɪʃən] N **1** (*wish*) tendenza, inclinazione *f*; **he felt no inclination to join in the fun** non aveva nessuna voglia di unirsi alla gazzarra; **her inclination was to ignore him** avrebbe voluto ignorarlo; **against my inclination** controvoglia; **to follow one's inclination** seguire le proprie inclinazioni **2** (*slope*) pendio, china **3** (*bow*) cenno
in·cline [*n* ˈɪnklaɪn; *vb* ɪnˈklaɪn] N pendenza, pendio
■ VT (*bend: head, body*) chinare, inclinare
■ VI **1** (*slope*) declinare **2** (*tend to*): **to incline to(wards)** tendere a; **I incline to the belief/opinion that ...** sono propenso a credere che...
in·clined [ɪnˈklaɪnd] ADJ **1** (*liable, apt*): **to be inclined to do sth** essere incline a fare qc; (*: out of habit*) tendere a fare qc; (*: from preference*) essere propenso(-a) a fare qc; **he was inclined to self-pity** tendeva ad autocommiserarsi; **it is inclined to break** ha la tendenza a rompersi **2** (*gifted*): **artistically/musically inclined** portato(-a) per l'arte/la musica **3** (*disposed*): **if you feel so inclined** se lo desideri, se ne hai voglia; **to be well inclined towards sb** essere ben disposto(-a) verso qn; **I'm inclined to agree with you** in linea di massima sono d'accordo con te; **nobody seemed inclined to argue with Steve** nessuno sembrava propenso a litigare con Steve
◎**in·clude** [ɪnˈkluːd] VT comprendere, includere; **your name is not included in the list** il tuo nome non è incluso nella lista; **he sold everything, books included** ha venduto tutto, compresi i libri; **service is/is not included** il servizio è compreso/escluso
◎**in·clud·ing** [ɪnˈkluːdɪŋ] PREP compreso(-a), incluso(-a); **including VAT** IVA compresa; **seven books including this one** sette libri compreso *or* incluso questo; **up to and including Chapter 12** fino al capitolo 12 compreso *or* incluso; **it will be two**

hundred pounds, including tax** sono duecento sterline, tasse comprese

in·clu·sion [ɪn'klu:ʒən] N inclusione *f*

in·clu·sive [ɪn'klu:sɪv] ADJ *(sum, price)* tutto compreso *inv*; **the inclusive price is two hundred pounds** il prezzo tutto compreso è di duecento sterline; **inclusive of** incluso(-a); **£500, inclusive of VAT** 500 sterline, IVA compresa
■ ADV: **from the 10th to the 15th inclusive** dal 10 al 15 incluso *or* compreso

in·clu·sive·ly [ɪn'klu:sɪvlɪ] ADV inclusivamente

inclusive terms NPL *(Brit)* (prezzo *m*) tutto compreso *inv*

in·cog·ni·to [ˌɪnkɒg'ni:təʊ] ADV *(travel)* in incognito; **to remain incognito** mantenere l'incognito

in·co·her·ence [ˌɪnkəʊ'hɪərəns] N incoerenza

in·co·her·ent [ˌɪnkəʊ'hɪərənt] ADJ *(person)* incoerente; **he was incoherent with rage** non connetteva per la rabbia

in·co·her·ent·ly [ˌɪnkəʊ'hɪərəntlɪ] ADV incoerentemente

in·com·bus·tible [ˌɪnkəm'bʌstəbl] ADJ incombustibile

◎ **in·come** ['ɪnkʌm] N *(gen)* reddito; *(from receipts)* introito; **gross/net income** reddito lordo/netto; **private income** rendita; **to live within/beyond one's income** vivere secondo i propri mezzi/al di sopra dei propri mezzi; **low income families** famiglie a basso reddito

income and expenditure account N conto entrate e uscite

in·comer ['ɪnˌkʌməʳ] N nuovo(-a) venuto(-a)

incomes policy N politica dei redditi

income support N *(Brit)* sussidio di indigenza *or* povertà

income tax N imposta sul reddito

income tax inspector N ispettore *m* delle imposte sul reddito

income tax return N dichiarazione *f* dei redditi

in·com·ing ['ɪnˌkʌmɪŋ] ADJ *(passengers)* in arrivo; *(tide)* montante; *(government)* entrante; *(tenant)* subentrante

in·com·mu·ni·ca·do [ˌɪnkəˌmju:nɪ'kɑ:dəʊ] ADJ: **to hold sb incommunicado** tenere segregato(-a) qn

in·com·pa·rable [ɪn'kɒmpərəbl] ADJ incomparabile

in·com·pa·rably [ɪn'kɒmpərəblɪ] ADV incomparabilmente

in·com·pat·ibil·ity ['ɪnkəmˌpætə'bɪlɪtɪ] N incompatibilità

in·com·pat·ible [ˌɪnkəm'pætəbl] ADJ incompatibile

in·com·pe·tence [ɪn'kɒmpɪtəns] N incompetenza

in·com·pe·tent [ɪn'kɒmpɪtənt] ADJ *(work)* da incompetenti; *(person)*: **incompetent (at)** incompetente (in fatto di)

in·com·plete [ˌɪnkəm'pli:t] ADJ *(partial)* incompleto(-a); *(unfinished: work)* non finito(-a); *(: book, painting)* incompiuto(-a)

in·com·pre·hen·sible [ɪnˌkɒmprɪ'hɛnsəbl] ADJ incomprensibile

in·com·pre·hen·sibly [ɪnˌkɒmprɪ'hɛnsəblɪ] ADV incomprensibilmente

in·com·pre·hen·sion [ˌɪnkɒmprɪ'hɛnʃən] N: **he gave me a look of incomprehension** mi fissava senza capire

in·con·ceiv·able [ˌɪnkən'si:vəbl] ADJ inconcepibile

in·con·ceiv·ably [ˌɪnkən'si:vəblɪ] ADV *(stupid, long)* incredibilmente

in·con·clu·sive [ˌɪnkən'klu:sɪv] ADJ *(debate, discussion)* inconcludente, non risolutivo(-a); *(evidence, experiment)* che lascia dubbi, inconcludente; *(argument)* poco convincente

in·con·gru·ity [ˌɪnkɒŋ'gru:ɪtɪ] N assurdità *f inv*

in·con·gru·ous [ɪn'kɒŋgrʊəs] ADJ *(appearance, behaviour)* inadeguato(-a), assurdo(-a); *(remark, act)* fuori luogo; **the top hat looked incongruous at such an occasion** il cilindro sembrava inadeguato per quell'occasione; **an Indian temple is an incongruous sight in a Welsh village** è atipico vedere un tempio indiano in un paesino gallese

in·con·gru·ous·ly [ɪn'kɒŋgrʊəslɪ] ADV assurdamente

in·con·sequen·tial [ɪnˌkɒnsɪ'kwɛnʃəl], **in·con·sequent** [ɪn'kɒnsɪkwənt] ADJ *(conversation)* senza importanza; *(remark)* irrilevante

in·con·sid·er·able [ˌɪnkən'sɪdərəbl] ADJ: **not inconsiderable** non trascurabile

in·con·sid·er·ate [ˌɪnkən'sɪdərɪt] ADJ *(person)* privo(-a) di riguardo; *(behaviour)* poco gentile

in·con·sist·en·cy [ˌɪnkən'sɪstənsɪ] N **1** *(of actions)* contraddizione *f*, incoerenza; *(of work)* irregolarità **2** *(of statement)* incongruenza

> DID YOU KNOW ...?
> **inconsistency** is not translated by the Italian word ***inconsistenza***

in·con·sist·ent [ˌɪnkən'sɪstənt] ADJ *(contradictory: action)* contraddittorio(-a), incoerente; *(uneven: work)* irregolare, incostante; **your work this year has been very inconsistent** il tuo rendimento quest'anno è stato incostante; **to be inconsistent with** essere in contraddizione con; **that is inconsistent with what you told me earlier** questo è in contraddizione con quanto mi avevi riferito prima; **his actions were inconsistent with his principles** le sue azioni non erano coerenti con i suoi principi

> DID YOU KNOW ...?
> **inconsistent** is not translated by the Italian word ***inconsistente***

in·con·sol·able [ˌɪnkən'səʊləbl] ADJ inconsolabile

in·con·spicu·ous [ˌɪnkən'spɪkjʊəs] ADJ *(place)* che non dà nell'occhio, poco in vista; *(colour)* poco appariscente; *(person, dress)* dimesso(-a); **to make o.s. inconspicuous** cercare di passare inosservato(-a); **an inconspicuous grey building** un edificio grigio che non si nota

in·con·spicu·ous·ly [ˌɪnkən'spɪkjʊəslɪ] ADV *(behave, move)* senza dare nell'occhio; *(dress)* in modo poco appariscente, modestamente; *(marked, placed)* in modo da non attirare l'attenzione

in·con·stan·cy [ɪn'kɒnstənsɪ] N incostanza

in·con·stant [ɪn'kɒnstənt] ADJ incostante, volubile

in·con·test·able [ˌɪnkən'tɛstəbl] ADJ incontestabile

in·con·ti·nence [ɪn'kɒntɪnəns] N *(Med)* incontinenza

in·con·ti·nent [ɪn'kɒntɪnənt] ADJ *(Med)* incontinente

in·con·tro·vert·ible [ɪnˌkɒntrə'vɜ:təbl] ADJ incontrovertibile

in·con·ven·ience [ˌɪnkən'vi:nɪəns] N *(see adj)* scomodità *f inv*; scarsa funzionalità; inopportunità; **not having a car was a great inconvenience** non aver la macchina era una gran scomodità; **to put sb to great inconvenience** creare problemi *mpl* a qn, recare disturbo a qn; **I don't want to cause any inconvenience** non vorrei dare disturbo
■ VT disturbare, incomodare; **don't inconvenience yourself** non si disturbi *or* incomodi

> DID YOU KNOW ...?
> **inconvenience** is not translated by the Italian word ***inconveniente***

Ii

in·con·ven·ient [ˌɪnkənˈviːnɪənt] ADJ *(time, appointment, location)* scomodo(-a); *(house, design)* poco funzionale; *(arrival)* inopportuno(-a); **is it an inconvenient time for you?** ti è scomodo a quest'ora?; **that time is very inconvenient for me** non è un'ora adatta per me; **if it is not inconvenient (to you)** se non è un problema; **could you let me have the key tomorrow, if it is not inconvenient** mi puoi dare la chiave domani, se non è un problema?

in·con·vert·ible [ˌɪnkənˈvɜːtəbl] ADJ inconvertibile

in·cor·po·rate [ɪnˈkɔːpəˌreɪt] VT *(include)* includere, comprendere; *(integrate)* incorporare

in·cor·po·rat·ed [ɪnˈkɔːpəˌreɪtɪd] ADJ *(Am Comm)*: **incorporated company** ≈ società *f inv* per azioni

in·cor·rect [ˌɪnkəˈrɛkt] ADJ *(statement, fact)* inesatto(-a); *(conclusion)* errato(-a); *(behaviour)* scorretto(-a); *(dress)* sconveniente; **that is incorrect** questo è inesatto; **the information he gave me was incorrect** le informazioni che mi ha dato erano inesatte; **you are incorrect in stating that ...** ti sbagli quando dici che...; **his backache is caused by incorrect posture** il suo mal di schiena è causato dalla postura scorretta

in·cor·rect·ly [ˌɪnkəˈrɛktlɪ] ADV *(state)* in modo inesatto; *(conclude)* in modo errato; *(behave, dress)* in modo sconveniente

in·cor·ri·gible [ɪnˈkɒrɪdʒəbl] ADJ incorreggibile

in·cor·rupt·ible [ˌɪnkəˈrʌptəbl] ADJ incorruttibile

◎**in·crease** [*vb* ɪnˈkriːs; *n* ˈɪnkriːs] VI *(prices, salaries)* aumentare; *(population, demand, supply, sales)* aumentare, crescere; *(excitement, tension)* farsi più intenso(-a); *(rain, wind)* aumentare, intensificarsi; **to increase in number/size** crescere di numero/di dimensioni; **to increase in volume/weight** aumentare di volume/di peso; **to increase in value** aumentare di valore; **to increase by 100** aumentare di 100; **the number increased** il numero è aumentato; **the hole is increasing in size** il buco si sta allargando
■VT *(see vi)* aumentare; accrescere; intensificare; **to increase speed** aumentare la velocità; **they've increased the price** hanno aumentato il prezzo; **to increase one's efforts** moltiplicare *or* intensificare i propri sforzi
■N *(see vi)* aumento; crescita; intensificazione *f*; **an increase in size/volume** un aumento di dimensioni/di volume; **an increase of £5/10%** un aumento di 5 sterline/del 10%; **an increase in road accidents** un aumento degli incidenti stradali; **a salary increase** un aumento di stipendio; **to be on the increase** essere in aumento; *(prices)* essere in aumento *or* in rialzo; *(sales, trade)* essere in aumento *or* in fase di espansione

in·creas·ing [ɪnˈkriːsɪŋ] ADJ *(number)* crescente, in aumento

◎**in·creas·ing·ly** [ɪnˈkriːsɪŋlɪ] ADV sempre più

◎**in·cred·ible** [ɪnˈkrɛdəbl] ADJ incredibile

in·cred·ibly [ɪnˈkrɛdəblɪ] ADV incredibilmente

in·cre·du·lity [ˌɪnkrɪˈdjuːlɪtɪ] N incredulità

in·credu·lous [ɪnˈkrɛdjʊləs] ADJ incredulo(-a)

in·credu·lous·ly [ɪnˈkrɛdjʊləslɪ] ADV incredulamente

in·cre·ment [ˈɪnkrɪmənt] N *(in salary)* aumento; *(Math)* incremento

in·cre·men·tal [ˌɪnkrɪˈmɛntl] ADJ *(increase)* progressivo(-a)

in·crimi·nate [ɪnˈkrɪmɪˌneɪt] VT incriminare

in·crimi·na·ting [ɪnˈkrɪmɪˌneɪtɪŋ] ADJ incriminante

in·cu·bate [ˈɪnkjʊˌbeɪt] VT *(eggs)* covare
■VI *(egg)* essere in incubazione; *(disease)* avere un'incubazione

in·cu·ba·tion [ˌɪnkjʊˈbeɪʃən] N incubazione *f*

incubation period N (periodo di) incubazione *f*

in·cu·ba·tor [ˈɪnkjʊˌbeɪtə^r] N *(for eggs, baby)* incubatrice *f*

in·cul·cate [ˈɪnkʌlˌkeɪt] VT *(frm)*: **to inculcate sth in(to) sb** inculcare qc a qn

in·cum·ben·cy [ɪnˈkʌmbənsɪ] N *(tenure)* incarico

in·cum·bent [ɪnˈkʌmbənt] *(frm)* ADJ: **it is incumbent on him to do it ...** spetta a lui farlo...
■N *(gen)* titolare *m/f*; *(Rel)* beneficiato

> **DID YOU KNOW ...?**
> **incumbent** is not translated by the Italian word *incombente*

in·cur [ɪnˈkɜː^r] VT *(debt, obligation)* contrarre; *(expenses)* andare incontro a; *(loss)* subire; *(anger)* attirarsi; *(risk)* esporsi a

in·cur·able [ɪnˈkjʊərəbl] ADJ *(disease)* incurabile; *(habit)* incorreggibile; *(fig: optimist)* inguaribile

in·cur·ably [ɪnˈkjʊərəblɪ] ADV: **the incurably ill** i malati incurabili; **to be incurably optimistic** essere un(a) inguaribile ottimista

in·cu·ri·ous [ɪnˈkjʊərɪəs] ADJ indifferente

in·cur·sion [ɪnˈkɜːʃən] N incursione *f*

in·debt·ed [ɪnˈdɛtɪd] ADJ *(fig)*: **to be indebted to sb (for sth)** essere molto obbligato(-a) a qn (per *or* di qc)

in·debt·ed·ness [ɪnˈdɛtɪdnɪs] N l'essere in debito; *(Fin)* indebitamento

in·de·cen·cy [ɪnˈdiːsnsɪ] N indecenza

in·de·cent [ɪnˈdiːsnt] ADJ *(dress, behaviour)* indecente

indecent assault N *(Brit Law)* atti *mpl* di libidine violenta

indecent behaviour N *(Brit Law)* oltraggio al pudore

indecent exposure N esibizionismo (di organi genitali)

in·de·cent·ly [ɪnˈdiːsntlɪ] ADV *(dress, behave)* indecentemente

in·de·ci·pher·able [ˌɪndɪˈsaɪfərəbl] ADJ indecifrabile

in·de·ci·sion [ˌɪndɪˈsɪʒən] N indecisione *f*

in·de·ci·sive [ˌɪndɪˈsaɪsɪv] ADJ *(person)* indeciso(-a), esitante; *(result, discussion)* non decisivo(-a)

in·de·ci·sive·ly [ˌɪndɪˈsaɪsɪvlɪ] ADV *(act)* con indecisione *or* esitazione; *(finish: game, argument)* in modo inconcludente; **the discussion ended indecisively** la discussione è finita senza un risultato preciso

in·deco·rous [ɪnˈdɛkərəs] ADJ indecoroso(-a)

in·deco·rous·ly [ɪnˈdɛkərəslɪ] ADV indecorosamente

◎**in·deed** [ɪnˈdiːd] ADV **1** veramente, infatti, in effetti; **I feel, indeed I know he is wrong** ho l'impressione, anzi sono certo che si sbaglia; **there are indeed mistakes, but ...** ci sono certamente degli errori, però...; **thank you very much indeed** grazie infinite; **that is praise indeed** questa è decisamente una lode; **it's very hard indeed** è veramente molto difficile; **thank you very much indeed!** grazie infinite! **2** *(in answer to question)*: **yes indeed!** certamente!; **isn't that right? — indeed it is** non è vero? — altroché; **are you coming? — indeed I am** vieni? — certo; **was I mistaken? — indeed you weren't** mi sbagliavo? — no, per niente; **know what I mean? – indeed I do** sai cosa intendo? – certamente

in·de·fati·gable [ˌɪndɪˈfætɪgəbl] ADJ infaticabile, instancabile

in·de·fati·gably [ˌɪndɪˈfætɪgəblɪ] ADV infaticabilmente, instancabilmente

in·de·fen·sible [ˌɪndɪˈfɛnsəbl] ADJ (*town*) indifendibile; (*conduct*) ingiustificabile
in·de·fin·able [ˌɪndɪˈfaɪnəbl] ADJ indefinibile
in·defi·nite [ɪnˈdɛfɪnɪt] ADJ (*answer, plans*) vago(-a); (*time, period, number*) indeterminato(-a), indefinito(-a); (*Gram*) indefinito(-a)
indefinite article N (*Gram*): **the indefinite article** l'articolo indeterminativo
in·defi·nite·ly [ɪnˈdɛfɪnɪtlɪ] ADV (*postpone*) a tempo indeterminato; (*wait*) indefinitamente, all'infinito
in·del·ible [ɪnˈdɛləbl] ADJ (*also fig*) indelebile
in·del·ibly [ɪnˈdɛləblɪ] ADV (*also fig*) indelebilmente
in·deli·ca·cy [ɪnˈdɛlɪkəsɪ] N (*lack of tact*) indelicatezza, mancanza di tatto; (*impoliteness*) indelicatezza
in·deli·cate [ɪnˈdɛlɪkɪt] ADJ (*tactless*) indelicato(-a), privo(-a) di tatto; (*not polite*) indelicato(-a)
in·dem·ni·fi·able [ɪnˌdɛmnɪˈfaɪəbl] ADJ indennizzabile, risarcibile
in·dem·ni·fy [ɪnˈdɛmnɪˌfaɪ] VT (*compensate*): **to indemnify sb for sth** indennizzare qn per qc, risarcire qn di qc; **to indemnify sb against sth** (*safeguard*) assicurare qn contro qc
in·dem·nity [ɪnˈdɛmnɪtɪ] N (*see vb*) indennizzo, risarcimento; assicurazione *f*
in·dent [ɪnˈdɛnt] VT (*Typ: text*) far rientrare dal margine
■ VI (*Comm*): **to indent for sth** ordinare *or* commissionare qc
in·den·ta·tion [ˌɪndɛnˈteɪʃən] N (*dent, hollow mark*) tacca; (*: in metal, car*) ammaccatura; (*Typ*) rientranza, rientro; (*notched edge*) dentellatura; (*in coastline*) frastagliatura
in·dent·ed [ɪnˈdɛntɪd] ADJ (*Typ*) rientrante; (*surface*) intaccato(-a), ammaccato(-a); (*coastline*) frastagliato(-a)
in·den·ture [ɪnˈdɛntʃəʳ] N contratto *m* formazione *inv*
◎ **in·de·pend·ence** [ˌɪndɪˈpɛndəns] N indipendenza; **the country gained independence in 1964** il paese ha conquistato l'indipendenza nel 1964
Independence Day N (*Am*) *festa nazionale americana*

INDEPENDENCE DAY

Negli Stati Uniti il 4 luglio si festeggia l'**Independence Day**, il giorno in cui è stata firmata, nel 1776, la Dichiarazione di Indipendenza con la quale tredici colonie britanniche dichiaravano la propria indipendenza dalla Gran Bretagna e la propria appartenenza agli Stati Uniti d'America.
▷ www.holidays.net/independence/story.htm
▷ www.archives.gov/national_archives_experience/charters/declaration.html

◎ **in·de·pend·ent** [ˌɪndɪˈpɛndənt] ADJ indipendente, autonomo(-a); **of independent means** finanziariamente indipendente; **to ask for an independent opinion** chiedere un parere imparziale; **two independent studies have been carried out** sono stati condotti due studi indipendenti; **independent suspension** (*Aut*) sospensioni *fpl* indipendenti; **an independent school** una scuola privata
in·de·pen·dent·ly [ˌɪndɪˈpɛndəntlɪ] ADV (*move, decide*) indipendentemente, autonomamente; (*arrive*) separatamente; **independently of** indipendentemente da
in-depth [ɪnˈdɛpθ] ADJ (*investigation, study*) approfondito(-a)
in·de·scrib·able [ˌɪndɪsˈkraɪbəbl] ADJ indescrivibile
in·de·scrib·ably [ˌɪndɪsˈkraɪbəblɪ] ADV indescrivibilmente; **indescribably horrible/beautiful** di una bruttezza/bellezza indescrivibile
in·de·struct·ible [ˌɪndɪsˈtrʌktəbl] ADJ indistruttibile
in·de·ter·mi·nable [ˌɪndɪˈtɜːmɪnəbl] ADJ indeterminabile
in·de·ter·mi·nate [ˌɪndɪˈtɜːmɪnɪt] ADJ (*gen*) indeterminato(-a), indefinito(-a); (*plans, ideas*) indefinito(-a), vago(-a)
In·dex [ˈɪndɛks] N (*Rel*): **the Index** l'indice dei libri proibiti
◎ **in·dex** [ˈɪndɛks] N **1** (*pl* **indexes**) (*in book*) indice *m*; (*: in library*) catalogo; **look in the index** guarda nell'indice **2** (*pl* **indices**) (*pointer, sign*) indicazione *f*, indizio; (*: Math*) indice *m*, esponente *m*; **standard index form** forma esponenziale
index card N scheda
index finger N (dito) indice *m*
index-link [ˌɪndɛksˈlɪŋk] VT indicizzare
index-linked [ˌɪndɛksˈlɪŋkt], (*Am*) **in·dexed** [ˈɪndɛkst] ADJ indicizzato(-a)
In·dia [ˈɪndɪə] N India
In·dian [ˈɪndɪən] ADJ **1** (*from India*) indiano(-a) **2** (*American Indian*) indiano(-a) (d'America)
■ N **1** (*from India*) indiano(-a) **2** (*American Indian*) indiano(-a) (d'America)
In·di·ana [ˌɪndɪˈænə] N Indiana *m*
▷ www.state.in.us/ai/
Indian elephant N elefante *m* indiano
Indian ink N (inchiostro di) china
Indian Ocean N: **the Indian Ocean** l'Oceano Indiano
Indian summer N (*fig*) estate *f* di San Martino
India paper N carta d'India, carta bibbia
India rubber N (*material*) caucciù *m*; (*eraser*) gomma da cancellare
◎ **in·di·cate** [ˈɪndɪˌkeɪt] VT **1** (*point out: place*) indicare; (*: with finger*) additare; (*register: temperature, speed*) segnare, indicare **2** (*show: feelings*) denotare; (*suggest*) indicare, lasciar intendere; **this indicates a change in US policy** questo indica un cambiamento della politica statunitense
■ VI (*Brit Aut*) segnalare (il cambiamento di direzione), mettere la freccia; **to indicate left/right** mettere la freccia a sinistra/a destra
◎ **in·di·ca·tion** [ˌɪndɪˈkeɪʃən] N indicazione *f*; **there is no indication that** non c'è niente che faccia pensare che; **this is some indication that** questo fa pensare *or* sembra indicare che; **he gave no indication he was unhappy** nulla faceva pensare che fosse infelice
in·dica·tive [ɪnˈdɪkətɪv] ADJ **1** **to be indicative of sth** essere indicativo(-a) *or* un indice di qc **2** (*Gram*) indicativo(-a)
■ N (*Gram*) indicativo; **in the indicative** all'indicativo
in·di·ca·tor [ˈɪndɪˌkeɪtəʳ] N (*sign*) segno; (*: fig*) indice *m*; (*in station, airport*) tabellone *m*; (*Brit Aut*) indicatore *m* di direzione, freccia; (*Chem*) indicatore
in·di·ces [ˈɪndɪsiːz] NPL *of* **index 2**
in·dict [ɪnˈdaɪt] VT (*Law*): **to indict sb for** incriminare qn per
in·dict·able [ɪnˈdaɪtəbl] ADJ (*Law*): **indictable offence** reato perseguibile a norma di legge
in·dict·ment [ɪnˈdaɪtmənt] N (*Law*) atto d'accusa, imputazione *f*; **to bring an indictment against sb** formulare un'accusa *or* imputazione contro qn
in·die [ˈɪndɪ] ADJ indipendente
in·die band [ˈɪndɪˌbænd] N (*Mus*) gruppo indie

Ii

in·die label [ˈɪndɪˌleɪbl] N (*Mus*) etichetta indipendente
in·dif·fer·ence [ɪnˈdɪfrəns] N (*see adj*) indifferenza; mediocrità
in·dif·fer·ent [ɪnˈdɪfrənt] ADJ **1** (*apathetic*): **indifferent (to)** indifferente (a); **he was indifferent to my feelings** era indifferente ai miei sentimenti **2** (*mediocre*) mediocre; **indifferent marks** voti mediocri
in·dif·fer·ent·ly [ɪnˈdɪfrəntlɪ] ADV (*apathetically*) con indifferenza; (*not well*) mediocremente
in·dig·enous [ɪnˈdɪdʒɪnəs] ADJ indigeno(-a)
in·di·gent [ˈɪndɪdʒənt] ADJ (*frm*) indigente
in·di·gest·ible [ˌɪndɪˈdʒɛstəbl] ADJ (*food*) indigesto(-a), poco digeribile; (*fig: style*) indigesto(-a)
in·di·ges·tion [ˌɪndɪˈdʒɛstʃən] N cattiva digestione *f*; (*chronic*) dispepsia; **to have indigestion** non riuscire a digerire, avere qualcosa sullo stomaco
in·dig·nant [ɪnˈdɪgnənt] ADJ indignato(-a); **to be indignant at** *or* **about sth/with sb** essere indignato(-a) per qc/contro qn; **to make sb indignant** far indignare qn
in·dig·nant·ly [ɪnˈdɪgnəntlɪ] ADV con indignazione
in·dig·na·tion [ˌɪndɪgˈneɪʃən] N indignazione *f*
in·dig·nity [ɪnˈdɪgnɪtɪ] N umiliazione *f*
in·di·go [ˈɪndɪgəʊ] N indaco
■ ADJ (color) indaco *inv*
in·di·rect [ˌɪndɪˈrɛkt] ADJ (*gen, Gram*) indiretto(-a); (*road, route, answer*) non diretto(-a)
indirect costs NPL (*Comm*) costi *mpl* indiretti
in·di·rect·ly [ˌɪndɪˈrɛktlɪ] ADV indirettamente
indirect object N (*Gram*) complemento indiretto
indirect question N (*Brit: Gram*) interrogativa indiretta
indirect speech N (*Brit: Gram*) discorso indiretto
in·dis·cern·ible [ˌɪndɪˈsɜːnəbl] ADJ indiscernibile
in·dis·ci·pline [ɪnˈdɪsɪplɪn] N indisciplina
in·dis·creet [ˌɪndɪsˈkriːt] ADJ (*tactless*) indiscreto(-a); (*incautious*) imprudente
in·dis·creet·ly [ˌɪndɪsˈkriːtlɪ] ADV (*tactlessly*) indiscretamente; (*incautiously*) imprudentemente
in·dis·cre·tion [ˌɪndɪsˈkrɛʃən] N **1** (*see adj*) indiscrezione *f*; imprudenza **2** (*action, remark*) indiscrezione
in·dis·crimi·nate [ˌɪndɪsˈkrɪmɪnɪt] ADJ (*killings*) indiscriminato(-a); (*person*) che non fa distinzioni; (*admiration*) cieco(-a)
in·dis·crimi·nate·ly [ˌɪndɪsˈkrɪmɪnɪtlɪ] ADV indiscriminatamente
in·dis·pen·sable [ˌɪndɪsˈpɛnsəbl] ADJ indispensabile; **no-one is indispensable** nessuno è indispensabile
in·dis·posed [ˌɪndɪsˈpəʊzd] ADJ (*frm*) **1** (*unwell*) indisposto(-a) **2** (*unwilling*) poco incline
in·dis·po·si·tion [ˌɪndɪspəˈzɪʃən] N (*frm*) **1** (*illness*) indisposizione *f* **2** (*unwillingness*) poca inclinazione *f*
in·dis·put·able [ˌɪndɪsˈpjuːtəbl] ADJ (*evidence*) inconfutabile, incontestabile; (*fact*) indiscutibile, incontestabile; (*winner*) incontestabile
in·dis·put·ably [ˌɪndɪsˈpjuːtəblɪ] ADV (*demonstrate*) indiscutibilmente, inconfutabilmente, incontestabilmente; **indisputably the winner** senza dubbio il vincitore
in·dis·sol·uble [ˌɪndɪˈsɒlʊbl] ADJ indissolubile
in·dis·sol·ubly [ˌɪndɪˈsɒljʊblɪ] ADV indissolubilmente
in·dis·tinct [ˌɪndɪsˈtɪŋkt] ADJ (*voice, words*) indistinto(-a); (*memory, noise*) vago(-a)
in·dis·tinct·ly [ˌɪndɪsˈtɪŋktlɪ] ADV (*mumble, appear*) indistintamente
in·dis·tin·guish·able [ˌɪndɪsˈtɪŋgwɪʃəbl] ADJ indistinguibile
◎ **in·di·vid·ual** [ˌɪndɪˈvɪdjʊəl] ADJ **1** (*separate: member, case*) (ogni) singolo(-a) **2** (*own, personal: taste, style*) personale, individuale; (*for one person: portion*) individuale
■ N individuo
in·di·vidu·al·ism [ˌɪndɪˈvɪdjʊəˌlɪzəm] N individualismo
in·di·vidu·al·ist [ˌɪndɪˈvɪdjʊəlɪst] N individualista *m/f*
in·di·vidu·al·is·tic [ˌɪndɪˌvɪdjʊəˈlɪstɪk] ADJ individualistico(-a)
in·di·vidu·al·ity [ˌɪndɪˌvɪdjʊˈælɪtɪ] N individualità *f inv*
in·di·vidu·al·ize [ˌɪndɪˈvɪdjʊəlaɪz] VT (*frm*) caratterizzare
in·di·vid·ual·ly [ˌɪndɪˈvɪdjʊəlɪ] ADV singolarmente, uno(-a) per uno(-a)
individual savings account N (*Brit: Fin*) pacchetto finanziario non tassato
in·di·vis·ible [ˌɪndɪˈvɪzəbl] ADJ indivisibile
Indo- [ˈɪndəʊ] PREF indo...
Indo·china [ˌɪndəʊˈtʃaɪnə] N l'Indocina
in·doc·tri·nate [ɪnˈdɒktrɪˌneɪt] VT indottrinare
in·doc·tri·na·tion [ɪnˌdɒktrɪˈneɪʃən] N indottrinamento
in·do·lence [ˈɪndələns] N indolenza
in·do·lent [ˈɪndələnt] ADJ indolente
in·do·lent·ly [ˈɪndələntlɪ] ADV indolentemente
in·domi·table [ɪnˈdɒmɪtəbl] ADJ (*spirit, character*) indomabile
In·do·nesia [ˌɪndəʊˈniːzɪə] N l'Indonesia
In·do·nesian [ˌɪndəʊˈniːzɪən] ADJ indonesiano(-a)
■ N (*person*) indonesiano(-a); (*language*) indonesiano
in·door [ˈɪnˌdɔː[r]] ADJ (*shoes*) da casa; (*plant*) da appartamento; (*sport: table tennis, squash*) praticato(-a) al coperto; (*: athletics*) indoor *inv*; (*tennis court*) al coperto; (*swimming pool*) coperto(-a); (*photography*) di interni; (*hobby*) da praticare a casa; **indoor aerial** antenna interna; **indoor sports stadium** palasport *m inv*
in·doors [ˌɪnˈdɔːz] ADV (*in building*) all'interno; (*at home*) in casa; (*under cover*) al coperto; **to go indoors** rientrare, andar dentro; **they're indoors** sono dentro
in·du·bi·table [ɪnˈdjuːbɪtəbl] ADJ indubitabile
in·du·bi·tably [ɪnˈdjuːbɪtəblɪ] ADV indubbiamente
in·duce [ɪnˈdjuːs] VT (*persuade*) persuadere, convincere; (*bring about: sleep*) provocare; (*: birth*) indurre; **to induce sb to do sth** persuadere *or* convincere qn a fare qc
in·duce·ment [ɪnˈdjuːsmənt] N (*incentive*) incentivo
in·duct [ɪnˈdʌkt] VT (*frm: install*) insediare; (*Am Mil*) reclutare
in·duc·tion [ɪnˈdʌkʃən] N (*Elec, Philosophy*) induzione *f*; (*Med: of birth*) parto indotto
induction course N (*Brit*) corso introduttivo
in·duc·tive [ɪnˈdʌktɪv] ADJ induttivo(-a)
in·duc·tor [ɪnˈdʌktə[r]] N (*Phys*) induttore *m*
in·dulge [ɪnˈdʌldʒ] VT (*give into: desire, appetite*) soddisfare, appagare; (*: person*) assecondare (i desideri di), accontentare; (*spoil: child*) viziare; **why not indulge yourself and have an ice-cream?** dai, concediti un gelato
▸ **indulge in** VI + PREP (*activity*) darsi a; (*emotion*) lasciarsi andare a; (*chocolate, sweets*) concedersi
in·dul·gence [ɪnˈdʌldʒəns] N (*extravagance*) piccolo lusso (che ci si concede); (*habit*) vizio; (*leniency, Rel*) indulgenza

in·dul·gent [ɪn'dʌldʒənt] ADJ: **indulgent (to** *or* **towards sb)** indulgente (con *or* verso qn)
in·dul·gent·ly [ɪn'dʌldʒəntlɪ] ADV con indulgenza
◎**in·dus·trial** [ɪn'dʌstrɪəl] ADJ (*area, town, processes*) industriale; (*worker*) dell'industria; (*accident, injury*) sul lavoro; (*disease*) del lavoro; **industrial machinery** macchinari *mpl* industriali
industrial action N (*strikes, working to rule*) agitazione *f* sindacale
industrial estate, (*Am*) **industrial park** N zona industriale
in·dus·tri·al·ism [ɪn'dʌstrɪə,lɪzəm] N industrialismo
in·dus·tri·al·ist [ɪn'dʌstrɪəlɪst] N industriale *m/f*
in·dus·tri·ali·za·tion [ɪn,dʌstrɪəlaɪ'zeɪʃən] N industrializzazione *f*
in·dus·tri·al·ize [ɪn'dʌstrɪə,laɪz] VT industrializzare
◎**in·dus·tri·al·ized** [ɪn'dʌstrɪə,laɪzd] ADJ industrializzato(-a)
in·dus·tri·al·ly [ɪn'dʌstrɪəlɪ] ADV industrialmente
industrial park (*Am*) N = **industrial estate**
industrial relations NPL relazioni *fpl* sindacali ■ N (*field of study*) relazioni *fpl* industriali
Industrial Revolution N: **the Industrial Revolution** la rivoluzione industriale
industrial tribunal N (*Brit*) *organo competente a decidere le controversie di lavoro*
industrial unrest N (*Brit*) agitazione *f* sindacale
in·dus·tri·ous [ɪn'dʌstrɪəs] ADJ diligente
in·dus·tri·ous·ly [ɪn'dʌstrɪəslɪ] ADV diligentemente
in·dus·tri·ous·ness [ɪn'dʌstrɪəsnɪs] N diligenza, zelo
◎**in·dus·try** ['ɪndəstrɪ] N **1** l'industria; **light/heavy industry** industria leggera/pesante; **the tourist industry** il turismo; **the oil industry** l'industria petrolifera **2** (*frm: industriousness*) operosità ▷ www.cbi.org.uk
in·ebri·at·ed [ɪ'ni:brɪ,eɪtɪd] ADJ (*frm*) ubriaco(-a)
in·ed·ible [ɪn'ɛdɪbl] ADJ (*not to be eaten*) non commestibile; (*not fit to be eaten*) immangiabile
in·ef·fable [ɪn'efəbl] ADJ (*frm*) ineffabile
in·ef·fec·tive [,ɪnɪ'fɛktɪv] ADJ (*remedy*) inefficace; (*minister, leader*) poco capace
in·ef·fec·tive·ly [,ɪnɪ'fɛktɪvlɪ], **in·ef·fec·tu·al·ly** [,ɪnɪ'fɛktjʊəlɪ] ADV inefficacemente
in·ef·fec·tual [,ɪnɪ'fɛktʊəl] ADJ (*policy*) inefficace; (*person*) inetto(-a); **to be ineffectual** essere un(-a) incapace
in·ef·fi·cien·cy [,ɪnɪ'fɪʃənsɪ] N inefficienza
in·ef·fi·cient [,ɪnɪ'fɪʃənt] ADJ inefficiente
in·ef·fi·cient·ly [,ɪnɪ'fɪʃəntlɪ] ADV inefficientemente
in·el·egant [ɪn'ɛlɪgənt] ADJ poco elegante
in·el·egant·ly [ɪn'ɛlɪgəntlɪ] ADV poco elegantemente
in·eli·gible [ɪn'ɛlɪdʒəbl] ADJ: **to be ineligible for sth/to do sth** non avere diritto a qc/a fare qc; **they are ineligible for unemployment benefit** non hanno diritto all'indennità di disoccupazione
in·eluc·table [,ɪnɪ'lʌktəbl] ADJ (*frm*) ineluttabile
in·ept [ɪ'nɛpt] ADJ (*person*) inetto(-a); (*remark, behaviour*) inopportuno(-a); (*management, handling*) poco abile
in·epti·tude [ɪ'nɛptɪtju:d] N (*see adj*) inettitudine *f*; inopportunità; scarsa abilità
in·equal·ity [,ɪnɪ'kwɒlɪtɪ] N (*gen*) ineguaglianza, disuguaglianza; (*Math*) disuguaglianza
in·equi·table [ɪn'ɛkwɪtəbl] ADJ iniquo(-a)
in·equi·ty [ɪn'ɛkwɪtɪ] N (*frm*) ingiustizie *fpl*
in·eradi·cable [,ɪnɪ'rædɪkəbl] ADJ (*frm: feeling*) tenace; (*: sign, memory*) incancellabile
in·ert [ɪ'nɜ:t] ADJ inerte
inert gas N gas *m* inerte *or* nobile
in·er·tia [ɪ'nɜ:ʃə] N inerzia
inertia-reel seat belt [ɪ,nɜ:ʃə,ri:l'si:t,bɛlt] N cintura di sicurezza con pretensionatore
in·es·cap·able [,ɪnɪs'keɪpəbl] ADJ ineluttabile, inevitabile
in·es·sen·tial [,ɪnɪ'sɛnʃl] ADJ superfluo(-a)
in·es·ti·mable [ɪn'ɛstɪməbl] ADJ inestimabile, incalcolabile
in·evi·tabil·ity [ɪn,ɛvɪtə'bɪlɪtɪ] N inevitabilità
◎**in·evi·table** [ɪn'ɛvɪtəbl] ADJ inevitabile; **I was offered the inevitable cup of tea** mi venne offerta l'immancabile tazza di tè
in·evi·tably [ɪn'ɛvɪtəblɪ] ADV inevitabilmente; **as inevitably happens ...** come immancabilmente succede...
in·ex·act [,ɪnɪg'zækt] ADJ inesatto(-a), impreciso(-a)
in·ex·act·ly [,ɪnɪg'zæktlɪ] ADV in modo inesatto, in modo impreciso
in·ex·cus·able [,ɪnɪks'kju:zəbl] ADJ imperdonabile
in·ex·cus·ably [,ɪnɪks'kju:zəblɪ] ADV imperdonabilmente; **inexcusably lazy** di una pigrizia imperdonabile
in·ex·haust·ible [,ɪnɪg'zɔ:stəbl] ADJ (*patience, supply*) inesauribile; (*person*) instancabile, infaticabile
in·exo·rable [ɪn'ɛksərəbl] ADJ inesorabile
in·exo·rably [ɪn'ɛksərəblɪ] ADV inesorabilmente
in·ex·pen·sive [,ɪnɪks'pɛnsɪv] ADJ a buon mercato, poco costoso(-a)
in·ex·pen·sive·ly [,ɪnɪks'pɛnsɪvlɪ] ADV (*buy*) a buon mercato; (*dress*) con poca spesa; (*live*) frugalmente
in·ex·pe·ri·ence [,ɪnɪks'pɪərɪəns] N inesperienza
in·ex·pe·ri·enced [,ɪnɪks'pɪərɪənst] ADJ inesperto(-a); **to be inexperienced in sth** essere poco pratico(-a) di qc
in·ex·pert [ɪn'ɛkspɜ:t] ADJ (*attempt*) maldestro(-a)
in·ex·pert·ly [ɪn'ɛkspɜ:tlɪ] ADV in modo poco esperto
in·ex·pli·cable [,ɪnɪks'plɪkəbl] ADJ inesplicabile
in·ex·pli·cable·ness [,ɪnɪks'plɪkəblnɪs] N inesplicabilità
in·ex·pli·cably [,ɪnɪks'plɪkəblɪ] ADV inesplicabilmente
in·ex·press·ible [,ɪnɪks'prɛsəbl] ADJ inesprimibile
in·ex·pres·sive [,ɪnɪks'prɛsɪv] ADJ (*style*) piatto(-a), inespressivo(-a); (*look, face*) senza espressione
in·ex·tri·cable [,ɪnɪks'trɪkəbl] ADJ inestricabile
in·ex·tri·cably [,ɪnɪks'trɪkəblɪ] ADV inestricabilmente
in·fal·libil·ity [ɪn,fælə'bɪlɪtɪ] N infallibilità
in·fal·lible [ɪn'fæləbl] ADJ infallibile
in·fal·libly [ɪn'fæləblɪ] ADV infallibilmente; **she's infallibly correct** ha sempre ragione; **he infallibly arrives just as we are sitting down to eat** arriva puntualmente quando stiamo per sederci a tavola
in·fa·mous ['ɪnfəməs] ADJ (*person*) famigerato(-a); (*crime*) infame
in·fa·my ['ɪnfəmɪ] N infamia
in·fan·cy ['ɪnfənsɪ] N (*childhood*) infanzia; (*Law*) minore età *f inv*; **in its infancy** (*fig: early stage*) ai primi passi
in·fant ['ɪnfənt] N bambino(-a); (*Law*) minorenne *m/f*, minore *m/f*
in·fan·ti·cide [ɪn'fæntɪsaɪd] N infanticidio
in·fan·tile ['ɪnfən,taɪl] ADJ infantile
infant mortality N mortalità infantile
in·fan·try ['ɪnfəntrɪ] N fanteria
in·fantry·man ['ɪnfəntrɪmən] N (*pl* **-men**) fante *m*
infant school N (*Brit*) scuola elementare (*per bambini dai 5 ai 7 anni*)
in·fatu·at·ed [ɪn'fætjʊ,eɪtɪd] ADJ: **infatuated (with sb)**

Ii

infatuato(-a) (di qn); **to become infatuated (with sb)** infatuarsi (di qn)
in·fat·ua·tion [ɪnˌfætjʊˈeɪʃən] N infatuazione *f*
◎**in·fect** [ɪnˈfɛkt] VT (*wound*) infettare; (*person*) contagiare; (*food, air*) contaminare; (*fig: poison*) corrompere; (*: influence*) influenzare; **to infect sb with a disease** trasmettere una malattia a qn; **he's infected everybody with his enthusiasm** ha contagiato tutti con il suo entusiasmo
in·fect·ed [ɪnˈfɛktɪd] ADJ (*wound*) infetto(-a); (*person*) contagiato(-a); **people infected with HIV** persone contagiate dall'HIV; **to become infected** (*wound*) infettarsi; **infected with measles** affetto(-a) da morbillo
◎**in·fec·tion** [ɪnˈfɛkʃən] N infezione *f*; **an ear infection** un'infezione all'orecchio; **a throat infection** un'angina
in·fec·tious [ɪnˈfɛkʃəs] ADJ (*disease*) infettivo(-a), contagioso(-a); (*person, laughter*) contagioso(-a)
in·fer [ɪnˈfɜːʳ] VT: **to infer (from)** dedurre (da)
in·fer·ence [ˈɪnfərəns] N deduzione *f*, illazione *f*
in·fe·ri·or [ɪnˈfɪərɪəʳ] ADJ (*in quality, rank*): **inferior (to)** inferiore (a); (*work, goods*) scadente; **of inferior quality** di qualità inferiore; **to feel inferior** sentirsi inferiore; **their status is inferior to that of men** si trovano in una condizione di inferiorità rispetto agli uomini
■ N inferiore *m/f*; (*in rank*) subalterno(-a)
in·fe·ri·or·ity [ɪnˌfɪərɪˈɒrɪtɪ] N inferiorità
inferiority complex N complesso di inferiorità
in·fer·nal [ɪnˈfɜːnl] ADJ (*fires*) dell'inferno; (*spirit, powers*) infernale; (*fig: cruelty*) diabolico(-a); (*fam: noise*) infernale, terribile
in·fer·nal·ly [ɪnˈfɜːnəlɪ] ADV (*difficult*) terribilmente; **it is infernally hot** fa un caldo infernale
in·fer·no [ɪnˈfɜːnəʊ] N inferno
in·fer·tile [ɪnˈfɜːtaɪl] ADJ sterile
in·fer·til·ity [ˌɪnfɜːˈtɪlɪtɪ] N sterilità
in·fest [ɪnˈfɛst] VT infestare
in·fes·ta·tion [ˌɪnfɛsˈteɪʃən] N infestazione *f*
in·fest·ed [ˌɪnˈfɛstɪd] ADJ: **infested (with)** infestato(-a) (di *or* da)
in·fi·del [ˈɪnfɪdəl] (*liter*) N infedele *m/f*
■ ADJ miscredente
in·fi·del·ity [ˌɪnfɪˈdɛlɪtɪ] N infedeltà *f inv*
in-fighting [ˈɪnfaɪtɪŋ] N lotte *fpl* interne *or* intestine
in·fil·trate [ˈɪnfɪlˌtreɪt] VT (*troops*) far penetrare; (*enemy line, political organization*) infiltrarsi in; **a detective infiltrated the group** un investigatore si infiltrò nel gruppo
■ VI: **to infiltrate (into)** infiltrarsi (in)
in·fil·tra·tion [ˌɪnfɪlˈtreɪʃən] N infiltrazione *f*
in·fi·nite [ˈɪnfɪnɪt] ADJ infinito(-a); **we haven't got an infinite amount of time/money** non abbiamo un'illimitata quantità di tempo/denaro
in·fi·nite·ly [ˈɪnfɪnɪtlɪ] ADV infinitamente
in·fini·tesi·mal [ˌɪnfɪnɪˈtɛsɪməl] ADJ infinitesimale
in·fini·tive [ɪnˈfɪnɪtɪv] ADJ (*Gram*) infinito(-a)
■ N infinito; **in the infinitive** all'infinito
in·fini·tude [ɪnˈfɪnɪtjuːd] N (*frm*) infinità *f inv*
in·fin·ity [ɪnˈfɪnɪtɪ] N (*infiniteness*) infinità; (*in time, space, Math*) infinito
in·firm [ɪnˈfɜːm] ADJ infermo(-a)
in·fir·ma·ry [ɪnˈfɜːmərɪ] N (*hospital*) ospedale *m*; (*in school, prison, barracks*) infermeria
in·fir·mity [ɪnˈfɜːmɪtɪ] N infermità *f inv*
in·flame [ɪnˈfleɪm] VT **1** (*Med: wound*) infiammare; **to become inflamed** infiammarsi **2** (*fig: feelings, passions*) accendere; (*: person*) far incollerire
in·flamed [ɪnˈfleɪmd] ADJ (*Med*) infiammato(-a)
in·flam·mable [ɪnˈflæməbl] ADJ (*substance, fabric*) infiammabile; (*fig: situation*) esplosivo(-a)
in·flam·ma·tion [ˌɪnfləˈmeɪʃən] N infiammazione *f*
in·flam·ma·tory [ɪnˈflæmətərɪ] ADJ (*speech*) incendiario(-a)
in·flat·able [ɪnˈfleɪtəbl] ADJ gonfiabile
in·flate [ɪnˈfleɪt] VT (*tyre, balloon*) gonfiare; (*fig: prices, profits*) gonfiare, far salire; (*: idea, opinion*) esagerare, gonfiare
■ VI (*tyre, balloon*) gonfiarsi; (*fig: prices, profits*) salire
in·flat·ed [ɪnˈfleɪtɪd] ADJ (*price, fee*) gonfiato(-a); (*idea, opinion, value*) esagerato(-a), gonfiato(-a); (*style, language*) ampolloso(-a); (*tyre*) gonfio(-a)
◎**in·fla·tion** [ɪnˈfleɪʃən] N (*Econ*) inflazione *f*
in·fla·tion·ary [ɪnˈfleɪʃnərɪ] ADJ inflazionistico(-a)
in·flect [ɪnˈflɛkt] VT (*voice*) modulare; (*Gram*) flettere
■ VI (*Gram*) flettersi
in·flec·tion [ɪnˈflɛkʃən] N (*of voice*) intonazione *f*, modulazione *f*; (*Gram*) flessione *f*; **the inflection of nouns/verbs** la flessione nominale/verbale; **point of inflection** (*Math*) punto di flesso
in·flex·ibil·ity [ɪnˌflɛksɪˈbɪlɪtɪ] N (*see adj*) rigidità; inflessibilità
in·flex·ible [ɪnˈflɛksəbl] ADJ (*object*) rigido(-a); (*fig: person, ideas*) inflessibile, rigido(-a)
in·flict [ɪnˈflɪkt] VT: **to inflict (on)** (*penalty*) infliggere (a); (*tax*) imporre (a); (*suffering, damage*) procurare (a); **to inflict a blow/wound on sb** assestare un colpo a/ferire qn; **to inflict o.s. on sb** imporre la propria presenza a qn
in·flic·tion [ɪnˈflɪkʃən] N l'infliggere *m*
in-flight [ˈɪnˌflaɪt] ADJ a bordo; **in-flight service** servizio a bordo
in·flow [ˈɪnˌfləʊ] N afflusso
◎**in·flu·ence** [ˈɪnflʊəns] N influenza; **to have an influence on sb/sth** (*subj: person*) avere un'influenza su qn/qc; (*: event*) influenzare qn/qc; (*: weather*) influire su qn/qc; **to have influence with sb** avere un ascendente su qn; **to be a good/bad influence on sb** avere *or* esercitare una buona/cattiva influenza su qn; **he's a bad influence on her** ha una cattiva influenza su di lei; **under the influence of drugs** sotto l'effetto della droga; **under the influence of drink** sotto l'effetto dell'alcol; (*Law*) in stato di ebbrezza; **he was under the influence** (*fam*) aveva alzato il gomito
■ VT (*person*) influenzare; (*action, decision*) influire su, influenzare; **to be easily influenced** essere facilmente influenzabile
in·flu·en·tial [ˌɪnfluˈɛnʃəl] ADJ influente
in·flu·en·za [ˌɪnfluˈɛnzə] N (*Med*) influenza
in·flux [ˈɪnflʌks] N (*of people, objects*) afflusso; (*of ideas*) flusso

DID YOU KNOW ...?
influx is not translated by the Italian word *influsso*

in·fo [ˈɪnfəʊ] N (*fam*) informazione *f*
◎**in·form** [ɪnˈfɔːm] VT informare, avvertire; **to inform sb about/of sth** informare *or* avvertire qn di qc; **nobody informed me of the change of plan** nessuno mi ha informato del cambiamento di programma; **I am happy to inform you that** sono lieto di comunicarle che; **keep me informed** tienimi informato; **a well-informed person** una persona di cultura

■ VI: **to inform on sb** denunciare qn

in·for·mal [ɪn'fɔ:məl] ADJ (*person, manner*) semplice, alla mano; (*tone: of letter*) non formale; (*language, style*) colloquiale; (*dinner, party*) fra amici; (*visit, announcement, invitation*) non ufficiale; (*meeting, arrangement, discussion*) informale; **"dress informal"** "non è richiesto l'abito da sera"

in·for·mal·ity [,ɪnfɔ:'mælɪtɪ] N (*of person, manner*) semplicità; (*of tone*) mancanza di formalità; (*of language, style*) tono colloquiale; (*of occasion*) tono familiare; (*of meeting, negotiations, announcement*) carattere *m* non ufficiale

in·for·mal·ly [ɪn'fɔ:məlɪ] ADV (*discuss, chat*) alla buona; (*invite, meet*) in modo non ufficiale; **the Queen visited the hospital informally** la regina ha visitato l'ospedale in forma privata; **I have been informally told that ...** mi è stato comunicato ufficiosamente che...

in·form·ant [ɪn'fɔ:mənt] N informatore(-trice)

in·for·mat·ics [,ɪnfə'mætɪks] NSG informatica

◎ **in·for·ma·tion** [,ɪnfə'meɪʃən] N: **information (about *or* on)** informazioni *fpl* (riguardo a *or* su); **a piece of information** un'informazione; **to give sb information about *or* on sb/sth** dare a qn informazioni su qn/qc; **to get information on** informarsi su; **where did you get this information?** dove hai avuto questa informazione?; **could you give me some information about ...** potrebbe darmi qualche informazione su...; **for further information contact the number below** per ulteriori informazioni contattare il numero sottostante; **for your information** (*on document*) a titolo d'informazione; (*fam iro*) per tua norma e regola

information bureau N ufficio *m* informazioni *inv*

information processing N (*Comput*) elaborazione *f* delle informazioni

information retrieval N (*Comput*) ricupero delle informazioni

information science N scienza dell'informazione

information superhighway N: **the information superhighway** (*Comput*) l'autostrada informatica

information technology N informatica
▷ www.itaa.org
▷ www.crito.uci.edu
▷ www.socitm.gov.uk/Public/default.htm

in·forma·tive [ɪn'fɔ:mətɪv] ADJ (*speech, book*) istruttivo(-a); **she wasn't very informative about it** non si è sbottonata sulla faccenda

in·formed [ɪn'fɔ:md] ADJ (*observer*) (ben) informato(-a); **an informed guess** un'ipotesi *f* fondata

in·form·er [ɪn'fɔ:məʳ] N informatore(-trice); **to turn informer** (*Police*) diventare un informatore(-trice)

in·fra dig ['ɪnfrə'dɪg] ADJ poco dignitoso(-a); **it would be infra dig for him to ...** non si abbasserebbe mai a...

infra·red [,ɪnfrə'rɛd] ADJ infrarosso(-a)
■ N (*beam*) infrarosso

infra·sound ['ɪnfrə,saʊnd] N (*Phys*) infrasuono

infra·struc·ture ['ɪnfrə,strʌktʃəʳ] N infrastruttura

in·fre·quen·cy [ɪn'fri:kwənsɪ] N rarità

in·fre·quent [ɪn'fri:kwənt] ADJ poco frequente, raro(-a)

in·fre·quent·ly [ɪn'fri:kwəntlɪ] ADV raramente

in·fringe [ɪn'frɪndʒ] VT (*law*) infrangere, violare; (*rights, copyright*) violare; **they infringed the copyright** hanno violato il copyright
■ VI (*encroach*): **to infringe on *or* upon** (*rights*) violare; (*privacy*) invadere

in·fringe·ment [ɪn'frɪndʒmənt] N (*of law, rule*) infrazione *f*, violazione *f*; (*of rights, copyright*) violazione *f*

in·furi·ate [ɪn'fjʊərɪ,eɪt] VT far infuriare, rendere furioso(-a); **to become infuriated** infuriarsi, andare in bestia

in·furi·at·ing [ɪn'fjʊərɪ,eɪtɪŋ] ADJ esasperante, estremamente irritante

in·furi·at·ing·ly [ɪn'fjʊərɪeɪtɪŋlɪ] ADV in modo esasperante, in modo estremamente irritante

in·fuse [ɪn'fju:z] VT **1** (*with courage, enthusiasm*): **to infuse sb with sth** infondere qc a qn; **to infuse courage into sb** infondere coraggio a qn **2** (*Culin: herbs, tea*) lasciare in infusione

in·fu·sion [ɪn'fju:ʒən] N (*tea*) infuso

in·gen·ious [ɪn'dʒi:nɪəs] ADJ ingegnoso(-a)

in·gen·ious·ly [ɪn'dʒi:nɪəslɪ] ADV ingegnosamente

in·genu·ity [,ɪndʒɪ'nju:ɪtɪ] N ingegnosità

in·genu·ous [ɪn'dʒɛnjʊəs] ADJ ingenuo(-a)

in·genu·ous·ly [ɪn'dʒɛnjʊəslɪ] ADV ingenuamente

in·genu·ous·ness [ɪn'dʒɛnjʊəsnɪs] N ingenuità

in·glo·ri·ous [ɪn'glɔ:rɪəs] ADJ inglorioso(-a)

in-goal ['ɪn'gəʊl] ADJ (*Rugby*): **in-goal area** area di meta

in·got ['ɪŋgət] N lingotto

in·grained ['ɪn'greɪnd] ADJ (*dirt*) incrostato(-a); (*fig: ideas, tradition*) radicato(-a); (*habit, prejudice*) inveterato(-a)

in·gra·ti·ate [ɪn'greɪʃɪ,eɪt] VT: **to ingratiate o.s. with sb** ingraziarsi qn

in·gra·ti·at·ing [ɪn'greɪʃɪ,eɪtɪŋ] ADJ (*smile, speech*) suadente, accattivante; (*person*) compiacente

in·grati·tude [ɪn'grætɪtju:d] N ingratitudine *f*

◎ **in·gre·di·ent** [ɪn'gri:dɪənt] N (*Culin*) ingrediente *m*; (*fig*) fattore *m*, elemento

in·grow·ing ['ɪngrəʊɪŋ], **in·grown** ['ɪn,grəʊn] ADJ: **ingrowing (toe)nail** unghia incarnita

in·gulf [ɪn'gʌlf] VT = **engulf**

in·hab·it [ɪn'hæbɪt] VT (*house*) abitare (in); (*town, country*) vivere in

in·hab·it·able [ɪn'hæbɪtəbl] ADJ abitabile

in·hab·it·ant [ɪn'hæbɪtənt] N abitante *m/f*

in·hab·it·ed [ɪn'hæbɪtɪd] ADJ abitato(-a)

in·hal·ant [ɪn'heɪlənt] N inalante *m*

in·ha·la·tion [,ɪnhə'leɪʃən] N inalazione *f*

in·hale [ɪn'heɪl] VT (*gas, smoke, air*) respirare; (*Med*) inalare
■ VI (*smoker*) aspirare; (*Med*) inspirare

in·hal·er [ɪn'heɪləʳ], **in·ha·la·tor** ['ɪnhə,leɪtəʳ] N inalatore *m*

in·her·ent [ɪn'hɪərənt] ADJ: **inherent (in)** intrinseco(-a) (a); (*kindness, cruelty*) innato(-a) (a)

in·her·ent·ly [ɪn'hɪərəntlɪ] ADV (*easy, difficult*) di per se stesso(-a), di per sé; **inherently inefficient** sostanzialmente inefficiente

in·her·it [ɪn'hɛrɪt] VT ereditare

in·her·it·ance [ɪn'hɛrɪtəns] N eredità *f inv*; (*fig*) retaggio

in·heri·tor [ɪn'hɛrɪtəʳ] N erede *m/f*

in·hib·it [ɪn'hɪbɪt] VT inibire; **to inhibit sb from doing sth** impedire a qn di fare qc

in·hib·it·ed [ɪn'hɪbɪtɪd] ADJ (*person*) inibito(-a)

in·hi·bit·ing [ɪn'hɪbɪtɪŋ] ADJ inibitorio(-a)

in·hi·bi·tion [,ɪnhɪ'bɪʃən] N inibizione *f*

in·hos·pi·table [,ɪnhɒs'pɪtəbl] ADJ inospitale

in-house ['ɪn'haʊs] ADJ (*magazine, video*) per il personale, aziendale; (*training*) all'interno dell'azienda
■ ADV (*train, produce*) all'interno dell'azienda

Ii

in·hu·man [ɪn'hjuːmən] ADJ (*cruelty, conditions, treatment*) disumano(-a); (*appearance*) non umano(-a)
in·hu·mane [ˌɪnhjuː'meɪn] ADJ inumano(-a)
in·hu·mane·ly [ˌɪnhjuː'meɪnlɪ] ADV inumanamente, disumanamente
in·hu·man·ity [ˌɪnhjuː'mænɪtɪ] N inumanità *f inv*, disumanità *f inv*
in·imi·cal [ɪ'nɪmɪkəl] ADJ ostile
in·imi·table [ɪ'nɪmɪtəbl] ADJ inimitabile
in·imi·tably [ɪ'nɪmɪtəblɪ] ADV in modo inimitabile
in·iqui·tous [ɪ'nɪkwɪtəs] ADJ iniquo(-a); **it's an iniquitous system** è un sistema di un'ingiustizia mostruosa
in·iqui·tous·ly [ɪ'nɪkwɪtəslɪ] ADV iniquamente
in·iquity [ɪ'nɪkwɪtɪ] N iniquità *f inv*
◎**ini·tial** [ɪ'nɪʃəl] ADJ iniziale; **in the initial stages** nella fase iniziale; **in the initial stages of their relationship** agli inizi della loro storia
■ N iniziale *f*; **to sign sth with one's initials** siglare qc con le proprie iniziali
■ VT siglare
ini·tial·ize [ɪ'nɪʃəˌlaɪz] VT (*Comput*) inizializzare
◎**ini·tial·ly** [ɪ'nɪʃəlɪ] ADV all'inizio, inizialmente
ini·ti·ate [ɪ'nɪʃɪˌeɪt] VT **1** (*begin*) iniziare; (: *talks*) iniziare, avviare; (: *reform*) promuovere; **to initiate proceedings against sb** (*Law*) intentare causa a *or* contro qn **2** (*admit*): **to initiate sb (into sth)** iniziare qn (a qc)
ini·tia·tion [ɪˌnɪʃɪ'eɪʃən] N iniziazione *f*
initiation ceremony N rito iniziatico
◎**ini·tia·tive** [ɪ'nɪʃətɪv] N iniziativa; **on one's own initiative** di propria iniziativa, da sé; **to take the initiative** prendere l'iniziativa; **she's got initiative** è una che ha spirito d'iniziativa; **an important initiative** un'importante iniziativa
ini·tia·tor [ɪ'nɪʃɪˌeɪtəʳ] N promotore(-trice)
in·ject [ɪn'dʒɛkt] VT (*drug*) iniettare; (*person*) fare un'iniezione a; (*fig: money*): **to inject into** immettere in; **to inject with** fare un'iniezione di; **they injected me with antibiotics** mi hanno fatto un'iniezione di antibiotici; **to inject o.s.** farsi un'iniezione; **he needs to inject himself twice a day** deve farsi un'iniezione due volte al giorno; **to inject enthusiasm into sb** dare una carica di entusiasmo a qn
in·jec·tion [ɪn'dʒɛkʃən] N (*Med*) iniezione *f*, puntura; (*Tech, fig*) iniezione; **to give sb an injection** fare un'iniezione *or* una puntura a qn; **the doctor gave me an injection** il dottore mi ha fatto un'iniezione; **to have an injection** farsi fare un'iniezione *or* una puntura
in·jec·tor [ɪn'dʒɛktəʳ] N (*Tech*) iniettore *m*
in·ju·di·cious [ˌɪndʒʊ'dɪʃəs] ADJ (*frm*) poco saggio(-a)
in·ju·di·cious·ly [ˌɪndʒʊ'dɪʃəslɪ] ADV (*frm*) poco saggiamente
in·junc·tion [ɪn'dʒʌŋkʃən] N (*Law*) ingiunzione *f*, intimazione *f*, ordinanza
in·jure ['ɪndʒəʳ] VT **1** (*physically*) ferire; **he injured his arm** si è fatto male a *or* si è ferito a un braccio; **to injure o.s.** farsi male, ferirsi **2** (*fig: reputation, trade etc*) nuocere a; (: *feelings*) offendere; (: *wrong: person*) fare (un) torto a

> DID YOU KNOW ...?
> **injure** is not translated by the Italian word *ingiuriare*

◎**in·jured** ['ɪndʒəd] ADJ (*person, leg*) ferito(-a); (*tone, feelings*) offeso(-a)
■ NPL: **the injured** i feriti
injured party N (*Law*) parte *f* lesa
in·ju·ri·ous [ɪn'dʒʊərɪəs] ADJ: **injurious (to)** nocivo(-a) (a), pregiudizievole (per)
◎**in·ju·ry** ['ɪndʒərɪ] N (*physical*) ferita, lesione *f*; (*fig: to reputation*) danno; (: *to feelings*) offesa; (: *wrong*) torto; **a serious injury** una ferita grave; **to escape without injury** rimanere illeso(-a)

> DID YOU KNOW ...?
> **injury** is not translated by the Italian word *ingiuria*

injury time N (*Sport*) (minuti *mpl* di) recupero
in·jus·tice [ɪn'dʒʌstɪs] N ingiustizia; **you do me an injustice** sei ingiusto verso di me
ink [ɪŋk] N inchiostro; **in ink** a penna
ink-cap ['ɪŋk,kæp] N (*Bot*) fungo dell'inchiostro
ink-jet printer ['ɪŋk,dʒɛt'prɪntəʳ] N stampante *f* a getto d'inchiostro
ink·ling ['ɪŋklɪŋ] N (*hint*) indizio; (*suspicion, vague idea*) mezza idea; **to give sb an inkling that** lasciar capire *or* intuire a qn che; **I had no inkling that** non avevo la minima idea che
ink pad N tampone *m or* cuscinetto per timbri
ink·stand ['ɪŋk,stænd] N calamaio
ink·well ['ɪŋk,wɛl] N calamaio
inky ['ɪŋkɪ] ADJ (*comp* **-ier**, *superl* **-iest**) macchiato(-a) *or* sporco(-a) d'inchiostro; (*fig: darkness*) nero(-a) come l'inchiostro
INLA [ˌaɪenɛl'eɪ] N ABBR (= **Irish National Liberation Army**) *organizzazione paramilitare repubblicana irlandese*
in·laid ['ɪn'leɪd] ADJ (*table, box*): **inlaid (with)** intarsiato(-a) (di)
in·land ['ɪnlænd] ADJ (*town*) dell'interno; (*mail*) nazionale, interno(-a); (*sea, waterway*) interno(-a); **inland areas** zone interne
■ ADV (*location*) nell'entroterra; (*travel*) verso l'interno
Inland Revenue N (*Brit*): **the Inland Revenue** il fisco ▷ www.hmrc.gov.uk
in-laws ['ɪn,lɔːz] (*fam*) NPL (*parents-in-law*) suoceri *mpl*; (*other family members*) famiglia del marito (*or* della moglie)
in·let ['ɪn,lɛt] N **1** (*Geog*) insenatura, baia; (*of sea*) braccio di mare **2** (*Tech*) apertura di ammissione
inlet pipe N (*Tech*) tubo d'immissione
inlet valve N valvola d'aspirazione
in loco pa·ren·tis [ɪn'ləukəupə'rɛntɪs] ADV (*frm*): **to be in loco parentis** fare le veci dei genitori
in·mate ['ɪn,meɪt] N (*of prison*) detenuto(-a), carcerato(-a); (*of asylum*) internato(-a); (*of hospital*) ricoverato(-a)
in·most ['ɪn,məʊst] ADJ più profondo(-a), più intimo(-a); **one's inmost being** il proprio intimo; **in one's inmost heart** nel profondo del proprio cuore, nel proprio intimo
inn [ɪn] N locanda
in·nards ['ɪnədz] NPL (*fam*) budella *fpl*
in·nate [ɪ'neɪt] ADJ innato(-a)
◎**in·ner** ['ɪnəʳ] ADJ (*place*) interno(-a), interiore; (*thoughts, emotions*) intimo(-a), profondo(-a); **an inner office** un ufficio interno; **her inner sense of security** il suo profondo senso di sicurezza
inner child N (*Psych*) bambino interiore; **my inner child** il bambino che c'è in me
inner city N centro di una zona urbana (*in degrado socio-economico*)
inner·most ['ɪnə,məʊst] ADJ = **inmost**
inner sole N (*in shoe*) soletta
inner tube N camera d'aria

◎**in·ning** [ˈɪnɪŋ] N (*Baseball*) inning *m inv*
in·ning [ˈɪnɪŋ] N (*Baseball*) inning, ripresa
in·nings [ˈɪnɪŋz] NSG (*in cricket*) turno di battuta; **he has had a good innings** (*Brit fig*) ha vissuto bene e a lungo; **that car has had a good innings** quella macchina ha fatto i suoi anni
in·nit (*Brit fam*) = **isn't it**
inn·keeper [ˈɪnˌkiːpəʳ] N locandiere(-a)
in·no·cence [ˈɪnəsns] N innocenza
◎**in·no·cent** [ˈɪnəsnt] ADJ innocente; **to put on an innocent air** fare l'innocente *or* l'ingenuo(-a)
in·no·cent·ly [ˈɪnəsntlɪ] ADV innocentemente
in·nocu·ous [ɪˈnɒkjʊəs] ADJ innocuo(-a)
in·no·vate [ˈɪnəʊˌveɪt] VI introdurre delle innovazioni
in·no·va·tion [ˌɪnəʊˈveɪʃən] N innovazione *f*
in·no·va·tive [ˈɪnəʊˌveɪtɪv] ADJ innovativo(-a)
in·no·va·tor [ˈɪnəʊˌveɪtəʳ] N innovatore(-trice)
in·nu·en·do [ˌɪnjʊˈɛndəʊ] N (*insinuation*) insinuazione *f*; (*sexual*) allusione *f*
in·nu·mer·able [ɪˈnjuːmərəbl] ADJ innumerevole
in·ocu·late [ɪˈnɒkjʊˌleɪt] VT: **to inoculate sb with sth** inoculare qn con qc; **to inoculate sb against sth** vaccinare qn contro qc
in·ocu·la·tion [ɪˌnɒkjʊˈleɪʃən] N inoculazione *f*
in·of·fen·sive [ˌɪnəˈfɛnsɪv] ADJ inoffensivo(-a), innocuo(-a)
in·op·er·able [ɪnˈɒpərəbl] ADJ **1** (*Med*) inoperabile **2** (*regulation, plan*) inattuabile; **this machine is inoperable without the help of a technician** questa macchina non può essere messa in funzione senza l'aiuto di un tecnico
in·op·era·tive [ɪnˈɒpərətɪv] ADJ (*plan, rule*) inoperante
in·op·por·tune [ɪnˈɒpətjuːn] ADJ inopportuno(-a)
in·op·por·tune·ly [ɪnˈɒpətjuːnlɪ] ADV inopportunamente
in·op·por·tune·ness [ɪnˈɒpəˌtjuːnnɪs] N inopportunità
in·or·di·nate [ɪˈnɔːdɪnɪt] ADJ esagerato(-a)
in·or·di·nate·ly [ɪˈnɔːdɪnɪtlɪ] ADV: **an inordinately large sum of money** una cifra esorbitante *or* astronomica; **an inordinately large amount of food** una quantità esagerata di cibo; **an inordinately long time** un'infinità di tempo
in·or·gan·ic [ˌɪnɔːˈɡænɪk] ADJ inorganico(-a)
inorganic chemistry N chimica inorganica
in·pa·tient [ˈɪnˌpeɪʃənt] N degente *m/f*, ricoverato(-a)
in·put [ˈɪnpʊt] N **1** (*outlay: of funds, labour, energy*) impiego; (*contribution: of ideas, work*) contributo; **thank you for your input** grazie per il tuo contributo; **they need more input and advice** hanno bisogno di ulteriori informazioni e consigli **2** (*Comput*) dati *mpl*, input *m inv* **3** (*Elec*) alimentazione *f*; (*in amplifiers*) ingresso
■VT (*Comput*) introdurre
input device N (*Comput*) periferica di input
input/output [ˌɪnpʊtˈaʊtpʊt] (*Comput*) N input/output *m inv*
■ADJ (*system*) di input/output
in·quest [ˈɪnkwɛst] N (*Law*) inchiesta giudiziaria
in·quire [ɪnˈkwaɪəʳ] VT: **to inquire when/where/whether** domandare quando/dove/se; **to inquire sth of sb** domandare qc a qn; **"is something wrong?" he inquired** "c'è qualcosa che non va?", domandò
■VI: **to inquire (about sth)** informarsi (di *or* su qc), chiedere informazioni (su qc)
▸ **inquire after** VI + PREP (*person*) chiedere di; (*sb's health*) informarsi di
▸ **inquire into** VI + PREP indagare su, svolgere delle indagini su
in·quir·er [ɪnˈkwaɪərəʳ] N (*frm*): **we told all inquirers to phone again later** abbiamo detto a tutti quelli che chiedevano informazioni di ritelefonare più tardi
in·quir·ing [ɪnˈkwaɪərɪŋ] ADJ (*mind*) pieno(-a) di curiosità; (*look*) interrogativo(-a), indagatore(-trice)
in·quir·ing·ly [ɪnˈkwaɪərɪŋlɪ] ADV (*look*) interrogativamente, con aria interrogativa
◎**in·quiry** [ɪnˈkwaɪərɪ] N **1** (*question*) domanda, richiesta di informazioni; **"Inquiries"** (*on sign*) "Informazioni"; **on inquiry he found that ...** essendosi informato scoprì che...; **to make inquiries (about sth)** chiedere informazioni (su qc), informarsi (di *or* su qc) **2** (*Admin, Law*) inchiesta; **committee of inquiry** commissione *f* d'inchiesta; **to hold an inquiry into sth** svolgere un'inchiesta su qc; **the police are making inquiries** la polizia sta indagando, la polizia sta svolgendo delle indagini; **there will be an inquiry into the accident** ci sarà un'inchiesta sull'incidente
inquiry desk N (*Brit*) (banco delle) informazioni *fpl*
inquiry office N (*Brit*) ufficio *m* informazioni *inv*
In·qui·si·tion [ˌɪnkwɪˈzɪʃən] N (*Rel*): **the Inquisition** l'Inquisizione *f*
in·qui·si·tion [ˌɪnkwɪˈzɪʃən] N inquisizione *f*
in·quisi·tive [ɪnˈkwɪzɪtɪv] ADJ (troppo) curioso(-a)
in·quisi·tive·ly [ɪnˈkwɪzɪtɪvlɪ] ADV con troppa curiosità
in·quisi·tive·ness [ɪnˈkwɪzɪtɪvnɪs] N indiscrezione *f*
in·quisi·tor [ɪnˈkwɪzɪtəʳ] N (*Rel*) inquisitore *m*
in·quisi·to·rial [ɪnˌkwɪzɪˈtɔːrɪəl] ADJ inquisitorio(-a)
in·roads [ˈɪnˌrəʊdz] NPL: **to make inroads into** (*savings, supplies*) intaccare (seriamente)
ins ABBR *of* **inches**
in·sa·lu·bri·ous [ˌɪnsəˈluːbrɪəs] ADJ (*frm*) insalubre
in·sane [ɪnˈseɪn] ADJ (*person*) pazzo(-a), matto(-a); (*Med*) malato(-a) di mente; (*act*) folle, demenziale; **to drive sb insane** (*fig*) far impazzire *or* far diventar matto(-a) qn
■NPL: **the insane** i malati di mente; **an asylum for the insane** un manicomio
in·sane·ly [ɪnˈseɪnlɪ] ADV (*behave*) da pazzo(-a); **insanely jealous** follemente geloso(-a)
in·sani·tary [ɪnˈsænɪtərɪ] ADJ malsano(-a), antigienico(-a)
in·san·ity [ɪnˈsænɪtɪ] N (*Med*) infermità mentale; (*gen*) pazzia, follia
in·sa·tiable [ɪnˈseɪʃəbl] ADJ insaziabile
in·sa·tiably [ɪnˈseɪʃəblɪ] ADV insaziabilmente
in·scribe [ɪnˈskraɪb] VT **1** (*engrave*) incidere; (*write*) scrivere **2** (*dedicate: book*) scrivere una dedica su; **to inscribe sth to sb** dedicare qc a qn
in·scrip·tion [ɪnˈskrɪpʃən] N (*on stone*) iscrizione *f*; (*in book*) dedica
in·scru·table [ɪnˈskruːtəbl] ADJ (*person*) imperscrutabile; (*face, eyes, gaze*) impenetrabile
in·sect [ˈɪnsɛkt] N insetto
insect bite N puntura *or* morsicatura di insetto
in·sec·ti·cide [ɪnˈsɛktɪsaɪd] N insetticida *m*
in·sec·ti·vore [ɪnˈsɛktɪˌvɔːʳ] N insettivoro
in·sec·tivo·rous [ˌɪnsɛkˈtɪvərəs] ADJ insettivoro(-a)
insect powder N polvere *f* insetticida
insect repellent N insettifugo
in·secure [ˌɪnsɪˈkjʊəʳ] ADJ (*structure, lock, door*) malsicuro(-a); (*Psych: person*) insicuro(-a)

Ii

in·secu·rity [ˌɪnsɪˈkjʊərɪtɪ] N (*of person*) insicurezza; (*of lock, employment, finances*) scarsa sicurezza
in·semi·nate [ɪnˈsɛmɪˌneɪt] VT inseminare
in·semi·na·tion [ɪnˌsɛmɪˈneɪʃən] N inseminazione *f*
in·sen·sibil·ity [ɪnˌsɛnsəˈbɪlɪtɪ] N **1** (*Med: unconsciousness*) incoscienza **2** (*fig: unfeelingness*): **insensibility (towards)** indifferenza (di fronte a)
in·sen·sible [ɪnˈsɛnsəbl] ADJ **1** (*unconscious*) privo(-a) di sensi *or* di conoscenza **2** (*unaware*): **insensible of** ignaro(-a) di

DID YOU KNOW ...?
insensible is not translated by the Italian word *insensibile*

in·sen·sibly [ɪnˈsɛnsəblɪ] ADV (*imperceptibly*) impercettibilmente
in·sen·si·tive [ɪnˈsɛnsɪtɪv] ADJ (*person*): **insensitive (to)** insensibile (a); (*action, behaviour*) privo(-a) di sensibilità
in·sen·si·tive·ly [ɪnˈsɛnsɪtɪvlɪ] ADV insensibilmente, senza sensibilità
in·sen·si·tiv·ity [ɪnˌsɛnsɪˈtɪvɪtɪ] N mancanza di sensibilità
in·sepa·rable [ɪnˈsɛpərəbl] ADJ inseparabile
in·sepa·rably [ɪnˈsɛpərəblɪ] ADV indissolubilmente
in·sert [*n* ˈɪnsɜːt; *vb* ɪnˈsɜːt] N inserto
■VT inserire; (*needle*) introdurre
in·ser·tion [ɪnˈsɜːʃən] N inserimento
in-service [ˌɪnˈsɜːvɪs] ADJ: **in-service training** corso di aggiornamento
in·shore [ˈɪnˈʃɔːʳ] ADV (*fish*) sotto costa; (*sail*) verso riva; (*blow*) dal mare
■ADJ (*fishing*) costiero(-a); (*wind*) dal mare
in·shrine [ɪnˈʃraɪn] VT = **enshrine**
◎**in·side** [ˈɪnˈsaɪd] N **1** interno, parte *f* interiore; (*of road: Brit*) sinistra; (*: Am, in Europe etc*) destra; **to overtake on the inside** (*Brit*) sorpassare a sinistra; (*Am, Europe etc*) sorpassare a destra; **to know sth from the inside** conoscere qc per esperienza diretta **2** **inside out** alla rovescia; **he put his jumper on inside out** si è messo il maglione alla rovescia; **to turn sth inside out** rivoltare qc; **to know sth inside out** conoscere qc a fondo; (*place*) conoscere qc come le proprie tasche **3** (*fam: stomach*): **insides** NPL budella *fpl*, pancia
■ADV dentro, all'interno; **to be inside** (*fam: in prison*) essere dentro *or* al fresco
■PREP **1** (*of place*) dentro, all'interno di; **inside the house** in casa; **come inside!** vieni dentro! **2** (*of time*) nel giro di; **inside 10 minutes** nel giro di 10 minuti; **he is inside the record** sta battendo il record; **just inside the speed limit** sotto il limite di velocità
■ADJ interno(-a)
inside forward N (*Sport*) mezzala
inside information N informazioni *fpl* riservate
inside job N (*fam: robbery*) *rapina organizzata con l'aiuto di un complice interno*
inside lane N (*Brit*) corsia di sinistra; (*Am, Europe*) corsia di destra
inside left N mezzala sinistra
inside leg measurement N (*Brit*) *lunghezza della gamba dei pantaloni partendo dal cavallo*
in·sid·er [ɪnˈsaɪdəʳ] N uno(-a) degli addetti ai lavori
insider dealing [-ˈdiːlɪŋ], **insider trading** N (*Stock Exchange*) insider trading *m inv*
inside right N mezzala destra
inside story N storia segreta
in·sidi·ous [ɪnˈsɪdɪəs] ADJ insidioso(-a)
in·sidi·ous·ly [ɪnˈsɪdɪəslɪ] ADV insidiosamente

in·sight [ˈɪnˌsaɪt] N (*perception*) perspicacia, intuito; (*glimpse, idea*) intuizione *f*; **to gain** *or* **get an insight into sth** potersi render conto di qc; **to give sb an insight into sth** permettere a qn di capire qc
in·sig·nia [ɪnˈsɪgnɪə] NPL insegne *fpl*
in·sig·nifi·cance [ˌɪnsɪgˈnɪfɪkəns] N scarsa importanza
in·sig·nifi·cant [ˌɪnsɪgˈnɪfɪkənt] ADJ insignificante
in·sin·cere [ˌɪnsɪnˈsɪəʳ] ADJ (*person*) falso(-a), insincero(-a), ipocrita; (*smile, behaviour*) falso(-a), ipocrita
in·sin·cer·ity [ˌɪnsɪnˈsɛrɪtɪ] N falsità, ipocrisia
in·sinu·ate [ɪnˈsɪnjʊˌeɪt] VT insinuare; **to insinuate o.s. into sb's favour** insinuarsi nelle grazie di qn
in·sin·ua·tion [ɪnˌsɪnjʊˈeɪʃən] N insinuazione *f*
in·sip·id [ɪnˈsɪpɪd] ADJ (*food, drink*) insipido(-a); (*fig*) insulso(-a), insipido(-a)
◎**in·sist** [ɪnˈsɪst] VI: **to insist (on sth/on doing sth)** insistere (su qc/nel fare qc); **I didn't want to, but he insisted** non volevo, ma ha insistito; **she insists on leaving tomorrow** vuole assolutamente partire domani, insiste nel voler partire domani
■VT: **to insist that** (*order*) insistere che + *sub*; (*maintain*) sostenere *or* affermare di; **I insist that you let me pay** insisto che tu mi lasci pagare; **he insists that he is innocent** sostiene di essere innocente
in·sist·ence [ɪnˈsɪstəns] N insistenza; **at her insistence** dietro sua insistenza, perché lei ha insistito (molto)
in·sist·ent [ɪnˈsɪstənt] ADJ insistente
in·sist·ent·ly [ɪnˈsɪstəntlɪ] ADV insistentemente, con insistenza
in·so·far as [ˌɪnsəʊˈfɑːrəz] CONJ in quanto, nella misura in cui
in·sole [ˈɪnˌsəʊl] N soletta; **orthopaedic insole** plantare *m*
in·so·lence [ˈɪnsələns] N insolenza
in·so·lent [ˈɪnsələnt] ADJ insolente
in·sol·uble [ɪnˈsɒljʊbl] ADJ insolubile
in·sol·ven·cy [ɪnˈsɒlvənsɪ] N insolvenza
in·sol·vent [ɪnˈsɒlvənt] ADJ insolvente
in·som·nia [ɪnˈsɒmnɪə] N insonnia
in·som·ni·ac [ɪnˈsɒmnɪæk] N chi soffre di insonnia
in·sou·ci·ant [ɪnˈsuːsɪənt] ADJ (*liter*) noncurante
◎**in·spect** [ɪnˈspɛkt] VT (*examine*) ispezionare; (*Brit: ticket*) controllare; (*Mil: troops*) passare in rassegna; **to inspect sth for faults** sottoporre qc a controllo *or* verifica; **the kitchens are inspected regularly** le cucine vengono ispezionate regolarmente; **my ticket was inspected twice** mi hanno controllato il biglietto due volte
in·spec·tion [ɪnˈspɛkʃən] N (*of goods*) controllo, ispezione *f*; (*of ticket, document*) controllo; (*Mil: of school*) ispezione; **on inspection it was found that** ad un controllo si scoprì che
◎**in·spec·tor** [ɪnˈspɛktəʳ] N (*police inspector*) ispettore(-trice) (di polizia); (*schools inspector*) ispettore(-trice) scolastico(-a); (*on bus, train*) controllore *m*; **inspector of taxes** ispettore *m* del fisco
in·spec·tor·ate [ɪnˈspɛktərɪt] N ispettorato
in·spi·ra·tion [ˌɪnspɪˈreɪʃən] N ispirazione *f*; **to have a sudden inspiration** avere un lampo di genio; **to be an inspiration to sb** ispirare qn, essere una fonte d'ispirazione per qn; **you've been an inspiration to us all** sei stato di esempio per tutti noi
in·spi·ra·tion·al [ˌɪnspɪˈreɪʃənəl] ADJ ispiratore(-trice)
in·spire [ɪnˈspaɪəʳ] VT: **to inspire sth in sb, to inspire**

sb with sth ispirare qc a qn; **to inspire sb (to do sth)** ispirare qn (a fare qc)

in·spired [ɪn'spaɪəd] ADJ (*writer, book etc*) ispirato(-a); **in an inspired moment** in un momento d'ispirazione

in·spir·ing [ɪn'spaɪərɪŋ] ADJ ispiratore(-trice), stimolante

inst. ABBR (*Brit Comm:* = **instant:** *of the present month*) c.m. (= *corrente mese*)

in·stabil·ity [ˌɪnstə'bɪlɪtɪ] N instabilità

◎**in·stall** [ɪn'stɔ:l] VT (*machine, equipment, telephone*) installare; (*mayor, official etc*) insediare

in·stal·la·tion [ˌɪnstə'leɪʃən] N (*see vb*) installazione *f*; insediamento

in·stal·ment, (*Am*) **in·stall·ment** [ɪn'stɔ:lmənt] N **1** (*Comm: part payment*) rata, pagamento rateale; **to pay in instalments** pagare a rate **2** (*of serial, story*) puntata, episodio; (*of publication*) dispensa

instalment plan N (*Am Comm*) sistema *m* di vendita rateale

◎**in·stance** ['ɪnstəns] N (*example*) esempio, caso; **for instance** per *or* ad esempio; **in that instance** in quel caso; **in the first instance** in primo luogo; **in many instances** in molti casi

◎**in·stant** ['ɪnstənt] ADJ **1** (*reply, reaction, success*) immediato(-a); (*food*) liofilizzato(-a); **instant coffee** caffè *m* solubile; **instant potatoes** fiocchi *mpl* di patate; **it was an instant success** è stato un successo immediato **2** (*Comm: of the present month*) corrente mese *inv*; **the 10th instant** il 10 corrente mese

■N istante *m*, attimo; **come here this instant** vieni immediatamente *or* subito qui; **in an instant** in un attimo; **I came the instant I got the news** sono venuto non appena ho ricevuto la notizia

instant access N (*Fin: to cash*) disponibilità *f inv* immediata

in·stan·ta·neous [ˌɪnstən'teɪnɪəs] ADJ istantaneo(-a)

in·stan·ta·neous·ly [ˌɪnstən'teɪnɪəslɪ] ADV istantaneamente

in·stant·ly ['ɪnstəntlɪ] ADV immediatamente, subito

instant messaging N (*Comput*) messaggistica immediata

instant replay N (*Am TV*) replay *m inv*

◎**in·stead** [ɪn'stɛd] ADV invece; **don't take Tom, take Fred instead** non prendere Tom, prendi piuttosto Fred; **I haven't got any coffee, will cocoa do instead?** non ho caffè, va bene lo stesso il cacao?; **if you're not going, I'll go instead** se non vai tu, andrò io al posto tuo

■PREP: **instead of** invece di; **instead of sb** al posto di qn; **instead of doing sth** invece di fare qc; **we played tennis instead of going swimming** abbiamo giocato a tennis invece di andare a nuotare

in·step ['ɪnˌstɛp] N (*of foot*) collo del piede; (*of shoe*) collo della scarpa

in·sti·gate ['ɪnstɪˌgeɪt] VT (*rebellion, strike, crime*) istigare a; (*new ideas*) promuovere

in·sti·ga·tion [ˌɪnstɪ'geɪʃən] N istigazione *f*; **at sb's instigation** per *or* in seguito al suggerimento di qn

in·sti·ga·tor ['ɪnstɪgeɪtə^r] N istigatore(-trice)

in·stil, (*Am*) **in·still** [ɪn'stɪl] VT: **to instil sth into sb** instillare qc a qn

in·stinct ['ɪnstɪŋkt] N istinto; **by instinct** per istinto, istintivamente

in·stinc·tive [ɪn'stɪŋktɪv] ADJ istintivo(-a)

in·stinc·tive·ly [ɪn'stɪŋktɪvlɪ] ADV istintivamente, per istinto

◎**in·sti·tute** ['ɪnstɪtju:t] N istituto, ente *m*

■VT (*start: reform*) introdurre; (*: inquiry, investigation*) avviare, aprire; (*: legal proceedings*) intentare

◎**in·sti·tu·tion** [ˌɪnstɪ'tju:ʃən] N **1** (*organization*) istituzione *f*; (*charitable institution*) istituto di beneficenza; (*mental institution*) istituto psichiatrico **2** (*custom, tradition*) istituzione *f*

in·sti·tu·tion·al [ˌɪnstɪ'tju:ʃənl] ADJ **1** (*reforms*) istituzionale **2** (*food, furniture*) tipico(-a) degli istituti assistenziali; **institutional care** (*for children*) ricovero presso un istituto; (*for handicapped people*) assistenza medica presso un istituto; **institutional life** la vita all'interno di un istituto

in·sti·tu·tion·al·ized [ˌɪnstɪ'tju:ʃnəˌlaɪzd] ADJ **1** (*procedure, religion*) istituzionalizzato(-a) **2** (*pej*): **the prisoner had become institutionalized** il detenuto era incapace di provvedere a se stesso a causa della lunga permanenza in carcere

in·struct [ɪn'strʌkt] VT **1** (*teach*) istruire; **to instruct sb in sth/in how to do sth** insegnare qc a qn/a qn come fare qc **2** (*order*): **to instruct sb to do sth** dare istruzioni *or* ordini a qn di fare qc; **she instructed us to wait outside** ci ha ordinato di aspettare fuori

◎**in·struc·tion** [ɪn'strʌkʃən] N **1** (*teaching*) istruzione *f* **2 instructions** NPL (*orders, directions*) istruzioni *fpl*; **to give sb instructions (to do sth)** dare istruzioni a qn (di fare qc); **instructions for use** istruzioni per l'uso

instruction book N libretto di istruzioni

in·struc·tive [ɪn'strʌktɪv] ADJ istruttivo(-a)

in·struc·tor [ɪn'strʌktə^r] N (*gen*) istruttore(-trice); (*Skiing*) maestro(-a); **my driving instructor** il mio istruttore di guida

◎**in·stru·ment** ['ɪnstrəmənt] N (*also Mus*) strumento; **do you play an instrument?** suoni qualche strumento?; **to fly on instruments** (*Aer*) fare il volo strumentale

in·stru·men·tal [ˌɪnstrə'mɛntl] ADJ **1 to be instrumental in sth/in doing sth** avere un ruolo importante in qc/nel fare qc **2** (*music etc*) strumentale

in·stru·men·tal·ist [ˌɪnstrə'mɛntəlɪst] N strumentista *m/f*

instrument panel N (*Aer*) quadro degli strumenti di bordo

in·sub·or·di·nate [ˌɪnsə'bɔ:dənɪt] ADJ insubordinato(-a)

in·sub·or·di·na·tion ['ɪnsəˌbɔ:dɪ'neɪʃən] N insubordinazione *f*

in·sub·stan·tial [ˌɪnsəb'stænʃəl] ADJ (*structure*) poco solido(-a); (*evidence*) inconsistente; (*vision*) irreale

in·suf·fer·able [ɪn'sʌfərəbl] ADJ intollerabile

in·suf·fer·ably [ɪn'sʌfərəblɪ] ADV intollerabilmente; **she's insufferably rude** è di una maleducazione intollerabile

in·suf·fi·ciency [ˌɪnsə'fɪʃənsɪ] N insufficienza

in·suf·fi·cient [ˌɪnsə'fɪʃənt] ADJ insufficiente

in·suf·fi·cient·ly [ˌɪnsə'fɪʃəntlɪ] ADV insufficientemente, in modo insufficiente

in·su·lar ['ɪnsjʊlə^r] ADJ (*climate*) insulare; (*fig: person*) di mentalità ristretta; **insular attitude** chiusura mentale, ristrettezza di idee

in·su·late ['ɪnsjʊˌleɪt] VT (*against cold*) isolare termicamente; (*against noise*) isolare acusticamente; (*Elec: wire*) isolare; (*fig: person*): **to insulate sb (from)** tener qn lontano (da)

in·su·lat·ing tape ['ɪnsjʊˌleɪtɪŋˌteɪp] N nastro isolante

in·su·la·tion [ˌɪnsjʊ'leɪʃən] N (*see vb*) isolamento termico; isolamento acustico; isolamento (elettrico); (*material*) (materiale *m*) isolante

Ii

in·su·la·tor ['ɪnsjʊˌleɪtəʳ] N isolante *m*
in·su·lin ['ɪnsjʊlɪn] N insulina; **insulin injection** iniezione *f* d'insulina
in·sult [*n* 'ɪnsʌlt; *vb* ɪn'sʌlt] N insulto
■ VT insultare, offendere
in·sult·ing [ɪn'sʌltɪŋ] ADJ offensivo(-a)
in·sult·ing·ly [ɪn'sʌltɪŋlɪ] ADV in modo offensivo
in·su·per·able [ɪn'suːpərəbl] ADJ insormontabile
in·sup·port·able [ˌɪnsə'pɔːtəbl] ADJ insopportabile
◎**in·sur·ance** [ɪn'ʃʊərəns] N assicurazione *f*; **life insurance** assicurazione sulla vita; **fire insurance** assicurazione contro gli incendi; **car insurance** assicurazione della macchina; **to take out insurance (against)** fare un'assicurazione (contro), assicurarsi (contro)
■ ADJ (*certificate, company*) di assicurazione
▹ www.lloydsoflondon.co.uk
insurance agent N agente *m/f* d'assicurazioni
insurance broker N broker *m inv* d'assicurazioni
insurance policy N polizza d'assicurazione
insurance premium N premio assicurativo
in·sure [ɪn'ʃʊəʳ] VT (*house, car, parcel*): **to insure (against)** assicurare (contro); **to insure o.s.** *or* **one's life** assicurarsi (sulla vita); **to insure sb** *or* **sb's life** assicurare qn sulla vita; **to be insured for £50,000** essere assicurato(-a) per 50.000 sterline
in·sured [ɪn'ʃʊəd] N: **the insured** l'assicurato(-a)
in·sur·er [ɪn'ʃʊərəʳ] N assicuratore(-trice)
in·sur·gent [ɪn'sɜːdʒənt] ADJ ribelle
■ N insorto(-a), rivoltoso(-a)
in·sur·mount·able [ˌɪnsə'maʊntəbl] ADJ insormontabile
in·sur·rec·tion [ˌɪnsə'rɛkʃən] N insurrezione *f*
in·tact [ɪn'tækt] ADJ intatto(-a)
in·take ['ɪnˌteɪk] N **1** (*Tech: of air, water, gas*) immissione *f* **2** (*quantity: of pupils*) (numero di) iscrizioni *fpl*; (*: of workers*) (numero di) assunzioni *fpl*; (*: of food*) consumo; **try to limit your intake of salt** cerchi di limitare il consumo di sale; **this year's intake of students** gli studenti iscritti quest'anno
in·tan·gible [ɪn'tændʒəbl] ADJ **1** (*fears, hopes*) indefinibile **2** (*Comm: asset*) immateriale
in·te·ger ['ɪntɪdʒəʳ] N (*Math*) intero
in·te·gral ['ɪntɪgrəl] ADJ (*essential: part*) integrante; **to be an integral part of** essere parte integrante di
■ N (*Math*) integrale *m*
integral calculus N (*Math*) calcolo integrale
◎**in·te·grate** ['ɪntɪˌgreɪt] VT (*gen: Math*) integrare; (*Am: school, community*) operare l'integrazione razziale in
in·te·grat·ed ['ɪntɪˌgreɪtɪd] ADJ (*population, school*) in cui si è operata l'integrazione razziale; (*personality*) equilibrato(-a); **integrated steelworks** impianto metallurgico a ciclo integrale
integrated circuit N (*Comput*) circuito integrato
in·te·gra·tion [ˌɪntɪ'greɪʃən] N integrazione *f*; **racial integration** integrazione razziale
in·teg·rity [ɪn'tɛgrɪtɪ] N integrità
in·tegu·ment [ɪn'tɛgjʊmənt] N tegumento
in·tel·lect ['ɪntɪlɛkt] N intelletto
◎**in·tel·lec·tual** [ɪntɪ'lɛktjʊəl] ADJ (*person*) intellettuale; (*interests*) culturale
■ N intellettuale *m/f*
in·tel·lect·u·al·ize [ɪntɪ'lɛktjʊəlaɪz] VT intellettualizzare
in·tel·lec·tu·al·ly [ɪntɪ'lɛktjʊəlɪ] ADV intellettualmente
intellectual property N (*Law*) proprietà intellettuale
◎**in·tel·li·gence** [ɪn'tɛlɪdʒəns] N (*cleverness*) intelligenza; (*information*) informazioni *fpl*
intelligence quotient N quoziente *m* d'intelligenza
Intelligence Service N servizio segreto
intelligence test N test *m inv* d'intelligenza
◎**in·tel·li·gent** [ɪn'tɛlɪdʒənt] ADJ intelligente
in·tel·li·gent·ly [ɪn'tɛlɪdʒəntlɪ] ADV intelligentemente
in·tel·li·gent·sia [ɪnˌtɛlɪ'dʒɛntsɪə] N intellighenzia
in·tel·li·gibil·ity [ɪnˌtɛlɪdʒə'bɪlɪtɪ] N intelligibilità
in·tel·li·gi·ble [ɪn'tɛlɪdʒəbl] ADJ intelligibile
in·tel·li·gibly [ɪn'tɛlɪdʒəblɪ] ADV intelligibilmente
in·tem·per·ate [ɪn'tɛmpərɪt] (*frm*) ADJ (*remarks, response, opinion*) privo(-a) di autocontrollo; (*climate*) rigido(-a); (*habits*) smoderato(-a); (*person: lacking moderation*) intemperante; (*: drinking too much*) intemperante nel bere
◎**in·tend** [ɪn'tɛnd] VT (*mean*): **to intend to do sth** avere (l')intenzione di fare qc, intendere fare qc; (*remark, gift*): **to intend sth for sb/sth** destinare qc a qn/qc; **I intend to do languages at university** ho intenzione di fare lingue all'università; **I intend him to come too** voglio che venga anche lui; **it was intended as a compliment** voleva essere un complimento; **I intended no harm** non intendevo fare del male; **did you intend that?** (*do on purpose*) l'hai fatto intenzionalmente?
in·tend·ed [ɪn'tɛndɪd] ADJ **1** (*deliberate: insult*) intenzionale **2** (*planned: effect*) voluto(-a); (*: journey, route*) programmato(-a); **he was not the intended victim** non era lui la vittima designata
■ N (*old often hum*) fidanzato(-a)
◎**in·tense** [ɪn'tɛns] ADJ (*heat, cold, expression*) intenso(-a); (*interest, enthusiasm*) vivo(-a), profondo(-a); (*person*) di forti sentimenti
in·tense·ly [ɪn'tɛnslɪ] ADV (*difficult, hot, cold*) estremamente; (*moved*) profondamente
in·ten·si·fi·er [ɪn'tɛnsɪfaɪəʳ] N (*Gram*) rafforzativo
in·ten·si·fy [ɪn'tɛnsɪˌfaɪ] VT intensificare
■ VI intensificarsi
in·ten·sity [ɪn'tɛnsɪtɪ] N intensità *f inv*
in·ten·sive [ɪn'tɛnsɪv] ADJ (*study*) intenso(-a); (*course*) intensivo(-a); (*bombing*) a tappeto; **intensive farming** agricoltura intensiva
intensive care N rianimazione *f*; **to be in intensive care** essere in rianimazione; **intensive care unit** reparto *or* centro di rianimazione
in·ten·sive·ly [ɪn'tɛnsɪvlɪ] ADV (*study*) intensamente; (*farm*) intensivamente
in·tent [ɪn'tɛnt] ADJ **1** (*determined*): **to be intent on doing sth** essere deciso(-a) a fare qc **2** (*absorbed*) assorto(-a); **to be intent on sth** essere intento(-a) a qc; **intent stare** sguardo attento
■ N (*frm*) intenzione *f*, intento; **with intent to kill** con l'intento di uccidere; **to all intents and purposes** praticamente, a tutti gli effetti
◎**in·ten·tion** [ɪn'tɛnʃən] N intenzione *f*; **I have no intention of going** non ho nessuna intenzione di andare; **I have every intention of going** ho proprio intenzione di andare; **with the best of intentions** con le migliori intenzioni del mondo
in·ten·tion·al [ɪn'tɛnʃənl] ADJ intenzionale, deliberato(-a); **it wasn't intentional** non l'ho (*or* l'ha *etc*) fatto apposta
in·ten·tion·al·ly [ɪn'tɛnʃnəlɪ] ADV intenzionalmente, deliberatemente
in·tent·ly [ɪn'tɛntlɪ] ADV attentamente
in·ter [ɪn'tɜːʳ] VT (*frm*) seppellire

inter... [ˈɪntəʳ] PREF inter...
inter·act [ˌɪntərˈækt] VI interagire
inter·ac·tion [ˌɪntərˈækʃən] N interazione *f*
inter·ac·tive [ˌɪntərˈæktɪv] ADJ *(gen, Comput)* interattivo(-a)
interactive computing N elaborazione *f* conversazionale
interactive video N *(Comput)* video interattivo
inter·ac·tiv·ity [ˌɪntərækˈtɪvɪtɪ] N *(Comput)* interattività *f inv*
inter·cede [ˌɪntəˈsiːd] VI: **to intercede with sb/on behalf of sb** intercedere presso qn/a favore di qn
inter·cept [*vb* ˌɪntəˈsɛpt; *n* ˈɪntəˌsɛpt] VT intercettare
■ N *(Math)* intersezione *f*
inter·cep·tion [ˌɪntəˈsɛpʃən] N intercettazione *f*
inter·ces·sion [ˌɪntəˈsɛʃən] N intercessione *f*
inter·change [*n* ˈɪntəˌtʃeɪndʒ; *vb* ˌɪntəˈtʃeɪndʒ] N **1** *(of views, ideas)* scambio **2** *(on motorway)* interscambio, svincolo
■ VT *(views)* scambiarsi
inter·change·abil·ity [ˌɪntəˌtʃeɪndʒəˈbɪlɪtɪ] N intercambiabilità
inter·change·able [ˌɪntəˈtʃeɪndʒəbl] ADJ intercambiabile
inter·city [ˌɪntəˈsɪtɪ] ADJ: **intercity (train)** (treno) intercity *m inv*
inter·com [ˈɪntəˌkɒm] N *(fam)* interfono
inter·con·nect [ˌɪntəkəˈnɛkt] VI *(rooms)* essere in comunicazione
inter·con·nect·ed [ˌɪntəkəˈnɛktɪd] ADJ interconnesso(-a); **interconnected parts** parti *fpl* legate tra loro
inter·con·ti·nen·tal [ˈɪntəˌkɒntɪˈnɛntl] ADJ intercontinentale
inter·con·ver·sion [ˌɪntəkənˈvɜːʃən] N *(Comput)* transcodificazione *f*
inter·cos·tal [ˌɪntəˈkɒstəl] ADJ *(Anat)* intercostale
inter·course [ˈɪntəˌkɔːs] N **1** *(also:* **sexual intercourse***)* rapporti *mpl* sessuali; **to have (sexual) intercourse with sb** avere rapporti sessuali con qn **2** *(frm: communication)* rapporti *mpl*, relazioni *fpl*
inter·de·nomi·na·tion·al [ˈɪntədɪˌnɒmɪˈneɪʃənl] ADJ interconfessionale
inter·de·part·ment·al [ˈɪntəˌdiːpɑːtˈmɛntl] ADJ interdipartimentale
inter·de·pend·ent [ˌɪntədɪˈpɛndənt] ADJ interdipendente
inter·dict [ˈɪntədɪkt] N interdizione *f*
inter·dis·ci·pli·nary [ˌɪntəˈdɪsɪˌplɪnərɪ] ADJ interdisciplinare
◎ **in·ter·est** [ˈɪntrɪst] N **1** *(involvement, curiosity)* interesse *m*; **she has a wide range of interests** ha moltissimi interessi; **to have** *or* **take an interest in sth** interessarsi di *or* a qc; **to have** *or* **take no interest in sth** non interessarsi di qc; **to be of interest to sb** interessare qn; **to lose interest in sth** perdere l'interesse per qc; **I have lost interest in motor racing** le corse automobilistiche non mi interessano più **2** *(profit, advantage)* interesse *m*; **in one's own interest(s)** nel proprio interesse; **to act in sb's interest(s)** agire nell'interesse di qn; **to have a vested interest in sth** essere direttamente interessato(-a) in *or* a qc; **in the public interest** nell'interesse pubblico **3** *(Comm: stake, share)* interessi *mpl*; **business interests** attività *fpl* commerciali; **British interests in the Middle East** gli interessi britannici nel Medio Oriente **4** *(Comm: on loan, shares etc)* interesse *m*; **compound/simple interest** interesse composto/semplice; **5% interest** un interesse del 5%; **at an interest of 5%** all'interesse del 5%; **to bear interest at 5%** fruttare il 5% (di interesse); **to lend at interest** prestare denaro a interesse
■ VT interessare; **to interest o.s. in sth** interessarsi a qc; **to interest sb in sth** (fare) interessare qn a qc
◎ **in·ter·est·ed** [ˈɪntrɪstɪd] ADJ *(expression)* interessato(-a), pieno(-a) di interesse; *(person)* che s'interessa; **to be interested in sth** interessarsi di qc; **he's interested in buying a car** è interessato all'acquisto di una macchina; **I'm not interested in politics** non mi interesso di politica; **interested party** parte *f* interessata
interest-free [ˈɪntrɪstˈfriː] ADJ *(loan)* senza interesse
◎ **in·ter·est·ing** [ˈɪntrɪstɪŋ] ADJ interessante
in·ter·est·ing·ly [ˈɪntrɪstɪŋlɪ] ADV in modo interessante; **interestingly enough ...** la cosa interessante è che...
interest rate N tasso di interesse
inter·face [ˈɪntəˌfeɪs] N *(Comput)* interfaccia
inter·fere [ˌɪntəˈfɪəʳ] VI **1 to interfere (in sth)** *(quarrel, other people's business)* interferire (in qc), intromettersi (in qc); **to interfere with sth** *(object)* manomettere qc; *(plans)* intralciare qc; *(process, activity)* interferire con qc; *(Radio, TV)* causare delle interferenze in qc; **he is always interfering** si intromette sempre in tutto; **stop interfering!** smettila di immischiarti!; **he didn't want his work to interfere with his family** non voleva che il lavoro interferisse con la famiglia **2** *(euph: sexually)*: **to interfere with sb** molestare sessualmente qn
inter·fer·ence [ˌɪntəˈfɪərəns] N interferenza, intromissione *f*; *(Radio, TV, Phys)* interferenza
inter·fer·ing [ˌɪntəˈfɪərɪŋ] ADJ invadente
◎ **in·ter·im** [ˈɪntərɪm] N: **in the interim** nel frattempo
■ ADJ *(report)* provvisorio(-a); *(government)* ad interim; **interim dividend** *(Comm)* acconto di dividendo
◎ **in·te·ri·or** [ɪnˈtɪərɪəʳ] ADJ interno(-a); *(life, world, monologue)* interiore
■ N interno; *(of country)* entroterra *m*; **Department of the Interior** Ministero degli Interni
interior decorator N *(designer)* arredatore(-trice); *(painter)* imbianchino; *(wallpaper hanger)* tappezziere
inter·ject [ˌɪntəˈdʒɛkt] VT intervenire (con)
inter·jec·tion [ˌɪntəˈdʒɛkʃən] N interiezione *f*
inter·link [ˌɪntəˈlɪŋk] VT: **to be interlinked (with)** essere connesso(-a) (con)
inter·lock [ˌɪntəˈlɒk] VI ingranarsi
■ VT ingranare
inter·locu·tor [ˌɪntəˈlɒkjʊtəʳ] N *(frm)* interlocutore(-trice)
inter·lop·er [ˈɪntələʊpəʳ] N intruso(-a)
inter·lude [ˈɪntəluːd] N parentesi *f inv*, intervallo; *(Theatre)* intermezzo; **musical interlude** interludio
inter·mar·ry [ˈɪntəˈmærɪ] VI *(races, groups)* fare matrimoni misti; *(blood relations)* sposarsi tra consanguinei
inter·medi·ary [ˌɪntəˈmiːdɪərɪ] N mediatore(-trice), intermediario(-a)
inter·medi·ate [ˌɪntəˈmiːdɪət] ADJ *(stage, position: course, level)* intermedio(-a); *(student)* che frequenta un corso intermedio
in·ter·ment [ɪnˈtɜːmənt] N *(frm)* inumazione *f*
in·ter·mi·nable [ɪnˈtɜːmɪnəbl] ADJ interminabile
in·ter·mi·nably [ɪnˈtɜːmɪnəblɪ] ADV interminabilmente

Ii

inter·min·gle [ˌɪntəˈmɪŋgl] VI: **to intermingle (with)** mescolarsi (a)
inter·mis·sion [ˌɪntəˈmɪʃən] N *(pause)* interruzione *f*, pausa; *(Theatre, Cine)* intervallo
inter·mit·tent [ˌɪntəˈmɪtənt] ADJ intermittente
inter·mit·tent·ly [ˌɪntəˈmɪtəntlɪ] ADV a intermittenza
in·tern N *(Am: student)* stagista *m/f*; (: *doctor*) (medico) interno
◎ **in·ter·nal** [ɪnˈtɜːnl] ADJ interno(-a); **internal injuries** lesioni *fpl* interne; **internal processes** *(Geol)* fenomeni *mpl* endogeni
internal-combustion engine [ɪnˌtɜːnlkəmˈbʌstʃənˌendʒɪn] N motore *m* a combustione interna *or* a scoppio
in·ter·nal·ize [ɪnˈtɜːnəˌlaɪz] VT *(frm)* interiorizzare
in·ter·nal·ly [ɪnˈtɜːnəlɪ] ADV internamente; **to bleed internally** avere un'emorragia interna; **"not to be taken internally"** "per uso esterno"
Internal Revenue Service N *(Am: Fin)* Fisco
◎ **inter·na·tion·al** [ˌɪntəˈnæʃnəl] ADJ internazionale
■ N *(Sport: game)* incontro internazionale; (: *player*) giocatore(-trice) della squadra nazionale
International Court of Justice N Corte *f* Internazionale di Giustizia
International Date Line N linea del cambiamento di data
inter·na·tion·al·ly [ˌɪntəˈnæʃnəlɪ] ADV: **internationally famous** di fama internazionale; **internationally, the situation is even worse** a livello internazionale la situazione è anche peggiore
International Monetary Fund N Fondo monetario internazionale
international relations NPL rapporti *mpl* internazionali
inter·necine [ˌɪntəˈnisaɪn] ADJ distruttivo(-a) per entrambe le parti
in·ternee [ˌɪntɜːˈniː] N internato(-a)
Inter·net [ˈɪntənɛt] N: **the Internet** Internet *m*; **on the Internet** in Internet
Internet cafe, **Internet café** N Internet café *m inv*
Internet service provider [-prəˈvaɪdəʳ] N *(Comput)* provider *m inv*
in·tern·ist [ɪnˈtɜːnɪst] N *(Am Med)* internista *m/f*
in·tern·ment [ɪnˈtɜːnmənt] N internamento
in·tern·ship [ˈɪntɜːnˌʃɪp] N *(Am)* stage *m inv*; *(Med)* internato
inter·per·son·al [ˌɪntəˈpɜːsnl] ADJ interpersonale
inter·play [ˈɪntəˌpleɪ] N interazione *f*
Inter·pol [ˈɪntəˌpɒl] N Interpol *f*
in·ter·po·late [ɪnˈtɜːpəˌleɪt] VT *(frm: remark)* interpolare; **to interpolate (into)** *(phrase, passage)* inserire (in)
in·ter·po·la·tion [ɪnˌtɜːpəˈleɪʃən] N *(frm)* interpolazione *f*
inter·pose [ˌɪntəˈpəʊz] VT intervenire; **to interpose oneself between** frapporsi fra
in·ter·pret [ɪnˈtɜːprɪt] VT **1** *(translate orally)*: **to interpret sth (into)** tradurre qc (in) **2** *(explain, understand)* interpretare
■ VI fare da interprete
in·ter·pre·ta·tion [ɪnˌtɜːprɪˈteɪʃən] N interpretazione *f*
in·ter·pret·er [ɪnˈtɜːprɪtəʳ] N interprete *m/f*
in·ter·pret·ing [ɪnˈtɜːprɪtɪŋ] N *(profession)* interpretariato
inter·reg·num [ˌɪntəˈrɛgnəm] N interregno
inter·re·late [ˌɪntərɪˈleɪt] VT mettere in connessione, connettere; **interrelated facts** fatti *mpl* connessi fra loro
■ VI essere connesso(-a)
inter·re·lat·ed [ˌɪntərɪˈleɪtɪd] ADJ correlato(-a), in relazione (l'uno(-a) con l'altro(-a))
in·ter·ro·gate [ɪnˈtɛrəˌgeɪt] VT interrogare
in·ter·ro·ga·tion [ɪnˌtɛrəˈgeɪʃən] N *(of suspect, witness)* interrogatorio
in·ter·rogative [ˌɪntəˈrɒgətɪv] ADJ interrogativo(-a)
■ N *(Gram)* interrogativo
in·ter·roga·tive·ly [ˌɪntəˈrɒgətɪvlɪ] ADV interrogativamente, con aria interrogativa; *(Gram)* in forma interrogativa
in·ter·ro·ga·tor [ɪnˈtɛrəˌgeɪtəʳ] N interrogatore(-trice)
in·ter·rupt [ˌɪntəˈrʌpt] VT, VI interrompere
in·ter·rup·tion [ˌɪntəˈrʌpʃən] N interruzione *f*
inter·sect [ˌɪntəˈsɛkt] VT *(Math)* intersecare
■ VI *(Math)* intersecarsi; *(roads)* incrociarsi, intersecarsi
inter·sec·tion [ˌɪntəˈsɛkʃən] N *(crossroads)* incrocio; *(Math)* intersezione *f*
inter·sperse [ˌɪntəˈspɜːs] VT: **to intersperse sth with sth** inframmezzare qc con qc
inter·state [ˌɪntəˈsteɪt] ADJ fra stati
inter·stel·lar [ˌɪntəˈstɛləʳ] ADJ *(frm)* interstellare
inter·twine [ˌɪntəˈtwaɪn] VT intrecciare
■ VI intrecciarsi
in·ter·val [ˈɪntəvəl] N intervallo; **at intervals** di tanto in tanto, a tratti; **at regular intervals** a intervalli regolari; **sunny intervals** *(Met)* schiarite *fpl*
inter·vene [ˌɪntəˈviːn] VI *(event, circumstances)* sopraggiungere; *(time)* intercorrere; *(person)*: **to intervene (in)** intervenire (in); **in the intervening years** negli anni che sono intercorsi
◎ **inter·ven·tion** [ˌɪntəˈvɛnʃən] N intervento
inter·ven·tion·ism [ˌɪntəˈvɛnʃənɪzəm] N interventismo
inter·ven·tion·ist [ˌɪntəˈvɛnʃənɪst] ADJ, N interventista *(m/f)*
◎ **inter·view** [ˈɪntəˌvjuː] N *(for job, position)* colloquio; *(in paper, on radio, TV)* intervista; **to have an interview with the director** avere un colloquio con il direttore
■ VT *(see n)* sottoporre a colloquio; intervistare; **I seized the chance to interview one of the actors** ho colto l'opportunità per intervistare uno degli attori; **to be interviewed for a job** avere un colloquio di lavoro
inter·viewee [ˌɪntəvjuːˈiː] N *(Media)* intervistato(-a); *(for job) chi viene sottoposto ad un colloquio di lavoro*
inter·view·er [ˈɪntəvjuːəʳ] N *(on radio, TV)* intervistatore(-trice)
inter·weave [ˌɪntəˈwiːv] VT intrecciare
■ VI intrecciarsi
in·tes·tate [ɪnˈtɛstɪt] ADJ *(Law)*: **to die intestate** morire intestato(-a)
in·tes·ti·nal [ɪnˈtɛstɪnl] ADJ intestinale
in·tes·tine [ɪnˈtɛstɪn] N intestino; **large intestine** (intestino) crasso; **small intestine** (intestino) tenue *m*
in·ti·ma·cy [ˈɪntɪməsɪ] N *(friendship)* intimità; *(sexual intimacy)* rapporti *mpl* intimi
in·ti·mate [*adj* ˈɪntɪˌmɪt; *vb* ˈɪntɪmeɪt] ADJ intimo(-a); *(knowledge)* profondo(-a); **to be/become intimate with sb** *(friendly)* essere/diventare amico(-a) intimo(-a) di qn; *(sexually)* avere rapporti intimi con qn
■ VT: **to intimate (that)** far *or* lasciar capire (che)

DID YOU KNOW ...?
intimate is not translated by the Italian word *intimare*

in·ti·mate·ly [ˈɪntɪmɪtlɪ] ADV intimamente; **to talk intimately with sb** scambiare confidenze con qn; **to be intimately involved in sth** essere direttamente coinvolto(-a) in qc

in·ti·ma·tion [ˌɪntɪˈmeɪʃən] N (*hint*) accenno

> DID YOU KNOW ...?
> **intimation** is not translated by the Italian word *intimazione*

in·timi·date [ɪnˈtɪmɪˌdeɪt] VT intimorire; (*witness*) minacciare, sottoporre ad intimidazione; **he tried to intimidate me** ha cercato di intimorirmi

in·timi·da·tion [ɪnˌtɪmɪˈdeɪʃən] N intimidazione *f*

◎**into** [ˈɪntu:] PREP **1** (*of place*) in, dentro; **put it into the box** mettilo nella *or* dentro la scatola; **come into the house** vieni dentro casa; **to go into the wood** entrare nel bosco; **to walk into a wall** sbattere contro un muro; **he drove into a tree** andò a sbattere contro un albero; **to go into town/the country** andare in città/in campagna; **to get into the car** salire in macchina **2** (*change in condition*) in; **to translate sth into Italian** tradurre qc in italiano; **to burst into tears** scoppiare in lacrime; **to change pounds into dollars** cambiare delle sterline in dollari; **to cut into pieces** tagliare a pezzi; **to change into clean clothes** mettersi dei vestiti puliti; **he is really into jazz** (*fam*) è un appassionato di jazz, ha la passione del jazz **3** (*Math*): **2 into 6 goes 3 times** il 2 nel 6 sta 3 volte; **to divide 3 into 12** dividere 12 per 3

in·tol·er·able [ɪnˈtɒlərəbl] ADJ intollerabile

in·tol·er·ably [ɪnˈtɒlərəblɪ] ADV intollerabilmente

in·tol·er·ance [ɪnˈtɒlərəns] N intolleranza

in·tol·er·ant [ɪnˈtɒlərənt] ADJ: **intolerant (of)** intollerante (verso)

in·tol·er·ant·ly [ɪnˈtɒlərəntlɪ] ADV in modo intollerante

in·to·na·tion [ˌɪntəʊˈneɪʃən] N (*Linguistics*) intonazione *f*

in·toxi·cant [ɪnˈtɒksɪkənt] N (*frm*) bevanda alcolica

in·toxi·cate [ɪnˈtɒksɪˌkeɪt] VT (*subj: alcohol*) ubriacare; (*subj: success*) inebriare

> DID YOU KNOW ...?
> **intoxicate** is not translated by the Italian word *intossicare*

in·toxi·cat·ed [ɪnˈtɒksɪˌkeɪtɪd] ADJ ubriaco(-a); **intoxicated (with)** (*fig*) inebriato(-a) (di); **to become intoxicated** ubriacarsi

> DID YOU KNOW ...?
> **intoxicated** is not translated by the Italian word *intossicato*

in·toxi·ca·tion [ɪnˌtɒksɪˈkeɪʃən] N (*see adj*) ubriachezza; ebbrezza

intra... [ˈɪntrə] PREF intra...

in·trac·table [ɪnˈtræktəbl] (*frm*) ADJ (*person, mood*) intrattabile; (*illness*) difficile da curare; (*problem*) insolubile

intra·mus·cu·lar [ˌɪntrəˈmʌskjʊləʳ] ADJ intramuscolare

intra·net [ˈɪntrənet] N intranet *m inv*

in·tran·si·gence [ɪnˈtrænsɪdʒəns] N intransigenza

in·tran·si·gent [ɪnˈtrænsɪdʒənt] ADJ intransigente

in·tran·si·tive [ɪnˈtrænsɪtɪv] ADJ (*Gram*) intransitivo(-a)

intra-uterine device [ˌɪntrəˈju:təraɪndɪˈvaɪs] N dispositivo anticoncezionale intrauterino, spirale *f*

intra·venous [ˌɪntrəˈvi:nəs] ADJ endovenoso(-a)

intra·venous·ly [ˌɪntrəˈvi:nəslɪ] ADV endovena

in-tray [ˈɪnˌtreɪ] N vassoio della corrispondenza in arrivo

in·trep·id [ɪnˈtrɛpɪd] ADJ intrepido(-a)

in·tre·pid·ity [ˌɪntrɪˈpɪdɪtɪ] N intrepidezza

in·tri·ca·cy [ˈɪntrɪkəsɪ] N complessità *f inv*

in·tri·cate [ˈɪntrɪkɪt] ADJ (*plot, problem*) intricato(-a), complicato(-a); (*pattern, machinery, mechanism*) complicato(-a), complesso(-a)

in·tri·cate·ly [ˈɪntrɪkɪtlɪ] ADV (*see adj*) in modo intricato; in modo complesso

in·trigue [ɪnˈtri:g] N (*plot*) intrigo; (*amorous*) tresca
■ VT (*fascinate*) intrigare, affascinare; (*make curious*) incuriosire
■ VI complottare, tramare

in·tri·guer [ɪnˈtri:gəʳ] N cospiratore(-trice)

in·tri·guing [ɪnˈtri:gɪŋ] ADJ (*fascinating*) affascinante, intrigante; (*arousing curiosity*) che suscita curiosità
■ N intrighi *mpl*

in·trin·sic [ɪnˈtrɪnsɪk] ADJ intrinseco(-a)

in·trin·si·cal·ly [ɪnˈtrɪnsɪklɪ] ADV intrinsecamente

in·tro [ˈɪntrəʊ] N (*fam*: = **introduction**) introduzione *f*

◎**intro·duce** [ˌɪntrəˈdju:s] VT **1** (*bring in: reform, new fashion, idea*) introdurre; (*: Pol: bill*) (*TV, Radio: programme*) presentare; **to introduce sb into a firm** far entrare qn in una ditta; **a new system is to be introduced** verrà introdotto un nuovo sistema **2** (*make acquainted*): **to introduce sb to sb** presentare qn a qn; **he introduced me to his parents** mi ha presentato ai suoi genitori; **to introduce sb to sth** (*pastime, technique*) far conoscere qc a qn, iniziare qn a qc; **she introduced us to the delights of Indian cookery** ci ha iniziato ai piaceri della cucina indiana; **may I introduce ...?** permette che le presenti...?

intro·duc·tion [ˌɪntrəˈdʌkʃən] N (*see vb*) introduzione *f*; presentazione *f*; **my introduction to maths** il mio primo contatto con la matematica; **a letter of introduction** una lettera di presentazione; **the introduction of the new system** l'introduzione del nuovo sistema

intro·duc·tory [ˌɪntrəˈdʌktərɪ] ADJ introduttivo(-a); **introductory remarks** osservazioni *fpl* preliminari; **an introductory offer** un'offerta di lancio; **an introductory course** un corso introduttivo

intro·spec·tion [ˌɪntrəʊˈspɛkʃən] N introspezione *f*

intro·spec·tive [ˌɪntrəʊˈspɛktɪv] ADJ introspettivo(-a)

intro·ver·sion [ˌɪntrəʊˈvɜ:ʃən] N introversione *f*

intro·vert [ˈɪntrəʊˌvɜ:t] N, ADJ introverso(-a)

intro·ver·ted [ˈɪntrəʊˌvɜ:tɪd] ADJ ≈ introvert

in·trude [ɪnˈtru:d] VI intromettersi; **to intrude on** *or* **upon** (*person*) importunare; (*conversation*) intromettersi in; **I hope I'm not intruding** spero di non disturbare

in·trud·er [ɪnˈtru:dəʳ] N (*trespasser*) intruso(-a); (*burglar*) ladro(-a)

in·tru·sion [ɪnˈtru:ʒən] N intrusione *f*

in·tru·sive [ɪnˈtru:sɪv] ADJ importuno(-a)

in·tui·tion [ˌɪntju:ˈɪʃən] N (*no pl: power*) intuito, intuizione *f*; (*feeling*) intuito

in·tui·tive [ɪnˈtju:ɪtɪv] ADJ intuitivo(-a)

in·tui·tive·ly [ɪnˈtju:ɪtɪvlɪ] ADV intuitivamente

Inu·it [ˈɪnju:ɪt] N (*people*) inuit *m/f inv*; (*language*) lingua inuit

in·un·date [ˈɪnʌnˌdeɪt] VT: **to inundate (with)** inondare (di); (*fig*) sommergere (di)

in·ure [ɪnˈjʊəʳ] VT: **to inure (to)** assuefare (a)

in·vade [ɪnˈveɪd] VT (*Mil, gen, fig*) invadere; (*privacy, sb's rights*) violare

in·vad·er [ɪnˈveɪdəʳ] N invasore *m*

Ii

in·vad·ing [ɪn'veɪdɪŋ] ADJ (*army, troops*) d'invasione
in·va·lid¹ ['ɪnvəlɪd] N (*sick person*) infermo(-a); (*disabled person*) invalido(-a)
■ ADJ (*see n*) infermo(-a); invalido(-a)
▸ **invalid out** VT + ADV (*Mil*) congedare per invalidità
in·val·id² [ɪn'vælɪd] ADJ (*document, cheque*) invalido(-a), non valido(-a); (*excuse, argument*) non valido(-a); (*marriage*) nullo(-a)
in·vali·date [ɪn'vælɪ,deɪt] VT (*law, contract*) invalidare; (*argument, conclusion*) smentire; **the will was invalidated** il testamento è stato invalidato
invalid chair N (*Brit*) sedia a rotelle
in·valu·able [ɪn'væljʊəbl] ADJ estremamente prezioso(-a); **your help has been invaluable** il tuo aiuto è stato estremamente prezioso
in·vari·able [ɪn'vɛərɪəbl] ADJ costante, invariabile
in·vari·ably [ɪn'vɛərɪəblɪ] ADV invariabilmente; **she is invariably late** è immancabilmente in ritardo; **they almost invariably get it wrong** sbagliano quasi sempre
in·vari·ant [ɪn'vɛərɪənt] ADJ (*Math*) invariante *f*
◎**in·va·sion** [ɪn'veɪʒən] N invasione *f*; **an invasion of sb's privacy** una violazione della privacy di qn
in·vec·tive [ɪn'vɛktɪv] N invettiva; **a stream of invective** una sfilza d'ingiurie, una sequela di improperi
in·veigh [ɪn'veɪ] VI: **to inveigh against** (*frm*) inveire contro
in·vei·gle [ɪn'vi:gl] VT: **to inveigle sb into (doing) sth** circuire qn per fargli/farle fare qc
in·vent [ɪn'vɛnt] VT inventare
in·ven·tion [ɪn'vɛnʃən] N invenzione *f*
in·ven·tive [ɪn'vɛntɪv] ADJ (*genius*) inventivo(-a), creativo(-a); (*mind*) ricco(-a) d'inventiva
in·ven·tive·ness [ɪn'vɛntɪvnɪs] N inventiva
in·ven·tor [ɪn'vɛntə^r] N inventore(-trice)
in·ven·tory ['ɪnvəntrɪ] N inventario; **to draw up/take an inventory** fare l'inventario
inventory control N (*Comm*) controllo delle giacenze
in·verse ['ɪn'vɜ:s] ADJ inverso(-a); **in inverse proportion (to)** inversamente proporzionale (a); **to be in inverse proportion** essere inversamente proporzionale
■ N inverso, contrario
in·verse·ly [ɪn'vɜ:slɪ] ADV all'inverso; **inversely proportionate** inversamente proporzionale
in·ver·sion [ɪn'vɜ:ʃən] N (*of elements, words, roles*) inversione *f*; (*of object*) capovolgimento, ribaltamento; (*of values*) rovesciamento, capovolgimento
in·vert [ɪn'vɜ:t] VT (*object*) capovolgere, rovesciare; (*elements, words*) invertire
in·ver·tebrate [ɪn'vɜ:tɪbrɪt] N, ADJ invertebrato(-a)
in·vert·ed com·mas [ɪn,vɜ:tɪd'kɒməz] NPL (*Brit*) virgolette *fpl*; **in inverted commas** tra virgolette
◎**in·vest** [ɪn'vest] VT **1** (*money, capital*) investire; (*fig: time, effort*) impiegare **2** (*endow*): **to invest sb with sth** investire qn di qc
■ VI: **to invest in** (*company, property*) investire in, fare (degli) investimenti in; (*acquire*) comprarsi
◎**in·ves·ti·gate** [ɪn'vɛstɪ,geɪt] VT (*crime, motive*) indagare su, investigare su; (*possibilities*) studiare, esaminare; **the police are investigating the murder** la polizia sta indagando sull'omicidio
in·ves·ti·ga·tion [ɪn,vɛstɪ'geɪʃən] N (*of crime*) indagine *f*, investigazione *f* giudiziaria; **police investigations** le indagini della polizia
in·ves·ti·gative [ɪn'vɛstɪgətɪv] ADJ: **investigative journalism** giornalismo investigativo
in·ves·ti·ga·tor [ɪn'vɛstɪ,geɪtə^r] N investigatore (-trice); **a private investigator** un investigatore privato, un detective
in·ves·ti·ture [ɪn'vɛstɪtʃə^r] N investitura
◎**in·vest·ment** [ɪn'vɛstmənt] N (*Comm*) investimento
▹ www.eib.org/
investment grant N incentivo agli investimenti
investment income N reddito da investimenti
investment trust N fondo comune di investimento
◎**in·ves·tor** [ɪn'vɛstə^r] N (*gen*) investitore(-trice); (*shareholder*) azionista *m/f*
in·vet·er·ate [ɪn'vɛtərɪt] ADJ (*habit, gambler*) inveterato(-a); (*liar, smoker*) incallito(-a)
in·vidi·ous [ɪn'vɪdɪəs] ADJ (*comparison*) ingiusto(-a); (*task*) poco invidiabile, antipatico(-a); (*choice*) imbarazzante, difficile

DID YOU KNOW ...?
invidious is not translated by the Italian word *invidioso*

in·vigi·late [ɪn'vɪdʒɪ,leɪt] VT, VI (*Brit Scol*) sorvegliare
in·vigi·la·tor [ɪn'vɪdʒɪ,leɪtə^r] N (*Brit*) chi sorveglia agli esami
in·vig·or·ate [ɪn'vɪgə,reɪt] VT (*subj: exercise, air*) tonificare, invigorire
in·vig·or·at·ing [ɪn'vɪgə,reɪtɪŋ] ADJ (*exercise, walk, air, breeze*) tonificante
in·vin·cible [ɪn'vɪnsəbl] ADJ invincibile
in·vio·lable [ɪn'vaɪələbl] ADJ (*frm*) inviolabile
in·vio·late [ɪn'vaɪəlɪt] ADJ inviolato(-a)
in·vis·ibil·ity [ɪn,vɪzə'bɪlɪtɪ] N invisibilità
in·vis·ible [ɪn'vɪzəbl] ADJ invisibile
invisible assets NPL (*Brit: Econ*) beni *mpl* immateriali
invisible earnings NPL (*Econ*) partite *fpl* invisibili
invisible export N (*Econ*) esportazione *f* di beni immateriali
invisible import N (*Econ*) importazione *f* di beni immateriali
invisible ink N inchiostro simpatico
invisible mending N rammendo invisibile
in·vis·ibly [ɪn'vɪzəblɪ] ADV in modo invisibile
◎**in·vi·ta·tion** [,ɪnvɪ'teɪʃən] N invito; **by invitation only** esclusivamente su invito; **at sb's invitation** dietro *or* su invito di qn
◎**in·vite** [ɪn'vaɪt] VT (*person*): **to invite sb (to do)** invitare qn (a fare); (*subscriptions, applications*) sollecitare, richiedere (cortesemente); (*opinions*) chiedere; (*discussion*) invitare a; (*ridicule*) provocare, suscitare; (*disbelief*) incoraggiare; **to invite sb to dinner** invitare qn a cena; **to invite sb in/up** invitare qn a entrare/salire; **you're invited to a party at Claire's house** sei invitato ad una festa a casa di Claire; **to invite trouble** cercare guai
▸ **invite out** VT + ADV invitare fuori; **he invited us out to dinner** ci ha invitato a cena fuori
▸ **invite over** VT + ADV invitare (a casa)
in·vit·ing [ɪn'vaɪtɪŋ] ADJ (*prospect, goods*) invitante, allettante; (*smile*) invitante; (*food, smell*) invitante, appetitoso(-a)
in·vit·ing·ly [ɪn'vaɪtɪŋlɪ] ADV (*smile, describe*) in modo invitante
in vitro [ɪn'vi:trəʊ] ADJ, ADV in vitro
in vitro fertilization N (*Med*) fecondazione *f* in vitro
in·vo·ca·tion [,ɪnvəʊ'keɪʃən] N invocazione *f*
in·voice ['ɪnvɔɪs] N fattura

■VT (*goods*) fatturare; **to invoice sb for goods** intestare a qn la fattura per le *or* delle merci

invoice clerk N fatturista *m/f*

in·voke [ɪnˈvəʊk] VT invocare

in·vol·un·tari·ly [ɪnˈvɒləntərɪlɪ] ADV involontariamente

in·vol·un·tary [ɪnˈvɒləntərɪ] ADJ involontario(-a)

◎**in·volve** [ɪnˈvɒlv] VT **1** (*associate*) coinvolgere; (*implicate*) implicare, coinvolgere; **to be/become involved in sth** essere/rimanere coinvolto(-a) in qc; **I don't want to be involved in the argument** non voglio essere coinvolto nella discussione; **to involve o.s./sb in sth** (*politics etc*) impegnarsi/coinvolgere qn in qc; **we won't involve him** non lo coinvolgeremo; **don't involve me in your quarrels!** non tiratemi in mezzo alle vostre beghe!; **don't involve yourself in unnecessary expense** non metterti a fare spese inutili; **how did he come to be involved?** come ha fatto a trovarcisi in mezzo?; **the factors involved** i fattori in causa *or* in gioco; **the persons involved** le persone in questione *or* coinvolte; **to feel involved** sentirsi coinvolto(-a); **to become** *or* **get involved with sb** (*socially*) legarsi a qn; (*emotionally*) legarsi sentimentalmente a qn; **to be involved with sb** avere una relazione con qn; **she was involved with a married man** aveva una relazione con un uomo sposato **2** (*entail*) implicare, comportare; **it involves a lot of expense/trouble** comporta un mucchio di spese/difficoltà

◎**in·volved** [ɪnˈvɒlvd] ADJ (*situation, discussion*) complicato(-a), complesso(-a); *see also* **involve**

◎**in·volve·ment** [ɪnˈvɒlvmənt] N **1** (*being involved*) impegno, partecipazione *f*, coinvolgimento; (*emotional*) legame *m*, relazione *f*; **we don't know the extent of his involvement** non sappiamo fino a che punto sia coinvolto; **their involvement in the deal** il loro coinvolgimento nell'affare; **his involvement in the activities of the group** la sua partecipazione alle attività del gruppo; **financial involvements** impegni *mpl* finanziari **2** (*complexity*) complessità

in·vul·ner·abil·ity [ɪn,vʌlnərəˈbɪlɪtɪ] N invulnerabilità

in·vul·ner·able [ɪnˈvʌlnərəbl] ADJ invulnerabile

in·ward [ˈɪnwəd] ADJ (*peace, happiness*) interiore; (*thought, feeling*) intimo(-a); (*movement*) verso l'interno

■ADV = **inwards**

inward investment N (*Econ*) investimenti *mpl* da capitale estero

inward-looking [ˈɪnwədˈlʊkɪŋ] ADJ (*society*) chiuso(-a); **an inward-looking individual** un introverso

in·ward·ly [ˈɪnwədlɪ] ADV (*feel, think*) nel proprio intimo, dentro di sé

in·wards [ˈɪnwədz] ADV verso l'interno

I/O ABBR (*Comput:* = **input/output**) I/O

IOC [,aɪəʊˈsiː] N ABBR (= **International Olympic Committee**) CIO *m* (= *Comitato olimpico internazionale*)

iodide [ˈaɪə,daɪd] N ioduro

iodine [ˈaɪə,diːn] N iodio

IOM ABBR (*Brit*) = **Isle of Man**

ion [ˈaɪən] N ione *m*

ion exchange N scambio ionico

Ionian Sea [aɪˈəʊnɪənˈsiː] N: **the Ionian Sea** il mar Ionio

Ion·ic [aɪˈɒnɪk] ADJ (*Archit*) ionico(-a)

ion·ic [aɪˈɒnɪk] ADJ (*Phys, Chem*) ionico(-a)

ioni·za·tion [,aɪənaɪˈzeɪʃən] N ionizzazione *f*

ion·iz·er [ˈaɪən,aɪzəʳ] N ionizzatore *m*

iono·sphere [aɪˈɒnə,sfɪəʳ] N ionosfera

iota [aɪˈəʊtə] N (*letter*) iota; (*of truth, commonsense*) briciolo

IOU [,aɪəʊˈjuː] N ABBR (= **I owe you**) pagherò *m inv*

IOW ABBR (*Brit*) = **Isle of Wight**

Iowa [ˈaɪəʊə] N Iowa *m*

▷ www.iowa.gov/state/main/index.html

IPA [,aɪpiːˈeɪ] N ABBR (= **International Phonetic Alphabet**) AFI *m* (= *Alfabeto Fonetico Internazionale*)

IP address [aɪˈpiːə,drɛs] N (*Comput:* = **Internet Protocol address**) indirizzo IP

Iphigenia [,ɪfɪdʒɪˈnaɪə] N Ifigenia

iPod® [ˈaɪpɒd] N iPOD *m inv*, lettore *m* MP3

ipso fac·to [,ɪpsəʊˈ fæktəʊ] ADV (*frm*) ipso facto

IQ [,aɪˈkjuː] N ABBR (= **intelligence quotient**) QI *m*

IRA [,aɪɑːrˈeɪ] N ABBR (= **Irish Republican Army**) IRA *f*

Iran [ɪˈrɑːn] N l'Iran *m*

Ira·nian [ɪˈreɪnɪən] ADJ iraniano(-a)

■N (*person*) iraniano(-a); (*language*) iranico

Iraq [ɪˈrɑːk] N l'Iraq *m*

Ira·qi [ɪˈrɑːkɪ] ADJ iracheno(-a)

■N (*person*) iracheno(-a)

iras·cibil·ity [ɪ,ræsɪˈbɪlɪtɪ] N irascibilità

iras·cible [ɪˈræsɪbl] ADJ irascibile

irate [aɪˈreɪt] ADJ irato(-a), infuriato(-a)

Ire·land [ˈaɪələnd] N l'Irlanda; **Northern Ireland** l'Irlanda del Nord; **Republic of Ireland** la Repubblica d'Irlanda, l'Eire *f*

▷ www.irlgov.ie/

▷ www.ireland.travel.ie

iri·des·cent [,ɪrɪˈdɛsnt] ADJ (*frm*) iridescente

iris [ˈaɪərɪs] N **1** (*Anat*) iride *f* **2** (*Bot*) iris *f inv*, giaggiolo

Irish [ˈaɪərɪʃ] ADJ irlandese

■N **1** (*language*) irlandese *m* **2** (*people*): **the Irish** NPL gli irlandesi

Irish·man [ˈaɪərɪʃmən] N (*pl* **-men**) irlandese *m*

Irish Sea N: **the Irish Sea** il mar d'Irlanda

Irish·woman [ˈaɪərɪʃ,wʊmən] N (*pl* **-women**) irlandese *f*

irk [ɜːk] VT seccare

irk·some [ˈɜːksəm] ADJ noioso(-a), seccante

IRO [,aɪɑːrˈəʊ] N ABBR (*Am*) = *International Refugee Organization*

◎**iron** [ˈaɪən] N (*also fig*) ferro; (*Golf*) mazza da golf di ferro; (*for ironing clothes*) ferro (da stiro); **a will of iron** una volontà ferrea *or* di ferro; **he rules his children with a rod of iron** comanda a bacchetta i figli; **to strike while the iron is hot** (*fig*) battere finché il ferro è caldo; **to have a lot of/too many irons in the fire** (*fig*) avere molta/troppa carne al fuoco; *see also* **irons**

■VT (*clothes*) stirare

■VI: **this dress irons well** questo vestito è facile da stirare

■ADJ (*bridge, bar, tool etc*) di ferro; (*fig: will, determination*) ferreo(-a), di ferro; **an iron gate** un cancello di ferro; **an iron fist in a velvet glove** un pugno di ferro in un guanto di velluto

▶ **iron out** VT + ADV (*creases*) far sparire col ferro; (*fig: problems, disagreements*) appianare

Iron Age N: **the Iron Age** l'età del ferro

iron and steel industry N l'industria siderurgica, la siderurgia

iron chloride N cloruro di ferro

iron constitution N (*fig*) costituzione *f* robusta

Iron Curtain N (*Pol*): **the Iron Curtain** la cortina di

Ii

ferro; **Iron Curtain countries** *or* **countries behind the Iron Curtain** gli stati d'oltrecortina
iron foundry N fonderia
iron·ic [aɪˈrɒnɪk], **ironi·cal** [aɪˈrɒnɪkəl] ADJ ironico(-a); **it's ironic that ...** è un'ironia (della sorte) che...; **an ironic remark** un commento ironico
ironi·cal·ly [aɪˈrɒnɪkəlɪ] ADV ironicamente; **ironically ...** per ironia...
iron·ing [ˈaɪənɪŋ] N (*act*) stirare *m*; (*clothes*) roba da stirare; **to do the ironing** stirare; **Mother is doing the ironing** la mamma sta stirando; **I hate ironing** odio stirare
ironing board N asse *f* da stiro
iron lung N (*Med*) polmone *m* d'acciaio
iron·monger [ˈaɪən,mʌŋgəʳ] N (*Brit*): **ironmonger's (shop)** (negozio di) ferramenta
iron·mongery [ˈaɪən,mʌŋgərɪ] N (*goods*) ferramenta
iron ore N minerale *m* di ferro
iron oxide N ossido di ferro
iron rations NPL viveri *mpl* di riserva
irons [ˈaɪənz] NPL (*chains*) catene *fpl*
iron·stone [ˈaɪənstəʊn] N minerale *m* di ferro
iron sulphate N solfato ferroso
iron·works [ˈaɪən,wɜːks] NSG stabilimento siderurgico
iro·ny [ˈaɪərənɪ] N ironia; **the irony of it is that ...** l'ironia maggiore è che...; **it's one of life's ironies** è un'ironia della sorte *or* del destino
ir·ra·di·ate [ɪˈreɪdɪ,eɪt] VT (*Phys*) irradiare
ir·ra·dia·tion [ɪ,reɪdɪˈeɪʃən] N (*Phys*) irradiazione *f*
ir·ra·tion·al [ɪˈræʃənl] ADJ irrazionale; **an irrational fear** una paura irrazionale; **he had become quite irrational about it** era diventato piuttosto irragionevole al riguardo
ir·ra·tion·al·ly [ɪˈræʃnəlɪ] ADV irrazionalmente
ir·rec·on·cil·able [ɪ,rɛkənˈsaɪləbl] (*frm*) ADJ (*persons*) irreconciliabile; (*foes, enemies*) irriducibile; **irreconcilable with** (*opinion, proposal, view*) inconciliabile con
ir·re·deem·able [,ɪrɪˈdiːməbl] ADJ **1** (*failing*) incorreggibile; (*selfishness*) assoluto(-a) **2** (*Comm*) irredimibile
ir·re·den·tist [,ɪrɪˈdɛntɪst] N irredentista *m/f*
ir·refu·table [,ɪrɪˈfjuːtəbl] ADJ irrefutabile
ir·regu·lar [ɪˈrɛgjʊləʳ] ADJ irregolare
ir·regu·lar·ity [ɪ,rɛgjʊˈlærɪtɪ] N irregolarità *f inv*
ir·rel·evance [ɪˈrɛləvəns] N non pertinenza
ir·rel·evant [ɪˈrɛləvənt] ADJ non pertinente; **if he has the qualifications, his age is irrelevant** se ha i titoli la sua età non ha importanza; **he either ignored the questions or gave irrelevant answers** o ignorava le domande o dava risposte non pertinenti; **that's irrelevant** non c'entra
ir·re·li·gious [,ɪrɪˈlɪdʒəs] ADJ irreligioso(-a)
ir·re·medi·able [,ɪrɪˈmiːdɪəbl] ADJ (*frm*) irreparabile
ir·repa·rable [ɪˈrɛpərəbl] ADJ irrimediabile, irreparabile
ir·repa·rably [ɪˈrɛpərəblɪ] ADV (*damage, harm*) irrimediabilmente, irreparabilmente
ir·re·place·able [,ɪrɪˈpleɪsəbl] ADJ insostituibile
ir·re·press·ible [,ɪrɪˈprɛsəbl] ADJ irrefrenabile
ir·re·proach·able [,ɪrɪˈprəʊtʃəbl] ADJ (*conduct*) irreprensibile
ir·re·sist·ible [,ɪrɪˈzɪstəbl] ADJ irresistibile
ir·re·sist·ibly [,ɪrɪˈzɪstəblɪ] ADV irresistibilmente
ir·reso·lute [ɪˈrɛzəluːt] ADJ (*person, character*) irresoluto(-a), indeciso(-a)
ir·re·spec·tive [,ɪrɪˈspɛktɪv] **irrespective of** PREP a prescindere da; **irrespective of the weather** qualunque tempo faccia
ir·re·spon·sible [,ɪrɪsˈpɒnsəbl] ADJ (*person, behaviour*) irresponsabile
ir·re·spon·sibly [,ɪrɪsˈpɒnsəblɪ] ADV irresponsabilmente
ir·re·triev·able [,ɪrɪˈtriːvəbl] ADJ (*object*) irrecuperabile; (*loss, damage*) irreparabile
ir·rev·er·ence [ɪˈrɛvərəns] N irriverenza
ir·rev·er·ent [ɪˈrɛvərənt] ADJ irriverente
ir·rev·er·ent·ly [ɪˈrɛvərəntlɪ] ADV in modo irriverente
ir·re·vers·ible [,ɪrɪˈvɜːsəbl] ADJ irreversibile
ir·revo·cable [ɪˈrɛvəkəbl] ADJ irrevocabile
ir·revo·cably [ɪˈrɛvəkəblɪ] ADV irrevocabilmente
ir·ri·gate [ˈɪrɪ,geɪt] VT irrigare
ir·ri·ga·tion [,ɪrɪˈgeɪʃən] N irrigazione *f*
ir·ri·tabil·ity [,ɪrɪtəˈbɪlɪtɪ] N irritabilità
ir·ri·table [ˈɪrɪtəbl] ADJ irritabile
ir·ri·tably [ˈɪrɪtəblɪ] ADV (*speak*) con tono irritato; (*shrug*) in modo scontroso
ir·ri·tant [ˈɪrɪtənt] N (*annoyance*) fastidio; (*substance*) sostanza irritante
ir·ri·tate [ˈɪrɪ,teɪt] VT (*annoy*) irritare, seccare; (*skin*) irritare
ir·ri·tat·ing [ˈɪrɪ,teɪtɪŋ] ADJ (*annoying*) irritante, seccante; (*itchy*) irritante
ir·ri·ta·tion [,ɪrɪˈteɪʃən] N (*gen, Med*) irritazione *f*; (*fig: irritating thing*) seccatura
IRS [,aɪɑːrˈɛs] N ABBR (*Am*) = **Internal Revenue Service**
is [ɪz] 3RD PERS SG PRESENT *of* **be**
ISA [ˈaɪsə] N ABBR = **individual savings account**
Isaac [ˈaɪzək] N Isacco
Isaiah [aɪˈzaɪə] N Isaia *m*
ISBN [,aɪɛsbiːˈɛn] N ABBR (= **International Standard Book Number**) ISBN *m*
ISDN [,aɪɛsdiːˈɛn] N ABBR (= **Integrated Service Digital Network**) ISDN *m inv*
Is·lam [ˈɪzlɑːm] N Islam *m inv*
▹ www.bbc.co.uk/religion/religions/islam/
▹ www.islam-guide.com/
Is·lam·ic [ɪzˈlæmɪk] ADJ islamico(-a); **Islamic countries** paesi islamici
Is·lam·ist [ˈɪzləmɪst] N attivista *m/f* islamico(-a)
◎ **is·land** [ˈaɪlənd] N isola; (*also:* **traffic island**) isola *f* spartitraffico *inv*, salvagente *m*
is·land·er [ˈaɪləndəʳ] N isolano(-a)
island people NPL isolani *mpl*
isle [aɪl] N (*liter*) isola; **the Isle of Man** l'isola di Man; **the Isle of Wight** l'isola di Wight
isn't [ˈɪznt] = **is not**
iso·bar [ˈaɪsəʊ,bɑːʳ] N (*Phys*) elemento isobaro; (*Met*) isobara
iso·hy·et [,aɪsəʊˈhaɪɪt] N isoieta
iso·late [ˈaɪsə,leɪt] VT (*gen*) (*Med*): **to isolate (from)** isolare (da); (*pinpoint: cause*) individuare, isolare
iso·lat·ed [ˈaɪsə,leɪtɪd] ADJ isolato(-a)
iso·la·tion [,aɪsəˈleɪʃən] N isolamento
iso·la·tion·ism [,aɪsəˈleɪʃə,nɪzəm] N isolazionismo
iso·la·tion·ist [,aɪsəˈleɪʃənɪst] ADJ, N isolazionista (*m/f*)
isolation ward N reparto d'isolamento
iso·mer [ˈaɪsəməʳ] N isomero
iso·met·ric [,aɪsəʊˈmɛtrɪk] ADJ (*Math, Geog, Poetry*) isometrico(-a)
isom·etry [aɪˈsɒmɪtrɪ] N (*Math*) isometria

iso·mor·phic [ˌaɪsəʊˈmɔːfɪk], **iso·mor·phous** [ˌaɪsəʊˈmɔːfəs] ADJ isomorfo(-a)
iso·mor·phism [ˌaɪsəʊˈmɔːfɪzəm] N isomorfismo
isos·celes [aɪˈsɒsɪˌliːz] ADJ isoscele
iso·therm [ˈaɪsəʊˌθɜːm] N isoterma
iso·tope [ˈaɪsəˌtəʊp] N isotopo
ISP [ˌaɪɛsˈpiː] N (= **Internet service provider**) provider *m inv*
Is·ra·el [ˈɪzreɪəl] N Israele *m*
Is·rae·li [ɪzˈreɪlɪ] ADJ israeliano(-a), d'Israele
■ N israeliano(-a)
Is·rael·ite [ˈɪzrɪəˌlaɪt] N israelita *m/f*
◎**is·sue** [ˈɪʃjuː] N **1** (*matter, question*) questione *f*, problema *m*; **a political issue** una questione politica; **a controversial issue** una questione controversa; **the (real/main) issue is whether ...** la questione (reale/fondamentale) è quella di sapere se...; **to confuse** *or* **obscure the issue** confondere le acque; **to avoid the issue** eludere il (vero) problema; **to face the issue** affrontare la questione; **to make an issue of sth** fare un problema di qc; **the point/matter at issue** il punto in discussione; **to take issue with sb (over sth)** prendere posizione contro qn (riguardo a qc); **I must take issue with you over your last remark** mi dispiace, ma non sono affatto d'accordo sulla tua ultima osservazione **2** (*fam: problem*) problema; **to have issues (with)** avere problemi (con) **3** (*of stamps, banknotes, shares*) emissione *f*; (*of passports, driving licences*) rilascio; (*of rations*) distribuzione *f*; **these coins are a new issue** queste monete sono di recente emissione **4** (*copy: of newspaper, magazine etc*) numero; **back issue** (numero) arretrato; **the March issue** il numero di marzo **5** (*frm: outcome*) risultato, esito **6** (*Law: offspring*) prole *g*, discendenti *mpl*; **to die without issue** morire senza lasciare discendenti
■ VT (*book*) pubblicare; (*stamps, cheques, banknotes, shares*) emettere; (*passports, documents*) rilasciare; (*rations, goods, equipment*) distribuire; (*tickets for performance*) mettere in vendita; (*orders*) dare, impartire; (*statement*) rilasciare, diramare; (*warrant, writ, summons*) spiccare, emettere; **the minister issued a statement yesterday** ieri il ministro ha rilasciato una dichiarazione; **to issue sth to sb** *or* **to issue sb with sth** consegnare qc a qn; **the police issued a warning to people to remain indoors** la polizia ha raccomandato alla popolazione di rimanere in casa; **staff will be issued with new uniforms** al personale verranno consegnate nuove uniformi
■ VI: **to issue (from)** uscire (da), venir fuori (da)
issue price N (*Fin*) prezzo di emissione (*di azioni*)
Is·tan·bul [ˌɪstænˈbuːl] N Istanbul *f*
isth·mus [ˈɪsməs] N istmo
IT [ˌaɪˈtiː] N ABBR = **information technology**

◎**it** [ɪt] PRON KEYWORD
1 (*specific: subject*) esso(-a) (*often not translated*); (*: direct object*) lo/la, l' (*before vowel*); (*: indirect object*) gli/le; **I spoke to him about it** gliene ho parlato; **she asked him about it yesterday** glielo ha chiesto ieri; **I didn't expect to meet her at it** non mi aspettavo di incontrarci lei; **what's behind it?** cosa ci sta dietro?, cosa c'è lì dietro?; **I doubt it** ne dubito; **I've come from it** vengo da lì; **there's a mistake in it** c'è un errore; **you're just in front of it** ci stai di fronte; **I'm afraid of it** ne ho paura, mi spaventa; **I'm proud of it** ne sono fiero; **it's on it** è lì sopra; **where's my book? — it's on the table** dov'è il mio libro? — è sul tavolo; **you won't get anything out of it** non ne ricaverai niente; **put a cover over it** mettici sopra una coperta; **he agreed to it** ha acconsentito; **did you go to it?** ci sei andato?; **there's nothing under it** non ci sta niente sotto, sotto non c'è niente; **have you seen my pen/book? — I can't find it anywhere** hai visto la mia penna/il mio libro? — non la/lo trovo da nessuna parte; **here's the book — give it to me** ecco il libro — dammelo
2 (*impersonal*): **it's the 10th of October** è il 10 ottobre; **I'm against it** sono contrario; **it's cold today** oggi fa freddo; **it's easy to talk** parlare è facile; **I'm (all) for it** sono pro; **it's Friday tomorrow** domani è venerdì; **it's 2 hours on the train** sono *or* ci vogliono 2 ore di treno; **it was kind of you** è stato gentile da parte tua; **it's me** sono io; **how far is it? — it's 10 miles** quanto dista? — 10 miglia; **it's 6 o'clock** sono le 6; **it was Peter who phoned** è Peter che ha telefonato; **I like it here, it's quiet** qui mi piace, è tranquillo; **it's raining** sta piovendo, piove; **that's it!** (*approval, agreement*) ecco!, è proprio così!; (*disapproval*) basta!; (*finishing*) (questo) è tutto; **it's no use worrying** preoccuparsi è inutile; **what is it?** (*what do you want?*) cosa c'è?; **where is it?** dov'è?; **who is it?** chi è?
3 (*in games*): **you're it!** tocca a te!
ITA [ˌaɪtiːˈeɪ] N ABBR (*Brit*: = **initial teaching alphabet**) *alfabeto fonetico semplificato per insegnare a leggere*
Ital·ian [ɪˈtæljən] ADJ italiano(-a); (*lesson, teacher, dictionary*) d'italiano; (*king*) d'Italia; **our Italian teacher** il nostro insegnante di italiano
■ N (*person*) italiano(-a); (*language*) italiano; **the Italians** gli italiani; **can you speak Italian?** parli italiano?
ital·ic [ɪˈtælɪk] ADJ (*handwriting*) corsivo(-a)
ital·ics [ɪˈtælɪks] NPL (*Typ*) (carattere *m*) corsivo; **in italics** in corsivo
Ita·ly [ˈɪtəlɪ] N l'Italia; **in Italy** in Italia; **do you like Italy?** ti piace l'Italia?
itch [ɪtʃ] N prurito; **to have an itch to do sth** (*fig*) avere la smania di fare qc
■ VI (*person*) avere prurito; (*part of body*) prudere; **my leg itches** mi prude la gamba; **to be itching for sth/to do sth** (*fig fam*) aver una gran voglia di qc/di fare qc
itch·ing [ˈɪtʃɪŋ] ADJ: **itching powder** polverina che dà prurito
itchy [ˈɪtʃɪ] ADJ (*comp* **-ier**, *superl* **-iest**) (*feeling*) di prurito; **my leg is itchy** ho prurito alla gamba; **I've got itchy feet** (*fig*) mi scotta la terra sotto i piedi
it'd [ˈɪtd] PRON = **it would, it had**
◎**item** [ˈaɪtəm] N (*in list, catalogue, newspaper*) articolo; (*in bill, account*) voce *f*; (*on agenda*) argomento *or* punto all'ordine del giorno; (*in programme*) numero; **items of clothing** capi *mpl* di abbigliamento; **an item of news** una notizia; **the main item of news** la notizia più importante; **a collector's item** un articolo da collezione; **the first item he bought was an alarm clock** il primo oggetto che ha comprato è stato una sveglia; **he checked the items on his bill** ha controllato le voci del conto; **the next item on the agenda is ...** il prossimo punto all'ordine del giorno è...
item·ize [ˈaɪtəˌmaɪz] VT specificare (uno(-a) per uno(-a)), dettagliare
item·ized bill [ˈaɪtəˌmaɪzdˈbɪl] N (*of restaurant etc*) conto dettagliato; (*Telec*) bolletta con documentazione del traffico telefonico

Ii

it·er·ate ['ɪtəˌreɪt] VT (*frm*) iterare
it·era·tive ['ɪtərətɪv] ADJ iterativo(-a)
itin·er·ant [ɪ'tɪnərənt] ADJ (*actors*) girovago(-a); (*seller*) ambulante; (*preacher*) itinerante
itin·er·ary [aɪ'tɪnərərɪ] N itinerario
it'll ['ɪtl] PRON = **it will, it shall**
ITN [ˌaɪti:'ɛn] N ABBR (*Brit*: = **Independent Television News**) *agenzia d'informazioni per la televisione*
◎**its** [ɪts] POSS ADJ il suo/la sua PL i suoi/le sue; **the dog hurt its paw** il cane si è fatto male alla zampa; **this doll has lost its leg** questa bambola ha perso una gamba; **the party has concluded its annual conference** il partito ha concluso la sua conferenza annuale; **the dog is losing its hair** il cane sta perdendo il pelo
it's [ɪts] PRON = **it is, it has**
◎**it·self** [ɪt'sɛlf] PRON **1** (*reflexive*) si; **the dog injured itself** il cane si è fatto male; **the cat is washing itself** il gatto si pulisce; **the door closed by itself** la porta si è chiusa da sé; **the heating switches itself off** il riscaldamento si spegne da solo **2** (*emphatic*): **by itself** da solo; **in itself** di per sé; **it's not a problem in itself** non è un problema di per sé; **the theatre itself** il teatro stesso; **life itself** la vita stessa; **Barra, itself a beautiful island ...** Barra, di per sé un'isola bellissima...; **she is kindness itself** è la bontà fatta persona

ITV [ˌaɪti:'vi:] N ABBR (*Brit*: = **Independent Television**) *emittente televisiva indipendente*

ITV

La **ITV** è un'azienda televisiva privata che comprende una serie di canali regionali, nazionali e digitali, la prima delle quali è stata aperta nel 1955. Si autofinanzia tramite la pubblicità ed è sottoposta al controllo di un ente ufficiale, l'"Ofcom".
▷ www.itv.co.uk

IUD [ˌaɪju:'di:] N ABBR (= **intra-uterine device**) IUD *m inv*
I've [aɪv] = **I have**
ivo·ry ['aɪvərɪ] N avorio
■ADJ (*colour*) avorio *inv*; (*object*) d'avorio
Ivory Coast N: **the Ivory Coast** la Costa d'Avorio
ivory tower N torre *f* d'avorio
ivy ['aɪvɪ] N (*Bot*) edera
Ivy League N *le otto università più prestigiose del Nord-Est degli Stati Uniti (Brown, Columbia, Cornell, Dartmouth College, Harvard, Princeton, University of Pennsylvania e Yale)*
▷ www.miskatonic.net/university/ivy.html

J, j [dʒeɪ] N *(letter)* J, j *f or m inv*; **J for Jack**, *(Am)*: **J for Jig** ≈ J come jolly

J/A ABBR = **joint account**

jab [dʒæb] N *(poke)* colpo (di punta); *(Boxing)* diretto; *(fam: injection)* puntura
■ VT: **to jab sth into** conficcare qc in; **she jabbed the needle into my arm** mi ha conficcato l'ago nel braccio; **to jab a finger at sb** puntare un dito contro qn
■ VI: **to jab at** dare colpi a

jab·ber ['dʒæbəʳ] VI *(person)* ciarlare, chiacchierare; *(monkey)* schiamazzare; **they were jabbering away in Russian** parlavano fitto fitto in russo
■ VT farfugliare, borbottare
■ N *(of person)* chiacchierio, cicaleccio; *(of monkey)* schiamazzo

jack [dʒæk] N *(Tech, Aut)* cric *m inv*; *(Cards)* fante *m*; *(Bowls)* boccino, pallino; **the jack's in the boot** il cric è nel cofano; **before you could say Jack Robinson** *(fam)* in men che non si dica; **every man jack of them** *(fam)* ognuno di loro
▸ **jack in** VT + ADV *(fam)* piantare; **I've had enough: let's jack it in** smettiamo, non ne posso più
▸ **jack up** VT + ADV **1** *(Tech, Aut)* sollevare con il cric **2** *(fam: raise: prices, wages)* alzare

jack·al ['dʒækɔːl] N sciacallo

jack·ass ['dʒæk,æs] N *(also fig: old)* asino, somaro

jack·boots ['dʒæk,buːts] NPL *(Mil)* stivali *mpl* alti

jack·daw ['dʒæk,dɔː] N taccola

◎**jack·et** ['dʒækɪt] N *(garment)* giacca; *(of book)* sovraccopertina; *(of boiler)* incamiciatura; *(of potato)* buccia; **wool jacket** giacca di lana

jacket potato N *patata cotta al forno con la buccia*

jack-in-the-box ['dʒækɪnðə,bɒks] N *(toy) scatola con pupazzo a molla*; **she popped up like a jack-in-the-box** è saltata fuori dal nulla

jack-knife ['dʒæk,naɪf] N coltello a serramanico
■ VI: **the lorry jack-knifed** il rimorchio del camion si è messo di traverso

jack-of-all-trades [,dʒækəv'ɔːl,treɪdz] N uno(-a) che sa fare un po' di tutto

jack plug N *(Brit)* jack *m inv*

jack·pot ['dʒæk,pɒt] N primo premio (in denaro); **he won the jackpot** ha vinto il primo premio; **to hit the jackpot** *(fam)* vincere il primo premio; (: *fig*) fare centro

Jaco·bean [,dʒækə'biːən] ADJ *(Brit)* dell'epoca di Giacomo I

ja·cuz·zi® [dʒə'kuːzi] N vasca per idromassaggio

jade [dʒeɪd] N *(stone)* giada; *(colour: jade green)* verde *m* giada *inv*
■ ADJ *(statue, carving, necklace)* di giada; *(also:* **jade-green***)* verde giada *inv*

Jj

jad·ed ['dʒeɪdɪd] ADJ *(person)* annoiato(-a), sfibrato(-a); **to have a jaded appetite** essere un po' svogliato(-a) nel mangiare

jag·ged ['dʒægɪd] ADJ *(edge)* dentellato(-a), irregolare; *(rock, cliffs)* frastagliato(-a)

jagu·ar ['dʒægjuəʳ] N giaguaro

◎**jail**, *(Brit)* **gaol** [dʒeɪl] N carcere *m*, prigione *f*; **in jail** in prigione; **to go to jail** andare in prigione; **to send sb to jail** mandare qn in prigione
■ VT mandare in prigione; **he was jailed for 10 years** è stato condannato a 10 anni di carcere

jail·bird, *(Brit)* **gaol·bird** ['dʒeɪl,bɜːd] N *(fam old)* avanzo di galera

jail·break ['dʒeɪl,breɪk] N evasione *f*

jail·breaker ['dʒeɪl,breɪkəʳ] N evaso(-a)

jail·er, *(Brit)* **gaol·er** ['dʒeɪləʳ] N carceriere *m*

ja·la·pe·no (pepper) [,hælə'peɪnjəʊ] N peperoncino piccante

ja·lopy [dʒə'lɒpɪ] N *(fam: old car)* macinino, carretta

jam¹ [dʒæm] N *(food)* marmellata, confettura; **strawberry jam** marmellata di fragole; **you want jam on it!** *(fig fam)* vuoi troppo!, sei incontentabile!; **that's money for jam!** *(fig fam)* ti *(or* lo *etc)* pagano per far niente!
■ ADJ *(tart)* alla marmellata; *(sandwich)* con la marmellata

jam² [dʒæm] VT **1** *(block: mechanism, drawer)* bloccare; (: *machine*) far inceppare; *(subj: people, cars: passage, exit)* bloccare, ingombrare, ostruire; *(Radio: station, broadcast)* disturbare con interferenze; **to jam a door open (***or* **shut)** bloccare una porta; **streets jammed with**

people strade molto affollate; **streets jammed with cars** strade congestionate; **demonstrators jammed the city centre** i manifestanti hanno bloccato il centro; **the telephone lines are jammed** le linee sono sovraccariche; **to jam one's brakes on** frenare bruscamente **2** (*cram*): **to jam sth into sth** (*drawer, suitcase*) ficcare *or* infilare qc a forza dentro qc; (*room, vehicle*) far entrare qc dentro qc; **he jammed his hat on his head** si è ficcato il cappello in testa; **I jammed my finger in the door** mi sono schiacciato il dito nella porta
■ VI **1** (*get stuck: mechanism, sliding part*) bloccarsi, incepparsi; (*: gun*) incepparsi **2** (*press tightly: people*): **to jam into** affollare; **twenty people jammed into the tiny office** venti persone erano ammassate nel piccolo ufficio **3** (*Mus fam*) improvvisare
■ N **1** (*of people*) folla, calca; (*of shoppers*) ressa; (*of cars: traffic jam*) ingorgo **2** (*fig fam*): **to be in/get into a jam** essere/ficcarsi nei pasticci; **to get sb out of a jam** tirare qn fuori dai pasticci

Ja·mai·ca [dʒəˈmeɪkə] N la Giamaica
Ja·mai·can [dʒəˈmeɪkən] ADJ, N giamaicano(-a)
jamb [dʒæm] N stipite *m*
jam·bo·ree [ˌdʒæmbəˈriː] N (*party, merrymaking*) baldoria; (*of scouts*) raduno
jam jar N barattolo *or* vasetto da marmellata
jam·ming [ˈdʒæmɪŋ] N (*Radio*) jamming *m inv*; *disturbo intenzionale di una trasmissione*
jam-packed [ˌdʒæmˈpækt] ADJ: **jam-packed (with)** pieno(-a) zeppo(-a) (di), strapieno(-a) (di)
jam session N (*Mus fam*) jam-session *f inv*
Jan. ABBR (= **January**) gen., genn. (= *gennaio*)
jan·gle [ˈdʒæŋgl] VI (*bells*) scampanellare; (*bracelets, keys, chains*) tintinnare
■ VT far risuonare
■ N (*see vi*) scampanio; tintinnio
jan·gled [ˈdʒæŋgld] ADJ (*nerves*) scosso(-a)
jan·gling [ˈdʒæŋglɪŋ] ADJ (*bells*) scampanellante; (*bracelets, keys*) tintinnante; (*nerves*) scosso(-a)
jani·tor [ˈdʒænɪtəʳ] (*esp Am, Scot*) N (*caretaker*) custode *m*; (*Scol*) bidello
Janu·ary [ˈdʒænjʊərɪ] N gennaio; **in January** in gennaio; *for usage see* **July**
Janus [ˈdʒeɪnəs] N Giano
Ja·pan [dʒəˈpæn] N il Giappone *m*
Japa·nese [ˌdʒæpəˈniːz] ADJ giapponese
■ N (*person: pl inv*) giapponese *m/f*; (*language*) giapponese *m*; **the Japanese** i giapponesi
ja·poni·ca [dʒəˈpɒnɪkə] N cotogno del Giappone
jar¹ [dʒɑːʳ] N (*container*) vasetto; (*: of glass*) barattolo; (*: of earthenware*) vaso; **jar of honey** vasetto di miele
jar² [dʒɑːʳ] VI (*clash: sounds*) stridere; **to jar (with)** (*colours*) stonare (con); (*opinions*) discordare (da); **to jar on sb's nerves** dare ai nervi a qn; **to jar on sb's ears** dar fastidio alle orecchie di qn
■ VT (*also fig*) scuotere; (*elbow*) urtare
■ N (*jolt*) scossa, scossone *m*; (*fig*) colpo, scossone
jar·gon [ˈdʒɑːgən] N gergo
jar·ring [ˈdʒɑːrɪŋ] ADJ (*sound, colour*) stonato(-a); **to strike a jarring note (in, at)** (*fig*) portare una nota stonata (in, a)
Jas. ABBR = *James*
jas·mine [ˈdʒæzmɪn] N gelsomino
Jason [ˈdʒeɪsən] N Giasone *m*
jaun·dice [ˈdʒɔːndɪs] N itterizia
jaun·diced [ˈdʒɔːndɪst] ADJ (*fig: cynical*) cinico(-a); (*Med*) itterico(-a); **with a jaundiced eye** con occhio cinico; **to have** *or* **take a jaundiced view of things** vedere le cose cinicamente
jaunt [dʒɔːnt] N gita; **to go for a jaunt** fare una gita
jaun·ti·ly [ˈdʒɔːntɪlɪ] ADV con fare baldanzoso; **his hat was perched jauntily on his head** portava il cappello sulle ventitré
jaun·ty [ˈdʒɔːntɪ] ADJ baldanzoso(-a); **at a jaunty angle** (*hat*) sulle ventitré
Java [ˈdʒɑːvə] N (*Geog*) Giava; (*Comput*) Java *m*
jave·lin [ˈdʒævlɪn] N giavellotto; **to throw the javelin** (*Sport*) lanciare il giavellotto; **javelin throwing** lancio del giavellotto
jaw [dʒɔː] N **1** (*Anat*) mascella; **my jaw dropped** sono rimasto a bocca aperta; **the jaws of death** le braccia della morte; **to snatch victory from the jaws of defeat** strappare una vittoria ormai insperata **2 jaws** NPL (*Tech: of vice, machine*) ganascia
jaw·bone [ˈdʒɔːˌbəʊn] N mandibola
jay [dʒeɪ] N ghiandaia
jay·walk·er [ˈdʒeɪˌwɔːkəʳ] N pedone *m* indisciplinato (*nell'attraversare la strada*)
◎**jazz** [dʒæz] N (*Mus*) jazz *m*; **... and all that jazz** (*fig fam usu pej*) ...eccetera eccetera
▸ **jazz up** VT + ADV **1** (*party, room, outfit*) vivacizzare **2** (*Mus: play*) suonare a ritmo di jazz; (*: arrange*) adattare a ritmo di jazz
▹ www.bbc.co.uk/radio2/soldonsong/genres/jazz.shtml
▹ www.apassion4jazz.net
▹ www.jazzinamerica.org
jazz band N banda *f* jazz *inv*
jazzy [ˈdʒæzɪ] ADJ (*comp* **-ier**, *superl* **-iest**) (*pattern, design*) vistoso(-a), chiassoso(-a); (*rhythm*) jazzistico(-a)
JCB® [ˌdʒeɪsiːˈbiː] N ABBR scavatrice *f*
JCS [ˌdʒeɪsiːˈɛs] N ABBR (*Am*) = **Joint Chiefs of Staff**
JD [ˌdʒeɪˈdiː] N ABBR (*Am*) **1** (= **Doctor of Laws**) ≈ dottore *m* in legge **2** (= **Justice Department**) ≈ Ministero della Giustizia
jeal·ous [ˈdʒɛləs] ADJ: **jealous (of)** geloso(-a) (di); **to make sb jealous** far ingelosire qn
jeal·ous·ly [ˈdʒɛləslɪ] ADV (*enviously*) con gelosia; (*possessively*) gelosamente
jeal·ousy [ˈdʒɛləsɪ] N gelosia
jeans [dʒiːnz] NPL jeans *mpl*
Jeep® [dʒiːp] N jeep *f inv*
jeer [dʒɪəʳ] N grido di scherno
■ VI: **to jeer (at sb)** schernire (qn)
jeer·ing [ˈdʒɪərɪŋ] ADJ (*crowd*) che lancia grida di scherno; (*remark, laughter*) di scherno
■ N grida *fpl* di scherno
Je·ho·vah [dʒɪˈhəʊvə] N Geova *m*
Jehovah's Witness N testimone *m/f* di Geova
▹ www.watchtower.org/
jell [dʒɛl] VI, N = **gel**
Jell-O® [ˈdʒɛləʊ] N (*Am*) gelatina di frutta
jel·ly [ˈdʒɛlɪ] N gelatina; **fruit jelly** gelatina di frutta
jelly·fish [ˈdʒɛlɪˌfɪʃ] N medusa
jelly roll N (*Am: Culin*) *rotolo di pan di Spagna farcito di marmellata*
jem·my, (*Am*) **jim·my** [ˈdʒɛmɪ] N piede *m* di porco
jeop·ard·ize [ˈdʒɛpəˌdaɪz] VT mettere in pericolo, mettere a repentaglio
jeop·ardy [ˈdʒɛpədɪ] N: **in jeopardy** a rischio, in pericolo; **to place** *or* **put in jeopardy** mettere a repentaglio *or* in pericolo
Jeremiah [ˌdʒɛrɪˈmaɪə] N Geremia *m*
Jeri·cho [ˈdʒɛrɪˌkəʊ] N Gerico *f*

jerk [dʒɜ:k] VT (*pull*) tirare con uno strattone; **he jerked it away from me** me l'ha strappato di mano
■VI muoversi a scatti; **to jerk along** procedere a sbalzi; **the bus jerked to a halt** l'autobus si fermò con un sobbalzo
■N **1** (*movement*) sobbalzo, scossa; (*reflex*) spasmo muscolare, contrazione *f* nervosa; **he sat up with a jerk** balzò a sedere di scatto **2** (*esp Am fam*) stronzo

jerki·ly ['dʒɜ:kɪlɪ] ADV (*move*) a scatti; (*speak, laugh*) in modo convulso

jer·kin ['dʒɜ:kɪn] N gilè *m inv*

jerky ['dʒɜ:kɪ] ADJ (*comp* **-ier**, *superl* **-iest**) (*motion, speech*) convulso(-a), a scatti; (*ride*) pieno(-a) di scossoni

jerry-build ['dʒɛrɪˌbɪld] (*pt, pp* **jerry-built**) VT *costruire utilizzando materiali e tecnologie scadenti*

jerry-built ['dʒɛrɪˌbɪlt] ADJ *costruito con materiali scadenti*

jer·ry can ['dʒɛrɪˌkæn] N tanica

Jer·sey ['dʒɜ:zɪ] N (*island*) Jersey *f*; **a Jersey (cow)** una mucca di razza Jersey

◎**jer·sey** ['dʒɜ:zɪ] N (*garment*) maglia; (*fabric*) jersey *m*

Je·ru·sa·lem [dʒə'ru:sələm] N Gerusalemme *f*

jest [dʒɛst] N scherzo, facezia; **in jest** per scherzo
■VI scherzare

jest·er ['dʒɛstəʳ] N (*also:* **court jester**) buffone *m* (di corte)

Jesu·it ['dʒɛzjʊɪt] ADJ, N gesuita (*m*)

◎**Jesus** ['dʒi:zəs] N Gesù *m*; **Jesus Christ** Gesù Cristo

◎**jet¹** [dʒɛt] N **1** (*plane*) jet *m inv*, aereo a reazione **2** (*of liquid, steam, gas*) getto; (*of fountain*) zampillo **3** (*nozzle: of gas burner*) becco, ugello; (*Aut*) spruzzatore *m*
■ADJ (*aircraft, propulsion*) a reazione; (*fuel*) per aviogetto
■VI (*fam: fly*) volare

jet² [dʒɛt] N (*mineral*) giaietto

jet-black [ˌdʒɛt'blæk] ADJ nero(-a) come l'ebano; **jet-black hair** capelli *mpl* corvini

jet engine N motore *m* a reazione

jet lag N jet lag *m inv*; **to be suffering from jet lag** essere scombussolato(-a) per il cambiamento di fuso orario

jet-propelled [ˌdʒɛtprə'pɛld] ADJ (*aeroplane*) a reazione

jet·sam ['dʒɛtsəm] N *oggetti gettati in mare e portati a riva dalla corrente; see also* **flotsam**

jet set N: **the jet set** il jet-set *m inv*

jet-setter ['dʒɛtˌsɛtəʳ] N membro del jet set

Jet Ski ® N acquascooter *m inv*, moto *f inv* d'acqua

jet·ti·son ['dʒɛtɪsn] VT (*burden*) alleggerirsi di; (*hopes, chances*) abbandonare; (*Naut*) gettare in mare

jet·ty ['dʒɛtɪ] N (*landing pier*) imbarcadero; (*breakwater*) molo

◎**Jew** [dʒu:] N ebreo(-a); **the Jews** gli ebrei

jew·el ['dʒu:əl] N (*stone*) pietra preziosa; (*ornament*) gioiello; (*of watch*) rubino; (*fig*) gioiello, perla

jewel box, jewel case N (*for jewels*) portagioie *m inv*; (*for CDs*) astuccio *m* porta-CD *inv*

jew·elled, (*Am*) **jew·eled** ['dʒu:əld] ADJ ornato(-a) di pietre preziose

jew·el·ler, (*Am*) **jew·el·er** ['dʒu:ələʳ] N gioielliere(-a), orefice *m*; **jeweller's (shop)** gioielleria, oreficeria

jew·el·lery, (*Am*) **jew·el·ry** ['dʒu:əlrɪ] N gioielli *mpl*, gioie *fpl*; **a piece of jewellery** un gioiello; **jewellery box** (cofanetto) portagioie *m inv*

Jew·ess ['dʒu:ɪs] N (*offensive*) ebrea

◎**Jew·ish** ['dʒu:ɪʃ] ADJ (*mother, people*) ebreo(-a); (*festival, religion, tradition*) ebraico(-a); **he's Jewish** è ebreo; **Jewish festival** festività ebraica; **Jewish joke** *battuta improntata al tipico umorismo degli ebrei*

Jew·ry ['dʒuərɪ] N (*frm*) il popolo ebraico, gli ebrei, la comunità ebraica

jew's-harp [ˌdʒu:z'hɑ:p] N scacciapensieri *m inv*

JFK [ˌdʒeɪɛf'keɪ] N ABBR (*Am*) **1** = *John Fitzgerald Kennedy* **2** = *John Fitzgerald Kennedy International Airport*

jib¹ [dʒɪb] VI (*horse*) impennarsi; (*person*) impuntarsi, recalcitrare; **to jib at doing sth** essere restio(-a) a fare qc

jib² [dʒɪb] N (*Naut*) fiocco; (*of crane*) braccio

jibe [dʒaɪb] N = **gibe**
■VI (*Am*) combaciare, corrispondere

jif·fy ['dʒɪfɪ] N (*fam*): **in a jiffy** in un baleno, in un batter d'occhio; **wait a jiffy** aspetta un attimo

Jiffy bag ® N busta imbottita

jig [dʒɪg] N (*dance, tune*) giga

jig·ger ['dʒɪgəʳ] N bicchierino da liquore

jig·gle ['dʒɪgl] VT muovere a scatti
■VI: **jiggle around/about** muoversi a scatti

jig·saw ['dʒɪgˌsɔ:] N **1** (*also:* **jigsaw puzzle**) puzzle *m inv* **2** (*tool*) sega da traforo

ji·had [dʒɪ'hæd] N (*Rel*) jihad *f*, gihad *f*

jilt [dʒɪlt] VT piantare (*fidanzato(a)*)

jim·my ['dʒɪmɪ] N (*Am*) = **jemmy**

jin·gle ['dʒɪŋgl] N (*of keys, coins*) tintinnio; (*of bells*) scampanellio; (*advert*) jingle *m inv*, ritornello pubblicitario
■VT (*see n*) far tintinnare; far scampanellare
■VI (*see n*) tintinnare; scampanellare

jin·go·ism ['dʒɪŋgəʊˌɪzəm] N sciovinismo

jin·go·is·tic [ˌdʒɪŋgəʊ'ɪstɪk] ADJ sciovinista

jinx [dʒɪŋks] (*fam*) N (*curse*) malocchio; (*person*) iettatore(-trice); (*thing*) cosa che porta sfortuna; **to be a jinx** portare iella; **there's a jinx on him** è iellato; **to put a jinx on sb** gettare il malocchio su qn

jit·ters ['dʒɪtəz] NPL (*fam*) fifa *fsg*; **to have the jitters** avere fifa; **to get the jitters** prendersi uno spavento

jit·tery ['dʒɪtərɪ] ADJ (*fam*) nervoso(-a), agitato(-a)

jiu·jit·su [dʒu:'dʒɪtsu:] N = **jujitsu**

Jnr ABBR = **junior**

Job [dʒəʊb] N Giobbe *m*; **to have the patience of Job** avere la pazienza di Giobbe

◎**job** [dʒɒb] N **1** (*work*) lavoro; (*post*) posto, impiego; **to look for a job** cercare lavoro; **to be out of a job** essere disoccupato(-a) *or* senza lavoro; **a part-time job** un lavoro part-time *or* a mezza giornata; **a full-time job** un lavoro a tempo pieno; **this is a case of jobs for the boys** (*fam pej*) questo è il modo di sistemare amici e parenti; **the government is creating new jobs** il governo sta creando nuovi posti di lavoro **2** (*piece of work*) lavoro; (*task*) compito; **on the job** sul lavoro; **to make a good/bad job of sth** fare bene/male qc; **you've done a good job!** hai fatto un ottimo lavoro!; **he's done a good job of work** ha fatto un buon lavoro; **that's not my job** non è compito mio; **it's not my job to make the tea** fare il tè non è compito mio; **to know one's job** conoscere il proprio mestiere; **he's only doing his job** sta solo facendo il suo dovere; **I had the job of telling him** è stato compito mio dirglielo; **that car is a nice little job** (*fam*) quella macchina è un gioiellino **3** **that's just the job!** è proprio quello che ci vuole!; **to give sth up as a bad job** lasciar perdere qc perché è un'impresa impossibile; **it's a good job that ...** meno male che...; **a good job too!** meno male!; **we had quite a job getting here** *or* **to get here** è stata un'impresa arrivare qui; **he was caught doing a bank**

Jj

job (*fam*) l'hanno preso mentre faceva un colpo alla banca

job·ber ['dʒɒbəʳ] N (*Brit Stock Exchange*) jobber *m/f inv*; *intermediario tra agenti di cambio*

job·bing ['dʒɒbɪŋ] ADJ (*Brit: worker, gardener*) a cottimo

Job·centre ['dʒɒb,sɛntəʳ] N (*Brit*) ufficio di collocamento

job creation scheme N (*Brit*) programma *m* per la creazione di posti di lavoro

job description N mansionario, descrizione *f* delle mansioni (*relative ad un lavoro*)

job evaluation N valutazione *f* delle mansioni (*relative ad un lavoro*)

job hunting N: **to go job hunting** cercare lavoro

job·less ['dʒɒblɪs] ADJ disoccupato(-a)
■ NPL: **the jobless** i disoccupati, i senza lavoro *m inv*

job lot N partita di articoli disparati

job satisfaction N soddisfazione *f* nel lavoro

job security N sicurezza del posto di lavoro

job·seek·er's allowance [ˌdʒɒbsiːkəzə'laʊəns] N (*Brit*) sussidio di disoccupazione (*pagato a chi può dimostrare di aver cercato un lavoro senza successo*)

job share VI fare un lavoro ripartito
■ N lavoro ripartito

job sharing ['dʒɒb,ʃɛərɪŋ] N job sharing *m inv*; *suddivisione di un posto di lavoro tra due persone che lavorano part-time*

job specification N specifica (*relativa ad un lavoro*)

jobs·worth ['dʒɒbz,wɜːθ] N (*Brit fam*) *persona che segue pedissequamente i regolamenti sul lavoro*

Jock [dʒɒk] N (*Brit fam pej*) *termine spregiativo usato dagli inglesi per chiamare uno scozzese*

jock [dʒɒk] N (*Am fam*) *studente universitario che si distingue in campo sportivo*

jock·ey ['dʒɒkɪ] N fantino
■ VI: **to jockey for position** (*fig*) manovrare per mettersi in una posizione vantaggiosa
■ VT: **to jockey sb into doing sth** indurre qn a fare qc (con manovre)

jockey cap N berretto da fantino

Jockey shorts ® NPL boxer *mpl*

jock·strap ['dʒɒk,stræp] N sospensorio, conchiglia

jocu·lar ['dʒɒkjʊləʳ] ADJ (*person*) gioviale; (*remark*) scherzoso(-a)

jodh·purs ['dʒɒdpəz] NPL calzoni *mpl* alla cavallerizza

jog [dʒɒg] VI (*Sport*) fare jogging
■ VT (*push*) urtare, spingere; (*fig*): **to jog sb's memory** rinfrescare la memoria a qn; **to jog sb into doing sth** (*fig*) spingere qn a fare qc
■ N **1** (*pace: jog trot*) passo lento di corsa; (*: of horse*) piccolo trotto; (*run*): **to go for a jog** andare a fare jogging **2** (*push*) spinta, colpetto
▸ **jog along** VI + ADV (*vehicle*) procedere con leggeri scossoni; (*fig*): **we're jogging along** si tira avanti; **the work is jogging along nicely** il lavoro procede senza alti né bassi

jog·ger ['dʒɒgəʳ] N persona che fa jogging

jog·ging ['dʒɒgɪŋ] N (*Sport*) jogging *m*; **to go jogging** andare a fare jogging

jog·gle ['dʒɒgl] VT (*fam*) scuotere leggermente

John [dʒɒn] N (*Bible*) Giovanni

john [dʒɒn] N (*esp Am fam*): **the john** il gabinetto

◎**join** [dʒɔɪn] VT **1** (*fasten*): **to join (together)** unire, congiungere; (*link*) collegare; (*: fig*) unire; **to join hands** prendersi per mano; **to join battle (with)** (*frm*) attaccare battaglia (con); **to join A and B** *or* **A to B** unire A e B *or* A a B; **to join forces (with)** allearsi (con or a); (*fig*) mettersi insieme (a) **2** (*procession*) unirsi a; (*club*) divenire socio(-a) di; (*university*) entrare a; (*army, navy, religious order, firm*) entrare in; (*political party*) iscriversi a; **to join a queue** mettersi in fila; **to join one's ship** imbarcarsi; **to join one's regiment** raggiungere il proprio reggimento; **I'm going to join a ski club** ho intenzione di iscrivermi ad uno sci club **3** (*person*) unirsi a; **may I join you?** *or* **do you mind if I join you?** posso?, permette?; **will you join us?** (*come with us*) viene con noi?; (*in restaurant, bar*) vuole sedersi con noi?; **will you join us for dinner?** viene a cena con noi?; **hi Tony, come and join us!** ciao Tony, siediti qui con noi!; **will you join me for a coffee?** vieni a bere un caffè?; **will you join me in a drink?** posso offrirle qualcosa da bere?; **I'll join you later** vi raggiungo più tardi; **they joined us in protesting** si sono uniti a noi nel protestare **4** (*river*) confluire in, gettarsi in; (*road*) immettersi in
■ VI **1** **to join (together)** (*parts, people*) unirsi; (*lines*) incontrarsi; (*roads*) congiungersi; (*rivers*) confluire; **the car parks are joined by a footpath** i parcheggi sono collegati da un sentiero **2** (*club member*) divenire socio(-a)
■ N (*in wood, wallpaper*) giuntura; (*Sewing*) cucitura
▸ **join in** VI + PREP (*game, discussion, protest*) prendere parte a, partecipare a; **they all joined in the chorus** tutti si unirono al ritornello
■ VI + ADV partecipare; (*in singing*): **join in!** cantate con noi!
▸ **join on** VT + ADV fissare, attaccare
■ VI + ADV (*in queue*) mettersi in coda; (*part*) unirsi
▸ **join up** VI + ADV (*Mil*) arruolarsi
■ VT + ADV (*wires*) unire, collegare

joined-up ['dʒɔɪndʌp] ADJ (*writing*) corsivo(-a); (*government, thinking*) coerente ed equilibrato(-a)

join·er ['dʒɔɪnəʳ] N falegname *m*

join·ery ['dʒɔɪnərɪ] N falegnameria

◎**joint** [dʒɔɪnt] ADJ (*action, effort, work*) comune; (*responsibility*) collettivo(-a); (*committee*) misto(-a); **joint authors** coautori(-trici); **to make a joint declaration on sth** rilasciare una dichiarazione congiunta su qc
■ N **1** (*Anat*) articolazione *f*, giuntura; **I' ve got pains in my joints** ho dolori alle articolazioni; **out of joint** slogato(-a); **to put sb's nose out of joint** (*fig fam*) far indispettire qn **2** (*join*) giuntura, giunto **3** (*Brit: of meat*) pezzo di carne; (*: cooked*) arrosto (*al forno*); **joint of pork** pezzo di maiale da arrosto **4** (*fam: place: esp Am*) locale *m* **5** (*fam: cannabis cigarette*) spinello
■ VT (*chicken*) tagliare a pezzi

joint account N (*at bank*) conto comune

Joint Chiefs of Staff N (*Am*) *gabinetto del ministero della difesa*

JOINT CHIEFS OF STAFF

Si chiama **Joint Chiefs of Staff** l'organismo al vertice del ministero della difesa americano che ha il compito di coadiuvare in materia militare il presidente, il consiglio nazionale di sicurezza e il ministro della Difesa. L'organismo, fondato nel 1942, è composto da un presidente e da un vicepresidente, dai capi di stato maggiore della Difesa (aviazione, marina ed esercito) e dal comandante del corpo dei Marines.

joint·ed ['dʒɔɪntɪd] ADJ **1** (*doll*) snodabile; (*fishing rod, tent poles*) smontabile **2** (*chicken*) (tagliato(-a)) a pezzi

joint·ly ['dʒɔɪntlɪ] ADV *(held, funded)* in comune; *(agree, organize, act)* di comune accordo
joint ownership N comproprietà
joint-stock company [ˌdʒɔɪnt'stɒkˌkʌmpənɪ] N società *f inv* per azioni
joint venture N joint venture *f inv*, società *f inv* a capitale misto
joist [dʒɔɪst] N trave *f*
◎**joke** [dʒəʊk] N *(verbal)* battuta; *(practical joke)* scherzo; *(funny story)* barzelletta; **to tell a joke** raccontare una barzelletta; **to make a joke about sth** fare una battuta su qc; **for a joke** per scherzo; **what a joke!** *(iro)* bello scherzo!; **it's no joke** non è uno scherzo; **the joke is that ...** la cosa buffa è che...; **the joke is on you** chi ci perde, comunque, sei tu; **it's (gone) beyond a joke** lo scherzo sta diventando pesante; **to play a joke on sb** fare uno scherzo a qn; **I don't see the joke** non capisco cosa ci sia da ridere; **he can't take a joke** non sa stare allo scherzo; **don't get upset, it was only a joke** non prendertela, era solo uno scherzo
■VI scherzare; **I was only joking** stavo solo scherzando; **you're** *or* **you must be joking!** stai scherzando!, scherzi!
jok·er ['dʒəʊkəʳ] N **1** *(amusing)* burlone(-a); *(fam pej)* buffone(-a) **2** *(Cards)* jolly *m inv*, matta
jok·ing ['dʒəʊkɪŋ] ADJ scherzoso(-a)
■N scherzi *mpl*
jok·ing·ly ['dʒəʊkɪŋlɪ] ADV scherzosamente
jol·li·fi·ca·tion [ˌdʒɒlɪfɪ'keɪʃən] N *(hum)* festeggiamento
jol·lity ['dʒɒlɪtɪ] N allegria
jol·ly ['dʒɒlɪ] ADJ *(comp* **-ier**, *superl* **-iest**) *(person)* allegro(-a), gioviale; *(laugh)* allegro(-a), gioioso(-a); *(old: party)* piacevole
■ADV *(Brit fam)* veramente, proprio; **he's jolly lucky!** è fortunatissimo!; **you were jolly unlucky** sei stato(-a) molto sfortunato(-a); **you've jolly well got to** devi assolutamente *or* proprio farlo; **it jolly well serves you right** te lo meriti proprio; **jolly good!** *(old)* benissimo!
■VT: **to jolly sb along** *(Brit: cheer up)* cercare di tenere qn su di morale; *(: encourage)* incoraggiare dolcemente qn
jolt [dʒəʊlt] VT *(gen)* urtare; *(fig)* scuotere; **to jolt sb into doing sth** spingere qn a fare qc
■VI *(vehicle)* sobbalzare; **to jolt along** avanzare a sbalzi
■N *(jerk)* scossa, sobbalzo; *(fig)* colpo; **it gave me a jolt** *(fig)* mi ha fatto venire un colpo
Jonah ['dʒəʊnə] N Giona *m*; *(fig)* iettatore(-trice)
jon·quil ['dʒɒŋkwɪl] N giunchiglia
Jor·dan ['dʒɔːdn] N *(country)* la Giordania; *(river)* Giordano
Jor·da·nian [dʒɔː'deɪnɪən] ADJ, N giordano(-a)
Joshua ['dʒɒʃʊə] N Giosuè *m*
joss stick ['dʒɒsˌstɪk] N bastoncino d'incenso
jos·tle ['dʒɒsl] VT urtare, spintonare
■VI darsi gomitate; **to jostle against sb** urtare qn; **to jostle for a place** farsi largo a gomitate
jos·tling ['dʒɒslɪŋ] ADJ *(crowd)* che spinge
■N pigia pigia *m*
jot [dʒɒt] N briciolo; **there's not a jot of evidence** non c'è la ben che minima prova; **not one jot** nemmeno un po'
▸**jot down** VT + ADV *(ideas, notes)* buttar giù; *(address, number)* prendere
jot·ter ['dʒɒtəʳ] N *(Brit)* blocchetto
jot·tings ['dʒɒtɪŋz] NPL appunti *mpl* disordinati
◎**jour·nal** ['dʒɜːnl] N *(periodical)* rivista (specializzata); *(newspaper)* giornale *m*; *(diary)* diario; *(Book-keeping)* brogliaccio; **scientific journal** rivista scientifica; **he keeps a journal** tiene un diario
jour·nal·ese [ˌdʒɜːnə'liːz] N *(pej)* giornalese
jour·nal·ism ['dʒɜːnəˌlɪzəm] N giornalismo
▷ www.pa.press.net
▷ www.ifj.org
▷ www.icfj.org
▷ www.pulitzer.org
◎**jour·nal·ist** ['dʒɜːnəlɪst] N giornalista *m/f*
jour·nal·is·tic [ˌdʒɜːnə'lɪstɪk] ADJ giornalistico(-a)
◎**jour·ney** ['dʒɜːnɪ] N *(trip)* viaggio; *(distance, time)* tragitto; **to go on a journey** fare un viaggio; **a 5-hour journey** un viaggio *or* un tragitto di 5 ore; **my journey to school takes about half an hour** mi ci vuole una mezz'ora per andare a scuola; **to reach one's journey's end** *(liter)* giungere a destinazione; **the outward/return journey** il viaggio di andata/di ritorno; **the journey there and back** il viaggio di andata e ritorno
■VI viaggiare
journey·man ['dʒɜːnɪmən] N *(pl* **-men**) *(old)* operaio qualificato
joust [dʒaʊst] N giostra
■VI giostrare
Jove [dʒəʊv] N Giove *m*; **by Jove!** *(old)* per Giove!
jo·vial ['dʒəʊvɪəl] ADJ gioviale
jo·vi·al·ity [ˌdʒəʊvɪ'ælɪtɪ] N giovialità
jo·vi·al·ly ['dʒəʊvɪəlɪ] ADV giovialmente, con giovialità
jowl [dʒaʊl] N *(cheek)* guancia; *(jaw)* mandibola; **a man with heavy jowls** un uomo con le guance cascanti
◎**joy** [dʒɔɪ] N gioia; **to jump for joy** fare salti di gioia; **I wish you joy of it!** *(iro)* buon pro ti faccia!; **the joys of camping** *(also iro)* i piaceri del campeggio; **it's a joy to hear him** è un piacere ascoltarlo; **did you have any joy?** ci sei riuscito?; **no joy!** *(fam)* niente da fare!
joy·ful ['dʒɔɪfʊl] ADJ *(happy)* lieto(-a); *(cheerful)* gioioso(-a)
joy·ful·ly ['dʒɔɪfəlɪ] ADV *(see adj)* lietamente; gioiosamente
joy·ous ['dʒɔɪəs] ADJ *(liter)* = **joyful**
joy·ride ['dʒɔɪˌraɪd] VI: **to go joy-riding** *rubare una macchina per farsi un giro*
■N: **to go for a joy-ride** *rubare una macchina per farsi un giro*
joy·rider ['dʒɔɪˌraɪdəʳ] N *chi ruba una macchina per farsi un giro*
joy·stick ['dʒɔɪˌstɪk] N *(Aer)* barra di comando; *(Comput)* joystick *m inv*
JP [ˌdʒeɪ'piː] N ABBR = **Justice of the Peace**
JPEG ['dʒeɪpɛg] N *(Comput)* JPEG *m*
Jr ABBR = **junior**
ju·bi·lant ['dʒuːbɪlənt] ADJ giubilante; **to be jubilant** essere esultante
ju·bi·la·tion [ˌdʒuːbɪ'leɪʃən] N *(emotion)* giubilo; **she was full of jubilation at the news of her win** esultò quando seppe di aver vinto
ju·bi·lee ['dʒuːbɪˌliː] N giubileo; **silver jubilee** venticinquesimo anniversario
Ju·da·ism ['dʒuːdeɪˌɪzəm] N giudaismo
▷ www.jewfaq.org/
Judas ['dʒuːdəs] N Giuda *m*; *(fig: traitor)* giuda *m*
Ju·dea [dʒuː'diːə] N Giudea
◎**judge** [dʒʌdʒ] N giudice *m*; **to be a good/bad judge of sth** sapere/non sapere giudicare qc; **I'm no judge of wines** non sono un intenditore di vini; **he's no judge**

Jj

of character non sa giudicare le persone
■VT (*Law: assess*) giudicare; (*estimate: weight, size*) calcolare, valutare; (*consider*) ritenere; **he judged the moment well** ha saputo scegliere il momento giusto; **I judged it necessary to inform him** ho ritenuto necessario informarlo; **I judged it to be right** l'ho ritenuto giusto
■VI (*act as judge*) fare da giudice; **judging** *or* **to judge by his expression** a giudicare dalla sua espressione; **to judge for o.s.** giudicare da sé; **as far as I can judge** a mio giudizio

judge advocate N (*Brit Mil*) magistrato militare

Judge Advocate General N (*Brit Mil*) *consigliere principale in materia di diritto militare*

◎**judg·ment, judge·ment** [ˈdʒʌdʒmənt] N giudizio; **error of judgement** errore *m* di valutazione; **to pass judgement (on)** (*Law*) pronunciare una sentenza (nei confronti di); (*fig*) giudicare; **in my judgement** a mio giudizio; **it's against my better judgement, but ...** non ne sono affatto convinto, ma...

judg(e)·men·tal [dʒʌdʒˈmɛntəl] ADJ critico(-a) nei confronti degli altri

judg(e)ment call N decisione *f* ragionata

Judgment Day N il giorno del giudizio

ju·di·cial [dʒuːˈdɪʃəl] ADJ **1** (*enquiry, decision*) giudiziario(-a); **to bring judicial proceedings against sb** procedere per vie legali contro qn **2** (*mind, faculty*) critico(-a)

ju·di·ci·ary [dʒuːˈdɪʃɪərɪ] N: **the judiciary** la magistratura

ju·di·cious [dʒuːˈdɪʃəs] ADJ (*frm*) giudizioso(-a)

ju·di·cious·ly [dʒuːˈdɪʃəslɪ] ADV (*frm*) giudiziosamente

judo [ˈdʒuːdəʊ] N judo

jug [dʒʌg] N **1** (*container*) brocca, caraffa; (*for milk*) lattiera, bricco **2** (*fam: prison*) gattabuia

jugged hare [ˌdʒʌgdˈhɛəʳ] N (*Brit*) lepre *f* in salmì

jug·ger·naut [ˈdʒʌgəˌnɔːt] N (*Brit: lorry*) bisonte *m* della strada

jug·gle [ˈdʒʌgl] VI fare giochi di destrezza
■VT fare giochi di destrezza con; (*fig*) manipolare

jug·gler [ˈdʒʌgləʳ] N giocoliere *m*

jug·gling [ˈdʒʌglɪŋ] N giochi *mpl* di destrezza; (*fig*) manipolazione *f*

Ju·go·slav [ˈjuːgəʊˌslɑːv] ADJ, N = **Yugoslav**

Ju·go·sla·via [ˈjuːgəʊˈslɑːvɪə] N = **Yugoslavia**

jugu·lar [ˈdʒʌgjʊləʳ] N (*also:* **jugular vein**) (vena) giugulare *f*

◎**juice** [dʒuːs] N **1** (*of fruit*) succo; (*of meat*) sugo; **orange juice** succo d'arancia **2** (*in stomach*): **juices** NPL succhi *mpl* gastrici **3** (*fam: petrol*) benzina; (: *electricity*) corrente *f*; **turn on the juice** accendi la luce

juice extractor, (*Am*) **jui·cer** [ˈdʒuːsəʳ] N centrifuga elettrica

juici·ness [ˈdʒuːsɪnɪs] N (*of fruit*) succosità, succulenza; (*of meat*) succulenza; (*of story*) succosità

juicy [ˈdʒuːsɪ] ADJ (*comp* **-ier**, *superl* **-iest**) (*fruit*) succoso(-a); (*meat*) sugoso(-a); (*story*) piccante

ju·jit·su [ˌdʒuːˈdʒɪtsuː] N jujitsu *m*

juke·box [ˈdʒuːkˌbɒks] N juke-box *m inv*

Jul. ABBR (= **July**) lug., lu. (= *luglio*)

July [dʒuːˈlaɪ] N luglio; **the first of July** il primo luglio; **(on) the eleventh of July** l'undici luglio; **in July** in luglio; **in the month of July** nel mese di luglio; **at the beginning/end of July** all'inizio/alla fine di luglio; **in the middle of July** a metà luglio; **during July** durante (il mese di) luglio; **in July of next year** a luglio dell'anno prossimo; **each** *or* **every July** ogni anno a luglio; **July was wet this year** è piovuto molto a luglio, quest'anno

jum·ble [ˈdʒʌmbl] N **1** (*of objects, ideas*) miscuglio, accozzaglia; **a meaningless jumble of words** un miscuglio di parole senza senso **2** (*old clothes etc*) roba usata
■VT (*also:* **jumble together, jumble up**) mettere alla rinfusa

jumble sale N (*Brit*) *vendita di roba usata*

JUMBLE SALE

La **jumble sale** è un mercatino dove vengono venduti vari oggetti, per lo più di seconda mano; viene organizzata in chiese, scuole o circoli ricreativi. I proventi delle vendite vengono devoluti in beneficenza o usati per una giusta causa.

jum·bo [ˈdʒʌmbəʊ] ADJ (*fam*) maxi *inv*; **jumbo size** formato gigante
■N (*also:* **jumbo jet**) jumbo *m inv* (jet *m inv*)

◎**jump** [dʒʌmp] VI (*gen Sport*) saltare; (*in fright*) fare un salto, trasalire; (*prices*) aumentare di colpo; **to jump about** fare salti, saltellare; **to jump over sth** saltare oltre qc; **they jumped over the wall** hanno saltato oltre il muro; **to jump in/out** saltare dentro/fuori; **to jump off/on(to) sth** saltare giù da/su qc; **to jump out (of) the window** saltare giù dalla finestra; **to jump out of bed** saltare fuori dal letto; **he jumped into a taxi** è saltato su un tassì ; **she jumped to her feet** si alzò di scatto, balzò in piedi; **to jump up** saltare in piedi; **to jump down** saltare giù; **to jump up and down** saltellare; **there's no need to jump down my throat!** (*fam*) non è il caso di aggredirmi così !; **you made me jump!** mi hai spaventato!; **I almost jumped out of my skin!** (*fam*) ho fatto un salto!; **jump to it!** (*fam*) presto, sbrigati!; **to jump to conclusions** arrivare a conclusioni affrettate
■VT (*ditch, fence*) saltare; (*horse*) far saltare; (*fig: company etc*) mollare; **to jump the rails** (*train*) deragliare; **to jump bail** (*Law*) *scappare quando si è in libertà provvisoria sotto cauzione*; **don't jump the gun!** (*fig fam*) non correre troppo!; **to jump the lights** (*Aut*) passare con il (semaforo) rosso; **to jump the queue** (*Brit*) passare davanti agli altri (*in una coda*); **to jump ship** lasciare la nave senza permesso; **to jump sb** (*fam*) assalire qn
■N **1** (*gen: Sport*) salto; **to give a jump** (*also fig: nervously*) fare un salto; **my heart gave a jump** ho provato un tuffo al cuore; **in** *or* **at one jump** in un salto; **a jump in prices** un'impennata dei prezzi; **to be one jump ahead of sb** (*fig*) essere un passo avanti a qn **2** (*Showjumping*) salto; (: *fence*) ostacolo
▶ **jump at** VI + PREP (*fig*) cogliere *or* afferrare al volo; **he jumped at the offer** si affrettò ad accettare l'offerta

jumped-up [ˈdʒʌmptˈʌp] ADJ (*Brit pej*) presuntuoso(-a)

jump·er [ˈdʒʌmpəʳ] N (*Brit: sweater*) maglione *m*; (*Am: pinafore dress*) scamiciato; (*Sport*) saltatore(-trice)

jump jet N aereo a decollo verticale

jump jockey N fantino (in corsa a ostacoli)

jump leads, (*Am*) **jumper cables** NPL (*Aut*) cavi *mpl* per batteria

jump-off [ˈdʒʌmpˌɒf] N (*Horse-riding*) barrage *m inv*

jump rope N (*Am*) corda per saltare

jump seat N (*Aut*) strapuntino, seggiolino (pieghevole)

jump-start ['dʒʌmp,stɑ:t] N: **to give the car a jump-start** dare una spinta alla macchina per farla partire; (*with jump leads*) mettere in moto una macchina usando i cavi per la batteria
■ VT: **to jump-start the car** far partire la macchina spingendola; **to jump-start the economy** dare una spinta all'economia

jump suit N tuta intera

jumpy ['dʒʌmpɪ] ADJ (*comp* **-ier**, *superl* **-iest**) nervoso(-a), agitato(-a)

Jun. ABBR **1** (= **June**) giu. (= *giugno*) **2** = **junior**

junc·tion ['dʒʌŋkʃən] N (*Brit: of roads*) bivio, incrocio; (*: Rail*) nodo ferroviario

junc·ture ['dʒʌŋktʃə^r] N (*fig: critical point*) momento critico; **at this juncture** in questo frangente

June [dʒu:n] N giugno; **in June** in giugno; *for usage see* July

jun·gle ['dʒʌŋgl] N giungla
■ ADJ della giungla

◎**jun·ior** ['dʒu:nɪə^r] ADJ (*on staff, in rank*) subalterno(-a); (*section: in competition*) per ragazzi; (*with name*): **Roy Smith, Junior** Roy Smith junior; **he's junior to me** ho più anzianità di lui; **junior sizes** (*Comm*) taglie *fpl* per ragazzi
■ N (*in organization*) persona più giovane; (*Brit: schoolchild*) ≈ allievo delle scuole elementari (*da 7 a 11 anni*); **3 years my junior** *or* **my junior by 3 years** è più giovane di me di 3 anni, ha tre anni meno di me

junior executive N dirigente *m/f* di livello inferiore

junior high school N (*Am*) ≈ scuola media (*da 11 a 14 anni*)

junior minister N (*Brit Pol*) ≈ sottosegretario (di Stato)

junior miss N (*Comm: junior miss size*) misura per giovanette (*11-14 anni*)

junior partner N socio meno anziano

junior school N (*Brit*) ≈ scuola elementare (*da 7 a 11 anni*)

ju·ni·per ['dʒu:nɪpə^r] N ginepro; **juniper berry** bacca di ginepro

junk¹ [dʒʌŋk] N (*stuff*) roba; (*fam: goods of poor quality*) porcherie *fpl*; **the attic's full of junk** la soffitta è piena di cianfrusaglie
■ VT disfarsi di

junk² [dʒʌŋk] N (*boat*) giunca

junk bond N (*Fin*) junk bond *m inv*, titolo *m* spazzatura *inv*

junk dealer N rigattiere *m*, robivecchi *m inv*

jun·ket ['dʒʌŋkɪt] N **1** (*fam pej*): **to go on a junket** fare bisboccia; (*trip*) farsi un viaggetto pagato (*dallo stato*) **2** (*Culin*) giuncata

jun·ket·ing ['dʒʌŋkɪtɪŋ] N (*fam pej*): **to go junketing** fare bisboccia; (*trip*) farsi un viaggetto pagato (*dallo stato*)

junk food N cibo a scarso valore nutritivo; **to eat junk food** mangiare porcherie

junkie, junky ['dʒʌŋkɪ] N (*fam*) tossico(-a)

junk mail N posta spazzatura *f inv*

junk room N ripostiglio

junk shop N (*fam*) (bottega di) rigattiere

junky ['dʒʌŋkɪ] N (*fam*) = **junkie**

junk·yard ['dʒʌŋk,jɑ:d] N deposito di robivecchi e anticaglie

Juno ['dʒu:nəʊ] N (*Myth, Astron*) Giunone *f*

Junr, junr ABBR = **junior**

jun·ta ['dʒʌntə] N giunta

Ju·pi·ter ['dʒu:pɪtə^r] N (*Myth, Astron*) Giove *m*

ju·ris·dic·tion [,dʒʊərɪs'dɪkʃən] N (*frm*) giurisdizione *f*; **it falls** *or* **comes within/outside our jurisdiction** è/non è di nostra competenza

jur·is·pru·dence [,dʒʊərɪs'pru:dəns] N giurisprudenza

ju·ror ['dʒʊərə^r] N (*Law*) giurato(-a); (*for contest*) membro della giuria

◎**jury** ['dʒʊərɪ] N (*Law: for contest*) giuria; **to serve on a jury** far parte di una giuria

jury box N banco dei giurati

jury·man ['dʒʊərɪmən] N (*pl* **-men**) giurato

jury system N (*Law*) *sistema giuridico in cui la giuria ha un'influenza decisiva sull'esito del processo*

jury·woman ['dʒʊərɪ,wʊmən] N (*pl* **-women**) giurata

just¹ [dʒʌst] ADJ (*fair*) giusto(-a)

◎**just²** [dʒʌst] ADV
1 (*exactly*) proprio, esattamente; **just here/there** proprio qui/là; **just behind/in front of/near** proprio dietro a/davanti a/vicino a; **just when it was going well ...** proprio quando tutto andava a gonfie vele...; **just then** *or* **just at that moment** proprio in quel momento; **it's just on 10 o'clock** sono le 10 in punto *or* precise; **it costs just (on) £20** costa 20 sterline tonde tonde; **it's just what I wanted** è proprio quello che volevo; **just right** proprio giusto; **just what did he say?** cosa ha detto esattamente?; **come just as you are** vieni così come sei; **leave it just as it is** lascialo esattamente com'è; **they are just like brothers** sono proprio come fratelli; **that's just it!** *or* **that's just the point!** precisamente!, proprio così !, per l'appunto!; **that's just (like) him, always late** è proprio da lui arrivare sempre in ritardo; **just as I thought/expected** proprio come pensavo/mi aspettavo; **just as he was leaving** proprio mentre se ne stava andando; **just as you like** come vuoi; **he likes everything just so** (*fam*) gli piace che tutto sia fatto a puntino
2 (*recently, soon*) appena, or ora; **he's just done it/left** lo ha appena fatto/è appena partito; **just this minute** proprio adesso; **the book is just out** il libro è appena stato pubblicato; **we were just going** stavamo giusto andando; **just about** quasi; **I've just about finished here** qui ho quasi finito; **I was just about to phone** stavo proprio per telefonare; **I'm just coming!** arrivo subito!
3 (*only*) soltanto, solo; **it's just me** sono solo io; **just the two of us** soltanto noi due; **it's just 3 o'clock** sono le 3; **just yesterday/this morning** soltanto ieri/stamattina; **just for a laugh** tanto per ridere; **it's just around the corner** è appena dietro l'angolo; **just a minute!** *or* **just one moment!** un attimo!
4 (*simply*) semplicemente, soltanto; **it's just a mistake** non è che uno sbaglio; **I just told him to go away** gli ho semplicemente detto di andarsene; **just ask someone the way** basta che tu chieda la strada a qualcuno; **I just thought that ...** pensavo solo che...; **I just wanted to say that ...** volevo solo dire che...; **I just can't imagine** non riesco proprio a immaginare; **it's just that I don't like it** il fatto è che non mi piace; **it's just one of those things** (*fam*) così è la vita
5 (*slightly*) poco; **just over/under 2 kilos** un po' più/meno di 2 chili; **just before 5 o'clock** poco prima delle 5; **just after 5 o'clock** poco dopo le 5; **it's just after 10 (o'clock)** sono le 10 passate; **just after I arrived** subito dopo il mio arrivo; **it's just to the left/right** è subito a sinistra/destra; **just after Christmas** poco dopo Natale
6 (*barely*) appena; (*almost not*) per un pelo; **just in time** giusto *or* appena in tempo; **I had just enough money** avevo giusto i soldi che mi servivano; **just enough**

Jj

money for sth/to do sth soldi appena sufficienti per qc/per fare qc; **he (only) just caught/missed it** *or* **he caught/missed it, but only just** l'ha preso/perso proprio per un pelo
7 (*in comparison*): **it's just as good** è altrettanto buono; **it's just as good as ...** è buono quanto...; **he speaks Italian just as well as I do** il suo italiano è buono almeno quanto il mio
8 (*with imperatives*) un po'; **just imagine!** pensa un po'!; **just look at this mess!** guarda un po' che disordine!; **just wait a minute!** aspetta un momento!; **just let me get my hands on him!** (*fam*) se lo prendo!
9 (*emphatic*) veramente, proprio; **that's just fine!** va bene così !; **so you regret buying it? — don't I just!** ti sei pentito di averlo comprato? — eccome!
10 (*phrases*): **I've had just about enough of this noise!** (*fam*) ne ho proprio avuto abbastanza di questo rumore!; **it's just as well you didn't go** per fortuna non ci sei andato; **it would be just as well if you didn't mention it** faresti bene a non parlarne; **not just yet** non ancora; **just now** proprio ora; **I did it just now** l'ho fatto proprio adesso; **I' m rather busy just now** in questo momento sono molto occupato; **not just now** non proprio ora; **take an umbrella just in case** prendi un'ombrello, che non si sa mai; **just in case I don't see you** caso mai non ti vedessi; **just the same, I'd rather ...** ciononostante, preferirei...; **I'd just as soon not go** preferirei non andarci; **just my luck!** la mia solita sfortuna!

◎**jus·tice** ['dʒʌstɪs] N 1 (*Law*) giustizia; **to bring sb to justice** consegnare qn alla giustizia; **justice system** sistema *m* giudiziario 2 (*fairness*): **in justice to her, she ...** per essere giusti, lei...; **there's no justice in this world!** non c'è giustizia a questo mondo!; **she never does herself justice** non dimostra mai quello che vale; **this biography doesn't do him justice** questa biografia non gli rende giustizia; **this photo doesn't do you justice** questa foto non ti fa giustizia; **to do justice to** rendere giustizia a; **to do justice to a meal** fare onore a un pranzo 3 (*judge*) giudice *m*; **Lord Chief Justice** (*Brit*) ≈ presidente *m* della Corte d'Appello

Justice of the Peace N (*Brit*) giudice *m* di pace

jus·ti·fi·able [,dʒʌstɪ'faɪəbl] ADJ giustificabile

jus·ti·fi·ably [,dʒʌstɪ'faɪəblɪ] ADV legittimamente, a ragione

jus·ti·fi·ca·tion [,dʒʌstɪfɪ'keɪʃən] N giustificazione *f*; **in justification of** *or* **for** a giustificazione di

◎**jus·ti·fy** ['dʒʌstɪ,faɪ] VT (*behaviour, action: also Typ*) giustificare; **to be justified in doing sth** avere ragione di fare qc; **am I justified in thinking that ...?** mi sbaglio o...?

just·ly ['dʒʌstlɪ] ADV giustamente

just·ness ['dʒʌstnɪs] N (*of decision*) giustezza

jut [dʒʌt] VI (*also:* **jut out**) sporgere; **a cliff jutting out over the sea** una scogliera a strapiombo sul mare

jute [dʒu:t] N iuta

ju·venile ['dʒu:və,naɪl] ADJ (*offender*) minorenne; (*crime*) minorile; (*books, sports*) per ragazzi; (*pej*) puerile, infantile
■ N (*Law*) minorenne *m/f*

juvenile court N tribunale *m* dei minori

juvenile delinquency N delinquenza minorile

juvenile delinquent N delinquente *m/f* minorenne

jux·ta·pose [,dʒʌkstə'pəʊz] VT giustapporre

jux·ta·po·si·tion [,dʒʌkstəpə'zɪʃən] N giustapposizione *f*; **to be in juxtaposition** essere in giustapposizione

Kk

K, k [keɪ] N *(letter)* K, k *f or m inv*; **K for King** ≈ K come kursaal

K [keɪ] ABBR (= **kilo**) kg
■ N ABBR **1** *(fam: one thousand)*: **he's on 35k** prende 35.000 (sterline) **2** *(Comput: =* **kilobyte**) kB *m inv*

kaf·tan ['kæftæn] N caffettano

Ka·la·ha·ri [ˌkælə'hɑːrɪ] N: **the Kalahari (Desert)** il deserto del Kalahari

kale [keɪl] N cavolo verde

ka·lei·do·scope [kə'laɪdəˌskəʊp] N caleidoscopio

ka·lei·do·scopic [kəˈlaɪdəˌskɒpɪk] ADJ caleidoscopico(-a)

ka·mi·ka·ze [ˌkæmɪ'kɑːzɪ] N *(also:* **kamikaze pilot**) kamikaze *m inv*
■ ADJ da kamikaze

Kam·pa·la [kæm'pɑːlə] N Kampala

Kam·pu·chea [ˌkæmpʊ'tʃɪə] N la Cambogia

kan·ga·roo [ˌkæŋgə'ruː] N canguro

kangaroo court N *commissione giudicante (in carcere o all'interno di un sindacato) che si arroga il diritto di far giustizia sommaria, normalmente su questioni disciplinari*

Kan·sas ['kænzəs] N Kansas *m*
▷ www.accesskansas.org/

kao·lin ['keɪəlɪn] N caolino

ka·pok ['keɪpɒk] N kapok *m*

ka·put [kə'pʊt] ADJ *(fam)* kaputt *inv*

kara·oke [ˌkɑːrɪ'əʊkɪ] N karaoke *m inv*

ka·ra·te [kə'rɑːtɪ] N karatè *m*

kart [kɑːt] N go-kart *m inv*
■ VI: **to go karting** andare in go-kart

kas·bah ['kæzbɑː] N casba

Kash·mir [kæʃ'mɪəʳ] N Kashmir *m*

kay·ak ['kaɪæk] N kayak *m inv*

Ka·zakh·stan [ˌkæzæk'stɑːn] N Kazakistan *m*

KB [ˌkeɪ'biː] ABBR (= **kilobyte**) Kb

Kbps [ˌkeɪbiːpiː'ɛs] ABBR (= **kilobits per second**) Kbps

KC [ˌkeɪ'siː] N ABBR *(Brit Law: =* **King's Counsel**) avvocato della Corona

KD [ˌkeɪ'diː] ABBR *(Comm: =* **knocked down**) da montare

ke·bab [kə'bæb] N kebab *m inv (spiedino di carne e verdura)*; **a lamb kebab** uno spiedino di agnello

ked·geree [ˌkɛdʒə'riː] N *riso pilaf con pesce e uova sode*

keel [kiːl] N *(Naut)* chiglia; **on an even keel** *(Naut)* di pescaggio uniforme; **to keep things on an even keel** *(fig)* mantenere un certo equilibrio; **to get back on an even keel** ritornare alla normalità
▸ **keel over** VI + ADV *(person)* crollare; *(Naut)* capovolgersi

◎ **keen** [kiːn] ADJ *(comp* **-er**, *superl* **-est**) **1** *(Brit: person)* entusiasta; **he doesn't seem very keen** non sembra molto entusiasta; **she's a keen student** è una studentessa attenta e interessata; **he's a keen gardener** è un appassionato di giardinaggio; **to be keen on sth** *(opera, theatre)* essere appassionato(-a) di qc; *(plan, idea)* essere entusiasta di qc; **she's keen on the music master** il maestro di musica le piace molto; **she's very keen on pop music** le piace molto la musica pop; **to be keen to do** *or* **on doing sth** avere una gran voglia di fare qc; **I'm not keen on going** non mi va di andare; **I'm not keen to do it** non ci tengo a farlo **2** *(edge, blade)* affilato(-a), tagliente; *(wind, air)* tagliente; *(hearing)* fine; *(appetite)* robusto(-a); *(intelligence, eyesight, observation)* acuto(-a); *(desire, delight, sense)* intenso(-a), forte; *(interest)* vivo(-a); *(price, rate)* competitivo(-a); *(competition, match, struggle)* duro(-a)

keen·ly ['kiːnlɪ] ADV **1** *(acutely)* intensamente; *(deeply)* profondamente; *(fiercely)* duramente; **to feel sth keenly** sentire qc profondamente; **he looked at her keenly** le rivolse uno sguardo penetrante
2 *(enthusiastically)* con entusiasmo

keen·ness ['kiːnnɪs] N *(eagerness)* entusiasmo

◎ **keep** [kiːp] *(vb: pt, pp* **kept**) VT
1 *(retain, maintain)* tenere; **keep the change** tenga il resto; **you can keep it** lo puoi tenere; **he keeps himself to himself** se ne sta per conto suo; **to keep sb busy** tenere qn occupato(-a); **the noise kept him awake** il rumore lo teneva sveglio; **to keep time** *(clock)* andar bene; **to keep sth clean** tenere qc pulito(-a); **to keep a place tidy** tenere un posto in ordine; **she keeps herself fit** si tiene *or* si mantiene in forma; **the garden is well kept** il giardino è tenuto bene; **he has kept his looks** è ancora un bell'uomo; **to keep sb waiting** far aspettare qn; **sorry to keep you ...** scusate il ritardo...; **keep him at it!** spingilo a continuare!; **to**

Kk

keep the engine running tenere il motore acceso; **I'll keep you to your promise** ti farò mantenere la promessa; **to keep sth from sb** (*fig*) tenere qc nascosto(-a) a qn; **to keep sth to o.s.** tenere qc per sé; **keep it to yourself** *or* **under your hat** (*fam*) tienilo per te
2 (*put aside*) mettere da parte; (*store*) tenere, conservare; **keep it in a safe place** *or* **somewhere safe** tienilo in un posto sicuro; **"keep in a cool place"** "conservare in un luogo fresco"
3 (*detain, restrain*) trattenere; **to keep sb in prison** tenere qn in prigione; **I mustn't** *or* **don't let me keep you** non voglio trattenerti; **what kept you?** come mai sei in ritardo?; **to keep sb from doing sth** impedire a qn di fare qc; **to keep sth from happening** impedire che qc succeda; **to keep o.s. from doing sth** trattenersi dal fare qc; **you're keeping me from my work** mi stai impedendo di lavorare, così non riesco a lavorare; **keep him from school** non mandarlo a scuola
4 (*fulfil, observe*: *promise, vow*) mantenere; (: *law, rule, Lent*) osservare; (: *treaty, agreement*) rispettare; (: *Christmas, Easter*) celebrare; **to keep a secret** tenere un segreto; **to keep an appointment** rispettare un appuntamento
5 (*own, have*: *also Comm*: *stock*) avere; (*Agr*: *animals*) allevare
6 (*support*: *family*) mantenere; **he earns enough to keep himself** guadagna abbastanza per mantenersi da solo; **to keep sb in food and clothing** nutrire e vestire qn
7 (*accounts, diary*) tenere; **to keep a record** *or* **note of sth** prendere nota di qc; **keep a note of how much you spend** segnati quanto spendi
■ VI
1 (*continue*) continuare; (*remain*) stare, restare; **to keep (to the) left/right** tenere la sinistra/la destra; **to keep straight on** continuare dritto(-a); **to keep to** (*promise*) mantenere; (*subject, text*) attenersi a; **to keep doing sth** continuare a fare qc; **I keep forgetting my keys** continuo a dimenticare le chiavi; **to keep fit** tenersi *or* mantenersi in forma; **to keep in good health** mantenersi in buona salute; **keep trying!** prova ancora!; **keep going!** forza!; **to keep at sb** (*fam*: *pester*) non dare pace a qn; **to keep at sth** (*fam*: *continue*) continuare a fare qc; **keep at it!** (*fam*) continua, dai!; **to keep still** stare *or* rimanere fermo(-a); **to keep quiet** stare zitto(-a); **to keep together** rimanere insieme; **to keep from doing sth** trattenersi *or* frenarsi dal fare qc; **to keep to one's room/bed** rimanere in camera/a letto; **they keep to themselves** si tengono in disparte, stanno per conto loro
2 (*in health*): **how are you keeping?** come stai?; **I hope you're keeping well** spero che tu stia bene; **she's keeping better** sta meglio
3 (*food*) mantenersi, conservarsi; (*fig*: *wait*): **this business can keep** quest'affare può aspettare
■ N
1 (*livelihood*) vitto e alloggio; **to earn one's keep** guadagnarsi di che vivere
2 (*of castle*) torrione *m*, maschio; *see also* **keeps**
▸ **keep away** VT + ADV: **to keep sth/sb away from sb** tenere qc/qn lontano(-a) da qn; **they kept him away from school** non l'hanno mandato a scuola
■ VI + ADV: **to keep away (from)** stare lontano(-a) (da)
▸ **keep back** VT + ADV
1 (*crowds, tears, money*) trattenere
2 (*conceal*: *information*): **keep back some of the strawberries to decorate the cake** tieni da parte qualche fragola per guarnire la torta; **to keep sth back from sb** nascondere qc a qn
■ VI + ADV tenersi indietro; **please keep back!** indietro per favore!
▸ **keep down** VT + ADV
1 (*control*: *prices, spending*) contenere; (: *anger*) controllare, contenere; (: *dog*) tenere a bada; (*rebellion*) soffocare, reprimere; (*population*) opprimere; **you can't keep a good man down** una persona valida prima o poi emerge
2 (*food*) trattenere, ritenere
3 (*Scol*): **he was kept down a year** gli hanno fatto ripetere l'anno
■ VI + ADV tenersi giù, stare giù
▸ **keep in** VT + ADV (*invalid, child*) tenere a casa; (*Scol*) *trattenere un alunno oltre l'orario scolastico, per punizione*; (*stomach*) tenere dentro; (*elbows*) tenere giù
■ VI + ADV (*fam*): **to keep in with sb** tenersi buono(-a) qn
▸ **keep off** VT + ADV: **keep your hands off!** giù le mani!, non toccare!
■ VT + PREP (*dog, person*) tenere lontano(-a) da; **keep your hands off that cake** non toccare quella torta
■ VI + PREP: **"keep off the grass"** "non calpestare l'erba"
■ VI + ADV: **if the rain keeps off** se non piove
▸ **keep on** VI + ADV (*continue*) continuare; **keep on along this road until ...** continui per questa strada finché...; **to keep on doing sth** continuare a fare qc; **the car keeps on breaking down** la macchina continua a rompersi; **to keep on at sb about sth** (*nag*) non dare pace a qc per qc; **don't keep on so!** *or* **don't keep on about it!** basta! smettila!
■ VT + ADV (*hat, employee*) tenere; (*light*) tenere acceso(-a)
▸ **keep out** VI + ADV (*not enter*) restare fuori; **"keep out"** "vietato l'ingresso"; **to keep out of trouble** tenersi fuori dai guai; **to keep out of a quarrel** non immischiarsi in una lite; **you keep out of this!** non immischiarti!
■ VT + ADV (*exclude*: *person, dog*) tenere fuori; **this coat keeps out the cold** questo cappotto protegge dal freddo; **to keep sb out of trouble** tenere qn lontano dai guai
▸ **keep up** VT + ADV
1 (*continue*: *tradition, subscription*) mantenere; **I did French at school, but I haven't kept it up** non ho più studiato francese dai tempi della scuola; **keep up the good work!** bravo, continua così !; **he'll never keep it up!** non ce la farà mai!
2 (*maintain*: *property*) mantenere
3 (*hold up*) tenere su, sorreggere; **to keep up one's spirits** (*fig*) tenersi su di morale, non perdersi d'animo; **the noise kept me up all night** il rumore mi ha tenuto sveglio tutta la notte
■ VI + ADV
1 **to keep up with sb** (*in race*) mantenersi al passo con qn; (*fig*: *in comprehension*) seguire qn; (: *by correspondence*) mantenere i rapporti con qn; **Matthew walks so fast I can't keep up** Matthew cammina così veloce che non riesco a stargli dietro; **to keep up with sth** (*work, payments, price rises*) tener dietro a qc; **to keep up with the times** mantenersi al passo con i tempi; **to keep up with the Joneses** (*fig*) non essere da meno dei vicini

2 (*weather*) continuare; (*prices*) mantenersi allo stesso livello

keep·er ['ki:pə^r] N **1** (*in park, zoo*) guardiano; (*in museum*) custode *m* **2** (*also:* **gamekeeper**) guardacaccia *m inv* **3** (*also:* **goalkeeper**) portiere *m*

keep-fit [,ki:p'fɪt] N ginnastica
■ ADJ (*class, exercises*) di ginnastica; **I go to keep-fit classes** vado ad un corso di ginnastica

keep·ing ['ki:pɪŋ] N **1** **in keeping/out of keeping (with)** in armonia/disaccordo (con); **that modern building is out of keeping with the houses round about** quella costruzione moderna stona con le case intorno **2** (*care*) custodia; **in the keeping of** in custodia a; **in his keeping** sotto la sua custodia; **in safe keeping** al sicuro

keeps [ki:ps] N: **for keeps** (*fam*) per sempre

keep·sake ['ki:p,seɪk] N ricordo

keg [kɛg] N barile *m*, fusto

keg beer N birra alla spina

kelp [kɛlp] N (*seaweed*) laminaria

ken [kɛn] N (*old*): **beyond one's ken** al di là della propria comprensione

ken·nel ['kɛnl] N **1** (*dog house*) canile *m* **2** **kennels** NPL OR NSG (*establishment: for boarding*) canile; (: *for breeding*) allevamento di cani; **to put a dog in kennels** portare un cane al canile

Ken·tucky [kɛn'tʌkɪ] N Kentucky *m*
▷ http://kentucky.gov/

Ken·ya ['kɛnjə] N il Kenia *m*

Ken·yan ['kɛnjən] ADJ, N keniano(-a), keniota (*m/f*)

kept [kɛpt] PT, PP *of* **keep**
■ ADJ: **a kept woman/man** un(-a) mantenuto(-a)

kera·tin ['kɛrətɪn] N cheratina

kerb [kɜ:b] N (*Brit*) bordo *or* orlo del marciapiede

kerb crawler ['kɜ:b,krɔ:lə^r] N (*Brit*) *chi va in macchina in cerca di una prostituta*

kerb crawling ['kɜ:b,krɔ:lɪŋ] N: **to go kerb crawling** *andare in macchina in cerca di una prostituta*

ker·chief ['kɜ:tʃɪf] N (*old*) foulard *m inv*

ker·fuf·fle [kə'fʌfl] N (*Brit*) bagarre *f inv*

ker·nel ['kɜ:nl] N (*of nut*) gheriglio; (*of fruit stone*) nocciolo, seme *m*

kero·sene, kero·sine ['kɛrəsi:n] N (*esp Am*) cherosene *m*

kes·trel ['kɛstrəl] N gheppio

ketch·up ['kɛtʃəp] N (*also:* **tomato ketchup**) ketchup *m inv*

ket·tle ['kɛtl] N bollitore *m*; **that's a different** *or* **another kettle of fish** (*fig*) questo è un altro paio di maniche

kettle·drum ['kɛtl,drʌm] N timpano

◎ **key** [ki:] N **1** (*also fig*) chiave *f*; (*for winding clock, toy*) chiave, chiavetta; (*can opener*) chiavetta; (*on map*) leg(g)enda; **a bunch of keys** un mazzo di chiavi; **the key to success** la chiave del successo **2** (*of piano, computer, typewriter*) tasto; (*of wind instrument*) chiave *f* **3** (*Mus*) chiave *f*; **in the key of C/F** in chiave di do/fa; **major/minor key** tonalità maggiore/minore; **to change key** cambiare tonalità; **to be in/off key** essere in/fuori tono
■ ADJ (*vital: position, industry, man*) chiave *inv*; **yes, this is a key point** sì, è un punto chiave
▸ **key in** VT + ADV (*on computer: text*) digitare, battere

key·board ['ki:,bɔ:d] N tastiera
■ VT (*text*) digitare, battere

key·board·er ['ki:,bɔ:də^r] N (*on typewriter*) dattilografo(-a); (*on computer*) tastierista *m/f*

key card N scheda magnetica; (*in hotels*) chiave *f* a scheda magnetica

keyed up ['ki:d'ʌp] ADJ: **to be (all) keyed up** essere (tutto(-a)) agitato(-a)

key·hole ['ki:,həʊl] N buco della serratura

keyhole surgery N chirurgia mininvasiva

key·note ['ki:,nəʊt] N (*Mus*) tonica; (*fig*) nota dominante
■ ADJ (*speech*) programmatico(-a)

key·pad ['ki:,pæd] N tastiera numerica

key ring N portachiavi *m inv*

key signature N (*Mus*) armatura

key stage N (*Brit: Scol*) *ciclo di studi del sistema scolastico obbligatorio inglese e gallese*

key·stone ['ki:,stəʊn] N chiave *f* di volta

key·stroke ['ki:,strəʊk] N (*on keyboard*) battuta

kg ABBR (= **kilogram**) kg

KGB [,keɪdʒi:'bi:] N ABBR: **the KGB** il KGB

kha·ki ['kɑ:kɪ] N (*cloth*) tela cachi; (*colour*) cachi *m*
■ ADJ cachi *inv*

Khmer [kmεə^r] ADJ khmer *inv*
■ N (*person*) khmer *m/f inv*; (*language*) khmer *m*

Khmer Rouge N, PL INV **the Khmer Rouge** i khmer *mpl* rossi

kib·butz [kɪ'bʊts] N (*pl* **kibbutzim**) kibbutz *m inv*

ki·bosh ['kaɪ,bɒʃ] N (*fam*): **to put the kibosh on sth** mettere fine a qc

◎ **kick** [kɪk] VT (*person*) dare *or* tirare calci a; (*ball*) calciare; (*subj: horse*) tirare un calcio a; **he kicked me** mi ha dato un calcio; **he kicked the ball hard** ha dato un forte calcio alla palla; **to kick sb downstairs** scaraventare qn giù per le scale; **to kick sth out of the way** spostare qc con un calcio; **I could have kicked myself** (*fig fam*) mi sarei preso a schiaffi; **to kick the bucket** (*fig fam*) tirare le cuoia; **to kick a habit** (*fig fam*) liberarsi da un vizio
■ VI (*person*) dare calci, tirare calci; (*baby, horse*) scalciare; **to kick at sth** dare *or* tirare un calcio a qc
■ N **1** (*action*) calcio; (*of firearm*) contraccolpo, rinculo; **to take a kick at sth/sb** tirare un calcio a qc/qn; **to give sth/sb a kick** dare un calcio a qc/qn; **this cocktail's got a kick to it** (*fam*) è forte questo cocktail; **it was a kick in the teeth for him** (*fig fam*) per lui è stato uno schiaffo morale; **he needs a kick in the pants** (*fig fam*) ha bisogno di un bel calcio nel sedere **2** (*fam: thrill*): **he gets a kick out of it** ci prova un gusto matto; **to do something for kicks** fare qc per divertimento
▸ **kick about, kick around** VT + ADV: **to kick a ball about** *or* **around** giocare a pallone
■ VI + ADV (*fam: object*) essere in giro
▸ **kick against** VI + PREP lottare contro
▸ **kick back** VI + ADV (*gun*) rinculare
■ VT + ADV (*ball*) rinviare, rimandare
▸ **kick down** VT + ADV abbattere a calci
▸ **kick in** VT + ADV abbattere, sfasciare; **to kick sb's teeth in** (*fam*) spaccare la faccia a qn
▸ **kick off** VI + ADV (*Ftbl*) dare il calcio d'inizio; (*fig fam: meeting etc*) cominciare
▸ **kick out** VI + ADV: **to kick out (at)** tirare calci (a)
■ VT + ADV (*fig fam*): **to kick sb out (of)** cacciare qn via (da), buttare qn fuori (da)
▸ **kick up** VT + ADV (*fig fam*): **to kick up a row** *or* **a din** scatenare un putiferio; **to kick up a fuss about** *or* **over sth** piantare un casino per qc

kick·back ['kɪk,bæk] N tangente *f*

kick boxing N (*Sport*) kick boxing *f*

Kk

kick·er ['kɪkə^r] N (*Rugby*) *giocatore che effettua un calcio piazzato*
kick·off ['kɪk,ɒf] N (*Ftbl*) calcio d'inizio; (*fig*) inizio
kick·stand ['kɪk,stænd] N cavalletto
kick-start ['kɪk,stɑ:t] (*Brit*) N (*also:* **kick-starter**) pedale *m* d'avviamento
■VT mettere in moto (col pedale); (*fig*): **to kick-start the economy** dare una spinta all'economia
kick turn N (*Skiing*) dietro-front *m inv* da fermo
◎**kid** [kɪd] N **1** (*fam: child*) bambino(-a); (: *teenager*) ragazzo(-a); (: *son, daughter*) figlio(-a); **one of the kids was crying** uno dei bambini stava piangendo; **a gang of kids on motorbikes** una banda di ragazzi in motorino; **they've got three kids** hanno tre figli **2** (*goat, leather*) capretto
■VT (*fam*): **to kid sb (on) that ...** dar da bere a qn che...; **to kid sb about sth** prendere in giro qn per qc; **don't kid yourself!** non illuderti!
■VI (*fam: kid on*) scherzare; **I'm only kidding** sto solo scherzando; **no kidding!** sul serio!
■ADJ **1** (*fam: brother, sister*) più giovane **2** (*gloves, leather*) di capretto
kid·die ['kɪdɪ] N (*fam*) bambino(-a)
kid·do ['kɪdəʊ] N (*fam*) ragazzo(-a)
kid gloves NPL: **to treat sb with kid gloves** trattare qn coi guanti
kid·nap ['kɪdnæp] VT rapire, sequestrare
kid·nap·per ['kɪdnæpə^r] N rapitore(-trice), sequestratore(-trice)
kid·nap·ping ['kɪdnæpɪŋ] N sequestro di persona
kid·ney ['kɪdnɪ] N (*Anat*) rene *m*; (*Culin*) rognone *m*; **he's got kidney trouble** ha disturbi ai reni
■ADJ (*disease, failure, transplant*) renale, del rene
kidney bean N fagiolo comune
kidney machine N rene *m* artificiale
kidney-shaped ['kɪdnɪ,ʃeɪpt] ADJ a forma di fagiolo
kidney stone N calcolo renale
Kili·man·ja·ro [,kɪlɪmən'dʒɑ:rəʊ] N (*also:* **Mount Kilimanjaro**) il Kilimangiaro
◎**kill** [kɪl] VT **1** uccidere, ammazzare; **she killed her husband** ha ucciso suo marito; **sixteen people were killed in the accident** nell'incidente sono rimaste uccise sedici persone; **he was killed in a car accident** è morto in un incidente stradale; **luckily, nobody was killed** fortunatamente non ci sono state vittime; **to be killed in action** essere ucciso(-a) in combattimento; **to kill two birds with one stone** (*fig*) prendere due piccioni con una fava; **this heat is killing me** (*fig fam*) sto morendo di caldo; **my feet are killing me** (*fam*) i piedi mi fanno male da morire; **he killed himself** si è ucciso; **he was killing himself laughing** (*fam*) moriva dal ridere *or* dalle risate; **he certainly wasn't killing himself!** (*fig hum*) di sicuro non si ammazzava di fatica! **2** (*fig: pain*) togliere; (: *rumour*) mettere fine a; (: *story*) rovinare, guastare; (: *paragraph, line*) sopprimere; (*newspaper article*) impedire la pubblicazione di, far saltare; (: *feeling, hope*) distruggere; (: *flavour, smell*) soffocare; (: *sound*) attutire, smorzare; (: *engine, motor*) fermare, spegnere; **to kill time** ammazzare il tempo
■N (*Hunting, Bullfighting*) uccisione *f*; **to be in at the kill** (*fig*) essere presente al colpo di grazia
▸ **kill off** VT + ADV sterminare; (*fig*) eliminare; (: *rumour*) soffocare
◎**kill·er** ['kɪlə^r] N (*murderer*) assassino(-a); (: *hired*) killer *m/f inv*; **the police are searching for the killer** la polizia sta cercando l'assassino; **flu can be a killer** si può morire per un'influenza
■ADJ (*disease*) mortale
killer app N (*Comput:* = **killer application**) applicazione *f* estremamente diffusa
killer instinct N (*fig*): **he has the killer instinct** sa essere spietato
killer whale N orca
◎**kill·ing** ['kɪlɪŋ] N (*murder*) uccisione *f*; (*massacre*) strage *f*; (*fam*) (: *profit*) colpaccio; **a brutal killing** un brutale assassinio; **to make a killing** fare un colpaccio
■ADJ (*blow*) mortale; (*fig: work*) estenuante; (*fam: funny*) divertentissimo(-a)
kill·joy ['kɪl,dʒɔɪ] N guastafeste *m/f*
kiln [kɪln] N fornace *f*
kilo ['ki:ləʊ] N chilo; **£5 a kilo** cinque sterline al chilo
kilo·byte ['kɪləʊbaɪt] N kilobyte *m inv*
kilo·gram, **kilo·gramme** ['kɪləʊgræm] N chilogrammo
kilo·hertz ['kɪləʊ,hɜ:ts] N chilohertz *m inv*
◎**kilo·metre** ['kɪləʊ,mi:tə^r], (*Am*) **kilo·meter** [kɪ'lɒmɪtə^r] N chilometro
kilo·watt ['kɪləʊwɒt] N chilowatt *m inv*
kilt [kɪlt] N kilt *m inv*
kilt·ed ['kɪltɪd] ADJ (*man*) in kilt; **a kilted skirt** un kilt *m inv*
kil·ter ['kɪltə^r] N (*fam*): **out of kilter** fuori fase
ki·mo·no [kɪ'məʊnəʊ] N chimono
kin [kɪn] N parenti *mpl*, familiari *mpl*; *see also* **kith, next of kin**
◎**kind** [kaɪnd] N (*species*) sorta, specie *f*, genere *m*; **all kinds of things** ogni genere di cose; **some kind of fish** qualche tipo di pesce; **it's a kind of sausage** è una specie di salsiccia; **he's not the kind of person to ...** non è il tipo da...; **what kind of an answer is that?** *or* **what kind of an answer do you call that?** che razza di risposta è questa?; **what kind of person do you take me for?** per chi mi prendi?; **I had a kind of feeling that would happen** avevo come il presentimento che sarebbe successo; **you know the kind of thing I mean** sai cosa intendo *or* voglio dire; **something of the kind** qualcosa del genere; **nothing of the kind!** niente affatto!; **it's not his kind of film** non è il tipo *or* genere di film che piace a lui, non è il suo genere di film; **they're two of a kind** (*pej*) sono della stessa pasta; **it's the only one of its kind** è l'unico nel suo genere; **it was tea of a kind** (*pej*) era una sottospecie di tè; **I kind of thought this would happen** (*fam*) quasi me l'aspettavo; **she looked kind of worried** (*fam*) sembrava come preoccupata; **payment in kind** pagamento in natura; **to repay sb in kind** (*after good deed*) ricambiare la cortesia a qn; (*after bad deed*) ripagare qn con la stessa moneta
■ADJ (*comp* **-er**, *superl* **-est**) gentile, buono(-a); **to be kind to sb** essere gentile con qn; **would you be kind enough to ...?** sarebbe così gentile da...?; **would you be so kind as to ...?** le spiacerebbe...?; **thank you for being so kind** grazie mille; **it's very kind of you (to do ...)** è molto gentile da parte sua (fare...); **thank you for your kind assistance** (*frm*) la ringrazio per il gentile aiuto
kin·der·gar·ten ['kɪndə,gɑ:tn] N asilo
kind-hearted [,kaɪnd'hɑ:tɪd] ADJ buono(-a), di buon cuore
kind-heartedness [,kaɪnd'hɑ:tɪdnɪs] N bontà, buon cuore *m*
kin·dle ['kɪndl] VT (*wood*) appiccare il fuoco a; (*fire*) accendere; (*emotion, interest*) suscitare
kind·li·ness ['kaɪndlɪnɪs] N gentilezza

kin·dling ['kındlıŋ] N frasche *fpl*, ramoscelli *mpl*

kind·ly ['kaındlı] ADJ (*comp* **-ier**, *superl* **-iest**) (*person, smile, tone*) benevolo(-a), affabile; (*gesture*) gentile
■ ADV (*speak, act*) con gentilezza, gentilmente; **they kindly offered to lend me some money** si sono offerti gentilmente di prestarmi del denaro; **kindly wait a moment** abbia la cortesia *or* gentilezza di aspettare un momento; **will you kindly ...** vuole... per cortesia; **kindly refrain from smoking** si prega di non fumare; **he doesn't take kindly to being kept waiting** non gli piace affatto dover aspettare; **he didn't take it kindly** non l'ha presa molto bene

kind·ness ['kaındnıs] N (*towards sb*) gentilezza, bontà; (*act*) gentilezza; **out of the kindness of her heart** per bontà d'animo; **to do sb a kindness** fare una cortesia *or* una gentilezza a qn

kin·dred ['kındrıd] ADJ (*tribes, peoples*) imparentato(-a); (*language*) affine; **to have a kindred feeling for sb** sentirsi molto vicino(-a) a qn
■ N (*relations*) familiari *mpl*, parenti *mpl*

kindred spirit N spirito affine

ki·net·ic [kı'nɛtık] ADJ cinetico(-a)

ki·net·ics [kı'nɛtıks] NSG cinetica

◎ **king** [kıŋ] N (*also fig: Chess, Cards*) re *m inv*; (*Draughts*) dama

king·cup ['kıŋ,kʌp] N (*flower*) botton *m* d'oro

king·dom ['kıŋdəm] N regno, reame *m*; **the Kingdom of Heaven** il Regno dei Cieli; **till kingdom come** (*fam*) fino al giorno del giudizio

king·fisher ['kıŋ,fıʃə^r] N martin *m inv* pescatore

king·ly ['kıŋlı] ADJ (*virtues, bearing*) regale; (*palace*) reale

king·pin ['kıŋ,pın] N (*Tech, fig*) perno

king-size ['kıŋ,saız], **king-sized** ['kıŋ,saızd] ADJ (*gen: object, bed*) king size *inv*, più grande del normale; (*packet*) formato gigante *inv*; (*cigarette*) king size, lungo(-a)

kink [kıŋk] N (*in rope*) attorcigliamento; (*in hair*) riccio; (*fig: emotional, psychological, sexual*) aberrazione *f*
■ VI attorcigliarsi

kinky ['kıŋkı] ADJ (*comp* **-ier**, *superl* **-iest**) (*hair*) crespo(-a); (*fam: sexually*) dai gusti particolari; (*: person, idea, fashion*) stravagante, eccentrico(-a)

kin·ship ['kınʃıp] N parentela

kins·man ['kınzmən] N (*pl* **-men**) (*old*) congiunto

kins·woman ['kınz,wʊmən] N (*pl* **-women**) (*old*) congiunta

ki·osk ['ki:ɒsk] N (*gen*) chiosco; (*Brit: also:* **telephone kiosk**) cabina telefonica; (*also:* **newspaper kiosk**) edicola

kip [kıp] (*fam*) VI dormire
■ N dormita; **to get some kip** fare una dormita

kip·per ['kıpə^r] N aringa affumicata

Kir·ghi·zia [,kɜ:'gızıə] N Kirghizistan *m*

kirk [kɜ:k] N (*Scot*) chiesa; **the Kirk** *la Chiesa presbiteriana scozzese*

◎ **kiss** [kıs] VT baciare; **he kissed her passionately** l'ha baciata appassionatamente; **to kiss sb goodbye** congedarsi da qn con un bacio; **to kiss sb goodnight** dare a qn il bacio della buonanotte; **to kiss sb's hand** baciare la mano a qn
■ VI: **to kiss (each other)** baciarsi; **they kissed** si sono baciati
■ N bacio

kissa·gram ['kısə,græm] N *servizio-burla in cui un(a) modello(a) viene incaricato(a) di porgere gli auguri baciando il(la) festeggiato(a)*

kiss of death N (*fam*): **the kiss of death** il colpo di grazia

kiss of life N (*esp Brit*): **to give the kiss of life** fare la respirazione bocca a bocca

kit [kıt] N **1** (*equipment: gen*) kit *m inv*, attrezzatura; (*Mil*) equipaggiamento; (*Sport: outfit*) tenuta; (*: gear*) attrezzi *mpl*; (*tools*) arnesi *mpl*; **I've forgotten my gym kit** ho dimenticato la roba da ginnastica; **a tool kit** un kit di attrezzi; **a sewing kit** un kit da cucito; **a first aid kit** una cassetta del pronto soccorso; **a puncture repair kit** l'attrezzatura per riparare la gomma; **a drum kit** una batteria **2** (*parts for assembly*) kit *m inv* di montaggio; **kitchen units in kit form** mobili *mpl* per cucina in kit di montaggio; **toy aircraft kit** kit per aeromodellismo
▸ **kit out** VT + ADV (*Brit*) attrezzare, equipaggiare

kit·bag ['kıt,bæg] N (*Mil*) sacco militare; (*Sport*) sacca sportiva

◎ **kitch·en** ['kıtʃın] N cucina; **a fitted kitchen** una cucina componibile; **the kitchen units** gli elementi della cucina
■ ADJ (*cupboard, equipment etc*) da cucina; **a kitchen knife** un coltello da cucina

kitchen cabinet N **1** (*cupboard*) mobile della cucina **2** (*fig: Pol: Brit*) stretti collaboratori del Primo Ministro; (*: Am*) stretti collaboratori del Presidente

kitch·en·ette [,kıtʃı'nɛt] N cucinino

kitchen foil N carta di alluminio

kitchen garden N orto

kitchen knife N coltello da cucina

kitchen roll, kitchen paper, kitchen towel (*Brit*) N Scottex® *f inv*, carta assorbente (da cucina)

kitchen sink N lavello, acquaio; **to take everything but the kitchen sink** (*fam hum*) portarsi dietro tutta la casa

kitchen sink drama N (*fam*) *teatro degli anni '50 rappresentante gli aspetti quotidiani della vita della classe operaia*

kitchen unit N (*Brit*) (mobile *m*) componibile *m* da cucina

kitchen·ware ['kıtʃın,wɛə] N (*dishes*) stoviglie *fpl*; (*equipment*) utensili *mpl* da cucina

kite [kaıt] N (*toy*) aquilone *m*; (*bird*) nibbio

kith [kıθ] N: **kith and kin** (*old*) amici *mpl* e parenti *mpl*

kitsch [kıtʃ] N kitsch *m inv*
■ ADJ kitsch *inv*

kit·ten ['kıtn] N gattino(-a); **I had kittens when ...** (*fig fam*) mi è venuto un colpo quando...

kit·ten·ish ['kıtənıʃ] ADJ da gattina

kit·ti·wake ['kıtı,weık] N gabbiano tridattilo

kit·ty ['kıtı] N **1** (*funds*) cassa comune; (*: Cards*) posta **2** (*fam: cat*) micio(-a), micino(-a)

kiwi ['ki:wi:] N kiwi *m inv*; (*fam: New Zealander*) neozelandese *m/f*

kiwi fruit N kiwi *m inv*

KKK [,keıkeı'keı] N ABBR = **Ku Klux Klan**

Kleen·ex® ['kli:neks] N kleenex® *m inv*, fazzoletto di carta

klep·to·ma·nia [,klɛptəʊ'meınıə] N (*Psych*) cleptomania

klep·to·ma·ni·ac [,klɛptəʊ'meınıæk] N cleptomane *m/f*

kludge [klʌdʒ] N (*Comput*) soluzione *f* poco ortodossa ma efficace

klutz [klʌts] N (*Am fam*) imbranato(-a)

km ABBR (= **kilometre**) km

km/h ABBR (= **kilometres per hour**) km/h

knack [næk] N abilità, capacità; **to get the knack of sth** farsi la mano in qc; **to have the knack of doing**

Kk

sth avere l'abilità di fare qc; **to learn the knack of doing sth** imparare la tecnica per fare qc; **there's a knack to doing this** c'è un trucco per fare questo

knack·ered ['nækəd] ADJ (*Brit fam*) fuso(-a)

knap·sack ['næp,sæk] N (*rucksack*) zainetto; (*shoulder bag*) tascapane *m*

knave [neɪv] N (*old*) furfante *m*; (*Cards*) fante *m*

knead [ni:d] VT (*dough, clay*) impastare, lavorare; (*muscle*) massaggiare

◎ **knee** [ni:] N (*Anat: of garment*) ginocchio; **I've hurt my knee** mi sono fatto male al ginocchio; **on one's knees** in ginocchio; **on one's hands and knees** carponi; **to go down on one's knees (to sb)** inginocchiarsi (davanti a qn)

knee-bend ['ni:,bɛnd] N flessione *f or* piegamento delle ginocchia

knee·cap ['ni:,kæp] N (*Anat*) rotula
■ VT gambizzare

knee·cap·ping ['ni:,kæpɪŋ] N gambizzazione *f*

knee-deep ['ni:'di:p] ADJ fino al ginocchio; **the water was knee-deep** l'acqua ci arrivava alle ginocchia

knee-high ['ni:'haɪ] ADJ che arriva al ginocchio

kneel [ni:l] (*pt, pp* **knelt**) VI (*also:* **kneel down**) inginocchiarsi

knee·pad ['ni:,pæd] N ginocchiera

knees-up ['ni:zʌp] N (*Brit*): **to have a knees-up** (*old: to dance*) fare quattro salti; (*drink*) farsi una bevuta

knell [nɛl] N (*liter: death knell*) campana a morto

knelt [nɛlt] PT, PP *of* **kneel**

knew [nju:] PT *of* **know**

knick·er·bock·ers ['nɪkə,bɒkəz] N knickerbockers *mpl*

knick·ers ['nɪkəz] NPL (*Brit*) slip *m inv* (*da donna*), mutandine *fpl*; **a pair of knickers** un paio di slip

knick-knack ['nɪk,næk] N ninnolo

◎ **knife** [naɪf] N (*pl* **knives**) (*gen*) coltello; (*also:* **penknife**) temperino; **a sharp knife** un coltello affilato; **knife, fork and spoon** coperto; **I can't wait to get my knife into him** (*fig*) non vedo l'ora di cavargli gli occhi
■ VT (*stab*) accoltellare; **to knife sb to death** uccidere qn a coltellate

knife edge N: **to be on a knife edge** (*fig: person*) stare *or* camminare sul filo del rasoio; (*: hope, result*) essere appeso(-a) a un filo; **the success of the scheme was balanced on a knife edge** la riuscita del progetto era appesa ad un filo

knife grinder N arrotino

knife pleat N: **a skirt with knife pleats** una gonna a pieghe sovrapposte

knife-sharpener ['naɪf,ʃɑ:pnəʳ] N (*tool*) affilacoltelli *m inv*

knight [naɪt] N cavaliere *m*; (*Chess*) cavallo
■ VT nominare cavaliere

knight·hood ['naɪthud] N (*Brit: title*) cavalierato; **to get a knighthood** essere nominato cavaliere

knit [nɪt] VT (*garment*) lavorare a maglia *or* a ferri; **to knit together** (*fig*) unire; **to knit one's brows** aggrottare le sopracciglia
■ VI **1** (*make garment*) lavorare a maglia **2** (*also:* **knit together**: *broken bones*) saldarsi; (*: people*) andare d'accordo

knit·ted ['nɪtɪd] ADJ lavorato(-a) a maglia

knit·ting ['nɪtɪŋ] N (*activity*) il lavorare *m* a maglia; (*product*) lavoro a maglia; **I like knitting** mi piace lavorare a maglia
▷ www.woolworks.org
▷ www.knitting-and-crochet-guild.org.uk

knitting machine N macchina per maglieria

knitting needle N ferro da calza

knitting pattern N modello per maglia

knit·wear ['nɪt,wɛəʳ] N maglieria

knives [naɪvz] NPL *of* **knife**

knob [nɒb] N pomo, pomello; (*on radio, TV*) manopola; **a knob of butter** (*Brit*) una noce *f* di burro; (*Brit fam!*) cazzo

knob·bly ['nɒblɪ], (*Am*) **knob·by** ['nɒbɪ] ADJ (*comp* **-ier**, *superl* **-iest**) (*wood, surface*) nodoso(-a); (*knee*) ossuto(-a)

◎ **knock** [nɒk] VT
1 (*strike*) colpire; **to knock a nail into sth** conficcare un chiodo in qc; **to knock sb on the head** colpire qn in *or* alla testa; **to knock one's head on/against sth** battere *or* sbattere la testa su/contro qc; **to knock sb unconscious** *or* **out** *or* **cold** tramortire qn; **to knock the bottom out of sth** (*box*) sfondare qc; (*fig: argument*) demolire qc; **he knocked the knife out of her hand** con un colpo le ha fatto cadere il coltello di mano; **to knock spots off sb/sth** (*fig fam*) dare dei punti a qn/qc; **to knock sb sideways** *or* **for six** (*fig fam*) lasciare qn di stucco; **to knock some sense into sb** (*fam*) far entrare un po' di buonsenso in testa a qn
2 (*fam: criticize*) criticare
■ VI
1 (*strike*) bussare; **he knocked at** *or* **on the door** ha bussato alla porta; **his knees were knocking** gli tremavano le ginocchia
2 (*bump*): **to knock into** *or* **against sb/sth** sbattere *or* urtare contro qn/qc
3 (*engine*) battere in testa
■ N
1 (*blow*) colpo; (*in collision*) botta; **there was a knock at the door** hanno bussato alla porta; **I heard a knock** ho sentito bussare; **his pride took a knock** il suo orgoglio ha subito un duro colpo
2 (*in engine*) battito in testa

▶ **knock about, knock around** VT + ADV (*person, object*) maltrattare
■ VI + ADV (*fam: person*) vagabondare; (*: thing*): **it's knocking around here somewhere** è qui in giro, da qualche parte

▶ **knock back** VT + ADV (*fam*)
1 (*drink*) scolare, tracannare
2 (*cost*): **it knocked me back £100** mi è costato la bellezza di 100 sterline

▶ **knock down** VT + ADV
1 (*building*) demolire; (*person*) gettare a terra, stendere; (*pedestrian*) investire; (*tree*) abbattere; (*door*) buttare giù; **she was knocked down by a car** è stata investita da una macchina; **you could have knocked me down with a feather!** mi sono cadute le braccia!
2 (*price*) abbassare; (*object at auction*) aggiudicare

▶ **knock in** VT + ADV (*nail*) conficcare

▶ **knock off** VT + ADV
1 (*strike off: vase on shelf*) far cadere; (*fig: from price, record*): **to knock off £10** *or* **knock £10 off the price** fare uno sconto di 10 sterline
2 (*fam: steal*) sgraffignare, fregare
3 (*fam: do quickly*) buttare giù
4 (*fam: stop*): **knock it off!** piantala!
■ VI + ADV (*fam: stop work*) smontare, staccare

▶ **knock out** VT + ADV
1 (*stun*) stordire, stendere; (*Boxing*) mettere k.o. *or* fuori combattimento; **they knocked out the watchman** hanno stordito il guardiano
2 (*nails*) far uscire, levare; (*in fight: teeth*) spaccare; **to knock out one's pipe** svuotare la pipa

3 (*eliminate: in competition*) eliminare; **they were knocked out early in the tournament** sono stati eliminati all'inizio del torneo

▸ **knock over** VT + ADV (*object*) far cadere; (*pedestrian*) investire

▸ **knock together** VT + ADV

1 (*two objects*) battere uno contro l'altro

2 (*make hastily*) mettere insieme alla svelta, arrangiare alla meglio

▸ **knock up** VT + ADV

1 (*handle, lever*) tirare in alto

2 (*Brit: waken*) svegliare bussando alla porta

3 (*make hastily*) = **knock together 2**

knock·down ['nɒk,daʊn] ADJ (*price*) stracciato(-a)

knock·er ['nɒkə^r] N (*on door*) battente *m*; **knockers** NPL (*fam!*) tette *fpl*

knock-for-knock agree·ment ['nɒkfə'nɒkə'gri:mənt] N (*Brit*) *accordo fra assicurazioni auto per risarcire i propri clienti indipendentemente dalla responsabilità*

knock·ing ['nɒkɪŋ] N colpi *mpl*

knocking-off time ['nɒkɪŋ'ɒf,taɪm] N: **knocking-off time is six o'clock** si stacca *or* si smonta alle sei

knock-kneed [,nɒk'ni:d] ADJ che ha le gambe a X

knock·off ['nɒkɒf] N (*Brit fam*) imitazione *f*

knock-on ['nɒk'ɒn] ADJ: **knock-on effect** reazione *f* a catena

knock·out ['nɒk,aʊt] N 1 (*Boxing*) knock out *m inv*- (*fam: person*) schianto, cannonata

knockout competition N gara ad eliminazione

knockout drops NPL (*fam*) sonnifero

knock-up ['nɒk,ʌp] N (*Tennis*) palleggio; **to have a knock-up** palleggiare

knoll [nəʊl] N poggio

knot [nɒt] N (*in rope, wood: also Naut: speed*) nodo; (*group: of people*) capannello; **to tie a knot** fare un nodo; **to tie o.s. up in knots** (*fig*) ingarbugliarsi

■ VT fare un nodo a, annodare; **to knot together** annodare insieme

knot·grass ['nɒt,grɑ:s] N centinodia

knot·ty ['nɒtɪ] ADJ (*comp* **-ier**, *superl* **-iest**) (*wood*) nodoso(-a); (*fig: problem*) spinoso(-a)

◎ **know** [nəʊ] (*vb: pt* **knew**, *pp* **known**) VT

1 (*facts, dates*) sapere; **to know that ...** sapere che...; **to get to know sth** venire a sapere qc; **to know how to do sth** saper fare qc; **I don't know any German** non so una parola di tedesco; **he knows a lot about cars** sa molte cose sulle macchine; **he knows all the answers** sa rispondere a tutte le domande; (*pej*) sa sempre tutto; **he knows what he's talking about** parla con cognizione di causa; **to know one's (own) mind** sapere ciò che si vuole; **I know nothing about it** non ne so niente; **there's no knowing what may happen** chissà cosa succederà; **it soon became known that ...** si è presto venuto a sapere che...; **to make sth known to sb** far sapere qc a qn; **he is known to have been there** si sa che c'è stato; **it's worth knowing what/how** *etc* **...** vale la pena sapere che cosa/come *etc*...; **to know sth backwards** conoscere qc a menadito; **let me know how you get on** fammi sapere come va; **you know how it is** sai com'è; **I knew it!** lo sapevo!

2 (*be acquainted with: person, place, author, subject*) conoscere; **I don't know him** non lo conosco; **I know London well** conosco bene Londra; **to know sb by sight/by name** conoscere qn di vista/di nome; **to get to know sb** (*gradually*) conoscere meglio qn; (*for the first time*) conoscere qn; **I don't know him to speak to** lo conosco solo di vista; **to make o.s. known to sb** presentarsi a qn; **he is known as X** è conosciuto con *or* sotto il nome di X

3 (*recognize*) riconoscere; **I knew him by his voice** l'ho riconosciuto dalla voce; **she knows a good painting when she sees one** sa riconoscere un buon dipinto; **to know the difference between ...** saper distinguere fra...; **to know right from wrong** distinguere il bene dal male

■ VI sapere; **as far as I know ...** che io sappia..., per quanto ne so io...; **we'll let you know** le faremo sapere; **how should I know?** come vuoi che lo sappia?; **you never know!** non si sa mai!; **no, not that I know of** no, che io sappia; **there's no (way of) knowing** non c'è modo di saperlo; **it's not easy, you know** non è facile, sai; **yes, I know** sì , lo so; **I don't know** non lo so; **you ought to know better (than to ...)** dovresti saperlo da solo (che non è il caso di...); **she says she didn't do it, but I know better** ha detto che non è stata lei, ma a me non la fa; **he doesn't know any better** non ha criterio *or* giudizio; **you know best** nessuno può saperlo meglio di te; **(well,) what do you know!** (*fam*) chi l'avrebbe mai detto!; **to know about** *or* **of sth** essere a conoscenza di qc; **to know about** *or* **of sb** aver sentito parlare di qn; **to get to know about sth** venire a sapere qc; **how many "don't knows" are there?** quanti sono gli incerti?

■ N: **to be in the know** (*fam*) essere al corrente, essere beninformato(-a)

know·able ['nəʊəbl] ADJ conoscibile

know-all ['nəʊɔ:l] N (*Brit pej*) sapientone(-a); **he's such a know-all!** è un gran sapientone!

◎ **know-how** ['nəʊ,haʊ] N know-how *m inv*

know·ing ['nəʊɪŋ] ADJ (*look, smile*) d'intesa; (*shrewd*) scaltro(-a)

know·ing·ly ['nəʊɪŋlɪ] ADV (*intentionally*) deliberatamente; (*smile, look*) con aria d'intesa

know-it-all ['nəʊɪt,ɔ:l] N (*Am*) = **know-all**

◎ **knowl·edge** ['nɒlɪdʒ] N 1 (*information, awareness, understanding*) conoscenza; **to have no knowledge of** ignorare, non sapere; **not to my knowledge** non che io sappia; **without my knowledge** a mia insaputa; **to (the best of) my knowledge** per quanto io ne sappia; **it is common knowledge that ...** è risaputo che...; **it has come to my knowledge that ...** sono venuto a sapere che... 2 (*learning*) conoscenza, sapere *m*; **to have a working knowledge of Italian** avere una conoscenza pratica dell'italiano; **to have a thorough knowledge of sth** conoscere qc a fondo

knowl·edge·able ['nɒlɪdʒəbl] ADJ (*person*) ben informato(-a); (*remark*) pertinente

knowledge economy N *economia basata sulla creatività e la condivisione di idee piuttosto che sulla produzione*

knowledge management N gestione *f* che incoraggia la creatività e la condivisione di idee

knowledge worker N impiegato(-a) di concetto

known [nəʊn] PP *of* **know**

■ ADJ (*thief, facts*) noto(-a); (*expert*) riconosciuto(-a), famoso(-a)

knuck·le ['nʌkl] N (*Anat*) nocca

▸ **knuckle down** VI + ADV (*fam*): **to knuckle down to some hard work** mettersi sotto a lavorare

▸ **knuckle under** VI + ADV (*fam*) cedere

knuckle·duster ['nʌkl,dʌstə^r] N tirapugni *m inv*

KO, k.o. ['keɪ'əʊ] N ABBR (*pl* **KO's**) (= **knockout**) KO, k.o.

■ VT (*pt, pp* **KO'd**) (= **knock out**) mettere k.o.

koa·la [kəʊ'ɑ:lə] N (*also:* **koala bear**) koala *m inv*

Kk

kohl [kəʊl] N kajal *m inv*
kook [ku:k] N (*Am fam*) svitato(-a)
kooky ['ku:kɪ] ADJ (*fam*) folle
Ko·ran [kɒ'rɑ:n] N: **the Koran** il Corano
▷ www.quran.org.uk/
Ko·ran·ic [kɒ'rænɪk] ADJ coranico(-a)
Ko·rea [kə'rɪə] N Corea; **North/South Korea** Corea del Nord/del Sud
Ko·rean [kə'ri:ən] ADJ, N coreano(-a)
ko·sher ['kəʊʃəʳ] ADJ kasher *inv*
kow·tow [ˌkaʊ'taʊ] VI (*fam*): **to kowtow to sb** prostrarsi davanti a qn (*fig*)
kph [ˌkeɪpi:'aɪtʃ] N km/h
◎ **Krem·lin** ['krɛmlɪn] N: **the Kremlin** il Cremlino
kremlin·olo·gist [ˌkrɛmlɪ'nɒlədʒɪst] N cremlinologo(-a)
kremlin·ol·ogy [krɛmlɪ'nɒlədʒɪ] N cremlinologia
kryp·ton ['krɪptɒn] N cripto
KS ABBR (*Am Post*) = **Kansas**
Kt ABBR (*Brit*) = **knight**
Kua·la Lum·pur ['kwɑ:lə'lʊmpʊəʳ] N Kuala Lumpur *f*
ku·dos ['kju:dɒs] NSG gloria, fama
Ku Klux Klan ['ku:'klʌks'klæn] N: **the Ku Klux Klan** il Ku Klux Klan
kung fu ['kʌŋ'fu:] N kung fu *m*
Kurd [kɜ:d] N curdo(-a)
Kurd·ish ['kɜ:dɪʃ] ADJ curdo(-a)
■ N (*language*) curdo
Ku·wait [kʊ'weɪt] N il Kuwait *m*
Ku·wai·ti [kʊ'weɪtɪ] ADJ, N kuwaitiano(-a)
kW ABBR (= **kilowatt**) kW
KwaZulu/Natal [kwɑ:ˌzu:lu:nə'tæl] N Kwa Zulu/ Natal *m*
▷ www.kwazulunatal.gov.za
▷ www.kzn.org.za
KY ABBR (*Am Post*) = **Kentucky**

Ll

L, **l** [ɛl] N (*letter*) L, l *f or m in*; **L for Lucy**, (*Am*): **L for Love** ≈ L come Livorno

L [ɛl] ABBR **1** (= **large**) L *f inv* **2** (*Brit Aut*: = **learner**) P (= *principiante*); *see also* **L-plates**

■ N ABBR (*Am fam*): **the L** (= **the elevated (railroad)**) la soprelevata

L., **l.** ABBR **1** (*lake*) L **2** (*left*) sin.

l ABBR (= **litre**) l.

L8R ['leɪtəʳ] ADV ABBR (= **later**) + tardi

LA [,ɛl'eɪ] (*Am*) N ABBR = **Los Angeles**; (*Post*) = **Louisiana**

la [lɑː] N (*Mus*) = **lah**

lab [læb] N ABBR (*fam*: = **laboratory**) laboratorio

◎ **la·bel** ['leɪbl] N etichetta, cartellino; (*brand*: *of record*) casa discografica, etichetta; **he records on the E.M.I. label** incide per la E.M.I.

■ VT **1** (*goods*) mettere l'etichetta su, marcare; (*fig*) classificare, etichettare; **a bottle labelled "poison"** una bottiglia con l'etichetta "veleno"

la·bor *etc* ['leɪbəʳ] (*Am*) = **labour** *etc*

◎ **la·bora·tory** [lə'bɒrətərɪ] N laboratorio

■ ADJ di laboratorio

Labor Day N festa del lavoro

LABOR DAY

La festa del lavoro, **Labor Day**, viene celebrata negli Stati Uniti e in Canada il primo lunedì di settembre. Nel 1894, dopo 12 anni di richieste da parte dei lavoratori, il Congresso americano stabilì ufficialmente la festività; oggi le implicazioni politiche sono praticamente dimenticate e i festeggiamenti consistono in genere in gite e picnic, parate e discorsi ufficiali.

> www.dol.gov/opa/aboutdol/laborday.htm

la·bo·ri·ous [lə'bɔːrɪəs] ADJ faticoso(-a), laborioso(-a)

la·bo·ri·ous·ly [lə'bɔːrɪəslɪ] ADV faticosamente, laboriosamente

labor union (*Am*) N sindacato

La·bour ['leɪbəʳ] N (*Brit Pol*: *the Labour Party*) il partito laburista, i laburisti; **she votes Labour** vota (per il partito) laburista

■ ADJ laburista; **official Labour policy** politica ufficiale dei laburisti

◎ **la·bour**, (*Am*) **la·bor** ['leɪbəʳ] N **1** (*toil, task*) lavoro; **hard labour** (*Law*) lavori forzati; **labour of love** lavoro fatto per il puro piacere di farlo **2** (*workforce*) manodopera **3** (*Med*) doglie *fpl*, travaglio (del parto); **to be in labour** avere le doglie

■ VT (*point*) insistere su

■ VI: **to labour at** (*with effort*) lavorare sodo *or* duro a; (*with difficulty*) faticare a fare; (*engine, motor*) essere sotto sforzo; **to labour under a delusion/ misapprehension** essere vittima di un'illusione/di un malinteso; **to labour up a hill** arrancare su per una collina

■ ADJ di lavoro

labour camp, (*Am*) **labor camp** N campo di lavoro

labour cost, (*Am*) **labor cost** N costo del lavoro

labour dispute, (*Am*) **labor dispute** N conflitto tra lavoratori e datori di lavoro

la·boured, (*Am*) **la·bored** ['leɪbəd] ADJ (*breathing*) affannoso(-a); (*style*) pesante

la·bour·er, (*Am*) **la·bor·er** ['leɪbərəʳ] N (*on building site*) manovale *m*; (*on farm*) bracciante *m*

labour exchange N (*Brit old*) ufficio di collocamento

labour force, (*Am*) **labor force** N manodopera

labour-intensive, (*Am*) **labor-intensive** ['leɪbərɪn,tɛnsɪv] ADJ che assorbe molta manodopera

La·bour·ite ['leɪbə,raɪt] N laburista *m/f*

labour market, (*Am*) **labor market** N mercato del lavoro

labour pains, (*Am*) **labor pains** NPL doglie *fpl*

labour relations, (*Am*) **labor relations** NPL relazioni *fpl* industriali

labour-saving, (*Am*) **labor-saving** ['leɪbə,seɪvɪŋ] ADJ che fa risparmiare fatica *or* lavoro

labour unrest, (*Am*) **labor unrest** N agitazioni *fpl* operaie

lab technician N tecnico di laboratorio

la·bur·num [lə'bɜːnəm] N maggiociondolo

laby·rinth ['læbɪrɪnθ] N labirinto

laby·rin·thine [,læbə'rɪnθaɪn] (*frm*) ADJ labirintico(-a)

lace [leɪs] N **1** (*fabric*) pizzo, merletto **2** (*of shoe*) laccio,

stringa; (*of corset*) laccio; **a pair of laces** un paio di lacci
■ ADJ di pizzo; **a lace collar** un colletto di pizzo
■ VT **1** (*also:* **lace up**: *shoes etc*) allacciare **2** (*drink: with spirits*) correggere; (*: with poison*) avvelenare

lace·ma·ker ['leɪs,meɪkəʳ] N merlettaia

lace·making ['leɪs,meɪkɪŋ] N fabbricazione *f* dei pizzi *or* dei merletti

lac·er·ate ['læsə,reɪt] VT lacerare

lac·era·tion [,læsə'reɪʃən] N lacerazione *f*

lace-up ['leɪs,ʌp] ADJ (*shoes*) con i lacci *or* le stringhe

lace-ups ['leɪs,ʌps] NPL scarpe *fpl* con i lacci *or* le stringhe

◎**lack** [læk] N mancanza, scarsità; **for** *or* **through lack of** per mancanza *or* scarsità di; **there is no lack of money** i soldi non mancano; **he got the job, despite his lack of experience** ha ottenuto il lavoro nonostante la mancanza d'esperienza
■ VT: **we lack (the) time to do it** ci manca il tempo di *or* per farlo; **he lacks confidence** non è sicuro di sé
■ VI: **to be lacking in** mancare di; **he is lacking in confidence** non è sicuro di sé; **he lacks for nothing** non gli manca niente

lacka·dai·si·cal [,lækə'deɪzɪkəl] ADJ (*careless*) noncurante; (*lacking enthusiasm*) svogliato(-a)

lacka·dai·si·cal·ly [,lækə'deɪzɪkəlɪ] ADV (*see adj*) con noncuranza; svogliatamente

lack·ey ['lækɪ] N (*also pej*) lacchè *m inv*

lack·lustre, (*Am*) **lack·luster** ['læk,lʌstəʳ] ADJ (*performance*) scialbo(-a); (*eyes*) spento(-a)

la·con·ic [lə'kɒnɪk] ADJ laconico(-a)

la·coni·cal·ly [lə'kɒnɪkəlɪ] ADV laconicamente

lac·quer ['lækəʳ] N (*for wood, hair*) lacca
■ VT (*wood*) laccare; (*hair*) mettere la lacca su

la·crosse [lə'krɒs] N (*sport*) lacrosse *m inv*
▷ www.lacrosse.ca

lac·tic ['læktɪk] ADJ lattico(-a)

lac·tose ['læktəʊs] N lattosio

lacy ['leɪsɪ] ADJ (*comp* **-ier**, *superl* **-iest**) (*made of lace*) di pizzo; (*like lace*) che sembra un pizzo

◎**lad** [læd] N ragazzo, giovanotto; (*Brit: in stable*) mozzo *or* garzone *m* di stalla; **when I was a lad** quand'ero ragazzo *or* giovane; **come on, lads!** forza, *or* dai, ragazzi!; **a drink with the lads** una bevuta con gli amici; **he's a bit of a lad** (*fam*) è uno a cui piace far bisboccia

lad·der ['lædəʳ] N scala a pioli; (*stepladder*) scala a libretto; (*Brit: in tights*) smagliatura; **social ladder** scala sociale; **it's the first step up the ladder** è il primo passo sulla via del successo
■ VT (*Brit: tights*) smagliare
■ VI (*Brit: tights*) smagliarsi

lad·der·proof ['lædə,pru:f] ADJ (*Brit*) indemagliabile

lad·dish ['lædɪʃ] ADJ (*Brit*) macho *inv*

lad·en ['leɪdn] ADJ: **laden (with)** carico(-a) *or* caricato(-a) (di); **fully laden** (*truck, ship*) a pieno carico

lad·ette [læ'dɛt] N (*Brit*) maschiaccio

la-di-da [,lɑ:dɪ'dɑ:] ADJ (*fam: person*) affettato(-a) e pretenzioso(-a); (*: voice*) affettato(-a)

la·dies ['leɪdɪz] NSG, **ladies' room** N (*lavatory*): **the ladies** i gabinetti per signore, la toilette *f inv*; **"Ladies"** "signore"; **where is the Ladies?** dov'è la toilette? (*per signore*)

ladies' man N *uomo premuroso con le donne e che si trova bene in loro compagnia*

la·dle ['leɪdl] N (*Culin*) mestolo
■ VT (*soup*) servire con il mestolo
▸ **ladle out** VT + ADV (*soup*) servire con il mestolo; (*fig: advice*) elargire, distribuire; **to ladle out money to sb** dare un sacco di soldi a qn

lad lit N (*Brit*) *romanzi diretti a un pubblico giovane maschile*

lad mag N (*Brit*) rivista maschile

◎**lady** ['leɪdɪ] N **1** signora; **the lady of the house** la padrona di casa; **young lady** (*married*) signora; (*unmarried*) signorina; **ladies' hairdresser** parrucchiere *m* per signora; **Ladies and Gentlemen!** signore e signori! **2 Our Lady** (*Rel*) la Madonna **3 Lady Jane Grey** lady Jane Grey

lady·bird ['leɪdɪ,bɜ:d], (*Am*) **lady·bug** ['leɪdɪ,bʌg] N coccinella

Lady Day N Annunciazione *f*

lady doctor N dottoressa

lady friend N (*old*) (*hum*) amica

lady-in-waiting ['leɪdɪɪn'weɪtɪŋ] N dama di corte

lady·killer ['leɪdɪ,kɪləʳ] N dongiovanni *m inv*, rubacuori *m inv*

lady·like ['leɪdɪ,laɪk] ADJ (*person*) ben educato(-a), distinto(-a); (*manners*) da signora, distinto(-a)

lady mayoress N (*Brit*) moglie *f* (*or* figlia) del Lord Mayor

lady·ship ['leɪdɪʃɪp] N: **Her Ladyship the Countess** la signora contessa; **Your Ladyship** signora contessa

lag¹ [læg] VI (*also:* **lag behind**) restare indietro; **we lag behind in space exploration** siamo ancora indietro nel campo dell'esplorazione spaziale
■ N (*also:* **time-lag**) lasso *or* intervallo di tempo; *see also* **jet lag**

lag² [læg] VT (*boiler, pipes*) rivestire con *or* di materiale isolante

lag³ [læg] N (*fam*): **old lag** vecchia conoscenza della polizia

la·ger ['lɑ:gəʳ] N birra chiara, birra bionda

la·ger lout ['lɑ:gə,laʊt] N (*Brit fam*) giovinastro ubriaco

lag·gard ['lægəd] N (*old*) lento(a); tiratardi ***m/f inv***

lag·ging ['lægɪŋ] N (*Tech*) rivestimento termo-isolante

la·goon [lə'gu:n] N laguna

La·gos ['leɪgɒs] N Lagos *f*

lah [lɑ:] N (*Mus*) la *m inv*

lah-di-dah [,lɑ:dɪ'dɑ:] = **la-di-da**

laid [leɪd] PT, PP *of* **lay³**

laid-back [,leɪd'bæk] ADJ (*fam*) rilassato(-a); **his laid-back attitude** il suo atteggiamento tranquillo e rilassato

lain [leɪn] PP *of* **lie²**

lair [lɛəʳ] N (*of animal*) tana, covo; (*of thieves*) covo

laissez-faire [,leseɪ'fɛəʳ] N liberismo
■ ADJ liberistico(-a)

la·ity ['leɪɪtɪ] COLLECTIVE N: **the laity** (*as opposed to the clergy*) i laici, il laicato; (*as opposed to professionals*) i non appartenenti ad una categoria professionale

◎**lake** [leɪk] N lago

Lake District N: **the Lake District** (*Brit*) la regione dei laghi (nel nord dell'Inghilterra)
▷ www.lake-district.gov.uk/

◎**lama** ['lɑ:mə] N (*Rel*) lama *m inv*

lamb [læm] N (*animal, meat*) agnello; **my poor lamb!** oh, povero tesoro!; **he took it like a lamb** ha accettato docilmente; **Lamb of God** Agnello di Dio
■ VI figliare, partorire (*di pecora*)

lamb chop N cotoletta d'agnello

lamb·ing ['læmɪŋ] N agnellatura

lamb·skin ['læm,skɪn] N (pelle *f* d') agnello

lambs·wool ['læmz,wʊl] N lambswool *m inv*

lame [leɪm] ADJ (*comp* **-r**, *superl* **-st**) zoppo(-a); (*also fig: argument, excuse*) zoppicante; **to be lame** zoppicare,

essere zoppo(-a); **to be lame in one foot** esser zoppo da un piede
■ VT (*person*) rendere zoppo(-a); (*horse*) azzoppare
lamé ['lɑːmeɪ] N lamé *m inv*
lame duck N (*person*) persona inetta; (*firm*) azienda traballante; **a lame duck president** (*Am*) presidente uscente
lame·ly ['leɪmlɪ] ADV (*fig*) in modo poco convincente
lame·ness ['leɪmnɪs] N zoppia
la·ment [lə'mɛnt] VT lamentare, piangere; **to lament sb** piangere qn
■ VI: **to lament over sth** lamentarsi di qc; **to lament for sb** affliggersi per qn
■ N (*poet*) lamento, elegia
lam·en·table ['læməntəbl] ADJ (*performance*) penoso(-a); (*disregard, waste*) deplorevole
lam·en·tably ['læməntəblɪ] ADV deplorevolmente; **we are lamentably short of good staff** purtroppo siamo veramente a corto di personale in gamba
la·men·ta·tion [ˌlæmən'teɪʃən] N (*frm*) lamento; **there was much lamentation over the news that the president had died** la notizia della morte del presidente ha causato profonda afflizione
lami·na·ted ['læmɪˌneɪtɪd] ADJ (*gen*) laminato(-a); (*card*) plastificato(-a)
lamp [læmp] N (*for table*) lampada; (*in street*) lampione *m*; (*Aut*) faro, luce *f*; (*Rail*) lanterna; (*bulb*) lampadina
lamp·light ['læmpˌlaɪt] N: **by lamplight** a lume della lampada
lam·poon [læm'puːn] N satira
■ VT fare oggetto di satira, satireggiare
lamp·post ['læmpˌpəʊst] N lampione *m*
lamp·shade ['læmpʃeɪd] N paralume *m*
lamp·stand ['læmpˌstænd] N base *f* (di lampada)
lamp standard N palo della luce
LAN [læn] N (*Comput*: = **local area network**) rete *f* LAN *inv*
lance [lɑːns] N lancia
■ VT (*Med*) incidere
lance corporal N (*Brit*) caporale *m*
lanc·er ['lɑːnsəʳ] N (*Mil*) lanciere *m*
lan·cet ['lɑːnsɪt] N (*Med*) bisturi *m inv*
Lancs [læŋks] N ABBR (*Brit*) = *Lancashire*
◎ **land** [lænd] N **1** terra; (*soil, ground*) terreno; (*estate*) terreni *mpl*, terre *fpl*; **to go/travel by land** andare/viaggiare per via di terra; **(dry) land** terraferma; **to work on the land** lavorare la terra; **fewer people work on the land now** oggi c'è meno gente che lavora la terra; **to live off the land** vivere dei prodotti della terra; **to own land** possedere dei terreni, avere delle proprietà (terriere); **to see how the land lies** (*fig*) tastare il terreno **2** (*nation, country*) paese *m*; **throughout the land** in tutto il paese; **to be in the land of the living** essere nel mondo dei vivi
■ VT **1** (*cargo, goods*) scaricare, (far) sbarcare; (*passengers*) (far) sbarcare; (*aircraft*) far atterrare; (*catch: fish*) tirare in secco; (*fig: job, contract*) accaparrarsi **2** (*fam: place*): **to land a blow on sb** assestare un colpo a qn; **it landed him in jail** gli è costato la galera; **to land sb in trouble** cacciare qn nei guai; **to land sb in debt** far indebitare qn; **I got landed with the job** è toccato a me fare il lavoro; **I got landed with him** mi è toccato restare con lui, me lo sono dovuto sorbire io
■ VI **1** (*plane, passenger*) atterrare; (*from boat, ship*) sbarcare; **the plane landed at five o'clock** l'aereo è atterrato alle cinque **2** (*after fall, jump*) atterrare; (*fig: fall*) cadere; **to land on** (*bird*) posarsi su; **to land on one's feet** (*to be lucky*) cadere in piedi; **the hat landed in my lap** il cappello è finito sulle mie ginocchia; **the bomb landed on the building** la bomba è caduta sul palazzo; **the first man to land on the moon** il primo uomo a mettere piede sulla luna
▶ **land up** VI + ADV (*fig fam*) andare a finire
lan·dau ['lændɔː] N landò *m inv*
land defences NPL difese *fpl* terrestri
land·ed ['lændɪd] ADJ (*estate*) terriero(-a)
landed gentry N proprietari *mpl* terrieri
land·fall ['lændˌfɔːl] N: **to make landfall** approdare, toccare terra
land·fill site ['lændfɪlˌsaɪt] N discarica pubblica (*in cui i rifiuti vengono interrati*)
land forces NPL (*Mil*) forze *fpl* terrestri
land·ing ['lændɪŋ] N **1** (*of aircraft*) atterraggio; (*of troops*) sbarco **2** (*in house*) pianerottolo
landing card N carta di sbarco
landing craft N mezzo da sbarco
landing fees NPL (*Aer*) diritti *mpl* d'atterraggio
landing gear N (*Aer*) carrello d'atterraggio
landing net N (*Fishing*) retino (da pesca)
landing party N (*Naut*) reparto da sbarco
landing stage N pontile *m* da sbarco
landing strip N pista d'atterraggio
land·lady ['lændˌleɪdɪ] N (*of flat, house*) padrona di casa; (*of pub*) proprietaria
land·locked ['lændˌlɒkt] ADJ senza sbocco sul mare
land·lord ['lændˌlɔːd] N (*landowner*) proprietario (di beni immobili); (*of flat*) padrone *m* di casa; (*of pub*) proprietario
land·lub·ber ['lændˌlʌbəʳ] N (*fam*) marinaio d'acqua dolce
land·mark ['lændˌmɑːk] N punto di riferimento; (*event*) pietra miliare; **a landmark in history** una pietra miliare nella storia; **Big Ben is a London landmark** la torre del Big Ben è un punto di riferimento a Londra
land mass N continente *m*
land·mine ['lændˌmaɪn] N mina terrestre
land·owner ['lændˌəʊnəʳ] N proprietario(-a) terriero(-a)
land reform N riforma fondiaria
Land·rover® ['lændˌrəʊvəʳ] N Land Rover® *f inv*
◎ **land·scape** ['lændˌskeɪp] N paesaggio
■ VT abbellire con criteri architettonici
landscape architect N architetto del paesaggio
landscape architecture N architettura del paesaggio
landscape gardener N architetto dei giardini, paesaggista *m/f*
landscape gardening N architettura dei giardini
landscape painter N (*Art*) paesaggista *m/f*, paesista *m/f*
landscape painting N (*Art*) paesaggistica
land·scap·ing ['lændˌskeɪpɪŋ] N architettura del paesaggio
land·slide ['lændˌslaɪd] N (*Geol*) frana; (*fig: Pol*) valanga di voti, maggioranza schiacciante
landslide victory N (*Pol*) vittoria schiacciante
land·slip ['lændˌslɪp] N smottamento
land tax N tassa *or* imposta fondiaria
◎ **lane** [leɪn] N (*in country*) stradina, viottolo; (*in town*) stradina, viuzza; (*Sport, Aut*) corsia; **a country lane** una stradina di campagna; **the outside lane** la corsia esterna; **"keep in lane"** (*Aut*) "divieto di sorpasso"; **"get into lane"** (*Aut*) "immettersi in corsia"; **I'm in**

Ll

the wrong lane (*Aut*) sono sulla corsia sbagliata; **a 3-lane motorway** un'autostrada a 3 corsie

DID YOU KNOW ...?
lane is not translated by the Italian word *lana*

lang·lauf ['lɑ:ŋ,laʊf] N (*Skiing*) sci *m* di fondo

◎ **lan·guage** ['læŋgwɪdʒ] N (*faculty, style of speech*) linguaggio; (*national tongue, also fig*) lingua; **the Italian language** la lingua italiana; **a foreign language** una lingua straniera; **legal/scientific language** linguaggio legale/scientifico; **we don't speak the same language** (*fig*) non parliamo la stessa lingua; **to use bad language** dire parolacce, usare un linguaggio volgare; **watch your language!** attento a come parli!

▹ www.britac.ac.uk/portal/
▹ www.collins.co.uk/wordexchange/
▹ www.ilovelanguages.com
▹ www.ethnologue.com/

language degree N laurea in lingue

language laboratory N laboratorio linguistico

language school N scuola di lingue

language studies NPL studi *mpl* linguistici

lan·guid ['læŋgwɪd] ADJ (*liter: graceful, affected*) languido(-a); (: *indolent*) fiacco(-a)

lan·guid·ly ['læŋgwɪdlɪ] ADV (*liter*) languidamente

lan·guish ['læŋgwɪʃ] VI: **to languish for love/over sb/in prison** languire d'amore/per qn/in prigione

lan·guish·ing ['læŋgwɪʃɪŋ] ADJ languido(-a)

lan·guor ['læŋgə^r] N (*liter*) languore *m*

lan·guor·ous ['læŋgərəs] ADJ (*liter*) languido(-a)

lank [læŋk] ADJ (*hair*) diritto(-a) e opaco(-a)

lanky ['læŋkɪ] ADJ (*comp* **-ier**, *superl* **-iest**) (*person*) allampanato(-a)

lano·lin, lano·line ['lænəlɪn] N lanolina

lan·tern ['læntən] N lanterna

lantern-jawed ['læntən,dʒɔ:d] ADJ con il volto affilato e incavato

Laocoon [leɪ'ɒkəʊ,ɒn] N Laocoonte

Laos [laʊs] N Laos *m*

Lao·tian ['laʊʃɪən] ADJ, N laotiano(-a)

◎ **lap¹** [læp] N (*Anat*) grembo, ginocchia *fpl*; **to sit in** *or* **on sb's lap** sedersi in grembo a *or* sulle ginocchia di qn; **on his mother's lap** in grembo a sua madre; **to live in the lap of luxury** vivere nel lusso; **in the lap of the gods** (*fig*) nelle mani di Dio

▸ **lap up** VT + ADV (*milk: cat*) leccare; (: *dog*) lappare; (*fig: compliments, attention*) bearsi di

lap² [læp] N (*Sport*) giro; **to run a lap** fare un giro della pista; **I ran ten laps** ho fatto dieci giri di corsa; **we're on the last lap now** (*fig*) siamo quasi arrivati al traguardo

lap³ [læp] VT = **lap up**

■ VI (*waves*) sciabordare; **to lap against** lambire

La Paz [læ'pæz] N La Paz *f*

lap dancer N ballerina di lap dance

lap dancing N lap dance *f inv*

lap·dog ['læp,dɒg] N cagnolino da salotto; (*fig: person*) cagnolino

la·pel [lə'pɛl] N risvolto

lap·is lazu·li ['læpɪs 'læzjʊlaɪ] N lapislazzuli *m inv*

Lap·land ['læp,lænd] N Lapponia

Lap·land·er ['læp,lændə^r] N lappone *m/f*

lap of honour N giro d'onore

Lapp [læp] ADJ lappone

■ N (*person*) lappone *m/f*; (*language*) lappone *m*

Lapp·ish ['læpɪʃ] ADJ Lappone

■ N (*language*) lappone *m*

lapse [læps] N **1** (*fault*) mancanza; (*in behaviour*) scorrettezza; **a lapse (of memory)** un vuoto (di memoria); **through a lapse of concentration** per mancanza di concentrazione; **a lapse into bad habits** un ritorno alle cattive abitudini **2** (*of time*) intervallo

■ VI **1** (*err*) sgarrare; **to lapse in one's duty** mancare al proprio dovere **2** (*fall slowly*): **to lapse into bad habits** prendere cattive abitudini; **to lapse into one's old ways** ritornare a poco a poco alle vecchie abitudini; **to let one's attention lapse** distrarsi; **to lapse into silence** tacere; **to lapse into English** cominciare a parlare inglese; **she lapsed into unconsciousness** scivolò in uno stato di incoscienza **3** (*law, act*) cadere, andare in prescrizione; (*membership, passport, ticket*) scadere

lapsed [læpst] ADJ (*contract, law, passport*) scaduto(-a); **lapsed Catholic** cattolico(-a) non praticante

lap·top ['læp,tɒp] N (*also:* **laptop computer**) laptop *m inv*

lap·wing ['læp,wɪŋ] N pavoncella

lar·ceny ['lɑ:sənɪ] N (*Law*) furto

larch [lɑ:tʃ] N larice *m*

lard [lɑ:d] N strutto

■ VT (*speech, writing*): **to lard with** infarcire di

lar·der ['lɑ:də^r] N dispensa

◎ **large** [lɑ:dʒ] ADJ (*comp* **-r**, *superl* **-st**) (*gen*) grande; (*item of clothing*) di taglia grande; (*garden, room*) grande, ampio(-a); (*person*) grande e grosso(-a); (*animal*) grosso(-a); (*sum, loss*) grosso(-a), ingente; (*family, population*) numeroso(-a); (*meal*) lauto(-a); **a large house** una casa grande; **a large amount** una grossa cifra; **a large, cheerful woman** un donnone allegro; **a large number of people** molta gente, molte persone; **we had a large meal** abbiamo mangiato tanto; **on a large scale** su vasta scala; **as large as life** in carne e ossa; **larger than life** portato(-a) all'estremo; **to grow large(r)** ingrandirsi; **to make large(r)** ingrandire

■ N: **at large** (*criminal, dangerous animal*) in libertà; (*generally*) in generale, nell'insieme; **the world at large** il mondo nel complesso

■ ADV: **by and large** generalmente

◎ **large·ly** ['lɑ:dʒlɪ] ADV in gran parte, per la maggior parte

DID YOU KNOW ...?
largely is not translated by the Italian word *largamente*

large·ness ['lɑ:dʒnɪs] N grandezza

large-scale [,lɑ:dʒ'skeɪl] ADJ (*map, drawing*) a larga scala; (*reforms, business activities*) su vasta *or* larga scala; **a large-scale operation** un'operazione su vasta scala

large-size [,lɑ:dʒ'saɪz], **large-sized** [,lɑ:dʒ'saɪzd] ADJ grande

lar·gesse, lar·gess [lɑ:'dʒɛs] N (*frm*) generosità

lark¹ [lɑ:k] N (*bird*) allodola

lark² [lɑ:k] N (*Brit fam: joke*) scherzo, gioco; **for a lark** per scherzo; **what a lark!** che spasso!

▸ **lark about, lark around** VI + ADV: **to lark about (with)** (*Brit fam*) divertirsi (con)

lark·spur ['lɑ:k,spɜ:^r] N delfinio

lar·va ['lɑ:və] N (*pl* **larvae** ['lɑ:vi:]) larva

lar·val ['lɑ:vəl] ADJ larvale

lar·yn·gi·tis [,lærɪn'dʒaɪtɪs] N laringite *f*

lar·ynx ['lærɪŋks] N (*Anat*) laringe *f*

la·sa·gne [lə'zænja] N lasagne *fpl*

las·civi·ous [lə'sɪvɪəs] ADJ lascivo(-a)

las·civi·ous·ly [lə'sɪvɪəslɪ] ADV lascivamente

la·ser ['leɪzə^r] N laser *m inv*

laser beam N raggio *m* laser *inv*
laser printer N stampante *f* laser *inv*
lash [læʃ] N **1** (*also:* **eye lash**) ciglio; **long lashes** ciglia *fpl* lunghe **2** (*thong*) laccio (di cuoio); (*stroke*) frustata, colpo di frusta; (*of tail*) colpo
■ VT **1** (*beat etc*) frustare; (*subj: rain, waves: lash against*) picchiare (contro), sbattere (contro); **the wind lashed the sea into a fury** il vento ha trasformato il mare in una furia **2** (*esp Naut: tie*) legare
▸ **lash down** VT + ADV assicurare (con corde)
■ VI + ADV (*rain*) scrosciare
▸ **lash out** VI + ADV **1** **to lash out (at** *or* **against sb/sth)** menare colpi (contro qn/a qc); (*fig*) attaccare violentemente (qn/qc), inveire (contro qn/qc); **he lashed out against the government** ha inveito contro il governo **2** (*fam*): **to lash out (on sth)** (*spend*) spendere un sacco di soldi (per qc)
lash·ing ['læʃɪŋ] N **1** (*beating*) frustata, sferzata **2** **lashings of** (*Brit fam*) un mucchio di, una montagna di
lass [læs] N (*esp in Northern Britain*) ragazza
las·si·tude ['læsɪtju:d] N (*frm*) apatia
las·so [læ'su:] N lazo *m inv*, laccio
■ VT prendere al lazo *or* al laccio
◎ **last**[1] [lɑ:st] ADJ **1** (*most recent*) ultimo(-a); (*week, month, year*) scorso(-a), passato(-a); **last Monday** lunedì scorso; **last night** ieri sera *or* notte, la notte scorsa; **I got home at midnight last night** ieri sera sono arrivata a casa a mezzanotte; **I couldn't sleep last night** ieri notte non sono riuscito a dormire; **during (the) last week** nel corso della settimana scorsa; **during the last 2 years** negli ultimi 2 anni; **the night before last** l'altro ieri sera *or* notte; **(the) last time** l'ultima volta **2** (*final: in series*) ultimo(-a); **the last page** l'ultima pagina; **the last slice of cake** l'ultima fetta di torta; **last thing at night** prima di andare a letto; **that was the last thing I expected** era l'ultima cosa che mi sarei aspettato; **you're the last person I'd trust with it** sei l'ultima persona al mondo di cui mi fiderei per questo; **last but one** *or* **second last** penultimo(-a)
■ N: **the last of the wine/bread** quello che resta del vino/del pane; **they were the last to arrive** erano gli ultimi arrivati, sono arrivati per ultimi; **the last in the series** l'ultimo della serie; **each one better than the last** uno meglio dell'altro; **I shall be glad to see the last of this** sarò contento di vederne la fine; **we'll never hear the last of it** chissà per quanto ne sentiremo parlare; **at (long) last** finalmente; **to the last** fino all'ultimo
■ ADV (per) ultimo; **to do/come/arrive last (of all)** fare come/venire per/arrivare ultimo(-a); **he arrived last** è arrivato ultimo; **last but not least ...** come ultimo, ma non per questo meno importante...; **when I last saw them** *or* **saw them last** l'ultima volta che li ho visti; **I've lost my bag. – When did you see it last?** ho perso la borsa. – Dove l'hai vista per l'ultima volta?
last[2] [lɑ:st] VI (*rain, film, pain*) durare; (*also:* **last out**: *person*) resistere; (*: money, resources*) durare, bastare; **the concert lasts two hours** il concerto dura due ore; **this material will last (for) years** questa stoffa durerà degli anni; **he didn't last long in the job** non ha resistito a lungo in quell'impiego; **it's too good to last** *or* **it can't last** è troppo bello per durare
■ VT durare; **he won't last the winter** non sopravviverà all'inverno; **it will last you a lifetime** ti durerà una vita
last-ditch ['lɑ:st,dɪtʃ] ADJ (*attempt*) ultimo(-a) e disperato(-a)
last-gasp ['lɑ:st,gɑ:sp] ADJ (*fam: attempt*) dell'ultima ora; (*: victory, defeat*) all'ultimo minuto
last·ing ['lɑ:stɪŋ] ADJ duraturo(-a), durevole; **to his lasting shame** con sua profonda vergogna
Last Judgement, **Last Judgment** N: **the Last Judgement** il Giudizio Universale
last·ly ['lɑ:stlɪ] ADV infine, per finire, per ultimo; **lastly I'd like to mention ...** infine vorrei accennare a...
last-minute ['lɑ:st,mɪnɪt] ADJ (*decision*) dell'ultimo momento; (*preparation*) fatto(-a) all'ultimo momento; **last-minute changes** cambiamenti fatti all'ultimo momento
last post N (*Mil*): **the last post** il silenzio
latch [lætʃ] N (*metal bar*) chiavistello; (*lock*) serratura a scatto; **the door is on the latch** la porta non è chiusa a chiave
▸ **latch on to** VI + ADV + PREP **1** (*cling to: person*) attaccarsi a, appiccicarsi a **2** (*idea*) afferrare, capire
latch·key ['lætʃ,ki:] N chiave *f* di casa
latchkey child, **latchkey kid** N *bambino i cui genitori lavorano e che perciò ha le chiavi per rientrare a casa*
◎ **late** [leɪt] (*comp* **-r**, *superl* **-st**) ADJ **1** (*not on time*) in ritardo; **to be (10 minutes) late** essere in ritardo (di 10 minuti); **hurry up or you'll be late!** sbrigati o farai tardi!; **to be late arriving** arrivare tardi *or* in ritardo; **to make sb late** far fare tardi a qn; **to be late with one's work** essere in ritardo con il proprio lavoro; **the late arrival of the flight** il ritardo del volo; **late delivery** consegna ritardata **2** (*towards end of period*) tardivo(-a); (*far on in day etc*) tardo(-a); (*composition, concerto*) ultimo(-a); **to be/be getting late** essere/farsi tardi; **to keep late hours** stare alzato(-a) fino a tardi, fare le ore piccole; **at this late hour** a un'ora così tarda, a quest'ora; **at this late stage** al punto in cui stanno ormai le cose; **in the late afternoon** nel tardo pomeriggio; **in late May** verso la fine di maggio; **in (the) late spring** nella tarda primavera, a fine primavera; **she's in her late sixties** è vicina ai settanta **3** (*recent*) recente; **his late remarks on industry** le sue recenti osservazioni sull'industria **4** (*euph: dead*) defunto(-a); **the late Mrs Smith** la defunta signora Smith; **my late-lamented husband** il mio povero marito **5** (*former*) ex *inv*; **our late prime minister** il nostro ex primo ministro
■ ADV **1** (*not on time*) in ritardo, tardi; **to arrive/leave 10 minutes late** arrivare/partire con 10 minuti di ritardo; **to arrive/leave too late** arrivare/partire troppo tardi; **I'm often late for school** arrivo spesso in ritardo a scuola; **better late than never** meglio tardi che mai **2** (*towards end of period*) tardi; **to work late** lavorare fino a tardi; **I went to bed late** sono andato a letto tardi; **late at night** a tarda notte; **late into the night** fino a tarda notte, fino a notte fonda; **in the late afternoon** nel tardo pomeriggio; **in late May** verso la fine di maggio; **late in life** in età avanzata; **late in 1978** verso la fine del 1978 **3** (*recently*): **as late as 1991** ancora nel 1991; **of late** negli ultimi tempi, di recente, recentemente
late·comer ['leɪt,kʌmə^r] N ritardatario(-a)
late·ly ['leɪtlɪ] ADV ultimamente, di recente, recentemente; **till lately** fino a poco *or* non molto tempo fa; **I haven't seen him lately** ultimamente non l'ho visto

Ll

late·ness ['leɪtnɪs] N (*of person, vehicle*) ritardo; (*of event*) ora tarda
late-night ['leɪt'naɪt] ADJ: **a late-night movie** l'ultimo spettacolo; **late-night shopping is on Thursdays** i negozi chiudono più tardi del solito il giovedì
la·tent ['leɪtənt] ADJ latente
◎ **lat·er** ['leɪtəʳ] ADV (*comp of* **late**) **1** (*not on time*) più tardi **2** (*after*) dopo, più tardi; **a few years later** pochi anni dopo *or* più tardi **3 later on** (*in series of events*) più avanti; (*in time*) più tardi; **later on today** più tardi; **I'll do it later** lo farò più tardi; **see you later!** ci vediamo dopo!
■ ADJ (*comp of* **late**) (*meeting, train*) successivo(-a); (*edition, version*) più recente, successivo(-a); (*date etc*) posteriore; **he was later than usual** è arrivato più tardi del solito; **Easter is later this year** Pasqua cade più tardi quest'anno; **at a later stage** *or* **date** in un secondo momento; **his later symphonies** le sue ultime sinfonie; **this version is later than that one** questa versione è posteriore a *or* più recente di quella
lat·er·al ['lætərəl] ADJ laterale
lateral thinking N pensiero laterale
◎ **lat·est** ['leɪtɪst] ADJ (*superl of* **late**) (*gen*) ultimo(-a), più recente; **her latest exhibition** la sua ultima mostra; **their latest album** il loro ultimo album; **the latest news** le ultime notizie
■ N **1** (*fam: most recent*) ultima novità; **the latest in skin care** l'ultima novità nel campo della cosmesi; **have you heard the latest?** (*news*) hai sentito l'ultima? **2 at the latest** al più tardi; **it'll arrive tomorrow at the latest** arriverà al più tardi domani; **by ten o'clock at the latest** alle dieci al più tardi
la·tex ['leɪtɛks] N latice *m*
lath [lɑːθ] N (*pl* **laths**) listello, assicella
lathe [leɪð] N tornio
lath·er ['lɑːðəʳ] N (*soap*) schiuma (di sapone); **in a lather of sweat** tutto(-a) sudato(-a); **the horse was in a lather** il cavallo era coperto di sudore; **in a lather** (*fig*) tutto affannato(-a) *or* scalmanato(-a)
■ VT (*one's face*) insaponarsi, insaponare
■ VI (*soap*) far schiuma
◎ **Lat·in** ['lætɪn] ADJ (*language, temperament*) latino(-a); (*textbook, scholar, lessons*) di latino
■ N (*language*) latino; **I do Latin** studio latino
Latin America ['lætɪnə'mɛrɪkə] N America Latina
Latin American ['lætɪnə'mɛrɪkən] ADJ dell'America Latina, latino-americano(-a)
■ N latino-americano(-a)
lati·tude ['lætɪtjuːd] N **1** (*Geog*) latitudine *f* **2** (*fig: freedom*) libertà d'azione; **artistic latitude** libertà artistica
la·trine [lə'triːn] N latrina
lat·te ['lɑːteɪ] N latte *m* macchiato; **a skinny latte** un latte macchiato con latte scremato
◎ **lat·ter** ['lætəʳ] N: **the latter** quest'ultimo(-a); **of the two, the latter is better** fra i due è meglio il secondo; **the former ..., the latter ...** il primo..., il secondo...
■ ADJ **1** (*later*) ultimo(-a); **the latter years of his life** gli ultimi anni della sua vita **2** (*of two*): **the latter part of the story** la seconda *or* l'ultima parte della storia; **the latter part of the match** l'ultima parte della partita
latter-day ['lætə,deɪ] ADJ moderno(-a), del giorno d'oggi
lat·ter·ly ['lætəlɪ] ADV negli ultimi tempi
lat·tice ['lætɪs] N (*gen*) reticolato; (*for plants*) graticcio, traliccio; (*Chem*) reticolo cristallino
lattice window N finestra con vetrata a losanghe
lattice work N graticcio
Lat·via ['lætvɪə] N Lettonia
Lat·vian ['lætvɪən] ADJ lettone
■ N (*person*) lettone *m/f*; (*language*) lettone *m*
laud·able ['lɔːdəbl] ADJ (*frm*) lodevole, degno(-a) di lode
lau·da·num ['lɔːdənəm] N laudano
lauda·tory ['lɔːdətərɪ] ADJ (*frm*) elogiativo(-a)
◎ **laugh** [lɑːf] VI ridere; **to laugh over** *or* **about sth** ridere di *or* per qc; **we all laughed about it later** più tardi ci abbiamo riso sopra; **it's nothing to laugh about** non c'è niente da ridere; **to laugh to o.s.** ridere dentro di sé *or* fra sé e sé; **I laughed till I cried** ho riso fino alle lacrime; **to laugh in sb's face** ridere in faccia a qn; **then we'll be laughing** (*fig*) poi saremo tranquilli; **to laugh up one's sleeve** ridere sotto i baffi
■ VT: **to laugh sb/sth out of court** ridicolizzare qn/qc; **they tried to laugh me out of my fears** hanno cercato di farmi passare la paura ridendo; **to laugh sb to scorn** deridere qn
■ N risata; **to get** *or* **raise a laugh (from sb)** far ridere (qn); **to have a good laugh at sth** farsi una bella risata su *or* sopra qc; **do you want a laugh?** vuoi farti due risate?; **to do sth for a laugh** (*fam*) fare qc per scherzo *or* per ridere; **what a laugh!** che ridere!; (*iro*) che ridicolo!; **with a laugh** con una risata; **it was a good laugh** è stato molto divertente; **good for a laugh** divertente; **he's always good for a laugh** ci fa sempre fare due risate; **we'll see who has the last laugh** (*fig*) staremo a vedere chi l'avrà vinta
▶ **laugh at** VI + PREP (*person, sb's behaviour: also fig*) ridere di; **I laughed at his joke** la sua barzelletta mi fece ridere
▶ **laugh off** VT + ADV (*pain, accusation*) ridere sopra, prendere alla leggera; **to laugh one's head off** (*fam*) sbellicarsi dalle risate
laugh·able ['lɑːfəbl] ADJ ridicolo(-a)
laugh·ing ['lɑːfɪŋ] ADJ (*face*) ridente; **this is no laughing matter** non è una cosa da ridere
laughing gas N gas *m* esilarante
laugh·ing·ly ['lɑːfɪŋlɪ] ADV ridendo allegramente; **it is laughingly called ...** viene scherzosamente chiamato...
laughing stock N zimbello; **to make a laughing stock of o.s.** rendersi ridicolo(-a)
◎ **laugh·ter** ['lɑːftəʳ] N risata; (*laughing*) riso; **he roared with laughter** si è fatto una fragorosa risata; **hysterical laughter** risate isteriche; **tears and laughter** lacrime e risa
◎ **launch** [lɔːntʃ] VT (*gen, also fig*) lanciare; (*ship, plan*) varare; (*shore lifeboat*) far uscire; (*ship's boat*) calare (in mare); **they're about to launch the new model** stanno per lanciare il nuovo modello
■ N **1** (*of rocket, product*) lancio; (*of boat*) varo **2** (*also:* **motor launch**) motolancia; (*pleasure boat*) battello
▶ **launch into** VI + ADV (*speech, task*) lanciarsi in
▶ **launch out** VI + ADV: **to launch out (into)** lanciarsi (in)
launch·er ['lɔːntʃəʳ] N (*Aer*) lanciamissili *m inv*
launch·ing ['lɔːntʃɪŋ] N lancio; (*of ship*) varo; (*of shore lifeboat*) uscita; (*of ship's boat*) calo, calata (in mare)
launching pad, launch pad N rampa di lancio
laun·der ['lɔːndəʳ] VT lavare e stirare; (*fig: money*) riciclare
Laun·der·ette®, laun·drette [,lɔːndə'rɛt],

(*Am*) **Laun·dro·mat®** ['lɔːndrəˌmæt] N lavanderia (automatica)
laun·dry ['lɔːndrɪ] N (*establishment*) lavanderia; (*clothes*) bucato, biancheria; **to do the laundry** fare il bucato, lavare la biancheria; **she does my laundry** mi fa lei il bucato
laundry bag N sacca portabiancheria
lau·reate ['lɔːrɪɪt] N: **Nobel laureate in Physics** insignito(-a) del Nobel per la fisica; *see also* **poet laureate**
lau·rel ['lɒrəl] N alloro, lauro; **to rest on one's laurels** riposare *or* dormire sugli allori
Lau·sanne [ləʊ'zæn] N Losanna
lava ['lɑːvə] N lava
lava flow N effusione *f* lavica
lava plateau N altopiano basaltico
lava·tory ['lævətrɪ] N (*Brit: room*) gabinetto, toilette *f inv*; (: *appliance*) water *m inv*, gabinetto
lavatory brush N (*Brit*) scopino del gabinetto
lavatory paper N (*Brit*) carta igienica
lavatory seat N (*Brit*) sedile *m* del gabinetto
lav·en·der ['lævɪndə^r] N lavanda
lavender bag N sacchettino di lavanda
lavender water N (acqua di) lavanda
lav·ish ['lævɪʃ] ADJ (*person*) prodigo(-a); (*meal*) lauto(-a); (*surroundings, apartment*) sontuoso(-a), lussuoso(-a); (*expenditure*) considerevole; (: *excessive*) eccessivo(-a); **a lavish production of Tosca** una ricca messa in scena della Tosca; **to be lavish with one's gifts** non badare a spese in fatto di regali; **to bestow lavish praise on sb** coprire qn di elogi *or* lodi
■ VT: **to lavish sth on sb/on sth** colmare qn/qc di qc; **to lavish money on sth** spendere molto denaro per qc
lav·ish·ly ['lævɪʃlɪ] ADV (*give, spend*) generosamente; (*furnished*) sontuosamente, lussuosamente
lav·ish·ness ['lævɪʃnɪs] N (*of person*) prodigalità; (*of meal*) abbondanza; (*of surroundings, apartment*) sontuosità, lusso
◎ **law** [lɔː] N legge *f*; **law of gravity** legge di gravità; **law of constant energy** legge della conservazione dell'energia; **against the law** contro la legge; **by law** a norma di *or* per legge; **by British law** secondo la legge britannica; **civil/criminal law** diritto civile/penale; **to study law** studiare giurisprudenza *or* legge; **Faculty of Law** facoltà di giurisprudenza; **court of law** corte *f* di giustizia, tribunale *m*; **to go to law** ricorrere alle vie legali; **to have the law on one's side** avere la legge dalla propria (parte); **to be above the law** essere al di sopra della legge; **to be a law unto o.s.** non conoscere altra legge che la propria; **there's no law against it** nessuna legge lo vieta *or* impedisce; **to take the law into one's own hands** farsi giustizia da sé; **his word is law** la sua parola è legge
law-abiding ['lɔːəˌbaɪdɪŋ] ADJ rispettoso(-a) delle leggi
law and order N l'ordine *m* pubblico
law·breaker ['lɔːˌbreɪkə^r] N persona che viola la legge
law court N (aula del) tribunale *m*, corte *f* di giustizia
law-enforcement [lɔːɪn'fɔːsmənt] N (*Am*): **law-enforcement agency/official** organismo/ funzionario preposto al controllo della corretta appplicazione delle leggi
law·ful ['lɔːfʊl] ADJ legale
law·ful·ly ['lɔːfəlɪ] ADV legalmente
law·giver ['lɔːˌgɪvə^r], **law·maker** ['lɔːˌmeɪkə^r] N legislatore *m*
law·less ['lɔːlɪs] ADJ (*time, place*) privo(-a) di legge; (*action*) illegale
Law Lords NPL (*Brit Pol*) ≈ Corte *f* Suprema
lawn¹ [lɔːn] N prato all'inglese
lawn² [lɔːn] N (*fabric*) batista
lawn·mower, lawn mower ['lɔːnˌməʊə^r] N tagliaerba *m inv*, tosaerba *m inv*
lawn tennis N tennis *m* sull'erba
law school N (*Am*) facoltà *f inv* di giurisprudenza *or* legge
law student N studente(-essa) di giurisprudenza *or* legge
law·suit ['lɔːˌsuːt] N causa, processo; **to bring a lawsuit against** intentare causa a; **to end in a lawsuit** finire in tribunale
◎ **law·yer** ['lɔːjə^r] N (*in court*) avvocato(-essa); (*consultant*) legale *m/f*; (*for sales, wills*) notaio; **I have put the matter in the hands of my lawyer** ho affidato la questione al mio avvocato

LAWYER

In Gran Bretagna gli avvocati, i **lawyers**, si distinguono in: "solicitors" e "barristers" (chiamati "advocates" in Scozia). I "solicitors" di solito forniscono assistenza legale in materia di compravendita di immobili, testamenti, recupero crediti e istanze di divorzio e ci si può rivolgere a loro direttamente. Alcuni sono qualificati a rappresentare i propri assistiti sia nelle cause civili che in quelle penali. I "barristers" non trattano direttamente con i clienti ma intervengono dietro richiesta del "solicitor": sono qualificati per esercitare nei tribunali di grado superiore, mentre i "solicitors" in quelli di grado inferiore.
Negli Stati Uniti gli avvocati sono di solito chiamati "attorneys"; si occupano di qualunque tipo di causa, civile o penale, e possono rappresentare i loro assistiti in tutti i gradi di giudizio, sia nelle "state courts" che nelle "federal courts". *Vedi anche* **solicitor; barrister**
▷ www.lawsociety.org.uk/home.law
▷ www.barcouncil.org.uk/
▷ www.advocates.org.uk/
▷ www.scotland.gov.uk/About/Factsheets/Legal-System-Factsheet
▷ www.loc.gov/law/guide/usintro.html

lax [læks] ADJ (*comp* **-er**, *superl* **-est**) (*conduct*) lassista; (*person: careless*) negligente; (: *on discipline*) permissivo(-a); **to be lax about punctuality** non tenere *or* badare alla puntualità
laxa·tive ['læksətɪv] N lassativo
lax·ity ['læksɪtɪ], **lax·ness** ['læksnɪs] N (*see adj*) lassismo; negligenza; permissività
lay¹ [leɪ] ADJ (*Rel*) laico(-a), secolare; (: *brother, sister*) laico(-a); (*fig: non-specialist*) profano(-a)
lay² [leɪ] PT *of* **lie²**
◎ **lay³** [leɪ] (*pt, pp* **laid**) VT
1 (*put, set*) mettere, posare; (*carpet*) stendere; (*bricks*) posare; (*cable, pipe*) installare, fare la posa di; (*trail*) lasciare; (*subj: bird: egg*) deporre, fare; **to lay sth over sth** stendere qc su qc; **to lay sth on sth** coprire qc con qc; **he laid a sheet of newspaper on the floor** ha posato un foglio di giornale sul pavimento; **she laid the baby in her cot** ha messo la bambina nel suo lettino; **to lay the facts/one's proposals before sb** presentare i fatti/delle proposte a qn; **to be laid low with flu** essere costretto(-a) a letto con l'influenza; **to**

Ll

be laid to rest (*euph: buried*) essere sepolto(-a); **to get laid** (*fam!*) scopare (*fam!*); **I don't know where to lay my hands on it** non saprei dove trovarlo; **to lay o.s. open to attack/criticism** esporsi agli attacchi/alle critiche; **to lay the blame (for sth) on sb** dar la colpa (di qc) a qn; **to lay claim to sth** reclamare qc, accampare diritti *mpl* su qc; **to lay odds** *or* **a bet on sth** scommettere su qc
2 (*prepare: fire*) preparare; (*: trap, snare*) tendere; (*: mine*) posare, piantare; (*: table*) apparecchiare; **I haven't laid the table yet** non ho ancora apparecchiato la tavola
3 (*settle: ghost*) placare, esorcizzare; (*: doubts, fears*) eliminare, dissipare
■ VI (*bird*) fare le uova, deporre le uova
▸ **lay alongside** VI + ADV (*Naut*) affiancarsi
▸ **lay aside** VT + ADV mettere da parte
▸ **lay by** VT + ADV mettere da parte
▸ **lay down** VT + ADV
1 (*put down: luggage*) posare, metter giù; (*: arms*) deporre, posare; (*: wine*) mettere in cantina; **to lay down one's life for sb/sth** sacrificare la propria vita per qn/qc
2 (*dictate: conditions*) stabilire, fissare; (*: principle, rule, policy*) formulare, fissare; **to lay down the law** (*fig*) dettar legge
▸ **lay in** VT + ADV fare una scorta di
▸ **lay into** VI + PREP (*fam: attack, scold*) aggredire
▸ **lay off** VT + ADV (*permanently*) licenziare; (*temporarily*) ≈ mettere in cassa integrazione; **my father's been laid off** mio padre è stato licenziato
■ VI + ADV (*fam*) smettere
■ VI + PREP (*fam*): **lay off it!** piantala!; **lay off him!** non rompergli le scatole!, lascialo in pace!
▸ **lay on** VT + ADV (*provide: water, electricity, gas*) installare, mettere; (*: meal etc*) fornire; (*paint*) applicare; **to lay on (for)** (*meal, entertainment*) offrire (a); (*facilities*) mettere a disposizione (di); **they laid on extra buses** hanno fornito autobus supplementari; **they laid on a special meal** hanno organizzato un pranzo speciale; **to lay it on thick** (*fam: flatter*) andarci pesante con i complimenti; (*: exaggerate*) metterla giù dura
▸ **lay out** VT + ADV
1 (*plan: garden, house, town*) pianificare, progettare; (*: page, letter*) impostare; **the way the house is laid out** la disposizione della casa
2 (*put ready: clothes*) preparare; (*display: goods for sale*) sistemare, disporre, presentare; (*make ready: body for burial*) preparare, comporre
3 (*spend*) sborsare
4 (*knock out*) stendere
▸ **lay over** VI + ADV (*Am*) fermarsi, far tappa
▸ **lay up** VT + ADV
1 (*store: provisions*) far scorta *or* provvista di, accumulare; **to lay up trouble for o.s.** crearsi dei guai
2 (*put out of service: boat*) mettere in disarmo, ritirare in cantiere; (*subj: illness*) costringere a letto; **to be laid up with flu** essere costretto(-a) a letto con l'influenza

lay·about ['leɪə,baʊt] N (*fam*) sfaccendato(-a), fannullone(-a)
lay-by ['leɪ,baɪ] N (*Brit Aut*) piazzola (di sosta)
lay days NPL (*Naut*) giorni di stallia
◎ **lay·er** ['leɪəʳ] N strato
lay·ered ['leɪəd] ADJ (*rocks*) stratificato(-a); (*potatoes, mushrooms*) a strati
lay·ette [leɪ'ɛt] N corredino (per neonato)
lay·man ['leɪmən] N (*pl* **-men**) (*Rel*) laico; (*fig: non-professional*) profano; **science for the layman** la scienza per i profani; **in layman's terms** detto con parole semplici
lay-off ['leɪ,ɒf] N (*permanent*) licenziamento; (*temporary*) ≈ messa in cassa integrazione
lay·out ['leɪ,aʊt] N (*of town*) piano urbanistico; (*of house, garden*) disposizione *f*; (*Typing*) impostazione *f*; (*Press*) impaginazione *f*
lay·over ['leɪ,əʊvəʳ] N (*Am*) sosta
Lazarus ['læzərəs] N Lazzaro
laze [leɪz] VI (*also:* **laze around** *or* **about**) oziare
la·zi·ly ['leɪzɪlɪ] ADV pigramente
la·zi·ness ['leɪzɪnɪs] N pigrizia
lazy ['leɪzɪ] ADJ (*comp* **-ier**, *superl* **-iest**) pigro(-a)
lazy·bones ['leɪzɪ,bəʊnz] N (*fam*) poltrone(-a)
lb ABBR (= libra: **pound**) lb.
lbw [,ɛlbi:'dʌbəlju:] N ABBR (*Cricket:* = **leg before wicket**) *fallo dovuto al fatto che il giocatore ha la gamba davanti alla porta*
LC [,ɛl'si:] N ABBR (*Am*) = *Library of Congress*
L/C, **l/c** ABBR = **letter of credit**
lc ABBR (*Typ*) = **lower-case**
LCD [,ɛlsi:'di:] N ABBR = **liquid crystal display**
Ld ABBR (*Brit:* = **lord**) *titolo*
LDS [,ɛldi:'ɛs] N ABBR (= **Licentiate in Dental Surgery**) specializzato(-a) in odontoiatria
LEA [,ɛli:'eɪ] N ABBR (*Brit:* = **Local Education Authority**) ≈ Provveditorato agli Studi
◎ **lead**[1] [li:d] (*vb: pt, pp* **led**) VT
1 (*conduct*) condurre; **to lead the way** fare strada; **to lead astray** sviare; **he is easily led** si lascia facilmente convincere *or* influenzare
2 (*be the leader of: government*) essere a capo di; (*: party*) essere alla guida *or* a capo di; (*: expedition, movement*) guidare; (*: revolution*) capeggiare; (*: team*) capitanare; (*: league, procession*) essere in testa a; (*: orchestra: Brit*) essere il primo violino di; (*: Am*) dirigere; **he led the party for five years** ha guidato il partito per cinque anni; **to lead the field** essere in testa; (*fig*) essere all'avanguardia nel campo
3 (*life, existence*) condurre
4 (*induce*) indurre, portare; **to lead sb to do sth** portare qn a fare qc; **to lead sb to believe that ...** far credere a qn che...; **it led me to the conclusion that ...** mi ha portato alla conclusione che...
■ VI
1 (*go in front*) andare avanti; (*Cards*) essere di mano
2 (*in match, race*) essere in testa; **to lead by 3 goals** avere 3 gol di vantaggio
3 (*street, corridor*) portare; **where does this door lead?** cosa c'è oltre questa porta?; **the street that leads to the station** la strada che porta alla stazione
4 (*result in*): **to lead to** portare a; **one thing led to another ...** una cosa tira l'altra...; **the incident led to serious trouble** l'incidente ha portato a problemi seri
■ N
1 (*front position*) posizione *f* di testa; (*distance, time ahead*) vantaggio; **to be in the lead** (*Sport*) essere in testa; (*fig*) essere all'avanguardia; **to be in the lead by 5 points to 4** condurre *or* essere in testa per 5 a 4; **to take the lead** (*Sport*) passare in testa; (*fig*) prendere l'iniziativa; **to have a 3-second lead** avere un vantaggio di 3 secondi; **to follow sb's lead** seguire l'esempio di qn; **it's your lead** (*Cards*) sei tu di mano
2 (*Elec*) filo (elettrico)
3 (*for dog*) guinzaglio
4 (*clue*) indizio, pista

5 (*Theatre*) parte *f or* ruolo principale; **male/female lead** protagonista *m/f* maschile/femminile
▸ **lead away** VT + ADV condurre via, portar via
▸ **lead back** VT + ADV riportare, ricondurre
▸ **lead off** VT + ADV
1 portare; **he led us off on a visit of the museum** ci ha portato a visitare il museo
2 (*fig: begin*) dare inizio a, cominciare
■ VI + PREP partire da; **a street leading off the main road** una traversa della strada principale
▸ **lead on** VT + ADV
1 (*deceive*) prendere in giro, ingannare
2 (*incite*): **to lead sb on (to do sth)** incoraggiare *or* spingere *or* trascinare qn (a fare qc)
▸ **lead up to** VI + ADV + PREP portare (a); (*fig*) preparare la strada per; **what's all this leading up to?** dove vuoi andare a parare?

lead² [lɛd] N (*metal*) piombo; (*in pencil*) mina; (*for sounding*) scandaglio
■ ADJ (*pipes*) di piombo; (*paint*) a base di piombo

lead·ed ['lɛdɪd] ADJ: **leaded windows** vetrate *fpl* (artistiche)

lead·en ['lɛdn] ADJ (*colour, sky*) plumbeo(-a); (*fig: atmosphere*) teso(-a); (: *silence*) opprimente; **with a leaden heart** con la morte nel cuore

◎ **lead·er** ['li:dəʳ] N 1 (*of group, expedition*) capo; (*of party, union*) capo, leader *m/f inv*; (*Mus: of orchestra: Brit*) primo violino; (: *Am*) direttore *m* d'orchestra; (*guide*) guida; (*Mountaineering*) capocordata *m inv*; **he's a born leader** è nato per comandare 2 (*Sport: in race*) chi è in testa, leader *m/f inv*; **the leaders of the First Division** (*Ftbl*) la squadra in testa alla classifica di serie A; **they are leaders in their field** (*fig*) sono all'avanguardia nel loro campo 3 (*Brit: in newspaper*) articolo di fondo, editoriale *m*

lead·er·board ['li:dəbɔ:d] N (*Sport*): **the leaderboard** tabellone *m* dei primi in classifica

leader of the house N capo della maggioranza ministeriale alla Camera

LEADER OF THE HOUSE

Nel parlamento britannico il **Leader of the House of Commons** nella Camera dei Comuni e il **Leader of the House** of Lords in quella dei Lord hanno il compito di preparare e annunciare il calendario settimanale dei lavori dell'assemblea, di concerto con i rappresentanti dell'opposizione. I due **Leader of the House** sono membri del governo.
▷ www.commonsleader.gov.uk/output/page1.asp

◎ **lead·er·ship** ['li:dəʃɪp] N 1 direzione *f*, leadership *f inv*; **under the leadership of ...** sotto la direzione *or* guida di...; **qualities of leadership** qualità *fpl* di un capo; **the leadership of the Conservative Party** la leadership del partito conservatore 2 (*leaders*) dirigenti *mpl*, dirigenza

lead-free ['lɛd'fri:] ADJ (*petrol*) senza piombo, verde

lead-in ['li:d,ɪn] N introduzione *f*, presentazione *f*

◎ **lead·ing** ['li:dɪŋ] ADJ (*horse, car: in race*) (che è) in testa, di testa; (: *in procession*) che apre la sfilata; (*chief: member etc*) principale, preminente; (: *Theatre etc: role, character*) principale, di primo piano; **one of the leading figures of this century** una delle più importanti figure di questo secolo

leading article N = leader 3

leading edge N avanguardia; **the leading edge of technology** la tecnologia di punta
■ ADJ di punta, all'avanguardia

leading lady N (*Theatre*) prima attrice

leading light N (*person*) personaggio di primo piano

leading man N (*Theatre*) primo attore

leading question N domanda tendenziosa

lead pencil [,lɛd'pɛnsəl] N matita con la mina di grafite

lead poisoning ['lɛd,pɔɪzənɪŋ] N saturnismo

lead time ['li:d,taɪm] N (*Comm*) tempo di consegna

lead weight [,lɛd'weɪt] N piombino, piombo

◎ **leaf** [li:f] N (*pl* **leaves**) 1 (*of plant*) foglia 2 (*of book*) foglio, pagina; **to turn over a new leaf** (*fig*) voltare pagina, cambiar vita; **to take a leaf out of sb's book** (*fig*) prendere esempio da qn 3 (*of table: fold-down*) ribalta; (: *extending*) asse *f* estraibile
▸ **leaf through** VT + PREP (*book*) sfogliare

leaf·let ['li:flɪt] N (*gen*) dépliant *m inv*; (*single sheet*) volantino

leaf spring N (*Tech*) molla a balestra

leafy ['li:fɪ] ADJ (*comp* **-ier**, *superl* **-iest**) (*suburb*) ricco(-a) di verde; (*branch*) ricco(-a) di foglie

◎ **league** [li:g] N 1 (*alliance*) associazione *f*, lega; **to be in league with** essere in associazione con; (*pej*) essere in combutta con, essere in lega con; **to form a league against** far lega contro 2 (*Ftbl, Rugby*) campionato; **they are at the top of the league** sono in testa al campionato; **the Premier League** ≈ la Serie A; **they're not in the same league** (*fig fam*) non c'è paragone

league champions NPL (*Brit: Ftbl*) vincitori del campionato

league championship N (*Brit: Ftbl*) campionato

league match N (*Brit: Ftbl*) partita di campionato

league table N (*Brit: Ftbl*) classifica del campionato; (*of schools etc*) classifica (*ordinata per livello qualitativo, pubblicata dal governo*)

◎ **leak** [li:k] N (*in pipe*) perdita, fuoriuscita; (*in boat*) falla; (*in roof, wall*) infiltrazione *f*; (*of gas*) fuga, perdita, fuoriuscita; (*fig: of information*) fuga di notizie; **a leak in the radiator** una perdita del radiatore; **to have** *or* **take a leak** (*fam*) andare al bagno, andare a far pipì
■ VI (*roof, bucket*) perdere; (*ship*) far acqua; (*shoes*) lasciar passare l'acqua; **the pipe is leaking** il tubo perde; **water was leaking into the cellar** l'acqua si stava infiltrando nella cantina
■ VT (*liquid*) gocciolare, perdere; (*fig: information*) divulgare
▸ **leak out** VI + ADV (*liquid*) uscire (fuori); (*gas*) esalare, uscire; (*fig: news*) trapelare

leak·age ['li:kɪdʒ] N (*of water, gas etc*) perdita

leaky ['li:kɪ] ADJ (*comp* **-ier**, *superl* **-iest**) (*pipe, bucket, roof*) che perde; (*shoe*) che lascia passare l'acqua; (*boat*) che fa acqua

lean¹ [li:n] ADJ (*comp* **-er**, *superl* **-est**) magro(-a); **the lean years** i tempi di magra
■ N (*of meat*) magro, parte *f* magra (della carne)

◎ **lean²** [li:n] (*pt, pp* **leaned** *or* **leant**) VI 1 (*gatepost, wall, slope*) essere inclinato(-a), pendere; **to lean to(wards) the left/right** (*Pol*) avere tendenze di sinistra/di destra 2 (*for support: person*): **to lean on, lean against** appoggiarsi a; **to be leaning against** (*ladder*) essere appoggiato(-a) a *or* contro; **the ladder was leaning against the wall** la scala era appoggiata al muro; **to lean on sb** (*also fig: for support*) appoggiarsi a qn; (*fig: put pressure on*) far pressione su qn; **she leant on his arm** si appoggiò al suo braccio; **she leant on him to**

Ll

contribute to the fund lo ha spinto a contribuire alla raccolta di fondi

■ VT (*ladder, bicycle*): **to lean sth against/on sth** appoggiare qc a *or* contro/su qc; **he leaned the ladder against the wall** ha appoggiato la scala al muro; **to lean one's head on sth** appoggiare la testa su qc

▶ **lean back** VI + ADV sporgersi indietro; (*against sth*) appoggiarsi all'indietro; **she leaned back against the pillows** si è adagiata sui cuscini

▶ **lean forward** VI + ADV piegarsi in avanti

▶ **lean out** VI + ADV: **to lean out (of)** sporgersi (da); **she leant out of the window** si è sporta dal finestrino

▶ **lean over** VI + ADV (*person*) chinarsi; (*thing*) piegarsi, inclinarsi; **don't lean over too far** non chinarti troppo; **to lean over backwards to help sb** (*fig fam*) farsi in quattro per aiutare qn

■ VI + PREP (*balcony, gate*) sporgersi da, affacciarsi a; (*desk*) piegarsi su, chinarsi su

lean·ing ['li:nɪŋ] N: **leaning (towards)** tendenza (a), propensione *f* (per)

■ ADJ inclinato(-a), pendente; **the leaning Tower of Pisa** la torre (pendente) di Pisa

leant [lɛnt] PT, PP *of* **lean²**

lean-to ['li:n,tu:] N (*roof*) tettoia; (*building*) *edificio con tetto appoggiato ad altro edificio*

◎ **leap** [li:p] (*vb: pp, pt* **leaped** *or* **leapt**) VI saltare, balzare; **he leapt into/out of the train** saltò sul/giù dal treno; **to leap to one's feet** scattare in piedi; **he leapt out of his chair when his team scored** è saltato in piedi quando la sua squadra ha segnato; **to leap about** saltellare qua e là; **to leap out** saltare fuori; **to leap out at sb** saltare addosso a qn; **to leap over sth** saltare qc con un balzo; **my heart leapt** ho avuto un tuffo al cuore; **to leap at an offer** afferrare al volo una proposta

■ VT (*fence, ditch*) saltare

■ N salto, balzo; **a leap in the dark** (*fig*) un salto nel buio; **by leaps and bounds** a passi da gigante

▶ **leap up** VI + ADV (*person*) balzare in piedi; (*flames*) divampare

leap·frog ['li:p,frɒg] N gioco della cavallina

■ VI: **to leapfrog over sb/sth** saltare (alla cavallina) qn/qc

leapt [lɛpt] PT, PP *of* **leap**

leap year N anno bisestile

◎ **learn** [lɜ:n] (*pt, pp* **learned** *or* **learnt**) VT (*study*) imparare; (*hear*) (venire a) sapere; **to learn (how) to do sth** imparare a fare qc; **I'm learning to ski** sto imparando a sciare; **to learn that ...** apprendere che..., venire a sapere che...; **we were sorry to learn that it was closing down** la notizia della chiusura ci ha fatto dispiacere; **I think he's learnt his lesson** (*fig*) penso che gli sia servito di lezione

■ VI: **to learn about sth** (*study*) studiare qc, imparare qc; (*hear*) sentire qc, apprendere qc; **I've learnt from experience not to trust him** l'esperienza mi ha insegnato a non fidarmi di lui; **you learn from your mistakes** sbagliando s'impara; **you'll learn!** un giorno capirai!

▶ **learn off** VT + ADV imparare a memoria

learn·ed ['lɜ:nɪd] ADJ (*person*) erudito(-a), dotto(-a); (*book*) dotto(-a); **a member of the learned profession** un principe del foro

learn·er ['lɜ:nəʳ] N principiante *m/f*; **she's a fast learner** è una che impara subito *or* con facilità; **slow learner** (*Scol*) alunno(-a) che ha difficoltà di apprendimento; **he's a learner (driver)** (*Brit*) sta imparando a guidare, è un principiante

learn·ing ['lɜ:nɪŋ] N cultura, erudizione *f*, sapere *m*

learnt [lɜ:nt] PT, PP *of* **learn**

◎ **lease** [li:s] N contratto di affitto (*a lungo termine con responsabilità simili a quelle di un proprietario*); **on lease** in affitto; **to give sb a new lease of life** (*fig*) ridare nuova vita a qn

■ VT (*take*) affittare, prendere in affitto; (*give*: *lease out*) affittare, dare in affitto

▶ **lease back** VT + ADV effettuare un lease-back *inv*

lease·back ['li:s,bæk] N lease-back *m inv*

lease·hold ['li:s,həʊld] ADJ in affitto

■ N (*property*) proprietà *f inv* in affitto; (*tenure*) diritto di godimento (della proprietà)

lease·holder ['li:s'həʊldəʳ] N locatario(-a), affittuario(-a) (*in possesso di un contratto a lungo termine e con diritti simili a quelli del proprietario*)

leash [li:ʃ] N guinzaglio; **on a leash** al guinzaglio

◎ **least** [li:st] (*superl of* **little**) ADJ minimo(-a), più piccolo(-a); **I haven't the least idea** non ne ho la minima idea; **it takes the least time** è quello per cui ci vuole meno tempo; **go for the ones with least fat** scegli quelli con meno grassi; **she wasn't in the least bit interested** non era minimamente interessata; **she always orders whatever costs the least money** ordina sempre quello che costa di meno; **that's the least of my worries** è la cosa che mi preoccupa di meno *or* che meno mi preoccupa, quella è l'ultima delle mie preoccupazioni

■ N minimo; **it's the least I can do** è il minimo che possa fare; **to say the least** a dir poco; **the least said about the meeting, the better** meno parliamo della riunione e meglio è; **at least** almeno; **I can at least try** posso sempre *or* almeno provarci; **...but at least nobody was hurt** ...ma almeno nessuno si è fatto male; **at the very least** come minimo; **not in the least** per nulla *or* niente, affatto

■ ADV meno; **the least expensive car** l'auto meno cara; **the least expensive hotel** l'albergo meno costoso; **the least qualified girl** la ragazza meno qualificata; **she is least able to afford it** è quella che se lo può permettere meno di tutti; **least of all me** e men che meno io, tanto meno io; **for a number of reasons, not least ...** per una serie di motivi, non ultimo il fatto che...; **history is the subject I like the least** la storia è la materia che mi piace di meno

◎ **leath·er** ['lɛðəʳ] N (*hide*: *soft*) pelle *f*; (: *hard*) cuoio; (*wash leather*) pelle di daino

■ ADJ (*see n*) di *or* in pelle; di *or* in cuoio; **leather goods** (articoli di) pelletteria; **a black leather jacket** una giacca di pelle nera

Leath·er·ette® [,lɛðə'rɛt] N similpelle *f*, vinilpelle® *f*

leath·er·ing ['lɛðərɪŋ] N: **to give sb a leathering** (*fam*) prendere qn a cinghiate

leath·ery ['lɛðərɪ] ADJ (*meat, substance, skin*) coriaceo(-a)

◎ **leave** [li:v] (*vb: pt, pp* **left**) VT

1 (*go away from*: *town*) lasciare, andarsene da; (: *room*) lasciare, uscire da; (: *station*) partire da; (: *hospital*) uscire da; (: *person*) lasciare; **to leave school** (*complete studies*) finire la scuola; (*prematurely*) lasciare la scuola; **to leave home** uscire di casa; (*permanently*) andarsene di casa; **she left home when she was sixteen** se n'è andata di casa quando aveva sedici anni; **we leave London at six o'clock** partiamo da Londra alle sei; **they have left this address** se ne sono andati da qui; **may I leave the room?** (*Scol euph*: *to go to the lavatory*)

posso uscire?; **to leave the table** alzarsi da tavola; **the car left the road** la macchina è uscita di strada; **the train is leaving in 10 minutes** il treno parte fra 10 minuti
2 (*forget*) lasciare, dimenticare; (*give: in will, as tip*) lasciare; **don't leave your wallet in the car** non lasciare il portafoglio in macchina
3 (*allow to remain*) lasciare; **to leave the window open** lasciare la finestra aperta; **let's leave it at that** per ora basta (così); **leave it to me!** ci penso io!, lascia fare a me!; **leave it with me** lascia che me ne occupi io; **I'll leave it to you to decide** decidi tu, lo lascio decidere a te; **she left him to it** lo ha lasciato alle sue occupazioni; **he leaves a wife and a child** lascia la moglie e un figlio; **to leave sb alone** lasciare qn (da) solo(-a); **leave me alone** *or* **in peace!** lasciami in pace!; **don't leave anything to chance** non lasciar niente al caso; **it leaves much to be desired** lascia molto a desiderare; **take it** *or* **leave it!** prendere o lasciare!; **3 from 10 leaves 7** 10 meno 3 fa 7
4 (*remaining*): **to be left (over)** rimanere, restare, avanzare; **all the money I have left (over)** tutti i soldi che mi restano *or* che mi sono avanzati; **there's some milk left over** c'è rimasto del latte; **how many are (there) left?** quanti ne restano?, quanti ce ne sono ancora?; **nothing was left for me (to do) but to sell it** non mi rimaneva *or* restava altro (da fare) che venderlo
■ VI (*plane, train*) partire; (*person*) uscire, andarsene; **the bus leaves at eight** l'autobus parte alle otto; **they left yesterday** sono partiti ieri; **she's just left** è appena andata via; **he's already left for the airport** è già uscito per andare all'aeroporto
■ N
1 (*permission*) permesso, autorizzazione *f*; **without so much as a "by your leave"** senza nemmeno chiedere il permesso
2 (*permission to be absent*) permesso; (: *of public employee*) congedo; (: *Mil*) licenza; **unpaid leave** ≈ aspettativa; **on leave** in congedo; **on leave of absence** in permesso; (*public employee*) in congedo; (*Mil*) in licenza; **my brother is on leave for a week** mio fratello è in licenza per una settimana
3 to take (one's) leave of sb accomiatarsi da qn, congedarsi da qn; **have you taken leave of your senses?** ma sei uscito di senno?, ma sei impazzito?
▸ **leave about, leave around** VT + ADV lasciare in giro
▸ **leave behind** VT + ADV (*also fig*) lasciare indietro; (*forget*) dimenticare; **I left my umbrella behind in the shop** ho dimenticato l'ombrello nel negozio; **she leaves everybody else behind** è superiore a tutti gli altri; **you'll be left behind by the rest** rimarrai indietro rispetto agli altri
▸ **leave in** VT + ADV lasciare, non togliere
▸ **leave off** VT + ADV
1 (*cover, lid, clothes*) non mettere; (*heating, light*) non accendere; (*name: from list*) non inserire
2 (*fam: stop*): **to leave off doing sth** smetterla *or* piantarla di fare qc
■ VI + ADV (*Brit fam: stop*) smetterla
▸ **leave on** VT + ADV (*lid*) lasciare su; (*light, fire, cooker*) lasciare acceso(-a); (*coat*) non togliersi
▸ **leave out** VT + ADV
1 (*omit*) tralasciare; (: *in reading etc*) saltare; **he feels left out** si sente escluso *or* lasciato in disparte; **not knowing the language, I felt really left out** mi sentivo proprio escluso dato che non sapevo la lingua
2 (*not put back*) lasciare fuori
▸ **leave over** VT + ADV (*postpone*) rimandare
leav·en ['lɛvn] N lievito
■ VT far lievitare
leaves [li:vz] NPL *of* **leaf**
leave·taking ['li:v,teɪkɪŋ] N commiato, addio
leav·ings ['li:vɪŋz] NPL avanzi *mpl*, rimasugli *mpl*
Leba·nese [,lɛbə'ni:z] ADJ libanese
■ N, PL INV libanese *m/f*
Leba·non ['lɛbənən] N: **(the) Lebanon** (il) Libano
lech·er ['lɛtʃəʳ] N satiro (*fig*)
lech·er·ous ['lɛtʃərəs] ADJ lascivo(-a)
lech·er·ous·ly ['lɛtʃərəslɪ] ADV in modo lascivo
lech·ery ['lɛtʃərɪ] N lascivia
lec·tern ['lɛktən] N leggio
◎ **lec·ture** ['lɛktʃəʳ] N **1** (*Univ*) lezione *f*; (*by visitor*) conferenza; **a public lecture** una conferenza pubblica; **to deliver** *or* **give a lecture on** tenere una conferenza *or* una lezione su **2** (*reproof*) paternale *f*, predica; **to give sb a lecture** fare la predica a qn
■ VI: **to lecture (in sth)** essere professore incaricato (di qc); **to lecture (to sb on sth)** (*Univ*) fare lezione (a qn di qc); (: *visiting lecturer*) tenere una conferenza (a qn su qc); **she lectures at the technical college** insegna all'istituto tecnico
■ VT (*reprove*) rimproverare, fare una ramanzina a; **he's always lecturing us** ci rimprovera sempre

DID YOU KNOW ...?
lecture is not translated by the Italian word *lettura*

lecture hall, lecture theatre N aula magna
lecture notes NPL appunti *mpl* (del corso *or* delle lezioni)
lec·tur·er ['lɛktʃərəʳ] N (*Brit: Univ*) professore(-essa), docente *m/f* (universitario(-a)); (*speaker*) conferenziere(-a); **assistant lecturer** (*Brit*) ≈ professore(-essa) associato(-a); **senior lecturer** (*Brit*) ≈ professore(-essa) ordinario(-a)
lec·ture·ship ['lɛktʃəʃɪp] N docenza
LED [,ɛli:'di:] N ABBR (*Elec*: = **light-emitting diode**) LED *m inv*
led [lɛd] PT, PP *of* **lead**
ledge [lɛdʒ] N (*on wall etc*) sporgenza; (*of window*) davanzale *m*; (*of mountain*) cengia, cornice *f*
ledg·er ['lɛdʒəʳ] N libro mastro, registro
◎ **lee** [li:] N lato *m* sottovento *inv*; **in the lee of** a ridosso di, al riparo di
■ ADJ sottovento *inv*; **to have a lee helm** (*ship*) essere poggiero(-a)
leech [li:tʃ] N sanguisuga
leek [li:k] N porro
leer [lɪəʳ] N (*lustful*) espressione *f* libidinosa; (*evil*) espressione *f* malvagia
■ VI: **to leer at sb** (*lustfully*) guardare qn con occhi vogliosi; (*cruelly*) guardare qn con malvagità
leery ['lɪərɪ] ADJ: **to be leery of** (*fam*) essere sospettoso(-a) di
lee·ward ['li:wəd] (*Naut*) ADJ sottovento *inv*
■ ADV sottovento; **to drift leeward** scarrocciare
■ N lato sottovento; **to leeward** sottovento
lee·way ['li:,weɪ] N (*Naut*) deriva; (*fig*) margine *m*; **they gave him a great deal of leeway** gli hanno lasciato ampia libertà di azione
left[1] [lɛft] PT, PP *of* **leave**
◎ **left**[2] [lɛft] ADJ sinistro(-a); **my left hand** la mia mano sinistra

Ll

■ ADV a sinistra; **turn left at the traffic lights** volta a sinistra al semaforo
■ N sinistra; **on my left, to my left** sulla *or* alla mia sinistra; **on the left, to the left** sulla *or* a sinistra; **the Left** (*Pol*) la sinistra; **he has always been on the Left** ha sempre avuto idee di sinistra

left-click ['lɛftklɪk] VI (*Comput*): **to left-click on** fare clic con il pulsante sinistro del mouse su

left-field [ˌlɛft'fi:ld] ADJ (*fam*) anticonformista, fuori dagli schemi

left-hand ['lɛftˌhænd] ADJ a sinistra; **left-hand page** pagina a *or* di sinistra; **left-hand side** (parte *f*) sinistra; **on the left-hand side** sulla *or* a sinistra, sul lato sinistro

left-hand drive ADJ (*Brit*) guida a sinistra

left-handed [ˌlɛft'hændɪd] ADJ mancino(-a); (*fig: compliment*) ambiguo(-a); **left-handed scissors** forbici *fpl* per mancini

left-hander [ˌlɛft'hændəʳ] N mancino(-a)

leftie ['lɛftɪ] N (*fam*) uno(-a) di sinistra

left·ist ['lɛftɪst] (*Pol*) ADJ di sinistra
■ N uno(-a) di sinistra

left-luggage [ˌlɛft'lʌgɪdʒ] N: **left-luggage office** deposito *m* bagagli *inv*; **left-luggage locker** armadietto per depositare i bagagli

left-of-centre [lɛftəv'sɛntəʳ] ADJ di centro sinistra

left·over ['lɛftəʊvəʳ] ADJ: **leftover food/chicken** avanzi *mpl* di cibo/pollo

left-overs ['lɛftˌəuvəz] NPL avanzi *mpl*

left-wing [ˌlɛft'wɪŋ] ADJ (*Pol*) di sinistra

left wing N (*Mil, Sport*) ala sinistra; (*Pol*) sinistra

left-winger [ˌlɛft'wɪŋəʳ] N (*Sport*) ala sinistra; (*Pol*) uno(-a) di sinistra

lefty ['lɛftɪ] N = **leftie**

◎ **leg** [lɛg] N **1** (*gen*) gamba; (*of animal, bird*) zampa; (*Culin: of chicken, turkey*) coscia; (*: of lamb, pork*) cosciotto; (*of furniture*) piede *m*; **she's broken her leg** si è rotta la gamba; **to be on one's last legs** (*person, animal*) stare in piedi per miracolo; (*machine, car*) funzionare per miracolo; **he hasn't got a leg to stand on** (*fig*) non ha una scusa *or* una ragione che stia in piedi; **to pull sb's leg** (*fig*) prendere in giro qn; **to stretch one's legs** sgranchirsi le gambe; **to give sb a leg up** aiutare qn a salire; (*fig*) dare una mano a qn; **I got a leg up** mi hanno dato una mano; **shake a leg!** (*Brit fam*) muoviti!, sbrigati!; **show a leg!** (*fam*) alzati!; **break a leg!** in bocca al lupo!; **to get one's leg over** (*Brit fam*) scopare
2 (*stage: of journey*) tappa; (*of relay race*) frazione *f*; (*of competition*) girone *m*
■ VT: **to leg it** (*fam*) darsela a gambe

lega·cy ['lɛgəsɪ] N eredità *f inv*; (*fig*) retaggio; **a small legacy** una piccola eredità; **a legacy from the past** un retaggio del passato

legacy system N (*Comput*) sistema *m* superato ma ancora in uso

◎ **le·gal** ['li:gəl] ADJ **1** (*lawful*) legale; (*: requirement*) di legge; **these coins are no longer legal currency** queste monete sono fuori corso **2** (*relating to the law: gen*) legale; (*: error*) giudiziario(-a); **as a member of the legal profession** come legale; **to take legal action** *or* **proceedings against sb** intentare un'azione legale contro qn, far causa a qn; **legal department** (*of a firm*) ufficio legale, contenzioso; **legal aid** assistenza legale gratuita, patrocinio legale gratuito

legal adviser N consulente *m/f* legale

le·gal·is·tic [ˌli:gə'lɪstɪk] ADJ legalista

le·gal·ity [lɪ'gælɪtɪ] N legalità

le·gali·za·tion [ˌli:gəlaɪ'zeɪʃən] N legalizzazione *f*

le·gal·ize ['li:gəˌlaɪz] VT legalizzare

le·gal·ly ['li:gəlɪ] ADV legalmente; **to be legally binding** essere (legalmente) vincolante

legal tender N moneta in corso legale

le·ga·tion [lɪ'geɪʃən] N legazione *f*

leg·end ['lɛdʒənd] N leggenda

leg·end·ary ['lɛdʒəndərɪ] ADJ leggendario(-a)

-legged ['lɛgɪd] SUFF: **two-legged** a due gambe (*or* zampe), bipede

leg·gings ['lɛgɪŋz] NPL (*women's*) pantacollant *mpl*, fuseaux *mpl*; (*men's*) gambali *mpl*

leg·gy ['lɛgɪ] ADJ (*comp* **-ier**, *superl* **-iest**) dalle gambe lunghe

leg·ibil·ity [ˌlɛdʒɪ'bɪlɪtɪ] N leggibilità

leg·ible ['lɛdʒəbl] ADJ leggibile

leg·ibly ['lɛdʒəblɪ] ADV in modo leggibile

le·gion ['li:dʒən] N legione *f*; (*fig*) schiera, stuolo
■ ADJ (*frm: very many*) innumerevole

le·gion·ary ['li:dʒənərɪ] N (*Roman history*) legionario

le·gion·naire [ˌli:dʒə'nɛəʳ] N (*French Foreign Legion*) legionario

legionnaire's disease, legionnaires' disease N morbo *or* malattia del legionario, legionellosi *f inv*

leg·is·late ['lɛdʒɪsˌleɪt] VI legiferare, promulgare delle leggi

◎ **leg·is·la·tion** [ˌlɛdʒɪs'leɪʃən] N legislazione *f*; **a piece of legislation** una legge; **legislation to protect women's rights** leggi in difesa dei diritti delle donne

leg·is·la·tive ['lɛdʒɪslətɪv] ADJ legislativo(-a)

leg·is·la·tor ['lɛdʒɪsˌleɪtəʳ] N legislatore *m*

leg·is·la·ture ['lɛdʒɪslətʃəʳ] N organi *mpl* legislativi, potere *m* legislativo

le·giti·ma·cy [lɪ'dʒɪtɪməsɪ] N (*gen*) legittimità; (*of argument, excuse*) validità

le·giti·mate [lɪ'dʒɪtɪmɪt] ADJ (*lawful*) legittimo(-a); (*argument, cause, excuse*) buono(-a), valido(-a); (*complaint*) legittimo(-a); (*conclusion*) logico(-a)

le·giti·mize [lɪ'dʒɪtɪˌmaɪz] VT (*gen*) convalidare, rendere legittimo(-a)

leg·less ['lɛglɪs] ADJ (*Brit fam*) sbronzo(-a), fatto(-a)

leg-pull ['lɛgˌpʊl] N (*fam*) scherzo

leg-pulling ['lɛgˌpʊlɪŋ] N (*fam*) scherzi *mpl*

leg-room ['lɛgˌrʊm] N spazio per le gambe

leg-warmers ['lɛgˌwɔ:məz] NPL scaldamuscoli *mpl*

Leics ABBR (*Brit*) = *Leicestershire*

lei·sure ['lɛʒəʳ] N svago, tempo libero; **a life of leisure** una vita comoda; **to be a lady of leisure** (*hum*) fare la bella vita; **do it at your leisure** fallo con comodo
■ ADJ: **leisure activities** attività ricreative; **in one's leisure time** durante il proprio tempo libero

leisure centre N (*Brit*) centro sportivo e ricreativo

lei·sure·ly ['lɛʒəlɪ] ADJ (*day, stroll, trip*) tranquillo(-a); **in a leisurely way** (fatto(-a)) con comodo *or* senza fretta

leisure suit N (*Am*) tuta da ginnastica

leisurewear ['lɛʒəwɛəʳ] N abbigliamento per il tempo libero

leit·mo·tiv, leit·mo·tif ['laɪtməʊˌti:f] N (*Mus, fig*) leitmotiv *m inv*

lem·ming ['lɛmɪŋ] N lemming *m inv*

lem·on ['lɛmən] N (*fruit*) limone *m*
■ ADJ (*colour*) giallo limone *inv*

lem·on·ade [ˌlɛmə'neɪd] N (*fizzy drink*) gassosa; (*: with lemon flavour*) limonata

lemon cheese, lemon curd N crema di limone (*da spalmare sul pane*)

lemon juice N succo di limone

lemon sole N sogliola limanda
lem·on squeez·er ['lɛmən,skwi:zəʳ] N spremilimoni *m inv*, spremiagrumi *m inv*
lemon tea N tè *m inv* al limone
lemon tree N (albero di) limone *m*
lem·on zest·er ['lɛmən,zɛstəʳ] N rigalimoni *m inv*
le·mur ['li:məʳ] N lemuride *m*
◎ **lend** [lɛnd] (*pt, pp* **lent**) VT (*gen*) prestare; (*fig: impart: importance, mystery, authority*) conferire; **I can lend you some money** posso prestarti del denaro; **he lent me £10** mi ha prestato dieci sterline; **to lend out** prestare, dare in prestito; **to lend a hand** dare una mano; **to lend an ear to sb/sth** prestare ascolto a qn/qc; **it does not lend itself to being filmed** non si presta ad essere filmato
lend·er ['lɛndəʳ] N chi presta, prestatore(-trice)
lend·ing ['lɛndɪŋ] N prestito
lending library N biblioteca (*con servizio di prestito di libri*)
lending rate N tasso di interesse
◎ **length** [lɛŋθ] N **1** (*size, extent*) lunghezza; (*duration*) durata; **it is 2 metres in length** è lungo 2 metri; **what is its length?** *or* **what length is it?** quant'è lungo?; **throughout the length and breadth of Italy** in tutta Italia; **to fall full length** cadere lungo(-a) disteso(-a); **length of time** periodo (di tempo); **for what length of time?** per quanto tempo?; **1000 words in length** di 1000 parole; **their team won the boat race by 2 lengths** (*Sport*) la loro squadra ha vinto la gara di canottaggio per 2 lunghezze; **at length** (*at last*) finalmente; (*lengthily*) a lungo; **to speak at length** dilungarsi, parlare a lungo; **I even went to the length of sending her flowers** sono perfino arrivato al punto di mandarle i fiori; **to go to any lengths to do sth** fare qualsiasi cosa pur di *or* per fare qc; **she went to great lengths to make sure that ...** fece di tutto per assicurarsi che... **2** (*piece: of road, pipe etc*) pezzo, tratto; (*: material*) taglio, altezza; **a dress/skirt length** un taglio per vestito/gonna
length·en ['lɛŋθən] VT (*distance*) allungare; (*time*) prolungare; **he lengthened his stride** ha allungato il passo
■ VI allungarsi; **the days are lengthening** le giornate si stanno allungando
lengthi·ly ['lɛŋθɪlɪ] ADV a lungo
length·ways ['lɛŋθ,weɪz], **length·wise** ['lɛŋθ,waɪz] ADV per la lunghezza, per lungo
lengthy ['lɛŋθɪ] ADJ (*comp* **-ier**, *superl* **-iest**) lungo(-a); (*tedious*) interminabile
le·ni·ence ['li:nɪəns], **le·ni·en·cy** ['li:nɪənsɪ] N (*of person*) clemenza, indulgenza; (*of sentence, punishment*) mitezza
le·ni·ent ['li:nɪənt] ADJ (*person*) indulgente, clemente; (*sentence, punishment*) mite; **to be lenient with sb** essere indulgente con qn
le·ni·ent·ly ['li:nɪəntlɪ] ADV con indulgenza
Len·in·ism ['lɛnɪ,nɪzəm] N leninismo
Len·in·ist ['lɛnɪ,nɪst] ADJ, N leninista (*m/f*)
◎ **lens** [lɛnz] N (*Anat: of the eye*) cristallino; (*of spectacles*) lente *f*; (*of camera etc*) obiettivo; **contact lenses** lenti a contatto
lens holder N (*Phot*) portaobiettivi *m inv*
lens hood N (*Phot*) paraluce *m inv*
Lent [lɛnt] N Quaresima; **I'm giving it up for Lent** vi rinuncio come fioretto (quaresimale)
lent [lɛnt] PT, PP *of* **lend**
len·ten ['lɛntən] ADJ (*Rel*) quaresimale
len·til ['lɛntl] N lenticchia
Leo ['li:əʊ] N (*Astron, Astrol*) Leone *m*; **to be Leo** essere del Leone; **I'm Leo** sono del Leone
leop·ard ['lɛpəd] N leopardo; **the leopard cannot** *or* **doesn't change its spots** il lupo perde il pelo ma non il vizio
leop·ard·ess [,lɛpə'dɛs] N femmina del leopardo
leo·tard ['li:əta:d] N body *m inv* (*per ginnastica, danza*)
lep·er ['lɛpəʳ] N lebbroso(-a)
leper colony N lebbrosario
lep·ro·sy ['lɛprəsɪ] N lebbra
lep·rous ['lɛprəs] ADJ lebbroso(-a)
◎ **les·bian** ['lɛzbɪən] ADJ lesbico(-a)
■ N lesbica
les·bi·an·ism ['lɛzbɪə,nɪzəm] N lesbismo
le·sion ['li:ʒən] N (*Med*) lesione *f*
Le·so·tho [lə'səʊtəʊ] N Lesotho *m*
◎ **less** [lɛs] (*comp of* **little**) ADJ meno; **now we eat less bread** ora mangiamo meno pane; **she has less time to spare** ha meno tempo a disposizione; **of less importance** di minor importanza
■ PRON meno; **a bit less, please** un po' meno, per favore; **we see less of them now** li vediamo di meno adesso; **the less you read the less you learn** meno leggi meno impari; **can't you let me have it for less?** mi potrebbe fare un piccolo sconto?; **the less said about it the better** meno se ne parla e meglio è; **less than half** meno della metà; **less than £1/a kilo/3 metres** meno di una sterlina/un chilo/3 metri; **it's less than a kilometre from here** è a meno di un chilometro da qui; **less than you think** meno di quanto tu creda; **less than you/ever** meno di te/che mai; **the holiday was less than perfect** la vacanza non è stata proprio stupenda; **it's nothing less than a disaster** è un disastro bell'e buono; **a tip of £10, no less!** (*fam*) nientemeno che 10 sterline di mancia!
■ ADV meno, di meno; **to go out less (often)** uscire di meno; **less and less** sempre meno; **still less** ancora meno; **none the less ...** ugualmente..., lo stesso...
■ PREP meno; **less 5%** meno il 5%
-less SUFF senza; **breathless** senza fiato; **meaningless** privo(-a) di significato, senza senso
les·see [lɛ'si:] N affittuario(-a), locatario(-a)
less·en ['lɛsn] VT (*gen*) diminuire, ridurre; (*pain*) alleviare; (*cost, tension*) ridurre; (*shock*) attutire, attenuare
■ VI (*gen*) diminuire, ridursi; (*shock*) attenuarsi
less·en·ing ['lɛsnɪŋ] N diminuzione *f*
less·er ['lɛsəʳ] ADJ (*importance, degree*) minore; (*size*) più piccolo(-a); **to a lesser extent** *or* **degree** in grado *or* misura minore; **the lesser of two evils** il minore dei due mali
◎ **les·son** ['lɛsn] N lezione *f*; **to give lessons in** dare *or* impartire lezioni di; **a French lesson** una lezione di francese; **to teach sb a lesson** (*fig*) dare una lezione a qn; **it taught him a lesson** (*fig*) gli è servito di lezione
les·sor [lɛ'sɔ:ʳ] N locatore(-trice)
lest [lɛst] CONJ (*old*) (*frm*) nel timore che + *sub*, per paura che + *sub*; **lest we forget** per non dimenticare
◎ **let**[1] [lɛt] (*pt, pp* **let**) VT
1 (*permit*) lasciare, permettere; **to let sb past** lasciar *or* far passare qn; **to let sb do sth** lasciar fare qc a qn, lasciare che qn faccia qc; **let him come** lascialo venire; **let me have a look** fammi vedere; **to let sb have sth** dare qc a qn; **to let sb know sth** far sapere qc a qn; **I'll let you know our decision as soon as possible** ti farò sapere cosa abbiamo deciso il prima possibile; **don't let him get away with it** (*fam*) non lasciare che la

Ll

passi liscia; **I'll let you have it back tomorrow** te lo ridò *or* restituisco domani; **don't let me catch** *or* **see you copying again!** che non ti peschi *or* sorprenda mai più a copiare!; **let him alone** *or* **be** lascialo stare *or* in pace; **to let go of sb/sth** mollare *or* lasciar andare qn/qc; **he let me go** mi ha lasciato andare; **let me go!** lasciami andare!; **let the water boil then ...** fate bollire l'acqua e quindi...

2 (*in verb forms*): **let's** *or* **let us go!** andiamo!; **let's go to the cinema!** andiamo al cinema!; **let's have a break!** – **yes, let's** facciamo una pausa! – va bene; **let's see, what was I saying?** dunque, cosa stavo dicendo?; **let them wait** che aspettino (pure); **let that be a warning to you!** che questo ti serva di lezione!; **let x=1 and y=2** sia x=1 e y=2

3 (*Brit: rent out*) affittare, dare in affitto; **"To Let"** "Affittasi"

▸ **let away** VT + ADV lasciare andare (via)

▸ **let down** VT + ADV

1 (*lower*) abbassare; (*dress*) allungare; (*hem*) allungare, lasciar giù; (*Brit: tyre*) sgonfiare; (*one's hair*) sciogliersi; (*on rope*) calare (giù)

2 (*disappoint*) deludere; **I won't let you down** non ti deluderò; **that car always lets me down** quella macchina mi molla sempre in asso

▸ **let go** VI + ADV mollare

■ VT + ADV mollare; (*allow to go*) lasciare andare

▸ **let in** VT + ADV far *or* lasciar entrare, far *or* lasciar passare; **to let sb in** far *or* lasciar entrare qn; **they wouldn't let me in because I'm under 18** non mi hanno fatto entrare perché sono minorenne; **shoes which let the water in** scarpe che lasciano passare l'acqua; **to let sb in for a lot of trouble** procurare *or* dare un mucchio di fastidi a qn; **what have you let yourself in for?** in che guai *or* pasticci sei andato a cacciarti?; **to let sb in on a secret** rivelare *or* confidare un segreto a qn

▸ **let into** VT + PREP

1 (*allow in*) lasciar entrare in

2 (*allow to share*): **to let sb into** far partecipe qn di

3 (*inset*) inglobare

▸ **let off** VT + ADV

1 (*explode*) far esplodere; (*fireworks*) accendere, lasciar partire; (*smell etc*) emettere; **to let off steam** (*fig fam*) sfogarsi, scaricarsi

2 (*allow to go*) lasciar andare *or* uscire; (*not punish*) non punire; **to let sb off lightly** non calcare la mano nel punire qn; **to let sb off with a warning** limitarsi ad ammonire qn

3 (*subj: taxi driver, bus driver*) far scendere

▸ **let on** VI + ADV (*fam*) dire, lasciar capire; **to let on to sb about sth** far capire qc a qn; **to let on (that ...)** dare a intendere (che...)

▸ **let out** VT + ADV

1 (*gen*) far *or* lasciare uscire; (*secret*) spifferare; (*news*) divulgare; **don't get up, I'll let myself out** non occorre che mi accompagni alla porta; **to let out a cry/sigh/scream** emettere un grido/un sospiro/un urlo; **to let the air out of a tyre** sgonfiare una gomma; **that lets her out** questo la esonera

2 (*dress, seam*) allargare

3 (*rent out*) affittare, dare in affitto

▸ **let up** VI + ADV (*bad weather*) diminuire; (*talker, worker*) smettere, fermarsi

■ VT + ADV far alzare

let² [lɛt] N (*Tennis*) colpo nullo

let-down [ˈlɛt,daʊn] N (*disappointment*) delusione *f*

le·thal [ˈliːθəl] ADJ: **lethal (to)** (*gen*) letale (per); (*wound, blow*) mortale (per)

le·thar·gic [lɪˈθɑːdʒɪk] ADJ (*physically*) fiacco(-a); (*mentally*) apatico(-a)

leth·ar·gy [ˈlɛθədʒɪ] N (*see adj*) fiacchezza; apatia

◎ **let·ter** [ˈlɛtəʳ] N **1** (*missive*) lettera; **by letter** per lettera; **letter of introduction/application/protest** lettera di presentazione/di domanda/di protesta **2** (*of alphabet*) lettera; **the letter G** la (lettera) G; **small/capital letter** lettera minuscola/maiuscola; **she's got a lot of letters after her name** ha un mucchio di titoli; **the letter of the law** (*fig*) la lettera della legge; **to follow instructions to the letter** seguire alla lettera le istruzioni

letter bomb [ˈlɛtə,bɒm] N lettera esplosiva

letter·box [ˈlɛtə,bɒks] N cassetta *or* buca delle lettere; **she pushed the key through the letterbox** infilò la chiave nella buca delle lettere sulla porta

letter card N biglietto postale

letter·head [ˈlɛtə,hɛd] N intestazione *f*

let·ter·ing [ˈlɛtərɪŋ] N (*engraving*) iscrizione *f*; (*letters*) caratteri *mpl*; **a blue sign with white lettering** un cartello blu con i caratteri bianchi

letter of credit N lettera di credito; **documentary letter of credit** lettera di credito documentata

letter-opener [ˈlɛtər,əʊpnəʳ] N tagliacarte *m inv*

letter-perfect [,lɛtəˈpɜːfɪkt] ADJ (*Am*): **to be letter-perfect in sth** conoscere qc a menadito

letter·press [ˈlɛtə,prɛs] (*Typ*) N (*method*) rilievografia; (*printed page*) testo

letter quality printer N stampante *f* ad alta definizione

let·ters [ˈlɛtəz] NPL (*Literature*): **man of letters** uomo di lettere

letter scales NPL pesalettere *m inv*

letters patent NPL brevetto di invenzione

letter tray N cestello per la corrispondenza

letter-writer [ˈlɛtə,raɪtəʳ] N corrispondente *m/f*

let·ting [ˈlɛtɪŋ] N affitto

let·tuce [ˈlɛtɪs] N lattuga

let-up [ˈlɛt,ʌp] N (*fam*) rallentamento; **without (a) let-up** ininterrottamente, senza smettere

leu·co·cyte [ˈluːkə,saɪt] N leucocita *m*

leu·kae·mia, (*Am*) **leu·ke·mia** [luːˈkiːmɪə] N leucemia

levee [ˈlɛvɪ] N (*esp Am*) argine *m*

◎ **lev·el** [ˈlɛvl] ADJ **1** (*flat: ground, surface*) piano(-a), piatto(-a); (*: shelf*) diritto(-a), orizzontale; **a level surface** una superficie piana; **I'll do my level best** (*fam*) farò del mio meglio, farò tutto il possibile; **a level spoonful** (*Culin*) un cucchiaio raso **2** (*steady: voice, tone*) pacato(-a); (*: gaze*) diretto(-a), sicuro(-a); **to keep a level head** mantenere il sangue freddo *or* la calma **3** (*equal*) alla pari; **to be level with sb** (*in race, league, studies*) essere allo stesso livello di; (*in rank*) avere lo stesso grado di qn; **to draw level with** (*team*) mettersi alla pari di; (*runner, car*) affiancarsi a

■ N **1** livello; **above/at/below sea level** sotto il/sul/al livello del mare; **the level of the river is rising** il livello del fiume sta salendo; **talks at ministerial level** colloqui a livello ministeriale; **to be on a level with** essere al livello di; (*fig*) essere allo stesso livello di; **to come down to sb's level** (*fig*) scendere *or* abbassarsi al livello di qn; **to find one's own level** trovare la giusta dimensione; **on the level** piatto(-a); (*fig*) onesto(-a); **he's on the level** (*fig fam*) è a posto **2** (*also:* **spirit level**) livella (a bolla d'aria) **3** (*Brit Scol*):

A-levels *diploma di studi superiori*; **O-levels** *(formerly) esame che si sosteneva in Inghilterra a 16 anni, ora sostituito dal GCSE*

■VT **1** *(make level: ground, site)* livellare, spianare; *(raze: building)* radere al suolo; *(fig)* livellare **2** *(aim)*: **to level (at)** *(blow)* tirare (a), allungare (a); *(gun)* puntare (verso); **to level an accusation against** lanciare un'accusa contro

▸ **level off, level out** VI + ADV *(prices, curve on graph etc)* stabilizzarsi; *(ground)* diventare pianeggiante; *(aircraft)* volare in quota

▸ **level with** VI + PREP *(fam)*: **to level with sb** esser franco(-a) con qn

level crossing N *(Brit)* passaggio a livello

level-headed [ˌlɛvl'hɛdɪd] ADJ equilibrato(-a), con la testa a posto *or* sulle spalle

lev·el·ling, *(Am)* **lev·el·ing** ['lɛvəlɪŋ] ADJ *(process, effect)* di livellamento

level playing field N: **to compete on a level playing field** competere ad armi pari

lev·er ['li:vəʳ, *Am* 'lɛvəʳ] N *(also fig)* leva

■VT: **to lever sth up/off/out** sollevare/togliere/estrarre qc (con una leva)

lev·er·age ['li:vərɪdʒ, *Am* 'lɛvərɪdʒ] N: **leverage (on)** forza (su); *(fig)* ascendente *m* (su); **to exert leverage on sth/sb** far leva su qc/qn

lever arch file N cartella con macchinetta a leva

levi·tate ['lɛvɪˌteɪt] VI levitare

Le·viti·cus [lɪ'vɪtɪkəs] N Levitico

lev·ity ['lɛvɪtɪ] *(frm)* N *(frivolity)* frivolezza; *(flippancy)* leggerezza

levy ['lɛvɪ] N *(amount)* imposta, tassa; *(collection)* riscossione *f*

■VT *(tax, contributions)* imporre; *(fine)* elevare; *(army)* arruolare

lewd [lu:d] ADJ *(comp* **-er**, *superl* **-est**) osceno(-a)

lewd·ness ['lu:dnɪs] N oscenità

lexi·cal ['lɛksɪkəl] ADJ lessicale

lexi·cog·ra·pher [ˌlɛksɪ'kɒgrəfəʳ] N lessicografo(-a)

lexi·cog·ra·phy [ˌlɛksɪ'kɒgrəfɪ] N lessicografia

▷ www.euralex.org/

▷ www.australex.org/

▷ http://polyglot.lss.wisc.edu/dsna/

lexi·colo·gist [ˌlɛksɪ'kɒlədʒɪst] N lessicologo(-a)

lexi·col·ogy [ˌlɛksɪ'kɒlədʒɪ] N lessicologia

lexi·con ['lɛksɪkən] N lessico

LI ABBR *(Am)* = *Long Island*

liabil·ities [ˌlaɪə'bɪlɪtɪz] NPL *(Comm)* debiti *mpl*; *(on balance sheet)* passivo *msg*, passività *f inv*

lia·bil·ity [ˌlaɪə'bɪlɪtɪ] N *(Law: responsibility)* responsabilità *f inv*; *(burden)* peso; *(person)* peso morto; *see also* **liabilities**; **he's becoming a liability** sta diventando un peso; **they disclaimed liability** hanno declinato ogni responsabilità

lia·ble ['laɪəbl] ADJ **1** *(likely)*: **liable to do** propenso(-a) a fare; **she's liable to get cross** è probabile che si arrabbi; **it's liable to break** è probabile che si rompa; **we are liable to get shot at here** qui c'è il rischio che ci sparino; **he's liable to colds** è soggetto a frequenti raffreddori, prende facilmente il raffreddore; **he's liable to panic** è facile che si lasci prendere dal panico **2** *(subject)*: **to be liable for military service** essere tenuto(-a) a svolgere il servizio militare; **to be liable to a fine** essere passibile di multa **3** *(responsible)*: **to be liable for** essere responsabile di

li·aise [li:'eɪz] VI: **to liaise (with)** mantenere i contatti (con)

liai·son [li:'eɪzɒn] N *(also euph)* relazione *f*; *(coordination)* coordinamento; *(Mil)* collegamento

liaison committee N comitato di coordinamento

liaison officer N ufficiale *m* di collegamento

lia·na [lɪ'ɑ:nə] N liana

liar ['laɪəʳ] N bugiardo(-a)

li·bel ['laɪbəl] N *(Law: crime)* diffamazione *f*; *(: written statement)* libello

■VT diffamare

li·bel·lous, *(Am)* **li·bel·ous** ['laɪbələs] ADJ diffamatorio(-a)

Lib·er·al ['lɪbərəl] N *(Pol)* liberale *m/f*

◎ **lib·er·al** ['lɪbərəl] ADJ *(generous)* liberale, generoso(-a); *(views)* liberale; **to be liberal with** essere prodigo(-a) di

liberal arts NPL *(Am)* materie *fpl* umanistiche

Liberal Democrat ADJ, N liberaldemocratico(-a)

lib·er·al·ism ['lɪbərəˌlɪzəm] N liberalismo

lib·er·al·ity [ˌlɪbə'rælɪtɪ] N *(generosity)* liberalità, generosità

lib·er·al·ize ['lɪbərəˌlaɪz] VT liberalizzare

lib·er·al·ly ['lɪbərəlɪ] ADV generosamente

liberal-minded [ˌlɪbərəl'maɪndɪd] ADJ tollerante

◎ **lib·er·ate** ['lɪbəˌreɪt] VT liberare; **a liberated woman** una donna emancipata

lib·er·at·ed ['lɪbəˌreɪtɪd] ADJ *(woman, lifestyle)* emancipato(-a)

lib·era·tion [ˌlɪbə'reɪʃən] N liberazione *f*

liberation theology N teologia della liberazione

lib·era·tor ['lɪbəˌreɪtəʳ] N liberatore(-trice)

Li·beria [laɪ'bɪərɪə] N Liberia

Li·berian [laɪ'bɪərɪən] ADJ, N liberiano(-a)

lib·er·tar·ian [ˌlɪbə'tɛərɪən] ADJ *(frm)* libertario(-a)

■N liberale *m/f*

◎ **lib·er·ty** ['lɪbətɪ] N libertà *f inv*; **liberty of conscience** libertà di coscienza; **at liberty** *(not detained)* in libertà; **to be at liberty to do sth** essere libero(-a) di fare qc; **to take the liberty of doing sth** prendersi la libertà di fare qc, permettersi di fare qc; **to take liberties** prendersi delle libertà; **what a liberty!** *(fam)* come ti permetti? *(or si permette? etc)*

li·bidi·nous [lɪ'bɪdɪnəs] ADJ *(frm)* libidinoso(-a)

li·bi·do [lɪ'bi:dəʊ] N *(Psych)* libido *f inv*

Li·bra ['li:brə] N *(Astron, Astrol)* Bilancia; **to be Libra** essere della Bilancia; **I'm Libra** sono della Bilancia

li·brar·ian [laɪ'brɛərɪən] N bibliotecario(-a)

li·brar·ian·ship [laɪ'brɛərɪənʃɪp] N biblioteconomia

◎ **li·brary** ['laɪbrərɪ] N biblioteca

▷ www.bl.uk/index.shtml

▷ www.loc.gov

DID YOU KNOW ...?
library is not translated by the Italian word *libreria*

library book N libro della biblioteca

library ticket N tesserino della biblioteca

li·bret·tist [lɪ'brɛtɪst] N librettista *m/f*

li·bret·to [lɪ'brɛtəʊ] N libretto

Libya ['lɪbɪə] N Libia

Liby·an ['lɪbɪən] ADJ, N libico(-a)

lice [laɪs] NPL *of* **louse**

◎ **li·cence,** *(Am)* **li·cense**[1] ['laɪsəns] N **1** *(permit)* autorizzazione *f*, permesso; *(for car)* bollo, tassa di circolazione; *(also:* **driving licence**; *Am: also:* **driver's licence**) patente *f* di guida; *(Comm)* licenza; *(for dog)* tassa; *(TV, Radio)* abbonamento; *(: amount paid)* canone *m*, abbonamento; **they were married by special licence** si sono sposati con dispensa; **provisional driving licence** ≈ foglio rosa; **pilot's licence** brevetto

LI

(di pilota); **import licence** licenza di importazione; **produced under licence** prodotto(-a) su licenza; **he lost his licence for a year** gli hanno ritirato la patente per un anno **2** *(freedom)* libertà; *(excessive freedom)* licenza, eccessiva libertà

licence number N *(Brit Aut)* numero di targa

li·cense² ['laɪsəns] VT **1** *(person)*: **to license sb to do** autorizzare qn a fare **2** *(car: subj: owner)* pagare la tassa di circolazione; (: *subj: licensing authority*) rilasciare il bollo (di circolazione)

li·censed ['laɪsənst] ADJ *(restaurant, premises)* autorizzato(-a) alla vendita di bevande alcoliche

licensed trade N commercio di bevande alcoliche con licenza speciale

li·cen·see [ˌlaɪsən'si:] N *(in pub)* titolare *m/f* di licenza per la vendita di bevande alcoliche

license plate N *(esp Am Aut)* targa (automobilistica)

li·cens·ing laws [laɪsənsɪŋlɔ:z] N *(Brit)* leggi *fpl* che regolamentano la vendita di alcolici

li·cen·tious [laɪ'sɛnʃəs] ADJ *(frm)* licenzioso(-a)

li·chee [ˌlaɪ'tʃi:] N = **lychee**

li·chen ['laɪkən] N lichene *m*

lick [lɪk] VT **1** *(with tongue)* leccare; *(subj: flames)* lambire; **to lick one's plate clean** pulire il piatto con la lingua; **to lick one's lips** leccarsi le labbra; *(hungrily)* leccarsi i baffi; **to lick one's wounds** *(also fig)* leccarsi le ferite; **to lick sb's boots** *(fig fam)* leccare i piedi a qn; **to lick sth into shape** *(fig fam)* mettere a punto qc **2** *(fam: defeat)* suonarle a, stracciare
■ N **1** leccata; **a lick of paint** una passata di vernice; **a lick and a promise** *(fig fam)* una pulitina sommaria **2** *(fam: speed)*: **at full lick** a tutta birra

lick·ing ['lɪkɪŋ] N *(fam: beating)* pestata, botte *fpl*; (: *defeat*) batosta

lico·rice ['lɪkərɪs] N = **liquorice**

lid [lɪd] N coperchio; **to take the lid off sth** *(fig)* smascherare qc; **that puts the lid on it** *(fam)* ci mancava solo questo

lido ['li:dəʊ] N *(esp Brit: swimming pool)* piscina (all'aperto); *(part of the beach)* lido, stabilimento balneare

lie¹ [laɪ] N bugia, menzogna; **to tell lies** raccontare *or* dir bugie; **to give the lie to** smentire
■ VI *(prp* **lying***)* mentire; **I know she's lying** so che sta mentendo; **you lied to me!** mi hai mentito!

◎ **lie²** [laɪ] *(pt* **lay**, *pp* **lain***)* *(prp* **lying***)* VI **1** *(also:* **lie down***)* sdraiarsi, distendersi; *(be lying)* essere sdraiato(-a) *or* disteso(-a), giacere; *(dead body)* giacere; **he was lying on the sofa** era disteso sul divano; **he had lain there for hours** è rimasto disteso lì per ore; **he lay where he had fallen** giaceva a terra nel punto in cui era caduto; **to lie still** giacere immobile; **she lay in bed until 10 o'clock** è rimasta a letto fino alle 10; **to lie low** *(fig)* tenersi nell'ombra; (: *hide*) nascondersi **2** *(be situated)* trovarsi, essere; *(remain)* rimanere; **the book lay on the table** il libro giaceva sul tavolo; **the snow lay half a metre deep** la neve formava una coltre di mezzo metro; **the town lies in a valley** la città è situata *or* si trova in una valle; **the plain lay before us** la pianura si stendeva dinanzi a noi; **in spite of the obstacles lying in his way** nonostante gli ostacoli che aveva di fronte; **where does the difficulty/difference lie?** dov'è *or* qual è la difficoltà/differenza?; **the fault lies with you** l'errore è tuo; **the challenge lies in ...** la difficoltà sta nel...; **the best remedy lies in ...** il miglior rimedio consiste nel...
▸ **lie about, lie around** VI + ADV *(things)* essere in giro; *(person)* bighellonare; **it must be lying about somewhere** dev'essere in giro da qualche parte
▸ **lie back** VI + ADV stendersi; **lie back and enjoy yourself!** rilassati e divertiti!
▸ **lie behind** VI + PREP essere dietro; **what lies behind his refusal?** cosa c'è dietro il suo rifiuto?; **the real cause that lay behind the rise in divorce** la vera causa all'origine dell'incremento dei divorzi
▸ **lie down** VI + ADV stendersi, sdraiarsi; **lie down!** *(to dog)* cuccia!; **why not go and lie down for a bit?** perché non vai a distenderti per un po'?; **to take sth lying down** *(fig)* accettare supinamente qc
▸ **lie in** VI + ADV *(stay in bed)* rimanere a letto *(al mattino)*
▸ **lie up** VI + ADV *(hide)* nascondersi

Liech·ten·stein ['lɪktən,staɪn] N Liechtenstein *m*

lie detector N macchina della verità

lie-down ['laɪ,daʊn] N *(Brit fam)* riposino

lie-in ['laɪ,ɪn] N: **to have a lie-in** *(Brit fam)* rimanere a letto *(al mattino)*

lieu [lu:] N: **in lieu of** invece di, al posto di

Lieut. ABBR (= **lieutenant**) Ten.

lieu·ten·ant [lɛf'tɛnənt, *Am* lu:'tɛnənt] N *(Mil)* tenente *m*; *(Naut)* tenente *m* di vascello

lieutenant-colonel [lɛf'tɛnənt'kɜ:nl, *Am* lu:'tɛnənt'kɜ:nl] N tenente *m* colonnello

lieutenant-general [lɛf'tɛnənt'dʒɛnərəl, *Am* lu:'tɛnənt'dʒɛnərəl] N tenente *m* generale, generale *m* di divisione

lieutenant governor N vicegovernatore *m*

◎ **life** [laɪf] N *(pl* **lives***)* **1** *(gen)* vita; **life on earth** vita terrestre *or* sulla terra; **bird life** gli uccelli; **a matter of life and death** una questione di vita o di morte; **to bring sb back to life** riportare in vita qn; **to come to life** rianimarsi, riprendere vita **2** *(existence)* vita; *(of battery etc)* durata; **to spend one's life doing sth** passare la vita a fare qc; **during the life of this government** durante questo governo, nel corso di questa amministrazione; **to begin life as** cominciare come; **to be sent to prison for life** essere condannato(-a) all'ergastolo; **in early life** in gioventù; **in later life** nella maturità; **all my life** tutta la vita; **a quiet/hard life** una vita tranquilla/dura; **country/city life** vita di campagna/di città; **how's life?** *(fam)* come va (la vita)?; **that's life** così è la vita; **to lose one's life** perdere la vita; **three lives were lost** tre persone sono morte *or* hanno perso la vita; **to take one's own life** *(euph: commit suicide)* togliersi la vita; **a danger to life and limb** un pericolo mortale; **to risk life and limb** rischiare l'osso del collo; **you'll be taking your life in your hands if you climb up there** *(fam)* rischi la pelle se ti arrampichi lassù; **his life won't be worth living** rimpiangerà di esser nato; **not on your life!** *(fam)* neanche morto!, fossi matto!; **to see life** vedere il mondo; **to run for one's life** correre per mettersi in salvo; **I can't for the life of me imagine ...** *(fam)* non riesco assolutamente a immaginare...; **true to life** fedele alla realtà; **to paint from life** dipingere dal vero **3** *(liveliness: of place)* vita, animazione *f*; (: *of person*) vita, vivacità; **the life and soul of the party** l'anima della festa; **to put** *or* **breathe new life into** *(person)* ridare entusiasmo a; *(project, area etc)* ridare nuova vita a
■ ADJ *(for life: membership)* a vita; *(in life: chances)* di vita

life-and-death ['laɪfən,dɛθ] ADJ: **life-and-death struggle** lotta all'ultimo sangue

life annuity N rendita vitalizia

life assurance N (*Brit*) = **life insurance**
life belt, life buoy N salvagente *m*
life·blood ['laɪf,blʌd] N (*fig*) linfa vitale
life·boat ['laɪf,bəʊt] N (*from shore*) lancia di salvataggio; (*from ship*) scialuppa di salvataggio
life cycle N ciclo vitale
life expectancy N durata media della vita
life form N forma di vita
life·guard ['laɪf,gɑːd] N (*on beach*) bagnino(-a)
life history N (*Bio*) ciclo biologico; **a significant event in his life history** un avvenimento importante nella sua vita
life imprisonment N ergastolo
life insurance, (*Brit*) **life assurance** N assicurazione *f* sulla vita
life jacket N giubbotto di salvataggio
life·less ['laɪflɪs] ADJ (*body*) privo(-a) di vita, inanimato(-a); (*fig*: *person*) privo(-a) di energia; (: *style*) piatto(-a); (: *hair*) senza corpo
life·less·ness ['laɪflɪsnɪs] N (*fig*) mancanza di vigore
life·like ['laɪf,laɪk] ADJ che sembra vero(-a), realistico(-a)
life·line ['laɪf,laɪn] N (*on ship*) sagola di salvataggio; (*for diver*) cavo di recupero *or* di salvataggio; **it was his lifeline** (*fig*) era vitale per lui
life·long ['laɪf,lɒŋ] ADJ (*ambition etc*) di tutta la mia *or* sua *etc* vita; (*friend*) di sempre
lifelong learning N formazione *f* permanente
▷ www.lifelonglearning.co.uk/
life member N membro a vita
life partner N compagno(-a), partner *m/f inv* (*in relazione a lungo termine*)
life peer N pari *m inv* a vita
life peerage N titolo di pari a vita
life pre·serv·er ['laɪfprɪ,zɜːvə^r] N **1** (*Am*: *life belt*) salvagente *m*; (: *life jacket*) giubbotto di salvataggio **2** (*Brit*: *bludgeon*) sfollagente *m inv*
lif·er ['laɪfə^r] N (*fam*) ergastolano(-a)
life raft N zattera di salvataggio
life-saver ['laɪf,seɪvə^r] N (*person*) bagnino(-a); **it/he** *etc* **was a life-saver** (*fig*) mi ha salvato la vita
life-saving ['laɪf,seɪvɪŋ] N (*rescuing*) salvataggio; **I've done a course in life-saving** ho fatto un corso di salvataggio
■ ADJ (*treatment, drug*) che salva (*or* salvano *etc*) la vita
life science N scienze *fpl* naturali
▷ www.sciencekomm.at/
▷ www.biologybrowser.org
▷ http://biotech.icmb.utexas.edu
life sentence N condanna all'ergastolo
life-size(d) ['laɪf,saɪz(d)] ADJ in *or* a grandezza naturale
life span N (durata della) vita
life story N biografia; **her life story** la sua biografia, la storia della sua vita
life style N stile *m* di vita
life·style ['laɪfstaɪl] ADJ (*change, choices*) di stile di vita; (*magazine, show*) sullo stile di vita
life support system N (*Med*) respiratore *m* automatico
life·time ['laɪf,taɪm] N vita; **a lifetime's work** *or* **the work of a lifetime** il lavoro di tutta una vita; **in my lifetime** nel corso della mia vita, durante la mia vita; **I don't think it will happen in my lifetime** non credo che succederà finché sono vivo; **in a lifetime** nell'arco della vita, in tutta la vita; **a trip of a lifetime** un viaggio memorabile; **the chance of a lifetime** un'occasione unica *or* che capita una sola volta nella vita; **it seemed a lifetime** sembrò (che fosse passata) un'eternità *or* una vita
LIFO ['laɪfəʊ] N ABBR (= **last in first out**) lifo *m inv*
◎ **lift** [lɪft] VT **1** (*thing, person*) sollevare, alzare; **it's too heavy, I can't lift it** è troppo pesante, non riesco a sollevarlo; **to lift sb over sth** far passare qn sopra qc; **to lift one's head** alzare *or* sollevare la testa; **she never lifts a finger to help** non alza *or* muove mai neanche un dito per aiutare **2** (*fig*: *restrictions, ban*) revocare **3** (*fam*: *steal*: *idea, quotation*) riprendere *or* copiare pari pari
■ VI sollevarsi, alzarsi; (*fog*) alzarsi
■ N **1** (*Brit*: *elevator*) ascensore *m*; (*for goods*) montacarichi *m inv*; **the lift isn't working** l'ascensore non funziona **2** (*esp Brit*: *in car*) passaggio; **to give sb a lift** dare un passaggio a qn; **he gave me a lift to the cinema** mi ha dato un passaggio al cinema **3** (*Aer*) spinta; **it gave him a tremendous lift** (*fig*) lo ha tirato su moltissimo
▸ **lift down** VT + ADV tirar giù
▸ **lift off** VT + ADV togliere
■ VI + ADV (*aircraft, rocket*) decollare
▸ **lift out** VT + ADV tirar fuori; (*troops, evacuees etc*) far evacuare per mezzo di elicotteri (*or* aerei)
▸ **lift up** VT + ADV sollevare, alzare
lift attendant N ascensorista *m/f*
lift·boy ['lɪft,bɔɪ], **lift·man** ['lɪft,mæn] N (*pl* **-boys** *or* **-men**) lift *m inv*, ascensorista *m/f*
lift-off ['lɪft,ɒf] N decollo
lift-off tape N (*for typewriter*) nastrino *m* correttore *inv* per macchina da scrivere
lift shaft N tromba dell'ascensore
liga·ment ['lɪgəmənt] N legamento
◎ **light**[1] [laɪt] (*vb*: *pt, pp* **lit** *or* **lighted**) N
1 (*gen*) luce *f*; **electric light** illuminazione *f or* luce elettrica; **at first light** alle prime luci dell'alba; **by the light of the moon** alla luce della luna, al chiaro di luna; **in the cold light of day** (*also fig*) alla luce del giorno; **you're (standing) in my light** mi fai ombra; **to hold sth up to** *or* **against the light** tenere qc controluce
2 (*fig*): **in the light of** alla luce di; **to bring to light** portare alla luce; **to come to light** venire in luce, emergere; **to cast** *or* **shed** *or* **throw light on** gettare *or* far luce su; **I was hoping that you could shed some light on it (for me)** speravo che tu potessi darmi dei chiarimenti su questo; **to see the light** (*Rel*) convertirsi; (*fig*) ravvedersi; **to reveal sb/sth in a new light** mostrare qn/qc sotto una nuova luce; **according to my lights** (*frm*) secondo quanto mi è dato di capire
3 (*single light*) luce *f*; (*lamp*) luce, lampada; (*Aut, Aer*) fanale *m*, faro, luce; **to turn the light on/off** accendere/spegnere la luce; **he switched on the light** ha acceso la luce; **he switched off the light** ha spento la luce; **rear lights** luci di posizione posteriori; **the (traffic) lights were red** il semaforo era rosso
4 (*flame*) fiamma; **pilot light** (*on stove, water heater*) fiammella di sicurezza; **have you got a light?** (*for cigarette*) hai da accendere?; **to put a light to sth** dar fuoco a qc
■ ADJ (*comp* **-er**, *superl* **-est**)
1 (*bright*) chiaro(-a); **to get lighter** rischiararsi, schiarirsi
2 (*colour, skin, hair, room*) chiaro(-a); **light yellow** giallo chiaro *inv*; **a light blue sweater** una maglia azzurro chiaro

LI

■VT
1 (*illuminate*) illuminare, rischiarare; **to light sb's way** far luce a qn; **lit by electricity** illuminato(-a) elettricamente
2 (*cigarette, fire, candle*) accendere; **to light a bonfire** accendere un falò; **to light the fire** accendere il fuoco; **she lit the candles on the cake** ha acceso le candeline sulla torta
■VI (*ignite*) accendersi
▶ **light up** VI + ADV
1 (*lamp*) accendersi; (*face, eyes*) illuminarsi
2 (*fam: smoke*) accendersi una sigaretta (*or* la pipa *etc*)
■VT + ADV illuminare, rischiarare
▶ **light upon** VI + PREP: **her eyes lit upon the jewels** il suo sguardo cadde sui gioielli

light² [laɪt] ADJ (*comp* **-er**, *superl* **-est**) (*gen*) leggero(-a); **a light jacket** una giacca leggera; **a light meal** un pasto leggero; **light ale** birra chiara; **some light reading** una lettura leggera; **she is a light sleeper** ha il sonno leggero; **as light as a feather** leggero(-a) come una piuma; **to be light on one's feet** avere il passo leggero; **with a light heart** a cuor leggero; **to make light work of sth** fare qc con molta facilità; **to make light of sth** (*fig*) prendere alla leggera qc, non dar peso a qc
■ADV (*travel*) leggero, con poco bagaglio

light bulb N lampadina

light-coloured ['laɪt'kʌləd] ADJ di colore chiaro

light·en¹ ['laɪtn] VT (*darkness*) rischiarare, illuminare; (*hair, colour*) schiarire
■VI schiarirsi; (*room*) rischiararsi

light·en² ['laɪtn] VT (*load*) alleggerire; (*fig: make cheerful: heart, atmosphere*) sollevare

light·er ['laɪtə^r] N **1** (*also:* **cigarette lighter**) accendino, accendisigari *m inv* **2** (*boat*) chiatta

lighter fuel N gas *m inv* per accendini

light-fingered ['laɪt'fɪŋgəd] ADJ lesto(-a) di mano

light-haired [ˌlaɪt'hɛəd] ADJ dai capelli chiari

light-headed [ˌlaɪt'hɛdɪd] ADJ (*by temperament*) svampito(-a); (*dizzy*) intontito(-a), stordito(-a); (*with fever*) vaneggiante; (*with excitement*) eccitato(-a); **the drink made him feel light-headed** il liquore gli ha fatto girare la testa

light-hearted ['laɪt'hɑːtɪd] ADJ (*person, laugh*) spensierato(-a), gaio(-a); (*discussion*) non impegnato(-a)

light·house ['laɪtˌhaʊs] N faro

light·ing ['laɪtɪŋ] N (*system*) illuminazione *f*; (*in theatre*) luci *fpl*

lighting-up time [ˌlaɪtɪŋ'ʌpˌtaɪm] N (*Brit Aut*) ora in cui bisogna accendere i fari

light·ly ['laɪtlɪ] ADV leggermente; **to fry sth lightly** (*Culin*) far soffriggere qc; **to sleep lightly** avere il sonno leggero; **to get off lightly** cavarsela a buon mercato; **lightly salted** leggermente salato; **to take sth lightly** prendere qc alla leggera

light meter N (*Phot*) esposimetro

light·ness ['laɪtnɪs] N **1** (*brightness*) chiarezza **2** (*in weight etc*) leggerezza

light·ning ['laɪtnɪŋ] N fulmine *m*, lampo; **a lot of lightning** molti lampi; **thunder and lightning** tuoni *mpl* e fulmini; **a flash of lightning** un fulmine; **as quick as lightning** *or* **like (greased) lightning** (*fam*) (veloce) come un fulmine, in un lampo

lightning attack N incursione *f* lampo

lightning conductor, (*Am*) **lightning rod** N parafulmine *m*

lightning strike N sciopero a sorpresa *or* a gatto selvaggio

light opera N operetta

light pen N (*Comput*) penna ottica

light pollution N inquinamento luminoso

light rail N metropolitana leggera
▷ www.lrta.org
▷ www.tfl.gov.uk/dlr/

lights [laɪts] NPL (*old: of animal*) polmone *m*

light·ship ['laɪtˌʃɪp] N battello *m* faro *inv*

light·weight ['laɪtˌweɪt] ADJ (*also fig*) leggero(-a); (*Boxing*) dei pesi leggeri; **a lightweight suit** un vestito leggero
■N (*Boxing*) peso leggero

light year ['laɪtˌjɪə^r] N anno *m* luce *inv*

lig·nite ['lɪgnaɪt] N lignite *f*

Li·gu·rian [lɪ'gjʊərɪən] ADJ, N ligure (*m/f*)

◎**like¹** [laɪk] PREP
1 (*similar to*) come, uguale a; (*in comparisons*) come; **to be like sb/sth** essere come qn/qc; **they are very like each other** si somigliano molto; **a house like mine** una casa come la mia; **people like that** tipi del genere; **what's he like?** che tipo è?, com'è?; **what's the weather like?** che tempo fa?; **what was Turkey like?** com'era la Turchia?; **this portrait is not like him** questo ritratto non gli somiglia affatto; **it's a bit like salmon** assomiglia un po' al salmone; **to look like sb** assomigliare a qn; **you look like my brother** assomigli a mio fratello; **what does she look like?** che aspetto ha?; **he thinks like us** la pensa come noi; **she behaved like an idiot** si è comportata come una *or* da cretina; **that's just like him** è proprio da lui; **it's not like him to do that** non è da lui fare così , non è tipo da fare cose del genere; **I never saw anything like it** non ho mai visto una cosa simile, non ho mai visto niente di simile; **that's more like it** (*fam*) così va meglio; **it's fine like that** così va bene; **that's nothing like it** non ha niente a che vedere con quello; **something like that** qualcosa del genere; **don't talk like that** non parlare così ; **do it like this** fallo così ; **there's nothing like a holiday** non c'è niente di meglio di una vacanza; **it happened like this ...** è andata così ...; **like father like son** tale padre tale figlio; **we ran like mad** (*fam*) abbiamo fatto una corsa pazzesca; **it rained like mad** (*fam*) ha piovuto a dirotto; **I feel like a drink** avrei voglia di bere qualcosa, berrei volentieri qualcosa; **it looks like a diamond** sembra un diamante
2 (*such as*) come; **a city like Paris** una città come Parigi
■ADJ simile, uguale; **in like cases** in casi simili *or* analoghi; **rabbits, mice and like creatures** conigli, topi e animali simili; **to be as like as two peas (in a pod)** essere come due gocce d'acqua
■ADV: **it's nothing like as hot as it was** non fa più così caldo come faceva prima; **as like as not** (molto) probabilmente
■CONJ (*as*) come; **like we used to (do)** come facevamo una volta
■N: **we shall not see his like again** non ci sarà mai più uno come lui; **did you ever see the like (of it)?** hai mai visto niente del genere?; **the like of which I never saw** come non ne avevo mai visti; **sparrows, blackbirds and the like** passeri, merli e altri uccelli simili; **the likes of him** (*fam pej*) quelli come lui

like² [laɪk] VT **1** **I like swimming/that book/**

chocolate mi piace nuotare/quel libro/il cioccolato; **I like hats** mi piacciono i cappelli; **I don't like dogs** non mi piacciono i cani; **I like Mary** Mary mi è simpatica; **he likes Mary and wants to ask her out** gli piace Mary e vuole chiederle di uscire con lui; **which do you like best?** quale preferisci?; **how did you like the trip?** ti è piaciuto il viaggio?; **well, I like that!** (*fam hum*) questa sì che è bella! **2** (*want*) desiderare, volere; **I would like** *or* **I'd like** mi piacerebbe, vorrei; **would you like ...?** vuoi...?; **would you like to come?** vuoi venire?; **what would you like?** cosa vuoi?; **if you like** se vuoi; **would you like a coffee?** vuole un caffè?, gradirebbe un caffè?; **I'd like an orange juice, please** vorrei un'aranciata, per favore; **I'd like to wash my hands** vorrei lavarmi le mani; **he'd like to leave early** vorrebbe andarsene presto; **I would like more time** vorrei *or* mi piacerebbe avere più tempo; **I should like to know why** vorrei *or* mi piacerebbe sapere perché; **would you like me to wait outside?** vuoi *or* desideri che aspetti fuori?; **I didn't like to (do it)** non volevo (farlo); **as you like** come vuoi; **if you like** se vuoi; **whenever you like** quando vuoi
■ **likes** NPL gusti *mpl*, preferenze *fpl*; **his likes and dislikes** i suoi gusti

like·able ['laɪkəbl] ADJ simpatico(-a)

like·li·hood ['laɪklɪˌhʊd] N probabilità; **in all likelihood** con ogni probabilità, molto probabilmente; **there is no likelihood of that** è da escludersi; **there is little likelihood that he'll come** è difficile che venga

◎ **like·ly** ['laɪklɪ] ADJ (*comp* **-ier**, *superl* **-iest**) (*outcome, winner*) probabile; (*place*) adatto(-a), buono(-a); (*story, explanation*) plausibile; **a likely explanation** una spiegazione attendibile *or* plausibile; **that's not very likely** non è molto probabile; **a likely story!** (*iro*) ma a chi la racconti?, e io dovrei crederci?; **when is the likeliest time to find you at home?** quando è più probabile trovarti a casa?; **it's likely that I'll be late** molto probabilmente sarò in ritardo; **an incident likely to cause trouble** un incidente che probabilmente causerà dei problemi; **it's not likely that he'll come** *or* **he is not likely to come** è difficile che venga; **he's likely to leave** è probabile che parta, probabilmente partirà
■ ADV probabilmente; **most** *or* **very likely they've lost it** con molta probabilità *or* molto probabilmente l'hanno perso; **not likely!** (*fam*) neanche per sogno!

like-minded [ˌlaɪk'maɪndɪd] ADJ che la pensa allo stesso modo

lik·en ['laɪkən] VT: **to liken sth to** paragonare qc a

like·ness ['laɪknɪs] N **1** (*similarity*) somiglianza; **there is a family likeness** ci sono tratti caratteristici della famiglia; **she saw a family likeness** vedeva una somiglianza con gli altri membri della famiglia; **that's a good likeness of you** ti rassomiglia molto **2** (*form*): **in the likeness of** sotto le apparenze *or* l'aspetto di

like·wise ['laɪkˌwaɪz] ADV (*similarly*) nello *or* allo stesso modo; (*also*) anche; (*moreover*) inoltre, per di più; **to do likewise** fare altrettanto, fare lo stesso

lik·ing ['laɪkɪŋ] N (*for person*) simpatia; (*for thing*) predilezione *f*; **to have a liking for sb/sth** avere un debole per qn/qc; **she had a liking for good clothes** le piacevano i bei vestiti; **to be to sb's liking** essere di gusto *or* gradimento di qn; **to take a liking to sb** prendere qn in simpatia; **to take a liking to sth/to doing sth** scoprire il piacere di qc/di fare qc; **is the meal to your liking?** è di tuo gradimento il pranzo?

li·lac ['laɪlək] N (*flower*) lillà *m inv*; (*colour*) lilla *m inv*
■ ADJ lilla *inv*

Lil·li·pu·tian [ˌlɪlɪ'pjuːʃɪən] ADJ, N (*liter*) lillipuziano(-a)

Lilo® ['laɪləʊ] N (*Brit*) *materassino gonfiabile*

lilt [lɪlt] N cadenza

lilt·ing ['lɪltɪŋ] ADJ melodioso(-a)

lily ['lɪlɪ] N giglio

lily-livered ['lɪlɪˌlɪvəd] ADJ (*old*) codardo(-a)

lily of the valley N mughetto

Lima ['liːmə] N Lima

limb [lɪm] N (*Anat*) arto; (*of tree*) (grosso) ramo; **a man with strong limbs** un uomo dalle membra robuste; **to be out on a limb** (*fig*) trovarsi in difficoltà; **to go out on a limb** (*fig*) esporsi; **to tear limb from limb** sbranare, fare a pezzettini

> DID YOU KNOW ...?
> **limb** is not translated by the Italian word *lembo*

lim·ber up [ˌlɪmbər'ʌp] VI + ADV scaldarsi (i muscoli)

limbo ['lɪmbəʊ] N (*Rel: also fig*) limbo

lime¹ [laɪm] N (*Chem, Geol*) calce *f*; **slaked lime** calce spenta

lime² [laɪm] N (*Bot: linden*) tiglio

lime³ [laɪm] N (*Bot: citrus fruit*) limetta; **lime green** giallo-verdino

lime juice N succo di limetta

lime·light ['laɪmˌlaɪt] N: **to be in the limelight** essere alla ribalta, essere in vista

lim·er·ick ['lɪmərɪk] N *poesiola umoristica di 5 versi*

lime·stone ['laɪmˌstəʊn] N (*Geol*) calcare *m*, pietra calcarea; **limestone cliffs** scogliere *fpl* di pietra calcarea

limestone pavement N (*Geol*) campi *mpl* solcati

lime·water ['laɪmˌwɔːtə^r] N acqua di calce

◎ **lim·it** ['lɪmɪt] N limite *m*; **weight/speed limit** limite di peso/di velocità; **there's a limit to my patience** la mia pazienza ha un limite; **within limits** entro certi limiti; **there is a limit to what one can do** c'è un limite a quello che si può fare; **he's the limit!** (*fam*) lui passa tutti i limiti!; **well, that's the limit!** (*fam*) questo è il massimo *or* il colmo!
■ VT limitare; **to limit o.s. to a few remarks** limitarsi ad alcune osservazioni; **I limit myself to 10 cigarettes a day** mi limito a (fumare) 10 sigarette al giorno

limi·ta·tion [ˌlɪmɪ'teɪʃən] N limitazione *f*, restrizione *f*; **he has/knows his limitations** ha/conosce i suoi limiti; **the limitation of nuclear weapons** la limitazione delle armi nucleari

◎ **lim·it·ed** ['lɪmɪtɪd] ADJ limitato(-a), ristretto(-a); (*means, income*) scarso(-a); **a limited amount** una quantità limitata; **to a limited extent** entro certi limiti, fino a un certo punto; **they are limited in what they can do** hanno una possibilità di agire limitata; **limited edition** edizione a bassa tiratura

limited company, limited liability company N (*Brit*) ≈ società *f inv* a responsabilità limitata

lim·it·less ['lɪmɪtlɪs] ADJ illimitato(-a)

lim·ou·sine ['lɪməziːn] N limousine *f inv*

limp¹ [lɪmp] VI zoppicare; **to limp in/out** entrare/uscire zoppicando; **the ship limped home** la nave è tornata faticosamente in porto
■ N: **to walk with** *or* **have a limp** zoppicare

limp² [lɪmp] ADJ (*gen*) molle; (*dress*) floscio(-a); (*person*) fiacco(-a); **she went limp** si afflosciò; **let your arm go**

Ll

limp rilassa completamente il braccio; **limp cover(s)** (*on book*) rilegatura in brossura

lim·pet ['lɪmpɪt] N (*Zool*) patella; (*fig*) persona appiccicosa

limpet mine N (*Mil*) mignatta

lim·pid ['lɪmpɪd] ADJ (*liter*) limpido(-a)

limp·ly ['lɪmplɪ] ADV (*see adj*) mollemente; flosciamente; fiaccamente

limp·ness ['lɪmpnɪs] N (*see adj*) mollezza; flaccidità; fiacchezza

Lim·po·po [lɪm"əʊpəʊ] N Limpopo
▷ www.limpopo.gov.za

linch·pin ['lɪntʃ,pɪn] N (*in axle*) acciarino, bietta; (*fig*) perno

Lincs [lɪŋks] ABBR (*Brit*) = *Lincolnshire*

linc·tus ['lɪŋktəs] N (*Med*) sciroppo per la tosse

lin·den ['lɪndən] N = **lime²**

◎**line¹** [laɪn] N
1 (*gen*) linea; (*pen stroke*) tratto; (*wrinkle*) ruga; **a straight line** una linea retta; **to draw a line under sth** sottolineare qc; (*fig*) dimenticare qc; **I want to draw a line under the experience** voglio dimenticare quell'esperienza; **to draw a line through sth** tirare una riga sopra qc; **to draw the line at (doing) sth** rifiutarsi di fare qc; **to know where to draw the line** (*fig*) saper rispettare i limiti; **in line to the throne** nella linea di successione al trono; **she comes from a long line of teachers** i suoi sono insegnanti da generazioni
2 (*rope*) corda, fune *f*; (*fishing line*) lenza; (*wire*) filo; (*Elec*) linea; **clothes line** filo *or* corda del bucato
3 (*Telec*) linea; **the line went dead** è caduta la linea; **hold the line please** resti in linea per cortesia, attenda in linea, per favore; **Mr Smith is on the line** c'è in linea il signor Smith; **it's a very bad line** la comunicazione è disturbata
4 (*row, series*) fila; (*queue*) fila, coda; **a line of people** una fila di persone; **to stand in line** mettersi in fila; **to be in line for sth** (*fig*) essere in lista per qc; **to bring sth into line with sth** mettere qc al passo con qc; **to fall into line with sb/sth** adeguarsi a qn/qc; **to step out of line** (*fig*) sgarrare; **to cut in line** (*Am*) passare avanti
5 (*direction, course*) linea, direzione *f*; **line of inquiry** pista; **in the line of fire** (*Mil*) sulla linea di tiro; **line of attack** (*Mil*) piano d'attacco; (*fig*) piano d'azione; **to follow** *or* **take the line of least resistance** seguire la via più facile; **in the line of duty** nell'esercizio delle proprie funzioni; **line of argument** filo del ragionamento; **line of research/business** settore *m* di ricerca/d'attività; **in his line of business** nel suo ramo (di affari); **line of interest** sfera di interesse; **it's not my line** (*fam: speciality*) non sono un esperto in materia; **to take a strong** *or* **firm line on sth** essere deciso(-a) per quanto riguarda qc; **to take the line that ...** essere del parere che...; **to toe** *or* **follow the party line** attenersi alla *or* seguire la linea politica del partito; **in line with** in linea con, d'accordo con; **along the same lines** dello stesso tipo *or* genere; **we are thinking along the same lines** la pensiamo più o meno allo stesso modo; **to be on the right lines** andare tutto sommato bene
6 (*of print*) riga; (*of verse*) verso; **he wrote a few lines** ha scritto qualche riga; **to learn one's lines** (*Theatre*) imparare le battute; **to read between the lines** (*fig*) leggere fra le righe; **drop me a line** scrivimi due righe
7 (*Rail: route*) linea; (*shipping company*) compagnia di navigazione; **all along the line** (*fig*) fin da principio; **to reach** *or* **come to the end of the line** (*fig: relationship*) arrivare a un punto di rottura
8 (*Comm*) linea; **a new line in cosmetics** una nuova linea di cosmetici; **our best-selling line** la linea che vendiamo di più
▶ **line up** VT + ADV (*people, objects*) allineare, mettere in fila; **have you got anyone lined up for the job?** hai già in mente qualcuno per quel posto?; **to have sth lined up** avere qc in programma
■ VI + ADV (*in queue*) mettersi in fila; (*in row*) allinearsi; **line up in twos** mettetevi in fila per due

line² [laɪn] VT: **to line (with)** (*clothes*) foderare (di); (*box*) rivestire (di), foderare (di); (*subj: trees, crowd*) fiancheggiare; **line the tin with greaseproof paper** rivesti la tortiera con carta oleata; **crowds lined the street** c'erano molte persone ai bordi della strada; **the street was lined with trees** la strada era alberata

lin·eage ['lɪnɪɪdʒ] N (*frm*) stirpe *f*, lignaggio, schiatta

lin·ear ['lɪnɪəʳ] ADJ lineare

line·backer ['laɪnbækəʳ] N (*American football*) difensore *m*

lined¹ [laɪnd] ADJ (*paper*) a righe, rigato(-a); (*face*) rugoso(-a)

lined² [laɪnd] ADJ (*clothes*) foderato(-a)

line dancing N *danza di tipo country*
▷ www.uk250.co.uk/linedancing

line drawing N disegno a tratteggio

line feed N (*Comput*) avanzamento di una interlinea

line·man ['laɪnmən] N (*pl* **-men**) (*Am Elec*) guardafili *m inv*; (*Rail*) guardalinee *m inv*; (*American Football*) attaccante *m*

line manager N (*Brit*) responsabile *m/f* in linea diretta

lin·en ['lɪnɪn] N (*cloth*) (tela di) lino; (*sheets, tablecloth etc*) biancheria; **embroidered linen** biancheria per la casa ricamata; **to wash one's dirty linen in public** (*fig*) lavare i panni sporchi in pubblico
■ ADJ (*garment*) di lino; (*basket, cupboard*) della biancheria; **a linen jacket** una giacca di lino

line of sight, line of vision N visuale *f*

line-out ['laɪn,aʊt] N (*Rugby*) touche *f inv*

line printer N stampante *f* parallela

lin·er ['laɪnəʳ] N **1** (*ship*) nave *f* di linea, transatlantico
2 dustbin liner sacchetto per la pattumiera

lines·man ['laɪnzmən] N (*pl* **-men**) (*Sport*) guardalinee *m inv*, segnalinee *m inv*; (*Telec*) guardafili *m inv*

line-up ['laɪn,ʌp] N (*row*) fila, allineamento; (*Sport*) formazione *f*; (*Am: identity parade*) confronto all'americana

ling¹ [lɪŋ] N (*Bot*) brugo

ling² [lɪŋ] N (*fish*) molva

lin·ger ['lɪŋgəʳ] VI (*person: dawdle*) indugiare; (*: wait*) attardarsi; (*: be on the point of death*) trascinarsi; (*smell, memory, tradition*) persistere; **to linger over a meal** attardarsi a tavola; **to linger on a subject** dilungarsi su un argomento; **I was tempted to linger in the sunshine** ero tentato di rimanere ancora un po' al sole; **the smell lingered for weeks** l'odore è rimasto per settimane

lin·gerie ['lænʒəri:] N lingerie *f inv*, biancheria intima (femminile)

lin·ger·ing ['lɪŋgərɪŋ] ADJ (*smell, doubt*) persistente; (*look*) insistente, lungo(-a); (*death*) lento(-a)

lin·go ['lɪŋgəʊ] N (*fam pej*) *qualunque lingua straniera che risulti incomprensibile*; (*: jargon*) gergo

lin·gua fran·ca ['lɪŋgwə'fræŋkə] N lingua franca

lin·guist ['lɪŋgwɪst] N (*academic*) linguista *m/f*; **I'm no linguist** sono negato per le lingue; **to be a good linguist** essere portato per le lingue; **he's an excellent linguist** è molto portato per le lingue
lin·guis·tic [lɪŋ'gwɪstɪk] ADJ linguistico(-a)
lin·guis·tics [lɪŋ'gwɪstɪks] NSG linguistica
▷ www.britac.ac.uk/portal/
▷ http://linguistlist.org/sp/LangAnalysis.html
lini·ment ['lɪnɪmənt] N linimento
lin·ing ['laɪnɪŋ] N (*of clothes etc*) fodera; (*Tech*) rivestimento (interno); (*of brake*) guarnizione *f*
◎ **link** [lɪŋk] N (*of chain*) anello; (*fig: connection*) legame *m*, collegamento, rapporto; (*Comput*) link *m inv*, collegamento; **cultural links** rapporti culturali; **rail link** collegamento ferroviario; **the link between smoking and cancer** il collegamento tra fumo e cancro; **there's a link to another site** c'è un collegamento ad un altro sito; *see also* **links**
■ VT (*also fig*) collegare, congiungere, unire; (*Comput*) creare un collegamento con; **to link arms with sb** prendere sottobraccio qn
■ VI: **to link to a site** creare un collegamento con un sito
▶ **link up** VI + ADV (*people: meet*) ritrovarsi, riunirsi; (*: join*) unirsi, associarsi; (*spaceships etc*) agganciarsi; (*railway lines, roads*) congiungersi
■ VT collegare, unire
link·age ['lɪŋkɪdʒ] N connessione *f*; **the linkage between cause and effect** il nesso fra causa ed effetto
link·man ['lɪŋkmən] N (*pl* **-men**) annunciatore
links [lɪŋks] NPL (*golf links*) terreno *or* campo da golf
link-up ['lɪŋk,ʌp] N legame *m*; (*of roads*) nodo; (*of spaceships*) aggancio; (*Radio, TV*) collegamento
lin·net ['lɪnɪt] N fanello
lino ['laɪnəʊ], **li·no·leum** [lɪ'nəʊlɪəm] N linoleum *m inv*
Li·no·type® ['laɪnəʊ,taɪp] N linotype® *f inv*
lin·seed oil ['lɪnsi:d'ɔɪl] N olio di semi di lino
lint [lɪnt] N (*Med*) garza
lin·tel ['lɪntl] N architrave *m*
lion ['laɪən] N leone *m*; (*fig: person*) celebrità *f inv*; **to get** *or* **take the lion's share** fare la parte del leone; **to put one's head in the lion's mouth** (*fig*) cacciarsi nei guai
lion cub N leoncino
li·on·ess ['laɪənɪs] N leonessa
lion-hearted ['laɪən,hɑ:tɪd] ADJ molto coraggioso(-a)
lion-tamer ['laɪən,teɪmə^r] N domatore(-trice) di leoni
◎ **lip** [lɪp] N (*Anat*) labbro; (*of jug*) beccuccio; (*of glass, of cup etc*) orlo; (*fam: insolence*) sfacciataggine *f*; **red lips** labbra rosse
lip gloss N lucidalabbra *m inv*
li·pid ['laɪpɪd] N (*Biochemistry*) lipide *m*
lipo·suc·tion ['lɪpəʊ,sʌkʃən] N liposuzione *f*
lip·py ['lɪpɪ] (*Brit fam*) ADJ insolente
■ N rossetto
lip-read ['lɪp,ri:d] VI, VT leggere (sul)le labbra
lip-reading ['lɪp,ri:dɪŋ] N lettura delle labbra, labiolettura
lip salve N burro di cacao
lip service N: **to pay lip service to sth** essere favorevole a qc solo a parole; **he pays lip service to environmentalism but ...** si professa ambientalista ma...
lip·stick ['lɪp,stɪk] N rossetto

liq·ue·fac·tion [,lɪkwɪ'fækʃən] N (*Tech*) liquefazione *f*
liq·ue·fy ['lɪkwɪ,faɪ] VT liquefare; **liquefied gas** gas *m* liquido
■ VI liquefarsi
li·queur [lɪ'kjʊə^r] N liquore *m*
▷ www.liqueurweb.com
liq·uid ['lɪkwɪd] ADJ (*gen*) liquido(-a)
■ N liquido
liquid assets NPL (*Fin*) attività *fpl* liquide
liq·ui·date ['lɪkwɪdeɪt] VT liquidare
liq·ui·da·tion [,lɪkwɪ'deɪʃən] N liquidazione *f*; **to go into liquidation** (*Fin*) andare in liquidazione
liquidation sale N (*Am*) liquidazione *f*
liq·ui·da·tor ['lɪkwɪ,deɪtə^r] N (*Fin*) liquidatore *m*
liquid crystal display N visualizzatore *m* a cristalli liquidi
li·quid·ity [lɪ'kwɪdɪtɪ] N (*Fin*) liquidità
liquidity ratio N (*Fin*) rapporto di liquidità
liq·uid·ize ['lɪkwɪ,daɪz] VT (*Brit Culin*) passare al frullatore
liq·uid·iz·er ['lɪkwɪ,daɪzə^r] N (*Brit Culin*) frullatore *m* (a brocca)
liquid paraffin N olio di paraffina
liq·uor ['lɪkə^r] N (*esp Am*) bevanda alcolica, alcolico
liquo·rice ['lɪkərɪs] N liquirizia
liquor store N (*Am*) negozio di alcolici
lira ['lɪərə] N lira
Lis·bon ['lɪzbən] N Lisbona
lisle [laɪl] N filo di Scozia
■ ADJ (*socks*) di filo di Scozia
lisp [lɪsp] N lisca (*fam*); **with a lisp** con la lisca (*fam*)
■ VI parlare con la lisca (*fam*)
lis·som ['lɪsəm] ADJ (*liter*) leggiadro(-a)
◎ **list[1]** [lɪst] N lista, elenco; (*Comm*) listino; **shopping list** lista *or* nota della spesa
■ VT (*include in list*) mettere in lista; (*write down*) fare una lista di; (*: expenses etc*) fare la nota di; (*enumerate*) elencare; (*Comput*) listare; **it is not listed** non è *or* non figura nell'elenco
list[2] [lɪst] VI (*ship*) inclinarsi, sbandare
■ N (*of ship*) sbandamento
list·ed build·ing ['lɪstɪd'bɪldɪŋ] N (*Brit Archit*) edificio sotto la protezione delle Belle Arti
list·ed com·pa·ny ['lɪstɪd'kʌmpənɪ] N società *f inv* le cui azioni sono quotate in Borsa
◎ **lis·ten** ['lɪsn] VI ascoltare; **to listen to sb/sth** ascoltare qn/qc; **listen!** ascolta!, senti!; **he wouldn't listen to me** non mi ha voluto dar retta *or* ascolto; **he wouldn't listen to reason** non ha voluto sentire ragione; **listen (out) for the car** senti se arriva la macchina; **listen (out) for your name** aspetta che ti chiamino; **to listen in on a conversation** ascoltare di nascosto una conversazione
lis·ten·able ['lɪsənəbl] ADJ piacevole da ascoltare
lis·ten·er ['lɪsnə^r] N (*to speaker*) ascoltatore(-trice); (*to radio*) radioascoltatore(-trice); **to be a good listener** saper ascoltare
lis·teria [,lɪs'tɪərɪə] N listeria
list·ing ['lɪstɪŋ] N (*entry*) voce *f*; (*Comput*) lista stampata
list·less ['lɪstlɪs] ADJ (*gen*) fiacco(-a), svogliato(-a); (*uninterested*) apatico(-a)
list·less·ly ['lɪstlɪslɪ] ADV (*see adj*) fiaccamente, svogliatamente; apaticamente
list·less·ness ['lɪstlɪsnɪs] N (*see adj*) fiacchezza, svogliatezza; apatia
list price N prezzo di listino

Ll

lists [lɪsts] NPL (*History*) lizza; **to enter the lists (against sb/sth)** (*fig*) entrare in lizza (contro qn/qc)

lit [lɪt] PT, PP *of* **light**[1]

lita·ny ['lɪtənɪ] N litania

lite [laɪt] ADJ (*cigarettes, soft drink etc*) light *inv* (*fig: after n*) leggero(-a)

li·ter ['li:tə^r] N (*Am*) = **litre**

lit·era·cy ['lɪtərəsɪ] N il saper leggere e scrivere

literacy campaign N lotta contro l'analfabetismo

lit·er·al ['lɪtərəl] ADJ (*meaning, translation*) letterale; (*account*) testuale; (*person*) prosaico(-a)
■ N (*Brit: Typ*) refuso

lit·er·al·ly ['lɪtərəlɪ] ADV (*gen*) letteralmente; (*interpret*) alla lettera; **it was literally impossible to work there** era letteralmente impossibile lavorare lì

◎ **lit·er·ary** ['lɪtərərɪ] ADJ letterario(-a); **a literary man** un letterato

literary criticism N critica letteraria

lit·er·ate ['lɪtərɪt] ADJ che sa leggere e scrivere; **highly literate** molto colto(-a), molto istruito(-a)

◎ **lit·era·ture** ['lɪtərɪtʃə^r] N (*publications: Literature*) letteratura; (*brochures etc*) opuscoli *mpl*, materiale *m*, informativo
▹ www.britac.ac.uk/portal/
▹ http://etext.lib.virginia.edu/modeng/modengo.browse.html
▹ www.themodernword.com/themodword.cfm

lithe [laɪð] ADJ (*frm*) agile, flessuoso(-a)

lith·ium ['lɪθɪəm] N litio

litho·graph ['lɪθəʊgrɑ:f] N litografia

li·thog·ra·pher [lɪ'θɒgrəfə^r] N litografo(-a)

li·thog·ra·phy [lɪ'θɒgrəfɪ] N litografia

Lithua·nia [ˌlɪθjʊ'eɪnɪə] N Lituania

Lithua·nian [ˌlɪθjʊ'eɪnɪən] ADJ lituano(-a)
■ N lituano(-a); (*language*) lituano

liti·gant ['lɪtɪgənt] N litigante *m/f*

liti·gate ['lɪtɪˌgeɪt] VI essere in causa

liti·ga·tion [ˌlɪtɪ'geɪʃən] N causa (giudiziaria)

li·ti·gious [lɪ'tɪdʒəs] ADJ (*frm: person*) *che fa eccessivo ricorso all'autorità giudiziaria*

lit·mus pa·per ['lɪtməsˌpeɪpə^r] N (*also fig*) cartina al tornasole

lit·mus test ['lɪtməsˌtɛst] N (*also fig*) cartina al tornasole

li·tre ['li:tə^r] N litro

lit·ter ['lɪtə^r] N **1** (*rubbish*) rifiuti *mpl*; (*papers*) cartacce *fpl* **2** (*young animals*) nidiata, figliata; (: *of dogs*) cucciolata **3** (*Agr: bedding*) lettiera
■ VT (*subj: person*) lasciare rifiuti in; (: *books, rubbish*) coprire; **littered with** coperto(-a) di; **the room was littered with books** nella stanza c'erano libri dappertutto; **a pavement littered with papers** un marciapiede pieno di cartacce

litter bin, litter basket N cestino dei rifiuti

litter lout, (*Am*) **litter·bug** ['lɪtəˌbʌg] N *persona che butta per terra le cartacce o i rifiuti*

◎ **lit·tle**[1] ['lɪtl] ADJ **1** (*small: gen*) piccolo(-a); **a little chair** una seggiolina; **a little cup** una tazzina; **my little brother** il mio fratellino; **a little girl** una bambina; **little finger** mignolo; **poor little thing!** poverino!
2 (*short*) breve; **we went for a little ride/walk** siamo andati a fare un giretto/una passeggiatina; **for a little while** per un po'; **it's only a little way to the station** la stazione non è lontana; **a little holiday** una breve vacanza

lit·tle[2] ['lɪtl] (*comp* **less**, *superl* **least**) ADJ, PRON (*not much*) poco(-a); (*some*) un poco *or* un po' di; **a little milk** un po' di latte; **how much would you like? – just a little** quanto ne vuoi? – solo un po'; **it's okay, we've still got a little time** va bene, abbiamo ancora un po' di tempo; **little money** pochi soldi; **with little difficulty** senza fatica *or* difficoltà; **it makes little difference** fa poca differenza; **we've got very little time** abbiamo molto poco tempo; **little is known about his childhood** si sa poco della sua infanzia; **to see/do little** non vedere/fare molto, vedere/fare molto poco; **we did what little we could** abbiamo fatto quel poco che abbiamo potuto; **little or nothing** poco o nulla; **that has little to do with it!** questo c'entra ben poco!; **as little as £5** soltanto 5 sterline; **to make little of sth** (*fail to understand*) capire poco di qc; (*belittle*) tenere qc in poco conto, dare poca importanza a qc; **little by little** poco a poco
■ ADV **1** **a little** un po'; **a little too big** un po' troppo grande; **a little longer** un po' più a lungo; **we were a little surprised** eravamo un po' sorpresi; **a little more milk** un po' più di latte; **a little more** ancora un po' **2** (*not much*): **a little-known fact** un fatto poco noto; **it's little better** non va molto meglio; **it's changed very little** è cambiato molto poco; **as little as possible** il meno possibile; **little more than a month ago** appena più di un mese fa; **I like it as little as you do** non mi piace più di quanto piaccia a te; **little does he know that ...** quello di cui non si rende conto è che...

Little League N *campionato di baseball per ragazzi sotto i 12 anni*

li·tur·gi·cal [lɪ'tɜ:dʒɪkəl] ADJ liturgico(-a)

lit·ur·gy ['lɪtədʒɪ] N liturgia

liv·able ['lɪvəbl] ADJ (*gen*) vivibile; (*house*) abitabile; **he's not livable with** (*fam*) è insopportabile

◎ **live**[1] [lɪv] VI
1 (*exist, survive*) vivere; **to live to be 100** vivere fino all'età di *or* a 100 anni; **he hasn't long to live** non gli resta molto da vivere; **as long as I live** finché vivo *or* campo; **to live through an experience** sopravvivere a un'esperienza; **he lived through two wars** ha visto due guerre; **to live like a lord** vivere da signore *or* come un re; **how can people live like that?** come si può vivere così ?; **she lives for her family** vive solo per la famiglia; **I'm living for the day when ...** vivo solo nell'attesa del giorno in cui...; **the doctors have given her three months to live** i medici le hanno dato tre mesi di vita; **you'll live!** (*iro*) vedrai che non morirai!; **to live with a memory** essere perseguitato(-a) da un ricordo; **he's not easy to live with** non è facile vivere con lui; **you live and learn** c'è sempre qualcosa da imparare; **live and let live** vivi e lascia vivere; **to live by .../by doing ...** guadagnarsi da vivere con.../facendo...; **long live the King!** viva il re!
2 (*reside*) abitare, vivere; **where do you live?** dove abiti?; **I live in Edinburgh** abito ad Edimburgo; **to live in London** abitare *or* vivere a Londra; **I live in Grange Road** abito in Grange Road; **I live with my grandmother** vivo con mia nonna
■ VT: **to live a happy life/a life of hardship** avere una vita felice/dura; **to live life to the full** godersi la vita; **to live a life of luxury** vivere nel lusso; **to live the part** (*Theatre: fig*) immedesimarsi nella parte
▸ **live down** VT + ADV (*disgrace*) far dimenticare (alla gente)
▸ **live in** VI + ADV (*students, nurses*) essere interno(-a); (*servants*) avere vitto e alloggio

▸ **live off** VI + PREP (*land, food*) vivere di; (*pej*: *parents*) vivere alle spalle *or* a spese di
▸ **live on** VI + PREP (*food, fruit, salary*) vivere di; **to live on £50 a week** vivere con 50 sterline la settimana; **enough to live on** abbastanza per vivere
■ VI + ADV continuare a vivere, sopravvivere
▸ **live out** VI + ADV (*Brit*: *students*) essere esterno(-a); (*housekeeper*) essere a mezzo servizio
■ VT + ADV: **to live out one's days** *or* **life** trascorrere gli ultimi anni
▸ **live together** VI + ADV (*cohabit*) vivere insieme, convivere
▸ **live up** VT + ADV: **to live it up** (*fam*) fare la bella vita
▸ **live up to** VI + ADV + PREP (*principles*) tenere fede a, non venir meno a; (*reputation*) essere all'altezza di; **the film didn't live up to our expectations** il film ci ha deluso
▸ **live with** VI + PREP (*cohabit with*) vivere con; (*put up with*): **I'll learn to live with it** mi ci abituerò; **I can't live with that pink door any more** non sopporto più quella porta rosa

live² [laɪv] ADJ **1** (*animal*) vivo(-a); (*issue*) scottante, d'attualità; (*Radio, TV*: *broadcast*) in diretta; (*music, concert*) dal vivo; **a real live crocodile** un coccodrillo in carne e ossa; **I'm against tests on live animals** sono contrario agli esperimenti su animali vivi; **live yoghurt** yogurt ricco di fermenti lattici vivi **2** (*shell, ammunition*: *not blank*) carico(-a); (: *unexploded*) inesploso(-a); (*Elec*: *rail*) sotto tensione; (: *wire*) ad alta tensione; (*still burning*: *coal*) ardente
■ ADV: **to be broadcast live** essere trasmesso(-a) in diretta

◎ **live-in** ['lɪvɪn] ADJ (*fam*: *partner*) convivente; (: *servant*) che vive in casa; **he has a live-in girlfriend** la sua ragazza vive con lui

live·li·hood ['laɪvlɪˌhʊd] N mezzi *mpl* di sostentamento; **to earn one's livelihood** guadagnarsi da vivere; **fishermen who depend on the sea for their livelihood** pescatori che dipendono dal mare per il loro sostentamento

live·li·ness ['laɪvlɪnɪs] N vivacità, brio

live·long ['lɪvˌlɒŋ] ADJ (*liter*): **all the livelong day** tutto il santo giorno

live·ly ['laɪvlɪ] ADJ (*comp* **-ier**, *superl* **-iest**) (*gen*) vivace, vivo(-a); (*imagination*) fervido(-a); (*conversation, argument*) animato(-a); (*interest*) vivo(-a); (*party, scene etc*) movimentato(-a); (*pace*) sostenuto(-a); **things are getting lively** l'ambiente *or* l'atmosfera comincia a scaldarsi; **she's got a lively personality** è una persona vivace

liv·en up [ˌlaɪvən'ʌp] VT + ADV (*room etc*) ravvivare; (*discussion, evening*) animare
■ VI + ADV animarsi

liv·er ['lɪvəʳ] N (*Anat, Culin*) fegato
■ ADJ di fegato

liver fluke N distoma *m* epatico

liv·er·ish ['lɪvərɪʃ] ADJ: **to be liverish** *or* **feel liverish** sentirsi il fegato ingrossato, avere mal di fegato; (*fig*) scontroso(-a)

Liv·er·pud·lian [ˌlɪvə'pʌdlɪən] ADJ di Liverpool
■ N abitante *m/f or* originario(-a) di Liverpool

liv·ery ['lɪvərɪ] N livrea

livery stable N scuderia (di cavalli da nolo)

lives [laɪvz] NPL *of* **life**

live·stock ['laɪvˌstɒk] N bestiame *m*

live wire ['laɪvwaɪəʳ] N (*fam*): **to be a live wire** essere pieno(-a) di vitalità

liv·id ['lɪvɪd] ADJ **1** (*furious*) furioso(-a), livido(-a) di rabbia, furibondo(-a) **2** (*in colour*: *complexion*) livido(-a); (: *sky*) plumbeo(-a); (: *bruise*) bluastro(-a); **she was absolutely livid** era assolutamente furibonda

◎ **liv·ing** ['lɪvɪŋ] ADJ (*alive*: *gen*) vivo(-a); (: *person*) vivente, in vita; **within living memory** a memoria d'uomo; **the greatest living pianist** il più grande pianista vivente; **there wasn't a living soul** non c'era anima viva
■ N vita; **what do you do for a living?** come ti guadagni da vivere?; **to earn** *or* **make a living** guadagnarsi da vivere; **the living** (*people*) i vivi

living conditions NPL condizioni *fpl* di vita

living expenses NPL spese *fpl* di mantenimento

living quarters NPL alloggi *mpl*

living room N soggiorno, salotto

living space N spazio per vivere

living standards NPL tenore *m or* livello di vita

living wage N salario sufficiente per vivere

living will N testamento biologico

Livy ['lɪvɪ] N Tito Livio

liz·ard ['lɪzəd] N lucertola

lla·ma ['lɑːmə] N lama *m inv*

LLB [ˌɛlɛl'biː] N ABBR (= **Bachelor of Laws**) laurea in legge

LLD [ˌɛlɛl'diː] N ABBR (= **Doctor of Laws**) ≈ dottorato in Giurisprudenza

LMT [ɛlˌɛm'tiː] ABBR (*Am*: = **Local Mean Time**) tempo medio locale

lo [ləʊ] EXCL (*old*): **lo and behold ...** quand'ecco che...

◎ **load** [ləʊd] N **1** (*Elec, Tech, burden*) carico; (*weight*) peso; **a heavy load** un pesante carico **2** (*fig*): **that's (taken) a load off my mind** mi sono tolto un peso; **loads of, a load of** (*fam*) un sacco *or* un mucchio di; **they've got loads of money** hanno un sacco di soldi; **it's a load of old rubbish** (*fam*) sono un mucchio di sciocchezze; **you're talking a load of rubbish!** stai dicendo un mucchio di sciocchezze!
■ VT (*also*: **load up**): **to load (with)** (*lorry, ship*) caricare (di); (*gun, camera*): **to load (with)** caricare (con); **he's loaded (down) with debts/worries** è carico di debiti/preoccupazioni; **to load a program** (*Comput*) caricare un programma; **I can't load the program** non riesco a caricare il programma

load·ed ['ləʊdɪd] ADJ **1 a loaded question** una domanda tendenziosa **2** (*dice*) truccato(-a); **the dice are loaded against him** (*fig*) ha tutto contro di lui **3 to be loaded** (*fam*: *rich*) essere pieno(-a) di soldi; **he's loaded** è pieno di soldi **4 loaded with** carico(-a) di; **a cart loaded with hay** un carro carico di fieno; **loaded with responsibilities** pieno(-a) di responsabilità

load·er ['ləʊdəʳ] N caricatore *m*

load·ing bay ['ləʊdɪŋˌbeɪ] N piazzola di carico

loaf¹ [ləʊf] N (*pl* **loaves**) pagnotta, pane *m*; **half a loaf is better than no bread** (*Proverb*) meglio poco che niente

loaf² [ləʊf] VI (*also*: **loaf about, loaf around**) oziare, bighellonare

loaf·er ['ləʊfəʳ] N (*fam*) scansafatiche *m/f inv*; (*shoes*): **loafers** mocassini *mpl*

loaf tin N stampo (per il pane)

loam [ləʊm] N terriccio (fertile)

◎ **loan** [ləʊn] N prestito; **to give sb the loan of sth** prestare *or* dare in prestito qc a qn; **to ask for the loan of** chiedere in prestito; **on loan** (*book, painting*) in prestito; (*employee*) distaccato(-a); **to raise a loan** (*money*) ottenere un prestito *or* un mutuo

Ll

■VT prestare, dare in prestito
loan capital N capitale *m* di prestito
loan-shark [ˈləʊnʃɑːk] N (*fam pej*) strozzino(-a)
loan word N prestito linguistico
loath [ləʊθ] ADJ: **to be loath to do sth** essere riluttante *or* restio(-a) a fare qc
loathe [ləʊð] VT (*thing, person*) detestare, odiare; **I loathe her** la detesto; **I loathe doing it** detesto farlo; **to loathe sb's doing sth** detestare che qn faccia qc
loath·ing [ˈləʊðɪŋ] N (*hatred*) odio; (*disgust*) ribrezzo, disgusto; **it fills me with loathing** mi riempie di disgusto, mi fa ribrezzo
loath·some [ˈləʊðsəm] ADJ (*gen*) ripugnante, disgustoso(-a); (*person*) detestabile, odioso(-a)
loaves [ləʊvz] NPL *of* **loaf**
lob [lɒb] VT (*ball*) lanciare; **to lob sth over to sb** lanciare qc a qn
◎**lob·by** [ˈlɒbɪ] N **1** atrio, hall *f inv*; **the lobby of the museum** l'atrio del museo **2** (*Pol: pressure group*) gruppo di pressione, lobby *f inv*; **a powerful lobby** una lobby potente
■VT (*Pol*) far pressione su
■VI fare pressioni; **to lobby for a reform** fare pressioni per ottenere una riforma
lob·by·ist [ˈlɒbɪɪst] N appartenente *m/f* ad un gruppo di pressione, lobbista *m/f*
lobe [ləʊb] N (*Anat*) lobo
lo·belia [ləʊˈbiːlɪə] N lobelia
lo·boto·my [ləʊˈbɒtəmɪ] N (*Med*) lobotomia
lob·ster [ˈlɒbstəʳ] N aragosta
lobster pot N nassa per aragoste
◎**lo·cal** [ˈləʊkəl] ADJ (*gen*) locale; (*resident, shop*) del posto; **the local paper** il giornale locale; **local doctor** medico della zona
■N (*fam*) **1 he's a local** è uno del posto; **the locals** la gente del posto **2** (*Brit: pub*) ≈ bar *m inv* sotto casa
local anaesthetic, (*Am*) **local anesthetic** N anestesia locale
local area network N (*Comput*) rete *f* LAN *inv*
◎**local authority** N autorità *f inv* locale; **local education authority** ≈ provveditorato agli studi; **local health authority** ≈ unità *f inv* sanitaria locale
local call N (*Telec*) telefonata urbana, chiamata urbana
local colour N colore *m* locale
lo·cale [ləʊˈkɑːl] N (*frm: gen*) ambiente *m*; (: *of film, book*) ambientazione *f*
local government N amministrazione *f* locale; **local government officer** *or* **official** funzionario dell'amministrazione locale; **local government elections** elezioni *fpl* amministrative
lo·cal·ity [ləʊˈkælɪtɪ] N (*place*) località *f inv*; (*neighbourhood*) vicinanze *fpl*
lo·cal·ize [ˈləʊkəlaɪz] VT localizzare
lo·cal·ly [ˈləʊkəlɪ] ADV (*nearby*) nei paraggi, nelle vicinanze; (*in the locality*) sul posto, in loco; **there will be showers locally** il tempo sarà localmente piovoso, ci saranno locali rovesci; **he lives locally** vive nei paraggi; **the money will be spent locally** il denaro verrà speso a livello locale
local time N ora locale
lo·cate [ləʊˈkeɪt] VT (*situate*) situare, collocare; (*find*) trovare; (: *cause*) individuare, trovare; **where can he be located?** dove lo si può rintracciare?; **we're trying to locate him** stiamo cercando di trovarlo; **to be located** essere situato; **the office is located in York** l'ufficio è situato a York
◎**lo·ca·tion** [ləʊˈkeɪʃən] N **1** (*place*) posto; (*placing*) posizione *f*, ubicazione *f*; (*Geog*) localizzazione *f*; **a beautiful location** una bellissima posizione **2** (*Cine*): **on location** in esterni; **film shot on location** film girato in esterni; **to be on location in Mexico** girare gli esterni in Messico
loch [lɒx] N (*Scot*) lago
lock¹ [lɒk] N (*of hair*) ciocca; **locks** (*liter*) chioma
◎**lock²** [lɒk] N **1** (*on door, box*) serratura; **under lock and key** sotto chiave; **lock stock and barrel** (*fig*) in blocco; **he moved out, lock stock and barrel** se n'è andato con armi e bagagli **2** (*of canal*) chiusa **3** (*Brit: Aut: turning*) sterzo; **on full lock** a tutto sterzo
■VT (*door*) chiudere a chiave; (*Tech: immobilize*) bloccare; **make sure you lock your door** non dimenticare di chiudere la porta a chiave; **she locked the steering mechanism** ha messo il bloccasterzo; **to lock sb/sth in a place** chiudere qn/qc in un posto; **behind locked doors** a porte chiuse; **they were locked in each other's arms** erano abbracciati stretti; **to be locked in combat** lottare corpo a corpo
■VI (*door etc*) chiudersi; (*wheels*) bloccarsi, incepparsi
▶ **lock away** VT + ADV (*valuables*) tenere (rinchiuso(-a)) al sicuro; (*criminal*) mettere dentro; (*mental patient*) rinchiudere
▶ **lock in** VT + ADV chiudere dentro (a chiave)
▶ **lock out** VT + ADV chiudere fuori; **the door slammed and I was locked out** la porta si è chiusa di colpo e sono rimasto chiuso fuori; **to lock workers out** (*Industry*) fare una serrata
▶ **lock up** VT + ADV (*object*) mettere al sicuro, chiudere (a chiave); (*criminal*) mettere dentro; (*mental patient*) rinchiudere; (*funds*) vincolare, immobilizzare; **she checked that the house was properly locked up** ha controllato che tutto fosse ben chiuso
■VI + ADV chiudere tutto (a chiave)
lock·er [ˈlɒkəʳ] N armadietto; (*Naut*) gavone *m*; **left-luggage lockers** armadietti per deposito bagagli
locker room N spogliatoio
lock·et [ˈlɒkɪt] N medaglione *m* (*portaritratti*)
lock·jaw [ˈlɒkˌdʒɔː] N tetano
lock-keeper [ˈlɒkˌkiːpəʳ] N guardiano(-a) di chiusa
lock·out [ˈlɒkˌaʊt] N (*Industry*) serrata
lock·smith [ˈlɒkˌsmɪθ] N fabbro
lock-up [ˈlɒkˌʌp] N (*prison*) prigione *f*; (*cell*) guardina; (*Brit: also:* **lock-up garage**) box *m inv*
lo·co·mo·tion [ˌləʊkəˈməʊʃən] N locomozione *f*
lo·co·mo·tive [ˌləʊkəˈməʊtɪv] N (*Rail*) locomotiva
lo·cum [ˈləʊkəm] N (*doctor*) medico sostituto; (*priest*) vicario
lo·cus [ˈləʊkəs] N (*pl* **loci** [ˈləʊsaɪ]) (*Math*) luogo geometrico
lo·cust [ˈləʊkəst] N locusta, cavalletta
locust tree N robinia
lo·cu·tion [ləʊˈkjuːʃən] N (*frm*) locuzione *f*
lodge [lɒdʒ] N (*house*) casetta del guardiano; (*porter's lodge*) portineria, guardiola; (*Freemasonry*) loggia; **a ski lodge** uno chalet in montagna
■VT (*person: give lodging*) dare alloggio a; (: *find lodging*) trovare alloggio per; (*money*) depositare; (*complaint, appeal etc*) fare, presentare; (*statement*) rilasciare; **to lodge an appeal** (*Law*) ricorrere in corte d'appello; **we lodged a complaint** abbiamo presentato un reclamo
■VI **1** (*person*): **to lodge (with)** (*landlady*) essere a pensione (presso *or* da); (*friends*) alloggiare (con); **I'd rather lodge with a family** preferirei alloggiare presso una famiglia **2** (*bullet*) conficcarsi; **to lodge**

(itself) in/between piantarsi dentro/fra; **a bullet lodged in his leg** una pallottola gli si è conficcata nella gamba

lodg·er ['lɒdʒəʳ] N (*with room and meals*) pensionante *m/f*; (*room only*) persona che ha una camera in affitto; **she takes in lodgers** fa l'affittacamere

lodg·ing ['lɒdʒɪŋ] N (*accommodation*) alloggio; *see also* board **board and lodging** vitto e alloggio

lodging house N (*Brit*) casa con camere in affitto

lodg·ings ['lɒdʒɪŋz] NPL (*room*) camera in affitto, camera ammobiliata; (*small flat*) appartamentino; **to look for lodgings** cercarsi un alloggio

loft [lɒft] N soffitta, solaio; (*also*: **hayloft**) granaio, fienile *m*; (*Am*) loft *m inv*

lofti·ly ['lɒftɪlɪ] ADV (*frm*) altezzosamente

lofty ['lɒftɪ] ADJ (*comp* **-ier**, *superl* **-iest**) (*frm*: *sentiments, aims*) nobile; (: *haughty*: *manner*) di superiorità, altezzoso(-a); (*liter*: *mountain*) alto(-a); **a lofty ceiling** un soffitto alto; **lofty ambitions** grandi ambizioni *fpl*; **lofty ideals** ideali *mpl* nobili

log [lɒg] N **1** (*for fire*) ceppo; (*tree trunk*) tronco **2** = **logbook**

■ N ABBR (= **logarithm**) log

■ VT **1** (*Naut, Aer*) annotare *or* registrare sul giornale di bordo **2** (*Aut*: *log up*: *speed*) fare; (*distance*) coprire; **to log 50 mph** ≈ fare 80 km/h

▸ **log in, log on** VI + ADV (*Comput*) aprire una sessione (con codice di riconoscimento)

▸ **log off, log out** VI + ADV (*Comput*) fare il log-off

logan·berry ['ləʊgənbərɪ] N mora

loga·rithm ['lɒgəˌrɪðəm] N logaritmo; **common logarithm** logaritmo decimale *or* volgare

log·book ['lɒgˌbʊk] N (*Naut, Aer*) giornale *m or* diario di bordo; (*Aut*: *registration document*) libretto di circolazione; (*of events, movement of goods*) registro

log cabin N capanna di tronchi

log fire N fuoco di legna

log·ger ['lɒgəʳ] N boscaiolo, taglialegna *m inv*

log·ger·heads ['lɒgəˌhɛdz] NPL: **at loggerheads (with sb)** in violento contrasto (con qn), ai ferri corti (con)

log·ging ['lɒgɪŋ] N disboscamento

log·ic ['lɒdʒɪk] N logica

logi·cal ['lɒdʒɪkəl] ADJ logico(-a)

logi·cal·ly ['lɒdʒɪkəlɪ] ADV logicamente; **logically, we should ...** a rigor di logica, dovremmo...

logic bomb N (*Comput*) *programma che entra in azione al verificarsi di un determinato evento, danneggiando il computer*

lo·gi·cian [lɒ'dʒɪʃən] N logico

lo·gis·tic [lɒ'dʒɪstɪk] N logistica

■ ADJ logistico(-a)

lo·gis·tics [lɒ'dʒɪstɪks] NSG logistica

log·jam ['lɒgˌdʒæm] N: **to break the logjam** superare l'impasse *f inv*

logo ['ləʊgəʊ] N logo *m inv*

loin [lɔɪn] N (*of meat*) lombata

loin chop N (*Culin*) lombatina, bistecca di lombo

loin cloth N perizoma *m*

loins [lɔɪnz] NPL (*frm*) reni *fpl*, fianchi *mpl*

loi·ter ['lɔɪtəʳ] VI (*idle*) bighellonare; (*lag behind*) attardarsi, fermarsi (ad ogni passo); **to loiter (about)** indugiare, bighellonare; **to loiter (with intent)** (*Law*) aggirarsi (con intenzioni sospette); **I loitered in the airport shops** ho gironzolato per i negozi dell'aeroporto

loll [lɒl] VI (*head, tongue*) ciondolare; **to loll about** *or* **around** starsene pigramente sdraiato(-a), essere stravaccato(-a); **to loll against sth, loll back on sth** appoggiarsi pigramente a qc

lol·li·pop ['lɒlɪˌpɒp] N lecca lecca *m inv*

lollipop man, lollipop lady N (*Brit fam*) *vigilatore del traffico*

LOLLIPOP MAN, LOLLIPOP LADY

In Gran Bretagna il **lollipop man** e la **lollipop lady** sono persone incaricate di regolare il traffico in prossimità delle scuole e di aiutare i bambini ad attraversare la strada; usano una paletta la cui forma ricorda quella di un lecca lecca, in inglese, appunto, "lollipop".

lol·lop ['lɒləp] VI (*Brit*) camminare (*or* correre) goffamente

lol·ly ['lɒlɪ] N (*Brit fam*) **1** (*lollipop*) lecca lecca *m inv*; (*also*: **ice lolly**) ghiacciolo **2** (*money*) grana, quattrini *mpl*

Lom·bardy ['lɒmbədɪ] N Lombardia

Lon·don ['lʌndən] N Londra; **I'm from London** sono di Londra

▷ www.cityoflondon.gov.uk

▷ www.visitlondon.com

Lon·don·er ['lʌndənəʳ] N londinese *m/f*

London Eye N ruota panoramica di Londra

▷ www.londoneye.com/

lone [ləʊn] ADJ (*frm*: *person*) solitario(-a), solo(-a); (: *house*) solitario(-a); **to play a lone hand** (*fig*) agire da solo

lone·li·ness ['ləʊnlɪnɪs] N solitudine *f*

lone·ly ['ləʊnlɪ] ADJ (*comp* **-ier**, *superl* **-iest**) (*person*) solitario(-a); (*place*: *isolated*) isolato(-a); (: *deserted*) deserto(-a); **to be** *or* **feel lonely** sentirsi solo(-a); **I sometimes feel lonely** qualche volta mi sento solo; **a lonely cottage** una villetta isolata

lonely hearts ADJ: **lonely hearts ad** annuncio per cuori solitari; **lonely hearts column** messaggi *mpl* personali; **lonely hearts club** club *m inv* dei cuori solitari

lone parent N (*mother*) madre single (*or* divorziata *or* vedova); (*father*) padre single (*or* divorziato *or* vedovo)

lon·er ['ləʊnəʳ] N tipo solitario, persona solitaria, solitario(-a)

lone·some ['ləʊnsəm] ADJ (*esp Am*) solo(-a); **to feel lonesome** sentirsi solo

lone wolf N (*fig*) tipo solitario

◎ **long**[1] [lɒŋ] ADJ (*comp* **-er**, *superl* **-est**)

1 (*in size*) lungo(-a); **she's got long hair** ha i capelli lunghi; **how long is it?** quant'è lungo?; **how long is this river?** quanto è lungo questo fiume?; **it is 6 metres long** è lungo 6 metri; **to get longer** allungarsi **2** (*in time*) lungo(-a); **(for) a long time** (per) molto tempo; **it takes a long time** ci vuole molto tempo; **I've been waiting a long time** aspetto da molto tempo; **how long is the film?** quanto dura il film?; **how long will it take?** quanto ci vorrà?; **how long did you stay there?** per quanto tempo sei rimasto lì ?; **2 hours long** che dura 2 ore, di 2 ore; **a long walk/holiday** una lunga camminata/vacanza; **a long job** un lavoro lungo; **to have a long memory** avere buona memoria; **it's been a long day** (*fig*) è stata una giornata lunga; **to take a long look at sth** esaminare ben bene qc; **at long last** finalmente

■ ADV a lungo, per molto tempo; **I shan't be long** non ne avrò per molto; **he won't be long finishing** non ci

Ll

metterà molto a finire; **we didn't stay (for) long** non ci siamo fermati a lungo; **I have long believed that ...** è da molto tempo che credo che...; **he had long understood that ...** aveva capito da molto tempo che...; **long before** molto tempo prima; **long before now** molto prima; **long before you came** molto prima che tu arrivassi; **before long** (*+ future*) presto, fra poco; (*+ past*) poco tempo dopo; **he's long since departed** se n'è andato molto tempo fa; **how long is it since you saw them?** da quant'è che non li vedi?; **how long have you been here?** da quanto sei qui?; **how long has he been learning Italian?** da quanto studia l'italiano?; **long ago** molto tempo fa; **how long ago?** quanto tempo fa?; **as long ago as 1960** nientemeno che nel 1960; **he no longer comes** non viene più; **all day long** tutto il giorno; **so long as, as long as** (*while*) finché; (*provided that*) sempre che + *sub*; **I'll come as long as it's not too expensive** verrò, sempre che non costi troppo; **so long!** (*fam esp Am*) ciao!; **don't be long!** fai presto!; **it won't take long** è questione di poco

■ N: **the long and the short of it is that ...** (*fig*) a farla breve...

long² [lɒŋ] VI: **to long for sth/sb** desiderare molto qc/qn; **to long to do sth** morire dalla voglia di fare qc; **to long for sb to do sth** desiderare tanto che qn faccia qc

long-awaited [ˈlɒŋəˌweɪtɪd] ADJ tanto atteso(-a), sospirato(-a)

long·bow [ˈlɒŋˌbəʊ] N arco

long-distance [ˌlɒŋˈdɪstəns] ADJ (*Telec: call*) interurbano(-a); (*race*) di fondo; **long-distance runner** fondista *m/f*

long division N divisione *f* scritta per esteso

long-drawn-out [ˌlɒŋdrɔːnˈaʊt] ADJ che va per le lunghe, interminabile

long drink N long drink *m inv*

longed-for [ˈlɒŋdˌfɔːˈ] ADJ tanto sospirato(-a)

lon·gev·ity [lɒŋˈdʒɛvɪtɪ] N longevità

long face N: **to pull a long face** fare il muso (lungo)

long-forgotten [ˈlɒŋˌfəˈgɒtn] ADJ dimenticato(-a) da tempo

long-haired [ˈlɒŋˈhɛəd] ADJ (*person*) dai capelli lunghi; (*animal*) dal pelo lungo

long·hand [ˈlɒŋˌhænd] N scrittura (normale)

long haul N lungo periodo di superlavoro; **to be in sth for the long haul** essere determinato(-a) a fare qc, per quanto tempo occorra

■ ADJ a lunga distanza; **long-haul flight** volo transoceanico

long-hours culture N (*Comm*) *cultura dellorario lungo*

long·ing [ˈlɒŋɪŋ] N desiderio; (*for food*) voglia; (*nostalgia*) nostalgia; **a longing for affection** un desiderio d'affetto

■ ADJ (*look*) pieno(-a) di desiderio *or* di nostalgia

long·ing·ly [ˈlɒŋɪŋlɪ] ADV con desiderio (*or* nostalgia)

lon·gi·tude [ˈlɒŋgɪtjuːd] N longitudine *f*

long johns NPL (*fam*) mutandoni *mpl*

long jump N salto in lungo

long jumper N (*Sport*) saltatore(-trice) in lungo

long-legged [ˈlɒŋˌlɛgd] ADJ (*person*) dalle gambe lunghe; (*animal*) con le zampe lunghe

long-life [ˈlɒŋˈlaɪf] ADJ a lunga conservazione; **long-life milk** latte *m* a lunga conservazione

long-list [ˈlɒŋlɪst] N prima lista, lista preliminare

■ VT: **be longlisted for sth** essere incluso(-a) nella lista preliminare

long-lived [ˈlɒŋˈlɪvd] ADJ longevo(-a); **women are longer-lived** *or* **more long-lived than men** le donne vivono più a lungo degli uomini

long-lost [ˈlɒŋˈlɒst] ADJ perduto(-a) da tempo; (*friend*) che non si vede da molto tempo

long-playing [ˈlɒŋˈpleɪɪŋ] ADJ: **long-playing record** (disco a) 33 giri *m inv*, long-playing *m inv*

long-range [ˈlɒŋˈreɪndʒ] ADJ (*gun, missile*) a lunga portata *or* gittata; (*aircraft*) a lungo raggio d'azione; (*weather forecast*) a lungo termine

long·shore [ˈlɒnʃɔːˈ] ADJ litoraneo(-a); **longshore drift** trasporto litoraneo

long·shore·man [ˈlɒŋʃɔːmən] N (*pl* **-men**) (*Am*) portuale *m*, scaricatore *m* di porto

long shot N: **it's a long shot** (*fam*) le probabilità sono minime

long-sighted [ˌlɒŋˈsaɪtɪd] ADJ presbite; (*Med*) ipermetrope; (*fig*) lungimirante

long-sightedness [ˌlɒŋˈsaɪtɪdnɪs] N presbiopia; (*Med*) ipermetropia; (*fig*) lungimiranza

long-sleeved [ˈlɒŋˌsliːvd] ADJ a maniche lunghe

long-standing [ˈlɒŋˈstændɪŋ] ADJ di vecchia data

long-suffering [ˈlɒŋˈsʌfərɪŋ] ADJ estremamente paziente, infinitamente tollerante

◎ **long-term** [ˈlɒŋˈtɜːm] ADJ (*plans, effects*) a lungo termine; **to take a long-term view of sth** proiettare qc nel futuro

◎ **long-time** [ˈlɒŋˌtaɪm] ADJ (*friend*) di vecchia data

long vacation N (*Univ*) vacanze *fpl* estive

long wave N (*Radio*) onde *fpl* lunghe

long·ways [ˈlɒŋˌweɪz] ADV longitudinalmente

long-winded [ˌlɒŋˈwɪndɪd] ADJ (*speaker*) prolisso(-a); (*account, explanation*) interminabile

loo [luː] N (*Brit fam: toilet*) gabinetto, cesso

loo·fah, loo·fa [ˈluːfə] N luffa

◎ **look** [lʊk] VI

1 (*see, glance*) guardare; **I'm just looking** (*in shop*) sto solo dando un'occhiata; **I'll look and see** vado a vedere; **look who's here!** (ma) guarda chi si vede!; **to look the other way** guardare dall'altra parte; (*fig*) far finta di non vedere; **to look ahead** guardare avanti; (*fig*) cominciare a pensare al futuro; **to look south** (*building etc*) essere esposto(-a) a sud, dare a sud; **look before you leap** (*fig*) non buttarti alla cieca

2 (*seem, appear*) sembrare, aver l'aria; **she looks surprised** sembra sorpresa; **that cake looks nice** la torta sembra buona; **he looks (as if he's) happy** sembra *or* ha l'aria felice; **she looked prettier than ever** era più graziosa che mai; **he looks about 60 (years old)** dimostra una sessantina d'anni; **it looks about 4 metres long** sarà lungo un 4 metri; **you don't look yourself** non mi sembri in forma; **you look** *or* **you're looking well** ti trovo bene; **it looks good on you** ti sta bene, ti dona; **it makes you look younger** ti ringiovanisce, ti fa sembrare più giovane; **it looks all right to me** a me pare che vada bene

3 **to look like** assomigliare a; **he looks like his brother** assomiglia a suo fratello; **what does she look like?** che aspetto ha?; **this photo doesn't look like him** in questa foto non sembra lui; **it looks like cheese to me** mi sembra formaggio; **it certainly looks like it** ne ha tutta l'aria; **the party looks like being fun** la festa promette bene; **it looks like rain** mi sa che sta per piovere; **it looks as if** *or* **as though the train will be late** mi sa tanto che il treno sarà in ritardo

■ VT guardare; **to look sb (straight) in the eye** *or* **in the face** guardare qn (dritto) negli occhi *or* in faccia;

to look sb up and down squadrare qn da capo a piedi; **look where you're going!** guarda dove vai!; **to look one's best** essere in gran forma; **you must look your best for this interview** dovresti cercare di presentarti a questo colloquio ben vestito e ben curato; **to look one's age** dimostrare la propria età

■ N

1 (*glance*) occhiata; (*expression*) sguardo, aria; **with a look of despair** con un'aria *or* un'espressione disperata; **to have a look at sth** dare un'occhiata a qc; **have a look at this!** dai un'occhiata a questo!; **let me have a look** fammi vedere; **to take a good look at sb/sth** guardare (per) bene qn/qc; **to have a look for sth** cercare qc; **shall we have a look round the town?** andiamo a visitare la città?; **she gave me a dirty look** mi ha lanciato un'occhiataccia

2 (*air, appearance*) aspetto, aria; **he has a look of his mother about him** ha qualcosa di sua madre; **there's a mischievous look about that child** quel bambino ha un'aria birichina; **by the look of things it's going to rain** ha tutta l'aria di (voler) piovere; **by the look of him** a vederlo; **I don't like the look of him** ha un'aria che non mi piace; **I don't like the look of it** non mi piace per niente; **the new look for summer** (*Fashion*) il nuovo look *m inv* per l'estate; *see also* **looks**

▸ **look after** VI + PREP (*gen*) occuparsi di; (*possessions*) prendersi cura di; (*keep an eye on*) guardare, badare a; **I look after my little sister** mi occupo della mia sorellina; **to look after sth for sb** dare un'occhiata a qc per qn; **he doesn't look after himself** si trascura; **she's old enough to look after herself** è abbastanza grande per badare a se stessa

▸ **look around** VI + ADV guardarsi intorno; **to look around for sb/sth** cercare qn/qc

▸ **look at** VI + PREP (*person, object*) guardare; (*problem, situation*) considerare; **look at the picture on page three** guardate la figura a pagina tre; **it isn't much to look at but ...** (*fam*) non è bellissimo(-a) ma...; **could you look at the engine for me?** puoi dare un'occhiata al motore?; **I wouldn't even look at such a low offer** non prenderei nemmeno in considerazione un'offerta così bassa

▸ **look away** VI + ADV distogliere lo sguardo

▸ **look back** VI + ADV girarsi *or* voltarsi indietro; (*remember*) ripensare al passato; **to look back at sth/sb** voltarsi a guardare qc/qn; **he's never looked back** (*fig*) non ha fatto che migliorare; **to look back on** (*event, period*) ripensare a

▸ **look down** VI + ADV abbassare gli occhi *or* lo sguardo; (*from height*) guardare giù; **to look down at sb/sth** guardare giù verso qn/qc

▸ **look down on** VI + ADV + PREP guardare giù verso; (*fig*) guardare dall'alto in basso, disprezzare

▸ **look for** VI + PREP cercare; **to look for sb/sth** cercare qn/qc; **I'm looking for my passport** sto cercando il mio passaporto

▸ **look forward to** VI + ADV + PREP: **to look forward to doing sth** non veder l'ora di fare qc; **I'm looking forward to his visit/the film** non vedo l'ora che venga/di vedere il film; **I'm looking forward to meeting you** non vedo l'ora di incontrarti; **I'm looking forward to the holidays** non vedo l'ora che arrivino le vacanze; **I'm not looking forward to it** non ne ho nessuna voglia; **looking forward to hearing from you** (*in letter*) aspettando tue notizie

▸ **look in** VI + ADV guardar dentro

▸ **look in on** VI + ADV + PREP (*visit*) fare un salto da

▸ **look into** VI + PREP (*matter, possibility*) esaminare

▸ **look on** VI + ADV rimanere a guardare, fare da spettatore

■ VI + PREP considerare

▸ **look onto** VI + PREP dare su, affacciarsi su; **to look onto the sea** dare sul mare; **my room looks onto the garden** la mia camera si affaccia *or* dà sul giardino

▸ **look out** VI + ADV

1 (*watch*) guardar fuori

2 **to look out (for)** stare attento(-a) (a); **look out!** attento!

■ VT + ADV (*find*) tirar fuori

▸ **look out for** VI + PREP (*seek*) cercare; **to look out for sb/sth** (*watch out for*) guardare se arriva qn/qc

▸ **look over** VT + ADV (*essay*) dare un'occhiata a, riguardare; (*building*) ispezionare; (*person*) esaminare

▸ **look upon** VT + PREP considerare, ritenere

▸ **look round** VI + ADV (*turn*) girarsi, voltarsi; (*in shops*) dare un'occhiata; **I shouted and he looked round** ho gridato e lui si è voltato; **I'm just looking round** sto solo dando un'occhiata; **to look round for sb/sth** guardarsi intorno per cercare qn/qc

■ VI + PREP (*museum, factory*) visitare; (*shops*) dare un'occhiata a; **to look round an exhibition** visitare una mostra

▸ **look through** VI + PREP

1 (*papers, book*) esaminare; (: *briefly*) scorrere; (: *revise*) rivedere

2 (*telescope*) guardare attraverso

▸ **look to** VI + PREP (*turn to*) rivolgersi a; (*look after*) badare a, stare attento(-a) a; (*rely on*) contare su

▸ **look up** VI + ADV

1 (*glance*) alzare gli occhi

2 (*improve: prospects*) migliorare; (: *business*) riprendersi; (: *sales*) aumentare; (: *shares*) essere in rialzo; (: *weather*) mettersi al bello; **things are looking up** le cose stanno migliorando

■ VT + ADV

1 (*information, word*) cercare; **if you don't know a word, look it up in the dictionary** se non conosci qualche parola cercala sul dizionario

2 (*visit: friend*) andare a trovare

▸ **look up to** VI + ADV + PREP avere rispetto per

look·alike [ˈlʊkəˌlaɪk] N sosia *m/f*

looker-on [ˌlʊkərˈɒn] N (*pl* **lookers-on**) astante *m/f*

look-in [ˈlʊkˌɪn] N (*fam*): **not to get a look-in** non avere la minima possibilità di (partecipare, vincere *etc*)

looking-glass [ˈlukɪŋˌglɑːs] N (*old*) specchio

look-out [ˈlʊkˌaʊt] N **1** **to keep a look-out** fare la guardia; **keep a look-out for a post box** guarda se vedi una buca per le lettere; **to be on the look-out for sth** cercare qc **2** (*viewpoint*) posto di vedetta, posto d'osservazione; (*person: thief*) palo; (: *Mil*) sentinella; (: *Naut*) vedetta **3** (*prospect*) prospettiva; **it's a grim** *or* **poor look-out** è una prospettiva poco allegra; **that's his look-out!** questo è affar suo!

look-out post N posto di vedetta, posto di osservazione

look-out tower N torre *f* di osservazione

looks [lʊks] NPL (*appearance*) aspetto; (*attractiveness*) bellezza; **she has kept her (good) looks** è rimasta bella; **you can't go by looks** non si può giudicare dalle apparenze

loom[1] [luːm] N (*weaving loom*) telaio

loom[2] [luːm] VI (*also:* **loom up**: *building, mountain*) apparire in lontananza; **the ship loomed (up) out of the mist** nella nebbia apparve la nave; **to loom large**

Ll

(*fig*) essere imminente, incombere; **the threat of a war is looming** incombe la minaccia di una guerra; **a new crisis is looming** si profila all'orizzonte una nuova crisi

loony ['lu:nɪ] ADJ, N (*fam*) pazzo(-a), matto(-a)

loony bin N (*fam*) manicomio

loop [lu:p] N (*in string etc*) cappio; (*fastening*) asola; (*for belt*) passante *m*; (*bend: in river*) ansa; (*Comput*) loop *m inv*, sequenza ciclica di istruzioni
■ VT: **to loop a rope round a post** passare una corda intorno a un palo; **to loop the loop** (*Aer*) fare il giro della morte

loop·hole ['lu:pˌhəʊl] N (*fig*) scappatoia, via d'uscita; **a legal loophole** una scappatoia legale

◎ **loose** [lu:s] ADJ (*comp* **-r**, *superl* **-st**) **1** (*not firm, attached: plaster, button*) che si stacca; (*: knot, shoelace, screw*) allentato(-a); (*: hair*) sciolto(-a); (*: skin*) floscio(-a); (*: tooth*) che tentenna; (*: page*) staccato(-a); (*: sheet of paper*) volante; (*: stone*) sconnesso(-a); (*animal*) in libertà, scappato(-a); **a loose screw** una vite allentata; **to come** *or* **work loose** allentarsi; **to turn** *or* **let loose** (*animal*) lasciare in libertà; **to get loose** (*animal*) scappare; **loose chippings** (*Aut*) ghiaino; **loose connection** (*Elec*) filo che fa contatto **2** (*not tight: clothes*) ampio(-a), largo(-a); **a loose shirt** una camicia larga; **loose weave** a trama *or* maglia larga **3** (*not packed: fruit, cheese*) non confezionato(-a), sfuso(-a) **4** (*fig: translation*) libero(-a); (*: style*) prolisso(-a); (*: discipline*) rilassato(-a); (*: associations, links, thinking*) vago(-a), poco rigoroso(-a); (*: life, morals*) dissoluto(-a); **loose living** vita dissipata
■ N (*fam*): **to be on the loose** (*criminal, animal*) essere in libertà
■ VT (*frm: free*) liberare; (*: untie*) sciogliere; (*: slacken*) allentare; (*also:* **loose off**: *arrow*) scoccare; **to loose one's gun (off) at** sparare a *or* contro; **to loose the dogs on** *or* **at sb** sguinzagliare i cani dietro a *or* contro qn

loose change N spiccioli *mpl*, moneta

loose cover N (*on settee, chair*) foderina

loose end N dettaglio in sospeso; **to tie up loose ends** (*fig*) sistemare gli ultimi dettagli; **to be at a loose end**, (*Am*): **to be at loose ends** (*fig*) non saper cosa fare

loose-fitting ['lu:sˌfɪtɪŋ] ADJ ampio(-a), largo(-a)

loose-leaf ['lu:s'li:f] ADJ: **loose-leaf binder** *or* **folder** raccoglitore *m* a fogli mobili

loose-limbed ['lu:s'lɪmd] ADJ snodato(-a), agile

loose·ly ['lu:slɪ] ADV (*hold, tie*) senza stringere; (*associate*) vagamente; (*translate*) liberamente; (*use word*) in modo improprio

loosely-knit ['lu:slɪ'nɪt] ADJ non rigidamente strutturato(-a)

loos·en ['lu:sn] VT (*slacken: screw, belt, knot*) allentare; (*: rope, grip*) mollare; (*: clothing*) slacciare; (*untie*) disfare; (*fig: tongue*) sciogliere
■ VI (*all senses*) allentarsi
▸ **loosen up** VI + ADV (*before game*) sciogliere i muscoli, scaldarsi; (*fam: relax*) rilassarsi

loose·ness ['lu:snɪs] N (*of knot, screw*) lentezza; (*of rope*) scarsa tensione *f*; (*of clothes*) ampiezza; (*of translation*) approssimazione *f*; (*of behaviour*) dissipazione *f*, dissolutezza

loot [lu:t] N bottino
■ VT saccheggiare, depredare
■ VI: **to go looting** darsi al saccheggio

loot·er ['lu:təʳ] N saccheggiatore(-trice)

loot·ing ['lu:tɪŋ] N saccheggio

lop [lɒp] VT (*also:* **lop off**) tagliar (via), recidere

lope [ləʊp] VI: **to lope along/off** *etc* procedere/partire *etc* a grandi balzi

lop-eared ['lɒpˌɪəd] ADJ dalle orecchie pendenti

lop-sided ['lɒp'saɪdɪd] ADJ (*smile*) di traverso; (*structure*) sbilenco(-a)

lo·qua·cious [lə'kweɪʃəs] ADJ (*frm*) loquace

lo·qua·cious·ly [lə'kweɪʃəslɪ] ADV (*frm*) loquacemente

lo·quac·ity [lə'kwæsɪtɪ] N (*frm*) loquacità

◎ **lord** [lɔ:d] N **1** signore *m*; **lord of the manor** signore del castello; **lord and master** signore e padrone; **to live like a lord** vivere da signore *or* come un re **2** (*Brit*): **Lord Smith** Lord Smith; **my Lord** (*to bishop, noble*) Eccellenza; (*to judge*) signor giudice **3 Our Lord** (*Rel*) Nostro Signore; **the Lord** il Signore; **the Lord's prayer** il Padrenostro; **good Lord!** Dio mio!
■ VT: **to lord it over sb** (*fam*) darsi arie da gran signore con qn

lord·li·ness ['lɔ:dlɪnɪs] N altezzosità

lord·ly ['lɔ:dlɪ] ADJ (*pej: person, manner*) altero(-a), altezzoso(-a); (*bearing, castle*) nobile, maestoso(-a)

Lords [lɔ:dz] NPL: **the Lords** = **House of Lords**

lord·ship ['lɔ:dʃɪp] N: **his lordship the Count** *etc* Sua Signoria il conte *etc*; **your Lordship** (*Brit*) Vostra Signoria

lore [lɔ:ʳ] N tradizioni *fpl*; **plant/weather lore** cognizioni *fpl* sulle piante/sul tempo

Lor·raine [lɒ'reɪn] N Lorena

lor·ry ['lɒrɪ] N (*Brit*) camion *m inv*

lorry driver N (*Brit*) camionista *m/f*

lorry load N (*Brit*) carico (*di camion*)

Los An·ge·les [lɒs'ændʒɪˌli:z] N Los Angeles *f*
▷ www.ci.la.ca.us/

◎ **lose** [lu:z] (*pt, pp* **lost**) VT **1** (*gen*) perdere; **I've lost my purse** ho perso il portamonete; **to get lost** (*object*) andare perso(-a) *or* perduto(-a) *or* smarrito(-a); (*person*) perdersi, smarrirsi; **I was afraid I'd get lost** avevo paura di perdermi; **get lost!** (*fam*) vattene!, sparisci!; **to lose one's life** perdere la vita; **many lives were lost** ci sono state molte vittime; **there were no lives lost** non ci sono stati morti, non ci sono state vittime; **he's lost his licence** (*Aut*) gli è stata ritirata la patente; **you've got nothing to lose** non hai niente da perdere; **to lose one's way** perdersi; **to lose interest/one's appetite** perdere interesse/l'appetito; **to lose weight** dimagrire; **to lose patience** perdere la pazienza, spazientirsi; **to lose no time (in doing sth)** non perdere tempo (a fare qc); **there's no time to lose** non c'è tempo da perdere; **he managed to lose his pursuers** è riuscito a seminare i suoi inseguitori; **you've lost me there** (*fig*) ho perso il filo **2 that mistake lost us the game** quell'errore ci ha fatto perdere il gioco; **they lost the match** hanno perso la partita **3 this watch loses 5 minutes every day** quest'orologio resta indietro di 5 minuti al giorno
■ VI perdere; **they lost (by) 3 goals to 2** hanno perso (per) 3 a 2; **to lose to sb** perdere contro qn; **to lose (out) on sth** (*deal*) rimetterci in qc; (*trip*) perdersi; **you can't lose** in tutti i casi ci guadagni; **the clock is losing** l'orologio resta indietro

los·er ['lu:zəʳ] N perdente *m/f*; **he's a born loser** è un perdente nato; **to be a good/bad loser** saper/non saper perdere

los·ing ['lu:zɪŋ] ADJ perdente; **to fight a losing battle** (*fig*) combattere una battaglia perduta; **on a losing streak** in un periodo nero

◎ **loss** [lɒs] N **1** perdita; **heavy losses** (*Mil*) gravi perdite;

without loss of life senza perdita di vite umane; **to cut one's losses** rimetterci il meno possibile; **it's your loss!** quello che ci rimette sei tu!; **he's a dead loss** (*fam*) è un disastro; **he's no great loss** (*fam*) nessuno lo rimpiange di certo; **to make a loss** perderci; (*Comm*) subire una perdita; **to sell sth at a loss** vendere qc perdendoci **2 to be at a loss** essere perplesso(-a); **to be at a loss to explain sth** non saper come fare a spiegare qc; **to be at a loss for words** essere senza parole

loss adjuster N (*Insurance*) liquidatore *m/f*

loss leader N (*Comm*) articolo *m* civetta *inv*

◎**lost** [lɒst] PT, PP *of* **lose**
■ADJ (*gen: fig*) perso(-a); (*bewildered*) smarrito(-a); **I realized I was lost** ho capito che mi ero perso; **a lost sheep** una pecorella smarrita; **some lost children** dei bambini che si erano smarriti; **lost in thought** immerso(-a) *or* perso(-a) nei propri pensieri; **to feel a bit lost** sentirsi smarrito(-a); **the remark/joke was lost on him** non ha capito l'osservazione/la barzelletta; **my advice was lost on her** non ha ascoltato il mio consiglio; **I feel lost without my car/him** mi sento perso senza la mia macchina/di lui; **to make up for lost time** recuperare il tempo perduto; **to give sth up for lost** dare qc per perso(-a); **lost baggage claim** ritiro bagagli smarriti; **lost at sea** perito(-a) in mare

lost cause N causa persa

lost property, (*Am*) **lost and found** N oggetti *mpl* smarriti; **lost property office** *or* **department** ufficio oggetti smarriti

◎**lot** [lɒt] N **1** (*large amount*) molto; **a lot of money** *or* (*fam*) **lots of money** un sacco di soldi; **I drink a lot of coffee** bevo molto caffè; **we saw a lot of interesting things** abbiamo visto molte cose interessanti; **a lot of people** *or* (*fam*) **lots of people** molta gente, molti; **he's got lots of friends** ha molti amici; **she's got lots of self-confidence** ha molta fiducia in se stessa; **she talks a lot** parla molto; **do you like football? – not a lot** ti piace il calcio? – non molto; **quite a lot of noise** parecchio rumore; **such a lot of people** talmente tanta gente; **there was not a lot we could say/do** c'era ben poco da dire/da fare; **I'd give a lot to know ...** darei non so cosa per sapere...; **I read a lot** leggo molto; **he feels a lot** *or* (*fam*) **lots better** si sente molto meglio; **thanks a lot!** (*also: iro*) grazie tante! **2** (*fam*): **the lot** (*all, everything*) tutto(-a) (quanto(-a)); **he took the lot** ha preso tutto (quanto); **that's the lot** (questo) è tutto; **the (whole) lot of them** tutti quanti **3** (*destiny*) sorte *f*, destino; **the common lot** il destino comune; **it fell to my lot to do it** è toccato a me farlo; **to throw in one's lot with sb** unirsi a qn **4** (*random selection*) sorte *f*; **to draw lots (for sth)** tirare a sorte (per qc) **5** (*at auction*) lotto, partita; **he's a bad lot** (*fig*) è un pessimo soggetto **6** (*plot of land*) lotto di terreno; **building lot** lotto edificabile

lo·tion ['ləʊʃən] N lozione *f*

lot·tery ['lɒtərɪ] N lotteria; **to win the lottery** vincere alla lotteria

lo·tus ['ləʊtəs] N loto

lotus position N posizione *f* del loto

◎**loud** [laʊd] ADJ (*comp* **-er**, *superl* **-est**) (*gen*) forte; (*laugh, applause, thunder*) fragoroso(-a), forte; (*noisy: behaviour, party, protests*) rumoroso(-a); (*pej: gaudy: colour, clothes*) chiassoso(-a), vistoso(-a), sgargiante; **the radio's too loud** il volume della radio è troppo alto
■ADV (*speak etc*) forte; **out loud** ad alta voce; **loud and clear** chiaro e forte, molto chiaramente

loud·hailer [ˌlaʊd'heɪləʳ] N megafono

loud·ly ['laʊdlɪ] ADV (*gen*) forte; (*laugh, applaud*) fragorosamente; (*protest*) rumorosamente; (*proclaim: out loud*) ad alta voce; (*: on banner etc*) a lettere cubitali

loud-mouthed [ˌlaʊd'maʊðd] ADJ (*person*) sguaiato(-a); (*protests*) rumoroso(-a)

loud·ness ['laʊdnɪs] N (*see adj*) forza; fragorosità; rumorosità, chiassosità

loud·speaker [ˌlaʊd'spiːkəʳ] N altoparlante *m*

Loui·si·ana [luːˌiːzɪ'ænə] N Lousiana
▷ www.louisiana.gov/wps/portal/

lounge [laʊndʒ] N soggiorno, salotto; (*of hotel*) salone *m*; (*of airport*) sala d'attesa; **in the lounge** nel soggiorno; **the departure lounge** la sala attesa per l'imbarco
■VI (*also:* **lounge about**) oziare, poltrire, starsene colle mani in mano

lounge bar N (*Brit*) bar *m inv* con servizio a tavolino

loung·er ['laʊndʒəʳ] N lettino da spiaggia

lounge suit N (*Brit*) completo da uomo

louse [laʊs] N (*pl* **lice**) pidocchio; (*pej fam: person*) verme *m*
▶ **louse up** VT + ADV (*Am fam*) rovinare

lousy ['laʊzɪ] ADJ (*Med*) pidocchioso(-a); (*fam: very bad*) schifoso(-a); (*: headache, cough*) orrendo(-a); **to feel lousy** stare da cani; **I feel lousy** sto da cani; **she's a lousy cook** fa schifo come cuoca; **a lousy trick** uno sporco trucco; **the food's lousy** il cibo è pessimo

lout [laʊt] N giovinastro

lout·ish ['laʊtɪʃ] ADJ rozzo(-a), da zotico(-a)

lou·vre, (*Am*) **lou·ver** ['luːvəʳ] ADJ (*door, window*) con apertura a gelosia

lov·able ['lʌvəbl] ADJ adorabile, carino(-a)

◎**love** [lʌv] N **1 love (of, for)** amore *m* (di, per); (*of hobby, object*) passione *f* (per); **true love** vero amore; **it was love at first sight** è stato amore a prima vista *or* un colpo di fulmine; **he studies history for the love of it** studia storia per il puro piacere di farlo; **to be in love (with sb)** essere innamorato(-a) (di qn); **she's in love with Paul** è innamorata di Paul; **to fall in love (with sb)** innamorarsi (di qn); **to make love** fare l'amore; **to make love to sb** (*old: woo*) fare la corte a qn; **there is no love lost between them** non si possono soffrire; **love from Anne** *or* **love, Anne** (*in letter*) con affetto, Anne; **to send one's love to sb** mandare i propri saluti a qn; **give Gloria my love** salutami Gloria **2 (my) love** amore *m* (mio), tesoro (mio) **3** (*Tennis etc*): **love all** zero a zero; **"15 love"** "15 a zero"
■VT (*person: spouse, child*) amare; (*: relative, friend*) voler bene a; (*food, activity, place*) amare, adorare; **I love you** ti amo; **everybody loves her** tutti le vogliono bene; **I love chocolate** mi piace molto la cioccolata; **he loves tennis/Florence** gli piace (molto) il tennis/Firenze; **he loves swimming** *or* **to swim** gli piace (molto) nuotare; **I'd love to...** mi piacerebbe molto...; **I'd love to come** mi piacerebbe molto venire; **would you like to come? – I'd love to** vuoi venire? – mi piacerebbe molto

love affair N relazione *f*

love·bird ['lʌvˌbɜːd] N (*fig*) piccioncino(-a)

love child N (*euph*) figlio(-a) dell'amore

loved ones ['lʌvd'wʌnz] NPL: **my loved ones** i miei cari

loved-up [ˌlʌvd'ʌp] ADJ (*fam*) felice ed eccitato(-a)

love-hate relationship ['lʌvˌheɪtrɪ'leɪʃənʃɪp] N rapporto *m* amore-odio *inv*

love·less ['lʌvlɪs] ADJ senza amore

Ll

love letter N lettera d'amore
love life N vita sentimentale
love·li·ness ['lʌvlɪnɪs] N (*of person*) grazia
love·lorn ['lʌv,lɔ:n] ADJ infelice in amore
◎ **love·ly** ['lʌvlɪ] ADJ (*comp* **-ier**, *superl* **-iest**) (*beautiful: gen*) bello(-a); (*delightful: meal, voice*) delizioso(-a); (*: evening, party*) bellissimo(-a); (*: holiday, weather*) bello(-a); (*delicious: smell, meal, food*) buono(-a); **what a lovely surprise!** che bella sorpresa!; **they've got a lovely house** hanno una bella casa; **is your meal okay? – yes, it's lovely** ti piace il pranzo? – sì , è buonissimo; **she's a lovely person** è una persona deliziosa; **it's lovely and warm** fa un bel calduccio; **it's been lovely seeing you** è stato un vero piacere vederti; **have a lovely time!** divertiti!; **we had a lovely time** ci siamo divertiti molto
love-making ['lʌv,meɪkɪŋ] N il fare l'amore
love match N matrimonio d'amore
love nest N nido d'amore
◎ **lov·er** ['lʌvə^r] N **1** (*sexually*) amante *m/f*; (*romantically*) innamorato(-a) **2** **lover (of)** (*enthusiast*) appassionato(-a) (di); **he's a lover of good food** è un buongustaio, è un amante della buona tavola
love·sick ['lʌv,sɪk] ADJ malato(-a) d'amore
love·song ['lʌv,sɒŋ] N canzone *f* d'amore
love story N storia d'amore, love story *f inv*
love-stricken ['lʌv,strɪkən] ADJ, **lovestruck** ['lʌv,strʌk] ADJ perdutamente innamorato(-a)
lovey-dovey ['lʌvɪ'dʌvɪ] ADJ (*fam*) melenso(-a)
lov·ing ['lʌvɪŋ] ADJ affettuoso(-a); (*care*) tenero(-a), amoroso(-a); **loving parents** genitori affettuosi
lov·ing·ly ['lʌvɪŋlɪ] ADV affettuosamente; (*stronger*) amorosamente
◎ **low**[1] [ləʊ] ADJ (*comp* **-er**, *superl* **-est**) (*gen*) basso(-a); (*bow*) profondo(-a); (*murmur*) sommesso(-a); (*intelligence*) scarso(-a); (*quality*) scadente; (*Bio, Zool: form of life*) primitivo(-a); (*pej: opinion, taste*) cattivo(-a); (*: character*) pessimo(-a); (*: behaviour*) ignobile; (*: café, place*) malfamato(-a); **a low trick** un tiro mancino, uno scherzo ignobile; **to feel low** (*depressed*) sentirsi (un po') giù; **he was feeling a bit low** era un po' giù; **he's very low** (*ill*) è molto debole; **supplies are low** le scorte si stanno esaurendo; **we are low on flour** non c'è rimasta molta farina; **in a low voice** a bassa voce; **in low gear** (*Aut*) in una marcia bassa; **on low ground** in pianura; **lower down** più in basso; **lower deck/floor** ponte/piano inferiore
■ ADV (*aim*) in basso; (*sing*) a bassa voce; (*fly*) a bassa quota, basso; (*bow*) profondamente; **that plane is flying very low** quell'aereo vola molto basso; **to sink lower** sprofondare sempre di più; **to fall** *or* **sink low** (*fig*) cadere in basso; **to turn sth down low** (*gas, radio etc*) abbassare qc; **supplies are running** *or* **getting low** le scorte stanno per finire
■ N **1** (*Met*) depressione *f*, zona di bassa pressione **2** (*fig: low point*): **to reach a new** *or* **an all-time low** toccare il livello più basso *or* il minimo
low[2] [ləʊ] VI (*cow*) muggire
low-alcohol ['ləʊ'ælkə,hɒl] ADJ a basso contenuto alcolico
low·brow ['ləʊ,braʊ] ADJ (*pej: person*) poco colto(-a); (*: interests, entertainment*) senza pretese intellettuali
■ N persona poco colta *or* senza pretese intellettuali
low-budget ['ləʊ'bʌdʒɪt] ADJ a basso costo
low-calorie ['ləʊ'kælərɪ] ADJ a basso contenuto calorico
low-cost ['ləʊ'kɒst] ADJ a basso prezzo

Low Countries N: **the Low Countries** i Paesi Bassi
low-cut ['ləʊ'kʌt] ADJ (*dress*) scollato(-a)
low-down ['ləʊ,daʊn] N (*fam*): **he gave me the low-down on it** mi ha messo al corrente dei fatti
■ ADJ (*mean*) ignobile
◎ **low·er**[1] ['ləʊə^r] ADJ (*comp of* **low**)
■ ADV (*comp of* **low**)
■ VT (*gen*) calare; (*flag, sail*) ammainare; (*reduce: price*) abbassare, ridurre; (*resistance*) indebolire; **they have lowered interest rates** hanno abbassato i tassi d'interesse; **to lower sb's morale** demoralizzare qn; **to lower one's guard** (*Boxing, also fig*) abbassare la guardia; **to lower one's voice** abbassare la voce; **to lower o.s. to do sth** (*fig*) abbassarsi a fare qc
low·er[2] ['laʊə^r] VI (*person*): **to lower (at sb)** dare un'occhiataccia (a qn); (*sky*) oscurarsi, essere minaccioso(-a)
lower-case ['ləʊə'keɪs] ADJ (*Typ*) minuscolo(-a)
Lower Chamber N (*Pol*): **the Lower Chamber** la Camera Bassa
lower-class [,ləʊə'klɑ:s] ADJ proletario(-a)
lower classes NPL: **the lower classes** le classi inferiori
low·er·ing[1] ['ləʊərɪŋ] N (*of price*) riduzione *f*, diminuzione *f*; (*of temperature, pressure*) abbassamento; (*of resistance*) indebolimento; (*of boat*) messa in acqua; **the lowering of morale** il calo del morale; **the lowering of the flag** l'ammainabandiera
■ ADJ umiliante, degradante
low·er·ing[2] ['laʊərɪŋ] ADJ (*look, sky*) minaccioso(-a)
low·est com·mon de·nomi·nat·or ['ləʊɪst,kɒməndɪ'nɒmɪ,neɪtə^r] N minimo comune denominatore *m*
low·est com·mon multi·ple ['ləʊɪst,kɒmən'mʌltɪpl] N minimo comune multiplo
low-fat ['ləʊ'fæt] ADJ magro(-a)
low-flying ['ləʊ,flaɪɪŋ] ADJ che vola a bassa quota
low-grade ['ləʊ,greɪd] ADJ di qualità inferiore
low-heeled ['ləʊ'hi:ld] ADJ basso(-a), coi tacchi bassi
low-impact [,ləʊ'ɪmpækt] ADJ (*exercise*) dolce, a basso impatto; (*holiday, activity*) ecologico(-a), nel rispetto dell'ambiente
low·ing ['ləʊɪŋ] N muggito
low-key [,ləʊ'ki:] ADJ moderato(-a); (*operation*) condotto(-a) con discrezione; **to keep sth low-key** fare qc con discrezione
low·land ['ləʊlənd] N bassopiano, pianura; **the Lowlands of Scotland** le Lowlands scozzesi
Low Latin N basso latino
low-level ['ləʊ,lɛvl] ADJ a basso livello; (*flying*) a bassa quota
low-loader [,ləʊ'ləʊdə^r] N camion *m inv* a pianale basso
low·ly ['ləʊlɪ] ADJ modesto(-a), umile
low-lying ['ləʊ,laɪɪŋ] ADJ (*land*) a basso livello
low-necked ['ləʊ'nɛkt] ADJ (*dress*) scollato(-a)
low·ness ['ləʊnɪs] N (*gen*) bassezza
low-paid [,ləʊ'peɪd] ADJ mal pagato(-a)
low-priced [,ləʊ'praɪst] ADJ a buon prezzo, a basso prezzo
low-rent ['ləʊrɛnt] ADJ (*house, apartment*) dall'affitto basso; (*fig*) da quattro soldi
low-rise ['ləʊ'raɪz] ADJ (*Archit*) di altezza contenuta, basso(-a)
low season N: **the low season** la bassa stagione
low-spirited [,ləʊ'spɪrɪtɪd] ADJ abbacchiato(-a), giù (di morale)
Low Sunday N Domenica in Albis

low-tech ['ləʊ'tɛk] ADJ a basso contenuto tecnologico
low tide, low water N: **at low tide** quando c'è la bassa marea
loy·al ['lɔɪəl] ADJ (*comp* **-er**, *superl* **-est**) leale, fedele
loy·al·ist ['lɔɪəlɪst] N, ADJ lealista (*m/f*)
loy·al·ly ['lɔɪəlɪ] ADV con lealtà, lealmente
loy·al·ty ['lɔɪəltɪ] N lealtà *f inv*, fedeltà *f inv*; **undying loyalty** fedeltà eterna
loyalty card N carta *f* fedeltà *inv*
loz·enge ['lɒzɪndʒ] N (*Med*) pastiglia; (*Geom*) losanga
LP [,ɛl'pi:] N ABBR (= **long-playing record**) LP *m inv*, ellepi *m inv*
LPG [,ɛlpi:'dʒi:] N ABBR (= **liquefied petroleum gas**) GPL *m inv* (= *gas di petrolio liquefatto*)
L-plates ['ɛl,pleɪts] NPL (*Brit*) ≈ cartello con P di principiante

L-PLATE

Le **L-plates** sono delle tabelle bianche con una L rossa che in Gran Bretagna i guidatori principianti, "learners", in possesso di una "provisional licence", che corrisponde al nostro foglio rosa, devono applicare davanti e dietro alla loro autovettura finché non ottengono la patente.
▷ www.dvla.gov.uk/drivers/drivers.htm

LPN [,ɛlpi:'ɛn] N ABBR (*Am*: = **Licensed Practical Nurse**) ≈ infermiere(-a) diplomato(-a)
LRAM [,ɛlɑ:reɪ'ɛm] N ABBR (*Brit*: = **Licentiate of the Royal Academy of Music**) *diplomato(-a) al conservatorio*
LSD [,ɛlɛs'di:] N ABBR **1** (= **lysergic acid diethylamide**) LSD *m* **2** (*Brit*: = **pounds, shillings and pence**) *sistema monetario in vigore in Gran Bretagna fino al 1971*
LSE [,ɛlɛs'i:] N ABBR = *London School of Economics*
LT [,ɛl'ti:] N ABBR (*Elec*: = **low tension**) BT (= *bassa tensione*)
Lt. ABBR (= **lieutenant**) Ten.
◎ **Ltd** ABBR (*Comm*: = **limited**) ≈ S.r.l.
lub·ri·cant ['lu:brɪkənt] N lubrificante *m*
lu·bri·cate ['lu:brɪ,keɪt] VT lubrificare; **lubricating oil** lubrificante *m*
lu·bri·ca·tion [,lu:brɪ'keɪʃən] N lubrificazione *f*
lu·bri·ca·tor ['lu:brɪ,keɪtəʳ] N (*liquid*) lubrificante *m*; (*device*) ingrassatore *m*
lu·cerne [lu:'sɜ:n] N erba medica
lu·cid ['lu:sɪd] ADJ (*person*) lucido(-a); (*instructions*) chiaro(-a); (*moments*) di lucidità
lu·cid·ity [lu:'sɪdɪtɪ] N (*of person*) lucidità; (*of instructions*) chiarezza
lu·cid·ly ['lu:sɪdlɪ] ADV (*think*) con lucidità; (*explain*) con chiarezza
◎ **luck** [lʌk] N fortuna, sorte *f*; **good luck** (buona) fortuna; **bad luck** mala sorte, sfortuna; **good luck!** buona fortuna!; **bad luck!** che sfortuna!; **just my luck!** la mia solita sfortuna!; **it's good/bad luck to do ...** porta fortuna/sfortuna fare...; **no such luck!** magari!, purtroppo no!; **with any luck** con un po' di fortuna; **to be in luck** essere fortunato(-a); **to be out of luck** essere sfortunato(-a); **to be down on one's luck** essere scalognato(-a); **I had the luck to** ho avuto la fortuna di; **better luck next time!** andrà meglio la prossima volta!; **he's got the luck of the devil!** (*fam*) ha una fortuna sfacciata!; **to trust to luck** affidarsi al caso; **as luck would have it** come volle il caso; **it's the luck of the draw** (*fig*) è una questione di fortuna
lucki·ly ['lʌkɪlɪ] ADV per fortuna, fortunatamente
luck·less ['lʌklɪs] ADJ (*liter*) sfortunato(-a)
◎ **lucky** ['lʌkɪ] ADJ (*comp* **-ier**, *superl* **-iest**) (*gen*) fortunato(-a); (*horseshoe, number*) portafortuna *inv*, che porta fortuna; **he's lucky, he's got a job** è fortunato, ha un lavoro; **lucky break** colpo di fortuna; **lucky charm** portafortuna *m inv*; **black cats are lucky in Britain** i gatti neri portano fortuna in Gran Bretagna; **that was lucky!** per fortuna!; **it was a lucky guess** è stata tutta fortuna; **he's lucky to be alive** è vivo per miracolo; **lucky you!** *or* **you lucky thing!** beato te!; **it was very lucky for you (that ...)** per fortuna (che...)
lucky dip N (*at fair*) pesca miracolosa
luc·ra·tive ['lu:krətɪv] ADJ lucrativo(-a), redditizio(-a)
lu·cre ['lu:kəʳ] N (*old*) lucro
Lud·dite ['lʌdaɪt] N, ADJ (*frm*) luddista (*m/f*)
lu·di·crous ['lu:dɪkrəs] ADJ ridicolo(-a), assurdo(-a)
lu·di·crous·ly ['lu:dɪkrəslɪ] ADV in modo ridicolo
ludo ['lu:dəʊ] N (*Brit*) ≈ gioco dell'oca
luff [lʌf] VI (*Naut*) fileggiare
lug [lʌg] VT (*fam*) trascinare
luge [lu:ʒ] N (*Sport*) luge *m inv*, slittino
lug·gage ['lʌgɪdʒ] N bagagli *mpl*, bagaglio; **my luggage was left behind** hanno dimenticato i miei bagagli
luggage rack N (*on train etc*) reticella (per i bagagli); (*Aut*) portapacchi *m inv*, portabagagli *m inv*
luggage van N (*Brit Rail*) bagagliaio
lug·hole ['lʌg,həʊl] N (*Brit*) orecchio
lu·gu·bri·ous [lʊ'gu:brɪəs] ADJ (*liter*) lugubre
lu·gu·bri·ous·ly [lʊ'gu:brɪəslɪ] ADV (*liter*) lugubremente
lug·worm ['lʌg,wɜ:m] N arenicola
luke·warm [,lu:k'wɔ:m] ADJ **1** (*tepid*: *water*) tiepido(-a) **2** (*unenthusiastic*: *support, response*) tiepido(-a); (: *person*) poco entusiasta
lull [lʌl] N (*gen*) momento di calma; (*in business*) periodo di stasi; (*in conversation*) pausa; (*in fighting*) tregua
■ VT (*fear*) calmare; (*person*) calmare, acquietare; (*child*) cullare; **to lull a baby to sleep** cullare un bambino finché si addormenta; **to be lulled into a false sense of security** illudersi che tutto vada bene; **to lull sb into a false sense of security** dare a qn un falso senso di sicurezza
lulla·by ['lʌlə,baɪ] N ninnananna
lum·ba·go [lʌm'beɪgəʊ] N lombaggine *f*
lum·bar ['lʌmbəʳ] ADJ (*Med*) lombare
lum·ber¹ ['lʌmbəʳ] N (*wood*: *esp Am*) legname *m*; (*junk*: *esp Brit*) roba vecchia
■ VT (*Brit*: *fam*): **to lumber sb with sth/sb** affibbiare *or* rifilare qc/qn a qn; **he got lumbered with the job** è toccato a lui fare quel lavoro; **I got lumbered with him for the evening** me lo sono dovuto sorbire per tutta la serata
lum·ber² ['lʌmbəʳ] VI (*also*: **lumber about, lumber along**) muoversi pesantemente; **to lumber past** (*vehicle*) passare facendo fracasso
lum·ber·ing ['lʌmbərɪŋ] ADJ goffo(-a)
lumber·jack ['lʌmbə,dʒæk] N taglialegna *m inv*, boscaiolo
lumber room N ripostiglio, sgabuzzino
lumber yard N (*Am*) segheria
lu·mi·nary ['lu:mɪnərɪ] N (*liter*) luminare *m/f*
lu·mi·nous ['lu:mɪnəs] ADJ luminoso(-a)
lump [lʌmp] N (*gen*) pezzo; (*of earth*) zolla; (*of sugar*) zolletta; (*in sauce*) grumo; (*swelling*) gonfiore *m*; (*hard swelling*) nodulo; (*bump*) bernoccolo; (*person*: *fam pej*) bestione *m*; **a lump of butter** un pezzo di burro; **he's got a lump on his forehead** ha un bernoccolo sulla

Ll

fronte; **with a lump in one's throat** (*fig*) con un nodo alla gola
■ VT (*fam: endure*): **if he doesn't like it he can lump it** dovrà mandarla giù, che gli piaccia o no
▶ **lump together** VT + ADV mettere insieme, riunire

lump sugar N zucchero in zollette

lump sum N somma globale; (*payment*) pagamento unico

lumpy ['lʌmpɪ] ADJ (*comp* **-ier**, *superl* **-iest**) (*sauce*) grumoso(-a); (*mattress*) bitorzoluto(-a)

lu·na·cy ['lu:nəsɪ] N demenza; (*fig*) pazzia, follia; **it's sheer lunacy!** ma è una vera pazzia!

lu·nar ['lu:nə^r] ADJ lunare; **lunar landing** allunaggio; **lunar module** modulo lunare

lu·na·tic ['lu:nətɪk] N (*idiot*) pazzo(-a); (*old: mentally-ill person*) matto(-a); **he's an absolute lunatic** è completamente pazzo
■ ADJ (*person*) pazzo(-a); (*idea: crazy*) pazzo(-a), pazzesco(-a); (*: stupid*) idiota; (*driving*) da pazzi

> DID YOU KNOW ...?
> **lunatic** is not translated by the Italian word *lunatico*

lunatic asylum N (*old offensive*) manicomio

lunatic fringe N: **the lunatic fringe** la frangia estremista

◎ **lunch** [lʌntʃ] N pranzo, (seconda) colazione *f*; **a delicious lunch** un pranzo squisito; **to invite sb to** *or* **for lunch** invitare qn a pranzo; **to have lunch** pranzare; **we have lunch at 12 30** pranziamo a mezzogiorno e mezza

lunch break N intervallo del pranzo

lunch·eon ['lʌntʃən] N (*frm*) pranzo

luncheon meat N ≈ mortadella

luncheon voucher N buono *m* pasto *inv*

lunch hour N = **lunch break**

lunch·time ['lʌntʃ,taɪm] N ora di pranzo

lung [lʌŋ] N polmone *m*; **to shout at the top of one's lungs** gridare a squarciagola

lung cancer N cancro del polmone

lung disease N malattia polmonare *or* dei polmoni

lunge [lʌndʒ] N balzo (in avanti); (*Fencing*) affondo
■ VI (*also:* **lunge forward**) fare un balzo in avanti; **to lunge at sb** balzare su qn; **to lunge out with one's fists/feet** tirare dei pugni/calci

lu·pin, (*Am*) **lu·pine** ['lu:pɪn] N lupino

lurch[1] [lɜ:tʃ] N sobbalzo; (*of ship, plane*) rollata; **a lurch forward** un improvviso scatto in avanti
■ VI (*person, car*) avere un sobbalzo; (*ship, plane*) rollare; **she lurched forward** è scattata in avanti; **to lurch along** (*person*) procedere barcollando; (*car*) procedere a scatti

lurch[2] [lɜ:tʃ] N scatto improvviso; **to leave sb in the lurch** (*fam*) piantare in asso qn

lure [ljʊə^r] N (*decoy, bait*) richiamo, esca; (*fig: charm*) attrazione *f*, lusinga; **the lure of country life** il richiamo della vita di campagna
■ VT attirare (con l'inganno); **to lure sb into a trap** attirare qn in una trappola; **they were lured into an ambush** sono stati attirati in un'imboscata; **to lure out** far uscire con l'inganno

lur·gy ['lɜ:gɪ] N (*Brit*): **I've got the dreaded lurgy again** mi sento di nuovo poco bene

lu·rid ['ljʊərɪd] ADJ **1** (*details, description etc: gruesome*) impressionante, sconvolgente; (*: sensational*) sensazionale, scandalistico(-a) **2** (*colour*) violento(-a), sgargiante; (*sunset*) fiammeggiante

> DID YOU KNOW ...?
> **lurid** is not translated by the Italian word *lurido*

lurk [lɜ:k] VI (*person: hide*) stare in agguato, appostarsi; (*: creep about*) girare furtivamente; (*danger*) stare in agguato; (*doubt*) persistere

lurk·ing ['lɜ:kɪŋ] ADJ (*fear, suspicion etc*) vago(-a)

lus·cious ['lʌʃəs] ADJ (*food*) appetitoso(-a), succulento(-a); (*taste, smell*) delizioso(-a); **a luscious blonde** una bionda appetitosa

lush [lʌʃ] ADJ rigoglioso(-a), lussureggiante

lust [lʌst] N (*sexual*) libidine *f*, desiderio; **lust for** (*greed*) sete *f* di
▶ **lust after, lust for** VI + PREP (*person*) desiderare; (*power, wealth etc*) aver sete di

lust·ful ['lʌstfʊl] ADJ pieno(-a) di desiderio

lus·tre, (*Am*) **lus·ter** ['lʌstə^r] N lustro, splendore *m*

lus·trous ['lʌstrəs] ADJ lucente, splendente

lusty ['lʌstɪ] ADJ (*comp* **-ier**, *superl* **-iest**) (*person*) vigoroso(-a), robusto(-a); (*cry etc*) forte

lute [lu:t] N liuto

Luther ['lu:θə^r] N Lutero

Lu·ther·an ['lu:θərən] ADJ, N luterano(-a)
▷ www.lutheranworld.org/Who_We_Are/LWF-Welcome.html

Lu·ther·an·ism ['lu:θərənɪzəm] N luteranesimo

luv [lʌv] N gioia

Lux·em·bourg ['lʌksəm,bɜ:g] N (*city*) Lussemburgo *f*; (*state*) Lussemburgo *m*

luxu·ri·ance [lʌg'zjʊərɪəns] N (*of growth*) rigoglio; (*of beard*) foltezza

luxu·ri·ant [lʌg'zjʊərɪənt] ADJ (*growth, jungle*) lussureggiante, rigoglioso(-a); (*beard*) folto(-a); (*fig: imagination*) ricco(-a), fervido(-a)

luxu·ri·ant·ly [lʌg'zjʊərɪəntlɪ] ADV (*grow*) rigogliosamente

luxu·ri·ate [lʌg'zjʊərɪ,eɪt] VI: **to luxuriate in** indulgere in, abbandonarsi al piacere di

luxu·ri·ous [lʌg'zjʊərɪəs] ADJ (*gen*) lussuoso(-a), di lusso; (*surroundings*) di lusso; (*meal, tastes*) raffinato(-a), di lusso

> DID YOU KNOW ...?
> **luxurious** is not translated by the Italian word *lussurioso*

luxu·ri·ous·ly [lʌg'zjʊərɪəslɪ] ADV lussuosamente

◎ **luxu·ry** ['lʌkʃərɪ] N (*gen*) lusso; (*article*) (oggetto di) lusso; **it was luxury!** è stato un vero lusso!
■ ADJ (*goods, apartment*) di lusso; **a luxury hotel** un albergo di lusso

> DID YOU KNOW ...?
> **luxury** is not translated by the Italian word *lussuria*

LV ABBR (*Brit*) = **luncheon voucher**

LW ABBR (*Radio:* = **long wave**) OL (= *onde lunghe*)

ly·chee, li·chee [,laɪ'tʃi:] N litchi *m inv*

Ly·cra® ['laɪkrə] N lycra®
■ ADJ di lycra

ly·ing ['laɪɪŋ] ADJ (*statement, story*) falso(-a); (*person*) bugiardo(-a)
■ N bugie *fpl*, menzogne *fpl*

lying-in [,laɪɪŋ'ɪn] N (*old*): **the lying-in period** la degenza post-natale

lymph [lɪmf] N linfa

lym·phat·ic [lɪm'fætɪk] ADJ linfatico(-a)

lymph nodes NPL linfonodi *mpl*

lynch [lɪntʃ] VT linciare

lynch·ing ['lɪntʃɪŋ] N linciaggio

lynch mob N folla pronta al linciaggio
lynch·pin ['lɪntʃpɪn] N = **linchpin**
lynx [lɪŋks] N lince *f*
Ly·ons [' laɪənz] N Lione *f*
lyre ['laɪə^r] N lira
lyre·bird ['laɪəˌbɜːd] N uccello *m* lira *inv*
lyr·ic ['lɪrɪk] ADJ lirico(-a)
■ N (*poem*) lirica; **lyrics** NPL (*words of song*) parole *fpl*
lyri·cal ['lɪrɪkəl] ADJ lirico(-a); (*fig*) entusiasta; **to wax** *or* **become lyrical about sth** infervorarsi a parlare di qc
lyri·cal·ly ['lɪrɪkəlɪ] ADV liricamente
lyri·cism ['lɪrɪˌsɪzəm] N lirismo
lyri·cist ['lɪrɪsɪst] N paroliere(-a)

Ll

Mm

M, m [ɛm] N (*letter*) M, m *f or m inv*; **M for Mary** (*Am*): **M for Mike** ≈ M come Milano
M [ɛm] ABBR **1** (*Brit*: = **motorway**) ≈ A *f* (= *autostrada*) **on the M6** sulla M6 **2** (= **medium**) M *f inv* (*taglia media*)
m [ɛm] ABBR **1** (= **metre**) m **2** = **mile 3** = **million**
MA [ɛm'eɪ] N ABBR **1** (*Univ*: = **Master of Arts**) master *m inv* in materie umanistiche **2** (*Am*) = **Military Academy**; *see* **academy**
■ ABBR (*Am Post*) = **Massachusetts**
ma [mɑː] N (*fam*) mamma
mac [mæk] N ABBR (*Brit fam*: = **mackintosh**) impermeabile *m*
ma·ca·bre [mə'kɑːbrə] ADJ macabro(-a)
mac·ad·am [mə'kædəm] N macadam *m*
mac·ad·am·ize [mə'kædə,maɪz] VT macadamizzare
ma·caque [mə'kɑːk] N (*animal*) macaco
maca·ro·ni [,mækə'rəʊnɪ] N maccheroni *mpl*
macaroni cheese N *pasta con formaggio gratinata al forno*
maca·roon [,mækə'ruːn] N ≈ amaretto (*biscotto*)
ma·caw [mə'kɔː] N (*bird*) ara
mace[1] [meɪs] N (*weapon, ceremonial*) mazza
mace[2] [meɪs] N (*spice*) macis *m or f*
mace·bearer ['meɪs,bɛərə^r] N mazziere *m*
Mac·edo·nia [,mæsɪ'dəʊnɪə] N la Macedonia
Mac·edo·nian [,mæsɪ'dəʊnɪən] ADJ macedone
■ N (*person*) macedone *m/f*; (*language*) macedone *m*
mac·er·ate ['mæsə,reɪt] VT macerare
■ VI macerarsi
Mach [mæk] N (*Aer*: *also*: **Mach number**) (numero di) mach *m inv*
ma·chete [mə'ʃɛtɪ] N machete *m inv*
Machia·vel·lian [,mækɪə'vɛlɪən] ADJ machiavellico(-a)
machi·na·tions [,mækɪ'neɪʃənz] NPL macchinazioni *fpl*, intrighi *mpl*
◎ **ma·chine** [mə'ʃiːn] N (*gen*) macchina; (*Pol*) apparato, macchina; (*washing machine*) lavatrice *f*; **it's a complicated machine** è una macchina complicata; **I put clothes in the machine** ho messo i vestiti in lavatrice
■ VT (*Tech*) lavorare (a macchina); (*Sewing*) cucire a macchina
machine code N (*Comput*) codice *m* (di) macchina
machine-gun [mə'ʃiːn,gʌn] VT mitragliare
machine gun N mitragliatrice *f*
machine-gunner [mə'ʃiːn,gʌnə^r] N mitragliere *m*
machine language N (*Comput*) linguaggio *m* macchina *inv*
machine operator N = **machinist**
machine-readable [mə'ʃiːn,riːdəbl] ADJ (*Comput*) leggibile dalla macchina
ma·chin·ery [mə'ʃiːnərɪ] N (*machines*) macchine *fpl*, macchinari *mpl*; (*mechanism*) meccanismo; (*fig*) macchina, apparato; **a piece of machinery** un macchinario; **the machinery in the factory was outdated** i macchinari della fabbrica erano superati
machine shop N officina meccanica
machine-stitch [mə'ʃiːn,stɪtʃ] VT cucire a macchina
machine tool N macchina utensile
machine washable ADJ lavabile in lavatrice
ma·chin·ist [mə'ʃiːnɪst] N (*Tech*) macchinista *m/f*; (*Sewing*) operaio(-a) addetto(-a) alla macchina da cucire
ma·chis·mo [mæ'kɪzməʊ] N atteggiamenti *mpl* da macho, machismo
macho ['mætʃəʊ] ADJ (da) macho *inv*
macke·rel ['mækrəl] N, PL INV sgombro
mack·in·tosh ['mækɪn,tɒʃ] N impermeabile *m*
mac·ra·me [mə'krɑːmɪ] N macramè *m*
macro... ['mækrəʊ] PREF macro...
macro ['mækrəʊ] ADJ (*lens*) macro
■ N (*Comput*) macro *f inv*
macro·bi·ot·ic [,mækrəʊbaɪ'ɒtɪk] ADJ macrobiotico(-a)
macro·bi·ot·ics [,mækrəʊbaɪ'ɒtɪks] NSG macrobiotica
macro·cosm ['mækrə,kɒzəm] N macrocosmo
macro·eco·nom·ics [,mækrəʊ,iːkə'nɒmɪks] NSG macroeconomia
macro·mol·ecule [,mækrəʊ'mɒlɪ,kjuːl] N macromolecola
◎ **mad** [mæd] ADJ (*comp* **-der**, *superl* **-dest**) **1** (*deranged*: *person*) pazzo(-a), matto(-a); (*: bull*) furioso(-a); (*: dog*) rabbioso(-a); (*foolish*) sciocco(-a); (*rash*: *person, idea, plan*) folle; **to go mad** impazzire, diventare matto(-a); **to drive sb mad** far diventare matto(-a) qn, far impazzire qn; **as mad as a hatter** *or* **a March hare** matto(-a) da

legare; **are you mad?** sei matto?, sei impazzito?; **have you gone mad?** sei impazzito?; **you're mad!** tu sei pazzo!; **mad with grief** pazzo(-a) di dolore; **I'm in a mad rush** ho una fretta terribile; **like mad** (*adv phrase: fam*) come un*a* pazzo(-a); **to be mad (keen) about** *or* **on sth** (*fam*) andar pazzo(-a) *or* matto(-a) per qc; **he's mad about football** va matto per il calcio **2** (*fam: angry*): **mad (at** *or* **with sb)** furioso(-a) *or* furibondo(-a) (con qn); **he's hopping mad** (*fam*) è furibondo

mad·am ['mædəm] N **1** signora; **can I help you madam?** (la signora) desidera?; **Madam Chairman** Signora Presidentessa; **a little madam** una bambinetta prepotente **2** (*of brothel*) tenutaria

mad·cap ['mæd,kæp] ADJ (*fam*) senza senso, assurdo(-a)

mad cow disease N morbo della mucca pazza

mad·den ['mædn] VT (*infuriate*) far impazzire, esasperare

mad·den·ing ['mædnɪŋ] ADJ esasperante

mad·den·ing·ly ['mædnɪŋlɪ] ADV in modo esasperante; **he's maddeningly slow** è di una lentezza esasperante; **she's maddeningly well-organized** è così organizzata che dà sui nervi

made [meɪd] PT, PP *of* **make**

Ma·dei·ra [mə'dɪərə] N (*Geog*) Madera; (*wine*) madera *m*

made-to-measure [,meɪdtə'mɛʒə[r]] ADJ (*Brit*) (fatto(-a)) su misura

made-to-order [,meɪdtə'ɔ:də[r]] ADJ fatto(-a) su ordinazione

◎ **made-up** [,meɪd'ʌp] ADJ (*story*) inventato(-a); (*face, person, eyes*) truccato(-a)

mad·house ['mædhaʊs] N (*also fig*) manicomio

mad·ly ['mædlɪ] ADV (*behave*) come un(-a) pazzo(-a); (*love*) alla follia; **to be madly in love with sb** essere follemente innamorato(-a) di qn; **I'm not madly keen on the idea** l'idea non mi entusiasma

mad·man ['mædmən] N (*pl* **-men**) pazzo, folle *m*

mad·ness ['mædnɪs] N pazzia, follia; **it's absolute madness** è pura pazzia

Ma·drid [mə'drɪd] N Madrid *f*

mad·ri·gal ['mædrɪgəl] N madrigale *m*

mad·woman ['mæd,wʊmən] N (*pl* **-women**) pazza, folle *f*

mael·strom ['meɪlstrəʊm] N (*frm*) turbine *m*, vortice *m*

maes·tro ['maɪstrəʊ] N maestro

Ma·fia ['mæfɪə] N: **the Mafia** la mafia

mag [mæg] N ABBR (*Brit fam*: = **magazine**) rivista

◎ **maga·zine** [,mægə'zi:n] N **1** (*Press*) rivista **2** (*of firearm*) caricatore *m*; (*Mil: store*) deposito, magazzino

ma·gen·ta [mə'dʒɛntə] N, ADJ (color *m*) magenta *inv*

mag·got ['mægət] N verme *m*, baco

mag·goty ['mægətɪ] ADJ bacato(-a), con i vermi

◎ **mag·ic** ['mædʒɪk] ADJ (*spell*) magico(-a); (*beauty*) straordinario(-a); **a magic potion** una pozione magica; **there's no magic solution** non ci sono soluzioni miracolose; **to say the magic word** pronunciare la parola magica; **it was magic!** è stato fantastico!

■ N magia; (*conjuring tricks*) giochi *mpl* di prestigio; **like magic** come per magia *or* per incanto

▷ www.themagiccircle.co.uk

▷ www.magic.rufy.com/

magi·cal ['mædʒɪkəl] ADJ magico(-a)

magi·cal·ly ['mædʒɪkəlɪ] ADV magicamente

magic bullet N panacea

magic carpet N tappeto volante

ma·gi·cian [mə'dʒɪʃən] N mago(-a); (*conjuror*) illusionista *m/f*

magic lantern N lanterna magica

magic mushroom N fungo allucinogeno

magic realism, magical realism N realismo magico

magic wand N bacchetta magica

mag·is·te·rial [,mædʒɪ'stɪərɪəl] ADJ (*frm*) di magistrato; (: *authoritative*) autorevole

mag·is·trate ['mædʒɪ,streɪt] N magistrato

mag·ma ['mægmə] N magma *m*

mag·na·nim·ity [,mægnə'nɪmətɪ] N magnanimità *f inv*

mag·nani·mous [mæg'nænɪməs] ADJ magnanimo(-a)

mag·nani·mous·ly [mæg'nænɪməslɪ] ADV con magnanimità, magnanimamente

mag·nate ['mægneɪt] N magnate *m*

mag·ne·sia [mæg'ni:ʃə] N magnesia

mag·ne·sium [mæg'ni:zɪəm] N magnesio

mag·net ['mægnɪt] N calamita, magnete *m*

mag·net·ic [mæg'nɛtɪk] ADJ magnetico(-a)

mag·neti·cal·ly [mæg'nɛtɪkəlɪ] ADV magneticamente

magnetic disk N (*Comput*) disco magnetico

magnetic field N campo magnetico

magnetic tape N nastro magnetico

mag·net·ism ['mægnɪ,tɪzəm] N magnetismo

mag·net·ize ['mægnɪ,taɪz] VT magnetizzare

mag·ne·to [mæg'ni:təʊ] N (*Elec*) magnete *m*

mag·ni·fi·ca·tion [,mægnɪfɪ'keɪʃən] N ingrandimento

mag·nifi·cence [mæg'nɪfɪsəns] N magnificenza

mag·nifi·cent [mæg'nɪfɪsənt] ADJ magnifico(-a); **a magnificent view** una vista magnifica; **it is a magnificent achievement** è un grosso risultato

mag·nifi·cent·ly [mæg'nɪfɪsəntlɪ] ADV magnificamente

mag·ni·fy ['mægnɪ,faɪ] VT **1** (*gen*) ingrandire; (*sound*) amplificare **2** (*exaggerate*) esagerare

mag·ni·fy·ing glass ['mægnɪfaɪɪŋ,glɑ:s] N lente *f* d'ingrandimento

mag·ni·tude ['mægnɪtju:d] N (*gen*) vastità *f inv*, grandezza, ampiezza; (*importance*) importanza; (*Astron*) magnitudine *f*; **an operation of this magnitude** un'operazione di questa importanza

mag·no·lia [mæg'nəʊlɪə] N magnolia

mag·num ['mægnəm] N (*bottle*) magnum *m inv*

mag·pie ['mæg,paɪ] N gazza

ma·ha·ra·jah, ma·ha·ra·ja [,mɑ:hə'rɑ:dʒə] N maragià *m inv*

ma·hoga·ny [mə'hɒgənɪ] N mogano

■ ADJ di *or* in mogano

Mahomet [mə'hɒmɪt] N = **Mohammed**

maid [meɪd] N **1** (*servant*) domestica; (*in hotel*) cameriera **2** (*old, liter: young girl*) ragazza, fanciulla

maid·en ['meɪdn] N (*old, liter*) fanciulla, ragazza

■ ADJ (*flight, voyage*) inaugurale

maiden aunt N zia nubile; (*pej*) zia zitella

maiden·hair ['meɪdn,hɛə[r]] N (*also:* **maidenhair fern**) capelvenere *m*

maiden name N nome *m* da ragazza *or* da nubile

maiden speech N primo discorso (*in Parlamento*)

maid of honour N damigella d'onore

◎ **mail** [meɪl] N posta; **by mail** per posta

■ VT spedire (per posta), inviare (per posta); **he mailed me the contract** mi ha spedito il contratto per posta; **I forgot to mail the letter** ho dimenticato di imbucare la lettera

mail·bag ['meɪl,bæg] N sacco postale, sacco delle poste

mail·box ['meɪl,bɒks] N (*Am*) cassetta delle lettere;

Mm

(*Comput*) mailbox *m or f inv*; **the newspaper is still in the mailbox** il giornale è ancora nella cassetta delle lettere

mail car N (*Am Rail*) carrozza *or* vagone *m* postale

mail carrier N (*Am*) postino(-a), portalettere *m/f inv*

mail clerk N (*Am*) impiegato(-a) delle poste

mail·ing list ['meɪlɪŋ,lɪst] N elenco di indirizzi, indirizzario (*per l'invio di materiale pubblicitario*)

mail·man ['meɪl,mæn] N (*pl* **-men**) (*Am*) portalettere *m inv*, postino

mail-order ['meɪl,ɔːdəʳ] ADJ: **mail-order firm** *or* **house** ditta di vendita per corrispondenza

mail order ['meɪl,ɔːdəʳ] N (*selling*) vendita per corrispondenza; (*buying*) acquisto per corrispondenza

mail server N (*Comput*) mail server *m inv*, server *m inv* per la posta elettronica

mail·shot ['meɪlʃɒt] N campagna promozionale a mezzo posta, mailing *m inv*

mail train N treno postale

mail truck N (*Am*: *Aut*) furgone *m* postale

mail van N (*Brit*: *Aut*) furgone *m* postale; (: *Rail*) vagone *m* postale

maim [meɪm] VT storpiare, mutilare

◎ **main** [meɪn] ADJ (*gen*) principale; **the main body of an army** il grosso di un esercito; **the main points** i punti principali; **the main thing is to ...** l'essenziale è...; **the main thing to remember is ...** soprattutto non bisogna dimenticare che...

■ N **1** (*pipe*: *for water, gas*) conduttura *or* tubatura principale; (*Elec*) linea principale; **main (sewer)** collettore *m*; *see also* **mains** **2** **in the main** nel complesso, nell'insieme

main clause N (*Gram*: *sentence*) proposizione *f* principale

main course N (*Culin*) piatto principale, piatto forte, secondo

main deck N (*of ship*) ponte *m* principale; (: *Mil*) ponte di batteria

Maine [meɪn] N Maine *m*

▷ www.state.me.us/

main·frame ['meɪn,freɪm] N (*also*: **mainframe computer**) mainframe *m inv*

main·land ['meɪnlənd] N continente *m*, terraferma; **the Greek mainland** la Grecia continentale

main·line ['meɪn,laɪn] (*slang*) VT (*heroin*) bucarsi di

■ VI bucarsi

main-line ['meɪn,laɪn] ADJ (*Rail*) della linea principale

main line N (*Rail*) linea principale

◎ **main·ly** ['meɪnlɪ] ADV principalmente, soprattutto

main·mast ['meɪn,mɑːst] N albero maestro

main memory N (*Comput*) memoria principale

main road N strada principale

mains [meɪnz] NPL: **the mains** (*supply*: *gas, water, electricity*) le condutture; **water from the mains** acqua delle condutture; **mains operated** che funziona a elettricità; **it works by battery or from the mains** funziona a pile o a corrente; **to turn sth off at the mains** (*water*) chiudere le condutture; (*electricity, gas*) chiudere il contatore

main·sail ['meɪn,seɪl] N randa

main·spring ['meɪn,sprɪŋ] N (*of clock, watch*) molla principale; (*fig*) molla

main·stay ['meɪn,steɪ] N (*support*) sostegno, pilastro

main·stream ['meɪn,striːm] N (*fig*) corrente *f* principale

Main Street (*Am*) N via principale; (*people*) l'americano medio che vive in una piccola città

◎ **main·tain** [meɪn'teɪn] VT **1** (*keep up*: *gen*) mantenere; (: *attack*) continuare; (: *lead in race*) mantenere, conservare; **if the improvement is maintained** se il miglioramento continua; **teachers try hard to maintain standards** gli insegnanti ce la mettono tutta per mantenere un certo livello scolastico **2** (*support*: *family, army*) mantenere **3** (*keep in good condition*) mantenere in buono stato **4** (*claim*): **to maintain that ...** sostenere che...; **she had always maintained her innocence** aveva sempre sostenuto la propria innocenza

main·te·nance ['meɪntɪnəns] N (*gen*) mantenimento; (*of car, building*) manutenzione *f*; (*alimony*) alimenti *mpl*; **his father has to pay maintenance** suo padre deve pagare gli alimenti

maintenance contract N contratto di manutenzione

maintenance costs NPL spese *fpl* di manutenzione

maintenance grant N (*for student*) presalario; (*for worker*) indennità *f inv* di trasferta

maintenance order N (*Law*) obbligo degli alimenti

mai·son·ette [,meɪzə'nɛt] N (*Brit*) appartamentino su due piani

maize [meɪz] N granturco, mais *m*

maize flour N farina di granturco *or* di mais

Maj. ABBR (*Mil*) = **major**

ma·jes·tic [mə'dʒɛstɪk] ADJ maestoso(-a)

ma·jes·ti·cal·ly [mə'dʒɛstɪkəlɪ] ADV maestosamente

maj·es·ty ['mædʒɪstɪ] N maestà *f inv*; **His Majesty** Sua Maestà

◎ **ma·jor** ['meɪdʒəʳ] ADJ (*greater, also Math, Mus*) maggiore; (*in importance*) principale, importante; (*repairs*) grosso(-a), sostanziale; (*disaster, loss*) grave; (*interest, artist, success*) grande; **a major operation** (*Med*) un complesso intervento chirurgico; (*undertaking*) un'operazione considerevole; **major road** strada con diritto di precedenza; **drugs are a major problem** la droga è un grosso problema; **a major new film** un importante nuovo film

■ N **1** (*Mil*) maggiore *m* **2** (*Law*) maggiorenne *m/f* **3** (*Am Univ*) materia di specializzazione

■ VI (*Am Univ*): **to major (in)** specializzarsi (in)

Ma·jor·ca [mə'jɔːkə] N Maiorca

major general N (*Mil*) generale *m* di divisione

◎ **ma·jor·ity** [mə'dʒɒrɪtɪ] N **1** maggioranza; **the majority of people** la maggior parte della gente; **elected by a majority of two** eletto con una maggioranza di due voti; **to be in the majority** essere in maggioranza; **the vast majority of our products** la grande maggioranza dei nostri prodotti **2** (*Law*): **the age of majority** la maggiore età

■ ADJ (*verdict*) maggioritario(-a); (*government*) di maggioranza

majority holding N (*Fin*): **to have a majority holding** essere il/la maggiore azionista

majority leader N (*Am*: *Pol*) leader *m/f inv* della maggioranza

major league ADJ (*Sport*) di serie A; (*fig*: *movie star*) di successo, importante; **a major league criminal** una persona colpevole di gravi crimini

◎ **make** [meɪk] (*pt, pp* **made**) VT

1 (*gen*) fare; (*Comm*) produrre, fabbricare; (*building*) costruire; (*points, score*) fare, segnare; **God made the world** Dio creò il mondo; **she made the material into a dress** con la stoffa ha fatto un vestito; **made of silver** (fatto(-a)) d'argento; **made in Italy** fabbricato(-a) in Italia; (*on label*) made in Italy; **it's well**

made è ben fatto; **I'd like to make a phone call** vorrei fare una telefonata; **I make my bed every morning** mi faccio il letto ogni mattina; **to show what one is made of** far vedere di che tempra *or* che stoffa si è fatti; **they were made for each other** erano fatti l'uno per l'altra
2 (*cause to be or become*) fare; (*+ adj*) rendere; **to make sb happy/sad** rendere *or* far felice/triste qn; **to make sb angry** far arrabbiare qn; **to make sth difficult** render difficile qc; **to make sth into sth else** fare di qc qualcos'altro; **to make sb a judge** nominare qn giudice; **let's make it 6 o'clock** facciamo alle 6; **to make o.s. heard** farsi sentire; **make yourself comfortable** si accomodi; **you'll make yourself ill!** starai male!
3 (*cause to do*) fare; (*: stronger*) costringere; **to make sb do sth** far fare qc a qn; costringere *or* obbligare qn a fare qc; **my mother makes me do my homework** mia madre mi obbliga a fare i compiti; **to make sb wait** far aspettare qn; **to make o.s. do sth** sforzarsi a fare qc; **if you don't want to I can't make you** se non vuoi non posso costringerti; **this made him leave** questo lo ha fatto partire, questo ha fatto sì che partisse; **what made you say that?** perché hai detto questo?; **what makes you think that?** cosa te lo fa pensare?; **to make sth do** *or* **to make do with sth** accontentarsi di qc; (*because it's the only available*) arrangiarsi con qc; **you'll have to make do with a cheaper alternative** dovrai accontentarti di qualcosa che costi meno
4 (*earn*) guadagnare; **to make money** far soldi; **he makes a lot of money** guadagna un sacco di soldi; **to make a profit of £500** ricavare un profitto di 500 sterline; **to make a loss of £500** subire una perdita di 500 sterline; **he made a profit/loss** ci ha rimesso/ guadagnato; **he made £500 on the deal** l'affare gli ha fruttato 500 sterline
5 (*reach: destination*) arrivare a; (*catch: bus, train*) prendere; **we made Exeter by seven o'clock** siamo arrivati ad Exeter alle sette; **they made (it to) the finals** sono entrati in finale; **to make it** (*in time*) arrivare; (*achieve sth*) farcela; **can you make it for four o'clock?** ce la fai per le quattro?; **sorry, I can't make it to the party** mi dispiace, ma non riesco a venire alla festa; **to make it in life** riuscire nella vita; **to make good** (*succeed*) aver successo; **to make port** raggiungere il porto
6 (*cause to succeed*): **he's made for life** il suo avvenire è assicurato, è a posto per sempre; **this film made her** questo film l'ha resa celebre; **that's made my day!** questo ha trasformato la mia giornata!; **to make or break sb** essere il successo o la rovina di qn
7 (*equal, constitute*) fare; **2 and 2 make 4** 2 più 2 fa 4; **that makes 20** questo fa 20; **does that book make good reading?** è un libro interessante?; **these records make a set** questi dischi formano un set; **he made a good husband** è stato un buon marito
8 (*estimate*): **how far do you make it to the village?** quanto pensi che ci sia da qui al paese?; **what time do you make it? — I make it six o'clock** che ora fai? — io faccio le sei; **what do you make of this?** cosa pensi che voglia dire questo?; **what do you make of him?** che te ne pare di lui?; **I make the total cost £1200** penso che il costo complessivo sia di milleduecento sterline
■ VI
1 (*go*): **to make towards the door** dirigersi verso la porta; **to make after sb** inseguire qn
2 **to make as if to do sth** fare (come) per fare qc
■ N
1 (*action*) fabbricazione f; (*brand*) marca; **it's our own make** è di nostra produzione
2 **to be on the make** (*fam*) essere a caccia di successo
▸ **make away** VI + ADV = make off
▸ **make away with** VI + ADV + PREP (*kill*) far fuori, togliere di mezzo
▸ **make for** VI + PREP
1 (*place*) essere diretto(-a) a, avviarsi verso; (*subj: ship*) far rotta verso
2 (*fig: result in*) produrre; (*: contribute to*) contribuire a
▸ **make off** VI + ADV svignarsela; **to make off with sth** svignarsela con qc
▸ **make out** VT + ADV
1 (*write out: cheque, receipt, list*) fare; (*: document*) redigere; (*: form*) riempire, compilare; **to make a cheque out to sb** intestare un assegno a qn; **to make out a case for sth** presentare delle valide ragioni in favore di qc
2 (*see, discern*) riuscire a vedere, distinguere; (*decipher*) decifrare; (*understand*) (riuscire a) capire; **I can't make out the address on the label** non riesco a decifrare l'indirizzo sull'etichetta; **how do you make that out?** che cosa te lo fa pensare?; **I can't make her out at all** non riesco proprio a capirla
3 (*claim, imply*): **to make out (that ...)** voler far credere (che...), darla ad intendere (che...); **to make sb out to be stupid** far passare qn per stupido; **they're making out it was my fault** vogliono far credere che sia colpa mia
■ VI + ADV (*fam: get on*) cavarsela
▸ **make out with** VI + ADV + PREP (*fam*): **to make out with sb** farsi qn; **did you make out with her, then?** sei poi riuscito a fartela?
▸ **make over** VT + ADV (*assign*): **to make over (to)** passare (a), trasferire (a)
▸ **make up** VT + ADV
1 (*invent: story*) inventare; **he made up the whole story** ha inventato tutta la storia
2 (*put together, prepare: list, parcel, bed*) fare; (*food, medicine*) preparare; **she made the books up into a parcel** ha impacchettato i libri
3 (*settle: dispute*) mettere fine a; **to make it up with sb** far la pace con qn
4 (*complete: total, quantity*) completare; **I need £5 to make up the sum we require** mi occorrono 5 sterline per raggiungere la somma stabilita
5 (*compensate for: loss, deficit, lost time*) recuperare, compensare, colmare; **to make it up to sb (for sth)** compensare qn (per qc); **I'll make it up to you somehow, I promise** ti ricompenserò in qualche modo, prometto
6 (*constitute*) comporre; **to be made up of** essere composto(-a) di *or* formato(-a) da; **women make up thirteen per cent of the police force** il tredici percento del corpo di polizia è formato da donne
7 (*apply cosmetics to*) truccare
■ VI + ADV
1 (*after quarrelling*) fare la pace, riconciliarsi; **they had a quarrel, but soon made up** hanno litigato, ma hanno subito fatto la pace
2 (*apply cosmetics*) truccarsi; **she spends hours making herself up** passa delle ore a truccarsi
3 (*catch up*): **to make up on sb** riprendere qn
▸ **make up for** VI + ADV + PREP (*lost time*) recuperare; (*trouble caused*) farsi perdonare; (*mistake*) rimediare a;

Mm

(*loss, injury*) compensare; **money can't make up for the stress I've suffered** il denaro non può compensare lo stress che ho subito
▶ **make up to** VI + ADV + PREP (*fam: curry favour with*) cercare di entrare nelle simpatie di *or* di accattivarsi il favore di, lisciare

make-believe ['meɪkbɪˌliːv] N: **the land of make-believe** il mondo delle favole; **it's just make-believe** (*activity*) è solo per finta; (*story*) sono frottole, è tutta un'invenzione

◎ **mak·er** ['meɪkəʳ] N (*manufacturer*) fabbricante *m*; (*creator*) creatore(-trice); (*originator*) autore(-trice); (*Rel*): **our Maker** il Creatore; **Italy's biggest car maker** il più grosso fabbricante di automobili in Italia

make·shift ['meɪkˌʃɪft] ADJ di fortuna, improvvisato(-a)

◎ **make-up** ['meɪkˌʌp] N **1** (*cosmetics*) trucco, cosmetici *mpl*; **to put on one's make-up** truccarsi; **she put on her make-up** si è truccata **2** (*nature: of object, group*) composizione *f*; (*: of football team*) formazione *f*; (*: of person*) carattere *m*

make-up artist N truccatore(-trice)

make-up bag N borsa del trucco

make-up remover N struccante *m*

make·weight ['meɪkˌweɪt] N (*thing*) *cosa aggiunta per completare un insieme*; (*person*): **I'm only in the team as a sort of makeweight** sono nella squadra solo per far numero

mak·ing ['meɪkɪŋ] N **1** (*Comm, gen*) fabbricazione *f*; (*of dress, food*) confezione *f*; **it's still in the making** non è ancora finito; **it's history in the making** è un momento storico; **it was the making of him** ha fatto di lui un uomo **2** **he has the makings of an actor** (*qualities, potential*) ha la stoffa dell'attore; **the makings of a good film** quello che ci vuole per fare un buon film

mala·chite ['mæləˌkaɪt] N malachite *f*

mal·ad·just·ed [ˌmælə'dʒʌstɪd] ADJ (*Psych*) disadattato(-a)

mala·droit [ˌmælə'drɔɪt] ADJ maldestro(-a)

mala·dy ['mælədɪ] N (*old*) male *m*, malattia

ma·laise [mæ'leɪz] N malessere *m*

ma·laria [mə'lɛərɪə] N malaria

ma·lar·ial [mə'lɛərɪəl] ADJ malarico(-a)

Ma·la·wi [mə'lɑːwɪ] N il Malawi

Ma·lay [mə'leɪ] ADJ malese
■ N (*person*) malese *m/f*; (*language*) malese *m*

Ma·la·ya [mə'leɪə] N la Malesia

Ma·lay·an [mə'leɪən] ADJ, N = **Malay**

Ma·lay·sia [mə'leɪzɪə] N la Malaysia

Ma·lay·sian [mə'leɪzɪən] ADJ, N malaysiano(-a)

mal·con·tent ['mælkənˌtɛnt] N (*frm*) malcontento(-a), insoddisfatto(-a)

Mal·dive Islands ['mɔːldaɪvˌaɪləndz], **Mal·dives** ['mɔːldaɪvz] NPL: **the Maldive Islands, the Maldives** le (isole *fpl*) Maldive

◎ **male** [meɪl] ADJ (*gen, sex*) maschile; (*animal, child*) maschio *inv*; **most football players are male** quasi tutti i giocatori di calcio sono maschi; **sex: Male** sesso: Maschile; **male and female students** studenti e studentesse
■ N (*Bio, Elec*) maschio

male chauvinism N maschilismo

male chauvinist N maschilista *m*

male chauvinist pig N (*fam*) sporco maschilista *m*

mal·efac·tor ['mælɪˌfæktəʳ] N (*frm*) malfattore *m*

male nurse N infermiere *m*

ma·levo·lence [mə'lɛvələns] N malevolenza, malanimo

ma·levo·lent [mə'lɛvələnt] ADJ malevolo(-a)

ma·levo·lent·ly [mə'lɛvələntlɪ] ADV con malevolenza

mal·for·ma·tion [ˌmælfɔː'meɪʃən] N malformazione *f*

mal·func·tion [ˌmæl'fʌŋkʃən] N cattivo funzionamento

mal·ice ['mælɪs] N cattiveria, malevolenza; **I bear him no malice** non gli serbo nessun rancore

mal·ice afore·thought [ˌmælɪsə'fɔːˌθɔːt] N (*Law*) premeditazione *f*

ma·li·cious [mə'lɪʃəs] ADJ cattivo(-a), malevolo(-a); (*Law*) doloso(-a); **malicious gossip** malignità *fpl*

ma·li·cious·ly [mə'lɪʃəslɪ] ADV con cattiveria, malignamente; (*Law*) dolosamente

ma·li·cious·ness [mə'lɪʃəsnɪs] N cattiveria, malignità *f inv*

ma·lign [mə'laɪn] ADJ malefico(-a), nocivo(-a)
■ VT diffamare, calunniare, malignare su

ma·lig·nan·cy [mə'lɪgnənsɪ] N (*of person, remark*) malignità *f inv*; (*of tumour*) carattere *m* maligno

ma·lig·nant [mə'lɪgnənt] ADJ maligno(-a), malevolo(-a); (*Med: tumour*) maligno(-a)

ma·lin·ger [mə'lɪŋgəʳ] VI fingersi malato(-a) (*per non lavorare*)

ma·lin·ger·er [mə'lɪŋgərəʳ] N uno(-a) che si finge malato(-a) (*per non lavorare*), scansafatiche *m/f inv*

mall [mɔːl] N (*Am: also:* **shopping mall**) centro commerciale

mal·lard ['mæləd] N (*duck*) germano reale

mal·le·able ['mælɪəbl] ADJ malleabile

mal·let ['mælɪt] N (*tool*) mazzuolo; (*in croquet*) maglio; (*in polo*) mazza

mal·low ['mæləʊ] N (*plant*) malva

mal·nour·ished [mæl'nʌrɪʃt] ADJ (*frm*) denutrito(-a)

mal·nu·tri·tion [ˌmælnjʊ'trɪʃən] N denutrizione *f*, malnutrizione *f*

mal·odor·ous [mæl'əʊdərəs] ADJ (*liter*) maleodorante

mal·prac·tice [ˌmæl'præktɪs] N (*by doctor*) negligenza (colposa); (*by minister, lawyer*) prevaricazione *f*

malt [mɔːlt] N malto; (*also:* **malt whisky**) whisky di malto
■ ADJ (*vinegar, whisky*) di malto

Mal·ta ['mɔːltə] N Malta

malt bread N pane *m* al malto

malt·ed milk ['mɔːltɪdˌmɪlk] ADJ latte *m* al malto

Mal·tese [ˌmɔːl'tiːz] ADJ maltese
■ N INV (*person*) maltese *m/f*; (*language*) maltese *m*

Maltese cross N croce di Malta

mal·treat [ˌmæl'triːt] VT maltrattare

mal·treat·ment [ˌmæl'triːtmənt] N maltrattamento

mama, mam·ma [mə'mɑː] N (*fam*) mamma

mam·mal ['mæməl] N mammifero

mam·ma·lian [mæ'meɪlɪən] ADJ (*Bio: species, behaviour*) dei mammiferi

mam·mon ['mæmən] N (*pej: money*) mammona *m or f*

mam·moth ['mæməθ] N mammut *m inv*
■ ADJ colossale, mostruoso(-a), enorme, gigantesco(-a); **a mammoth task** un lavoro mostruoso

◎ **man** [mæn] N (*pl* **men**) **1** (*gen, Mil, Sport*) uomo; (*in office, shop*) impiegato; (*Chess*) pezzo; (*Draughts*) pedina; **an old man** un vecchio; **a blind man** un cieco; **man and wife** marito e moglie; **her man is in the army** il suo uomo è nell'esercito; **the man in the street** l'uomo della strada; **he was man enough to apologize** ha avuto il coraggio di scusarsi; **he's a man about town** è un uomo di mondo; **a man of the world**

un uomo di mondo *or* di grande esperienza; **men say that ...** si dice che...; **no man** nessuno; **any man** chiunque; **that man Jones** quel Jones; **as one man** come un sol uomo; **they're communists to a man** sono tutti comunisti, dal primo all'ultimo; **he's not the man for the job** non è l'uomo adatto per questo lavoro; **I'm not a drinking man** non sono un bevitore; **he's a family man** è un uomo tutto casa e famiglia; **he's a Glasgow man** è di Glasgow; **the ice-cream man** il gelataio; **come on, man!** dai, forza!; **good man!** bravo! **2** (*humanity*): **Man** l'uomo, l'umanità *f inv*
■ VT (*ship, fortress*) fornire di uomini; (*fleet*) armare; **the ship is manned by Americans** l'equipaggio della nave è americano; **the telephone is manned all day** c'è sempre una persona che risponde al telefono; **man the guns!** uomini ai cannoni!

mana·cle ['mænəkl] VT ammanettare, mettere le manette a

mana·cles ['mænəklz] NPL manette *fpl*

◎ **man·age** ['mænɪdʒ] VT **1** (*direct: company, organization, hotel*) dirigere; (*: shop, restaurant*) gestire; (*: household, property, affairs*) amministrare; (*: football team, pop star*) essere il manager di; **the election was managed** (*pej*) le elezioni erano truccate; **she manages a big store** dirige un grande negozio **2** (*handle, control: tool*) maneggiare; (*: ship, vehicle*) manovrare; (*: person, child*) saper prendere *or* trattare; **I can manage him** so come trattarlo *or* prenderlo **3 to manage to do sth** riuscire a fare qc; **luckily I managed to pass the exam** fortunatamente sono riuscito a passare l'esame; **he managed not to get his feet wet** è riuscito a non bagnarsi i piedi; **£5 is the most I can manage** posso metterci 5 sterline ma non di più; **I shall manage it** ce la farò; **can you manage the cases?** ce la fai a portare le valigie?; **can you manage 8 o'clock?** alle 8 ti va bene?; **can you manage a bit more?** posso mettertene ancora un po'?
■ VI farcela; **can you manage?** ce la fai?; **how do you manage?** come riesci a farcela?; **I have to manage on £20** mi devo arrangiare con 20 sterline; **to manage without sb/sth** fare a meno di qn/qc; **we haven't got much money, but we manage** non abbiamo molto denaro, ma ci arrangiamo

man·age·able ['mænɪdʒəbl] ADJ (*car, boat, size, proportions*) maneggevole; (*person*) trattabile, arrendevole; (*task*) fattibile; **it was a manageable task** era fattibile; **manageable hair** capelli *mpl* docili al pettine

◎ **man·age·ment** ['mænɪdʒmənt] N **1** (*act: see* VT) direzione *f*; gestione *f*; amministrazione *f* **2** (*persons: of business, firm*) dirigenti *mpl*, direzione *f*; (*: of hotel, shop, theatre*) direzione *f*; **"under new management"** "nuova gestione"; **the restaurant is under new management** il ristorante ha una nuova gestione; **management and workers** dirigenti e lavoratori

management accounting N contabilità *f inv* di gestione

management buyout N *acquisto di una società da parte dei suoi dirigenti*

management consultant N consulente *m/f* aziendale

management potential N potenzialità *fpl* manageriali

◎ **man·ag·er** ['mænɪdʒə^r] N (*gen*) direttore *m*; (*of shop, restaurant*) gestore *m*, gerente *m*; (*of football team, pop star, artiste*) manager *m inv*; (*of estate*) amministratore *m*; **sales manager** direttore *m* delle vendite; **I complained to the manager** mi sono lamentato con il direttore; **the England manager** il commissario tecnico dell'Inghilterra

man·ag·er·ess [,mænɪdʒə'rɛs] N (*gen*) direttrice *f*; (*of shop, restaurant*) gerente *f*

mana·gerial [,mænə'dʒɪərɪəl] ADJ (*class*) dirigente, manageriale, dirigenziale; (*ability, post*) direttivo(-a), manageriale, dirigenziale

man·ag·ing di·rec·tor ['mænɪdʒɪŋ,dɪ'rɛktə^r] N amministratore *m* delegato

mana·tee [,mænə'ti:] N (*mammal*) lamantino

Man·cu·nian [mæŋ'kju:nɪən] ADJ di Manchester
■ N (*resident*) abitante *m/f* di Manchester; (*native*) originario(-a) di Manchester

man·da·rin ['mændərɪn] N **1** (*person*) mandarino **2** (*also:* **mandarin orange**) mandarino

man·date ['mændeɪt] N delega, mandato

man·da·tory ['mændətərɪ] ADJ obbligatorio(-a)

man·do·lin, man·do·line ['mændəlɪn] N mandolino

man·drill ['mændrɪl] N (*monkey*) mandrillo

mane [meɪn] N criniera

man-eater ['mæn,i:tə^r] N (*animal*) mangiatore *m* di uomini; (*person*) cannibale *m/f*, antropofago(-a)

man-eating ['mæn,i:tɪŋ] ADJ (*animal*) che si nutre di carne umana; (*tribe*) antropofago(-a)

ma·neu·ver *etc* [mə'nu:və^r] (*Am*) = **manoeuvre** *etc*

man·ful ['mænfʊl] ADJ coraggioso(-a), valoroso(-a)

man·ful·ly ['mænfəlɪ] ADV coraggiosamente, valorosamente

man·ga·nese [,mæŋgə'ni:z] N manganese *m*

man·gel·wur·zel ['mæŋgəl,wɜ:zəl], **man·gel** ['mæŋgəl] N bietola da foraggio

man·ger ['meɪndʒə^r] N mangiatoia

mange·tout ['mɑ̃ʒ'tu:] N pisello dolce, taccola

Mm

man·gle[1] ['mæŋgl] VT (*mutilate: body*) straziare, maciullare; (*: object*) stritolare

man·gle[2] ['mæŋgl] N strizzatoio

man·go ['mæŋgəʊ] N mango

mango chutney N *salsa piccante a base di mango*

man·grove ['mæŋ,grəʊv] N mangrovia

man·gy ['meɪndʒɪ] ADJ rognoso(-a)

man·handle ['mæn,hændl] VT (*treat roughly*) malmenare; (*move by hand: goods*) spostare a mano

man·hole ['mæn,həʊl] N botola stradale

manhole cover N tombino, chiusino

man·hood ['mænhʊd] N **1** (*state*) età *f inv* virile **2** (*manliness*) virilità *f inv* **3** (*men*) uomini *mpl*

man-hour ['mæn,aʊə^r] N (*Industry*) ora di lavoro

man·hunt ['mæn,hʌnt] N caccia all'uomo

ma·nia ['meɪnɪə] N mania; **to have a mania for (doing) sth** avere la mania di (fare) qc

ma·ni·ac ['meɪnɪæk] N maniaco(-a); **sports maniac** (*fig fam*) maniaco(-a) dello sport; **a dangerous maniac** un pericoloso maniaco; **he drives like a maniac!** guida come un pazzo!

ma·nia·cal [mə'naɪəkəl] ADJ (*behaviour*) da folle

man·ic ['mænɪk] ADJ (*Psych*) maniaco(-a), maniacale

manic depression N (*Psych*) psicosi *f inv* maniaco-depressiva

manic-depressive [,mænɪkdɪ'prɛsɪv] (*Psych*) ADJ maniaco-depressivo(-a)
■ N persona affetta da psicosi maniaco-depressiva

mani·cure ['mænɪ,kjʊə^r] N manicure *f inv*
■ VT: **to manicure one's hands (***or* **one's nails)** fare manicure; **well-manicured hands** mani ben curate

manicure set N trousse *f inv* della manicure

mani·cur·ist ['mænɪ,kjʊərɪst] N manicure *f inv*

mani·fest ['mænɪ,fɛst] ADJ evidente, manifesto(-a), palese
■ VT manifestare
■ N (*Aer, Naut*) manifesto
mani·fes·ta·tion [,mænɪfɛs'teɪʃən] N manifestazione *f*
mani·fest·ly ['mænɪ,fɛstlɪ] ADV manifestamente, palesemente
mani·fes·to [,mænɪ'fɛstəʊ] N (*pl* **manifestoes**) manifesto
mani·fold ['mænɪ,fəʊld] ADJ molteplice
■ N (*Aut*): **exhaust manifold** collettore *m* di scarico; **intake manifold** collettore *m* di aspirazione
Ma·nila [mə'nɪlə] N Manila
ma·nila, ma·nil·la [mə'nɪlə] ADJ (*paper, envelope*) manilla *inv*
ma·nipu·late [mə'nɪpjʊleɪt] VT (*tool*) maneggiare; (*controls*) azionare; (*Med, fig: person*) manipolare; (*situation, system*) manovrare; **she used her position to manipulate people** usava la sua posizione per manipolare le persone; **he tried to manipulate the situation** ha cercato di pilotare la situazione a proprio vantaggio
ma·nipu·la·tion [mə,nɪpjʊ'leɪʃən] N (*see vb*) maneggiare *m*; capacità *f inv* di azionare; manipolazione *f*; capacità *f inv* di manovrare
ma·nipu·la·tive [mə'nɪpjʊ,lətɪv] ADJ: **to be manipulative** (*person*) cercare di manipolare gli altri; **manipulative behaviour** comportamento teso alla manipolazione altrui
Mani·to·ba [,mænɪ'təʊbə] N Manitoba
▷ www.gov.mb.ca
▷ www.travelmanitoba.com
man·kind [mæn'kaɪnd] N l'umanità *f inv*, il genere *m* umano
man·like ['mæn,laɪk] ADJ (*appearance, qualities*) umano(-a); (*pej: woman*) mascolino(-a)
man·li·ness ['mænlɪnɪs] N virilità *f inv*
man·ly ['mænlɪ] ADJ (*comp* **-ier**, *superl* **-iest**) virile, coraggioso(-a)
man-made ['mæn,meɪd] ADJ artificiale, sintetico(-a)
man·na ['mænə] N manna
manned ['mænd] ADJ pilotato(-a) da un equipaggio (a bordo)
man·ne·quin ['mænɪkɪn] N (*dummy*) manichino; (*fashion model*) indossatrice *f*
◎ **man·ner** ['mænə^r] N **1** (*mode*) modo, maniera; **in this manner** in questo modo, così ; **she was behaving in an odd manner** si comportava in modo strano; **in such a manner that** in modo tale che + *indic* (*actual result*) *or* + *sub* (*intended result*); **he spoke in such a manner as to offend them** ha parlato in modo tale da offenderli *or* che li ha offesi; **after** *or* **in the manner of X** alla maniera di X, nello stile di X; **in a manner of speaking** per così dire; **(as) to the manner born** come se ce l'avesse nel sangue **2** (*behaviour*) comportamento; (*attitude*) atteggiamento; **I don't like his manner** ha un modo di fare che non mi piace; **a confident manner** un modo di fare molto sicuro **3** **(good) manners** buona educazione *f*, buone maniere *fpl*; **bad manners** maleducazione *f*; **it's bad manners to talk with your mouth full** è da maleducati parlare con la bocca piena; **she has no manners** non conosce le buone maniere; **to teach sb manners** insegnare l'educazione a qn; **a novel of manners** un romanzo di costume **4** (*class, type*): **all manner of** ogni sorta di
man·nered ['mænəd] ADJ affettato(-a)
man·ner·ism ['mænə,rɪzəm] N **1** (*habit*) vezzo, tic *m inv* **2** (*Art*) manierismo
man·ner·ly ['mænəlɪ] ADJ educato(-a), civile
man·nish ['mænɪʃ] ADJ (*pej*) mascolino(-a)
ma·noeu·vrabil·ity [mə,nu:vrə'bɪlɪtɪ] N manovrabilità *f inv*, maneggevolezza
ma·noeu·vrable, (*Am*) **ma·neu·ver·able** [mə'nu:vrəbl] ADJ (*gen*) facile da manovrare; (*car*) maneggevole; (*ship, plane*) manovriero(-a)
ma·noeu·vre, (*Am*) **ma·neu·ver** [mə'nu:və^r] N manovra; **the soldiers were out on manoeuvres** i soldati stavano facendo le manovre *or* le esercitazioni
■ VT (*also Mil*) manovrare; **I couldn't manoeuvre the settee through the door** non sono riuscito a far passare il divano attraverso la porta; **they manoeuvred the statue into position** hanno messo la statua in posizione; **he manoeuvred himself into a job** è riuscito a ottenere un posto con abili manovre; **to manoeuvre sb into doing sth** costringere abilmente qn a fare qc
■ VI (*Mil, fig*) manovrare; (*Aut*) far manovra
man·oeu·vring, man·euve·ring (*Am*) [mə'nu:vərɪŋ] N manovre *fpl*
ma·nom·eter [mə'nɒmɪtə^r] N manometro
man·or ['mænə^r] N (*also:* **manor house**) maniero
man·power ['mæn,paʊə^r] N (*gen, Industry*) manodopera; (*Mil*) effettivi *mpl*
man·sard ['mænsɑ:d] N **1** (*also:* **mansard roof**) tetto mansardato **2** (*attic*) mansarda
manse [mæns] N canonica
man·servant ['mæn,sɜ:vənt] N (*pl* **manservants**) servitore *m*, domestico
man·sion ['mænʃən] N (*in town*) palazzo (signorile); (*in country*) villa, maniero

DID YOU KNOW ...?
mansion is not translated by the Italian word *mansione*

man-sized ['mæn,saɪzd] ADJ (*fig*) grande
man·slaughter ['mæn,slɔ:tə^r] N omicidio colposo
man·ta ['mæntə] N (*also:* **manta ray**) manta
mantel·piece ['mæntl,pi:s] N mensola del caminetto
man·til·la [mæn'tɪlə] N mantiglia
man·tle ['mæntl] N (*old: garment*) mantello, manto; (*also:* **gas mantle**) reticella; (*Geol*) mantello; **a mantle of snow** un manto di neve
man-to-man [,mæntə'mæn] ADJ, ADV da uomo a uomo
man·trap ['mæn,træp] N trappola per l'uomo
Man·tua ['mæntjʊə] N Mantova
manu·al ['mænjʊəl] ADJ manuale
■ N (*book*) manuale *m*
manu·al·ly ['mænjʊəlɪ] ADV manualmente
manual worker N manovale *m*; **manual workers** la manovalanza
manu·fac·tur·able [,mænjʊ'fæktʃərəbl] ADJ fabbricabile
◎ **manu·fac·ture** [,mænjʊ'fæktʃə^r] N (*act*) fabbricazione *f*, manifattura; (*of clothes*) confezione *f*; (*product*) manufatto
■ VT (*gen*) fabbricare; (*clothes*) confezionare; (*fig: excuse, lie*) architettare, inventare
manu·fac·tured goods [,mænjʊ'fæktʃəd'gʊdz] NPL manufatti *mpl*
◎ **manu·fac·tur·er** [,mænjʊ'fæktʃərə^r] N fabbricante *m*

manu·fac·tur·ing in·dus·tries [ˌmænjʊˈfæktʃərɪŋˈɪndəstrɪz] NPL industrie *fpl* manifatturiere

ma·nure [məˈnjʊəʳ] N concime *m*; (*organic*) letame *m*
■ VT concimare

manu·script [ˈmænjʊˌskrɪpt] N manoscritto

Manx [mæŋks] ADJ dell'isola di Man

◎ **many** [ˈmɛnɪ] ADJ, PRON molti(-e), tanti(-e); **many a ...** più di un(a)..., molti(-e)...; **a great many** un gran numero (di), moltissimi(-e); **so many** tanti; **he told so many lies** ha detto tante bugie; **so many books** (così) tanti libri; **many people** molta *or* tanta gente, molte persone; **he hasn't got many friends** non ha molti amici; **as many as** quanti; **take as many as you like** prendine quanti ne vuoi; **he has as many as I have** ne ha tanti quanti ne ho io; **there were as many as 100 at the meeting** alla riunione c'erano ben 100 persone; **as many again** altrettanti; **twice as many** due volte tanto; **many a man** più d'uno, molti; **many a time** più volte; **a good** *or* **great many houses** moltissime case, un gran numero di case; **how many?** quanti(-e)?; **how many do you want?** quanti ne vuoi?; **how many people?** quanta gente?, quante persone?; **too many** troppi(-e); **too many difficulties** troppe difficoltà; **sixteen people? that's too many** sedici persone? sono troppe; **there are too many of you** siete (in) troppi; **there's one too many** ce n'è uno in più; **he's had one too many** ha bevuto un bicchiere di troppo; **however many there may be** per quanti ce ne siano; **many of them came** molti di loro sono venuti

many-coloured [ˌmɛnɪˈkʌləd] ADJ multicolore

many-sided [ˌmɛnɪˈsaɪdɪd] ADJ (*object*) che ha molti lati; (*fig: problem, question*) complesso(-a), che ha molte sfaccettature

Mao·ri [ˈmaʊrɪ] ADJ, N maori (*m/f*) *inv*
▷ www.maori.org.nz/

◎ **map** [mæp] N (*gen*) carta (geografica); (*of town*) pianta; **maps and guide books** cartine *fpl* e guide *fpl*; **a map of the city** una pianta della città; **treasure map** mappa del tesoro; **this will put Eastdean on the map** (*fig*) questo renderà famoso *or* farà conoscere Eastdean; **off the map** (*fig*) in capo al mondo
■ VT tracciare una carta (*or* una pianta *or* una mappa) di
▸ **map out** VT + ADV tracciare una carta (*or* una pianta *or* una mappa) di; (*fig: career, holiday, essay*) pianificare
▷ www.cartography.org.uk/
▷ www.ordnancesurvey.co.uk/
▷ www.usgs.gov/

ma·ple [ˈmeɪpl] N acero; **field maple** acero campestre

map·ping [ˈmæpɪŋ] N (*Math*) funzione *f*

Mar. ABBR (= March) mar. (= *marzo*)

mar [mɑːʳ] VT sciupare, guastare

mara·bou [ˈmærəˌbuː] N (*bird*) marabù *m inv*

ma·ras·ca [məˈræskə] N (*tree*) marasco

mara·schi·no [ˌmærəˈskiːnəʊ] N (*liqueur*) maraschino

maraschino cherry N marasca

mara·thon [ˈmærəθən] N maratona
■ ADJ (*debate*) lunghissimo; **a marathon session** una seduta fiume

marathon runner N maratoneta *m/f*

ma·raud [məˈrɔːd] VI darsi al saccheggio

ma·raud·er [məˈrɔːdəʳ] N predone *m*, saccheggiatore(-trice), predatore(-trice)

ma·raud·ing [məˈrɔːdɪŋ] ADJ che si dà al saccheggio

mar·ble [ˈmɑːbl] N **1** (*material, sculpture*) marmo; **a marble statue** una statua di marmo **2** (*toy*) bilia, biglia; **to play marbles** giocare a bilie
■ ADJ di marmo

March [mɑːtʃ] N marzo; **in March** in marzo; *for usage see* **July**

◎ **march** [mɑːtʃ] N (*gen*) marcia; (*demonstration*) marcia, dimostrazione *f*; **on the march** in marcia; **a day's march** una giornata di marcia
■ VI (*Mil*) marciare; **quick march!** avanti, marsc!; **the soldiers marched 50 miles** i soldati hanno marciato per cinquanta miglia; **the demonstrators were marching along the main street** i dimostranti stavano sfilando sulla via principale; **to march into a room** entrare a passo deciso in una stanza; **to march past** sfilare; **to march past sb** sfilare davanti a qn; **to march up to sb** andare risolutamente da qn
■ VT (*Mil*) far marciare; **to march sb off to prison/to bed** spedire qn in prigione/a letto

march·er [ˈmɑːtʃəʳ] N dimostrante *m/f*

marching band [ˈmɑːtʃɪŋ-] N banda

march·ing or·ders [ˈmɑːtʃɪŋ ˈɔːdəz] NPL (*Mil*) ordini *mpl* di partenza; **to give sb his marching orders** (*fig*) dare il benservito a qn

mar·chion·ess [ˈmɑːʃənɪs] N marchesa

march past N (*Mil*) sfilata

Mardi Gras [ˌmɑːdɪˈgrɑː] N (*Am: Rel*) martedì *m inv* grasso

mare [mɛəʳ] N giumenta, cavalla

> DID YOU KNOW ...?
> **mare** is not translated by the Italian word *mare*

marg, **marge** [mɑːdʒ] N ABBR (*Brit fam*) = **margarine**

mar·ga·rine [ˌmɑːdʒəˈriːn] N margarina

◎ **mar·gin** [ˈmɑːdʒɪn] N (*gen, fig*) margine *m*; **to win by a wide/narrow margin** vincere con largo margine/di stretta misura

mar·gin·al [ˈmɑːdʒɪnl] ADJ marginale
■ N (*Brit Pol: also:* **marginal seat**) *collegio elettorale con una stretta maggioranza a favore del partito al governo*

mar·gin·al·ly [ˈmɑːdʒɪnəlɪ] ADV (*bigger, better*) lievemente, di poco; (*different*) un po'

mar·gue·rite [ˌmɑːgəˈriːt] N margherita

mari·gold [ˈmærɪˌgəʊld] N calendola

ma·ri·jua·na, **ma·ri·hua·na** [ˌmærɪˈhwɑːnə] N marijuana

ma·ri·na [məˈriːnə] N porticciolo, marina

mari·nade [ˌmærɪˈneɪd] N marinata
■ VT = **marinate**

mari·nate, **mari·nade** [ˈmærɪˌneɪt] VT marinare

◎ **ma·rine** [məˈriːn] ADJ (*animal, plant*) marino(-a); (*products*) del mare; (*vegetation, forces*) marittimo(-a); (*engineering*) navale
■ N **1 merchant** *or* **mercantile marine** marina mercantile **2** (*Mil*) fante *m* di marina; (*Am*) marine *m inv*; **tell that to the marines!** (*fam*) va' a raccontarla a un altro!

marine insurance N assicurazione *f* marittima

mari·ner [ˈmærɪnəʳ] N marinaio

mari·on·ette [ˌmærɪəˈnɛt] N marionetta

mari·tal [ˈmærɪtl] ADJ coniugale, maritale

marital status N stato civile

mari·time [ˈmærɪˌtaɪm] ADJ (*climate, nation, museum*) marittimo(-a); (*plant, creature*) marino(-a)

maritime law N diritto marittimo

mar·jo·ram [ˈmɑːdʒərəm] N maggiorana

◎ **mark¹** [mɑːk] N
1 (*gen*) segno; (*stain*) macchia; (*of shoes, fingers: in mud*)

Mm

impronta; (*of skid*) traccia; **to leave a mark on sth** lasciare un segno su qc; **to leave one's mark on sth** (*fig*) lasciare un segno in qc; **there wasn't a mark on him** *or* **on his body** non aveva nemmeno un graffio; **there were red marks all over his back** aveva segni rossi su tutta la schiena; **you've got a mark on your shirt** hai una macchia sulla camicia; **it's the mark of a gentleman** è da gentiluomo; **it bears the mark of genius** ha l'impronta del genio; **to make one's mark (as)** (*fig*) farsi un nome (come); **as a mark of my gratitude** come segno della mia gratitudine; **punctuation marks** segni di punteggiatura
2 (*instead of signature*) croce *f*; **to make one's mark** fare una croce
3 (*Brit Scol*) voto; **good/bad mark** buon *or* bel/brutto voto; **I get good marks for French** prendo bei voti in francese; **he failed by 2 marks** l'hanno bocciato per 2 punti; **full marks for trying!** un bravo per aver tentato!; **there are no marks for guessing where I've been!** non ci vuole un genio per sapere dove sono stato!
4 (*Brit Tech*): **Mark 1/2** prima/seconda serie *f*
5 (*Sport: target*) bersaglio; **to hit the mark** far centro; (*fig*) azzeccare in pieno; **to be wide of the mark** essere lontano(-a) dal bersaglio; (*fig*) essere lontano(-a) dal vero
6 (*Sport: starting line*) linea di partenza; **on your marks! get set! go!** ai vostri posti! pronti! (attenti!) via!; **to be quick off the mark (in doing sth)** (*fig*) non perdere tempo (per fare qc); **up to the mark** (*in health*) in forma; (*in efficiency*) all'altezza
■VT
1 (*make a mark on*) segnare; (*stain*) macchiare, lasciare dei segni su
2 (*indicate: score*) segnare; (*: price*) mettere; (*: place*) indicare, segnare; (*: change, improvement*) indicare; **this marks the frontier** questo segna la frontiera; **mark its position on the map** segna il posto in cui si trova sulla cartina; **the qualities which mark a good swimmer** le qualità che contraddistinguono un buon nuotatore
3 (*heed*): **mark my words** fa' attenzione a quello che ti dico
4 (*Brit Scol: correct*) correggere; (*: exam*) dare un voto a; **the teacher hasn't marked my homework yet** il professore non mi ha ancora corretto il compito; **to mark sth wrong** segnare qc come errore
5 (*Sport: player*) marcare
6 **to mark time** (*Mil, fig*) segnare il passo
■VI macchiarsi
▶ **mark down** VT + ADV
1 (*reduce: prices, goods*) ribassare, ridurre; **the shirts were marked down at the beginning of the week** le camicie sono state ribassate all'inizio della settimana
2 (*note down*) prendere nota di
▶ **mark off** VT + ADV
1 (*separate*) dividere, separare
2 (*tick off*) spuntare, cancellare
▶ **mark out** VT + ADV
1 (*zone, road*) delimitare
2 (*single out: for promotion*) designare; (*characterize*) distinguere
▶ **mark up** VT + ADV
1 (*write up*) segnare
2 (*increase: goods*) aumentare il prezzo di; (*: price*) aumentare

DID YOU KNOW ...?
mark is not translated by the Italian word *marca*

mark² [mɑːk] N (*currency*) marco; **three million marks** tre milioni di marchi
mark·down [ˈmɑːkdaʊn] N ribasso
◎ **marked** [mɑːkt] ADJ (*accent, contrast, bias*) marcato(-a); (*improvement, increase*) sensibile, spiccato(-a), chiaro(-a); **he's a marked man** è sotto tiro
mark·ed·ly [ˈmɑːkɪdlɪ] ADV visibilmente, notevolmente, marcatamente
mark·er [ˈmɑːkəʳ] N (*stake*) paletto; (*pen*) pennarello; (*sign*) segno; (*in book*) segnalibro; (*Brit Scol*) *persona addetta a correggere le prove d'esame*; (*scorekeeper in games*) segnapunti *m inv*
◎ **mar·ket** [ˈmɑːkɪt] N (*gen*) mercato; (*also:* **stock market**) mercato azionario *or* dei titoli; **to go to market** andare al mercato; **open market** mercato libero; **there is a good market for videos** c'è una grossa richiesta di video; **is there a market for that?** c'è uno sbocco sul mercato per quello?; **it appeals to the Italian market** è richiesto sul mercato italiano; **to be in the market for sth** avere intenzione di comprare qc; **to be on the market** essere (messo(-a)) in vendita *or* in commercio; **to come on(to) the market** essere introdotto(-a) sul mercato; **to play the market** giocare *or* speculare in borsa
■VT (*Comm: sell*) vendere, mettere in vendita; (*: promote*) lanciare sul mercato
mar·ket·abil·ity [ˌmɑːkɪtəˈbɪlɪtɪ] N commerciabilità *f inv*
mar·ket·able [ˈmɑːkɪtəbl] ADJ commercializzabile
market analysis N analisi *f inv* di mercato
market day N giorno di mercato
market demand N domanda del mercato
market-driven [ˈmɑːkɪtˌdrɪvn] ADJ determinato(-a) dal mercato
market economy N economia di mercato
market forces NPL forze *fpl* di mercato
market garden N (*Brit*) orto (industriale)
market gardener N (*Brit*) ortofrutticoltore *m*
market gardening N (*Brit*) ortofrutticoltura
◎ **mar·ket·ing** [ˈmɑːkɪtɪŋ] N marketing *m inv*
▷ www.marketing.org
▷ www.marketingpower.com/
marketing manager N direttore *m* del marketing
market leader N leader *m inv* del mercato
market-led [ˈmɑːkɪtˌlɛd] ADJ = **market-driven**
market·place [ˈmɑːkɪtˌpleɪs] N (*square*) (piazza del) mercato; (*world of trade*) piazza, mercato
market potential N possibilità *f inv* di mercato
market price N prezzo di mercato
market research N indagini *fpl or* ricerche *fpl* di mercato
market share N quota di mercato
market test N indagine *f* di mercato
■VT sottoporre a un'indagine di mercato
market town N città dove si tiene (*or* si teneva) un mercato
market trend N tendenza del mercato
market value N valore *m* di mercato
mark·ing [ˈmɑːkɪŋ] N **1** (*on animal*) marcatura di colore; (*on road*) segnaletica orizzontale **2** (*Brit Scol*) correzione *f* (dei compiti) **3** (*Ftbl*) marcamento, marcatura
marking ink N inchiostro indelebile
marks·man [ˈmɑːksmən] N (*pl* **-men**) tiratore *m* scelto

marks·man·ship ['mɑːksmənʃɪp] N abilità *f inv* nel tiro
mark-up ['mɑːkˌʌp] N (*Comm: margin*) margine *m* di vendita; (*: increase*) aumento
marl [mɑːl] N (*Geol*) marna
mar·ma·lade ['mɑːməˌleɪd] N marmellata d'arance
marmalade orange N arancia amara
mar·mo·set ['mɑːməʊˌzɛt] N callitricide *m*
mar·mot ['mɑːmət] N marmotta
ma·roon¹ [mə'ruːn] ADJ, N (*colour*) bordeaux (*m*) *inv*

DID YOU KNOW ...?
maroon is not translated by the Italian word *marrone*

ma·roon² [mə'ruːn] VT (*on island*) abbandonare; (*subj: sea, traffic, snow*) bloccare; **to be marooned (in** *or* **at)** (*fig*) essere abbandonato(-a) (in)
mar·quee [mɑː'kiː] N grande tenda, padiglione *m*
mar·quis, **mar·quess** ['mɑːkwɪs] N marchese *m*
Mar·ra·kech, **Mar·ra·kesh** [ˌmærə'kɛʃ] N Marrakesh *f*
◎ **mar·riage** ['mærɪdʒ] N matrimonio; **he's my uncle by marriage** è uno zio acquisito
■ ADJ (*vows*) di matrimonio; (*bed*) coniugale
mar·riage·able ['mærɪdʒəbl] ADJ: **of marriageable age** (*woman*) da marito, in età da marito; (*man*) che deve prendere moglie
marriage bureau N agenzia matrimoniale
marriage certificate N certificato di matrimonio
marriage guidance, (*Am*) **marriage counseling** N consulenza matrimoniale
marriage licence N licenza matrimoniale
marriage lines NPL (*Brit old*) certificato di matrimonio
marriage of convenience N matrimonio di convenienza
◎ **mar·ried** ['mærɪd] ADJ (*person*) sposato(-a); (*life, love*) coniugale, matrimoniale; (*name*) da sposata
mar·row ['mærəʊ] N **1** (*Anat*) midollo; **bone marrow** il midollo osseo; **to be frozen to the marrow** sentirsi il gelo *or* il freddo nelle ossa **2** (*vegetable*) zucca; **baby marrow** zucchino
marrow·bone ['mærəʊˌbəʊn] N ossobuco, osso con il midollo
◎ **mar·ry** ['mærɪ] VT (*take in marriage*) sposare, sposarsi con; (*subj: father, priest*) dare in matrimonio; **he wants to marry her** vuole sposarla
■ VI (*also: to get married*) sposarsi; **my sister's getting married in June** mia sorella si sposa in giugno; **to marry again** risposarsi; **to marry into a rich family** imparentarsi con una famiglia ricca
▸ **marry up** VT + ADV (*pattern*) far combaciare
Mars [mɑːz] N (*Astron, Myth*) Marte *m*
Mar·seilles [mɑː'seɪlz] N Marsiglia
marsh [mɑːʃ] N palude *f*
mar·shal ['mɑːʃəl] N (*Mil*) maresciallo; (*for demonstration, meeting*) membro del servizio d'ordine; (*Am: also:* **fire marshal**) capo; (*: also:* **police marshal**) capitano
■ VT (*soldiers, procession*) schierare, adunare; (*fig: facts*) ordinare
mar·shal·ling yard ['mɑːʃəlɪŋˌjɑːd] N (*Brit*) scalo smistamento
marsh gas N gas *m inv* delle paludi
marsh harrier [-'hærɪəʳ] N (*bird*) falco di palude
marsh·mal·low ['mɑːʃˌmæləʊ] N (*sweet*) *caramella soffice e gommosa*
marsh mallow N (*plant*) altea
marsh marigold N (*plant*) calta, farferugine *f* di palude
marshy ['mɑːʃɪ] ADJ (*comp* **-ier**, *superl* **-iest**) paludoso(-a)
mar·su·pial [mɑː'suːpɪəl] ADJ, N marsupiale (*m*)
mar·ten ['mɑːtɪn] N (*animal*) martora; **pine marten** martora degli alberi; **stone marten** faina
mar·tial ['mɑːʃəl] ADJ marziale
martial art N arte *f* marziale
martial law N legge *f* marziale
Mar·tian ['mɑːʃən] N marziano(-a)
mar·tin ['mɑːtɪn] N (*bird, also:* **house martin**) balestruccio; **sand martin** topino
mar·ti·net [ˌmɑːtɪ'nɛt] N: **to be a martinet** essere molto rigido(-a), essere molto intransigente
mar·tyr ['mɑːtəʳ] N martire *m/f*; **to be a martyr to arthritis** essere torturato(-a) dall'artrite
■ VT martirizzare
mar·tyr·dom ['mɑːtədəm] N martirio
mar·tyred ['mɑːtəd] ADJ (*look, expression, sigh*) da martire
mar·vel ['mɑːvəl] N (*of nature*) meraviglia; (*of science, skill*) prodigio; **if she gets there it will be a marvel** (*fam*) se ci arriva è un miracolo; **it's a marvel to me how she does it** (*fam*) non so proprio come riesca a farlo; **you're a marvel!** (*fam*) sei un fenomeno!
■ VI: **to marvel (at)** (*awestruck*) rimanere incantato(-a) (davanti a); (*surprised*) stupirsi (di fronte a), meravigliarsi (di)
mar·vel·lous, (*Am*) **mar·ve·lous** ['mɑːvələs] ADJ meraviglioso(-a); **the weather was marvellous** il tempo era stupendo
mar·vel·lous·ly ['mɑːvələslɪ] ADV meravigliosamente
Marx·ism ['mɑːksɪzəm] N marxismo
Marx·ist ['mɑːksɪst] ADJ, N marxista (*m/f*)
Mary ['mɛərɪ] N Maria
Mary·land ['mɛərɪlænd] N Maryland *m*
▷ www.maryland.gov/
Mary Mag·da·lene ['mɛərɪ'mægdəˌliːn] N Maria Maddalena, Maria di Magdala
mar·zi·pan [ˌmɑːzɪ'pæn] N marzapane *m*
mas·cara [mæs'kɑːrə] N mascara *m inv*
mas·cot ['mæskət] N mascotte *f inv*, portafortuna *m inv*
mas·cu·line ['mæskjʊlɪn] ADJ (*also Gram*) maschile; (*pej: woman*) mascolino(-a)
■ N (*Gram*) (genere *m*) maschile *m*
mas·cu·lin·ity [ˌmæskjʊ'lɪnɪtɪ] N virilità *f inv*, mascolinità *f inv*; (*pej: of woman*) mascolinità *f inv*
MASH [mæʃ] N ABBR (*Am Mil:* = **Mobile Army Surgical Hospital**) *ospedale da campo di unità mobile dell'esercito*
mash [mæʃ] N **1** (*Brit fam: also:* **mashed potatoes**) purè *m* (di patate) **2** (*for animals*) pastone *m*
■ VT (*Culin*) passare, schiacciare
◎ **mask** [mɑːsk] N (*gen, Elec*) maschera
■ VT mascherare
masked ball ['mɑːsktˌbɔːl] N ballo in maschera, ballo mascherato
mask·ing tape ['mɑːskɪŋˌteɪp] N (*during painting, spraying*) nastro adesivo di carta
maso·chism ['mæsəʊˌkɪzəm] N masochismo
maso·chist ['mæsəʊkɪst] N masochista *m/f*
maso·chis·tic [ˌmæsəʊ'kɪstɪk] ADJ masochistico(-a)
ma·son ['meɪsn] N **1** (*builder*) muratore *m*; (*also:* **stonemason**) scalpellino **2** (*also:* **freemason**) massone *m*
ma·son·ic [mə'sɒnɪk] ADJ massonico(-a)
ma·son·ry ['meɪsnrɪ] N **1** (*stonework*) muratura; (*skill*) arte *f* muratoria **2** (*also:* **freemasonry**) massoneria
mas·quer·ade [ˌmæskə'reɪd] N (*fig: pretence*)

Mm

mascherata, finzione *f*, montatura; (*masked ball*) ballo in maschera
■VI: **to masquerade as** farsi passare per

mass¹ [mæs] N (*Rel*) messa; **to say mass** dire (la) messa; **to go to mass** andare a *or* alla messa; **Sunday mass** messa della domenica

◎**mass²** [mæs] N (*gen*) massa, moltitudine *f*; (*Phys*) massa; **a mass of books and papers** una massa di libri e carte; **he's a mass of bruises** è coperto di lividi; **in the mass** nella gran maggioranza; **the masses** le masse; **masses (of)** (*fam*) un sacco (di), un mucchio (di)
■VI (*Mil*) adunarsi, concentrarsi; (*crowd*) radunarsi, ammassarsi; (*clouds*) addensarsi
■VT adunare
■ADJ (*culture, demonstration*) di massa; (*education*) delle masse; (*hysteria*) collettivo(-a); (*murders*) in massa; **mass grave** fossa comune

Mas·sa·chu·setts [ˌmæsəˈtʃuːsɪts] N Massachusetts *m*
▷ www.mass.gov/

mas·sa·cre [ˈmæsəkəʳ] N massacro
■VT massacrare

mas·sage [ˈmæsɑːʒ] N massaggio
■VT massaggiare

massage parlour N centro *m* massaggi *inv*; (*fig*) casa d'appuntamenti

massed [mæst] ADJ (*bands, troops*) radunato(-a) in massa; (*artillery*) ammassato(-a)

mas·seur [mæˈsɜːʳ] N massaggiatore *m*

mas·seuse [mæˈsɜːz] N massaggiatrice *f*

◎**mas·sive** [ˈmæsɪv] ADJ massiccio(-a), enorme

mass market N mercato di massa

mass-market [ˈmæˌmɑːkɪt] ADJ per il gran pubblico

mass media NPL mass media *mpl*, mezzi *mpl* di comunicazione *f* di massa

mass meeting N (*of everyone concerned*) riunione *f* generale; (*huge*) adunata popolare

mass number N (*Phys*) numero di massa

mass-produce [ˈmæsprəˌdjuːs] VT produrre in serie

mass production N produzione *f* in serie

mast [mɑːst] N (*Naut*) albero; (*flagpole*) asta; (*Radio, TV*) pilone *m* (a traliccio)

mastectomy [ˌmæsˈtɛktəmɪ] N mastectomia

◎**mas·ter** [ˈmɑːstəʳ] N **1** (*of servant, dog*) padrone *m*; **the master of the house** il padrone di casa; **to be one's own master** non aver padroni; **I am (the) master now** ora comando io; **to be master of the situation** essere padrone della situazione **2** (*Naut: of ship*) capitano **3** (*musician, painter*) maestro **4** (*Brit: teacher: in primary school*) maestro; (*: in secondary school*) professore *m*; **fencing master** maestro di scherma **5** (*title for boys*): **Master Paul Moran** il signorino Paul Moran; (*on letters*) (il) signor Paul Moran
■VT **1** (*animal*) domare; (*person*) dominare; (*one's emotions*) controllare **2** (*theory: understand*) conoscere a fondo; (*learn: subject, skill*) imparare a fondo; **she soon mastered the technique** si è impadronita rapidamente della tecnica

master baker N mastro pasticciere

master bedroom N camera da letto principale

master builder N capomastro

master cylinder N (*Tech*) pompa idraulica

master disk N (*Comput*) disco *m* master *inv*, disco principale

mas·ter·ful [ˈmɑːstəfʊl] ADJ (*imperious*) imperioso(-a); (*authoritative*) magistrale

mas·ter·ful·ly [ˈmɑːstəfəlɪ] ADV (*see adj*) imperiosamente; magistralmente

master key N passe-partout *m inv*

mas·ter·ly [ˈmɑːstəlɪ] ADJ magistrale, da maestro

master·mind [ˈmɑːstəˌmaɪnd] N (*genius*) mente *f* superiore; (*in crime*) cervello
■VT ideare e dirigere, essere il cervello di

Master of Arts/Science N (*degree*) master *m inv* in materie umanistiche/scienze; (*person*) *titolare di un master in lettere/scienze*

master of ceremonies N maestro di cerimonie

master·piece [ˈmɑːstəˌpiːs] N capolavoro

master plan N piano generale, progetto di massima

master race N razza superiore

mas·ter's [ˈmɑːstəz] N (*also:* **master's degree**) master *m inv*

MASTER'S DEGREE

Il **Master's degree** è il riconoscimento che viene conferito a chi segue un corso di specializzazione dopo aver conseguito un "Bachelor's degree". Vi sono diversi tipi di **Master's Degree**; i più comuni sono il "Master of Arts (MA)" e il "Master of Science (MSc)" che si ottengono dopo aver seguito un corso e aver presentato una tesi originale. Per il "Master of Letters (MLitt)" e il "Master of Philosophy (MPhil)" è invece sufficiente presentare la tesi. In Scozia il sistema universitario è un po' diverso e MA e MSc possono essere anche lauree di primo grado. *Vedi anche* **Bachelor's degree; doctorate**

▷ www.dfes.gov.uk/hegateway/
▷ http://educationusa.state.gov/graduate/about/degrees.htm
▷ www.aucc.ca/can_uni/general_info/overview_e.html
▷ www.internationaleducationmedia.com/newzealand/
▷ www.southafrica.info/ess_info/sa_glance/education/education.htm

master·stroke [ˈmɑːstəˌstrəʊk] N colpo magistrale *or* da maestro

master switch N interruttore *m* centrale

mas·tery [ˈmɑːstərɪ] N: **mastery (of)** (*subject, musical instrument*) padronanza (di); (*of the seas*) dominio (su), supremazia (su); **mastery (at)** (*skill*) virtuosità *f inv* (a *or* in), maestria (a *or* in); **mastery (over)** (*competitors*) superiorità *f inv* (su)

mas·ti·cate [ˈmæstɪˌkeɪt] VT, VI masticare

mas·tiff [ˈmæstɪf] N mastino

mas·toid [ˈmæstɔɪd] N **1** (*also:* **mastoide bone**) mastoide *f* **2** (*Med fam: inflammation*) = **mastoiditis**

mas·toid·itis [ˌmæstɔɪˈdaɪtɪs] N mastoidite *f*

mas·tur·bate [ˈmæstəˌbeɪt] VI masturbarsi
■VT masturbare

mas·tur·ba·tion [ˌmæstəˈbeɪʃən] N masturbazione *f*

mat¹ [mæt] N (*on floor*) tappetino; (*: of straw*) stuoia; (*also:* **doormat**) zerbino, stoino; (*on table*) tovaglietta all'americana

mat² [mæt] ADJ = **matt**

◎**match¹** [mætʃ] N **1** (*of colours*): **to be a good match (for)** intonarsi a, andar bene con; **Paul and Jane make a good match** Paul e Jane sono una bella coppia; **it's an exact match** è identico **2** (*equal*) uguale *m/f*, pari *m/f inv*; **to be a match/no match for sb** riuscire/non riuscire a tenere testa a qn; **to meet one's match** trovare pane per i propri denti **3** (*marriage*) partito **4** (*game*) incontro; (*: Ftbl, Rugby*) partita, incontro; **are**

you going to the match? vai alla partita?
■ VT **1** (*find similar to: also:* **match up**): **can you match this wool for me?** ha della lana che vada bene con questa?; **to match sb against sb** opporre qn a qn; **they are well matched** (*opponents*) son ben assortiti; (*two friends*) sono una coppia bene assortita; (*husband and wife*) sono una bella coppia; **match the pictures to the titles** fai corrispondere le immagini ai titoli **2** (*equal*) uguagliare; **the results did not match our hopes** i risultati non hanno corrisposto alle nostre speranze; **I can't match that** per me è troppo **3** (*go well with: colours*) intonarsi a; (*: clothes*) andare benissimo con; **his tie matches his socks** la sua cravatta s'intona ai calzini
■ VI (*colours, materials*) intonarsi; **with a skirt to match** *or* **with a matching skirt** con una gonna adatta *or* intonata; **the jacket matches the trousers** la giacca si intona con i pantaloni
▸ **match up to** VI + ADV + PREP essere all'altezza di

match² [mætʃ] N fiammifero; **a box of matches** una scatola di fiammiferi; **to put a match to sth** dar fuoco a qc

match·box ['mætʃ,bɒks] N scatola di fiammiferi

match·ing ['mætʃɪŋ] ADJ (*colours*) intonato(-a), ben assortito(-a); **with matching shoes and bag** con scarpe e borsa intonate

match·less ['mætʃlɪs] ADJ senza pari

match·make ['mætʃ,meɪk] VI: **she's always matchmaking** cerca sempre di combinare matrimoni

match·maker ['mætʃ,meɪkəʳ] N (*arranger of marriages*) sensale *m/f* di matrimoni; (*Sport*) organizzatore(-trice) di incontri sportivi; **she is a great matchmaker** ha combinato molte unioni felici

match play N (*Sport*) *tipo di golf in cui vince chi fa il maggior numero di buche, indipendentemente dal numero di colpi dati alla pallina*

match point N (*Tennis*) match point *m inv*

match·stick ['mætʃ,stɪk] N fiammifero

match·wood ['mætʃ,wud] N legno per fiammiferi; **the boat was smashed to matchwood** (*fig*) la barca fu completamente sfasciata

◎ **mate¹** [meɪt] N **1** (*at work*) compagno(-a) di lavoro; (*fam: friend*) amico(-a); **he always goes on holiday with his mates** va sempre in vacanza con i suoi amici; **look here, mate** ehi tu, senti **2** (*assistant*) aiutante *m/f* **3** (*Zool*) compagno(-a), maschio (*or* femmina) **4** (*in merchant navy*) secondo
■ VT (*Zool*) accoppiare
■ VI (*Zool*) accoppiarsi

mate² [meɪt] N (*Chess*) scaccomatto

◎ **ma·terial** [mə'tɪərɪəl] ADJ **1** (*things, needs, success*) materiale **2** (*important*) sostanziale, essenziale; (*relevant*): **material to** pertinente a; (*Law: evidence*) determinante; **a material witness** un testimone chiave
■ N **1** (*substance*) materiale *m*, materia; (*cloth*) stoffa, tessuto; **the curtains are made of thin material** le tende sono fatte di una stoffa sottile; **she is university material** è una che dovrebbe continuare gli studi; **he is officer material** ha la stoffa dell'ufficiale **2** (*equipment*): **materials**
■ NPL occorrente *m*; **building materials** materiali *mpl* da costruzione; **raw materials** materie prime; **have you any writing materials?** hai l'occorrente per scrivere? **3** (*for novel, report*) materiale *m*, documentazione *f*; **I'm collecting material for my project** sto raccogliendo materiale per la mia ricerca

ma·teri·al·ism [mə'tɪərɪə,lɪzəm] N materialismo

ma·teri·al·ist [mə'tɪərɪəlɪst] N materialista *m/f*

ma·teri·al·is·tic [mə,tɪərɪə'lɪstɪk] ADJ materialista

ma·teri·al·ize [mə'tɪərɪə,laɪz] VI materializzarsi; (*idea, hope*) avverarsi, realizzarsi; **so far he hasn't materialized** (*fam*) per ora non si è visto

ma·teri·al·ly [mə'tɪərɪəlɪ] ADV (*see adj*) dal punto di vista materiale; sostanzialmente

ma·ter·nal [mə'tɜ:nl] ADJ materno(-a)

ma·ter·nal·ly [mə'tɜ:nəlɪ] ADV maternamente

ma·ter·nity [mə'tɜ:nɪtɪ] N maternità *f inv*
■ ADJ di maternità

maternity benefit N sussidio di maternità

maternity dress N vestito *m* pre-maman *inv*

maternity home, maternity hospital N ≈ clinica ostetrica

maternity leave N congedo per maternità

maternity ward N reparto *m* maternità *inv*

matey ['meɪtɪ] ADJ (*Brit fam*) amicone(-a)

math [mæθ] N ABBR (*Am:* = **mathematics**) matematica

math·emati·cal [,mæθə'mætɪkəl] ADJ matematico(-a)

math·emati·cal·ly [,mæθə'mætɪkəlɪ] ADV matematicamente

math·ema·ti·cian [,mæθəmə'tɪʃən] N matematico(-a)

math·emat·ics [,mæθə'mætɪks] NSG matematica
▷ http://carbon.cudenver.edu/~hgreenbe/glossary/index.php
▷ www.nrich.maths.org.uk

maths [mæθs] N ABBR (*Brit* = **mathematics**) matematica

mati·née ['mætɪ,neɪ] N matinée *f inv*

mat·ing ['meɪtɪŋ] N accoppiamento
■ ADJ dell'accoppiamento

mating call N chiamata all'accoppiamento

mating season N stagione *f* degli amori

mat·ins ['mætɪnz] NSG OR NPL mattutino

ma·tri·arch ['meɪtrɪɑ:k] N matriarca

ma·tri·ar·chal [,meɪtrɪ'ɑ:kl] ADJ matriarcale

ma·tri·ar·chy ['meɪtrɪɑ:kɪ] N matriarcato

ma·tri·ces ['meɪtrɪsi:z] NPL *of* **matrix**

mat·ri·cide ['mætrɪ,saɪd] N (*crime*) matricidio; (*person*) matricida *m/f*

ma·tricu·late [mə'trɪkjʊ,leɪt] VI immatricolarsi

ma·tricu·la·tion [mə,trɪkjʊ'leɪʃən] N immatricolazione *f*

mat·ri·mo·nial [,mætrɪ'məʊnɪəl] ADJ (*vows*) di matrimonio; (*state, troubles*) coniugale, matrimoniale

mat·ri·mo·ny ['mætrɪmənɪ] N matrimonio

ma·trix ['meɪtrɪks] N (*pl* **matrices** *or* **matrixes**) matrice *f*

ma·tron ['meɪtrən] N (*Brit: in hospital*) capoinfermiera; (*: in school*) infermiera; (*older woman*) matrona

ma·tron·ly ['meɪtrənlɪ] ADJ (*figure, behaviour*) da matrona; (*woman*) imponente e di una certa età

matron-of-honour [,meɪtrənəv'ɒnəʳ] N dama d'onore

matt [mæt] ADJ opaco(-a)

mat·ted ['mætɪd] ADJ (*hair*) arruffato(-a); (*sweater*) infeltrito(-a)

◎ **matter** ['mætəʳ] N
1 (*substance: gen: Phys*) materia, sostanza; **colouring matter** colorante *m*; **foreign matter** sostanza estranea; **advertising matter** pubblicità *f inv*; **reading matter** (*Brit*) qualcosa da leggere
2 (*content*) contenuto
3 (*question, affair*) questione *f*, faccenda; **money**

Mm

matters questioni finanziarie; **the matter in hand** l'argomento *or* la faccenda in questione; **there's the matter of my wages** ci sarebbe la questione del mio stipendio; **and to make matters worse ...** e come se non bastasse...; **that will only make matters worse** questo servirà solo a peggiorare la situazione; **it's a matter of great concern to us** è una cosa che ci preoccupa molto; **it's no laughing matter** è una cosa *or* faccenda seria; **it's a matter of life and death** è una questione di vita o di morte; **it will be a matter of a few weeks** ci vorrà qualche settimana; **it's a matter of a few pounds** si tratta di poche sterline; **in the matter of** in fatto di, per quanto riguarda; **for that matter** peraltro; **as a matter of course** di conseguenza, come cosa naturale; **as a matter of fact** per (dire) la verità, in verità; **it's a matter of opinion** è una questione di punti di vista; **that's another matter** quella è un'altra faccenda; **it's a matter of habit** è una questione di abitudine
4 (*importance*): **no matter!** non importa!; **do it, no matter how** non importa come, basta che tu lo faccia; **no matter how you do it** comunque tu lo faccia; **no matter what** qualsiasi cosa accada; **no matter what he says** qualsiasi *or* qualunque cosa dica; **no matter how big it is** per quanto grande sia; **no matter when** in qualunque momento, non importa quando; **no matter who** chiunque
5 (*difficulty, problem*): **what's the matter?** cosa c'è (che non va)?; **what's the matter with you?** cos'hai?; **what's the matter with my hair?** cos'hanno i miei capelli che non va?; **there's something the matter with my arm** c'è qualcosa che non va al braccio; **as if nothing was the matter** come se niente fosse; **something's the matter with the lights** le luci hanno qualcosa che non va; **nothing's the matter** non è successo niente; **nothing's the matter with me** non ho niente
6 (*Med: pus*) pus *m*
■ VI importare; **it doesn't matter** (*I don't mind*) non importa, non fa niente; **I can't give you the money today — it doesn't matter** non ti posso dare i soldi oggi — non importa; **what does it matter?** cosa importa?, che importanza ha?; **what does it matter to you?** ma a te che te ne importa?; **why should it matter to me?** e perché dovrebbe importarmi?; **it matters a lot to me** è molto importante per me

Mat·ter·horn [ˈmætəˌhɔːn] N: **the Matterhorn** il Cervino

matter-of-fact [ˌmætərəvˈfækt] ADJ (*person, attitude*) pratico(-a), prosaico(-a); (*tone, voice*) neutro(-a), piatto(-a); (*account*) che si limita ai fatti

mat·ting [ˈmætɪŋ] N stuoia

mat·tins [ˈmætɪnz] NSG OR PL = **matins**

mat·tress [ˈmætrɪs] N materasso

ma·ture [məˈtjʊə^r] ADJ (*comp* **-r**, *superl* **-st**) (*gen*) maturo(-a); (*cheese*) stagionato(-a); **he's much more mature** è molto più maturo
■ VI (*gen*) maturarsi, maturare; (*Fin*) maturare, scadere; (*cheese*) stagionarsi, stagionare

mature student N studente(-essa) universitario(-a) di età superiore ai 25 anni

ma·tur·ity [məˈtjʊərɪtɪ] N maturità *f inv*

maud·lin [ˈmɔːdlɪn] ADJ piagnucoloso(-a)

maul [mɔːl] VT (*subj: tiger*) dilaniare, sbranare; **mauled to death** sbranato(-a) vivo(-a)

Maun·dy Thurs·day [ˈmɔːndɪˈθɜːzdɪ] N giovedì *m inv* santo

Mau·ri·ta·nia [ˌmɔːrɪˈteɪnɪə] N la Mauritania

Mau·ri·tius [məˈrɪʃəs] N (l'isola di) Maurizio *f*

mau·so·leum [ˌmɔːsəˈlɪəm] N mausoleo

mauve [məʊv] ADJ (color) malva *inv*

mav·er·ick [ˈmævərɪk] N chi sta fuori del branco
■ ADJ anticonformista

mawk·ish [ˈmɔːkɪʃ] ADJ svenevole, sdolcinato(-a), insipido(-a)

max. ABBR (= **maximum**) max

max·im [ˈmæksɪm] N massima

maxi·ma [ˈmæksɪmə] NPL *of* **maximum**

maxi·mal·ism [ˈmæksɪməˌlɪzəm] N massimalismo

max·im·ize [ˈmæksɪˌmaɪz] VT (*profits*) massimizzare; (*chances*) aumentare al massimo; (*Comput: window*) ingrandire a pieno schermo

◎ **maxi·mum** [ˈmæksɪməm] N (*pl* **maxima** *or* **maximums**) massimo
■ ADJ massimo(-a)

May [meɪ] N maggio; **in May** in maggio; *for usage see* **July**

◎ **may** [meɪ] (*pt* **might**) MODAL AUX VB **1** (*possibility*): **she may come** può darsi che venga, può venire; **he might come** potrebbe venire, può anche darsi che venga; **it may rain** potrebbe piovere; **are you going to the party? — I don't know, I may ...** vai alla festa? – non so, forse...; **they may have thought you were joking** forse hanno pensato che scherzassi; **I might well go** potrei anche andare; **he might be there** può darsi che ci sia; **he may not be hungry** potrebbe non aver fame, può darsi che non abbia fame; **they may well be connected** può darsi benissimo che ci sia un legame; **that's as may be** può anche darsi; **be that as it may** comunque sia, sia come sia; **you may well ask!** è quello che mi chiedo anch'io! **2** (*of permission*): **may I smoke?** posso fumare?; **may I have a cigarette? — yes, of course** potrei avere una sigaretta? — sì, prego; **may I sit here?** le dispiace se mi siedo qua?; **if I may say so** se mi è concesso dirlo; **may I?** permette?; **might I suggest that ...?** con il suo permesso suggerirei che...; **he said I might leave** mi ha detto che potevo andare **3** **I hope he may succeed** (*frm*) spero che ci riesca; **I hoped he might succeed this time** speravo che stavolta ci sarebbe riuscito; **we may** *or* **might as well go** tanto vale che ci andiamo; **he might have offered to help** avrebbe potuto offrirsi di aiutare; **as you might expect** come c'era da aspettarsi; **you might like to try** forse le piacerebbe provare **4** (*in wishes*): **may you have a happy life together** possiate vivere insieme felici; **may God bless you!** (che) Dio la benedica!

◎ **may·be** [ˈmeɪbiː] ADV forse, può darsi; **maybe not** forse no, può darsi di no; **maybe tomorrow** forse *or* magari domani; **maybe he'll come** può darsi che venga, magari *or* forse verrà

May Day N il primo maggio (*in cui si festeggia l'arrivo della primavera*)

May·day [ˈmeɪˌdeɪ] N (*Aer, Naut*) mayday *m inv*, S.O.S. *m inv*

may·fly [ˈmeɪˌflaɪ] N efemera

may·hem [ˈmeɪhɛm] N cagnara

may·on·naise [ˌmeɪəˈneɪz] N maionese *f*

◎ **mayor** [mɛə^r] N sindaco

mayor·ess [ˈmɛərɛs] N (*wife*) moglie *f* del sindaco; (*holding office*) sindaco (*donna*)

may·pole [ˈmeɪˌpəʊl] N *palo ornato di fiori attorno a cui si danza durante la festa del primo maggio*

maze [meɪz] N dedalo, labirinto

ma·zur·ka [mə'zɜ:kə] N mazurca
MB [ˌɛm'bi:] N ABBR **1** (*Med:* = **Bachelor of Medicine**) laurea in Medicina **2** (*Comput*) = **megabyte**
■ ABBR = *Manitoba*
MBA [ˌɛmbi:'eɪ] N ABBR (= **Master of Business Administration**) master *m inv* in gestione aziendale
⊳ www.mba.com/mba
⊳ www.mbaworld.com/
MBBS [ˌɛmbi:bi:'ɛs], **MBChB** N ABBR (*Brit:* = **Bachelor of Medicine and Surgery**) laurea in Medicina e Chirurgia
MBE [ˌɛmbi:'i:] N ABBR (*Brit:* = **Member of the Order of the British Empire**) *titolo onorifico*
MBO [ˌɛmbi:'əʊ] N ABBR = **management buyout**
MC [ˌɛm'si:] N ABBR **1** = **master of ceremonies** **2** (*Am:* = **Member of Congress**) membro del Congresso
MCAT [ˌɛmsi:eɪ'ti:] N ABBR (*Am:* = **Medical College Admissions Test**) *esame di ammissione alla Facoltà di Medicina*
McCoy [mə'kɔɪ] (*fam*): **this is the real McCoy!** questo è quello originale!
MCP [ˌɛmsi:'pi:] N ABBR (*Brit fam:* = **male chauvinist pig**) sporco maschilista *m*
MD [ˌɛm'di:] N ABBR **1** (= **Doctor of Medicine**) Dottore *m* in Medicina **2** (*Comm:* = **managing director**) AD *m* (= *Amministratore Delegato*)
■ ABBR (*Am Post*) = *Maryland*
MDT [ˌɛmdi:'ti:] ABBR (*Am:* = **Mountain Daylight Time**) *ora estiva nel fuso delle Montagne Rocciose*
ME [ˌɛm'i:] N ABBR (*Med*) **1** (= **myalgic encephalomyelitis**) sindrome *f* da affaticamento cronico **2** = **medical examiner**
■ ABBR (*Am Post*) = *Maine*
◎ **me** [mi:] PERS PRON **1** (*direct: unstressed*) mi, m' + *vowel or silent 'h'*; (*: stressed*) me; **he can hear me** mi sente; **excuse me!** mi scusi!; **it's me** sono io; **he heard me** mi ha *or* m'ha sentito; **he heard ME!** ha sentito ME! **2** (*indirect*) mi, m'+ *vowel or silent 'h'*; **he gave me the money, he gave the money to me** mi ha *or* m'ha dato i soldi; **he gave them to me** me li ha dati; **give them to me** dammeli; **could you lend me your pen?** puoi prestarmi la penna? **3** (*stressed, after prep*) me; **it's for me** è per me; **without me** senza (di) me; **look at me!** guardami!; **come with me!** vieni con me!; **without me** senza di me
mead¹ [mi:d] N idromele *m*
mead² [mi:d] N (*liter: meadow*) prato
mead·ow ['mɛdəʊ] N prato, pascolo
meadow·sweet ['mɛdəʊˌswi:t] N (*plant*) olmaria, barba di capra
mea·gre, (*Am*) **mea·ger** ['mi:gəʳ] ADJ magro(-a)
meal¹ [mi:l] N (*flour*) farina
◎ **meal²** [mi:l] N pasto; **to have a meal** mangiare; **to have a good meal** mangiar bene; **to go out for a meal** mangiare fuori; **what a lovely meal** che pranzo delizioso (*or* cena deliziosa); **to make a meal of sth** (*fam*) fare di qc un affare di stato; **before meals** prima dei pasti; **enjoy your meal!** buon appetito!
meals on wheels NSG (*Brit*) *distribuzione di pasti caldi a domicilio a persone malate o anziane*
meal ticket N (*Am*) buono *m* pasto *inv*; (*fig fam: job*) che dà di che vivere; **a meal ticket for life** (*fig*) la pagnotta assicurata a vita
meal·time ['mi:lˌtaɪm] N ora di mangiare; **at mealtimes** all'ora dei pasti
mealy ['mi:lɪ] ADJ farinoso(-a)
mealy-mouthed ['mi:lɪˌmaʊðd] ADJ evasivo(-a)

◎ **mean¹** [mi:n] (*pt, pp* **meant**) VT **1** (*signify*) significare, voler dire; **what does that word mean?** che significa quella parola?; **what does "trap" mean?** cosa significa "trap"?; **what do you mean by that?** cosa vuoi dire con questo?; **you don't mean that, do you?** non parli sul serio, vero?; **do you really mean it?** dici sul serio?; **he said it as if he meant it** l'ha detto senza scherzare *or* sul serio; **I mean what I say** parlo sul serio; **it means a lot of expense for us** per noi questo vuol dire una grossa spesa; **the play didn't mean a thing to me** la commedia non mi ha detto niente; **her name means nothing to me** il suo nome non mi dice niente; **you mean a lot to me** significhi molto per me; **your friendship means a lot to me** la tua amicizia è molto importante per me; **he means nothing to me** non conta niente per me **2** (*intend*) intendere; **to mean to do sth** aver l'intenzione di fare qc, intendere fare qc; **to be meant for** essere destinato(-a) a; **I meant it for her** era destinato a lei; **that's not what I meant** non era quello che intendevo; **I meant it as a joke** volevo solo scherzare; **he means what he says** parla sul serio; **do you really mean it?** parli sul serio?; **what do you mean to do?** cosa intendi fare?, cosa pensi di fare?; **he didn't mean to do it** non intendeva *or* non era sua intenzione farlo; **I didn't mean to hurt you** non volevo farti del male; **do you mean me?** (*are you speaking to me?*) dici a me?; (*about me*) ti riferisci a me?, intendi me?; **was that remark meant for me?** quell'osservazione era diretta a me?; **Roberta is meant to do it** è Roberta che lo deve fare; **I mean to be obeyed** intendo essere ubbidito; **he means well** le sue intenzioni sono buone
mean² [mi:n] ADJ (*comp* **-er**, *superl* **-est**) **1** (*with money*) avaro(-a), spilorcio(-a), gretto(-a); **mean with** avaro(-a) con; **he's too mean to buy presents** è troppo avaro per comprare regali **2** (*unkind, spiteful*) meschino(-a), maligno(-a); **a mean trick** uno scherzo ignobile; **that's a really mean thing to say!** che cosa meschina da dire!; **you're being mean to me** sei cattivo con me; **you mean thing!** (*fam*) che meschino!; **it made me feel mean** mi ha fatto sentire un verme **3** (*Am: vicious: animal*) cattivo(-a); (*: person*) perfido(-a) **4** (*poor: appearance, district*) misero(-a); **she's no mean cook** è una cuoca tutt'altro che disprezzabile
mean³ [mi:n] N (*middle term*) mezzo; (*Math*) media; **the golden** *or* **happy mean** il giusto mezzo; *see also* **means**
■ ADJ (*average*) medio(-a)
me·ander [mɪ'ændəʳ] N meandro
■ VI (*river*) serpeggiare; (*person*) girovagare; (*fig*) divagare
mean deviation N (*Statistics*) scarto medio
◎ **mean·ing** ['mi:nɪŋ] N significato, senso; **a look full of meaning** uno sguardo eloquente; **do you get my meaning?** capisci cosa voglio dire?; **what's the meaning of this?** (*as reprimand*) e questo cosa significa?
mean·ing·ful ['mi:nɪŋfʊl] ADJ (*word, look*) significativo(-a), eloquente; (*relationship*) profondo(-a)
mean·ing·ful·ly ['mi:nɪŋfəlɪ] ADV (*look, speak*) eloquentemente
mean·ing·less ['mi:nɪŋlɪs] ADJ senza senso; **your remarks are quite meaningless** i tuoi commenti non vogliono dire niente
mean·ly ['mi:nlɪ] ADV **1** (*stingily*) avaramente **2** (*unkindly*) meschinamente, grettamente **3** (*Am: viciously*) perfidamente
mean·ness ['mi:nnɪs] N (*see adj*) avarizia, spilorceria; meschinità *f inv*; cattiveria; perfidia

◉ **means** [mi:nz] N INV *(method or way of doing)* mezzo, modo; **a means of transport** un mezzo di trasporto; **to find a means to do** *or* **of doing sth** trovare il modo per fare qc; **there is no means of doing it** non c'è mezzo *or* modo di farlo; **he'll do it by any possible means** lo farà con ogni mezzo possibile; **a means to an end** un modo *or* mezzo per raggiungere i propri fini; **by means of** per mezzo di; **by this means** in questo modo, così ; **by some means or other** in un modo o nell'altro; **by all means!** ma certamente!; **can I come? – by all means!** posso venire? – ma certamente!; **by no means** *or* **not by any means** per niente, niente affatto; **by all manner of means** in tutti i modi
■ NPL *(Fin)* mezzi *mpl*; **private means** rendite *fpl*; **to live within/beyond one's means** vivere secondo i/al di sopra dei propri mezzi

means test N *(Admin)* accertamento dei redditi *(per concedere di prestito)*

means-tested ['mi:nz,tɛstɪd] ADJ basato(-a) sul reddito; **the grant is not means-tested** la borsa di studio non dipende dal reddito

meant [mɛnt] PT, PP *of* mean

mean·time ['mi:n,taɪm], **mean·while** ['mi:n,waɪl] ADV *(also:* **in the meantime***)* nel frattempo, (e) intanto

mea·sles ['mi:zlz] N morbillo

mea·sly ['mi:zlɪ] ADJ *(comp* **-ier**, *superl* **-iest***)* *(fam)* misero(-a), miserabile

meas·ur·able ['mɛʒərəbl] ADJ misurabile

◉ **meas·ure** ['mɛʒə^r] N **1** *(gen)* misura; *(also:* **tape measure***)* metro; **a litre measure** una misura da un litro; **to give full measure** dare il peso giusto *(or* la quantità giusta); **for good measure** *(fig)* in più, in aggiunta; **to be a measure of ...** essere un sintomo di...; **her happiness was beyond measure** era immensamente felice; **in some/large measure** in parte/gran parte; **some measure of success** un certo successo; **I've got her measure** *(fig)* so quanto vale **2** *(step, action)* misura, provvedimento; **to take measures to do sth** prendere provvedimenti per fare qc; **to take measures against ...** prendere provvedimenti contro...
■ VT misurare; *(take sb's measurements)* prendere le misure di *or* a; **to measure one's length** *(fig: fall)* cadere lungo(-a) disteso(-a)
▸ **measure against** VT + PREP: **to measure sb/sth against sb/sth** valutare qn/qc confrontandolo a qn/qc
▸ **measure off** VT + ADV misurare
▸ **measure out** VT + ADV dosare
▸ **measure up** VI + ADV: **to measure up (to)** dimostrarsi *or* essere all'altezza (di)

meas·ured ['mɛʒəd] ADJ misurato(-a)

meas·ure·ment ['mɛʒəmənt] N *(act)* misurazione *f*; *(measure)* misura; **to take sb's measurements** prendere le misure di *or* a qn; **chest/hip measurement** giro petto/fianchi; **are you sure the measurements are correct?** sei sicuro che le misure siano giuste?; **the measurement of blood pressure** la misurazione della pressione sanguigna

meas·ur·ing ['mɛʒərɪŋ] N misurazione *f*

measuring jug N bicchiere *m* graduato

measuring tape N metro a nastro

◉ **meat** [mi:t] N carne *f*; **cold meats** *(Brit)* affettati *mpl*; **I don't eat meat** non mangio carne; **meat and drink** da mangiare e da bere; **this is meat and drink to them** *(fig)* questo per loro è una delizia; **one man's meat is another man's poison** *(proverb)* ciò che giova a uno nuoce a un altro
▹ www.meatuk.com

meat·ball ['mi:t,bɔ:l] N polpetta di carne

meat-eater ['mi:t,i:tə^r] N carnivoro(-a)

meat-eating ['mi:t,i:tɪŋ] ADJ carnivoro(-a)

meat extract N estratto di carne

meat pie N *torta salata in pasta frolla con ripieno di carne*

meaty ['mi:tɪ] ADJ *(comp* **-ier**, *superl* **-iest***)* *(flavour)* di carne; *(fig: book, talk)* sostanzioso(-a)

Mec·ca ['mɛkə] N La Mecca; **it has become a Mecca for tourists** *(fig)* è diventato la mecca dei turisti

me·chan·ic [mɪ'kænɪk] N meccanico; **motor mechanic** motorista *m*

me·chani·cal [mɪ'kænɪkəl] ADJ *(also fig)* meccanico(-a)

mechanical engineer N ingegnere *m* meccanico

mechanical engineering N *(science)* ingegneria meccanica; *(industry)* costruzioni *fpl* meccaniche
▹ www.imeche.org.uk/
▹ www.asme.org/

me·chani·cal·ly [mɪ'kænɪkəlɪ] ADV meccanicamente

me·chan·ics [mɪ'kænɪks] N **1** *(sg: science)* meccanica **2** *(pl: of car)* meccanismo, meccanica; *(: fig: of legal system)* meccanismo; *(: of writing, novel, plot)* meccanismo

◉ **mecha·nism** ['mɛkə,nɪzəm] N meccanismo

mecha·nis·tic [,mɛkə'nɪstɪk] ADJ *(Philosophy)* meccanicistico(-a)

mecha·ni·za·tion [mɛkənaɪ'zeɪʃən] N *(see vb)* meccanizzazione *f*; motorizzazione *f*

mecha·nize ['mɛkə,naɪz] VT *(process, industry)* meccanizzare; *(troops)* motorizzare

MEd [,ɛm'ɛd] N ABBR (= **Master of Education**) master *m inv* in pedagogia

◉ **med·al** ['mɛdl] N medaglia

me·dal·lion [mɪ'dæljən] N medaglione *m*

med·al·list, *(Am)* **med·al·ist** ['mɛdəlɪst] N *(Sport)*: **to be a gold/silver medallist** essere medaglia d'oro/ d'argento

med·dle ['mɛdl] VI *(interfere)*: **to meddle (in)** immischiarsi (in); **to meddle with sth** *(tamper)* toccare qc; **stop meddling!** smettila di impicciarti!

med·dler ['mɛdlə^r] N *(busybody)* impiccione(-a)

med·dle·some ['mɛdlsəm], **med·dling** ['mɛdlɪŋ] ADJ *(interfering)* impiccione(-a), ficcanaso *m/f*

Medea [mɪ'dɪə] N Medea

◉ **me·dia** ['mi:dɪə] NPL **1** *(Press, Radio, TV)*: **the media** i mass media; **all the media were there** stampa, radio e televisione erano tutte sul posto **2** *(frm)* PL *of* medium N **2**

media circus N carrozzone *m* dell'informazione

me·di·aeval [,mɛdɪ'i:vəl] ADJ = **medieval**

me·dian ['mi:dɪən] N *(Math, Statistics)* mediana; *(Am: also:* **median strip***)* banchina *f* spartitraffico *inv*

media research N sondaggio tra gli utenti dei mass media

media studies N studi *mpl* in scienze della comunicazione

me·di·ate ['mi:dɪ,eɪt] VI fare da mediatore(-trice)
■ VT *(settlement)* mediare

me·dia·tion [,mi:dɪ'eɪʃən] N mediazione *f*

me·dia·tor ['mi:dɪeɪtə^r] N mediatore(-trice)

med·ic ['mɛdɪk] N *(fam: doctor)* dottore(-essa); *(: student)* studente(-essa) di medicina; **a final year medic** uno studente all'ultimo anno di medicina

Medi·caid ['mɛdɪˌkeɪd] N *(Am) programma di assistenza medica ai poveri*

MEDICAID, MEDICARE

Negli Stati Uniti si chiama **Medicaid** l'assistenza medica e ospedaliera sovvenzionata congiuntamente dal governo federale e da quello statale. Ne hanno diritto i cittadini al di sotto dei 65 anni in base a fasce di reddito stabilite dal governo federale; i criteri di valutazione e il tipo di servizi offerti variano da stato a stato e possono comprendere cure non coperte dal **Medicare**.
Il **Medicare** è l'assistenza sanitaria sovvenzionata dal governo federale che copre parzialmente le spese mediche per i cittadini oltre i 65 anni, per i dializzati e i disabili. Gli assistiti versano un contributo mensile e possono usufruire dei servizi ospedalieri e medici convenzionati. Esiste inoltre un tipo di assistenza privata parallela e supplementare al **Medicare**, il "Medigap". Chi non è coperto dal **Medicare** o dal **Medicaid** paga di tasca propria l'assistenza sanitaria attraverso assicurazioni sanitarie private.
▷ www.cms.hhs.gov/about/default.asp
▷ www.medicare.gov/
▷ www.cms.hhs.gov/medicaid/

◎ **medi·cal** ['mɛdɪkəl] ADJ *(school, ward)* di medicina; *(test, treatment)* medico(-a); **the medical profession** il corpo dei medici; **medical treatment** cure *fpl* mediche; **a medical student** uno studente di medicina
■ N visita medica; **he had his medical last week** ha fatto una visita medica la settimana scorsa
medical board N commissione *f* sanitaria
medical certificate N certificato medico
medical examination N visita medica
medical examiner N *(Am)* medico legale
medical jurisprudence N medicina legale
medi·cal·ly ['mɛdɪkəlɪ] ADV dal punto di vista medico; **medically treated** curato(-a) da un medico
medical officer N *(Mil)* medico militare; *(Admin)* ufficiale *m* sanitario
medical school N facoltà *f inv* di medicina
medical student N studente(-essa) di medicina
Medi·care ['mɛdɪˌkɛəʳ] N *(Am) programma di assistenza medica agli anziani*
medi·ca·ted ['mɛdɪˌkeɪtɪd] ADJ medicato(-a)
medi·ca·tion [ˌmɛdɪ'keɪʃən] N *(medicine)* medicinali *mpl*, farmaci *mpl*; **to be on medication** prendere medicinali
me·dici·nal [mɛ'dɪsɪnl] ADJ medicinale, medicamentoso(-a)
◎ **medi·cine** ['mɛdsɪn, 'mɛdɪsɪn] N **1** *(drug)* medicina; **to give sb a taste of his own medicine** *(fig)* rendere pan per focaccia a qn **2** *(science)* medicina
medicine cabinet, medicine chest N armadietto farmaceutico *or* dei medicinali
medicine man N stregone *m*
me·di·eval [ˌmɛdɪ'iːvəl] ADJ medievale, del medio evo; **medieval studies** medievalistica *sg*
me·dio·cre [ˌmiːdɪ'əʊkəʳ] ADJ mediocre
me·di·oc·rity [ˌmiːdɪ'ɒkrɪtɪ] N mediocrità *f inv*
medi·tate ['mɛdɪˌteɪt] VI: **to meditate (on *or* about)** meditare (su)
■ VT meditare
medi·ta·tion [ˌmɛdɪ'teɪʃən] N meditazione *f*
medi·ta·tive ['mɛdɪtətɪv] ADJ meditativo(-a)
Medi·ter·ra·nean [ˌmɛdɪtə'reɪnɪən] ADJ mediterraneo(-a); **the Mediterranean (Sea)** il (mar) Mediterraneo
◎ **me·dium** ['miːdɪəm] ADJ medio(-a); **small, medium or large?** piccola, media o grande?; **medium walk/trot** *(Horse-riding)* passo/trotto ordinario
■ N **1** *(spiritualist)* medium *m/f inv* **2** *(pl* **media** *or* **mediums***)* *(gen, Phys)* mezzo; **through the medium of the press** per mezzo della stampa; **an advertising medium** un organo di pubblicità; **the artist's medium** i mezzi espressivi dell'artista; *see also* media **3** *(midpoint)*: **a happy medium** una giusta misura *or* una via di mezzo **4** *(environment)* ambiente *m*, habitat *m inv*
medium-dry ['miːdɪəm'draɪ] ADJ *(wine)* semisecco(-a), demi-sec *inv*
medium-sized ['miːdjəmˌsaɪzd] ADJ *(tin, packet)* di grandezza media; *(clothes)* di taglia media
medium-term ['miːdɪəm'tɜːm] N: **to look at the medium term** fare una valutazione a medio termine
medium term ADJ a medio termine
medium wave N *(Radio)* onde *fpl* medie
med·lar ['mɛdləʳ] N *(also:* **medlar tree***)* nespolo; *(fruit)* nespola
med·ley ['mɛdlɪ] N *(mixture)* miscuglio, accozzaglia; *(Mus)* pot-pourri *m inv*, selezione *f*
me·dul·la [mɪ'dʌlə] N *(Anat: also:* **medulla oblungata***)* midollo allungato
Medusa [mɪ'djuːzə] N Medusa
meek [miːk] ADJ *(comp* **-er**, *superl* **-est***)* mite, umile; **meek and mild** mite come un agnello
meek·ly ['miːklɪ] ADV docilmente, umilmente
meek·ness ['miːknɪs] N mitezza, umiltà *f inv*
◎ **meet** [miːt] *(pt, pp* **met***)* VT
1 *(gen)* incontrare; *(coming in opposite direction)* incrociare; *(by arrangement)* rivedere, ritrovare; **to arrange to meet sb** dare appuntamento a qn; **I met Paul in town** ho incontrato Paul in città; **I'm going to meet my friends at the swimming pool** mi trovo con i miei amici in piscina; **she ran out to meet us** ci è corsa incontro; **to meet sb off the train** (andare a) aspettare *or* andare a prendere qn al treno; **the car will meet the train** ci sarà una macchina all'arrivo del treno; **I'll meet you at the station** verrò a prenderla (*or* a prenderti) alla stazione; **to meet sb's eye *or* gaze** incrociare lo sguardo di qn; **a terrible sight met him *or* his eyes** gli si presentò un orrendo spettacolo; **there's more to this than meets the eye** è molto più complicato di quanto possa sembrare a prima vista
2 *(for the first time)* fare la conoscenza di, essere presentato(-a) a; **meet my brother** le presento mio fratello; **come and meet my dad** vieni che ti presento mio padre; **pleased to meet you!** lieto di conoscerla!, piacere (di conoscerla)!
3 *(encounter: team, difficulty)* incontrare; *(face: enemy, danger, death)* affrontare; **to meet one's death** trovare la morte
4 *(satisfy: requirement, demand, need)* soddisfare, andare incontro a; *(: criticism, objection)* ribattere a; *(pay: bill, expenses)* far fronte a; **we agree to meet your expenses** siamo d'accordo a rimborsarle le spese
■ VI
1 *(gen)* incontrarsi; *(by arrangement)* darsi appuntamento, trovarsi; *(committee, society)* riunirsi; **we met by chance** ci siamo incontrati per caso; **until we**

Mm

meet again! arrivederci (alla prossima volta)!; **haven't we met before?** non ci conosciamo già?
2 *(join: rivers, teams, armies)* incontrarsi
■N *(Brit Hunting)* raduno *(dei partecipanti alla caccia alla volpe)*; *(Am Sport)* raduno (sportivo)
▸ **meet up** VI + ADV incontrarsi, vedersi; **to meet up with sb** incontrare qn; **they arranged to meet up with the others at eight o'clock** hanno stabilito di incontrarsi con gli altri alle otto
▸ **meet with** VI + PREP
1 *(success, difficulties, praise)* incontrare; *(welcome)* ricevere; **they met with an accident** hanno avuto un incidente
2 *(have meeting with)* incontrarsi con

◎**meet·ing** ['mi:tɪŋ] N 1 *(between individuals)* incontro; *(arranged)* appuntamento; *(interview)* intervista, colloquio; **their first meeting** il loro primo incontro; **the minister had a meeting with the ambassador** il ministro ha avuto un colloquio con *or* si è incontrato con l'ambasciatore 2 *(session: of club, committee, council)* riunione *f*: *of members, citizens, employees,* assemblea; **to call a meeting** convocare una riunione; **a business meeting** una riunione di lavoro; **Mrs Stark is in a meeting** la signora Stark è in riunione 3 *(Sport: rally)* raduno; *(Horse-racing)* riunione *f* ippica

meeting place N luogo d'incontro

meeting point area N *(at airport, station)* area *f* convocazione gruppi *inv*, meeting point *m inv*

mega... ['mɛgə] PREF mega...

mega·bit ['mɛgə,bɪt] N *(Comput)* megabit *m inv*

mega·bucks ['mɛgə,bʌks] NPL *(fam)* cifre *fpl* astronomiche

mega·byte ['mɛgə,baɪt] N megabyte *m inv*

mega·hertz ['mɛgə,hɜ:ts] N megahertz *m inv*

mega·lith ['mɛgəlɪθ] N megalite *m*

mega·lo·ma·nia [,mɛgələʊ'meɪnjə] N megalomania

mega·lo·ma·ni·ac [,mɛgələʊ'meɪnɪæk] N megalomane *m/f*

mega·phone ['mɛgə,fəʊn] N megafono

mega·star ['mɛgə,stɑ:ʳ] N *(fam)* famosissima star *f inv*

mega·store ['mɛgəstɔ:ʳ] N megastore *m inv*

mega·ton ['mɛgə,tʌn] N megaton *m inv*

mega·watt ['mɛgə,wɒt] N megawatt *m inv*

meio·sis [maɪ'əʊsɪs] N meiosi *f*

mela·mine ['mɛlə,mi:n] N melammina

mel·an·cho·lia [,mɛlən'kəʊljə] N *(old Psych)* malinconia

mel·an·chol·ic [,mɛlən'kɒlɪk] ADJ malinconico(-a)

mel·an·choly ['mɛlənkəlɪ] ADJ *(person)* malinconico(-a); *(duty, subject)* triste
■N malinconia

Mel·bourne ['mɛlbən] N Melbourne *f*
▹ www.melbourne.vic.gov.au
▹ www.melbourne.com.au

mê·lée ['mɛleɪ] N confusione *f*, mischia

mel·low ['mɛləʊ] *(comp* **-er**, *superl* **-est**) ADJ *(fruit)* ben maturo(-a); *(wine)* maturo(-a) e pastoso(-a); *(colour, light)* caldo(-a) e morbido(-a); *(person, character)* addolcito(-a) dall'età; *(sound)* melodioso(-a); **after a few glasses of wine he was quite mellow** dopo qualche bicchiere di vino era piuttosto brillo
■VI *(fruit, wine)* maturare, maturarsi; *(colour, sound)* attenuarsi, smorzarsi; *(person, character)* addolcirsi
■VT: **old age has mellowed him** con l'età si è addolcito

mel·low·ness ['mɛləʊnɪs] N *(of wine)* pastosità *f inv*; *(of colour, character)* dolcezza

me·lo·dious [mɪ'ləʊdɪəs] ADJ melodioso(-a)

me·lo·di·ous·ly [mɪ'ləʊdɪəslɪ] ADV melodiosamente

melo·dra·ma ['mɛləʊ,drɑ:mə] N melodramma *m*

melo·dra·mat·ic [,mɛləʊdrə'mætɪk] ADJ melodrammatico(-a)

melo·dra·mati·cal·ly [,mɛləʊdrə'mætɪkəlɪ] ADV in modo melodrammatico

melo·dy ['mɛlədɪ] N melodia

mel·on ['mɛlən] N melone *m*

melt [mɛlt] VT 1 *(gen)* sciogliere, struggere; *(metal)* fondere; **melted butter** burro fuso; **melt two ounces of butter in a saucepan** sciogliete sessanta grammi di burro in una casseruola 2 *(fig: heart)* intenerire; *(: anger)* far svanire; *(: person)* commuovere
■VI 1 *(gen)* sciogliersi, struggersi; *(metals)* fondersi; **it melts in the mouth** si scioglie in bocca; **the snow is melting** la neve si sta sciogliendo 2 *(fig: anger, determination)* svanire; *(: heart)* intenerirsi; **he melted into the crowd** si confuse tra la folla
▸ **melt away** VI + ADV *(snow, ice)* sciogliersi completamente; *(fog)* dileguarsi; *(fig: anger, anxiety, opposition)* svanire; *(: savings)* andare in fumo; *(: crowd)* disperdersi; **he melted away into the crowd** svanì tra la folla
▸ **melt down** VT + ADV fondere

melt·down ['mɛlt,daʊn] N melt-down *m inv*

melt·ing ['mɛltɪŋ] ADJ *(snow)* che si scioglie *(or* scioglieva *etc)*: *voice, look,* tenero(-a)
■N *(Chem)* fusione *f*

melting point N punto di fusione

melting pot N *(fig)* crogiolo; **to be in the melting pot** essere ancora in discussione

melt·water ['mɛlt,wɔ:təʳ] N acque *fpl* di fusione

◎**mem·ber** ['mɛmbəʳ] N *(gen)* membro; *(of club)* socio(-a), iscritto(-a); *(of political party)* iscritto(-a); **a member of NATO** un membro della NATO; **she's like a member of the family** è come una di famiglia; **"members only"** "riservato ai soci"; **member of staff** *(Scol, Univ)* insegnante *m/f*; **a member of the staff** *(gen)* una dipendente *m/f*; **member of the public** privato(-a) cittadino(-a)

member countries NPL paesi *mpl* membri

Member of Parliament N *(Brit)* deputato(-a)

Member of the European Parliament N eurodeputato(-a)

Member of the House of Representatives N *(Am)* membro della Camera dei Rappresentanti

◎**mem·ber·ship** ['mɛmbəʃɪp] N 1 *(state)*: **membership (of)** iscrizione *f* (a), adesione *f* (a); **I'm going to apply for membership** farò domanda d'iscrizione
2 *(number of members)*: **the club has a membership of 950** il club ha 950 iscritti

membership card N tessera (di iscrizione)

membership fee N tassa d'iscrizione

member state N stato membro

mem·brane ['mɛmbreɪn] N membrana

me·men·to [mə'mɛntəʊ] N ricordo, souvenir *m inv*

memo ['mɛməʊ] N ABBR (= **memorandum**) promemoria *m inv*; *(to staff)* comunicazione *f* interna *or* di servizio

> DID YOU KNOW ...?
> **memo** is not translated by the Italian word *memo*

mem·oir ['mɛmwɑ:ʳ] N *(essay)* saggio monografico; *(biography)* nota biografica

mem·oirs ['mɛmwɑ:z] NPL memorie *fpl*

memo pad N blocchetto per appunti

memo·ra·bilia [,mɛmərə'bɪlɪə] NPL cimeli *mpl*

memo·rable [ˈmɛmərəbl] ADJ *(day)* memorabile; *(beauty)* notevole
memo·ran·dum [ˌmɛməˈrændəm] N *(pl* **memoranda***)* *(gen)* promemoria *m inv*; *(Diplomacy, Comm)* memorandum *m inv*; *(within company)* comunicazione *f* interna *or* di servizio
me·mo·rial [mɪˈmɔːrɪəl] ADJ commemorativo(-a)
■ N monumento commemorativo; **as a memorial to** in commemorazione di; **a memorial service** una funzione commemorativa; **a war memorial** un monumento ai caduti
Memorial Day N *(Am)* *festa dei caduti in guerra*

MEMORIAL DAY

Negli Stati Uniti il **Memorial Day** è una festa nazionale per la commemorazione di tutti i soldati americani caduti in guerra. Le celebrazioni sono tenute ogni anno l'ultimo lunedì di maggio.
▷ www.usmemorialday.org/

memo·rize [ˈmɛməˌraɪz] VT imparare a memoria, memorizzare
◎ **memo·ry** [ˈmɛmərɪ] N **1** *(faculty, of computer)* memoria; **to have a good/bad memory** aver buona/cattiva memoria; **I've got a terrible memory** ho una pessima memoria; **loss of memory** amnesia, perdita di memoria; **I have a bad memory for faces** non sono molto fisionomista; **he recited the poem from memory** ha recitato la poesia a memoria
2 *(recollection)* ricordo; **happy memories** bei ricordi; **I have no memory of it** non me lo ricordo affatto **3** **in memory of** in memoria *or* ricordo di; **to the memory of** alla memoria di
memory bank N *(Comput)* blocco di memoria
memory card N *(Comput)* espansione *f* di memoria
memory chip N *(Comput)* scheda di memoria
memory loss N perdita della memoria
men [mɛn] NPL *of* **man**
men·ace [ˈmɛnɪs] N *(threat)* minaccia; *(fam: nuisance)* peste *f*; **he's a menace** è una peste; **a public menace** un pericolo pubblico
■ VT minacciare
men·ac·ing [ˈmɛnɪsɪŋ] ADJ minaccioso(-a)
men·ac·ing·ly [ˈmɛnɪsɪŋlɪ] ADV minacciosamente
me·nage [meɪˈnɑːʒ] N *(frm)* ménage *m inv*
me·nag·erie [mɪˈnædʒərɪ] N serraglio
mend [mɛnd] VT *(repair: fence, car, clothes)* aggiustare, riparare; *(darn)* rammendare; **to mend one's ways** *(improve)* correggersi; **to mend matters** risolvere le cose
■ VI *(broken bone)* rimettersi a posto
■ N: **to be on the mend** star migliorando, essere in via di guarigione
mend·ing [ˈmɛndɪŋ] N *(act)* rammendo; *(items to be mended)* cose *fpl* da rammendare
Menelaus [ˌmɛnɪˈleɪəs] N Menelao
men·folk [ˈmɛnˌfəʊk] NPL uomini *mpl*
me·nial [ˈmiːnɪəl] ADJ *(position)* subalterno(-a); *(work, task)* umile, servile
men·in·gi·tis [ˌmɛnɪnˈdʒaɪtɪs] N meningite *f*
me·nis·cus [mɪˈnɪskəs] N *(pl* **meniscuses** *or* **menisci** [mɪˈnɪsaɪ]*)* menisco
meno·pau·sal [ˌmɛnəʊˈpɔːzəl] ADJ *(woman)* in menopausa; *(symptoms, problems)* della menopausa
meno·pause [ˈmɛnəʊpɔːz] N menopausa
men·or·rha·gia [ˌmɛnɔːˈreɪdʒɪə] N menorragia
men·servants [ˈmɛnˌsɜːvənts] NPL *of* **manservant**
men's room N *(esp Am)*: **the men's room** la toilette degli uomini
men·strual [ˈmɛnstrʊəl] ADJ mestruale
men·stru·ate [ˈmɛnstrʊˌeɪt] VI avere le mestruazioni, mestruare
men·strua·tion [ˌmɛnstrʊˈeɪʃən] N mestruazione *f*
men·su·ra·tion [ˌmɛnsjʊəˈreɪʃən] N *(also Math)* misurazione *f*
mens·wear [ˈmɛnzˌwɛəʳ] N *(Comm: clothing)* abbigliamento maschile; *(also:* **menswear department***)* (reparto) abbigliamento uomo
◎ **men·tal** [ˈmɛntl] ADJ **1** *(gen)* mentale, della mente; *(ability, powers)* intellettuale; *(treatment)* psichiatrico(-a); **to make a mental note of sth** prendere mentalmente nota di qc; **mental patient** malato(-a) di mente; **mental strain** tensione *f* **2** *(fam: mad)* pazzo(-a)
mental age N età *f inv* mentale
mental arithmetic N calcolo mentale
mental defective N *(offensive)* ritardato(-a) mentale
mental handicap N handicap *m inv* mentale
mental hospital, mental home, mental institution N ospedale *m* psichiatrico
mental illness N malattia mentale
men·tal·ity [mɛnˈtælɪtɪ] N mentalità *f inv*
men·tal·ly [ˈmɛntəlɪ] ADV *(calculate)* mentalmente, a mente; **to be mentally handicapped** avere un handicap mentale; **she is mentally ill** è malata di mente; **the mentally handicapped** i portatori di handicap mentale
men·thol [ˈmɛnθɒl] N mentolo
■ ADJ al mentolo
◎ **men·tion** [ˈmɛnʃən] N menzione *f*, accenno; **it's hardly worth a mention** non è neanche il caso di parlarne
■ VT *(gen)* accennare a; *(name, person)* fare il nome di, menzionare; **I mentioned it to him** gliel'ho accennato; **he didn't mention it to me** non me ne ha parlato; **she didn't mention her unpleasant experience** non ha accennato alla sua spiacevole esperienza; **just mention my name** basta che tu faccia il mio nome; **all those people, too numerous to mention, who ...** tutti coloro che qui sarebbe troppo lungo elencare, i quali...; **I need hardly mention that ...** inutile dire che...; **I mentioned she might come later** ho detto che poteva passare più tardi; **not to mention** *or* **without mentioning** per non parlare di, senza contare; **don't mention it!** non c'è di che!, prego!
men·tor [ˈmɛntɔː] N mentore *m*
menu [ˈmɛnjuː] N *(also Comput)* menù *m inv*; **a set menu** un menù a prezzo fisso
menu bar N *(Comput)* barra degli strumenti
menu-driven [ˈmɛnjuːˌdrɪvn] ADJ *(Comput)* guidato(-a) da menù
MEP [ˌɛmiːˈpiː] N ABBR = **Member of the European Parliament**
mer·can·tile [ˈmɜːkənˌtaɪl] ADJ mercantile; *(law)* commerciale
mer·ce·nary [ˈmɜːsɪnərɪ] ADJ *(person)* mercenario(-a); *(motive)* venale
■ N mercenario
mer·cer·ize [ˈmɜːsəˌraɪz] VT mercerizzare
mer·cer·ized cot·ton [ˈmɜːsəˌraɪzdˈkɒtn] N cotone *m* mercerizzato
mer·chan·dise [ˈmɜːtʃənˌdaɪz] N merce *f*, merci *fpl*
■ VT commercializzare

Mm

mer·chan·dis·er ['mɜːtʃən,daɪzəʳ] N merchandiser *m inv*

mer·chan·dis·ing ['mɜːtʃən,daɪzɪŋ] N (*goods*) *articoli riportanti un logo pubblicitario, oppure i personaggi di un film, di un fumetto o simili*; (*Comm*) merchandising *m*

◎ **mer·chant** ['mɜːtʃənt] N (*trader*) commerciante *m/f*; (*shopkeeper*) negoziante *m/f*, commerciante *m/f*; **timber/wine merchant** commerciante di legname/vino

merchant bank N (*Brit*) banca d'affari

merchant banker N (*Fin*) dirigente *m/f* di una banca d'affari

mer·chant·man ['mɜːtʃəntmən] N (*pl* **-men**) (*ship*) mercantile *m*

merchant navy, (*Am*) **merchant marine** N marina mercantile
▷ www.mna.org.uk

merchant seaman N marinaio (di nave mercantile)

mer·ci·ful ['mɜːsɪfʊl] ADJ (*Rel*) misericordioso(-a); (*person*) compassionevole, pietoso(-a), clemente; **it was a merciful release** è stata una vera liberazione

mer·ci·ful·ly ['mɜːsɪfəlɪ] ADV (*act*) con clemenza, con misericordia; (*fortunately*) per fortuna

mer·ci·less ['mɜːsɪlɪs] ADJ spietato(-a)

mer·ci·less·ly ['mɜːsɪlɪslɪ] ADV spietatamente

mer·cu·rial [mɜː'kjʊərɪəl] ADJ (*unpredictable*) volubile

Mer·cu·ry ['mɜːkjʊrɪ] N (*Astron, Myth*) Mercurio

mer·cu·ry ['mɜːkjʊrɪ] N (*Chem*) mercurio

mer·cy ['mɜːsɪ] N pietà *f inv*, clemenza; (*Rel*) misericordia; **to be at the mercy of sb/sth** essere alla mercé *or* in balia di qn/qc; **to have mercy on sb** avere pietà di qn; **to be left to the tender mercies of sb** essere lasciato(-a) alle buone cure di qn; **it's a mercy that** è una fortuna che *+ sub*

mercy killing N eutanasia

◎ **mere** [mɪəʳ] ADJ (*formality*) semplice, puro(-a) (*before n*); (*thought*) solo(-a) (*before n*); (*chance, coincidence*) puro(-a) (*before n*); **she's a mere child** non è che una bambina, è solo una bambina; **the mere sight of him irritates her** solo a vederlo s'arrabbia; **she's a mere secretary** è una semplice segretaria; **by the merest chance** per mero caso; **it's a mere formality** è una semplice formalità; **a mere five percent** solo il cinque per cento; **the merest** il minimo; **the merest hint of criticism** il minimo accenno di critica

◎ **mere·ly** ['mɪəlɪ] ADV soltanto, semplicemente, non... che; **I merely said that ...** ho semplicemente detto che...

merge [mɜːdʒ] VT (*Comm*) fondere, unire; (*Comput*: *files, text*) unire
■VI **1** (*colours, sounds, shapes*): **to merge (into, with)** fondersi (con), confondersi (con); **to merge (with)** (*roads*) unirsi (a); (*river*) confluire (in); **the rivers merge here** i fiumi confluiscono qui **2** (*Comm*) fondersi, unirsi; **the companies merged last year** le compagnie si sono fuse lo scorso anno

◎ **mer·ger** ['mɜːdʒəʳ] N (*Comm*) fusione *f*

me·rid·ian [mə'rɪdɪən] N meridiano

me·ringue [mə'ræŋ] N meringa

me·ri·no [mə'riːnəʊ] N merino

mer·it ['mɛrɪt] N merito, valore *m*; **to look** *or* **inquire into the merits of sth** valutare *or* pesare i pro e i contro di qc; **to treat a case on its merits** trattare un caso con obiettività; **the idea has some merit** l'idea ha qualche valore
■VT meritare

meri·toc·ra·cy [,mɛrɪ'tɒkrəsɪ] N meritocrazia

meri·to·ri·ous [,mɛrɪ'tɔːrɪəs] ADJ (*frm*: *deed, service*) meritorio(-a)

mer·maid ['mɜːmeɪd] N sirena

mer·ri·ly ['mɛrɪlɪ] ADV allegramente

mer·ri·ment ['mɛrɪmənt] N allegria, gaiezza; (*laughter*) ilarità *f inv*

mer·ry ['mɛrɪ] ADJ (*comp* **-ier**, *superl* **-iest**) (*cheerful*) allegro(-a), gaio(-a), festoso(-a); (*Brit fam*: *tipsy*) brillo(-a); **Merry Christmas!** Buon Natale!

merry-go-round ['mɛrɪgəʊ,raʊnd] N giostra, carosello

merry·making ['mɛrɪ,meɪkɪŋ] N festeggiamenti *mpl*

me·sa ['meɪsə] N (*tableland*) mesa

mes·ca·line ['mɛskə,liːn] N mescalina

mesh [mɛʃ] N **1** (*in net*) maglia; **a 6-cm mesh net** una rete con maglie di 6 cm **2** (*network, net*) rete *f*; **wire mesh** rete *f* metallica **3** (*gears*): **in mesh** ingranato(-a)
■VI (*gears*) ingranare

mes·mer·ize ['mɛzmə,raɪz] VT ipnotizzare; **she was mesmerized** (*fig*) non riusciva a distogliere lo sguardo

◎ **mess** [mɛs] N **1** (*confusion of objects*) disordine *m*, confusione *f*; (*dirt*) sporcizia; (*awkward predicament*) pasticcio; **you look a mess!** guarda in che stato sei!; **to be (in) a mess** (*house, room*) essere in disordine, essere molto sporco(-a); (*fig*: *marriage, life*) essere un caos *or* un disastro; **my hair's a mess, it needs cutting** ho i capelli in disordine: devo tagliarli; **I'll be in a mess if I fail the exam** sarò in un bel guaio se non passerò l'esame; **to make a mess** fare un gran disordine dappertutto, sporcare dappertutto; **the dog has made a mess** il cane ha sporcato; **to make a mess of** (*dirty*) sporcare; (*tear*) strappare; (*wreck*) sfasciare; **to make a mess of one's life/career** rovinarsi la vita/la carriera; **I made a mess of the exam** ho fatto un pasticcio all'esame; **to be/get (o.s.) in a mess** (*fig*) essere/cacciarsi in un pasticcio **2** (*Mil*) mensa
▸ **mess about**, **mess around** (*fam*) VI + ADV (*waste time*) perdere tempo, trastullarsi; (*play the fool*) far confusione; (*in water, mud*) pasticciare; **what are you doing? — just messing about** cosa fai? — niente di speciale
■VT + ADV (*person*) menare per il naso; (*plans*) scombinare; **stop messing me about!** smettila di farmi perdere tempo!
▸ **mess about with**, **mess around with** (*fam*) VI + ADV + PREP (*plans*) fare un pasticcio di; **to mess about with sth** armeggiare *or* trafficare con qc; **stop messing about with my computer!** smettetela di trafficare con il mio computer!; **to mess about with sb** divertirsi con qn
▸ **mess up** VT + ADV (*room*) mettere sottosopra; (*dress*) sporcare; (*hair*) scompigliare; (*fig*: *plan, marriage, situation*) mandare a monte, rovinare; **you've messed up my cassettes!** hai incasinato le mie cassette!; **I messed up my chemistry exam** mi è andato male l'esame di chimica

DID YOU KNOW ...?
mess is not translated by the Italian word *massa*

◎ **mes·sage** ['mɛsɪdʒ] N messaggio; **to get the message** (*fig fam*) capire l'antifona

message board N (*Comput*) bacheca elettronica

message switching [-swɪtʃɪŋ] N (*Comput*) smistamento messaggi

mes·sag·ing ['mɛsɪdʒɪŋ] N (*Comput, Telec*) invio di messaggi

mes·sen·ger ['mɛsɪndʒəʳ] N (*gen*) messaggero(-a); (*in office*) messo
messenger boy N fattorino
mess hall N (*Mil*) mensa
Mes·si·ah [mɪ'saɪə] N Messia *m*
Messrs ['mɛsəz] MPL ABBR (*on letters*: = **messieurs**) Spett.
messy ['mɛsɪ] ADJ (*comp* **-ier**, *superl* **-iest**) (*dirty*: *clothes*) sporco(-a); (: *job*) che insudicia; (*untidy*) disordinato(-a); (*confused*: *situation*) ingarbugliato(-a); **she's such a messy person!** è una persona talmente pasticciona!; **painting can be a messy activity** dipingere è un'attività con cui ci si può sporcare molto; **her writing is very messy** ha una scritturaccia
Met [mɛt] N ABBR: **the Met** **1** (*Am*) = *the Metropolitan Opera* **2** (*Brit*) = **the Metropolitan Police**
met [mɛt] PT, PP *of* **meet**
meta·bol·ic [ˌmɛtə'bɒlɪk] ADJ metabolico(-a)
me·tabo·lism [mə'tæbəˌlɪzəm] N metabolismo
◎ **met·al** ['mɛtl] N metallo; **road metal** pietrisco
■ ADJ in metallo
■ VT massicciare
metal detector N metaldetector *m inv*
metal fatigue N fatica del metallo
me·tal·lic [mɪ'tælɪk] ADJ metallico(-a)
met·al·loid ['mɛtəˌlɔɪd] N metalloide *m*
met·al·lur·gist [mɛ'tælədʒɪst] N metallurgista *m*
met·al·lur·gy [mɛ'tælədʒɪ] N metallurgia
metal polish N lucido per metalli
metal·work ['mɛtlˌwɜːk] N (*craft*) lavorazione *f* del metallo
meta·mor·phic [ˌmɛtə'mɔːfɪk] ADJ metamorfico(-a)
meta·mor·phose [ˌmɛtə'mɔːfəʊz] VI: **to metamorphose into** (*frm*) trasformarsi in
meta·mor·pho·sis [ˌmɛtə'mɔːfəsɪs] N (*pl* **metamorphoses** [ˌmɛtə'mɔːfəsiːz]) metamorfosi *f inv*
meta·phor ['mɛtəfəʳ] N metafora
meta·phor·ic [ˌmɛtə'fɒrɪk], **meta·phor·ical** [ˌmɛtə'fɒrɪkəl] ADJ metaforico(-a)
meta·phori·cal·ly [ˌmɛtə'fɒrɪkəlɪ] ADV metaforicamente
meta·physi·cal [ˌmɛtə'fɪzɪkəl] ADJ metafisico(-a)
meta·physi·cal·ly [ˌmɛtə'fɪzɪkəlɪ] ADV metafisicamente
meta·phys·ics [ˌmɛtə'fɪzɪks] NSG metafisica
me·tas·ta·sis [mɪ'tæstəsɪs] N metastasi *f inv*
meta·tar·sus [ˌmɛtə'tɑːsəs] N metatarso
mete [miːt] VI: **to mete out** (*punishment*) infliggere
me·teor ['miːtɪəʳ] N meteora
me·teor·ic [ˌmiːtɪ'ɒrɪk] ADJ meteorico(-a); (*fig*) fulmineo(-a)
me·teor·ite ['miːtɪəˌraɪt] N meteorite *m*
me·teoro·logi·cal [ˌmiːtɪərə'lɒdʒɪkəl] ADJ meteorologico(-a)
me·teor·olo·gist [ˌmiːtjə'rɒlədʒɪst] N meteorologo(-a)
me·teor·ol·ogy [ˌmiːtɪə'rɒlədʒɪ] N meteorologia
▷ http://sciencepolicy.colorado.edu/socasp/toc_img.html
▷ www.worldweather.org
me·ter[1] ['miːtəʳ] N (*gen*) contatore *m*; (*parking meter*) parchimetro; **electricity meter** contatore dell'elettricità
me·ter[2] ['miːtəʳ] N (*Am*) = **metre**
meter maid N (*Brit*, *old fam*) vigilessa
me·thane ['miːθeɪn] N metano
metha·nol ['mɛθəˌnɒl] N metanolo
◎ **meth·od** ['mɛθəd] N **1** (*manner, way*) metodo, sistema *m*; **my method of working** il mio metodo di lavoro; **method of payment** modo *or* modalità *fpl* di pagamento **2** (*orderliness*) metodo; **there's method in his madness** la sua follia non è priva di logica
me·thodi·cal [mɪ'θɒdɪkəl] ADJ metodico(-a)
me·thodi·cal·ly [mɪ'θɒdɪkəlɪ] ADV metodicamente, con metodo, con ordine
Meth·od·ism ['mɛθədɪzəm] N metodismo
Meth·od·ist ['mɛθədɪst] ADJ, N metodista (*m/f*)
▷ www.methodist.org.uk/
meth·od·ol·ogy [ˌmɛθə'dɒlədʒɪ] N metodologia
meths [mɛθs] N ABBR (*Brit fam*) = **methylated spirit(s)**
me·thyl ['mɛθɪl] N metile *m*
meth·yl·at·ed spir·it(s) ['mɛθɪˌleɪtɪd'spɪrɪt(s)] N(PL) (*Brit*) alcol *m inv* denaturato
me·ticu·lous [mɪ'tɪkjʊləs] ADJ meticoloso(-a)
me·ticu·lous·ly [mɪ'tɪkjʊləslɪ] ADV meticolosamente
Met Office N ABBR (*Brit*): **the Met Office** (= the Meteorological Office) l'Ufficio meteorologico
◎ **me·tre**, (*Am*) **me·ter** ['miːtəʳ] N metro
met·ric ['mɛtrɪk] ADJ metrico(-a); **to go metric** adottare il sistema metrico decimale
met·ri·cal ['mɛtrɪkəl] ADJ (*also Poetry*) metrico(-a)
met·ri·ca·tion [ˌmɛtrɪ'keɪʃən] N conversione *f* al sistema metrico decimale
metric system N sistema *m* metrico decimale
metric ton N tonnellata
met·ro·nome ['mɛtrəˌnəʊm] N metronomo
me·tropo·lis [mɪ'trɒpəlɪs] N metropoli *f inv*
met·ro·poli·tan [ˌmɛtrə'pɒlɪtən] ADJ metropolitano(-a)
Metropolitan Police N (*Brit*): **the Metropolitan Police** la polizia di Londra
met·tle ['mɛtl] N: **to be on one's mettle** essere pronto(-a) a dare il meglio di se stesso(-a)
mew [mjuː] N miagolio
■ VI miagolare
mews flat [mjuːz flæt] N (*Brit*) *appartamentino ricavato da una vecchia scuderia*
Mexi·can ['mɛksɪkən] ADJ, N messicano(-a)
Mexican stand-off N (*Am*) punto morto, stallo
Mexican wave N (*Brit*) ola
Mexi·co ['mɛksɪkəʊ] N il Messico
Mexico City N Città *f inv* del Messico
mez·za·nine ['mɛzəniːn] N (*also*: **mezzanine floor**) mezzanino
mezzo-soprano [ˌmɛtsəʊsə'prɑːnəʊ] N (*voice, singer*) mezzosoprano *sm*
MFA [ˌɛmɛf'eɪ] N ABBR (*Am*: = **Master of Fine Arts**) master *m inv* in Belle Arti
mfr ABBR **1** = **manufacture** **2** = **manufacturer**
mg ABBR (= **milligram**) mg
Mgr ABBR **1** (= **Monseigneur, Monsignor**) mons. **2** (*Comm*) = **manager**
MHR [ˌɛmeɪtʃ'ɑːʳ] N ABBR (*Am*) = **Member of the House of Representatives**
MHz ABBR (= **megahertz**) MHz
MI ABBR (*Am Post*) = *Michigan*
mi [miː] N (*Mus*) mi *m inv*
MI5 [ˌɛmaɪ'faɪv] N ABBR (*Brit*: = **Military Intelligence 5**) *agenzia di controspionaggio*
MI6 [ˌɛmaɪ'sɪks] N ABBR (*Brit*: = **Military Intelligence 6**) *agenzia di spionaggio*
MIA [ˌɛmaɪ'eɪ] ABBR (*Am*: = **missing in action**); *see* **missing**
mi·aow [miː'aʊ] N miao
■ VI miagolare
mica ['maɪkə] N mica

Mm

mice [maɪs] NPL *of* **mouse**
Mich·ael·mas ['mɪklməs] N festa di San Michele
Michaelmas daisy N margherita settembrina
Michi·gan ['mɪʃɪgən] N Michigan *m*
▷ www.michigan.gov/
mick·ey ['mɪkɪ] N (*Brit fam*): **to take the mickey out of sb** prendere qn per i fondelli *or* in giro
mi·cro ['maɪkrəʊ] N microcomputer *m inv*
micro... ['maɪkrəʊ] PREF micro...
mi·crobe ['maɪkrəʊb] N microbio, microbo
micro·bi·ol·ogist [ˌmaɪkrəʊbaɪ'ɒlədʒɪst] N microbiologo(-a)
micro·bi·ol·ogy [ˌmaɪkrəʊbaɪ'ɒlədʒɪ] N microbiologia
▷ www.ishs.org/
micro-brewery ['maɪkrəʊˌbru:ərɪ] N piccola fabbrica di birra
micro·chip ['maɪkrəʊˌtʃɪp] N (*Elec*) microcircuito integrato, microchip *m inv*
micro·cir·cuit ['maɪkrəʊˌsɜ:kɪt] N microcircuito
micro·cli·mate ['maɪkrəʊˌklaɪmɪt] N microclima *m*
micro·com·put·er [ˌmaɪkrəʊkəm'pju:təʳ] N microcomputer *m inv*
micro·cosm ['maɪkrəʊˌkɒzəm] N microcosmo
micro·cred·it ['maɪkrəʊˌkredɪt] N (*Fin*) microcredito
micro·eco·nom·ic [ˌmaɪkrəʊˌi:kə'nɒmɪk] ADJ microeconomico(-a)
micro·eco·nom·ics [ˌmaɪkrəʊˌi:kə'nɒmɪks] NSG microeconomia
micro·elec·tron·ics [ˌmaɪkrəʊɪlɛk'trɒnɪks] NSG microelettronica
micro·fi·bre ['maɪkrəʊˌfaɪbəʳ] N microfibra
micro·fiche ['maɪkrəʊˌfi:ʃ] N microfiche *f inv*
micro·film ['maɪkrəʊˌfɪlm] N microfilm *m inv*
■ VT microfilmare
micro·graph ['maɪkrəʊˌgræf] N microfotografia
mi·crog·ra·phy [maɪ'krɒgrəfɪ] N microfotografia
micro·light ['maɪkrəʊˌlaɪt] N aereo *m* biposto *inv*
micro·man·age ['maɪkrəʊˌmænɪdʒ] VT (*business*) dirigere in modo troppo capillare
micro·mesh ['maɪkrəʊˌmɛʃ] ADJ (*stockings*) a rete finissima, velato(-a)
mi·crom·eter [maɪ'krɒmɪtəʳ] N micrometro, palmer *m inv*
mi·cron ['maɪkrɒn] N micron *m inv*
micro·or·gan·ism [ˌmaɪkrəʊ'ɔ:gəˌnɪzəm] N microorganismo
micro·phone ['maɪkrəˌfəʊn] N microfono
micro·pro·ces·sor [ˌmaɪkrəʊ'prəʊsɛsəʳ] N microprocessore *m*
micro-scooter ['maɪkrəʊˌsku:təʳ] N monopattino
micro·scope ['maɪkrəskəʊp] N microscopio; **light microscope** microscopio ottico; **electron microscope** microscopio elettronico; **under the microscope** al microscopio
micro·scop·ic [ˌmaɪkrə'skɒpɪk], **micro·scop·ical** [ˌmaɪkrə'skɒpɪkəl] ADJ microscopico(-a)
micro·sec·ond ['maɪkrəʊˌsɛkənd] N microsecondo
micro·site ['maɪkrəʊˌsaɪt] N (*Comput*) microsito
micro·sur·gery ['maɪkrəʊˌsɜ:dʒərɪ] N (*Med*) microchirurgia
micro·wav·able, **microwaveable** ['maɪkrəʊˌweɪvəbl] ADJ adatto(-a) al forno a microonde
micro·wave ['maɪkrəʊˌweɪv] N microonda; (*also:* **microwave oven**) (forno a) microonde *m*
mid [mɪd] ADJ: **mid morning** a metà (della) mattina; **mid afternoon** metà pomeriggio; **in mid journey** a metà del viaggio; **in mid June** a metà giugno; **in mid air** a mezz'aria; **to leave sth in mid air** (*fig*) lasciare qc in sospeso; **in mid Atlantic** in mezzo all'Atlantico; **he's in his mid thirties** avrà circa trentacinque anni
Midas ['maɪdəs] N Mida *m*; **he has the Midas touch** (*fig*) tutto ciò che tocca si trasforma in oro
mid·day [ˌmɪd'deɪ] N mezzogiorno; **at midday** a mezzogiorno
■ ADJ di mezzogiorno
◎ **mid·dle** ['mɪdl] ADJ (*of place*) di mezzo, centrale; (*in quality, size*) medio(-a); **the middle seat** il sedile di mezzo; **the middle chair in the row** la sedia nel centro della fila
■ N (*centre*) mezzo, centro; (*fam: waist*) vita, cintura; **in the middle** in mezzo; **in the middle let's put ...** e in mezzo mettiamo...; **in the middle of** in mezzo a; **the car was in the middle of the road** la macchina era in mezzo alla strada; **the potatoes were still raw in the middle** le patate erano ancora crude dentro; **she was in the middle of her exams** era sotto esame; **in the middle of the field** in mezzo al campo; **a village in the middle of nowhere** un paese sperduto; **in the middle of summer** in piena estate; **in the middle of the night** nel cuore della notte, a notte fonda; **I'm in the middle of reading it** sto proprio leggendolo ora
middle age N mezza età *f inv*
middle-aged [ˌmɪdl'eɪdʒd] ADJ di mezza età
Middle Ages NPL: **the Middle Ages** il Medioevo
▷ www.mnsu.edu/emuseum/history/middleages
▷ www.learner.org/exhibits/middleages/feudal.html
Middle America N ceto medio americano
middle·brow ['mɪdəlˌbraʊ] (*pej*) ADJ (*fiction, play, film*) *per il lettore or spettatore ecc medio*
■ N chi ha una cultura media
middle C N (*Mus*) do sotto il rigo
middle-class [ˌmɪdl'klɑ:s] ADJ borghese, della borghesia
◎ **middle class** N: **the middle class(es)** ≈ la borghesia
middle-distance [ˌmɪdl'dɪstəns] ADJ (*runner*) di mezzofondo
middle distance N (*Art*): **in the middle distance** in secondo piano
◎ **Middle East** N: **the Middle East** il Medio Oriente
Middle England N ceto medio inglese
middle finger N medio
middle·man ['mɪdlˌmæn] N (*pl* **-men**) (*gen*) intermediario; (*Comm*) (agente *m*) rivenditore *m*
middle management N quadri *mpl* intermedi
middle name N secondo nome *m*
middle-of-the-road [ˌmɪdləvðə'rəʊd] ADJ moderato(-a)
middle school N ≈ scuola media (*per ragazzi dagli 8 o 9 anni ai 12 o 13 anni in Gran Bretagna e dagli 11 anni ai 14 anni negli Stati Uniti*)
middle·weight ['mɪdlˌweɪt] (*Boxing*) ADJ dei pesi medi
■ N peso medio
Middle West N (*Am*): **the Middle West** = **Midwest**
mid·dling ['mɪdlɪŋ] ADJ così così, medio(-a)
Middx. ABBR (*Brit*) = *Middlesex*
midge [mɪdʒ] N moscerino; (*biting*) pappataci *m inv*
midg·et ['mɪdʒɪt] N nano(-a)
MIDI ['mɪdɪ] N ABBR (*Comput* = **musical instrument digital interface**) interfaccia per collegare al computer strumenti musicali
midi system ['mɪdɪˌsɪstəm] N compatto
Mid·lands ['mɪdləndz] NPL: **the Midlands** *le contee del centro dell'Inghilterra*

mid·life crisis [ˌmɪdlaɪfˈkraɪsɪs] N crisi *f inv* di mezza età

◎ **mid·night** [ˈmɪdˌnaɪt] N mezzanotte *f*; **at midnight** a mezzanotte
■ ADJ (*gen*) di mezzanotte; (*attack*) a mezzanotte

midnight oil N: **to burn the midnight oil** lavorare *or* studiare fino a tarda notte

mid·point [ˈmɪdpɔɪnt] N: **at the midpoint of** (*road, event*) nel mezzo di

mid-range [mɪdˈreɪndʒ] ADJ di qualità media

mid·riff [ˈmɪdrɪf] N (*diaphragm*) diaframma *m*; (*stomach*) stomaco

mid·ship·man [ˈmɪdʃɪpmən] N (*pl* **-men**) aspirante guardiamarina *m inv*

midst [mɪdst] N: **in the midst of** in mezzo a; (*during*) durante; **in our midst** tra di noi, in mezzo a noi

mid·stream [ˈmɪdˌstriːm] N: **in midstream** (*of river*) al centro della corrente; **she paused** *or* **stopped midstream** (*fig*) si interruppe nel bel mezzo del discorso

mid·sum·mer [ˈmɪdˌsʌməʳ] N piena estate *f*

Midsummer('s) Day [ˈmɪdˌsʌmə(z)deɪ] N festa di San Giovanni (*24 giugno*)

mid·term [ˈmɪdˈtɜːm] N (*Scol, Univ: holiday*) *vacanza a metà trimestre*

mid·way [ˌmɪdˈweɪ] ADV, ADJ: **midway (between)** a metà strada (fra); **midway between London and Worcester** a metà strada tra Londra e Worcester; **midway through the afternoon** a metà pomeriggio; **a midway point** un punto a metà strada

mid·week [ˌmɪdˈwiːk] ADV, ADJ a metà settimana

Mid·west [ˌmɪdˈwɛst] N (*Am*): **the Midwest** il Midwest *m* (*regione medio-occidentale degli Stati Uniti*)

mid·wife [ˈmɪdˌwaɪf] N (*pl* **-wives**) ostetrica

mid·wife·ry [ˈmɪdˌwɪfərɪ] N ostetricia

mid·win·ter [ˌmɪdˈwɪntəʳ] N pieno inverno

mien [miːn] N (*liter*) contegno

miffed [mɪft] ADJ (*fam*) seccato(-a), stizzito(-a)

◎ **might¹** [maɪt] PT *of* **may**

might² [maɪt] N forza, potere *m*, forze *fpl*; **with all one's might** con tutte le proprie forze

mighty [ˈmaɪtɪ] ADJ (*comp* **-ier**, *superl* **-iest**) (*ruler, nation*) forte, potente; (*warrior*) possente; (*ocean*) vasto(-a); **a mighty bang** un forte colpo
■ ADV (*fam*) molto; **I'm mighty proud of it** ne sono molto orgoglioso

mi·graine [ˈmiːgreɪn] N emicrania

mi·grant [ˈmaɪgrənt] ADJ (*bird, animal*) migratore(-trice); (*worker*) emigrante, emigrato(-a); (*herdsman*) nomade
■ N (*see adj*) migratore(-trice); emigrante *m/f*; nomade *m/f*

mi·grate [maɪˈgreɪt] VI (*bird*) migrare; (*worker*) emigrare

mi·gra·tion [maɪˈgreɪʃən] N (*see vb*) migrazione *f*; emigrazione *f*

mike [maɪk] N ABBR (*fam*: = **microphone**) microfono

Mi·lan [mɪˈlæn] N Milano *f*

Mil·an·ese [ˌmɪləˈniːz] ADJ milanese, alla milanese
■ N INV milanese *m/f*

◎ **mild** [maɪld] ADJ (*comp* **-er**, *superl* **-est**) (*climate, punishment, weather*) mite; (*character, person, cheese, voice*) dolce; (*flavour, taste*) delicato(-a), non piccante; (*curry*) non piccante; (*illness, sedative, beer, cigar*) leggero(-a); (*effect*) blando(-a); **it's mild today** non fa freddo oggi; **the winters are quite mild** gli inverni sono abbastanza miti; **mild soap** sapone neutro
■ N (*Brit*) birra leggera

mil·dew [ˈmɪldjuː] N muffa

mil·dewed [ˈmɪlˌdjuːd] ADJ ammuffito(-a)

mild·ly [ˈmaɪldlɪ] ADV (*gently*) gentilmente, dolcemente, delicatamente; (*slightly*) vagamente; **to put it mildly** (*fam*) per usare un eufemismo, a dir poco

mild-mannered [ˌmaɪldˈmænəd] ADJ: **to be mild-mannered** essere dal carattere docile

mild·ness [ˈmaɪldnɪs] N (*of climate, punishment, weather, effect*) mitezza; (*of character, person*) mitezza, dolcezza; (*of cheese, dish*) sapore *m* delicato, delicatezza; (*of sedative, beer, cigar*) leggerezza; (*of illness*) non gravità *f inv*

◎ **mile** [maɪl] N miglio (*1609,33 m*); **nautical mile** miglio nautico; **to do 20 miles per gallon** ≈ fare cento chilometri con 14 litri; **miles and miles** ≈ chilometri e chilometri; **we walked for miles!** abbiamo fatto chilometri a piedi!; **they live miles away** abitano lontanissimo; **it stands** *or* **sticks out a mile** si capisce *or* si vede lontano un miglio; **you were miles better than him!** eri cento volte più bravo di lui!

mile·age [ˈmaɪlɪdʒ] N ≈ chilometraggio; **what mileage does your car do?** ≈ quanti chilometri al litro fa la tua macchina?

mileage allowance N ≈ rimborso per chilometro

mile·om·eter [maɪˈlɒmɪtəʳ] N (*Brit*) = **milometer**

mile·stone [ˈmaɪlˌstəʊn] N (*also fig*) pietra miliare

mi·lieu [ˈmiːljɜː] N ambiente *m* sociale

mili·tan·cy [ˈmɪlɪtənsɪ] N militanza

◎ **mili·tant** [ˈmɪlɪtənt] ADJ, N militante (*m/f*)

mili·ta·rism [ˈmɪlɪtəˌrɪzəm] N militarismo

mili·ta·ris·tic [ˌmɪlɪtəˈrɪstɪk] ADJ militaristico(-a)

◎ **mili·tary** [ˈmɪlɪtərɪ] ADJ militare
■ NPL: **the military** i militari, l'esercito

military service N servizio militare

mili·tate [ˈmɪlɪˌteɪt] VI: **to militate against** pregiudicare, essere di ostacolo a

mi·li·tia [mɪˈlɪʃə] N milizia, milizie *fpl*

◎ **milk** [mɪlk] N latte *m*; **tea with milk** tè con il latte; **it's no good crying over spilt milk** (*Proverb*) è inutile piangere sul latte versato
■ VT (*cow*) mungere; (*fig: person*) spillare quattrini a; (*: situation*) sfruttare fino in fondo

milk chocolate N cioccolato al latte

milk churn N bidone *m* per il latte

milk float N (*Brit*) furgone *m* del lattaio

milk·ing [ˈmɪlkɪŋ] N mungitura

milking machine N mungitrice *f*

milking parlour N sala di mungitura

milk jug N bricco del latte

milk·man [ˈmɪlkmən] N (*pl* **-men**) lattaio

milk of magnesia N latte di magnesia

milk pan N bollilatte *m inv*

milk pudding N budino al latte

milk round N (*Brit*) **1** (*delivery route*) consegna del latte a domicilio **2** (*Univ*): **the milk round** incontro tra aziende e studenti

milk shake N frappé *m inv*, frullato

milk tooth N dente *m* di latte

milk truck N (*Am*) = **milk float**

milky [ˈmɪlkɪ] ADJ (*comp* **-ier**, *superl* **-iest**) (*substance*) lattiginoso(-a); (*colour*) latteo(-a); (*coffee*) con tanto latte

Milky Way N: **the Milky Way** la Via Lattea

◎ **mill** [mɪl] N **1** (*gen*) mulino; (*Industry: for grain*) macina; (*also:* **windmill**) mulino a vento; (*small: for coffee, pepper*) macinino; **to go through the mill** (*fig*) passare un

Mm

periodo duro; **to put sb through the mill** (*fig*) mettere qn sotto torchio **2** (*factory*) fabbrica, stabilimento; **a woollen mill** un lanificio
■VT (*coffee, pepper, flour*) macinare; (*metal*) laminare; (*coin*) zigrinare
▸ **mill about**, **mill around** VI + ADV (*crowd*) brulicare, formicolare

mil·len·nium [mɪ'lɛnɪəm] N (*pl* **millennia**) (*period*) millennio; (*anniversary*) millenario; **the millennium** periodo (futuro) di pace e felicità; **millennium bug** baco del millennio

mil·ler ['mɪlə^r] N mugnaio

mil·let ['mɪlɪt] N miglio

milli... ['mɪlɪ] PREF milli...

mil·li·bar ['mɪlɪˌbɑː^r] N millibar *m inv*

mil·li·gram, **mil·li·gramme** ['mɪlɪˌɡræm] N milligrammo

mil·li·li·tre, (*Am*) **mil·li·li·ter** ['mɪlɪˌliːtə^r] N millilitro

mil·li·metre, (*Am*) **mil·li·meter** ['mɪlɪˌmiːtə^r] N millimetro

mil·li·ner ['mɪlɪnə^r] N modista

mil·li·nery ['mɪlɪnərɪ] N (articoli *mpl* di) modisteria

mill·ing ['mɪlɪŋ] ADJ: **the milling crowd** la folla in movimento

◎**mil·lion** ['mɪljən] N milione *m*; **a million women** un milione di donne; **two million euros** due milioni di euro; **thanks a million!** (*fam*) grazie mille!; **she's one in a million** (*fam*) come lei ce ne sono poche; **millions of** (*fam*) migliaia di, miliardi di; **you look like a million dollars** (*fam*) sei in forma smagliante

mil·lion·aire [ˌmɪljə'nɛə^r] N ≈ miliardario(-a)

◎**mil·lionth** ['mɪljənθ] ADJ milionesimo(-a)
■N (*in series*) milionesimo(-a); (*fraction*) milionesimo

mil·li·pede ['mɪlɪˌpiːd] N millepiedi *m inv*

mill·pond ['mɪlˌpɒnd] N: **the sea is like a millpond** il mare è liscio come l'olio

mill·race ['mɪlˌreɪs] N *corrente d'acqua che fa girare la ruota di un mulino*

mill·stone ['mɪlˌstəʊn] N macina, mola; **it's a millstone round his neck** è un grosso peso per lui, è una palla al piede per lui

mill·wheel ['mɪlˌwiːl] N ruota di mulino

mill worker N operaio(-a) di cotonificio

mi·lom·eter, **mile·om·eter** [maɪ'lɒmətə^r] N (*Brit*) ≈ contachilometri *m inv*

mime [maɪm] N (*play*) mimo; (*skill, gestures*) mimica; (*actor*) mimo(-a)
■VT, VI mimare
▹ www.mime.info

mim·ic ['mɪmɪk] N imitatore(-trice)
■VT (*subj: comedian*) imitare; (*: animal, person*) scimmiottare

mim·ic·ry ['mɪmɪkrɪ] N imitazioni *fpl*; (*Zool*) mimetismo

Min. ABBR (*Brit Pol:* = **ministry**) Min.

min. ABBR **1** (= **minute** or **minutes**) min
2 (= **minimum**) min

mina·ret [ˌmɪnə'rɛt] N minareto

mince [mɪns] N (*Brit Culin*) macinato, carne *f* macinata; **lean mince** carne macinata magra
■VT tritare, macinare; **he does not mince (his) words** non ha peli sulla lingua
■VI (*in walking*) camminare a passettini; (*in talking*) parlare con affettazione

mince·meat ['mɪnsˌmiːt] N *composto di frutta secca tritata e spezie usato in pasticceria*; **to make mincemeat of** (*fig: person*) ridurre in polpette; (*: argument*) demolire

mince pie N *tortino ripieno di frutta secca*
▹ www.britainexpress.com/articles/Food/mince-pies.htm

minc·er ['mɪnsə^r] N (*for meat*) tritacarne *m inv*; (*all-purpose*) tritatutto *m inv*

minc·ing ['mɪnsɪŋ] ADJ affettato(-a), lezioso(-a)

◎**mind** [maɪnd] N
1 (*gen*) mente *f*; (*intellect*) intelletto; **a case of mind over matter** una vittoria dello spirito sulla materia; **one of Britain's finest minds** uno dei più grandi cervelli della Gran Bretagna; **I am not clear in my mind about the idea** non ho le idee chiare in proposito; **to be uneasy in one's mind** avere dei dubbi, essere un po' preoccupato(-a); **what's on your mind?** cosa c'è che ti preoccupa?; **I can't get it out of my mind** non riesco a togliermelo dalla mente; **to put** *or* **set** *or* **give one's mind to sth** concentrarsi su qc, applicarsi a qc; **that will take your mind off it** questo ti aiuterà a non pensarci (più); **it'll keep your mind off the exam** ti distrarrà dall'esame; **to bear** *or* **keep sth in mind** (*take account of*) tener presente qc; (*remember*) tenere a mente qc, non dimenticare qc; **I'll bear that in mind** lo terrò presente; **it went right out of my mind** mi è completamente passato di mente, me ne sono completamente dimenticato; **to bring** *or* **call sth to mind** riportare *or* richiamare qc alla mente
2 (*inclination, intention*) intenzione *f*, idea; **to have sb/sth in mind** avere in mente qn/qc; **to have in mind to do sth** avere intenzione *or* in mente di fare qc; **what have you got in mind?** che cos'hai in mente?; **I have a good mind to do it** avrei molta voglia di farlo; **I have half a mind to do it** ho una mezza idea di farlo; **nothing was further from my mind** non mi era nemmeno passato per l'anticamera del cervello; **it never crossed my mind** non mi ha mai sfiorato la mente; **to change one's mind** cambiare idea; **he's changed his mind** ha cambiato idea
3 (*opinion*): **to make up one's mind** decidersi; decidere; **I haven't made up my mind yet** non ho ancora deciso; **to be in two minds about sth** essere incerto(-a) *or* indeciso(-a) su qc; **to be in two minds about doing sth** non sapersi decidere se fare qc o no; **of one mind** della stessa idea; **I am still of the same mind** sono ancora dello stesso parere; **to have a mind of one's own** (*person: think for o.s.*) saper pensare con la propria testa; (*: not conform*) avere delle idee proprie; **she's got a mind of her own** pensa con la sua testa; **my car has a mind of its own** la mia macchina fa un po' quello che vuole lei; **to my mind** a mio parere, secondo me
4 (*sanity*) cervello, mente *f*, testa; **to go out of** *or* **lose one's mind** impazzire, perdere la testa; **to be out of one's mind** essere pazzo(-a), essere uscito(-a) di senno, essere fuori di sé; **are you out of your mind?** sei impazzito?
■VT
1 (*pay attention to, be careful of*) fare attenzione a, stare attento(-a) a; **never mind** (*don't worry*) non preoccuparti; (*it makes no difference*) non importa, non fa niente; **"please mind the step"** "attenti *or* attenzione al gradino"; **mind you don't fall** attento a non cadere, fa' attenzione a non cadere; **mind your language!** bada a come parli!, controlla le tue parole!; **mind you, ...** (*fam*) sì , però va detto che...; **mind your own business!** (*fam*) fatti gli affari tuoi!; **never mind him** non badargli, non fargli caso; **never mind the**

expense se costa caro, pazienza!; **don't mind me!** (*iro*) per carità, non fare caso a me!
2 (*attend to, look after: shop, machine, children*) occuparsi di, badare a; **could you mind the baby this afternoon?** puoi occuparti del bambino questo pomeriggio?; **could you mind my bags for a few minutes?** può guardarmi le borse per qualche minuto?
3 (*be put out by, object to*): **I don't mind what he does** non m'importa cosa fa; **which? — I don't mind** quale? — è indifferente; **I don't mind the cold/noise** il freddo/rumore non mi dà noia *or* fastidio; **I don't mind getting up early** non mi dispiace alzarmi presto; **would you mind opening the door?** le dispiace aprire la porta?; **do you mind if I open the window? — I don't mind** le dispiace se apro la finestra? — faccia pure!; **I wouldn't mind a cup of tea** prenderei volentieri una tazza di tè

mind-altering ['maɪnd,ɒltərɪŋ] ADJ psicotropo(-a)

mind-bending ['maɪnd,bendɪŋ] ADJ (*substance*) psicotropo(-a); (*idea, concept etc*) difficile da comprendere

mind-blowing ['maɪnd,bləʊɪŋ] ADJ (*fam*) allucinante, che fa sballare

mind-boggling ['maɪnd,bɒglɪŋ] ADJ (*fam*) inconcepibile, incredibile

mind·ed ['maɪndɪd] ADJ (*frm*): **to be minded to do sth** essere intenzionato(-a) a fare qc

-minded ['maɪndɪd] ADJ SUFF: **fair-minded** imparziale; **an industrially-minded nation** una nazione orientata verso l'industria

mind·er ['maɪndə^r] N (*Brit: child minder*) bambinaia; (*: bodyguard*) guardia del corpo

mind·ful ['maɪndfʊl] ADJ: **mindful of** conscio(-a) *or* consapevole di, attento(-a) a, memore di

mind·less ['maɪndlɪs] ADJ (*violence, crime*) insensato(-a); (*task*) che non richiede nessuna intelligenza, idiota; **mindless vandals** vandali idioti

mind-numbing ['maɪnd,nʌmɪŋ] ADJ (*boredom, tedium*) mortale

mind-numbingly ['maɪnd,nʌmɪŋlɪ] ADV (*boring, tedious*) da morire

mind-reader ['maɪnd,ri:də^r] N chi legge nel pensiero; **you must be a mind-reader!** mi devi aver letto nel pensiero!

◎ **mine**[1] [maɪn] POSS PRON il/la mio(-a)
■ PL i/le miei/mie; **he's a friend of mine** è un mio amico; **is this your coat? – no, mine's black** è tuo questo cappotto? – no, il mio è nero; **this is mine** questo è (il) mio; **this book is mine** questo libro è mio; **these pencils are mine** queste matite sono mie; **your marks are better than mine** i tuoi voti sono migliori dei miei; **her shoes are nicer than mine** le sue scarpe sono più belle delle mie

mine[2] [maɪn] N **1** (*pit*) miniera; **a coal mine** una miniera di carbone; **to work down the mines** lavorare in miniera; **a mine of information** (*fig*) una miniera di informazioni **2** (*explosive*) mina; **to lay mines** posare delle mine; **there are still many unexploded mines in Kosovo** ci sono ancora molte mine inesplose in Kosovo
■ VT **1** (*coal, metal*) estrarre **2** (*Mil, Naut*) minare
■ VI fare degli scavi minerari; **to mine for sth** estrarre qc

mine detector N rivelatore *m* di mine

mine disposal N disinnesco di mine

mine·field ['maɪn,fi:ld] N (*also fig*) campo minato

mine·layer ['maɪn,leɪə^r] N posamine *m or f inv*

◎ **min·er** ['maɪnə^r] N minatore *m*

min·er·al ['mɪnərəl] ADJ (*substance, kingdom*) minerale; (*wealth, deposits, ore*) minerario(-a); **mineral salts** sali *mpl* minerali
■ N minerale *m*; (*Brit: soft drink*): **minerals** NPL bevande *fpl* gasate

min·er·al·ogic [,mɪnərə'lɒdʒɪk], **min·er·al·ogical** [,mɪnərə'lɒdʒɪkl] ADJ mineralogico(-a)

min·er·alo·gist [,mɪnə'rælədʒɪst] N mineralogista *m/f*

min·er·al·ogy [,mɪnə'rælədʒɪ] N mineralogia

mineral water N acqua minerale

Minerva [mɪ'nɜ:və] N Minerva

mine·sweeper ['maɪn,swi:pə^r] N dragamine *m inv*

mine sweep·ing ['maɪn,swi:pɪŋ] N dragaggio di mine

ming·er ['mɪŋə^r] N (*fam: ugly woman*) cozza

ming·ing ['mɪŋɪŋ] ADJ (*fam*) orribile

min·gle ['mɪŋgl] VT: **to mingle (with)** mescolare *or* mischiare (a *or* con); **excitement mingled with fear** eccitazione mescolata a paura
■ VI: **to mingle (with)** (*sounds*) mescolarsi *or* mischiarsi (a *or* con); **to mingle with one's guests** mescolarsi agli ospiti; **they ate and mingled** mangiarono e si mescolarono agli ospiti

min·gy ['mɪndʒɪ] ADJ (*Brit fam: person*) tirchio(-a), spilorcio(-a); (*: share, portion, amount*) misero(-a), scarso(-a)

mini ['mɪnɪ] N (*also:* **miniskirt**) mini *f inv*

mini... ['mɪnɪ] PREF mini...

minia·ture ['mɪnɪtʃə^r] N miniatura; **in miniature** in miniatura
■ ADJ (*gen*) in miniatura; (*poodle*) nano(-a)

minia·tur·ist ['mɪnɪtʃərɪst] N miniaturista *m/f*

minia·turi·za·tion [,mɪnɪtʃəraɪ'zeɪʃən] N miniaturizzazione *f*

minia·tur·ize ['mɪnɪtʃə,raɪz] VT miniaturizzare

minia·tur·iz·ed ['mɪnɪtʃə,raɪzd] ADJ miniaturizzato(-a)

mini·bar ['mɪnɪbɑ:^r] N minibar *m inv*, frigobar *m inv*

mini-break ['mɪnɪbreɪk] N breve vacanza

mini·bus ['mɪnɪ,bʌs] N minibus *m inv*, pulmino

mini·cab ['mɪnɪ,kæb] N (*Brit*) ≈ taxi *m inv*

mini·cam ['mɪnɪkæm] N piccola telecamera

mini·com·put·er [,mɪnɪkəm'pju:tə^r] N minielaboratore *m*, minicomputer *m inv*

Mini·disc® ['mɪnɪdɪsk] N minidisc *m inv*

mini·dish ['mɪnɪdɪʃ] N (*Telec*) antenna parabolica

min·im ['mɪnɪm] N (*Brit: Mus*) minima

mini·ma ['mɪnɪmə] NPL *of* **minimum**

mini·mal ['mɪnɪməl] ADJ minimo(-a)

mini·mal·ism ['mɪnɪməlɪzəm] N minimalismo

mini·mal·ist ['mɪnɪməlɪst] ADJ, N minimalista (*m/f*)

mini·market ['mɪnɪ,mɑ:kɪt] N minimarket *m inv*

mini·mize ['mɪnɪ,maɪz] VT minimizzare; (*Comput: window*) ridurre

minim rest N (*Mus*) pausa di minima

◎ **mini·mum** ['mɪnɪməm] N (*pl* **minimums** *or* **minima**) minimo; **he does the minimum of work** lavora il meno possibile *or* il minimo indispensabile; **to reduce to a minimum** ridurre al minimo
■ ADJ minimo(-a); **the minimum temperature** la (temperatura) minima; **minimum wage** salario minimo garantito

minimum lending rate N (*Brit*) ≈ tasso ufficiale di sconto

minimum wage N salario minimo

min·ing ['maɪnɪŋ] N **1** estrazione *f* mineraria, industria mineraria **2** (*Mil, Naut*) posa di mine

Mm

■ADJ (*industry, engineer, area*) minerario(-a); (*community, family*) di minatori
minion ['mɪnjən] N (*pej*) galoppino
mini-roundabout [,mɪnɪ'raʊndəbaʊt] N piccola rotonda
mini-series ['mɪnɪ,sɪəri:z] NSG miniserie *fsg*
mini-ski ['mɪnɪ,ski:] N minisci *m inv*
mini·skirt ['mɪnɪ,skɜ:t] N minigonna
◎**min·is·ter** ['mɪnɪstəʳ] N (*Brit Pol*) ministro; (*Rel*) pastore *m*; **Minister for Defence** Ministro della Difesa; **the Education Minister** il ministro della Pubblica Istruzione
■VI: **to minister to** (*sick person*) assistere; **to minister to sb's needs** provvedere ai bisogni di qn; **ministering angel** (*fig*) angelo del paradiso
min·is·terial [,mɪnɪs'tɪərɪəl] ADJ (*Brit Pol*) ministeriale
mini·stra·tions [,mɪnɪ'streɪʃənz] NPL assistenza, cure *fpl*
◎**min·is·try** ['mɪnɪstrɪ] N **1** (*Brit Pol*) ministero; **Ministry of Defence** Ministero della Difesa **2** (*Rel*): **the ministry** il ministero sacerdotale; **to go into** *or* **enter the ministry** diventare sacerdote (*or* pastore)
mini·van ['mɪnɪvæn] N (*Auto*) furgoncino
mink [mɪŋk] N visone *m*; **European mink** lutreola
mink coat N pelliccia di visone
Min·ne·so·ta [,mɪnɪ'səʊtə] N Minnesota *m*
▷ www.state.mn.us/
min·now ['mɪnəʊ] N *pesciolino d'acqua dolce*
◎**mi·nor** ['maɪnəʳ] ADJ (*also Math, Mus*) minore; (*detail, role*) secondario(-a), di poca importanza; (*importance*) secondario(-a); (*repairs, operation, expense*) piccolo(-a); **a minor problem** un problema secondario; **a minor operation** una piccola operazione
■N **1** (*Law*) minore *m/f*, minorenne *m/f* **2** (*Am Univ*) materia complementare
Mi·nor·ca [mɪ'nɔ:kə] N Minorca
◎**mi·nor·ity** [maɪ'nɒrɪtɪ] N minoranza; **to be in a minority** essere in minoranza
■ADJ (*verdict*) minoritario(-a); (*government*) di minoranza
Minos ['maɪnɒs] N Minosse *m*
Minotaur ['maɪnətɔ:ʳ] N Minotauro
min·ster ['mɪnstəʳ] N (*Brit*) cattedrale *f* (*annessa a monastero*)
min·strel ['mɪnstrəl] N giullare *m*, menestrello
mint¹ [mɪnt] N (*Fin*) zecca; **to be worth a mint (of money)** valere un patrimonio; **the (Royal) Mint** (*Brit*) *or* **the (US) Mint** (*Am*) la Zecca
■ADJ: **in mint condition** in perfette condizioni, che sembra nuovo(-a) di zecca
■VT (*coins*) battere, coniare; **he's minting money** (*fig*) sta facendo soldi a palate
mint² [mɪnt] N (*plant*) menta; (*sweet*) mentina, caramella di menta; **would you like a mint?** vuoi una mentina?
■ADJ alla menta
mint·ing ['mɪntɪŋ] N coniazione *f*
mint sauce N salsa di menta
minu·et [,mɪnjʊ'ɛt] N minuetto
mi·nus ['maɪnəs] PREP (*Math*) meno; (*fam: without*) senza; **sixteen minus three** sedici meno tre; **I got a B minus for my French** ho ricevuto B meno in francese; **minus two degrees** due gradi sotto zero; **I found my wallet, minus the money** ho ritrovato il mio portafoglio, ma senza il denaro
■ADJ: **minus quantity** (*Math*) quantità *f inv* negativa; **minus sign** (segno) meno *inv*
■N (segno) meno *inv*

mi·nus·cule ['mɪnəskju:l] ADJ piccolissimo(-a), minuscolo(-a)
◎**min·ute¹** ['mɪnɪt] N **1** (*of time*) minuto; (*of degree*) minuto, primo; **ten minutes** dieci minuti; **it is 5 minutes past 3** sono le 3 e 5 (minuti); **I'll come in a minute** vengo subito *or* tra un attimo; **wait a minute!** (aspetta) un momento!; **come here this minute!** vieni subito!; **I won't be a minute** vengo (*or* torno) subito; (*I've nearly finished*) faccio subito; **at the last minute** all'ultimo momento; **at that minute the phone rang** in quel (preciso) istante suonò il telefono; **tell me the minute he arrives** (non) appena arriva dimmelo; **up to the minute** (*fashions, news*) ultimissimo; (*equipment*) modernissimo **2 minutes** NPL (*of meeting*) verbale *m*, verbali *mpl*; **to take the minutes of a meeting** redigere i verbali di una riunione
min·ute² [maɪ'nju:t] ADJ (*small*) minuscolo(-a); (: *change, improvement*) piccolissimo(-a); (*detailed, exact*) minuzioso(-a); **in minute detail** minuziosamente; **her flat is minute** il suo appartamento è minuscolo; **a minute amount** una quantità minima
minute book ['mɪnɪt,bʊk] N libro dei verbali
minute hand ['mɪnɪt,hænd] N lancetta dei minuti
mi·nute·ly [maɪ'nju:tlɪ] ADV (*by a small amount*) di poco; (*in detail*) minuziosamente
minute steak ['mɪnɪt,steɪk] N fettina (di carne), paillard *f inv*
mi·nu·tiae [mɪ'nju:ʃɪ,i:] NPL minuzie *fpl*
mips [mɪps] NPL ABBR (*Comput* = **million instructions per second**) mips *mpl*
mira·cle ['mɪrəkl] N (*also fig*) miracolo; **it's a miracle that** è un miracolo che + *sub*; **by some miracle** per qualche miracolo; **to work miracles** (*also fig*) far miracoli
miracle cure N cura miracolosa
miracle drug N medicina miracolosa
miracle play N (*Theatre*) miracolo
miracle worker N: **I'm not a miracle worker** non posso fare miracoli
mi·racu·lous [mɪ'rækjʊləs] ADJ miracoloso(-a)
mi·racu·lous·ly [mɪ'rækjʊləslɪ] ADV miracolosamente
mi·rage ['mɪrɑ:ʒ] N miraggio
mire [maɪə] N pantano, melma
◎**mir·ror** ['mɪrəʳ] N specchio; (*Aut*) specchietto (retrovisore); **she got in the car and adjusted the mirror** è entrata in macchina e ha regolato lo specchietto; **hand mirror** specchio a mano; **pocket mirror** specchietto da borsetta; **to look at o.s. in the mirror** guardarsi allo specchio; **she looked at herself in the mirror** si è guardata allo specchio
■VT riflettere, rispecchiare
mirror image N immagine *f* speculare
mirror site N (*Comput*) sito *m* mirror *inv*
mirth [mɜ:θ] N ilarità *f inv*, gaiezza
mirth·less ['mɜ:θlɪs] ADJ (*smile, laugh*) mesto(-a)
mis·ad·ven·ture [,mɪsəd'vɛntʃəʳ] N sfortuna, disavventura; **death by misadventure** (*Brit Law*) morte *f* accidentale
mis·an·throp·ic [,mɪzən'θrɒpɪk] ADJ misantropico(-a)
mis·an·thro·pist [mɪ'zænθrəpɪst] N misantropo(-a)
mis·an·thro·py [mɪ'zænθrəpɪ] N misantropia
mis·ap·pli·ca·tion [,mɪsæplɪ'keɪʃən] N (*of technique*) uso improprio; (*of resources*) cattivo uso
mis·ap·ply [,mɪsə'plaɪ] VT impiegare male, usare erroneamente
mis·ap·pre·hen·sion ['mɪs,æprɪ'hɛnʃən] N equivoco,

malinteso; **to be (labouring) under a misapprehension** sbagliarsi
mis·ap·pro·pri·ate [ˌmɪsəˈprəʊprɪˌeɪt] VT appropriarsi indebitamente di
mis·ap·pro·pria·tion [ˈmɪsəˌprəʊprɪˈeɪʃən] N appropriazione *f* indebita
mis·be·have [ˌmɪsbɪˈheɪv] VI comportarsi male
mis·be·hav·iour, (*Am*) **mis·be·hav·ior** [ˌmɪsbɪˈheɪvjəʳ] N comportamento scorretto
misc. ABBR = miscellaneous
mis·cal·cu·late [ˌmɪsˈkælkjʊˌleɪt] VT, VI calcolare male
mis·cal·cu·la·tion [ˈmɪsˌkælkjʊˈleɪʃən] N errore *m* di calcolo
mis·car·riage [ˌmɪsˈkærɪdʒ] N **1** (*Med*) aborto spontaneo **2** **miscarriage of justice** (*fig*) errore *m* giudiziario
mis·car·ry [ˌmɪsˈkærɪ] VI **1** (*Med*) abortire **2** (*fail: plans*) andare a monte, fallire
mis·cast [ˌmɪsˈkɑːst] ADJ: **to be miscast** non essere adatto(-a) al ruolo
mis·cel·la·neous [ˌmɪsəˈleɪnɪəs] ADJ (*items*) vario(-a), diverso(-a); (*collection*) misto(-a), eterogeneo(-a); **miscellaneous expenses** spese *fpl* varie; **miscellaneous items** articoli *mpl* vari
mis·cel·la·ny [mɪˈsɛlənɪ] N misto; (*Literature*) miscellanea, raccolta; (*Radio, TV*) selezione *f*
mis·chance [ˌmɪsˈtʃɑːns] N: **by (some) mischance** per sfortuna
mis·chief [ˈmɪstʃɪf] N (*roguishness*) furberia; (*naughtiness*) birichinate *fpl*; (*maliciousness*) cattiveria, malizia; (*harm*) male *m*, danno; **he's always getting into mischief** ne combina sempre una; **to keep sb out of mischief** tenere qn occupato(-a) così che non possa combinare guai; **full of mischief** birichino(-a); **to make mischief (for sb)** rendere la vita difficile (a qn); **to make mischief between** seminare zizzania tra; **to do o.s. a mischief** (*Brit: hum*) farsi male
mischief-maker [ˈmɪstʃɪfˌmeɪkəʳ] N (*troublemaker*) chi semina discordia; (*gossip*) maldicente *m/f*
mis·chie·vous [ˈmɪstʃɪvəs] ADJ (*roguish*) malizioso(-a); (*: child*) birichino(-a); (*harmful*) pieno(-a) di cattiveria; **mischievous rumours** (*troublemaking*) malignità *fpl*
mis·chie·vous·ly [ˈmɪstʃɪvəslɪ] ADV (*roguishly*) maliziosamente; (*naughtily*) con aria birichina
mis·chie·vous·ness [ˈmɪstʃɪvəsnɪs] N (*roguishness*) maliziosità *f inv*; (*naughtiness*) birbanteria
mis·cible [ˈmɪsɪbəl] ADJ miscibile
mis·con·ceived [ˌmɪskənˈsiːvd] ADJ (*plan*) sbagliato(-a)
mis·con·cep·tion [ˌmɪskənˈsɛpʃən] N (*false idea/opinion*) idea/convinzione *f* sbagliata; (*misunderstanding*) malinteso
mis·con·duct [ˌmɪsˈkɒndʌkt] N cattiva condotta, comportamento scorretto; (*sexual*) adulterio; **professional misconduct** reato professionale
mis·con·struc·tion [ˌmɪskənˈstrʌkʃən] N interpretazione errata *f*
mis·con·strue [ˌmɪskənˈstruː] VT interpretare male
mis·count [ˌmɪsˈkaʊnt] N (*gen*) calcolo errato; (*in election*) conteggio erroneo
■ VT contare male
■ VI sbagliare il conto
mis·deed [ˌmɪsˈdiːd] N (*old*) misfatto
mis·de·mean·our, (*Am*) **mis·de·mean·or** [ˌmɪsdɪˈmiːnəʳ] N infrazione *f*, trasgressione *f*, misfatto
mis·di·rect [ˌmɪsdɪˈrɛkt] VT (*letter*) mettere l'indirizzo sbagliato su; (*person*) dare indicazioni sbagliate a, mal indirizzare; (*operation*) organizzare male; (*Law: jury*) dare istruzioni sbagliate a
mis·di·rect·ed [ˌmɪsdɪˈrɛktd] ADJ (*energies*) mal indirizzato(-a)
mi·ser [ˈmaɪzəʳ] N avaro(-a)
mis·er·able [ˈmɪzərəbl] ADJ **1** (*unhappy*) infelice; (*deplorable: sight, failure*) penoso(-a); **to feel miserable** sentirsi avvilito(-a) *or* giù di morale; (*physically*) sentirsi a terra; **don't look so miserable!** non fare quella faccia da funerale!; **a miserable life** una vita infelice **2** (*filthy, wretched*) miserabile; **miserable weather** brutto tempo **3** (*contemptible*) miserabile; **a miserable £2** 2 miserabili sterline; **a miserable failure** un fiasco
mis·er·ably [ˈmɪzərəblɪ] ADV (*smile, answer*) tristemente; (*fail, live, pay*) miseramente; **the attempt failed miserably** il tentativo è fallito miseramente
mi·ser·li·ness [ˈmaɪzəlɪnɪs] N taccagneria
mi·ser·ly [ˈmaɪzəlɪ] ADJ taccagno(-a), avaro(-a)

DID YOU KNOW ...?
miserly is not translated by the Italian word ***miserabile***

mis·ery [ˈmɪzərɪ] N (*unhappiness*) tristezza; (*pain*) sofferenza, tormento, dolore *m*; (*wretchedness*) miseria; (*fam: person*) lagna; **she's a real misery** è proprio una lagna; **all that money brought nothing but misery** tutto quel denaro non ha portato che tristezza; **to put an animal out of its misery** uccidere un animale (per non farlo soffrire più); **to put sb out of his misery** (*fig*) mettere fine alle sofferenze di qn; **to make sb's life a misery** rovinare la vita a qn
mis·fire [ˌmɪsˈfaɪəʳ] VI (*gun, plan, joke*) far cilecca; (*engine*) perdere colpi
mis·fit [ˈmɪsˌfɪt] N (*person*) disadattato(-a), spostato(-a)
mis·for·tune [mɪsˈfɔːtʃən] N disgrazia, sventura, sfortuna; **she has the misfortune to be blind** ha la sventura di essere cieca; **that's YOUR misfortune!** peggio per te!
mis·giv·ing [mɪsˈgɪvɪŋ] N (*often pl*) diffidenza, apprensione *f*, dubbi *mpl*, sospetti *mpl*; **to have misgivings about sth** essere diffidente verso qc, avere dei dubbi su qc
mis·guid·ed [ˌmɪsˈgaɪdɪd] ADJ (*person*) malaccorto(-a); (*conduct*) poco assennato(-a); **a misguided belief** una convinzione sbagliata
mis·guid·ed·ly [ˌmɪsˈgaɪdɪdlɪ] ADV (*attempt, try*) malaccortamente; (*believe, think*) in modo poco assennato
mis·han·dle [ˌmɪsˈhændl] VT (*object*) maneggiare senza precauzioni; (*person*) non prendere per il verso giusto; (*mismanage*) condurre male; **he mishandled the whole situation** ha sbagliato tutto
mis·hap [ˈmɪsˌhæp] N incidente *m*; **without mishap** senza incidenti; **a minor mishap** una piccola disavventura
mis·hear [ˈmɪsˈhɪəʳ] (*pt, pp* **misheard**) VT, VI capire male
mis·hit [ˌmɪsˈhɪt] (*Sport*) VT colpire male
■ N tiro sbagliato
mish·mash [ˈmɪʃˌmæʃ] N (*fam*) minestrone *m*, guazzabuglio
mis·in·form [ˌmɪsɪnˈfɔːm] VT informare male, dare informazioni erronee
mis·in·for·ma·tion [ˌmɪsɪnfəˈmeɪʃən] N disinformazione *f*
mis·in·ter·pret [ˌmɪsɪnˈtɜːprɪt] VT interpretare male
mis·in·ter·pre·ta·tion [ˈmɪsɪnˌtɜːprɪˈteɪʃən] N interpretazione errata *f*; **open to misinterpretation** che dà adito ad un'interpretazione errata

Mm

mis·judge [ˌmɪsˈdʒʌdʒ] VT *(distance, amount)* calcolare male; *(person)* giudicare male; **I may have misjudged him** posso averlo giudicato male; **the driver misjudged the bend** il guidatore ha valutato male la curva

mis·judge·ment, mis·judg·ment [ˌmɪsˈdʒʌdʒmənt] N errore *m* di valutazione

mis·kick [ˌmɪsˈkɪk] *(Sport)* VI sbagliare il tiro
■VT *(ball)* colpire male; *(penalty)* sbagliare
■N tiro sbagliato

mis·lay [ˌmɪsˈleɪ] *(pt, pp* **mislaid***)* VT smarrire

mis·lead [ˌmɪsˈliːd] *(pt, pp* **misled***)* VT trarre in inganno, sviare; **to mislead sb into thinking that ...** far credere a qn che..., indurre qn a credere che...

mis·lead·ing [ˌmɪsˈliːdɪŋ] ADJ ingannevole, fuorviante

mis·led [mɪsˈlɛd] PT, PP *of* **mislead**

mis·man·age [ˌmɪsˈmænɪdʒ] VT amministrare *or* gestire *or* condurre male

mis·man·age·ment [ˌmɪsˈmænɪdʒmənt] N cattiva amministrazione *f or* gestione *f*

mis·no·mer [ˌmɪsˈnəʊməʳ] N: **to call her a cook is a misnomer** non si può certo definirla una cuoca

mi·sogy·nist [mɪˈsɒdʒɪnɪst] N misogino

mi·sogy·nis·tic [mɪˌsɒdʒɪˈnɪstɪk] ADJ misogino(-a)

mis·place [ˌmɪsˈpleɪs] VT **1** *(mislay)* smarrire **2 to be misplaced** *(trust)* essere malriposto(-a)

mis·print [ˈmɪsˌprɪnt] N errore *m* di stampa, refuso

mis·pro·nounce [ˌmɪsprəˈnaʊns] VT pronunciare male

mis·pro·nun·cia·tion [ˈmɪsprəˌnʌnsɪˈeɪʃən] N pronuncia errata; **a mispronunciation** un errore di pronuncia

mis·quo·ta·tion [ˌmɪskwəʊˈteɪʃən] N citazione *f* errata

mis·quote [ˌmɪsˈkwəʊt] VT citare erroneamente

mis·read [ˌmɪsˈriːd] *(pt, pp* **misread***)* VT leggere male; *(misinterpret)* interpretare male

mis·re·mem·ber [ˌmɪsrɪˈmɛmbəʳ] VT sbagliarsi su

mis·rep·re·sent [ˈmɪsˌrɛprɪˈzɛnt] VT *(facts)* travisare; *(person)* dare un'impressione sbagliata di

◎**miss¹** [mɪs] N *(shot)* colpo mancato *or* a vuoto; **it was a near miss** *(fig)* c'è mancato poco *or* un pelo; **we had a near miss** per poco non ci è successo un incidente; **to give sth a miss** *(fam)* lasciar perdere qc; **he decided to give the film a miss** ha deciso di non andare a vedere quel film
■VT
1 *(gen: train, opportunity, film)* perdere; *(appointment, class)* mancare a, saltare; *(target)* mancare; *(remark: not hear)* non sentire; *(: not understand)* non capire; *(omit: meal, page)* saltare; **hurry or you'll miss the bus** affrettati o perderai l'autobus; **it's too good an opportunity to miss** è un'opportunità da non perdere assolutamente; **you haven't missed much!** non hai perso molto!; **he missed the target** ha mancato il bersaglio; **you've missed a page** hai saltato una pagina; **I missed you at the station** non ti ho visto alla stazione; **sorry to have missed you** mi dispiace di non averti trovato; **to miss the boat** *or* **bus** *(fig)* perdere il treno, lasciarsi sfuggire (di mano) l'occasione; **we must have missed the sign for London** ci dev'essere sfuggito il cartello per Londra; **you can't miss our house, it's ...** non puoi sbagliarti: la nostra casa è...; **don't miss this film** non perderti questo film; **I missed what you said** mi è sfuggito quello che hai detto; **you're missing the point** non capisci
2 *(escape or avoid: accident, bad weather)* evitare, scampare; **the bus just missed the wall** l'autobus per un pelo non è andato a finire contro il muro; **he narrowly missed being run over** per poco non è stato investito
3 *(notice loss of: money)* accorgersi di non avere più; **then I missed my wallet** allora mi sono accorto che mi mancava *or* che non avevo più il portafoglio
4 *(regret the absence of: person)*: **I miss you so** mi manchi tanto; **I miss him/it** sento la sua mancanza, mi manca; **I miss my family** sento la mancanza della mia famiglia; **do you miss Trieste?** senti la mancanza di *or* ti manca Trieste?
■VI *(person, shot)* mancare il bersaglio; **you can't miss!** non puoi fallire!
▸ **miss out** VT + ADV *(Brit)* saltare, omettere; **what about Sally? you've missed her out** e Sally? l'hai saltata
▸ **miss out on** VI + ADV + PREP *(fun, party)* perdersi; *(chance, bargain)* lasciarsi sfuggire; **I feel I've been missing out on life** sento di non aver goduto la vita come avrei potuto

miss² [mɪs] N **1** signorina; **the modern miss** la ragazza moderna **2 Miss Smith** la signorina Smith; *(on envelope)* Sig.na Smith; *(in letter)*: **Dear Miss Smith** Cara Signorina Smith; *(more frm)* Gentile Signorina Smith; **Miss World 1994** Miss Mondo 1994

mis·sal [ˈmɪsəl] N messale *m*

mis-sell [ˌmɪsˈsel] VT: **to mis-sell a pension** vendere un piano pensione inadatto alle esigenze del cliente

mis·shap·en [ˌmɪsˈʃeɪpən] ADJ deforme

◎**mis·sile** [ˈmɪsaɪl] N *(Mil)* missile *m*; *(frm: projectile)* proiettile *m*

missile base N base *f* missilistica

mis·sile launch·er [ˈmɪsaɪlˌlɔːntʃəʳ] N lanciamissili *m inv*

◎**mis·sing** [ˈmɪsɪŋ] ADJ *(not able to be found)* smarrito(-a), perso(-a); *(not there)* mancante; *(person: also Mil)* disperso(-a); **to be missing** *(thing)* mancare; *(persona)* mancare all'appello; **to go missing** sparire; **there are several books missing** mancano diversi libri; **the missing link** l'anello mancante; **missing in action** *(Mil)* disperso(-a) durante un'azione militare; **missing person** disperso(-a), scomparso(-a); **reported missing** *(Mil)* dato(-a) per disperso

◎**mis·sion** [ˈmɪʃən] N *(all senses)* missione *f*; **on a mission to sb** in missione da qn; **it's her mission in life** è la sua missione nella vita

mis·sion·ary [ˈmɪʃənrɪ] N *(Rel)* missionario(-a)

missionary position N: **the missionary position** la posizione del missionario

mission control N centro di controllo

mission statement N dichiarazione *f* di intenti

Mis·sis·sip·pi [ˌmɪsɪˈsɪpɪ] N *(state)* Mississippi *m*; *(river)*: **the Mississippi** il Mississippi
▷ www.mississippi.gov/index.jsp

mis·sive [ˈmɪsɪv] N *(old)* missiva

Mis·souri [mɪˈzʊərɪ] N Missouri *m*
▷ www.state.mo.us/

mis·spell [ˌmɪsˈspɛl] *(pt, pp* **misspelled** *or* **misspelt***)* VT sbagliare l'ortografia di

mis·spell·ing [ˌmɪsˈspɛlɪŋ] N errore *m* di ortografia

mis·spent [ˈmɪsˌspɛnt] ADJ: **his misspent youth** la sua gioventù dissoluta

mis·sus [ˈmɪsɪz] N *(fam)* **1 the missus** *(wife)* mia moglie; **how's your missus?** come sta tua moglie?
2 *(Brit: term of address)* signora

mist [mɪst] N *(Met)* foschia, nebbia, nebbiolina; *(on glass)* appannamento; *(of perfume)* nuvola; **through a mist of tears** attraverso un velo di lacrime; **lost in the**

mists of time (*fig*) perduto nella notte dei tempi
■ VI (*also:* **mist over**: *eyes*) velarsi; (*also:* **mist over** *or* **up**: *scene, landscape*) annebbiarsi, offuscarsi; (: *mirror, window, windscreen*) appannarsi

DID YOU KNOW ...?
mist is not translated by the Italian word *misto*

◎ **mis·take** [mɪs'teɪk] (*vb: pt* **mistook**, *pp* **mistaken**)
N errore *m*, sbaglio; **to make a mistake** (*in writing, calculating*) fare uno sbaglio *or* un errore; **he makes a lot of mistakes when he speaks English** fa molti errori quando parla in inglese; **a spelling mistake** un errore di ortografia; **to make a mistake (about sb/sth)** sbagliarsi (sul conto di qn/su qc); **my mistake!** è colpa mia!; **you're making a big mistake** commetti un grosso *or* grave errore; **I made the mistake of trusting him** ho fatto l'errore di fidarmi di lui; **by mistake** per sbaglio; **he took my hat in mistake for his** ha preso il mio cappello credendo fosse il suo; **there must be some mistake** ci dev'essere un errore; **make no mistake (about it)** non aver paura, sta' tranquillo; **she's pretty and no mistake** (*fam*) è proprio una bella ragazza
■ VT (*meaning, remark*) capir male, fraintendere; (*road*) sbagliare; (*time*) sbagliarsi su; **to mistake A for B** prendere *or* scambiare A per B; **he mistook me for my sister** mi ha scambiato per mia sorella

mis·tak·en [mɪs'teɪkən] PP *of* **mistake**
■ ADJ (*wrong: idea, conclusion*) sbagliato(-a), errato(-a); (*misplaced: loyalty, generosity*) malriposto(-a); **in the mistaken belief that ...** credendo erroneamente che...; **to be mistaken** sbagliarsi; **if I'm not mistaken** se non sbaglio; **if you think I'm going to pay, you're mistaken** se pensi che ho intenzione di pagare ti sbagli

mistaken identity N errore *m* di persona

mis·tak·en·ly [mɪs'teɪkənlɪ] ADV (*believe*) erroneamente; (*by mistake*) per errore

mis·ter ['mɪstəʳ] N (*fam*) signore *m*; *see also* **Mr**

mis·time [ˌmɪs'taɪm] VT (*action, blow*) calcolare male; **to mistime one's arrival** (*arrive inopportunely*) arrivare al momento sbagliato; (*miscalculate time*) sbagliarsi su *or* calcolare male il proprio orario d'arrivo; **the government mistimed its announcement** il governo ha emesso il comunicato al momento sbagliato; **a mistimed remark** un'osservazione poco opportuna

mis·tle thrush ['mɪsl,θrʌʃ] N tordela

mis·tle·toe ['mɪsl,təʊ] N vischio

mis·took [mɪs'tʊk] PT *of* **mistake**

mis·tral ['mɪstrəl] N: **the mistral** il mistral

mis·trans·late [ˌmɪstræns'leɪt] VT tradurre in modo sbagliato

mis·trans·la·tion [ˌmɪstrænz'leɪʃən] N errore *m* di traduzione, traduzione *f* errata

mis·treat [ˌmɪs'tri:t] VT maltrattare, trattare male

mis·tress ['mɪstrɪs] N **1** (*of servant*) padrona; **the mistress of the house** la padrona di casa **2** (*lover*) amante *f*; **he's got a mistress** ha un'amante **3** (*Brit Scol: teacher*) insegnante *f*, professoressa; **our English mistress** la nostra professoressa di inglese

mis·trust [ˌmɪs'trʌst] N: **mistrust (of)** diffidenza (nei confronti di); **a deep mistrust of politicians** una profonda diffidenza nei confronti dei politici
■ VT (*person, motives*) diffidare di; (*one's own abilities*) dubitare di

mis·trust·ful [mɪs'trʌstfʊl] ADJ: **mistrustful (of)** diffidente (nei confronti di)

mis·trust·ful·ly [mɪs'trʌstfəlɪ] ADV con diffidenza

misty ['mɪstɪ] ADJ (*comp* **-ier**, *superl* **-iest**) (*day, morning*) brumoso(-a), nebbioso(-a); (*mirror, window*) appannato(-a); **it's misty today** c'è foschia oggi

misty-eyed [ˌmɪstɪ'aɪd] ADJ trasognato(-a)

mis·under·stand [ˌmɪsʌndə'stænd] (*pt, pp* **misunderstood**) VT fraintendere, capire male; **maybe I misunderstood you** forse ho frainteso

mis·under·stand·ing [ˌmɪsʌndə'stændɪŋ] N malinteso, equivoco; **I think there's been some misunderstanding** penso che ci sia stato un malinteso

mis·under·stood [ˌmɪsʌndə'stʊd] PT, PP *of* **misunderstand**
■ ADJ incompreso(-a)

mis·use [*n* ˌmɪs'ju:s; *vb* ˌmɪs'ju:z] N (*of power, authority*) abuso; (*of word, tool*) uso improprio; (*of resources, time, energies*) cattivo uso
■ VT (*see n*) abusare di; usare impropriamente; fare cattivo uso di; **he misuses his position** abusa della sua posizione

MIT [ˌɛmaɪ'ti:] N ABBR (*Am*) = *Massachusetts Institute of Technology*

mite [maɪt] N **1** (*small quantity*) briciolo; **the widow's mite** (*Bible*) l'obolo della vedova **2** (*Brit: small child*): **poor mite!** povera creaturina! **3** (*Zool*) acaro

mi·ter ['maɪtəʳ] N (*Am*) = **mitre**

miti·gate ['mɪtɪ,geɪt] VT (*punishment*) mitigare; (*suffering*) alleviare

miti·gat·ing cir·cum·stances ['mɪtɪ,geɪtɪŋ 'sɜ:kəmstənsɪz] NPL circostanze *fpl* attenuanti

miti·ga·tion [ˌmɪtɪ'geɪʃən] N (*see vb*) mitigazione *f*; alleviamento

mi·to·sis [maɪ'təʊsɪs] N (*Bio*) mitosi *f*

mi·tral ['maɪtrəl] ADJ (*Anat*) mitralico(-a); **mitral valve** valvola mitrale

mi·tre, (*Am*) **mi·ter** ['maɪtəʳ] N **1** (*Rel*) mitra **2** (*Tech: also:* **mitre joint**) giunto ad angolo retto

mitt [mɪt] N **1** (*also:* **mitten**: *with cut-off fingers*) mezzo guanto; (: *no separate fingers*) muffola, manopola **2** (*baseball glove*) guantone *m* **3** (*fam*) zampa; **keep your dirty mitts off my stuff!** giù le zampe dalla mia roba!

◎ **mix** [mɪks] N mescolanza; **the school has a good social mix** gli studenti di questa scuola provengono da diverse classi sociali; **the film is a mix of science fiction and comedy** il film è un misto di fantascienza e commedia; **a cake mix** un preparato per torte
■ VT mescolare; (*cocktail, sauce*) preparare (mescolando); **mix to a smooth paste** mescolare fino ad ottenere una pasta omogenea; **to mix sth with sth** mischiare qc a qc; **to mix business with pleasure** unire l'utile al dilettevole; **mix the flour with the sugar** mescolate la farina con lo zucchero
■ VI mescolarsi; **he doesn't mix well** non riesce a legare; **he mixes with all sorts of people** ha a che fare con persone di ogni tipo; **they just don't mix** (*people*) non legano fra di loro; (*patterns*) non stanno bene insieme; **he doesn't mix much** non lega molto con gli altri
▸ **mix in** VT + ADV (*eggs*) incorporare
▸ **mix together** VT + ADV mescolare
▸ **mix up** VT + ADV **1** (*prepare: drink, medicine*) preparare **2** (*get in a muddle: documents*) confondere, mescolare;

Mm

(*confuse*): **to mix sb/sth up (with)** scambiare qn/qc (per); **the travel agent mixed up the bookings** l'agente di viaggio ha confuso le prenotazioni **3 to mix sb up in sth** (*involve*) coinvolgere *or* immischiare qn in qc; **to be mixed up in sth** essere coinvolto(-a) in qc; **she got herself mixed up with some shady characters** ha avuto a che fare con dei tipi loschi

◎**mixed** [mɪkst] ADJ (*biscuits, nuts*) assortito(-a); (*school*) misto(-a); **in mixed company** in presenza di persone di entrambi i sessi; **we had mixed weather** il tempo è stato un po' bello e un po' brutto; **I've got mixed feelings about it** ho dei sentimenti contrastanti a riguardo; **the announcement got a mixed reception** non tutti hanno accolto favorevolmente l'annuncio; **mixed metaphor** metafora che non sta in piedi; **I'm getting mixed up** sono disorientato

mixed-ability [ˌmɪkstˈbɪlɪtɪ] ADJ (*class, teaching*) alunni di capacità diverse

mixed bag N miscuglio, accozzaglia; **it's a mixed bag** (*fig fam*) c'è un po' di tutto

mixed blessing N: **it's a mixed blessing** è una cosa buona che ha il suo risvolto negativo

mixed doubles NPL (*Sport*) doppio misto

mixed economy N economia mista

mixed farming N agricoltura e allevamento di bestiame insieme

mixed grill N (*Brit*) grigliata mista

mixed marriage N matrimonio misto

mixed-up [ˌmɪkstˈʌp] ADJ (*person, ideas*) confuso(-a); (*papers*) mescolato(-a), in disordine; **I'm all mixed-up** sono disorientato

mix·er [ˈmɪksəʳ] N **1** (*for food: electric*) frullatore *m*, mixer *m inv*; (*: hand*) frullino **2** (*person*): **he's a good mixer** è molto socievole

mixer tap N (*Brit*) miscelatore *m*

mix·ing bowl [ˈmɪksɪŋˌbəʊl] N terrina

◎**mix·ture** [ˈmɪkstʃəʳ] N mistura, miscuglio, mescolanza; (*Med*) sciroppo; (*blend: of tobacco*) miscela; **a mixture of spices** un miscuglio di spezie

mix-up [ˈmɪksʌp] N (*fam*) confusione *f*

MK [ˌɛmˈkeɪ] ABBR (*Brit Tech*) = **mark¹** N **4**

mk ABBR = **mark²**

mkt ABBR = **market**

MLitt [ˈɛmˈlɪt] N ABBR (= **Master of Literature, Master of Letters**) master *m inv* in lettere

MLR [ˌɛmɛlˈɑːʳ] N ABBR (*Brit Fin*: = **minimum lending rate**) TUS *m* (= *Tasso Ufficiale di Sconto*)

◎**mm** ABBR (= **millimetre**) mm

MN [ˌɛmˈɛn] N ABBR **1** (*Brit*) = **Merchant Navy 2** (*Am Post*) = **Minnesota**

MO [ˌɛmˈəʊ] N ABBR **1** (*Brit*) = **medical officer 2** (*fam*) (= **modus operandi**) modo d'agire
■ABBR (*Am Post*) = **Missouri**

m.o. [ˌɛmˈəʊ] N ABBR = **money order**

moan [məʊn] N (*gen*) gemito, lamento; (*complaint*) lamentela, lagna
■VI (*gen*) gemere; **to moan (about)** (*fam: complain*) lamentarsi (di); **she's always moaning about sth** ha sempre qc di cui lamentarsi

moan·er [ˈməʊnəʳ] N (*fam*) brontolone(-a)

moan·ing [ˈməʊnɪŋ] N gemiti *mpl*, lamenti *mpl*

moat [məʊt] N fossato

mob [mɒb] N (*of people*) folla, massa; (*disorderly*) calca; (*rioting, violent*) folla inferocita; (*fam: criminal gang*) cricca, banda; **the mob** (*pej: Mafia*) la Mafia; (*: rabble*) la plebaglia
■VT (*person*) assalire, accalcarsi intorno a; (*place*) prendere d'assalto, accalcarsi intorno a; **to be mobbed** essere assalito(-a)

mob·cap [ˈmɒbˌkæp] N cuffia (*da donna*) con pizzi

◎**mo·bile** [ˈməʊbaɪl] ADJ (*gen*) mobile; **the old man is no longer mobile** il vecchio non può più muoversi; **she's ninety, but still mobile** ha novant'anni ma riesce ancora a camminare; **are you mobile today?** hai un mezzo oggi?; **applicants must be mobile** (*Brit*) i candidati devono essere disposti a viaggiare; **mobile studio** (*Radio, TV*) studio mobile
■N (*Art*) mobile *m inv*; (*Brit*) (telefono) cellulare *m*, telefonino

mobile home N grande roulotte *f inv* (*utilizzata come domicilio*)

mobile library N (*Brit*) biblioteca ambulante

mobile phone N telefonino

mobile phone operator N società *f inv* di fornitura servizi di telefonia mobile

mobile shop N (*Brit*) negozio ambulante

mobile unit N unità *f inv* mobile

mo·bil·ity [məʊˈbɪlɪtɪ] N mobilità *f inv*; (*of applicant*) disponibilità *f inv* a viaggiare

mobility allowance N *indennità che i portatori di handicap in Gran Bretagna ricevono dallo stato come rimborso alle spese sostenute per spostarsi o viaggiare*

mo·bi·li·za·tion [ˌməʊbɪlaɪˈzeɪʃən] N mobilitazione *f*

mo·bi·lize [ˈməʊbɪˌlaɪz] VT mobilitare
■VI mobilitarsi

mob·ster [ˈmɒbstəʳ] N (*Am*) gangster *m inv*

moc·ca·sin [ˈmɒkəsɪn] N mocassino

mock [mɒk] ADJ (*gen*) finto(-a), falso(-a); (*battle*) simulato(-a); **a mock exam** una simulazione d'esame; **mock Tudor** in stile Tudor
■VT (*ridicule: person*) canzonare, deridere, farsi beffe di; (*: plan, efforts*) ridicolizzare, farsi beffe di; (*mimic*) scimmiottare
■VI: **to mock at** farsi beffe di
▸ **mock up** VT + ADV costruire un modello di

mock·er [ˈmɒkəʳ] N chi prende in giro

mock·ery [ˈmɒkərɪ] N (*derision*) scherno, derisione *f*; **it was a mockery of a trial** il processo è stato tutto una farsa; **to make a mockery of** rendere ridicolo(-a)

mock·ing [ˈmɒkɪŋ] ADJ (*gen*) beffardo(-a), derisorio(-a), di scherno

mocking·bird [ˈmɒkɪŋˌbɜːd] N mimo (*uccello*)

mock·ing·ly [ˈmɒkɪŋlɪ] ADV (*smile*) beffardamente; (*speak*) con tono di scherno

mock turtle soup N *zuppa di testina di vitello, a imitazione della zuppa di tartaruga*

mock-up [ˈmɒkˌʌp] N modello dimostrativo, abbozzo

MOD [ˌɛməʊˈdiː] N ABBR (*Brit*) = **Ministry of Defence**; *see* **ministry**

mod [mɒd] N ABBR (*fam: person*: = **modernist**) mod *inv*

mod·al [ˈməʊdl] ADJ modale

mod cons [ˌmɒdˈkɒnz] NPL ABBR = *modern conveniences*; **all mod cons** (*fam*) tutti i comfort

mode [məʊd] N **1** (*gen*) modo, maniera; (*of transport*) mezzo; (*Mus*) modo; (*Comput*) modalità *f inv* **2** (*fashion, Math*) moda

◎**mod·el** [ˈmɒdl] N (*gen, fig, Archit*) modello; (*small-scale*) modellino; (*also:* **fashion model**) indossatore(-trice), modello(-a); (*also:* **artist's model**) modello(-a); **she's a famous model** è una modella famosa; **male model** indossatore, modello; **a model of the castle** un modellino del castello; **it's the basic model** è il modello base; **4-door model** (*of car*) versione *f* 4 porte
■VT **1 to model sth on** modellare qc su; **to model sb**

on prendere a modello per qn; **to model o.s. on sb** prendere a modello qn **2** (*make a model: in clay*) modellare, plasmare; (*: in wood*) scolpire **3** (*clothes*) indossare
■ VI (*Art, Phot*) fare da modello(-a), posare; (*fashion*) sfilare, fare l'indossatore(-trice) *or* il/la modello(-a)
■ ADJ **1** (*small-scale: village, aircraft*) in miniatura **2** (*prison, school, husband*) modello *inv*

model car N modellino di auto

mod·el·ling, (*Am*) **mod·el·ing** ['mɒdlɪŋ] N **1** (*Fashion*) professione *f* d'indossatore(-trice) *or* modello(-a) **2** (*Sculpture*) modellamento

modelling clay N creta per modellare

model railway N modellino di ferrovia, trenino in miniatura
▹ www.modelmaking.co.uk

mo·dem ['məʊdɛm] N modem *m inv*

◎ **mod·er·ate** [*adj* 'mɒdərɪt; *vb* 'mɒdə,reɪt] ADJ (*gen*) moderato(-a); (*climate*) temperato(-a); (*size, income*) medio(-a); (*demands, price*) modico(-a), ragionevole; (*language, terms*) misurato(-a); (*quality, ability*) mediocre, modesto(-a); **his views are quite moderate** ha opinioni abbastanza moderate; **a moderate amount of** un po' di; **I do a moderate amount of exercise** faccio un po' di ginnastica
■ N (*Pol*) moderato(-a)
■ VT moderare
■ VI (*pain, wind, anger*) calmarsi, attenuarsi, placarsi

mod·er·ate·ly ['mɒdərɪtlɪ] ADV (*act*) con moderazione; (*expensive, difficult*) non troppo, moderatamente; (*pleased, happy*) abbastanza, discretamente; **moderately priced** a prezzo modico; **it was moderately successful** ha avuto un discreto successo

mod·era·tion [,mɒdə'reɪʃən] N moderazione *f*, misura; **in moderation** (*eat, drink*) in quantità moderata, con moderazione; **patience and moderation** pazienza e moderazione

moderator ['mɒdə,reɪtə^r] N (*gen*) moderatore(-trice); (*Rel*) *moderatore in importanti riunioni della chiesa presbiteriana*

◎ **mod·ern** ['mɒdən] ADJ moderno(-a); **all modern conveniences** tutti i comfort

mod·ern·ism ['mɒdənɪzəm] N (*Art*) modernismo
▹ www.artsmia.org/modernism

mo·der·nity [mɒ'dɜ:nɪtɪ] N modernità *f inv*

mod·erni·za·tion [,mɒdənaɪ'zeɪʃən] N rimodernamento, modernizzazione *f*

mod·ern·ize ['mɒdə,naɪz] VT modernizzare

modern languages NPL lingue *fpl* moderne

◎ **mod·est** ['mɒdɪst] ADJ (*all senses*) modesto(-a); **to be modest about sth** non vantarsi di qc

mod·est·ly ['mɒdɪstlɪ] ADV modestamente

mod·es·ty ['mɒdɪstɪ] N modestia; **in all modesty** in tutta modestia

modi·cum ['mɒdɪkəm] N: **a modicum of** un minimo di

modi·fi·ca·tion [,mɒdɪfɪ'keɪʃən] N: **modification (to, in)** modifica (a); **to make modifications** fare *or* apportare delle modifiche

modi·fi·er ['mɒdɪ,faɪə^r] N (*Gram*) modificatore *m*

modi·fy ['mɒdɪ,faɪ] VT (*change: also Gram*) modificare; (*moderate: demands*) moderare

mod·ish ['məʊdɪʃ] ADJ (*liter*) à la page *inv*

Mods [mɒdz] N ABBR (*Brit*: = **(Honour) Moderations**) *primo esame all'università di Oxford*

modu·lar ['mɒdjʊlə^r] ADJ (*furniture, unit*) modulare

modu·late ['mɒdjʊ,leɪt] VT modulare

modu·la·tion [,mɒdjʊ'leɪʃən] N modulazione *f*

mod·ule ['mɒdju:l] N modulo

modu·lus ['mɒdjʊləs] N (*Math, Phys*) modulo

Moga·dishu [,mɒgə'dɪʃu:] N Mogadiscio *f*

mog·gy, mog·gie ['mɒgɪ] N (*Brit*) micio

mo·gul ['məʊgəl] N **1** (*fig*) magnate *m*, pezzo grosso **2** (*Skiing*) cunetta

MOH [,ɛməʊ'eɪtʃ] N ABBR (*Brit*: = **Medical Officer of Health**) ≈ ufficiale *m* sanitario

mo·hair ['məʊ,hɛə^r] N mohair *m*

Mohammed [məʊ'hæmɪd] N Maometto

Mo·ham·med·an [məʊ'hæmɪdən] ADJ, N maomettano(-a)

Mo·ham·med·an·ism [məʊ'hæmɪdə,nɪzəm] N maomettismo

moi·ré ['mwɑ:reɪ] ADJ moiré *inv*, marezzato(-a)

moist [mɔɪst] ADJ (*comp* **-er**, *superl* **-est**) (*gen*) umido(-a); (*cake*) soffice; **eyes moist with tears** occhi umidi di lacrime; **sow the seeds in moist soil** piantate i semi nel terreno umido; **this cake is very moist** questa torta è molto soffice

mois·ten ['mɔɪsn] VT inumidire; **to moisten one's lips** umettarsi le labbra

moist·ness ['mɔɪstnɪs] N (*see adj*) umidità *f inv*; sofficità *f inv*

mois·ture ['mɔɪstʃə^r] N (*gen*) umidità *f inv*; (*on glass*) vapore *m* condensato

mois·tur·ize ['mɔɪstʃə,raɪz] VT (*skin*) idratare

mois·tur·iz·er ['mɔɪstʃə,raɪzə^r] N (prodotto) idratante *m*

mo·lar ['məʊlə^r] ADJ, N molare (*m*)

mo·las·ses [məʊ'læsɪz] NSG melassa

mold *etc* [məʊld] (*Am*) = **mould** *etc*

Mol·da·via [,mɒl'deɪvɪə], **Mol·dova** [mɒl'dəʊvə] N la Moldavia

Mol·da·vian [,mɒl'deɪvɪən], **Mol·dovan** [mɒl'dəʊvən] ADJ, N moldavo(-a)

mole[1] [məʊl] N (*Zool*: *fig*) talpa

DID YOU KNOW ...?
mole is not translated by the Italian word *mole*

mole[2] [məʊl] N (*on skin*) neo; **I've got a mole on my back** ho un neo sulla schiena

mole[3] [məʊl] N (*Chem*) mole *f*

mole[4] [məʊl] N (*breakwater*) frangiflutti *m inv*

mo·lecu·lar [məʊ'lɛkjʊlə^r] ADJ molecolare

mol·ecule ['mɒlɪkju:l] N molecola

mole·hill ['məʊl,hɪl] N *cumulo di terra vicino alla tana scavata da una talpa*

mole·skin ['məʊl,skɪn] N (*fur*) (pelliccia di) talpa; (*Textiles*) fustagno

mo·lest [məʊ'lɛst] VT (*trouble*) importunare; (*harm*: *Law*: *sexually*) molestare

mol·li·fy ['mɒlɪ,faɪ] VT rabbonire, ammansire

mol·lusc, (*Am*) **mol·lusk** ['mɒləsk] N mollusco

molly·coddle ['mɒlɪ,kɒdl] VT (*pej*) coccolare, vezzeggiare

Molotov cock·tail ['mɒlə,tɒf'kɒk,teɪl] N (bottiglia) Molotov *f inv*

molt [məʊt] VI (*Am*) = **moult**

mol·ten ['məʊltən] ADJ (*metal*) fuso(-a); (*lava*) allo stato liquido

mom [mɒm] N (*Am fam*) = **mum**

◎ **mo·ment** ['məʊmənt] N **1** momento, istante *m*; **(at) any moment** *or* **any moment now** da un momento all'altro; **at the (present) moment** *or* **at this moment in time** al momento, in questo momento; **at the last moment** all'ultimo momento; **for a** *or* **one moment**

Mm

per un momento; **for the moment** per il momento, per ora; **not for a** *or* **one moment** neanche per un istante; **in a moment** *(very soon)* tra un momento; *(quickly)* in un attimo; **one moment!** *or* **wait a moment!** (aspetta) un momento *or* un attimo!; **I won't be a moment** vengo (*or* torno) subito; *(I've nearly finished)* faccio subito; **it won't take a moment** è (solo) questione di un attimo; **I've just this moment heard about it** l'ho saputo in questo (preciso) istante; **the moment he arrives** (non) appena arriva; **from the moment I saw him** dal primo momento in cui l'ho visto; **the man of the moment** l'uomo del momento; **"one moment please"** *(Telec)* "attenda, prego" **2** *(Phys)* momento **3** *(frm: importance)* importanza, rilievo

mo·men·tari·ly ['məʊməntərɪlɪ] ADV *(for a second)* per un momento; *(Am: very soon)* da un momento all'altro

mo·men·tary ['məʊməntərɪ] ADJ momentaneo(-a), passeggero(-a)

moment of truth N: **the moment of truth** il momento della verità

mo·men·tous [məʊ'mɛntəs] ADJ (molto) importante, di grande importanza

mo·men·tum [məʊ'mɛntəm] N *(Phys)* momento, quantità *f inv* di moto; *(fig)* slancio, impeto, velocità *f inv* acquisita; **to gather** *or* **gain momentum** *(vehicle, person)* acquistare *or* prendere velocità, aumentare di velocità; *(fig)* prendere *or* guadagnare terreno; **to lose momentum** *(vehicle, person)* perdere velocità; *(fig)* perdere vigore

mom·ma ['mɒmə] N *(Am fam)* mamma

mom·my ['mɒmɪ] N *(Am)* = **mummy**

Mon. ABBR (= **Monday**) lun. (= *lunedì*)

Mona·co ['mɒnə,kəʊ] N Monaco *f (Principato)*

mon·ad ['mɒnæd] N *(Chem, Philosophy)* monade *f*

mon·arch ['mɒnək] N monarca *m*

mon·ar·chism ['mɒnəkɪzəm] N monarchia

mon·ar·chist ['mɒnəkɪst] ADJ, N monarchico(-a)

mon·ar·chy ['mɒnəkɪ] N monarchia

mon·as·tery ['mɒnəstərɪ] N monastero

mo·nas·tic [mə'næstɪk] ADJ monastico(-a)

mo·nas·ti·cism [mə'næstɪ,sɪzəm] N monachesimo

Mon·day ['mʌndɪ] N lunedì *m inv*; *for usage see* **Tuesday**

Mon·egasque [,mɒnə'gæsk] ADJ, N monegasco(-a)

mon·etar·ism ['mʌnɪtə,rɪzəm] N monetarismo

mon·etar·ist ['mʌnɪtərɪst] ADJ monetaristico(-a)
■N monetarista *m/f*

◎**mon·etary** ['mʌnɪtərɪ] ADJ monetario(-a)

◎**mon·ey** ['mʌnɪ] N denaro, soldi *mpl*; **paper money** banconote *fpl*; **Italian money** moneta italiana; **I need to change some money** devo cambiare dei soldi; **there's money in it** c'è da farci i soldi; **I've got no money left** non ho più neanche una lira; **to make money** *(person)* fare (i) soldi; *(business)* rendere; **we didn't make any money on that deal** in quell'affare non ci abbiamo guadagnato niente; **that's the one for my money!** *(fam)* è quello su cui sono pronto a scommettere!; **it's money for jam** *or* **old rope** *(fam)* son soldi guadagnati senza fatica; **to be in the money** nuotare nell'oro, essere pieno(-a) di soldi; **to get one's money's worth** spender bene i propri soldi; **to earn good money** guadagnare bene; **money doesn't grow on trees!** non me li tirano mica dietro i soldi!; **I'm not made of money** non nuoto nell'oro; **your money or your life!** o la borsa o la vita!; **danger money** *(Brit)* indennità *f inv* di rischio

money·bags ['mʌnɪ,bægz] N *(fam pej)* riccone(-a)

money-box ['mʌnɪbɒks] N salvadanaio

mon·eyed ['mʌnɪd] ADJ danaroso(-a), ricco(-a); **the moneyed classes** le classi più abbienti

money-grubbing ['mʌnɪ,grʌbɪŋ] ADJ *(pej)* avido(-a) di denaro

money laundering N riciclaggio di denaro sporco

money·lender ['mʌnɪ,lɛndə^r] N chi presta soldi; *(pej)* usuraio(-a)

money·maker ['mʌnɪ,meɪkə^r] N *(Brit fam: business)* affare *m* d'oro

money·making ['mʌnɪ,meɪkɪŋ] ADJ che rende (bene *or* molto), lucrativo(-a)

money market N mercato monetario

money order N vaglia *m inv* (postale)

money-spinner ['mʌnɪ,spɪnə^r] N *(fam)* miniera d'oro *(fig)*

money supply N liquidità *f inv* monetaria

Mon·gol ['mɒŋgəl] N *(person)* mongolo(-a); *(language)* mongolo
■ADJ mongolo(-a)

mon·gol ['mɒŋgəl] N, ADJ *(offensive)* mongoloide *(m/f)*

Mon·go·lia [mɒŋ'gəʊlɪə] N la Mongolia

Mon·go·lian [mɒŋ'gəʊlɪən] ADJ *(people, tribe)* mongolo(-a); *(language)* mongolico(-a)
■N *(person)* mongolo(-a)

mon·go·lism ['mɒŋgə,lɪzəm] N *(offensive)* mongolismo

mon·goose ['mɒŋgu:s] N mangusta

mon·grel ['mʌŋgrəl] N *(dog)* (cane *m*) bastardo; **my dog's a mongrel** il mio cane è un bastardo

◎**moni·tor** ['mɒnɪtə^r] N **1** *(Brit Scol)* ≈ capoclasse *m/f (Am Scol)* chi sorveglia agli esami **2** *(TV, Tech: screen)* monitor *m inv*; *(Radio: person)* addetto(-a) all'ascolto delle trasmissioni dall'estero
■VT *(foreign station, broadcast)* ascoltare le trasmissioni di; *(machine, progress)* controllare; *(discussion)* dirigere, fare da moderatore(-trice) in *or* di

monk [mʌŋk] N frate *m*, monaco

mon·key ['mʌŋkɪ] N scimmia; *(fig: child)* birbante *m*
► **monkey about, monkey around** VI + ADV *(fam)* far lo/la scemo(-a); **to monkey about with sth** armeggiare con qc

monkey business N, **monkey tricks** NPL *(fam)* scherzi *mpl*

monkey nut N *(Brit)* nocciolina americana, arachide *f*

monkey puzzle N *(tree)* araucaria

monkey wrench N chiave *f* inglese a rullino

monk·ish ['mʌŋkɪʃ] ADJ da monaco

mono ['mɒnəʊ] ADJ mono *inv*; *(broadcast)* in mono
■N: **in mono** in mono

mono... ['mɒnəʊ] PREF mono...

mono·atom·ic [,mɒnəʊə'tɒmɪk] ADJ monoatomico(-a)

mono·ba·sic [,mɒnəʊ'beɪsɪk] ADJ monobasico(-a)

mono·chro·ma·tism [,mɒnəʊ'krəʊmə,tɪzəm] N monocromatismo

mono·chrome ['mɒnə,krəʊm] ADJ *(painting, print)* monocromatico(-a), monocromo(-a); *(television)* in bianco e nero

mono·cle ['mɒnəkl] N monocolo

mono·coque ['mɒnə,kɒk] ADJ, N monoscocca *(f) inv*

mono·coty·ledon [,mɒnəʊ,kɒtɪ'li:dən] N *(Bot)* monocotiledone *m*

mono·cul·ture ['mɒnəʊ,kʌltʃə^r] N monocoltura

mo·noga·mous [mɒ'nɒgəməs] ADJ monogamo(-a)

mo·noga·my [mɒ'nɒgəmɪ] N monogamia

mono·gram ['mɒnə,græm] N monogramma *m*

mono·grammed ['mɒnəgræmd] ADJ *(shirt, handkerchief)* con il monogramma

mono·graph ['mɒnəˌgrɑːf] N monografia
mono·lith ['mɒnəʊlɪθ] N monolito
mono·lithic ['mɒnəʊˌlɪθɪk] ADJ *(also fig)* monolitico(-a)
mono·logue ['mɒnəlɒg] N monologo
mono·ma·nia [ˌmɒnəʊ'meɪnjə] N monomania
mono·ma·ni·ac [ˌmɒnəʊ'meɪnɪæk] N monomaniaco(-a)
mono·mer ['mɒnəməʳ] N *(Chem)* monomero
mo·no·mial [mɒ'nəʊmɪəl] ADJ monomiale
■N monomio
mono·plane ['mɒnəʊpleɪn] N monoplano
Monopolies and Mergers Commission N *(Brit)* commissione *f* antimonopoli
mo·nopo·lize [mə'nɒpəˌlaɪz] VT monopolizzare
Mo·nopo·ly® [mə'nɒpəlɪ] N *(game)* monopoli® *m*
mo·nopo·ly [mə'nɒpəlɪ] N monopolio; **a state monopoly** un monopolio di stato
mono·rail ['mɒnəʊˌreɪl] N monorotaia
▷ http://faculty.washington.edu/~jbs/itrans/itrans2.htm
▷ www.monorails.org/
mono·sac·cha·ride [ˌmɒnəʊ'sækəˌraɪd] N monosaccaride *m*
mono·so·dium glu·ta·mate [ˌmɒnəʊ'səʊdɪəm'gluːtəˌmeɪt] N glutammato di sodio
mono·syl·lab·ic [ˌmɒnəʊsɪ'læbɪk] ADJ *(word, reply)* monosillabico(-a); *(person)* che parla a monosillabi
mono·syl·la·ble ['mɒnəˌsɪləbl] N monosillabo; **to speak/answer in monosyllables** parlare/rispondere a monosillabi
mono·theism ['mɒnəʊθɪˌɪzəm] N monoteismo
mono·theis·tic [ˌmɒnəʊθɪ'ɪstɪk] ADJ monoteistico(-a)
mono·tone ['mɒnəˌtəʊn] N: **in a monotone** con voce monotona, con tono monotono
mo·noto·nous [mə'nɒtənəs] ADJ monotono(-a)
mo·noto·nous·ly [mə'nɒtənəslɪ] ADV in modo monotono, monotonamente
mo·noto·ny [mə'nɒtənɪ] N monotonia
Mono·type® ['mɒnəˌtaɪp] N monotype® *f inv*
mon·ox·ide [mɒ'nɒksaɪd] N monossido
mon·soon [mɒn'suːn] N monsone *m*
mon·ster ['mɒnstəʳ] N mostro
■ADJ *(enormous)* gigantesco(-a)
mon·strance ['mɒnstrəns] N ostensorio
mon·stros·ity [mɒns'trɒsɪtɪ] N mostruosità *f inv*
mon·strous ['mɒnstrəs] ADJ *(huge)* colossale, enorme; *(dreadful)* mostruoso(-a); **it is monstrous that ...** è scandaloso *or* pazzesco che... + *sub*
mon·strous·ly ['mɒnstrəslɪ] ADV mostruosamente
mon·tage [mɒn'tɑːʒ] N montaggio
Mon·tana [mɒn'tænə] N Montana *m*
▷ www.discoveringmontana.com/
Mont Blanc [mɔ̃'blɑ̃] N il Monte Bianco
◎**month** [mʌnθ] N mese *m*; **last month** il mese scorso; **in the month of May** nel mese di maggio, in maggio; **300 dollars a month** 300 dollari al mese; **paid by the month** pagato(-a) mensilmente; **which day of the month is it?** quanti ne abbiamo (oggi)?; **every month** *(happen)* tutti i mesi; *(pay)* mensilmente, ogni mese
◎**month·ly** ['mʌnθlɪ] ADJ *(gen)* mensile; *(ticket)* valevole per un mese
■ADV mensilmente, ogni mese, al mese; **twice monthly** due volte al mese
■N *(magazine)* (rivista) mensile *m*
Mont·real [ˌmɒntrɪ'ɔːl] N Montreal *f*
▷ www.tourism-montreal.org
monu·ment ['mɒnjʊmənt] N monumento
monu·men·tal [ˌmɒnjʊ'mentl] ADJ *(also: fig)* monumentale, colossale
monumental mason, monumental sculptor N marmista *m*
moo [muː] N muggito
■VI muggire, mugghiare
mooch [muːtʃ] VI *(fam)*: **to mooch about** *or* **around** bighellonare
◎**mood¹** [muːd] N umore *m*; **what kind of mood are you in?** di che umore sei?; **to be in a good/bad mood** essere di buonumore/di cattivo umore; **he was in a bad mood** era di cattivo umore; **to be in a generous mood** sentirsi generoso(-a); **she's in one of her moods** ha la luna; **to be in the mood for sth/to do sth** sentirsi in vena *or* aver voglia di qc/di fare qc; **I'm not in the mood** non mi sento in vena; **I'm in no mood to argue** non ho voglia di discutere
mood² [muːd] N *(Gram)* modo
moodi·ly ['muːdɪlɪ] ADV *(reply)* sgarbatamente; *(stare)* con aria imbronciata
moodi·ness ['muːdɪnɪs] N *(changeability)* volubilità *f inv*; *(sulkiness)* malumore *m*
moody ['muːdɪ] ADJ *(comp* **-ier**, *superl* **-iest**) *(variable)* lunatico(-a), capriccioso(-a); *(morose)* imbronciato(-a), intrattabile; **he's moody and unpredictable** è lunatico e imprevedibile; **moody lyrics** parole malinconiche
◎**moon** [muːn] N luna; **full/new moon** luna piena/nuova; **there's a full moon tonight** stanotte c'è la luna piena; **by the light of the moon** al chiaro di luna; **once in a blue moon** a ogni morte di papa; **to be over the moon** *(fam)* essere al settimo cielo; **she's over the moon about it** è al settimo cielo
▶ **moon about, moon around** VI + ADV aggirarsi con aria trasognata
▶ **moon over** VI + PREP: **to moon over sb** sospirare per qn
moon·beam ['muːnˌbiːm] N raggio di luna
moon landing N allunaggio
moon·light ['muːnˌlaɪt] N chiaro di luna; **in the moonlight** al chiaro di luna
■VI *(fam)* fare del lavoro nero
■ADJ *(walk)* al chiaro di luna; **to do a moonlight flit** *(Brit fam) traslocare di notte per non pagare l'affitto*
moon·light·ing ['muːnˌlaɪtɪŋ] N lavoro nero
moon·lit ['muːnˌlɪt] ADJ illuminato(-a) dalla luna; **on a moonlit night** in una notte rischiarata dalla luna
moon·rise ['muːnˌraɪz] N il sorgere della luna
moon·shine ['muːnˌʃaɪn] N *(fam: nonsense)* fandonie *fpl*; *(Am: liquor: illegally made) liquore distillato clandestinamente*; *(: smuggled) liquore di contrabbando*
moon·shot ['muːnˌʃɒt] N lancio sulla luna
moon·stone ['muːnˌstəʊn] N lunaria, pietra della luna
moon·struck ['muːnˌstrʌk] ADJ pazzo(-a)
moony ['muːnɪ] ADJ *(comp* **-ier**, *superl* **-iest**) *(eyes)* sognante
Moor [mʊəʳ] N moro(-a)
moor¹ [mʊəʳ] N *(land)* brughiera
moor² [mʊəʳ] VT *(ship)* ormeggiare
■VI ormeggiarsi, attraccare
moor·hen ['mʊəˌhen] N gallinella d'acqua
moor·ing ['mʊərɪŋ] N *(place)* ormeggio
mooring buoy N gavitello
moor·ings ['mʊərɪŋz] NPL *(chains, ropes)* ormeggi *mpl*; *(place)* ormeggio
Moor·ish ['mʊərɪʃ] ADJ moresco(-a)

Mm

moor·land ['mʊələnd] N brughiera
moose [mu:s] N, PL INV alce *m*
moot [mu:t] ADJ: **it's a moot point** è un punto discutibile *or* controverso
■ VT: **it has been mooted whether ...** è stata sollevata la questione se...
mop [mɒp] N (*for floor*) mocio *m* Vileda® *inv*; (*for dishes*) spazzolino per i piatti; (*fam: hair*) cespuglio *or* testa di capelli
■ VT (*floor*) lavare; **to mop one's brow** asciugarsi la fronte
▸ **mop up** VT + ADV **1** asciugare con uno straccio **2** (*Mil*) eliminare
mope [məʊp] VI essere depresso(-a) *or* avvilito(-a)
▸ **mope about, mope around** VI + ADV trascinarsi *or* aggirarsi con aria avvilita
mo·ped ['məʊpɛd] N (*Brit*) ciclomotore *m*
mopping-up op·era·tions [mɒpɪŋ'ʌp,ɒpə'reɪʃəns] NPL (*Mil*) operazioni *fpl* di rastrellamento
MOR [,ɛməʊ'ɑ:ʳ] ADJ ABBR (*Mus*) = **middle-of-the-road**; **MOR music** musica melodica
■ N ABBR (= **middle-of-the-road**) per il gran pubblico
mo·raine [mɒ'reɪn] N morena
◎ **mor·al** ['mɒrəl] ADJ (*gen*) morale; (*person*) di saldi principi morali; **to lower moral standards** rilassare i costumi
■ N **1** (*lesson*) morale *f*; **the moral of the story is ...** la morale della storia è... **2 morals** NPL principi *mpl* morali, moralità *f inv*
mo·rale [mɒ'rɑ:l] N morale *m*; **to raise sb's morale** risollevare il morale di qn; **morale was low** il morale era basso
morale booster N: **to be a morale booster (for sb)** tirare (qn) su di morale
morale-boosting [mə'rɒ:l,bu:stɪŋ] ADJ che tira su di morale
mor·al·ist ['mɒrəlɪst] N moralista *m/f*
mor·al·is·tic [mɒrə'lɪstɪk] ADJ (*pej: attitude*) moralistico(-a)
mo·ral·ity [mə'rælɪtɪ] N moralità *f inv*
morality play N (*Theatre*) moralità *f inv*
mor·al·ize ['mɒrə,laɪz] VI: **to moralize (about)** fare il/la moralista (riguardo a), moraleggiare (riguardo a)
mor·al·ly ['mɒrəlɪ] ADV (*act*) moralmente; **morally wrong** moralmente sbagliato(-a)
moral philosophy N filosofia morale
moral support N appoggio morale
moral victory N vittoria morale
mo·rass [mə'ræs'] N pantano, palude *f*; (*fig*) pantano
mora·to·rium [,mɒrə'tɔ:rɪəm] N moratoria
mor·bid ['mɔ:bɪd] ADJ morboso(-a)

> **DID YOU KNOW ...?**
> **morbid** is not translated by the Italian word *morbido*

mor·bid·ly ['mɔ:bɪdlɪ] ADV morbosamente
mor·dant ['mɔ:dənt] ADJ (*frm: wit, humour*) mordace

◎ **more** [mɔ:ʳ] **KEYWORD**
(*comp of* **many, much**)
■ ADJ (*greater in number*) più *inv*; (*in addition*) altro(-a), ancora *inv*; **is there any more wine?** c'è ancora del vino?, c'è dell'altro vino?; **a few more weeks** ancora qualche settimana, qualche altra settimana; **many more people** molta più gente; **I have no more pennies** non ho più un penny; **do you want some more tea?** vuoi ancora un po' di tè?, vuoi dell'altro tè?; **I have more wine/money than you** ho più vino/soldi di te; **I have more wine than beer** ho più vino che birra; **there was more snow this winter than last** c'è stata più neve quest'inverno che l'inverno scorso; **more letters than we expected** più lettere di quante ne aspettavamo; **the more fool you for giving her the money** sei ancora più stupido tu che le hai dato i soldi
■ PRON
1 (*greater amount*) più *inv*; (*further amount*) ancora; **4 more** ancora 4; **a few more** ancora qualcuno; **a little more** ancora un po', un altro po'; **is there any more?** ce n'è ancora?, ce n'è dell'altro?; **you couldn't ask for more** non potresti chiedere di più; **it cost more than we had expected** è costato (di) più di quanto pensavamo; **many more** molti altri; **much more** molto di più; **there's no more** non ce n'è più; **let's say no more about it** non parliamone più; **more than 10** più di 10; **more than ever** più che mai; **I want more** ne voglio ancora *or* di più; **and what's more ...** e per di più...
2 (all) the more (molto) di più; **the more you give him the more he wants** più gliene dai e più ne vuole; **the more the merrier** più gente c'è, meglio è
■ ADV (di) più; **more and more** sempre di più; **it's more and more difficult to ...** è sempre più difficile...; **I don't want to go any more** non ci voglio più andare; **more dangerous than** più pericoloso(-a) di *or* che; **more difficult** più difficile; **more easily** più facilmente; **no more** non... più; **not any more** non... più; **once more** ancora (una volta), un'altra volta; **(all) the more so as ...** tanto più che...; **he was more surprised than angry** era più sorpreso che arrabbiato; **it will more than meet the demand** supererà ampiamente la richiesta; **more** *or* **less** più o meno

more·ish ['mɔ:rɪʃ] ADJ (*fam*) così buono(-a) che se ne vuole mangiare ancora
mo·rel [mɒ'rɛl] N (*mushroom*) morchella
◎ **more·over** [mɔ:'rəʊvəʳ] ADV per di più, inoltre
mor·es ['mɔ:reɪz] NPL (*frm*) costumi *mpl*
mor·ga·nat·ic [,mɔ:gə'nætɪk] ADJ morganatico(-a)
morgue [mɔ:g] N obitorio
MORI ['mɔ:rɪ] N ABBR (*Brit*: = **Market & Opinion Research Institute**) *istituto di sondaggio*
mori·bund ['mɒrɪ,bʌnd] ADJ moribondo(-a)
Mor·mon ['mɔ:mən] N, ADJ mormone (*m/f*)
▹ www.mormon.org/
◎ **morn·ing** ['mɔ:nɪŋ] N (*part of day*) mattina, mattino; (*expressing duration*) mattinata; **this morning** stamattina, questa mattina; **yesterday morning** ieri mattina; **tomorrow morning** domani mattina, domattina; **on Monday morning** lunedì mattina; **a morning's work** il lavoro di una mattinata; **in the morning** di mattina, la mattina; (*tomorrow*) domattina; **I work in the mornings** lavoro la mattina; **at 7 o'clock in the morning** alle 7 di *or* del mattino; **on the morning of September 19th** la mattina del 19 settembre; **I'll do it first thing in the morning** lo farò domani mattina appena mi sveglio
■ ADJ (*walk*) mattutino(-a); (*papers*) del mattino
morning-after pill [,mɔ:nɪŋ'ɑ:tə,pɪl] N pillola del giorno dopo
morning dress N frac *m inv*
morning prayer, morning service N mattutino
morning sickness N (*Med*) nausee *fpl* mattutine
morning star N stella del mattino
Mo·roc·can [mə'rɒkən] ADJ, N marocchino(-a)

Mo·roc·co [məˈrɒkəʊ] N **1** il Marocco **2** (*also:* **Morocco leather**) marocchino
mor·on [ˈmɔːrɒn] N (*fam*) idiota *m/f*, deficiente *m/f*
mo·ron·ic [mɒˈrɒnɪk] ADJ cretino(-a), idiota, deficiente
mo·rose [məˈrəʊs] ADJ cupo(-a), tetro(-a), imbronciato(-a)

> DID YOU KNOW ...?
> **morose** is not translated by the Italian word *moroso*

mo·rose·ly [məˈrəʊslɪ] ADV cupamente
morph [mɔːf] VI tramutarsi
■VT tramutare
mor·pheme [ˈmɔːfiːm] N morfema *m*
mor·phine [ˈmɔːfiːn], **mor·phia** [ˈmɔːfɪə] N morfina
morphine addict, morphia addict N morfinomane *m/f*
mor·pho·logi·cal·ly [ˌmɔːfəˈlɒdʒɪkəlɪ] ADV morfologicamente
mor·phol·ogy [mɔːˈfɒlədʒɪ] N morfologia
mor·ris danc·ing [ˈmɒrɪsˌdɑːnsɪŋ] N (*Brit*) *antica danza tradizionale inglese*
▷ www.streetswing.com/histmain/z3moris.htm
▷ http://web.syr.edu/~rsholmes/morris/rich
mor·row [ˈmɒrəʊ] N: **the morrow** (*old*) domani *m inv*; **on the morrow** domani
Morse [mɔːs] N (*also:* **Morse code**) alfabeto Morse
mor·sel [ˈmɔːsl] N (*of food*) boccone *m*; (*fig*) briciolo
mor·tal [ˈmɔːtl] ADJ, N mortale (*m/f*)
mor·tal·ity [mɔːˈtælɪtɪ] N mortalità *f inv*
mortality rate N tasso di mortalità
mor·tal·ly [ˈmɔːtəlɪ] ADV mortalmente
mor·tar [ˈmɔːtə^r] N **1** (*cannon, bowl*) mortaio; **pestle and mortar** pestello e mortaio **2** (*cement*) malta; **bricks and mortar** mattoni e malta
mortar·board [ˈmɔːtəˌbɔːd] N *tradizionale copricapo nero, con cupola piatta e quadrata, indossato da studenti e docenti universitari a cerimonie ufficiali*
◎**mort·gage** [ˈmɔːgɪdʒ] N (*in house buying*) mutuo ipotecario; (*second loan*) ipoteca; **to take out a mortgage** contrarre un mutuo (*or* un'ipoteca); **to pay off a mortgage** pagare un mutuo (*or* un'ipoteca); **I've got a mortgage** ho un mutuo
■VT ipotecare
mortgage company N (*Am*) società *f inv* immobiliare
mort·ga·gee [ˌmɔːgɪˈdʒiː] N creditore *m* ipotecario
mort·gag·or [ˈmɔːgɪdʒə^r] N debitore *m* ipotecario
mor·tice [ˈmɔːtɪs] N = **mortise**
mor·ti·cian [mɔːˈtɪʃən] N (*Am*) impresario di pompe funebri
mor·ti·fi·ca·tion [ˌmɔːtɪfɪˈkeɪʃən] N mortificazione *f*
mor·ti·fied [ˈmɔːtɪˌfaɪd] ADJ mortificato(-a)
mor·ti·fy [ˈmɔːtɪˌfaɪ] VT mortificare
mor·ti·fy·ing [ˈmɔːtɪˌfaɪɪŋ] ADJ mortificante
mor·tise, **mor·tice** [ˈmɔːtɪs] N mortasa
mortise lock N serratura incastrata
mor·tu·ary [ˈmɔːtjʊərɪ] N camera mortuaria
mo·sa·ic [məʊˈzeɪɪk] N mosaico
Mos·cow [ˈmɒskəʊ] N Mosca; **he's in Moscow** è a Mosca
Moses [ˈməʊzɪs] N (*Brit*) Mosè *m*
Moses basket N (*Brit*) culla di vimini
mosh [mɒʃ] VI (*fam*) dimenarsi, ballare
Mos·lem [ˈmɒzləm] ADJ, N = **Muslim**
mosque [mɒsk] N moschea
mos·qui·to [mɒsˈkiːtəʊ] N (*pl* **mosquitoes**) zanzara; **a mosquito bite** una puntura di zanzara
mosquito net N zanzariera
moss [mɒs] N (*Bot*) muschio
mossy [ˈmɒsɪ] ADJ (*comp* **-ier**, *superl* **-iest**) muscoso(-a)
◎**most** [məʊst] (*superl of* **many, much**) ADJ **1** più (di tutti); **the most pleasure** il piacere più grande; **who has (the) most money?** chi ha più soldi (di tutti)?; **for the most part** in gran parte, per la maggior parte; **he won the most votes** ha avuto più voti degli altri **2** (*the majority of*): **most men** la maggior parte *or* la grande maggioranza degli uomini; **most fish** la maggior parte dei pesci; **most people** quasi tutti; **most people go out on Friday night** quasi tutti escono venerdì sera
■PRON: **most of it/them** quasi tutto/tutti; **most of the money/her friends/the time** la maggior parte dei soldi/dei suoi amici/del tempo; **I know most of them** conosco gran parte di loro; **do the most you can** fai più che puoi; **I did most of the work** ho fatto gran parte del lavoro; **at most** *or* **at the (very) most** al massimo; **two hours at the most** due ore al massimo; **to make the most of sth** sfruttare al massimo qc, trarre il massimo vantaggio da qc; **he made the most of his holiday** ha sfruttato al massimo la vacanza; **make the most of it!** approfittane!
■ADV **1** (*spend, eat, work, sleep*) di più; **I saw most** ho visto più io; **the most attractive/difficult/comfortable** il/la più attraente/difficile/confortevole; **the most expensive restaurant** il ristorante più caro; **which one did it most easily?** chi ha avuto più facilità a farlo?; **the thing she most feared** la cosa che temeva di più; **he's the one who talks most** lui è quello che parla di più **2** (*very*): **most likely** molto probabilmente; **a most interesting book** un libro estremamente interessante; **a most unusual choice** una scelta estremamente insolita
◎**most·ly** [ˈməʊstlɪ] ADV (*chiefly*) per lo più; (*usually*) in genere; **the teachers are mostly quite nice** in genere gli insegnanti sono abbastanza gentili
MOT [ˌɛməʊˈtiː] N ABBR (*Brit:* = **Ministry of Transport test**) *revisione obbligatoria degli autoveicoli*; **the car passed/failed its MOT** ≈ la macchina ha passato/non ha passato la revisione
mo·tel [məʊˈtɛl] N motel *m inv*
moth [mɒθ] N falena, farfalla notturna; (*also:* **clothes moth**) tarma
moth·ball [ˈmɒθˌbɔːl] N pallina di naftalina
moth-eaten [ˈmɒθˌiːtn] ADJ tarmato(-a)
◎**moth·er** [ˈmʌðə^r] N madre *f*; **my mother** mia madre
■VT (*care for*) fare da madre a; (*spoil*) essere troppo chioccia con
moth·er·board [ˈmʌðəˌbɔːd] N (*Comput*) scheda *f* madre *inv*
moth·er·hood [ˈmʌðəˌhʊd] N maternità *f inv*
Moth·er·ing Sun·day [ˈmʌðərɪŋˌsʌndɪ] N (*Brit*) ≈ la festa della mamma
mother-in-law [ˈmʌðərɪnlɔː] N (*pl* **mothers-in-law**) suocera
mother·land [ˈmʌðəˌlænd], **mother country** N madrepatria, patria
mother love N amore *m* materno
moth·er·ly [ˈmʌðəlɪ] ADJ materno(-a)
Mother Nature N madre *f* natura
mother-of-pearl [ˌmʌðərəvˈpɜːl] N madreperla
Mother's Day N la festa della mamma
mother's help N bambinaia
Mother Superior N madre superiora

mother-to-be [ˌmʌðətəˈbiː] N (*pl* **mothers-to-be**) futura mamma
mother tongue N lingua materna, madrelingua
moth·proof [ˈmɒθˌpruːf] ADJ antitarmico(-a)
mo·tif [məʊˈtiːf] N motivo
◎ **mo·tion** [ˈməʊʃən] N **1** (*movement*) moto, movimento; **circular motion** movimento circolare; **perpetual motion** moto perpetuo; **to be in motion** (*vehicle*) essere in moto; (*machine*) essere in funzione; **to set in motion** avviare; **to go through the motions of doing sth** (*fig*) fare qc pro forma **2** (*gesture*) cenno, gesto; (*proposal: at meeting*) mozione *f* **3** (*Brit: also:* **bowel motion**) evacuazione *f* (intestinale)
■ VT, VI: **to motion (to) sb to do sth** far cenno *or* segno a qn di fare qc
mo·tion·less [ˈməʊʃənlɪs] ADJ immobile
motion picture N (*Am*) film *m inv*
motion-picture in·dus·try [ˌməʊʃənˈpɪktʃərˌɪndəstrɪ] N (*Am*) l'industria cinematografica
motion sickness N mal *m* d'auto (*or* d'aria *or* di mare)
◎ **mo·ti·vate** [ˈməʊtɪˌveɪt] VT (*act, decision*) dare origine a, motivare; (*person*) spingere, motivare
mo·ti·vat·ed [ˈməʊtɪˌveɪtɪd] ADJ motivato(-a); **he's highly motivated** è fortemente motivato
mo·ti·va·tion [ˌməʊtɪˈveɪʃən] N motivazione *f*
mo·tive [ˈməʊtɪv] N (*gen*) motivo, ragione *f*; (*for crime*) movente *m*; **the motive for the killing** il movente dell'omicidio; **from the best motives** con le migliori intenzioni; **an ulterior motive** un secondo fine
■ ADJ motore(-trice)
mot·ley [ˈmɒtlɪ] ADJ (*many-coloured*) variopinto(-a); (*mixed*) eterogeneo(-a), molto vario(-a); **a motley crew** una banda eterogenea
mo·to·cross [ˈməʊtəˌkrɒs] N motocross *m*
◎ **mo·tor** [ˈməʊtə^r] N **1** (*engine*) motore *m*; **a boat with a motor** una barca a motore **2** (*Brit fam: car*) macchina
■ VI andare in automobile
■ ADJ motore(-trice)
motor accident N incidente *m* automobilistico
motor·bike [ˈməʊtəˌbaɪk] N moto *f inv*
motor·boat [ˈməʊtəˌbəʊt] N motoscafo
motor·cade [ˈməʊtəˌkeɪd] N corteo di auto
motor·car [ˈməʊtəkɑː^r] N (*Brit frm*) automobile *f*
motor caravan N (*Brit*) camper *m inv*
motor·coach [ˈməʊtəˌkəʊtʃ] N (*Brit*) pullman *m inv*
motor·cycle [ˈməʊtəˌsaɪkl] N motocicletta
▷ www.ama-cycle.org/
motor·cycling [ˈməʊtəˌsaɪklɪŋ] N motociclismo
motor·cyclist [ˈməʊtəˌsaɪklɪst] N motociclista *m/f*
motor home N (*Auto*) camper *m inv*
motor industry N industria automobilistica
mo·tor·ing [ˈməʊtərɪŋ] ADJ (*accident*) d'auto, automobilistico(-a); (*offence*) di guida; **motoring holiday** vacanza in macchina; **the motoring public** gli automobilisti
■ N (*Brit*) turismo automobilistico; **the hazards of motoring** i rischi dell'andare in macchina
mo·tor·ist [ˈməʊtərɪst] N automobilista *m/f*
mo·tori·za·tion [ˌməʊtəraɪˈzeɪʃən] N motorizzazione *f*
mo·tor·ize [ˈməʊtəˌraɪz] VT motorizzare
motor·man [ˈməʊtəˌmæn] N (*pl* **-men**) (*Am: of electric train*) macchinista *m*
motor mechanic N meccanico
motor·mouth [ˈməʊtəmaʊθ] N (*fam*) chiacchierone(-a)
motor muscle N muscolo motore
motor oil N olio lubrificante
motor racing N (*Brit*) corse *fpl* automobilistiche
motor scooter N motorscooter *m inv*
motor show N salone *m* dell'automobile
motor vehicle N (*frm*) automezzo, autoveicolo
motor·way [ˈməʊtəˌweɪ] N (*Brit*) autostrada; **on the motorway** in autostrada
mott·led [ˈmɒtld] ADJ (*leaves, bird*) variopinto(-a), variegato(-a), screziato(-a); (*marble*) variegato(-a); (*animal*) pezzato(-a), marezzato(-a); (*complexion*) a chiazze, chiazzato(-a)
mot·to [ˈmɒtəʊ] N (*pl* **mottoes**) motto
mouf·lon [ˈmuːflɒn] N (*sheep*) muflone *m*
mould[1] (*Am*) **mold** [məʊld] N (*fungus*) muffa; **jam covered with mould** marmellata coperta di muffa
mould[2] (*Am*) **mold** [məʊld] N (*Art, Culin, Tech*) stampo, forma
■ VT (*clay, figure*) plasmare, modellare; (*fig: character*) plasmare, formare, foggiare; **parents try to mould their children** i genitori cercano di plasmare i propri figli; **mould the mixture into balls** forma delle palline con l'impasto
mould·er, (*Am*) **mold·er** [ˈməʊldə^r] VI (*decay*) ammuffire; (*building*) sgretolarsi, andare in rovina
mould·ing, (*Am*) **mold·ing** [ˈməʊldɪŋ] N (*Archit*) modanatura
mouldy, (*Am*) **moldy** [ˈməʊldɪ] ADJ (*comp* **-ier**, *superl* **-iest**) ammuffito(-a); **to smell mouldy** avere odore di muffa; **to go mouldy** ammuffire
moult, (*Am*) **molt** [məʊlt] VI far la muta
mound [maʊnd] N rialzo, collinetta
◎ **mount**[1] [maʊnt] N (*liter*) monte *m*, montagna; **Mount Everest** il monte Everest; **Mount of Olives** (*Rel*) il Monte degli Ulivi
mount[2] [maʊnt] N **1** (*horse*) cavalcatura **2** (*support, base*) piedistallo; (*of machine*) incastellatura di sostegno; (*of jewel, photo*) montatura; (*of slide*) telaietto
■ VT **1** (*horse*) montare; (*platform*) salire su; (*stairs*) salire **2** (*exhibition*) organizzare; (*play*) metter su; (*attack*) sferrare, condurre; **they're mounting a publicity campaign** stanno organizzando una campagna pubblicitaria **3** (*picture, stamp*) sistemare; (*jewel*) montare **4 to mount guard (on** *or* **over)** fare la guardia a; (*Mil*) montare la guardia a
■ VI **1** (*get on a horse*) montare a cavallo **2** (*quantity, price: also:* **mount up**) aumentare, salire; **tension is mounting** la tensione sta aumentando; **letters and bills mounted up while we were on holiday** lettere e fatture si sono accumulate mentre eravamo in vacanza; **my savings are mounting up gradually** i miei risparmi aumentano a poco a poco
◎ **moun·tain** [ˈmaʊntɪn] N (*also fig*) montagna; **in the mountains** sulle montagne, in montagna; **to have a holiday in the mountains** fare una vacanza in montagna; **to make a mountain out of a molehill** fare di una mosca un elefante; **butter mountain** (*Econ*) montagna di burro
■ ADJ (*people*) montanaro(-a), di montagna; (*shoes*) da montagna; (*animal, plant, path*) di montagna
mountain bike N mountain bike *f inv*
mountain breed N razza montana
mountain cat, mountain lion N puma *m inv*
moun·tain·eer [ˌmaʊntɪˈnɪə^r] N alpinista *m/f*
moun·tain·eer·ing [ˌmaʊntɪˈnɪərɪŋ] N alpinismo; **to go mountaineering** fare dell'alpinismo
moun·tain·ous [ˈmaʊntɪnəs] ADJ (*country*) montagnoso(-a), montuoso(-a); (*fig*) gigantesco(-a)
mountain range N catena montuosa *or* di montagne

mountain rescue team N ≈ squadra di soccorso alpino

moun·tain·side ['maʊntɪn,saɪd] N fianco della montagna

mount·ed ['maʊntɪd] ADJ a cavallo

mourn [mɔːn] VT piangere, lamentare; **to mourn sb** piangere la morte di qn; **she's still mourning her father** sta ancora piangendo la morte del padre; **she mourns the loss of her idealism** rimpiange la perdita del proprio idealismo
■ VI: **to mourn (for sb)** piangere (la morte di qn)

mourn·er ['mɔːnəʳ] N chi piange un defunto

mourn·ful ['mɔːnfʊl] ADJ *(person)* triste, malinconico(-a); *(tone, sound)* lugubre, funereo

mourn·ful·ly ['mɔːnfəlɪ] ADV *(gaze, speak)* tristemente, malinconicamente

mourn·ful·ness ['mɔːnfʊlnɪs] N tristezza, malinconia

mourn·ing ['mɔːnɪŋ] N lutto; **to be in mourning** essere in lutto; **to wear mourning** portare il lutto
■ ADJ *(dress)* da lutto

mouse [maʊs] N *(pl* **mice***)* *(gen)* topo; *(Comput)* mouse *m inv*; **house mouse** topo domestico

mous·er ['maʊzəʳ] N *(cat)* cacciatore *m* di topi

mouse·trap ['maʊs,træp] N trappola per i topi

mous·sa·ka [,mʊ'sɑːkə] N moussaka; *sorta di parmigiana di melanzane con ragù di carne, specialità greca*

mousse [muːs] N mousse *f inv*; **chocolate mousse** mousse al cioccolato

mous·tache [mə'stɑːʃ] N baffi *mpl*

mousy, **mousey** ['maʊsɪ] ADJ *(comp* **-ier**, *superl* **-iest***)* *(person)* timido(-a), schivo(-a); **mousy hair** capelli color castano spento

◎ **mouth** [*n* maʊθ; *vb* maʊð] N *(pl* **mouths** [maʊðz]*)* *(gen)* bocca; *(of cave)* imboccatura, imbocco; *(of river)* foce *f*, bocca; *(opening)* orifizio; **to keep one's mouth shut** *(fig)* tener la bocca chiusa; **shut your mouth!** ma sta' un po' zitto!
■ VT *(insincerely)* blaterare; *(soundlessly)* esprimere col semplice movimento delle labbra

mouth·ful ['maʊθfʊl] N *(of food)* boccone *m*; *(of drink)* sorsata

mouth organ N armonica (a bocca)

mouth·piece ['maʊθ,piːs] N *(Mus)* imboccatura, bocchino; *(of breathing apparatus)* boccaglio; *(of telephone)* microfono; *(fig: person)* portavoce *m/f*

mouth-to-mouth ['maʊθtə'maʊθ], **mouth-to-mouth resuscitation** N respirazione *f* bocca a bocca

mouth·wash ['maʊθ,wɒʃ] N collutorio

mouth·water·ing ['maʊθ,wɔːtərɪŋ] ADJ che fa venire l'acquolina in bocca

mov·able ['muːvəbl] ADJ mobile, movibile

◎ **move** [muːv] N
1 *(movement)* movimento, mossa; **to be on the move** *(travelling)* spostarsi; *(active, busy)* essere indaffarato(-a); *(fig: developments)* essere in continuo progresso; **to get a move on** *(fam)* affrettarsi, sbrigarsi; **get a move on (with that)!** *(fam)* sbrigati (con quello)!, datti una mossa (con quello)!; **to make a move** *(start to leave, go)* andarsene; *(begin to take action)* muoversi; **he made a move towards her** fece un passo verso di lei
2 *(in game)* mossa; *(: turn to play)* turno; *(fig: step, action)* passo; **it's my move** tocca a me; **a good/bad move** una mossa buona/sbagliata; **what's the next move?** e adesso cosa facciamo?; **to make the first move** *(fig)* fare il primo passo; **his first move after his victory** la prima cosa che ha fatto dopo la sua vittoria; **there was a move to oust him from the party** ci fu un tentativo di estrometterlo dal partito
3 *(change of house)* trasloco; *(to different job)* trasferimento; **our move from Oxford to Luton** il nostro trasloco da Oxford a Luton
■ VT
1 *(change place of)* spostare; *(: limbs, chesspiece)* muovere; *(transport)* trasportare; *(transfer: employee, troops)* trasferire; **move those children off the grass!** fate andare via i bambini dal prato!; **could you move your stuff please?** può spostare le sue cose per favore?; **to move house** traslocare, cambiar casa; **we asked a (removal) firm to move us** abbiamo chiesto a una ditta (di traslochi) di farci il trasloco
2 *(fig: sway)*: **to move somebody from an opinion** smuovere qn da un'idea; **to move sb to do sth** indurre *or* spingere qn a fare qc; **he will not be easily moved** non cambierà facilmente idea
3 *(cause emotion in)* commuovere; **to be moved** essere commosso(-a); **to move sb to tears** commuovere qn fino alle lacrime; **to move sb to anger/pity** far arrabbiare/impietosire qn; **the book moved me deeply** il libro mi ha commossa profondamente
4 *(frm: propose)*: **to move a resolution** avanzare una proposta; **to move that ...** proporre che... *+ sub*
■ VI
1 *(gen)* muoversi; *(traffic)* circolare; *(from a place)* spostarsi; **move!** muoviti!, spostati!; **let's move!** andiamo!; **don't move!** non muovetevi!; **to move towards** andare verso; **she moves beautifully** si muove con molta grazia; **I'll not move from here** di qui non mi muovo; **the car was moving very slowly** la macchina avanzava molto lentamente; **to move freely** *(piece of machinery)* aver gioco; *(person)* circolare liberamente; *(traffic)* scorrere; **the policeman kept the traffic moving** il vigile ha fatto scorrere il traffico; **things are moving at last** finalmente qualcosa si è mosso; **to move in high society** frequentare l'alta società
2 *(move house)* cambiar casa, traslocare; **the family moved to a new house** la famiglia è andata ad abitare in una nuova casa; **we're moving in July** traslochiamo in luglio; **we're moving to Scotland** ci trasferiamo in Scozia
3 *(in games)* muovere; **it's you to move** tocca a te
4 *(take steps)* intervenire
▸ **move about**, **move around** VT + ADV *(furniture)* spostare; *(person)* far spostare
■ VI + ADV *(fidget)* agitarsi; *(walk about)* muoversi; *(travel)* spostarsi, viaggiare
▸ **move along** VT + ADV *(crowd)* far circolare; *(car)* far spostare
■ VI + ADV spostarsi in avanti, scorrere
▸ **move away** VT + ADV *(demonstrators)* allontanare; *(employee)* trasferire; *(object)* spostare
■ VI + ADV, VI *(move aside)* spostarsi; *(leave)* allontanarsi, andarsene; *(move house)* traslocare; **our neighbours are moving away** i nostri vicini se ne vanno
▸ **move back** VT + ADV
1 *(to former place: person)* far tornare; *(: object)* rimettere dov'era
2 *(cause to give ground: crowd)* sospingere indietro; *(: troops)* far indietreggiare
■ VI + ADV
1 *(return)* ritornare; **they had no intention of moving back to Britain** non avevano intenzione di ritornare in Gran Bretagna

Mm

2 (*give ground*) indietreggiare

▸ **move down** VT + ADV (*person*) far scendere; (*object*) spostare in basso; (*demote*) far retrocedere

■ VI + ADV scendere; (*be demoted*) retrocedere

▸ **move forward** VT + ADV (*object*) spostare in avanti; (*people, troops, chesspiece*) far avanzare; (*fig: date*) anticipare

■ VI + ADV avanzare

▸ **move in** VT + ADV (*police*) far intervenire; (*take inside*) portar dentro; **we haven't moved the furniture in yet** non ci abbiamo ancora messo i mobili

■ VI + ADV

1 (*to a house*) traslocare, andare ad abitare; **when are the new neighbours moving in?** quando arrivano i nuovi vicini?

2 (*police*) intervenire; (*pej: try to take control*) cercare di imporsi

▸ **move off** VT + ADV (*object*) togliere

■ VI + ADV

1 (*go away*) allontanarsi

2 (*start moving*) partire

▸ **move on** VT + ADV (*crowd*) far circolare; (*hands of clock*) spostare in avanti

■ VI + ADV ripartire, riprendere la strada; **I felt it was time to move on** sentii che era arrivato il momento di cambiare; **the policeman asked them to move on** il poliziotto ha ordinato loro di andare via; **to move on to** (*fig: point*) passare a; **let's move on to the next question** passiamo alla prossima domanda

▸ **move out** VT + ADV (*gen*) portar fuori; (*person*) mandare fuori; (*troops*) far ritirare; **move the chair out of the corner** togli la sedia dall'angolo

■ VI + ADV (*of house*) sgombrare, trasferirsi; (*withdraw: troops*) ritirarsi

▸ **move over** VT + ADV spostare

■ VI + ADV spostarsi; **could you move over a bit?** puoi spostarti un po'?

▸ **move up** VT + ADV (*person*) portare su; (*object*) spostare in alto; (*promote: employee*) promuovere

■ VI + ADV

1 (*move along*) andare avanti, avanzare

2 (*fig: shares*) salire; (*: rates*) aumentare; (*be promoted*) passare di grado

◎ **move·ment** ['mu:vmənt] N (*gen*) movimento; (*gesture*) gesto; (*of stars, water, physical*) moto; **movement (of the bowels)** (*Med*) evacuazione *f* (intestinale); **a sudden movement** un movimento brusco; **the police questioned him about his movements** la polizia lo ha interrogato circa i suoi spostamenti; **he was asked to account for his movements** gli è stato chiesto di rendere conto dei suoi spostamenti

mov·er ['mu:vəʳ] N proponente *m/f*

◎ **movie** ['mu:vɪ] (*esp Am*) N film *m inv*; **the movies** il cinema *m inv*; **to go to the movies** andare al cinema

■ ADJ (*star*) del cinema; (*industry*) cinematografico(-a)

movie camera N (*Am*) cinepresa

movie·goer ['mu:vɪ,gəʊəʳ] N (*Am*) frequentatore(-trice) di cinema

mov·ing ['mu:vɪŋ] ADJ 1 (*parts, staircase*) mobile; (*vehicle*) in movimento; **a moving bus** un autobus in movimento 2 (*fig: instigating*) animatore(-trice) 3 (*causing emotion*) commovente, toccante; **a moving story** una storia commovente

mov·ing·ly ['mu:vɪŋlɪ] ADV in modo commovente

mow [məʊ] (*pt* **mowed**, *pp* **mown** *or* **mowed**) VT (*corn*) falciare; (*grass*) tagliare; **I sometimes mow the lawn** a volte taglio l'erba del prato

▸ **mow down** VT + ADV falciare

mow·er ['məʊəʳ] N (*machine: Agr*) falciatrice *f*; (*also:* **lawn mower**) tagliaerba *m inv*, tosaerba *m inv*

Mo·zam·bique [,məʊzəm'bi:k] N il Mozambico

◎ **MP** [,ɛm'pi:] N ABBR 1 = *Military Police* 2 (*Canada*) = *Mounted Police* 3 (*Brit:* = **Member of Parliament**) deputato(-a); (*on envelope*): **Paul Smith, MP** ≈ On. Paul Smith

MP3 [,ɛmpi:'θri:] N ABBR (= **MP(EG-Audio Layer-)3**) MP3 *m inv*

MP3 player N lettore *m* MP3

MPEG ['ɛmpɛg] N ABBR (*Comput* = **Motion Picture Experts Group**) MPEG *m*

mpg [,ɛmpi:'dʒi:] N ABBR (= **miles per gallon**) ≈ km/l

mph [,ɛmpi:'eɪtʃ] N ABBR (= **miles per hour**) ≈ km/h

MPhil [,ɛm'fɪl] N ABBR (= **Master of Philosophy**) ≈ diploma *m inv* post-laurea

Mpu·ma·lan·ga [m'pʌmə,lɑ:ngə] N Mpumalanga

⊳ www.mpumalanga.gov.za/

MPV [,ɛmpi:'vi:] N ABBR (*Auto* = **multi-purpose vehicle**) monovolume *f inv*

Mr ['mɪstəʳ] N signore *m*; **Mr Smith** il signor Smith; (*on letter*) Sig. Smith; (*direct address*) signor Smith

MRC [,ɛmɑ:'si:] N ABBR (*Brit:* = **Medical Research Council**) *ufficio governativo per la ricerca medica in Gran Bretagna e nel Commonwealth*

MRCP [,ɛmɑ:si:'pi:] N ABBR (*Brit*) = *Member of the Royal College of Physicians*

MRCS [,ɛmɑ:si:'ɛs] N ABBR (*Brit*) = *Member of the Royal College of Surgeons*

MRCVS [,ɛmɑ:si:vi:'ɛs] N ABBR (*Brit*) = *Member of the Royal College of Veterinary Surgeons*

MRI [,ɛmɑ:r'aɪ] N ABBR = *magnetic resonance imaging*; **an MRI scan** una risonanza magnetica

Mrs ['mɪsɪz] N signora; **Mrs Black** la signora Black; (*on letter*) Sig.ra Black; (*direct address*) signora Black

MS [,ɛm'ɛs] N ABBR 1 (*Am:* = **Master of Science**) master *m inv* in scienze 2 (*Med*) = **multiple sclerosis**

■ ABBR (*Am: Post*) = *Mississippi*

MS., ms. (*pl* **MSS., mss.**) ABBR (= **manuscript**) ms

Ms [mɪz] N ABBR *termine usato per evitare di distinguere tra signora e signorina*

MSA [,ɛmɛs'eɪ] N ABBR (*Am:* = **Master of Science in Agriculture**) master *m inv* in scienze agrarie

MSc [,ɛmɛs'si:] N ABBR (= **Master of Science**) master *m inv* in scienze; **she's got an MSc** ha un Master in scienze naturali

MSG [,ɛmɛs'dʒi:] ABBR = **monosodium glutamate**

MSP [,ɛmɛs'pi:] N ABBR (= **Member of the Scottish Parliament** *Pol*) deputato(-a) del parlamento scozzese

MST [,ɛmɛs'ti:] ABBR (*Am:* = **Mountain Standard Time**) *ora (invernale) nel fuso orario delle Montagne Rocciose*

MT [,ɛm'ti:] N ABBR = *machine translation*

■ ABBR (*Am Post*) = **Montana**

Mt ABBR (*Geog:* = **mount**) M.

mth ABBR (= **month**) m.

MTV [,ɛmti:'vi:] N ABBR (= **music television**) MTV *f*

much [mʌtʃ] KEYWORD

(*comp* **more**, *superl* **most**)

■ ADJ, PRON

1 molto(-a); **how much money?** quanti soldi?; **how much is it?** quanto costa?; **it's not much** non è tanto; **there's not much to do** non c'è molto da fare; **much of this is true** molto di questo è vero; **I'm not much of a cook/singer** non sono un granché come cuoco/cantante; **that wasn't much of a party** la festa non è

stata un granché; **we don't see much of each other** non ci vediamo molto spesso; **he/it isn't up to much** (*fam*) non vale granché

2 as much *or* **as much again** altrettanto(-a); **as much as you want** (tanto) quanto vuoi; **he drinks as much beer as I do** beve tanta birra quanto me; **it's as much as he can do to stand up** stare in piedi è il massimo che riesce a fare; **he spends as much as he earns** spende tanto quanto guadagna; **he has (just) as much money as you** ha tanti soldi quanto te; **I thought as much** c'era da aspettarselo; **three times as much tea** tre volte tanto tè

3 so much talmente tanto(-a), così (tanto(-a)); **at so much a pound** un tot *or* un tanto alla libbra; **so much for that!** pazienza!; **the problem is not so much one of money as time** non è tanto una questione di soldi quanto di tempo

4 too much troppo(-a); **that's too much!** *or* **a bit (too) much!** (*fam*) questo è (un po') troppo!; **the job is too much for her** quel lavoro è al di sopra delle sue capacità

5 to make much of sb (*treat as important*) coprire qn di attenzioni; **to make much of** (*success, failure*) fare un sacco di storie per; (*item of news, scandal*) dare rilievo a; **I couldn't make much of that** (*fam*) non ci ho capito molto

■ ADV

1 molto; **much as I would like to go I can't** per quanto abbia *or* anche se ho una gran voglia di andarci, non posso; **he was much embarrassed** era molto imbarazzato; **how much?** quanto?; **however much he tries** per quanto ci provi; **I hardly know her, much less her mother** conosco appena lei e ancora meno sua madre; **it doesn't much matter** non ha molta importanza; **much to my surprise** con mia grande sorpresa, con mio grande stupore; **too much** troppo; **I like it very much** mi piace moltissimo; **thank you very much** molte grazie

2 (*by far*) di gran lunga; **much the biggest** di gran lunga il/la più grande; **I would much rather stay** preferirei di gran lunga restare

3 (*almost*) pressappoco, quasi; **they're much the same** sono praticamente uguali

much·ness ['mʌtʃnɪs] N (*fam*): **they're much of a muchness** sono più o meno uguali

mu·ci·lage ['mju:sɪlɪdʒ] N mucillagine *f*

muck [mʌk] N **1** (*dirt*) sporcizia, sudiciume *m*; (*mud*) fango; (*manure*) letame *m*; **shoes covered with muck** scarpe coperte di fango; **muck in the engine** sporcizia nel motore; **a load of muck** un mucchio di letame **2** (*fig*) porcherie *fpl*

▸ **muck about, muck around** (*fam*) VT + ADV: **to muck sb about** complicare la vita a qn

■ VI + ADV **1** (*lark about*) fare lo/la stupido(-a); (*do nothing in particular*) non fare niente di speciale, gingillarsi; **stop mucking about!** finiscila di fare lo stupido! **2** (*tinker*) armeggiare; **to muck about with sth** trafficare con qc

▸ **muck in** VI + ADV (*Brit fam*) mettersi insieme

▸ **muck out** VT + ADV (*stable*) pulire

▸ **muck up** VT + ADV (*fam*) **1** (*dirty*) sporcare **2** (*spoil*) rovinare; **he's mucked up our plans** ci ha incasinato i piani

mucki·ness ['mʌkɪnɪs] N (*see adj*) fangosità; sporcizia

muck·rak·ing ['mʌk,reɪkɪŋ] (*fig fam*) N scandalismo

■ ADJ scandalistico(-a)

muck-up ['mʌk,ʌp] N (*fam*) casino, pasticcio

mucky ['mʌkɪ] ADJ (*comp* **-ier**, *superl* **-iest**) (*muddy*) fangoso(-a); (*filthy*) sudicio(-a), sporco(-a), lordo(-a)

mu·cous ['mju:kəs] ADJ (*of mucus*) mucoso(-a); (*producing mucus*) muciparo(-a)

mu·cus ['mju:kəs] N muco

mud [mʌd] N **1** fango **2** (*fig*): **his name is mud** non è molto ben visto; **to sling mud at sb** gettar fango addosso a qn

mud bath N: **to have a mud bath** fare i fanghi

mud·di·ness ['mʌdɪnɪs] N (*of road, ground*) fangosità *f inv*; (*of liquid*) torbidità *f inv*; (*of complexion*) colore *m* terreo

mud·dle ['mʌdl] N (*perplexity*) confusione *f*; (*disorder*) disordine *m*; **to be in a muddle** (*room, books*) essere in disordine; (*person*) essere molto confuso(-a), non riuscire a raccapezzarsi; (*plan, arrangements*) essere per aria; **to get into a muddle** (*person: while explaining*) imbrogliarsi, fare confusione; (*things*) finire sottosopra; **the photos are in a muddle** le foto sono in disordine; **there's been a muddle over the seats** è successo un pasticcio con i posti

■ VT (*also:* **muddle up**) **1** (*papers*) mettere sottosopra; **you've muddled up A and B** hai confuso A con B **2** (*person, story, details*) confondere; **he muddles me up with my sister** mi confonde con mia sorella; **to get muddled up** essere confuso(-a); **I'm getting muddled up** sono confuso

▸ **muddle along, muddle on** VI + ADV andare avanti a casaccio

▸ **muddle through** VI + ADV cavarsela alla meno peggio

muddle-headed ['mʌdl,hɛdɪd] ADJ (*person*) confusionario(-a); (*ideas*) confuso(-a)

mud·dler ['mʌdləʳ] N confusionario(-a), pasticcione(-a)

mud·dy ['mʌdɪ] ADJ (*comp* **-ier**, *superl* **-iest**) (*road, ground, field*) fangoso(-a); (*hands*) coperto(-a) di fango; (*clothes, shoes*) infangato(-a); (*liquid*) torbido(-a); (*complexion*) smorto(-a), terreo(-a)

mud flap N (*Aut, Brit*) paraspruzzi *m inv*

mud flat N distesa fangosa

mud·guard ['mʌd,gɑ:d] N (*Brit*) parafango

mud hut N capanna di fango

mud·pack ['mʌd,pæk] N maschera di fango

mud pie N formina di fango

mud-slinging ['mʌd,slɪŋɪŋ] N (*fig*) infangamento

mues·li ['mju:zlɪ] N müsli *msg*

mu·ez·zin [mu:'ɛzɪn] N muezzin *m inv*

muff¹ [mʌf] N manicotto

muff² [mʌf] VT (*shot, catch*) mancare, sbagliare; **to muff it** sbagliare tutto; **to muff one's lines** (*actor*) impappinarsi

muf·fin ['mʌfɪn] N (*Brit*) *specie di pasticcino soffice da tè*

muf·fle ['mʌfl] VT **1** (*wrap warmly: also:* **muffle up**) imbacuccare **2** (*deaden: sound*) smorzare, attutire; (*: screams*) soffocare

muf·fled ['mʌfld] ADJ (*sound*) attutito(-a), smorzato(-a)

muf·fler ['mʌfləʳ] N (*scarf*) sciarpa (pesante); (*Am: Aut*) marmitta; (*: on motorbike*) silenziatore *m*; **a woollen muffler** una sciarpa di lana

muf·ti ['mʌftɪ] N: **in mufti** in borghese

mug [mʌg] N **1** (*cup*) tazzone *m*; (*for beer*) boccale *m*; **a mug of coffee** una tazza grande di caffè **2** (*Brit fam: fool*) salame *m*, scemo(-a); **it's a mug's game** è proprio (una cosa) da fessi **3** (*fam: face*) muso

■ VT (*attack and rob*) aggredire, assalire; **he was mugged in the city centre** è stato aggredito in centro

Mm

▸ **mug up** VT + ADV (*Brit fam: also:* **mug up on**) studiare bene
mug·ger ['mʌgəʳ] N aggressore *m*, rapinatore(-trice)
mug·ging ['mʌgɪŋ] N aggressione *f* (*a scopo di rapina*)
mug·gins ['mʌgɪnz] NSG (*Brit fam*) fesso(-a), salame *m*; (*: oneself*): **muggins had to do it** come sempre è toccato a me
mug·gy ['mʌgɪ] ADJ (*comp* **-ier**, *superl* **-iest**) (*weather*) afoso(-a); **it's muggy today** oggi c'è afa
mug shot N (*fam*) foto *f inv* segnaletica
mu·lat·to [mju:'lætəʊ] N (*pl* **mulattoes**) (*offensive*) mulatto(-a)
mul·berry ['mʌlbərɪ] N (*fruit*) mora (di gelso); (*tree*) gelso, moro; **black mulberry** gelso nero
mulch [mʌltʃ] N pacciame *m*
mule [mju:l] N mulo(-a); **(as) stubborn as a mule** testardo(-a) come un mulo
mul·ish ['mju:lɪʃ] ADJ testardo(-a)
mull [mʌl] VT (*wine*) scaldare con aromi e zucchero
▸ **mull over** VT + ADV rimuginare
mul·lah ['mʌlə] N mullah *m inv*
mulled wine ['mʌld,waɪn] N vin brûlé *m inv*, vino caldo
mul·let ['mʌlɪt] N: **red mullet** triglia; **grey mullet** muggine *m*, cefalo
mul·li·ga·taw·ny [,mʌlɪgə'tɔ:nɪ] N minestra al curry
multi... ['mʌltɪ] PREF multi...
multi·ac·cess [,mʌltɪ'æksɛs] ADJ (*Comput*) ad accesso multiplo
multi·cel·lu·lar [mʌltɪ'sɛljʊləʳ] ADJ pluricellulare
multi·col·oured, (*Am*) **multi·col·ored** ['mʌltɪ'kʌləd] ADJ multicolore, variopinto(-a)
multi·fari·ous [,mʌltɪ'fɛərɪəs] ADJ molteplice, svariato(-a)
multi·hull ['mʌltɪ,hʌl] N multiscafo
multi·lat·er·al [,mʌltɪ'lætərəl] ADJ (*Pol*) multilaterale; **multilateral trade** interscambio
multi-level ['mʌltɪ,lɛvl] ADJ (*Am*) = **multistorey**
multi·lin·gual [,mʌltɪ 'lɪŋgwəl] ADJ multilingue
multi·me·dia [,mʌltɪ'mi:dɪə] ADJ (*Comput*) multimediale
■ N multimediale *m*
multi·mil·lion·aire [,mʌltɪ,mɪljə'nɛəʳ] N multimiliardario(-a)
multi·na·tion·al [,mʌltɪ'næʃənl] N multinazionale *f*
■ ADJ multinazionale
multi·ple ['mʌltɪpl] ADJ **1**
■ WITH SG N multiplo(-a) **2** (*with pl n: many*) molteplici
■ N **1** (*Math*) multiplo **2** (*Brit: also:* **multiple store**) *grande magazzino che fa parte di una catena*
multiple choice N esercizi *mpl* a scelta multipla
multiple crash N serie *f inv* di incidenti a catena
multiple purpose resource management N gestione *f* multiuso delle risorse
multiple sclerosis N sclerosi *f* a placche
multiple socket N (*Elec*) presa multipla
multi·plex ['mʌltɪ,plɛks] N (*also:* **multiplex cinema**) cinema multisale *m inv*
multi·pli·ca·tion [,mʌltɪplɪ'keɪʃən] N moltiplicazione *f*
multiplication table N tavola pitagorica; **to learn one's multiplication tables** imparare le tabelline
multi·plic·ity [,mʌltɪ'plɪsɪtɪ] N molteplicità *f inv*; **for a multiplicity of reasons** per una serie di ragioni
multi·ply ['mʌltɪ,plaɪ] VT (*Math*) moltiplicare
■ VI **1** (*Math*) moltiplicare; **she can't multiply** non sa fare le moltiplicazioni **2** (*increase*) moltiplicarsi
multi·pur·pose [,mʌltɪ'pɜ:pəs] ADJ multiuso *inv*
multi·racial [,mʌltɪ'reɪʃəl] ADJ multirazziale
multi-skilled [,mʌltɪ'skɪld] ADJ versatile; **to be multi-skilled** essere versatile
multi-skilling [,mʌltɪ'skɪlɪŋ] N versatilità
multi·sto·rey [,mʌltɪ'stɔ:rɪ], (*Am*) **multi-level** ADJ (*building, car park*) a più piani
multi-tasking [,mʌltɪ'tɑ:skɪŋ] N (*of computer, person*) versatilità *f inv*
multi·tude ['mʌltɪ,tju:d] N moltitudine *f*
multi-user [,mʌltɪ'ju:zəʳ] ADJ multiutente *inv*
◎ **mum¹** [mʌm] N (*Brit fam: mother*) mamma; **I'll ask mum** chiederò alla mamma; **my mum** la mia mamma
mum² [mʌm] ADJ: **to keep mum (about sth)** non fare parola (di qc), non aprire bocca (su qc); **mum's the word!** acqua in bocca!
mum·ble ['mʌmbl] VT, VI borbottare
mum·bo jum·bo [,mʌmbəʊ'dʒʌmbəʊ] N (*pej*) sfilza di paroloni
mum·mi·fy ['mʌmɪ,faɪ] VT mummificare
mum·my¹ ['mʌmɪ] N (*Brit fam: mother*) mamma; **I want my mummy** voglio la mia mamma; **he's a mummy's boy** è un mammone
mum·my² ['mʌmɪ] N (*embalmed corpse*) mummia
mumps [mʌmps] NSG orecchioni *mpl*
munch [mʌntʃ] VT, VI sgranocchiare
munch·ies ['mʌntʃɪz] NPL (*Am*) qualcosa di sgranocchiare **to have the munchies** (*be hungry*) avere un buco nello stomaco
mun·dane [,mʌn'deɪn] ADJ (*worldly*) di questo mondo; (*pej: humdrum*) banale, terra terra *inv*
Mu·nich ['mju:nɪk] N Monaco *f* (di Baviera)
mu·nici·pal [mju:'nɪsɪpəl] ADJ municipale, comunale
mu·nici·pal·ity [mju:,nɪsɪ'pælɪtɪ] N (*place*) comune *m*, municipio
mu·nifi·cence [mju:'nɪfɪsns] N (*frm*) munificenza
mu·nifi·cent [mju:'nɪfɪsnt] ADJ munifico(-a)
mu·ni·tions [mju:'nɪʃənz] NPL munizioni *fpl*
munitions dump N deposito di munizioni
mu·ral ['mjʊərəl] ADJ murale
■ N dipinto murale
◎ **mur·der** ['mɜ:dəʳ] N **1** omicidio, assassinio; **to commit murder** commettere un omicidio; **a terrible murder** un terribile omicidio **2** (*fam*): **it was murder!** è stato pazzesco!; **to scream blue murder** strepitare; **she gets away with murder** se la cava sempre
■ VT (*person*) assassinare; (*fig, song*) massacrare
murder case N caso di omicidio
mur·der·er ['mɜ:dərəʳ] N assassino, omicida *m*
mur·der·ess ['mɜ:dərɪs] N assassina, omicida *f*
mur·der·ous ['mɜ:dərəs] ADJ (*intentions*) omicida; (*look*) assassino(-a); (*climate, road*) micidiale
murder weapon N arma del delitto
mu·rex ['mjʊərɛks] N murice *m*
murk [mɜ:k] N oscurità *f inv*, buio
murky ['mɜ:kɪ] ADJ (*comp* **-ier**, *superl* **-iest**) (*gen*) oscuro(-a), cupo(-a), tenebroso(-a), buio(-a); (*thick: darkness*) fitto(-a); (*: smoke*) denso(-a); (*fig*) torbido(-a)
mur·mur ['mɜ:məʳ] N (*soft speech*) mormorio; (*of traffic, voices*) brusio; (*of bees*) ronzio; (*of leaves*) fruscio; **there were murmurs of disagreement** c'era un mormorio di disapprovazione; **without a murmur** senza fiatare; **heart murmur** (*Med*) soffio al cuore
■ VT, VI borbottare, mormorare
Murphy's law [,mɜ:fɪz'lɔ:] N legge *f* di Murphy

MusB, MusBac N ABBR (= **Bachelor of Music**) *diploma universitario in musica*

◎**mus·cle** ['mʌsl] N muscolo; (*fig*) energia, forza; **to have muscle** avere potere e influenza; **he never moved a muscle** rimase fermo immobile
▸ **muscle in** VI + ADV: **to muscle in (on sth)** (*fam*) intromettersi *or* immischiarsi (in qc)

mus·cle·man ['mʌsl,mæn] N (*pl* **-men**) mister muscolo *m inv*

mus·cu·lar ['mʌskjʊlə^r] ADJ muscolare; (*person, arm*) muscoloso(-a); **he's got muscular legs** ha gambe muscolose

muscular dystrophy N distrofia muscolare

MusD, MusDoc N ABBR (= **Doctor of Music**) *titolare di un diploma universitario in musica*

Muse [mju:z] N (*Myth*) Musa

muse[1] [mju:z] N (*fig*) musa

muse[2] [mju:z] VI: **to muse on** *or* **about sth** rimuginare *or* meditare su qc

◎**mu·seum** [mju:'zɪəm] N museo

museum piece N pezzo da museo

mush [mʌʃ] [mʊʃ] N (*paste*) poltiglia, pappa; (*fig*) sdolcinatezza

mush·room ['mʌʃrum] N (*Bot*) fungo
■ ADJ (*soup, omelette*) ai *or* coi funghi; (*flavour*) di funghi; (*colour*) color beige rosato *inv*
■ VI **1** (*town*) svilupparsi rapidamente; (*houses*) spuntare come funghi; **the cloud of smoke went mushrooming up** la nuvola di fumo si alzò prendendo la forma di un fungo **2 to go mushrooming** andare per funghi, andare a cercare funghi

mushroom cloud N fungo di un'esplosione nucleare

mushy ['mʌʃɪ] ADJ (*comp* **-ier**, *superl* **-iest**) (*food*) spappolato(-a), come pappa; (*fig, film, novel*) sdolcinato(-a)

mushy peas NPL *piatto a base di piselli grandi stracotti e mescolati fino a ridurli in poltiglia*

◎**mu·sic** ['mju:zɪk] N musica; **to set to music** mettere in musica *or* musicare; **it was music to her ears** (*fig*) era musica per le sue orecchie
■ ADJ (*teacher, lesson*) di musica
▹ www.music.ucc.ie/wrrm
▹ www.classical.net
▹ www.essentialsofmusic.com/glossary/n.html

◎**mu·si·cal** ['mju:zɪkəl] ADJ (*gen*) musicale; **he's very musical** (*fond of*) è amante della musica; (*skilled*) è portato per la musica; **I'm not musical** non sono portato per la musica; **she comes from a musical family** viene da una famiglia di musicisti
■ N (*Cine, Theatre*) musical *m inv*, commedia musicale
▹ www.musicals101.com/musical.htm

musical chairs NSG gioco delle sedie (*in cui bisogna sedersi non appena cessa la musica*); (*fig*) scambio delle poltrone

musical instrument N strumento musicale

mu·si·cal·ly ['mju:zɪkəlɪ] ADV musicalmente

music box, musical box N carillon *m inv*

music centre N stereo *m inv* compatto

music critic N critico musicale

music festival N festival *m inv* musicale

music hall N teatro di varietà
▹ www.rfwilmut.clara.net/musichll/musich.html
▹ www.theatrelinks.com/hall.htm

◎**mu·si·cian** [mju:'zɪʃən] N musicista *m/f*

mu·si·cian·ship [mju:'zɪʃənʃɪp] N tecnica (musicale)

music lover N appassionato(-a) di *or* amante *m/f* della musica

mu·si·colo·gist [,mju:zɪ'kɒlədʒɪst] N musicologo(-a)

mu·si·col·ogy [,mju:zɪ'kɒlədʒɪ] N musicologia

music stand N leggio

musk [mʌsk] N muschio

mus·ket ['mʌskɪt] N moschetto

musk ox N bue *m* muschiato

musk·rat ['mʌsk,ræt] N (*animal*) topo muschiato, ondatra; (*fur*) rat musqué *m inv*

musk rose N (*Bot*) rosa muschiata

musky ['mʌskɪ] ADJ (*comp* **-ier**, *superl* **-iest**) muschiato(-a)

◎**Mus·lim, Mos·lem** ['mʊslɪm] ADJ, N musulmano(-a)

mus·lin ['mʌzlɪn] N mussola (di cotone)
■ ADJ di mussola

mus·quash ['mʌskwɒʃ] N (*fur*) rat musqué *m inv*

muss [mʌs] VT (*also:* **muss up**: *Am fam: hair*) scompigliare; (: *dress*) spiegazzare

mus·sel ['mʌsl] N cozza

◎**must**[1] [mʌst] MODAL AUX VB **1** (*obligation*) dovere; **I must do it** devo farlo; **if you must** se proprio devi; **one must not be too hopeful** non bisogna sperare troppo; **there must be a reason** ci deve (pur) essere un motivo; **I must say** francamente; **you mustn't forget to send her a card** non devi dimenticare di mandarle una cartolina; **you must come again next year** devi assolutamente tornare il prossimo anno; **you must be joking!** stai scherzando! **2** (*probability*): **he must be there by now** dovrebbe essere arrivato ormai; **it must be cold up there** dev'essere freddo lassù; **I must have made a mistake** devo essermi sbagliato; **there must be some problem** dev'esserci qualche problema
■ N (*fam*): **this programme/trip is a must** è un programma/viaggio da non perdere; **for a celebration champagne is a must** per celebrare qc lo champagne è d'obbligo

must[2] [mʌst] N = **mustiness**

must[3] [mʌst] N (*in wine-making*) mosto

mus·tache [mə'stɑ:ʃ] N (*Am*) = **moustache**

mus·tard ['mʌstəd] N senape *f*; (*also:* **grain mustard**) mostarda; **as keen as mustard** molto entusiasta

mustard gas N (*Chem*) iprite *f*

mustard plaster N senapismo

mus·ter ['mʌstə^r] N (*gathering*) adunata; (*roll-call*) appello; **to pass muster** (*fig*) essere (considerato(-a)) accettabile *or* passabile
■ VT (*men, helpers*) radunare, mettere insieme; (*money, sum*) mettere insieme; (*also:* **muster up**: *strength, courage*) fare appello a; **I can't muster up any enthusiasm** non riesco ad entusiasmarmi; **he mustered his troops** ha radunato le truppe; **he mustered his courage** ha fatto appello al proprio coraggio
■ VI radunarsi

musti·ness ['mʌstɪnɪs] N odor di muffa *or* di stantio

mustn't ['mʌsnt] = **must not**

mus·ty ['mʌstɪ] ADJ (*comp* **-ier**, *superl* **-iest**) (*smell*) (che sa) di stantio *or* di muffa; (*ideas*) ammuffito(-a), stantio(-a); **to smell musty** aver odore di stantio

mu·tant ['mju:tənt] ADJ, N mutante (*m/f*)

mu·tate [mju:'teɪt] VI subire una mutazione

mu·ta·tion [mju:'teɪʃən] N mutazione *f*

mute [mju:t] ADJ (*comp* **-r**, *superl* **-st**) muto(-a)
■ N (*person*) muto(-a); (*Mus*) sordina

mut·ed ['mju:tɪd] ADJ (*noise*) attutito(-a), smorzato(-a);

Mm

(*criticism*) attenuato(-a); (*Mus*) in sordina; (: *trumpet*) con sordina

mu·ti·late ['mju:tɪˌleɪt] VT mutilare

mu·ti·la·tion [ˌmju:tɪ'leɪʃən] N mutilazione *f*

mu·ti·neer [ˌmju:tɪ'nɪəʳ] N ammutinato(-a)

mu·ti·nous ['mju:tɪnəs] ADJ (*sailor, troops*) ammutinato(-a); (*attitude*) ribelle

mu·ti·ny ['mju:tɪnɪ] N ammutinamento
■ VI ammutinarsi

mut·ter ['mʌtəʳ] N borbottio
■ VT borbottare, bofonchiare
■ VI borbottare; (*thunder*) brontolare

mut·ton ['mʌtn] N carne *f* di montone, montone *m*; **a leg of mutton** un cosciotto di montone; **mutton dressed as lamb** (*fig*) *una vecchia che vuol sembrare una giovincella*

◎ **mu·tu·al** ['mju:tjʊəl] ADJ (*affection, suspicion*) reciproco(-a); (*interests*) mutuo(-a), reciproco(-a), comune; (*friend, cousin*) comune; **to our mutual satisfaction** in modo da soddisfare entrambi, con reciproca soddisfazione; **the feeling was mutual** il sentimento era reciproco

mu·tu·al·ism ['mju:tjʊəˌlɪzəm] N simbiosi *f* mutualistica

mu·tu·al·ly ['mju:tjʊəlɪ] ADV reciprocamente; **a mutually agreed solution** una soluzione soddisfacente per entrambe le parti

Mu·zak® ['mju:zæk] N *musica di sottofondo trasmessa in ristoranti, posti di lavoro ecc*

muz·zle ['mʌzl] N (*snout*) muso; (*of gun*) bocca (da fuoco); (*for dog*) museruola
■ VT (*dog*) mettere la museruola a; (*fig: person*) costringere a tacere

muz·zy ['mʌzɪ] ADJ (*comp* **-ier**, *superl* **-iest**) (*outline, ideas*) confuso(-a); (*person*) intontito(-a)

MV [ˌɛm'vi:] ABBR (= **motor vessel**) M/N, m/n (= *motonave*)

MVP [ˌɛmvi:'pi:] N (*Am: Sport* = **most valuable player**) miglior giocatore(-trice)

MW ABBR (*Radio:* = **medium wave**) OM

◎ **my** [maɪ] POSS ADJ il/la mio(-a), *pl* i/le miei(-mie); **this is my house** questa è la mia casa; **my brother** mio fratello; **my friend** il mio amico; **my parents** i miei genitori; **my car** la mia macchina; **my opinions** le mie opinioni; **I've lost my wallet** ho perduto il portafoglio; **with my hands in my pockets** con le mani in tasca; **I want to wash my hair** voglio lavarmi i capelli; **I've hurt my foot** mi sono fatto male ad un piede

Myanmar ['maɪænmɑ:ʳ] N la Myanma

my·co·sis [maɪ'kəʊsɪs] N micosi *f*

MYOB [ˌɛmwaɪəʊ'b:] ABBR (= **mind your own business**) fatti gli affari tuoi

myo·pia [maɪ'əʊpɪə] N (*frm*) miopia

my·op·ic [maɪ'ɒpɪk] ADJ miope

myri·ad ['mɪrɪəd] N miriade *f*

myr·tle ['mɜ:tl] N mirto

◎ **my·self** [maɪ'sɛlf] PERS PRON (*reflexive*) mi; (*emphatic*) io stesso(-a); (*after preposition*) me, me stesso(-a); **by myself** da solo; **I don't like travelling by myself** non mi piace viaggiare da solo; **I did it (all) by myself** l'ho fatto (tutto) da solo; **I'm not myself today** non mi sento in forma oggi; **I've hurt myself** mi sono fatto male; **I looked at myself in the mirror** mi sono guardato allo specchio; **a beginner like myself** un principiante come me; **I made it myself** l'ho fatto io; *see also* **oneself**

mys·teri·ous [mɪs'tɪərɪəs] ADJ misterioso(-a)

mys·teri·ous·ly [mɪs'tɪərɪəslɪ] ADV misteriosamente

◎ **mys·tery** ['mɪstərɪ] N mistero; **it's a mystery to me where it can have gone** dove sia finito (per me) è un mistero; **a murder mystery** un romanzo giallo
■ ADJ (*man, woman*) misterioso(-a)

mystery play N mistero

mystery ship N nave *f* fantasma *inv*

mystery story N racconto del mistero

mystery tour N *viaggio con destinazione a sorpresa*

mys·tic ['mɪstɪk] ADJ, N mistico(-a)

mys·ti·cal ['mɪstɪkəl] ADJ mistico(-a)

mys·ti·cism ['mɪˌstɪsɪzəm] N misticismo

mys·ti·fi·ca·tion [ˌmɪstɪfɪ'keɪʃən] N (*bewilderment*) perplessità *f inv*

mys·ti·fy ['mɪstɪˌfaɪ] VT (*bewilder*) lasciare perplesso(-a), disorientare; **I'm totally mystified!** sono totalmente confuso!

DID YOU KNOW ...?
mystify is not translated by the Italian word mistificare

mys·tique [mɪs'ti:k] N fascino

◎ **myth** [mɪθ] N mito; **a Greek myth** un mito greco; **that's a myth** è una credenza falsa

myth·ic ['mɪθɪk] ADJ mitico(-a)

mythi·cal ['mɪθɪkəl] ADJ mitico(-a)

mytho·logi·cal [ˌmɪθə'lɒdʒɪkəl] ADJ mitologico(-a)

my·thol·ogy [mɪ'θɒlədʒɪ] N mitologia
▷ www.pantheon.org/

mytho·ma·nia [ˌmɪθəʊ'meɪnɪə] N mitomania

myxo·ma·to·sis [ˌmɪksəʊmə'təʊsɪs] N mixomatosi *f*

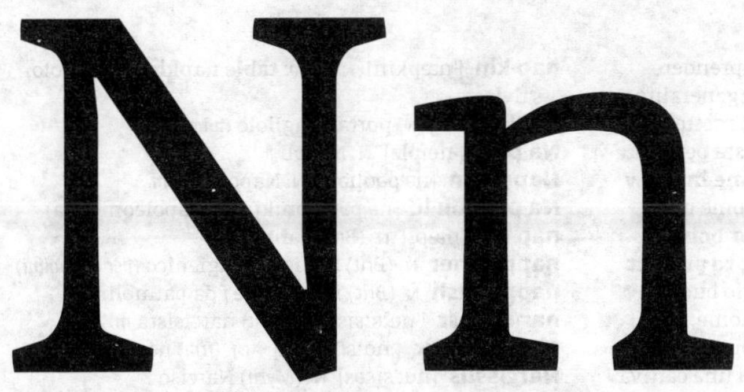

N, n [ɛn] N (*letter*) N, n *f or m inv*; **N for Nellie** (*Am*): **N for Nan** ≈ N come Napoli
N ABBR (= **north**) N (= *nord*)
NA [ˌɛn'eɪ] N ABBR **1** (*Am*: = **Narcotics Anonymous**) *associazione in aiuto dei tossicodipendenti* **2** (*Am*) = *National Academy*
n/a ABBR **1** (= **not applicable**) non pertinente **2** (*Comm etc*) = *no account*
NAACP [ˌɛneɪeɪsiː'piː] N ABBR (*Am*) = *National Association for the Advancement of Colored People*
NAAFI ['næfɪ] N ABBR (*Brit*: = **Navy, Army & Air Force Institute**) *organizzazione che fornisce negozi, mense ecc. per il personale militare*
nab [næb] VT (*fam*: *thief etc*) acciuffare, beccare; (: *person to speak to*) beccare, bloccare
NACU [ˌɛneɪsiː'juː] N ABBR (*Am*) = *National Association of Colleges and Universities*
na·dir ['neɪdɪəʳ] N (*Astron*) nadir *m*; (*fig*) punto più basso
naff [næf] ADJ kitsch
nag¹ [næg] N (*pej*: *horse*) ronzino
nag² [næg] VT (*also*: **nag at**) assillare, tormentare; **she's always nagging me** mi tormenta in continuazione; **the children nagged (at) their parents to take them to the fair** i bambini hanno tormentato i genitori per farsi portare alle giostre; **the family nagged me into buying a new car** a forza di insistere in famiglia mi hanno fatto comprare una macchina nuova
■ VI lagnarsi, brontolare in continuazione
■ N (*person*) brontolone(-a)
nag·ging ['nægɪŋ] ADJ (*person*) brontolone(-a); (*pain*) insistente, persistente; (*doubt, fear etc*) tormentoso(-a), angoscioso(-a)
■ N brontolii *mpl*, osservazioni *fpl* continue
nai·ad ['naɪæd] N (*Myth*) naiade *f*
nail [neɪl] N **1** (*Anat*) unghia; **to bite one's nails** mangiarsi le unghie **2** (*metal*) chiodo; **he hammered a nail into the wall** ha piantato un chiodo nel muro; **to hit the nail on the head** (*fig*) cogliere *or* colpire nel segno; **to pay cash on the nail** (*Brit*) pagare subito e in contanti, pagare sull'unghia (*fam*)
■ VT (*also fig fam*: *criminal*) inchiodare; **to nail the lid on a box** inchiodare il coperchio di una cassa
▸ **nail down** VT + ADV fissare con chiodi, inchiodare; (*fig*): **to nail sb down to a date** costringere qn a una data; **to nail sb down to a promise** costringere qn a fare una promessa; **to nail sb down to a price** costringere qn ad accettare un prezzo
▸ **nail up** VT + ADV (*picture, sign*) fissare con un chiodo; (*door*) chiudere con chiodi
nail bar N negozio (*or* bancone *m*) di manicure
nail·brush ['neɪlˌbrʌʃ] N spazzolino per unghie
nail·file ['neɪlˌfaɪl] N lima *or* limetta per unghie
nail polish N smalto per unghie
nail polish remover, nail varnish remover (*Brit*) N acetone *m*, solvente *m*
nail scissors NPL forbicine *fpl* per unghie
nail varnish N (*Brit*) = **nail polish**
Nai·ro·bi [naɪ'rəʊbɪ] N Nairobi *f*
na·ive [naɪ'iːv] ADJ ingenuo(-a)
na·ive·ly [naɪ'iːvlɪ] ADV ingenuamente
na·ive·ty [naɪ'iːvtɪ] N ingenuità *f inv*
na·ked ['neɪkɪd] ADJ (*person*) nudo(-a); (*hillside, trees*) spoglio(-a), nudo(-a); **the naked truth** la verità nuda e cruda; **visible to the naked eye** che si può vedere a occhio nudo; **with the naked eye** a occhio nudo
na·ked·ness ['neɪkɪdnɪs] N nudità
NAM [ˌɛneɪ'ɛm] N ABBR (*Am*) = *National Association of Manufacturers*
namby-pamby [ˌnæmbɪ'pæmbɪ] ADJ, N (*fam*) rammollito(-a)
◎ **name** [neɪm] N nome *m*; (*of book etc*) titolo; (*reputation*) (buon) nome, fama, reputazione *f*; **what's your name?** come ti chiami?; **my name is Peter** mi chiamo Peter; **his real name** il suo vero nome; **by the name of Jones** di nome Jones; **to go by** *or* **under the name of** farsi chiamare; **she knows them all by name** li conosce tutti per nome; **I know him only by name** lo conosco solo di nome; **in the name of the law/of God** in nome della legge/di Dio; **in the name of all those present** a nome di tutti i presenti; **in name only** solo

Nn

di nome; **to take sb's name and address** prendere nome e indirizzo di qn; (*Police*) prendere le generalità di qn; **to put one's name down for** (*ticket*) mettersi in lista per avere; (*school, course*) mettersi in lista per; **to call sb names** insultare qn; **he's a big name in show business** è una personalità *or* un grosso nome nel mondo dello spettacolo; **he has a name for being honest** è noto *or* famoso per la sua onestà; **to protect one's (good) name** salvaguardare il proprio buon nome; **to make a name for o.s.** farsi un nome; **the firm has a good name** l'azienda ha una buona reputazione; **to get (o.s.) a bad name** farsi una cattiva fama *or* una brutta reputazione

■ VT **1** (*baby etc*) chiamare; (*ship*) battezzare; **a man named Jones** un uomo di nome Jones; **he was named after his father** gli è stato dato il nome del padre; **they haven't named him yet** non gli hanno ancora dato un nome **2** (*mention*) nominare, fare il nome di; (*identify*) identificare; (: *accomplice*) fare il nome di, rivelare il nome di; **to name sb for a post** proporre la candidatura di qn a una carica, proporre qn per una carica; **you name it, we've got it** abbiamo tutto quello che vuoi **3** (*date, price etc*) stabilire, fissare; **have you named the day yet?** (*for wedding*) avete già fissato la data?

name·check ['neɪmtʃɛk] N menzione *f*, citazione *f*; **to have a name-check in** essere menzionato(-a) *or* citato(-a) in

■ VT menzionare, citare

name-drop ['neɪm,drɒp] VI: **he's always name-dropping** si dà tante arie vantando amicizie importanti

name-dropping ['neɪm,drɒpɪŋ] N: **there was a lot of name-dropping in his speech** il suo discorso era infarcito di nomi di gente famosa

name·less ['neɪmlɪs] ADJ (*unknown*) senza nome; (*anonymous*) ignoto(-a), anonimo(-a); (*indefinable: fears, crimes*) indescrivibile, indefinibile; **a certain person who shall be nameless** una persona di cui non verrà fatto il nome

name·ly ['neɪmlɪ] ADV vale a dire

name·plate ['neɪm,pleɪt] N (*on door etc*) targa, targhetta

name·sake ['neɪm,seɪk] N omonimo(-a)

nan bread ['nɑːn,brɛd] N *tipo di pane indiano poco lievitato di forma schiacciata*

nan·ny ['nænɪ] N (*children's*) bambinaia, tata (*fam*)

nanny goat N capra

nano·tech·nol·ogy [,nænəʊtɛk'nɒlədʒɪ] N nanotecnologia

▷ www.nano.org.uk/links.htm

▷ www.nano.gov

nap¹ [næp] N (*sleep*) sonnellino, pisolino; **to have** *or* **take a nap** fare *or* farsi un sonnellino, schiacciare un pisolino; **she likes to have a nap in the afternoon** le piace fare un pisolino di pomeriggio

■ VI: **to be caught napping** essere preso(-a) alla sprovvista

nap² [næp] N (*on cloth*) peluria; **against the nap** contropelo

NAPA [,ɛneɪpiː'eɪ] N ABBR (*Am*: = **National Association of Performing Arts**) *associazione nazionale degli artisti di palcoscenico*

na·palm ['neɪpɑːm] N napalm *m*

napalm bomb N bomba al napalm

nape [neɪp] N: **nape of the neck** nuca

naph·tha ['næfθə] N nafta

nap·kin ['næpkɪn] N (*also:* **table napkin**) tovagliolo, salvietta

napkin ring N portatovagliolo (*ad anello*)

Na·ples ['neɪplz] N Napoli *f*

Napoleon [nə'pəʊlɪən] N Napoleone *m*

Na·po·leon·ic [nə,pəʊlɪ'ɒnɪk] ADJ napoleonico(-a)

nap·py ['næpɪ] N (*Brit*) pannolino

nappy liner N (*Brit*) foglietto igienico (*per pannolini*)

nappy rash N (*Brit*) irritazione *f* da pannolino

nar·cis·sist ['nɑːsɪsɪst] N (*frm*) narcisista *m/f*

nar·cis·sis·tic [,nɑːsɪ'sɪstɪk] ADJ (*frm*) narcisistico(-a)

Narcissus [nɑː'sɪsəs] N (*Myth*) Narciso

nar·cis·sus [nɑː'sɪsəs] N (*pl* **narcissi** [nɑː'sɪsaɪ]) (*flower*) narciso

Narcissus complex N: **to have a Narcissus complex** essere narcisista

nar·cot·ic [nɑː'kɒtɪk] ADJ narcotico(-a)

■ N (*Med*) narcotico

narcotics NPL (*drugs*) narcotici *mpl*, stupefacenti *mpl*

nark [nɑːk] VT (*Brit fam*) scocciare

narked [nɑːkt] ADJ (*Brit fam*) scocciato(-a)

nar·rate [nə'reɪt] VT narrare, raccontare

nar·ra·tion [nə'reɪʃən] N narrazione *f*

nar·ra·tive ['nærətɪv] ADJ narrativo(-a)

■ N narrazione *f*; (*technique*) narrativa

nar·ra·tor [nə'reɪtə^r] N narratore(-trice)

◎ **nar·row** ['nærəʊ] ADJ (*comp* **-er**, *superl* **-est**) (*gen*) stretto(-a); (*advantage, majority*) scarso(-a); (*outlook, mind*) ristretto(-a), limitato(-a); (*interpretation*) limitato(-a); (*means*) limitato(-a), modesto(-a); **to have a narrow escape** farcela per un pelo, scamparla bella; **to take a narrow view of** avere una visione limitata di

■ VT **1** (*also:* **narrow down**) (: *road, investigations*) restringere; (: *choice*) restringere, ridurre; **to narrow sth down to** ridurre qc a; **we have narrowed the field (down) to three candidates** abbiamo ristretto la scelta a tre candidati **2** (*eyes*) stringere

■ VI (*road*) restringersi; (*majority*) ridursi; (*eyes*) stringersi; **so the question narrows down to this** la questione, quindi, si riduce a questo

narrow·band ['nærəʊ,bænd] (*Comput*) N banda stretta

■ ADJ a banda stretta

narrow-gauge ['nærəʊ,geɪdʒ] ADJ (*Rail*) a scartamento ridotto

nar·row·ly ['nærəʊlɪ] ADV **1** (*miss, escape etc*): **Maria narrowly escaped drowning** per un pelo Maria non è affogata; **he narrowly missed hitting the cyclist** per poco non ha investito il ciclista **2** (*interpret: rules etc*) rigorosamente

narrow-minded [,nærəʊ'maɪndɪd] ADJ (*pej: person*) di idee ristrette; (: *views, outlook etc*) ristretto(-a)

narrow-mindedness [,nærəʊ'maɪndɪdnɪs] N chiusura mentale

nar·row·ness ['nærəʊnɪs] N strettezza

nar·whal ['nɑːwəl] N narvalo

NAS [ɛneɪ'ɛs] N ABBR (*Am*) = *National Academy of Sciences*

NASA ['næsə] N ABBR (*Am*: = **National Aeronautics and Space Administration**) N.A.S.A. *f*

na·sal ['neɪzəl] ADJ nasale

na·sal·ize ['neɪzə,laɪz] VT nasalizzare

nas·cent ['næsnt] ADJ (*frm*) nascente

NASDAQ, Nasdaq ['næzdæk] N (*Fin*) Nasdaq *m*

▷ www.nasdaq.com

Nas·sau ['næsaʊ] N Nassau *f*

nas·ti·ly ['nɑːstɪlɪ] ADV (*unpleasantly*) sgradevolmente; (*spitefully*) malignamente, con cattiveria

nas·ti·ness ['nɑːstɪnɪs] N (*of person, remark*) malignità, cattiveria

na·stur·tium [nə'stɜːʃəm] N cappuccina, nasturzio (indiano)

nas·ty ['nɑːstɪ] ADJ (*comp* **-ier**, *superl* **-iest**) (*smell, taste*) cattivo(-a), sgradevole; (*moment, experience, situation*) brutto(-a), spiacevole; (*accident, wound, corner, trick*) brutto(-a); (*person*) antipatico(-a), villano(-a); (: *spiteful*: *also*: *remark, mind*) maligno(-a), cattivo(-a); (*temper, nature*) brutto(-a); (*weather*) brutto(-a), cattivo(-a); (*book, film etc*) di cattivo gusto; (: *violent*) violento(-a); **a nasty cold** un brutto raffreddore; **a nasty smell** un cattivo odore; **to smell nasty** avere un cattivo odore, non avere un buon odore; **to turn nasty** (*situation*) mettersi male; (*weather*) guastarsi; (*person*) incattivirsi; **he's a nasty piece of work** (*fam*) è un farabutto; **what a nasty mind you have!** quanto sei maligno!; **he had a nasty time of it** se l'è passata brutta; **she gave me a nasty look** mi ha dato un'occhiataccia; **it's a nasty business** è una brutta faccenda, è un brutto affare

NAS/UWT [ɛneɪ'ɛs,juːdʌbljuː'tiː] N ABBR (*Brit*: = **National Association of Schoolmasters/Union of Women Teachers**) *sindacato di insegnanti in Inghilterra e Galles*

◎ **na·tion** ['neɪʃən] N nazione *f*

◎ **na·tion·al** ['næʃənl] ADJ nazionale; **national news** notizie *fpl* dall'interno; **national press** stampa (a diffusione) nazionale
■ N cittadino(-a)

national anthem N inno nazionale

National Curriculum N (*Brit*) ≈ programma *m* (scolastico) ministeriale (*in Inghilterra e Galles*)

NATIONAL CURRICULUM

Il **National Curriculum**, il programma scolastico di base adottato nelle scuole inglesi e gallesi, comprende le seguenti materie: inglese, matematica, scienze, tecnologia, storia, geografia, educazione musicale e artistica, educazione fisica e lingue straniere (più il gallese, nelle scuole del Galles). L'apprendimento di inglese, matematica e scienze viene valutato periodicamente durante tutto il percorso scolastico. Nelle scuole primarie e secondarie si insegna inoltre educazione religiosa, e nelle scuole secondarie anche educazione sessuale; è consentito ai genitori dispensare i propri figli dall'insegnamento di queste materie, se lo desiderano.
Nell'Irlanda del Nord il sistema è simile a quello inglese e gallese, mentre in Scozia il programma è stabilito dagli organi scolastici regionali e da ciascun istituto.
▷ www.nc.uk.net/index.html

national debt N debito pubblico

national dress, national costume N costume *m* nazionale

National Gallery N (*in London*) National Gallery *f*
▷ www.nationalgallery.org.uk

national grid N: **the national grid** la rete elettrica nazionale

National Guard N (*Am*): **the National Guard** la milizia nazionale (*volontaria, in ogni stato*)

National Health N (*Brit*: *also*: **National Health Service**) *servizio nazionale di assistenza sanitaria*; **I got it on the National Health** l'ho avuto con la mutua

national income N (*Econ*) reddito nazionale

National Insurance N (*Brit*) ≈ Previdenza Sociale

na·tion·al·ism ['næʃnə,lɪzəm] N nazionalismo

◎ **na·tion·al·ist** ['næʃnəlɪst] ADJ nazionalista; (*sympathies*) nazionalistico(-a)
■ N nazionalista *m/f*

na·tion·al·is·tic [,næʃnə'lɪstɪk] ADJ (*pej*) nazionalistico(-a)

na·tion·al·ity [,næʃə'nælɪtɪ] N nazionalità *f inv*; (*citizenship*) cittadinanza, nazionalità

na·tion·ali·za·tion [,næʃnəlaɪ'zeɪʃən] N nazionalizzazione *f*

na·tion·al·ize ['næʃnə,laɪz] VT nazionalizzare

na·tion·al·ized ['næʃnə,laɪzd] ADJ nazionalizzato(-a)

na·tion·al·ly ['næʃnəlɪ] ADV (*consider*) da un punto di vista nazionale; (*broadcast*) in tutto il paese; (*apply etc*) a livello nazionale

national park N parco nazionale

National Security Council N (*Am*) consiglio nazionale di sicurezza

national service N (*Mil*) servizio militare

National Trust N (*Brit*): **the National Trust** ≈ soprintendenza ai beni culturali e ambientali

NATIONAL TRUST

Fondato nel 1895, il **National Trust** è un'organizzazione che si occupa della raccolta di fondi per la tutela e salvaguardia di edifici e monumenti di interesse storico e di territori di interesse ambientale nel Regno Unito.
▷ www.nationaltrust.org.uk/main

nation-state ['neɪʃənsteɪt] N stato-nazione *m*

nation-wide ['neɪʃən,waɪd] ADJ, ADV su scala nazionale

◎ **na·tive** ['neɪtɪv] ADJ **1** (*country, town*) natale, natio(-a), nativo(-a); (*dialect*) nativo(-a); **he's a native Italian speaker** è di madrelingua italiana; **native language** lingua materna, madrelingua; **native land** paese *m* natio, patria; **my native country** il mio paese natale **2** (*innate: ability*) innato(-a), naturale **3** (*indigenous: animal, plant*) indigeno(-a), originario(-a); (: *product, resources*) del luogo, del paese; **native to** originario(-a) di; **Britain's native red squirrel** lo scoiattolo rosso originario della Gran Bretagna **4** (*of the natives: customs, costume, rites*) del luogo, del paese **5** (*offensive: non-Western*) indigeno(-a)
■ N **1** (*of birth, nationality*) abitante *m/f* del luogo; **he's a native of Japan** è giapponese di nascita; **he's a native of Salzburg** è originario di Salisburgo; **he speaks Italian like a native** parla l'italiano come un madrelingua **2** (*offensive: esp in colonies*) indigeno(-a)

Native American N *discendente di tribù nordamericana dell'America settentrionale*
▷ www.americanindian.si.edu/

Na·tiv·ity [nə'tɪvɪtɪ] N (*Rel*): **the Nativity** la Natività

nativity play N rappresentazione *f* della Natività

◎ **NATO** ['neɪtəʊ] N ABBR (= **North Atlantic Treaty Organisation**) N.A.T.O. *f*

nat·ter ['nætəʳ] (*fam*) N chiacchierata; **to have a natter** fare quattro chiacchiere
■ VI chiacchierare

nat·ty ['nætɪ] ADJ (*comp* **-ier**, *superl* **-iest**) (*fam*) elegante, chic *inv*

◎ **natu·ral** ['nætʃrəl] ADJ (*gen*) naturale; (*ability*) innato(-a); (*manner*) semplice; **death from natural**

Nn

causes (*Law*) morte *f* per cause naturali; **he died a natural death** è morto di morte naturale; **a natural instinct** un istinto naturale; **in its natural state** allo stato naturale; **he never knew his natural parents** non ha mai conosciuto i suoi veri genitori; **it's natural to be tired after a long journey** è naturale essere stanchi dopo un lungo viaggio; **it seemed the natural thing to do** è sembrata la cosa più ovvia *or* più naturale da farsi; **it is natural that ...** è naturale che... + *sub*; **he's a natural painter** è un pittore nato; **C natural** (*Mus*) do naturale
■ N **1** (*Mus: sign*) bequadro **2 she's a natural!** ci è nata!

natural childbirth N parto naturale
natural gas N gas *m* metano
natural history N storia naturale
natu·ral·ism ['nætʃrə,lɪzəm] N (*Art, Literature*) naturalismo
natu·ral·ist ['nætʃrəlɪst] N naturalista *m/f*
natu·ral·is·tic [,nætʃrə'lɪstɪk] ADJ (*Art*) naturalistico(-a)
natu·rali·za·tion [,nætʃrəlaɪ'zeɪʃən] N (*see vb*) naturalizzazione *f*; acclimatazione *f*
natu·ral·ize ['nætʃrə,laɪz] VT: **to be naturalized** (*person*) naturalizzarsi; **to become naturalized** (*animal, plant*) acclimatarsi
◎ **natu·ral·ly** ['nætʃrəlɪ] ADV **1** (*gen*) naturalmente; **naturally, we were very disappointed** naturalmente siamo rimasti molto delusi **2** (*by nature: gifted*) di natura, per natura; **he is naturally lazy** è pigro per natura; **my hair is naturally curly** i miei capelli sono ricci per natura; **a naturally optimistic person** un ottimista per natura; **it comes naturally to him to do ...** gli viene spontaneo fare... **3** (*unaffectedly: behave, speak*) con naturalezza, in modo naturale **4** (*of course*) naturalmente, certo
natu·ral·ness ['nætʃrəlnɪs] N naturalezza
natural resources NPL risorse *fpl* naturali
natural selection N selezione *f* naturale
natural wastage N (*Industry*) naturale diminuzione *f* di personale (*per pensionamento, decesso, ecc.*)
◎ **na·ture** ['neɪtʃə^r] N **1** natura; **a law of nature** una legge di natura; **the laws of nature** le leggi naturali *or* della natura; **to draw/paint from nature** disegnare/dipingere dal vero **2** (*character: of person*) natura, indole *f*; (*: of thing*) natura; **by nature** per natura, di natura; **it is not in his nature to say that** non è nella sua natura *or* nel suo carattere parlare così ; **it's second nature to him to do that** gli viene quasi istintivo farlo **3** (*kind, type*) natura; **things of this nature** cose *fpl* di questo genere; **the ambitious nature of the project** la natura ambiziosa del progetto; **documents of a confidential nature** documenti *mpl* di natura riservata; **something in the nature of an apology** una specie di scusa
-natured ['neɪtʃəd] SUFF: **ill-natured** maldisposto(-a); **jealous-natured** geloso(-a) di natura, di temperamento geloso
nature lover N amante *m/f* della natura
nature reserve N (*Brit*) parco naturale
nature study N scienze *fpl* naturali
nature trail N *percorso tracciato in parchi nazionali ecc. con scopi educativi*
na·tur·ism ['neɪtʃə,rɪzm] N naturismo, nudismo
na·tur·ist ['neɪtʃə,rɪst] N naturista *m/f*, nudista *m/f*
naught [nɔ:t] N **1** (*Math*) = **nought 2** (*old liter: nothing*) niente *m*, nulla *m*; **to come to naught** finire in nulla

naugh·ti·ly ['nɔ:tɪlɪ] ADV (*behave*) male, con cattiveria; (*say*) maliziosamente
naugh·ti·ness ['nɔ:tɪnɪs] N cattiveria
naugh·ty ['nɔ:tɪ] ADJ (*comp* **-ier**, *superl* **-iest**) **1** (*child*) cattivo(-a), cattivello(-a), birichino(-a); **naughty girl!** cattiva!; **that was a naughty thing to do** non si fanno queste cose **2** (*joke, song, story, film*) spinto(-a)
nau·sea ['nɔ:zɪə] N (*Med*) nausea; (*fig: disgust*) schifo, disgusto
nau·seate ['nɔ:zɪ,eɪt] VT (*Med*) nauseare; (*fig*) far schifo a, disgustare; **I was nauseated by the smell** ero nauseato dall'odore
nau·seat·ing ['nɔ:zɪ,eɪtɪŋ] ADJ nauseante; (*fig*) disgustoso(-a)
nau·seous ['nɔ:zɪəs] ADJ (*Med, fig*) nauseabondo(-a); **to be nauseous** avere la nausea
nau·ti·cal ['nɔ:tɪkəl] ADJ nautico(-a)
nautical mile N miglio nautico *or* marino
◎ **na·val** ['neɪvəl] ADJ (*battle, strength, base, academy*) navale; (*affairs, barracks*) della marina; **naval forces** forze *fpl* navali, marina militare; **naval officer** ufficiale *m* di marina
nave [neɪv] N (*of church*) navata centrale

DID YOU KNOW ...?
nave is not translated by the Italian word ***nave***

na·vel ['neɪvəl] N ombelico
navi·gable ['nævɪgəbl] ADJ (*river etc*) navigabile
navi·gate ['nævɪ,geɪt] VT (*ship, plane*) pilotare, governare; (*seas, river*) navigare, percorrere navigando
■ VI navigare; (*Aut*) fare da navigatore
navi·ga·tion [,nævɪ'geɪʃən] N navigazione *f*
navi·ga·tor ['nævɪ,geɪtə^r] N (*Naut, Aer*) navigatore *m*, ufficiale *m* di rotta; (*explorer*) navigatore *m*; (*Aut*) secondo pilota *m*, copilota *m/f*
nav·vy ['nævɪ] N (*Brit*) sterratore *m*, manovale *m*
◎ **navy** ['neɪvɪ] N marina (militare *or* da guerra); **to join the navy** arruolarsi in marina; **Department of the Navy** (*Am*) Ministero della Marina; **he's in the navy** è in marina
navy-blue [,neɪvɪ'blu:] ADJ (*also:* **navy**) blu scuro *inv*; **a navy-blue skirt** una gonna blu scuro
nay [neɪ] ADV (*old: no*) no
Naza·rene [,næzə'ri:n] N: **Jesus the Nazarene** Gesù Nazareno, il Nazareno
Naza·reth ['næzərɪθ] N Nazareth f
◎ **Nazi** ['nɑ:tsɪ] ADJ, N nazista (*m/f*)
Na·zism ['nɑ:tsɪzəm] N nazismo
NB [,ɛn'bi:] N ABBR (= **nota bene**) N.B.
■ ABBR (*Canada*) = *New Brunswick*
NBA [,ɛnbi:'eɪ] N ABBR **1** (*Am:* = **National Basket Association**) ≈ F.I.P. *f* (= *Federazione Italiana Pallacanestro*) **2** (*Am*) = *National Boxing Association*
NBC [,ɛnbi:'si:] N ABBR (*Am:* = **National Broadcasting Company**) *rete televisiva americana*
NBS [,ɛnbi:'ɛs] N ABBR (*Am:* = **National Bureau of Standards**) *istituto per la normalizzazione*
NC ABBR **1** (*Comm:* = **no charge**) gratis **2** (*Am Post*) = *North Carolina*
NCC [,ɛnsi:'si:] N ABBR **1** (= **Nature Conservancy Council**) *organismo per la protezione dei beni naturali* **2** (*Am*) = *National Council of Churches*
NCO [,ɛnsi:'əʊ] N ABBR = **noncommissioned officer**
ND ABBR (*Am Post*) = **North Dakota**
NE ABBR **1** (*Am Post*) = **Nebraska,** = **New England**
2 (= **North East(ern)**) NE (= *nord est*)

NEA ['ɛni:'eɪ] N ABBR *(Am)* = *National Education Association*

Ne·an·der·thal [nɪ'ændə,tɑ:l] ADJ **1** *(Archeol)* neandertaliano(-a) **2** *(pej: brutish: person, behaviour)* da bruto; (: *reactionary: politician, attitude*) reazionario(-a)
■ N *(pej: brute)* bruto(-a); (: *reactionary*) reazionario(-a)

Neanderthal man N l'Uomo di Neandertal

neap [ni:p] N *(also:* **neap tide***)* marea di quadratura

Nea·poli·tan [nɪə'pɒlɪtən] ADJ, N napoletano(-a)

◎ **near** [nɪə^r] ADV vicino; **it's quite near** è abbastanza vicino; **I like to know that you are near** mi piace sapere che tu sei (qui) vicino *or* accanto; **near at hand** a portata di mano; *(event)* imminente, alle porte; **to come** *or* **draw near** *(person, event)* avvicinarsi; **come nearer** vieni più vicino, avvicinati; **to bring sth nearer (to)** portare qc più vicino (a); **he came near to being drowned** per poco non è annegato; **near to tears** sul punto di piangere; **that's near enough** va bene così ; **there were 100 people there, near enough** c'erano pressappoco 100 persone; **nowhere near full** ben lontano(-a) dall'essere pieno(-a)
■ PREP *(also:* **near to**: *of place)* vicino a, presso; *(in time)* circa, quasi; **it's very near to the school** è molto vicino alla scuola; **near here/there** qui/lì vicino; **is there a bank near here?** c'è una banca qui vicino?; **I live near Liverpool** abito vicino a Liverpool; **he was standing near the door** era in piedi vicino alla porta; **it was somewhere near midnight** era circa mezzanotte; **it's somewhere near here** dev'essere da queste parti; **the passage is near the end of the book** il brano è verso la fine del libro; **his views are very near my own** è di vedute molto simili alle mie; **nobody comes anywhere near her at cooking** nessuno può competere con lei in cucina
■ ADJ *(comp* **-er**, *superl* **-est***)* **1** *(in space, time)* vicino(-a); **where's the nearest service station?** dov'è la stazione di servizio più vicina?; **the nearest shops were three kilometres away** i negozi più vicini erano a tre chilometri di distanza; **in the near distance** a breve distanza; **the nearest way** la via *or* strada più breve; **£25,000 or nearest offer** *(Brit)* 25.000 sterline trattabili; **in the near future** in un prossimo futuro **2** *(relation)* stretto(-a), prossimo(-a) **3** **their win was a near thing** hanno vinto di misura; **that was a near thing!** per un pelo!
■ VT *(place, event)* avvicinarsi a; **the building is nearing completion** il palazzo è quasi terminato *or* ultimato

◎ **near·by** [nɪə'baɪ] ADV (qui *or* lì) vicino; **there's a supermarket nearby** c'è un supermercato qui vicino
■ ADJ vicino(-a); **a nearby village** un paese vicino

Near East N: **the Near East** il Medio Oriente

◎ **near·ly** ['nɪəlɪ] ADV **1** *(gen)* quasi; **I'm nearly fifteen** ho quasi quindici anni; **dinner's nearly ready** la cena è quasi pronta; **not nearly** non… affatto; **it's not nearly ready** non è affatto pronto; **that's not nearly enough** non basta per niente **2** *(with vb)*: **I nearly lost it** per poco non lo perdevo; **she was nearly crying** era lì lì per piangere; **he very nearly died** ha rischiato di morire; **did you win? — very nearly!** hai vinto? — c'è mancato poco!

nearly new ADJ *(clothes)* quasi nuovo(-a), seminuovo(-a); **a nearly new shop** un negozio di abiti usati quasi nuovi

near miss N *(Aer)* incidente mancato; **that was a near miss** *(fig)* c'è mancato poco; **he had a near miss with that car** per un pelo non ha investito quella macchina

near·ness ['nɪənɪs] N prossimità, vicinanza

near·side ['nɪə,saɪd] N *(Aut: right-hand drive)* lato sinistro; (: *left-hand drive*) lato destro
■ ADJ *(see n)* sinistro(-a); destro(-a)

near-sighted [,nɪə'saɪtɪd] ADJ miope

◎ **neat** [ni:t] ADJ *(comp* **-er**, *superl* **-est***)* **1** *(tidy: person, handwriting)* ordinato(-a); (: *room, house, desk*) ordinato(-a), in ordine; (: *work*) accurato(-a), pulito(-a); *(well-dressed)* curato(-a) nel vestire; *(skilful)* (: *plan, solution*) indovinato(-a), azzeccato(-a); *(Am fam: excellent)* figo(-a); **she is a neat worker** è molto accurata nel lavoro; **he has made a neat job of the bathroom** ha fatto un buon lavoro *or* un lavoro accurato nel bagno; **she has a neat figure** è ben proporzionata; **a neat little car** una bella macchinetta **2** *(undiluted: spirits)* liscio(-a)

neat·ly ['ni:tlɪ] ADV **1** *(tidily: fold, wrap, dress)* accuratamente, con cura; (: *write*) bene, in bella calligrafia **2** *(skilfully)* abilmente; **neatly put** ben espresso(-a)

neat·ness ['ni:tnɪs] N **1** *(tidiness)* ordine *m* **2** *(skilfulness)* abilità

Ne·bras·ka [nɪ'bræskə] N Nebraska *m*
▷ www.nebraska.gov/index.phtml

nebu·la ['nɛbjʊlə] N nebulosa

nebu·lous ['nɛbjʊləs] ADJ nebuloso(-a); *(fig)* nebuloso(-a), vago(-a)

◎ **nec·es·sari·ly** ['nɛsɪsərɪlɪ] ADV necessariamente, per forza; *(lead to, give rise to)* inevitabilmente; **not necessarily** non necessariamente, non è detto

◎ **nec·es·sary** ['nɛsɪsərɪ] ADJ *(gen)* necessario(-a); *(result, effect)* inevitabile; **a necessary evil** un male necessario; **is it necessary to make so much noise?** è proprio necessario *or* indispensabile far tanto rumore?; **it is necessary for you to go** *or* **that you go** è necessario che *or* bisogna che tu vada; **don't do more than is necessary** non fare più del necessario; **if necessary** se necessario; **the necessary qualifications (for)** i requisiti necessari (per); **necessary to health** necessario(-a) alla salute
■ N *(fam: what is needed)*: **to do the necessary** fare il necessario; **the necessary** *(money)* i quattrini

ne·ces·si·tate [nɪ'sɛsɪ,teɪt] VT rendere necessario(-a)

ne·ces·sity [nɪ'sɛsɪtɪ] N **1** necessità; **there is no necessity for you to do that** non è necessario che *or* non c'è bisogno che tu lo faccia; **the necessity of doing sth** la necessità di fare qc; **is there any necessity?** è proprio necessario?, c'è proprio bisogno?; **of necessity** di necessità, necessariamente; **from** *or* **out of necessity** per necessità *or* bisogno; **in case of necessity** in caso di necessità **2** *(necessary thing)* cosa indispensabile, necessità *f inv*; **the bare necessities** lo stretto necessario, il minimo indispensabile

◎ **neck** [nɛk] N *(Anat, of bottle)* collo; *(of garment)* collo, colletto; (: *Dressmaking*) scollo; **to break one's neck** rompersi il collo; *(fig)* affannarsi; **to have a stiff neck** avere il torcicollo; **a V-neck sweater** un maglione con il collo a V; **the favourite won by a neck** *(Horseracing)* il favorito ha vinto per un'incollatura; **neck and neck** testa a testa; **to be up to one's neck in work** *(fam)* essere immerso(-a) nel lavoro fino al collo; **he is in it up to his neck** *(fam)* c'è dentro fino al collo; **to risk one's neck** rischiare l'osso del collo, rischiare la pelle; **to save one's neck** salvare la pelle; **to stick one's neck out** *(fam)* rischiare (forte); **in this neck of the woods** *(fam)* in questi paraggi, da queste parti; **dress with a low neck** *or* **low-necked dress** vestito scollato

Nn

■VI (*fam*) pomiciare, sbaciucchiarsi
neck·ing ['nɛkɪŋ] N (*fam*) pomiciate *fpl*
neck·lace ['nɛklɪs] N collana; **pearl necklace** collana di perle
neck·line ['nɛk,laɪn] N scollatura
neck·tie ['nɛk,taɪ] N (*esp Am*) cravatta
nec·ro·man·cy ['nɛkrəʊ,mænsɪ] N (*frm*) negromanzia
nec·ro·philia [,nɛkrəʊ'fɪlɪə] N necrofilia
nec·ro·phili·ac [,nɛkrəʊ'fɪlɪæk] N necrofilo(-a)
ne·cro·sis [nɛ'krəʊsɪs] N necrosi *f inv*
nec·tar ['nɛktə^r] N nettare *m*
nec·tar·ine ['nɛktərɪn] N nocepesca
née [neɪ] ADJ nata; **Mary Green neé Smith** Mary Green nata Smith
◎**need** [ni:d] N
1 (*necessity, obligation*) bisogno, necessità *f inv*; **if need(s) be** se necessario; **in case of need** in caso di bisogno *or* necessità; **there's no need to worry** non c'è bisogno di preoccuparsi; **there's no need for you to come too** non c'è bisogno *or* non occorre che venga anche tu; **what need is there to buy it?** che bisogno c'è di comprarlo?
2 (*want, lack*) bisogno; (*poverty*) povertà, bisogno; **to be in need of** *or* **to have need of** aver bisogno di; **it's in need of a wash** ha bisogno di una lavata; **she felt in need of a friend** sentiva il bisogno di un amico; **there's a great need for a book on this subject** c'è molto bisogno di un libro su questo argomento; **in times of need** nei momenti difficili; **to be in need** essere bisognoso(-a)
3 (*thing needed*) bisogno, necessità *f inv*; **£100 will meet my immediate needs** 100 sterline mi basteranno per le necessità più urgenti; **his needs are few** non ha grosse esigenze; **the needs of industry** le esigenze dell'industria
■VT aver bisogno di; **he needs money** ha bisogno di soldi, gli occorrono soldi; **I need it** ne ho bisogno, mi serve; **it's just what I need** è proprio quel che mi ci vuole; **a signature is needed** occorre *or* ci vuole una firma; **a much needed holiday** una vacanza di cui si ha proprio bisogno; **all that you need** tutto ciò che occorre; **he doesn't need me to tell him what to do** non c'è bisogno che sia io a dirgli cosa deve fare; **he needs watching** *or* **to be watched** va tenuto d'occhio; **this book needs careful reading** questo libro richiede un'attenta lettura; **the report needs no comment** il rapporto non ha bisogno di commenti; **he needs to have everything explained to him** bisogna spiegargli proprio tutto; **he doesn't need to be told all the details** non c'è bisogno di *or* non occorre dirgli tutti i particolari; **you only needed to ask** bastava che lo chiedessi; **it needed a war to alter things** c'è voluta una guerra per cambiare le cose
■MODAL AUX VB: **need I go?** devo (proprio) andarci?; **I need hardly tell you that ...** non c'è bisogno che io le dica *or* di dirle che...; **I need to do it** bisogna che io lo faccia, lo devo fare; **you don't need to go** non c'è bisogno che *or* non è necessario che tu vada, non devi andare per forza; **you needn't wait** non c'è bisogno che *or* non è necessario che aspetti; **you needn't have bothered to come** non occorreva che venissi; **it need not be done now** non c'è bisogno di farlo ora; **it need not follow that ...** non ne consegue necessariamente che... *+ sub*
need·ful ['ni:dfʊl] ADJ (*old*) necessario(-a)
nee·dle ['ni:dl] N ago; (*on record player*) puntina; **knitting needle** ferro (da calza); **it's like looking for a needle in a haystack** è come cercare un ago in un pagliaio; **to give sb the needle** (*fam: annoy*) dare ai nervi a qn
■VT (*fam: annoy*) irritare, dare ai nervi a; (: *tease, provoke*) punzecchiare; **she was needled into replying** punzecchiata, ha risposto
needle·cord ['ni:dl,kɔ:d] N (*Brit*) velluto a coste sottili
needle·point ['ni:dl,pɔɪnt] N ricamo ad ago
need·less ['ni:dlɪs] ADJ inutile; **needless to say he didn't keep his promise** inutile dire che non ha mantenuto la promessa
need·less·ly ['ni:dlɪslɪ] ADV inutilmente
needle·woman ['ni:dəl,wʊmən] N (*pl* **-women**) (*old*) cucitrice *f*
needle·work ['ni:dl,wɜ:k] N cucito; (*embroidery*) ricamo
needn't ['ni:dnt] = **need not**
needy ['ni:dɪ] ADJ (*comp* **-ier**, *superl* **-iest**) bisognoso(-a)
ne'er [nɛə^r] ADV (*poetic*) = **never**
ne'er-do-well ['nɛədu:,wɛl] N buono(-a) a nulla
ne·fari·ous [nɪ'fɛərɪəs] ADJ (*liter*) scellerato(-a)
ne·gate [nɪ'geɪt] VT (*frm: nullify*) annullare; (: *deny*) negare
ne·ga·tion [nɪ'geɪʃən] N negazione *f*
◎**nega·tive** ['nɛgətɪv] ADJ negativo(-a); **he's got a very negative attitude** ha un atteggiamento molto negativo
■N **1** (*answer*): **his answer was a firm negative** ha risposto con un fermo no *or* con un fermo diniego; **an answer in the negative** una risposta negativa; **to answer in the negative** rispondere negativamente *or* di no **2** (*Gram*) negazione *f*; **to put a sentence into the negative** mettere una frase in forma negativa **3** (*Phot*) negativa, negativo **4** (*Elec*) polo negativo
negative equity N *situazione in cui l'ammontare del mutuo su un immobile supera il suo valore sul mercato*
nega·tive·ly ['nɛgətɪvlɪ] ADV negativamente
ne·glect [nɪ'glɛkt] VT (*friends, children, garden*) trascurare; (*opportunity*) lasciarsi sfuggire; (*obligations*) mancare a; **to neglect to do sth** trascurare *or* tralasciare di fare qc
■N (*lack of care*) trascuratezza; (*of child*) il trascurare; (*of duty*) negligenza; (*of rule etc*) mancata osservanza; **neglect of one's appearance** trascuratezza nel vestire; **his neglect of his friends** l'aver trascurato gli amici; **in a state of neglect** (*house, garden*) in stato di abbandono
ne·glect·ed [nɪ'glɛktɪd] ADJ trascurato(-a)
ne·glect·ful [nɪ'glɛktfʊl] ADJ (*gen*) negligente; (*parent*) che trascura; **to be neglectful of sb/sth** trascurare qn/qc
neg·li·gee ['nɛglɪ,ʒeɪ] N négligé *m inv*
neg·li·gence ['nɛglɪdʒəns] N negligenza; **through negligence** per negligenza; **criminal negligence** (*Law*) reato d'omissione
neg·li·gent ['nɛglɪdʒənt] ADJ **1** (*careless*) negligente; **she has become negligent in her work** è diventata trascurata nel lavoro **2** (*offhand: gesture, manner*) noncurante, disinvolto(-a)
neg·li·gent·ly ['nɛglɪdʒəntlɪ] ADV con negligenza
neg·li·gible ['nɛglɪdʒəbl] ADJ trascurabile, insignificante
ne·go·tiable [nɪ'gəʊʃɪəbl] ADJ **1** (*Comm etc*) negoziabile; (: *cheque*) trasferibile; **not negotiable** non trasferibile **2** (*road*) transitabile; (*river*) navigabile; (*hill*) valicabile
◎**ne·go·ti·ate** [nɪ'gəʊʃɪ,eɪt] VT **1** (*Comm: treaty, loan, sale*)

negoziare, trattare **2** (*obstacle, difficulty, hill*) superare; (*river*) passare; (*bend in road*) prendere
■VI trattare, condurre (le) trattative; **to negotiate with sb for sth** trattare con qn per ottenere qc

ne·go·tiat·ing ta·ble [nɪˈgəʊʃɪˌeɪtɪŋˈteɪbl] N tavolo delle trattative

◎ **ne·go·tia·tion** [nɪˌgəʊʃɪˈeɪʃən] N (*gen*) trattativa; (*Pol*) negoziato, trattativa; **to enter into negotiations with sb** entrare in trattative *or* intavolare i negoziati con qn

ne·go·tia·tor [nɪˈgəʊʃɪˌeɪtəʳ] N negoziatore(-trice)

Ne·gress [ˈniːgrɪs] N (*old offensive*) negra

Ne·gro [ˈniːgrəʊ] (*offensive*) ADJ negro(-a)
■N (*pl* **-es**) negro(-a)

ne·groid [ˈniːgrɔɪd] ADJ negroide

neigh [neɪ] VI nitrire
■N nitrito

◎ **neigh·bour**, (*Am*) **neigh·bor** [ˈneɪbəʳ] N vicino(-a); (*Bible etc*) prossimo(-a)

neigh·bour·hood, (*Am*) **neigh·bor·hood** [ˈneɪbəˌhʊd] N (*district*) quartiere *m*, vicinato; (*surrounding area*) vicinanze *fpl*; **the whole neighbourhood knows her** tutto il vicinato *or* il quartiere la conosce; **in the neighbourhood of the station** nelle vicinanze *or* nei paraggi della stazione; **(something) in the neighbourhood of £1,000** qualcosa come 1.000 sterline

neighbourhood watch N (*Brit*: *also*: **neighbourhood watch scheme**) *sistema di vigilanza reciproca in un quartiere*

neigh·bour·ing, (*Am*) **neigh·bor·ing** [ˈneɪbərɪŋ] ADJ vicino(-a), confinante, limitrofo(-a)

neigh·bour·ly, (*Am*) **neigh·bor·ly** [ˈneɪbəlɪ] ADJ (*action*) da buon vicino; (*feelings*) amichevole; **people here aren't very neighbourly** la gente qua non ha il senso del vicinato

◎ **nei·ther** [ˈnaɪðəʳ] ADV né; **neither he nor I can go** né io né lui possiamo andare; **neither good nor bad** né buono(-a) né cattivo(-a); **he neither smokes nor drinks** non fuma né beve; **he likes neither the house nor the people** non gli piace né la casa né la gente; **neither Sarah nor Tamsin is coming to the party** alla festa non vengono né Sarah né Tamsin; **that's neither here nor there** (*fig*) questo non c'entra
■CONJ neanche, nemmeno, neppure; **if you aren't going, neither am I** se tu non ci vai, non ci vado neanch'io *or* nemmeno io; **I don't like it — neither do I** non mi piace — nemmeno a me; **I didn't move and neither did he** io non mi mossi e nemmeno lui; **... neither did I refuse** ...ma non ho nemmeno rifiutato
■ADJ: **on neither side** né da una parte né dall'altra; **neither story is true** nessuna delle due storie è vera
■PRON né l'uno(-a) né l'altro(-a), nessuno(-a) dei/delle due; **neither of them has any money** né l'uno né l'altro *or* nessuno dei due ha soldi, non hanno soldi né l'uno né l'altro; **carrots or peas? — neither, thanks** vuoi carote o piselli? — nessuno dei due, grazie; **neither of them is coming** non viene nessuno dei due

Nemesis [ˈnɛmɪsɪs] N (*Myth*) Nemesi *f*; (*fig*): **nemesis** nemesi *f*

neo... [ˈniːəʊ] PREF neo...

neo·clas·si·cal [ˌniːəʊˈklæsɪkl] ADJ neoclassico(-a)

neo·co·lo·ni·al·ism [ˌniːəʊkəˈləʊnɪəˌlɪzəm] N neocolonialismo

neo·con [ˈniːəʊˌkɒn] N (*fam: Pol*) neoconservatore(-trice)

neo·con·serva·tive [ˌniːəʊkənˈsɜːvətɪv] N (*Pol*) neoconservatore(-trice)

neo·fasc·ism [ˌniːəʊˈfæʃɪzəm] N neofascismo

neo·fasc·ist [ˌniːəʊˈfæʃɪst] ADJ, N neofascista (*m/f*)

neo·lith·ic [ˌniːəʊˈlɪθɪk] ADJ neolitico(-a)

ne·olo·gism [nɪˈɒləˌdʒɪzəm] N neologismo

neon [ˈniːɒn] N neon *m inv*
■ADJ al neon; **a neon light** una luce al neon

neo·nazi [ˌniːəʊˈnɑːtsɪ] ADJ, N neonazista (*m/f*)

neo·nazism [ˌniːəʊˈnɑːtsɪzəm] N neonazismo

neon light N luce *f* al neon

neon sign N insegna al neon

neo·prene [ˈniːəʊˌpriːn] N neoprene *m*

Ne·pal [nɪˈpɔːl] N il Nepal *m*

neph·ew [ˈnɛvjuː] N nipote *m* (*di zii*)

ne·phrit·ic [nɪˈfrɪtɪk] ADJ (*Med*) nefritico(-a)

ne·phri·tis [nɪˈfraɪtɪs] N (*Med*) nefrite *f*

nepo·tism [ˈnɛpətɪzəm] N nepotismo

Nep·tune [ˈnɛptjuːn] N (*Myth, Astron*) Nettuno

nerd [nɜːd] N (*fam pej*) sfigato(-a)

nerdy [ˈnɜːdɪ] ADJ (*fam*) sfigato(-a)

Ne·reid [ˈnɪərɪɪd] N (*Myth*) nereide *f*

Nero [ˈnɪərəʊ] N Nerone *m*

◎ **nerve** [nɜːv] N **1** (*Anat*) nervo; (*Bot*) nervatura; **she suffers from nerves** soffre di nervi; **my nerves are on edge** ho i nervi tesi; **a fit of nerves** una crisi di nervi; **it/he gets on my nerves** mi dà ai nervi, mi fa venire i nervi **2** (*fig: courage*) coraggio; (: *calm*) sangue *m* freddo; (: *self-confidence*) fiducia in se stesso(-a); (*fam: impudence*) sfacciataggine *f*, faccia tosta; **a man of nerve** un uomo che ha fegato; **to lose one's nerve** (*self-confidence*) perdere la fiducia in se stesso(-a); **I lost my nerve** (*courage*) mi è mancato il coraggio; **I hadn't the nerve to do it** non ho avuto il coraggio di farlo; (*cheek*) non ho avuto la faccia tosta di farlo; **he's got a nerve!** ha una bella faccia tosta!
■VT: **to nerve o.s. to do sth** farsi coraggio *or* animo per fare qc, armarsi di coraggio per fare qc

nerve agent N agente *m* nervino

nerve cell N cellula nervosa, neurone *m*

nerve centre N (*Anat*) centro nervoso; (*fig*) cervello, centro vitale

nerve gas N gas *m* nervino

nerve·less [ˈnɜːvlɪs] ADJ (*without strength*) privo(-a) di forza; (*calm*) che ha sangue freddo

nerve-racking [ˈnɜːvˌrækɪŋ] ADJ logorante

◎ **nerv·ous** [ˈnɜːvəs] ADJ (*Anat, Med*) nervoso(-a); (*edgy*) nervoso(-a), agitato(-a), teso(-a); (*apprehensive*) ansioso(-a), apprensivo(-a); **he's full of nervous energy** è tutto nervi; **he is making me nervous** mi innervosisce; **I was nervous about speaking to her** (*apprehensive*) l'idea di parlarle mi agitava; (*excited*) ero emozionato all'idea di parlarle; **I'm nervous about flying** ho un po' paura di volare; **I bite my nails when I'm nervous** quando sono teso mi mangio le unghie; **I'm a bit nervous about the exams** sono un po' tesa per gli esami

nervous breakdown N esaurimento nervoso

nerv·ous·ly [ˈnɜːvəslɪ] ADV nervosamente; (*apprehensively*) con ansia

nerv·ous·ness [ˈnɜːvəsnɪs] N nervosismo; (*anxiousness*) ansia

nervous system N sistema *m* nervoso

nervous wreck N (*fam*): **to be a nervous wreck** avere i nervi a pezzi

nervy [ˈnɜːvɪ] ADJ (*comp* **-ier**, *superl* **-iest**) (*fam: Brit: tense*) teso(-a), nervoso(-a); (: *Am: cheeky*) sfacciato(-a)

nest [nɛst] N **1** nido **2** **nest of tables** tris *m* di tavolini

Nn

■VI fare il nido, nidificare
nest egg N (*fig*) gruzzolo
nes·tle ['nɛsl] VI accoccolarsi; **to nestle up to** *or* **against sb** accoccolarsi vicino a qn, rannicchiarsi accanto a qn; **to nestle down in bed** sistemarsi ben bene nel letto; **a village nestling among hills** un paesetto annidato tra le colline
nest·ling ['nɛslɪŋ] N uccellino di nido, nidiaceo
Net [nɛt] N (= **the Net**) la Rete
◎**net**[1] [nɛt] N **1** (*gen, fig*) rete *f*; (*for hair*) retina (per capelli); (*fabric*) tulle *m*; **a fishing net** una rete da pesca **2** (*Geom*) sviluppo
■VT (*fish, game*) prendere con la rete
net[2] [nɛt] ADJ (*weight, price, salary*) netto(-a); **net assets** patrimonio netto, attività *fpl* nette; **he earns £30,000 net per year** guadagna 30.000 sterline nette all'anno; **net of tax** al netto delle tasse
■VT (*get, obtain*) ottenere; (*make: profit*) fare; (*subj: deal, sale*) dare un utile netto di
net·ball ['nɛt,bɔ:l] N *sport simile alla pallacanestro*
▷ www.netball.org
net call judge N (*Tennis*) giudice *m* di rete
net curtains NPL tende *fpl* di tulle
net·head ['nɛthɛd] N (*fam*) fanatico(-a) di Internet
neth·er ['nɛðə^r] ADJ (*old*): **the nether regions** *or* **world** gli inferi
Neth·er·lands ['nɛðələndz] NPL: **the Netherlands** i Paesi Bassi
neti·quette ['nɛtɪkɛt] N netiquette *f*; *norme di comportamento per gli utenti di Internet*
net margin N (*Econ*) (percentuale *f* di) utile *m* netto
net profit N utile *m* netto
net·speak ['nɛtspi:k] N gergo usato in Internet
net·surf·er ['nɛtsɜ:fə^r] N navigatore(-trice) in Internet
net·surf·ing ['nɛtsɜ:fɪŋ] N navigazione *f* in Internet
nett [nɛt] ADJ = **net**[2]
net·ting ['nɛtɪŋ] N (*nets*) reti *fpl*; (*mesh*) rete; (*also:* **wire netting**: *for fence etc*) rete metallica, reticolato; (*fabric*) tulle *m*
net·tle ['nɛtl] N ortica
■VT esasperare; **he is easily nettled** è una persona facilmente irritabile
nettle rash N orticaria
◎**net·work** ['nɛt,wɜ:k] N **1** (*Elec, TV, fig*) rete *f*; **network of roads** rete stradale; **spy network** rete spionistica *or* di spie **2** (*Comput*) rete *f*, network *m inv*
■VT (TV) trasmettere su rete nazionale
network administrator N (*Comput*) amministratore *m* di rete
net·work·ing ['nɛt,wɜ:kɪŋ] N (*Comput*) collegamenti *mpl* in rete; (*fig*) lo stabilire una rete di contatti
network (interface) card N (*Comput*) scheda di rete
neu·ral ['njʊərəl] ADJ (*Anat*) neurale
neu·ral·gia [njʊə'rældʒə] N nevralgia
neural net N, **neural network**
■N (*Comput*) rete *f* neuronale
neuro... ['njʊərəʊ] PREF neuro...
neu·ro·logi·cal [njʊərəʊ'lɒdʒɪkəl] ADJ neurologico(-a)
neu·rolo·gist [njʊ'rɒlədʒɪst] N neurologo(-a)
neu·rol·ogy [njʊ'rɒlədʒɪ] N neurologia
neu·ron ['njʊərɒn] N (*Bio*) neurone *m*
neu·ro·path ['njʊərəʊ,pæθ] N neuropatico(-a)
neu·ro·path·ic [,njʊərəʊ'pæθɪk] ADJ neuropatico(-a)
neu·ropa·thy [njʊ'rɒpəθɪ] N neuropatia
neu·ro·psy·chia·trist [,njʊərəʊsaɪ'kaɪətrɪst] N neuropsichiatra *m/f*
neu·ro·psy·chia·try [,njʊərəʊsaɪ'kaɪətrɪ] N neuropsichiatria
neu·ro·sis [njʊ'rəʊsɪs] N (*pl* **neuroses** [njʊ'rəʊsi:z]) nevrosi *f inv*
neu·ro·sur·geon [,njʊərəʊ'sɜ:dʒən] N neurochirurgo
neu·ro·sur·gery [,njʊərəʊ'sɜ:dʒərɪ] N neurochirurgia
neu·rot·ic [njʊ'rɒtɪk] ADJ (*person, disease*) nevrotico(-a); **she's getting quite neurotic about it** (*fig*) se ne sta facendo un'ossessione
■N nevrotico(-a)
neu·ter ['nju:tə^r] ADJ neutro(-a)
■N (*Gram*) neutro
■VT (*cat etc*) castrare
neu·tral ['nju:trəl] ADJ **1** (*person, country, opinion*) neutrale **2** (*Chem, colour*) neutro(-a)
■N (*Aut*) folle *f*; **in neutral** in folle
neu·tral·ity [nju:'trælɪtɪ] N neutralità
neu·trali·za·tion [,nju:trəlaɪ'zeɪʃən] N neutralizzazione *f*
neu·tral·ize ['nju:trə,laɪz] VT neutralizzare
neu·tri·no [nju:'tri:nəʊ] N neutrino
neu·tron ['nju:trɒn] N neutrone *m*
neutron bomb N bomba al neutrone
Ne·va·da [nɪ'vɑ:də] N Nevada *m*
▷ www.nebraska.gov/index.phtml
◎**nev·er** ['nɛvə^r] ADV **1** non... mai; **they never go out** non escono mai; **I have never read it** non l'ho mai letto; **have you been to Rome? — never** è mai stato a Roma? — no, mai; **never before had he been so bored** non si era mai annoiato tanto; **she's never been here before** non è mai venuta qui prima; **never again!** mai più!; **I'll never go there again** non ci andrò mai più; **never in my life** mai in vita mia **2** (*emphatic negative*): **I never slept a wink all night** non ho chiuso occhio per tutta la notte; **he never so much as smiled** non ha nemmeno accennato un sorriso; **I told the boss what I thought of him — never!** *or* **you never did!** ho detto al capo quel che pensavo di lui — no, non mi dire! *or* non ci credo!; **well I never!** chi l'avrebbe (mai) detto!, ma guarda un po'!; **never mind** non fa niente
never-ending [,nɛvər'ɛndɪŋ] ADJ interminabile
never-never [,nɛvə'nɛvə^r] N: **to buy sth on the never-never** (*Brit fam*) comprare qc a rate
never-never land N mondo dei sogni
◎**never·the·less** [,nɛvəðə'lɛs] ADV tuttavia, ciononondimeno, ciononostante
never-to-be-forgotten [,nɛvətəbi:fə'gɒtən] ADJ indimenticabile
◎**new** [nju:] ADJ (*comp* **-er**, *superl* **-est**) nuovo(-a); (*brand new*) nuovo(-a) di zecca; (*different*) nuovo(-a), altro(-a); (*bread*) fresco(-a); **he buys a new car every year** (*brand-new*) si compra una macchina nuova ogni anno; **her new boyfriend** il suo nuovo ragazzo; (*different*) si compra una nuova macchina *or* una macchina diversa ogni anno; **bring me a new glass** portami un altro bicchiere; **new potatoes** patate *fpl* novelle; **as good as new** come nuovo(-a); **that's nothing new** non è una novità; **what's new?** ci sono novità?; **are you new here?** sei nuovo di qui?; **I'm new to this job** sono nuovo del mestiere; **the idea was quite new to him** l'idea gli risultava nuova
New Age ADJ, N New Age *(f) inv*
new·bie ['nju:bɪ] N (*Comput*) utilizzatore(-trice) inesperto(-a)
new·born ['nju:,bɔ:n] ADJ neonato(-a); **newborn baby** neonato(-a)
new boy N (*Scol*) nuovo scolaro

new broom N (*Brit*): **this firm needs a new broom** questa azienda ha bisogno di qualcuno che introduca dei cambiamenti; **a new broom sweeps clean** (*Proverb*) tutti sono bravi all'inizio

New Bruns·wick N New Brunswick *m*
▷ www.gnb.ca
▷ www.tourismenouveau-brunswick.ca/Cultures/en-CA/welcome.htm

new·comer ['nju:ˌkʌməʳ] N nuovo(-a) venuto(-a)

New England N New England *m*

new-fangled ['nju:ˌfæŋgld] ADJ (*pej*) stramoderno(-a)

new-found ['nju:ˌfaʊnd] ADJ nuovo(-a)

New·found·land ['nju:fəndlənd] N Newfoundland *m*
▷ www.gov.nf.ca

new girl N (*Scol*) nuova scolara

New Guinea N la Nuova Guinea

New Hamp·shire N New Hampshire *m*
▷ www.state.nh.us/

New Jersey N New Jersey *m*
▷ www.state.nj.us/

new-laid ['nju:ˌleɪd] ADJ (*egg*) fresco(-a)

◎ **new·ly** ['nju:lɪ] ADV (*recently*) appena, da poco, di recente; (*in a new way*) in modo nuovo; **newly made** appena fatto(-a)

newly-weds ['nju:lɪˌwɛdz] NPL sposini *mpl*, sposi *mpl* novelli

New Mexico N Nuovo Messico
▷ www.state.nm.us/

new moon N luna nuova

new·ness ['nju:nɪs] N novità

◎ **news** [nju:z] NSG (*gen, Press*) notizie *fpl*; (*report*: *on radio*) notiziario, giornale *m* radio; (: *on TV*) notiziario, telegiornale *m*; **a piece of** *or* **an item of news** una notizia; (*in newspaper*) un articolo; **have you heard the news?** hai saputo la notizia?; **have you heard the news about Maria?** hai saputo di Maria?; **have you any news of Maria/of her?** hai notizie di Maria/sue notizie?; **it was nice to have your news** mi ha fatto piacere avere tue notizie; **that's wonderful news!** che bella notizia!; **what's your news?** (ci sono) novità?; **what's the latest news about the earthquake?** si sa qualcosa di nuovo sul terremoto?; **is there any news?** ci sono notizie?; **good/bad news** buone/cattive notizie; **I've got news for you!** non sai l'ultima!; **this is news to me** questo mi giunge nuovo; **it's in the news** (*newspapers*) è su tutti i giornali; (*radio, TV*) è in tutti i notiziari; **home/foreign news** notizie dall'interno/dall'estero; **financial news** (*Press*) pagina economica e finanziaria; (*Radio, TV*) notiziario economico

◎ **news agency** N agenzia di stampa

news·agent ['nju:zˌeɪdʒənt] N (*Brit*) giornalaio(-a)

news bulletin N (*Radio, TV*) notiziario

news·cast ['nju:zˌkɑ:st] N (*esp Am Radio, TV*) notiziario

news·caster ['nju:zˌkɑ:stəʳ] N (*Radio*) annunciatore(-trice); (*TV*) presentatore(-trice)

news conference N (*Am*) conferenza *f* stampa *inv*

news·dealer ['nju:zˌdi:ləʳ] N (*Am*) giornalaio(-a)

news·flash ['nju:zˌflæʃ] N (notizia *f*) flash (*m*) *inv*

news·group ['nju:zgru:p] N (*Comput*) newsgroup *m inv*, gruppo di discussione

news headlines N titoli *mpl* delle principali notizie

news·hound ['nju:zˌhaʊnd] N (*esp Am fam*) reporter *m/f inv*

news·letter ['nju:zˌlɛtəʳ] N bollettino (*di ditta, associazione*)

news·man ['nju:zˌmæn] N (*pl* **-men**) reporter *m inv*

New South Wales N Nuovo Galles *m* del Sud
▷ www.nsw.gov.au
▷ www.tourism.nsw.gov.au

◎ **news·paper** ['nju:zˌpeɪpəʳ] N giornale *m*; **daily newspaper** quotidiano; **weekly newspaper** settimanale *m*

news·paper·man ['nju:zˌpeɪpəmən] N (*pl* **-men**) giornalista *m*

news·print ['nju:zˌprɪnt] N carta da giornale

news·reader ['nju:zˌri:dəʳ] N (*esp Brit*) = newscaster

news·reel ['nju:zˌri:l] N cinegiornale *m*

news·room ['nju:zˌrʊm] N redazione *f*

news sheet N notiziario, bollettino

news·stand ['nju:zˌstænd] N edicola

news·worthy ['nju:zˌwɜ:ðɪ] ADJ che vale la pena pubblicare

newsy ['nju:zɪ] ADJ (*fam*) ricco(-a) di notizie

newt [nju:t] N tritone *m*

New Testament N: **the New Testament** il Nuovo Testamento

new town N (*Brit*) nuovo centro urbano (*creato con fondi pubblici*)

new wave N new wave *f inv*
▷ www.nyfavideo.com

New World N: **the New World** il Nuovo Mondo

New Year N anno nuovo; **Happy New Year!** Buon anno!; **to wish sb a happy New Year** augurare buon anno a qn; **to bring in the New Year** brindare all'anno nuovo; **to celebrate New Year** festeggiare l'anno nuovo
■ ADJ (*party etc*) di Capodanno; (*resolution*) per l'anno nuovo

New Year's Day N Capodanno

New Year's Eve N la vigilia di Capodanno, la notte di San Silvestro

New York N New York *f*, Nuova York *f*; **New York State** stato di New York
▷ www.nycvisit.com
▷ www.state.ny.us/
▷ www.nyc.gov/
▷ www.statueofliberty.org/

New Zea·land [ˌnju:'zi:lənd] N Nuova Zelanda
■ ADJ neozelandese
▷ www.govt.nz/en/aboutnz
▷ www.purenz.com
▷ www.newzealandnz.co.nz

New Zea·land·er [ˌnju:'zi:ləndəʳ] N neozelandese *m/f*

◎ **next** [nɛkst] ADJ
1 (*immediately adjoining*: *house, street, room*) vicino(-a), accanto *inv*; (*immediately following*: *bus stop, turning*: *in future*) prossimo(-a); (: *in past*) successivo(-a), (subito) dopo; **"turn to the next page"** "vedi pagina seguente"; **the next size (up)** la misura più grande; **get off at the next stop** scendi alla prossima fermata; **he got off at the next stop** è sceso alla fermata successiva; **I arrived at 3 and Mary was next to arrive** io sono arrivato alle 3 e dopo di me è arrivata Mary; **the next room** la stanza accanto; **it's the next door but one on the right** è la seconda porta a destra; **who's next?** a chi tocca?; **you're next** tocca a lei
2 (*in time*: *day, week etc*: *in future*) prossimo(-a); (: *in past*) successivo(-a); **next time** la prossima volta; **next year** l'anno prossimo *or* venturo; **next month** il mese prossimo; **the next month** il mese dopo *or* successivo; **the week after next** fra due settimane; **(the) next time you come** quando vieni la prossima volta, la prossima volta che vieni; **this time next year** in

Nn

questo periodo fra un anno; **the next day** il giorno dopo, l'indomani; **the next morning** l'indomani mattina, la mattina dopo *or* seguente
■ADV
1 (*in time*) dopo, poi; **first he opened his letters and next he read the paper** prima ha aperto la corrispondenza e dopo *or* poi ha letto il giornale; **what will you do next?** e adesso che farai?; **when you next see him** quando lo vedi la prossima volta, la prossima volta che lo vedi; **when next I saw him** quando l'ho visto la volta dopo *or* una seconda volta; **when do we meet next?** quando ci rincontriamo?; **what comes next?** che cosa viene dopo?; **what next?** e poi?; (*expressing surprise etc*) e che altro mai?; **the next best thing would be ...** la migliore alternativa sarebbe...; **the next to last** il/la penultimo(-a)
2 **next to** (*nearly*) quasi, pressocché; **next to nothing** quasi niente; **we got it for next to nothing** non ci è costato quasi niente, l'abbiamo comprato per una sciocchezza; **there is next to no news** non si sa quasi niente
■PREP: **next to** (*beside*) di fianco a, accanto a; **his room is next to mine** la sua stanza è accanto alla mia; **next to the bank** accanto alla banca; **I don't like wearing synthetics next to the skin** non mi piacciono le fibre sintetiche a contatto della pelle
■N prossimo(-a); **next please!** (avanti) il prossimo!; **the next to speak is Carla** Carla è la prossima a parlare

next-door [ˌnɛks'dɔːʳ] ADJ: **the next-door house** la casa accanto; **my next-door neighbour** il/la mio(-a) vicino(-a) di casa

next door ADV accanto; **next door to us** accanto a noi, nella casa accanto; **the girl next door** la ragazza della porta accanto
■N la casa accanto; **from next door** della casa accanto

next of kin N parente *m/f* prossimo(-a)

NF [ˌɛn'ɛf] N ABBR (*Brit Pol:* = **National Front**) *partito di estrema destra*
■ABBR (*Canada*) = **Newfoundland**

NFL [ˌɛnɛf'ɛl] N ABBR (*Am*) = **National Football League**

NG [ˌɛn'dʒiː] N ABBR (*Am*) = **National Guard**

NGO [ˌɛndʒiː'əʊ] N ABBR (= **non-governmental organization**) ONG *f inv* (= *organizzazione non governativa*)

NH ABBR (*Am Post*) = **New Hampshire**

NHL [ˌɛneɪtʃ'ɛl] N ABBR (*Am:* = **National Hockey League**) ≈ F.I.H.P. *f* (= *Federazione Italiana Hockey e Pattinaggio*)

◎**NHS** [ˌɛneɪtʃ'ɛs] N ABBR (*Brit*) = **National Health Service**

NHS

Dal 1948 il servizio sanitario nazionale, **National Health Service** o **NHS**, fornisce assistenza medica gratuita a tutti i residenti in Gran Bretagna. Il servizio sanitario è finanziato attraverso il gettito fiscale, i contributi previdenziali e le entrate provenienti da ticket sui farmaci e dalle cure dentistiche.

▷ www.nhs.uk/

NI ABBR 1 = **Northern Ireland** 2 (*Brit*) = **National Insurance**

Ni·aga·ra Falls [naɪ'ægrə'fɔːls] NPL: **the Niagara Falls** le cascate del Niagara

nib [nɪb] N (*of pen*) pennino

nib·ble ['nɪbl] VT (*also:* **nibble at**) 1 (*subj: mouse*) rosicchiare; (: *fish*) mordicchiare; (: *person: biscuit, nuts*) sgranocchiare; (: *bread, cheese*) sbocconcellare 2 (*fig: offer*) mostrarsi tentato(-a) da
■VI (*person*) mangiucchiare

Nica·ra·gua [ˌnɪkə'rægjʊə] N Nicaragua *m*

Nica·ra·guan [ˌnɪkə'rægjʊən] ADJ, N nicaraguense (*m/f*)

Nice [niːs] N Nizza

◎**nice** [naɪs] ADJ (*comp* **-r**, *superl* **-st**) 1 (*gen: pleasant*) bello(-a), piacevole, gentile; (: *person*) simpatico(-a), piacevole; (: *taste, smell, meal*) buono(-a); (*attractive, pretty*) carino(-a), bello(-a); **he's a nice man** è una brava persona, è un uomo simpatico; **your parents are very nice** i tuoi genitori sono molto simpatici; **he was very nice about it** è stato molto gentile; **she was always very nice to me** è sempre stata gentile con me; **be nice to him** sii gentile con lui; **it was nice of you to remember my birthday** sei stata carina a ricordarti del mio compleanno; **that's a nice dress!** che vestito carino!; **how nice you look!** come stai bene!; **did you have a nice time?** ti sei divertito?; **it's nice here** si sta bene qui; **this pasta is very nice** questa pasta è molto buona; **Pisa is a nice town** Pisa è una bella città; **nice weather** bel tempo; **it's a nice day** è una bella giornata 2 (*iro*) bello(-a); **that's a nice thing to say!** sono cose da dirsi, queste?; **you've got us into a nice mess!** ci hai messo in un bel pasticcio! 3 (*refined, polite*) gentile, garbato(-a); **he has nice manners** ha modi gentili *or* garbati; **nice girls don't go out at night on their own** le ragazze perbene non escono da sole la sera; **that's not nice** non sta bene
4 (*intensifier: fam*) bello(-a) + *adj*; **he gets nice long holidays** le sue vacanze sono belle lunghe; **it's nice and warm here** è bello caldo qui, c'è un bel calduccio qui; **nice and early** di buon'ora; **a nice cup of coffee** una bella tazza di caffè 5 (*frm: subtle: distinction*) sottile, fine

nice-looking ['naɪsˌlʊkɪŋ] ADJ bello(-a)

nice·ly ['naɪslɪ] ADV bene; (*kindly*) gentilmente; **that will do nicely** andrà benissimo; **he's getting on nicely in his new job** se la cava bene nel nuovo lavoro

ni·cety ['naɪsɪtɪ] N (*of judgment*) accuratezza; **niceties** NPL particolari *mpl*, finezze *fpl*; **a question of some nicety** una questione piuttosto delicata; **to a nicety** alla perfezione

niche [niːʃ] N (*Archit*) nicchia; (*Ecology*) nicchia ecologica; (*fig*): **to find a niche for o.s.** trovare una propria collocazione

nick [nɪk] N 1 (*in wood, blade*) tacca; (*in skin*) taglietto; (*in plate*) scheggiatura; **in the nick of time** appena in tempo 2 (*fam*): **in good nick** decente, in buono stato 3 (*Brit fam: prison*) galera; (: *police station*) centrale *f* (di polizia); **in the nick** in galera
■VT 1 (*see n*) intaccare; tagliare; scheggiare, scalfire; **to nick o.s.** farsi un taglietto 2 (*fam: steal*) fregare; **somebody's nicked it** qualcuno l'ha fregato 3 (*Brit fam: arrest*) beccare; **to get nicked** farsi beccare

nick·el ['nɪkl] N (*metal*) nichel *m*; (*Am: coin*) (moneta da) cinque centesimi *mpl* di dollaro

nickel-plate [nɪkl'pleɪt] VT nichelare

nickel-plated [nɪkl'pleɪtɪd] ADJ nichelato(-a)

nick·name ['nɪkˌneɪm] N soprannome *m*; (*humorous, malicious*) nomignolo
■VT: **to nickname sb sth** soprannominare qn qc

Nico·sia [ˌnɪkə'siːə] N Nicosia

nico·tine ['nɪkəˌtiːn] N nicotina

nicotine patch N cerotto antifumo (a base di nicotina)

nicotine poisoning N nicotinismo
niece [ni:s] N nipote *f* (*di zii*)
Nie·tzschean ['ni:tʃɪən] ADJ nietzschiano(-a)
nif·ty ['nɪftɪ] ADJ (*comp* **-ier**, *superl* **-iest**) (*fam: car, jacket*) chic *inv*; (*: gadget, tool*) ingegnoso(-a); **that was a nifty piece of work** è stato un bel lavoretto
Ni·ger ['naɪdʒə] N (*country, river*) il Niger *m*
Ni·geria [naɪ'dʒɪərɪə] N la Nigeria
Ni·gerian [naɪ'dʒɪərɪən] ADJ, N nigeriano(-a)
nig·gard·ly ['nɪgədlɪ] ADJ (*person*) tirchio(-a), spilorcio(-a); (*allowance, amount*) misero(-a)
nig·ger ['nɪgəʳ] N (*fam!: highly offensive*) negro(-a)
nig·gle ['nɪgl] VT assillare
■ VI fare il/la pignolo(-a)
nig·gling ['nɪglɪŋ] ADJ (*detail*) insignificante; (*doubt, pain*) persistente; (*person*) pignolo(-a)
nigh [naɪ] (*old*) ADV **1** (*close*) prossimo(-a), vicino(-a) **2 well nigh** (*virtually*) praticamente; **it's well nigh impossible** è praticamente impossibile
■ PREP: **nigh on** (*nearly*) quasi; **he is nigh on forty** ha quasi quarant'anni
◎ **night** [naɪt] N notte *f*; (*evening*) sera; **good night!** buona notte!; **at night** di notte, la notte; **in the night** *or* **during the night** durante la notte; **by night** di notte; **last night** la notte scorsa, ieri notte, stanotte; **we went to a party last night** ieri sera siamo andati ad una festa; **Tuesday night** martedì notte, la notte di martedì, la notte fra martedì e mercoledì; (*evening*) martedì sera, la sera di martedì; **the night before** la notte prima; (*evening*) la sera prima; **the night before last** l'altro ieri notte; (*evening*) l'altro ieri sera; **11 o'clock at night** le 11 di sera; **the last 3 nights of** (*Theatre etc*) le 3 ultime serate *or* rappresentazioni di; **to have a night out** uscire la sera; **we had a lovely night out** abbiamo passato una bellissima serata fuori; **to spend the night** passare la notte; **I spent the night studying** ho passato la notte a studiare; **to have a good/bad night** dormire bene/male; **to have a late night** andare a letto tardi; **he's working nights** fa il turno di notte; **I want a single room for two nights** vorrei una camera singola per due notti
■ ADJ (*work, nurse, train etc*) di notte; **night flight** volo notturno
night-bird ['naɪt,bɜ:d] N uccello notturno; (*fig*) nottambulo(-a)
night·cap ['naɪt,kæp] N papalina, berretto da notte; (*drink*) *bicchierino prima di andare a letto*
night·clothes ['naɪt,kləʊðz] NPL (*pyjamas*) pigiama *m*; (*nightdress*) camicia da notte
night·club ['naɪt,klʌb] N locale *m* notturno, night(-club) *m inv*
night·dress ['naɪt,drɛs] N camicia da notte
night·fall ['naɪt,fɔ:l] N crepuscolo; **at nightfall** al calar della notte
night·gown ['naɪt,gaʊn] N (*frm*) camicia da notte
nightie ['naɪtɪ] N (*fam*) camicia da notte
night·in·gale ['naɪtɪŋ,geɪl] N usignolo
night·jar ['naɪt,dʒɑ:ʳ] N (*Zool*) caprimulgo nostrano
night·life ['naɪt,laɪf] N vita notturna
night-light ['naɪt,laɪt] N lumino da notte
night·ly ['naɪtlɪ] ADV ogni notte, tutte le notti; (*evening*) ogni sera, tutte le sere; **she appears nightly on the news** c'è ogni sera al telegiornale
■ ADJ di ogni notte, di tutte le notti; (*evening*) di ogni sera, di tutte le sere; (*by night*) notturno(-a)
◎ **night·mare** ['naɪt,mɛəʳ] N incubo; **the whole trip was a nightmare** il viaggio è stato un vero incubo
nightmare scenario N scenario peggiore che si possa immaginare
night·mar·ish ['naɪt,mɛərɪʃ] ADJ da incubo
night owl N (*fig*) nottambulo(-a)
night porter N portiere *m* di notte
night safe N cassa continua
night school N scuola serale
night·shade ['naɪt,ʃeɪd] N (*Bot*): **deadly nightshade** belladonna
night shift N turno di notte; **to be on night shift** fare il turno di notte, essere di notte
night·shirt ['naɪt,ʃɜ:t] N camicia da notte (*da uomo*)
night·spot ['naɪtspɒt] N (*fam*) night *m inv*, locale *m* notturno
night stick N (*Am*) manganello
night-time ['naɪt,taɪm] N notte *f*; **at night-time** di notte, la notte
night vision N visione *f* notturna; **night vision goggles** occhiali *mpl* per visione notturna
night watchman N (*pl* **-men**) guardiano notturno
night·wear ['naɪt,wɛəʳ] N indumenti *mpl* per la notte
ni·hil·ism ['naɪɪ,lɪzəm] N nichilismo
ni·hil·ist ['naɪɪlɪst] N nichilista *m/f*
ni·hil·is·tic [,naɪɪ'lɪstɪk] ADJ nichilista
nil [nɪl] N nulla *m*; (*Sport*) zero; **we won one-nil** abbiamo vinto uno a zero
Nile [naɪl] N: **the Nile** il Nilo
nim·ble ['nɪmbl] ADJ (*comp* **-r**, *superl* **-st**) (*in moving*) agile; (*mentally*) vivace, sveglio(-a)
nim·bly ['nɪmblɪ] ADV agilmente
nim·bus ['nɪmbəs] N nembo
nin·com·poop ['nɪŋkəm,pu:p] N (*fam*) scemo(-a)
◎ **nine** [naɪn] ADJ, N nove (*m*) *inv*; **nine times out of ten** (*fig*) nove volte su dieci; **they were dressed up to the nines** si erano messi in pompa magna; *for usage see* **five**
9-11 [,naɪnɪ'lɛvn] N 11 settembre
nine·pins ['naɪn,pɪnz] NPL birilli *mpl*; **to go down like ninepins** cadere come birilli
◎ **nine·teen** [,naɪn'ti:n] ADJ, N diciannove (*m*) *inv*; **to talk nineteen to the dozen** (*fam*) parlare come una mitragliatrice; *for usage see* **five**
◎ **nine·teenth** [,naɪn'ti:nθ] ADJ diciannovesimo(-a)
■ N (*in series*) diciannovesimo(-a); (*fraction*) diciannovesimo; *for usage see* **fifth**
◎ **nine·ti·eth** ['naɪntɪɪθ] ADJ novantesimo(-a)
■ N (*in series*) novantesimo(-a); (*fraction*) novantesimo; *for usage see* **fifth**
◎ **nine·ty** ['naɪntɪ] ADJ, N novanta (*m*) *inv*; *for usage see* **fifty**
nin·ny ['nɪnɪ] N (*fam*) sciocco(-a)
◎ **ninth** ['naɪnθ] ADJ nono(-a)
■ N (*in series*) nono(-a); (*fraction*) nono; *for usage see* **fifth**
nip¹ [nɪp] N (*pinch*) pizzico; (*bite*) morso; **there's a nip in the air** l'aria è pungente
■ VT (*pinch*) pizzicare; (*bite*) morsicare; (*prune: bud, shoot*) spuntare; (*subj: cold: plant*) assiderare; (*: face*) pungere; **to nip sth in the bud** (*fig*) stroncare qc sul nascere
■ VI (*Brit fam*): **to nip inside** andar dentro un attimo; **to nip out/down/up** fare un salto fuori/giù/di sopra; **where has she nipped off to?** dov'è sparita?; **I nipped round to the shop** ho fatto un salto al negozio
nip² [nɪp] N (*drink*) goccio, bicchierino; **a nip of brandy** un goccio di brandy
nip·per ['nɪpə] N (*Brit fam*) bambino(-a)
nip·ple ['nɪpl] N (*Anat*) capezzolo
nip·py ['nɪpɪ] ADJ (*comp* **-ier**, *superl* **-iest**) (*fam*) **1** (*Brit:*

Nn

person, car) svelto(-a); **be nippy about it!** sbrigati!, fa' alla svelta! **2** *(wind, weather)* pungente; **it's nippy** l'aria è pungente

nit [nɪt] N **1** *(of louse)* lendine *m* **2** *(fam: idiot)* cretino(-a), scemo(-a)

nit-pick ['nɪt,pɪk] VI *(fam)* cercare il pelo nell'uovo

nit-picking ['nɪt,pɪkɪŋ] N *(fam)* il cercare il pelo nell'uovo

ni·trate ['naɪtreɪt] N nitrato

ni·tric ['naɪtrɪk] ADJ nitrico(-a)

ni·tri·fi·ca·tion [,naɪtrɪfɪ'keɪʃən] N nitrificazione *f*

ni·trite ['naɪtraɪt] N nitrito

ni·tro·gen ['naɪtrədʒən] N azoto; **nitrogen cycle** ciclo dell'azoto

ni·tro·glyc·er·ine [,naɪtrəʊ'glɪsə,ri:n], **ni·tro·glyc·er·in** [,naɪtrəʊ'glɪsərɪn] N nitroglicerina

ni·trous ['naɪtrəs] ADJ nitroso(-a)

nitty-gritty ['nɪtɪ'grɪtɪ] N *(fam)*: **to get down to the nitty-gritty** venire al sodo

nit·wit ['nɪt,wɪt] N *(fam)* imbecille *m/f*, scemo(-a)

NJ ABBR *(Am Post)* = **New Jersey**

NLF [,ɛnɛl'ɛf] N ABBR (= **National Liberation Front**) ≈ F.L.N. *m* (= *Fronte di Liberazione Nazionale)*

NLQ [,ɛnɛl'kju:] ABBR (= **near letter quality**) stampa di qualità

NLRB [,ɛnɛla:'bi:] N ABBR *(Am*: = **National Labor Relations Board)** *organismo per la tutela dei lavoratori*

NM ABBR *(Am Post)* = **New Mexico**

◎ **no** [nəʊ] KEYWORD

■ ADV

1 *(opposite of "yes")* no; **are you coming? — no** vieni? — no; **would you like some more? — no thank you** ne vuoi ancora? — no grazie

2 *(emphatic)*: **it is no easy task** non è un'impresa facile; **it is no small matter** non è una cosa da poco; **there is no such thing** una cosa simile non esiste; **in no uncertain terms** in termini tutt'altro che ambigui

3 *(in comparatives)*: **there were no fewer than 100 people** c'erano non meno di 100 persone; **he wants to become prime minister, no less!** vuole diventare nientemeno che primo ministro!; **I can stand it no longer** non ne posso più; **I am no taller than you** non sono più alto di te

■ ADJ

1 *(not any)* nessuno(-a); **there's no denying it** non si può negarlo; **"no dogs"** "vietato l'accesso ai cani"; **"no entry"** "vietato l'accesso"; **she has no furniture** non ha mobili, non ha nessun mobile; **it is of no interest to us** non siamo interessati; **I have no money** non ho soldi; **there is no more coffee** non c'è più caffè; **who's going with you? — no one** chi ti accompagna? — nessuno; **no other man** nessun altro; **"no parking"** "divieto di sosta"; **there is no reason to believe ...** non c'è ragione di credere che...; **"no smoking"** "vietato fumare"; **it's no trouble** non c'è problema; **no two houses are alike** le case sono tutte diverse l'una dall'altra; **no two people think alike** non ci sono due persone che la pensino allo stesso modo

2 *(quite other than)*: **she's no beauty** non è certo una bellezza; **he's no fool** è tutt'altro che stupido, non è affatto (uno) stupido; **he's no friend of mine** non è affatto un mio amico

■ N *(pl* **noes)** no *m inv*; **I won't take no for an answer** non accetterò un rifiuto

No., no. ABBR *(pl* **Nos.)** (= **number**) n. (= *numero)*

Noah ['nəʊə] N Noè *m*; **Noah's ark** l'arca di Noè

nob [nɒb] N *(old fam)* persona altolocata

nob·ble ['nɒbl] VT *(Brit fam)* **1** *(bribe: person)* comprare, corrompere **2** *(catch: thief)* beccare; (: *person to speak to)* bloccare, beccare **3** *(Racing) impedire illegalmente a un cane/cavallo di partecipare a una gara*

Nobel prize ['nəʊbɛl'praɪz] N premio Nobel

▷ www.nobel.se

no·bil·ity [nəʊ'bɪlɪtɪ] N nobiltà

no·ble ['nəʊbl] ADJ *(comp* **-r**, *superl* **-st)** nobile; *(also iro)* generoso(-a); **of noble birth** di nobili natali

■ N nobile *m/f*

noble·man ['nəʊblmən] N *(pl* **-men)** nobile *m*, nobiluomo

noble·woman ['nəʊbl,wʊmən] N *(pl* **-women)** nobile *f*, nobildonna

no·bly ['nəʊblɪ] ADV *(selflessly)* generosamente

◎ **no·body** ['nəʊbədɪ] PRON nessuno; **I saw nobody** non ho visto nessuno; **nobody spoke** nessuno ha parlato, non ha parlato nessuno; **there was nobody in the office** in ufficio non c'era nessuno; **nobody likes him** non è simpatico a nessuno; **nobody else** nessun altro/nessun'altra

■ N: **he's a nobody** è una nullità

no-brainer [,nəʊ'breɪnə^r] *(fam)* N *(easy: question, decision)* scelta ovvia *or* scontata; *(stupid: action)* cosa stupida da fare; **he's a no-brainer** è uno stupido

no-claims bonus [,nəʊ'kleɪmz ,bəʊnəs] N *riduzione del premio assicurativo qualora l'assicurato non abbia provocato incidenti nel corso di un determinato periodo de tempo*

noc·tur·nal [nɒk'tɜ:nl] ADJ notturno(-a)

noc·turne ['nɒktɜ:n] N *(Mus)* notturno

◎ **nod** [nɒd] N cenno del capo; **to give sb a nod** fare un cenno col capo a qn; *(answering yes)* accennare di sì a qn, fare di sì col capo a qn

■ VT: **to nod one's head** fare di sì col capo; **he nodded a greeting** accennò un saluto col capo; **they nodded their agreement** accennarono di sì (col capo)

■ VI **1** fare un cenno col capo; *(say yes)* far segno di sì col capo, annuire; **he nodded to me in a friendly way** mi ha salutato cordialmente con un cenno del capo; **we have a nodding acquaintance** ci conosciamo solo di vista **2** *(doze)* ciondolare il capo (per il sonno); *(sleep)* sonnecchiare

▶ **nod off** VI + ADV appisolarsi, assopirsi

nod·dle ['nɒdəl] N *(old fam)* zucca *(testa)*; **use your noddle!** usa il cervello!

node [nəʊd] N *(Math, Bot)* nodo

nod·ule ['nɒdju:l] N nodulo

no-fly zone [,nəʊ'flaɪ,zəʊn] N zona di interdizione aerea

no-go area [,nəʊ'gəʊ,ɛərɪə] N zona proibita

◎ **noise** [nɔɪz] N *(sound)* rumore *m*; *(din)* rumore, chiasso, fracasso; *(Telec, Radio, TV)* disturbo, interferenza; **to make a noise** fare un rumore; **stop making a noise!** smettila di far rumore!; **my wife's making noises about starting a family** mia moglie sembra farmi capire che vuole avere un bambino; **a big noise** *(fam: person)* un pezzo grosso

noise·less ['nɔɪzlɪs] ADJ silenzioso(-a)

noise·less·ly ['nɔɪzlɪslɪ] ADV senza far rumore, silenziosamente

noisi·ly ['nɔɪzɪlɪ] ADV rumorosamente

noisy ['nɔɪzɪ] ADJ *(comp* **-ier**, *superl* **-iest)** *(street, car)* rumoroso(-a); *(child, party)* rumoroso(-a), chiassoso(-a); **stop being noisy!** smettila di far rumore!; **the**

noisiest city in the world la città più rumorosa del mondo

DID YOU KNOW ...?
noisy is not translated by the Italian word *noioso*

no·mad ['nəʊmæd] N nomade *m/f*
no·mad·ic [nəʊ'mædɪk] ADJ nomade
no·mad·ism ['nəʊmædɪzəm] N nomadismo
no-man's-land ['nəʊmænz,lænd] N terra di nessuno
nom de plume ['nɒmdə'plu:m] N (*Literature*) pseudonimo
no·men·cla·ture [nəʊ'mɛnklətʃə^r] N (*frm*) nomenclatura
nomi·nal ['nɒmɪnl] ADJ (*Gram, Econ*) nominale; (*ostensible*) nominale, di nome
nomi·nal·ly ['nɒmɪnəlɪ] ADV nominalmente
nomi·nate ['nɒmɪ,neɪt] VT: **to nominate sb (for sth)** (*propose*) proporre qn come candidato (a qc); (*appoint*) nominare *or* designare qn (a qc)
nomi·na·tion [,nɒmɪ'neɪʃən] N (*see vb*) candidatura; nomina
nomi·na·tive ['nɒmɪnətɪv] ADJ, N (*Gram*) nominativo(-a)
nomi·nee [,nɒmɪ'ni:] N (*see vb*) candidato(-a); persona nominata
non... [nɒn] PREF non
non·ag·gres·sion [,nɒnə'grɛʃən] N non aggressione *f*
nona·gon ['nɒnəgɒn] N nonagono
non-alcoholic ['nɒnælkə'hɒlɪk] ADJ analcolico(-a)
non·aligned [,nɒnə'laɪnd] ADJ non allineato(-a)
non·ar·ri·val ['nɒnə'raɪvəl] N mancato arrivo
non·be·liev·er ['nɒnbɪ'li:və^r] N non credente *m/f*
non·break·able ['nɒn'breɪkəbl] ADJ infrangibile
nonce word ['nɒns,wɜ:d] N parola coniata per l'occasione
non·cha·lance ['nɒnʃələns] N disinvoltura, indifferenza
non·cha·lant ['nɒnʃələnt] ADJ disinvolto(-a), indifferente, incurante
non·cha·lant·ly ['nɒnʃələntlɪ] ADV con disinvoltura, con indifferenza
non·com·bat·ant ['nɒn'kɒmbətənt] N militare *m* non combattente
non·com·mis·sioned of·fic·er ['nɒnkə'mɪʃənd'ɒfɪsə^r] N sottufficiale *m*
non·com·mit·tal ['nɒnkə'mɪtl] ADJ (*statement*) non impegnativo(-a), evasivo(-a); (*person*) che non si compromette, evasivo(-a)
Non·con·form·ism ['nɒnkən'fɔ:mɪzəm] N (*Brit Rel*) movimento protestante
non·con·form·ism ['nɒnkən'fɔ:mɪzəm] N anticonformismo
Non·con·form·ist ['nɒnkən'fɔ:mɪst] ADJ, N (*Brit Rel*) *protestante non appartenente alla Chiesa Anglicana*
non·con·form·ist ['nɒnkən'fɔ:mɪst] ADJ anticonformista
■ N anticonformista *m/f*
non·con·tribu·tory [,nɒnkən'trɪbjʊtərɪ] ADJ: **noncontributory pension scheme** *sistema di pensionamento con i contributi interamente a carico del datore di lavoro*
non·co·op·era·tion ['nɒnkəʊ,ɒpə'reɪʃən] N non cooperazione *f*, non collaborazione *f*
non-custodial [,nɒnkʌs'təʊdɪəl] (*Law*) ADJ: **a non-custodial sentence** una condanna che non prevede il carcere; **non-custodial parent** genitore *m* che non ha la custodia

non·de·script ['nɒndɪ,skrɪpt] ADJ (*person, clothes*) qualunque *inv*; (*colour*) indefinito(-a)
◎ **none** [nʌn] PRON nessuno(-a), nemmeno uno(-a), neanche uno(-a); **none of them wants to go** nessuno di loro vuole andarci; **none of the machines is working** nessuna delle macchine funziona, non c'è neanche una macchina che funzioni; **I have none of the books** non ho nessuno dei libri; **I have none** non ne ho nemmeno uno; **none of this is yours** niente di questo è tuo; **none of this money** neanche un centesimo di questi soldi; **none of this wine** neanche una goccia di questo vino; **I have none left** non ne ho più; **any news? — none** ci sono novità? — niente *or* nessuna; **how many sisters have you got? — none** quante sorelle hai? — neanche una *or* nessuna; **there's none left** non ce n'è più; **none of that!** basta!; **he would have none of it** non ne ha voluto sapere; **none at all** (*nothing*) proprio niente; (*not one*) nemmeno uno; **our host was none other than the president** il nostro ospite era nientemeno che il presidente
■ ADV: **I was none too comfortable** non ero per niente a mio agio; **it's none too warm** non fa molto caldo; **and none too soon!** ed era ora!; **I like him none the worse for it** non per questo mi piace di meno; **he is none the worse for his experience** non sembra aver risentito di quell'esperienza
non·en·tity [nɒn'ɛntɪtɪ] N persona insignificante, nullità *f inv*
non·es·sen·tial ['nɒnɪ'sɛnʃəl] ADJ non essenziale; **nonessentials** NPL superfluo *sg*, cose *fpl* superflue
none·the·less [,nʌnðə'lɛs] ADV nondimeno
non-event ['nɒnɪ'vent] N delusione *f*; **the party turned out to be a non-event** la festa è stata deludente *or* una delusione
non·ex·ecu·tive [,nɒnɪg'zɛkjʊtɪv] ADJ: **nonexecutive director** direttore *m* senza potere esecutivo
non·ex·ist·ence [,nɒnɪg'zɪstəns] N inesistenza
non·ex·ist·ent [,nɒnɪg'zɪstənt] ADJ inesistente
non·fic·tion ['nɒn'fɪkʃən] N *qualunque pubblicazione non di narrativa*
non·flam·mable ['nɒn'flæməbl] ADJ non infiammabile
non·gov·ern·men·tal [,nɒngʌvən'mEntl] ADJ non governativo(-a)
non·inter·ven·tion ['nɒn,ɪntə'venʃən] N non intervento
non·iron ['nɒn'aɪən] ADJ che non si stira
non·mem·ber ['nɒn'mɛmbə^r] N non socio(-a)
non·met·al ['nɒn'mɛtl] N (*Chem*) non metallo
non-nuclear ['nɒn'nju:klɪə^r] ADJ (*country*) che non dispone di armi nucleari; **non-nuclear weapons** armi *mpl* convenzionali
no-no ['nəʊ,nəʊ] N: **it's a no-no!** (*undesirable*) è inaccettabile!; (*forbidden*) non si può fare!
non obst. ABBR (*notwithstanding*) (= **non obstante**) nonostante
no-nonsense [,nəʊ'nɒnsɛns] ADJ che va al sodo
non-partisan [,nɒnpɑ:tɪ'zæn] ADJ no partisan *inv*
non·par·ty ['nɒn'pɑ:tɪ] ADJ (*decision, vote*) indipendente
non·pay·ment ['nɒn'peɪmənt] N mancato pagamento
non·plus ['nɒn'plʌs] (*pt, pp* **nonplussed**) VT sconcertare
non·plussed ['nɒn'plʌst] ADJ sconcertato(-a)
non·pro·fes·sion·al ['nɒnprə'fɛʃənl] ADJ, N dilettante (*m/f*)
non-profit-making ['nɒn'prɒfɪt,meɪkɪŋ], (*Am*) **non-profit** ['nɒn'prɒfɪt] ADJ senza scopo di lucro

Nn

non·resi·dent ['nɒn'rɛzɪdənt] N non residente *m/f*; (*in hotel*) ospite *m/f* di passaggio
non·re·turn·able [,nɒnrɪ'tɜ:nəbl] ADJ: **nonreturnable bottle** vuoto a perdere
non·sense ['nɒnsəns] N sciocchezze *fpl*, assurdità *fpl*; **(what) nonsense!** che sciocchezze!, che assurdità!; **it is nonsense to say that ...** è un'assurdità *or* non ha senso dire che...; **to talk nonsense** dire sciocchezze *or* assurdità; **that's a piece of nonsense!** è una sciocchezza!; **to make (a) nonsense of sth** rendere assurdo qc; **he stands no nonsense** con lui non si scherza
non·sen·si·cal [nɒn'sɛnsɪkəl] ADJ assurdo(-a), ridicolo(-a)
non se·qui·tur [,nɒn'sɛkwɪtə^r] N: **it is a non sequitur** è illogico
non·shrink ['nɒn'ʃrɪŋk] ADJ (*Brit*) irrestringibile
non·skid ['nɒn'skɪd], **non·slip** ['nɒn'slɪp] ADJ antisdrucciolo *inv*, antisdrucciolevole
non·smok·er ['nɒn'sməʊkə^r] N **1** (*person*) non fumatore(-trice); **I'm a nonsmoker** non fumo **2** (*Rail*) scompartimento per non fumatori
non·smok·ing ['nɒn'sməʊkɪŋ] ADJ (*person*) che non fuma; (*area, section*) per non fumatori
non-standard ['nɒn'stændəd] ADJ (*word, pronunciation*) che non fa parte della lingua standard
non·start·er [,nɒn'stɑ:tə^r] N: **it's a nonstarter** è fallito in partenza
non·stick ['nɒn'stɪk] ADJ (*saucepan*) (con rivestimento) antiaderente
non·stop ['nɒn'stɒp] ADJ continuo(-a), senza sosta; (*train, bus*) diretto(-a), direttissimo(-a); (*flight*) diretto(-a), senza scalo; **nonstop entertainment** spettacolo continuo
■ ADV ininterrottamente, senza sosta; (*Rail*) diretto; **I flew non-stop to New York** ho preso un volo diretto per New York
non·tax·able ['nɒn'tæksəbl] ADJ: **non-taxable income** reddito non imponibile
non-U [,nɒn'ju:] ADJ ABBR (*Brit fam*: = **non-upper class**) poco fine
non·un·ion [,nɒn'ju:njən] ADJ (*workers, labour*) non appartenente al sindacato
non-violence ['nɒn'vaɪələns] N non violenza
non·vio·lent ['nɒn'vaɪələnt] ADJ non violento(-a)
non·vola·tile [,nɒn'vɒlətaɪl] ADJ (*Comput*): **non-volatile memory** memoria permanente
non·vola·tile memory [nɔn'vɔlətaɪl'mɛmərɪ] ADJ (*Comput*) memoria non volatile
non·voting [,nɒn'vəʊtɪŋ] ADJ: **non-voting shares** azioni *fpl* senza diritto di voto
non·white [,nɒn'waɪt] ADJ di colore
■ N persona di colore
noo·dles ['nu:dlz] NPL taglierini *mpl*, tagliatelle *fpl*; **egg noodles** pasta all'uovo
nook [nʊk] N angolino; **we searched every nook and cranny** abbiamo frugato dappertutto *or* in ogni angolo
noon [nu:n] N mezzogiorno; **at noon** a mezzogiorno
noon·day ['nu:n,deɪ] (*old*) ADJ (*meal, sun*) di mezzogiorno
■ N: **at noonday** a mezzogiorno
◎ **no-one** ['nəʊ,wʌn] PRON = **nobody**
noose [nu:s] N (*loop*) nodo scorsoio, cappio; (*for animal trapping*) laccio; (*hangman's*) cappio; **to put one's head in the noose** (*fig*) scavarsi la fossa con le proprie mani
nope [nəʊp] ADV (*fam*) no
◎ **nor** [nɔ:^r] ADV *see* **neither**
■ CONJ = **neither**
Nor·dic ['nɔ:dɪk] ADJ nordico(-a); **nordic skiing** sci *m* nordico
norm [nɔ:m] N norma
◎ **nor·mal** ['nɔ:məl] ADJ normale; **it was quite normal for him to object** era perfettamente normale che obiettasse; **it is perfectly normal to be left-handed** è perfettamente normale *or* naturale essere mancini
■ N **1 to return to normal** tornare alla normalità; **above/below normal** al disopra/al disotto della norma **2** (*Math*) normale *f*
nor·mal·ity [nɔ:'mælɪtɪ] N normalità
nor·mali·za·tion [,nɔ:məlaɪ'zeɪʃən] N normalizzazione *f*
nor·mal·ize ['nɔ:mə,laɪz] VT normalizzare
◎ **nor·mal·ly** ['nɔ:məlɪ] ADV normalmente
Nor·man ['nɔ:mən] N, ADJ normanno(-a)
▷ www.bbc.co.uk/history/war/normans/index.shtml
▷ www.spartacus.schoolnet.co.uk/Normans.htm
Nor·man·dy ['nɔ:məndɪ] N Normandia
Norse [nɔ:s] N lingua norrena
▷ www.windows.ucar.edu/tour/link=/mythology/norse_culture.html
◎ **north** [nɔ:θ] N nord *m*, settentrione *m*; **(to the) north of** a nord di; **the town lies north of the border** la città si trova a nord del confine; **in the north** al nord; **in the north of** nel nord di; **the wind is from the north** il vento soffia da nord; **to veer to the north** (*wind*) girare verso nord; **a house facing north** una casa esposta a nord
■ ADJ (*gen*) nord *inv*; (*wind*) del nord, settentrionale; (*coast*) settentrionale
■ ADV verso nord; **to sail north** navigare verso nord; **we were travelling north** viaggiavamo verso nord
North Africa N l'Africa del Nord
North African ADJ, N nordafricano(-a)
North America N l'America del Nord
North American ADJ, N nordamericano(-a)
Northants [nɔ:'θænts] ABBR (*Brit*) = *Northamptonshire*
north·bound ['nɔ:θ,baʊnd] ADJ (*traffic*) diretto(-a) a nord; (*carriageway*) nord *inv*
North Caro·li·na N Carolina del Nord
▷ www.ncgov.com/
north-country ['nɔ:θ,kʌntrɪ] ADJ del nord, settentrionale
Northd ABBR (*Brit*) = *Northumberland*
North Da·ko·ta N Nord Dakota *m*
▷ http://discovernd.com/
◎ **north·east** [,nɔ:θ'i:st] N nordest *m*
■ ADJ di nordest
■ ADV verso nordest
north·easter·ly [,nɔ:θ'i:stəlɪ] ADJ (*wind*) che viene dal nordest; (*direction*) verso nordest
north·eastern [,nɔ:ð'i:stən] ADJ di nordest
nor·ther·ly ['nɔ:ðəlɪ] ADJ (*wind*) del nord; (*direction*) verso nord; **house with a northerly aspect** casa esposta a nord; **a northerly wind** un vento settentrionale
◎ **north·ern** ['nɔ:ðən] ADJ (*region*) del nord, settentrionale; (*wall*) (esposto(-a) a) nord *inv*; (*coast*) settentrionale; **in northern Spain** nel nord della Spagna, nella Spagna settentrionale; **Northern Europe** l'Europa settentrionale

Northern Cape N Capo settentrionale
▷ www.northern-cape.gov.za
▷ www.northerncape.org.za

north·ern·er [ˈnɔːðənəʳ] N settentrionale *m/f*, abitante *m/f* del nord

northern hemisphere N: **the northern hemisphere** l'emisfero settentrionale *or* boreale

Northern Ireland N Irlanda del Nord
▷ www.discovernorthernireland.com/discover.aspx

northern lights NPL: **the northern lights** l'aurora boreale

north·ern·most [ˈnɔːðənˌməʊst] ADJ (il/la) più a nord; **the northernmost town in Europe** la città più a nord dell'Europa

Northern Territory N Territorio del Nord
▷ www.nt.gov.au

north-northeast [ˌnɔːθˌnɔːθˈiːst] N nord-nordest *m*

north-northwest [ˌnɔːθˌnɔːθˈwɛst] N nord-nordovest *m*

North Pole N: **the North Pole** il Polo Nord

North Sea N: **the North Sea** il mare del Nord

North Sea gas N gas del mare del Nord

North Sea oil N petrolio del mare del Nord

North Star N: **the North Star** la stella polare

north·wards [ˈnɔːθwədz], **north·ward** [ˈnɔːθwəd] ADV verso nord

North West N (*Geog*) Nord-Ovest

◎ **north·west** [ˌnɔːθˈwɛst] N nordovest *m*
■ ADJ di nordovest
■ ADV verso nordovest

north·wester·ly [ˌnɔːθˈwɛstəlɪ] ADJ (*wind*) che viene da nordovest; (*direction*) verso nordovest

north·western [ˌnɔːθˈwɛstən] ADJ di nordovest

Northwest Territories NPL Territori *mpl* del Nord-Ovest
▷ www.gov.nt.ca/
▷ www.nwttravel.nt.ca

Nor·way [ˈnɔːˌweɪ] N Norvegia

Nor·we·gian [nɔːˈwiːdʒən] ADJ norvegese
■ N (*person*) norvegese *m/f*; (*language*) norvegese *m*

Nos., nos. ABBR (= **numbers**) nn (= *numeri*)

no-score draw [ˌnəʊskɔːˈdrɔː] N (*Sport*): **a no-score draw** un pareggio zero a zero

◎ **nose** [nəʊz] N naso; (*of animal, plane*) muso; **to speak through one's nose** parlare col naso; **to blow one's nose** soffiarsi il naso; **my nose is bleeding** perdo sangue dal naso; **nose drops** gocce *fpl* per il naso; **right under my nose** (*fig*) proprio sotto il naso; **to follow one's nose** andare a naso; **to pay through the nose (for sth)** (*fam*) pagare (qc) un occhio della testa; **to poke** *or* **stick one's nose into sth** (*fam*) ficcare *or* cacciare il naso in qc; **to turn up one's nose (at sth)** arricciare il naso (di fronte a qc); **to look down one's nose at** disprezzare; (*person*) guardare dall'alto in basso; **to have a (good) nose for** aver buon fiuto *or* buon naso per
■ VI: **to nose (one's way)** avanzare cautamente; **the car nosed (its way) into the stream of traffic** l'auto si è infilata poco a poco nella corrente del traffico
▶ **nose about, nose around** VI + ADV curiosare
▶ **nose out** VT + ADV (*subj: dog, fig*) fiutare

nose·bag [ˈnəʊzˌbæg] N sacchetto per il foraggio

nose·bleed [ˈnəʊzˌbliːd] N emorragia nasale

-nosed [nəʊzd] SUFF dal naso...; **red-nosed** dal naso rosso

nose-dive [ˈnəʊzˌdaɪv] N (*Aer*) picchiata; (*fig*) calo vertiginoso
■ VI (*see n*) scendere in picchiata; calare vertiginosamente

nose·gay [ˈnəʊzˌgeɪ] N (*gen*) mazzolino (di fiori); (*at wedding*) piccolo bouquet *m inv*

nos·ey [ˈnəʊzɪ] ADJ = **nosy**

nosey parker [-ˈpɑːkəʳ] N (*Brit*) = **nosy parker**

nosh [nɒʃ] N (*Brit fam*) cibo

nosh-up [ˈnɒʃˌʌp] N (*Brit fam*) mangiata, abbuffata

nos·tal·gia [nɒsˈtældʒɪə] N nostalgia

nos·tal·gic [nɒsˈtældʒɪk] ADJ nostalgico(-a)

nos·tril [ˈnɒstrəl] N narice *f*; (*of horse*) frogia

nosy, nos·ey [ˈnəʊzɪ] ADJ (*comp* **-ier**, *superl* **-iest**) (*fam*) curioso(-a); **don't be so nosy** non fare il ficcanaso; **she's a nosy girl** è una ficcanaso

nosy parker N (*Brit fam*) ficcanaso *m/f*

◎ **not** [nɒt] ADV non; **he is not here** non è qui, non c'è; **I haven't seen anybody** non ho visto nessuno; **it's too late, isn't it?** è troppo tardi, vero? *or* no?; **she will not** *or* **won't go** non ci andrà; **he isn't coming** non viene; **I'm not sure** non sono sicuro; **he asked me not to do it** mi ha chiesto di non farlo; **whether you go or not** che tu ci vada o no; **not that I don't like him** non che (lui) non mi piaccia; **big, not to say enormous** grosso, per non dire enorme; **why not?** perché no?; **are you coming or not?** vieni o no?; **I hope not** spero di no; **not at all** niente affatto, per niente; (*after thanks*) prego, s'immagini; **I'm not at all sure it's a good idea** non sono affatto sicuro che sia una buona idea; **you must not** *or* **mustn't do this** non deve fare questo; **not one book** neanche un libro; **not me/you** *etc* io/tu *etc* no; **not yet** non ancora; **have you finished? — not yet** hai finito? — non ancora; *see also* **even, much, only** *etc*

no·table [ˈnəʊtəbl] ADJ (*person*) eminente; (*event*) notevole, degno(-a) di nota
■ N notabile *m*, persona importante

no·tably [ˈnəʊtəblɪ] ADV (*noticeably*) notevolmente; (*in particular*) in particolare

no·ta·ry [ˈnəʊtərɪ] N (*also:* **notary public**) notaio

no·ta·tion [nəʊˈteɪʃən] N notazione *f*

notch [nɒtʃ] N (*in wood, blade*) tacca; (*in wheel, saw*) dente *m*; (*in belt*) buco
■ VT (*stick, blade*) intagliare, fare tacche in
▶ **notch up** VT + ADV (*score, victory*) marcare, segnare

◎ **note** [nəʊt] N **1** (*gen, Diplomacy*) nota; **to take** *or* **make notes** prendere appunti; **remember to take notes** ricordati di prendere appunti; **I'll drop her a note** le lascerò una nota; **Italian lecture notes** appunti *mpl* di italiano; **to take** *or* **make a note of sth** prendere nota di qc, prendere atto di qc; **I must make a note to buy some more** devo tenere a mente di comprarne di più; **to compare notes** (*fig*) scambiarsi le impressioni **2** (*informal letter*) biglietto, due righe; **just a quick note to let you know ...** ti scrivo solo due righe per informarti... **3** (*Mus, of bird*) (*fig*) nota; **to play** *or* **sing a wrong note** prendere una stecca; **to strike the right/wrong note (with)** (*fig*) intonarsi (a)/stonare (con); **with a note of anxiety in his voice** con una nota di ansia nella voce **4** (*Comm*) nota; (*also:* **banknote**) banconota, biglietto di banca; **delivery note** bolletta di consegna; **five-pound note** biglietto da cinque sterline **5** (*of person*): **of note** eminente, importante **6** (*notice*): **worthy of note** degno(-a) di nota
■ VT (*observe*) notare, osservare; (*also:* **note down**) annotare, prendere nota di

note·book [ˈnəʊtˌbʊk] N taccuino; (*Scol*) blocco per appunti; (*for shorthand*) bloc-notes *m inv*

Nn

note·case ['nəʊt,keɪs] N (*Brit*) portafoglio

◎ **not·ed** ['nəʊtɪd] ADJ (*Brit*): **noted (for)** celebre (per), famoso(-a) (per)

note·pad ['nəʊt,pæd] N bloc-notes *m inv*, blocchetto

note·paper ['nəʊt,peɪpə^r] N carta da lettere

note·worthy ['nəʊt,wɜ:ðɪ] ADJ degno(-a) di nota, importante

◎ **noth·ing** ['nʌθɪŋ] N **1** niente *m*, nulla *m*; (*Math, Sport*) zero; **nothing happened** non è successo niente *or* nulla; **I've eaten nothing** non ho mangiato niente *or* nulla; **there is nothing to eat** non c'è niente *or* nulla da mangiare **2** (*in phrases*): **as if nothing had happened** come se niente fosse; **nothing at all** proprio niente; **nothing else** nient'altro; **nothing much/new** *etc* niente di speciale/nuovo *etc*; **nothing but** nient'altro che; **she does nothing but sleep** non fa altro che dormire; **there is nothing for it but to go** non c'è altra scelta che andare; **there is nothing in it** (*not true*) non c'è niente di vero; (*not interesting*) non è per niente interessante; (*nearly the same*) non c'è una grande differenza; **there's nothing in it for us** non ci guadagniamo niente; **there's nothing to it!** (*it's easy*) è una cosa da niente!; **to have nothing on** (*naked*) non aver niente addosso; (*not busy*) non aver niente in programma; **for nothing** (*free, unpaid*) per niente, gratis; (*in vain*) per niente, inutilmente; (*for no reason*) senza ragione; **he is nothing if not careful** è soprattutto attento; **I can do nothing about it** non posso farci nulla; **to come to nothing** finire in nulla; **to say nothing of ...** per non parlare di...; **to think nothing of doing sth** non farsi nessun problema nel fare qc; **think nothing of it!** s'immagini!, si figuri!; **I can make nothing of it** non ci capisco niente; **a mere nothing** una cosa da nulla *or* da niente; **to whisper sweet nothings to sb** sussurrare tenerezze a qn; **nothing doing!** (*fam*) niente da fare!
■ ADV per niente, niente affatto; **it was nothing like as expensive as we thought** era molto meno caro di quanto credessimo

noth·ing·ness ['nʌθɪŋnɪs] N (*non-existence*) nulla *m*; (*worthlessness, insignificance*) nullità

◎ **no·tice** ['nəʊtɪs] N **1** (*intimation, warning*) avviso; (*period*) preavviso; **without notice** senza preavviso; **he was transferred without notice** è stato trasferito senza preavviso; **advance** *or* **previous notice** preavviso; **a week's notice** una settimana di preavviso; **at short notice** con un breve preavviso; **at a moment's notice** immediatamente, all'istante; **until further notice** fino a nuovo avviso; **to give notice to** (*to tenant*) dare la disdetta a; (*to landlord*) dare il preavviso a; **to give sb notice** (*Admin: inform*) notificare a qn; (*: sack*) licenziare qn; **to give notice** *or* **to hand in one's notice** (*subj: employee*) licenziarsi; **she handed in her notice yesterday** ha dato le dimissioni ieri; **to give notice of sth** annunciare qc; **to give sb notice of sth** avvisare qn di qc **2** (*announcement*) avviso; (*Press*) annuncio; (*sign*) cartello; (*poster*) manifesto, cartellone *m*; **to put a notice in the paper** mettere un annuncio sul giornale; **there's a notice on the board about the trip** in bacheca c'è un avviso a proposito del viaggio
3 (*Brit: review: of play etc*) critica, recensione *f*
4 (*attention*): **to bring sth to sb's notice** far notare qc a qn; **to take notice of sb/sth** notare qn/qc, fare caso a qn/qc; **to take no notice of sb/sth** non prestare attenzione a qn/qc; **he keeps waving at me — take no notice!** continua a farmi dei cenni — ignoralo!; **it has come to my notice that ...** sono venuto a sapere che...; **to escape** *or* **avoid notice** passare inosservato(-a); **it escaped my notice that ...** non ho notato che...
■ VT accorgersi di, notare; **he pretended not to notice us** ha fatto finta di non vederci; **I notice you have a new car** vedo che ha una macchina nuova

> DID YOU KNOW ...?
> **notice** is not translated by the Italian word *notizia*

no·tice·able ['nəʊtɪsəbl] ADJ (*perceptible*) percettibile; (*obvious*) evidente; (*considerable*) notevole; **the scar is hardly noticeable** la cicatrice si vede appena; **there has been a noticeable increase in prices** c'è stato un notevole aumento dei prezzi

no·tice·ably ['nəʊtɪsəblɪ] ADV (*perceptibly*) sensibilmente; (*obviously*) evidentemente; (*considerably*) notevolmente

notice board N (*Brit*) bacheca

no·ti·fi·able ['nəʊtɪ,faɪəbəl] ADJ (*disease, crime*) che deve essere notificato(-a) *or* denunciato(-a) alle autorità

no·ti·fi·ca·tion [,nəʊtɪfɪ'keɪʃən] N (*see vb*) notifica; denuncia; (*announcement*) annuncio

no·ti·fy ['nəʊtɪ,faɪ] VT: **to notify sb of sth** informare *or* avvisare qn di qc; (*police*) denunciare qc a qn; **to notify sth to sb** notificare qc a qn; **you should notify the police that your car has been stolen** deve denunciare il furto della macchina alla polizia

◎ **no·tion** ['nəʊʃən] N **1** idea; (*concept*) nozione *f*; **to have no notion of time** non avere la nozione del tempo; **I haven't the slightest** *or* **foggiest notion** non ho la più pallida idea; **I have no notion of what you mean** non ho la più vaga idea di cosa tu voglia dire
2 notions NPL (*Am: haberdashery*) merceria

no·tion·al ['nəʊʃənəl] ADJ (*figure, amount, price*) simbolico(-a)

no·to·ri·ety [,nəʊtə'raɪətɪ] N notorietà

no·to·ri·ous [nəʊ'tɔ:rɪəs] ADJ (*thief, criminal, prison etc*) famigerato(-a); (*liar*) ben noto(-a); (*place, crime*) tristemente famoso(-a); **a town notorious for its fog** una città tristemente famosa per la nebbia

no·to·ri·ous·ly [nəʊ'tɔ:rɪəslɪ] ADV notoriamente

Notts [nɒts] ABBR (*Brit*) = *Nottinghamshire*

not·with·stand·ing [,nɒtwɪð'stændɪŋ] PREP nonostante, malgrado
■ CONJ: **international agreements notwithstanding ...** malgrado gli accordi internazionali...

nou·gat ['nu:gɑ:] N torrone *m*

nought [nɔ:t] N (*Math*) zero

noughts and crosses NSG (*Brit*) tris (*giocata segnando "x" e "o" su un quadrato con 9 caselle*)

noun [naʊn] N sostantivo, nome *m*

nour·ish ['nʌrɪʃ] VT nutrire

nour·ish·ing ['nʌrɪʃɪŋ] ADJ nutriente

nour·ish·ment ['nʌrɪʃmənt] N nutrimento

nous [naʊs] N (*Brit fam*) buonsenso; **to have the nous to do sth** avere il buonsenso di fare qc

nou·veau riche [,nu:vəʊ'ri:ʃ] N (*pl* **nouveaux riches**) nuovo(-a) ricco(-a), arricchito(-a)

Nov. ABBR (= **November**) nov. (= *novembre*)

Nova Scotia ['nəʊvə'skəʊʃə] N Nuova Scozia
▷ www.gov.ns.ca

◎ **nov·el** ['nɒvəl] ADJ originale, nuovo(-a) *after n*
■ N (*Literature*) romanzo

> DID YOU KNOW ...?
> **novel** is not translated by the Italian word *novella*

nov·el·ette [ˌnɒvəˈlɛt] N (*usu pej*) romanzetto
nov·el·ist [ˈnɒvəlɪst] N romanziere(-a)
nov·el·ty [ˈnɒvəltɪ] N **1** NO PL novità **2** (*Comm*) oggettino, ninnolo
No·vem·ber [nəʊˈvɛmbəʳ] N novembre *m*; *for usage see* July
no·vena [nəʊˈviːnə] N novena
nov·ice [ˈnɒvɪs] N principiante *m/f*; (*Rel*) novizio(-a)
NOW [naʊ] N ABBR (*Am*: = **National Organization for Women**) ≈ U.D.I. *f* (= *Unione Donne Italiane*)
◎ **now** [naʊ] ADV **1** (*at present, these days*) adesso, ora; (*at that time*) allora; **right now** subito, immediatamente; **now is the time to do it** questo è il momento per farlo; **they won't be long now** ormai non tarderanno; **I saw her just now** l'ho vista proprio adesso; **that's the fashion just now** è la moda del momento; **I'm very busy just now** in questo momento sono molto occupato; **I'll read it just now** lo leggo subito; **(every) now and then** *or* **now and again** ogni tanto, di tanto in tanto; **it's now or never** ora o mai più **2** (*with prep*): **between now and Monday** entro lunedì , da qui a lunedì ; **I couldn't do it before now** non potevo farlo prima; **long before now** molto tempo fa; **by now** ormai; **it should be ready by now** ormai dovrebbe essere pronto; **the train should have arrived by now** il treno dovrebbe essere già arrivato; **in 3 days from now** fra 3 giorni; **from now on** d'ora in poi; **from now until then** da adesso fino a quel momento; **that's all for now** per ora basta; **until now** *or* **up to now** fino ad ora **3** (*without temporal force*): **now (then)!** dunque!, allora!; **now then, no more quarrelling** ora *or* adesso basta con i litigi; **well now** vediamo, dunque; **well now, look who it is!** ma guarda un po' chi si vede!; **be careful now!** ma sta' attento!
■ CONJ: **now (that)** adesso che, ora che
nowa·days [ˈnaʊəˌdeɪz] ADV al giorno d'oggi, oggi, oggigiorno, oggidì ; **nowadays I haven't got time to watch television** attualmente non ho il tempo per guardare la televisione
◎ **no·where** [ˈnəʊˌwɛəʳ] ADV in nessun posto *or* luogo, da nessuna parte; **I went nowhere** non sono andato in nessun posto *or* da nessuna parte; **nowhere in Italy** in nessuna parte d'Italia, da nessuna parte in Italia; **nowhere else** in nessun altro posto; **it/he is nowhere to be found** non si riesce a trovarlo da nessuna parte; **we're getting nowhere** non stiamo concludendo nulla; **that will get you nowhere** ciò non le servirà a nulla; **he appeared from nowhere** è saltato fuori da chissà dove; **Paul is nowhere near as tall as John** Paul non è neanche lontanamente alto come John; **it's nowhere near as good** non vale neanche la metà; **nowhere near enough** ben lontano dall'essere sufficiente
no-win situation [ˌnəʊwɪnsɪtjʊˈeɪʃən] N: **to be in a no-win situation** aver perso in partenza
nowt [naʊt] N (*Brit dial*) = **nothing**
nox·ious [ˈnɒkʃəs] ADJ nocivo(-a)
noz·zle [ˈnɒzl] N (*of hose, vacuum cleaner, syringe*) bocchetta, boccaglio; (*of fire extinguisher*) lancia
NP [ˌɛnˈpiː] N ABBR = **notary public**
NS [ˌɛnˈɛs] ABBR (*Canada*) = **Nova Scotia**
NSC [ˌɛnɛsˈsiː] N ABBR (*Am*) = **National Security Council**
NSF [ˌɛnɛsˈɛf] N ABBR (*Am*) = *National Science Foundation*
NSPCC [ˌɛnɛspiːsiːˈsiː] N ABBR (*Brit*) = *National Society for the Prevention of Cruelty to Children*
NSW ABBR (*Australia*) = **New South Wales**
NT [ˌɛnˈtiː] N ABBR (= **New Testament**) N.T. (= *Nuovo Testamento*)
nth [ɛnθ] ADJ (*Math*): **to the nth power** *or* **degree** all'ennesima potenza; **for the nth time** (*fam*) per l'ennesima volta
nu·ance [ˈnjuːɑːns] N sfumatura
nub [nʌb] N: **the nub of the matter** il nocciolo del problema
nu·bile [ˈnjuːbaɪl] ADJ nubile; (*attractive*) giovane e desiderabile
◎ **nu·clear** [ˈnjuːklɪəʳ] ADJ nucleare; (*warfare*) atomico(-a); **nuclear power** energia nucleare
nuclear capability N capacità nucleare
nuclear disarmament N disarmo nucleare
nuclear family N famiglia nucleare
nuclear-free [ˈnjuːklɪəfriː] ADJ (*zone*) denuclearizzato(-a)
nuclear-free zone [ˌnjuːklɪəfriːˈzəʊn] N zona denuclearizzata
nuclear fuel N combustibile *m* nucleare
nuclear physicist N fisico nucleare
nuclear physics N fisica nucleare
▷ http://ie.lbl.gov/education/glossary/glossaryf.htm
▷ www.atomicarchive.com
▷ www.visionlearning.com/library/module_viewer.php?mid=59
▷ www.iaea.org/inis/ws/
nuclear power N energia nucleare, nucleare *m*
nuclear-powered [ˌnjuːklɪəˈpaʊəd] ADJ nucleare
nuclear power station N centrale *f* termonucleare
nuclear reactor N reattore *m* nucleare
nu·cleic [njuːˈkliːɪk] ADJ nucleico(-a)
nu·cleon [ˈnjuːklɪɒn] N nucleone *m*
nu·cleus [ˈnjuːklɪəs] N (*pl* **nuclei** [ˈnjuːklɪaɪ]) nucleo
nude [njuːd] ADJ nudo(-a)
■ N (*Art*) nudo; **in the nude** nudo(-a), tutto(-a) nudo(-a)
nudge [nʌdʒ] N gomitata
■ VT dare un colpetto col gomito a; **he nudged me out of the way** mi ha spinto via con una gomitata
nud·ism [ˈnjuːdɪzəm] N nudismo
nud·ist [ˈnjuːdɪst] ADJ (*colony*) nudista; (*camp, beach*) di nudisti
■ N nudista *m/f*
nu·dity [ˈnjuːdɪtɪ] N nudità
nug·get [ˈnʌgɪt] N pepita
nui·sance [ˈnjuːsns] N (*state of affairs, thing*) fastidio, seccatura; (*person*) peste *f*; **what a nuisance!** che seccatura!; **it's a nuisance having to shave** doversi radere è una (gran) seccatura; **to make a nuisance of o.s.** rendersi insopportabile; **he's a nuisance** dà fastidio
NUJ [ˌɛnjuːˈdʒeɪ] N ABBR (*Brit*: = **National Union of Journalists**) *sindacato nazionale dei giornalisti*
nuke [njuːk] (*esp Am fam*) VT attaccare con armi atomiche
■ N bomba atomica
null [nʌl] ADJ: **null and void** (*Law*) nullo(-a)
nul·li·fy [ˈnʌlɪˌfaɪ] VT annullare
nul·lity [ˈnʌlɪtɪ] N nullità
NUM [ˌɛnjuːˈɛm] N ABBR (*Brit*: = **National Union of Mineworkers**) *sindacato nazionale dei minatori*
numb [nʌm] ADJ **1** (*fingers etc*) intorpidito(-a); **numb with cold** intirizzito(-a) (dal freddo); **my leg has gone numb** mi si è intorpidita una gamba **2** (*fig*): **numb with** (*fear, grief*) paralizzato(-a) da, impietrito(-a) da

Nn

■VT **1** intorpidire; **the cold numbs you as soon as you step outside** appena si esce si resta paralizzati dal freddo **2** (*fig*) rendere insensibile; **she drinks to numb her grief** beve per attenuare il dolore

◎**num·ber** ['nʌmbəʳ] N **1** (*Math*) numero; (*figure*) cifra, numero; **in round numbers** in cifra tonda; **even/odd number** numero pari/dispari; **the Book of Numbers** (*Bible*) i Numeri **2** (*quantity*) numero, quantità *f inv*; **a number of people** un certo numero di persone, diversa gente; **a fair number of** (*reasons, mistakes, people*) una buona quantità di; **on a number of occasions** diverse volte, in diverse occasioni; **any number of** una gran quantità di, moltissimi; **they were 15 in number** erano in 15; **times without number** tantissime volte; **one of their number** uno di loro **3** (*of house etc*) numero; **at number 15** al (numero) 15; **what's your phone number?** qual è il tuo numero di telefono?; **you've got the wrong number** ha sbagliato numero; **his number's up!** (*fam*) è venuta la sua ora!; **to look after number one** (*fam*) fare solo i propri interessi; **he's my number two** è il mio vice **4** (*issue: of magazine etc*) numero **5** (*song, act etc*) numero; (*piece of music*) pezzo

■VT **1** (*count, include*) contare; **to number sb among one's friends** considerare qn un amico **2** (*amount to*) ammontare a; **they numbered 10 in all** erano 10 in tutto **3** (*assign number to*) numerare; **his days are numbered** (*fig*) ha i giorni contati

num·bered ac·count [,nʌmbədə'kaʊnt] N (*in bank*) conto numerato

num·ber·ing ['nʌmbərɪŋ] N numerazione *f*

num·ber·less ['nʌmbəlɪs] ADJ innumerevole, senza numero

number plate N (*Brit Aut*) targa

Number Ten N (*Brit: 10 Downing Street*) *residenza del Primo Ministro del Regno Unito*

numb·ness ['nʌmnɪs] N intorpidimento; (*due to cold*) intirizzimento

numb·skull ['nʌm,skʌl] N (*fam*) imbecille *m/f*, idiota *m/f*

nu·mera·cy ['nju:mərəsɪ] N il saper far di conto

nu·mer·al ['nju:mərəl] N numero, cifra

nu·mer·ate ['nju:mərɪt] ADJ: **to be numerate** (*Brit*) saper far di conto

nu·mera·tor ['nju:mə,reɪtəʳ] N numeratore *m*

nu·meri·cal [nju:'mɛrɪkəl] ADJ numerico(-a); **in numerical order** in ordine numerico

nu·meri·cal·ly [nju:'mɛrɪkəlɪ] ADV numericamente

◎**nu·mer·ous** ['nju:mərəs] ADJ numeroso(-a)

nu·mis·mat·ics [,nju:mɪz'mætɪks] NSG numismatica
▷ http://numis.org/about.htm

nump·ty ['nʌmptɪ] N (*fam*) stupidone(-a)

nun [nʌn] N suora, monaca

Nunavut ['nʊnəvʊt] N Territori *mpl* del Nunavut
▷ www.gov.nu.ca
▷ www.nunavuttourism.com

nun·nery ['nʌnərɪ] N convento

nup·tial ['nʌpʃəl] ADJ nuziale

◎**nurse** [nɜ:s] N **1** (*in hospital etc*) infermiere(-a); **student nurse** allievo(-a) infermiere(-a); **male nurse** infermiere *m* **2** (*also:* **nursemaid**: *children's*) bambinaia

■VT **1** (*patient*) assistere, curare; (*cold*) curare; **she nursed him back to health** è guarito grazie alle sue cure; **to nurse a cold** curarsi un raffreddore **2** (*suckle: baby*) allattare, dare il latte a **3** (*cradle*) cullare; (*fig: hope*) nutrire, cullare; (*: anger, grudge*) covare

nurse·maid ['nɜ:s,meɪd] N bambinaia

nurse·ry ['nɜ:sərɪ] N **1** (*room*) stanza dei bambini; (*institution*) asilo, nido **2** (*Agr*) vivaio

nursery education N istruzione *f* prescolastica

nursery nurse N (*Brit*) puericultrice *f*

nursery rhyme N filastrocca

nursery school N scuola materna, asilo infantile

nursery slope N (*Brit Skiing*) pista per principianti

nurs·ing ['nɜ:sɪŋ] N (*care of invalids*) assistenza; (*profession*) professione *f* di infermiere (*or* di infermiera); **she's going in for nursing** ha deciso di fare l'infermiera

■ADJ **1** (*mother*) che allatta **2** (*of hospital*): **the nursing staff** gli infermieri, il personale infermieristico; **nursing auxiliary** infermiere(-a) non diplomato(-a)

nursing home N casa di cura, clinica

nur·ture ['nɜ:tʃəʳ] VT (*rear*) allevare con amore; (*feed*) nutrire

NUS [,ɛnju:'ɛs] N ABBR (*Brit:* = **National Union of Students**) *organizzazione nazionale degli studenti universitari*

NUT [,ɛnju:'ti:] N ABBR (*Brit:* = **National Union of Teachers**) *sindacato nazionale degli insegnanti*

nut [nʌt] N **1** (*Bot*) noce *f* (*or* nocciola *or* mandorla *etc*) (*no generic term in Italian*); **nuts** NPL frutta *sg* secca; **a bag of mixed nuts** un sacchetto di frutta secca mista **2** (*Tech*) dado; (*Mountaineering*) nut *m inv* **3** (*fam: head*) zucca; **he is off his nut** gli manca una rotella, è svitato **4** (*fam: person*) pazzo(-a), matto(-a); **he's nuts** è pazzo

■ADJ (*chocolate etc*) alle noci (*or* alla nocciola *or* alla mandorla *etc*); *see also* **nuts**

nut·case ['nʌt,keɪs] N (*fam*) matto(-a), pazzo(-a), pazzerello(-a)

nut·crackers ['nʌt,krækəz] NPL schiaccianoci *m inv*

nut·hatch ['nʌt,hætʃ] N (*bird*) picchio muratore

nut·house ['nʌt,haʊs] N (*fam*) manicomio

nut·meg ['nʌt,mɛg] N noce *f* moscata

nu·tria ['nju:trɪə] N nutria

nu·tri·ent ['nju:trɪənt] N sostanza nutritiva

■ADJ nutriente; **nutrient cycle** (*Geol*) ciclo pedogenetico

nu·tri·tion [nju:'trɪʃən] N nutrizione *f*, alimentazione *f*

nu·tri·tion·al [nju:'trɪʃənl] ADJ (*value*) nutritivo(-a)

nu·tri·tion·ist [nju:'trɪʃənɪst] N nutrizionista *m/f*

nu·tri·tious [nju:'trɪʃəs], **nu·tri·tive** ['nju:trɪtɪv] ADJ nutriente, nutritivo(-a)

nuts [nʌts] (*fam*) ADJ matto(-a), pazzo(-a); **to be nuts about sb** essere pazzo(-a) di qn; **to be nuts about sth** andare matto(-a) per qc; **to go nuts** impazzire, dare i numeri

■EXCL (*nonsense*) col cavolo!

nut·shell ['nʌtʃɛl] N guscio di noce (*or* nocciola *etc*) (*no generic term in Italian*); **in a nutshell** in poche parole; **to put it in a nutshell** per farla breve

nut·ter ['nʌtəʳ] N (*Brit fam*) matto(-a)

nut·ty ['nʌtɪ] ADJ (*comp* **-ier**, *superl* **-iest**) **1** (*flavour, taste*) di noce (*or* nocciola *or* mandorla *etc*); (*cake*) di frutta secca; (*chocolate*) alla nocciola *etc* **2** (*fam*) pazzo(-a), matto(-a)

nuz·zle ['nʌzl] VI: **to nuzzle up to** strofinare il muso contro

NV ABBR (*Am*) = **Nevada**

NVQ [,ɛnvi:'kju:] N ABBR (= **National Vocational Qualification**) *diploma di istruzione secondaria in materie tecnico-pratiche*

NVQ

In Gran Bretagna, Galles e Irlanda del Nord si chiamano **National Vocational Qualifications** o **NVQs** i diplomi rilasciati da alcuni istituti tecnici professionali al termine di corsi indirizzati principalmente a chi è già inserito nel mondo del lavoro e desidera un riconoscimento 'formale'; tuttavia anche in alcune scuole secondarie è possibile prepararsi agli **NVQs** in alternativa o in aggiunta ai "GCSEs" e agli "A levels". La valutazione viene effettuata attraverso test pratici e esami orali e scritti. In Scozia il diploma equivalente si chiama "Scottish Vocational Qualifications" (o "SVQs").
Vedi anche **A LEVEL; GCSE**
▷ www.dfes.gov.uk/nvq/

NW ABBR (= **North West(ern)**) NO (= *nord ovest*)
NWT [ˌɛndʌblju:'ti:] ABBR (*Canada*) = **Northwest Territories**
NY [ˌɛn'waɪ] N ABBR (*Am Post*) = **New York**
NYC [ˌɛnwaɪ'si:] N ABBR (*Am Post*) = *New York City*
ny·lon ['naɪlɒn] N nailon *m*; **nylons** NPL calze *fpl* di nailon
■ ADJ di nailon
nymph [nɪmf] N ninfa
nymph·et ['nɪmfɪt] N ninfetta
nym·pho·ma·nia [ˌnɪmfəʊ'meɪnɪə] N ninfomania
nym·pho·ma·ni·ac [ˌnɪmfəʊ'meɪnɪæk] ADJ, N ninfomane (*f*)
NYSE [ˌɛnwaɪɛs'i:] N ABBR (*Am*) = *New York Stock Exchange*
NZ ABBR = **New Zealand**

O, o [əʊ] N **1** (*letter*) O, o *f or m inv*; **O for Oliver** (*Am*): **O for Oboe** ≈ O come Otranto **2** (*number*: *Telec etc*) zero **3** (*Am Scol*: = **outstanding**) ≈ ottimo

O, o [əʊ] EXCL (*liter*) oh!

oaf [əʊf] N zoticone(-a)

oaf·ish ['əʊfɪʃ] ADJ (*behaviour*) da zoticone(-a); **an oafish person** uno(-a) zoticone(-a)

oak [əʊk] N quercia; **common oak** farnia; **English oak** rovere *m*; **red oak** quercia rossa
■ ADJ di quercia

oak apple N galla di quercia

oakum ['əʊkəm] N stoppa per calafataggio

OAP [ˌəʊeɪ'piː] N ABBR (*Brit*) = **old-age pensioner**

oar [ɔː'] N remo; **to put** *or* **shove one's oar in** (*fig fam*) impicciarsi

oar·lock ['ɔːˌlɒk] N (*Am*) scalmiera

oars·man ['ɔːzmən] N (*pl* **-men**) rematore *m*; (*Sport*) vogatore *m*

oars·woman ['ɔːzwʊmən] N (*pl* **-women**) rematrice *f*; (*Sport*) vogatrice *f*

OAS [ˌəʊeɪ'ɛs] N ABBR (= **Organization of American States**) OSA *f* (= *Organizzazione degli Stati Americani*)

oasis [əʊ'eɪsɪs] N (*pl* **oases** [əʊ'eɪsiːz]) oasi *f inv*

oat·cake ['əʊtˌkeɪk] N biscotto d'avena

oath [əʊθ] N **1** (*solemn promise*) giuramento; **under** *or* **on oath** sotto giuramento; **to put sb on** *or* **under oath to do sth** far giurare a qn di fare qc; **to take the oath** giurare; **to swear on oath** *or* **on one's oath** giurare solennemente **2** (*swear word*) imprecazione *f*; **a string of oaths** una sequela di imprecazioni

oat·meal ['əʊtmiːl] N farina d'avena
■ ADJ (*colour*) beige *inv*

oats ['əʊts] NPL avena

OAU [ˌəʊeɪ'juː] N ABBR (= **Organization of African Unity**) OUA *f* (= *Organizzazione dell'Unità Africana*)

ob·du·ra·cy ['ɒbdjʊrəsɪ] N (*frm*) caparbietà, pervicacia

ob·du·rate ['ɒbdjʊrɪt] (*frm*) ADJ (*unyielding*) irremovibile; (*stubborn*) caparbio(-a), pervicace; (*hard-hearted*) insensibile

OBE [ˌəʊbiː'iː] N ABBR (*Brit*: = **Order of the British Empire**) *titolo onorifico*

obedi·ence [ə'biːdɪəns] N ubbidienza; **in obedience to your orders** (*frm*) conformemente ai vostri ordini

obedi·ent [ə'biːdɪənt] ADJ ubbidiente; **to be obedient to sb/sth** ubbidire a qn/qc

obedi·ent·ly [ə'biːdɪəntlɪ] ADV docilmente

ob·elisk ['ɒbɪlɪsk] N obelisco

obese [əʊ'biːs] ADJ (*frm*) obeso(-a)

obesity [əʊ'biːsɪtɪ] N (*frm*) obesità

obey [ə'beɪ] VT (*person*) ubbidire a; (*instructions*) seguire; (*regulations*) osservare; **to obey the rules** rispettare il regolamento; **to obey one's conscience** seguire i dettami della propria coscienza
■ VI ubbidire

obi·tu·ary [ə'bɪtjʊərɪ] N necrologio

obituary column N colonna degli annunci mortuari

obituary notice N necrologio

◎ **ob·ject¹** ['ɒbdʒɪkt] N **1** (*gen*) oggetto; **she was an object of ridicule** era oggetto di scherno **2** (*aim*) scopo, intento, obiettivo; **the object of the exercise** lo scopo dell'esercizio; **with this object in view** *or* **in mind** in vista di questo scopo; **with the object of doing** al fine di fare; **what's the object of doing that?** a che serve farlo?; **expense is no object** non si bada a spese **3** (*Gram*) complemento; **direct/indirect object** complemento oggetto/indiretto

ob·ject² [əb'dʒɛkt] VT: **to object that** obiettare che
■ VI avere da obiettare su; **if you don't object** se non hai obiezioni; **to object to sb doing sth** disapprovare che qn faccia qc; **she objects to my behaviour** lei disapprova il mio comportamento; **a lot of people objected to the proposal** molti hanno obiettato alla proposta; **do you object to my smoking?** la disturba se fumo?; **I object!** (*frm*) mi oppongo!

ob·jec·tion [əb'dʒɛkʃən] N obiezione *f*; **to make** *or* **raise an objection** sollevare un'obiezione; **there is no objection to your going** non c'è alcuna obiezione alla tua partenza; **are there any objections?** ci sono obiezioni?; **have you any objection to my smoking?** la disturba se fumo?; **if you have no objection** se non hai nulla in contrario

ob·jec·tion·able [əb'dʒɛkʃnəbl] ADJ (*person*) antipatico(-a); (*conduct, method*) discutibile; (*language, attitude*) riprovevole; (*smell, colour*) sgradevole; **why are**

you being so objectionable? perché sei così antipatico?; **morally objectionable** moralmente discutibile

◎ **ob·jec·tive** [əbˈdʒɛktɪv] ADJ **1** (*impartial*) obiettivo(-a) **2** (*Gram, Philosophy*) oggettivo(-a)
■ N (*aim*) obiettivo

ob·jec·tive·ly [əbˈdʒɛktɪvlɪ] ADV (*see adj*) obiettivamente; oggettivamente

ob·jec·tiv·ity [ˌɒbdʒɛkˈtɪvɪtɪ] N (*see adj*) obiettività; oggettività

object lesson N (*fig*): **object lesson (in)** dimostrazione *f* (di)

ob·jec·tor [əbˈdʒɛktəʳ] N oppositore(-trice); **a conscientious objector** un obiettore di coscienza

object-oriented [ˌɒbdʒɪktˈɔːrɪəntɪd] ADJ (*Comput*) object-oriented

ob·jet d'art [ɔbʒɛdar] N oggetto artistico

ob·li·gat·ed [ˈɒblɪˌgeɪtɪd] ADJ (*Am, frm*): **to feel obligated to do sth** sentirsi in dovere di fare qc

ob·li·ga·tion [ˌɒblɪˈgeɪʃən] N (*duty*) obbligo; (*compulsion*) impegno; **"without obligation"** "senza impegno"; **to be under an obligation to sb/to do sth** essere in dovere verso qn/di fare qc; **I'm under no obligation to do it** non sono tenuto(-a) a farlo; **to meet one's obligations** rispettare i propri impegni; **to fail to meet one's obligations** venire meno ai propri impegni

ob·liga·tory [ɒˈblɪgətərɪ] ADJ obbligatorio(-a), d'obbligo; **to make it obligatory for sb to do sth** imporre a qn l'obbligo di fare qc

oblige [əˈblaɪdʒ] VT **1** (*compel*) obbligare, costringere; **to oblige sb to do sth** obbligare *or* costringere qn a fare qc; **to be obliged to do sth** essere obbligato(-a) *or* costretto(-a) a fare qc; **to feel obliged to do sth** sentirsi in dovere di fare qc **2** (*do a favour to*) fare una cortesia a; **anything to oblige!** (*fam*) questo e altro!; **will you oblige?** farai questa cortesia?; **to be obliged to sb for sth** essere grato(-a) a qn per qc; **much obliged!** (*old*) molto grato!, obbligato!; **I am obliged to you for your help** ti sono grato per il tuo aiuto

oblig·ing [əˈblaɪdʒɪŋ] ADJ gentile, servizievole; **it was very obliging of them** è stato molto gentile da parte loro

oblig·ing·ly [əˈblaɪdʒɪŋlɪ] ADV cortesemente, gentilmente

oblique [əˈbliːk] ADJ (*angle*) obliquo(-a); (*fig: allusion*) indiretto(-a)
■ N (*Brit Typ*): **oblique (stroke)** barra

oblique·ly [əˈbliːklɪ] ADV (*move*) obliquamente; (*mention, allude*) indirettamente

oblit·erate [əˈblɪtəˌreɪt] VT cancellare completamente

oblivi·on [əˈblɪvɪən] N oblio; **to fall** *or* **sink into oblivion** cadere nell'oblio

oblivi·ous [əˈblɪvɪəs] ADJ: **oblivious of** *or* **to** ignaro(-a) di

ob·long [ˈɒblɒŋ] ADJ oblungo(-a)
■ N rettangolo

ob·nox·ious [əbˈnɒkʃəs] ADJ (*person, behaviour*) detestabile, odioso(-a); (*fumes, smell*) pestifero(-a), pestilenziale

o.b.o. [ˌəʊbiːˈəʊ] ABBR (*Am: in classified ads*: = **or best offer**) o al miglior offerente

oboe [ˈəʊbəʊ] N oboe *m*

obo·ist [ˈəʊbəʊɪst] N oboista *m/f*

ob·scene [əbˈsiːn] ADJ osceno(-a)

ob·scene·ly [əbˈsiːnlɪ] ADV oscenamente

ob·scen·ity [əbˈsɛnɪtɪ] N oscenità *f inv*

ob·scu·rant·ism [ˌɒbskjʊəˈræntɪzəm] N oscurantismo

ob·scure [əbˈskjʊəʳ] ADJ (*comp* **-r**, *superl* **-st**) (*gen*) oscuro(-a); (*feeling, memory*) vago(-a)
■ VT (*darken*) oscurare; (*hide: sun*) coprire; (*issue, idea*) confondere; **trees obscured his vision** degli alberi gli oscuravano la visione; **the mountain is obscured by fog** la montagna è nascosta dalla nebbia

ob·scure·ly [əbˈskjʊəlɪ] ADV in modo oscuro

ob·scu·rity [əbˈskjʊərɪtɪ] N (*also fig*) oscurità *f inv*

ob·se·qui·ous [əbˈsiːkwɪəs] ADJ (*pej*) ossequioso(-a)

ob·se·qui·ous·ly [əbˈsiːkwɪəslɪ] ADV (*pej*) ossequiosamente

ob·serv·able [əbˈzɜːvəbl] ADJ osservabile, riscontrabile; (*appreciable*) notevole

ob·ser·vance [əbˈzɜːvəns] N osservanza; **religious observances** pratiche *fpl* religiose

ob·ser·vant [əbˈzɜːvənt] ADJ (*watchful*) che ha spirito d'osservazione; **observant (of)** (*Rel, Law*) osservante (di); **you're very observant!** hai molto spirito di osservazione!

ob·ser·va·tion [ˌɒbzəˈveɪʃən] N **1** (*gen*) osservazione *f*; (*of the law*) osservanza; **the police are keeping him under observation** la polizia lo tiene sotto sorveglianza; **he is under observation in hospital** è in ospedale sotto osservazione; **powers of observation** spirito d'osservazione; **to escape observation** sfuggire alla sorveglianza **2** (*remark*) osservazione *f*, commento

ob·ser·va·tion·al [ˌɒbzəˈveɪʃənl] ADJ (*frm: device*) per l'osservazione; (*: abilities, faculties*) di osservazione

observation car N (*Rail*) carrozza *f* belvedere *inv*

observation post N (*Mil*) osservatorio (militare)

observation tower N torre *f* di osservazione

ob·ser·va·tory [əbˈzɜːvətrɪ] N osservatorio

◎ **ob·serve** [əbˈzɜːv] VT osservare

◎ **ob·serv·er** [əbˈzɜːvəʳ] N osservatore(-trice)

ob·sess [əbˈsɛs] VT ossessionare; **to be obsessed by** *or* **with sb/sth** essere ossessionato(-a) da *or* con qn/qc

ob·ses·sion [əbˈsɛʃən] N ossessione *f*; **football is an obsession with him** è maniaco del calcio; **his obsession with her** la sua fissazione per lei; **his obsession about cleanliness** la sua mania della pulizia; **it's getting to be an obsession with you** sta diventando una fissazione per te

ob·ses·sive [əbˈsɛsɪv] ADJ ossessivo(-a)

obsessive-compulsive disorder [əbˌsɛsɪvkəmˈpʌlsɪvdɪsˌɔːdəʳ] N (*Med*) disturbi *mpl* ossessivo-compulsivi

ob·ses·sive·ly [əbˈsɛsɪvlɪ] ADV ossessivamente

ob·sid·ian [ɒbˈsɪdɪən] N ossidiana

ob·so·les·cence [ˈɒbsəˈlɛsns] N obsolescenza; **built-in** *or* **planned obsolescence** (*Comm*) obsolescenza programmata

ob·so·les·cent [ˌɒbsəˈlɛsnt] ADJ obsolescente

ob·so·lete [ˈɒbsəˌliːt] ADJ obsoleto(-a), in disuso; (*word*) desueto(-a)

ob·sta·cle [ˈɒbstəkl] N ostacolo; **to be an obstacle to sb/sth** essere di ostacolo a qn/qc; **to put an obstacle in the way of sb** ostacolare qn; **that is no obstacle to our doing it** questo non ci impedisce affatto di farlo

obstacle course N (*Sport, fig*) percorso a ostacoli

obstacle race N (*Sport*) corsa ad ostacoli

ob·stet·ric [ɒbˈstɛtrɪk], **ob·stet·rical** [ɒbˈstɛtrɪkəl] ADJ ostetrico(-a)

ob·ste·tri·cian [ˌɒbstəˈtrɪʃən] N ostetrico

ob·stet·rics [ɒbˈstɛtrɪks] NSG ostetricia

ob·sti·na·cy [ˈɒbstɪnəsɪ] N ostinazione *f*

Oo

ob·sti·nate [ˈɒbstɪnɪt] ADJ (*gen*) ostinato(-a); (*resistance*) strenuo(-a); (*illness*) persistente; **as obstinate as a mule** testardo(-a) come un mulo
ob·sti·nate·ly [ˈɒbstɪnɪtlɪ] ADV ostinatamente
ob·strep·er·ous [əbˈstrɛpərəs] ADJ turbolento(-a)
ob·struct [əbˈstrʌkt] VT (*block: pipe, artery*) ostruire; (*: traffic, road, Sport*) bloccare; (*hinder*) ostacolare; **a lorry was obstructing the traffic** un camion bloccava il traffico; **you're obstructing my view** mi impedisci la visuale
ob·struc·tion [əbˈstrʌkʃən] N (*sth which obstructs*) ostacolo; (*: in pipe, artery*) ostruzione *f*; **an obstruction in the pipe** un'ostruzione nel tubo; **to cause an obstruction** (*in road*) bloccare la strada; **the lorry was causing an obstruction** il camion stava ostruendo il traffico
ob·struc·tion·ist [əbˈstrʌkʃənɪst] ADJ ostruzionistico(-a)
■ N ostruzionista *m/f*
ob·struc·tive [əbˈstrʌktɪv] ADJ che crea impedimenti; **stop being obstructive!** smettila di fare ostruzionismo!
◎ **ob·tain** [əbˈteɪn] VT (*gen*) ottenere; **to obtain sth (for o.s.)** (*goods*) procurarsi qc; **to obtain sth for sb** procurare qc a qn
■ VI (*frm: circumstances, custom*) esistere
ob·tain·able [əbˈteɪnəbl] ADJ: **where is that obtainable?** dove si può trovare?
ob·trude [əbˈtruːd] (*frm*) VI imporsi
■ VT imporre
ob·tru·sive [əbˈtruːsɪv] ADJ (*person*) invadente, importuno(-a); (*opinions*) ostentato(-a); (*smell*) pungente; (*building*) che disturba la visuale
ob·tru·sive·ly [əbˈtruːsɪvlɪ] ADV in modo invadente
ob·tuse [əbˈtjuːs] ADJ (*gen, Math*) ottuso(-a); (*remark*) stolto(-a)
ob·tuse·ly [əbˈtjuːslɪ] ADV ottusamente
ob·tuse·ness [əbˈtjuːsnɪs] N ottusità
ob·verse [ˈɒbvɜːs] N (*frm*) opposto, inverso
ob·vi·ate [ˈɒbvɪˌeɪt] (*frm*) VT (*danger, objection*) evitare; (*necessity*) ovviare a
◎ **ob·vi·ous** [ˈɒbvɪəs] ADJ (*clear, perceptible*) ovvio(-a), evidente; (*unsubtle*) scontato(-a), banale; **it's obvious that ...** è ovvio che...; **she's the obvious person for the job** è chiaramente la persona che ci vuole per quel lavoro; **the obvious thing to do is to leave** la cosa più logica da fare è andarsene; **try not to make it obvious that you're bored** cerca di non farti vedere annoiato
◎ **ob·vi·ous·ly** [ˈɒbvɪəslɪ] ADV ovviamente, evidentemente; **he was obviously not drunk** si vedeva che non era ubriaco; **he was not obviously drunk** non si vedeva che era ubriaco; **she was obviously exhausted** si vedeva che era stanca; **obviously!** certo!; **obviously not!** certo che no!; **obviously I'd be sorry if we didn't go** ovviamente mi dispiacerebbe non andarci
oca·ri·na [ˌɒkəˈriːnə] N ocarina
◎ **oc·ca·sion** [əˈkeɪʒən] N **1** (*point in time*) occasione *f*, circostanza; **on occasion** di tanto in tanto; **on several occasions** in varie occasioni; **on that occasion** in quell'occasione, quella volta **2** (*special occasion*) occasione *f*, avvenimento; **an important occasion** un avvenimento importante; **it was quite an occasion** è stato un avvenimento; **music written for the occasion** musica scritta per l'occasione; **on the occasion of** in occasione di; **to rise to the occasion** mostrarsi all'altezza della situazione **3** (*frm: reason*) motivo, ragione *f*; **there was no occasion for it** non ce n'era motivo; **to have occasion to do sth** avere l'occasione di fare qc; **if you ever have occasion to be in London** se ti capita di essere a Londra
■ VT (*frm*) causare; (*: remark*) dare origine a
◎ **oc·ca·sion·al** [əˈkeɪʒənl] ADJ (*gen*) occasionale; (*showers*) sporadico(-a); **I like the occasional cigarette** ogni tanto mi piace fumare una sigaretta
oc·ca·sion·al·ly [əˈkeɪʒnəlɪ] ADV ogni tanto; **very occasionally** molto raramente
occasional table N tavolino (*che si usa saltuariamente*)
oc·ci·den·tal [ˌɒksɪˈdɛntəl] ADJ (*frm*) occidentale
oc·cipi·tal [ɒkˈsɪpɪtəl] ADJ: **occipital bone** osso occipitale
oc·cult [ɒˈkʌlt] ADJ occulto(-a)
■ N: **the occult** l'occulto
oc·cult·ism [ˈɒkʌlˌtɪzəm] N occultismo
oc·cu·pan·cy [ˈɒkjʊpənsɪ] N (*of house*) occupazione *f*, presa di possesso; **to take up occupancy of a house** prendere possesso di una casa
oc·cu·pant [ˈɒkjʊpənt] N (*of house*) inquilino(-a); (*of boat, car*) persona a bordo; (*of job, post*) titolare *m/f*
◎ **oc·cu·pa·tion** [ˌɒkjʊˈpeɪʃən] N **1** (*job*) mestiere *m*, professione *f*; (*pastime*) occupazione *f*; **he's a joiner by occupation** è falegname di mestiere **2** (*gen, Mil*) occupazione *f*; **army of occupation** esercito d'occupazione; **the occupation of Paris** l'occupazione di Parigi; **the house is ready for occupation** la casa è pronta per essere abitata
oc·cu·pa·tion·al [ˌɒkjʊˈpeɪʃənl] ADJ (*group, disease*) professionale; **occupational accident** infortunio sul lavoro
occupational guidance N (*Brit*) orientamento professionale
occupational hazard N rischio professionale
occupational pension scheme N *sistema pensionistico a disposizione di una determinata categoria di lavoratori*
occupational therapy N ergoterapia
oc·cu·pi·er [ˈɒkjʊˌpaɪə^r] N (*of house*) inquilino(-a); (*of post*) titolare *m/f*
◎ **oc·cu·py** [ˈɒkjʊˌpaɪ] VT occupare; **this job occupies all my time** questo lavoro occupa *or* prende tutto il mio tempo; **to be occupied with sth** essere preso(-a) da qc; **to be occupied in doing sth** essere occupato(-a) a fare qc; **she occupies herself by knitting** si tiene occupata lavorando a maglia; **to keep one's mind occupied** tenere la mente occupata; **the toilet was occupied** il bagno era occupato
◎ **oc·cur** [əˈkɜː^r] VI **1** (*event*) accadere; (*difficulty, opportunity*) presentarsi; (*phenomenon*) aver luogo; (*error, word, plant*) essere presente, trovarsi; **the accident occurred yesterday** l'incidente è successo ieri; **to occur again** ripetersi **2** (*come to mind*): **to occur to sb** venire in mente a qn; **it suddenly occurred to me that ...** improvvisamente mi è venuto in mente che...; **such an idea would never have occurred to her** una tale idea non le sarebbe mai venuta in mente

> DID YOU KNOW ...?
> **occur** is not translated by the Italian word *occorrere*

oc·cur·rence [əˈkʌrəns] N evento; **an everyday occurrence** un fatto quotidiano; **this is a common occurrence** è una cosa che capita spesso; **the greatest occurrence of heart attack is in those over 65** l'infarto ha la massima incidenza nelle persone sopra i 65

DID YOU KNOW ...?
occurrence is not translated by the Italian word *occorrenza*

OCD [ˌəʊsiːˈdiː] N ABBR (*Med* = **obsessive-compulsive disorder**) disturbi *mpl* ossessivo-compulsivi

◎ **ocean** [ˈəʊʃən] N oceano; **oceans of** (*fam*) fiumi *mpl* di

ocean bed N fondale *m* oceanico

ocean cruise N crociera sull'oceano

ocean-going [ˈəʊʃənˌɡəʊɪŋ] ADJ d'alto mare

Oceania [ˌəʊʃɪˈɑːnɪə] N l'Oceania

ocean·ic [ˌəʊʃɪˈænɪk] ADJ oceanico(-a)

ocean liner N transatlantico

ocean·og·ra·pher [ˌəʊʃəˈnɒɡrəfəʳ] N oceanografo(-a)

oceano·graph·ic [ˌəʊʃənəˈɡræfɪk] ADJ oceanografico(-a)

ocean·og·ra·phy [ˌəʊʃəˈnɒɡrəfɪ] N oceanografia

oc·elot [ˈɒsɪˌlɒt] N ocelot *m inv*

ochre, (*Am*) **ocher** [ˈəʊkəʳ] N ocra *f inv*
■ ADJ (color) ocra *inv*

◎ **o'clock** [əˈklɒk] ADV: **it is one o'clock** è l'una; **it's five o'clock** sono le cinque; **at 9 o'clock** alle 9; **at twelve o'clock** (*midday*) a mezzogiorno; (*midnight*) a mezzanotte

OCR [ˌəʊsiːˈɑːʳ] N ABBR **1** = **optical character reader** **2** = **optical character recognition**

Oct. ABBR (= **October**) ott. (= *ottobre*)

oc·ta·gon [ˈɒktəɡən] N ottagono

oc·tago·nal [ɒkˈtæɡənl] ADJ ottagonale

oc·tane [ˈɒkteɪn] N ottano
■ ADJ: **high-octane petrol,** (*Am*) **high-octane gas** benzina ad alto numero di ottani

octane rating N numero di ottani

oc·tave [ˈɒktɪv] N (*Mus*) ottava

oc·ta·vo [ɒkˈteɪvəʊ] N volume *m* in-ottavo

oc·tet [ɒkˈtɛt] N ottetto

Oc·to·ber [ɒkˈtəʊbəʳ] N ottobre *m*; **in October** in ottobre; *for usage see* **July**

oc·to·genar·ian [ˌɒktəʊdʒɪˈnɛərɪən] N ottuagenario(-a)

oc·to·pus [ˈɒktəpəs] N (*gen*) polpo; (*larger*) piovra

ocu·list [ˈɒkjʊlɪst] N oculista *m/f*

OD [ˌəʊˈdiː] N ABBR (= **overdose**) overdose *f inv*
■ VI: **to OD on** farsi un'overdose di

◎ **odd** [ɒd] ADJ (*comp* **-er**, *superl* **-est**) **1** (*strange*) strano(-a); **how** *or* **that's odd!** che strano!; **he says some odd things** dice delle cose strane **2** (*number*) dispari *inv*; **an odd number** un numero dispari **3** (*extra, left over*) in più; (*unpaired: sock*) spaiato(-a); **if you have an odd minute** se hai un momento libero; **the odd man** *or* **one out** l'eccezione *f* **4** (*occasional*) occasionale; **at odd moments** in certi momenti; **he has written the odd article** ha scritto qualche articolo **5** (*and more*): **30 odd** 30 e rotti, poco più di 30; *see also* **odds**

odd·ball [ˈɒdˌbɔːl] N, ADJ (*fam*) eccentrico(-a)

odd·ity [ˈɒdɪtɪ] N **1** (*also:* **oddness**) stranezza, bizzarria **2** (*person*) originale *m/f*

odd-job man [ɒdˈdʒɒbˈmæn] N (*pl* **-men**) tuttofare *m inv*

odd jobs NPL lavori *mpl* occasionali

odd-looking [ɒdˈlʊkɪŋ] ADJ dall'aria strana

odd·ly [ˈɒdlɪ] ADV stranamente; **they are oddly similar** tra di loro c'è una strana somiglianza; **oddly enough you are right** stranamente hai ragione

odd·ments [ˈɒdmənts] NPL (*Brit Comm*) avanzi *mpl* di magazzino

odd·ness [ˈɒdnɪs] N = **oddity 1**

odds [ɒdz] NPL **1** (*Betting*) probabilità *fpl*; **odds of 10 to 1** una probabilità di 10 a 1; **the odds on the horse are 5 to 1** danno il cavallo 5 a 1; **short/long odds** alta/bassa probabilità; **the odds are in his favour** i pronostici sono a suo favore; **to fight against overwhelming odds** lottare contro enormi difficoltà; **to succeed against all the odds** riuscire contro ogni aspettativa; **the odds are that ...** è facile *or* probabile che...; **the odds are against his coming** è poco probabile che venga **2** (*difference*): **what's the odds?** (*fam*) che differenza fa?, cosa cambia?; **it makes no odds** non fa differenza, non importa **3** (*variance, strife*): **at odds** ai ferri corti; **to be at odds with sb over sth** essere in disaccordo con qn su qc

odds and ends (*fam*) NPL (*assorted objects*) oggetti *mpl* vari; (*junk*) cianfrusaglie *fpl*; **I'll finish the last few odds and ends tomorrow** le ultime due o tre cosette le finisco domani

odds-on [ɒdzˈɒn] ADJ (*fam*) probabile; **it's odds-on that ...** è quasi certo che...; **odds-on favourite** (*Horse-racing*) gran favorito(-a)

ode [əʊd] N ode *f*

odi·ous [ˈəʊdɪəs] ADJ odioso(-a)

odium [ˈəʊdɪəm] N (*frm*) odio

odom·eter [ɒˈdɒmɪtəʳ] N (*Aut*) odometro

odor·ous [ˈəʊdərəs] ADJ (*liter*) odoroso(-a)

odour, (*Am*) **odor** [ˈəʊdəʳ] N odore *m*; **to be in bad odour with sb** (*fig*) essere malvisto(-a) da qn

odour·less, (*Am*) **odor·less** [ˈəʊdəlɪs] ADJ inodore

Odysseus [əˈdiːsɪəs] N Ulisse

od·ys·sey [ˈɒdɪsɪ] N odissea

OECD [ˌəʊiːsiːˈdiː] N ABBR (= **Organization for Economic Cooperation and Development**) OCSE *f* (= *Organizzazione per la Cooperazione e lo Sviluppo Economico*)
▷ www.oecd.org

Oedipus [ˈiːdɪpəs] N Edipo

Oedipus complex N (*Psych*) complesso di Edipo

OEM [ˌəʊiːˈɛm] N ABBR (*Comput* = **original equipment manufacturer**) azienda che si occupa di assemblaggio di computer

oesopha·gus, (*Am*) **esopha·gus** [iːˈsɒfəɡəs] N esofago

oes·tro·gen, (*Am*) **es·tro·gen** [ˈiːstrəʊdʒən] N estrogeno

◎ **of** [ɒv, əv] PREP **1** (*gen*) di; **the house of my uncle** la casa di mio zio; **the love of God** l'amore di Dio; **a friend of mine** un mio amico; **that was very kind of you** è stato molto carino da parte tua; **free of charge** gratis; **the 5th of July** il 5 luglio; **loss of appetite** perdita dell'appetito; **south of Glasgow** a sud di Glasgow; **a quarter of 4** (*Am: time*) le 4 meno un quarto; **the City of New York** la città di New York; **a boy of 8** un ragazzo di 8 anni; **a man of great ability** un uomo di grande abilità; **that idiot of a minister** quell'idiota di ministro **2** (*cause*) di, per; **of necessity** necessariamente, per necessità; **to die of pneumonia** morire di polmonite **3** (*material*) di, in; **made of steel** (fatto(-a)) di *or* in acciaio; **it's made of wood** è di legno **4** (*concerning*) di; **what do you think of him?** cosa pensi di lui?; **what of it?** e allora? **5** (*partitive*) di; **how much of this do you need?** quanto te ne serve?; **a kilo of flour** un chilo di farina; **a handful of coins** una manciata di monete; **there were four of us** eravamo in quattro; **four of us went** quattro di noi sono andati; **there were four of them** (*people*) erano in quattro; (*things*) ce n'erano quattro

Of·com [ˈɒfkɒm] N ABBR (*Brit:* = **Office of**

Oo

Communications) *organismo di regolamentazione delle telecomunicazioni*

◎**off** [ɒf] **KEYWORD**

■ADV

1 (*distance, time*): **the game was/is three days off** la gara era dopo/è fra tre giorni; **5 km off (the road)** a 5 km (dalla strada); **a place 2 miles off** un posto distante 2 miglia; **it's a long way off** è molto lontano
2 (*departure*): **I must be off** devo andare; **off we go** via, partiamo; **he's gone off to see the boss** è andato a parlare col capo; **he's off to Paris tonight** parte per Parigi stasera
3 (*removal*): **5% off** (*Comm*) sconto del 5%; **a button came off** è venuto via un bottone; **with his hat off** senza cappello; **the lid was off** non c'era il coperchio; **off with those wet clothes!** togliti quei vestiti bagnati!
4 (*not at work*): **to take a day off** prendersi una giornata di vacanza; **I'm off on Fridays** il venerdì non lavoro; **he's off sick** è in malattia
5 (*in phrases*): **off and on, on and off** di tanto in tanto; **right** *or* **straight off** subito

■ADJ

1 (*inoperative*): **to be off** (*machine, light, engine*) essere spento(-a); (*water, gas, tap*) essere chiuso(-a)
2 (*cancelled*) sospeso(-a); (*Brit: not available: in restaurant*) finito(-a); **I'm afraid the chicken is off** purtroppo il pollo è finito; **the play is off** la commedia è sospesa; **the wedding is off** il matrimonio è saltato
3 (*not fresh*) andato(-a) a male; **this cheese is off** questo formaggio è andato a male; **that's a bit off, isn't it?** (*fig fam*) non è molto carino, vero?
4 **to be badly off** non essere benestante; **you'd be better off staying where you are** faresti meglio a rimanere dove sei; **how are you off for cash?** come stai a soldi?; **to be well off** essere benestante; **the less well off** i meno abbienti
5 **to have an off day** (*fam*) avere una giornata no

■PREP

1 (*indicating motion, removal*) da; **there are two buttons off my coat** al mio cappotto mancano due bottoni; **to fall off a cliff** cadere da una scogliera; **he knocked £20 off the price** (*fam*) mi ha fatto uno sconto di 20 sterline; **she took the picture off the wall** tolse il quadro dalla parete; **he was off work for three weeks** è stato in malattia per tre settimane
2 (*distant from*): **his flat is somewhere off Baker Street** il suo appartamento è dalle parti di Baker Street; **off the coast** al largo della costa; **height off the ground** altezza dal suolo; **it's just off the M1** è appena fuori della M1; **a house off the main road** una casa poco lontana della strada principale; **a street off the square** una strada che parte dalla piazza
3 **I've gone off fried food** non mi piacciono più i fritti; **I'm off meat** non mangio più la carne
■N: **from the off** (*fam*) dall'inizio

of·fal [ˈɒfəl] N frattaglie *fpl*
off·beat [ˌɒfˈbiːt] ADJ (*fig*) originale, anticonvenzionale
off-centre, (*Am*) **off-center** [ˌɒfˈsɛntəʳ] ADJ storto(-a), fuori centro
off-chance [ˈɒfˌtʃɑːns] N: **on the off-chance of seeing him** nella vaga speranza di incontrarlo
off-colour, (*Am*) **off-color** [ˌɒfˈkʌləʳ] ADJ **1** (*Brit: ill*) malato(-a), indisposto(-a); **to feel off-colour** sentirsi poco bene **2** (*joke, remark*) spinto(-a), osé *inv*
off-duty [ˌɒfˈdjuːtɪ] ADJ (*policeman*) non in servizio
◎**of·fence**, (*Am*) **of·fense** [əˈfɛns] N **1** (*crime*) infrazione *f*, contravvenzione *f*, reato; **first offence** primo reato; **to commit an offence** commettere un reato; **it is an offence to ...** è vietato dalla legge... **2** (*moral*) offesa; **to give offence (to sb)** offendere (qn); **to take offence (at sth)** offendersi (per qc)
of·fend [əˈfɛnd] VT (*person*) offendere; (*ears, eyes*) ferire; **I don't want to offend you** non voglio offenderti; **it offends my sense of justice** è un'offesa al mio senso di giustizia; **to be offended (at)** offendersi (per)
■VI: **to offend against** (*law, rule*) trasgredire, contravvenire a; (*God*) disubbidire a; (*common sense*) andare contro; (*good taste*) offendere; **boys are more likely to offend than girls** è più facile che siano i ragazzi, piuttosto che le ragazze, a trasgredire la legge
of·fend·er [əˈfɛndəʳ] N (*frm: criminal*) delinquente *m/f*; (*culprit*) reo(-a), colpevole *m/f*
of·fend·ing [əˈfɛndɪŋ] ADJ (*often hum: word, object*) incriminato(-a)
of·fense [əˈfɛns] N (*Am*) = **offence**
◎**of·fen·sive** [əˈfɛnsɪv] ADJ **1** (*causing offence, unpleasant: behaviour, remark*) offensivo(-a); (*: person*) antipatico(-a); (*: smell, sight*) sgradevole; **to be offensive to sb** offendere qn **2** (*attacking*) offensivo(-a)
■N (*Mil, Sport*) offensiva; **to go over to** *or* **go on** *or* **take the offensive** passare all'offensiva
of·fen·sive·ly [əˈfɛnsɪvlɪ] ADV (*unpleasantly etc*) in modo offensivo
◎**of·fer** [ˈɒfəʳ] N (*gen*) offerta, proposta; **offer of marriage** proposta di matrimonio; **to make an offer for sth** fare un'offerta per qc; **offers over £25** offerte dalle 25 sterline in su; **to be on offer** (*Comm*) essere in offerta (speciale); **"on special offer"** "in offerta speciale"
■VT (*gen*) offrire; (*apology*) presentare; (*comment, opinion*) dare; **to offer sth to sb** *or* **sb sth** offrire qc a qn; **can I offer you a drink?** posso offrirti qc da bere?; **to offer to do sth** offrirsi di fare qc; **he offered to help me** si è offerto di aiutarmi; **to offer resistance** opporre resistenza
◎**of·fer·ing** [ˈɒfərɪŋ] N offerta
offer price N (*Fin*) prezzo di offerta
of·fer·tory [ˈɒfətərɪ] N (*Rel: part of service*) offertorio; (*: collection*) questua
off-guard [ɒfˈgɑːd] ADJ: **to be taken off-guard** essere colto(-a) alla sprovvista
off·hand [ˈɒfˈhænd] ADJ (*casual*) disinvolto(-a); (*curt*) sgarbato(-a); **an offhand attitude** un atteggiamento noncurante
■ADV: **I can't tell you offhand** non posso dirtelo su due piedi
off·handed·ly [ˈɒfˈhændɪdlɪ] ADV (*see adj*) con disinvoltura; sgarbatamente
off·handed·ness [ˈɒfˈhændɪdnɪs] N (*see adj*) disinvoltura; sgarbatezza
◎**of·fice** [ˈɒfɪs] N **1** (*place*) ufficio; (*: of lawyer, doctor*) studio; **ticket office** biglietteria; **head office** sede *f* centrale **2** (*public position*) ufficio, carica; (*duty, function*) incarico, compito; **to be in** *or* **to hold office** (*person*) essere in carica; (*political party*) essere al potere; **to come into office** *or* **to take office** (*person*) assumere la carica; (*political party*) salire al potere **3** **through his good offices** con il suo prezioso aiuto; **through the offices of** grazie all'aiuto di **4** (*Rel*) ufficio, funzione *f*

■ ADJ (*staff*) d'ufficio; (*furniture*) da ufficio; (*supplies*) per ufficio
office automation N automazione *f* d'ufficio, burotica
office bearer N (*of club etc*) membro dell'amministrazione
office block, (*Am*) **office building** N complesso di uffici
office boy N fattorino
office-holder ['ɒfɪs,həʊldə^r] N (*frm*) funzionario(-a)
office hours NPL orario d'ufficio; (*Am Med*) orario delle visite
office manager N capoufficio *m/f*
Office of Fair Trading N (*Brit*) *organismo di tutela contro pratiche commerciali abusive*
◎ **of·fic·er** ['ɒfɪsə^r] N **1** (*Mil, Naut, Aer*) ufficiale *m*; **officers' mess** mensa degli ufficiali **2** (*official*) funzionario; **police officer** agente *m* di polizia; **excuse me, officer** mi scusi, agente
office work N lavoro d'ufficio
office worker N impiegato(-a)
◎ **of·fi·cial** [ə'fɪʃəl] ADJ (*authorized*) ufficiale; (*formal*) ufficiale, formale; **to make official** (*position, agreement*) ufficializzare
■ N (*civil servant*) funzionario, impiegato(-a) statale; (*of club, organization*) dirigente *m/f*
of·fi·cial·dom [ə'fɪʃəldəm] N (*pej*) burocrazia
of·fi·cial·ese [ə,fɪʃə'li:z] N (*pej*) burocratese *m*
of·fi·cial·ly [ə'fɪʃəlɪ] ADV ufficialmente
Official Receiver N: **the Official Receiver** il curatore fallimentare
of·fi·ci·ate [ə'fɪʃɪ,eɪt] VI (*Rel*) ufficiare; **to officiate as Mayor** esplicare le funzioni di sindaco; **to officiate at a marriage** celebrare un matrimonio
of·fi·cious [ə'fɪʃəs] ADJ invadente

DID YOU KNOW ...?
officious is not translated by the Italian word ***ufficioso***

of·fi·cious·ly [ə'fɪʃəslɪ] ADV con invadenza
of·fi·cious·ness [ə'fɪʃəsnɪs] N invadenza
of·fing ['ɒfɪŋ] N: **in the offing** (*fig*) in vista
off-key [,ɒf'ki:] ADJ stonato(-a)
■ ADV fuori tono
off-licence ['ɒf,laɪsns] N (*Brit*) bottiglieria

OFF-LICENCE
In Gran Bretagna e in Irlanda, gli **off-licences** sono esercizi pubblici specializzati nella vendita strettamente regolamentata di bevande alcoliche, per la quale è necessario avere un'apposita licenza. In genere sono aperti fino a tarda sera.

off-limits [,ɒf'lɪmɪts] ADJ (*Am Mil*) vietato(-a) (al personale militare), off-limits *inv*; (: *not to be entered*) off-limits
off-line ['ɒf,laɪn] (*Comput*) ADJ off-line *inv*, fuori linea; (*switched off*) spento(-a)
■ ADV: **to go off-line** andare off-line *or* fuori linea
off-load ['ɒf,ləʊd] VT scaricare
off-message ['ɒf,mɛsɪdʒ] ADJ (*Pol*) non allineato(-a), che non segue la linea del partito
off-peak ['ɒf'pi:k] ADJ (*time*) non di punta; (*ticket, heating*) a tariffa ridotta; (*tariff*) ridotto(-a); **it's cheaper to go on holiday off-peak** costa meno andare in vacanza in bassa stagione; **train tickets are cheaper off-peak** i biglietti ferroviari sono più economici al di fuori dell'ora di punta
off-piste ['ɒf'pi:st] (*Skiing*) N fuoripista *m*
■ ADV: **to ski off-piste** fare del fuoripista
off-putting ['ɒf,pʊtɪŋ] ADJ (*Brit fam: person, manner*) antipatico(-a), scostante; (*appearance*) sgradevole; **I find her manner off-putting** trovo scostante il suo modo di fare; **I hope you won't find my presence off-putting** spero che la mia presenza non ti crei problemi
off-road vehicle [,ɒfrəʊd'vi:ɪkl] N, **off-roader**
■ N (*Auto*) fuoristrada *m inv*
off-season ['ɒf,si:zn] N: **the off-season** la bassa stagione
■ ADJ di bassa stagione *f*
off·set ['ɒf,sɛt] (*vb: pt, pp* **offset**) VT bilanciare, compensare
■ N (*Typ*) offset *m inv*
offset printing N stampa in offset
off·shoot ['ɒf,ʃu:t] N (*fig*) diramazione *f*; (*Bot*) germoglio
off·shore ['ɒf'ʃɔ:'] ADJ (*breeze*) di terra; (*island*) vicino(-a) alla costa; (*fishing*) costiero(-a); (*oil rig*) off-shore *inv*
off·side ['ɒf'saɪd] ADJ **1** (*Sport*) in fuorigioco **2** (*Aut: right-hand drive*) destro(-a); (: *left-hand drive*) sinistro(-a)
■ N (*Aut: see adj*) destra; sinistra
off·spring ['ɒf,sprɪŋ] N (*pl inv: of person*) rampollo; (: *with pl sense*) prole *f*; (*of animal*) piccolo(-a); (: *with pl sense*) piccoli(-e)
off·stage [,ɒf'steɪdʒ] ADJ, ADV dietro le quinte
off-street [,ɒf'stri:t] ADJ: **off-street parking** parcheggio fuori della strada principale
off-the-cuff [,ɒfðə'kʌf] ADV a braccio, improvvisando
■ ADJ (*speech*) a braccio, improvvisato(-a); (*remark*) spontaneo(-a)
off-the-job ['ɒfðə'dʒɒb] ADJ (*course, training*) fuori sede *inv*
off-the-peg ['ɒfðə'pɛg], (*Am*) **off-the-rack** ['ɒfðə'ræk] ADJ (*clothes*) prêt-à-porter *inv*, confezionato(-a)
■ ADV: **to buy a dress off-the-peg** comprare un abito confezionato
off-the-record [,ɒfðə'rɛkəd] ADJ ufficioso(-a)
■ ADV in via ufficiosa
off-the-shelf [,ɒfðə'ʃɛlf] ADJ, ADV (*Brit*) preconfezionato(-a)
off-the-wall [,ɒfðə'wɔ:l] ADJ (*humor, idea*) bizzarro(-a)
off-white ['ɒf,waɪt] ADJ bianco sporco *inv*
Ofgem N ABBR (*Brit:* = **Office of Gas and Electricity Markets**) *ente di vigilanza dei servizi di erogazione di gas ed elettricità*
Of·sted ['ɒfstɛd] N ABBR (= **Office for Standards in Education**) *organo di controllo degli istituti scolastici inglesi e gallesi*
▷ www.ofsted.gov.uk
OFT N ABBR (*Brit:* = **Office of Fair Trading**) *organo di controllo della correttezza commerciale a tutela dei consumatori*
◎ **of·ten** ['ɒfən] ADV spesso; **it often rains** spesso piove; **as often as not** il più delle volte; **more often than not** quasi sempre; **every so often** (*of time*) una volta ogni tanto; (*of distance, spacing*) regolarmente, a intervalli regolari; **how often?** ogni quanto?; **how often do you see him?** ogni quanto lo vedi?; **her behaviour is often disappointing** il suo comportamento è spesso deludente; **it's not often that I ask you to help me** non è che ti chieda spesso di aiutarmi
Ofwat ['ɒfwɒt] N ABBR (*Brit:* = **Office of Water Services**) *in Inghilterra e Galles, ente di vigilanza dei servizi di erogazione dell'acqua*

Oo

ogle ['əʊgl] VT mangiarsi con gli occhi
ogre ['əʊgə^r] N orco
OH ABBR *(Am Post)* = **Ohio**
◎ **oh** [əʊ] EXCL oh!
Ohio [əʊ'haɪəʊ] N Ohio
▷ http://ohio.gov/
OHMS [ˌəʊeɪtʃɛm'ɛs] ABBR *(Brit:* = **On His** *(or* **Her)** **Majesty's Service**) al servizio di Sua Maestà britannica
◎ **oil** [ɔɪl] N **1** *(Art, Aut, Culin)* olio; **fried in oil** fritto(-a) nell'olio **2** *(petroleum)* petrolio; *(for central heating)* nafta; **to pour oil on troubled waters** placare le acque
■ VT *(machine)* oliare, lubrificare; **to oil the wheels** *(fig)* appianare la difficoltà
■ ADJ *(lamp, stove)* a olio
oil-burning ['ɔɪlˌbɜːnɪŋ] ADJ *(lamp)* a petrolio
oil·can ['ɔɪlˌkæn] N oliatore *m*; *(for storing)* latta da olio
oil change N *(Aut)* cambio dell'olio
oil·cloth ['ɔɪlˌklɒθ] N tela cerata
oil colours NPL colori *mpl* a olio
oil·field ['ɔɪlˌfiːld] N giacimento petrolifero
oil filter N *(Aut)* filtro dell'olio
oil-fired ['ɔɪlˌfaɪəd] ADJ a nafta
oil gauge N indicatore *m* del livello dell'olio
oil industry N industria petrolifera
oili·ness ['ɔɪlɪnɪs] N *(of liquid, consistency)* oleosità; *(of hands, skin also fig, pej)* untuosità
oil level N livello dell'olio
oil paint N colore *m* a olio
oil painting N quadro a olio; **she's no oil painting** *(fam)* non è una bellezza
oil refinery N raffineria di petrolio
oil rig N derrick *m inv*; *(at sea)* piattaforma per trivellazioni subacquee
oil·skin ['ɔɪlˌskɪn] N tela cerata
■ ADJ *(hat, tablecloth)* di tela cerata
oil·skins ['ɔɪlˌskɪnz] NPL indumenti *mpl* di tela cerata
oil slick N chiazza di petrolio
oil tanker N petroliera
oil well N pozzo petrolifero
oily ['ɔɪlɪ] ADJ *(comp* **-ier**, *superl* **-iest**) *(liquid, consistency)* oleoso(-a); *(hands)* unto(-a); *(fig pej)* untuoso(-a)
oint·ment ['ɔɪntmənt] N unguento
O.K., okay [əʊ'keɪ] *(fam)* EXCL OK!, okay!, va bene!
■ ADJ: **the film was O.K.** il film non era male; **are you O.K. for money?** sei a posto coi soldi?; **it's O.K. with** *or* **by me** per me va bene; **is it O.K. with you if ...?** ti va bene se...?; **is it O.K.?** *or* **are you O.K.?** tutto OK?; **did you hurt yourself? — no, I'm O.K.** ti sei fatto male? — no, sto bene; **is the car O.K.?** è a posto la macchina?; **that may have been O.K. last year** questo poteva forse andar bene l'anno scorso
■ N: **to give sth one's O.K.** dare l'okay a qc
■ VT *(pt, pp* **O.K.'d** *or* **okayed**) dare l'okay a, approvare
OK ABBR *(Am Post)* = **Oklahoma**
oka·pi [əʊ'kɑːpɪ] N okapi *m inv*
Ok·la·ho·ma [əʊklə'həʊmə] N Oklahoma *m*
▷ www.ok.gov/
◎ **old** [əʊld] ADJ *(comp* **-er**, *superl* **-est**) **1** *(gen)* vecchio(-a), anziano(-a); *(ancient)* antico(-a), vecchio(-a); **an old man** un vecchio; **old people** *or* **folk(s)** i vecchi, gli anziani; **my grandfather is very old** mio nonno è molto vecchio; **to grow** *or* **get old(er)** invecchiare; **he's old for his years** è maturo per la sua età; **the old country** la madrepatria; **as old as the hills** vecchio(-a) come Matusalemme *or* come il cucco; **the old part of Glasgow** la zona vecchia di Glasgow; **an old friend of mine** un mio vecchio amico; **here's old Peter coming!** *(fam)* ecco che arriva il vecchio Peter!; **she's a funny old thing** *(fam)* è un tipetto buffo; **we had a high old time** *(fam)* ci siamo divertiti un sacco; **any old thing will do** *(fam)* va bene qualsiasi cosa; **I say, old man** *or* **old boy!** *(old)* vecchio mio!; **my old man** *(fam: father)* il (mio) vecchio **2** **how old are you?** quanti anni hai?; **she is 8 years old** ha 8 anni; **an 8-year-old boy** un bambino di 8 anni; **she is 2 years older than you** ha 2 anni più di te; **he's older than me** è più vecchio di me; **older brother/sister** fratello/sorella maggiore; **my older brother** mio fratello maggiore; **the older generation** i vecchi; **he's old enough to look after himself** è grande abbastanza per sbrigarsela da solo; **to be old enough to vote** avere l'età per votare; **you're old enough to know better!** alla tua età dovresti avere più senno!; **when you're older** *(to child)* quando sarai grande; **if I were 20 years older** se avessi 20 anni di più **3** *(former)* precedente; **my old school** la mia vecchia scuola; **in the old days** una volta, ai vecchi tempi; **it's not as good as our old one** non è buono come quello vecchio
■ N **1** **the old** NPL i vecchi, gli anziani **2** **of old** da tempo; **in days of old** nei tempi passati
old age N vecchiaia; **in one's old age** nella vecchiaia
old-age pension [ˌəʊldeɪdʒ'pɛnʃən] N pensione *f* di vecchiaia
old-age pensioner [ˌəʊldeɪdʒ'pɛnʃənə^r] N *(Brit)* pensionato(-a)
old boy N *(Scol)* ex alunno; *(fam)* vecchio
old·en ['əʊldən] ADJ: **in the olden days** nei tempi antichi, nei giorni passati
Old English N inglese *m* antico
old-established ['əʊldɪs'tæblɪʃt] ADJ di vecchia data
old-fashioned ['əʊld'fæʃnd] ADJ antiquato(-a), fuori moda; *(person)* all'antica; **my parents are rather old-fashioned** i miei sono un po' all'antica
old flame N *(fam)* vecchia fiamma
old girl *(Brit)* N **1** *(former pupil)* ex alunna **2** *(old woman)* vecchia
old guard N: **the old guard** la vecchia guardia
old maid N *(pej)* vecchia zitella
old master N *(artist) grande pittore europeo del periodo compreso tra il 16° e il 19° secolo*; *(painting)* dipinto *(di un grande pittore europeo dal 16° al 19° secolo)*
old people's home N casa di riposo (per anziani)
old school tie N *(pej)*: **the old school tie** *(Brit) legame che resta tra ex compagni di studi che, arrivati a posizioni di potere, usano la propria influenza per aiutarsi a vicenda*
old-style ['əʊld'staɪl] ADJ (di) vecchio stampo *inv*
Old Testament N: **the Old Testament** il Vecchio Testamento
old-time ['əʊldˌtaɪm] ADJ di una volta
old-timer [ˌəʊld'taɪmə^r] N veterano(-a)
old wives' tale N vecchia superstizione *f*
Old World N: **the Old World** il Vecchio mondo
old-world ['əʊld'wɜːld] ADJ di vecchio stile, di vecchio stampo
oleagi·nous [ˌəʊlɪ'ædʒɪnəs] ADJ oleaginoso(-a), oleoso(-a)
olean·der [ˌəʊlɪ'ændə^r] N oleandro
O-level ['əʊˌlɛvl] N *(Brit: formerly) diploma di istruzione secondaria conseguito a 16 anni in Inghilterra e Galles, ora sostituito dal GCSE*
oli·gar·chic [ˌɒlɪ'gɑːkɪk] ADJ oligarchico(-a)
oli·gar·chy ['ɒlɪˌgɑːkɪ] N oligarchia

ol·ive ['ɒlɪv] N (*fruit*) oliva; (*also:* **olive tree**) olivo ■ ADJ (*skin*) olivastro(-a); (*also:* **olive-green**) verde oliva *inv*

olive branch N ramoscello d'olivo

olive oil N olio d'oliva
▷ www.internationaloliveoil.org

Olym·pic [əʊ'lɪmpɪk] ADJ olimpico(-a)

Olympic Games NPL: **the Olympic Games** i giochi *mpl* olimpici

Olym·pics NPL: **the Olympics** le Olimpiadi *fpl*

Olym·pus [əʊ'lɪmpəs] N (*Geog, Myth*) Olimpo

OM [ˌəʊ'ɛm] N ABBR (*Brit:* = **Order of Merit**) *titolo onorifico*

Oman [əʊ'mɑːn] N l'Oman *m*

om·buds·man ['ɒmbʊdzmən] N (*pl* **-men**) difensore *m* civico
▷ www.ombudsman.org.uk/

ome·lette, **ome·let** ['ɒmlɪt] N frittata, omelette *f inv*; **ham/cheese omelette** omelette al prosciutto/al formaggio

omen ['əʊmən] N presagio, auspicio; **a bad omen** un cattivo presagio; **a good omen** un buon auspicio

omi·nous ['ɒmɪnəs] ADJ (*sign*) minaccioso(-a), infausto(-a); (*event*) di malaugurio; (*look, smile, silence*) sinistro(-a); **ominous black clouds** nuvole nere minacciose; **the reappearance of tuberculosis is an ominous development** la ricomparsa della tubercolosi è un fatto preoccupante

omi·nous·ly ['ɒmɪnəslɪ] ADV minacciosamente

omis·sion [əʊ'mɪʃən] N omissione *f*

omit [əʊ'mɪt] VT omettere; **to omit to do sth** tralasciare *or* trascurare di fare qc; **his name was omitted from the list** il suo nome fu omesso dalla lista

om·ni·bus ['ɒmnɪbəs] N (*old: bus*) autobus *m inv*; (*book*) raccolta; **omnibus edition** (*TV, Radio*) replica delle puntate precedenti

om·nipo·tence [ɒm'nɪpətəns] N onnipotenza

om·nipo·tent [ɒm'nɪpətənt] ADJ onnipotente

om·ni·pres·ent [ˌɒmnɪ'prezənt] ADJ (*frm*) onnipresente

om·nis·ci·ent [ɒm'nɪsɪənt] ADJ onnisciente

om·ni·vore ['ɒmnɪˌvɔːʳ] N onnivoro

om·niv·or·ous [ɒm'nɪvərəs] ADJ onnivoro(-a)

ON ABBR (*Canada Post*) = **Ontario**

◎ **on** [ɒn] KEYWORD

■ PREP

1 (*position*) su; (*on top of*) sopra; **on the Continent** nell'Europa continentale; **with her hat on her head** col cappello in testa; **on the left** sulla *or* a sinistra; **I haven't any money on me** non ho soldi con me; **on page 2** a pagina 2; **on the right** sulla *or* a destra; **the house is on the main road** la casa è sulla strada principale; **on the table** sul tavolo; **hanging on the wall** appeso(-a) al muro

2 (*fig*): **an attack on the government** un attacco al governo; **we did it on his authority** l'abbiamo fatto dietro sua autorizzazione; **based on fact** basato(-a) sui fatti; **he's away on business** è via per affari; **on Channel 4** su Canale 4; **he is on the committee** fa parte della commissione; **on foot** a piedi; **he's on heroin** si fa di eroina; **to be on holiday** (*Brit*) essere in vacanza; **she lives on cheese** vive di formaggio; **the march on Rome** la marcia su Roma; **have it on me** offro io; **this round's on me** questo giro lo offro io; **on the plane** sull'*or* in aereo; **he played it on the violin/piano** l'ha suonato al violino/al pianoforte; **on the radio** alla radio; **on the telephone** al telefono; **on the television** alla televisione; **on the train** sul *or* in treno; **prices are up on last year('s)** i prezzi sono rincarati rispetto all'anno scorso; **to be on vacation** (*Am*) essere in vacanza; **we're on irregular verbs** stiamo facendo i verbi irregolari; **he's on £16,000 a year** guadagna 16.000 sterline all'anno

3 (*of time*): **on May 9th** il 9 maggio; **on my arrival** al mio arrivo; **on a day like this** in una giornata come questa; **on Friday** venerdì ; **a week on Friday** venerdì a otto; **on Fridays** il *or* di venerdì ; **on seeing him** nel vederlo, vedendolo

4 (*about, concerning*) su, di; **a book on physics** un libro di *or* sulla fisica; **he lectured on Keats** tenne un corso su Keats; **have you read Purnell on Churchill?** hai letto cosa scrive Purnell su Churchill?; **while we're on the subject** visto che siamo in argomento

■ ADV

1 (*covering*): **what's she got on?** cosa indossa?; **to have one's coat on** avere indosso il cappotto; **she put her boots on** si mise gli stivali; **screw the lid on tightly** avvita il coperchio ben stretto; **on with your coat!** mettiti il cappotto!

2 (*forward*): **from that day on** da quel giorno in poi; **it's getting on for ten o'clock** sono quasi le dieci; **it was well on in the evening** era sera inoltrata; **it was well on in May** era maggio avanzato; **they talked well on into the night** continuarono a parlare fino a notte inoltrata

3 (*continuation*): **to go on, walk on, carry on** continuare, proseguire; **on and off** ogni tanto; **he rambled on and on** continuava nei suoi discorsi sconclusionati; **to read on** continuare a leggere, proseguire nella lettura; **and so on** e così via

4 (*in phrases*): **what are you on about?** cosa vai dicendo?; **my father's always on at me to get a job** (*fam*) mio padre mi sta sempre addosso perché trovi un lavoro; **the police are on to him** la polizia lo tiene d'occhio

■ ADJ

1 (*functioning, in operation: radio, light, oven*) acceso(-a); (*: tap*) aperto(-a); (*: machine*) in moto; (*: brake*) inserito(-a); **when is this film on?** quand'è che danno questo film?; **there's a good film on at the cinema** danno un buon film al cinema; **the meeting is still on** la riunione è ancora in corso; **is the meeting still on tonight?** è confermata la riunione di stasera?; **the programme is on in a minute** il programma inizia tra un minuto; **sorry, I've got something on tonight** mi spiace, stasera sono impegnato

2 (*fam*): **you're on!** d'accordo!; **that's not on!** (*not acceptable*) non si fa così !; (*not possible*) non se ne parla neanche!

onan·ism ['əʊnəˌnɪzəm] N onanismo

◎ **once** [wʌns] ADV **1** (*on one occasion*) una volta; **I've been to Italy once before** sono già stato in Italia una volta; **I've only met him once before** prima d'ora l'ho incontrato una volta sola; **once only** solo una volta; **once or twice** un paio di volte; **once again** *or* **once more** ancora una volta; **(every) once in a while** (una volta) ogni tanto; **once a week** una volta alla settimana; **once and for all** una volta per tutte; **just this once** solo (per) questa volta; **for once** una volta tanto; **it never once occurred to me** non mi è mai venuto in mente **2** (*formerly*) un tempo; **I knew him**

once un tempo *or* in passato lo conoscevo; **once upon a time there was ...** c'era una volta... **3 at once** (*immediately*) subito, immediatamente; (*simultaneously*) contemporaneamente, a un tempo; **all at once** (*suddenly*) tutt'a un tratto, improvvisamente; (*in one go*) tutto in una volta

■ CONJ una volta che, quando, non appena; **once he had finished he left** una volta che *or* non appena ebbe finito andò via

once-over ['wʌns,əʊvəʳ] N (*fam*): **to give sb/sth the once-over** dare una sbirciata a qn/qc

on·col·ogy [ɒŋ'kɒlədʒɪ] N (*Med*) oncologia

on·coming ['ɒn,kʌmɪŋ] ADJ (*traffic*) in senso contrario

◎ **one** [wʌn] KEYWORD

■ ADJ

1 uno(-a); **one day** un giorno; **one cold winter's day** una fredda giornata d'inverno; **one hundred and fifty** centocinquanta; **the baby is one (year old)** il bambino ha un anno; **it's one (o'clock)** è l'una; **one or two people** una o due persone, un paio di persone; **for one reason or another** per un motivo o per l'altro; **twenty-one years ago** ventun'anni fa; **that's one way of doing it** questo è uno dei modi per farlo

2 (*sole*) unico(-a), solo(-a); **his one worry** la sua unica *or* sola preoccupazione; **no one man could do it** nessuno potrebbe farlo da solo; **one and only** unico(-a); **the one and only Charlie Chaplin** l'inimitabile Charlie Chaplin; **the one man who** il solo *or* l'unico che; **the one book which ...** l'unico libro che...

3 (*same*) stesso(-a); **they are one and the same person** sono la stessa persona; **it is one and the same thing** è la stessa cosa; **in the one car** nella stessa macchina

■ N uno(-a); **one after the other** uno(-a) dopo l'altro(-a); **one and all** tutti; **to be at one (with sb)** andare d'accordo (con qn); **I belted him one** (*fam*) gli ho mollato un cazzotto; **to go one better than sb** fare meglio di qn; **one by one** a uno(-a) a uno(-a); **I for one am not going** per quanto mi riguarda non ci vado; **to have one for the road** bere il bicchiere della staffa; **one hundred and one** cento uno; **in ones and twos** a piccoli gruppi; **she's cook and housekeeper in one** è contemporaneamente cuoca e governante; **twenty-one** ventuno; **to be one up on sb** essere avvantaggiato(-a) rispetto a qn

■ PRON

1 this one questo(-a); **any one of us** chiunque *or* uno qualsiasi di noi; **our dear ones** i nostri cari; **that's a difficult one** quello è un osso duro; **you're a fine one!** (*fam*) sei un bel tipo!; **he's a great one for chess** va matto per gli scacchi; **I'll have the grey one** prenderò quello grigio; **have you got one?** ne hai uno?; **what about this little one?** cosa ne dici di questo piccolino?; **the little ones** i bambini, i piccoli; **he is not one to protest** non è il tipo che protesta; **one or two of the books were damaged** c'erano un paio di libri rovinati; **one of them** uno(-a) di loro; **I lost one of them** ne ho perso uno; **one or two** uno(-a) o due; **that one** quello(-a); **the one on the floor** quello(-a) sul pavimento; **the one who (*or* that *or* which)** quello(-a) che; **the ones who (*or* that *or* which)** quelli(-e) che; **which one do you want?** quale vuoi?

2 one another l'un l'altro(-a); **they all kissed one another** si baciarono tutti a vicenda; **do you see one another much?** vi vedete spesso?

3 (*impersonal*): **to cut one's finger** tagliarsi un dito; **one never knows** non si sa mai; **one must eat** bisogna mangiare; **to express one's opinion** esprimere la propria opinione

one-armed [,wʌn'ɑːmd] ADJ con un braccio solo

one-armed bandit N slot-machine *f inv*

one-day excursion [,wʌndeɪɪks'kɜːʃən] N (*Am*) biglietto giornaliero di andata e ritorno

one-dimensional [,wʌndaɪ'mɛnʃənl] ADJ **1** (*Math*) unidimensionale **2** (*character*) monocorde

one-eyed [,wʌn'aɪd] ADJ con un occhio solo

one-horse ['wʌn,hɔːs] ADJ: **one-horse town** (*fam*) piccola città di provincia

one-legged [,wʌn'lɛgɪd] ADJ con una gamba sola

one-man ['wʌn'mæn] ADJ (*business*) gestito(-a) da una sola persona; (*art exhibition*) personale; (*boat*) a un posto; **one-man show** recital *m inv*; **she's a one-man woman** è tendenzialmente monogama, è una donna fedele

one-man band ['wʌn,mæn'bænd] N (*Mus: person*) *suonatore ambulante con vari strumenti*; **it's a one-man band** (*fig fam*) c'è solo una persona a mandare avanti la baracca

one-night ['wʌn,naɪt] ADJ: **one-night stand** (*Theatre*) spettacolo unico; (*sexual*) avventura di una notte

one-off [,wʌn'ɒf] N (*Brit fam*) fatto eccezionale

■ ADJ eccezionale, più unico(-a) che raro(-a)

one-on-one [,wʌnɒn'wʌn] ADJ, ADV = **one-to-one**

one-parent family ['wʌn,pɛərənt'fæmɪlɪ] N famiglia *f* monogenitore *inv*

one-piece ['wʌn,piːs] ADJ (*bathing suit*) intero(-a), monopezzo *inv*

on·er·ous ['ɒnərəs] (*frm*) ADJ (*task, duty*) oneroso(-a); (*responsibility*) pesante

one·self [wʌn'sɛlf] PERS PRON (*reflexive*) si; (*after prep*) se stesso(-a), sé; (*emphatic*) da sé; **to hurt oneself** farsi male; **to be by oneself** stare da solo(-a), stare per conto proprio; **to do sth by oneself** fare qc da solo(-a) *or* da sé; **to keep sth for oneself** tenere qc per sé; **to see for oneself** vedere con i propri occhi; **to say to oneself** dirsi; **to talk to oneself** parlare da solo *or* tra sé e sé; **one asks oneself how it could happen** ci si chiede come sia potuto succedere; **it's quicker to do it oneself** si fa più in fretta a farlo da solo

one-shot [,wʌn'ʃɒt] N (*Am*) = **one-off**

one-sided [,wʌn'saɪdɪd] ADJ (*decision, view*) unilaterale; (*judgment, account*) parziale; (*game, contest*) impari *inv*; **his account was one-sided** il suo resoconto non è stato obiettivo; **the match was one-sided** l'incontro era impari

one-stop ['wʌn,stɒp] ADJ: **one-stop shop** *negozio che fornisce tutti i beni e i servizi necessari a un determinato scopo*

one-time ['wʌn,taɪm] ADJ ex *inv*

one-to-one [,wʌntə'wʌn] ADJ **1** (*correlation*) univoco(-a); (*relationship*) tra due persone; (*interview, talk*) a quattr'occhi, faccia a faccia; (*training, therapy*) individuale; **teaching is on a one-to-one basis** l'insegnamento è organizzato in lezioni individuali

■ ADV (*talk, discuss*) faccia a faccia, a quattr'occhi

one-track ['wʌn,træk] ADJ: **to have a one-track mind** essere fissato(-a), avere la mente a senso unico

one-upmanship [,wʌn'ʌpmənʃɪp] N: **the art of one-upmanship** l'arte *f* di primeggiare

one-way ['wʌn,weɪ] ADJ (*traffic, street*) a senso unico; (*ticket*) di sola andata

one-woman ['wʌn,wʊmən] ADJ: **one-woman show**

(*Art*) mostra personale; **one-woman business** impresa individuale gestita da una donna

on·going ['ɒn,gəʊɪŋ] ADJ (*in progress*) in corso; (*continuing*) che si sviluppa; **the ongoing debate** il dibattito in corso; **the club's ongoing financial problems** gli attuali problemi finanziari del club

on·ion ['ʌnjən] N cipolla

onion rings NPL *rondelle di cipolla passate in pastella e fritte*

onion soup N zuppa di cipolle

on·line ['ɒn,laɪn] ADJ (*Comput*) on line *inv*, in linea; (: *switched on*) acceso(-a); **on-line banking** servizi *mpl* bancari on-line; **online shopping** shopping *m* on-line
■ADV on-line

on·looker ['ɒn,lʊkə^r] N astante *m/f*, spettatore(-trice)

◎**only** ['əʊnlɪ] ADJ solo(-a), unico(-a); **it's the only one left** è l'unico rimasto; **your only hope is to hide** la tua unica speranza sta nel nasconderti; **you are the only one who can help us** sei l'unico che possa *or* che può aiutarci; **you are not the only one** non sei l'unico; **an only child** un(-a) figlio(-a) unico(-a); **the only thing I don't like about it is ...** l'unica cosa che non mi va è...
■ADV solo, soltanto, solamente; **we have only five** ne abbiamo solo cinque; **how much was it? — only ten pounds** quanto è costato? — solo dieci sterline; **only one choice** una sola possibilità, un'unica scelta; **only time will tell** chi vivrà vedrà; **I'm only the porter** io sono solo il portinaio; **I only touched it** l'ho soltanto toccato; **I only took one** ne ho preso soltanto uno; **we only want to stay for one night** vorremmo stare solo una notte; **only when I ...** solo quando io...; **not only A but also B** non solo A ma anche B; **I saw her only yesterday** l'ho vista appena ieri; **we can only hope** non possiamo far altro che sperare; **I'd be only too pleased to help** sarei proprio felice di essere d'aiuto; **it's only too true** è proprio vero; **only just** appena; **I only just passed the exam** ho appena passato l'esame
■CONJ solo che, ma (purtroppo); **I would come, only I'm very busy** verrei volentieri, solo che sono molto occupato

on-message ['ɒn,mɛsɪdʒ] ADJ (*Pol*) allineato(-a), che segue la linea del partito

o.n.o. ABBR = or nearest offer; *see* near

ono·mato·poeia [,ɒnəʊmætəʊ'pi:ə] N onomatopea

ono·mato·poe·ic [,ɒnəʊmætəʊ'pi:ɪk] ADJ onomatopeico(-a)

on·rush ['ɒn,rʌʃ] N ondata

on·set ['ɒn,sɛt] N (*of winter*) arrivo; (*of illness, old age*) inizio, principio; **the onset of winter** l'arrivo dell'inverno; **the onset of war** l'inizio della guerra

on·shore ['ɒn'ʃɔ:^r] ADJ (*wind*) di mare; (*job*) a terra

on·side [ɒn'saɪd] ADJ (*Sport*): **to be onside** non essere in fuorigioco; **to bring sb onside** portare qn dalla propria parte

on·slaught ['ɒn,slɔ:t] N (*Mil, fig*) attacco

On·tario [ɒn'tɛərɪəʊ] N Ontario
▷ www.gov.on.ca
▷ www.tourism.gov.on.ca/english

on-the-job ['ɒnðə'dʒɒb] ADJ (*course, training*) in sede

on-the-spot ['ɒnðə'spɒt] ADJ (*investigations*) sul posto

◎**onto** ['ɒntʊ] PREP su, sopra; **he climbed onto the table** è salito sopra il tavolo; **to be onto sb** (*fam: suspect*) scoprire qn; **I'm onto something** (*fam*) sono su una buona pista; **to be onto a good thing** (*fam*) trovare l'America; **I'll get onto him about it** gliene parlerò io

on·tol·ogy [ɒn'tɒlədʒɪ] N (*Philosophy*) ontologia

onus ['əʊnəs] N, NO PL onere *m*; **the onus is on him to prove it** sta a lui dimostrarlo; **to shift the onus for sth onto sb** scaricare la responsabilità di qc su qn; **the onus of proof is on the prosecution** l'onere della prova spetta all'accusa

on·ward ['ɒnwəd] ADJ in avanti
■ADV (*also:* **onwards**) in avanti; **she stumbled onward** è caduta in avanti; **from this time onward** d'ora in poi; **from the 12th century onward(s)** dal XII secolo in poi

onyx ['ɒnɪks] N onice *f*

oodles ['u:dəlz] N (*old fam*): **oodles (of)** un sacco (di)

oomph [ʊmf] N (*fam*) verve *f inv*

oops [ʊps] EXCL ops! (*esprime rincrescimento per un piccolo contrattempo*)

oops-a-daisy! ['ʊpsə,deɪzɪ] EXCL oplà!

ooze [u:z] N melma
■VI (*water*) filtrare; (*gum, resin*) trasudare; (*pus*) fuoriuscire
■VT: **the wound oozed blood** la ferita stillava sangue; **he simply oozes confidence** (*pej*) sprizza sicurezza da tutti i pori

opa·city [əʊ'pæsɪtɪ] N opacità

opal ['əʊpəl] N opale *m or f*

opal·es·cence [,əʊpə'lɛsns] N opalescenza

opal·ine ['əʊpə,laɪn] N opalina

opaque [əʊ'peɪk] ADJ opaco(-a)

OPEC ['əʊpɛk] N ABBR (= **Organization of Petroleum-Exporting Countries**) OPEC *f*
▷ www.opec.org

op-ed [,ɒp'ɛd] ADJ (*Am*): **op-ed piece** *articolo che riporta l'opinione di un giornalista o un commentatore autorevole*

◎**open** ['əʊpən] ADJ
1 (*gen*) aperto(-a); (*flower*) aperto(-a), sbocciato(-a); **wide open** (*door, window*) spalancato(-a); **half open** *or* **slightly open** socchiuso(-a); **open at the neck** col colletto sbottonato; **to welcome with open arms** accogliere a braccia aperte; **to cut a sack open** aprire un sacco con un taglio; **to keep open house** (*fig*) aprire la propria casa a tutti; **open to the public on Mondays** aperto(-a) al pubblico di lunedì ; **the shop's open on Sunday morning** il negozio è aperto la domenica mattina
2 (*fig: letter*) aperto(-a); (: *water, channel*) navigabile; (: *cheque*) in bianco; **in the open air** all'aria aperta, all'aperto; **on the open road** su autostrada; **road open to traffic** strada aperta al traffico *or* transitabile; **open to the elements/to attack** esposto(-a) alle intemperie/all'attacco; **open country** aperta campagna; **open ground** (*among trees*) radura; (*waste ground*) terreno non edificato; **the open sea** il mare aperto; **to lay o.s. open to criticism** esporsi alle critiche; **open to persuasion** disposto(-a) a lasciarsi convincere; **it is open to doubt whether ...** è in dubbio se...
3 (*competition, scholarship*) aperto(-a) a tutti; (*meeting*) pubblico(-a); (*trial*) a porte aperte; **what choices are open to me?** che scelta ho?; **the post is still open** il posto è sempre vacante; **in open court** (*Law*) a porte aperte
4 (*person, face*) aperto(-a); (*hatred, admiration*) evidente, palese; (*enemy*) dichiarato(-a); **it's an open secret that ...** è il segreto di Pulcinella che...; **in open revolt** in aperta rivolta; **to be open with sb** essere franco(-a) con qn
5 (*undecided: question*) aperto(-a); **the race was still wide open** la gara era ancora tutta da giocare; **open verdict** dichiarazione di morte per cause non

Oo

accertate; **open ticket** biglietto aperto; **to have an open mind (on sth)** non avere ancora deciso (su qc); **to leave the matter open** lasciare la faccenda in sospeso
■ N 1: **out in the open** (*out of doors*) fuori, all'aperto; (*in the country*) in campagna, all'aperto; **their true feelings came into the open** vennero a galla i loro veri sentimenti
2 (*Golf, Tennis*): **the Australian Open** l'open *m inv* di Australia
■ VT (*gen*) aprire; (*legs*) divaricare; **to open sth wide** spalancare qc; **to open a road to traffic** aprire al traffico una strada; **to open a road through a forest** aprire una strada nella foresta; **to open Parliament** aprire i lavori parlamentari; **to open a bank account** aprire un conto in banca; **to open fire** (*Mil*) aprire il fuoco; **I didn't open my mouth** non ho aperto bocca; **to open one's heart to sb** confidarsi con qn; **to open one's mind to sth** aprirsi con qc
■ VI
1 (*eyes, door, debate*) aprirsi; (*shop, bank, museum*) aprire; **what time do the shops open?** a che ora aprono i negozi?; **the shops open at 9** i negozi aprono alle 9; **the door opens automatically** la porta si apre automaticamente; **to open onto** *or* **into** dare su
2 (*begin: book, film*) cominciare; (*Cards, Chess*) aprire; **the play opens next Monday** la prima della commedia è lunedì prossimo; **the book opens with a long description** il libro comincia con una lunga descrizione
▸ **open out** VT + ADV (*unfold*) aprire, spiegare
■ VI + ADV aprirsi, dischiudersi
▸ **open up** VT + ADV aprire; (*blocked road*) sgombrare; **to open up a country for trade** aprire il mercato di un paese
■ VI + ADV
1 (*flower, shop*) aprirsi
2 (*start shooting*) aprire il fuoco

open-air [ˌəʊpnˈɛəʳ] ADJ all'aperto

open-and-shut [ˌəʊpnənˈʃʌt] ADJ: **open-and-shut case** caso di facile soluzione

open·cast [ˈəʊpnˌkɑːst] ADJ: **opencast mine/mining** miniera/estrazione *f* a cielo aperto

open day N (*Brit: in school, institution*) giornata di apertura al pubblico

open-ended [ˌəʊpnˈɛndɪd] ADJ (*question*) aperto(-a); (*discussion*) senza conclusioni

open·er [ˈəʊpnəʳ] N: **bottle-opener** apribottiglie *m inv*; (*also:* **can opener** *or* **tin opener**) apriscatole *m inv*

open-handed [ˌəʊpnˈhændɪd] ADJ generoso(-a)

open-heart [ˈəʊpnˌhɑːt] ADJ: **open-heart surgery** intervento *m* (chirurgico) a cuore aperto *inv*

open-hearted [ˌəʊpnˈhɑːtɪd] ADJ sincero(-a), franco(-a)

◎ **open·ing** [ˈəʊpnɪŋ] ADJ (*gen*) d'apertura; (*ceremony, speech*) d'apertura, inaugurale
■ N 1 (*gap*) apertura; (: *in wall*) breccia; **a narrow opening** una stretta apertura 2 (*beginning*) inizio; (*also:* **official opening**: *of factory, hospital*) inaugurazione *f*; (*first performance: of film, play*) prima (rappresentazione *f*); **the opening of the book** l'inizio del libro 3 (*opportunity*) occasione *f*, possibilità *f inv*; (*post*) posto vacante; **to give one's opponent an opening** offrire il fianco all'avversario; **she needed an opening to show her capabilities** le occorreva un'occasione per dimostrare le proprie capacità

opening hours NPL orario *msg* d'apertura

opening night N (*Theatre*) prima

opening time N (*Brit*) orario d'apertura (*dei pub*)

open learning N *sistema educativo nel quale lo studente ha maggior controllo e gestione delle modalità di apprendimento*

open letter N lettera aperta

open·ly [ˈəʊpənlɪ] ADV apertamente

open market N: **on the open market** sul libero mercato

open-minded [ˌəʊpnˈmaɪndɪd] ADJ aperto(-a), dalla mentalità aperta

open-mouthed [ˌəʊpnˈmaʊðd] ADJ a bocca aperta

open-necked [ˈəʊpnˌnɛkt] ADJ (*shirt, blouse*) col colletto slacciato *or* sbottonato

open·ness [ˈəʊpnnɪs] N (*frankness*) franchezza, sincerità

open-plan [ˈəʊpnˌplæn] ADJ senza pareti divisorie

open prison N (*Brit*) istituto di pena per detenuti in semilibertà

open sandwich N tartina

open secret N segreto di Pulcinella

open shop N (*Industry*) *impresa che assume anche operai non iscritti ai sindacati*

open source N (*Comput*) open source *m inv*

open system N (*Comput*) open system *m inv*, sistema *m* aperto

Open University N (*Brit*): **the Open University** *corsi universitari a distanza*

OPEN UNIVERSITY

La **Open University** (**OU**), fondata in Gran Bretagna nel 1969, organizza corsi universitari per corrispondenza o via Internet, basati anche su lezioni che vengono trasmesse dalla BBC per radio e per televisione e su corsi estivi.
▷ www.open.ac.uk/

◎ **op·era** [ˈɒpərə] N (*work*) opera (lirica); (*genre*) opera, (musica) lirica
▷ www.operabase.com/index.cgi?lang=en
▷ www.aria-database.com/index2.html
▷ www.royalopera.org
▷ www.eno.org
▷ www.metopera.org/
▷ www.sydneyoperahouse.com/

op·er·able [ˈɒpərəbl] ADJ (*Med*) operabile

opera glasses NPL binocolo da teatro

opera house N teatro lirico *or* dell'opera, opera

opera singer N cantante *m/f* d'opera *or* lirico(-a)

◎ **op·er·ate** [ˈɒpəˌreɪt] VT 1 (*machine, switchboard, brakes*) azionare, far funzionare; **a machine operated by electricity** una macchina funzionante a corrente (elettrica); **can you operate this tool?** sai usare questo strumento?; **can you operate the video?** sai far funzionare il videoregistratore? 2 (*company*) dirigere, gestire; (*service*) gestire; (*system, law*) applicare
■ VI 1 (*function: machine, mind*) funzionare; **I don't know how the electoral system operates in Italy** non so come funziona il sistema elettorale italiano
2 (*drug, propaganda*) agire 3 (*company, firm*) operare; (*bus, airport*) essere in funzione; (*person*) agire 4 (*Med*) operare, intervenire (su); **to operate on sb** operare qn; **to be operated on** subire un'operazione *f or* un intervento (chirurgico); **she was operated on for appendicitis** fu operata di appendicite

op·er·at·ic [ˌɒpəˈrætɪk] ADJ operistico(-a), lirico(-a)

op·er·at·ing [ˈɒpəˌreɪtɪŋ] ADJ 1 (*Comm: costs*) di

gestione, d'esercizio **2** (*Med*) operatorio(-a); (: *nurse*) di sala operatoria
operating costs NPL costi *mpl* di esercizio
operating profit N utile *m* d'esercizio
operating room N (*Am*) = operating theatre
operating system N (*Comput*) sistema *m* operativo
operating table N (*Med*): **the operating table** il tavolo operatorio
operating theatre N (*Med*) sala operatoria
◎ **op·era·tion** [ˌɒpəˈreɪʃən] N **1** (*gen, Mil*) operazione *f*; (*Med*) operazione *f*, intervento (chirurgico); **a minor operation** una piccola operazione; **to have an operation for appendicitis** essere operato(-a) di appendicite; **to undergo an operation** subire un'operazione *or* un intervento (chirurgico); **I've never had an operation** non sono mai stato operato; **the company's operations during the year** le operazioni dell'azienda durante l'anno **2 to be in operation** (*machine*) essere in funzione; (*plan, system*) essere in azione; (*law*) essere in vigore; **to come into operation** entrare in funzione (*or* in azione *etc*), diventare operativo(-a); **to bring** *or* **put into operation** mettere in funzione (*or* in azione); (*law*) far entrare in vigore
op·era·tion·al [ˌɒpəˈreɪʃənl] ADJ (*relating to operations*) operativo(-a); (*Comm*) di gestione, d'esercizio; (*ready for use or action*) in attività, in funzione; **operational research** ricerca operativa; **when the service is fully operational** quando il servizio sarà completamente operante
op·era·tive [ˈɒpərətɪv] ADJ **1** (*law, measure*) in vigore, operativo(-a), operante; **the operative word** la parola chiave **2** (*Med*) operatorio(-a)
■ N (*in factory*) operaio(-a)
◎ **op·era·tor** [ˈɒpəˌreɪtə^r] N (*of machine*) operatore(-trice); (*Telec*) centralinista *m/f*; **tour operator** operatore(-trice) turistico(-a); **a smooth operator** (*fam*) uno(-a) che ci sa fare
oper·cu·lum [əʊˈpɜːkjʊləm] N opercolo
op·er·et·ta [ˌɒpəˈrɛtə] N operetta
oph·thal·mia [ɒfˈθælmɪə] N oftalmia
oph·thal·mic [ɒfˈθælmɪk] ADJ oftalmico(-a)
oph·thal·molo·gist [ˌɒfθælˈmɒlədʒɪst] N oculista *m/f*
oph·thal·mol·ogy [ˌɒfθælˈmɒlədʒɪ] N oculistica
oph·thal·mo·scope [ɒfˈθælməˌskəʊp] N oftalmoscopio
opi·ate [ˈəʊpɪɪt] N oppiaceo
opine [əʊˈpaɪn] VT (*frm old*) opinare
◎ **opin·ion** [əˈpɪnjən] N (*belief, view*) opinione *f*, parere *m*; **public opinion** opinione pubblica; **in my opinion** secondo me, a mio avviso; **in the opinion of those who know** secondo gli esperti; **it's a matter of opinion** è discutibile *or* opinabile; **what's your opinion?** cosa ne pensi?; **what is your opinion of him?** tu che cosa pensi di lui?; **to be of the opinion that ...** essere dell'opinione che..., ritenere che...; **to ask sb's opinion** chiedere il parere di qn, consultare qn; **to give one's opinion** dare il proprio parere; **to form an opinion of sb/sth** farsi un'opinione di qn/qc; **to have a high/poor opinion of sb** avere/non avere un'alta opinione di qn, stimare molto/poco qn; **to have a high opinion of o.s.** (*pej*) avere un'alta opinione di sé, credersi chissà chi; **to seek a second opinion** (*Med*) consultare un altro medico
opin·ion·at·ed [əˈpɪnjəˌneɪtɪd] ADJ dogmatico(-a)
opinion poll N sondaggio di opinione
opium [ˈəʊpɪəm] N oppio
opium addict N oppiomane *m/f*
opium den N fumeria d'oppio
opos·sum [əˈpɒsəm] N opossum *m inv*
◎ **op·po·nent** [əˈpəʊnənt] N avversario(-a); (*in debate, discussion*) oppositore(-trice); **I have always been an opponent of privatization** sono sempre stato un accanito oppositore delle privatizzazioni
op·por·tune [ˈɒpəˌtjuːn] ADJ opportuno(-a); **to be opportune** capitare a proposito
op·por·tune·ly [ˈɒpəˌtjuːnlɪ] ADV opportunamente
op·por·tune·ness [ˈɒpəˌtjuːnnɪs] N opportunità
op·por·tun·ism [ˌɒpəˈtjuːnɪzəm] N (*frm pej*) opportunismo
op·por·tun·ist [ˌɒpəˈtjuːnɪst] N (*frm pej*) opportunista *m/f*
op·por·tun·is·tic [ˌɒpətjʊˈnɪstɪk] ADJ (*frm*) opportunistico(-a)
◎ **op·por·tu·nity** [ˌɒpəˈtjuːnɪtɪ] N opportunità *f inv*, occasione *f*; **to have the opportunity to do** *or* **of doing** avere l'opportunità di fare; **I've never had the opportunity to go to Spain** non ho mai avuto l'opportunità di andare in Spagna; **to take the opportunity to do** *or* **of doing** cogliere l'occasione per fare; **at the earliest opportunity** appena possibile, alla prima occasione; **when I (***or* **you** *etc***) get the opportunity** quando capita l'occasione; **to miss one's opportunity** perdere l'occasione; **opportunities for promotion** possibilità *fpl* di carriera
◎ **op·pose** [əˈpəʊz] VT (*gen*) opporsi a; **she opposes my leaving** è contraria alla mia partenza
◎ **op·posed** [əˈpəʊzd] ADJ (*conflicting: ideas*) contrastante, opposto(-a); **to be opposed to** essere contrario(-a) a, essere contro; **ideas opposed to mine** idee contrarie alle mie; **I am opposed to hunting** sono contro la caccia; **as opposed to** (*in contrast to*) in confronto a, rispetto a, in contrasto con; (*instead of*) invece che *or* di; **how important is financial success, as opposed to job satisfaction?** quanto è importante il successo in termini economici rispetto alla soddisfazione che dà il lavoro?
op·pos·ing [əˈpəʊzɪŋ] ADJ (*tendencies, points of view*) opposto(-a); (*team*) avversario(-a); **the opposing team** la squadra avversaria
◎ **op·po·site** [ˈɒpəzɪt] ADV di fronte, dirimpetto; **they live directly opposite** abitano proprio di fronte
■ PREP di fronte a; **opposite one another** l'uno(-a) di fronte all'altro(-a); **a house opposite the school** una casa di fronte alla scuola; **to play opposite sb** (*Theatre, Cine*) essere co-protagonista *m/f* insieme a qn
■ ADJ (*house*) di fronte; (*end, direction, side*) opposto(-a); (*point of view*) opposto(-a), contrario(-a); **on the opposite side of the road** dall'altro lato della strada; **"see opposite page"** "vedere pagina a fronte"
■ N (*reverse*) contrario, opposto; (*of word*) contrario; **quite the opposite!** al contrario!; **she said just the opposite** lei ha detto esattamente il contrario; **the opposite is true** è vero l'opposto
opposite number N omologo(-a), controparte *f*
opposite sex N: **the opposite sex** l'altro sesso
◎ **op·po·si·tion** [ˌɒpəˈzɪʃən] N **1** (*resistance*) opposizione *f*; (*people opposing*) avversari *mpl*; **in opposition to** in contrasto con; **the plan met considerable opposition** il progetto ha incontrato una notevole opposizione; **what are the opposition like?** com'è la squadra avversaria? **2** (*Brit Pol*): **the Opposition** l'opposizione *f*; **leader of the Opposition** leader *m/f*

Oo

inv dell'opposizione; **to be in opposition** essere all'opposizione

op·press [ə'prɛs] VT opprimere

op·pres·sion [ə'prɛʃən] N oppressione *f*

op·pres·sive [ə'prɛsɪv] ADJ (*regime, system*) oppressivo(-a); (*fig: heat, thought*) opprimente

op·pres·sive·ly [ə'prɛsɪvlɪ] ADV (*see adj*) oppressivamente; in modo opprimente; **it was oppressively hot** faceva un caldo opprimente

op·pres·sor [ə'prɛsə^r] N oppressore *m*

op·pro·brium [ə'prəʊbrɪəm] N (*frm*) vituperio

◎ **opt** [ɒpt] VI: **to opt for** optare per; **to opt to do** scegliere di fare, optare per fare

▸ **opt out (of)** VI + ADV (+ PREP) **1** (*of agreement, arrangement*) scegliere di non partecipare a; **I think I'll opt out of going** penso che non ci andrò; **we went to the match, but Fred opted out** noi siamo andati alla partita ma Fred non è venuto **2** (*Brit: of NHS*) scegliere di non far più parte di

op·ta·tive ['ɒptətɪv] ADJ ottativo(-a)

■ N ottativo

op·tic ['ɒptɪk] ADJ ottico(-a)

op·ti·cal ['ɒptɪkəl] ADJ ottico(-a)

optical character reader N lettore *m* ottico di caratteri

optical character recognition N lettura ottica di caratteri

optical disk N (*Comput*) disco ottico

optical fibre N fibra ottica

optical illusion N illusione *f* ottica

optical pen N (*Comput*) penna ottica

op·ti·cian [ɒp'tɪʃən] N (*also:* **ophthalmic optician**) optometrista *m/f*; (*also:* **dispensing optician**) ottico

op·tics ['ɒptɪks] NSG ottica

op·ti·mism ['ɒptɪˌmɪzəm] N ottimismo

op·ti·mist ['ɒptɪmɪst] N ottimista *m/f*; **I'm an optimist** sono ottimista

◎ **op·ti·mis·tic** [ˌɒptɪ'mɪstɪk] ADJ (*attitude*) ottimistico(-a); (*person*) ottimista; **let's be optimistic** cerchiamo di essere ottimisti

op·ti·mis·ti·cal·ly [ˌɒptɪ'mɪstɪklɪ] ADV ottimisticamente

op·ti·mum ['ɒptɪməm] ADJ ottimale

■ N (*pl* **optimums** *or* **optima** ['ɒptɪmə]) optimum *m inv*, condizioni *fpl* ottimali

◎ **op·tion** ['ɒpʃən] N **1** (*choice*) scelta; **I have** *or* **I've got no option** non ho scelta; **she had no option but to leave** non poteva far altro che partire; **to keep one's options open** non precludersi alcuna possibilità; **imprisonment without the option of bail** (*Law*) carcerazione *f* senza possibilità di libertà provvisoria **2** (*Comm*) opzione *f*; **with the option to buy** con opzione di acquisto **3** (*Scol, Univ*) materia facoltativa; **I'm doing geology as my option** come materia facoltativa studio geologia

op·tion·al ['ɒpʃənl] ADJ (*course, subject, ingredient*) facoltativo(-a); **optional extra** (*Comm*) optional *m inv*

op·tom·etry [ɒp'tɒmɪtrɪ] N optometria

opu·lence ['ɒpjʊləns] N opulenza

opu·lent ['ɒpjʊlənt] ADJ opulento(-a)

opu·lent·ly ['ɒpjʊləntlɪ] ADV (*furnish etc*) con opulenza; (*live*) nell'opulenza

opus ['əʊpəs] N (*pl* **opuses** *or* **opera** ['ɒpərə]) (*Mus*) opera

OR ABBR (*Am Post*) = **Oregon**

◎ **or** [ɔː^r] CONJ (*gen*) o; **or rather** o meglio, o piuttosto; **or else** oppure, se no, altrimenti; **do it or else!** (*fam*) fallo, altrimenti...!; **20 or so** circa 20; **hurry up or you'll miss the bus** sbrigati, altrimenti perdi l'autobus; **let me go or I'll scream!** lasciami andare o mi metto a urlare!; **would you like tea or coffee?** vuoi del tè o del caffè?; **I don't eat meat or fish** non mangio né carne né pesce; **without relatives or friends** senza (né) parenti né amici; **he can't read or write** non sa né leggere né scrivere; **he hasn't seen or heard anything** non ha (né) visto né sentito niente

ora·cle ['ɒrəkl] N oracolo

oral ['ɔːrəl] ADJ orale

■ N (*also:* **oral exam**) (esame *m*) orale *m*; **I've got my Italian oral soon** tra poco avrò l'orale d'italiano

oral history N la tradizione orale

oral·ly ['ɔːrəlɪ] ADV oralmente; (*take medicine*) per via orale

oral sex N sesso orale

◎ **or·ange** ['ɒrɪndʒ] N (*fruit*) arancia; (*tree*) arancio; (*colour*) arancione *m*

■ ADJ (*in colour*) arancione; (*juice, jelly*) d'arancia; (*marmalade*) di arance; (*cake*) all'arancia; **an orange juice** un succo d'arancia; **an orange jumper** un maglione arancione

or·ange·ade [ˌɒrɪndʒ'eɪd] N aranciata

orange blossom N fiori *mpl* d'arancio

Orange·man ['ɒrɪndʒmən] N (*pl* **-men**) *protestante militante dell'Irlanda del Nord*

orange squash N succo d'arancia (*da diluire con acqua*)

orange stick N bastoncino d'arancio (*per manicure*)

orang-utan [ɔːˌræŋuː'tæn] N orango, orangutan *m inv*

ora·tion [ɔː'reɪʃən] N orazione *f*; **funeral oration** orazione funebre

ora·tor ['ɒrətə^r] N oratore(-trice)

ora·tori·cal [ˌɒrə'tɒrɪkəl] ADJ oratorio(-a)

ora·to·rio [ˌɒrə'tɔːrɪəʊ] N (*Mus*) oratorio

ora·tory[1] ['ɒrətərɪ] N (*public speaking*) oratoria

ora·tory[2] ['ɒrətərɪ] N (*Rel*) oratorio

orb [ɔːb] N (*frm: sphere*) orbe *m*; (*liter: celestial body*) astro; (*in regalia*) globo (*simbolo del potere reale e imperiale*)

or·bit ['ɔːbɪt] N orbita; **to be in/go into orbit (round)** essere/entrare in orbita (attorno a); **it's outside my orbit** (*fig*) non rientra nel mio campo

■ VI (*satellite, astronaut*) orbitare

■ VT (*earth, moon*) orbitare attorno a

or·bit·al ['ɔːbɪtəl] N (*also:* **orbital motorway**) raccordo anulare

Or·cad·ian [ɔː'keɪdɪən] ADJ delle Orcadi

■ N abitante *m/f* delle Orcadi

or·chard ['ɔːtʃəd] N frutteto; **apple orchard** meleto

or·ches·tra ['ɔːkɪstrə] N orchestra; (*Am: seating*) platea

or·ches·tral [ɔː'kɛstrəl] ADJ (*music, style*) orchestrale; (*concert*) sinfonico(-a)

orchestra pit N fossa dell'orchestra

or·ches·trate ['ɔːkɪsˌtreɪt] VT (*Mus, fig*) orchestrare

or·ches·tra·tion [ˌɔːkɪs'treɪʃən] N orchestrazione *f*

or·chid ['ɔːkɪd] N orchidea; **common spotted orchid** orchidea maculata

or·dain [ɔː'deɪn] VT **1** (*decree*) decretare; **it was ordained that ...** (*fig*) era destino che... **2** (*Rel*) ordinare

or·deal [ɔː'diːl] N esperienza traumatica

◎ **order** ['ɔːdə^r] N

1 (*sequence*) ordine *m*; **in alphabetical order** in ordine alfabetico; **in order of merit** in ordine di merito; **in order of size** in ordine di grandezza; **put these in the right order** mettili nell'ordine giusto; **to be in the wrong order** *or* **out of order** non essere in ordine; **she**

had no order in her life aveva una vita disordinata; **in the order of things** nell'ordine delle cose
2 (*also:* **good order**) ordine *m*; **in order** (*room*) in ordine; (*documents*) in regola; **a machine in working order** un macchinario funzionante; **to be out of order** (*machine, toilets*) essere guasto(-a); (*telephone, lift*) essere fuori servizio
3 (*peace, control*) ordine *m*; **to keep order** mantenere l'ordine; **to keep children in order** tenere i bambini sotto controllo
4 (*command*) ordine *m*, comando; (*of court: for search, arrest*) mandato; (: *for payment of fine, maintenance*) ingiunzione *f*; **by order of** per ordine di; **on the orders of** agli ordini di; **to be under orders to do sth** avere l'ordine di fare qc; **to give sb orders to do sth** dare a qn l'ordine di fare qc; **to take orders from sb** prendere ordini da qn; **to obey orders** ubbidire agli ordini; **order of the day** ordine del giorno; **violence is the order of the day** (*fig*) la violenza è all'ordine del giorno
5 (*correct procedure: at meeting, Parliament*) procedura; **order (order)!** (*in Parliament*) ordine, signori!; **order in court!** silenzio!; **to call sb to order** richiamare qn all'ordine; **a point of order** una questione di procedura; **to be out of order** non (essere) regolamentare; **is it in order for me to go to Rome?** mi è permesso andare a Roma?
6 (*Comm*) ordinazione *f*, ordinativo; **to be on order** essere stato(-a) ordinato(-a); **to ask for a repeat order** chiedere che venga rinnovata un'ordinazione; **rush order** ordinazione urgente; **tall order** (*fig fam*) un'impresa ardua; **made to order** fatto(-a) su ordinazione, fatto(-a) su misura; **to place an order for sth with sb** fare un'ordinazione di qc a qn; **the waiter took our order** il cameriere ha preso la nostra ordinazione; **to the order of** (*Banking*) all'ordine di; **payment order** (*social security*) mandato (di pagamento)
7 **in order to do sth** per fare qc; **in order that** perché + *sub*, affinché + *sub*; **he does it in order to earn money** lo fa per guadagnare qualcosa; **they cancelled their holiday in order to go to the wedding** hanno cancellato la vacanza per andare al matrimonio; **in order there should be no misunderstanding** affinché non ci siano equivoci
8 **of** *or* **in the order of** (*approximately*) nell'ordine di; **his income is of the order of £40,000 per year** il suo reddito annuale è nell'ordine delle 40.000 sterline
9 (*of society, also Bio*) ordine *m*; **the lower orders** (*pej*) i ceti inferiori; **Benedictine Order** ordine benedettino; **holy orders** ordini (sacri); **to be in/take orders** (*Rel*) aver ricevuto/prendere gli ordini
■ VT
1 (*command*) ordinare; **to order sb to do sth** ordinare a qn di fare qc; **the referee ordered the player off the field** l'arbitro espulse il giocatore dal campo
2 (*put in order*) ordinare, fare ordine in, mettere in ordine
3 (*meal*) ordinare; (*goods*) ordinare, commissionare; (*taxi*) chiamare; **we ordered steak and chips** abbiamo ordinato bistecca e patatine
■ VI ordinare; **are you ready to order?** volete ordinare?
▸ **order about, order around** VT + ADV comandare, dare ordini a; **he tries to order me about** cerca di darmi ordini

order book N copiacommissione *m inv*; **to have a full order book** avere molte ordinazioni
or·dered [ˈɔːdəd] ADJ (*organized*) ordinato(-a)
order form N modulo di ordinazione; modulo d'ordine
or·der·li·ness [ˈɔːdəlɪnɪs] N ordine *m*
or·der·ly [ˈɔːdəlɪ] ADJ (*person*) ordinato(-a); (*mind*) metodico(-a); (*room*) in ordine, ordinato(-a); (*meeting, crowd*) disciplinato(-a)
■ N (*Mil*) attendente *m*; (*Med*) inserviente *m*
orderly room N (*Mil*) fureria
order number N numero di commissione
or·di·nal [ˈɔːdɪnl] ADJ (*number*) ordinale
■ N (numero) ordinale *m*
or·di·nance [ˈɔːdɪnəns] N (*frm*) ordinanza
or·di·nari·ly [ˈɔːdnrɪlɪ] ADV normalmente, di solito
◎ **or·di·nary** [ˈɔːdnrɪ] ADJ 1 (*usual*) abituale, solito(-a); **in the ordinary way** (*in the normal fashion*) nel solito modo; (*generally*) normalmente, di norma; **in ordinary use** usato(-a) normalmente; **it has 25 calories less than ordinary ice cream** ha 25 calorie in meno rispetto a un gelato normale 2 (*average*) comune, normale; (*pej*) mediocre, ordinario(-a); **an ordinary day** una giornata come tante; **he's just an ordinary guy** è uno come tanti; **the ordinary Italian** l'italiano qualunque; **the meal was very ordinary** il pranzo non era niente di speciale
■ N: **out of the ordinary** diverso(-a) dal solito, fuori dell'ordinario
ordinary degree N *laurea*

ORDINARY DEGREE

In Gran Bretagna esistono titoli universitari di diverso livello. Se uno studente non approfondisce i propri studi in alcuna materia, ottiene un **ordinary degree**. *Vedi anche* **Bachelor's degree**
▷ www.dfes.gov.uk/hegateway/
▷ http://educationusa.state.gov/undergrad/about/degrees.htm
▷ www.aucc.ca/can_uni/general_info/overview_e.html
▷ www.internationaleducationmedia.com/newzealand/
▷ www.southafrica.info/ess_info/sa_glance/education/education.htm

ordinary seaman N (*Brit*) marinaio semplice
ordinary shares NPL (*Fin*) azioni *fpl* ordinarie
or·di·nate [ˈɔːdɪnɪt] N ordinata
or·di·na·tion [ˌɔːdɪˈneɪʃən] N (*Rel*) ordinazione *f*
ord·nance [ˈɔːdnəns] (*Mil*) N (*guns*) artiglieria; (*supplies*) materiale *m* militare; **the ordnance** (*department*) il reparto di sussistenza
Ordnance Survey map N (*Brit*) ≈ carta topografica dell'Istituto Geografico Militare
ore [ɔːʳ] N minerale *m* grezzo; **copper ore** minerale grezzo di rame
orega·no [ˌɒrɪˈgɑːnəʊ] N origano
Or·egon [ˈɒrɪgən] N Oregon *m*
▷ www.oregon.gov/
Orestes [ɒˈrɛstiːz] N Oreste
or·gan [ˈɔːgən] N (*all senses*) organo
or·gan·die, or·gan·dy [ɔːˈɔːgəndɪ] N (*Am*) organdi *m*
organ-grinder [ˈɔːgənˌgraɪndəʳ] N suonatore(-trice) di organetto
organic [ɔːˈgænɪk] ADJ 1 (*gen, also fig*) organico(-a)
2 (*free of chemicals: vegetables, food, farming*) biologico(-a)

Oo

or·gani·cal·ly [ɔːˈgænɪkəlɪ] ADV *(affect, develop)* organicamente; *(farm, cultivate)* biologicamente
organic chemistry N chimica organica
or·gan·ism [ˈɔːgəˌnɪzəm] N *(Bio)* organismo
or·gan·ist [ˈɔːgənɪst] N organista *m/f*
◎**or·gani·za·tion** [ˌɔːgənaɪˈzeɪʃən] N organizzazione *f*; **a charitable organization** un'organizzazione filantropica
or·gani·za·tion·al [ˌɔːgənaɪˈzeɪʃənl] ADJ organizzativo(-a)
organization chart N organigramma *m*
◎**or·gan·ize** [ˈɔːgəˌnaɪz] VT organizzare; **to get organized** organizzarsi
◎**or·gan·ized** [ˈɔːgəˌnaɪzd] ADJ organizzato(-a)
organized crime N criminalità organizzata
organized labour N manodopera organizzata (in sindacati)
◎**or·gan·iz·er** [ˈɔːgəˌnaɪzəʳ] N organizzatore(-trice)
or·gan·iz·ing [ˈɔːgəˌnaɪzɪŋ] ADJ organizzativo(-a)
organ loft N *(Mus)* tribuna dell'organo
or·gasm [ˈɔːgæzəm] N orgasmo
or·gas·mic [ɔːˈgæzmɪk] ADJ *(Med)* orgasmico(-a); *(fam: exciting)* eccitante
orgy [ˈɔːdʒɪ] N *(also fig)* orgia
Ori·ent [ˈɔːrɪənt] N: **the Orient** l'Oriente *m*
ori·ent [ˈɔːrɪənt], **ori·en·tate** [ˈɔːrɪənˌteɪt] VT orientare; **to orient o.s.** orientarsi
ori·en·tal [ˌɔːrɪˈɛntəl] ADJ orientale
■ N: **Oriental** orientale *m/f*
Ori·en·tal·ist [ˌɔːrɪˈɛntəlɪst] N orientalista *m/f*
ori·en·ta·tion [ˌɔːrɪənˈteɪʃən] N orientamento
ori·en·teer·ing [ˌɔːrɪənˈtɪərɪŋ] N *(sport)* gara di orientamento
ori·fice [ˈɒrɪfɪs] N orifizio
ori·ga·mi [ˌɒrɪˈgɑːmɪ] N origami *m inv*
▷ www.origami.com
▷ www.paperfolding.com/history/
◎**ori·gin** [ˈɒrɪdʒɪn] N origine *f*; **country of origin** paese *m* d'origine; **to be of humble origin** *or* **have humble origins** essere di umili origini
◎**origi·nal** [əˈrɪdʒɪnl] ADJ *(gen)* originale; *(inhabitant, form, splendour)* originario(-a); **it's very original** è molto originale; **the original inhabitants** gli abitanti originari
■ N *(manuscript, painting etc)* originale *m*; *(garment)* modello originale; *(person)* originale *m/f*; **he reads Homer in the original** legge Omero in lingua originale
origi·nal·ity [əˌrɪdʒɪˈnælɪtɪ] N originalità
◎**origi·nal·ly** [əˈrɪdʒənəlɪ] ADV *(at first)* originariamente, all'inizio; *(in an original way)* originalmente
original sin N *(Rel)* peccato originale
origi·nate [əˈrɪdʒɪˌneɪt] VT dare origine a
■ VI: **to originate (from)** *(gen)* avere origine (da); *(suggestion, idea)* derivare (da); *(goods)* provenire (da); **to originate (in)** *(river)* nascere (in); *(custom)* avere origine (in); **most of these problems originate in childhood** la maggior parte di questi problemi hanno origine nell'infanzia
origi·na·tor [əˈrɪdʒɪˌneɪtəʳ] N ideatore(-trice)
Orion [əˈraɪən] N *(Myth, Astron)* Orione *m*
Ork·neys [ˈɔːknɪz] NPL: **the Orkneys, the Orkney Islands** le (isole) Orcadi *fpl*
Or·lon® [ˈɔːlɒn] N orlon® *m inv*
or·na·ment [*n* ˈɔːnəmənt; *vb* ˈɔːnəˌmɛnt] N *(gen)* ornamento; *(vase, figurine)* soprammobile *m*; *(trinket)* ninnolo; **a glass ornament** un soprammobile di vetro; **architectural ornaments** ornamenti architettonici; **Christmas tree ornaments** decorazioni *fpl* per l'albero di Natale
■ VT ornare, decorare
or·na·men·tal [ˌɔːnəˈmɛntl] ADJ ornamentale
or·na·men·ta·tion [ˌɔːnəmɛnˈteɪʃən] N *(act)* ornamentazione *f*; *(ornaments)* decorazione *f*
or·nate [ɔːˈneɪt] ADJ *(decor)* ricco(-a); *(style in writing)* ornato(-a)
or·ni·tho·logi·cal [ˌɔːnɪθəˈlɒdʒɪkəl] ADJ ornitologico(-a)
or·ni·tholo·gist [ˌɔːnɪˈθɒlədʒɪst] N ornitologo(-a)
or·ni·thol·ogy [ˌɔːnɪˈθɒlədʒɪ] N ornitologia
oro·graph·ic [ˌɒrəʊˈgræfɪk] ADJ orografico(-a)
orog·ra·phy [ɒˈrɒgrəfɪ] N orografia
or·phan [ˈɔːfən] ADJ, N orfano(-a)
■ VT: **to be orphaned** restare orfano(-a)
or·phan·age [ˈɔːfənɪdʒ] N orfanotrofio
Orpheus [ˈɔːfɪəs] N Orfeo
ortho·cen·tre, *(Am)* **ortho·cen·ter** [ˈɔːθəʊˌsɛntəʳ] N ortocentro
ortho·don·tics [ˌɔːθəʊˈdɒntɪks] NSG ortodonzia
ortho·dox [ˈɔːθəˌdɒks] ADJ ortodosso(-a)
ortho·doxy [ˈɔːθəˌdɒksɪ] N ortodossia
or·thogo·nal [ɔːˈθɒgənəl] ADJ ortogonale
or·thog·ra·phy [ɔːˈθɒgrəfɪ] N ortografia
ortho·paedic, *(Am)* **ortho·pedic** [ˌɔːθəʊˈpiːdɪk] ADJ ortopedico(-a)
ortho·paedics, *(Am)* **ortho·pedics** [ˌɔːθəʊˈpiːdɪks] NSG ortopedia
ortho·paedist, *(Am)* **ortho·pedist** [ˌɔːθəʊˈpiːdɪst] N ortopedico
OS [ˌəʊˈɛs] ABBR *(Brit)* **1** (= **Ordnance Survey**) ≈ IGM *m* (= *Istituto Geografico Militare*) **2** *(Naut)* = **ordinary seaman 3** *(clothes)* = **outsize**
O/S ABBR = *out of stock*; *see* **stock**
Os·car [ˈɒskəʳ] N *(film award)* Oscar *m inv*
os·cil·late [ˈɒsɪˌleɪt] VI oscillare
os·cil·lat·ing [ˈɒsɪˌleɪtɪŋ] ADJ oscillante
os·cil·la·tion [ˌɒsɪˈleɪʃən] N oscillazione *f*
os·cil·la·tor [ˈɒsɪˌleɪtəʳ] N oscillatore *m*
os·cil·lo·scope [ɒˈsɪləˌskəʊp] N oscilloscopio
osier [ˈəʊzɪəʳ] N vinco
Oslo [ˈɒzləʊ] N Oslo *f*
os·mium [ˈɒzmɪəm] N osmio
os·mo·sis [ɒzˈməʊsɪs] N osmosi *f*
os·mot·ic [ɒzˈmɒtɪk] ADJ osmotico(-a)
os·prey [ˈɒspreɪ] N falco pescatore
os·si·cle [ˈɒsɪkəl] N ossicino
os·si·fi·ca·tion [ˌɒsɪfɪˈkeɪʃən] N ossificazione *f*; *(fig: of ideas)* fossilizzazione *f*
os·si·fy [ˈɒsɪˌfaɪ] VI ossificarsi
os·ten·sible [ɒsˈtɛnsəbl] ADJ apparente; **ostensible reason** pretesto
os·ten·sibly [ɒsˈtɛnsəblɪ] ADV apparentemente
os·ten·ta·tion [ˌɒstɛnˈteɪʃən] N ostentazione *f*
os·ten·ta·tious [ˌɒstɛnˈteɪʃəs] ADJ *(lifestyle)* pretenzioso(-a); *(gesture, wealth)* ostentato(-a); **to be ostentatious about sth** ostentare qc
os·ten·ta·tious·ly [ˌɒstɛnˈteɪʃəslɪ] ADV con ostentazione
osteo... [ˈɒstɪəʊ] PREF osteo...
os·teo·ar·thri·tis [ˌɒstɪəʊɑːˈθraɪtɪs] N osteoartrite *f*
os·teo·my·eli·tis [ˌɒstɪəʊˌmaɪɪˈlaɪtɪs] N osteomielite *f*
os·teo·path [ˈɒstɪəpæθ] N chiroterapista *m/f*
os·teopa·thy [ˌɒstɪˈɒpəθɪ] N chiroterapia

os·tra·cism ['ɒstrəsɪzəm] N (*frm*) ostracismo
os·tra·cize ['ɒstrəsaɪz] VT (*frm*) ostracizzare
os·trich ['ɒstrɪtʃ] N struzzo

DID YOU KNOW ...?
ostrich is not translated by the Italian word *ostrica*

OT ABBR (*Bible*: = **Old Testament**) VT *m* (= *Vecchio Testamento*)
OTB N ABBR (*Am*: = **off-track betting**) *puntate effettuate fuori dagli ippodromi*
OTC [ˌəʊtiː'siː] ADJ ABBR (*drugs* = **over-the-counter**) da banco
OTE ABBR (= **on-target earnings**) *stipendio (comprese le commissioni) obiettivo di un addetto alle vendite*
◎ **oth·er** ['ʌðəʳ] ADJ altro(-a); **the other one** l'altro(-a); **this one? — no, the other one** questo? no, l'altro; **other people** altri, altre persone *fpl*; **have you got these jeans in other colours?** avete questi jeans in altri colori?; **some other people have still to arrive** deve ancora arrivare altra gente; **the other day** l'altro giorno; **some other time** un'altra volta, un altro momento; **if there are no other questions ...** se non ci sono altre domande...; **some actor or other** un certo attore; **other people's property** la proprietà altrui
■ PRON: **the other** l'altro(-a); **the others** gli altri/le altre; **the others are going but I'm not** gli altri ci vanno ma io no; **one after the other** uno(-a) dopo l'altro(-a); **are there any others?** ce ne sono altri?; **one or other of them will come** o uno o l'altro verrà; **somebody or other** qualcuno(-a); **no other** (*nobody else*) nessun altro/nessun'altra; (*old: nothing else*) nient'altro
■ ADV: **other (than)** (*differently*) diversamente (da); **he could not act other than as he did** non poteva agire diversamente (da come fece); **somewhere or other** da qualche parte
■ PREP: **other (than)** (*except*) tranne (che); **nothing other than** nient'altro che; **she never discussed it with anyone other than David** non ne ha parlato con nessun altro a parte *or* all'infuori di David; **none other than** (*no less than*) nientemeno che; **the car was none other than Roberta's** la macchina era proprio di Roberta
oth·er·ness ['ʌðənɪs] N diversità
◎ **other·wise** ['ʌðəˌwaɪz] ADV **1** (*in another way*) diversamente; **it cannot be otherwise** non può essere diversamente *or* altrimenti; **she was otherwise engaged** aveva già altri impegni; **except where otherwise stated** salvo indicazione contraria; **whether sold or otherwise** venduto o no **2** (*in other respects*) altrimenti, a parte ciò; **I'm tired, but otherwise I'm fine** sono stanco, ma a parte ciò sto bene; **an otherwise good piece of work** un lavoro per il resto buono
■ CONJ (*if not*) altrimenti, se no; **note down the number, otherwise you'll forget it** scriviti il numero, altrimenti te lo dimentichi
other-worldly [ˌʌðə'wɜːldlɪ] ADJ (*person*) disinteressato(-a) alle cose materiali
OTOH [ˌəʊtiːəʊ'eɪtʃ] ABBR (= **on the other hand**) d'altra parte
OTT [ˌəʊtiː'tiː] ABBR (*fam*) (= **over the top**) *see* **top**
Ot·ta·wa ['ɒtəwə] N Ottawa
▷ www.city.ottawa.on.ca
ot·ter ['ɒtəʳ] N lontra
OU [ˌəʊ'juː] N ABBR (*Brit*) = **Open University**
ouch [aʊtʃ] EXCL ohi!, ahi!
ought¹ [ɔːt] N = **aught**
◎ **ought²** [ɔːt] (*pt* **ought**) MODAL AUX VB **1** (*moral obligation*): **I ought to do it** dovrei farlo; **one ought not to do it** non lo si dovrebbe fare; **I ought to phone my parents** dovrei telefonare ai miei; **this ought to have been corrected** questo avrebbe dovuto essere corretto **2** (*vague desirability*): **you ought to go and see it** dovresti andare a vederlo, faresti bene ad andarlo a vedere **3** (*probability*): **that ought to be enough** quello dovrebbe bastare; **he ought to have arrived by now** dovrebbe essere arrivato, ormai; **he ought to win** dovrebbe vincere
Ouija board® ['wɪdʒəˌbɔːd] N *tavoletta con le lettere per le sedute spiritiche*
ounce [aʊns] N oncia (= *28,35 grammi; 16 in una libbra*)
◎ **our** ['aʊəʳ] POSS ADJ il nostro/la nostra, i nostri/le nostre *pl*; **this is our house** questa è la nostra casa; **at our house** a casa nostra; **our brother** nostro fratello; **our dog** il nostro cane; **we took off our coats** ci siamo tolti i cappotti; **we washed our hair** ci siamo lavati i capelli
ours ['aʊəz] POSS PRON il/la nostro(-a), i/le nostri(-e) *pl*; **a friend of ours** un nostro amico; **theirs is red, ours is green** il loro è rosso, il nostro è verde; **this is ours** questo è (il) nostro
◎ **our·selves** [ˌaʊə'sɛlvz] PERS PRON (*reflexive*) ci; (*emphatic, after preposition*) noi stessi(-e); **we did it (all) by ourselves** l'abbiamo fatto (tutto) da soli; **we really enjoyed ourselves** ci siamo divertiti moltissimo; **we built our garage ourselves** il garage l'abbiamo costruito noi; **by ourselves** da soli; **we don't like travelling by ourselves** non ci piace viaggiare da soli; *see also* **oneself**
oust [aʊst] VT: **to oust sb from sth** spodestare qn da qc

Oo

◎ **out** [aʊt] KEYWORD
■ ADV
1 (*gen*) fuori; **to be out and about again** (*Brit*) *or* **to be out and around again** (*Am*) essere di nuovo in piedi; **the ball is out** (*Sport*) la palla è fuori; **out here** qui fuori; **they're out in the garden** sono fuori in giardino; **Mr Green is out** il signor Green non c'è *or* è uscito; **the journey out** l'andata; **to have a night out** passare una serata fuori; **speak out (loud)!** parla forte!; **out there** là fuori; **out with it!** sputa fuori!; **out!** (*Tennis*) fuori!
2 (*indicating distance*): **three days out from Plymouth** (*Naut*) a tre giorni di navigazione da Plymouth; **she's out in Kuwait** è via in Kuwait; **the boat was 10 miles out** la barca era a 10 miglia dalla costa; **it carried us out to sea** ci portò al largo
3 (*fig*): **to be out** (*person: unconscious*) essere privo(-a) di sensi; (*: on strike*) essere in sciopero; (*: out of game etc*) essere eliminato(-a); (*out of fashion*) essere out *inv or* passato(-a) di moda; (*have appeared: sun, moon*) splendere; (*: flowers*) sbocciare; (*: news, secret*) essere rivelato(-a); (*: book*) uscire; (*extinguished: fire, light, gas*) essere spento(-a); **she is out and away the best** è di gran lunga la migliore; **it's the biggest swindle out** è la truffa più grossa che ci sia; **I was not far out** non mi sbagliavo di tanto; **he was out in his reckoning (by 5%)** si sbagliava nei suoi calcoli (del 5%); **the tide is out** c'è bassa marea; **before the week was out** prima della fine della settimana
4 **to be out for sth** cercare qc, volere qc; **he's out for all he can get** sta cercando di trarne il massimo profitto; **I'm out for a good time** voglio divertirmi

5 **to be out to do sth** essere deciso(-a) a far qc, cercare di far qc; **they're out to get me** mi danno la caccia; **he's out to make money** il suo unico scopo è quello di fare soldi

■ **out of** prep

1 (*outside, beyond*) fuori; **to be out of danger** essere fuori pericolo; **to disappear out of sight** sparire alla vista; **to feel out of it** (*fam*) sentirsi escluso(-a); **to go out of the house** uscire di casa; **to look out of the window** guardare fuori dalla finestra; **to be out of sight** non essere visibile; **we're well out of it** (*fam*) per fortuna ne siamo fuori

2 (*cause, motive*) per; **out of curiosity** per curiosità

3 (*origin, source*) da; **to copy sth out of a book** copiare qc da un libro; **to drink sth out of a cup** bere qc da una tazza; **Blue Ribbon, by Black Rum out of Grenada** (*esp Horse-breeding*) Blue Ribbon, figlio di Black Rum e Grenada; **a box made out of wood** una scatola di *or* in legno; **it was like something out of a nightmare** era come in un incubo; **to take sth out of a drawer** prendere qc da un cassetto

4 (*from among*) su; **1 out of every 3 smokers** 1 fumatore su 3; **9 marks out of 10** 9 punti su 10

5 (*without*) senza; **to be out of sth** essere rimasto(-a) senza qc; **to be out of breath** essere senza fiato; **to be out of petrol** essere (rimasto(-a)) senza benzina; **it's out of stock** (*Comm*) non è disponibile

■ N *see* **in** N

■ VT: **to out sb** rivelare pubblicamente l'omosessualità di qn

out·age ['aʊtɪdʒ] N (*esp Am: power failure*) black-out *m inv*, interruzione *f* (dell'erogazione) della corrente elettrica

out-and-out ['aʊtən'aʊt] ADJ vero(-a) e proprio(-a)

out·back ['aʊt,bæk] N (*in Australia*) entroterra *m*

out·bid [,aʊt'bɪd] (*pt, pp* **outbid**) VT offrire di più di

out·board ['aʊt,bɔːd] ADJ, N: **outboard (motor)** (motore *m*) fuoribordo *inv*

out·bound ['aʊt,baʊnd] ADJ: **outbound (for** *or* **from)** in partenza (per *or* da)

out·box ['aʊt,bɒks] N (*Comput*) (cartella della) posta in uscita

out·break ['aʊt,breɪk] N (*of war*) scoppio; (*of disease*) insorgenza; (*of food poisoning*) epidemia; (*of crime*) ondata; **an outbreak of cholera** un'epidemia di colera; **at the outbreak of war** allo scoppio della guerra

out·build·ing ['aʊt,bɪldɪŋ] N costruzione *f* annessa

out·burst ['aʊt,bɜːst] N (*of anger*) scoppio; (*of applause*) scroscio

out·cast ['aʊt,kɑːst] N reietto(-a); (*socially*) emarginato(-a)

out·class [,aʊt'klɑːs] VT surclassare

◎ **out·come** ['aʊt,kʌm] N esito, risultato

out·crop ['aʊt,krɒp] N affioramento

out·cry ['aʊt,kraɪ] N protesta; **to raise an outcry about sth** protestare contro qc; **the incident caused an international outcry** l'incidente sollevò una protesta internazionale

out·dat·ed [,aʊt'deɪtɪd] ADJ (*idea*) antiquato(-a), sorpassato(-a); (*custom, clothes*) fuori moda; **outdated equipment** attrezzature sorpassate

out·did [,aʊt'dɪd] PT *of* **outdo**

out·distance [,aʊt'dɪstəns] VT distanziare

out·do [,aʊt'duː] (*pt* **outdid**, *pp* **outdone** [,aʊt'dʌn]) VT: **to outdo sb (in)** superare qn (in); **he was not to be outdone** non voleva essere da meno

out·door ['aʊt'dɔːʳ] ADJ (*activity*) all'aperto; (*life*) all'aria aperta; (*swimming pool*) scoperto(-a); (*clothes*) pesante; **an outdoor swimming pool** una piscina scoperta; **outdoor activities** attività *fpl* all'aperto

out·doors [,aʊt'dɔːz] ADV (*go*) fuori; (*live, sleep*) all'aria aperta

■ NSG: **the great outdoors** l'aria aperta

out·er ['aʊtəʳ] ADJ esterno(-a); **the outer wall** il muro esterno; **outer suburbs** estrema periferia

outer·most ['aʊtə,məʊst] ADJ estremo(-a), più lontano(-a)

outer space N spazio cosmico; **a creature from outer space** un/una extraterrestre *m/f*

out·field ['aʊt,fiːld] N (*Sport*) outfield *m inv*; *parte del campo distante dal battitore*

out·field·er ['aʊt,fiːldəʳ] N (*Sport*) esterno

out·fit ['aʊt,fɪt] N **1** (*clothes*) completo; (*for sports*) tenuta; (*for dressing up*) costume *m* **2** (*equipment*) attrezzatura **3** (*fam: organization*) organizzazione *f*

out·fit·ter ['aʊt,fɪtəʳ] N: **"(gent's) outfitters"** (*Brit*) "confezioni *mpl* da uomo"; **sports outfitter's** negozio di articoli sportivi

out·flank [,aʊt'flæŋk] VT (*Mil*) aggirare; (*outdo*) prendere in contropiede

out·flow ['aʊt,fləʊ] N (*for liquid*) scarico

out·fox [,aʊt'fɒks] VT superare in astuzia

out·go·ing ['aʊt,gəʊɪŋ] ADJ **1** (*president, tenant*) uscente; (*means of transport*) in partenza **2** (*character*) socievole, estroverso(-a); **she's very outgoing** è molto estroversa

out·go·ings ['aʊt,gəʊɪŋz] NPL (*Brit: expenses*) spese *fpl*, uscite *fpl*

out·grow [,aʊt'grəʊ] VT (*pt* **outgrew** [,aʊt'gruː], *pp* **outgrown** [,aʊt'grəʊn]) (*clothes*) diventare troppo grande per; (*habit, attitude*) perdere (col tempo)

out·growth ['aʊt,grəʊθ] N sviluppo

out·house ['aʊt,haʊs] N = **outbuilding**

out·ing ['aʊtɪŋ] N gita, escursione *f*; **to go on an outing** andare in gita

out·land·ish [aʊt'lændɪʃ] ADJ (*dress, person*) bizzarro(-a)

out·last [,aʊt'lɑːst] VT sopravvivere a

out·law ['aʊt,lɔː] N fuorilegge *m/f inv*

■ VT (*person, practice*) bandire

out·lay ['aʊt,leɪ] N spesa

out·let ['aʊtlɛt] N (*for water, sewage*) scarico; (*for air*) sfogo; (*of river*) foce *f*; (*Comm*) mercato; (*also:* **retail outlet**) punto *m* (di) vendita *inv*; (*Am Elec*) presa di corrente; (*fig: for emotion, talents*) (valvola di) sfogo; **the washing machine outlet** lo scarico della lavatrice; **an outlet for his incredible energy** una valvola di sfogo per la sua incredibile energia; **there was only one outlet on the wall** c'era una sola presa di corrente nel muro

■ ADJ (*Tech*) di scarico

◎ **out·line** ['aʊt,laɪn] N (*of object*) contorno; (*of face, building*) profilo; (*summary, general idea*) abbozzo; **outlines** NPL aspetti *mpl* generali; **the outline of the building** il contorno dell'edificio; **give me the broad outline(s)** spiegamelo a grandi linee; **this is an outline of the plan** questo è un abbozzo del progetto

■ VT (*theory, plan, idea*) abbozzare; (*book, event, facts*) descrivere a grandi linee; **to be outlined against sth** (*in silhouette*) stagliarsi contro qc

out·live [,aʊt'lɪv] VT sopravvivere a

out·look [ˈaʊtˌlʊk] N (*view*) vista, veduta; (*prospects*) prospettive *fpl*; (*opinion*) visione *f*, concezione *f*; **the outlook for next Saturday is sunny** si prevede bel tempo per sabato prossimo; **it changed my outlook on life** ha cambiato la mia visione della vita; **the uncertain outlook of the motor industry** le prospettive incerte dell'industria automobilistica; **weather outlook** previsioni *fpl* meteorologiche

out·ly·ing [ˈaʊtˌlaɪɪŋ] ADJ (*distant*) fuori mano; (*outside town boundary*) periferico(-a)

out·ma·noeu·vre, (*Am*) **out·ma·neu·ver** [ˌaʊtməˈnuːvəʳ] VT (*Mil*) superare strategicamente; (*fig: rival, opposition*) surclassare

out·mod·ed [ˌaʊtˈməʊdɪd] ADJ = **outdated; an outmoded system** un sistema superato

out·num·ber [ˌaʊtˈnʌmbəʳ] VT superare numericamente

out-of-court [ˈaʊtəvˈkɔːt] ADJ (*settlement*) extragiudiziale
■ ADV (*settle*) senza ricorrere al tribunale

out-of-date [ˌaʊtəvˈdeɪt] ADJ (*passport, ticket*) scaduto(-a); (*theory, idea*) sorpassato(-a), superato(-a); (*custom*) antiquato(-a); (*clothes*) fuori moda; **your credit card is out-of-date** la sua carta di credito è scaduta; **out-of-date medical knowledge** conoscenze *fpl* mediche superate; **out-of-date power stations** centrali *fpl* elettriche obsolete

out-of-doors [ˌaʊtəvˈdɔːz] ADV = **outdoors**

out-of-pocket [ˌaʊtəvˈpɒkɪt] ADJ (*person*) a corto di soldi; **out-of-pocket expenses** spese *fpl* extra *inv*

out-of-the-way [ˌaʊtəvðəˈweɪ] ADJ (*remote*) fuori mano; (*unusual*) insolito(-a)

out-of-work [ˌaʊtɒvˈwɜːk] ADJ (*actor*) disoccupato(-a)

out·pace [ˌaʊtˈpeɪs] VT distanziare

out·pa·tient [ˈaʊtˌpeɪʃənt] N paziente *m/f* esterno(-a); **outpatients' department** ambulatorio (*all'interno di un ospedale*)

out·post [ˈaʊtˌpəʊst] N (*Mil, fig*) avamposto

out·pour·ing [ˈaʊtˌpɔːrɪŋ] N (*fig*) torrente *m*

◎ **out·put** [ˈaʊtˌpʊt] N (*of machine, factory*) produzione *f*; (*of person*) rendimento; (*of computer*) output *m inv*, dati *mpl* in uscita; (*Elec*) erogazione *f*; **their industrial output** la loro produzione industriale
■ VT (*Comput*) emettere

out·rage [ˈaʊtˌreɪdʒ] N (*wicked, violent deed*) atrocità *f inv*; (*emotion*) sdegno; **bomb outrage** attentato dinamitardo; **who would have committed this latest outrage?** chi può aver commesso le ultime atrocità?; **it caused a public outrage** ha provocato uno scandalo; **an outrage against good taste** un oltraggio al buon gusto; **an outrage against humanity** un crimine contro l'umanità; **it's an outrage!** è una vergogna!, è uno scandalo!
■ VT offendere; **to be outraged by sth** essere scandalizzato(-a) da qc

out·ra·geous [aʊtˈreɪdʒəs] ADJ (*language, joke: offensive*) scioccante; (*price*) esorbitante; (*clothes*) stravagante; (*crime*) atroce; **it's outrageous that ...** è scandaloso che...; **her behaviour was outrageous** il suo comportamento è stato scandaloso; **the prices they charge are outrageous** hanno prezzi esorbitanti

out·ra·geous·ly [aʊtˈreɪdʒəslɪ] ADV (*see adj*) in modo scioccante; in modo stravagante; in modo atroce; (*expensive*) terribilmente

out·ran [ˌaʊtˈræn] PT *of* **outrun**

out·reach [ˈaʊtriːtʃ] N: **outreach programme** *programma mirante a diffondere la conoscenza dei servizi sociali disponibili a chi potrebbe averne bisogno*

out·rid·er [ˈaʊtˌraɪdəʳ] N (*on motorcycle*) battistrada *m inv*

out·right [*adv* ˌaʊtˈraɪt; *adj* ˈaʊtˌraɪt] ADV (*kill*) sul colpo; (*win*) nettamente; (*own*) completamente; (*buy*) tutto(-a) in una volta; (*refuse, reject*) categoricamente; **he was killed outright** è morto sul colpo
■ ADJ (*winner, refusal*) netto(-a); (*liar, selfishness*) bell'e buono(-a)

out·run [ˌaʊtˈrʌn] (*pt* **outran**, *pp* **outrun**) VT superare (nella corsa); (*fig*) superare

out·sell [ˌaʊtˈsɛl] VT (*product*): **to outsell sth** vendersi meglio di qc

out·set [ˈaʊtˌsɛt] N: **at the outset** all'inizio

out·shine [ˌaʊtˈʃaɪn] (*pt, pp* **outshone** [ˌaʊtˈʃɒn]) VT (*fig*) eclissare

◎ **out·side** [ˌaʊtˈsaɪd] ADV fuori, all'esterno; **to be/go outside** stare/andare fuori; **seen from outside** visto(-a) dall'esterno *or* da fuori; **it's very cold outside** fa molto freddo fuori
■ PREP **1** fuori di, all'esterno di; **the car outside the house** la macchina fuori della casa; **he waited outside the door** aspettò fuori della porta; **outside the city/school** fuori (della) città/scuola; **don't go outside the garden** non uscire dal giardino **2** (*not included in*) al di fuori di; **outside school hours** al di fuori dell'orario scolastico; **he has no interests outside his job** non ha altri interessi al di fuori del lavoro; **it's outside my experience** non ne ho una conoscenza diretta
■ ADJ **1** (*exterior*) esterno(-a); **an outside seat** (*in bus, plane*) un posto vicino al corridoio; **outside contractor** appaltatore *m* esterno; **the outside walls** le mura esterne; **to get an outside opinion** chiedere un parere imparziale **2** (*maximum: price*) massimo(-a), massimale **3** (*remote, unlikely*): **an outside chance** una vaga possibilità
■ N esterno; **the outside of the house** l'esterno della casa; **to overtake on the outside** (*Aut*) ≈ sorpassare sulla sinistra; **judging from the outside** (*fig*) a giudicare dalle apparenze; **at the (very) outside** (*fig*) al massimo

outside broadcast N (*Radio, TV*) trasmissione *f* in esterni

outside lane N (*Aut*) ≈ corsia di sorpasso

outside left N (*Ftbl*) ala sinistra

outside line N (*Telec*) linea esterna

out·sid·er [ˌaʊtˈsaɪdəʳ] N (*stranger*) estraneo(-a); (*in racing, contest*) outsider *m/f inv*; **he felt an outsider** si sentiva un estraneo; **the race was won by an outsider** la corsa è stata vinta da un outsider

outside right N (*Ftbl*) ala destra

out·size [ˈaʊtˌsaɪz] ADJ (*gen*) gigante; (*clothes*) per taglie forti; **outsize department** reparto taglie forti

out·sized [ˈaʊtˌsaɪzd] ADJ enorme, gigantesco(-a)

out·skirts [ˈaʊtˌskɜːts] NPL (*of town*) sobborghi *mpl*, periferia *fsg*; (*of wood*) limitare *msg*, margine *msg*; **on the outskirts of town** in periferia

out·smart [ˌaʊtˈsmɑːt] VT superare in astuzia

out·source [ˌaʊtˈsɔːs] VT esternalizzare

out·sourcing [ˌaʊtˈsɔːsɪŋ] N (*Econ*) esternalizzazione *f*

out·spo·ken [ˌaʊtˈspəʊkən] ADJ franco(-a), senza peli sulla lingua (*fam*)

out·spo·ken·ly [ˌaʊtˈspəʊkənlɪ] ADV (*support, condemn*) apertamente; **outspokenly in favour of** apertamente in favore di

out·spo·ken·ness [ˌaʊtˈspəʊkənnɪs] N il parlare franco

Oo

out·spread ['aʊt,sprɛd] ADJ (*gen*) aperto(-a); (*wings*) spiegato(-a)

◎**out·stand·ing** [,aʊt'stændɪŋ] ADJ **1** (*exceptional*) eccezionale; (*: feature*) saliente **2** (*not settled: bill*) non pagato(-a); (*: problem*) irrisolto(-a); **the work is still outstanding** il lavoro non è ancora stato finito; **your account is still outstanding** deve ancora saldare il conto

out·stand·ing·ly [,aʊt'stændɪŋlɪ] ADV eccezionalmente

out·stay [,aʊt'steɪ] VT: **to outstay sb** trattenersi più a lungo di qn; **to outstay one's welcome** abusare dell'ospitalità di qn

out·stretched [,aʊt'strɛtʃt] ADJ (*body, legs*) disteso(-a), steso(-a); (*hand*) teso(-a); **with outstretched arms** a braccia aperte

out·strip [,aʊt'strɪp] VT (*also fig*) superare

out-take ['aʊt,teɪk] N *pezzo di pellicola scartato di un film o di un programma televisivo che normalmente non viene mostrato al pubblico*

out-tray ['aʊt,treɪ] N *vassoio per la corrispondenza e gli ordini da evadere*

out·vote [,aʊt'vəʊt] VT: **it was outvoted (by ...)** fu respinto (con una maggioranza di...); **I wanted to go dancing but I was outvoted** volevo andare a ballare ma mi hanno messo in minoranza

out·ward ['aʊtwəd] ADJ **1** (*movement*) verso l'esterno; **on the outward journey** durante il viaggio di andata **2** (*sign, appearances*) esteriore; **with an outward show of interest** mostrando un apparente interesse

out·ward·ly ['aʊtwədlɪ] ADV (*on the surface*) esteriormente; (*apparently*) apparentemente; **worried but outwardly calm** preoccupato(-a) ma all'apparenza calmo(-a)

out·wards, out·ward ['aʊtwəd(z)] ADV verso l'esterno; **outward bound** in partenza

out·wash ['aʊt,wɒʃ] N depositi *mpl* fluvio-glaciali

out·weigh [,aʊt'weɪ] VT avere maggior peso di

out·wit [,aʊt'wɪt] VT essere più furbo(-a) di

out·with [,aʊt'wɪθ] PREP (*Scot*) = **outside**

out·work ['aʊt,wɜːk] N lavoro a domicilio

out·work·er ['aʊt,wɜːkə^r] N lavoratore(-trice) a domicilio

out·worn ['aʊtwɔːn] ADJ (*idea, expression*) trito(-a); (*custom*) sorpassato(-a)

ouzo ['uːzəʊ] N *liquore greco a base di anice*

oval ['əʊvəl] ADJ, N ovale (*m*)

Oval Office N *ufficio del Presidente degli Stati Uniti*

OVAL OFFICE

L'**Oval Office** è una grande stanza di forma ovale nella "White House", la Casa Bianca, dove ha sede l'ufficio del Presidente degli Stati Uniti. Spesso il termine è usato per indicare la stessa presidenza degli Stati Uniti.

▷ www.whitehouse.gov/president/

ovar·ian [,əʊ'vɛərɪən] ADJ ovarico(-a)

ova·ry ['əʊvərɪ] N (*Anat*) ovaia; (*Bot*) ovario

ova·tion [əʊ'veɪʃən] N ovazione *f*

oven ['ʌvn] N forno; **in the oven** al forno; **it's like an oven in there** è un forno lì dentro

oven glove N guanto da forno

oven·proof ['ʌvn,pruːf] ADJ: **ovenproof dish** pirofila

oven-ready [,ʌvn'rɛdɪ] ADJ pronto(-a) da infornare

oven·ware ['ʌvn,wɛə^r] N pirofile *fpl*

◎**over** ['əʊvə^r] ADV KEYWORD

1 (*across*): **over here** qui; **over there** laggiù, là; **over in France** in Francia; **he's over from France for a few days** è venuto dalla Francia per alcuni giorni; **over against the wall** (lì *or* là) contro il muro; **the little boy went over to his mother** il bambino andò da sua madre; **to drive over to the other side of town** andare (in macchina) dall'altra parte della città; **can you come over tonight?** puoi venire da me (*or* noi) stasera?; **over to you!** (*TV, Radio*) a te (la linea)!; **now over to our Paris correspondent** diamo ora la linea al nostro corrispondente da Parigi; **to go over to the enemy** passare al nemico

2 (*everywhere*): **the world over** in tutto il mondo; **I ache all over** mi fa male dappertutto; **I looked all over for you** ti ho cercato dappertutto; **that's him all over** è proprio da lui

3 (*indicating movement from one side to another, from upright position*): **to turn sth over (and over)** girare (e rigirare) qc; **she hit me and over I went** mi ha colpito e sono caduto

4 (*finished*) finito(-a); **the rain is over** la pioggia è cessata; **the danger was soon over** il pericolo cessò presto; **I'll be happy when the exams are over** sarò contento quando gli esami saranno finiti; **it's all over between us** tra noi è tutto finito

5 (*again*): **to tell over and over** dire mille volte; **to start (all) over again** ricominciare da capo; **several times over** diverse volte

6 (*excessively*) molto, troppo; **she's not over intelligent** (*Brit*) non è molto intelligente

7 (*remaining*) rimasto(-a); **there are three over** ne sono rimasti tre; **is there any cake left over?** è rimasta della torta?

8 (*more*): **persons of 21 and over** persone dai 21 anni in su

9 (*esp in signalling and radio*): **over and out** passo e chiudo

■ PREP

1 (*on top of, above*) su; **to spread a sheet over sth** stendere un lenzuolo su qc; **there's a mirror over the washbasin** sopra il lavandino c'è uno specchio; **over my head** sopra la mia testa; **his speech went over my head** (*fig*) il suo discorso era troppo complicato per me; **he's over me** è un mio superiore; **to have an advantage over sb** avere un vantaggio su qn

2 (*across*): **the pub over the road** il pub di fronte; **it's over the river** è al di là del fiume; **the shop is over the road** il negozio è dall'altra parte della strada; **the bridge over the river** il ponte sul fiume; **the ball went over the wall** la palla andò al di là del muro, la palla è andata oltre il muro; **over the page** alla pagina seguente

3 (*everywhere in/on*): **all over the world** in tutto il mondo; **all over Scotland** in tutta la Scozia; **you've got mud all over your shoes** hai le scarpe tutte infangate

4 (*more than*): **over 200** più di 200; **he must be over 60** deve aver superato i 60; **it's over twenty kilos** pesa oltre venti chili; **over and above normal requirements** oltre ai soliti requisiti; **an increase of 5% over last year's total** un aumento del 5% rispetto al totale dell'anno scorso

5 (*during*) durante, nel corso di; **over the last few years** nel corso degli ultimi anni; **over the summer/ winter** durante l'estate/l'inverno; **over Christmas** durante il periodo natalizio; **let's discuss it over**

dinner discutiamone a cena; **how long will you be over it?** quanto tempo ti prenderà?
6 *(means)*: **I heard it over the radio** l'ho sentito alla radio
7 *(about, concerning)*: **they fell out over money** litigarono per una questione di denaro

over... ['əʊvəʳ] PREF, E.G. **overabundance** N sovrabbondanza; **overprotective** ADJ superprotettivo(-a)
over·abun·dant [,əʊvərə'bʌndənt] ADJ sovrabbondante
over·achieve [,əʊvərə'tʃi:v] VI andare troppo oltre le aspettative
over·achiev·er [,əʊvərə'tʃi:vəʳ] N *persona che ottiene risultati troppo superiori alle aspettative*
over·act [,əʊvər'ækt] VI recitare con troppa enfasi
over·ac·tive [,əʊvər'æktɪv] ADJ troppo attivo(-a); *(imagination)* sbrigliato(-a); **she's got an overactive thyroid** soffre di ipertiroidismo
over-age [,əʊvər'eɪdʒ] ADJ che ha superato il limite d'età; *(fig)* troppo vecchio(-a)
◎ **over·all** [,əʊvər'ɔ:l] ADJ *(improvement)* generale; *(width, length)* totale; **overall dimensions** *(Aut)* ingombro; **overall placings** *(Sport)* classifica generale; **overall improvement** miglioramento generale; **overall majority** maggioranza assoluta; **overall total** somma complessiva; **what was your overall impression?** nel complesso che impressione ti ha fatto?
■ ADV nell'insieme, complessivamente; **overall I was disappointed** nel complesso sono rimasto deluso
■ N *(Brit)* camice *m*
overall majority N maggioranza assoluta
over·alls ['əʊvərɔ:lz] NPL tuta (da lavoro)
over·anx·ious [,əʊvər'æŋkʃəs] ADJ troppo ansioso(-a)
over·arch [,əʊvər'ɑ:tʃ] VT formare un arco sopra
over·ate [,əʊvər'eɪt] PT *of* **overeat**
over·awe [,əʊvər'ɔ:] VT intimidire
over·bal·ance [,əʊvə'bæləns] VI sbilanciarsi
■ VT sbilanciare
over·bear·ing [,əʊvə'bɛərɪŋ] ADJ autoritario(-a), prepotente
over·board ['əʊvə,bɔ:d] ADV *(Naut)* fuori bordo; **to fall overboard** cadere in mare; **man overboard!** uomo in mare!; **to go overboard for sth** *(fig)* impazzire per qc
over·book [,əʊvə'bʊk] VI, VT *accettare troppe prenotazioni rispetto alla disponibilità di posti*
over·bur·den [,əʊvə'bɜ:dn] VT sovraccaricare
over·came [,əʊvə'keɪm] PT *of* **overcome**
over·ca·pac·ity [,əʊvəkə'pæsɪtɪ] N eccesso di capacità produttiva
over·capi·tal·ize [,əʊvə'kæpɪtə,laɪz] VT *(Fin)* sovracapitalizzare
over·cast ['əʊvə,kɑ:st] ADJ nuvoloso(-a), coperto(-a)
over·cau·tious [,əʊvə'kɔ:ʃəs] ADJ troppo cauto(-a)
over·cau·tious·ness [,əʊvə'kɔ:ʃəsnɪs] N eccessiva cautela
over·charge [,əʊvə'tʃɑ:dʒ] VT **1 to overcharge sb for sth** far pagare troppo qc a qn; **they overcharged us for the meal** ci hanno fatto pagare troppo per il pranzo **2** *(Elec)* sovraccaricare
over·coat ['əʊvə,kəʊt] N *(light)* soprabito; *(heavy)* cappotto
◎ **over·come** [,əʊvə'kʌm] *(pt* **overcame**, *pp* **overcome**) VT *(enemies)* sopraffare; *(obstacle, difficulty)* superare; *(rage, temptation)* vincere; *(sb's doubts)* dissolvere; **to be overcome by the heat** essere sopraffatto(-a) dall'afa; **to be overcome by remorse** essere preso(-a) dal rimorso; **overcome with grief** sopraffatto(-a) dal dolore; **she was quite overcome by the occasion** era oltremodo emozionata per l'evento; **I'm sure we can overcome these difficulties** sono certo che possiamo superare queste difficoltà; **they were overcome by fumes** sono stati sopraffatti dai vapori
over·con·fi·dence [,əʊvə'kɒnfɪdəns] N eccessiva sicurezza (di sé), presunzione *f*
over·con·fi·dent [,əʊvə'kɒnfɪdənt] ADJ troppo sicuro(-a) (di sé), presuntuoso(-a)
over·cook [,əʊvə'kʊk] VT far cuocere troppo
over·crowd·ed [,əʊvə'kraʊdɪd] ADJ sovraffollato(-a)
over·crowd·ing [,əʊvə'kraʊdɪŋ] N *(in prison, housing)* sovraffollamento; *(in bus)* calca
over·do [,əʊvə'du:] *(pt* **overdid** [,əʊvə'dɪd], *pp* **overdone**) VT **1** *(exaggerate)* esagerare; **don't overdo these exercises** cerca di non strafare con questi esercizi (di ginnastica); **to overdo it** *or* **things** *(work too hard)* lavorare troppo; *(convalescent)* affaticarsi troppo
2 *(cook too long)* (far) cuocere troppo
over·done [,əʊvə'dʌn] PP *of* **overdo**
■ ADJ *(exaggerated)* esagerato(-a); *(overcooked)* troppo cotto(-a)
over·dose ['əʊvə,dəʊs] N overdose *f inv*
■ VI: **to overdose on** farsi un'overdose di
over·draft ['əʊvə,drɑ:ft] N *(Fin)* scoperto (di conto); **to have an overdraft at the bank** avere il conto scoperto
over·draw [,əʊvə'drɔ:] *(pt* **overdrew** [,əʊvə'dru:], *pp* **overdrawn** [,əʊvə'drɔ:n]) VI avere il conto scoperto
over·drawn [,əʊvə'drɔ:n] ADJ *(account)* scoperto(-a); **to be overdrawn** avere il conto scoperto; **I'm £200 overdrawn** sono in rosso di 200 sterline
over·dress [,əʊvə'drɛs] VI vestirsi in modo troppo elegante; **don't you think you're a bit overdressed?** non pensi di essere un po' troppo elegante?
over·drive ['əʊvə,draɪv] N *(Aut)* overdrive *m inv*
over·due [,əʊvə'dju:] ADJ *(bill, rent)* arretrato(-a); *(library book)* col prestito scaduto; *(train, bus)* in ritardo; *(recognition)* tardivo(-a); *(fam: baby, period)* in ritardo; **she's a week overdue** *(pregnant woman)* è in ritardo di una settimana *(sulla data prevista del parto)*; **this work is 2 days overdue** questo lavoro andava consegnato 2 giorni fa; **that change was long overdue** quel cambiamento ci voleva da tempo
over·eat [,əʊvər'i:t] *(pt* **overate**, *pp* **overeaten**) VI mangiare troppo
over·eat·ing [,əʊvər'i:tɪŋ] N iperalimentazione *f*; **obesity is only partly caused by overeating** l'obesità è causata solo parzialmente dall'iperalimentazione
over·em·pha·sis [,əʊvər'ɛmfəsɪs] N: **overemphasis on sth** importanza eccessiva data a qc
over·em·pha·size [,əʊvər'ɛmfə,saɪz] VT dare troppa enfasi a; **to overemphasize the importance of sth** esagerare l'importanza di qc
over·es·ti·mate [,əʊvər'ɛstɪ,meɪt] VT *(value, amount)* sovrastimare; *(fig: person, qualities)* sopravvalutare
over·es·ti·ma·tion [,əʊvərɛstɪ'meɪʃən] N sopravvalutazione *f*
over·ex·cit·ed [,əʊvərɪk'saɪtɪd] ADJ sovraeccitato(-a)
over·ex·ert [,əʊvərɪg'zɜ:t] VI: **to overexert o.s.** sovraffaticarsi
over·ex·er·tion [,əʊvərɪg'zɜ:ʃən] N iperaffaticamento, surmenage *m inv*
over·ex·pose [,əʊvərɪks'pəʊz] VT *(Phot)* sovraesporre
over·feed [,əʊvə'fi:d] *(pt, pp* **overfed** [,əʊvə'fɛd]) VT sovralimentare

Oo

over·feed·ing [ˌəʊvəˈfiːdɪŋ] N sovralimentazione *f*

over·flow [*n* ˈəʊvəˌfləʊ; *vb* ˌəʊvəˈfləʊ] N (*also:* **overflow pipe**) troppopieno; (*fig: people*): **the overflow filled the courtyard** quelli che non riuscirono ad entrare si accalcarono nel cortile
■ VI (*gen*) traboccare; (*river*) straripare; (*people*) riversarsi; **the theatre was overflowing with people** il teatro traboccava di gente

over·fly [ˌəʊvəˈflaɪ] (*pt* **overflew** [ˌəʊvəˈfluː], *pp* **overflown** [ˌəʊvəˈfləʊn]) VT sorvolare

over·full [ˌəʊvəˈfʊl] ADJ troppo pieno(-a)

over·gen·er·ous [ˌəʊvəˈdʒɛnərəs] ADJ troppo generoso(-a)

over·grown [ˈəʊvəˈgrəʊn] ADJ (*garden*): **overgrown with weeds/ivy** coperto(-a) di erbacce/edera; **he's just an overgrown schoolboy** è proprio un bambinone

over·hang [*vb* ˈəʊvəˈhæŋ; *n* ˈəʊvəˌhæŋ] (*vb: pt, pp* **overhung**) VT sporgere da
■ VI sporgere
■ N strapiombo

over·hang·ing [ˈəʊvəˈhæŋɪŋ] ADJ sporgente

over·haul [*n* ˈəʊvəˌhɔːl; *vb* ˌəʊvəˈhɔːl] N revisione *f*
■ VT (*service: machine*) revisionare; (*revise: system, method*) rivedere

over·head [*adv* ˌəʊvəˈhɛd; *adj* ˈəʊvəˌhɛd] ADV in alto
■ ADJ (*railway*) sopraelevato(-a); (*cable*) aereo(-a); **overhead shot** (*Tennis*) schiacciata; **overhead valve** (*Aut*) valvola in testa

overhead projector N lavagna luminosa

over·heads [ˈəʊvəˌhɛdz] NPL (*Brit*) costi *mpl* di gestione

over·hear [ˌəʊvəˈhɪəʳ] (*pt, pp* **overheard** [ˌəʊvəˈhɜːd]) VT (*accidentally*) sentire per caso; (*deliberately*) ascoltare; **she was overheard complaining** qualcuno l'ha sentita lamentarsi

over·heat [ˌəʊvəˈhiːt] VI (*engine, brakes*) surriscaldarsi
■ VT surriscaldare

over·heat·ed [ˌəʊvəˈhiːtɪd] ADJ (*debate*) surriscaldato(-a); (*person: angry*) arrabbiato(-a)

over·hung [ˈəʊvəˈhʌŋ] PT, PP *of* **overhang**

over·joyed [ˌəʊvəˈdʒɔɪd] ADJ: **overjoyed (at)** pazzo(-a) di gioia (per)

over·kill [ˈəʊvəˌkɪl] N (*Mil*) potenziale *m* (nucleare) superiore al necessario; (*fig*) esagerazione *f*

over·land [ˈəʊvəˌlænd] ADV, ADJ per via di terra

over·lap [*n* ˈəʊvəˌlæp; *vb* ˌəʊvəˈlæp] N sovrapposizione *f*; (*fig*) coincidenza
■ VI sovrapporsi; (*fig*) coincidere
■ VT sovrapporre

over·lay [ˌəʊvəˈleɪ] (*pt, pp* **overlaid** [ˌəʊvəˈleɪd]) VT ricoprire

over·leaf [ˌəʊvəˈliːf] ADV a tergo

over·load [*n* ˈəʊvəˌləʊd; *vb* ˌəʊvəˈləʊd] N sovraccarico
■ VT sovraccaricare

over·look [ˌəʊvəˈlʊk] VT **1** (*subj: building*) dare su; **the hotel overlooked the beach** l'albergo dava sulla spiaggia; **our garden is not overlooked** nel nostro giardino nessuno ci può vedere **2** (*not notice*) lasciarsi sfuggire, trascurare; (*tolerate*) chiudere un occhio su, passare sopra a; **he had overlooked one important problem** aveva trascurato un problema importante; **I'll overlook it just this once** ci passerò sopra solo per questa volta

over·lord [ˈəʊvəˌlɔːd] N capo supremo

over·ly [ˈəʊvəlɪ] ADV troppo

over·manned [ˌəʊvəˈmænd] ADJ: **to be overmanned** avere un'eccedenza di personale

over·man·ning [ˌəʊvəˈmænɪŋ] N esubero di manodopera

over·much [ˌəʊvəˈmʌtʃ] (*frm*) ADV troppo
■ ADJ troppo(-a)

◎ **over·night** [ˈəʊvəˈnaɪt] ADV (*happen*) durante la notte; (*travel*) di notte; (*fig: quickly*) da un giorno all'altro; **to stay overnight** fermarsi a dormire; **he stayed there overnight** ha passato la notte lì ; **he'll be away overnight** passerà la notte fuori; **the weather remained calm overnight** il tempo è rimasto sereno durante la notte; **we can't solve this one overnight** non possiamo risolvere questo da un giorno all'altro; **things won't change overnight** le cose non cambieranno tutto ad un tratto
■ ADJ (*journey*) di notte; (*fig: success*) istantaneo(-a), fulmineo(-a); **this'll mean an overnight stay at Calais** questo significa che dovremo passare la notte a Calais; **an overnight success** un successo fulmineo

over·night bag N borsa da viaggio

over·paid [ˌəʊvəˈpeɪd] PT, PP *of* **overpay**

over·par·ticu·lar [ˌəʊvəpəˈtɪkjʊləʳ] ADJ (*on rules*) pignolo(-a); **not to be overparticular about sth** (*be indifferent*) non badare molto *or* troppo a qc

over·pass [ˈəʊvəˌpɑːs] N (*Am*) cavalcavia *m inv*

over·pay [ˌəʊvəˈpeɪ] (*pt, pp* **overpaid**) VT strapagare; **to overpay sb by £50** pagare 50 sterline in più a qn

over·pay·ment [ˌəʊvəˈpeɪmənt] N pagamento eccessivo

over·play [ˌəʊvəˈpleɪ] VT dare troppa importanza a; **to overplay one's hand** sopravvalutare la propria posizione

over·popu·lated [ˌəʊvəˈpɒpjʊˌleɪtɪd] ADJ sovrappopolato(-a)

over·popu·la·tion [ˌəʊvəˌpɒpjʊˈleɪʃən] N sovrappopolazione *f*

over·pow·er [ˌəʊvəˈpaʊəʳ] VT sopraffare

over·pow·er·ing [ˌəʊvəˈpaʊərɪŋ] ADJ (*smell, heat*) asfissiante, soffocante; (*desire*) irrefrenabile, irresistibile

over·priced [ˌəʊvəˈpraɪst] ADJ (*pej*): **it's overpriced** costa troppo per quello che è

over·pro·duc·tion [ˌəʊvəprəˈdʌkʃən] N sovrapproduzione *f*

over·rate [ˌəʊvəˈreɪt] VT sopravvalutare

over·reach [ˌəʊvəˈriːtʃ] VT: **to overreach o.s.** volere strafare

over·react [ˌəʊvəriːˈækt] VI reagire in modo esagerato

over·ride [ˌəʊvəˈraɪd] (*pt* **overrode** [ˌəʊvəˈrəʊd], *pp* **overridden** [ˌəʊvəˈrɪdn]) VT (*law*) calpestare; (*person*) scavalcare; (*decision*) annullare; (*sb's wishes, orders*) non tener conto di; (*Tech: cancel*) annullare

over·rid·ing [ˌəʊvəˈraɪdɪŋ] ADJ (*factor*) preponderante; (*importance*) essenziale

over·ripe [ˌəʊvəˈraɪp] ADJ troppo maturo(-a)

over·rule [ˌəʊvəˈruːl] VT (*person*) prevalere su; (*request, claim*) respingere; (*decision*) annullare

over·run [ˌəʊvəˈrʌn] (*pt* **overran** [ˌəʊvəˈræn], *pp* **overrun**) VT (*Mil: country*) invadere, occupare; (*time limit*) superare; **the town is overrun with tourists** la città è invasa dai turisti
■ VI (*meeting, event*) protrarsi

◎ **over·seas** [ˈəʊvəˈsiːz] ADV (*abroad*) all'estero; **visitors from overseas** visitatori stranieri
■ ADJ (*countries*) d'oltremare; (*foreign*) straniero(-a); (*: trade, market*) estero(-a)

over·see [ˌəʊvəˈsiː] (*pt* **oversaw** [ˌəʊvəˈsɔː], *pp* **overseen** [ˌəʊvəˈsiːn]) VT sorvegliare

over·seer ['əʊvə,sɪəʳ] N sorvegliante *m/f*; (*foreman*) caposquadra *m*
over·sell [,əʊvə'sɛl] VT (*praise excessively*) dare eccessivo valore a
over·sexed [,əʊvə'sɛkst] ADJ (*pej*): **he's oversexed** pensa solo al sesso
over·shad·ow [,əʊvə'ʃædəʊ] VT (*fig*) eclissare; **her childhood was overshadowed by her mother's illness** la sua infanzia è stata offuscata dalla malattia della madre; **Hester is overshadowed by her younger sister** Hester è messa in ombra dalla sorella più giovane
over·shoot [,əʊvə'ʃu:t] (*pt, pp* **overshot** [,əʊvə'ʃɒt]) VT (*destination*) superare
over·sight ['əʊvə,saɪt] N (*omission*) svista; **due to an oversight** per una svista
over·sim·pli·fi·ca·tion [,əʊvə,sɪmplɪfɪ'keɪʃən] N eccessiva semplificazione *f*
over·sim·pli·fy [,əʊvə'sɪmplɪ,faɪ] VT semplificare troppo
over·size(d) [,əʊvə'saɪz(d)] ADJ (*gen*) troppo grande; (*class, family*) troppo numeroso(-a)
over·sleep [,əʊvə'sli:p] (*pt, pp* **overslept** [,əʊvə'slɛpt]) VI non svegliarsi in tempo; **I overslept this morning** non mi sono svegliato in tempo stamattina
over·spend [,əʊvə'spɛnd] (*pt, pp* **overspent** [,əʊvə'spɛnt]) VI spendere troppo; **we have overspent by 5,000 dollars** abbiamo speso 5.000 dollari di troppo
over·spill ['əʊvə,spɪl] N (*Brit: population*) eccedenza di popolazione; **an overspill town** ≈ una città satellite
over·staffed [,əʊvə'stɑ:ft] ADJ: **to be overstaffed** avere troppo personale
over·staffing [,əʊvə'stɑ:fɪŋ] N eccedenza di personale
over·state [,əʊvə'steɪt] VT: **to overstate one's case** esagerare nel presentare le proprie ragioni
over·state·ment [,əʊvə'steɪtmənt] N esagerazione *f*
over·stay [,əʊvə'steɪ] VT: **to overstay one's welcome** trattenersi troppo a lungo (come ospite)
over·steer [,əʊvə'stɪəʳ] VI (*Aut*) sovrasterzare
over·step [,əʊvə'stɛp] VT: **to overstep the mark** superare ogni limite
over·stock [,əʊvə'stɒk] VT sovrapprovvigionare, sovraimmagazzinare
over·stretched [,əʊvə'strɛtʃt] ADJ (*person*) sovraccarico(-a); (*resources, budget*) arrivato(-a) al limite
over·strike ['əʊvə,straɪk] N (*Typ*) sovrapposizione *f* (di caratteri)
■ VT sovrapporre
overt [əʊ'vɜ:t] ADJ evidente, aperto(-a)
over·take [,əʊvə'teɪk] (*pt* **overtook** [,əʊvə'tʊk], *pp* **overtaken** [,əʊvə'teɪkən]) VT (*catch up*) raggiungere; (*pass*) superare; **events have overtaken us** gli eventi ci hanno colto di sorpresa; **tragedy was shortly to overtake him** una disgrazia stava per travolgerlo
■ VI sorpassare
over·tak·ing [,əʊvə'teɪkɪŋ] N (*Aut*) sorpasso; **"no overtaking"** "divieto di sorpasso"
over·tax [,əʊvə'tæks] VT (*Fin*) imporre tasse eccessive a; (*fig: strength, patience*) mettere a dura prova; **to overtax o.s.** abusare delle proprie forze
over·throw [*n* 'əʊvə,θrəʊ; *vb* ,əʊvə'θrəʊ] (*vb: pt* **overthrew** [,əʊvə'θru:], *pp* **overthrown** [,əʊvə'θrəʊn]) N (*of government etc*) rovesciamento
■ VT (*king, system, government*) rovesciare
over·time ['əʊvə,taɪm] N (lavoro) straordinario; **to do** *or* **work overtime** fare lo straordinario; **your imagination has been working overtime!** (*fam*) corri un po' troppo con la fantasia!
overtime ban N *rifiuto sindacale di fare gli straordinari*
over·tired [,əʊvə'taɪəd] ADJ stanchissimo(-a), sovraffaticato(-a)
overt·ly [əʊ'vɜ:tlɪ] ADV apertamente
over·tone ['əʊvə,təʊn] N **1** OFTEN PL (*fig*) sfumatura **2** (*Mus*): **overtones** NPL armoniche *fpl* superiori, ipertoni *mpl*
over·took [,əʊvə'tʊk] PT *of* **overtake**
over·ture ['əʊvə,tjʊəʳ] N **1** (*Mus*) ouverture *f inv* **2 to make overtures to sb** (*fig: friendly*) comportarsi amichevolmente verso qn; (*: romantic*) tentare un approccio con qn, fare delle avances a qn
over·turn [,əʊvə'tɜ:n] VT (*car, boat, chair*) capovolgere, ribaltare; (*government, regime*) rovesciare; (*Law: decision*) annullare, cassare; **the decision was overturned** la decisione è stata annullata
■ VI (*car, boat*) rovesciarsi, ribaltarsi; **the car overturned** la macchina si è rovesciata
over·use [,əʊvə'ju:z] VT (*chemicals, medication*) fare uso eccessivo di
over·value [,əʊvə'vælju:] VT sopravvalutare
over·view ['əʊvə,vju:] N visione *f* d'insieme
over·ween·ing [,əʊvə'wi:nɪŋ] ADJ (*frm pej: pride, arrogance, ambition, self-confidence*) smodato(-a), eccessivo(-a), smisurato(-a)
over·weight [,əʊvə'weɪt] ADJ: **to be overweight** (*person*) essere sovrappeso; (*luggage*) superare il peso consentito; **the parcel is a kilo overweight** il pacco pesa un chilo di troppo
over·whelm [,əʊvə'wɛlm] VT (*opponent, team*) schiacciare; (*with questions, requests, work*) sommergere; **to be overwhelmed by grief** essere sopraffatto(-a) dal dolore; **sorrow overwhelmed him** il dolore lo sopraffece; **overwhelmed by her kindness** confuso dalla sua gentilezza; **to be overwhelmed** (*touched, impressed*) rimanere colpito(-a); **we have been overwhelmed with offers of help** siamo stati sommersi da offerte di aiuto
◎ **over·whelm·ing** [,əʊvə'wɛlmɪŋ] ADJ (*victory, majority*) schiacciante; (*defeat*) pesante; (*pressure, heat, desire, emotion*) intenso(-a); **one's overwhelming impression is of heat** l'impressione dominante è quella di caldo
over·whelm·ing·ly [,əʊvə'wɛlmɪŋlɪ] ADV (*win*) in modo schiacciante; (*defeat*) pesantemente; (*vote*) in massa
over·work [,əʊvə'wɜ:k] N lavoro eccessivo; **a heart attack caused by overwork** un infarto causato dal superlavoro
■ VI lavorare troppo, strapazzarsi
■ VT (*staff, servants*) far lavorare troppo
over·write [,əʊvə'raɪt] VT (*Comput*) sovrascrivere
over·wrought [,əʊvə'rɔ:t] ADJ estremamente agitato(-a)
over·zeal·ous [,əʊvə'zɛləs] ADJ troppo zelante
Ovid ['ɒvɪd] N Ovidio
ovi·duct ['ɒvɪ,dʌkt] N ovidotto
ovipa·rous [əʊ'vɪpərəs] ADJ oviparo(-a)
ovo·vi·vipa·rous [,əʊvəʊvaɪ'vɪpərəs] ADJ ovoviviparo(-a)
ovu·late ['ɒvjʊ,leɪt] VI ovulare
ovu·la·tion [,ɒvjʊ'leɪʃən] N ovulazione *f*
ovule ['ɒvju:l] N ovulo
ovum ['əʊvəm] N (*pl* **ova** ['əʊvə]) ovocito
◎ **owe** [əʊ] VT (*gen*): **to owe sb sth, to owe sth to sb** dovere qc a qn; **how much do I owe you?** quanto le

Oo

devo?; **to what do I owe the honour of your visit?** (*iro*) a che devo l'onore della visita?; **you owe it to yourself to come** è per te stesso che devi venire

ow·ing ['əʊɪŋ] ADJ da pagare; **how much is owing to you now?** quanto ti devono (*or* devo *or* deve) adesso?

owing to PREP a causa di; **owing to the bad weather** a causa del maltempo

owl [aʊl] N (*small*) civetta; (*big*) gufo; **little owl** civetta notturna; **long-eared owl** gufo comune; **short-eared owl** gufo di palude

owl·et ['aʊlɪt] N giovane gufo

owl·ish ['aʊlɪʃ] ADJ da gufo

owl·ish·ly ['aʊlɪʃlɪ] ADV con uno sguardo da gufo

◎ **own** [əʊn] ADJ proprio(-a); **this is my own recipe** è una mia ricetta; **I made it with my own hands** l'ho fatto con le mie mani; **it's all my own money** sono tutti soldi miei; **the house has its own garage** la casa ha il suo garage; **he can't trust his own judgement** non si può fidare del proprio giudizio
■ PRON: **he has a style all his own** ha uno stile tutto suo; **of my own** tutto(-a) per me; **I'll give you a copy of your own** ti darò una copia tutta per te; **a room of my own** una camera tutta per me; **a place of one's own** una casa tutta per sé; **can I have it for my (very) own?** posso averlo tutto per me?; **the house is her (very) own** la casa è di sua proprietà; **she has money of her own** è ricca di suo; **to come into one's own** mostrare le proprie qualità; **to be on one's own** stare per conto proprio; **on his own** da solo; **on their own** da soli; **from now on, you're on your own** (*fam*) d'ora in poi te la dovrai cavare da solo; **if I can get him on his own** se riesco a beccarlo da solo; **to do sth on one's own** (*unaided*) fare qualcosa da solo(-a); **I am so busy I have scarcely any time to call my own** sono così occupato che non ho tempo per me stesso; **without a chair to call my own** senza una sedia che possa chiamare mia; **to get one's own back** rendere pan per focaccia
■ VT **1** (*possess*) possedere, essere proprietario(-a) di; **everything I own** tutto ciò che possiedo; **does anybody own this pen?** è di qualcuno questa penna?; **the golf course is owned by a Japanese company** il campo da golf appartiene ad una società giapponese; **he acts as if he owns the place** si comporta come se fosse il padrone; **you don't own me!** non sei il mio padrone! **2** (*old: admit*) ammettere
■ VI (*Brit*): **to own to sth** ammettere qc; **to own to having done sth** ammettere di aver fatto qc
▸ **own up** VI + ADV: **to own up (to sth)** confessare (qc), ammettere (qc); **to own up to having done sth** ammettere di aver fatto qc

own-brand [əʊn,brænd] ADJ: **our own-brand products** i prodotti *mpl* con il nostro marchio

own brand N (*Comm*) marchio proprio

◎ **own·er** ['əʊnəʳ] N proprietario(-a)

owner-occupier [,əʊnər'ɒkjʊ,paɪəʳ] N proprietario(-a) della casa in cui abita

◎ **own·er·ship** ['əʊnəʃɪp] N proprietà; **it's under new ownership** ha un nuovo proprietario; **under his ownership the business flourished** nelle sue mani la ditta prosperava; **car ownership** il possesso di una macchina

own goal N (*Sport, fig*) autogol *m inv*, autorete *f*

own label N = own-brand

ox [ɒks] N (*pl* **oxen** ['ɒksən]) bue *m*

oxa·lis [ɒk'sælɪs] N ossalide *f*

ox·bow ['ɒks,bəʊ] N (*also:* **oxbow lake**) *lago di meandro abbandonato*

Ox·bridge ['ɒks,brɪdʒ] (*Brit*) N *le università di Oxford e/o Cambridge*
■ ADJ (*education, accent, attitudes*) *di chi ha studiato a Oxford o Cambridge*

> **OXBRIDGE**
>
> La parola **Oxbridge** deriva dalla fusione dei nomi Ox(ford) e (Cam)bridge e fa riferimento a queste due antiche università.
> ▷ www.ox.ac.uk
> ▷ www.cam.ac.uk

ox·eye daisy ['ɒks,aɪ'deɪzɪ] N margherita

Ox·fam ['ɒksfæm] N ABBR (*Brit:* = **Oxford Committee for Famine Relief**) *organizzazione no-profit per aiuti al Terzo Mondo*

oxi·da·tion [,ɒksɪ'deɪʃən] N ossidazione *f*

ox·ide ['ɒksaɪd] N ossido

oxi·dize ['ɒksɪ,daɪz] VI ossidare

Oxon ABBR = *Oxfordshire*

Oxon. ['ɒksən] ABBR (*Brit:* = **Oxoniensis**) (dell')Università di Oxford

oxo·nium [ɒk'səʊnɪəm] **oxonium ion** N ione *m* ossonio

ox·tail ['ɒks,teɪl] N: **oxtail soup** zuppa di coda di bue

oxy·acety·lene [,ɒksɪə'setɪli:n] ADJ (*torch, burner*) ossiacetilenico(-a)

oxy·gen ['ɒksɪdʒən] N ossigeno

oxy·gen·ate ['ɒksɪdʒɪ,neɪt] VT ossigenare

oxy·gena·tion [,ɒksɪdʒɪ'neɪʃən] N ossigenazione *f*

oxygen mask N maschera a ossigeno

oxy·gen re-breather ['ɒksɪdʒən,ri:'bri:ðəʳ] N (*Diving*) autorespiratore *m* ad ossigeno

oxygen tent N tenda a ossigeno

oys·ter ['ɔɪstəʳ] N ostrica; **the world is your oyster** il mondo è tuo

oyster bed N banco di ostriche

oyster-catcher ['ɔɪstə,kætʃəʳ] N beccaccia di mare

oyster shell N conchiglia di ostrica

oz. ABBR = **ounce**

ozone ['əʊzəʊn] N ozono

ozone-friendly [,əʊzəʊn'frendlɪ] ADJ che rispetta l'ozono, che non danneggia lo strato d'ozono

ozone layer N fascia d'ozono; strato d'ozono; **the hole in the ozone layer** il buco nell'ozono

ozo·no·sphere [əʊ'zəʊnə,sfɪəʳ] N ozonosfera

P, p [piː] N *(letter)* P, p *f or m inv*; **P for Peter** ≈ P come Padova; **mind your p's and q's!** bada a come parli!

p [piː] ABBR *(Brit)* = **penny, pence**

p. [piː] ABBR (= **page**) p. (= *pagina*)

◎ **PA** [piːˈeɪ] N ABBR **1** (= **personal assistant**) assistente *m/f* personale **2** = **public address system; the PA system** l'impianto di amplificazione

■ ABBR *(Am Post)* = **Pennsylvania**

pa [pɑː] N *(fam)* papà *m inv*, babbo

p.a. ABBR = **per annum**

◎ **pace** [peɪs] N **1** *(step)* passo; **30 paces away** a 30 passi di distanza; **to put sb through his paces** *(fig)* mettere qn alla prova **2** *(speed)* passo, andatura; **at a good pace** *(walk)* di buon passo; *(work)* ad un buon ritmo; **at a slow pace** lentamente; **he was walking at a brisk pace** camminava a passo spedito; **the pace of life** il ritmo di vita; **to keep pace with** *(person)* andare di pari passo con; *(fig: technology)* procedere di pari passo con; (: *events*) tenersi al corrente di; **to set the pace** *(running)* fare l'andatura; *(fig)* dare il la *or* il tono

■ VT *(room)* andare su e giù per; **to pace sth off** *or* **out** misurare a passi qc

■ VI: **to pace up and down** camminare su e giù *or* avanti e indietro

pace·maker [ˈpeɪsˌmeɪkəʳ] N **1** *(Med)* pacemaker *m inv* **2** *(Sport)* chi fa l'andatura, battistrada *m inv*

pac·er [ˈpeɪsəʳ] N *(Am Sport)* = **pacemaker 2**

pace·setter [ˈpeɪsˌsɛtəʳ] N *(Am Sport)* = **pacemaker 2**

pacey ADJ = **pacy**

Pa·cif·ic [pəˈsɪfɪk] N: **the Pacific (Ocean)** il Pacifico, l'Oceano Pacifico

■ ADJ del Pacifico

pa·cif·ic [pəˈsɪfɪk] ADJ *(frm)* pacifico(-a)

paci·fi·ca·tion [ˌpæsɪfɪˈkeɪʃən] N pacificazione *f*

paci·fi·er [ˈpæsɪˌfaɪəʳ] N *(Am fam: dummy)* succhiotto, ciuccio

paci·fism [ˈpæsɪˌfɪzəm] N pacifismo

paci·fist [ˈpæsɪfɪst] N pacifista *m/f*

paci·fy [ˈpæsɪˌfaɪ] VT *(person)* calmare; *(country)* riportare la calma in, pacificare; *(fears)* placare; *(creditors)* ammansire

◎ **pack** [pæk] N **1** *(packet)* pacco; *(Comm)* confezione *f*; *(of cotton, wool)* balla; *(Am: of cigarettes)* pacchetto; *(rucksack, Mil)* zaino; *(of cards)* mazzo; *(Rugby)* pacchetto; **he was carrying a heavy pack on his back** portava un grosso zaino sulle spalle; **an information pack** una serie di opuscoli informativi; **a six-pack** una confezione da sei; **a pack of cigarettes** un pacchetto di sigarette; **a pack of cards** un mazzo di carte; **a pack of lies** *(fig)* un mucchio *or* sacco di bugie **2** *(of hounds)* muta; *(of wolves)* branco; *(of thieves)* banda; *(of fools)* massa

■ VT **1** *(objects, goods)* imballare; **packed in dozens** *(Comm)* in confezioni da dodici; **to pack one's bags** *or* **one's case** fare le valigie *or* i bagagli; *(fig)* far fagotto; **I've already packed my case** ho già fatto la valigia; **I still have a few things to pack** ho ancora qualcosa da mettere in valigia; **pack your swimming costume** metti il costume da bagno in valigia **2** *(cram full)*: **to pack (with)** *(container)* riempire di; *(room, car)* stipare di; **can you pack two more into your car?** riesci a infilarcene ancora due nella tua macchina?

3 *(Comput)* comprimere, impaccare **4** *(make firm: soil etc)* comprimere, pressare

■ VI **1** *(do one's luggage)* fare le valigie *or* i bagagli; **I'll help you pack** ti aiuto a fare i bagagli; **to send sb packing** *(fam)* dare il benservito a qn **2** *(people)*: **to pack (into)** accalcarsi (in), pigiarsi (in); **thousands packed into the square** erano a migliaia stipati nella piazza; **packed like sardines** pigiati(-e) come sardine

► **pack away** VT + ADV riporre

► **pack in** *(Brit fam)* VI + ADV *(break down: watch, car)* guastarsi

■ VT + ADV mollare, piantare; **pack it in!** piantala!

► **pack off** VT + ADV: **to pack sb off to school/bed** spedire qn a scuola/letto

► **pack up** VI + ADV *(person)* far fagotto; *(Brit fam: machine)* guastarsi

■ VT + ADV **1** *(belongings, clothes)* mettere in una valigia; *(goods, presents)* imballare **2** = **pack in** VT + ADV

◎ **pack·age** [ˈpækɪdʒ] N *(parcel)* pacco; *(smaller)* pacchetto; *(fig: terms of agreement)* pacchetto; **a small package** un piccolo pacco

■ VT *(Comm: goods)* confezionare

package deal N *(Comm)* offerta *f* tutto compreso *inv*

Pp

package holiday N (*Brit*) vacanza organizzata
package tour N (*Brit*) viaggio organizzato
pack·ag·ing ['pækɪdʒɪŋ] N confezione *f*, imballo
pack animal N bestia da soma
packed [pækt] ADJ (*crowded*) affollato(-a); **the place was packed** il posto era affollato
packed lunch N (*for walker*) pranzo al sacco; (*for traveller*) cestino da viaggio; **I always take a packed lunch to work** al lavoro mi porto sempre il pranzo da casa
packed out ['pækt'aʊt] ADJ (*Brit fam*) strapieno(-a)
pack·er ['pækəʳ] N (*person*) imballatore(-trice); (*machine*) imballatrice *f*
pack·et ['pækɪt] N (*gen*) pacchetto; (*of sweets, crisps*) sacchetto; (*of needles, seeds*) bustina; **to make a packet** (*fam*) fare un mucchio *or* un sacco di soldi; **that must have cost a packet** (*fam*) dev'essere costato un sacco di soldi; **a packet of cigarettes** un pacchetto di sigarette; **a packet of crisps** un sacchetto di patatine
pack ice N banchisa, pack *m inv*
pack·ing ['pækɪŋ] N **1** (*of luggage*): **to do one's packing** fare le valigie *or* i bagagli **2** (*material*) (materiale *m* da) imballaggio
packing case N cassa da imballaggio
◎ **pact** [pækt] N patto, trattato, accordo; **he has signed a pact** ha firmato un accordo; **a non-aggression pact** un patto di non aggressione
pacy, pacey ['peɪsɪ] ADJ (*Brit: sports person*) veloce; (*film, story*) con un buon ritmo
pad [pæd] N **1** (*to prevent friction etc*) cuscinetto; (*Ftbl*) parastinco; (*Hockey*) gambiera; (*brake pad*) pastiglia; (*for ink*) tampone *m*; **shoulder pads** spalline imbottite **2** (*writing pad*) blocco di carta da lettere; (*notepad*) bloc-notes *m inv*, blocchetto **3** (*launch pad*) rampa di lancio **4** (*of animal's foot*) cuscinetto **5** (*fam: flat*) appartamentino
■ VT (*cushion, shoulders etc*) imbottire
■ VI: **to pad about/in** *etc* camminare/entrare *etc* a passi felpati
▶ **pad out** VT + ADV (*speech etc*) farcire
pad·ded ['pædɪd] ADJ imbottito(-a)
padded cell N cella con le pareti imbottite (*in carceri, ospedali psichiatrici*)
pad·ding ['pædɪŋ] N (*material*) imbottitura; (*fig: in speech, essay*) riempitivo; **it means nothing, it's just padding** non vuol dire niente, è solo un riempitivo; **protective padding** imbottitura protettiva
pad·dle ['pædl] N **1** (*oar*) pagaia; (*blade of wheel*) pala **2 to have a paddle** sguazzare nell'acqua bassa
■ VT (*boat*) fare andare a colpi di pagaia
■ VI **1** (*in boat*) pagaiare **2** (*walk in water*) sguazzare
paddle boat, paddle steamer (*Brit*) N battello a ruote
pad·dling pool ['pædlɪŋ,pu:l] N piscina per bambini
pad·dock ['pædək] N (*field*) recinto; (*of racecourse*) paddock *m inv*
pad·dy ['pædɪ]: **paddy field** N risaia
pad·lock ['pæd,lɒk] N lucchetto
■ VT chiudere con il lucchetto
pa·dre ['pɑ:drɪ] N **1** (*Mil, Naut*) cappellano **2** (*fam: clergyman*) padre *m*
Pad·ua ['pædʒʊə] N Padova
pae·di·at·ric, (*Am*) **pe·di·at·ric** [,pi:dɪ'ætrɪk] ADJ pediatrico(-a)
pae·dia·tri·cian, (*Am*) **pe·dia·tri·cian** [,pi:dɪə'trɪʃən] N pediatra *m/f*
pae·di·at·rics, (*Am*) **pe·di·at·rics** [,pi:dɪ'ætrɪks] NSG pediatria
pae·do·phile, (*Am*) **pe·do·phile** ['pi:dəʊ,faɪl] ADJ, N pedofilo(-a)
pagan ['peɪgən] ADJ, N pagano(-a)
◎ **page¹** [peɪdʒ] N (*of book etc*) pagina; **on page 2** a pagina 2; **on both sides of the page** su tutt'e due le facciate (del foglio)
page² [peɪdʒ] N (*also:* **pageboy**: *servant*) fattorino; (: *at wedding*) paggetto
■ VT: **to page sb** (far) chiamare qn
pag·eant ['pædʒənt] N (*show*) spettacolo di rievocazione storica; (*procession*) corteo in costume
pag·eant·ry ['pædʒəntrɪ] N sfarzo, pompa
page·boy ['peɪdʒ,bɔɪ] N (*attendant*) paggio; (*hairstyle*) pettinatura alla paggetto
page impression N (*Comput*) *numero delle volte in cui una particolare pagina Web all'interno di un sito viene visitata*
pag·er ['peɪdʒəʳ] N cercapersone *m*
page rate N (*Press*) tariffa inserzioni per pagina
pagi·nate ['pædʒɪ,neɪt] VT (*Typ*) impaginare; (*Comput*) paginare
pagi·na·tion [,pædʒɪ'neɪʃən] N (*see vb*) impaginazione *f*; paginazione *f*
pa·go·da [pə'gəʊdə] N pagoda
paid [peɪd] PT, PP *of* **pay**
■ ADJ (*work, official*) rimunerato(-a); **to put paid to sth** (*ruin*) metter fine a qc; **three weeks' paid holiday** tre settimane di ferie pagate
paid-up ['peɪd,ʌp] ADJ, (*Am*) **paid-in** ['peɪd,ɪn] ADJ (*member*) che ha pagato la sua quota; (*share*) interamente pagato(-a); **paid-up capital** capitale *m* interamente versato
pail [peɪl] N secchio
◎ **pain** [peɪn] N **1** dolore *m*; **to cause pain to** (*physical*) provocare dolori a; (*mental*) far soffrire; **to be in pain** soffrire; **she's in a lot of pain** soffre molto; **I have a pain in my leg** ho male *or* un dolore a una gamba; **a terrible pain** un dolore insopportabile; **he's a real pain (in the neck)** (*fam*) è un gran rompiscatole **2**: **pains** NPL (*efforts*) sforzi *mpl*; **and all I got for my pains was ...** e come ringraziamento ho avuto...; **to take pains over sth** mettercela tutta in qc; **to be at (great) pains to do sth** fare di tutto per fare qc **3** (*penalty*): **on pain of death** sotto pena di morte
■ VT (*mentally*) addolorare, affliggere
pained [peɪnd] ADJ: **a pained expression** un'aria seccata; **a pained silence** un silenzio amareggiato
◎ **pain·ful** ['peɪnfʊl] ADJ (*wound*) doloroso(-a); (*leg*) che fa male; (*task, sight, also fam*) penoso(-a); (*difficult*) difficile; **it is my painful duty to tell you that ...** purtroppo ho il dovere di informarla che...; **it was painful to watch** (*fam*) era penoso (a vedersi)
pain·ful·ly ['peɪnfəlɪ] ADV (*walk, breathe*) a fatica; (*thin*) penosamente; **the cut throbbed painfully** la ferita pulsava e faceva male; **it was painfully clear that ...** era fin troppo chiaro che...
pain·killer ['peɪn,kɪləʳ] N analgesico, antidolorifico
pain·less ['peɪnlɪs] ADJ (*gen*) indolore; (*fig: exam*) non troppo difficile; (: *interview*) non spiacevole
pain·less·ly ['peɪnlɪslɪ] ADV in modo indolore
pains·taking ['peɪnz,teɪkɪŋ] ADJ (*person*) coscienzioso(-a), diligente; (*work*) accurato(-a); (*accuracy*) minuzioso(-a)
pains·taking·ly ['peɪnz,teɪkɪŋlɪ] ADV (*work*) accuratamente, diligentemente; (*research*) minuziosamente
◎ **paint** [peɪnt] N (*Art*) colore *m*; (*for house etc*) tinta,

vernice *f*; **a tin of paint** un barattolo di tinta *or* vernice; **a box of paints** una scatola di colori
■VT (*house, also Art*) dipingere; (*door*) verniciare; **to paint sth blue/red** dipingere (*or* verniciare) qc di blu/rosso; **he decided to paint it green** ha deciso di verniciarlo di verde; **when did he paint the picture?** quando ha dipinto il quadro?; **to paint the town red** (*fig*) far baldoria; **he's not as black as he's painted** è meno cattivo di quanto si dica in giro
■VI dipingere; **to paint in oils** dipingere a olio

paint·ball·ing ['peɪnt,bɔ:lɪŋ] N *gioco di guerra in cui ci si spara con pallottole che contengono pittura*

paint·box ['peɪnt,bɒks] N scatola di colori

paint·brush ['peɪnt,brʌʃ] N pennello

paint·er¹ ['peɪntəʳ] N (*Art*) pittore(-trice); (*decorator*) imbianchino(-a); **a famous 13th century painter** un famoso pittore del XIII secolo; **the painter is coming tomorrow to redecorate the house** domani viene l'imbianchino per ridipingere la casa

paint·er² ['peɪntəʳ] N (*Naut*) fune *f* d'ormeggio

◎ **paint·ing** ['peɪntɪŋ] N (*Art: picture*) dipinto, quadro; (*: activity*) pittura; (*decorating: of doors etc*) verniciatura; (*: of walls*) imbiancatura; **a painting by Picasso** un quadro di Picasso; **my hobby is painting** il mio hobby è la pittura

paint·pot ['peɪnt,pɒt] N latta di tinta *or* vernice *f*

paint stripper, **paint remover** N prodotto sverniciante

paint·work ['peɪnt,wɜ:k] N (*gen*) pittura; (*of car*) vernice *f*

◎ **pair** [pɛəʳ] N (*of gloves, shoes etc*) paio; (*of people*) coppia; **a pair of scissors/trousers/shoes** un paio di forbici/pantaloni/scarpe; **in pairs** a coppie; **we work in pairs** lavoriamo a coppie; **arranged in pairs** disposti(-e) a due a due; **ordered pair** (*Math*) coppia ordinata
■VT accoppiare, appaiare
▶ **pair off** VT + ADV trovar marito (*or* moglie) a
■VI + ADV: **to pair off (with sb)** fare coppia (con qn)
▶ **pair up** VI + ADV: **to pair up (with sb)** mettersi in coppia (con qn)

pais·ley ['peɪzlɪ] ADJ: **paisley pattern** disegno cachemire

pa·jam·as [pə'dʒɑ:məz] NPL (*Am*) = **pyjamas**

Paki ['pækɪ] N (*Brit*) *termine spregiativo usato dagli inglesi per definire i pakistani*

Paki-bashing ['pækɪ,bæʃɪŋ] N (*Brit fam*) *atti di violenza contro la minoranza pakistana*

Pa·ki·stan [,pɑ:kɪs'tɑ:n] N Pakistan *m*

Pa·ki·stani [,pɑ:kɪs'tɑ:nɪ] ADJ, N pakistano(-a)

pa·ko·ra [pə'kɔ:rə] N (*Culin*) *polpettine fritte di verdura e spezie tipiche della cucina indiana*

PAL [pæl] N ABBR (TV: = **phase alternation line**) PAL *m*

pal [pæl] N (*fam*) amico(-a)
▶ **pal up** VI + ADV (*fam*) far amicizia

◎ **pal·ace** ['pælɪs] N palazzo

palae·on·tol·ogy, (*Am*) **pale·on·tol·ogy** [,pælɪɒn'tɒlədʒɪ] N paleontologia

pal·at·able ['pælətəbl] ADJ (*tasty*) gradevole (al palato); (*fig*) piacevole, gradevole

pala·tal ['pælətl] ADJ palatale

pal·ate ['pælɪt] N (*Anat, fig*) palato

pa·la·tial [pə'leɪʃəl] ADJ sontuoso(-a), sfarzoso(-a)

pala·tine ['pælə,taɪn] ADJ palatino(-a)

palaver [pə'lɑ:vəʳ] N (*fam: fuss*) storie *fpl*; (*: talk*) tiritera

◎ **pale¹** [peɪl] ADJ (*comp* **-r**, *superl* **-st**) (*gen*) pallido(-a); (*colour*) chiaro(-a), pallido(-a); **pale blue** azzurro pallido *inv*, celeste; **pale pink** rosa pallido; **pale green** verdolino; **to grow** *or* **turn pale** diventare pallido(-a), impallidire; **she still looks very pale** è ancora molto pallida
■VI impallidire; **to pale into insignificance (beside)** perdere d'importanza (nei confronti di)

pale² [peɪl] N: **to be beyond the pale** aver oltrepassato ogni limite

pale·ly ['peɪllɪ] ADV pallidamente

pale·ness ['peɪlnɪs] N pallore *m*

Pal·es·tine ['pælɪ,staɪn] N Palestina

Pal·es·tin·ian [,pæləs'tɪnɪən] ADJ, N palestinese (*m/f*)

pal·ette ['pælɪt] N tavolozza

palette knife N (*Art, Culin*) spatola di metallo

pali·mo·ny ['pælɪmənɪ] N (*fam*) *alimenti pagati a exconvivente dopo la separazione*

palings ['peɪlɪŋz] NPL (*fence*) palizzata *fsg*; (*boards*) assi *fpl*

pali·sade [,pælɪ'seɪd] N palizzata

pall¹ [pɔ:l] N (*on coffin*) drappo funebre; (*of smoke*) coltre *f*, cappa; **a pall of smoke** una cappa di fumo

pall² [pɔ:l] VI: **to pall (on)** perdere il proprio fascino (per), diventare noioso(-a) (per)

pall·bearer ['pɔ:l,bɛərəʳ] N persona che porta la bara

pal·let ['pælɪt] N (*for goods*) pallet *m inv*

pal·lia·tive ['pælɪətɪv] N palliativo

pal·lid ['pælɪd] ADJ pallido(-a), smorto(-a)

pal·lor ['pæləʳ] N pallore *m*

pal·ly ['pælɪ] ADJ (*comp* **-ier**, *superl* **-iest**) (*fam*): **to be pally with sb** essere molto amico (*or* amica) di qn

palm¹ [pɑ:m] N (*Bot: also:* **palm tree**) palma
▶ **palm off** VT + ADV: **to palm sth off on sb** (*fam*) rifilare qc a qn

palm² [pɑ:m] N (*Anat*) palma, palmo; **to read sb's palm** leggere la mano a qn; **to grease sb's palm** (*fig*) dare una bustarella a qn; **to have sb in the palm of one's hand** avere *or* tenere in pugno qn

palm·ist ['pɑ:mɪst] N chiromante *m/f*

palm·is·try ['pɑ:mɪstrɪ] N chiromanzia

palm oil N olio di palma

Palm Sunday N Domenica delle Palme

palm·top ['pɑ:mtɒp] N (*Comput*) palmtop *m inv*, palmare *m*

pal·pable ['pælpəbl] ADJ (*lie, mistake*) palese, evidente

pal·pably ['pælpəblɪ] ADV palesemente, evidentemente

pal·pi·tate ['pælpɪ,teɪt] VI palpitare

pal·pi·ta·tion [,pælpɪ'teɪʃən] N: **to have palpitations** avere le palpitazioni

pal·sied ['pɔ:lzɪd] ADJ paralitico(-a)

pal·try ['pɔ:ltrɪ] ADJ (*meagre*) irrisorio(-a); (*unworthy of consideration*) insignificante; **a paltry sum** una somma insignificante; **for a paltry £5** per la somma irrisoria di 5 sterline

pam·pas ['pæmpəs] NPL pampas *fpl*

pam·per ['pæmpəʳ] VT viziare, coccolare; **he's been pampered all his life** è stato viziato tutta la vita

pam·phlet ['pæmflɪt] N (*informative brochure*) opuscolo, dépliant *m inv*; (*political, handed out in street*) volantino, manifestino

Pan [pæn] N Pan

◎ **pan** [pæn] N (*Culin: also:* **saucepan**) casseruola; (*frying pan*) padella; (*milk pan*) pentolino; (*of scales*) piatto; (*of lavatory*) tazza; **roasting pan** teglia per arrosti
■VT **1** (*gold etc*) passare al vaglio **2** (*fam: play*) stroncare

Pp

■VI **1** **to pan for gold** (lavare le sabbie aurifere per) cercare l'oro **2** *(Cine)* fare una panoramica
▸ **pan out** VI + ADV *(develop)* andare; *(turn out well)* riuscire
pan- [pæn] PREF pan...
pana·cea [pænə'sɪə] N panacea
pa·nache [pə'næʃ] N stile *m*
Pan-African ADJ panafricano(-a)
Pana·ma ['pænə,mɑ:] N Panama *f*
pana·ma ['pænə,mɑ:] N *(also:* **panama hat***)* (cappello di) panama *m inv*
Panama Canal N canale *m* di Panama
Pana·ma·nian [,pænə'meɪnɪən] ADJ, N panamense *(m/f)*
Pan-American [,pænə'mɛrɪkən] ADJ panamericano(-a)
Pan-Asian ['pæn'eɪʃən] ADJ panasiatico(-a)
pan·cake ['pæn,keɪk] N frittella, crêpe *f inv*; **as flat as a pancake** *(fig)* piatto(-a) come una tavola
Pancake Day N *(Brit)* martedì *m* grasso
pancake roll N *crêpe ripiena di verdure alla cinese*
pan·chro·mat·ic [,pænkrəʊ'mætɪk] ADJ pancromatico(-a)
pan·cre·as ['pæŋkrɪəs] N pancreas *m inv*
pan·da ['pændə] N panda *m inv*
panda car N *(Brit)* auto *f* della polizia; ≈ pantera
pan·dem·ic [pæn'dɛmɪk] N *(frm, Med)* pandemia
■ADJ *(Med)* pandemico(-a)
pan·de·mo·nium [,pændɪ'məʊnɪəm] N pandemonio
pan·der ['pændə^r] VI: **to pander to** *(person, whims)* assecondare; **the government must not pander to terrorists** il governo non deve assecondare i terroristi; **to pander to sb's tastes** piegarsi ai gusti di qn
p&h [,pi:ənd'eɪtʃ] N ABBR *(Am:* = **postage and handling***)* affrancatura e trasporto
P & L ABBR (= **profit and loss**) P.P. (= *profitti e perdite*)
Pandora's box [pæn,dɔ:rəz'bɒks] N il vaso di Pandora
p & p [,pi:ənd'pi:] N ABBR *(Brit:* = **postage and packing***)* affrancatura ed imballaggio
pane [peɪn] N vetro
pan·egyr·ic [,pænɪ'dʒɪrɪk] N *(frm)* panegirico
◎**pan·el** ['pænl] N **1** *(gen)* pannello; *(of triptych)* tavola; *(of ceiling)* cassettone *m*; *(of instruments, switches)* quadro; **oak panels** pannelli *mpl* di quercia **2** *(Radio, TV: of judges)* giuria; *(of experts, researchers etc)* gruppo; *(in market research)* panel *m inv*; **the only woman on the panel** l'unica donna della giuria
■VT *(wall, door)* rivestire di *or* con pannelli
panel beater N battilastra *m inv*
panel discussion N tavola rotonda
panel game N *(Brit)* quiz *m inv* a squadre
pan·elled, *(Am)* **pan·eled** ['pænəld] ADJ *(door etc)* a pannelli
panelling, *(Am)* **pan·el·ing** ['pænəlɪŋ] N rivestimento di *or* a pannelli
pan·el·list, *(Am)* **pan·el·ist** ['pænəlɪst] N partecipante *m/f (al quiz, alla tavola rotonda etc)*
pang [pæŋ] N: **a pang of guilt/sadness** un senso di colpa/tristezza; **without a pang** senza rimpianti; **the pangs of hunger** i morsi della fame; **pangs of conscience** rimorsi *mpl* di coscienza; **to feel pangs of remorse** essere torturato(-a) dal rimorso
pan·han·dler ['pæn,hændlə^r] N *(Am fam)* accattone(-a)
◎**pan·ic** ['pænɪk] N panico; **to get into a panic about sth** farsi prendere dal panico per qc; **to throw into a panic** *(crowd)* seminare il panico tra; *(person)* gettare in uno stato di agitazione
■VI lasciarsi prendere dal panico; **he panicked when he saw the blood** quando ha visto il sangue si è fatto prendere dal panico; **don't panic!** non agitarti!; **don't panic!** non agitarti!
panic buying ['pænɪk'baɪɪŋ] N accaparramento *(di generi alimentari)*
pan·icky ['pænɪkɪ] ADJ *(person)* che si lascia prendere dal panico; *(report)* allarmista; *(decision)* dettato(-a) dal panico
panic stations N: **when he realized he'd lost the key it was panic stations** fu preso dal panico quando si accorse di aver perso la chiave
panic-stricken ['pænɪk,strɪkən] ADJ *(person)* preso(-a) dal panico, in preda al panico; *(look)* terrorizzato(-a)
pan·ni·er ['pænɪə^r] N *(gen)* paniere *m*; *(on bicycle)* borsa; *(on animal)* bisaccia
pano·ply ['pænəplɪ] N: **the whole panoply of** *(frm)* l'intera collezione di
pano·ra·ma [,pænə'rɑ:mə] N panorama *m*
pano·ram·ic [,pænə'ræmɪk] ADJ panoramico(-a)
pano·rami·cal·ly [,pænə'ræmɪkəlɪ] ADV panoramicamente
pan·pipes ['pæn,paɪps] NPL flauto *msg* di Pan, siringa *fsg*
pan·sy ['pænzɪ] N *(Bot)* viola del pensiero, pensée *f inv*; *(fam pej)* checca
pant [pænt] VI ansimare, avere il fiatone; **he was panting for a drink** moriva dalla voglia di bere; **she panted up the stairs** salì le scale ansimando
pan·tech·ni·con [pæn'tɛknɪkən] N *(Brit)* grosso furgone *m* per traslochi
pan·theism ['pænθɪ,ɪzəm] N panteismo
pan·theis·tic [,pænθɪ'ɪstɪk] ADJ panteistico(-a)
pan·the·on ['pænθɪən] N pantheon *m inv*
pan·ther ['pænθə^r] N pantera
panties ['pæntɪz] NPL mutandine *fpl*
pan·ti·hose ['pæntɪ,həʊz] N *(Am)* collant *m inv*
pan·to ['pæntəʊ] N *(Brit fam)* = **pantomime 1**
pan·to·graph ['pæntə,grɑ:f] N *(Rail, Tech)* pantografo
pan·to·mime ['pæntə,maɪm] N **1** *(at Christmas)* spettacolo natalizio **2** *(mime)* pantomima

PANTOMIME

In Gran Bretagna la **pantomime** (abbreviata in **panto**) è una sorta di libera interpretazione delle favole più conosciute che vengono messe in scena nei teatri durante il periodo natalizio. Gli attori principali sono la dama, "dame", che è un uomo vestito da donna, il protagonista, "principal boy", che è una donna travestita da uomo, e il cattivo, "villain". È uno spettacolo per tutta la famiglia, che prevede la partecipazione del pubblico.
▹ www.its-behind-you.com/

pan·try ['pæntrɪ] N dispensa
pants [pænts] NPL *(Brit: underwear)* mutande *fpl*, slip *m inv*; *(Am: trousers)* pantaloni *mpl*, calzoni *mpl*; **bra and pants** reggiseno e mutande; **to catch sb with his pants down** *(fam)* beccare qn in una situazione imbarazzante
pant·suit ['pænt,su:t] N *(Am)* completo *m* pantalone *inv*
pan·ty·hose ['pæntɪ,həʊz] N = **pantihose**
pan·zer ['pænzə^r] N panzer *m inv*
pap [pæp] N *(pej: drivel)* stupidaggini *fpl*; *(food)* pappa
pa·pa·cy ['peɪpəsɪ] N papato

pa·pal ['peɪpəl] ADJ papale, pontificio(-a)
pa·pa·raz·zi [,pæpə'rætsi:] NPL paparazzi *mpl*
pa·pa·ya [pə'paɪə] N papaia
◎ **pa·per** ['peɪpə^r] N **1** *(material)* carta; *(wallpaper)* carta da parati, tappezzeria; **a piece of paper** *(odd bit)* un pezzo di carta; *(sheet)* un foglio (di carta); **on paper** sulla carta; **to put sth down on paper** mettere qc per iscritto **2** *(exam questions)* prova scritta, scritto; *(lecture)* relazione *f* **3** *(newspaper)* giornale *m*; **the papers** i giornali; **it was in the papers** era su tutti giornali; **I saw an advert in the paper** ho visto un annuncio sul giornale; **to write to the papers about sth** scrivere una lettera aperta *or* ai giornali su qc
■ VT *(wall, room)* tappezzare
■ ADJ *(towel, cup)* di carta; *(industry)* cartario(-a), della carta; *see also* **papers**
▸ **paper over** VI + PREP: **to paper over the cracks** *(fig)* appianare le divergenze
paper advance N *(on printer)* avanzamento della carta
paper·back ['peɪpə,bæk] N tascabile *m*, paperback *m inv*
paperback edition N edizione *f* economica
paper bag N sacchetto di carta
paper·boy ['peɪpə,bɔɪ] N *(selling)* strillone *m*; *(delivering)* ragazzo che recapita i giornali
paper chase N *(game) corsa campestre in cui i partecipanti seguono una scia di pezzetti di carta*
paper·clip ['peɪpə,klɪp] N graffetta, clip *f inv*
paper-cutter ['peɪpə,kʌtə^r] N taglierina
paper handkerchief N *(also:* **paper hankie***)* fazzoletto *or* fazzolettino di carta
paper knife N tagliacarte *m inv*
paper·less ['peɪpəlɪs] ADJ: **the paperless office** l'ufficio informatizzato; **paperless trading** *(Fin)* contrattazioni *fpl* elettroniche
paper mill N cartiera
paper money N cartamoneta, moneta cartacea
paper profit N *(Fin)* utile *m* sulla carta
paper round N: **to do a paper round** recapitare i giornali a domicilio
papers ['peɪpəz] NPL *(writings, documents)* carte *fpl*; *(identity papers)* documenti *mpl* (di riconoscimento); **old papers** scartoffie *fpl*; **Churchill's private papers** gli scritti *or* i documenti privati di Churchill
paper shop N giornalaio *(negozio)*
paper tiger N tigre *f* di carta
paper towel N salvietta di carta
paper·weight ['peɪpə,weɪt] N fermacarte *m inv*
paper·work ['peɪpə,wɜ:k] N parte *f* amministrativa di un lavoro; **I've got a lot of paperwork to do** ho un sacco di pratiche da sbrigare
papier-mâché [,pæpjeɪ'mæʃeɪ] N cartapesta
pa·pist ['peɪpɪst] N *(pej)* papista *m/f*
pap·ri·ka ['pæprɪkə] N *(spice)* paprica; *(vegetable)* peperoncino rosso
Pap test ['pæp,tɛst], *(Am)* **Pap smear** ['pæp,smɪə^r] N *(Med)* pap-test *m inv*
par [pɑ:^r] N **1** *(equality of value)* parità, pari *f*; *(Fin: of shares)* valore *m* nominale; **to be on a par with sb/sth** essere allo stesso livello di qn/qc; **at/above/below par** *(Fin)* alla/sopra la/sotto la pari **2** *(average)*: **to feel below** *or* **under** *or* **not up to par** *(ill)* non essere *or* non sentirsi in forma; **that's par for the course** *(fig)* è normale; **to be above/below par** *(gen, Golf)* essere al di sopra/al di sotto della norma
para ['pærə] N *(fam)* parà *m inv*
para·ble ['pærəbl] N parabola *(Rel)*
pa·rabo·la [pə'ræbələ] N parabola *(Mat)*
para·chute ['pærəʃu:t] N paracadute *m inv*
■ VT paracadutare
■ VI *(also:* **parachute down***)* paracadutarsi
parachute jump N lancio col paracadute
para·chut·ist ['pærəʃu:tɪst] N paracadutista *m/f*
pa·rade [pə'reɪd] N *(procession)* sfilata; *(Mil: marchpast)* parata; *(: ceremony, inspection)* rivista; **to be on parade** *(Mil: marching)* sfilare; *(: for inspection)* essere schierato(-a); **a fashion parade** *(Brit)* una sfilata di moda
■ VT *(troops: in ceremonial order)* schierare in parata; *(: for a march)* far sfilare; *(placard etc)* portare in giro *or* in corteo; *(show off: learning, wealth, new clothes)* fare sfoggio di, sfoggiare, ostentare
■ VI *(Mil: march)* sfilare; *(: in ceremonial order)* schierarsi in parata; *(boy scouts, demonstrators)* marciare in corteo; **to parade about** *or* **around** *(fam)* pavoneggiarsi; **the strikers paraded through the town** gli scioperanti hanno attraversato la città in corteo
parade ground N piazza d'armi
para·digm ['pærə,daɪm] N paradigma *m*
para·dig·mat·ic [,pærədɪg'mætɪk] ADJ paradigmatico(-a)
para·dise ['pærə,daɪs] N paradiso
para·dox ['pærə,dɒks] N paradosso
para·doxi·cal [,pærə'dɒksɪkəl] ADJ paradossale
para·doxi·cal·ly [,pærə'dɒksɪkəlɪ] ADV paradossalmente
par·af·fin ['pærəfɪn], *(Am)* **par·af·fin oil** N cherosene *m*; **liquid paraffin** olio di paraffina
paraffin heater N *(Brit)* stufa al cherosene
paraffin lamp N *(Brit)* lampada a petrolio
paraffin wax N paraffina solida
para·glide ['pærəglaɪd] VI *(Sport)* fare parapendio
para·glid·er ['pærə,glaɪdə^r] N *(parachute)* parapendio; *(person)* parapendista *m/f*
para·glid·ing ['pærə,glaɪdɪŋ] N *(Sport)* parapendio; **to go paragliding** fare parapendio
para·gon ['pærəgən] N: **paragon of virtue** modello di virtù

DID YOU KNOW ...?
paragon is not translated by the Italian word *paragone*

para·graph ['pærəgrɑ:f] N *(gen)* paragrafo; *(in newspaper)* trafiletto; **to begin a new paragraph** andare a capo
Para·guay ['pærə,gwaɪ] N Paraguay *m*
Para·guay·an [,pærə'gwaɪən] ADJ, N paraguaiano(-a)
para·keet ['pærəki:t] N parrocchetto
par·al·lel ['pærəlɛl] ADJ: **parallel (with, to)** parallelo(-a) (a); **the road runs parallel to the railway** la strada corre parallela alla ferrovia
■ N *(Geom)* parallela; *(Geog)* parallelo; *(Horse-riding)* largo; *(fig)* confronto, paragone *m*, parallelo; **to draw a parallel between** *(fig)* fare un parallelo fra
■ VT *(fig: equal)* uguagliare; *(: be similar to)* essere analogo(-a) *or* parallelo(-a) a
parallel bars NPL parallele *fpl*
par·al·lel·epi·ped [,pærə,lɛlə'paɪpɛd] N parallelepipedo
par·al·lelo·gram [,pærə'lɛləʊ,græm] N parallelogramma *m*
parallel port N *(Comput)* porta parallela
parallel processing N *(Comput)* processo in parallelo
parallel turn N *(Skiing)* curva a sci uniti
pa·raly·sis [pə'ræləsɪs] N *(pl* **paralyses***)* paralisi
para·lyt·ic [,pærə'lɪtɪk] ADJ *(Med: person)* paralitico(-a);

Pp

(*: stroke*) di paralisi; (*Brit fam: drunk*) ubriaco(-a) fradicio(-a)
para·lyze, para·lyse ['pærə,laɪz] VT (*Med, fig*) paralizzare; **paralyzed with fear** paralizzato(-a) dalla paura; **his leg is paralyzed** ha la gamba paralizzata
para·lyzed ['pærə,laɪzd] ADJ **1** (*Med*) paralizzato **2** (*fig: immobilized*) paralizzato; **paralyzed with fear** paralizzato dalla paura
para·medic [,pærə'mɛdɪk], **para·medi·cal** [,pærə'mɛdɪkəl] N paramedico
para·medi·cal [,pærə'mɛdɪkəl] ADJ paramedico(-a)
pa·ram·eter [pə'ræmɪtə^r] N parametro
para·mili·tary [,pærə'mɪlɪtərɪ] ADJ paramilitare
para·mount ['pærə,maʊnt] ADJ: **of paramount importance** di importanza capitale
para·noia [,pærə'nɔɪə] N paranoia
para·noi·ac [,pærə'nɔɪɪk] ADJ paranoico(-a)
para·noid ['pærə,nɔɪd] ADJ (*Psych*) paranoico(-a); **paranoid (about)** (*fig*) ossessionato(-a) (da)
para·nor·mal [,pærə'nɔːməl] N: **the paranormal** i fenomeni paranormali
■ ADJ paranormale
para·pet ['pærəpɪt] N parapetto
para·pher·na·lia [,pærəfə'neɪlɪə] N armamentario
para·phrase ['pærə,freɪz] N parafrasi *f inv*
■ VT parafrasare
para·plegia [,pærə'pliːdʒə] N paraplegia
para·plegic [,pærə'pliːdʒɪk] ADJ, N paraplegico(-a)
para·psy·chol·ogy [,pærəsaɪ'kɒlədʒɪ] N parapsicologia
para·site ['pærə,saɪt] N parassita *m*
para·sit·ic [,pærə'sɪtɪk], **para·siti·cal** [,pærə'sɪtɪkəl] ADJ (*gen*) parassita; (*disease*) parassitario(-a)
para·sit·ism ['pærəsaɪ,tɪzəm] N parassitismo
para·sol [,pærə'sɒl] N parasole *m inv*
para·trooper ['pærə,truːpə^r] N (*Mil*) paracadutista *m*, parà *m inv*
para·troops ['pærə,truːps] NPL paracadutisti *mpl*
par·boil ['pɑː,bɔɪl] VT sbollentare
par·cel ['pɑːsl] N (*gen*) pacchetto; (*larger*) pacco; (*of land*) appezzamento; (*fig: of fools, liars*) branco; (*: of lies*) mucchio
▸ **parcel out** VT + ADV (*inheritance*) dividere; (*land*) distribuire, spartire
▸ **parcel up** VT + ADV impacchettare, fare un pacco di

> DID YOU KNOW ...?
> **parcel** is not translated by the Italian word ***parcella***

parcel bomb N (*Brit*) pacchetto esplosivo
parcel office N ufficio *m* spedizioni *inv*
parcel post N servizio pacchi
parch [pɑːtʃ] VT riardere
parched [pɑːtʃt] ADJ (*land, garden*) disseccato(-a), riarso(-a); (*person*) assetato(-a); **parched earth** terra arsa; **I'm parched!** (*fam*) muoio di sete!
parch·ment ['pɑːtʃmənt] N pergamena
par·don ['pɑːdn] N perdono, scusa; (*Rel*) indulgenza; (*Law*) condono della pena, grazia; **general pardon** amnistia; **a presidential pardon** una grazia del presidente
■ VT (*forgive*) perdonare; (*Law*) graziare; **to pardon sb for sth/doing sth** perdonare qc a qn/qn per aver fatto qc
■ EXCL (*apologizing*) mi scusi!; (*not hearing*) scusi?, come?, prego?; **(I beg your) pardon?** (*Am*): **pardon me?** prego?
par·don·able ['pɑːdnəbl] ADJ perdonabile
par·don·ably ['pɑːdnəblɪ] ADV comprensibilmente

pare [pɛə^r] VT (*nails*) tagliarsi; (*fruit*) sbucciare, pelare
▸ **pare down** VT + ADV (*costs*) ridurre, limitare
◎ **par·ent** ['pɛərənt] N padre *m* (*or* madre *f*); **his parents** i suoi genitori; **she changed when she became a parent** è cambiata quando è diventata madre

> DID YOU KNOW ...?
> **parent** is not translated by the Italian word ***parente***

par·ent·age ['pɛərəntɪdʒ] N natali *mpl*; **of unknown parentage** di genitori sconosciuti
pa·ren·tal [pə'rɛntl] ADJ dei genitori; (*Bio*) parentale
parental leave N congedo parentale
parent company N società *f inv* madre *inv*
pa·ren·thesis [pə'rɛnθɪsɪs] N (*pl* **parentheses** [pə'rɛnθɪsiːz]) parentesi *f inv*; **in parentheses** fra parentesi
par·en·theti·cal [,pærən'θɛtɪkəl] ADJ (*clause*) parentetico(-a); (*statement*) fra parentesi
par·en·theti·cal·ly [,pærən'θɛtɪkəlɪ] ADV tra parentesi
par·ent·hood ['pɛərənthʊd] N paternità (*or* maternità)
par·ent·ing ['pɛərəntɪŋ] N: **parenting is a full-time occupation** allevare i figli è un lavoro a tempo pieno; **young couples lacking parenting skills** giovani coppie che non riescono ad essere bravi genitori
parent-teacher association [,pɛərənt'tiːtʃə əsəʊsɪ'eɪʃən] N ≈ consiglio di classe
pa·resis [pə'riːsɪs] N paresi *f*
par ex·cel·lence [,pɑːr'ɛksələːns] ADV per eccellenza
pa·ri·ah [pə'raɪə] N (*frm*) paria *m inv*
Par·is[1] ['pærɪs] N Parigi *f*
Par·is[2] ['pærɪs] N (*Myth*) Paride
par·ish ['pærɪʃ] N (*Rel*) parrocchia; (*Brit: civil*) ≈ comune *m*
■ ADJ (*church*) parrocchiale; (*hall*) parrocchiale *or* municipale
parish council N (*Brit*) ≈ consiglio comunale
pa·rish·ion·er [pə'rɪʃənə^r] N parrocchiano(-a)
parish priest N parroco
Pa·ris·ian [pə'rɪzɪən] ADJ, N parigino(-a)
par·ity ['pærɪtɪ] N parità
◎ **park** [pɑːk] N (*gen*) parco; (*public*) giardino pubblico; **why don't we go for a walk in the park?** perché non andiamo al parco a fare una passeggiata?; **a national park** un parco nazionale; **theme park** parco divertimenti; **car park** parcheggio
■ VT (*Aut*) parcheggiare; **where can I park my car?** dove posso parcheggiare l'auto?
■ VI (*Aut*) parcheggiare, parcheggiarsi
par·ka ['pɑːkə] N eskimo
park·ing ['pɑːkɪŋ] N (*act*) parcheggiare *m*; (*parking space*) parcheggio; **parking is difficult in the city centre** è difficile trovare parcheggio in centro; **"no parking"** "divieto di sosta"
■ ADJ (*space*) di parcheggio
parking attendant N custode *m/f* di posteggio, posteggiatore(-trice)
parking fine N multa per sosta vietata
parking lights NPL luci *fpl* di posizione
parking lot N (*Am*) posteggio, parcheggio
parking meter N parchimetro
parking offence, (*Am*) **parking violation** N infrazione *f* al divieto di sosta
parking place N posto di parcheggio
parking ticket N multa per sosta vietata
Parkinson's ['pɑːkɪnsənz] N (*also:* **Parkinson's disease**) morbo di Parkinson

Parkinson's Law ['pɑ,kınsənz,lɔː] N legge *f* di Parkinson (*secondo la quale il tempo necessario a fare qualcosa tende ad allungarsi per riempire il tempo a disposizione*)
park·land ['pɑːk,lænd] N parco
park·way ['pɑːk,weı] N (*Am*) viale *m*
parky ['pɑːkı] ADJ (*comp* **-ier**, *superl* **-iest**) (*Brit fam*) freddino(-a)
par·lance ['pɑːləns] N: **in common/modern parlance** nel linguaggio comune/moderno
par·ley ['pɑːlı] (*old*) N colloquio
■ VI conferire, parlamentare
◎ **par·lia·ment** ['pɑːləmənt] N parlamento; **to get into parliament** essere eletto(-a) al parlamento
▷ www.parliament.uk/
▷ www.scottish.parliament.uk/
▷ www.aph.gov.au/
▷ www.parl.gc.ca/
▷ www.parliament.govt.nz/
▷ www.parliament.gov.za/
▷ www.europarl.eu.int/home/default_en.htm
▷ www.ipu.org/english/parlweb.htm

PARLIAMENT

Nel Regno Unito il Parlamento, **Parliament**, è formato da due camere: la "House of Commons", e la "House of Lords". Nella "House of Commons" siedono 650 parlamentari, chiamati "MPs", eletti per votazione diretta del popolo nelle rispettive circoscrizioni elettorali, le "constituencies". Le sessioni del Parlamento sono presiedute e moderate dal presidente della Camera, lo "Speaker". Alla "House of Lords", i cui poteri sono più limitati, in passato si accedeva per nomina o per carica ereditaria mentre ora le cariche ereditarie sono state ridotte e in futuro verranno abolite.
▷ www.parliament.uk/

par·lia·men·tar·ian [,pɑːləmen'tɛərıən] N parlamentare *m/f*
◎ **par·lia·men·ta·ry** [,pɑːlə'mentərı] ADJ parlamentare
parliamentary secretary N sottosegretario
parlour, (*Am*) **par·lor** ['pɑːləʳ] N (*in house*) salotto; **ice-cream parlour** gelateria
par·lous ['pɑːləs] ADJ (*old, liter*) periglioso(-a)
Par·me·san [,pɑːmı'zæn] N (*also:* **Parmesan cheese**) parmigiano
Par·nas·sus [pɑː'næsəs] N (*Geog, Myth*) Parnaso
pa·ro·chial [pə'rəʊkıəl] ADJ (*of parish*) parrocchiale; (*fig pej*) provinciale, ristretto(-a)
pa·ro·chi·al·ly [pə'rəʊkıəlı] ADV (*fig pej*). campanilisticamente
paro·dy ['pærədı] N parodia
■ VT parodiare
pa·role [pə'rəʊl] N (*Law*) libertà condizionale; **on parole** in libertà condizionale; **to break (one's) parole** *commettere un atto che ha per conseguenza la revoca della libertà condizionale*
par·ox·ysm ['pærək,sızəm] N (*Med*) parossismo; (*of laughter, coughing*) convulso; (*of grief, anger*) attacco
par·quet ['pɑːkeı] N (*also:* **parquet floor**) parquet *m inv*
par·rot ['pærət] N pappagallo
parrot-fashion ['pærət,fæʃən] ADV (*learn*) a pappagallo, in modo pappagallesco
par·ry ['pærı] VT (*blow*) parare; (*fig: question*) eludere
parse [pɑːs] VT analizzare dal punto di vista grammaticale
par·si·mo·ni·ous [,pɑːsı'məʊnıəs] ADJ parsimonioso(-a)
par·si·mo·ni·ous·ly [,pɑːsı'məʊnıəslı] ADV con parsimonia
par·si·mo·ny ['pɑːsımənı] N parsimonia
pars·ley ['pɑːslı] N prezzemolo
parsley sauce N besciamella con prezzemolo
pars·nip ['pɑːsnıp] N pastinaca
par·son ['pɑːsn] N (*gen*) parroco, prete *m*; (*Church of England*) pastore *m*
par·son·age ['pɑːsənıdʒ] N canonica, casa parrocchiale
parson's nose N boccone *m* del prete
◎ **part** [pɑːt] N
1 (*portion, fragment*) parte *f*; (*of serial*) episodio; **in part** in parte; **it was funny in parts** è stato divertente a tratti; **the first part of the play was boring** la prima parte della commedia era noiosa; **for the most part** nell'insieme, per lo più; **the greater part of it is done** il più è fatto; **for the better part of the day** per la maggior parte della giornata; **two parts of sand to one of cement** due parti di sabbia e una (parte) di cemento; **to be part and parcel of** essere parte integrante di
2 (*Tech: component*) pezzo *or* parte *f* (di ricambio); (*Mus*) parte; **soprano part** la parte del soprano; **2-part song** canto a 2 voci; **moving part** parte meccanica; **spare parts** pezzi di ricambio
3 (*role: also Theatre*) parte *f*, ruolo; **to take part in sth** prendere parte *or* partecipare a qc; **a lot of people took part in the demonstration** alla manifestazione ha partecipato molta gente; **to have no part in sth** non aver nulla a che fare con qc; **to play a part in sth/doing sth** avere un certo ruolo in qc/nel fare qc; **to look the part** essere perfetto(-a) nella parte; **she got a part in the film** ha ottenuto una parte nel film
4 (*region*) parte *f*; **in these parts** da queste parti; **a lovely part of the country** una bella regione
5 (*behalf, side*) parte *f*; **on his part** da parte sua; **to take sb's part** prendere le parti di qn, parteggiare per qn; **for my part** da parte mia, per quanto mi riguarda; **a mistake on the part of my brother** un errore da parte di mio fratello; **to take sth in good/bad part** prendere bene/male qc
6 (*Am: in hair*) scriminatura, riga
■ ADV (*partly*) in parte; **a part eaten apple** una mela mezza mangiata
■ VT (*curtains, branches*) scostare; (*lovers*) dividere, separare; (*boxers*) separare; **to part one's hair** farsi la riga *or* la scriminatura (nei capelli)
■ VI (*boxers*) separarsi; (*curtains*) aprirsi; (*roads*) dividersi; (*rope: break*) spezzarsi, rompersi; (*friends, lovers*) lasciarsi; **to part (from sb)** separarsi (da qn); **they parted friends** si sono lasciati da buoni amici
▸ **part with** VI + PREP (*possessions*) separarsi da, disfarsi di; (*money*) sborsare; **I hate parting with it** mi dispiace disfarmene
par·take [pɑː'teık] (*pt* **partook**, *pp* **partaken** [pɑː'teıkən]) VI (*frm*) **1** **to partake of sth** consumare qc, prendere qc **2** **to partake in an activity** partecipare *or* prender parte ad una attività
part exchange N (*Brit*): **in part exchange** in pagamento parziale; **we will take your car in part exchange for a new one** detrarremo il valore della sua vecchia auto da quello della nuova
par·tial ['pɑːʃəl] ADJ (*gen*) parziale; **to be in partial agreement** essere parzialmente *or* in parte d'accordo;

Pp

to be partial to sth *(like)* avere un debole per qc; **partial blindness** cecità *f inv* parziale

par·tial·ity [ˌpɑːʃɪ'ælɪtɪ] N **1** *(bias)*: **partiality (towards)** parzialità (verso) **2** *(liking)*: **partiality (for)** predilezione *f* (per); debole *m* (per)

par·tial·ly ['pɑːʃəlɪ] ADV *(partly)* parzialmente, in parte

par·tici·pant [pɑː'tɪsɪpənt] N: **participant (in)** partecipante *m/f* (a)

◎ **par·tici·pate** [pɑː'tɪsɪˌpeɪt] VI: **to participate (in)** partecipare (a), prendere parte (a)

par·tici·pa·tion [pɑːˌtɪsɪ'peɪʃən] N: **partecipation (in)** partecipazione *f* (a)

par·ti·ci·ple [pɑː'tɪsɪpl] N participio; **past/present participle** participio passato/presente

par·ti·cle ['pɑːtɪkl] N *(Gram, Phys)* particella; *(of dust)* granello; *(of food)* pezzettino; *(fig: of truth, sense)* briciolo

◎ **par·ticu·lar** [pə'tɪkjʊlə^r] ADJ **1** *(specific, special)* particolare; **that particular house/train** quella casa/quel treno in particolare; **to pay particular attention to** *or* **to take particular care over** fare molta attenzione a; **to place particular emphasis on sth** dare particolare importanza a qc; **in this particular case** in questo caso particolare; **for no particular reason** senza una ragione precisa *or* particolare; **she's a particular friend of mine** è una mia carissima amica **2** *(fastidious, fussy)* pignolo(-a), difficile; *(painstaking)* meticoloso(-a); **to be very particular about** essere molto pignolo(-a) su; **he's particular about his food** è molto difficile nel mangiare; **I'm not particular** per me va bene tutto

■ N **1** *(detail)* particolare *m* **2** **in particular** in particolare, particolarmente; **nothing in particular** nulla in *or* di particolare; *see also* **particulars**

par·ticu·lar·ity [pəˌtɪkjʊ'lærɪtɪ] N particolarità *f inv*; *(detail)* particolare *m*; *(fastidiousness)* pignoleria

par·ticu·lar·ize [pə'tɪkjʊləˌraɪz] VT, VI particolareggiare

◎ **par·ticu·lar·ly** [pə'tɪkjʊləlɪ] ADV *(especially)* particolarmente; **I particularly wanted it for tomorrow** lo volevo proprio per domani; **particularly since ...** soprattutto perché...

par·ticu·lars [pə'tɪkjʊləz] NPL *(information)* particolari *mpl*, dettagli *mpl*; *(personal details)* dati *mpl*; **full particulars** informazioni *fpl* complete

par·ticu·lates [pɑː'tɪkjʊləts] NPL *(Chem)* polveri *fpl* sottili

part·ing ['pɑːtɪŋ] ADJ *(kiss etc)* d'addio; **his parting words** le sue ultime parole; **parting shot** *(fig)* battuta finale; **and with this parting shot he left** e detto ciò se ne andò

■ N **1** separazione *f*; **we have reached the parting of the ways** *(fig)* a questo punto le nostre strade si dividono **2** *(Brit: in hair)* scriminatura, riga

par·ti·san [ˌpɑːtɪ'zæn] ADJ *(gen)* fazioso(-a); *(fighter)* partigiano(-a); **partisan spirit** spirito di parte

■ N *(fighter)* partigiano(-a)

par·ti·tion [pɑː'tɪʃən] N **1** *(wall)* parete *f* divisoria, tramezzo **2** *(of country)* suddivisione *f*, divisione *f*

■ VT *(country etc)* suddividere, dividere

▸ **partition off** VT + ADV separare con una parete divisoria

par·ti·tive ['pɑːtɪtɪv] ADJ partitivo(-a)

■ N partitivo

◎ **part·ly** ['pɑːtlɪ] ADV parzialmente, in parte

◎ **part·ner** ['pɑːtnə^r] N *(gen)* compagno(-a), partner *m/f inv*; *(Comm)* socio(-a); *(in crime)* complice *m/f*; *(Sport)* compagno(-a); *(at dance: male)* cavaliere *m*; (: *female)* dama

■ VT *(Sport)* essere in coppia con; *(at dance)* accompagnare; *(in individual dance)* ballare con

◎ **part·ner·ship** ['pɑːtnəʃɪp] N *(gen)* associazione *f*; *(Comm)* società *f inv*; **a global partnership of environmental groups** un'associazione mondiale di gruppi ambientalisti; **to take sb into partnership** prendere qn come socio(-a); **to go into partnership (with)** *or* **form a partnership (with)** mettersi in società (con), associarsi (a); **the two lawyers went into partnership ten years ago** i due avvocati si sono messi in società due anni fa

part of speech N *(Gram)* parte del discorso

par·took [pɑː'tʊk] PT *of* **partake**

part owner N comproprietario(-a)

part payment N acconto

par·tridge ['pɑːtrɪdʒ] N pernice *f*

part-time ['pɑːt'taɪm] ADV, ADJ part-time *inv*; **a part-time job** un lavoro part time; **she works part-time** lavora part time

part-timer [ˌpɑːt'taɪmə^r] N *(also:* **part-time worker)** impiegato(-a) *or* lavoratore(-trice) part-time *inv*

part·way ['pɑːtweɪ] ADV: **partway through sth** *(fam)* a metà di qc

◎ **par·ty** ['pɑːtɪ] N **1** *(Pol)* partito; **the Conservative/Labour Party** il partito conservatore/laburista **2** *(group)* gruppo; *(Mil, team)* squadra; **a party of travellers/tourists** una comitiva di viaggiatori/turisti **3** *(celebration)* festa; **to have** *or* **give** *or* **throw a party** dare una festa *or* un party; **birthday party** festa di compleanno **4** *(Law)* parte *f* (in causa); **the parties to a dispute** le parti in causa; **to be a party to a crime** essere coinvolto(-a) in un reato; **he refused to be a party to such an agreement** si è rifiutato di entrare in un accordo del genere

■ ADJ *(leader)* del *or* di partito; *(dress, finery)* della festa

par·ty·ing ['pɑːtɪɪŋ] N *(fam)*: **he loves partying** gli piace far baldoria

party line N **1** *(Pol)* linea del partito **2** *(Telec)* duplex *m inv*

party piece N *(Brit fam)*: **to do one's party piece** *esibirsi nel proprio pezzo forte per divertire gli altri*

party political broadcast N *comunicato radiotelevisivo di propaganda*

party politics N *(Pol)* propaganda di partito

party wall N muro di confine *or* divisorio

par value ['pɑːˌvæljuː] N *(of share, bond)* valore *m* nominale

par·venu ['pɑːvənˌjuː] N *(frm)* parvenu *m inv*

◎ **pass** [pɑːs] N

1 *(permit)* lasciapassare *m inv*; *(for bus, train)* tesserino; *(Mil etc)* permesso; **bus pass** abbonamento dell'autobus

2 *(Geog: in mountains)* passo, gola, valico; **the pass was blocked with snow** il valico era bloccato dalla neve

3 *(Sport)* passaggio

4 *(in exams)* sufficienza; **to get a pass in German** prendere la sufficienza in tedesco; **I got six passes** ho preso la sufficienza in sei materie

5 **things have come to a pretty pass** ecco a cosa siamo arrivati

6 **to make a pass at sb** *(fam)* fare delle proposte *or* delle avances a qn

■ VT

1 *(move past)* passare, oltrepassare; *(in opposite direction)* incrociare; *(Aut: overtake)* sorpassare, superare; **they**

passed each other on the way si sono incrociati per strada; **I pass his house on my way to school** passo davanti a casa sua andando a scuola
2 (*hand, give*) (far) passare; (*Sport: ball*) passare; **could you pass me the salt, please?** mi passeresti il sale, per favore?; **he passed his hand over his forehead** si passò la mano sulla fronte; **to pass a thread through a hole** far passare un filo attraverso un foro; **to pass sb sth** *or* **sth to sb** passare qc a qn
3 (*Scol: exam*) superare, passare; (*: candidate*) promuovere; **I hope I'll pass the exam** spero di passare l'esame
4 (*approve: motion, plan*) approvare, votare
5 (*spend: time*) passare, trascorrere; **we passed the weekend pleasantly** abbiamo trascorso *or* passato piacevolmente il fine settimana; **it passes the time** fa passare il tempo
6 (*express: remark*) fare; (*: opinion*) esprimere; **to pass the time of day with sb** scambiarsi i (soliti) convenevoli
■ VI
1 (*come, go*): **to pass (through)** passare (per); (*Aut: overtake*) sorpassare; **he passed by the cinema** è passato davanti al cinema; **sales have passed the £1 million mark** le vendite hanno superato il milione di sterline; **to pass out of sight** sparire alla vista; **to pass into oblivion** cadere nell'oblio; **to pass into history** passare alla storia
2 (*be accepted: behaviour*) essere accettabile; (*: plan*) essere approvato(-a); **she could pass for twenty-five** potrebbe passare per una venticinquenne; **what passes for art these days** quel che si definisce arte oggigiorno; **is this okay? — oh, it'll pass** questo va bene? — sì , può andare; **I decided to let it pass** ho deciso di lasciar correre
3 (*time, day*) passare; **the time has passed quickly** il tempo è passato in fretta; **how time passes!** come passa il tempo!
4 (*pain*) passare; (*memory, opportunity*) sfuggire
5 (*in exam*) essere promosso(-a)
6 (*happen*) accadere; **all that passed between them** tutto quello che c'è stato fra loro; **should it come to pass that ...** (*frm*) dovesse accadere che...
7 (*Cards*) passare
▶ **pass along** VT + ADV far passare
▶ **pass around** VT + ADV = pass round
▶ **pass away** VI + ADV (*euph: die*) mancare, spegnersi
▶ **pass back** VT + ADV (*object*) passare indietro; **I will now pass you back to the studio** (*Radio, TV*) e ora ridiamo la linea allo studio
▶ **pass by** VI + ADV passare (di qui *or* lì)
■ VT + ADV (*ignore*) ignorare, passar sopra a; **life has passed her by** non ha davvero vissuto
▶ **pass down** VT + ADV (*customs, inheritance*) tramandare, trasmettere
▶ **pass off** VI + ADV (*happen*) svolgersi, andare; (*wear off: faintness, headache*) passare
■ VT + ADV: **to pass sb/sth off as** far passare qn/qc per
▶ **pass on** VI + ADV (*euph: die*) spegnersi, mancare; (*proceed*): **to pass on (to)** passare (a)
■ VT + ADV (*hand on*): **to pass on (to)** (*news, information, object*) passare (a); (*cold, illness*) attaccare (a); (*benefits*) trasmettere (a); (*price rises*) riversare (su)
▶ **pass out** VI + ADV (*become unconscious*) svenire; (*Brit Mil*) uscire dall'accademia
▶ **pass over** VI + ADV (*euph: die*) spirare
■ VT + ADV (*topic*) ignorare; (*employee, candidate*) non prendere in considerazione
▶ **pass round, pass around** VT + ADV (*bottle, photographs*) far girare; **could you pass the vegetables round?** potrebbe far passare la verdura?
▶ **pass through** VI + ADV essere di passaggio
■ VT + ADV (*country, city*) passare per; (*hardships*) attraversare
▶ **pass up** VT + ADV (*opportunity*) lasciarsi sfuggire, perdere

pass·able ['pɑːsəbl] ADJ **1** (*tolerable*) passabile; (*work*) accettabile; **his French is passable** il suo francese è passabile **2** (*road*) transitabile, praticabile; (*river*) attraversabile

pass·ably ['pɑːsəblɪ] ADV (*tolerably*) discretamente, passabilmente

◎ **pas·sage** ['pæsɪdʒ] N **1** (*way through*) passaggio; (*corridor*) corridoio **2** (*Naut: voyage*) traversata; **to grant sb safe passage** garantire a qn di passare incolume **3** (*passing*) passare *m*; (*: of bill through parliament*) iter *m inv*; **with the passage of time** (*frm*) col passar del tempo **4** (*section: of book*) brano, passo; (*of music*) brano; **read the passage carefully** leggi attentamente il brano

passage·way ['pæsɪdʒˌweɪ] N passaggio

pass·book ['pɑːsˌbʊk] N libretto di risparmio

pass degree N laurea col minimo dei voti

pas·sé ['pæseɪ] ADJ sorpassato(-a), fuori moda

◎ **pas·sen·ger** ['pæsɪndʒəʳ] N (*in boat, plane, car*) passeggero(-a); (*on train*) viaggiatore(-trice), passeggero(-a)
■ ADJ (*aircraft, liner*) di linea, passeggeri *inv*; (*train*) viaggiatori *inv*

passenger list N lista dei passeggeri

passenger seat N (*Aut*) posto di fianco al guidatore

passenger traffic N movimento passeggeri

passer-by ['pɑːsə'baɪ] N (*pl* **passers-by**) passante *m/f*

pass·ing ['pɑːsɪŋ] ADJ (*fleeting: fancy, thought*) passeggero(-a); (*: moment*) fuggevole; (*glance, remark*) di sfuggita; (*car, person*) di passaggio
■ N (*of customs, euph: death*) scomparsa; **with the passing of the years** col passar degli anni; **to mention sth in passing** accennare a qc di sfuggita; **to mention sth in passing** accennare a qc di sfuggita

passing-out parade [ˌpɑːsɪŋ'aʊtpəˌreɪd] N (*Mil, Police*) parata finale

passing place N (*Aut*) piazzola (di sosta)

◎ **pas·sion** ['pæʃən] N **1** passione *f*; **to have a passion for sth** aver la passione di qc, avere una passione per qc; **his passion for seafood** la sua passione per i frutti di mare; **his passion for accuracy** il suo amore per la precisione; **to get into a passion (about sth)** andare su tutte ie furie (per qc) **2** (*Rel*): **the Passion** la Passione

pas·sion·ate ['pæʃənɪt] ADJ (*embrace, speech*) appassionato(-a); (*temperament, person*) passionale; (*believer*) convinto(-a); (*desire*) ardente

pas·sion·ate·ly ['pæʃənɪtlɪ] ADV (*embrace, speak*) appassionatamente; (*believe, desire*) ardentemente; **to be passionately fond of** adorare

passion·flower ['pæʃənˌflaʊəʳ] N passiflora, fiore *m* della passione

passion fruit N frutto della passione

Passion Play N rappresentazione *f* della Passione di Cristo

Passion Sunday N domenica di Passione

pas·sive ['pæsɪv] ADJ (*gen, Gram*) passivo(-a)
■ N passivo; **in the passive** al passivo

pas·sive·ly ['pæsɪvlɪ] ADV passivamente

Pp

pas·sive·ness ['pæsɪvnɪs], **pas·siv·ity** [pæ'sɪvɪtɪ] N passività
passive smoker N fumatore(-trice) passivo(-a)
passive smoking N fumo passivo
pass·key ['pɑ:s,ki:] N passe-partout *m inv*
pass mark N punteggio minimo (*per la promozione*)
Pass·over ['pɑ:s,əʊvə^r] N Pasqua ebraica
pass·port ['pɑ:spɔ:t] N passaporto; (*fig*): **passport (to)** chiave *f* (di)
passport control N controllo *m* passaporti *inv*
pass·word ['pɑ:s,wɜ:d] N (*also Comput*) parola *f* d'ordine
◎ **past** [pɑ:st] ADV: **to walk past, go past** passare; **to run** *or* **dash past** passare di corsa; **the days flew past** i giorni sono volati (via)
■ PREP **1** (*in place: in front of*) davanti a; (: *beyond*) oltre, di là di, dopo; **I go past the school every day** passo davanti alla scuola ogni giorno; **it's just past the church** è appena oltre la chiesa **2** (*in time*) passato(-a); **it's past midnight** è mezzanotte passata; **quarter/half past four** le quattro e un quarto/e mezzo; **at twenty past four** alle quattro e venti **3** (*beyond the limits of*) al di là di, oltre; **it's past belief** è assolutamente incredibile; **I'm past caring** non me ne importa più nulla; **she's past forty** ha passato i quaranta; **to be past it** (*fam: person*) essere finito(-a); (: *object*) essere da buttar via; **I wouldn't put it past her to do it** (*fam*) non sarei affatto sorpreso se lo facesse
■ ADJ (*gen, Gram*) passato(-a); (*president, pupil*) ex *inv*; **for some time past** da qualche tempo; **for the past few days** da qualche giorno, in questi ultimi giorni; **for the past 3 days** negli ultimi 3 giorni; **in the past 5 years** negli ultimi 5 anni; **in past years** negli anni passati; **those days are past now** è passato quel tempo
■ N passato; **in the past** in *or* nel passato; (*Gram*) al passato; **it's a thing of the past** è una cosa del passato
pas·ta ['pæstə] N (*Culin*) pasta
paste [peɪst] N **1** (*substance, consistency*) impasto; (*glue*) colla; **fish paste** pâté *m inv* di pesce **2** (*gems*) strass *m inv*
■ ADJ (*jewellery*) di strass
■ VT (*put glue on*) spalmare di colla, collare; (*fasten with glue*) incollare; **to paste sth to the wall** appiccicare qc al muro
paste·board ['peɪst,bɔ:d] N cartone *m*
pas·tel ['pæstəl] N (*crayon, drawing*) pastello; (*colour*) colore *m* pastello *inv*
■ ADJ (*colour*) pastello *inv*; (*drawing*) a pastello
paste-up ['peɪst,ʌp] N collage *m inv*
pas·teur·ize ['pæstə,raɪz] VT pastorizzare
pas·teur·ized ['pæstə,raɪzd] ADJ pastorizzato(-a)
past historic N (*Gram*) passato remoto
pas·tiche [pæ'sti:ʃ] N (*frm*) pastiche *m inv*
pas·tille ['pæstɪl] N pastiglia
pas·time ['pɑ:s,taɪm] N passatempo
past·ing ['peɪstɪŋ] N (*fam: thrashing*) battuta, botte *fpl*
past master N: **to be a past master at** essere molto esperto(-a) in
pas·tor ['pɑ:stə^r] N (*Rel*) pastore *m*
pas·to·ral ['pɑ:stərəl] ADJ (*land*) da pascolo; (*scene, poetry, also Rel*) pastorale
past participle N participio passato
past perfect N: **the past perfect** il piuccheperfetto, il trapassato (*prossimo e remoto*)
pas·try ['peɪstrɪ] N (*dough*) pasta; per rustici, dolci (*cake*) pasta, pasticcino
▷ www.basic-recipes.com/r/pas
pastry board N spianatoia
pastry case N base *f* di (*or* per) pasticcino
pastry cook N pasticciere(-a)
pastry cutter N stampino per biscotti
pastry fork N forchetta da dolce
pastry wheel N rotella
past tense N passato; **in the past tense** al passato
pas·ture ['pɑ:stʃə^r] N pascolo; **to put animals out to pasture** condurre gli animali al pascolo; **to move on to pastures new** (*fig*) cambiare aria
pasture land N pascolo
pasty[1] ['pæstɪ] N (*pie*) *sfogliatina salata ripiena di carne e patate*
pasty[2] ['peɪstɪ] ADJ (*comp* **-ier**, *superl* **-iest**) (*complexion*) smorto(-a)
pat[1] [pæt] N **1** (*with hand*) colpetto (affettuoso); (*to animal*) carezza; **to give sb/o.s. a pat on the back** (*fig*) congratularsi *or* compiacersi con qn/se stesso; **he deserves a pat on the back** bisogna congratularsi con lui **2** (*of butter*) panetto
■ VT (*hair, face etc*) dare dei colpetti leggeri a; (*dog*) accarezzare; (*sb's shoulder etc*) dare un colpetto (affettuoso) su; **he patted her knee** le ha dato un colpetto sul ginocchio
pat[2] [pæt] ADJ, ADV: **the answer came** *or* **was too pat** la risposta è stata troppo pronta; **he knows it (off) pat** *or* (*Am*) **he has it down pat** lo conosce *or* sa a menadito
patch [pætʃ] N (*piece of cloth, material*) toppa, pezza; (*on tyre*) toppa; (*eye patch*) benda; (*area of colour, spot*) macchia; (*piece of land*) appezzamento, pezzo; **a jacket with patches on the elbows** una giacca con le toppe sui gomiti; **a patch of blue sky** un pezzetto di cielo azzurro; **a patch of grass** uno spiazzo erboso; **a vegetable patch** un orticello; **a bald patch** una calvizie incipiente; **a bad patch** un brutto periodo; **the team is going through a bad patch** la squadra sta attraversando un brutto periodo; **it's not a patch on the other one** (*fam*) non vale neanche la metà dell'altro
■ VT (*garment, hole*) rattoppare, mettere una pezza a
▶ **patch together** VT + ADV (*cobble together: agreement, strategy*) mettere insieme alla meglio; (*article, report*) cucire insieme alla meglio
▶ **patch up** VT + ADV (*clothes*) rattoppare; (*car, machine*) riparare alla meglio; (*quarrel*) appianare; (*marriage*) rimettere in sesto
patch·work ['pætʃ,wɜ:k] N patchwork *m inv*; **a patchwork of fields** (*fig*) un mosaico di campi
■ ADJ (*quilt*) patchwork *inv*
patchy ['pætʃɪ] ADJ (*comp* **-ier**, *superl* **-iest**) (*performance etc*) pieno(-a) di alti e bassi; (*knowledge*) incompleto(-a); (*fog*) a banchi; (*colour*) irregolare
pate [peɪt] N: **a bald pate** una testa pelata
pâté ['pæteɪ] N pâté *m inv*
pat·en ['pætən] N patena
pa·tent ['peɪtənt] ADJ (*obvious*) evidente, palese
■ N brevetto; **to take out a patent on sth** far brevettare qc
■ VT brevettare

DID YOU KNOW ...?
patent is not translated by the Italian word *patente*

patent leather N vernice *f* (*pellame*)
pa·tent·ly ['peɪtəntlɪ] ADV palesemente
patent medicine N prodotto medicinale
Patent Office N: **the Patent Office** l'ufficio brevetti
pa·ter·nal [pə'tɜ:nl] ADJ paterno(-a)

pa·ter·nal·ism [pə'tɜːnəlɪzm] N paternalismo
pa·ter·nal·ist [pə'tɜːnəlɪst], **pa·ter·nal·is·tic** [pə'tɜːnə'lɪstɪk] ADJ paternalistico(-a)
pa·ter·nal·ly [pə'tɜːnəlɪ] ADV paternamente, in modo paterno
pa·ter·nity [pə'tɜːnɪtɪ] N paternità
paternity suit N (*Law*) causa di paternità
paternity test N test *m inv* di paternità
◎**path** [pɑːθ] N (*pl* **paths** [pɑːðz]) **1** (*gen*) sentiero, viottolo; (*in garden*) vialetto; (*fig*) strada, via; **a forest path** un sentiero nella foresta; **some men blocked my path** degli uomini mi bloccavano la strada **2** (*of river*) corso; (*of sun, missile, planet*) traiettoria
pa·thet·ic [pə'θɛtɪk] ADJ **1** (*pitiful*) patetico(-a), toccante **2** (*very bad*) penoso(-a), pietoso(-a); **a pathetic sight** uno spettacolo patetico; **his pathetic excuses** le sue scuse penose
pa·theti·cal·ly [pə'θɛtɪklɪ] ADV da far pena, da far pietà; **pathetically thin/weak** spaventosamente magro(-a)/debole; **a pathetically inadequate answer** una risposta da far cascar le braccia
path name N (*Comput*) path name, percorso del file
patho·gen ['pæθəˌdʒɛn] N agente *m* patogeno
patho·gen·ic [ˌpæθə'dʒɛnɪk] ADJ patogeno(-a)
patho·logi·cal [ˌpæθə'lɒdʒɪkəl] ADJ (*also fig*) patologico(-a)
pa·tholo·gist [pə'θɒlədʒɪst] N patologo(-a)
pa·thol·ogy [pə'θɒlədʒɪ] N patologia
▷ www.medbioworld.com/home/lists/diseases.html
▷ www.cdc.gov/health
pa·thos ['peɪθɒs] N pathos *m inv*
path·way ['pɑːθˌweɪ] N sentiero, viottolo
pa·tience ['peɪʃəns] N **1** pazienza; **to lose one's patience** spazientirsi; **to lose one's patience with sb/sth** perdere la pazienza con qn/qc; **he hasn't got much patience** non ha molta pazienza; **he has no patience with children** non ha pazienza con i bambini **2** (*Brit Cards*) solitario; **to play patience** fare un solitario
◎**pa·tient** ['peɪʃənt] ADJ paziente; **to be patient with sb** essere paziente *or* aver pazienza con qn
■ N (*Med*) paziente *m/f*, malato(-a)
pa·tient·ly ['peɪʃəntlɪ] ADV pazientemente
pa·tio ['pætɪəʊ] N terrazza
pa·tri·arch ['peɪtrɪˌɑːk] N patriarca *m*
pa·tri·ar·chal [peɪtrɪ'ɑːkəl] ADJ (*society, role*) patriarcale; (*man, figure*) dall'aspetto patriarcale
pa·tri·cian [pə'trɪʃən] (*frm*) ADJ (*family, looks, features*) aristocratico(-a)
■ N nobile *m/f*
pa·tri·ot ['peɪtrɪət] N patriota *m/f*
pat·ri·ot·ic [ˌpætrɪ'ɒtɪk] ADJ patriottico(-a)
pat·ri·oti·cal·ly [ˌpætrɪ'ɒtɪkəlɪ] ADV patriotticamente, con patriottismo
pat·ri·ot·ism ['pætrɪəˌtɪzəm] N patriottismo
pa·trol [pə'trəʊl] N **1** (*gen*) ronda, giro d'ispezione; (*by plane*) ricognizione *f*; (*by boat*) perlustrazione *f*; **to be on patrol** essere di pattuglia; essere in ricognizione; essere in perlustrazione **2** (*patrol unit*) pattuglia
■ VT pattugliare
■ VI essere di pattuglia; **to patrol up and down** andare avanti e indietro
patrol boat N guardacoste *m inv*
patrol car N autopattuglia (della polizia)
patrol leader N capopattuglia *m*
patrol·man [pə'trəʊlmən] N (*pl* **-men**) **1** (*Am*) agente *m* di polizia **2** (*Aut*) membro del personale del soccorso stradale
patrol wagon N (*Am*) (furgone *m*) cellulare
pa·tron ['peɪtrən] N (*of artist*) mecenate *m/f*; (*of charity*) benefattore(-trice); (*of society*) patrono(-essa); (*of shop, hotel*) cliente *m/f* abituale; **patron of the arts** mecenate *m/f*
pat·ron·age ['pætrənɪdʒ] N (*gen*) patrocinio; (*of shop etc*) frequentazione *f*; **under the patronage of** sotto l'alto patrocinio *or* patronato di; **patronage of the arts** mecenatismo
pat·ron·ize ['pætrəˌnaɪz] VT **1** (*fig: treat condescendingly*) trattare con condiscendenza; **don't patronize me!** non trattarmi con condiscendenza! **2** (*shop*) essere cliente abituale di; (*cinema*) frequentare
pat·ron·iz·ing ['pætrəˌnaɪzɪŋ] ADJ condiscendente
pat·ron·iz·ing·ly ['pætrəˌnaɪzɪŋlɪ] ADV con condiscendenza
patron saint N patrono(-a)
pat·ro·nym·ic [ˌpætrə'nɪmɪk] ADJ, N patronimico(-a)
pat·ter[1] ['pætəʳ] N (*comedian's*) monologo; (*conjuror's*) chiacchiere *fpl*; (*sales talk*) discorsetto imbonitore
pat·ter[2] ['pætəʳ] N (*of feet*) scalpiccio; (*of rain*) picchiettio
■ VI (*person*) trotterellare; (*rain*) picchiettare
◎**pat·tern** ['pætən] N **1** (*design*) motivo, disegno; **a geometric pattern** un motivo geometrico **2** (*Sewing*) modello (di carta), cartamodello; (*fig*) modello; **pattern of events** sequenza degli avvenimenti; **behaviour patterns** tipi *mpl* di comportamento; **the three attacks follow the same pattern** le tre aggressioni seguono lo stesso schema **3** (*sample*) campione *m*
■ VT (*model*): **to pattern a dress on** fare un vestito sul modello di; **to pattern o.s. on sb/sth** prendere a modello qn/qc
pattern book N album *m inv* di modelli
pat·terned ['pætənd] ADJ a disegni, a motivi; (*material*) fantasia *inv*
pau·city ['pɔːsɪtɪ] N (*frm*) scarsità
paunch [pɔːntʃ] N pancia
paunchy ['pɔːntʃɪ] ADJ (*comp* **-ier**, *superl* **-iest**) pancione(-a)
pau·per ['pɔːpəʳ] N indigente *m/f*; **pauper's grave** fossa comune
pau·per·ize ['pɔˌpəˌraɪz] VT ridurre in miseria
◎**pause** [pɔːz] N pausa; (*Mus*) pausa; (*: sign*) corona; **there was a pause while ...** ci fu un momento di attesa mentre...
■ VI (*gen*) fermarsi un momento; (*in speech*) fare una pausa; **to pause for breath** fermarsi un attimo per riprendere fiato
pave [peɪv] VT (*gen*) lastricare; (*road*) pavimentare, lastricare; **the street was paved last year** la strada è stata pavimentata l'anno scorso; **to pave the way for** (*fig: person*) spianare la strada a; (*: changes, reforms*) aprire la via a
pave·ment ['peɪvmənt] N (*Brit*) marciapiede *m*; (*Am*) pavimentazione *f* stradale

> DID YOU KNOW ...?
> **pavement** is not translated by the Italian word *pavimento*

pa·vil·ion [pə'vɪlɪən] N (*gen*) padiglione *m*; (*Sport*) *tribuna annessa ad un campo da cricket in cui sono anche alloggiati gli spogliatoi*
pav·ing ['peɪvɪŋ] N pavimentazione *f*
paving stone N lastra di pavimentazione

Pp

paw [pɔː] N (*of animal, also fam: hand*) zampa
■VT **1** (*subj: animal*) dare una zampata a; **to paw the ground** (*also fig*) scalpitare **2** (*pej: sexually*) palpare, mettere le zampe addosso a
pawn¹ [pɔːn] N (*Chess*) pedone *m*; (*fig*) pedina; **to be sb's pawn** lasciarsi manovrare da qn
pawn² [pɔːn] N: **in pawn** impegnato(-a) al monte di pietà; (*article pledged*) pegno; **to leave** *or* **put sth in pawn** impegnare qc
■VT impegnare, dare in pegno
pawn·broker ['pɔːn,brəʊkəʳ] N prestatore(-trice) su pegno
pawn·shop ['pɔːn,ʃɒp] N monte *m* di pietà
◎ **pay** [peɪ] (*vb: pt, pp* **paid**) N (*gen*) paga; **to be in sb's pay** essere pagato(-a) da *or* essere al servizio di qn
■VT
1 (*gen*) pagare; (*debt, account*) saldare, pagare; **he paid him £10** gli ha dato 10 sterline; **to pay for sth** pagare qc; **I paid £15 for that record** quel disco l'ho pagato 15 sterline; **how much did you pay for it?** quanto l'hai pagato?; **to be** *or* **get paid on Fridays** prendere *or* riscuotere la paga il venerdì ; **a badly paid worker** un(-a) lavoratore(-trice) mal pagato(-a); **they pay me more on Sundays** la domenica mi pagano di più; **that's what you're paid for** sei pagato per questo; **to pay one's way** (*to contribute one's share*) pagare la propria parte; (*to remain solvent: company*) coprire le spese; **to put paid to** (*plan, person*) rovinare; (*trip*) impedire; **to pay the penalty** (*fig*) pagare le conseguenze; **to pay dividends** (*Fin*) pagare dividendi; (*fig*) dare buoni frutti
2 (*be profitable to: also fig*) convenire a; **it won't pay you to do that** non ti conviene farlo
3 (*attention*) fare, prestare; (*homage*) rendere; (*respects*) porgere; **I wasn't paying attention to what the teacher was saying** non stavo prestando attenzione a quello che diceva l'insegnante; *see* **visit**
■VI
1 pagare; **to pay in advance** pagare in anticipo; **don't worry, I'll pay** non preoccuparti, pagherò io; **can I pay by cheque?** posso pagare con un assegno?; **I paid by credit card** ho pagato con la carta di credito; **they paid for her to go to Italy** le hanno pagato il viaggio in Italia
2 (*be profitable*) rendere, convenire; **the business doesn't pay** l'attività non rende *or* non è redditizia; **it pays to be courteous** ci si guadagna sempre ad essere gentile; **it pays to advertise** far pubblicità conviene sempre; **it pays to shop around** conviene confrontare i prezzi; **crime doesn't pay** il delitto non paga
3 (*fig: to suffer*) pagare; **she paid for it with her life** le è costato la vita, ha pagato con la vita; **I'll make you pay for this!** te la farò pagare!
▸ **pay back** VT + ADV
1 restituire; **to pay sb back** rimborsare qn; **I'll pay you back tomorrow** ti restituisco i soldi domani
2 (*in revenge*) farla pagare a qn; **to pay sb back for doing sth** farla pagare a qn per aver fatto qc
▸ **pay down** VT + ADV versare un acconto di
▸ **pay for** VI + PREP pagare
▸ **pay in** VT + ADV versare, depositare
▸ **pay off** VT + ADV
1 (*debts*) saldare; (*creditor*) pagare; (*mortgage*) estinguere; **to pay sth off in instalments** pagare qc a rate
2 (*discharge*) licenziare
■VI + ADV (*scheme, ruse*) funzionare; (*patience, decision*) dare dei frutti
▸ **pay out** VT + ADV
1 (*money*) sborsare, tirar fuori; (*subj: cashier*) pagare
2 (*rope*) far allentare
▸ **pay up** VT + ADV, VI + ADV saldare, pagare
pay·able ['peɪəbl] ADJ pagabile; **to make a cheque payable to sb** intestare un assegno a (nome di) qn
pay-and-display [,peɪəndɪs'pleɪ] ADJ (*Brit*): **pay-and-display parking** parcheggio a pagamento (*con parcometro*)
pay-as-you-go [,peɪəzjə'gəʊ] N: **pay-as-you-go phone** telefono con scheda prepagata
pay award N aumento salariale
pay-bed ['peɪ,bɛd] N (*Brit*) *posto letto a pagamento in un ospedale pubblico*
pay·day ['peɪ,deɪ] N giorno di paga
pay desk N cassa
PAYE [,piːeɪwaɪ'iː] N ABBR (*Brit:* = **pay as you earn**) *sistema di pagamento delle imposte mediante ritenuta alla fonte*
payee [peɪ'iː] N beneficiario(-a)
pay envelope N (*Am*) = **pay packet**
pay increase N (*for individual*) aumento di stipendio; (*for group of workers*) aumento salariale
pay·ing ['peɪɪŋ] ADJ (*business, scheme*) redditizio(-a)
paying guest N ospite *m/f* pagante, pensionante *m/f*
paying-in book [,peɪɪŋ'ɪnbʊk] N (*Brit*) *carnet di distinte di versamento*
paying-in slip [,peɪɪŋ'ɪn,slɪp] N modulo di versamento
pay·load ['peɪ,ləʊd] N carico utile
pay·master ['peɪ,mɑːstəʳ] N (*Mil*) ufficiale *m* pagatore
◎ **pay·ment** ['peɪmənt] N (*gen*) pagamento; (*of debt, account, interest*) saldo, pagamento; (*fig: reward*) ricompensa; **advance payment** (*part sum*) anticipo, acconto; (*total sum*) pagamento anticipato; **deferred payment** *or* **payment by instalments** pagamento dilazionato *or* a rate; **payment in full** (pagamento a) saldo; **payment on account** acconto; **payment by results** ≈ premio di produzione; **in payment of** (*sum owed*) come saldo di; **in payment for** *or* **as payment for** (*goods*) come pagamento di; (*help, efforts, kindness*) in cambio di, come ricompensa per; **on payment of £5** dietro pagamento di 5 sterline
pay·off ['peɪ,ɒf] N (*fam: payment*) saldo; (: *reward*) ricompensa; (: *retribution*) resa dei conti; (: *of joke*) finale *m*
pay packet, pay envelope (*Am*) N busta *f* paga *inv*
pay-per-view [,peɪpə'vjuː] N pay tv *f inv*
■ADJ (*TV*) a pagamento
pay·phone ['peɪ,fəʊn], (*Am*) **pay station** N cabina telefonica
pay rise N = **pay increase**
pay·roll ['peɪ,rəʊl] N (*list*) lista del personale; (*money*) paga (di tutto il personale); (*employees*) personale *m*; **to be on a firm's payroll** far parte dell'organico di una ditta
pay slip N (*Brit*) busta *f* paga *inv*
pay station N (*Am*) = **payphone**
PBS [,piːbiː'ɛʃ] N ABBR (*Am:* = **Public Broadcasting Service**) *servizio che collabora alla realizzazione di programmi per la rete televisiva nazionale*
PBX [,piːbiː'ɛks] ABBR (*Telec:* = **private branch exchange**) *sistema telefonico con centralino*
◎ **PC** [,piː'siː] N ABBR **1** (= **personal computer**) PC *m inv*
2 (*Brit*) = **police constable**
■ABBR (*Brit*) = **Privy Councillor**
■ADJ ABBR = **politically correct**
pc [,piː'siː] ABBR **1** (= **postcard**) CP (= *cartolina postale*)
2 = **per cent**

p/c ABBR = **petty cash**
pcm [ˌpi:si:ˈɛm] ABBR = *per calendar month*
PD [ˌpi:ˈdi:] N ABBR (*Am*) = **police department**
pd ABBR = **paid**
PDA [ˌpi:di:ˈeɪ] N ABBR (*Comput*: = **personal digital assistant**) PDA *m inv*
PDF [ˌpi:di:ˈɛf] N (*Comput*: = *Portable Document Format*) PDF *m inv*
pdq [ˌpi:di:ˈkju:] ADV ABBR (*fam*: = **pretty damn quick**) subito
PDSA [ˌpi:di:ɛsˈeɪ] N ABBR (*Brit*: = **People's Dispensary for Sick Animals**) *assistenza veterinaria pubblica*
PDT [ˌpi:di:ˈti:] ABBR (*Am*: = **Pacific Daylight Time**) *ora estiva nel fuso orario del Pacifico*
PE [ˌpi:ˈi:] N ABBR (= **physical education**) educazione fisica
■ ABBR (*Canada*) = **Prince Edward Island**
pea [pi:] N pisello; **green peas** pisellini *mpl*
◎ **peace** [pi:s] N (*gen*) pace *f*; **to be at peace with sb/sth** essere in pace con qn/qc; **he is at peace** (*euph*: *dead*) riposa in pace; **to make peace between** rappacificare; **to make one's peace with** fare la pace con; **peace of mind** tranquillità di spirito; **peace and quiet** pace e tranquillità; **to keep the peace** (*subj*: *policeman*) mantenere l'ordine pubblico; (: *citizen*) rispettare l'ordine pubblico; (*fig*) calmare le acque
peace·able [ˈpi:səbl] ADJ pacifico(-a)
peace·ably [ˈpi:səblɪ] ADV in pace, pacificamente
peace conference N conferenza per la pace
Peace Corps NSG (*Am*) *organizzazione che invia giovani volontari in paesi sottosviluppati*
◎ **peace·ful** [ˈpi:sfʊl] ADJ (*person, coexistence*) pacifico(-a); (*demonstration*) non violento(-a); (*period*) di pace; (*place, life, sleep*) tranquillo(-a); **a peaceful demonstration** una manifestazione pacifica; **a peaceful afternoon** un pomeriggio tranquillo
peace·ful·ly [ˈpi:sfəlɪ] ADV (*coexist, reign*) in pace; (*demonstrate*) senza violenza; (*sleep, work, live*) tranquillamente
peace·ful·ness [ˈpi:sfʊlnɪs] N tranquillità, pace *f*
peace·keep·ing [ˈpi:sˌki:pɪŋ] ADJ (*operation, force*) di pace; **peacekeeping force** forza di pace
■ N mantenimento della pace; **troops responsible for peacekeeping** truppe *fpl* responsabili del mantenimento della pace
peace-loving [ˈpi:sˌlʌvɪŋ] ADJ pacifico(-a)
peace·maker [ˈpi:sˌmeɪkə^r] N (*between nations*) mediatore(-trice) di pace; (*between individuals*) conciliatore(-trice) *m/f*
peace offering N (*fig*) dono in segno di riconciliazione
peace pipe N calumet *m inv* (della pace)
peace process N processo di pace
peace talks NPL negoziati *mpl* per la pace
peace·time [ˈpi:sˌtaɪm] N: **in peacetime** in tempo di pace
peace treaty N trattato di pace
peach [pi:tʃ] N **1** (*fruit*) pesca; (*tree*) pesco **2** (*fam*): **she's a peach** è un amore
■ ADJ (*blossom*) di pesco; (*colour*) (color) pesca *inv*
peach melba [ˈpi:tʃˈmɛlbə] N pesche *fpl* melba *inv*
pea·cock [ˈpi:ˌkɒk] N pavone *m*
peacock blue ADJ, N azzurro pavone (*m*) *inv*
pea green ADJ, N verde pisello (*m*) *inv*
pea·hen [ˈpi:ˌhɛn] N pavona, pavonessa
◎ **peak** [pi:k] N (*of mountain*) vetta, cima; (*mountain itself*) picco; (*of roof etc*) cima; (*of cap*) visiera; (*on graph*) vertice *m*; (*fig*: *of power, career*) apice *m*, vertice; **to be at its peak** (*fame, career, empire*) essere all'apice; (*business*) essere nella fase culminante; (*traffic, demand*) aver raggiunto il livello massimo; **he was at the peak of fitness** era al massimo della forma fisica
■ ADJ (*demand, production*) massimo(-a)
peaked [pi:kt] ADJ **1** (*cap*) con visiera **2** = **peaky**
peak hours NPL ore *fpl* di punta
peak period N periodo di punta
peak rate N tariffa ore di punta
peak season N l'alta stagione *f*
peak time N (*Brit*: *TV*) orario di massimo ascolto
peak-time [ˈpi:ktaɪm] ADJ (*Brit*: *TV programme*) di fascia oraria con picco d'ascolto
peaky [ˈpi:kɪ] ADJ (*comp* **-ier**, *superl* **-iest**) (*Brit fam*) sbattuto(-a); **I'm feeling a bit peaky** mi sento un po' giù
peal [pi:l] N (*sound of bells*) scampanio; **peal of thunder** fragore *m* di tuono; **peals of laughter** scoppi *mpl* di risa
■ VT suonare (a distesa)
■ VI (*also*: **peal out**: *bell*) suonare (a distesa); (: *thunder*) rimbombare
pea·nut [ˈpi:ˌnʌt] N arachide *f*, nocciolina americana; **a packet of peanuts** un pacchetto di noccioline americane; **to work for peanuts** (*fam*) lavorare per una miseria
peanut butter N burro di arachidi
peanut oil N olio di semi di arachide
pear [pɛə^r] N (*fruit*) pera; (*tree*) pero
pearl [pɜ:l] N perla; **pearl of wisdom** (*fig*) perla di saggezza; **to cast pearls before swine** (*fig*) gettare le perle ai porci
■ ADJ (*necklace, brooch*) di perle; (*buttons*) di madreperla
pearl barley N orzo perlato
pearl diver N pescatore(-trice) di perle
pearl oyster N ostrica perlifera
pearly [ˈpɜ:lɪ] ADJ (*comp* **-ier**, *superl* **-iest**) (*teeth*) come perle; (*buttons*) a perla; **pearly white** bianco perla *inv*; **the Pearly Gates** (*hum*) le porte del paradiso
pear-shaped [ˈpɛəʃeɪpt] ADJ a forma di pera; (*woman*) con le spalle strette e i fianchi larghi
peas·ant [ˈpɛzənt] N contadino(-a)
■ ADJ (*life*) dei contadini; (*societies*) contadino(-a); (*dress*) da contadino(-a)
peasant farmer N contadino(-a)
pea·shooter [ˈpi:ˌʃu:tə^r] N cerbottana
pea soup N passato *or* crema di piselli
peat [pi:t] N torba
peat bog N torbiera
peaty [ˈpi:tɪ] ADJ (*comp* **-ier**, *superl* **-iest**) torboso(-a)
peb·ble [ˈpɛbl] N ciottolo; **you're not the only pebble on the beach** (*fam*) non ci sei mica solo tu
pebble dash N (*Brit*) intonaco a pinocchino
peb·bly [ˈpɛblɪ] ADJ (*beach*) di ciottoli
pe·can [pɪˈkæn] N pecan *m inv*
pec·ca·dil·lo [ˌpɛkəˈdɪləʊ] N peccatuccio
peck [pɛk] N (*of bird*) beccata; (*fam*: *kiss*) bacetto; **to take a peck at** beccare; **he gave me a peck on the cheek** mi ha dato un bacetto sulla guancia
■ VT (*subj*: *bird*: *grain*) beccare; (: *person*) dare una beccata a; (*hole*) fare a furia di beccate
■ VI: **to peck at** (*subj*: *bird*) beccare; (: *person*: *food*) mangiucchiare; **he pecked at his food** sbocconcellò il suo cibo
peck·ing or·der [ˈpɛkɪŋˌɔ:də^r] N (*fig*) ordine *m* gerarchico

Pp

peck·ish ['pɛkɪʃ] ADJ (*Brit fam*): **to feel a bit peckish** avere un languorino

pecs [pɛks] NPL, **pectoral muscles** NPL (*fam*) (muscoli *mpl*) pettorali *mpl*

pec·tin ['pɛktɪn] N pectina

pec·to·ral ['pɛktərəl] ADJ pettorale; **pectoral fins** pinne *fpl* ventrali

pe·cu·li·ar [pɪ'kju:lɪəʳ] ADJ **1** (*strange: idea, smell*) strano(-a), curioso(-a); **he's a peculiar person** è un tipo strano; **it tastes peculiar** ha un sapore strano **2** (*particular: importance, qualities*) particolare; **it has its own peculiar beauty** ha una sua bellezza particolare; **peculiar to** caratteristico(-a) di, tipico(-a) di; **it is a phrase peculiar to him** è un modo di dire tutto suo

pe·cu·li·ar·ity [pɪ,kju:lɪ'ærɪtɪ] N peculiarità *f inv*

pe·cu·liar·ly [pɪ'kju:lɪəlɪ] ADV **1** (*exceptionally*) particolarmente; **to be peculiarly American** essere tipicamente americano **2** (*strangely*) in un modo peculiare, in un modo curioso

pe·cu·ni·ary [pɪ'kju:nɪərɪ] ADJ pecuniario(-a)

peda·gog·ic [,pɛdə'gɒdʒɪk], **peda·gogi·cal** [,pɛdə'gɒdʒɪkəl] ADJ pedagogico(-a)

peda·gogi·cal·ly [,pɛdə'gɒdʒɪkəlɪ] ADV pedagogicamente

peda·gogue ['pɛdə,gɒg] N pedagogo(-a)

peda·go·gy ['pɛdə,gɒgɪ] N pedagogia

ped·al ['pɛdl] N pedale *m*
■VI pedalare; **to pedal up/down** pedalare su per/giù per
■VT: **she pedalled her bicycle up the hill** salì la collina in bicicletta

pedal bin N (*Brit*) pattumiera a pedale

pedal car N automobilina a pedali

peda·lo ['pɛdələʊ] N pedalò *m inv*

ped·ant ['pɛdənt] N pedante *m/f*

pe·dan·tic [pɪ'dæntɪk] ADJ pedante, pedantesco(-a)

pe·dan·ti·cal·ly [pɪ'dæntɪkəlɪ] ADV pedantemente, con pedanteria

ped·ant·ry ['pɛdəntrɪ] N pedanteria

ped·dle ['pɛdl] VT (*goods*) andare in giro a vendere; (*drugs*) spacciare; (*gossip*) mettere in giro

ped·dler ['pɛdləʳ] N (*esp Am*) = **pedlar**

ped·er·ast ['pɛdəræst] N pederasta *m*

ped·er·as·ty ['pɛdəræstɪ] N pederastia

ped·es·tal ['pɛdɪstl] N piedistallo; **to put sb on a pedestal** (*fig*) mettere qn su un piedistallo

pe·des·trian [pɪ'dɛstrɪən] N pedone *m*; **cyclists and pedestrians** ciclisti e pedoni
■ADJ **1** (*pej: style, speech*) prosaico(-a), pedestre **2** (*access*) pedonale

pedestrian crossing N (*Brit*) passaggio pedonale

pe·des·tri·an·ize [pɪ'dɛstrɪənaɪz] VT pedonalizzare

pedestrian mall N (*Am*) zona pedonale

pedestrian precinct N (*Brit*) zona pedonale

pe·di·at·ric *etc* [,pi:dɪ'ætrɪk] = **paediatric** *etc*

pedi·cel ['pɛdɪ,sɛl] N pedicello

pedi·cure ['pɛdɪ,kjʊəʳ] N pedicure *m/f inv*

pedi·gree ['pɛdɪ,gri:] N (*of person*) discendenza, stirpe *f*; (*of animal*) pedigree *m inv*
■ADJ di razza (pura); **a pedigree dog** un cane di razza

ped·lar ['pɛdləʳ] N venditore(-trice) ambulante; (*of drugs*) spacciatore(-trice)

pe·dom·eter [pɪ'dɒmɪtəʳ] N pedometro, contapassi *m inv*

pe·dun·cle [pɪ'dʌŋkəl] N peduncolo

pee [pi:] N (*fam*): **to have a pee** fare la pipì

peek [pi:k] N sbirciatina; **to take** *or* **have a peek at** dare una sbirciatina a; **I had a peek at his diary** ho dato una sbirciatina al suo diario
■VI sbirciare

peel [pi:l] N (*gen*) buccia; (*of orange, lemon etc*) scorza, buccia; **apple peel** buccia di mela; **orange peel** scorza d'arancia
■VT (*fruit etc*) sbucciare; (*shrimps etc*) sgusciare; **shall I peel the potatoes?** sbuccio le patate?; **to keep one's eyes peeled** (*fam*) stare all'erta
■VI (*wallpaper*) staccarsi; (*paint etc*) scrostarsi; (*skin*) squamarsi; (*person*) spellarsi; **my nose is peeling** mi si sta spellando il naso
▸ **peel away** VI + ADV (*skin*) squamarsi; (*paint*) scrostarsi; (*wallpaper*) staccarsi
■VT + ADV (*gen*) staccare; (*paint*) scrostare; (*wrapper*) togliere
▸ **peel back** VT + ADV togliere, levare
▸ **peel off** VT + ADV **1** = **peel away** VT + ADV **2** (*clothes*) togliersi, sfilarsi
■VI + ADV = **peel away** VI + ADV

peel·er ['pi:ləʳ] N (*potato knife*) pelapatate *m inv*

peel·ings ['pi:lɪŋz] NPL bucce *fpl*

peep¹ [pi:p] N (*of bird*) squittio; (*of chick*) pigolio; (*of whistle*) trillo; **we haven't heard a peep out of them** (*fam*) non hanno aperto bocca
■VI (*bird*) squittire; (*whistle*) trillare

peep² [pi:p] N (*Brit: look*) sbirciata, sguardo furtivo; **to take** *or* **have a peep (at sth)** dare una sbirciata (a qc); **he took a peep at his watch** ha dato un'occhiata all'orologio
■VI: **to peep at sth** sbirciare qc; **she peeped to see what he was doing** ha dato un'occhiata per vedere cosa stava facendo
▸ **peep out** VI + ADV (*Brit*) far capolino; **the sun peeped out from behind the clouds** il sole fece capolino da dietro le nuvole

peep·hole ['pi:p,həʊl] N spioncino

Peep·ing Tom [,pi:pɪŋ'tɒm] N guardone *m*

peep·show ['pi:pʃəʊ] N peep-show *m inv*

peer¹ [pɪəʳ] N (*noble*) pari *m inv*; (*equal*) pari *m/f inv*, uguale *m/f*; **they get on well with their peers** vanno d'accordo con i loro pari; **children who are cleverer than their peers** bambini più intelligenti dei loro coetanei

◎ **peer²** [pɪəʳ] VI: **to peer at sth** aguzzare gli occhi per vedere qc; **to peer into a room** guardare in una stanza

peer·age ['pɪərɪdʒ] N dignità di pari; **he was given a peerage** gli è stato conferito il titolo di pari

peer·ess ['pɪərɪs] N *nobildonna che ha diritto al titolo di pari*

peer group N (*contemporaries*) gruppo di coetanei; (*from same social class, background*) persone *fpl* del proprio ambiente

peer·less ['pɪəlɪs] ADJ (*frm*) impareggiabile, senza pari

peeved [pi:vd] ADJ (*fam*) seccato(-a), stizzito(-a)

peev·ish ['pi:vɪʃ] ADJ scontroso(-a), stizzoso(-a)

peev·ish·ly ['pi:vɪʃlɪ] ADV stizzosamente

pee·wit ['pi:,wɪt] N pavoncella

◎ **peg** [pɛg] N (*for tent*) picchetto; (*Brit: also*: **clothes peg**) molletta; (*for coat, hat*) attaccapanni *m inv*; **to take sb down a peg (or two)** far abbassare la cresta a qn; **a peg on which to hang a theory** un pretesto per presentare una teoria
■VT (*clothes*) appendere con le mollette; (*groundsheet, tent*) fissare con i picchetti; (*fig: prices, wages*) fissare, stabilizzare
▸ **peg away** VI + ADV: **to peg away at sth** (*fam*) incaponirsi su qc

▶ **peg down** VT + ADV (*tent*) fissare con i picchetti
▶ **peg out** VI + ADV (*fam: die*) crepare, tirare le cuoia

Pega·sus ['pɛgəsəs] N (*Myth, Astron*) Pegaso

pe·jo·ra·tive [pɪ'dʒɒrɪtɪv] ADJ spregiativo(-a), peggiorativo(-a)

pe·jo·ra·tive·ly [pɪ'dʒɒrɪtɪvlɪ] ADV spregiativamente

Pe·kin·ese [ˌpi:kɪ'ni:z] N (cane) pechinese *m*

Pe·king [pi:'kɪŋ], **Pekin** N = **Beijing**

pe·lag·ic [pɛ'lædʒɪk] ADJ pelagico(-a)

pel·ar·go·nium [ˌpɛlə'gəʊnɪəm] N pelargonio

peli·can ['pɛlɪkən] N pellicano

pelican crossing N (*Brit Aut*) *attraversamento pedonale con semaforo a controllo manuale*

pel·let ['pɛlɪt] N (*of paper, bread*) pallina; (*for gun*) pallino

pell-mell ['pɛl'mɛl] ADV disordinatamente, alla rinfusa

pel·met ['pɛlmɪt] N (*wooden*) cassonetto; (*cloth*) mantovana

pelt¹ [pɛlt] VT: **to pelt sb with sth** tirare qc addosso a qn; **to pelt sth with sth** colpire qc con qc; **the crowd pelted the car with stones** la folla ha tempestato la macchina di pietre; **they pelted him with questions** lo hanno tempestato *or* bombardato di domande
■ VI **1 the rain is pelting (down)** (*fam*) piove a dirotto **2** (*fam: go fast*): **she pelted across the road** ha attraversato sparata la strada

pelt² [pɛlt] N (*of animal*) pelliccia, pelle *f*

pel·vic ['pɛlvɪk] ADJ pelvico(-a)

pelvis ['pɛlvɪs] N bacino, pelvi *f inv*

pen¹ [pɛn] N (*for animals*) recinto, chiuso; (*playpen*) box *m inv*; (*Am fam: prison*) gattabuia
■ VT (*also:* **pen in, pen up**) rinchiudere

◎ **pen²** [pɛn] N (*gen*) penna; (*felt-tip pen*) pennarello; **I haven't got a pen** non ho una penna; **to put pen to paper** prendere la penna in mano
■ VT (*frm*) scrivere

pe·nal ['pi:nl] ADJ (*gen*) penale; (*tax, fine*) oneroso(-a)

pe·nal·ize ['pi:nəˌlaɪz] VT **1** (*punish*) punire; **bad spelling will be penalized** gli errori di ortografia verranno penalizzati **2** (*Sport*) penalizzare **3** (*handicap*) handicappare

penal servitude N lavori *mpl* forzati

◎ **pen·al·ty** ['pɛnəltɪ] N **1** (*punishment*) pena; (*fig: disadvantage*) svantaggio; (*fine*) ammenda; **those who break the rules do so on penalty of dismissal** coloro che infrangono il regolamento verranno puniti con il licenziamento; **the penalty for this offence is life imprisonment** la pena per questo reato è l'ergastolo; **a penalty of £1000** un'ammenda di 1000 sterline; **to pay the penalty for sth** pagare le conseguenze di qc; **I paid the penalty for her mistake** ho pagato io le conseguenze del suo errore; **the death penalty** la pena di morte **2** (*Sport*) penalità *f inv*; (*Ftbl*) (calcio di) rigore *m*

penalty area, penalty box N (*Brit Ftbl*) area di rigore

penalty clause N (*in contract*) penale *f*

penalty goal N goal *m inv* su calcio di rigore

penalty kick N (*Ftbl*) calcio di rigore

penalty shoot-out [ˌpɛnəltɪ'ʃu:tˌaʊt] N (*Ftbl*) rigori *mpl*; **to beat a team in a penalty shoot-out** battere una squadra ai rigori

pen·ance ['pɛnəns] N penitenza; **to do penance for** fare la penitenza per

pen-and-ink [ˌpɛnənd'ɪŋk] ADJ: **pen-and-ink drawing** disegno a penna

pence [pɛns] NPL *of* **penny**

pen·chant ['pɒŋʃɒŋ] N (*frm*) debole *m*, penchant *m inv*

pen·cil ['pɛnsl] N matita
■ ADJ (*drawing, line*) a matita; **in pencil** a matita
▶ **pencil in** VT + ADV (*note*) scrivere a matita; (*fig: date*) segnarsi provvisoriamente

pencil case N astuccio per matite

pen·cil sharp·en·er ['pɛnslʃɑ:pnəʳ] N temperamatite *m inv*

pen·dant ['pɛndənt] N pendaglio

pend·ing ['pɛndɪŋ] ADJ in sospeso
■ PREP in attesa di; **pending the arrival of** in attesa dell'arrivo di; **pending an enquiry** in attesa di indagini

pen·du·lum ['pɛndjʊləm] N pendolo

pen·etrable ['pɛnɪtrəbl] ADJ penetrabile

pen·etrate ['pɛnɪˌtreɪt] VT (*gen, Mil*) penetrare in; (*infiltrate*) infiltrarsi in; (*understand: meaning, mystery*) penetrare; (*: truth*) afferrare
■ VI (*go right through*) penetrare; **the significance of what he was saying finally penetrated** il significato delle sue parole fu finalmente chiaro

pen·etrat·ing ['pɛnɪˌtreɪtɪŋ] ADJ (*look, sound*) penetrante; (*question etc*) acuto(-a); (*person, mind etc*) perspicace

pen·etrat·ing·ly ['pɛnɪˌtreɪtɪŋlɪ] ADV (*look, scream*) in modo penetrante

pen·etra·tion [ˌpɛnɪ'treɪʃən] N penetrazione *f*

pen·friend ['pɛnˌfrɛnd] N amico(-a) di penna

pen·guin ['pɛŋgwɪn] N pinguino

peni·cil·lin [ˌpɛnɪ'sɪlɪn] N penicillina

pen·in·su·la [pɪ'nɪnsjʊlə] N penisola

pe·nis ['pi:nɪs] N pene *m*

peni·tence ['pɛnɪtəns] N penitenza

peni·tent ['pɛnɪtənt] ADJ pentito(-a)
■ N penitente *m/f*

peni·ten·tial [ˌpɛnɪ'tɛnʃəl] ADJ (*frm: tone, look*) contrito(-a); (*psalm*) penitenziale

peni·ten·tia·ry [ˌpɛnɪ'tɛnʃərɪ] N (*esp Am: prison*) penitenziario, carcere *m*

peni·tent·ly ['pɛnɪtəntlɪ] ADV (*act, look*) con (un')aria contrita; (*say*) con tono pentito

pen·knife ['pɛnˌnaɪf] N (*pl* **-knives** ['pɛnˌnaɪvz]) temperino

pen name N pseudonimo

pen·nant ['pɛnənt] N bandierina

pen·nies ['pɛnɪz] NPL *of* **penny**

pen·ni·less ['pɛnɪlɪs] ADJ senza un soldo *or* una lira

Pen·nines ['pɛnaɪnz] NPL: **the Pennines** i Pennini

Penn·syl·va·nia [ˌpɛnsɪl'veɪnɪə] N Pennsylvania
▷ www.state.pa.us/

◎ **pen·ny** ['pɛnɪ] N (*pl* **pennies** *or* **pence**) (*Brit*) penny *m inv*; (*Am*) centesimo; **24 pence** 24 penny; **it won't cost you a penny** non ti costerà un soldo; **in for a penny, in for a pound** abbiamo fatto trenta, facciamo trentuno; **I'm not a penny the wiser** continuo a capirci quanto prima; **she hasn't a penny to her name** non ha un soldo bucato; **he turns up like a bad penny** te lo ritrovi sempre tra i piedi; **a penny for your thoughts** a che pensi?; **and then the penny dropped!** (*fig*) improvvisamente ci sono arrivato!

penny-pinching ['pɛnɪ'pɪntʃɪŋ] N: **there should be no penny-pinching** non si dovrebbe stare a lesinare il centesimo
■ ADJ (*person*) taccagno(-a), spilorcio(-a)

pen pal N (*fam*) amico(-a) di penna

pen·pusher ['pɛnˌpʊʃəʳ] N (*pej*) scribacchino(-a)

◎ **pen·sion** ['pɛnʃən] N pensione *f*

Pp

▸ **pension off** VT + ADV mandare in pensione
pen·sion·able ['pɛnʃənəbl] ADJ pensionabile
pension book N (*Brit*) libretto della pensione
pen·sion·er ['pɛnʃənə'] N pensionato(-a)
pension fund N fondo pensioni
pension plan N piano pensionistico
pension scheme N sistema *m* di pensionamento
pen·sive ['pɛnsɪv] ADJ pensoso(-a)
pen·sive·ly ['pɛnsɪvlɪ] ADV pensosamente
Pentagon ['pɛntəgən] N (*Am Pol*): **the Pentagon** il Pentagono

PENTAGON

Il **Pentagon** è un edificio a pianta pentagonale che si trova ad Arlington, in Virginia, nel quale hanno sede gli uffici del Ministero della Difesa degli Stati Uniti. Il termine **Pentagon** è usato anche per indicare la dirigenza militare del paese.
▹ www.defenselink.mil/pubs/pentagon/

pen·ta·gon ['pɛntəgən] N pentagono
pen·tago·nal [pɛn'tægənl] ADJ pentagonale
pen·tam·eter [pɛn'tæmɪtə'] N pentametro
pen·tath·lon [pɛn'tæθlən] N pentathlon *m inv*
Pen·tecost ['pɛntɪˌkɒst] N (*Rel*) Pentecoste *f*
pent·house ['pɛntˌhaʊs] N attico
pent-up [ˌpɛnt'ʌp] ADJ (*emotions, feelings*) represso(-a)
pe·nul·ti·mate [pɪ'nʌltɪmɪt] ADJ penultimo(-a)
pe·nu·ri·ous [pɪ'njʊərɪəs] ADJ (*frm*) indigente
penu·ry ['pɛnjʊrɪ] N (*frm*) indigenza

DID YOU KNOW ...?
penury is not translated by the Italian word *penuria*

peo·ny ['pɪənɪ] N peonia
◎ **peo·ple** ['pi:pl] N **1** (*pl: persons*) persone *fpl*, gente *fsg*; **old people** i vecchi; **young people** i giovani; **some people** alcuni *mpl*, certa gente; **several people** diverse persone; **a lot of people** un sacco di gente; **six people** sei persone; **four/several people came** sono venute quattro/parecchie persone; **the people were nice** la gente era simpatica; **the room was full of people** la stanza era piena di gente; **how many people are there in your family?** quanti siete in famiglia?; **what do you people think?** e voi (altri) cosa ne pensate?; **some people are born lucky** c'è chi nasce con la camicia; **you of all people should ...** se c'è uno che dovrebbe... quello sei tu **2** (*pl: in general*) gente *fsg*; **many people think that ...** molti pensano che..., molta gente pensa che...; **people say that ...** si dice *or* la gente dice che... **3** (*pl: inhabitants*) abitanti *mpl*; **Italian people** gli italiani; **the people of London** i londinesi; **country people** la gente di campagna; **town people** la gente di città; **the native peoples of Central America** le popolazioni originarie dell'America centrale **4** (*pl: Pol: citizens*) popolo; (*: general public*) pubblico; **the people** il popolo; **people at large** il grande pubblico; **a man of the people** un uomo del popolo **5** (*pl: family*) famiglia *fsg* **6** (*sg: nation, race*) popolo, nazione *f*
■ VT: **to people (with)** popolare (con); **to be peopled with** essere popolato(-a) di
people carrier N, **people mover** N (*Auto*) monovolume *f inv*
PEP [pɛp] N ABBR (*Fin*) = **personal equity plan**; *piano d'investimento azionario personale con incentivi fiscali, sostituito nel 1999 dall'ISA*

pep [pɛp] N (*fam*) dinamismo, vitalità; **to put some pep in** vivacizzare
▸ **pep up** VT + ADV (*person*) tirar su; (*party*) animare, vivacizzare; (*food*) rendere più gustoso(-a); (*drink*) correggere
◎ **pep·per** ['pɛpə'] N **1** (*spice*) pepe *m*; **white/black pepper** pepe bianco/nero; **pass the pepper, please** mi passi il pepe, per favore? **2** (*vegetable*) peperone *m*; **a green pepper** un peperone verde
■ VT pepare; **to pepper an essay with quotations** (*fig*) infarcire un saggio di citazioni
pepper-and-salt [ˌpɛpərən'sɔ:lt] ADJ (*hair*) brizzolato(-a), sale e pepe *inv*
pepper·corn ['pɛpəˌkɔ:n] N grano di pepe
pepper mill N macinapepe *m inv*
pepper·mint ['pɛpəˌmɪnt] N (*Bot*) menta peperita; (*sweet*) caramella alla menta; **would you like a peppermint?** vuoi una caramella alla menta?; **peppermint tea** il tè alla menta
pep·pero·ni [ˌpɛpə'rəʊnɪ] N salsiccia piccante
pepper·pot ['pɛpəˌpɒt] N pepaiola
pep·pery ['pɛpərɪ] ADJ pepato(-a); (*fig*) irascibile
pep pill N stimolante *m*
pep·sin ['pɛpsɪn] N pepsina
pep talk N (*fam*) discorso d'incoraggiamento
pep·tic ['pɛptɪk] ADJ: **peptic ulcer** ulcera peptica
pep·tide ['pɛptaɪd] N peptide *m*
◎ **per** [pɜ:'] PREP per, a; **£7 per week/dozen** 7 sterline la *or* alla settimana/dozzina; **per day** al giorno; **per week** alla settimana; **per head** *or* **person** a testa, a *or* per persona; **per hour** all'ora, orario(-a); **30 miles per hour** 30 miglia all'ora; **per kilo** al *or* il chilo; **per pro** (*by proxy*) per procura; **as per your instructions** secondo le vostre istruzioni
per annum [ˌpər'ænəm] ADV all'anno
per·bo·rate [pə'bɔ:reɪt] N perborato
per·cale [pə'keɪl] N percalle *m*
per capita [pə'kæpɪtə] ADJ, ADV pro capite (*inv*)
per·ceive [pə'si:v] VT (*sound, meaning, change*) percepire; (*person, object*) notare; (*realize*) accorgersi di
◎ **per cent** [pə'sɛnt] N per cento; **50 per cent** 50 per cento
■ ADV per cento; **a 20 per cent discount** uno sconto del 20 per cento
◎ **per·cent·age** [pə'sɛntɪdʒ] N percentuale *f*; **as a percentage** in percentuale; **to get a percentage on all sales** avere una percentuale sulle vendite; **on a percentage basis** a percentuale
percentage point N punto percentuale
per·cen·tile [pə'sɛntaɪl] N percentile *m*
per·cep·tible [pə'sɛptəbl] ADJ percettibile
per·cep·tibly [pə'sɛptɪblɪ] ADV visibilmente
per·cep·tion [pə'sɛpʃən] N (*gen*) percezione *f*; (*sensitiveness*) sensibilità; (*insight*) perspicacia; **one's perception of a situation** il proprio modo di vedere una situazione
per·cep·tive [pə'sɛptɪv] ADJ (*gen*) perspicace; (*analysis*) acuto(-a)
per·cep·tive·ly [pə'sɛptɪvlɪ] ADV acutamente, con perspicacia
perch¹ [pɜ:tʃ] N (*fish*) pesce *m* persico
perch² [pɜ:tʃ] N (*of bird*) pertica, posatoio; (*in tree*) ramo; (*fig: for person etc*) posto di vedetta
■ VT poggiare
■ VI (*bird, person*) appollaiarsi
per·chance [pə'tʃɑ:ns] ADV (*old: perhaps*) forse

per·co·late [ˈpɜːkəˌleɪt] VT filtrare; **percolated coffee** caffè filtrato
■VI (*water, coffee*) passare, filtrare; (*fig: news*) filtrare

per·co·la·tor [ˈpɜːkəˌleɪtəʳ] N caffettiera a filtro

per·cus·sion [pəˈkʌʃən] N **1** percussione *f* **2** (*Mus*) percussioni *fpl*; **I play percussion** suono le percussioni

percussion instrument N strumento a percussione

per·cus·sion·ist [pəˈkʌʃənɪst] N percussionista *m/f*

per diem [ˌpɜːˈdiːɛm] N (*Am frm*) diaria

per·egri·na·tion [pɛrɪgrɪˈneɪʃən] N (*frm*) peregrinazione *f*

per·egrine [ˈpɛrɪgrɪn]: **peregrine falcon** N falco pellegrino

per·emp·to·ri·ly [pəˈrɛmptərɪlɪ] ADV perentoriamente

per·emp·tory [pəˈrɛmptərɪ] ADJ perentorio(-a)

per·en·nial [pəˈrɛnɪəl] ADJ perenne
■N (*Bot*) pianta perenne

per·en·ni·al·ly [pəˈrɛnɪəlɪ] ADV perennemente

◎**per·fect** [*adj* ˈpɜːfɪkt; *vb* pəˈfɛkt] ADJ (*gen, Gram*) perfetto(-a); **that's perfect!** perfetto!; **it's a perfect day for skiing** è una giornata ideale per sciare; **he's a perfect stranger to me** mi è completamente sconosciuto
■N (*Gram: also*: **perfect tense**) perfetto; passato prossimo
■VT perfezionare; (*skill, technique*) mettere a punto

per·fect·ible [pəˈfɛktɪbl] ADJ perfettibile

per·fec·tion [pəˈfɛkʃən] N perfezione *f*; **to perfection** a *or* alla perfezione

per·fec·tion·ism [pəˈfɛkʃəˌnɪzm] N perfezionismo

per·fec·tion·ist [pəˈfɛkʃənɪst] N perfezionista *m/f*

◎**per·fect·ly** [ˈpɜːfɪktlɪ] ADV (*gen*) perfettamente, alla perfezione; **perfectly normal** perfettamente normale; **she's perfectly lovely** è una bellezza; **I'm perfectly happy with the situation** sono completamente soddisfatta della situazione; **you know perfectly well** sai benissimo

perfect pitch N (*Mus*) intonazione *f* giusta

per·fidi·ous [pɜːˈfɪdɪəs] ADJ perfido(-a)

per·fidi·ous·ly [pɜːˈfɪdɪəslɪ] ADV perfidamente

per·fi·dy [ˈpɜːfɪdɪ] N perfidia

per·fo·rate [ˈpɜːfəˌreɪt] VT perforare; **perforated line** linea perforata

per·fo·rat·ed ul·cer [ˈpɜːfəˌreɪtɪdˈʌlsəʳ] N (*Med*) ulcera perforata

per·fo·ra·tion [ˌpɜːfəˈreɪʃən] N (*act*) perforazione *f*; (*in stamps*) dentellatura; (*hole*) foro

per·force [pəˈfɔːs] ADV (*old*) per forza

◎**per·form** [pəˈfɔːm] VT **1** (*function, task*) svolgere, eseguire; (*duty*) adempiere a; (*miracles, experiments*) fare, compiere; (*ceremony*) celebrare; **to perform an operation** (*Med*) operare; **to perform a task** svolgere un compito; **he performed many acts of bravery** ha compiuto molti atti di coraggio **2** (*play, ballet, opera*) rappresentare; (*duet, symphony*) eseguire, suonare; (*acrobatics*) fare; **this play was first performed in 1890** questa commedia è stata rappresentata per la prima volta nel 1890
■VI **1** (*theatre company*) dare una rappresentazione; (*person*) esibirsi **2** (*vehicle, machine, also fig: student*) comportarsi; **to perform brilliantly** fornire un'ottima prestazione; **if you want a car that performs really well ...** se volete una macchina che dia ottime prestazioni...

◎**per·for·mance** [pəˈfɔːməns] N **1** (*see vt 1*) svolgimento; adempimento; celebrazione *f*; **in the performance of his duties** nell'adempimento dei suoi doveri **2** (*presentation: of play, opera*) rappresentazione *f*; (: *of film, ballet*) spettacolo; (*by actor, of a part*) interpretazione *f*; **the performance lasts two hours** lo spettacolo dura due ore; **he gave a splendid performance as Hamlet** la sua interpretazione di Amleto è stata magnifica; **a fine performance of the Ninth Symphony** un'ottima esecuzione della Nona sinfonia; **what a performance!** (*fam*) quante scene *or* storie! **3** (*effectiveness: of machine etc*) prestazioni *fpl*; (: *of company*) rendimento; (: *of racehorse, athlete*) performance *f inv*; **the team put up a good performance** la squadra ha giocato una bella partita; **the team's disappointing performance** la deludente prestazione della squadra

performance related pay N retribuzione commensurata al rendimento

per·form·er [pəˈfɔːməʳ] N artista *m/f*

per·form·ing [pəˈfɔːmɪŋ] ADJ (*animal*) ammaestrato(-a); **a performing seal** una foca ammaestrata

performing arts NPL: **the performing arts** le arti *fpl* dello spettacolo

per·fume [*n* ˈpɜːfjuːm; *vb* pəˈfjuːm] N profumo
■VT profumare

per·fum·ery [pəˈfjuːmərɪ] N profumeria

per·func·to·ri·ly [pəˈfʌŋktərɪlɪ] ADV (*inspect, enquire*) superficialmente; (*agree, answer*) senza convinzione; (*greet, smile*) meccanicamente

per·func·tory [pəˈfʌŋktərɪ] ADJ (*inspection, inquiry*) superficiale, pro forma *inv*; (*nod*) meccanico(-a)

per·go·la [ˈpɜːgələ] N pergola

◎**per·haps** [pəˈhæps, præps] ADV forse; **perhaps so/not** forse sì /no, può darsi di sì /di no; **perhaps he'll come** magari *or* forse verrà, può darsi che venga; **perhaps he's ill** forse è malato

peri·gla·cial [ˌpɛrɪˈgleɪʃəl] ADJ periglaciale

per·il [ˈpɛrɪl] N pericolo; **at your peril** a tuo rischio e pericolo

peri·lous [ˈpɛrɪləs] ADJ pericoloso(-a)

peri·lous·ly [ˈpɛrɪləslɪ] ADV pericolosamente; **they came perilously close to being caught** sono stati a un pelo dall'esser presi

pe·rim·eter [pəˈrɪmɪtəʳ] N perimetro

perimeter wall N muro di cinta

◎**pe·ri·od** [ˈpɪərɪəd] N **1** (*length of time*) periodo; (*stage: in career, development etc*) periodo, momento; (*Am Ftbl*) tempo; **for a period of three weeks** per un periodo di *or* per la durata di tre settimane; **for a limited period** per un periodo limitato; **at that period (of my life)** in quel periodo (della mia vita); **the holiday period** (*Brit*) il periodo delle vacanze; **the Victorian period** l'epoca *or* l'età vittoriana; **a painting of his early period** un dipinto del suo primo periodo **2** (*Scol*) ora; **each period lasts forty minutes** ogni lezione dura quaranta minuti **3** (*Am: full stop*) punto; **comma or period?** virgola o punto? **4** (*menstruation*) mestruazioni *fpl*; **I'm having my period** ho le mestruazioni
■ADJ (*costume*) d'epoca

period dress N costume *m* d'epoca

period furniture N (*genuine*) mobili *mpl* d'epoca; (*copy*) mobili in stile

pe·ri·od·ic [ˌpɪərɪˈɒdɪk] ADJ periodico(-a)

pe·ri·odi·cal [ˌpɪərɪˈɒdɪkəl] ADJ periodico(-a)
■N periodico

pe·ri·odi·cal·ly [ˌpɪərɪˈɒdɪkəlɪ] ADV periodicamente

Pp

periodic table N (*Chem*): **the periodic table** la tavola periodica degli elementi
▷ www.webelements.com/
▷ www.colorado.edu/physics/2000/applets/a2.html
period pains NPL (*Brit*) dolori *mpl* mestruali
period piece N bell'esemplare *m* d'epoca
peri·pa·tet·ic [ˌpɛrɪpəˈtɛtɪk] ADJ (*salesman*) ambulante; (*Brit: teacher*) *che insegna in varie scuole*
pe·riph·er·al [pəˈrɪfərəl] ADJ (*gen*) periferico(-a); (*interest*) marginale
■ N (*Comput*) unità *f inv* periferica
pe·riph·ery [pəˈrɪfərɪ] N periferia
peri·scope [ˈpɛrɪˌskəʊp] N periscopio
per·ish [ˈpɛrɪʃ] VI (*person etc*) perire, morire; (*material*) deteriorarsi; **hundreds perished in the earthquake** centinaia di persone sono morte a causa del terremoto; **the rubber had perished** la gomma si era deteriorata
per·ish·able [ˈpɛrɪʃəbl] ADJ deperibile
per·ish·ables [ˈpɛrɪʃəblz] NPL merci *fpl* deperibili
per·ished [ˈpɛrɪʃt] ADJ (*fam: cold*) gelato(-a), intirizzito(-a)
per·ish·ing [ˈpɛrɪʃɪŋ] ADJ (*Brit fam*): **it's perishing (cold)** fa un freddo da morire
peri·stal·sis [ˌpɛrɪˈstælsɪs] N peristalsi *f*
peri·to·ni·tis [ˌpɛrɪtəˈnaɪtɪs] N peritonite *f*
peri·win·kle[1] [ˈpɛrɪˌwɪŋkl] N (*Bot*) pervinca
peri·win·kle[2] [ˈpɛrɪˌwɪŋkl] N (*Zool*) littorina
per·jure [ˈpɜːdʒəʳ] VT: **to perjure o.s.** spergiurare; (*Law*) giurare il falso
per·jury [ˈpɜːdʒərɪ] N (*breach of oath*) spergiuro; (*Law*) falso giuramento; **to commit perjury** spergiurare; (*Law*) giurare il falso
perk [pɜːk] N (*fam*) vantaggio
perki·ly [ˈpɜːkɪlɪ] ADV (*see adj*) con aria allegra, con tono allegro; vivacemente; con impertinenza
perk up VT + ADV (*cheer up*) tirar su di morale; **he tried to perk up her appetite** cercava di stimolarle l'appetito
■ VI + ADV (*cheer up*) tirarsi su di morale; (*show interest*) animarsi; **the dog's ears perked up** il cane drizzò le orecchie
perky [ˈpɜːkɪ] ADJ (*comp* **-ier**, *superl* **-iest**) (*cheerful*) allegro(-a); (*bright*) vivace; (*cheeky*) impertinente
perm [pɜːm] N permanente *f*; **she's got a perm** ha la permanente
■ VT: **to perm sb's hair** fare la permanente a qn; **to have one's hair permed** farsi fare la permanente
per·ma·frost [ˈpɜːməˌfrɒst] N permafrost *m inv*
per·ma·nence [ˈpɜːmənəns] N permanenza
per·ma·nen·cy [ˈpɜːmənənsɪ] N **1** (*person*) figura sempre presente **2** (*job*) occupazione *f* fissa, lavoro fisso
◎ **per·ma·nent** [ˈpɜːmənənt] ADJ (*state, building, agreement*) permanente; (*job, position*) fisso(-a); (*dye, ink*) indelebile; **a permanent ban** un divieto permanente; **I'm not permanent here** non sono fisso qui; **permanent address** residenza fissa; **permanent job** lavoro fisso
per·ma·nent·ly [ˈpɜːmənəntlɪ] ADV (*stay, leave*) definitivamente; **he is permanently drunk** è perennemente ubriaco
permanent wave N permanente *f*
per·man·ga·nate [pɜːˈmæŋgənɪt] N permanganato
per·me·abil·ity [ˌpɜːmɪəˈbɪlɪtɪ] N permeabilità
per·me·able [ˈpɜːmɪəbl] ADJ permeabile; **selectively permeable** semipermeabile
per·me·ate [ˈpɜːmɪˌeɪt] VT (*gen*) filtrare attraverso; (*Tech*) permeare; (*subj: smell*) pervadere; (: *fig: ideas etc*) diffondersi in; **permeated with** impregnato(-a) di
■ VI filtrare; (*fig*) diffondersi
per·mis·sible [pəˈmɪsɪbl] ADJ (*action*) permesso(-a); (*behaviour*) accettabile; (*attitude*) ammissibile, permissibile; **it is not permissible to do that** non è permesso farlo
◎ **per·mis·sion** [pəˈmɪʃən] N permesso; (*official*) autorizzazione *f*; **with your permission** se mi permette, con il suo permesso; **to ask permission to do sth** chiedere il permesso di fare qc; **you'll have to ask permission** dovrai chiedere il permesso; **to give sb permission to do sth** dare a qn il permesso di fare qc
per·mis·sive [pəˈmɪsɪv] ADJ (*parents, society*) permissivo(-a), tollerante
per·mis·sive·ness [pəˈmɪsɪvnɪs] N permissività
◎ **per·mit** [*n* ˈpɜːmɪt; *vb* pəˈmɪt] N (*gen*) autorizzazione *f* (scritta); (*for specific activity*) permesso; (*entrance pass*) lasciapassare *m*; **fishing permit** licenza di pesca; **building/export permit** permesso *or* licenza di costruzione/di esportazione; **work permit** permesso di lavoro
■ VT permettere; **to permit sb to do sth** permettere a qn di fare qc; **to permit sth to take place** permettere che qc avvenga
■ VI permettere; **to permit of** (*frm*) ammettere, consentire; **weather permitting** tempo permettendo
per·mu·ta·tion [ˌpɜːmjʊˈteɪʃən] N permutazione *f*
per·ni·cious [pɜːˈnɪʃəs] ADJ nocivo(-a), dannoso(-a); (*Med*) pernicioso(-a)
per·nick·ety [pəˈnɪkətɪ] ADJ (*fam: person*) pignolo(-a); (: *job*) da certosino
per·ox·ide [pəˈrɒksaɪd] N perossido
peroxide blonde N bionda ossigenata
per·pen·dicu·lar [ˌpɜːpənˈdɪkjʊləʳ] ADJ (*gen, Math*) perpendicolare; (*cliff*) a picco
■ N perpendicolare *f*
per·pen·dicu·lar·ly [ˌpɜːpənˈdɪkjʊləlɪ] ADV perpendicolarmente
per·pe·trate [ˈpɜːpɪˌtreɪt] VT perpetrare, commettere
per·pe·tra·tor [ˈpɜːpɪˌtreɪtəʳ] N (*of crime*) autore(-trice)
per·pet·ual [pəˈpɛtjʊəl] ADJ (*gen, motion*) perpetuo(-a); (*ice, snow*) perenne; (*continuous: noise, complaining*) incessante, continuo(-a)
per·pet·ual·ly [pəˈpɛtjʊəlɪ] ADV eternamente, perennemente
per·petu·ate [pəˈpɛtjʊˌeɪt] VT perpetuare
per·pe·tu·ity [ˌpɜːpɪˈtjuːɪtɪ] N: **in perpetuity** in perpetuo
per·plex [pəˈplɛks] VT lasciare perplesso(-a); **I was perplexed by his behaviour** il suo comportamento mi ha lasciato perplesso
per·plexed [pəˈplɛkst] ADJ perplesso(-a)
per·plex·ed·ly [pəˈplɛksɪdlɪ] ADV con perplessità
per·plex·ing [pəˈplɛksɪŋ] ADJ che lascia perplesso(-a)
per·plex·ity [pəˈplɛksɪtɪ] N perplessità
per·qui·site [ˈpɜːkwɪzɪt] N (*frm*) = **perk**
per·secute [ˈpɜːsɪkjuːt] VT perseguitare
per·secu·tion [ˌpɜːsɪˈkjuːʃən] N persecuzione *f*
persecution complex N (*Psych*) mania di persecuzione
per·secu·tor [ˈpɜːsɪkjuːtəʳ] N persecutore(-trice)
Persephone [pəˈsɛfənɪ] N Persefone *f*
Perseus [ˈpɜːsjuːs] N Perseo
per·sever·ance [ˌpɜːsɪˈvɪərəns] N perseveranza

per·severe [ˌpɜːsɪˈvɪəʳ] VI perseverare
per·sever·ing [ˌpɜːsɪˈvɪərɪŋ] ADJ perseverante, assiduo(-a)
per·sever·ing·ly [ˌpɜːsɪˈvɪərɪŋlɪ] ADV con perseveranza, assiduamente
Per·sia [ˈpɜːʃə] N Persia
Per·sian [ˈpɜːʃən] ADJ persiano(-a)
■ N **1** (*person*) persiano(-a) **2** (*language*) persiano
Persian carpet N tappeto persiano
Persian cat N (gatto) persiano
Persian Gulf N Golfo Persico
Persian lamb N (*animal*) karakul *m inv*; (*skin*) astrakan *m inv*
per·sim·mon [pɜːˈsɪmən] N cachi *m inv*
per·sist [pəˈsɪst] VI (*person*) persistere, ostinarsi; (*custom, rain*) persistere, durare; **to persist in sth/in doing sth** ostinarsi in qc/a fare qc, persistere in qc/nel *or* a fare qc; **why do they persist in wasting money?** perché continuano a buttar via soldi?; **if the cough persists, contact your doctor** se la tosse persiste, contattare il medico
per·sis·tence [pəˈsɪstəns] N (*tenacity*) perseveranza; (*obstinacy*) ostinazione *f*, persistenza; (*continued existence*) persistere *m*
per·sis·tent [pəˈsɪstənt] ADJ (*person, attempt, questions*) insistente, ostinato(-a); (*cough, pain, smell*) persistente; (*lateness, rain*) continuo(-a); **persistent offender** (*Law*) delinquente *m/f* abituale
per·sis·tent·ly [pəˈsɪstəntlɪ] ADV con insistenza; (*continuously*) continuamente
per·snick·ety [pəˈsnɪkɪtɪ] ADJ (*Am*) = **pernickety**
◎ **per·son** [ˈpɜːsn] N **1** (*pl* **people** *or (frm)*: **persons**) persona; **a person to person call** (*Telec*) una chiamata con preavviso **2** (*pl* **persons:** *Gram, Law*) persona **3** (*body, physical presence*) figura, personale *m*; (*appearance*) aspetto; **in person** di *or* in persona, personalmente; **in the person of my uncle** nella persona di mio zio; **on** *or* **about one's person** (*weapon*) su di sé; (*money*) con sé
per·son·able [ˈpɜːsnəbl] ADJ di bell'aspetto, prestante
per·son·age [ˈpɜːsnɪdʒ] N personaggio
◎ **per·son·al** [ˈpɜːsnl] ADJ (*gen, Gram*) personale; (*application*) (fatto(-a)) di persona; **personal belongings** oggetti d'uso personale; **a personal opinion** un'opinione personale; **a personal question** una domanda indiscreta; **a personal interview** un incontro privato; **for personal reasons** per motivi personali; **to make a personal appearance** apparire di persona; **to have personal knowledge of sth** conoscere qc per esperienza personale; **don't get personal!** non entriamo nel personale!; **one's personal habits** le proprie piccole manie; **"personal"** (*on letter*) "riservata", "personale"
personal allowance N (*Tax*) quota non imponibile
personal assistant N assistente *m/f* personale
personal call N (*Brit Telec: person to person*) chiamata con preavviso; (*: private*) telefonata personale
personal column N colonna degli annunci personali, colonna dei piccoli annunci
personal computer N personal computer *m inv*
personal details NPL dati *mpl* personali
personal digital assistant N (*Comput*) PDA *m inv*
personal equity plan N *deposito a risparmio per investimento azionario con agevolazioni fiscali*
personal identification number N (*Comput, Banking*) numero di codice segreto
◎ **per·son·al·ity** [ˌpɜːsəˈnælɪtɪ] N (*nature*) personalità *f inv*; (*famous person*) personalità, personaggio; **let's not indulge in personalities** lasciamo da parte i commenti personali
personality cult N culto della personalità
per·son·al·ize [ˈpɜːsənəˌlaɪz] VT personalizzare
per·son·al·ized [ˈpɜːsənəˌlaɪzd] ADJ personalizzato(-a)
personal loan N credito *or* prestito personale, prestito privato
◎ **per·son·al·ly** [ˈpɜːsnəlɪ] ADV **1** (*for my part*) personalmente; **I feel personally responsible** mi sento personalmente responsabile; **personally I think that ...** personalmente penso che...; **personally I don't agree** personalmente non sono d'accordo; **don't take it too personally** non prenderla come un'offesa *or* una critica personale **2** (*in person*) personalmente, di persona; **to hand sth over personally** consegnare qc di persona
personal organizer N (*book*) agenda; (*electronic*) agenda elettronica
personal property N (*Law*) beni *mpl* personali
personal shopper N *assistente personale che si occupa degli acquisti*
personal stereo N Walkman® *m inv*
personal trainer N personal trainer *m/f inv*, allenatore(-trice) personale
per·so·na non gra·ta [pɜːˈsəʊnənɒnˈgrɑːtə] N (*frm*) persona non grata
per·soni·fi·ca·tion [pɜːˌsɒnɪfɪˈkeɪʃən] N personificazione *f*
per·soni·fy [pɜːˈsɒnɪˌfaɪ] VT personificare
◎ **per·son·nel** [ˌpɜːsəˈnɛl] N personale *m*
personnel department N ufficio del personale
personnel management N direzione *f* del personale
personnel manager N direttore(-trice) del personale
personnel officer N addetto(-a) all'ufficio del personale
◎ **per·spec·tive** [pəˈspɛktɪv] N prospettiva; **a new perspective** una nuova prospettiva; **to see** *or* **look at sth in perspective** (*fig*) vedere qc nella giusta prospettiva; **to get sth into perspective** ridimensionare qc
Per·spex® [ˈpɜːspɛks] N plexiglas® *m*
per·spi·ca·cious [ˌpɜːspɪˈkeɪʃəs] ADJ (*frm*) perspicace
per·spi·cac·ity [ˌpɜːspɪˈkæsɪtɪ] N (*frm*) perspicacia
per·spi·ra·tion [ˌpɜːspəˈreɪʃən] N traspirazione *f*, sudore *m*; **bathed in perspiration** in un bagno di sudore, bagnato(-a) di sudore; **excessive perspiration** sudorazione eccessiva
per·spire [pəˈspaɪəʳ] VI traspirare, sudare
◎ **per·suade** [pəˈsweɪd] VT persuadere; **to persuade sb of sth/that** persuadere qn di qc/che; **to persuade sb to do sth** persuadere qn a fare qc; **she persuaded me to go with her** mi ha convinto ad andare con lei; **but they persuaded me not to** ma mi hanno persuaso a non farlo; **she is easily persuaded** si lascia facilmente persuadere *or* convincere; **I am persuaded that ...** (*frm*) sono persuaso *or* convinto che... + *sub*
per·sua·sion [pəˈsweɪʒən] N **1** (*persuading*) persuasione *f*; **her powers of persuasion** la sua capacità di persuasione **2** (*creed*) convinzione *f*, credo; **people of all political persuasions** gente di tutte le convinzioni politiche
per·sua·sive [pəˈsweɪsɪv] ADJ (*person*) convincente; (*argument*) persuasivo(-a), convincente
per·sua·sive·ly [pəˈsweɪsɪvlɪ] ADV in modo persuasivo
per·sua·sive·ness [pəˈsweɪsɪvnɪs] N (*of person, argument*) potere *or* forza di convinzione

Pp

pert [pɜːt] ADJ (*comp* **-er**, *superl* **-est**) (*girl, answer*) impertinente, sfacciato(-a); (*hat*) spiritoso(-a)
per·tain [pɜːˈteɪn] VI (*frm*): **to pertain to** (*concern*) riferirsi a, riguardare; (*belong to*) appartenere a; **documents pertaining to the case** documenti relativi al caso
per·ti·na·cious [ˌpɜːtɪˈneɪʃəs] ADJ ostinato(-a), pertinace
per·ti·na·cious·ly [ˌpɜːtɪˈneɪʃəslɪ] ADV con ostinazione, con pertinacia
per·ti·nac·ity [ˌpɜːtɪˈnæsɪtɪ] N pertinacia
per·ti·nence [ˈpɜːtɪnəns] N pertinenza
per·ti·nent [ˈpɜːtɪnənt] ADJ pertinente
per·ti·nent·ly [ˈpɜːtɪnəntlɪ] ADV in modo pertinente; **he very pertinently said that ...** disse molto a proposito che...
pert·ly [ˈpɜːtlɪ] ADV (*reply, smile*) impudentemente
per·turb [pəˈtɜːb] VT turbare, agitare; **I was perturbed to learn that ...** fui sconvolto nello scoprire che...
per·turb·ing [pəˈtɜːbɪŋ] ADJ inquietante
Peru [pəˈruː] N Perù *m*
pe·rus·al [pəˈruːzəl] N lettura
pe·ruse [pəˈruːz] VT leggere
Pe·ru·vian [pəˈruːvɪən] ADJ, N peruviano(-a)
per·vade [pɜːˈveɪd] VT (*subj*: *smell, feeling, atmosphere*) pervadere; (: *influence, ideas*) insinuarsi in, diffondersi in
per·va·sive [pɜːˈveɪsɪv] ADJ (*smell*) penetrante; (*influence*) dilagante; (*gloom, feelings, ideas*) diffuso(-a)
per·verse [pəˈvɜːs] ADJ (*contrary*: *behaviour*) da bastian contrario; (*wicked*) cattivo(-a); (*desires*) perverso(-a); (*circumstances*) avverso(-a); **to be perverse** (*person*) essere un bastian contrario
per·verse·ly [pəˈvɜːslɪ] ADV (*see adj*) da bastian contrario; con cattiveria; perversamente
per·ver·sion [pəˈvɜːʃən] N (*Psych*) perversione *f*; (*of justice, truth*) travisamento, pervertimento
per·ver·sity [pəˈvɜːsɪtɪ] N (*wickedness*) perversità, malvagità; (*contrariness*) spirito di contraddizione
per·vert [*vb* pəˈvɜːt; *n* ˈpɜːvɜːt] VT (*mind*) pervertire, corrompere; (*speech, truth etc*) travisare; **to pervert the course of justice** deviare il corso della giustizia
■ N pervertito(-a)
per·ver·ted [pəˈvɜːtɪd] ADJ (*person*) pervertito(-a); (*behaviour, logic, imagination*) perverso(-a)
pesky [ˈpɛskɪ] ADJ (*comp* **-ier**, *superl* **-iest**) (*Am*: *fam*) fastidioso(-a), noioso(-a)
pes·sa·ry [ˈpɛsərɪ] N pessario; (*contraceptive*) diaframma *m*
pes·si·mism [ˈpɛsɪˌmɪzəm] N pessimismo
pes·si·mist [ˈpɛsɪmɪst] N pessimista *m/f*
pes·si·mis·tic [ˌpɛsɪˈmɪstɪk] ADJ (*attitude, forecast*) pessimistico(-a); (*person*) pessimista
pes·si·mis·ti·cal·ly [ˌpɛsɪˈmɪstɪkəlɪ] ADV pessimisticamente
pest [pɛst] N **1** (*Zool*) insetto (*or* animale *m*) nocivo; **garden pests** gli insetti nocivi del giardino **2** (*fig*: *person*) peste *f*; (: *thing*) rottura; **he's a real pest!** è un gran rompiscatole!
pest control N disinfestazione *f*
pest control officer N funzionario responsabile della disinfestazione
pes·ter [ˈpɛstəʳ] VT tormentare, molestare; **he's always pestering me** mi tormenta in continuazione; **stop pestering me!** smettila di scocciarmi!
pes·ti·cide [ˈpɛstɪˌsaɪd] N pesticida *m*
pes·ti·lence [ˈpɛstɪləns] N pestilenza
pes·ti·lent [ˈpɛstɪlənt], **pes·ti·len·tial** [ˌpɛstɪˈlɛnʃəl] ADJ (*fam*: *exasperating*) pestifero(-a)
pes·tle [ˈpɛsl] N pestello
◎ **pet** [pɛt] N **1** (*animal*) animale *m* domestico; **have you got any pets?** hai qualche animale domestico?; **my dad won't let me have any pets** il mio papà non mi lascia tenere (in casa) nessun animale **2** (*favourite*) preferito(-a), favorito(-a), beniamino(-a); **the teacher's pet** il cocco dell'insegnante; **come here pet** (*fam*) vieni qua tesoro
■ VT (*indulge*) coccolare; (*fondle*) accarezzare
■ VI (*sexually*) pomiciare, fare il petting
■ ADJ **1** (*monkey*) ammaestrato(-a); (*food*) per animali domestici; **we have a pet dog** abbiamo un cane; **pet mouse** topo addomesticato **2** (*favourite*: *pupil, subject etc*) preferito(-a), prediletto(-a); **my pet aversion** la cosa che detesto di più
pet·al [ˈpɛtl] N petalo
pe·tard [pɪˈtɑːd] N: **to be hoist with one's own petard** essere preso(-a) nelle proprie reti
pe·ter [ˈpiːtəʳ] VI: **to peter out** (*supply*) esaurirsi, estinguersi; (*stream*) perdersi; (*plan*) andare in fumo; (*interest, excitement*) svanire; (*conversation*) spegnersi; (*song, noise*) cessare; (*track, path*) finire
peti·ole [ˈpɛtɪˌəʊl] N picciolo
pe·tite [pəˈtiːt] ADJ (*woman*) minuta e graziosa
pe·ti·tion [pəˈtɪʃən] N (*list of names*) petizione *f*; (*frm*: *request*) richiesta, istanza
■ VT (*person*) presentare una petizione a
■ VI richiedere; **to petition for divorce** (*Law*) presentare un'istanza di divorzio
pet name N (*Brit*) nomignolo
Petrarch [ˈpɛtrɑːk] N Petrarca *m*
pet·ri·fied [ˈpɛtrɪˌfaɪd] ADJ terrorizzato(-a); **I was petrified** ero terrorizzato(-a); **to be petrified (with fear)** restare impietrito(-a) (per la paura)
pet·ri·fy [ˈpɛtrɪˌfaɪ] VT (*fig*) terrorizzare
■ VI (*turn to stone*) pietrificarsi; (*frm*: *stagnate*) sclerotizzarsi
pet·ro·chemi·cal [ˌpɛtrəʊˈkɛmɪkl] ADJ petrolchimico(-a)
■ N prodotto petrolchimico
pet·ro·dol·lar [ˈpɛtrəʊˌdɒləʳ] N petrodollaro
pet·rol [ˈpɛtrəl] (*Brit*) N benzina; **unleaded petrol** la benzina verde; **high-octane petrol** (benzina) super *f inv*; **to be heavy on petrol** (*car*) bere molta benzina; **to run out of petrol** restare senza benzina; **they spend a lot on petrol** spendono molto per la benzina
■ ADJ (*leak, stain*) di benzina

DID YOU KNOW ...?
petrol is not translated by the Italian word ***petrolio***

petrol bomb N (bottiglia *or* bomba) molotov *f inv*
petrol can N tanica per benzina
petrol engine N motore *m* a benzina
pe·tro·leum [pɪˈtrəʊlɪəm] N petrolio
petroleum jelly N vaselina
petrol gauge N spia della benzina
petrol pump N (*at garage, in car*) pompa della benzina
petrol station N stazione *f* di servizio *or* rifornimento
petrol tank N serbatoio della benzina
pet shop N negozio di animali domestici
pet·ti·coat [ˈpɛtɪˌkəʊt] N (*full-length*) sottoveste *f*; (*waist*) sottogonna *f*
pet·ti·fog·ging [ˈpɛtɪˌfɒgɪŋ] ADJ (*details*) insignificante; (*objections*) cavilloso(-a)
pet·ti·ly [ˈpɛtɪlɪ] ADV (*small-mindedly*) meschinamente

pet·ti·ness ['pɛtɪnɪs] N (*small-mindedness*) meschinità *f inv*

pet·ting ['pɛtɪŋ] N petting *m inv*

pet·ty ['pɛtɪ] ADJ (*comp* **-ier**, *superl* **-iest**) **1** (*trivial: detail, complaint*) insignificante, di poca importanza; **petty crime** reati *mpl* minori; **petty problems** problemi *mpl* insignificanti **2** (*minor: official*) subalterno(-a) **3** (*small-minded, spiteful*) meschino(-a); **you're being petty** sei meschino(-a)

petty cash N piccola cassa

petty cash book N primanota

petty officer N (*Naut*) sottufficiale *m* di marina

petu·lance ['pɛtjʊləns] N irritabilità

petu·lant ['pɛtjʊlənt] ADJ irritabile

petu·lant·ly ['pɛtjʊləntlɪ] ADV con irritazione

pew [pju:] N (*in church*) banco; **take a pew!** (*fig fam*) accomodati!, siediti!

pew·ter ['pju:tə^r] N peltro

PFI [ˌpi:ɛf'aɪ] N ABBR (*Brit*) = **Private Finance Initiative**

PG [ˌpi:'dʒi:] N ABBR (*Cinema:* = **parental guidance**) *classificazione di film la cui visione è a discrezione dei genitori date le scene poco adatte ai bambini*

PG 13 [-θɜ:'ti:n] ABBR (*Am: Cine:* = **Parental Guidance 13**) vietato ai minori di 13 anni non accompagnati dai genitori

PGA [ˌpi:dʒi:'eɪ] N ABBR (= **Professional Golfers' Association**) *associazione dei giocatori di golf professionisti*

PGCE [ˌpi:dʒi:si:'i:] N ABBR (*Brit:* = **Postgraduate Certificate in Education**) *diploma post-laurea di abilitazione all'insegnamento*

PH [ˌpi:'eɪtʃ] N ABBR (*Am Mil*) = **Purple Heart**

pH [ˌpi:'eɪtʃ] N ABBR (*Chem*) pH *m*

PHA [ˌpi:eɪtʃ'eɪ] N ABBR (*Am:* = **Public Housing Administration**) amministrazione per l'edilizia pubblica

Phaedra ['fi:drə] N Fedra

phal·lic ['fælɪk] ADJ fallico(-a)

phan·tom ['fæntəm] ADJ fantasma *inv*
■ N fantasma *m*

Phar·aoh ['fɛərəʊ] N faraone *m*

phar·ma·ceu·ti·cal [ˌfɑ:mə'sju:tɪkəl] ADJ farmaceutico(-a)

phar·ma·ceu·tics [ˌfɑ:mə'sju:tɪks] NPL prodotti *mpl* farmaceutici

phar·ma·cist ['fɑ:məsɪst] N farmacista *m/f*

phar·ma·col·ogy [ˌfɑ:mə'kɒlədʒɪ] N farmacologia
▷ www.pharmweb.net
▷ www.medbioworld.com/home/lists/medications.html

phar·ma·cy ['fɑ:məsɪ] N farmacia

phar·yn·gi·tis [ˌfærɪn'dʒaɪtɪs] N faringite *f*

phar·ynx ['færɪŋks] N faringe *f*

◎ **phase** [feɪz] N fase *f*, periodo; **to be out of phase** (*Tech, Elec*) essere sfasato(-a) *or* fuori fase; **she's just going through a phase** sta attraversando un periodo difficile, le passerà; **it's a phase all children go through** è una fase che tutti i bambini attraversano
■ VT (*stagger*) introdurre gradualmente; (*coordinate*) sincronizzare; **the redundancies will be phased** i licenziamenti verranno effettuati gradualmente; **phased withdrawal** ritirata progressiva
▸ **phase in** VT + ADV introdurre gradualmente
▸ **phase out** VT + ADV eliminare gradualmente

phase change N (*Chem*) passaggio di stato; (*Phys*) cambiamento di fase

Ph.D. [ˌpi:eɪtʃ'di:] N ABBR (= **Doctor of Philosophy**) ≈ dottorato di ricerca

pheas·ant ['fɛznt] N fagiano

phe·no·bar·bi·tone [ˌfi:nəʊ'bɑ:bɪˌtəʊn] N fenilbarbiturico, luminal® *m*

phe·nol ['fi:nɒl] N fenolo

phe·nom·enal [fɪ'nɒmɪnl] ADJ fenomenale

phe·nom·enal·ly [fɪ'nɒmɪnəlɪ] ADV straordinariamente

phe·nom·enon [fɪ'nɒmɪnən] N (*pl* **phenomena** [fɪ'nɒmɪnə]) fenomeno

phe·no·type ['fi:nəʊˌtaɪp] N fenotipo

phew [fju:] EXCL (*heat, tiredness*) uff!; (*relief, surprise*) uh!

phial ['faɪəl] N fiala

Phidias ['fɪdɪæs] N Fidia *m*

phi·lan·der [fɪ'lændə^r] VI (*pej*): **to philander (with)** amoreggiare (con)

phi·lan·der·er [fɪ'lændərə^r] N (*pej*) libertino

phi·lan·der·ing [fɪ'lændərɪŋ] N (*pej*) libertinaggio

phil·an·throp·ic [ˌfɪlən'θrɒpɪk] ADJ filantropico(-a)

phil·an·thropi·cal·ly [ˌfɪlən'θrɒpɪkəlɪ] ADV filantropicamente

phi·lan·thro·pist [fɪ'lænθrəpɪst] N filantropo(-a)

phi·lan·thro·py [fɪ'lænθrəpɪ] N filantropia

phi·lat·elist [fɪ'lætəlɪst] N filatelista *m/f*, filatelico(-a)

phi·lat·ely [fɪ'lætəlɪ] N filatelia

phil·har·mon·ic [ˌfɪlhɑ:'mɒnɪk] ADJ filarmonico(-a)

Phil·ip·pines ['fɪlɪˌpi:nz] NPL: **the Philippines** le Filippine

Phil·is·tine ['fɪlɪˌstaɪn] ADJ filisteo(-a)

Phil·is·tin·ism ['fɪlɪstɪˌnɪzəm] N mancanza di raffinatezza culturale

philo·den·dron [ˌfɪlə'dɛndrən] N filodendro

philo·logi·cal [ˌfɪlə'lɒdʒɪkəl] ADJ filologico(-a)

philo·logi·cal·ly [ˌfɪlə'lɒdʒɪkəlɪ] ADV filologicamente

phi·lolo·gist [fɪ'lɒlədʒɪst] N filologo(-a)

phi·lol·ogy [fɪ'lɒlədʒɪ] N filologia
▷ www.britac.ac.uk/portal/

phi·loso·pher [fɪ'lɒsəfə^r] N filosofo(-a)

philo·sophi·cal [ˌfɪlə'sɒfɪkəl] ADJ (*also fig*) filosofico(-a); **he's been very philosophical about it** l'ha presa con molta filosofia

philo·sophi·cal·ly [ˌfɪlə'sɒfɪkəlɪ] ADV filosoficamente

phi·loso·phize [fɪ'lɒsəˌfaɪz] VI: **to philosophize (about *or* on)** filosofare (su)

◎ **phi·loso·phy** [fɪ'lɒsəfɪ] N filosofia; **her philosophy of life** la sua massima *or* filosofia
▷ www.philosophypages.com
▷ www.utm.edu/research/iep/

phle·bi·tis [flɪ'baɪtɪs] N flebite *f*

phlegm [flɛm] N flemma

phleg·mat·ic [flɛg'mætɪk] ADJ flemmatico(-a)

phleg·mati·cal·ly [flɛg'mætɪkəlɪ] ADV flemmaticamente

pho·bia ['fəʊbɪə] N fobia; **to have a phobia about sth** avere la fobia di qc

pho·bic ['fəʊbɪk] ADJ: **to be phobic about sth** avere una fobia per qc
■ N fobico(-a)

Phoebus ['fi:bəs] N Febo

phoe·nix ['fi:nɪks] N fenice *f*

◎ **phone** [fəʊn] N telefono; **to be on the phone** avere il telefono; (*be calling*) essere al telefono; **she's on the phone at the moment** in questo momento è al telefono; **by phone** per telefono
■ VT telefonare a; **I'll phone the station** telefono alla stazione
■ VI telefonare
▸ **phone back** VT + ADV, VI + ADV richiamare

Pp

▸ **phone up** VT + ADV: **to phone sb up** dare un colpo di telefono a qn
phone book N guida del telefono, elenco telefonico
phone booth N cabina telefonica (*in luogo pubblico*)
phone box N cabina telefonica (*per strada*)
phone call N telefonata; **to make a phone call** fare una telefonata
phone·card [ˈfəʊn,kɑːd] N scheda telefonica
phone-in [ˈfəʊn,ɪn] N (*Radio, TV*) *trasmissione con telefonate in diretta*
pho·neme [ˈfəʊniːm] N (*Ling*) fonema *m*
phone tap·ping [ˈfəʊn,tæpɪŋ] N intercettazioni *fpl* telefoniche
pho·net·ic [fəʊˈnɛtɪk] ADJ fonetico(-a)
pho·neti·cal·ly [fəˈnɛtɪkəlɪ] ADV foneticamente
pho·neti·cian [,fəʊnɪˈtɪʃən], **pho·net·ist** [ˈfəʊnɪtɪst] N fonetista *m/f*
pho·net·ics [fəʊˈnɛtɪks] NSG fonetica
▹ http://www2.arts.gla.ac.uk/IPA/ipa.html
▹ http://faculty.washington.edu/dillon/PhonResources
pho·ney [ˈfəʊnɪ] (*fam*) ADJ (*comp* **-ier**, *superl* **-iest**) (*gen*) falso(-a), fasullo(-a); (*accent*) fasullo(-a)
■ N (*person*) venditore(-trice) di fumo, ciarlatano(-a)
pho·no·graph [ˈfəʊnə,grɑːf] (*old*) N fonografo; (*Am*) giradischi *m inv*
pho·no·logi·cal [,fəʊnəˈlɒdʒɪkəl] ADJ (*Ling*) fonologico(-a)
pho·nol·ogy [fəʊˈnɒlədʒɪ] N (*Ling*) fonologia
pho·ny [ˈfəʊnɪ] (*Am*) = **phoney**
phoo·ey [ˈfuːɪ] EXCL (*fam: to express disbelief*) ma dai!, ma va'!
phos·phate [ˈfɒsfeɪt] N fosfato
phos·pho·res·cence [,fɒsfəˈrɛsns] N fosforescenza
phos·pho·res·cent [,fɒsfəˈrɛsnt] ADJ fosforescente
phos·phor·ic [fɒsˈfɒrɪk] ADJ fosforico(-a)
phos·pho·rus [ˈfɒsfərəs] N fosforo
◎ **pho·to** [ˈfəʊtəʊ] N foto *f inv*; **to take a photo** fare una foto; **I took a photo of the bride and groom** ho fatto una foto agli sposi
photo... [ˈfəʊtəʊ] PREF foto...
photo album N album *m inv* fotografico (*or* di fotografie)
photo booth N cabina automatica per fototessere
photo·call [ˈfəʊtəʊ,kɔːl] N *convocazione di fotoreporter a scopo pubblicitario*
photo·cell [ˈfəʊtəʊ,sɛl] N fotocellula
photo·chemi·cal [,fəʊtəʊˈkɛmɪkəl] ADJ fotochimico(-a)
photo·copi·er [ˈfəʊtəʊ,kɒpɪəʳ] N fotocopiatrice *f*
photo·copy [ˈfəʊtəʊ,kɒpɪ] N fotocopia
■ VT fotocopiare
photo·copy·ing [ˈfəʊtəʊ,kɒpɪɪŋ] N fotocopiatura
photo·elec·tric [,fəʊtəʊɪˈlɛktrɪk] ADJ fotoelettrico(-a)
photoelectric cell N = **photocell**
photo·elec·tric·ity [,fəʊtəʊɪlɛkˈtrɪsɪtɪ] N fotoelettricità
photo finish N (*Sport*) fotofinish *m inv*
Photo·fit® [ˈfəʊtəʊ,fɪt] N photofit *m inv*
photo·gen·ic [,fəʊtəʊˈdʒɛnɪk] ADJ fotogenico(-a)
◎ **photo·graph** [ˈfəʊtə,græf] N fotografia; **to take a photograph of sb** fare una fotografia a *or* fotografare qn; **to take a photograph of sth** fotografare qc
■ VT fotografare
photograph album N (*new*) album *m inv* per fotografie; (*containing photos*) album delle fotografie
◎ **pho·tog·ra·pher** [fəˈtɒgrəfəʳ] N fotografo(-a); **she's a photographer** fa la fotografa; **newspaper photographer** fotoreporter *m/f inv*; **street photographer** fotografo di piazza; **he's a keen photographer** è appassionato di fotografia
photo·graph·ic [,fəʊtəˈgræfɪk] ADJ fotografico(-a); **to have a photographic memory** avere una memoria fotografica
photo·graphi·cal·ly [,fəʊtəˈgræfɪkəlɪ] ADV fotograficamente
pho·tog·ra·phy [fəˈtɒgrəfɪ] N fotografia; **my hobby is photography** il mio hobby è la fotografia
▹ www.nmpft.org.uk/photography/
▹ www.photography-museum.com/
▹ www.nyip.com
photo·gra·vure [,fəʊtəʊgrəˈvjʊəʳ] N fotoincisione *f*
photo·jour·nal·ism [,fəʊtəʊˈdʒɜːnəlɪzəm] N fotogiornalismo
photo·jour·nal·ist [,fəʊtəʊˈdʒɜːnəlɪst] N fotogiornalista *m/f inv*
pho·ton [ˈfəʊtɒn] N (*Phys*) fotone *m*
photo opportunity N *opportunità di scattare delle foto ad un personaggio importante*
photo·sen·si·tive [,fəʊtəʊˈsɛnsɪtɪv] ADJ (*gen*) fotosensibile; (*lens*) fotocromatico(-a)
photo shoot N sessione *f* fotografica
photo·stat® [ˈfəʊtəʊ,stæt] N = **photocopy**
photo·syn·the·sis [,fəʊtəʊˈsɪnθəsɪs] N fotosintesi *f*
photo·trop·ism [,fəʊtəʊˈtrəʊpɪzəm] N fototropismo
phras·al verb [,freɪzəlˈvɜːb] N (*Gram*) *verbo seguito da preposizione o avverbio*
◎ **phrase** [freɪz] N **1** (*Gram*) locuzione *f*; (*saying*) espressione *f*; **noun phrase** sintagma *m* nominale **2** (*Mus*) frase *f*
■ VT **1** (*thought*) esprimere; (*letter*) redigere **2** (*Mus*) dividere in frasi
phrase book N vocabolarietto
phra·seol·ogy [,freɪzɪˈɒlədʒɪ] N fraseologia
phras·ing [ˈfreɪzɪŋ] N (*of thought, request, letter*) formulazione *f*; (*Mus*) fraseggio
phre·nol·ogy [frɪˈnɒlədʒɪ] N frenologia
phut [fʌt] ADV: **to go phut** (*fam*) andare in tilt; **the TV's gone phut** è saltata la tivù
◎ **physi·cal** [ˈfɪzɪkəl] ADJ **1** (*of the body*) fisico(-a) **2** (*world, object*) materiale; (*of physics*) fisico(-a); **physical change** reazione *f* fisica; **physical stocktaking** (*Comm*) inventario fisico; **it's a physical impossibility** è un'impossibilità materiale
physical education N educazione *f* fisica
physical examination N visita medica
physical jerks (*fam*), **physical exercises** NPL ginnastica *fsg*
physi·cal·ly [ˈfɪzɪkəlɪ] ADV fisicamente; **it's physically impossible** è materialmente impossibile
physical sciences NPL: **the physical sciences** le scienze fisiche
phy·si·cian [fɪˈzɪʃən] N medico
physi·cist [ˈfɪzɪsɪst] N fisico; **nuclear physicist** fisico nucleare
phys·ics [ˈfɪzɪks] NSG fisica; **she teaches physics** insegna fisica
▹ www.physlink.com
▹ www.physicsweb.org
physio [ˈfɪsɪəʊ] N (*fam: person*) fisioterapista *m/f*; (*: treatment*) fisioterapia
physi·og·no·my [,fɪzɪˈɒnəmɪ] N (*person's features, Geog etc*) fisionomia; (*art of judging character*) fisiognomia
physio·logi·cal [,fɪzɪəˈlɒdʒɪkəl] ADJ fisiologico(-a)

physio·logi·cal·ly [ˌfɪzɪəˈlɒdʒɪkəlɪ] ADV fisiologicamente

physi·olo·gist [ˌfɪzɪˈɒlədʒɪst] N fisiologo(-a)

physi·ol·ogy [ˌfɪzɪˈɒlədʒɪ] N fisiologia
▷ www.physoc.org/links/

physio·thera·pist [ˌfɪzɪʊˈθɛrəpɪst] N fisioterapista *m/f*

physio·thera·py [ˌfɪzɪʊˈθɛrəpɪ] N fisioterapia

phy·sique [fɪˈziːk] N fisico

pi [paɪ] N (*Math*) pi greco *m*

pia·nist [ˈpɪənɪst] N pianista *m/f*

pia·no [piːˈænəʊ] N piano(forte) *m*
■ ADJ (*lesson, teacher*) di piano(forte); (*concerto, stool*) per piano(forte)

piano accordion N fisarmonica (a tastiera)

Pia·no·la® [pɪəˈnəʊlə] N pianola®

piano tuner N accordatore(-trice) di pianoforti

Pic·ar·dy [ˈpɪkədɪ] N Piccardia

pica·resque [ˌpɪkəˈrɛsk] ADJ (*liter*) picaresco(-a)

pic·co·lo [ˈpɪkələʊ] N (*pl* **-s**) (*Mus*) ottavino

◎**pick** [pɪk] N
1 (*also:* **pickaxe**) piccone *m*; **pick and shovel** pala e piccone
2 (*choice, right to choose*) scelta; **take your pick!** scegli quello che vuoi!, prendi quello che ti pare!; **it's the pick of the bunch** è il migliore di tutti
■ VT
1 (*choose*) scegliere; **to pick a winner** puntare sul vincente; (*fig*) fare un ottimo affare, imbroccarla giusta; **to pick one's way through** attraversare stando ben attento(-a) a dove mettere i piedi; **to pick a fight/quarrel with sb** attaccar rissa/briga con qn; **I picked the biggest piece** ho scelto il pezzo più grosso
2 (*flowers*) cogliere; (*fruit*) raccogliere; **I picked some strawberries** ho raccolto delle fragole
3 (*scab, spot*) grattarsi; **to pick one's nose** mettersi le dita nel naso; **to pick one's teeth** pulirsi i denti con uno stuzzicadenti, stuzzicarsi i denti; **to pick a lock** far scattare una serratura; **to pick a bone** spolpare un osso; **I've got a bone to pick with you!** devo fare i conti con te; **to pick holes in sth** (*fig*) trovare i punti deboli in qc; **to pick sb's pocket** alleggerire qn del portafoglio; **to pick sb's brains** farsi dare dei suggerimenti da qn
■ VI: **to pick and choose** scegliere con cura

▶ **pick at** VI + PREP (*food, meal*) mangiare contro voglia; (*scab*) grattarsi

▶ **pick off** VT + ADV
1 (*remove: fluff*) togliere; (: *flower, leaf*) cogliere
2 (*shoot*) abbattere (uno(-a) dopo l'altro(-a))

▶ **pick on** VI + PREP
1 (*fam: harass*) avercela con, prendersela con; **she's always picking on me** se la prende sempre con me
2 (*single out*) beccare; **they always pick on him to do it** lo fanno sempre fare a lui

▶ **pick out** VT + ADV
1 (*choose*) scegliere; **I like them all – it's difficult to pick one out** mi piacciono tutti, è difficile sceglierne uno
2 (*place: on map*) trovare; (*person: in crowd, photo*) individuare; (: *in identification parade*) identificare; **four victims picked him out on identity parades** quattro vittime lo hanno identificato in un confronto
3 (*Mus*): **to pick out a tune on the piano** trovare gli accordi di un motivo al piano

▶ **pick over** VT + ADV (*fruit, vegetables*) selezionare, scegliere; (*rice, lentils*) mondare

▶ **pick up** VT + ADV
1 (*lift: sth dropped*) raccogliere, raccattare; (: *sb fallen*) tirar su; **could you help me pick up the toys?** mi aiuti a raccogliere i giocattoli?; **to pick o.s. up** rialzarsi; **to pick up a child** prendere in braccio un bambino; **to pick up the phone** alzare il ricevitore; **to pick up the bill** (*fig*) pagare (il conto); **to pick sb up for having made a mistake** riprendere qn per aver fatto uno sbaglio
2 (*collect: goods, person*) passare a prendere; **we'll come to the airport to pick you up** veniamo a prenderti all'aeroporto; (*subj: bus etc*) far salire, caricare; (*rescue*) raccogliere; (: *from sea*) ripescare; (*arrest*) arrestare; **the car picked up speed** la macchina ha acquistato velocità *or* ha accelerato
3 (*acquire: sale bargain*) trovare; (: *information, points in exam, germ*) prendere; (*learn: habit, ideas*) prendere; (: *skill, language, tricks*) imparare; **they picked up a nasty infection** si sono presi una brutta infezione; **can you pick up some information while you're there?** puoi prendere delle informazioni mentre sei lì ?; **I picked up some Spanish during my holiday** ho imparato un po' di spagnolo in vacanza; **he picked up a girl at the disco** (*fam*) ha rimorchiato una ragazza in discoteca
4 (*Radio, TV, Telec*) captare
■ VI + ADV
1 (*improve: gen*) migliorare; (: *wages*) aumentare; (: *invalid, business*) riprendersi; (: *weather*) rimettersi; **things are picking up** le cose stanno migliorando
2 (*continue*) continuare, riprendere; **to pick up where one left off** riprendere dal punto in cui ci si era fermati

picka·back [ˈpɪkəˌbæk] N = **piggyback**

pickaxe, (*Am*) **pick·ax** [ˈpɪkˌæks] N piccone *m*

pick·er [ˈpɪkə^r] N (*of fruit etc*) raccoglitore(-trice)

pick·et [ˈpɪkɪt] N **1** (*stake*) picchetto **2** (*striker, band of strikers*) picchetto; (*Mil: sentry*) sentinella; (: *group*) picchetto
■ VT picchettare
■ VI picchettare

picket duty N: **to be on picket duty** (*Mil, Industry*) essere di picchetto

picket fence N steccato, palizzata

picket line N cordone *m* degli scioperanti

pick·ings [ˈpɪkɪŋz] NPL (*profits*): **there are good pickings to be had here** qui si possono fare dei guadagni facili

pick·le [ˈpɪkl] N (*brine*) salamoia; (*vinegar*) aceto; **pickles** NPL (*preserved vegetables*) sottaceti *mpl*; **mixed pickles** giardiniera *fsg*; **to be in a pickle** (*fig fam*) essere in un guaio *or* pasticcio
■ VT mettere sott'aceto; **pickled onions** cipolline *fpl* sott'aceto

pick-me-up [ˈpɪkmiːˌʌp] N (*fam: drink*) goccetto; (: *tonic*) tonico

pick·pocket [ˈpɪkˌpɒkɪt] N borsaiolo(-a), borseggiatore(-trice)

◎**pick-up** [ˈpɪkˌʌp] N **1** (*Brit: on record player: also:* **pick-up arm**) pick-up *m inv* **2** (*also:* **pick-up truck**) camioncino

picky [ˈpɪkɪ] ADJ (*comp* **-ier**, *superl* **-iest**) (*fam pej: person*) difficile; **to be a picky eater** essere schizzinoso(-a) nel mangiare

pic·nic [ˈpɪknɪk] (*vb: pt, pp* **picnicked**) N picnic *m inv*; **to have a picnic** fare un picnic; **to go on a picnic** andare a fare un picnic; **it was no picnic** (*fig fam*) non è stata una passeggiata
■ VI fare un picnic

Pp

picnic basket N cestino per il picnic
pic·nick·er ['pɪknɪkəʳ] N chi partecipa a un picnic
pic·to·gram ['pɪktəˌgræm] N pittogramma *m*
pic·to·rial [pɪk'tɔ:rɪəl] ADJ (*magazine*) illustrato(-a); (*representation*) pittoresco(-a); (*masterpiece*) di pittura; **a pictorial record of one's travels** una serie di immagini in ricordo dei propri viaggi
pic·to·ri·al·ly [pɪk'tɔ:rɪəlɪ] ADV (*record, express*) per immagini; (*describe*) pittorescamente
◎ **pic·ture** ['pɪktʃəʳ] N **1** (*Art: painting*) quadro, pittura, dipinto; (*: drawing*) disegno; (*: portrait*) ritratto; (*photo*) fotografia; (*in book*) illustrazione *f*; **to paint a picture of sth** dipingere qc; **there were pictures on the walls** c'erano dei quadri alle pareti; **a picture of Queen Elizabeth I** un ritratto della regina Elisabetta I; **to draw a picture of sth** disegnare qc; **to take a picture of sb/sth** fare una foto a qn/di qc; **children's books have lots of pictures** ci sono molte illustrazioni nei libri per bambini; **my picture was in the paper** c'era la mia foto sul giornale; **he looked the picture of health** sembrava il ritratto della salute; **you're the picture of your mother** sei (proprio) il ritratto di tua madre; **the garden is a picture in June** il giardino in giugno è uno spettacolo; **his face was a picture!** avresti dovuto vedere la sua faccia!; **to be in/out of the picture** essere/non essere coinvolto(-a) **2** (*TV*) immagine *f*; **we get a good picture here** la ricezione qui è buona **3** (*Cine*) film *m inv*; **the pictures** (*esp Brit*) il cinema; **to go to the pictures** andare al cinema; **shall we go to the pictures?** andiamo al cinema? **4** (*mental image*) immagine *f*, idea; **the other side of the picture** il rovescio della medaglia; **he painted a black picture of the future** ha dipinto il futuro a tinte fosche; **to get the picture** afferrare l'idea; **the overall picture** il quadro generale; **to put sb in the picture** mettere qn al corrente
■ VT (*imagine*) immaginare; (*remember*) ricordare; **I can just picture it!** me lo immagino!
picture book N libro illustrato
picture frame N cornice *f*
picture gallery N (*public*) pinacoteca; (*private*) galleria (d'arte)
picture library N archivio fotografico
picture messaging N picture messaging *m*, invio di messaggini con disegni
picture postcard N cartolina illustrata
pic·tur·esque [ˌpɪktʃə'rɛsk] ADJ pittoresco(-a)
picture window N finestra panoramica
pid·dle ['pɪdl] (*Brit*) VI (*fam*) fare pipì
■ N: **to have a piddle** fare pipì
pid·dling ['pɪdlɪŋ] ADJ (*fam*) insignificante
pidg·in Eng·lish ['pɪdʒɪn'ɪŋglɪʃ] N pidgin english *m inv*
pie [paɪ] N (*of fruit*) torta; (*of fish, meat*) pasticcio in crosta; **apple pie** torta di mele; **as easy as pie** (*fam*) (facile) come bere un bicchier d'acqua; **that's pie in the sky** sono castelli in aria
pie·bald ['paɪˌbɔ:ld] ADJ (*horse*) pezzato(-a)
◎ **piece** [pi:s] N **1** (*gen, also Chess*) pezzo; (*smaller*) pezzetto; (*of land*) appezzamento; (*fragment*) frammento; (*Draughts*) pedina; (*item*): **a piece of furniture/clothing/advice** un mobile/indumento/consiglio; **a piece of news/poetry** una notizia/poesia; **a piece of luck** un colpo di fortuna; **a 10p piece** (*Brit*) una moneta da 10 pence; **a six-piece band** un complesso di sei strumentisti; **a 21-piece tea set** ≈ un servizio da tè per 6 persone; **a piano piece** un pezzo *or* componimento per piano; **a small piece, please** un pezzo piccolo, per favore; **it is made all in one piece** è fatto in un pezzo solo; **in one piece** (*object*) intatto(-a); **to get back all in one piece** (*person*) tornare a casa incolume *or* sano(-a) e salvo(-a); **piece by piece** poco alla volta; **to be in pieces** (*taken apart*) essere smontato(-a); (*broken*) essere a pezzi; **to take sth to pieces** smontare qc; **to come** *or* **fall to pieces** sfasciarsi; **to smash sth to pieces** mandare in frantumi *or* in mille pezzi qc; **to go to pieces** (*fig*) crollare; **to say one's piece** dire la propria; **to give sb a piece of one's mind** dire a qn il fatto suo **2** (*fam*): **she was a flighty piece** era una donna volubile
▸ **piece together** VT + ADV (*also fig*) ricostruire
pièce de ré·sis·tance [pjɛsdərezistãs] N cavallo di battaglia
piece·meal ['pi:sˌmi:l] ADV poco alla volta
■ ADJ (*approach, process*) graduale
piece rate N (*Industry*) tariffa a cottimo
piece·work ['pi:sˌwɜ:k] N (*Industry*) (lavoro a) cottimo
piece·worker ['pi:sˌwɜ:kəʳ] N (*Industry*) cottimista *m/f*
pie chart N areogramma *m*, grafico a torta
pie·crust ['paɪˌkrʌst] N crosta di torta
pied-à-terre [ˌpjeɪtɑ:'tɛəʳ] N pied-à-terre *m inv*
pie dish N terrina, tegame da forno
Pied·mont ['pi:dmɒnt] N Piemonte *m*
pie-eyed [ˌpaɪ'aɪd] ADJ (*fam: drunk*) sbronzo(-a)
pier [pɪəʳ] N pontile *m*; (*landing stage*) imbarcadero, pontile; (*of bridge*) pila
pierce [pɪəs] VT (*gen*) bucare, forare; (*subj: cold, wind*) penetrare; (*: shriek, light*) squarciare; (*: arrow*) trafiggere; **a bullet pierced his chest** un proiettile gli ha perforato il petto; **to have one's ears pierced** farsi fare i buchi per gli orecchini
pierc·ing ['pɪəsɪŋ] ADJ (*gen*) penetrante; (*cry*) lacerante, acuto(-a); (*wind, sarcasm*) pungente
■ N (*of body part*) piercing *m inv*; **she has several piercings** ha diversi piercing
pi·etism ['paɪɪˌtɪzəm] N pietismo
pi·ety ['paɪətɪ] N pietà, devozione *f*
pif·fle ['pɪfl] N (*Brit old fam*) sciocchezze *fpl*
pif·fling ['pɪflɪŋ] (*fam*) ADJ insignificante
pig [pɪg] N **1** maiale *m*, porco; **to buy a pig in a poke** (*fig*) fare un acquisto alla cieca *or* a scatola chiusa **2** (*fam: person: nasty*) stronzo(-a); (*: greedy, dirty*) porco, maiale *m*; **to make a pig of o.s.** mangiare (e bere) come un porco; *see also* **piggy in the middle**
pi·geon ['pɪdʒən] N piccione *m*; **that's your pigeon** (*fig*) sono affari tuoi
pigeon fancier [-'fænsɪəʳ] N colombicoltore(-trice)
▹ www.ifpigeon.com/
pigeon·hole ['pɪdʒənˌhəʊl] N (*also fig*) casella
■ VT (*fig*) etichettare, catalogare
pigeon loft N piccionaia
pigeon-toed ['pɪdʒən'təʊd] ADJ: **to be pigeon-toed** camminare con i piedi in dentro
pig·gery ['pɪgərɪ] N allevamento di maiali
piggy·back ['pɪgɪˌbæk] N: **to give sb a piggyback** portare qn in groppa; portare qn a cavalluccio; **I can't give you a piggyback, you're too heavy** non posso portarti in groppa *or* a cavalluccio, sei troppo pesante
pig·gy bank ['pɪgɪˌbæŋk] N salvadanaio
pig·gy in the middle ['pɪgɪ-], **pig in the middle** N (*game*) ≈ palla prigioniera; **to be piggy in the middle** trovarsi fra due fuochi
pig-headed [pɪg'hɛdɪd] ADJ testardo(-a), cocciuto(-a)
pig-headedly [ˌpɪg'hɛdɪdlɪ] ADV caparbiamente, con testardaggine

pig-headedness [ˌpɪgˈhɛdɪdnɪs] N caparbietà, testardaggine *f*

pig in the mid·dle N = **piggy in the middle**

pig iron N ghisa

pig·let [ˈpɪglɪt] N maialino, porcellino

pig·meat [ˈpɪgˌmiːt] N = **pork**

pig·ment [ˈpɪgmənt] N pigmento

pig·men·ta·tion [ˌpɪgmənˈteɪʃən] N pigmentazione *f*

pig·my [ˈpɪgmɪ] N = **pygmy**

pig·skin [ˈpɪgˌskɪn] N cinghiale *m*

pig·sty [ˈpɪgˌstaɪ] N (*also fig*) porcile *m*

pig·tail [ˈpɪgˌteɪl] N (*plaited*) treccina; (*loose*) codino

pike[1] [paɪk] N (*fish*) luccio; **he caught a pike** ha preso un luccio

pike[2] [paɪk] N (*spear*) picca

pil·af(f) [ˈpɪlæf], **pilau** [pɪˈlaʊ] N pilaf *m inv*

Pilate [ˈpaɪlət] N: **Pontius Pilate** Ponzio Pilato

pilchard [ˈpɪltʃəd] N sardina

◎ **pile**[1] [paɪl] N **1** (*heap: of books, records*) pila; (*less tidy*) mucchio, cumulo; **he put his things in a pile** ha ammucchiato le sue cose; **there were piles of dirty dishes in the kitchen** c'erano pile di piatti sporchi in cucina **2** (*fam: large amount*) mucchio, sacco; **piles of** un mucchio di; **I've got piles of work to do** ho un mucchio di lavoro da fare; **a pile of** una montagna di **3** (*fam: fortune*) fortuna; **my brother made a pile selling videos** mio fratello ha fatto una barca di soldi vendendo video

■ VT (*stack*) impilare; (*heap*) ammucchiare; **a table piled high with books** un tavolo coperto da pile di libri

■ VI (*fam*): **pile in!** salta su!; **to pile into a car** stiparsi *or* ammucchiarsi in una macchina; **to pile on/off a bus** far ressa per salire sull'autobus/scendere dall'autobus

► **pile on** VT + ADV: **to pile on the pressure** (*fam*) fare pressione; **to pile it on** (*fam*) esagerare, drammatizzare; **to pile work on sb** caricare qn di lavoro

► **pile up** VI + ADV (*also fig*) accumularsi, ammucchiarsi

■ VT + ADV ammucchiare, accumulare

pile[2] [paɪl] N (*of carpet, cloth*) pelo

pile[3] [paɪl] N (*Constr*) palo

piles [paɪlz] NPL (*Med*) emorroidi *fpl*

pile-up [ˈpaɪlˌʌp] N (*Aut fam*) tamponamento a catena

pil·fer [ˈpɪlfəʳ] VT rubacchiare

■ VI fare dei furtarelli

pil·fer·er [ˈpɪlfərəʳ] N ladruncolo(-a)

pil·fer·ing [ˈpɪlfərɪŋ] N furtarelli *mpl*

pil·grim [ˈpɪlgrɪm] N pellegrino(-a)

pil·grim·age [ˈpɪlgrɪmɪdʒ] N pellegrinaggio; **to go on a pilgrimage** andare in pellegrinaggio

Pilgrim Fathers N: **the Pilgrim Fathers** i Padri Pellegrini

▷ www.usahistory.info/New-England/Pilgrims.html

▷ www.mayflowersteps.co.uk

◎ **pill** [pɪl] N pillola; **to be on the pill** (*contraceptive*) prendere la pillola; **to sweeten** *or* **sugar the pill** (*fig*) indorare la pillola

pil·lage [ˈpɪlɪdʒ] VT saccheggiare

■ VI darsi al saccheggio

pil·lar [ˈpɪləʳ] N (*round*) colonna; (*square*) pilastro; **a pillar of smoke** una colonna di fumo; **a pillar of the church** (*fig*) uno dei pilastri della chiesa; **to be driven from pillar to post** essere sballottato(-a) a destra e a manca

pillar box N (*Brit*) buca delle lettere (a colonnina)

pillar-box red [ˌpɪləbɒksˈrɛd] N rosso fiammante

Pillars of Hercules N: **the Pillars of Hercules** (*Geog*) le Colonne d'Ercole

pill·box [ˈpɪlbɒks] N (*Mil*) casamatta; (*for pills*) scatolina per pastiglie; (*also:* **pillbox hat**) toque *f inv*

pil·lion [ˈpɪljən] N sellino posteriore (*di moto*); **on the pillion** sul sellino posteriore

■ ADV: **to ride pillion** viaggiare dietro

pillion passenger N passeggero(-a) (*che viaggia sul sellino posteriore*)

pil·lo·ry [ˈpɪlərɪ] N berlina

■ VT (*fig*) mettere alla berlina

pil·low [ˈpɪləʊ] N cuscino, guanciale *m*

pillow·case [ˈpɪləʊˌkeɪs], **pillow·slip** [ˈpɪləʊˌslɪp] N federa

pillow talk N chiacchiere *fpl* fra le lenzuola

◎ **pi·lot** [ˈpaɪlət] N (*Aer, Naut*) pilota *m/f*; **he's a pilot** fa il pilota

■ VT (*Aer, Naut*) pilotare; (*fig: guide*) guidare, dirigere

■ ADJ (*scheme*) pilota *inv*

pilot boat N pilotina

pilot certificate N brevetto di pilota

pilot light N (*on cooker etc*) fiammella di sicurezza

pilot study N studio *m* pilota *inv*

pi·men·to [pɪˈmɛntəʊ] N peperoncino

pimp [pɪmp] N ruffiano, protettore

pim·per·nel [ˈpɪmpəˌnɛl] N: **scarlet pimpernel** primula rossa

pim·ple [ˈpɪmpl] N foruncolo

pim·ply [ˈpɪmplɪ] ADJ (*comp* **-ier**, *superl* **-iest**) foruncoloso(-a)

PIN [pɪn] N ABBR (= **personal identification number**) PIN *m inv*

◎ **pin** [pɪn] N (*gen, as ornament*) spillo; (*safety pin*) spillo di sicurezza; (*Tech*) perno; (*in grenade*) spoletta; (*Med*) chiodo; (*Elec: of plug*) spinotto; (*Bowling*) birillo; **fastened with a pin** fissato(-a) con uno spillo; **as neat as a (new) pin** (*room*) lucido(-a) come uno specchio; (*person*) impeccabile; **you could have heard a pin drop** non si sentiva volare una mosca; **for two pins I'd have hit him!** (*fam*) per poco non l'avrei picchiato!

■ VT **1** (*with drawing pin*) attaccare con una puntina; (*sewing*) attaccare con gli spilli; **they pinned a notice on the board** hanno appuntato un avviso in bacheca **2** (*fig*): **to pin sb against a wall** mettere qn con le spalle al muro; **to pin sb's arms to his sides** immobilizzare le braccia di qn contro i fianchi

► **pin down** VT + ADV **1** (*fasten or hold down*) immobilizzare **2** (*fig*): **to pin sb down to a date** far fissare una data a qn; **to pin sb down to their promise** costringere qn a mantenere una promessa; **to pin sb down about his beliefs** far dire a qn quello che pensa; **there's something strange here but I can't quite pin it down** c'è qualcosa di strano qua ma non riesco a capire cos'è

► **pin on** VT + PREP attaccare con uno spillo (*or* una puntina) a; **to pin one's hopes on sth** riporre le proprie speranze in qc; **to pin a crime on sb** (*fam*) addossare a qn la colpa di un delitto

■ VT + ADV attaccare con uno spillo (*or* una puntina)

► **pin up** VT + ADV (*notice*) attaccare (al muro) con una puntina; (*hair*) appuntare con le forcine; (*hem*) appuntare con gli spilli

pina·fore [ˈpɪnəˌfɔːʳ] N (*apron*) grembiule *m*

pinafore dress N scamiciato

pin·ball [ˈpɪnˌbɔːl] N (*also:* **pinball machine**) flipper *m inv*; **they're playing pinball** giocano a flipper

Pp

pince-nez ['pæns,neɪ] N pince-nez *m inv*
pin·cers ['pɪnsəz] NPL (*of crab etc*) pinze *fpl*, chele *fpl*; (*tool*) tenaglie *fpl*
pinch [pɪntʃ] N **1** (*with fingers*) pizzicotto, pizzico; **to feel the pinch** (*fig*) trovarsi nelle ristrettezze; **at a pinch** (*fig*) se è proprio necessario; **if it comes to the pinch** se le cose si mettono male **2** (*small quantity*) pizzico, presa; **to take sth with a pinch of salt** (*fig*) prendere qc con un grano di sale
■VT **1** (*with fingers*) pizzicare; **he pinched me!** mi ha pizzicato!; **my shoes are pinching me** le scarpe mi vanno strette **2** (*fam: steal*) fregare, grattare; (*: idea*) rubare; **who's pinched my pen?** chi mi ha fregato la penna? **3** (*fam: arrest*) pizzicare
■VI (*shoe*) essere (troppo) stretto(-a), stringere; **to pinch and scrape** fare economia (su tutto)
pinched ['pɪntʃt] ADJ (*face*) dai lineamenti tirati; **pinched with cold** raggrinzito(-a) dal freddo; **pinched with hunger** scavato(-a) dalla fame
pinch-hit ['pɪntʃ,hɪt] VI (*Baseball*) battere la palla al posto di un altro giocatore; (*fam fig*): **to pinch hit for sb** sostituire qn
pinch-hitter ['pɪntʃ,hɪtə^r] N (*Baseball*) giocatore(-trice) che sostituisce un altro(-a) alla battuta
pin·cushion ['pɪn,kʊʃn] N (cuscinetto) puntaspilli *m inv*
pine[1] [paɪn] N (*also:* **pine tree**) pino
pine[2] [paɪn] VI: **to pine for sb/sth** sentire tanto la mancanza di qn/qc
▸ **pine away** VI + ADV languire, deperire
pine·apple ['paɪn,æpl] N ananas *m inv*
pine cone N pigna
pine needle N ago di pino
pine nut, pine kernel N pinolo
pine·wood ['paɪn,wʊd] N (*grove of trees*) pineta; (*material*) (legno di) pino
ping [pɪŋ] N suono metallico; (*of bell*) tintinnio
■VI (*see n*) produrre un suono metallico; tintinnare
ping-pong® ['pɪŋ,pɒŋ] N ping-pong® *m*
pin·ion ['pɪnjən] N (*Tech*) pignone *m*
◎**pink**[1] [pɪŋk] N **1** (*colour*) rosa *m inv* **2** (*Bot*) garofano a piumino rosa **3** **to be in the pink (of health)** essere in perfetta salute
■ADJ **1** (*colour*) rosa *inv*; **to turn** *or* **go pink** (*flush*) arrossire **2** (*Pol fam*) con tendenze di sinistra
pink[2] [pɪŋk] VT (*Sewing*) dentellare
pinkie ['pɪŋkɪ] N (*Scot fam, Am fam*) mignolo
pink·ing shears ['pɪŋkɪŋ ʃɪəz], **pinking scissors** NPL forbici *fpl* a zigzag
pin money N (*Brit*) denaro per spese superflue; **most women work from economic necessity, not for pin money** la maggior parte delle donne lavora per ragioni economiche, non per procurarsi il superfluo
pin·na·cle ['pɪnəkl] N (*Archit*) pinnacolo; (*of rock*) guglia; (*top of mountain*) vetta, cima; (*fig*) apice *m*, vertice *m*
pin·ny ['pɪnɪ] N (*fam*) grembiule *m*
pin·point ['pɪn,pɔɪnt] VT (*on map*) localizzare con esattezza; (*problem*) mettere a fuoco, individuare con esattezza
pin·prick ['pɪn,prɪk] N puntura di spillo
pins and needles NPL formicolio *msg*; **I've got pins and needles** ho un formicolio
pin·stripe ['pɪn,straɪp] ADJ: **pinstripe suit** (abito) gessato
pint [paɪnt] N (*measure*) pinta (*Brit=0,568 litri; Am=0,4732 litri*); (*Brit fam: of beer*) ≈ boccale *m* di birra; **half a pint of beer** una birra piccola; **to have a pint** bere una birra; **to go out for a pint** uscire a bere una birra
pin·ta ['paɪntə] N (*Brit fam*) pinta di latte
pint-size ['paɪnt,saɪz], **pint-sized** ['paɪnt,saɪzd] ADJ minuscolo(-a); **he's a pint-sized version of his father** è suo padre in versione ridotta
pin-up ['pɪn,ʌp] N pin-up (girl) *f inv*
pio·neer [,paɪə'nɪə^r] N pioniere(-a)
■VT (*technique, invention*) essere l'ideatore(-trice) di; **he pioneered DNA tests** è stato uno dei primi a fare i test sul DNA
pio·neer·ing [,paɪə'nɪərɪŋ] ADJ (*work, spirit*) pionieristico(-a)
pi·ous ['paɪəs] ADJ pio(-a); (*pej*) bigotto(-a); **a pious hope** una vana speranza
pi·ous·ly ['paɪəslɪ] ADV piamente, con devozione; (*pej*) in modo bigotto
pip[1] [pɪp] N: **to give sb the pip** (*Brit fam*) far venire i nervi a qn
pip[2] [pɪp] N (*seed*) seme *m*; (*on card*) seme *m*; (*on dice*) punto; (*Brit Mil fam: on uniform*) stelletta; (*on radar screen*) segnale *m*; **an orange pip** un seme d'arancia; **the pips** NPL (*Telec*) il segnale acustico; (*Radio*) il segnale orario
pip[3] [pɪp] VT (*Brit fam*): **to be pipped at the post** essere battuto(-a) sul traguardo
◎**pipe** [paɪp] N **1** (*tube*) tubo; **pipes** NPL (*piping*) tubatura *fsg*, conduttura *fsg*; **a plastic pipe** un tubo di plastica **2** (*Mus: of organ*) canna; (*: wind instrument*) piffero; **pipes** NPL (*also:* **bagpipes**) cornamusa *fsg*; **he plays the pipes** suona la cornamusa **3** (*smoker's*) pipa; **to smoke a pipe** fumare la pipa; **put that in your pipe and smoke it!** (*fam*) che ti piaccia o no, è così !
■VT **1** (*water, oil etc*) portare per mezzo di tubature **2** (*Mus*) suonare (col piffero *or* con la cornamusa); (*speak or sing in high voice*) dire (*or* cantare) con un tono di voce acuto; **to pipe sb aboard** (*Naut*) accogliere qn a bordo al suono di una banda **3** (*Culin*): **to pipe icing on a cake** decorare un dolce con la glassa
▸ **pipe down** VI + ADV (*fam*) fare silenzio
▸ **pipe up** VI + ADV (*fam*) farsi sentire
pipe cleaner N scovolino
piped mu·sic ['paɪpt,mju:zɪk] N musica di sottofondo
pipe dream N sogno impossibile
pipe·line ['paɪp,laɪn] N (*gen*) conduttura; (*also:* **oil pipeline**) oleodotto; (*also:* **gas pipeline**) metanodotto; **to be in the pipeline** (*fig*) essere in arrivo; **these changes are in the pipeline** questi cambiamenti sono in arrivo
pip·er ['paɪpə^r] N (*on bagpipes*) suonatore(-trice) di cornamusa
pipe tobacco N tabacco da pipa
pi·pette [pɪ'pɛt] N pipetta
pip·ing ['paɪpɪŋ] N (*tubing*) tubature *fpl*; (*Sewing*) cordoncino
piping bag N (*Culin*) tasca da pasticciere
piping hot ADJ (*food, water*) bollente
pip·it ['pɪpɪt] N: **meadow pipit** prispola; **tree pipit** prispolone *m*
pip·pin ['pɪpɪn] N renetta
pi·quan·cy ['pi:kənsɪ] N (*of food*) gusto piccante; (*of situation*) aspetto intrigante
pi·quant ['pi:kənt] ADJ (*sauce*) piccante; (*situation*) intrigante; **a piquant charm** un fascino strano
pique [pi:k] N dispetto, picca
■VT indispettire
pi·ra·cy ['paɪrəsɪ] N pirateria
pi·ra·nha [pɪ'rɑ:njə] N piranha *m inv*

pi·rate ['paɪrɪt] N (*also fig*) pirata *m*
■VT (*product*) contraffare; (*idea*) impossessarsi di; (*record, video, book*) riprodurre abusivamente
pi·rat·ed ['paɪrɪtɪd] ADJ (*book, record etc*) riprodotto(-a) abusivamente; **a pirated video** una videocassetta pirata
pirate radio N radio *f inv* pirata
pirou·ette [,pɪrʊ'ɛt] N piroetta
■VI piroettare
Pi·sces ['paɪsi:z] N Pesci *mpl*; **to be Pisces** essere dei Pesci
piss [pɪs] VI (*fam!*) pisciare (*fam!*)
▶ **piss about, piss around** VI + ADV (*fam!*) far cazzate (*fam!*)
▶ **piss down** VI + ADV (*fam: rain*) piovere a catinelle
▶ **piss off** (*fam!*) VI + ADV: **piss off!** levati dalle palle! (*fam!*); vaffanculo! (*fam!*)
■VT + ADV: **I'm pissed off with it** ne ho le palle piene (*fam!*)
pissed [pɪst] ADJ (*Brit fam!: drunk*) sbronzo(-a); (*Am fam!*) incazzato(-a); **to be pissed at sb** essere incazzato(-a) con qn
piss-poor [,pɪs'pʊəʳ] ADJ (*Brit: fam!*) terribile
pissy ['pɪsɪ] ADJ (*Am fam!*) incazzato(-a); (: *in a bad mood*) nero(-a)
pis·ta·chio [pɪs'tɑ:ʃɪəʊ] N pistacchio
piste [pi:st] N (*Skiing*) pista
pis·tol ['pɪstl] N pistola
pistol point N: **at pistol point** sotto la minaccia della pistola
pistol shot N colpo di pistola
pis·ton ['pɪstən] N (*gen*) stantuffo; (*Aut*) pistone *m*
piston engine N (*Aut*) motore *m* a pistoni
piston ring N (*Aut*) fascia elastica
piston rod N (*Aut*) biella
◎**pit¹** [pɪt] N **1** (*hole in ground*) buca, fossa; (*on moon*) cratere *m*; (*coalmine*) miniera di carbone; (*quarry*) cava; (*to trap animals*) buca; **in the pit of one's stomach** alla bocca dello stomaco; **he used to work down the pit** lavorava in miniera; **the last pit was closed twenty years ago** l'ultima miniera di carbone è stata chiusa vent'anni fa; **they dug a large pit** hanno scavato una grande buca **2** (*Aut: in garage*) fossa; (: *Motor Racing: also:* **the pits**) i box **3** (*Brit Theatre*) platea; **orchestra pit** golfo mistico
■VT **1** (*subj: chickenpox*) butterare; (: *rust*) corrodere in più punti **2** **to pit A against B** contrapporre A a B; **to pit one's wits against sb** misurarsi contro qn
pit² [pɪt] N (*in fruit*) nocciolo, seme *m*
pita·pat ['pɪtə'pæt] ADV: **to go pitapat** (*heart*) palpitare; (*rain*) picchiettare
pitch¹ [pɪtʃ] N (*tar*) pece *f*
◎**pitch²** [pɪtʃ] N **1** (*esp Brit Sport*) campo; **football pitch** campo di calcio **2** (*angle, slope: of roof*) inclinazione *f* **3** (*Naut, Aer*) beccheggio **4** (*of note, voice, instrument*) intonazione *f*, altezza; (*fig: degree*) grado, punto; **I can't keep working at this pitch** non posso continuare a lavorare a questo ritmo; **at its (highest) pitch** al massimo, al colmo; **his anger reached such a pitch that ...** la sua furia raggiunse un punto tale che... **5** (*fam: also:* **sales pitch**) discorsetto imbonitore **6** (*Mountaineering*) tiro di corda **7** (*throw*) lancio
■VT **1** (*throw: ball, object*) lanciare; (: *hay*) sollevare col forcone; **he pitched the bottle into the lake** ha lanciato la bottiglia nel lago; **he was pitched off his horse** fu sbalzato da cavallo *or* disarcionato **2** (*Mus: song*) intonare; (: *note*) dare; **she can't pitch a note properly** non riesce a prendere una nota giusta; **to pitch one's aspirations too high** mirare troppo in alto; **to pitch it too strong** (*fam*) esagerare, calcare troppo la mano **3** (*set up: tent*) piantare; **we pitched our tent near the beach** abbiamo piantato la tenda vicino alla spiaggia
■VI **1** (*fall*) cascare, cadere; **to pitch forward** essere catapultato(-a) in avanti **2** (*Naut, Aer*) beccheggiare
▶ **pitch in** VI + ADV (*fam*) darci dentro *or* sotto
▶ **pitch into** VI + PREP (*attack*) saltare addosso a; (*start: work, food*) attaccare, buttarsi su
pitch-black [,pɪtʃ'blæk] (*also:* **pitch-dark**) ADJ nero(-a) come la pece; **the room was pitch-black** nella stanza c'era un buio pesto
pitched battle [,pɪtʃt'bætl] N (*Mil, also fig*) battaglia campale
pitch·er¹ ['pɪtʃəʳ] N (*jar*) brocca
pitch·er² ['pɪtʃəʳ] N (*Baseball*) lanciatore *m*
pitch·fork ['pɪtʃ,fɔ:k] N forcone *m*
■VT: **to pitchfork sb into a job** (*fig*) costringere qn ad accettare un lavoro di punto in bianco
pitch inspection N (*Brit Sport*) ispezione *f* del campo
pitch pine N pitch pine *m*
pit·eous ['pɪtɪəs] ADJ pietoso(-a)
pit·eous·ly ['pɪtɪəslɪ] ADV pietosamente
pit·fall ['pɪt,fɔ:l] N (*fig*) tranello, trappola
pith [pɪθ] N (*of plant*) midollo; (*of oranges, lemons*) parte *f* bianca della scorza; (*fig: core: of argument*) nocciolo, essenza, succo; (: *force*) vigore *m*
pit·head ['pɪt,hɛd] N imbocco della miniera
pithy ['pɪθɪ] ADJ (*comp* **-ier**, *superl* **-iest**) (*fig: argument*) vigoroso(-a); (: *remarks*) arguto(-a); (: *account*) conciso(-a)
piti·able ['pɪtɪəbl] ADJ pietoso(-a)
piti·ful ['pɪtɪfʊl] ADJ **1** (*sight, story*) pietoso(-a); (*person*) che fa pietà *or* compassione **2** (*pej: attempt*) pietoso(-a); (: *cowardice*) deplorevole; (: *sum*) miserabile
piti·ful·ly ['pɪtɪfəlɪ] ADV (*gen*) pietosamente; (*thin etc*) da far pietà; **it's pitifully obvious** è penosamente chiaro
piti·less ['pɪtɪlɪs] ADJ spietato(-a)
piti·less·ly ['pɪtɪlɪslɪ] ADV spietatamente, senza pietà
pi·ton ['pi:tɒn] N chiodo
pit pony N *pony impiegato in una miniera*
pit·tance ['pɪtəns] N miseria, somma miserabile; **they work for a pittance** lavorano per una miseria
pit·ted ['pɪtɪd] ADJ: **pitted with** (*potholes*) pieno(-a) di; (*chickenpox*) butterato(-a) da
pitter-patter ['pɪtə'pætəʳ] = **patter²**
pi·tui·tary [pɪ'tju:ɪtərɪ] N (*also:* **pituitary gland**) ghiandola pituitaria
pit worker N minatore *m*
pity ['pɪtɪ] N **1** compassione *f*, pietà; **to feel pity for sb** provare compassione per qn; **for pity's sake!** per amor del cielo!; (*pleading*) per pietà!; **to have** *or* **take pity on sb** aver pietà di qn **2** (*cause of regret*) peccato; **what a pity!** che peccato!; **more's the pity** purtroppo; **it is a pity that you can't come** è un peccato che tu non possa venire
■VT compatire, commiserare; **I don't hate him, I pity him** non lo odio, lo compatisco
pity·ing ['pɪtɪɪŋ] ADJ compassionevole; (*with contempt*) di commiserazione
pity·ing·ly ['pɪtɪɪŋlɪ] ADV (*see adj*) pietosamente; con aria (*or* tono) di commiserazione
piv·ot ['pɪvət] N (*Mil, Tech, fig*) perno
■VT imperniare
■VI girare su se stesso(-a)
piv·ot·al ['pɪvətl] ADJ essenziale, centrale

Pp

pix·el ['pɪksəl] N (*Comput*) pixel *m inv*
pixie ['pɪksɪ] N folletto
piz·za ['pitsə] N pizza
piz·zazz [pə'zæz] N: **to have pizzazz** (*fam*) essere pieno(-a) di verve
piz·zi·ca·to [ˌpɪtsɪ'kɑːtəʊ] ADV (*Mus*) pizzicato
plac·ard ['plækɑːd] N cartello
pla·cate [plə'keɪt] VT placare, calmare
placa·tory [plə'keɪtərɪ] ADJ (*gesture, tone, words etc*) tranquillizzante, conciliante
◎**place** [pleɪs] N
1 (*in general*) posto; (*more formally*) luogo; **it's a quiet place** è un posto tranquillo; **there are a lot of interesting places to visit** ci sono tanti posti interessanti da vedere; **to take place** (*incident*) succedere, accadere; (*meeting*) avere luogo; **elections will take place on November 25th** le elezioni avranno luogo il 25 novembre; **we came to a place where ...** siamo arrivati in un posto dove...; **from place to place** da un posto all'altro; **this is no place for you** questo non è un posto per te; **place of business** posto di lavoro; **place of worship/birth** luogo di culto/nascita; **all over the place** dappertutto; **to go places** (*travel*) andare in giro (per il mondo); **he's going places** (*fig fam*) si sta facendo strada; **we're going places at last** (*fig fam*) finalmente abbiamo sfondato; **it's only a small place** (*town*) è solo un paesino; (*house*) è piccolina; **his place in the country** la sua villa in campagna; **at your place** a casa tua; **shall we meet at your place?** ci incontriamo a casa tua?; **come to our place** venite da noi *or* a casa nostra; **to put sth back in its place** rimettere qc al suo posto; **that remark was quite out of place** quell'osservazione era proprio fuori luogo; **I feel rather out of place here** qui mi sento un po' fuori posto; **this isn't the place to discuss politics!** questo non è il posto giusto per discutere di politica!; **to change places with sb** scambiarsi di posto con qn; **to take the place of sb/sth** sostituire qn/qc, prendere il posto di qn/qc; **in place of** al posto di, invece di
2 (*in street names*) via; **market place** piazza del mercato
3 (*in book*): **to find one's place** trovare la pagina giusta; **to lose one's place** perdere il segno
4 (*seat*) posto (a sedere); (: *at table*) posto (a tavola); (: *in restaurant*) coperto; **to lay an extra place for sb** aggiungere un posto a tavola per qn
5 (*job, vacancy in team, school*) posto; **he found a place for his nephew in the firm** ha trovato un posto a suo nipote nella ditta; **a university place** un posto all'università
6 (*social position*) posizione *f*, rango; **friends in high places** amici altolocati *or* nelle alte sfere; **to know one's place** (*fig*) sapere stare al proprio posto; **it is not my place to do it** non sta a me farlo; **to put sb in his place** (*fig*) mettere a posto qn, mettere qn al suo posto
7 (*in series, rank etc*): **in the first/second place** in primo/secondo luogo; **she took second place in the race** si è piazzata *or* è arrivata seconda nella gara; **she took second place in the exam** ha preso il secondo miglior voto all'esame; **A won, with B in second place** A ha vinto e B è finito secondo
■VT
1 (*put: gen*) posare, mettere; (*on wall*) mettere; **place it on the table** mettilo *or* posalo sul tavolo; **he placed his hand on hers** ha posato la mano sulla sua; **we should place no trust in that** non dovremmo farci nessun affidamento
2 (*situate: town*) situare; (: *person*) piazzare; **we are better placed than a month ago** siamo in una situazione migliore *or* siamo messi meglio di un mese fa; **awkwardly placed** (*shop*) piazzato(-a) male; (*fig: person*) messo(-a) male; (: *in embarrassing situation*) in una posizione delicata
3 (*contract, bet*) fare; (*goods*) piazzare; **to place an order with sb (for)** fare un'ordinazione a qn (di); **to place a book with a publisher** trovare un editore per un libro; **to place sth in sb's hands** mettere qc nelle mani di qn; **we could place 200 men** possiamo procurare lavoro a 200 uomini
4 (*in exam, race etc*) classificare; **to be placed second** classificarsi *or* piazzarsi al secondo posto
5 (*recall, identify: person*) ricordarsi di; (: *face, accent*) riconoscere; **I can't place him** non riesco a ricordarmi dove l'ho visto
pla·cebo [plə'siːbəʊ] N placebo *m inv*
place card N (*on table*) segnaposto
place mat N (*cork*) sottopiatto; (*linen*) tovaglietta
place·ment ['pleɪsmənt] N (*in group, accommodation*) collocamento; (*of trainee*) stage *m inv*; **to do a work placement** fare uno stage
place name N toponimo
pla·cen·ta [plə'sɛntə] N placenta
place setting N coperto
plac·id ['plæsɪd] ADJ placido(-a), calmo(-a)
pla·cid·ity [plə'sɪdɪtɪ] N placidità
pla·cid·ly ['plæsɪdlɪ] ADV placidamente
pla·gia·rism ['pleɪdʒjəˌrɪzəm] N plagio
pla·gia·rist ['pleɪdʒjərɪst] N plagiario(-a)
pla·gia·rize ['pleɪdʒjəˌraɪz] VT plagiare
plague [pleɪg] N (*disease, also fig*) peste *f*; (*of rats, locusts*) invasione *f*; **to avoid sb/sth like the plague** evitare qn/qc come la peste
■VT (*fig*) tormentare; **she's plagued with money worries** è tormentata da problemi economici; **to plague sb with questions** assillare qn di domande
plaice [pleɪs] N platessa, passera di mare
plaid [plæd] N (*material*) tessuto scozzese *or* a scacchi; (*cloak*) mantellina scozzese; **a plaid shirt** una camicia a scacchi; **a plaid sports jacket** una giacca sportiva a scacchi
◎**plain** [pleɪn] ADJ (*comp* **-er**, *superl* **-est**) **1** (*clear, obvious*) chiaro(-a), palese, evidente; (*path, track*) ben segnato(-a); **it's as plain as a pikestaff** *or* **as the nose on your face** (*fam*) è chiaro come il sole; **you have made your feelings plain** ti sei spiegato benissimo; **to make sth plain to sb** far capire chiaramente qc a qn; **do I make myself plain?** mi sono spiegato?; **he's lying, that's plain** è chiaro che mente **2** (*outspoken, honest, frank*) franco(-a), aperto(-a), schietto(-a); **plain dealing** sincerità, franchezza; **in plain language** *or* **English** in parole povere; **I shall be plain with you** sarò franco con te **3** (*simple, with nothing added*) semplice; (*paper: unlined*) non rigato(-a); (*fabric: in one colour*) in tinta unita *inv*; (*without seasoning*) scondito(-a); **the plain truth** la pura verità; **he's a plain man** è un uomo semplice; **plain stitch** (*Knitting*) maglia a diritto; **a plain tie** una cravatta in tinta unita; **a plain white blouse** una camicetta bianca, semplice; **it's just plain commonsense** (*fam*) è una questione di semplice buon senso; **to send sth under plain cover** spedire qc in busta riservata **4** (*not pretty*) insignificante, scialbo(-a)
■ADV **1** (*fam: simply, completely*) semplicemente

2 *(clearly)*: **I can't put it plainer than that** non potrei esprimermi più chiaramente
■ N **1** *(Geog)* pianura **2** *(Knitting)* (maglia a) diritto
plain chocolate N cioccolato fondente
plain clothes NPL: **in plain clothes** in borghese
plain flour N farina
plain·ly ['pleɪnlɪ] ADV *(clearly)* chiaramente; *(speak)* con franchezza, francamente; *(dress)* con semplicità, sobriamente; **he was plainly embarrassed** era chiaramente imbarazzato
plain·ness ['pleɪnnɪs] N *(simplicity)* semplicità; *(lack of beauty)* insignificanza
plain sailing N *(fam)*: **it'll be plain sailing from now on** d'ora in poi andrà tutto liscio
plain·song ['pleɪn,sɒŋ] N canto piano
plain speak·ing N [,pleɪn'spi:kɪŋ] **there has been some plain speaking between the two leaders** i due leader si sono parlati chiaro
plain-spoken [,pleɪn'spəʊkən] ADJ *(person)* franco(-a), schietto(-a); *(criticism)* senza mezze parole
plain text N *(Comput)* testo non formattato
plain·tiff ['pleɪntɪf] N *(Law)* attore(-trice)
plain·tive ['pleɪntɪv] ADJ *(voice, song)* lamentoso(-a); *(look)* struggente; **plaintive cry** lamento
plain·tive·ly ['pleɪntɪvlɪ] ADV *(speak)* lamentosamente; *(look)* malinconicamente
plait [plæt] N treccia
■ VT *(raffia)* intrecciare; **to plait one's hair** farsi una treccia (*or* le trecce)
◎ **plan** [plæn] N **1** *(scheme)* piano, progetto; *(Pol, Econ)* piano; **plan of campaign** *(Mil, also fig)* piano di battaglia; **development plan** piano *or* progetto di sviluppo; **to draw up a plan** fare *or* elaborare un programma; **if everything goes according to plan** se tutto va secondo le previsioni *or* il previsto; **everything went according to plan** è andato tutto come previsto; **to make plans** far programmi *or* progetti; **the best plan would be to ...** la cosa migliore sarebbe...; **have you got any plans for today?** che programmi hai per oggi?; **what are your plans for the holidays?** che programmi hai per le vacanze? **2** *(diagram, map: of building, town)* pianta; *(: for essay, speech)* schema *m*; **a plan of the campsite** una piantina del campeggio
■ VT **1** *(arrange: robbery, holiday, campaign)* organizzare; *(economy, research)* pianificare; *(essay)* fare lo schema di; **we're planning a trip to France** stiamo progettando un viaggio in Francia; **plan your revision carefully** organizza bene il ripasso; **to plan one's family** pianificare le nascite **2** *(intend)* avere in progetto; **to plan to do** avere l'intenzione di fare; **I'm planning to get a job in the holidays** ho intenzione di trovare un lavoro per le vacanze; **how long do you plan to stay?** quanto conti di restare? **3** *(design)* progettare; **a well-planned town** una città che ha un buon piano urbanistico
■ VI: **to plan (for)** far piani *or* progetti (per); **one has to plan months ahead** bisogna cominciare a pensarci diversi mesi prima; **to plan on sth/on doing sth** contare su qc/di fare qc
▸ **plan out** VT + ADV organizzare nei particolari
pla·nar ['pleɪnə^r] ADJ planare
◎ **plane¹** [pleɪn] N aereo; **by plane** in aereo
plane² [pleɪn] ADJ *(Geom)* piano(-a)
■ N **1** *(Art, Math)* piano **2** *(fig)* piano, livello
plane³ [pleɪn] N *(tool)* pialla
■ VT *(also: **plane down**)* piallare; **to plane sth smooth** levigare qc con la pialla
plane⁴ [pleɪn] N *(tree)* platano; **London plane** platano di Londra
plane⁵ [pleɪn] VI *(bird, glider, boat)* planare
◎ **plan·et** ['plænɪt] N pianeta *m*
plan·etar·ium [,plænɪ'tɛərɪəm] N planetario
plan·etary ['plænɪtərɪ] ADJ planetario(-a)
plani·sphere ['plænɪ,sfɪə^r] N planisfero
plank [plæŋk] N *(of wood)* tavola, asse *f*
plank·ton ['plæŋktən] N plancton *m inv*
planned economy [,plændɪ'kɒnəmɪ] N economia pianificata
plan·ner ['plænə^r] N *(Econ)* pianificatore(-trice); *(Industry)* progettista *m/f*; *(also: **forward planner**)* calendario; **town planner** urbanista
◎ **plan·ning** ['plænɪŋ] N *(Pol, Econ)* pianificazione *f*; *(Industry)* progettazione *f*; **the trip needs careful planning** bisogna organizzare bene il viaggio; **family planning** pianificazione *f* familiare
planning committee N *(in local government)* commissione *f* urbanistica
planning permission N *(Brit)* licenza edilizia; permesso di costruzione
◎ **plant** [plɑ:nt] N **1** *(Bot)* pianta; **I water my plants every week** annaffio le piante ogni settimana **2** *(no pl: machinery etc)* impianto; *(factory)* stabilimento; **a chemical plant** uno stabilimento chimico
■ VT **1** *(trees, seeds, flowers)* piantare; **to plant a field with corn** piantare *or* coltivare un terreno a grano **2** *(position: pole)* piantare, conficcare; *(bomb)* mettere; *(kiss)* stampare; **to plant an idea in sb's mind** ficcare *or* cacciare in testa un'idea a qn; **he planted himself right in her path** le si è piantato di fronte; **to plant sth on sb** *(fam)* nascondere qc su qn *(per incriminarlo)*
▸ **plant out** VT + ADV *(seedlings)* trapiantare
plan·tain ['plæntɪn] N *(banana) varietà di banana con la buccia verde*
plan·ta·tion [plæn'teɪʃən] N piantagione *f*
plant·er ['plɑ:ntə^r] N *(person)* piantatore(-trice); *(machine)* piantatrice *f*
plant life N flora
plant pot N vaso (per piante)
plaque [plæk] N *(on building)* placca, targa; *(on teeth)* placca batterica
plas·ma ['plæzmə] N plasma *m*
plasma proteins NPL proteine *fpl* plasmatiche
plasma screen N schermo al plasma
plasma TV N TV *f inv* al plasma
plas·ter ['plɑ:stə^r] N **1** *(Constr)* intonaco **2** *(Med)* gesso; **with his leg in plaster** con la gamba ingessata **3** *(Brit: also: **sticking plaster**)* cerotto; **have you got a plaster, by any chance?** hai un cerotto, per caso?
■ VT **1** *(Constr)* intonacare **2** *(fam: cover)* impiastricciare; **to be plastered with** *(mud)* essere impiastricciato(-a) di; **to plaster a wall with posters** tappezzare un muro di manifesti **3** *(Med)* ingessare
plaster·board ['plɑ:stə,bɔ:d] N lastra di cartongesso
plaster cast N *(Med)* ingessatura, gesso; *(model, statue)* modello in gesso
plas·tered ['plɑ:stəd] ADJ *(fam: drunk)* ubriaco(-a) fradicio(-a)
plas·ter·er ['plɑ:stərə^r] N intonacatore *m*
plaster of Paris N gesso
◎ **plas·tic** ['plæstɪk] N plastica, materia plastica; **plastics** materie *fpl* plastiche
■ ADJ **1** *(made of plastic)* di plastica **2** *(flexible)*

Pp

plastico(-a); **plastic behaviour** (*Phys*) plasticità; **the plastic arts** le arti plastiche
plastic bag N sacchetto di plastica
plastic bullet N pallottola di plastica
plastic explosive N (esplosivo al) plastico
Plas·ti·cine® ['plæstɪsi:n] N plastilina®
plas·tic·ity [plæs'tɪsɪtɪ] N plasticità
plastics industry N industria delle materie plastiche
plastic surgeon N specialista *m/f* in chirurgia plastica *or* estetica
plastic surgery N chirurgia plastica, chirurgia estetica
◎ **plate** [pleɪt] N **1** (*flat dish, plateful*) piatto; (*for church collection*) piatto delle elemosine; **to hand sb sth on a plate** (*fig fam*) offrire qc a qn su un piatto d'argento; **to have a lot on one's plate** (*fig fam*) avere un sacco di cose da fare **2** **gold/silver plate** vasellame *m* d'oro/d'argento; (*electroplated*) metallo placcato in oro/in argento **3** (*Phot*) lastra; (*Tech*) placca; (*on door*) targa, targhetta; (*Aut*: *number plate*) targa; (*on cooker*: *hot plate*) piastra **4** (*dental plate*) dentiera **5** (*book illustration*) tavola (fuori testo) **6** (*Geol*) zolla **7** (*sheet of metal*) lamiera **8** (*Typ*) cliché *m inv*
■ VT (*gen*) placcare; (*with gold*) dorare; (*with silver*) argentare
plat·eau ['plætəʊ] N (*pl* **plateaus** *or* **plateaux**) (*Geog*) altopiano
plate·ful ['pleɪtfʊl] N piatto
plate glass N vetro piano
plate·layer ['pleɪt,leɪəʳ] N (*Brit Rail*) armatore *m*
plate·let ['pleɪtlɪt] N (*Bio*) piastrina
plat·en ['plætən] N (*of typewriter, printer etc*) rullo
plate rack N scolapiatti *m inv*
plate warmer [-,wɔ:məʳ] N scaldapiatti *m inv*
◎ **plat·form** ['plæt,fɔ:m] N (*Brit*: *on bus*) piattaforma; (*at meeting, for band, stage*) palco; (*Pol*: *manifesto*) piattaforma, programma *m* (di base); (*Rail*) marciapiede *m*, banchina; **the soloist had just left the platform** il solista aveva appena lasciato il palco; **the train leaves from platform 7** il treno parte dal binario 7; **they were waiting on the platform** aspettavano sulla banchina
platform shoe N scarpa con la zeppa
platform ticket N (*Brit*) biglietto d'ingresso ai binari
plat·ing ['pleɪtɪŋ] N (*gold/silver plating*) placcatura; (*chrome plating*) cromatura
plati·num ['plætɪnəm] N platino
platinum blond ADJ: **a platinum blonde** una bionda platinata
plati·tude ['plætɪtju:d] N luogo comune, banalità *f inv*
Plato ['pleɪtəʊ] N Platone *m*
pla·ton·ic [plə'tɒnɪk] ADJ platonico(-a)
pla·toni·cal·ly [plə'tɒnɪkəlɪ] ADV platonicamente
pla·toon [plə'tu:n] N (*Mil*) plotone *m*
plat·ter ['plætəʳ] N piatto da portata
plau·dits ['plɔ:dɪts] NPL plauso *msg*
plau·sibil·ity [,plɔ:zə'bɪlɪtɪ] N (*of argument, story*) plausibilità; **he lacks plausibility** non è convincente
plau·sible ['plɔ:zəbl] ADJ (*argument, story*) plausibile, credibile; (*person*) convincente; **a plausible excuse** una scusa plausibile; **he seemed plausible** sembrava convincente
plau·sibly ['plɔ:zəblɪ] ADV in modo convincente
Plautus ['plɔ:təs] N Plauto
◎ **play** [pleɪ] N
1 (*recreation*) gioco; **the children were at play** i bambini giocavano; **to do/say sth in play** fare/dire qc per scherzo; **work and play** lavoro e svago; **a play on words** un gioco di parole
2 (*Sport*) gioco; **play began at 3 o'clock** la partita è cominciata alle 3; **there was some good play in the first half** ci sono state delle belle azioni nel primo tempo; **to be in/out of play** (*ball*) essere in/fuori gioco
3 (*Theatre*) opera teatrale; **radio/television play** commedia radiofonica/per la televisione; **a play by Shakespeare** una commedia di Shakespeare; **to put on a play** mettere in scena una commedia
4 (*Tech*: *movement, give*) gioco; **there's not enough play in the rope** la fune non ha abbastanza gioco
5 (*fig phrases*): **to bring** *or* **call into play** (*plan*) mettere in azione; (*emotions*) esprimere; **to give full play to one's imagination** dare libero sfogo alla propria fantasia; **to make great play of sth** giocare molto su qc; **to make a play for sb** fare il filo a qn; **to make a play for sth** darsi da fare per ottenere qc; **the play of light on the water** i giochi di luce sull'acqua
■ VT
1 (*match, card*) giocare; (*cards, chess, tennis*) giocare a; (*opponent*) giocare contro; (*chesspiece*) muovere; **to play a game of tennis** giocare una partita a tennis; **I play hockey** gioco a hockey; **can you play pool?** sai giocare a biliardo?; **to play sb at chess** giocare contro qn a scacchi; **Italy will play Scotland next month** il mese prossimo l'Italia giocherà contro la Scozia; **they played him in goal** l'hanno fatto giocare in porta; **don't play games with me** (*fam*) non prendermi in giro; **to play a trick on sb** fare uno scherzo a qn; **my eyes must be playing tricks on me** devo avere le traveggole; **to play the field** (*sexually*) darsi da fare in campo amoroso; **to play a fish** (*Angling*) stancare un pesce
2 (*perform*: *role*) interpretare; (*: play*) rappresentare, dare; (*perform in*: *town*) esibirsi a, dare uno spettacolo (*or* una serie di spettacoli) a; **I would like to play Cleopatra** mi piacerebbe interpretare Cleopatra; **to play sth for laughs** interpretare qc in chiave comica
3 (*instrument, piece of music*) suonare; (*record*) mettere; (*radio*) ascoltare; **I play the guitar** suono la chitarra; **she's always playing that record** ascolta sempre quel disco
4 (*direct*: *light, hose*) puntare, dirigere
■ VI
1 (*gen*) giocare; **to play at tennis** giocare a tennis; **to go out to play** andar fuori a giocare; **to play with a stick** giocherellare con un bastone; **he's playing with his friends** sta giocando con gli amici; **they're playing at soldiers** stanno giocando ai soldati; **to play with fire** (*fig*) scherzare col fuoco; **to play for money** giocare a soldi; **to play for time** (*fig*) cercare di guadagnar tempo; **to play into sb's hands** (*fig*) fare il gioco di qn; **to play safe** giocare sul sicuro; **to play hard to get** fare il/la prezioso(-a); **what are you playing at?** (*fam*) cosa cavolo stai facendo?; **he's just playing at it** non lo sta prendendo sul serio
2 (*move about, form patterns*): **we watched the fountains playing** guardavamo i giochi d'acqua delle fontane; **the sun was playing on the water** il sole creava giochi di luce sull'acqua; **a smile played on his lips** un sorriso gli sfiorò le labbra
3 (*Mus*) suonare; (*radio*) essere acceso(-a); **to play on the piano** suonare il piano
4 (*Theatre, Cine*) recitare (una parte); **to play dead** (*fig*) fingere di essere morto(-a)
► **play about, play around** VI + ADV (*person*)

divertirsi; **to play about** *or* **around with** (*fiddle with*) giocherellare con; (*idea*) accarezzare
▸ **play along** VI + ADV: **to play along with** (*fig: person*) stare al gioco di; (*: plan, idea*) fingere di assecondare
■ VT + ADV: **to play sb along** (*fig*) illudere qn
▸ **play around** VI = play about
▸ **play back** VT + ADV riascoltare, risentire
▸ **play down** VT + ADV minimizzare
▸ **play off** VT + ADV: **to play X off against Y** mettere X e Y l'uno(-a) contro l'altro(-a)
■ VI + ADV (*Sport*) giocare lo spareggio
▸ **play on** VI + ADV (*Sport*) continuare a giocare; (*Mus*) continuare a suonare
■ VI + PREP (*sb's feelings, credulity*) giocare su; **to play on sb's nerves** dare sui nervi a qn
▸ **play out** VT + ADV (*enact*) mettere in atto
▸ **play through** VT + ADV (*piece*) suonare
▸ **play up** VI + ADV
1 (*Brit fam: cause trouble: child, engine*) fare i capricci; (*: leg, ulcer*) farsi sentire
2 (*fam: flatter*): **to play up to sb** arruffianarsi qn
■ VT + ADV
1 (*fam: cause trouble to*): **to play sb up** (*subj: child*) combinarne di tutti i colori a qn; (*: leg*) fare male a qn
2 (*exaggerate*) esagerare, gonfiare

play·act ['pleɪ,ækt] VI (*fig*) fare la commedia

play-acting ['pleɪ,æktɪŋ] N (*fig*): **it's only play-acting** è tutta una commedia

play·back ['pleɪ,bæk] N playback *m inv*

play·bill ['pleɪ,bɪl] N manifesto (di teatro), locandina

play·boy ['pleɪ,bɔɪ] N playboy *m inv*

play date N (*Am*): **to have a play date** incontrarsi per giocare

played out ['pleɪd'aʊt] ADJ (*exhausted: person*) spossato(-a); (*: vein in mine*) esaurito(-a); (*: argument*) superato(-a)

◎ **play·er** ['pleɪəʳ] N (*Sport*) giocatore(-trice); (*Mus*) musicista *m/f*; (*Theatre*) attore(-trice); **players of musical instruments** suonatori di strumenti musicali; **football player** calciatore(-trice); **piano player** pianista *m/f*; **saxophone player** sassofonista *m/f*

play·fellow ['pleɪ,fɛləʊ] N = playmate

play·ful ['pleɪfʊl] ADJ (*child, puppy*) giocherellone(-a); (*mood, smile, remark*) scherzoso(-a)

play·ful·ly ['pleɪfəlɪ] ADV giocosamente; (*remark, smile*) scherzosamente

play·ful·ness ['pleɪfʊlnɪs] N (*of child, puppy*) carattere *m* giocoso; (*of remark, mood, smile*) scherzosità

play·goer ['pleɪ,gəʊəʳ] N appassionato(-a) di teatro; **an actor well-loved by playgoers** un attore molto amato dal pubblico

play·ground ['pleɪ,graʊnd] N (*in school*) cortile *m* per la ricreazione; (*in park*) parco *m* giochi *inv*

play·group ['pleɪ,gru:p] N ≈ asilo

play·house ['pleɪ,haʊs] N (*theatre*) teatro; (*for children*) casetta per i giochi

play·ing ['pleɪɪŋ] N: **some fine playing** (*Mus*) dei passaggi ben eseguiti

playing card N carta da gioco

playing field N campo sportivo

playing field N (*Sport*) campo sportivo; **to compete on a level playing field** combattere ad armi pari

play·list ['pleɪ,lɪst] N playlist *f inv*; *raccolta di brani musicali trasmessi da una stazione radiofonica*

play·maker ['pleɪ,meɪkəʳ] N (*Sport*) playmaker *m/f inv*

play·mate ['pleɪ,meɪt] N compagno(-a) di gioco

play-off ['pleɪ,ɒf] N (*Sport*) (partita di) spareggio, bella

play park N parco giochi

play·pen ['pleɪ,pɛn] N box *m inv* (*per bambini*)

play·room ['pleɪ,rʊm] N stanza dei giochi

play scheme N attività *fpl* ricreative per ragazzi

play·school ['pleɪsku:l] N ≈ asilo

play·thing ['pleɪ,θɪŋ] N (*also fig*) giocattolo

play·time ['pleɪ,taɪm] N (*Scol*) ricreazione *f*

play·wright ['pleɪ,raɪt] N commediografo(-a), drammaturgo(-a)

plc, **PLC** [,pi:ɛl'si:] ABBR = **public limited company**

plea [pli:] N **1** (*entreaty: for donations*) appello; (*: for leniency*) supplica; (*excuse*) scusa, pretesto; **a plea to mankind** un appello all'umanità; **a plea for help** una richiesta di aiuto; **to make a plea for sth** chiedere qc; **he made a plea for understanding** chiedeva comprensione; **on the plea of** con la scusa di **2** (*Law*): **to enter a plea of guilty** dichiararsi colpevole; **to put forward a plea of self-defence** invocare la legittima difesa

plea bargaining N (*Law*) patteggiamento (della pena)

plead [pli:d] (*pt, pp* **pleaded**, (*esp Am*) **pled**) VT **1 to plead sb's case** (*Law*) *or* **to plead sb's cause** (*fig*) perorare la causa di qn **2** (*as excuse: ignorance*) addurre come (*or* a) pretesto; **to plead insanity** (*Law*) invocare l'infermità mentale
■ VI **1** (*beg*): **to plead with sb (to do sth)** supplicare *or* implorare qn (di fare qc); **to plead for sth** (*beg for*) implorare qc; (*make speech in favour of*) parlare in favore di qc; **he was pleading for mercy** chiedeva pietà
2 (*Law: lawyer*): **to plead for** perorare in favore di; **to plead guilty/not guilty** (*defendant*) dichiararsi colpevole/innocente

plead·ing ['pli:dɪŋ] N (*entreaties*) suppliche *fpl*
■ ADJ supplichevole

plead·ing·ly ['pli:dɪŋlɪ] ADV supplichevolmente

◎ **pleas·ant** ['plɛznt] ADJ (*gen*) piacevole, gradevole; (*surprise, news*) bello(-a); (*smell*) gradevole, buono(-a); (*people, smile*) simpatico(-a); (*weather*) bello(-a); **we had a pleasant time** ci siamo divertiti

pleas·ant·ly ['plɛzntlɪ] ADV (*smile, greet*) cordialmente; **I am pleasantly surprised** sono piacevolmente sorpreso

pleas·ant·ness ['plɛzntnɪs] N (*of person*) amabilità; (*of place*) amenità

pleas·ant·ry ['plɛzntrɪ] N (*joke*) battuta di spirito, spiritosaggine *f*; (*polite remark*): **to exchange pleasantries** scambiarsi convenevoli

◎ **please** [pli:z] EXCL per piacere, per favore; **(yes,) please** sì , grazie; **come in, please** entrate, prego; **please pass the salt** *or* **pass the salt please** per piacere *or* per favore, mi passi il sale?; **two coffees, please** due caffè, per favore; **my bill, please** il conto, per piacere; **please don't cry!** ti prego, non piangere!
■ VI **1 if you please** (*frm: in request*) per piacere, per favore; **he wanted ten, if you please!** (*iro*) ne voleva dieci, figurati!; **he does as he pleases** fa come gli pare
2 (*cause satisfaction*) far piacere, piacere; **anxious** *or* **eager to please** desideroso(-a) di piacere; **a gift that is sure to please** un dono sicuramente gradito
■ VT (*give pleasure to*) far piacere a; (*satisfy*) accontentare; **I did it to please you** l'ho fatto per farti piacere; **there's no pleasing him** non c'è verso di accontentarlo; **to please o.s.** far come si vuole; **please yourself!** come vuoi!, come ti pare!

◎ **pleased** [pli:zd] ADJ (*happy*) felice, lieto(-a); (*satisfied*) contento(-a), soddisfatto(-a); **to be pleased (about**

Pp

sth) essere contento(-a) (di qc); **pleased to meet you!** piacere!; **my mother's not going to be very pleased** mia madre non sarà molto contenta; **I am not pleased at your decision** la tua decisione non mi ha fatto piacere; **to be pleased with sb/sth** essere contento(-a) *or* soddisfatto(-a) di qn/qc; **it's beautiful: she'll be pleased with it** è bellissimo, ne sarà contenta; **to be pleased with o.s.** compiacersi, essere compiaciuto(-a) di sé; **we are pleased to inform you that ...** abbiamo il piacere di informarla che...

pleas·ing ['pli:zɪŋ] ADJ *(person)* simpatico(-a); *(news, sight)* piacevole, che fa piacere; **it's pleasing that ...** fa piacere che...

pleas·ing·ly ['pli:zɪŋlɪ] ADV *(arranged, performed etc)* gradevolmente, in modo gradevole

pleas·ur·able ['plɛʒərəbl] ADJ (molto) piacevole *or* gradevole

pleas·ur·ably ['plɛʒərəblɪ] ADV (molto) gradevolmente; *(anticipate)* con piacere

◎ **pleas·ure** ['plɛʒə^r] N **1** *(satisfaction, happiness)* piacere *m*; **with pleasure** con piacere, volentieri; **it's a pleasure!** *or* **my pleasure!** *or* **the pleasure is mine!** *(frm: returning thanks)* prego!, il piacere è (tutto) mio!; **I have much pleasure in informing you that ...** sono lieto di informarla che...; **may I have the pleasure?** *(frm: at dance)* mi concede l'onore di questo ballo?; **Mr and Mrs Smith request the pleasure of your company** *(frm)* i Signori Smith gradirebbero averla come ospite **2** *(source of pleasure)* piacere *m*; **all the pleasures of London** tutti i divertimenti di Londra; **is this trip for business or pleasure?** è un viaggio d'affari o di piacere? **3** *(frm: will)* desiderio, volontà; **at sb's pleasure** secondo i desideri di qn; **we await your pleasure** *(Comm)* siamo a vostra disposizione; **to be detained during her Majesty's pleasure** *(Law) essere condannato ad una pena detentiva di durata illimitata (prevista per i reati più gravi)*
■ ADJ *(cruise)* di piacere

pleasure boat N battello da diporto

pleasure-loving ['plɛʒə,lʌvɪŋ] ADJ: **she's a pleasure-loving person** è amante dei piaceri

pleasure steamer N vapore *m* da diporto

pleat [pli:t] N piega
■ VT pieghettare

ple·beian [plɪ'bi:ən] ADJ, N plebeo(-a)

plebi·scite ['plɛbɪsɪt] N plebiscito; **to hold a plebiscite** fare un referendum

plebs [plɛbz] NPL *(pej)* plebe *fsg*

plec·trum ['plɛktrəm] N plettro

pled [plɛd] *(esp Am)* PT, PP *of* **plead**

◎ **pledge** [plɛdʒ] N *(promise)* promessa solenne; *(security, token)* pegno; **to be under a pledge of secrecy** aver promesso di mantenere il segreto; **as a pledge of** come pegno *or* testimonianza di; **to sign** *or* **take the pledge** *(hum fam)* promettere solennemente di non toccare alcolici
■ VT **1** *(promise)*: **to pledge sth/to do sth** promettere qc/di fare qc; **the US has pledged thirty million dollars** gli USA hanno promesso trenta milioni di dollari; **to pledge sb to secrecy** far promettere a qn di mantenere il segreto; **to pledge support for sb** impegnarsi a sostenere qn **2** *(pawn)* impegnare

ple·na·ry ['pli:nərɪ] ADJ plenario(-a); **in plenary session** in seduta plenaria

pleni·po·ten·ti·ary [,plɛnɪpə'tɛnʃərɪ] N plenipotenziario
■ ADJ plenipotenziario(-a)

plen·ti·ful ['plɛntɪfʊl] ADJ abbondante; **to be in plentiful supply** abbondare, esserci in gran quantità

◎ **plen·ty** ['plɛntɪ] N **1** abbondanza; **in plenty** *(in large quantities)* in abbondanza; **land of plenty** paese *m* di cuccagna *or* di bengodi **2** **plenty of** *(lots of)* molto(-a), tanto(-a); *(enough)* abbastanza; **he has plenty of friends** ha tanti amici; **we've got plenty of time** abbiamo un sacco di tempo; **I've got plenty** ne ho abbastanza; **there's plenty to go on** *(information)* ci sono indizi più che sufficienti; **we've got plenty of time** abbiamo un sacco di tempo

pletho·ra ['plɛθərə] N pletora, sovrabbondanza

pleu·ra ['plʊərə] N *(pl* **pleurae** ['plʊəri:]) pleura

pleu·ral ['plʊərəl] ADJ pleurico(-a)

pleu·ri·sy ['plʊərɪsɪ] N pleurite *f*

Plexi·glas® ['plɛksɪ,glɑ:s] N plexiglas® *m*

pli·abil·ity [,plaɪə'bɪlɪtɪ] N *(see adj)* flessibilità; malleabilità

pli·able ['plaɪəbl], **pli·ant** ['plaɪənt] ADJ *(substance)* pieghevole, flessibile; *(fig: person)* malleabile

pli·ers ['plaɪəz] NPL *(also:* **pair of pliers***)* pinze *fpl*

plight [plaɪt] N situazione *f* (critica); **their desperate plight** la loro situazione disperata; **the country's economic plight** le gravi condizioni economiche del paese

plim·soll ['plɪmsəl] N *(Brit)* scarpa da tennis

Plimsoll line N *(Naut)* linea di immersione massima

plinth [plɪnθ] N plinto

Pliny ['plɪnɪ] N: **Pliny the Younger/the Elder** Plinio il Giovane/il Vecchio

PLO [,pi:ɛl'əʊ] N ABBR (= **Palestine Liberation Organization**) OLP *f*

plod [plɒd] VI: **to plod up/down** *etc* trascinarsi su per/giù per *etc*; **to plod away at sth** *(fig)* sgobbare su qc; **we must plod on** *(fig)* dobbiamo farci forza e tirare avanti

plod·der ['plɒdə^r] N sgobbone(-a)

plod·ding ['plɒdɪŋ] ADJ *(gait)* pesante; *(pace of work)* lento(-a) e pesante; *(fig: person)* che sgobba

plonk¹ [plɒŋk] N *(Brit fam: wine)* vino ordinario

plonk² [plɒŋk] N *(sound)* tonfo
■ ADV: **plonk in the middle** nel bel mezzo
■ VT *(fam: also:* **plonk down***)* appoggiare pesantemente; **to plonk o.s. down** lasciarsi cadere (di peso); **he plonked himself down on the sofa** è crollato sul sofà

plop [plɒp] N plop *m inv*
■ VI *(stone)* fare plop

plo·sive ['pləʊsɪv] *(Phonetics)* ADJ occlusivo(-a)
■ N occlusiva

plot¹ [plɒt] N *(of land)* appezzamento, lotto; **a vegetable plot** un orticello; **building plot** lotto edificabile

◎ **plot²** [plɒt] N **1** *(conspiracy)* complotto, cospirazione *f*, congiura; **a plot against the president** un complotto contro il presidente **2** *(of story, play)* intreccio, trama; **a complicated plot** una trama complicata
■ VT **1** *(mark out: course, graph, diagram etc)* tracciare; **to plot one's position** *(Naut)* fare il punto **2** *(plan secretly)* complottare, cospirare, congiurare
■ VI complottare, congiurare

plot·ter ['plɒtə^r] N **1** *(conspirator)* cospiratore(-trice) **2** *(Naut, Comput)* plotter *m inv*

plot·ting ['plɒtɪŋ] N *(conspiracy)* cospirazione *f*

Plough [plaʊ] N *(Astron)*: **the Plough** il Gran Carro

plough, *(Am)* **plow** [plaʊ] N aratro
■ VT *(field)* arare; *(furrow)* scavare; **they plough the fields in the autumn** arano i campi in autunno; **to**

plough one's way through a book (*fig*) leggere con fatica un libro
■VI (*Agr*) arare; **the car ploughed into the wall** l'auto ha sfondato il muro
▸ **plough back** VT (*profits*) reinvestire
▸ **plough in** VT + ADV sotterrare arando
▸ **plough through** VI + PREP (*snow, mud*) procedere a fatica in; (*work*) procedere metodicamente in; (*speech*) leggere monotonamente; **he ploughed through a plate of spaghetti** macinò a fatica un piattone di spaghetti
▸ **plough up** VT + ADV (*field*) arare

ploughing ['plaʊɪŋ], (*Am*) **plow·ing** N aratura

plough·man, (*Am*) **plow·man** ['plaʊmən] N (*pl* **-men**) aratore *m*

ploughman's lunch ['plaʊmənz 'lʌntʃ] N (*Brit*) *semplice pasto a base di pane e formaggio*

plov·er ['plʌvəʳ] N piviere *m*; **ringed plover** corriere *m* grosso; **golden plover** piviere dorato

plow [plaʊ] (*Am*) = **plough**

plowing N (*Am*) = **ploughing**

plowman N (*Am*) = **ploughman**

ploy [plɔɪ] N stratagemma *m*, manovra

pls ABBR = **please**

pluck [plʌk] N (*courage*) coraggio, fegato
■VT (*fruit, flower*) cogliere; (*also:* **pluck out**) strappare; (*Mus: strings*) pizzicare; (*: guitar*) pizzicare le corde di; (*Culin: bird*) spennare; **to pluck one's eyebrows** depilarsi le sopracciglia; **to pluck up (one's) courage** farsi coraggio, armarsi di coraggio
■VI: **to pluck at sb's sleeve** tirare qn per la manica

plucki·ly ['plʌkɪlɪ] ADV coraggiosamente

plucky ['plʌkɪ] ADJ (*comp* **-ier**, *superl* **-iest**) coraggioso(-a)

plug [plʌg] N **1** (*of bath, basin, barrel, volcano*) tappo; (*for stopping a leak*) tampone *m* **2** (*Elec*) spina; (*Aut: also:* **spark(ing) plug**) candela; **the plug is faulty** la spina è difettosa **3** (*fam: piece of publicity*) pubblicità *f inv*, réclame *f inv*; **to give sb/sth a plug** fare pubblicità a qn/qc
■VT **1** (*also:* **plug up**: *hole*) tappare; (*tooth*) otturare **2** (*insert*) infilare, cacciare; **to plug a lead into a socket** inserire un filo (elettrico) in una presa di corrente **3** (*fam: publicize*) fare pubblicità a; (*: push, put forward*) fare propaganda a
▸ **plug away** VI + ADV (*fam*): **to plug away (at sth)** sgobbare (su qc)
▸ **plug in** (*Elec*) VI + ADV collegarsi; **the TV plugs in behind the table** la presa per la TV è dietro il tavolo
■VT + ADV (*appliance*) attaccare; **is the iron plugged in?** è attaccato il ferro da stiro?

plug-and-play [ˌplʌgən'pleɪ] ADJ plug-and-play *inv*, che può essere connesso(-a) senza installazione

plug·hole ['plʌgˌhəʊl] N scarico; **it went down the plughole** è caduto nel buco del lavandino (*or* della vasca)

plug-in ['plʌgɪn] **1** ADJ (*radio*) a corrente **2** (*Comput*): **plug-in memory card** scheda di memoria plug-in; **plug-in software module** applicativo plug-in

plum [plʌm] N (*fruit*) prugna, susina; (*also:* **plum tree**) prugno, susino; **a real plum (of a job)** (*fig fam*) un lavoro favoloso
■ADJ **1** (*tart, tree*) di prugne; (*plum-coloured*) (color) prugna *inv* **2** (*fig fam*): **a plum role** un ruolo ambito

plum·age ['plu:mɪdʒ] N piume *fpl*, piumaggio

plumb [plʌm] N piombo
■ADV (*fam*): **plumb in the middle** esattamente nel centro; **he's plumb stupid** (*Am fam*) è proprio stupido
■VT scandagliare; (*sb's mind*) sondare; **to plumb the depths** scandagliare gli abissi; (*fig*) toccare il fondo
▸ **plumb in** VT + ADV (*washing machine*) collegare all'impianto idraulico

plumb bob N piombino

plumb·er ['plʌməʳ] N idraulico; **he's a plumber** fa l'idraulico

plumb·ing ['plʌmɪŋ] N (*craft*) lavoro *or* mestiere *m* di idraulico; (*piping*) impianto idraulico, tubature *fpl*; **the plumbing's okay** le tubature sono a posto; **bricklaying and plumbing** lavori *mpl* di muratura e di idraulica

plumb line N (*builder's*) filo a piombo; (*Naut*) scandaglio

plume [plu:m] N piuma, penna; (*on hat, helmet*) penna, pennacchio; **a plume of smoke** un pennacchio di fumo

plumed [plu:md] ADJ (*helmet*) chiomato(-a)

plum·met ['plʌmɪt] VI (*bird*) calare a piombo; (*plane*) precipitare; (*temperature, price, sales*) calare bruscamente; (*spirits, morale*) calare a zero

plum·my ['plʌmɪ] ADJ (*comp* **-ier**, *superl* **-iest**) **1** (*Brit: voice, accent*) (esageratamente) aristocratico(-a) **2** (*colour*) (color *m*) prugna *inv*

plump [plʌmp] ADJ (*comp* **-er**, *superl* **-est**) (*person, chicken*) bene in carne; (*cheeks, face*) paffuto(-a); (*wallet, cushion*) (bello(-a)) gonfio(-a); (*arms, child, hands*) grassoccio(-a), grassottello(-a)
▸ **plump down** VT + ADV lasciar cadere di peso; **to plump sth (down) on** lasciar cadere qc di peso su
■VI + ADV lasciarsi cadere di peso *or* di schianto
▸ **plump for** VI + PREP (*fam*) decidersi per
▸ **plump up** VT + ADV (*cushion*) sprimacciare

plump·ness ['plʌmpnɪs] N (*of person, arms*) rotondità; (*of cheeks, face*) paffutezza

Pp

plum pudding N *specie di budino a base di farina, grasso di rognone, zucchero e frutta secca cotto a vapore*

plun·der ['plʌndəʳ] N (*act*) saccheggio; (*loot*) bottino
■VT (*gen*) saccheggiare; (*villagers*) depredare; (*objects*) far man bassa di

plun·der·er ['plʌndərəʳ] N predone *m*, saccheggiatore(-trice)

plun·der·ing ['plʌndərɪŋ] ADJ saccheggiatore(-trice)
■N saccheggio

◎**plunge** [plʌndʒ] N (*dive*) tuffo; (*fig: into debt, of currency*) caduta; **to take the plunge** (*fig*) buttarsi, saltare il fosso, fare il gran passo
■VT **1** (*immerse*) immergere, tuffare; (*thrust: knife*) conficcare; (*: hand*) ficcare, tuffare; **to plunge a dagger into sb's chest** conficcare un pugnale nel petto di qn **2** (*fig*): **to plunge a room into darkness** far piombare una stanza nel buio; **we were plunged into gloom by the news** la notizia ci ha gettato nella costernazione; **to plunge sb into debt** precipitare qn nei debiti
■VI **1** (*dive*) tuffarsi; **she plunged into the pool** si è tuffata nella piscina **2** (*fall*) precipitare, cadere; **he plunged to his death** ha fatto una caduta mortale **3** (*share prices, currency*) calare precipitosamente; **to plunge into debt** riempirsi di debiti **4** (*fig: rush*): **he plunged into trade union activites** si buttò anima e corpo in attività sindacali; **to plunge heedlessly into danger** buttarsi allo sbaraglio

plung·er ['plʌndʒəʳ] N (*for clearing drain*) sturalavandini *m inv*

plung·ing ['plʌndʒɪŋ] ADJ (*neckline*) profondo(-a); (*back of dress*) profondamente scollato(-a)

plu·per·fect [ˌplu:'pɜ:fɪkt] N (*Gram*) piuccheperfetto

plu·ral ['plʊərəl] ADJ (*Gram: form*) plurale, del plurale; (*: noun, verb*) plurale, al plurale
■ N (*Gram*) plurale *m*; **in the plural** al plurale
plu·ral·ism ['plʊərə,lɪzm] N pluralismo
plu·ral·ist ['plʊərə,lɪst] ADJ pluralistico(-a)
◎ **plus** [plʌs] PREP più; **4 plus 3 equals 7** 4 più 3 fa 7; **three children plus a dog** tre bambini e un cane
■ ADJ (*Math, Elec*) positivo(-a); **ten/twenty plus** più di dieci/venti; **you must be 20 plus** devi avere vent'anni compiuti; **I got B plus for my essay** ho ricevuto B più nel tema; **a plus factor** (*fig*) un vantaggio
■ N (*Math: plus sign*) più *m inv*; (*fig: advantage*) vantaggio
plus fours NPL calzoni *mpl* alla zuava
plush [plʌʃ] N felpa
■ ADJ (*also:* **plushy**: *fam*) sontuoso(-a), lussuoso(-a)
Plutarch ['plu:tɑ:k] N Plutarco
Plu·to ['plu:təʊ] N (*Astron, Myth*) Plutone *m*
plu·toc·ra·cy [,plu:'tɒkrəsɪ] N plutocrazia
plu·to·crat ['plu:təʊ,kræt] N plutocrate *m/f*
plu·ton·ic [plu:'tɒnɪk] ADJ plutonico(-a)
plu·to·nium [plu:'təʊnɪəm] N plutonio
ply¹ [plaɪ] N (*of wool*) capo; (*of wood*) strato
■ ADJ: **three-ply wood** compensato a tre strati; **three-ply wool** lana a tre capi
ply² [plaɪ] VT (*knitting needle, tool etc*) maneggiare; (*sea, river, route*) viaggiare regolarmente su; **to ply one's trade** esercitare il proprio mestiere; **to ply sb with questions** continuare a far domande a qn; **to ply sb with drink** continuare a offrir da bere a qn
■ VI: **to ply between** far la spola fra, fare servizio regolare fra; **to ply for hire** (*taxi*) andare avanti e indietro in attesa di clienti
ply·wood ['plaɪ,wʊd] N (legno) compensato
◎ **PM** [,pi:'ɛm] N ABBR (*Brit fam*) = **Prime Minister**
p.m. ['pi:'ɛm] ADV ABBR (*in the afternoon*) del pomeriggio; (*in the evening*) di sera; **at 8 p.m.** alle otto di sera; **at 2 p.m.** alle quattordici
PMS [,pi:ɛm'ɛs] N ABBR (= **premenstrual syndrome**) sindrome *f* premestruale
PMT [,pi:ɛm'ti:] N ABBR (= **premenstrual tension**) sindrome *f* premestruale
pneu·mat·ic [nju:'mætɪk] ADJ pneumatico(-a); **pneumatic drill** martello pneumatico
pneu·mo·nia [nju:'məʊnɪə] N polmonite *f*
pneu·mo·tho·rax [,nju:məʊ'θɔ:ræks] N pneumotorace *m*
PO [,pi:'əʊ] N ABBR (= **Post Office**) ≈ PT *fpl*
■ ABBR (*Naut*) = **petty officer**
p.o. [,pi:'əʊ] ABBR = **postal order**
POA [,pi:əʊ'eɪ] N ABBR (*Brit*: = **Prison Officers' Association**) ≈ sindacato degli agenti di custodia
poach¹ [pəʊtʃ] VT (*Culin: fish*) cuocere in bianco; **poached egg** uovo affogato *or* in camicia
poach² [pəʊtʃ] VT (*hunt: game*) cacciare di frodo; (*fish*) pescare di frodo; (*fig fam: steal*) soffiare, portar via
■ VI cacciare (*or* pescare) di frodo; **to poach on sb's preserves** (*fig*) invadere il campo di qn
poach·er ['pəʊtʃəʳ] N (*of game*) bracconiere *m*
poach·ing ['pəʊtʃɪŋ] N bracconaggio, caccia (*or* pesca) di frodo
PO Box N ABBR (= **Post Office Box**) C.P. (= *casella postale*)
◎ **pock·et** ['pɒkɪt] N (*in garment etc*) tasca; **breast pocket** taschino; **with his hands in his pockets** con le mani in tasca; **to have sb in one's pocket** (*fig*) tenere in pugno qn; **to have sth in one's pocket** (*fig*) avere qc (già) in tasca; **to be in pocket** guadagnarci; **to be out of pocket** rimetterci; **to line one's pockets** arricchirsi, fare i soldi; **to put one's hand in one's pocket** (*fig*) metter mano al portafoglio; **to go through sb's pockets** frugare le tasche di qn; **to live in each other's pockets** rimanere *or* essere sempre appiccicati; **pocket of resistance/warm air** sacca di resistenza/di aria calda
■ VT (*fig: gain, take*) intascare; **to pocket one's pride** (*fig*) metter da parte l'orgoglio
■ ADJ (*edition, calculator*) tascabile
pocket·book ['pɒkɪt,bʊk] N (*wallet*) portafoglio; (*notebook*) taccuino; (*Am: handbag*) borsetta; (*paperback*) tascabile *m*
pock·et·ful ['pɒkɪtfʊl] N tascata
pocket handkerchief N fazzoletto da taschino
pocket·knife ['pɒkɪtnaɪf] N (*pl* **-knives**) temperino
pocket money N (*of child*) paghetta; **£8 a week pocket money** una paghetta settimanale di otto sterline
pocket-size, pocket-sized ['pɒkɪtsaɪz(d)] ADJ (*book*) tascabile; (*garden*) piccolissimo(-a)
pock·marked ['pɒk,mɑ:kt] ADJ (*face*) butterato(-a); (*surface*) bucherellato(-a)
pod [pɒd] N baccello, guscio
■ VT sgusciare
podgy ['pɒdʒɪ] ADJ (*comp* **-ier**, *superl* **-iest**) tracagnotto(-a)
po·dia·trist [pɒ'di:ətrɪst] N (*Am*) callista *m/f*, pedicure *m/f*
po·dia·try [pɒ'di:ətrɪ] N (*Am*) mestiere *m* di callista
po·dium ['pəʊdɪəm] N podio
POE [,pi:əʊ'i:] ABBR = *port of entry*
◎ **poem** ['pəʊɪm] N poesia
◎ **poet** ['pəʊɪt] N poeta(-essa)
po·et·ess ['pəʊɪtɛs] N poetessa
po·et·ic [pəʊ'ɛtɪk] ADJ poetico(-a)
po·eti·cal·ly [pəʊ'ɛtɪkəlɪ] ADV poeticamente
po·eti·cize [pəʊ'ɛtɪ,saɪz] VT poeticizzare
poetic justice N: **poetic justice!** giustizia fatta!
poetic licence N licenza poetica
poet lau·reate [,pəʊɪt'lɔ:rɪɪt] N (*Brit*) *poeta di corte*

POET LAUREATE

In Gran Bretagna il **poet laureate** è un poeta di corte con nomina a vita. Riceve un vitalizio dalla casa reale britannica e ha l'incarico di scrivere delle poesie commemorative in occasione delle festività ufficiali.
Negli Stati Uniti il **poet laureate** ha incarico annuale, da ottobre a maggio, e riceve uno stipendio. Nominato dal bibliotecario del Congresso, detiene il titolo di "Poet Laureate Consultant in Poetry" e il suo compito è quello di stimolare la lettura e la scrittura di poesie.
▷ www.poetsgraves.co.uk/poets_laureate%20uk.htm
▷ www.loc.gov/poetry/

◎ **po·et·ry** ['pəʊɪtrɪ] N poesia; **to write poetry** scrivere (delle) poesie
▷ www.loc.gov/poetry/180/
▷ www.bbc.co.uk/bbcfour/audiointerviews/professions/poets.shtml
▷ www.ibiblio.org/ipa/
poetry reading N reading *m inv* di poesia
po-faced [,pəʊ'feɪst] ADJ (*Brit*) serioso(-a)
pog·rom ['pɒgrəm] N pogrom *m inv*
poign·an·cy ['pɔɪnjənsɪ] N (*of grief*) intensità; **it was a**

moment of extraordinary poignancy fu un attimo di grande commozione

poign·ant [ˈpɔɪnjənt] ADJ commovente, toccante

poign·ant·ly [ˈpɔɪnjəntlɪ] ADV (*feel*) intensamente; (*describe*) in modo toccante

◎**point** [pɔɪnt] N

1 (*dot, punctuation mark, Geom*) punto; (*decimal point*) virgola; **2 point 6 (2.6)** 2 virgola 6 (2,6)

2 (*on scale, compass etc*) punto; **freezing point** punto di congelamento; **from all points of the compass** da tutte le parti del mondo; **up to a point** (*fig*) fino a un certo punto

3 (*of needle, pencil, knife*) punta; **a pencil with a sharp point** una matita appuntita; **on points** (*Ballet*) sulle punte; **at the point of a gun/sword** sotto la minaccia di un fucile/una spada; **not to put too fine a point on it** (*fig*) parlando chiaro

4 (*place*) punto; **the train stops at Carlisle and all points south** il treno ferma a Carlisle e in tutte le stazioni a sud di Carlisle; **point of contact** punto d'incontro; **point of departure** (*also fig*) punto di partenza; **a point on the horizon** un punto all'orizzonte; **at this point** (*spatially*) in questo punto; (*in time*) a questo punto; **at that point, we decided to leave** a quel punto abbiamo deciso di andarcene; **from that point on** (*in time*) da quel momento in poi; (*in space*) da quel punto in poi; **to be on the point of doing sth** essere sul punto di *or* stare (proprio) per fare qc; **when it comes to the point** quando si arriva al dunque; **when it came to the point of leaving** quando giunse il momento di partire; **abrupt to the point of rudeness** brusco al punto di essere villano

5 (*counting unit: Sport, in test, Stock Exchange*) punto; **to win on points** vincere ai punti; **they scored five points** hanno segnato cinque punti; **the index is down 3 points** l'indice è sceso di 3 punti

6 (*purpose*) scopo, motivo; (*matter*) questione *f*, argomento; (*main idea, important part: of argument, joke*) nocciolo; **there's no point in staying** è inutile *or* non ha senso restare; **I don't see** *or* **get the point** (*of joke*) mi sfugge; **I don't see the point of** *or* **in doing that** non vedo il motivo di farlo; **what's the point?** perché?; **what's the point of leaving so early?** perché partire così presto?; **the point is that ...** il fatto è che...; **that's the whole point!** precisamente!, sta tutto lì !; **the point at issue** l'argomento in discussione *or* questione; **a 5-point plan** un piano articolato in 5 punti; **she described the process point by point** descrisse il processo punto per punto; **in point of fact** a dire il vero; **to be beside the point** non entrarci; **to get off the point** divagare; **to come** *or* **get to the point** venire al punto *or* al dunque, arrivare al punto; **to keep** *or* **stick to the point** restare in argomento; **to make a point of doing sth** non mancare di fare qc; **to make a point** fare un'osservazione; **he made some interesting points** ha fatto delle osservazioni interessanti; **to make one's point** dimostrare la propria tesi; **I take your point** so che hai ragione; **to win one's point** averla vinta; **to stretch a point** fare uno strappo (alla regola) *or* un'eccezione; **his remarks were to the point** le sue osservazioni erano pertinenti *or* a proposito; **to get sb's point** capire ciò che qn vuole dire; **yes, I get your point** sì , capisco quello che vuoi dire; **you've got a point there!** giusto!, hai ragione!; **that's a good point!** giusto!; **I missed the point of that joke** non ho afferrato quella battuta; **you've missed the whole point!** non hai capito niente!; **a point of principle** una questione di principio

7 (*characteristic*) caratteristica, qualità *f inv*; **good/bad points** lati positivi/negativi; **tact isn't one of his strong points** il tatto non è il suo forte; **what points should I look for?** a cosa devo stare attento?

8 (*Brit Rail*): **points** NPL scambio *msg*

9 (*Aut*): **points** NPL puntine *fpl*

10 (*Brit Elec: also*: **power point**) presa (di corrente)

■VT

1 (*aim, direct: gun, hosepipe etc*): **to point sth (at sb/sth)** puntare qc (contro *or* su qn/qc); **to point a gun at sb** puntare una pistola contro qn; **she pointed the car at the gap in the traffic** diresse la macchina verso un varco nel traffico; **to point one's finger at sb** indicare qn con il dito, additare; **to point one's toes** stendere il piede

2 (*indicate, show*) indicare, mostrare; **to point the way** (*also fig*) indicare la strada *or* la direzione da seguire

3 (*Constr*) riempire gli interstizi di

■VI

1 indicare (con il dito), additare; **don't point!** non indicare col dito!; **to point at** *or* **to** *or* **towards sth/sb** indicare qc/qn

2 (*indicate: signpost, hand*) indicare, segnare; **everything points to him being guilty** tutti gli indizi fanno pensare che sia colpevole; **it points (to the) north** (*compass needle*) segna *or* indica il nord; **this points to the fact that ...** questo fa pensare che...

▸ **point out** VT + ADV

1 (*show*) additare, indicare; **the guide pointed out Big Ben to us** la guida ci ha indicato il Big Ben

2 (*mention*) far notare, far presente; **I'd like to point out that...** vorrei far notare che...; **she pointed out our mistakes** ci ha fatto presente i nostri errori

▸ **point up** VT + ADV sottolineare, mettere in evidenza

point-blank [ˌpɔɪntˈblæŋk] ADJ (*shot, question*) a bruciapelo; (*refusal*) categorico(-a), secco(-a); **at point-blank range** a bruciapelo

■ADV (*fire*) a bruciapelo; (*refuse*) categoricamente; **he was asked point-blank if he would resign** gli fu chiesto a bruciapelo se intendeva dimettersi

point-by-point [ˈpɔɪntˌbaɪˈpɔɪnt] ADJ (*analysis etc*) particolareggiato(-a)

point duty N (*Brit: Police*) servizio di controllo del traffico; **to be on point duty** dirigere il traffico

point·ed [ˈpɔɪntɪd] ADJ **1** (*sharp: stick, chin*) appuntito(-a), aguzzo(-a); (*beard*) a punta; (*roof*) aguzzo(-a); (*arch*) a sesto acuto **2** (*obvious in intention: remark, question*) pregno(-a) di significati; **a pointed remark** un'osservazione critica; **in a pointed manner** in modo significativo

point·ed·ly [ˈpɔɪntɪdlɪ] ADV (*look*) in modo significativo; (*say*) in un tono pieno di sottintesi

point·er [ˈpɔɪntəʳ] N **1** (*indicator*) lancetta; (*stick*) bacchetta **2** (*dog*) pointer *m inv* **3** (*clue*) indizio; (*advice*) consiglio; **to give sb some pointers on ...** consigliare qn su...; **a useful pointer** un consiglio utile; **a pointer to the likely outcome** un indizio del probabile risultato; **this is a pointer to the guilty man** questo è un indizio che ci aiuta ad identificare il colpevole

point·ing [ˈpɔɪntɪŋ] N (*Constr*) fissaggio (con la malta)

point·less [ˈpɔɪntlɪs] ADJ (*suffering, existence, journey*) inutile, vano(-a); (*crime*) senza senso, gratuito(-a);

Pp

(*remark*) superfluo(-a); (*story, joke*) senza capo né coda; **it is pointless to refuse** è inutile rifiutarsi

point·less·ly ['pɔɪntlɪslɪ] ADV (*suffer, live, remark*) inutilmente, senza scopo; (*destroy, kill*) inutilmente, senza motivo

point·less·ness ['pɔɪntlɪsnɪs] N (*gen*) inutilità, futilità; (*of crime*) gratuità

point of no return N: **to reach the point of no return** (*also fig*) arrivare a un punto da cui non è più possibile tornare indietro

point of order N (*in debate*) mozione *f* d'ordine

point of presence N (*Comput*) numero telefonico del provider

point of reference N punto di riferimento

point of sale N (*Comm*) punto di vendita

◎ **point of view** N punto di vista

points·man ['pɔɪnts,mæn] N (*pl* **-men**) (*Rail*) scambista *m*

point-to-point [,pɔɪnttə'pɔɪnt] N *steeplechase per dilettanti*

poise [pɔɪz] N (*carriage of head, body*) portamento; (*balance*) equilibrio; (*composure, dignity of manner*) padronanza di sé; (*calmness*) calma
■ VT (*balance*) mettere in equilibrio; (*hold balanced*) tenere in equilibrio

poised [pɔɪzd] ADJ **1** (*suspended*) sospeso(-a); **her pen was poised over the paper** teneva la penna sospesa sul foglio; **he sat at the keyboard, fingers poised** era seduto alla tastiera con le dita pronte; **poised on the brink of success/disaster** sull'orlo del successo/della rovina **2** (*ready*): **to be poised for sth/to do sth** essere pronto(-a) per/a fare qc; **they are poised to attack** *or* **for the attack** sono *or* si tengono pronti ad attaccare **3** (*self-possessed*) posato(-a)

poi·son ['pɔɪzn] N (*also fig*) veleno; **they hate each other like poison** si odiano a morte; **what's your poison?** (*fam*) cosa bevi?
■ VT **1** (*person, food*) avvelenare; (*air, atmosphere*) inquinare, avvelenare **2** (*fig*): **to poison sb's mind** corrompere qn; **to poison sb's mind against sb/sth** sobillare qn contro qn/qc

poi·son·er ['pɔɪznəʳ] N avvelenatore(-trice)

poison gas N gas *m inv* tossico

poi·son·ing ['pɔɪznɪŋ] N (*also fig*) avvelenamento; **arsenic poisoning** avvelenamento da arsenico; **food poisoning** intossicazione *f* alimentare; **to die of poisoning** morire avvelenato(-a)

poison ivy N edera velenosa

poi·son·ous ['pɔɪznəs] ADJ **1** (*snake, plant*) velenoso(-a); (*fumes*) venefico(-a), tossico(-a) **2** (*fig: tongue*) velenoso(-a); (*: propaganda*) venefico(-a); (*: ideas, literature*) pernicioso(-a); (*: rumours, individual*) perfido(-a); (*: fam: coffee etc*) schifoso(-a)

poison-pen letter [,pɔɪzən'pɛn,lɛtəʳ] N lettera (anonima) diffamatoria

poke [pəʊk] N (*jab*) colpetto; (*with elbow*) gomitata; **to give the fire a poke** attizzare il fuoco
■ VT **1** (*jab with stick, finger etc*) dare un colpetto a; **to poke sb with one's umbrella** dare un colpetto con l'ombrello a qn; **you poked me in the eye** mi hai messo *or* ficcato un dito nell'occhio; **to poke the fire** attizzare il fuoco **2** **to poke fun at sb** (*mock*) prendere in giro qn **3** (*Am fam: punch*) dare un pugno a **4** (*thrust*) cacciare, ficcare; **to poke one's head out of the window** mettere la testa fuori dalla finestra; **to poke sth in(to) sth** spingere qc dentro qc **5** (*make by poking*): **to poke a hole in sth** fare un buco in qc (*con il dito, un bastone etc*)
■ VI: **to poke at** dare dei colpetti a
▶ **poke about, poke around** VI + ADV (*fam: in drawers, attic*) frugare, rovistare; (*: in shop*) curiosare
▶ **poke out** VI + ADV spuntar fuori, sporger fuori
■ VT + ADV: **to poke sb's eye out** cavare un occhio a qn

pok·er¹ ['pəʊkəʳ] N (*for fire*) attizzatoio

pok·er² ['pəʊkəʳ] N (*Cards*) poker *m inv*; **I play poker** gioco a poker

poker-faced ['pəʊkə,feɪst] ADJ dal viso impassibile

poky, pok·ey ['pəʊkɪ] ADJ (*comp* **-ier**, *superl* **-iest**) (*pej*) angusto(-a)

Po·land ['pəʊlənd] N Polonia

po·lar ['pəʊləʳ] ADJ (*Elec, Geog*) polare

polar bear N orso(-a) bianco(-a)

po·lar·ity [pəʊ'lærɪtɪ] N polarità *f inv*

po·lari·za·tion [,pəʊləraɪ'zeɪʃən] N polarizzazione *f*

polarize ['pəʊlə,raɪz] (*also fig*) VT polarizzare
■ VI polarizzarsi

Po·lar·oid® ['pəʊlə,rɔɪd] N **1** (*also:* **Polaroid photograph**) foto *f inv* polaroid®; (*also:* **Polaroid camera**) (macchina fotografica) polaroid® *f inv* **2**: **Polaroids** NPL (*also:* **Polaroid sunglasses**) occhiali *mpl* polaroid® *inv* **3** (*material*) polaroid® *m inv*

Pole [pəʊl] N polacco(-a)

◎ **pole¹** [pəʊl] N (*gen*) palo; (*flagpole, for vaulting*) asta; (*of tent, fence*) paletto; (*for punting*) pertica; (*curtain pole*) bastone *m*; **telegraph pole** palo del telegrafo; **tent pole** paletto per la tenda; **ski pole** racchetta da sci; **up the pole** (*fig fam: mad*) fuori di testa; **to send** *or* **drive sb up the pole** (*infuriate*) far uscire dai gangheri qn

pole² [pəʊl] N (*Elec, Geog, Astron*) polo; **the earth's poles** i poli terrestri; **the North Pole** il polo nord; **the South Pole** il polo sud; **poles apart** (*fig*) agli antipodi

pole·axe, (*Am*) **pole·ax** ['pəʊl,æks] VT (*person*) atterrare, stendere

pole·cat ['pəʊl,kæt] N (*Brit*) puzzola; (*Am*) moffetta

po·lem·ic [pə'lɛmɪk] N polemica

po·lemi·cal [pə'lɛmɪkəl] ADJ polemico(-a)

Pole Star N stella polare

pole vault N salto con l'asta

◎ **po·lice** [pə'liːs] NPL (*organization*) polizia *fsg*; (*policemen*) poliziotti *mpl*; **the railway/river police** la polizia ferroviaria/fluviale; **we called the police** abbiamo chiamato la polizia; **a large number of police were hurt** molti poliziotti sono rimasti feriti; **the police have caught him** è stato preso dalla polizia; **extra police were brought in** sono state fatte intervenire forze di polizia supplementari; **to join the police** arruolarsi nella polizia
■ VT (*streets, city, frontier*) presidiare; (*fig: agreements, prices*) controllare; **to police a football match** presidiare lo stadio durante un incontro di calcio
■ ADJ (*escort, protection*) di agenti di polizia

police car N macchina della polizia

police constable N (*Brit*) agente *m* di polizia

police department N (*Am*) dipartimento di polizia

police dog N cane *m* poliziotto *inv*

police force N corpo di polizia, polizia

police inspector N ispettore *m* di polizia

◎ **police·man** [pə'liːsmən] N (*pl* **-men**) poliziotto, agente *m* di polizia

◎ **police officer** N (*man*) agente *m* di polizia; (*woman*) donna *f* poliziotto *inv*

police record N: **to have a police record** avere precedenti penali

police state N stato di polizia
police station N ≈ commissariato di Pubblica Sicurezza
police superintendent N ≈ commissario di Pubblica Sicurezza
police·woman [pəˈliːsˌwʊmən] N (*pl* **-women**) donna *f* poliziotto *inv*
◎ **poli·cy**[1] [ˈpɒlɪsɪ] N (*gen*) politica; (*of newspaper, company*) linea di condotta, prassi *f inv*; **it is our policy to do that** fa parte della nostra prassi *or* politica fare questo; **to follow a policy of** seguire una politica di; **the government's policies** la politica del governo; **their economic policy** la loro politica economica; **foreign policy** politica estera; **it's a matter of policy** è una questione di principio; **it would be good/bad policy to do that** sarebbe una buona/cattiva politica fare questo
■ ADJ (*discussion, statement*) sulla linea di condotta
poli·cy[2] [ˈpɒlɪsɪ] N (*also:* **insurance policy**) polizza (d'assicurazione); **to take out a policy** fare *or* stipulare un'assicurazione; **the terms of the policy** le condizioni della polizza
policy holder N assicurato(-a)
policy-making [ˈpɒlɪsɪˌmeɪkɪŋ] N messa a punto di programmi
po·lio [ˈpəʊlɪəʊ] N polio *f*; **polio victim** vittima *m/f* della polio
po·lio·my·eli·tis [ˈpəʊlɪəʊˌmaɪəˈlaɪtɪs] N poliomielite *f*
Po·lish [ˈpəʊlɪʃ] ADJ polacco(-a)
■ N (*language*) polacco
pol·ish [ˈpɒlɪʃ] N **1** (*for shoes, car*) lucido; (*for furniture, floor*) cera; **shoe polish** lucido per scarpe **2** (*act*) lucidata; **to give sth a polish** dare una lucidata *or* lustrata a qc **3** (*shine*) lucido, lucentezza; **it has a very high polish** è molto lucido; **to put a polish on sth** far brillare qc **4** (*fig: of person*) raffinatezza; (*: of style, performance*) eleganza
■ VT (*wood, leather*) lucidare; (*stones, glass*) levigare; (*style*) perfezionare, raffinare
▸ **polish off** VT + ADV (*food, drink*) far fuori; (*work, correspondence*) sbrigare
▸ **polish up** VT + ADV (*skill, ability*) perfezionare; (*shoes, metal objects*) lucidare, lustrare

DID YOU KNOW ...?
polish is not translated by the Italian word ***pulizia***

pol·ished [ˈpɒlɪʃt] ADJ (*surface*) lucidato(-a); (*stone*) levigato(-a); (*fig: person, manner, performer*) raffinato(-a); (*: performance*) impeccabile; **a polished performance** un'esecuzione impeccabile
pol·ish·er [ˈpɒlɪʃəʳ] N (*machine*) levigatrice *f*; (*floor polisher*) lucidatrice *f*
po·lite [pəˈlaɪt] ADJ (*comp* **-r**, *superl* **-st**) educato(-a); **it's not polite to do that** non è educato *or* buona educazione fare questo; **to be polite to sb/about sth** essere cortese con qn/riguardo a qc; **in polite society** nella buona società
po·lite·ly [pəˈlaɪtlɪ] ADV educatamente, cortesemente
po·lite·ness [pəˈlaɪtnɪs] N educazione *f*, cortesia; **out of politeness** per educazione
poli·tic [ˈpɒlɪtɪk] ADJ (*frm*) prudente
◎ **po·liti·cal** [pəˈlɪtɪkəl] ADJ politico(-a); **I'm not at all political** non mi interesso di politica; **political analyst** politologo(-a)
▹ www.political-theory.org/
▹ www.politicalresources.net
political asylum N asilo politico
po·liti·cal·ly [pəˈlɪtɪkəlɪ] ADV politicamente
politically correct ADJ politicamente corretto(-a)

POLITICALLY CORRECT

Si dicono **politically correct** (o **PC**) persone, termini e attività che sostituiscono espressioni considerate sessiste, razziste ecc. con altre più accettabili e non offensive. L'appellativo **politically correct** viene usato quasi come un insulto da coloro che invece ridicolizzano questo tipo di atteggiamento. Alcuni esempi di termini **politically correct** sono: "Native American" invece di "Red Indian" e "visually impaired" invece di "blind".

political science N scienze *fpl* politiche
◎ **poli·ti·cian** [ˌpɒlɪˈtɪʃən] N politico
po·liti·cize [pəˈlɪtɪˌsaɪz] VT politicizzare
poli·tick·ing [ˈpɒlɪˌtɪkɪŋ] N (*pej*) *il fare politica per vantaggio personale*
◎ **poli·tics** [ˈpɒlɪtɪks] N (*sg: career*) politica; (*: subject*) scienze *fpl* politiche; (*pl: views, policies*) tendenze *fpl*, idee *fpl* politiche; **to talk politics** parlare di politica; **to go into politics** darsi alla politica; **I'm not interested in politics** non m'interesso di politica
pol·ka [ˈpɒlkə] N (*dance*) polca
polka dot N pois *m inv*
◎ **poll** [pəʊl] N **1** (*voting*) votazione *f*, votazioni *fpl*; (*election*) elezioni *fpl*; **to take a poll (on sth)** mettere (qc) ai voti; **they got 65% of the poll** hanno ottenuto il 65% dei voti; **to go to the polls** (*voters*) andare alle urne; (*government*) indire le elezioni; **a defeat at the polls** una sconfitta alle elezioni **2** (*also:* **opinion poll**) sondaggio (d'opinione); **to conduct a poll** fare un sondaggio; **a recent poll revealed that ...** un recente sondaggio ha rivelato che...
■ VT **1** (*votes*) ottenere **2** (*in opinion poll*) interrogare nel corso di un sondaggio
pol·len [ˈpɒlən] N polline *m*
pollen count N *indice ufficiale della quantità di polline nell'aria*
pol·li·nate [ˈpɒlɪˌneɪt] VT impollinare
pol·li·na·tion [ˌpɒlɪˈneɪʃən] N impollinazione *f*
pol·ling [ˈpəʊlɪŋ] N **1** (*Brit Pol*) votazioni *fpl*; **polling has been heavy** c'è stata un'alta percentuale di votanti **2** (*Comput*) interrogazione *f* ciclica, polling *m*
polling booth N (*Brit*) cabina elettorale
polling day N (*Brit*) giorno delle elezioni
polling station N (*Brit*) seggio *or* sezione *f* elettorale
poll·ster [ˈpəʊlstəʳ] N chi esegue sondaggi d'opinione
poll tax N (*Brit fam*) *imposta locale sulla persona fisica (non più in vigore)*
pol·lu·tant [pəˈluːtənt] N sostanza inquinante
pol·lute [pəˈluːt] VT inquinare; (*fig*) inquinare, corrompere
◎ **pol·lu·tion** [pəˈluːʃən] N (*see vb*) inquinamento; corruzione *f*
Pollux [ˈpɒləks] N (*Myth, Astron*) Polluce *m*
polo [ˈpəʊləʊ] N (*sport*) polo
▹ www.fippolo.com/aboutpolo/index.asp
polo neck N (*collar*) collo alto; (*also:* **polo neck sweater**) dolcevita
■ ADJ a collo alto
pol·ter·geist [ˈpɒltəˌgaɪst] N poltergeist *m inv*
poly [ˈpɒlɪ] N ABBR (*Brit*) = **polytechnic**
poly... [ˈpɒlɪ] PREF poli...
poly·am·ide [ˌpɒlɪˈæmaɪd] N poliammide *f*

Pp

poly·an·dry ['pɒlɪændrɪ] N poliandria
poly·an·thus [,pɒlɪ'ænθəs] N *specie di primula*
poly·chro·mat·ic [,pɒlɪkrəʊ'mætɪk] ADJ policromatico(-a)
poly·chro·my ['pɒlɪ,krəʊmɪ] N policromia
poly·es·ter [,pɒlɪ'ɛstə^r] N poliestere *m*
poly·eth·yl·ene [,pɒlɪ'ɛθɪ,li:n] N = **polythene**
po·lyga·my [pɒ'lɪgəmɪ] N poligamia
poly·glot ['pɒlɪ,glɒt] ADJ, N poliglotta *(m/f)*
poly·gon ['pɒlɪgən] N poligono
po·lygo·nal [pɒ'lɪgənl] ADJ poligonale
poly·graph ['pɒlɪ,grɑ:f] N macchina della verità
poly·he·dral [,pɒlɪ'hi:drəl] ADJ poliedrico(-a)
poly·he·dron [,pɒlɪ'hi:drən] N poliedro
poly·mer ['pɒlɪmə^r] N polimero
po·lym·eri·za·tion [pə,lɪmərаɪ'zeɪʃən] N polimerizzazione *f*
Poly·nesia [,pɒlɪ'ni:zɪə] N Polinesia
Poly·nesian [,pɒlɪ'ni:ʒən] ADJ, N polinesiano(-a)
poly·no·mial [,pɒlɪ'nəʊmɪəl] N polinomio
pol·yp ['pɒlɪp] N *(Zool, Med)* polipo
poly·pep·tide [,pɒlɪ'pɛptaɪd] N polipeptide *m*
Polyphemus [,pɒlɪ'fi:məs] N Polifemo
poly·phon·ic [,pɒlɪ'fɒnɪk] ADJ *(Mus)* polifonico(-a)
po·lypho·ny [pə'lɪfənɪ] N *(Mus)* polifonia
poly·pro·pyl·ene [,pɒlɪ'prəʊpɪ,li:n] N polipropilene *m*
poly·semous [,pɒlɪ'si:məs] ADJ polisemico(-a)
poly·sty·rene [,pɒlɪ'staɪri:n] N polistirolo; **polystyrene chips** palline *fpl* di polistirolo
poly·syl·lab·ic [,pɒlɪsɪ'læbɪk] ADJ polisillabo(-a)
poly·syl·la·ble ['pɒlɪ,sɪləbl] N polisillabo
poly·tech·nic [,pɒlɪ'tɛknɪk] N *(Brit) istituto superiore ora inglobato nella struttura universitaria*
poly·theism ['pɒlɪθi:,ɪzəm] N politeismo
poly·theis·tic [,pɒlɪθi:'ɪstɪk] ADJ politeistico(-a)
poly·thene ['pɒlɪ,θi:n] N *(Brit)* polietilene *m*, politene *m*
polythene bag N sacchetto di plastica
poly·to·nal [,pɒlɪ'təʊnəl] ADJ *(Mus)* politonale
poly·un·satu·rat·ed [,pɒlɪʌn'sætʃə,reɪtɪd] ADJ *(Chem, Culin)* polinsaturo(-a)
poly·urethane [,pɒlɪ'jʊərɪ,θeɪn] N poliuretano
pom·egran·ate ['pɒmɪ,grænɪt] N *(tree)* melograno; *(fruit)* melagrana
pom·mel ['pʌml] N pomo
■ VT = **pummel**
pom·my ['pɒmɪ] ADJ, N *termine leggermente spregiativo usato dagli australiani per definire gli inglesi*
pomp [pɒmp] N pompa, fasto; **pomp and circumstance** grande *or* magnifico apparato
Pompey ['pɒmpɪ] N: **Pompey the Great** Pompeo Magno
pom·pon ['pɒmpɒn], **pom·pom** ['pɒmpɒm] N *(on hat)* pompon *m inv*
pom·pos·ity [pɒm'pɒsɪtɪ] N pomposità
pomp·ous ['pɒmpəs] ADJ *(pej: speech, attitude)* pomposo(-a); *(: person)* pieno(-a) di boria
pomp·ous·ly ['pɒmpəslɪ] ADV pomposamente
ponce [pɒns] *(fam)* VI *(pimp)* fare il magnaccia
■ N **1** *(pimp)* magnaccia *m inv* **2** *(Brit pej: effeminate man)* damerino
pon·cho ['pɒntʃəʊ] N poncho *m inv*
pond [pɒnd] N stagno; *(in park)* laghetto **the pond** *(ocean)* l'Atlantico
pon·der ['pɒndə^r] VT ponderare, riflettere su
■ VI: **to ponder (on** *or* **upon)** riflettere (su), meditare (su); **they're pondering how to improve profits** stanno riflettendo su come aumentare i profitti
pon·der·ous ['pɒndərəs] ADJ pesante, ponderoso(-a)
pon·der·ous·ly ['pɒndərəslɪ] ADV pesantemente, ponderosamente
pong [pɒŋ] *(Brit fam)* N puzzo
■ VI puzzare
pon·tiff ['pɒntɪf] N pontefice *m*
pon·tifi·cal [pɒn'tɪfɪkəl] ADJ pontificio(-a); *(pej: speech, gesture, manner)* pontificante
pon·tifi·cate [pɒn'tɪfɪ,keɪt] VI: **to pontificate about** *or* **on** pontificare su
pon·toon¹ [pɒn'tu:n] N pontone *m*
pon·toon² [pɒn'tu:n] N *(Cards)* ventuno
pony ['pəʊnɪ] N pony *m inv*
pony·tail ['pəʊnɪ,teɪl] N *(hairstyle)* coda di cavallo; **she's got a ponytail** ha la coda di cavallo
pony trekking [-'trekɪŋ] N: **to go pony trekking** fare un'escursione a cavallo
poo·dle ['pu:dl] N barboncino
poof [pʊf] N *(Brit offensive)* finocchio
pooh [pu:] EXCL puah!
pooh-pooh ['pu:'pu:] VT *(fam)* farsi beffe di
◎ **pool¹** [pu:l] N *(of water, rain, blood)* pozza; *(of light)* cerchio; *(pond)* stagno: *artificial, vasca; (swimming pool)* piscina; *(in river)* tonfano
pool² [pu:l] N **1** *(common fund)* cassa comune; *(at poker)* piatto **2** *(supply, source: of money, goods, workers)* riserva; *(: of experience, ideas)* fonte *f*; *(: of experts)* équipe *f inv*; *(of cars)* parco **3** *(game)* biliardo; **let's play pool** giochiamo a biliardo **4** *(Comm: consortium)* pool *m inv*; *(Am: monopoly trust)* trust *m inv*
■ VT *(money, resources)* mettere insieme, mettere in un fondo comune; *(efforts, knowledge)* mettere insieme
pool·room ['pu:l,rʊm] N sala da biliardo
pools [pu:lz] NPL: **to do the (football) pools** ≈ giocare la schedina, ≈ giocare al totocalcio
◎ **poor** [pʊə^r] ADJ *(comp* **-er**, *superl* **-est**) *(gen)* povero(-a); *(crop, light, visibility)* scarso(-a); *(effort, excuse)* misero(-a); *(memory, health, quality)* cattivo(-a); *(mark)* mediocre; **a poor family** una famiglia povera; **he's a poor loser** non sa perdere; **I'm a poor traveller** sopporto male i viaggi; **it has a poor chance of success** ha scarse possibilità di successo; **it's a poor thing when ...** è deplorevole che... + *sub*; **to be poor at maths** essere debole in matematica; **as poor as a church mouse** povero(-a) in canna; **you poor thing!** poverino!; **poor David, he's very unlucky!** povero David, è proprio sfortunato!; **you poor fool!** povero scemo!
■ NPL: **the poor** i poveri
poor box N cassetta per i poveri
poor·ly ['pʊəlɪ] ADV *(badly)* male; **a poorly paid job** un lavoro mal retribuito; **a poorly furnished room** una stanza arredata squallidamente; **to be poorly off** non avere molti soldi
■ ADJ *(ill)* indisposto(-a); **to be poorly** sentirsi poco bene; **I'm a bit poorly today** oggi mi sento poco bene
poor·ness ['pʊənɪs] N *(lack of wealth)* povertà; *(of crop, light)* scarsità; *(of effort, excuse, accommodation)* insufficienza, inadeguatezza; *(of health)* debolezza
poor relation N parente *m/f* povero(-a)
POP [,pi:əʊ'pi:] N ABBR *(Comput)* = **point of presence**
◎ **pop¹** [pɒp] N **1** *(sound)* schiocco; **to go pop** schioccare **2** *(fam: drink)* bevanda gasata
■ VT **1** *(balloon)* far scoppiare; *(cork)* far saltare **2** *(fam: put)* mettere; **I'll just pop my coat on** m'infilo il cappotto; **she popped her head out** *(of the window)* sporse fuori la testa; *(from under the blankets)* fece capolino; **he popped a sweet into his mouth** si è

messo una caramella in bocca; **to pop the question** (*fig*) fare la proposta di matrimonio

■ VI **1** (*balloon*) scoppiare; (*cork, buttons*) saltare; (*ears*) sbloccarsi; (*corn*) scoppiettare **2** (*fam: go quickly*): **she's just popped upstairs** è andata di sopra un attimo; **I'll just pop to the toilet** farò un salto alla toilette; **let's pop round to Joe's** facciamo un salto da Joe

▸ **pop in** VI + ADV (*fam*) fare un salto, entrare un attimo

▸ **pop off** VI + ADV (*Brit fam*) **1** (*die*) tirar le cuoia **2** (*leave*) scappare

▸ **pop out** VI + ADV (*person*) fare un salto fuori; **to pop out to the shops** fare un salto ai negozi; **his eyes nearly popped out of his head** sgranò tanto d'occhi

▸ **pop up** VI + ADV (*fam*) apparire

pop³ [pɒp] N (*Am fam: dad*) papà *m inv*

pop² [pɒp] ABBR *of* **popular**

■ N (*pop music*) musica pop; **it's top of the pops** è in testa alla hit parade

■ ADJ pop *inv*

▹ www.bbc.co.uk/radio2/soldonsong/genres/pop.shtml

▹ www.dotmusic.com

▹ www.nme.com

pop art N pop art *f inv*

pop concert N concerto *m* pop *inv*

pop·corn ['pɒp,kɔ:n] N popcorn *m inv*

pope [pəʊp] N: **the Pope** il Papa

pop·ery ['pəʊpərɪ] N (*pej*) papismo

pop-eyed ['pɒp,aɪd] ADJ con gli occhi sbarrati

pop group N gruppo *m* pop *inv*

pop·gun ['pɒp,gʌn] N fucile *m* (*or* pistola) giocattolo *inv* (*che spara tappi di sughero*)

pop·ish ['pəʊpɪʃ] ADJ (*pej*) papistico(-a)

pop·lar ['pɒplə^r] N pioppo; **black poplar** pioppo nero europeo

pop·lin ['pɒplɪn] N popeline *f*

pop·pa·dum, pop·pa·dom ['pɒpədəm] N *tipo di pane sottile e croccante, rotondo, tipico della cucina indiana*

pop·per ['pɒpə^r] N (*Brit*) (bottone *m*) automatico

pop·pet ['pɒpɪt] N (*fam*) tesoro, amore *m*

pop·py ['pɒpɪ] N papavero

poppy·cock ['pɒpɪ,kɒk] N (*fam*) scempiaggini *fpl*

Poppy Day N (*Brit*) *giorno della commemorazione dei caduti delle due guerre mondiali*

poppy seed N seme *m* di papavero

Pop·sicle® ['pɒpsɪkl] N (*Am*) ghiacciolo

popu·lace ['pɒpjʊlɪs] N popolo, popolino

◎ **popu·lar** ['pɒpjʊlə^r] ADJ **1** (*well-liked*): **to be popular (with)** (*person*) essere benvoluto(-a) *or* ben visto(-a) (da); (*decision*) essere gradito(-a) (a); (*product*) essere molto richiesto(-a) (da); **she's a very popular girl** è molto simpatica a tutti; **he's the most popular politician in France** è il personaggio politico più popolare in Francia; **a popular song** una canzone di successo; **a popular colour** un colore che va di moda; **this is a very popular style** questo stile è molto in voga **2** (*for the layman*) popolare; **the popular press** la stampa popolare **3** (*widespread: theory, fallacy*) comune; (: *support*) popolare; **by popular request** a richiesta generale

popu·lar·ity [,pɒpjʊ'lærɪtɪ] N popolarità

popu·lar·ize ['pɒpjʊlə,raɪz] VT **1** (*make well-liked: person*) rendere popolare; (*make fashionable: product, fashion*) diffondere **2** (*make accessible to laymen*) rendere accessibile ai più, divulgare; (*science*) volgarizzare

popu·lar·iz·er ['pɒpjʊlə,raɪzə^r] N divulgatore(-trice)

popu·lar·ly ['pɒpjʊləlɪ] ADV comunemente

popu·late ['pɒpjʊ,leɪt] VT popolare

◎ **popu·la·tion** [,pɒpjʊ'leɪʃən] N popolazione *f*

population explosion N boom *m inv* demografico

population growth N incremento demografico

population pyramid N piramide *f* d'età

popu·lism ['pɒpjʊlɪzm] N (*frm*) populismo

popu·list ['pɒpjʊlɪst] ADJ (*frm*) populistico(-a)

popu·lous ['pɒpjʊləs] ADJ popoloso(-a), densamente popolato(-a)

pop-up ['pɒpʌp] **1** ADJ: **pop-up book** libro per bambini con le figure a comparsa; **pop-up menu** (*Comput*) menu *m inv* a comparsa; **pop-up toaster** tostapane *m inv* a espulsione automatica

2 ■ N pubblicità a comparsa (sullo schermo)

porce·lain ['pɔ:səlɪn] N porcellana; **a piece of porcelain** una porcellana

▹ www.gotheborg.com

▹ www.worcesterporcelainmuseum.org.uk/collections/galleries

porch [pɔ:tʃ] N veranda; (*of church*) sagrato

por·cu·pine ['pɔ:kjʊ,paɪn] N porcospino

pore¹ [pɔ:^r] N (*Anat*) poro

pore² [pɔ:^r] VI: **to pore over** (*map, problem*) studiare attentamente; (*book*) essere immerso(-a) in

pork [pɔ:k] N (carne *f* di) maiale *m*; **I don't eat pork** non mangio carne di maiale; **a pork chop** una braciola di maiale

pork butcher N ≈ salumiere *m*

pork chop N braciola di maiale

pork pie N pasticcio di maiale in crosta

porn [pɔ:n], **porno** ['pɔ:nəʊ] (*fam*) N porno *m inv*; **hard/soft porn** pornografia hard-core/soft-core

■ ADJ (*film*) porno *inv*

porn merchant N commerciante *m/f* di pornografia

por·no·graph·ic [,pɔ:nə'græfɪk] ADJ pornografico(-a)

por·no·graphi·cal·ly [,pɔ:nə'græfɪkəlɪ] ADV pornograficamente

por·nog·ra·phy [pɔ:'nɒgrəfɪ] N pornografia

porn shop N sex shop *m inv*

porous ['pɔ:rəs] ADJ poroso(-a); (*fig: border*) permeabile, facilmente oltrepassabile

por·poise ['pɔ:pəs] N focena

por·ridge ['pɒrɪdʒ] N porridge *m*

porridge oats NPL fiocchi *mpl* d'avena

◎ **port¹** [pɔ:t] N (*harbour*) porto; (*town*) città *f inv* portuale; **naval/fishing port** porto militare/per pescherecci; **to come into port** entrare in porto; **any port in a storm** (*fig*) in tempo di tempesta ogni buco è porto

▹ www.iaphworldports.org/top.htm

▹ www.abports.co.uk/index.htm

port² [pɔ:t] N (*Naut, Aer: left side*) babordo; **to port** a babordo

■ ADJ (*cabin*) di sinistra; **on the port side** a babordo

port³ [pɔ:t] N (*wine*) porto

port⁴ [pɔ:t] N (*Naut: access to hold*) portello; (*Comput*) porta

port·able ['pɔ:təbl] ADJ portatile; **a portable TV** una TV portatile

Porta·kab·in® ['pɔ:tə,kæbɪn] N prefabbricato; (*for builders etc*) box *m inv* prefabbricato, baracca

por·tal ['pɔ:tl] N portale *m*

port authorities NPL capitaneria *fsg* di porto

port·cul·lis [pɔ:t'kʌlɪs] N saracinesca

por·tend [pɔ:'tɛnd] VT (*frm*) far presagire

por·tent ['pɔ:tɛnt] N presagio

Pp

por·ten·tous [pɔː'tɛntəs] ADJ *(frm: ominous)* funesto(-a); *(: grave)* solenne, grave; *(pompous)* pomposo(-a)
por·ter ['pɔːtə^r] N *(of office etc)* portinaio(-a), portiere(-a); *(of hotel)* portiere(-a); *(Rail, Aer)* facchino, portabagagli *m inv*; *(Am Rail)* addetto ai vagoni letto
por·ter·age ['pɔːtərɪdʒ] N facchinaggio
porter·house ['pɔːtəˌhaʊs] N *(also:* **porterhouse steak**) lombata
port·fo·lio [ˌpɔːt'fəʊlɪəʊ] N *(case)* cartella; *(Fin, Pol: office)* portafoglio; *(of artist, designer etc)* portfolio *m inv*; **at the interview she showed them her portfolio** al colloquio mostrò loro la raccolta dei suoi lavori; **portfolio of shares** portafoglio *m* titoli *inv*; **portfolio of investments** portafoglio di investimenti
port·hole ['pɔːtˌhəʊl] N oblò *m inv*
por·ti·co ['pɔːtɪkəʊ] N *(pl* **porticos** *or* **porticoes**) portico
por·tion ['pɔːʃən] N *(part, piece)* parte *f*; *(of food)* porzione *f*
▶ **portion out** VT + ADV distribuire
port·ly ['pɔːtlɪ] ADJ *(comp* **-ier**, *superl* **-iest**) corpulento(-a)
port·man·teau [ˌpɔːt'mæntəʊ] N baule *m* portabiti
portmanteau word N parola macedonia
port of call N (porto di) scalo
◎ **por·trait** ['pɔːtrɪt] N ritratto
portrait gallery N galleria di ritratti
portrait painter N ritrattista *m/f*
por·trai·ture ['pɔːtrɪtʃə^r] N *(Art)* ritrattistica
por·tray [pɔː'treɪ] VT *(painter, writer, novel)* ritrarre; *(painting)* raffigurare; *(actor)* interpretare; **journalists portray him as a despot** i giornalisti lo dipingono come un tiranno; **he portrayed the king in "Hamlet"** ha interpretato il re nell'"Amleto"
por·tray·al [pɔː'treɪəl] N *(see vb)* ritratto; rappresentazione *f*; interpretazione *f*
Por·tu·gal ['pɔːtjʊgəl] N Portogallo
Por·tu·guese [ˌpɔːtjʊ'giːz] ADJ portoghese
■ N *(person: pl inv)* portoghese *m/f*; *(language)* portoghese *m*; **the Portuguese** i portoghesi
Portuguese man-of-war [ˌpɔːtjʊ'giːzˌmænəv'wɔː^r] N *(jellyfish)* fisalia, caravella portoghese
◎ **pose** [pəʊz] N posa; **to strike a pose** mettersi in posa; **it's only a pose** *(fig)* è tutta una posa
■ VT **1** *(person)* mettere in posa **2** *(problem, difficulty)* porre, creare; *(question)* fare; **nobody dared pose the question** nessuno osò porre la domanda
■ VI *(for artist, also fig: attitudinize)* posare; **she posed for Dalí** ha posato per Dalí ; **to pose as** *(pretend to be)* atteggiarsi a, posare a; fingere di essere; **to pose as a policeman** farsi passare per un poliziotto
Poseidon [pɒ'saɪdən] N Poseidone *m*
pos·er ['pəʊzə^r] *(fam)* N *(problem)* domanda difficile; *(pej: person)* posatore(-trice)
po·seur [pəʊ'zɜː^r] N *(pej)* persona affettata
posh [pɒʃ] *(fam)* ADJ *(comp* **-er**, *superl* **-est**) *(people, neighbourhood, family)* per bene; *(car, hotel, clothes)* elegante
■ ADV: **to talk posh** *(pej)* parlare in modo snob
▶ **posh up** *(fam)* VT + ADV *(decorate, improve)* abbellire; *(clean up)* pulire; **to posh o.s. up** agghindarsi
pos·it ['pɒzɪt] VT *(frm)* postulare
◎ **po·si·tion** [pə'zɪʃən] N **1** *(gen)* posizione *f*; *(of furniture etc)* disposizione *f*; *(in class, league, job)* posizione, posto; **to be in/out of position** essere/non essere al proprio posto; **in an uncomfortable position** *(also fig)* in una posizione scomoda; **in a reclining position** *(of chair)* reclinato(-a); *(of person)* semisdraiato(-a); **what position do you play?** *(Sport)* in che posizione giochi?; **he's lying in second position** si trova al secondo posto *or* in seconda posizione; **to jockey** *or* **manoeuvre for position** *(also fig)* dare l'assalto ai posti **2** *(post)* posto, impiego; **to have a good position in a bank** avere un buon posto in banca; **a position of trust** un posto di fiducia **3** *(fig: situation, standing)* posizione *f*; **a man in his position** un uomo nella sua posizione; **to be in a position to do sth** essere nella posizione di fare qc; **he's in no position to criticize** non sta proprio a lui criticare; **put yourself in my position** si metta al mio posto; **I am in an awkward position** sono in una posizione difficile **4** *(fig: point of view, attitude)* posizione *f*; **to take up a position on sth** prendere posizione su qc; **what's your position on this?** qual è la tua posizione riguardo a questo?; **do I make my position clear?** sono stato sufficientemente chiaro?
■ VT *(place in position: chairs, lamp)* sistemare; *(: model)* mettere in posa; *(: soldiers)* disporre; **I positioned myself to get the best view** mi sono piazzato in modo da poter vedere bene
position paper N *rapporto dettagliato sulla situazione nel quale si raccomanda una certa linea d'azione*
◎ **posi·tive** ['pɒzɪtɪv] ADJ **1** *(gen, also Elec, Math, Phot)* positivo(-a); *(constructive: advice, help, criticism)* costruttivo(-a); **a positive attitude** un atteggiamento positivo; **we look forward to a positive reply** *(Comm)* in attesa di una risposta favorevole **2** *(definite: gen)* positivo(-a), preciso(-a); *(: improvement, increase)* deciso(-a); *(: proof)* inconfutabile; **I'm positive** ne sono sicuro; **are you sure? — yes, positive** sei sicuro? — sicurissimo; **to make a positive contribution to sth** dare un contributo effettivo a qc; **he's a positive nuisance** è un vero rompiscatole
positive discrimination N discriminazione a favore di minoranze
posi·tive·ly ['pɒzɪtɪvlɪ] ADV *(approach)* positivamente; *(decisively)* decisamente; *(effectively)* concretamente; *(fam: really, absolutely)* assolutamente; **to respond positively** rispondere positivamente; **to think positively** pensare in modo costruttivo; **this is positively the last time I'll do this** è decisamente l'ultima volta che lo faccio; **it looks positively frightening** fa decisamente paura; **she was positively delighted** era assolutamente entusiasta
posi·tiv·ism ['pɒzɪtɪvɪzm] N positivismo
pos·se ['pɒsɪ] N *(Am)* gruppo armato di volontari
pos·sess [pə'zɛs] VT possedere; **everything they possess** tutto ciò che possiedono; **like one possessed** come un ossesso; **to be possessed by an idea** essere ossessionato(-a) da un'idea; **whatever (can have) possessed you?** cosa ti ha preso?
pos·ses·sion [pə'zɛʃən] N **1** *(ownership)* possesso; **in possession of** in possesso di; **house with vacant possession** casa libera subito; **to have sth in one's possession** avere qc in proprio possesso; **to get possession of** entrare in possesso di; **to take possession of sth** impossessarsi *or* impadronirsi di qc; **to take possession of a house** prendere possesso di una casa; **to get/have possession of the ball** *(Sport)* impossessarsi/essere in possesso della palla **2** *(thing possessed)* bene *m*, avere *m*; **one's possessions** le sue cose; **have you got all your possessions?** hai tutte le tue cose?; **her most treasured possession** la cosa più cara che ha
pos·ses·sive [pə'zɛsɪv] ADJ *(gen, also Gram)* possessivo(-a); **an over-possessive wife** una moglie

troppo possessiva; **to be possessive about sth/ towards sb** essere possessivo(-a) nei confronti di qc/qn
■ N (*Gram*) possessivo
pos·ses·sive·ly [pəˈzɛsɪvlɪ] ADV in modo possessivo
pos·ses·sive·ness [pəˈzɛsɪvnɪs] N possessività
pos·ses·sor [pəˈzɛsəʳ] N possessore *m*, proprietario(-a); **to be the proud possessor of sth** essere orgoglioso(-a) di possedere qc
◎ **pos·sibil·ity** [ˌpɒsəˈbɪlɪtɪ] N possibilità *f inv*; **the possibility of a strike** la possibilità di uno sciopero; **it's a distinct possibility** è molto probabile; **there is no possibility of his agreeing to it** non c'è la minima possibilità *or* probabilità che accetti; **there is some possibility of success** c'è qualche probabilità di successo *or* riuscita; **he's a possibility for the part** è uno dei candidati per la parte; **to foresee all the possibilities** prevedere tutte le eventualità; **to have possibilities** (*person*) avere delle (buone) possibilità; **your idea has possibilities** la tua idea ha delle buone possibilità di successo; **this job has possibilities** questo lavoro offre molte possibilità
◎ **pos·sible** [ˈpɒsəbl] ADJ possibile; **it is possible that he'll come** può darsi che *or* è possibile che venga; **it is possible to do it** è possibile farlo, è fattibile; **it will be possible for you to leave early** potrai uscire prima; **as soon as possible** appena possibile, al più presto possibile; **as big as possible** il più grande possibile; **as far as possible** nei limiti del possibile; **if (at all) possible** se (appena è) possibile; **the best possible result** il miglior risultato possibile; **to make sth possible for sb** rendere qc possibile a qn; **what possible excuse can you have for your behaviour?** che giustificazione puoi trovare per il tuo comportamento?; **a possible candidate** un possibile candidato
■ N: **a list of possibles for the job** una lista dei possibili candidati al posto; **he's a possible for Saturday's match** è uno dei possibili giocatori per la partita di sabato
◎ **pos·sibly** [ˈpɒsəblɪ] ADV **1 he did all he possibly could** ha fatto tutto il possibile; **as often as I possibly can** quanto più spesso posso; **how can I possibly?** come posso?; **I cannot possibly do it** non posso assolutamente *or* proprio farlo; **I can't possibly come** non posso proprio venire; **could you possibly ...?** potresti...?; **if you possibly can** se le è possibile
2 (*perhaps*) forse; **are you coming to the party?** – **possibly** vieni alla festa? – forse

DID YOU KNOW ...?
possibly is not translated by the Italian word *possibilmente*

pos·sum [ˈpɒsəm] N (*fam*) = **opossum**
post... [pəʊst] PREF post...; **post-1980** dopo il 1980
post¹ [pəʊst] N (*pole*) palo; **the ball hit the post** la palla ha colpito il palo; **starting/finishing post** (*for race*) palo di partenza/arrivo; **to be left at the post** rimanere indietro alla partenza; **to be pipped at the post** essere battuto(-a) sul filo del traguardo; (*fig*) perdere per un pelo
■ VT **1** (*also:* **post up**: *notice, list*) affiggere
2 (*announce*) annunciare; **to post sb/sth (as) missing** (*Mil*) dare qn/qc per disperso(-a)
◎ **post²** [pəʊst] N (*Brit: mail*) posta; **by post** per posta; **by return of post** a giro di posta; **to catch/miss the post** arrivare/non arrivare in tempo per la levata; **it's in the post** è stato spedito; **to take sth to the post** andare a spedire qc; **has the post come yet?** è già arrivata la posta?; **is there any post for me?** c'è posta per me?; **it went first post this morning** è partito stamattina con la prima posta
■ VT **1** (*send*) spedire per posta, mandare per posta; (*Brit: put in mailbox*) impostare, imbucare; **I've got some cards to post** devo imbucare delle cartoline
2 (*inform*): **to keep sb posted** tenere qn al corrente
post³ [pəʊst] N **1** (*job*) posto; **to take up one's post** assumere la propria carica **2** (*Mil*) posto; **at one's post** al proprio posto
■ VT **1** (*position: sentry*) piazzare **2** (*Brit: send, assign*) inviare; (*: Mil*) assegnare
post·age [ˈpəʊstɪdʒ] N affrancatura; **"postage: 50p"** "spese di spedizione: 50 penny"; **postage due 40p** soprattassa (*per affrancatura insufficiente*) di 40 penny
postage stamp N francobollo
post·al [ˈpəʊstəl] ADJ (*service, charges*) postale; (*vote*) per posta; **postal worker** postelegrafonico(-a)
postal order N vaglia *m inv* postale
post·bag [ˈpəʊstˌbæg] N (*Brit*) sacco postale, sacco della posta
post·box [ˈpəʊstˌbɒks] (*Brit*) N (*in street*) buca delle lettere; (*in entrance hall*) cassetta per le lettere
post·card [ˈpəʊstˌkɑːd] N cartolina (postale)
post·code [ˈpəʊstˌkəʊd] N (*Brit*) codice *m* (di avviamento) postale
post·date [ˌpəʊstˈdeɪt] VT (*cheque*) postdatare
post·er [ˈpəʊstəʳ] N (*for advertising*) manifesto, affisso; (*for decoration*) poster *m inv*; **there are posters all over town** ci sono manifesti in tutta la città; **I've got posters on my bedrooms walls** ho dei poster sulle pareti di camera mia
poster child N, **poster boy/girl** N bambino(-a) testimonial *inv*; (*fig*) esempio tipico
poste res·tante [ˌpəʊstˈrɛstɑ̃nt] N (*Brit*) fermo posta *m*
pos·teri·or [pɒsˈtɪərɪəʳ] N (*hum*) deretano, didietro
■ ADJ (*Tech*) posteriore
pos·ter·ity [pɒsˈtɛrɪtɪ] N posterità
poster paint N tempera
post·femi·nist [ˌpəʊstˈfɛmɪnɪst] ADJ, N post-femminista *m/f*
post-free [ˌpəʊstˈfriː] ADJ, ADV franco di porto
post·gradu·ate [ˈpəʊstˈgrædjʊɪt] ADJ (*studies, course*) successivo(-a) alla laurea; **a postgraduate course** un corso post-laurea
■ N *laureato che continua gli studi*
post·haste [ˌpəʊstˈheɪst] ADV in gran fretta
post·hu·mous [ˈpɒstjʊməs] ADJ postumo(-a)
post·hu·mous·ly [ˈpɒstjʊməslɪ] ADV dopo la sua (loro *etc*) morte
postie [ˈpəʊstɪ] N (*Brit fam*) postino(-a)
post·im·pres·sion·ism [ˈpəʊstɪmˈprɛʃəˌnɪzəm] N postimpressionismo
post·in·dus·trial [ˌpəʊstɪnˈdʌstrɪəl] ADJ postindustriale
post·ing [ˈpəʊstɪŋ] N (*Brit*) incarico; (*Comput*) messaggio lanciato in Internet
Post-it (Note)® [ˈpəʊstɪt] N Post-it® *m inv*
post·man [ˈpəʊstmən] N (*pl* **-men**) (*Brit*) postino; **he's a postman** fa il postino
post·mark [ˈpəʊstˌmɑːk] N bollo *or* timbro postale
■ VT timbrare; **it was postmarked Rome** il timbro postale era di Roma
post·master [ˈpəʊstˌmɑːstəʳ] N direttore *m* di un ufficio postale
postmaster general N ≈ ministro delle Poste

Pp

post·mistress ['pəʊst,mɪstrɪs] N direttrice *f* di un ufficio postale
post·mor·tem [,pəʊst'mɔ:təm] N (*also:* **postmortem examination**) autopsia; (*fig*) analisi *f inv* a posteriori
post·na·tal [,pəʊst'neɪtl] ADJ post-parto *inv*
postnatal depression N (*Med*) depressione *f* postparto
Post Office N (*institution*): **the Post Office** ≈ le Poste e Telecomunicazioni
post office N (*place*) ufficio postale, posta
post office box N casella postale
post office worker N impiegato(-a) delle poste
post-paid ['pəʊst'peɪd] ADJ già affrancato(-a)
post·pone [,pəʊst'pəʊn] VT: **to postpone sth for a month/until Monday** rimandare *or* rinviare *or* posticipare qc di un mese/a lunedì ; **the match has been postponed until next Saturday** la partita è stata rinviata a sabato prossimo
post·pone·ment [,pəʊst'pəʊnmənt] N rinvio
post·script ['pəʊs,skrɪpt] N poscritto
post-traumatic stress disorder [,pəʊsttrɔ:,mætɪk'strɛsdɪs,ɔ:dəʳ] N (*Med*) nevrosi *f* posttraumatica
pos·tu·late ['pɒstjʊ,leɪt] VT (*frm*) postulare
pos·ture ['pɒstʃəʳ] N posizione *f*; (*carriage*) portamento; (*pose*) posa, atteggiamento; **bad posture** postura scorretta
■VI (*pej*) mettersi in posa, posare
post-viral fatigue syndrome [,pəʊst,vaɪərəlfə'ti:g,sɪndrəʊm] N (*Med*) sindrome *f* da affaticamento postvirale
post·war ['pəʊst'wɔ:ʳ] ADJ del dopoguerra; **the postwar period** il periodo postbellico *or* del dopoguerra
post·woman ['pəʊst,wʊmən] N (*Brit*) postina
posy ['pəʊzɪ] N mazzolino (di fiori)
◎**pot** [pɒt] N **1** (*for cooking*) pentola, casseruola; (*teapot*) teiera; (*coffeepot*) caffettiera; (*for jam*) vasetto, barattolo; (*piece of pottery*) ceramica; (*for plants*) vaso; **pots and pans** pentole; **to go to pot** (*fam: plans, business*) andare in malora; (*: person*) lasciarsi andare **2** (*potful*): **a pot of jam** un vasetto di marmellata; **a pot of soup** una pentola di zuppa; **a pot of tea for two, please** tè per due, per piacere **3** **pots of** (*fam*) un sacco di; **to have pots of money** avere quattrini a palate **4** (*fam: marijuana*) erba; **to smoke pot** fumare erba
■VT **1** (*plant*) mettere in un vaso, invasare; (*jam*) mettere nei vasetti **2** (*shoot: pheasant, rabbit*) ammazzare **3** (*Billiards*) mandare in buca *or* biglia
pot·ash ['pɒt,æʃ] N potassa
po·tas·sium [pə'tæsɪəm] N potassio
po·tas·sium per·man·ga·nate N permanganato di potassio
◎**po·ta·to** [pə'teɪtəʊ] N (*pl* **potatoes**) patata; **baked potato** patata cotta al forno con la buccia; **mashed potatoes** purè *m inv* di patate
potato crisps, potato chips NPL patatine *fpl*
potato flour N fecola di patate
potato peeler N (*knife*) pelapatate *m inv*; (*machine*) pelapatate *m inv*
pot·bel·lied ['pɒt,bɛlɪd] ADJ (*from overeating*) panciuto(-a); (*from malnutrition*) dal ventre gonfio
pot·belly ['pɒt,bɛlɪ] N: **to have a potbelly** (*from overeating*) avere la pancia; (*from malnutrition*) avere il ventre gonfio
pot·boiler ['pɒt,bɔɪləʳ] N (*pej: novel, musical*) opera commerciale
pot·bound ['pɒt,baʊnd] ADJ: **this plant is potbound** il vaso è ormai troppo piccolo per questa pianta
po·ten·cy ['pəʊtənsɪ] N (*see adj*) potenza; validità; (*of drink*) forza
po·tent ['pəʊtənt] ADJ (*gen*) potente, forte; (*fig: argument, reason*) validissimo(-a)
po·ten·tate ['pəʊtən,teɪt] N potentato
◎**po·ten·tial** [pəʊ'tɛnʃəl] ADJ potenziale; **a potential problem** un potenziale problema
■N **1** (*possibilities*) potenziale *m*; **to realize one's full potential** realizzarsi pienamente; **sales potential** potenziale di vendita; **to show potential** promettere bene; **to have potential** essere promettente **2** (*Elec, Math, Phys*) potenziale *m*
potential difference N (*Math, Phys*) differenza di potenziale
po·ten·tial·ly [pəʊ'tɛnʃəlɪ] ADV potenzialmente
po·ten·til·la [,pəʊtən'tɪlə] N potentilla, cinquefoglie *m inv*
po·ten·ti·om·eter [pə,tɛnʃɪ'ɒmɪtəʳ] N (*Elec*) potenziometro
pot·ful ['pɒtfʊl] N pentola (piena)
pot·herb ['pɒt,hɜ:b] N erba aromatica
pot holder N (*Culin*) presina
pot·hole ['pɒt,həʊl] N (*in road*) buca; (*Brit Geol*) marmitta
pot·holer ['pɒt,həʊləʳ] N (*Brit*) speleologo(-a)
pot·hol·ing ['pɒt,həʊlɪŋ] N (*Brit*) esplorazione *f* speleologica; **to go potholing** fare della speleologia
po·tion ['pəʊʃən] N pozione *f*, filtro
pot·luck [,pɒt'lʌk] N: **to take potluck** (*for food*) mangiare quel che passa il convento; (*for other things*) tentare la sorte
pot plant N pianta in vaso
pot·pour·ri [,pəʊ'pʊri:] N **1** (*flowers*) *miscuglio di petali essiccati per profumare un ambiente* **2** (*fig: of music, writing*) pot-pourri *m inv*
pot roast N (*Culin*) brasato
pot scourer N spugnetta abrasiva
pot·sherd ['pɒt,ʃɜ:d] N (*Archeol*) frammento di vaso
pot shot N: **to take a potshot at sth** sparare a casaccio contro qc
pot·ted ['pɒtɪd] ADJ **1** (*fish, meat*) conservato(-a) in vaso; (*plant*) in vaso **2** (*fig: shortened*) condensato(-a)
pot·ter[1] ['pɒtəʳ] N ceramista *m/f*
pot·ter[2] ['pɒtəʳ] VI, (*Am*) **put·ter** ['pʌtəʳ] VI: **to potter round the shops** fare un tranquillo giretto per i negozi; **to potter round the house** sbrigare con calma le faccende di casa; **he likes pottering about in the garden** gli piace fare qualche lavoretto in giardino
potter's wheel N tornio (da vasaio)
pot·tery ['pɒtərɪ] N (*workshop*) fabbrica *or* laboratorio di ceramiche; (*craft*) ceramica; (*pots*) ceramiche *fpl*; **a piece of pottery** una ceramica
■ADJ (*dish, jug*) di ceramica; **pottery classes** un corso di ceramica
▷ www.ceramicstoday.com
▷ www.studiopottery.com
▷ www.potterymaking.org/pmionline.html
pot·ty[1] ['pɒtɪ] N (*fam*) vasino
pot·ty[2] ['pɒtɪ] ADJ (*comp* **-ier**, *superl* **-iest**) (*Brit fam: mad*) matto(-a), tocco(-a); (*: idea*) balordo(-a); **you're driving me potty!** mi fai diventare matto!
potty-trained ['pɒtɪ,treɪnd] ADJ che ha imparato a farla nel vasino
pouch [paʊtʃ] N (*Anat, for tobacco*) borsa; (*for money*) borsellino; (*Zool*) marsupio; **my money was in a pouch**

i miei soldi erano in un borsellino; **in their mother's pouch** nel marsupio della madre
pouf, pouffe [pu:f] N **1** (*seat*) pouf *m inv* **2** (*Brit offensive*) = **poof**
poul·ter·er ['pəʊltərə^r] N (*Brit*) pollivendolo(-a)
poul·tice ['pəʊltɪs] N impiastro, cataplasma *m*
poul·try ['pəʊltrɪ] N pollame *m*
poultry farm N azienda avicola
poultry farmer N pollicoltore(-trice)
poultry farming N avicoltura
pounce [paʊns] N balzo
■ VI (*cat, tiger*) balzare (sulla preda); (*bird*) piombare (sulla preda); **to pounce on sb/sth** (*animal*) balzare su qn/qc; (*bird*) piombare su qn/qc; (*person*) piombare *or* balzare su qn/qc; **she pounced on my offer of help** ha colto al volo la mia offerta di aiuto; **he pounced on my suggestion that ...** (*attack*) è saltato su quando ho proposto che...
◎ **pound¹** [paʊnd] N **1** (*weight = 453g, 16 ounces*) libbra; **sold by the pound** venduto(-a) alla libbra; **half a pound** mezza libbra; **a pound of carrots** mezzo chilo di carote **2** (*money = 100 pence*) (lira) sterlina; **twenty pounds** venti sterline; **one pound sterling** una sterlina; **a pound coin** una moneta da una sterlina; **a ten-pound note** una banconota da dieci sterline
pound² [paʊnd] VT (*hammer, strike: door, table, person*) picchiare; (*: piano*) pestare i tasti di; (*: typewriter*) battere sui tasti di; (*subj: sea, waves*) sbattere contro; (*: guns, bombs*) martellare; (*pulverize: drug, spices, nuts*) pestare, polverizzare; (*knead: dough*) lavorare; **to pound sth to pieces** fare a pezzi qc; **to pound sth to a pulp** ridurre qc in poltiglia
■ VI **1** (*heart*) battere forte; (*drums*) rullare; (*sea*) sbattere; (*person*): **to pound at** *or* **on** dare dei gran colpi a *or* su; (*piano*) pestare i tasti di; **to pound on the door** battere alla porta; **my heart was pounding** mi batteva forte il cuore **2** (*run, walk heavily*): **to pound in/out** entrare/uscire a passi pesanti
pound³ [paʊnd] N (*enclosure: for dogs*) canile *m*: *for cars* municipale, deposito *m* auto *inv* (*per auto sottoposte a rimozione forzata*)
pound·ing ['paʊndɪŋ] N: **to take a pounding** (*team*) prendere una batosta; (*ship*) essere sbattuto(-a) violentemente dalle onde; (*town: in war*) venire duramente colpito(-a)
pound sterling N lira sterlina
◎ **pour** [pɔ:^r] VT versare; **to pour sth off** buttar via qc, versar fuori qc; **let me pour you a drink** lascia che ti versi da bere; **shall I pour you a cup of tea?** ti verso del tè?; **she poured some water into the pan** ha versato dell'acqua nella pentola; **to pour money into a project** investire molti soldi in un progetto
■ VI **1** **to come pouring in** (*water*) entrare a fiotti; (*letters*) arrivare a valanghe; (*cars, people*) affluire in gran quantità; **the sweat is pouring off you!** sei grondante di sudore! **2** **it's pouring (with rain)** sta piovendo a dirotto; sta diluviando
▸ **pour away** VT + ADV buttar via
▸ **pour in** VI + ADV (*people*) entrare a frotte; **tourists are pouring in** i turisti stanno arrivando in massa; **the sunshine poured into the room** la luce del sole inondava la stanza
▸ **pour out** VT + ADV (*drink*) versare; (*dirty water*) buttar via; (*fig: feelings*) sfogare; (*: troubles*) sfogarsi parlando di; (*: story*) raccontare tutto d'un fiato; **she poured out her complaints** si lanciò in una serie di lamentele
pour·ing ['pɔ:rɪŋ] ADJ **1** (*rain*) battente; **in the pouring rain** sotto la pioggia battente; **a pouring wet day** una giornata molto piovosa **2** (*custard*) liquido(-a)
pout [paʊt] N broncio
■ VI fare il broncio, mettere il muso
◎ **pov·er·ty** ['pɒvətɪ] N miseria, povertà; **poverty of resources** mancanza di risorse; **to live in poverty** vivere in miseria
poverty line N: **below the poverty line** sotto la soglia di povertà
poverty-stricken ['pɒvətɪˌstrɪkən] ADJ (*gen*) poverissimo(-a); (*hum: hard up*) al verde; **the most poverty-stricken areas of the city** le zone più povere della città
poverty trap N (*Econ*) *circolo vizioso nel quale, accettando un lavoro si perderebbe parte dell'assegno di disoccupazione*
POW [ˌpi:əʊ'dʌblju:] N ABBR = **prisoner of war**
pow·der ['paʊdə^r] N (*gen*) polvere *f*; (*face powder*) cipria; (*medicine*) polverina; **white powder** polvere bianca
■ VT **1** (*reduce to powder*) ridurre in polvere **2** (*apply powder to: face*) incipriarsi; **to powder one's body** mettersi il talco; **to powder one's nose** incipriarsi il naso; (*euph*) andare alla toilette
powder compact N portacipria *m inv*
pow·dered ['paʊdəd] ADJ: **powdered milk** latte *m* in polvere; **powdered sugar** (*Am*) zucchero a velo
powder keg N (*fig: area*) polveriera; (*: situation*) situazione *f* esplosiva
powder puff N piumino della cipria
powder room N toilette *f inv* (*per signore*)
pow·dery ['paʊdərɪ] ADJ (*substance*) come polvere; (*surface*) impolverato(-a), polveroso(-a); (*snow*) farinoso(-a)
◎ **pow·er** ['paʊə^r] N **1** (*physical strength, also fig*) forza; (*energy*) energia; (*force: of engine, blow, explosion*) potenza; (*: of sun*) intensità; (*electricity*) elettricità; **to cut off the power** (*Elec*) togliere la corrente; **the power's off** la corrente è staccata; **the ship returned under its own power** la nave è tornata con i propri mezzi; **more power to your elbow!** (*fam*) dacci dentro!; **nuclear power** energia nucleare; **solar power** energia solare **2** (*ability, capacity*) capacità *f inv*, potere *m*; (*faculty*) facoltà *f inv*; **mental powers** capacità *fpl* mentali; **it is beyond his power to save her** non può far nulla per salvarla; **to do all in one's power to help sb** fare tutto quello che si può per aiutare qn; **the power of speech** la facoltà *or* l'uso della parola; **powers of persuasion/imagination** forza di persuasione/immaginazione **3** (*Pol: authority*) potere *m*, autorità *f inv*; **the power of the Church** l'autorità della Chiesa; **that is beyond my power(s)** questo è al di là dei miei poteri; **to have power over sb** aver potere su qn; **to have sb in one's power** avere qn in proprio potere; **to be in sb's power** essere in potere di qn; **to be in power** essere al potere; **the Tories were in power for 18 years** i conservatori sono stati al potere per diciotto anni; **to come to power** salire al potere; **the power behind the throne** l'eminenza grigia; **the world powers** le grandi potenze; **the powers that be** le autorità costituite; **the powers of darkness** *or* **evil** le forze del male **4** (*Math*) potenza; **7 to the power (of) 3** 7 al cubo *or* alla terza **5** (*fam: a lot of*): **it did me a power of good** mi ha fatto un bene enorme
■ VT azionare; **plane powered by 4 jets** aereo azionato da 4 motori a reazione; **nuclear-powered submarine** sottomarino a propulsione atomica
■ ADJ (*saw, also Elec: cable*) elettrico(-a); (*supply, consumption*) di energia elettrica

Pp

power-assisted ['paʊərəˌsɪstɪd] ADJ (*Auto*) servoassistito(-a); **power-assisted brakes** servofreno *sg*; **power-assisted steering** servosterzo
power base N (*of politician*) sostenitori *mpl*
power·boat ['paʊəˌbəʊt] N (*Brit*) motobarca, imbarcazione *f* a motore
power broker N persona molto influente in politica
power cut N (*Brit*) interruzione *f or* mancanza di corrente
power dressing N *modo di vestire sobrio ed elegante di chi vuole sottolineare il proprio ruolo dirigenziale*
power drill N trapano elettrico
power-driven ['paʊəˌdrɪvn] ADJ a motore; (*Elec*) elettrico(-a)
-powered ['paʊəd] SUFF: **nuclear powered submarine** sommergibile *m* nucleare; **battery-powered appliances** apparecchi *mpl* a batteria
power failure N guasto alla linea elettrica
◎ **pow·er·ful** ['paʊəfʊl] ADJ (*gen*) potente, forte; (*person: physically*) possente; (*film, actor, speech*) formidabile
pow·er·ful·ly ['paʊəfəlɪ] ADV: **to be powerfully built** essere di costituzione robusta
power·house ['paʊəˌhaʊs] N (*fig: person*) persona molto dinamica; **a powerhouse of ideas** una miniera di idee
pow·er·less ['paʊəlɪs] ADJ impotente, senza potere; **to be powerless to do sth** essere impossibilitato a fare qc; **I felt totally powerless** mi sentivo totalmente impotente
pow·er·less·ly ['paʊəlɪslɪ] ADV con impotenza
pow·er·less·ness ['paʊəlɪsnɪs] N impotenza
power line N linea elettrica
power of attorney N (*Law*) procura
power pack N (*Elec*) alimentatore
power plant N centrale *f* elettrica
power play N (*Ice Hockey*) (gioco con) superiorità numerica; (*fig*) prova di forza
power point N (*Elec*) presa di corrente
power politics NPL politica *fsg* della forza
power-sharing ['paʊəˈʃeərɪŋ] N partecipazione *f* al potere
power station N centrale *f* elettrica
power steering N (*Aut: also:* **power-assisted steering**) servosterzo
power structure N gerarchia di poteri
power surge N sovratensione *f*
power tool N strumento elettrico (*or* a motore)
power walking N camminata sportiva
pow·wow ['paʊˌwaʊ] N (*fam*) riunione *f*
pox [pɒks] N: **the pox** (*fam*) il mal francese; *see also* **chickenpox**
◎ **pp** ['pi:'pi:] ABBR (= *per procurationem: by proxy*): **pp J Smith** per il Signor J. Smith
pp. ABBR (= **pages**) pp. (= *pagine*)
PPE [ˌpi:pi:'i:] N ABBR (*Brit Univ:* = **philosophy, politics and economics**) *corso di laurea in filosofia, scienze politiche ed economia*
PPP [ˌpi:pi:'pi:] N ABBR (= **private-public partnership**) *accordo con il quale una società privata si impegna a finanziare un progetto pubblico*
◎ **PR** [ˌpi:'ɑʳ] **1** N ABBR (= **public relations**) PR; = **proportional representation**
prac·ti·cabil·ity [ˌpræktɪkə'bɪlɪtɪ] N praticabilità, attuabilità
prac·ti·cable ['præktɪkəbl] ADJ (*scheme*) praticabile, attuabile
◎ **prac·ti·cal** ['præktɪkəl] ADJ (*gen*) pratico(-a); **a practical suggestion** un consiglio pratico; **for all practical purposes** in pratica, agli effetti pratici; **he's very practical** è un tipo molto pratico
prac·ti·cal·ity [ˌpræktɪ'kælɪtɪ] N (*of person*) senso pratico; (*of scheme, idea*) aspetto pratico; **practicalities** dettagli *mpl* pratici
practical joke N burla
prac·ti·cal·ly ['præktɪklɪ] ADV **1** (*almost*) praticamente, quasi; **it's practically impossible** è praticamente impossibile **2 practically based** (*education, training*) basato(-a) sulla pratica
◎ **prac·tice** ['præktɪs] N **1** (*habit*) abitudine *f*, consuetudine *f*; **it's common practice** è d'uso; **it is not our practice to do that** generalmente non lo facciamo; **to make a practice of doing sth** avere l'abitudine di fare qc **2** (*exercise*) esercizio; (*training*) allenamento; (*rehearsal*) prove *fpl*; **target practice** pratica di tiro; **piano practice** esercizi *mpl* al piano; **football practice** allenamento di calcio; **to be out of practice** esser fuori esercizio (*or* allenamento); **I'm out of practice** sono fuori allenamento; **practice makes perfect** le cose si imparano a forza di pratica **3** (*not theory*) pratica; **in practice** in pratica; **in practice it's more difficult** in pratica è più difficile; **to put sth into practice** mettere qc in pratica **4** (*of doctor, lawyer*): **to be in practice** esercitare la professione; **he has a small practice** (*doctor*) ha un numero ristretto di pazienti; (*lawyer*) ha un numero ristretto di clienti; **his practice is in Trieste** il suo studio è a Trieste; **to set up in practice as** cominciare ad esercitare la professione di; **a medical practice** uno studio medico
■ VT, VI (*Am*) = **practise**
practice match N partita di allenamento
practice session N (*Sport*) (seduta di) allenamento
prac·tise, (*Am*) **prac·tice** ['præktɪs] VT **1 to practise patience/self-control** cercare di avere pazienza/ di controllarsi; **to practise charity** essere caritatevole; **to practise what one preaches** mettere in pratica ciò che si predica **2** (*train o.s. at: piano*) esercitarsi a; (*: song*) esercitarsi per imparare; **to practise a shot** (*Golf, Tennis*) esercitarsi in un tiro; **to practise doing sth** esercitarsi a fare qc; **I practise the flute every evening** mi esercito al flauto ogni sera; **I practised my Italian on her** ho fatto pratica d'italiano con lei **3** (*follow, exercise: profession*) esercitare; (*: sport, religion*) praticare; (*: method*) seguire, usare; (*custom*) seguire
■ VI **1** (*in order to acquire skill: gen, Mus*) esercitarsi; (*: Sport*) allenarsi; **I ought to practise more** dovrei esercitarmi di più; **the team practises on Thursdays** la squadra si allena di giovedì **2** (*lawyer, doctor*) esercitare
practised, (*Am*) **prac·ticed** ['præktɪst] ADJ (*person*) esperto(-a), provetto(-a); (*performance*) da virtuoso(-a); (*liar*) matricolato(-a); **with a practised eye** con occhio esperto
practising, (*Am*) **prac·tic·ing** ['præktɪsɪŋ] ADJ (*lawyer*) che esercita (la professione); (*Jew, Catholic etc*) praticante; (*homosexual*) che è attivo(-a); **she's a practising Catholic** è cattolica praticante
prac·ti·tion·er [præk'tɪʃənəʳ] N (*of an art*) professionista *m/f*; (*Med*) medico
Prae·to·rian Guard [prɪˌtɔ:rɪən'gɑ:d] N (*History, fig*) guardia pretoriana
prag·mat·ic [præg'mætɪk] ADJ pragmatico(-a)
prag·ma·tism ['prægməˌtɪzəm] N pragmatismo
Prague [prɑ:g] N Praga
prai·rie ['prɛərɪ] N prateria; **the prairies** le grandi praterie

prairie dog N cane *m* delle praterie
prairie oyster N (*Culin*) uovo all'ostrica
◎ **praise** [preɪz] N elogio, lode *f*; **he spoke in praise of their achievements** ha elogiato i loro risultati; **I have nothing but praise for her** non posso che lodarla; **praise be to God!** sia lodato Iddio!; **praise be!** (*fam*) sia ringraziato il cielo!
■ VT lodare, elogiare; (*God*) render lode a; **to praise sb for sth/for doing sth** lodare *or* elogiare qn per qc/per aver fatto qc
praise·worthy ['preɪz,wɜːðɪ] ADJ lodevole, degno(-a) di lode
pra·line ['prɑːliːn] N pralina
pram [præm] N (*Brit*) carrozzina
prance [prɑːns] VI (*horse*) caracollare; (*person: proudly*) pavoneggiarsi; (*: gaily*) saltellare; **to prance in/out** entrare/uscire pavoneggiandosi (*or* saltellando)
prank [præŋk] N scherzetto, burla; **a childish prank** una birichinata; **to play a prank on sb** giocare un tiro a qn, fare uno scherzo a qn
prank·ster ['præŋkstəʳ] N burlone(-a)
prat [præt] N (*Brit fam!*) cretino(-a)
prate [preɪt] VI cicalare; **to prate on about sth** parlare a più non posso di qc
prat·tle ['prætl] VI chiacchierare, cianciare
prawn [prɔːn] N gambero, gamberetto
prawn cocktail N cocktail *m inv* di gamberetti
prax·is ['præksɪs] N (*frm*) prassi *f*
pray [preɪ] VI (*say prayers*) pregare; **to pray to God** pregare Dio; **to pray for sb/sth** pregare per qn/qc; **to pray for forgiveness** implorare il perdono; **we are praying for good weather** preghiamo che faccia bello
prayer [prɛəʳ] N preghiera; **to say one's prayers** dire *or* recitare le preghiere
prayer beads NPL corona *fsg* del rosario
prayer book N libro di preghiere
prayer mat N tappeto da preghiera (*usato dagli Islamici*)
prayer meeting N incontro di preghiera
prayer wheel N mulino da preghiere (*nella religione buddista*)
pray·ing ['preɪɪŋ] N preghiere *fpl*
pray·ing man·tis [,preɪɪŋ'mæntɪs] N mantide *f* religiosa
pre... [priː] PREF pre...; **pre-1970** prima del 1970
preach [priːtʃ] VT (*gen*) predicare; (*sermon*) fare
■ VI predicare; **to preach at sb** far la predica a qn; **to preach to the converted** (*fig*) cercare di convincere chi è già convinto
preach·er ['priːtʃəʳ] N (*of sermon*) predicatore *m*; (*Am: minister*) pastore *m*
pre·am·ble [priː'æmbl] N preambolo
pre·ar·range [,priːə'reɪndʒ] VT prestabilire
pre·ar·ranged [,priːə'reɪndʒd] ADJ organizzato(-a) in anticipo
pre·cari·ous [prɪ'kɛərɪəs] ADJ precario(-a)
pre·cari·ous·ly [prɪ'kɛərɪəslɪ] ADV precariamente
pre·cari·ous·ness [prɪ'kɛərɪəsnɪs] N precarietà
pre·cast ['priː,kɑːst] ADJ prefabbricato(-a)
pre·cau·tion [prɪ'kɔːʃən] N precauzione *f*; **as a precaution** per precauzione; **to take precautions** prendere precauzioni; **to take the precaution of doing** prendere la precauzione di fare
pre·cau·tion·ary [prɪ'kɔːʃənərɪ] ADJ (*measure*) precauzionale
pre·cede [prɪ'siːd] VT (*in space, time*) precedere; **he preceded me as chairman of the Society** è stato il mio predecessore nella presidenza della Società
prec·edence ['prɛsɪdəns] N (*in rank*) precedenza; (*in importance*) priorità; **to take precedence over sb/sth** avere la precedenza su qn/qc
prec·edent ['prɛsɪdənt] N (*also Law*) precedente *m*; **without precedent** senza precedenti; **to establish** *or* **set a precedent** creare un precedente
pre·ced·ing [prɪ'siːdɪŋ] ADJ precedente
pre·cept ['priːsɛpt] N precetto
pre·cinct ['priːsɪŋkt] N **1** (*also:* **shopping precinct**) zona dei negozi (*chiusa al traffico automobilistico*); centro commerciale; **pedestrian precinct** zona pedonale **2** (*of cathedral*) recinto; **precincts** NPL (*environs*) dintorni *mpl* **3** (*Am: district*) circoscrizione *f*
pre·cious ['prɛʃəs] ADJ prezioso(-a); **a precious resource** una risorsa preziosa; **it's very precious to me** mi è molto caro; **your precious dog** (*iro*) il tuo amatissimo cane
■ ADV (*fam*): **precious little/few** ben poco/pochi
precious stone N pietra preziosa
preci·pice ['prɛsɪpɪs] N precipizio; **on the edge of a precipice** sull'orlo del precipizio
pre·cipi·tate [*adj, n* prɪ'sɪpɪtɪt; *vb* prɪ'sɪpɪteɪt] ADJ (*hasty*) precipitoso(-a), affrettato(-a)
■ N (*Chem*) precipitato
■ VT **1** (*bring on: crisis*) accelerare **2** (*Chem*) precipitare; (*Met*) far condensare
pre·cipi·tate·ly [prɪ'sɪpɪtɪtlɪ] ADV precipitosamente
pre·cipi·ta·tion [prɪ,sɪpɪ'teɪʃən] N precipitazione *f*
pre·cipi·tous [prɪ'sɪpɪtəs] ADJ (*slope, path*) a precipizio; (*decision, action*) precipitoso(-a)
pre·cipi·tous·ly [prɪ'sɪpɪtəslɪ] ADV precipitosamente
pré·cis ['preɪsiː] N (*pl* **précis**) riassunto
pre·cise [prɪ'saɪs] ADJ (*gen*) preciso(-a); (*pej: over precise*) pignolo(-a), pedante; **there were 5, to be precise** ce n'erano 5, per essere precisi; **at that precise moment** in quel preciso istante; **he's very precise in everything he does** è sempre molto preciso in quello che fa; **a precise old lady** una vecchietta meticolosa
◎ **pre·cise·ly** [prɪ'saɪslɪ] ADV con precisione; **at 4 o'clock precisely** *or* **at precisely 4 o'clock** alle 4 precise *or* in punto; **what precisely is her job?** che lavoro fa esattamente?; **precisely!** precisamente!, proprio così!
pre·ci·sion [prɪ'sɪʒən] N precisione *f*
precision bombing N bombardamento di precisione
precision instrument N strumento di precisione
pre·clude [prɪ'kluːd] (*frm*) VT (*possibility*) precludere, impedire; (*misunderstanding, doubt*) non lasciar adito a; **we are precluded from doing that** siamo impossibilitati a farlo; **to preclude sb from doing** impedire a qn di fare; **his age precludes travel** l'età gli impedisce di viaggiare
pre·co·cious [prɪ'kəʊʃəs] ADJ precoce
pre·co·cious·ly [prɪ'kəʊʃəslɪ] ADV precocemente
pre·co·cious·ness [prɪ'kəʊʃəsnɪs], **pre·coc·ity** [prɪ'kɒsɪtɪ] N precocità
pre·con·ceived [,priːkən'siːvd] ADJ (*idea*) preconcetto(-a); **preconceived notions** idee preconcette
pre·con·cep·tion [,priːkən'sɛpʃən] N preconcetto
pre·con·di·tion [,priːkən'dɪʃən] N condizione *f* indispensabile; **to set preconditions** stabilire le condizioni necessarie
pre·cooked [,priː'kʊkt] ADJ precotto(-a)
pre·cur·sor [,priː'kɜːsəʳ] N precursore *m*
pre·date [,priː'deɪt] VT (*precede*) precedere; (*put earlier date on*) retrodatare
preda·tor ['prɛdətəʳ] N predatore(-trice)

Pp

preda·tory ['prɛdətərɪ] ADJ (*animal*) rapace, predatore(-trice); (*habits, army*) rapace; (*person, look*) avido(-a), cupido(-a)
predatory pricing [-'praɪsɪŋ] N politica dei prezzi stracciati
pre·de·cease [ˌpri:dɪ'si:s] VT morire prima di
pre·de·ces·sor ['pri:dɪˌsɛsəʳ] N predecessore *m*
pre·des·ti·na·tion [pri:ˌdɛstɪ'neɪʃən] N predestinazione *f*
pre·des·tine [ˌpri:'dɛstɪn] VT predestinare
pre·de·ter·mine [ˌpri:dɪ'tɜ:mɪn] VT predeterminare, determinare in anticipo
pre·dica·ment [prɪ'dɪkəmənt] N situazione *f* difficile (*or* imbarazzante); **I'm in a bit of a predicament** sono in una situazione un po' imbarazzante
predi·cate [*n, adj* 'prɛdɪkɪt; *vb* 'prɛdɪˌkeɪt] N (*Gram*) predicato
■ ADJ (*Gram*) predicativo(-a)
■ VT **1** (*frm: imply*) asserire **2** (*frm: idea*): **to be predicated on sth** dipendere da qc
pre·dica·tive [prɪ'dɪkətɪv] ADJ (*Gram*) predicativo(-a)
pre·dica·tive·ly [prɪ'dɪkətɪvlɪ] ADV (*Gram*) in funzione di predicato
◎ **pre·dict** [prɪ'dɪkt] VT predire
pre·dict·able [prɪ'dɪktəbl] ADJ prevedibile
pre·dict·ably [prɪ'dɪktəblɪ] ADV (*behave, react*) in modo prevedibile; **predictably she didn't turn up** come era da prevedere, non è arrivata
pre·dic·tion [prɪ'dɪkʃən] N predizione *f*
pre·di·gest·ed [ˌpri:daɪ'dʒɛstɪd] ADJ (*pej*) predigerito(-a)
pre·di·lec·tion [ˌpri:dɪ'lɛkʃən] N predilezione *f*
pre·dis·pose [ˌpri:dɪs'pəʊz] VT predisporre
pre·dis·po·si·tion [ˌpri:dɪspə'zɪʃən] N predisposizione *f*
pre·domi·nance [prɪ'dɒmɪnəns] N predominanza
pre·domi·nant [prɪ'dɒmɪnənt] ADJ predominante
pre·domi·nant·ly [prɪ'dɒmɪnəntlɪ] ADV prevalentemente, per lo più; **it's a predominantly female profession** è una professione prevalentemente femminile
pre·domi·nate [prɪ'dɒmɪˌneɪt] VI predominare
pre-eminence [ˌpri:'ɛmɪnəns] N preminenza
pre-eminent [ˌpri:'ɛmɪnənt] ADJ eccezionale, preminente
pre-eminently [ˌpri:'ɛmɪnəntlɪ] ADV soprattutto, preminentemente
pre-empt [ˌpri:'ɛmpt] VT acquistare per diritto di prelazione; (*fig*) anticipare
pre-emptive [ˌpri:ɛmptɪv] ADJ: **pre-emptive strike** (*Mil*) azione *f* preventiva
preen [pri:n] VT **1** (*feathers*) lisciare (con il becco); **the bird was preening itself** l'uccello si stava lisciando le piume; **he was preening himself in front of the mirror** (*fig pej*) stava lisciandosi davanti allo specchio **2 to preen o.s. on sth/on doing sth** (*liter pej*) compiacersi di qc/di fare qc
pre·es·tab·lish [ˌpri:ɪs'tæblɪʃ] VT prestabilire
pre·fab ['pri:ˌfæb] N (*fam*) casetta prefabbricata
pre·fab·ri·ca·ted [ˌpri:'fæbrɪˌkeɪtɪd] ADJ prefabbricato(-a)
pref·ace ['prɛfɪs] N prefazione *f*; (*to speech*) introduzione *f*
pre·fect ['pri:fɛkt] N (*Brit: Scol*) *allievo delle classi superiori che è incaricato della disciplina e gode di alcuni privilegi*; (*Admin: in Italy, France*) prefetto
pre·fec·ture ['pri:fɛktjʊəʳ] N prefettura
◎ **pre·fer** [prɪ'fɜ:ʳ] VT **1** preferire; **which would you prefer?** quale preferisci?; **to prefer coffee to tea** preferire il caffè al tè; **I prefer chemistry to maths** preferisco la chimica alla matematica; **I prefer walking to going by car** preferisco camminare piuttosto che andare in macchina; **I prefer to stay home** preferisco restare a casa **2** (*Law: charges, complaint*) sporgere; (: *action*) intentare
pref·er·able ['prɛfərəbl] ADJ preferibile
pref·er·ably ['prɛfərəblɪ] ADV di preferenza, preferibilmente
pref·er·ence ['prɛfərəns] N preferenza; **my preference is for ...** *or* **I have a preference for ...** preferisco...; **in preference to sth** piuttosto che qc; **to give preference to sb/sth** dare la preferenza a qn/qc
preference shares NPL (*Brit Fin*) azioni *fpl* privilegiate
pref·er·en·tial [ˌprɛfə'rɛnʃəl] ADJ preferenziale; **preferential treatment** trattamento di favore
pre·ferred stock [prɪ'fɜ:d'stɒk] NPL (*Am Fin*) = preference shares
pre·fig·ure [pri:'fɪgəʳ] VT (*Art*) prefigurare
pre·fix ['pri:fɪks] N (*Gram*) prefisso
◎ **preg·nan·cy** ['prɛgnənsɪ] N gravidanza
pregnancy test N test *m inv* (di gravidanza)
◎ **preg·nant** ['prɛgnənt] ADJ (*woman*) incinta; (*animal*) gravida; (*liter: remark, pause*) significativo(-a); **she's 3 months pregnant** è incinta di 3 mesi; **pregnant with meaning** (*liter*) pregno(-a) di significato
pre·heat [pri:'hi:t] VT far riscaldare; **bake in a preheated oven at 250°** cucinare nel forno già riscaldato a 250°
pre·hen·sile [prɪ'hɛnsaɪl] ADJ (*Zool*) prensile
pre·his·tor·ic [ˌpri:hɪ'stɒrɪk] ADJ preistorico(-a)
pre·his·to·ry [ˌpri:'hɪstərɪ] N preistoria
pre·in·dus·trial [ˌpri:ɪn'dʌstrɪəl] ADJ preindustriale
pre·judge [ˌpri:'dʒʌdʒ] VT farsi a priori un giudizio di
preju·dice ['prɛdʒʊdɪs] N **1** (*biased opinion*) pregiudizio
■ COLLECTIVE N pregiudizi *mpl*; **his prejudice against sb/sth** i suoi pregiudizi nei riguardi di qn/qc **2** (*Law: injury, detriment*) pregiudizio; **without prejudice to** (*frm*) senza pregiudicare
■ VT **1** (*bias*): **to prejudice sb in favour of/against** disporre bene/male qn verso **2** (*frm: injure*) pregiudicare, ledere, compromettere
preju·diced ['prɛdʒʊdɪst] ADJ (*person*) pieno(-a) di pregiudizi, prevenuto(-a); (: *racially*) pieno(-a) di pregiudizi; (*view, opinion*) preconcetto(-a); **to be prejudiced against sb/sth** essere prevenuto(-a) contro qn/qc; **to be prejudiced in favour of sb/sth** essere ben disposto(-a) verso qn/qc
preju·di·cial [ˌprɛdʒʊ'dɪʃəl] ADJ: **prejudicial (to)** pregiudizievole (per *or* a)
prel·ate ['prɛlɪt] N prelato
pre·limi·naries [prɪlɪmɪnərɪz] NPL preliminari *mpl*
pre·limi·nary [prɪ'lɪmɪnərɪ] ADJ preliminare
■ PREP: **preliminary to sth/doing sth** prima di qc/fare qc
prel·ude ['prelju:d] N preludio
pre·mari·tal [ˌpri:'mærɪtl] ADJ prematrimoniale
prema·ture ['prɛməˌtjʊəʳ] ADJ (*baby, birth, decision*) prematuro(-a); (*arrival*) (molto) anticipato(-a); **you are being a little premature** sei un po' troppo precipitoso; **premature baby** neonato prematuro
prema·ture·ly ['prɛməˌtjʊəlɪ] ADV prematuramente, prima del tempo
pre·medi·tate [ˌpri:'mɛdɪteɪt] VT premeditare
pre·medi·tat·ed [ˌpri:'mɛdɪteɪtɪd] ADJ premeditato(-a)

pre·medi·ta·tion [pri:ˌmɛdɪˈteɪʃən] N premeditazione *f*

pre·men·stru·al [ˌpri:ˈmɛnstrʊəl] ADJ (*Med*) premestruale

premenstrual tension, premenstrual syndrome N (*Med*) sindrome *f* premestruale

◎ **prem·ier** [ˈprɛmɪəʳ] N (*Pol*) premier *m inv*, primo ministro; **the Australian premier** il primo ministro australiano
■ ADJ primo(-a); **the Premier League** la prima divisione

premiere [ˈprɛmɪɛəʳ] N prima

prem·ier·ship [ˈprɛmɪəʃɪp] N carica di premier

prem·ise [ˈprɛmɪs] N (*hypothesis*) premessa

prem·ises [ˈprɛmɪsɪz] NPL locale *msg*; **on the premises** sul posto; **he was asked to leave the premises** l'hanno invitato ad abbandonare il locale; **business premises** locali commerciali; **they're moving to new premises** si trasferiscono in nuovi locali

◎ **pre·mium** [ˈpri:mɪəm] N (*gen*) premio; (*additional charge*) maggiorazione *f*; **insurance companies charge high premiums** le compagnie assicurative fanno pagare premi elevati; **you have to pay a premium for a sea view** bisogna pagare una maggiorazione per avere la vista sul mare; **to sell at a premium** (*shares*) vendere sopra la pari; **to be at a premium** (*fig*) essere ricercatissimo(-a), scarseggiare; **in Hong Kong accommodation is at a premium** a Hong Kong le case scarseggiano

premium bond N (*Brit*) *obbligazione emessa dal Tesoro britannico che non frutta interessi ma un premio periodico di denaro*

premium deal N (*Comm*) offerta speciale

premium gasoline N (*Am*) super *f*

premo·ni·tion [ˌprɛːməˈnɪʃən] N presentimento, premonizione *f*

pre·moni·tory [prɪˈmɒnɪtərɪ] ADJ (*frm*) premonitore(-trice)

pre·na·tal [ˌpri:ˈneɪtl] ADJ prenatale

pre·nup [ˈpri:nʌp] N (*fam*) accordo prematrimoniale

pre·nup·tial agreement [ˌpri:ˌnʌpʃələˈgri:mənt] N accordo prematrimoniale

pre·oc·cu·pa·tion [pri:ˌɒkjʊˈpeɪʃən] N preoccupazione *f*; **his preoccupation with death** la sua ossessione della morte; **in his preoccupation with ...** dato che era tutto preso da...

pre·oc·cu·pied [ˌpri:ˈɒkjʊpaɪd] ADJ (*absorbed*) assorto(-a); **they're preoccupied with the forthcoming wedding** sono tutti presi dall'imminente matrimonio

> DID YOU KNOW ...?
> **preoccupied** is not translated by the Italian word *preoccupato*

pre·oc·cu·py [ˌpri:ˈɒkjʊpaɪ] VT (*absorb*) assorbire; (*mind, thoughts*) occupare

> DID YOU KNOW ...?
> **preoccupy** is not translated by the Italian word *preoccupare*

pre·or·dained [pri:ɔ:ˈdeɪnd] ADJ (*frm*) predestinato(-a)

prep [prɛp] (*fam Scol*) N ABBR (*in private schools*) compiti *mpl*; **history prep** compiti di storia
■ ADJ ABBR: **prep school** = preparatory school

pre·pack [ˌpri:ˈpæk], **pre·pack·age** [ˌpri:ˈpækɪdʒ] VT preconfezionare

pre·packed [ˌpri:ˈpækt], **pre·pack·aged** ADJ preconfezionato(-a)

pre·paid [ˌpri:ˈpeɪd] ADJ pagato(-a) in anticipo; (*envelope*) già affrancato(-a)

◎ **prepa·ra·tion** [ˌprɛpəˈreɪʃən] N **1** (*preparing*) preparazione *f*; **in preparation for sth** in vista di qc; **to be in preparation** essere in (corso di) preparazione; **months of preparation** mesi di preparazione
2: **preparations** NPL (*preparatory measures*) preparativi *mpl*; **to make preparations** fare i preparativi; **preparations are being made for the visit of the Queen** sono in atto i preparativi per la visita della regina **3** (*Brit Scol*) compiti *mpl*

pre·para·tory [prɪˈpærətərɪ] ADJ (*work*) preparatorio(-a); (*measure*) preliminare; **preparatory to sth/to doing sth** prima di qc/di fare qc

preparatory school N *tipo di scuola privata*

> **PREPARATORY SCHOOL**
> In Gran Bretagna, la **prep(aratory) school** è una scuola privata frequentata da bambini dai 7 ai 13 anni in vista dell'iscrizione alla "public school". Negli Stati Uniti, invece, è una scuola superiore privata che prepara i ragazzi che si iscriveranno al "college".
> ▷ www.isc.co.uk/index.php/68

◎ **pre·pare** [prɪˈpɛəʳ] VT preparare; **teachers have to prepare lessons in the evening** la sera gli insegnanti devono preparare le lezioni; **prepare yourself for a shock** preparati a uno shock; **to prepare the way for sth** preparare il terreno per qc; **to prepare to do sth** prepararsi a fare qc
■ VI: **to prepare for** (*journey, party, sb's arrival*) fare dei preparativi per; (*exam, future*) prepararsi per; **we're preparing for our skiing holiday** stiamo facendo i preparativi per le vacanze in montagna; **to prepare for war** prepararsi alla guerra

◎ **pre·pared** [prɪˈpɛəd] ADJ **1** (*speech, answer*) preparato(-a) in anticipo; (*food*) pronto(-a) **2** (*in state of readiness*) pronto(-a); **to be prepared to do sth** essere pronto(-a) a fare qc; **to be prepared for anything** essere pronto(-a) a tutto; **we were not prepared for this** questo ci ha colto alla sprovvista *or* non ce lo aspettavamo **3** (*willing*): **to be prepared to help sb** essere disposto(-a) *or* pronto(-a) ad aiutare qn; **I'm prepared to help you** sono pronto(-a) *or* disposto(-a) ad aiutarti

pre·par·ed·ness [prɪˈpɛərɪdnɪs] N preparazione *f*

pre·pon·der·ance [prɪˈpɒndərəns] N preponderanza

pre·pon·der·ant [prɪˈpɒndərənt] ADJ preponderante

pre·pon·der·ant·ly [prɪˈpɒndərəntlɪ] ADV in modo preponderante

prepo·si·tion [ˌprɛpəˈzɪʃən] N preposizione *f*

pre·pos·sess·ing [ˌpri:pəˈzɛsɪŋ] ADJ attraente

pre·pos·ter·ous [prɪˈpɒstərəs] ADJ ridicolo(-a), assurdo(-a)

pre·pos·ter·ous·ly [prɪˈpɒstərəslɪ] ADV ridicolmente, assurdamente

Pre-Raphaelite [pri:ˈræfəlaɪt] N, ADJ preraffaellita (*m/f*)

pre·re·cord [ˌpri:rɪˈkɔ:d] VT registrare in anticipo; **prerecorded broadcast** trasmissione *f* registrata; **prerecorded cassette** (musi)cassetta

pre·requi·site [ˌpri:ˈrɛkwɪzɪt] N prerequisito

pre·roga·tive [prɪˈrɒgətɪv] N prerogativa

Pres·by·ter·ian [ˌprɛzbɪˈtɪərɪən] ADJ, N presbiteriano(-a)

Pp

Pres·by·teri·an·ism [ˌprɛzbɪˈtɪərɪəˌnɪzəm] N presbiterianesimo
pres·by·tery [ˈprɛzbɪtərɪ] N presbiterio
pre·school [ˈpriːˌskuːl] ADJ *(child)* in età prescolastica; *(age)* prescolastico(-a); **preschool children** bambini in età prescolare
pres·ci·ence [ˈprɛsɪəns] N *(frm)* preveggenza
pres·ci·ent [ˈprɛsɪənt] ADJ *(frm)* preveggente
pre·scribe [prɪˈskraɪb] VT *(gen, Med)* prescrivere, ordinare; *(fig)* consigliare; **prescribed books** *(Scol, Univ)* testi *mpl* in programma
pre·scribed [prɪˈskraɪbd] ADJ **1** *(drugs, dose, treatment)* prescritto **2** *(period)* prestabilito
pre·scrip·tion [prɪˈskrɪpʃən] N *(Med)* ricetta (medica); **to make up a prescription** *or (Am)* **fill a prescription** preparare *or* fare una ricetta; **to make out a prescription for sb** fare una ricetta a qn; **only available on prescription** ottenibile solo dietro presentazione di ricetta medica
prescription charges NPL *(Brit)* ≈ ticket *m inv*
pre·scrip·tive [prɪˈskrɪptɪv] ADJ normativo(-a)
◎**pres·ence** [ˈprɛzns] N presenza; **in the presence of** in presenza di, davanti a; **to make one's presence felt** far sentire la propria presenza
presence of mind N presenza di spirito
◎**pres·ent** [*adj, n* ˈprɛznt; *vb* prɪˈzɛnt] ADJ **1** *(in attendance)* presente; **to be present at** *(gen)* essere presente a; *(officially)* presenziare a; **he wasn't present at the meeting** non era presente alla riunione; **those present** i presenti **2** *(of the moment)* attuale; **the present situation** la situazione attuale; **in the present circumstances** date le circostanze attuali; **at the present moment** al momento attuale; **its present value** il suo valore attuale **3** *(Gram)* presente
■N **1** *(present time)* presente *m*; *(Gram: also:* **present tense***)* (tempo) presente *m*; **the past and the present** il passato e il presente; **at present** al momento; **for the present** per il momento, per adesso, per ora; **up to the present** fino a questo momento, finora **2** *(gift)* regalo; **to give sb a present** fare un regalo a qn; **he gave me a lovely present** mi ha fatto un bel regalo; **I got this watch as a present** questo orologio mi è stato regalato; **to make sb a present of sth** regalare qc a qn
■VT **1** *(hand over: gen)* presentare; *(: prize, certificate)* consegnare; *(give as gift)* offrire (in omaggio); *(proof, evidence)* fornire; *(Law: case)* esporre; **to present sb with sth** *or* **present sth to sb** fare dono di qc a qn; *(prize)* consegnare qc a qn; **the Mayor presented the winner with a medal** il sindaco ha consegnato una medaglia al vincitore; **to present arms** *(Mil)* presentare le armi; **to present o.s. for an interview** presentarsi per un colloquio **2** *(offer: difficulty, problem, opportunity)* presentare; *(: features)* offrire; **if the opportunity presents itself** se si presenterà l'opportunità **3** *(put on: play, concert, film)* dare; *(TV, Radio: act as presenter of)* presentare; **to present the news** *(TV, Radio)* leggere le notizie; **presenting Jack Nicholson as ...** con Jack Nicholson nella parte di... **4** *(frm: introduce)*: **to present sb to sb** presentare qn a qn; **may I present Miss Clark?** permette che le presenti la signorina Clark?
pre·sent·able [prɪˈzɛntəbl] ADJ presentabile; **to make o.s. presentable** rendersi presentabile, mettersi in ordine
pres·en·ta·tion [ˌprɛzənˈteɪʃən] N **1** *(act of presenting)* presentazione *f*; *(report)* relazione; *(Law: of case)* esposizione *f*; **he gave an interesting presentation** ha fatto una presentazione interessante; **on presentation of the voucher** dietro presentazione del buono; **to make a presentation of sth** *(plan, report)* presentare **2** *(Radio, TV, Theatre)* rappresentazione *f* **3** *(of prizes etc)* consegna ufficiale; *(gift)* regalo, dono; **to make the presentation** fare la consegna ufficiale; **the winners went to London for the presentation of prizes** i vincitori si sono recati a Londra per la consegna ufficiale dei premi
present-day [ˈprɛzntˌdeɪ] ADJ attuale, d'oggigiorno, di oggi
pre·sent·er [prɪˈzɛntəʳ] N *(Radio, TV)* presentatore(-trice)
pre·sen·ti·ment [prɪˈzɛntɪmənt] N presentimento
pres·ent·ly [ˈprɛzntlɪ] ADV *(shortly)* tra poco, a momenti; *(esp Am: now)* adesso, ora; **you'll feel better presently** tra poco ti sentirai meglio; **presently a secretary came in** poco dopo è entrata una segretaria; **they're presently on tour** al momento sono in tournée

> **DID YOU KNOW ...?**
> **presently** is not translated by the Italian word ***presentemente***

present perfect N *(Gram)* passato prossimo
pres·er·va·tion [ˌprɛzəˈveɪʃən] N conservazione *f*; *(of peace, one's dignity)* mantenimento
preservation order N *(on building, tree)* ordinanza per la salvaguardia *(di beni artistici e naturali)*
pre·serva·tive [prɪˈzɜːvətɪv] N *(Culin)* conservante *m*

> **DID YOU KNOW ...?**
> **preservative** is not translated by the Italian word ***preservativo***

◎**pre·serve** [prɪˈzɜːv] VT **1** *(maintain: traditions)* conservare, mantenere; *(: dignity, peace)* mantenere; *(keep intact: buildings, memory)* conservare; **they will strive to preserve peace** lotteranno per mantenere la pace **2** *(keep from decay)* preservare, proteggere; **well preserved** ben conservato(-a); **he is well preserved** *(hum)* si conserva bene **3** *(Culin)* conservare, mettere in conserva; **to preserve fruit** fare conserve di frutta **4** *(keep from harm, save)* proteggere; **efforts to preserve the forest** sforzi per preservare la foresta; **preserve me from that!** (che) Dio mi scampi!
■N **1** *(domain)* dominio **2** *(reservation)* riserva **3** *(often pl: jam)* marmellata; *(bottled fruit)* frutta sciroppata
preset [*vb* priːˈsɛt; *adj* ˈpriːsɛt] VT programmare
■ADJ *(oven)* programmato(-a) (col timer)
pre·shrunk [ˌpriːˈʃrʌŋk] ADJ *(fabric, garment)* irrestringibile
pre·side [prɪˈzaɪd] VI: **to preside (at** *or* **over)** presiedere (a)
◎**presi·den·cy** [ˈprɛzɪdənsɪ] N *(Pol)* presidenza; *(Am: of company)* direzione *f*
◎**presi·dent** [ˈprɛzɪdənt] N *(Pol)* presidente *m*; *(Am: of company)* direttore(-trice) generale
president-elect [ˈprɛzɪdəntɪˈlɛkt] N presidente *m* designato
◎**presi·den·tial** [ˌprɛzɪˈdɛnʃəl] ADJ *(Pol)* presidenziale
◎**press** [prɛs] N
1 *(apparatus, machine: gen)* pressa; *(: for wine)* torchio **2** *(printing press)* torchio da stampa; *(: place)* tipografia; **to go to press** *(newspaper)* andare in macchina; **to be in the press** *(being printed)* essere in (corso di) stampa; *(in the newspapers)* essere sui giornali; **the press** *(newspapers)* la stampa, i giornali; **to get a good/bad**

press avere una buona/cattiva stampa; **a member of the press** un rappresentante della stampa

■ VT

1 (*push: button*) premere, schiacciare; (*: doorbell*) suonare; (*: trigger*) premere; (*squeeze: grapes, olives*) pigiare; (*: flowers*) pressare; (*: hand*) stringere; **to press sb/sth to one's heart** stringersi qn/qc al petto *or* al cuore; **don't press so hard!** non premere così forte!

2 (*iron*) stirare; **she was pressing her blouse** si stava stirando la camicetta

3 (*urge, entreat*): **to press sb to do** *or* **into doing sth** fare pressione su qn affinché faccia qc; **they pressed me to stay** hanno insistito perché restassi; (*force*): **to press sth on sb** (*food, gift*) insistere perché qn accetti qc; (*one's opinions*) voler imporre qc su qn; (*insist on: attack*) rendere più pressante; (*: claim, demands*) insistere su *or* in; **to press sb for an answer** insistere perché qn risponda; **to be hard pressed** essere alle strette; **to press one's opponent** incalzare l'avversario; **to press home an advantage** sfruttare al massimo un vantaggio; **to press the point** insistere sul punto; **to be pressed for time** aver poco tempo; **to be pressed for money** essere a corto di soldi; **to press sb into service** obbligare qn a lavorare; **to press sth into service** far uso di qc; **to press charges against sb** (*Law*) sporgere una denuncia contro qn

■ VI

1 (*in physical sense*) spingere, premere; **the people pressed round him** la gente gli si è accalcata intorno; **the crowd pressed towards the exit** la folla si accalcava all'uscita; **to press ahead** *or* **forward (with sth)** (*fig*) proseguire (in qc)

2 (*urge, agitate*): **to press for sth** fare pressioni per ottenere qc; **time presses** il tempo stringe

▶ **press down** VI + ADV: **to press down (on)** premere (su)

■ VT + ADV premere

▶ **press on** VI + ADV continuare

press agency N agenzia di stampa

press agent N press agent *m/f*

press box N tribuna (della) stampa (*in manifestazioni sportive*)

press card N tessera di giornalista

press conference N conferenza *f* stampa *inv*

press corps N: **the White House press corps** i giornalisti accreditati presso la Casa Bianca

press cutting, **press clipping** N ≈ ritaglio di giornale

press gallery N tribuna (della) stampa (*in tribunale, parlamento*)

press-gang ['prɛs,gæŋ] VT: **to press-gang sb into doing sth** costringere qn a viva forza a fare qc

press·ing ['prɛsɪŋ] ADJ (*matter, problem*) urgente, pressante; (*request, invitation*) insistente, pressante; **he was very pressing** era molto insistente

■ N stiratura

press·man ['prɛs,mæn] N (*pl* **-men**) giornalista *m*, cronista *m*

press·mark ['prɛs,mɑːk] N (*on library book*) segnatura

press officer N addetto(-a) stampa

press photographer N fotoreporter *m/f inv*

press release N comunicato *m* stampa *inv*

press report N servizio giornalistico

press reporter N reporter *m/f inv*

press stud N (bottone *m*) automatico

press-up ['prɛs,ʌp] N (*Brit*) flessione *f* sulle braccia; **to do press-ups** fare flessioni sulle braccia

◎ **pres·sure** ['prɛʃəʳ] N 1 (*Phys, Tech, Met*) pressione *f*; **at full pressure** (*Tech*) al livello massimo di pressione

2 (*compulsion, influence*) pressione *f*, pressioni *fpl*; **to be under pressure** essere sotto pressione; **he's been under a lot of pressure recently** ultimamente ha dovuto sopportare molta pressione; **he's under pressure from his wife to give up smoking** sua moglie fa pressione perché lui smetta di fumare; **to put pressure on sb** fare pressione su qn; **they are really putting the pressure on** ci (*or* vi *etc*) stanno assillando; **to use pressure to obtain sth** far pressione per ottenere qc; **to work under pressure** lavorare sotto pressione; **she's under a lot of pressure** è sotto un'enorme pressione; **the pressure of these events** la tensione creata da questi avvenimenti; **pressure of work prevented her from going** non è potuta andare per via del troppo lavoro

■ VT = **pressurize 2**

pressure cabin N cabina pressurizzata

pressure cooker N pentola a pressione

pressure gauge N manometro

pressure group N (*Pol*) gruppo di pressione

pressure plate N (*Aut: of clutch*) spingidisco

pressure point N (*Med*) punto di compressione emostatica

pres·suri·za·tion [,prɛʃəraɪ'zeɪʃən] N pressurizzazione *f*

pres·sur·ize ['prɛʃə,raɪz] VT 1 (*Tech*) pressurizzare

2 (*fig*): **to pressurize sb to do sth** fare pressioni su qn perché faccia qc; **my parents are pressurizing me to stay on at school** i miei mi stanno facendo pressione perché continui gli studi

pres·sur·ized ['prɛʃə,raɪzd] ADJ pressurizzato(-a)

pres·tige [prɛs'tiːʒ] N prestigio

pres·tig·ious [prɛs'tɪdʒəs] ADJ prestigioso(-a), di grande prestigio

pre·stressed con·crete ['priː,strɛst'kɒnkriːt] N cemento armato precompresso

◎ **pre·sum·ably** [prɪ'zjuːməblɪ] ADV: **presumably he did it** penso *or* presumo che l'abbia fatto

pre·sume [prɪ'zjuːm] VT 1 (*suppose*): **to presume (that)** supporre (che), presumere (che); **I presume she'll come** suppongo che verrà; **I presume so** presumo di sì ; **I presume he did it** suppongo che l'abbia fatto 2 (*frm: venture*): **to presume to do sth** permettersi di fare qc

■ VI (*frm: take liberties*) prendersi troppe libertà; **to presume on sb's friendship** approfittarsi dell'amicizia di qn

pre·sump·tion [prɪ'zʌmpʃən] N 1 (*arrogance*) presunzione *f*; (*impudence*) audacia 2 (*thing presumed*) supposizione *f*; **there is a strong presumption that ...** tutto fa supporre *or* presumere che...

pre·sump·tu·ous [prɪ'zʌmptjʊəs] ADJ presuntuoso(-a)

pre·sump·tu·ous·ly [prɪ'zʌmptjʊəslɪ] ADV presuntuosamente

pre·sup·pose [,priːsə'pəʊz] VT presupporre

pre·sup·po·si·tion [,priːsʌpə'zɪʃən] N presupposto

pre-tax ['priː'tæks] ADJ al lordo d'imposta

pre·tence, (*Am*) **pre·tense** [prɪ'tɛns] N 1 **his pretence of innocence/sympathy** la sua finta *or* falsa innocenza/comprensione; **she is devoid of all pretence** non si nasconde dietro false apparenze; **to make a pretence of doing sth** far finta di fare qc; **he made a pretence of listening** fece finta di ascoltare; **it's all (a) pretence** è tutta una finta, è tutta scena

2 (*claim*) pretesa 3 (*pretext*) pretesto, scusa; **on** *or* **under the pretence of doing sth** con il pretesto *or*

Pp

la scusa di fare qc; **under false pretences** con l'inganno

pre·tend [prɪ'tɛnd] VT **1** (*feign*): **to pretend illness/ ignorance** fingersi malato(-a)/ignorante, far finta di essere malato(-a)/ignorante; **to pretend to do sth** far finta *or* fingere di fare qc; **she's pretending she can't hear us** fa finta di non sentirci; **he was pretending to be a lawyer** si spacciava per avvocato **2** (*claim*): **to pretend to do/that** pretendere di fare/che + *sub*
■ VI (*feign*) far finta, fingere; **she is only pretending** sta solo facendo finta
■ ADJ (*fam: gun, money*) finto(-a)

pre·tend·ed [prɪ'tɛndɪd] ADJ falso(-a), finto(-a)

pre·tend·er [prɪ'tɛndə^r] N (*to the throne*) pretendente *m/f*

pre·tense [prɪ'tɛns] N (*Am*) = **pretence**

pre·ten·sion [prɪ'tɛnʃən] N (*claim*) pretesa; **to have no pretensions to sth/to being sth** non avere la pretesa di avere qc/di essere qc

pre·ten·tious [prɪ'tɛnʃəs] ADJ pretenzioso(-a)

pre·ten·tious·ly [prɪ'tɛnʃəslɪ] ADV pretenziosamente

pre·ten·tious·ness [prɪ'tɛnʃəsnɪs] N pretenziosità

pret·er·ite ['prɛtərɪt] N (tempo) passato, preterito

pre·ter·natu·ral [,pri:tə'nætʃrəl] ADJ (*frm*) soprannaturale

pre·text ['pri:tɛkst] N pretesto; **on** *or* **under the pretext of doing sth** col pretesto di fare qc

Pre·to·ria [prɪ'tɔ:rɪə] N Pretoria
▷ www.sa-venues.com/attractionsga/pretoria-metro.htm

pret·ti·ly ['prɪtɪlɪ] ADV graziosamente

◎ **pret·ty** ['prɪtɪ] ADJ (*comp* **-ier**, *superl* **-iest**) grazioso(-a), carino(-a); **she's very pretty** è molto carina; **he wasn't a pretty sight** non era bello da vedersi; **it'll cost you a pretty penny!** (*fam*) ti costerà una bella sommetta!; **pretty weather** (*Am*) bel tempo
■ ADV (*rather*) piuttosto; (*very*) molto; **the weather was pretty awful** il tempo era piuttosto brutto; **pretty well** (*not badly*) piuttosto bene; **pretty nearly** (*almost*) quasi, praticamente; **pretty much** praticamente; **it's pretty much the same** (*fam*) è praticamente uguale

pretty-pretty ['prɪtɪ'prɪtɪ] ADJ (*pej*) un po' troppo grazioso(-a)

pret·zel ['prɛtsl] N salatino

pre·vail [prɪ'veɪl] VI **1** (*gain mastery*): **to prevail (against, over)** prevalere (su); **in the end his view prevailed** alla fine è prevalsa la sua opinione **2** (*be current: fashion, belief etc*) essere diffuso(-a); **the conditions that prevail** le condizioni attuali; **the fashion which prevailed at that time** la moda che era diffusa a quel tempo **3** (*persuade*): **to prevail (up)on sb to do sth** convincere qn a fare qc, persuadere qn a fare qc

pre·vail·ing [prɪ'veɪlɪŋ] ADJ (*conditions*) attuale; (*belief, customs, attitude*) predominante, prevalente; (*wind*) dominante

preva·lence ['prɛvələns] N (*of crime, customs, attitude*) larga diffusione *f*; (*of conditions*) prevalere *m*

preva·lent ['prɛvələnt] ADJ (*belief, disease, fashion etc*) diffuso(-a), comune, predominante; **the conditions which are prevalent in ...** le condizioni esistenti in...

pre·vari·cate [prɪ'værɪ,keɪt] VI tergiversare

> DID YOU KNOW ...?
> **prevaricate** is not translated by the Italian word *prevaricare*

pre·vari·ca·tion [prɪ,værɪ'keɪʃən] N tergiversazione *f*

> DID YOU KNOW ...?
> **prevarication** is not translated by the Italian word *prevaricazione*

◎ **pre·vent** [prɪ'vɛnt] VT (*crime, accidents, fire*) prevenire; **to prevent sb/sth (from doing sth)** impedire a qn/qc (di fare qc); **the police prevented the protesters from entering the building** la polizia ha impedito ai dimostranti di entrare nell'edificio; **to prevent sth happening again** fare in modo che qc non si ripeta; **to prevent sb's doing sth** (*frm*) impedire che qn faccia qc

pre·vent·able [prɪ'vɛntəbl] ADJ che può essere prevenuto(-a), evitabile

pre·ven·ta·tive [prɪ'vɛntətɪv] ADJ = **preventive**

pre·ven·tion [prɪ'vɛnʃən] N prevenzione *f*; **the prevention of cruelty to animals** la protezione degli animali

pre·ven·tive [prɪ'vɛntɪv] ADJ preventivo(-a)

pre·view ['pri:vju:] N (*of film etc*) anteprima; **to give sb a preview of sth** (*fig*) dare a qn un'idea di qc

◎ **pre·vi·ous** ['pri:vɪəs] ADJ precedente; **the previous day** il giorno prima *or* precedente; **previous experience** precedente esperienza; **he has no previous experience in that field** non ha esperienza in quel campo; **I have a previous engagement** ho già (preso) un impegno; **on a previous occasion** in precedenza; **in a previous life** in un'altra vita; **to have no previous convictions** (*Law*) non aver precedenti penali; **to have 5 previous convictions** essere già stato(-a) condannato(-a) 5 volte

◎ **pre·vi·ous·ly** ['pri:vɪəslɪ] ADV (*before*) prima; (*in the past*) in precedenza; (*already*) già

pre·war ['pri:'wɔ:^r] ADJ dell'anteguerra, anteguerra *inv*

prey [preɪ] N (*also fig*) preda; **to be prey to** (*fig*) essere in preda a; **tourists are easy prey** i turisti sono una facile preda; **bird of prey** uccello rapace
▸ **prey on** VI + PREP (*subj: animals*) predare, far preda di; (*: person*) depredare; **to prey on sb's mind** ossessionare qn; **it was preying on his mind** gli rodeva la mente

Priam ['praɪəm] N Priamo

pria·pism ['praɪə,pɪzəm] N priapismo

◎ **price** [praɪs] N **1** (*also fig*) prezzo; **to go up** *or* **rise in price** salire *or* aumentare di prezzo; **to go down** *or* **fall in price** scendere *or* calare di prezzo; **I got a good price for it** me lo hanno pagato bene; **what is the price of that painting?** quanto costa quel quadro?; **at a reduced price** a prezzo ribassato; **we pay top prices for silver** offriamo ottimi prezzi per l'argento; **every man has his price** ogni uomo ha il suo prezzo; **the price of fame** il prezzo del successo; **it's a small price to pay for it** (*fig*) non è che un piccolo sacrificio; **to pay a high price for sth** (*also fig*) pagare caro qc; **peace at any price** pace ad ogni costo *or* costi quello che costi; **not at any price** per nessuna cosa al mondo; **he regained his freedom, but at a price** ha riconquistato la sua libertà, ma a caro prezzo **2** (*value, valuation*) valore *m*; **to put a price on sth** valutare *or* stimare qc; **to put a price on sb's head** mettere una taglia sulla testa di qn; **what price his promises now?** a che valgono ora le sue promesse?; **you can't put a price on it** (*fig: friendship, loyalty*) è inestimabile **3** (*Betting: odds*) quotazione *f*, quota
■ VT (*fix price of*) fissare il prezzo di; (*put price label on*) prezzare, mettere il prezzo su; (*ask price of*) chiedere il prezzo di; **we price the components separately** fissiamo il prezzo dei componenti separatamente; **it**

was priced at £20 il prezzo era di 20 sterline; **it was priced too high/low** aveva un prezzo troppo alto/ basso; **to be priced out of the market** (*article*) essere così caro(-a) da diventare invendibile; (*producer, nation*) non poter sostenere la concorrenza
■ ADJ (*index*) dei prezzi; **prices and incomes policy** politica dei prezzi e dei salari

price control N calmiere *m* dei prezzi, controllo dei prezzi

price cut N ribasso

price cutting N riduzione *f* dei prezzi

price-earnings ratio [ˌpraɪs'ɜːnɪŋz,reɪʃɪəʊ] N (*Fin*) rapporto prezzo-utile

price-fixing ['praɪs,fɪksɪŋ] N controllo dei prezzi

price freeze N congelamento dei prezzi

price·less ['praɪslɪs] ADJ (*jewels, necklace*) di valore inestimabile; (*fam: amusing*) impagabile, spassosissimo(-a); **friendship is priceless** l'amicizia è un bene inestimabile

price limit N limite *m* di prezzo

price list N listino (dei) prezzi

price point N prezzo di vendita

price range N gamma di prezzi; **it's within my price range** rientra nelle mie possibilità

price tag N cartellino del prezzo

price war N guerra dei prezzi

pricey ['praɪsɪ] ADJ (*comp* **-ier**, *superl* **-iest**) (*Brit fam*) caruccio(-a)

prick [prɪk] N **1** (*act, sensation*) puntura; (*mark*) buco; **pricks of conscience** rimorsi *mpl* di coscienza
2 (*fam!: penis*) cazzo; (: *person*) testa di cazzo (*fam!*)
■ VT (*puncture: balloon, blister*) bucare; (*subj: thorn, needle*) pungere; (: *conscience*) rimordere; **to prick a hole in sth** fare un buco in qc; **to prick one's finger (with/on sth)** pungersi un dito (con/su qc); **I've pricked my finger** mi sono punto un dito
▸ **prick out, prick off** VT + ADV (*seedlings*) trapiantare
▸ **prick up** VT + ADV: **to prick up one's ears** (*also fig*) drizzare le orecchie

prick·ing ['prɪkɪŋ] N (*feeling*) prurito, pizzicore *m*; **to feel prickings of conscience** avere dei rimorsi di coscienza

prick·le ['prɪkl] N **1** (*on plant, animal etc*) spina; **cactus prickles** spine di cactus **2** (*sensation*) sensazione *f* di prurito, pizzicore *m*; (: *of fear*) brivido

prick·ly ['prɪklɪ] ADJ (*comp* **-ier**, *superl* **-iest**) **1** (*plant*) spinoso(-a); (*animal*) pieno(-a) di spine; (*beard*) ispido(-a); (*wool*) che dà prurito **2** (*fig: person*) permaloso(-a); (: *subject*) spinoso(-a)

prickly heat N (*Med*) sudamina

prickly pear N (*plant, fruit*) fico d'India

◎ **pride** [praɪd] N **1** (*arrogance*) superbia, orgoglio; (*self-respect*) orgoglio, amor proprio; (*satisfaction*) fierezza; **his pride may be his downfall** la superbia potrebbe essere la sua rovina; **false pride** falso orgoglio; **wounded pride** orgoglio ferito; **to take (a) pride in** (*appearance, punctuality*) tenere molto a; (*children, achievements*) essere orgoglioso(-a) di; **she takes (a) pride in arriving on time** ci tiene molto ad essere sempre puntuale; **his pride was hurt** fu ferito nell'orgoglio; **she is a (great) source of pride to him** è (molto) fiero *or* orgoglioso di lei; **her plants are her pride and joy** le sue piante sono il suo orgoglio *or* vanto; **to have pride of place** essere al primo posto
2 (*of lions*) branco
■ VT: **to pride o.s. on sth** essere orgoglioso(-a) di qc

◎ **priest** [priːst] N prete *m*, sacerdote *m*

priest·ess ['priːstɪs] N sacerdotessa

priest·hood ['priːst,hʊd] N: **to enter the priesthood** farsi prete

priest·ly ['priːstlɪ] ADJ sacerdotale

prig [prɪg] N: **don't be such a prig!** non fare il(la) moralista!; **what a prig she is!** ma chi si crede di essere!

prig·gish ['prɪgɪʃ] ADJ (*person*) moralista; (*behaviour, attitude*) moraleggiante

prig·gish·ness ['prɪgɪʃnɪs] N (*of person*) atteggiamento moraleggiante; **the priggishness of his behaviour** il suo atteggiamento moraleggiante; **the priggishness of his remarks** il suo tono moraleggiante

prim [prɪm] ADJ (*comp* **-mer**, *superl* **-mest**) (*demure: person, dress*) per benino; (: *house, garden*) in cui nulla è fuori posto; (*manner, smile*) compassato(-a); (*prudish: also:* **prim and proper**) per benino

pri·ma·cy ['praɪməsɪ] N (*frm*) suprema importanza

pri·ma don·na ['priːmə'dɒnə] N primadonna; **she is a real prima donna** (*pej*) fa la primadonna

pri·ma fa·cie [ˌpraɪmə'feɪʃɪ] ADV a prima vista
■ ADJ (*assumption*) (a prima vista) legittimo(-a); (*evidence*) (a prima vista) convincente; **to have a prima facie case** (*Law*) presentare una causa in apparenza fondata

pri·mal ['praɪməl] ADJ (*origins, matter, world*) originario(-a); (*religion, music*) primitivo(-a); (*first in importance*) primario(-a)

pri·mari·ly ['praɪmərɪlɪ] ADV (*chiefly*) principalmente, essenzialmente

◎ **pri·ma·ry** ['praɪmərɪ] ADJ (*chief, main: gen*) principale, primario(-a); **of primary importance** di primaria *or* fondamentale importanza; **the primary reason for my choice was ...** la principale ragione della mia scelta è stata...
■ N (*Am: election*) primarie *fpl*

PRIMARY

Negli Stati Uniti, tramite le **primaries** (le primarie) viene fatta una prima scrematura dei candidati dei partiti alle elezioni presidenziali. La scelta definitiva del candidato da presentare alla presidenza si basa sui risultati delle primarie e ha luogo durante le "Conventions" dei partiti, che si tengono in luglio e in agosto.
▷ http://fpc.state.gov/fpc/c9810.htm
▷ www.historylearningsite.co.uk/primaries.htm

primary colour N colore *m* primario

primary education N istruzione *f* elementare *or* primaria

primary products NPL prodotti *mpl* del settore primario

primary school N (*Brit*) scuola elementare

PRIMARY SCHOOL

In Gran Bretagna la **primary school** è la scuola elementare, frequentata dai bambini dai 5 agli 11 anni di età. È suddivisa in "infant school" (5-7 anni) e "junior school" (7-11 anni). *Vedi anche* **secondary school**
▷ www.rmplc.co.uk/orgs/nape/

primary sector N settore *m* primario

primary teacher N insegnante *m/f* di scuola elementare, maestro(-a)

Pp

pri·mate [1 'praImeIt, 2 'praImIt] N 1 (*Zool*) primate *m* 2 (*Rel*) primate *m*

◎**prime** [praɪm] ADJ 1 (*chief, major: gen*) principale, primario(-a), fondamentale; (: *cause, reason*) primo(-a), fondamentale; **of prime importance** della massima importanza; **my prime concern** la mia preoccupazione principale 2 (*excellent: example*) superbo(-a); (: *meat*) di prima scelta; **of prime quality** di prima scelta; **in prime condition** (*car, athlete*) in perfette condizioni; (*fruit*) in condizioni perfette
■ N: **in the prime of life, in one's prime** nel fiore della vita; **to be past one's prime** non essere più quello(-a) di una volta
■ VT (*wood*) preparare; (*gun*) innescare; (*pump*) adescare; (*fig: instruct*) istruire, mettere al corrente; **he arrived well primed** è arrivato ben preparato

◎**prime minister** N primo ministro

prime mover N primo motore *m*

prime number N (*Math*) numero primo

prim·er ['praɪmə^r] N 1 (*textbook*) testo elementare 2 (*paint*) vernice *f* base *inv*

prime time N (*Radio, TV*) fascia di massimo ascolto, prime time *m*

pri·meval [praɪ'mi:vəl] ADJ primordiale, primitivo(-a); **primeval forests** foreste originarie

primi·tive ['prɪmɪtɪv] ADJ, N primitivo(-a)

prim·ly ['prɪmlɪ] ADV (*smile, behave*) da persona per benino

prim·ness ['prɪmnɪs] N (*of person*) comportamento da persona per benino; (*of dress*) eccessiva modestia; (*of house, garden*) eccessivo ordine *m*; (*prudishness*) pudore *m* eccessivo

pri·mor·dial [praɪ'mɔ:dɪəl] ADJ primordiale

prim·rose ['prɪm,rəʊz] N (*Bot*) primula (gialla)
■ ADJ (*also:* **primrose yellow**) giallo canarino *inv*

primu·la ['prɪmjʊlə] N (*Bot*) primula

Pri·mus® ['praɪməs] N (*also:* **Primus stove**) fornello a petrolio

◎**prince** [prɪns] N principe *m*; **Prince Charles** il principe Carlo

prince charming N il principe *m* azzurro

prince consort N principe *m* consorte

Prince Edward Island N Prince Edward Island *f*
▷ www.gov.pe.ca

prince·ly ['prɪnslɪ] ADJ (*also fig*) principesco(-a)

Prince of Wales N il principe di Galles

prince regent N principe *m* reggente

◎**prin·cess** [prɪn'sɛs] N principessa

◎**prin·ci·pal** ['prɪnsɪpəl] ADJ principale; **the principal violin** il primo violino
■ N 1 (*of school, college*) preside *m/f*; (*in play*) protagonista *m/f*; (*in orchestra*) primo(-a) strumentista *m/f* 2 (*Fin*) capitale *m*

prin·ci·pal·ity [,prɪnsɪ'pælɪtɪ] N principato

prin·ci·pal·ly ['prɪnsɪpəlɪ] ADV principalmente

principal parts NPL (*Gram*) paradigma *msg*

◎**prin·ci·ple** ['prɪnsəpl] N principio; **in principle** in linea di principio; **on principle** per principio; **it's a matter of principle** *or* **it's the principle of the thing** è una questione di principio; **a man of principle** un uomo di saldi principi; **it's against my principles** è contrario ai miei principi; **to go back to first principles** (*fig*) tornare alle origini

prin·ci·pled ['prɪnsɪpəld] ADJ (*person, position*) di principio; **I didn't know you were so high principled** non ti facevo uno di così elevati principi

◎**print** [prɪnt] N 1 (*mark, imprint: of foot, tyre, finger*) impronta; **the policeman took his prints** il poliziotto gli ha preso le impronte digitali 2 (*typeface, characters*) caratteri *mpl*; (*printed matter*) stampa; **that book is in/out of print** quel libro è disponibile/esaurito; **to see o.s. in print** vedere il proprio nome stampato; **in small/large print** stampato(-a) a caratteri piccoli/grandi 3 (*fabric*) (tessuto) stampato 4 (*Art*) stampa; (*Phot*) fotografia; **a framed print** una stampa incorniciata; **colour prints** foto *fpl* a colori
■ VT 1 (*Typ, Textiles, Phot*) stampare; (*fig: on memory*) imprimere 2 (*publish*) pubblicare, stampare; **it was printed in Hong Kong** è stato stampato a Hong Kong 3 (*write in block letters*) scrivere in stampatello; **please print your name and address** per favore scrivere nome e indirizzo in stampatello
▸ **print out** VT + ADV (*Comput*) stampare

print·able ['prɪntəbl] ADJ stampabile; **what he said is not printable!** (*hum*) ciò che ha detto non è ripetibile!

print·ed ['prɪntɪd] ADJ stampato(-a); **the power of the printed word** il potere di tutto ciò che è stampato

printed circuit board N circuito stampato

printed matter N stampe *fpl*

print·er ['prɪntə^r] N (*person*) tipografo(-a); (*machine*) stampante *m*; **at the printer's** (*book*) in tipografia; **printer's error** errore *m* di stampa; **printer's ink** inchiostro tipografico

print·head ['prɪnt,hɛd] N (*Comput*) testina di stampa

print·ing ['prɪntɪŋ] N 1 (*process, also Phot*) stampa; **a printing error** un errore di stampa 2 (*block writing*) stampatello; (*characters*) caratteri *mpl*; (*print*) stampa 3 (*number printed*) tiratura; **the next printing** la prossima tiratura
▷ www.fontscape.com

printing press N pressa tipografica

printing works N tipografia, stamperia

print-out ['prɪnt,aʊt] N (*Comput*) tabulato, stampato

print wheel N margherita

◎**pri·or**[1] ['praɪə^r] ADJ precedente; **without prior notice** senza preavviso; **without prior knowledge** senza saperlo prima; **prior approval is required** occorre prima avere l'approvazione; **to have a prior claim to sth** avere un diritto di precedenza su qc
■ PREP: **prior to sth/to doing sth** prima di qc/di fare qc; **prior to this date** prima di questa data

pri·or[2] ['praɪə^r] N (*Rel*) priore *m*

pri·or·ess ['praɪərɪs] N priora

◎**pri·or·ity** [praɪ'ɒrɪtɪ] N priorità *f inv*, precedenza; **my first priority** la mia priorità; **to have** *or* **take priority over sth** avere la precedenza su qc; **my family takes priority over my work** la mia famiglia ha la precedenza sul lavoro; **we must get our priorities right** dobbiamo decidere quali sono le cose più importanti per noi; **to treat sth as a priority** dare la precedenza a qc; **the government's priority is to build more power plants** la priorità del governo è quella di costruire più centrali elettriche

pri·ory ['praɪərɪ] N priorato

prise, (*Am*) **prize** [praɪz] VT: **to prise sth open** aprire qc (forzando il coperchio); **to prise a lid up/off** aprire/togliere un coperchio facendo leva
▸ **prise out**, (*Am*) **prize out** VT + ADV: **to prise sth out (of sb)** (*secret*) tirar fuori qc (da qn)

prism ['prɪzəm] N (*Geom, Tech*) prisma *m*

pris·mat·ic [prɪz'mætɪk] ADJ prismatico(-a)

◎**pris·on** ['prɪzn] N prigione *f*, carcere *m*; **to be in prison** essere in prigione; **to go to prison for 5 years** essere condannato(-a) a 5 anni di carcere *or* di reclusione; **to**

send sb to prison for 2 years condannare qn a 2 anni di reclusione
■ ADJ (*system*) carcerario(-a); (*conditions, food*) nelle *or* delle prigioni

prison camp N campo di prigionia

◎ **pris·on·er** ['prɪznəʳ] N (*under arrest*) arrestato(-a); (*convicted*) detenuto(-a); (*Mil, fig*) prigioniero(-a); **prisoners have to share cells** i detenuti devono dividere le celle; **the prisoner at the bar** l'accusato(-a), l'imputato(-a); **to take sb prisoner** far prigioniero(-a) qn

prisoner of war N prigioniero(-a) di guerra

prisoner of war camp N campo di prigionia

prison life N vita carceraria

prison officer N agente *m/f* di custodia

pris·sy ['prɪsɪ] ADJ (*pej*) per benino

pris·tine ['prɪstaɪn] ADJ (*unspoiled*) immacolato(-a), puro(-a); (*original*) originario(-a)

pri·va·cy ['prɪvəsɪ] N privacy *f*; **his desire for privacy** il suo desiderio di stare da solo; (*actor, popstar*) il suo desiderio di privacy; **in the privacy of one's own home** nell'intimità della propria casa; **in the strictest privacy** nella massima segretezza

◎ **pri·vate** ['praɪvɪt] ADJ **1** (*not public: conversation, meeting, land*) privato(-a); (*: funeral, wedding*) in forma privata; (*: showing*) a inviti; (*confidential: letter*) personale; (*: agreement, information*) confidenziale; **"private"** (*on door*) "privato"; (*on envelope*) "riservata"; **this information must be kept private** quest'informazione deve rimanere strettamente confidenziale; **he is a very private person** è una persona molto riservata; **in (his) private life** nella vita privata; **private place** posto segreto; **private hearing** (*Law*) udienza a porte chiuse **2** (*for one person: car, house, secretary*) privato(-a), personale; (*: lessons*) privato(-a); (*personal: bank account, reasons*) personale; **a man of private means** un uomo che vive di rendita **3** (*not state-owned: company, army*) privato(-a); (*: doctor, nursing home*) non convenzionato(-a), privato(-a)
■ N **1** (*Mil*) soldato semplice **2 in private** = **privately 1, 2**

private citizen N privato (cittadino)

private detective, private investigator N investigatore(-trice) *or* detective *m/f inv* privato(-a)

private enterprise N l'iniziativa privata

private eye N (*Am fam*) investigatore(-trice) *or* detective *m/f inv* privato(-a)

Private Finance Initiative N (*Brit*) *programma governativo di incentivazione degli investimenti privati in progetti pubblici*

private limited company N società *f inv* a responsabilità limitata non quotata in borsa

pri·vate·ly ['praɪvɪtlɪ] ADV **1** (*not publicly*) privatamente, in privato **2** (*secretly*) in privato; (*personally*) personalmente; (*within o.s.*) dentro di sé **3** (*unofficially*) a titolo personale

private member N (*Parliament*) deputato(-a) (*senza incarichi di governo*)

private member's bill N (*Parliament*) progetto di legge ad iniziativa personale

private parts NPL (*euph*) parti *fpl* intime

private practice N (*Brit*) studio *or* ambulatorio privato; **to be in private practice** essere medico non convenzionato (con la mutua)

private property N proprietà *f inv* privata

private school N scuola privata

private sector N: **the private sector** il settore privato

private view N (*Art*) vernissage *m inv*

pri·va·tion [praɪ'veɪʃən] N **1** (*state*) privazione *f* **2** (*hardship*) privazioni *fpl*, stenti *mpl*

◎ **pri·va·tize** ['praɪvɪˌtaɪz] VT privatizzare

priv·et ['prɪvɪt] N ligustro

privet hedge N siepe *f* di ligustro

privi·lege ['prɪvɪlɪdʒ] N privilegio; (*Parliament*) prerogativa; **I had the privilege of meeting her** ho avuto il privilegio *or* l'onore di incontrarla
■ VT: **to be privileged to do sth** avere il privilegio *or* l'onore di fare qc

privi·leged ['prɪvɪlɪdʒd] ADJ privilegiato(-a); **a privileged few** pochi privilegiati; **the privileged few** la minoranza dei privilegiati

privy ['prɪvɪ] ADJ: **to be privy to sth** essere a conoscenza *or* al corrente di qc
■ N (*old: toilet*) gabinetto, ritirata

Privy Council N (*Brit*): **the Privy Council** il Consiglio della Corona

PRIVY COUNCIL

Il **Privy Council**, un gruppo di consiglieri del re, era il principale organo di governo durante il regno dei Tudor e degli Stuart. Col tempo ha perso la sua importanza e oggi è un organo senza potere effettivo formato da ministri e altre personalità politiche ed ecclesiastiche.

▷ www.privy-council.org.uk/

Privy Councillor N (*Brit*) Consigliere *m* della Corona

◎ **prize**[1] [praɪz] N (*gen*) premio; **to win first prize** (*in game, race, lottery*) vincere il primo premio; (*Scol*) ottenere il primo premio
■ ADJ **1** (*awarded a prize*) premiato(-a); (*worthy of a prize*) eccellente; (*example*) perfetto(-a); **a prize idiot** (*fam*) un(-a) cretino(-a) patentato(-a) **2** (*awarded as a prize: cup, medal*) premio *inv (after n)*
■ VT (*honesty, friendship*) stimare, valutare; **he prizes his medals** è molto orgoglioso delle sue medaglie; **her most prized possession** il suo avere più prezioso; **a rare model, now much prized** un modello raro che oggi ha una valutazione molto alta

prize[2] [praɪz] VT (*Am*) = **prise**

prize draw N estrazione *f* a premi *or* a premio

prize fight N (*Boxing*) incontro di pugilato fra professionisti

prize fighter N (*Am*) pugile *m* professionista

prize fighting N pugilato professionistico

prize-giving ['praɪzˌgɪvɪŋ] N premiazione *f*

prize money N soldi *mpl* del premio

prize·winner ['praɪzˌwɪnəʳ] N (*in competition, lottery*) vincitore(-trice); (*Scol, in show*) premiato(-a)

prize·winning ['praɪzˌwɪnɪŋ] ADJ (*gen*) vincente; (*novel, essay*) premiato(-a)

pro- [prəʊ] PREF (*in favour of*) filo...; **pro-American** filoamericano(-a)

pro[1] [prəʊ] N: **the pros and cons** i pro e i contro; **we weighed up the pros and cons** abbiamo valutato i pro e i contro

pro[2] [prəʊ] N (*fam: Sport*) professionista *m/f*

pro-active [ˌprəʊ'æktɪv] ADJ: **to be pro-active** avere iniziativa

prob·abil·ity [ˌprɒbə'bɪlɪtɪ] N probabilità *f inv*; **in all probability** con ogni probabilità

prob·able ['prɒbəbl] ADJ probabile; **it is probable/**

Pp

hardly probable that ... è probabile/poco probabile che... + *sub*

◎ **prob·ably** ['prɒbəblɪ] ADV probabilmente

pro·bate ['prəʊbɪt] N (*Law*) omologazione *f* (di un testamento)

pro·ba·tion [prə'beɪʃən] N: **to be on probation** (*Law*) essere in libertà vigilata; (*gen: in employment*) essere in prova, fare un periodo di prova; **to put sb on probation** (*Law*) sottoporre qn a libertà vigilata

pro·ba·tion·ary [prə'beɪʃnərɪ] ADJ (*year, period*) di prova; (*teacher, nurse*) in prova; (*Law*) di libertà vigilata

pro·ba·tion·er [prə'beɪʃnəʳ] N (*Law*) persona sottoposta a libertà vigilata; (*in employment*) persona in prova; (*novice*) novizio(-a)

probation officer N (*Law*) *funzionario incaricato della sorveglianza delle persone sottoposte a libertà vigilata*

probe [prəʊb] N **1** (*Med, Space*) sonda **2** (*inquiry*) indagine *f*, investigazione *f*
■ VT (*hole, crack*) tastare; (*Med*) esplorare, sondare; (*Space*) esplorare; (*also:* **probe into**) indagare su; **the policeman kept probing me** il poliziotto continuò a farmi domande

prob·ing ['prəʊbɪŋ] ADJ (*look*) penetrante; (*question*) sottile; (*interrogation, study*) approfondito(-a)

pro·bity ['prəʊbɪtɪ] N probità, rettitudine *f*

◎ **prob·lem** ['prɒbləm] N (*also Math*) problema *m*; **to have problems with the car** avere dei problemi con la macchina; **my son is a problem** mio figlio è un problema; **the housing problem** la crisi degli alloggi; **to have a drinking problem** avere il vizio del bere; **I had no problem in finding her** non mi è stato difficile trovarla; **what's the problem?** che cosa c'è?; **no problem!** ma certamente!, non c'è problema!; **it's not my problem** è un affare che non mi riguarda; **that's no problem for/to him** per lui non è un problema
■ ADJ (*child, family*) difficile

prob·lem·at·ic [ˌprɒblɪ'mætɪk], **prob·lem·at·ical** [ˌprɒblɪ'mætɪkəl] ADJ problematico(-a), dubbio(-a); **it is problematic whether ...** è in dubbio se...

prob·lem page N posta del cuore

problem-solving N risoluzione *f* di problemi

pro·cedur·al [prə'si:djʊrəl] ADJ procedurale

◎ **pro·cedure** [prə'si:dʒəʳ] N (*Admin, Law*) procedura; **the usual procedure is to ...** la procedura normale *or* prassi è di...; **cashing a cheque is a simple procedure** riscuotere un assegno è un'operazione semplice

◎ **pro·ceed** [prə'si:d] VI **1** (*move forward*) procedere; **to proceed with sth** continuare qc; **let us proceed with caution** procediamo con cautela; **let us proceed to the next item** passiamo al prossimo punto; **things are proceeding according to plan** tutto procede *or* si svolge secondo i piani; **work was proceeding normally** il lavoro procedeva normalmente; **I am not sure how to proceed** non so bene come fare; **please proceed to gate 32** vi preghiamo di recarvi all'uscita 32 **2** (*originate*): **to proceed from** (*sound*) provenire da; (*fear*) derivare da **3 to proceed against sb** (*Law*) procedere contro qn
■ VT: **to proceed to do sth** cominciare *or* mettersi a fare qc; **he then proceeded to tell me the whole story** quindi cominciò a raccontarmi tutta la storia

pro·ceed·ing [prə'si:dɪŋ] N (*action, course of action*) modo d'agire

proceedings ['prə'si:dɪŋz] NPL **1** (*events*) avvenimenti *mpl*; (*manoeuvres*) manovre *fpl*; (*function*) cerimonia *fsg*; (*meeting*) riunione *fsg*, seduta *fsg*; (*discussions*) dibattito *msg* **2** (*esp Law: measures*) provvedimenti *mpl*, misure *fpl*; **to take proceedings (in order to do sth)** prendere i provvedimenti necessari (per fare qc); **to institute proceedings (against sb)** (*Law*) promuovere un'azione legale (contro qn) **3** (*records: of learned society*) atti *mpl*, rendiconti *mpl*

pro·ceeds ['prəʊsi:dz] NPL proventi *mpl*, ricavato *msg*; **the proceeds from the concert will go to charity** il ricavato del concerto sarà devoluto in beneficenza

◎ **pro·cess¹** ['prəʊsɛs] N **1** processo; **the whole process** l'intera operazione; **a lengthy process** un lungo procedimento; **in the process of restoring the picture he discovered ...** stava restaurando il quadro quando ha scoperto...; **in process of construction** in (corso di) costruzione; **the process of growing up** il processo della crescita; **we are in the process of moving to ...** stiamo per trasferirci a...; **the peace process** il processo di pace **2** (*specific method*) procedimento, sistema *m*, metodo; **the Bessemer process** il metodo Bessemer **3** (*Law: action*) processo; (*: summons*) mandato di comparizione, citazione *f* in giudizio
■ VT (*Tech*) trattare; (*Phot*) sviluppare e stampare; (*Admin: application etc*) sbrigare; (*Comput*) elaborare

pro·cess² [prə'sɛs] VI (*Brit frm: go in procession*) sfilare, procedere in corteo

pro·cessed cheese [ˌprəʊsɛst'tʃi:z], (*Am*) **process cheese** N formaggio fuso

pro·cess·ing ['prəʊsɛsɪŋ] N (*of data*) elaborazione *f*; (*of food*) trattamento; (*of film*) sviluppo e stampa; (*of application*) disbrigo

pro·ces·sion [prə'sɛʃən] N (*of people, cars*) processione *f*, corteo; (*Rel*) processione; **funeral procession** corteo funebre

pro·ces·sor ['prəʊsɛsəʳ] N (*Comput*) processore *m*

pro-choice ['prəʊ'tʃɔɪs] ADJ per la libertà di scelta di gravidanza

pro·claim [prə'kleɪm] VT **1** (*gen*) proclamare, dichiarare; (*peace, public holiday*) dichiarare; **to proclaim sb king/that** proclamare qn re/che **2** (*fig: reveal*) dimostrare, rivelare

proc·la·ma·tion [ˌprɒklə'meɪʃən] N proclama *m*, proclamazione *f*

pro·cliv·ity [prə'klɪvɪtɪ] N (*frm*) tendenza, propensione *f*

pro·cras·ti·nate [prəʊ'kræstɪˌneɪt] VI procrastinare

pro·cras·ti·na·tion [prəʊˌkræstɪ'neɪʃən] N procrastinazione *f*

pro·cre·ate ['prəʊkrɪˌeɪt] VI procreare

pro·crea·tion [ˌprəʊkrɪ'eɪʃən] N procreazione *f*

Procu·ra·tor Fis·cal ['prɒkjʊˌreɪtə'fɪskəl] N (*in Scotland*) ≈ procuratore *m*

pro·cure [prə'kjʊəʳ] VT **1** procurare, ottenere; **it's difficult to procure food and fuel** è difficile procurarsi cibo e carburante; **to procure sb sth** *or* **to procure sth for sb** procurare qc a qn, ottenere qc per qn; **I managed to procure a copy for myself** sono riuscito a procurarmene una copia **2** (*prostitute*) procurare

pro·cure·ment [prə'kjʊəmənt] N (*of goods*) rifornimento, approvvigionamento

pro·cur·er [prə'kjʊərəʳ] N (*Law*) prosseneta *m*, lenone *m*

pro·cur·ing [prə'kjʊərɪŋ] N (*Law*) lenocinio

prod [prɒd] N (*push, jab*) colpetto; (*with elbow*) gomitata
■ VT (*jab: with stick, finger*) dare un colpetto a; **he prodded the page with his finger** ha puntato il dito

sulla pagina; **he has to be prodded along** (*fig*) ha bisogno di essere pungolato
■ VI: **she prodded at the picture with a finger** ha puntato il dito sul quadro

prodi·gal ['prɒdɪgəl] ADJ prodigo(-a)

prodi·gal·ity [ˌprɒdɪ'gælɪtɪ] N prodigalità

pro·di·gious [prə'dɪdʒəs] ADJ prodigioso(-a), straordinario(-a)

pro·di·gious·ly [prə'dɪdʒəslɪ] ADV prodigiosamente

prodi·gy ['prɒdɪdʒɪ] N prodigio; **child prodigy** *or* **infant prodigy** bambino(-a) prodigio *inv*

pro·drome ['prəʊˌdrəʊm] N (*Med*) prodromo

◎ **pro·duce** [*n* 'prɒdju:s; *vb* prə'dju:s] N (*Agr*) prodotto
■ COLLECTIVE N prodotti *mpl*
■ VT **1** (*manufacture: gen*) produrre; (*create: book, essay*) scrivere; (*: work of art*) fare; (*: meal*) preparare; (*: ideas, profit*) dare; (*give birth to*) partorire **2** (*bring, show: gen*) tirar fuori; (*: tickets*) esibire, mostrare; (*: proof of identity*) produrre, fornire; **I can't suddenly produce £500!** da dove le tiro fuori 500 sterline? **3** (*film*) produrre; (*play*) mettere in scena **4** (*cause: gen*) causare, provocare; (*: results*) produrre; (*: interest*) suscitare; **this produced a stir** ha fatto sensazione

◎ **pro·duc·er** [prə'dju:sə^r] N (*Agr, Cine, TV, Theatre*) produttore(-trice)

◎ **prod·uct** ['prɒdʌkt] N (*also Math*) prodotto; (*fig*) frutto

◎ **pro·duc·tion** [prə'dʌkʃən] N **1** (*manufacture*) produzione *f*; **to put into production** mettere in produzione; **to take out of production** togliere dalla produzione; **the country's steel production** la produzione siderurgica del paese; **they're increasing production of luxury models** stanno aumentando la produzione di modelli di lusso **2** (*showing*) presentazione *f*; (*: of documents*) produzione *f*; **on production of this ticket** dietro presentazione di questo biglietto **3** (*of film, show*) produzione *f*; (*of play*) messa in scena; (*work produced*) realizzazione *f* teatrale (*or* cinematografica); **a production of "Hamlet"** una rappresentazione di "Amleto"

production agreement N (*Am*) accordo sui tempi di produzione

production control N controllo di produzione

production line N linea di produzione

production manager N direttore *m* di produzione, production manager *m/f inv*

production overheads NPL costi *mpl* indiretti di produzione

pro·duc·tive [prə'dʌktɪv] ADJ (*gen*) produttivo(-a); (*meeting, discussion*) fruttuoso(-a); (*enterprise, business*) che rende; (*writer*) prolifico(-a); (*land, imagination*) fertile; **he had a very productive day** ha avuto una giornata molto soddisfacente

prod·uc·tiv·ity [ˌprɒdʌk'tɪvɪtɪ] N produttività

productivity agreement N (*Brit*) accordo sui tempi di produzione

productivity bonus N premio di produzione

product line N linea di prodotti

product placement N pubblicità *f inv* occulta

product range N gamma di prodotti

pro·fane [prə'feɪn] ADJ **1** (*secular*) profano(-a) **2** (*irreverent*) irriverente; (*: language*) sacrilego(-a)
■ VT profanare

pro·fane·ly [prə'feɪnlɪ] ADV (*behave, speak*) in modo irriverente

pro·fan·ity [prə'fænɪtɪ] N (*oath*) imprecazione *f*

pro·fess [prə'fɛs] VT **1** (*faith, belief etc*) professare **2** (*claim*) dichiarare; **he professes extreme regret** si dichiara molto dispiaciuto; **he professed interest in my opinion** ha dichiarato di essere interessato alla mia opinione; **I do not profess to be an expert** non pretendo di essere un esperto

pro·fessed [prə'fɛst] ADJ (*Rel*) professo(-a); (*self-declared*) dichiarato(-a)

◎ **pro·fes·sion** [prə'fɛʃən] N **1** (*gen*) professione *f*; **the professions** le professioni liberali; **by profession** di professione; **the medical profession** (*calling*) la professione medica; (*doctors collectively*) i medici **2** (*declaration*) dichiarazione *f*; **profession of faith** (*Rel*) professione *f* di fede

◎ **pro·fes·sion·al** [prə'fɛʃənl] ADJ **1** (*capacity*) professionale; (*diplomat, soldier*) di carriera; **a professional man** un professionista; **to take professional advice** consultare un esperto; **to be a professional singer** essere un(-a) cantante *m/f* professionista *or* di professione; **to turn** *or* **go professional** (*Sport*) passare al professionismo **2** (*competent, skilled: worker*) esperto(-a); (*: piece of work, approach*) da professionista; (*: attitude*) professionale; **a very professional piece of work** un lavoro da professionista; **it's not up to professional standards** non è da professionista
■ N professionista *m/f*

pro·fes·sion·al·ism [prə'fɛʃnəˌlɪzəm] N professionismo

pro·fes·sion·al·ly [prə'fɛʃnəlɪ] ADV (*play*) come professionista; (*sing*) per professione; (*expertly*) professionalmente, in modo professionale; **she sings professionally** è una cantante professionista; **I only know him professionally** lo conosco solo per motivi di lavoro; **to be professionally qualified** essere abilitato(-a) alla professione

◎ **pro·fes·sor** [prə'fɛsə^r] N (*Univ: Brit*) docente *m/f*; (*: Am: teacher*) professore(-essa)

prof·es·so·rial [ˌprɒfə'sɔ:rɪəl] ADJ professorale

pro·fes·sor·ship [prə'fɛsəʃɪp] N cattedra

prof·fer ['prɒfə^r] VT (*remark*) profferire; (*hand*) porgere; (*apologies*) porgere, presentare; (*advice*) fornire

pro·fi·cien·cy [prə'fɪʃənsɪ] N competenza, abilità

pro·fi·cient [prə'fɪʃənt] ADJ provetto(-a), competente

pro·fi·cient·ly [prə'fɪʃəntlɪ] ADV abilmente

◎ **pro·file** ['prəʊfaɪl] N profilo; **in profile** di profilo; **to keep a low profile** (*fig*) cercare di non farsi notare troppo, cercare di passare inosservato(-a); **to maintain a high profile** mettersi in mostra; **low-profile tyre** (*Aut*) pneumatico a basso profilo

◎ **prof·it** ['prɒfɪt] N (*Comm*) profitto, utile *m*, guadagno; (*fig*) profitto, vantaggio, beneficio; **a profit of £10,000** un guadagno di 10.000 sterline; **to my profit** a mio vantaggio; **profit and loss account** conto profitti e perdite; **to make a profit out of** *or* **on sth** ricavare un utile da qc; **to sell sth at a profit** vendere qc con un utile
■ VI: **to profit by** *or* **from sth** ricavare beneficio da qc

> DID YOU KNOW ...?
> **profit** is not translated by the Italian word *approfittare*

prof·it·abil·ity [ˌprɒfɪtə'bɪlɪtɪ] N redditività

prof·it·able ['prɒfɪtəbl] ADJ (*Comm*) remunerativo(-a), redditizio(-a); (*fig: beneficial: scheme*) vantaggioso(-a); (*meeting, visit*) fruttuoso(-a)

prof·it·ably ['prɒfɪtəblɪ] ADV (*Comm*) con profitto; (*fig*) vantaggiosamente; (*: spend time*) utilmente

profit centre N centro di profitto

Pp

profi·teer [ˌprɒfɪ'tɪəʳ] VI speculare
■ N profittatore(-trice), speculatore(-trice)
profi·teer·ing [ˌprɒfɪ'tɪərɪŋ] N (*pej*) affarismo
prof·it·less ['prɒfɪtlɪs] ADJ (*fig*) inutile
profit-making ['prɒfɪtˌmeɪkɪŋ] ADJ (*industry*) rimunerativo(-a)
profit margin N margine *m* di profitto
profit-sharing ['prɒfɪtʃɛərɪŋ] N compartecipazione *f* agli utili
profits tax N (*Brit*) imposta sugli utili
profit-taking ['prɒfɪtteɪkɪŋ] N (*Econ*) presa di beneficio su un valore mobiliare
prof·li·ga·cy ['prɒflɪgəsɪ] N (*debauchery*) dissolutezza; (*extravagance*) grande prodigalità
prof·li·gate ['prɒflɪgɪt] ADJ (*dissolute*: *behaviour, act*) dissipato(-a); (: *person*) dissoluto(-a); **he's very profligate with his money** è uno che sperpera i suoi soldi
pro for·ma ['prəʊ'fɔːmə] ADV: **pro forma invoice** fattura proforma
pro·found [prə'faʊnd] ADJ profondo(-a)
pro·found·ly [prə'faʊndlɪ] ADV profondamente
pro·fun·dity [prə'fʌndɪtɪ] N profondità
pro·fuse [prə'fjuːs] ADJ (*tears, bleeding*) copioso(-a); (*vegetation*) abbondante; (*thanks, praise, apologies*) infinito(-a); **she was profuse in her thanks** si è profusa in ringraziamenti
pro·fuse·ly [prə'fjuːslɪ] ADV (*sweat, bleed*) abbondantemente; (*praise*) con grande effusione; (*grow*) rigogliosamente; **he apologized profusely** si è profuso in scuse
pro·fu·sion [prə'fjuːʒən] N profusione *f*, abbondanza; **in profusion** a profusione
pro·geni·tor [prəʊ'dʒɛnɪtəʳ] N (*frm*) progenitore(-trice), antenato(-a)
prog·eny ['prɒdʒɪnɪ] N (*frm*) progenie *f*, discendenti *mpl*
pro·ges·ter·one [prəʊ'dʒɛstəˌrəʊn] N progesterone *m*
prog·no·sis [prɒg'nəʊsɪs] N (*pl* **prognoses** [prɒg'nəʊsiːz]) (*Med*) prognosi *f inv*
prog·nos·ti·cate [prɒg'nɒstɪˌkeɪt] VT pronosticare, predire
prog·nos·ti·ca·tion [prɒgˌnɒstɪ'keɪʃən] N pronostico
◎ **program** ['prəʊgræm] N (*Comput*) programma *m*
■ VT (*computer, machine*) programmare
◎ **pro·gramme**, (*Am*) **pro·gram** ['prəʊgræm] N (*gen, Pol*) programma *m*; (*Radio, TV*: *broadcast*) programma, trasmissione *f*; (: *station*) canale *m*; **what's the programme for today?** che cosa facciamo oggi?
■ VT (*arrange*) programmare, stabilire
pro·grammed learn·ing [ˌprəʊgræmd'lɜːnɪŋ] N apprendimento graduale
programme editor N (*Radio, TV*) curatore(-trice) di un programma
programme music N musica a programma
programme note N programma *m* di sala
pro·gram·mer ['prəʊgræməʳ] N (*Comput*) programmatore(-trice); **she's a programmer** fa la programmatrice
programme seller N (*Theatre*) venditore(-trice) di programmi
pro·gram·ming, (*Am*) **pro·gram·ing** ['prəʊgræmɪŋ] N (*Comput*) programmazione *f*
programming language N (*Comput*) linguaggio di programmazione
◎ **pro·gress** [*n* 'prəʊgrɛs; *vb* prəʊ'grɛs] N (*gen*) progresso, progressi *mpl*; **to make progress** (*gen*) fare progressi; (*walk forward*) avanzare; **you're making progress!** stai facendo progressi!; **the pupil is making good progress** l'allievo fa dei buoni progressi; **the work is making little progress** il lavoro procede lentamente; **the progress of events** il corso degli avvenimenti; **in progress** (*meeting, work etc*) in corso; **that's progress!** questo è il progresso!
■ VI **1** (*go forward*) avanzare, procedere **2** (*in time*) procedere; **as the match progressed** man mano che la partita procedeva **3** (*improve, make progress*: *person*) fare progressi; (: *investigation, studies*) progredire
pro·gres·sion [prə'grɛʃən] N progresso; (*Math*) progressione *f*; **arithmetic/geometric progression** progressione aritmetica/geometrica
pro·gres·sive [prə'grɛsɪv] ADJ **1** (*increasing*: *disease, taxation*) progressivo(-a); **a progressive loss of memory** una progressiva perdita della memoria
2 (*favouring progress*: *idea, party*) progressista
pro·gres·sive·ly [prə'grɛsɪvlɪ] ADV progressivamente, gradualmente
progress report N (*Med*) bollettino medico; (*Admin*) rendiconto dei lavori; (*Scol*) pagella, scheda di valutazione
pro·hib·it [prə'hɪbɪt] VT **1** (*forbid*) proibire, vietare; **to prohibit sb from doing sth** vietare *or* proibire a qn di fare qc; **"smoking prohibited"** "vietato fumare"
2 (*prevent*: *thing*) impedire
pro·hi·bi·tion [ˌprəʊɪ'bɪʃən] N proibizione *f*, divieto; **Prohibition** (*esp Am*: *of alcohol*) proibizionismo
pro·hibi·tive [prə'hɪbɪtɪv] ADJ (*price*) proibitivo(-a)
pro·hibi·tive·ly [prə'hɪbɪtɪvlɪ] ADV in modo proibitivo; **it's prohibitively expensive** il costo è proibitivo
◎ **proj·ect** [*n* 'prɒdʒɛkt; *vb* prə'dʒɛkt] N (*scheme, plan, venture*) progetto, piano; (*study*) progetto, lavoro di ricerca; (: *Scol, Univ*) ricerca; **a development project** un piano di sviluppo; **a major project** un importante progetto; **I'm doing a project on the greenhouse effect** sto facendo una ricerca sull'effetto serra; studio
■ VT (*film*) proiettare; (*voice*) spiegare; (*one's personality*) mettere in luce; (*visit*) progettare
■ VI (*jut out*) sporgere in fuori
proj·ect·ed [prə'dʒɛktɪd] ADJ (*predicted*) previsto(-a); (*planned*) progettato(-a); **a population rise of 5% is projected** è previsto un aumento della popolazione del 5%
pro·jec·tile [prə'dʒɛktaɪl] N proiettile *m*
pro·jec·ting [prə'dʒɛktɪŋ] ADJ sporgente
pro·jec·tion [prə'dʒɛkʃən] N **1** (*of films, figures*) proiezione *f*; **sales projections** le proiezioni di vendita
2 (*forecast*: *of cost*) preventivo **3** (*overhang, protrusion*) sporgenza, prominenza
pro·jec·tion·ist [prə'dʒɛkʃənɪst] N (*Cine*) proiezionista *m/f*
projection room N (*Cine*) cabina di proiezione
pro·jec·tor [prə'dʒɛktəʳ] N (*Cine*) proiettore *m*
pro·lapse ['prəʊlæps] N (*Med*) prolasso
pro·letar·ian [ˌprəʊlə'tɛərɪən] ADJ, N proletario(-a)
pro·letari·at [ˌprəʊlə'tɛərɪət] N proletariato
pro-life ['prəʊ'laɪf] ADJ per il diritto alla vita
pro·lif·er·ate [prə'lɪfəˌreɪt] VI (*Bio, fig*) proliferare; (*animals*) prolificare
pro·lif·era·tion [prəˌlɪfə'reɪʃən] N (*see vb*) proliferazione *f*; prolificazione *f*
pro·lif·ic [prə'lɪfɪk] ADJ (*animal*) prolifico(-a); (*crop*) abbondante; (*writer*) fecondo(-a)
pro·lix ['prəʊlɪks] ADJ (*frm*) prolisso(-a)
prologue, (*Am*) **pro·log** ['prəʊlɒg] N prologo

pro·long [prəˈlɒŋ] VT prolungare
pro·lon·ga·tion [ˌprəʊlɒŋˈgeɪʃən] N prolungamento
prom [prɒm] N ABBR **1** (*Brit fam*) = **promenade** **2** (*Brit fam*) = **promenade concert**
■ N (*Am*) ballo studentesco

PROM

In Gran Bretagna i **Proms** (= promenade concerts) sono concerti di musica classica, i più noti dei quali sono quelli eseguiti nella Royal Albert Hall a Londra. Prendono il nome dal fatto che in origine il pubblico li ascoltava stando in piedi o passeggiando. È possibile acquistare biglietti molto economici per assistere ai concerti stando in piedi o sedendosi per terra di fronte all'orchestra. Negli Stati Uniti, invece, con prom si intende il ballo studentesco di una high school o di un college.
▷ www.bbc.co.uk/proms/

prom·enade [ˌprɒmɪˈnɑːd] N (*at seaside*) lungomare *m*
■ VI (*stroll*) passeggiare
promenade concert N (*Brit Mus*) concerto di musica classica (*che fa parte di una rassegna che si tiene ogni anno a Londra*)
promenade deck N (*Naut*) ponte *m* di passeggio
prom·enad·er [ˌprɒmɪˈnɑːdəʳ] N (*Brit Mus*) spettatore(-trice) (*di un concerto*)
Prometheus [prəˈmiːθɪəs] N Prometeo
promi·nence [ˈprɒmɪnəns] N (*of ridge*) prominenza; (*conspicuousness*) imponenza; (*of role*) importanza; **to come into prominence** (*person*) venire alla ribalta
◎ **promi·nent** [ˈprɒmɪnənt] ADJ **1** (*projecting: ridge*) prominente; (*: teeth*) sporgente; (*: cheekbones*) marcato(-a) **2** (*conspicuous*) che spicca; **put it in a prominent position** mettilo ben in vista **3** (*leading: role, feature*) di rilievo **4** (*well-known: personality*) molto in vista; **she is prominent in the field of ...** è un'autorità nel campo di...; **prominent people** gente *f* importante
promi·nent·ly [ˈprɒmɪnəntlɪ] ADV (*display, set*) ben in vista; **he figured prominently in the case** ha avuto una parte di primo piano nella faccenda
promis·cu·ity [ˌprɒmɪsˈkjuːɪtɪ] N (*sexual*) promiscuità
pro·mis·cu·ous [prəˈmɪskjʊəs] ADJ (*sexually*) promiscuo(-a)
pro·mis·cu·ous·ly [prəˈmɪskjʊəslɪ] ADV (*behave*) promiscuamente, in modo promiscuo
◎ **prom·ise** [ˈprɒmɪs] N promessa; **to make sb a promise** fare una promessa a qn; **he made me a promise** mi ha fatto una promessa; **to keep one's promise** mantenere la propria promessa; **it's a promise!** promesso!; **a young man of promise** un giovane promettente; **to show promise** promettere bene
■ VT promettere; **to promise (sb) to do sth** promettere (a qn) di fare qc; **she promised to write** ha promesso di scrivere; **to promise sb sth** *or* **to promise sth to sb** promettere qc a qn; **to promise sb the earth** *or* **the moon** (*fig*) promettere a qn mari e monti; **to promise o.s. sth** promettere a se stesso(-a) qc
■ VI: **I can't promise, but ...** non te (*or* ve *etc*) lo prometto, ma...; **to promise well** promettere bene
prom·is·ing [ˈprɒmɪsɪŋ] ADJ promettente; **it doesn't look promising** non sembra promettente; **the future is promising** il futuro promette bene; **a promising player** un giocatore promettente
prom·is·ing·ly [ˈprɒmɪsɪŋlɪ] ADV in modo promettente
prom·is·sory note [ˈprɒmɪsərɪˌnəʊt] N pagherò *m inv*
prom·on·tory [ˈprɒməntrɪ] N promontorio
◎ **pro·mote** [prəˈməʊt] VT **1** (*in job*): **to be promoted** avere una promozione; **she was promoted after six months** ha avuto una promozione dopo sei mesi; (*in rank*): **to promote sb (from sth) to sth** promuovere qn (da qc) a qc; **the team was promoted to the second division** (*Brit Ftbl*) la squadra è stata promossa in serie B **2** (*encourage: trade, plan, concert, campaign*) promuovere; (*: product*) lanciare, reclamizzare
pro·mot·er [prəˈməʊtəʳ] N (*gen*) promotore(-trice); (*of sporting event*) promoter *m inv*, organizzatore(-trice), fondatore(-trice); (*of cause*) sostenitore(-trice)
◎ **pro·mo·tion** [prəˈməʊʃən] N (*gen*) promozione *f*; **to get promotion** ottenere la promozione
pro·mo·tion·al [prəˈməʊʃənl] ADJ promozionale
◎ **prompt** [prɒmpt] ADJ (*comp* **-er**, *superl* **-est**) (*action*) tempestivo(-a); (*delivery*) immediato(-a); (*payment*) pronto(-a), immediato(-a); **a prompt reply** una risposta sollecita; **to be prompt to do sth** essere sollecito(-a) nel fare qc; **he's always very prompt** (*punctual*) è sempre molto puntuale, è sempre puntualissimo
■ ADV: **at 6 o'clock prompt** alle 6 in punto
■ N **1** (*Theatre*) imbeccata **2** (*Comput*) prompt *m inv*
■ VT **1** **to prompt sb to do sth** spingere qn a fare qc; **it prompts the thought that ...** questo fa pensare che... **2** (*Theatre*) suggerire a
prompt·er [ˈprɒmptəʳ] N (*Theatre*) suggeritore(-trice)
prompt·ing [ˈprɒmptɪŋ] N imbeccata, suggerimento
prompt·ly [ˈprɒmptlɪ] ADV (*speedily*) prontamente; (*punctually*) puntualmente; **we left promptly at seven** siamo partiti puntualmente alle sette
prompt·ness [ˈprɒmptnɪs] N (*speed*) prontezza, sollecitudine *f*; (*punctuality*) puntualità
prone [prəʊn] ADJ **1** (*face down*) a faccia in giù, prono(-a); **he lay prone on the floor** giaceva prono sul pavimento **2** (*liable*): **prone to** incline a, propenso(-a) a, soggetto(-a) a; **people with fair skin are prone to skin cancer** le persone di pelle chiara sono più soggette al cancro della pelle; **to be prone to illness** essere *or* andare soggetto(-a) a malattie; **she is prone to burst into tears if ...** scoppia facilmente in lacrime se...
prong [prɒŋ] N (*of fork*) rebbio, dente *m*; **three-pronged** (*fork*) a tre rebbi *or* denti; (*attack*) su tre fronti, triplice
pro·noun [ˈprəʊˌnaʊn] N pronome *m*
pro·nounce [prəˈnaʊns] VT **1** (*letter, word*) pronunciare; **how do you pronounce that word?** come si pronuncia quella parola? **2** (*declare*) dichiarare; **they pronounced him unfit to drive** lo hanno dichiarato inabile alla guida; **to pronounce o.s. for/against sth** dichiararsi in favore di/contro qc; **to pronounce sentence** (*Law*) pronunziare la sentenza
■ VI: **to pronounce in favour of/against sth** pronunciarsi in favore di/contro qc; **to pronounce on sth** pronunciarsi su qc
pro·nounce·able [prəˈnaʊnsəbl] ADJ pronunciabile
pro·nounced [prəˈnaʊnst] ADJ (*marked: improvement*) netto(-a), spiccato(-a); (*: views*) preciso(-a); **he has a pronounced limp** zoppica in modo molto pronunciato
pro·nounce·ment [prəˈnaʊnsmənt] N dichiarazione *f*

Pp

pron·to ['prɒntəʊ] ADV (*fam*) subito, immediatamente

DID YOU KNOW ...?
pronto is not translated by the Italian word *pronto*

pro·nun·cia·tion [prə,nʌnsɪ'eɪʃən] N pronuncia

◎**proof** [pru:f] N **1** (*evidence*) prova; (*Math*) dimostrazione *f*; **proof of identity** documento d'identità; **I have proof that he did it** ho le prove che è stato lui a farlo; **as** *or* **in proof of** come prova *or* testimonianza di; **to give** *or* **show proof of** dar prova di **2** (*test, trial*): **to put sth to the proof** mettere alla prova qc **3** (*Typ*) bozza, prova di stampa; (*Phot*) provino **4** (*of alcohol*): **70% proof** ≈ 40° (alcolici)
■ ADJ: **to be proof against** essere a prova di
■ VT (*tent, anorak*) impermeabilizzare

proof·read ['pru:f,ri:d] VT correggere le bozze di

proof·reader ['pru:f,ri:dəʳ] N correttore(-trice) di bozze

proof·read·ing ['pru:f,ri:dɪŋ] N correzione *f* di bozze

prop¹ [prɒp] N sostegno, appoggio, puntello; (*fig*) sostegno; **the army is the government's main prop** l'esercito è il principale sostegno del governo
■ VT (*also:* **prop up**) **1** (*rest, lean: ladder*) appoggiare; **to prop sth against** appoggiare qc contro *or* a; **she propped her bike against the wall** appoggiò la bicicletta al muro **2** (*support*) sostenere, puntellare; (*fig*) tenere su, tenere in piedi

prop² [prɒp] N ABBR (*Theatre*) (*elemento del*) *materiale m* di scena

propa·gan·da [,prɒpə'gændə] N propaganda
■ ADJ (*campaign, leaflets*) propagandistico(-a)

propa·gan·dist [,prɒpə'gændɪst] N (*pej*) persona che fa propaganda politica
■ ADJ (*activities, literature*) di propaganda politica

propa·gate ['prɒpə,geɪt] VT propagare
■ VI (*plants, theories*) propagarsi; (*birds*) riprodursi

propa·ga·tion [,prɒpə'geɪʃən] N (*see vb*) propagazione *f*; riproduzione *f*

pro·pane ['prəʊpeɪn] N propano

pro·pel [prə'pɛl] VT spingere

pro·pel·lant [prə'pɛlənt] N (*in rocket*) propellente *m*

pro·pel·ler [prə'pɛləʳ] N elica

pro·pel·ling pen·cil [prə,pɛlɪŋ'pɛnsl] N (*Brit*) portamina *m inv*

pro·pen·sity [prə'pɛnsɪtɪ] N tendenza; **propensity (for)** propensione *f* (per)

◎**prop·er** ['prɒpəʳ] ADJ **1** (*suitable, appropriate: clothes, tools*) adatto(-a), appropriato(-a); (*correct, right: order, way, method*) giusto(-a); (*seemly: behaviour, person*) decente, perbene; **the proper time** il momento adatto *or* giusto; **if you had come at the proper time ...** se fossi venuto all'ora giusta...; **in the proper way** come si deve; **this is the proper way to do it** questo è il modo giusto di farlo; **to go through the proper channels** (*Admin*) seguire la regolare procedura; **you have to have the proper equipment** bisogna avere l'attrezzatura adatta; **do as you think proper** fa' come ritieni opportuno; **it isn't proper to do that** non sta bene fare così ; **to do the proper thing by sb** agire bene verso qn; **proper to** (*Chem, Philosophy*) proprio di **2** (*actual, authentic*) vero(-a) e proprio(-a); **physics proper** la fisica propriamente detta; **he isn't a proper doctor** non è un medico come si deve; **in the proper sense of the word** nel vero senso della parola; **in the city proper** nella città vera e propria **3** (*fam: real: lady, gentleman*) vero(-a), autentico(-a); (*: thorough: mess*) vero(-a), bello(-a); **it's a proper nuisance** è proprio una bella scocciatura; **we didn't have a proper lunch, just sandwiches** non abbiamo mangiato un vero pranzo, solo dei panini
■ ADV (*Brit fam: very*) proprio; **to talk proper** (*correctly*) parlare bene

proper fraction N (*Math*) frazione *f* propria

◎**prop·er·ly** ['prɒpəlɪ] ADV **1** (*correctly: speak, write*) bene, come si deve; (*: use*) in modo giusto; **you're not doing it properly** non lo stai facendo come si deve; **she very properly refused** ha giustamente rifiutato; **properly speaking** propriamente parlando **2** (*in seemly fashion*) correttamente, decentemente; **not properly dressed** vestito(-a) in maniera sconveniente; **dress properly for your interview** vestiti in modo adeguato per il colloquio **3** (*fam: really, thoroughly*) veramente

proper noun N nome *m* proprio

prop·er·tied ['prɒpətɪd] ADJ: **a propertied man** un possidente

◎**prop·er·ty** ['prɒpətɪ] N **1** (*quality*) proprietà *f inv*, caratteristica **2** (*possessions*) beni *mpl*; (*land, building, Chem*) proprietà *f inv*; **a new property** una nuova casa; **he owns property in Spain** ha delle proprietà in Spagna; **personal property** beni *mpl* mobili; **"private property"** "proprietà privata"; **a man of property** un possidente; **is this your property?** è tuo?; **lost property** oggetti *mpl* smarriti **3** (*Theatre*) (elemento del) materiale *m* di scena

property developer N (*Brit*) costruttore *m* edile

property man, property manager N (*Theatre*) trovarobe *m inv*

property owner N proprietario(-a)

property tax N imposta patrimoniale

proph·ecy ['prɒfɪsɪ] N profezia

proph·esy ['prɒfɪ,saɪ] VT predire, profetizzare

proph·et ['prɒfɪt] N profeta *m*

proph·et·ess ['prɒfɪtɪs] N profetessa

pro·phet·ic [prə'fɛtɪk] ADJ profetico(-a)

pro·pheti·cal·ly [prə'fɛtɪkəlɪ] ADV profeticamente

prophy·lac·tic [,prɒfɪ'læktɪk] ADJ (*Med*) profilattico(-a)
■ N profilattico

pro·pi·ti·ate [prə'pɪʃɪ,eɪt] VT propiziarsi

pro·pi·tia·tion [prə,pɪʃɪ'eɪʃən] N propiziazione *f*

pro·pi·tious [prə'pɪʃəs] ADJ propizio(-a)

pro·pi·tious·ly [prə'pɪʃəslɪ] ADV in modo propizio

pro·po·nent [prə'pəʊnənt] N fautore(-trice)

◎**pro·por·tion** [prə'pɔ:ʃən] N **1** (*ratio*) proporzione *f*, pro rata; **the proportion of boys to girls** la proporzione dei ragazzi rispetto alle ragazze; **to be in proportion** (*numbers*) essere proporzionali; **in proportion to** in relazione a; **your weight in proportion to your height** il peso in relazione alla statura; **to be in/out of proportion (to one another)** essere proporzionati/sproporzionati (tra di loro); **to be in/out of proportion to** *or* **with sth** essere in proporzione/sproporzionato(-a) rispetto a qc; **to see sth in proportion** (*fig*) dare il giusto peso a qc; **sense of proportion** (*fig*) senso della misura **2** (*part, amount, share*) parte *f*; **they keep a proportion of the profits** si tengono una parte dei profitti **3**: **proportions** NPL (*size, dimensions*) proporzioni *fpl*
■ VT proporzionare, commisurare; **well-proportioned** ben proporzionato(-a)

pro·por·tion·al [prə'pɔ:ʃənl] ADJ: **proportional (to)** proporzionale (a)

pro·por·tion·al·ly [prə'pɔ:ʃnəlɪ] ADV proporzionalmente

proportional representation N *(Pol)* rappresentanza proporzionale

pro·por·tion·ate [prə'pɔːʃnɪt] ADJ: **proportionate (to)** proporzionato(-a) (a)

◎**pro·po·sal** [prə'pəuzl] N *(offer)* offerta, proposta; (: *of marriage*) proposta di matrimonio; *(suggestion)*: **proposal (for sth/to do sth)** proposta (di qc/di fare qc); *(plan)* progetto, proposta

◎**pro·pose** [prə'pəuz] VT **1** proporre; **to propose doing sth** proporre di fare qc; **what do you propose to do?** cosa proponi di fare?; **to propose that sth should be done** proporre che sia fatto qc; **I propose that we go by bus** propongo di andare con l'autobus; **to propose marriage to sb** fare una proposta di matrimonio a qn; **to propose sb for a job/as treasurer** proporre qn per un posto/come tesoriere; **to propose a toast to sb** proporre un brindisi a qn **2** *(have in mind)*: **to propose sth/to do** *or* **doing sth** proporsi qc/di fare qc
■VI *(offer marriage)* fare una proposta di matrimonio

pro·pos·er [prə'pəuzə^r] N *(Brit: of motion)* proponente *m/f*

propo·si·tion [ˌprɒpə'zɪʃən] N **1** *(statement, Math, Logic)* proposizione *f* **2** *(proposal)* proposta; **to make sb a proposition** proporre qc a qn; **a business proposition** una proposta d'affari **3** *(person or thing to be dealt with)*: **he's a tough proposition** è un osso duro; **that's a tough proposition** è un'impresa; **early retirement may seem an attractive proposition** il prepensionamento può sembrare una prospettiva allettante

pro·pound [prə'paund] VT *(idea, scheme, theory)* proporre, presentare; *(problem, question)* porre

pro·pri·etary [prə'praɪətərɪ] ADJ *(Comm)*: **proprietary article** prodotto con marchio depositato; **proprietary brand** marchio di fabbrica; **proprietary medicine** specialità farmaceutica; **proprietary name** nome depositato *or* registrato

pro·pri·etor [prə'praɪətə^r] N proprietario(-a)

pro·pri·etorial [prɒpraɪə'tɔːrɪəl] *(frm)* ADJ **1** *(behaviour, attitude)* possessivo(-a) **2** *(duties, rights)* del proprietario

pro·pri·ety [prə'praɪətɪ] N *(seemliness)* decoro, rispetto delle convenienze sociali; *(appropriateness)* convenienza; **the proprieties** le convenzioni sociali

pro·pul·sion [prə'pʌlʃən] N: **jet propulsion** propulsione *f* a getto

pro rata ['prəu'rɑːtə] ADV in proporzione, pro rata

pro·sa·ic [prəu'zeɪɪk] ADJ *(dull)* prosaico(-a), banale

pro·sai·cal·ly [prəu'zeɪɪkəlɪ] ADV prosaicamente

pro·scribe [prəus'kraɪb] VT proscrivere

pro·scrip·tion [prəus'krɪpʃən] N proscrizione *f*

prose [prəuz] N prosa; *(Scol: translation)* traduzione *f* dalla lingua madre *or* madrelingua

pros·ecute ['prɒsɪkjuːt] VT **1** *(Law)* intentare azione contro; **"trespassers will be prosecuted"** "i trasgressori saranno perseguiti a norma di legge"; **"shoplifters will be prosecuted"** "i taccheggiatori saranno perseguiti a norma di legge" **2** *(frm: carry on: inquiry)* proseguire

pros·ecut·ing at·tor·ney ['prɒsɪkjuːtɪŋə'tɜːnɪ] N *(Am)* ≈ procuratore *m*

◎**pros·ecu·tion** [ˌprɒsɪ'kjuːʃən] N *(Law: act, proceedings)* azione *f* giudiziaria; *(accusing side)* accusa; **witness for the prosecution** testimone per l'accusa; **the prosecution** ≈ il pubblico ministero

pros·ecu·tor ['prɒsɪkjuːtə^r] N *(Law)*: **public prosecutor** ≈ procuratore *m* della Repubblica

pros·elyt·ize ['prɒsɪlɪˌtaɪz] VI *(frm)* fare del proselitismo

prose writer N prosatore(-trice)

proso·dy ['prɒsədɪ] N prosodia

◎**pros·pect** [*n* 'prɒspɛkt; *vb* prə'spɛkt] N *(outlook)* vista; *(fig)* prospettiva; (: *hope*) speranza; (: *chance*) probabilità *f inv*; **future prospects** *(of person, country)* prospettive *fpl*; **it's a grim prospect** è una prospettiva poco allegra; **we are faced with the prospect of leaving** rischiamo di dovercene andare; **there's little prospect of its happening** ci sono poche probabilità che accada; **what have you got in prospect?** cos' hai in vista?; **there is every prospect of an early victory** tutto lascia prevedere una rapida vittoria; **what are his prospects?** che prospettiva ha?; **his future prospects are good** ha delle buone prospettive; **a job with no prospects** un lavoro che non offre nessuna prospettiva; **he is a good prospect for the team** è una speranza per la squadra; **to seem a good prospect** sembrare promettente
■VT esplorare
■VI: **to prospect for gold** cercare l'oro

pros·pect·ing [prəs'pɛktɪŋ] N *(Mining)* prospezione *f*

pro·spec·tive [prəs'pɛktɪv] ADJ *(buyer)* probabile; *(legislation, son-in-law)* futuro(-a); **a prospective buyer** un probabile acquirente; **the terms of the prospective deal** le condizioni della futura transazione

pro·spec·tor [prəs'pɛktə^r] N prospettore *m*; **gold prospector** cercatore *m* d'oro

pro·spec·tus [prəs'pɛktəs] N prospetto

pros·per ['prɒspə^r] VI *(person)* raggiungere il benessere (economico); *(business, trade)* prosperare

pros·per·ity [prɒs'pɛrɪtɪ] N benessere *m*, prosperità

pros·per·ous ['prɒspərəs] ADJ *(industry)* prospero(-a), fiorente; *(businessman)* di successo

pros·per·ous·ly ['prɒspərəslɪ] ADV in modo prospero; **to live prosperously** vivere agiatamente

pros·ta·glan·din [ˌprɒstə'glændɪn] N prostaglandina

pros·tate ['prɒsteɪt] N *(also:* **prostate gland***)* prostata, ghiandola prostatica

pros·the·sis [prɒs'θiːsɪs] N *(Med)* protesi *f inv*

pros·thet·ic [prɒs'θɛtɪk] ADJ *(Med, artificial)* artificiale

pros·ti·tute ['prɒstɪˌtjuːt] N prostituta; **male prostitute** prostituto
■VT prostituire

pros·ti·tu·tion [ˌprɒstɪ'tjuːʃən] N prostituzione *f*

pros·trate [*adj* 'prɒstreɪt; *vb* prɒ'streɪt] ADJ bocconi *inv*; *(in respect, submission)* prosternato(-a), prostrato(-a); *(exhausted)*: **prostrate (with)** prostrato(-a) (da)
■VT: **to prostrate o.s.** *(before sb)* prostrarsi, prosternarsi; *(on the floor)* stendersi bocconi; *(fig)* abbattersi

pros·tra·tion [prɒs'treɪʃən] N *(Med: exhaustion)* spossatezza

pro·tago·nist [prəu'tægənɪst] N protagonista *m/f*

◎**pro·tect** [prə'tɛkt] VT *(gen)* proteggere, salvaguardare; *(from cold, heat)* riparare; *(interests, rights)* salvaguardare

◎**pro·tec·tion** [prə'tɛkʃən] N **1** protezione *f*; *(against cold, wind)* riparo; **to be under sb's protection** essere sotto la protezione di qn **2** = **protection money**

pro·tec·tion·ism [prə'tɛkʃəˌnɪzəm] N protezionismo

pro·tec·tion·ist [prə'tɛkʃənɪst] ADJ protezionista
■N protezionista *m/f*

protection money N pizzo

protection racket N racket *m inv*

Pp

pro·tec·tive [prəˈtɛktɪv] ADJ *(gen)* protettivo(-a); **protective custody** *(Police)* protezione *f*
pro·tec·tive·ly [prəˈtɛktɪvlɪ] ADV *(say, act)* in modo protettivo
pro·tec·tor [prəˈtɛktəʳ] N protettore(-trice)
pro·tec·tor·ate [prəˈtɛktərɪt] N protettorato
pro·té·gé(e) [ˈprəʊtɪʒeɪ] N protetto(-a)
◎ **pro·tein** [ˈprəʊtiːn] N proteina
pro tem [prəʊˈtɛm] ADV ABBR (= **pro tempore**: *for the time being*) pro tempore
◎ **pro·test** [*n* ˈprəʊtɛst; *vb* prəˈtɛst] N protesta; **to do sth under protest** fare qc protestando; **he ignored their protests** ha ignorato le loro proteste; **a protest march** una manifestazione di protesta
■ VT protestare
■ VI: **to protest against/about** protestare contro/per; **to protest to sb** fare le proprie rimostranze a qn
Prot·es·tant [ˈprɒtɪstənt] ADJ, N protestante *(m/f)*
Prot·es·tant·ism [ˈprɒtɪstənˌtɪzəm] N protestantesimo
pro·tes·ta·tion [ˌprɒtɛsˈteɪʃən] N *(frm)* protesta
pro·test·er, **pro·tes·tor** [prəˈtɛstəʳ] N contestatore(-trice); *(in demonstration)* dimostrante *m/f*
protest march N marcia di protesta
protest meeting N manifestazione *f or* dimostrazione *f* di protesta
protest vote N voto di protesta
proto·col [ˈprəʊtəˌkɒl] N protocollo
pro·ton [ˈprəʊtɒn] N protone *m*
proton number N numero protonico
proto·plasm [ˈprəʊtəʊˌplæzəm] N protoplasma *m*
proto·type [ˈprəʊtəʊˌtaɪp] N prototipo
pro·tract [prəˈtrækt] VT protrarre
pro·tract·ed [prəˈtræktɪd] ADJ protratto(-a), prolungato(-a)
pro·trac·tor [prəˈtræktəʳ] N *(Geom)* goniometro
pro·trude [prəˈtruːd] VI sporgere
pro·trud·ing [prəˈtruːdɪŋ] ADJ sporgente
pro·tu·ber·ance [prəˈtjuːbərəns] N protuberanza, sporgenza
pro·tu·ber·ant [prəˈtjuːbərənt] ADJ *(eyes)* sporgente
◎ **proud** [praʊd] ADJ *(comp* **-er**, *superl* **-est)** **1** *(person)* orgoglioso(-a), fiero(-a); *(pej: arrogant)* superbo(-a); **to be proud to do sth** essere fiero di fare qc; **her parents are proud of her** i suoi sono orgogliosi di lei; **he was as proud as a peacock** si è gonfiato come un tacchino; **that's nothing to be proud of!** non mi pare che sia il caso di vantarsene! **2** *(splendid: ship)* superbo(-a), splendido(-a)
■ ADV: **to do sb proud** non far mancare nulla a qn; **to do o.s. proud** non farsi mancare nulla
proud·ly [ˈpraʊdlɪ] ADV *(see adj)* orgogliosamente, con fierezza; superbamente
◎ **prove** [pruːv] *(pt* **proved**, *pp* **proved** *or* **proven** [ˈpruːvən]) VT **1** *(verify)* provare, dimostrare; **to prove sb innocent** provare *or* dimostrare l'innocenza di qn; **he was proved right in the end** alla fine i fatti gli hanno dato ragione; **the police couldn't prove it** la polizia non è riuscita a dimostrarlo **2** *(put to the test: courage, usefulness etc)* dimostrare, mettere alla prova; **to prove o.s.** dar prova di sé **3** *(turn out)*: **to prove (to be) useful** rivelarsi utile; **to prove correct** risultare vero(-a); **if it proves (to be) otherwise** dovesse rivelarsi altrimenti
■ VI = VT **3**
prov·enance [ˈprɒvɪnəns] N *(frm)* provenienza, origine *f*

Pro·vence [prɒˈvɑ̃ːns] N Provenza
prov·erb [ˈprɒvɜːb] N proverbio
pro·ver·bial [prəˈvɜːbɪəl] ADJ proverbiale
pro·ver·bi·al·ly [prəˈvɜːbɪəlɪ] ADV proverbialmente
◎ **pro·vide** [prəˈvaɪd] VT **1** *(supply)* fornire; **it provides plenty of scope for development** offre molte possibilità di sviluppo; **to provide sb with sth** *or* **provide sth for sb** fornire qc a qn; **they provided us with maps** ci hanno fornito delle cartine; **to be provided with** essere dotato(-a) *or* munito(-a) di **2** *(legislation)* prevedere
■ VI: **the Lord will provide** Dio provvederà
▸ **provide for** VI + PREP **1** *(financially)* provvedere a; (: *in the future*) provvedere al futuro di; **he can't provide for his family any more** non è più in grado di mantenere la famiglia **2** **the treaty does not provide for that** il trattato non lo contempla; **we have provided for that** vi abbiamo provveduto
pro·vid·ed [prəˈvaɪdɪd] CONJ: **provided (that)** sempre che *+ sub*, a patto che *+ sub*, purché *+sub*, a condizione che *+sub*; **he'll play in the next match provided he's fit** giocherà nella prossima partita sempre che sia in forma
provi·dence [ˈprɒvɪdəns] N provvidenza
provi·den·tial [ˌprɒvɪˈdɛnʃəl] ADJ provvidenziale
provi·den·tial·ly [ˌprɒvɪˈdɛnʃəlɪ] ADV provvidenzialmente
pro·vid·ing [prəˈvaɪdɪŋ] CONJ: **providing (that)** *see* provided
◎ **prov·ince** [ˈprɒvɪns] N provincia; **they live in the provinces** vivono in provincia; **it's not (within) my province** *(fig)* questo non rientra nel mio campo
pro·vin·cial [prəˈvɪnʃəl] ADJ *(gen)* di provincia; *(pej)* provinciale
■ N *(usu pej)* provincialotto(-a)
pro·vin·cial·ism [prəˈvɪnʃəˌlɪzəm] N *(pej)* provincialismo
◎ **pro·vi·sion** [prəˈvɪʒən] N **1** *(supplying: of power, water)* fornitura; (: *of food)* approvvigionamento; (: *of hospitals, housing)* costruzione *f* **2** *(supply)* provvista, riserva, rifornimento, scorta; **the provision of health care** la fornitura di prestazioni sanitarie; **provisions** *(food)* provviste, scorte; **to get** *or* **lay in provisions** fare provviste; **provisions are running short** le provviste stanno finendo; **provision of capital** *(Fin)* apporto di capitale **3** *(preparation)*: **to make provision for** *(one's family, future)* pensare a; *(journey)* fare i preparativi per; **he made provision for his nephew in his will** ha pensato a suo nipote nel testamento **4** *(stipulation)* disposizione *f*, clausola; **there's no provision for this in the contract** il contratto non lo prevede; **with the provision that** a condizione che; **there's no provision for this in the contract** il contratto non lo prevede
Provisional ADJ, N *(Ir Pol)* provisional *m inv (membro dell'ala estremista dell'IRA)*
pro·vi·sion·al [prəˈvɪʒənl] ADJ provvisorio(-a)
provisional licence N *(Brit Aut)* ≈ foglio *m* rosa *inv*
pro·vi·sion·al·ly [prəˈvɪʒnəlɪ] ADV *(accept)* provvisoriamente; *(appoint)* a titolo provvisorio
pro·vi·so [prəˈvaɪzəʊ] N condizione *f*; **with the proviso that** a condizione che *+sub*, a patto che *+sub*
pro·vi·sory [prəˈvaɪzərɪ] ADJ *(provisional)* provvisorio(-a); *(Law)* condizionale
Pro·vo [ˈprəʊvəʊ] N *membro dell'ala estremista dell'IRA*
provo·ca·tion [ˌprɒvəˈkeɪʃən] N provocazione *f*; **she acted under provocation** ha agito così perché è stata provocata

pro·voca·tive [prəˈvɒkətɪv] ADJ *(causing anger)* provocatorio(-a); *(seductive)* provocante; *(thought-provoking)* stimolante

pro·voca·tive·ly [prəˈvɒkətɪvlɪ] ADV *(see adj)* provocatoriamente, in modo provocatorio; in modo provocante; in modo stimolante

◎ **pro·voke** [prəˈvəʊk] VT *(gen)* provocare, incitare; **to provoke sb to sth/to do** *or* **into doing sth** spingere qn a qc/a fare qc

pro·vok·ing [prəˈvəʊkɪŋ] ADJ irritante, esasperante

prov·ost [ˈprɒvəst] N *(Brit Univ)* rettore *m*; *(Scot)* sindaco

prow [praʊ] N prua

prow·ess [ˈpraʊɪs] N *(skill)*: **his prowess as a footballer** le sue capacità di calciatore

prowl [praʊl] VI *(also:* **prowl about** *or* **around***)* aggirarsi
■ N: **on the prowl** in cerca di preda

prowl·er [ˈpraʊləʳ] N: **there was a prowler in the garden** c'era un tipo sospetto che si aggirava in giardino

prox·im·ity [prɒkˈsɪmɪtɪ] N vicinanza, prossimità; **in the proximity of** in prossimità di

proxy [ˈprɒksɪ] N *(power)* procura, delega; *(person)* mandatario(-a); **by proxy** per procura

Pro·zac® [ˈprəʊzæk] N *(Med)* Prozac *m inv*

PRP [ˌpiːɑːˈpiː] N ABBR = **performance related pay**

prude [pruːd] N puritano(-a), prude *m/f*

pru·dence [ˈpruːdəns] N prudenza

pru·dent [ˈpruːdənt] ADJ prudente

pru·dent·ly [ˈpruːdəntlɪ] ADV prudentemente

prud·ish [ˈpruːdɪʃ] ADJ puritano(-a), che si scandalizza facilmente

prud·ish·ness [ˈpruːdɪʃnɪs] N puritanesimo

prune¹ [pruːn] N *(fruit)* prugna (secca)

prune² [pruːn] VT *(tree)* potare; *(size, cost)* ridurre

prun·ing [ˈpruːnɪŋ] N potatura

pruning knife N falcetto

pruning shears NPL cesoie *fpl*, forbici *fpl* da giardiniere

pru·ri·ence [ˈprʊərɪəns] N *(unhealthy interest)* curiosità morbosa, lascivia

pru·ri·ent [ˈprʊərɪənt] ADJ *(person)* lascivo(-a); *(interest)* morboso(-a)

Prus·sia [ˈprʌʃə] N Prussia

Prus·sian [ˈprʌʃən] ADJ, N prussiano(-a)

prus·sic acid [ˈprʌsɪkˈæsɪd] N acido prussico

pry¹ [praɪ] VI essere troppo curioso(-a); **to pry into sb's affairs** cacciare il naso negli affari di qn; **he's always prying into other people's affairs** s'impiccia sempre degli affari altrui

pry² [praɪ] VT *(Am)* = **prise**

pry·ing [ˈpraɪɪŋ] ADJ curioso(-a), indiscreto(-a)

PS, ps. ABBR (= **postscript**) PS

psalm [sɑːm] N salmo

psalm·ist [ˈsɑːmɪst] N salmista *m*

psal·ter [ˈsɔːltəʳ] N salterio

pseud [ˈsjuːd] N *(fam: poser)* intellettualoide *m/f*

pseu·do [ˈsjuːdəʊ] ADJ *(fam)* fasullo(-a), finto(-a)

pseudo... [ˈsjuːdəʊ] PREF pseudo...

pseudo·bio·graph·ic, pseudo·bio·graph·ical [ˌsjuːdəʊˌbaɪəʊˈgræfɪk(əl)] ADJ pseudobiografico(-a)

pseudo-intellectual [ˌsjuːdəʊˌɪntɪˈlɛktjʊəl] ADJ, N pseudointellettuale *(m/f)*

pseudo·nym [ˈsjuːdəˌnɪm] N pseudonimo

pseudo·sci·ence [ˈsjuːdəʊˌsaɪəns] N pseudoscienza

pseudo·sci·en·tif·ic [ˌsjuːdəʊˌsaɪənˈtɪfɪk] ADJ pseudoscientifico(-a)

PSNI [ˈpiːɛsɛnˌaɪ] N ABBR *(Brit:* = **Police Service of Northern Ireland***)* forze *fpl* di polizia dell'Irlanda del Nord

pso·ria·sis [sɒˈraɪəsɪs] N psoriasi *f*

psyche [ˈsaɪkɪ] N *(Psych)* psiche *f*

psychedel·ic [ˌsaɪkɪˈdɛlɪk] ADJ psichedelico(-a)

psy·chi·at·ric [ˌsaɪkɪˈætrɪk] ADJ *(treatment, hospital)* psichiatrico(-a); *(disease, illness)* mentale

psy·chia·trist [saɪˈkaɪətrɪst] N psichiatra *m/f*

psy·chia·try [saɪˈkaɪətrɪ] N psichiatria
▹ www.nmha.org
▹ www.psych.org/

psy·chic [ˈsaɪkɪk] ADJ **1** *(supernatural)* metapsichico(-a), paranormale; *(telepathic)* che ha dei poteri telepatici; **you must be psychic!** *(fam)* devi essere un indovino!, devi avere poteri telepatici!; **psychic powers** poteri paranormali **2** *(Psych)* psichico(-a), della psiche

psy·cho [ˈsaɪkəʊ] N *(Am fam)* folle *m/f*, psicopatico(-a)

psycho·ac·tive [ˌsaɪkəʊˈæktɪv] ADJ psicoattivo(-a)

psychoanalyse, *(Am)* **psycho·ana·lyze** [ˌsaɪkəʊˈænəˌlaɪz] VT psicanalizzare

psy·cho·analy·sis [ˌsaɪkəʊəˈnælɪsɪs] N psicanalisi *f inv*
▹ http://aapsa.org/
▹ www.psychoanalysis.org.uk/

psycho·ana·lyst [ˌsaɪkəʊˈænəlɪst] N psicanalista *m/f*

psycho·ana·lyt·ic, psycho·ana·lyt·ical [ˈsaɪkəʊˌænəˈlɪtɪk(əl)] ADJ psicanalitico(-a)

psychoanalyze [ˌsaɪkəʊˈænəlaɪz] VT = **psychoanalyse**

psycho·bab·ble [ˈsaɪkəʊˌbæbl] N *(fam)* linguaggio da psicanalista

psycho·dra·ma [ˈsaɪkəʊˌdrɑːmə] N *(Psych)* psicodramma *m*

psycho·dy·nam·ic [ˌsaɪkəʊdaɪˈnæmɪk] ADJ psicodinamico(-a)

psycho·dy·nam·ics [ˌsaɪkəʊdaɪˈnæmɪks] N psicodinamica

psycho·ki·nesis [ˌsaɪkəʊkɪˈniːsɪs] N psicocinesi *f*

psycho·lin·guis·tic [ˈsaɪkəʊlɪŋˈgwɪstɪk] ADJ psicolinguistico(-a)

psycho·lin·guis·tics [ˌsaɪkəʊlɪŋˈgwɪstɪks] N psicolinguistica

◎ **psycho·logi·cal** [ˌsaɪkəˈlɒdʒɪkəl] ADJ psicologico(-a)

psycho·logi·cal·ly [ˌsaɪkəˈlɒdʒɪkəlɪ] ADV psicologicamente

psychological warfare N guerra psicologica

psy·cholo·gist [saɪˈkɒlədʒɪst] N psicologo(-a)

psy·chol·ogy [saɪˈkɒlədʒɪ] N psicologia
▹ www.apa.org/

psycho·met·ric [ˌsaɪkəʊˈmɛtrɪk] ADJ psicometrico(-a)

psycho·met·rics [ˌsaɪkəʊˈmɛtrɪks] N psicometria

psycho·path [ˈsaɪkəʊˌpæθ] N psicopatico(-a)

psycho·path·ic [ˌsaɪkəʊˈpæθɪk] ADJ psicopatico(-a)

psycho·physi·cal [ˌsaɪkəʊˈfɪzɪkəl] ADJ psicofisico(-a)

psycho·phys·ics [ˌsaɪkəʊˈfɪzɪks] NSG psicofisica

psy·cho·sis [saɪˈkəʊsɪs] N *(pl* **psychoses** [saɪˈkəʊsiːz]*)* psicosi *f inv*

psycho·so·mat·ic [ˌsaɪkəʊsəʊˈmætɪk] ADJ psicosomatico(-a)

psycho·thera·pist [ˌsaɪkəʊˈθɛrəpɪst] N psicoterapeuta *m/f*, psicoterapista *m/f*

psycho·thera·py [ˌsaɪkəʊˈθɛrəpɪ] N psicoterapia

psy·chot·ic [saɪˈkɒtɪk] ADJ, N psicotico(-a)

psycho·trop·ic [ˌsaɪkəʊˈtrɒpɪk] ADJ psicotropo(-a)

psych out [saɪk-] VT + ADV *(fam: frighten)* intimidire

psych up VT + ADV *(fam)*: **to psych oneself up** caricarsi, prepararsi psicologicamente

Pp

pt ABBR **1** = **pint** **2** = **point**
PTA [ˌpi:ti:ˈeɪ] N ABBR = **parent-teacher association**
ptar·mi·gan [ˈtɑ:mɪgən] N pernice *f* bianca
ptero·dac·tyl [ˌtɛrəʊˈdæktɪl] N pterodattilo
PTO [ˌpi:ti:ˈəʊ] ABBR (= **please turn over**) v.r. (= *vedi retro*)
PTSD [ˌpi:ti:ɛsˈdi:] N ABBR = **post-traumatic stress disorder**
pub [pʌb] N (*Brit*) pub *m inv*

PUB

In Gran Bretagna e in Irlanda i **pubs** sono locali dove vengono servite bibite alcoliche ed analcoliche e dove è anche possibile mangiare. Sono punti di ritrovo dove spesso si può giocare a biliardo, a freccette o guardare la televisione. Le leggi che regolano la vendita degli alcolici sono molto severe in Gran Bretagna e quindi gli orari di apertura e di chiusura vengono osservati scrupolosamente.

pub-crawl [ˈpʌbˌkrɔ:l] N (*Brit fam*): **to go on a pub-crawl** fare il giro dei pub
pu·ber·ty [ˈpju:bətɪ] N pubertà
pu·bes·cent [pju:ˈbɛsənt] ADJ (*girl, boy*) pubere, nell'età puberale; (*age*) puberale
pu·bic [ˈpju:bɪk] ADJ pubico(-a), del pube
pu·bis [ˈpju:bɪs] N pube *m*
pub·lic [ˈpʌblɪk] ADJ (*gen*) pubblico(-a); (*Comm: industry*) statale; **in the public interest** nel pubblico interesse; **to be public knowledge** essere di pubblico dominio; **he's a public figure** *or* **he's in public life** è un personaggio della vita pubblica; **a public place** un luogo pubblico; **this place is too public to discuss it** c'è troppa gente qui per poterne discutere; **to make sth public** render noto *or* di pubblico dominio qc; **to be in the public eye** essere una persona molto in vista, essere un personaggio in vista; **her public support of** il suo aperto appoggio a; **to create more public awareness (of)** focalizzare l'attenzione del pubblico (su); **to go public** (*Comm*) immettere le azioni sul mercato
■ N: **the public** il pubblico; **open to the public** aperto al pubblico; **in public** in pubblico; **the sporting/reading public** il pubblico sportivo/dei lettori
public address system [ˌpʌblɪkəˈdrɛsˌsɪstəm] N impianto di amplificazione
pub·li·can [ˈpʌblɪkən] N (*Brit*) gestore *m* (*or* proprietario) di un pub
pub·li·ca·tion [ˌpʌblɪˈkeɪʃən] N pubblicazione *f*
public company N società *f inv* per azioni quotata in borsa
public convenience N (*Brit*) gabinetti *mpl* pubblici
public enemy N nemico *or* pericolo pubblico
public holiday N giorno festivo, festa nazionale
public house N (*Brit*) pub *m inv*
pub·li·cist [ˈpʌblɪsɪst] N pubblicitario(-a)
pub·lic·ity [pʌbˈlɪsɪtɪ] N **1** pubblicità **2** (*Comm: advertising, advertisements*) pubblicità *f inv*, réclame *f inv*
■ ADJ (*campaign, material, budget*) pubblicitario(-a); (*manager*) della pubblicità
pub·li·cize [ˈpʌblɪˌsaɪz] VT **1** (*make public*) far sapere in giro **2** (*advertise*) fare (della) pubblicità a, reclamizzare
Public Lending Right N *diritti d'autore sul prestito bibliotecario*
public limited company N ≈ società *f inv* a responsabilità limitata quotata in Borsa
pub·lic·ly [ˈpʌblɪklɪ] ADV (*say, do etc*) pubblicamente; **a publicly-owned company** una società nazionalizzata
public opinion N opinione *f* pubblica
public opinion poll N sondaggio d'opinione
public ownership N: **to be taken into public ownership** essere statalizzato(-a)
public prosecutor N (*Brit*) ≈ pubblico ministero; **public prosecutor's office** l'ufficio del pubblico ministero
public relations NPL relazioni *fpl* pubbliche
public relations officer N addetto(-a) alle pubbliche relazioni
public school N (*Brit*) scuola superiore privata; (*Am*) scuola statale

PUBLIC SCHOOL

In Inghilterra le **public schools** sono scuole o collegi privati di istruzione secondaria, spesso di un certo prestigio. In Scozia e negli Stati Uniti, invece, le **public school** sono scuole pubbliche gratuite amministrate dallo stato.
▷ www.publicschools.co.uk

public sector N settore *m* pubblico
public servant N funzionario(-a) della pubblica amministrazione
public service N (*Civil Service*) amministrazione *f* pubblica
public service announcement N (*Am*) importante annuncio trasmesso per radio o per televisione
public service broadcasting N (*TV, Radio*) servizio radiotelevisivo pubblico
public speaking N arte *f* oratoria
public-spirited [ˌpʌblɪkˈspɪrɪtɪd] ADJ (*attitude*) che denota senso civico; (*act*) di civismo; (*person*) che ha senso civico
public transport, (*Am*) **public transportation** N mezzi *mpl* pubblici
public utility N servizio pubblico
public works NPL lavori *mpl* pubblici
pub·lish [ˈpʌblɪʃ] VT pubblicare; **who publishes Moravia?** chi è l'editore di Moravia?; **"published weekly"** "edito settimanalmente", "pubblicato settimanalmente"
pub·lish·er [ˈpʌblɪʃə^r] N (*person*) editore *m*; (*firm*) casa editrice
pub·lish·ing [ˈpʌblɪʃɪŋ] N (*industry*) editoria, industria editoriale; (*of book*) pubblicazione *f*
▷ www.publishers.org
▷ www.publishers.org.uk/
publishing company, publishing house N casa *or* società editrice
puce [pju:s] ADJ color pulce *inv*
puck [pʌk] N (*Ice Hockey*) disco
puck·er [ˈpʌkə^r] VT (*also:* **pucker up**: *lips*) increspare; (: *brow*) aggrottare, corrugare; (: *Sewing*) increspare
pud·ding [ˈpʊdɪŋ] N (*dessert*) dolce *m*, dessert *m inv*; **what's for pudding?** cosa c'è per dessert?; (*steamed pudding*) *dolce cotto a bagnomaria a base di uova, burro, farina e latte*; **black pudding** *or* (*Am*) **blood pudding** sanguinaccio; **rice pudding** budino di riso
pudding basin N terrina
pud·dle [ˈpʌdl] N pozzanghera, pozza
pu·er·ile [ˈpjʊəraɪl] ADJ puerile, infantile
Puer·to Rico [ˈpwɜ:təʊˈri:kəʊ] N Portorico

puff [pʌf] N **1** (*of breath*) soffio; (*of engine*) sbuffare *m*; (*of air, wind*) folata, soffio; (*of smoke*) sbuffo; (*of cigarette*) tiro, boccata; **I'm out of puff** (*fam*) sono senza fiato
2 (*powder puff*) piumino della cipria **3** (*Culin*): **cream puff** sfogliatina alla panna
■VT **1** **to puff (out) smoke** *etc* mandar fuori (sbuffi di) fumo *etc* **2** (*also:* **puff out**: *sails, cheeks*) gonfiare; **his face was all puffed up** la sua faccia era tutta gonfia
■VI (*breathe heavily*) ansimare; (*blow*) soffiare; **he started puffing, and pedalled more slowly** cominciò ad ansimare e a pedalare più piano; **the train puffed into the station** il treno entrò sbuffando in stazione; **to puff (away) at** *or* **on one's pipe** tirare boccate di fumo dalla pipa

puff adder N vipera del deserto

puff·ball ['pʌf,bɔ:l] N (*mushroom*) vescia

puffed ['pʌft] ADJ (*fam*: *out of breath*): **I'm puffed (out)** sono senza fiato

puf·fin ['pʌfɪn] N pulcinella *m* di mare, puffino

puffi·ness ['pʌfɪnɪs] N gonfiore *m*

puff pastry, (*Am*) **puff paste** N pasta sfoglia

puff sleeves NPL maniche *fpl* a sbuffo

puffy ['pʌfɪ] ADJ (*comp* **-ier**, *superl* **-iest**) gonfio(-a)

pug [pʌg] N (*also:* **pug dog**) carlino

pu·gi·lism ['pju:dʒɪ,lɪzəm] N (*frm*) pugilato, boxe *f*

pu·gi·list ['pju:dʒɪlɪst] N (*frm*) pugile *m*

pug·na·cious [pʌg'neɪʃəs] ADJ bellicoso(-a), battagliero(-a)

pug·na·cious·ly [pʌg'neɪʃəslɪ] ADV in modo battagliero

pug·nac·ity [pʌg'næsɪtɪ] N combattività, bellicosità

pug-nosed [,pʌg'nəʊzd] ADJ dal naso rincagnato

puke [pju:k] VI (*fam*) rigettare

puk·ka ['pʌkə] ADJ (*fam*: *genuine*) originale, autentico(-a); (*excellent*) eccellente, di prim'ordine; **he's a pukka sahib** (*Brit*) è un vero gentleman

◎ **pull** [pʊl] N
1 (*tug*) strattone *m*, tirata, strappo; (*of moon, magnet, the sea*) attrazione *f*; (*fig*: *attraction*: *of personality*) forza di attrazione; (: *of family ties*) forza; **I felt a pull at my sleeve** ho sentito qualcuno che mi tirava per la manica; **to give sth a pull** dare uno strattone a qc; **he has some pull with the manager** (*fam*: *influence*) ha dell'influenza sul direttore
2 (*at pipe*) boccata, tirata; (*at beer*) sorsata; **he took a pull at the bottle** ha bevuto un sorso dalla bottiglia
3 (*handle of drawer*) maniglia, pomolo; (*of bell*) cordone *m*
■VT
1 (*draw*: *cart*) tirare, trascinare; (: *curtains*) tirare; (: *fig*: *crowd*) attirare; **to pull a door shut/open** chiudere/aprire la porta tirandola
2 (*tug*: *handle, rope*) tirare; (*press*: *trigger*) premere; **to pull sb's hair** tirare i capelli a qn; **she pulled my hair** mi ha tirato i capelli; **to pull to pieces** *or* **to bits** (*toy*) fare a pezzi; (*argument*) demolire; (*person, play*) stroncare; **to pull one's punches** (*Boxing*) risparmiare l'avversario; **she didn't pull any punches** (*fig*) non ha risparmiato nessun colpo; **to pull sb's leg** prendere in giro qn; **you're pulling my leg!** mi stai prendendo in giro!; **to pull strings (for sb)** muovere qualche pedina (per qn); **to pull one's weight** fare la propria parte, dare il proprio contributo; **to pull a face** fare una smorfia
3 (*extract, draw out*: *gen*) togliere; (: *gun, knife*) tirar fuori; (: *weeds*) strappare; (: *leeks, rhubarb*) raccogliere; (: *beer*) spillare; **to pull a gun on sb** estrarre una pistola e puntarla contro qn
4 (*tear*: *thread*) tirare; **to pull a muscle** farsi uno strappo muscolare; **to pull a tendon** farsi uno stiramento
5 (*fam*: *carry out, do*: *robbery*) fare; **to pull a fast one on sb** combinarla a qn
■VI
1 (*tug*) tirare; **pull!** tira!; **to pull at sb's sleeve** tirare qn per la manica; **the car is pulling to the right** lo sterzo *or* la macchina tira a destra; **to pull at** *or* **on one's pipe** tirare boccate dalla pipa
2 (*move*): **to pull for the shore** remare verso la riva; **the train pulled into/out of the station** il treno è entrato in/è partito dalla stazione; **he pulled alongside the kerb** ha accostato al marciapiede; **we pulled clear of the traffic** ci siamo lasciati il traffico alle spalle

▸ **pull about** VT + ADV (*handle roughly*: *object*) strapazzare; (: *person*) malmenare

▸ **pull along** VT + ADV trascinare; **to pull o.s. along** trascinarsi

▸ **pull apart** VT + ADV
1 (*pull to pieces*) smontare; (*break*) fare a pezzi, sfasciare; (*separate*) separare
2 (*fig fam*: *search thoroughly*) frugare dappertutto in; (: *criticize*: *novel, theory*) demolire

▸ **pull away** VT + ADV strappare via
■VI + ADV (*move off*: *vehicle*) muoversi, partire; **to pull away from** (*kerb*) allontanarsi da; (*quay*) staccarsi da; (*platform*) muoversi da; (*subj*: *runner*: *competitors*) distanziare

▸ **pull back** VT + ADV (*person, lever*) tirare indietro; (*curtains*) aprire
■VI + ADV tirarsi indietro; (*Mil*) ritirarsi

▸ **pull down** VT + ADV
1 (*gen*) tirar giù; (*opponent*) stendere a terra
2 (*demolish*: *buildings*) demolire, buttar giù; **the old school was pulled down last year** la vecchia scuola fu demolita l'anno scorso

▸ **pull in** VT + ADV
1 (*rope, fishing line*) tirare su; (*Naut*: *sail*) cazzare; (*person*: *into car, room*) tirare dentro; (*stomach*) tirare in dentro
2 (*rein in*: *horse*) trattenere
3 (*attract*: *crowds*) attirare
4 (*fam*: *take into custody*) mettere dentro; **the police pulled him in for questioning** la polizia l'ha fermato per interrogarlo
■VI + ADV (*Aut*: *arrive*) arrivare; (: *stop*) fermarsi; **she pulled in at the side of the road** si fermò a lato della strada

▸ **pull off** VT + ADV
1 (*remove*: *wrapping paper*) strappare; (: *clothes, shoes, gloves*) levarsi, togliersi
2 (*fam*: *succeed in*: *plan, attack etc*) portare a termine; **he didn't pull it off** non gli è riuscito il colpo

▸ **pull on** VT + ADV (*clothes*) mettersi

▸ **pull out** VT + ADV
1 (*take out*: *tooth, splinter*) togliere; (: *gun, knife, person*) tirare fuori
2 (*withdraw*: *troops, police*) (far) ritirare
■VI + ADV
1 (*withdraw*) ritirarsi; **she pulled out of the tournament** si è ritirata dal torneo
2 (*leave*: *train, car*) uscire; **he pulled out to overtake** si è spostato per sorpassare

▸ **pull over** VT + ADV
1 (*box, table*): **pull it over here/there** tiralo in qua/in là; **pull it over to the window** tiralo vicino alla finestra

Pp

2 (*topple*) far cascare, tirar giù
■VI + ADV accostare
▸ **pull round** VI + ADV (*unconscious person*) rinvenire; (*sick person*) ristabilirsi
▸ **pull through** VT + ADV
1 tirare dall'altra parte
2 (*fig*) aiutare a venirne fuori
■VI + ADV (*fig*) cavarsela; **they think he'll pull through** pensano che se la caverà
▸ **pull together** VT + ADV (*fig*): **to pull o.s. together** ricomporsi; **pull yourself together!** datti una regolata!
■VI + ADV (*make common effort*) cooperare, mettersi insieme
▸ **pull up** VT + ADV
1 (*raise by pulling*) tirar su
2 (*uproot: weeds*) sradicare
3 (*stop: horse, car*) fermare
4 (*scold*) riprendere
■VI + ADV (*stop*) fermarsi; **a black car pulled up beside me** una macchina nera si è fermata accanto a me

pull-down menu [ˌpʊldaʊnˈmɛnjuː] N (*Comput*) menu *m inv* a tendina

pul·let [ˈpʊlɪt] N pollastra, gallina giovane

pul·ley [ˈpʊlɪ] N puleggia, carrucola

Pull·man [ˈpʊlmən] N (*also:* **Pullman car**) pullman *m inv*

pull-out [ˈpʊlˌaʊt] N inserto
■ADJ staccabile

pull·over [ˈpʊlˌəʊvəʳ] N pullover *m inv*

pul·mo·nary [ˈpʌlmənərɪ] ADJ polmonare

pulp [pʌlp] N **1** (*for paper*) pasta (di legno *or* stracci *etc*); **to reduce sth to pulp** spappolare qc **2** (*of fruit, vegetable*) polpa **3** (*fiction*) romanzi di qualità scadente
■VT (*fruit, vegetables*) spappolare; (*paper, book*) mandare al macero

pul·pit [ˈpʊlpɪt] N pulpito

pul·sar [ˈpʌlsəʳ] N pulsar *m or f inv*

pul·sate [pʌlˈseɪt] VI (*heart, blood*) pulsare; (*music*) vibrare

pul·sat·ing [pʌlˈseɪtɪŋ] ADJ pulsante

pul·sa·tion [pʌlˈseɪʃən] N pulsazione *f*

pulse [pʌls] N (*Anat*) polso; (*Phys*) impulso; (*fig: of drums, music*) vibrazione *f*; **to feel** *or* **take sb's pulse** sentire *or* tastare il polso a qn; **the nurse took his pulse** l'infermiera gli ha tastato il polso

pulse rate N (*Med*) (numero di) pulsazioni *fpl*

pulses [ˈpʌlsɪz] NPL (*Culin*) legumi *mpl* secchi

pul·ver·ize [ˈpʌlvəˌraɪz] VT (*also fig*) polverizzare

puma [ˈpjuːmə] N puma *m inv*

pum·ice [ˈpʌmɪs] N (*also:* **pumice stone**) (pietra) pomice *f*

pum·mel [ˈpʌml] VT prendere a pugni

pum·mel·ling [ˈpʌməlɪŋ] N scarica di pugni

◎**pump[1]** [pʌmp] N pompa; **bicycle pump** pompa da bicicletta; **petrol pump** distributore *m* (di benzina)
■VT **1** pompare; **to pump sth dry** prosciugare qc con una pompa; **to pump air into a tyre** gonfiare uno pneumatico; **to pump money into a project** immettere capitali in un progetto; **to pump sb for information** cercare di strappare delle informazioni a qn **2** (*handle*) alzare e abbassare vigorosamente; **to pump sb's hand up and down** dare una vigorosa stretta di mano a qn
▸ **pump in** VT + ADV (*water*) far passare (con una pompa); (*foam into walls*) iniettare; (*fig: money*) immettere
▸ **pump out** VT + ADV pompare fuori; **to pump out sb's stomach** fare la lavanda gastrica a qn
▸ **pump up** VT + ADV (*tyre*) gonfiare

pump[2] N (*sports shoe*) scarpa da ginnastica; (*dancing shoe*) scarpetta da ballo; (*slip-on shoe*) ballerina; **she was wearing a leotard and black pumps** indossava un body e scarpe da ginnastica nere

pump·kin [ˈpʌmpkɪn] N zucca

pumpkin pie N torta di zucca

pump·kin·seed [ˈpʌmpkɪnˌsiːd] N seme *m* di zucca

pun [pʌn] N gioco di parole

Punch [pʌntʃ] N Pulcinella *m*; **Punch and Judy show** spettacolo di burattini

◎**punch[1]** [pʌntʃ] N **1** (*for making holes: in metal, leather*) punzonatrice *f*; (*: in paper*) perforatore *m*; (*: in tickets*) pinza per forare; (*for stamping metal*) punzone *m* **2** (*blow*) pugno; (*fig: vigour*) mordente *m*, forza
■VT **1** (*with tool: gen*) punzonare; (*: ticket*) forare; **he forgot to punch my ticket** si è dimenticato di forarmi il biglietto; **to punch a hole in sth** forare qc **2** (*with fist*): **to punch sb/sth** dare un pugno a qn/qc; **he punched me!** mi ha dato un pugno!; **to punch a ball** colpire una palla con un pugno; **to punch sb's nose** dare un pugno sul naso a qn
▸ **punch in** VI + ADV (*Am*) timbrare il cartellino (all'entrata)
▸ **punch out** VI + ADV (*Am*) timbrare il cartellino (all'uscita)

punch[2] [pʌntʃ] N (*drink*) punch *m inv*, ponce *m inv*

punch bag N (*Brit Sport*) punching bag *m inv*

punch·ball [ˈpʌntʃˌbɔːl] N punching ball *m inv*

punch·bowl [ˈpʌntʃˌbəʊl] N grande coppa da punch

punch-drunk [ˌpʌntʃˈdrʌŋk] ADJ (*Boxing*) groggy; (*fig: stupefied*) stordito(-a)

punched card [ˌpʌntʃtˈkɑːd], **punch card** (*esp Am*) N (*Comput*) scheda perforata

punch·ing bag [ˈpʌntʃɪŋˌbæg] N (*Am*) = **punchball**

punch line N (*of joke*) battuta finale; (*of story*) finale *m*

punch-up [ˈpʌntʃˌʌp] N (*Brit fam*) scazzottata, rissa

punchy [ˈpʌntʃɪ] ADJ (*comp* **-ier**, *superl* **-iest**) (*fam*)
1 (*prose, writing, article*) incisivo(-a) **2** (*punch-drunk: person*) stordito(-a)

punc·tili·ous [pʌŋkˈtɪlɪəs] ADJ scrupoloso(-a), meticoloso(-a)

punc·tili·ous·ly [pʌŋkˈtɪlɪəslɪ] ADV scrupolosamente, meticolosamente

punc·tili·ous·ness [pʌŋkˈtɪlɪəsnɪs] N scrupolosità, meticolosità

punc·tu·al [ˈpʌŋktjʊəl] ADJ (*person*) puntuale; (*train*) in orario

punc·tu·al·ity [ˌpʌŋktjʊˈælɪtɪ] N puntualità

punc·tu·al·ly [ˈpʌŋktjʊəlɪ] ADV (*see adj*) puntualmente; in orario; **it will start punctually at 6** comincerà alle 6 precise *or* in punto

punc·tu·ate [ˈpʌŋktjʊˌeɪt] VT (*Gram*) mettere la punteggiatura a *or* in; **his speech was punctuated by bursts of applause** il suo discorso fu ripetutamente interrotto da scrosci di applausi

punc·tua·tion [ˌpʌŋktjʊˈeɪʃən] N (*Gram*) punteggiatura, interpunzione *f*

punctuation mark N segno d'interpunzione

punc·ture [ˈpʌŋktʃəʳ] N (*in tyre*) foratura; (*in balloon*) foratura, buco; (*in skin*) puntura; **I have a puncture** (*Aut*) ho forato (una gomma)
■VT bucare, forare
■VI bucarsi, forarsi

pun·dit [ˈpʌndɪt] N (*iro*) esperto(-a), sapientone(-a)

pun·gen·cy ['pʌndʒənsɪ] N (*see adj*) asprezza; acredine *f*; sapore *m* piccante; causticità

pun·gent ['pʌndʒənt] ADJ (*smell, taste*) pungente, aspro(-a); (*smoke*) acre; (*sauce*) piccante; (*remark, satire*) caustico(-a), mordace

pun·gent·ly ['pʌndʒəntlɪ] ADV (*gen*) aspramente; (*seasoned*) in modo piccante; (*remark*) causticamente

pun·ish ['pʌnɪʃ] VT **1** **to punish sb for sth/for doing sth** punire qn per qc/per aver fatto qc **2** (*fig fam: car*) mettere a dura prova; (*: horse*) sfiancare; (*: opposition*) dare una bella batosta a; (*: meal, bottle of whisky*) far fuori

pun·ish·able ['pʌnɪʃəbl] ADJ punibile

pun·ish·ing ['pʌnɪʃɪŋ] ADJ (*fig: exhausting*) sfiancante
■ N punizione *f*

pun·ish·ment ['pʌnɪʃmənt] N **1** (*punishing*) punizione *f*, castigo; (*penalty*) pena; **to take one's punishment** subire il castigo; **to make the punishment fit the crime** punire secondo il reato **2** (*fig fam*): **to take a lot of punishment** (*boxer*) incassare parecchi colpi; (*car*) essere messo(-a) a dura prova; (*furniture*) essere maltrattato(-a)

pu·ni·tive ['pju:nɪtɪv] ADJ (*action, measures*) punitivo(-a)

punitive damages NPL (*Law*) risarcimento esemplare

Pun·ja·bi [pʌn'dʒɑ:bɪ] N **1** abitante *m/f* or nativo(-a) del Punjab **2** (*language*) lingua parlata nel Punjab
■ ADJ del Punjab

punk [pʌŋk] N **1** (*person: also:* **punk rocker**) punk *m/f inv*; (*music: also:* **punk rock**) musica punk, punk rock *m* **2** (*Am fam: hoodlum*) teppista *m*
▹ www.punk77.co.uk
▹ www.bbc.co.uk/dna/h2g2/A791336

pun·net ['pʌnɪt] N cestello; **a punnet of strawberries** un cestino di fragole

punt¹ [pʌnt] N (*boat*) barchino; (*Ftbl*) calcio al volo; **we hired a punt** abbiamo noleggiato un barchino
■ VT (*boat*) spingere con la pertica; (*ball*) calciare al volo
■ VI: **to go punting** andare in barchino

punt² [pʌnt] N (*in Ireland*) sterlina irlandese; **10 Irish punts** 10 sterline irlandesi

punt·er ['pʌntəʳ] N (*Brit fam: gambler*) scommettitore(-trice); (*: customer*) cliente *m/f*; **to pull in the punters** attirare clienti

puny ['pju:nɪ] ADJ (*comp* **-ier**, *superl* **-iest**) (*person*) gracile, striminzito(-a); (*effort*) penoso(-a)

pup [pʌp] N (*dog*) cagnolino(-a), cucciolo(-a); (*seal*) cucciolo(-a)

pupa ['pju:pə] N (*pl* **pupae** ['pju:pi:]) pupa

◎ **pu·pil¹** ['pju:pl] N (*Scol*) allievo(-a), scolaro(-a)

pu·pil² ['pju:pl] N (*Anat*) pupilla

pupil power N potere *m* studentesco

pup·pet ['pʌpɪt] N (*glove puppet*) burattino; (*string puppet*) marionetta; (*fig*) burattino, fantoccio
▹ www.punchandjudy.org/mainframesethistory.htm
▹ www.cln.org/themes/puppetry.html
▹ www.puppetryindia.org/

pup·pet·eer [pʌpɪ'tɪəʳ] N burattinaio(-a)

puppet government N governo *m* fantoccio *inv*

puppet show N spettacolo di burattini (*or* di marionette)

pup·py ['pʌpɪ] N cucciolo(-a), cagnolino(-a)

puppy fat N pinguedine *f* infantile

puppy love N infatuazione *f* giovanile

◎ **pur·chase** ['pɜ:tʃɪs] N **1** (*act*) acquisto; (*thing purchased*) acquisto, compera **2** (*grip*) presa; **to get a purchase on** trovare un appoggio su
■ VT (*frm*) acquistare, comprare

purchase order N ordine *m* d'acquisto, ordinazione *f*

purchase price N prezzo d'acquisto

pur·chas·er ['pɜ:tʃɪsəʳ] N acquirente *m/f*, compratore(-trice)

purchase tax N (*Brit*) imposta sugli acquisti

pur·chas·ing pow·er ['pɜ:tʃɪsɪŋ,paʊəʳ] N potere *m* d'acquisto

◎ **pure** [pjʊəʳ] ADJ (*comp* **-r**, *superl* **-st**) puro(-a); **the pure in heart** i puri di cuore; **as pure as the driven snow** innocente come un bambino; **a pure wool jumper** un golf di pura lana; **pure mathematics** matematica pura; **pure orange juice** puro succo d'arancia; **it's laziness pure and simple** è pura pigrizia; **by pure chance** per puro caso

pure·bred ['pjʊə,brɛd] ADJ di razza pura

pu·rée ['pjʊəreɪ] N purè *m inv*, purea
■ VT schiacciare, passare

pure·ly ['pjʊəlɪ] ADV puramente

pure·ness ['pjʊənɪs] N = purity

pur·ga·tive ['pɜ:gətɪv] N (*Med*) purgante *m*
■ ADJ purgativo(-a)

pur·ga·tory ['pɜ:gətərɪ] N (*Rel, fig*) purgatorio

purge [pɜ:dʒ] N (*gen, Med*) purga; (*Pol*) epurazione *f*, purga
■ VT **1** (*Med*) purgare; (*Pol*): **to purge (of)** epurare (da); **to purge one's sins** espiare i propri peccati; **to purge o.s. of sth** liberarsi da qc **2** (*Law: offence, crime*) espiare

pu·ri·fi·ca·tion [,pjʊərɪfɪ'keɪʃən] N (*see vb*) depurazione *f*; purificazione *f*

pu·rifi·ca·tory [,pjʊərɪfɪ'keɪtərɪ] ADJ purificatorio(-a)

pu·ri·fi·er ['pjʊərɪ,faɪəʳ] N (*see vb*) depuratore *m*

pu·ri·fy ['pjʊərɪ,faɪ] VT (*water, air*) depurare; (*person*) purificare

pur·ist ['pjʊərɪst] N purista *m/f*

pu·ri·tan ['pjʊərɪtən] ADJ, N puritano(-a)

pu·ri·tani·cal [,pjʊərɪ'tænɪkəl] ADJ puritano(-a)

pu·ri·tan·ism ['pjʊərɪtən,ɪzəm] N puritanesimo

pu·rity ['pjʊərɪtɪ] N purezza

purl [pɜ:l] N (maglia *or* punto a) rovescio
■ VT lavorare a rovescio

pur·loin [pɜ:'lɔɪn] VT (*frm*) sottrarre, rubare

◎ **pur·ple** ['pɜ:pl] ADJ viola *inv*; **to go purple (in the face)** diventare paonazzo(-a), farsi di porpora
■ N (*colour*) viola *m inv*; (*Rel*): **the purple** la porpora

Purple Heart N (*Am*) *medaglia per ferite riportate in battaglia*

purple heart N (*fam*) pillola di amfetamina

purple patch, purple passage N brano ornato

pur·port [*n* 'pɜ:pət; *vb* pɜ:'pɔ:t] N significato, senso generale
■ VT: **to purport to be/do** pretendere di essere/fare

◎ **pur·pose** ['pɜ:pəs] N **1** (*intention*) scopo, intenzione *f*; (*use*) uso; **she has a purpose in life** ha uno scopo nella vita; **for our purposes** per i nostri scopi; **for teaching purposes** per l'insegnamento; **for the purposes of this meeting** agli effetti di questa riunione; **for all practical purposes** a tutti gli effetti pratici, in pratica; **on purpose** di proposito, apposta; **he did it on purpose** l'ha fatto apposta; **for illustrative purposes** a titolo illustrativo; **to the purpose** a proposito, pertinente; **with the purpose of** con il proposito di; **to some purpose** con qualche risultato; **to no purpose** senza nessun risultato, inutilmente; **to good purpose** con buoni risultati; **what is the purpose of these changes?** qual è lo scopo di questi cambiamenti? **2** (*resolution, determination*): **sense of purpose** risolutezza

Pp

purpose-built ['pɜ:pəs,bɪlt] ADJ (*Brit*) costruito(-a) appositamente
pur·pose·ful ['pɜ:pəsfʊl] ADJ deciso(-a), risoluto(-a)
pur·pose·ful·ly ['pɜ:pəsfəlɪ] ADV con uno scopo preciso, deliberatamente
pur·pose·ly ['pɜ:pəslɪ] ADV di proposito, apposta
purr [pɜ:ʳ] N (*of cat*) le fusa *fpl*
■VI far le fusa
purse [pɜ:s] N (*for money*) borsellino, portamonete *m inv*; (*Am*: *handbag*) borsetta, borsa; (*esp Sport*: *prize*) montepremi *m inv*; **I've got 10 pounds in my purse** ho 10 sterline nel portamonete
■VT: **to purse one's lips** increspare le labbra
purs·er ['pɜ:səʳ] N (*Naut*) commissario di bordo
purse snatch·er ['pɜ:s,snætʃəʳ] N (*Am*) scippatore *m*
purse strings NPL: **to hold the purse strings** (*fig*) tenere i cordoni della borsa
◎**pur·sue** [pə'sju:] VT **1** (*chase*) inseguire; (: *pleasures*) andare in cerca di; (*subj*: *bad luck*) perseguitare **2** (*carry on*: *studies*) proseguire; (: *career*) intraprendere; (: *inquiry, matter*) portare avanti; (: *plan*) andare avanti con
pur·su·er [pə'sju:əʳ] N inseguitore(-trice)
pur·suit [pə'sju:t] N **1** (*chase*) inseguimento; (*fig*: *of pleasure, happiness, knowledge*) ricerca; **the pursuit of success** la ricerca del successo; **in (the) pursuit of sb** all'inseguimento di qn; **in (the) pursuit of sth** alla ricerca di qc; **with two policemen in hot pursuit** con due poliziotti alle calcagna **2** (*occupation*) attività *f inv*, occupazione *f*; (*pastime*) svago, passatempo; **scientific pursuits** ricerche *fpl* scientifiche; **outdoor pursuits** attività *fpl* all'aperto
pur·vey·or [pɜ:'veɪəʳ] N (*frm*) fornitore(-trice)
pus [pʌs] N pus *m inv*
◎**push** [pʊʃ] N
1 (*shove*) spinta, spintone *m*; **to give sb/sth a push** dare una spinta a qn/qc; **to give sb the push** (*Brit fam*) dare il benservito a qn
2 (*drive, aggression*) iniziativa, energia
3 (*effort*) grande sforzo; (*Mil*: *offensive*) offensiva
4 (*fam*): **at a push** in caso di necessità; **if** *or* **when it comes to the push** al momento critico
■VT
1 (*shove, move by pushing*) spingere; (*press*: *button*) schiacciare, premere; **to push a door open/shut** aprire/chiudere una porta con una spinta *or* spingendola; **he pushed it into my hands** me lo ha cacciato in mano; **the accident pushed everything else out of my mind** l'incidente mi ha fatto dimenticare tutto il resto
2 (*fig*: *press, advance*: *views*) imporre; (: *claim*) far valere; (: *product*) spingere le vendite di; (: *candidate*) appoggiare; **to push home an advantage** sfruttare a fondo un vantaggio; **to push home an attack** portare a conclusione un attacco; **to push drugs** spacciare droga; **don't push your luck!** (*fam*) non sfidare la fortuna!, non tirare troppo la corda!
3 (*fig*: *put pressure on*): **to push sb into doing sth** costringere qn a fare qc; **to push sb to do sth** spingere qn a fare qc; **my parents are pushing me to go to university** i miei mi spingono ad andare all'università; **don't push her too far** non esigere troppo da lei; **that's pushing it a bit** (*fam*) è un po' troppo; **to be pushed for time/money** essere a corto di tempo/soldi; **I'm hard pushed to understand how ...** mi riesce difficile capire come...; **I'm really pushed today** oggi non ho un minuto di tempo
■VI spingere; **to push for** (*better pay, conditions*) fare pressione per ottenere; **to push past sb** spingere qn per passare; **to push into a room** entrare in una stanza facendosi largo; **"push"** (*on door*) "spingere"; (*on bell*) "suonare"
▸ **push about, push around** VT + ADV (*fig fam*: *bully*) fare il prepotente con; **he likes pushing people around** gli piace dare ordini a tutti
▸ **push ahead** VI + ADV: **to push ahead (with sth)** andare avanti (con qc)
▸ **push aside** VT + ADV spingere da parte, scostare; (*fig*: *suggestions*) scartare; (: *problems*) accantonare
▸ **push away** VT + ADV respingere
▸ **push back** VT + ADV (*blankets*) spingere via, buttare all'indietro; (*curtains*) aprire; (*lock of hair*) ricacciare all'indietro; (*enemy forces*) respingere
▸ **push down** VI + ADV: **to push down on** schiacciare, premere
■VT + ADV (*switch, knob*) abbassare, tirare giù; (*knock over*: *fence, person*) buttare giù
▸ **push forward** VI + ADV (*Mil*) avanzare
■VT + ADV spingere in avanti; **he tends to push himself forward** (*fig*) cerca sempre di mettersi in mostra
▸ **push in** VT + ADV
1 (*person*) spingere dentro; (*stick, rag*: *into hole*) ficcare dentro, cacciare dentro; **to push sb in(to) the water** spingere qn in acqua; **she pushed her way in** è entrata facendosi largo
2 (*break*: *door etc*) sfondare
■VI + ADV introdursi a forza
▸ **push off** VT + ADV (*gen*) buttare giù; (*lid, top*) spingere via; **he pushed me off the wall** mi ha spinto giù dal muretto
■VI + ADV
1 (*in boat*) prendere il largo
2 (*fam*: *leave*) filare, smammare; **push off!** sparisci!
▸ **push on** VI + ADV (*with journey*) continuare; (*with job*) perseverare; **I've got a lot to do, so I must push on now** ho molto da fare, quindi devo andare avanti
■VT + ADV (*fig*: *incite, urge on*) spronare, spingere
▸ **push out** VT + ADV (*car, person*) spingere fuori; (*cork*) far uscire
▸ **push over** VT + ADV
1 (*over cliff etc*) spingere giù; **to push sth over the edge** spingere qc oltre il bordo
2 (*knock over*) far cadere
▸ **push through** VT + ADV
1 (*gen*) spingere dall'altra parte; **to push one's way through** farsi largo; **I pushed my way through till I reached the front** mi sono fatto largo fino ad arrivare davanti
2 (*force acceptance of*: *decision*) far accettare; (: *Parliament*: *bill*) riuscire a far votare
■VI + ADV farsi strada, farsi largo; (*troops*) aprirsi un varco; **to push through a crowd** farsi largo *or* aprirsi un varco tra la folla
▸ **push to** VT + ADV (*door*) socchiudere
▸ **push up** VT + ADV
1 spingere in su
2 (*fig*: *raise, increase*) far salire
push-bike ['pʊʃ,baɪk] N (*Brit*) bicicletta
push-button ['pʊʃ,bʌtn] ADJ a tastiera; **push-button warfare** guerra dei bottoni
push·chair ['pʊʃ,tʃɛəʳ] N (*Brit*) passeggino
push·er ['pʊʃəʳ] N (*fam*) **1** (*also*: **drug pusher**) spacciatore(-trice) (di droga) **2** (*ambitious person*) arrivista *m/f*

push·ing ['pʊʃɪŋ] PREP (*fam: almost*) quasi; **she is pushing 50** (*fam*) va per i 50
■ ADJ (*enterprising*) intraprendente; (*pej*) arrivista
push·over ['pʊʃ,əʊvəʳ] N (*fam*): **it's a pushover** è un gioco da ragazzi; **she's a pushover** si lascia convincere facilmente
push technology N (*Comput*) tecnologia push (*con invio automatico di aggiornamenti all'utente*)
push-up ['pʊʃ,ʌp] N (*Am*) flessione *f* sulle braccia; **to do push-ups** fare flessioni sulle braccia
pushy ['pʊʃɪ] ADJ (*comp* **-ier**, *superl* **-iest**) (*fam pej*) troppo intraprendente
pu·sil·lani·mous [,pju:sɪ'lænɪməs] ADJ pusillanime
puss [pʊs], **pus·sy** ['pʊsɪ] N (*fam*) micio(-a)
pussy·cat ['pʊsɪ,kæt] N = **puss**
pussy·foot ['pʊsɪ,fʊt] VI (*fam pej*) tentennare
pussy willow ['pʊsɪ,wɪləʊ] N salicone *m*
◎ **put** [pʊt] (*pt, pp* **put**) VT
1 (*place*) mettere; (*put down*) posare, metter giù; **where shall I put my things?** dove metto le mie cose?; **she's putting the baby to bed** sta mettendo a letto il bambino; **my brother put me on the train** mio fratello mi ha messo sul treno; **to put the ball in the net** mandare la palla in rete; **to put sth to one's ear** avvicinarsi qc all'orecchio; **she put her head on my shoulder** appoggiò la testa sulla mia spalla; **to put one's signature to sth** apporre la propria firma a qc; **to put a lot of time into sth** dedicare molto tempo a qc; **she has put a lot into her marriage** ha fatto molto per la riuscita del suo matrimonio; **to put money into a company** investire *or* mettere dei capitali in un'azienda; **to put money on a horse** scommettere su un cavallo
2 (*thrust, direct*) cacciare; **he put his finger right in my eye** mi ha cacciato un dito nell'occhio; **I put my fist through the window** sfondai la finestra con il pugno; **to put one's pen through sth** cancellare qc con un frego; **he put his head round the door** fece capolino dalla porta; **to put the shot** (*Sport*) lanciare il peso
3 (*cause to be*): **to put sb in a good/bad mood** mettere qn di buon/cattivo umore; **to put sb in charge of sth** incaricare qn di qc; **to put sb to a lot of trouble** dare un sacco da fare a qn; **I put her to answering the phone** le ho dato l'incarico di rispondere al telefono; **he put her to work immediately** l'ha messa subito al lavoro
4 (*express*) esprimere, dire; **let me put it another way** te lo spiego in un altro modo; **how shall I put it?** come dire?; **let me put it this way** diciamo così ; **as Dante puts it** come dice Dante; **to put it bluntly** per parlar chiaro; **put it to him gently** diglielo senza spaventarlo; **to put sth into French** tradurre qc in francese; **to put the words to music** mettere in musica *or* musicare le parole
5 (*expound: case, problem*) esporre, presentare; **I put it to you that ...** io sostengo che...; **to put a question to sb** rivolgere una domanda a qn
6 (*estimate*) valutare, stimare; **what would you put it at?** quanto pensi che valga?; **I'd put his age at 40** direi che ha 40 anni
■ VI (*Naut*): **to put to sea** prendere il mare; **to put into port** entrare in porto
■ ADV: **to stay put** (*fam*) non muoversi
▸ **put about** VT + ADV (*circulate: news, rumour*) mettere in giro
■ VI + ADV (*Naut*) virare di bordo, invertire la rotta
▸ **put across** VT + ADV
1 (*communicate: ideas, opinion*) comunicare, far capire; (*: new product*) propagandare; **he finds it hard to put his ideas across** trova difficile riuscire a comunicare le proprie idee; **she can't put herself across** non sa far valere le sue doti
2 (*fam: play trick*): **to put one across on sb** darla a bere a qn
▸ **put aside** VT + ADV
1 (*lay down: book, game*) mettere da una parte, posare
2 (*save*) mettere da parte; (*in shop*) tenere da parte; **can you put this aside for me till tomorrow?** me lo può tenere da parte fino a domani?
3 (*fig: abandon: idea, hope, doubt*) mettere da parte, dimenticare
▸ **put away** VT + ADV
1 (*clothes, toys, dishes*) mettere via, riporre; **can you put away the dishes, please?** ti dispiace riporre i piatti?
2 = **put aside 2**
3 (*fam: consume: food, drink*) far fuori
4 (*fam: lock up in prison*) mettere dentro; (*: in mental hospital*) rinchiudere; **I hope they put him away for a long time** spero che lo mettano dentro per un bel pezzo
▸ **put back** VT + ADV
1 (*replace*) rimettere (a posto); **put it back when you've finished with it** rimettilo a posto quando hai finito
2 (*postpone*) rimandare, rinviare; (*slow down: production*) rallentare; (*set back: watch, clock*) mettere indietro; **the meeting's been put back till two o'clock** la riunione è stata rinviata alle due; **remember to put your watch back** ricorda di mettere indietro l'orologio; **this will put us back 10 years** questo ci farà tornare indietro di 10 anni; **you can't put the clock back** (*fig*) non si può tornare indietro
■ VI + ADV (*Naut*) rientrare (in porto)
▸ **put by** VT + ADV = **put aside 1, 2**
▸ **put down** VT + ADV
1 (*set down*) mettere giù, posare; (*passenger*) far scendere; **I'll put these bags down for a minute** poso un attimo queste borse; **I couldn't put that book down** (*fig*) non riuscivo a smettere di leggere quel libro
2 (*lower: umbrella*) chiudere; (*: car roof*) abbassare
3 (*crush: revolt*) reprimere; (*: gambling, prostitution*) abolire; (*: rumour*) mettere a tacere; (*humiliate*) mortificare
4 (*pay: deposit*) versare
5 (*destroy: pet*) abbattere; **we had to have our dog put down** abbiamo dovuto far abbattere il cane
6 (*write down*) scrivere; **I've put down a few ideas** ho buttato giù alcune idee; **to put sth down in writing** mettere qc per iscritto; **put it down on my account** (*Comm*) me lo addebiti *or* metta in conto; **put me down for £15** segnami *or* mettimi in lista per 15 sterline; **he's put his son down for Harrow** ha iscritto suo figlio nella lista d'attesa per Harrow
7 (*classify*) considerare; **I'd put her down as about forty** le darei una quarantina d'anni; **I put him down as a troublemaker** lo considero un elemento disturbatore
8 (*attribute*): **to put sth down to sth** attribuire qc a qc
■ VI + ADV (*Aer*) atterrare
▸ **put forward** VT + ADV
1 (*propose: gen*) proporre; (*: theory*) avanzare; (*: opinion*) esprimere

Pp

2 (*advance*: *date, meeting, function*) anticipare; (: *clock*) mettere avanti
▸ **put in** VT + ADV
1 (*place inside*: *drawer, bag*) metter dentro
2 (*insert*: *in book, speech*) aggiungere, inserire
3 (*interpose*: *remark*) fare; **she put in her piece** ha detto la sua
4 (*enter*: *application, complaint*) presentare; **to put in a plea of not guilty** (*Law*) dichiararsi innocente; **to put sb in for an exam** presentare qn a un esame; **to put sb in for an award** proporre qn per un premio
5 (*install*: *central heating*) mettere, installare
6 (*Pol*: *elect*) eleggere
7 (*devote, expend*: *time*) passare, dedicare; **to put in a few extra hours** fare qualche ora in più; **to put in a lot of work** lavorare sodo; **to put in a good day's work** fare una bella giornata di lavoro
■ VI + ADV (*Naut*) fare scalo
▸ **put in for** VI + ADV + PREP (*job*) far domanda per; (*promotion*) far domanda di; **he's put in a request for an assistant** ha presentato richiesta per avere un assistente
▸ **put off** VT + ADV
1 (*set down*: *passenger*) far scendere
2 (*pospone, delay*: *match, decision*) rimandare, rinviare; (: *guest*) chiedere di rimandare la visita; **to put off doing sth** rimandare qc a più tardi; **I keep putting it off** continuo a rimandarlo; **to put sb off with an excuse** liberarsi di qn con una scusa
3 (*discourage*) far passare la voglia a; **he's not easily put off** non si lascia scoraggiare facilmente; **to put sb off their food** far passare a qn la voglia di mangiare
4 (*distract*) distrarre; **stop putting me off!** smettila di distrarmi!
5 (*repel*: *smell*) disgustare
6 (*switch off*) spegnere; **shall I put the light off?** spengo la luce?
▸ **put on** VT + ADV
1 (*clothes, lipstick, shoes*) mettere, mettersi; **I'll put my coat on** mi metto il cappotto
2 (*assume*: *accent, manner*) affettare; (: *airs*) darsi; (*fam*: *kid, have on*: *esp Am*) prendere in giro; **to put on airs** darsi delle arie; **to put on an innocent expression** assumere un'aria innocente; **she's just putting it on** sta solo facendo finta
3 (*add, increase*: *speed, pressure*) aumentare; **to put on weight** aumentare di peso, ingrassare; **he's put on a lot of weight** è ingrassato parecchio; **I put on four pounds** sono ingrassata di due chili
4 (*concert, exhibition*) allestire, organizzare; (*play*) mettere in scena; (*extra bus, train*) mettere in servizio; **we're putting on "Bugsy Malone"** stiamo mettendo in scena "Bugsy Malone"
5 (*on telephone*): **put me on to Mr Strong please** mi passi il signor Strong per favore
6 (*switch on*: *light etc*) accendere; (*kettle, meal*) metter su; **to put on the brakes** frenare; **shall I put the heating on?** accendo il riscaldamento?; **I'll put the potatoes on** metto a cuocere le patate
7 (*inform, indicate*): **to put sb on to sb/sth** indicare qn/qc a qn; **she put us on to you** è lei che ci ha detto di rivolgerci a te; **who put the police on to him?** chi lo ha segnalato alla polizia?; **what put you on to it?** cosa te lo ha fatto capire?
▸ **put out** VT + ADV
1 (*place outside*) mettere fuori; **to put clothes out to dry** stendere la biancheria ad asciugare; **to be put out** (*asked to leave*) essere buttato(-a) fuori; **she couldn't put him out of her head** non riusciva a non pensare a lui
2 (*stretch out*: *arm, foot, leg*) allungare; (: *one's hand*) porgere; (*tongue*) tirare fuori; (*push out*: *leaves etc*) spuntare; **to put one's head out of the window** metter fuori *or* sporgere la testa dalla finestra; **he smiled and put out his hand** ha sorriso tendendo la mano
3 (*lay out in order*) disporre
4 (*circulate*: *propaganda*) fare; (: *news*) annunciare; (: *rumour*) mettere in giro; (*bring out*: *new book*) pubblicare; (: *regulation*) emettere
5 (*extinguish*: *fire, cigarette, light*) spegnere; **it took them five hours to put out the fire** ci sono volute cinque ore per spegnere l'incendio
6 (*discontent, vex*) contrariare, seccare; **to be put out** essere seccato(-a); **he's a bit put out that nobody came** è un po' seccato che non sia venuto nessuno; **to be put out by sth/sb** essere contrariato(-a) da qn/qc
7 (*inconvenience*): **to put o.s. out (for sb)** scomodarsi *or* disturbarsi per qn
8 (*dislocate*: *shoulder, knee*) lussarsi; (: *back*) farsi uno strappo a
9 (*subcontract*) subappaltare
■ VI + ADV (*Naut*): **to put out to sea** prendere il largo; **to put out from Plymouth** partire da Plymouth
▸ **put over** VT + ADV = put across
▸ **put through** VT + ADV
1 (*complete*: *business, deal*) concludere; (*have accepted*: *reform, bill*) far approvare, far passare
2 (*Telec*: *connect*: *caller*) mettere in comunicazione; (*call*) passare; **can you put me through to the manager?** mi passa il direttore, per favore?; **I'm putting you through** le passo la comunicazione
▸ **put together** VT + ADV
1 mettere insieme, riunire; **she is worth more than all the others put together** vale più lei da sola che tutte le altre messe insieme
2 (*assemble*: *furniture*) montare; (: *model*) fare; (: *essay*) comporre; (: *meal*) improvvisare; (: *evidence*) raccogliere; (: *team*) mettere insieme, formare
▸ **put up** VT + ADV
1 (*raise, lift up*: *hand*) alzare; (: *umbrella*) aprire; (: *collar*) rialzare; (*hoist*: *flag, sail*) issare; **put 'em up!** (*fam*: *hands*: *in surrender*) arrenditi!; (: *in robbery*) mani in alto!; (: *fists*: *to fight*) forza, difenditi!; **if you have any questions, put up your hand** se avete domande alzate la mano
2 (*fasten up*): **to put up (on)** attaccare (su), appendere (su); (*notice*) affiggere (su)
3 (*erect*: *building, barrier, fence*) costruire, erigere; (: *tent*) montare; **we put up our tent in a field** abbiamo montato la tenda in un prato
4 (*send up*: *space probe, missile*) lanciare, mettere in orbita
5 (*increase*) aumentare; **they've put up the price** hanno aumentato il prezzo
6 = put forward 1
7 (*offer*): **to put sth up for sale** mettere in vendita qc; **they're going to put their house up for sale** metteranno in vendita la casa; **they put up a struggle** hanno opposto resistenza
8 (*give accommodation to*) ospitare; **a friend will put me up for the night** un amico mi ospita per la notte
9 (*provide*: *money, funds*) fornire; (: *reward*) offrire
10 (*incite*): **to put sb up to doing sth** istigare qn a fare qc

■VI + ADV
1 **to put up (at)** (*at hotel*) alloggiare (in); (: *for the night*) pernottare (in)
2 (*offer o.s.*): **to put up (for)** presentarsi come candidato(-a) (per)
▸ **put upon** VI + PREP: **to be put upon** (*imposed on*) farsi mettere sotto i piedi
▸ **put up with** VI + ADV + PREP sopportare; **she has a lot to put up with** ha un sacco di problemi; **I'm not going to put up with it any longer** non ho intenzione di sopportarlo oltre

pu·ta·tive ['pju:tətɪv] ADJ (*frm*): **the putative father** il padre putativo

pu·tre·fac·tion [ˌpju:trɪ'fækʃən] N putrefazione *f*

pu·tre·fy ['pju:trɪˌfaɪ] VI putrefarsi

pu·tre·fy·ing ['pju:trɪˌfaɪɪŋ] ADJ putrescente

pu·trid ['pju:trɪd] ADJ putrido(-a); **to turn putrid** putrefarsi

putsch [pʊtʃ] N putsch *m inv*, colpo di Stato

putt [pʌt] N (*Golf*) putting *m*
■VT (*ball*) colpire leggermente

put·ter[1] ['pʌtə^r] N (*Golf*) putter *m inv*

put·ter[2] ['pʌtə^r] VI (*Am*) = **potter**

putt·ing ['pʌtɪŋ] N (*game*) *un tipo di golf*; **putting green** green *m inv* di pratica

put·ty ['pʌtɪ] N (*for windows*) stucco, mastice *m* da vetrai; **to be putty in sb's hands** (*fig*) essere come la creta nelle mani di qn

put-up ['pʊtˌʌp] ADJ: **put-up job** (*fam*) montatura

put-you-up ['pʊtju:ˌʌp] N poltrona *f* (*or* divano *m*) letto *inv*

puz·zle ['pʌzl] N 1 (*game*) rompicapo; (*word game*) rebus *m inv*; (*crossword*) parole *fpl* incrociate, cruciverba *m inv*; (*riddle*) indovinello; (*also*: **jigsaw puzzle**) puzzle *m inv*
2 (*mystery*) enigma *m*, mistero; **she was a puzzle** era un mistero; **it's a puzzle to me how it happened** non so come sia successo, per me resta un enigma
■VT lasciar perplesso(-a)
▸ **puzzle out** VT + ADV (*problem*) risolvere; (*mystery, person, attitude*) capire; (*writing, instructions*) decifrare; (*answer, solution*) trovare; **I'm trying to puzzle out why** sto cercando di scoprire il perché
▸ **puzzle over, puzzle about** VT + ADV (*sb's actions*) cercare di capire; (*mystery, problem*) cercare di risolvere
▹ www.puzzles.com

puz·zled ['pʌzld] ADJ perplesso(-a); **to be puzzled about sth** domandarsi il perché di qc; **you look puzzled!** hai un'aria perplessa!

puz·zle·ment ['pʌzlmənt] N perplessità

puz·zler ['pʌzlə^r] N mistero, enigma *m*

puz·zling ['pʌzlɪŋ] ADJ (*question*) poco chiaro(-a); (*attitude, set of instructions*) incomprensibile

PVC [ˌpi:vi:'si:] N ABBR (= **polyvinyl chloride**) PVC

p.w. ABBR = **per week**

pyg·my ['pɪgmɪ] N pigmeo(-a)

py·ja·mas, (*Am*) **pa·jam·as** [pə'dʒɑ:məz] NPL pigiama *msg*; **a pair of pyjamas** un pigiama; **my pyjamas** il mio pigiama

py·lon ['paɪlən] N pilone *m*

pyra·mid ['pɪrəmɪd] N piramide *f*

py·rami·dal [pɪ'ræmɪdl] ADJ piramidale

pyramid selling N sistema *m* di vendita piramidale

pyre ['paɪə^r] N pira

Pyr·enean [pɪrə'ni:ən] ADJ pirenaico(-a), dei Pirenei

Pyr·enees [pɪrə'ni:z] NPL: **the Pyrenees** i Pirenei

Py·rex® ['paɪrɛks] N pirex® *m inv*

Pyrex dish N pirofila

pyro... ['paɪərəʊ] PREF piro...

pyro·clasts [ˌpaɪrəʊ'klæsts] NPL materiali *mpl* piroclastici

py·roly·sis [paɪ'rɒlɪsɪs] N pirolisi *f*

pyro·ma·nia [ˌpaɪərəʊ'meɪnɪə] N piromania

pyro·ma·ni·ac [ˌpaɪərəʊ'meɪnɪæk] N piromane *m/f*

pyro·tech·nics [ˌpaɪrəʊ'tɛknɪks] N 1 (*sg: Phys*) pirotecnica 2 (*pl: fireworks display*) spettacolo *msg* pirotecnico

Pythagoras [paɪ'θægərəs] N Pitagora *m*; **Pythagoras' theorem** teorema *m* di Pitagora

py·thon ['paɪθən] N pitone *m*

Q, q [kjuː] N (*letter*) Q, q *f or m inv*; **Q for Queen** ≈ Q come Quarto

Q & A [ˌkjuːənd'eɪ] N ABBR (= *question and answer*): **Q & A session** dibattito

Qa·tar [kæ'tɑːʳ] N il Qatar *m*

QC [ˌkjuː'siː] N ABBR (*Brit*: = **Queen's Counsel**) *avvocato della Corona, nominato dietro raccomandazione del capo della magistratura*

QED [ˌkjuːiː'diː] ABBR (= **quod erat demonstrandum**) qed

QM [ˌkjuː'ɛm] N ABBR = **quartermaster**

q.t. [kjuː'tiː] N ABBR (*fam*) = **quiet; on the q.t.** di nascosto

qty ABBR = **quantity**

qua [kwɑː] PREP (*frm*) in quanto

quack[1] [kwæk] N (*of duck*) qua qua *m inv*
■ VI fare qua qua

quack[2] [kwæk] N (*pej*: *bogus doctor*) ciarlatano(-a); (*hum*: *doctor*) dottore(-essa)

quad [kwɒd] N ABBR = **quadrangle 2, quadruplet**

quad bike N quad *m inv*; *specie di moto con quattro ruote*

Quad·ra·gesi·ma [ˌkwɒdrə'dʒɛsɪmə] N (*also*: **Quadragesima Sunday**) domenica di quadragesima

quad·ran·gle ['kwɒdˌræŋgl] N **1** (*Math*) quadrangolo, quadrilatero **2** (*courtyard*) cortile *m* (*di collegio, scuola*)

quad·rant ['kwɒdrənt] N quadrante *m*

quad·rat·ic [kwɒ'drætɪk] ADJ (*equation*) di secondo grado, quadratico(-a)

quad·ri·lat·er·al [ˌkwɒdrɪ'lætərəl] ADJ quadrilatero(-a)

quad·ri·no·mial [ˌkwɒdrɪ'nəʊmɪəl] N quadrinomio

quad·ro·phon·ic [ˌkwɒdrə'fɒnɪk] ADJ quadrifonico(-a); **in quadrophonic sound** in quadrifonia

quad·ru·ped ['kwɒdrʊˌpɛd] N quadrupede *m*

quad·ru·ple ['kwɒdrʊpl] ADJ quadruplo(-a), quadruplice
■ VT quadruplicare
■ VI quadruplicarsi; **the number has quadrupled** il numero è quadruplicato
■ N quadruplo

quad·ru·plet [kwɒ'druːplɪt] N uno(-a) di quattro gemelli

quads [kwɒdz] NPL quadricipiti

quaff [kwɑːf] VT (*old*) tracannare

quag·mire ['kwægˌmaɪəʳ] N pantano; (*fig*) caos *m inv*

quail[1] [kweɪl] N (*bird*) quaglia

quail[2] [kweɪl] VI (*flinch*): **to quail at** *or* **before** perdersi d'animo davanti a

quaint [kweɪnt] ADJ (*comp* **-er**, *superl* **-est**) (*odd*) strano(-a), bizzarro(-a); (*picturesque*) pittoresco(-a); (*old-fashioned*) antiquato(-a) e pittoresco(-a)

quaint·ly ['kweɪntlɪ] ADV (*see adj*) in modo strano; in modo bizzarro; pittorescamente

quake [kweɪk] VI: **to quake (with)** tremare (di)
■ N (*earthquake*) terremoto

Quak·er ['kweɪkəʳ] N quacchero(-a)
▷ http://quakerinfo.org/beliefs.html

quali·fi·ca·tion [ˌkwɒlɪfɪ'keɪʃən] N **1**: **qualifications** NPL (*gen*) qualifiche *fpl*, requisiti *mpl*; (*paper qualifications*) titoli *mpl* di studio; **what are your qualifications?** quali sono le sue qualifiche?; (*paper qualifications*) quali sono i suoi titoli di studio?; **what qualifications do they require?** che qualifiche richiedono?; **I've got a teaching qualification** sono abilitato *or* ho l'abilitazione all'insegnamento; **he left school without any qualifications** ha lasciato la scuola senza alcun titolo di studio; **reliability is a necessary qualification** l'affidabilità è un requisito necessario; **vocational qualifications** qualifiche professionali **2** (*reservation*) riserva, restrizione *f*; **without qualification(s)** senza condizioni *or* riserve; **I agree, with one qualification** sono d'accordo, ma con una riserva

◎ **quali·fied** ['kwɒlɪˌfaɪd] ADJ **1** (*engineer, doctor, teacher*) abilitato(-a); (*nurse*) diplomato(-a); **qualified for/to do** qualificato(-a) per/per fare; **to be well qualified** avere tutti i requisiti necessari; **he's not qualified for the job** non ha i requisiti necessari per questo lavoro **2** (*support*) condizionato(-a); (*acceptance*) con riserva; **it was a qualified success** è stato un successo parziale; **the film has received qualified praise** il film non è stato accolto proprio favorevolmente

quali·fi·er ['kwɒlɪˌfaɪəʳ] N (*Gram*) aggettivo qualificativo; (*Sport*) chi si è qualificato(-a)

◎ **quali·fy** [ˈkwɒlɪˌfaɪ] VT **1** *(make competent)* qualificare; **his experience in South Africa qualified him to speak on apartheid** la sua esperienza in Sudafrica lo autorizzava a parlare dell'apartheid **2** *(modify)* modificare; (: *support, approval*) porre delle condizioni a **3** *(Gram)* qualificare
■ VI *(professionally)* abilitarsi, essere abilitato(-a); *(in competition)* qualificarsi; *(be eligible)* avere i requisiti necessari; **to qualify as an engineer** diventare un perito tecnico; *(with degree)* laurearsi in ingegneria; **to qualify for a job** avere i requisiti necessari per un lavoro; **she qualified as a teacher last year** ha ottenuto l'abilitazione all'insegnamento l'anno scorso; **he hardly qualifies as a major dramatist** non si può certamente definirlo un grande drammaturgo; **our team didn't qualify for the finals** la nostra squadra non si è qualificata per le finali; **they qualify for benefit** hanno diritto al sussidio

quali·fy·ing [ˈkwɒlɪˌfaɪɪŋ] ADJ *(Gram)* qualificativo(-a); *(exam)* di ammissione; *(round)* eliminatorio(-a)

quali·ta·tive [ˈkwɒlɪtətɪv] ADJ qualitativo(-a)

◎ **qual·ity** [ˈkwɒlɪtɪ] N qualità *f inv*; **of good quality** di buona qualità; **of poor quality** scadente
■ ADJ di qualità; **good-quality paper** carta di buona qualità

quality control N controllo (di) qualità

quality of life N qualità *f inv* della vita

quality papers NPL, **quality press** N *(Brit)* stampa *fsg* d'informazione

QUALITY PAPERS

Il termine **quality press** si riferisce ai quotidiani o ai settimanali che offrono un'informazione seria ed approfondita. Questi giornali si differenziano da quelli popolari, i "tabloid", per contenuti e spesso anche per formato. *Vedi anche* **tabloid press**
▷ www.totaltravel.co.uk/library/britain/uk-newspapers/

quality time N tempo di qualità

qualm [kwɑːm] N *(often pl: fear)* apprensione *f*; (: *scruple*) scrupolo, esitazione *f*; **to have qualms about sth** avere degli scrupoli per qc; **to have no qualms about sth** non avere degli scrupoli su qc

quan·da·ry [ˈkwɒndərɪ] N: **in a quandary** in un dilemma; **to be in a quandary (about sth)** essere molto incerto(-a) (su qc)

quango [ˈkwæŋgəʊ] N ABBR *(Brit:* = **quasi-autonomous nongovernmental organization**) *organizzazione autonoma di nomina governativa, dotata di fondi, che agisce in vari settori (salute, scuola ecc)*

quan·ti·fi·able [ˈkwɒntɪfaɪəbl] ADJ quantificabile

quan·ti·fi·er [ˈkwɒntɪˌfaɪəʳ] N *(Gram)* quantificatore *m*

quan·ti·fy [ˈkwɒntɪˌfaɪ] VT quantificare

quan·ti·ta·tive [ˈkwɒntɪtətɪv] ADJ quantitativo(-a)

quan·ti·ta·tive·ly [ˈkwɒntɪtətɪvlɪ] ADV quantitativamente

◎ **quan·tity** [ˈkwɒntɪtɪ] N quantità *f inv*; *(Comm)* quantità, quantitativo; **in quantity** in grande quantità

quantity discount N sconto sulla quantità

quantity surveyor N geometra *m (che valuta il costo del materiale e della manodopera necessari per una costruzione)*

quan·tum [ˈkwɒntəm] *(Phys)* N quanto
■ ADJ *(number)* quantico(-a); *(mechanics)* quantistico(-a)

quantum leap N *(fig)* enorme cambiamento

quantum theory N *(Phys)* teoria quantistica *or* dei quanti

quar·an·tine [ˈkwɒrəntiːn] N quarantena; **in quarantine** in quarantena
■ VT mettere in quarantena

quark [kwɑːk] N *(Phys)* quark *m inv*

quar·rel [ˈkwɒrəl] N *(argument)* litigio, lite *f*; **to have a quarrel (with sb)** litigare (con qn); **we had a quarrel** abbiamo litigato; **to pick a quarrel (with sb)** attaccar briga (con qn); **I've no quarrel with him** non ho niente contro di lui; **after their last quarrel** dopo la loro ultima lite
■ VI: **to quarrel (with sb about** *or* **over sth)** litigare (con qn per qc); **they quarrelled about** *or* **over money** hanno litigato per i soldi; **I can't quarrel with that** non ho niente da ridire su questo

quar·relling, *(Am)* **quar·rel·ing** [ˈkwɒrəlɪŋ] N litigi *mpl*

quar·rel·some [ˈkwɒrəlsəm] ADJ litigioso(-a)

quar·ry¹ [ˈkwɒrɪ] N *(Hunting, fig)* preda

quar·ry² [ˈkwɒrɪ] N *(mine)* cava
■ VT cavare

quarry·man [ˈkwɒrɪmən] N *(pl* **-men**) cavapietre *m inv*

quarry-tiled [ˈkwɒrɪˌtaɪld] ADJ *(floor)* di quadrelli

quart [kwɔːt] N quarto di gallone *(Brit = 1,136 litri; Am = 0,964 litri)*; **a quart** due pinte

◎ **quar·ter** [ˈkwɔːtəʳ] N **1** *(fourth part)* quarto; *(of year)* trimestre *m*; **three quarters** tre quarti; **a quarter (of a pound) of tea** ≈ un etto di tè; **a quarter of a century** un quarto di secolo; **to divide sth into quarters** dividere qc in quattro (parti); **to pay by the quarter** pagare trimestralmente; **we expect fewer orders in the next quarter** ci aspettiamo meno ordini nel prossimo trimestre **2** *(Am, Canada: 25 cents)* quarto di dollaro, 25 centesimi **3** *(time)*: **a quarter of an hour** un quarto d'ora; **an hour and a quarter** un'ora e un quarto; **it's a quarter to** *or (Am)* **of 3** sono le 3 meno un quarto, manca un quarto alle 3; **it's a quarter past** *or (Am)* **after 3** sono le 3 e un quarto **4** *(district)* quartiere *m* **5** *(direction)*: **from all quarters** da tutte le parti *or* direzioni; **at close quarters** a distanza ravvicinata; **you won't get any help from that quarter** non otterrai nessun aiuto da quella parte **6**: **quarters** NPL *(accommodation)* alloggio; *(Mil)* quartiere *m*; (: *temporary*) alloggiamento **7 to give sb no quarter** essere implacabile verso qn
■ VT **1** *(divide into four)* dividere in quattro (parti) **2** *(Mil)* alloggiare

Qq

quarter·back [ˈkwɔːtəˌbæk] N *(Am Ftbl)* quarterback *m inv*

quarter-deck [ˈkwɔːtəˌdɛk] N *(Naut)* cassero

quarter·final [ˈkwɔːtəˌfaɪnl] N quarti *mpl* di finale

quarter finalist N *(Sport)* partecipante *m/f* ai quarti di finale

quar·ter·ing [ˈkwɔːtərɪŋ] N *(Mil)* accantonamento

quar·ter·ly [ˈkwɔːtəlɪ] ADJ trimestrale
■ N periodico trimestrale
■ ADV trimestralmente

quarter·master [ˈkwɔːtəˌmɑːstəʳ] N *(Mil)* furiere *m*; *(Naut)* timoniere *m*

quarter pounder N *(Culin)* hamburger *m inv (che pesa poco più di un etto)*

quar·tet, **quar·tette** [kwɔːˈtɛt] N quartetto; **string quartet** quartetto di archi

quar·tile [ˈkwɔːtaɪl] N quartile *m*

quar·to [ˈkwɔːtəʊ] ADJ in quarto

quartz [kwɔ:ts] N quarzo
■ADJ di quarzo; (*clock, watch*) al quarzo
quartz·ite ['kwɔ:tsaɪt] N quarzite *f*
qua·sar ['kweɪzɑ:ʳ] N (*Astron*) quasar *f inv*
quash [kwɒʃ] VT **1** (*reject*) respingere; (*: Law: sentence, conviction*) revocare, annullare **2** (*destroy: enemies, rebellion*) stroncare; (*: emotion*) reprimere
quasi- ['kwɑ:zɪ] PREF semi...; (*pej*) pseudo...; **quasi-official** ADJ semiufficiale; **quasi-religious** ADJ quasi religioso(-a); **quasi-revolutionary** ADJ, N pseudorivoluzionario(-a)
qua·ver ['kweɪvəʳ] N (*when speaking*) tremolio; (*Brit Mus: note*) croma
■VI (*voice*) tremare, tremolare
qua·ver·ing ['kweɪvərɪŋ] ADJ (*voice*) tremulo(-a), tremolante
quay [ki:] N molo, banchina
quay·side ['ki:ˌsaɪd] N banchina
quea·si·ness ['kwi:zɪnɪs] N nausea
quea·sy ['kwi:zɪ] ADJ (*comp* **-ier**, *superl* **-iest**) (*stomach*) nauseato(-a); **to feel queasy** avere la nausea
Que·bec [kwɪ'bɛk] N il Quebec *m*
▷ www.gouv.qc.ca/index_en.html
▷ www.tourisme.gouv.qc.ca/anglais
◎**queen** [kwi:n] N regina; (*Cards, Chess*) regina, donna; **Queen Elizabeth** la regina Elisabetta; **the queen of hearts** la regina di cuori
queen bee N ape *f* regina *inv*
queen·ly ['kwi:nlɪ] ADJ regale, da regina
queen mother N regina madre
queen-size ['kwi:nˌsaɪz], **queen-sized** ['kwi:nˌsaɪzd] ADJ (*bed, bed linen*) un po' più grande del normale
Queens·land ['kwi:nzlənd] N Queensland *m*
▷ www.qld.gov.au
▷ www.qttc.com.au
Queen's speech N (*Brit*): **the Queen's speech** *discorso letto dalla regina in occasione dell'apertura del parlamento*

QUEEN'S SPEECH

Durante la sessione di apertura del Parlamento britannico il sovrano legge un discorso redatto dal primo ministro, il **Queen's speech** (se si tratta della regina), che contiene le linee generali del nuovo programma politico.
▷ www.number-10.gov.uk/output/Page7488.asp

queer [kwɪəʳ] ADJ (*comp* **-er**, *superl* **-est**) **1** (*odd*) strano(-a), curioso(-a), singolare; **he's a queer customer** è un tipo strano; **there's something queer going on here** qui c'è qualcosa che non va, qui sta succedendo qc di strano; **queer in the head** (*fam*) tocco(-a), picchiato(-a) **2** (*ill*) strano(-a), non giusto(-a); **to feel queer** sentirsi poco bene **3** (*fam offensive: homosexual*) omosessuale; **he's queer** è gay **4** (*suspicious*) dubbio(-a), sospetto(-a)
■N (*old fam offensive: male homosexual*) finocchio
■VT: **to queer sb's pitch** (*fam*) rovinare tutto a qn, rompere le uova nel paniere a qn
queer-bashing ['kwɪəˌbæʃɪŋ] N (*fam offensive*) *atti di violenza contro gli omosessuali*
queer·ly ['kwɪəlɪ] ADV stranamente
queer·ness ['kwɪənɪs] N stranezza
quell [kwɛl] VT (*passion*) reprimere; (*fear*) dominare; (*rebellion*) soffocare; (*attempt*) sventare
quench [kwɛntʃ] VT (*thirst*) togliere, levare; (*flames*) spegnere; **to quench one's thirst** dissetarsi
queru·lous ['kwɛrʊləs] ADJ querulo(-a)
queru·lous·ly ['kwɛrʊləslɪ] ADV in tono querulo
que·ry ['kwɪərɪ] N (*question*) domanda; (*question mark*) punto interrogativo; (*fig: doubt*) interrogativo, dubbio
■VT **1** (*ask*): **to query sb about sth** rivolgere delle domande a qn riguardo a qc **2** (*doubt*) mettere in dubbio; (*disagree with, dispute*) sollevare (dei) dubbi su, contestare; **no one queried my decision** nessuno ha messo in dubbio la mia decisione; **they queried the bill** hanno chiesto spiegazioni sul conto
quest [kwɛst] N ricerca; **in quest of** alla ricerca di, in cerca di; **my quest for a better bank continues** la mia ricerca di una banca migliore continua; **the quest to boost sales** il tentativo di aumentare le vendite
◎**ques·tion** ['kwɛstʃən] N **1** (*enquiry*) domanda; **to ask sb a question** *or* **put a question to sb** fare una domanda a qn; **can I ask a question?** posso fare una domanda? **2** (*matter, issue*) questione *f*, argomento; **it is an open question whether ...** resta da vedere se..., è una questione aperta se...; **the question is ...** il problema è...; **that's a difficult question** è una questione difficile; **the person/night in question** la persona/la notte in questione; **it is a question of whether ...** si tratta di sapere se...; **it's a question of doing ...** si tratta di fare...; **that is not the question** non è questo il problema; **there is no question of outside help** non c'è nessuna possibilità di aiuto esterno; **there can be no question of your resigning** che lei dia le dimissioni non è nemmeno da prendersi in considerazione; **it's out of the question** è fuori discussione; **there's some question of closing the shop** c'è chi suggerisce di chiudere il negozio **3** (*doubt*): **beyond** *or* **past question** fuori discussione *or* questione; **in question** in discussione, in dubbio; **there is no question about it** su questo non c'è (assolutamente) nessun dubbio; **to bring** *or* **call sth into question** mettere in dubbio qc
■VT **1** (*interrogate: person*) interrogare; **he was questioned by the police** è stato interrogato dalla polizia **2** (*doubt*) mettere in dubbio, dubitare di; **I question whether it is worthwhile** mi domando se ne vale *or* valga la pena; **nobody questions his loyalty** nessuno mette in dubbio la sua lealtà
ques·tion·able ['kwɛstʃənəbl] ADJ discutibile
ques·tion·er ['kwɛstʃənəʳ] N interrogante *m/f*
ques·tion·ing ['kwɛstʃənɪŋ] ADJ (*mind*) inquisitore(-trice), indagatore(-trice); (*expression*) interrogativo(-a)
■N interrogatorio
question mark N punto interrogativo
question master N presentatore *m* (*di un quiz*)
ques·tion·naire [ˌkwɛstʃə'nɛəʳ] N questionario
queue [kju:] N coda, fila; **to form a queue** mettersi in fila *or* in coda; **to stand in a queue** essere in fila *or* in coda, fare la fila *or* la coda; **people were standing in a queue outside the cinema** la gente era in fila fuori dal cinema; **to jump the queue** passare davanti agli altri (*in coda*)
■VI (*also:* **queue up**) fare la fila, fare la coda; **we had to queue for tickets** abbiamo dovuto fare la fila per i biglietti
quib·ble ['kwɪbl] N cavillo, sottigliezza
■VI cavillare, sottilizzare
quiche [ki:ʃ] N quiche *f inv*
◎**quick** [kwɪk] ADJ (*comp* **-er**, *superl* **-est**) (*fast: in motion*)

veloce, rapido(-a); (: *in time*) svelto(-a), veloce; (*agile: reflexes*) pronto(-a); (: *in mind*) svelto(-a); **a quick temper** un temperamento irascibile; **a quick lunch** un pranzo veloce; **it's quicker by train** è più veloce in treno; **the quickest method** il metodo più rapido; **a quick reply** una risposta pronta; **be quick about it!** fa' presto!, sbrigati!; **she's a quick learner** impara presto; **she was quick to see that ...** ha visto subito che...; **to be quick to act** agire prontamente; **to be quick to take offence** essere permaloso(-a), offendersi subito; **do you fancy a quick one?** (*fam: drink*) andiamo a bere qualcosa?

■ ADV in fretta, rapidamente; **come quick!** vieni subito!; **as quick as a flash** *or* **as lightning** veloce come un fulmine

■ N: **to cut sb to the quick** pungere qn sul vivo

quick·en ['kwɪkən] VT affrettare, accelerare; (*fig: feelings*) stimolare; **to quicken one's pace** affrettare *or* allungare il passo

■ VI: **the pace quickened** il ritmo divenne più veloce

quick fix N soluzione *f* tampone *inv*

quick-freeze [ˌkwɪk'fri:z] VT sottoporre a congelamento rapido

quickie ['kwɪkɪ] N (*fam*) cosa fatta velocemente; (*question*) domanda veloce; **do you fancy a quickie?** (*drink*) andiamo a bere qualcosa?

quick·lime ['kwɪkˌlaɪm] N calce *f* viva

quick·ly ['kwɪklɪ] ADV velocemente, rapidamente; **"certainly not" she said quickly** "certo che no" disse velocemente; **we must act quickly** dobbiamo agire tempestivamente; **as quickly as possible** più velocemente possibile

quick·ness ['kwɪknɪs] N velocità, rapidità; (*of mind, intellect*) prontezza; (*of eye*) acutezza

quick·sand ['kwɪkˌsænd] N sabbie *fpl* mobili

quick·silver ['kwɪkˌsɪlvə^r] N argento vivo, mercurio

quick·step ['kwɪkˌstɛp] N (*dance*) quick step *m inv*

quick-tempered [ˌkwɪk'tɛmpəd] ADJ che si arrabbia facilmente

quick-witted [ˌkwɪk'wɪtɪd] ADJ sveglio(-a)

quick-wittedly [ˌkwɪk'wɪtɪdlɪ] ADV (*act, answer*) prontamente

quid [kwɪd] N (*Brit fam: pl inv*) sterlina; **ten quid** dieci sterline

quid pro quo [ˌkwɪdprəʊ'kwəʊ] N (*reciprocal exchange*) contraccambio; **his promotion was the quid pro quo for his support** venne promosso in cambio del suo appoggio

qui·es·cent [kwɪ'ɛsənt] (*frm*) ADJ (*person: passive*) passivo(-a); (: *quiet*) tranquillo(-a); (*symptoms, disease, problem*) latente; **in a quiescent state** allo stato latente; **quiescent minorities** le minoranze per ora silenziose

◎ **qui·et** ['kwaɪət] ADJ (*comp* **-er**, *superl* **-est**) **1** (*person: silent*) silenzioso(-a), tranquillo(-a); (: *reserved*) quieto(-a), taciturno(-a); (: *calm*) tranquillo(-a), calmo(-a); **quiet!** silenzio!; **be quiet!** *or* **keep quiet!** silenzio!, sta' zitto!; (*when moving about*) non far rumore!, fa' piano!; **you're very quiet today** sei molto silenzioso oggi; **to keep sb quiet** tener tranquillo(-a) qn; **they paid him £1,000 to keep him quiet** gli hanno dato 1.000 sterline perché stesse zitto **2** (*not noisy: engine*) silenzioso(-a); (: *music, voice, laugh*) sommesso(-a); (: *sound*) basso(-a), leggero(-a); **the engine's very quiet** il motore è molto silenzioso **3** (*not busy: day*) calmo(-a), tranquillo(-a); (: *place*) tranquillo(-a); **a quiet little town** una cittadina tranquilla; **a quiet weekend** un tranquillo fine settimana; **the shops/trains are always quiet on a Monday** i negozi/treni non sono mai affollati di lunedì ; **business is quiet at this time of year** questa è la stagione morta **4** (*discreet: manner*) dolce, garbato(-a); (: *colours*) tenue, smorzato(-a); (: *humour*) garbato(-a); (*private, intimate*) intimo(-a); **I'll have a quiet word with him** gli dirò due parole in privato; **to lead a quiet life** fare una vita tranquilla; **he managed to keep the whole thing quiet** è riuscito a tener segreta tutta la faccenda; **we had a quiet wedding** abbiamo avuto un matrimonio semplice

■ N (*silence*) silenzio; (*calm*) pace *f*, calma, tranquillità; **on the quiet** (*fam: act*) di nascosto; (: *tell*) in confidenza

■ VT (*Am*) = **quieten** VT

qui·et·en ['kwaɪətən] VT (*also:* **quieten down**) calmare, placare; **to quieten sb down** calmare qn

■ VI (*also:* **quieten down**) calmarsi

qui·et·ly ['kwaɪətlɪ] ADV (*softly, silently*) silenziosamente, senza far rumore; (*not loudly: speak, sing*) in modo sommesso; (*calmly*) tranquillamente, con calma; **to be quietly dressed** essere vestito(-a) in modo sobrio; **to be quietly situated** (*house*) trovarsi in un posto tranquillo; **let's get married quietly** sposiamoci con una cerimonia semplice; **he slipped off quietly to avoid being noticed** se n'è andato alla chetichella per non essere notato; **he quietly opened the door** ha aperto la porta senza far rumore; **"she's dead," he said quietly** "è morta," disse piano; **he lives quietly in the country** conduce una vita tranquilla in campagna

qui·et·ness ['kwaɪətnɪs] N (*silence*) silenzio; (*peacefulness*) tranquillità, calma, quiete *f*; (*softness: of voice, music*) dolcezza

quill [kwɪl] N (*feather*) penna; (*pen*) penna d'oca; (*of porcupine*) aculeo

quilt [kwɪlt] N (*traditional*) trapunta; (*continental quilt*) piumino

■ VT trapuntare

quilt·ed ['kwɪltɪd] ADJ trapuntato(-a)

quilt·ing ['kwɪltɪŋ] N (*material*) stoffa trapuntata; (*craft*) trapunto

▷ www.quilts.com

▷ www.pbs.org/americaquilts

quin [kwɪn] N ABBR = **quintuplet**

quince [kwɪns] N (*fruit*) (mela) cotogna; (*tree*) cotogno

quince jelly N cotognata

qui·nine [kwɪ'ni:n] N chinino

quin·tes·sence [kwɪn'tɛsns] N (*frm*) quintessenza

quin·tes·sen·tial [ˌkwɪntɪ'sɛnʃəl] ADJ (*frm*) per eccellenza; **the quintessential Renaissance man** l'uomo rinascimentale per eccellenza

quin·tet, **quin·tette** [kwɪn'tɛt] N quintetto

quin·tu·plet [kwɪn'tju:plɪt] N uno(-a) di cinque gemelli

quip [kwɪp] N battuta di spirito

quire ['kwaɪə^r] N ventesima parte di una risma; (*Bookbinding*) segnatura di 16 pagine

quirk [kwɜ:k] N (*oddity*) stranezza, bizzarria; **by some quirk of fate** per un capriccio della sorte; **one of his quirks** una delle sue stranezze

quirky ['kwɜ:kɪ] ADJ (*comp* **-ier**, *superl* **-iest**) stravagante, capriccioso(-a)

quis·ling ['kwɪzlɪŋ] N (*old*) collaborazionista *m/f*

◎ **quit** [kwɪt] (*vb: pt, pp* **quit** *or* **quitted**) VT **1** (*cease: work*) lasciare, piantare; **to quit doing sth** smettere di fare qc; **I've quit smoking** ho smesso di fumare; **I quit my**

Qq

job last week ho lasciato il lavoro la settimana scorsa; **quit stalling!** (*Am fam*) non tirarla per le lunghe! **2** (*leave*: *place*) lasciare; **notice to quit** (*Brit*) preavviso (*dato all'inquilino*); **I've been given notice to quit** mi hanno dato lo sfratto
■ VI (*resign*) dare le dimissioni, dimettersi; (*give up*: *in game*) abbandonare, mollare; (*accept defeat*) darsi per vinto(-a)
■ ADJ: **quit of** sbarazzato(-a) di, liberato(-a) di

◎ **quite** [kwaɪt] ADV **1** (*rather*) abbastanza, piuttosto; **I quite like that idea** è un'idea che non mi dispiace; **quite a few of them** non pochi di loro; **quite a few people** un bel po' di gente; **she's quite pretty** è piuttosto carina; **he's quite a good writer** è uno scrittore abbastanza bravo; **it's quite warm today** fa piuttosto caldo oggi; **it's quite a long way** è piuttosto lontano; **quite a lot** un bel po'; **it costs quite a lot to go abroad** costa un bel po' andare all'estero; **quite a lot of money** un bel po' di denaro; **there were quite a few people there** c'era un bel po' di gente; **I quite liked the film, but...** il film mi è piaciuto abbastanza, ma... **2** (*completely*) proprio, perfettamente; (*entirely*) completamente, del tutto; **quite new** proprio nuovo(-a); **quite (so)!** appunto!, proprio (così)!, precisamente!; **that's quite enough** è più che abbastanza, basta così ; **that's not quite right** non è proprio esatto; **I can quite believe that ...** non faccio fatica a credere che...; **not quite as many as last time** non proprio così tanti come l'ultima volta; **I quite understand** capisco perfettamente; **I'm not quite sure** non sono del tutto sicuro; **it's quite empty** è completamente vuoto

Qui·to ['ki:təʊ] N Quito *f*

quits [kwɪts] ADV: **to be quits (with sb)** essere pari (con qn); **let's call it quits** adesso siamo pari

quit·ter ['kwɪtə^r] N rinunciatario(-a)

quiv·er¹ ['kwɪvə^r] N (*for arrows*) faretra, turcasso

quiv·er² ['kwɪvə^r] VI (*person, voice, lips*): **to quiver (with)** tremare (per *or* da)

quix·ot·ic [kwɪk'sɒtɪk] ADJ (*frm*) donchisciottesco(-a)

quix·oti·cal·ly [kwɪk'sɒtɪkəlɪ] ADV (*frm*) alla don Chisciotte

quiz [kwɪz] N (*game*) quiz *m inv*
■ VT (*old*): **to quiz sb about** interrogare qn su

quiz·master ['kwɪz,mɑ:stə^r] N (*TV, Radio*) presentatore *m* (*di quiz*)

quiz·zi·cal ['kwɪzɪkəl] ADJ (*glance*) interrogativo(-a) (e beffardo(-a))

quiz·zi·cal·ly ['kwɪzɪkəlɪ] ADV con aria interrogativa (e beffarda)

quoit [kɔɪt] N anello (*per il gioco degli anelli*); **to play quoits** giocare agli anelli

quor·um ['kwɔ:rəm] N quorum *m inv*

quo·ta ['kwəʊtə] N quota

quo·ta·tion [kwəʊ'teɪʃən] N **1** (*words*) citazione *f*; **a quotation from Shakespeare** una citazione da Shakespeare **2** (*estimate*) preventivo; (*of shares*) quotazione *f*; **I asked the firm to give me a quotation** ho chiesto alla ditta di farmi un preventivo

quotation marks NPL (*Typ*) virgolette *fpl*; **in quotation marks** tra virgolette

◎ **quote** [kwəʊt] VT **1** (*words, author*) citare; **can you quote me an example?** puoi citarmi *or* farmi un esempio? **2** (*Comm*: *sum, figure, price*) indicare, fissare; (*shares*) quotare; **to quote for a job** dare un preventivo per un lavoro; **the figure quoted for the repairs** il preventivo per le riparazioni
■ VI: **to quote from** citare; **and I quote** (*from text*) cito testualmente; (*sb's words*) riferisco *or* ripeto testualmente; **quote ...unquote** (*in dictation*) aprire le virgolette... chiudere le virgolette; (*in lecture, report*) cito... fine della citazione
■ N **1** = quotation 1 **2**: **quotes** NPL (*inverted commas*) virgolette *fpl*; **in quotes** tra virgolette

quoted company ['kwəʊtɪd-] N società *f inv* quotata in borsa

quoth [kwəʊθ] VT: **quoth he** disse

quo·tient ['kwəʊʃənt] N quoziente *m*

R, r [ɑːʳ] N (*letter*) R, r *f or m inv*; **the three Rs** leggere, scrivere e far di conto; **R for Robert**, (*Am*): **R for Roger** ≈ R come Roma

RA [ˌɑːr'eɪ] N ABBR (*Brit*) = **Royal Academy, *Royal Academician***
■ ABBR = **rear admiral**

RAAF [ˌɑːreɪeɪ'ɛf] N ABBR = *Royal Australian Air Force*

Ra·bat [rə'bɑːt] N Rabat *f*

rab·bi ['ræbaɪ] N rabbino

rab·bit ['ræbɪt] N coniglio; **doe rabbit** coniglia
■ VI: **to rabbit (on)** (*Brit fam*) blaterare

rabbit hole N tana di coniglio

rabbit hutch N conigliera

rabble ['ræbl] N confusione *f* di gente; **the rabble** (*pej*) il popolino, la plebaglia

rabble-rouser ['ræbəlraʊzəʳ] N agitatore(-trice)

rab·id ['ræbɪd] ADJ (*dog*) idrofobo(-a), rabbioso(-a); (*fig: furious*) arrabbiato(-a); (*: fanatical*) fanatico(-a)

ra·bies ['reɪbiːz] N rabbia, idrofobia; **a dog with rabies** un cane con la rabbia

rabies virus N virus *m inv* rabbico

RAC [ˌɑːreɪ'siː] N ABBR (*Brit*: = **Royal Automobile Club**) ≈ ACI *m* (= *Automobile Club d'Italia*)

rac·coon [rə'kuːn] N procione *m*, orsetto lavatore

◎ **race¹** [reɪs] N (*competition, rush*) corsa; **the 100 metres race** la corsa sui 100 metri, i 100 metri (piani); **a race against time** una corsa contro il tempo; **a cycle race** una gara ciclistica; **the arms race** la corsa agli armamenti
■ VT **1** (*horse*) far gareggiare, far correre **2** (*person*) correre contro, gareggiare contro; **I'll race you!** facciamo a gara!; **I'll race you around the block** ti sfido a una corsa intorno all'isolato **3** (*engine*) imballare
■ VI **1 to race (against sb)** correre (contro qn) **2** (*rush*) correre; **to race in/out** *etc* precipitarsi dentro/fuori *etc*; **he raced across the road** ha attraversato la strada di corsa; **we raced to catch the bus** abbiamo corso per prendere l'autobus **3** (*pulse*) battere precipitosamente; (*engine*) imballarsi

race² [reɪs] N razza; **students of all races** studenti di tutte le razze; **the human race** l'umanità, il genere umano
■ ADJ (*hatred, riot*) razziale

race car N (*Am*) = **racing car**

race car driver N (*Am*) = **racing driver**

race·course ['reɪsˌkɔːs] N ippodromo

race·horse ['reɪsˌhɔːs] N cavallo da corsa

rac·er ['reɪsəʳ] N **1** (*person*) corridore *m* **2** (*bike*) bicicletta da corsa

race relations NPL rapporti *mpl* interrazziali

race·track ['reɪsˌtræk] N (*for horses, Aut*) pista

◎ **ra·cial** ['reɪʃəl] ADJ (*tension*) razziale; (*harmony, equality*) fra le razze

racial discrimination N discriminazione *f* razziale

ra·cial·ism ['reɪʃəˌlɪzəm] N (*Brit old*) razzismo

ra·cial·ist ['reɪʃəlɪst] ADJ, N razzista (*m/f*)

◎ **rac·ing** ['reɪsɪŋ] N corsa; (*horse-racing*) corse *fpl*
■ ADJ (*cycle*) da corsa

racing car N (*Brit*) macchina da corsa

racing driver N (*Brit*) corridore *m* automobilista

racing stables NPL scuderia di cavalli da corsa

racing yacht N yacht *m inv* da competizione

rac·ism ['reɪsɪzəm] N razzismo

rac·ist ['reɪsɪst] ADJ, N razzista (*m/f*)

rack¹ [ræk] N **1** (*storage framework*) rastrelliera; (*for luggage*) rete *f* portabagagli *inv*; (*for hats, coats*) appendiabiti *m inv*; (*in shops*) scaffale *m*; **magazine rack** portariviste *m inv*; **shoe rack** scarpiera; **toast rack** portatoast *m inv* **2** (*for torture*) cavalletto
■ VT (*subj: pain, cough*) torturare, tormentare; **racked by remorse** roso(-a) dal rimorso; **to rack one's brains** scervellarsi
▸ **rack up** VT + ADV accumulare

rack² [ræk] N: **to go to rack and ruin** (*building*) andare in rovina; (*business*) andare in malora *or* a catafascio; (*country*) andare a catafascio; (*person*) lasciarsi andare completamente

rack-and-pinion [ˌrækən'pɪnjən] N (*Tech*) rocchetto *m* cremagliera *inv*

rack·et¹ ['rækɪt] N (*for tennis*) racchetta

rack·et² ['rækɪt] N **1** (*din*) baccano, fracasso; **they were making a terrible racket** stavano facendo un

Rr

terribile baccano **2** (*organised fraud*) traffico, racket *m inv*; (*swindle*) imbroglio, truffa; **he's on to quite a racket** (*fam*) gli sta andando bene con il suo giochetto
rack·et·eer [ˌrækɪ'tɪəʳ] N (*esp Am*) trafficante *m/f*
rack·et·eer·ing [ˌrækə'tɪərɪŋ] N traffici *mpl*
racket press N (*Tennis*) tendiracchetta *m inv*
rack·ing [rækɪŋ] ADJ (*pain*) atroce
rac·on·teur [ˌrækɒn'tɜːʳ] N narratore(-trice)
ra·coon [rə'kuːn] N = **raccoon**
rac·quet ['rækɪt] N = **racket'**
racy ['reɪsɪ] ADJ (*comp* **-ier**, *superl* **-iest**) (*style*) spigliato(-a), brioso(-a); (*humour, talk*) un po' spinto(-a)
RADA ['rɑːdə] N ABBR (*Brit*) = *Royal Academy of Dramatic Art*
ra·dar ['reɪdɑːʳ] N radar *m inv*
■ ADJ (*station, screen*) radar *inv*
radar operator N radarista *m/f*
radar trap N (*Aut*) multanova® *m*
ra·dial ['reɪdɪəl] ADJ (*also*: **radial-ply**: *tyre*) radiale
ra·dian ['reɪdɪən] N radiante *m*
ra·di·ance ['reɪdɪəns] N (*brilliance*) splendore *m*, fulgore *m*; (*fig*) radiosità
ra·di·ant ['reɪdɪənt] ADJ (*Phys*: *heat*) radiante; (*light*) sfolgorante; (*fig*): **radiant (with)** raggiante (di); **the bride was radiant** la sposa era raggiante
ra·di·ant·ly ['reɪdɪəntlɪ] ADV (*smile*) radiosamente; **to be radiantly happy** essere raggiante di gioia
ra·di·ate ['reɪdɪˌeɪt] VT (*heat*) irraggiare, irradiare; (*fig*: *happiness*) irraggiare; **she radiates happiness** sprizza felicità da tutti i pori
■ VI: **to radiate from** irraggiarsi da, irradiarsi da; **the streets that radiate from the centre** le strade che si irradiano dal centro
ra·dia·tion [ˌreɪdɪ'eɪʃən] N (*nuclear*) radiazione *f*; (*of heat*) irradiamento
radiation sickness N malattia da radiazioni
radiation treatment N (*Med*) radioterapia
ra·dia·tor ['reɪdɪeɪtəʳ] N radiatore *m*
radiator cap N (*Aut*) tappo del radiatore
radiator grill N (*Aut*) mascherina, calandra
◎ **radi·cal** ['rædɪkəl] ADJ radicale
■ N **1** (*person*) radicale *m/f* **2** (*Math, Chem*) radicale *m*
radi·cal·ism ['rædɪkəˌlɪzəm] N radicalismo
radi·cal·ize ['rædɪkəlaɪz] VT (*frm*) radicalizzare
radi·cal·ly ['rædɪkəlɪ] ADV radicalmente
radi·cle ['rædɪkəl] N **1** (*Bot*) radichetta **2** (*Math, Chem*) = **radical** N **2**
ra·dii ['reɪdɪˌaɪ] NPL *of* **radius**
◎ **ra·dio** ['reɪdɪəʊ] N (*Telec*) radio *f*; (*radio set*) radio *f inv*, apparecchio *m* radio *inv*; **by radio** per radio; **on the radio** alla radio
■ VI: **to radio to sb** comunicare via radio con qn
■ VT (*information*) trasmettere per radio; (*one's position*) comunicare via radio; (*person*) chiamare via radio
■ ADJ (*programme*) radiofonico(-a); (*frequency*) radio *inv*
▷ www.ebu.ch
▷ www.nexus.org
▷ http://radio-locator.com
radio... ['reɪdɪəʊ] PREF radio...
radio·ac·tive [ˌreɪdɪəʊ'æktɪv] ADJ radioattivo(-a)
radio·ac·tiv·ity [ˌreɪdɪəʊæk'tɪvɪtɪ] N radioattività
radio alarm N radiosveglia
radio announcer N annunciatore(-trice) radiofonico(-a)
radio beacon N radiofaro
radio·bi·ol·ogy [ˌreɪdɪəʊbaɪ'ɒlədʒɪ] N radiobiologia
radio·car·bon [ˌreɪdɪəʊ'kɑːbən] N radiocarbonio
radiocarbon dating [-'deɪtɪŋ] N prova del carbonio 14
radio cassette N radioriproduttore *m*
radio cassette recorder N radioregistratore *m*
radio·com·mu·ni·ca·tion [ˌreɪdɪəʊkəˌmjuːnɪ'keɪʃən] N radiocomunicazione *f*
radio compass N radiobussola
radio-controlled [ˌreɪdɪəʊkən'trəʊld] ADJ radiocomandato(-a), radioguidato(-a)
radio·elec·tric·ity [ˌreɪdɪəʊɪlɛk'trɪsɪtɪ] N radioelettricità
radio·gram ['reɪdɪəʊˌgræm] N **1** (*combined radio and gramophone*) radiogrammofono **2** (*Med*) radiografia, radiogramma *m*
ra·di·og·ra·pher [ˌreɪdɪ'ɒgrəfəʳ] N radiologo(-a) (*tecnico*)
ra·di·og·ra·phy [ˌreɪdɪ'ɒgrəfɪ] N radiografia
radio·iso·tope [ˌreɪdɪəʊ'aɪsətəʊp] N radioisotopo
radio link N ponte *m* radio *inv*
ra·di·olo·gist [ˌreɪdɪ'ɒlədʒɪst] N radiologo(-a) (*medico*)
ra·di·ol·ogy [ˌreɪdɪ'ɒlədʒɪ] N radiologia
radio navigation N navigazione *f* radioassistita
radio operator N operatore *m* radio *inv*
ra·di·os·co·py [ˌreɪdɪ'ɒskəpɪ] N radioscopia
radio station N stazione *f* radio *inv*
radio taxi N radiotaxi *m inv*
radio·teleg·ra·phy [ˌreɪdɪəʊtɪ'lɛgrəfɪ] N radiotelegrafia
radio·tele·phone [ˌreɪdɪəʊ'tɛlɪˌfəʊn] N radiotelefono
radio telescope N radiotelescopio
radio·thera·pist [ˌreɪdɪəʊ'θɛrəpɪst] N radioterapista *m/f*
radio·thera·py [ˌreɪdɪəʊ'θɛrəpɪ] N radioterapia
radio wave N radioonda
rad·ish ['rædɪʃ] N ravanello
ra·dium ['reɪdɪəm] N radio
ra·dius ['reɪdɪəs] N (*pl* **radii** ['reɪdɪaɪ]) (*Math, fig*) raggio; (*Anat*) radio; **within a radius of 50 miles** in un raggio di 50 miglia
RAF [ˌɑːreɪ'ɛf] N ABBR (*Brit*) = **Royal Air Force**
raf·fia ['ræfɪə] N rafia
raff·ish ['ræfɪʃ] ADJ (*liter*) dissipato(-a)
raf·fle ['ræfl] N lotteria, riffa
■ VT (*object*) mettere in palio
raffle ticket N biglietto della lotteria *or* della riffa
raft [rɑːft] N zattera; **a raft of** un sacco di; **a raft of proposals** un sacco di proposte
raft·er ['rɑːftəʳ] N trave *f* (del tetto), puntone *m* (*Archit*)
raft·ing ['rɑːftɪŋ] N rafting *m*
rag[1] [ræg] N **1** (*piece of cloth*) straccio, cencio; **rags** NPL (*old clothes*) stracci *mpl*; **in rags** stracciato(-a); **dressed in rags** vestito(-a) di stracci; **to feel like a wet rag** (*fam*) sentirsi uno straccio **2** (*fam*: *newspaper*) giornalaccio
rag[2] [ræg] VT (*Brit old*: *tease*) prendere in giro
raga ['rɑːgə] N (*Mus*) raga *m inv*
raga·muf·fin ['rægəˌmʌfɪn] N (*old*) monello(-a)
rag-and-bone man [ˌrægənd'bəʊnˌmæn] N (*pl* **-men**) straccivendolo
rag·bag ['rægˌbæg] N (*fig*: *mixture*) guazzabuglio, accozzaglia
rag doll N bambola di pezza
◎ **rage** [reɪdʒ] N **1** (*anger*) collera, furia; **to fly into a rage** andare *or* montare su tutte le furie; **to be in a rage** essere furioso(-a) *or* su tutte le furie; **he was trembling with rage** tremava dalla rabbia; **mad with rage** arrabbiatissimo(-a) **2** (*fashion, trend*) mania; **it's all the rage** fa furore

■ VI (*person*) essere furioso(-a), andare su tutte le furie, infuriarsi; (*sea, fire, plague, wind*) infuriare

DID YOU KNOW ...?
rage is not translated by the Italian word *raggio*

rag·ga [ˈræɡə] N (*Mus*) ragga *m*

rag·ged [ˈræɡɪd] ADJ (*dress*) stracciato(-a); (*cuff*) logoro(-a); (*person*) lacero(-a), cencioso(-a); (*edge*) irregolare; **ragged children** bambini cenciosi; **ragged clothes** vestiti logori

rag·ged·ly [ˈræɡɪdlɪ] ADV **1** **raggedly dressed** vestito(-a) di stracci **2** (*engine*): **to run raggedly** funzionare irregolarmente

ragged robin N (*Bot*) garofano di prato, fior *m* di cuculo

rag·ing [ˈreɪdʒɪŋ] ADJ (*all senses*) furioso(-a); **in a raging temper** su tutte le furie; **I've got a raging thirst/toothache** muoio di sete/dal mal di denti

rag·lan [ˈræɡlən] ADJ (alla) raglan *inv*
■ N raglan *f*

rag·man [ˈræɡˌmæn] N (*pl* **-men**) = **rag-and-bone man**

rag·tag [ˈræɡˌtæɡ] (*pej*) N: **ragtag and bobtail** marmaglia
■ ADJ (*group, organization, collection*) di bassa lega; **a ragtag army** un'armata brancaleone

rag·time [ˈræɡˌtaɪm] N ragtime *m inv*
▷ www.jazzinamerica.org

rag trade N (*fam*): **the rag trade** (il settore *m* del)l'abbigliamento

rag week N *settimana di festa studentesca*

RAG WEEK

Durante la **rag week**, gli studenti universitari organizzano vari spettacoli e manifestazioni i cui proventi vengono devoluti in beneficenza.

rag·wort [ˈræɡˌwɜːt] N erba di San Giacomo

◎ **raid** [reɪd] N (*Mil*) incursione *f*; (*by police*) irruzione *f*; (*by bandits*) razzia; (*by criminals*) rapina; **a police raid** un raid della polizia; **a bank raid** una rapina in banca
■ VT (*see n*) fare un'incursione in; fare irruzione in; fare razzia in; rapinare; **the police raided a club in Soho** la polizia ha fatto irruzione in una discoteca di Soho; **the boys raided the orchard** i ragazzi hanno saccheggiato il frutteto

raid·er [ˈreɪdəʳ] N (*bandit*) bandito; (*bank raider etc*) rapinatore(-trice); (*plane*) aeroplano da incursione

◎ **rail** [reɪl] N **1** (*bar*) sbarra, traversa; (*banister*) corrimano; (*on bridge, balcony*) parapetto; (*of ship*) battagliola; **he climbed the stairs, holding the rail** salì le scale tenendosi al corrimano; **he leaned over the rail** si è sporto dal parapetto; **towel rail** portasciugamani *m inv*; **bath rail** maniglia del bagno **2** (*for train*) rotaia; **to go off the rails** (*train*) deragliare, uscire dal binario; (*fig: be confused*) uscire di carreggiata; (*: err*) sviarsi; **by rail** in treno, per ferrovia; **between the rails** tra le rotaie
▸ **rail off** VT + ADV recintare una ringhiera

rail·card [ˈreɪlˌkɑːd] N (*Brit*) tessera di riduzione ferroviaria

rail·ing [ˈreɪlɪŋ] N (*also:* **railings**) ringhiera, inferriata

rail·road [ˈreɪlˌrəʊd] N (*Am*) = **railway**
■ VT (*fig*): **to railroad sb into doing sth** costringere velocemente qn a fare qc

rail strike N sciopero dei treni

rail transport N trasporto ferroviario

◎ **rail·way** [ˈreɪlˌweɪ] N (*system*) ferrovia; (*track*) strada ferrata
■ ADJ (*bridge, timetable, network*) ferroviario(-a)
▷ www.heritagerailways.com/

railway engine N (*Brit*) locomotiva

railway line N (*Brit*) linea ferroviaria

rail·way·man [ˈreɪlˌweɪmən] N (*pl* **-men**) (*Brit*) ferroviere *m*

railway station N (*Brit*) stazione *f* ferroviaria

rail workers NPL ferrovieri *mpl*

◎ **rain** [reɪn] N pioggia; **in the rain** sotto la pioggia; **it looks like rain** per me si mette a piovere, c'è aria di pioggia; **heavy/light rain** pioggia forte/leggera; **come rain** *or* **shine** qualunque tempo faccia, col bello o col cattivo tempo; (*fig*) qualunque cosa succeda
■ VI piovere; **it's raining** piove; **it's raining cats and dogs** piove a catinelle; **it never rains but it pours** (*Proverb*) piove sempre sul bagnato; **to rain down (on sb)** (*blows*) piovere (addosso a qn)
▸ **rain off**
▸ **rain out** (*Am*) VT + ADV: **the match has been rained off** l'incontro è stato sospeso per la pioggia

rain·bow [ˈreɪnˌbəʊ] N arcobaleno

rain·check [ˈreɪnˌtʃɛk] N: **I'll take a raincheck** (*Am fam*) sarà per un'altra volta

rain·coat [ˈreɪnˌkəʊt] N impermeabile *m*

rain·drop [ˈreɪnˌdrɒp] N goccia di pioggia

rain·fall [ˈreɪnˌfɔːl] N (*amount*) piovosità, precipitazioni *fpl*

rain·for·est [ˈreɪnˌfɒrɪst] N foresta pluviale *or* equatoriale

rain gauge N pluviometro

rain·proof [ˈreɪnˌpruːf] ADJ impermeabile
■ VT impermeabilizzare

rain·storm [ˈreɪnˌstɔːm] N temporale *m*, pioggia torrenziale

rain·water [ˈreɪnˌwɔːtəʳ] N acqua piovana

rainy [ˈreɪnɪ] ADJ (*comp* **-ier**, *superl* **-iest**) (*climate*) piovoso(-a); (*season*) delle piogge; **rainy day** giorno piovoso; **to save** *or* **keep sth for a rainy day** (*fig*) mettere qc da parte per i tempi di magra

◎ **raise** [reɪz] VT **1** (*lift: gen*) sollevare, alzare; (*: shipwreck*) riportare alla superficie; (*: flag*) alzare, issare; (*: dust*) sollevare; (*fig: spirits, morale*) risollevare, tirar su; (*: to power, in rank*) elevare; (*Math*): **to raise to the third power** elevare alla terza potenza; **to raise o.s. up on one's elbows** sollevarsi sui gomiti; **he raised his hat to me** si è tolto il cappello per salutarmi; **to raise one's glass to sb/sth** brindare a qn/qc; **to raise one's voice** alzare la voce; **he didn't raise an eyebrow** non ha battuto ciglio; **he raised his hand** sollevò la mano; **to raise sb's hopes** accendere le speranze di qn; **to raise from the dead** risuscitare **2** (*erect: building, statue*) erigere **3** (*increase: salary, production*) aumentare; (*: price*) aumentare, alzare; **they want to raise standards in schools** vogliono migliorare il livello qualitativo delle scuole **4** (*crop*) coltivare; (*bring up, breed: family, livestock*) allevare **5** (*produce: question, objection*) sollevare; (*: problem*) porre; (*: doubts, suspicions*) far sorgere, far nascere; **to raise a laugh/a smile** far ridere/sorridere; **to raise hell** *or* **the roof** (*fam*) fare il diavolo a quattro; **she raised the question of unemployment** ha sollevato la questione della disoccupazione **6** (*get together: funds, army*) raccogliere; (*: taxes*) imporre; (*: money*) procurarsi; **to raise a loan** ottenere un prestito **7** (*end: siege, embargo*) togliere
■ N (*Am: payrise*) aumento

Rr

rai·sin ['reɪzən] N uvetta
rai·son d'être [ˌreɪzø:n'deɪtrə] N ragione *f* di vita
Raj [rɑ:dʒ] N: **the Raj** l'impero britannico (*in India*)
rajah ['rɑ:dʒə] N ragià *m inv*
rake¹ [reɪk] N (*tool*) rastrello
■VT (*sand, leaves, soil*) rastrellare; (*strafe: ship, row of men*) spazzare
▸ **rake in** VT + ADV (*fam: money*) fare; **they raked in a profit of £1,000** ci hanno fatto un guadagno di 1.000 sterline
▸ **rake off** VT + ADV (*fam: share of profit*) intascare
▸ **rake out** VT + ADV (*fire*) spegnere facendo cadere la brace
▸ **rake over** VT + ADV (*fig*) rivangare
▸ **rake through** VI + PREP rovistare in, frugare in
▸ **rake up** VT + ADV (*subject, memories*) rivangare, riesumare
rake² [reɪk] N (*old: dissolute man*) libertino
raked [reɪkd] ADJ in pendenza
rake-off ['reɪkˌɒf] N (*fam: share of profit*) parte *f*, fetta
rak·ish ['reɪkɪʃ] ADJ **1** (*person*) libertino(-a), dissoluto(-a) **2 at a rakish angle** (*hat*) sulle ventitré
◎**ral·ly** ['rælɪ] N (*of troops, people, also Pol*) raduno, riunione *f*; (*Aut*) rally *m inv*; (*Tennis*) lungo scambio di colpi; **a pre-election rally** un raduno pre-elettorale; **rally driver** pilota *m/f* di rally
■VT (*troops, supporters*) riunire, radunare
■VI (*troops, supporters*) riunirsi; (*revive, recover: patient, strength, share prices*) riprendersi
▸ **rally round** VI + ADV (*fig: cause*) far fronte comune
■VI + PREP (*person needing help*) stringersi intorno a
ral·ly·ing point ['rælɪɪŋˌpɔɪnt] N (*Pol, Mil*) punto di raduno
RAM [ræm] N ABBR (*Comput:* = **random access memory**) RAM *f inv*
ram [ræm] N (*Zool*) montone *m*, ariete *m*; (*Astrol, Mil*) ariete
■VT **1 to ram (into)** (*pack tightly*) calcare (in), pigiare (in); (*push down*) ficcare (in); (*stick into*) conficcare; **to ram one's hat down on one's head** calcarsi il cappello in testa; **they rammed their ideas down my throat** hanno cercato di imbottirmi la testa con le loro idee **2** (*collide with: ship*) speronare; (*: car*) cozzare, sbattere contro; **the car rammed the lamppost** la macchina è andata a sbattere con il muso contro il lampione

> DID YOU KNOW ...?
> **ram** is not translated by the Italian word *ramo*

Rama·dan [ˌræmə'dɑ:n] N (*Rel*) ramadan *m inv*
ram·ble ['ræmbl] N (lunga) passeggiata; (*hike*) escursione *f*; **to go for a ramble** fare un'escursione
■VI **1** (*walk*) gironzolare, vagare; (*hike*) fare escursioni **2** (*fig: in speech*) divagare, dilungarsi; **to ramble on** sproloquiare; **his mind has started to ramble** è un po' svanito
ram·bler ['ræmblə^r] N **1** (*hiker*) escursionista *m/f* **2** (*Bot*) rosa rampicante
ram·bling ['ræmblɪŋ] ADJ (*plant*) rampicante; (*speech, book*) sconnesso(-a); (*house*) tutto(-a) nicchie e corridoi
■N escursionismo
ram·bunc·tious [ræm'bʌŋkʃəs] ADJ (*Am*) = **rumbustious**
RAMC [ˌɑ:reɪem'si:] N ABBR (*Brit*) = *Royal Army Medical Corps*
rami·fi·ca·tion [ˌræmɪfɪ'keɪʃən] N ramificazione *f*
rami·fy ['ræmɪˌfaɪ] VI (*tree, problem*) ramificare; (*system*) ramificarsi
ramp [ræmp] N (*on road etc*) rampa; (*in garage*) ponte *m* idraulico; (*Aer*) scala d'imbarco; **"ramp"** (*Aut*) "fondo stradale in rifacimento"
ram·page [ræm'peɪdʒ] N: **to go on the rampage** scatenarsi (in modo violento)
■VI scatenarsi; **they went rampaging through the town** si sono scatenati in modo violento per la città
ram·pant ['ræmpənt] ADJ **1** (*fig: crime, disease*): **to be rampant** dilagare; **rampant corruption** corruzione *f* dilagante **2** (*Heraldry*) rampante
ram·part ['ræmpɑ:t] N terrapieno, bastione *m*
ram raid·ing ['ræmˌreɪdɪŋ] N *il rapinare un negozio o una banca sfondandone la vetrina con un'auto-ariete*
ram·shack·le ['ræmˌʃækl] ADJ (*house*) cadente, malandato(-a); (*car, table*) sgangherato(-a); **the present ramshackle system** l'attuale sistema sgangherato
RAN [ˌɑ:reɪ'ɛn] N ABBR = *Royal Australian Navy*
ran [ræn] PT *of* **run**
ranch [rɑ:ntʃ] N ranch *m inv*
ranch·er ['rɑ:ntʃə^r] N (*owner*) proprietario di un ranch; (*ranch hand*) cowboy *m inv*
ran·cid ['rænsɪd] ADJ rancido(-a); **to smell rancid** avere odore di rancido
ran·cor·ous ['ræŋkərəs] ADJ (*frm*) pieno(-a) di rancore
ran·cour, (*Am*) **ran·cor** ['ræŋkə^r] N (*frm*) rancore *m*
R&B [ˌɑ:rən'bi:] N ABBR = *rhythm and blues*
▷ www.rhythm-n-blues.org
R&D [ˌɑ:rən'di:] N ABBR = **research and development**
ran·dom ['rændəm] ADJ (*arrangement*) casuale, fortuito(-a); (*selection, shot, killing*) a caso; **a random selection** una selezione effettuata a caso
■N: **at random** a caso, a casaccio
random access N (*Comput*) accesso casuale
R&R [ˌɑ:rən'ɑ:] N ABBR (= **rest and recreation**) ricreazione *f*; (*Mil*) permesso
randy ['rændɪ] ADJ (*comp* **-ier**, *superl* **-iest**) (*Brit fam*) arrapato(-a)
rang [ræŋ] PT *of* **ring²**
◎**range** [reɪndʒ] N **1** (*distance attainable, scope: of gun, missile*) portata, gittata; (*: of ship, plane*) autonomia; **within (firing) range** a portata (di tiro); **out of (firing) range** fuori portata (di tiro); **at short/long range** a breve/lunga distanza; **range of vision** campo visivo **2** (*extent between limits: of temperature*) variazioni *fpl*; (*: of salaries, prices*) scala; (*: Mus: of instruments, voice*) gamma, estensione *f*; (*selection: of colours, feelings, speeds*) gamma; (*: of goods*) assortimento, gamma; (*domain, sphere*) raggio, sfera; **the range of sb's mind** le capacità mentali di qn; **a range of subjects** diverse materie; **she has a wide range of interests** ha interessi molto vari; **there's a wide range of colours** c'è una vasta gamma di colori; **price range** gamma di prezzi; **it's out of my price range** è fuori dal mio budget; **do you have anything else in this price range?** ha nient'altro più o meno a questo prezzo? **3** (*row*) serie *f inv*, fila; (*of mountains*) catena **4** (*Am Agr*) prateria **5** (*also:* **shooting range**: *in open*) poligono di tiro; (*: at fair*) tiro a segno **6** (*also:* **kitchen range**) cucina economica
■VT (*arrange, place*) disporre, allineare; **ranged left/right** (*text*) allineato(-a) a destra/sinistra
■VI **1** (*mountains, discussion, search*) estendersi; (*numbers, opinions, results*) variare; **they were ranged along the perimeter** furono disposti lungo il perimetro; **the discussion ranged over a wide number of topics** la

discussione ha toccato vari argomenti **2** *(roam)*: **to range over** vagare per; **to range from … to** andare da… a; **tickets range from four pounds to twenty pounds** i prezzi dei biglietti vanno dalle quattro alle venti sterline

range·finder ['reɪndʒˌfaɪndəʳ] N telemetro

rang·er ['reɪndʒəʳ] N *(also:* **forest ranger***)* guardia forestale; *(Am: mounted policeman)* poliziotto a cavallo

Ran·goon [ræŋ'guːn] N Rangoon *f*

◎**rank¹** [ræŋk] N **1** *(row)* fila; **taxi rank** posteggio di taxi **2** *(status: also Mil)* grado; **the rank of captain** il grado di capitano; **people of all ranks** gente *fsg* di tutti i ceti **3** *(Mil)*: **the ranks** la truppa; **he rose from the ranks** è venuto dalla gavetta; **to close ranks** *(Mil)* serrare le righe; *(fig)* serrare i ranghi; **to break rank(s)** rompere le righe; **I've joined the ranks of the unemployed** mi sono aggiunto alla massa dei disoccupati **4** *(Math)* posizione *f*

■VT considerare, ritenere; **I rank him 6th** gli dò il sesto posto, lo metto al sesto posto

■VI: **to rank 4th** essere quarto(-a), essere al quarto posto; **to rank above sb** essere superiore a qn; *(Mil)* essere superiore in grado a qn; **he ranks among the best** è uno dei migliori

rank² [ræŋk] ADJ **1** *(hypocrisy, injustice etc)* bello(-a) e buono(-a), vero(-a) e proprio(-a); *(traitor)* sporco(-a) **2** *(smell)* puzzolente, fetido(-a); *(fats)* rancido(-a) **3** *(frm: plants)* troppo rigoglioso(-a); **rank outsider** outsider *m/f inv*

rank and file N: **the rank and file** *(of political party)* la base

◎**rank·ing** ['ræŋkɪŋ] N posizione *f*, posto *(in classifica)*; **he holds the number two ranking** è in seconda posizione, è al secondo posto

■ADJ *(Am)*: **ranking officer** ufficiale di grado più elevato

ran·kle ['ræŋkl] VI: **to rankle (with sb)** bruciare (a qn); **this rejection still rankles** questo rifiuto brucia ancora

ran·sack ['rænsæk] VT *(drawer, room)* frugare, rovistare; *(town)* saccheggiare; **the burglars ransacked the house** i ladri hanno rovistato in casa; **embassies and homes were ransacked** le ambasciate e le case furono saccheggiate

ran·som ['rænsəm] N riscatto; **to hold sb to ransom** tenere in ostaggio qn *(per denaro)*; *(fig)* tenere qn in scacco

■VT riscattare

ransom demand N richiesta di riscatto

rant [rænt] VI *(pej)*: **to rant (at sb)** inveire (contro qn)

rant·ing ['ræntɪŋ] N *(pej)* invettiva

rap [ræp] N **1** *(noise)* colpetti *mpl*; *(at the door)* bussata; **there was a rap at the door** hanno bussato con un colpo secco alla porta; **to take the rap** *(fam)* pagare di persona **2** *(Mus)* rap *m*

■VT *(window)* dare dei colpetti su; *(door)* bussare a; **to rap sb's knuckles** dare un colpo secco sulle nocche di qn; *(fig)* dare una tirata d'orecchi a qn

■VI **1 to rap (at)** *(see vt)* dare dei colpetti (su); bussare (a) **2** *(Am fam: talk)* chiacchierare

▸ **rap out** VT + ADV *(order)* dire bruscamente

ra·pa·cious [rə'peɪʃəs] ADJ *(frm)* rapace

ra·pa·cious·ly [rə'peɪʃəslɪ] ADV *(frm)* rapacemente

ra·pa·city [rə'pæsɪtɪ] N *(frm)* rapacità

◎**rape¹** [reɪp] N *(also Law)* stupro, violenza carnale

■VT violentare, stuprare

DID YOU KNOW ...?
rape is not translated by the Italian word *rapire*

rape² [reɪp] N *(Bot)* colza

rape·seed oil ['reɪpˌsiːd'ɔɪl] N olio di colza

Raphael ['ræfeɪəl] N *(Art)* Raffaello

◎**rap·id** ['ræpɪd] ADJ rapido(-a)

ra·pid·ity [rə'pɪdɪtɪ] N rapidità

rap·id·ly ['ræpɪdlɪ] ADV rapidamente

rap·ids ['ræpɪdz] NPL *(in river)* rapide *fpl*

ra·pi·er ['reɪpɪəʳ] N spadino

rap·ist ['reɪpɪst] N violentatore *m*, stupratore *m*

rap·pel [ræ'pɛl] VI *(Am: Mountaineering)* discendere a corda doppia

rap·port [ræ'pɔːʳ] N intesa

rap·proche·ment [raprɔʃmɑ̃] N *(frm)*: **rapprochment (with/of/between)** riavvicinamento (a/di/fra)

rapt [ræpt] ADJ *(person, face, expression)* rapito(-a); *(silence, attention)* profondo(-a); **to be rapt in contemplation** essere in estatica contemplazione

rap·ture ['ræptʃəʳ] N *(liter)* estasi *f inv*; **in rapture** in estasi; **to be in raptures over sth/sb** essere estasiato(-a) di fronte a qc/qn; **to go into raptures over sth/sb** andare in estasi per qc/qn, rimanere estasiato(-a) da qc/qn

rap·tur·ous ['ræptʃərəs] *(liter)* ADJ *(smile)* estatico(-a); *(welcome, praise, applause)* entusiastico(-a)

rap·tur·ous·ly ['ræptʃərəslɪ] *(liter)* ADV *(smile)* estaticamente; *(welcome, praise, applaud)* entusiasticamente

◎**rare** [rɛəʳ] ADJ *(comp* **-r**, *superl* **-st***)* **1** raro(-a); **in a rare moment of generosity** in un raro momento di generosità; **it is rare to find that …** capita raramente *or* di rado che… *+ sub*; **a rare disease** una malattia rara **2** *(air)* rarefatto(-a) **3** *(meat)* al sangue, poco cotto(-a)

rare·bit ['rɛəbɪt] N: **Welsh rarebit** toast *m inv* al formaggio fuso

rar·efied ['rɛərɪˌfaɪd] ADJ *(atmosphere, air)* rarefatto(-a); *(fig)* raffinato(-a)

◎**rare·ly** ['rɛəlɪ] ADV di rado, raramente

rar·ing ['rɛərɪŋ] ADJ: **to be raring to go** *(fam)* non veder l'ora di cominciare

rar·ity ['rɛərɪtɪ] N **1** *(also:* **rareness***)* rarità **2** *(rare thing)* rarità *f inv*

ras·cal ['rɑːskəl] N *(scoundrel)* mascalzone *m*; *(child)* birbante *m*

ras·cal·ly ['rɑːskəlɪ] ADJ briccone(-a)

rash¹ [ræʃ] ADJ avventato(-a)

rash² [ræʃ] N *(Med: gen)* eruzione *f*, sfogo; *(: from food, allergy)* orticaria; **to come out in a rash** *(gen)* avere uno sfogo; **strawberries bring me out in a rash** le fragole mi fanno venire l'orticaria; **I've got a rash on my chest** ho un'eruzione sul petto

rash·er ['ræʃəʳ] N: **a rasher of bacon** una fetta di pancetta

rash·ly ['ræʃlɪ] ADV avventatamente

rash·ness ['ræʃnɪs] N avventatezza

rasp [rɑːsp] N *(tool)* raspa, lima; *(sound)* stridio, suono stridulo

■VT *(file)* raspare, raschiare; *(speak: also:* **rasp out***)* gracchiare

rasp·berry ['rɑːzbərɪ] N *(fruit)* lampone *m*; **to blow a raspberry** *(fam)* fare una pernacchia

■ADJ *(jam)* di lamponi; *(ice cream, syrup)* di lampone

raspberry bush N lampone *m (pianta)*

rasp·ing ['rɑːspɪŋ] ADJ stridulo(-a), stridente

Rr

Ras·ta·far·ian [ˌræstəˈfɛərɪən] ADJ, N rastafariano(-a)
rat [ræt] N ratto; **black rat** ratto comune; **brown rat** topo delle chiaviche; **you dirty rat!** (*fam*) brutta carogna!
■ VI: **to rat on sb** (*fam*) fare una spiata *or* una soffiata su qn; **to rat on a deal** (*fam*) rimangiarsi la parola; **to smell a rat** subodorare qualcosa
rat·able [ˈreɪtəbl] ADJ = **rateable**
rat-catcher [ˈræt,kætʃə^r] N *addetto alla derattizzazione*
ratch·et [ˈrætʃɪt] N arpionismo
ratchet wheel N ruota dentata
◎ **rate** [reɪt] N **1** (*ratio*) tasso, percentuale *f*; (*speed*) velocità *f inv*; **at a rate of 60 kph** alla velocità di 60 km all'ora; **at a great rate** *or* **at a rate of knots** (*fam*) a tutta velocità; **at a slow rate** a bassa velocità; **rate of growth** tasso di crescita; **at a steady rate** a un ritmo costante; **birth/death rate** tasso *or* indice *m* di natalità/di mortalità; **failure rate** percentuale *f* dei bocciati; **rate of flow/consumption** flusso/ consumo medio; **rate of reaction** (*Chem*) velocità *f inv* di reazione; **pulse rate** frequenza delle pulsazioni; **at this rate** di questo passo, con questo ritmo; **at any rate** in *or* ad ogni modo, comunque **2** (*price, charge*) tariffa; (*Comm, Fin*) tasso; **at a rate of 5% per annum** al tasso (annuo) del 5%; **postage rates** tariffe postali; **insurance rates** premi *mpl* assicurativi; **rate of exchange** tasso di cambio; **rate of pay** compenso medio; **bank rate** tasso d'interesse bancario; **a high rate of interest** un alto tasso d'interesse; **there are reduced rates for students** ci sono tariffe ridotte per gli studenti; *see also* **rates**
■ VT (*evaluate, appraise*) valutare; **to rate sb/sth highly** stimare molto qn/qc; **how do you rate that film?** cosa pensi di quel film?; **I rate it as one of the best** lo considero uno fra i migliori
■ VI: **it rates as one of the worst** è fra i peggiori; **to rate sb/sth among** annoverare qn/qc tra; **how does it rate among the critics?** che cosa ne hanno detto i critici?; **he was rated the best** era considerato il migliore
rate·able, **rat·able** [ˈreɪtəbl] ADJ (*property*) soggetto(-a) a tassazione
rat(e)able value N (*Brit old*) valore *m* imponibile (*agli effetti delle imposte comunali*)
rate of return N (*Fin*) tasso di rendimento
rate·payer [ˈreɪt,peɪə^r] N (*Brit old*) contribuente *m/f* (*di imposte comunali*)
rates [ˈreɪts] NPL (*Brit old*) imposte *fpl* comunali sugli immobili
◎ **ra·ther** [ˈrɑːðə^r] ADV **1** (*preference*) piuttosto; **rather than wait, she ...** piuttosto che aspettare, lei...; **I'd rather have this one than that** preferirei avere questo piuttosto che quello; **would you rather stay here?** preferisci rimanere qui?; **I'd rather you didn't come** preferirei che tu non venissi; **I'd rather not** preferirei di no; **I'd rather not come** preferirei non venire; **I would** *or* **I'd rather go** preferirei andare **2** (*to a considerable degree*) piuttosto; (*somewhat*) abbastanza; (*to some extent*) un po'; **it's rather expensive** (*quite*) è piuttosto caro; (*excessively*) è un po' troppo caro; **there's rather a lot** ce n'è parecchio; **I've got rather a lot of homework to do** ho molti compiti da fare; **I was rather disappointed** ero piuttosto deluso(-a); **a rather difficult task** un compito piuttosto difficile; **I feel rather more happy today** oggi mi sento molto più contento; **it's rather a pity** è proprio *or* davvero un peccato **3 or rather** (*more accurately*) anzi, per essere (più) precisi
■ EXCL eccome!
rati·fi·ca·tion [ˌrætɪfɪˈkeɪʃən] N (*frm*) ratifica
rati·fy [ˈrætɪ,faɪ] VT (*frm*) ratificare
◎ **rat·ing** [ˈreɪtɪŋ] N **1** (*assessment*) valutazione *f*; **it got a rating of ten out of ten** ha ottenuto una valutazione di dieci su dieci; **their popularity rating is at an all-time low** la loro popolarità ha raggiunto i minimi storici **2** (*Naut*) marinaio semplice
rat·ings [ˈreɪtɪŋz] NPL (*Radio, TV*) indice *msg* di ascolto
ra·tio [ˈreɪʃɪəʊ] N rapporto, proporzione *f*; **in the ratio of 2 to 1** in rapporto di 2 a 1
ra·tion [ˈræʃən] N razione *f*; **to be on ration** (*food*) essere razionato(-a); **to be on short rations** (*person*) essere a razioni ridotte
■ VT (*also:* **ration out**) razionare; **to ration sb to sth** imporre a qn un limite di qc
ra·tion·al [ˈræʃənl] ADJ (*being*) razionale; (*Med: lucid*) lucido(-a); (*faculty, action, argument*) razionale; (*solution, explanation, reasoning*) logico(-a), razionale
ra·tion·ale [ræʃəˈnɑːl] N fondamento logico
ra·tion·al·ism [ˌræʃənə,lɪzəm] N razionalismo
ra·tion·al·ist [ˈræʃnəlɪst] ADJ, N razionalista (*m/f*)
ra·tion·ali·za·tion [ˌræʃnəlaɪˈzeɪʃən] N razionalizzazione *f*
ra·tion·al·ize [ˈræʃnə,laɪz] VT **1** (*action, attitude*) (cercare di) spiegare razionalmente **2** (*reorganize: industry*) razionalizzare **3** (*Math*) razionalizzare
ra·tion·al·ly [ˈræʃnəlɪ] ADV (*behave, speak, think*) razionalmente
ration book N tessera annonaria
ra·tion·ing [ˈræʃnɪŋ] N razionamento
rat·pack [ˈræt,pæk] N (*Brit fam*) stampa scandalistica
rat poison N veleno per topi
rat race N (*pej*) corsa al successo
rat·tan [ræˈtæn] N malacca
rat-tat-tat [ˈrætəˈtæt] N (*on door*) toc-toc *m*; (*of machine gun*) ta-ta-ta *m*
rat·tle [ˈrætl] N **1** (*of train, car*) rumore *m* di ferraglia; (*of stone in tin, of windows*) tintinnio; (*of typewriter*) ticchettio; (*of hail, rain, bullets*) crepitio; **a rattle of bottles/chains** un rumore di bottiglie/catene; **death rattle** rantolo **2** (*instrument: used by football fan*) raganella; (: *child's*) sonaglio
■ VT **1** (*shake*) agitare; (: *moneybox*) far tintinnare **2** (*fam: person*) innervosire; **to get rattled** innervosirsi
■ VI (*box, objects in box, machinery*) far rumore; (*bullets, hailstones*) crepitare; (*window*) vibrare; **the train rattled over the crossing** il treno passò sferragliando al passaggio a livello
▸ **rattle off** VT + ADV (*poem, speech*) snocciolare
▸ **rattle on** VI + ADV blaterare
rattle·snake [ˈrætl,sneɪk] N crotalo, serpente *m* a sonagli
rat-trap [ˈræt,træp] N trappola per topi
rat·ty [ˈrætɪ] ADJ (*comp* **-ier**, *superl* **-iest**) (*Brit fam*) incavolato(-a); **to get ratty** incavolarsi
rau·cous [ˈrɔːkəs] ADJ (*voice, person*) rauco(-a); (*laughter*) sguaiato(-a)
rau·cous·ly [ˈrɔːkəslɪ] ADV (*see adj*) raucamente, con voce roca; sguaiatamente
raun·chy [ˈrɔːntʃɪ] ADJ (*comp* **-ier**, *superl* **-iest**) (*fam*) sexy *inv*
rav·age [ˈrævɪdʒ] VT (*frm*) devastare
rav·ages [ˈrævɪdʒɪz] NPL (*frm*) danni *mpl*; **the ravages of time** le offese *or* ingiurie del tempo

rave [reɪv] VI (*be delirious*) delirare; (*talk wildly*) farneticare; (*rant*) infuriarsi, fare una sfuriata; (*talk enthusiastically*): **to rave (about)** andare in estasi (per); essere assolutamente entusiasta (di); **they raved about the film** erano assolutamente entusiasti del film; **she cried and raved for weeks** ha urlato e farneticato per settimane
■ N rave *m inv*
■ ADJ (*scene, culture, music*) rave *inv*

ra·ven ['reɪvn] N corvo (imperiale)

raven-haired [ˌreɪvn'hɛəd] ADJ (*liter*) dai capelli corvini

rav·en·ous ['rævənəs] ADJ (*person*) affamato(-a); (*appetite, animal*) famelico(-a), vorace; **to be ravenous** avere una fame da lupi

rav·en·ous·ly ['rævənəslɪ] ADV voracemente

rav·er ['reɪvəʳ] N (*Brit fam*) festaiolo(-a)

rave review N (*fam*) critica entusiastica

rave-up ['reɪvʌp] N (*Brit fam*): **to have a rave-up** dare una grande festa

ra·vine [rə'vi:n] N burrone *m*

rav·ing ['reɪvɪŋ] ADJ: **raving lunatic** pazzo(-a) furioso(-a); **you must be raving mad!** sei matto da legare!

rav·ings ['reɪvɪŋz] NPL vaneggiamenti *mpl*

ra·vio·li [ˌrævɪ'əʊlɪ] N ravioli *mpl*

rav·ish ['rævɪʃ] VT **1** (*liter: enchant, delight*) estasiare, rapire **2** (*old: rape*) violentare; (*: carry off*) rapire

rav·ish·ing ['rævɪʃɪŋ] ADJ (*sight, beauty*) incantevole

rav·ish·ing·ly ['rævɪʃɪŋlɪ] ADV: **ravishingly beautiful** di incantevole bellezza

◎**raw** [rɔ:] ADJ **1** (*food*) crudo(-a); (*spirit*) puro(-a); (*silk, leather, cotton, ore*) greggio(-a); (*sugar*) non raffinato(-a); **to get a raw deal** (*fam: bad bargain*) prendere un bidone; (*: harsh treatment*) venire trattato(-a) ingiustamente; **raw carrots** carote *fpl* crude **2** (*wind, weather*) gelido(-a) **3** (*wound: open*) aperto(-a); (*: sore*) vivo(-a); (*skin*) screpolato(-a) **4** (*person: inexperienced*) inesperto(-a); **he's still raw** è ancora un pivello *or* un novellino
■ N: **it got him on the raw** (*fig*) lo ha punto sul vivo; **life in the raw** la vita così com'è

Ra·wal·pin·di [rɔ:l'pɪndɪ] N Rawalpindi *f*

raw·boned [ˌrɔ:'bəʊnd] ADJ scarno(-a)

raw·hide ['rɔ:ˌhaɪd] N **1** cuoio non conciato **2** (*whip*) frusta di cuoio

Rawl·plug® ['rɔ:lˌplʌg] N tassello

raw material N materia prima

raw·ness ['rɔ:nɪs] N **1** (*of weather, wind*) freddezza **2** (*of skin*) screpolature *fpl* **3** (*lack of experience*) inesperienza

◎**ray¹** [reɪ] N **1** raggio; (*of hope*) barlume *m*, raggio; **a ray of comfort** un po' di conforto **2** (*Geom*) semiretta

ray² [reɪ] N (*fish*) razza

ray·on ['reɪɒn] N raion *m*

raze [reɪz] VT (*also:* **raze to the ground**) radere al suolo

ra·zor ['reɪzəʳ] N rasoio; **disposable razor** rasoio usa e getta

razor·bill ['reɪzəˌbɪl] N gazza marina

razor blade N lametta (da barba)

razor-sharp ['reɪzə'ʃɑ:p] ADJ (*edge*) tagliente come un rasoio; (*mind*) molto acuto(-a); (*wit*) tagliente

razor shell NPL cannolicchio

razzle-dazzle ['ræzl'dæzl] N (*Brit fam*) brio; **to be/go on the razzle(-dazzle)** fare/andare a fare baldoria

razz·ma·tazz ['ræzmə'tæz] N (*fam*) clamore *m*

◎**R.C.** [ˌɑ:'si:] ABBR = **Roman Catholic**

RCAF [ˌɑ:si:eɪ'ɛf] N ABBR = *Royal Canadian Air Force*

RCMP [ˌɑ:si:ɛm'pi:] N ABBR = *Royal Canadian Mounted Police*

RCN [ˌɑ:si:'ɛn] N ABBR = *Royal Canadian Navy*

RD [ˌɑ:'di:] ABBR (*New Zealand Post*) = *rural delivery*

Rd ABBR = **Road**

RDA [ˌɑ:di:'eɪ] N ABBR (= **recommended daily amount** *or* **allowance**) dose *f* giornaliera consigliata

RDC [ˌɑ:di:'si:] N ABBR (*Brit*) = **rural district council**

RE [ˌɑ:r'i:] N ABBR **1** (*Brit Mil:* = **Royal Engineers**) ≈ GM (= *Genio Militare*) **2** = **religious education**

re¹ [ri:] PREP (*Comm: with regard to*) oggetto, con riferimento a

re² [reɪ] N (*Mus*) re *m inv*

re... [ri:] PREF ri..., re...

re·ab·sorp·tion [ˌri:əb'sɔ:pʃən] N riassorbimento

◎**reach** [ri:tʃ] N **1** portata; **within (easy) reach** a portata di mano, vicino(-a); **it's within easy reach by bus** lo si raggiunge facilmente in autobus; **the hotel is within easy reach of the town centre** l'albergo è vicino al centro; **out of reach** fuori portata; **keep medicine out of reach of children** non lasciare medicinali alla portata dei bambini **2** (*of river*) tratto; **the upper reaches of the Thames** l'alto corso del Tamigi **3** (*Naut*): **on a beam reach** al traverso; **on a broad reach** al gran lasco, al giardinetto; **on a close reach** al lasco
■ VT (*arrive at, attain*) arrivare a; (*: goal, limit, person*) raggiungere; **to reach a conclusion** arrivare ad una conclusione; **when the news reached my ears** quando mi è arrivata all'orecchio la notizia; **to reach a compromise** arrivare a *or* raggiungere un compromesso; **we reached the hotel at seven o'clock** siamo arrivati all'albergo alle sette; **eventually they reached an agreement** alla fine hanno raggiunto un accordo; **can I reach you at your hotel?** posso trovarla al suo albergo?; **to reach sb by phone** contattare qn per telefono; **we need to be able to reach him in an emergency** dobbiamo essere in grado di contattarlo in caso di emergenza
■ VI **1** (*stretch out hand: also:* **reach down, reach over, reach across** *etc*) allungare una mano; **he reached (over) for the book** si è allungato per prendere il libro; **he reached for his gun** fece per prendere la pistola **2** (*stretch: land etc*) estendersi; (*: wire, rope*) arrivare; (*voice, sound*) giungere
▸ **reach out** VI + ADV: **to reach out for** stendere la mano per prendere

◎**re·act** [ri:'ækt] VI: **to react (against/to)** reagire (contro/a)

◎**re·ac·tion** [ri:'ækʃən] N reazione *f*

re·ac·tion·ary [ri:'ækʃənrɪ] ADJ, N reazionario(-a)

re·ac·tive [ri:'æktɪv] ADJ reattivo(-a)

re·ac·tiv·ity [ˌri:æk'tɪvɪtɪ] N (*Chem*) reattività

re·ac·tor [ri:'æktəʳ] N reattore *m*

◎**read** [ri:d] (*vb: pt, pp* **read** [rɛd]) VT **1** (*gen*) leggere; **to read o.s. to sleep** leggere per addormentarsi; **I read a lot** leggo molto; **to take sth as read** (*fig*) dare qc per scontato; **to take the minutes as read** (*Admin*) passare subito all'ordine del giorno; **do you read me?** (*Telec*) mi ricevete? **2** (*Univ: study*) studiare; **to read Chemistry** fare *or* studiare chimica **3** (*interpret: dream, signal*) interpretare; (*: hand*) leggere; **she can read me like a book** mi legge nel cuore, per lei sono come un libro aperto; **to read sb's thoughts** leggere nel pensiero di qn; **to read between the lines** leggere tra

Rr

le righe; **to read too much into sth** attribuire troppa importanza a qc

■VI **1** leggere; **I read about him in the paper** ho letto qualcosa su di lui sul giornale; **I read about it in the paper** l'ho letto sul giornale; **to read to sb** leggere qualcosa a qn; **the book reads well** è un libro che si legge bene **2** (*indicate: meter, clock*) segnare; **the inscription reads "To my son"** la dedica dice "A mio figlio"

■N: **to have a quiet read** leggersi qualcosa in santa pace; **that book's a good read** quel libro è una buona lettura

▸ **read back** VT + ADV rileggere

▸ **read off** VT + ADV **1** (*without pause*) leggere tutto d'un fiato; **he read off the figures from the printout** (*at sight*) ha letto le cifre dal tabulato **2** (*instrument readings*) leggere

▸ **read on** VI + ADV continuare a leggere

▸ **read out** VT + ADV leggere (ad alta voce)

▸ **read over** VT + ADV rileggere attentamente

▸ **read through** VT + ADV (*quickly*) dare una scorsa a; (*thoroughly*) leggere da cima a fondo

▸ **read up (on)** VT + ADV (+PREP) studiare bene

read·able ['ri:dəbl] ADJ (*book*) che si legge volentieri; (*writing*) leggibile; **her latest book is very readable** il suo ultimo libro si legge molto volentieri

re·address [ˌri:ə'drɛs] VT (*letter*) cambiare indirizzo a

◎**read·er** ['ri:dəʳ] N **1** lettore(-trice); **she's a great reader** adora leggere **2** (*Brit Univ*) ≈ (docente *m/f*) incaricato(-a) **3** (*book*) libro di lettura; (: *anthology*) antologia

read·er·ship ['ri:dəʃɪp] N (numero di) lettori *mpl*

read·ily ['rɛdɪlɪ] ADV (*quickly*) prontamente; (*willingly*) volentieri; (*easily*) con facilità, facilmente; **she readily accepted** ha accettato prontamente; **the ingredients are readily available** gli ingredienti si trovano facilmente

readi·ness ['rɛdɪnɪs] N prontezza; **to be in readiness for** essere pronto(-a) per; **their readiness to co-operate** la loro disponibilità a collaborare; **in readiness for the president's arrival** in preparazione all'arrivo del presidente

◎**read·ing** ['ri:dɪŋ] N **1** (*gen*) lettura; (*of proofs*) correzione *f*; **I like reading** mi piace leggere; **reading and writing** leggere e scrivere **2** (*interpretation*) interpretazione *f*; (*of original text, manuscript*) lezione *f* **3** (*of thermometer etc*) lettura; **to take a reading** prendere *or* fare una lettura **4** (*recital: of play, poem*) reading *m inv*; **to give a poetry reading** tenere un reading di poesia

reading book N libro di lettura

reading glasses NPL occhiali *mpl* per leggere

reading group N *gruppo di persone che si riunisce regolarmente per discutere dei libri letti*

reading knowledge N: **to have a reading knowledge of Russian** essere capace di leggere il russo

reading lamp N lampada da scrivania

reading list N (*Scol*) lista dei libri da leggere; (*Univ*) bibliografia

reading matter N qualcosa da leggere

reading room N sala di lettura

re·adjust [ˌri:ə'dʒʌst] VT regolare (di nuovo); **they are now readjusting their policy** ora stanno rivedendo la loro politica; **the brakes need readjusting** i freni devono essere regolati

■VI (*person*): **to readjust (to)** riadattarsi (a); **astronauts find it difficult to readjust to life on Earth** gli astronauti fanno difficoltà a riabituarsi alla vita sulla Terra

re·adjust·ment [ˌri:ə'dʒʌstmənt] N **1** (*to situation, change*) riadattamento; **a period of readjustment** un periodo di riadattamento **2** (*of mechanism*) regolazione *f*

READ-ME file ['ri:dmi:ˌfaɪl] N (*Comput*) file *m inv* di sola lettura

read-only [ˌri:d'əʊnlɪ] ADJ (*Comput: file*) read-only

read only memory N (*Comput*) memoria di sola lettura

read-write memory [ˌri:dˌraɪt'mɛmərɪ] N (*Comput*) memoria read and write

◎**ready** ['rɛdɪ] ADJ (*comp* **-ier**, *superl* **-iest**) pronto(-a); (*willing*) pronto(-a), disposto(-a); (*quick*) rapido(-a); (*available*) disponibile; **are you ready?** sei pronto?; **ready for use** pronto per l'uso; **ready for anything** pronto(-a) a tutto; **ready money** denaro contante, contanti *mpl*; **to be ready to do sth** essere pronto a fare qc; **she was always ready to help** era sempre pronta ad aiutare; **to get ready** prepararsi; **to get ready to do** prepararsi a fare; **ready to serve** (*food*) già pronto; **to get sth ready** preparare qc; **ready, steady, go!** pronti, attenti, via!; **I'm ready for him!** lo sto aspettando!; **we were ready to give up there and then** eravamo sul punto di piantare lì tutto

■N: **at the ready** (*Mil*) pronto(-a) (a far fuoco *or* sparare); (*fig*) (tutto(-a)) pronto(-a)

■VT preparare

ready cash N contanti *mpl*

ready-cooked [ˌrɛdɪ'kʊkt] ADJ già cucinato(-a) *or* cotto(-a)

ready-made [ˌrɛdɪ'meɪd] ADJ (*clothes*) confezionato(-a); (*excuses, solution*) bell'e pronto(-a); (*ideas*) banale; **ready-made meals** pasti *mpl* pronti; **ready-made curtains** tende *fpl* confezionate; **a ready-made topic** un argomento bell'e pronto

ready-mix [ˌrɛdɪ'mɪks] N (*Culin*) miscela pronta; (*concrete*) calcestruzzo

ready reck·on·er ['rɛdɪ'rɛkənəʳ] N (*Brit*) prontuario di calcolo

ready-to-wear [ˌrɛdɪtə'wɛəʳ] ADJ prêt-à-porter *inv*

re·affirm [ri:ə'fɜ:m] VT riaffermare

re·agent [ri:'eɪdʒənt] N: **chemical reagent** reagente *m* chimico

◎**real** [rɪəl] ADJ (*gen*) vero(-a); (*reason, motive*) reale, vero(-a); (*Philosophy*) reale; **in real life** nella realtà; **in real terms** (*Fin*) in termini effettivi; **real account** (*Fin: in ledger*) conto patrimoniale; **he's a real villain** è un vero mascalzone; **he wasn't a real policeman** non era un vero poliziotto; **she has no real authority** in pratica non ha alcuna autorità; **once you've tasted the real thing ...** una volta provato l'originale...

■ADV (*Am fam*) veramente, proprio

■N: **for real** (*fam*) per davvero, sul serio

real ale N *tipo di birra scura prodotta secondo il metodo tradizionale*

real estate N (*Am*) beni *mpl* immobili

re·align·ment [ri:ə'laɪnmənt] N (*frm*): **realignment (of)** riallineamento (di)

re·al·ism ['rɪəˌlɪzəm] N (*also Art*) realismo

re·al·ist ['rɪəlɪst] N realista *m/f*

re·al·is·tic [rɪə'lɪstɪk] ADJ (*thing*) realistico(-a); (*person*) realista

re·al·is·ti·cal·ly [ˌrɪə'lɪstɪkəlɪ] ADV realisticamente

◎**re·al·ity** [ri:'ælɪtɪ] N realtà *f inv*; **in reality** in realtà, in effetti

reality TV N reality TV *f inv*
re·ali·za·tion [ˌrɪəlaɪˈzeɪʃən] N *(awareness)* presa di coscienza; *(frm: of hopes, plans, assets)* realizzazione *f*; **there is a growing realization that ...** sempre più ci si rende conto che...; **at the realization that ...** quando si rese conto che...; **the realization of their worst fears** la materializzazione delle loro peggiori paure; **the realization of their dreams** la realizzazione dei loro sogni
◎**re·al·ize** [ˈrɪəˌlaɪz] VT **1** *(become aware of)* rendersi conto di, accorgersi di; *(understand)* capire; **to realize sth** rendersi conto di qc; **I suddenly realized he was lying** improvvisamente mi sono reso conto che stava mentendo; **I realize that ...** mi rendo conto *or* capisco che...; **she hadn't fully realized the gravity of the situation** non si era resa completamente conto della gravità della situazione; **once they realized their mistake ...** dopo che si erano resi conto del loro errore...; **without realizing it** senza rendersene conto, senza accorgersene; **he realized how/why** ha capito come/perché **2** *(frm: hopes, ambitions, assets, project)* realizzare; (: *plan*) attuare, realizzare
◎**re·al·ly** [ˈrɪəlɪ] ADV davvero, veramente; **I don't really know** a dire la verità non lo so; **he doesn't really speak Chinese, does he?** non parla cinese sul serio, vero?; **I really ought to go home** devo proprio andare a casa; **I really don't like Tom** Tom non mi piace proprio; **a really good party** una festa bellissima; **she's really nice** è proprio simpatica; **did he hurt you? – not really** ti ha fatto male? – non è niente di grave; **I'm learning German – really?** sto studiando tedesco – davvero?
realm [rɛlm] N *(frm)* regno; **the realm of politics** il regno della politica; **within the realms of possibility** nel possibile
real number N *(Math)* numero reale
real time N *(Comput)* tempo reale; **in real time** in tempo reale
real-time [ˈrɪəltaɪm] ADJ *(Comput)* in tempo reale
re·al·tor [ˈrɪəltɔːʳ] N *(Am)* agente *m/f* immobiliare
ream [riːm] N risma; **reams** NPL *(fig fam)* pagine e pagine *fpl*
reap [riːp] VT mietere; *(fig: profit, benefit)* raccogliere; **to reap the benefit of sth** trarre beneficio da qc
reap·er [ˈriːpəʳ] N *(person)* mietitore(-trice); *(machine)* mietitrice *f*
re·appear [ˌriːəˈpɪəʳ] VI ricomparire, riapparire
re·appear·ance [ˌriːəˈpɪərəns] N ricomparsa, riapparizione *f*
re·apply [ˌriːəˈplaɪ] VI: **to reapply for** fare nuovamente domanda per
re·apprais·al [ˌriːəˈpreɪzəl] N riesame *m*
◎**rear¹** [rɪəʳ] ADJ *(gen)* di dietro, posteriore; *(Aut: door, window, wheel)* posteriore
■N *(back part)* didietro, parte *f* posteriore; *(Anat fam: buttocks)* didietro, sedere *m*; *(Mil)* retroguardia; **in** *or* **at the rear (of)** dietro (a), didietro (a); **to bring up the rear** venire per ultimo; *(Mil)* formare la retroguardia; **the rear of the building** il retro dell'edificio; **at the rear of the train** in coda al treno
rear² [rɪəʳ] VT **1** *(raise: cattle, family)* allevare **2** *(one's head)* drizzare
■VI *(also:* **rear up**: *esp horse)* impennarsi
rear admiral N contrammiraglio
rear-engined [ˌrɪərˈɛndʒɪnd] ADJ *(Aut)* con motore posteriore
rear·guard [ˈrɪəgɑːd] N *(Mil)* retroguardia
rearguard action N *(Mil)* azione *f* di retroguardia; *(fig)* azione *f* dilatoria
re·arm [ˌriːˈɑːm] VT riarmare
■VI riarmarsi
re·arma·ment [ˌriːˈɑːməmənt] N riarmo
rear·most [ˈrɪəˌməʊst] ADJ ultimo(-a)
re·arrange [ˌriːəˈreɪndʒ] VT *(objects)* ridisporre, riordinare; *(appointment)* fissare di nuovo, spostare; **a waiter was rearranging the tables** un cameriere riordinava i tavoli; **the meeting will have to be rearranged** la data dell'incontro dovrà essere spostata
re·arrange·ment [ˌriːəˈreɪndʒmənt] N *(see vt)* ridisposizione *f*; cambiamento
rear-view mirror [ˈrɪəˌvjuːˈmɪrəʳ] N *(Aut)* specchietto retrovisore
rear wheel N ruota posteriore
◎**rea·son** [ˈriːzn] N **1** *(motive, cause)* ragione *f*, motivo; **the reason for/why** la ragione *or* il motivo di/per cui; **the reason (why) I'm late is ...** sono in ritardo perché...; **don't ask the reason why** non chiedere il perché; **for no reason** senza ragione; **she claims with good reason that she's underpaid** si lamenta, e a ragione, di essere sottopagata; **all the more reason why you should not sell it** ragione di più per non venderlo; **we have reason to believe that ...** abbiamo motivo di ritenere che...; **by reason of** a causa di; **for security reasons** per ragioni di sicurezza **2** *(faculty, good sense)* ragione *f*; **to lose one's reason** perdere la ragione; **to listen to reason** ascoltare (la voce della) ragione; **it stands to reason** è logico; **within reason** entro limiti ragionevoli, entro certi limiti
■VT: **to reason that** concludere che, fare il ragionamento che
■VI: **to reason (with sb)** far ragionare qn
▶ **reason out** VT + ADV: **to reason sth out** risolvere qc ragionandoci su
◎**rea·son·able** [ˈriːznəbl] ADJ *(person, price)* ragionevole; *(behaviour, decision)* sensato(-a); *(standard)* accettabile; **be reasonable!** sii ragionevole!; **a perfectly reasonable thing to do** una cosa perfettamente sensata da farsi; **it is reasonable to conclude that ...** si può logicamente concludere che...; **he wrote a reasonable essay** ha fatto un tema discreto
rea·son·able·ness [ˈriːznəblnɪs] N ragionevolezza
rea·son·ably [ˈriːznəblɪ] ADV *(fairly, quite)* abbastanza; *(in a reasonable way)* ragionevolmente; **reasonably well** discretamente; **the team played reasonably well** la squadra ha giocato discretamente; **a reasonably accurate report** una relazione abbastanza accurata; **one can reasonably suppose that ...** si può logicamente supporre che...; **reasonably priced accommodation** alloggi *mpl* a prezzi ragionevoli
rea·soned [ˈriːznd] ADJ *(discussion, approach)* ragionato(-a); *(argument, opinion)* ponderato(-a)
rea·son·ing [ˈriːznɪŋ] N ragionamento
re·as·semble [ˌriːəˈsɛmbl] VT *(machine)* rimontare, riassemblare
■VI *(reconvene)* tornare a riunirsi
re·as·sert [ˌriːəˈsɜːt] VT riaffermare
re·as·sess [ˌriːəˈsɛs] VT *(situation)* riesaminare
re·assur·ance [ˌriːəˈʃʊərəns] N rassicurazione *f*
re·assure [ˌriːəˈʃʊəʳ] VT: **to reassure sb (of)** rassicurare qn (di *or* su)
re·assur·ing [ˌriːəˈʃʊərɪŋ] ADJ rassicurante
re·assur·ing·ly [ˌriːəˈʃʊərɪŋlɪ] ADV in modo rassicurante

Rr

re·awak·en [ˌriːəˈweɪkən] VT risvegliare, ridestare
■VI risvegliarsi, ridestarsi
re·awak·en·ing [ˌriːəˈweɪkənɪŋ] N risveglio
re·badge [ˌriːˈbædʒ] VT (*Brit*) rilanciare con un nuovo nome
re·bate [ˈriːbeɪt] N rimborso
◎ **re·bel** [*adj, n* ˈrɛbl; *vb* rɪˈbɛl] ADJ, N ribelle (*m/f*)
■VI: **to rebel (against sb/sth)** ribellarsi (a qn/contro qc)
re·bel·lion [rɪˈbɛljən] N ribellione *f*
re·bel·lious [rɪˈbɛljəs] ADJ ribelle
re·bel·lious·ness [rɪˈbɛljəsnɪs] N spirito di ribellione
re·birth [ˌriːˈbɜːθ] N rinascita
re·born [ˌriːˈbɔːn] ADJ **1** (*Rel: reincarnated*): **to be reborn** (*person*) rinascere **2** (*rejuvenated*): **to feel reborn** sentirsi rinascere
re·bound [*n* ˈriːbaʊnd; *vb* rɪˈbaʊnd] N: **on the rebound** per ripicca
■VI (*ball*) rimbalzare
▸ **rebound on** VI + PREP ricadere su, ritorcersi contro
re·brand [ˌriːˈbrænd] VT dare un nuovo nome e una nuova immagine a
re·brand·ing [ˌriːˈbrændɪŋ] N rinnovamento dell'immagine di un'azienda
re·buff [rɪˈbʌf] N secco rifiuto
■VT rifiutare, respingere
re·build [ˌriːˈbɪld] (*pt, pp* **rebuilt** [ˌriːˈbɪlt]) VT ricostruire
re·buke [rɪˈbjuːk] N rimprovero
■VT rimproverare; **to rebuke sb for sth/for doing sth** rimproverare qn per qc/per aver fatto qc
re·but [rɪˈbʌt] VT (*frm*) confutare
re·but·tal [rɪˈbʌtl] N (*frm*) confutazione *f*
re·cal·ci·trance [rɪˈkælsɪtrəns] N (*frm*) riluttanza
re·cal·ci·trant [rɪˈkælsɪtrənt] ADJ (*frm*) riluttante
◎ **re·call** [rɪˈkɔːl] N richiamo; **beyond recall** irrimediabilmente; per sempre; **the ground has been polluted beyond recall** il terreno è stato inquinato irrimediabilmente; **those days are gone beyond recall** quei tempi sono passati per sempre; **the recall of the ambassador** il richiamo in patria dell'ambasciatore; **he has total recall of what she said** ricorda perfettamente ciò che lei ha detto
■VT **1** (*call back: gen, Comput*) richiamare; (*: parliament*) riconvocare; (*: past*) far rivivere; **the ambassador has been recalled** l'ambasciatore è stato richiamato **2** (*remember*) ricordare, ricordarsi di; **I don't recall where we met** non ricordo dove ci siamo incontrati
re·cant [rɪˈkænt] (*frm*) VT (*religious belief*) abiurare; (*statement*) ritrattare
■VI fare abiura
re·cap¹ [ˈriːˌkæp] (*fam*) N riepilogo
■VT, VI riepilogare, ricapitolare; **to recap briefly ...** per ricapitolare brevemente...
re·cap² [ˈriːˌkæp] N (*Am: tyre*) pneumatico rigenerato
re·ca·pitu·late [ˌriːkəˈpɪtjʊˌleɪt] VT, VI riepilogare, ricapitolare
re·ca·pitu·la·tion [ˈriːkəˌpɪtjʊˈleɪʃən] N (*summary*) ricapitolazione *f*
re·cap·ture [ˈriːˈkæptʃəʳ] VT (*prisoner etc*) ricatturare; (*town*) riconquistare, riprendere; (*memory, scene*) ritrovare; (*atmosphere*) ricreare
re·cast [ˌriːˈkɑːst] VT **1** (*play, film*) cambiare il cast di; (*actor*) dare una parte diversa a; (*part*) dare ad un altro attore **2** (*rewrite: sentence*) rimaneggiare
recd ABBR = **received**
re·cede [rɪˈsiːd] VI (*tide, flood*) abbassarsi; (*view*) allontanarsi; (*danger, threat*) diminuire; **the threat of an epidemic is now receding** la minaccia di un'epidemia si sta allontanando; **his hair is starting to recede** sta cominciando a stempiarsi
re·ced·ing [rɪˈsiːdɪŋ] ADJ (*forehead, chin*) sfuggente; **he's got a receding hairline** è stempiato
re·ceipt [rɪˈsiːt] N **1** (*slip of paper*) ricevuta **2** (*frm esp Comm*) ricevimento; **to acknowledge receipt of** accusare ricevuta di; **we are in receipt of ...** abbiamo ricevuto... **3** (*money taken*): **receipts** NPL incassi *mpl*, introiti *mpl*
receipt book N blocchetto delle ricevute
re·ceiv·able [rɪˈsiːvəbl] ADJ (*Comm*) esigibile; (*: owed*) dovuto(-a)
◎ **re·ceive** [rɪˈsiːv] VT (*gen, Radio, TV*) ricevere; (*stolen goods*) ricettare; **"received with thanks"** (*Comm*) "per quietanza"; **to receive sb into one's home** ricevere qn in casa; **the book was not well received** il libro non ha avuto *or* ricevuto un'accoglienza favorevole
re·ceived [rɪˈsiːvd] ADJ (*opinion*) generalmente accettato(-a)
Received Pronunciation N pronuncia standard (*dell'inglese*)

RECEIVED PRONUNCIATION

Si chiama **Received Pronunciation (RP)** l'accento dell'inglese parlato in alcune parti del sud-est dell'Inghilterra. In esso si identifica l'inglese "standard" delle classi colte, privo di inflessioni regionali e adottato tradizionalmente dagli annunciatori della BBC. La Received Pronunciation è anche l'accento standard dell'inglese insegnato come lingua straniera.

▷ www.bbc.co.uk/dna/h2g2/classic/A657560

re·ceiv·er [rɪˈsiːvəʳ] N **1** (*gen*) persona che riceve qualcosa; (*of letter*) destinatario(-a); (*of stolen goods*) ricettatore(-trice); **(official) receiver** (*liquidator*) curatore *m* fallimentare **2** (*Radio*) apparecchio ricevente; (*Telec*) ricevitore *m*, cornetta (*fam*); **she picked up the receiver** ha sollevato la cornetta
re·ceiv·er·ship [ˌrɪˈsiːvəʃɪp] N curatela; **to go into receivership** andare in amministrazione controllata
◎ **re·cent** [ˈriːsnt] ADJ recente; **in recent memory** in tempi recenti; **in recent years** negli ultimi anni; **in recent weeks** nelle ultime settimane; **recent events** avvenimenti *mpl* recenti
◎ **re·cent·ly** [ˈriːsntlɪ] ADV di recente, recentemente, ultimamente; **as recently as 1990** soltanto nel 1990; **until recently** fino a poco tempo fa; **I haven't seen him recently** non l'ho visto di recente
re·cep·ta·cle [rɪˈsɛptəkl] N (*frm*) recipiente *m*
reception [rɪˈsɛpʃən] N **1** (*ceremony*) ricevimento; (*welcome*) accoglienza; **to get a warm reception** avere *or* ricevere un'accoglienza calorosa; **his speech got a cool reception** il suo discorso ha ricevuto una fredda accoglienza; **the reception will be at a big hotel** il ricevimento si terrà in un grande albergo **2** (*desk: in hotel*) reception *f inv*; (*: in hospital, at doctor's*) accettazione *f*; (*: in large building, offices*) portineria; **please leave your key at reception** si prega di lasciare le chiavi alla reception **3** (*Radio, TV*) ricezione *f*; **4** (*Brit: Scol*) ≈ primina
reception centre N (*Brit*) centro di raccolta
reception desk N = **reception 2**
re·cep·tion·ist [rɪˈsɛpʃənɪst] N (*in hotel, offices*)

receptionist *m/f inv*; (*at doctor's*) addetto(-a) alla ricezione, assistente *m/f* di studio

re·cep·tive [rɪ'sɛptɪv] ADJ ricettivo(-a)

re·cep·tive·ness [rɪ'sɛptɪvnɪs], **re·cep·tiv·ity** [ˌriːsɛp'tɪvɪtɪ] N ricettività

re·cep·tor [rɪ'sɛptəʳ] N recettore *m*

re·cess [rɪ'sɛs] N **1** (*Law, Parliament: cessation of business*) ferie *fpl*, vacanza; (*Am Law: short break*) sospensione *f*; (*Scol: esp Am*) intervallo; **a ten-minute recess** una sospensione di dieci minuti; **after the summer recess** dopo le vacanze estive **2** (*for bed*) rientranza; (*for statue*) nicchia; (*fig: of mind*) recesso; **a recess beside the fireplace** una nicchia accanto al caminetto

◎ **re·ces·sion** [rɪ'sɛʃən] N (*Econ*) recessione *f*

re·ces·sive [rɪ'sɛsɪv] ADJ (*Bio*) recessivo(-a)

re·charge [riː'tʃɑːdʒ] VT (*battery*) ricaricare

re·charge·able [rɪː'tʃɑːdʒəbl] ADJ (*battery*) ricaricabile

re·cher·ché [rə'ʃɛəʃeɪ] ADJ ricercato(-a)

re·cidi·vism [rɪ'sɪdɪˌvɪzəm] N recidività

re·cidi·vist [rɪ'sɪdɪvɪst] N recidivo(-a)

reci·pe ['rɛsɪpɪ] N (*also fig*) ricetta

re·cipi·ent [rɪ'sɪpɪənt] N (*of letter*) destinatario(-a); (*of cheque*) beneficiario(-a); (*of award*) assegnatario(-a)

> DID YOU KNOW ...?
> **recipient** is not translated by the Italian word *recipiente*

re·cip·ro·cal [rɪ'sɪprəkəl] ADJ reciproco(-a); **reciprocal trading** scambio commerciale

re·cip·ro·cal·ly [rɪ'sɪprəkəlɪ] ADV reciprocamente

re·cip·ro·cate [rɪ'sɪprəˌkeɪt] VT, VI ricambiare, contraccambiare

reci·proc·ity [ˌrɛsɪ'prɒsətɪ] N reciprocità

re·cit·al [rɪ'saɪtl] N (*Mus*) recital *m inv*; (*of poetry*) recita; (*account*) resoconto

reci·ta·tion [ˌrɛsɪ'teɪʃən] N recitazione *f*; **to give recitations from Shakespeare** recitare brani da Shakespeare

re·cite [rɪ'saɪt] VT (*poem*) recitare; (*facts, details*) elencare, enumerare
■ VI recitare

reck·less ['rɛklɪs] ADJ (*driver, driving, speed*) spericolato(-a); (*disregard, pursuit*) incosciente; (*action, decision*) avventato(-a)

reck·less·ly ['rɛklɪslɪ] ADV (*drive*) in modo spericolato; (*gamble, bet, plunge*) avventatamente

reck·less·ness ['rɛklɪsnɪs] N (*of driving*) spericolatezza; (*of person, behaviour*) incoscienza, avventatezza

◎ **reck·on** ['rɛkən] VT (*calculate*) calcolare; (*believe*) pensare, credere; (*judge*) considerare, stimare; **I reckon him to be one of the best** lo considero uno dei migliori, per me è uno dei migliori; **I reckon (that) we'll be late** prevedo che saremo in ritardo; **what do you reckon?** cosa ne pensi?
■ VI contare, calcolare; **to reckon with sb** fare i conti con qn; **he is somebody to be reckoned with** è uno da non sottovalutare; **to reckon without sb/sth** non tener conto di qn/qc; **to reckon without doing sth** non calcolare di fare qc
▸ **reckon in** VT + ADV considerare; **when everything is reckoned in ...** a conti fatti...
▸ **reckon on** VI + PREP (*bank on*) contare su; (*expect*) prevedere; **to reckon on doing sth** far conto di fare qc
▸ **reckon up** VT + ADV (*frm: cost, losses*) calcolare; **to reckon up the bill** fare il conto

reck·on·ing ['rɛknɪŋ] N calcoli *mpl*, conti *mpl*; **by my reckoning** secondo i miei calcoli; **to be out in one's reckoning** aver sbagliato *or* fatto male i propri conti; **the day of reckoning** (*fig*) il momento della resa dei conti

re·claim [rɪ'kleɪm] VT (*baggage, waste materials*) ricuperare; (*money*) richiedere, reclamare; (*land*) bonificare; **before leaving I reclaimed my passport** prima di partire ho chiesto indietro il passaporto; **large areas were reclaimed** ampie zone sono state bonificate

rec·la·ma·tion [ˌrɛklə'meɪʃən] N (*of waste materials*) ricupero; (*of land*) bonifica

re·cline [rɪ'klaɪn] VI (*person*) essere sdraiato(-a); **the seat reclines** il sedile è reclinabile *or* ribaltabile

re·clin·ing [rɪ'klaɪnɪŋ] ADJ: **reclining seat** sedile reclinabile *or* ribaltabile

re·cluse [rɪ'kluːs] N recluso(-a), eremita *m*

re·clu·sive [riː'kluːsɪv] ADJ (*frm*) recluso(-a); **to become reclusive** fare vita da recluso(-a), far vita appartata

◎ **rec·og·ni·tion** [ˌrɛkəg'nɪʃən] N riconoscimento; **in recognition of** in *or* come segno di riconoscimento per; **to gain recognition** ottenere un riconoscimento, essere riconosciuto(-a); **to change/change sth beyond recognition** diventare/rendere qc irriconoscibile; **transformed** *or* **changed beyond recognition** irriconoscibile; **a sign of recognition** un segno di riconoscimento

rec·og·niz·able ['rɛkəgˌnaɪzəbl] ADJ: **recognizable (by)** riconoscibile (a *or* da)

rec·og·niz·ably ['rɛkəgˌnaɪzəblɪ] ADV riconoscibilmente

◎ **rec·og·nize** ['rɛkəgˌnaɪz] VT (*all senses*) riconoscere; **to recognize (by/as)** riconoscere (a *or* da/come)

rec·og·nized ['rɛkəgnaɪzd] ADJ (*technique, authority*) riconosciuto(-a)

re·coil [rɪ'kɔɪl] VI **1** (*person: draw back*) tirarsi indietro; **to recoil (from) sth** indietreggiare (di fronte *or* davanti a) qc; **to recoil from doing sth** rifuggire dal fare qc **2** (*gun*) rinculare
■ N (*of gun*) rinculo

rec·ol·lect [ˌrɛkə'lɛkt] VT rammentare, ricordare

rec·ol·lec·tion [ˌrɛkə'lɛkʃən] N memoria, ricordo; **to the best of my recollection** per quello che mi ricordo

◎ **rec·om·mend** [ˌrɛkə'mɛnd] VT (*course of action*) consigliare; (*product, doctor*) raccomandare, consigliare; (*person: for job*) raccomandare; **I recommend that he sees a doctor** (*frm*) gli consiglierei di vedere un medico; **what do you recommend?** che cosa ci consiglia?; **to recommend sb for sth** raccomandare qn per qc; **she has a lot to recommend her** ha molti elementi a suo favore

◎ **rec·om·men·da·tion** [ˌrɛkəmɛn'deɪʃən] N (*of person, product*) raccomandazione *f*; (*of course of action*) consiglio; **to do sth on sb's recommendation** fare qc su *or* dietro consiglio di qn; **the committee's recommendations will be made public** le raccomandazioni della commissione verranno rese pubbliche; **on his recommendation I visited Conwy** su suo consiglio ho visitato Conwy

rec·om·men·ded [ˌrɛkə'mɛndɪd] ADJ consigliato(-a); **highly recommended** vivamente consigliato(-a); **recommended retail price** prezzo (di vendita) consigliato

rec·om·pense ['rɛkəmpɛns] N ricompensa; (*Law: for damage*) risarcimento
■ VT ricompensare; **to recompense sb (for sth)** (*Law*) risarcire qn (di qc)

Rr

rec·on·cil·able ['rɛkən,saɪləbl] ADJ: **reconcilable (with)** conciliabile (con)

rec·on·cile ['rɛkən,saɪl] VT *(persons)* riconciliare; *(theories, contradictions)* conciliare; **to become reconciled** *(people)* riconciliarsi; **the couple have now been reconciled** la coppia ora si è riconciliata; **to reconcile o.s. to sth** rassegnarsi a qc; **she had reconciled herself to never seeing him again** si è rassegnata a non rivederlo più; **how can you reconcile your ideals with your lifestyle?** come riesci a conciliare i tuoi ideali con il tuo stile di vita?

rec·on·cilia·tion [,rɛkənsɪlɪ'eɪʃən] N *(of people)* riconciliazione *f*; *(of contradictions, attitudes)* conciliazione *f*; **her husband wants a reconciliation** suo marito vuole una riconciliazione

re·con·dite [rɪ'kɒndaɪt] ADJ *(frm)* recondito(-a)

re·con·di·tion [,ri:kən'dɪʃən] VT *(engine)* ricondizionare

re·con·nais·sance [rɪ'kɒnɪsəns] N *(Mil)* ricognizione *f*

reconnaissance flight N volo di ricognizione

re·con·noi·tre, *(Am)* **re·con·noi·ter** [,rɛkə'nɔɪtə^r] *(Mil)* VT fare una ricognizione di
■ VI fare una ricognizione

re·con·sid·er [,ri:kən'sɪdə^r] VT riconsiderare

re·con·sid·era·tion [,ri:kən,sɪdə'reɪʃən] N riconsiderazione *f*

re·con·sti·tute [ri:'kɒnstɪ,tju:t] VT ricostituire

re·con·struct [,ri:kən'strʌkt] VT ricostruire

re·con·struc·tion [,ri:kən'strʌkʃən] N ricostruzione *f*

re·con·vene [,ri:kən'vi:n] VT riconvocare
■ VI radunarsi

re·con·ver·sion [,ri:kən'vɜ:ʃən] N *(Fin)* riconversione *f*

◎ **rec·ord** [*n, adj* 'rɛkɔ:d; *vb* rɪ'kɔ:d] N **1** *(report, note)* rapporto; *(file)* pratica, dossier *m inv*; *(minutes: of meeting)* verbale *m*; *(Law)* registro; *(historical report)* documento; *(Comput)* record *m inv*, registrazione *f*; **record of attendance** registro delle presenze; **public records** archivi *mpl*; **I'll check in the records** controllo in archivio; **there is no record of it** non c'è niente che lo possa comprovare; **there is no record of your booking** non c'è traccia della vostra prenotazione; **to keep a record of sth** tener nota di qc; **just for the record** tanto per mettere le cose in chiaro; **he is on record as saying that ...** ha dichiarato pubblicamente che...; **it is on record that ...** è stato registrato che...; **to place** *or* **put sth on record** mettere qc agli atti; **he told me off the record** *(fam)* me l'ha detto ufficiosamente; **to set the record straight** mettere le cose in chiaro **2** *(person's past in general)* precedenti *mpl*; *(as dossier)* resoconto; *(also:* **criminal record***)* menzione *f* nel casellario giudiziale; **to have a criminal record** avere precedenti penali; **he has a clean record** ha la fedina penale pulita, non ha precedenti penali; **police records** schedario *msg* della polizia; **Italy's excellent record** i brillanti successi italiani; **the school has a poor record of exam passes** in quella scuola si registra una bassa percentuale di promozioni **3** *(Sport)* record *m inv*, primato; **to beat** *or* **break a record** battere un record *or* un primato; **to hold the record (for sth)** detenere il primato (di qc); **the world record** il record mondiale **4** *(Mus)* disco; **one of my favourite records** uno dei miei dischi preferiti
■ ADJ ATTR record *inv*; **in record time** a tempo di record
■ VT **1** *(set down)* registrare, prendere nota di; *(relate)* raccontare; **to record one's vote** votare **2** *(Mus)* registrare, incidere; *(Comput)* registrare **3** *(subj: thermometer)* registrare

> DID YOU KNOW ...?
> **record** is not translated by the Italian word *ricordare*

record-breaking ['rɛkɔ:d,breɪkɪŋ] ADJ che batte tutti i record

record card ['rɛkɔ:d,kɑ:d] N *(index card)* scheda

record-changer ['rɛkɔ:d,tʃeɪndʒə^r] N cambiadischi *m inv* automatico

rec·ord·ed de·liv·ery [rɪ'kɔ:dɪddɪ'lɪvərɪ] N *(Brit Post)* raccomandata; **to send sth recorded delivery** spedire qc per raccomandata

re·cord·er [rɪ'kɔ:də^r] N **1** *(tape recorder)* registratore *m* **2** *(Mus)* flauto diritto *or* dolce; **to play the recorder** suonare il flauto dolce **3** *(Law: in England and Wales) avvocato che funge da giudice*

record holder ['rɛkɔ:d,həʊldə^r] N *(Sport)* primatista *m/f*, detentore(-trice) di (un) record

◎ **re·cord·ing** [rɪ'kɔ:dɪŋ] N *(of programme, song)* registrazione *f*

recording session N seduta di registrazione

recording studio N sala di registrazione

record library ['rɛkɔ:d,laɪbrərɪ] N discoteca *(raccolta)*

record player ['rɛkɔ:d,pleɪə^r] N giradischi *m inv*

record token ['rɛkɔ:dtəʊkən] N *buono per l'acquisto di dischi*

re·count [rɪ'kaʊnt] VT *(narrate)* raccontare

re-count [*n* 'ri:,kaʊnt; *vb* ,ri:'kaʊnt] N *(of votes)* nuovo conteggio
■ VT ricontare, rifare il conteggio di

re·coup [rɪ'ku:p] VT ricuperare; **to recoup one's losses** ricuperare le perdite, rifarsi

re·course [rɪ'kɔ:s] N *(frm)*: **to have recourse to** ricorrere a, far ricorso a

◎ **re·cov·er** [rɪ'kʌvə^r] VT *(belongings, goods, wreck, lost time)* ricuperare; *(reclaim: money)* ottenere il rimborso di; *(Law: damages)* ottenere il risarcimento di; *(balance, appetite, health etc)* ritrovare, ricuperare; **to recover one's senses** riprendere i sensi; *(fig)* ritornare in sé
■ VI *(all senses)* riprendersi; *(from illness)* ristabilirsi; **it took her half an hour to recover** le ci è voluta mezz'ora per riprendersi

> DID YOU KNOW ...?
> **recover** is not translated by the Italian word *ricoverare*

re-cover [,ri:'kʌvə^r] VT *(chair, settee)* ricoprire

re·cov·er·able [ri'kʌvərəbl] ADJ *(debt, loss)* ricuperabile

◎ **re·cov·ery** [rɪ'kʌvərɪ] N **1** *(see vt)* ricupero; rimborso; risarcimento **2** *(see vi)* ripresa; **to make a recovery** *(Med)* avere *or* fare un miglioramento; *(Sport, Fin)* avere una ripresa; **to be on the way to recovery** *(Med)* essere in via di guarigione; *(Sport, Fin)* essere in ripresa

> DID YOU KNOW ...?
> **recovery** is not translated by the Italian word *ricovero*

recovery position N *(Med)* posizione laterale di sicurezza; **to put sb in the recovery position** mettere qn in posizione laterale di sicurezza

recovery room N *(Med)* sala rianimazione

re·cre·ate [,ri:krɪ'eɪt] VT ricreare

rec·rea·tion [**1** ,rɛkrɪ'eɪʃən; **2** ,ri:krɪ'eɪʃən] N **1** *(leisure)* ricreazione *f*; **interests and recreations** interessi *mpl* e svaghi *mpl* **2** *(restoration)* restaurazione *f*; **the recreation of the original theatre** la ricostruzione del teatro originale

rec·rea·tion·al [,rɛkrɪ'eɪʃənəl] ADJ ricreativo(-a)

recreational drug N *sostanza stupefacente usata a scopo ricreativo*

recreational vehicle N (*Am: motorhome*) camper *m inv*; (*: trailer*) roulotte *f inv*
recreation ground N campo *m* giochi *inv*
re·crimi·na·tion [rɪˌkrɪmɪˈneɪʃən] N recriminazione *f*
◎ **re·cruit** [rɪˈkruːt] N (*Mil*) recluta; (*new member: of club*) nuovo(-a) iscritto(-a); (*: of staff*) nuovo(-a) assunto(-a) ■ VT (*staff, members, soldiers*) reclutare
re·cruit·ing of·fice [rɪkruːtɪŋˌɒfɪs] N ufficio di reclutamento
re·cruit·ment [rɪˈkruːtmənt] N reclutamento
recruitment consultant N consulente *m/f* occupazionale
rec·tan·gle [ˈrɛkˌtæŋgl] N rettangolo
rec·tan·gu·lar [rɛkˈtæŋgjʊləʳ] ADJ rettangolare
rec·ti·fi·er [ˈrɛktɪˌfaɪəʳ] N (*Elec*) raddrizzatore *m*
rec·ti·fy [ˈrɛktɪˌfaɪ] VT (*error*) rettificare; (*omission*) riparare a
rec·ti·lin·ear [ˌrɛktɪˈlɪnɪəʳ] ADJ rettilineo(-a); **rectilinear motion** moto rettilineo
rec·ti·tude [ˈrɛktɪˌtjuːd] N (*frm*) rettitudine *f*
rec·tor [ˈrɛktəʳ] N (*Rel*) parroco (*anglicano*); (*Univ*) rettore *m*; (*in Scottish universities*) *personalità eletta dagli studenti per rappresentarli*; (*of school*) preside *m/f*
rec·tory [ˈrɛktərɪ] N casa parrocchiale (*anglicana*)
rec·tum [ˈrɛktəm] N (*Anat*) retto
re·cum·bent [rɪˈkʌmbənt] ADJ (*frm*) giacente
re·cu·per·ate [rɪˈkuːpəˌreɪt] VI (*Med*) ristabilirsi ■ VT (*losses*) ricuperare
re·cu·pera·tion [rɪˌkuːpəˈreɪʃən] N (*after illness*) convalescenza; (*of losses*) ricupero
re·cu·pera·tive [rɪˈkuːpərətɪv] ADJ (*powers*) di ricupero
re·cur [rɪˈkɜːʳ] VI (*pain, event, mistake*) ripetersi; (*idea, theme*) ricorrere, riapparire; (*difficulty, opportunity, symptoms*) ripresentarsi, ripetersi; **such a disaster could recur** questo disastro potrebbe riaccadere; **if the symptoms recur ...** se i sintomi si ripresentano...
re·cur·rence [rɪˈkʌrəns] N (*of pain, dream, violence*) ripetersi *m*; (*of injury, problem*) ripresentarsi *m*; (*of disease, symptoms*) ricomparsa; (*of idea, theme*) ricorrenza
re·cur·rent [rɪˈkʌrənt] ADJ ricorrente
re·cur·ring [rɪˈkɜːrɪŋ] ADJ (*Math*) periodico(-a)
re·cy·cle [ˌriːˈsaɪkl] VT riciclare
re·cy·cling [ˌriːˈsaɪklɪŋ] N riciclaggio
◎ **red** [rɛd] ADJ (*comp* **-der**, *superl* **-dest**) (*all senses*) rosso(-a); **to be red in the face** (*from physical effort*) essere tutto(-a) rosso(-a), avere il viso rosso; (*embarrassed*) essere rosso(-a) (in viso); **to roll out the red carpet (for sb)** (*fig*) accogliere qn in pompa magna; **it's like a red rag to a bull with him** è una cosa che gli fa vedere rosso ■ N (*colour*) rosso; (*Pol pej*) rosso(-a); **in the red** (*Fin: account*) in rosso, scoperto(-a); (*: firm*) in deficit, in rosso; **to see red** (*fig*) vedere rosso
red alert N allarme rosso
red-blooded [ˌrɛdˈblʌdɪd] ADJ (*fam*) gagliardo(-a)
red·breast [ˈrɛdˌbrɛst] N (*bird*) pettirosso
red·brick [ˈrɛdˌbrɪk] ADJ: **redbrick university** (*Brit*) *università istituita alla fine del diciannovesimo secolo*

RED-BRICK UNIVERSITY

In Gran Bretagna, con il termine **red-brick university** (letteralmente, università di mattoni rossi) si indicano le università istituite tra la fine dell'Ottocento e i primi del Novecento, per contraddistinguerle dalle università più antiche, i cui edifici sono di pietra. *Vedi anche* **Oxbridge**

red card N (*Sport*) cartellino rosso
red carpet treatment N trattamento d'onore
Red Crescent N: **the Red Crescent** la Mezzaluna Rossa
Red Cross N: **the Red Cross** la Croce Rossa
red·cur·rant [ˌrɛdˈkʌrənt] N ribes *m inv* rosso; **redcurrant jelly** marmellata di ribes rosso
red deer N, PL INV cervo(-a)
red·den [ˈrɛdn] VT arrossare, tingere di rosso ■ VI (*sky, leaves*) diventar rosso, tingersi di rosso; (*person*) arrossire
red·dish [ˈrɛdɪʃ] ADJ rossiccio(-a), rossastro(-a); (*hair*) rossiccio(-a)
re·deco·rate [ˌriːˈdɛkəˌreɪt] VT tinteggiare (e tappezzare) di nuovo
re·deem [rɪˈdiːm] VT (*Rel: sinner*) redimere; (*buy back: pawned goods*) disimpegnare, riscattare; (*Fin: debt, mortgage*) estinguere, ammortare; (*fulfil: promise*) mantenere; (*: obligation*) adempiere a; (*compensate for: fault*) compensare; **to redeem o.s.** farsi perdonare
re·deem·able [rɪˈdiːməbl] ADJ (*bonds, shares*) redimibile
Re·deem·er [rɪˈdiːməʳ] N Redentore *m*
re·deem·ing [rɪˈdiːmɪŋ] ADJ: **redeeming feature** unico aspetto positivo
re·de·fine [ˌriːdɪˈfaɪn] VT ridefinire
re·demp·tion [rɪˈdɛmpʃən] N (*Rel*) redenzione *f*; **past** *or* **beyond redemption** irrecuperabile
re·deploy [ˌriːdɪˈplɔɪ] VT (*troops: send elsewhere*) trasferire in un altro settore; (*: reorganize*) riorganizzare lo schieramento di; (*workers*) reimpiegare; (*resources*) ridistribuire
re·deploy·ment [ˌriːdɪˈplɔɪmənt] N (*of resources*) ridistribuzione *f*
re·deve·lop [riːdɪˈvɛləp] VT (*area*) ristrutturare
re·devel·op·ment [ˌriːdɪˈvɛləpmənt] N (*of area*) ristrutturazione *f*
red-eye [ˈrɛdaɪ] N **1** (*fam: flight*) volo notturno **2** (*Phot*) effetto occhi rossi ■ ADJ **1** (*fam: flight*) notturno **2** (*Phot*): **red-eye reduction** riduzione effetto occhi rossi; **red-eye reduction facility** dispositivo per la riduzione dell'effetto occhi rossi
red-eyed [ˌrɛdˈaɪd] ADJ con gli occhi rossi *or* arrossati
red-faced [ˌrɛdˈfeɪst] ADJ (*also fig*) rosso(-a) in viso
red-haired [ˌrɛdˈhɛəd] ADJ con i *or* dai capelli rossi
red-handed [ˌrɛdˈhændɪd] ADJ: **to catch sb red-handed** prendere qn con le mani nel sacco, cogliere qn in flagrante
red·head [ˈrɛdˌhɛd] N (*person with red hair*) rosso(-a)
red herring N (*fig*) falsa pista
red-hot [ˌrɛdˈhɒt] ADJ arroventato(-a), rovente
re·did [ˌriːˈdɪd] PT *of* **redo**
Red Indian N (*offensive*) pellerossa *m/f*
re·di·rect [ˌriːdaɪˈrɛkt] VT (*letter*) rispedire (*a un nuovo indirizzo*)
re·dis·count [ˌriːˈdɪskaʊnt] VT (*Fin*) riscontare
re·dis·trib·ute [ˌriːdɪsˈtrɪbjuːt] VT ridistribuire
red-letter day [ˌrɛdˈlɛtəˌdeɪ] N giorno memorabile
red light N (*Aut*) (semaforo) rosso; **to go through a red light** passare col rosso
red-light district [ˌrɛdˈlaɪtˌdɪstrɪkt] N quartiere *m* a luce rossa
red meat N carne *f* rossa
red·ness [ˈrɛdnɪs] N (*of skin*) rossore *m*; (*of hair, colour*) rosso
re·do [ˌriːˈduː] VT (*pt* **redid**, *pp* **redone**) rifare

Rr

redo·lent ['rɛdəʊlənt] ADJ (*liter*): **redolent of** fragrante di, profumato(-a) di; (*fig*) evocativo(-a) di

re·done [ˌri:'dʌn] PP *of* **redo**

re·dou·ble [ˌri:'dʌbl] VT raddoppiare; **to redouble one's efforts** intensificare *or* raddoppiare gli sforzi

re·doubt·able [rɪ'daʊtəbl] ADJ (*frm*) formidabile, temibile

re·dound [rɪ'daʊnd] VI: **to redound upon sb** riversarsi su qn; **to redound to sb's credit** tornare a credito di qn

red pepper N (*capsicum*) peperone *m*; (*cayenne pepper*) peperoncino rosso

re·draft [*n* 'ri:ˌdrɑ:ft; *vb* ˌri:'drɑ:ft] N nuova stesura
■VT stendere di nuovo, fare una nuova stesura di

re·dress [rɪ'drɛs] (*frm*) N riparazione *f*
■VT riparare; **to redress the balance** ristabilire l'equilibrio

Red Sea N: **the Red Sea** il mar Rosso

red·shank ['rɛdˌʃæŋk] N (*Zool*) pettegola

red shift N (*Phys*) spostamento verso il rosso

red·skin ['rɛdˌskɪn] N (*offensive*) pellerossa *m/f*

red tape N lungaggini *fpl* burocratiche

red-throated diver [ˌrɛdθrəʊtɪd'daɪvəʳ] N tuffatore *m* stellato

◎**re·duce** [rɪ'dju:s] VT **1** (*gen*) ridurre; (*prices, taxes*) abbassare, ridurre, diminuire; (*speed, voltage, expenses, Med: swelling*) ridurre, diminuire; (*temperature*) far diminuire, far scendere; **to reduce sth by/to** ridurre qc di/a; **"reduce speed now"** (*Aut*) "rallentare"; **to reduce sth to ashes** ridurre qc in cenere; **to reduce sb to silence/despair/tears** ridurre qn al silenzio/alla disperazione/in lacrime; **we were reduced to begging** eravamo ridotti all'elemosina; **reduced to nothing** ridotto(-a) a zero **2** (*Mil*): **to reduce sb to the ranks** degradare qn a soldato semplice
■VI (*slim*) dimagrire

re·duced [rɪ'dju:st] ADJ (*decreased*) ridotto(-a); **at a reduced price** a prezzo ribassato *or* ridotto; **"greatly reduced prices"** "grandi ribassi"; **in reduced circumstances** nelle ristrettezze

◎**re·duc·tion** [rɪ'dʌkʃən] N (*see vt 1*) riduzione *f*; diminuzione *f*; **reductions in staff** riduzioni di personale; **reductions for cash** sconto per (il pagamento in) contanti; **"huge reductions!"** "grandi sconti!"

re·dun·dan·cy [rɪ'dʌndənsɪ] N (*Industry*) licenziamento (*per esubero di personale*); (*frm: profusion*) superfluità; (*Literature*) ridondanza; **compulsory redundancy** licenziamento (*per esubero*); **voluntary redundancy** *forma di cassa integrazione volontaria*

redundancy payment N (*Brit*) indennità *f inv* di licenziamento

re·dun·dant [rɪ'dʌndənt] ADJ (*Brit: worker*) licenziato(-a) (*per esubero di personale*); (*detail, object*) superfluo(-a); (*Literature*) ridondante; **to be made redundant** (*worker*) essere licenziato(-a) (*perché in esubero*); **these skills are now redundant** queste capacità sono ormai superflue

red·wood ['rɛdˌwʊd] N sequoia

reed [ri:d] N (*Bot*) canna; (*Mus: in mouthpiece*) ancia; (*: instrument*) strumento a fiato munito di ancia

re-educate [ˌri:'ɛdjʊˌkeɪt] VT rieducare

reedy ['ri:dɪ] ADJ (*comp* **-ier**, *superl* **-iest**) (*voice, instrument*) acuto(-a)

reef¹ [ri:f] N (*Geog*) scogliera, banco di scogli; **coral reef** barriera corallina; **the ship ran onto a reef** la nave si è incagliata su una scogliera

reef² [ri:f] (*Naut*) N terzarolo; **to take in a reef** (*Naut*) prendere una mano di terzaroli
■VT terzarolare

reef·er ['ri:fəʳ] N **1** (*jacket*) giacca da pescatore a doppiopetto **2** (*old fam: joint*) spinello

reef knot N nodo piano

reef point N (*Naut*) matafione *m*

reek [ri:k] VI: **to reek of sth** puzzare di qc

◎**reel** [ri:l] N **1** (*in fishing etc*) mulinello; (*cotton reel*) rocchetto, spoletta; (*Tech*) aspo; (*for tape recorder*) bobina; (*Phot: for small camera*) rotolino, rullino; (*: of cine film*) bobina, pizza **2** (*dance*) *danza scozzese o irlandese molto vivace*
■VI (*sway*) vacillare, barcollare; **my head is reeling** mi gira la testa
■VT (*Tech*) annaspare; (*wind up*) avvolgere
▸ **reel in** VT + ADV (*fish*) tirare su
▸ **reel off** VT + ADV snocciolare, sciorinare

re-elect [ˌri:ɪ'lekt] VT rieleggere

re-election [ˌri:ɪ'lɛkʃən] N rielezione *f*

re-enact [ˌri:ɪ'nækt] VT (*crime, scene*) ricostruire

re-enter [ˌri:'ɛntəʳ] VI rientrare; **to re-enter for an exam** ripresentarsi a un esame
■VT rientrare in

re-entry [ˌri:'ɛntrɪ] N rientro

re-examine [ˌri:ɪg'zæmɪn] VT (*person, proposal, evidence*) riesaminare; (*witness*) interrogare di nuovo

re-export [ˌri:ɪkspɔ:t] VT riesportare
■N (*trading activity*) riesportazione *f*; (*goods*) merce *f* riesportata

ref [rɛf] N ABBR (*Sport fam:* = **referee**) arbitro

ref. ABBR (*Comm*) = **reference**

re·fec·tory [rɪ'fɛktərɪ] N refettorio

◎**re·fer** [rɪ'fɜ:ʳ] VT (*gen*): **to refer sth to** (*matter, decision*) sottoporre qc a qn, deferire qc a qn; **to refer sb to sth** richiamare l'attenzione di qn su qc; **he referred me to the manager** mi ha detto di rivolgermi al direttore; **to refer sb to a specialist** mandare qn da uno specialista; **"refer to drawer"** (*on cheque*) "rivolgersi al traente"
■VI: **to refer to 1** (*relate to*) riferirsi a; **does that refer to me?** vale anche per me? **2** (*allude to: directly*) fare riferimento a; (*: indirectly*) fare allusione *or* accenno a; **he referred to a recent trip to Canada** ha fatto accenno ad un recente viaggio in Canada; **referring to your letter** (*Comm*) in riferimento alla Vostra lettera; **we will not refer to it again** non ne riparleremo più **3** (*turn attention to, see*) consultare; (*consult: person*) rivolgersi a; **please refer to section 3** vedi sezione 3

ref·eree [ˌrɛfə'ri:] N **1** (*in dispute, Sport*) arbitro; (*Tennis*) giudice *m* di gara **2** (*Brit: for job application*) referenza; **to give sb as a referee** dare il nome di qn per referenze; **to be referee for sb** scrivere una lettera di referenze per qn
■VT arbitrare

◎**ref·er·ence** ['rɛfrəns] N **1** (*allusion: direct*) riferimento, menzione *f*; (*: indirect*) allusione *f*; (*relation, connection*) rapporto; (*Comm: in letter*): **with reference to** in *or* con riferimento a; **without reference to any particular case** senza nessun riferimento specifico **2** (*from book, list*) rimando; (*on letter*) numero di riferimento; (*on map*) coordinate *fpl*; **"please quote this reference"** (*Comm*) "si prega di far riferimento al numero di protocollo"; **our reference is A32** il nostro numero di riferimento è A32 **3** (*testimonial*): **reference(s)** referenze *fpl*; **they require references** chiedono delle referenze; **may I**

give you as a reference? posso dare il suo nome per referenze?
■ ADJ *(library)* di consultazione; *(point)* di riferimento
reference book N libro *or* testo di consultazione
reference library N biblioteca per la consultazione
reference number N *(Comm)* numero di riferimento; numero di protocollo
◎ **ref·er·en·dum** [ˌrɛfəˈrɛndəm] N *(pl* **referendums** *or* **referenda** [ˌrɛfəˈrɛndə]) referendum *m inv*
refer·ral [rɪˈfɜːrəl] N deferimento; *(Med)*: **she got a referral to a specialist** l'hanno mandata da uno specialista
re·fill [*n* ˈriːˌfɪl; *vb* ˌriːˈfɪl] N *(for pen etc)* ricambio
■ VT *(gen)* riempire (di nuovo); *(pen, lighter)* ricaricare
re·fine [rɪˈfaɪn] VT *(sugar, oil, tastes, style)* raffinare; *(design, technique, machine)* perfezionare
▸ **refine on, refine upon** VI + PREP perfezionare, migliorare
re·fined [rɪˈfaɪnd] ADJ raffinato(-a)
re·fine·ment [rɪˈfaɪnmənt] N *(of person, language)* raffinatezza, finezza; *(in machine, system)* miglioramento
re·fin·er [rɪˈfaɪnəʳ] N raffinatore *m*
re·fin·ery [rɪˈfaɪnərɪ] N raffineria; **oil/sugar refinery** raffineria di petrolio/zucchero
re·fit [*n* ˈriːˌfɪt; *vb* ˌriːˈfɪt] N *(Naut)* raddobbo
■ VT *(ship)* raddobbare
re·flate [ˌriːˈfleɪt] VT *(Econ)* reflazionare
re·fla·tion [ˌriːˈfleɪʃən] N *(Econ)* reflazione *f*
re·fla·tion·ary [ˌriːˈfleɪʃənərɪ] ADJ *(Econ: programme)* reflazionistico(-a)
◎ **re·flect** [rɪˈflɛkt] VT **1** *(light, image, heat)* riflettere; *(fig)* rispecchiare; **to reflect credit on sb** fare onore a qn **2** *(think)*: **to reflect that** riflettere sul fatto che
■ VI **1** *(think, meditate)*: **to reflect (on sth)** riflettere (su qc) **2** *(discredit)*: **to reflect (up)on sb/sth** ripercuotersi su qn/qc
re·flec·tion [rɪˈflɛkʃən] N **1** *(act)* riflessione *f*; *(in mirror etc)* riflesso **2** *(thought)* riflessione *f*; **on reflection** dopo aver riflettuto, pensandoci sopra **3** *(aspersion, doubt)* dubbio; **this is no reflection on your honesty** questa non è un'insinuazione sulla tua onestà **4** *(Math)* riflessione *f*
re·flec·tive [rɪˌflɛktɪv] ADJ **1** *(pensive)* pensoso(-a) **2** *(indicative)*: **to be reflective of** *(frm)* riflettere **3** *(light, surface)* riflettente **4** *(jacket, belt)* lucido(-a)
re·flec·tor [rɪˈflɛktəʳ] N *(Aut: also:* **rear reflector)** catarifrangente *m*
re·flex [ˈriːflɛks] N riflesso
■ ADJ *(Math)* concavo(-a)
reflex action N azione *f* riflessa
reflex camera N *(Phot)* reflex *f inv*
re·flex·ive [rɪˈflɛksɪv] ADJ *(Gram)* riflessivo(-a); **reflexive verb** verbo riflessivo
re·float [ˌriːˈfləʊt] VT *(ship, business)* rimettere a galla
re·for·est [riːˈfɒrɪst] VT rimboscare
◎ **re·form** [rɪˈfɔːm] N riforma
■ VT *(society, morals)* riformare; *(criminal)* rieducare, ricuperare socialmente; *(person's character)* correggere
■ VI *(person)* emendarsi
re·for·mat [ˌriːˈfɔːmæt] VT *(Comput)* riformattare
Ref·or·ma·tion [ˌrɛfəˈmeɪʃən] N *(Rel)*: **the Reformation** la Riforma
▹ www.bbc.co.uk/history/state/church_reformation/index.shtml
▹ www.lepg.org/religion.htm

re·forma·tory [rɪfɔːmətərɪ] N *(Am)* riformatorio
re·formed [rɪˈfɔːmd] ADJ *(criminal)* rieducato(-a), ricuperato(-a) alla società; *(morals)* riformato(-a)
re·form·er [rɪˈfɔːməʳ] N riformatore(-trice)
re·form·ist [rɪˈfɔːmɪst] ADJ, N riformista *(m/f)*
re·fract [rɪˈfrækt] VT rifrangere
re·frac·tion [rɪˈfrækʃən] N rifrazione *f*
re·frac·tive [rɪˈfræktɪv] ADJ di *or* della rifrazione; **refractive constant** indice *m* di rifrazione costante
re·frac·tory [rɪˈfræktərɪ] ADJ *(frm)* refrattario(-a)
re·frain[1] [rɪˈfreɪn] N *(Mus)* ritornello, refrain *m inv*
re·frain[2] [rɪˈfreɪn] VI: **to refrain from sth/from doing sth** astenersi *or* trattenersi da qc/dal fare qc; **she refrained from making any comment** si astenne dal fare qualsiasi commento
re·fresh [rɪˈfrɛʃ] VT *(subj: drink)* rinfrescare; (: *food, sleep, bath)* ristorare; *(fig: memory)* rinfrescare; **this will refresh your memory** questo ti rinfrescherà la memoria
re·fresh·er course [rɪˈfrɛʃəˌkɔːs] N *(Brit)* corso di aggiornamento
re·fresh·ing [rɪˈfrɛʃɪŋ] ADJ *(drink)* rinfrescante; *(sleep)* ristoratore(-trice); *(change)* piacevole; *(idea, point of view)* originale; **it was a refreshing change** è stato un piacevole cambiamento
re·fresh·ment [rɪˈfrɛʃmənt] N *(eating, resting)* ristoro; **refreshments** NPL *(food and drink)* rinfreschi *mpl*
refreshment room N posto di ristoro
re·frig·er·ate [rɪˈfrɪdʒəˌreɪt] VT refrigerare
re·frig·era·tion [rɪˌfrɪdʒəˈreɪʃən] N refrigerazione *f*
re·frig·era·tor [rɪˈfrɪdʒəˌreɪtəʳ] N frigorifero
re·fu·el [ˌriːˈfjʊəl] VI rifornirsi di carburante, fare rifornimento (di carburante)
■ VT rifornire di carburante
re·fu·el·ling [ˌriːˈfjʊəlɪŋ] N rifornimento di carburante
refuelling stop N scalo tecnico
ref·uge [ˈrɛfjuːdʒ] N *(shelter)* riparo; *(for climbers, battered wives, fig)* rifugio; **place of refuge** rifugio; **to take refuge in** *(also fig)* rifugiarsi in
◎ **refu·gee** [ˌrɛfjʊˈdʒiː] N rifugiato(-a), profugo(-a)
refugee camp N campo *m* profughi *inv*
re·fund [*n* ˈriːˌfʌnd; *vb* rɪˈfʌnd] N rimborso
■ VT rimborsare; **to refund sb's expenses** rimborsare qn
re·fur·bish [ˌriːˈfɜːbɪʃ] VT *(frm)* rimettere a nuovo
re·fur·nish [ˌriːˈfɜːnɪʃ] VT ammobiliare di nuovo
re·fus·al [rɪˈfjuːzəl] N: **refusal (to do)** rifiuto (di *or* a fare); **to have first refusal on sth** avere il diritto d'opzione su qc
◎ **re·fuse**[1] [rɪˈfjuːz] VT *(all senses)* rifiutare; **to refuse sb sth** rifiutare qc a qn; **to refuse to do sth** rifiutare *or* rifiutarsi di fare qc
■ VI rifiutarsi; *(horse)* rifiutare (l'ostacolo)
ref·use[2] [ˈrɛfjuːs] N rifiuti *mpl*; **garden refuse** rifiuti del giardino
refuse collection [ˈrɛfjuːzkəˌlɛkʃən] N raccolta dei rifiuti
refuse collector [ˈrɛfjuːzkəˌlɛktəʳ] N netturbino
refuse disposal [ˈrɛfjuːzdɪspˌəʊzl] N smaltimento dei rifiuti
refuse dump [ˈrɛfjuːzˌdʌmp] N discarica (di rifiuti)
refuse lorry [ˈrɛfjuːzˌlɒrɪ] N camion *m inv* della spazzatura
re·fuse·nik [rɪˈfjuːznɪk] N *(old) ebreo a cui il governo sovietico impediva di lasciare il paese*
refu·ta·tion [ˌrɛfjuːˈteɪʃən] N *(frm)* confutazione *f*

Rr

re·fute [rɪ'fju:t] VT (*frm*) confutare
re·gain [rɪ'geɪn] VT (*gen*) riguadagnare; (*balance, consciousness*) riprendere; (*confidence*) riacquistare; (*health*) ricuperare; **to regain possession of sth** rientrare in possesso di qc; **to regain one's composure** ricomporsi; **to regain control** riacquistare il controllo; **to regain consciousness** riprendere conoscenza
re·gal ['ri:gəl] ADJ (*bearing, manners*) regale; (*person*) dal portamento regale
re·gale [rɪ'geɪl] VT deliziare, intrattenere; **to regale sb with sth** intrattenere qn con qc

DID YOU KNOW ...?
regale is not translated by the Italian word ***regalare***

re·ga·lia [rɪ'geɪlɪə] N (*royal trappings*) insegne *fpl* reali; (*gen: insignia*) abiti *mpl* da cerimonia
re·gal·ly ['ri:gəlɪ] ADV regalmente
◎ **re·gard** [rɪ'gɑ:d] N **1** (*relation*): **in** *or* **with regard to** per quanto riguarda, riguardo a; **in this regard** (*frm*) a questo riguardo *or* proposito **2** (*esteem, concern*) riguardo, stima; **out of regard for** per riguardo a; **to have a high regard for sb** *or* **hold sb in high regard** aver molta stima per qn, tenere qn in grande considerazione; **he shows little regard for their feelings** dimostra scarsa considerazione per loro **3** (*in messages*): **regards to Maria, please give my regards to Maria** salutami Maria, da' i miei saluti a Maria; (*as letter-ending*): **(kind) regards** cordiali saluti
■ VT **1** (*consider*) considerare, stimare; **to regard sth as** considerare qc come; **we don't regard it as necessary** non lo riteniamo necessario **2** (*concern*) riguardare; **as regards ...** per quel che riguarda..., riguardo a...
re·gard·ing [rɪ'gɑ:dɪŋ] PREP riguardo a, per quanto riguarda; **the laws regarding the export of animals** le leggi riguardanti l'esportazione di animali
re·gard·less [rɪ'gɑ:dlɪs] ADJ: **regardless of** (*heedless of*) senza preoccuparsi di; (*in spite of*) a dispetto di; **regardless of rank** senza distinzioni; **regardless of race** senza distinzioni di razza
■ ADV (*fam*): **to carry on regardless** continuare come se niente fosse; **she did it regardless** l'ha fatto lo stesso
re·gat·ta [rɪ'gætə] N regata
Re·gen·cy ['ri:dʒənsɪ] N: **the Regency** (*in England*) *la reggenza del principe di Galles, futuro Giorgio IV*; (*in France*) la Reggenza
■ ADJ (*style*) reggenza *inv*; (*house, furniture*) (in) stile reggenza *inv*
re·gen·cy ['ri:dʒənsɪ] N reggenza
re·gen·er·ate [rɪ'dʒɛnə,reɪt] (*frm*) VT (*Bio, fig: society*) rigenerare; (*: feelings, enthusiasm*) far rinascere
■ VI (*see vt*) rigenerarsi; rinascere
re·gen·era·tion [rɪ,dʒɛnə'reɪʃən] N (*frm: of economy, society*) rigenerazione *f*; (*: of feelings, enthusiasm*) rinnovamento
re·gen·era·tive [rɪ'dʒɛnərətɪv] ADJ (*frm: tissue*) rigenerativo(-a); (*: climate, air*) rigeneratore(-trice)
re·gent ['ri:dʒənt] N reggente *m/f*
reg·gae ['rɛgeɪ] N (*Mus*) reggae *m*
▷ www.bbc.co.uk/radio2/soldonsong/genres/reggae.shtml
regi·cide ['rɛdʒɪ,saɪd] N (*frm: crime*) regicidio; (*: person*) regicida *m/f*
◎ **ré·gime** [reɪ'ʒi:m] N regime *m*
regime change N cambio di regime
regi·men ['rɛdʒɪ,mɛn] N (*frm*) regime *m*
regi·ment [*n* 'rɛdʒɪmənt; *vb* 'rɛdʒɪ,mɛnt] N (*Mil*) reggimento
■ VT (*fig*) irreggimentare
regi·men·tal [,rɛdʒɪ'mɛntl] ADJ reggimentale
regi·men·ta·tion [,rɛdʒɪmɛn'teɪʃən] N (*pej*) irreggimentazione *f*
regi·men·ted ['rɛdʒɪ,mɛntɪd] ADJ (*pej: way of life, institution*) irregimentato(-a)
◎ **re·gion** ['ri:dʒən] N (*all senses*) regione *f*; **in the region of 40** (*fig*) circa 40, intorno a 40
◎ **re·gion·al** ['ri:dʒənl] ADJ regionale; **regional development** (*Brit Admin*) sviluppo economico delle regioni; **regional development fund** fondo per lo sviluppo regionale
re·gion·al·ism ['ri:dʒənəlɪzəm] N regionalismo
re·gion·al·ly ['ri:dʒənəlɪ] ADV (*vary*) da regione a regione; (*collaborate, manage*) regionalmente; (*based, organized*) a livello regionale
◎ **reg·is·ter** ['rɛdʒɪstə^r] N (*gen*) registro; (*of members*) elenco; **the register of births, marriages and deaths** l'anagrafe *f*; **the hotel register** il registro dell'albergo; **to call the register** fare l'appello
■ VT **1** (*fact, birth, death*) registrare; (*vehicle*) immatricolare; (*trademark*) depositare; (*complaint, dissatisfaction*) sporgere; **to register a protest** presentare un esposto; **he registered the birth of his son** ha denunciato all'anagrafe la nascita del figlio **2** (*Post: letter*) assicurare; (*Rail: luggage*) spedire assicurato(-a) **3** (*indicate: speed, temperature*) registrare, segnare; (*: dismay, disbelief, surprise*) dar segno di, mostrare
■ VI **1** (*for class*) iscriversi; (*for work*) mettersi in lista; (*at hotel*) firmare il registro; **to register with a doctor** mettersi nella lista di un medico come paziente; **to register for a course** iscriversi a un corso **2** (*have impact, become clear*): **it didn't register (with me)** non me ne sono reso conto
reg·is·tered ['rɛdʒɪstəd] ADJ **1** (*student, voter*) iscritto(-a); (*car*) immatricolato(-a); (*Comm: design*) depositato(-a); (*charity*) riconosciuto(-a) **2** (*Brit: letter, luggage*) assicurato(-a); **a registered letter** un'assicurata
registered company N società *f inv* iscritta all'Ufficio del Registro
Registered General Nurse N (*Brit*) infermiere(-a) generico(-a) diplomato(-a)
registered nurse N (*Am*) infermiere(-a) diplomato(-a)
registered office N sede *f* legale
registered trademark N marchio registrato
reg·is·trar [,rɛdʒɪs'trɑ:^r] N (*of births, deaths, marriages*) ufficiale *m* di stato civile; (*Univ*) direttore *m* amministrativo; (*Med*) *medico ospedaliero superiore ad un interno*; **Registrar of Companies** ≈ Ufficio del Registro
reg·is·tra·tion [,rɛdʒɪs'treɪʃən] N (*gen*) registrazione *f*; (*of vehicle*) immatricolazione *f*; (*of voters, members*) iscrizione *f*; (*Scol*) appello; **during registration** durante l'appello; **English is the first lesson after registration** la prima lezione dopo l'appello è quella d'inglese; **L-/M-** *etc* **registration** *dicitura su targhe automobilistiche che ne indica l'anno di fabbricazione*; **registration of voters** iscrizione alle liste elettorali dei votanti
registration number N (*Aut*) (numero di) targa
reg·is·try ['rɛdʒɪstrɪ] N (*record office*) archivio; (*in university*) segreteria
registry office N (*Brit*) anagrafe *f*; **to get married in a registry office** ≈ sposarsi in municipio

re·gress [rɪˈgrɛs] VI (*frm*) regredire
re·gres·sion [rɪˈgrɛʃən] N (*frm*) regresso
re·gres·sive [rɪˈgrɛsɪv] ADJ (*frm*) regressivo(-a); **a regressive step** (*fig*) un passo indietro; **regressive tax** (*Econ*) imposta regressiva
◎ **re·gret** [rɪˈgrɛt] N **1** rimpianto, rammarico; **much to my regret** *or* **to my great regret** con mio grande dispiacere; **I have no regrets** non ho rimpianti **2**: **regrets** NPL (*excuses*) scuse *fpl*
■ VT (*news, death*) essere dispiaciuto(-a) per, essere desolato(-a) per; **to regret doing sth** rimpiangere di aver fatto qc; **try it, you won't regret it!** provalo, non te ne pentirai!; **he is very ill, I regret to say** purtroppo è molto malato; **I regret that I will be unable to attend your party** (*frm*) mi rincresce (di) non poter venire alla vostra festa; **we regret to inform you that ...** (*frm*) siamo spiacenti di informarla che...; **I regret that I/he cannot help** mi rincresce (di) non poter aiutare/che lui non possa aiutare
re·gret·ful [rɪˈgrɛtfʊl] ADJ (*person*) spiacente, dispiaciuto(-a); (*look*) dispiaciuto(-a)
re·gret·ful·ly [rɪˈgrɛtfəlɪ] ADV (*sadly*) con molto rimpianto, con rincrescimento; (*unwillingly*) a malincuore
re·gret·table [rɪˈgrɛtəbl] ADJ (*deplorable*) increscioso(-a), deplorevole; (*unfortunate*): **her absence is regrettable** ci rincresce che sia assente
re·gret·tably [rɪˈgrɛtəblɪ] ADV (*unfortunately*) purtroppo, sfortunatamente; **regrettably few** pochi, purtroppo
re·group [ˌriːˈgruːp] VI raggrupparsi (di nuovo)
■ VT raggruppare (di nuovo)
Regt ABBR = **regiment**
◎ **regu·lar** [ˈrɛgjʊləʳ] ADJ **1** (*gen: shape, employment, army, verb*) regolare; **as regular as clockwork** (*person, event*) puntuale come un orologio; (*visits*) molto regolare; **at regular intervals** a intervalli regolari **2** (*habitual: visitor, client*) fisso(-a); (*: listener, reader*) fedele; (*Comm: size, price*) normale; **he's a regular customer** è un cliente abituale; **a regular portion of fries** una porzione media di patatine fritte; **you need to take regular exercise** devi fare moto regolarmente **3** (*permissible: action, procedure*) corretto(-a) **4** (*fam: intensive*): **it's a regular nuisance** è una solenne scocciatura
■ N (*customer, client*) habitué *m/f inv*, cliente *m/f* abituale; (*Mil*) soldato regolare
regu·lar·ity [ˌrɛgjʊˈlærɪtɪ] N regolarità
regu·lar·ize [ˈrɛgjʊləˌraɪz] VT regolarizzare
regu·lar·ly [ˈrɛgjʊləlɪ] ADV regolarmente
regu·late [ˈrɛgjʊˌleɪt] VT regolare
◎ **regu·la·tion** [ˌrɛgjʊˈleɪʃən] N (*rule*) regolamento, regola; (*adjustment*) regolazione *f*; **safety regulations** norme *fpl* di sicurezza; **the regulation of nurseries** la regolamentazione degli asili
■ ADJ (*item, clothing*) di ordinanza
◎ **regu·la·tor** [ˈrɛgjʊleɪtəʳ] N (*Tech*) regolatore *m*
re·gur·gi·tate [rɪgɜːdʒɪˌteɪt] VT (*vomit*) rigurgitare; (*ideas, facts*) ripetere automaticamente
re·ha·bili·tate [ˌriːəˈbɪlɪˌteɪt] VT (*criminal, drug addict, invalid*) recuperare, reinserire
re·ha·bili·ta·tion [ˈriːəˌbɪlɪˈteɪʃən] N (*of offender, of disabled*) ricupero, reinserimento
rehabilitation centre N centro di ricupero
re·hash [ˌriːˈhæʃ] (*pej*) N rimaneggiamento
■ VT rimaneggiare
re·hears·al [rɪˈhɜːsəl] N prova; **dress rehearsal** prova generale
re·hearse [rɪˈhɜːs] VT (*Mus, Theatre*) provare; (*: one's part*) ripassare; (*what one is going to say*) ripetere
re·house [ˌriːˈhaʊz] VT rialloggiare
reign [reɪn] N regno; **in the reign of** sotto *or* durante il regno di; **reign of terror** regno del terrore
■ VI (*also fig*) regnare; **the reigning champion** il campione in carica; **to reign supreme** (*champion*) non avere rivali; (*justice, peace etc*) regnare sovrano(-a)
reign·ing [ˈreɪnɪŋ] ADJ (*monarch*) regnante; (*champion*) in carica
re·im·burse [ˌriːɪmˈbɜːs] VT: **to reimburse sb for sth** rimborsare qc a qn
re·im·burse·ment [ˌriːɪmˈbɜːsmənt] N rimborso
rein [reɪn] N (*for horse*) redine *f*, briglia; **to keep a tight rein on sb** (*fig*) tenere a freno qn; **to give sb free rein** (*fig*) lasciare completa libertà a qn
▸ **rein back** VI + ADV indietreggiare
▸ **rein in** VT + ADV trattenere (tirando le briglie); (*expenditure*) limitare
re·incar·nat·ed [riːˈɪnkɑːneɪtɪd] ADJ: **to be reincarnated (as)** reincarnarsi (in)
re·incar·na·tion [ˌriːɪnkɑːˈneɪʃən] N reincarnazione *f*
rein·deer [ˈreɪnˌdɪəʳ] N, PL INV renna
re·inforce [ˌriːɪnˈfɔːs] VT (*army, material, structure*) rinforzare; (*fig: theory, belief*) rafforzare
re·inforced con·crete [ˌriːɪnfɔːstˈkɒnkriːt] N cemento armato
re·inforce·ment [ˌriːɪnˈfɔːsmənt] N **1** (*action*) rinforzo, rafforzamento; (*thing*) rinforzo **2** (*Mil*): **reinforcements** NPL rinforzi *mpl*
re·instate [ˌriːɪnˈsteɪt] VT (*employee, official*) reintegrare
re·instate·ment [ˌriːɪnˈsteɪtmənt] N reintegrazione *f*
re·invent [ˌriːɪnˈvɛnt] VT reinventare
re·invest [ˌriːɪnˈvɛst] VT reimpiegare
re·issue [ˌriːˈɪʃjuː] VT (*book*) fare una ristampa di, ristampare; (*record, film*) rimettere in circolazione, distribuire di nuovo
re·it·er·ate [riːˈɪtəˌreɪt] VT (*frm*) ripetere, reiterare
re·it·era·tion [riːˌɪtəˈreɪʃən] N (*frm*) reiterazione *f*
◎ **re·ject** [*n* ˈriːdʒɛkt; *vb* rɪˈdʒɛkt] N (*person, thing, also Comm*) scarto
■ VT (*offer etc*) rifiutare, respingere; (*applicant etc*) scartare, respingere; (*subj: body: food*) rifiutare; **the patient's body rejected the new organ** il paziente ha avuto una crisi di rigetto; **to feel rejected** sentirsi respinto(-a)
reject goods NPL prodotti *mpl* di scarto
re·jec·tion [rɪˈdʒɛkʃən] N (*of offer, applicant*) rifiuto; (*of new organ*) rigetto
re·jig [ˌriːˈdʒɪg] VT **1** (*fam: rearrange, improve*) riorganizzare **2** (*factory etc*) riequipaggiare
re·joice [rɪˈdʒɔɪs] VI (*frm*) rallegrarsi; **to rejoice in sth** godere di qc; **to rejoice (at** *or* **over)** provare diletto (in); **they had no cause to rejoice** non avevano motivo di rallegrarsi
re·joic·ing [rɪˈdʒɔɪsɪŋ] (*liter*) N (*jubilation*) festeggiamenti *mpl*; **rejoicings** NPL (*festivities*) festività *f inv*
re·join[1] [ˌriːˈdʒɔɪn] VT (*Mil: ship, regiment*) raggiungere; (*club, library*) iscriversi di nuovo a
re·join[2] [rɪˈdʒɔɪn] VI (*frm: retort*) replicare
re·join·der [rɪˈdʒɔɪndəʳ] N (*frm: retort*) replica
re·ju·venate [rɪˈdʒuːvɪˌneɪt] VT (far) ringiovanire
re·ju·vena·tion [rɪˌdʒuːvɪˈneɪʃən] N ringiovanimento

Rr

re·kindle [ˌri:ˈkɪndl] VT (*also fig*) riaccendere

re·lapse [rɪˈlæps] N (*Med*) ricaduta; **to have a relapse** avere una ricaduta
■ VI (*gen*): **to relapse (into)** ricadere (in); (*Med*) avere una ricaduta

◎ **re·late** [rɪˈleɪt] VT **1** (*tell: story*) raccontare, riferire; **he related the whole story** ha raccontato tutta la storia **2** (*establish relation between*) collegare
■ VI: **to relate to 1** (*connect*) riferirsi a; riguardare; **these recommendations relate to road safety** queste raccomandazioni riguardano la sicurezza sulle strade; **how does your religion relate to your politics?** che rapporto c'è tra la tua religione e la politica? **2** (*get on with*) stabilire un rapporto con; **he can't relate to older people** non riesce a stabilire un rapporto con le persone più anziane

◎ **re·lat·ed** [rɪˈleɪtɪd] ADJ **1** (*connected: subject*) connesso(-a), collegato(-a); (*: substances, languages*) affine; **the two events were not related** non c'è alcun rapporto tra i due avvenimenti **2** (*attached by family: person*): **related to** imparentato(-a) con; **we are distantly related** siamo parenti alla lontana

re·lat·ing [rɪˈleɪtɪŋ]: **relating to** PREP relativo(-a) a, che riguarda

◎ **re·la·tion** [rɪˈleɪʃən] N **1** (*relationship*) rapporto, relazione *f*; (*Math*) relazione; **to bear a relation to** corrispondere a; **it has no relation to reality** non ha nessun rapporto con la realtà; **in relation to** con riferimento a; **to have good relations with sb** essere in *or* avere buoni rapporti con qn; **diplomatic/ international relations** rapporti diplomatici/ internazionali; **sexual relations** rapporti sessuali **2** (*family: relative*) parente *m/f*; (*: kinship*) parentela; **what relation is she to you?** che legami di parentela ha con te?; **he's a distant relation** è un lontano parente

re·la·tion·al database [rɪˌleɪʃənlˈdeɪtəbeɪs] N (*Comput*) database *m inv* relazionale

◎ **re·la·tion·ship** [rɪˈleɪʃənʃɪp] N **1** (*family ties*) legami *mpl* di parentela **2** (*connection: between two things*) rapporto, nesso; (*: with sb*) rapporti *mpl*; **to see a relationship between** vedere un nesso fra; **to have a relationship with sb** (*sexual*) avere una relazione con qn; **I'm not in a relationship at the moment** al momento non ho una relazione; **they have a good relationship** vanno molto d'accordo, hanno un bel rapporto

◎ **rela·tive** [ˈrɛlətɪv] ADJ (*comparative, Gram*) relativo(-a); (*connected*): **relative to** legato(-a) a; **the relative merits of X and Y** i meriti rispettivi di X e Y
■ N parente *m/f*

◎ **rela·tive·ly** [ˈrɛlətɪvlɪ] ADV relativamente; (*fairly, rather*) abbastanza

rela·tiv·ity [ˌrɛləˈtɪvɪtɪ] N relatività

re·launch [ri:ˈlɔ:ntʃ] VT rilanciare
■ N rilancio

◎ **re·lax** [rɪˈlæks] VT (*muscles, person*) rilassare; (*restrictions*) diminuire; (*discipline*) allentare; **to relax one's hold on sth** allentare la presa di qc
■ VI (*rest*) rilassarsi; (*amuse oneself*) svagarsi; (*slacken: sb's grip*) allentarsi; (*calm down*): **relax!** calma!; **his face relaxed into a smile** il suo viso si distese in un sorriso

re·lax·ant [rɪˈlæksənt] ADJ, N (*Med*) calmante (*m*)

re·laxa·tion [ˌri:lækˈseɪʃən] N (*rest*) relax *m*; (*of muscles*) rilassamento, rilasciamento; (*entertainment*) svago; **she plays the piano for relaxation** suona il piano per rilassarsi

re·laxed [rɪˈlækst] ADJ (*muscles*) rilassato(-a), rilasciato(-a); (*person, mood*) disteso(-a), rilassato(-a)

re·lax·ing [rɪˈlæksɪŋ] ADJ rilassante

re·lay [*n* ˈri:leɪ; *vb* rɪˈleɪ] N **1** (*of workmen, horses*) ricambio; **to work in relays** lavorare a squadre (*dandosi il cambio*) **2** (*Radio, TV*) ripetitore *m*; (*Elec*) relé *m inv*; (*Sport: also:* **relay race**) (corsa a) staffetta
■ VT (*Radio, TV*) ripetere; (*pass on: message*) passare, trasmettere

◎ **re·lease** [rɪˈli:s] N **1** (*gen*) rilascio; (*from army*) congedo; (*from suffering, obligation*) liberazione *f*; **the release of Nelson Mandela** la liberazione di Nelson Mandela **2** (*of gas*) emissione *f*; (*of film, record*) uscita, distribuzione *f*; (*of book*) pubblicazione *f*; **on general release** (*film*) in distribuzione **3** (*record, film etc*): **new release** nuovo disco (*or* film *etc*); **his latest release** il suo ultimo disco (*or* film *etc*) **4** (*also:* **release switch**) disinnesto
■ VT **1** (*let go*) lasciare andare, mollare; (*: bomb*) sganciare; (*: fig: tension*) allentare; **to release one's hold of** *or* **one's grip on sth** allentare la presa di qc **2** (*set free*) rilasciare; (*: Law*) rimettere in libertà; (*: from wreckage*) liberare; (*: from promise, vow*) sciogliere **3** (*issue: gas*) emettere; (*: book, record*) mettere in circolazione, fare uscire; (*: film*) distribuire; (*: statement*) rilasciare; (*: news*) rendere pubblico(-a) **4** (*Tech: catch, clasp, spring*) liberare; (*Phot: shutter*) far scattare; (*handbrake*) togliere; **to release the clutch** (*Aut*) staccare la frizione

rel·egate [ˈrɛlɪˌgeɪt] VT (*demote*) relegare; (*Sport*) (far) retrocedere; **to be relegated** (*team*) essere retrocesso(-a)

rel·ega·tion [ˌrɛlɪˈgeɪʃən] N (*see vb*) relegazione *f*; retrocessione *f*

re·lent [rɪˈlɛnt] VI (*frm*) cedere

> DID YOU KNOW ...?
> **relent** is not translated by the Italian word ***rallentare***

re·lent·less [rɪˈlɛntlɪs] ADJ implacabile

rel·evance [ˈrɛləvəns] N pertinenza; **relevance of sth to sth** rapporto tra qc e qc

rel·evant [ˈrɛləvənt] ADJ: **relevant (to)** (*remark, fact*) pertinente (a); (*information, papers, chapter*) relativo(-a) (a); (*course of action*) adeguato(-a) (a); **make sure that what you say is relevant** cerca di dire qualcosa di pertinente; **education should be relevant to real life** l'istruzione dovrebbe avere un riscontro nella vita reale; **they passed all relevant information to the police** hanno passato tutte le informazioni del caso alla polizia; **that's not relevant** questo non c'entra

> DID YOU KNOW ...?
> **relevant** is not translated by the Italian word ***rilevante***

re·li·abil·ity [rɪˌlaɪəˈbɪlɪtɪ] N (*see adj*) attendibilità; affidabilità; capacità; sicurezza; (*of person*) serietà

◎ **re·li·able** [rɪˈlaɪəbl] ADJ (*report, source*) attendibile; (*machine*) affidabile; (*person: trustworthy*) fidato(-a), che dà affidamento; (*: capable*) capace; (*method*) sicuro(-a); **a reliable source of information** una fonte attendibile

re·li·ably [rɪˈlaɪəblɪ] ADV: **I am reliably informed that ...** so da fonti sicure che...

re·li·ance [rɪˈlaɪəns] N: **reliance (on)** dipendenza (da)

re·li·ant [rɪˈlaɪənt] ADJ: **to be reliant on sth/sb** dipendere da qc/qn

rel·ic [ˈrɛlɪk] N (*Rel*) reliquia; (*fig: of the past*) retaggio

◎ **re·lief** [rɪˈli:f] N **1** (*from pain, anxiety*): **relief (from)** sollievo (a); **by way of light relief** come diversivo;

that's a relief! che sollievo! **2** (*Mil: of besieged town*) liberazione *f*; (*help, supplies*) soccorsi *mpl* **3** (*also:* **tax relief**) sgravio fiscale **4** (*Art, Geog*) rilievo; **to throw sth into relief** (*fig*) mettere qc in evidenza *or* in risalto **5** (*of guard*) cambio
■ ADJ (*bus*) supplementare; (*driver*) che da il cambio a un collega; (*work, organization, troops*) di soccorso

relief map N carta in rilievo

relief road N (*Brit*) circonvallazione *f*

re·lieve [rɪ'li:v] VT **1** (*pain, anxiety, boredom*) alleviare; (*person*) sollevare; (*bring help*) soccorrere; **I am relieved to hear you are better** sono sollevato dalla notizia che stai meglio; **to relieve sb of sth** (*load*) alleggerire qn di qc; (*anxiety*) sollevare qn da qc; (*duty*) esonerare qn da qc; **to relieve sb of his command** (*Mil*) esonerare qn dal comando; **to relieve one's anger** sfogare la propria rabbia; **to relieve congestion in sth** (*Med*) decongestionare qc; **to relieve o.s.** (*euph: go to lavatory*) fare i propri bisogni **2** (*take over from*) sostituire; (*replace, also Mil*) dare il cambio a; (*Mil: town*) liberare

re·lieved [rɪ'li:vd] ADJ sollevato(-a); **to be relieved that ...** essere sollevato(-a) (dal fatto) che...; **I'm relieved to hear it** mi hai tolto un peso con questa notizia

◎ **re·li·gion** [rɪ'lɪdʒən] N religione *f*

◎ **re·li·gious** [rɪ'lɪdʒəs] ADJ (*gen*) religioso(-a); (*conscientious*) scrupoloso(-a)

religious education N istruzione *f* religiosa

re·li·gious·ly [rɪ'lɪdʒəslɪ] ADV (*see adj*) religiosamente; scrupolosamente

re·line [,ri:'laɪn] VT (*coat, jacket*) rifare la fodera a; (*brakes*) cambiare *or* sostituire le guarnizioni di

re·lin·quish [rɪ'lɪŋkwɪʃ] VT (*frm: right, control, responsibility*) rinunciare a; (*: post*) lasciare, abbandonare; **to relinquish one's hold on sth** lasciare andare qc

reli·quary ['rɛlɪkwərɪ] N reliquiario

rel·ish ['rɛlɪʃ] N **1 relish (for)** gusto (per); **to do sth with relish** fare qc con diletto **2** (*sauce*) condimento, salsa
■ VT (*food, wine*) gustare; (*fig: like*): **I don't relish the idea** l'idea non è allettante; **I relish the challenge of difficult tasks** la sfida di un'impresa difficile mi attrae; **he didn't relish the prospect** la prospettiva non lo allettava

re·live [,ri:'lɪv] VT rivivere

re·load [,ri:'ləʊd] VT ricaricare

re·load·ing [,ri:'ləʊdɪŋ] N ricarica

re·lo·cate [,ri:ləʊ'keɪt] VT (*business, person*) trasferire
■ VI: **to relocate to** trasferire la propria sede a; **rising costs forced us to relocate** l'aumento dei costi ci ha costretti a trasferire la sede

relocation N (*of premises*) trasloco; (*of employee*) trasferimento

relocation expenses NPL spese *fpl* di trasloco

re·luc·tance [rɪ'lʌktəns] N riluttanza

◎ **re·luc·tant** [rɪ'lʌktənt] ADJ (*person*) riluttante, restio(-a); (*praise, consent*) concesso(-a) a malincuore; **to be reluctant to do sth** essere restio(-a) a fare qc

re·luc·tant·ly [rɪ'lʌktəntlɪ] ADV a malincuore, di mala voglia

◎ **rely** [rɪ'laɪ] VI: **to rely on sb/sth** (*count on*) contare su qn/qc; (*be dependent on*) dipendere da qn/qc; **I'm relying on you** conto su di te; **you can rely on my discretion** puoi fidarti della mia discrezione; **you can't rely on the trains** non si può fare affidamento sui treni; **she relies on him for financial support** dipende da lui finanziariamente

◎ **re·main** [rɪ'meɪn] VI rimanere, restare; **it remains to be seen whether ...** resta da vedere se...; **it will remain in my memory** resterà sempre impresso nel mio ricordo; **the fact remains that ...** resta il fatto che...; **to remain faithful to sb** rimanere fedele a qn; **to remain silent** restare in silenzio; **to remain behind** restare indietro; **I remain, yours faithfully** (*Brit: in letters*) distinti saluti

re·main·der [rɪ'meɪndə^r] N: **the remainder** (*amount, also Math*) il resto, l'avanzo; (*people*) i/le rimanenti *pl*; **remainders** NPL (*Comm: books*) remainder *mpl*; (*: other goods*) giacenze *fpl* di magazzino

◎ **re·main·ing** [rɪ'meɪnɪŋ] ADJ che rimane; **the three remaining possibilities** le tre possibilità che restano *or* che rimangono; **the remaining ingredients** il resto degli ingredienti

re·mains [rɪ'meɪnz] NPL (*gen*) resti *mpl*; (*of food*) avanzi *mpl*; **the remains of his fortune** ciò che restava del suo patrimonio; **the remains of the picnic** i resti del picnic; **human remains** resti umani; **Roman remains** le rovine romane

re·make ['ri:meɪk] N (*Cine*) remake *m inv*

re·mand [rɪ'mɑ:nd] (*Law*) N: **on remand** in custodia cautelare
■ VT rinviare a giudizio; **to remand sb in custody** ordinare la custodia cautelare di qn

remand home N (*Brit*) riformatorio, casa di correzione

◎ **re·mark** [rɪ'mɑ:k] N osservazione *f*, commento; **worthy of remark** (*frm*) degno(-a) di nota
■ VT (*say, notice*) osservare, notare
■ VI: **to remark on sth** commentare qc

◎ **re·mark·able** [rɪ'mɑ:kəbl] ADJ notevole

re·mark·ably [rɪ'mɑ:kəblɪ] ADV notevolmente

re·mar·riage [,ri:'mærɪdʒ] N seconde (*or* terze) nozze *fpl*

re·marry [,ri:'mærɪ] VI risposarsi

re·medial [rɪ'mi:dɪəl] ADJ (*Med*) correttivo(-a); (*action*) atto(-a) a porre rimedio; (*school, teaching*) speciale; (*class, tuition*) di ricupero

rem·edy ['rɛmədɪ] N: **remedy (for)** rimedio (contro *or* per)
■ VT (*situation, problem, defect*) rimediare a; (*loss*) porre riparo a

◎ **re·mem·ber** [rɪ'mɛmbə^r] VT ricordare, ricordarsi di; **I can't remember his name** non mi ricordo come si chiama; **I remember seeing it** *or* **I remember having seen it** (mi) ricordo di averlo visto; **she remembered to do it** si è ricordata di farlo; **remember to post that letter** ricordati di imbucare la lettera; **I don't remember saying that** non mi ricordo di aver detto una cosa del genere; **give me sth to remember you by** lasciami un tuo ricordo; **to remember sb in one's prayers** ricordare qn nelle proprie preghiere; **remember me to your wife and children!** saluta tua moglie e i bambini da parte mia!; **that's worth remembering** buono a sapersi

re·mem·brance [rɪ'mɛmbrəns] N (*frm*) ricordo, memoria; **in remembrance of** in memoria di

Remembrance Sunday, Remembrance Day N *giorno della commemorazione dei caduti in guerra*

REMEMBRANCE SUNDAY

Nel Regno Unito la domenica più vicina all'11 di novembre, data in cui fu firmato l'armistizio con la

Rr

Germania nel 1918, ricorre il **Remembrance Sunday**, giorno in cui vengono commemorati i caduti in guerra. In questa occasione molti portano un papavero di carta appuntato al petto in segno di rispetto.

▷ www.army.mod.uk/ceremonialandheritage/household/Remembrance.htm
▷ www.britishlegion.org.uk/who/remember_sunday.asp

◎ **re·mind** [rɪ'maɪnd] VT ricordare, rammentare; **to remind sb of sth/to do sth** ricordare *or* rammentare a qn qc/di fare qc; **he reminds me of Brian** mi ricorda Brian; **the scenery here reminds me of Scotland** il paesaggio mi ricorda la Scozia; **remind me to speak to Daniel** ricordami di parlare a Daniel; **that reminds me!** a proposito!

re·mind·er [rɪ'maɪndəʳ] N **1** (*note*) promemoria *m inv*; (*Comm: letter*) (lettera di) sollecito; **to serve as a reminder of sth** servire a ricordare qc; **as a reminder that** per ricordarsi che; **the final reminder for the gas bill** l'ultimo sollecito della bolletta del gas **2** (*memento*) ricordo

remi·nisce [ˌrɛmɪ'nɪs] VI: **to reminisce (about)** abbandonarsi ai ricordi (di)

remi·nis·cence [ˌrɛmɪ'nɪsəns] N (*usu pl*) reminiscenza

remi·nis·cent [ˌrɛmɪ'nɪsənt] ADJ: **to be reminiscent of** richiamare (alla mente)

remi·nis·cent·ly [ˌrɛmɪ'nɪsəntlɪ] ADV (*smile*) in preda ai ricordi; **to talk reminiscently of** parlare nostalgicamente di

re·miss [rɪ'mɪs] ADJ (*frm*) negligente; **it was remiss of me** è stata una negligenza da parte mia

re·mis·sion [rɪ'mɪʃən] N (*gen, Rel, Med*) remissione *f*; (*Law: of debts, fee*) condono

re·mit [rɪ'mɪt] VT (*frm*) **1** (*send: amount due*) rimettere **2** (*refer: decision*) rimettere **3** (*Rel: sins*) rimettere, perdonare; (*fee, penalty*) condonare

re·mit·tal [rɪ'mɪtl] N (*Law*) rinvio

re·mit·tance [rɪ'mɪtəns] N (*frm*) rimessa (di pagamento)

rem·nant ['rɛmnənt] N (*remainder*) resto; **remnants** NPL (*of food*) avanzi *mpl*; (*of cloth*) scampoli *mpl*; **the remnants of Roman flooring** i resti della pavimentazione romana; **the remnants of the defeated army** ciò che restava dell'esercito sconfitto

remnant sale N svendita di scampoli

re·mod·el [ˌri:'mɒdl] VT ristrutturare

re·mon·strance [rɪ'mɒnstrəns] N (*frm: complaint*) rimostranza, protesta

re·mon·strate ['rɛmənˌstreɪt] VI (*frm*) protestare; **to remonstrate with sb about sth** fare le proprie rimostranze a qn circa qc

re·morse [rɪ'mɔ:s] N rimorso; **without remorse** senza pietà

re·morse·ful [rɪ'mɔ:sfʊl] ADJ pieno(-a) di rimorsi

re·morse·ful·ly [rɪ'mɔ:sfəlɪ] ADV con rimorso

re·morse·less [rɪ'mɔ:slɪs] ADJ (*person*) spietato(-a); (*wind, noise*) implacabile

re·morse·less·ly [rɪ'mɔ:slɪslɪ] ADV implacabilmente

◎ **re·mote** [rɪ'məʊt] ADJ (*comp* **-r**, *superl* **-st**) **1** (*place, period*) remoto(-a); (*ancestor*) lontano(-a); (*in concept: idea*) lontano(-a); (*person: aloof*) distante; (*: uninvolved*) distaccato(-a); (*Comput*) a distanza; **a remote village** un paesino isolato; **remote from the matter in hand** non pertinente alla questione **2** (*slight: possibility, resemblance*) vago(-a); **not the remotest idea/hope** neanche la più vaga idea/speranza; **there is a remote possibility that ...** c'è una vaga possibilità che... + *sub*

remote access N (*Comput*) accesso remoto

remote central locking [-'lɒkɪŋ] N (*Auto*) chiusura centralizzata con telecomando

remote control N (*TV*) telecomando

remote-controlled [rɪˌməʊtkən'trəʊld] ADJ telecomandato(-a)

re·mote·ly [rɪ'məʊtlɪ] ADV **1** (*distantly*) lontanamente, alla lontana; **remotely situated** in una posizione isolata **2** (*slightly*) vagamente; **there was nobody remotely resembling this description** non c'era nessuno che corrispondesse neanche vagamente alla descrizione; **I suppose it is remotely possible that ...** suppongo che ci sia una remota possibilità che...

re·mote·ness [rɪ'məʊtnɪs] N **1** (*of ancestor*) antichità; (*of place, period, concept*) lontananza; (*aloofness*) distacco **2** (*of possibility, resemblance*) vaghezza

remote sensing [-'sɛnsɪŋ] N telerilevamento

re·mould ['ri:ˌməʊld] N (*Brit: tyre*) pneumatico rigenerato

re·mount [ˌri:'maʊnt] VI (*on horse, on bicycle*) rimontare in sella
■ VT: **to remount a horse/bicycle** rimontare a cavallo/in bicicletta

re·mov·able [rɪ'mu:vəbl] ADJ (*detachable*) staccabile

re·mov·al [rɪ'mu:vəl] N **1** (*of person*) allontanamento; (*: from post*) rimozione *f*, destituzione *f*; (*of problem*) allontanamento; (*of doubt, fear, obstacle, stain*) eliminazione *f*; (*Med*) asportazione *f*; **the removal of a small lump in her breast** l'asportazione di un piccolo nodulo al seno **2** (*move from house*) trasloco

removal expenses NPL spese *fpl* di trasloco

removal man N (*Brit*) addetto ai traslochi

removal van N (*Brit*) camion *m inv* per *or* dei traslochi

◎ **re·move** [rɪ'mu:v] VT (*gen*) togliere, levare; (*person*) allontanare; (*: from post*) rimuovere; (*stain*) togliere, eliminare; (*problem*) allontanare; (*doubt, fear*) eliminare, dissipare; (*obstacle*) rimuovere, eliminare; (*Med*) asportare; **to remove from** togliere da; **please remove your bag from my seat** le dispiace togliere la borsa dal mio sedile?, levare da; **to remove one's make-up** struccarsi; **first cousin once removed** cugino(-a) di secondo grado; **far removed from** (*fig*) ben lontano(-a) da
■ VI traslocare; **to remove from London to the country** trasferirsi da Londra in campagna

re·mov·er [rɪ'mu:vəʳ] N **1** (*removal man*) addetto ai traslochi; **removers** NPL (*Brit: firm*) ditta *fsg or* impresa *fsg* di traslochi **2** (*of stains*) smacchiatore *m*; (*of nail varnish*) solvente *m*; (*of paint, varnish*) sverniciatore *m*; **make-up remover** struccatore *m*

re·mu·ner·ate [rɪ'mju:nəˌreɪt] VT (*frm*) retribuire, rimunerare

re·mu·nera·tion [rɪˌmju:nə'reɪʃən] N (*frm*) rimunerazione *f*

re·mu·nera·tive [rɪ'mju:nərətɪv] ADJ (*frm*) rimunerativo(-a)

Remus ['ri:məs] N Remo

Re·nais·sance [rɪ'neɪsɑ̃:ns] N: **the Renaissance** il Rinascimento
■ ADJ (*style*) (del) Rinascimento; (*palace, art*) rinascimentale, del Rinascimento

▷ www.learner.org/exhibits/renaissance
▷ www.ibiblio.org/wm/paint/glo/renaissance

Renaissance man N persona eclettica

re·nal [ˈriːnl] ADJ (*Med*) renale
re·name [ˌriːˈneɪm] VT ribattezzare
rend [rɛnd] VT (*pt, pp* **rent**) (*liter*) lacerare
ren·der [ˈrɛndəʳ] VT **1** (*thanks, honour, service*) rendere; (*account*) presentare **2** (*make*) rendere; **this renders it impossible for me to leave** questo rende impossibile la mia partenza **3** (*interpret: sonata, role, play*) interpretare; (*translate: text*) tradurre **4** (*Culin: fat*) sciogliere
ren·der·ing [ˈrɛndərɪŋ] N (*translation*) traduzione *f*; (*of song, role*) interpretazione *f*
ren·dez·vous [ˈrɒndɪˌvuː] N (*meeting*) appuntamento; (*meeting place*) punto *or* luogo di ritrovo
■VI ritrovarsi; (*spaceship*) effettuare un rendez-vous
ren·di·tion [rɛnˈdɪʃən] N (*Mus*) interpretazione *f*
ren·egade [ˈrɛnɪˌgeɪd] N (*pej*) rinnegato(-a)
re·nege [rɪˈniːg], **re·negue** [rɪˈneɪg] VI (*frm*) mancare alla parola; **to renege on** (*agreement, deal*) venire meno a; (*promise*) mancare a, venire meno a
◎ **re·new** [rɪˈnjuː] VT (*gen*) rinnovare; (*negotiations, discussion, strength*) riprendere; **to renew one's acquaintance with sb** riprendere contatto con qn
renewable [rɪˈnjuːəbl] ADJ rinnovabile; **renewable resources** fonti *fpl* di energia rinnovabili
■**renewables** NPL fonti di energia rinnovabili
re·new·al [rɪˈnjuːəl] N (*see vb*) rinnovo; ripresa; **urban renewal** rinnovamento urbano; **a renewal of hostilities** una ripresa delle ostilità
re·newed [rɪˈnjuːd] ADJ rinnovato(-a)
ren·net [ˈrɛnɪt] N caglio
re·nounce [rɪˈnaʊns] VT (*right, claim, title*) rinunciare a; (*violence, terrorism*) abbandonare; **to renounce one's faith** abiurare la fede
reno·vate [ˈrɛnəʊˌveɪt] VT (*house*) rimettere a nuovo; (*furniture, building, art work*) restaurare

> DID YOU KNOW ...?
> **renovate** is not translated by the Italian word *rinnovare*

reno·va·tion [ˌrɛnəʊˈveɪʃən] N (*see vb*) rimessa a nuovo; restauro
re·nown [rɪˈnaʊn] N rinomanza, fama
re·nowned [rɪˈnaʊnd] ADJ famoso(-a), rinomato(-a)
◎ **rent** [rɛnt] PT, PP *of* **rend**
■N (canone *m* di) affitto, pigione *f*
■VT **1** (*take for rent: house*) affittare, prendere in affitto; (*: car, TV*) noleggiare, prendere a noleggio **2** (*also:* **rent out**) affittare, dare in affitto; (*: car, TV*) noleggiare, dare a noleggio
rent·al [ˈrɛntl] N (*charge: on TV, telephone*) abbonamento; (*: on car*) nolo, noleggio
rent book N *libretto di ricevute dell'affitto*
rent boy N (*Brit fam*) giovane prostituto
rent collector N esattore *m* dell'affitto
rent-free [ˌrɛntˈfriː] ADJ (*accommodation*) gratuito(-a)
■ADV (*live*) senza pagare l'affitto
rent rebate N rimborso parziale dell'affitto
re·nun·cia·tion [rɪˌnʌnsɪˈeɪʃən] N (*of right, claim, title*) rinuncia; (*of violence, terrorism*) abbandono; (*of faith*) abiura
re·open [ˌriːˈəʊpən] VT (*gen*) riaprire; (*discussion, hostilities*) riaprire, riprendere
■VI riaprirsi
re·open·ing [ˌriːˈəʊpnɪŋ] N riapertura
re·or·der [ˌriːˈɔːdəʳ] N (*Comm*) riordino
■VT **1** (*goods, supplies*) ordinare di nuovo **2** (*reorganize*) riorganizzare; (*rearrange*) rimettere in ordine
re·or·gani·za·tion [ˌriːˌɔːgənaɪˈzeɪʃən] N riorganizzazione *f*
re·or·gan·ize [ˈriːˈɔːgənaɪz] VT riorganizzare
Rep ABBR (*Am Pol*) **1** = **Representative** **2** = **Republican**
rep [rɛp] (*fam*) N ABBR **1** (*Comm:* = **representative**) rappresentante *m/f* **2** (*Theatre:* = **repertory**) teatro di repertorio
re·packing [ˌriːˈpækɪŋ] N reimballaggio
re·paid [rɪˈpeɪd] PT, PP *of* **repay**
re·paint [ˌriːˈpeɪnt] VT ridipingere
◎ **re·pair** [rɪˈpɛəʳ] N riparazione *f*; **under repair** in riparazione; **in good repair** *or* **in a good state of repair** in buono stato; **it is damaged beyond repair** è irrimediabilmente rovinato; **closed for repairs** chiuso(-a) per restauro
■VT (*car, shoes etc*) aggiustare, riparare; (*fig: wrong*) rimediare a; **to get sth repaired** far aggiustare qc; **I got the washing machine repaired** ho fatto aggiustare la lavatrice
re·pair·er [rɪˈpɛərəʳ] N riparatore(-trice)
repair kit N attrezzatura per riparazioni
repair man N (*pl* **repair men**) riparatore *m*
repair shop N negozio di riparazioni; (*Aut*) officina
repa·ra·tion [ˌrɛpəˈreɪʃən] N (*frm*) riparazione *f*; **to make reparation for sth** riparare a qc
rep·ar·tee [ˌrɛpɑːˈtiː] N botta e risposta *m inv*
re·past [rɪˈpɑːst] N (*frm*) pranzo
re·pat·ri·ate [riːˈpætrɪˌeɪt] VT rimpatriare
re·pat·ria·tion [riːˌpætrɪˈeɪʃən] N rimpatrio
re·pay [riːˈpeɪ] VT (*pt, pp* **repaid**) (*money*) restituire; (*debt*) pagare; (*lender*) rimborsare, restituire i soldi a; (*sb's kindness etc*) ricambiare; **how can I ever repay you?** come potrò mai ricompensarti?, come potrò mai sdebitarmi?
re·pay·able [riːˈpeɪəbl] ADJ rimborsabile
re·pay·ment [riːˈpeɪmənt] N (*of money*) pagamento; (*of expenses*) rimborso; (*compensation*) ricompensa; **debt repayment** il rimborso del debito pubblico; **mortgage repayments** le rate del mutuo
re·peal [rɪˈpiːl] VT (*law*) abrogare; (*sentence*) annullare; (*decree*) revocare
■N (*see vb*) abrogazione *f*; annullamento; revoca
◎ **re·peat** [rɪˈpiːt] VT (*gen*) ripetere; (*pattern*) riprodurre; (*promise, attack*) rinnovare; **don't repeat it to anybody** non riferirlo a nessuno; **this offer cannot be repeated** questa è un'offerta irripetibile; **to repeat an order** (*Comm*) rinnovare un'ordinazione; **to get repeat business** fidelizzare la clientela; **in spite of repeated reminders** malgrado diversi *or* ripetuti solleciti
■VI ripetersi
■N ripetizione *f*; (*Radio, TV*) replica; **there are too many repeats on TV** ci sono troppe repliche in TV
repeat customer N cliente *m/f* fedele
re·peat·ed·ly [rɪˈpiːtɪdlɪ] ADV ripetutamente
repeat offender N (*Law*) recidivo(-a)
repeat order N (*Comm*): **to place a repeat order (for)** rinnovare l'ordinazione (di)
repeat performance N (*fig*): **I don't want a repeat performance of that** non vorrei che questo si ripetesse
repeat prescription N ricetta medica ripetibile
repeat purchasing [-ˈpɜːtʃɪsɪŋ] N (*Comm*) riordino continuo
re·pel [rɪˈpɛl] VT (*frm: force back*) respingere; (*disgust*) ripugnare a

Rr

re·pel·lent [rɪ'pɛlənt] ADJ (*disgusting*) ripugnante, repellente
■ N: **insect repellent** insettifugo; **moth repellent** antitarmico
re·pent [rɪ'pɛnt] VI (*frm*): **to repent (of)** pentirsi (di)
re·pent·ance [rɪ'pɛntəns] N (*frm*) pentimento
re·pent·ant [rɪ'pɛntənt] ADJ (*frm*) pentito(-a)
re·per·cus·sions [ˌriːpə'kʌʃnz] NPL ripercussioni *fpl*
rep·er·toire ['rɛpətwɑːʳ] N repertorio
rep·er·tory ['rɛpətərɪ] N (*Theatre, fig: of jokes, songs*) repertorio; **to act in repertory** far parte di una compagnia di repertorio
repertory company N compagnia di repertorio
repertory theatre N teatro di repertorio
rep·eti·tion [ˌrɛpɪ'tɪʃən] N ripetizione *f*
rep·eti·tious [ˌrɛpɪ'tɪʃəs] ADJ (*frm: speech*) pieno(-a) di ripetizioni
repetitive [rɪ'pɛtɪtɪv] ADJ (*work*) ripetitivo(-a), monotono(-a); (*movement*) che si ripete
repetitive strain injury N (*Med*) lesione *f* da sforzo ripetuto
re·phrase [riː'freɪz] VT formulare in modo diverso
◎ **re·place** [rɪ'pleɪs] VT **1** (*put back*) rimettere (a posto); (: *Telec: receiver*) riattaccare **2** (*get replacement for, take the place of*): **to replace (by, with)** rimpiazzare (con), sostituire (con); **computers have replaced typewriters** i computer hanno rimpiazzato le macchine da scrivere
re·place·able [rɪ'pleɪsəbl] ADJ sostituibile
◎ **re·place·ment** [rɪ'pleɪsmənt] N (*substitute: thing*) pezzo *or* parte *f* di ricambio; (: *person*) sostituto(-a); (*act*) sostituzione *f*; **my replacement at work** il mio sostituto al lavoro; **the replacement of faulty goods** la sostituzione di articoli difettosi
replacement cost N (*Insurance*) costo della sostituzione
replacement value N valore *m* di sostituzione
re·play [*vt, vi* ˌriː'pleɪ; *n* 'riːpleɪ] (*Sport*) VT (*match*) ripetere
■ VI ripetere l'incontro
■ N (*of match*) partita ripetuta; (*TV: playback*) replay *m inv*; **to hold a replay** ripetere l'incontro
re·plen·ish [rɪ'plɛnɪʃ] VT (*frm: tank, glass*) riempire (di nuovo); (: *one's wardrobe*) rifare; **to replenish one's supplies of sth** rifornirsi di qc
re·plen·ish·ment [rɪ'plɛnɪʃmənt] N (*frm: gen*) rifornimento
re·plete [rɪ'pliːt] ADJ (*frm*): **replete (with)** sazio(-a) (di)
re·ple·tion [rɪ'pliːʃən] N (*frm*) sazietà
rep·li·ca ['rɛplɪkə] N replica, copia
rep·li·cate ['rɛplɪˌkeɪt] VT (*frm*) replicare
◎ **re·ply** [rɪ'plaɪ] N risposta; **in reply** in risposta; **what did you say in reply?** cos'hai risposto?; **there's no reply** (*Telec*) non risponde (nessuno)
■ VT, VI rispondere
reply coupon N (*Post*) tagliando per la risposta
reply-paid [rɪ'plaɪˌpeɪd] ADJ: **reply-paid postcard** cartolina postale con risposta pagata
◎ **re·port** [rɪ'pɔːt] N **1** (*account: written*) rapporto, relazione *f*; (: *spoken*) resoconto; (*Press, Radio, TV*) reportage *m inv*, servizio; (*Brit Scol*) pagella (scolastica); **annual report** (*Comm*) relazione annuale; **weather report** bollettino meteorologico; **to give a report on sth** fare una relazione *or* un rapporto su qc, fare un resoconto di qc; **the committee will today publish its report** la commissione pubblicherà oggi la sua relazione; **there's a report in today's paper** c'è un articolo sul giornale di oggi; **to submit a progress report on sth/sb** fare un rapporto periodico su qc/qn; **I have heard a report that ...** ho sentito (dire) che...; **he got a terrible report** ha ricevuto una bruttissima pagella **2** (*frm: bang*) detonazione *f*; (: *shot*) sparo
■ VT (*gen, Press, TV*) riportare; (*notify: accident, culprit*) denunciare; (*bring to notice: occurrence*) segnalare; **it is reported from Berlin that ...** ci è stato riferito da Berlino che...; **what have you to report?** che cos'ha da riferire?; **to report progress** riferire sugli sviluppi della situazione; **to report one's findings** riferire sulle proprie conclusioni; **I reported the theft to the police** ho denunciato il furto alla polizia
■ VI **1** **to report (on)** fare un rapporto (su); (*Press, Radio, TV*) fare un reportage (su) **2** (*present oneself*): **to report (to)** presentarsi (a); **report to reception when you arrive** si presenti alla reception al suo arrivo; **to report for duty** presentarsi al lavoro; **to report sick** darsi malato(-a)
▸ **report back** VI + ADV **1** (*come back*) ritornare **2** (*make report*) tornare a riferire; **I'll report back as soon as I hear anything** appena ho notizie te lo faccio sapere
report card N (*Am, Scot*) pagella
re·port·ed·ly [rɪ'pɔːtɪdlɪ] ADV secondo le testimonianze; **it's reportedly the best restaurant in town** si dice che sia il miglior ristorante della città; **she is reportedly living in Spain** si dice che viva in Spagna
re·port·ed speech [rɪpɔːtɪd'spiːtʃ] N (*Gram*) discorso indiretto
◎ **re·port·er** [rɪ'pɔːtəʳ] N (*Press*) cronista *m/f*, reporter *m/f inv*; (*Radio*) radiocronista *m/f*; (*TV*) telecronista *m/f*
◎ **re·port·ing** [rɪ'pɔːtɪŋ] N (*TV, Radio*) servizi *mpl*
re·pose [rɪ'pəuz] (*frm*) N riposo; **in repose** in riposo
■ VI riposare
re·po·si·tion [ˌriːpə'zɪʃən] VT (*object*) riposizionare, ricollocare; (*product, service etc*) ricreare un'immagine a
re·posi·tory [rɪ'pɒzɪtərɪ] N (*of facts, information*) miniera; (*warehouse*) deposito
re·pos·sess [ˌriːpə'zɛs] VT (*property*) rientrare in possesso di
re·pos·ses·sion or·der [ˌriːpə'zɛʃnˌɔːdəʳ] N (*for house*) ordine *m* di espropriazione
re-pot [riː'pɒt] VT (*plant*) rinvasare
rep·re·hend [ˌrɛprɪ'hɛnd] VT (*frm*) rimproverare, riprendere
rep·re·hen·sible [ˌrɛprɪ'hɛnsɪbl] ADJ (*frm*) riprovevole
rep·re·hen·sibly [ˌrɛprɪ'hɛnsəblɪ] ADV (*frm*) riprovevolmente, in modo riprovevole
◎ **re·pre·sent** [ˌrɛprɪ'zɛnt] VT (*all senses*) rappresentare
rep·re·sen·ta·tion [ˌrɛprɪzɛn'teɪʃən] N **1** (*Pol*) rappresentanza; (*portrayal*) rappresentazione *f* **2** **representations** NPL (*frm: statements, protests*) rimostranze *fpl*; **to make representations to sb** fare delle rimostranze a qn
rep·re·sen·ta·tion·al [ˌrɛprɪzɛn'teɪʃənəl] ADJ (*frm: art, painting*) figurativo(-a)
◎ **rep·re·senta·tive** [ˌrɛprɪ'zɛntətɪv] ADJ: **representative (of)** rappresentativo(-a) (di)
■ N (*gen*) rappresentante *m/f*, delegato(-a); (*Comm*) rappresentante *m/f* (di commercio); (*Am Pol*): **Representative** deputato
re·press [rɪ'prɛs] VT reprimere
re·pressed [rɪ'prɛst] ADJ represso(-a)
re·pres·sion [rɪ'prɛʃən] N repressione *f*
re·pres·sive [rɪ'prɛsɪv] ADJ repressivo(-a)

re·pres·sive·ly [rɪˈprɛsɪvlɪ] ADV in modo repressivo

re·prieve [rɪˈpriːv] N (*Law: cancellation*) commutazione *f* della pena capitale; (*: postponement*) sospensione *f* dell'esecuzione della condanna; (*delay: also gen*) proroga; **a temporary reprieve** una dilazione temporanea; **a last-minute reprieve** una sospensione all'ultimo momento dell'esecuzione della condanna
■ VT (*Law: for good*) rinviare l'esecuzione di; (*: for a time*) sospendere l'esecuzione di; (*grant a delay*) concedere una proroga a; (*: fig*) dare tregua a

rep·ri·mand [ˈrɛprɪˌmɑːnd] N rimprovero
■ VT redarguire, rimproverare

re·print [*n* ˈriːˌprɪnt; *vb* ˌriːˈprɪnt] N ristampa
■ VT ristampare

re·pris·al [rɪˈpraɪzəl] N: **reprisals** NPL rappresaglie *fpl*; **to take reprisals** fare delle rappresaglie; **as a reprisal for** come rappresaglia per

re·proach [rɪˈprəʊtʃ] (*frm*) N rimprovero; **to look at sb with reproach** guardare qn con aria di rimprovero; **above** *or* **beyond reproach** irreprensibile
■ VT: **to reproach sb with** *or* **for sth** rimproverare qc a qn; **to reproach sb with** *or* **for doing sth** rimproverare a qn di *or* per aver fatto qc; **don't reproach yourself for what happened** non devi sentirti in colpa per quello che è successo

re·proach·ful [rɪˈprəʊtʃfʊl] ADJ (*look*) di rimprovero

re·proach·ful·ly [rɪˈprəʊtʃfəlɪ] ADV con aria di rimprovero

rep·ro·bate [ˈrɛprəʊˌbeɪt] N (*hum*) canaglia

re·pro·duce [ˌriːprəˈdjuːs] VT riprodurre
■ VI riprodursi

re·pro·duc·tion [ˌriːprəˈdʌkʃən] N (*all senses*) riproduzione *f*

reproduction furniture N riproduzioni *fpl* di mobili antichi

re·pro·duc·tive [ˌriːprəˈdʌktɪv] ADJ riproduttore(-trice)

re·proof [rɪˈpruːf], **re·prov·al** [rɪˈpruːvəl] N (*frm*) riprovazione *f*

re-proof [riːˈpruːf] VT (*garment*) impermeabilizzare di nuovo

re·prove [rɪˈpruːv] VT (*person*): **to reprove (for)** rimproverare (di *or* per), biasimare (per)

re·prov·ing [rɪˈpruːvɪŋ] ADJ (*frm: look, frown*) di rimprovero, di disapprovazione

re·prov·ing·ly [rɪˈpruːvɪŋlɪ] ADV (*frm*) con aria di rimprovero

rep·tile [ˈrɛptaɪl] N rettile *m*

Repub. ABBR (*Am Pol*) = **Republican**

◎ **re·pub·lic** [rɪˈpʌblɪk] N repubblica

◎ **republican** [rɪˈpʌblɪkən] ADJ, N **1** repubblicano(-a) **2 a Republican** (*Am: Pol*) un(-a) repubblicano(-a)

re·pub·li·can·ism [rɪˈpʌblɪkəˌnɪzəm] N repubblicanesimo

re·pub·lish [ˌriːˈpʌblɪʃ] VT ripubblicare

re·pu·di·ate [rɪˈpjuːdɪˌeɪt] (*frm*) VT (*charge, offer of friendship*) respingere; (*debt, treaty*) disconoscere, rifiutarsi di onorare; (*one's wife*) ripudiare

re·pu·dia·tion [rɪˌpjuːdɪˈeɪʃən] N (*frm*) ripudio

re·pug·nance [rɪˈpʌgnəns] N ripugnanza

re·pug·nant [rɪˈpʌgnənt] ADJ ripugnante; **to be repugnant to sb** ripugnare a qn

re·pulse [rɪˈpʌls] VT respingere

re·pul·sion [rɪˈpʌlʃən] N ripulsione *f*, ribrezzo

re·pul·sive [rɪˈpʌlsɪv] ADJ ripugnante, ripulsivo(-a), ributtante

re·pul·sive·ness [rɪˈpʌlsɪvnɪs] N (*ugliness*) aspetto ripugnante

repu·table [ˈrɛpjʊtəbl] ADJ (*firm, supplier*) degno(-a) di fiducia, serio(-a); (*occupation*) rispettabile

◎ **repu·ta·tion** [ˌrɛpjʊˈteɪʃən] N reputazione *f*; **he has a reputation for being awkward** ha la fama di essere un tipo difficile; **to live up to one's reputation** non smentirsi, non smentire la propria reputazione

re·pute [rɪˈpjuːt] N (*frm*) reputazione *f*; **of (good) repute** (*person*) che ha una buona reputazione; (*place*) che ha un buon nome; **by repute** di fama

re·put·ed [rɪˈpjuːtɪd] ADJ reputato(-a); **to be reputed to be rich/intelligent** essere ritenuto(-a) ricco(-a)/ intelligente; **he is reputed to earn £500,000 a year** si dice che guadagni 500.000 sterline all'anno

re·put·ed·ly [rɪˈpjuːtɪdlɪ] ADV (stando) a quel che si dice, secondo quanto si dice

◎ **re·quest** [rɪˈkwɛst] N (*formal*) richiesta, domanda; **to make a request for sth** fare richiesta di qc; **at the request of** su richiesta di; **on** *or* **by request** a *or* su richiesta; **by popular request** a grande richiesta
■ VT: **to request sth from** *or* **of sb/sb to do sth** richiedere qc a qn/a qn di fare qc; **"you are requested not to smoke"** "si prega di non fumare"

request stop N (*Brit: for bus*) fermata facoltativa *or* a richiesta

requi·em [ˈrɛkwɪɛm] N requiem *m inv*

requiem mass N messa di requiem

◎ **re·quire** [rɪˈkwaɪəʳ] (*frm*) VT **1** (*subj: person*) aver bisogno di; (*: thing, action*) richiedere; **it requires careful thought** richiede un attento esame; **what qualifications are required?** che requisiti sono richiesti?, che qualifiche si richiedono?; **if required** se necessario; **when required** quando è necessario **2** (*demand, order*): **to require sb to do sth/sth of sb** esigere che qn faccia qc/qc da qn; **to require that sth be done** esigere che qc sia fatto; **passengers are required to show their tickets** i passeggeri devono esibire i biglietti; **required by law** prescritto(-a) dalla legge

re·quired [rɪˈkwaɪəd] ADJ (*qualifications, exams*) richiesto(-a); (*amount*) voluto(-a); **in the required time** nel tempo prescritto

◎ **re·quire·ment** [rɪˈkwaɪəmənt] N (*need*) esigenza; (*condition*) requisito, condizione *f* (richiesta); **to meet sb's requirements** soddisfare le esigenze di qn; **she meets all the requirements for the job** risponde a tutti i requisiti (necessari per il lavoro); **entry requirements** criteri *mpl* d'ammissione

requi·site [ˈrɛkwɪzɪt] N occorrente *m*, necessario; **toilet requisites** articoli *mpl* da bagno
■ ADJ (*frm*) necessario(-a), richiesto(-a)

requi·si·tion [ˌrɛkwɪˈzɪʃən] N **1** (*Mil*) requisizione *f* **2** (*request for supply*) richiesta
■ VT (*see n*) requisire; richiedere

rere·dos [ˈrɪədɒs] N (*Art*) dossale *m*

re·route [ˌriːˈruːt] VT (*train*) deviare (il percorso di); **the train was rerouted through Blackpool** hanno fatto passare il treno per Blackpool

re-run [riːˈrʌn] N (*Cine, TV, Theatre*) replica
■ VT **1** (*film: at cinema*) ridare; (*: on TV*) trasmettere la replica di; (*Theatre*) rimettere in scena **2** (*race*) rifare

re·sale [ˈriːseɪl] N rivendita

resale price maintenance N prezzo minimo di vendita imposto

re·sat [ˌriːˈsæt] PT, PP *of* **resit**

re·scind [rɪˈsɪnd] VT (*law*) abrogare; (*contract*) rescindere; (*order*) annullare

◎ **res·cue** [ˈrɛskjuː] N (*saving*) salvataggio; (*help*) soccorso;

Rr

to come/go to sb's rescue venire/andare in aiuto a *or* di qn; **a mountain rescue team** una squadra di soccorso alpino
■VT salvare

rescue attempt N tentativo di salvataggio

rescue operation N operazione *f* di salvataggio

rescue party N squadra di salvataggio

res·cu·er ['rɛskjʊəʳ] N soccorritore(-trice)

rescue team N squadra di soccorso *or* di salvataggio

◎ **re·search** [rɪ'sɜ:tʃ] N ricerca, ricerche *fpl*; **a piece of research** un lavoro di ricerca; **to do research** fare ricerca; **she's doing some research in the library** sta facendo delle ricerche in biblioteca
■VI: **to research (into sth)** fare ricerca (su qc)
■VT documentarsi su; **a well researched book** un libro ben documentato
■ADJ (*centre, laboratory*) di ricerca

research and development N (*Industry*) ricerca e sviluppo

re·search·er [rɪ'sɜ:tʃəʳ] N ricercatore(-trice)

research establishment N centro di ricerca

research fellow N (*Univ*) ricercatore(-trice)

research student N studente(-essa) che fa della ricerca

research work N lavoro di ricerca, ricerche *fpl*

research worker N ricercatore(-trice)

re·sell [ˌri:'sɛl] VT rivendere

re·sem·blance [rɪ'zɛmbləns] N somiglianza; **to bear a strong resemblance to** somigliare moltissimo a

re·sem·ble [rɪ'zɛmbl] VT (as)somigliare a

re·sent [rɪ'zɛnt] VT risentirsi per; **to resent sb** provare risentimento nei confronti di qn; **he resents my being here** è contrariato dalla mia presenza; **I resent your remarks** le tue osservazioni mi offendono; **I resent being dependent on her** non sopporto di dipendere da lei

re·sent·ful [rɪ'zɛntfʊl] ADJ (*person*) pieno(-a) di risentimento; (*tone*) risentito(-a); **to be** *or* **feel resentful of sb** provare del risentimento per qn, essere pieno di risentimento nei confronti di qn

re·sent·ful·ly [rɪ'zɛntfəlɪ] ADV con risentimento

re·sent·ment [rɪ'zɛntmənt] N risentimento

res·er·va·tion [ˌrɛzə'veɪʃən] N **1** (*booking*) prenotazione *f*; **to make a reservation** prenotare, fare una prenotazione; **I've got a reservation for two nights** ho una prenotazione per due notti **2** (*doubt*) riserva; **without reservation** senza riserve; **with reservations** con le dovute riserve; **I've got reservations about it** ho delle riserve a riguardo **3** (*area of land*) riserva; (*Brit Aut: also:* **central reservation**) spartitraffico *m inv*

reservation desk N (*Am: in hotel*) reception *f inv*

◎ **re·serve** [rɪ'zɜ:v] N **1** (*most senses*) riserva; (*hiding one's feelings*) riserbo; **keep/have in reserve** tenere/avere di riserva; **without reserve** senza riserve **2**: **the reserves** NPL (*Mil*) le riserve
■VT **1** (*table, seat*) prenotare, riservare; (*set aside*) riservare; **to reserve one's strength** risparmiarsi le forze; **I'd like to reserve a table for tomorrow evening** vorrei riservare un tavolo per domani sera **2** **to reserve judgment (on)** (*fig*) riservarsi di decidere in merito (a); **to reserve the right to do** riservarsi il diritto di fare

reserve currency N (*Fin*) valuta di riserva

re·served [rɪ'zɜ:vd] ADJ (*booked: table, seat*) prenotato(-a), riservato(-a); (*shy*) riservato(-a)

reserve fund N fondo di riserva

reserve player N (giocatore(-trice) di) riserva

reserve price N (*Brit: at auction*) prezzo minimo, prezzo *m* base *inv*

reserve tank N (*Aut*) serbatoio di riserva

reserve team N (*Brit Sport*) seconda squadra

re·serv·ist [rɪ'zɜ:vɪst] N (*Mil*) riservista *m*

res·er·voir ['rɛzəˌvwɑ:ʳ] N (*artificial lake*) bacino idrico; (*tank etc*) serbatoio

reset [ˌri:'sɛt] VT (*Comput*) azzerare

re·set·tle [ˌri:'sɛtl] VT (*refugees*) far insediare; (*land*) ripopolare
■VI stabilirsi, insediarsi

re·set·tle·ment [ˌri:'sɛtlmənt] N (*see vt*) insediamento; ripopolamento

re·shape [ˌri:'ʃeɪp] VT (*policy*) ristrutturare

re·shuf·fle [ˌri:'ʃʌfl] N: **Cabinet reshuffle** (*Pol*) rimpasto ministeriale *or* governativo

re·side [rɪ'zaɪd] VI (*frm*) risiedere; (: *fig: power, authority*): **to reside in** *or* **with** essere nelle mani di

resi·dence ['rɛzɪdəns] (*frm*) N (*gen*) residenza; (*stay*) permanenza, soggiorno; **"desirable residence for sale"** "abitazione signorile vendesi"; **to take up residence** prendere residenza; **in residence** (*queen*) in sede; **artist/writer in residence** *artista/scrittore che insegna presso una scuola o università*

residence permit N (*Brit*) permesso di soggiorno

resi·den·cy ['rɛzɪdənsɪ] N residenza

◎ **resi·dent** ['rɛzɪdənt] N abitante *m/f*; (*of hotel*) cliente *m/f*; **local residents** abitanti della zona
■ADJ (*tutor, specialist*) interno(-a); (*population*) stabile; **to be resident in a town/in London** risiedere in una città/a Londra

resi·den·tial [ˌrɛzɪ'dɛnʃəl] ADJ (*area*) residenziale; **residential course** corso con pernottamento; **residential nurse** infermiere(-a) interno(-a)

re·sid·ual [rɪ'zɪdjʊəl] ADJ residuo(-a)

re·sidu·ary [rɪ'zɪdjʊərɪ] ADJ residuo(-a); **residuary legatee** (*Law*) legatario(-a) universale

resi·due ['rɛzɪdju:] N (*frm*) residuo, residui *mpl*

◎ **re·sign** [rɪ'zaɪn] VT (*office, leadership*) lasciare; (*frm: claim*) rinunciare a; **to resign one's post** dimettersi; **he resigned his post** ha lasciato l'impiego; **to resign one's commission** (*Mil*) rassegnare le dimissioni; **to resign o.s. to (doing) sth** rassegnarsi a (fare) qc
■VI: **to resign (from)** dimettersi (da), dare le dimissioni (da); **I resigned** ho dato le dimissioni

◎ **res·ig·na·tion** [ˌrɛzɪg'neɪʃən] N **1** (*from job*) dimissioni *fpl*; **to tender one's resignation** dare le dimissioni **2** (*mental state*) rassegnazione *f*; **a feeling of resignation** un senso di rassegnazione

re·signed [rɪ'zaɪnd] ADJ rassegnato(-a)

re·sign·ed·ly [rɪ'zaɪnɪdlɪ] ADV con rassegnazione

re·sili·ence [rɪ'zɪlɪəns] N (*see adj*) elasticità; capacità di ripresa

re·sili·ent [rɪ'zɪlɪənt] ADJ (*substance, material*) elastico(-a); (*fig: person*) che ha buone capacità di ripresa; **polyester is more resilient than cotton** il poliestere è più elastico del cotone

res·in ['rɛzɪn] N resina

res·in·ous ['rɛzɪnəs] ADJ resinoso(-a)

◎ **re·sist** [rɪ'zɪst] VT (*attack*) resistere a; (*change*) opporsi a; **he couldn't resist taking a quick look** non ha resistito alla tentazione di dare un'occhiata
■VI resistere

◎ **re·sist·ance** [rɪ'zɪstəns] N (*all senses*) resistenza; **to offer resistance (to)** opporre resistenza a; **to take the**

line of least resistance scegliere la strada più facile
■ADJ (*fighter, movement*) della resistenza
re·sist·ant [rɪ'zɪstənt] ADJ: **resistant (to)** resistente (a)
re·sit [*vb* ˌri:'sɪt; *n* 'ri:ˌsɪt] (*vb: pt, pp* **resat**) VT (*exam*) ripresentarsi a; **I'm resitting the exam in December** mi ripresento all'esame in dicembre
■N: **when are the resits?** quando è la prossima sessione?; **I've got three resits** devo ripresentarmi a tre esami
re·skill [ri:'skɪl] VT riqualificare
■VI riqualificarsi
reso·lute ['rɛzəlu:t] ADJ (*frm*) risoluto(-a)
reso·lute·ly ['rɛzəlu:tlɪ] ADV (*frm*) risolutamente
reso·lute·ness ['rɛzəlu:tnɪs] N (*frm*) risolutezza
◎**reso·lu·tion** [ˌrɛzə'lu:ʃən] N **1** (*determination*) risolutezza; (*resolve*) fermo proposito, risoluzione *f*; **to make a resolution** fare un proposito; **have you made any New Year resolutions?** hai fatto dei buoni propositi per l'anno nuovo? **2** (*of problem, Chem*) soluzione *f* **3** (*on screen, Pol: motion*) risoluzione *f*; **a UN resolution** una risoluzione dell'ONU
◎**re·solve** [rɪ'zɒlv] (*frm*) N (*resoluteness*) risolutezza; **to make a resolve to do sth** risolversi a fare qc
■VT **1** (*sort out*) risolvere; **the only way to resolve the problem** l'unico modo di risolvere il problema **2** (*decide*): **to resolve to do sth/that** decidere di fare qc/che; **the committee resolved against appointing him** il comitato ha deliberato contro la sua nomina
re·solved [rɪ'zɒlvd] ADJ risoluto(-a)
reso·nance ['rɛzənəns] (*frm*) N (*see adj*) risonanza; sonorità
reso·nant ['rɛzənənt] (*frm*) ADJ (*sound*) risonante; (*voice*) sonoro(-a), risonante
reso·nate ['rɛzəˌneɪt] (*frm*) VI (*voice, room*) risonare
◎**re·sort** [rɪ'zɔ:t] N **1** (*recourse*) ricorso; (*thing resorted to*) risorsa; **without resort to force** senza ricorrere *or* far ricorso alla forza; **in the last resort** *or* **as a last resort** come ultima risorsa **2** (*place*) località *f inv*; **holiday resort** località di villeggiatura; **seaside/winter sports resort** stazione *f* balneare/di sport invernali
■VI: **to resort to** (*violence, treachery*) far ricorso a; **to resort to drink/stealing** *etc* mettersi *or* ridursi a bere/rubare *etc*
re·sound [rɪ'zaʊnd] VI (*frm*): **to resound (with)** risonare (di)
re·sound·ing [rɪ'zaʊndɪŋ] ADJ (*noise*) fragoroso(-a), risonante; (*victory, defeat*) clamoroso(-a); **a resounding slap** un ceffone sonoro; **a resounding victory** una vittoria clamorosa
re·sound·ing·ly [rɪ'zaʊndɪŋlɪ] ADV clamorosamente
◎**re·source** [rɪ'sɔ:s] N (*asset*) risorsa; **resources** NPL (*wealth*) mezzi *mpl*; **natural resources** risorse naturali
re·source·ful [rɪ'sɔ:sfʊl] ADJ (*person*) pieno(-a) di risorse, intraprendente
re·source·ful·ly [rɪ'sɔ:sfəlɪ] ADV ingegnosamente
re·source·ful·ness [rɪ'sɔ:sfʊlnɪs] N (*of person*) ingegnosità
◎**re·spect** [rɪs'pɛkt] N **1** (*gen*) rispetto; **respects** NPL (*regards*) ossequi *mpl*; **to have** *or* **show respect for** aver rispetto per; **I have tremendous respect for Dean** ho un grandissimo rispetto per Dean; **out of respect for** per rispetto *or* riguardo a; **with due respect (for)** con tutto il rispetto (per); **with (all) due respect I think you're mistaken** con rispetto parlando, penso che si sbagli; **to pay one's respects to sb** (*frm*) rendere omaggio a qn **2** (*point, detail*): **in some respects** sotto certi aspetti; **I like the town except in one respect** la città mi piace salvo che per una cosa **3** (*reference, regard*): **in respect of** quanto a; **with respect to** per quanto riguarda
■VT rispettare
re·spect·abil·ity [rɪsˌpɛktə'bɪlɪtɪ] N rispettabilità
re·spect·able [rɪs'pɛktəbl] ADJ **1** (*decent*) rispettabile; **for perfectly respectable reasons** per motivi più che leciti; **in respectable society** nella società bene; **a respectable family** una famiglia rispettabile **2** (*quite big: amount, number*) considerevole; (*quite good: player, result*) niente male *inv*; **my marks were respectable** i miei voti erano discreti
re·spect·ably [rɪs'pɛktəblɪ] ADV (*dress, behave*) perbene; (*quite well: perform, sing*) (piuttosto) bene
re·spect·er [rɪs'pɛktə^r] N: **he's no respecter of persons** non guarda in faccia a nessuno
re·spect·ful [rɪs'pɛktfʊl] ADJ rispettoso(-a)
re·spect·ful·ly [rɪs'pɛktfəlɪ] ADV rispettosamente; **respectfully yours** (*in letter*) con rispetto
re·spect·ing [rɪs'pɛktɪŋ] PREP riguardante, concernente
re·spec·tive [rɪs'pɛktɪv] ADJ rispettivo(-a)
re·spec·tive·ly [rɪs'pɛktɪvlɪ] ADV rispettivamente
res·pi·ra·tion [ˌrɛspɪ'reɪʃən] N respirazione *f*
res·pi·ra·tor ['rɛspəreɪtə[r]] N (*Med*) respiratore *m*; (*Mil*) maschera *f* antigas *inv*
res·pira·tory [rɪs'paɪərətərɪ] ADJ respiratorio(-a)
re·spire [rɪs'paɪə[r]] VT (*frm*)
■VI respirare
res·pite ['rɛspaɪt] N (*frm*) tregua, requie; **without respite** senza tregua *or* requie; **they gave us no respite** non ci hanno dato tregua
respite care N assistenza temporanea (*a malato, persona anziana ecc*)
re·splend·ent [rɪs'plɛndənt] ADJ (*frm*) risplendente
◎**re·spond** [rɪ'spɒnd] VI rispondere; **to respond to treatment** (*Med*) reagire (bene) alla cura; **he did not respond** non rispose; **the army responded with gunfire** l'esercito ha risposto sparando; **the government was slow to respond to the crisis** la risposta del governo alla crisi è stata lenta; **teachers strive to respond to students' needs** gli insegnanti cercano di far fronte alle necessità degli studenti
re·spond·ent [rɪ'spɒndənt] N (*Law*) convenuto(-a)
◎**re·sponse** [rɪ'spɒns] N (*answer*) risposta; (*reaction*) reazione *f*; **in response to** in risposta a
response time N tempo di risposta
◎**re·spon·sibil·ity** [rɪˌspɒnsə'bɪlɪtɪ] N responsabilità *f inv*; **to place the responsibility for sth on sb** ritenere qn responsabile di qc; **on one's own responsibility** di propria iniziativa; **to take responsibility for sth/sb** assumersi *or* prendersi la responsabilità di qc/per qn; **that's his responsibility** è compito suo
responsibility payment N *premio per mansioni di responsabilità*
◎**re·spon·sible** [rɪ'spɒnsəbl] ADJ responsabile; (*trustworthy*) fidato(-a); **to be responsible for sth** essere responsabile di qc; **to be responsible to sb (for sth)** dover rispondere a qn (di qc); **to hold sb responsible for** ritenere qn responsabile di; **it's a responsible job** è un posto di responsabilità
re·spon·sibly [rɪ'spɒnsəblɪ] ADV responsabilmente
re·spon·sive [rɪ'spɒnsɪv] ADJ (*audience, class, pupil*) che reagisce bene; (*to affection*) affettuoso(-a); (*to needs*): **responsive to** sensibile a; **he has a very responsive nature** è un tipo molto aperto; **the students are**

Rr

responsive and full of ideas gli studenti rispondono positivamente e sono pieni di idee

re·spray [ˌriːˈspreɪ] [ˈriːˌspreɪ] VT *(car)* riverniciare
■ N riverniciatura

◎**rest[1]** [rɛst] N **1** *(repose)* riposo; *(break)* pausa; (: *in walking*) sosta, tappa; **to come to rest** *(object)* fermarsi; **to have a rest** riposarsi; **to have a good night's rest** farsi una buona *or* bella dormita; **five minutes' rest** cinque minuti di riposo; **at rest** *(not moving)* fermo(-a); *(euph: dead)* in pace; **to set sb's mind at rest** tranquillizzare qn **2** *(Mus)* pausa **3** *(support)* sostegno, supporto
■ VT **1** *(animal, dough)* (far) riposare; **God rest his soul!** pace all'anima sua!; **to rest one's eyes** *or* **gaze on** posare lo sguardo su; **he has to rest his knee** non deve affaticare il ginocchio **2** *(support: ladder, bicycle, head)*: **to rest on/against** appoggiare su/contro; **I rested my bike against the window** ho appoggiato la bici alla finestra
■ VI **1** *(repose)* riposarsi, riposare; **she's resting in her room** è in camera sua a riposare; **I feel quite rested** mi sento molto riposato; **may she rest in peace** riposi in pace; **we shall not rest until it is settled** non avremo pace finché la cosa non sarà sistemata **2** *(remain)* stare; **it rests with him to decide** sta a lui decidere; **it doesn't rest with me** non dipende da me; **rest assured that ...** stia tranquillo che...; **let the argument rest there** lascia le cose come stanno **3** **to rest on** *(perch)* posarsi su; *(be supported)* poggiare su, appoggiarsi su; *(Law: case)* basarsi su; **her head rested on my shoulder** il suo capo era appoggiato alla mia spalla; **a heavy responsibility rests on her** ha una grossa responsabilità sulle spalle

> DID YOU KNOW ...?
> **rest** is not translated by the Italian word *restare*

rest[2] [rɛst] N *(remainder)*: **the rest** *(of money, substance)* il resto; *(of people, things)* gli altri/le altre *pl*; **the rest of the money** il resto dei soldi; **the rest of them** gli altri; **the rest of them went swimming** gli altri sono andati a nuotare; **the rest of us will go later** noialtri ci andiamo più tardi; **I'll do the rest** faccio io il resto; **can you carry the rest?** porti tu quello che rimane?

rest area N *(Am)* area di sosta

re·start [ˌriːˈstɑːt] VT *(engine)* rimettere in marcia; *(work)* ricominciare

re·state [riːˈsteɪt] VT *(frm: case, problem, reasons)* reiterare; (: *argument, theory*) enunciare nuovamente; **to restate one's position/one's opposition** riaffermare la propria posizione/la propria opinione

◎**res·tau·rant** [ˈrɛstəˌrɒŋ] N ristorante *m*

restaurant car N *(Brit Rail)* vagone *m* ristorante

restaurant owner N proprietario(-a) di ristorante

rest cure N cura del riposo

rest day N giorno di riposo

rest·ed [ˈrɛstɪd] ADJ riposato(-a); **to feel rested** sentirsi riposato(-a); **to look rested** avere un'aria riposata

rest·ful [ˈrɛstfʊl] ADJ riposante

rest home N casa di riposo

rest·ing place [ˈrɛstɪŋpleɪs] N **1** *(gen)* posto *or* luogo dove riposarsi **2** *(grave)* ultima dimora

res·ti·tu·tion [ˌrɛstɪˈtjuːʃən] N *(act)* restituzione *f*; *(reparation)* riparazione *f*

res·tive [ˈrɛstɪv] ADJ *(person)* irrequieto(-a), nervoso(-a), agitato(-a); *(horse)* restio(-a)

rest·less [ˈrɛstlɪs] ADJ *(gen)* irrequieto(-a), agitato(-a); *(crowd etc)* inquieto(-a); **to get restless** spazientirsi; **I had a restless night** ho passato una notte agitata; **if you're restless why not read for a while?** se non riesci a dormire perché non leggi per un po'?

rest·less·ly [ˈrɛstlɪslɪ] ADV *(gen)* irrequietamente; *(fidget)* nervosamente

rest·less·ness [ˈrɛstlɪsnɪs] N *(of person)* irrequietezza; *(of crowd)* agitazione *f*, nervosismo

re·stock [ˌriːˈstɒk] VT rifornire

res·to·ra·tion [ˌrɛstəˈreɪʃən] N **1** *(repair: of building, monument)* restauro **2** *(return: of land, property)* restituzione *f*, riconsegna; *(reintroduction: of law and order)* ripristino; (: *of confidence*) ristabilimento; *(History)*: **the Restoration** la Restaurazione
▷ www.bbc.co.uk/history/timelines/britain/stu_charles_ii.shtml
▷ www.britainexpress.com/History/Cromwell_and_Restoration.htm

re·stora·tive [rɪˈstɔːrətɪv] ADJ *(powers, effect)* corroborante
■ N *(tonic)* ricostituente *m*; *(hum: alcoholic drink)* cordiale *m*

◎**re·store** [rɪˈstɔːʳ] VT **1** *(repair: building)* restaurare; **the picture has been restored** il quadro è stato restaurato **2** *(give back: gen)* restituire; *(introduce again: confidence, custom, law and order)* ripristinare; **to restore sb's confidence** far riacquistare fiducia a qn; **restored to health** ristabilito(-a); **they restored order** hanno ripristinato l'ordine

re·stor·er [rɪˈstɔːrəʳ] N *(Art)* restauratore(-trice)

rest period N riposo

re·strain [rɪˈstreɪn] VT *(feeling)* contenere, frenare; *(dog etc)* tenere sotto controllo; **to restrain o.s.** controllarsi, trattenersi; **to restrain sb (from doing sth)** trattenere qn (dal fare qc)

re·strained [rɪˈstreɪnd] ADJ *(person, style etc)* contenuto(-a), sobrio(-a); *(manner)* riservato(-a)

restraining order N *(Am: Law)* ordinanza restrittiva

re·straint [rɪˈstreɪnt] N **1** *(check, control)* limitazioni *fpl*, restrizioni *fpl*; **wage restraint** contenimento salariale **2** *(constraint, moderation: of manner)* ritegno, riservatezza; *(self-control)* autocontrollo; **without restraint** senza reticenze, liberamente

re·strict [rɪˈstrɪkt] VT limitare, restringere

re·strict·ed [rɪˈstrɪktɪd] ADJ *(gen)* limitato(-a); *(by law)* soggetto(-a) a restrizioni; **he has rather a restricted outlook** *(fig)* ha una visione piuttosto limitata delle cose

restricted area N *(Brit Aut)* zona con limitazione di velocità

restricted zone N *(Mil)* zona militare

◎**re·stric·tion** [rɪˈstrɪkʃən] N limitazione *f*, restrizione *f*; **to place restrictions on sth** imporre delle restrizioni su qc; **speed restriction** *(Aut)* limite *m* di velocità

re·stric·tive [rɪˈstrɪktɪv] ADJ restrittivo(-a)

restrictive practices NPL *(Industry)* pratiche *fpl* restrittive di produzione

rest room N *(Am)* toilette *f inv*

re·struc·ture [ˌriːˈstrʌktʃəʳ] VT ristrutturare

re·struc·tur·ing [ˌriːˈstrʌktʃərɪŋ] N *(also Econ)* ristrutturazione *f*

◎**re·sult** [rɪˈzʌlt] N risultato; **as a result (of)** in *or* di conseguenza (a), in seguito (a); **as a result of the strike ...** in seguito allo sciopero...; **... and as a result, morale is low** ...e di conseguenza il morale è basso; **to get results** *(fam: person)* rendere; (: *action*) dare dei risultati; **an excellent result** un risultato eccellente

■VI: **to result (from)** essere una conseguenza (di), essere causato(-a) (da); **to result in** avere come conseguenza; **if the police leave, disorder will result** se la polizia se ne andrà, ci saranno dei disordini; **the inquiry resulted in several dismissals** l'inchiesta ha portato a diversi licenziamenti

re·sult·ant [rɪ'zʌltənt] ADJ (*frm*) risultante, conseguente
■N (*Phys, Math*) risultante *m/f*

◎**re·sume** [rɪ'zju:m] VT (*start again*) riprendere; **to resume one's seat** rimettersi a sedere; **they've resumed work** hanno ripreso il lavoro
■VI (*class, meeting*) riprendere

ré·su·mé ['rɛzjʊ,meɪ] N **1** (*summary*) sommario; **a quick résumé** un breve riassunto **2** (*Am*: *CV*) curriculum vitae *m inv*

re·sump·tion [rɪ'zʌmpʃən] N ripresa

re·sur·face [,ri:'sɜ:fɪs] VT (*road*) rifare il manto stradale di
■VI (*submarine*) riaffiorare; (*fig*: *problem*) ripresentarsi; (*fam*: *person*) rispuntare

re·sur·gence [rɪ'sɜ:dʒəns] N (*frm*) rinascita

re·sur·gent [rɪ'sɜ:dʒənt] ADJ (*frm*) in fase di ripresa

res·ur·rect [,rɛzə'rɛkt] VT risuscitare; (*fig*: *ideas, fashion*) riesumare

Res·ur·rec·tion [,rɛzə'rɛkʃən] N (*Rel*): **the Resurrection** la Risurrezione

res·ur·rec·tion [,rɛzə'rɛkʃən] N risurrezione *f*

re·sus·ci·tate [rɪ'sʌsɪ,teɪt] VT (*Med*) rianimare

re·sus·ci·ta·tion [rɪ,sʌsɪ'teɪʃən] N (*frm*) rianimazione *f*

◎**re·tail** ['ri:,teɪl] ADJ (*price, trade*) al dettaglio, al minuto
■ADV al dettaglio, al minuto; **to sell retail** vendere al dettaglio
■VT (*Comm*) vendere al minuto *or* al dettaglio; (*gossip*) riferire
■VI (*Comm*): **to retail at** essere in vendita al pubblico al prezzo di

re·tail·er ['ri:,teɪləʳ] N dettagliante *m/f*, commerciante *m/f* al minuto *or* al dettaglio

retail outlet N punto di vendita al minuto *or* al dettaglio

retail park N ≈ centro commerciale

retail price N prezzo al minuto *or* al dettaglio

retail price index N indice *m* dei prezzi al consumo

◎**re·tain** [rɪ'teɪn] VT (*hold*) tenere; (*keep*) conservare, serbare; (*remember*) tenere a mente; (*sign up*: *lawyer*) impegnare (*pagando una parte dell'onorario in anticipo*)

re·tain·er [rɪ'teɪnəʳ] N **1** (*fee*) onorario (*versato in anticipo*) **2** (*servant*) servitore *m*

re·take ['ri:teɪk] (*vb*:*pt* **retook**, *pp* **retaken**) VT **1** (*city, hall*) riprendere, riconquistare; (*prisoner*) ricatturare **2** (*Cine*) nuova ripresa; (*scene*) girare di nuovo **3** (*exam*) ridare
■N **1** (*exam*) ≈ esame *m* di riparazione

re·tali·ate [rɪ'tælɪ,eɪt] VI: **to retaliate (against sb/sth)** vendicarsi (contro qn/di qc)

re·talia·tion [rɪ,tælɪ'eɪʃən] N rappresaglie *fpl*; **by way of retaliation** *or* **in retaliation** per rappresaglia; **in retaliation for** per vendicarsi di

re·talia·tory [rɪ'tælɪətərɪ] ADJ di rappresaglia, di ritorsione

re·tard [rɪ'tɑ:d] VT ritardare

re·tard·ed [rɪ'tɑ:dɪd] ADJ (*Med*) ritardato(-a); **to be mentally retarded** essere (un*a*) ritardato(-a) mentale

retch [rɛtʃ] VI avere (dei) conati di vomito

re·ten·tion [rɪ'tɛnʃən] N (*frm*: *gen*) conservazione *f*; (: *of facts, faces, names*) memorizzazione *f*; (*Med*) ritenzione *f*

re·ten·tive [rɪ'tɛntɪv] ADJ (*memory*) ritentivo(-a)

re·think [,ri:'θɪŋk] VT ripensare

reti·cence ['rɛtɪsəns] N reticenza

reti·cent ['rɛtɪsənt] ADJ reticente, riservato(-a)

reti·na ['rɛtɪnə] N retina

reti·nue ['rɛtɪ,nju:] N seguito, scorta

◎**re·tire** [rɪ'taɪəʳ] VI **1** (*give up work*) andare in pensione; (*quit business*) ritirarsi **2** (*withdraw, go to bed, Sport*) ritirarsi
■VT **1** (*Fin*: *bill of exchange*) ritirare **2** (*person*) mandare in pensione

re·tired [rɪ'taɪəd] ADJ **1** (*no longer working*) in pensione, pensionato(-a); **a retired person** un*a* pensionato(-a); **a retired teacher** un insegnante in pensione **2** (*liter*: *quiet, secluded*) ritirato(-a), appartato(-a)

◎**re·tire·ment** [rɪ'taɪəmənt] N: **to look forward to one's retirement** non vedere l'ora di andare in pensione; **on her retirement she hopes to ...** quando va in pensione spera di...; **since his retirement** da quando è andato in pensione; **early retirement** prepensionamento

retirement age N età del pensionamento

retirement home N casa di riposo

re·tir·ing [rɪ'taɪərɪŋ] ADJ **1** (*frm*: *shy*) riservato(-a) **2** (*departing*: *chairman*) uscente; (*age*) pensionabile

re·tort [rɪ'tɔ:t] N **1** (*answer*) risposta (per le rime) **2** (*Chem*) storta
■VT (*answer*) ribattere
■VI rimbeccare, rispondere per le rime

re·trace [rɪ'treɪs] VT ripercorrere; (*recall*) ricostruire; **to retrace one's steps** (ri)tornare sui propri passi

re·tract [rɪ'trækt] VT (*statement*) ritrattare; (*draw in*: *claws*) ritrarre; (: *aerial*) ritirare; (: *wheels of plane*) far rientrare; **he later retracted the statement** in seguito ha ritrattato la dichiarazione; **when the wheels were retracted** quando le ruote furono fatte rientrare
■VI (*claws*) ritrarsi; (*aerial, wheels*) rientrare

re·tract·able [rɪ'træktəbl] ADJ (*undercarriage, nib*) retrattile

re·trac·tile [rɪ'træktaɪl] ADJ (*Zool*) retrattile

re·train [,ri:'treɪn] VT (*worker*) riqualificare
■VI riqualificarsi

re·train·ing [,ri:'treɪnɪŋ] N riqualificazione *f*

retread [*n* 'ri:,trɛd; *vb* ,ri:'trɛd] N gomma rigenerata; (*of book, film*) rifacimento; (*of themes*) ripetizione *f*
■VT (*Aut*: *tyre*) rigenerare

◎**re·treat** [rɪ'tri:t] N **1** (*place*) rifugio; (*Rel*) ritiro (spirituale); **a country retreat** una tranquilla casa in campagna, un rifugio di campagna; **to go into retreat** (*Rel*) andare in ritiro **2** (*Mil*) ritirata; **to be in retreat** essere in ritirata *or* rotta; **to beat a hasty retreat** (*fig*) battersela
■VI (*Mil*) ritirarsi, battere in ritirata; (*flood*) ritirarsi; (*move back*) ritrarsi; **the army retreated** l'esercito batté in ritirata

re·trench [rɪ'trɛntʃ] VI fare delle economie

re·trench·ment [rɪ'trɛntʃmənt] N riduzione *f* delle spese

re·tri·al [,ri:'traɪəl] N (*Law*) nuovo processo

ret·ri·bu·tion [,rɛtrɪ'bju:ʃən] N castigo

re·triev·able [rɪ'tri:vəbl] ADJ (*see vb*) ricuperabile; riconquistabile; rimediabile; richiamabile

re·triev·al [rɪ'tri:vəl] N (*Comput*) richiamo; (*see vb*) ricupero; riconquista; rimedio, richiamo

re·trieve [rɪ'tri:v] VT **1** (*get back*: *object, money*)

Rr

ricuperare; (: *honour, position*) riconquistare; (*set to rights: error, loss, situation*) rimediare a; **we retrieved our luggage** abbiamo ritrovato i nostri bagagli; **the one person who could retrieve the situation ...** la sola persona che poteva salvare la situazione... **2** (*Comput*) richiamare; **to retrieve information** reperire informazioni

re·triev·er [rɪ'tri:vəʳ] N cane *m* da riporto

retro·ac·tive [ˌrɛtrəʊ'æktɪv] ADJ retroattivo(-a)

retro·ac·tive·ly [ˌrɛtrəʊ'æktɪvlɪ] ADV in modo retroattivo, retroattivamente

retro·fit ['rɛtrəʊˌfɪt] VT (*machine, building*) rimodernare
■N rimodernamento

retro·grade ['rɛtrəʊˌgreɪd] ADJ (*frm*): **a retrograde step** (*fig*) un passo (all')indietro

retro·gress [ˌrɛtrəʊ'grɛs] VI (*frm*) regredire

retro·gres·sive [ˌrɛtrəʊ'grɛsɪv] ADJ (*frm: change*) retrogrado(-a)

retro·rock·et ['rɛtrəʊˌrɒkɪt] N retrorazzo

retro·spect ['rɛtrəʊˌspɛkt] N: **in retrospect** ripensandoci

retro·spec·tive [ˌrɛtrəʊ'spɛktɪv] ADJ (*gen*) retrospettivo(-a); (*pay rise, Law*) retroattivo(-a)
■N (*Art*) retrospettiva

retro·spec·tive·ly [ˌrɛtrəʊ'spɛktɪvlɪ] ADV retrospettivamente

retro·vi·ral ['rɛtrəʊˌvaɪərəl] ADJ retrovirale

retro·vi·rus ['rɛtrəʊˌvaɪərəs] N retrovirus *m inv*

re·tune [ˌri:'tju:n] VI risintonizzarsi
■VT risintonizzare

◎**re·turn** [rɪ'tɜ:n] N **1** (*going, coming back*) ritorno; (*sending back*) rinvio; (*reappearance: of illness etc*) ricomparsa; **on my return** al mio ritorno; **by return of post** a stretto giro di posta; **many happy returns (of the day)!** cento di questi giorni! **2** (*of thing borrowed, lost, stolen*) restituzione *f*; (*of money*) rimborso; (*Comm: of merchandise*) reso **3** (*Fin: profit*) profitto, guadagno; **to bring in a good return** *or* **good returns** fruttare *or* dare un buon guadagno **4** (*exchange*): **in return (for)** in cambio (di); **... and I help her in return** ...e io in cambio aiuto lei **5** (*declaration*): **tax return** dichiarazione *f* dei redditi; **census/election returns** risultati *mpl* del censimento/delle elezioni **6** (*Brit: return ticket*) (biglietto di) andata e ritorno; **a return to Bangor, please** un biglietto di andata e ritorno per Bangor, per favore **7** (*Sport*) risposta; **return of serve** (*Tennis*) risposta al servizio **8** (*key*) (tasto di) invio; **hit return** premere invio
■VT **1** (*give back*) restituire, rendere; (*bring back*) riportare; (*put back*) rimettere; (*send back*) rinviare, mandare indietro; (: *by post*) rispedire; (*Mil: gunfire*) rispondere a; (*favour, love, sb's visit*) ricambiare; **she borrows my things and doesn't return them** prende le mie cose e poi non le restituisce; **"return to sender"** "rispedire al mittente" **2** (*Law*): **to return a verdict of guilty/not guilty** pronunciare un verdetto di colpevolezza/di innocenza **3** (*Pol: elect*) eleggere
■VI (*go, come back*) (ri)tornare; (*illness, symptoms etc*) ricomparire; **to return home** (ri)tornare a casa; **to return to** (*room, office*) (ri)tornare in; (*school, work*) (ri)tornare a; (*subject, argument*) (ri)tornare su; **I've just returned from holiday** sono appena tornato dalle vacanze
■ADJ (*Brit: ticket, fare*) di andata e ritorno; (*journey, flight*) di ritorno; **the return journey** il viaggio di ritorno

re·turn·able [rɪ'tɜ:nəbl] ADJ: **returnable bottle** vuoto a rendere

re·turn·er [rɪ'tɜ:nəʳ] N (*Brit*) *donna che ritorna a lavoro dopo la maternità*

re·turn·ing of·fic·er [rɪˌtɜ:nɪŋ'ɒfɪsəʳ] N (*Brit Pol*) *funzionario addetto all'organizzazione e alla presentazione dei risultati delle elezioni in un distretto*

return key N (*on computer*) tasto di invio

return match N (*Sport*) (partita di) ritorno

return stroke N (*Tech*) corsa di ritorno

re·uni·fi·ca·tion [ˌri:ju:nɪfɪ'keɪʃən] N riunificazione *f*

re·union [rɪ'ju:njən] N riunione *f*

re·unite [ˌri:ju:'naɪt] VT riunire
■VI riunirsi

re-use [*n* ri:'ju:s; *vt* ˌri:'ju:z] N riutilizzazione *f*
■VT riusare, riutilizzare

Rev, Revd. ABBR = **Reverend**

rev [rɛv] (*fam*) N (*Aut*) giro; **3,000 revs per minute** 3.000 giri al minuto; **to keep the revs up** tenere il motore su di giri
■VT (*engine*) mandare su di giri
■VI (*also:* **rev up**: *car*) andar su di giri, imballarsi; (: *driver*) tenere il motore su di giri

re·valua·tion [ˌri:væljʊ'eɪʃən] N rivalutazione *f*

re·value [ˌri:'vælju:] VT rivalutare

re·vamp [ˌri:'væmp] VT (*methods, system*) modernizzare; (*company, organization*) rinnovare; (*play*) rendere di nuovo attuale

re·vanch·ism [rɪ'væntʃɪzəm] N revanscismo

rev counter N (*Aut*) contagiri *m inv*

◎**re·veal** [rɪ'vi:l] VT (*make known*) rivelare, svelare; (*uncover: hidden object*) scoprire

re·veal·ing [rɪ'vi:lɪŋ] ADJ (*remarks, action*) rivelatore(-trice); (*dress*) scollato(-a)

re·veil·le [rɪ'vælɪ] N (*Mil*) sveglia

rev·el ['rɛvl] VI far baldoria; **to revel in sth/in doing sth** godere di qc/nel fare qc

rev·ela·tion [ˌrɛvə'leɪʃən] N rivelazione *f*; **(the Book of the) Revelation** (*Bible*) l'Apocalisse *f*

rev·el·ler, (*Am*) **rev·eler** ['rɛvləʳ] N chi fa baldoria

rev·el·ry ['rɛvlrɪ] N baldoria

re·venge [rɪ'vɛndʒ] N vendetta; (*in game etc*) rivincita; **to get one's revenge (for sth)** vendicarsi (di qc); **to take revenge on sb (for sth)** vendicarsi su qn (per qc); **this is my revenge** questa è la mia vendetta
■VT vendicare; **to be revenged (on sb)** prendersi la vendetta (su qn); **to revenge o.s. (on sb)** vendicarsi (su qn)

re·venge·ful [rɪ'vɛndʒfʊl] ADJ vendicativo(-a)

◎**rev·enue** ['rɛvənju:] N entrate *fpl*, reddito

re·ver·ber·ate [rɪ'vɜ:bəˌreɪt] VI (*frm: sound*) rimbombare; (: *fig*) ripercuotersi

re·ver·bera·tion [rɪˌvɜ:bə'reɪʃən] (*frm*) N (*see vb*) rimbombo; ripercussione *f*

re·vere [rɪ'vɪəʳ] VT (*frm*) venerare

rev·er·ence ['rɛvərəns] N venerazione *f*, riverenza
■VT venerare

Rev·er·end ['rɛvərənd] ADJ (*in titles*) reverendo(-a)

rev·er·ent ['rɛvərənt] ADJ riverente

rev·er·en·tial [ˌrɛvə'rɛnʃəl] ADJ (*frm: awe, bow*) riverente

rev·er·ent·ly ['rɛvərəntlɪ] ADV rispettosamente

rev·erie ['rɛvərɪ] N fantasticheria

re·ver·sal [rɪ'vɜ:səl] N (*of roles, tendencies*) inversione *f*; (*of situation, fortunes*) capovolgimento; (*of decision*) revoca; **the reversal of industrial decline** il risollevamento delle sorti dell'industria

◎**re·verse** [rɪ'vɜ:s] ADJ (*order*) inverso(-a); (*direction*) opposto(-a); (*side*) altro(-a); **in reverse order** in ordine inverso

■ N **1** (*opposite*): **the reverse** il contrario, l'opposto; **quite the reverse** al contrario **2** (*face: of coin, paper*) rovescio **3** (*Aut*) retromarcia, marcia indietro; **to go into reverse** fare marcia indietro *or* retromarcia
■ VT (*turn the other way round*) invertire; (*situation, position*) capovolgere, rovesciare; (*movement*) invertire la direzione di; (*garment*) rivoltare; (*Law*) cassare; **to reverse the charges** (*Brit Telec*) fare una telefonata a carico (del destinatario); **to reverse one's car** fare marcia indietro
■ VI (*Brit Aut*) fare marcia indietro; **I reversed into the car behind** facendo retromarcia ho urtato la macchina di dietro

DID YOU KNOW ...?
reverse is not translated by the Italian word *riversare*

re·verse-charge call [rɪˌvɜːstʃɑːdʒˈkɔːl] N (*Brit Telec*) telefonata a carico (del destinatario)
reverse engineering N *analisi di un prodotto di un'altra azienda allo scopo di replicarlo e immetterlo sul mercato a costi inferiori*
reverse gear N (*Aut*) marcia indietro
reverse video N (*Comput*) inversione *f* dei colori del video
re·vers·ible [rɪˈvɜːsəbl] ADJ (*garment*) double-face *inv*; (*procedure*) reversibile
re·vers·ing lights [rɪˈvɜːsɪŋˌlaɪts] NPL (*Brit Aut*) luci *fpl* di retromarcia
re·ver·sion [rɪˈvɜːʃən] N (*return to previous state*) ritorno; (*Bio*) reversione *f*
re·vert [rɪˈvɜːt] VI (*gen*): **to revert (to)** ritornare (a); **to revert to type** (*Bio*) ritornare allo stato primitivo; (*fig*) tornare alla propria natura
◎ **re·view** [rɪˈvjuː] N **1** (*survey, taking stock*) revisione *f*; (*Mil: of troops*) rivista; (*critique*) critica, recensione *f*; **to come** *or* **be under review** essere preso(-a) in esame; **the play got good reviews** lo spettacolo ha ricevuto critiche favorevoli, lo spettacolo ha avuto recensioni favorevoli **2** (*journal*) rivista, periodico
■ VT (*take stock of*) fare una revisione di; (*situation*) fare il punto di; (*Mil: troops*) passare in rivista; (*book, play, film*) fare la recensione di
review board N commissione *f* di valutazione
review copy N copia per la stampa
re·view·er [rɪˈvjuːəʳ] N recensore *m*; **book/film reviewer** critico letterario/cinematografico
re·vile [rɪˈvaɪl] VT (*frm*) insultare
re·vise [rɪˈvaɪz] VT **1** (*look over: subject, notes*) ripassare **2** (*alter: text*) emendare; (*decision, opinion*) modificare; **to revise one's opinion** cambiare idea; **revised edition** edizione *f* riveduta e corretta
■ VI (*for exams*) ripassare; **I haven't started revising yet** non ho ancora cominciato a ripassare
Re·vised Ver·sion [rɪˌvaɪzdˈvɜːʃən] N (*Brit: of Bible*): **the Revised Version** *la traduzione inglese della Bibbia effettuata nel 1884*
re·vi·sion [rɪˈvɪʒən] N **1** (*before exam*) ripasso; (*of text*) revisione *f* **2** (*revised version*) versione *f* riveduta e corretta
re·vi·sion·ism [rɪˈvɪʒəˌnɪzəm] N (*Pol*) revisionismo
re·vi·sion·ist [rɪˈvɪʒənɪst] ADJ, N (*Pol*) revisionista *m/f*
re·vis·it [ˌriːˈvɪzɪt] VT rivisitare
re·vi·tal·ize [ˌriːˈvaɪtəˌlaɪz] VT ravvivare
re·viv·al [rɪˈvaɪvəl] N (*of person, business, play*) ripresa; (*of faith, religion*) risveglio; (*of custom, usage: restoration*) ripristino; (*: reappearance*) rinascita; **a revival in car sales** una ripresa delle vendite di automobili; **a revival of 'The Seagull'** un revival de 'Il gabbiano'
re·viv·al·ism [rɪˈvaɪvəˌlɪzəm] N (*Rel*) revivalismo
re·viv·al·ist [rɪˈvaɪvəlɪst] N (*Rel*) revivalista *m/f*
revival meeting N (*Rel*) *incontro per il rinnovamento della fede religiosa*
re·vive [rɪˈvaɪv] VT (*person*) rianimare; (*: from faint*) far riprendere i sensi a; (*fig: spirits*) risollevare; (*old customs*) far tornare di moda, far rivivere; (*hopes, courage*) riaccendere; (*suspicions*) risvegliare, ridestare; (*Theatre: play*) riprendere; **the nurses tried to revive him** gli infermieri cercarono di rianimarlo
■ VI (*person, business, trade, activity*) riprendersi, rianimarsi; (*hope, emotions*) riaccendersi, rinascere
revo·ca·tion [ˌrɛvəˈkeɪʃən] (*frm*) N (*of law*) abrogazione *f*; (*of order, decision*) revoca
re·voke [rɪˈvəʊk] (*frm*) VT (*law*) abrogare; (*: order, decision*) revocare
re·volt [rɪˈvəʊlt] N rivolta, ribellione *f*; **to be in open revolt** essere in aperta rivolta
■ VT (far) rivoltare; **to be revolted by sth** provare disgusto per qc
■ VI **1** (*rebel*): **to revolt (against sb/sth)** ribellarsi (a qn/qc) **2** (*feel disgust*): **to revolt at** *or* **against** rivoltarsi (a *or* di fronte a)
re·volt·ing [rɪˈvəʊltɪŋ] ADJ rivoltante, ripugnante
re·volt·ing·ly [rɪˈvəʊltɪŋlɪ] ADV in modo rivoltante, disgustosamente
◎ **revo·lu·tion** [ˌrɛvəˈluːʃən] N (*movement, change, Pol*) rivoluzione *f*; (*of record, engine, wheel*) giro
◎ **revo·lu·tion·ary** [ˌrɛvəˈluːʃnərɪ] ADJ, N rivoluzionario(-a)
revo·lu·tion·ize [ˌrɛvəˈluːʃəˌnaɪz] VT rivoluzionare
re·volve [rɪˈvɒlv] VT (far) girare
■ VI girare; **to revolve around sth** girare *or* ruotare intorno a qc; **the Earth revolves on its own axis** la Terra ruota intorno al proprio asse; **he thinks everything revolves round him** si crede il centro dell'universo
re·volv·er [rɪˈvɒlvəʳ] N rivoltella
re·volv·ing [rɪˈvɒlvɪŋ] ADJ girevole; **revolving light** (*on police car*) lampeggiatore *m*
revolving credit N (*Fin*) credito a termine rinnovabile automaticamente
revolving door N porta girevole
re·vue [rɪˈvjuː] N (*Theatre*) rivista
re·vul·sion [rɪˈvʌlʃən] N ripugnanza
◎ **re·ward** [rɪˈwɔːd] N ricompensa, premio; **as a reward for (doing) sth** in premio *or* come ricompensa per (aver fatto) qc
■ VT: **to reward (for)** ricompensare (per), premiare (per)
re·ward·ing [rɪˈwɔːdɪŋ] ADJ (*activity*) di grande soddisfazione, gratificante; (*book*) che vale la pena di leggere; **a rewarding job** un lavoro gratificante; **financially rewarding** conveniente dal punto di vista economico
re·wind [ˌriːˈwaɪnd] VT **1** (*ball of wool etc*) riavvolgere, riarrotolare; (*tape, cassette*) far tornare indietro **2** (*clock, toy*) ricaricare
re·wire [ˌriːˈwaɪəʳ] VT (*house*) rifare l'impianto elettrico di
re·word [ˌriːˈwɜːd] VT formulare *or* esprimere con altre parole
re·work [riːˈwɜːk] VT (*idea, novel*) modificare
re·writ·able [ˌriːˈraɪtəbl] ADJ riscrivibile
re·write [ˌriːˈraɪt] VT riscrivere
Rey·kja·vik [ˈreɪkjəˌvɪk] N Reykjavik *f*

Rr

RFD [ˌɑːrɛfˈdiː] ABBR (*Am Post*) = *rural free delivery*

RGN [ˌɑːrdʒiːˈɛn] N ABBR (*Brit*: = **Registered General Nurse**) infermiere(-a) diplomato(-a); dopo corso triennale

Rh ABBR (= **rhesus**) Rh

rhap·sod·ic [ræpˈsɒdɪk] ADJ (*account, description, praise*) entusiastico(-a); (*Mus*) rapsodico(-a)

rhap·so·dize [ˈræpsəˌdaɪz] VI: **to rhapsodize (about), rhapsodize (over)** parlare entusiasticamente (di)

rhap·so·dy [ˈræpsədɪ] N (*Mus*) rapsodia; **to go into rhapsodies over sth** (*fig*) andare in estasi per qc

rheo·stat [ˈrɪəʊˌstæt] N (*Elec*) reostato

rhe·sus [ˈriːsəs] N (*also*: **rhesus monkey**) reso

rhesus factor N (*Med*) fattore *m* Rh

rhesus negative ADJ (*Med*) Rh-negativo(-a)

rhesus positive ADJ (*Med*) Rh-positivo(-a)

rheto·ric [ˈrɛtərɪk] N retorica

rhe·tori·cal [rɪˈtɒrɪkəl] ADJ (*style, question*) retorico(-a)

rhe·tori·cal·ly [rɪˈtɒrɪkəlɪ] ADV (*ask, declaim*) in modo retorico

rheu·mat·ic [ruːˈmætɪk] ADJ reumatico(-a)

rheumatic fever N febbre *f* reumatica

rheu·mat·ics [ruːˈmætɪks] NSG (*old*) reumatismi *mpl*

rheu·ma·tism [ˈruːməˌtɪzəm] N reumatismo

rheu·ma·toid ar·thri·tis [ˈruːmətɔɪdɑːˈθraɪtɪs] N artrite *f* reumatoide

Rhine [raɪn] N: **the Rhine** il Reno

rhine·stone [ˈraɪnˌstəʊn] N strass *m inv*

rhino [ˈraɪnəʊ] N ABBR (*fam*) rinoceronte *m*

rhi·noc·er·os [raɪˈnɒsərəs] N rinoceronte *m*

rhi·zome [ˈraɪzəʊm] N rizoma *m*

Rhode Island [ˌrəʊdˈaɪlənd] N Rhode Island *m* ▷ www.state.pa.us/

Rhodes [rəʊdz] N Rodi *f*

Rho·desia [rəʊˈdiːʃə] N la Rodesia

Rho·desian [rəʊˈdiːʃən] ADJ, N Rodesiano(-a)

rho·do·den·dron [ˌrəʊdəˈdɛndrən] N rododendro

rhom·bus [ˈrɒmbəs] N rombo

Rhone [rəʊn] N: **the Rhone** il Rodano

rhu·barb [ˈruːbɑːb] N rabarbaro
■ ADJ (*jam, pie, tart*) di rabarbaro

rhyme [raɪm] N rima; (*verse*) poesia; **in rhyme** in rima; **a little rhyme** una breve poesia; **without rhyme** *or* **reason** senza capo né coda
■ VI: **to rhyme (with)** fare rima (con); **'Moon' rhymes with 'June'** 'Moon' fa rima con 'June'

rhym·ing [ˈraɪmɪŋ] ADJ rimato(-a), in rima; **rhyming couplet** rima baciata

rhyming slang N *gergo Cockney che sostituisce una certa parola con altre che con questa fanno rima*

◎ **rhythm** [ˈrɪðəm] N ritmo

rhyth·mic, rhyth·mi·cal [ˈrɪðmɪk(əl)] ADJ ritmico(-a)

rhyth·mi·cal·ly [ˈrɪðmɪkəlɪ] ADV ritmicamente

rhythm method N (*Med*): **the rhythm method** il metodo Ogino-Knaus

RI [ˌɑːrˈaɪ] ABBR (*Am Post*) = **Rhode Island**
■ N ABBR (*Brit*) = *religious instruction*

rib [rɪb] N (*Anat*) costola; (*Culin*) costata; (*of umbrella*) stecca; (*of leaf*) nervatura; (*Knitting*) costa; **to dig** *or* **poke sb in the ribs** dare una gomitata nelle costole a qn
■ VT (*fam*: *tease*) punzecchiare

rib·ald [ˈrɪbəld] ADJ (*old*: *person*) sguaiato(-a); (*: joke*) licenzioso(-a)

rib·ald·ry [ˈrɪbəldrɪ] N (*old*) sguaiataggine *f*

ribbed [rɪbd] ADJ (*knitting*) a coste

rib·bon [ˈrɪbən] N (*gen, of typewriter*) nastro; (*Mil*) nastrino; **to tear sth to ribbons** ridurre qc a brandelli; (*fig*) demolire qc

ribbon development N (*Brit*) *sviluppo urbano lineare sul bordo delle strade periferiche*

rib cage N (*Anat*) gabbia toracica

ri·bo·fla·vin [ˌraɪbəʊˈfleɪvɪn] N (*Chem*) riboflavina

◎ **rice** [raɪs] N riso

rice field N risaia

rice growing N risicoltura

rice paper N (*for art*) carta di riso; (*Culin*) ≈ ostie *fpl*

rice pudding N budino di riso

◎ **rich** [rɪtʃ] ADJ (*comp* **-er**, *superl* **-est**) (*gen*) ricco(-a); (*food*) con molti grassi; (*colour*) intenso(-a); (*clothes*) sontuoso(-a); **it was lovely but rather rich** era buono ma un po' troppo sostanzioso; **that's rich!** (*fam iro*) questa sì che è bella!; **the rich** i ricchi; **to be rich in sth** essere ricco(-a) di qc; **to become** *or* **get** *or* **grow rich(er)** arricchirsi, diventar ricco(-a)

riches [ˈrɪtʃɪz] NPL ricchezze *fpl*

rich·ly [ˈrɪtʃlɪ] ADV (*rewarded*) lautamente; (*endowed*) abbondantemente; (*dressed*) sontuosamente; (*deserved*) pienamente; **richly deserved** pienamente meritato

rich·ness [ˈrɪtʃnɪs] N (*see adj*) ricchezza; (alto) contenuto di grassi; intensità *f inv*; sontuosità *f inv*

Richter scale [ˈrɪxtər skeɪl] N: **the Richter scale** la scala Richter

rick [rɪk] N covone *m*, pagliaio
■ VT (*Brit fam*: *one's neck, back*) farsi uno strappo muscolare a

rick·ets [ˈrɪkɪts] NSG rachitismo

rick·ety [ˈrɪkɪtɪ] ADJ (*furniture, structure*) traballante

rick·shaw [ˈrɪkʃɔː] N risciò *m inv*

rico·chet [ˈrɪkəʃeɪ] N rimbalzo
■ VI: **to ricochet (off)** rimbalzare (contro)

◎ **rid** [rɪd] (*pt, pp* **rid** *or* **ridded**) VT: **to rid sb/sth of** sbarazzare qn/qc di, liberare qn/qc da; **an attempt to rid the house of mice** un tentativo di liberare la casa dai topi; **to get rid of sb/sth** *or* **rid o.s. of sb/sth** sbarazzarsi *or* liberarsi di qn/qc

rid·dance [ˈrɪdəns] N: **good riddance!** (*fam*) che liberazione!

rid·den [ˈrɪdn] PP *of* **ride**

rid·dle¹ [ˈrɪdl] N (*puzzle*) indovinello; **to speak in riddles** parlare per enigmi

rid·dle² [ˈrɪdl] VT (*soil, coal*) setacciare, vagliare; (*fig*): **to riddle with** (*bullets*) crivellare di; **riddled with holes** bucherellato(-a); **the council was riddled with corruption** la corruzione dilagava nel consiglio
■ N (*sieve*) setaccio, vaglio

◎ **ride** [raɪd] (*vb*: *pt* **rode**, *pp* **ridden**) N (*on horse*) cavalcata; (*in car, on bike*) giro, corsa; (*esp Am*: *lift*) passaggio, strappo; **to go for a ride** (*on horse*) andare a fare una cavalcata; (*on bike*) andare a fare un giro; **it was a rough ride** è stato un viaggio scomodo; **he got** *or* **was given a rough ride** (*fig*) passò un momentaccio; **it's a 10-minute ride on the bus** ci vogliono 10 minuti in autobus; **he gave me a ride into town** (*in car*) mi ha dato un passaggio in città; **it's a short bus ride to the town centre** in autobus il centro non è lontano; **to take sb for a ride** (*in car, on horseback*) portare qn a fare un giro; (*fig*: *make fool of, swindle*) prendere in giro qn
■ VT: **to ride a horse** andare a cavallo; cavalcare; (*subj*: *jockey*) montare un cavallo; **to ride a donkey/camel** cavalcare un asino/cammello; **to ride a bicycle** andare in bicicletta; **can you ride a bike?** sai andare in bicicletta?; **he rode his horse into town** è venuto in città a cavallo; **we rode 10 km yesterday** ieri abbiamo

fatto 10 km a cavallo (*or* in bicicletta); **to ride a good race** fare un'ottima gara; **to ride the bus** (*Am*) prendere l'autobus

■VI (*ride a horse*) andare a cavallo; (*go by car/bicycle etc*) andare in macchina/in bicicletta *etc*; **to ride along/through** *etc* passare/attraversare *etc* a cavallo (*or* in macchina *etc*); **can you ride?** (*ride a horse*) sai andare a cavallo?, sai cavalcare?; **I'm learning to ride** sto imparando a cavalcare; **he rode to school on his new bike** è andato a scuola con la bici nuova; **he's riding high at the moment** in questo momento è sulla cresta dell'onda; **to ride at anchor** (*ship*) essere all'ancora *or* alla fonda; **to let things ride** lasciare che le cose seguano il loro corso

▸ **ride out** VT + ADV (*Naut: storm*) sostenere; (*fig: difficult period*) superare; **to ride out the storm** (*fig*) mantenersi a galla

▸ **ride up** VI + ADV (*skirt, dress*) salire

◎ **rid·er** ['raɪdə[r]] N **1** (*horse rider*) uomo/donna a cavallo; (*: skilled man*) cavallerizzo; (*: skilled woman*) cavallerizza, amazzone *f*; (*jockey*) fantino(-a); (*cyclist*) ciclista *m/f*; (*motorcyclist*) motociclista *m/f*; **she's a good rider** è una buona cavallerizza **2** (*addition to document*) clausola addizionale

ridge [rɪdʒ] N (*of mountain, hill*) cresta; (*of chain of mountains*) crinale *m*; (*of roof*) colmo; (*in ploughed field*) porca; (*Met*): **ridge of high pressure** fascia di alta pressione; **we walked along the ridge** camminammo lungo la cresta

ridge·pole ['rɪdʒpəʊl] N (*on tent*) asta di colmo

ridge tent N (tenda) canadese *f*

ridi·cule ['rɪdɪkjuːl] N ridicolo; **to hold sb/sth up to ridicule** mettere in ridicolo qn/qc

■VT ridicolizzare

ri·dicu·lous [rɪ'dɪkjʊləs] ADJ ridicolo(-a); **to make o.s. (look) ridiculous** rendersi ridicolo(-a)

ri·dicu·lous·ly [rɪ'dɪkjʊləslɪ] ADV (*stupidly*) in modo ridicolo; (*disproportionately*) incredibilmente; **a ridiculously large/small amount** una quantità enorme/irrisoria

ri·dicu·lous·ness [rɪ'dɪkjʊləsnɪs] N ridicolaggine *f*

rid·ing ['raɪdɪŋ] N (*horse-riding*) equitazione *f*; **to go riding** fare equitazione

riding breeches NPL pantaloni *mpl or* calzoni *mpl* da cavallerizzo

riding crop, **riding whip** N frustino

riding habit N amazzone *f*, abito da cavallerizza

riding school N scuola di equitazione

rife [raɪf] ADJ (*frm*): **to be rife** (*corruption, disease*) dilagare; abbondare; **speculation is rife** abbondano le congetture; **to be rife with** abbondare di; **corruption is rife** c'è molta corruzione

riff [rɪf] N (*Mus*) riff *m inv*

riff·raff ['rɪf,ræf] N gentaglia, canaglia

ri·fle¹ ['raɪfl] VT (*house, till etc*) ripulire, svuotare

▸ **rifle through** VI + PREP frugare

ri·fle² ['raɪfl] N fucile *m*, carabina

rifle range N (*Mil*) poligono di tiro; (*at fair*) tiro a segno

rift [rɪft] N (*in family, between friends*) incrinatura; (*Pol: in party*) spaccatura; (*in rock, ground*) crepa, fessura; (*in clouds*) squarcio; **a serious rift between the President and the government** una grave incrinatura tra il Presidente e il governo

rift valley N fossa tettonica

rig [rɪg] N (*also:* **oil rig**) impianto di trivellazione (per il petrolio); (*: offshore*) piattaforma petrolifera *or* di trivellazione

■VT **1** (*election, competition*) truccare; (*prices*) manipolare; (*also:* **rig up**: *equipment, device*) improvvisare, mettere su **2** (*boat*) armare

▸ **rig out** VT + ADV (*Brit*) attrezzare; (*pej*) abbigliare, agghindare; **to rig out (as/in)** vestire (da/in)

▸ **rig up** VT + ADV (*also fig*) improvvisare, mettere su

rig·ging ['rɪgɪŋ] N (*Naut*) attrezzatura; **standing/running rigging** manovre *fpl* fisse/correnti

◎ **right** [raɪt] ADJ

1 (*morally good*) retto(-a), onesto(-a); (*just*) giusto(-a); **it's not right to behave like that** non sta bene fare così ; **it's not right to leave children alone in a house** non è ammissibile lasciare i bambini da soli a casa; **it's not right!** non è giusto!; **it is only right that ...** è più che giusto che...; **to do what is right** fare ciò che si crede giusto; **I thought it right to warn him** mi è sembrato giusto avvertirlo

2 (*suitable: person, clothes, time*) adatto(-a), appropriato(-a); **to choose the right moment for sth/to do sth** scegliere il momento giusto *or* adatto per qc/per fare qc; **that's the right attitude!** così va bene!; **to say the right thing** dire la cosa giusta; **you did the right thing** hai fatto bene; **what's the right thing to do?** qual è la cosa migliore da farsi?; **to know the right people** conoscere la gente giusta

3 (*correct: answer, solution etc*) giusto(-a), esatto(-a), corretto(-a); (*: size*) giusto(-a); **right first time!** hai azzeccato al primo colpo!; **to get sth right** far giusto qc; **I got every question right** ho risposto esattamente a tutte le domande; **let's get it right this time!** cerchiamo di farlo bene stavolta!; **to get one's facts right** sapere di che cosa si parla; **get your facts right!** non parlare se non sei sicuro di quello che dici!; **(yes,) that's right** sì , esatto; **the right answer** la risposta esatta; **the right road** la strada buona; **the right time** l'ora esatta; **do you have the right time?** hai l'ora esatta?; **it isn't the right size** non è la taglia giusta; **to get on the right side of sb** (*fig*) entrare nelle grazie di qn; **to put a clock right** rimettere (all'ora esatta) un orologio; **to put a mistake right** (*Brit*) correggere un errore; **right you are!** *or* **right-oh!** (*fam*) va bene!

4 to be right (*person*) aver ragione; (*answer, behaviour*) essere giusto(-a) *or* corretto(-a); **you're quite right** *or* (*fam*) **you're dead right** hai proprio *or* perfettamente ragione; **you were right to come to me** hai fatto bene a venire da me

5 (*well, in order*): **to be/feel as right as rain** essere/sentirsi completamente ristabilito(-a); **he is not quite right in the head** gli manca una rotella; **I don't feel quite right** non mi sento del tutto a posto; **all's right with the world** tutto va bene; **the stereo still isn't right** lo stereo ha ancora qualcosa che non va

6 (*not left*) destro(-a); **my right hand** la mano destra; **I'd give my right arm to know ...** darei un occhio per sapere...

7 (*Math: angle*) retto(-a)

8 (*fam: intensive*): **a right idiot** un perfetto idiota

■ADV

1 (*directly, exactly*): **right now** (*at this moment*) in questo momento, proprio adesso; (*immediately*) subito; **right away** subito; **I'll do it right away** lo faccio subito; **right off** subito; (*at the first attempt*) al primo colpo; **right here** proprio qui; **she (just) went right on talking** ha continuato a parlare lo stesso; **right against the wall** proprio contro il muro; **right ahead** sempre diritto, proprio davanti; **right behind/in**

Rr

front of proprio dietro/davanti a; **right before/after** subito prima/dopo; **right after the summer** subito dopo l'estate; **right in the middle** proprio nel (bel) mezzo; (*of target*) in pieno centro; **right round sth** tutt'intorno a qc; **right at the end** proprio alla fine
2 (*completely*) completamente; **to go right back to the beginning of sth** ricominciare qc da capo; **to go right to the end of sth** andare fino in fondo a qc; **to push sth right in** spingere qc fino in fondo; **to read a book right through** leggere un libro dall'inizio alla fine
3 (*correctly*) giusto, bene; (*well*) bene; **if I remember right** se mi ricordo bene; **if everything goes right** se tutto va bene; **did I pronounce it right?** l'ho pronunciato bene?
4 (*properly, fairly*) giustamente, con giustizia; **to treat sb right** trattare qn in modo giusto; **you did right not to go** hai fatto bene a non andarci
5 (*not left*) a destra; **turn right at the traffic lights** al semaforo gira a destra; **right, left and centre** (*fig*) da tutte le parti
6 **right, who's next?** bene, chi è il prossimo?; **right then, let's begin!** (va) bene allora, cominciamo!
7 **all right!** va bene!, d'accordo!; (*that's enough*) va bene!; **it's all right** (*don't worry*) va (tutto) bene; **it's all right for you!** già, facile per te!; **is it all right for me to go at 4?** va bene se me ne vado alle 4?; **I'm/I feel all right now** adesso sto/mi sento bene
■ N
1 **right and wrong** il bene e il male; **to be in the right** essere nel giusto; **to know right from wrong** distinguere il bene dal male; **I want to know the rights and wrongs of it** voglio sapere chi ha ragione e chi ha torto; **two wrongs don't make a right** due errori non ammontano a una cosa giusta
2 (*claim, authority*) diritto; **film rights** diritti *mpl* di riproduzione cinematografica; **to have a right to sth** aver diritto a qc; **you have a right to your own opinions** è tuo diritto pensarla come vuoi; **the right to be/say/do sth** il diritto di essere/dire/fare qc; **what right have you got to ...?** che diritto hai di...?; **you've got no right to do that** non hai diritto di farlo; **by rights** di diritto; **to be within one's rights** avere tutti i diritti; **to own sth in one's own right** possedere qc per conto proprio; **she's a good actress in her own right** è una brava attrice anche per conto suo
3 (*not left*) destra; (*Boxing: punch*) destro; **the Right** (*Pol*) la destra; **to the right (of)** sul lato destro (di); **on the right (of)** a destra (di)
4 **to set** *or* **put to rights** mettere a posto
■ VT (*correct: balance*) ristabilire; (*: wrong, injustice*) riparare a; (*vehicle, vessel*) raddrizzare; **to right itself** (*vehicle, vessel*) raddrizzarsi; (*situation*) risolversi da solo *or* da sé
■ EXCL bene!

right angle N angolo retto; **at right angles (to)** ad angolo retto (con)

right-angled ['raɪt,æŋgld] ADJ ad angolo retto; (*triangle*) rettangolo(-a)

right-click ['raɪtklɪk] VI (*Comput*) fare clic con il pulsante destro del mouse

right·eous ['raɪtʃəs] ADJ (*person*) virtuoso(-a), retto(-a); (*indignation, anger: moralistic*) un po' troppo virtuoso(-a); (*: justified*) giustificato(-a); **righteous indignation** giusta indignazione *f*

right·eous·ness ['raɪtʃəsnɪs] N rettitudine *f*, virtù

right·ful ['raɪtfʊl] ADJ (*heir*) legittimo(-a)

right·ful·ly ['raɪtfəlɪ] ADV legittimamente, a buon diritto

right-hand ['raɪt,hænd] ADJ (*side*) destro(-a); **right-hand drive** (*Aut*) guida a destra

right-handed [,raɪt'hændɪd] ADJ (*person*) destrimano(-a); **I'm right-handed** uso la destra

right-hander [,raɪt'hændə^r] N (*person*) chi usa *or* adopera la mano destra; (*blow*) destro

right-hand man N (*pl* **-men**) (*personal aide*) braccio destro

right-hand side N lato destro; **to be on the right-hand side** essere sulla destra

right·ist ['raɪtist] N persona di destra
■ ADJ di destra

right·ly ['raɪtlɪ] ADV (*correctly*) correttamente; (*with reason*) a ragione, giustamente; **she rightly decided that he was lying** concluse, giustamente, che lui mentiva; **I don't rightly know** non so di preciso; **if I remember rightly** se mi ricordo bene; **rightly or wrongly** a torto o a ragione

right-minded [,raɪt'maɪndɪd], **right-thinking** ['raɪt,θɪŋkɪŋ] ADJ di buon senso, sensato(-a)

righto, right oh ['raɪt'əʊ] EXCL (*Brit fam*) OK

right-of-centre [raɪtɒf'sɛntə^r] ADJ di centrodestra

right of way N (*across property*) diritto di accesso; (*Aut: precedence*) precedenza; **to have right of way** avere la precedenza

◎ **right-on** [,raɪt'ɒn] ADJ politicamente corretto(-a)

rights issue N (*Fin*) emissione *f* di azioni riservate agli azionisti, emissione *f* riservata agli azionisti

right to life N diritto alla vita

right·ward ['raɪtwəd], **rightwards** (*Pol*) ADJ (*trend, shift*) a destra
■ ADV a destra

right wing N: **the right wing** (*Pol*) la destra; (*Sport, Mil: position, person*) l'ala destra

◎ **right-wing** [,raɪt'wɪŋ] ADJ (*Pol*) di destra

right-winger [,raɪt'wɪŋə^r] N (*Pol*) uno(-a) di destra; (*Sport*) ala destra

rig·id ['rɪdʒɪd] ADJ (*material*) rigido(-a); (*discipline, specifications, principle*) rigoroso(-a); (*rules*) severo(-a); (*pej: person, ideas*) inflessibile; **rigid with fear** impietrito(-a) dalla paura

ri·gid·ity [rɪ'dʒɪdɪtɪ] N (*see adj*) rigidità; rigorosità; severità; inflessibilità

rig·id·ly ['rɪdʒɪdlɪ] ADV (*strictly*) rigorosamente; (*inflexibly*) inflessibilmente; (*closely*) rigidamente; **to stand rigidly to attention** stare impalato(-a) sull'attenti

rig·ma·role ['rɪgmə,rəʊl] N (*pej: speech*) storia, tiritera; (*: complicated procedure*) trafila

ri·gor ['rɪgə^r] N (*Am*) = **rigour**

rig·or mor·tis [,rɪgɔː'mɔːtɪs] N rigor mortis *m inv*

rig·or·ous ['rɪgərəs] ADJ rigoroso(-a)

rig·or·ous·ly ['rɪgərəslɪ] ADV (*apply, test*) rigorosamente

rig·our, (*Am*) **rig·or** ['rɪgə^r] N rigore *m*

rig·out ['rɪg,aʊt] N (*Brit fam old*) tenuta; **where are you going in that rigout?** dove vai conciato così ?

rile [raɪl] VT (*fam*) irritare, seccare

rim [rɪm] N (*of cup etc*) orlo; (*of wheel*) cerchione *m*; **the rim of a cup** l'orlo di una tazza; **rims** NPL (*of spectacles*) montatura *sg*; **glasses with wire rims** occhiali con montatura metallica

rim·less ['rɪmlɪs] ADJ (*spectacles*) senza montatura

rimmed ['rɪmd] ADJ (*with colour*) bordato(-a)

rind [raɪnd] N (*of fruit*) buccia; (*of lemon*) scorza; (*of cheese*) crosta; (*of bacon*) cotenna

ring[1] [rɪŋ] N **1** (*gen*) anello; (*for napkin*) portatovagliolo; **wedding ring** fede *f*; (*of smoke*) spirale *f*; **he gave her a silver ring** le ha regalato un anello d'argento; **the rings of Saturn** gli anelli di Saturno; **to run rings round sb** (*fig*) surclassare qn **2** (*of people, objects*) cerchio; (*gang*) cricca, banda; (*of spies*) rete *f*; **they were sitting in a ring** erano seduti in circolo *or* in cerchio **3** (*arena etc: Boxing*) ring *m inv*, quadrato; (: *at circus*) pista, arena
■VT (*surround*) circondare, accerchiare; (*mark with ring*) fare un cerchietto intorno a

◎**ring**[2] [rɪŋ] (*vb: pt* **rang**, *pp* **rung**) N **1** (*of bell*) trillo; (*of telephone*) squillo; (*tone of voice*) tono; **he answered at the first ring** ha risposto al primo squillo; **that has the ring of truth about it** questo ha l'aria d'essere vero **2** (*Brit Telec*): **to give sb a ring** dare un colpo di telefono a qn; telefonare a qn
■VT **1** (*bell, doorbell*) suonare; **to ring the bell** suonare il campanello; **to ring the changes** (*fig*) variare; **the name doesn't ring a bell (with me)** (*fig*) questo nome non mi dice niente **2** (*Brit Telec*): **to ring sb (up)** telefonare a qn, dare un colpo di telefono a qn
■VI **1** (*bell, telephone etc*) suonare; **the phone's ringing** sta squillando il telefono; **to ring for sb/sth** (suonare il campanello per) chiamare qn/chiedere qc **2** (*telephone*) telefonare; **your mother rang this morning** stamattina ha telefonato tua madre; **several friends have rung to congratulate me** mi hanno telefonato diversi amici per congratularsi **3** (*words, voice*) risuonare; (*blast*) rimbombare; (*ears*) fischiare; **their laughter rang through the room** le loro risate risuonavano nella stanza; **my ears are still ringing from the blast** mi fischiano ancora le orecchie per via dell'esplosione; **to ring true/false** (*fig*) suonare vero(-a)/falso(-a)
▸ **ring around** VI + ADV = **ring round** VI + ADV
▸ **ring back** VT + ADV (*Brit Telec*) richiamare; **I'll ring back later** richiamerò più tardi
▸ **ring in** VI + ADV (*Brit Telec*) telefonare
▸ **ring off** VI + ADV (*Brit Telec*) mettere giù, riattaccare
▸ **ring out** VI + ADV risuonare, riecheggiare
▸ **ring round** VI + ADV fare un giro di telefonate
■VT + ADV: **to ring round one's friends** telefonare a tutti gli amici
▸ **ring up** VT + ADV = **ring**[2] VT

ring binder N classificatore *m* ad anelli
ring finger N anulare *m*
ring·ing [ˈrɪŋɪŋ] ADJ (*voice, tone*) sonoro(-a)
■N (*of church bells*) scampanio; (*of door bell*) scampanellata; (*of telephone*) squillo; (*in ears*) fischio, ronzio
ringing tone N (*Brit Telec*) segnale *m* di libero
ring·leader [ˈrɪŋˌliːdəʳ] N (*of gang*) capobanda *m/f*
ring·let [ˈrɪŋlɪt] N boccolo
ring·master [ˈrɪŋˌmɑːstəʳ] N direttore *m* del circo
ring road N (*Brit*) circonvallazione *f*
ring·side [ˈrɪŋˌsaɪd] N prima fila
■ADJ in prima fila
ring tone N suoneria
ring·worm [ˈrɪŋˌwɜːm] N tigna
rink [rɪŋk] N (*for ice-skating*) pista di pattinaggio (su ghiaccio); (*for roller-skating*) pista di pattinaggio (a rotelle)
rinse [rɪns] N (ri)sciacquatura; (*quick*) (ri)sciacquata; (*hair-colouring*) cachet *m inv*; **to give sth a rinse** dare una sciacquata a qc
■VT (ri)sciacquare; **to rinse (the soap off) one's hands** sciacquarsi le mani
▸ **rinse out** VT + ADV sciacquare; **to rinse out one's mouth** sciacquarsi la bocca

Rio de Ja·nei·ro [ˌriːəʊdədʒəˈnɪərəʊ] N Rio de Janeiro *f*
◎**riot** [ˈraɪət] N disordini *mpl*; **a riot of colour(s)** un'orgia di colori; **to put down a riot** sopprimere i disordini; **to read sb the riot act** (*fam*) dare una lavata di capo a qn; **to run riot** (*out of control*) scatenarsi
■VI tumultuare, manifestare violentemente
ri·ot·er [ˈraɪətəʳ] N dimostrante *m/f* (*durante dei disordini*)
riot gear N (*Police*): **in riot gear** in assetto antisommossa
ri·ot·ing [ˈraɪətɪŋ] N disordini *mpl*
ri·ot·ous [ˈraɪətəs] ADJ (*person, mob, party*) scatenato(-a); (*living*) sfrenato(-a); (*very funny*) esilarante
ri·ot·ous·ly [ˈraɪətəslɪ] ADV sfrenatamente; **riotously funny** esilarante
riot police N ≈ la Celere
RIP [ˌɑːraɪˈpiː] ABBR (= **requiescat** *or* **requiescant in pace**: *may he, she, or they rest in peace*) RIP
rip [rɪp] N strappo
■VT strappare; **to rip sth to pieces** stracciare in mille pezzi qc; **to rip open** strappare (per aprire); **I accidentally ripped the envelope** senza volere ho strappato la busta; **I've ripped my jeans** mi si sono strappati i jeans
■VI strapparsi; **to let rip** (*fig*) scatenarsi; **to let rip at sb** dirne di tutti di colori a qn
▸ **rip off** VT + ADV **1** strappare **2** (*fam: overcharge*) pelare; (: *cheat*) fregare; **the hotel ripped us off** all'albergo ci hanno pelato
▸ **rip up** VT + ADV stracciare; **he read the note and then ripped it up** ha letto il biglietto e poi l'ha strappato

Rr

rip·cord [ˈrɪpˌkɔːd] N (*Aer*) cavo di spiegamento
ripe [raɪp] ADJ (*comp* **-r**, *superl* **-st**) (*gen, fruit*) maturo(-a); (*cheese*) stagionato(-a); **to be ripe for sth** (*fig*) essere pronto(-a) per qc; **to live to a ripe old age** vivere fino a una bella età
rip·en [ˈraɪpən] VT maturare
■VI maturarsi; (*cheese*) stagionarsi
ripe·ness [ˈraɪpnɪs] N maturazione *f*
rip-off [ˈrɪpˌɒf] N (*fam*): **it's a rip-off!** è un furto!
ri·poste [rɪˈpɒst] (*liter*) N replica
■VI replicare
ripper [ˈrɪpəʳ] N (*fam: murderer*) squartatore *m*; **Jack the Ripper** Jack lo squartatore; (*Comput*) programma *m* in grado di estrarre le tracce audio dai CD;
rip·ple [ˈrɪpl] N (*of water*) ondulazione *f*; (*small wave*) increspatura; (*noise: of voices*) mormorio; (: *of laughter*) fremito; **ripples on the lake** increspature sul lago; **a ripple of laughter** delle risate
■VT increspare; **the breeze rippled the water** la brezza increspava l'acqua
■VI incresparsi; **murmurs rippled through the audience** mormorii echeggiavano tra il pubblico
ripple tank N (*Phys*) serbatoio ad increspatura
rip-roaring [ˈrɪpˈrɔːrɪŋ] ADJ (*party, success*) travolgente
rip·tide [ˈrɪpˌtaɪd] N corrente *f* di ritorno
◎**rise** [raɪz] (*vb: pt* **rose**, *pp* **risen**) [rɪzn] N **1** (*increase: in prices, wages, inflation*): **rise (in)** aumento (di); **to ask for a rise** chiedere un aumento **2** (*of sun*) sorgere *m*; (*of theatre curtain*) alzarsi *m*; (*fig: ascendancy*) ascesa; **rise to power** ascesa al potere; **to take a rise out of sb** (*fam*) stuzzicare qn **3** (*upward slope*) salita, pendio; (*small hill*)

altura **4** (*origin: of river*) sorgente *f*; **to give rise to** (*fig*) dar origine a

■VI **1** (*get up*) alzarsi; (*fig: building*) sorgere; **to rise to one's feet** alzarsi in piedi; **he rose to his feet** si alzò in piedi; **the House rose** (*Parliament*) la seduta della Camera è stata tolta; **to rise to the occasion** dimostrarsi all'altezza della situazione **2** (*go higher: sun*) sorgere, levarsi; (*: smoke*) alzarsi, levarsi; (*: dough, cake*) crescere (di volume), lievitare; (*: ground*) salire; (*fig: spirits*) sollevarsi; **the plane rose to 4,000 metres** l'aereo si è alzato a 4.000 metri; **to rise from the ranks** (*Mil*) venir su dalla gavetta; **to rise from nothing** venir su dal niente; **he rose to be President** ascese alla carica di Presidente; **to rise to the surface** (*also fig*) venire a galla, affiorare; **to rise above sth** (*fig*) essere al di sopra di qc; **to rise to a higher sum** offrire di più, fare un'offerta più alta **3** (*increase: prices*) aumentare, rincarare; (*temperature, shares, numbers*) salire; (*wind, sea*) alzarsi; **prices rose sharply last month** i prezzi sono aumentati notevolmente il mese scorso; **his voice rose in anger** alzò la voce per la rabbia **4** (*river*) nascere; (*water*) salire

▸ **rise up** VI + ADV (*rebel*) sollevarsi, insorgere

ris·en [rɪzn] PP *of* **rise**

ris·er [ˈraɪzəʳ] N: **to be an early riser** essere mattiniero(-a); **to be a late riser** alzarsi sempre tardi

ris·ing [ˈraɪzɪŋ] ADJ **1** (*increasing: number*) sempre crescente; (*: prices*) in aumento; (*: tide*) montante; (*: anger, alarm, doubt*) crescente **2** (*getting higher: sun, moon*) nascente, che sorge; (*: ground*) in salita; (*fig: promising*) promettente

■N (*uprising*) sommossa

rising damp N infiltrazioni *fpl* d'umidità (*dal sottosuolo*)

rising star N (*also fig*) astro nascente

◎**risk** [rɪsk] N rischio; **fire/health/security risk** rischio d'incendio/per la salute/per la sicurezza; **to be a fire risk** essere una potenziale causa d'incendio; **there's not much risk of rain** non c'è pericolo che piova; **to take a risk** *or* **risks** correre un rischio *or* dei rischi, rischiare; **to run the risk of sth** correre il rischio di qc; **it's not worth the risk** non vale la pena di correre il rischio; **at risk** in pericolo; **to put sth at risk** mettere a repentaglio qc; **he put his job at risk** ha rischiato di giocarsi il posto; **at one's own risk** a proprio rischio e pericolo; **it's at your own risk** è a tuo rischio e pericolo; **at the risk of seeming stupid** a costo di sembrare stupido

■VT (*life, health, money*) rischiare, arrischiare; (*criticism, anger, defeat*) rischiare; **I'll risk it** ci proverò lo stesso; **to risk losing/being caught** rischiare di perdere/di esser preso(-a); **to risk one's neck** rischiare la pelle

risk capital N (*Fin*) capitale *m* di rischio

riski·ness [ˈrɪskɪnɪs] N rischiosità

risk management N gestione *f* del rischio

risky [ˈrɪskɪ] ADJ (*comp* **-ier**, *superl* **-iest**) rischioso(-a)

ris·qué [ˈriːskeɪ] ADJ audace, spinto(-a), osé *inv*

ris·sole [ˈrɪsəʊl] N (*Culin*) crocchetta

rite [raɪt] N rito; (*Rel*): **the last rites** l'estrema unzione *fsg*; **rite of passage** rito di passaggio

ritu·al [ˈrɪtjʊəl] ADJ, N rituale (*m*)

ritu·al·is·tic [ˌrɪtjʊəˈlɪstɪk] ADJ (*ritual*) rituale; (*nonsense*) di rito

ritu·al·ly [ˈrɪtjʊəlɪ] ADV ritualmente

◎**ri·val** [ˈraɪvəl] ADJ (*team*) rivale; (*firm*) concorrente; (*claim, attraction*) in concorrenza; **a rival gang** una banda rivale; **a rival company** una ditta concorrente

■N (*see adj*) rivale *m/f*; concorrente *m/f*

■VT rivaleggiare con; **to rival sb/sth in** competere con qn/qc in; **cassette recorders cannot rival the sound quality of CD players** i registratori a cassette non possono competere con la qualità del suono dei lettori CD

ri·val·ry [ˈraɪvəlrɪ] N rivalità *f inv*; (*in business*) concorrenza

riv·en [ˈrɪvən] ADJ (*old, frm*): **riven by** spaccato(-a) in due da

◎**riv·er** [ˈrɪvəʳ] N fiume *m*; **up/down river** a monte/valle; **across the river** dall'altra parte del fiume; **the River Thames** il Tamigi

■ADJ (*port, police, basin, traffic*) fluviale

river·bank [ˈrɪvəˌbæŋk] N sponda (del fiume), argine *m*

river·bed [ˈrɪvəˌbɛd] N letto del fiume

river fish N pesce *m* d'acqua dolce

river fishing N pesca fluviale

river head N sorgente *f* (del fiume)

river horse N (*fam*) ippopotamo

river·side [ˈrɪvəˌsaɪd] N: **the riverside** la riva *or* la sponda (del fiume); **by the riverside** in riva al fiume; **along the riverside** lungo il fiume

■ADJ: **a riverside café** un bar sul fiume

riv·et [ˈrɪvɪt] N ribattino, rivetto

■VT rivettare; (*fig: attention*) attirare; (*: audience*) inchiodare; **to be riveted by sth** essere terribilmente attratto(-a) da qc

riv·et·er [ˈrɪvɪtəʳ] N (*machine*) rivettatrice *f*

riv·et·ing [ˈrɪvɪtɪŋ] ADJ (*gripping*) avvincente

Rivi·era [ˌrɪvɪˈɛərə] N: **the Italian Riviera** la Riviera; la riviera ligure; **the French Riviera** la Costa Azzurra

rivu·let [ˈrɪvjʊlɪt] N (*frm*) rivolo

Ri·yadh [rɪˈjɑːd] N Riad *f*

RMT [ˌɑːrɛmˈtiː] N ABBR (= **Rail, Maritime and Transport**) *sindacato degli autoferrotranvieri e dei marittimi*

RN [ˌɑːrˈɛn] N ABBR **1** (*Brit*) = **Royal Navy** **2** (*Am*) = **registered nurse**

RNA [ˌɑːrɛnˈeɪ] N ABBR (*Biochemistry*: = **ribonucleic acid**) RNA

RNLI [ˌɑːrɛnˈɛlˈaɪ] N ABBR (*Brit*: = **Royal National Lifeboat Institution**) *associazione volontaria che organizza e dispone di scialuppe di salvataggio*

RNZAF [ˌɑːrɛnzɛdeɪˈɛf] N ABBR = *Royal New Zealand Air Force*

RNZN [ˌɑːrɛnzɛdˈɛn] N ABBR = *Royal New Zealand Navy*

◎**road** [rəʊd] N (*route, fig*) strada, via; (*residential: Road*) via; **main road** strada principale; **A-/B-road** ≈ strada statale/secondaria; **country road** strada di campagna; **it takes 4 hours by road** sono 4 ore di macchina (*or* in camion *etc*); **just across the road (from)** proprio di fronte a; **to be off the road** (*car: for repairs*) essere in riparazione; (*: laid up*) essere fuori uso; **he shouldn't be allowed on the road** dovrebbero togliergli la patente; **that car shouldn't be allowed on the road** non dovrebbero lasciar circolare quella macchina; **to hold the road** (*Aut*) tenere la strada; **"road up"** "attenzione: lavori in corso"; **to be on the road** (*pop group*) essere in tournée; (*salesman*) viaggiare; **on the road to success** sulla via del successo; **to take to the road** (*tramp*) darsi al vagabondaggio; **to have one for the road** (*fam*) bere il bicchiere della staffa; **somewhere along the road** (*fig*) a un certo punto

■ADJ (*accident, sign*) stradale

road·block [ˈrəʊdˌblɒk] N blocco stradale

road haulage N autotrasporti *mpl*
road haulier N autotrasportatore *m*
road·hog ['rəʊd,hɒg] N *(fam pej) automobilista che guida tenendosi al centro della strada così da impedire il sorpasso*
road·hold·ing ['rəʊd,həʊldɪŋ] N *(Auto)* tenuta di strada
road·house ['rəʊd,haʊs] N *posto di ristoro lungo la strada*
roadie ['rəʊdɪ] N *incaricato del trasporto e del montaggio delle attrezzature di un gruppo musicale*
road kill N *animale o uccello ucciso accidentalmente da un veicolo*
road manager N *(of singer)* organizzatore(-trice) di tournée; *(of sports player)* organizzatore(-trice) di trasferte
road map N carta stradale, carta automobilistica; *(fig)* piano dettagliato; **a road map to peace** un piano di pace
road movie N road movie *m inv*
road pricing [-'praɪsɪŋ] N *sistema elettronico di pagamento di pedaggio per autoveicoli*
road racer, road rider N *(Cycling)* stradista *m/f*
road rage N aggressività al volante
road·roller ['rəʊd,rəʊlə^r] N rullo compressore
road safety N sicurezza sulle strade
road sense N attitudine *f* alla guida; **to teach a child road sense** insegnare a un bambino a guardarsi dai pericoli della strada
road show N spettacolo di tournée
road·side ['rəʊd,saɪd] N ciglio della strada; **by the roadside** a lato della strada
road sign N cartello stradale
road·sweeper ['rəʊd,swi:pə^r] N *(Brit: person)* spazzino; *(: vehicle)* autospazzatrice *f*
road tax N *(Auto)* tassa di circolazione
road tax disk N *(Auto)* bollo (di circolazione)
road test N prova su strada
road-test ['rəʊd,tɛst] VT provare su strada
road transport N autotrasporti *mpl*
road user N utente *m/f* della strada
road·way ['rəʊdweɪ] N carreggiata
road works NPL lavori *mpl* stradali; *(on road sign)* "lavori in corso"
road·worthy ['rəʊd,wɜ:ðɪ] ADJ *(vehicle)* in buono stato di marcia
roam [rəʊm] VT *(streets)* vagabondare per, gironzolare per, vagare per; **children who roamed the streets** bambini che vagavano per le vie
■ VI *(person)* vagabondare, errare, gironzolare; *(thoughts)* vagare; **we roamed far and wide** abbiamo vagato in lungo e in largo
roaming ['rəʊmɪŋ] ADJ vagabondo(-a); *(Telec, Comput)* roaming *m*
roan [rəʊn] ADJ roano(-a)
■ N *(horse)* roano
roar [rɔ:^r] N *(of lion)* ruggito; *(of bull)* mugghio; *(of crowd)* urlo, tumulto; *(of waves)* fragore *m*; *(of wind, storm)* muggito; *(of thunder)* rimbombo; **the roar of the crowd** il tumulto della folla; **the roar of a lion** il ruggito di un leone; **with great roars of laughter** con fragorose risate
■ VI *(lion)* ruggire; *(bull)* mugghiare; *(crowd, audience)* urlare, fare tumulto; *(wind, storm)* muggire; *(thunder)* rimbombare; *(guns)* tuonare; **to roar with laughter** ridere fragorosamente; **the lorry roared past** il camion passò rombando; **the crowd roared** la folla era in tumulto; **lions roar** il leone ruggisce
roar·ing ['rɔ:rɪŋ] ADJ *(lion)* ruggente; *(bull)* mugghiante; *(crowd)* urlante; *(sea, thunder)* fragoroso(-a); **a roaring fire** un bel fuoco, una bella fiammata; **a roaring success** un successo strepitoso; **to do a roaring trade** fare affari d'oro; **roaring drunk** ubriaco(-a) fradicio(-a)
roast [rəʊst] N arrosto
■ ADJ arrosto *inv*; **roast beef** arrosto di manzo; **roast chicken** pollo arrosto; **roast pork** arrosto di maiale
■ VT *(meat)* arrostire; *(coffee)* tostare
■ VI arrostire; **I'm roasting!** *(fam)* sto crepando dal caldo!
roast beef N arrosto di manzo
roast·ing ['rəʊstɪŋ] ADJ **1** *(chicken)* da fare arrosto; *(pan)* per arrosti **2** *(fam)*: **a roasting (hot) day** una giornata torrida
■ N *(fam)*: **to give sb a roasting** dare una lavata di capo a qn
rob [rɒb] VT *(person)* derubare; *(with weapon)* rapinare; *(till, bank)* svaligiare; **to rob sb of sth** *(money)* derubare qn di qc, rubare qc a qn; *(fig: happiness, right)* privare qn di qc; **he was robbed of his wallet** gli hanno rubato il portafoglio; **I've been robbed!** mi hanno derubato!; **to rob a bank** rapinare una banca
rob·ber ['rɒbə^r] N ladro(-a); *(armed)* rapinatore(-trice)
rob·bery ['rɒbərɪ] N furto; *(armed robbery)* rapina (a mano armata); **robbery with violence** *(Law)* furto con aggressione; **a bank robbery** una rapina in banca; **he was arrested for robberies on trains** è stato arrestato per aver commesso vari furti sui treni; **it's daylight robbery!** *(fam)* (ma) è una rapina!
robe [rəʊb] N *(garment)* tunica; *(also:* **bathrobe***)* accappatoio; *(also:* **robes***)* abiti *mpl* da cerimonia; *(lawyer's, Univ)* toga; **scarlet robes** abiti *mpl* scarlatti; **a towelling robe** un accappatoio di spugna
■ VT *(frm)* vestire

DID YOU KNOW ...?
robe is not translated by the Italian word *roba*

rob·in ['rɒbɪn] N pettirosso
Robin Hood [,rɒbɪn'hʊd] N Robin Hood *m*
▷ www.legends.dm.net/robinhood/
ro·bot ['rəʊbɒt] N robot *m inv*, automa *m*
ro·bot·ics [rəʊ'bɒtɪks] NSG robotica
ro·bust [rəʊ'bʌst] ADJ robusto(-a); *(material)* solido(-a)
◎ **rock** [rɒk] N **1** *(gen)* roccia; *(large stone, boulder)* roccia, masso; *(in sea)* scoglio; **the Rock of Gibraltar** la Rocca di Gibilterra; **I sat on a rock** mi sono seduto(-a) su una roccia; **the crowd started to throw rocks** la folla cominciò a lanciare sassi; **on the rocks** *(drink)* con ghiaccio; **their marriage is on the rocks** il loro matrimonio sta naufragando **2 stick of rock** *(Brit: sweet)* bastoncino di zucchero caramellato **3** *(Mus)* rock *m*
■ VT *(gently: cradle, boat)* far dondolare; *(: baby)* cullare; *(violently: boat)* sballottare; *(subj: earthquake)* squassare; *(fig: shake, startle)* sconvolgere, far tremare; **to rock the boat** *(fig fam)* piantare grane; **the tremor rocked the building** la scossa ha fatto oscillare l'edificio
■ VI *(gently)* dondolare; *(violently)* oscillare
rock and roll N rock and roll *m*
▷ www.bbc.co.uk/radio2/soldonsong/genres/rock.shtml
rock-bottom ['rɒk'bɒtəm] N *(fig)*: **to reach** *or* **touch rock-bottom** *(person)* toccare il fondo; *(price)* raggiungere il livello più basso; **morale was at rock-bottom** il morale era a terra; **prices have hit rock-bottom** i prezzi sono scesi tantissimo

Rr

rock cake N (*Brit*: *bun*) brutto ma buono
rock climber N rocciatore(-trice), scalatore(-trice)
rock climbing N (*Sport*) roccia
rock concert N concerto *m* rock *inv*
rock crystal N cristallo di roccia
rock·er ['rɒkəʳ] N (*chair*) sedia a dondolo; **to be off one's rocker** (*fam*) essere pazzo(-a)
rock·ery ['rɒkərɪ] N giardino roccioso
◎ **rock·et[1]** ['rɒkɪt] N razzo; **to fire** *or* **send up a rocket** lanciare un razzo; **to give sb a rocket** (*fig fam*) fare un cicchetto a qn
■ VI (*prices*) salire alle stelle
rock·et[2] ['rɒkɪt] **1** N (*Bot*) ruchetta, rucola **2** (*Culin*) rucola
rocket launcher N lanciarazzi *m inv*
rock·et·ry ['rɒkɪtrɪ] N (*science*) missilistica; (*rockets collectively*) missili *mpl*
rocket science N: **it's not rocket science** non è niente di trascendentale
rocket scientist N (*scientist*) ingegnere *m* astronautico; (*fig*) esperto(-a); **it doesn't take a rocket scientist to...** non ci vuole un esperto per ...
rock face N parete *f* di roccia
rock fall N caduta (di) massi
rock garden N = **rockery**
rock-hard [rɒk'hɑːd] ADJ duro(-a) come la pietra
rock·ing chair ['rɒkɪŋ,tʃɛəʳ] N sedia a dondolo
rock·ing horse ['rɒkɪŋ,hɔːs] N cavallo a dondolo
rock plant N pianta rupestre
rock salmon N blennio
rock salt N salgemma *m*
rock star N rock star *f inv*
rocky[1] ['rɒkɪ] ADJ (*comp* **-ier**, *superl* **-iest**) (*hill*) roccioso(-a); (*path*) sassoso(-a)
rocky[2] ['rɒkɪ] ADJ (*comp* **-ier**, *superl* **-iest**) (*shaky, unsteady*) malfermo(-a), traballante; (*fig: situation, marriage*) instabile; **their relationship got off to a rocky start** la loro relazione ha avuto un inizio difficile
Rocky Mountains NPL: **the Rocky Mountains** le Montagne Rocciose
▷ www.nps.gov/romo/
ro·co·co [rəʊ'kəʊkəʊ] ADJ, N rococò (*m*) *inv*
rod [rɒd] N (*wooden, plastic*) bacchetta; (*metallic, Tech*) asta, sbarra; (*fishing rod*) canna da pesca; (*curtain rod*) bastone *m*; **to rule with a rod of iron** comandare a bacchetta
rode [rəʊd] PT *of* ride
ro·dent ['rəʊdənt] N roditore *m*
ro·deo ['rəʊdɪəʊ] N rodeo
roe [rəʊ] N (*of fish*): **hard roe** uova *fpl* di pesce; **soft roe** latte *m* di pesce
roe·buck ['rəʊ,bʌk] N capriolo maschio
roe deer ['rəʊ,dɪəʳ] N (*species*) capriolo; (*female deer*: *pl inv*) capriolo femmina
rogue [rəʊg] N mascalzone *m*; **rogues' gallery** foto *fpl* di pregiudicati
■ ADJ (*elephant*) solitario(-a)
rogue state N (*Pol*) stato *m* canaglia *inv*
ro·guish ['rəʊgɪʃ] ADJ (*look, smile*) malizioso(-a); (*child*) birichino(-a)
ro·guish·ly ['rəʊgɪʃlɪ] ADV (*smile, wink*) maliziosamente
◎ **role** [rəʊl] N ruolo
role-model ['rəʊl,mɒdl] N modello (di comportamento)
role play, role playing N il recitare un ruolo, role-playing *m inv*; **to do a role play** fare un gioco di ruolo

◎ **roll** [rəʊl] N
1 (*of paper, wire*) rotolo; (*of hair*) chignon *m inv*; (*of banknotes*) mazzo; (*of film*) rullino; (*of cloth*) pezza, rotolo; (*of fat, flesh*) cuscinetto; **a roll of film** un rullino fotografico; **a toilet roll** un rotolo di carta igienica
2 (*also:* **bread roll**) panino; **cheese roll** panino al formaggio
3 (*list*) lista; **to have 500 pupils on the roll** avere 500 iscritti (alla scuola)
4 (*sound*: *of thunder*) rombo; (*of drums*) rullio, rullo
5 (*movement*: *of ship, plane*) rollio
■ VT (*ball*) (far) rotolare; (*road, lawn, pitch*) cilindrare, rullare; (*cigarette*) rollare; (*also:* **roll out**: *pastry*) spianare, stendere; (: *metal*) laminare; **roll the meatballs in breadcrumbs** passare le polpette nel pangrattato; **to roll one's eyes** roteare gli occhi; **to roll one's r's** arrotare la erre; **he can't roll his r's** ha la erre moscia
■ VI
1 (*turn over*) rotolare; (*dog, horse*) rotolarsi; (*in pain*) contorcersi; **it rolled under the chair** è rotolato sotto la seggiola; **tears rolled down her cheeks** le lacrime le scendevano sulle guance; **the ball rolled into the net** la palla rotolò in rete; **they're rolling in money** *or* **they're rolling in it** (*fam*) sono ricchi sfondati
2 (*sound*: *thunder*) rombare; (: *drum*) rullare
3 (*ship*) rollare
▸ **roll about, roll around** VI + ADV (*ball, coin*) rotolare qua e là; (*person, dog*) rotolarsi; (*in pain*) contorcersi
▸ **roll away** VI + ADV (*ball*) rotolare (via); (*clouds, vehicle*) allontanarsi
▸ **roll back** VT + ADV arrotolare, togliere arrotolando
▸ **roll by** VI + ADV (*vehicle, years*) passare
▸ **roll in** VI + ADV (*money, letters*) continuare ad arrivare; (*fam: person*) arrivare
▸ **roll on** VI + ADV (*time*) passare; **roll on the holidays!** venite presto, vacanze!
▸ **roll out** VT + ADV (*pastry*) spianare; (*carpet, map*) srotolare, spiegare
▸ **roll over** VI + ADV (*object*) rotolare; (*person, animal*) (ri)girarsi, (ri)voltarsi
▸ **roll up** VI + ADV
1 (*animal*): **to roll up into a ball** appallottolarsi
2 (*arrive*) arrivare; **roll up!** venite, venite!
■ VT + ADV (*cloth, map, carpet*) arrotolare; (*sleeves*) rimboccare; **to roll o.s. up into a ball** raggomitolarsi
roll bar N (*Auto*) roll bar *m inv*
roll call N appello; **a roll call of** un elenco di
rolled gold [,rəʊld'gəʊld] N oro laminato
■ ADJ laminato(-a) oro *inv*
roll·er ['rəʊləʳ] N **1** (*gen*) rullo, cilindro; (*in metallurgy*) laminatoio; (*roadroller*) rullo compressore; (*castor*) rotella; (*for hair*) bigodino **2** (*wave*) cavallone *m*
Roller·blades® ['rəʊlə,bleɪdz] NPL pattini *mpl* in linea
roller blind N (*Brit*) avvolgibile *m*
roller coaster N montagne *fpl* russe
roller·skate ['rəʊlə,skeɪt] VI pattinare a rotelle
roller skates NPL pattini *mpl* a rotelle
roller skating N pattinaggio a rotelle
roller towel N asciugamano a rullo
rol·lick·ing ['rɒlɪkɪŋ] ADJ (*person*) incredibilmente esuberante; (*party*) allegro(-a) e chiassoso(-a); **to have a rollicking time** divertirsi pazzamente
roll·ing ['rəʊlɪŋ] ADJ (*waves, sea*) ondeggiante; (*countryside*) ondulato(-a)
rolling mill N fabbrica di laminati
rolling pin N matterello
rolling stock N (*Rail*) materiale *m* rotabile

rolling stone N (*fig*) vagabondo(-a)
roll·neck ['rəʊl,nɛk] ADJ a dolce vita
■ N dolcevita
roll of honour N (*Brit*) albo d'onore
roll-on ['rəʊl,ɒn] N (*corset*) panciera
roll-on-roll-off [,rəʊlɒnrəʊl'ɒf] ADJ (*Brit: ferry*) roll-on roll-off *inv*
roll·over ['rəʊl,əʊvəʳ] N (*prize*) premio rimesso in gioco; (*Fin*) rifinanziamento; **it's a rollover week** il premio della scorsa settimana è stato rimesso in gioco
roll-top ['rəʊl,tɒp] ADJ: **roll-top desk** scrittoio con alzata avvolgibile
roll-up ['rəʊl,ʌp] N sigaretta fatta a mano; **to make a roll-up** arrotolarsi una sigaretta
roly-poly ['rəʊlɪ'pəʊlɪ] N (*Brit Culin*) *rotolo di pasta con ripieno di marmellata*
ROM [rɒm] N ABBR (*Comput:* = **read-only memory**) ROM *f inv*
Ro·man ['rəʊmən] ADJ romano(-a); **the Roman empire** l'impero romano
■ N (*person*) Romano(-a); (*Typ*): **roman** (carattere *m*) romano; **the Romans** i romani
Roman alphabet N: **the Roman alphabet** l'alfabeto latino
Roman Catholic ADJ, N cattolico(-a)
▷ www.vatican.va/phome_en.htm
Ro·mance [rəʊ'mæns] ADJ (*language*) romanzo(-a)
ro·mance [rəʊ'mæns] N **1** (*love affair*) storia d'amore; **a holiday romance** un amore estivo **2** (*romantic character*) fascino, romanticismo; **the romance of Paris** il fascino di Parigi **3** (*love story*) romanzo *m* rosa *inv*; (*film*) film *m inv* d'amore; (*medieval*) romanzo (cavalleresco); (*Mus*) romanza; **she writes romances** scrive romanzi rosa
Ro·man·esque [,rəʊmə'nɛsk] ADJ (*Archit*) romanico(-a)
Ro·ma·nia, **Ru·ma·nia**, **Rou·ma·nia** [rəʊ'meɪnɪə] N Romania
Ro·ma·nian, **Ru·ma·nian**, **Rou·ma·nian** [rəʊ'meɪnɪən] ADJ romeno(-a)
■ N (*person*) romeno(-a); (*language*) romeno
Ro·man·ism ['rəʊmə,nɪzəm] N romanismo
Roman nose N naso aquilino
Roman numerals N numeri *mpl* romani
◎ **ro·man·tic** [rəʊ'mæntɪk] ADJ, N romantico(-a)
ro·man·ti·cal·ly [rəʊ'mæntɪkəlɪ] ADV romanticamente
ro·man·ti·cism [rəʊ'mæntɪ,sɪzəm] N (*Art*) romanticismo
ro·man·ti·cize [rəʊ'mæntɪ,saɪz] VT romanzare
Roma·ny ['rɒmənɪ] ADJ zingaresco(-a)
■ N (*person*) zingaro(-a); (*language*) lingua degli zingari
rom·com ['rɒm,kɒm] N (*fam:* = **romantic comedy**) commedia romantica
Rome [rəʊm] N Roma *f*; **the Church of Rome** la Chiesa Romana; **when in Rome (do as the Romans do)** paese che vai usanze che trovi
romp [rɒmp] N gioco chiassoso
■ VI (*also:* **romp about**: *children, puppies*) giocare chiassosamente; **she romped through the examination** (*fig*) ha passato l'esame a occhi chiusi; **to romp home** (*horse*) vincere senza difficoltà, stravincere

DID YOU KNOW ...?
romp is not translated by the Italian word *rompere*

romp·ers ['rɒmpəz] NPL tutina, pagliaccetto
Romulus ['rɒmjʊləs] N Romolo
ron·do ['rɒndəʊ] N (*Mus*) rondò *m inv*
◎ **roof** [ru:f] N tetto; (*of tunnel, cave*) volta; **a sloping roof** un tetto spiovente; **roof of the mouth** palato; **to have a roof over one's head** avere un tetto sopra la testa; **we live under the same roof** viviamo sotto lo stesso tetto; **to go through the roof** (*fig: person*) andare su tutte le furie; (*: price*) salire alle stelle
■ VT (*also:* **roof in, roof over**) mettere *or* fare il tetto a
roof garden N giardino pensile
roof·ing ['ru:fɪŋ] N materiale *m* per copertura
roof rack N (*Aut*) portapacchi *m inv*, portabagagli *m inv*
roof terrace N tetto a terrazza
roof·top ['ru:f,tɒp] N tetto
rook¹ [rʊk] N (*bird*) corvo
■ VT (*fam: swindle*) imbrogliare, truffare
rook² [rʊk] N (*Chess*) torre *f*
rook·ery ['rʊkərɪ] N colonia di corvi
rookie ['rʊkɪ] N (*Mil fam*) burba
◎ **room** [rʊm] N **1** (*in house*) stanza, camera; (*in property adverts*) locale *m*, vano; (*bedroom, in hotel*) camera; (*large, public, in school*) sala; **rooms** NPL (*lodging*) alloggio *msg*; **"rooms to let"** (*Am*): **"rooms for rent"** "si affittano camere"; **a 5-roomed house** una casa di 5 locali; **the biggest room in the house** la stanza più grande della casa; **she's in her room** è in camera sua; **a single room** una camera singola; **a double room** una camera doppia; **the music room** la sala musica; **they've always lived in rooms** hanno sempre abitato in camere ammobiliate **2** (*space*) spazio, posto; **is there room for this?** c'è spazio per questo?, ci sta anche questo?; **is there room for me?** c'è posto per me?, ci sto anch'io?; **there's no room for that box** non c'è posto per quella scatola; **to make room for sb** far posto a qn; **standing room only** solo posti in piedi; **there is no room for doubt** non c'è nessuna possibilità di dubbio; **there is room for improvement** si potrebbe migliorare
room·ful ['rʊmfʊl] N stanza piena
room·ing house ['rʊmɪŋ,haʊs] N (*Am*) casa con camere ammobiliate
room·mate ['rʊm,meɪt] N compagno(-a) di stanza
room service N servizio in camera
room temperature N temperatura ambiente
roomy ['rʊmɪ] ADJ (*comp* **-ier**, *superl* **-iest**) (*flat, cupboard etc*) spazioso(-a); (*garment*) ampio(-a)
roost [ru:st] N posatoio; **to rule the roost** dettar legge
■ VI appollaiarsi; **now the chickens are coming home to roost!** (*fig*) ora arriva il momento della resa dei conti!
roost·er ['ru:stəʳ] N gallo
◎ **root** [ru:t] N (*gen, Math*) radice *f*; **repeated root** (*Math*) radice *f* multipla; **to pull up by the roots** sradicare; **to take root** (*plant*) attecchire, prendere; (*idea*) far presa; **the root of the problem is that ...** il problema deriva dal fatto che...; **to put down roots in a country** mettere radici in un paese
■ VT (*plant*) far fare le radici a, far radicare; **to be rooted to the spot** (*fig*) rimanere inchiodato(-a) sul posto
■ VI (*Bot*) attecchire, mettere radici
▸ **root about**, **root around** VI + ADV (*fig*) frugare, rovistare
▸ **root for** VI + PREP (*Am fam*) fare il tifo per
▸ **root out** VT + ADV (*find*) scovare, pescare; (*remove*) eradicare, estirpare; **they are determined to root out corruption** sono decisi a eliminare la corruzione
▸ **root up** VT + ADV sradicare
root beer N (*Am*) *bibita dolce a base di estratti di erbe e radici*

Rr

root canal N (*Med*) canale *m* radicolare; **root canal work** (*of tooth*) devitalizzazione *f*, cura canalare
root cause N causa prima
root crops NPL tuberi *mpl or* radici *fpl* commestibili
root hairs NPL (*Bot*) peli *mpl* radicali
root·less ['ru:tlɪs] ADJ (*person*) senza radici
root nodules NPL (*Bot*) noduli *mpl* radicali
root word N radice *f*
rope [rəʊp] N fune *f*, corda; (*Naut*) cima, cavo; **to give sb more rope** (*fig*) allentare le redini a qn; **to know/learn the ropes** (*fig*) conoscere/imparare i segreti *or* i trucchi del mestiere; **a rope of pearls** una lunga collana di perle; **a rope of climbers** una cordata di alpinisti
■VT legare (con una fune *or* una corda); **the climbers were roped together** i rocciatori erano legati assieme
▶ **rope in** VT + ADV (*fam fig*): **to rope sb in to help** tirar dentro qn per aiutare; **I was roped in to help with the refreshments** mi hanno tirato dentro a dare una mano con i rinfreschi
▶ **rope off** VT + ADV isolare con dei cordoni
▶ **rope up** VI + ADV (*Mountaineering*) legarsi in cordata
rope ladder N scala di corda
ropy, ropey ['rəʊpɪ] ADJ (*comp* **-ier**, *superl* **-iest**) (*fam*) scadente; **to feel rop(e)y** (*ill*) sentirsi male
ro·sary ['rəʊzərɪ] N **1** (*Rel*) rosario; **to say** *or* **recite the rosary** dire *or* recitare il rosario **2** (*rose garden*) roseto
rose¹ [rəʊz] N **1** (*flower, colour*) rosa; (*also:* **rose bush**) rosaio; **my life isn't all roses** (*fam*) la mia vita non è tutta rose e fiori **2** (*on shower, watering can*) bulbo (forato); (*on ceiling*) rosone *m*
■ADJ (*rose-coloured*) rosa *inv*
◎**rose²** [rəʊz] PT *of* **rise**
rosé ['rəʊzeɪ] N, ADJ rosé (*m*) *inv*
rose·bay ['rəʊz,beɪ] N (*Bot*): **rosebay willowherb** camenerio, epilobio
rose·bed ['rəʊz,bɛd] N rosaio, roseto
rose·bud ['rəʊz,bʌd] N bocciolo di rosa
rose-coloured ['rəʊz,kʌləd] ADJ color rosa *inv*; **to see sth through rose-coloured spectacles** (*fig*) vedere tutto rosa
rose garden N roseto
rose grower N rosicoltore *m*
rose·hip ['rəʊz,hɪp] N frutto della rosa canina
rose·mary ['rəʊzmərɪ] N rosmarino
rose quartz N quarzo rosa
rose-red ['rəʊz'rɛd] ADJ vermiglio(-a)
ro·sette [rəʊ'zɛt] N (*emblem, as prize*) coccarda; (*Archit*) rosone *m*
rose window N rosone *m* (*vetrata*)
rose·wood ['rəʊz,wʊd] N palissandro
ROSPA ['rɒspə] N ABBR (*Brit*) = *Royal Society for the Prevention of Accidents*
ros·ter ['rɒstə^r] N = **rota**
ros·trum ['rɒstrəm] N podio, tribuna
rosy ['rəʊzɪ] ADJ (*comp* **-ier**, *superl* **-iest**) roseo(-a); **to paint a rosy picture of sth** (*fig*) dipingere qc a tinte rosa
rot [rɒt] N (*decay*) putrefazione *f*, marciume *m*; (*fam: nonsense*) fesserie *fpl*, stupidaggini *fpl*; **the rot has set in** (*fig*) le cose hanno cominciato a guastarsi; **to stop the rot** (*Brit fig*) salvare la situazione; **dry/wet rot** *funghi parassiti del legno*
■VT far marcire; **sugar rots your teeth** lo zucchero caria i denti
■VI: **to rot (away)** marcire, imputridire; **the wood had rotted** il legno era marcito

Rota ['rəʊtə] N (*Rel*): **the Rota** il Tribunale della Sacra Rota
rota ['rəʊtə] N tabella dei turni; **on a rota basis** a turno; **we worked out a rota** abbiamo elaborato una tabella di turni
ro·ta·ry ['rəʊtərɪ] ADJ (*movement*) rotatorio(-a); (*blades*) rotante
ro·tate [rəʊ'teɪt] VT (*revolve*) far girare; (*change round: crops, staff*) avvicendare, fare la rotazione di; **rotate your hips** fai ruotare i fianchi; **to rotate crops** fare la rotazione delle colture
■VI (*wheel, Earth*) ruotare, girare; (*staff etc*) alternarsi, avvicendarsi; **the earth rotates round the sun** la terra ruota intorno al sole; **the presidency rotates** vi è un avvicendamento della presidenza
ro·tat·ing [rəʊ'teɪtɪŋ] ADJ (*revolving*) rotante
ro·ta·tion [rəʊ'teɪʃən] N rotazione *f*; **in rotation** a turno, in rotazione; **rotation of crops** rotazione *f* delle colture
rote [rəʊt] N: **to learn sth by rote** imparare qc a memoria; **rote learning** l'imparare *m* a memoria
ro·tor ['rəʊtə^r] N rotore *m*
rotor arm N (*Aut*) spazzola rotante
rot·ten ['rɒtn] ADJ **1** (*fruit, eggs*) marcio(-a); (*meat*) andato(-a) a male; (*tooth*) cariato(-a); (*wood*) marcio(-a), marcito(-a); (*fig: morally*) corrotto(-a), marcio(-a); **rotten to the core** completamente marcio(-a) **2** (*fam: bad*) schifoso(-a), brutto(-a); (*action*) vigliacco(-a); **rotten weather** tempo da cani; **what rotten luck!** che scalogna!; **what a rotten thing to do!** che vigliaccata!, che carognata!; **I feel rotten** (*ill*) mi sento da cani; (*mean*) mi sento un verme

DID YOU KNOW ...?
rotten is not translated by the Italian word *rotto*

rotten apple N mela marcia
rot·ter ['rɒtə^r] N (*Brit old fam*) mascalzone(-a)
rot·ting ['rɒtɪŋ] ADJ in putrefazione
ro·tund [rəʊ'tʌnd] ADJ (*frm: person*) pingue; (*: object*) arrotondato(-a)
ro·tun·da [rəʊ'tʌndə] N rotonda
rou·ble, (*Am*) **ru·ble** ['ru:bl] N rublo
rouge [ru:ʒ] N belletto
◎**rough** [rʌf] ADJ (*comp* **-er**, *superl* **-est**) **1** (*uneven: ground, road, path, edge*) accidentato(-a); (*not smooth: skin, cloth, surface, hands*) ruvido(-a); **my hands are rough** ho le mani ruvide **2** (*voice*) rauco(-a); (*taste, wine*) aspro(-a); (*coarse, unrefined: person, manners, life*) rozzo(-a); (*harsh: person, game*) violento(-a); (*neighbourhood*) poco raccomandabile, malfamato(-a); (*sea crossing, weather*) brutto(-a); **rugby's a rough sport** il rugby è uno sport violento; **the sea is rough today** c'è mare grosso oggi, il mare è mosso oggi; **I don't want any rough stuff!** (*fam*) niente risse!; **it's a rough area** è una zona poco raccomandabile; **a rough customer** (*fam*) un duro; **to have a rough time (of it)** passare un periodaccio; **to give sb a rough time (of it)** rendere la vita dura a qn; **it's rough on him** che sfortuna per lui; **to feel rough** (*Brit fam*) sentirsi male **3** (*calculation, figures*) approssimativo(-a), approssimato(-a); (*plan*) sommario(-a); **rough work** *or* **rough draft** *or* **rough copy** brutta copia; **rough sketch** schizzo; **rough estimate** approssimazione *f*; **at a rough guess** *or* **estimate** ad occhio e croce; **I've got a rough idea** ne ho un'idea approssimativa; **he's a rough diamond** sotto quei modi un po' grezzi si nasconde un cuore d'oro

■ ADV: **to play rough** (*Sport*) giocare pesante; (*children*) fare dei giochi violenti; **to sleep rough** (*Brit*) dormire all'addiaccio, dormire per strada; **a lot of people sleep rough in London** a Londra tanta gente dorme per strada; **to live rough** vivere in strada
■ N **1** (*fam: person*) duro **2 to take the rough with the smooth** prendere le cose come vengono **3** (*Golf*) erba alta, macchia
■ VT: **to rough it** (*fam*) far vita dura
▸ **rough out** VT + ADV (*draft, plan*) fare un abbozzo di, abbozzare
▸ **rough up** VT + ADV (*fam*): **to rough sb up** malmenare qn
rough·age ['rʌfɪdʒ] N fibre *fpl*
rough-and-ready [,rʌfənd'rɛdɪ] ADJ rudimentale
rough-and-tumble [,rʌfən'tʌmbl] N zuffa
rough·cast ['rʌf,kɑːst] N intonaco grezzo
rough·en ['rʌfn] VT (*a surface*) rendere ruvido(-a), irruvidire
rough-hewn [,rʌf'hjuːn] ADJ (*stone*) sgrossato(-a)
rough-house ['rʌf,haʊs] N (*fam*) zuffa, baruffa
rough justice N giustizia sommaria
rough·ly ['rʌflɪ] ADV **1** (*not gently: push, handle*) brutalmente; (*: speak, order*) bruscamente; **to treat sb/sth roughly** maltrattare qn/qc **2** (*not finely: make, sew*) grossolanamente; **to chop roughly** tagliare a pezzi grossi; **roughly chop the tomatoes and peppers** tagliare i pomodori e i peperoni a pezzi grossi; **to sketch sth roughly** fare uno schizzo di qc **3** (*approximately*) grosso modo, approssimativamente, pressappoco; **roughly speaking** grosso modo, ad occhio e croce; **there were roughly 50 people** c'erano pressappoco 50 persone; **it weighs roughly twenty kilos** pesa pressapoco venti chili
rough·neck ['rʌf,nɛk] N (*Am fam*) duro, bestione *m*
rough·ness ['rʌfnɪs] N (*of hands, surface*) ruvidità, ruvidezza; (*of person: abruptness*) modi *mpl* bruschi; (*: harshness*) durezza, brutalità; (*of sea*) violenza; (*of road*) cattive condizioni *fpl*; (*of terrain*) asprezza
rough·shod ['rʌfʃɒd] ADV: **to ride roughshod over** (*person*) mettere sotto i piedi; (*objection*) non badare minimamente a
rough-spoken [,rʌf'spəʊkən] ADJ sboccato(-a)
rou·lette [ruː'lɛt] N roulette *f inv*
Rou·ma·nia *etc* [ruː'meɪnɪə] N = **Romania** *etc*
◎ **round** [raʊnd] ADJ rotondo(-a); (*arms, body*) grassoccio(-a); (*cheeks*) paffuto(-a); **to have round shoulders** avere le spalle tonde; **a round table** un tavolo rotondo; (*fig*) un'associazione; **a round number** una cifra tonda; **in round figures** in cifra tonda; **a round dozen** una dozzina completa
■ ADV: **all round** *or* **right round** tutt'intorno, tutt'in giro; **there were vineyards all round** c'erano vigne tutt'intorno; **the wheels go round** le ruote girano; **all year round** (durante) tutto l'anno; **round here** da queste parti; **is there a chemist's round here?** c'è una farmacia da queste parti?; **to ask sb round** invitare qn (a casa propria); **to go round to sb's house** andare a casa di qn; **we were round at my sister's** eravamo da mia sorella; **I'll be round at 6 o'clock** ci sarò alle 6; **to take the long way round** fare il giro più lungo
■ PREP intorno a, attorno a; **round the table** intorno alla tavola; **we were sitting round the table** eravamo seduti intorno alla tavola; **all round the house** (*inside*) dappertutto in casa; (*outside*) tutt'intorno alla casa; **round about** circa; **it costs round about a hundred pounds** costa circa cento sterline; **round about eight o'clock** verso le otto; **she arrived round (about) noon** è arrivata verso mezzogiorno; **it's just round the corner** (*also fig*) è dietro l'angolo; **to look round a house/a town** visitare una casa/una città; **to have a look round** dare un'occhiata in giro; **I've been round all the shops** ho fatto il giro di tutti i negozi; **to go round a museum** visitare un museo; **round the clock** ininterrottamente, 24 ore su 24; **wrap a blanket round him** avvolgilo in una coperta
■ N
1 (*circle*) cerchio, tondo; (*Brit: slice: of bread, meat*) fetta; **a few rounds of cucumber** alcune fettine di cetriolo; **a round (of sandwiches)** due tramezzini
2 the daily round (*fig*) la routine quotidiana
3 (*of watchman, postman, milkman*) giro; **I've got a paper round** consegno i giornali a domicilio; **the doctor's on his rounds** il dottore sta facendo il suo giro di visite; **to go the rounds** (*illness*) diffondersi; (*story*) passare di bocca in bocca, circolare
4 (*Boxing*) round *m inv*; (*Golf*) partita; (*Showjumping*) percorso; (*in tournament, competition*) incontro; **he was knocked out in the tenth round** è andato al tappeto al decimo round; **a round of golf** una partita di golf; **another round of talks** un altro giro di consultazioni; **in the first round of the elections** nella prima tornata elettorale; **to buy a round of drinks** offrire un giro (di bevute); **I think it's my round** tocca a me offrire da bere; **a round of ammunition** un colpo; **a round of applause** un applauso
■ VT
1 (*make round: lips*) arrotondare; (*: edges*) smussare
2 (*go round: corner*) girare, voltare; (*: bend*) superare; (*: Naut*) doppiare
▸ **round off** VT + ADV (*speech, series, meal, evening*) finire in bellezza; **they rounded off the meal with liqueurs** hanno terminato il pranzo con dei liquori
▸ **round on** VI + PREP (*attacker, critic*) aggredire verbalmente
▸ **round up** VT + ADV
1 (*cattle*) radunare; (*friends etc*) riunire; (*criminals*) fare una retata di
2 (*figures*) arrotondare
round·about ['raʊndə,baʊt] ADJ (*route, means*) indiretto(-a); **I heard the news in a roundabout way** ho saputo la notizia per vie traverse; **to refer in a roundabout way to sth** accennare indirettamente a qc
■ N (*Brit: at fair*) giostra; (*: Aut*) rotatoria
round·ed ['raʊndɪd] ADJ (*shape*) arrotondato(-a); (*fig: sentence*) forbito(-a); (*style*) armonioso(-a)
round·ers ['raʊndəz] NPL (*Brit: game*) *gioco simile al baseball*
▷ www.roundersonline.net
round-eyed [,raʊnd'aɪd] ADJ (*fig*) con gli occhi sbarrati
round-faced [,raʊnd'feɪst] ADJ dalla faccia tonda
round·ly ['raʊndlɪ] ADV (*say, tell*) chiaro e tondo; (*condemn*) senza mezzi termini; **I cursed him roundly** gliene ho dette di tutti i colori
round-necked [,raʊnd'nɛkt] ADJ (*pullover*) a girocollo
round·ness ['raʊndnɪs] N rotondità
round robin N petizione *f*
round-robin [,raʊnd'rɒbɪn] ADJ (*Sport: also:* **round-robin tournament**) torneo round robin
round-shouldered [,raʊnd'ʃəʊldəd] ADJ con le spalle curve

Rr

rounds·man ['raʊndzmən] N (*pl* **-men**) (*Brit*) garzone *m* (*che esegue le consegne a domicilio*)
round trip N (viaggio di) andata e ritorno
round·up ['raʊnd,ʌp] N (*of cattle, people*) raduno; (*of suspects*) retata; **a roundup of the latest news** un sommario *or* riepilogo delle ultime notizie
rouse [raʊz] VT (*person: from sleep*) svegliare; (*: from apathy*) scuotere; (*interest, suspicion, admiration*) suscitare, destare; **they roused me at six** mi hanno svegliato alle sei; **to rouse sb to action** spronare qn ad agire; **to rouse sb to fury** far infuriare qn; **to rouse o.s. from** scuotersi di dosso; **I couldn't rouse myself from my apathy** non riuscivo a scuotermi di dosso l'apatia
rous·ing ['raʊzɪŋ] ADJ (*cheer*) entusiasmante; (*welcome, applause*) entusiastico(-a); (*speech, song*) trascinante
rout[1] [raʊt] N (*defeat*) disfatta, rotta
■VT mettere in rotta, sbaragliare
▸ **rout out** VT + ADV (*find*) scovare; (*force out*) (far) sloggiare
rout[2] [raʊt] VI (*search*): **to rout about** frugare, rovistare
◎**route** [ru:t] N (*gen*) itinerario; **shipping/air routes** rotte *fpl* marittime/aeree; **bus route** percorso dell'autobus; **we're on the main bus route** abitiamo vicino alla linea dell'autobus; **the best route to London** la strada migliore per andare a Londra; **en route** per strada; **en route from ...to** viaggiando da... a; **en route for** in viaggio verso; **"all routes"** (*Aut*) "tutte le direzioni"
route map N (*Brit: for journey*) cartina di itinerario; (*for trains*) pianta dei collegamenti
rout·er ['ru:tə^r] N (*Comput*) router *m inv*
◎**rou·tine** [ru:'ti:n] N (*normal procedure*) ordinaria amministrazione *f*; (*study routine, work routine*) ritmo di lavoro; (*Theatre*) numero; (*Comput*) sottoprogramma *m*; **daily routine** routine *f*, tran tran *m*; **my daily routine** il tran tran quotidiano
■ADJ (*duties, work*) abituale; (*inspection, medical examination*) periodico(-a); (*questions*) di prammatica; **a routine check** un controllo di routine; **the meeting was just routine** si è trattato di un incontro di normale amministrazione; **routine procedure** prassi *f*
rou·tine·ly [ru:'ti:nlɪ] ADV regolarmente; **vitamin K is routinely given to new-born babies** la vitamina K viene regolarmente somministrata ai neonati
rov·ing ['rəʊvɪŋ] ADJ (*person*) vagabondo(-a); (*life*) itinerante; **he has a roving eye** gli piace adocchiare le donne; **to have a roving commission** avere piena libertà d'azione *or* di manovra
roving reporter N reporter *m inv* volante
◎**row**[1] [rəʊ] N (*line*) fila; (*: of plants*) fila, filare *m*; (*Knitting*) ferro; (*Math*) riga; **a row of houses** una fila di case; **in a row** in fila; **in the front row** in prima fila; **for five days in a row** per cinque giorni di fila
row[2] [rəʊ] VT (*boat*) remare; **to row sb across a river** trasportare qn dall'altra parte di un fiume su una barca a remi
■VI remare; (*Sport*) vogare; **to go rowing** andare a fare una remata
row[3] [raʊ] N (*noise*) baccano, fracasso; (*quarrel*) lite *f*, litigio; (*scolding*) sgridata; **to make a row** far baccano; **what's that terrible row?** cos'è quel baccano?; **to have a row** litigare; **they've had a row** hanno litigato; **their latest row** il loro ultimo litigio; **to get (into) a row** prendersi una sgridata; **to give sb a row** sgridare qn
■VI litigare

ro·wan ['raʊən] N (*also:* **rowan tree**) sorbo
row·boat ['rəʊ,bəʊt] N (*Am*) = **rowing boat**
row·di·ness ['raʊdɪnɪs] N baccano; (*fighting*) zuffa
row·dy ['raʊdɪ] ADJ (*comp* **-ier**, *superl* **-iest**) (*noisy*) chiassoso(-a); (*rough*) turbolento(-a)
■N teppista *m/f*
row·dy·ism ['raʊdɪɪzəm] N teppismo
row·er ['rəʊə^r] N rematore(-trice); (*Sport*) vogatore(-trice)
row·ing ['rəʊɪŋ] N remare *m*; (*Sport*) canottaggio; **I like rowing** mi piace il canottaggio
▹ www.worldrowing.com
▹ www.theboatrace.org
rowing boat N (*Brit*) barca a remi
rowing club N circolo di canottaggio
row·lock ['rɒlək] N scalmo
◎**roy·al** ['rɔɪəl] ADJ reale; **the royal household** la famiglia reale e il seguito; **the royal we** il pluralis maiestatis; **they gave us a royal welcome** ci hanno fatto un'accoglienza principesca
■N: **the Royals** (*fam*) i reali, la famiglia reale
Royal Academy N (*Brit*) Accademia Reale d'Arte britannica

ROYAL ACADEMY

L'Accademia Reale d'Arte britannica, **Royal Academy (of the Arts)**, è un'istituzione fondata nel 1768 al fine di incoraggiare la pittura, la scultura e l'architettura. Ogni anno organizza una mostra estiva d'arte contemporanea.
▹ www.royalacademy.org.uk/

Royal Air Force N (*Brit*) *areonautica militare britannica*
royal blue ADJ azzurro reale *inv*
Royal Commission N *commissione d'inchiesta di nomina reale*
Royal Family N: **the Royal Family** la famiglia reale
▹ www.royal.gov.uk/
royal icing N (*Culin*) glassa reale
roy·al·ist ['rɔɪəlɪst] N realista *m/f*
roy·al·ly ['rɔɪəlɪ] ADV da re
Royal Mail N: **the Royal Mail** (*Brit*) la Posta
Royal Navy N (*Brit*) *marina militare britannica*
roy·al·ty ['rɔɪəltɪ] N **1** (*people*) reali *mpl*; **royalty and government leaders from all over the world** rappresentanti delle monarchie e dei governi di tutto il mondo **2** (*payment: royalties*) diritti *mpl* d'autore; (*from oil well, to inventor*) royalty *f inv*; **the royalties on a book** i diritti d'autore su un libro
RP [,ɑ:'pi:] N ABBR (*Brit:* = **received pronunciation**) pronuncia standard
rpm [,ɑ:pi:'ɛm] N ABBR **1** = **resale price maintenance** **2** (= **revolutions per minute**) giri/minuto
RRP [,ɑ:rɑ:'pi:] N ABBR (*Brit*) = **recommended retail price**
RSA [,ɑ:rɛs'eɪ] N ABBR (*Brit*) **1** = *Royal Society of Arts* **2** = *Royal Scottish Academy*
RSI [,ɑ:rɛs'aɪ] N ABBR (*Med:* = **repetitive strain injury**) lesione *f* da sforzo ripetuto
RSPB [,ɑ:rɛspi:'bi:] N ABBR (*Brit:* = **Royal Society for the Protection of Birds**) ≈ LIPU *f* (= *Lega Italiana Protezione Uccelli*)
RSPCA [,ɑ:rɛspi:si:'eɪ] N ABBR (*Brit:* = **Royal Society for the Prevention of Cruelty to Animals**) ≈ ENPA *m* (= *Ente Nazionale Protezione Animali*)

RSVP [ˌɑːrɛsviːˈpiː] ABBR (= **répondez s'il vous plaît**) RSVP

RTA [ˌɑːtiːˈeɪ] N ABBR = *road traffic accident*

RTF [ˌɑːtiːˈɛf] N ABBR (*Comput*: = **rich text format**) RTF *m*

Rt Hon. ABBR (*Brit*: = **Right Honourable**) ≈ On. (= *Onorevole*)

Rt Rev. ABBR (= **Right Reverend**) Rev.

rub [rʌb] N (*with cloth*) fregata, strofinata; (*on person*) frizione *f*, massaggio; **to give sth a rub** (*furniture, mark*) strofinare qc; (*sore place*) massaggiare qc; **there's the rub!** (*liter*) qui sta il problema!
■ VT sfregare, fregare, strofinare; **to rub one's hands together/one's nose** sfregarsi le mani/il naso; **she rubbed her eyes** si sfregò gli occhi; **to rub lotion into one's skin** frizionare la pelle con una lozione; **to rub sth dry** asciugare qc sfregando; **to rub a hole in sth** fare un buco in qc strofinando; **she gently rubbed the stain** ha sfregato leggermente la macchia; **there is no need to rub my nose in it!** (*fig*) non c'è bisogno che continui a ricordarmelo!; **to rub shoulders with sb** (*fig*) venire a contatto con qn
■ VI: **to rub against sth, rub on sth** strofinarsi contro *or* su qc
▸ **rub along** VI + ADV (*fam: two people*) andare d'accordo nonostante le difficoltà
▸ **rub away** VT + ADV togliere (sfregando)
▸ **rub down** VT + ADV **1** (*body*) strofinare, frizionare; (*horse*) strigliare **2** (*door, wall*) levigare
▸ **rub in** VT + ADV (*ointment*) far penetrare (massaggiando *or* frizionando); (*cream, polish: into leather etc*) far penetrare (strofinando); **don't rub it in!** (*fam*) non rivoltare il coltello nella piaga!
▸ **rub off** VI + ADV venire (*or* andare) via; **to rub off onto sth** restare attaccato(-a) a qc; **his opinions have rubbed off on me** ho finito col pensarla come lui
■ VT + PREP (*writing*) cancellare; (*dirt*) togliere *or* levare (strofinando)
▸ **rub out** VT + ADV cancellare
▸ **rub up** VT + ADV (*silver, vase*) lucidare; **to rub sb up the wrong way** (*Am*): **rub sb the wrong way** (*fig*) prendere qn per il verso sbagliato, lisciare qn contropelo

rub·ber¹ [ˈrʌbəʳ] N (*material*) gomma, caucciù *m*; (*eraser*) gomma (da cancellare); **you'll need a pencil and a rubber** ti occorre una matita e una gomma da cancellare
■ ADJ (*ball, dinghy, gloves*) di gomma; **rubber soles** suole *fpl* di gomma

rub·ber² [ˈrʌbəʳ] N (*Bridge*) rubber *m inv*

rubber band N elastico

rubber bullet N pallottola di gomma

rubber industry N industria della gomma

rub·ber·ized [ˈrʌbəˌraɪzd] ADJ gommato(-a)

rubber·neck [ˈrʌbənɛk] VI (*fam*) curiosare

rubber plant N ficus *m inv*

rubber plantation N piantagione *f* di gomma

rubber ring N (*for swimming*) ciambella

rubber stamp N timbro di gomma

rubber-stamp [ˌrʌbəˈstæmp] VT (*fig*) approvare senza discussione

rub·bery [ˈrʌbərɪ] ADJ gommoso(-a)

rub·bing [ˈrʌbɪŋ] N sfregamento; (*Art*) rilievo (*ottenuto sfregando colore su un foglio sovrapposto*)

rub·bish [ˈrʌbɪʃ] N (*waste material*) rifiuti *mpl*; (*household rubbish*) spazzatura, immondizia; (*nonsense*) sciocchezze *fpl*, fesserie *fpl*; (*worthless stuff*) cose *fpl* senza valore, robaccia; **the rubbish is collected on Mondays** la raccolta dei rifiuti è di lunedì; **he threw the bottle in the rubbish** ha buttato la bottiglia nelle immondizie; **children today eat a lot of rubbish** oggigiorno i bambini mangiano un sacco di porcherie; **the film was rubbish** il film non valeva niente; **rubbish!** (*fam*) sciocchezze!, fesserie!; **don't talk rubbish!** non dire sciocchezze!; **that's a load of rubbish!** tutte sciocchezze!
■ ADJ (*Brit fam*): **they're a rubbish team!** è una squadra che non vale niente!
■ VT (*fam*) sputtanare

rubbish bin N (*Brit*) pattumiera; (: *outside house*) bidone *m* (per la spazzatura)

rubbish collection N raccolta dei rifiuti

rubbish dump N discarica (delle immondizie)

rub·bishy [ˈrʌbɪʃɪ] ADJ (*Brit fam*) scadente, che non vale niente

rub·ble [ˈrʌbl] N detriti *mpl*; (*smaller*) pietrisco; (*of building*) macerie *fpl*; **the building was reduced to a heap of rubble** l'edificio era ridotto a un cumulo di macerie

ru·bel·la [ruːˈbɛlə] N (*Med*) rosolia

ru·ble [ˈruːbl] N (*Am*) = **rouble**

ruby [ˈruːbɪ] N rubino
■ ADJ (*colour*) (color) rubino *inv*; (*lips*) rosso(-a); (*made of rubies: necklace, ring*) di rubini

RUC [ˌɑːjuːˈsiː] N ABBR (*Brit*: = **Royal Ulster Constabulary**) *forze di polizia dell'Irlanda del Nord sostituite nel 2000 dal PSNI*

ruck [rʌk] N **1** (*Brit: scrap*) zuffa **2** (*Rugby*) mischia aperta **3** (*crease: in clothing, carpet*) piega
▸ **ruck up** VI sollevarsi facendo una piega

ruck·sack [ˈrʌkˌsæk] N zaino

ruck up [ˌrʌkˈʌp] VI + ADV (*skirt, coat*) fare le grinze

ruc·tions [ˈrʌkʃənz] NPL (*fam*) putiferio *msg*, finimondo *msg*; **there will be ructions if** succederà il finimondo se

rud·der [ˈrʌdəʳ] N (*Naut*) timone *m*; (*Aer*) timone di direzione

rud·dy¹ [ˈrʌdɪ] ADJ (*comp* **-ier**, *superl* **-iest**) (*complexion*) rubicondo(-a); (*sky*) rossastro(-a)

rud·dy² [ˈrʌdɪ] ADJ (*comp* **-ier**, *superl* **-iest**) (*Brit fam*) dannato(-a)

rude [ruːd] ADJ (*comp* **-r**, *superl* **-st**) **1** (*impolite*) villano(-a), maleducato(-a); (*indecent*) indecente, volgare; **to be rude to sb** essere maleducato con qn; **he was very rude to me** è stato molto maleducato nei miei confronti; **it's rude to interrupt** è maleducato interrompere; **it's rude to talk with your mouth full** è cattiva educazione parlare con la bocca piena; **a rude word** una parolaccia; **a rude joke** una barzelletta sporca **2** **a rude awakening** (*fig*) una doccia fredda; **to be in rude health** essere in ottima salute **3** (*liter: primitive*) rudimentale

rude·ly [ˈruːdlɪ] ADV **1** (*impolitely*) villanamente, maleducatamente; (*indecently*) indecentemente, volgarmente **2** **to be rudely awoken** (*fig*) tornare bruscamente alla realtà

rude·ness [ˈruːdnɪs] N (*impoliteness*) villania, maleducazione *f*; (*indecency*) indecenza, volgarità

ru·di·men·ta·ry [ˌruːdɪˈmɛntərɪ] ADJ rudimentale

ru·di·ments [ˈruːdɪmənts] NPL: **the rudiments** i (primi) rudimenti *mpl*

rue¹ [ruː] VT (*liter*) pentirsi amaramente di; **I rue the day that ...** maledico il giorno in cui...

rue² [ruː] N (*Bot*) ruta

rue·ful [ˈruːfʊl] ADJ (*liter*) mesto(-a)

Rr

rue·ful·ly ['ru:fʊlɪ] ADV *(liter)* mestamente

ruff [rʌf] N *(Dressmaking)* gorgiera; *(Zool)* collare *m*

ruf·fian ['rʌfɪən] N *(old)* manigoldo

DID YOU KNOW ...?
ruffian is not translated by the Italian word *ruffiano*

ruf·fle ['rʌfl] VT *(surface)* (far) increspare; *(hair, feathers)* arruffare, scompigliare; *(fig: person)* (far) agitare, turbare, (far) innervosire; **nothing ruffles him** non si scompone mai

rug [rʌg] N *(floor mat)* tappeto; *(bedside rug)* scendiletto; *(travelling rug)* coperta (da viaggio); *(in tartan)* plaid *m inv*

◎**rug·by** ['rʌgbɪ] N rugby *m*
■ADJ *(team, player)* di rugby
▷ www.irb.com/
▷ http://world.rleague.com
▷ www.rfu.com/

rugby league N rugby a tredici

rugby tackle N placcaggio
■VT placcare

rug·ged ['rʌgɪd] ADJ *(terrain)* accidentato(-a); *(coastline, mountains)* frastagliato(-a); *(character)* rude; *(features)* marcato(-a), duro(-a); *(landscape)* aspro(-a); **rugged terrain** un terreno aspro; **rugged features** lineamenti *mpl* marcati

rug·ged·ness ['rʌgɪdnɪs] N *(of terrain, coastline, mountain)* asprezza, asperità; *(of character)* rudezza; *(of features)*: **the ruggedness of his face** i lineamenti marcati del suo volto

rug·ger ['rʌgəʳ] N *(Brit fam)* = **rugby**

◎**ruin** ['ru:ɪn] N **1** rudere *m*; **ruins** NPL *(architectural remains)* rovine *fpl*; **the ruins of the castle** le rovine del castello; **in ruins** in rovina; **to fall into ruin** cadere in rovina **2** *(fig)* rovina
■VT rovinare

ru·ina·tion [ˌru:ɪ'neɪʃən] N rovina

ruined ['ru:ɪnd] ADJ *(person)* rovinato(-a); *(castle)* in rovina

ru·in·ous ['ru:ɪnəs] ADJ *(expensive)* costoso(-a)

ru·in·ous·ly ['ru:ɪnəslɪ] ADV: **ruinously expensive** costosissimo(-a)

◎**rule** [ru:l] N **1** *(gen)* regola; *(regulation)* regola, regolamento; **the rules of the road** le norme della circolazione stradale; **rules and regulations** norme e regolamenti; **it's against the rules** è contro le regole *or* il regolamento; **as a rule** normalmente, di regola; **to make it a rule to do sth** essersi imposto(-a) la regola di fare qc; **by rule of thumb** a lume di naso
2 *(dominion)*: **under British rule** sotto il dominio britannico; **majority rule** *(Pol)* governo di maggioranza **3** *(for measuring)* riga; **slide rule** regolo (calcolatore)
■VT **1** *(govern: also:* **rule over**: *country)* governare; **he has ruled the country since 1996** governa il paese dal 1996; **he's ruled by his wife** è sua moglie che comanda
2 *(subj: umpire, judge)*: **to rule (that)** decretare (che), decidere (che) **3** *(paper, page)* rigare
■VI **1** *(monarch)* regnare **2** *(Law)*: **to rule against/in favour of/on** pronunciarsi a sfavore di/in favore di/su
▸ **rule out** VT + ADV escludere; **murder cannot be ruled out** non si esclude che si tratti di omicidio

rule book N regolamento

ruled [ru:ld] ADJ *(paper)* vergato(-a), a righe

rule of law N *(frm)*: **the rule of law** il principio di legalità

rul·er ['ru:ləʳ] N **1** *(sovereign)* sovrano(-a); *(in a republic)* capo **2** *(for measuring)* righello, riga

◎**rul·ing** ['ru:lɪŋ] ADJ *(passion, idea)* grande, dominante; *(party)* al potere; **the ruling classes** la classe dirigente
■N *(Law)* decisione *f*

rum¹ [rʌm] N *(drink)* rum *m inv*

rum² [rʌm] ADJ *(comp* **-mer**, *superl* **-mest**) *(Brit fam)* strambo(-a)

Ru·ma·nia *etc* [ru:'meɪnɪə] N = **Romania** *etc*

rum·ble¹ ['rʌmbl] N *(of traffic etc)* rombo; *(thunder)* brontolio; **a rumble of thunder** il rimbombo di un tuono
■VI *(thunder, cannon etc)* rimbombare; *(stomach)* brontolare; *(pipe)* gorgogliare; **the train rumbled past** il treno passò sferragliando; **voices rumbled in the next room** nella stanza accanto rimbombavano delle voci; **my stomach is rumbling** il mio stomaco brontola

rum·ble² ['rʌmbl] VT *(Brit fam)* scoprire

rum·bling ['rʌmblɪŋ] N *(of stomach, thunder, pipe)* brontolio; *(of traffic)* ronzio

rum·bus·tious [rʌm'bʌstʃəs] ADJ *(person)*: **to be rumbustious** essere un terremoto

ru·mi·nant ['ru:mɪnənt] *(Zool)* ADJ ruminante
■N ruminante *m*

ru·mi·nate ['ru:mɪˌneɪt] VI *(frm)* meditare

ru·mi·na·tive ['ru:mɪnətɪv] ADJ *(liter)* meditativo(-a)

ru·mi·na·tive·ly ['ru:mɪnətɪvlɪ] ADV *(liter: nod, say)* con aria meditabonda

rum·mage ['rʌmɪdʒ] VI: **to rummage (about** *or* **around)** rovistare, frugare; **to rummage about in sth/for sth** rovistare *or* frugare in qc/per trovare qc

rum·my ['rʌmɪ] N ramino

◎**ru·mour**, *(Am)* **ru·mor** ['ru:məʳ] N voce *f*; **rumour has it that ...** *or* **there's a rumour that ...** corre voce che... *+ sub*
■VT: **it is rumoured that ...** si dice in giro che... *+ sub*

DID YOU KNOW ...?
rumour is not translated by the Italian word *rumore*

rumour mill N fonte *f* di chiacchiere

rumour-monger ['ru:məˌmʌŋgəʳ] N persona che mette in giro delle chiacchiere

rump [rʌmp] N *(of horse)* groppa (posteriore), culatta; *(Culin)* scamone *m*

rum·ple ['rʌmpl] VT *(clothes)* spiegazzare, sgualcire; *(hair)* arruffare, scompigliare

rump steak N bistecca di girello

rum·pus ['rʌmpəs] N *(fam)* putiferio, casino; **to kick up a rumpus** scatenare un putiferio

◎**run** [rʌn] *(vb: pt* **ran**, *pp* **run**) VI
1 correre; *(flee)* scappare; **run and see** corri a vedere; **to run in/out** *etc* entrare/uscire *etc* di corsa; **to run for the bus** fare una corsa per prendere l'autobus; **to run to help sb** accorrere in aiuto di qn, correre ad aiutare qn; **don't come running to me when you've got problems** non correre da me quando avrai dei problemi; **we shall have to run for it** ci toccherà tagliare la corda; **to run for President** candidarsi per la Presidenza; **he's running for the Presidency** si è presentato come candidato per la presidenza; **a rumour ran through the town that ...** si è sparsa la voce in città che...; **that tune keeps running through my head** continua a venirmi in mente quel motivetto; **it runs in the family** è un tratto di famiglia
2 the train runs between Gatwick and Victoria il treno fa servizio tra Gatwick e la stazione Victoria; **the bus runs every 20 minutes** c'è un autobus ogni 20

minuti; **to be running late** essere in ritardo
3 (*function*) funzionare, andare; **to run the engine** tenere acceso il motore; **leave the engine running** lascia il motore acceso; **to run on petrol/on diesel/off batteries** andare a benzina/a diesel/a batterie; **things did not run smoothly for him** (*fig*) le cose non gli sono andate molto bene
4 (*extend: contract*) essere valido(-a); **it has another 5 years to run** vale per altri 5 anni; **the play ran for 2 years** lo spettacolo ha tenuto cartellone per 2 anni; **the cost ran to hundreds of pounds** alla fine la spesa è stata di centinaia di sterline; **their losses run into millions** hanno avuto una perdita di milioni
5 (*river, tears, curtains, drawer*) scorrere; (*nose*) colare; (*eyes*) lacrimare; (*tap*) perdere; (*sore, abscess*) spurgare; (*melt: butter, icing*) fondere; (*colour, ink*) sbavare; (*colour: in washing*) stingere; **the tears ran down her cheeks** le lacrime le scorrevano sulle guance; **you left the tap running** hai lasciato il rubinetto aperto; **the river runs into the sea** il fiume sfocia nel mare; **the road runs into the square** la strada sbocca nella piazza; **the milk ran all over the floor** il latte si è sparso sul pavimento; **to run high** (*river, sea*) ingrossarsi; (*feelings*) inasprirsi; **my nose is running** mi cola il naso; **his face was running with sweat** il sudore gli colava sul viso; **his blood ran cold** gli si è gelato il sangue
6 (*with adv or prep*): **to run across the road** attraversare di corsa la strada; **the road runs along the river** la strada corre lungo il fiume; **the road runs by our house** la strada passa davanti a casa nostra; **the path runs from our house to the station** il sentiero va da casa nostra fino alla stazione; **the car ran into the lamppost** la macchina è andata a sbattere contro il lampione; **he was running towards her** correva verso di lei; **he ran up to me** mi corse incontro; **she ran up the stairs** salì su per le scale di corsa
■ VT
1 correre; (*race*) partecipare a; **I ran five kilometres** ho corso cinque chilometri; **to run a marathon** partecipare ad una maratona; **she ran a good race** ha fatto una buona gara; **the race is run over 4 km** la gara si svolge su un percorso di 4 km; **to let things run their course** lasciare che le cose seguano il loro corso; **to run a horse** far correre un cavallo
2 (*move*): **to run sb into town** accompagnare *or* portare qn in città; **I'll run you to the station** ti porto io alla stazione; **to run the car into a lamppost** andare a sbattere con la macchina contro un lampione; **to run errands** andare a fare commissioni
3 (*organize, manage: business, hotel*) dirigere, gestire; (*: country*) governare; (*: campaign*) organizzare; **he runs a large company** dirige una grossa società; **they run music courses in the holidays** organizzano corsi di musica durante le vacanze; **are they running any trains today?** ci sono treni oggi?; **they ran an extra train** hanno messo un treno straordinario; **she runs everything** è lei che manda avanti tutto; **I want to run my own life** voglio essere io a gestire la mia vita
4 (*operate: machine*) usare; **to run a program** (*Comput*) eseguire un programma; **we run two cars** abbiamo due macchine; **it's a very cheap car to run** è una macchina economica
5 **to be run off one's feet** doversi fare in quattro; **to run it close** *or* **fine** ridursi all'ultimo momento; **their win was a close run thing** hanno vinto per il rotto della cuffia; **to run a (high) temperature** avere la febbre (alta); **to run a risk** correre un rischio
6 (*with adv or prep*): **to run one's eye over a letter** dare una scorsa a una lettera; **to run a fence round a field** costruire un recinto intorno a un campo; **to run a pipe through a wall** far passare un tubo attraverso un muro; **to run one's fingers through sb's hair** passare le dita fra i capelli di qn; **he ran his fingers through her hair** le passò le dita tra i capelli; **to run a comb through one's hair** darsi una pettinata; **to run water into the bath** far correre l'acqua nella vasca; **to run a bath for sb** preparare un bagno a qn
■ N
1 (*act of running*) corsa; **to go for a run** andare a correre; **I go for a run every morning** vado a correre ogni mattina; **at a run** di corsa; **to break into a run** mettersi a correre; **he's on the run from the police** è ricercato dalla polizia; **a prisoner on the run** un evaso; **the criminals are still on the run** i criminali sono ancora latitanti; **to keep the enemy on the run** premere il nemico in fuga; **we've got them on the run now** adesso sono ridotti allo sbando; **he's on the run from his creditors** cerca di sfuggire ai creditori; **to make a run for it** scappare, tagliare la corda; **to give sb a run for his money** non darla vinta a qn prima del tempo; **she's had a good run** (*on death, retirement*) ha avuto il suo; **to have the run of sb's house** utilizzare la casa altrui come casa propria
2 (*outing*) giro; **to go for a run in the car** fare un giro in macchina
3 (*Rail*) percorso, tragitto; **it's a 10-minute bus run** è un tragitto di 10 minuti in autobus; **boats on the Calais run** navi che fanno il servizio per Calais
4 (*sequence*) serie *f inv*; (*Cards*) scala; **a run of luck** un periodo di fortuna; **he's different from the common run of men** è fuori dall'ordinario; **it stands out from the general run of books** è un libro fuori dal comune; **the play had a long run** lo spettacolo ha tenuto a lungo il cartellone; **in the long run** alla lunga; **in the short run** sulle prime
5 (*Comm etc*): **there's been a run on ...** c'è stata una forte richiesta di...
6 (*for animals*) recinto
7 (*for skiing, bobsleighing*) pista
8 (*in stocking, tights*) smagliatura
▶ **run about** VI + ADV correre (di) qua e (di) là
▶ **run across** VI + PREP (*meet, find*) incontrare per caso, imbattersi in
▶ **run along** VI + ADV correre, andare; **run along and play** su, vai a giocare
▶ **run away** VI + ADV
1 scappare di corsa, fuggire; **they ran away before the police came** sono scappati prima che arrivasse la polizia; **to run away from home** scappare di casa
2 (*water*) scolare
▶ **run away with** VI + ADV + PREP scappare con; (*fig*): **he let his imagination run away with him** si lasciò trasportare dalla fantasia; **don't run away with the idea that ...** non credere che...
▶ **run down** VT + ADV
1 (*Aut*) investire, mettere sotto
2 (*reduce: production*) ridurre gradualmente; (*: factory, shop*) rallentare l'attività di
3 (*disparage*) parlar male di, denigrare
4 (*battery*) scaricare
■ VI + ADV (*battery, watch*) scaricarsi
▶ **run in** VT + ADV
1 (*car*) rodare, fare il rodaggio di
2 (*fam: arrest*) mettere dentro

Rr

▶ **run into** VI + PREP *(meet: person)* incontrare per caso; *(difficulties, troubles etc)* incontrare, trovare; *(collide with)* andare a sbattere contro; **to run into debt** trovarsi nei debiti

▶ **run off** VI + ADV = **run away**

■ VT + ADV *(copies)* fare

▶ **run off with** VI + ADV + PREP = **run away with**

▶ **run on** VI + ADV

1 *(fam: person)* parlare senza tregua; *(talk, meeting)* protrarsi (oltre il previsto)

2 *(Typ)* continuare senza andare a capo

▶ **run out** VI + ADV *(contract, lease)* scadere; *(food, money etc)* finire, esaurirsi; *(person)* uscire di corsa; *(liquid)* colare; **the supplies have run out** le provviste sono finite; **time is running out** ormai c'è poco tempo

▶ **run out of** VI + ADV + PREP non avere più; **to run out of** rimanere senza; **I ran out of petrol** *(Am)*: **I ran out of gas** sono rimasto senza benzina

▶ **run out on** VI + ADV + PREP *(abandon)* piantare

▶ **run over** VI + ADV *(overflow)* traboccare

■ VI + PREP *(reread)* rileggere; *(recapitulate)* ricapitolare

■ VT + PREP *(Aut)* investire, mettere sotto; **to get run over** essere investito(-a)

▶ **run through** VI + PREP

1 *(use up: fortune)* far fuori, dilapidare

2 *(read quickly: notes etc)* dare un'occhiata a; *(list)* scorrere

3 *(rehearse: play)* riprovare, ripetere; *(recapitulate)* ricapitolare

▶ **run to** VI + PREP *(be sufficient for)* essere sufficiente per; **my salary won't run to a car** col mio stipendio non posso permettermi una macchina

▶ **run up** VT + ADV

1 *(debt)* accumulare

2 *(dress)* mettere insieme

▶ **run up against** VI + ADV + PREP *(person, problem)* imbattersi in; *(difficulties)* incontrare

run·about [ˈrʌnəˌbaʊt] N *(car)* utilitaria

run·around [ˈrʌnəˌraʊnd] N *(fam)*: **to give sb the runaround** far girare a vuoto qn

run·away [ˈrʌnəˌweɪ] ADJ *(slave, person)* in fuga; *(child)* scappato(-a) di casa; *(truck, train)* fuori controllo; *(horse)* imbizzarrito(-a); *(success, victory)* trascinante; **runaway inflation** inflazione *f* galoppante

■ N fuggitivo(-a), fuggiasco(-a)

run-down [ˈrʌnˌdaʊn] ADJ *(person)* debilitato(-a); *(building)* fatiscente, in rovina

■ N 1 *(Brit: of industry)* riduzione *f* graduale dell'attività di 2 **to give sb a run-down on sth** *(fam)* mettere qn al corrente di qc

rung[1] [rʌŋ] N *(of ladder)* piolo; *(of chair)* traversa

rung[2] [rʌŋ] PP *of* **ring**

run-in [ˈrʌnˌɪn] N *(fam)* scontro

◎ **run·ner** [ˈrʌnə^r] N 1 *(athlete)* corridore *m*; *(horse)* partente *m* 2 *(of sledge, aircraft)* pattino; *(of skate)* lama; *(of car seat, drawer)* guida 3 *(hall carpet)* guida, passatoia 4 *(Bot)* stolone *m*

runner bean N *(Brit)* fagiolino

runner-up [ˌrʌnərˈʌp] N secondo(-a) arrivato(-a)

◎ **run·ning** [ˈrʌnɪŋ] ADJ *(water)* corrente; *(tap)* che cola; *(sore)* che spurga; **a running stream** un corso d'acqua; **running battle** lotta continua; **to be in good running order** *(car)* essere in buone condizioni di marcia; **for five days running** per cinque giorni consecutivi; **for the sixth time running** per la sesta volta di fila *or* di seguito

■ N *(of business, hotel)* gestione *f*, direzione *f*; *(of campaign)* organizzazione *f*; *(of machine)* funzionamento; *(of race)* corsa; **to be in/out of the running for sth** essere/non essere più in lizza per qc; **to make the running** *(Sport fig)* imporre il ritmo

running board N *(Aut)* predellino

running commentary N *(Radio)* radiocronaca; *(TV)* telecronaca

running costs NPL *(of business)* costi *mpl* d'esercizio; *(of car)* spese *fpl* di mantenimento

running head N *(Typ, Word Processing)* testata, titolo corrente

running mate N *(Am Pol)* candidato(-a) alla vicepresidenza

running time N *(of video, film etc)* durata

run·ny [ˈrʌnɪ] ADJ *(comp* **-ier**, *superl* **-iest**) *(butter)* sciolto(-a); *(sauce)* troppo liquido(-a); *(nose)* che cola, che gocciola

run-off [ˈrʌnˌɒf] N *(in contest, election)* ballottaggio finale; *(extra race)* spareggio

run-of-the-mill [ˌrʌnəvðəˈmɪl] ADJ banale, solito(-a)

run-out [ˈrʌnˌaʊt] N *(Horse-riding)* scarto

runt [rʌnt] N *(Zool)*: **the runt of the litter** *(puppy)* il cucciolo più piccolo della figliata; *(pej: person)* omuncolo

run-through [ˈrʌnˌθruː] N *(rehearsal)* prova generale

run time N *(Comput)* tempo di esecuzione

run-up [ˈrʌnˌʌp] N: **the run-up to Christmas** *(Brit)* il periodo che precede natale

run·way [ˈrʌnˌweɪ] N *(Aer)* pista

ru·pee [ruːˈpiː] N rupia

rup·ture [ˈrʌptʃə^r] N rottura; *(Med: hernia)* ernia

■ VT *(blood vessel etc)* far scoppiare; **to rupture o.s.** farsi venire un'ernia; **the tank ruptured** il serbatoio si è rotto

◎ **ru·ral** [ˈrʊərəl] ADJ *(gen)* rurale; *(scene)* campestre; *(life)* di campagna; **rural depopulation** deruralizzazione *f*

rural district council N *(Brit) fino al 1974 consiglio amministrativo di distretto rurale*

ruse [ruːz] N *(frm)* stratagemma *m*, astuzia

rush[1] [rʌʃ] N *(Bot)* giunco

◎ **rush**[2] [rʌʃ] N

1 *(of people)* affollamento, ressa; **the Christmas rush** la ressa di Natale; **gold rush** corsa all'oro; **there was a rush to** *or* **for the door** tutti si precipitarono verso la porta; **we've had a rush of orders** abbiamo avuto una valanga di ordinazioni

2 *(hurry)* fretta, premura; **in a rush** in fretta; **to be in a rush** avere fretta; **I'm in a rush (to do)** ho fretta *or* premura (di fare); **there's no rush** non c'è fretta; **it was all done in a rush** è stato fatto tutto in gran fretta; **it got lost in the rush** nella fretta è andato perso; **what's all the rush about?** cos'è tutta questa fretta?; **is there any rush for this?** è urgente?; **we had a rush to get it ready in time** abbiamo dovuto affrettarci per prepararlo in tempo

3 *(current)*: **a rush of air** una corrente d'aria; **a rush of water** un flusso d'acqua

■ VT

1 *(person)* far fretta *or* premura a; *(work, order)* fare in fretta; **to rush sth off** spedire con urgenza qc; **I hate being rushed** non mi piace che mi si faccia premura; **we were rushed off our feet** abbiamo dovuto correre come i matti; **he was rushed (off) to hospital** lo hanno portato d'urgenza all'ospedale

2 *(attack: town)* prendere d'assalto; *(: person)* precipitarsi contro; **the crowd rushed the barriers** la folla ha dato l'assalto ai cancelli

■VI (*person: run*) precipitarsi; (: *be in a hurry*) essere di corsa; (*car*) andare veloce; **there's no need to rush** non c'è bisogno di affrettarsi; **don't rush at it, take it slowly** non farlo in fretta, prenditela con comodo; **to rush up/down** *etc* precipitarsi su/giù *etc*; **everyone rushed outside** tutti si precipitarono fuori; **I rushed to her side** sono corso subito da lei; **I was rushing to finish it** mi affrettavo a finirlo

▸ **rush about**, **rush around** VI + ADV correre su e giù

▸ **rush out** VT + ADV (*product*) immettere velocemente sul mercato; (*book*) pubblicare in tutta fretta

■VI + ADV precipitarsi fuori

▸ **rush over** VI + ADV: **to rush over (to sb/to do sth)** precipitarsi (da qn/a fare qc)

▸ **rush up** VI + ADV = rush over

▸ **rush through** VT + PREP (*meal*) mangiare in fretta; (*book*) dare una scorsa frettolosa a; (*work*) sbrigare frettolosamente; (*town*) attraversare in fretta

■VT + ADV (*Comm: order*) eseguire d'urgenza; (*supplies*) mandare d'urgenza

rush hour N ora di punta; **the rush hour traffic** il traffico delle ore di punta

rush job N (*urgent*) lavoro urgente; (*botched, hurried*) lavoro fatto in fretta

rush matting N stuoia

rusk [rʌsk] N fetta biscottata

rus·set ['rʌsɪt] ADJ (*colour*) marrone rossiccio *inv*

Rus·sia ['rʌʃə] N Russia

Rus·sian ['rʌʃən] ADJ russo(-a)

■N (*person*) russo(-a); (*language*) russo; **the Russians** i russi

Russian Orthodox Church N Chiesa russo-ortodossa

▹ www.russian-orthodox-church.org.ru/en.htm

Russian roulette N roulette russa

rust [rʌst] N ruggine *f*

■VI arrugginire, arrugginirsi

■VT (far) arrugginire

rust-coloured ['rʌst,kʌləd] ADJ (color) ruggine *inv*

rustic ['rʌstɪk] ADJ (*gen*) rustico(-a); (*scene*) campestre

■N (*pej*) cafone(-a)

rus·tle[1] ['rʌsl] N fruscio

■VT (*paper*) far frusciare

■VI frusciare; **the leaves rustled** le foglie frusciavano

▸ **rustle up** (*fam*) VT + ADV (*find*) ripescare; (: *money*) racimolare; (*meal*) rimediare, mettere insieme

rus·tle[2] ['rʌsl] VT (*Am: cattle*) rubare

rus·tler ['rʌslə'] N ladro di bestiame

rus·tling[1] ['rʌslɪŋ] N (*noise*) fruscio

rus·tling[2] ['rʌslɪŋ] N (*of cattle*) furto di bestiame

rust·proof ['rʌst,pru:f], **rust-resistant** ['rʌstrɪ,zɪstənt] ADJ inattaccabile dalla ruggine

rust·proofing ['rʌst,pru:fɪŋ] N trattamento antiruggine

rusty ['rʌstɪ] ADJ (*comp* **-ier**, *superl* **-iest**) rugginoso(-a), arrugginito(-a); **my Greek is pretty rusty** (*fig*) il mio greco è molto arrugginito

rut[1] [rʌt] N solco; **to get into a rut** (*fig*) fossilizzarsi; **to be in a rut** (*fig*) essersi fossilizzato(-a)

rut[2] (*Zool*) N: **the rut** la fregola, il calore *m*

■VI andare in calore

ru·ta·ba·ga [,ru:tə'beɪgə] N (*Am*) rapa svedese

ruth·less ['ru:θlɪs] ADJ spietato(-a)

ruth·less·ly ['ru:θlɪslɪ] ADV spietatamente

ruth·less·ness ['ru:θlɪsnɪs] N spietatezza

rut·ted ['rʌtɪd] ADJ (*road, lane*) con solchi (delle ruote)

RV [,ɑ:'vi:] N ABBR (= **Revised Version**) *versione riveduta della Bibbia anglicana*; (*Am*) = **recreational vehicle**

rye [raɪ] N segale *f*; (*Am: whisky*) whisky *m inv* di segale

rye bread N pane *m* di segale

rye-grass ['raɪ,grɑ:s] N loglio perenne

Rr

S

S, s [ɛs] N (*letter*) S, s *f or m inv*; **S for sugar** ≈ S come Savona

S ABBR **1** (*on clothes*) (= **small**) S *f inv* **2** (= **south**) S **3** (*Scol:* = **satisfactory**) ≈ sufficiente

S. (*pl* **SS.**) ABBR (= **Saint**) S., SS. *pl*

SA ABBR = **South Africa, South America**

Sab·bath [ˈsæbəθ], **Sab·bath Day** [ˈsæbəθˈdeɪ] N (*Jewish*) sabato; (*Christian old*) domenica

sab·bati·cal [səˈbætɪkəl] (*Univ*) N anno sabbatico; **to take a sabbatical** prendere un anno sabbatico
■ ADJ sabbatico(-a); **sabbatical year** anno sabbatico

sa·ble [ˈseɪbl] N **1** (*animal, fur*) zibellino **2** (*liter: colour*) nero
■ ADJ (*fur*) di zibellino; (*brush*) di martora

sabo·tage [ˈsæbəˌtɑːʒ] N sabotaggio
■ VT sabotare

sabo·teur [ˌsæbəˈtɜːʳ] N sabotatore(-trice)

sa·bre, (*Am*) **sa·ber** [ˈseɪbəʳ] N sciabola

sac [sæk] N (*Anat*) sacco; **honey sac** cestella (del polline)

sac·cha·rine, (*Am*) **sac·cha·rin** [ˈsækərɪn] N saccarina

sa·chet [ˈsæʃeɪ] N bustina

◎**sack¹** [sæk] N **1** (*bag*) sacco; **sack of potatoes** sacco di patate; **coal sack** sacco per il carbone; **sack of coal** sacco di carbone **2** (*fam*): **to get the sack** essere licenziato(-a); **to give sb the sack** licenziare qn **3** (*esp Am fam: bed*) letto
■ VT (*fam: dismiss*) licenziare

sack² [sæk] N (*plundering*) saccheggio; **the sack of Rome** il sacco di Roma
■ VT (*plunder*) saccheggiare

sack·cloth [ˈsækˌklɒθ] N tela di sacco; **sackcloth and ashes** (*Rel*) il sacco e la cenere; **to be in sackcloth and ashes** (*fig*) avere l'aria contrita

sack dress N vestito a sacco

sack·ful [ˈsækˌfʊl] N sacco (pieno)

sack·ing [ˈsækɪŋ] N **1** (*cloth*) tela di sacco **2** (*fam: dismissal*) licenziamento

sack·load [ˈsækləʊd] N sacco

sack race N corsa coi sacchi

sac·ra·ment [ˈsækrəmənt] N sacramento; **the Blessed Sacrament** l'Eucaristia; **to receive the sacraments** ricevere i sacramenti

sa·cred [ˈseɪkrɪd] ADJ (*holy*) sacro(-a); **sacred to the memory of** dedicato(-a) alla memoria di; **a sacred promise** (*fig*) una promessa solenne; **is nothing sacred?** non c'è più religione!

sacred cow N (*fig: person*) intoccabile *m/f*; (: *institution*) caposaldo; (: *idea, belief*) dogma *m*

Sacred Heart N (*Rel*): **the Sacred Heart** il Sacro Cuore

◎**sac·ri·fice** [ˈsækrɪˌfaɪs] N sacrificio; **to make sacrifices (for sb)** fare (dei) sacrifici (per qn)
■ VT sacrificare

sac·ri·fi·cial [ˌsækrɪˈfɪʃəl] ADJ (*act, altar*) sacrificale; (*lamb*) destinato(-a) al sacrificio

sac·ri·lege [ˈsækrɪlɪdʒ] N sacrilegio

sac·ri·legious [ˌsækrɪˈlɪdʒəs] ADJ sacrilego(-a)

sac·ris·tan [ˈsækrɪstən] N sagrestano

sac·ris·ty [ˈsækrɪstɪ] N sagrestia

sac·ro·sanct [ˈsækrəʊˌsæŋkt] ADJ sacrosanto(-a)

SAD [sæd] N ABBR (= **seasonal affective disorder**) stato depressivo causato dalla mancanza di luce solare

◎**sad** [sæd] ADJ (*comp* **-der**, *superl* **-dest**) **1** (*sorrowful, depressing*) triste; **to make sb sad** rattristare qn; **how sad!** che tristezza!; **sadder but wiser** maturato(-a) dall'esperienza **2** (*deplorable*) deplorevole; **sad but true** è triste ma è così ; **it's a sad state of affairs when ...** la situazione è proprio triste quando...

sad·den [ˈsædn] VT rattristare

sad·dle [ˈsædl] N (*of horse, also Culin*) sella; (*of bicycle*) sellino, sella; **in the saddle** in sella; **when he was in the saddle** (*fig*) quando aveva le redini (del potere); **saddle of lamb** sella d'agnello
■ VT (*horse: also:* **saddle up**) sellare; **to saddle sb with sth** (*fam: task, bill, name*) appioppare qc a qn; (: *responsibility*) accollare qc a qn; **I got saddled with him again** me lo sono dovuto sorbire di nuovo

saddle·bag [ˈsædlˌbæg] N bisaccia; (*on bicycle*) borsa

sad·dler [ˈsædləʳ] N sellaio

sad·do [ˈsædəʊ] N (*Brit fam*) sfigato(-a)

sad·ism [ˈseɪdɪzəm] N sadismo

sad·ist [ˈseɪdɪst] N sadico(-a)

sa·dis·tic [səˈdɪstɪk] ADJ sadico(-a), sadistico(-a)

sa·dis·ti·cal·ly [sə'dɪstɪkəlɪ] ADV sadisticamente, in modo sadico

sad·ly ['sædlɪ] ADV (*unhappily*) tristemente; (*regrettably*) sfortunatamente; **sadly lacking in ...** completamente privo(-a) di...; **"she's gone," he said sadly** "se n'è andata" disse tristemente; **sadly, it was too late** sfortunatamente era troppo tardi

sad·ness ['sædnɪs] N tristezza

sado·maso·chism [,seɪdəʊ'mæsə,kɪzəm] N sadomasochismo

sado·maso·chist [,seɪdəʊ'mæsəkɪst] N sadomasochista *m/f*

sado·maso·chist·ic [,seɪdəumæsə'kɪstɪk] ADJ sadomasochistico(-a)

s.a.e. [,ɛseɪ'i:] N ABBR (*Brit*) = **stamped addressed envelope**

sa·fa·ri [sə'fɑ:rɪ] N safari *m inv*; **to be on safari** fare un safari

safari park N zoosafari *m inv*

◎ **safe** [seɪf] ADJ (*comp* **-r**, *superl* **-st**) **1** (*not in danger: person*) salvo(-a); (*: money, jewels, secret*) al sicuro; (*out of danger: person*) fuori pericolo; **safe and sound** sano(-a) e salvo(-a); **as safe as houses** sicurissimo(-a); **he didn't feel very safe up there** non si sentiva molto (al) sicuro lassù; **to be safe from** essere al sicuro da; **to feel safe** sentirsi al sicuro; **you'll be safe here** qui sarai al sicuro; **no woman is safe with you** (*hum*) non ti si può lasciare una donna vicino **2** (*not dangerous: toy, beach, animal*) non pericoloso(-a); (*: ladder*) sicuro(-a); (*secure: hiding place, investment*) sicuro(-a); (*prudent: choice*) prudente; **that dog isn't safe with children** non si dovrebbe lasciare quel cane coi bambini; **(have a) safe journey!** buon viaggio!; **in safe hands** in buone mani; **just to be on the safe side** per andare sul sicuro, per precauzione, per non correre rischi; **better safe than sorry!** meglio essere prudenti!; **it's a safe bet** è praticamente certo; **safe to drink** potabile; **is the water safe to drink?** è potabile l'acqua?; **it is safe to say that ...** si può affermare con sicurezza che...; **to play safe** giocare sul sicuro; **this car isn't safe** questa macchina non è sicura; **it might not be safe to leave your car here** potrebbe non essere prudente lasciare la macchina qui

safe bet N: **it's a safe bet** è una cosa sicura

safe-breaker ['seɪf,breɪkə^r], **safe-cracker** ['seif,krækə^r] (*Am*) N scassinatore(-trice)

safe-conduct [,seɪf'kɒndʌkt] N salvacondotto

safe-deposit ['seɪfdɪ,pɒzɪt], **safety-deposit** ['seiftɪdɪ,pɒzɪt] N (*vault*) caveau *m inv*; (*box*) cassetta di sicurezza

safe·guard ['seɪf,gɑ:d] N salvaguardia
■ VT salvaguardare

safe haven N zona sicura *or* protetta

safe·keeping ['seɪf'ki:pɪŋ] N custodia; **to give sb sth for safekeeping** dare qc in custodia a qn; **I gave it to him for safekeeping** gliel'ho dato in custodia; **the key is in his safekeeping** gli è stata affidata la custodia della chiave

safe·ly ['seɪflɪ] ADV (*securely*) al sicuro; (*without danger*) senza (correre) rischi, tranquillamente; (*without accident*): **to arrive safely** arrivare sano(-a) e salvo(-a); **I can safely say ...** posso tranquillamente asserire...

safe·ness ['seɪfnɪs] N (*of construction, machine*) sicurezza

safe passage N passaggio sicuro

safe period N: **the safe period** (*fam: of menstrual cycle*) il periodo non fecondo

safe seat N (Pol) seggio sicuro

safe sex N sesso sicuro

◎ **safe·ty** ['seɪftɪ] N sicurezza; **to reach safety** mettersi in salvo; **in a place of safety** al sicuro; **there's safety in numbers** l'unione fa la forza; **safety first!** la prudenza innanzitutto!; **for safety's sake** per (maggior) sicurezza
■ ADJ (*device, measure, margin*) di sicurezza

safety belt N (*Aut, Aer*) cintura di sicurezza

safety catch N sicura

safety curtain N (*Theatre*) (sipario) spartifuoco

safety-deposit ['seɪftɪdɪ,pɒzɪt] N = **safe-deposit**

safety glass N cristallo di sicurezza

safety lock N chiusura *or* serratura di sicurezza

safety match N (fiammifero) svedese *m*

safety net N (*in circus*) rete *f* di protezione; (*fig: safeguard*) ancora di salvezza; **to slip through the social security safety net** (*fig*) scivolare attraverso le maglie dell'assistenza sociale

safety pin N spilla da balia *or* di sicurezza

safety valve N valvola di sicurezza

saf·fron ['sæfrən] N zafferano
■ ADJ (*colour*) (color) zafferano *inv*

sag [sæg] VI (*hang down: ceiling, awning, bed*) incurvarsi; (*: breasts*) afflosciarsi; (*slacken: rope*) allentarsi; (*fig: spirits*) deprimersi; **his knees sagged** gli hanno ceduto le ginocchia; **the roof sags at one corner** il tetto è incurvato ad un'estremità; **muscles start to sag when you get to a certain age** i muscoli cominciano ad afflosciarsi ad una certa età

saga ['sɑ:gə] N saga

sa·ga·cious [sə'geɪʃəs] ADJ sagace

sa·ga·cious·ly [sə'geɪʃəslɪ] ADV sagacemente, in modo sagace

sa·gac·ity [sə'gæsɪtɪ] N sagacia

sage[1] [seɪdʒ] ADJ (*liter*) saggio(-a)
■ N (*man*) saggio

sage[2] [seɪdʒ] N (*herb*) salvia; **sage and onion stuffing** ripieno di salvia e cipolla; **chopped sage** salvia tritata

sage green ADJ, N verde salvia (*m*) *inv*

sage·ly ['seɪdʒlɪ] ADV saggiamente

sag·ging ['sægɪŋ] ADJ (*ceiling*) incurvato(-a); (*rope*) allentato(-a); (*breasts*) cadente; (*fig: spirits*) a terra

Sag·it·ta·rius [,sædʒɪ'tɛərɪəs] N (*Astron, Astrol*) Sagittario; **to be Sagittarius** essere del Sagittario; **I'm Sagittarius** sono del Sagittario

sago ['seɪgəʊ] N sagù *m inv*

Sa·ha·ra [sə'hɑ:rə] N: **the Sahara (Desert)** il (deserto del) Sahara

sa·hib ['sɑ:hɪb] N sahib *m inv*

said [sɛd] PT, PP *of* **say**
■ ADJ (*aforementioned*): **the said** il/la suddetto(-a)

Sai·gon [saɪ'gɒn] N Saigon *f*

◎ **sail** [seɪl] N (*of boat*) vela; (*of windmill*) pala; (*trip*): **to go for a sail** fare un giro in barca a vela; **to set sail** salpare; **under sail** a vela
■ VT **1** (*ship*) condurre, governare; **to sail a boat** condurre una barca **2** (*travel over*): **to sail the Atlantic** attraversare l'Atlantico; **to sail the seas** solcare i mari
■ VI **1** (*travel: ship*) navigare; (*: person*) viaggiare per mare; **to sail into harbour** entrare in porto; **the ship sailed into Naples** la nave è arrivata a Napoli; **to sail round the Cape** doppiare il Capo; **to sail away/back** *etc* allontanarsi/rientrare *etc* in barca; **they sailed into Genoa** sono entrati nel porto di Genova; **to sail round the world** fare il giro del mondo in barca a vela; **to sail close to the wind** (*fig*) tirare troppo la corda **2** (*set off*) salpare; **the ship sails at 5 o'clock** la nave

Ss

salpa alle 5 **3** (*Sport*) fare della vela **4** (*fig: clouds*) veleggiare; (: *swan*) incedere maestosamente; **she sailed into the room** fece il suo ingresso solenne nella stanza; **the plate sailed over my head** il piatto è volato al di sopra della mia testa
▶ **sail through** VI + ADV (*fig*) farcela senza difficoltà ■VI + PREP (*fig*) fare qc senza difficoltà; (*pass: exam, driving text*) superare senza difficoltà

sail·cloth ['seɪl,klɒθ] N tela da vela

sail·ing ['seɪlɪŋ] N (*sport*) vela; (*departure*) partenza; **(pleasure) sailing** navigazione *f* da diporto; **to go sailing** fare vela; **now it's all plain sailing** il resto è liscio come l'olio

sailing boat, (*Am*) **sail·boat** ['seɪl,bəʊt] N barca a vela

sailing dinghy N deriva

sailing ship N veliero

sail·maker ['seɪl,meɪkəʳ] N velaio; **sailmaker's (shop)** veleria

sail·or ['seɪləʳ] N marinaio; **to be a bad sailor** soffrire il mal di mare

sailor hat N berretto da marinaio

sailor suit N divisa da marinaio; (*for children*) vestito alla marinara

sail·plane ['seɪl,pleɪn] N (*Aer*) veleggiatore *m*

sain·foin ['sænfɔɪn] N fieno santo

◎ **saint** [seɪnt] N (*also fig*) santo(-a); **Saint John** San Giovanni; **Saint Mark's (Church)** (la chiesa di) San Marco

Saint Bernard [sənt'bɜːnəd] N (*dog*) sanbernardo, San Bernardo

saint·hood ['seɪnthʊd] N santità

Saint John's wort N (*Bot*) erba di San Giovanni

saint·li·ness ['seɪntlɪnɪs] N santità

saint·ly ['seɪntlɪ] ADJ (*comp* **-ier**, *superl* **-iest**) (*expression, life*) da santo(-a); **a saintly person** una santa persona

saint's day N *giorno dedicato a un santo*

Saint Vitus's (dance) [sənt'vaɪtəsɪz('dɑːns)] N (*Med*) ballo di San Vito

◎ **sake** [seɪk] N: **for the sake of sb/sth** per amor di qn/qc; **for my sake** per amor mio, per me; **for the sake of the children** per il bene dei bambini; **for God's/for heaven's sake!** per amor di Dio!/del cielo!; **art for art's sake** l'arte per l'arte; **for your own sake** per te (stesso), per il tuo bene; **for pity's sake** per pietà; **for old times' sake** in ricordo del passato; **for argument's sake** *or* **for the sake of argument** a titolo d'esempio

sa·la·cious [sə'leɪʃəs] ADJ (*joke, remark*) salace; (*book, film*) scabroso(-a); (*look, smile*) lascivo(-a)

sa·la·cious·ness [sə'leɪʃəsnɪs] N (*see adj*) salacità; scabrosità; lascivia

sal·ad ['sæləd] N insalata; **tomato salad** insalata di pomodori; **ham salad** prosciutto e insalata; **green salad** insalata verde

salad bowl N insalatiera

salad cream N (*esp Brit*) *tipo di maionese con cui si condisce l'insalata*

salad days NPL (*liter*) anni *mpl* verdi; **in my salad days** quand'ero giovane e inesperto

salad dressing N condimento per l'insalata

salad oil N olio da tavola

salad servers NPL posate *fpl* da insalata

salad spinner N centrifuga scolaverdure

sala·man·der ['sælə,mændəʳ] N salamandra

sa·la·mi [sə'lɑːmɪ] N salame *m*

sala·ried ['sælərɪd] ADJ (*person, post*) stipendiato(-a)

◎ **sala·ry** ['sælərɪ] N stipendio

salary earner N stipendiato(-a)

salary range N fascia salariale

salary review N revisione *f* degli stipendi

salary scale N scala salariale

◎ **sale** [seɪl] N **1** (*of article*) vendita; (*also:* **auction sale**) vendita all'asta; **"for sale"** (*one article*) "vendesi"; (*two or more articles*) "vendonsi"; **for sale** in vendita; **to put a house up for sale** mettere in vendita una casa; **the house is for sale** la casa è in vendita; **to be on sale** essere in vendita; **the sale of the company** la vendita della ditta **2** (*Comm: sales*) svendita, saldi *mpl*; **to be on sale** (*Am*) essere in saldi *or* in svendita; **she bought a dress in the sale(s)** ha comprato un vestito nei saldi; **the January sales** ≈ i saldi di fine anno; **there's a sale on at Harrods** da Harrods ci sono i saldi

> DID YOU KNOW ...?
> **sale** is not translated by the Italian word *sale*

sale·able, **sal·able** ['seɪləbl] ADJ vendibile

sale and lease back N (*Fin*) vendita con patto di locazione

sale of work N vendita di beneficenza

sale or return, **sale and return** N conto a deposito; **on sale or return** *or* **on a sale or return basis** in conto a deposito; **sale or return goods** merce *f* in conto a deposito

sale price N prezzo di liquidazione

sale·room ['seɪl,rʊm] N (*esp Brit*) sala di vendite all'asta

sales analysis N analisi *f inv* delle vendite

sales assistant N (*Brit*) commesso(-a)

sales budget N bilancio preventivo delle vendite

sales campaign N campagna di vendita

sales clerk N (*Am*) commesso(-a)

sales conference N riunione *f* marketing e vendite

sales department N reparto vendite

sales drive N campagna promozionale

sales executive N (*in shop*) addetto(-a) alle vendite; (*representative*) agente *m/f* di commercio

sales figures N fatturato

sales force N forza di vendita

sales forecast N previsione *f* delle vendite

sales·girl ['seɪlz,gɜːl] N commessa

sales incentive N incentivo sulle vendite

sales inquiry N richiesta d'offerta

sales literature N dépliant *mpl* illustrativi

sales·man ['seɪlzmən] N (*pl* **-men**) (*representative*) rappresentante *m* di commercio; (*in shop*) commesso; **car salesman** rivenditore di auto

sales manager N direttore(-trice) delle vendite

sales·man·ship ['seɪlzmənʃɪp] N arte *f* del vendere

sales manual N manuale *m* di vendita

sales·person ['seɪlz,pɜːsən] N (*in shop*) commesso(-a); (*representative*) rappresentante *m/f* di commercio

sales pitch N *dichiarazioni e promesse fatte allo scopo di persuadere qualcuno a comprare qualcosa*

sales promotion N promozione *f* delle vendite

sales prospect N possibile cliente *m/f*

sales quota N quota stabilita di vendite

sales rep(resentative) N rappresentante *m/f* (di commercio)

sales resistance N resistenza del consumatore all'acquisto

sales revenue N incassi *mpl* delle vendite

sales·room ['seɪlz,rʊm] N (*Am*) sala di vendite all'asta

sales slip N (*Am*) scontrino

sales talk N discorso imbonitore

sales tax N (*Am*) imposta sulle vendite
sales territory N zona di vendite
sales volume N volume *m* delle vendite
sales·woman ['seɪlz,wʊmən] N (*pl* **-women**) (*in shop*) commessa; (*representative*) rappresentante *f* di commercio
sa·li·ent ['seɪlɪənt] ADJ (*frm*) saliente
sa·line ['seɪlaɪn] ADJ salino(-a)
sa·li·va [sə'laɪvə] N saliva
sali·vate ['sælɪ,veɪt] VI salivare
sal·low ['sæləʊ] ADJ (*comp* **-er**, *superl* **-est**) (*complexion*) giallastro(-a)
sal·low·ness ['sæləʊnɪs] N colore *m* giallastro
sal·ly ['sælɪ] N (*witty remark*) battuta
▸ **sally forth, sally out** VI + ADV (*old*) uscire di gran carriera
salm·on ['sæmən] N salmone *m*; **salmon fishing** pesca del salmone; **salmon steak** trancio di salmone
sal·mo·nel·la [,sælmə'nɛlə] N salmonella
salmon pink ADJ, N rosa salmone (*m*) *inv*
salmon trout N trota salmonata, trota di mare
sa·lon ['sælɒn] N (*all senses*) salone *m*; **hair salon** il salone da parrucchiere; **beauty salon** istituto di bellezza
sa·loon [sə'lu:n] N **1** (*on ship*) sala, salone *m* **2** (*Brit: car*) berlina; **a family saloon** una berlina familiare **3** (*Am: bar*) saloon *m inv*, bar *m inv*; (*Brit: also:* **saloon bar**) bar (*in pub, hotel*)
saloon car N (*Brit Aut*) berlina; (*Am Rail*) vettura *or* carrozza salone
Sal·op ['sæləp] N ABBR (*Brit*) = *Shropshire*
sal·sa ['s[ae]l,sə] N salsa
sal·si·fy ['sælsɪfɪ] N (*Bot*) salsefica
SALT [sɔ:lt] N ABBR (= **Strategic Arms Limitation Talks** *or* **Treaty**) SALT *m*
◎**salt** [sɔ:lt] N sale *m*; **to rub salt into the wound** (*fig*) rigirare il coltello nella piaga; **not to be worth one's salt** non valere un granché; **he's the salt of the earth** è un brav'uomo; **an old salt** un lupo di mare; *see also* salts
■ VT (*flavour*) salare; (*preserve*) conservare sotto sale
■ ADJ (*water*) salato(-a); (*beef, meat*) salato(-a), sotto sale; (*mine*) di sale; (*spoon*) per il sale
▸ **salt away** VT + ADV (*fam*) mettere da parte
salt·cellar ['sɔ:lt,sɛləʳ], (*Am*) **salt shaker** N saliera
salt·ed [sɔ:ltɪd] ADJ salato
salt flats NPL saline *fpl*
salt-free [,sɔ:lt'fri:] ADJ senza sale
sal·tine [sɔ:l'ti:n] N (*Am: Culin*) cracker *m inv*
salti·ness ['sɔ:ltɪnɪs] N (*of water*) salsedine *f*; (*of food*) sapore *m* salato
salt lake N lago salato
salt·pan ['sɔ:lt,pæn] N (bacino di) salina
salt·pe·tre, (*Am*) **salt·pe·ter** ['sɔ:lt,pi:təʳ] N salnitro
salts [sɔ:lts] NPL (*Med*) sali *mpl*
salt shaker N (*Am*) = saltcellar
salt·water ['sɔ:lt,wɔ:təʳ] ADJ (*fish*) di mare
salty ['sɔ:ltɪ] ADJ (*comp* **-ier**, *superl* **-iest**) (*taste*) salato(-a); (*fig: humour, remark*) piccante
sa·lu·bri·ous [sə'lu:brɪəs] (*frm*) ADJ salubre; (*fig: district*) raccomandabile
salu·tary ['sæljʊtərɪ] ADJ salutare
salu·ta·tion [,sæljʊ'teɪʃən] N (*old, frm*) saluto
sa·lute [sə'lu:t] N (*Mil: with hand*) saluto; (*: with gunfire*) salva; **to take the salute** passare in rassegna le truppe
■ VT (*Mil, fig*) salutare; **to salute the flag** salutare la bandiera

DID YOU KNOW ...?
salute is not translated by the Italian word *salute*

sal·vage ['sælvɪdʒ] N **1** (*saving: of ship etc*) salvataggio; (*: for re-use*) ricupero **2** (*things saved*) oggetti *mpl* salvati *or* ricuperati; (*: for re-use*) materiale *m* di ricupero **3** (*compensation*) compenso
■ VT (*boat, cargo, goods*) ricuperare; (*fig*) salvare
■ ADJ (*operation*) di salvataggio; (*goods*) di ricupero
salvage vessel N nave *f* di salvataggio
sal·va·tion [sæl'veɪʃən] N salvezza
Salvation Army N: **the Salvation Army** l'Esercito della Salvezza
▷ http://www.salvationarmy.org/
sal·va·tion·ist, Sal·va·tion·ist [sæl'veɪʃənɪst] N salutista *m/f*
salve [sælv] VT: **to salve one's conscience** mettersi la coscienza in pace
■ N balsamo
sal·ver ['sælvəʳ] N vassoio (*d'argento o altro metallo*)
sal·vo ['sælvəʊ] N (*Mil*) salva; (*outburst: of applause*) scroscio
Sa·mari·tan [sə'mærɪtən] N **1** **the Good Samaritan** il buon Samaritano **2** **the Samaritans** (*organisation*) ≈ Telefono Amico
sam·ba ['sæmbə] N samba
sam·bo ['sæmbəʊ] N (*offensive*) negro(-a)
◎**same** [seɪm] ADJ stesso(-a), medesimo(-a); **the same book as/that** lo stesso libro di/che; **the same model** lo stesso modello; **the same table as usual** il solito tavolo; **on the same day** lo stesso giorno; **the** *or* **that same day** il *or* quel giorno stesso; **at the same time** allo stesso tempo; **it comes to the same thing** è la stessa cosa; **in the same way** allo stesso modo; **to go the same way as sb** (*fig pej*) seguire le orme di qn; **they're exactly the same** sono esattamente uguali
■ PRON: **the same** (*sg*) lo(-a) stesso(-a); (*pl*) gli/le stessi(-e); **it's all the same to me** per me fa lo stesso; **just the same as usual** come al solito; **same again, please** (*in pub*) un altro, per favore; **it was wrong but I did it all** *or* **just the same** non era giusto ma l'ho fatto lo stesso; **they're one and the same** (*person*) sono la stessa persona; (*thing*) sono la stessa cosa; **it's not the same** non è lo stesso; **to do the same** fare la stessa cosa; **I'll do the same for you** farò altrettanto per te; **I would do the same again** rifarei quello che ho fatto; **to do the same as sb** fare come qn; **do the same as your father** fa' come tuo padre; **and the same to you!** altrettanto a te!; **I don't feel the same about it** non la vedo allo stesso modo; **I still feel the same about you** i miei sentimenti nei tuoi confronti non sono cambiati; **same here!** (*fam*) anch'io!
same·ness ['seɪmnɪs] N (*monotony*) monotonia
same-sex ['seɪm,sɛks] ADJ (*people, friends*) dello stesso sesso; (*same-sex marriage, relationship*) tra due persone dello stesso sesso
samey ['seɪmɪ] ADJ (*Brit fam: unvaried*) tutto(-a) uguale
sa·mo·sa [sə'məʊsə] N *triangolo di sfoglia ripieno di verdure o carne fritto, specialità della cucina indiana*
◎**sam·ple** ['sɑ:mpl] N (*gen*) campione *m*; (*fig*) saggio; **to take a sample** prelevare un campione; **to take a blood sample** fare un prelievo di sangue; **free sample** campione omaggio; **a free sample of perfume** un campione gratuito di profumo
■ VT (*food, wine*) assaggiare, degustare; (*fig: experience*) provare; (*Market Research: people*) usare come campione
■ ADJ (*bottle*) campione *inv*; **sample line/verse**

Ss

esempio; **sample selection** campioni *mpl*; **sample copy** copia saggio; **sample survey** indagine *f* su campione

sam·pler [ˈsɑːmpləʳ] N (*Sewing*) saggio di ricamo; (*Mus*) *strumento elettronico per la campionatura di pezzi musicali*

samu·rai [ˈsæmʊˌraɪ] N samurai *m inv*

sana·to·rium [ˌsænəˈtɔːrɪəm] N (*pl* **sanatoria** [ˌsænəˈtɔːrɪə] *or* **sanatoriums**) **1** casa di cura; (*for tuberculosis*) sanatorio **2** (*Brit Scol*) ≈ infermeria

sanc·ti·fy [ˈsæŋktɪˌfaɪ] VT santificare

sanc·ti·mo·ni·ous [ˌsæŋktɪˈməʊnɪəs] ADJ (*pej: person*) bigotto(-a), bacchettone(-a); (*: tone*) moraleggiante

sanc·ti·mo·ni·ous·ly [ˌsæŋktɪˈməʊnɪəslɪ] ADV (*pej: say*) con tono moraleggiante

◎**sanc·tion** [ˈsæŋkʃən] N (*gen*) sanzione *f*; **economic sanctions** sanzioni *fpl* economiche; **to impose economic sanctions on** *or* **against** adottare sanzioni economiche contro
■VT sancire, sanzionare

sanc·tity [ˈsæŋktɪtɪ] N (*of person, marriage*) santità; (*of oath, place*) sacralità

sanc·tu·ary [ˈsæŋktjʊərɪ] N (*Rel*) santuario; (*fig, Pol: refuge*) asilo; (*for wildlife, birds*) riserva; **a wildlife sanctuary** una riserva naturale; **to seek sanctuary** cercare asilo; **they sought sanctuary in the church** hanno cercato rifugio nella chiesa

◎**sand** [sænd] N sabbia; *see also* **sands**
■VT **1** (*road*) cospargere di sabbia **2** (*also:* **sand down:** *wood*) levigare, smerigliare

san·dal [ˈsændl] N sandalo

sandal·wood [ˈsændlˌwʊd] N (*wood*) legno di sandalo; (*oil*) olio di sandalo
■ADJ (*soap, perfume*) al sandalo

sand·bag [ˈsændˌbæg] N sacchetto di sabbia
■VT (*protect*) proteggere con sacchetti di sabbia; (*hit*) colpire (con un sacchetto di sabbia)

sand·bank [ˈsændˌbæŋk] N banco di sabbia

sand·blast [ˈsændˌblɑːst] VT sabbiare

sand·blast·er [ˈsændˌblɑːstəʳ] N (*machine*) sabbiatrice *f*

sand·box [ˈsændˌbɒks] N (*Am*) buca della sabbia (*per i giochi dei bambini*)

sand·boy [ˈsændˌbɔɪ] N: **(as) happy as a sandboy** contento(-a) come una Pasqua

sand·castle [ˈsændˌkɑːsl] N castello di sabbia

sand dune N duna

sand eel N anguilla della sabbia

sand·er [ˈsændəʳ] N (*machine*) levigatrice *f*

sand flea, **sand hopper** N pulce *f* di mare

sand·fly [ˈsændˌflaɪ] N pappataci *m inv*

S & L [ˌɛsəndˈɛl] N ABBR (*Am: Fin*) = **savings and loan association**

S & M [ˌɛsənˈɛm] N ABBR = **sadomasochism**

sand·man [ˈsændˌmæn] N: **the sandman** *personaggio fantastico che fa addormentare i bambini spargendo sabbia sui loro occhi*

sand·paper [ˈsændˌpeɪpəʳ] N carta vetrata
■VT cartavetrare

sand·piper [ˈsændˌpaɪpəʳ] N (*also:* **common sandpiper**) piro piro piccolo

sand·pit [ˈsændˌpɪt] N cava di sabbia; (*Brit: for children*) buca della sabbia (*per i giochi dei bambini*); **they're playing in the sandpit** giocano nella buca della sabbia

sands [sændz] NPL spiaggia *fsg*; **the sands of time** (*fig*) lo scorrere del tempo

sand·shoe [ˈsændˌʃuː] N scarpa di tela

sand·stone [ˈsændˌstəʊn] N arenaria

sand·storm [ˈsændˌstɔːm] N tempesta di sabbia

sand·wich [ˈsænwɪdʒ] N tramezzino, sandwich *m inv*; **cheese/ham sandwich** panino al formaggio/ prosciutto
■VT (*also:* **sandwich in:** *person, appointment etc*) infilare; **to be sandwiched between** essere incastrato(-a) fra

sandwich bar N snack bar *m inv*

sandwich board N cartello pubblicitario (*portato da uomo sandwich*)

sandwich cake N torta farcita (*di marmellata o panna*)

sandwich course N (*Brit*) *corso che alterna lo studio a periodi di pratica presso aziende o fabbriche*

sandwich loaf N pane *m* a cassetta

sandwich man N uomo *m* sandwich *inv*

sandy [ˈsændɪ] ADJ (*comp* **-ier**, *superl* **-iest**) (*gen*) sabbioso(-a); (*colour*) color sabbia *inv*; (*hair*) biondo rossiccio *inv*; **a sandy beach** una spiaggia sabbiosa

sane [seɪn] ADJ (*comp* **-r**, *superl* **-st**) (*person*) sano(-a) di mente; (*judgment, outlook*) sensato(-a); **he seemed perfectly sane** sembrava assolutamente sano di mente; **no sane person wants conflict** nessuna persona sensata vorrebbe un conflitto

sane·ly [ˈseɪnlɪ] ADV (*act, speak*) in modo sensato

San Fran·cis·co [ˌsænfrænˈsɪskəʊ] N San Francisco *f*
▷ www.sfvisitor.org
▷ www.ci.sf.ca.us/

sang [sæŋ] PT *of* **sing**

sang·froid [ˌsɑ̃ːŋˈfrwɑː] N sangue *m* freddo

san·gria [sæŋˈgrːə] N sangria

san·guine [ˈsæŋgwɪn] ADJ ottimista

san·guine·ly [ˈsæŋgwɪnlɪ] ADV ottimisticamente

San·hed·rin [ˈsænɪdrɪn] N sinedrio

sani·ta·rium [ˌsænɪˈtɛərɪəm] N (*pl* **sanitaria** [ˌsænɪˈtɛərɪə] *or* **sanitariums**) (*Am*) = **sanatorium**

sani·tary [ˈsænɪtərɪ] ADJ (*clean*) igienico(-a); (*system, arrangements, fittings*) sanitario(-a)

sanitary towel, (*Am*) **sanitary napkin** N assorbente *m* (igienico)

sani·ta·tion [ˌsænɪˈteɪʃən] N (*plumbing: in house*) impianti *mpl* igienici; (*: in town*) fognature *fpl*; (*hygiene*) igiene *f*; **poor sanitation** qualità scadente delle strutture per l'igiene pubblica

sanitation department N (*Am*) ≈ assessorato alla nettezza urbana

sani·tize [ˈsænɪˌtaɪz] VT sanitizzare; (*fig: make inoffensive*) espurgare

san·ity [ˈsænɪtɪ] N (*of person*) sanità mentale; (*of judgment*) buonsenso; **sanity prevailed** il buonsenso ha avuto la meglio

sank [sæŋk] PT *of* **sink**[1]

San Ma·ri·no [ˌsænməˈriːnəʊ] N San Marino *f*

San·skrit [ˌsænskrɪt] N sanscrito

Santa Claus [ˌsæntəˈklɔːz] N ≈ Babbo Natale

San·tia·go [ˌsæntɪˈɑːgəʊ] N (*also:* **Santiago de Chile**) Santiago *f* (del Cile)

sap[1] [sæp] N (*of plants*) linfa

sap[2] [sæp] VT (*strength*) fiaccare; (*confidence*) minare

sap·ling [ˈsæplɪŋ] N alberello

sa·poni·fi·ca·tion [səˌpɒnɪfɪˈkeɪʃən] N saponificazione *f*

sap·per [ˈsæpəʳ] N **1** (*Mil*) geniere *m* **2** **the Sappers** (*Brit*) il Genio

sap·phire [ˈsæfaɪəʳ] N zaffiro
■ADJ (*necklace*) di zaffiri; (*colour*) blu zaffiro *inv*

sapphire ring N anello di zaffiri (*or* con uno zaffiro)

Sara·cen [ˈsærəsn] N (*History*) saraceno(-a)

sar·casm [ˈsɑːkæzəm] N sarcasmo

sar·cas·tic [sɑːˈkæstɪk] ADJ sarcastico(-a); **to be sarcastic** fare del sarcasmo
sar·cas·ti·cal·ly [sɑːˈkæstɪkəlɪ] ADV sarcasticamente, in modo sarcastico
sar·copha·gus [sɑːˈkɒfəgəs] N (*pl* **sarcophaguses** *or* **sarcophagi**) sarcofago
sar·dine [sɑːˈdiːn] N sardina
Sar·dinia [sɑːˈdɪnɪə] N la Sardegna
Sar·din·ian [sɑːˈdɪnɪən] ADJ, N (*person*) sardo(-a)
sar·don·ic [sɑːˈdɒnɪk] ADJ sardonico(-a)
sar·doni·cal·ly [sɑːˈdɒnɪkəlɪ] ADV in modo sardonico, sardonicamente
sari, **saree** [ˈsɑːrɪ] N sari *m inv*
sar·in [ˈsɑːrɪn] N Sarin *m inv*®
sa·rong [səˈrɒŋ] N sarong *m inv*
SARS [sɑːz] N ABBR (= **severe acute respiratory syndrome**) SARS *f*, polmonite *f* atipica
sar·to·rial [sɑːˈtɔːrɪəl] ADJ (*frm*) sartoriale
SAS [ˌɛseɪˈɛs] N ABBR (*Brit Mil:* = **Special Air Service**) *reparto militare britannico specializzato in operazioni segrete*
SASE [ˌɛseɪɛsˈiː] N ABBR (*Am:* = **self-addressed stamped envelope**) *busta già affrancata e indirizzata a se stessi*
sash¹ [sæʃ] N (*of dress*) fusciacca; (*on uniform*) fascia
sash² [sæʃ] N (*also:* **window sash**) telaio
sash window N finestra a ghigliottina
Sas·katch·ewan [sæˈskætʃɪwən] N Saskatchewan *m*
▷ www.gov.sk.ca
▷ www.sasktourism.com
Sas·se·nach [ˈsæsənæk] N (*pej*) *termine usato dagli scozzesi per definire gli inglesi*
SAT [ˌɛseɪˈtiː] N ABBR (*Am:* = **Scholastic Aptitude Test**) *esami attitudinali per l'iscrizione all'università*

SAT

Negli Stati Uniti gli **Scholastic Aptitude Tests** o **SAT** sono gli esami di cultura generale sostenuti all'ultimo anno di scuola superiore che consentono di accedere al college o all'università. La votazione massima è 1600, con una media intorno a 900. I risultati vengono comunicati al college presso cui si fa domanda ma l'ammissione dipende anche dall'andamento complessivo degli studi. Gli esami **SAT** possono essere sostenuti più volte, fino a raggiungere un risultato accettabile, ma sono soggetti ogni volta al pagamento di una tassa.
▷ www.ed.gov/help/site/index/topics_az.jsp

Sat. ABBR (= **Saturday**) sab. (= *sabato*)
sat [sæt] PT, PP *of* **sit**
Satan [ˈseɪtn] N Satana *m*
sa·tan·ic [səˈtænɪk] ADJ satanico(-a)
satch·el [ˈsætʃəl] N cartella (*per la scuola*)
sa·ted [ˈseɪtɪd] ADJ (*frm*) sazio(-a)
sa·teen [sæˈtiːn] N rasatello
◎ **sat·el·lite** [ˈsætəˌlaɪt] N (*all senses*) satellite *m*
■ ADJ satellite *inv*
satellite dish N antenna parabolica
satellite television N televisione *f* via satellite
satellite town N città satellite *f inv*
sa·ti·ate [ˈseɪʃɪˌeɪt] VT (*frm*) saziare
sa·ti·ety [səˈtaɪətɪ] N (*frm*) sazietà
sat·in [ˈsætɪn] N raso, satin *m*
■ ADJ (*dress, blouse*) di raso *or* di satin; (*paper*) satinato(-a); **with a satin finish** satinato(-a)
sat·ire [ˈsætaɪəʳ] N: **satire (on)** satira (di, su)
sa·tiri·cal [səˈtɪrɪkəl] ADJ satirico(-a)
sa·tiri·cal·ly [səˈtɪrɪkəlɪ] ADV satiricamente
sati·rist [ˈsætərɪst] N (*writer etc*) scrittore(-trice) satirico(-a); (*cartoonist*) caricaturista *m/f*
sati·rize [ˈsætəˌraɪz] VT satireggiare
sat·is·fac·tion [ˌsætɪsˈfækʃən] N (*gen*) soddisfazione *f*; (*of ambitions, hopes*) realizzazione *f*; **has it been done to your satisfaction?** ne è rimasto soddisfatto?; **it gives me great satisfaction to learn that ...** è con immenso piacere che apprendo che...; **both sides expressed satisfaction** entrambe le parti hanno espresso soddisfazione
sat·is·fac·to·ri·ly [ˌsætɪsˈfæktərɪlɪ] ADV in modo soddisfacente
sat·is·fac·tory [ˌsætɪsˈfæktərɪ] ADJ soddisfacente; (*Scol*) sufficiente; **to bring sth to a satisfactory conclusion** concludere qc in modo soddisfacente
sat·is·fied [ˈsætɪsˌfaɪd] ADJ (*person, voice, customer*) soddisfatto(-a); **I'm not satisfied with that** ciò non mi basta; **I am satisfied that ...** sono convinto *or* sicuro che...
sat·is·fy [ˈsætɪsˌfaɪ] VT **1** (*make content*) soddisfare, contentare; **the offer won't satisfy everyone** l'offerta non soddisferà tutti **2** (*need, condition, creditor*) soddisfare; (*hunger*) calmare; **to satisfy the requirements** rispondere ai requisiti **3** (*convince*): **to satisfy sb (that)** convincere qn (che); **they must satisfy us that things will be different in future** devono convincerci che le cose andranno diversamente in futuro; **to satisfy o.s. of sth** accertarsi di qc; **to satisfy o.s. that** accertarsi che; **he wanted to satisfy himself that everyone was safe** voleva accertarsi che tutti fossero al sicuro
sat·is·fy·ing [ˈsætɪsˌfaɪɪŋ] ADJ (*gen*) soddisfacente; (*food, meal*) sostanzioso(-a)
SATs [sæts] NPL ABBR (*Brit:* = **standard assessment tests**) *test scritti a cui si sottopongono i ragazzi inglesi e gallesi all'età di 7, 11 e 14 anni*
sat·su·ma [ˌsætˈsuːmə] N satsuma; *tipo di mandarino*
satu·rate [ˈsætʃəˌreɪt] VT: **to saturate (with)** (*soak*) inzuppare (di); (*Chem, fig*) saturare (di); **to saturate the market** (*Comm*) saturare il mercato
satu·rat·ed [ˈsætʃəˌreɪtɪd] ADJ (*see vb*) inzuppato(-a); saturo(-a)
saturated fat N grassi *mpl* saturi
satu·ra·tion [ˌsætʃəˈreɪʃən] N saturazione *f*
saturation bombing N bombardamento a tappeto
saturation point N punto di saturazione; **to reach ~ saturation point** (*Chem*) raggiungere il punto di saturazione; (*fig*) arrivare a saturazione
Sat·ur·day [ˈsætədɪ] N sabato; *for usage see* **Tuesday**
Saturday night special N (*Am*) piccola pistola facile da nascondere
Saturn [ˈsætɜːn] N (*Myth, Astron*) Saturno
sat·ur·nine [ˈsætəˌnaɪn] ADJ (*liter*) malinconico(-a), taciturno(-a)
sa·tyr [ˈsætəʳ] N (*liter*) satiro
◎ **sauce** [sɔːs] N **1** (*containing meat, fish*) sugo; **tomato sauce** salsa di pomodoro **2** (*fam: impudence*) faccia tosta
sauce boat N salsiera
sauce·pan [ˈsɔːspən] N pentola, casseruola
sau·cer [ˈsɔːsəʳ] N piattino
sau·ci·ly [ˈsɔːsɪlɪ] ADV (*see adj*) sfacciatamente; in modo provocante
sau·ci·ness [ˈsɔːsɪnɪs] N sfacciataggine *f*
saucy [ˈsɔːsɪ] ADJ (*comp* **-ier**, *superl* **-iest**) (*impertinent*) sfacciato(-a), impertinente; (*look*) provocante

Ss

Sau·di Ara·bia ['saʊdɪə'reɪbɪə] N Arabia Saudita
Sau·di Ara·bian ['saʊdɪə'reɪbɪən] ADJ, N (*also:* **Saudi**) saudita (*m/f*)
sau·er·kraut ['saʊə,kraʊt] N crauti *mpl*
sau·na ['sɔ:nə] N sauna
saun·ter ['sɔ:ntəʳ] VI: **to saunter in/out** entrare/uscire con disinvoltura; **to saunter up and down** passeggiare su e giù
sau·sage ['sɒsɪdʒ] N (*to be cooked*) salsiccia; (*salami etc*) salame *m*
sausage dog N (*Brit fam*) bassotto
sausage meat N *carne macinata per salsicce*
sausage roll N *involtino di pasta sfoglia ripieno di salsiccia*
sau·té ['səʊteɪ] ADJ (*Culin: potatoes*) sauté *inv*
■VT (*potatoes, meat*) saltare; (*onions*) soffriggere
sav·age ['sævɪdʒ] ADJ **1** (*gen*) violento(-a); (*animal, murderer, attack*) feroce; **a savage attack** un feroce attacco **2** (*primitive: custom, tribe*) selvaggio(-a)
■N selvaggio(-a)
■VT (*subj: dog*) sbranare; (*fig*) fare a pezzi, attaccare violentemente
sav·age·ly ['sævɪdʒlɪ] ADV (*attack*) selvaggiamente; (*maul, criticize*) ferocemente
sav·age·ry ['sævɪdʒrɪ] N ferocia
sa·van·nah, sa·van·na [sə'vænə] N savana
◎**save¹** [seɪv] VT **1** (*rescue, Rel*): **to save (from)** salvare (da); **to save sb from falling** impedire a qn di cadere; **to save sb's life** salvare la vita a qn; **she saved his life** gli ha salvato la vita; **I couldn't do it to save my life** (*fig fam*) sono completamente negato per quello; **to save the situation** *or* **the day** salvare la situazione; **to save one's (own) skin** (*fam*) salvare la (propria) pelle; **to save face** salvare la faccia; **to save a goal** (*Ftbl*) parare un goal; **God save the Queen!** Dio salvi la Regina! **2** (*put aside: money: also:* **save up**) risparmiare, mettere da parte; (: *food, newspapers*) conservare, tenere da parte; (*collect: stamps*) raccogliere; (*Comput*) memorizzare; **I've saved fifty pounds already** ho già messo da parte cinquanta sterline; **I saved you a piece of cake** ti ho tenuto da parte una fetta di dolce; **save me a seat** prendimi un posto; **to save sth till last** tenere qc per ultimo(-a); **I saved the file onto a diskette** ho memorizzato il file su un dischetto; **I'm saving up for a new bike** sto risparmiando per comprare una bici nuova **3** (*avoid using: money, effort*) risparmiare; **it saved us a lot of trouble/another journey** ci ha risparmiato una bella seccatura/un altro viaggio; **I saved money by staying in youth hostels** ho risparmiato alloggiando negli ostelli della gioventù; **it will save me an hour** mi farà risparmiare un'ora; **it saved us time** ci ha fatto risparmiare tempo; **to save time ...** per risparmiare *or* guadagnare tempo...; **save your breath** risparmia il fiato
■VI **1** (*also:* **save up**): **to save (for)** risparmiare (per) **2 to save on time** risparmiare tempo; **to save on food/transport** risparmiare *or* economizzare sul vitto/trasporto
■N (*Sport*) parata
save² [seɪv] PREP (*liter, old*) salvo, a eccezione di
sav·eloy ['sævəlɔɪ] N cervellata
sav·er ['seɪvəʳ] N risparmiatore(-trice)
◎**sav·ing** ['seɪvɪŋ] N (*of time, money*): **saving of** *or* **in** risparmio di; **to make savings** fare economia; **savings** NPL (*in bank*) risparmi *mpl*; **life savings** i risparmi di tutta una vita; **to live on** *or* **off one's savings** vivere dei propri risparmi
saving grace N: **her kindness is her saving grace** si salva grazie alla sua gentilezza
savings account N libretto di risparmio
savings and loan association N (*Am: Fin*) società *f inv* immobiliare e finanziaria
savings bank N cassa di risparmio
sav·iour, (*Am*) **sav·ior** ['seɪvjəʳ] N salvatore(-trice)
savoir-faire ['sævwɑ:'fɛəʳ] N (*frm*) savoir-faire *m inv*
sa·vory ['seɪvərɪ] N **1** (*Bot*) satureia **2** (*Am*) = **savoury**
sa·vour, (*Am*) **sa·vor** ['seɪvəʳ] N sapore *m*, gusto
■VT (*also fig*) assaporare, gustare
■VI: **to savour of sth** sapere di qc
sa·voury, (*Am*) **sa·vory** ['seɪvərɪ] ADJ (*not sweet*) salato(-a); (*appetizing*) saporito(-a), appetitoso(-a); **savoury flan** *or* **tart** torta salata; **is it sweet or savoury?** è dolce o salato?; **not very savoury** (*fig: district*) poco raccomandabile; (: *subject*) scabroso(-a)
■N (*Culin*) piatto salato; (: *on toast*) crostino
sav·vy ['sævɪ] N (*fam*) comprendonio
saw¹ [sɔ:] (*vb: pt* **sawed**, *pp* **sawed** *or* **sawn**) N (*tool*) sega
■VT segare; **to saw sth up** fare a pezzi qc con la sega; **to saw sth off** segare via qc
■VI: **to saw through** segare
saw² [sɔ:] PT *of* see
saw·dust ['sɔ:,dʌst] N segatura
saw·mill ['sɔ:,mɪl] N segheria
sawn [sɔ:n] PP *of* saw¹
sawn-off shotgun [,sɔ:nɒfʃɒtgʌn], **sawed-off shotgun** [,sɔ:dɒfʃɒtgʌn] N fucile *m* a canne mozze
sax [sæks] N sax *m*
saxi·frage ['sæksɪ,freɪdʒ] N sassifraga
Sax·on ['sæksən] ADJ, N sassone *m/f*
▷ www.bbc.co.uk/history/ancient/anglo_saxons/index.shtml
saxo·phone ['sæksə,fəʊn] N sassofono
sax·opho·nist [sæk'sɒfənɪst] N sassofonista *m/f*
◎**say** [seɪ] (*vb: pt, pp* **said**) VT, VI
1 (*gen*) dire; (*subj: dial, gauge*) indicare; **he said (that) he'd do it** ha detto che l'avrebbe fatto; **David said he'd come** David ha detto che sarebbe venuto; **she said (that) I was to give you this** mi ha detto di darti questo; **what did he say?** cos'ha detto?; **my watch says 3 o'clock** il mio orologio fa le 3; **the rules say that ...** il regolamento dice che...; **to say mass/a prayer** dire messa/una preghiera; **to say yes/no** dire di sì /di no; **to say yes/no to a proposal** accettare/rifiutare una proposta; **I wouldn't say no** (*Brit fam*) non mi dispiacerebbe; **to say goodbye/goodnight to sb** dire arrivederci/buonanotte a qn; **to say sth again** ripetere qc; **could you say that again?** potrebbe ripetere?; **say after me ...** ripetete con me...; **I've nothing more to say** non ho altro da dire; **I'll say more about it later** ne riparlerò più tardi; **let's say no more about it** non ne parliamo più; **I'd rather not say** preferisco non pronunciarmi; **I should say it's worth about £100** direi che vale sulle 100 sterline; **(let's) say it's worth £20** diciamo *or* ammettiamo che valga 20 sterline; **shall we say Tuesday?** facciamo martedì ?; **will you take an offer of, say, £50?** accetta un'offerta di, diciamo, 50 sterline?
2 (*in phrases*): **that is to say** vale a dire, cioè; **to say nothing of** per non parlare di; **to say the least** a dir poco; **she hasn't much** *or* **has nothing to say for herself** (*by way of conversation*) non sa dire due parole; **what have you got to say for yourself?** (*by way of excuse*) qual è la tua giustificazione?; **that doesn't say much for him** non torna a suo credito; **it goes**

without saying (that) va da sé (che); **there's no saying what he'll do** Dio solo sa cosa farà; **it's not for me to say** non sta a me dirlo; **what do** *or* **would you say to a walk?** che ne dici *or* diresti di una passeggiata?; **when all is said and done** in fin dei conti; **let's say that ...** mettiamo *or* diciamo che...; **it is said that** si dice che *+ sub*; **they say that** dicono che *+ sub*; **there is something** *or* **a lot to be said for it** ha i suoi lati positivi; **it must be said that ...** bisogna ammettere che...; **he is said to have ...** si dice che abbia...; **it is easier** *or* **sooner said than done** è più facile a dirsi che a farsi; **I say!** *or* *(Am)* **Say!** *(calling attention)* senta!, scusi!; *(in surprise, appreciation)* perbacco!; **I'll say!** *(fam)* eccome!; **I should say it is** *or* **so!** *or* **you can say THAT again!** *(fam)* altroché!; **you don't say!** *(fam: often iro)* ma va'!, ma che dici!; **you('ve) said it!** *(fam: emphatic)* l'hai detto!; **say no more!** *(fam: often hum)* non aggiungere altro!

■ N: **to have one's say** dire la propria; **to have a say/no say in the matter** avere/non avere voce in capitolo

say·ing ['seɪɪŋ] N detto; **as the saying goes** come dice il proverbio

say-so ['seɪˌsəʊ] N *(fam: authority)*: **to do sth on sb's say-so** fare qc col permesso di qn; **why should I believe it just on your say-so?** perché dovrei crederci, solo perché lo dici tu?

SBA [ˌɛsbiː'eɪ] N ABBR *(Am:* = **Small Business Administration)** *organismo ausiliario per piccole imprese*

SC ABBR *(Am)* **1** = **Supreme Court** **2** *(Post)* = **South Carolina**

s/c ABBR *(Brit)* = **self-contained**

scab [skæb] N **1** *(Med)* crosta **2** *(fam pej: strikebreaker)* crumiro(-a)

scab·bard ['skæbəd] N fodero

scab·by ['skæbɪ] ADJ *(comp* **-ier**, *superl* **-iest)** crostoso(-a)

sca·bies ['skeɪbiːz] N *(Med)* scabbia

sca·bi·ous ['skeɪbɪəs] N *(Bot)*: **field scabious** scabiosa

scaf·fold ['skæfəld] N *(Constr)* impalcatura, ponteggio; *(for execution)* patibolo

scaf·fold·ing ['skæfəldɪŋ] N impalcatura

sca·lar ['skeɪlə^r] *(Math, Phys)* ADJ scalare

■ N scalare *m*

scala·wag ['skæləˌwæg] N *(Am)* = **scallywag**

scald [skɔːld] N scottatura

■ VT *(gen)* scottare; *(Culin: milk)* sbollentare; *(sterilize)* sterilizzare

> DID YOU KNOW ...?
> **scald** is not translated by the Italian word *scaldare*

scald·ing ['skɔːldɪŋ] ADJ: **scalding hot** bollente

◎ **scale¹** [skeɪl] N *(of fish, reptile etc)* squama, scaglia; *(flake: of rust, chalk)* scaglia; (: *of skin)* squama

■ VT *(fish)* squamare

◎ **scale²** [skeɪl] N **1** *(on ruler, thermometer)* scala graduata; *(of model, map)* scala; **pay scale** scala salariale; **scale of charges** tariffario; **on a scale of 1 cm to 5 km** in scala di 1 a 500.000; **on a large scale** su vasta scala; **on a small scale** su scala ridotta; **small-scale model** modello in scala ridotta; **large-scale map** carta geografica su larga scala; **to draw sth to scale** disegnare qc in scala; **he underestimated the scale of the problem** ha sottovalutato la portata del problema **2** *(Mus)* scala; *see also* **scales**

■ VT *(wall, mountain)* scalare

▸ **scale down** VT + ADV ridurre proporzionalmente

scaled-down ['skeɪldˌdaʊn] ADJ su scala ridotta

scale drawing N disegno in scala

scale factor N *(Math)* fattore *m* di scala

scale model N modellino in scala

sca·lene ['skeɪliːn] ADJ *(Geom)*: **scalene triangle** triangolo scaleno

scales [skeɪlz] NPL **1** **(pair** *or* **set of) scales** bilancia; **he tips the scales at 70 kilos** pesa 70 chili; **to turn** *or* **tip the scales in sb's/sth's favour** far pendere la bilancia dalla parte di qn/qc; **to turn** *or* **tip the scales against sb** giocare a sfavore di qn; **the scales of justice** la bilancia della giustizia **2** *(also:* **bathroom scales)** bilancia *f* pesapersone *inv*

scal·lion ['skælɪən] N cipollotto; *(Am: shallot)* scalogno

scal·lop ['skɒləp] N **1** *(Zool)* pettine *m* **2** *(Culin)* cappa santa **3** *(Sewing)* smerlo

scal·loped ['skɒləpt] ADJ *(edge)* a smerlo; *(neck)* smerlato(-a)

scallop shell N conchiglia di pettine

scal·ly·wag ['skælɪˌwæg] N *(fam)* briccone(-a)

scalp [skælp] N cuoio capelluto; *(as trophy)* scalpo

■ VT scotennare; *(Am: Stock Exchange)* speculare in Borsa

scal·pel ['skælpəl] N bisturi *m inv*

scalp·er ['skælpə^r] N *(Am fam: of tickets)* bagarino

scaly ['skeɪlɪ] ADJ *(comp* **-ier**, *superl* **-iest)** squamoso(-a)

scam [skæm] N *(fam)* truffa

scamp¹ [skæmp] N *(fam: child)* peste *f*

scamp² VT *(one's work)* fare in fretta e male

scamp·er ['skæmpə^r] VI + ADV *(child)*: **to scamper about** scorrazzare; **to scamper in/out** *etc* entrare/uscire *etc* di corsa; **to scamper away** *or* **scamper off** darsela a gambe

scam·pi ['skæmpɪ] NPL scampi *mpl*

scan [skæn] VT **1** *(inspect closely: horizon, sb's face, crowd)* scrutare; (: *newspaper)* leggere attentamente; **he scans the papers for European news** legge con attenzione i giornali alla ricerca di notizie dall'Europa; **she scanned the crowd for Matt** ha scrutato la folla alla ricerca di Matt **2** *(glance at quickly)* dare un'occhiata a, scorrere; **she scanned the advertisement pages** ha dato una scorsa alle pagine degli annunci pubblicitari **3** *(machine)* leggere; *(Radar: sea bed)* scandagliare; (: *sky)* esplorare; *(immagine)* scannerizzare; **all luggage is scanned before loading** i bagagli vengono passati ai raggi x prima di essere caricati; **I had trouble scanning this photo** ho avuto delle difficoltà nello scannerizzare questa foto

■ VI *(Poetry)* scandire

■ N *(Med)* ecografia

◎ **scan·dal** ['skændl] N **1** *(public furore, disgrace)* scandalo; **it's a scandal that** è uno scandalo *or* è scandaloso che *+ sub*; **it caused a scandal** ha fatto scandalo **2** *(gossip)* chiacchiere *fpl*, pettegolezzi *mpl*; **have you heard the latest scandal about ...?** hai sentito l'ultima su...?

scan·dal·ize ['skændəˌlaɪz] VT scandalizzare

scandal·monger ['skændlˌmʌŋgə^r] N malalingua

scan·dal·ous ['skændələs] ADJ scandaloso(-a)

scan·dal·ous·ly ['skændələslɪ] ADV scandalosamente, in modo scandaloso

Scan·di·na·via [ˌskændɪ'neɪvɪə] N la Scandinavia

Scan·di·na·vian [ˌskændɪ'neɪvɪən] ADJ, N scandinavo(-a)

scan·ner ['skænə^r] N *(Radar, Med)* scanner *m inv*; *(for bar codes)* lettore *m* di codice a barre

scan·sion ['skænʃən] N *(Literature)* scansione *f*

scant [skænt] ADJ *(comp* **-er**, *superl* **-est)** scarso(-a); **with scant courtesy** poco cortesemente; **to pay scant attention to** prestare poca attenzione a; **they have**

Ss

scant respect for him hanno scarsa considerazione per lui

scanti·ly ['skæntɪlɪ] ADV: **scantily clad** *or* **dressed** succintamente vestito(-a)

scanti·ness ['skæntɪnɪs] N scarsezza; **the scantiness of her clothes** i suoi abiti succinti

scanty ['skæntɪ] ADJ (*comp* **-ier**, *superl* **-iest**) (*meal etc*) scarso(-a); (*clothing*) succinto(-a); (*swimsuit*) ridotto(-a)

scape·goat ['skeɪp,gəʊt] N capro espiatorio

scapu·la ['skæpjʊlə] N (*pl* **scapulas** *or* **scapulae**) (*Med*) scapola

scar[1] [skɑː'] N (*Med*) cicatrice *f*; (*on face*) sfregio, cicatrice; (*fig: on landscape etc*) segno; **it left a deep scar on his mind** gli ha lasciato il segno
■VT (*gen*) lasciare delle cicatrici su; (*face*) sfregiare; (*fig*) segnare, lasciare il segno su; **scarred by acne** butterato(-a) dall'acne; **a battle-scarred town** una città segnata dalla guerra
■VI (*also:* **scar over**: *heal*) cicatrizzarsi

scar[2] [skɑː'] N (*Geog*) rupe *f*

scarce [skɛəs] ADJ (*comp* **-r**, *superl* **-st**) (*money, food, resources*) scarso(-a); (*copy, edition*) raro(-a); **to be scarce** scarseggiare; **to grow** *or* **become scarce** diventare raro(-a); **to make o.s. scarce** (*fig fam*) squagliarsela

scarce·ly ['skɛəslɪ] ADV (*barely*) appena; **scarcely anybody** quasi nessuno; **scarcely ever** quasi mai; **I scarcely know what to say** non so proprio che dire; **I can scarcely believe it** faccio fatica a crederci; **I've scarcely seen him** l'ho visto raramente; **I scarcely knew him** lo conoscevo appena; **it can scarcely be a coincidence** non può essere una coincidenza

> DID YOU KNOW ...?
> **scarcely** is not translated by the Italian word *scarsamente*

scar·city ['skɛəsɪtɪ], **scarce·ness** ['skɛəsnɪs] N (*of jobs, accommodation*) scarsezza, scarsità; (*of food*) penuria

scarcity value N: **this item has a certain scarcity value** questo oggetto ha un certo valore grazie alla sua rarità

scare ['skɛə'] N spavento, paura; **to cause a scare (amongst)** creare il panico (tra); **to give sb a scare** far prendere uno spavento a qn, mettere paura a qn; **we had a bit of a scare** abbiamo preso uno spavento; **a bomb scare** un allarme per sospetta presenza di una bomba
■VT spaventare, impaurire; **you scared me!** mi hai spaventato!; **to scare sb to death** *or* **scare sb stiff** (*fam*) spaventare qn a morte
▸ **scare away, scare off** VT + ADV (*dog*) mettere in fuga; (*fig: subj: price*) far scappare; **the price scared him away** il prezzo l'ha scoraggiato

scare·crow ['skɛəkrəʊ] N (*also fig*) spaventapasseri *m inv*

scared [skɛəd] ADJ impaurito(-a), spaventato(-a); **to be scared (of)** aver paura (di); **are you scared of him?** hai paura di lui?; **to be scared to death** *or* **be scared stiff** essere spaventato(-a) a morte, essere mezzo(-a) morto(-a) di paura; **to be scared out of one's wits** (*fam*) non capire più niente dalla paura

scare·monger ['skɛə,mʌŋgə'] N allarmista *m/f*

scare·monger·ing ['skɛə,mʌŋgərɪŋ] N allarmismo

scare story N notizie *fpl* allarmistiche

scarf [skɑːf] N (*pl* **scarfs** *or* **scarves**) **1** (*long*) sciarpa **2** (*also:* **headscarf**) foulard *m inv*

scar·la·ti·na [,skɑːlə'tiːnə] N (*Med*) scarlattina

scar·let ['skɑːlɪt] N scarlatto
■ADJ scarlatto(-a); **a scarlet ribbon** un nastro scarlatto

scarlet fever N scarlattina

scarp [skɑːp] N scarpata

scarp·er ['skɑːpə'] VI (*Brit fam*) darsela a gambe

Scart, SCART [skɑːt] N (*Elec*): **a Scart cable/socket** un cavo/una presa Scart

scarves [skɑːvz] NPL *of* **scarf**

scary ['skɛərɪ] ADJ (*comp* **-ier**, *superl* **-iest**) (*fam*) che fa paura; **to be scary** fare paura; **it was really scary** faceva veramente paura; **a scary film** un film del brivido

scath·ing ['skeɪðɪŋ] ADJ (*remark, criticism*) aspro(-a); (*look*) sprezzante; **to be scathing about sth** essere molto critico(-a) nei confronti di qc; **a scathing attack** un duro attacco

scath·ing·ly ['skeɪðɪŋlɪ] ADV sprezzantemente, in modo sprezzante

scat·ter ['skætə'] VT **1** (*gen*) spargere; (*papers*) sparpagliare **2** (*disperse: crowd, clouds*) disperdere; (*: enemy*) mettere in fuga; **her relatives are scattered about the world** la sua famiglia è sparsa per il mondo; **toys were scattered everywhere** c'erano giocattoli sparsi dappertutto
■VI (*crowd*) disperdersi; **the crowd scattered** la folla si disperse

scatter·brain ['skætə,breɪn] N (*fam*) sventato(-a), sbadato(-a)

scatter·brained ['skætə,breɪnd] ADJ (*fam*) sventato(-a), sbadato(-a)

scatter cushion N cuscino (*decorativo*)

scatter diagram N diagramma *m* di dispersione

scat·tered ['skætəd] ADJ (*books, houses*) sparso(-a), sparpagliato(-a); (*population*) sparso(-a); **scattered showers** precipitazioni *fpl* sparse; **scattered with** (*strewn*) cosparso(-a) di

scat·ty ['skætɪ] ADJ (*comp* **-ier**, *superl* **-iest**) (*Brit fam*) svitato(-a)

scav·enge ['skævɪndʒ] VT (*food*) cercare; (*streets*) pulire
■VI (*hyenas, birds*) nutrirsi di carogne; **to scavenge (for)** (*person*) frugare tra i rifiuti (alla ricerca di)

scav·en·ger ['skævɪndʒə'] N (*animal*) insetto (*or* animale *m*) necrofago; (*person*) *chi fruga nei rifiuti alla ricerca di qualcosa*

SCE [,ɛssiː'iː] N ABBR (= **Scottish Certificate of Education**) *diploma di scuola secondaria superiore*

sce·nario [sɪ'nɑːrɪəʊ] N scenario; **try to imagine all possible scenarios** cerca di immaginare tutte le possibili situazioni

◎**scene** [siːn] N **1** (*gen, Theatre, Cine, TV*) scena; **indoor/outdoor scenes** interni/esterni *mpl*; **the scene is set in a castle** la scena si svolge in un castello; **to set the scene** (*fig*) creare l'atmosfera; **behind the scenes** (*also fig*) dietro le quinte; **the political scene in Italy** il quadro politico in Italia; **the Punk scene** il mondo dei punk; **the music scene** il mondo della musica; **scenes of violence** scene di violenza; **to make a scene** (*fam: fuss*) fare una scenata **2** (*of crime, accident*) luogo, scena; **at the scene of the crime** sul luogo *or* sulla scena del delitto; **she needs a change of scene** ha bisogno di cambiare aria; **to appear** *or* **come on the scene** (*also fig*) entrare in scena; **it's not my scene** (*fam*) non è il mio genere **3** (*sight*) scena, spettacolo; (*view*) vista, spettacolo; **a scene of utter destruction** una scena di totale distruzione; **it was an amazing scene** è stata una scena incredibile

scene change N (*Theatre*) cambio di scena

scene painter N scenografo(-a)
scen·ery ['si:nərɪ] N (*landscape*) paesaggio, panorama *m*; (*Theatre*) scenario, scenari *mpl*
scene shift·er ['si:nʃɪftə^r] N (*Theatre*) macchinista *m* di scena
sce·nic ['si:nɪk] ADJ (*postcard, view*) pittoresco(-a); (*road, railway*) panoramico(-a)
scent [sɛnt] N **1** (*smell, perfume*) profumo **2** (*track*) tracce *fpl*, pista; **to follow/lose the scent** seguire/perdere le tracce *or* la pista; **to pick up the scent** fiutare le tracce; **to put** *or* **throw sb off the scent** (*fig*) far perdere le tracce a qn, sviare qn
■ VT **1 to scent (with)** (*make sth smell nice*) profumare (di *or* con) **2** (*smell*) fiutare
scent·ed ['sɛntɪd] ADJ profumato(-a)
scep·ter ['sɛptə^r] (*Am*) N = **sceptre**
scep·tic, (*Am*) **skep·tic** ['skɛptɪk] N scettico(-a)
scep·ti·cal, (*Am*) **skep·ti·cal** ['skɛptɪkəl] ADJ: **sceptical (of** *or* **about)** scettico(-a) (su *or* circa)
scep·ti·cal·ly, (*Am*) **skep·ti·cal·ly** ['skɛptɪkəlɪ] ADV scetticamente
scep·ti·cism, (*Am*) **skep·ti·cism** ['skɛptɪˌsɪzəm] N scetticismo
scep·tre, (*Am*) **scep·ter** ['sɛptə^r] N scettro
◎ **sched·ule** ['ʃɛdju:l, *Am* 'skɛdju:l] N **1** (*timetable: of work, visits, events*) programma *m*, tabella *or* ruolino di marcia; **the work is behind/ahead of schedule** il lavoro è in ritardo/in anticipo sul previsto; **on schedule** in orario; **we are working to a very tight schedule** il nostro programma di lavoro è molto intenso; **a busy schedule** un programma fitto d'impegni; **everything went according to schedule** tutto è andato secondo i piani *or* secondo il previsto **2** (*list: of contents, goods*) lista; (*Customs, Tax etc*) tabella
■ VT (*date, time*) fissare, stabilire; (*visit, event*) programmare; **as scheduled** come stabilito; **scheduled flight** volo di linea; **the meeting is scheduled for 7.00** *or* **to begin at 7.00** la riunione è fissata per le 7; **this building is scheduled for demolition** questo edificio è destinato alla demolizione
sched·uled ['ʃɛdju:ld, *Am* 'skɛdju:ld] ADJ (*date, time*) fissato(-a); (*meeting, event*) programmato(-a); (*programme*) in programma
sche·ma ['ski:mə] N (*pl* **schemata**) (*frm*) schema
sche·mat·ic [skɪ'mætɪk] ADJ schematico(-a)
sche·mati·cal·ly [skɪ'mætɪklɪ] ADV schematicamente
◎ **scheme** [ski:m] N **1** (*plan*) piano; (*method*) sistema *m*; **a scheme to rebuild** *or* **for rebuilding sth** un piano per la ricostruzione di qc; **a scheme of work** un piano *or* programma *m* di lavoro; **a road-widening scheme** un progetto di ampliamento della strada; **it's some crazy scheme of his** è una delle sue idee balzane **2** (*dishonest plan, plot*): **scheme (to do** *or* **for doing sth/for sth)** piano (per fare qc/per qc); **a scheme for making money quickly** un piano per far soldi velocemente **3** (*arrangement*) sistemazione *f*; **colour scheme** combinazione *f* di colori; **man's place in the scheme of things** (*fig*) il posto dell'uomo nell'ordine delle cose
■ VI: **to scheme (to do)** (*intrigue*) tramare (per fare), complottare (per fare)
schem·er ['ski:mə^r] N intrigante *m/f*
schem·ing ['ski:mɪŋ] ADJ intrigante
■ N intrighi *mpl*, macchinazioni *fpl*
schism ['sɪzəm, 'skɪzəm] N scisma *m*
schiz·oid ['skɪtsɔɪd] ADJ, N schizoide (*m/f*)
schizo·phre·nia [ˌskɪtsəʊ'fri:njə] N schizofrenia
schizo·phren·ic [ˌskɪtsəʊ'frɛnɪk] ADJ, N schizofrenico(-a)
schlep [ʃlɛp] (*Am fam*) VT trascinare
■ VI (*to place*) trascinarsi
schmaltz, **schmalz** [ʃmɔ:lts] N (*fam*) sdolcinatezza
schmaltzy, **schmalzy** ['ʃmɔ:ltsɪ] ADJ (*fam*) sdolcinato(-a)
schnau·zer ['ʃnaʊtsə^r] N (*dog*) schnauzer *m inv*
schol·ar ['skɒlə^r] N (*learned person*) erudito(-a), studioso(-a); **a famous Dickens scholar** un noto studioso di Dickens; **he's never been much of a scholar** non è mai stato portato per gli studi

DID YOU KNOW ...?
scholar is not translated by the Italian word *scolaro*

schol·ar·ly ['skɒləlɪ] ADJ dotto(-a), erudito(-a)
schol·ar·ship ['skɒləʃɪp] N **1** (*learning*) erudizione *f*, cultura **2** (*award, grant*) borsa di studio; **to win a scholarship** vincere una borsa di studio
scholarship holder N borsista *m/f*
scho·las·tic [skə'læstɪk] ADJ scolastico(-a)
◎ **school¹** [sku:l] N **1** (*gen*) scuola; **to be at/go to school** frequentare la/andare a scuola; **to leave school** terminare gli studi; **school of motoring** scuola guida, autoscuola; **the Dutch school** (*Art*) la scuola olandese; **school of thought** corrente *f* di pensiero; **of the old school** (*fig*) di vecchio stampo **2** (*Univ*) facoltà *f inv*; **medical/law school** facoltà di medicina/giurisprudenza; **art school** istituto d'arte; **she's at law school** studia legge; **School of Interpreters** Scuola Interpreti
■ VT (*animal*) addestrare; (*reaction, voice etc*) controllare; **he schooled himself in patience** *or* **to be patient** ha imparato ad essere paziente
■ ADJ (*year, fees etc*) scolastico(-a); **during school hours** *or* **in school time** durante l'orario scolastico
▷ www.learningcurve.gov.uk
school² [sku:l] N (*of fish*) banco
school age N età *f inv* scolare
school attendance N frequenza scolastica
school attendance officer N *funzionario addetto al controllo della frequenza scolastica*
school·bag ['sku:lˌbæg] N cartella
school·book ['sku:lˌbʊk] N libro scolastico, libro di scuola
school·boy ['sku:lˌbɔɪ] N scolaro
schoolboy slang N gergo studentesco
school bus N scuolabus *m inv*
school·child ['sku:lˌtʃaɪld] N (*pl* **-children**) scolaro(-a)
school·days ['sku:lˌdeɪz] NPL tempi *mpl* della scuola
school·girl ['sku:lˌgɜ:l] N scolara
school·house ['sku:lˌhaʊs] N (*school building*) scuola (*edificio*); (*head teacher's house*) residenza del preside
school·ing ['sku:lɪŋ] N istruzione *f*; **compulsory schooling** istruzione *f* obbligatoria, scuola dell'obbligo
school-leaver ['sku:lˌli:və^r] N (*Brit: about to leave*) ≈ maturando(-a) (: *having recently left*) ≈ neo-diplomato(-a)
school-leaving age [ˌsku:l'li:vɪŋˌeɪdʒ] N età *f* in cui termina l'obbligo scolastico
school·marm ['sku:lˌmɑ:m] N (*pej*) maestrina
school·mar·mish ['sku:lˌmɑ:mɪʃ] ADJ (*pej*) pedante
school·master ['sku:lˌmɑ:stə^r] N (*in primary school*) maestro; (*in secondary school*) professore *m*
school·mate ['sku:lˌmeɪt] N compagno(-a) di scuola

Ss

school·mistress ['sku:lˌmɪstrɪs] N *(in primary school)* maestra; *(in secondary school)* professoressa
school report N *(Brit)* scheda di valutazione scolastica, pagella
school·room ['sku:lˌrʊm] N aula
school·teacher ['sku:lˌti:tʃəʳ] N insegnante *m/f*
school·teach·ing ['sku:lˌti:tʃɪŋ] N insegnamento
school uniform N uniforme *f* scolastica
school·work ['sku:lˌwɜ:k] N studio
school·yard ['sku:lˌjɑ:d] N *(Am)* cortile *m* della scuola
school year N anno scolastico
schoon·er ['sku:nəʳ] N **1** *(Naut)* schooner *m inv*, goletta **2** *(Brit: sherry glass)* bicchiere *m* da sherry; *(Am: beer glass)* boccale *m* da birra
schtick, **shtick** [ʃtɪk] N *(Am fam: of entertainer)* numero
sci·ati·ca [saɪ'ætɪkə] N *(Med)* sciatica
◎ **sci·ence** ['saɪəns] N scienza; *(Scol)* le materie scientifiche; **the sciences** le scienze; **the natural/ social sciences** le scienze naturali/sociali
■ ADJ *(teacher, exam)* di scienze; *(subject, equipment, laboratory)* scientifico(-a)
▷ www.scicentral.com
▷ www.100TopScienceSites.com
▷ www.sciencedaily.com
▷ www.treasure-troves.com
science faculty N *(Univ)* facoltà *f inv* di scienze *fpl*
science fiction N fantascienza
science park N polo di ricerca scientifica applicata
◎ **sci·en·tif·ic** [ˌsaɪən'tɪfɪk] ADJ scientifico(-a)
sci·en·tifi·cal·ly [ˌsaɪən'tɪfɪkəlɪ] ADV scientificamente
◎ **sci·en·tist** ['saɪəntɪst] N scienziato(-a)
sci-fi ['saɪˌfaɪ] N ABBR *(fam)* = **science fiction**
Scil·ly Isles ['sɪlɪˌaɪlz] NPL: **the Scilly Isles, the Scillies** le isole *fpl* Scilly
scimi·tar ['sɪmɪtəʳ] N scimitarra
scin·til·late ['sɪntɪˌleɪt] VI *(star, jewel)* brillare, scintillare; *(fig: person)* brillare
scin·til·lat·ing ['sɪntɪˌleɪtɪŋ] ADJ *(jewels, chandelier)* scintillante; *(wit, conversation, company)* brillante
scion ['saɪən] N **1** *(descendant)* rampollo **2** *(Bot)* pollone *m*
scis·sors ['sɪzəz] NPL forbici *fpl*; **a pair of scissors** un paio di forbici
scissors kick N *(Ftbl, Swimming)* sforbiciata
scle·ro·sis [sklɪ'rəʊsɪs] N *(Med)* sclerosi *f*
scle·rot·ic [sklɪ'rɒtɪk] ADJ *(Anat)* sclerale; *(Med)* sclerotico(-a); *(Bot)* scleroso(-a)
■ N sclera
scoff [skɒf] VI: **to scoff (at sb/sth)** *(mock)* farsi beffe (di qn/qc); **my friends scoffed at the idea** i miei amici hanno riso dell'idea
■ VT *(Brit fam: eat)* papparsi, spazzolare; **he scoffed the lot** si è pappato tutto, ha spazzolato tutto quello che c'era
scold [skəʊld] VT: **to scold sb (for doing sth)** sgridare qn (per aver fatto qc)
scold·ing ['skəʊldɪŋ] N lavata di capo, sgridata
scol·lop ['skɒləp] N = **scallop**
scone [skɒn, skəʊn] N *tipo di focaccina da tè*
scoop [sku:p] N **1** *(for flour etc)* paletta; *(for ice cream)* cucchiaio dosatore; *(for water)* mestolo, ramaiolo **2** *(also:* **scoopful***)* palettata; cucchiaiata; mestolata; **three scoops of ice-cream** tre palline di gelato **3** *(Press)* scoop *m inv*, colpo giornalistico; *(Comm)* affarone *m*; **a wonderful scoop** un ottimo scoop
■ VT *(Comm: market)* accaparrarsi; *(: profit)* intascare; *(Comm, Press: competitors)* battere sul tempo; *(Press)*: **to scoop an exclusive (about)** accaparrarsi l'esclusiva (su)
▶ **scoop out** VT + ADV *(flour, water etc)* svuotare *(con paletta, cucchiaio etc)*; *(hole)* scavare
▶ **scoop up** VT + ADV *(child)* sollevare (tra le braccia); *(books)* raccogliere; **he scooped her up into his arms** l'ha sollevata tra le braccia
scoop neck ADJ *(top, vest, T-shirt)* scollatura a barchetta
scoot [sku:t] VI *(fam)*: **to scoot in/out** entrare/uscire di corsa
scoot·er ['sku:təʳ] N scooter *m inv*; *(child's)* monopattino; **he was riding a scooter** era in sella ad uno scooter
scope [skəʊp] N *(opportunity: for action)* possibilità *fpl*; *(range: of law, activity)* ambito; *(capacity: of person)* capacità *fpl*; *(: of plan, undertaking)* portata; **the scope of the plan is limited** la portata del piano à limitata; **it's beyond the scope of a child's mind** è al di sopra delle capacità di un bambino; **it's well within his scope to ...** è perfettamente in grado di...; **there is plenty of scope for improvement** *(Brit)* ci sono notevoli possibilità di miglioramento; **it is within/beyond the scope of this book** rientra/non rientra nei limiti di questo libro

DID YOU KNOW ...?
scope is not translated by the Italian word *scopo*

scorch [skɔ:tʃ] N *(also:* **scorch mark***)* bruciacchiatura
■ VT *(fabric)* bruciacchiare; *(subj: sun, fire: earth, grass)* bruciare; **hot sun will scorch the leaves** il calore del sole seccherà le foglie; **the bomb scorched one side of the building** la bomba ha bruciacchiato un lato dell'edificio
■ VI *(esp Brit fam: car)* andare a tutta velocità
scorched earth policy [ˌskɔ:tʃt'ɜ:θˌpɒlɪsɪ] N tattica del fare terra bruciata
scorch·er ['skɔ:tʃəʳ] N *(fam: hot day)* giornata torrida
scorch·ing ['skɔ:tʃɪŋ] ADJ *(also:* **scorching hot***)* rovente; *(day)* torrido(-a); *(sun)* che spacca le pietre; *(sand)* bollente; **it's scorching** fa un caldo pazzesco
◎ **score** [skɔ:ʳ] N **1** *(Sport, Cards)* punteggio, punti *mpl*; **to keep (the) score** segnare i punti; **there's no score yet** *(Sport)* finora nessuno ha segnato (un punto); **there was no score in the match** *(Sport)* hanno finito zero a zero; *(Sport)*: **the score was three nil** il punteggio era tre a zero; **to know the score** *(fig fam)* sapere come stanno le cose; **to have an old score to settle with sb** *(fig)* avere un vecchio conto da saldare con qn **2** *(account)* motivo, titolo; **on that score** a questo riguardo **3** *(cut, mark: on wood)* scalfittura; *(: on leather, card)* incisione *f* **4** *(Mus: of opera)* partitura, spartito; *(: of film)* colonna sonora **5** *(twenty)*: **a score** venti; **a score of people** una ventina di persone; **scores of** *(fig)* molti(-e); **scores of times** molte volte; **scores of people** *(fig)* un sacco di gente
■ VT **1** *(goal, point, runs)* segnare; *(success)* ottenere; **to score 75% in an exam** prendere 75 su 100 a *or* in un esame; **to score a hit** *(Fencing)* fare una stoccata; *(Shooting)* centrare il bersaglio; **to score a hit with sth** *(fig)* far centro con qc; **to score a hit with sb** *(fig)* far colpo su qn; **he scored a goal** ha segnato una rete **2** *(cut: leather, wood, card)* incidere **3** *(music: for piano etc)* comporre; *(: for film)* comporre la colonna sonora
■ VI **1** *(Sport: footballer)* segnare; *(: player)* totalizzare; *(: keep score)* tenere il punteggio; **to score 6 out of 10** *(in exam, test)* prendere 6 su 10; **to score over sb** *(fig)* dare dei punti a qn; **who's going to score?** chi tiene il

punteggio? **2** *(fam!: have sex with)*: **to score (with sb)** portarsi a letto qn
▸ **score off** VT + ADV **1** *(name, item on list)* cancellare, spuntare **2** *(fig: in argument)*: **to score points off sb** avere la meglio su qn
▸ **score out, score through** VT + ADV cancellare, cancellare (con un segno)

score·board ['skɔː,bɔːd] N tabellone *m* segnapunti *inv*

score·card ['skɔː,kɑːd] N cartoncino *m* segnapunti *inv*

score draw N *(Brit: Sport)* pareggio *(con almeno un gol per squadra)*

score·line ['skɔːlaɪn] N *(Sport)* risultato

scor·er ['skɔːrəʳ] N *(keeping score)* segnapunti *m/f inv*; *(player)* marcatore(-trice); **the scorer of the winning goal** il marcatore del gol vincente; **I'll be the scorer** segno io i punti

scor·ing ['skɔːrɪŋ] N *(Sport)* punteggio

scorn ['skɔːn] N disprezzo, scherno; **to pour scorn on sb/sth** deridere qn/qc
■ VT *(gen)* disprezzare; *(attempt)* ridicolizzare; *(advice, offer)* respingere con sdegno; **to scorn to tell a lie** *(frm)* rifiutarsi sdegnosamente di dire una bugia

scorn·ful ['skɔːnfʊl] ADJ sprezzante; **to be scornful about sth** parlare con disprezzo di qc

scorn·ful·ly ['skɔːnfəlɪ] ADV sprezzantemente, in modo sprezzante

Scor·pio ['skɔːpɪəʊ] N *(Astron, Astrol)* Scorpione *m*; **to be Scorpio** essere dello Scorpione; **I'm Scorpio** sono dello Scorpione

scor·pi·on ['skɔːpɪən] N scorpione *m*

Scot [skɒt] N scozzese *m/f*; **the Scots** gli scozzesi

Scotch [skɒtʃ] N *(also: **Scotch whisky**)* scotch *m inv*

scotch [skɒtʃ] VT *(attempt, plan)* bloccare; *(revolt, uprising)* stroncare; *(rumour, claim)* mettere a tacere

Scotch broth N *(Brit) minestra fatta con brodo di manzo o montone, verdure e orzo*

Scotch egg N *(Brit) uovo sodo ricoperto di salsiccia, impanato e fritto*

Scotch mist N nebbia densa accompagnata da pioggia

Scotch tape ® N *(Am)* scotch® *m*

scot-free [,skɒt'friː] ADJ: **to get off scot-free** *(unpunished)* farla franca; *(unhurt)* uscire illeso(-a)

Scot·land ['skɒtlənd] N la Scozia
▹ www.scotland.gov.uk/
▹ www.visitscotland.com

Scotland Yard N Scotland Yard

Scots [skɒts] ADJ scozzese; **a Scots accent** un accento scozzese

Scots·man ['skɒtsmən] N *(pl **-men**)* scozzese *m*

Scots pine N pino silvestre

Scots·woman ['skɒts,wʊmən] N *(pl **-women**)* scozzese *f*

Scot·tish ['skɒtɪʃ] ADJ scozzese; **the Scottish Parliament** il Parlamento scozzese

Scottish Executive N: **the Scottish Executive** *(Brit: Pol)* il governo scozzese *(con mansioni che escludono la difesa e la politica estera)*

Scottish National Party N: **the Scottish National Party** il partito nazionalista scozzese

Scottish Office N *(Brit Pol)*: **the Scottish Office** *il ministero degli Affari scozzesi, attualmente sostituito dallo Scottish Executive*

scoun·drel ['skaʊndrəl] N *(old)* canaglia, furfante *m/f*; *(hum: child)* furfantello(-a), birba

scour ['skaʊəʳ] VT **1** *(clean: pan, floor etc)* sfregare **2** *(search: area, countryside)* setacciare, perlustrare, battere palmo a palmo; **he scoured the phone book** ha esaminato attentamente l'elenco telefonico; **rescue crews scoured a large area** i soccorritori hanno perlustrato una vasta zona

scour·er ['skaʊərəʳ] N *(pad)* paglietta

scourge [skɜːdʒ] N *(also fig)* flagello
■ VT *(beat)* flagellare; *(fig: bedevil)* tormentare

scour·ing pow·der ['skaʊərɪŋ,paʊdəʳ] N detergente *m* in polvere

scout [skaʊt] N *(Mil)* ricognitore *m (persona)*; *(boy)* boy-scout *m inv*
▸ **scout around** VI + ADV andare alla ricerca

scout·ing ['skaʊtɪŋ] N scoutismo

scout·master ['skaʊt,mɑːstəʳ] N capogruppo dei boy-scout

scowl [skaʊl] N espressione *f* accigliata; **with a scowl** con lo sguardo torvo
■ VI accigliarsi; **to scowl at sb** guardare qn in malo modo, guardare qn torvo; **he scowled but said nothing** ha aggrottato le sopracciglia senza dire nulla

Scrab·ble® ['skræbl] N Scarabeo®
▹ www.scrabble.com
▹ www.collins.co.uk/wordexchange/

scrab·ble ['skræbl] VI *(claw)*: **to scrabble (at)** raspare, grattare; **to scrabble about** *or* **around for sth** cercare a tastoni qc

scrag·gly ['skræglɪ] ADJ *(Am)*: **scraggly hair** capelli *mpl* sottili e incolti

scrag·gy ['skrægɪ] ADJ *(comp **-ier**, superl **-iest**)* *(neck, limb)* scheletrico(-a); *(animal)* pelle e ossa *inv*

scram [skræm] VI *(fam)* filare, filarsela

scram·ble ['skræmbl] VI **1 to scramble down/along** scendere/avanzare a fatica; **to scramble out** uscire in fretta; **to scramble for** *(coins, seats, job)* azzuffarsi per prendere; **he scrambled up (the hill)** si è inerpicato su (per la collina); **we scrambled over the rocks** ci siamo inerpicati sulle rocce **2** *(Sport)*: **to go scrambling** fare il motocross
■ VT **1** *(Culin: eggs)* strapazzare **2** *(Telec: message)* disturbare con interferenze
■ N **1** *(rush)* corsa; **the scramble to obtain funding** la corsa ai finanziamenti **2** *(Sport: motorcycle meeting)* gara di motocross

scram·bled eggs [,skræmbld'ɛgz] NPL uova *fpl* strapazzate

scram·bler ['skræmbləʳ] N *(Telec) dispositivo per il disturbo di trasmissioni radio o telefoniche*

scram·bling ['skræmblɪŋ] N motocross *m*

scrap[1] [skræp] N **1** *(small piece)* pezzo, pezzetto; *(fig: of truth)* briciolo; **a scrap of paper** un pezzo di carta; **a scrap of conversation** un frammento di conversazione; **there's not a scrap of proof** non c'è la benché minima prova; **it's not a scrap of use** non serve a un bel niente **2 scraps** NPL *(left-overs)* avanzi *mpl* **3** *(iron, gold)* scarti *mpl*; **to sell sth for scrap** vendere qc come rottame
■ VT *(gen)* buttar via; *(ship, car)* demolire; *(fig: plan)* scartare; **in the end the plan was scrapped** alla fine il progetto venne scartato

scrap[2] [skræp] *(fam)* N *(fight)* bisticcio, zuffa; **he got into a scrap with a bigger boy** si è azzuffato con un ragazzo più grande
■ VI: **to scrap (with sb)** bisticciare *or* azzuffarsi (con qn)

scrap·book ['skræp,bʊk] N album *m inv* per ritagli *(di giornali, fotografie etc)*

Ss

scrap dealer, **scrap merchant** N rottamaio(-a), commerciante *m/f* in rottami
scrape [skreɪp] N **1** (*act*) raschiatura; (*sound*) stridio; (*mark*) graffio; (*on leg, elbow*) scorticatura, sbucciatura **2** (*fig*) pasticcio, guaio; **to get into a scrape** mettersi nei pasticci *or* nei guai; **to get out of a scrape** tirarsi fuori dai pasticci *or* dai guai
■VT (*knee*) scorticare, sbucciare; (*clean: vegetables*) raschiare, grattare; (*: walls, woodwork*) raschiare; **the lorry scraped the wall** il camion ha strisciato il muro; **to scrape a living** sbarcare il lunario; **we managed to scrape enough money together** siamo riusciti a racimolare abbastanza soldi; **to scrape the bottom of the barrel** (*fig*) raschiare il fondo del barile
■VI (*make sound*) grattare; (*rub*): **to scrape (against)** strusciare (contro)
▸ **scrape along**, **scrape by** VI + ADV (*fam: manage*) cavarsela; (*: live*) tirare avanti
▸ **scrape off**, **scrape away** VT + ADV grattare via, raschiare via; **she scraped the ice off the car windows** ha grattato via il ghiaccio dai finestrini della macchina
■VT + PREP grattare via
▸ **scrape through** VI + ADV (*succeed*) farcela per un pelo, cavarsela
■VI + PREP (*exam*) passare per il rotto della cuffia; **I managed to scrape through the last exam** sono riuscito a passare l'ultimo esame per il rotto della cuffia
scrap·er ['skreɪpəʳ] N raschietto
scrap·heap ['skræp,hiːp] N ammasso di rottami; **to throw on the scrapheap** (*fig*) mettere nel dimenticatoio; (*person*) privare del posto di lavoro; **fit for the scrapheap** da buttare via
scrap metal N rottami *mpl*
scrap paper N (*for scribbling on*) (fogli *mpl* di) carta per appunti; (*for recycling*) carta da destinare al riciclo
scrap·py ['skræpɪ] ADJ (*comp* **-ier**, *superl* **-iest**) (*essay etc*) senza capo né coda; (*knowledge, education*) lacunoso(-a); (*meal*) arrangiato(-a)
scrap yard N deposito di rottami; (*for cars*) cimitero delle macchine
scratch [skrætʃ] N **1** (*mark*) graffio, graffiatura; **it's just a scratch** è solo un graffio; **without a scratch** (*unharmed*) illeso(-a), senza un graffio **2** (*noise*): **I heard a scratch at the door** ho sentito grattare alla porta **3** **to start from scratch** (*fig*) cominciare *or* partire da zero; **his work wasn't** *or* **didn't come up to scratch** il suo lavoro non è stato all'altezza; **to keep sth up to scratch** mantenere qc al livello desiderato
■VT **1** (*gen*) graffiare; (*one's name*) incidere; **we've barely scratched the surface** (*fig: of problem, topic*) l'abbiamo appena sfiorato; **the cat scratched me** il gatto mi ha graffiato **2** (*to relieve itch*) grattare; **he scratched his head** si è grattato la testa; **you scratch my back and I'll scratch yours** (*fig*) una mano lava l'altra **3** (*cancel: meeting, game, Comput*) cancellare; (*cross off list: horse, competitor*) eliminare
■VI (*person, dog*) grattarsi; (*hens*) razzolare, raspare; (*pen*) raschiare; (*clothing*) pungere; **the dog scratched at the door** il cane raspava alla porta
▸ **scratch out** VT + ADV (*from list*) cancellare; **to scratch sb's eyes out** cavare gli occhi a qn
scratch card N (*card*) gratta e vinci *m inv*
scratch file N (*Comput*) file *m inv* temporaneo
scratch meal N pranzo arrangiato
scratch pad N (*Am*) bloc-notes *m inv*
scratch team N squadra raccogliticcia
scratchy ['skrætʃɪ] ADJ (*comp* **-ier**, *superl* **-iest**) (*fabric*) ruvido(-a); (*pen*) che raschia; (*record*) graffiato(-a)
scrawl [skrɔːl] N (*handwriting*) scrittura illeggibile; (*brief note*) messaggio scarabocchiato
■VT scarabocchiare
■VI scarabocchiare
scrawny ['skrɔːnɪ] ADJ (*comp* **-ier**, *superl* **-iest**) (*neck, limb*) scheletrico(-a); (*animal, person*) pelle e ossa *inv*
◎**scream** [skriːm] N (*of pain, fear*) grido, urlo; **screams of laughter** grasse risate *fpl*; **he let out a scream** cacciò un urlo; **it was a scream** (*fig fam*) era da crepar dal ridere; **he's a scream** (*fig fam*) è una sagoma, è uno spasso
■VT (*subj: person: abuse, insults*) urlare; (*subj: poster, headlines*) strombazzare
■VI gridare, urlare; **to scream at sb (to do sth)** gridare a qn (di fare qc); **to scream (out) with pain** gridare di *or* dal dolore; **to scream for help** gridare aiuto; **to scream with laughter** sbellicarsi dalle risa
scream·ing·ly ['skriːmɪŋlɪ] ADV: **screamingly funny** spassosissimo(-a)
scree [skriː] N ghiaione *m*
screech [skriːtʃ] N (*of brakes, tyres*) stridio, stridore *m*; (*of owl*) strido; (*of person*) strillo; **a screech of laughter** una risata stridula
■VI (*person*) strillare; (*owl, brakes*) stridere; **"get out of here!" she screeched** "esci di qui!" strillò
screech owl N gufo comune
screeds [skriːdz] NPL (*fam*): **to write screeds** scrivere un romanzo (*iro*)
◎**screen** [skriːn] N **1** (*in room*) paravento; (*for fire*) parafuoco; (*fig: of trees*) barriera; (*: of smoke*) cortina **2** (*Cine, TV, Radar*) schermo; **stars of the big/small screen** divi(-e) del grande/piccolo schermo
■VT **1** **to screen (from)** (*hide: from view, sight*) nascondere (da); (*protect*) schermire (da), riparare (da); **he screened his eyes (from the sun) with his hand** si schermiva gli occhi (dal sole) con la mano **2** (*TV: film, programme*) mandare in onda; (*: Cine: film*) dare al cinema; **his earlier films were only screened in France** i suoi primi film sono usciti solo in Francia **3** (*sieve: coal*) setacciare; (*fig: person: for security*) passare al vaglio; (*: for job*) selezionare; (*: for illness*) fare uno screening
screen door N porta a zanzariera
screen dump N (*Comput*) stampa della videata
screen editing ['skriːn,edɪtɪŋ] N (*Comput*) editing *m inv* su schermo
screen·ing ['skriːnɪŋ] N **1** (*of film*) proiezione *f*; (*TV*) messa in onda **2** (*also:* **medical screening**) screening *m inv* **3** (*for security*) controlli *mpl* (di sicurezza)
screen memory N (*Psych*) ricordi *mpl* di copertura
screen name N (*Comput: on the Internet*) pseudonimo
screen·play ['skriːn,pleɪ] N sceneggiatura
screen·sav·er ['skriːn,seɪvəʳ] N (*Comput*) screen saver *m inv*, salvaschermo
screen test N provino cinematografico
screen writer N sceneggiatore(-trice)
screw [skruː] N **1** vite *f*; (*Brit old: of sweets*) cartoccio; **he's got a screw loose** (*fig fam*) gli manca una rotella; **to put the screws on sb** (*fig fam*) far pressione su qn **2** (*propeller*) elica **3** (*fam: prison officer*) secondino **4** (*fam!: sexual intercourse*) chiavata (*fam!*)
■VT **1** avvitare; **to screw sth to the wall** fissare qc al muro con viti; **I screwed the shelf to the wall** ho avvitato lo scaffale al muro; **to screw sth (up) tight**

avvitare bene qc; **to screw money out of sb** (*fam*) far scucire soldi a qn; **to screw one's head round** storcere la testa; **to have one's head screwed on** avere la testa sulle spalle; **he screwed the letter into a ball** ha appallottolato la lettera **2** (*fam!: have sex with*) chiavare (*fam!*); **screw you!** va' a farti fottere!
■ VI (*fam!: have sex*) chiavare (*fam!*)
▸ **screw off** VI + ADV svitarsi
■ VT + ADV svitare
▸ **screw together** VI + ADV avvitarsi
■ VT + ADV (*kit*) montare con viti; (*two pieces*) avvitare
▸ **screw up** VT + ADV **1** (*paper, material*) spiegazzare; **to screw up one's eyes** strizzare gli occhi; **to screw up one's face** fare una smorfia; **to screw up one's courage** (*fig*) armarsi di coraggio **2** (*fam: ruin*) mandare all'aria; **he really screwed it up this time!** stavolta ha fatto davvero un casino!; **I've screwed everything up** ho rovinato tutto; **to screw sb up** (*fig fam*) incasinare qn; **to be screwed up (about sth)** (*fig fam*) essere incasinato(-a) (per qc)

screw·ball ['skru:ˌbɔ:l] (*fam: esp Am*) N testa matta, svitato(-a)
■ ADJ mezzo matto(-a), svitato(-a)

screw·driver ['skru:ˌdraɪvəʳ] N cacciavite *m inv*

screwed-up [ˌskru:d'ʌp] ADJ (*fam*): **she's totally screwed-up** è nel pallone

screw-top, screw-topped ['skru:ˌtɒp(d)] ADJ con il tappo (*or* coperchio) a vite

screwy ['skru:ɪ] ADJ (*comp* **-ier**, *superl* **-iest**) (*fam: mad*) strambo(-a), svitato(-a)

scrib·ble ['skrɪbl] N scarabocchio
■ VT scribacchiare, scarabocchiare; **to scribble sth down** scribacchiare qc
■ VI scarabocchiare

scrib·bler ['skrɪbləʳ] N (*pej*) scribacchino(-a)

scrib·bling ['skrɪblɪŋ] N scarabocchi *mpl*

scribbling pad N bloc-notes *m inv*

scribe [skraɪb] N scriba *m*

scrim·mage ['skrɪmɪdʒ] N tafferuglio

scrimp [skrɪmp] VI: **to scrimp and save** risparmiare fino all'ultimo centesimo

scrip [skrɪp] N (*Fin*) certificato azionario provvisorio

◎ **script** [skrɪpt] N **1** (*Cine, Theatre*) copione *m*, sceneggiatura; (*Brit: answer paper*) elaborato; (*writing system*) caratteri *mpl*, sistema di scrittura; **Arabic script** caratteri arabi **2** (*writing*) scrittura

script·ed ['skrɪptɪd] ADJ (*Radio, TV*) preparato(-a)

scrip·tur·al ['skrɪptʃərəl] ADJ scritturale

Scrip·ture ['skrɪptʃəʳ] N (*also:* **Holy Scripture**) Sacre Scritture *fpl*

script·writer ['skrɪptˌraɪtəʳ] N sceneggiatore(-trice), soggettista *m/f*

scroll [skrəʊl] N (*roll of parchment*) rotolo (di pergamena); (*ancient manuscript*) papiro, pergamena; (*Archit*) voluta
■ VT (*Comput: text*) far scorrere su video; **I scrolled through the text looking for the sentence** ho scorso il testo alla ricerca della frase

scroll bar N (*Comput*) barra di scorrimento

scro·tum ['skrəʊtəm] N (*pl* **scrota** *or* **scrotums**) scroto

scrounge [skraʊndʒ] (*fam*) N: **to be on the scrounge (for sth)** scroccare (qc); **here he comes, on the scrounge again** eccolo, il solito scroccone
■ VT (*gen*) scroccare; **to scrounge sth off** *or* **from sb** scroccare qc a qn
■ VI: **to scrounge on** *or* **off sb** vivere alle spalle di qn

scroung·er ['skraʊndʒəʳ] N (*fam*) scroccone(-a); (*on society*) parassita *m*

scrub¹ [skrʌb] N (*brushwood*) macchia

scrub² [skrʌb] N (*clean*) strofinata
■ VT **1** (*clean*) strofinare con lo spazzolone; (*hands etc*) pulire con lo spazzolino; **to scrub sth clean** pulire qc strofinandolo(-a) **2** (*fam: cancel*) annullare; (*: holiday, plan*) cancellare
▸ **scrub down** VT + ADV (*room, wall*) pulire a fondo con lo spazzolone
▸ **scrub off** VT + ADV (*mark, stain*) togliere strofinando
▸ **scrub up** VI + ADV (*doctor etc*) lavarsi le mani

scrub·ber¹ ['skrʌbəʳ] N (*also:* **pan-scrubber**) paglietta di ferro

scrub·ber² ['skrʌbəʳ] N (*Brit, Australia fam pej*) puttanella (*fam!*)

scrubbing-brush ['skrʌbɪŋˌbrʌʃ] N spazzolone *m*

scruff [skrʌf] N **1 by the scruff of the neck** per la collottola **2** (*fam: untidy person*) sciattone(-a)

scruffi·ness ['skrʌfɪnɪs] N (*of appearance, person, clothes*) trasandatezza, sciatteria

scruffy ['skrʌfɪ] ADJ (*comp* **-ier**, *superl* **-iest**) (*person, clothes, appearance*) trasandato(-a), sciatto(-a); (*building*) squallido(-a); (*paintwork*) malandato(-a)

scrum [skrʌm], **scrum·mage** ['skrʌmɪdʒ] N (*Rugby*) mischia; **loose/set scrum** mischia aperta/chiusa

scrum half N mediano di mischia

scrump·tious ['skrʌmpʃəs] ADJ (*fam: food, smell*) delizioso(-a)

scrunch ['skrʌntʃ] = **crunch**

scru·ple ['skru:pl] N scrupolo; **to have no scruples about doing sth** non avere scrupoli a fare qc

scru·pu·lous ['skru:pjʊləs] ADJ scrupoloso(-a)

scru·pu·lous·ly ['skru:pjʊləslɪ] ADV scrupolosamente; **he tries to be scrupulously fair/honest** cerca di essere più imparziale/onesto che può

scru·pu·lous·ness ['skru:pjʊləsnɪs] N scrupolosità

scru·ti·nize ['skru:tɪˌnaɪz] VT (*work etc*) esaminare accuratamente; (*person's face*) scrutare; (*votes*) scrutinare

scru·ti·ny ['skru:tɪnɪ] N esame *m* accurato; (*Pol: of votes*) scrutinio; **under the scrutiny of sb** sotto la sorveglianza di qn; **to come under scrutiny** essere sottoposto(-a) ad un esame accurato; **it does not stand up to scrutiny** non regge ad un esame accurato

SCSI ['skʌzɪ] N ABBR (*Comput:* = **small computer system interface**) SCSI *m inv; interfaccia per il collegamento di periferiche*

scu·ba ['sku:bə] N autorespiratore *m*

scuba diving N immersioni *fpl* subacquee (*con autorespiratore*)

scud [skʌd] VI: **clouds were scudding across the sky** (*liter*) le nuvole si rincorrevano nel cielo

scuff [skʌf] VT (*shoes*) scorticare; (*floor*) segnare; (*feet*) strascicare

scuf·fle ['skʌfl] N tafferuglio, zuffa
■ VI: **to scuffle (with sb)** venire alle mani *or* azzuffarsi (con qn)

scull [skʌl] N bratto
■ VI, VT vogare (a bratto)

scul·lery ['skʌlərɪ] N retrocucina *m or f inv*

scul·ling ['skʌlɪŋ] N: **to go sculling** remare

sculpt [skʌlpt] VT, VI scolpire

sculp·tor ['skʌlptəʳ] N scultore *m*

sculp·tress ['skʌlptrɪs] N scultrice *f*

sculp·ture ['skʌlptʃəʳ] N scultura

Ss

■VT, VI scolpire
▷ www.bluffton.edu/~sullivanm/index

scum [skʌm] N (*on liquid*) schiuma; (*fig pej: people*) feccia; **the scum of the earth** la feccia della società; **to remove the scum (from sth)** schiumare (qc)

scup·per ['skʌpəʳ] VT (*Naut*) autoaffondare; (*Brit fig: plan*) far naufragare

scurf [skɜ:f] N forfora

scur·ril·ity [skə'rɪlɪtɪ] N (*frm*) scurrilità

scur·ril·ous ['skʌrɪləs] ADJ (*remark*) scurrile; (*attack*) di bassa lega

scur·ri·lous·ly ['skʌrɪləslɪ] ADV in modo scurrile

scur·ry ['skʌrɪ] VI: **to scurry along/away** *etc* procedere/andarsene *etc* a tutta velocità; **to scurry about** aggirarsi frettolosamente

scur·vy ['skɜ:vɪ] N scorbuto

scut·tle¹ ['skʌtl] VT (*ship*) autoaffondare
■N **1** (*Naut*) portellino **2** (*also:* **coal scuttle**) secchio del carbone

scut·tle² ['skʌtl] VI: **to scuttle away** *or* **off** filare via; **to scuttle in** entrare precipitosamente

scuzzy ['skʌzɪ] ADJ lurido(-a)

Scylla ['sɪlə] N Scilla

scythe [saɪð] N falce *f*
■VT falciare

SD ABBR (*Am Post*) = **South Dakota**

SDI [ˌɛsdi:'aɪ] N ABBR (= **Strategic Defense Initiative**) *programma di difesa strategica spaziale*

SDLP [ˌɛsdi:ɛl'pi:] N ABBR (*Brit Pol*) = *Social Democratic and Labour Party*

SDP [ˌɛsdi:'pi:] N ABBR (*Brit Pol:* = **Social Democratic Party**) *partito unitosi con i Liberals nel 1988*

SE ABBR (= **South East(ern)**) SE (= *sud est*)

◎**sea** [si:] N mare *m*; **by** *or* **beside the sea** (*holiday*) al mare; (*village*) sul mare; **on the sea** (*boat*) sul mare, in mare; (*village, town*) sul mare; **to go by sea** andare per mare; **to go to sea** (*person*) diventare marinaio; **to put to sea** (*sailor*) uscire in mare; (*boat*) salpare; **to spend 3 years at sea** passare 3 anni in mare; **(out) at sea** al largo; **to look out to sea** guardare il mare; **heavy** *or* **rough sea(s)** mare grosso *or* agitato; **a delay caused by rough seas** un ritardo causato dalle cattive condizioni del mare; **to be all at sea (about** *or* **with sth)** (*fig*) non capirci niente (di qc); **a sea of faces** (*fig*) una marea di gente
■ADJ (*salt*) marino(-a); (*fish, air*) di mare; (*route, transport, port*) marittimo(-a); (*battle, power*) navale

sea anchor N ancora galleggiante

sea anemone N anemone *m* di mare, attinia

sea bathing N bagni *mpl* di mare

sea bed N fondale *m* marino

sea bird N uccello marino

sea·board ['si:ˌbɔ:d] N litorale *m*

sea·borne ['si:ˌbɔ:n] ADJ via mare; **the arrival of seaborne reinforcements** l'arrivo di rinforzi via mare

sea breeze N brezza marina

sea captain N capitano di lungo corso (*nella marina mercantile*)

sea coast N costa

sea dog N (*sometimes hum*) lupo di mare

sea·farer ['si:ˌfɛərəʳ] N navigatore *m*, navigante *m*

sea·faring ['si:ˌfɛərɪŋ] ADJ (*community*) marinaro(-a); (*life*) da marinaio

sea floor N fondo marino

sea·floor spread·ing [ˌsi:flɔ:'sprɛdɪŋ] N (*Geog*) espansione *f* del fondo marino

sea·food ['si:ˌfu:d] N frutti *mpl* di mare
▷ www.aboutseafood.com

sea front N lungomare *m*

sea·going ['si:ˌgəʊɪŋ] ADJ (*nation*) marinaro(-a); (*ship*) d'alto mare

sea-green [ˌsi:'gri:n] ADJ verde mare *inv*

sea·gull ['si:ˌgʌl] N gabbiano

sea horse N cavalluccio marino

seal¹ [si:l] N (*Zool*) foca

◎**seal²** [si:l] N (*gen*) sigillo; (*on parcel*) piombino; (*of door, lid*) chiusura ermetica; **to set one's seal to sth** *or* **to give the** *or* **one's seal of approval to sth** dare il proprio beneplacito a qc; **to set the seal on** (*bargain*) concludere; (*friendship*) suggellare
■VT **1** (*put seal on: document*) sigillare; (*close: envelope*) chiudere, incollare; (*: jar, tin*) chiudere ermeticamente; (*Culin: meat*) rosolare; **to seal an envelope** chiudere una busta; **my lips are sealed** (*fig*) sarò una tomba **2** (*decide: sb's fate*) segnare; (*: bargain*) concludere
▸ **seal off** VT + ADV (*close up: building, room*) sigillare; (*forbid entry to: area*) bloccare l'accesso a
▸ **seal up** VT + ADV (*parcel*) sigillare; (*jar, door*) chiudere ermeticamente

sea lane N linea marittima, rotta

sealed-bid [ˌsi:ld'bɪd] ADJ (*Comm*): **sealed-bid tender** offerta in busta chiusa

sea legs NPL: **to find one's sea legs** abituarsi al mare

seal·er ['si:ləʳ] N nave *f* per la pesca delle foche

sea level N livello del mare

seal·ing ['si:lɪŋ] N (*seal hunting*) caccia alla foca

seal·ing wax ['si:lɪŋˌwæks] N ceralacca

sea lion N leone *m* marino, otaria

sea loch N braccio di mare

seal·skin ['si:lˌskɪn] N pelle *f* di foca

seam [si:m] N **1** (*Sewing*) cucitura; (*Welding*) saldatura; **to come apart at the seams** scucirsi; **trouser seams** le cuciture dei pantaloni; **my dress is bursting at the seams** scoppio dentro questo vestito; **the hall was bursting at the seams** (*fig*) l'aula era piena zeppa **2** (*Geol: of coal*) filone *m*, vena

sea·man ['si:mən] N (*pl* **-men**) marinaio

sea·man·ship ['si:mənʃɪp] N tecnica di navigazione

seam·less ['si:mlɪs] ADJ senza cucitura

seam·stress ['sɛmstrɪs] N sarta

seamy ['si:mɪ] ADJ (*comp* **-ier**, *superl* **-iest**) (*fam: district*) malfamato(-a); **the seamy side of life** gli aspetti più squallidi della vita

se·ance, sé·ance ['seɪɑ̃:ns] N seduta spiritica

sea pink N (*Bot*) statice

sea·plane ['si:ˌpleɪn] N idrovolante *m*

sea·port ['si:ˌpɔ:t] N porto di mare *or* marittimo

sear [sɪəʳ] VT (*Culin: meat*) scottare; (*scorch*) bruciare

◎**search** [sɜ:tʃ] N **1** (*for sth lost*) ricerca; **in search of** alla ricerca di; **to make a search for sb/sth** fare delle ricerche per trovare qn/qc; **the search was abandoned** la ricerca fu abbandonata **2** (*of person, building etc*) perquisizione *f*; **to carry out a search of sth** (*subj: police, customs official*) eseguire una perquisizione di qc; (*: thief*) frugare in qc **3** (*Comput*) ricerca; **"search and replace"** "ricerca e sostituzione"
■VT **1 to search (for)** (*subj: police etc*) perquisire (alla ricerca di); (*: thief*) frugare (alla ricerca di); (*area, woods etc*) perlustrare *or* setacciare (alla ricerca di); **the police searched him for drugs** la polizia l'ha perquisito alla ricerca di droga; **they searched the woods for the little girl** hanno perlustrato i boschi alla ricerca della bambina; **search me!** (*fig fam*) e che ne so io? **2** (*scan:*

records, documents, photograph) esaminare minuziosamente; (: *notice-board, newspaper*) leggere attentamente; (: *Comput*) ricercare; (: *one's conscience*) interrogare; (: *one's memory*) frugare in; **he searched her face for some sign of affection** scrutava il suo viso in cerca di un segno di affetto

■VI **1** (*gen*) cercare; **to search after** *or* **for sb/sth** cercare qn/qc; **they're searching for the missing climbers** stanno cercando gli alpinisti dispersi; **to search through** *or* **in sth for sth** frugare *or* rovistare qc alla ricerca di qc **2** (*Comput*): **to search for** ricercare

▸ **search out** VT + ADV scovare; **the library eventually searched out the book I wanted** la biblioteca alla fine ha rintracciato il libro che cercavo

search engine N (*Comput*) motore *m* di ricerca

search·er ['sɜːtʃəʳ] N chi cerca

search·ing ['sɜːtʃɪŋ] ADJ (*look*) indagatore(-trice); (*examination*) minuzioso(-a); (*question*) pressante

search·light ['sɜːtʃˌlaɪt] N riflettore *m*

search party N squadra di soccorso

search warrant N mandato di perquisizione

sear·ing ['sɪərɪŋ] ADJ (*heat*) rovente; (*pain*) acuto(-a)

sea·scape ['siːˌskeɪp] N (*Art*) paesaggio marino

sea·shell ['siːˌʃɛl] N conchiglia

sea·shore ['siːˌʃɔːʳ] N riva del mare; **by the seashore** in riva al mare; **on the seashore** sulla riva del mare

sea·sick ['siːˌsɪk] ADJ: **to be seasick** avere *or* soffrire il mal di mare

sea·sick·ness ['siːˌsɪknɪs] N mal *m* di mare

sea·side ['siːˌsaɪd] N: **at the seaside** al mare; **to go to the seaside** andare al mare

■ADJ (*town*) di mare; (*holiday*) al mare

seaside resort N centro *or* stazione *f* balneare

sea slug N lumaca di mare

◎ **sea·son** ['siːzn] N (*gen*) stagione *f*; **to be in/out of season** essere di/fuori stagione; **the Christmas season** il periodo natalizio; **"Season's Greetings"** "Buone Feste"; **the busy season** (*for shops*) il periodo di punta; (*for hotels etc*) l'alta stagione; **during the holiday season** nel periodo delle vacanze; **football/fishing season** stagione calcistica/della pesca; **the open season** (*Hunting*) la stagione della caccia; **it's against the law to hunt during the closed season** è proibito dalla legge andare a caccia quando la stagione è chiusa; **in season** (*Zool*) in calore

■VT **1** (*wood*) stagionare **2** (*Culin*) condire; **season with salt and pepper** condite con sale e pepe

sea·son·able ['siːznəbl] ADJ (*weather*) di stagione; (*advice*) opportuno(-a)

sea·son·al ['siːzənl] ADJ stagionale; **after seasonal adjustment** (*Econ*) dopo la destagionalizzazione

sea·soned ['siːznd] ADJ (*wood*) stagionato(-a); (*fig: worker, troops*) con esperienza; (: *actor*) consumato(-a); **a seasoned campaigner** un*a* veterano(-a); **a seasoned traveller** un *un'* esperto(-a) viaggiatore(-trice)

sea·son·ing ['siːznɪŋ] N condimento

season ticket N (*Theatre, Rail etc*) abbonamento

◎ **seat** [siːt] N **1** (*chair*) sedia; (*in theatre etc*) posto; (*in bus, train, car etc*) posto, sedile *m*; (*on cycle*) sella, sellino; **are there any seats left?** ci sono posti?; **to take one's seat** prendere posto; **do take a seat** prego, si accomodi; **to take a back seat** (*fig*) restare in secondo piano **2** (*Pol*) seggio; **to keep/lose one's seat** essere/non essere rieletto(-a); **to win four seats from the nationalists** strappare quattro seggi ai nazionalisti; **to take one's seat in the (House of) Commons** iniziare la propria carriera di parlamentare **3** (*of chair*) sedile *m*; (*buttocks*) didietro; (*of trousers*) fondo **4** (*centre: of government etc, of infection*) sede *f*; (: *of learning*) centro **5** (*Horse-riding*) assetto

■VT **1** (*person etc*) far sedere; **to be seated** essere seduto(-a); **please be seated** accomodatevi per favore; **please remain seated** rimanete ai vostri posti per cortesia **2** (*subj: hall, cinema etc*) essere fornito(-a) di posti a sedere per; **the theatre seats 500** il teatro può accogliere 500 persone

seat belt N (*Aut, Aer*) cintura di sicurezza

seat cover N (*Aut*) coprisedile *m*

-seater ['siːtəʳ] SUFF: **a three-seater settee** un divano a tre posti

seat·ing ['siːtɪŋ] N posti *mpl* a sedere

seating arrangements NPL sistemazione *fsg or* disposizione *fsg* dei posti

seating capacity N posti *mpl* a sedere

SEATO ['siːtəʊ] N ABBR (= **South East Asia Treaty Organization**) SEATO *f*

sea urchin N riccio di mare

sea wall N diga marittima

sea·wards ['siːwədz] ADV verso il mare

sea water N acqua di mare

sea·way ['siːˌweɪ] N rotta marittima

sea·weed ['siːˌwiːd] N alghe *fpl*; **a strand of seaweed** un'alga

sea·worthiness ['siːˌwɜːðɪnɪs] N idoneità alla navigazione

sea·worthy ['siːˌwɜːðɪ] ADJ idoneo(-a) alla navigazione

se·ba·ceous [sɪ'beɪʃəs] ADJ sebaceo(-a)

se·bum ['siːbəm] N sebo

SEC [ˌɛsiː'siː] N ABBR (*Am*: = **Securities and Exchange Commission**) *commissione di controllo sulle operazioni in Borsa*

Sec. ABBR = **Secretary**

sec [sɛk] N ABBR (*fam*: = **second**) attimo, secondo

sec. ABBR = **second**

se·cant ['siːkənt] N secante *f*

seca·teurs [ˌsɛkə'tɜːz] NPL cesoie *fpl*

se·cede [sɪ'siːd] VI (*frm*): **to secede (from)** staccarsi (da)

se·ces·sion [sɪ'sɛʃən] N (*frm*): **secession (from)** secessione *f* (da)

se·clud·ed [sɪ'kluːdɪd] ADJ (*house*) appartato(-a), isolato(-a); (*life*) ritirato(-a)

se·clu·sion [sɪ'kluːʒən] N isolamento; **to live in seclusion** fare vita ritirata

◎ **sec·ond**[1] [*adj, adv, n, vt* **1** 'sɛkənd; *vt* **2** sɪ'kɒnd]

ADJ secondo(-a); **he's a second Beethoven** è un nuovo Beethoven; **give him a second chance** dagli un'altra opportunità; **second floor** (*Brit*) secondo piano; (*Am*) primo piano; **in second gear** (*Aut*) in seconda; **to travel second class** viaggiare in seconda classe; **to ask for a second opinion** (*Med*) chiedere un altro consulto; **second person** (*Gram*) seconda persona; **Charles the Second** Carlo II; **every second day/week** ogni due giorni/settimane; **to be second to none** non essere inferiore a nessuno; **to have second thoughts (about doing sth)** avere dei ripensamenti (quanto a fare qc); **we had second thoughts about it** ci abbiamo ripensato; **on second thoughts ...** ripensandoci meglio...

■ADV **1** (*in race, competition etc*) al secondo posto; **to come second** arrivare secondo(-a), piazzarsi al secondo posto; **it's the second largest fish I've ever caught** ho preso soltanto un pesce più grosso di

Ss

questo, finora **2** (*secondly*) in secondo luogo, secondo
■N **1** (*Boxing, in duel*) secondo **2** **in second** (*Aut*) in seconda **3** **he came a good second** (*in race*) è arrivato secondo con un buon tempo; **he came a poor second** è arrivato secondo ma con notevole scarto **4** (*Brit Univ*) ≈ laurea con punteggio discreto **5** (*Comm: imperfect goods*): **seconds** NPL merce *fsg* di seconda scelta **6** (*fam: second helping*): **seconds** NPL bis *m inv*
■VT **1** (*motion, statement*) appoggiare; **I'll second that** (*fig*) l'appoggio, sono a favore **2** (*Brit: employee*) distaccare

sec·ond² ['sɛkənd] N (*in time, Geog, Math*) (minuto) secondo; **at that very second** (proprio) in quell'istante; **just a second!** un attimo!; **it won't take a second** ci vuole un attimo

sec·ond·ary ['sɛkəndərɪ] ADJ secondario(-a); **secondary sector** (*Industry*) settore *m* secondario; **presentation is of secondary importance** la presentazione ha un'importanza secondaria

secondary modern (school) N (*Brit*) *scuola media superiore ad indirizzo tecnico, ora non più esistente*

secondary picket N picchetto di solidarietà

secondary school N scuola secondaria

> **SECONDARY SCHOOL**
>
> In Gran Bretagna la **secondary school** è la scuola frequentata dai ragazzi dagli 11 ai 18 anni. Nel paese è obbligatorio andare a scuola fino a 16 anni. *Vedi anche* **primary school; high school**
> ▷ www.parentscentre.gov.uk/choosingaschool/typesofschool/

secondary stress N (*Ling*) accento secondario

second-best [ˌsɛkənd'bɛst] N ripiego; **as a second-best** in mancanza di meglio
■ADV: **to come off second-best** avere la peggio

second childhood N seconda infanzia

second-class [ˌsɛkənd'klɑːs] ADJ **1** (*mail*) ordinario(-a); (*ticket, carriage*) di seconda classe **2** (*pej: goods, quality*) scadente
■ADV: **to send sth second-class** spedire qc per posta ordinaria; **to travel second-class** viaggiare in seconda classe

second-class citizen N cittadino di serie B

second coming N (*Rel: Christ*): **the second coming** secondo avvento

second cousin N cugino(-a) di secondo grado

sec·ond·er ['sɛkəndə^r] N sostenitore(-trice)

second-guess [ˌsɛkənd'gɛs] (*fam*) VT (*sb's reaction*) cercare di anticipare

second-half ['sɛkəndˌhɑːf] ADJ (*Sport: goal, try, substitution*) del secondo tempo

second-hand [ˌsɛkənd'hænd] ADJ di seconda mano, usato(-a); **second-hand bookshop** negozio di libri usati
■ADV: **to buy sth second-hand** comprare qc di seconda mano; **second-hand news** notizie *fpl* di seconda mano; **to hear sth second-hand** venire a sapere qc da terze persone

second hand N lancetta dei secondi

second-in-command [ˌsɛkəndɪnkə'mɑːnd] N (*Mil*) comandante *m* in seconda; (*Admin*) aggiunto

sec·ond·ly ['sɛkəndlɪ] ADV secondo, in secondo luogo, secondariamente; **firstly ..., secondly ...** in primo luogo..., in secondo luogo...

se·cond·ment [sɪ'kɒndmənt] N (*Brit: of employee*) distaccamento

second name N cognome *m*

second nature N: **to be second nature to sb** essere naturale per qn; **it was second nature for him to help his friends** gli veniva naturale aiutare gli amici

second person N (*Gram*): **the second person singular** la seconda persona singolare; **the second person plural** la seconda persona plurale

second-rate [ˌsɛkənd'reɪt] ADJ di second'ordine, scadente

second sight N chiaroveggenza; **to have second sight** essere chiaroveggente

Second World War N: **the Second World War** la seconda guerra mondiale

se·cre·cy ['siːkrəsɪ] N segretezza; **there's no secrecy about ...** non si fa mistero di...; **in secrecy** in segreto, in tutta segretezza

◎**se·cret** ['siːkrɪt] ADJ segreto(-a); **to keep sth secret (from sb)** tenere qc nascosto (a qn); **keep it secret** che rimanga un segreto; **a secret mission** una missione segreta
■N segreto; **in secret** in segreto; **to keep a secret** mantenere un segreto; **can you keep a secret?** sai tenere un segreto?; **to let sb into a secret** mettere qn a parte di un segreto, confidare un segreto a qn; **to make no secret of sth** non far mistero di qc; **to do sth in secret** fare qc in segreto *or* segretamente

secret agent N agente *m* segreto

sec·re·taire [ˌsɛkrɪ'tɛə^r] N secrétaire *m inv*

sec·re·tar·ial [ˌsɛkrə'tɛərɪəl] ADJ (*work*) di segreteria; (*college, course*) di segretariato; **secretarial work** lavoro di segreteria; **secretarial training** corso di addestramento per segretarie

sec·re·tari·at [ˌsɛkrə'tɛərɪət] N segretariato

◎**sec·re·tary** ['sɛkrətrɪ] N segretario(-a)

◎**secretary-general** [ˌsɛkrətrɪ'dʒɛnərəl] N segretario generale

◎**Secretary of State** N (*Brit*) ministro; (*Am*) segretario di Stato; ≈ ministro degli Esteri; **Secretary of State for Education** (*Brit*) ministro della Pubblica Istruzione

se·crete [sɪ'kriːt] VT **1** (*Med, Anat, Bio*) secernere **2** (*frm: hide*) nascondere

se·cre·tion [sɪ'kriːʃən] N secrezione *f*

se·cre·tive ['siːkrətɪv] ADJ riservato(-a); **to be secretive about sth** essere riservato(-a) a proposito di qc

se·cret·ly ['siːkrətlɪ] ADV in segreto, segretamente

secret police N: **the secret police** la polizia segreta

secret service N servizi *mpl* segreti: **the Secret Service** (*Am*) *servizi segreti incaricati di salvaguardare l'incolumità del presidente*

secret weapon N arma segreta

sect [sɛkt] N setta

sec·tar·ian [sɛk'tɛərɪən] ADJ settario(-a)

sec·tari·an·ism [sɛk'tɛərɪəˌnɪzəm] N settarismo

◎**sec·tion** ['sɛkʃən] N **1** (*part: gen*) sezione *f*, parte *f*; (*of community, population*) settore *m*, fascia; (*: of town: esp Am*) quartiere *m*; (*of document, law etc*) articolo; (*of pipeline, road etc*) tratto; (*of machine, furniture*) pezzo; **the business section** (*Press*) la pagina economica **2** (*department*) sezione *f* **3** (*cut*) sezione *f*; **vertical section** sezione verticale, spaccato
■VT (*cut*) sezionare, dividere in sezioni

sec·tion·al ['sɛkʃənl] ADJ **1** (*bookcase etc*) scomponibile, smontabile **2** *(interests)* settoriale **3** *(drawing etc)* in sezione

◎**sec·tor** ['sɛktəʳ] N *(gen)* settore *m*; *(Geom)* settore *m* circolare

secu·lar ['sɛkjʊləʳ] ADJ *(authority, school)* laico(-a); *(writings, music)* profano(-a); *(clergy)* secolare

secu·lar·ism ['sɛkjʊlə,rɪzəm] N secolarismo

secu·lar·ize ['sɛkjʊlə,raɪz] VT secolarizzare

◎**se·cure** [sɪ'kjʊəʳ] ADJ *(comp* **-r**, *superl* **-st)** **1** *(firm: knot)* saldo(-a), sicuro(-a); (: *nail)* ben piantato(-a); (: *rope)* ben fissato(-a); (: *door)* ben chiuso(-a); (: *ladder, chair)* stabile; (: *hold)* saldo(-a); **to make sth secure** fissare bene qc; **make sure the load is secure** assicurati che il carico sia ben fissato **2** *(safe: place, container)* sicuro(-a); *(certain: career, success)* assicurato(-a); *(victory)* certo(-a); **secure from** *or* **against sth** al sicuro da qc; **a secure job** un lavoro sicuro **3** *(free from anxiety)* sicuro(-a), tranquillo(-a); **to rest secure in the knowledge that ...** stare tranquillo(-a) sapendo che...; **to feel secure** sentirsi sicuro(-a)

■VT **1** *(fix: rope)* assicurare; (: *door, window)* chiudere bene; *(tie up: person, animal)* legare; **secure the bike to the back of the car** fissa la bici dietro la macchina **2** *(make safe)*: **to secure (from** *or* **against)** proteggere (da) **3** *(frm: obtain: job, staff etc)* assicurarsi; **to secure sth for sb** procurare qc per *or* a qn; **his experience helped secure him the job** ha avuto il lavoro anche grazie alla sua esperienza **4** *(Fin: loan)* garantire

se·cured credi·tor [sɪ,kʊəd'krɛdɪtəʳ] N *(Fin)* creditore *m* privilegiato

se·cure·ly [sɪ'kjʊəlɪ] ADV *(firmly)* saldamente, bene; *(safely)* in modo sicuro

secure unit N *(in prison, hospital)* reparto di isolamento *(per pazienti con problemi psichiatrici)*

◎**se·cu·rity** [sɪ'kjʊərɪtɪ] N **1** *(safety, stability)* sicurezza; **job security** sicurezza dell'impiego; **security of tenure** garanzia di titolo *or* di godimento; *(in job)* garanzia del posto di lavoro; *(in property)*: **they have security of tenure** non possono essere sfrattati fino al termine del contratto **2** *(against theft etc)* misure *fpl* di sicurezza; **to increase/tighten security** aumentare/intensificare la sorveglianza **3** *(Fin: on loan)* garanzia; **to lend money on security** prestare denaro su *or* dietro garanzia **4** *(Stock Exchange)*: **securities** NPL titoli *mpl*

security camera N telecamera a circuito chiuso

security check N controllo di sicurezza

◎**Security Council** N: **the Security Council** il Consiglio di Sicurezza

security forces NPL forze *fpl* dell'ordine

security guard N guardia giurata

security leak N fuga di notizie

security police NPL servizi *mpl* di sicurezza

security risk N *persona che costituisce una minaccia per la sicurezza dello stato*

secy. ABBR = **secretary**

se·dan [sɪ'dæn] N *(Am Aut)* berlina

sedan chair N *(History)* portantina

se·date [sɪ'deɪt] ADJ posato(-a), pacato(-a)

■VT *(Med)* somministrare sedativi a

se·date·ly [sɪ'deɪtlɪ] ADV in modo posato

se·da·tion [sɪ'deɪʃən] N *(Med)*: **to be under sedation** essere sotto l'effetto di sedativi

seda·tive ['sɛdətɪv] ADJ calmante, sedativo(-a)

■N sedativo, calmante *m*

sed·en·tary ['sɛdntrɪ] ADJ sedentario(-a)

sedi·ment ['sɛdɪmənt] N *(in liquids, boiler)* deposito, fondo; *(Geol)* sedimento

sedi·men·tary [,sɛdɪ'mɛntərɪ] ADJ sedimentario(-a)

se·di·tion [sə'dɪʃən] N sedizione *f*

se·di·tious [sə'dɪʃəs] ADJ sedizioso(-a)

se·di·tious·ly [sə'dɪʃəslɪ] ADV sediziosamente

se·duce [sɪ'dju:s] VT sedurre

se·duc·er [sɪ'dju:səʳ] N seduttore(-trice)

se·duc·tion [sɪ'dʌkʃən] N seduzione *f*

se·duc·tive [sɪ'dʌktɪv] ADJ *(gen)* seducente; *(dress)* sexy *inv*; *(offer)* allettante

se·duc·tive·ly [sɪ'dʌktɪvlɪ] ADV in modo seducente

sedu·lous ['sɛdjʊləs] ADJ *(frm)* diligente

se·dum ['si:dəm] N *(Bot)* sedo

◎**see**[1] [si:] *(pt* **saw**, *pp* **seen)** VT, VI

1 *(gen)* vedere; **I can't see him** non lo vedo; **I saw him writing the letter** l'ho visto scrivere *or* mentre scriveva la lettera; **I saw him write the letter** l'ho visto scrivere la lettera; **have you seen that film?** hai visto quel film?; **there was nobody to be seen** non c'era anima viva; **I can't see anything** non vedo niente; **I can't see to read** non ci vedo abbastanza per leggere; **let me see** *(show me)* fammi vedere; *(let me think)* vediamo (un po'); **can you see your way to helping us?** *(fig)* puoi trovare il modo di aiutarci?; **to go and see sb** andare a trovare qn; **see you soon/later/tomorrow!** a presto/più tardi/domani!; **see you!** ci vediamo!; **now see here!** *(in anger)* ma insomma!; **so I see** sì , vedo; **see for yourself!** guarda qua!; **as you can see** come vedi; **I must be seeing things** *(fam)* devo avere le allucinazioni *or* le traveggole; **I see in the paper that ...** vedo che sul giornale è scritto che...; **I see nothing wrong in it** non ci trovo niente di male; **I don't know what she sees in him** non so che cosa ci trova in lui; **(go and) see who it is** vai a vedere chi è, vedi chi è; **this car has seen better days** questa macchina ha conosciuto tempi migliori; **I never thought I'd see the day when ...** non avrei mai creduto che un giorno...

2 *(understand, perceive)* vedere, capire; (: *joke)* afferrare; **to see the funny side of sth** vedere il lato comico di qc; **I see!** capisco!; **I don't** *or* **can't see how/why** *etc* **...** non vedo come/perché *etc*...; **as far as I can see** da quanto posso vedere; **the way I see it** a parer mio, a mio giudizio

3 *(accompany)* accompagnare; **to see sb to the door/home** accompagnare qn alla porta/a casa; **I'll see you to your car** ti accompagno alla macchina

4 *(ensure, check)* vedere, assicurarsi; **to see if** vedere se + *indic*; **to see that** vedere *or* badare che + *sub*; **see that he has all he needs** vedi che non gli manchi nulla; **I'll see that he gets it** farò in modo che lo riceva

5 *(imagine)* vedere; **I can just see him as a teacher** lo vedo benissimo nei panni dell'insegnante; **I can't see myself as ...** non mi vedo come...; **I can't see him winning** non credo che lui vincerà

▶ **see about** VI + PREP

1 *(deal with)* occuparsi di

2 *(consider)*: **I'll see about it** ci penserò, vedrò; **we'll see about it** si vedrà; **we'll see about that!** *(iro)* vedremo!

▶ **see in** VT + ADV: **to see the New Year in** festeggiare l'Anno Nuovo

▶ **see off** VT + ADV salutare alla partenza

▶ **see out** VT + ADV *(person)* accompagnare alla porta; **I'll see myself out** *(fam)* non c'è bisogno che mi

Ss

accompagni; **I'm afraid she won't see the week out** (*survive*) temo che non passerà la settimana
▸ **see over, see round** VI + PREP (*visit*) visitare
▸ **see through** VI + PREP (*promises, behaviour*) non lasciarsi ingannare da; **I finally saw through him** finalmente ho capito che tipo è
■ VT + ADV (*project, deal*) portare a termine; **we'll see him through** lo aiuteremo noi
■ VT + PREP: **£100 will see him through the week** 100 sterline gli basteranno ad arrivare alla fine della settimana
▸ **see to** VI + PREP (*deal with*) occuparsi di; (: *work-load*) sbrigare; (*mend*) mettere a posto; **please see to it that you lock all doors** si assicuri di aver chiuso tutte le porte; **the shower isn't working. can you see to it please?** la doccia non funziona. se ne può occupare, per favore?

see² [si:] N (*Rel*) sede *f* vescovile; **the Holy See** la Santa Sede

◎ **seed** [si:d] N **1** (*Bot*) seme *m*; (*for sowing*) semi *mpl*, semente *f*; **sunflower seeds** semi di girasole; **to go** *or* **run to seed** (*plant*) fare seme; **to go to seed** (*fig: person*) ridursi male **2** (*fig: origin*): **the seeds of** il seme di, il germe di; **the seeds of discontent** il seme del malcontento **3** (*Tennis: player*) testa di serie
■ VT **1** (*lawn etc*) seminare **2** (*remove the seed: raisins, grapes*) togliere i semi a **3** (*Tennis*): **he was seeded fifth** è stato classificato quinta testa di serie
■ VI fare seme
■ ADJ (*potato, corn*) da semina

seed·bed ['si:d,bɛd] N semenzaio

seed·ed ['si:dɪd] ADJ (*Sport*): **a seeded player** una testa di serie; **to be seeded second** classificarsi seconda testa di serie

seed·less ['si:dlɪs] ADJ senza semi

seed·ling ['si:dlɪŋ] N semenzale *m*

seed money N (*Fin*) capitale *m* di avviamento

seed pearls NPL semenza *fsg*

seedy ['si:dɪ] ADJ (*comp* **-ier**, *superl* **-iest**) (*fam: sordid, shabby*) squallido(-a); **I feel decidedly seedy today** non mi sento affatto bene oggi

see·ing ['si:ɪŋ] CONJ: **seeing (that)** visto che

◎ **seek** [si:k] (*pt, pp* **sought**) VT (*gen*): **to seek (sth/to do sth)** cercare (qc/di fare qc); **people seeking work** le persone che cercano lavoro; **they are seeking a solution to the problem** cercano di trovare una soluzione al problema; **he sought to calm them down** ha cercato di tranquillizzarli; **to seek shelter (from)** cercar riparo (da); **to seek one's fortune** cercar fortuna; **to seek advice/help from sb** chiedere consiglio/aiuto a qn
■ VI: **to seek after, seek for** cercare
▸ **seek out** VT + ADV (*person*) andare a cercare

seek·er ['si:kəʳ] N cercatore(-trice)

◎ **seem** [si:m] VI sembrare, parere; **she seems capable** sembra (essere) in gamba; **he seemed to be in difficulty** sembrava (trovarsi) in difficoltà; **she seems to know you** sembra *or* pare che lei ti conosca; **she seems not to want to leave** non dà segno di voler andar via; **I seemed to be sinking** mi sembrava di affondare; **I seem to have heard that before** questa mi pare di averla già sentita; **I can't seem to do it** a quanto pare non ci riesco; **how did he seem to you?** come ti è sembrato?; **it seems (that)** sembra *or* pare che + *sub*; **it seems she's getting married** pare che si sposi; **so it seems** così pare *or* sembra; **it seems not** pare di no; **it seems you're right** pare che tu abbia ragione; **it seems ages since ...** mi sembra una vita da quando...; **what seems to be the trouble?** cosa c'è che non va?; **there seems to be a mistake** ci dev'essere un errore, sembra *or* pare che ci sia un errore; **that seems like a good idea** mi sembra una buona idea; **she died yesterday, it seems** pare che sia morta ieri; **I did what seemed best** ho fatto quello che sembrava più opportuno

seem·ing ['si:mɪŋ] ADJ apparente

seem·ing·ly ['si:mɪŋlɪ] ADV (*evidently*) a quanto pare; (*from appearances*) in apparenza, apparentemente

seem·ly ['si:mlɪ] ADJ (*comp* **-ier**, *superl* **-iest**) (*frm: behaviour, language, dress*) decoroso(-a)

seen [si:n] PP *of* **see¹**

seep [si:p] VI: **to seep (through/from/into)** filtrare (attraverso/da/in *or* dentro)
▸ **seep away** VI + ADV scolare a poco a poco
▸ **seep in** VI + ADV infiltrarsi
▸ **seep out** VI + ADV trapelare

seep·age ['si:pɪdʒ] N infiltrazione *f*

seer [sɪəʳ] N (*old, liter*) veggente *m/f*

seer·sucker ['sɪə,sʌkəʳ] N crespo di cotone a strisce

see·saw ['si:,sɔ:] N altalena (a bilico)
■ VI (*fig*) oscillare

seethe [si:ð] VI (*liquid*) ribollire, gorgogliare; (*street*): **to seethe (with)** brulicare (di); **to seethe** *or* **be seething with anger** schiumare *or* fremere di rabbia

see-through ['si:,θru:] ADJ trasparente

◎ **seg·ment** [*n* 'sɛgmənt; *vb* ,sɛg'mɛnt] N (*section*) parte *f*; (*of orange*) spicchio; (*Geom*) segmento circolare; **line segment** (*Geom*) segmento
■ VT segmentare

seg·men·ta·tion [,sɛgmɛn'teɪʃən] N segmentazione *f*

seg·re·gate ['sɛgrɪ,geɪt] VT: **to segregate (from)** separare (da), segregare (da)

seg·re·ga·ted ['sɛgrɪ,geɪtɪd] ADJ (*Pol*) in cui vige la segregazione

seg·re·ga·tion [,sɛgrɪ'geɪʃən] N segregazione *f*

seg·re·ga·tion·ist ['sɛgrɪ'geɪʃnɪst] ADJ, N segregazionista (*m/f*)

Seine [sɛn] N: **the Seine** la Senna

seis·mic ['saɪzmɪk] ADJ sismico(-a)

seis·mo·graph ['saɪzmə,grɑ:f] N sismografo

seis·mol·ogy [saɪz'mɒlədʒɪ] N sismologia

◎ **seize** [si:z] VT (*clutch, grasp*) afferrare; (*Mil, Law: person, territory, power*) prendere; (: *articles*) sequestrare; (*opportunity*) cogliere; **to seize hold of sth/sb** afferrare qc/qn; **he seized my hand** mi ha afferrato la mano; **to seize an opportunity** cogliere un'opportunità; **troops have seized the airport** le truppe si sono impadronite dell'aeroporto; **to seize power** impadronirsi del potere; **he was seized with a fit of coughing** gli è venuto un accesso di tosse; **she was seized with fear/rage** è stata presa dalla paura/rabbia; **I was seized by the desire to laugh** mi è venuta una gran voglia di ridere
▸ **seize on, seize upon** VI + PREP (*chance, mistake*) non lasciarsi sfuggire; (*idea*) sfruttare prontamente
▸ **seize up** VI + ADV (*muscle, back*) bloccarsi; (*Tech: machine*) grippare; **my back seized up** mi si è bloccata la schiena

sei·zure ['si:ʒəʳ] N **1** (*of goods*) sequestro, confisca; (*of land, city, ship*) presa **2** (*Med*) attacco; **he had a seizure** ha avuto un attacco

sel·dom ['sɛldəm] ADV di rado, raramente

◎ **se·lect** [sɪ'lɛkt] VT (*team, candidate*) scegliere,

selezionare; (*book, gift etc*) scegliere; **selected works** opere *fpl* scelte
■ ADJ (*hotel, restaurant*) chic *inv*; (*club*) esclusivo(-a); (*group*) ristretto(-a); (*audience*) scelto(-a); **a select few** pochi eletti *mpl*
select committee N (*Brit Pol*) commissione *f* d'inchiesta parlamentare
◎**se·lec·tion** [sɪ'lɛkʃən] N (*gen*) scelta; (*of goods etc*) scelta, selezione *f*; **selections from** (*Mus, Literature*) brani scelti da
selection committee N comitato di selezione
se·lec·tive [sɪ'lɛktɪv] ADJ (*gen*) selettivo(-a)
se·lec·tively [sɪ'lɛktɪvlɪ] ADV (*used, applied*) in modo selettivo
selective service N (*Am*) servizio militare obbligatorio
se·lec·tiv·ity [ˌsɪlɛk'tɪvɪtɪ] N selettività
se·lec·tor [sɪ'lɛktə^r] N (*person*) selezionatore(-trice); (*Tech*) selettore *m*
◎**self** [sɛlf] N (*pl* **selves**): **the self** l'io *m inv*; **my better self** la parte migliore di me stesso; **my inner self** il mio io; **his true self** il suo vero io; **he's quite his old self again** è tornato quello di una volta; **you're looking more like your usual self** sembri essere tornata quella di sempre
self- [sɛlf] PREF auto...
self-absorbed [ˌsɛlfəb'zɜːbd] ADJ egocentrico(-a)
self-addressed envelope [ˌsɛlfə'drɛst'ɛnvələʊp] N busta col proprio nome e indirizzo
self-adhesive [ˌsɛlfəd'hiːsɪv] ADJ autoadesivo(-a)
self-adjusting [ˌsɛlfə'dʒʌstɪŋ] ADJ autoregolante
self-appointed [ˌsɛlfə'pɔɪntɪd] ADJ (*usu pej*): **self-appointed leader** leader autonominatosi tale
self-assertive [ˌsɛlfə'sɜːtɪv] ADJ che si fa valere
self-assessment [ˌsɛlfə'sɛsmənt] N autovalutazione *f*; (*for taxes*) sistema di autodichiarazione del reddito
self-assurance [ˌsɛlfə'ʃʊərəns] N sicurezza di sé
self-assured [ˌsɛlfə'ʃʊəd] ADJ sicuro(-a) di sé
self-aware [ˌsɛlfə'wɛə^r] ADJ: **to be self-aware** avere coscienza di sé
self-awareness [ˌsɛlfə'wɛənɪs] N coscienza di sé
self-belief [ˌsɛlfbɪ'liːf] N fiducia in se stesso(-a)
self-catering [ˌsɛlf'keɪtərɪŋ] ADJ (*Brit*): **self-catering apartment** appartamento indipendente (con cucina)
self-centred, (*Am*) **self-centered** [ˌsɛlf'sɛntəd] ADJ egocentrico(-a)
self-cleaning [ˌsɛlf'kliːnɪŋ] ADJ (*oven*) autopulente
self-coloured, (*Am*) **self-colored** [ˌsɛlf'kʌləd] ADJ monocromatico(-a)
self-confessed [ˌsɛlfkən'fɛst] ADJ (*alcoholic, cheat*) dichiarato(-a); **he's a self-confessed thief/liar** ha ammesso di essere un ladro/bugiardo
self-confidence [ˌsɛlf'kɒnfɪdəns] N fiducia in se (me, te *etc*) stesso(-a)
self-confident [ˌsɛlf'kɒnfɪdənt] ADJ sicuro(-a) di sé
self-congratulation ['sɛlfkənˌgrætjʊ'leɪʃən] N autocompiacimento
self-conscious [ˌsɛlf'kɒnʃəs] ADJ a disagio, impacciato(-a); **she was very self-conscious at first** all'inizio era molto impacciata; **she was self-conscious about her height** era complessata per la statura
self-consciousness [ˌsɛlf'kɒnʃəsnɪs] N disagio, imbarazzo
self-contained [ˌsɛlfkən'teɪnd] ADJ (*Brit: flat*) indipendente
self-contradictory [ˌsɛlfkɒntrə'dɪktərɪˌs] ADJ contraddittorio(-a)
self-control [ˌsɛlfkən'trəʊl], **self-restraint** [ˌsɛlfrɪ'streɪnt] N self-control *m inv*, autocontrollo, padronanza di sé
self-controlled [ˌsɛlfkən'trəʊld] ADJ padrone(-a) di sé
self-deception [ˌsɛlfdɪ'sɛpʃən] N l'ingannare se stesso(-a)
self-declared [ˌsɛlfdɪ'klɛəd] ADJ = **self-proclaimed**
self-defeating [ˌsɛlfdɪ'fiːtɪŋ] ADJ controproducente
self-defence, (*Am*) **self-defense** [ˌsɛlfdɪ'fɛns] N autodifesa; **to act in self-defence** (*Law*) agire per legittima difesa; **she killed him in self-defence** l'ha ucciso per legittima difesa; **self-defence classes** corso di difesa personale
self-denial [ˌsɛlfdɪ'naɪəl] N abnegazione *f*, sacrificio
self-destructive [ˌsɛlfdɪs'trʌktɪv] ADJ autodistruttivo(-a)
self-determination [ˌsɛlfdɪˌtɜːmɪ'neɪʃən] N autodeterminazione *f*
self-discipline [ˌsɛlf'dɪsɪplɪn] N autodisciplina
self-drive [ˌsɛlf'draɪv] ADJ: **self-drive car** vettura da noleggio senza autista
self-educated [ˌsɛlf'ɛdjʊˌkeɪtɪd] ADJ: **to be self-educated** essere un(-a) autodidatta
self-effacing [ˌsɛlfɪ'feɪsɪŋ] ADJ schivo(-a) e modesto(-a)
self-employed [ˌsɛlfɪm'plɔɪd] ADJ (*worker*) autonomo(-a), che lavora in proprio; **to be self-employed** lavorare in proprio
■ NPL: **the self-employed** i lavoratori autonomi
self-employment [ˌsɛlfɪm'plɔɪmənt] N lavoro autonomo
self-esteem [ˌsɛlfɪs'tiːm] N stima di sé
self-evident [ˌsɛlf'ɛvɪdənt] ADJ evidente, lampante
self-explanatory [ˌsɛlfɪks'plænətərɪ] ADJ ovvio(-a), che non ha bisogno di spiegazioni
self-expression [ˌsɛlfɪk'sprɛʃən] N espressione *f* della propria personalità
self-governing [ˌsɛlf'gʌvənɪŋ] ADJ autonomo(-a)
self-government [ˌsɛlf'gʌvənmənt] N autogoverno
self-help [ˌsɛlf'hɛlp] N autoaiuto; **a self-help group** un gruppo di autoaiuto
self-image [ˌsɛlf'ɪmɪdʒ] N immagine *f* di se stesso
self-importance [ˌsɛlfɪm'pɔːtəns] N presunzione *f*, boria
self-important [ˌsɛlfɪm'pɔːtənt] ADJ presuntuoso(-a), borioso(-a)
self-imposed [ˌsɛlfɪm'pəʊzd] ADJ autoimposto(-a)
self-indulgence [ˌsɛlfɪn'dʌldʒəns] N indulgenza verso le proprie passioni
self-indulgent [ˌsɛlfɪn'dʌldʒənt] ADJ indulgente verso le proprie passioni
self-inflicted [ˌsɛlfɪn'flɪktɪd] ADJ: **self-inflicted wound** autolesione *f*; **your problems are self-inflicted** ti sei creato da solo i tuoi problemi
self-interest [ˌsɛlf'ɪntrɪst] N interesse *m* personale
self-interested [ˌsɛlf'ɪntrɪstɪd] ADJ egoistico(-a)
self·ish ['sɛlfɪʃ] ADJ egoista
self·ish·ly ['sɛlfɪʃlɪ] ADV egoisticamente
self·ish·ness ['sɛlfɪʃnɪs] N egoismo
self·less ['sɛlflɪs] ADJ altruista, altruistico(-a)
self·less·ly ['sɛlflɪslɪ] ADV altruisticamente
self·less·ness ['sɛlflɪsnɪs] N altruismo
self-made [ˌsɛlf'meɪd] ADJ che si è fatto(-a) da sé
self-made man N self-made man *m inv*, uomo che si è fatto da sé

Ss

self-obsessed [ˌsɛlfəb'sɛst] ADJ egocentrico(-a)
self-opinionated [ˌsɛlfə'pɪnjəneɪtɪd] ADJ convinto(-a) di avere sempre ragione
self-pity [ˌsɛlf'pɪtɪ] N autocommiserazione *f*
self-portrait [ˌsɛlf'pɔ:trɪt] N autoritratto
self-possessed [ˌsɛlfpə'zɛst] ADJ padrone(-a) di sé, composto(-a)
self-possession [ˌsɛlfpə'zɛʃən] N padronanza di sé
self-preservation ['sɛlfˌprɛzə'veɪʃən] N istinto di conservazione
self-proclaimed [ˌsɛlfprə'kleɪmd] ADJ che si è autoproclamato(-a); **to be a self-proclaimed fascist** ammettere con orgoglio di essere fascista
self-raising [ˌsɛlf'reɪzɪŋ], *(Am)* **self-rising** [ˌsɛlf'raɪzɪŋ] ADJ: **self-raising flour** *miscela di farina e lievito*
self-regulation [ˌsɛlfrɛgjʊ'leɪʃən] N autoregolamentazione *f*
self-regulatory [ˌsɛlf'rɛgjʊlətərɪ] ADJ di autoregolamentazione
self-reliant [ˌsɛlfrɪ'laɪənt] ADJ indipendente
self-respect [ˌsɛlfrɪs'pɛkt] N dignità, amor proprio *m*
self-respecting [ˌsɛlfrɪs'pɛktɪŋ] ADJ dignitoso(-a); **no self-respecting Englishman would do such a thing** nessun inglese che si rispetti farebbe una cosa simile
self-restraint [ˌsɛlfrɪ'streɪnt] N = **self-control**
self-righteous [ˌsɛlf'raɪtʃəs] ADJ *(pej)* presuntuoso(-a)
self-righteousness [ˌsɛlf'raɪtʃəsnɪs] N presunzione *f*
self-rising [ˌsɛlf'raɪzɪŋ] ADJ *(Am)* = **self-raising**
self-sacrifice [ˌsɛlf'sækrɪfaɪs] N abnegazione *f*
self-sacrificing [ˌsɛlf'sækrɪfaɪsɪŋ] ADJ altruista
self-same ['sɛlfˌseɪm] ADJ stesso(-a)
self-satisfied [ˌsɛlf'sætɪsfaɪd] ADJ soddisfatto(-a) di sé
self-sealing [ˌsɛlf'si:lɪŋ] ADJ autosigillante
self-seeking ['sɛlf'si:kɪŋ] ADJ egoista
■N egoismo
self-service [ˌsɛlf'sɜ:vɪs] ADJ self-service *inv*
self-starter [ˌsɛlf'stɑ:təʳ] N *(Aut)* motorino d'avviamento; *(fig: worker with initiative)* lavoratore(-trice) pieno(-a) d'iniziativa
self-study [ˌsɛlf'stʌdɪ] N autoapprendimento
self-styled [ˌsɛlf'staɪld] ADJ sedicente
self-sufficiency [ˌsɛlfsə'fɪʃənsɪ] N autosufficienza
self-sufficient [ˌsɛlfsə'fɪʃənt] ADJ autosufficiente
self-supporting [ˌsɛlfsə'pɔ:tɪŋ] ADJ economicamente indipendente
self-taught [ˌsɛlf'tɔ:t] ADJ autodidatta
self-test [ˌsɛlf'tɛst] N *(Comput)* test *m inv* autodiagnostico
self-torture [ˌsɛlf'tɔ:tʃəʳ], **self-torment** [ˌsɛlf'tɔmɛnt] N il tormentarsi *m*
self-willed [ˌsɛlf'wɪld] ADJ ostinato(-a)
self-winding [ˌsɛlf'waɪndɪŋ] ADJ a carica automatica
self-worship [ˌsɛlf'wɜ:ʃɪp] N narcisismo
self-worth [ˌsɛlf'wɜ:θ] N autostima
◎**sell** [sɛl] *(pt, pp* **sold***)* VT vendere; **to sell sth for £150** vendere qc per 150 sterline; **to sell sth at £10 per dozen** vendere qc a 10 sterline la dozzina; **to sell sth to sb** vendere qc a qn; **I was sold this in London** questo me l'hanno venduto a Londra; **to sell sb down the river** *(fig)* vendere qn; **to sell sb an idea** *(fig)* far accettare un'idea a qn; **to sell sb a pup** *(fig old)* imbrogliare qn; **to be sold on sb/sth** *(fam)* essere entusiasta di qn/qc; **he doesn't sell himself very well** non si sa vendere bene; **they're selling the house** stanno vendendo la casa; **he sold his car to his sister** ha venduto la macchina alla sorella
■VI essere in vendita; **they sell at** *or* **for 15p each** sono in vendita a 15p l'uno
▸ **sell off** VT + ADV *(stocks and shares, goods)* svendere, liquidare
▸ **sell out** VI + ADV: **to sell out (to sb/sth)** *(Comm)* vendere (tutto) (a qn/qc); **to sell out to the enemy** *(fig)* passare al nemico
■VT + ADV esaurire; **the tickets are all sold out** i biglietti sono esauriti; **we're** *or* **we've sold out of bread** il pane è tutto finito *(in negozio)*
▸ **sell up** VI + ADV *(esp Brit)* vendere (tutto)
■VT + ADV vendere
sell-by date ['sɛlbaɪˌdeɪt] N data di scadenza
sell·er ['sɛləʳ] N **1** venditore(-trice); **seller's market** mercato favorevole ai venditori; **a hot-dog seller** un venditore di hot-dog **2** *(product)*: **this item's a good seller** questo articolo (si) vende molto
seller's market N *(Fin)* mercato del venditore
sell·ing ['sɛlɪŋ] N *(act, business)* vendita
selling point N *(Comm)* caratteristica che fa vendere bene un prodotto; *(fig: advantage)* vantaggio
selling price N prezzo di vendita
Sel·lo·tape® ['sɛləʊˌteɪp] *(Brit)* N scotch® *m inv*
■VT attaccare con lo scotch
sell·out ['sɛlˌaʊt] N **1** *(Theatre)* **to be a sellout registrare il tutto esaurito; it was a sellout** ha fatto registrare il tutto esaurito **2** *(betrayal: to enemy)* tradimento
Selt·zer ['sɛltsəʳ] N seltz *m inv*
sel·vage, sel·vedge ['sɛlvɪdʒ] N *(Sewing)* cimosa
selves [sɛlvz] NPL *of* self
se·man·tic [sɪ'mæntɪk] ADJ semantico(-a)
se·man·ti·cal·ly [sɪ'mæntɪkəlɪ] ADV semanticamente
se·man·tics [sɪ'mæntɪks] NSG semantica
sema·phore ['sɛməˌfɔ:ʳ] N **1** *(system)* segnalazioni *fpl* con bandierine **2** *(Rail: signal post)* semaforo ferroviario
sem·blance ['sɛmbləns] N parvenza, apparenza
se·men ['si:mən] N seme *m*, sperma *m*
se·mes·ter [sɪ'mɛstəʳ] N *(Am)* semestre *m*
semi ['sɛmɪ] N *(Brit fam)* casetta a schiera
semi- ['sɛmɪ] PREF semi-
semi-annual [ˌsɛmɪ'ænjʊəl] ADJ *(Am)* biennale
semi·auto·mat·ic [ˌsɛmɪˌɔ:tə'mætɪk] ADJ semiautomatico(-a)
semi·breve ['sɛmɪˌbri:v] N *(Brit Mus)* semibreve *f*
semi·cir·cle ['sɛmɪˌsɜ:kl] N semicerchio
semi·cir·cu·lar [ˌsɛmɪ'sɜ:kjʊləʳ] ADJ semicircolare
semi·co·lon [ˌsɛmɪ'kəʊlən] N punto e virgola
semi·con·duc·tor [ˌsɛmɪkən'dʌktəʳ] N semiconduttore *m*
semi·con·scious [ˌsɛmɪ'kɒnʃəs] ADJ parzialmente cosciente
semi·dark·ness [ˌsɛmɪ'dɑ:knɪs] N semioscurità
semi·de·tached [ˌsɛmɪdɪ'tætʃt] ADJ: **semidetached house** casetta a schiera
semi·fi·nal [ˌsɛmɪ'faɪnl] N semifinale *f*
semi·fi·nal·ist [ˌsɛmɪ'faɪnəlɪst] N semifinalista *m/f*
semi·nal ['sɛmɪnl] ADJ *(fig: book, film)* che ha fatto scuola
semi·nar ['sɛmɪnɑ:ʳ] N *(Univ)* seminario
semi·nar·ist ['sɛmɪnərɪst] N seminarista *m*
semi·nary ['sɛmɪnərɪ] N *(Rel)* seminario
semi·of·fi·cial [ˌsɛmɪə'fɪʃəl] ADJ semiufficiale
se·mio·logi·cal [ˌsɛmɪə'lɒdʒɪkəl] ADJ semiologico(-a)
se·mi·ol·ogy [ˌsɛmɪ'ɒlədʒɪ] N semiologia

se·mi·ot·ics, se·mei·ot·ics [ˌsɛmɪˈɒtɪks] NSG (*Ling*) semiotica; (*Med*) semeiotica
semi·precious [ˈsɛmɪˌprɛʃəs] ADJ semiprezioso(-a)
semi·qua·ver [ˈsɛmɪˌkweɪvəʳ] N (*Brit Mus*) semicroma
semi·skilled [ˌsɛmɪˈskɪld] ADJ (*worker*) parzialmente qualificato(-a); (*work*) che richiede una specializzazione parziale
semi-skimmed [ˌsɛmɪˈskɪmd] ADJ parzialmente scremato(-a)
Se·mit·ic [sɪˈmɪtɪk] ADJ (*language*) semitico(-a); (*people*) semita
semi·tone [ˈsɛmɪˌtəʊn] N (*Mus*) semitono
semo·li·na [ˌsɛməˈliːnə] N semolino
semolina pudding N dolce *m* di semolino
Sen., sen. ABBR **1** = **senator 2** = **senior**
sen·ate [ˈsɛnɪt] N (*Pol*) senato; (*Univ*) senato accademico
◎ **sena·tor** [ˈsɛnɪtəʳ] N (*Pol*) senatore(-trice)
sena·to·rial [ˌsɛnəˈtɔːrɪəl] ADJ (*frm*) senatoriale
◎ **send** [sɛnd] (*pt, pp* **sent**) VT
1 (*gen*) mandare; (*letter, telegram*) mandare, spedire; (*arrow, rocket, ball*) lanciare; **to send by post** (*Am*): **send by mail** spedire per posta; **to send by telex/fax** mandare via telex/fax; **have you sent the letter?** hai spedito la lettera?; **she sent me a birthday card** mi ha mandato un biglietto d'auguri; **she sent out a hundred invitations** ha inviato cento inviti; **to send word that ...** mandare a dire che...; **she sends (you) her love** ti saluta affettuosamente; **to send sb for sth** mandare qn a prendere qc; **to send sb to do sth** mandare qn a fare qc; **to send sb home** mandare qn a casa; (*from abroad*) rimpatriare qn; **to send sb to prison/bed/school** mandare qn in prigione/a letto/a scuola; **to send sb to sleep** (*bore*) far addormentare qn; **send sb into fits of laughter** far scoppiare dal ridere qn; **the explosion sent a cloud of dust into the air** l'esplosione ha sollevato una nuvola di polvere; **to send a shiver down sb's spine** far venire i brividi a qn; **to send sb flying** mandare qn a gambe all'aria; **to send sth flying** far volare via qc; **to send sb to Coventry** (*Brit*) dare l'ostracismo a qn
2 (*cause to become*): **to send sb mad** far impazzire qn; **that really sends me** (*fam old*) mi manda in visibilio
▸ **send away** VT + ADV (*person*) mandare; (*: get rid of*) mandare via
▸ **send away for, send off for** VI + ADV + PREP richiedere per posta, farsi spedire; **I'll send away for a brochure** mi farò spedire un depliant
▸ **send back** VT + ADV rimandare
▸ **send down** VT + ADV (*person, prices*) far scendere; (*Brit: student*) cacciare, mandar via; (*fam: imprison*) mandare in galera
▸ **send for** VI + PREP
1 (*doctor, police*) (mandare a) chiamare, far venire
2 (*by post*) ordinare per posta
▸ **send in** VT + ADV (*person*) far entrare; (*troops*) inviare; (*report, application, resignation*) presentare
▸ **send off** VT + ADV (*person*) mandare; (*letter, goods*) spedire; (*Ftbl: player*) espellere; **we sent off your order yesterday** ieri abbiamo spedito il suo ordinativo; **he was sent off** l'hanno espulso; **to send sb off to do sth** mandare qn a fare qc
▸ **send off for** VI + ADV + PREP = **send away for**
▸ **send on** VT + ADV (*Brit: letter*) inoltrare; (*luggage etc: in advance*) spedire in anticipo; (*: afterwards*) mandare, spedire
▸ **send out** VI + ADV: **to send out for sth** mandare a prendere qc; farsi portare qc; **let's send out for a pizza** facciamoci portare una pizza
■ VT + ADV
1 (*person*) mandar fuori; (*troops*) inviare
2 (*post: invitations*) mandare, spedire
3 (*emit: light, heat*) mandare, emanare; (*: signals*) emettere
▸ **send round** VT + ADV (*letter, document etc*) far circolare; **to send sb round (to sb)** mandare qn (da qn); **I'll send it round later** te lo farò pervenire più tardi
▸ **send up** VT + ADV
1 (*person, luggage*) mandar su; (*balloon, rocket, flare*) lanciare; (*smoke, dust*) sollevare; (*prices*) far salire
2 (*Brit fam: make fun of: person, book*) fare la parodia di
send·er [ˈsɛndəʳ] N mittente *m/f*
send·off [ˈsɛndˌɒf] N: **to give sb a sendoff** festeggiare la partenza di qn
send-up [ˈsɛndˌʌp] N (*Brit fam*) parodia
Seneca [ˈsɛnɪkə] N Seneca *m*
Sen·egal [ˌsɛnɪˈgɔːl] N il Senegal
Sen·ega·lese [ˌsɛnɪgəˈliːz] ADJ, N, PL INV senegalese (*m/f*)
se·nile [ˈsiːnaɪl] ADJ senile; **I'm not senile yet!** non sono ancora rimbambito!
se·nil·ity [sɪˈnɪlɪtɪ] N senilità
◎ **sen·ior** [ˈsiːnɪəʳ] ADJ **1** (*in age*) maggiore, più anziano(-a); **she is 10 years senior to me** ha 10 anni più di me; **P. Jones senior** P. Jones senior *or* padre; **senior year** (*Am Univ, Scol*) ultimo anno di studi; **senior pupils** gli studenti delle classi superiori **2** (*of higher rank: employee, officer*) di grado superiore; (*: partner*) più anziano(-a); **senior management** i dirigenti di grado superiore; **he holds a senior position in the company** occupa una posizione di responsabilità nell'azienda; **he is senior to me in the firm** ha più anzianità di me nella ditta
■ N **1** (*in age*) persona più anziana; **he is my senior by 2 years** ha 2 anni più di me **2** (*Am Univ*) studente(-essa) dell'ultimo anno
senior citizen N (*euph: old person*) anziano(-a); (*: pensioner*) pensionato(-a)
senior high school N (*Am*) ≈ liceo
sen·ior·ity [ˌsiːnɪˈɒrɪtɪ] N (*in age, years of service*) anzianità; (*in rank*) superiorità
senior moment N (*hum: memory lapse*) momento di defaillance
sen·sa·tion [sɛnˈseɪʃən] N **1** (*physical feeling, impression*) sensazione *f*; **a strange sensation** una strana sensazione; **he is completely without sensation in that leg** ha perso completamente la sensibilità della gamba **2** (*excitement*) sensazione *f*, scalpore *m*; **to be** *or* **cause a sensation** fare sensazione, destare scalpore
sen·sa·tion·al [sɛnˈseɪʃənl] ADJ (*gen, also fam: marvellous*) sensazionale; (*newspaper*) sensazionalistico(-a); (*novel etc*) a sensazione; (*account, description*) a forti tinte
sen·sa·tion·al·ism [sɛnˈseɪʃnəˌlɪzəm] N (*pej: of reporting*) sensazionalismo
sen·sa·tion·al·ly [sɛnˈseɪʃnəlɪ] ADV (*see adj*) sensazionalmente; a forti tinte
◎ **sense** [sɛns] N **1** (*faculty*) senso; **a keen sense of smell/hearing** un olfatto/udito fine; **to come to one's senses** (*regain consciousness*) riprendere i sensi; **the five senses** i cinque sensi; **sixth sense** sesto senso; **sense of direction** senso di orientamento; **to lose all sense of time** perdere la nozione del tempo;

Ss

sense of humour (senso dell') umorismo **2** (*feeling*) senso, sensazione *f*; **sense of duty/guilt** senso del dovere/di colpa; **a sense of well-being** una sensazione di benessere **3** (*also*: **common sense**) buonsenso; **he should have had more sense than to do it** avrebbe dovuto avere il buonsenso di non farlo; **have a bit of sense!** un po' di buonsenso, via!; **there is no sense in (doing) that** non ha senso (farlo); **she had the sense to call the doctor** ha avuto il buonsenso di chiamare il medico; **to make sb see sense** far ragionare qn, far intendere ragione a qn **4** (*sanity*): **senses** NPL ragione *fsg*, senno *msg*; **to come to one's senses** (*become reasonable*) tornare in sé; **to bring sb to his senses** riportare qn alla ragione, far rinsavire qn; **to take leave of one's senses** perdere il lume *or* l'uso della ragione **5** (*meaning*) senso, significato; **it makes sense** ha senso; **it doesn't make sense** non ha senso; **I can't make (any) sense of this** non ci capisco niente; **in one** *or* **a sense** in un certo senso; **in every sense (of the word)** in tutti i sensi (del termine) **6** (*Math*) verso
■VT (*presence, interest*) avvertire, intuire; (*danger*) sentire, percepire; **to sense that all is not well** sentire che c'è qualcosa che non va

sense·less ['sɛnslɪs] ADJ **1** (*stupid*: *action*) insensato(-a); (: *idea*) assurdo(-a); **acts of senseless violence** atti di violenza insensata **2** (*unconscious*) privo(-a) di sensi *or* di conoscenza; **she fell senseless to the ground** cadde a terra priva di sensi

sense·less·ly ['sɛnslɪslɪ] ADV in modo insensato

sense·less·ness ['sɛnslɪsnɪs] N (*of person*) mancanza di buon senso; (*of action, idea*) insensatezza, assurdità

sen·sibil·ities [ˌsɛnsɪ'bɪlɪtɪz] NPL (*frm*) suscettibilità *fsg*

sen·sibil·ity [ˌsɛnsɪ'bɪlɪtɪ] N (*delicacy of feeling*) sensibilità *f inv* **2** (*sensitivity*) suscettibilità *f inv*

◎**sen·sible** ['sɛnsəbl] ADJ **1** (*having good sense*: *person*) assennato(-a) **2** (*act, decision, choice*) sensato(-a), ragionevole; (*clothing, shoes*) pratico(-a); **be sensible!** sii ragionevole!; **it would be more sensible (to do)** avrebbe più senso (fare) **3** (*frm*: *noticeable*) sensibile, rilevante

sen·sibly ['sɛnsəblɪ] ADV (*reasonably*: *behave, talk*) assennatamente, con molto buon senso

◎**sen·si·tive** ['sɛnsɪtɪv] ADJ (*person, tooth, instrument, film*): **sensitive (to)** sensibile (a); (*delicate*: *skin, question*) delicato(-a); (*easily offended*) suscettibile; **he is very sensitive about it** è meglio non toccare quel tasto con lui

sen·si·tiv·ity [ˌsɛnsɪ'tɪvɪtɪ] N (*see adj*) sensibilità; delicatezza; suscettibilità

sen·si·tized ['sɛnsɪˌtaɪzd] ADJ sensibilizzato(-a)

sen·sor ['sɛnsə^r] N (*Tech*) sensore *m*

sen·so·ry ['sɛnsərɪ] ADJ sensorio(-a)

sen·sual ['sɛnsjʊəl] ADJ (*gen*) sensuale; (*pleasures*) dei sensi

sen·su·al·ity [ˌsɛnsjʊ'ælɪtɪ] N sensualità

sen·su·ous ['sɛnsjʊəs] ADJ sensuoso(-a)

sen·su·ous·ness ['sɛnsjʊəsnɪs] N l'essere sensuoso(-a)

sent [sɛnt] PT, PP *of* **send**

◎**sen·tence** ['sɛntəns] N **1** (*gen*) frase *f*; (*Gram*) proposizione *f*; (: *complex sentence*) periodo; **he wrote a sentence** ha scritto una frase **2** (*Law*: *verdict*) sentenza; (: *punishment*) condanna; **to pass sentence on sb** condannare qn; (*fig*) giudicare qn; **sentence of death** condanna a morte; **under sentence of death** condannato(-a) a morte; **the judge gave him a 6-month sentence** il giudice lo ha condannato a 6 mesi di prigione; **he served a long sentence** ha scontato una lunga condanna; **he got a life sentence** ha avuto l'ergastolo
■VT: **to sentence sb to death/to 5 years (in prison)/to life imprisonment** condannare qn a morte/a 5 anni (di prigione)/all'ergastolo

sentence adverb N (*Ling*) avverbio frasale

sen·ten·tious [sɛn'tɛnʃəs] ADJ (*frm*) sentenzioso(-a)

sen·ten·tious·ly [sɛn'tɛnʃəslɪ] ADV (*frm*) in modo sentenzioso

sen·ti·ent ['sɛntɪənt] ADJ (*frm*: *creature, being*) sensibile, senziente

sen·ti·ment ['sɛntɪmənt] N **1** (*feeling*) sentimento; (*opinion*) opinione *f*; **the sentiments expressed by the previous speaker** le opinioni espresse dall'oratore precedente; **nationalist sentiments** sentimenti nazionalisti **2** (*sentimentality*) sentimentalismo

sen·ti·ment·al [ˌsɛntɪ'mɛntl] ADJ (*emotional*) sentimentale; (*pej*: *film, love story*) troppo sentimentale; **I have a sentimental attachment to this pen** sono attaccato a questa penna per motivi sentimentali

sen·ti·men·tal·ity [ˌsɛntɪmɛn'tælɪtɪ] N (*pej*) sentimentalismo

sen·ti·men·tal·ize [ˌsɛntɪ'mɛntəˌlaɪz] (*frm pej*) VT fare del sentimentalismo su

sen·ti·men·tal·ly [ˌsɛntɪ'mɛntəlɪ] ADV sentimentalmente; (*pej*) con sentimentalismo

sentimental value N valore *m* affettivo

sen·ti·nel ['sɛntɪnl] N (*old*) sentinella

sen·try ['sɛntrɪ] N sentinella

sentry box N garitta

sentry duty N: **to be on sentry duty** essere di sentinella

Seoul [səʊl] N Seul *f*

sep·al ['sɛpəl] N sepalo

sepa·rable ['sɛpərəbl] ADJ separabile

◎**sepa·rate** [*adj* 'sɛprɪt; *vb* 'sɛpəˌreɪt] ADJ (*gen*) separato(-a); (*organization, career*) indipendente; (*occasion, issue*) diverso(-a); **they went their separate ways** (*also fig*) sono andati ognuno per la propria strada; **we sat at separate tables** ci siamo seduti a tavoli diversi; **it was discussed at a separate meeting** è stato discusso in un'altra riunione; **they have separate rooms** hanno camere separate; **on separate occasions** in diverse occasioni; **I wrote it on a separate sheet** l'ho scritto su un altro foglio di carta; **separate from** separato(-a) da; **under separate cover** (*Comm*) in plico a parte
■VT (*gen*) separare, dividere; (*divide up*): **to separate into** dividere in; **to separate sth from sth** separare qc da qc; **he is separated from his wife, but not divorced** è separato dalla moglie ma non divorziato; **the police tried to separate the two groups** la polizia ha cercato di separare i due gruppi
■VI (*mixture, milk*) separarsi; (*married couple, boxers*) separarsi, dividersi; (*unmarried couple, friends*) lasciarsi; *see also* **separates they separated seven years ago** si sono separati sette anni fa

sepa·rate·ly ['sɛprɪtlɪ] ADV separatamente

sepa·rates ['sɛprɪts] NPL (*clothes*) coordinati *mpl*

sepa·ra·tion [ˌsɛpə'reɪʃən] N separazione *f*

sepa·ra·tism ['sɛpərəˌtɪzəm] N separatismo

sepa·ra·tist ['sɛpərətɪst] ADJ, N separatista (*m/f*)

se·pia ['siːpjə] N nero di seppia

Sept. ABBR (= **September**) sett., set. (= *settembre*)

Sep·tem·ber [sɛp'tɛmbə^r] N settembre *m*; *for usage see* **July**

sep·tic ['sɛptɪk] ADJ settico(-a); (*wound*) infetto(-a); **to go septic** infettarsi; **a septic finger** un dito infettato
sep·ti·cae·mia, (*Am*) **sep·ti·cemia** [,sɛptɪ'si:mɪə] N setticemia
septic tank N fossa settica
sep·tua·genar·ian [,sɛptjʊədʒɪ'nɛərɪən] N (*frm*) settuagenario(-a)
sepulchral [sɪ'pʌlkrəl] ADJ (*liter: tone, gloom*) sepolcrale
sep·ul·chre, (*Am*) **sep·ul·cher** ['sɛpəlkəʳ] N (*liter*) sepolcro
se·quel ['si:kwəl] N (*of film, book*): **sequel (to)** seguito (di); (*of event*) conseguenza (di), strascico (di)
se·quence ['si:kwəns] N **1** (*order*) successione *f*, ordine *m*; **in sequence** in ordine, di seguito; **sequence of tenses** (*Gram*) concordanza dei tempi **2** (*series*) serie *f inv*; (*Mus, Cards, film sequence*) sequenza; **the sequence of events that led to the murder** la serie di avvenimenti che ha portato all'omicidio
se·quen·tial [sɪ'kwɛnʃəl] ADJ sequenziale; **sequential access** (*Comput*) accesso sequenziale
se·ques·ter [sɪ'kwɛstəʳ] VT (*Law: property*) sequestrare, confiscare
se·ques·tered [sɪ'kwɛstəd] ADJ **1** (*liter: place*) isolato(-a); (: *life*) ritirato(-a), appartato(-a) **2** (*Law: property*) sequestrato(-a)
se·ques·trate [sɪ'kwɛstreɪt] VT sequestrare, confiscare
se·quin ['si:kwɪn] N paillette *f inv*, lustrino
ser·aph ['sɛrəf] N (*pl* **seraphs** *or* **seraphim**) serafino
Serb [s3:b] ADJ, N = Serbian
Ser·bia ['s3:bɪə] N Serbia
Ser·bian ['s3:bɪən] ADJ serbo(-a)
■ N (*person*) serbo(-a); (*language*) serbo
Serbo-Croat ['s3:bəʊ'krəʊæt] N (*language*) serbocroato
ser·enade [,sɛrə'neɪd] N serenata
■ VT fare la serenata a
ser·en·dip·ity [,sɛrən'dɪpɪtɪ] N (*frm*) serendipità
se·rene [sə'ri:n] ADJ (*person, sky*) sereno(-a); (*sea*) calmo(-a)
se·rene·ly [sə'ri:nlɪ] ADV (*smile, say*) serenamente
se·ren·ity [sɪ'rɛnɪtɪ] N serenità
serf [s3:f] N servo(-a) della gleba
serf·dom ['s3:fdəm] N servitù della gleba
serge [s3:dʒ] N serge *f*
ser·geant ['sɑ:dʒənt] N (*Mil*) sergente *m*; (*Police*) ≈ brigadiere *m*
sergeant major N (*Mil*) sergente *m* maggiore
se·rial ['sɪərɪəl] N (*in magazine*) romanzo a puntate; (*TV*) teleromanzo a puntate, serial *m inv* televisivo; (*Radio*) commedia radiofonica a puntate
■ ADJ (*Comput*) seriale
se·riali·za·tion [,sɪərɪəlaɪ'zeɪʃən] N (*publishing in instalments*) pubblicazione a puntate; (*TV, Radio: adapting*) adattamento e trasmissione a puntate; (: *series of broadcasts*): **a new serialization of a novel by Jane Austen** un nuovo teleromanzo a puntate tratto da un'opera di Jane Austen
se·rial·ize ['sɪərɪə,laɪz] VT (*Press*) pubblicare a puntate; (*TV, Radio*) trasmettere a puntate
serial killer N serial-killer *m/f inv*
serial number N (*of goods, machinery, banknotes etc*) numero di serie
serial port N (*Comput*) porta seriale
◎ **se·ries** ['sɪərɪz] N, PL INV (*gen, Radio, TV*) serie *f inv*; (*set of books*) collana
series elements NPL (*Phys*) elementi *mpl* in serie
seri·graph ['sɛrɪ,græf] N serigrafia (*stampa*)
se·rig·ra·phy [sə'rɪgrəfɪ] N serigrafia (*metodo*)
◎ **se·ri·ous** ['sɪərɪəs] ADJ **1** (*earnest*) serio(-a); **to give serious thought to sth** considerare seriamente qc; **he's a serious student of jazz** s'interessa seriamente di jazz; **she's getting serious about him** si sta innamorando sul serio di lui; **are you serious (about it)?** parli sul serio?; **you can't be serious!** stai scherzando!; **you're looking very serious** hai un'aria molto seria **2** (*causing concern*) serio(-a), grave; **the patient's condition is serious** il paziente versa in gravi condizioni; **a serious illness** una grave malattia
◎ **se·ri·ous·ly** ['sɪərɪəslɪ] ADV **1** (*in earnest*) seriamente; **to take sth/sb seriously** prendere qc/qn sul serio; **seriously though ...** scherzi a parte..., sul serio...; **we'll have to think about it seriously** dovremo pensarci seriamente **2** (*wounded*) gravemente; (*worried*) seriamente; **seriously injured** gravemente ferito(-a) **3** (*fam: extremely*): **he's seriously rich** ha un casino di soldi
se·ri·ous·ness ['sɪərɪəsnɪs] N (*gen*) serietà, gravità; (*of error*) gravità; **in all seriousness** in tutta sincerità; **the seriousness of the situation** la gravità della situazione
ser·mon ['s3:mən] N (*in church*) sermone *m*; (*pej: lecture*) predica
ser·mon·ize ['s3:mə,naɪz] VI (*fig pej*) fare la predica
sero·thera·py [,sɪərəʊ'θɛrəpɪ] N sieroterapia
sero·to·nin [,sɛrə'təʊnɪn] N (*Med*) serotonina
ser·pent ['s3:pənt] N (*liter*) serpente *m*
ser·pen·tine ['s3:pən,taɪn] N (*liter: sinuous*) sinuoso(-a)
ser·rat·ed [sɛ'reɪtɪd] ADJ seghettato(-a)

DID YOU KNOW ...?
serrated is not translated by the Italian word *serrato*

ser·ra·tion [sɛ'reɪʃən] N seghettatura
ser·ried ['sɛrɪd] ADJ (*liter*) serrato(-a); **in serried ranks** in ranghi serrati
se·rum ['sɪərəm] N siero
◎ **serv·ant** ['s3:vənt] N (*domestic*) domestico(-a); (*fig: of the public, one's country*) servitore *m*
◎ **serve** [s3:v] VT **1** (*work for: employer*) servire; (: *God, one's country*) servire, essere al servizio di **2** (*be used for or useful as*): **to serve (as)** servire (da); **that serves to explain ...** così si spiega...; **it serves a variety of purposes** ha svariati usi; **it serves my purpose** fa al caso mio, serve al mio scopo; **it serves its purpose** serve allo scopo; **it serves no useful purpose** non serve a niente; **it serves you right** (*fam*) ben ti sta; **his knowledge served him well** la sua preparazione gli è tornata utile **3** (*in shop, restaurant*) servire; (*food, meal, also Tennis*) servire; **to serve sb (with) sth** servire qc a qn; **are you being served?** la stanno servendo?; **dinner is served** la cena è servita; **this dish should be served hot** è un piatto che va servito caldo; **the power station serves the entire region** la centrale elettrica alimenta l'intera regione; **the railway line serves five cities** la ferrovia serve cinque città **4** (*complete*): **to serve an apprenticeship** fare tirocinio; **to serve a prison sentence** scontare una condanna; **to serve time** (*fam*) essere in prigione; **he has served time (in prison)** è stato in prigione; **he has served his time** (*prisoner*) ha scontato la sua condanna; (*apprentice*) ha finito il periodo di prova **5** (*Law: summons, writ*): **to serve sth on sb** notificare qc a qn; **to serve a summons on sb** (*Law*) spiccare un mandato di comparizione contro qn
■ VI **1** (*servant, soldier*) prestare servizio; (*shop assistant,*

Ss

waiter) servire; (*Tennis*) servire, battere; **to serve on a committee/jury** far parte di un comitato/una giuria; **she served for 2 years as chairwoman** è stata in carica come presidente per 2 anni **2** (*be useful*): **to serve as/for/to do** servire da/per/per fare
■ N (*Tennis*) servizio, battuta
▸ **serve out, serve up** VT + ADV (*food*) servire; (*meal*) servire in tavola

serv·er ['sɜ:vəʳ] N **1** (*Comput*) server *m inv* **2** (*Rel*) chierichetto; (*Tennis*) chi ha il servizio, battitore(-trice) **3** (*piece of cutlery*) posata di servizio; (*tray*) vassoio, piatto da portata

server farm N (*Comput*) fattoria di server

◎ **ser·vice** ['sɜ:vɪs] N **1** (*gen, also Mil*) servizio; **to see service** (*Mil*) prestare servizio; **military service** servizio militare; **at your service** al suo (*or* vostro) servizio; **to be of service (to sb)** essere utile (a qn); **to do sb a service** fare un (gran) favore a qn; **this old chair has seen a lot of service** questa vecchia sedia ne ha viste tante; **in service** (*domestic*) a servizio; **On Her (or His) Majesty's Service** al servizio di Sua Maestà (Britannica); **in the service of one's country** al servizio della patria; **service is included** il servizio è compreso **2** (*department, system*) servizio; **medical/ social services** servizi sanitari/sociali; **the postal service** il servizio postale; **the essential services** i servizi primari; **goods and services** (*Econ*) beni *mpl* e servizi; **the train service to London** il servizio di treni per Londra; **the number 13 bus service** la linea del 13 **3 the Services** (*Mil*) le Forze Armate **4** (*Rel*) funzione *f*; **funeral service** rito funebre; **to hold a service** celebrare una funzione **5** (*maintenance work*) revisione *f* (periodica); **to put the car in for a service** portare la macchina in officina per una revisione **6** (*set of crockery*) servizio; **a tea/coffee/dinner service** un servizio da tè/da caffè/da tavola **7** (*on motorway*): **services** NPL stazione *fsg* di servizio **8** (*Tennis etc*) servizio, battuta
■ VT (*car, washing machine*) revisionare; (*group, organization*) dare assistenza a; (*Fin: debt*) pagare gli interessi su

ser·vice·able ['sɜ:vɪsəbl] ADJ (*practical: clothes, shoes*) pratico(-a); (*usable, functioning*) usabile

service area N (*on motorway*) area di servizio

service charge N (*in restaurant*) servizio; **there's no service charge** il servizio è compreso

service court N (*Tennis*) rettangolo di battuta

service flat N (*Brit*) ≈ appartamento in un residence

service industries NPL settore *msg* terziario

service line N (*Tennis*) linea di battuta

ser·vice·man ['sɜ:vɪsmən] N (*pl* **-men**) militare *m*

service provider N provider *m inv*

service sector N settore *m* dei servizi

service station N (*Aut*) stazione *f* di servizio

ser·vice·woman ['sɜ:vɪsˌwʊmən] N (*pl* **-women**) militare *m* donna *inv*

ser·vi·cing ['sɜ:vɪsɪŋ] N (*of car*) revisione *f*

ser·vi·ette [ˌsɜ:vɪ'ɛt] N (*Brit*) tovagliolo, salvietta

serviette ring N portatovagliolo

ser·vile ['sɜ:vaɪl] ADJ (*pej*) servile

ser·vile·ly ['sɜ:vaɪllɪ] ADV (*pej*) servilmente

ser·vil·ity [sɜ:'vɪlɪtɪ] N (*pej*) servilismo

serv·ing ['sɜ:vɪŋ] N (*portion*) porzione; **serving dish** piatto da portata

ser·vi·tude ['sɜ:vɪtju:d] N servitù *f*

ser·vo·mecha·nism ['sɜ:vəʊˌmɛkəˌnɪzəm] N servomeccanismo

sesa·me ['sɛsəmɪ] N **1** (*plant*) sesamo **2** (*Arabian Nights*): **open sesame** apriti sesamo; (*fig*): **an open sesame to sth** un biglietto d'ingresso per qc (*fig*)

sesame oil N olio di sesamo

sesame seeds NPL (*Culin*) semi *mpl* di sesamo

ses·sile ['sɛsaɪl] ADJ (*Bot*) sessile

◎ **ses·sion** ['sɛʃən] N **1** (*sitting*) seduta, sessione *f*; (*meeting*) riunione *f*; **to be in session** (*parliament, court*) essere in seduta; **the court is now in session** l'udienza è aperta; **I had a long session with her** (*talk*) ho avuto un lungo colloquio con lei; (*work*) ho avuto una lunga riunione di lavoro con lei **2** (*esp Am, Scot Scol, Univ: year*) anno scolastico (*or* accademico); (*: term*) trimestre *m or* quadrimestre *m*; **the new parliamentary session begins in October** l'attività parlamentare riprenderà a ottobre

session musician N musicista *m/f* di studio

◎ **set** [sɛt] (*vb: pt, pp* **set**) N
1 (*gen*) serie *f inv*; (*of kitchen tools, saucepans*) batteria; (*of books*) raccolta, collezione *f*; (*of dishes*) servizio; **a set of false teeth** una dentiera; **he still has a full set of teeth** ha ancora una dentatura completa; **a set of dining-room furniture** una camera da pranzo; **a chess/draughts set** un gioco di scacchi/dama; **a painting/writing set** l'occorrente *m* per dipingere/ per scrivere; **these articles are sold in sets** questi articoli si vendono in serie complete
2 (*Tennis*) set *m inv*
3 (*Math*) insieme *m*; **closed set** insieme chiuso; **empty set** insieme vuoto
4 (*Elec*) apparecchio; **television set** televisore *m*
5 (*Cine*) set *m inv*; (*Theatre*) scena
6 (*Hairdressing*) messa in piega
7 (*group: often pej*) cerchia; **the smart set** il bel mondo
■ ADJ
1 (*unchanging: gen*) fisso(-a); (*smile*) artificiale; (*purpose*) definito(-a), preciso(-a); (*lunch*) a prezzo fisso; (*speech, talk*) preparato(-a); (*date, time*) preciso(-a), stabilito(-a); (*Scol: subjects*) obbligatorio(-a); (*: books*) in programma (per l'esame); **set in one's ways** abitudinario(-a); **set in one's opinions** rigido(-a) nelle proprie convinzioni; **a set phrase** una frase fatta; **at a set time** a un'ora stabilita
2 (*determined*) deciso(-a); (*ready*) pronto(-a); **he is (dead) set on doing it** è deciso a farlo; **he is (dead) set on a new car** si è ficcato in testa di comprare una nuova macchina; **to be (dead) set against (doing) sth** essere assolutamente contrario(-a) a (fare) qc; **to be all set to do sth** essere pronto(-a) a fare qc; **the scene was set for ...** (*fig*) tutto era pronto per...
■ VT
1 (*place, put*) mettere; **a novel set in Rome** un romanzo ambientato a Roma; **to set a higher value on happiness than on wealth** dar più valore alla felicità che alla ricchezza; **to set the value of a ring at £500** valutare un anello 500 sterline; **to set sb free** liberare qn, mettere qn in libertà; **to set fire to sth** dare *or* appiccare fuoco a qc; **to set a dog on sb** aizzare un cane contro qn
2 (*arrange, adjust: clock, mechanism*) regolare; (*: alarm clock*) mettere, puntare; (*: trap*) mettere, tendere; (*: hair*) fissare, mettere in piega; (*: broken arm, leg: in plaster*) ingessare; (*: with splint*) mettere una stecca a; (*: type*) comporre; **to set a poem to music** mettere in musica

una poesia; **I set the alarm for seven o'clock** ho messo la sveglia alle sette
3 (*fix, establish: date, limit*) fissare, stabilire; (*: record*) stabilire; (*: fashion*) lanciare; (*dye, colour*) fissare; **to set course for** (*Naut*) far rotta per; **the world record was set last year** il record mondiale è stato stabilito l'anno scorso
4 (*gem*) montare
5 (*assign: task, homework*) dare, assegnare; **to set sb a problem** porre un problema a qn; **to set sb an exam in Italian** far fare un esame d'italiano a qn; **to set an exam in Italian** preparare il testo *or* le domande di un esame d'italiano; **we'll set you a task** ti daremo un compito
6 (*start, cause to start*): **to set sth going** mettere in moto qc; **it set me thinking** mi ha fatto pensare; **to set sb to work** mettere qn al lavoro; **to set to work** mettersi al lavoro
■ VI
1 (*sun, moon*) tramontare; **the sun was setting** il sole stava tramontando
2 (*broken bone, limb*) saldarsi; (*jelly, jam*) rapprendersi; (*concrete, glue*) indurirsi, fare presa; (*fig: face*) irrigidirsi; *see also* **sail, table, example, heart**
▸ **set about** VI + PREP
1 (*task*): **to set about doing sth** intraprendere qc, mettersi a fare qc; **I don't know how to set about it** non so da che parte cominciare
2 (*attack*) assalire
▸ **set against** VT + PREP
1 (*make hostile to*): **to set sb against sb/sth** mettere qn contro qn/qc
2 (*balance against*): **to set sth against sth** contrapporre qc a qc
▸ **set apart** VT + ADV (*object*) mettere da parte; (*fig: person*) distinguere
▸ **set aside** VT + ADV
1 (*book, work*) mettere via; (*money, time*) mettere da parte; (*differences, quarrels, principles*) accantonare; (*land*) mettere a riposo
2 (*reject: objection*) respingere; (*: will, judgement*) invalidare, annullare
▸ **set back** VT + ADV
1 (*clock*) mettere indietro; (*progress*) ritardare; **to set back the clock (by one hour)** mettere l'orologio indietro (di un'ora); **the strike has set us back 6 months** lo sciopero ci ha fatto perdere 6 mesi
2 a house set back from the road una casa a una certa distanza dalla strada
3 (*fam: cost*): **it set me back £900** mi è costato la bellezza di 900 sterline
▸ **set down** VT + ADV
1 (*put down: object*) posare; (*: passenger*) lasciare, far scendere
2 (*record*) prendere nota di; **to set sth down in writing** *or* **on paper** mettere qc per iscritto *or* sulla carta
▸ **set forth** VT + ADV (*frm: facts, reasons, arguments*) esporre
■ VI + ADV (*liter: set off*) mettersi in viaggio
▸ **set in** VI + ADV (*infection*) svilupparsi; (*complications*) intervenire; **the rain has set in for the day** ormai pioverà tutto il giorno; **before the rot sets in** prima che la situazione degeneri
▸ **set off** VI + ADV (*leave*) mettersi in cammino, partire; **to set off on a journey (to)** mettersi in viaggio (per); **we set off after breakfast** siamo partiti dopo colazione
■ VT + ADV
1 (*bomb*) far scoppiare *or* esplodere; (*mechanism, burglar alarm*) azionare; (*process, chain of events*) mettere in moto, scatenare
2 (*enhance*) mettere in risalto, far risaltare
▸ **set out** VI + ADV: **to set out (for)** avviarsi (verso, a); (*city*) partire (per); **we set out for London at nine o'clock** siamo partiti per Londra alle nove; **to set out (from)** partire (da); **to set out in search of sb/sth** mettersi alla ricerca di qn/qc; **to set out to do sth** proporsi di fare qc
■ VT + ADV (*goods etc, fig: reasons, ideas*) esporre, presentare; (*chess pieces*) schierare, disporre
▸ **set to** VI + ADV: **to set to (and do sth)** mettersi all'opera (e fare qc)
▸ **set up** VI + ADV: **to set up (in business) as a baker/lawyer** aprire una panetteria/uno studio legale; **when did you set up in business?** quand'è che ti sei messo in proprio?
■ VT + ADV
1 (*place in position: chairs, stalls, road blocks*) disporre; (*tent*) rizzare, piantare; (*monument*) innalzare
2 (*start: firm, business etc*) avviare; (*: school, organization*) fondare; (*: fund*) costituire; (*: inquiry*) aprire; (*: infection*) provocare; (*: record*) stabilire; **to set up house** trovarsi una casa; **to set up camp** accamparsi; **to set up shop** mettersi in proprio; **to set sb up in business** avviare qn agli affari; **to set o.s. up as sth** (*fig*) pretendere di essere qc
▸ **set upon** VI + PREP (*attack*) assalire

set-aside ['sɛtəsaɪd] N (*of land*) messa a riposo; (*land*) terreno messo a riposo
set·back ['sɛt,bæk] N (*hitch*) contrattempo, inconveniente *m*; (*more serious*) momento di crisi; (*in health*) ricaduta; **a setback for the peace process** un intoppo al processo di pace; **he suffered a setback in his career** la sua carriera ha avuto un momento di crisi
set menu N menù *m inv* fisso *or* turistico
set piece N (*Mus, Literature: part of work, piece of music*) brano famoso; (*in music competition*) brano obbligatorio; (*Sport*) tattica di gioco
set-piece ['sɛt,pi:s] ADJ (*offensive, manoeuvre*) accuratamente programmato(-a)
set point N (*Tennis*) set point *m inv*
set square N squadra da disegno
set·tee [sɛ'ti:] N divano
set·ter ['sɛtəʳ] N (*dog*) setter *m inv*
set theory N (*Math*) teoria degli insiemi, insiemistica
set·ting ['sɛtɪŋ] N **1** (*of novel*) ambiente *m*, ambientazione *f*; (*scenery*) sfondo; (*of jewels*) montatura; **a house in a beautiful setting** una casa in una posizione meravigliosa **2** (*Mus*) adattamento (musicale) **3** (*of controls*) posizione *f*; **the heating was on the highest setting** il termosifone era fissato sulla regolazione più alta **4** (*of sun*) tramonto
setting lotion N fissatore *m* (*per messa in piega*)
set·tle¹ ['sɛtl] N cassapanca con schienale alto
◎ **set·tle²** ['sɛtl] VT
1 (*place carefully*) sistemare; **to settle o.s.** *or* **get settled** sistemarsi
2 (*decide, finalize: details, date*) definire, concordare; (*pay: bill, account*) regolare, saldare; (*solve: problem*) risolvere; (*: difficulty*) appianare; (*: dispute, argument*) comporre; **to settle a case** *or* **claim out of court** definire una causa in via amichevole; **that should settle the problem** questo dovrebbe risolvere il

Ss

problema; **I'll settle the bill tomorrow** salderò il conto domani; **that's settled then** allora è deciso; **that settles it!** (*I've decided*) ecco, ho deciso!; (*indignant*) questo è il colmo!
3 (*calm down*: *nerves*) distendere; (: *doubts*) dissipare; **to settle one's stomach** calmare il mal di stomaco
4 (*colonize*: *land*) colonizzare
5 (*Law*): **to settle sth on sb** intestare qc a qn
■ VI
1 (*bird, insect*) posarsi; (*sediment, dust, snow*) depositarsi; (*building*) assestarsi; (*conditions, situation*) stabilizzarsi; (*weather*) mettersi al bello; (*emotions*) calmarsi; (*nerves*) distendersi; **to settle to sth** applicarsi a qc; **I couldn't settle to anything** non riuscivo a concentrarmi
2 (*go to live*: *in town, country*) stabilirsi; (: *in new house*) sistemarsi, installarsi; (: *as colonist*) insediarsi; **to feel settled** (*in a place*) sentirsi a casa
3 **to settle with sb for the price of sth** concordare il prezzo di qc con qn; **can I settle with you later?** posso darti i soldi più tardi?; **to settle out of court** (*Law*) giungere a un accordo in via amichevole; **to settle on sth** (*choose*) decidere *or* optare per qc
► **settle down** VI + ADV (*person*: *in house, armchair etc*) sistemarsi; (: *become calmer*) calmarsi; (: *after wild youth*) mettere la testa a posto; (*situation*) sistemarsi, tornare alla normalità; **to settle down to work** mettersi a lavorare; **has he settled down in his new job?** si è adattato bene al nuovo lavoro?; **things will settle down eventually** le cose si sistemeranno alla fine; **I want to settle down and start a family** voglio sistemarmi e metter su famiglia; **to get married and settle down** mettere su casa (e famiglia)
► **settle for** VI + PREP: **to settle for sth** accontentarsi di qc; **he settled for £100** ha accettato 100 sterline
► **settle in** VI + ADV (*in new house*) sistemarsi, installarsi; (*in new job, neighbourhood*) ambientarsi
► **settle up** VI + ADV: **to settle up (with sb)** saldare *or* regolare i conti (con qn)

◉ **set·tle·ment** ['sɛtlmənt] N **1** (*of bill, debt*) pagamento, saldo; (*of question*) soluzione *f*; (*of dispute*) composizione *f*; **in settlement of our account** (*Comm*) a saldo del nostro conto **2** (*agreement*) accordo; **a peace settlement** un accordo di pace **3** (*village*) insediamento, comunità *f inv*; (*colony*) colonia

set·tler ['sɛtləʳ] N colonizzatore(-trice)

set-to ['sɛt'tu:] N (*fam*: *fight*) zuffa; (: *quarrel*) baruffa

set-top box ['sɛttɒp,bɒks] N (*TV*) decodificatore *m*, decoder *m inv*

◉ **set-up**, **setup** ['sɛt,ʌp] N (*fam*: *situation*) situazione *f*; (*Comput*) setup *m inv*

setup costs [-,kɒsts] NPL (*Comm*) costi *mpl* d'avviamento

setup file N (*Comput*) file *m inv* di configurazione

◉ **sev·en** ['sɛvn] ADJ, N sette *(m) inv*; *for usage see* **five**

◉ **sev·en·teen** [,sɛvn'ti:n] ADJ, N diciassette *(m) inv*; *for usage see* **five**

◉ **sev·en·teenth** [,sɛvn'ti:nθ] ADJ diciassettesimo(-a)
■ N (*in series*) diciassettesimo(-a); (*fraction*) diciassettesimo; *for usage see* **fifth**

◉ **sev·enth** ['sɛvnθ] ADJ settimo(-a)
■ N (*in series*) settimo(-a); (*fraction*) settimo; *for usage see* **fifth**

◉ **sev·en·ti·eth** ['sɛvntɪɪθ] ADJ settantesimo(-a)
■ N (*in series*) settantesimo(-a); (*fraction*) settantesimo; *for usage see* **fifth**

◉ **sev·en·ty** ['sɛvntɪ] ADJ, N settanta *(m) inv*; *for usage see* **fifty**

sev·er ['sɛvəʳ] VT (*rope*) tagliare, recidere; (*limb*) staccare, mozzare; (*fig*: *relations*) troncare, rompere; (: *communications*) interrompere; **he severed an artery** ha reciso un'arteria; **she severed all ties with her family** ha troncato tutti i legami con la famiglia

◉ **sev·er·al** ['sɛvrəl] ADJ parecchi(-ie) *pl*, diversi(-e) *pl*; **several times** diverse volte
■ PRON parecchi(-ie) *pl*, alcuni(-e) *pl*; **several of us** parecchi di noi, alcuni di noi

sev·er·al·ly ['sɛvrəlɪ] ADV (*liter*) separatamente, individualmente

sev·er·ance ['sɛvərəns] N (*frm*: *of relations*) rottura

severance pay N (*Industry*) indennità di licenziamento

◉ **se·vere** [sɪ'vɪəʳ] ADJ (*comp* **-r**, *superl* **-st**) (*problem, case, flooding, injuries*) grave; (*climate, winter, restrictions*) rigido(-a); (*frost, cold*) intenso(-a); (*punishment, person*) severo(-a); (*examination*) rigoroso(-a); (*damage*) ingente; (*blow, criticism*) duro(-a); (*pain, headache, pressure*) forte; (*symptoms*) acuto(-a); **to be severe (with sb)** essere severo(-a) (con qn); **a severe cold** un forte raffreddore; **children with severe handicaps** bambini con gravi handicap; **a severe shortage of staff** una forte carenza di personale; **a severe punishment** una punizione severa; **a severe blow** un duro colpo

se·vere·ly [sɪ'vɪəlɪ] ADV (*damage, affect, injure*) gravemente; (*criticise, speak, strain*) duramente; (*punish, reprimand*) severamente; (*test*) rigorosamente; (*curtail, restrict, reduce*) seriamente; **to leave severely alone** (*object*) non toccare mai; (*person*) ignorare completamente; (*politics etc*) non interessarsi assolutamente a

se·ver·ity [sɪ'vɛrɪtɪ] N (*gen*) gravità; (*of punishment*) severità; (*of criticism*) durezza; (*of climate, weather*) rigore *m*; (*of damage*) ingenza; (*of pain*) intensità; (*of symptoms*) acutezza

Seville [sə'vɪl] N Siviglia

Seville orange N arancia amara

sew [səʊ] (*pt* **sewed**, *pp* **sewn** *or* **sewed**) VT, VI cucire; **to sew a button on sth** attaccare un bottone a qc; **she was sewing** cuciva; **it was sewn by hand** era cucito a mano
► **sew up** VT + ADV (*tear*) rammendare; (*wound*) ricucire; (*hem*) cucire; (*seam*) fare; **it's all sewn up** (*fig fam*) è tutto a posto

sew·age ['sju:ɪdʒ] N acque *fpl* di scolo, liquami *mpl*

sewage discharge N scarico di liquami

sewage farm N impianto per il riciclaggio delle acque di scolo

sewage works N stabilimento per la depurazione dei liquami

sew·er ['sjʊəʳ] N fogna

sew·er·age ['su:ərɪdʒ] N rete *f* fognaria

sew·ing ['səʊɪŋ] N (*skill, activity*) (il) cucire *m*; (*piece of work*) cucito; **I like sewing** mi piace cucire

sewing basket N cestino del cucito

sewing cotton N (filo) cucirino

sewing machine N macchina da cucire

sewn [səʊn] PP *of* **sew**

◉ **sex** [sɛks] N (*gender*) sesso; (*sexual intercourse*) rapporti *mpl* sessuali; **to have sex with sb** avere rapporti sessuali con qn; **the opposite sex** l'altro sesso; **all he ever thinks about is sex** non pensa che al sesso *or* a quello
■ ADJ (*discrimination*) sessuale

sex act N atto sessuale

sex aid N gadget *m inv* erotico

sex appeal N sex appeal *m inv*
sex change N: **to have a sex change** cambiare sesso
sex drive N impulso sessuale
sex education N educazione *f* sessuale
sex industry N: **the sex industry** l'industria del sesso
sex·ism ['sɛksɪzəm] N sessismo
sex·ist ['sɛksɪst] N, ADJ sessista *(m/f)*
sex·less ['sɛkslɪs] ADJ *(neuter)* asessuato(-a); *(incapable of sexual feeling)* frigido(-a); *(not sexually attractive)* per niente sensuale
sex life N vita sessuale
sex link·age ['sɛksˌlɪŋkɪdʒ] N *(Genetics)* eredità *f inv* biologica legata al sesso
sex maniac N maniaco sessuale
sex object N oggetto sessuale; **to be treated as a sex object** *(woman)* essere trattata da donna oggetto; *(man)* essere trattato da uomo oggetto
sex offender N colpevole *m/f* delitto a sfondo sessuale
sex·olo·gist [sɛk'sɒlədʒɪst] N sessuologo(-a)
sex·ol·ogy [sɛk'sɒlədʒɪ] N sessuologia
sex organ N organo sessuale
sex·pot ['sɛkspɒt] N *(fam: woman)* vamp *f inv*
sex shop N sex-shop *m inv*
sex symbol N sex symbol *m/f inv*
sex·tet [sɛks'tɛt] N sestetto
sex·ton ['sɛkstən] N sagrestano
sex toy N gadget *m inv* erotico
sex·tup·let [sɛks'tju:plɪt] N **1** uno(-a) di sei gemelli **2** *(Mus)* sestina
◎ **sex·ual** ['sɛksjʊəl] ADJ sessuale; **sexual discrimination** discriminazione *f* sessuale; **sexual assault** violenza carnale
sexual abuse N violenza sessuale
sexual harassment N molestie *fpl* sessuali
sexual intercourse N rapporti *mpl* sessuali
sexu·al·ity [ˌsɛksjʊ'ælɪtɪ] N sessualità
sex·ual·ize ['sɛksjʊəlaɪz] VT considerare sessualmente
sex·ual·ly ['sɛksjʊəlɪ] ADV *(attract)* dal punto di vista sessuale; *(reproduce)* sessualmente
sexual orientation, sexual preference N orientamento sessuale
sex urge N pulsione *f* sessuale
sexy ['sɛksɪ] ADJ *(comp* **-ier**, *superl* **-iest)** sexy *inv*, provocante; *(fam: subject etc)* stuzzicante
Sey·chelles [seɪ'ʃɛlz] NPL: **the Seychelles** le Seychelles
SF [ɛs'ɛf] N ABBR = **science fiction**
SG [ˌɛs'dʒi:] N ABBR *(Brit:* = **Solicitor General)** *assistente del Procuratore Generale*
SGML [ˌɛsdʒi:em'ɛl] N *(Comput:* = **standard generalized mark-up language)** SGML *m*; *linguaggio per la creazione di file*
Sgt. ABBR = **sergeant**
sh [ʃ:] EXCL sss
shab·bi·ness ['ʃæbɪnɪs] N *(of dress, person)* trasandatezza; *(of building)* squallore *m*; *(of treatment)* meschinità
shab·by ['ʃæbɪ] ADJ *(comp* **-ier**, *superl* **-iest)** *(building)* malandato(-a), squallido(-a); *(clothes)* sciatto(-a); *(person: also:* **shabby-looking)** trasandato(-a); *(behaviour)* meschino(-a); **a shabby trick** un tiro mancino
shack [ʃæk] N capanno; *(in slum)* baracca
■ VI: **to shack up with sb** *(fam)* convivere (con qn)
shack·le ['ʃækl] VT *(bind)* mettere i ferri *or* i ceppi a; *(fig: restrict)* ostacolare; *see also* **shackles**
shackles ['ʃæklz] NPL ceppi *mpl*, ferri *mpl*; *(fig: constraints)* impacci *mpl*
◎ **shade** [ʃeɪd] N **1** ombra; **in the shade** all'ombra; **to put in the shade** *(fig)* mettere in ombra, oscurare **2** *(also:* **lampshade)** paralume *m* **3** *(also:* **eyeshade)** visiera **4** *(Am: window shade)* tapparella **5** **shades** NPL *(Am: sunglasses)* occhiali *mpl* da sole **6** *(of colour)* tonalità *f inv*, sfumatura; *(fig: of meaning, opinion)* sfumatura; **several shades darker/lighter** di tonalità parecchio più scura/chiara; **this lipstick comes in several shades** questo rossetto è disponibile in diverse gradazioni di colore; **a beautiful shade of blue** una bella tonalità d'azzurro **7** *(small quantity)*: **just a shade more** un tantino di più; **a shade bigger** un tantino più grande
■ VT *(from sun, light)* riparare; **to shade one's eyes from the sun** ripararsi gli occhi dal sole
▶ **shade in** VT + ADV *(drawing)* ombreggiare
shad·ing ['ʃeɪdɪŋ] N **1** *(in drawing, painting)* ombreggiatura **2** *(gradation)* sfumatura
◎ **shad·ow** ['ʃædəʊ] N ombra; **in shadow** in ombra, all'ombra; **in the shadow (of)** all'ombra (di); **without** *or* **beyond a shadow of a doubt** senz'ombra di dubbio; **to cast a shadow over** proiettare *or* fare ombra su; *(fig)* gettare un'ombra su, offuscare; **he's only a shadow of his former self** è diventato l'ombra di se stesso; **to have shadows under one's eyes** avere le occhiaie
■ VT *(follow)* pedinare
■ ATTR: **the Shadow Foreign Secretary** il ministro degli Esteri del governo ombra
shadow boxing N allenamento con l'ombra
Shadow Cabinet N *(Pol Brit)* governo *m* ombra *inv*

SHADOW CABINET

Nel sistema parlamentare britannico il governo ombra, **Shadow Cabinet**, rappresenta il gruppo di parlamentari che nel partito di opposizione svolge compiti analoghi a quelli dei ministri del governo in carica. Si hanno così , ad esempio, uno "Shadow Home Secretary" (omologo del ministro degli Interni) e uno "Shadow Chancellor" (omologo del ministro delle Finanze). Sta ai membri del governo ombra, portavoce ufficiali per ciascun dipartimento governativo, interpellare il governo nelle rispettive aree di competenza. *Vedi anche* **Cabinet**
▷ www.parliament.uk/directories/hciolists/opp.cfm

shad·owy ['ʃædəʊɪ] ADJ *(form, figure)* indistinto(-a), vago(-a); *(place)* pieno(-a) di ombre
shady ['ʃeɪdɪ] ADJ *(comp* **-ier**, *superl* **-iest)** *(place)* ombreggiato(-a); *(tree)* ombroso(-a); *(fig: person, deal)* losco(-a), equivoco(-a); **a wide, shady street** una larga strada ombrosa; **shady dealings** affari loschi
shaft [ʃɑ:ft] N **1** *(of arrow, spear)* asta; *(of tool)* manico; *(of cart etc)* stanga; *(Aut, Tech)* albero; **shaft of light/sunlight** raggio di luce/sole **2** *(of mine, lift etc)* pozzo; **ventilator shaft** condotto di ventilazione
shag [ʃæg] N **1** *(bird)* cormorano **2** *(tobacco)* trinciato forte
■ ADJ: **shag pile rug/carpet** tappeto folto/moquette *f inv* folta
■ VT *(Brit fam!)* scopare *(fam!)*
shagged [ʃægd], **shagged out** ADJ *(Brit fam!)* distrutto(-a), a pezzi
shag·gy ['ʃægɪ] ADJ *(comp* **-ier**, *superl* **-iest)** *(mane, hair)* ispido(-a), arruffato(-a); *(dog)* a pelo lungo e arruffato
shaggy dog story N storiella interminabile senza capo né coda

Ss

shah [ʃɑː] N scià *m inv*

◎**shake** [ʃeɪk] (*vb: pt* **shook**, *pp* **shaken**) N scossa, scrollata; **with a shake of her head ...** scuotendo *or* scrollando la testa *or* il capo...; **to give a rug a good shake** dare una bella sbattuta ad un tappeto; **he's no great shakes at swimming** (*fam*) nel nuoto non è che brilli; **in two shakes** (*fam*) in quattro e quattr'otto; **to have the shakes** avere la tremarella; **he gets the shakes when ...** gli viene la tremarella quando ...

■VT

1 (*person, object*) scuotere; (*building, windows*) far tremare; (*bottle, dice*) agitare; (*cocktail*) shakerare; **to shake one's fist at sb** minacciare qn col pugno; **to shake hands** stringersi la mano, darsi una stretta di mano; **they shook hands** si strinsero la mano; **to shake hands with sb** stringere la mano a qn; **to shake one's head** (*in refusal, dismay*) scuotere la testa *or* il capo; **Donald shook his head** Donald scosse il capo

2 (*harm: confidence, belief, opinion*) scuotere; (*: reputation*) minare; (*amaze, disturb*) scuotere, sconvolgere; **nothing will shake our resolve** niente ci smuoverà; **even torture did not shake him** nemmeno la tortura riuscì a farlo vacillare; **he needs to be shaken out of his apathy** bisogna scuoterlo dalla sua apatia; **I was feeling a bit shaken** ero un po' scosso(-a)

■VI (*person, building, voice etc*) tremare; **to shake with fear/cold** tremare di paura/freddo; **he was shaking with cold** tremava di freddo; **to shake with laughter** essere scosso(-a) dalle risate; **the walls shook at the sound** il fragore ha fatto tremare i muri

▶ **shake down** VT + ADV: **to shake down apples from a tree** scuotere un albero per far cadere le mele

■VI + ADV (*fam: sleep*) dormire

▶ **shake off** VT + ADV (*raindrops, snow*) scrollarsi di dosso; (*dust*) scuotersi di dosso; (*fig: cold, cough*) sbarazzarsi di; (*: habit*) togliersi; (*: pursuer*) seminare

▶ **shake out** VT + ADV (*sail*) sciogliere; (*blanket etc*) scuotere; (*bag*) svuotare scuotendo

▶ **shake up** VT + ADV

1 (*bottle*) agitare; (*pillow*) sprimacciare

2 (*upset: person*) sconvolgere, scuotere

3 (*rouse, stir: person, company etc*) scuotere, dare una scossa salutare a

shake·down ['ʃeɪkdaʊn] N (*of plane, car*) test *m inv* finale

shak·en ['ʃeɪkən] PP *of* **shake**

Shak·er [ʃeɪkə^r] N *membro di un gruppo religioso americano i cui appartenenti vivono in comunità e conducono una vita molto semplice*

■ADJ (*furniture*) di legno e di stile essenziale

shak·er ['ʃeɪkə^r] N **1** (*also:* **cocktail shaker**) shaker *m inv* **2** (*also:* **salt shaker**) spargisale *m inv*, saliera

Shake·spear·ean, **Shake·spear·ian** [ʃeɪks'pɪərɪən] ADJ shakespeariano(-a)

shake-up ['ʃeɪk,ʌp] N (*fig*) cambiamento

shaki·ly ['ʃeɪkɪlɪ] ADV (*reply*) con voce tremante; (*walk*) con passo malfermo; (*write*) con mano tremante

shaky ['ʃeɪkɪ] ADJ (*comp* **-ier**, *superl* **-iest**) (*table, building*) traballante; (*trembling: voice*) tremulo(-a); (*: hands*) tremante; (*: handwriting*) tremolante; (*fig: health*) vacillante, malfermo(-a); (*: memory*) labile; (*: knowledge*) incerto(-a); (*: start*) incerto(-a); **I feel a bit shaky** mi gira un po' la testa; **my Spanish is rather shaky** il mio spagnolo lascia un po' a desiderare; **the team got off to a shaky start** la partita ha avuto un avvio incerto per la squadra; **he answered in a shaky voice** ha risposto con voce tremante

shale [ʃeɪl] N scisto

◎**shall** [ʃæl] AUX VB **1** (*used to form 1st person in future tense and questions*): **I shall** *or* **I'll go tomorrow** ci andrò domani, ci vado domani; **I shall know more next week, I hope** ne saprò qc di più la prossima settimana, spero; **shall I open the door or will you?** devo aprire io la porta o lo fai tu?; **shall I shut the window?** chiudo la finestra?; **shall we ask him to come with us?** gli chiediamo di venire con noi?; **shall we hear from you soon?** ci manderà presto sue notizie?; **I'll get some, shall I?** ne prendo un po', che ne dici?; **let's go out, shall we?** usciamo, vuoi? **2** (*in commands, promises: emphatic*): **you shall pay for this!** questa la pagherai!; **it shall be done** sarà fatto; **but I wanted to see him — and so you shall** ma volevo vederlo! — lo vedrai!

shal·lot [ʃə'lɒt] N scalogno

shal·low ['ʃæləʊ] ADJ (*comp* **-er**, *superl* **-est**) (*water etc*) basso(-a), poco profondo(-a); (*dish*) piano(-a); (*breathing*) leggero(-a); (*fig: person*) superficiale, leggero(-a); (*: conversation*) futile, frivolo(-a)

■**shallows** NPL secche *fpl*

shalt [ʃælt] (*old*) 2ND PERS SG *of* **shall**

sham [ʃæm] ADJ (*piety*) falso(-a); (*politeness*) finto(-a); (*elections*) fasullo(-a); (*battle, illness*) simulato(-a); **a sham marriage** un falso matrimonio; **sham promises** promesse vuote e false

■N **1** (*imposture*) messinscena, finta **2** (*person*) ciarlatano(-a), impostore *m*

■VT fingere, simulare; **to sham illness** fingersi malato(-a)

■VI fingere, far finta; **he's just shamming** fa solo finta

sham·an ['ʃæmən] N sciamano

sham·ble ['ʃæmbl] VI: **to shamble in/out** *etc* entrare/uscire *etc* trascinando i piedi

sham·bles ['ʃæmblz] NSG (*scene of confusion*) macello, baraonda; **the area was (in) a shambles after the earthquake** dopo il terremoto la zona era nella distruzione più totale; **the economy is (in) a complete shambles** l'economia è nel caos più totale; **the place was (in) a shambles** c'era un macello; **the game was a shambles** la partita è stata un disastro; **it's a complete shambles** è un disastro totale

sham·bo·lic [ʃæm'bɒlɪk] ADJ (*Brit fam*) incasinato(-a)

◎**shame** [ʃeɪm] N **1** (*feeling*) vergogna, pudore *m*; (*humiliation*) vergogna; **shame on you!** vergognati!, vergogna!; **to put sb/sth to shame** (*fig*) far sfigurare qn/qc; **I'd die of shame!** morirei di vergogna! **2** (*pity*): **it's a shame (that/to do)** è un peccato (che + *sub*/fare); **what a shame!** che peccato!

■VT (*make ashamed*) far vergognare; (*bring disgrace on*) disonorare; **to shame sb into doing sth** far vergognare qn a tal punto da fargli fare qc

shame·faced ['ʃeɪm,feɪst] ADJ (*ashamed*) tutto(-a) vergognoso(-a); (*confused*) confuso(-a), timido(-a)

shame·fac·ed·ly ['ʃeɪm,feɪsɪdlɪ] ADV (*see adj*) vergognosamente; timidamente

shame·fac·ed·ness ['ʃeɪm,feɪstɪdnɪs] N (*see adj*) aria vergognosa; timidezza

shame·ful ['ʃeɪmfʊl] ADJ vergognoso(-a)

shame·less ['ʃeɪmlɪs] ADJ (*unashamed, brazen*) svergognato(-a), sfrontato(-a); (*immodest*) spudorato(-a)

shame·less·ly ['ʃeɪmlɪslɪ] ADV (*see adj*) sfrontatamente; spudoratamente

shame·less·ness ['ʃeɪmlɪsnɪs] N (*see adj*) sfrontatezza; spudoratezza

sham·my, **cha·mois** [ˈʃæmɪ] N (*also:* **shammy leather**) pelle *f* di camoscio
sham·poo [ʃæmˈpuː] N (*for hair*) shampoo *m inv*; (*for carpet*) detersivo liquido; **shampoo and set** shampoo e messa in piega
■VT (*hair*) lavare (*con shampoo*); (*carpet*) lavare (*con detersivo liquido*); **to shampoo one's hair** farsi lo shampoo
sham·rock [ˈʃæm,rɒk] N trifoglio
shan·dy [ˈʃændɪ] N (*Brit*) birra con gazzosa
shank [ʃæŋk] N (*of person*) stinco; (*of animal*) garretto; (*of tool*) manico
shan't [ʃɑːnt] = **shall not**
shan·tung [ʃænˈtʌŋ] N sciantung *m*
shan·ty[1] [ˈʃæntɪ] N (*also:* **sea shanty**) canzone *f* marinaresca
shan·ty[2] [ˈʃæntɪ] N baracca
shanty·town [ˈʃæntɪ,taʊn] N bidonville *f inv*, baraccopoli *f inv*
SHAPE [ʃeɪp] N ABBR (= **Supreme Headquarters Allied Powers Europe**) quartier *m* generale delle forze NATO in Europa
◎ **shape** [ʃeɪp] N forma; **what shape is it?** di che forma è?, che forma ha?; **in the shape of a heart** a forma di cuore; **it is rectangular in shape** è di forma rettangolare; **his ears are a funny shape** le sue orecchie hanno una forma buffa; **a strange shape** una strana forma; **in all shapes and sizes** d'ogni forma e dimensione, di tutti i tipi; **I can't bear gardening in any shape or form** detesto il giardinaggio di qualunque specie; **to take shape** prendere forma; **to take the shape of** prendere la forma di; **the news reached him in the shape of a telegram** ha ricevuto la notizia sotto forma di telegramma; **the shape of things to come** il volto del futuro; **to lose its shape** (*sweater etc*) sformarsi; **to be in good/poor shape** (*person*) essere in (ottima) forma/giù di forma; (*object*) essere in buone/cattive condizioni; **to knock** *or* **hammer sth into shape** dar forma a qc a colpi di martello; **to knock** *or* **lick into shape** (*fig: business etc*) rimettere in sesto; (*: plan, team*) mettere a punto; (*: athlete*) rimettere in forma; **to get o.s. into shape** rimettersi in forma; **a shape loomed up out of the fog** una forma indistinta emerse dalla nebbia
■VT (*clay, stone*) dar forma a; (*fig: ideas, character*) formare; (*: course of events*) determinare, condizionare
■VI (*fig: also:* **shape up**): **things are shaping (up) well** le cose si mettono bene; **he's shaping (up) nicely** sta facendo dei progressi
-shaped [seɪpt] SUFF: **heart-shaped** a forma di cuore; **diamond-shaped** a forma di losanga
◎ **shaped** ADJ: **shaped like a ...** con la forma di...; **oddly shaped** con una strana forma
shape·less [ˈʃeɪplɪs] ADJ informe, senza forma
shape·less·ness [ˈʃeɪplɪsnɪs] N mancanza di forma
shape·ly [ˈʃeɪplɪ] ADJ (*comp* **-ier**, *superl* **-iest**) (*woman*) ben fatto(-a)
shard [ʃɑːd] N (*frm*) coccio
◎ **share** [ʃɛəʳ] N **1** parte *f*; **to have a share in the profits** partecipare agli utili; **to have a share in sth** aver parte in qc; **he has a 50% share in a new business venture** è socio al 50% in una nuova impresa commerciale; **he had a share in it** (*fig*) c'è entrato anche lui; **to take a share in sth** partecipare a qc; **fair shares for all** parti giuste *or* uguali per tutti; **she's had more than her (fair) share of suffering** ha avuto la sua buona dose di sofferenze; **I want a fair share** ne voglio una parte equa; **the minister came in for his share of criticism** il ministro ha avuto la sua parte di critiche; **he refused to pay his share of the bill** ha rifiutato di pagare la sua quota del conto; **to do one's (fair) share** fare la propria parte **2** (*Fin*) azione *f*, titolo; **he has 500 shares in an oil company** possiede 500 azioni di una compagnia di petrolio; **they've got shares in British Gas** hanno delle azioni della British Gas; **ordinary/preference shares** azioni ordinarie/privilegiate
■VT **1** (*also:* **share out**) spartirsi; **to share (out) among** *or* **between** dividere tra; **they shared the sweets out among the children** hanno distribuito le caramelle ai bambini; **the thieves shared (out) the money** i ladri si sono spartiti i soldi **2** (*use jointly*): **to share (with)** dividere (con); **I share the room with Helen** divido la stanza con Helen; **shall we share the last bottle of wine?** ci beviamo insieme l'ultima bottiglia di vino?; **shared line** (*Telec*) duplex *m inv*
3 (*fig: have in common*) condividere, avere in comune; **she shares his love of gardening** hanno in comune la passione del giardinaggio
■VI: **children must learn to share** i bambini devono imparare a dividere ciò che hanno; **share and share alike** un po' per uno non fa male a nessuno; **to share in** (*gen*) partecipare a; (*blame*) prendersi la propria parte di

DID YOU KNOW ...?
share is not translated by the Italian word *share*

share capital N (*Fin*) capitale *m* azionario
share certificate N (*Fin*) certificato azionario
◎ **share·holder** [ˈʃɛə,həʊldəʳ] N azionista *m/f*
share·holding [ˈʃɛə,həʊldɪŋ] N (quota di) azioni *fpl*
share index N (*Fin*) indice *m* azionario
share issue N (*Fin*) emissione *f* di azioni
share option N (*Fin*) diritto di opzione su azioni (*da parte dei dipendenti di un'azienda*)
share-out [ˈʃɛər,aʊt] N spartizione *f*, ripartizione *f*
share price N (*Fin*) valore *m* azionario
share·ware [ˈʃɛə,wɛəʳ] (*Comput*) N shareware *m inv*
sha·ria [ʃəˈriːə] N sharia, legge *f* islamica
shark [ʃɑːk] N (*fish*) squalo, pescecane *m*; (*fam: swindler*) pirata *m*; (*: a successful and rich one*) pescecane *m*
◎ **sharp** [ʃɑːp] ADJ (*comp* **-er**, *superl* **-est**) **1** (*edge, razor, knife*) tagliente, affilato(-a); (*point*) acuminato(-a); (*pencil*) appuntito(-a); (*needle, stone*) aguzzo(-a); (*angle*) acuto(-a); (*curve, bend*) stretto(-a), a gomito; (*features*) spigoloso(-a); (*nose, chin*) affilato(-a), aguzzo(-a); **be careful, that knife's sharp!** stai attento, quel coltello è affilato!; **a sharp bend** una curva a gomito
2 (*abrupt: change, halt*) brusco(-a); (*: descent*) ripido(-a); (*: rise, fall*) improvviso(-a) e marcato(-a); **a sharp rise in prices** un brusco e notevole aumento dei prezzi
3 (*well-defined: outline*) nitido(-a), netto(-a); (*: contrast*) spiccato(-a), marcato(-a); (TV: *picture*) chiaro(-a)
4 (*harsh: smell, taste*) acuto(-a), aspro(-a); (*: pain, cry*) acuto(-a); (*: blow*) violento(-a); (*: tone, voice*) secco(-a), aspro(-a); (*: wind, frost*) penetrante, pungente; (*: rebuke*) aspro(-a); (*: retort, tongue*) tagliente, duro(-a); (*: words*) pungente; **to be sharp with sb** rimproverare aspramente qn **5** (*acute: eyesight, hearing, sense of smell*) acuto(-a), fine; (*: mind, intelligence*) acuto(-a); (*: person*) sveglio(-a), svelto(-a); **she's very sharp** è molto sveglia
6 (*Mus*): **C sharp** do diesis
■ADV **1** (*Mus*) in diesis **2** **at 5 o'clock sharp** alle 5 in punto; **turn sharp left** gira tutto a sinistra; **look**

Ss

sharp! sbrigati!, spicciati!
■ N (*Mus*) diesis *m inv*
sharp·en ['ʃɑ:pən] VT **1** (*tool, blade etc*) affilare; (*pencil*) temperare **2** (*outline*) mettere in risalto, far spiccare; (*contrast, difference*) sottolineare, evidenziare; (*TV picture*) mettere a fuoco; (*conflict*) intensificare; (*desire, pain*) acuire; (*appetite*) aguzzare, stuzzicare; **to sharpen one's wits** aguzzare l'ingegno
sharp·en·er ['ʃɑ:pnəʳ] N (*for pencils*) temperamatite *m inv*; (*for knives*) affilacoltelli *m inv*
sharp-eyed [ʃɑ:p'aɪd], **sharp-sighted** [ʃɑ:p'saɪtɪd] ADJ dalla vista acuta
sharp-faced [ʃɑ:p'feɪst], **sharp-featured** [ʃɑ:p'fi:tʃəd] ADJ dal volto affilato
sharp·ish ['ʃɑ:pɪʃ] ADV (*Brit fam: quickly*) subito
sharp·ly ['ʃɑ:plɪ] ADV **1** (*abruptly: turn, rise, stop*) bruscamente **2** (*clearly: stand out, contrast*) nettamente **3** (*harshly: criticize, retort*) duramente, aspramente
sharp practice N pratiche *fpl* poco oneste
sharp·shooter ['ʃɑ:pˌʃu:təʳ] N tiratore *m* scelto
sharp-sighted [ʃɑ:p'saɪtɪd] ADJ = **sharp-eyed**
sharp-tempered [ʃɑ:p'tɛmpəd] ADJ irascibile
sharp-witted [ʃɑ:p'wɪtɪd] ADJ sveglio(-a)
shat·ter ['ʃætəʳ] VT (*glass, window*) frantumare, mandare in frantumi; (*door*) fracassare; (*health*) rovinare; (*career*) compromettere definitivamente; (*nerves*) mandare in pezzi; (*self-confidence, hope*) distruggere; **the bullet shattered his skull** la pallottola gli ha frantumato il cranio; **his death shattered all their hopes** la sua morte ha mandato in fumo tutte le loro speranze
■ VI frantumarsi, andare in frantumi; **it shattered into a thousand pieces** è andato in mille pezzi; **the windscreen shattered** il parabrezza è andato in pezzi
shat·tered ['ʃætəd] ADJ (*grief-stricken*) sconvolto(-a); (*fam: exhausted*) a pezzi, distrutto(-a); **I'm absolutely shattered!** sono proprio distrutto!; **I was shattered to hear this news** la notizia mi ha sconvolto
shat·ter·ing ['ʃætərɪŋ] ADJ (*attack*) schiacciante; (*defeat, news*) disastroso(-a); (*experience*) traumatico(-a); (*day, journey*) faticoso(-a); **it was a shattering blow to his hopes** è stato un colpo tremendo per le sue speranze
shatter·proof ['ʃætəˌpru:f] ADJ infrangibile
shave [ʃeɪv] N: **to have a shave** farsi la barba; **I need a shave** devo farmi la barba; **to have a close shave** (*fig*) cavarsela per un pelo; **that was a close shave!** ce la siamo cavata per un pelo!
■ VT (*person, legs, head*) radere, rasare; (*wood*) piallare; (*fig: graze*) sfiorare, rasentare; **to shave off one's beard** tagliarsi la barba; **to shave one's legs** depilarsi le gambe
■ VI (*person*) farsi la barba, radersi, sbarbarsi; **he's shaving** si sta facendo la barba
shav·en ['ʃeɪvn] ADJ (*head*) rasato(-a), rapato(-a) (a zero)
shav·er ['ʃeɪvəʳ] N (*also:* **electric shaver**) rasoio elettrico
shav·ing ['ʃeɪvɪŋ] N, GEN PL (*of wood etc*) truciolo
shaving brush N pennello da barba
shaving cream N crema da barba
shaving soap N sapone *m* da barba
shawl [ʃɔ:l] N scialle *m*
◎ **she** [ʃi:] PERS PRON **1** (*used of people, animals*) lei; **she has gone out** è uscita; **she was fifteen then** allora lei aveva quindici anni; **she's very tall** è molto alta; **there she is** eccola; **SHE didn't do it** non è stata lei a farlo **2** (*used of countries, cars, ships*): **she does 0 to 60 in 10 seconds** ha un'accelerazione da 0 a 60 in 10 secondi
■ N: **it's a she** (*animal, fam: baby*) è una femmina
sheaf [ʃi:f] N (*pl* **sheaves**) (*Agr*) covone *m*; (*of papers*) fascio
shear [ʃɪəʳ] (*pt* **sheared**, *pp* **sheared** *or* **shorn**) VT (*sheep*) tosare
▸ **shear off** VI + ADV (*break off*) spezzarsi
shear·er ['ʃɪərəʳ] N (*person*) tosatore(-trice); (*machine*) tosatrice *f*
shear·ing ['ʃɪərɪŋ] N tosatura
shears [ʃɪəz] NPL (*for gardening*) cesoie *fpl*; (*for dressmaking*) forbici *fpl*; (*for sheep*) forbici *fpl* da tosatore
sheath [ʃi:θ] N (*gen*) guaina; (*for sword*) guaina, fodero; (*contraceptive*) preservativo
sheathe [ʃi:ð] VT ricoprire; (*sword*) rinfoderare
sheath knife N coltello con fodero
sheaves [ʃi:vz] NPL *of* **sheaf**
she-bear ['ʃi:ˌbɛəʳ] N orsa
she'd [ʃi:d] = **she had, she would**
shed¹ [ʃɛd] (*pt, pp* **shed**) VT **1** (*get rid of: gen*) perdere; (*: clothes*) togliersi; (*: employees*) disfarsi di, licenziare; **a lorry shed its load on the motorway** un camion ha perso il carico sull'autostrada; **to shed leaves** perdere foglie **2** (*tears*) versare; (*blood*) spargere **3** (*send out: light, warmth*) diffondere; **to shed light on** (*problem, mystery*) far luce su
◎ **shed²** [ʃɛd] N (*in garden*) capanno; (*for bicycles*) rimessa; (*Industry, Rail*) capannone *m*; (*for cattle*) stalla
she-elephant ['ʃi:ˌɛlɪfənt] N elefantessa
sheen [ʃi:n] N lucentezza
sheep [ʃi:p] N, PL INV pecora; **to make sheep's eyes at sb** (*fig*) fare gli occhi dolci a qn
sheep·dog ['ʃi:pˌdɒg] N cane *m* (da) pastore
sheep farm N allevamento di pecore
sheep farmer N allevatore *m* di pecore
sheep farming N pastorizia
sheep·fold ['ʃi:pˌfəʊld] N ovile *m*
sheep·ish ['ʃi:pɪʃ] ADJ (*look, smile*) imbarazzato(-a), mortificato(-a)
sheep·ish·ly ['ʃi:pɪʃlɪ] ADV (*look, smile*) in modo imbarazzato, con aria mortificata
sheep·skin ['ʃi:pˌskɪn] N pelle *f* di pecora *or* di montone
■ ADJ (*gloves*) di montone
sheepskin jacket N (giacca di) montone *m*
sheer¹ [ʃɪəʳ] ADJ (*comp* **-er**, *superl* **-est**) **1** (*utter: madness, greed*) puro(-a); (*: waste of time*) totale; (*: necessity*) assoluto(-a); **that's sheer robbery!** è un furto bello e buono!; **it's sheer greed** è pura avidità; **the sheer impossibility of ...** l'assoluta impossibilità di...; **by sheer chance** *or* **by a sheer accident** per puro caso *or* pura combinazione **2** (*transparent*) trasparente **3** (*precipitous*) a picco; **a sheer drop** uno strapiombo
■ ADV a picco, a perpendicolo
sheer² [ʃɪəʳ] VI (*also:* **to sheer off**: *gen, Naut*) deviare
◎ **sheet¹** [ʃi:t] N (*on bed*) lenzuolo; (*also:* **dust sheet**) telo; (*of paper, plastic*) foglio; (*of metal, glass, ice*) lastra; (*of water*) distesa; (*of flame*) muro; **cotton sheets** lenzuola di cotone; **a sheet of paper** un foglio di carta
▸ **sheet down** VI + ADV (*rain*) piovere a dirotto
sheet² [ʃi:t] N (*Naut*) scotta
sheet anchor N ancora di speranza *or* di riserva
sheet feed N (*on printer*) alimentazione *f* di fogli
sheet lightning N lampeggio diffuso
sheet metal N lamiera
sheet music N spartito (*non rilegato*)
sheik, **sheikh** [ʃeɪk] N sceicco
sheik·dom, **sheikh·dom** ['ʃeɪkdəm] N sceiccato
shel·duck ['ʃɛlˌdʌk] N volpoca (*femmina*)

shelf [ʃɛlf] N (*pl* **shelves**) **1** (*in cupboard, oven*) ripiano; (*fixed to wall*) mensola; **to be on the shelf** (*fig fam: woman*) essere zitella **2** (*in rock face, underwater*) piattaforma

shelf life N (*Comm*) durata di conservazione

shelf mark N (*in libraries*) collocazione *f*, segnatura

shelf unit N scaffalatura

she'll [ʃi:l] = **she will, she shall**

◎ **shell** [ʃɛl] N **1** (*of egg, nut, tortoise*) guscio; (*of oyster, mussel*) conchiglia; (*of lobster*) corazza, guscio; (*Phys*) guscio elettronico; **to come out of one's shell** (*fig*) uscire dal (proprio) guscio; **an egg shell** un guscio d'uovo **2** (*of building*) struttura, scheletro; (*of ship*) ossatura **3** (*Mil*) granata; **an unexploded shell** una granata inesplosa

■ VT **1** (*nuts*) sgusciare; (*peas, beans*) sgranare **2** (*Mil*) bombardare

▸ **shell out** (*fam*) VI + ADV: **to shell out (for)** sganciare soldi (per)

■ VT + ADV: **to shell out (for)** (*money*) sganciare (per)

shell·fire [ˈʃɛl,faɪəʳ] N bombardamento

shell·fish [ˈʃɛl,fɪʃ] N, PL INV (*crab etc*) crostaceo; (*mollusc*) mollusco; (*Culin*) frutti *mpl* di mare

shell·ing [ˈʃɛlɪŋ] N bombardamento

shell program N (*Comput*) programma shell *m*

shell·proof [ˈʃɛl,pru:f] ADJ a prova di bomba

shell shock N (*old*) psicosi traumatica (da bombardamento)

shell-shocked [ˈʃɛl,ʃɒkt] ADJ **1** (*soldier*) traumatizzato(-a) da un bombardamento **2** (*stunned, dazed*) sotto shock

shell·suit [ˈʃɛl,su:t] N tuta di acetato

◎ **shel·ter** [ˈʃɛltəʳ] N **1** (*protection*) riparo; **under the shelter of** al riparo di; **to seek shelter (from)** cercare riparo (da *or* contro), ripararsi (da); **to take shelter (from)** mettersi al riparo (da) **2** (*construction: on mountain etc*) rifugio; **bus shelter** pensilina; **air-raid shelter** rifugio antiaereo

■ VT **1** (*protect*): **to shelter (from)** riparare (da); (*from blame etc*) proteggere (da) **2** (*give lodging to: homeless, criminal etc*) dare rifugio *or* asilo a

■ VI ripararsi, mettersi al riparo; **to shelter from the rain** ripararsi dalla pioggia; **to shelter under a tree** ripararsi sotto un albero

shel·tered [ˈʃɛltəd] ADJ (*place*) riparato(-a); (*childhood*) sereno(-a), senza problemi; (*environment*) protetto(-a); **she has led a very sheltered life** è vissuta nella bambagia

shelve [ʃɛlv] VT (*fig: postpone*) accantonare

shelves [ʃɛlvz] NPL *of* **shelf**

shelv·ing [ˈʃɛlvɪŋ] N scaffalature *fpl*

shep·herd [ˈʃɛpəd] N pastore *m*; **the Good Shepherd** (*Rel*) il buon Pastore; **a shepherd with his dog** un pastore con il suo cane

■ VT: **to shepherd sb in/out** accompagnare qn dentro/fuori; **she shepherded the children across the road** ha aiutato i bambini ad attraversare la strada

shep·herd·ess [ˈʃɛpədɪs] N pastorella

shepherd's pie N (*Culin*) *timballo di carne macinata e purè di patate*

sher·bet [ˈʃɜ:bət] N (*Brit: powder*) *polvere effervescente al gusto di frutta*; (*Am: water ice*) sorbetto

sher·iff [ˈʃɛrɪf] N sceriffo

Sher·pa [ˈʃɜ:pə] N sherpa *m inv*

sher·ry [ˈʃɛrɪ] N sherry *m inv*

she's [ʃi:z] = **she is, she has**

Shet·land [ˈʃɛtlənd] N: **the Shetlands** *or* **the Shetland Islands** le (isole) Shetland

Shetland pony N pony *m inv* delle Shetland

Shetland wool N (lana) Shetland

shi·at·su [ʃi:ˈætsu:] N shiatsu *m*

shield [ʃi:ld] N (*armour*) scudo; (*on machine etc*) schermo (di protezione)

■ VT: **to shield sb from sth** riparare qn da qc; **to shield sb with one's body** fare scudo a qn con il proprio corpo

◎ **shift** [ʃɪft] N **1** (*change: in wind, opinion etc*) cambiamento; (*movement: of load*) spostamento; (*Comm: in demand*) variazione *f* (della domanda); **a shift in government policy** un cambiamento nella politica del governo **2** (*period of work, group of workers*) turno; **to work in shifts** fare i turni (di lavoro); **the night shift** il turno di notte; **to work on night/day shift** fare il turno di notte/di giorno **3** (*old: expedient*) espediente *m*; **to make shift with/without sth** arrangiarsi con/senza qc **4** (*Am Aut: also:* **gear shift**) cambio

■ VT (*gen*) spostare; (*sth stuck*) smuovere; (*dirt, stain*) togliere; (*employee*) trasferire; (*change: position etc*) cambiare; **to shift scenery** (*Theatre*) cambiare le scene; **to shift the blame on to sb** scaricare la colpa su qn; **I couldn't shift the wardrobe on my own** non riuscivo a spostare l'armadio da solo

■ VI **1** (*gen*) spostarsi; (*opinions*) mutare; (*change one's mind*) cambiare idea; **the wind has shifted to the south** il vento ha girato verso sud; **he shifted over to the door** si è avvicinato alla porta; **shift off the sofa!** togliti dal divano!; **shift up** *or* **over** *or* **along!** spostati!; **that car's certainly shifting** (*fam*) quella macchina va molto forte; **to shift into second gear** (*Aut*) innestare la seconda (marcia) **2 to shift for o.s.** arrangiarsi da sé, cavarsela da solo(-a)

shifti·ly [ˈʃɪftɪlɪ] ADV (*behave*) in modo equivoco, in modo losco; (*answer*) evasivamente

shifti·ness [ˈʃɪftɪnɪs] N (*of behaviour*) equivocità; (*of answer*) evasività

shift·ing [ˈʃɪftɪŋ] ADJ (*sand*) mobile; (*crowd*) in movimento; (*opinion, scene*) mutevole

shifting cultivation N agricoltura itinerante

shift key N (*on typewriter*) tasto delle maiuscole

shift·less [ˈʃɪftlɪs] ADJ: **a shiftless person** un(-a) inetto(-a)

shift·less·ness [ˈʃɪftlɪsnɪs] N inettitudine *f*

shift work N: **to do shift work** fare i turni

shifty [ˈʃɪftɪ] ADJ (*comp* **-ier**, *superl* **-iest**) (*person*) losco(-a), equivoco(-a); (*behaviour*) equivoco(-a); (*eyes*) sfuggente; **he looked shifty** aveva un'aria losca

Shi·ite [ˈʃi:aɪt] ADJ, N sciita (*m/f*)

shil·ling [ˈʃɪlɪŋ] N (*Brit*) scellino

shilly·shally [ˈʃɪlɪ,ʃælɪ] VI (*fam*) tentennare, esitare; **don't shillyshally!** *or* **stop shillyshallying!** deciditi una buona volta!

shim·mer [ˈʃɪməʳ] VI (*gen*) luccicare, scintillare; (*heat haze*) tremolare

shim·mer·ing [ˈʃɪmərɪŋ] ADJ (*gen*) luccicante, scintillante; (*haze*) tremolante; (*satin etc*) cangiante

shin [ʃɪn] N stinco

■ VI: **to shin up a tree** arrampicarsi in cima a un albero

shin·bone [ˈʃɪn,bəʊn] N tibia

shin·dig [ˈʃɪn,dɪg] N (*fam*) festa indiavolata

shin·dy [ˈʃɪndɪ] N (*fam: noise*) gazzarra, casino; (*: brawl*) rissa; **to kick up a shindy** fare casino

shine [ʃaɪn] (*pt, pp* **shone**) VI (ri)splendere, brillare; **the**

Ss

sun was shining splendeva il sole; **the light was shining in his eyes** aveva la luce negli occhi; **the light was shining under the door** si vedeva la luce sotto la porta; **the metal shone in the sun** il metallo risplendeva al sole; **her face shone with happiness** il suo viso splendeva di felicità; **her eyes shone with joy** i suoi occhi brillavano di gioia; **to shine at maths** (*fig*) brillare in matematica

■ VT (*pt, pp* **shone** *or* **shined**) **1** **shine the light** *or* **your torch over here** fai luce (con la pila) in questa direzione **2** (*pt, pp* **shined**) (*polish*) lucidare, lustrare

■ N (*of sun, metal*) lucentezza, splendore *m*; **to give sth a shine** dare una lucidata a qc; **those shoes have got a good shine** quelle scarpe luccicano; **to take the shine off sth** far perdere il lucido a qc; (*fig*) offuscare qc; **to take a shine to sb** (*fig*) prendere qn in simpatia; **come rain or shine ...** qualunque tempo faccia..., col bello o col cattivo tempo...

shin·gle ['ʃɪŋgl] N **1** (*on beach*) ciottoli *mpl* **2** (*on roof*) scandola **3** (*Am: signboard*) insegna

shin·gles ['ʃɪŋglz] NSG (*Med*) fuoco di Sant'Antonio

shin·gly ['ʃɪŋglɪ] ADJ (*beach*) ciottoloso(-a)

shin·ing ['ʃaɪnɪŋ] ADJ (*surface, hair*) lucente; (*light*) brillante; (*eyes*) splendente; **a shining example** (*fig*) un fulgido esempio

shiny ['ʃaɪnɪ] ADJ (*comp* **-ier**, *superl* **-iest**) lucido(-a)

◎ **ship** [ʃɪp] N nave *f*; **Her (***or* **His) Majesty's Ship Ark Royal** l'Ark Royal *f*; **on board ship** a bordo; **ship's company** equipaggio; **ship's papers** carte *fpl* di bordo; **ship's stores** riserve *fpl* di bordo

■ VT **1** (*take on board: goods, water*) imbarcare; (*: oars*) tirare in barca **2** (*transport: usu by ship*) spedire (*via mare*); **a new engine had to be shipped out to them** hanno dovuto spedire loro un motore nuovo

ship·builder ['ʃɪp,bɪldəʳ] N costruttore *m* navale

ship·building ['ʃɪp,bɪldɪŋ] N costruzione *f* navale

ship chan·dler ['ʃɪp,tʃændləʳ] N (*person*) fornitore *m* marittimo; (*company*) società *f inv* di forniture navali

ship·load ['ʃɪp,ləʊd] N carico; (*fig fam*) marea

ship·mate ['ʃɪp,meɪt] N compagno di bordo

ship·ment ['ʃɪpmənt] N (*act*) spedizione *f*; (*quantity*) carico

ship·owner ['ʃɪp,əʊnəʳ] N armatore *m*

ship·per ['ʃɪpəʳ] N spedizioniere *m* (marittimo)

ship·ping ['ʃɪpɪŋ] N (*ships*) imbarcazioni *fpl*; (*traffic*) navigazione *f*; **a danger to shipping** un pericolo per la navigazione; **shipping is extra** i costi di trasporto sono a parte

shipping agent N agente *m* marittimo

shipping company, shipping line N compagnia di navigazione

shipping lane N rotta (di navigazione)

ship·shape ['ʃɪpʃeɪp] ADJ in perfetto ordine

ship-to-shore [ʃɪptə'ʃɔːʳ] ADJ (*radio*) per le comunicazioni da bordo a terra

ship·wreck ['ʃɪp,rɛk] N (*ship*) relitto; (*event*) naufragio

■ VT: **to be shipwrecked** naufragare, fare naufragio

ship·yard ['ʃɪp,jɑːd] N cantiere *m* navale

shire ['ʃaɪəʳ] N (*Brit*) contea

shirk [ʃɜːk] VT (*duty*) sottrarsi a, sfuggire a; (*issue*) ignorare; (*work*) scansare; **to shirk doing sth** evitare di fare qc

■ VI fare lo(-a) scansafatiche

shirk·er ['ʃɜːkəʳ] N scansafatiche *m/f inv*

◎ **shirt** [ʃɜːt] N (*man's*) camicia; (*woman's*) camicetta, camicia; **in one's shirt sleeves** in maniche di camicia; **to put one's shirt on sth** (*fig: Betting*) giocarsi anche la camicia su qc; **keep your shirt on!** (*fig fam*) non ti scaldare!

shirt front N sparato

shirt·lifter ['ʃɜː,lɪftəʳ] N (*fam!*) checca (*fam!*)

shirty ['ʃɜːtɪ] ADJ (*comp* **-ier**, *superl* **-iest**) (*fam*): **he was pretty shirty about it** si è incavolato abbastanza per questa storia

shit [ʃɪt] (*fam!*) EXCL merda (*fam!*)

■ N (*excrement*) merda (*fam!*); (*rubbish*) porcheria; (*worthless person*) pezzo di merda (*fam!*); **to be in the shit** (*fig*) essere nella merda (*fam!*)

■ VI cacare

shit·bag ['ʃɪtbæg] N (*fam!*) pezzo di merda (*fam!*)

shite [ʃaɪt] N (*Brit fam!*) merda (*fam!*)

shit-faced ['ʃɪtfeɪst] ADJ (*fam!: drunk*) completamente fatto(-a)

shit·hole ['ʃɪthəʊl] N (*fam!*) buco di culo (*fam!*)

shit-hot [ʃɪt'hɒt] ADJ (*fam!*): **to be shit-hot** (*person*) essere una spada; (*thing*) essere una figata

shit·house ['ʃɪthaʊs] (*fam!*) N cesso; **to be built like a brick shithouse** (*person*) essere un armadio

shit·less ['ʃɪtlɪs] (*fam!*) ADJ: **to be scared shitless** farsela sotto; **to be bored shitless** essere stufo(-a) marcio

shit·load ['ʃɪtləʊd] N (*fam!*): **to be in a shitload of trouble** essere nella merda fino al collo

shit-stirrer ['ʃɪt,stɜːrəʳ] N (*fam!*) testa calda

shit·ty ['ʃɪtɪ] ADJ (*comp* **-tier**, *superl* **-tiest**) (*fam!*) di merda (*fam!*)

shiv·er[1] ['ʃɪvəʳ] N brivido; **it sends shivers down my spine** *or* **it gives me the shivers** mi fa venire i brividi

■ VI: **to shiver (with)** (*cold, fear*) rabbrividire (da), tremare (da)

shiv·er[2] ['ʃɪvəʳ] (*liter*) VT frantumare

■ VI frantumarsi

■ N (*of glass*) scheggia

shiv·ery ['ʃɪvərɪ] ADJ (*from cold*) che ha i brividi; (*from fear*) tremante; **I feel shivery** ho i brividi

shoal [ʃəʊl] N (*of fish*) banco

◎ **shock** [ʃɒk] N **1** (*Elec, of earthquake*) scossa; (*of explosion*) scossone *m*; (*of collision*) urto; **an electric shock** una scossa elettrica; **to get a shock** (*Elec*) prendere la scossa; **I got a shock when I touched the switch** quando ho toccato l'interruttore ho preso la scossa **2** (*emotional*) shock *m inv*, colpo; **the shock was too much for him** non ha sopportato il colpo *or* lo shock; **the news came as a shock** la notizia è stata uno shock; **it came as a shock to hear that ...** è stato uno shock venire a sapere che...; **it may come as a shock to you, but ...** per quanto possa sorprenderti...; **to give sb a shock** far venire un colpo a qn **3** (*Med*) shock *m inv*; **to be suffering from shock** essere in stato di shock

■ VT (*affect emotionally, scandalize*) sciоccare; **he is easily shocked** si scandalizza facilmente; **they were shocked by what happened** erano sciоccati per ciò che era successo; **after twenty years in the police nothing shocks him** dopo vent'anni di lavoro in polizia non lo scandalizza più niente; **to shock sb out of his complacency** far perdere a qn un po' della sua boria

■ VI far scandalo, destare scalpore

shock absorber [-əb'sɔːbəʳ] N (*Aut*) ammortizzatore *m*

shock·er ['ʃɒkəʳ] N (*fam*): **it was a real shocker** è stata una vera bomba

shock·ing ['ʃɒkɪŋ] ADJ (*appalling: news*) sciоccante; (*: sight, crime*) agghiacciante; (*causing scandal: behaviour,* *film*) scandaloso(-a); (: *price*) sbalorditivo(-a); (: *waste*) vergognoso(-a); (*very bad*: *weather, handwriting*) orribile; (: *results*) disastroso(-a); **it's shocking!** è scandaloso!; **a shocking waste** uno spreco vergognoso; **the weather was shocking** il tempo era orribile

shocking pink ADJ rosa shocking *inv*

shock jock N (*fam*: *Radio*) *presentatore radiofonico che, esprimendo idee estremiste, cerca di provocare le reazioni degli ascoltatori*

shock·proof ['ʃɒk,pruːf] ADJ antiurto *inv*

shock reaction N grande scalpore *m*

shock tactics NPL (*in war, struggle*) tattica *fsg* d'urto

shock therapy, shock treatment N (*Med*) trattamento con elettroshock

shock troops NPL truppe *fpl* d'assalto

shock wave N (*of explosion, earthquake*) onda d'urto; (*fig*): **shock waves** NPL impatto *msg*

shod [ʃɒd] PT, PP *of* **shoe**

shod·dy ['ʃɒdɪ] ADJ (*comp* **-ier**, *superl* **-iest**) scadente

◎ **shoe** [ʃuː] (*vb*: *pt, pp* **shod**) N **1** scarpa, calzatura; **I wouldn't like to be in his shoes** non vorrei essere nei suoi panni **2** (*horseshoe*) ferro di cavallo **3** (*also:* **brake shoe**) ganascia (del freno)

■ VT (*horse*) ferrare

shoe·brush ['ʃuː,brʌʃ] N spazzola per le scarpe

shoe·horn ['ʃuː,hɔːn] N calzante *m*, calzascarpe *m inv*

shoe·lace ['ʃuː,leɪs] N laccio (di scarpa), stringa

shoe·maker ['ʃuː,meɪkə[r]] N calzolaio

shoe polish N lucido da *or* per scarpe

shoe rack N scarpiera

shoe repairs NPL calzoleria *fsg*

shoe shop ['ʃuː,ʃɒp] N negozio di scarpe *or* di calzature

shoe·string ['ʃuː,strɪŋ] N (*Am*) stringa (di scarpa); **on a shoestring** (*fig*: *do sth*) con quattro soldi; (: *live*) contando il centesimo

shoe·tree ['ʃuː,triː] N forma per scarpe

shone [ʃɒn] PT, PP *of* **shine**

shoo [ʃuː] EXCL sciò!, via!

■ VT (*also*: **shoo away, shoo off**) cacciare (via)

shoo-in ['ʃuːɪn] N (*Am fam*): **he looks like a shoo-in for the presidency** è facile che ottenga la presidenza

shook [ʃʊk] PT *of* **shake**

◎ **shoot** [ʃuːt] (*vb*: *pt, pp* **shot**) VT

1 (*hit*) colpire, sparare a; (*hunt*) cacciare, andare a caccia di; (*execute*) fucilare; (*kill*) uccidere; **he was shot in the arm** gli hanno sparato al braccio; **he was shot by a sniper** è stato colpito da un cecchino; **he was shot at dawn** è stato fucilato all'alba; **he shot himself with a revolver** si è sparato con un revolver; **to shoot sb dead** colpire a morte qn; **to shoot o.s. in the foot** (*fig*) darsi la zappa sui piedi; **you'll get shot if you do that!** (*fig fam*) puoi rimetterci le penne!

2 (*fire*: *bullet*) sparare; (: *arrow*) scoccare; (: *missile*) lanciare; **to shoot one's way out** farsi largo a colpi di pistola; **to shoot an arrow at sb** tirare una freccia contro qn; **to shoot dice** tirare i dadi

3 (*direct*: *look, smile*) lanciare; **to shoot a look at sb** lanciare uno sguardo a qn; **to shoot a question at sb** sparare una domanda a qn

4 (*Cine*: *film, scene*) girare; (: *person, object*) riprendere; **the film was shot in Prague** il film è stato girato a Praga

5 (*pass quickly*: *rapids*) scendere

■ VI

1 to shoot (at sb/sth) (*with gun*) sparare (a qn/qc); (*with bow*) tirare (su *or* contro qn/qc); **don't shoot!** non sparare!; **to shoot on sight** sparare a vista; **to shoot back** rispondere al fuoco; **to shoot wide** tirare a vuoto; **to shoot at goal** (*Ftbl etc*) tirare in porta *or* a rete

2 (*rush*): **to shoot in/out** entrare/uscire come una freccia; **to shoot across to** precipitarsi verso; **to shoot past sb** sfrecciare vicino a qn; **a car shot past me** una macchina mi è sfrecciata accanto; **the pain shot up his leg** sentì una fitta lancinante alla gamba; **the bullet shot past his head** il colpo gli ha sfiorato la testa

■ N

1 (*Bot*) germoglio

2 (*shooting party*) partita di caccia; (*competition*) gara di tiro; (*preserve*) riserva di caccia

3 (*fig fam*): **the whole shoot** tutto, ogni cosa

▸ **shoot down** VT + ADV (*aeroplane*) abbattere; (*person*) uccidere; (*fig*: *person*) distruggere; (: *argument*) demolire

▸ **shoot out** VT + ADV: **he shot out his arm and saved me** ha allungato prontamente il braccio e mi ha salvato; **to shoot it out** regolare una faccenda a colpi di pistola

■ VI + ADV (*water*) sprizzare; (*flames*) divampare

▸ **shoot up** VI + ADV

1 (*flames, rocket*) alzarsi; (*water*) scaturire con forza; (*price*) salire alle stelle

2 he's shooting up sta crescendo a vista d'occhio; **he has shot up** è cresciuto molto

■ VT + ADV (*fam*: *heroin*) bucarsi

shoot-em-up ['ʃuːtəmʌp] (*fam*) N (*game*) videogioco violento; (*film*) film *m inv* violento

shoot·ing ['ʃuːtɪŋ] N **1** (*shots*) spari *mpl*, colpi *mpl* d'arma da fuoco; (*continuous shooting*) sparatoria; **they heard shooting** hanno sentito degli spari **2** (*act*: *murder*) uccisione *f* (a colpi d'arma da fuoco); (: *wounding*) ferimento **3** (*Cine*) riprese *fpl* **4** (*Hunting*) caccia; **shooting and fishing** la caccia e la pesca

■ ADJ (*pain*) lancinante

shooting gallery N tiro a segno

shooting match N: **the whole shooting match** (*fig fam*) l'intera faccenda

shooting range N poligono di tiro

shooting star N stella cadente

shooting stick N *bastone da passeggio trasformabile in sgabello*

shoot-out ['ʃuːt,aʊt] N **1** (*fight*) sparatoria **2** (*Ftbl*: *also*: **penalty shoot-out**) rigori *mpl*; **to win in a shoot out** vincere ai rigori

◎ **shop** [ʃɒp] N **1** (*Comm*) negozio; **at the baker's shop** in panetteria; **a sports shop** un negozio di articoli sportivi; **to shut up shop** chiudere; (*fig*) chiudere bottega; **to talk shop** (*fig*) parlare di lavoro; **all over the shop** (*fig*: *fam*) dappertutto **2** (*Industry*: *workshop*) officina; **repair shop** officina di riparazione

■ VI (*gen*) fare acquisti, fare compere; (*for food*) fare la spesa; **to go shopping** andare a fare lo shopping, andare a fare la spesa; **they shop in expensive stores** vanno a fare compere in negozi costosi; **I was shopping for a dress** cercavo un vestito

■ VT (*fam*: *betray*) tradire

▸ **shop around** VI + ADV (*compare prices*) confrontare i prezzi; (*fig*: *weigh up alternatives*) confrontare diverse possibilità

shopa·holic [ʃɒpə'hɒlɪk] N (*fam*) maniaco(-a) dello shopping

shop assistant N (*Brit*) commesso(-a)

shop floor N (*Industry*): **the workers on the shop floor** gli operai; **he works on the shop floor** è un operaio

Ss

shop front N (*Brit*) facciata di negozio
shop girl N commessa
shop·keeper ['ʃɒp,ki:pəʳ] N negoziante *m/f*, bottegaio(-a)
shop·lift ['ʃɒp,lɪft] VI taccheggiare
shop·lifter ['ʃɒp,lɪftəʳ] N taccheggiatore(-trice)
shop·lifting ['ʃɒp,lɪftɪŋ] N taccheggio
shop·per ['ʃɒpəʳ] N **1** (*person*) acquirente *m/f* **2** (*bag*) borsa per la spesa
◎ **shop·ping** ['ʃɒpɪŋ] N (*goods*) acquisti *mpl*, compere *fpl*; (: *food*) spesa; **she loves shopping** adora lo shopping; **can you get the shopping from the car?** puoi prendere la spesa dalla macchina?
shopping bag N borsa per la spesa
shopping basket N cestino della spesa, sporta
shopping centre N centro commerciale
shopping channel N (TV) canale *m* televisivo di televendita
shopping list N lista della spesa
shopping precinct N zona dei negozi (*chiusa al traffico automobilistico*)
shop·soiled ['ʃɒp,sɔɪld] ADJ sciupato(-a) (*da lunga esposizione in vetrina*)
shop steward N (*Brit: Industry*) rappresentante *m/f* sindacale
shop·walker ['ʃɒp,wɔ:kəʳ] N (*Brit*) caporeparto *m/f*
shop window N vetrina
shore[1] [ʃɔ:ʳ] VT: **to shore up** (*tunnel, wall*) puntellare; (*fig*) consolidare; (: *prices*) mantenere
◎ **shore**[2] [ʃɔ:ʳ] N (*of sea*) riva; (*of lake*) sponda, riva; (*beach*) spiaggia; (*coast*) costa; **on shore** a terra; **to go on shore** sbarcare; **the ship hugged the shore** la nave navigava sotto costa; **boats on the shore** barche sulla riva
shore leave N (*Naut*) franchigia
shore·line ['ʃɔ:laɪn] N litorale *m*
shorn [ʃɔ:n] PP *of* **shear**
■ ADJ **1** (*grass*) tosato(-a); (*head*) rasato(-a) **2** (*fig*): **shorn of** (*power, glory*) privato(-a) di
◎ **short** [ʃɔ:t] ADJ (*comp* **-er**, *superl* **-est**)
1 (*in length, distance*) corto(-a); (*in time*) breve; (*person*) basso(-a); **a short skirt** una gonna corta; **short hair** capelli corti; **a short break** una breve pausa; **it was a great holiday, but too short** è stata una bella vacanza, ma troppo breve; **she's quite short** è piuttosto bassa; **the days are getting shorter** le giornate si stanno accorciando; **to be short in the leg** (*person*) avere le gambe corte; (*trousers*) essere corti di gamba; **to win by a short head** (*Racing*) vincere di mezza testa *or* incollatura; **a short time ago** poco tempo fa; **time is getting short** il tempo stringe; **that was short and sweet** è stato sbrigativo; **to make short work of sb** (*fig*) sistemare qn; **to make short work of sth** (*job*) sbrigare qc; (*cake, drink*) far fuori qc
2 (*insufficient*): **I'm £30 short** mi mancano 30 sterline; **to give short weight** *or* **short measure to sb** imbrogliare qn sul peso *or* sulla misura; **to be in short supply** scarseggiare; **to be short of sth** (*money*) essere a corto di qc; **I'm short of time** ho poco tempo; **short of breath** senza fiato, con il fiatone; **it's little short of madness** è pazzia bella e buona; **three miles short of home** a tre miglia da casa; **at short notice** con poco preavviso
3 (*concise*) breve; **short and to the point** breve e conciso; **"Pat" is short for "Patricia"** "Pat" è il diminutivo di "Patricia"; **in short** in breve, a farla breve; **in short, the answer is no** per farla breve, la risposta è no
4 (*reply, manner*) secco(-a), brusco(-a); **to have a short temper** essere irascibile; **to be short with sb** essere brusco(-a) con qn
■ ADV
1 (*suddenly, abruptly*): **to stop short** fermarsi di colpo; **I'd stop short of stealing** non arriverei mai a rubare; **he wouldn't stop short of murder** arriverebbe al punto di uccidere; **to pull up short** frenare bruscamente
2 (*insufficiently*): **to run short of sth** rimanere senza qc; **we never went short (of anything) as children** da bambini non ci è mai mancato nulla; **to come** *or* **fall short of** (*expectations*) venire meno a; (*needs*) non soddisfare; **to sell sb short** (*fig: belittle*) sminuire qn, buttar giù qn; **to be taken** *or* **caught short** (*fam*) avere un bisognino urgente
3 (*except*): **short of selling the house, what can we do?** non vedo cos'altro potremmo fare, a parte vendere la casa; **I'll do anything short of...** farò tutto tranne che...; **nothing short of a miracle can save him** solo un miracolo potrebbe salvarlo
■ N
1 (*Elec*) = **short circuit**
2 (*fam: drink*) superalcolico
3 (*also:* **short film**) cortometraggio; *see also* **shorts**
■ VT, VI (*Elec*) = **short-circuit**
◎ **short·age** ['ʃɔ:tɪdʒ] N carenza, scarsità *f inv*; **the housing shortage** la crisi degli alloggi
short back and sides N (*Brit*) *taglio di capelli corto sulla nuca e sulle tempie*
short·bread ['ʃɔ:t,brɛd] N frollino, biscotto di pasta frolla
short·cake ['ʃɔ:t,keɪk] N (*Am*) *torta di pasta frolla farcita con frutta e panna*; (*Brit*) frollino
short-change [ʃɔ:t'tʃeɪndʒ] VT: **to short-change sb** imbrogliare qn sul resto; (*fig*) fregare qn
short-circuit [ʃɔ:t'sɜ:kɪt] VT (*Elec*) mettere in cortocircuito
■ VI (*Elec*) fare cortocircuito
short circuit N (*Elec*) cortocircuito
short·coming [ʃɔ:t'kʌmɪŋ] N difetto
short crust pastry N (*Brit*) = **short pastry**
short cut N scorciatoia
short·en ['ʃɔ:tn] VT (*gen*) accorciare; **the article needs to be shortened** l'articolo deve essere accorciato
■ VI accorciarsi
short·en·ing ['ʃɔ:tnɪŋ] N (*Culin*) grasso (*usato in pasticceria*)
short·fall ['ʃɔ:t,fɔ:l] N (*Fin*) deficit *sm inv*; **there is a shortfall of £20,000** mancano 20.000 sterline
short·hand ['ʃɔ:t,hænd] N stenografia; **to take sth down in shorthand** stenografare qc
short-handed ['ʃɔ:t'hændɪd] ADJ a corto di personale
shorthand notebook N bloc-notes *m inv* per stenografia
shorthand typing N stenodattilografia
shorthand typist N stenodattilografo(-a)
short-haul ['ʃɔ:t'hɔ:l] ADJ a breve distanza
short-list ['ʃɔ:t,lɪst] VT includere nella graduatoria finale; (*Brit: for job*) includere nella rosa dei candidati
short list N graduatoria finale; (*Brit: for job*) rosa dei candidati
short-lived ['ʃɔ:t,lɪvd] ADJ (*fig*) di breve durata, effimero(-a)
◎ **short·ly** ['ʃɔ:tlɪ] ADV **1** (*soon*) tra poco, tra breve;

shortly before/after poco prima/dopo **2** (*curtly*) seccamente, bruscamente

short message service N (*Telec*) servizio di invio di sms

short·ness ['ʃɔːtnɪs] N (*of person*) bassa statura; (*of reply, manner*) bruschezza; **shortness of temper** irascibilità; **the shortness of her skirt** la sua gonna corta; **shortness of breath** affanno

short pastry, short crust pastry N (*Brit*) pasta frolla

short-range [ʃɔːt'reɪndʒ] ADJ (*gun*) a gittata corta; (*aircraft*) a corto raggio d'azione; (*plan*) a breve termine; **the short-range weather forecast is for ...** il bollettino meteorologico per le prossime dodici ore prevede...

shorts [ʃɔːts] NPL shorts *mpl*, calzoncini *mpl*

short sight N miopia

short-sighted [ʃɔːt'saɪtɪd] ADJ (*also fig: policy, decision*) miope

short-sightedness [ʃɔːt'saɪtɪdnɪs] N (*also fig: of policy, decision*) miopia

short-staffed [ʃɔːt'stɑːft] ADJ a corto di personale

short·stop ['ʃɔːtstɒp] N (*Baseball*) interbase *m/f inv*

short·stop ['ʃɔːt,stɒp] N (*Baseball*) interbase

short story N racconto, novella

short-tempered [ʃɔːt'tɛmpəd] ADJ (*in general*) irascibile; (*in a bad mood*) di cattivo umore

◎ **short-term** ['ʃɔːt,tɜːm] ADJ a breve scadenza; (*solution*) di *or* a breve durata

short term N: **in the short term** nell'immediato futuro

short-termism [ʃɔːt'tɜːmɪzəm] N ottica a breve termine

short time N: **to work short time, be on short time** (*Industry*) essere *or* lavorare a orario ridotto

short-wave ['ʃɔːt,weɪv] ADJ (*radio*) a onde corte

short wave N (*Radio*) onde *fpl* corte

◎ **shot** [ʃɒt] N **1** (*from gun, also sound*) sparo, colpo d'arma da fuoco; (*shotgun pellets*) pallottole *fpl*; **to fire a shot at sb/sth** sparare un colpo a qn/qc; **a warning shot** un colpo di avvertimento; **good shot!** bel colpo!; **a witness said he heard a shot** un testimone ha detto di aver sentito uno sparo; **he was off like a shot** (*fig*) è partito come un razzo; **it was a shot in the dark** (*fig*) è stata un'ipotesi azzardata **2** (*person*) tiratore(-trice); **he's a good/bad shot** è un buon/pessimo tiratore; **a big shot** (*fam*) un pezzo grosso *or* da novanta, un alto papavero **3** (*Ftbl, Golf, Tennis etc*) tiro; (*throw*) lancio; **to put the shot** lanciare il peso; **a shot at goal** un tiro in porta; **good shot!** bel tiro!, bel lancio!; **he had only one shot at goal** ha avuto solo una possibilità di segnare **4** (*attempt*) prova; (*turn to play*) turno; **to have a shot at sth/doing sth** provare a fare qc; **I'll have a shot at it** ci proverò **5** (*injection*) puntura, iniezione *f*; (*of alcohol*) bicchierino; **they gave him shots** gli hanno fatto delle iniezioni; **the economy needs a shot in the arm** (*fig*) l'economia ha bisogno di una sferzata **6** (*Phot*) foto *f inv*; (*Cine*) inquadratura; **a shot of Edinburgh castle** una foto del castello di Edimburgo

■ PT, PP *of* **shoot to get shot of sb/sth** (*fam*) sbarazzarsi di qn/qc

■ ADJ: **shot silk** seta cangiante; **shot with blue** screziato(-a) di blu

shot·gun ['ʃɒt,gʌn] N fucile *m* da caccia

shotgun wedding N (*fam*) matrimonio riparatore

shot put N: **the shot put** il lancio del peso

◎ **should** [ʃʊd] MODAL AUX VB **1** (*duty, advisability, desirability*): **all school buses should have seat belts** tutti gli autobus scolastici dovrebbero essere forniti di cinture di sicurezza; **I should go now** dovrei andare ora; **I should have been a doctor** avrei dovuto fare il medico; **I should have told you before** avrei dovuto dirtelo prima; **you shouldn't do that** non dovresti farlo; **you should take more exercise** dovresti fare più moto; **I should go if I were you** se fossi in te andrei; **I shouldn't if I were you** se fossi in te non lo farei; **how should I know?** e che ne so io?, e come faccio a saperlo?; **I should be so lucky!** sarebbe bello! **2** (*probability*): **he should pass his exams** dovrebbe superare gli esami; **they should have arrived by now** a quest'ora dovrebbero essere già arrivati; **he should be there now** dovrebbe essere arrivato ora; **that shouldn't be too hard** non dovrebbe essere troppo difficile; **this should be good** dovrebbe essere bello **3** (*conditional uses*): **if they invited me I should go** *or* **I'd go** se mi invitassero ci andrei; **I should like to** mi piacerebbe; **I should have liked to** mi sarebbe piaciuto; **I should think so!** mi pare!, direi!; **should he phone ...** (*frm*) se telefonasse..., se dovesse telefonare...; **who should I see but Maria!** e chi dovevo vedere se non Maria! **4** (*remote form of shall in indirect speech*): **I told you I should be late** ti ho detto che avrei fatto tardi

◎ **shoul·der** ['ʃəʊldə^r] N **1** (*gen*) spalla; **to carry sth over one's shoulder** portare qc a spalla; **to cry on sb's shoulder** piangere sulla spalla di qn; **to look over one's shoulder** guardarsi alle spalle; **to look over sb's shoulder** guardare da dietro le spalle di qn; (*fig*) stare addosso a qn; **shoulder to shoulder** spalla a spalla; **to have broad shoulders** (*also fig*) avere le spalle larghe; **to put one's shoulder to the wheel** (*fig*) mettersi all'opera; **to rub shoulders with sb** (*fig*) frequentare qn; **to give sb the cold shoulder** (*fig*) trattare qn con freddezza; **he stands head and shoulders above everybody else** è di gran lunga superiore a tutti gli altri

■ VT (*fig: responsibilities etc*) accollarsi, addossarsi; **to shoulder sb aside** spingere qn da parte a spallate; **to shoulder one's way through the crowd** farsi largo a spallate tra la folla

shoulder bag N borsa a tracolla

shoulder blade N scapola

shoulder-high ['ʃəʊldə'haɪ] ADV: **to carry sb shoulder-high** portare qn in trionfo

shoulder-length ['ʃəʊldə,lɛŋθ] ADJ (*hair*) (lungo(-a)) fino alle spalle

shoulder pad N spallina imbottita

shoulder strap N bretella, spallina

shouldn't ['ʃʊdnt] = **should not**

◎ **shout** [ʃaʊt] N (*gen*) urlo, grido; **a shout of laughter** una risata fragorosa; **to give sb a shout** dare una voce a qn

■ VT (*order, name*) gridare, urlare

■ VI gridare, urlare; **to shout to sb to do sth** gridare a qn di fare qc; **to shout with pain** urlare per il *or* di dolore; **to shout for help** gridare aiuto; **to shout with laughter** scoppiare a ridere; **don't shout!** non urlare!; **"Go away!" he shouted** "Vattene!" urlò

▸ **shout at** VI + PREP gridare a, urlare a; **to shout at sb** (*angrily*) sgridare qn

▸ **shout down** VT + ADV: **they shouted him down** gridavano così forte che non si sentiva ciò che diceva

▸ **shout out** VI + ADV emettere un grido

■ VT + ADV gridare

Ss

shout·ing ['ʃaʊtɪŋ] N grida *fpl*, urla *fpl*; **it's all over bar the shouting** (*fig*) il più è fatto

shouting match N (*fam*) vivace scambio di opinioni

shove [ʃʌv] N spintone *m*; **to give sb/sth a shove** dare uno spintone a qn/qc

■VT (*gen*) spingere; (*thrust*) cacciare, ficcare; **he shoved me out of the way** mi ha spinto da parte in malo modo; **he shoved a cloth into my hand** mi ha ficcato in mano uno straccio; **to shove in/out** *etc* spingere dentro/fuori *etc*; **he shoved his fist/stick into my face** mi ha minacciato con il pugno/bastone

■VI spingere; **he shoved (his way) through the crowd** si è fatto largo tra la folla a spintoni; **to shove past sb** passare davanti a qn con uno spintone

▸ **shove off** VI + ADV **1** (*fam*) sloggiare, smammare **2** (*Naut*) prendere il largo

▸ **shove over, shove up** VI + ADV (*fam*) farsi più in là

shov·el ['ʃʌvl] N pala

■VT (*coal, snow*) spalare; (*sth spilt*) raccogliere con una paletta; **he was shovelling food into his mouth** (*fig*) mangiava a quattro ganasce

shov·el·er ['ʃʌvləʳ] N (*Zool*) mestolone *m*

shov·el·ful ['ʃʌvlfʊl] N palata

◎**show** [ʃəʊ] (*vb: pt* **showed**, *pp* **shown**) N

1 (*of feeling, emotion*) manifestazione *f*; (*of strength, goodwill*) dimostrazione *f*, prova; (*ostentation*) mostra; **a show of strength** una dimostrazione di forza; **to ask for a show of hands** chiedere una votazione per alzata di mano

2 (*exhibition: Art*) mostra, esposizione *f*; (*: Comm, Tech*) salone *m*, fiera; (*: Agr*) fiera; **a fashion show** una sfilata di moda; **to be on show** essere esposto(-a); **the garden is a splendid show** il giardino offre uno spettacolo stupendo

3 (*Theatre, Cine etc*) spettacolo; (*variety show*) varietà *m inv*; **to go to a show** andare a vedere uno spettacolo; **we're seeing a show this evening** stasera andiamo a vedere uno spettacolo; **on with the show!** (*fig*) andiamo avanti!; **good show!** (*old fam*) bene, bravo(-a)!; **the last show** (*Theatre*) l'ultima rappresentazione; (*Cine*) l'ultimo spettacolo; **he's now got his own show** ora ha un suo programma; **she stole the show** tutti gli occhi erano puntati su di lei; **to put up a good show** (*fam*) difendersi bene; **to put up a poor show** (*fam*) essere una delusione; **it's a poor show when/if ...** (*fam*) siamo proprio ridotti male se...

4 (*outward appearance, pretence*) apparenza; **it's just for show** è solo per far scena; **to make a show of doing sth** far finta di fare qc; **to make a show of anger** far finta di essere arrabbiato(-a); **to make a show of resistance** accennare una qualche resistenza

5 (*fam: organization*) baracca; **who's running the show here?** chi è il padrone qui?; **this is my show** qui comando io

■VT

1 (*gen*) mostrare; (*film, slides*) proiettare; (*goods for sale, pictures*) esporre; (*animals*) presentare ad una mostra; **to show sb sth** mostrare qc a qn; **he showed me his new car** mi ha mostrato la sua macchina nuova; **have you shown the article to your boss?** hai mostrato l'articolo al tuo capo?; **to show a film at Cannes** presentare un film a Cannes; **what's showing at the Odeon?** cosa danno all'Odeon?; **white shoes soon show the dirt** le scarpe bianche si sporcano in fretta; **don't show your face here again!** non farti mai più vedere da queste parti!; **to show one's hand** *or* **one's cards** scoprire le carte; (*fig*) mettere le carte in tavola; **I have nothing to show for it** non ho niente a dimostrazione dei miei sforzi; **I'll show him!** (*fam*) gli faccio vedere io!

2 (*indicate*) indicare, segnare; **as shown in the illustration** come da illustrazione; **the motorways are shown in black** le autostrade sono segnate in nero; **to show a profit/loss** (*Comm*) registrare un utile/una perdita

3 (*reveal: interest, surprise*) (di)mostrare, dar prova di; **she showed great courage** ha dimostrato un gran coraggio; **her action showed intelligence** la sua azione ha dato prova di intelligenza; **her face showed her happiness/fear** le si leggeva la felicità/paura in viso; **the choice of dishes shows excellent taste** la scelta dei piatti rivela un ottimo gusto; **this shows him to be a coward** questo dimostra la sua vigliaccheria; **it just goes to show that ...** il che sta a dimostrare che...

4 (*direct, conduct: person*) accompagnare; **to show sb the way** indicare la strada a qn; **to show sb into a room** far entrare qn in una stanza; **to show sb to his seat/to the door** accompagnare qn al suo posto/alla porta; **to show sb the door** (*fig*) mettere qn alla porta; **to show sb round** *or* **over a house** far visitare *or* vedere la casa a qn; **to show sb in/out/up** far entrare/uscire/salire qn

■VI (*stain, emotion, underskirt*) vedersi, essere visibile; **it shows** si vede; **I've never been riding before – it shows** non sono mai andato a cavallo prima d'ora – si vede; **it doesn't show** non si vede; **don't worry, it won't show** sta' tranquillo, non si vedrà

▸ **show off** VI + ADV (*pej*) darsi delle arie, mettersi in mostra; **he's showing off again** ecco che ricomincia a darsi delle arie

■VT + ADV (*pej*) mettere in mostra; (*ability, one's figure*) mostrare; (*knowledge*) ostentare; (*subj: colour, dress: qualities, features*) mettere in risalto, valorizzare

▸ **show through** VI + ADV vedersi

■VI + PREP vedersi attraverso

▸ **show up** VI + ADV

1 (*be visible: gen*) risaltare; (*: mistake*) saltare all'occhio

2 (*fam: arrive*) farsi vivo(-a), farsi vedere; **he showed up late as usual** si è presentato in ritardo, come al solito

■VT + ADV

1 (*reveal: thief, fraud*) smascherare; (*: deception*) mettere a nudo; **he was shown up as an impostor** è stato smascherato per l'impostore che era; **the bright lighting showed up her scars** la forte luce metteva in evidenza le sue cicatrici

2 (*embarrass*) far fare una figuraccia a

show business ['ʃəʊ,bɪznɪs], **show biz** ['ʃəʊ,bɪz] (*fam*) N mondo dello spettacolo

show·case ['ʃəʊ,keɪs] N (*cabinet*) vetrina, bacheca; (*fig*) vetrina; **the tournament will be a showcase of European football** il torneo sarà la vetrina del calcio europeo

show·down ['ʃəʊ,daʊn] N regolamento di conti

show·er ['ʃaʊəʳ] N **1** (*of rain*) rovescio; **a shower of hail** una grandinata; **a snow shower** una nevicata **2** (*fig: of arrows, stones*) pioggia; (*: of blows*) gragnuola, scarica; (*: of bullets*) scarica; (*: of kisses, presents*) valanga **3** (*shower bath*) doccia; **to have** *or* **take a shower** fare una doccia **4** (*Am: party*) *festa di fidanzamento (in cui si fanno regali alla persona festeggiata)*

■VT (*fig*): **to shower sb with** (*gifts, abuse*) coprire qn di; (*blows*) riempire qn di; (*missiles*) bersagliare qn con una

pioggia di; **he was showered with invitations** è stato inondato di inviti
■VI *(take a shower)* fare la doccia
shower cap N cuffia da doccia
shower cubicle N box *m* doccia *inv*
shower curtain N tenda per doccia
shower gel N gel *m inv* doccia *inv*
shower·proof [ˈʃaʊə,pruːf] ADJ impermeabile
shower unit N blocco *m* doccia *inv*
show·ery [ˈʃaʊərɪ] ADJ *(weather)* con piogge intermittenti
show·girl [ˈʃəʊ,gɜːl] N show girl *f inv*
show·ground [ˈʃəʊ,graʊnd] N area di esposizione
show house N casa *f* tipo *inv*
show·ing [ˈʃəʊɪŋ] N *(of film)* proiezione *f*; *(cinema session)* spettacolo; **to make a poor showing in the opinion polls** avere un magro risultato al sondaggio d'opinione
showing off N *(pej)* esibizionismo
show·jumping [ˈʃəʊ,dʒʌmpɪŋ] N concorso ippico *(di salto ad ostacoli)*
show·man [ˈʃəʊmən] N *(pl* **-men***)* *(at fair, circus)* impresario; **he's a great showman** *(fig)* fa sempre un po' l'attore
show·man·ship [ˈʃəʊmənʃɪp] N *(fig)* abilità *or* capacità di intrattenere il pubblico
shown [ʃəʊn] PP *of* **show**
show-off [ˈʃəʊ,ɒf] N *(fam)* esibizionista *m/f*
show·piece [ˈʃəʊ,piːs] N *(of exhibition)* pezzo forte; **that hospital is a showpiece** quello è un ospedale modello
show·place [ˈʃəʊ,pleɪs] N: **the Lloyds Building is one of the showplaces of London** la sede dei Lloyds è una delle attrattive di Londra
show·room [ˈʃəʊ,rʊm] N *(Comm)* show-room *m inv*, salone *m* d'esposizione; *(Art)* sala d'esposizione
show stopper N *(fam)* scena *or* numero *etc* che strappa gli applausi
show trial N processo a scopo dimostrativo *(spesso ideologico)*
showy [ˈʃəʊɪ] ADJ *(comp* **-ier**, *superl* **-iest***)* vistoso(-a), appariscente
shrank [ʃræŋk] PT *of* **shrink**
shrap·nel [ˈʃræpnl] N shrapnel *m inv*
shred [ʃrɛd] N, GEN PL *(of cloth)* brandello; *(of paper)* strisciolina; *(fig: of truth, evidence)* briciolo; **not a shred of truth** neanche un briciolo di verità; **you haven't got a shred of evidence** non ne hai la benché minima prova; **in shreds** a brandelli; **to tear to shreds** fare a brandelli; *(fig: argument)* demolire; **to tear sb to shreds** fare a pezzi qn
■VT *(paper)* stracciare, strappare; *(mechanically)* trinciare; *(food: with grater)* grattugiare; *(: with knife)* tagliuzzare, sminuzzare; **shred the apples and carrots** sminuzzate le mele e le carote; **the documents were shredded** i documenti furono distrutti
shred·der [ˈʃrɛdəʳ] N *(for documents, papers)* distruttore *m* di documenti
shrew [ʃruː] N *(Zool)* toporagno; *(fig pej: woman)* strega
shrewd [ʃruːd] ADJ *(comp* **-er**, *superl* **-est***)* *(person, assessment)* acuto(-a), accorto(-a); *(lawyer, businessman)* scaltro(-a); *(plan, look)* astuto(-a); *(guess)* perspicace; **a shrewd businessman** uno scaltro uomo d'affari; **a shrewd investment** un investimento accorto; **I have a shrewd idea that ...** mi sa tanto che...
shrewd·ly [ˈʃruːdlɪ] ADV *(act)* con accortezza; *(reason)* con perspicacia; **to look at sb shrewdly** lanciare uno sguardo astuto a qn
shrewd·ness [ˈʃruːdnɪs] N *(see adj)* acume *m*; accortezza; astuzia; perspicacia
shrew·ish [ˈʃruːɪʃ] ADJ *(pej: woman, wife)* bisbetico(-a)
shriek [ʃriːk] N strillo; **a shriek of pain** un grido di dolore; **shrieks of laughter** risate *fpl* stridule
■VI strillare; **to shriek at sb** strillare a qn; **to shriek with laughter** sbellicarsi dalle risa
■VT strillare
shrift [ʃrɪft] N *(fig)*: **to give sb short shrift** trattare qn in modo sbrigativo; **to get short shrift from sb** essere trattato(-a) in modo sbrigativo da qn
shrike [ʃraɪk] N averla maggiore
shrill [ʃrɪl] ADJ *(comp* **-er**, *superl* **-est***)* *(bell, sound)* acuto(-a), penetrante; *(laugh, voice)* stridulo(-a); *(demand, protest)* insistente
shrill·ness [ˈʃrɪlnɪs] N *(of laugh, voice)* suono stridulo
shril·ly [ˈʃrɪlɪ] ADV in modo penetrante
shrimp [ʃrɪmp] N *(Zool)* gamberetto; *(fig: child)* scricciolo
shrine [ʃraɪn] N *(tomb)* sepolcro; *(place)* santuario; *(reliquary)* reliquiario, teca
shrink [ʃrɪŋk] *(vb: pt* **shrank**, *pp* **shrunk***)* VT *(wool)* far restringere
■VI **1** *(clothes)* restringersi, ritirarsi; *(metal)* contrarsi; *(gums)* ritirarsi; *(piece of meat)* ridursi; *(area, person)* rimpicciolirsi; **to shrink in the wash** restringersi con il lavaggio; **my sweater shrank in the wash** il mio maglione si è ristretto durante il lavaggio; **all my jumpers have shrunk** mi si sono ristretti tutti i maglioni; **the forests of West Africa have shrunk** le foreste dell'Africa occidentale si sono ridotte **2** *(also:* **shrink away, shrink back***)* ritrarsi, tirarsi indietro; **to shrink from doing sth** rifuggire dal fare qc; **he didn't shrink from telling her the truth** non ha esitato a dirle la verità
■N *(fam pej)* strizzacervelli *m/f inv*
shrink·age [ˈʃrɪŋkɪdʒ] N *(of clothes)* restringimento; *(Comm: in shops)* perdite *fpl (dovute a danno o taccheggio)*
shrink-wrap [ʃrɪŋkˈræp] VT cellofanare
shrink-wrapped [ˈʃrɪŋkræpt] ADJ incellofanato(-a)
shriv·el [ˈʃrɪvl] *(also:* **shrivel up***)* VT *(plant etc)* far rinsecchire; *(skin)* far raggrinzire, far avvizzire
■VI *(see vt)* rinsecchirsi; raggrinzirsi, avvizzire
shroud [ʃraʊd] N *(round corpse)* sudario; *(fig: of secrecy)* alone *m*
■VT *(fig)*: **shrouded in** *(mist, darkness)* circondato(-a) da; **shrouded in mystery** avvolto(-a) nel mistero
Shrove Tuesday [ʃrəʊvˈtjuːzdɪ] N martedì *m inv* grasso
shrub [ʃrʌb] N arbusto
shrub·bery [ˈʃrʌbərɪ] N arbusti *mpl*
shrug [ʃrʌg] N alzata di spalle; **a shrug of indifference** un gesto d'indifferenza; **to give a shrug of contempt** alzare le spalle con disprezzo; **...he said with a shrug** ... disse alzando le spalle
■VT, VI: **to shrug (one's shoulders)** alzare le spalle, fare spallucce
► **shrug off** VT + ADV *(danger)* prendere sottogamba; *(insult)* ignorare, passare sopra a; *(troubles)* minimizzare; *(cold, illness)* sbarazzarsi di
shrunk [ʃrʌŋk] PP *of* **shrink**
shrunk·en [ˈʃrʌŋkən] ADJ *(body)* rinsecchito(-a)
shtick [ʃtɪk] N *(Am)* = **schtick**
shucks [ʃʌks] EXCL *(Am fam)*: **shucks!** sciocchezze!
shud·der [ˈʃʌdəʳ] VI *(person)*: **to shudder (with)**

Ss

rabbrividire (per *or* da); *(machinery)* vibrare; **the car shuddered to a halt** dopo vari sussulti la macchina si fermò; **I shudder to think!** rabbrividisco al solo pensiero!
■ N *(of person)* brivido; *(of machinery)* vibrazione *f*; **to give a shudder** *(person)* rabbrividire; *(car)* sussultare

shuf·fle ['ʃʌfl] N **1** passo strascicato **2** *(Cards)* mescolata, scozzata; **to give the cards a shuffle** dare una mescolata alle carte
■ VT **1** *(feet)* strascicare **2** *(mix up: cards)* mescolare, scozzare; *(: papers)* mettere sottosopra
■ VI *(walk)* strascicare i piedi; **she shuffled along the corridor** strascicava i piedi lungo il corridoio; **to shuffle in/out** *etc* entrare/uscire *etc* con passo strascicato

shun [ʃʌn] VT *(person, work, publicity)* evitare, sfuggire; *(obligation)* sottrarsi a

shunt [ʃʌnt] VT *(Rail: direct)* smistare; *(: divert)* deviare; *(fig: from one place to another)* spostare
■ VI: **to shunt to and fro** fare la spola

shunt·er ['ʃʌntəʳ] N *(Rail: engine)* locomotiva da manovra

shunt·ing ['ʃʌntɪŋ] N *(Rail)* smistamento

shunting yard N fascio di smistamento

shush [ʃʊʃ] EXCL zitto(-a)!
■ VT *(fam)* zittire

◎ **shut** [ʃʌt] *(pt, pp* **shut***)* VT *(gen)* chiudere; **to shut the door in sb's face** sbattere la porta in faccia a qn; **to shut one's finger in the door** chiudersi un dito nella porta; **to shut sb in a room** rinchiudere qn in una stanza; **shut your mouth** *or* **face!** *(fam!)* chiudi il becco!
■ VI *(door, window)* chiudersi; *(shop, bank etc)* chiudere; **what time do the shops shut?** a che ora chiudono i negozi?
■ ADJ chiuso(-a); **to keep one's mouth shut** tenere la bocca chiusa
▸ **shut away** VT + ADV *(person, animal)* rinchiudere, chiudere; *(valuables)* mettere al sicuro
▸ **shut down** VI + ADV *(factory, shop)* chiudere i battenti; **the cinema shut down last year** il cinema ha chiuso i battenti l'anno scorso
■ VT + ADV *(factory, shop)* chiudere; *(machine)* fermare; *(nuclear reactor)* ridurre al minimo
▸ **shut in** VT + ADV rinchiudere
▸ **shut off** VT + ADV **1** *(stop: power)* staccare; *(: water)* chiudere; *(: engine)* spegnere **2** *(isolate)*: **to shut off (from)** tagliar fuori (da), isolare (da)
▸ **shut out** VT + ADV *(person, noise, cold)* non far entrare; *(block: view)* impedire, bloccare; *(: memory)* scacciare; **to be shut out of the house** rimanere chiuso(-a) fuori casa
▸ **shut up** VI + ADV *(fam: be quiet)* star zitto(-a); **shut up!** stai zitto!
■ VT + ADV **1** *(factory, business, house)* chiudere **2** *(person, animal)* rinchiudere, chiudere; *(valuables)* mettere al sicuro **3** *(fam: silence)* far stare zitto(-a)

shut·down ['ʃʌt,daʊn] N chiusura

shut-eye ['ʃʌtaɪ] N *(fam)* dormita; **to get some shut-eye** farsi una dormita

shut-in [ʃʌt'ɪn] ADJ *(feeling)* di soffocamento

shut·ter ['ʃʌtəʳ] N *(on window)* imposta; *(for shop)* battente *m*; *(Phot)* otturatore *m*; **shutter speed** tempo di apertura

shut·tered ['ʃʌtəd] ADJ con le imposte

shutter release N *(Phot)* bottone *m* dello scatto

shutter speed N *(Phot)* tempo di esposizione

shut·tle ['ʃʌtl] N **1** *(of loom)* spola, navetta; *(of sewing machine)* spoletta **2** *(fig: plane etc)* navetta
■ VI *(subj: vehicle, person)* fare la spola
■ VT *(to and fro: passengers)* portare avanti e indietro; **I was/the papers were shuttled from one department to another** sono stato sballottato/la pratica è stata mandata da un ufficio all'altro

shuttle·cock ['ʃʌtl,kɒk] N *(Badminton)* volano

shuttle diplomacy N *la gestione dei rapporti diplomatici caratterizzata dai frequenti viaggi e incontri dei rappresentanti del governo*

shuttle service N servizio *m* navetta *inv*

shy [ʃaɪ] ADJ *(comp* **-er**, *superl* **-est***)* timido(-a); *(unsociable)* schivo(-a); **to be shy of doing sth** esitare a fare qc; **don't be shy of asking for …** non esitare a chiedere…; **to fight shy of sth** tenersi alla larga da qc; **to fight shy of doing sth** cercare in tutti i modi di non fare qc
■ VI *(horse)*: **to shy (at)** fare uno scarto (davanti a); **the horse shied at the noise** il cavallo ha fatto uno scarto quando ha sentito il rumore; **to shy away from sth** evitare qc; **to shy away from doing sth** *(fig)* rifuggire dal fare qc
■ VT *(old: throw)* scagliare

shy·ly ['ʃaɪlɪ] ADV timidamente

shy·ness ['ʃaɪnɪs] N timidezza

shy·ster ['ʃaɪstəʳ] N *(Am fam)* lestofante *m*; *(lawyer, politician)* filibustiere *m*

SI [,ɛs'aɪ] N ABBR (= **Système International (d'unités)**) SI *m* (= *sistema internazionale (di unità di misura)*)

Siam [saɪ'æm] N il Siam

Sia·mese [,saɪə'mi:z] ADJ siamese
■ N *(person: pl inv)* siamese *m/f*; *(fam: cat)* siamese *m/f*; *(language)* siamese *m*

Siamese cat N gatto siamese

Siamese twins NPL fratelli *mpl (or* sorelle *fpl)* siamesi

Si·beria [saɪ'bɪərɪə] N la Siberia

sibi·lant ['sɪbɪlənt] ADJ sibilante
■ N sibilante *f*

sib·ling ['sɪblɪŋ] N *(frm)* fratello/sorella; **sibling rivalry** rivalità tra fratelli

sib·yl ['sɪbɪl] N sibilla

sic [sɪk] ADV: **(sic)** (sic)

Si·cil·ian [sɪ'sɪlɪən] ADJ, N siciliano(-a)

Sici·ly ['sɪsɪlɪ] N la Sicilia

◎ **sick** [sɪk] ADJ *(comp* **-er**, *superl* **-est***)* **1** *(ill)* malato(-a), ammalato(-a); **a sick person** una malato(-a); **to fall** *or* **take sick** ammalarsi; **to be (off) sick** *(from work)* essere assente (per malattia); **to go sick** mettersi in malattia; **to be sick** *(vomiting)* vomitare, rimettere; **I was sick twice last night** ho vomitato due volte, ieri notte; **to feel sick** avere la nausea; **I feel sick** ho la nausea; **she looks after her sick mother** si occupa della madre malata **2** *(fig: mind, imagination)* malato(-a); *(: humour)* macabro(-a); *(: joke)* di gusto macabro; **to be sick of sth** averne abbastanza di qc; **I'm sick of your lies** ne ho abbastanza delle tue bugie; **to be sick (and tired) of sb/sth** averne fin sopra i capelli di qn/qc; **to be sick to death of sb/sth** essere stufo(-a) marcio(-a) di qn/qc; **sick at heart** desolato(-a); **to be sick of the sight of sb/sth** non poterne più di qn/qc; **you make me sick!** mi fai schifo!; **that's really sick!** è veramente di cattivo gusto!
■ N **1** *(fam: vomit)* vomito **2 the sick** NPL i malati
▸ **sick up** VT + ADV *(fam)* vomitare, rimettere

sick·bag ['sɪk,bæg] N sacchetto *(da usarsi in caso di malessere)*

sick·bay ['sɪk,beɪ] N infermeria
sick·bed ['sɪk,bɛd] N letto di ammalato; **he rose from his sickbed to attend the meeting** fu costretto a lasciare il letto per partecipare alla riunione
sick benefit N = sickness benefit
sick building syndrome N *malattia causata dalla continua esposizione a ventilazione con sistemi di aria condizionata*
sick·en ['sɪkn] VT nauseare, stomacare; (*fig*) disgustare
■ VI sentirsi male, ammalarsi; **to sicken of sth** stufarsi di qc; **to be sickening for sth** (*cold, flu etc*) covare qc
sick·en·ing ['sɪknɪŋ] ADJ (*smell, sight*) nauseante; (*fig: crime, waste, behaviour*) disgustoso(-a), rivoltante; (*: crash*) pauroso(-a); (*fam: annoying*) esasperante
sick·en·ing·ly ['sɪknɪŋlɪ] ADV (*polite, cruel*) disgustosamente
sickie ['sɪkɪ] N (*Brit fam*) giorno di malattia (*preso anche senza che ce ne sia la necessità*)
sick·le ['sɪkl] N falcetto; **hammer and sickle** falce e martello
sick leave N: **on sick leave** in congedo per motivi di salute *or* per malattia
sickle-cell anaemia [,sɪklsɛlə'ni:mɪə] N anemia falciforme
sick·li·ness ['sɪklɪnɪs] N (*of person*) salute *f* malferma; (*of cake, sweet*) sapore *m* stucchevole
sick list N: **on the sick list** sulla lista dei malati
sick·ly ['sɪklɪ] ADJ (*comp* **-ier**, *superl* **-iest**) (*person*) malaticcio(-a); (*plant, animal*) malato(-a); (*smile*) stentato(-a); (*complexion*) giallastro(-a); (*taste, smell*) stomachevole; (*cake*) stucchevole; **sickly sweet** nauseante
sick·ness ['sɪknɪs] N malattia; **there's a lot of sickness about** c'è molta gente malata; **wave of sickness** ondata di malessere
sickness benefit N indennità di malattia
sick note N certificato di malattia
sick pay N *salario erogato al dipendente in caso di malattia*
sick·room ['sɪk,rʊm] N stanza di malato
◎ **side** [saɪd] N
1 (*of person, animal*) fianco; **side of beef** quarto di bue; **at** *or* **by sb's side** al fianco di qn, accanto a qn; **side by side** (*people*) fianco a fianco; (*objects*) uno(-a) accanto all'altro(-a); **she was lying on her side** era sdraiata su un fianco
2 (*edge: of box, square etc*) lato; (*: of buildings*) fianco, lato; (*: of boat, vehicle*) fiancata; (*: of ship*) murata, fianco; (*: of lake*) riva; (*: of road*) bordo, ciglio; **at the side of the road** sul bordo della strada; **by the side of the lake** sulla riva del lago
3 (*face, surface: gen*) faccia; (*: of paper*) facciata; (*: of slice of bread*) lato; (*fig: aspect*) aspetto, lato; **the right/wrong side** il dritto/rovescio; **the other side of the coin** (*fig*) il rovescio della medaglia; **to hear both sides of the question** sentire tutt'e due le campane
4 (*part*) parte *f*; **from all sides** *or* **from every side** da ogni parte; **from side to side** da una parte all'altra; **to move to one side** scostarsi, farsi *or* tirarsi da (una) parte; **he was driving on the wrong side of the road** guidava sul lato sbagliato della strada; **to take sb on one side** prendere qn da parte *or* in disparte; **to put sth to** *or* **on one side (for sb)** mettere qc da parte (per qn); **on the mother's side** per parte di madre; **to be on the wrong/right side of 30** aver/non aver superato la trentina; **to get on the wrong/right side of sb** prendere qn per il verso sbagliato/giusto; **on this side of town** da questa parte della città; **it's a bit on the large side** è un po' abbondante; **to make a bit (of money) on the side** (*fam*) farsi un po' di soldi extra
5 (*Sport: team*) squadra; (*Pol: faction*) parte *f*; **the other side** la parte opposta; **God is on our side** Dio è con noi; **to be on sb's side** essere dalla parte di *or* con qn; **I'm on your side** sto dalla tua parte; **to be on the side of moderation** essere per la moderazione; **to have age/the law** *etc* **on one's side** avere l'età/la legge *etc* dalla propria (parte); **to pick** *or* **choose sides** formare le squadre; **to take sides** prendere posizione; **to take sides with sb** schierarsi con qn; **to let the side down** (*Sport, fig*) deludere le aspettative di qn; **Arsenal was the stronger side** l'Arsenal era la squadra più forte
■ VI: **to side with sb** prendere le parti di qn, parteggiare per qn
■ ADJ (*door, entrance*) laterale; **a side entrance** un ingresso laterale; **a side issue** una questione secondaria
▶ **side against** VT + PREP schierarsi contro
side·board ['saɪd,bɔ:d] N credenza
side·boards ['saɪd,bɔ:dz], (*Am*) **side·burns** ['saɪd,bɜ:nz] NPL basette *fpl*
side·car ['saɪd,kɑ:ʳ] N sidecar *m inv*
-sided [saɪdɪd] SUFF: **a seven-sided coin** una moneta ettagonale; **a many-sided problem** un problema complesso
side dish N contorno
side drum N (*Mus*) piccolo tamburo
side effect N effetto collaterale
side-impact bars [,saɪd'ɪmpækt,bɑ:z] NPL (*Auto*) barre *fpl* antiurto *inv* laterali
side·kick ['saɪd,kɪk] N (*fam: esp Am: assistant*) braccio destro *m inv*; (*: friend*) amico(-a)
side·light ['saɪd,laɪt] N (*Aut*) luce *f* di posizione
side·line ['saɪd,laɪn] N **1** (*Ftbl etc*) linea laterale; **to watch from the sidelines** (*fig*) guardare dall'esterno; **to be on the sidelines of** (*fig*) non prendere parte alle decisioni di **2** (*Comm*) attività *f inv* collaterale; **a profitable sideline** un'attività secondaria redditizia; **to be on the sidelines** (*fig*) essere lasciato(-a) fuori; **to watch from the sidelines** (*fig*) essere uno(-a) spettatore(-trice) passivo(-a)
■ VT (*fig*) escludere
side·long ['saɪd,lɒŋ] ADJ: **to give a sidelong glance at sth** guardare qc con la coda dell'occhio
side plate N piattino
side road N strada secondaria
side·saddle ['saɪd,sædl] ADV: **to ride sidesaddle** cavalcare all'amazzone
side salad N (*Culin*) contorno di insalata
side·show ['saɪd,ʃəʊ] N (*at fair*) attrazione *f*
side·slip ['saɪd,slɪp] (*Skiing*) N derapata, dérapage *m inv*
■ VI derapare
side-splitting ['saɪd,splɪtɪŋ] ADJ (*fam*) da crepar dal ridere, esilarante
side·step ['saɪd,stɛp] VT (*question, problem*) eludere, scansare
■ VI (*Boxing*) schivare
side·step·ping ['saɪd,stɛpɪŋ] N (*Skiing*) salita a scaletta
side street N traversa
side·swipe ['saɪd,swaɪp] N frecciata en passant; **to take a sideswipe at** lanciare una frecciata en passant a
side·track ['saɪd,træk] VT (*person*) sviare, mettere fuori strada; **I got sidetracked** mi hanno distratto

Ss

side view N inquadratura di profilo
side·walk ['saɪd,wɔ:k] N (*Am: pavement*) marciapiede *m*
side·ways ['saɪd,weɪz] ADJ laterale; **to give a sideways glance at sth** guardare qc con la coda dell'occhio
■ADV (*move*) di lato, di fianco; (*look*) con la coda dell'occhio; **sideways on** di profilo; **I took a step sideways** ho fatto un passo di lato
side·winder ['saɪd,waɪndə^r] N (*snake*) crotalo ceraste
sid·ing ['saɪdɪŋ] N (*Rail*) binario di raccordo
si·dle ['saɪdl] VI: **to sidle up to sb** avvicinarsi furtivamente a qn; **to sidle out/past** *etc* uscire/passare *etc* furtivamente
SIDS [sɪdz] N ABBR (*Med:* = **sudden infant death syndrome**) morte *f* improvvisa del lattante
siege [si:dʒ] N assedio; **in a state of siege** in stato d'assedio; **to lay siege to** porre l'assedio a

DID YOU KNOW ...?
siege is not translated by the Italian word *seggio*

siege economy N economia da stato d'assedio
si·en·na [sɪ'ɛnə] N (*colour*) terra di Siena
Si·er·ra Leo·ne [sɪ'ɛərəlɪ'əʊnɪ] N Sierra Leone *f*
si·es·ta [sɪ'ɛstə] N siesta; **to have a siesta** schiacciare un pisolino
sieve [sɪv] N (*for flour*) setaccio; (*for coal, soil*) crivello; **to have a memory like a sieve** (*fam*) avere una memoria che fa acqua, essere smemorato(-a)
■VT (*soil, flour etc*) setacciare, passare al setaccio; (*coal etc*) passare al crivello
sift [sɪft] VT (*flour, sand etc*) setacciare; (*coal etc*) passare al crivello; (*fig: evidence*) vagliare; **to sift out** (*truth etc*) separare; **sift the flour and spices** setacciate la farina e le spezie; **after sifting the evidence ...** dopo aver vagliato le prove...
■VI (*fig*): **to sift through** esaminare minuziosamente; (*statement, evidence*) vagliare accuratamente
◎**sigh** [saɪ] N (*of person*) sospiro; (*of wind*) sussurro; **Daphne heaved a sigh of relief** Daphne tirò un sospiro di sollievo
■VI: **to sigh (with)** sospirare (di); **to sigh over** (*sth lost*) piangere su
sigh·ing ['saɪɪŋ] N sospiri *mpl*; (*of wind*) sussurrio
◎**sight** [saɪt] N **1** (*faculty, act of seeing*) vista; **to have good/poor (eye)sight** avere la vista buona/cattiva; **at first sight** a prima vista; **to know sb by sight** conoscere di vista qn; **I know her by sight** la conosco di vista; **payable at sight** (*Comm*) pagabile a vista; **to be within sight of** (*sea*) essere in vista di; (*victory*) essere vicino(-a) a; **in sight** visibile; **the bus was still in sight** l'autobus si vedeva ancora; **the end is in sight** si intravvede la fine; **a solution is in sight** è in vista una soluzione; **to come into sight** (*thing*) profilarsi all'orizzonte; **Janice came into sight** abbiamo scorto Janice; **to catch sight of sth/sb** scorgere qc/qn; **keep out of my sight!** sparisci!; **keep out of sight!** non farti vedere!; **don't let it out of your sight** non perderlo di vista; **when it's out of sight** quando non si vede più, quando non è più visibile; **out of sight out of mind** (*Proverb*) lontano dagli occhi lontano dal cuore; **to lose sight of sb/sth** perdere di vista qn/qc; **to hate the sight of sb/sth** non sopportare la vista di qn/qc; **my sight is failing** la vista mi sta calando **2** (*spectacle*) spettacolo; **the sights** le attrazioni turistiche; **to see the sights of Rome** vedere *or* visitare i monumenti di Roma; **it's not a pretty sight** non è uno spettacolo edificante; **you're a sight for sore eyes!** al solo vederti mi si allarga il cuore!; **you look a sight!** (*fam*) come sei conciato!; **it's a sight to be seen** è uno spettacolo da non perdere; **it was an amazing sight** era uno spettacolo incredibile **3** (*on gun: often pl*) mirino; **in one's sights** sotto mira; **to set one's sights on sth/on doing sth** (*fig*) mirare a qc/a fare qc; **to set one's sights too high** (*fig*) mirare troppo in alto **4** (*fam: a great deal*) molto; **a sight more** molto di più; **it isn't finished by a long sight** è ben lungi dall'essere finito; **a sight too clever** fin troppo furbo(-a)
■VT (*rare animal, land*) avvistare; (*person*) scorgere
sight·ed ['saɪtɪd] ADJ che ha il dono della vista; **partially sighted** parzialmente cieco(-a); **sighted people** i vedenti
sight·ing ['saɪtɪŋ] N avvistamento; **several sightings have been reported** si è avuta notizia di diversi avvistamenti
sight·less ['saɪtlɪs] ADJ (*person*) non vedente
sight-read ['saɪt,ri:d] VT, VI (*Mus*) suonare (*or* cantare) a prima vista
sight·see·ing ['saɪt,si:ɪŋ] N turismo; **to go sightseeing** *or* **to do some sightseeing** (*gen*) fare un giro turistico; (*in town*) visitare la città
sight·seer ['saɪt,si:ə^r] N turista *m/f*
sig·ma ['sɪgmə] N sigma *m or f inv*
◎**sign** [saɪn] N
1 (*with hand etc*) segno, gesto; **to communicate by signs** comunicare a gesti; **to make a sign to sb (to do sth)** far segno a qn (di fare qc); **to make the sign of the Cross** far(si) il segno della croce
2 (*indication*) segno, indizio; **as a sign of** in segno di; **it's a sign of the times** è sintomo dei tempi che corrono; **it's a good/bad sign** è buon/brutto segno; **all the signs are that ...** tutto fa prevedere che...; **at the first** *or* **slightest sign of** al primo *or* al minimo segno di; **to show signs/no sign of doing sth** accennare/non accennare a fare qc; **there was no sign of him anywhere** non c'era traccia di lui da nessuna parte; **there was no sign of life in the village** nel paesino non c'era segno di vita; **there's no sign of improvement** non c'è alcun segno di miglioramento
3 (*also:* **road sign**) segnale *m*
4 (*also:* **shop sign**) insegna; (*notice*) cartello, avviso; **there was a big sign saying "private"** c'era un grande cartello con la scritta "privato"
5 (*written symbol*) segno; **plus/minus sign** segno del più/meno
6 (*also:* **star sign**) segno zodiacale; **what sign are you?** di che segno sei?
■VT
1 (*letter, contract*) firmare; **to sign one's name** firmare, apporre la propria firma; **she signs herself B. Smith** si firma B. Smith
2 (*Ftbl: player*) ingaggiare
■VI
1 (*with signature*) firmare; (*Ftbl*) firmare un contratto; **sign here, please** firmi qui, per favore
2 (*signal*): **to sign to sb to do sth** far segno a qn di fare qc
3 (*deaf people*) usare il linguaggio dei segni
▸ **sign away** VT + ADV (*rights etc*) cedere (*con una firma*)
▸ **sign for** VI + PREP (*letter, goods*) firmare per l'accettazione di; (*football club, record company*) firmare un contratto con
▸ **sign in** VI + ADV (*in hotel*) firmare il registro (*all'arrivo*)

▸ **sign off** VI + ADV (*TV, Radio*) chiudere le trasmissioni
▸ **sign on** VI + ADV (*as unemployed*) iscriversi all'ufficio di collocamento; (*Mil etc: enlist*) arruolarsi; (*as worker*) prendere servizio; (*enrol*): **to sign on for a course** iscriversi a un corso
■ VT + ADV (*employees*) assumere; (*Mil: enlisted man*) arruolare
▸ **sign out** VI + ADV (*in hotel*) firmare il registro (*alla partenza*)
■ VT + ADV (*book*) firmare il registro per il prestito di un libro
▸ **sign over** VT + ADV (*rights etc*): **to sign sth over to sb** cedere qc con scrittura legale a qn
▸ **sign up** VI + ADV (*Mil: enlist*) arruolarsi; (*enrol: for course*) iscriversi
■ VT + ADV (*employee*) assumere; (*Mil*) arruolare

sign·age ['saɪnɪdʒ] N segnaletica stradale

◎ **sig·nal** ['sɪgnl] N: **signal (for)** segnale *m* (di); **at a prearranged signal** ad un segnale convenuto; **distress signal** segnale di soccorso; **traffic signals** semafori *mpl*; **railway signals** segnali *mpl* ferroviari; **the engaged signal** (*Telec*) il segnale di occupato; **the signal is very weak** (*TV*) la ricezione è molto debole
■ ADJ (*frm: success, importance*) notevole
■ VT **1** (*message*) comunicare per mezzo di segnali; **to signal a left/right turn** (*Aut*) segnalare una svolta a sinistra/destra; **to signal sb on/through** far segno a qn di avanzare/passare **2** (*signify*) indicare
■ VI (*gen*) segnalare; (*for help*) fare segnalazioni; **to signal to sb (to do sth)** far segno a qn (di fare qc)

signal box N (*Rail*) cabina di manovra

sig·nal·ly ['sɪgnəlɪ] ADV (*fail, lack*) completamente

signal·man ['sɪgnlmən] N (*pl* **-men**) (*Rail*) deviatore *m*

sig·na·tory ['sɪgnətərɪ] N firmatario(-a)

signature ['sɪgnətʃəʳ] N **1** (*of person*) firma; **to put one's signature to sth** firmare qc, apporre la propria firma a qc; **a petition containing one thousand signatures** una petizione con mille firme **2** (*Mus*): **key signature** segnatura in chiave; **time signature** indicazione *f* del tempo
■ ADJ tipico(-a)

signature tune N (*Brit*) sigla musicale

sign·board ['saɪn,bɔːd] N cartello

sign·er ['saɪnəʳ] N (*on TV, at theatre etc*) *chi usa il linguaggio dei segni*

sig·net ['sɪgnɪt] N sigillo

signet ring N anello con sigillo

sig·nifi·cance [sɪg'nɪfɪkəns] N (*of remark*) significato; (*of event, speech*) importanza; **that is of no significance** ciò non ha importanza

◎ **sig·nifi·cant** [sɪg'nɪfɪkənt] ADJ (*discovery, change, event*) importante; (*increase, improvement, amount*) notevole; (*evidence*) significativo(-a); (*look, smile*) eloquente; **it is significant that ...** è significativo che...; **a significant development** uno sviluppo importante; **a significant improvement** un miglioramento notevole

sig·nifi·cant·ly [sɪg'nɪfɪkəntlɪ] ADV (*smile*) in modo eloquente; (*improve, increase*) considerevolmente; **and, significantly, ...** e, fatto significativo, ...

significant other N partner *m/f inv* fisso(-a)

sig·ni·fi·ca·tion [,sɪgnɪfɪ'keɪʃən] N (*frm: of word*) significato

sig·ni·fy ['sɪgnɪ,faɪ] VT (*mean*) significare; (*indicate*) indicare; (*make known*) manifestare, esprimere
■ VI avere importanza

sign·ing ['saɪnɪŋ] N (*of document, letter etc*) firma; (*of deaf people*) linguaggio dei segni; (*Sport*): **a new signing** un nuovo ingaggio

sign language N linguaggio dei segni

sign off N conclusione *f* (*di lettera ecc*)

sign·post ['saɪn,pəʊst] N indicazione *f or* cartello stradale
■ VT (*fig*) indicare, segnalare

sign·post·ing ['saɪn,pəʊstɪŋ] N segnaletica

Sikh [siːk] ADJ, N sikh (*m/f*) *inv*
▷ www.sikhnet.com/s/SikhIntro

si·lage ['saɪlɪdʒ] N insilato

◎ **si·lence** ['saɪləns] N silenzio; **silence!** silenzio!; **in (dead** *or* **complete) silence** in (totale *or* perfetto) silenzio; **there was silence on** *or* **about the subject** non si è parlato dell'argomento; **to pass over sth in silence** passare qc sotto silenzio
■ VT (*person, critics*) ridurre al silenzio, far tacere; (*conscience*) mettere a tacere

si·lenc·er ['saɪlənsəʳ] N (*Aut*) marmitta; (*on motorbike, gun*) silenziatore *m*

◎ **si·lent** ['saɪlənt] ADJ (*person*) silenzioso(-a); (*film, prayer etc*) muto(-a); **silent "h"** "h" muta; **to fall silent** tacere; **to keep** *or* **remain silent** tacere, stare zitto(-a)

si·lent·ly ['saɪləntlɪ] ADV (*noiselessly*) silenziosamente; (*without speaking*) in silenzio

silent partner N (*Am*) = **sleeping partner**

sil·hou·ette [,sɪluː'ɛt] N (*gen*) sagoma; (*drawing*) silhouette *f inv*
■ VT: **to be silhouetted against** stagliarsi contro

sili·ca ['sɪlɪkə] N silice *f*

silica gel N gel *m inv* di silice

sili·con ['sɪlɪkən] N silicio

silicon chip N chip *m inv* al silicone

sili·cone ['sɪlɪ,kəʊn] N silicone *m*

sili·co·sis [,sɪlɪ'kəʊsɪs] N (*Med*) silicosi *f*

silk [sɪlk] N seta
■ ADJ (*blouse, stockings*) di seta; (*industry*) della seta; **a silk scarf** un foulard di seta

silk·en ['sɪlkən] (*liter*) ADJ (*dress, hair*) di seta; (*skin*) vellutato(-a); (*voice*) suadente, carezzevole

silk factory N setificio

silk manufacturer N fabbricante *m/f* di seta

silk-screen ['sɪlk,skriːn] N: **silk-screen printing** serigrafia

silk·worm ['sɪlk,wɜːm] N baco da seta

silky ['sɪlkɪ] ADJ (*comp* **-ier**, *superl* **-iest**) (*hair, dress*) di seta; (*skin*) vellutato(-a); (*voice*) suadente, carezzevole

sill [sɪl] N **1** (*also:* **windowsill**) davanzale *m* **2** (*Aut*) predellino **3** (*Geol: of corrie*) soglia

sil·li·ness ['sɪlɪnɪs] N stupidità

sil·ly ['sɪlɪ] ADJ (*comp* **-ier**, *superl* **-iest**) (*stupid*) sciocco(-a), stupido(-a); (*ridiculous*) ridicolo(-a); **don't be silly** non fare lo(-a) sciocco(-a), non essere stupido(-a); **to do something silly** fare una sciocchezza

silly season N: **the silly season** *periodo estivo in cui i giornali riportano notizie frivole perché l'attività parlamentare è sospesa*

silo ['saɪləʊ] N silo

silt [sɪlt] N limo
▸ **silt up** VI + ADV insabbiarsi
■ VT + ADV ostruire

◎ **sil·ver** ['sɪlvəʳ] N **1** (*metal*) argento **2** (*silverware, cutlery*) argenteria; **to polish the silver** lucidare l'argenteria **3** (*money*) *monete da 5, 10, 20 o 50 pence*; **£5 in silver** cinque sterline in moneta
■ ADJ (*ring, coin*) d'argento; **a silver medal** una medaglia d'argento

Ss

silver birch N betulla argentata *or* bianca
silver fir N abete *m* bianco
silver·fish ['sɪlvə,fɪʃ] N INV pesciolino d'argento (*insetto*)
silver foil, silver paper N carta argentata, (carta) stagnola
silver gilt N argento dorato
silver-grey [,sɪlvə'greɪ] ADJ grigio argento *inv*
silver-haired [,sɪlvə'hɛəd] ADJ dai capelli argentei
silver jubilee N venticinquesimo anniversario
silver lining N lato positivo; **every cloud has a silver lining** non tutto il male vien per nuocere
silver paper N = **silver foil**
silver plate N (*material*) argentatura; (*objects*) oggetti *mpl* placcati in argento
silver-plated [,sɪlvə'pleɪtɪd] ADJ placcato(-a) in argento, argentato(-a)
silver screen N: **the silver screen** il cinema (*attività*)
silver·side ['sɪlvə,saɪd] N (*Culin*) culaccio di manzo
silver·smith ['sɪlvə,smɪθ] N argentiere *m*
silver·ware ['sɪlvəwɛə^r] N argenteria; **jewellery and silverware** i gioielli e l'argenteria
silver wedding N nozze *fpl* d'argento
sil·very ['sɪlvərɪ] ADJ (*colour*) argenteo(-a); (*hair*) argentato(-a); (*sound*) argentino(-a)
sim [sɪm] N ABBR (= **simulation**) simulatore *m*
sim [sɪm] N (*Comput*) sim *f inv*
sima ['saɪmə] N (*Geol*) sima *m*
SIM card ['sɪmkɑ:d] N (*Telec*: = **Subscriber Identity Module card**) SIM card *f inv*
sim·ian ['sɪmɪən] ADJ scimmiesco(-a)
◎**simi·lar** ['sɪmɪlə^r] ADJ: **similar (to)** simile (a), dello stesso tipo (di); **similar in size** (*objects*) della stessa misura; (*people*) della stessa altezza; **...and similar products** ... e simili
simi·lar·ity [,sɪmɪ'lærɪtɪ] N (ras)somiglianza, similarità *f inv*
simi·lar·ly ['sɪmɪləlɪ] ADV (*in a similar way*) allo stesso modo; (*as is similar*) così pure; **and similarly, ...** e allo stesso modo,...; **similarly, the second plan too has defects** e analogamente anche il secondo piano ha dei difetti; **they were similarly dressed** erano vestiti allo stesso modo
simi·le ['sɪmɪlɪ] N similitudine *f*, paragone *m*
sim·mer ['sɪmə^r] VT cuocere a fuoco lento; **simmer the soup for ten minutes** cuocete la minestra a fuoco lento per dieci minuti
■VI (*water*) sobbollire; (*food*) cuocere a fuoco lento; (*fig: revolt*) covare; **to simmer with rage** ribollire dalla rabbia; **rebellion continued to simmer** la ribellione continuava a covare
▸ **simmer down** VI + ADV (*fig fam*) calmarsi
sim·per ['sɪmpə^r] N sorriso affettato
■VI fare lo(-a) smorfioso(-a)
sim·per·ing ['sɪmpərɪŋ] ADJ lezioso(-a), smorfioso(-a)
◎**sim·ple** ['sɪmpl] ADJ (*comp* **-r**, *superl* **-est**) (*gen*) semplice; (*foolish*) sempliciotto(-a), sprovveduto(-a); **to make simple(r)** semplificare; **it's as simple as ABC** è come bere un bicchier d'acqua; **to make it simple for you ...** per semplificarti le cose...; **the simple truth** la pura verità; **the answer is simple** la risposta è semplice; **in simple terms** *or* **in simple English** in parole povere; **for the simple reason that ...** per il semplice motivo che...; **the simple past** (*Gram*) il passato semplice; **simple equation** (*Math*) equazione *f* di primo grado; **a simple Simon** un*a* sempliciotto(-a); **he's a bit simple** (*fam euph*: *mentally impaired*) è poco sveglio
simple interest N (*Fin*) interesse *m* semplice
simple-minded [,sɪmpl'maɪndɪd] ADJ semplicione(-a)
simple-mindedness [,sɪmpl'maɪndɪdnɪs] N semplicioneria
sim·ple·ton ['sɪmpltən] N (*old*) semplicione(-a), sempliciotto(-a)
sim·plic·ity [sɪm'plɪsɪtɪ] N semplicità
sim·pli·fi·ca·tion [,sɪmplɪfɪ'keɪʃən] N semplificazione *f*
sim·pli·fy ['sɪmplɪ,faɪ] VT semplificare
sim·plis·tic [sɪm'plɪstɪk] ADJ (*pej*: *analysis, view*) semplicistico(-a)
◎**simp·ly** ['sɪmplɪ] ADV (*gen*) semplicemente; **I simply said that ...** ho semplicemente detto che...; **you simply MUST come!** devi assolutamente venire!; **a simply furnished room** una stanza arredata con semplicità
simu·late ['sɪmjʊ,leɪt] VT simulare
simu·la·tion [,sɪmjʊ'leɪʃən] N simulazione *f*
simu·lat·or ['sɪmjʊ,leɪtə^r] N simulatore *m*
simul·cast ['sɪməlkɑ:st] (*TV, Radio*) N programma *m* trasmesso contemporaneamente per radio e per televisione
■VT trasmettere contemporaneamente per radio e per televisione
sim·ul·ta·neity [,sɪməltə'nɪətɪ] N simultaneità
sim·ul·ta·neous [,sɪməl'teɪnɪəs] ADJ simultaneo(-a)
simultaneous equations NPL (*Math*) sistema *m* di equazioni
sim·ul·ta·neous·ly [,sɪməl'teɪnɪəslɪ] ADV simultaneamente, contemporaneamente; **simultaneously with** contemporaneamente a
sin [sɪn] N peccato; **sins of omission** peccati di omissione; **mortal sin** peccato mortale; **it would be a sin to do that** (*Rel*) sarebbe peccato farlo; (*fig*) sarebbe un peccato farlo
■VI peccare
Si·nai ['saɪnaɪ] N il Sinai
sin bin N (*Sport*): **to be in the sin bin** essere espulso(-a) temporaneamente
◎**since** [sɪns] ADV da allora; **ever since** da allora (in poi); **(not) long since** da (non) molto (tempo); **I haven't seen him since** non lo vedo da allora
■PREP da; **since Monday** da lunedì ; **since Christmas** da Natale; **(ever) since then/that ...** da allora...; **since leaving** da quando sono (*or* è *etc*) partito(-a); **how long is it since his last visit?** da quanto tempo non viene?; **I've been here since the beginning of June** sono qua dall'inizio di giugno; **we've been waiting for him since three o'clock** siamo qui ad aspettarlo dalle tre
■CONJ **1** (*time*) da quando; **(ever) since I arrived** (fin) da quando sono arrivato; **I haven't seen her since she left** non l'ho più vista da quando è partita; **how long is it since you last saw him?** da quando non lo vedi?, quant'è che non lo vedi? **2** (*because*) siccome, dato che; **since you're tired, let's stay at home** dato che sei stanco restiamo a casa
sin·cere [sɪn'sɪə^r] ADJ sincero(-a)
sin·cere·ly [sɪn'sɪəlɪ] ADV sinceramente; **Yours sincerely** (*at end of letter*) Distinti saluti
sin·cer·ity [sɪn'sɛrɪtɪ] N sincerità
sine [saɪn] N (*Math*) seno
si·necure ['saɪnɪkjʊə^r] N sinecura
sine curve N (*Math*) sinusoide *f*

sin·ew ['sɪnjuː] N (*tendon*) tendine *m*; **sinews** NPL (*muscles*) muscoli *mpl*; (*fig: strength*) forza

sin·ewy ['sɪnjuɪ] ADJ (*person*) muscoloso(-a); (*meat*) pieno(-a) di nervi

sin·ful ['sɪnfʊl] ADJ (*Rel*) peccaminoso(-a); (*waste, act*) vergognoso(-a)

sin·ful·ly ['sɪnfəlɪ] ADV (*see adj*) in modo peccaminoso; vergognosamente

sin·ful·ness ['sɪnfʊlnɪs] N (*Rel: of person, deeds*) peccaminosità

◎ **sing** [sɪŋ] (*pt* **sang**, *pp* **sung**) VT cantare; **to sing the tenor part** cantare come tenore; **to sing sb's praises** (*fig*) cantare le lodi di qn; **to sing a child to sleep** cantare la ninna nanna a un bambino

■ VI (*person, bird*) cantare; (*ears, kettle, bullet*) fischiare; **to sing like a lark** cantare come un usignolo; **she sang in the school choir** cantava nel coro della scuola; **he has sung in the choir for two years** canta nel coro da due anni

▸ **sing out** VI + ADV (*fam: call*) chiamare

Sin·ga·pore [ˌsɪŋgə'pɔːʳ] N Singapore *f*

singe [sɪndʒ] VT bruciacchiare

◎ **sing·er** ['sɪŋəʳ] N cantante *m/f*

Sin·gha·lese [ˌsɪŋə'liːz] ADJ, N = **Sinhalese**

sing·ing ['sɪŋɪŋ] N (*of person, bird*) canto; (*of kettle, bullet, in ears*) fischio

■ ADJ (*lessons, teacher*) di canto

◎ **sin·gle** ['sɪŋgl] ADJ **1** (*only one*) solo(-a), unico(-a) (*before n*); **a single tree in a garden** un solo albero in un giardino; **only on one single occasion** in una sola occasione; **he gave her a single rose** le ha dato una rosa; **I haven't a single moment to spare** non ho neanche un attimo di tempo; **not a single one was left** non ne è rimasto nemmeno uno; **she didn't see a single person** *or* **soul** non ha visto anima viva; **she hadn't said a single word** non aveva detto una sola parola; **every single day** tutti i santi giorni **2** (*not double*) unico(-a); (*: flower*) semplice; (*: ticket*) di (sola) andata; **down to single figures** (*inflation*) inferiore a dieci; **single spacing** (*Typ*) interlinea uno **3** (*not married: man*) celibe, single *inv*; (*: woman*) nubile, single *inv*

■ N **1** (*Rail etc*) biglietto di (sola) andata; **a single to Oxford, please** un biglietto di sola andata per Oxford, per favore **2** (*record*): **a single** un 45 giri; **a CD single** un CD singolo; *see also* **singles**

▸ **single out** VT + ADV (*choose*) scegliere; (*distinguish*) distinguere, isolare; **his boss singled him out for special mention** il suo capo lo ha scelto per una menzione d'onore

single bed N letto a una piazza

single-breasted ['sɪŋglˌbrestɪd] ADJ (*jacket*) a un petto

single cream N (*Brit*) panna liquida (da cucina)

single-decker [ˌsɪŋgl'dɛkəʳ] N (*Brit*) autobus *m inv* a un piano solo

single-engined [ˌsɪŋgl'ɛndʒɪnd] ADJ monomotore

Single European Market N: **the Single European Market** il Mercato Unico

single file N: **in single file** in fila indiana

single-handed [ˌsɪŋgl'hændɪd] ADJ (*voyage*) solitario(-a); (*achievement*) fatto(-a) da solo(-a)

■ ADV da solo(-a), senza aiuto

single honours N (*Brit Univ: also:* **single honours degree**) *laurea in una sola materia*

single-minded [ˌsɪŋgl'maɪndɪd] ADJ (*person*) deciso(-a), tenace, risoluto(-a); (*ambition, attempt*) ostinato(-a); **to be single-minded about sth** concentrare tutte le proprie forze in qc

single-mindedness [ˌsɪŋgl'maɪndɪdnɪs] N risolutezza

sin·gle·ness ['sɪŋglnɪs] N: **singleness of purpose** tenacia

single parent N genitore single

single-parent ['sɪŋgl'pɛərənt] ADJ: **a single-parent family** una famiglia monoparentale; **the problems of single-parent families** i problemi delle famiglie con un solo genitore

single-party ['sɪŋgl'pɑːtɪ] ADJ (*Pol*) monopartitico(-a); **single-party system** monopartitismo

single (person) supplement N (*of hotel room*) supplemento uso singola

single room N camera singola

singles ['sɪŋglz] NPL **1** (*Tennis*) singolo *msg*; **the women's singles** il singolare femminile **2** (*Am: single people*) single *m/fpl*

singles bar N (*esp Am*) *bar per single, dove è possibile fare amicizia*

single-seater [ˌsɪŋgl'siːtəʳ] ADJ: **single-seater aeroplane** aeroplano monoposto

single-sex school [ˌsɪŋglseks'skuːl] ADJ (*for boys*) scuola maschile; (*for girls*) scuola femminile

single-sided disk [ˌsɪŋglˌsaɪdɪd'dɪsk] N (*Comput*) disco a singola faccia

sin·glet ['sɪŋglɪt] N (*esp Brit*) canottiera

sin·gle·ton ['sɪŋgltən] N (*Cards*) singleton *m inv*; (*person*) single *m/f inv*

single-track ['sɪŋglˌtræk] ADJ (*Rail*) a un solo binario

sin·gly ['sɪŋglɪ] ADV singolarmente, uno(-a) a uno(-a)

sing·song ['sɪŋˌsɒŋ] ADJ (*tone*) cantilenante

■ N (*Brit fam*): **to have a singsong** farsi una cantata

sin·gu·lar ['sɪŋgjʊləʳ] ADJ **1** (*Gram*) singolare **2** (*frm: extraordinary*) strano(-a), singolare

■ N (*Gram*) singolare *m*; **in the singular** al singolare; **in the feminine singular** al femminile singolare

sin·gu·lar·ity [ˌsɪŋgjʊ'lærɪtɪ] N (*frm*) singolarità *f inv*

sin·gu·lar·ly ['sɪŋgjʊləlɪ] ADV (*frm*) singolarmente

singular noun N (*Gram*) sostantivo singolare

Sin·ha·lese [ˌsɪnhə'liːz] ADJ, N singalese (*m/f*)

sin·is·ter ['sɪnɪstəʳ] ADJ sinistro(-a)

sin·is·ter·ly ['sɪnɪstəlɪ] ADV sinistramente

◎ **sink**[1] [sɪŋk] (*pt* **sank**, *pp* **sunk**) VT

1 (*ship, object*) (far) affondare; (*fig: project*) far naufragare; (*: person*) distruggere; **the ship was sunk in the war** la nave venne affondata durante la guerra; **to be sunk** (*fam*) essere nei guai; **I'm sunk without it** se non ce l'ho sono perso; **to be sunk in thought** essere immerso(-a) nei propri pensieri; **to be sunk in despair** essere assolutamente disperato(-a); **let's sink our differences** accantoniamo le divergenze

2 (*mineshaft, well*) scavare; (*foundations*) gettare; (*stake*) piantare, conficcare; (*pipe etc*) interrare; **to sink the ball** (*Golf*) fare buca; **to sink money into an enterprise** investire denaro in un'impresa; **lets sink a few beers** (*Brit fam*) facciamoci un paio di birre

■ VI (*in water*) affondare; (*level of water, sun*) calare; (*ground*) cedere; (*value, voice*) abbassarsi; (*sales*) diminuire; **the ship sank** la nave è affondata; **to sink to the bottom** (*ship*) colare a picco; **to sink to one's knees** cadere in ginocchio; **he sank into a chair/the mud** sprofondò in una poltrona/nel fango; **the water sank slowly into the ground** l'acqua è penetrata lentamente nel terreno; **she's sinking fast** (*dying*) deperisce rapidamente; **he has sunk in my estimation** è scaduto ai miei occhi; **he was left to**

Ss

sink or swim (*fig*) fu lasciato a cavarsela da solo; **to sink like a stone** andar giù come un sasso; **to sink out of sight** scomparire alla vista; **the shares have** *or* **the share price has sunk to 3 dollars** le azioni sono crollate a 3 dollari; **my heart** *or* **spirits sank** mi sentii venir meno

▸ **sink back** VI + ADV (*in chair*) accomodarsi bene; (*under water*) affondare di nuovo

▸ **sink down** VI + ADV: **to sink down onto a chair** lasciarsi cadere su una poltrona; **to sink down on one's knees** cadere in ginocchio; **to sink down out of sight** scomparire

▸ **sink in** VI + ADV (*person, car*) sprofondare; (*liquid: into ground, carpet*) penetrare; (*remark, explanation*) essere capito(-a); **it hasn't sunk in yet** (*fig*) non mi rendo (*or* si rende *etc*) ancora conto; **it took a long time to sink in** ci ho (*or* ha *etc*) messo molto a capirlo

sink² [sɪŋk] N (*in kitchen*) lavello, acquaio; (*in bathroom*) lavandino

sink·ing [ˈsɪŋkɪŋ] N (*shipwreck*) naufragio
■ ADJ: **a** *or* **that sinking feeling** una stretta allo stomaco; **I have a sinking feeling that things have gone wrong** ho il brutto presentimento che le cose siano andate male; **with sinking heart** con la morte nel cuore

sinking fund N (*Comm*) fondo d'ammortamento

sink unit N blocco *m* lavello *inv*

sin·ner [ˈsɪnəʳ] N peccatore(-trice)

Sinn Féin [ʃɪnˈfeɪn] N Sinn Féin *m inv; braccio politico dei cattolici repubblicani*

Sino... [ˈsaɪnəʊ] PREF: **Sino-Russian relations** i rapporti Cina-Russia

sinu·ous [ˈsɪnjʊəs] ADJ (*course, route*) sinuoso(-a), tortuoso(-a); (*dance, movement*) flessuoso(-a)

si·nus [ˈsaɪnəs] N (*Anat*) seno, cavità *f inv*

si·nusi·tis [ˌsaɪnəˈsaɪtɪs] N sinusite *f*

si·nusoi·dal [ˌsaɪnəˈsɔɪdəl] ADJ sinusoidale

sip [sɪp] N sorso
■ VT sorseggiare, centellinare

si·phon [ˈsaɪfən] N sifone *m*
■ VT (*also:* **siphon off**: *liquid*) travasare (con un sifone); (*fig: funds, traffic*) deviare; **he siphoned the petrol out of the tank** ha travasato la benzina dal serbatoio; **they siphoned the money into their accounts** hanno dirottato il denaro nei loro conti correnti

◎ **sir** [sɜːʳ] N (*frm*) signore *m*; **yes, sir** sì, signore; (*Mil*) sissignore; **Dear Sir** (*in letter*) Egregio signor (+ *surname*); **Dear Sirs** Spettabile ditta; **Sir Winston Churchill** Sir Winston Churchill

sire [saɪəʳ] VT (*Zool*) (*old: child*) generare
■ N **1** (*old: to king*): **yes, sire** sì, maestà; (*: father*) padre *m* **2** (*Zool*) padre *m*

si·ren [ˈsaɪərən] N (*all senses*) sirena

sir·loin [ˈsɜːˌlɔɪn] N (*of beef*) controfiletto

sirloin steak N bistecca di controfiletto

si·roc·co [sɪrɒkəʊ] N scirocco

si·sal [ˈsaɪsəl] N sisal *f inv*

sis·sy [ˈsɪsɪ] N (*fam pej*) femminuccia

◎ **sis·ter** [ˈsɪstəʳ] N **1** (*relation*) sorella; **this is my sister** questa è mia sorella **2** (*Med*) (infermiera *f*) caposala *inv*; **she's a sister at the infirmary** è infermiera caposala all'ospedale **3** (*Rel*) suora; **Sister Mary** Suor Maria

sis·ter·hood [ˈsɪstəˌhʊd] N (*gen*) sorellanza; (*Rel*) congregazione *f* di suore

sister-in-law [ˈsɪstərɪnˌlɔː] N (*pl* **sisters-in-law**) cognata

sis·ter·ly [ˈsɪstəlɪ] ADJ fraterno(-a), da sorella

sister nations NPL nazioni *fpl* sorelle

sister organization N organizzazione *f* affine

sister ship N nave *f* gemella

Sisyphus [ˈsɪsɪfəs] N (*Myth*) Sisifo

◎ **sit** [sɪt] (*pt, pp* **sat**) VI
1 (*also:* **sit down**) sedersi, sedere; **sit!** (*to dog*) seduto!; **sit beside me** siediti accanto a me; **he just sits at home all day** sta a casa tutto il giorno senza far nulla; **he was sitting in front of the TV** era seduto davanti alla TV; **we sat in the front row** eravamo seduti in prima fila; **this unit sits on top of that one** questo pezzo poggia su quello; **to sit still/straight** stare seduto(-a) fermo(-a)/dritto(-a); **to sit tight** (*wait patiently*) starsene seduto(-a); **to be sitting pretty** (*fig fam*) passarsela bene; **to sit on a committee** far parte di una commissione; **to sit for** (*a constituency*) rappresentare; **to sit in Parliament** sedere in Parlamento; **to sit for a painter/portrait** posare per un pittore/ritratto; **to sit for an examination** (*esp Brit*) dare *or* sostenere un esame; **to sit through** (*a film, play*) resistere fino alla fine di; **to sit over one's work** *or* **books** stare con la testa sui libri
2 (*assembly, committee*) riunirsi, essere in seduta; **the committee is sitting now** il comitato è in riunione; **Parliament sits from November till June** i lavori parlamentari iniziano a novembre e terminano a giugno
3 (*bird, insect*) posarsi; (*on eggs*) covare
4 (*dress etc*) cadere; **that jacket sits well** quella giacca cade bene
■ VT
1 (*guest, child etc*) far sedere
2 (*exam*) dare, sostenere; **to sit an exam** sostenere un esame

▸ **sit about, sit around** VI + ADV star seduto(-a) senza far nulla

▸ **sit back** VI + ADV (*in seat*) appoggiarsi allo schienale; (*doing nothing*) stare con le mani in mano

▸ **sit by** VI + ADV: **to sit by while sb does sth** starsene a guardare mentre qn fa qc

▸ **sit down** VI + ADV sedersi; **he sat down at his desk** si sedette alla scrivania; **please sit down** prego, si accomodi; **to be sitting down** essere seduto(-a)
■ VT + ADV far sedere, far accomodare

▸ **sit in** VI + ADV
1 **to sit in on a discussion** assistere ad una discussione; **to sit in for sb** (*as substitute*) fare le veci di qn, sostituire qn
2 (*demonstrate*): **to sit in a building** occupare un edificio

▸ **sit on** VI + PREP (*fig fam*)
1 (*keep secret: news, information*) tenere segreto(-a); (*delay taking action on: document, application*) tenere nel cassetto
2 (*person: silence*) far tacere

▸ **sit out** VT + ADV (*dance etc*) non partecipare a, saltare; (*lecture, play*) restare fino alla fine di

▸ **sit up** VI + ADV
1 (*upright*) stare seduto(-a) diritto(-a); (*in bed*) tirarsi (su) a sedere; **to make sb sit up (and take notice)** (*fig*) far drizzare le orecchie a qn
2 (*stay up late*) restare alzato(-a); **to sit up with** (*invalid*) passare la notte al capezzale di; **to sit up for sb** aspettare qn alzato(-a)
■ VT + ADV (*baby, doll*) mettere a sedere, mettere seduto(-a)

si·tar [sɪˈtɑːʳ] N sitar *m inv*

sit·com ['sɪt,kɒm] N (*fam: Radio, TV*) situation comedy *f inv*

sit-down ['sɪt,daʊn] ADJ: **a sit-down strike** sciopero bianco (*con occupazione del posto di lavoro*); **a sit-down meal** un pranzo (a tavola)
■ N (*fam*): **to have a sit-down** sedersi un momento

◎ **site** [saɪt] N **1** (*of town, building*) ubicazione *f*; (*Archeol*) località *f inv*; **the site of the accident** il luogo dell'incidente; **the site of the battle** il teatro della battaglia; **an archaeological site** una zona archeologica **2** (*Constr: also:* **building site**) cantiere *m* **3** (*also:* **camp site**) campeggio **4** (*Comput*) sito; **to visit a site** visitare un sito
■ VT collocare, situare; **a badly sited building** un edificio in una brutta posizione

sit-in ['sɪt,ɪn] N (*demonstration*) sit-in *m inv*; **to hold a sit-in** fare un sit-in

sit·ing ['saɪtɪŋ] N ubicazione *f*

sit·ter ['sɪtəʳ] N (*Art*) modello(-a); (*also:* **babysitter**) baby-sitter *m/f inv*

sit·ting ['sɪtɪŋ] N (*of assembly, Parliament*) seduta; (*in canteen*) turno; (*for portrait*) seduta (di posa); **there are three sittings at lunchtime** ci sono tre turni per il pranzo; **an emergency sitting of the council** una seduta d'emergenza del consiglio
■ ADJ: **in a sitting position** seduto(-a)

sitting duck, **sitting target** N (*fig*) facile bersaglio

sitting member N (*Pol*) deputato in carica

sitting room N salotto, soggiorno

sitting tenant N (*Brit*) affittuario(-a), inquilino(-a)

situ·ate ['sɪtjʊ,eɪt] VT collocare, situare

situ·ated ['sɪtjʊ,eɪtɪd] ADJ situato(-a); **well situated** (*house*) in una bella posizione; **how are you situated for money?** (*fig*) come stai a soldi?

◎ **situa·tion** [,sɪtjʊ'eɪʃən] N (*position*) posizione *f*; (*fig*) situazione *f*; (*frm, old: job*) lavoro, impiego; **"situations vacant/wanted"** (*Brit*) "offerte *fpl*/domande *fpl* di impiego"; **to save the situation** salvare la situazione; **a difficult situation** una situazione difficile

situation comedy N (*TV, Radio, Theatre*) situation comedy *f inv*

sit-up ['sɪt,ʌp] N (*Gymnastics*): **to do sit-ups** *passare dalla posizione sdraiata a quella seduta*

◎ **six** [sɪks] ADJ sei *inv*
■ N sei *m inv*; **to be (all) at sixes and sevens** (*fig: person, things*) essere sottosopra; **it's six of one and half a dozen of the other** (*fig*) se non è zuppa è pan bagnato, siamo lì ; *for usage see* **five**

six-footer [,sɪks'fʊtəʳ] N: **he's a six-footer** ≈ sarà alto due metri

six-pack ['sɪks,pæk] N confezione *f* da sei (*di birra*); (*muscles*) potenti addominali *mpl*

six·pence ['sɪkspəns] N (*coin*) moneta da sei penny (*non più in circolazione legale*); (*value*) sei penny *mpl*

six-shooter ['sɪks,ʃu:təʳ] N rivoltella a sei colpi

◎ **six·teen** [,sɪks'ti:n] ADJ sedici *inv*
■ N sedici *m inv*; *for usage see* **five**

◎ **six·teenth** [,sɪks'ti:nθ] ADJ sedicesimo(-a)
■ N (*in series*) sedicesimo(-a); (*fraction*) sedicesimo; *for usage see* **fifth**

◎ **sixth** [sɪksθ] ADJ sesto(-a)
■ N (*in series*) sesto(-a); (*fraction*) sesto; **the upper/lower sixth** (*Brit Scol*) ≈ l'ultimo/il penultimo anno di scuola superiore *for usage see* **fifth**

sixth form N ≈ ultimo biennio delle superiori

sixth-form college ['sɪksθ,fɔ:m'kɒlɪdʒ] N (*Brit*) *istituto che offre corsi di preparazione all'esame di maturità*

sixth-former ['sɪksθ,fɔ:məʳ] N (*Brit*) ≈ studente(-essa) dell'ultimo biennio delle superiori

sixth sense N sesto senso

◎ **six·ti·eth** ['sɪkstɪɪθ] ADJ sessantesimo(-a)
■ N (*in series*) sessantesimo(-a); (*fraction*) sessantesimo; *for usage see* **fifth**

◎ **six·ty** ['sɪkstɪ] ADJ sessanta *inv*
■ N sessanta *m inv*; *for usage see* **fifty**

sixty-four thousand dollar question N: **that's the sixty-four thousand dollar question** (*fam*) questa è una domanda da mille punti

six-yard box [,sɪksjɑ:d'bɒks] N (*Ftbl*) area di porta

◎ **size¹** [saɪz] N (*gen*) dimensioni *fpl*; (*fig: of problem, operation etc*) proporzioni *fpl*; (*of garments*) taglia, misura; (*of shoes*) numero, misura; (*of hat*) misura; **I take size 5 shoes** ≈ porto il 38 di scarpe; **I take size 14 in a dress** ≈ porto la 44 di vestiti; **what size (of) collar?** che misura di collo?; **what size are you?** *or* **what size do you take?** che taglia porti?; **he's about your size** sarà più o meno come te; **to be the size of** essere grande come; **Leeds is about the size of Florence** Leeds è grande più o meno come Firenze; **it's the size of a brick/nut** sarà grande come un mattone/una noce; **I'd like the small/large size** (*of soap powder etc*) vorrei la confezione piccola/grande; (*of clothes*) vorrei la misura piccola/grande; **plates of various sizes** piatti di varie dimensioni; **to try sth for size** misurare qc per vedere se è della taglia giusta; **to cut sth to size** tagliare qc nella misura desiderata *or* voluta; **to cut sb down to size** (*fig fam*) ridimensionare qn; **that's about the size of it** (*fig*) le cose stanno più o meno così
▸ **size up** VT + ADV (*person, problem*) valutare, farsi un'idea di

size² [saɪz] N (*for walls*) colla; (*for fabric*) appretto
■ VT (*wall*) dare una mano di colla a; (*fabric*) apprettare

-size [saɪz], **-sized** [saɪzd] SUFF: **bite-size pieces** bocconcini *mpl*, pezzetti *mpl*

size·able ['saɪzəbl] ADJ (*house, diamond*) abbastanza grande; (*sum, problem*) considerevole, notevole; **a sizeable sum** una somma considerevole; **a sizeable property** una casa abbastanza grande

siz·zle ['sɪzl] VI sfrigolare

siz·zler ['sɪzləʳ] N (*fam*): **it's been a real sizzler today** ha fatto un caldo da morire, oggi

SK ABBR (*Canada*) = **Saskatchewan**

skate¹ [skeɪt] N (*pl inv: fish*) razza

skate² [skeɪt] N pattino; **to get one's skates on** (*fig: hurry up*) affrettarsi, sbrigarsi
■ VI pattinare; **to go skating** andare a pattinare; **to skate across/down** *etc* attraversare/scendere *etc* pattinando; **it went skating across the room** (*fig*) è scivolato lungo la stanza
▸ **skate over**, **skate around** VI + PREP (*problem, issue*) prendere alla leggera, prendere sottogamba

skate·board ['skeɪt,bɔ:d] N skateboard *m inv*

skate·board·ing ['skeɪt,bɔ:dɪŋ] N: **to go skateboarding** andare sullo skateboard

skat·er ['skeɪtəʳ] N pattinatore(-trice)

skat·ing ['skeɪtɪŋ] N pattinaggio; **figure skating** pattinaggio artistico

skating rink N pista di pattinaggio

skating turn N (*Skiing*) passo di pattinaggio

skein [skeɪn] N (*of wool*) matassa

skel·etal ['skɛlɪtl] ADJ (*Anat*) dello scheletro; (*like a skeleton*) scheletrico(-a)

skel·eton ['skɛlɪtn] N (*of person*) scheletro; (*of building*) struttura, ossatura; (*of novel, report*) schema *m*; **a**

Ss

walking skeleton (*fig*) uno scheletro ambulante; **the skeleton at the feast** (*fig*) il/la guastafeste; **skeleton in the cupboard** *or* **closet** (*fig*) scheletro nell'armadio
■ ADJ (*staff, service*) ridotto(-a)
skeleton key N passe-partout *m inv*
skeleton outline N schema *m*
skep·tic *etc* ['skɛptɪk] (*Am*) = **sceptic** *etc*
sketch [skɛtʃ] N **1** (*drawing*) schizzo, abbozzo; (*fig: rough draft: of ideas, plan*) abbozzo, schema *m*; (: *description*) schizzo **2** (*Theatre etc*) sketch *m inv*
■ VT (*draw*) schizzare, abbozzare; (*fig: ideas, plan*) abbozzare; **to sketch a map for sb** fare una piantina per qn
▸ **sketch in** VT + ADV (*details*) inserire, aggiungere
▸ **sketch out** VT + ADV (*plan, situation*) descrivere a grandi linee
sketch·book ['skɛtʃ,bʊk], **sketch·pad** ['skɛtʃ,pæd] N album *m inv or* blocco per schizzi
sketchi·ly ['skɛtʃɪlɪ] ADV (*answer, understand*) in modo incompleto; (*plan, recall*) a grandi linee
sketch map N carta (geografica) muta
sketchy ['skɛtʃɪ] ADJ (*comp* **-ier**, *superl* **-iest**) (*drawing, plan*) approssimato(-a); (*plans, knowledge*) vago(-a)
skew [skju:] ADJ storto(-a); **skew distribution** (*Math*) distribuzione *f* asimmetrica; **skew lines** (*Math*) rette *fpl* sghembe
■ VT: **to be skewed** essere inclinato(-a) *or* storto(-a)
■ N (*Brit*): **on the skew** storto(-a), di traverso
skew·er ['skjʊəʳ] N (*for roasts*) spiedo; (*for kebabs*) spiedino
■ VT infilzare in uno spiedo
skew-whiff ['skju:'wɪf] ADJ (*Brit fam*) a sghimbescio
◎ **ski** [ski:] N sci *m inv*
■ VI sciare; **to ski down a slope** fare una discesa con gli sci; **to go skiing** andare a sciare
ski binding N attacco degli sci
ski·bob ['ski:bɒb] N skibob *m inv*
ski boot N scarpone *m* da sci
skid [skɪd] N (*Aut*) slittamento; (: *sideways slip*) sbandamento; **to go into a skid** slittare; sbandare; **to get out of a skid** *or* **to correct a skid** riprendere controllo del veicolo; **on the skids** (*fig*) in difficoltà
■ VI (*Aut*) slittare; (: *slip sideways*) sbandare; (*person, object*) scivolare; **to skid into sth** (*car*) slittare e sbattere contro qc; (*person, object*) scivolare contro qc
skid·lid ['skɪd,lɪd] N (*fam*) casco da motociclista
skid mark N (*Aut*) segno della frenata
skid pan N *pista di materiale scivoloso dove ci si può esercitare nella guida*
skid·proof ['skɪd,pru:f] ADJ antiscivolo *inv*
skid row N (*fam*) quartiere *m* malfamato
ski·er ['ski:əʳ] N sciatore(-trice)
skiff [skɪf] N (*boat*) skiff *m inv*
ski·ing ['ski:ɪŋ] N sci *m* (*sport*)
■ ADJ (*holiday etc*) sciistico(-a); **to go on a skiing holiday** fare una vacanza sulla neve
ski instructor N maestro(-a) di sci
ski jump N **1** trampolino **2** (*also:* **ski jumping**) salto con gli sci
skil·ful, (*Am*) **skill·ful** ['skɪlfʊl] ADJ abile
skil·ful·ly, (*Am*) **skill·ful·ly** ['skɪlfəlɪ] ADV abilmente
skil·ful·ness, (*Am*) **skill·ful·ness** ['skɪlfʊlnɪs] N (*of person, handiwork*) abilità
ski lift N impianto di risalita
◎ **skill** [skɪl] N **1** (*gen*) capacità *f inv*, abilità *f inv*; (*talent*) talento; **her skill in dealing with people** la sua abilità nel trattare con le persone; **his skill as a mechanic** la sua abilità come meccanico; **a writer of great skill** uno scrittore di grande talento; **it requires a lot of skill** richiede molta abilità; **to make use of sb's skills** sfruttare le capacità di qn **2** (*technique*) tecnica; **there's a certain skill to doing it** ci vuole una certa tecnica *or* arte nel farlo
skilled [skɪld] ADJ **1** (*gen*) abile, esperto(-a) **2** (*job, work*) specializzato(-a); (*worker*) specializzato(-a), qualificato(-a); **a skilled worker** un operaio specializzato
skil·let ['skɪlɪt] N (*Am*) padella
skill·ful ['skɪlfʊl] ADJ (*Am*) = **skilful**
skill·fully ['skɪlfʊlɪ] ADJ (*Am*) = **skilfully**
skill·ful·ness ['skɪlfʊlnɪs] N (*Am*) = **skilfulness**
skim [skɪm] VT **1** (*soup*) schiumare; (*milk*) scremare; **to skim the fat off the soup** schiumare il brodo; **skim off the fat** schiuma via il grasso; **to skim the cream off the milk** scremare il latte **2** (*stone*) far rimbalzare; (*subj: bird, plane*): **to skim the water/ground** sfiorare *or* rasentare l'acqua/il suolo
■ VI: **to skim across** *or* **along** sfiorare; **the boat skimmed over the waves** la barca sfiorava le onde; **the stone skimmed across the ice** il sasso rimbalzò sul ghiaccio; **to skim through a book** (*fig*) scorrere *or* dare una scorsa a un libro
skimmed milk [,skɪmd'mɪlk] N latte *m* scremato
ski mountaineering N sci-alpinismo
skimp [skɪmp] VI: **to skimp on** (*material etc*) risparmiare; (*work*) raffazzonare; (*refreshments*) lesinare
skimpi·ly ['skɪmpɪlɪ] ADV (*dressed*) in modo succinto; (*provided*) insufficientemente
skimpi·ness ['skɪmpɪnɪs] N (*of skirt*) scarsa ampiezza; (*of allowance*) esiguità; (*of meal*) frugalità
skimpy ['skɪmpɪ] ADJ (*comp* **-ier**, *superl* **-iest**) (*skirt etc*) striminzito(-a), succinto(-a); (*hem*) piccolo(-a); (*allowance*) misero(-a); (*meal*) frugale
◎ **skin** [skɪn] N **1** (*gen*) pelle *f*; (*of fruit, vegetable*) buccia; (*of boat, aircraft*) rivestimento; (*for duplicating*) matrice *f* per duplicatori; (*crust: on paint, milk pudding: thin*) pellicola; (: *thick*) crosta; **next to the skin** a contatto con la pelle; **to have a thick/thin skin** (*fig*) non essere/essere suscettibile; **by the skin of one's teeth** (*fig*) per un pelo; **wet** *or* **soaked to the skin** bagnato(-a) fino al midollo; **to be (all) skin and bone** (*fig*) essere pelle e ossa; **to get under sb's skin** (*fig*) dare sui nervi a qn; **I've got you under my skin** (*fig*) ti ho nella pelle; **it's no skin off my nose** (*fig fam: does not concern me*) non sono affari miei; (: *does not hurt me*) non mi costa niente **2** (*fam*) = **skinhead**
■ VT (*animal*) spellare, scuoiare, scorticare; (*fruit etc*) sbucciare, pelare; **to skin one's knee/elbow** sbucciarsi *or* scorticarsi un ginocchio/gomito; **I'll skin him alive!** (*fig*) lo scortico vivo!; **keep your eyes skinned for a garage** tieni gli occhi aperti per un distributore
skin cancer N cancro alla pelle
skin care, **skincare** ['skɪnkɛəʳ] N cura della pelle; **skincare products** prodotti *mpl* per la cura della pelle
skin colour N colore *m* della pelle
skin cream N crema (per il viso)
skin-deep [,skɪn'di:p] ADJ (*also fig*) superficiale
skin disease N malattia della pelle, dermatosi *f inv*
skin diver N sub *m/f*
skin diving N nuoto subacqueo
skin·flick ['skɪn,flɪk] N (*fam*) film porno *inv*
skin·flint ['skɪn,flɪnt] N taccagno(-a), spilorcio(-a)

skin·ful ['skɪnfʊl] N (*fam*): **to have (had) a skinful** aver fatto il pieno
skin graft N innesto epidermico
skin·head ['skɪn,hɛd] N testa rasata, skinhead *m/f*
skin·ny ['skɪnɪ] ADJ (*comp* **-ier**, *superl* **-iest**) (*usu pej*: *person*) magro(-a), gracile, mingherlino(-a); (*jumper*) striminzito(-a); (*milk*) magro(-a), scremato(-a)
■ N: **the skinny** (*Am fam*) le ultime (notizie)
skinny dipping N bagno senza vestiti
skint [skɪnt] ADJ (*Brit fam*): **to be skint** essere in bolletta, essere al verde
skin test N prova di reazione cutanea
skin·tight ['skɪn,taɪt] ADJ aderente come una seconda pelle
skip[1] [skɪp] N saltello, balzo
■ VI saltellare, salterellare; (*with rope*) saltare con la corda; **to skip in/out** *etc* entrare/uscire *etc* saltellando; **to skip off** (*fig*) tagliare la corda; **to skip over sth** (*fig*) sorvolare su qc; **to skip from one subject to another** saltare da un argomento a un altro
■ VT (*fig*: *meal, lesson, page*) saltare; (: *school*) marinare, bigiare; **let's skip it!** (*fam*) sorvoliamo!; **you should never skip breakfast** non si dovrebbe mai saltare la colazione; **to skip school** marinare la scuola
skip[2] [skɪp] N benna
ski pants NPL pantaloni *mpl* da sci
ski pass N ski-pass *m inv*
ski·plane ['ski:,pleɪn] N aeroplano munito di sci
ski pole N = **ski stick**
skip·per ['skɪpəʳ] N (*Sport, Naut*) capitano; (*in boat race*) skipper *m inv*
■ VT (*boat*) essere al comando di; (*sports team*) capitanare
skip·ping ['skɪpɪŋ] N salto della corda
skipping rope N (*Brit*) corda per saltare
ski rack N (*Aut*) portascì *m inv*
ski resort N località *f inv or* stazione *f* sciistica
skir·mish ['skɜ:mɪʃ] N scaramuccia
skirt [skɜ:t] N gonna
■ VT **1** (*road, path*) fiancheggiare, costeggiare **2** (*person*: *also*: **skirt around**: *town, table*) girare intorno a; (: *obstacle, difficulty*) aggirare; (: *argument, subject*) schivare
skirt hanger N reggigonne *m inv*
skirt·ing ['skɜ:tɪŋ], **skirt·ing board** N (*Brit*) zoccolo, battiscopa *m inv*
ski run, ski slope N pista da sci
ski school N scuola di sci
ski stick, ski pole N racchetta da sci
ski suit N tuta da sci
skit [skɪt] N (*Theatre*) sketch *m inv* satirico
ski tow N sciovia, ski-lift *m inv*
skit·ter ['skɪtəʳ] VI: **to skitter around** *or* **about** (*bird, leaf*) svolazzare; (*dog*) scorrazzare
skit·tish ['skɪtɪʃ] ADJ (*horse, person*) ombroso(-a)
skit·tle ['skɪtl] N birillo; **skittles** NPL (*game*) (gioco dei) birilli *mpl*; **to play skittles** giocare a birilli; **it isn't all beer and skittles** (*fam*) non è tutto rose e fiori
skive [skaɪv] VI (*Brit fam*) fare il/la lavativo(-a); **it's Monday morning, and she's skiving as usual** è lunedì mattina e come al solito fa la lavativa; **to skive off** svignarsela, filarsela; **to skive off school** marinare la scuola
skiv·er ['skaɪvəʳ] N (*fam*) lavativo(-a), scansafatiche *m/f inv*
skiv·vy ['skɪvɪ] N (*esp Brit fam pej*) sguattera

skul·dug·gery, (*Am*) **skull·dug·gery** [skʌl'dʌgərɪ] N (*fam*) imbrogli *mpl*, manovre *fpl*
skulk [skʌlk] VI (*also*: **skulk about**) aggirarsi furtivamente; **to skulk into/out of** entrare/uscire furtivamente
skull [skʌl] N (*of live person*) cranio; (*of dead person*) teschio; (*fam*: *head*) testa, testona; **skull and crossbones** (*danger warning*) teschio; (*flag*) bandiera dei pirati
skull·cap ['skʌl,kæp] N (*worn by Jews*) zucchetto; (*worn by Pope*) papalina
skull·dug·gery [skʌl'dʌgərɪ] N (*Am*) = **skulduggery**
skunk [skʌŋk] N (*Zool*) moffetta, puzzola; **you skunk!** (*fam*) farabutto!, carogna!
◎ **sky** [skaɪ] N cielo; **to sleep under the open sky** dormire sotto le stelle *or* all'aperto; **to praise sb to the skies** portare alle stelle qn; **the sky's the limit** (*fig fam*) non ci sono limiti
sky-blue [,skaɪ'blu:] N azzurro
■ ADJ azzurro(-a)
sky·div·er ['skaɪdaɪvəʳ] N paracadutista *m/f* acrobatico(-a)
sky-diving ['skaɪ,daɪvɪŋ] N paracadutismo in caduta libera
sky-high [,skaɪ'haɪ] ADV (*throw*) molto in alto; **to blow sth sky-high** far saltare in aria qc; **to blow a theory sky-high** confutare una teoria; **prices have gone sky-high** i prezzi sono saliti alle stelle
■ ADJ (*fam*) esorbitante
sky·jack ['skaɪ,dʒæk] VT (*aircraft*) dirottare
sky·jack·er ['skaɪ,dʒækəʳ] N pirata *m* dell'aria, dirottatore(-trice)
Sky·lab ['skaɪlæb] N laboratorio spaziale
sky·lark ['skaɪ,lɑ:k] N (*bird*) allodola
■ VI (*fig fam*) fare il matto(-a)
sky·light ['skaɪ,laɪt] N lucernario
sky·line ['skaɪlaɪn] N (*horizon*) orizzonte *m*; (*of city*) profilo
sky marshal N agente *m/f* armato a bordo (*di aereo*)
sky·scraper ['skaɪ,skreɪpəʳ] N grattacielo
sky·ward(s) ['skaɪwəd(z)] ADJ (*glance*) al cielo; (*shot*) in aria
■ ADV (*look*) verso il cielo; (*shoot*) in aria
sky·writing ['skaɪ,raɪtɪŋ] N pubblicità aerea
slab [slæb] N (*of stone, metal*) lastra; (*of wood*) tavola; (*of chocolate*) tavoletta; (*of meat, cheese*) pezzo; (*fam*: *in mortuary*) tavolo anatomico; **a concrete slab** una lastra di cemento
slack [slæk] ADJ (*comp* **-er**, *superl* **-est**) **1** (*not tight*: *rope, knot*) lento(-a), allentato(-a); (: *grip*) debole **2** (*lax*: *work*) trascurato(-a); (: *student, worker*) negligente; (*lazy*) pigro(-a), fiacco(-a); **to be slack about one's work** essere negligente nel proprio lavoro; **to grow slack** lasciarsi andare **3** (*Comm*: *market*) stagnante; (: *demand*) scarso(-a); (*period*) morto(-a); **business is slack** si fanno pochi affari; **the slack season** la bassa stagione
■ N **1** (*part of rope etc*): **to take up the slack in a rope** tendere una corda **2** (*coal dust*) polvere *f* di carbone; *see also* **slacks**
■ VI (*fam*) fare il/la lavativo(-a)
■ VT (*Naut*: *sail*) lascare
▶ **slack off** VI + ADV (*fam*: *activity etc*) ridursi, calare
slack·en ['slækn] (*also*: **slacken off**) VT (*rope, grip, reins, nut*) allentare; (*pressure*) diminuire; **to slacken speed** ridurre la velocità; **to slacken one's pace** rallentare il passo

Ss

■VI (*gen*) allentarsi; (*pressure, speed, activity*) diminuire, rallentare; (*gale*) placarsi; (*trade*) calare, ridursi

slack·er ['slækəʳ] N (*fam*) lavativo(-a), pelandrone(-a)

slack·ness ['slæknɪs] N (*of rope, cable*) mancanza di tensione; (*of person*) negligenza; (*of trade*) ristagno

slacks [slæks] NPL pantaloni *mpl* casual *inv*

slag [slæg] N **1** (*waste: from coal mine, smelting*) scorie *fpl* **2** (*Brit fam offensive*) puttana

■VT (*Brit fam*): **to slag sb/sth off** sputtanare qn/qc

slag heap N cumulo di scorie

slain [sleɪn] PP *of* **slay**

■NPL (*liter*): **the slain** i caduti

slake [sleɪk] VT (*liter: one's thirst*) spegnere

sla·lom ['slɑːləm] (*Sport*) N slalom *m inv*; **special slalom** slalom speciale

■VI fare lo slalom

slam [slæm] N **1** (*of door*) colpo **2** (*Bridge*) slam *m inv*; **grand slam** (*Cards, Sport*) grande slam

■VT **1** (*door, lid*) sbattere; **to slam sth shut** chiudere qc sbattendolo(-a); **to slam down the phone** buttare giù la cornetta; **to slam sth (down) on the table** sbattere qc sul tavolo; **to slam on the brakes** frenare di colpo; **to slam the door (in sb's face)** sbattere la porta (in faccia a qn); **she slammed the door** ha sbattuto la porta **2** (*criticize*) stroncare

■VI (*door, lid*) sbattere

slam-dunk [ˌslæm'dʌŋk] (*Basketball*) VT schiacciare

■VI effettuare una schiacciata

slam·mer ['slæməʳ] N (*fam*): **the slammer** la gattabuia

slan·der ['slɑːndəʳ] N calunnia; (*Law*) diffamazione *f*

■VT calunniare; (*Law*) diffamare

slan·der·ous ['slɑːndərəs] ADJ calunnioso(-a); (*Law*) diffamatorio(-a)

slan·der·ous·ly ['slɑːndərəslɪ] ADV calunniosamente

slang [slæŋ] N (*gen*) slang *m inv*, gergo; **school/army slang** gergo studentesco/militare; **to talk slang** parlare in gergo

■ADJ (*word*) gergale

■VT (*fam: insult, criticize*) dirne di tutti i colori a

slang·ing match ['slæŋɪŋˌmætʃ] N (*Brit fam*) rissa verbale

slangy ['slæŋɪ] ADJ (*comp* **-ier**, *superl* **-iest**) (*fam*) gergale

slant [slɑːnt] N pendenza, inclinazione *f*; (*Geom*) apotema *m*; (*fig: point of view*) punto di vista, angolazione *f*; **to be on a slant** essere inclinato(-a); **the house is on a slant** la casa è in pendenza; **a different slant** un punto di vista diverso; **to give a new slant on sth** presentare qc sotto una nuova angolazione; **to get a new slant on sth** vedere qc da un'altra angolazione

■VT (*roof etc*) inclinare; **to slant a report** (*fig*) dare una versione distorta *or* tendenziosa dei fatti

■VI essere inclinato(-a), pendere

slant·ed ['slɑːntɪd] ADJ (*programme, report*) tendenzioso(-a)

slant-eyed ['slɑːntˌaɪd] ADJ (*pej*) dagli occhi a mandorla

slant·ing ['slɑːntɪŋ] ADJ (*handwriting*) inclinato(-a); (*roof*) spiovente; (*line*) obliquo(-a); (*rain*) che cade di traverso

slant·wise ['slɑːntˌwaɪz], **slant·ways** ['slɑːntˌweɪz] ADJ, ADV di traverso

slap [slæp] N schiaffo, ceffone *m*; **a slap in the face** uno schiaffo; (*fig*) uno schiaffo morale; **a slap on the wrist** (*fig*) una tirata d'orecchi; **a slap on the back** una pacca sulla spalla

■ADV (*fam*): **to run slap into** (*tree, lamppost*) colpire in pieno; (*person*) imbattersi in; **it fell slap in the middle** cadde proprio nel mezzo

■VT **1** schiaffeggiare; **to slap a child's bottom** sculacciare un bambino; **to slap sb on the back** dare una pacca sulla spalla a qn; **to slap sb down** (*fig: child*) zittire; (*: opposition*) stroncare **2** **he slapped the book on the table** ha sbattuto il libro sul tavolo; **slap a coat of paint on it** dagli una mano di vernice

■VI: **to slap against** andare a sbattere contro; **the waves slapped against the pier** le onde si infrangevano sul molo

slap-bang [ˌslæp'bæŋ] ADV (*esp Brit fam*): **he ran slap-bang into the door** ha preso in pieno la porta

slap·dash ['slæpˌdæʃ], **slap·happy** ['slæpˌhæpɪ] ADJ (*person*) negligente; (*work*) raffazzonato(-a); **a slapdash piece of work** un lavoro raffazzonato; **a slapdash person** una persona negligente

slap·head ['slæpˌhɛd] N (*Brit fam*): **to be a slaphead** essere pelato(-a)

slap·stick ['slæpˌstɪk] N (*also:* **slapstick comedy**) farsa grossolana

slap-up ['slæpˌʌp] ADJ (*Brit fam*): **a slap-up meal** un pasto coi fiocchi *or* da leccarsi i baffi

slash [slæʃ] N **1** (*slit*) taglio; (*: in dress, skirt*) spacco; (*stroke: of sword, whip*) colpo **2** (*Typ: also:* **slash mark**) barra

■VT (*with knife: gen*) tagliare, squarciare; (*: face, painting*) sfregiare; (*with whip, stick*) sferzare; (*fig: prices*) ridurre fortemente; **to slash one's wrists** tagliarsi le vene; **I found my tyres slashed** ho trovato le gomme tagliate; **they're slashing prices** stanno riducendo drasticamente i prezzi

slat [slæt] N (*of wood*) stecca; (*of plastic*) lamina

slate [sleɪt] N **1** (*rock*) ardesia; (*tile*) tegola (d'ardesia); (*writing tablet*) lavagnetta; **to wipe the slate clean** (*fig*) metterci una pietra sopra; **to put sth on sb's slate** mettere qc sul conto di qn; **a missing slate** una tegola d'ardesia mancante **2** (*Am Pol*) lista di candidati

■VT **1** (*roof*) coprire con tegole **2** (*fam: criticize*) criticare, stroncare

■ADJ di ardesia; **a slate roof** un tetto d'ardesia

slate-blue [ˌsleɪt'bluː] ADJ blu ardesia *inv*

slate-coloured ['sleɪt ˌkʌləd] ADJ plumbeo(-a)

slate-grey [ˌsleɪt'greɪ] ADJ grigio ardesia *inv*; (*sky, storm clouds*) plumbeo(-a)

slat·ted ['slætɪd] ADJ a stecche

slat·tern ['slætən] N (*old pej*) sciattona

slaugh·ter ['slɔːtəʳ] N (*of animals*) macellazione *f*; (*of people*) strage *f*, massacro, carneficina

■VT (*animals*) macellare; (*people*) trucidare, massacrare; (*fig*) distruggere, massacrare

slaughter·house ['slɔːtəˌhaʊs] N macello, mattatoio

Slav [slɑːv] ADJ, N slavo(-a)

slave [sleɪv] N schiavo(-a); **to be a slave to sth** (*fig*) essere schiavo(-a) di qc; **to be a slave of habit** essere schiavo(-a) delle abitudini

■VI: **to slave (away) at sth/at doing sth** sgobbare per qc/per fare qc

slave-driver ['sleɪvˌdraɪvəʳ] N sorvegliante *m* di schiavi; (*fig*) schiavista *m/f*

slave labour N lavoro fatto dagli schiavi; **we're just slave labour here** (*fig*) siamo solamente sfruttati qui dentro

slav·er¹ ['slævəʳ] VI (*dribble*) sbavare

slav·er² ['sleɪvəʳ] N (*person*) schiavista *m/f*

slav·ery ['sleɪvərɪ] N (*condition*) schiavitù *f*; (*system*) schiavismo; **to reduce to slavery** schiavizzare

slave trade N tratta degli schiavi
▷ www.spartacus.schoolnet.co.uk/slavery.htm
▷ http://webworld.unesco.org/slave_quest/en

slav·ey [sleɪvɪ] N (*old fam*) serva

slav·ish ['sleɪvɪʃ] ADJ (*pej: devotion*) servile; (*: imitation*) pedissequo(-a)

slav·ish·ly ['sleɪvɪʃlɪ] ADV (*see adj*) servilmente; pedissequamente

Sla·von·ic [slə'vɒnɪk], **Slav·ic** (*Am*) ['slɑ:vɪk] ADJ, N slavo(-a)

slaw [slɔ:] N (*Am*) insalata di cavolo bianco, carote e altre verdure con maionese

slay [sleɪ] (*pt* **slew**, *pp* **slain**) VT (*liter: kill*) uccidere

SLD [ˌɛsɛl'di:] N ABBR (*Brit Pol:* = **Social and Liberal Democrats**) *nome originario dei Liberal Democrats*

sleaze [sli:z] (*fam*) N (*corruption*) corruzione *f*; **the sleaze factor** la questione morale; (*sordidness*) sordidezza

slea·zy ['sli:zɪ] ADJ (*comp* **-ier**, *superl* **-iest**) squallido(-a), infimo(-a)

sledge [slɛdʒ] N (*also:* **sled**) slitta
■ VI: **to go sledging** andare in slitta; **to sledge down a hill** scendere in slitta giù per una collina

sledge·hammer ['slɛdʒˌhæməʳ] N mazza

sleek [sli:k] ADJ (*comp* **-er**, *superl* **-est**) (*shiny: hair, coat*) liscio(-a) e lucente; (*cat*) dal pelo lucido; (*person: in appearance*) azzimato(-a); (*: in manner*) untuoso(-a); (*car, boat*) elegante
■ VT: **to sleek one's hair down/back** lisciarsi i capelli

sleek·ly ['sli:klɪ] ADV (*answer*) in modo untuoso

◎ **sleep** [sli:p] (*vb: pt, pp* **slept**) N sonno; **deep** *or* **sound sleep** sonno profondo; **a couple of hours' sleep** un paio di ore di sonno; **to have a good night's sleep** farsi una bella dormita; **to drop off** *or* **go to sleep** addormentarsi; **to go to sleep** (*limb*) intorpidirsi; **to put to sleep** (*patient*) anestetizzare; (*animal: euph: kill*) abbattere; **to talk in one's sleep** parlare nel sonno; **to walk in one's sleep** camminare nel sonno; (*as a habit*) essere sonnambulo(-a); **to send sb to sleep** (*bore*) far addormentare qn; **I shan't lose any sleep over it** (*fig*) non starò a perderci il sonno
■ VT: **we can sleep four** abbiamo quattro posti letto, possiamo alloggiare quattro persone; **the villa sleeps ten** la villa può alloggiare dieci persone
■ VI dormire; **I couldn't sleep last night** ieri notte non riuscivo a dormire; **the baby slept during the journey** il bambino ha dormito lungo il tragitto; **to sleep like a log** *or* **top** dormire della grossa *or* come un ghiro; **he was sleeping soundly** *or* **deeply** era profondamente addormentato; **to sleep lightly** avere il sonno leggero; **let's sleep on it** (*fig*) la notte porta consiglio, dormiamoci sopra; **sleep tight!** sogni d'oro!; **I slept through the storm/alarm clock** non ho sentito il temporale/la sveglia; **he slept at his mother's** ha dormito dalla mamma; **to sleep with sb** (*euph: have sex*) andare a letto con qn
▸ **sleep around** VI + ADV (*fam*) andare a letto con tutti
▸ **sleep in** VI + ADV (*lie late*) alzarsi tardi; (*oversleep*) dormire fino a tardi
▸ **sleep off** VT + ADV: **to sleep sth off** smaltire qc dormendo
▸ **sleep out** VI + ADV dormire all'aperto

sleep·er ['sli:pəʳ] N **1** (*person*) dormiente *m/f*; **to be a heavy/light sleeper** avere il sonno pesante/leggero **2** (*Brit Rail: track*) traversina; (*: berth*) cuccetta; (*: coach*) vagone *m* letto *inv* **3** (*earring*) campanella

sleepi·ly ['sli:pɪlɪ] ADV con aria assonnata

sleepi·ness ['sli:pɪnɪs] N (*of person, village*) sonnolenza

sleep·ing ['sli:pɪŋ] ADJ addormentato(-a); **the Sleeping Beauty** la Bella Addormentata nel bosco; **let sleeping dogs lie** (*Proverb*) non svegliare il can che dorme

sleeping bag N sacco a pelo

sleeping car N (*Rail*) vagone *m* letto *inv*

sleeping partner N (*Brit Comm*) socio inattivo

sleeping pill N sonnifero

sleeping policeman N (*esp Brit*) dosso artificiale (*per far diminuire la velocità*)

sleeping quarters NPL dormitorio *msg*, camerata *fsg*

sleeping sickness N malattia del sonno

sleep·less ['sli:plɪs] ADJ (*person*) insonne; (*night*) in bianco, insonne

sleep·less·ly ['sli:plɪslɪ] ADV senza dormire

sleep·less·ness ['sli:plɪsnɪs] N insonnia

sleep·over ['sli:pəʊvəʳ] N *notte che un ragazzino o una ragazzina passa da amici*

sleep·walk ['sli:pˌwɔ:k] VI camminare nel sonno; (*as a habit*) essere sonnambulo(-a); **she sleepwalks** soffre di sonnambulismo, è sonnambula

sleep·walk·er ['sli:pˌwɔ:kəʳ] N sonnambulo(-a)

sleep·walk·ing ['sli:pˌwɔ:kɪŋ] N sonnambulismo

sleepy ['sli:pɪ] ADJ (*comp* **-ier**, *superl* **-iest**) (*person, voice, look*) assonnato(-a), sonnolento(-a); (*village*) addormentato(-a); **to be** *or* **feel sleepy** avere sonno

sleepy·head ['sli:pɪˌhɛd] N (*fam*) dormiglione(-a); **go to bed, sleepyhead!** va' a letto che stai dormendo in piedi!

sleet [sli:t] N nevischio
■ VI: **it was sleeting** nevischiava

sleeve [sli:v] N (*of garment*) manica; (*of record*) copertina; **to roll up one's sleeves** rimboccarsi le maniche; **to have sth up one's sleeve** (*fig*) avere in serbo qc

sleeve·board ['sli:vˌbɔ:d] N stiramaniche *m inv*

-sleeved [sli:vd] SUFF: **short/long-sleeved** con le maniche corte/lunghe

sleeve·less ['sli:vlɪs] ADJ (*garment*) senza maniche

sleigh [sleɪ] N slitta

sleight [slaɪt] N: **sleight of hand** (*trick*) gioco di destrezza; (*fig*) trucchetto

slen·der ['slɛndəʳ] ADJ (*person*) snello(-a), slanciato(-a); (*waist, neck, hand*) sottile; (*fig: resources, majority*) scarso(-a), esiguo(-a); (*: hope, chance*) piccolo(-a), scarso(-a)

slen·der·ness ['slɛndənɪs] N (*of person*) snellezza; (*of waist, neck, hand*) sottigliezza

slept [slɛpt] PT, PP *of* **sleep**

sleuth [slu:θ] N (*hum*) segugio

slew¹ [slu:] PT *of* **slay**

slew², (*Am*) **slue** [slu:] VI (*also:* **slew round**) rigirarsi

slewed [slu:d] ADJ (*Brit old fam*) sbronzo(-a)

◎ **slice** [slaɪs] N **1** (*of meat etc*) fetta; (*of lemon, cucumber*) fettina; **a slice of the profits** (*fig*) una fetta dei profitti; **a slice of life** (*fig*) uno scorcio di vita **2** (*tool*) paletta
■ VT (*meat etc*) affettare, tagliare a fette; (*rope etc*) tagliare di netto; (*Sport: ball*) tagliare; **to slice sth thickly/thinly** affettare qc grosso/sottile; **sliced loaf** *or* **bread** pane *m* a cassetta
▸ **slice off** VT + ADV tagliare (via)
▸ **slice through** VI + PREP tagliare di netto; (*fig: the air, waves*) fendere
▸ **slice up** VT + ADV affettare

slic·er ['slaɪsəʳ] N affettatrice *f*

Ss

slick [slɪk] ADJ (*comp* **-er**, *superl* **-est**) (*adroitly executed: show, performance*) brillante; (*pej: answer, excuse*) troppo pronto(-a); (*: person: glib*) dalla parlantina sciolta; (*: cunning*) scaltro(-a); (*: insincere*) untuoso(-a); **a slick character** una dritto(-a)
■ N (*also:* **oil slick**) chiazza di petrolio
■ VT (*also:* **slick down**: *hair: with comb*) lisciare; (*: with haircream*) impomatare

slick·ly [slɪklɪ] ADV (*answer*) abilmente, prontamente

slid PT, PP *of* **slide**

◎ **slide** [slaɪd] (*vb: pt, pp* **slid**) N **1** (*action: on ice, mud etc*) scivolone *m*; (*fig: in temperature, profits*) caduta; **the slide in share prices** la caduta del prezzo delle azioni **2** (*in playground, swimming pool*) scivolo; **some swings and a slide** alcune altalene ed uno scivolo **3** (*landslide*) frana **4** (*Brit: also:* **hair slide**) fermacapelli *m inv* **5** (*also:* **microscope slide**) vetrino; (*Phot*) diapositiva; **he showed us his slides** ci ha mostrato le sue diapositive
■ VI scivolare; **these drawers slide in and out easily** questi cassetti scorrono bene; **to slide down the banisters** scivolare giù per il corrimano; **to let things slide** (*fig*) trascurare tutto
■ VT (*box, case*) far scivolare; (*bolt*) far scorrere; **he slid the gun from its holster** ha tirato la pistola fuori dalla custodia

slide projector N (*Phot*) proiettore *m* per diapositive

slide rule N (*Math*) regolo calcolatore

slide show N (*Phot*) proiezione *f* di diapositive

slid·ing [ˈslaɪdɪŋ] ADJ (*part, seat*) mobile; (*door*) scorrevole; **sliding roof** (*Aut*) capotte *f inv*

sliding scale N (*Admin etc*) scala mobile

◎ **slight** [slaɪt] ADJ (*comp* **-er**, *superl* **-est**) **1** (*person: slim*) minuto(-a); (*: frail*) gracile, delicato(-a) **2** (*trivial: cold*) leggero(-a); (*: error*) piccolo(-a), insignificante; **a slight pain in the arm** un leggero dolore al braccio **3** (*small*) piccolo(-a), leggero(-a); **a slight improvement** un leggero miglioramento; **a slight problem** un piccolo problema; **there's not the slightest possibility** non c'è la minima possibilità; **there's not the slightest danger** non c'è il benché minimo pericolo; **not in the slightest** per nulla, niente affatto
■ N offesa, affronto
■ VT (*person*) snobbare, ignorare

slight·ed [ˈslaɪtɪd] ADJ offeso(-a); **to feel slighted** sentirsi offeso(-a)

slight·ing [ˈslaɪtɪŋ] ADJ offensivo(-a)

slight·ing·ly [ˈslaɪtɪŋlɪ] ADV offensivamente

◎ **slight·ly** [ˈslaɪtlɪ] ADV **1** (*better, nervous*) leggermente; **they are slightly more expensive** sono leggermente più costosi; **I know her slightly** la conosco appena **2** **slightly built** esile

◎ **slim** [slɪm] ADJ (*comp* **-mer**, *superl* **-mest**) **1** (*figure, person*) magro(-a), snello(-a); (*ankle, wrist, book*) sottile **2** (*fig: resources*) scarso(-a), magro(-a); (*: evidence*) insufficiente; (*: excuse*) magro(-a); (*: hope*) poco(-a); **a slim chance** una scarsa possibilità; **his chances are pretty slim** le sue possibilità sono molto scarse
■ VI dimagrire, fare *or* seguire una dieta dimagrante; **she's trying to slim** sta cercando di dimagrire

slime [slaɪm] N (*mud*) melma; (*sticky substance*) sostanza viscida; (*of snail*) bava

slimi·ness [ˈslaɪmɪnɪs] N (*also fig: of person*) viscidità

slim·mer [ˈslɪməʳ] N chi è a dieta

slim·ming [ˈslɪmɪŋ] ADJ (*diet, pills*) dimagrante; (*food*) ipocalorico(-a)

slim·ness [ˈslɪmnɪs] N (*goal of slimmer*) l'essere magro(-a); (*of ankle, wrist, book*) sottigliezza; (*fig: of resources*) scarsità, insufficienza

slimy [ˈslaɪmɪ] ADJ (*comp* **-ier**, *superl* **-iest**) (*also fig: person*) viscido(-a); (*covered with mud*) melmoso(-a)

sling [slɪŋ] (*vb: pt, pp* **slung**) N (*weapon*) fionda; (*catapult*) catapulta; (*Med*) fascia a tracolla; (*Mountaineering*) anello di fettuccia; **to have one's arm in a sling** avere un braccio al collo
■ VT (*fam: throw*) scagliare, buttare; (*hang: hammock*) appendere; **he slung his bag onto the back seat** ha buttato la borsa sul sedile posteriore; **to sling over** *or* **across one's shoulder** (*rifle, load*) mettere in spalla; (*coat, shawl*) buttarsi sulle spalle
▸ **sling out** VT + ADV (*fam: object*) buttare via; (*: person*) buttare fuori

slink [slɪŋk] (*pt, pp* **slunk**) VI: **to slink away, slink off** svignarsela

slinki·ly [ˈslɪŋkɪlɪ] ADV (*fam: dressed*) con abiti attillati

slink·ing [ˈslɪŋkɪŋ] ADJ (*movement*) furtivo(-a)

slinky [ˈslɪŋkɪ] ADJ (*comp* **-ier**, *superl* **-iest**) (*fam: dress*) aderente, attillato(-a); (*: movement*) sinuoso(-a)

◎ **slip** [slɪp] N **1** (*downward slide*) scivolata; (*trip*) scivolone *m* **2** (*also:* **landslip**) smottamento **3** (*mistake*) errore *m*, sbaglio; (*moral*) sbaglio; **a slip of the tongue** un lapsus linguae; **a slip of the pen** un lapsus calami; **a Freudian slip** un lapsus freudiano; **there must be no slips** non ci devono essere sbagli **4** (*petticoat*) sottoveste *f*; **a white slip** una sottoveste bianca **5** (*also:* **pillowslip**) federa **6** (*small receipt, bill*) scontrino; **a slip of paper** un foglietto; **pay slip** busta paga; **a slip of a girl** (*fig*) una ragazzina minuta **7** (*fam*): **to give sb the slip** seminare qn; *see also* **slips**
■ VI **1** (*slide*) scivolare; **I slipped** sono scivolato; **he slipped on the ice** è scivolato sul ghiaccio; **my foot slipped** mi è scivolato un piede; **it slipped from** *or* **out of her hand** le sfuggì di mano; **to slip into bad habits** prendere delle cattive abitudini; **he let (it) slip that ...** si è lasciato sfuggire che...; **to let a chance slip through one's fingers** lasciarsi scappare un'occasione; **you're slipping!** (*fig fam*) perdi colpi! **2** (*move quickly*): **to slip into/out of** sgattaiolare dentro/fuori da; **to slip into a dress** infilarsi un vestito; **the months/years have slipped by** i mesi/gli anni sono passati
■ VT **1** (*slide*) far scivolare; **to slip a coin into a slot** infilare una moneta in una fessura; **to slip sb a tenner** allungare dieci sterline a qn; **to slip an arm round sb's waist** mettere il braccio attorno alla vita di qn; **to slip on/off a jumper** infilarsi/sfilarsi un maglione **2** (*escape*) sfuggire a; **the dog slipped its collar** il cane si liberò dal collare; **it slipped my memory** *or* **attention** *or* **mind** mi è sfuggito
▸ **slip away, slip off** VI + ADV svignarsela
▸ **slip in** VT + ADV (*object*) far scivolare in (*or* dentro); (*reference, remark*) aggiungere en passant
▸ **slip out** VI + ADV (*thief*) svignarsela; (*guest*) andarsene alla chetichella; (*secret, word*) sfuggire; **to slip out to the shops** fare una scappatina per la spesa; **it slipped out that ...** è saltato fuori che...
▸ **slip up** VI + ADV (*fam*) sbagliarsi

slip·case [ˈslɪpˌkeɪs] N (*of book*) custodia

slip·cover [ˈslɪpˌkʌvəʳ] N (*Am*) fodera

slip·knot [ˈslɪpˌnɒt] N nodo scorsoio

slip-on [ˈslɪpˌɒn] ADJ (*gen*) comodo(-a) da mettere; (*shoes*) senza allacciatura

slip·over [ˈslɪpəʊvəʳ] N pullover *m inv* senza maniche

slipped disc [ˌslɪptˈdɪsk] N (*Med*) ernia del disco

slip·per ['slɪpə^r] N pantofola

slip·pery ['slɪpərɪ] ADJ sdrucciolevole, scivoloso(-a); (*fig pej: person*) viscido(-a); **it's slippery underfoot** il pavimento è scivoloso; **he's as slippery as they come** *or* **as an eel** è un tipo viscido

slip·py ['slɪpɪ] ADJ (*comp* **-ier**, *superl* **-iest**) (*fam*) scivoloso(-a)

slip road N (*Brit: to motorway*) rampa di accesso

slip·shod ['slɪpʃɒd] ADJ sciatto(-a), trascurato(-a)

slip·stream ['slɪp,stri:m] N (*Aer*) risucchio

slip-up ['slɪp,ʌp] N (*fam: mistake*) sbaglio; **there's been a slip-up somewhere** è stato fatto uno sbaglio da qualche parte

slip·way ['slɪp,weɪ] N (*Naut*) scalo

slit [slɪt] (*vb: pt, pp* **slit**) N (*opening*) fessura; (*cut*) taglio; (*tear*) strappo; (*in skirt*) spacco; **a skirt with a slit at the back** una gonna con lo spacco dietro; **she was watching through a slit in the curtains** guardava attraverso una fessura tra le tende

■VT tagliare; **to slit open** (*letter*) aprire; (*sack*) aprire con un taglio; **to slit sb's throat** tagliare la gola a qn

slith·er ['slɪðə^r] VI (*person*) scivolare; (*snake*) strisciare; **he was slithering about on the ice** avanzava slittando sul ghiaccio

sliv·er ['slɪvə^r] N (*of glass, wood*) scheggia; (*of cheese, sausage*) fettina

slob [slɒb] N (*fam*) sciattone(-a)

slob·ber ['slɒbə^r] VI (*pej*) sbavare

▸ **slobber over** VI + PREP sviolinare

sloe [sləʊ] N (*tree*) pruno selvatico; (*fruit*) prugnola

sloe gin N gin *m inv* alle di prugnole

slog [slɒg] N faticata; **it's a hard slog to the top** è una faticaccia arrivare in cima

■VI **1** (*work*) faticare, sgobbare; **to slog away at sth** sgobbare su qc **2** (*walk etc*): **to slog along** avanzare a fatica; **we slogged on for 8 kilometres** ci trascinammo per 8 chilometri

■VT (*ball, opponent*) colpire con forza

slo·gan ['sləʊgən] N slogan *m inv*

slog·ger ['slɒgə^r] N (*hard worker*) sgobbone(-a)

sloop [slu:p] N (*ship*) sloop *m inv*

slop [slɒp] VI (*also:* **slop over**) traboccare, versarsi; **the water was slopping about in the bucket** l'acqua quasi traboccava dal secchio

■VT versare, rovesciare; *see also* **slops**

slope [sləʊp] N **1** (*gen, of hill*) pendio; (*side of hill*) versante *m*; (*of roof*) pendenza; (*of floor*) inclinazione *f*; **a steep slope** un pendio ripido; **on the slopes of Mount Etna** alle falde *or* pendici dell'Etna; **the car got stuck on a slope** la macchina si è bloccata su una salita **2** (*also:* **ski slope**) pista (da sci)

■VI (*path, roof, handwriting*) essere inclinato(-a); **to slope up** essere in salita; **the garden slopes down to the stream** il giardino digrada verso il ruscello

▸ **slope off** VI + ADV (*fam*) filarsela, tagliare la corda

slop·ing ['sləʊpɪŋ] ADJ inclinato(-a)

slop·pi·ly ['slɒpɪlɪ] ADV **1** (*carelessly*) con trascuratezza; **to dress sloppily** essere sciatto(-a) nel vestire **2** (*sentimentally*) in modo sdolcinato

slop·pi·ness ['slɒpɪnɪs] N (*of work, appearance, dress*) sciatteria

slop·py ['slɒpɪ] (*fam*) ADJ (*comp* **-ier**, *superl* **-iest**) **1** (*work*) trascurato(-a); (*appearance, dress*) trasandato(-a), sciatto(-a) **2** (*book, film, letter*) sdolcinato(-a) **3** (*food*) brodoso(-a)

sloppy joe [-dʒəʊ] N (*fam*) maglione *m* informe

slops [slɒps] NPL (*for animals*) pastone *m*; (*dirty water*) acqua sporca; (*: in teacup*) rimasugli *mpl*

slosh [slɒʃ] (*fam*) VT **1** (*liquid*) spargere; **to slosh some water over sth** gettare dell'acqua su qc **2** (*hit: person*) colpire

■VI: **to slosh about in the puddles** sguazzare nelle pozzanghere

sloshed [slɒʃt] ADJ (*fam: drunk*) sbronzo(-a); **to get sloshed** prendere una sbronza

slot [slɒt] N (*in machine etc*) fessura; (*groove*) scanalatura; (*fig: in timetable, Radio, TV*) spazio; **put the money in the slot** inserite il denaro nella fessura

■VT (*object*) infilare; (*fig: activity, speech*) inserire

■VI: **to slot (into)** inserirsi (in)

sloth [sləʊθ] N **1** (*frm: vice*) indolenza **2** (*Zool*) bradipo

sloth·ful ['sləʊθfʊl] ADJ (*frm*) indolente

sloth·ful·ness ['sləʊθfʊlnɪs] N (*frm*) indolenza

slot machine N (*for cigarettes, food*) distributore *m* automatico; (*for amusement*) slot-machine *f inv*

slot meter N contatore *m* a monete

slouch [slaʊtʃ] VI (*when walking*) camminare dinoccolato(-a); **don't slouch!** raddrizza la schiena!, non stare con la schiena curva!; **to slouch in/out** trascinarsi dentro/fuori; **she was slouched in the chair** era stravaccata nella poltrona

■N: **to be no slouch at sth** (*fam*) cavarsela benino in qc

▸ **slouch about, slouch around** VI + ADV (*laze*) oziare

slough off [,slʌf'ɒf] VT + ADV **1** (*subj: snake*): **to slough off its skin** mutare pelle **2** (*liter: abandon: habit*) abbandonare

Slo·vak ['sləʊvæk] ADJ slovacco(-a)

■N (*person*) slovacco(-a); (*language*) slovacco

Slo·vakia [sləʊ'vækɪə] N Slovacchia

Slo·vak·ian [sləʊ'vækɪən] ADJ, N = **Slovak**

Slovak Republic N: **the Slovak Republic** la repubblica slovacca

Slo·vene ['sləʊvi:n] ADJ sloveno(-a)

■N (*person*) sloveno(-a); (*language*) sloveno

Slo·venia [sləʊ'vi:nɪə] N Slovenia

Slo·venian [sləʊ'vi:nɪən] ADJ, N = **Slovene**

slov·en·li·ness ['slʌvnlɪnɪs] N (*of person*) sciatteria; (*of work*) trascuratezza

slov·en·ly ['slʌvnlɪ] ADJ (*person*) sciatto(-a), trasandato(-a); (*work*) trascurato(-a), poco accurato(-a)

◎**slow** [sləʊ] (*comp* **-er**, *superl* **-est**) ADJ **1** (*gen*) lento(-a); **a slow lorry** un camion lento; **at a slow speed** a bassa velocità; **she's a slow worker** lavora lentamente; **this car is slower than my old one** questa macchina è meno veloce di quella che avevo; **to be slow to act/decide** essere lento(-a) ad agire/a decidere; **to be slow to anger** (*liter*) non arrabbiarsi facilmente **2** (*of clock*): **to be slow** essere *or* andare indietro; **the clock's slow** l'orologio è indietro; **my watch is 20 minutes slow** il mio orologio è indietro di 20 minuti **3** (*person: stupid*) lento(-a), tardo(-a); **slow to understand/notice** tardo(-a) a capire/notare; **he's a bit slow at maths** fa un po' di fatica in matematica **4** (*boring, dull: film, play*) lento(-a); (*: party*) poco movimentato(-a); **life here is slow** qui la vita scorre lenta; **the game is very slow** il gioco è molto lento; **business is slow** (*Comm*) gli affari procedono a rilento **5** (*slowing down movement: pitch, track, surface*) pesante; **bake for two hours in a slow oven** cuocere per due ore nel forno a bassa temperatura

■ADV lentamente; **to go slow** (*driver*) andare piano; (*in industrial dispute*) attuare uno sciopero bianco; (*be*

Ss

cautious) andare con i piedi di piombo; **go slower!** vai più piano!; **"(go) slow"** "rallentare"
■ VT (*also:* **slow down, slow up**: *progress, machine*) rallentare; (: *person*) far rallentare; (: *pace of novel etc*) rendere più lento(-a); **the interruptions have slowed us down** le interruzioni ci hanno fatto perdere tempo; **that car slows up the traffic** quella macchina fa rallentare il traffico
■ VI (*also:* **slow down, slow up**) rallentare; **production has slowed to almost nothing** la produzione si è ridotta a livelli minimi

slow-acting ['sləʊ,æktɪŋ] ADJ che agisce lentamente, ad azione lenta

slow·coach ['sləʊ,kəʊtʃ] N (*fam: dawdler*) lumaca; (: *dullard*) testone(-a)

slow·down ['sləʊ,daʊn] N rallentamento

slow food N slow food *m*

slow lane N (*Brit: on road*) corsia per il traffico lento; (*situation*): **to be in the slow lane** essere rallentato(-a)

slow·ly ['sləʊlɪ] ADV lentamente; **to drive slowly** andare piano; **slowly but surely** a poco a poco ma in modo certo; **work is proceeding slowly but surely** il lavoro procede piano ma bene; **to go more slowly** rallentare

slow motion N: **in slow motion** al rallentatore

slow-moving ['sləʊ'mu:vɪŋ] ADJ (*vehicle, traffic*) lento(-a)

slow·ness ['sləʊnɪs] N lentezza

slow·poke ['sləʊ,pəʊk] N (*Am fam*) = **slowcoach**

slow-witted [,sləʊ'wɪtɪd] ADJ tardo(-a), ottuso(-a)

slow·worm ['sləʊ,wɜ:m] N orbettino

sludge [slʌdʒ] N (*mud, sediment*) melma; (*sewage*) deposito di fognatura

slue [slu:] (*Am*) N = **slew²**

slug [slʌg] N (*Zool*) lumaca; (*esp Am fam: bullet*) pallottola; (*fam: blow*) colpo; (: *large mouthful*) sorsata; **a slug of whisky** (*fam*) un bicchierino di whisky
■ VT (*fam: hit*) colpire

slug·gish ['slʌgɪʃ] ADJ (*indolent*) pigro(-a), fiacco(-a); (*slow-moving: river, engine, car*) lento(-a); (: *business, market, sales*) stagnante, fiacco(-a); **the car is very sluggish** la macchina manca di ripresa

slug·gish·ly ['slʌgɪʃlɪ] ADV (*move*) lentamente, pigramente

slug·gish·ness ['slʌgɪʃnɪs] N (*gen*) lentezza; (*of business, sales*) stasi *f*, ristagno

sluice [slu:s] N (*also:* **sluicegate**) chiusa; (*also:* **sluiceway**) canale *m* di chiusa
■ VT: **to sluice down** *or* **out** lavare con abbondante acqua

slum [slʌm] N (*house*) catapecchia, tugurio; **to live in the slums** vivere nei quartieri bassi

slum area N quartiere *m* povero

slum·ber ['slʌmbəʳ] N (*often pl: liter*) sonno
■ VI dormire (tranquillamente)

slumber party N (*Am*) *notte che un ragazzino o una ragazzina passa da amici*

slum clearance N (*also:* **slum clearance programme**) (programma *m* di) risanamento edilizio

slum·my ['slʌmɪ] ADJ (*buildings*) povero(-a), squallido(-a); (*appearance*) misero(-a)

slump [slʌmp] N (*gen*) caduta, crollo; (*in production, sales*) calo, crollo; (*economic*) crisi *f inv*, depressione *f*; **the slump in the price of copper** il crollo del prezzo del rame; **a slump in property prices** un crollo dei prezzi delle case; **the slump of the early 1980s** la crisi dei primi anni '80
■ VI **1** (*price etc*) cadere, crollare; (*production, sales*) calare, diminuire; (*fig: morale etc*) abbassarsi; **profits have slumped** i profitti sono crollati **2** **to slump into a chair** lasciarsi cadere su una sedia; **he was slumped over the wheel** era accasciato sul volante

slung [slʌŋ] PT, PP *of* **sling**

slunk [slʌŋk] PT, PP *of* **slink**

slur [slɜ:ʳ] N **1** (*stigma*) macchia; (*insult*) diffamazione *f*; **racial slurs** insulti razzisti; **a slur on sb's reputation** una calunnia su qn; **to cast a slur on sb** calunniare qn; **without wishing to cast a slur on his character, I think ...** senza per questo volerlo denigrare, penso che... **2** (*Mus*) legatura
■ VT (*word etc*) farfugliare, pronunciare in modo inarticolato; (*Mus*) legare; **his speech was slurred** biascicava (*perché ubriaco*)

slurp [slɜ:p] VT, VI (*fam*) bere rumorosamente
■ N rumore fatto bevendo

slurred [slɜ:d] ADJ (*speech*) confuso(-a)

slurry ['slʌrɪ] N fanghiglia

slush [slʌʃ] N (*melting snow*) neve *f* sciolta, fanghiglia; (*fam: literature etc*) letteratura *etc* sdolcinata

slush fund N fondi *mpl* neri

slushy ['slʌʃɪ] ADJ (*comp* **-ier**, *superl* **-iest**) (*snow*) sciolto(-a), fangoso(-a); (*fam Brit: poetry*) sdolcinato(-a)

slut [slʌt] (*offensive*) N (*immoral*) donnaccia, sgualdrina; (*dirty, untidy*) sciattona

slut·tish ['slʌtɪʃ] ADJ (*immoral: behaviour*) immorale, dissoluto(-a); (*dirty, untidy: appearance*) sciatto(-a), disordinato(-a)

sly [slaɪ] ADJ (*comp* **-ier**, *superl* **-iest**) (*wily*) astuto(-a), scaltro(-a); (*secretive*) furtivo(-a); (*mischievous: trick*) birbone(-a: *smile*), *sornione(-a), malizioso(-a)*; **she's sly!** è scaltra!
■ N: **on the sly** di nascosto, di soppiatto

sly·ly ['slaɪlɪ] ADV (*see adj*) astutamente, scaltramente; furtivamente; (*smile, wink*) maliziosamente

sly·ness ['slaɪnɪs] N (*wiliness*) astuzia, scaltrezza; (*mischievousness: of trick, smile*) malizia

smack¹ [smæk] N (*slap: on buttocks*) pacca; (: *on face*) schiaffo, ceffone *m*; (*sound*) colpo secco; (: *of lips, whip*) schiocco; **it was a smack in the eye for them** è stato uno smacco *or* uno schiaffo morale per loro; **to give a child a smack** sculacciare un bambino; **to have a smack at doing sth** (*fig*) provare a fare qc
■ VT (*child*) sculacciare; (*face*) schiaffeggiare; **she smacked the child's bottom** sculacciò il bambino; **to smack one's lips** schioccare le labbra
■ ADV: **it fell smack in the middle** (*fam*) cadde giusto nel mezzo; **she ran smack into the door** andò a sbattere dritto contro la porta

smack² [smæk] VI: **to smack of** (*fig: intrigue etc*) puzzare di

smack³ [smæk] N (*also:* **fishing smack**) barca da pesca

smack·er ['smækəʳ] N (*fam: kiss*) bacio; (: *Brit old: pound note*) sterlina; (: *Am: dollar bill*) dollaro

smack·ing ['smækɪŋ] N sculacciata; **to give sb a smacking** sculacciare qn

◎ **small** [smɔ:l] ADJ (*comp* **-er**, *superl* **-est**) (*gen: in size, number*) piccolo(-a); (: *in height*) basso(-a); (*stock, supply, population*) scarso(-a); (*waist*) sottile; (*meal*) leggero(-a); (*letter*) minuscolo(-a); (*minor, unimportant*) da poco, insignificante; (: *increase, improvement*) piccolo(-a), leggero(-a); **a small car** una macchina piccola; **when we were small** quando eravamo piccoli; **there was only a small audience** c'era poco pubblico; **this house makes the other one look small** questa casa fa sembrare piccola l'altra; **the smallest possible number of books** il minor numero di libri possibile; **the smallest details** i minimi dettagli; **to have a small appetite** avere poco *or* scarso appetito; **in a small voice** con un filo di voce; **to feel small** *(fig)* sentirsi umiliato(-a) *or* sminuito(-a); **to get** *or* **grow smaller** *(stain, town)* rimpicciolire; *(debt, organization, numbers)* ridursi; **to make smaller** *(amount, income)* ridurre; *(garden, object, garment)* rimpicciolire; **to have small hope of success** avere scarse speranze di successo; **to have small cause** *or* **reason to do sth** non avere molti motivi per fare qc; **to start in a small way** cominciare da poco; **a small shopkeeper** una piccolo(-a) negoziante

■ N **1** **the small of the back** le reni **2** NPL: **smalls** *(fam: underwear)* biancheria intima

small ad N *(in newspaper)* annuncio economico

small arms NPL armi *fpl* leggere

small business N piccola impresa

small change N spiccioli *mpl*

small fry N: **he is small fry** è un pesce piccolo; **they are small fry** sono dei pesci piccoli

small·holder ['smɔːlˌhəʊldəʳ] N *(Brit)* piccolo proprietario

small·holding ['smɔːlˌhəʊldɪŋ] N *(Brit)* piccola tenuta

small hours NPL: **the small hours** le ore piccole; **in the small hours** alle ore piccole

small·ish ['smɔːlɪʃ] ADJ piccolino(-a)

small-minded [ˌsmɔːl'maɪndɪd] ADJ meschino(-a)

small-mindedness [ˌsmɔːl'maɪndɪdnɪs] N meschinità

small·ness ['smɔːlnɪs] N *(gen)* piccolezza; *(of person)* bassa statura; *(of income, sum)* scarsità

small·pox ['smɔːlˌpɒks] N *(Med)* vaiolo

small print N caratteri *mpl* piccoli; *(in contract etc)* parte *f* scritta in piccolo

small-scale ['smɔːlˌskeɪl] ADJ *(map, model)* in scala ridotta; *(business, farming)* modesto(-a)

small screen N: **the small screen** *(television)* il piccolo schermo

small talk N conversazione *f* mondana, chiacchiere *fpl*

small-time ['smɔːlˌtaɪm] ADJ *(fam)* da poco; **a small-time criminal** un delinquente di mezza tacca; **a small-time thief** un ladro di polli

small-town ['smɔːlˌtaʊn] ADJ *(pej)* provinciale

smarmy ['smɑːmɪ] ADJ *(comp* **-ier**, *superl* **-iest)** *(Brit fam)* untuoso(-a), servile

◎ **smart** [smɑːt] ADJ *(comp* **-er**, *superl* **-est)** **1** *(elegant)* elegante, chic *inv*; *(fashionable)* di moda; **the smart set** il bel mondo; **to look smart** essere elegante; **a smart navy blue suit** un elegante vestito blu; **that's a smart car** è una bella macchina **2** *(clever)* intelligente, brillante; *(quick-witted)* sveglio(-a), furbo(-a); **he thinks he's smarter than Sarah** pensa di essere più intelligente di Sarah; **that was pretty smart of you!** che furbo!; **smart work by the police led to ...** una brillante operazione della polizia ha portato a...
3 *(quick: pace, action)* svelto(-a), rapido(-a); **look smart about it!** sbrigati!, spicciati!

■ VI **1** *(cut, graze etc)* bruciare; **my eyes are smarting** mi bruciano gli occhi **2** *(fig)*: **she's still smarting from his remarks** le bruciano ancora le sue osservazioni; **to smart under an insult/a reproof** soffrire per un insulto/un rimprovero

■ N *(pain)* dolore *m* acuto

smart aleck ['smɑːtˌælɪk] N *(fam)* sapientone(-a), sputasentenze *m/f inv*

smart·card ['smɑːtˌkɑːd] N *(Comput)* smart card *f inv*, carta intelligente

smart·en ['smɑːtn] VT *(also:* **smarten up**: *room, house etc)* abbellire, ravvivare; *(: child)* far bello(-a); *(: o.s.)* farsi bello(-a); **I'll go and smarten up** andrò a farmi bella; **a plan to smarten up the station** un progetto per abbellire la stazione; **to smarten up one's ideas** darsi una mossa

■ VI *(also:* **smarten up)** abbellirsi, farsi bello(-a)

smart·ly ['smɑːtlɪ] ADV *(elegantly)* elegantemente; *(cleverly)* con arguzia *or* intelligenza; *(quickly: walk)* velocemente; *(: answer)* con prontezza

smart·ness ['smɑːtnɪs] N *(see adv)* eleganza; intelligenza; velocità; prontezza

smarty ['smɑːtɪ] N *(fam)* = **smart aleck**

◎ **smash** [smæʃ] N **1** *(sound)* fracasso **2** *(also:* **smash-up**: *collision)* scontro; *(Tennis etc)* schiacciata, smash *m inv*; *(powerful blow)* pugno; *(Fin)* crollo; **he died in a car smash** è morto in un incidente automobilistico; **the smash of plates** il rumore di piatti rotti

■ VT *(break)* rompere, fracassare; *(shatter)* infrangere, frantumare; *(beat: enemy, opponent)* schiacciare, annientare; *(: record)* polverizzare; *(wreck, also fig)* distruggere; *(Tennis etc)* schiacciare; **they smashed the windows** hanno rotto le finestre; **he smashed it against the wall** lo scagliò contro la parete; **we will smash this crime ring** distruggeremo quest'organizzazione criminale; **he smashed his way out of the building** uscì dall'edificio spaccando tutto quello che trovava davanti

■ VI *(break)* rompersi, andare in frantumi; **the glass smashed** il bicchiere si è rotto; **the car smashed into the wall** la macchina si schiantò contro il muro

▶ **smash down** VT + ADV *(door)* abbattere

▶ **smash in** VT + ADV *(door, window)* abbattere; **to smash one's way in** entrare con la forza; **to smash sb's face in** *(fam)* spaccare la faccia a qn

▶ **smash up** VT + ADV *(car)* sfasciare; *(room)* distruggere

smash-and-grab [ˌsmæʃənd'græb] ADJ *(fam)*: **smash-and-grab robbery** furto con scasso della vetrina

smashed [smæʃt] ADJ **1** *(fam: drunk)* sbronzo(-a), partito(-a); *(: stoned)* fatto(-a) **2** *(wrecked)* fracassato(-a)

smash·er ['smæʃəʳ] N *(fam)*: **she's a smasher** *(in appearance)* è una bomba; *(in character)* è fantastica

smash-hit [ˌsmæʃ'hɪt] N successone *m*

smash·ing ['smæʃɪŋ] ADJ *(fam)* formidabile; **we had a smashing time** ci siamo divertiti come pazzi; **I think he's smashing** io lo trovo formidabile

smat·ter·ing ['smætərɪŋ] N: **to have a smattering of** avere un'infarinatura di

smear [smɪəʳ] N *(smudge)* traccia; *(dirty mark, also fig)* macchia; *(insult)* calunnia; *(Med)* striscio; **a smear of grease** una macchia di grasso; **a smear against him** una calunnia nei suoi confronti

■ VT **1** *(butter etc)* spalmare; **to smear cream on one's hands** *or* **smear one's hands with cream** spalmarsi le mani di crema; **she smeared sun cream on his back** gli ha spalmato la crema solare sulla schiena **2** *(make dirty)* sporcare; *(smudge: ink, paint)* sbavare; **the page was smeared** c'erano delle sbavature sulla pagina; **his hands were smeared with oil/ink** aveva le mani sporche di olio/inchiostro **3** *(fig: libel)* calunniare, diffamare; **an attempt to smear the organization** un tentativo di infangare il nome dell'organizzazione

■ VI *(paint, ink etc)* sbavare

smear campaign N campagna diffamatoria

Ss

smear test N (*Brit Med*) Pap-test *m inv*, striscio (*fam*)

◎ **smell** [smɛl] (*vb: pt, pp* **smelled** *or* **smelt**) N **1** (*sense of smell*) olfatto, odorato; (*of animal, fig*) fiuto; **to have a keen sense of smell** (*person*) avere l'olfatto sviluppato; (*animal*) avere un fiuto finissimo **2** (*odour*) odore *m*; (*: pleasant*) profumo; (*stench*) puzza; **it has a nice smell** ha un buon odore; **there's a strong smell of gas here** qui c'è una forte puzza di gas

■ VT (*gas, cooking*) sentire odore di; (*flower*) annusare; **to smell something burning** sentire odore di bruciato; **to smell danger** (*fig*) fiutare un pericolo; **I smell a rat** (*fig*) qui gatta ci cova; **I can smell gas** sento odore di gas; **I took a rose and smelled it** ho preso una rosa e l'ho annusata

■ VI (*pleasantly*) sapere, odorare; (*unpleasantly*) puzzare; **to smell of sth** avere odore di qc; **it smells of petrol** ha odore di benzina; **my fingers smell of garlic** ho le dita che puzzano di aglio; **it smells like chicken** odora di pollo; **it smells good** ha un buon odore; **it smells damp in here** c'è odore di umidità qui dentro; **that dog smells!** quel cane puzza!; **his breath smells** gli puzza l'alito

▸ **smell out** VT + ADV **1** (*animal, prey, also fig*) fiutare **2** **your feet are smelling the room out!** i tuoi piedi appestano la stanza!

smell·ing salts ['smɛlɪŋ,sɔ:lts] NPL sali *mpl*

smelly ['smɛlɪ] ADJ (*comp* **-ier**, *superl* **-iest**) (*fam*) puzzolente; **it's smelly in here** qui c'è puzza

smelt[1] [smɛlt] PT, PP *of* **smell**

smelt[2] [smɛlt] VT (*ore*) fondere

smel·ter ['smɛltəʳ] N fonderia

smel·ting ['smɛltɪŋ] N fusione *f*

smelting works NPL fonderia

◎ **smile** [smaɪl] N sorriso; **she said with a smile** disse sorridendo; **with a smile on one's lips** col sorriso sulle labbra; **to be all smiles** essere raggiante; **to give sb a smile** sorridere a qn; **I'll soon wipe the smile off your face!** ti faccio io passare la voglia di ridere!

■ VI sorridere; **to smile at sb/sth** sorridere a qn/qc; **to keep smiling** continuare a sorridere; (*fig*) conservare l'allegria; **fortune smiled on him** la fortuna gli arrise

■ VT: **he smiled his appreciation** sorrise in segno di apprezzamento

smi·ley ['smaɪlɪ] N faccina

smil·ing ['smaɪlɪŋ] ADJ sorridente

smil·ing·ly ['smaɪlɪŋlɪ] ADV (*look, reply*) sorridendo

smirk [smɜ:k] N (*self-satisfied*) sorriso compiaciuto; (*knowing*) sorrisetto furbo; (*affected*) sorriso affettato

■ VI (*see n*) sorridere compiaciuto(-a); fare un sorriso furbo; sorridere in modo affettato

smite [smaɪt] (*pt* **smote**, *pp* **smitten**) VT (*old: strike*) colpire; (*: punish*) punire

smith [smɪθ] N fabbro

smith·er·eens [,smɪðə'ri:nz] NPL: **to be smashed to smithereens** andare in frantumi *or* in mille pezzi

smithy ['smɪðɪ] N fucina

smit·ten ['smɪtn] PP *of* **smite**

■ ADJ PRED: **to be smitten with** (*remorse, desire, fear*) essere preso(-a) da; (*idea*) entusiasmarsi per; **to be smitten (with sb)** avere una cotta (per qn); **to be smitten with flu** essere colpito(-a) dall'influenza

smock [smɒk] N (*loose shirt*) camiciotto; (*blouse*) blusa; (*to protect clothing*) grembiule *m*

smock·ing ['smɒkɪŋ] N ricamo a nido d'ape

smog [smɒg] N smog *m inv*

◎ **smoke** [sməʊk] N **1** fumo; **there's no smoke without fire** non c'è fumo senza arrosto; **to go up in smoke** (*house*) andare distrutto(-a) dalle fiamme; (*fig*) andare in fumo **2** **to have a smoke** (*cigarette, pipe*) fare una fumatina

■ VT **1** (*tobacco*) fumare **2** (*bacon, fish, cheese*) affumicare

■ VI (*gen*) fumare; (*chimney*) fare fumo; **do you smoke?** fumi?; **you should stop smoking** dovresti smettere di fumare

▸ **smoke out** VT + ADV (*insects etc*) snidare col fumo

smoke alarm, **smoke detector** N rivelatore *m* di fumo

smoke bomb N bomba fumogena, candelotto fumogeno

smoked [sməʊkt] ADJ (*bacon, fish, etc*) affumicato(-a); **smoked glass** vetro fumé

smoke detector N = **smoke alarm**

smoke·less fuel [,sməʊklɪs'fjʊəl] N combustibile *m* che non dà fumo

smoke·less zone [,sməʊklɪs'zəʊn] N (*Brit*) *zona in cui sono vietati gli scarichi di fumo*

smok·er ['sməʊkəʳ] N (*person*) fumatore(-trice), tabagista *m/f*; (*railway carriage*) carrozza (per) fumatori; **smoker's cough** tosse *f* da fumo

smoke ring N: **to blow smoke rings** fare anelli di fumo

smoke screen N (*Mil, fig*) cortina fumogena

smoke shop N (*Am*) tabaccheria

smoke signal N segnale *m* di fumo

smoke·stack ['sməʊk,stæk] N ciminiera

smokestack industry N industria pesante

◎ **smok·ing** ['sməʊkɪŋ] ADJ fumante

■ N fumo; **"no smoking"** "vietato fumare"; **he's given up smoking** ha smesso di fumare; **smoking can damage your health** il fumo può danneggiare la salute; **smoking is bad for you** il fumo fa male

> DID YOU KNOW ...?
> **smoking** is not translated by the Italian word *smoking*

smoking car, **smoking compartment** N carrozza (per) fumatori

smoking jacket N giacca da camera

smoky ['sməʊkɪ] ADJ (*comp* **-ier**, *superl* **-iest**) (*chimney, fire*) fumoso(-a), che fa fumo; (*room, atmosphere*) fumoso(-a), pieno(-a) di fumo; (*flavour*) affumicato(-a); **a smoky room** una stanza fumosa; **to have a smoky flavour** sapere di affumicato

smol·der ['sməʊldəʳ] VI (*Am*) = **smoulder**

smooch [smu:tʃ] VI (*fam*) sbaciucchiarsi, pomiciare

smoochy ['smu:tʃɪ] ADJ (*comp* **-ier**, *superl* **-iest**) (*fam*) romantico(-a)

◎ **smooth** [smu:ð] ADJ (*comp* **-er**, *superl* **-est**) **1** (*surface, skin*) liscio(-a); (*chin: hairless*) imberbe; (*sea*) liscio(-a), calmo(-a); **as smooth as silk** liscio(-a) come la seta; **it keeps your skin soft and smooth** mantiene la pelle morbida e liscia **2** (*in consistency: paste etc*) omogeneo(-a) **3** (*movement, breathing, pulse*) regolare; (*landing, take-off, flight*) senza problemi; (*crossing, trip, life*) tranquillo(-a) **4** (*not harsh: cigarette*) leggero(-a); (*: drink*) dal gusto morbido, amabile; (*: voice, sound*) carezzevole **5** (*pej: person*) mellifluo(-a); **he's a smooth operator** (*fam*) ci sa fare; **he's a smooth talker** ha la parola facile; **he's too smooth for my liking** è troppo mellifluo per i miei gusti

■ VT **1** (*also:* **smooth down**: *hair etc*) lisciare; **to smooth the way** *or* **path for sb** (*fig*) spianare la strada a qn **2** (*stone, wood*) levigare; **to smooth away wrinkles** far sparire le rughe **3** **to smooth cream**

into one's face massaggiarsi la crema sul viso
▸ **smooth out** VT + ADV (*fabric, creases*) lisciare, spianare; (*fig: difficulties*) appianare
▸ **smooth over** VT + ADV: **to smooth things over** (*fig*) sistemare le cose
smoothie, smoothy ['smu:ðɪ] N (*fam pej*): **to be a smoothie** essere anche troppo cortese e disinvolto(-a)
smooth·ly ['smu:ðlɪ] ADV (*easily*) liscio; (*gently*) dolcemente; (*move*) senza scosse; (*talk*) in modo mellifluo; **the engine is running smoothly** il motore non dà problemi; **everything went smoothly** tutto andò liscio
smooth·ness ['smu:ðnɪs] N (*of stone, wood*) levigatezza; (*of skin*) morbidezza; (*of sauce*) omogeneità; (*of sea*) calma; (*of trip, life*) tranquillità; (*of manner*) mellifluità
smooth-running [ˌsmu:ð'rʌnɪŋ] ADJ (*engine*) che non perde colpi; (*business, project*) che va bene
smooth-spoken [ˌsmu:ð'spəʊkən], **smooth-tongued** [ˌsmu:ð'tʌŋd] ADJ mellifluo(-a)
smote [sməʊt] PT *of* **smite**
smoth·er ['smʌðə^r] VT **1** (*stifle*) soffocare **2** (*cover*) ricoprire; **to smother sb with kisses** ricoprire qn di baci; **fruit smothered in cream** frutta ricoperta di panna
smoul·der, (*Am*) **smol·der** ['sməʊldə^r] VI (*fire*) covare sotto la cenere; (*fig: passion etc*) covare
SMS [ˌɛsɛm'ɛs] ABBR (*Telec*: = **short message service**) SMS (*servizio*)
smudge [smʌdʒ] N sbavatura, macchia
■ VT sporcare, imbrattare
■ VI sbavare
smug [smʌg] ADJ (*comp* **-ger**, *superl* **-gest**) compiaciuto(-a)
smug·gle ['smʌgl] VT (*tobacco, drugs*) contrabbandare; **to smuggle in/out** (*goods etc*) far entrare/uscire di contrabbando *or* clandestinamente; (*fig: person, letter etc*) far entrare/uscire di nascosto; **to smuggle sth past** *or* **through Customs** passare la dogana con qc senza dichiararlo
smug·gler ['smʌglə^r] N contrabbandiere(-a)
smug·gling ['smʌglɪŋ] N contrabbando
smug·ly ['smʌglɪ] ADV con sufficienza, con compiacimento
smug·ness ['smʌgnɪs] N (*of person, expression*) aria compiaciuta, aria di sufficienza
smut [smʌt] N (*grain of soot*) granello di fuliggine; (*mark*) segno nero; (*in conversation etc*) sconcezze *fpl*
smut·ty ['smʌtɪ] ADJ (*comp* **-ier**, *superl* **-iest**) (*crude*) osceno(-a), sconcio(-a); (*dirty*) sporco(-a), sudicio(-a); **a smutty magazine** un giornale sconcio
snack [snæk] N spuntino; **to have a snack** fare uno spuntino
snack bar N snack-bar *m inv*, tavola calda (*or* fredda)
snaf·fle ['snæfl] N (*also:* **snaffle bit**: *for horse*) filetto
sna·fu [snæ'fu:] ADJ (*Am fam*) incasinato(-a)
snag [snæg] N (*pulled thread*) filo tirato; (*difficulty*) intralcio, intoppo; **the snag is that ...** il guaio è che...; **the snag is that it costs £2000** il guaio è che costa 2000 sterline; **what's the snag?** qual è il problema?; **to run into** *or* **hit a snag** incontrare una difficoltà, trovare un intoppo
■ VT (*jumper*) tirare un filo a; (*tights*) smagliare
snail [sneɪl] N chiocciola; **at a snail's pace** a passo di lumaca
snail mail N posta tradizionale
snake [sneɪk] N serpente *m*, serpe *f*; **snake in the grass** (*fig*) traditore(-trice)
snake·bite ['sneɪkˌbaɪt] N morso di serpente
snake charmer N incantatore *m* di serpenti
snakes and ladders N ≈ gioco dell'oca
snake·skin ['sneɪkˌskɪn] N pelle *f* di serpente
■ ADJ (*bag, shoes*) di serpente
◎ **snap** [snæp] N **1** (*sound, action: of sth breaking, closing*) colpo secco; (*: of fingers*) schiocco; **a cold snap** (*fam*) un'improvvisa ondata di freddo; **the dog made a snap at the biscuit** il cane ha cercato di afferrare il biscotto; **with a snap of one's fingers** schioccando le dita **2** (*Cards*) rubamazzo **3** (*fam: photo*) foto *f inv*; **holiday snaps** foto delle vacanze
■ ADJ (*sudden: strike*) selvaggio(-a); (*: answer, judgement*) immediato(-a); (*: decision*) repentino(-a)
■ VT **1** (*break*) spezzare di netto **2** (*fingers*) schioccare; **to snap one's fingers at sb/sth** (*fig*) infischiarsi di qn/qc; **to snap a box shut** chiudere una scatola di colpo **3** **"be quiet!", she snapped** "sta' zitto!", sbottò **4** (*Phot*) fotografare, scattare una foto a
■ VI **1** (*break: elastic*) spezzarsi **2** (*whip*) schioccare; **it snapped shut** si chiuse di scatto; **to snap back into place** scattare di nuovo a posto; **everything snapped into place** (*fig*) tutto fu chiaro **3** **to snap at sb** (*dog*) cercare di mordere qn; (*person*) rivolgersi a qn con tono brusco
▸ **snap off** VT + ADV rompere con un colpo secco; **to snap sb's head off** (*fig*) aggredire qn
▸ **snap out** VI + ADV: **snap out of it!** (*fam*) non lasciarti andare!
■ VT + ADV (*order etc*) dare bruscamente
▸ **snap up** VT + ADV afferrare; **to snap up a bargain** (*fig*) accaparrarsi un affare, non lasciarsi sfuggire un affare
snap·dragon ['snæpˌdrægən] N bocca di leone
snap fastener N bottone *m* a pressione
snap·pish ['snæpɪʃ] ADJ irritabile, bisbetico(-a)
snap·py ['snæpɪ] ADJ (*comp* **-ier**, *superl* **-iest**) (*fam: slogan, answer*) d'effetto; (*: way of speaking*) sbrigativo(-a); (*: smart*) elegante; **he's a snappy dresser** è un elegantone; **make it snappy!** (*fam*) sbrigati!
snap·shot ['snæpʃɒt] N (*Phot*) istantanea
snare [snɛə^r] N trappola
■ VT prendere in trappola, intrappolare
snarl[1] [snɑ:l] N ringhio
■ VI: **to snarl (at sb)** ringhiare (a qn)
snarl[2] [snɑ:l] N (*in wool etc*) garbuglio
■ VT: **to get snarled up** (*wool, plans*) ingarbugliarsi; (*traffic*) intasarsi
snarl-up ['snɑ:lˌʌp] N (*of traffic*) intasamento
snatch [snætʃ] N **1** (*act of snatching*): **to make a snatch at sth** cercare di afferrare qc **2** (*fam: theft*) furto, rapina; (*: kidnapping*) rapimento; **there was a wages snatch** dei ladri hanno rubato le paghe **3** (*snippet*) pezzo; **snatches of conversation** frammenti *mpl* di conversazione; **to sleep in snatches** dormire a intervalli
■ VT (*grab: object*) strappare con violenza; (*: opportunity*) cogliere; (*: few days, short break*) prendersi; (*steal, also fig: kiss, victory*) rubare; (*kidnap*) rapire; **my bag was snatched** mi hanno scippato; **to snatch a sandwich** buttar giù in fretta un panino; **to snatch some sleep** riuscire a dormire un po'; **to snatch sth from sb** strappare qc a qn; **he snatched the keys from my hand** mi ha strappato di mano le chiavi; **to snatch a knife out of sb's hand** strappare di mano un coltello a qn
■ VI: **don't snatch!** non strappare le cose di mano!; **to**

Ss

snatch at (*object*) cercare di afferrare; (*opportunity*) cogliere al volo

▸ **snatch away** VT + ADV: **to snatch sth away from sb** strappare qc a qn

▸ **snatch up** VT + ADV raccogliere in fretta, afferrare

snaz·zy ['snæzɪ] ADJ (*comp* **-ier**, *superl* **-iest**) (*fam: clothes*) sciccoso(-a)

sneak [sni:k] VT: **to sneak sth out of a place** portare fuori qc di nascosto da un luogo; **to sneak a look at sth** dare una sbirciatina a qc; **to sneak a quick cigarette** fumarsi una sigaretta di nascosto
■VI **1 to sneak in/out** entrare/uscire di nascosto *or* di soppiatto; **to sneak away** *or* **off** allontanarsi di nascosto *or* di soppiatto, squagliarsela; **to sneak off with sth** portare via di soppiatto qc **2 to sneak on sb** (*fam*) fare la spia a qn
■N (*fam: telltale*) spione(-a)

sneak·ers ['sni:kəz] NPL (*Am*) scarpe *fpl* da ginnastica

sneak·ing ['sni:kɪŋ] ADJ (*dislike, preference*) segreto(-a); **I have a sneaking admiration for him** mio malgrado l'ammiro; **to have a sneaking feeling/suspicion that ...** avere la vaga impressione/il vago sospetto che...

sneak preview N anteprima non ufficiale

sneak thief N ladruncolo(-a)

sneaky ['sni:kɪ] ADJ (*comp* **-ier**, *superl* **-iest**) (*fam*) vile

sneer [snɪə^r] N (*expression*) sogghigno, ghigno; (*remark*) commento sarcastico
■VI sogghignare; **to sneer at sb/sth** farsi beffe di qn/qc; **you may sneer, but ...** puoi ridere, ma...

sneer·ing ['snɪərɪŋ] ADJ (*smile, remark*) beffardo(-a)
■N beffe *fpl*

sneer·ing·ly ['snɪərɪŋlɪ] ADV sarcasticamente

sneeze [sni:z] N starnuto
■VI starnutire; **an offer not to be sneezed at** (*fig fam*) un'offerta su cui non si può sputare

snick·er ['snɪkə^r] (*Am*) VI ridacchiare
■N risatina

snide [snaɪd] ADJ (*fam*) maligno(-a)

sniff [snɪf] N (*sound*) annusata, fiutata; **to have a sniff of sth** annusare qc; **one sniff of this is enough to kill you** un'annusata a questo e muori di sicuro; **he gave a sniff of contempt** ha arricciato il naso con disprezzo
■VT (*gen*) annusare, fiutare; (*glue, drug*) sniffare; (*inhalant*) fare inalazioni di; **the dog sniffed my hand** il cane mi ha annusato la mano; **to sniff glue** sniffare colla
■VI (*person*) tirare su col naso; (*: in contempt*) arricciare il naso; **stop sniffing!** smettila di tirare su col naso!

▸ **sniff at** VI + PREP annusare; **it's not to be sniffed at** non è da disprezzare

▸ **sniff out** VT + ADV fiutare; (*fig*) fiutare, subodorare

sniff·er dog ['snɪfə,dɒg] N cane *inv* poliziotto *m* (*antidroga o antiterrorismo*)

snif·fle ['snɪfl] = **snuffle**

snif·fy ['snɪfɪ] ADJ (*comp* **-ier**, *superl* **-iest**) (*fam: disdainful*) sprezzante

snif·ter ['snɪftə^r] N (*fam: of whisky etc*) cicchetto, goccetto

snig·ger ['snɪgə^r] (*pej*) N risolino
■VI ridacchiare, ridere sotto i baffi; **to snigger at** ridere sotto i baffi per

snig·ger·ing ['snɪgərɪŋ] (*pej*) N risatine *fpl*

snip [snɪp] N (*cut*) taglio; (*small piece*) ritaglio; (*Brit fam: bargain*) affare *m*, occasione *f*; **with a snip of the scissors** con un colpo di forbici
■VT tagliare; **to snip sth off** tagliare via qc

snipe [snaɪp] N, PL INV (*bird*) beccaccino
■VI: **to snipe at sb** sparare a qn da un nascondiglio; (*fig*) lanciare frecciatine a qn

snip·er ['snaɪpə^r] N franco tiratore *m*, cecchino

snip·pet ['snɪpɪt] N (*of cloth, paper*) ritaglio; (*of information, conversation etc*) frammento

snitch [snɪtʃ] (*fam*) VI (*inform*): **to snitch on sb** fare la spia a qn
■VT (*steal*) sgraffignare

sniv·el ['snɪvl] VI piagnucolare, frignare

sniv·el·ler, (*Am*) **sniv·el·er** ['snɪvlə^r] N piagnucolone(-a), frignone(-a)

sniv·el·ling, (*Am*) **sniv·el·ing** ['snɪvlɪŋ] ADJ piagnucoloso(-a)

snob [snɒb] N snob *m/f inv*; **he's an intellectual snob** è uno snob in fatto di cultura

snob·bery ['snɒbərɪ] N snobismo

snob·bish ['snɒbɪʃ] ADJ snob *inv*

snob·bish·ness ['snɒbɪʃnɪs] N snobismo

snob·by ['snɒbɪ] ADJ (*comp* **-ier**, *superl* **-iest**) (*fam*) = **snobbish**

snog [snɒg] (*Brit fam*) N pomiciata
■VI sbaciucchiarsi, pomiciare

snook [snu:k] N (*Brit fam*): **to cock a snook at sb** fare marameo a qn, prendere in giro qn

snook·er ['snu:kə^r] N ≈ (gioco del) biliardo
■VT: **to be properly snookered** (*fig fam*) essere in un bel casino

snoop [snu:p] (*fam pej*) N (*act*): **to have a snoop round** curiosare
■VI (*also:* **snoop about, snoop around**) curiosare; **to snoop into sb's affairs** ficcare il naso negli affari di qn; **to snoop on sb** spiare qn

snoop·er ['snu:pə^r] N ficcanaso *m/f*

snooty ['snu:tɪ] ADJ (*comp* **-ier**, *superl* **-iest**) (*fam pej*) snob *inv*, borioso(-a), altezzoso(-a)

snooze [snu:z] N sonnellino, pisolino; **to have a snooze** fare un sonnellino, schiacciare un pisolino
■VI sonnecchiare

snore [snɔ:^r] N: **to give a loud snore** russare sonoramente
■VI russare

snor·ing ['snɔ:rɪŋ] N il russare *m*

snor·kel ['snɔ:kl] N (*of submarine*) presa d'aria; (*of swimmer*) respiratore *m* subacqueo, boccaglio
■VI: **to go snorkelling** nuotare con il boccaglio

snort [snɔ:t] N sbuffata, sbuffo
■VI (*horse, person*) sbuffare; **to snort with laughter** soffocare dalle risate
■VT (*fam: drugs*) sniffare

snort·er ['snɔ:tə^r] N (*Brit fam*) **1 a real snorter of a problem** un bel rompicapo **2** (*drink*) bicchierino, goccio

snot [snɒt] N (*fam*) moccio

snot·ty ['snɒtɪ] ADJ (*comp* **-ier**, *superl* **-iest**) (*fam*) moccioso(-a); (*: fig: snooty*) borioso(-a), altezzoso(-a)

snout [snaʊt] N (*of animal*) muso; (*of pig*) grugno

◎**snow** [snəʊ] N **1** neve *f*; (*also:* **snowfall**) nevicata; (*fam: cocaine*) neve **2** (*on TV screen*) effetto neve
■VT: **to be snowed in** *or* **up** essere isolato(-a) a causa della neve; **to be snowed under with work** essere sommerso(-a) di lavoro
■VI nevicare; **it's snowing** nevica

snow·ball ['snəʊ,bɔ:l] N palla di neve
■VI (*fig: scheme, appeal*) crescere a vista d'occhio

snowball fight N: **to have a snowball fight** fare una battaglia a palle di neve

snow blindness N (*Med*) ambliopia da riflesso della neve
snow·board ['snəʊ,bɔ:d] N (*board*) snowboard *m*
snow·board·er ['snəʊ,bɔ:dəʳ] N *persona che fa snowboard*
snow·board·ing ['snəʊ,bɔ:dɪŋ] N (*Sport*) snowboard *m*
snow·boot ['snəʊ,bu:t] N doposcì *m inv*
snow·bound ['snəʊ,baʊnd] ADJ (*village*) isolato(-a) dalla neve; (*person, road*) bloccato(-a) dalla neve; (*countryside*) coperto(-a) di neve
snow cannon N (*Skiing*) cannone *m* per innevamento artificiale
snow-capped ['snəʊ,kæpt] ADJ (*mountain*) incappucciato(-a) di neve; (*peak*) coperto(-a) di neve
snow·cat ['snəʊ,kæt] N gatto delle nevi
snow chains NPL catene *fpl* da neve
snow-covered ['snəʊ,kʌvəd] ADJ coperto(-a) di neve
snow·drift ['snəʊ,drɪft] N cumulo di neve (*ammucchiato dal vento*)
snow·drop ['snəʊ,drɒp] N bucaneve *m inv*
snow·fall ['snəʊ,fɔ:l] N (*fall of snow*) nevicata; (*amount that falls*) nevosità *f inv*
snow·flake ['snəʊ,fleɪk] N fiocco di neve
snow job N (*Am fam*) chiacchiere *fpl* da imbonitore
snow line N limite *m* delle nevi perenni
snow·man ['snəʊ,mæn] N (*pl* **-men**) pupazzo di neve; **the abominable snowman** l'abominevole uomo delle nevi
snow·mobile ['snəʊmə,bi:l] N = **snowcat**
snow pea N (*Am*: *Culin*) pisello dolce, taccola
snow·plough, (*Am*) **snow·plow** ['snəʊ,plaʊ] N spazzaneve *m inv*
snowplough turn N (*Skiing*) curva a spazzaneve
snow report N (*Met*) bollettino della neve
snow·shoe ['snəʊʃu:] N racchetta da neve
snow·storm ['snəʊ,stɔ:m] N tormenta, tempesta di neve
snow·suit ['snəʊsu:t] N tutina termica
Snow White N Biancaneve *f*
snow-white [,snəʊ'waɪt] ADJ candido(-a)
snowy ['snəʊɪ] ADJ (*comp* **-ier**, *superl* **-iest**) (*climate, region, day etc*) nevoso(-a); (*hills, roof*) innevato(-a); (*white as snow*) candido(-a), niveo(-a); **it's been very snowy recently** ha nevicato parecchio, ultimamente
SNP [,ɛsɛn'pi:] N ABBR (*Brit Pol*: = **Scottish National Party**) *partito nazionalista scozzese*
Snr ABBR (*Am*) = **Senior**
snub [snʌb] N affronto, offesa
■VT (*person*) snobbare
snub-nosed [,snʌb'nəʊzd] ADJ con il naso a patata *or* patatina
snuff [snʌf] N tabacco da fiuto; **to take snuff** fiutare tabacco
■VT (*also*: **snuff out**: *candle*) spegnere; **to snuff it** (*Brit fam*) tirare le cuoia
snuff·box ['snʌf,bɒks] N tabacchiera
snuf·fle ['snʌfl] N: **I've got a snuffle** mi cola il naso; **I've got the snuffles** ho il raffreddore
■VI tirare su col naso
snuff movie N (*fam*) *film porno dove una persona viene uccisa realmente*
snug [snʌg] ADJ (*comp* **-ger**, *superl* **-gest**) (*cosy*: *room, house*) accogliente, comodo(-a); (*safe*: *harbour*) sicuro(-a); (*fitting closely*) attillato(-a); **a snug little house** una casetta accogliente; **warm and snug by the fire** accoccolato(-a) vicino al fuoco; **to be snug in bed** essere al calduccio nel letto; **it's a snug fit** è attillato(-a)

snug·gle ['snʌgl] VI: **to snuggle down in bed** rannicchiarsi nel letto; **to snuggle up to sb** stringersi a qn
snug·ly ['snʌglɪ] ADV comodamente; **it fits snugly** (*object in pocket etc*) ci sta giusto(-a) giusto(-a); (*garment*) sta ben attillato(-a)
SO ABBR (*Banking*) = **standing order**

◎ **so** [səʊ] KEYWORD
■ADV
1 (*in comparisons: before adjective and adverb*) così ; **so quickly** (*soon*) così presto; (*fast*) così in fretta; **it is so big that ...** è così grosso che...; **it was so much more difficult than I expected** era molto più difficile di quanto pensassi; **she's not so clever as him** lei non è intelligente come lui; **he's not so foolish as I thought** non è così scemo come pensavo; **I wish you weren't so clumsy** magari non fossi così maldestro
2 (*very*) così ; **so much** tanto; (*+ noun*) tanto(-a); **so many** tanti(-e); **I love you so much** ti voglio tanto bene; **I'm so worried** sono così preoccupato; **I'm so glad to see you again** sono così felice rivederti; **I've got so much to do** ho tanto da fare; **I've got so much to do that ...** ho così tanto da fare che...; **thank you so much** grazie infinite *or* mille
3 (*thus, in this way, likewise*) così , in questo modo; **the article is so written as to ...** l'articolo è scritto in modo da...; **if so** se è così , quand'è così ; **he likes things just so** vuole che tutto sia fatto a puntino; **I didn't do it — you DID so!** non l'ho fatto io — l'hai fatto tu eccome!; **so do I, so am I** *etc* anch'io; **he's wrong and so are you** lui si sbaglia e tu pure; **and so forth** *or* **and so on** e così via; **so it is!** *or* **so it does!** davvero!; **it so happens that ...** si dà il caso che... *+ sub*; **while she was so doing** mentre lo stava facendo; **you should do it so** dovresti farlo così ; **I hope so** lo spero; **I think so** penso di sì ; **I'm afraid so** temo di sì ; **so he says** così dice; **so to speak** per così dire; **don't worry so** non preoccuparti così tanto; **I told you so** te l'avevo detto io; **so saying he walked away** così dicendo se ne andò; **do so** fallo
4 (*phrases*): **she didn't so much as send me a birthday card** non mi ha neanche mandato un biglietto di auguri per il compleanno; **I haven't so much as a penny** non ho neanche una lira; **so much for her promises!** a fidarsi delle sue promesse!; **at so much per week** a un tot alla settimana; **ten or so** circa una decina; **just so!** *or* **so!** esattamente!; **even so** comunque; **so long!** (*fam*) ciao!, ci vediamo!; **so far** finora, fin qui; (*in past*) fino ad allora
■CONJ
1 (*expressing purpose*): **so as to do sth** in modo *or* così da fare qc; **we hurried so as not to be late** ci affrettammo per non fare tardi; **so (that)** perché *+ sub*; **I brought it so that you could see it** l'ho portato perché tu lo vedessi; **so as to prevent cheating** così da evitare imbrogli
2 (*expressing result*): **it was raining and so we could not go out** pioveva e così non potemmo uscire; **as her French improved so did her confidence** man mano che il suo francese migliorava acquistava più sicurezza; **so you see ...** così vedi...
3 (*in questions, exclamations*): **so you're Spanish?** e così sei spagnolo?; **so that's the reason!** allora è questo il motivo!, ecco perché!; **so there you are!** ah eccoti qua!; **so there!** (*fam*) ecco!; **so (what)?** (*fam*) e allora?, e con questo *or* ciò?

Ss

soak [səʊk] VT **1** (*bread etc*) inzuppare; (*clothes*) mettere a mollo; **soak it in cold water** mettilo in ammollo nell'acqua fredda; **to get soaked (to the skin)** bagnarsi *or* infradiciarsi (fino alle ossa); **to be soaked through** essere (bagnato(-a)) fradicio(-a) **2** (*fam*): **to soak the rich** mungere i ricchi
■ VI (*clothes*) inzupparsi; **to leave to soak** (*garment*) lasciare in ammollo; (*dishes*) lasciare a bagno
■ N **1** (*in water*): **to have a long soak in the bath** restare a lungo a mollo nella vasca **2** (*fam: drunkard*) spugna
▸ **soak in** VI + ADV penetrare; **it took a long time to soak in** (*fig*) ci è voluto tanto prima che mi (*or* gli *etc*) entrasse in testa
▸ **soak up** VT + ADV (*liquid, knowledge*) assorbire; **to soak up water** assorbire acqua; **to soak up the sunshine** (*fam*) crogiolarsi al sole
soaking ['səʊkɪŋ] ADJ (*also:* **soaking wet**) bagnato(-a) fradicio(-a); **your shoes are soaking** hai le scarpe zuppe
so-and-so ['səʊən,səʊ] N (*somebody*) un(-a) tale; **Mr/Mrs so-and-so** (*fam*) signor/signora tal dei tali; **he's a so-and-so!** (*fam*) che tipo odioso che è!
soap [səʊp] N sapone *m*; (*also:* **cake of soap**) saponetta; (*TV fam*) telenovela, soap opera *f inv*
■ VT insaponare
soap·box ['səʊp,bɒks] N palco improvvisato (*per orazioni pubbliche*)
soap·dish ['səʊp,dɪʃ] N portasapone *m inv*
soap·flakes ['səʊp,fleɪks] NPL sapone *msg* in scaglie
soap opera N telenovela, soap opera *f inv*
soap powder N detersivo in polvere
soap·suds ['səʊp,sʌdz] NPL saponata *fsg*
soap·wort ['səʊp,wɜ:t] N saponaria
soapy ['səʊpɪ] ADJ (*comp* **-ier**, *superl* **-iest**) (*covered in soap: person*) insaponato(-a); (*: water*) saponato(-a); (*like soap*) saponoso(-a); **to taste soapy** sapere di sapone
soar [sɔ:ʳ] VI **1** (*rise: bird*) librarsi; (*: plane, ball*) volare **2** (*fig: tower etc*) elevarsi, ergersi; (*: price, morale, spirits*) salire alle stelle; (*: ambitions, hopes*) aumentare notevolmente; **the price has soared** il prezzo è lievitato; **the temperature soared** la temperatura è salita moltissimo
soar·ing ['sɔ:rɪŋ] ADJ (*flight*) altissimo(-a); (*building*) slanciato(-a); (*prices*) alle stelle; (*hopes, imagination*) ardito(-a); **soaring inflation** inflazione *f* galoppante
sob [sɒb] N singhiozzo
■ VI singhiozzare
■ VT: **to sob one's heart out** piangere disperatamente
s.o.b. [,ɛsəʊ'bi:] N ABBR (*Am fam!*) (= **son of a bitch**) figlio di puttana (*fam!*)
sob·bing ['sɒbɪŋ] ADJ singhiozzante
■ N singhiozzi *mpl*
so·ber ['səʊbəʳ] ADJ **1** (*not drunk*) sobrio(-a); **to be far from sober** non essere affatto sobrio(-a); **to be as sober as a judge** *or* **be stone-cold sober** essere perfettamente sobrio(-a) **2** (*rational, sedate, dull: life, person, colour*) sobrio(-a); (*: opinion, statement, estimate*) ponderato(-a); (*: occasion*) solenne; **the sober truth** la verità pura e semplice; **in a sober mood** serio(-a)
■ VT (*also:* **sober up**) far passare la sbornia a; (*fig*) calmare
■ VI (*also:* **sober up**) smaltire la sbornia; (*fig*) calmarsi; **her mother's rebuke had a sobering effect on her** il rimprovero di sua madre la fece pensare
so·ber·ly ['səʊbəlɪ] ADV in modo sobrio, sobriamente
so·bri·ety [səʊ'braɪətɪ] N **1** (*not being drunk*) sobrietà **2** (*seriousness, sedateness*) sobrietà, pacatezza
sob story N (*fam pej*) storia lacrimosa
sob stuff N (*fam: in film etc*) sentimentalismo
Soc. ABBR (= **society**) Soc.
◎ **so-called** [,səʊ'kɔ:ld] ADJ cosiddetto(-a)
◎ **soc·cer** ['sɒkəʳ] N calcio
■ ADJ (*club, season, match*) calcistico(-a), di calcio; **a game of soccer** una partita di calcio
soccer mom N (*Am*) *mamma che dedica molto tempo ai propri figli*
soccer pitch N campo di calcio
soccer player N calciatore *m*
so·cia·bil·ity [,səʊʃə'bɪlɪtɪ] N (*of person*) socievolezza
so·cia·ble ['səʊʃəbl] ADJ (*person*) socievole, cordiale; (*evening, gathering*) amichevole, tra amici; **I don't feel very sociable** non ho molta voglia di vedere gente; **I'll have one drink, just to be sociable** berrò qualcosa, tanto per gradire
so·cia·bly ['səʊʃəblɪ] ADV (*behave*) in modo socievole; (*invite, say*) amichevolmente
◎ **so·cial** ['səʊʃəl] ADJ (*all senses*) sociale; **man is a social animal** l'uomo è un animale sociale *or* socievole
■ N festicciola
social anthropology N antropologia culturale
social class N classe *f* sociale
social climber N arrampicatore(-trice) sociale, arrivista *m/f*
social club N circolo
social column N (*Press*) cronaca mondana
social democrat N socialdemocratico(-a)
social disease N malattia sociale
social drinker N: **to be a social drinker** bere solo in compagnia
social engineering N manipolazione *f* a sfondo sociologico delle strutture sociali
social exclusion N (*Brit*) esclusione *f* sociale
social insurance N (*Am*) assicurazione *f* sociale
so·cial·ism ['səʊʃə,lɪzəm] N socialismo
◎ **so·cial·ist** ['səʊʃəlɪst] ADJ, N socialista (*m/f*)
so·cial·ite ['səʊʃə,laɪt] N persona mondana
so·ciali·za·tion [,səʊʃəlaɪ'zeɪʃən] N (*Psych*) socializzazione *f*
so·cial·ize ['səʊʃə,laɪz] VI (*be with people*) frequentare gente; (*make friends*) fare amicizia; (*chat*) chiacchierare; **he has to socialize a lot because he's a salesman** deve mantenere molti contatti a causa del suo lavoro di rappresentante; **the party will be an opportunity to socialize and relax** la festa è un'occasione per socializzare e rilassarsi; **to socialize with** socializzare con, frequentare; **she was sorry she and Charles no longer socialized with old friends** le dispiaceva che lei e Charles non frequentassero più i vecchi amici
■ VT (*Pol, Psych*) socializzare
social life N: **to have a good social life** avere un'intensa vita sociale
so·cial·ly ['səʊʃəlɪ] ADV (*gen*) socialmente, in società; **I know him socially** lo incontro in occasioni mondane
social mobility N capacità di salire nella scala sociale
social outcast N emarginato(-a)
social science N scienze *fpl* sociali
▹ http://bitbucket.icaap.org/
social scientist N specialista *m/f* in scienze sociali, sociologo(-a)
social security N previdenza sociale; **to be on social security** (*fam*) ricevere sussidi dalla previdenza sociale; **Department of Social Security** (*Brit*)

≈ Istituto di Previdenza Sociale
social services NPL servizi *mpl* sociali
social studies NPL scienze *fpl* sociali
social welfare N sicurezza sociale
▷ www.icsw.org/
▷ www.unfpa.org
social work N assistenza sociale
social worker N assistente *m/f* sociale
◎ **so·ci·ety** [sə'saɪətɪ] N **1** (*social community*) società *f inv*; **to live in society** vivere in società; **he was a danger to society** era un pericolo pubblico; **we live in a multicultural society** viviamo in una società multiculturale **2** (*club, organization*) società *f inv*, associazione *f*; **film society** cineclub *m inv*; **learned society** circolo culturale; **literary society** associazione letteraria **3** (*also*: **high society**) alta società; **polite society** società bene **4** (*frm*: *company*) compagnia; **in the society of** in compagnia di; **I enjoyed his society** ho gradito la sua compagnia
■ ADJ (*party, column*) mondano(-a)
Society of Friends N: **the Society of Friends** i Quaccheri
Society of Jesus N Compagnia di Gesù
society wedding N matrimonio nell'alta società
so·cio·biolo·gist [ˌsəʊsɪəʊbaɪ'ɒlədʒɪst] N sociobiologo(-a)
so·cio·biolo·gy [ˌsəʊsɪəʊbaɪ'ɒlədʒɪ] N sociobiologia
so·cio·eco·nom·ic [ˌsəʊsɪəʊˌiːkə'nɒmɪk] ADJ socioeconomico(-a)
so·cio·lin·guis·tic [ˌsəʊsɪəʊlɪŋ'gwɪstɪk] ADJ sociolinguistico(-a)
so·cio·lin·guis·tics [ˌsəʊsɪəʊlɪŋ'gwɪstɪks] N sociolinguistica
so·cio·logi·cal [ˌsəʊsɪə'lɒdʒɪkəl] ADJ sociologico(-a)
so·ci·olo·gist [ˌsəʊsɪ'ɒlədʒɪst] N sociologo(-a)
so·ci·ol·ogy [ˌsəʊsɪ'ɒlədʒɪ] N sociologia
▷ www.sociologyonline.co.uk/
▷ www.asanet.org/public/public.html
so·cio·path ['səʊsɪəʊˌpæθ] N disadattato(-a)
so·cio·po·liti·cal [ˌsəʊsɪəʊpə'lɪtɪkəl] ADJ sociopolitico(-a)
sock[1] [sɒk] N (*short*) calzino; (*long*) calzettone *m*; (*of horse*) balzana; **to pull one's socks up** (*fig*) darsi una regolata; **put a sock in it!** (*Brit fam*) chiudi il becco!
sock[2] [sɒk] (*fam*) N (*blow*) colpo, pugno; **to give sb a sock on the jaw** dare un pugno sul muso a qn
■ VT colpire, picchiare; **come on, sock him one!** dai, suonagliele!
sock·et ['sɒkɪt] N (*of eye*) orbita; (*of joint*) cavità *f inv*; (*Elec*: *for plug*) presa (di corrente); (: *for light bulb*) portalampada *m inv*
Socrates ['sɒkrəˌtiːz] N Socrate *m*
sod[1] [sɒd] N (*liter*: *of earth*) zolla erbosa
sod[2] [sɒd] N (*Brit fam!*) stronzo(-a) (*fam!*); **you lazy sod!** pezzo di sfaticato!; **poor sod!** povero diavolo!
▶ **sod off** VI + ADV (*Brit fam!*): **sod off!** levati dalle palle! (*fam!*)
soda ['səʊdə] N **1** (*Chem*) soda **2** (*drink*) seltz *m inv*; **whisky and soda** whisky e soda **3** (*Am*: *also*: **soda pop**) gassosa
soda fountain N (*Am*) chiosco delle bibite
soda siphon N sifone *m* del seltz
soda water N acqua di seltz
sod·den ['sɒdn] ADJ zuppo(-a)
sod·ding ['sɒdɪŋ] (*Brit fam!*) ADJ: **that sodding dog!** quel cane del cazzo! (*fam!*)
■ ADV: **don't be so sodding stupid!** non fare il coglione! (*fam!*)
so·dium ['səʊdɪəm] N sodio
sodium bicarbonate [-baɪ'kɑːbənɪt] N bicarbonato di sodio
sodium chloride N cloruro di sodio
sodium hydroxide N soda caustica
sodium lamp N lampada al sodio
sodo·my ['sɒdəmɪ] N sodomia
sofa ['səʊfə] N sofà *m inv*, divano
So·fia ['səʊfɪə] N Sofia (*città*)
◎ **soft** [sɒft] ADJ (*comp* **-er**, *superl* **-est**) **1** (*not hard, rough etc*: *gen*) morbido(-a); (: *snow, ground*) soffice; (: *metal, stone*) tenero(-a); (: *cheese*) a pasta molle; (: *pej*: *muscles*) flaccido(-a); **soft cheeses** formaggi a pasta molle; **a nice soft towel** un asciugamano bello morbido; **the mattress is too soft** il materasso è troppo soffice **2** (*gentle, not harsh*: *breeze, rain, pressure*) leggero(-a); (: *colour*) delicato(-a); (: *light*) tenue; (: *look, smile, answer*) dolce; (: *heart*) tenero(-a); (: *life, option*) facile; (: *job*) non pesante; (: *teacher, parent*) indulgente; **you're too soft with him** sei troppo indulgente con lui; **to have a soft spot for sb** avere un debole per qn; **to be soft on sb** essere cotto(-a) di qn; **he has a soft time of it** lui se la passa bene; **soft skills** capacità *fpl* relazionali **3** (*not loud*: *sound, laugh, voice*) sommesso(-a); (: *steps, whisper*) leggero(-a); **the music is too soft** il volume della musica è troppo basso **4** (*fam*: *person*: *no stamina*) smidollato(-a); (*stupid*): **to be soft (in the head)** essere un po' tocco(-a) **5** (*Ling*: *consonant*) dolce
soft·ball ['sɒftˌbɔːl] N (*game*) softball *m inv*; (*ball*) palla da softball
▷ www.internationalsoftball.com
soft-boiled ['sɒftˌbɔɪld] ADJ (*egg*) alla coque
soft copy N (*Comput*) copia in formato elettronico
soft currency N moneta debole
soft drink N bibita analcolica
soft drugs NPL droghe *fpl* leggere
sof·ten ['sɒfn] VT (*gen*) ammorbidire; (*light*) attenuare; (*sound, impression*) attutire; (*colour, anger*) smorzare; (*resistance*) fiaccare; (*person*: *weaken*) addolcire; **he became softened by luxurious living** vivendo nel lusso si è rammollito; **they have recently softened their position** recentemente hanno ammorbidito la loro posizione; **to soften the blow** (*fig*) attutire il colpo; **to soften the impact of** ridurre l'impatto di
■ VI (*see vt*) ammorbidirsi; attenuarsi; attutirsi; smorzarsi; fiaccarsi; (*person, character*) addolcirsi; **her heart softened** si intenerì ; **fry until the onion has softened** soffriggere finché la cipolla si ammorbidisce; **his voice softened** la sua voce si è addolcita
▶ **soften up** VT + ADV (*fam*): **to soften sb up** ammorbidire qn
sof·ten·er ['sɒfnə[r]] N ammorbidente *m*
soft fruit N (*Brit*) ≈ frutti *mpl* di bosco
soft furnishings NPL (*Brit*) tessuti *mpl* d'arredo
soft goods NPL (*Comm*) tessili *mpl*
soft-hearted [ˌsɒft'hɑːtɪd] ADJ dal cuore tenero
softie ['sɒftɪ] N = **softy**
soft landing N (*of spacecraft*: *on moon*) allunaggio morbido; (: *on earth*) atterraggio morbido; (*fig*: *easy answer*) soluzione *f* indolore; (*Econ*) situazione *f* di stallo dell'economia
soft·ly ['sɒftlɪ] ADV (*gen*) dolcemente; (*walk*) silenziosamente; (*gently*: *knock*) lievemente; **he**

Ss

laughed softly rise piano; **softly lit** debolmente illuminato
softly-softly ['sɒftlı'sɒftlı] ADJ *(approach)* cauto(-a); **a softly-softly approach** un approccio cauto
soft·ness ['sɒftnıs] N *(of skin, bed, snow, leather)* morbidezza; *(of voice, manner, glance)* dolcezza; *(indulgence)* indulgenza
soft option N soluzione (più) facile
soft palate N palato molle
soft-pedal [ˌsɒft'pɛdl] VT *(fig)* minimizzare
soft pedal N *(on piano)* sordina
soft porn N soft-core *inv*
soft sell N persuasione *f* (indiretta) all'acquisto
soft shoulder, soft verge N *(Aut)* banchina non transitabile
soft soap N *(fam)* saponata, lusinghe *fpl*
soft-soap [ˌsɒft'səʊp] VT *(fam)* dare del sapone a, lusingare
soft-spoken ['sɒftˌspəʊkən] ADJ dalla voce carezzevole
soft target N obiettivo civile *(e quindi facile da colpire)*
soft-top ['sftˌtɒp] N *(Auto)* (automobile *f*) decappottabile *f*
soft touch N *(fam)*: **to be a soft touch** lasciarsi mungere facilmente
soft toy N pupazzo di peluche
soft verge N *(Aut)* = **soft shoulder**
◎ **soft·ware** ['sɒftˌwɛəʳ] N *(Comput)* software *m inv*
software package N *(Comput)* pacchetto di software
soft water N acqua non calcarea, acqua dolce
soft·wood ['sɒftˌwʊd] N legno dolce
softy, softie ['sɒftı] N *(fam: weak)* pappamolle *m/f*; (: *tender-hearted)* tenerone(-a)
SOGAT ['səʊgæt] N ABBR *(Brit:* = **Society of Graphical and Allied Trades**) *sindacato dei lavoratori dell'industria della stampa*
sog·gy ['sɒgı] ADJ *(comp* **-ier**, *superl* **-iest**) fradicio(-a), inzuppato(-a); *(bread, cake)* molle, pesante
soh, so [səʊ] N *(Mus)* sol *m inv*
◎ **soil** [sɔıl] N *(earth)* terreno, terra, suolo; **chalky/poor soil** terreno calcareo/povero; **cover it with soil** coprilo di terra; **on British soil** sul suolo britannico; **the soil** *(fig: farmland)* la terra
■ VT *(dirty)* sporcare; *(fig: reputation, honour etc)* infangare, macchiare
soiled [sɔıld] ADJ sporco(-a), sudicio(-a)
so·journ ['sɒdʒɜ:n] *(liter)* N soggiorno
■ VI soggiornare
sol·ace ['sɒlıs] N consolazione *f*
so·lar ['səʊləʳ] ADJ solare
solar cell N cellula solare
so·lar·ium [səʊ'lɛərıəm] N *(pl* **solariums** *or* **solaria** [səʊ'lɛərıə]) solarium *m inv*
solar panel N pannello solare
so·lar plex·us [ˌsəʊlə'plɛksəs] N *(Anat)* plesso solare
solar power N energia solare
sold [səʊld] PT, PP *of* **sell**
sol·der ['səʊldəʳ] N lega per saldatura
■ VT saldare; **soldering iron** saldatore *m (attrezzo)*
◎ **sol·dier** ['səʊldʒəʳ] N soldato, militare *m*; **a girl soldier** una soldatessa; **toy soldier** soldatino; **an old soldier** *(also fig)* un veterano; **to play at soldiers** giocare alla guerra
■ VI fare il soldato
▶ **soldier on** VI + ADV perseverare
sol·dier·ly ['səʊldʒəlı] ADJ *(behaviour, appearance)* da soldato
sold out ADJ *(Comm)* esaurito

sole[1] [səʊl] N *(of foot)* pianta del piede; *(of shoe)* suola
■ VT risolare

DID YOU KNOW ...?
sole is not translated by the Italian word *sole*

sole[2] [səʊl] N *(pl* **sole** *or* **soles**) *(fish)* sogliola
sole[3] [səʊl] ADJ **1** *(only)* unico(-a), solo(-a); **the sole reason** la sola *or* l'unica ragione; **she was the sole woman in the group** era l'unica donna del gruppo **2** *(exclusive)* esclusivo(-a); **sole agent** agente *m or* rappresentante *m* esclusivo; **sole rights** diritti in esclusiva
sol·ecism ['sɒləˌsızəm] N *(frm: in grammar)* solecismo; (: *in behaviour)* scorrettezza
sole·ly ['səʊllı] ADV solamente, unicamente; **I will hold you solely responsible** ti considererò il solo responsabile
sol·emn ['sɒləm] ADJ solenne
so·lem·nity [sə'lɛmnıtı] N solennità *f inv*
sol·em·ni·za·tion [ˌsɒləmnaı'zeıʃən] *(frm)* N solennizzazione *f*; *(of marriage)* celebrazione *f*
sol·em·nize ['sɒləmˌnaız] *(frm)* VT solennizzare; *(marriage)* celebrare
sol·emn·ly ['sɒləmlı] ADV solennemente
so·lenoid ['səʊlıˌnɔıd] N *(Phys, Elec)* solenoide *m*
sole trader N titolare *m/f* unico(-a) di azienda
sol-fa ['sɒl'fɑ:] N *(Mus)* solfeggio
so·lic·it [sə'lısıt] VT *(frm: request)* richiedere, sollecitare
■ VI *(prostitute)* adescare
so·lic·it·ing [sə'lısıtıŋ] N *(Law)* adescamento
◎ **so·lici·tor** [sə'lısıtəʳ] N *(Brit: in court)* ≈ avvocato(-essa) (: *for wills etc)* ≈ notaio *(Am)* rappresentante *m* legale *(di una città o un ministero)*

SOLICITOR

Il **solicitor** appartiene a una delle due branche della professione legale britannica. È compito dei **solicitors** agire come consulenti in materia legale, redigere documenti legali, preparare i casi per i "barristers". Contrariamente a questi ultimi, i **solicitors** non sono qualificati a rappresentare una parte nelle corti investite della potestà di decidere sui reati più gravi. *Vedi anche* **solicitor**
▷ www.lawsociety.org.uk/home.law
▷ www.advocates.org.uk/
▷ www.scotland.gov.uk/About/Factsheets/Legal-System-Factsheet

Solicitor General N *(pl* **Solicitors General**) *(in GB)* ≈ sostituto procuratore *m* generale; *(in USA)* ≈ sottosegretario di stato al ministero di Grazia e Giustizia
so·lici·tous [sə'lısıtəs] ADJ *(frm: concerned, caring)* sollecito(-a); **solicitous (about** *or* **for)** preoccupato(-a) (per); **solicitous to please** ansioso(-a) di piacere
so·lici·tude [sə'lısıtju:d] N *(frm)* sollecitudine *f*
◎ **sol·id** ['sɒlıd] ADJ *(gen)* solido(-a); *(not hollow)* pieno(-a); *(gold, wood)* massiccio(-a); *(crowd, row)* compatto(-a); *(line)* ininterrotto(-a); *(vote)* unanime; *(meal)* sostanzioso(-a); **to become solid** solidificarsi; **cut out of solid rock** scolpito(-a) nella roccia viva; **a solid wall** un muro solido; **solid gold** oro massiccio; **as solid as a rock** solido come una roccia; **to be frozen solid** essere completamente ghiacciato(-a); **we waited two solid hours** abbiamo aspettato due ore filate; **a man of solid build** un uomo di corporatura massiccia; **the**

street was packed solid with people la strada era affollatissima; **a solid mass of colour** una massa uniforme di colore; **he's a good solid worker** è un lavoratore serio; **a solid argument** un argomento fondato *or* valido; **solid common sense** buon senso pratico; **the town is solid for Labour** nella città c'è una gran maggioranza laburista
■ N solido

soli·dar·ity [ˌsɒlɪ'dærɪtɪ] N solidarietà

solid fuel N combustibile *m* solido

solid geometry N geometria solida

solid ground N: **to be on solid ground** essere su terraferma; (*fig*) muoversi su un terreno sicuro

so·lidi·fi·ca·tion [səˌlɪdɪfɪ'keɪʃən] N solidificazione *f*

so·lidi·fy [sə'lɪdɪˌfaɪ] VT solidificare
■ VI solidificarsi

so·lid·ity [sə'lɪdɪtɪ] N solidità

sol·id·ly ['sɒlɪdlɪ] ADV (*gen*) solidamente; **a solidly-built house** una casa costruita solidamente; **to work solidly** lavorare sodo; **to vote solidly for sb** votare all'unanimità per qn; **they are solidly behind him** lo appoggiano all'unanimità

solid-state ['sɒlɪdˌsteɪt] ADJ (*Elec*) a stato solido; **solid-state physics** fisica dei solidi

so·lilo·quy [sə'lɪləkwɪ] N soliloquio

sol·ip·sism ['sɒlɪpˌsɪzəm] N solipsismo

soli·taire [ˌsɒlɪ'tɛə^r] N (*game, gem*) solitario

soli·tary ['sɒlɪtərɪ] ADJ (*alone, secluded*) solitario(-a); (*sole: example, case*) solo(-a), unico(-a); **a solitary figure** una figura solitaria; **not a solitary one** neanche uno(-a)

solitary confinement N: **to be in solitary confinement** essere in cella d'isolamento

soli·tude ['sɒlɪtju:d] N solitudine *f*

solo ['səʊləʊ] N (*pl* **solos**) (*Mus*) assolo; **a tenor solo** un assolo di tenore; **a guitar solo** un assolo di chitarra
■ ADJ: **solo flight** volo in solitario; **passage for solo violin** brano per violino solista
■ ADV (*Mus*): **to play (***or* **sing) solo** fare un assolo; **to fly solo** volare in solitario

so·lo·ist ['səʊləʊɪst] N solista *m/f*

Solo·mon ['sɒləmən] N Salomone *m*

Solomon Islands NPL: **the Solomon Islands** le isole Salomone

sol·stice ['sɒlstɪs] N solstizio

sol·ubil·ity [ˌsɒljʊ'bɪlɪtɪ] N solubilità

sol·uble ['sɒljʊbl] ADJ solubile

so·lute [sɒ'lju:t] N soluto

◎ **so·lu·tion** [sə'lu:ʃən] N soluzione *f*

solv·able ['sɒlvəbəl] ADJ (*problem*) risolvibile

◎ **solve** [sɒlv] VT risolvere

sol·ven·cy ['sɒlvənsɪ] N (*Fin*) solvibilità

sol·vent ['sɒlvənt] ADJ (*Fin*) solvibile; (*Chem*) solvente; **to be solvent** avere una discreta posizione economica
■ N (*Chem*) solvente *m*

solvent abuse N abuso di colle e solventi (*a scopo stupefacente*)

Som. ABBR (*Brit*) = *Somerset*

So·ma·li [səʊ'mɑ:lɪ] ADJ, N somalo(-a)

So·ma·lia [səʊ'mɑ:lɪə] N la Somalia

Somaliland [səʊ'mɑ:lɪˌlænd] N paesi *mpl* del Corno d'Africa

sombre, (*Am*) **som·ber** ['sɒmbə^r] ADJ (*mood, person*) triste, tetro(-a); (*colour*) scuro(-a); **a sombre prospect** una triste prospettiva

som·bre·ly, (*Am*) **som·ber·ly** ['sɒmbəlɪ] ADV (*reply, gaze etc*) tristemente; (*dressed*) di scuro; (*painted*) con colori scuri

◎ **some** [sʌm] KEYWORD

■ ADJ

1 (*a certain amount or number of*): **some tea/water/biscuits/girls** del tè/dell'acqua/dei biscotti/delle ragazze; **I have some books** ho qualche libro *or* alcuni libri; **some children came** sono venuti dei bambini; **all I have left is some chocolate** mi è rimasto solo un po' di cioccolato; **have some more crisps** prendi ancora delle patatine; **there's some milk in the fridge** c'è un po' del latte in frigo; **there were some people outside** c'era della gente fuori; **he asked me some questions about the accident** mi ha fatto qualche domanda *or* alcune domande *or* delle domande sull'incidente; **have some tea/ice-cream** prendi un po' di tè/gelato; **if you have some time to spare** se hai un po' di tempo a disposizione

2 (*certain: in contrast*) certo(-a), alcuni(-e) *pl*; **some people hate fish** certa gente odia il pesce; **some people say that ...** certa gente dice *or* alcuni dicono che...; **in some ways** per certi versi, in un certo senso

3 (*vague, indeterminate*) un(-a) certo(-a), qualche; **some day** un giorno; **some day next week** un giorno della prossima settimana; **in some form or other** in una qualche forma; **some man was asking for you** un tale chiedeva di te; **at some place in Sweden** da qualche parte in Svezia; **some politician or other** un qualche uomo politico; **some other time!** sarà per un'altra volta!

4 (*considerable amount of*): **it took some courage to do that** ci è voluto un bel coraggio per farlo; **some days ago** parecchi giorni fa; **some distance away** abbastanza lontano; **at some length** a lungo; **after some time** dopo un po'

5 (*emphatic: a few, a little*): **that's SOME consolation!** questo è già qualcosa!; **there's still SOME petrol in the tank** c'è ancora un po' di benzina nel serbatoio

6 (*fam: intensive*): **that's some fish!** questo sì che è un pesce!; **it was some party** è stata una grande festa; **you're some help!** (*iro*) sei proprio un bell'aiuto!

■ PRON

1 (*a certain number*) alcuni(-e) *pl*, certi(-e) *pl*; **some of them are crazy** alcuni di loro sono pazzi; **I've got some** (*books etc*) ne ho alcuni; (*milk, money*) ne ho un po'; **some (of them) have been sold** alcuni sono stati venduti; **would you like some?** ne vorresti qualcuno?; **do take some** prendine qualcuno; **some went this way and some that** alcuni andarono di qua e altri di là

2 (*a certain amount*) un po'; **could I have some of that cheese?** potrei avere un po' di quel formaggio?; **have some more** prendine ancora un po'; **have some!** prendine un po'!; **I've read some of the book** ho letto parte del libro; **some of what he said was true** parte di ciò che ha detto era vero; **some of it was left** ne è rimasto un po'

■ ADV: **some 20 people** circa 20 persone

◎ **some·body** ['sʌmbədɪ] PRON qualcuno; **there's somebody coming** sta arrivando qualcuno; **somebody knocked at the door** hanno bussato alla porta; **somebody else** qualcun altro; **somebody Italian** un italiano; **somebody told me so** me l'ha detto qualcuno; **somebody or other** qualcuno

Ss

■ N: **to be somebody** essere qualcuno; **she thinks she's somebody** si crede importante

some·day ['sʌm,deɪ] ADV uno di questi giorni, un giorno o l'altro

◎**some·how** ['sʌm,haʊ] ADV **1** (*in some way*) in qualche modo, in un modo o nell'altro; **it must be done somehow or other** bene o male va fatto; **we managed it somehow** non so come, ma ce l'abbiamo fatta; **we'll manage somehow** in un modo o nell'altro ce la faremo; **I'll do it somehow** lo farò, in un modo o nell'altro **2** (*for some reason*) per un motivo o per l'altro; **it seems odd somehow** non so perché, ma mi sembra strano; **somehow I've never succeeded** chissà perché non ce l'ho mai fatta; **somehow I don't think he believed me** qualcosa mi dice che non mi ha creduto

◎**some·one** ['sʌm,wʌn] PRON = somebody

some·place ['sʌm,pleɪs] ADV (*Am*) = somewhere

som·er·sault ['sʌmə,sɔːlt] N (*by person*) capriola; (: *in air*) salto mortale; (*by car etc*) ribaltamento, cappottamento
■ VI (*see n*: *also*: **turn a somersault**) fare una capriola; fare un salto mortale; cappottare, ribaltarsi

◎**some·thing** ['sʌm,θɪŋ] PRON qualche cosa, qualcosa; **something nice** (*pretty*) qualcosa di carino; (*to eat*) qualcosa di buono; (*to do*) qualcosa di bello; **something interesting** qualcosa di interessante; **something special** qualcosa di speciale; **something to do** qualcosa da fare; **something else** altro, qualcos'altro; **something has happened** è successo qualcosa; **something of the kind** qualcosa del genere; **she said something or other about it** mi ha detto qualcosa a tale proposito; **he's a lecturer in something or other** è professore di non so che; **he's a doctor or something** è dottore o qualcosa del genere; **wear something warm** mettiti qualcosa di pesante; **there's something the matter** c'è qualcosa che non va; **to have something to live for** avere uno scopo nella vita; **there's something in what you say** c'è del vero in quello che dici; **will you have something to drink?** vuoi qualcosa da bere?; **he's called John something** si chiama John vattelappesca; **give her something for herself** regalale qualcosa di personale; **here's something for your trouble** eccoti qualcosa per il disturbo; **I hope to see something of you** spero di vederti qualche volta; **I think you may have something there** penso che tu abbia ragione; (*good idea*) mi sembra una buona idea, la tua; **there's something about him that ...** c'è qualcosa in lui che...; **she has a certain something** ha un certo non so che; **that's really something!** mica male!; **it would be really something!** non sarebbe mica male!
■ ADV
1 something over/under 200 un po' più/meno di 200; **something like 200** circa 200; **... or something like that** ...o giù di lì ; **it cost a hundred pounds, or something like that** è costato cento sterline o giù di lì ; **he's something like me** mi assomiglia un po'; **now that's something like a rose!** (*approving comment*) questa sì che è una rosa!
2 it's something of a problem è un bel problema; **he is something of a liar** è un bel pezzo di bugiardo; **he's something of a musician** è un musicista abbastanza bravo
3 (*fam*): **the weather was something shocking** faceva un tempo da cani

some·time ['sʌm,taɪm] ADV un giorno, uno di questi giorni; **sometime last month** un giorno, il mese scorso; **sometime before tomorrow** prima di domani; **sometime next year** (nel corso del)l'anno prossimo; **sometime soon** presto, uno di questi giorni; **I'll finish it sometime** lo finirò uno di questi giorni; **I want to go to Spain sometime** voglio andare in Spagna un giorno o l'altro; **you must come and see us sometime** vieni a trovarci uno di questi giorni; **sometime or (an)other it will have to be done** bisognerà farlo prima o poi
■ ADJ (*frm*: *former*) ex

◎**some·times** ['sʌm,taɪmz] ADV qualche volta, a volte; **sometimes I think Carol hates me** a volte ho l'impressione che Carol mi detesti

◎**some·what** ['sʌm,wɒt] ADV piuttosto, alquanto

◎**some·where** ['sʌm,weə^r] ADV **1** (*in space*) da qualche parte, in qualche posto; **somewhere else** da qualche altra parte; **I lost it somewhere** l'ho perso da qualche parte; **I've left my keys somewhere** ho lasciato le chiavi da qualche parte; **somewhere in Wales** da qualche parte nel Galles; **somewhere or other in Scotland** da qualche parte in Scozia; **now we're getting somewhere!** ora stiamo facendo dei passi in avanti **2** (*approximately*) circa, all'incirca, più o meno; **he paid somewhere around £12** l'ha pagato circa 12 sterline; **he's somewhere in his fifties** è sulla cinquantina

som·nam·bu·lism [sɒm'næmbjʊ,lɪzəm] N (*frm*) sonnambulismo

som·nam·bu·list [sɒm'næmbjʊlɪst] N (*frm*) sonnambulo(-a)

som·no·lence ['sɒmnələns] N (*liter*) sonnolenza

som·no·lent ['sɒmnələnt] ADJ (*liter*) sonnolento(-a)

◎**son** [sʌn] N figlio; **come here son** (*fam*) vieni qui figliolo; **the Son of God/of Man** (*Rel*) il Figlio di Dio/dell'uomo

so·nar ['səʊnɑː^r] N sonar *m inv*

so·na·ta [sə'nɑːtə] N sonata

son et lu·mi·ère ['sɒneɪ'luːmɪ,ɛə^r] N (*Brit*) spettacolo "Suoni e Luci"

◎**song** [sɒŋ] N (*ballad etc*) canzone *f*; (*of birds*) canto; **give us a song!** cantaci una canzone!; **to burst into song** mettersi a cantare; **to make a great song and dance about sth** (*fig*) fare un sacco di storie per qc; **I got it for a song** (*fig*) l'ho avuto per quattro soldi

song·bird ['sɒŋ,bɜːd] N uccello canoro

song book N canzoniere *m*

song cycle N ciclo di canzoni

song·writer ['sɒŋ,raɪtə^r] N compositore(-trice) di canzoni

son·ic ['sɒnɪk] ADJ sonico(-a); **sonic depth finder** ecoscandaglio

sonic boom, sonic bang N bang *m inv* sonico

son-in-law ['sʌnɪn,lɔː] N (*pl* **sons-in-law**) genero

son·net ['sɒnɪt] N sonetto

son·ny ['sʌnɪ] N (*fam*) figlio mio, ragazzo mio

so·nor·ity [sə'nɒrɪtɪ] N (*frm*) sonorità *f inv*

so·no·rous ['sɒnərəs] ADJ (*frm*) sonoro(-a)

so·no·rous·ly ['sɒnərəslɪ] ADV (*frm*) sonoramente

◎**soon** [suːn] ADV **1** (*before long*) presto, fra poco; **come back soon!** torna presto!; **soon afterwards** poco dopo; **it will soon be summer** presto *or* fra poco sarà estate; **you would soon get lost** ti perderesti subito; **see you soon!** a presto!; **very/quite soon** molto/abbastanza presto; **he soon changed his mind** ha cambiato presto idea **2** (*early*) presto; **how soon can you be ready?** fra quanto tempo sarai pronto?; **Friday is too soon** venerdì è troppo presto; **it's too soon to tell** è troppo presto per dirlo; **all too soon** fin troppo presto; **we were none too soon** siamo arrivati appena in tempo; **an hour too soon** con un'ora di anticipo **3** (*with as*): **as soon as possible** prima possibile, il più presto possibile; **I'll do it as soon as I can** lo farò appena posso; **as soon as it was finished** appena finito **4** (*expressing preference*): **I would as soon not go** preferirei non andarci; **I would as soon he didn't know** preferirei che non lo sapesse

soon·er ['su:nəʳ] ADV **1** (*of time*) prima; **can't you come a bit sooner?** non puoi venire un po' prima?; **sooner or later** prima o poi; **the sooner the better** prima è meglio è; **when are you leaving? — the sooner the better** quando parti? — prima parto meglio è; **no sooner had we left than ...** eravamo appena partiti, quando...; **no sooner said than done** detto fatto **2** (*of preference*): **I'd** *or* **I would sooner not do it** preferirei non farlo; **I would sooner do something useful** preferirei fare qualcosa di utile; **I'd sooner die!** (*fam*) piuttosto morirei!

soot [sʊt] N fuliggine *f*

soothe [su:ð] VT (*gen*) calmare; (*pain, anxieties*) alleviare

sooth·ing ['su:ðɪŋ] ADJ (*ointment etc*) calmante; (*tone, words etc*) rassicurante; (*bath*) rilassante

sooth·ing·ly ['su:ðɪŋlɪ] ADV (*speak*) con tono rassicurante; (*stroke, caress*) in modo rassicurante

sooty ['sʊtɪ] ADJ (*comp* **-ier**, *superl* **-iest**) fuligginoso(-a)

SOP [ˌɛsəʊ'pi:] N ABBR (*Banking*) = *standard operating procedure*

sop [sɒp] N **1** (*concession*): **that's only a sop** è soltanto un contentino; **to give sb a sop** dare il contentino a qn; **as a sop to his pride** per lusingare il suo amor proprio **2** **sops** NPL (*food*) pappette *fpl*

▸ **sop up** VT + ADV (*fam*) assorbire, bere

◎ **so·phis·ti·cat·ed** [sə'fɪstɪˌkeɪtɪd] ADJ (*method, machine*) sofisticato(-a); (*person*) raffinato(-a), sofisticato(-a); (*clothes, room*) raffinato(-a); (*discussion*) sottile; (*mind, film*) complicato(-a); **a sophisticated machine** una macchina sofisticata; **sophisticated tastes** gusti raffinati

so·phis·ti·ca·tion [səˌfɪstɪ'keɪʃən] N (*of method, machine*) complessità; (*of person, clothes etc*) raffinatezza; (*of argument etc*) sottigliezza

soph·ist·ry ['sɒfɪstrɪ] N (*frm*) sofisma *m*

Sophocles ['sɒfəˌkli:z] N Sofocle *m*

sopho·more ['sɒfəˌmɔ:ʳ] N (*Am*) *studente del secondo anno di scuola superiore o dell'università*

sopo·rif·ic [ˌsɒpə'rɪfɪk] ADJ soporifero(-a)

sop·ping ['sɒpɪŋ] ADJ (*also:* **sopping wet**) bagnato(-a) fradicio(-a)

sop·py ['sɒpɪ] ADJ (*comp* **-ier**, *superl* **-iest**) (*Brit fam: sentimental*) sdolcinato(-a); (*: silly*) sciocco(-a)

so·pra·no [sə'prɑ:nəʊ] N (*pl* **sopranos**) (*Mus: singer*) soprano *m/f*; (*: voice*) soprano *m*

■ ADJ di soprano

sor·bet ['sɔ:bɪt] N sorbetto

sor·cer·er ['sɔ:sərəʳ] N stregone *m*

sor·cer·ess ['sɔ:sərɪs] N maga, fattucchiera

sor·cery ['sɔ:sərɪ] N stregoneria

sor·did ['sɔ:dɪd] ADJ (*place, room etc*) sordido(-a); (*deal, motive etc*) meschino(-a), sordido(-a)

sor·did·ly ['sɔ:dɪdlɪ] ADV (*see adj*) sordidamente; meschinamente

sore [sɔ:ʳ] ADJ (*comp* **-r**, *superl* **-st**) **1** (*painful*) dolorante; **I feel sore all over** sono tutto indolenzito; **sore throat** mal *m* di gola; **it's sore** mi fa male; **my eyes are sore** *or* **I have sore eyes** mi fanno male gli occhi; **he's like a bear with a sore head** (*fig*) è molto irascibile **2** (*fig*): **it's a sore point** è un punto delicato; **to touch on a sore point** mettere il dito sulla piaga; **to feel sore about sth** (*esp Am fam*) essere molto seccato(-a) per qc; **don't get sore!** (*esp Am fam*) non te la prendere!

■ N (*Med*) piaga

sore·ly ['sɔ:lɪ] ADV (*tempted*) fortemente; (*regretted*) amaramente; **it is sorely needed** ce n'è un estremo bisogno; **she is sorely missed by her family** la sua famiglia sente molto la sua mancanza; **he has been sorely tried** (*frm*) è stato duramente provato

sore·ness ['sɔ:nɪs] N (*painfulness*) indolenzimento; (*irritation*) irritazione *f*

sor·ghum ['sɔ:gəm] N sorgo comune, saggina

sor·rel ['sɒrəl] N **1** (*Bot*) acetosa **2** (*horse*) sauro; (*colour*) giallo bruno *inv*

■ ADJ (*colour*) giallo bruno *inv*

sor·row ['sɒrəʊ] N dolore *m*; **her sorrow at the death of her son** il suo dolore per la morte del figlio; **more in sorrow than in anger** più con dolore che con rabbia

■ VI: **to sorrow over sth** (*liter*) addolorarsi per qc

sor·row·ful ['sɒrəʊfʊl] ADJ addolorato(-a), triste

sor·row·ful·ly ['sɒrəʊfəlɪ] ADV tristemente, con aria triste *or* desolata

sor·row·ing ['sɒrəʊɪŋ] ADJ (*liter*) addolorato(-a), afflitto(-a)

◎ **sor·ry** ['sɒrɪ] ADJ (*comp* **-ier**, *superl* **-iest**) **1** (*in apologizing*): **sorry!** scusa! (*or* scusi! *or* scusate!); **awfully sorry!** *or* **so sorry!** *or* **very sorry!** (*more polite*) scusa (*or* scusi *or* scusate) tanto!; **to be sorry** essere spiacente *or* desolato(-a); **to say sorry (to sb for sth)** chiedere scusa (a qn per qc); **to be sorry about sth** essere dispiaciuto(-a) *or* spiacente di qc; **I'm sorry I'm late** scusa il ritardo; **I'm sorry about what happened last night** scusami per quello che è successo ieri sera; **I'm sorry, but you're wrong** scusa ma hai torto; **to be sorry to have to do sth** essere spiacente di dover fare qc **2** (*Brit: what did you say?*): **sorry?** come, scusa? **3** (*regretful, sad*) triste, addolorato(-a), desolato(-a); **I'm very sorry** mi dispiace tanto; **I'm sorry to hear that ...** mi dispiace (sapere) che...; **I'm sorry to tell you that ...** mi dispiace dirti che...; **it was a failure, I'm sorry to say** purtroppo è stato un fiasco; **I can't say I'm sorry** non posso dire che mi dispiaccia; **you'll be sorry for this!** te ne pentirai! **4** (*pitying*): **to be** *or* **feel sorry for sb** dispiacersi per qn; **to be** *or* **feel sorry for o.s.** compiangersi, piangersi addosso **5** (*condition, tale*) pietoso(-a); (*sight, failure*) triste; (*excuse*) misero(-a); **in a sorry state** in uno stato pietoso

Ss

◎ **sort** [sɔ:t] N

1 (*gen*) specie *f inv*, genere *m*, tipo; (*make: of coffee, car etc*) tipo; **what sort do you want?** che tipo vuole?; **I know his sort** conosco il suo tipo; **books of all sorts** libri di ogni genere; **he's a painter of sorts** è, per così dire, un pittore; **of the worst sort** della peggior specie; **something of the sort** qualcosa del genere; **it's tea of a sort** è una specie di tè; **I'll do nothing of the sort!** nemmeno per sogno!; **behaviour of that sort** comportamento del genere; **it takes all sorts (to make a world)** il mondo è bello perché è vario

2 sort of *or* **what sort of car?** che tipo di macchina?; **what sort of bike have you got?** che tipo di bici hai?; **what sort of man is he?** che tipo di uomo è?; **it's my sort of film** è il tipo di film che piace a me; **he's not the sort of man to say that** non è il tipo da dire cose del genere; **all sorts of dogs** cani di ogni tipo; **he's some sort of painter** è una specie di pittore; **it's a sort of dance** è una specie di danza; **and all that sort of thing** e così via; **what sort of an answer is that?** che razza di risposta è questa?; **that's the sort of person I am** io sono fatto così ; **you know the sort of thing I mean** sai cosa voglio dire; **it's sort of awkward** (*fam*) è piuttosto difficile; **it's sort of yellow** (*fam*) è giallastro; **aren't you pleased? — sort of** (*fam*) non sei contento? — insomma; **I sort of thought that would happen** (*fam*) quasi me lo sentivo che sarebbe successo

3 (*person*): **he's a good sort** è una brava persona; **he's not my sort** non è il mio tipo; **he's an odd sort** è un tipo strano

4 **to be out of sorts** (*in a bad temper*) avere la luna (storta *or* di traverso), non essere in vena; (*unwell*) non essere in forma

■ VT

1 (*classify: documents, stamps*) classificare; (*put in order: papers, clothes*) mettere in ordine; (*: letters*) smistare; (*separate*) separare, dividere; **the students are sorted into three groups** gli studenti sono suddivisi in tre gruppi

2 (*Comput*) ordinare

▸ **sort out** VT + ADV

1 = **sort** VT 1

2 (*straighten out: room*) riordinare, sistemare; (*: papers, one's ideas*) riordinare; (*solve: problem etc*) risolvere; **have you managed to sort out what's happening?** sei riuscito a sapere cosa succede?; **things will sort themselves out** le cose si sistemeranno da sole; **we've got it sorted out now** la faccenda è risolta

3 **I'll sort him out!** (*fam*) lo sistemo io!

sort code N codice *m* bancario

sor·tie ['sɔːtɪ] N (*Aer, Mil*) sortita

sort·ing of·fice ['sɔːtɪŋ,ɒfɪs] N (*Post*) ufficio di smistamento

SOS [,ɛsəʊ'ɛs] N S.O.S. *m inv*

so-so ['səʊsəʊ] ADJ, ADV (*fam*) così così ; **how are you feeling? – so-so** come ti senti? – così così

sot [sɒt] N (*old*) ubriacone(-a)

souf·flé ['suːfleɪ] N soufflé *m inv*; **cheese soufflé** soufflé di formaggio

soufflé dish N stampo per soufflé

sought [sɔːt] PT, PP *of* **seek**

sought-after ['sɔːt,ɑːftə'] ADJ richiesto(-a)

◎ **soul** [səʊl] N 1 anima; **with all one's soul** con tutta l'anima; **All Souls' Day** il giorno dei morti; **God rest his soul** pace all'anima sua; **he's the soul of discretion** è la discrezione in persona 2 (*person*) anima; **the ship sank with all souls** la nave affondò con tutti a bordo; **I didn't see a soul** non ho visto anima viva; **the poor soul had nowhere to sleep** il poveraccio non aveva dove dormire 3 (*also:* **soul music**) soul *m*

▹ www.bbc.co.uk/radio2/soldonsong/genres/soul.shtml

soul-destroying ['səʊldɪ'strɔɪɪŋ] ADJ (*fig: boring*) alienante; (*: depressing*) demoralizzante

soul·ful ['səʊlfʊl] ADJ (*gen*) pieno(-a) di sentimento; (*eyes, expression*) espressivo(-a)

soul·ful·ly ['səʊlfəlɪ] ADV (*gaze*) in modo meditabondo

soul·less ['səʊllɪs] ADJ (*task, factory*) alienante; (*person*) senza cuore, crudele

soul mate N anima gemella

soul-searching ['səʊl,sɜːtʃɪŋ] N: **after much soul-searching** dopo un profondo esame di coscienza

◎ **sound**[1] [saʊnd] N (*gen*) suono; (*of sea, breaking glass etc*) rumore *m*; (*volume of TV*) audio; **don't make a sound!** non fare rumore!; **the sound of footsteps** il rumore di passi; **can I turn the sound down?** posso abbassare l'audio?; **the speed of sound** la velocità del suono; **to the sound of the national anthem** al suono dell'inno nazionale; **not a sound was to be heard** non si sentiva volare una mosca; **a language with many consonant sounds** una lingua piena di consonanti; **I don't like the sound of it** (*fig: of film etc*) non mi dice niente; (*: of news*) è preoccupante

■ VT 1 (*alarm, bell, horn*) suonare; **to sound the retreat** (*Mil*) suonare la ritirata; **to sound a note of warning** (*fig*) dare un segnale d'allarme 2 **sound your "r"s more** pronuncia la r più chiaramente 3 (*Med*): **to sound sb's chest** auscultare il torace di qn

■ VI 1 (*trumpet, bell, alarm*) suonare; (*voice, siren*) risuonare; **a cannon sounded a long way off** si sentì un colpo di cannone in lontananza 2 **it sounds hollow** dal rumore sembra vuoto; **he sounds Italian to me** da come parla mi sembra italiano; **it sounds like French** (*similar*) somiglia al francese; **it sounds better like that** suona meglio così ; **that sounds like them arriving now** mi sembra di sentirli arrivare; **you sound like your mother** mi sembra di sentire parlare tua madre; **he sounded angry** (a giudicare) dalla voce sembrava arrabbiato 3 (*seem*): **that sounds interesting** mi sembra interessante; **that sounds very odd** sembra molto strano; **how does it sound to you?** che te ne pare?; **that sounds like a good idea** sembra una buona idea; **she sounds like a nice girl** sembra una brava ragazza; **it sounds as if she's doing well at school** sembra che stia andando bene a scuola; **it sounds as if she won't be coming** ho l'impressione che non verrà

▸ **sound off** VI + ADV (*fam*): **to sound off (about)** (*give one's opinions*) fare dei grandi discorsi (su); (*boast*) vantarsi (di); (*grumble*) brontolare (per)

▸ **sound out** VT + ADV sondare

sound[2] [saʊnd] ADJ (*comp* **-er**, *superl* **-est**) 1 (*in good condition, healthy*) sano(-a); (*: structure, organization, investment*) solido(-a); **to be of sound mind** essere sano(-a) di mente; **as sound as a bell** (*person*) sano(-a) come un pesce; (*thing*) in perfette condizioni; **a sound structure** una struttura solida 2 (*valid: argument, policy*) valido(-a); (*: move*) sensato(-a); (*dependable: person*) affidabile; **Julian gave me some sound advice** Julian mi ha dato un buon consiglio; **a sound conservative** un conservatore convinto; **he's sound on government policy** conosce molto bene la politica del governo 3 (*thorough*): **to give sb a sound beating** picchiare qn di santa ragione 4 (*sleep: deep, untroubled*) profondo(-a); **he's a sound sleeper** è uno che dorme sodo

■ ADV: **to be sound asleep** dormire sodo, dormire profondamente

sound[3] [saʊnd] VT (*Naut*) scandagliare, sondare; **to sound sb out about sth** sondare le opinioni di qn su qc

sound[4] [saʊnd] N (*Geog*) stretto

sound archives NPL (*Radio*) fonoteca

sound barrier N: **the sound barrier** la barriera *or* il muro del suono

sound·bite ['saʊnd,baɪt] N frase *f* incisiva (*trasmessa per radio o per TV*)

sound·card ['saʊndkɑːd] N (*Comput*) sound card *f inv*, scheda *f* audio *inv*
sound effects NPL effetti *mpl* sonori
sound engineer N tecnico del suono
sound·ing ['saʊndɪŋ] N (*Naut*) scandagliamento
sounding board N (*Mus*) tavola armonica; (*fig*) banco di prova
sound·less ['saʊndlɪs] ADJ silenzioso(-a)
sound·less·ly ['saʊndlɪslɪ] ADV (*move etc*) silenziosamente
sound·ly ['saʊndlɪ] ADV (*build*) solidamente; (*argue*) giudiziosamente; (*invest*) saggiamente; **to beat sb soundly** (*thrash*) picchiare qn di santa ragione; (*defeat*) battere duramente qn; **to sleep soundly** dormire profondamente
sound·ness ['saʊndnɪs] N (*of body, mind*) sanità; (*of argument, judgment*) validità; (*of business, building*) solidità; (*solvency*) solvibilità
sound·proof ['saʊnd,pruːf] ADJ insonorizzato(-a)
■ VT insonorizzare
sound·proof·ed ['saʊnd,pruːft] ADJ insonorizzato(-a)
sound·proofing ['saʊnd,pruːfɪŋ] N insonorizzazione *f*
sound system N impianto *m* audio *inv*
sound·track ['saʊnd,træk] N (*music*) colonna sonora; (*speech, noises*) sonoro
sound wave N (*Phys*) onda sonora
soup [suːp] N minestra; (*thick*) zuppa; (*clear*) brodo; **vegetable soup** minestra di verdura; **to be in the soup** (*fam*) essere *or* trovarsi nei pasticci
soup·çon ['suːpsøn] N (*frm, hum*) ombra
soup course N minestra
souped-up ['suːpt,ʌp] ADJ (*fam: car/motorbike engine*) truccato(-a)
soup kitchen N mensa dei poveri
soup plate N piatto fondo
soup spoon N cucchiaio da minestra
soup tureen N zuppiera
soupy ['suːpɪ] ADJ (*comp* **-ier**, *superl* **-iest**) **1** (*liquid, fog*) denso(-a) **2** (*Am fam: sentimental*) sdolcinato(-a)
sour ['saʊə[r]] ADJ (*comp* **-er**, *superl* **-est**) (*gen*) aspro(-a), agro(-a); (*milk, fig: person, remark*) acido(-a); (*smell*) acre; **whisky sour** *cocktail di whisky al limone*; **to go** *or* **turn sour** (*milk, wine*) inacidirsi; (*fig: relationship, plans*) guastarsi; **it was sour grapes on his part** (*fig*) ha fatto come la volpe con l'uva, è stata solo invidia da parte sua; **to be in a sour mood** (*fig*) essere di umore nero
◎ **source** [sɔːs] N (*of river*) sorgente *f*; (*fig: of problem, epidemic*) fonte *f*, origine *f*; **oranges are a source of vitamin C** le arance sono ricche di vitamina C; **I have it from a reliable source that ...** ho saputo da fonte sicura che...; **renewable sources of energy** fonti di energia rinnovabile; **the source of the Severn** la sorgente del fiume Severn
■ VT comperare; **they source their organic products from outside the UK** comperano i loro prodotti biologici da paesi al di fuori del Regno Unito
source code N (*Comput*) codice *m* sorgente
source language N (*Ling*) lingua di partenza; (*Comput*) linguaggio di programmazione *or* assoluto
sour cherry N visciola
sour(ed) cream ['saʊə(d)'kriːm] N (*Culin*) panna acida
sour-faced ['saʊə,feɪsd] ADJ (*person*) dal viso arcigno
sourly ['saʊəlɪ] ADV (*remark, look*) aspramente
sour·ness ['saʊənɪs] N (*see adj*) asprezza; acidità; acredine *f*

souse [saʊs] VT (*Culin: pickle*) marinare; (*plunge*) immergere; (*soak*) ammollare; **soused fish** (*Culin*) pesce *m* in carpione; **to souse sth with water** inzuppare qc d'acqua
◎ **south** [saʊθ] N sud *m*, meridione *m*, mezzogiorno; **(to the) south of** a sud di; **it's south of London** è a sud di Londra; **in the south of** nel sud di; **the wind is from the south** il vento soffia da sud *or* da mezzogiorno; **to veer to the south** (*wind*) girare verso sud; **the South of France** il sud della Francia, la Francia del sud *or* meridionale
■ ADJ (*gen*) sud *inv*; (*coast*) meridionale; (*wind*) del sud; **the south coast** la costa meridionale; **South Wales** il Galles del sud *or* meridionale
■ ADV verso sud; **south of the border** a sud del confine; **to sail due south** andare direttamente verso sud; **to travel south** viaggiare verso sud; **we were travelling south** viaggiavamo verso sud; **this house faces south** questa casa è esposta a sud *or* a mezzogiorno
South Africa N il Sudafrica
▷ www.gov.za
▷ www.southafrica.net
South African ADJ, N sudafricano(-a)
South America N il Sudamerica, l'America del sud
South American ADJ, N sudamericano(-a)
South Australia N Australia meridionale
▷ www.sa.gov.au
south·bound ['saʊθ,baʊnd] ADJ (*gen*) diretto(-a) a sud; (*carriageway*) sud *inv*
South Caro·li·na N Carolina del Sud
▷ www.myscgov.com/
South Da·ko·ta N Sud Dakota *m*
▷ www.state.sd.us/
◎ **south-east** [,saʊθ'iːst] N sud-est *m*
■ ADJ (*wind*) di sud-est; (*counties etc*) sudorientale
■ ADV verso sud-est
South-East Asia N l'Asia sudorientale
south-easterly [,saʊθ'iːstəlɪ] ADJ (*wind*) che viene da sud-est; (*direction*) verso sud-est
south-eastern [,saʊθ'iːstən] ADJ di sudest, sudorientale
south·er·ly ['sʌðəlɪ] ADJ (*wind*) del sud; (*direction*) verso sud; **house with a southerly aspect** casa esposta a sud
◎ **south·ern** ['sʌðən] ADJ (*region*) del sud, meridionale; (*coast*) meridionale; (*wall*) esposto(-a) a sud; **Southern Europe** l'Europa del sud *or* meridionale; **in southern Spain** nella Spagna del sud *or* meridionale, nel sud della Spagna; **the southern part of the island** la zona meridionale dell'isola
south·ern·er ['sʌðənə[r]] N abitante *m/f* del sud
southern hemisphere N: **the southern hemisphere** l'emisfero australe
south·ern·most ['sʌðən,məʊst] ADJ il/la più a sud
South Pole N: **the South Pole** il polo sud
South Sea Islands NPL: **the South Sea Islands** le isole dei Mari del Sud
South Seas NPL: **the South Seas** i Mari del Sud
south-south-east ['saʊθ,saʊθ'iːst] N sud sud-est *m*
■ ADJ di sud sud-est
■ ADV verso sud sud-est
south-south-west ['saʊθ,saʊθ'wɛst] N sud sud-ovest *m*
■ ADJ di sud sud-ovest
■ ADV verso sud sud-ovest
South Vietnam N Vietnam *m* del Sud

Ss

south·ward(s) ['saʊθwəd(z)] ADV verso sud
■ ADJ a sud
◎ **south-west** [ˌsaʊθ'wɛst] N sud-ovest *m*
■ ADJ di sud-ovest
■ ADV verso sud-ovest
south-westerly [ˌsaʊθ'wɛstəlɪ] ADJ (*wind*) che viene da sud-ovest; (*direction*) verso sud-ovest
south-western [ˌsaʊθ'wɛstən] ADJ di sud-ovest
sou·venir [ˌsu:və'nɪəʳ] N souvenir *m inv*, ricordo; **a souvenir shop** un negozio di souvenir
sou·west·er [saʊ'wɛstəʳ] N cappello di cerata
sov·er·eign ['sɒvrɪn] ADJ (*gen*) sovrano(-a); **with sovereign contempt** (*fig*) con sommo disprezzo; **a sovereign remedy** (*old*) un rimedio infallibile
■ N (*monarch*) sovrano(-a); (*coin*) sovrana
sov·er·eign·ty ['sɒvrəntɪ] N sovranità
so·vi·et ['səʊvɪət] N soviet *m inv*
■ ADJ sovietico(-a); **Soviet Russia** Russia Sovietica
Soviet Union N: **the Soviet Union** l'Unione *f* Sovietica
sow¹ [səʊ] (*pt* **sowed**, *pp* **sown**) VT seminare; **to sow (the seeds of) doubt in sb's mind** far sorgere dei dubbi a qn; **to sow (the seeds of) discord** seminare zizzania
sow² [saʊ] N scrofa
sow·er ['səʊəʳ] N (*person*) seminatore(-trice); (*machine*) seminatrice *f*
sow·ing ['səʊɪŋ] N semina
sown [səʊn] PP *of* **sow¹**
soya ['sɔɪə], (*Am*) **soy** [sɔɪ] N soia
soya bean, (*Am*) **soy bean** N seme *m* di soia
soy(a) flour N farina di soia
soya milk N latte *m* di soia
soy sauce [sɔɪ-] N salsa di soia
soz·zled ['sɒzld] ADJ (*Brit fam*) sbronzo(-a); **to get sozzled** sbronzarsi
spa [spɑ:] N (*resort*) stazione *f* termale, terme *fpl*; (*Am*: *also*: **health spa**) centro di cure estetiche
◎ **space** [speɪs] N (*all senses*) spazio; **to stare into space** guardare nel vuoto; **to clear a space for sth** fare posto per qc; **to take up a lot of space** occupare molto spazio, ingombrare; **to buy space in a newspaper** comprare spazio pubblicitario su un giornale; **blank space** spazio in bianco; **answer in the space provided** scrivere le risposte negli appositi spazi; **in a confined space** in un luogo chiuso; **there isn't enough space** non c'è abbastanza spazio; **I couldn't find a space for my car** non sono riuscito a trovare un posto per la macchina; **in a short space of time** in un breve lasso di tempo; **(with)in the space of an hour/three generations** nell'arco di un'ora/di tre generazioni; **for the space of a fortnight** per un periodo di due settimane; **after a space of two hours** dopo un intervallo di due ore
■ VT (*also*: **space out**: *gen*) distanziare; (: *payments*) scaglionare, dilazionare; (: *type*) spaziare
■ ADJ (*research, capsule, probe etc*) spaziale
space-age ['speɪsˌeɪdʒ] ADJ dell'era spaziale
space age N era spaziale
space-bar ['speɪsˌbɑ:ʳ] N (*on typewriter, computer*) barra spaziatrice
space·craft ['speɪsˌkrɑ:ft] N, PL INV veicolo spaziale
spaced out ADJ sballato(-a), suonato(-a); (*with drugs*) calato(-a)
space·man ['speɪsmən] N (*pl* **-men**) astronauta *m*, cosmonauta *m*
space-saving ['speɪsˌseɪvɪŋ] ADJ poco ingombrante
space·ship ['speɪʃɪp] N astronave *f*, navicella spaziale
space shuttle N shuttle *m inv*
space station N laboratorio spaziale
space·suit ['speɪsˌsu:t] N tuta spaziale
space·walk ['speɪsˌwɔ:k] N passeggiata spaziale
space·woman ['speɪsˌwʊmən] N (*pl* **-women**) astronauta *f*, cosmonauta *f*
spacey ['speɪsɪ] ADJ (*fam*: *person*) stranito(-a); (: *music, art*) strano(-a) e irreale
spac·ing ['speɪsɪŋ] N (*Typing etc*) spaziatura; **single/double spacing** spaziatura uno/due, spaziatura singola/doppia
spa·cious ['speɪʃəs] ADJ spazioso(-a)
spa·cious·ness ['speɪʃəsnɪs] N spaziosità
spade [speɪd] N **1** (*tool*) vanga; (*child's*) paletta; **to call a spade a spade** (*fig*) dire pane al pane (e vino al vino) **2** (*Cards*): **spades** NPL picche *fpl*; **the three of spades** il tre di picche; **the ace of spades** l'asso di picche; **to play spades** giocare picche; **to play a spade** giocare una carta di picche
spade·ful ['speɪdfʊl] N vangata
spade·work ['speɪdˌwɜ:k] N (*fig*) il grosso dei preparativi
spa·ghet·ti [spə'gɛtɪ] N spaghetti *mpl*
spaghetti western N (*Cine*) western *m inv* all'italiana
Spain [speɪn] N la Spagna
spam [spæm] (*Comput*) N spamming *m*
■ VT: **to spam sb** inviare a qn messaggi pubblicitari non richiesti via e-mail
span¹ [spæn] N (*of hand*) spanna; (*of bridge, arch, roof*) luce *f*, campata; (*of time*) periodo; **attention span** capacità di concentrazione; **a short attention span** una limitata capacità di concentrazione; **life span** durata; **the batteries have a life span of six hours** le batterie hanno una durata di sei ore; **time span** intervallo di tempo; **a span of ten years** un periodo di dieci anni
■ VT (*subj*: *bridge etc*) attraversare; **to span 3 decades** abbracciare un periodo di 30 anni; **his career spanned sixteen years** la sua carriera abbracciava un periodo di sedici anni; **her interests spanned every aspect of nature** i suoi interessi spaziavano in ogni aspetto della natura; **the bridge spanning the Avon** il ponte che attraversa il fiume Avon; **his memory spanned 50 years** i suoi ricordi risalivano a 50 anni fa
span² [spæn] PT *of* **spin**
span·gle ['spæŋgl] VT far brillare
■ N paillette *f inv*
Span·iard ['spænjəd] N spagnolo(-a)
span·iel ['spænjəl] N spaniel *m inv*
Span·ish ['spænɪʃ] ADJ (*gen*) spagnolo(-a); (*teacher, lesson, book*) di spagnolo; **Spanish America** America latina
■ N **1** (*language*) spagnolo **2** **the Spanish** NPL (*people*) gli Spagnoli
Spanish omelette N *frittata di patate*
Spanish onion N cipolla di Spagna
spank [spæŋk] VT sculacciare
spank·ing ['spæŋkɪŋ] N sculacciata
■ ADJ **1** (*breeze*) frizzante; (*pace*) svelto(-a) **2** (*fam*: *very*): **a spanking new car** una macchina nuova di zecca
spanner ['spænəʳ] N (*Brit*) chiave *f* inglese; **adjustable spanner** chiave *f* a rullino; **to throw a spanner in the works** (*fig*) mettere il bastone tra le ruote
spar¹ [spɑ:ʳ] N (*Naut*) asta, palo
spar² [spɑ:ʳ] VI: **to spar with sb** (*Boxing*) allenarsi (con qn); (*argue*) discutere (con qn)
◎ **spare** [spɛəʳ] ADJ **1** (*surplus*) in più, d'avanzo; (*reserve*) di

riserva, di scorta; **spare batteries** pile di scorta; **the spare wheel** la ruota di scorta; **I've lost my key. – have you got a spare?** ho perso la chiave. – ne hai un'altra?; **I haven't enough spare cash to go on holiday** non mi avanzano soldi per andare in vacanza; **any spare change, please?** ha qualche spicciolo, per favore?; **is there any string spare?** c'è rimasto un po' di spago?; **there are two going spare** (*Brit*) ce ne sono due in più; **to go spare** (*fam*) andare su tutte le furie **2** (*person: lean*) asciutto(-a); **she's tall and spare** è alta e asciutta
■ N (*part*) pezzo di ricambio
■ VT **1** (*be grudging with*): **she spared no effort** *or* **pains in helping me** ha fatto tutto il possibile per aiutarmi; **to spare no expense** non badare a spese **2** (*do without*) fare a meno di; **can you spare this for a moment?** puoi prestarmelo per un attimo?; **if you can spare it** se puoi farne a meno; **can you spare the time?** hai tempo?; **I can't spare the time** non ho tempo; **to spare a thought for** pensare a; **can you spare (me) £10?** puoi prestarmi 10 sterline?; **there is none to spare** ce n'è appena a sufficienza; **I've a few minutes to spare** ho un attimino di tempo; **I got to the station with 3 minutes to spare** sono arrivato alla stazione con 3 minuti di anticipo; **I had £1 to spare** mi avanzava 1 sterlina; **they've got no money to spare** non hanno poi tanti soldi; **there is no time to spare** non c'è tempo da perdere **3** (*refrain from hurting, using*) risparmiare; **to spare sb's feelings** avere riguardo per i sentimenti di qn; **she doesn't spare herself** non si risparmia **4** (*save from need or trouble*): **to spare sb the trouble of doing sth** risparmiare a qn la fatica di fare qc; **spare me the details** risparmiami i particolari

spare part N pezzo di ricambio

spare·rib ['spɛə,rɪb] N (*Culin*) costina di maiale

spare room N stanza degli ospiti

spare time N tempo libero

spare tyre N (*Aut*) gomma di scorta; (*fig*) maniglie *fpl* dell'amore

spare wheel N (*Aut*) ruota di scorta

spar·ing ['spɛərɪŋ] ADJ (*amount, use*) moderato(-a); **to be sparing of praise** essere avaro(-a) di lodi; **to be sparing with** essere parsimonioso(-a) con

spar·ing·ly ['spɛərɪŋlɪ] ADV (*eat, live*) frugalmente; (*use, drink*) con moderazione, moderatamente

◎ **spark** [spɑːk] N (*from fire*) scintilla; (*fig*): **there wasn't a spark of life in the battery** la batteria non dava segni di vita; **he didn't show a spark of interest** non ha mostrato il benché minimo interesse; **bright spark** (*iro*) genio
■ VT (*also:* **spark off**: *debate, quarrel, revolt*) provocare; (: *interest*) suscitare

spar·kle ['spɑːkl] N (*gen*) scintillio, sfavillio; (*fig: of person, conversation*) brio
■ VI (*flash, shine*) scintillare, sfavillare, luccicare; (: *eyes*) brillare, luccicare; (: *person, conversation*) brillare; (*wine*) frizzare, spumeggiare

spar·kler ['spɑːklə^r] N **1** bengala *m inv*, fuoco d'artificio **2** (*fam: diamond*) brillante *m*

spar·kling ['spɑːklɪŋ] ADJ (*gen*) scintillante, sfavillante; (*person, conversation*) brillante; (*wine*) frizzante

spark plug, sparking plug ['spɑːkɪŋ,plʌg] N (*Aut*) candela

spar·ring match ['spɑːrɪŋ'mætʃ] N disputa amichevole

spar·ring part·ner ['spɑːrɪŋ'pɑːtnə^r] N sparring partner *m inv*; (*fig*) *interlocutore abituale in discussioni, dibattiti, tavole rotonde ecc*

spar·row ['spærəʊ] N passero

sparrow·hawk ['spærəʊ,hɔːk] N sparviero

sparse [spɑːs] ADJ (*comp* **-r**, *superl* **-st**) (*vegetation, hair*) rado(-a); (*population*) scarso(-a)

sparse·ly ['spɑːslɪ] ADV poco, scarsamente

Spar·ta ['spɑːtə] N Sparta

Spar·tan, spar·tan ['spɑːtən] ADJ, N (*also fig*) spartano(-a)

spasm ['spæzəm] N (*Med*) spasmo; (*of coughing*) attacco, accesso; (*fig*) accesso; **there was a brief spasm of activity** c'è stato un momento di attività spasmodica; **a spasm of pain** uno spasmo di dolore

spas·mod·ic [spæz'mɒdɪk] ADJ (*Med*) spasmodico(-a); (*fig: growth*) irregolare; **she made spasmodic attempts to give up smoking** ha tentato più volte di smettere di fumare

spas·modi·cal·ly [spæz'mɒdɪkəlɪ] ADV (*fig: grow*) irregolarmente; (: *attempt, work*) in modo discontinuo

spas·tic ['spæstɪk] ADJ, N (*offensive*) spastico(-a)

spat¹ [spæt] PT, PP *of* **spit**

spat² [spæt] N (*Am*) battibecco

spate [speɪt] N (*of letters, orders*) valanga; (*of words, abuse*) torrente *m*; (*of accidents*) gran numero; **to be in spate** (*river*) essere in piena; **a spate of attacks** una lunga serie di attacchi

spa·tial ['speɪʃəl] ADJ spaziale

spat·ter ['spætə^r] VT: **to spatter (with)** schizzare (di); **spattered with mud** inzaccherato(-a)

spatu·la ['spætjʊlə] N spatola

spawn [spɔːn] N (*of fish, frogs*) uova *fpl*
■ VI deporre le uova
■ VT (*pej*) produrre

spay [speɪ] VT sterilizzare

◎ **speak** [spiːk] (*vb: pt* **spoke**, *pp* **spoken**) VT (*words, lines*) dire; (*language*) parlare; **she speaks Italian** parla italiano; **do you speak English?** parli inglese?; **to speak the truth** dire la verità; **to speak one's mind** dire quello che si pensa
■ VI
1 (*gen*) parlare; **to speak to sb** parlare a qn; (*converse with*) parlare con qn; **have you spoken to him?** gli hai parlato?; **I spoke to her yesterday** le ho parlato ieri; **I'll speak to him about it** (*problem, idea*) gliene parlerò; (*his lateness etc*) glielo farò presente; **to speak about (***or* **on** *or* **of) sth** parlare di qc; **to speak in a whisper** bisbigliare; **they haven't spoken to each other since they quarrelled** da quando hanno litigato non si rivolgono la parola; **to speak at a conference/in a debate** intervenire *or* prendere la parola ad una conferenza/in un dibattito; **he's very well spoken of** tutti ne parlano bene; **I don't know him to speak to** lo conosco solo di vista; **so to speak** per così dire; **it's nothing to speak of** non è niente di speciale; **he has no money to speak of** non si può proprio dire che sia ricco; **speaking of holidays** a proposito di vacanze; **roughly speaking** grosso modo; **speaking for myself** per quel che mi riguarda; **speaking as a student myself, I ...** in qualità di studente, io...; **generally speaking** generalmente parlando
2 (*Telec*): **speaking!** sono io!; **this is Peter speaking** sono Peter; **could I speak to Alison? – speaking!** posso parlare con Alison? – sono io!; **who's speaking?** chi parla?
▸ **speak for** VI + PREP: **to speak for sb** parlare a nome di qn; **speak for yourself!** (*fam*) parla per te!; **let her**

Ss

speak for herself lascia che dica la sua opinione; **it speaks for itself** parla da sé; **that picture is already spoken for** (*in shop*) quel quadro è già stato venduto

▶ **speak up** VI + ADV

1 (*raise voice*) parlare a voce alta; **speak up!** parli più forte!

2 (*fig: speak out*) parlare apertamente; **he finally decided to speak out** alla fine si è deciso a parlare; **to speak out against sth** dichiararsi pubblicamente contrario(-a) a qc; **to speak up for sb** parlare a favore di qn

Speak·er ['spi:kəʳ] N (*Brit Parliament*): **the Speaker** ≈ il presidente della Camera dei deputati

SPEAKER, SPEAKER OF THE HOUSE

Nel sistema parlamentare britannico la responsabilità generale per l'organizzazione e il buon funzionamento della Camera dei Comuni spetta al presidente della Camera, detto "**Speaker (of the House)**". Il presidente (non necessariamente appartenente al partito al governo) viene eletto all'inizio della legislatura; non ha diritto di voto e non partecipa al dibattito parlamentare se non nelle vesti di arbitro imparziale delle sedute.

Negli Stati Uniti il presidente della Camera dei Rappresentanti, o **Speaker of the House** è anche il leader del partito di maggioranza, fa parte della Camera ed è eletto dal partito a cui appartiene, di cui è il portavoce ufficiale. La carica di **Speaker** è tra le più importanti del governo federale e chi la ricopre rappresenta il successore in linea dopo il presidente e il vicepresidente.

▷ www.parliament.uk/works/speaker.cfm

◎ **speak·er** ['spi:kəʳ] N **1** (*gen*) chi parla; (*in discussion*) interlocutore(-trice); (*in public*) oratore(-trice); **he's a good/poor speaker** è un buon/pessimo oratore **2** (*of language*): **are you a Welsh speaker?** parla gallese?; **they're both English native speakers** sono tutti e due madrelingua inglesi **3** (*also:* **loudspeaker**) altoparlante *m*

speak·ing ['spi:kɪŋ] ADJ parlante; **Italian-speaking people** persone che parlano italiano; **I am not on speaking terms with her** la conosco solo di vista; **they are not on speaking terms** (*after quarrel*) non si rivolgono la parola

■ N (*skill*) arte *f* del parlare

spear [spɪəʳ] N lancia

spear·head ['spɪə,hɛd] N punta di lancia; (*Mil*) reparto d'assalto; (*fig*) avanguardie *mpl*

■ VT (*attack etc*) condurre

spear·mint ['spɪəmɪnt] N (*Bot etc*) menta verde

spec [spɛk] N (*Brit fam*): **to buy sth on spec** comprare qc sperando di fare un affare; **I went to the theatre on spec** sono andato al teatro nella speranza di trovare un biglietto

◎ **spe·cial** ['spɛʃəl] ADJ **1** (*specific*) particolare, speciale; **have you any special date in mind?** hai in mente una data particolare?; **I've no-one special in mind** non penso a nessuno in particolare **2** (*exceptional: price, favour, legislation*) speciale; (*: powers*) straordinario(-a); (*particular: care, situation, attention*) particolare; **take special care!** siate particolarmente prudenti!; **to make a special effort** fare del proprio meglio; **this is a special day for me** è una giornata speciale per me; **you're extra special** (*fam*) sei veramente speciale; **to expect special treatment** aspettarsi un trattamento speciale; **nothing special** niente di speciale; **what's so special about her?** che cosa ha di tanto speciale?

■ N (*train*) treno straordinario; (*newspaper*) edizione *f* straordinaria; **the chef's special** la specialità dello chef

special agent N agente *m* segreto

Special Branch N *serivizi segreti in Gran Bretagna*

special correspondent N (*Press*) inviato speciale

special delivery N (*Post*): **by special delivery** per espresso

special education N insegnamento di sostegno

special effects NPL (*Cine*) effetti *mpl* speciali

special feature N (*Press*) servizio speciale

spe·cial·ism ['spɛʃəlɪzəm] N (*subject, skill*) specialità *f inv*; (*specialization*) specializzazione *f*

◎ **spe·cial·ist** ['spɛʃəlɪst] N specialista *m/f*; **a heart specialist** (*Med*) un cardiologo

■ ADJ (*teacher*) specializzato(-a); (*dictionary*) specialistico(-a); (*knowlege, work*) da specialista

spe·ci·al·ity [,spɛʃɪ'ælɪtɪ], **spe·cial·ty** (*Am*) ['spɛʃəltɪ] N specialità *f inv*; **to make a speciality of sth** specializzarsi in qc

spe·ciali·za·tion [,spɛʃəlaɪ'zeɪʃən] N specializzazione *f*

◎ **spe·cial·ize** ['spɛʃə,laɪz] VI: **to specialize (in)** specializzarsi (in)

spe·cial·ized ['spɛʃə,laɪzd] ADJ (*work*) specialistico(-a); (*staff, worker*) specializzato(-a)

spe·cial·ly ['spɛʃəlɪ] ADV (*specifically*) specialmente; (*on purpose*) apposta; (*particularly*) particolarmente; **it can be very cold here, specially in January** qui può fare molto freddo, specialmente in gennaio; **not specially** non particolarmente; **do you like opera? – not specially** ti piace l'opera? – non particolarmente; **it's specially designed for teenagers** è concepito apposta per i giovani

special needs N: **with special needs** con difficoltà d'apprendimento; **special needs students** studenti con difficoltà d'apprendimento; **special needs education** insegnamento di sostegno; **to teach special needs** insegnare a ragazzi con difficoltà di apprendimento

special offer N (*Comm*) offerta speciale

spe·cial·ty ['spɛʃəltɪ] N (*Am*) = **speciality**

◎ **spe·cies** ['spi:ʃi:z] N, PL INV specie *f inv*

◎ **spe·cif·ic** [spə'sɪfɪk] ADJ **1** (*example, order etc*) preciso(-a); (*meaning*) specifico(-a); **certain specific issues** certi problemi specifici; **could you be more specific?** puoi essere più preciso?; **he was very specific about that** è stato molto chiaro in proposito; **to be specific to** avere un legame specifico con

2 (*Bio, Phys, Chem, Med*) specifico(-a); *see also* **specifics**

◎ **spe·cifi·cal·ly** [spə'sɪfɪkəlɪ] ADV (*explicitly: state, warn*) chiaramente, esplicitamente; (*especially: design, intend*) appositamente; **it's specifically designed for teenagers** è appositamente concepito per i giovani; **in Britain, or more specifically in England ...** in Gran Bretagna, o più specificamente in Inghilterra...; **I specifically said that...** avevo chiaramente detto che...

speci·fi·ca·tion [,spɛsɪfɪ'keɪʃən] N **1** (*gen*) specificazione *f* **2** **specifications** (*of car, machine*) dati *mpl* caratteristici; (*for building*) dettagli *mpl*; **the parts do not meet our specification** i pezzi non sono conformi alle nostre specifiche

specific gravity N (*Phys*) peso specifico

spec·if·ics [spəˈsɪfɪks] NPL: **the specifics** i dettagli, i particolari

speci·fy [ˈspɛsɪˌfaɪ] VT specificare, precisare; **unless otherwise specified** salvo indicazioni contrarie; **he hasn't specified what action he will take** non ha precisato quale iniziativa intende adottare

speci·men [ˈspɛsɪmɪn] N *(sample: gen)* campione *m*; *(: of rock, species)* esemplare *m*; **a rare specimen** un esemplare raro; **a specimen of urine** un campione di urina; **he's an odd specimen** *(fig)* è un tipo strano

specimen page N *(Typ)* prova di stampa

specimen signature N firma depositata

spe·cious [ˈspiːʃəs] ADJ *(frm)* specioso(-a)

speck [spɛk] N *(of dust, dirt)* granello; *(of ink, paint etc)* macchiolina, puntino; **it was just a speck on the horizon** era solo un puntino all'orizzonte

speck·led [ˈspɛkld] ADJ maculato(-a)

specs [spɛks] NPL *(fam)* occhiali *mpl*

spec·ta·cle [ˈspɛktəkl] N spettacolo; **to make a spectacle of o.s.** *(fig)* coprirsi di ridicolo; **a bizarre spectacle** uno spettacolo bizzarro; *see also* **spectacles**

spectacle case N *(Brit)* custodia degli occhiali

spec·ta·cles [ˈspɛktəklz] NPL *(Brit)* occhiali *mpl*

◎ **spec·tacu·lar** [spɛkˈtækjʊləʳ] ADJ *(gen)* spettacolare; *(view)* favoloso(-a)

■ N *(Cine, TV)* kolossal *m*, film *m inv etc* spettacolare

spec·tacu·lar·ly [spɛkˈtækjʊləlɪ] ADV in modo spettacolare

spec·ta·tor [spɛkˈteɪtəʳ] N spettatore(-trice)

spectator sport N sport *m inv* come spettacolo *inv*; **football is Britain's most popular spectator sport** in Gran Bretagna il calcio è lo sport più seguito dal pubblico

spec·tra [ˈspɛktrə] NPL *of* **spectrum**

spec·tral [ˈspɛktrəl] ADJ *(liter: ghostly)* spettrale

spec·tre, *(Am)* **spec·ter** [ˈspɛktəʳ] N spettro

spec·trum [ˈspɛktrəm] N *(pl* **spectra***)* *(Phys)* spettro; *(fig)* gamma; **a wide spectrum of problems** un'ampia gamma di problemi; **the colours of the spectrum** i colori dell'arcobaleno

◎ **specu·late** [ˈspɛkjʊˌleɪt] VI *(Fin)* speculare; *(wonder)*: **to speculate on the stock exchange** speculare in borsa; **to speculate (about** *or* **on sth/whether)** chiedersi (qc/se); **I can only speculate** posso solo fare congetture

■ VT: **to speculate that ...** ipotizzare che...; **they speculate that he had a heart attack** ipotizzano che abbia avuto un infarto

specu·la·tion [ˌspɛkjʊˈleɪʃən] N *(guessing)* congetture *fpl*; *(Fin)* speculazione *f*

specu·la·tive [ˈspɛkjʊlətɪv] ADJ *(Philosophy, Fin)* speculativo(-a); *(expression)* indagatore(-trice)

specu·la·tor [ˈspɛkjʊˌleɪtəʳ] N *(Fin)* speculatore(-trice)

sped [spɛd] PT, PP *of* **speed**

◎ **speech** [spiːtʃ] N **1** *(faculty)* parola; *(manner of speaking)* parlata, modo di parlare; **to lose the power of speech** perdere l'uso della parola; **freedom of speech** libertà di parola; **the development of speech in children** lo sviluppo del linguaggio nei bambini **2** *(language)* linguaggio; **children's speech** il linguaggio dei bambini **3** *(formal talk)* discorso, intervento; **to make a speech** fare un discorso; **he made a speech at the conference** ha fatto un discorso alla conferenza **4** *(Brit Gram)*: **direct/indirect speech** discorso diretto/indiretto

speech day N *(Brit Scol)* giorno della premiazione

speechi·fy [ˈspiːtʃɪˌfaɪ] VI *(pej)*: **to speechify (about)** sproloquiare (su)

speech impediment N difetto di pronuncia

speech·less [ˈspiːtʃlɪs] ADJ senza parole, ammutolito(-a); **to be speechless** rimanere senza parole

speech·less·ly [ˈspiːtʃlɪslɪ] ADV: **I watched speechlessly** rimasi a guardare senza riuscire a proferire parola

speech·mak·ing [ˈspiːtʃˌmeɪkɪŋ] N *(slightly pej)* discorsi *mpl* d'occasione

speech organ N organo vocale

speech therapist N logopedista *m/f*, logoterapista *m/f*

speech therapy N logoterapia

speech training N corso di dizione

◎ **speed** [spiːd] N **1** *(rate of movement)* velocità; *(rapidity, haste)* rapidità; *(promptness)* prontezza; **at speed** *(Brit)* velocemente; **at full speed** *or* **at top speed** a tutta velocità; **at a speed of 70 km/h** a una velocità di 70 km all'ora; **the speed of light/sound** la velocità della luce/del suono; **what speed were you doing?** *(Aut)* a che velocità andavi?; **to pick up** *or* **gather speed** *(car)* acquistare velocità; *(project, work)* procedere più speditamente; **the speed of his reactions** la sua prontezza di riflessi; **shorthand/typing speeds** numero di parole al minuto in stenografia/dattilografia **2** *(Aut, Tech: gear)* marcia; **a five-speed gearbox** un cambio a cinque marce; **a ten-speed bike** una bicicletta a dieci marce **3** *(Phot: of film)* sensibilità; *(: of shutter)* tempo di apertura

■ VI **1** *(pt, pp* **sped***)* **to speed along** *(car, work)* procedere velocemente; **to speed away** *or* **off** *(car, person)* sfrecciare via; **the years sped by** gli anni sono volati **2** *(pt, pp* **speeded***)* *(Aut: exceed speed limit)* andare a velocità eccessiva

▶ **speed up** *(pt, pp* **speeded up***)* VI + ADV *(gen)* andare più veloce; *(Aut)* accelerare; *(walker/worker/train etc)* camminare/lavorare/viaggiare più veloce; *(engine, machine)* girare più veloce; *(production)* accelerare

■ VT + ADV accelerare

speed·boat [ˈspiːdˌbəʊt] N motoscafo

speed bump N dissuasore *m* di velocità

speed camera N autovelox® *m inv*

speed cop N *(fam)* agente *m* della stradale

speed dating [-ˈdeɪtɪŋ] N *sistema di appuntamenti grazie al quale si possono incontrare in pochissimo tempo diverse persone e scegliere eventualmente chi frequentare*

speed dial N selezione *f* rapida *(di numero telefonico)*

speedi·ly [ˈspiːdɪlɪ] ADV *(see adj)* velocemente, rapidamente; prontamente

speed·ing [ˈspiːdɪŋ] N *(Aut)* eccesso di velocità; **he was fined for speeding** ha preso la multa per eccesso di velocità

speed limit N limite *m* di velocità; **to exceed the speed limit** superare il limite di velocità

speed merchant N *(fam)* amante *m/f* della velocità

speed·om·eter [spɪˈdɒmɪtəʳ] N tachimetro

speed restriction N limite *m* di velocità

speed trap N *(Aut)* *tratto di strada sul quale la polizia controlla la velocità dei veicoli*

speed·way [ˈspiːdˌweɪ] N: **speedway racing** corsa motociclistica su pista

speedy [ˈspiːdɪ] ADJ *(comp* **-ier**, *superl* **-iest***)* *(gen)* veloce, rapido(-a); *(reply)* pronto(-a)

spe·leolo·gist [ˌspiːlɪˈɒlədʒɪst] N speleologo(-a)

◎ **spell¹** [spɛl] *(pt, pp* **spelled** *or* **spelt***)* VT: **how do you spell**

Ss

your name? come si scrive il tuo nome?; **can you spell it for me?** me lo puoi dettare lettera per lettera?; **c-a-t spells "cat"** c-a-t formano la parola "cat"; **I can't spell** faccio errori di ortografia; **it spells disaster for us** (*fig*) significa la nostra rovina
▸ **spell out** VT + ADV (*fig*): **to spell sth out for sb** spiegare qc a qn per filo e per segno

spell[2] [spɛl] N (*also:* **magic spell**) incantesimo; (*words*) formula magica; **an evil spell** una stregoneria; **to cast** *or* **put a spell on sb** fare un incantesimo a qn; (*fig*) stregare qn; **to be under sb's spell** essere stregato(-a) da qn; **to fall under sb's spell** (*fig*) subire il fascino di qn; **to break the spell** (*also fig*) rompere l'incantesimo

spell[3] [spɛl] N (*period of time*) periodo; **cold spell** periodo di freddo; **a spell of dry weather** un periodo di tempo secco; **to do a spell of duty** fare un turno; **they're going through a bad spell** stanno attraversando un brutto periodo

spell·bind·ing [ˈspɛlˌbaɪndɪŋ] ADJ affascinante

spell·bound [ˈspɛlˌbaʊnd] ADJ incantato(-a), affascinato(-a); **to hold sb spellbound** affascinare qn

spell·check [ˈspɛlˌtʃɛk] VT (*Comput*) fare la correzione ortografica di

spell·check·er [ˈspɛlˌtʃɛkəʳ] N (*Comput*) correttore *m* ortografico

spell·er [ˈspɛləʳ] N **1** (*person*): **to be a bad/good speller** fare/non fare errori di ortografia **2** (*Am*: *book*) sillabario

spell·ing [ˈspɛlɪŋ] N ortografia; **my spelling is terrible** faccio molto errori di ortografia

spelling mistake N errore *m* di ortografia

spelt [spɛlt] PT, PP *of* **spell**[1]

spe·lunk·er [spɪˈlʌŋkəʳ] N (*Am*) speleologo(-a)

spe·lunk·ing [spɪˈlʌŋkɪŋ] N (*Am*) speleologia

◎ **spend** [spɛnd] (*pt, pp* **spent**) VT **1** (*money*) spendere; **to spend money on sb/sth** spendere soldi per qn/qc; **they spend an enormous amount of money on advertising** spendono grosse cifre per la pubblicità; **without spending a penny** senza spendere una lira; **to go to spend a penny** (*Brit fam euph*) ≈ andare a fare una telefonata (*fig fam*(**2** (*pass*) passare, trascorrere; **he spent a month in France** ha trascorso un mese in Francia; **he spends his time sleeping** passa il tempo dormendo **3** (*devote*): **to spend time/money/effort on sth** dedicare tempo/soldi/energie a qc; **I spent 2 hours writing that letter** ho passato 2 ore a scrivere quella lettera; **he spends a lot of time on his hobbies** dedica un sacco di tempo ai suoi hobby

spend·er [ˈspɛndəʳ] N: **to be a big spender** avere le mani bucate

spend·ing [ˈspɛndɪŋ] N spesa; **government spending** spesa pubblica

spending money N denaro per le piccole spese

spending power N potere *m* d'acquisto

spend·thrift [ˈspɛndˌθrɪft] ADJ spendereccio(-a)
■ N spendaccione(-a)

spent [spɛnt] PT, PP *of* **spend**
■ ADJ (*cartridge, bullets, match*) usato(-a); (*supplies*) esaurito(-a); **he's a spent force** è un uomo finito

sperm [spɜːm] N (*Bio*) sperma *m*

sper·ma·to·zo·on [ˌspɜːmətəʊˈzəʊɒn] N (*pl* **spermatozoa** [ˌspɜːmətəʊˈzəʊə]) spermatozoo

sperm bank N banca dello sperma

sperm count N numero di spermatozoi

sper·mi·ci·dal [ˌspɜːmɪˈsaɪdəl] ADJ spermicida

sper·mi·cide [ˈspɜːmɪˌsaɪd] N spermicida *m*

sperm whale N capodoglio

spew [spjuː] VT (*also:* **spew out**: *smoke, pollution*) emettere, vomitare
■ VI **1** (*subj*: *smoke, pollution*) fuoriuscire **2** (*also:* **to spew up**: *fam*: *vomit*) rigettare

sphere [sfɪəʳ] N (*gen*) sfera; **his sphere of interest** la sua sfera d'interessi; **his sphere of activity** il suo campo di attività; **within a limited sphere** in un ambito molto ristretto; **sphere of influence** sfera d'influenza; **that's outside my sphere** non rientra nelle mie competenze

spheri·cal [ˈsfɛrɪkəl] ADJ sferico(-a)

sphinx [sfɪŋks] N (*also fig*) sfinge *f*

spice [spaɪs] N (*Culin*) droga, spezia; (*fig*) sapore *m*; **mixed spice(s)** spezie miste; **variety is the spice of life** la varietà dà sapore alla vita
■ VT (*Culin*) condire (con spezie), aromatizzare; **a highly spiced account** un racconto molto gustoso
▷ www.culinarycafe.com/Spices_Herbs

spice rack N mensolina *f* portaspezie *inv*

spick-and-span [ˌspɪkənˈspæn] ADJ pulito(-a) come uno specchio

spicy [ˈspaɪsɪ] ADJ (*comp* **-ier**, *superl* **-iest**) (*Culin, fig*) piccante

spi·der [ˈspaɪdəʳ] N ragno; (*tool*) chiave *f* a croce; **spider's web** ragnatela

spider crab N grancevola

spider elastic N (*Aut*) elastico *m* fermabagagli *inv*

spider monkey N scimmia *f* ragno *inv*

spi·dery [ˈspaɪdərɪ] ADJ (*handwriting*) angoloso(-a)

spiel [ʃpiːl] N (*fam*) tiritera

spike [spaɪk] N **1** (*point*) punta; (*on shoe*) chiodo; **rocky spike** (*Mountaineering*) spuntone *m* **2** **spikes** NPL (*Sport*) scarpe *fpl* chiodate **3** (*Elec*) punta (di corrente) **4** (*in price, volume etc*) aumento improvviso
■ VT (*story, interview*) rifiutare di pubblicare; (*fig*): **to spike sb's guns** rompere le uova nel paniere a qn; **a spiked drink** (*fam*) una bevanda corretta
■ VI (*price, volume etc*) aumentare improvvisamente

spike heel N (*Am*) tacco a spillo

spiky [ˈspaɪkɪ] ADJ (*comp* **-ier**, *superl* **-iest**) (*bush, branch*) spinoso(-a); (*animal*) ricoperto(-a) di aculei; (*fig*: *person*) spigoloso(-a)

spill [spɪl] (*pt, pp* **spilled** *or* **spilt** [spɪlt]) VT (*gen*) rovesciare, versare; (*blood*) spargere; **he spilled coffee on his trousers** s'è rovesciato il caffè sui pantaloni; **to spill the beans** (*fam*) spiattellare tutto, vuotare il sacco
■ VI rovesciarsi, versarsi
▸ **spill out** VI + ADV uscire fuori; (*fall out*) cadere fuori; **the audience spilt out of the cinema** gli spettatori si riversarono fuori dal cinema
■ VT + ADV (*contents etc*) rovesciare; (*fig*: *story*) rivelare
▸ **spill over** VI + ADV: **to spill over (into)** (*liquid*) versarsi (in); (*crowd*) riversarsi (in)

spill·age [ˈspɪlɪdʒ] N (*event*) fuoriuscita; (*substance*) sostanza fuoriuscita

◎ **spin** [spɪn] (*vb*: *pt* **spun** *or* **span**, *pp* **spun**) N **1** (*revolution*) giro; **to give a wheel a spin** far girare una ruota; **to give sth a long/short spin** (*in washing machine*) fare una centrifuga completa/ridotta; **to be in a flat spin** (*fam*) essere in preda al panico; **to go into a flat spin** lasciarsi prendere dal panico **2** (*on ball*) effetto; **to put a spin on a ball** imprimere l'effetto a una palla **3** (*Aer*): **to go into a spin** discendere in avvitamento; (*Aut*) fare un testa-coda **4** (*ride*): **to go for a spin** fare un giretto **5** (*Pol*) reinterpretazione *f*; **to put a new/**

different spin on sth presentare qc da un'angolazione nuova/diversa
■VT **1** (*turn: wheel*) far girare; (*Brit: clothes*) mettere nella centrifuga; (*ball*) imprimere l'effetto a; **to spin a coin** (*Brit*) lanciare in aria una moneta; **he spun the wheel sharply** ha girato il volante bruscamente **2** (*cotton, wool*) filare; (*subj: spider*) tessere; **to spin a yarn** (*fig*) imbastire una storia; **she spins the wool from her own sheep** fila la lana delle sue pecore
■VI **1** filare **2** (*revolve: person*) girarsi; (*: ball*) ruotare; (*: wheel*) girare; **to spin round and round** girare su se stesso(-a); **the car spun out of control** la macchina ha sbandato e ha girato su se stessa; **to send sb spinning** mandare qn a gambe all'aria; **it makes my head spin** mi fa girare la testa
▶ **spin out** VT + ADV (*fam: visit, holiday*) prolungare; (*: speech, food*) far durare

spi·na bi·fi·da [ˌspaɪnəˈbɪfɪdə] N spina bifida

spin·ach [ˈspɪnɪdʒ] N spinaci *mpl*; **the spinach is delicious** gli spinaci sono ottimi

spi·nal [ˈspaɪnl] ADJ spinale; **spinal injury** lesione *f* alla spina dorsale

spinal column N colonna vertebrale, spina dorsale

spinal cord N midollo spinale

spin·dle [ˈspɪndl] N (*Tech*) perno, asse *m*; (*for spinning*) fuso

spin·dly [ˈspɪndlɪ] ADJ (*comp* **-ier**, *superl* **-iest**) (*legs, arms, plant*) stecchito(-a)

spin doctor N (*Pol*) *pierre addetto alla difesa di provvedimenti impopolari con interviste, interventi in TV ecc*

spin-dry [ˌspɪnˈdraɪ] VT strizzare con la centrifuga

spin-dryer [ˌspɪnˈdraɪəʳ] N (*Brit*) centrifuga

spine [spaɪn] N (*Anat*) spina dorsale; (*Zool*) aculeo; (*Bot*) spina; (*of book*) dorso; (*of mountain range*) cresta

spine-chiller [ˈspaɪnˌtʃɪləʳ] N (*film, book etc*) thriller *m inv*

spine-chilling [ˈspaɪnˌtʃɪlɪŋ] ADJ agghiacciante

spine·less [ˈspaɪnlɪs] ADJ (*fig*) smidollato(-a); (*animal*) invertebrato(-a)

spin·na·ker [ˈspɪnəkəʳ] N (*Naut*) spinnaker *m inv*

spin·ner [ˈspɪnəʳ] N (*of thread, yarn*) tessitore(-trice); (*Fishing*) cucchiaino; (*fam: spin-dryer*) centrifuga

spin·ney [ˈspɪnɪ] N boschetto

spin·ning [ˈspɪnɪŋ] N filatura; **spinning and weaving** la filatura e la tessitura

spinning mill N filanda

spinning top N trottola

spinning wheel N filatoio

spin-off [ˈspɪnˌɒf] N (*Tech, Industry*) applicazione *f* secondaria; (*product*) prodotto secondario; **this TV series is a spin-off from the famous film** questa serie televisiva è ispirata al famoso film

spin·ster [ˈspɪnstəʳ] N (*old*) zitella

spiny [ˈspaɪnɪ] ADJ coperto(-a) di spine

spi·ral [ˈspaɪərəl] ADJ a spirale
■N spirale *f*; **the inflationary spiral** la spirale dell'inflazione
■VI (*prices*) salire vertiginosamente; **to spiral up/down** (*also Aer*) salire/scendere a spirale

spiral staircase N scala a chiocciola

spire [ˈspaɪəʳ] N guglia

◎ **spir·it** [ˈspɪrɪt] N **1** (*soul*) spirito; **the human spirit** lo spirito umano; **I'll be with you in spirit** ti sarò vicino col pensiero; **one of the greatest spirits of the age** uno dei più grandi personaggi dell'epoca; **one of the leading spirits in the party** uno dei principali animatori del partito **2** (*ghost, supernatural being*) spirito; **Holy Spirit** Spirito Santo **3** (*courage*) coraggio; (*energy*) energia; (*vitality*) brio, vitalità; **everyone who knew her admired her spirit** tutti quelli che la conoscevano ammiravano il suo coraggio **4** (*attitude etc*) spirito; **community spirit** *or* **public spirit** senso civico; **in a spirit of optimism** con un atteggiamento ottimista; **to enter into the spirit of sth** entrare nello spirito di qc; **that's the spirit!** (*fam*) bravo!, così va bene!; **the spirit of the law** lo spirito della legge; **to take sth in the right/wrong spirit** prendere qc bene/male **5** **spirits** NPL (*state of mind*): **high spirits** buon umore *m*; **to be in low spirits** essere giù di morale; **we kept our spirits up by singing** ci siamo tenuti su di morale cantando; **my spirits rose somewhat** mi sono tirato un po' su **6** **spirits** NPL (*alcohol*) liquori *mpl*; **raw spirits** alcol *m* puro **7** (*Chem*) spirito, alcol *m inv*
▶ **spirit away, spirit off** VT + ADV far sparire misteriosamente

spir·it·ed [ˈspɪrɪtɪd] ADJ (*horse*) focoso(-a); (*conversation*) animato(-a); (*person, attack etc*) energico(-a); (*description*) vivace, vigoroso(-a); **he gave a spirited performance** (*Mus, Theatre*) ha dato una brillante interpretazione

> DID YOU KNOW ...?
> **spirited** is not translated by the Italian word *spiritato*

spirit lamp N lampada a spirito

spirit level N livella a bolla d'aria

◎ **spir·itu·al** [ˈspɪrɪtjʊəl] ADJ spirituale
■N (*Mus*) spiritual *m inv*

spir·itu·al·ism [ˈspɪrɪtjʊəˌlɪzəm] N (*occult*) spiritismo

spir·itu·al·ist [ˈspɪrɪtjʊəlɪst] N (*Rel*) spiritualista *m/f*

spir·itu·al·ity [ˌspɪrɪtjʊˈælɪtɪ] N spiritualità

spir·itu·al·ly [ˈspɪrɪtjʊəlɪ] ADV spiritualmente

spit¹ [spɪt] N (*Culin: for roasting*) spiedo; (*of land*) lingua di terra; **on the spit** allo spiedo

spit² [spɪt] (*vb: pt, pp* **spat**) N (*spittle*) sputo; (*saliva*) saliva; **a bit of spit and polish** (*fam*) una bella lucidata; **to be the dead spit of sb** (*fam*) essere il ritratto sputato di qn
■VT sputare
■VI: **to spit (at)** sputare (addosso a); (*cat*) soffiare (contro); **they spat at me** mi hanno sputato addosso; **to spit on the ground** sputare per terra; **it is spitting with rain** sta piovigginando
▶ **spit out** VT + ADV (*sparks*) sprigionare; (*fat*) schizzare; **spit it out!** (*fam: say it*) sputa il rospo!; **it tasted horrible and I spat it out** aveva un saporaccio e l'ho sputato

◎ **spite** [spaɪt] N **1** (*ill will*) dispetto; **out of spite** per dispetto; **to do sth out of (or from) spite** fare qc per dispetto **2** **in spite of** (*despite*) nonostante, malgrado; **in spite of the fact that** malgrado *or* nonostante (il fatto che) + *sub*; **she laughed in spite of herself** ha riso suo malgrado
■VT far dispetto a; **he just did it to spite me** l'ha fatto solo per farmi dispetto

spite·ful [ˈspaɪtfʊl] ADJ (*person, behaviour*) dispettoso(-a); (*tongue, remark*) maligno(-a), velenoso(-a)

spite·ful·ly [ˈspaɪtfəlɪ] ADV (*see adj*) dispettosamente; malignamente

spit·fire [ˈspɪtˌfaɪəʳ] N: **she's a real spitfire** è una persona molto irascibile

spit·roast [ˈspɪtˌrəʊst] VT cuocere allo spiedo

spit·ting [ˈspɪtɪŋ] N: **"spitting prohibited"** "vietato sputare"

Ss

■ADJ: **to be the spitting image of sb** essere il ritratto sputato di qn

spit·tle ['spɪtl] N (*ejected*) sputo; (*dribbled*) saliva; (*of animal*) bava

spit·toon [spɪ'tu:n] N sputacchiera

spiv [spɪv] N (*Brit fam*) imbroglione *m*

splash [splæʃ] N (*sound*) tonfo; (*series of splashes*) sciabordio; (*mark*) spruzzo, macchia; (*fig: of colour, light*) chiazza; **I heard a splash** ho sentito un tonfo; **a splash of colour** un tocco di colore; **to make a splash** (*fig*) far furore

■VT schizzare; **to splash sb with water** schizzare qn d'acqua; **to splash sth over sb** schizzare qc addosso a qn; **to splash one's face with water** spruzzarsi acqua sul viso; **he splashed water on his face** si spruzzò acqua sul viso; **to splash paint on the floor** schizzare il pavimento di vernice; **the story was splashed across the front page** (*fam*) la notizia è stata sbattuta in prima pagina; **don't splash me!** non schizzarmi!

■VI (*liquid, mud etc*) schizzare; (*person, animal in water*: *also*: **splash about**) sguazzare; **to splash across a stream** guadare un ruscello; **to splash into the water** (*stone*) cadere nell'acqua con un tonfo

▶ **splash down** VI + ADV ammarare

▶ **splash out** VI + ADV (*fam*) fare spese folli

▶ **splash up** VI + ADV schizzare; **the waves splashed up against the rocks** le onde s'infrangevano sugli scogli

splash·back ['splæʃ,bæk] N (*at sink etc*) pannello di protezione (contro gli spruzzi)

splash·down ['splæʃ,daʊn] N ammaraggio

splat·ter ['splætəʳ] VI schizzare; **mud had splattered onto our shoes** avevamo le scarpe inzaccherate di fango

■VT (*liquid*) schizzare; (*food*) spiaccicare; **an apron splattered with blood** un grembiule schizzato di sangue

■N (*sound*): **the splatter of rain on the windows** il tamburellare della pioggia sui vetri

splay [spleɪ] VI: **splayed fingers** dita allargate

spleen [spli:n] N (*Anat*) milza; **to vent one's spleen** (*fig*) sfogarsi

splen·did ['splɛndɪd] ADJ (*ceremony, clothes*) splendido(-a), magnifico(-a); (*idea, example*) eccellente, ottimo(-a); **that's splendid!** magnifico!, fantastico!

splen·did·ly ['splɛndɪdlɪ] ADV splendidamente, magnificamente

splen·dif·er·ous [splɛn'dɪfərəs] ADJ (*old, hum*) magnifico(-a), splendido(-a)

splen·dour, (*Am*) **splen·dor** ['splɛndəʳ] N splendore *m*, magnificenza

splice [splaɪs] VT (*rope, film*) giuntare; (*wood*) calettare

splint [splɪnt] N (*Med*) stecca; **to put sb's arm in splints** steccare il braccio di qn

splin·ter ['splɪntəʳ] N scheggia

■VI (*wood, glass*) scheggiarsi; (*fig: party*) staccarsi, scindersi

■VT (*wood, glass*) scheggiare; (*fig: party*) scindere

splinter group N gruppo scissionista

◎ **split** [splɪt] (*vb: pt, pp* **split**) N **1** (*in ground, wall, rock*) fessura, crepa; (*in wood*) spacco; (*in garment, fabric*) strappo **2** (*fig: division, quarrel*) scissione *f*, spaccatura; **there are fears of a split in the party** si teme una scissione nel partito **3** **to do the splits** fare la spaccata **4** (*cake etc*): **jam split** tortina farcita di marmellata; **banana split** banana-split *f inv*

■VT **1** (*cleave*) spaccare; (*tear*) strappare; **he split the wood with an axe** spaccava la legna con l'ascia; **to split the atom** scindere l'atomo; **to split sth open** aprire qc spaccandolo(-a); **he split his head open** si è spaccato la testa; **to split sth down the middle** (*also fig*) spaccare qc a metà; **to split hairs** (*fig*) spaccare il capello in quattro; **to split one's sides laughing** (*fig*) ridere a crepapelle **2** (*divide*: *also fig*) dividere, spartire; **to split sth into three parts** dividere qc in tre; **to split the profit five ways** dividere il guadagno in cinque parti; **they decided to split the profits** hanno deciso di dividere i guadagni; **to split the difference** (*agree price*) incontrarsi a metà strada; (*fig*) accettare una soluzione di compromesso

■VI **1** (*wood, stone*) spaccarsi; (*cloth*) strapparsi; (*fig: party, church*) spaccarsi, dividersi; **to split open** spaccarsi; **my head is splitting** mi scoppia la testa; **the ship hit a rock and split in two** la nave ha urtato contro una roccia e s'è spaccata in due **2** (*fam: tell tales*): **don't you split on me to the police!** non provarti a denunciarmi alla polizia!

▶ **split off** VI + ADV (*also fig*) staccarsi, separarsi

■VT + ADV (*also fig*) staccare, separare

▶ **split up** VI + ADV (*stone etc*) spaccarsi; (*ship on rocks*) schiantarsi; (*crowd*) disperdersi; (: *into groups*) dividersi; (*meeting*) sciogliersi; (*partners*) separarsi; (*couple*) separarsi, rompere; (*friends*) rompere

■VT + ADV (*stone etc*) spaccare; (*movement, money, work*) dividere; (*crowd*) disperdere; (*partners*) separare

split infinitive N (*Gram*) *infinito in cui un avverbio divide il 'to' dal verbo*

split-level ['splɪt,lɛvl] ADJ (*house*) a piani sfalsati

split peas NPL piselli *mpl* secchi spaccati

split personality N sdoppiamento della personalità

split screen N (*Cine, TV, Comput*) schermo diviso

split-screen ['splɪt'skri:n] ADJ (*Cine, TV, Comput: technique, facility*) di schermo diviso

split second N frazione *f* di secondo

split shifts NPL (*Industry*) turni *mpl* articolati

split·ting ['splɪtɪŋ] ADJ: **a splitting headache** un terribile mal di testa

split-up ['splɪt,ʌp] N (*of married couple*) separazione *f*; (*of friends, political group*) rottura

splodge [splɒdʒ], **splotch** [splɒtʃ] N macchia

splurge [splɜ:dʒ] (*fam*) VI fare una follia; **to splurge on sth** fare una follia comprando qc

■VT: **to splurge one's money (on sth)** fare una follia (comprando qc)

■N (*spending spree*) spese *fpl* folli; **to go on** *or* **have a splurge** darsi alle spese folli

splut·ter ['splʌtəʳ] VI (*person: spit*) sputacchiare; (: *stutter*) farfugliare; (*fire*) crepitare; (*fat*) schizzare; (*engine*) scoppiettare

spoil [spɔɪl] (*pt, pp* **spoiled** *or* **spoilt**) VT **1** (*ruin, detract from*) rovinare, sciupare; (*ballot paper*) annullare, invalidare; **don't spoil our fun** non fare il guastafeste; **to spoil one's appetite** guastarsi l'appetito; **don't let it spoil your holiday!** non lasciare che ti rovini la vacanza! **2** (*child*) viziare; **grandparents like to spoil their grandchildren** ai nonni piace viziare i nipotini

■VI **1** (*food*) guastarsi, andare a male; (: *while cooking*) rovinarsi **2** **to be spoiling for a fight** morire dalla voglia di litigare

spoil·er ['spɔɪləʳ] N (*Aut, Aer*) spoiler *m inv*

spoils [spɔɪlz] NPL: **the spoils** il bottino *msg*

spoil·sport ['spɔɪl,spɔ:t] N (*fam*) guastafeste *m/f inv*

spoilt [spɔɪlt] PT, PP *of* **spoil**

■ADJ (*child*) viziato(-a); (*meal*) rovinato(-a); (*ballot paper*) nullo(-a)

spoke[1] [spəʊk] N raggio; **to put a spoke in sb's wheel** mettere i bastoni fra le ruote a qn

spoke[2] [spəʊk] PT *of* **speak**

spo·ken ['spəʊkən] PP *of* **speak**

◎**spokes·man** ['spəʊksmən] N (*pl* **-men**) portavoce *m inv*

spokes·person ['spəʊks,pɜːsən] N portavoce *m/f inv*

spokes·woman ['spəʊks,wʊmən] N (*pl* **-women**) portavoce *f inv*

sponge [spʌndʒ] N spugna; (*Culin: also:* **sponge cake**) pan *m* di Spagna; **to throw in the sponge** (*fig*) gettare la spugna; **a wet sponge** una spugna bagnata

■VT (*wash*) lavare con una spugna; **to sponge a stain off** pulire una macchia con una spugna

■VI (*fam: scrounge*) scroccare; **to sponge off** *or* **on sb** vivere alle spalle di qn

▶ **sponge down** VT + ADV lavare con una spugna

sponge bag N (*Brit*) nécessaire *m inv*

sponge cake N (*Culin*) = **sponge** N

spong·er ['spʌndʒəʳ] N (*fam*) scroccone(-a); (*pej*) parassita *m inv*

spon·gy ['spʌndʒɪ] ADJ (*comp* **-ier**, *superl* **-iest**) spugnoso(-a)

◎**spon·sor** ['spɒnsəʳ] N (*of enterprise, bill, for fund raising*) promotore(-trice); (*for loan*) garante *m/f*; (*of member*) socio(-a) garante; (*Radio, TV, Sport etc*) sponsor *m inv*; (*godparent*) padrino/madrina

■VT (*enterprise etc*) promuovere, patrocinare; (*borrower, member of club*) garantire; (*Pol: Parliamentary bill*) presentare; (*Radio, TV, Sport etc*) sponsorizzare; (*as godparents*) tenere a battesimo; **the tournament was sponsored by local firms** il torneo è stato sponsorizzato da imprese locali; **I sponsored him at 50p a mile** (*in fund-raising race*) mi sono impegnato a donare 50 penny per ogni miglio

spon·sor·ship ['spɒnsəʃɪp] N (*financial backing*) promozione *f*; (*of arts, events*) sponsorizzazione *f*; (*of candidate*) sostegno

spon·ta·neity [,spɒntə'neɪətɪ] N spontaneità

spon·ta·neous [spɒn'teɪnɪəs] ADJ spontaneo(-a)

spontaneous combustion N autocombustione *f*

spon·ta·neous·ly [spɒn'teɪnɪəslɪ] ADV spontaneamente

spoof [spuːf] N (*fam*) parodia

spook [spuːk] N (*fam*) fantasma *m*, spettro

spooky ['spuːkɪ] ADJ (*comp* **-ier**, *superl* **-iest**) (*fam*) sinistro(-a); **the house has a spooky atmosphere** la casa ha un'atmosfera sinistra

spool [spuːl] N (*Phot, on sewing machine, on fishing line*) bobina; (*spool of thread*) rocchetto di filo

spoon [spuːn] N cucchiaio; **to be born with a silver spoon in one's mouth** essere nato(-a) con la camicia

■VT: **to spoon out** (*sauce, cream*) servire con il cucchiaio; **to spoon sth into a plate** versare qc in un piatto con il cucchiaio

spoon·bill ['spuːn,bɪl] N (*Zool*) spatola

spoon·er·ism ['spuːnə,rɪzəm] N *papera consistente nello scambio delle iniziali di due parole*

spoon-feed ['spuːn,fiːd] (*pt, pp* **spoon-fed** ['spuːn,fɛd]) VT imboccare; (*fig*) scodellare la pappa a

spoon·ful ['spuːnfʊl] N cucchiaiata

spoor [spʊəʳ] N traccia, pista

spo·rad·ic [spə'rædɪk] ADJ (*attempts, gunfire*) sporadico(-a); (*work*) discontinuo(-a)

spo·radi·cal·ly [spə'rædɪkəlɪ] ADV (*attempt, fire*) sporadicamente; (*work*) saltuariamente; (*function*) in modo discontinuo

spore [spɔːʳ] N spora

spor·ran ['spɒrən] N *borsello agganciato alla cintura del kilt, indossato con il tradizionale costume scozzese*

◎**sport** [spɔːt] N **1** sport *m inv*; **indoor/outdoor sports** sport al chiuso/all'aria aperta; **to be good at sport** riuscire bene nello sport; **I'm not interested in sport** lo sport non mi interessa; **sports** NPL (*meeting*) gare *fpl* **2** (*amusement*) divertimento **3** (*fam: person*) persona di spirito; **be a sport!** sii buono!

■VT sfoggiare

sport·ing ['spɔːtɪŋ] ADJ (*event, behaviour, attitude*) sportivo(-a); **there's a sporting chance that** c'è una buona probabilità che + *sub*; **to give sb a sporting chance** dare a qn una possibilità (di vincere)

sport·ing·ly ['spɔːtɪŋlɪ] ADV sportivamente

sports car N automobile *f* sportiva

sports·cast ['spɔːtskɑːst] N (*Am: TV, Radio*) trasmissione *f* sportiva

sports·cast·er ['spɔːtskɑːstəʳ] N (*Am: TV, Radio*) cronista *m/f* sportivo(-a)

sports desk N (*TV, Radio: department*) redazione *f* sportiva

sports ground N campo sportivo

sports jacket, (*Am*) **sport jacket** N giacca sportiva

sports·man ['spɔːtsmən] N (*pl* **-men**) sportivo

sportsmanlike ['spɔːtsmən,laɪk] ADJ sportivo(-a); **in a sportsmanlike fashion** sportivamente

sports·man·ship ['spɔːtsmənʃɪp] N spirito sportivo

sports page N pagina sportiva

sport(s) utility vehicle N (*esp Am*) fuoristrada *m inv*

sports·wear ['spɔːts,wɛəʳ] N abbigliamento sportivo

sports·woman ['spɔːts,wʊmən] N (*pl* **-women**) sportiva

sporty ['spɔːtɪ] ADJ (*comp* **-ier**, *superl* **-iest**) (*fam*) sportivo(-a)

◎**spot** [spɒt] N **1** (*dot*) puntino; (*on dress*) pois *m inv*, pallino; (*stain, also fig*) macchia; **a material with blue spots** una stoffa a pallini *or* pois blu; **there's a spot on your shirt** hai una macchia sulla camicia; **to knock spots off sb** (*fig fam*) dare dei punti a qn; **to have spots before one's eyes** vedere dei puntini **2** (*pimple*) foruncolo; **to break** *or* **come out in spots** coprirsi di foruncoli; **he's covered in spots** è pieno di brufoli **3** (*place*) posto; **a pleasant spot** un bel posto; **it's a lovely spot for a picnic** è un posto ideale per un picnic; **to have a tender spot on the arm** avere un punto dolorante nel braccio; **the reporter was on the spot** il reporter era sul posto; **the firemen were on the spot in 3 minutes** i pompieri sono arrivati sul posto in 3 minuti; **an on-the-spot broadcast** una trasmissione in diretta; **to do sth on the spot** fare qc immediatamente *or* lì per lì; **to be in a (tight) spot** (*fig*) essere nei guai *or* nei pasticci; **to put sb in a spot** *or* **on the spot** (*fig*) mettere in difficoltà qn; **that's my weak spot** (*fig*) è il mio punto debole **4** (*Brit fam: small amount*): **a spot of** un po' di; (: *of milk, wine etc*) un goccio di; **just a spot, thanks** solo un goccio, grazie; **we had a spot of rain yesterday** c'è stata qualche goccia di pioggia ieri; **would you like a spot of lunch?** vuoi mangiare un boccone?; **to have a spot of bother** avere noie **5** (*Radio, Theatre, TV: in show*) numero; (*Radio, TV: advertisement*) spot *m inv* (pubblicitario) **6** (*fam: also:* **spotlight**) faretto

■VT **1** (*speckle*): **to spot (with)** macchiare (di) **2** (*notice, see: mistake, person in a crowd*) notare; (: *car, person*

Ss

in the distance) scorgere; (*recognize: winner*) indovinare; (: *talent, sb's ability*) scoprire; (: *bargain*) riconoscere; **I spotted a mistake** ho notato un errore

spot check N controllo casuale

spot·less ['spɒtlɪs] ADJ pulitissimo(-a), immacolato(-a); (*fig: reputation*) senza macchia; (: *character*) retto(-a)

spot·less·ly ['spɒtlɪslɪ] ADV: **spotlessly clean** pulitissimo(-a)

spot·light ['spɒt,laɪt] N (*lamp*) spot *m inv*, faro; (*beam*) fascio luminoso; (*Aut*) faro, riflettore *m*; **in the spotlight** sotto la luce dei riflettori; (*fig*) al centro dell'attenzione; **to turn the spotlight on sb/sth** (*fig*) mettere in risalto qn/qc, richiamare l'attenzione su qn/qc

spot·lit ['spɒtlɪt] ADJ (*stage, building*) illuminato(-a) dai riflettori

spot-on ['spɒt'ɒn] ADJ (*Brit*) esatto(-a)

spot price N (*Comm*) prezzo per contanti

spot remover N smacchiatore *m*

spot·ted ['spɒtɪd] ADJ (*material*) a pois, a pallini; (*animal*) maculato(-a); **spotted with** punteggiato(-a) di; **a spotted tie** una cravatta a pallini

spot·ty ['spɒtɪ] ADJ (*comp* **-ier**, *superl* **-iest**) (*fam*) foruncoloso(-a)

spouse [spaʊs] N (*frm*) sposo(-a)

spout [spaʊt] N (*of teapot*) becco, beccuccio; (*of guttering*) scarico; (*for tap*) cannella; (*column of water*) getto, zampillo; **those figures are completely up the spout** (*fam*) quei dati sono completamente sballati
■ VT (*water*) gettare; (*lava*) eruttare; (*smoke*) emettere; (*fam pej: poetry*) declamare
■ VI (*liquid*) zampillare

sprain [spreɪn] N slogatura, storta, distorsione *f*; (*of muscle*) strappo muscolare
■ VT (*muscle*) stirarsi; **to sprain one's wrist/ankle** slogarsi un polso/una caviglia; **she's sprained her ankle** s'è slogata una caviglia

sprang [spræŋ] PT *of* **spring**

sprat [spræt] N (*fish*) spratto

sprawl [sprɔ:l] VI (*person: sit, lie*) stravaccarsi; (: *fall*) cadere scompostamente; (*town*) estendersi in modo incontrollato; (*plant*) crescere disordinatamente; **her handwriting sprawled all over the page** la sua scrittura copriva tutta la pagina; **he sprawled on the sofa, smoking** si stravaccò sul divano fumando; **to send sb sprawling** mandare qn a gambe all'aria
■ N: **urban sprawl** sviluppo urbanistico incontrollato, espansione urbana tentacolare; **a sprawl of buildings lay below them** un gruppo di edifici si estendeva disordinatamente dinanzi ai loro occhi

sprawl·ing ['sprɔ:lɪŋ] ADJ (*person*) sdraiato(-a); (: *in armchair*) stravaccato(-a); (*handwriting*) disordinato(-a); (*city*) tentacolare

◎ **spray¹** [spreɪ] N **1** (*from hosepipe*) getto; (*from wet road*) schizzi *mpl*; (*of sea, fountain*) spruzzi *mpl*; (*from atomizer, aerosol*) spruzzo **2** (*aerosol, atomizer*) spray *m inv*, bomboletta; (: *of perfume*) vaporizzatore *m*; (: *for paint, garden*) spruzzatore *m*, nebulizzatore *m*; (*Med*) spray
■ VT (*gen*) spruzzare; (*crops*) irrorare; **to spray sth/sb with water** spruzzare qc/qn d'acqua; **to spray sth/sb with bullets** sparare una scarica di proiettili contro qc/qn; **she sprayed perfume on my hand** mi ha spruzzato del profumo sulla mano
■ ADJ (*deodorant*) spray *inv*; (*gun, paint*) a spruzzo

spray² [spreɪ] N (*of greenery*) ramoscello; (*of flowers*) mazzolino; (*brooch*) spilla a forma di ramoscello

spray can N bombola *f* spray *inv*

spray·er ['spreɪəʳ] N = **spray** N **2**

spray·ing ma·chine ['spreɪɪŋ məʃi:n] N (*Agr*) irroratrice *f*

spray paint N vernice *f* in bomboletta spray
■ VT (*car*) verniciare a spruzzo; (*on wall*) scrivere con una bomboletta spray

◎ **spread** [sprɛd] (*vb: pt, pp* **spread**) N
1 (*of fire, infection*) propagazione *f*; (*of idea, knowledge*) diffusione *f*; (*of crime*) il dilagare; **the spread of nuclear weapons** la proliferazione delle armi nucleari; **the spread of modern technology** la diffusione della tecnologia moderna
2 (*extent: of bridge*) ampiezza; (: *of wings, arch*) apertura
3 (*range: of prices, figures, marks*) gamma; (: *on graph, scale*) distribuzione *f*; **middle-age spread** pancetta
4 (*fam: feast*) banchetto
5 (*also:* **bedspread**) copriletto
6 (*for bread*): **anchovy spread** ≈ pasta d'acciughe; **cheese spread** formaggio da spalmare; **chocolate spread** cioccolata da spalmare
7 (*Press, Typ: two pages*) doppia pagina; (: *across columns*) articolo a più colonne
■ VT
1 (*open or lay out: also:* **spread out**: *wings, sails etc*) spiegare; (: *cloth*) stendere; (: *fingers*) distendere; (: *arms*) allargare, spalancare; **to spread a map out on the table** spiegare una cartina sul tavolo; **he spread the map out on the table** ha spiegato la cartina sul tavolo; **to spread one's wings** (*fig*) spiccare il volo; **she spread the towel on the sand** ha steso l'asciugamano sulla sabbia
2 (*butter, cream etc*) spalmare; **spread the whipped cream on the top of the cake** spalma la panna montata sopra la torta; **to spread cream on one's face** spalmarsi la crema sul viso
3 (*distribute: also:* **spread out**: *sand, fertilizer*): **to spread sth on sth** cospargere qc di qc; (: *goods, objects*) disporre; (: *cards, toys*) spargere; (: *soldiers*) scaglionare; (: *payments*) rateizzare, scaglionare; (: *resources*) distribuire; **repayments will be spread over 18 months** i pagamenti saranno scaglionati lungo un periodo di 18 mesi
4 (*disseminate: germs, disease*) propagare, diffondere; (: *knowledge, panic etc*) diffondere; (: *news*) spargere, diffondere
■ VI (*news, rumour etc*) diffondersi, propagarsi, spargersi; (*pain, fire, flood etc*) estendersi; (*milk etc*) spargersi; (*disease, weeds*) propagarsi; **to spread into sth** estendersi fino a qc; **margarine spreads better than butter** la margarina si spalma meglio del burro; **the news spread rapidly** la notizia si diffuse rapidamente
▸ **spread out** VI + ADV (*view, valley*) stendersi; (*soldiers, police*) disporsi; **the soldiers spread out across the field** i soldati si sparpagliarono nel campo
■ VT + ADV = **spread** VT **1, 3**

spread betting N scommessa diversificata (*che non si limita a puntare su un solo risultato*)

spread-eagled [,sprɛd'i:gld] ADJ: **to be** *or* **lie spread-eagled** essere disteso(-a) a gambe e braccia aperte

spread·sheet ['sprɛdʃi:t] N (*Comput*) foglio elettronico

spree [spri:] N (*fam*): **to go on a spending spree** fare spese folli; **to go on a spree** darsi alla pazza gioia, fare baldoria

sprig [sprɪg] N ramoscello

spright·ly ['spraɪtlɪ] ADJ (*comp* **-ier**, *superl* **-iest**) vivace; **a sprightly old man** un vecchietto arzillo

◎**spring** [sprɪŋ] (*vb: pt* **sprang**, *pp* **sprung**) N **1** (*season*) primavera; **in spring** *or* **in the spring** in primavera; **spring is in the air** c'è aria di primavera **2** (*coiled metal, also Tech*) molla **3** **springs** NPL (*Aut*) sospensioni *fpl*, balestre *fpl* **4** (*of water*) sorgente *f*; **hot spring** sorgente termale **5** (*leap*) salto, balzo; **in one spring** in un salto **6** (*bounciness*) elasticità; **to walk with a spring in one's step** camminare con passo elastico
■VT (*trap, lock etc*) far scattare; **to spring a leak** (*pipe etc*) cominciare a perdere; **the boat has sprung a leak** s'è aperta una falla nella barca; **he sprang a question on me** (*fig*) mi ha fatto una domanda a bruciapelo; **to spring a surprise on sb** fare una sorpresa a qn; **he sprang the news on me** mi ha sorpreso con quella notizia; **he sprang it on me** mi ha preso alla sprovvista
■VI **1** (*leap*) saltare, balzare; **suddenly the cat sprang** il gatto improvvisamente spiccò un balzo; **to spring aside/forward** balzare da una parte/in avanti; **to spring back** saltare *or* scattare all'indietro; **the door sprang open** la porta si aprì di scatto; **where on earth did you spring from?** (*fam*) da dove spunti?; **to spring into the air** fare un balzo in aria; **to spring into action** entrare rapidamente in azione; **to spring to one's feet** scattare in piedi; **he sprang to his feet** è balzato in piedi; **to spring to mind** venire in mente; **nothing springs to mind** non mi viene in mente niente **2** (*originate: gen*) sorgere; (*: tears*) sgorgare
■ADJ **1** (*of season*) di primavera, primaverile **2** (*with springs: mattress*) a molle
▸ **spring up** VI + ADV (*person*) saltar su; (*plant, weeds, building*) spuntare; (*problem, obstacle*) presentarsi; (*wind, storm*) alzarsi, levarsi; (*doubt, friendship, rumour*) nascere

spring binder N (*file*) raccoglitore *m* a molla

spring·board ['sprɪŋˌbɔ:d] N trampolino

spring·bok ['sprɪŋˌbɒk] N (*Zool*) antidorcade *f*

spring-clean [ˌsprɪŋ'kli:n] VI fare le pulizie di primavera

spring-cleaning [ˌsprɪŋ'kli:nɪŋ] N pulizie *fpl* di primavera

spring·like ['sprɪŋˌlaɪk] ADJ (*day, weather*) primaverile

spring onion N (*Brit*) cipollina

spring-release ['sprɪŋrɪˌli:s] ADJ a cerniera; **spring-release tin** (*Culin*) stampo a cerniera

spring roll N involtino primavera; *involtino fritto farcito di verdure o carne, specialità cinese*

spring·time ['sprɪŋˌtaɪm] N primavera

springy ['sprɪŋɪ] ADJ (*comp* **-ier**, *superl* **-iest**) (*gen*) elastico(-a); (*carpet, turf*) morbido(-a); (*mattress*) molleggiato(-a)

sprin·kle ['sprɪŋkl] VT: **to sprinkle with** (*gen*) cospargere di; (*water*) spruzzare di; **they are sprinkled about here and there** sono sparsi un po' dovunque; **to sprinkle water** *etc* **on** spruzzare dell'acqua *etc* su; **to sprinkle sugar** *etc* **on** *or* **sprinkle with sugar** *etc* spolverizzare di zucchero *etc*; **sprinkled with mistakes** infarcito(-a) di errori

sprin·kler ['sprɪŋkləʳ] N (*for lawn etc*) irrigatore *m*; (*for fire-fighting*) sprinkler *m inv*

sprin·kling ['sprɪŋklɪŋ] N (*of water, snow*) spruzzatina; (*of salt, sugar*) pizzico; **there was a sprinkling of young people** c'era qualche giovane

sprint [sprɪnt] N (*in race*) sprint *m inv*, scatto; (*dash*) corsa; **in a sprint finish** con uno sprint finale; **the women's 100 metres sprint** i cento metri piani femminili; **the 200-metres sprint** i 200 metri piani
■VI (*in race*) scattare, sprintare; (*dash: for bus etc*) fare una corsa; **she sprinted for the bus** ha fatto una corsa per prendere l'autobus

sprint·er ['sprɪntəʳ] N (*Sport*) velocista *m/f*

sprint finish N (*Sport*) finale in volata

sprite [spraɪt] N elfo, folletto

spritz·er ['sprɪtsəʳ] N spritz *m inv*

sprock·et ['sprɒkɪt] N (*on printer, bicycle*) dente *m*, rocchetto

sprog [sprɒg] N (*Brit fam*) rampollo(-a)

sprout [spraʊt] N (*from bulb, seeds*) germoglio; *see also* **sprouts**
■VT (*leaves, shoots*) mettere, produrre; **to sprout a moustache** farsi crescere i baffi
■VI germogliare; **skyscrapers are sprouting up everywhere** i grattacieli spuntano dappertutto

sprouts [spraʊts] NPL (*also:* **Brussels sprouts**) cavoletti *mpl* di Bruxelles

spruce¹ [spru:s] N (*Bot*) abete *m*; **Norway spruce** abete norvegese *or* rosso

spruce² [spru:s] ADJ (*outfit*) elegante; (*lawn*) curato(-a); (*person*) azzimato(-a)
▸ **spruce up** VT + ADV (*tidy*) mettere in ordine; (*smarten up: room etc*) abbellire; **to spruce o.s. up** farsi bello(-a); **all spruced up** tutto(-a) azzimato(-a) *or* agghindato(-a)

sprung [sprʌŋ] PP *of* **spring**
■ADJ (*seat, mattress*) a molle; **interior-sprung mattress** materasso a molle

spry [spraɪ] ADJ (*comp* **-er**, *superl* **-est**) vivace, sveglio(-a), arzillo(-a)

SPUC [spʌk] N ABBR (= **Society for the Protection of the Unborn Child**) *associazione anti-abortista*

spud [spʌd] N (*fam: potato*) patata

spun [spʌn] PT, PP *of* **spin**

spunk [spʌŋk] N (*fam*): **she's got spunk** ha fegato

◎**spur** [spɜ:ʳ] N (*also Geog*) sperone *m*; (*fig*) sprone *m*; **to be a spur to** essere d'incentivo a; **on the spur of the moment** su due piedi, d'impulso
■VT (*also:* **spur on**: *horse, fig*) spronare; **to spur sb on to do sth** spronare qn a fare qc

spurge [spɜ:dʒ] N euforbia

spu·ri·ous ['spjʊərɪəs] ADJ (*gen*) falso(-a); (*affection, interest*) falso(-a), simulato(-a)

spurn [spɜ:n] VT respingere, sdegnare

spurt [spɜ:t] N (*of water, steam etc*) getto; (*of speed, energy, anger*) scatto; **to put on a spurt** (*runner*) fare uno scatto; (*fig: in work etc*) affrettarsi, sbrigarsi; **a spurt of water** un getto d'acqua; **a spurt of anger** uno scatto di rabbia
■VI (*gush: also:* **spurt out**) sgorgare

sput·nik ['spʊtnɪk] N sputnik *m inv*

sput·ter ['spʌtəʳ] VI = **splutter**

spy [spaɪ] N spia; **police spy** informatore(-trice) (della polizia)
■VT (*catch sight of*) scorgere
■VI spiare; **to spy on sb** spiare qn
■ADJ (*film, story*) di spionaggio
▸ **spy out** VT + ADV: **to spy out the land** (*fig*) tastare il terreno

spy·glass ['spaɪˌglɑ:s] N cannocchiale *m*

spy·hole ['spaɪˌhəʊl] N spioncino

spy·ing ['spaɪɪŋ] N spionaggio

Sq. ABBR (*in address*: = **Square**) p.zza

sq. ABBR (*Math*) *of* **square**

Ss

squab·ble ['skwɒbl] N battibecco
■ VI: **to squabble (over** *or* **about)** bisticciarsi (per); **stop squabbling!** smettetela di bisticciare!

squab·bling ['skwɒblɪŋ] N bisticci *mpl*; **stop that squabbling, you two!** smettetela di bisticciare voi due!

◎ **squad** [skwɒd] N (*Mil*) drappello, plotone *m*; (*of police, workmen etc*) squadra; **flying squad** (*Police*) (squadra) volante *f*, (squadra) mobile *f*; **a squad of soldiers** un drappello di soldati; **vice squad** buoncostume *f*; **the England World Cup squad was named today** (*Ftbl*) oggi è stata annunciata la formazione inglese convocata per i mondiali

squad car N (*Brit Police*) automobile *f* della polizia

squad·die ['skwɒdɪ] N (*Brit Mil fam*) burba

squad·ron ['skwɒdrən] N (*Mil*) squadrone *m*; (*Aer, Naut*) squadriglia

squadron leader N (*Brit: Aviation*) capitano

squal·id ['skwɒlɪd] ADJ squallido(-a), sordido(-a)

squall [skwɔ:l] N (*Met*) bufera, burrasca
■ VI (*baby*) strillare, urlare

squal·ling ['skwɔ:lɪŋ] ADJ (*baby*) che strilla, urlante

squal·or ['skwɒləʳ] N squallore *m*

squan·der ['skwɒndəʳ] VT (*money*) sperperare, dissipare, scialacquare; (*time, opportunity*) sprecare, perdere

◎ **square** [skwɛəʳ] N
1 (*gen*) quadrato; (*instrument*) squadra; (*check on material*) quadro; **a square and a triangle** un quadrato e un triangolo; **with red and blue squares** a quadri rossi e blu; **to cut into squares** tagliare in (pezzi) quadrati; **we're back to square one** (*fig*) siamo al punto di partenza
2 (*in town*) piazza; (*Am: block of houses*) isolato; **the town square** la piazza principale
3 (*Math*) quadrato; **16 is the square of 4** 16 è il quadrato di 4
4 (*fam: old-fashioned person*) matusa *m inv*; **he's a real square** è proprio un matusa
■ ADJ
1 (*in shape*) quadrato(-a); **a square table** un tavolo quadrato; **he's a square peg in a round hole in that job** non è tagliato per quel lavoro
2 (*Math*) quadrato(-a); **1 square metre** 1 metro quadrato; **two square metres** due metri quadrati; **it is less than a centimetre square** misura meno di un centimetro per lato; **2 metres square** di 2 metri per 2
3 a square meal un pasto sostanzioso
4 (*fair, honest*) onesto(-a), retto(-a); **to give sb a square deal** trattare qn onestamente; **I'll be square with you** sarò franco con te
5 (*even: accounts, figures*) in ordine; **to get one's accounts square** mettere in ordine i propri conti; **to get square with sb** (*also fig*) regolare i conti con qn; **now we're all square** (*fig*) adesso siamo pari
6 (*fam: old-fashioned: person*) all'antica; (*: idea*) sorpassato(-a); (*: style*) fuori moda
■ ADV: **square in the middle** esattamente *or* proprio nel centro; **to look sb square in the eye** guardare qn diritto negli occhi
■ VT
1 (*make square: stone, timber*) squadrare; (*: shape*) rendere quadrato(-a); **to square one's shoulders** raddrizzare le spalle
2 (*settle etc: accounts, books*) far quadrare; (*: debts*) saldare, regolare; **can you square it with your conscience?** riesci a conciliarlo con la tua coscienza?; **I'll square it with him** (*fam*) sistemo io le cose con lui
3 (*Math*) elevare al quadrato; **2 squared is 4** 2 al quadrato fa 4
■ VI (*agree*) accordarsi; **to square with** quadrare con
▸ **square off** VT + ADV (*wood, edges*) squadrare
▸ **square up** VI + ADV
1 (*Brit: settle*) saldare; **to square up with sb** regolare i conti con qn
2 to square up (to) (*opponent*) affrontare; (*fig: difficulties*) far fronte a

square-bashing ['skwɛə, bæʃɪŋ] N (*Brit Mil fam*) esercitazioni *fpl*

square bracket N (*Typ*) parentesi *f inv* quadra

square-built ['skwɛə'bɪlt] ADJ (*squat: person*) tarchiato(-a), tozzo(-a)

square dance N (*esp Am*) quadriglia
▹ www.dosado.com/articles/hist-maca.html

square·ly ['skwɛəlɪ] ADV **1** (*directly*) direttamente; **to place sth squarely in the middle of the table** mettere qc proprio in mezzo al tavolo; **to face sth squarely** affrontare qc con coraggio **2** (*honestly, fairly*) onestamente; **to deal squarely with sb** trattare qn onestamente

Square Mile N (*Fin*): **the Square Mile** la City di Londra

square root N radice *f* quadrata

squash¹ [skwɒʃ] N **1** (*Brit: drink*): **orange/lemon squash** ≈ sciroppo di arancia/limone **2** (*crowd*) ressa, calca
■ VT **1** (*squeeze*) schiacciare; **you're squashing me** mi stai schiacciando; **can you squash two more in?** (*passengers*) puoi farne entrare altri due?; **to be squashed together** essere schiacciati(-e) l'uno(-a) contro l'altro(-a) **2** (*fig: argument*) soffocare; (*: opposition*) mettere a tacere; (*: person*) umiliare, schiacciare
■ VI: **to squash in** riuscire a entrare; **to squash up to make room for sb** stringersi per fare posto a qn

squash² [skwɒʃ] N (*vegetable*) zucca

squash³ [skwɒʃ] N (*Sport*) squash *m*

squash ball N pallina da squash

squash court N campo da squash

squash racket N racchetta da squash

squashy ['skwɒʃɪ] ADJ (*fruit*) molle; (*cushion etc*) morbido(-a)

squat [skwɒt] ADJ (*comp* **-ter**, *superl* **-test**) (*person*) tarchiato(-a), tozzo(-a); (*building, shape etc*) tozzo(-a)
■ VI **1** (*also:* **squat down**) accovacciarsi, acquattarsi; **he squatted to examine the footprints** si accovacciò per esaminare le impronte **2** (*on property*) occupare abusivamente; **to squat in a house** occupare abusivamente una casa
■ N (*fam: house*) casa occupata

squat·ter ['skwɒtəʳ] N occupante *m/f* abusivo(-a)

squaw [skwɔ:] N squaw *f inv*

squawk [skwɔ:k] N strido rauco
■ VI (*parrot, baby, person*) strillare; (*fam: complain*) lamentarsi

squeak [skwi:k] N (*of hinge, wheel etc*) cigolio; (*of shoes*) scricchiolio; (*of mouse etc*) squittio; **a squeak of surprise** un gridolino di sorpresa; **I don't want to hear a squeak out of you!** non voglio sentire una parola!
■ VI (*see n*) cigolare; scricchiolare; squittire; emettere un gridolino; **the door squeaked as it opened** la porta scricchiolò aprendosi; **she squeaked with delight** ha lanciato un gridolino di gioia

squeaky ['skwi:kɪ] ADJ (*comp* **-ier**, *superl* **-iest**) (*hinge,* wheel) cigolante; (*shoes*) scricchiolante; **squeaky clean** (*hair*) splendente; (*fig: very clean: office, home*) tirato(-a) a specchio; (*: person: irreproachable*) dall'immagine cristallina

squeal [skwi:l] N (*gen*) strillo; (*of tyres, brakes*) stridore *m*; **a squeal of laughter** una risatina
■ VI (*see n*) strillare; stridere; (*fam: inform*): **to squeal (on sb)** fare una soffiata (a qn)

squeam·ish ['skwi:mɪʃ] ADJ (*easily nauseated*) facilmente impressionabile; **I was too squeamish to look** mi faceva troppa impressione guardare

squeam·ish·ness ['skwi:mɪʃnɪs] N impressionabilità

◎**squeeze** [skwi:z] N (*pressure*) pressione *f*; (*of hand*) stretta; (*crush, crowd*) ressa, calca; **credit squeeze** (*Fin*) stretta creditizia; **to give sb's hand a squeeze** dare una lieve stretta di mano a qn; **it was a tight squeeze to get through** c'era appena il posto per passare; **we're in a tight squeeze** (*fig fam*) ci troviamo in difficoltà; **a squeeze of lemon** una spruzzata di limone; **give me a squeeze of toothpaste** dammi un po' di dentifricio; **to put the squeeze on sb** far pressione su qn
■ VT (*gen*) premere; (*sponge*) strizzare; (*lemon etc*) spremere; (*hand, arm*) stringere; **to squeeze the juice out of a lemon** spremere un limone; **squeeze two large lemons** spremete due limoni grossi; **to squeeze toothpaste out of a tube** spremere il dentifricio da un tubetto; **to squeeze clothes into a case** pigiare i vestiti in una valigia; **to squeeze information out of sb** strappare delle informazioni a qn; **she squeezed my hand reassuringly** mi ha stretto la mano con fare rassicurante; **can you squeeze two more in?** riesci a farcene entrare altri due?; **I can squeeze you in at two o'clock** le posso dare un appuntamento alle due
■ VI: **to squeeze past/under sth** passare vicino/sotto a qc con difficoltà; **to squeeze in** infilarsi; **to squeeze through a hole** passare a forza attraverso un buco; **to squeeze through the crowd** riuscire ad aprirsi un varco tra la folla; **the thieves squeezed through a tiny window** i ladri si sono introdotti attraverso una finestrella
▶ **squeeze out** VT + ADV spremere

squeez·er ['skwi:zə^r] N: **lemon squeezer** spremiagrumi *m inv*

squelch [skwɛltʃ] VI: **to squelch in/out** *etc* entrare/ uscire sguazzando; **he squelched through the mud** faceva cic ciac nel fango

squib [skwɪb] N petardo

squid [skwɪd] N calamaro

squidgy ['skwɪdʒɪ] ADJ (*Brit fam: cake, fruit*) molliccio(-a); (*: sofa, armchair*) morbido(-a)

squig·gle ['skwɪgl] N scarabocchio
■ VI scarabocchiare

squint [skwɪnt] N (*Med*) strabismo; (*sidelong look*) occhiata, sbirciata; **to have a squint** (*Med*) essere strabico(-a); **let's have a squint** (*fam*) diamo un'occhiata
■ VI (*Med*) essere strabico(-a); **to squint at sth** guardare qc di traverso; (*quickly*) sbirciare qc; **he squinted in the sunlight** la luce del sole gli faceva strizzare gli occhi

squire ['skwaɪə^r] N (*old: landowner*) possidente *m*

squirm [skw3:m] VI contorcersi; **to squirm with embarrassment** sentirsi morire dall'imbarazzo

squir·rel ['skwɪrəl] N scoiattolo; **red squirrel** scoiattolo eurasiatico; **grey squirrel** scoiattolo grigio

squirt [skw3:t] N (*of water*) schizzo; (*of detergent, perfume*) spruzzo
■ VT spruzzare
■ VI schizzare

squishy ['skwɪʃɪ] ADJ (*fam: fruit*) molliccio(-a); (*: armchair*) morbido(-a)

Sr ABBR = **senior, sister 3**

Sri Lan·ka ['srɪ'læŋkə] N lo Sri Lanka

Sri Lan·kan ['srɪ'læŋkən] ADJ dello Sri Lanka
■ N abitante *m/f or* nativo(-a) dello Sri Lanka

SS [,ɛs'ɛs] ABBR = **steamship**

SSA [,ɛsɛs'eɪ] N ABBR (*Am:* = **Social Security Administration**) ≈ Previdenza Sociale

ST [,ɛs'ti:] ABBR (*Am*) = **standard time**

St ABBR = **Saint**

St. ABBR = **Street**

stab [stæb] N **1** (*with knife*) coltellata; (*with dagger*) pugnalata; (*of pain*) fitta; **a stab in the back** (*also fig*) una pugnalata alla schiena; **he felt a stab of remorse** gli rimordeva la coscienza **2** (*fam: try*): **to have a stab at (doing) sth** provare a fare qc
■ VT (*with dagger*) pugnalare; (*with knife*) accoltellare; **to stab sb to death** uccidere qn a coltellate; **to stab sb in the back** (*also fig*) pugnalare qn alla schiena; **he was stabbed through the heart** fu pugnalato al cuore

stab·bing ['stæbɪŋ] N: **there's been a stabbing** c'è stato un accoltellamento
■ ADJ (*pain, ache*) lancinante

sta·bil·ity [stə'bɪlɪtɪ] N (*structural, political, economic*) stabilità; (*mental, emotional*) equilibrio; (*of family, relationship*) solidità

sta·bi·li·za·tion [,steɪbəlaɪ'zeɪʃən] N stabilizzazione *f*

sta·bi·lize ['steɪbə,laɪz] VT stabilizzare; **stabilizing jacket** (*Skin diving*) giubbetto equilibratore
■ VI stabilizzarsi

sta·bi·li·zer ['steɪbə,laɪzə^r] N (*Aer, Naut*) stabilizzatore *m*

◎**sta·ble¹** ['steɪbl] ADJ (*comp* **-r**, *superl* **-st**) (*government, economy*) stabile; (*relationship*) solido(-a), stabile; (*person: emotionally, mentally*) equilibrato(-a); **a stable relationship** una relazione stabile; **the patient is stable** (*Med*) le condizioni del paziente sono stazionarie

sta·ble² ['steɪbl] N (*building*) stalla; (*establishment*) scuderia; **riding stables** maneggio
■ VT (*keep in stable*) tenere in una stalla

stable·boy ['steɪbl,bɔɪ], **stable·lad** ['steɪbl,læd] N garzone *m* di stalla

stab wound N ferita da taglio

stac·ca·to [stə'kɑ:təʊ] (*Mus*) ADV in staccato
■ ADJ staccato(-a); (*sound*) scandito(-a)

stack [stæk] N **1** (*pile*) pila, catasta; (*Brit fam*) mucchio, sacco; **there was a stack of books on the table** sul tavolo c'era una pila di libri; **stacks of** un sacco di; **they've got stacks of money** hanno un sacco di soldi; **there's stacks of time to finish it** abbiamo un sacco di tempo per finirlo **2** (*also:* **chimney stack**) comignolo; (*: of factory*) ciminiera **3** (*Geog*) faraglione *m*
■ VT (*books, boxes*) impilare, accatastare; (*chairs*) mettere l'uno(-a) sopra l'altro(-a); (*aircraft*) tenere a quote assegnate (*in attesa dell'atterraggio*); **the cards are stacked against us** (*fig*) tutto è contro di noi

stack·er ['stækə^r] N (*on printer*) casella di ricezione

◎**sta·dium** ['steɪdɪəm] N stadio

◎**staff** [stɑ:f] N **1** (*personnel: gen*) personale *m*; (*: servants*) personale di servizio; (*Mil*) Stato Maggiore; **the administrative staff** il personale amministrativo;

Ss

the teaching staff il corpo insegnante; **to be on the staff** far parte del personale *or* dell'organico; **a staff of 15** un personale *or* organico di 15 persone; **to join the staff** entrare a far parte del personale; **"staff only"** "passaggio di servizio" **2** (*old: stick*) bastone *m*; (*Rel*) bastone pastorale; (*of flag*) asta **3** (*Mus: stave*) pentagramma *m*, rigo
■ VT fornire di personale; **to be staffed by Asians/women** avere un personale asiatico/costituito da donne; **to be well staffed** essere ben fornito(-a) di personale

staff·ing ['stɑːfɪŋ] N dotazione *f* di personale
■ ADJ: **staffing problems** problemi *mpl* di personale

staff meeting N riunione *f* del personale; (*Scol*) riunione dei professori

staff nurse N (*Brit*) infermiere(-a)

staff officer N (*Mil*) ufficiale *m* di Stato Maggiore

staff room N sala dei professori

Staffs ABBR (*Brit*) = *Staffordshire*

stag [stæg] N (*Zool*) cervo; (*Brit Stock Exchange*) rialzista *m/f* su nuove emissioni

stag beetle N cervo volante

◎ **stage** [steɪdʒ] N **1** (*period, section: of process, development*) fase *f*, stadio; (*: of journey*) tappa; (*: of rocket*) stadio; **in stages** (*travel, work etc*) a tappe; **in** *or* **by easy stages** a piccole tappe; **in the early/final stages** negli stadi iniziali/finali; **at this stage in the negotiations** in questa fase dei negoziati; **the final stage of their world tour** la tappa conclusiva della loro tournée mondiale; **to go through a difficult stage** attraversare un periodo difficile **2** (*platform*) palco; (*: in theatre*) palcoscenico; **the stage** (*profession*) il teatro; **to go on the stage** entrare in scena; (*become an actor*) fare del teatro; **she went on stage and did her act** è salita sul palco e ha fatto il suo show
■ VT (*play*) mettere in scena, rappresentare; (*arrange: welcome, demonstration*) organizzare; (*fake: accident*) simulare; **to stage a scene** allestire una scena; (*fig*) fare una sceneggiata; **to stage a quick recovery** riprendersi subito; **to stage a comeback** fare ritorno

> DID YOU KNOW ...?
> **stage** is not translated by the Italian word *stage*

stage·coach ['steɪdʒ,kəʊtʃ] N diligenza

stage·craft ['steɪdʒ,krɑːft] N tecnica teatrale

stage direction N (*in text*) didascalie *fpl*

stage director N regista *m/f* teatrale

stage door N ingresso degli artisti

stage fright N panico prima di andare in scena; **to get stage fright** essere assalito(-a) dal panico prima di andare in scena

stage·hand ['steɪdʒ,hænd] N (*Theatre*) macchinista *m*

stage-manage ['steɪdʒ,mænɪdʒ] VT (*event, confrontation*) montare, inscenare; (*: pej*) orchestrare

stage manager N direttore(-trice) di scena

stage name N nome *m* d'arte

stage-struck ['steɪdʒ,strʌk] ADJ: **to be stage-struck** essere preso(-a) dal fuoco sacro del teatro

stage whisper N (*fig*) sussurro perfettamente udibile

stag·ey ['steɪdʒɪ] ADJ = **stagy**

stag·fla·tion [stæg'fleɪʃən] N stagflazione *f*

stag·ger ['stægə^r] VT **1** (*amaze: person*) sbalordire; **it staggered me** mi ha sbalordito **2** (*holidays, payments, hours*) scaglionare; (*objects*) disporre a intervalli
■ VI barcollare; **to stagger along/in/out** avanzare/entrare/uscire barcollando; **he staggered to the door** andò verso la porta barcollando

stag·gered ['stægəd] ADJ **1** (*amazed*) sbalordito(-a), stupefatto(-a) **2** (*hours, holidays etc*) scaglionato(-a); **staggered working hours** orario di lavoro scaglionato *or* diversificato

stag·ger·ing ['stægərɪŋ] ADJ (*amazing*) sbalorditivo(-a), incredibile

stag·ing post ['steɪdʒɪŋ,pəʊst] N tappa obbligata

stag·nant ['stægnənt] ADJ stagnante

stag·nate [stæg'neɪt] VI (*water*) stagnare; (*fig: economy*) ristagnare; (*: person*) vegetare; (*: mind*) intorpidirsi

stag·na·tion [stæg'neɪʃən] N (*of water, economy*) ristagno, stagnazione *f*; (*of mind*) intorpidimento

stag night, **stag party** N festa di addio al celibato

stagy, **stagey** ['steɪdʒɪ] ADJ (*comp* **-ier**, *superl* **-iest**) (*pej*) teatrale

staid [steɪd] ADJ (*comp* **-er**, *superl* **-est**) compassato(-a)

staid·ness ['steɪdnɪs] N eccessiva posatezza

stain [steɪn] N **1** (*also fig*) macchia; **grease stain** macchia di grasso; **a large stain** una grande macchia **2** (*dye*) colorante *m*
■ VT **1** (*also fig*) macchiare; **to stain with** macchiare di **2** (*wood*) tingere; (*: glass*) colorare
■ VI macchiarsi

stained glass [,steɪnd'glɑːs] N vetro colorato

stained-glass window [,steɪndglɑːs'wɪndəʊ] N vetrata colorata

stain·less ['steɪnlɪs] ADJ (*steel*) inossidabile

stain remover N smacchiatore *m*

stair [stɛə^r] N (*single step*) scalino, gradino; (*whole flight: usu pl*) scala; **he fell down the stairs** è caduto (giù) per le scale; **on the stairs** per le *or* sulle scale; **he left the bag on the bottom stair** ha lasciato la borsa sull'ultimo gradino

stair carpet N guida

stair·case ['stɛə,keɪs], **stair·way** ['stɛə,weɪ] N scala

stair rod N asta metallica per fissare la guida

stair·well ['stɛə,wɛl] N tromba delle scale

◎ **stake** [steɪk] N **1** (*share*) interesse *m*; (*bet*) puntata, scommessa; **to be at stake** essere in gioco; **to raise the stakes** alzare la posta in gioco; **to have a stake in sth** avere un interesse in qc **2** (*for fence, tree*) palo; (*for plant*) bastoncino; **a wooden stake** un palo di legno **3** (*for execution*): **to be burnt at the stake** essere bruciato(-a) sul rogo
■ VT **1** (*bet*): **to stake (on)** scommettere (su); **I'd stake my reputation on it** ci giocherei la reputazione **2** (*also:* **stake out**: *area*) delimitare con paletti; (*also:* **stake up**: *plant*) legare a un bastoncino; **to stake a claim (to sth)** rivendicare (qc)

stake·hold·er ['steɪk,həʊldə^r] N (*gen*) persona che ha un interesse in una ditta, un'organizzazione e simili; (*Fin*) azionista *m/f*

stakeholder pension N (*Brit: Fin*) *pensione integrativa a partecipazione statale*

stake·out ['steɪkaʊt] N (*esp Am Police*) sorveglianza

stal·ac·tite ['stæləktaɪt] N stalattite *f*

stal·ag·mite ['stæləg,maɪt] N stalagmite *f*

stale [steɪl] ADJ (*comp* **-r**, *superl* **-st**) (*food: gen*) stantio(-a); (*: bread*) stantio(-a), raffermo(-a); (*: beer*) svaporato(-a); (*air*) viziato(-a); (*news, joke*) vecchio(-a) come il cucco, trito(-a); (*Law: claim*) caduto(-a) in prescrizione, prescritto(-a); **stale bread** pane raffermo; **stale air** aria viziata; **I'm getting stale** non ho più entusiasmo

stale·mate ['steɪl,meɪt] N (*Chess*) stallo; (*fig*) punto morto; **to reach stalemate** (*fig*) arrivare a un punto morto; **the negotiations have reached a stalemate** i negoziati sono arrivati ad un punto morto

stale·ness ['steɪlnɪs] N (*of food*) mancanza di freschezza; (*of air*) pesantezza

Sta·lin·ism ['stɑːlɪ,nɪzəm] N stalinismo

Sta·lin·ist ['stɑːlɪnɪst] N stalinista *m/f*

stalk[1] [stɔːk] VT (*animal, person*) inseguire
■ VI: **to stalk in/out** *etc* entrare/uscire *etc* impettito(-a); **she stalked out of the room angrily** uscì furiosa dalla stanza

stalk[2] [stɔːk] N (*Bot*) gambo, stelo; (*of cabbage*) torsolo; (*of fruit*) picciolo

stall [stɔːl] N **1** (*Agr: stable*) stalla, box *m inv*; (*Brit: in market*) bancarella, banco; (*at exhibition, fair*) stand *m inv*; **a newspaper/flower stall** chiosco del giornalaio/del fioraio; **to set out your stall** (*Brit*) dire chiaramente le proprie intenzioni **2** (*Theatre*): **the stalls** la platea **3** (*Aer*) stallo
■ VT (*plane*) far andare in stallo; **he stalled the car** gli si è spento il motore
■ VI **1** (*car, engine*) bloccarsi; (*plane*) andare in stallo **2** (*fig: delay*): **to stall for time** prendere tempo, temporeggiare; **stop stalling!** smettila di menare il can per l'aia!

stall·holder ['stɔːl,həʊldəʳ] N (*Brit*) bancarellista *m/f*

stal·lion ['stæljən] N stallone *m*

stal·wart ['stɔːlwət] ADJ (*person: in spirit*) prode, coraggioso(-a); (*party member*) fidato(-a); (*supporter, opponent*) risoluto(-a), deciso(-a); **a party stalwart** un fedelissimo del partito
■ N prode *m*, persona coraggiosa

sta·men ['steɪmɛn] N stame *m*

stami·na ['stæmɪnə] N resistenza; **he's got stamina** ha molta resistenza

stam·mer ['stæməʳ] N balbuzie *f*; **he's got a stammer** è balbuziente
■ VI, VT balbettare

stam·mer·er ['stæmərəʳ] N balbuziente *m/f*

◎ **stamp** [stæmp] N **1** (*also:* **postage stamp**) francobollo; (*also:* **trading stamp**) bollino premio; ≈ marchetta; **I collect stamps** faccio collezione di francobolli **2** (*rubber stamp*) timbro; (*mark*) bollo; **an official stamp** un timbro ufficiale; **it bears the stamp of genius** porta l'impronta del genio **3** **with an angry stamp of her foot** battendo il piede per terra con rabbia
■ VT **1** **to stamp one's feet** battere i piedi; (*in anger*) pestare i piedi; **the audience stamped their feet** il pubblico batteva i piedi; **to stamp the ground** (*person*) pestare i piedi per terra; (*horse*) scalpitare **2** (*letter*) affrancare **3** (*mark with rubber stamp*) timbrare, bollare; (*emboss*) imprimere su; **they stamped my passport at the border** mi hanno timbrato il passaporto al confine; **he looked at her ticket, and stamped it** le ha guardato il biglietto e l'ha timbrato
■ VI (*single movement*) battere il piede per terra; **to stamp in/out** entrare/uscire infuriato(-a); **ouch, you stamped on my foot!** ahi, mi hai pestato un piede!
▸ **stamp out** VT + ADV (*fire*) estinguere; (*crime*) eliminare; (*opposition*) soffocare

DID YOU KNOW ...?
stamp is not translated by the Italian word *stampo*

stamp album N (*new*) album *m inv* per francobolli; (*containing stamps*) album *m inv* di francobolli

stamp collecting [-kə'lektɪŋ] N filatelia
▹ www.philately.com

stamp collection N collezione *f* di francobolli

stamp collector N collezionista *m/f* di francobolli

stamp dealer N commerciante *m/f* di francobolli da collezione, filatelico(-a)

stamp duty N (*Brit*) bollo

stamped addressed envelope ['stæmptəd,rest'ɛnvələʊp] N busta affrancata per la risposta

stam·pede [stæm'piːd] N (*of cattle*) fuga precipitosa; (*of people*) fuggi fuggi *m inv*; **a stampede for the exit** un fuggi fuggi verso l'uscita; **there was a sudden stampede for the door** ci fu un fuggi fuggi verso la porta
■ VT (*cattle*) far scappare; **to stampede sb into doing sth** (*pej*) spingere qn a fare qc senza dargli il tempo di riflettere
■ VI (*cattle*) fuggire precipitosamente; (*fig*) precipitarsi

stamp·ing ground ['stæmpɪŋ'graʊnd] N: **to be sb's (old) stamping ground** essere il ritrovo (favorito) di qn

stamp machine N distributore *m* automatico di francobolli

stance [stæns] N **1** (*way of standing*) posizione *f* **2** (*attitude*) presa di posizione *f*

DID YOU KNOW ...?
stance is not translated by the Italian word *stanza*

◎ **stand** [stænd] (*vb: pt, pp* **stood**) N
1 (*booth*) chiosco; (*market stall*) banco, bancarella; (*at exhibition, fair*) stand *m inv*; (*raised area: also:* **bandstand**) palco; (*: Sport*) tribuna; (*: Am Law: also:* **witness stand**) banco; **a music stand** un leggio; **our stand in the trade fair** il nostro stand alla fiera; **he kicked the ball into the stand** con un calcio ha tirato la palla in tribuna
2 (*position, also fig*) posizione *f*; (*resistance*) resistenza; **to take (up) one's stand at the door** prendere il proprio posto vicino alla porta; **to take a stand on an issue** prendere posizione su un problema; **to make a stand against sth** (*Mil, fig*) opporre resistenza contro qc
3 (*also:* **taxi stand**) posteggio di taxi
■ VT
1 (*place*) mettere, porre; **to stand sth against a wall** appoggiare qc a un muro; **to stand sth on end** mettere qc in piedi
2 (*withstand, bear: weight*) reggere a, resistere, sopportare; **it won't stand serious examination** non reggerà ad un esame accurato; **the troops stood heavy bombardment** le truppe hanno sopportato pesanti bombardamenti; **the company will have to stand the loss** la ditta dovrà sostenere la perdita; **to stand the cost of** sobbarcarsi le spese di
3 (*tolerate*) sopportare; **I can't stand him** non lo sopporto; **I can't stand this noise** non sopporto questo chiasso; **I can't stand the sight of him** non lo posso vedere; **I can't stand it any longer!** non ce la faccio più!; **I can't stand waiting for people** non sopporto aspettare la gente
4 (*fam: treat*): **to stand sb a drink/meal** offrire da bere/un pranzo a qn
5 (*phrases*): **to stand guard** *or* **watch** (*Mil*) essere di guardia *or* sentinella; **to stand guard over** (*Mil, fig*) fare la guardia a
■ VI
1 (*be upright*) stare in piedi; (*stay standing*) restare in piedi; (*get up*) alzarsi; **I had to stand** sono dovuto restare in piedi; **he could hardly stand** si reggeva a malapena; **the woman standing over there** la donna in piedi laggiù; **he was standing by the door** stava in piedi vicino alla porta; **don't just stand there – help**

Ss

me! non stare lì impalato – aiutami!; **the house is still standing** la casa è ancora in piedi; **they stood talking for hours** restarono a parlare per delle ore; **they kept us standing about** *or* **around for ages** ci hanno fatto aspettare in piedi per ore; **to stand on sb's foot** pestare il piede a qn; **to stand in sb's way** intralciare il passaggio a qn; **I won't stand in your way** (*fig*) non ti sarò d'ostacolo; **nothing stands in our way** la via è libera; **that was all that stood between him and ...** era tutto ciò che si frapponeva fra lui e...; **nothing stands between us** non c'è niente che ci separi; **to be left standing** (*building*) essere rimasto(-a) in piedi; (*fig: competitor*) essere bruciato(-a) in partenza; **it made my hair stand on end** mi ha fatto rizzare i capelli; **to stand still** stare fermo(-a) (in piedi); **to stand fast** tener duro; **to stand on one's own two feet** (*fig*) cavarsela da solo(-a); **to stand on one's head/hands** fare la verticale in appoggio/la verticale; **he could do the job standing on his head** potrebbe fare quel lavoro a occhi chiusi; **to stand a (good) chance of** avere una (buona) possibilità di; **to stand on the brakes** (*Aut*) frenare di colpo; **to stand on one's dignity** stare sulle sue
2 **he stands over 6 feet** è alto più di 2m; **the tower stands 50m high** la torre è alta 50m
3 (*be situated: building, tree*) trovarsi, stare; **the car stands outside all year round** la macchina sta fuori tutto l'anno; **the house stands on top of a hill** la casa è situata in cima ad una collina
4 (*Culin*): **to leave to stand** (*tea*) lasciare in infusione; (*batter*) (lasciar) riposare; **my objection still stands** la mia obiezione è ancora valida; **to let sth stand as it is** lasciare qc così com'è; **the theory stands or falls on this** è questo il presupposto su cui si basa la teoria; **it stands to reason that ...** è logico che...
5 (*fig: be placed*) stare; **to stand accused of** essere accusato(-a) di; **how do things stand?** come stanno le cose?; **as things stand** stando così le cose; **the peace process as it stands violates human rights** il processo di pace così com'è viola i diritti umani; **to stand at** (*thermometer, clock*) indicare, segnare; (*offer, price, sales*) ammontare a; (*score*) essere
6 (*Pol*): **to stand as a candidate** candidarsi; **to stand in an election** candidarsi ad un'elezione; **to stand for Parliament** candidarsi al Parlamento
7 (*Naut*): **to stand out to sea** stare al largo
▸ **stand aside** VI + ADV farsi da parte, scostarsi
▸ **stand back** VI + ADV tirarsi indietro; (*building: be placed further back*): **to stand back from** essere arretrato(-a) rispetto a
▸ **stand by** VI + ADV (*be onlooker*) stare là (a non far niente); (*be ready*) tenersi pronto(-a); **stand by for further news** tenetevi pronti a ricevere altre notizie
■ VI + PREP (*person*) rimanere vicino(-a) a; (*promise*) mantenere; (*opinion*) sostenere
▸ **stand down** VI + ADV (*withdraw*) ritirarsi; (*Mil*) smontare di guardia; (*Law*) lasciare il banco dei testimoni; **to stand down in favour of** (*fig*) farsi da parte a favore di
▸ **stand for** VI + PREP
1 (*represent: principle, honesty*) rappresentare; (*: subj: initials*) indicare, stare per; **"BT" stands for "British Telecom"** "BT" è l'abbreviazione di "British Telecom"
2 (*tolerate*) tollerare, sopportare; **I won't stand for that** non tollero una cosa del genere; **I won't stand for it any more!** non ho intenzione di tollerarlo oltre!
3 (*Pol*) = **stand** VI **6**
▸ **stand in** VI + ADV: **to stand in for sb** sostituire qn
▸ **stand out** VI + ADV
1 (*be noticeable: veins, eyes*) sporgere; (*: colours*) risaltare, spiccare; (*: person*) distinguersi; (*: mountains*) stagliarsi; **it stands out a mile!** si vede lontano un miglio!
2 (*be firm, hold out*) resistere, tener duro; **to stand out against sth** opporsi fermamente a qc; **to stand out for sth** rivendicare qc, insistere su qc
▸ **stand over** VI + ADV (*items for discussion*) rimanere in sospeso
■ VT + PREP (*person*) stare adosso a
▸ **stand to** VI + ADV (*Mil*) tenersi pronto(-a)
▸ **stand up** VI + ADV (*rise*) alzarsi in piedi; (*be standing*) stare in piedi; (*fig: argument*) reggersi
■ VT + ADV (*fam: girlfriend, boyfriend*): **she stood me up** non è venuta all'appuntamento
▸ **stand up for** VI + ADV + PREP difendere; **to stand up for sb/sth** difendere qn/qc; **stand up for your rights!** difendi i tuoi diritti!; **to stand up for o.s.** difendersi
▸ **stand up to** VI + ADV + PREP tenere testa a, resistere a; **to stand up to sb** tenere testa a qn, affrontare qn con coraggio; **it stands up to hard wear** è resistente (all'uso)

stand-alone [ˌstændəˈləʊn] ADJ (*business, organization*) indipendente; (*Comput*) a sé stante, non in rete

◎ **stand·ard** [ˈstændəd] N **1** (*norm*) standard *m inv*; (*intellectual standard*) livello culturale; **the gold standard** (*Fin*) il tallone aureo; **to be** *or* **come up to standard** rispondere ai requisiti; **to set a high standard** dare il buon esempio; **at first-year university standard** a livello del primo anno d'università; **of (a) high/low standard** di alto/basso livello; **the standard is very high** il livello qualitativo è molto alto; **below** *or* **not up to standard** (*work*) mediocre **2** (*moral: usu pl*) scala di valori; **moral standards** valori *mpl* morali; **to accept sb's standards** accettare la scala di valori di qn; **to apply a double standard** avere due pesi e due misure **3** (*flag*) insegna; (*Mil*) stendardo
■ ADJ (*size, quality*) standard *inv*; (*reference book*) classico(-a); **standard English** inglese standard

standard-bearer [ˈstændədˌbɛərəʳ] N (*Mil, fig*) portabandiera *m/f*

standard English N inglese *m* standard

stand·ardi·za·tion [ˌstændədaɪˈzeɪʃən] N standardizzazione *f*

stand·ard·ize [ˈstændəˌdaɪz] VT standardizzare

standard lamp N (*Brit*) lampada a stelo

standard model N modello di serie

standard of living N tenore *m or* standard *m inv* di vita

standard practice N procedura normale; **it's standard practice to do so** è d'ordinaria amministrazione fare così ; **to become standard practice** diventare normale

standard rate N (*Fin: of income tax*) aliquota di base

standard time N ora ufficiale

stand-by [ˈstændˌbaɪ] N **1** (*person*) riserva; **have you got a stand-by, should that fail?** ha qualcosa che lo rimpiazzi nel caso che non funzioni?; **to be on stand-by** (*gen*) tenersi pronto(-a); (*doctor*) essere di guardia **2** (*also:* **stand-by ticket**) biglietto *m* stand-by *inv*

stand-by generator N generatore *m* d'emergenza

stand-by passenger N (*Aer*) passeggero(-a) in lista d'attesa

stand-by ticket N (*Aer*) biglietto *m* stand-by *inv*

stand-in ['stænd,ɪn] N sostituto(-a); (*Cine*) controfigura

stand·ing ['stændɪŋ] ADJ **1** (*passenger*) in piedi; (*upright: corn*) non mietuto(-a); **he was given a standing ovation** tutti si alzarono per applaudirlo; **standing start** partenza da fermo; **standing waves** (*Phys*) onde *fpl* stazionarie **2** (*permanent: rule*) fisso(-a); (*: army*) regolare; (*grievance*) continuo(-a); **it's a standing joke** è diventato proverbiale

■ N **1** (*social position*) rango, condizione *f*, posizione *f*; (*repute*) reputazione *f*; **financial standing** standing *m*; **a man of some standing** un uomo di una certa importanza; **what is his standing locally?** che reputazione ha da queste parti?; **wealth and social standing** ricchezza e posizione sociale; **the Prime Minister's standing in the country** la reputazione del primo ministro nel paese **2** (*duration*): **of 6 months' standing** che dura da 6 mesi; **of long standing** di lunga data

standing committee N commissione *f* permanente

standing order N **1** (*Brit: at bank*) ordine *m* permanente (di pagamento) **2 standing orders** NPL (*Mil, Parliament*) regolamento

standing room N posto in piedi

standing stone N menhir *m inv*

stand-off ['stænd,ɒf] N (*stalemate*) situazione *f* di stallo

stand·offish [,stænd'ɒfɪʃ] ADJ (*fam pej*) scostante, freddo(-a)

stand·offish·ly [,stænd'ɒfɪʃlɪ] ADV (*fam pej*) in modo scostante, con freddezza

stand·out ['stændaʊt] (*Am fam*) N: **to be a standout** (*person*) essere un asso; (*thing*) essere eccezionale; **a standout performance** uno spettacolo eccezionale

stand·pat ['stænd'pæt] ADJ (*Am*) irremovibile

stand·pipe ['stænd,paɪp] N fontanella

stand·point ['stænd,pɔɪnt] N punto di vista

stand·still ['stænd,stɪl] N: **to bring a car to a standstill** fermare una macchina; **to be at a standstill** (*vehicle*) essere fermo(-a); (*industry etc*) ristagnare, essere paralizzato(-a), il traffico è fermo; **traffic is at a standstill** *or* **to come to a standstill** (*vehicle*) fermarsi; (*industry etc*) rimanere paralizzato(-a); (*production*) arrestarsi; (*talks, negotiations*) giungere a un punto morto; **the train came to a standstill** il treno si è fermato; **the talks came to a standstill** i colloqui erano ad un punto morto

stand-to ['stænd'tu:] N (*Mil: order*): **to give the stand-to** dare l'allerta

stand-up ['stænd,ʌp] ADJ (*fight, argument*) accanito(-a); (*meal*) in piedi; **stand-up comedian** ≈ comico da cabaret

stank [stæŋk] PT *of* **stink**

stan·za ['stænzə] N stanza (*Poesia*)

sta·ple¹ ['steɪpl] N (*for papers*) punto metallico

■ VT (*also:* **staple together**) cucire con punti metallici

sta·ple² ['steɪpl] ADJ (*diet, food, products*) base *inv*; (*crop, industry*) principale; **rice is their staple food** il loro alimento principale è il riso

■ N (*chief product*) prodotto principale; (*of diet*) alimento principale

staple extractor [-ɪks'træktəʳ] N levapunti *m inv*

staple gun N pistola *f* sparachiodi *inv*

sta·pler ['steɪpləʳ], **sta·pling ma·chine** ['steɪplɪŋmə∫i:n] N cucitrice *f*

◎ **star** [stɑ:ʳ] N **1** (*gen*) stella; (*Mil*) stelletta; (*Typ etc*) asterisco; **the moon and stars** la luna e le stelle; **four-star hotel** albergo a quattro stelle; **3-star petrol** (*Brit*) ≈ benzina normale; **4-star petrol** (*Brit*) ≈ (benzina) super *f*; **born under a lucky star** nato(-a) sotto una buona stella; **the stars** (*horoscope*) le stelle; **you can thank your lucky stars that** puoi ringraziare la tua buona stella che + *sub*; **to see stars** (*fig*) vedere le stelle **2** (*celebrity*) divo(-a); (*actress only*) stella; **a TV star** una star della TV

■ VT (*Cine etc*) essere interpretato(-a) da; **a film starring Greta Garbo** un film con Greta Garbo; **the film stars Sharon Stone** il film ha come protagonista Sharon Stone

■ VI (*Cine etc*): **to star in a film** essere il (*or* la) protagonista di un film; **he starred as Othello** ha interpretato il ruolo di Otello

star attraction N (*in show*) numero principale; (*in museum*) l'attrazione *f* principale

star·board ['stɑ:bəd] N tribordo; **on the starboard side** a dritta, a tribordo

starch [stɑ:tʃ] N amido

■ VT inamidare

starched [stɑ:tʃt] ADJ (*collar*) inamidato(-a)

starch-reduced [,stɑ:tʃrɪ'dju:sd] ADJ (*bread etc*) povero(-a) d'amido

starchy ['stɑ:tʃɪ] ADJ (*comp* **-ier**, *superl* **-iest**) (*food*) ricco(-a) di amido

star·dom ['stɑ:dəm] N celebrità

◎ **stare** [stɛəʳ] N sguardo fisso; **a vacant stare** uno sguardo assente

■ VT: **it's staring you in the face** (*obvious*) salta agli occhi; (*very near*) ce l'hai sotto il naso

■ VI: **to stare at sb/sth** fissare qn/qc; **to stare into space** fissare il vuoto; **to stare at sb in surprise** fissare qn con aria sorpresa; **it's rude to stare** non sta bene fissare la gente

▸ **stare out** VT + ADV (fissare fino a) fare abbassare gli occhi

DID YOU KNOW ...?
stare is not translated by the Italian word *stare*

star·fish ['stɑ:,fɪʃ] N stella di mare

star·gaz·ing ['stɑ:,geɪzɪŋ] N (*fig*): **to be stargazing** avere la testa nelle nuvole

stark [stɑ:k] ADJ (*comp* **-er**, *superl* **-est**) (*outline*) aspro(-a); (*landscape*) desolato(-a); (*simplicity, colour*) austero(-a); (*contrast*) forte; (*reality, poverty, truth*) crudo(-a)

■ ADV: **stark staring** *or* **raving mad** matto(-a) da legare; **stark naked** nudo(-a) come un verme

stark·ers ['stɑ:kəz] ADJ (*Brit fam*) nudo(-a) come un verme

star key N (*on phone, computer*) asterisco

star·let ['stɑ:lɪt] N (*Cine*) stellina

star·light ['stɑ:,laɪt] N: **in the starlight** alla luce delle stelle

star·ling ['stɑ:lɪŋ] N storno

star·lit ['stɑ:,lɪt] ADJ stellato(-a)

star part N ruolo principale

star player N giocatore(-trice) di prima grandezza

star prize N primo premio

starring role N ruolo da protagonista

starry ['stɑ:rɪ] ADJ (*comp* **-ier**, *superl* **-iest**) stellato(-a); **starry cast** cast *m inv* di prim'ordine

starry-eyed [,stɑ:rɪ'aɪd] ADJ (*idealistic, gullible*) ingenuo(-a); (*from wonder*) meravigliato(-a); (*from love*) perdutamente innamorato(-a)

Stars and Stripes NPL: **the Stars and Stripes** la bandiera a stelle e strisce

star sign N segno zodiacale

Ss

star·struck ['stɑːstrʌk] ADJ abbagliato(-a) dalla celebrità
star-studded ['stɑː,stʌdɪd] ADJ: **a star-studded cast** un cast di attori famosi
star system N **1** (*Astron*) galassia **2** (*Cine*) star system *m inv*
◎**start** [stɑːt] N
1 (*beginning*) inizio; (*in race*) partenza; (: *starting line*) linea di partenza; (*Mountaineering*) attacco; **at the start** all'inizio; **the start of the school year** l'inizio dell'anno scolastico; **from the start** dall'inizio; **for a start** tanto per cominciare; **for a start you need to check all the names** per cominciare devi controllare tutti i nomi; **to get off to a good** *or* **flying start** cominciare bene; **to make a start** cominciare; **shall we make a start on the washing-up?** cominciamo a lavare i piatti?; **to make an early start** partire di buon'ora; **to make a fresh (***or* **new) start in life** ricominciare daccapo *or* da zero; **it's not much, but it's a start** non è molto ma è pur sempre un inizio
2 (*advantage*) vantaggio; **the thieves had 3 hours' start** i ladri avevano 3 ore di vantaggio; **to give sb a 5-minute start** dare un vantaggio di 5 minuti a qn
3 (*sudden movement*) sussulto, sobbalzo; **to give a start** trasalire; **to give sb a start** far trasalire qn; **to wake with a start** svegliarsi di soprassalto
■VT
1 (*begin: gen*) cominciare, iniziare; (: *bottle*) aprire; (: *habit*) prendere; **to start doing sth** *or* **to do sth** iniziare a fare qc; **to start negotiations** avviare i negoziati; **he started life as a labourer** ha cominciato come operaio
2 (*cause to begin or happen: conversation, discussion*) iniziare; (: *quarrel*) cominciare, provocare; (: *rumour*) mettere in giro; (: *series of events, policy*) dare l'avvio a; (: *reform*) avviare; (: *fashion*) lanciare; (*found: business, newspaper*) fondare, creare; (*car, engine*) mettere in moto, avviare; **to start a fire** provocare un incendio; **to start a race** dare il via a una gara; **you started it!** hai cominciato tu!; **don't start anything!** non cominciare!; **don't start him on that!** non toccare quest'argomento in sua presenza!; **we'd like to start a family** ci piacerebbe avere un bambino subito; **he wants to start his own business** vuole avviare un'attività in proprio; **she started a campaign against drugs** ha lanciato una campagna contro la droga; **he couldn't start the car** non riusciva a far partire la macchina
■VI
1 (*begin: gen*) cominciare, iniziare; (: *rumour*) nascere; (*on journey*) partire, mettersi in viaggio; (*car, engine*) mettersi in moto, partire; **starting from Tuesday** a partire da martedì ; **to start on a task** cominciare un lavoro; **to start at the beginning** cominciare dall'inizio; **it started (off) well/badly** è cominciato bene/male; **she started (off) down the street** s'incamminò giù per la strada; **what time does it start?** a che ora inizia?; **what shall we start (off) with?** con che cosa cominciamo?; **she started (off) as a nanny** ha cominciato come bambinaia; **to start (off) with ...** (*firstly*) per prima cosa...; (*at the beginning*) all'inizio...; **he started (off) by saying (that) ...** cominciò col dire che...; **the car wouldn't start** la macchina non partiva; **we started off first thing in the morning** ci siamo messi in viaggio di buon mattino
2 (*in fright*): **to start (at)** trasalire (a), sobbalzare (a); **his eyes were starting out of his head** aveva gli occhi fuori dalle orbite
▸ **start off** VI + ADV (*leave*) partire; *see also* **start** VI **1**
■VT + ADV causare, far nascere; **to start sb off** (*on complaints, story etc*) far cominciare qn; (*give initial help*) aiutare qn a cominciare; **that was enough to start him off** è bastato questo a dargli il via
▸ **start out** VI + ADV (*begin journey*) partire; (*fig*): **to start out as** cominciare come; **to start out to do sth** cominciare con l'intenzione di fare qc
▸ **start over** VI + ADV (*Am*) ricominciare
▸ **start up** VI + ADV (*engine*) mettersi in moto; (*driver*) mettere in moto; (*music*) cominciare
■VT + ADV (*car, engine*) mettere in moto, avviare
start·er ['stɑːtə^r] N **1** (*Brit Culin*): **as a starter** come *or* per antipasto; **for starters** (*fig*) per cominciare
2 (*Aut etc: motor*) motorino d'avviamento; (*on machine*) pulsante *m* d'accensione **3** (*Sport: judge*) starter *m inv*; (: *competitor*) concorrente *m/f*; **he was a late starter** (*child*) ha cominciato tardi a leggere e a scrivere
starter home N prima casa (*abbastanza economica*)
start·ing ['stɑːtɪŋ] ADJ di partenza
starting handle N (*Brit*) manovella d'avviamento
starting point N punto di partenza
starting post N palo di partenza
starting price N (*Horse-racing*) ultima quotazione
star·tle ['stɑːtl] VT far trasalire, spaventare
star·tling ['stɑːtlɪŋ] ADJ (*surprising*) sorprendente, sbalorditivo(-a); (*alarming*) impressionante
start·up ['stɑːtʌp] ADJ: **startup costs** costi *mpl* di avviamento
■N (*also:* **startup company**) azienda appena avviata
star turn N (*Theatre, fig: person*) vedette *f inv*; (*act*) attrazione *f* principale
star·va·tion [stɑː'veɪʃən] N inedia, fame *f*; **to die of starvation** morire d'inedia; **they died of starvation** sono morti d'inedia; **poverty and starvation breed terrorism** il terrorismo nasce da povertà e fame; **it might be fuel starvation** (*Tech*) potrebbe essere un problema di alimentazione del carburante
starvation diet N dieta da fame
starvation wages NPL salario *msg* da fame
starve [stɑːv] VT far patire la fame a, affamare; **to starve sb to death** far morire qn di fame; **to starve o.s.** lasciarsi morire di fame; **to starve sb into submission** prendere qn per fame; **to be starved of affection** soffrire per mancanza di affetto
■VI (*lack food*) soffrire la fame; **to starve (to death)** morire di fame; **people are starving** la gente muore di fame; **I'm starving!** (*fam*) sto morendo di fame!
starv·ing ['stɑːvɪŋ] ADJ affamato(-a)
stash [stæʃ] VT (*fam*): **to stash sth away** nascondere qc
◎**state** [steɪt] N **1** (*condition*) stato, condizione *f*; **state of emergency** stato di emergenza; **state of mind** stato d'animo; **state of war** stato di guerra; **to be in a bad/good state** essere in cattivo/buono stato; **he's not in a (fit) state to do it** non è in condizioni di farlo; **he was in no state to drive** non era in condizioni di guidare; **to be in a state of shock** essere sotto shock; **he arrived home in a shocking state** è arrivato a casa ridotto proprio male **2** (*anxiety*) agitazione *f*; **to be in a real state** essere tutto agitato(-a); **now don't get into a state** non ti agitare **3** (*pomp*): **in state** in pompa; **to lie in state** essere esposto(-a) solennemente **4** (*Pol*): **the State** lo Stato; **it's an independent state** è uno stato indipendente
■VT (*gen*) dichiarare, affermare; (*time, place*) decidere,

fissare; *(conditions)* indicare; *(case, problem, theory, facts)* esporre; **as stated above** come indicato sopra; **state your name and address** fornisca nome e indirizzo; **cheques must state the amount clearly** gli assegni debbono indicare chiaramente la somma; **he stated his intention to resign** ha dichiarato di essere intenzionato a dimettersi

■ ADJ *(business)* di stato; *(control)* statale; *(security)* dello stato; **the State line** *(Am)* il confine (tra due stati); **to pay a state visit to a country** andare in visita ufficiale in un paese

state banquet N banchetto ufficiale

state-controlled [ˌsteɪtkən'trəʊld] ADJ parastatale

stat·ed ['steɪtɪd] ADJ stabilito(-a), fissato(-a); **within stated limits** entro i limiti stabiliti; **within the stated period** entro il periodo di tempo stabilito

◎ **State Department** N *(Am)*: **the State Department** il Dipartimento di Stato; ≈ Ministero degli Esteri

state education N *(Brit)* istruzione *f* pubblica *or* statale

state·less ['steɪtlɪs] ADJ apolide; **a stateless person** un(a) apolide

state·li·ness ['steɪtlɪnɪs] N maestosità

state·ly ['steɪtlɪ] ADJ *(comp* **-ier**, *superl* **-iest**) maestoso(-a)

stately home N *(Brit)* residenza nobiliare *(d'interesse storico e artistico)*

◎ **state·ment** ['steɪtmənt] N *(gen)* dichiarazione *f*; *(of views, facts)* esposizione *f*; *(Law)* deposizione *f*; *(Fin)* rendiconto; **statement of account** *or* **bank statement** estratto conto; **official statement** comunicato ufficiale; **to make a statement** rilasciare un(a) dichiarazione; *(Law)* fare una deposizione; **he made a statement to the police** ha fatto una dichiarazione alla polizia; **I found this statement vague and unclear** ho trovato vaga e poco chiara l'affermazione

state of affairs N circostanze *fpl*; situazione *f*

state of the art ADJ *(equipment)* dell'ultima generazione

■ N: **the state of the art** l'ultima generazione

State of the Union address N discorso annuale del Presidente degli Stati Uniti

STATE OF THE UNION ADDRESS

Si chiama **State of the Union address** il discorso pronunciato annualmente dal Presidente degli Stati Uniti e indirizzato al Congresso (l'organo legislativo americano). Il Presidente, coadiuvato da consiglieri specializzati nei diversi settori, prepara e presenta un rapporto sull'andamento degli affari pubblici: il messaggio offre una panoramica finanziaria, economica e sociale della situazione a livello nazionale e propone le misure legislative necessarie soprattutto in campo economico e militare. Al discorso viene data ampia copertura mediatica, per cui è in realtà indirizzato, oltre che al Congresso, anche al popolo americano; è previsto dalla costituzione e viene pronunciato a gennaio.

▷ www.gpoaccess.gov/sou/

state-owned ['steɪt'əʊnd] ADJ statale, pubblico(-a)

state·room ['steɪtˌrʊm] N *(in palace)* salone *m* di rappresentanza; *(on ship)* cabina

States [steɪts] NPL: **the States** *(USA)* gli Stati *mpl* Uniti

state school N *(Brit)* scuola statale

states·man ['steɪtsmən] N *(pl* **-men**) statista *m*

states·man·like ['steɪtsmənˌlaɪk] ADJ da statista

states·man·ship ['steɪtsmənʃɪp] N abilità *f inv* politica

state-subsidized [ˌsteɪt'sʌbsɪˌdaɪzd] ADJ sovvenzionato(-a) dallo stato

state trooper N *(Am)* agente *m* di polizia

stat·ic ['stætɪk] ADJ statico(-a); **static electricity** elettricità statica

■ N **1** *(Radio, TV)* scariche *fpl* **2 statics** NSG *(Phys)* statica

◎ **sta·tion** ['steɪʃən] N **1** *(gen, Rail)* stazione *f*; *(also:* **fire station**) caserma (dei pompieri); *(also:* **police station**) commissariato (di Pubblica Sicurezza), questura, caserma (dei Carabinieri); *(esp Mil: post)* base *f*; **action stations** posti *mpl* di combattimento **2** *(Radio)* stazione *f* **3** *(social position)* condizione *f* sociale, rango; **to have ideas above one's station** montarsi la testa

■ VT *(Mil: troops, sentry)* stanziare; *(fig)* piazzare; **to be stationed in** *(Mil)* essere di stanza in; **to station o.s. by the door** piazzarsi sulla porta

■ ADJ *(Rail: staff, bookstall)* della stazione

sta·tion·ary ['steɪʃənərɪ] ADJ *(gen)* fermo(-a), immobile; *(vehicle)* in sosta; *(temperature, condition)* stazionario(-a); *(not movable)* fisso(-a); **to remain stationary** rimanere fermo(-a); **stationary point** *(Math)* punto di stazionarietà

sta·tion·er ['steɪʃənəʳ] N cartolaio(-a); **stationer's shop** cartoleria

sta·tion·ery ['steɪʃənərɪ] N articoli *mpl* di cancelleria; *(writing paper)* carta da lettere

station master N *(Rail)* capostazione *m*

stationmaster ['steɪʃənˌmɑːstəʳ] N *(Railways)* capostazione *m/f*

station wagon N *(Am Aut)* station-wagon *f*, familiare *f*

◎ **sta·tis·tic** [stə'tɪstɪk] N statistica; *see also* **statistics**

sta·tis·ti·cal [stə'tɪstɪkəl] ADJ statistico(-a)

sta·tis·ti·cal·ly [stə'tɪstɪkəlɪ] ADV statisticamente

stat·is·ti·cian [ˌstætɪs'tɪʃən] N esperto(-a) di statistica

sta·tis·tics [stə'tɪstɪks] NSG *(science)* statistica

■ NPL *(numbers)* statistiche *fpl*; **statistics show that ...** la statistica dimostra che...; **official statistics** statistiche ufficiali

▷ www.statistics.gov.uk/
▷ www.statcan.ca/start.html
▷ www.bls.gov/

statu·ary ['stætjʊərɪ] N *(frm: technique, statues)* statuaria

statue ['stætjuː] N statua

Statue of Liberty N Statua della Libertà

▷ www.nps.gov/stli/

statu·esque [ˌstætjʊ'ɛsk] ADJ *(woman)* statuario(-a)

statu·ette [ˌstætjʊ'ɛt] N statuetta

stat·ure ['stætʃəʳ] N **1** *(build)* statura; **to be of short stature** essere basso(-a) *or* di bassa statura **2** *(fig)* importanza; **a woman of considerable intellectual stature** una donna di grande levatura

◎ **sta·tus** ['steɪtəs] N *(of person: legal, marital)* stato; *(: economic, official etc)* posizione *f*; *(of agreement etc)* validità; *(prestige)* prestigio; **social status** status *m inv*; **the status of children in society** la posizione dei bambini nella società; **men and women of wealth and status** uomini e donne benestanti e di una certa condizione sociale; **nurses do not have the same status as doctors** le infermiere non hanno il prestigio di un medico

status quo [-'kwəʊ] N: **the status quo** lo statu quo

status symbol N status symbol *m inv*

Ss

stat·ute ['stætju:t] N (*law*) legge *f*, statuto
statute book N codice *m*
statu·tory ['stætjʊtərɪ] ADJ (*right, wage, control etc*) stabilito(-a) dalla legge; (*offence*) legalmente punibile; **statutory meeting** (*Comm*) assemblea ordinaria
statutory rape N (*Am: Law*) violenza sessuale (*su minore consenziente*)
staunch¹ [stɔ:ntʃ] ADJ (*comp* **-er**, *superl* **-est**) (*supporter, friend*) fedele, leale; (*believer, Christian*) convinto(-a)
staunch² [stɔ:ntʃ] VT (*flow*) arrestare; (*blood*) tamponare
staunch·ly ['stɔ:ntʃlɪ] ADV (*defend, support*) fedelmente; (*deny, refuse*) recisamente; **they moved to a staunchly Republican area** si trasferirono in una zona ultrarepubblicana
stave [steɪv] N (*Mus*) = **staff** N **3**
▸ **stave in** VT + ADV (*pt, pp* **stove in**) sfondare
▸ **stave off** VT + ADV (*pt, pp* **staved off**) (*crisis, threat, illness*) evitare; (*attack*) respingere; (*: temporarily*) allontanare
◎**stay** [steɪ] N
1 (*period of time*) soggiorno, permanenza; (*in hospital*) degenza; **a stay of ten days** *or* **a ten-day stay** un soggiorno di dieci giorni; **my stay in Italy** il mio soggiorno in Italia
2 (*Law*): **stay of execution** sospensione *f* dell'esecuzione di una sentenza
■ VI
1 (*remain in a place or situation*) rimanere, restare; (*spend some time*) fermarsi, soggiornare; (*reside, visit: in hotel*) alloggiare, stare; (*: with friends*) stare; **you stay right there** stai fermo dove sei; **stay here!** resta qui!; **to stay to dinner** rimanere a cena; **how long can you stay?** quanto ti fermi?; **to stay with friends** stare con degli amici; **she's staying with friends** sta presso amici; **where are you staying?** dove alloggi?; **to stay the night** passare la notte; **to stay overnight with friends** passare la notte a casa di amici; **camcorders are here to stay** le videocamere non sono un fenomeno temporaneo
2 (*continue, remain: with adj*) rimanere; **if it stays fine** se il tempo si mantiene bello; **to stay put** non muoversi
■ VT
1 (*last out*): **to stay the course** (*also fig*) resistere fino alla fine
2 (*punishment*) sospendere; (*spread of disease, flow*) fermare; **to stay sb's hand** fermare la mano a qn
▸ **stay away** VI + ADV: **to stay away from** (*person*) stare lontano da; (*school, party etc*) non andare a; **to stay away for** (*period of time*) stare via per
▸ **stay behind** VI + ADV (*after school, work etc*) fermarsi, trattenersi; (*not to go*) non andare
▸ **stay down** VI + ADV (*downstairs*) rimanere giù, rimanere di sotto; (*crouching, lying*) rimanere a terra; (*under water*) rimanere sott'acqua
▸ **stay in** VI + ADV (*person*) rimanere a casa, non uscire; (*screw*) tenere
▸ **stay on** VI + ADV rimanere, restare; **he stayed on as manager** è rimasto in carica come direttore
▸ **stay out** VI + ADV (*overnight, outside*) rimanere fuori, restare fuori; (*strikers*) continuare lo sciopero; **to stay out late** stare fuori fino a tardi; **to stay out of trouble** tenersi fuori dai pasticci; **you stay out of this!** non ti immischiare!
▸ **stay over** VI + ADV fermarsi
▸ **stay up** VI + ADV (*trousers, tent*) tenersi su; (*person: wait up*) rimanere alzato(-a) *or* in piedi; **we stayed up till midnight** siamo rimasti alzati fino a mezzanotte; **to stay up late** fare tardi
stay-at-home ['steɪət,həʊm] N tipo(-a) casalingo(-a)
stay·er ['steɪəʳ] N (*in race*) persona (*or* cavallo *etc*) che ha resistenza; (*fig*) chi tiene duro, chi non si dà per vinto(-a)
stay·ing pow·er ['steɪɪŋ,paʊəʳ] N capacità di resistenza
STD [,ɛsti:'di:] N ABBR **1** = **subscriber trunk dialling**
2 (= **sexually transmitted disease**) malattia venerea
stead [stɛd] N: **to stand sb in good stead** essere utile a qn; **in sb's stead** (*Brit*) al posto di qn
stead·fast ['stɛdfəst] ADJ costante, risoluto(-a)
stead·fast·ly ['stɛdfəstlɪ] ADV fermamente
stead·fast·ness ['stɛdfəstnɪs] N (*of spirit, character*) costanza, risolutezza; (*of resolution*) fermezza
steadi·ly ['stɛdɪlɪ] ADV (*walk*) con passo sicuro; (*speak*) con tono risoluto; (*improve, decrease*) gradualmente; (*rain*) di continuo; **it is getting steadily worse** continua a peggiorare; **to gaze steadily at sb** guardare qn senza distogliere lo sguardo; **to work steadily** lavorare senza interruzione *or* costantemente; **to increase steadily** essere in costante crescita; **keep breathing steadily** continua a respirare normalmente
◎**steady** ['stɛdɪ] ADJ (*comp* **-ier**, *superl* **-iest**) (*not wobbling: gen*) fermo(-a), stabile; (*: voice, gaze*) sicuro(-a); (*: nerves*) saldo(-a); (*not fluctuating: prices, sales*) stabile; (*regular: temperature, demand, improvement, progress*) costante; (*reliable: person, character*) serio(-a); (*boyfriend, girlfriend*) fisso(-a); **a steady job** un lavoro *or* impiego fisso; **a steady income** un reddito regolare; **a steady hand** una mano ferma; **you need a steady hand for this job** ci vuole mano ferma per fare questo lavoro; **we were going at a steady 70 km/h** andavamo a una velocità costante di 70 km l'ora
■ ADV: **steady!** calma!, piano!; **they are going steady** (*old fam*) fanno coppia fissa, stanno insieme
■ VT stabilizzare; (*wobbling object*) tenere fermo(-a); (*nervous person*) calmare; **to steady o.s.** reggersi, tenersi in equilibrio; **she smokes to steady her nerves** fuma per calmarsi; **to have a steadying influence on sb** rendere più calmo(-a) qn
steak [steɪk] N (*beef*) carne *f* di manzo; (*piece of beef, pork etc*) bistecca; **a cod steak** un trancio di merluzzo; **steak and kidney pie** *pasticcio di carne e rognoni di manzo in pasta sfoglia*
steak hammer N batticarne *m inv*
steak·house ['steɪk,haʊs] N *ristorante specializzato in bistecche*
steak knife N coltello a lama seghettata (da bistecca)
◎**steal** [sti:l] (*pt* **stole**, *pp* **stolen**) VT (*also fig*) rubare; **to steal money/an idea from sb** rubare denaro/un'idea a qn; **to steal a glance at sb** dare un'occhiata furtiva a qn; **to steal a march on sb** battere qn sul tempo; **thieves broke in and stole the video** sono entrati i ladri e hanno rubato il videoregistratore; **my car was stolen last week** mi hanno rubato la macchina la settimana scorsa
■ VI **1** (*thieve*) rubare **2** (*move quietly*): **to steal in/out** *etc* entrare/uscire *etc* furtivamente; **to steal up on sb** avvicinarsi furtivamente a qn
▸ **steal away, steal off** VI + ADV svignarsela, andarsene alla chetichella
steal·ing ['sti:lɪŋ] N furto
stealth [stɛlθ] N: **by stealth** furtivamente, di nascosto
stealthi·ly ['stɛlθɪlɪ] ADV furtivamente

stealthy ['stɛlθɪ] ADJ (*comp* **-ier**, *superl* **-iest**) furtivo(-a)

◎**steam** [sti:m] N vapore *m*; **to get up steam** (*train, ship*) aumentare la pressione; (*worker, project*) mettersi in moto; **to let off steam** (*fig*) sfogarsi; **under one's own steam** (*fig*) da solo, con i propri mezzi; **to run out of steam** (*fig: person*) non farcela più; (*: project, movement*) perdere vigore; **full steam ahead!** (*Naut*) avanti tutta!; **to go full steam ahead** (*fig*) andare a tutto vapore
■VT (*Culin*) cuocere a vapore; **to steam open an envelope** aprire una busta con il vapore
■VI **1** (*give off steam: liquid, food etc*) fumare; **a steaming saucepan** una pentola fumante **2 the ship steamed into harbour** la nave entrò nel porto; **to steam along** filare; **to steam away** (*ship*) partire; (*fig: person, car*) partire a tutto gas
▶ **steam up** VI + ADV (*window*) appannarsi; **to get steamed up about sth** (*fig*) andare in bestia per qc

steam·boat ['sti:m,bəʊt] N nave *f* a vapore; (*small*) vaporetto

steam-driven ['sti:m,drɪvn] ADJ a vapore

steam engine N (*Rail*) locomotiva a vapore

steam·er ['sti:məʳ] N (*steamship*) nave *f* a vapore, piroscafo; (*Culin*) pentola per cottura a vapore

steam iron N ferro a vapore

steam·roller ['sti:m,rəʊləʳ] N rullo compressore

steam·ship ['sti:m,ʃɪp] N piroscafo, nave *f* a vapore

steamy ['sti:mɪ] ADJ (*comp* **-ier**, *superl* **-iest**) (*room*) pieno(-a) di vapore; (*window*) appannato(-a); (*atmosphere, heat*) umido(-a); (*fam: book, film, play*) erotico(-a)

stea·rin, stea·rine ['stɪərɪn] N stearina

steed [sti:d] N (*liter*) corsiero, destriero

◎**steel** [sti:l] N acciaio; **nerves of steel** nervi *mpl* di acciaio
■VT: **to steel one's heart against** corazzarsi contro; **to steel o.s. for sth/to do sth** armarsi di coraggio per affrontare qc/per fare qc
■ADJ (*knife, tool*) d'acciaio

steel band N banda di strumenti metallici a percussione (*tipica delle Antille*)

steel helmet N casco di protezione

steel mill N acciaieria

steel-plated [,sti:l'pleɪtɪd] ADJ rivestito(-a) d'acciaio

steel wool N lana d'acciaio

steel·worker ['sti:l,wɜ:kəʳ] N operaio(-a) di acciaieria

steel·works ['sti:l,wɜ:ks] N, PL INV acciaieria

steely ['sti:lɪ] ADJ (*comp* **-ier**, *superl* **-iest**) (*determination*) inflessibile; (*gaze*) duro(-a); (*eyes*) freddo(-a) come l'acciaio; **steely grey** color piombo *inv*

steel·yard ['sti:l,jɑ:d] N stadera

steep¹ [sti:p] ADJ (*comp* **-er**, *superl* **-est**) (*gen*) ripido(-a); (*cliff*) scosceso(-a); (*increase, drop*) drastico(-a); (*fig fam: price*) alto(-a); (*: demands*) eccessivo(-a); (*: story*) inverosimile; **it's a bit steep!** (*fig fam*) è un po' troppo!

steep² [sti:p] VT (*washing*): **to steep (in)** mettere a bagno (in); (*Culin*) lasciare in infusione; **a town steeped in history** (*fig*) una città impregnata di storia; **steeped in prejudice** pieno(-a) di pregiudizi

steep·en ['sti:pən] VI diventare *or* farsi più ripido(-a)

stee·ple ['sti:pl] N campanile *m*

steeple·chase ['sti:pl,tʃeɪs] N corsa ad ostacoli, steeplechase *m inv*

steeple·jack ['sti:pl,dʒæk] N chi ripara campanili e ciminiere

steep·ly ['sti:plɪ] ADV ripidamente; **to rise/fall steeply** (*road, hill*) salire/scendere ripidamente; (*fig: prices*) aumentare/diminuire vertiginosamente; **prices fell steeply** i prezzi sono diminuiti vertiginosamente

steep·ness ['sti:pnɪs] N (*of hill etc*) ripidezza

steer¹ [stɪəʳ] VT **1** (*car*) guidare; (*fig: conversation, person*) dirigere, condurre; (*ship, boat*) dirigere; **my father let me steer the car** mio padre mi ha lasciato guidare la macchina; **he steered us into the nearest seats** ci ha guidati fino ai posti più vicini **2** (*handle controls of: ship*) governare; (*: boat*) portare
■VI (*in car*) sterzare; (*on ship*) dirigere; **to steer towards** *or* **for sth** dirigersi verso qc; **to steer clear of sb/sth** (*fig*) tenersi alla larga da qn/qc

steer² [stɪəʳ] N (*animal*) manzo

steer·ing ['stɪərɪŋ] N (*Aut*) sterzo; **power steering** servosterzo

steering column N (*Aut*) piantone *m* dello sterzo

steering committee N (*Am*) comitato direttivo

steering lock N (*Aut*) bloccasterzo

steering wheel N (*Aut*) volante *m*, sterzo

stel·lar ['stɛləʳ] ADJ (*frm, also fig*) stellare

◎**stem** [stɛm] N (*of plant*) gambo, stelo; (*of fruit, leaf*) gambo, picciolo; (*of glass*) stelo; (*of word*) radice *f*
■VT (*check, stop*) frenare, arrestare; (*river*) arginare, contenere; (*disease*) contenere; **to stem the tide of events** arrestare il corso degli eventi; **attempts to stem the flow of illegal immigrants** tentativi di arginare l'afflusso di immigrati clandestini
▶ **stem from** VI + ADV derivare da

DID YOU KNOW ...?
stem is not translated by the Italian word *stemma*

stem cell N (*Bio*) cellula staminale

stench [stɛntʃ] N puzzo, fetore *m*

sten·cil ['stɛnsl] N (*for lettering etc*) stampino; (*in typing*) matrice *f*
■VT stampinare

ste·nog·ra·pher [stɛ'nɒgrəfəʳ] N (*Am*) stenografo(-a)

ste·nog·ra·phy [stɛ'nɒgrəfɪ] N (*Am*) stenografia

ste·no·sis [stɪ'nəʊsɪs] N stenosi *f*

sten·to·rian [stɛn'tɔ:rɪən] ADJ (*frm: voice*) stentoreo(-a)

◎**step** [stɛp] N **1** (*movement*) passo; (*fig: move*) mossa, passo; **to take a step back/forward** fare un passo indietro/avanti; **he took a step forward** fece un passo in avanti; **it's a great step forward** (*fig*) è un gran passo avanti; **a step in the right direction** (*fig*) un passo nella direzione giusta; **step by step** un passo dietro l'altro; (*fig*) poco a poco; **to be in/out of step with** (*also fig*) stare/non stare al passo con; **to keep in step (with)** (*also fig*) mantenersi al passo (con); **to watch one's step** guardare dove si mettono i piedi; (*fig*) fare attenzione **2** (*measure*) misura; **to take steps to solve a problem** prendere le misure necessarie per risolvere un problema **3** (*stair*) gradino, scalino; (*of ladder*) piolo; (*of vehicle*) predellino; (*fig: in scale*) gradino; **steps** NPL (*stairs*) scala *fsg*; (*: outside building*) scalinata *fsg*; **folding steps** *or* **pair of steps** scala a libretto; **a step up in his career** (*fig*) un passo avanti nella carriera; **she tripped over the step** ha inciampato sul gradino
■VI fare un passo, andare; **to step aside** farsi da parte, scansarsi; **to step inside** entrare; **she stepped out of the car** uscì dalla macchina; **to step back** tirarsi indietro; **step this way, please!** da questa parte, per favore!; **to step over sth** scavalcare qc; **to step off the pavement** scendere dal marciapiede; **to step on sth** calpestare qc; **step on it!** (*fam*) muoviti!; **to step out of line** (*fig*) sgarrare

Ss

▸ **step down** VI + ADV scendere; (*fig: resign*): **to step down (in favour of sb)** dimettersi *or* dare le dimissioni (a favore di qn)
▸ **step forward** VI + ADV fare un passo avanti; (*fig: volunteer*) farsi avanti; **I tried to step forward** ho cercato di fare un passo in avanti
▸ **step in** VI + ADV entrare, fare il proprio ingresso; (*fig*) intromettersi
▸ **step up** VT + ADV (*production*) aumentare; (*efforts, campaign*) intensificare; **to step up work on sth** accelerare i lavori per qc
step aerobics NPL step *msg*
step·brother ['stɛp,brʌðə^r] N fratellastro
step change N svolta
step·child ['stɛp,tʃaɪld] N (*pl* **-children**) figliastro(-a)
step·daughter ['stɛp,dɔːtə^r] N figliastra
step·father ['stɛp,fɑːðə^r] N patrigno
step·ladder ['stɛp,lædə^r] N scala a libretto
step·mother ['stɛp,mʌðə^r] N matrigna
step-parent ['stɛp,pɛərənt] N (*stepfather*) patrigno; (*stepmother*) matrigna
steppe [stɛp] N steppa
step·ping stone ['stɛpɪŋ,stəʊn] N pietra di un guado; (*fig*): **stepping stone (to)** trampolino di lancio (verso)
step·sister ['stɛp,sɪstə^r] N sorellastra
step·son ['stɛp,sʌn] N figliastro
ste·reo ['stɛrɪəʊ] N (*hi-fi equipment*) stereo *m inv*; (*sound*) stereofonia; **in stereo** in stereofonia
■ ADJ stereofonico(-a), stereo *inv*
ste·reo·phon·ic [,stɛrɪə'fɒnɪk] ADJ stereofonico(-a)
ste·reo·scope ['stɛrɪə,skəʊp] N stereoscopio
ste·reo·scop·ic [,stɛrɪə'skɒpɪk] ADJ stereoscopico(-a)
ste·reo·type ['stɛrɪə,taɪp] N stereotipo
ster·ile ['stɛraɪl] ADJ sterile
ste·ril·ity [stɛ'rɪlɪtɪ] N sterilità
steri·li·za·tion [,stɛrɪlaɪ'zeɪʃən] N sterilizzazione *f*
steri·lize ['stɛrɪ,laɪz] VT sterilizzare
◎ **ster·ling** ['stɜːlɪŋ] N (*Fin*) sterlina
■ ADJ **1** (*silver*) al titolo di 925/1000, di buona lega; (*Econ*): **pound sterling** lira sterlina **2** (*fig*): **of sterling qualities** di gran pregio; **he is of sterling character** è una persona fidata
sterling area N (*Fin*) area della sterlina
stern¹ [stɜːn] ADJ (*comp* **-er**, *superl* **-est**) (*discipline*) rigido(-a); (*person, warning*) severo(-a); **I thought he was made of sterner stuff** pensavo fosse più forte
stern² [stɜːn] N (*Naut*) poppa
stern·ly ['stɜːnlɪ] ADV (*warn, glare*) severamente
stern·ness ['stɜːnnɪs] N (*of discipline*) rigidità, rigore *m*; (*of person, warning, voice*) severità
ster·num ['stɜːnəm] N (*Anat*) sterno
ster·oid ['stɛrɔɪd] N steroide *m*
ster·to·rous ['stɜːtərəs] ADJ (*frm: breathing*) stertoroso(-a)
stet [stɛt] N (*Typ*) vive
stetho·scope ['stɛθə,skəʊp] N stetoscopio
stet·son® ['stɛtsən] N lobbia
ste·vedore ['stiːvɪ,dɔː^r] N scaricatore *m* di porto
stew [stjuː] N **1** (*Culin*) stufato **2** (*fig*): **to be in a stew (about sth)** essere agitato(-a) (per qc); **to get into a stew (about sth)** mettersi in agitazione (per qc)
■ VT (*meat*) stufare, cuocere in umido; **stewed fruit** frutta cotta
■ VI (*tea*) diventare troppo forte; **to let sb stew in his own juice** (*fig*) lasciar cuocere qn nel suo brodo
stew·ard ['stjuːəd] N (*Aer, Naut, Rail*) steward *m inv*; (*on estate*) fattore *m*; (*in club*) dispensiere *m*; (*butler*) maggiordomo; (*shop steward*) rappresentante *m/f* sindacale
stew·ard·ess ['stjʊədɛs] N (*Aer, Naut*) hostess *f inv*
stew·ard·ship ['stjʊədʃɪp] N (*frm: supervision, care*) amministrazione *f*
stew·ing steak ['stjʊɪŋ,steɪk], (*Am*) **stew meat** N carne *f* di manzo per stufato
stg ABBR = **sterling**
◎ **stick** [stɪk] (*vb: pt, pp* **stuck**) N (*gen*) bastone *m*; (*twig*) ramoscello; (*support for plants*) asticella, bastoncino; (*of celery, rhubarb*) gambo; (*of shaving soap*) stick *m inv*; (*of dynamite*) candelotto; **dried sticks** rametti secchi; **he walks with a stick** cammina con il bastone; **a stick of celery** un gambo di sedano; **to wave the big stick** (*fig*) fare il/la prepotente; **to get hold of the wrong end of the stick** (*fig*) fraintendere; **a few sticks of furniture** pochi mobili *mpl* sgangherati; **to live in the sticks** (*fam*) abitare a casa del diavolo; **to give sb stick** (*fig*) fare un cicchetto a qn
■ VT
1 (*with glue etc*) incollare; **to stick two things together** incollare due cose; **he was sticking stamps into his album** attaccava i francobolli nell'album; **she stuck the envelope down** incollò la busta
2 (*thrust, poke: hand etc*) ficcare; (*sth pointed: pin, needle*) conficcare, piantare; **he stuck his hand in his pocket** ficcò una mano in tasca; **to stick a knife into sb** accoltellare qn
3 (*fam: place, put*) mettere; **stick it in your case** mettilo *or* ficcalo nella borsa; **he picked up the papers and stuck them in his briefcase** ha raccolto i documenti e li ha ficcati nella valigetta
4 (*fam: tolerate*) sopportare; **I can't stick it any longer** non ne posso più
5 **to be stuck** (*door, window*) essere bloccato(-a); (*knife, screw*) essere incastrato(-a); **it's stuck in my throat** mi si è conficcato in gola; **to be stuck with sb/sth** (*fam*) doversi sorbire qn/qc, dover sopportare qn/qc; **I'm stuck in bed** sono inchiodato a letto; **I'm stuck at home all day** sono bloccato a casa tutto il giorno
■ VI (*glue, sticky object etc*) attaccarsi, appiccicarsi; (*food, sauce*) attaccarsi; (*get jammed: door, lift*) bloccarsi; (*: lock*) incepparsi; (*in mud etc*) impantanarsi; (*sth pointed*) conficcarsi; **it stuck to the wall** è rimasto attaccato al muro; **the rice stuck to the pan** il riso s'è attaccato; **the nickname seems to have stuck** (*fam*) sembra che il soprannome gli (*or* le *etc*) sia rimasto; **to stick to sb's wheel** (*Cycling*) incollarsi alla ruota di qn; **it stuck in my mind** mi è rimasto in mente; **she will stick at nothing to get what she wants** è capace di tutto per ottenere quello che vuole; **just stick at it and I'm sure you'll manage it** non mollare e sono sicuro che riuscirai a farlo
▸ **stick around** VI + ADV (*fam*) restare, rimanere, fermarsi
▸ **stick by** VI + PREP (*stand by*) stare vicino(-a); **we'll all stick by you** (*support you*) siamo tutti con te; **she stuck by him through it all** è sempre rimasta al suo fianco
▸ **stick in** VT + ADV (*knife*) affondare; (*pin, needle etc*) appuntare; (*photo in album etc*) incollare, attaccare; **to get stuck in** (*fam*) impegnarsi seriamente; **I stuck in a few quotations from Shakespeare** ho inserito qua e là delle citazioni di Shakespeare
▸ **stick on** VT + ADV (*stamp, label*) incollare
▸ **stick out** VI + ADV
1 (*protrude*) sporgere; (*be noticeable*) spiccare; **his teeth stick out** ha i denti sporgenti; **his ears stick out** ha le

orecchie a sventola; **to stick out like a sore thumb** essere un pugno nell'occhio; **it sticks out because of the colour** spicca a causa del colore; **it was sticking out of the back of the car** sporgeva dal retro della macchina
2 to stick out for sth battersi per qc
■ VT + ADV (*tongue*) tirar fuori; (*arm*) allungare; (*head*) sporgere; **to stick it out** (*fam*) tener duro; **the little girl stuck out her tongue** la bambina tirò fuori la lingua
▸ **stick to** VI + PREP (*one's word, promise*) mantenere; (*principles*) tener fede a; (*text*) rimanere fedele a; (*facts*) attenersi a; **decide what you're going to do, then stick to it** decidi il da farsi e poi fallo
▸ **stick together** VI + ADV (*people*) restare uniti; (*things*) attaccarsi
▸ **stick up** VI + ADV (*protrude*) rimanere diritto(-a); **to stick up out of the water** uscire dall'acqua
■ VT + ADV
1 (*fam: raise: hand*) alzare; (*: rob*) rapinare; **stick 'em up!** mani in alto!
2 (*notice*) affiggere
▸ **stick up for** VI + ADV + PREP difendere; **to stick up for sb/sth** (*fam*) battersi per qn/qc
▸ **stick with** VI + PREP (*carry on with*) attenersi a; **I'll stick with the job for another few months** continuerò a fare questo lavoro per qualche altro mese

stick·er ['stɪkə^r] N (*label*) etichetta; (*on car etc*) adesivo
sticki·ness ['stɪkɪnɪs] N (*of pastry*) collosità *f inv*; (*of mud*) vischiosità *f inv*; (*fam: of situation*) difficoltà *f inv*
stick·ing plas·ter ['stɪkɪŋˌplɑːstə^r] N cerotto adesivo
stick·ing point ['stɪkɪŋˌpɔɪnt] N (*fig*) punto di stallo, impasse *f inv*
stick insect N insetto stecco
stick-in-the-mud ['stɪkɪnðəˌmʌd] N (*fam*) retrogrado(-a)
stickle·back ['stɪklˌbæk] N spinarello
stick·ler ['stɪklə^r] N: **to be a stickler for** essere esigente in fatto di, essere pignolo(-a) su
stick-on ['stɪkˌɒn] ADJ (*label*) adesivo(-a)
stick pin N (*Am*) fermacravatta *m inv*
stick shift N (*Am Aut*) cambio manuale
stick-up ['stɪkˌʌp] N (*fam*) rapina a mano armata
sticky ['stɪkɪ] ADJ (*comp* **-ier**, *superl* **-iest**) appiccicoso(-a), vischioso(-a); (*label*) adesivo(-a); (*fam: situation*) difficile, imbarazzante; **a sticky label** un'etichetta adesiva; **my hands are sticky** ho le mani appiccicose; **a sticky situation** una situazione difficile; **he was a bit sticky about lending me the money** ha fatto un sacco di storie per prestarmi i soldi; **to come to a sticky end** (*fam*) fare una brutta fine; **sticky tape** nastro adesivo; **you're on a sticky wicket there** (*fam*) sei proprio nelle peste
stiff [stɪf] ADJ (*comp* **-er**, *superl* **-est**) **1** (*gen*) rigido(-a); (*starched: shirt*) inamidato(-a); (*brush*) duro(-a); (*dough*) compatto(-a), denso(-a); (*arm, joint*) rigido(-a), indolenzito(-a); (*muscle*) legato(-a); **stiff material** stoffa rigida; **to have a stiff neck/back** avere il torcicollo/mal di schiena; **to be** *or* **feel stiff** essere *or* sentirsi indolenzito(-a); **the door's stiff** la porta si apre (*or* si chiude) con difficoltà; **as stiff as a ramrod** *or* **a poker** dritto(-a) come un palo; **to keep a stiff upper lip** (*Brit fig*) restare impassibile **2** (*fig: climb, examination, test*) arduo(-a), difficile; (*: competition, breeze, drink*) forte; (*: resistance*) tenace; (*punishment*) severo(-a); (*price, fine*) salato(-a); (*manner, smile, reception*) freddo(-a); **that's a bit stiff!** (*fam*) è un po' troppo!; **it was a stiff price to pay** (*fig*) l'hanno pagata cara; **bored stiff** annoiato(-a) a morte; **frozen stiff** congelato(-a); **scared stiff** morto(-a) di paura
stiff·en ['stɪfn] VT (*legs etc*) irrigidire; (*with starch*) inamidare; (*fig: resistance etc*) rafforzare
■ VI (*person, manner*) irrigidirsi; (*determination*) rafforzarsi; (*morale*) risollevarsi
stiff·ly ['stɪflɪ] ADV (*walk, move*) rigidamente; (*smile, bow*) freddamente
stiff-necked ['stɪfˈnɛkt] ADJ (*pej*) ostinato(-a), cocciuto(-a)
stiff·ness ['stɪfnɪs] N (*gen*) rigidità; (*of punishment*) durezza; (*of climb*) difficoltà; (*of back etc*) indolenzimento; (*of manner*) freddezza; (*of resolution*) fermezza
sti·fle ['staɪfl] VT (*yawn, sob, anger*) soffocare; (*desire, smile*) reprimere; (*revolt, opposition*) stroncare
■ VI soffocare
sti·fled ['staɪfld] ADJ soffocato(-a)
sti·fling ['staɪflɪŋ] ADJ (*heat*) soffocante; **it's stifling in here** qui non si respira
stig·ma ['stɪgmə] N stigma *m*; **the stigma attached to illegitimacy** il marchio dell'essere figli illegittimi
stig·ma·ta [stɪg'mɑːtə] NPL (*Rel*) stigmate *fpl*
stig·ma·tize ['stɪgməˌtaɪz] VT stigmatizzare
stile [staɪl] N scaletta (*per scavalcare una siepe*)
sti·let·to [stɪ'lɛtəʊ] N (*knife*) stiletto; (*shoe*) scarpa con tacco a spillo
stiletto heel N tacco a spillo
◎ **still**[1] [stɪl] ADV **1** (*up to now*) ancora; **she's still in bed** è ancora a letto; **it's past midnight and he still hasn't arrived** è mezzanotte passata e non è ancora arrivato; **I still haven't finished!** non ho ancora finito!; **she still doesn't believe me** ancora non mi crede **2** (*with comp: even*) ancora; **still better** *or* **better still** meglio ancora **3** (*nevertheless*) tuttavia, nonostante ciò; **still, it was worth it** però, ne valeva la pena; **she's still your sister** è pur sempre tua sorella; **she knows I don't like it, but she still does it** sa che non mi piace, ma ciò nonostante lo fa lo stesso; **still, it's the thought that counts** in fondo è il pensiero che conta
still[2] [stɪl] ADJ (*comp* **-er**, *superl* **-est**) (*motionless*) fermo(-a), immobile; (*quiet*) tranquillo(-a), silenzioso(-a); (*orange juice*) non gassato(-a); **still mineral water** acqua minerale naturale; **still waters run deep** (*Proverb*) le acque chete rovinano i ponti
■ N **1 in the still of the night** nel silenzio della notte **2** (*Cine*) fotogramma *m*
■ ADV: **to stand still, sit still** stare fermo(-a); **to hold still** tenersi fermo(-a); **keep still!** stai fermo!
still[3] [stɪl] N (*for alcohol*) alambicco; (*: place*) distilleria
still·birth ['stɪlˌbɜːθ] N bambino(-a) nato(-a) morto(-a)
still·born ['stɪlˌbɔːn] ADJ nato(-a) morto(-a)
still life N (*Art*) natura morta
still·ness ['stɪlnɪs] N immobilità; (*quietness*) silenzio, tranquillità
stilt [stɪlt] N trampolo; (*pile*) palo; **to walk on stilts** camminare sui trampoli
stilt·ed ['stɪltɪd] ADJ (*style*) artificioso(-a); (*way of speaking*) formale; (*translation*) poco naturale
stimu·lant ['stɪmjʊlənt] N stimolante *m*
◎ **stimu·late** ['stɪmjʊˌleɪt] VT stimolare; **to stimulate sb to do sth** stimolare qn a fare qc
stimu·lat·ing ['stɪmjʊˌleɪtɪŋ] ADJ stimolante
stimu·la·tion [ˌstɪmjʊ'leɪʃən] N stimolazione *f*
stimu·lus ['stɪmjʊləs] N (*pl* **stimuli** ['stɪmjʊlaɪ]) stimolo; **it gave trade a new stimulus** ha dato un

Ss

nuovo impulso al commercio; **under the stimulus of** stimolato(-a) da

sting [stɪŋ] (*vb: pt, pp* **stung**) N (*Zool*) pungiglione *m*; (*Bot*) pelo urticante; (*pain, mark*) puntura; (*of iodine, antiseptic*) bruciore *m*; **a bee sting** una puntura d'ape; **to take the sting out of sth** (*fig*) rendere qc meno pungente; **but there was a sting in the tail** (*fig*) ma c'era una spiacevole sorpresa
■ VT **1** (*subj: insect, nettle*) pungere; (*: jellyfish*) pizzicare; (*: iodine*) bruciare; (*: cold wind*) tagliare; (*fig: remark, criticism*) pungere sul vivo; **he was stung into action** fu spronato all'azione; **she was stung by remorse** fu presa dal rimorso; **I got stung by a wasp** mi ha punto una vespa **2** (*fam*): **they stung me for £40** mi hanno scucito 40 sterline
■ VI (*iodine etc*) bruciare; (*remark, criticism*) ferire; **my eyes are stinging** mi bruciano gli occhi

stin·gi·ly ['stɪndʒɪlɪ] ADV (*pej: spend*) con parsimonia; (*: behave*) da avaro; **they rewarded him rather stingily** gli hanno dato una ben magra ricompensa

stin·gi·ness ['stɪndʒɪnɪs] N (*pej: of person*) avarizia, tirchieria; (*: of gift, contribution*) esiguità

sting·ray ['stɪŋreɪ] N (*fish*) pastinaca

stin·gy ['stɪndʒɪ] ADJ (*comp* **-ier**, *superl* **-iest**) (*pej: person*) avaro(-a), tirchio(-a), spilorcio(-a), taccagno(-a); (*: gift etc*) misero(-a); **to be stingy with** (*one's praise, money*) essere avaro(-a) di; (*food*) razionare

stink [stɪŋk] (*vb: pt* **stank**, *pp* **stunk**) N puzza, fetore *m*; **to raise** *or* **kick up a stink** (*fig fam*) scatenare un putiferio, piantare un casino
■ VI: **to stink (of)** puzzare (di); **the room stank of cigarettes** la stanza puzzava di fumo; **it stinks in here** che puzza c'è qui; **it stinks to high heaven** puzza tremendamente; **the whole thing stinks** (*fig fam*) tutta la faccenda puzza
■ VT (*also:* **stink out**: *room*) appestare

stink bomb N fialetta puzzolente

stink·er ['stɪŋkəʳ] N (*fam: person*) carogna, fetente *m/f*; **this problem is a stinker** questo problema è una bella rogna; **he wrote her a real stinker** gliene ha scritte di tutti i colori

stink·horn ['stɪŋk,hɔːn] N (*fungus*) satirione *m*

stink·ing ['stɪŋkɪŋ] ADJ: **a stinking cold** un raffreddore tremendo; **what stinking weather!** che tempo da cani!
■ ADV: **stinking rich** ricco(-a) sfondato(-a)

stint [stɪnt] N: **to do one's stint (at sth)** fare la propria parte (di qc); **I do a stint in the pool every day** faccio una nuotata in piscina ogni giorno; **to do a stint at the wheel** (*Aut*) fare il proprio turno al volante
■ VT: **he did not stint his praises** non è stato avaro di complimenti; **don't stint yourself!** (*iro*) non farti mancare niente!

sti·pend ['staɪpɛnd] N congrua

sti·pen·di·ary [staɪ'pɛndɪərɪ] ADJ: **stipendiary magistrate** magistrato stipendiato

stip·pled ['stɪpəld] ADJ punteggiato(-a)

stipu·late ['stɪpjʊ,leɪt] VT: **to stipulate (that)** stabilire (che)

> DID YOU KNOW ...?
> **stipulate** is not translated by the Italian word *stipulare*

stipu·la·tion [,stɪpjʊ'leɪʃən] N stipulazione *f*; **on the stipulation that** a condizione che + *sub*

◎ **stir** [stɜːʳ] N **1 to give sth a stir** mescolare qc **2** (*fig*) agitazione *f*, scalpore *m*; **to cause a stir** fare scalpore
■ VT **1** (*liquid etc*) mescolare; (*fire*) attizzare; **stir the mixture well** mescolare bene l'impasto **2** (*move*) muovere, agitare; **she didn't stir a finger** non ha mosso un dito; **the breeze stirred the leaves** la brezza muoveva le foglie **3** (*fig: emotions, interest*) risvegliare; (*: person*) commuovere; (*: imagination, curiosity*) eccitare, stimolare; **to stir sb to do sth** incitare qn a fare qc; **come on, stir yourself!** forza, muoviti!
■ VI (*move*) muoversi; **he never stirred from the spot** non si è mosso
▸ **stir in** VT + PREP aggiungere mescolando
▸ **stir up** VT + ADV (*memories*) risvegliare; (*hatred, revolt*) fomentare; (*trouble*) provocare; **he's always trying to stir things up** cerca sempre di creare problemi

stir-fry ['stɜː,fraɪ] VT saltare in padella
■ N pietanza al salto

stir·rer ['stɜːrəʳ] N (*Brit fam*) piantagrane *m/f*

stir·ring ['stɜːrɪŋ] ADJ (*exciting*) entusiasmante; (*moving*) commovente

stir·rup ['stɪrəp] N staffa

stirrup leather N staffile *m*

stitch [stɪtʃ] N (*Sewing*) punto; (*Med*) punto (di sutura); (*Knitting*) maglia, punto; (*pain in side*) fitta (al fianco); **to put a few stitches in sth** mettere due punti a qc; **a stitch in time saves nine** (*Proverb*) un punto in tempo ne salva cento; **to put stitches in a wound** cucire una ferita; **I had five stitches** mi hanno messo cinque punti; **she hadn't a stitch on** era completamente nuda; **we were in stitches** (*fam*) ridevamo a crepapelle
■ VT (*Sewing*) cucire; (*Med*) suturare, cucire; **to stitch up a hem/wound** cucire un orlo/una ferita
▸ **stitch down** VT + ADV cucire
▸ **stitch on** VT + ADV (*button etc*) attaccare; (*button that's come off*) riattaccare

stitch·ing ['stɪtʃɪŋ] N cucitura

stoat [stəʊt] N ermellino

◎ **stock¹** [stɒk] N **1** (*supply, store*) provvista, scorta; (*in bank: of money*) riserva; (*Comm*) stock *m inv*; **out of stock** esaurito(-a); **I'm sorry, they're both out of stock** mi dispiace, sono esauriti tutt'e due; **in stock** disponibile; **is it in stock?** è disponibile?; **to have sth in stock** avere qc in magazzino, avere disponibilità di qc; **yes, we've got your size in stock** sì , abbiamo la sua taglia; **to take stock** (*Comm*) fare l'inventario; **to take stock (of the situation)** fare il punto della situazione; **to lay in a stock of** fare una scorta di; **a small stock of medicines** una piccola scorta di medicine **2** (*Agr: also:* **livestock**) bestiame *m* **3** (*Culin*) brodo; **chicken stock** brodo di pollo **4** (*Rail: also:* **rolling stock**) materiale *m* rotabile **5** (*Fin: company's capital*) capitale *m* azionario; (*: investor's shares*) titoli *mpl*, azioni *fpl*; **stocks and shares** valori *mpl* di borsa; **government stock** titoli di Stato **6** (*descent, origin*) stirpe *f* **7 to be on the stocks** (*ship*) essere in cantiere; (*fig: piece of work*) essere in lavorazione; **the stocks** NPL (*History: for punishment*) la gogna
■ VT (*Comm: goods*) tenere, avere, vendere; (*supply: shop, library, freezer, cupboard*) rifornire; (*: lake, river*) ripopolare; (*: farm*) fornire di bestiame; (*: shelves*) riempire; **a well-stocked shop/library** un negozio/una biblioteca ben fornito(-a); **do you stock camping stoves?** vendete fornellini da campeggio?
■ ADJ (*Comm: size*) standard *inv*; (*fig: response, arguments, excuse*) solito(-a), consueto(-a); (*: greeting*) usuale
▸ **stock up** VI + ADV: **to stock up (on)** rifornirsi (di), fare provvista (di); **I must stock up on candles** devo fare provvista di candele

stock² [stɒk] N (*Bot*) violacciocca
stock·ade [stɒˈkeɪd] N palizzata
stock·breeder [ˈstɒk,bri:dəʳ] N allevatore(-trice) di bestiame
stock·breeding [ˈstɒk,bri:dɪŋ] N allevamento di bestiame
stock·broker [ˈstɒk,brəʊkəʳ] N agente *m* di cambio
stock car N (*Sport*) stock-car *m inv*
stock control N gestione *f* magazzino
stock cube N (*Brit Culin*) dado (da brodo)
◎**stock exchange** N (*Fin*) borsa valori
stock·holder [ˈstɒk,həʊldəʳ] N (*Fin*) azionista *m/f*
Stock·holm [ˈstɒkhəʊm] N Stoccolma
stock·ing [ˈstɒkɪŋ] N calza
■ ADJ: **in one's stocking(ed) feet** senza scarpe
stocking mask N calza di nylon (*di bandito mascherato*)
stocking stitch N (*Knitting*) maglia rasata
stock-in-trade [,stɒkɪnˈtreɪd] N (*goods*) merce *f* a magazzino; (*tools etc*) strumenti *mpl* di lavoro; (*fig*) ferri *mpl* del mestiere; **it's his stock-in-trade** è la sua specialità
stock·ist [ˈstɒkɪst] N (*Brit*) fornitore *m*
stock level N livello di magazzino
◎**stock market** N (*Brit Fin*) mercato azionario
stock option N (*Am Fin*) diritto di opzione su azioni (*da parte dei dipendenti di un'azienda*)
stock phrase N frase *f* fatta, cliché *m inv*
stock·pile [ˈstɒk,paɪl] N riserva, scorta
■ VT accumulare riserve di
stock·pot [ˈstɒk,pɒt] N (*Culin*) pentola per brodo
stock·room [ˈstɒ,krʊm] N magazzino
stock-still [,stɒkˈstɪl] ADV: **to be** *or* **stand stock-still** stare immobile; (*from shock, horror*) restare impietrito(-a)
stock·taking [ˈstɒk,teɪkɪŋ] N (*Brit Comm*) inventario
stock turnover N ricambio del magazzino
stocky [ˈstɒkɪ] ADJ (*comp* **-ier**, *superl* **-iest**) tarchiato(-a), tozzo(-a)
stodge [stɒdʒ] N (*fam*) cibo pesante
stodgy [ˈstɒdʒɪ] ADJ (*comp* **-ier**, *superl* **-iest**) (*food, book*) pesante, indigesto(-a); (*: person*) pesante
sto·ic [ˈstəʊɪk] N stoico(-a)
stoi·cal [ˈstəʊɪkəl] ADJ stoico(-a)
stoi·cal·ly [ˈstəʊɪkəlɪ] ADV stoicamente
stoi·chi·om·etry [,stɔɪkɪˈɒmɪtrɪ] N stechiometria
stoi·cism [ˈstəʊɪsɪzəm] N stoicismo
stoke [stəʊk] VT (*also:* **stoke up**: *fire*) attizzare; (*: furnace*) alimentare
stok·er [ˈstəʊkəʳ] N fuochista *m*
stole¹ [stəʊl] N stola
stole² [stəʊl] PT *of* **steal**
stol·en [ˈstəʊlən] PP *of* **steal**
stol·id [ˈstɒlɪd] ADJ flemmatico(-a)
sto·lid·ity [stɒˈlɪdɪtɪ] N flemma
stol·id·ly [ˈstɒlɪdlɪ] ADV flemmaticamente
sto·lon [ˈstəʊlən] N (*Bot, Zool*) stolone *m*
sto·ma [ˈstəʊmə] N stoma *m*
◎**stom·ach** [ˈstʌmək] N (*gen*) stomaco; (*abdomen*) ventre *m*; **it turns my stomach** mi rivolta lo stomaco; **they have no stomach for a fight** (*fig*) non hanno il fegato di battersi; **lie down on your stomach** stenditi sulla pancia
■ VT (*fig fam*) sopportare, digerire
stomach ache N mal *m* di stomaco; **to have stomach ache** avere mal di stomaco
stomach pump N lavanda gastrica
stomach trouble N disturbi *mpl* gastrici
stomach ulcer N ulcera gastrica
stomp [stɒmp] VI: **to stomp in/out** *etc* entrare/uscire *etc* con passo pesante
◎**stone** [stəʊn] N **1** (*material*) pietra; (*single pebble, rock*) sasso, ciottolo; (*also:* **gemstone**) pietra preziosa, gemma; (*of fruit*) nocciolo; (*Med*) calcolo; (*also:* **gravestone**) lastra tombale, lapide *f*; **to turn to stone** (*vt*) pietrificare; (*vi*) rimanere pietrificato(-a); **within a stone's throw of the station** a due passi dalla stazione, ad un tiro di schioppo dalla stazione; **to leave no stone unturned** non lasciare nulla d'intentato; **a peach stone** un nocciolo di pesca
2 (*Brit: weight: pl gen inv*) ≈ 6,348 kg
■ ADJ (*wall*) di pietra; **a stone wall** un muro di pietra
■ VT **1** (*person*) scagliare pietre contro; **to stone sb to death** lapidare qn **2** (*fruit*) snocciolare
Stone Age N: **the Stone Age** l'età della pietra
stone·chat [ˈstəʊn,tʃæt] N saltimpalo
stone-cold [ˈstəʊnˈkəʊld] ADJ ghiacciato(-a)
■ ADV: **stone-cold sober** perfettamente sobrio(-a)
stone·cutter [ˈstəʊn,kʌtəʳ] N (*person*) scalpellino; (*machine*) mola
stoned [stəʊnd] ADJ PRED (*fam: drunk, on drugs*) fatto(-a)
stone-dead [,stəʊnˈdɛd] ADJ morto(-a) stecchito(-a)
stone-deaf [,stəʊnˈdɛf] ADJ sordo(-a) come una campana
stone·ground [ˈstəʊngraʊnd] ADJ (*flour, wheat*) macinato(-a) con la mola
stone·mason [ˈstəʊn,meɪsn] N scalpellino
stone·wall [,stəʊnˈwɔ:l] VI (*fig*) fare ostruzionismo
■ VT ostacolare
stone·ware [ˈstəʊn,wɛəʳ] N articoli *mpl* di grès
stone·work [ˈstəʊn,wɜ:k] N lavoro in muratura
stoni·ly [ˈstəʊnɪlɪ] ADV (*fig: glance, reply*) freddamente
stony [ˈstəʊnɪ] ADJ (*comp* **-ier**, *superl* **-iest**) (*ground*) sassoso(-a); (*beach*) pieno(-a) di ciottoli; (*fig: glance, silence*) freddo(-a); **a stony heart** un cuore di pietra
stony-broke [,stəʊnɪˈbrəʊk] ADJ (*fam*): **to be stony-broke** essere al verde, essere in bolletta
stony-faced [,stəʊnɪˈfeɪst] ADJ dal volto impassibile
stood [stʊd] PT, PP *of* **stand**
stooge [stu:dʒ] N (*fam minion*) tirapiedi *m/f*; (*Theatre*) spalla
stool [stu:l] N (*seat*) sgabello; **to fall between two stools** (*fig*) fare come l'asino di Buridano
stool pigeon N (*fam*) informatore(-trice)
stoop [stu:p] N: **to have a stoop** avere la schiena curva; **to walk with a stoop** camminare curvo(-a)
■ VI **1** (*bend: also:* **stoop down**) chinarsi, curvarsi, abbassarsi; (*have a stoop*) essere curvo(-a); **he stooped down to pick up the letter** si è chinato per raccogliere la lettera **2** (*fig*): **to stoop to sth/doing sth** abbassarsi a qc/a fare qc; **I wouldn't stoop so low!** non mi abbasserei a tanto!
stoop·ing [ˈstu:pɪŋ] ADJ curvo(-a)
◎**stop** [stɒp] N
1 (*halt*) arresto; (*break, pause*) pausa; (*: overnight*) sosta; **a 20 minute stop for coffee** una pausa di 20 minuti per il caffè; **without a stop** senza fermarsi; **to come to a stop** (*traffic, production*) arrestarsi; (*work*) fermarsi; **to bring to a stop** (*traffic, production*) paralizzare; (*work*) fermare; **to make a stop** (*bus*) fare una fermata; (*train*) fermarsi; (*plane, ship*) fare scalo; **to put a stop to sth** mettere fine a qc
2 (*stopping place: for bus etc*) fermata; **a bus stop** una fermata d'autobus
3 (*Typ: also:* **full stop**) punto; (*in telegrams*) stop *m inv*

Ss

4 (*Mus: on organ*) registro; (*: on trombone etc*) chiave *f*; **to pull out all the stops** (*fig*) mettercela tutta
■VT
1 (*arrest movement of: runaway, engine, car*) fermare, bloccare; (*: blow, punch*) parare
2 (*put an end to: gen*) mettere fine a; (*: noise*) far cessare; (*: pain*) far passare; (*: production: permanently*) arrestare; (*: temporarily*) interrompere, sospendere; **she drew the curtains to stop the light coming in** tirò le tende per impedire che entrasse la luce; **rain stopped play** la partita è stata sospesa a causa del maltempo
3 (*prevent*) impedire; **to stop sb (from) doing sth** impedire a qn di fare qc; **to stop sth (from) happening** impedire che qc succeda; **can't you stop him?** non puoi fermarlo?; **to stop o.s. (from doing sth)** trattenersi (dal fare qc); **I managed to stop myself in time** sono riuscito a fermarmi in tempo
4 (*cease*) smettere; **to stop doing sth** smettere di fare qc; **I'm trying to stop smoking** sto cercando di smettere di fumare; **stop it!** smettila!; **I just can't stop it** (*help it*) proprio non riesco a smetterla
5 (*suspend: payments, wages*) sospendere; (*: subscription*) cancellare; (*: leave*) revocare; (*: cheque*) bloccare; **to stop £30 pound from sb's wages** trattenere trenta sterline dallo stipendio di qn
6 (*also:* **stop up**: *block: hole*) bloccare, otturare: *leak, flow of blood, arrestare, fermare;* **to stop one's ears** tapparsi *or* turarsi le orecchie
■VI
1 (*stop moving, pause: gen*) fermarsi; (*cease: gen*) cessare; (*machine, production*) arrestarsi; (*play, concert, speaker*) finire; **stop!** fermo!; **stop, thief!** al ladro!; **without stopping** senza fermarsi; **to stop to do sth** fermarsi per fare qc; **he stopped to look at the view** si è fermato per guardare il panorama; **to stop in one's tracks** *or* **stop dead** fermarsi di colpo; **to stop at nothing (to do sth)** non fermarsi davanti a niente (pur di fare qc); **to know where to stop** (*fig*) avere il senso della misura; **the bus doesn't stop there** l'autobus non si ferma lì
2 (*fam: stay*): **to stop (at/with)** fermarsi (a/da); **I'm not stopping** non mi fermo
▸ **stop away** VI + ADV (*fam*) stare via
▸ **stop by** VI + ADV (*fam*) passare, fare un salto
▸ **stop in** VI + ADV rimanere a casa
▸ **stop off** VI + ADV fermarsi, sostare brevemente
▸ **stop over** VI + ADV: **to stop over (in)** fermarsi (a), fare una sosta (a); (*Aer*) fare scalo (a)
▸ **stop up** VT + ADV = **stop** VT **1**
■VI + ADV (*fam*) stare alzato(-a)

stop·cock ['stɒp,kɒk] N rubinetto di arresto

stop·gap ['stɒpgæp] N (*person*) supplente, sostituto(-a) temporaneo(-a); (*measure*) palliativo; **a temporary stopgap** un ripiego temporaneo
■ADJ (*measures, solution*) tampone *inv*, sostitutivo(-a); **a stopgap solution** una soluzione tampone

stop·light ['stɒp,laɪt] N (*traffic light*) (semaforo) rosso

stop·over ['stɒp,əʊvəʳ] N sosta; (*Aer*) scalo intermedio; **during a stopover in London** durante una breve sosta a Londra

stop·page ['stɒpɪdʒ] N (*in pipe etc*) ostruzione *f*; (*of work*) interruzione *f*; (*strike*) interruzione *f* del lavoro; (*from wages*) detrazione *f*, trattenuta

stoppage time N (*Brit: Sport*) interruzione *f* del gioco

stop·per ['stɒpəʳ] N tappo

stop·ping ['stɒpɪŋ] N (*gen*) arresto; (*fam: in tooth*) otturazione *f*
■ADJ: **stopping place** (*lay-by*) piazzola di sosta; **we found a good stopping place** abbiamo trovato un bel posto per fare una sosta; **stopping train** ≈ (treno) locale *m*

stop press N ultimissime *fpl*

stop sign N (*Aut*) (segnale *m* di) stop *m inv*

stop·watch ['stɒp,wɒtʃ] N cronometro

stor·age ['stɔːrɪdʒ] N (*of goods, fuel*) immagazzinamento; (*of heat, electricity*) accumulazione *f*; (*of documents*) conservazione *f*; (*Comput*) memoria; **to put sth into storage** immagazzinare qc; **the cupboards provide ample storage** gli armadi offrono ampio spazio per tenere la roba; **the storage of information on computers** l'immagazzinamento di informazioni nei computer

storage battery N accumulatore *m*

storage capacity N (*Comput*) capacità *f inv* di memoria

storage charges NPL magazzinaggio *msg*

storage heater N (*Brit*) radiatore *m* elettrico che accumula calore

storage space N: **we haven't got much storage space** non abbiamo molto spazio per riporre la roba

storage tank N (*for rainwater, oil*) cisterna

◎**store** [stɔːʳ] N **1** (*stock*) provvista, scorta, riserva; (*fig: of knowledge etc*) bagaglio; **stores** NPL (*food*) provviste *fpl*, scorte *fpl*, rifornimenti *mpl*; **to lay in a store of sth** fare provvista di qc; **in store** di riserva, come provvista; **we had no idea what lay in store for us** non avevamo idea di cosa ci aspettasse; **who knows what is in store for us** chissà cosa ci riserva il futuro; **to set great/little store by sth** dare molta/poca importanza a qc; **my secret store of biscuits** la mia scorta segreta di biscotti **2** (*also:* **storehouse, storeroom**: *depot*) deposito; **to put one's furniture in(to) store** mettere i mobili in un deposito **3** (*Am: shop*) negozio; (*Brit: also:* **department store**) grande magazzino; **a furniture store** un negozio di mobili
■VT **1** (*also:* **store up**: *food, fuel, goods*) fare provvista di; (*: heat, electricity*) accumulare; (*: documents*) conservare
2 (*also:* **store away**: *food, fuel*) mettere da parte; (*: grain, goods*) immagazzinare; (*: information: in memory*) immagazzinare; (*: in filing system*) schedare
▸ **store up** VT + ADV conservare

store detective N sorvegliante *m/f* (*di negozio*)

store·front [,stɔː'frʌnt] N (*Am*) facciata di negozio

store·house ['stɔː,haʊs] N magazzino, deposito

store·keeper ['stɔː,kiːpəʳ] N (*Am: shopkeeper*) negoziante *m/f*

store·room ['stɔː,rʊm] N deposito; (*for food*) dispensa

stores requisition N (*Admin*) richiesta di materiale a magazzino

sto·rey, (*Am*) **sto·ry** ['stɔːrɪ] N piano; **a 9-stor(e)y building** un edificio a 9 piani

stork [stɔːk] N cicogna

storks·bill ['stɔːks,bɪl] N (*Bot*) becco di gru

◎**storm** [stɔːm] N **1** (*Met*) tempesta; (*: at sea*) burrasca, tempesta; (*: thunderstorm*) temporale *m*; (*fig: of applause*) scroscio; (*: of abuse*) torrente *m*; (*: of protests*) uragano; (*: of weeping, tears*) mare *m*; (*: uproar*) scompiglio; **it caused a storm** (*fig*) ha creato scompiglio; **a storm in a teacup** (*fig*) una tempesta in un bicchier d'acqua
2 (*Mil*): **to take a town by storm** prendere d'assalto una città; **the play took Paris by storm** (*fig*) la commedia ha trionfato a Parigi
■VT (*Mil*) prendere d'assalto; **to storm a building** irrompere in un edificio
■VI (*wind, rain*) infuriare; (*person*): **to storm in/out**

entrare/uscire come una furia; **she stormed up the stairs** si è precipitata di sopra furiosa; **"get out!" she stormed** "fuori!" urlò
■ ADJ (*signal, warning*) di burrasca

storm·bound ['stɔ:mbaʊnd] ADJ (*ship, plane, passengers*) bloccato(-a) dal maltempo

storm cloud N nube *f* temporalesca; **there are storm clouds on the horizon** (*fig*) c'è aria di burrasca

storm door N controporta

stormi·ly ['stɔ:mɪlɪ] ADV burrascosamente

storm jib N (*Naut: sail*) tormentina

storm pet·rel ['stɔ:m,pɛtrəl] N procellaria

storm troops NPL (*Mil: gen*) truppe *fpl* d'assalto; (*: Nazi*) reparti *mpl* d'assalto

storm window N controfinestra

stormy ['stɔ:mɪ] ADJ (*comp* **-ier**, *superl* **-iest**) (*also fig*) burrascoso(-a), tempestoso(-a)

◎ **sto·ry¹** ['stɔ:rɪ] N **1** (*account, lie*) storia; (*of book, film*) trama; (*tale, Literature*) racconto; **short story** (*Literature*) novella; **that's not the whole story** non è tutto; **it's the same old story** è sempre la solita storia; **to cut a long story short** per farla breve; **but that's another story** ma questa è un'altra storia; **that's the story of my life!** (*fam*) per me va sempre a finire così !; **to tell stories** (*fam: lies*) raccontare storie **2** (*Press*) articolo; **he covered the story of the earthquake** ha fatto il servizio sul terremoto

sto·ry² ['stɔ:rɪ] N (*Am*) = **storey**

story·board ['stɔ:rɪbɔ:d] N story board *m inv*; *serie di immagini che illustrano la trama di un film o uno spot pubblicitario*

story·book ['stɔ:rɪ,bʊk] N libro di racconti

story line N trama

story·teller ['stɔ:rɪ,tɛləʳ] N **1** narratore(-trice); **he's a good storyteller** è uno che sa raccontare bene le storie **2** (*fam: liar*) bugiardo(-a)

stout [staʊt] ADJ (*comp* **-er**, *superl* **-est**) (*sturdy: stick, shoes etc*) robusto(-a), solido(-a); (*fat: person*) corpulento(-a), robusto(-a); (*determined: supporter, resistance*) tenace; (*: refusal*) deciso(-a); (*brave*) coraggioso(-a); **with stout hearts** coraggiosamente, valorosamente; **a short, stout man** un uomo basso e robusto; **a stout fellow** (*old fig*) un tipo in gamba
■ N (*beer*) birra scura

stout-hearted [,staʊt'hɑ:tɪd] ADJ (*liter*) coraggioso(-a), valoroso(-a)

stout·ly ['staʊtlɪ] ADV (*defend, resist, fight*) valorosamente; (*deny*) categoricamente; (*believe, maintain*) fermamente

stout·ness ['staʊtnɪs] N (*of person*) corpulenza; (*of stick, shoes*) robustezza

stove¹ [stəʊv] N **1** (*for heating*) stufa **2** (*for cooking*) cucina; (*: small*) fornelletto; **gas/electric stove** cucina a gas/elettrica; **camping stove** fornello da campeggio

stove² [stəʊv]: **stove in** PT, PP *of* **stave in**

stow [stəʊ] VT (*Naut: cargo*) stivare
► **stow away** VT + ADV mettere via
■ VI + ADV imbarcarsi clandestinamente

stow·away ['stəʊə,weɪ] N passeggero(-a) clandestino(-a)

strad·dle ['strædl] VT (*subj: person: stream*) stare a gambe divaricate su; (*: chair*) stare a cavalcioni di; (*: horse*) stare in groppa a; (*subj: bridge: stream*) essere sospeso(-a) sopra; (*subj: town: border*) essere a cavallo di

Stradi·var·ius [,strædɪ'vɛərɪəs] N stradivario

strafe [strɑ:f] VT mitragliare

strag·gle ['strægl] VI (*lag behind*) rimanere indietro; (*spread untidily*) estendersi disordinatamente; **to straggle in/out** entrare/uscire uno ad uno; **they straggled back to the classroom** rientrarono in classe alla spicciolata

strag·gler ['stræglәʳ] N chi rimane indietro

strag·gling ['stræglɪŋ], **strag·gly** ['stræglɪ] ADJ (*village*) sparso(-a); (*hair*) scarmigliato(-a); (*line*) irregolare; (*plant*) che cresce in modo disordinato

◎ **straight** [streɪt] ADJ (*comp* **-er**, *superl* **-est**) **1** (*gen*) diritto(-a), dritto(-a); (*hair*) liscio(-a); (*Geom*) retto(-a); (*posture*) eretto(-a); **a straight road** una strada dritta; **the picture isn't straight** il quadro non è diritto; **to be (all) straight** (*tidy*) essere a posto, essere sistemato(-a); (*clarified*) essere chiaro(-a); **let's get this straight** mettiamo le cose in chiaro; **to put straight** (*picture*) raddrizzare; (*hat, tie*) aggiustare; (*house, room, accounts*) mettere in ordine; **to put things** *or* **matters straight** chiarire le cose; **he soon put me straight** mi ha corretto immediatamente; **I couldn't keep a straight face** *or* **I couldn't keep my face straight** non riuscivo a stare serio **2** (*continuous, direct*) diritto(-a); **ten straight wins** dieci vittorie di fila **3** (*honest, frank: person*) onesto(-a); (*: answer*) franco(-a); (*: denial*) netto(-a); **straight speaking** *or* **straight talking** franchezza; **I'll be straight with you** sarò franco con te **4** (*plain, uncomplicated*) semplice; (*drink*) liscio(-a); (*Theatre: part, play*) serio(-a); (*person: conventional*) normale; (*: heterosexual*) etero *inv*; **I'm sure he's straight** sono sicura che sia eterosessuale
■ ADV **1** (*in a straight line: gen*) dritto; **to go straight up/down** andare dritto su/giù; **it's straight across the road from us** è proprio di fronte a noi; **straight ahead** avanti dritto; **straight on** sempre dritto; **to go straight on** andare dritto; **to go straight** (*fig*) rigare dritto **2** (*directly, without diversion*) direttamente, diritto; **I went straight home** sono andato direttamente a casa; **to come straight to the point** venire al sodo **3** (*immediately*) subito, immediatamente; **straight away** *or* **straight off** subito; **I'll come straight back** torno subito **4** (*frankly*) chiaramente, francamente; **straight out** chiaro e tondo
■ N (*on racecourse*) dirittura d'arrivo; (*Rail*) rettilineo; **to cut sth on the straight** tagliare qc in drittofilo; **to keep to the straight and narrow** (*fig*) seguire la retta via

straight·away [,streɪtə'weɪ] ADV subito

straight·edge ['streɪt,ɛdʒ] N (*Carpentry*) regolo

straight·en ['streɪtn] VT (*sth bent: also:* **straighten out**) raddrizzare; (*hair*) stirare; (*tablecloth, tie*) aggiustare; (*tidy: also:* **straighten up**) mettere in ordine; (*fig: problem: also:* **straighten out**) spianare, risolvere; **to straighten things out** mettere le cose a posto; **to straighten one's shoulders** raddrizzarsi; **straighten your shoulders!** stai su dritto!
■ VI (*person: also:* **straighten (o.s.) up**) raddrizzarsi

straight-faced [,streɪt'feɪst] ADJ serio(-a)
■ ADV con espressione seria

straight·forward [,streɪt'fɔ:wəd] ADJ (*honest, frank*) franco(-a), diretto(-a); (*simple*) semplice; **the question seemed straightforward enough** la questione sembrava abbastanza semplice; **she's a very straightforward girl** è una ragazza molto onesta

straight·forward·ly [,streɪt'fɔ:wədlɪ] ADV (*behave*) onestamente; (*answer*) francamente; **to proceed straightforwardly** procedere senza intoppi

straight·forward·ness [,streɪt'fɔ:wədnɪs] N (*of reply*)

Ss

franchezza, schiettezza; (*of behaviour*) onestà

straight·laced [ˌstreɪtˈleɪst] = **strait-laced**

◎**strain**[1] [streɪn] N **1** (*Tech: on rope*) tensione *f*; (*: on beam*) sollecitazione *f*; (*on person: physical*) sforzo; (*: mental*) tensione *f*; (*: tiredness*) fatica; **to take the strain off sth** ridurre la tensione di (*or* la sollecitazione su) qc; **the bridge is showing signs of strain** il ponte mostra segni di deformazione; **the rope broke under the strain** la corda si è spezzata a causa della tensione; **she's under a lot of strain** è molto tesa, è sotto pressione; **it was a strain** è stata dura; **I can't stand the strain** non resisto, non ce la faccio più; **the strains of modern life** il logorio della vita moderna; **to put a great strain on** (*marriage, friendship*) mettere a dura prova; (*person, savings, budget*) pesare molto su **2** (*Med: sprain*) strappo **3 to the strains of** (*Mus*) sulle note di; **he continued in that strain** (*fig*) e continuò su questo tono

■VT **1** (*stretch*) tendere, tirare **2** (*put strain on*) sottoporre a sforzo; (*: fig: relationship, marriage*) mettere a dura prova; (*: resources etc*) gravare su; (*: meaning*) forzare; (*Med: back, muscle, ligament*) farsi uno stiramento a; (*: eyes, heart*) affaticare; **don't strain yourself!** (*also iro*) non affaticarti troppo!; **to strain one's back** farsi male alla schiena; **to strain a muscle** farsi uno strappo muscolare; **to strain the truth** deformare la verità; **to strain every nerve to do sth** fare ogni sforzo per fare qc; **to strain one's voice** sforzare la voce; **to strain one's ears** aguzzare le orecchie; **to strain (one's eyes) to see sth** aguzzare la vista per vedere qc **3** (*soup*) passare; (*tea*) filtrare; (*vegetables, pasta*) scolare

■VI: **to strain at sth** (*push/pull*) spingere/tirare qc con tutte le forze; **to strain against** (*ropes, bars*) far forza contro

▸ **strain off** VT + ADV (*liquid*) togliere

strain[2] [streɪn] N (*breed*) razza; (*lineage*) stirpe *f*; (*of virus*) tipo; (*streak, trace*) tendenza

strained [streɪnd] ADJ (*muscle*) stirato(-a); (*arm, ankle*) slogato(-a); (*heart, eyes*) affaticato(-a); (*laugh, smile etc*) forzato(-a); (*relations*) teso(-a); (*liquid*) filtrato(-a); (*solid food*) passato(-a); **a strained muscle** uno strappo muscolare

strain·er [ˈstreɪnəʳ] N (*Culin*) passino, colino

strait [streɪt] N (*Geog*) stretto; **the Straits of Dover** lo stretto di Dover; **to be in dire straits** (*fig*) essere nei guai

strait·ened [ˈstreɪtnd] ADJ: **to be in straitened circumstances** (*frm*) vivere nelle ristrettezze

strait·jacket [ˈstreɪtˌdʒækɪt] N camicia di forza

strait-laced [ˌstreɪtˈleɪst] ADJ puritano(-a)

strand [strænd] N (*of thread, pearls*) filo; (*of hair*) ciocca

strand·ed [ˈstrændɪd] ADJ: **to be (left) stranded** (*ship, fish*) essere arenato(-a); (*person: without transport*) essere lasciato(-a) a piedi; rimanere bloccato(-a); (*: without money etc*) trovarsi nei guai; **to leave sb stranded** lasciare qn nei guai

◎**strange** [streɪndʒ] ADJ (*comp* **-r**, *superl* **-st**) **1** (*odd*) strano(-a), bizzarro(-a); **it is strange that ...** è strano che...; **strange as it may seem ...** per quanto possa sembrare strano...; **I felt rather strange** mi sono sentito strano **2** (*unknown, unfamiliar*) sconosciuto(-a); **you'll feel rather strange at first** all'inizio ti sentirai un po' spaesato; **to wake up in a strange bed** svegliarsi in un letto che non è il proprio; **the work is strange to him** non è pratico di questo lavoro

strange·ly [ˈstreɪndʒlɪ] ADV stranamente; **strangely (enough), I've never met him** stranamente, non l'ho mai incontrato

stran·ger [ˈstreɪndʒəʳ] N (*unknown person*) sconosciuto(-a); (*from another place*) forestiero(-a), estraneo(-a); **don't speak to strangers** non parlare con gli sconosciuti; **I'm a stranger here** non sono del posto; **he's a complete stranger to me** non lo conosco affatto, per me è un perfetto sconosciuto; **I'm no stranger to Rome** conosco Roma

> **DID YOU KNOW ...?**
> **stranger** is not translated by the Italian word *straniero*

stran·gle [ˈstræŋgl] VT strangolare, strozzare

strangle·hold [ˈstræŋglˌhəʊld] N (*Wrestling*) presa di gola; **to have a stranglehold on sb/sth** (*fig*) tenere qn/qc in pugno

stran·gler [ˈstræŋgləʳ] N strangolatore(-trice)

stran·gling [ˈstræŋglɪŋ] N strangolamento

stran·gu·la·tion [ˌstræŋgjʊˈleɪʃən] N strangolamento

strap [stræp] N (*of watch, shoes*) cinturino; (*for suitcase*) cinghia; (*in bus etc*) maniglia a pendaglio; (*also:* **shoulder strap**: *of bra*) bretella, spallina; (*: of bag*) tracolla; **the strap of her bag** la tracolla della borsa; **I need a new strap for my watch** ho bisogno di un cinturino nuovo per l'orologio; **a top with thin straps** un top con le spalline strette; **to give sb the strap** punire qn con la cinghia

■VT **1** (*fasten*): **to strap down, strap in, strap on, strap up** legare; **to strap sb in** (*in car, plane*) allacciare la cintura di sicurezza a qn **2** (*Med: also:* **strap up**) fasciare

strap·hanger [ˈstræpˌhæŋəʳ] N chi viaggia in piedi (*su mezzi pubblici reggendosi a un sostegno*)

strap·less [ˈstræplɪs] ADJ (*bra, dress*) senza spalline

strapped [stræpt] ADJ: **strapped for cash** a corto di soldi; **financially strapped** messo(-a) male finanziariamente

strap·ping [ˈstræpɪŋ] ADJ (*person*) robusto(-a), ben piantato(-a)

Stras·bourg [ˈstræzbɜːg] N Strasburgo *f*

stra·ta [ˈstrɑːtə] NPL *of* **stratum**

strata·gem [ˈstrætɪdʒəm] N stratagemma *m*

◎**stra·tegic** [strəˈtiːdʒɪk] ADJ (*also fig*) strategico(-a)

stra·tegi·cal·ly [strəˈtiːdʒɪkəlɪ] ADV strategicamente

strat·egist [ˈstrætɪdʒɪst] N stratega *m*

◎**strat·egy** [ˈstrætɪdʒɪ] N (*also fig*) strategia

Stratford (up)on Avon [ˌstræfəd(əp)ɒnˈeɪvən] N Stratford *f* sull'Avon

▷ www.stratford-upon-avon.co.uk/

strati·fi·ca·tion [ˌstrætɪfɪˈkeɪʃən] N stratificazione *f*

strati·fied [ˈstrætɪfaɪd] ADJ stratificato(-a)

strato·sphere [ˈstrætəʊˌsfɪəʳ] N stratosfera

stra·tum [ˈstrɑːtəm] N (*pl* **strata**) (*also fig*) strato

stra·tus [ˈstreɪtəs] N (*pl* **strati** [ˈstreɪtaɪ]) (*Met*) strato

straw [strɔː] N paglia; (*drinking straw*) cannuccia; **he sucked the juice through a straw** ha bevuto il succo di frutta con la cannuccia; **that's the last straw!** questa è la goccia che fa traboccare il vaso!

straw·berry [ˈstrɔːbərɪ] N fragola; **wild strawberry** fragolina di bosco

■ADJ (*jam, tart*) di fragole; (*ice cream*) alla fragola

strawberry mark N voglia di fragola

straw-coloured [ˈstrɔːˌkʌləd] ADJ color paglia *inv*

straw hat N cappello di paglia, paglietta

straw poll N sondaggio d'opinione (*su un campione scelto a caso*)

stray [streɪ] ADJ (*dog, cat*) randagio(-a); (*person, cow,*

sheep) smarrito(-a); **a stray cat** un gatto randagio; **he was killed by a stray bullet** è stato ucciso da un proiettile vagante; **a few stray cars** qualche rara macchina
■ N (*animal*) randagio *m*
■ VI (*animal: get lost*) smarrirsi, perdersi; (*wander: person*) allontanarsi, staccarsi dal gruppo; (*: speaker*) divagare; (*: thoughts*) vagare; **some cows strayed into the garden** delle mucche hanno sconfinato nel giardino; **to stray into enemy territory** ritrovarsi in territorio nemico

streak [stri:k] N (*line*) striscia, riga; (*of mineral*) filone *m*, vena; **he had streaks of grey in his hair** aveva delle ciocche di capelli grigi; **to have streaks in one's hair** avere le mèches; **like a streak of lightning** come un fulmine; **to have a streak of madness** avere una vena di pazzia; **he had a cruel streak (in him)** c'era un che di crudele in lui; **lucky streak** periodo di fortuna; **a winning/losing streak** un periodo fortunato/sfortunato
■ VT rigare, screziare, striare; **streaked with** (*tears*) rigato(-a) di; (*subj: sky*) striato(-a) di; (*: clothes*) macchiato(-a) di
■ VI (*move quickly*): **to streak away/across/past** allontanarsi/attraversare/passare come un fulmine; (*run naked*) fare lo streaking

streak·er ['stri:kəʳ] N streaker *m/f*

streak·ing ['stri:kɪŋ] N streaking *m inv*

streaky ['stri:kɪ] ADJ (*colour, window, sky*) striato(-a); (*rock*) venato(-a), screziato(-a)

streaky bacon N (*Brit*) ≈ pancetta

◎ **stream** [stri:m] N (*brook*) ruscello; (*current*) corrente *f*; (*flow: of liquid, people, words*) fiume *m*; (*: of cars*) colonna; (*: of air*) soffio; (*: of light*) fascio; **against the stream** controcorrente; **a mountain stream** un ruscello di montagna; **a stream of visitors** una marea di visitatori; **an unbroken stream of cars** un fiume ininterrotto di macchine; **divided into three streams** (*Scol*) diviso in tre gruppi di diverso livello; **the B stream** (*Scol*) il gruppo di secondo livello; **to come on stream** (*oilwell, production line*) entrare in attività
■ VT **1** (*water etc*) scendere a fiumi; **his nose streamed blood** grondava sangue dal naso **2** (*Scol*) dividere in gruppi di diverso livello (*di rendimento e abilità*)
■ VI (*liquid*) scorrere; (*cars, people*) riversarsi; **her eyes were streaming** (*because of smoke*) le lacrimavano gli occhi; **her cheeks were streaming with tears** le lacrime le rigavano il volto; **cars kept streaming past me** fiumi di macchine continuavano a passarmi davanti; **to stream in/out** *etc* entrare/uscire *etc* a fiotti

stream·er ['stri:məʳ] N (*of paper, at parties etc*) stella filante

stream feed N (*on photocopier etc*) alimentazione *f* continua

stream·ing ['stri:mɪŋ] N (*Comput*) streaming *m*; *sistema di trasmissione di dati via Internet direttamente sullo schermo di un computer*; (*Scol*) suddivisione degli studenti in livelli (*di rendimento e abilità*)
■ ADJ: **I've got a streaming cold** ho il naso che cola per il raffreddore

stream·line ['stri:m,laɪn] VT dare una linea aerodinamica a; (*fig*) razionalizzare, snellire

stream·lined ['stri:m,laɪnd] ADJ (*see vb*) aerodinamico(-a); razionalizzato(-a), snellito(-a)

◎ **street** [stri:t] N strada, via; **the back streets** le strade secondarie; **a narrow street** una strada stretta; **to be on the streets** (*homeless*) essere senza tetto; (*as prostitute*) battere il marciapiede; **it's right up my street** (*fig: job*) è proprio quello che fa per me, è il mio forte; **to be streets ahead of sb** (*fam*) essere di gran lunga superiore a qn

street·car ['stri:t,kɑ:ʳ] N (*Am*) tram *m inv*

street child N bambino di strada

street cleaner, street sweeper N spazzino(-a), netturbino(-a)

street cred [-kred] N (*fam*) *credibilità presso i giovani*

street door N porta, portone *m*

street lamp N lampione *m*

street lighting N illuminazione *f* stradale

street map, street plan N pianta (della città), stradario

street market N mercato rionale

street musician N suonatore(-trice) ambulante

street people NPL i senzatetto

street-smart ['stri:tsmɑ:t] ADJ (*Am*) scafato(-a)

street style N modo di vestire originale (*non influenzato dai dettami della moda*)

street sweeper N = street cleaner

street theatre N teatro di piazza

street urchin N scugnizzo(-a)

street value N (*of drug*) valore *m* di mercato

street·walker ['stri:t,wɔ:kəʳ] N passeggiatrice *f*

street·wise ['stri:t,waɪz] ADJ (*fam*) scafato(-a); **to be streetwise** sapersela cavare

◎ **strength** [strɛŋθ] N **1** (*gen, fig*) forza; (*of wall, nail, wood etc*) solidità; (*of rope*) resistenza; (*of chemical solution*) concentrazione *f*; (*of wine*) gradazione *f* alcolica; **you'll soon get your strength back** presto ti rimetterai in forze; **his strength failed him** gli sono mancate le forze; **strength of character/mind** forza di carattere/d'animo; **strength of purpose** risolutezza; **on the strength of** sulla base di, in virtù di; **to go from strength to strength** andare di bene in meglio **2** (*Mil etc*) effettivo; **below/at full strength** con gli effettivi ridotti/al completo; **to come in strength** (*fig*) venire in gran numero

◎ **strength·en** ['strɛŋθən] VT (*person, muscles*) irrobustire; (*wall, building*) rinforzare; (*economy, currency*) consolidare; (*desire, determination*) rafforzare; **they are trying to strengthen their position** stanno cercando di rafforzare la loro posizione
■ VI (*economy, currency*) consolidarsi; (*wind*) aumentare di intensità; (*desire, determination*) rafforzarsi

strength·en·ing ['strɛŋθənɪŋ] N (*of structure*) rinforzo; (*of economy, currency*) consolidamento; (*of desire, determination*) rafforzamento

strenu·ous ['strɛnjʊəs] ADJ (*denial, attempt*) energico(-a), vigoroso(-a); (*game, match, day*) faticoso(-a); (*opposition, efforts, resistance*) accanito(-a); **strenuous exercise** esercizi *mpl* pesanti; **you mustn't do anything too strenuous** devi evitare di fare troppi sforzi

strenu·ous·ly ['strɛnjʊəslɪ] ADV (*deny*) energicamente; (*attempt, exercise, play*) con impegno; (*resist, oppose, attempt*) accanitamente

◎ **stress** [strɛs] N **1** (*Tech*) sforzo; (*force, pressure*) pressione *f*; (*psychological etc: strain*) tensione *f*, stress *m*; **to be under stress** essere stressato(-a); (*fig*) essere sotto pressione; **in times of stress** in momenti di grande tensione; **a stress-related illness** una malattia legata allo stress; **the stresses and strains of modern life** il logorio *or* lo stress della vita moderna

Ss

2 (*emphasis*) enfasi *f*; (*Ling, Poetry*) accento; **the stress is on the first syllable** l'accento cade sulla prima sillaba; **to lay great stress on sth** dare grande importanza a qc
■ VT (*emphasize*) sottolineare, mettere in rilievo; **I would like to stress that...** vorrei sottolineare che...

stressed [strɛst] ADJ (*syllable*) accentato(-a)

stress·ful ['strɛsfʊl] ADJ (*job*) difficile, stressante

stress mark N accento

◎**stretch** [strɛtʃ] N
1 (*distance*) tratto; (*expanse*) distesa; (*of time*) periodo; **a stretch of road** un pezzo di strada; **a stretch of time** un periodo; **for a long stretch it runs between ...** per un lungo *or* bel tratto passa fra...; **for three days at a stretch** per tre giorni di seguito *or* di fila; **he's done a five-year stretch** (*fam*: *in prison*) è stato dentro cinque anni
2 (*elasticity*) elasticità; **to have a stretch** (*person*) stiracchiarsi; **we'll begin with a few stretches** cominceremo con qualche esercizio di stretching; **to be at full stretch** lavorare a tutta forza; **by no stretch of the imagination** in nessun modo
■ VT
1 (*pull out*: *elastic*) tendere, tirare; (*make larger*: *pullover, shoes*) allargare; (*spread on ground etc*) stendere; **to stretch (between)** (*rope etc*) tendere (fra); **they stretched a rope between two trees** hanno teso una corda tra due alberi; **to stretch one's legs** sgranchirsi le gambe; **to stretch o.s.** (*after sleep etc*) stiracchiarsi
2 (*money, resources, meal*) far bastare
3 (*meaning*) forzare; (*truth*) esagerare; **to stretch a point** fare uno strappo alla regola
4 (*athlete, student etc*) far sforzare al massimo; **to be fully stretched** essere impegnato(-a) a fondo; **to stretch o.s.** mettercela tutta, impegnarsi a fondo
■ VI
1 (*reach, extend*: *area of land*): **to stretch to** *or* **as far as** estendersi fino a; (: *meeting*): **to stretch (into)** prolungarsi (fino a); (*reach*: *rope, power, influence*): **to stretch (to)** andare (fino a); (*be enough*: *money, food*) bastare (per)
2 (*stretch one's limbs*) stirarsi, stiracchiarsi; **the dog woke up and stretched** il cane s'è svegliato e s'è stiracchiato; **I stretched across for the book** mi sono allungato per prendere il libro
3 (*be elastic*) essere elastico(-a); (*become larger*: *clothes, shoes*) allargarsi; **my sweater stretched when I washed it** il maglione s'è allargato durante il lavaggio
■ ADJ (*fabric, trousers*) elasticizzato(-a)
▸ **stretch out** VI + ADV (*person*) allungarsi; (: *lie down*) stendersi; (*countryside etc*) estendersi, stendersi; **there wasn't enough room to stretch out** non c'era abbastanza spazio per distendersi; **to stretch out for sth** allungare la mano per prendere qc; **a life of unrelieved monotony stretched out before him** lo aspettava una vita di terribile monotonia
■ VT + ADV (*arm, leg*) allungare, tendere; (*net, blanket*) distendere, stendere; (*rope*) stendere; **she stretched out an arm and grabbed me** ha allungato un braccio per afferrarmi

stretch·er ['strɛtʃəʳ] N (*Med*) barella

stretcher-bearer ['strɛtʃə,bɛərəʳ] N barelliere *m*

stretcher case N ferito(-a) che dev'essere trasportato(-a) in barella

stretch limo [-'lɪməʊ] N (*Auto*) limousine *f inv* molto lunga

stretch marks NPL smagliature *fpl*

stretchy ['strɛtʃɪ] ADJ (*comp* **-ier**, *superl* **-iest**) (*fabric*) elastico(-a)

strew [stru:] (*pt* **strewed**, *pp* **strewed** *or* **strewn** [stru:n])
VT (*scatter*: *sand, straw, wreckage*) spargere; (*cover*): **to strew (with)** ricoprire (di); **to strew one's things about the room** disseminare la roba in giro per la stanza

strewn [stru:n] ADJ: **strewn with** cosparso(-a) di

stria·tion [straɪ'eɪʃən] N striatura; (*Geol*) striatura glaciale

strick·en ['strɪkən] (*old*) PP *of* **strike**
■ ADJ (*distressed, upset*) colpito(-a); (*wounded*) ferito(-a); (*damaged*: *ship etc*) in avaria; (: *city*) colpito(-a); **grief stricken** affranto(-a); **she was stricken with remorse** fu presa dal rimorso; **he was stricken with cancer** fu colpito dal cancro

◎**strict** [strɪkt] ADJ (*comp* **-er**, *superl* **-est**) **1** (*stern, severe*: *person, principles, views*) severo(-a), rigido(-a); (: *order, rule*) rigoroso(-a); (: *supervision*) stretto(-a); (: *discipline, ban*) rigido(-a) **2** (*precise*: *meaning, accuracy*) preciso(-a); (*absolute*: *secrecy, truth*) assoluto(-a); (: *time limit*) tassativo(-a); **in the strict sense of the word** nel senso stretto della parola; **in strict confidence** in assoluta confidenza

strict·ly ['strɪktlɪ] ADV (*see adj*) severamente; rigorosamente; strettamente; rigidamente; precisamente; assolutamente; tassativamente; **she was strictly brought up** ha ricevuto un'educazione rigida; **strictly confidential** strettamente confidenziale; **it is strictly forbidden** è severamente proibito; **strictly speaking** a rigor di termini; **strictly between ourselves ...** detto fra noi...; **strictly controlled** rigorosamente controllato; **that's not strictly true** questa non è proprio la verità

strict·ness ['strɪktnɪs] N (*of person*) severità

stric·ture ['strɪktʃəʳ] N (*usu pl*: *frm*: *criticism*) critica

stride [straɪd] (*vb*: *pt* **strode**, *pp* **stridden** ['strɪdn])
N passo, falcata; **to get into one's stride** (*fig*) trovare il ritmo giusto; **to take sth in one's stride** (*fig*: *changes etc*) prendere con tranquillità; (: *exam*) sostenere senza grossi problemi; **to make great strides** (*fig*) fare passi da gigante; **a few strides** alcuni lunghi passi
■ VI: **to stride in/out** *etc* entrare/uscire a grandi passi; **to stride along** camminare a grandi passi; **to stride up and down** camminare avanti e indietro

stri·dent ['straɪdənt] ADJ (*sound*) stridente, stridulo(-a); (*voice*) stridulo(-a); (*protest*) energico(-a)

strife [straɪf] N conflitto; **industrial strife** lotte *fpl* sindacali

◎**strike** [straɪk] (*vb*: *pt, pp* **struck**) N
1 (*by workers*) sciopero; **to be on strike** essere in sciopero; **to go on** *or* **come out on strike** entrare in sciopero; **to call a strike** organizzare uno sciopero
2 (*Mil*: *also*: **air strike**) attacco; **a military strike** un attacco militare
3 (*discovery*: *of oil, gold*) scoperta; **to make a strike** scoprire un giacimento
4 (*Baseball, Bowling*) strike *m inv*
■ VT
1 (*hit*: *gen*) colpire; **to strike a blow at sb** sferrare un colpo a qn; **who struck the first blow?** chi ha colpito per primo?; **to strike a blow for freedom** spezzare una lancia in favore della libertà; **to strike a man when he's down** (*fig*) uccidere un uomo morto; **the president was struck by two bullets** il presidente è stato colpito da due pallottole; **the clock struck nine o'clock** l'orologio ha suonato le nove; **to be struck by**

lightning essere colpito(-a) da un fulmine; **panic struck** preso(-a) dal panico; **to strike sth out of sb's hand** far cadere qc di mano a qn; **he struck the ball hard** ha colpito forte la palla
2 (*collide with*) urtare, sbattere contro; (: *rocks etc*) sbattere contro, cozzare contro; **she struck her head against the wall** ha battuto la testa contro il muro; **a ghastly sight struck our eyes** una scena orribile si presentò ai nostri occhi; **disaster struck us** siamo stati colpiti da una sciagura
3 (*produce, make: coin, medal*) coniare; (: *agreement, deal*) concludere; (: *a light, match*) accendere; (: *sparks*) far sprizzare; **to strike an attitude** assumere un atteggiamento; **to strike a balance** (*fig*) trovare il giusto mezzo; **to be struck dumb** ammutolire; **to strike terror into sb's heart** terrorizzare qn
4 (*occur to*) colpire; **the thought** *or* **it strikes me that ...** mi viene in mente che...; **it strikes me as being most unlikely** mi sembra molto improbabile; **how does it strike you?** che te ne pare?, che ne pensi?; **I'm not much struck with him** non mi ha fatto una buona impressione
5 (*find: gold, oil*) trovare; **he struck it rich** (*fig*) ha fatto fortuna, ha trovato l'America
6 (*pp: also* **stricken**) (*remove, cross out*): **to strike (from)** cancellare (da)
■ VI
1 (*workers*) scioperare; **to strike for higher wages** scioperare per rivendicazioni salariali; **they decided to strike** hanno deciso di fare sciopero
2 (*clock*) rintoccare, suonare
3 (*attack: Mil etc*) attaccare, sferrare un attacco; (: *tiger*) aggredire la preda; (: *snake*) mordere; (: *disease, disaster*) colpire, abbattersi; **now is the time to strike** questo è il momento di agire; **it strikes at our very existence** minaccia di distruggerci; **to strike at** (*person, evil*) colpire; **to strike at the root of a problem** intervenire alla radice di un problema; **they fear the killer may strike again** temono che il killer possa colpire di nuovo
4 **to strike on an idea** avere un'idea
■ ADJ (*pay, committee*) di sciopero
▸ **strike back** VI + ADV (*Mil*) fare rappresaglie; (*fig*) reagire
▸ **strike down** VT + ADV (*subj: illness etc: incapacitate*) colpire; (: *kill*) uccidere; **he was struck down in his prime** è morto nel fiore degli anni
▸ **strike off** VT + ADV (*from list*) cancellare; (: *doctor*) radiare
■ VT + PREP (*name off list*) depennare
■ VI + ADV: **he struck off across the fields** ha tagliato per i campi
▸ **strike out** VT + ADV (*cross out*) depennare
■ VI + ADV
1 (*hit out*): **to strike out (at)** tirare colpi (a), dare botte (a)
2 (*set out*): **to strike out (for)** dirigersi (verso); **to strike out across country** tagliare per la campagna; **to strike out on one's own** (*fig: in business*) mettersi in proprio
▸ **strike up** VT + ADV
1 (*friendship*) fare; **to strike up a conversation** attaccare discorso
2 (*tune*) attaccare
■ VI + ADV (*band*) attaccare

strike·bound ['straɪk,baʊnd] ADJ (*factory*) paralizzato(-a) da uno sciopero

strike·breaker ['straɪk,breɪkəʳ] N crumiro(-a)

strike·breaking ['straɪk,breɪkɪŋ] N: **he was accused of strikebreaking** l'hanno tacciato di crumiraggio

strike force N (*Mil, Aer*) distaccamento aereo

strik·er ['straɪkəʳ] N (*in industry*) scioperante *m/f*; (*Sport*) attaccante *m/f*; **the strikers wanted more money** gli scioperanti volevano più soldi; **the Arsenal striker** l'attaccante dell'Arsenal

◎ **strik·ing** ['straɪkɪŋ] ADJ (*arresting: picture, dress, colour*) che colpisce; (: *person*) che fa colpo; (*obvious: contrast, resemblance*) evidente, lampante; (*shocking: change, sight*) impressionante; **to be within striking distance of sth** (*Mil*) essere a portata di tiro da qc; (*fig*) essere a un tiro di schioppo da qc

strik·ing·ly ['straɪkɪŋlɪ] ADV (*different, original*) totalmente; (*pretty, handsome*) straordinariamente

Strim·mer® ['strɪməʳ] N tagliabordi

◎ **string** [strɪŋ] (*vb: pt, pp* **strung**) N **1** (*cord*) spago; (*of puppet*) filo; (*plait: of onions*) treccia; (*row: of beads*) filo; (: *of vehicles, people*) fila; (: *of excuses*) sfilza, serie *f inv*; (*Comput, Ling*) stringa, sequenza; **a piece of string** un pezzo di spago; **a string of victories** una serie di vittorie; **to pull strings for sb** raccomandare qn; **to get a job by pulling strings** ottenere un lavoro a forza di raccomandazioni; **with no strings attached** (*fig*) senza legami, senza obblighi **2** (*on musical instrument, racket*) corda; **the strings** (*Mus*) gli archi; **to have more than one string to one's bow** (*fig*) avere molte frecce al proprio arco
■ VT **1** (*pearls*) infilare; (*lights, decorations*) appendere; (*rope*): **to string across/between** tendere attraverso/tra **2** (*violin, bow*) incordare; (*tennis racket*) mettere le corde a; **he can't even string two sentences together** non sa mettere insieme due parole
▸ **string along** VT + ADV (*fam*) menare per il naso
▸ **string out** VT + ADV: **to be strung out behind sb/along sth** formare una fila dietro a qn/lungo qc
▸ **string up** VT + ADV (*object*) appendere a una corda; (*fam: hang*) appendere (per il collo); **to be strung up about sth** (*fig*) essere teso(-a) per qc

string bean N fagiolino

stringed in·stru·ment [,strɪŋd'ɪnstrʊmənt] N (*Mus*) strumento a corda

strin·gen·cy ['strɪndʒənsɪ] N rigore *m*

strin·gent ['strɪndʒənt] ADJ (*measures, economies, tests*) rigoroso(-a); **stringent rules** regolamento *msg* stretto

string·ing ['strɪŋɪŋ] N (*Tennis*) accordatura

string instrument N = **stringed instrument**

string·pulling ['strɪŋ,pʊlɪŋ] N: **to do some stringpulling for sb** raccomandare qn

string quartet N quartetto d'archi

string vest N canottiera a rete

stringy ['strɪŋɪ] ADJ (*comp* **-ier**, *superl* **-iest**) (*meat, celery*) filaccioso(-a); (*cooked cheese*) filante; (*plant, hair*) lungo(-a) e rado(-a)

◎ **strip** [strɪp] N **1** (*gen*) striscia; (*of metal*) nastro; (*Aer*) pista; **comic strip** fumetto; **a strip of material** una striscia di stoffa; **to tear a strip off sb** (*fig fam*) dare una lavata di capo a qn **2** (*Sport: clothes*) divisa; **wearing the Celtic strip** con la divisa del Celtic
■ VT **1** (*person, plants, bushes*) spogliare; (*bed*) disfare; (*house*) vuotare, svuotare; (*wallpaper*) staccare; (*paint*) togliere; (*furniture, woodwork*) sverniciare; **to strip from** staccare (*or* togliere) da; **to strip sb/sth of sth** spogliare qn/qc di qc; **he was stripped of his rank** (*Mil*) è stato degradato **2** (*Tech: also:* **strip down**: *engine*) smontare

Ss

■VI (*undress*) spogliarsi, svestirsi; (*do striptease*) fare lo spogliarello; **to strip to the waist** spogliarsi fino alla cintola
▸ **strip off** VI + ADV spogliarsi
strip cartoon N fumetto
strip club N (*Brit*) locale *m* di striptease
stripe [straɪp] N **1** riga, striscia; **white with green stripes** bianco(-a) a strisce verdi **2** (*Mil*) gallone *m*
striped [straɪpt] ADJ a strisce, a righe; **a striped skirt** una gonna a righe
strip joint N (*Am fam*) = **strip club**
strip light N (*Brit*) tubo al neon
strip lighting N illuminazione *f* al neon
strip·ling ['strɪplɪŋ] N (*esp hum*) giovanotto
strip·per ['strɪpəʳ] N (*also*: **paint stripper**) sverniciatore *m*; (*striptease*) spogliarellista *m/f*
strip poker N strip-poker *m*
strip-search [ˌstrɪp'sɜːtʃ] VT: **to strip-search sb** perquisire qn facendolo(-a) spogliare
■N perquisizione *f* (*facendo spogliare il perquisito*)
strip show N spettacolo di spogliarello
strip·tease ['strɪpˌtiːz] N spogliarello
stripy ['straɪpɪ] ADJ (*comp* **-ier**, *superl* **-iest**) (*shirt*) a righe
strive [straɪv] (*pt* **strove**, *pp* **striven** ['strɪvn]) VI sforzarsi; **strive as he might** per quanto si sforzasse; **to strive after** *or* **for sth** lottare per ottenere qc; **to strive to do sth** sforzarsi di fare qc, fare ogni sforzo per fare qc; **she strove to read the name on the pillar** si sforzò di leggere il nome sul pilastro
strobe [strəʊb], **strobe light** N luce *f* stroboscopica
strode [strəʊd] PT *of* **stride**
◎**stroke** [strəʊk] N **1** (*blow*) colpo; **at a stroke** *or* **at one stroke** d'un solo colpo **2** (*caress*) carezza **3** (*Med*) ictus *m inv* **4** (*of pen*) tratto; (*of brush*) pennellata **5** (*Cricket, Golf*) colpo; (*Rowing*) vogata, remata; (*Swimming: single movement*) bracciata; (*: style*) nuoto; **butterfly stroke** nuoto a farfalla; **he hasn't done a stroke (of work)** non ha fatto un bel niente; **a stroke of genius** un lampo di genio; **a stroke of luck** un colpo di fortuna; **to put sb off his stroke** (*Sport*) far perdere il ritmo a qn; (*fig*) far perdere la concentrazione a qn **6** (*of bell, clock*) rintocco; **on the stroke of 12** allo scoccare delle 12 **7** (*of piston*) corsa; **two-stroke engine** motore *m* a due tempi
■VT (*cat, sb's hair*) accarezzare
stroll [strəʊl] N passeggiata, giretto; **to go for a stroll** *or* **have** *or* **take a stroll** andare a fare un giretto *or* due passi
■VI andare a spasso; **to stroll around** *or* **through** gironzolare per; **to stroll in/out** *etc* entrare/uscire *etc* tranquillamente
stroll·er ['strəʊləʳ] N (*Am: pushchair*) passeggino
◎**strong** [strɒŋ] ADJ (*comp* **-er**, *superl* **-est**) (*gen*) forte; (*sturdy: table, shoes, fabric*) solido(-a), resistente; (*candidate*) che ha buone possibilità; (*protest, letter, measures*) energico(-a); (*concentrated, intense: bleach, acid*) concentrato(-a); (*marked, pronounced: characteristic*) marcato(-a); (*: accent*) marcato(-a), forte; **as strong as a horse** *or* **an ox** (*powerful*) forte come un toro; (*healthy*) sano(-a) come un pesce; **he's never been very strong** è sempre stato di salute cagionevole; **she's stronger than me** lei è più forte di me; **there's a strong possibility that ...** ci sono buone possibilità che...; **there are strong indications that ...** tutto sembra indicare che...; **to have a strong stomach** avere uno stomaco di ferro; **I have strong feelings on the matter** ho molto a cuore quel problema; **to be a strong believer in** credere fermamente in; **strong language** (*swearing*) linguaggio volgare; (*frank and critical*) linguaggio incisivo; **he's not very strong on grammar** non è molto forte in grammatica; **geography was never my strong point** la geografia non è mai stata il mio forte; **they are 20 strong** sono in 20
■ADV: **to be going strong** (*company, business*) andare a gonfie vele; (*song, singer*) andare forte, avere successo; (*old person*) essere attivo(-a)
strong-arm ['strɒŋˌɑːm] ADJ (*pej: methods*) brutale; **strong-arm tactics** le maniere forti
strong·box ['strɒŋˌbɒks] N cassaforte *f*
strong drink N alcolici *mpl*
strong·hold ['strɒŋˌhəʊld] N fortezza; **the last stronghold of ...** (*fig*) l'ultima roccaforte di...
strong·ly ['strɒŋlɪ] ADV (*made, built*) solidamente; (*tempted, influenced*) fortemente; (*remind*) moltissimo; (*protest, support, argue*) energicamente; (*believe*) fermamente; (*feel*) profondamente, intensamente; **to feel strongly about sth** avere molto a cuore qc; **I don't feel strongly about it** per me fa lo stesso; **she strongly resembles her mother** somiglia molto a sua madre; **to smell strongly of sth** avere un forte odore di qc; **it smells strongly of garlic** ha un forte odore di aglio; **a strongly-worded letter** una lettera dura; **we recommend strongly that ...** raccomandiamo vivamente di...; **strongly built** robusto(-a)
strong·man ['strɒŋˌmæn] N (*pl* **-men**) (*circus performer*) maciste
strong-minded [ˌstrɒŋ'maɪndɪd] ADJ deciso(-a), risoluto(-a)
strong-mindedly [ˌstrɒŋ'maɪndɪdlɪ] ADV fermamente, con decisione, con risolutezza
strong·room ['strɒŋˌrʊm] N camera blindata
strong verb (*Gram*) N verbo forte
strong-willed [ˌstrɒŋ'wɪld] ADJ prepotente
stron·tium ['strɒntɪəm] N stronzio
strop·py ['strɒpɪ] ADJ (*comp* **-ier**, *superl* **-iest**) (*Brit fam*) indisponente, scontroso(-a); **to get stroppy** mettersi a fare il/la difficile
strove [strəʊv] PT *of* **strive**
struck [strʌk] PT, PP *of* **strike**
struc·tur·al ['strʌktʃərəl] ADJ strutturale; **structural formula** (*Chem*) formula di struttura
struc·tur·al·ism ['strʌktʃərəˌlɪzəm] N strutturalismo
struc·tur·al·ist ['strʌktʃərəlɪst] ADJ strutturalistico(-a)
■N strutturalista *m/f*
struc·tur·al·ly ['strʌktʃərəlɪ] ADV strutturalmente
◎**struc·ture** ['strʌktʃəʳ] N (*gen, Chem, of building*) struttura; (*building itself*) costruzione *f*, fabbricato; **the structure of the organization** la struttura dell'organizzazione; **a four-storey structure** una costruzione di quattro piani
■VT (*essay, argument*) strutturare
◎**strug·gle** ['strʌgl] N (*fight*) lotta; (*effort*) sforzo; **he lost his glasses in the struggle** ha perso gli occhiali nella zuffa; **a violent struggle** una lotta violenta; **a power struggle** una lotta per il potere; **the struggle for survival** la lotta per la sopravvivenza; **without a struggle** (*surrender*) senza opporre resistenza; (*without difficulty*) senza problemi; **to have a struggle to do sth** avere dei problemi a fare qc; **it was a struggle** è stata dura
■VI (*physically*) lottare; **to struggle with sth/sb** lottare con qc/qn; **to struggle to one's feet** alzarsi con sforzo;

to struggle through the crowd avanzare a fatica tra la folla
■VT: **to struggle to do sth** lottare per fare qc; **he struggled to get custody of his daughter** ha lottato per ottenere la custodia della figlia; **they struggle to pay their bills** riescono a stento a pagare le bollette; **to struggle to make ends meet** *(fig)* faticare a sbarcare il lunario
▸ **struggle on** VI + ADV *(fighting)* continuare a lottare; *(walking)* avanzare a fatica; *(living)* tirare avanti
▸ **struggle through** VI + ADV *(fig)*: **they managed to struggle through** sono riusciti a farcela

strug·gling [ˈstrʌglɪŋ] ADJ *(artist, actor etc)* che lotta per affermarsi

strum [strʌm] VT *(guitar)* strimpellare

strung [strʌŋ] PT, PP *of* **string**; *see also* **highly**

strut[1] [strʌt] VI: **to strut about** *or* **around** pavoneggiarsi; **he strutted past** mi passò davanti impettito; **to strut into a room** entrare impettito(-a) in una stanza

strut[2] [strʌt] N *(beam)* supporto, sostegno

strych·nine [ˈstrɪkniːn] N stricnina

stub [stʌb] N *(of cigarette, pencil)* mozzicone *m*; *(of candle)* moccolo; *(of cheque, receipt, ticket)* matrice *f*, talloncino
■VT: **to stub one's toe (on sth)** urtare *or* sbattere il dito del piede (contro qc)
▸ **stub out** VT + ADV: **to stub out a cigarette** spegnere una sigaretta

stub·ble [ˈstʌbl] N *(in field)* stoppia; *(on chin)* barba di due giorni; **to have stubble** avere la barba di due giorni

stub·born [ˈstʌbən] ADJ *(gen)* ostinato(-a); *(person)* cocciuto(-a), testardo(-a)

stub·born·ly [ˈstʌbənlɪ] ADV ostinatamente, cocciutamente

stub·born·ness [ˈstʌbənnɪs] N testardaggine *f*, ostinazione *f*

stub·by [ˈstʌbɪ] ADJ tozzo(-a)

stuc·co [ˈstʌkəʊ] N stucco

stuck [stʌk] PT, PP *of* **stick**
■ADJ **1** *(jammed)* bloccato(-a); **to get stuck** bloccarsi, rimanere bloccato(-a); **we got stuck in a traffic jam** siamo rimasti bloccati nel traffico **2** *(stumped)*: **I'm stuck** *(fam: with crossword, puzzle)* non riesco ad andare avanti; **to be stuck for an answer** non sapere cosa rispondere; **he's never stuck for an answer** ha sempre la risposta pronta

stuck-up [ˌstʌkˈʌp] ADJ *(fam)* presuntuoso(-a), arrogante

stud[1] [stʌd] N *(in road)* chiodo; *(of football boots)* tacchetto; *(decorative)* borchia; *(earring)* orecchino *(a perno)*; *(also:* **collar stud, shirt stud***)* bottoncino
■VT: **studded with** *(fig)* ornato(-a) di, tempestato(-a) di; **studded tyre** pneumatico chiodato

stud[2] [stʌd] N *(stud farm)* scuderia di allevamento; *(also:* **stud horse***)* stallone *m*

stud·book [ˈstʌdˌbʊk] N registro di allevamento

◎**stu·dent** [ˈstjuːdənt] N *(Scol, Univ)* studente(-essa); *(of human nature etc)* studioso(-a); **a law/medical student** uno(-a) studente(-essa) di legge/di medicina
■ADJ *(life, unrest)* studentesco(-a); *(attitudes, opinions)* degli studenti; *(canteen)* universitario(-a)

student driver N *(Am)* conducente *m/f* principiante

stu·dent·ship [ˈstjuːdəntʃɪp] N borsa di studio

students' union N *(Brit: association)* associazione *f* universitaria; *(: building)* sede *f* dell'associazione universitaria

student teacher N *studente che fa il tirocinio di insegnamento*

stud·ied [ˈstʌdɪd] ADJ *(calm, simplicity)* studiato(-a), calcolato(-a); *(insult)* premeditato(-a), intenzionale; *(pose, style)* affettato(-a)

◎**stu·dio** [ˈstjuːdɪəʊ] N *(TV, Radio, Cine, of artist)* studio; *(also:* **recording studio***)* sala di registrazione; **a TV studio** uno studio televisivo

studio audience N *(TV, Radio)* pubblico in sala

studio couch N divano *m* letto *inv*

studio flat, *(Am)* **studio apartment** N monolocale *m*

studio portrait N fotoritratto

stu·di·ous [ˈstjuːdɪəs] ADJ *(person)* studioso(-a); *(attention to detail)* accurato(-a)

stu·di·ous·ly [ˈstjuːdɪəslɪ] ADV *(see adj)* studiosamente; accuratamente; *(deliberately)* studiatamente, deliberatamente

stu·di·ous·ness [ˈstjuːdɪəsnɪs] N amore *m* per lo studio

◎**study** [ˈstʌdɪ] N *(activity, room)* studio; **to make a study of sth** fare uno studio su qc; **his face was a study!** *(fig)* ha fatto una faccia!; **it repays closer study** vale la pena di studiarlo a fondo
■VT *(gen)* studiare; *(examine: evidence, painting)* esaminare, studiare
■VI studiare; **she's studying to be a doctor** studia medicina; **to study under sb** *(Univ)* essere uno degli studenti di qn; *(subj: artist, composer)* essere allievo(-a) di qn; **to study for an exam** prepararsi a un esame

◎**stuff** [stʌf] N **1** *(substance)* roba; **there is some good stuff in that book** ci sono delle buone cose in quel libro; **it's dangerous stuff** è roba pericolosa; **do you call this stuff beer?** questa robaccia la chiami birra?; **I can't read his stuff** non riesco a leggere quello che scrive; **he's the stuff that heroes are made of** ha la stoffa dell'eroe **2** *(possessions, equipment)* cose *fpl*, roba; **she leaves her stuff scattered about** lascia la sua roba sparsa in giro; **have you got all your stuff?** hai tutta la tua roba? **3** *(fam: nonsense)*: **all that stuff about her leaving** tutte quelle storie sulla sua partenza; **stuff and nonsense!** sciocchezze! **4** *(fam)*: **to do one's stuff** fare la propria parte; **go on, do your stuff!** forza, fai quello che devi fare!; **he certainly knows his stuff** sa il fatto suo
■VT *(fill)* riempire; *(: Culin)* farcire; *(: animal: for exhibition)* impagliare; **to stuff (with)** *(container)* riempire (di); *(cushion, toy)* imbottire (di); **to stuff into** *(stow: contents)* ficcare (in); **he stuffed it into his pocket** se lo ficcò in tasca; **my nose is stuffed up** ho il naso chiuso; **get stuffed!** *(offensive)* va' a farti fottere!; **stuffed shirt** *(fam)* pallone *m* gonfiato; **to stuff o.s. (with food)** rimpinzarsi, strafogarsi

stuffi·ly [ˈstʌfɪlɪ] ADV *(say)* con tono di disapprovazione

stuffi·ness [ˈstʌfɪnɪs] N **1** *(in room)* odore *m* di chiuso **2** *(of person)* ristrettezza di idee; *(of ideas)* arretratezza

stuff·ing [ˈstʌfɪŋ] N *(in cushion etc)* imbottitura; *(Culin)* farcia, ripieno; **to knock the stuffing out of sb** *(subj: boxer, blow)* mettere al tappeto; **a stuffing for peppers** il ripieno per i peperoni

stuffy [ˈstʌfɪ] ADJ *(comp* **-ier**, *superl* **-iest***)* **1** *(room)* mal ventilato(-a), senz'aria; **it's terribly stuffy in here** qui non si respira; **it smells stuffy** c'è odore di chiuso **2** *(ideas)* antiquato(-a), arretrato(-a); *(person)* all'antica

stul·ti·fy [ˈstʌltɪˌfaɪ] VT *(frm)* istupidire

stum·ble [ˈstʌmbl] VI inciampare; *(in speech)* incespicare; **to stumble against sth** inciampare

Ss

contro qc; **to stumble in/out** entrare/uscire barcollando; **to stumble on** *or* **across sth** (*fig: secret*) scoprire per caso; (*: photo etc*) trovare per caso

stum·bling block ['stʌmblɪŋ,blɒk] N ostacolo, scoglio

stump [stʌmp] N (*of limb*) moncone *m*; (*of pencil, tail*) mozzicone *m*; (*of tree*) troncone *m*; (*of tooth*) pezzo; (*Cricket*) paletto (*della porta*)
■VT (*perplex*) sconcertare, lasciare perplesso(-a); **to be stumped for an answer** essere incapace di rispondere
■VI: **to stump in/out** *etc* entrare/uscire *etc* con passo pesante
▶ **stump up** VT + ADV (*fam*) sganciare, sborsare
■VI + ADV (*fam*) sborsare i soldi, sganciare i soldi

stumpy ['stʌmpɪ] ADJ (*person*) tarchiato(-a)

stun [stʌn] VT (*subj: blow*) stordire, tramortire; (*fig: amaze*) sbalordire, stupefare; **the news stunned everybody** la notizia sbalordì tutti; **I was stunned by the news** sono rimasto sbalordito dalla notizia; **he was stunned by the blow** il colpo lo aveva stordito

stung [stʌŋ] PT, PP *of* **sting**

stunk [stʌŋk] PP *of* **stink**

stunned [stʌnd] ADJ (*by blow*) stordito(-a); (*fig*) sbalordito(-a); **in stunned silence** ammutolito(-a)

stun·ner ['stʌnəʳ] N (*fam*): **she's a stunner** è uno schianto

stun·ning ['stʌnɪŋ] ADJ (*news etc*) sbalorditivo(-a), stupefacente; (*dress, girl etc*) fantastico(-a), splendido(-a)

stunt¹ [stʌnt] N (*Aer, for film etc*) acrobazia; (*Comm*) trovata pubblicitaria; **it's just a stunt to get your money** è tutto un trucco per farti tirar fuori i soldi; **he performed his own stunts** ha girato personalmente le scene pericolose

stunt² [stʌnt] VT (*tree, person*) arrestare la crescita *or* lo sviluppo di; (*growth*) arrestare

stunt·ed ['stʌntɪd] ADJ (*tree*) striminzito(-a); (*person*) rachitico(-a)

stunt·man ['stʌnt,mæn] N (*pl* **-men**) stuntman *m inv*, cascatore *m*

stunt woman N (*pl* **stunt women**) stuntwoman *f inv*

stu·pefac·tion [,stju:pɪ'fækʃən] N stupefazione *f*, stupore *m*

stu·pefy ['stju:pɪ,faɪ] VT (*subj: tiredness, alcohol*) stordire, istupidire; (*fig: astound*) stupire, sbalordire

stu·pefy·ing ['stju:pɪ,faɪɪŋ] ADJ (*news*) sbalorditivo(-a), stupefacente; (*boredom*) che stupidisce

stu·pen·dous [stju:'pɛndəs] ADJ (*fam: film, holiday etc*) stupendo(-a), fantastico(-a); (*: price*) altissimo(-a); (*: mistake*) enorme

stu·pen·dous·ly [stju:'pɛndəslɪ] ADV stupendamente, fantasticamente; **a stupendously high price** un prezzo incredibilmente alto

◎**stu·pid** ['stju:pɪd] ADJ (*gen*) stupido(-a); (*person*) stupido(-a), sciocco(-a); (*: from sleep, drink*) intontito(-a), istupidito(-a); **that was stupid of you** *or* **that was a stupid thing to do** hai fatto una stupidaggine; **he drank himself stupid last night** era ubriaco fradicio ieri sera

stu·pid·ity [stju:'pɪdɪtɪ] N stupidità *f inv*

stu·pid·ly ['stju:pɪdlɪ] ADV (*smile, say*) stupidamente; **I stupidly forgot to lock the door** mi sono stupidamente dimenticato di chiudere la porta a chiave

stu·por ['stju:pəʳ] N (*from heat, alcohol*) intontimento, stordimento

DID YOU KNOW ...?
stupor is not translated by the Italian word *stupore*

stur·di·ly ['stɜ:dɪlɪ] ADV (*built, supported*) solidamente; (*fig: refuse*) energicamente, risolutamente

stur·di·ness ['stɜ:dɪnɪs] N (*see adj*) robustezza; solidità; risolutezza

stur·dy ['stɜ:dɪ] ADJ (*comp* **-ier**, *superl* **-iest**) (*person, tree*) robusto(-a), forte; (*boat, material*) resistente, solido(-a); (*fig: supporter*) accanito(-a); (*: refusal*) risoluto(-a)

stur·geon ['stɜ:dʒən] N storione *m*

stut·ter ['stʌtəʳ] N balbuzie *f*; **he has a bad stutter** ha una balbuzie pronunciata; **he's got a stutter** è balbuziente
■VI, VT balbettare

stut·ter·er ['stʌtərəʳ] N balbuziente *m/f*

stut·ter·ing ['stʌtərɪŋ] N balbuzie *f*

Stutt·gart ['stʊtgɑ:t] N Stoccarda

sty¹ [staɪ] N (*for pigs*) porcile *m*

sty², **stye** [staɪ] N (*Med*) orzaiolo

stye [staɪ] N (*Med*) orzaiolo

◎**style** [staɪl] N **1** (*gen*) stile *m*; **in the Renaissance style** in stile rinascimentale; **that's the style!** così va bene!; **that's not his style** non è nel suo stile **2** (*of dress etc*) modello, linea; (*also:* **hair style**) pettinatura; (*: more elaborate*) acconciatura; **in the latest style** all'ultima moda; **something in this style** qualcosa di questo tipo **3** (*elegance: of person, car, film*) classe *f*, stile *m*; **to dress with style** vestire con un certo stile; **she has style** ha classe *or* stile; **to live in style** avere un elevato tenore di vita; **to do things in style** fare le cose in grande stile **4** (*Bot*) stilo

sty·li ['staɪlaɪ] NPL *of* **stylus**

styl·ing ['staɪlɪŋ] N (*Hairdressing*) taglio

styl·ish ['staɪlɪʃ] ADJ (*person*) di classe; (*car, district, furniture*) elegante; (*film*) raffinato(-a)

styl·ish·ly ['staɪlɪʃlɪ] ADV (*dress, live, travel*) con stile, con classe

styl·ish·ness ['staɪlɪʃnɪs] N stile *m*, classe *f*

styl·ist ['staɪlɪst] N: **hair stylist** parrucchiere(-a); (*in advertising*) pubblicitario(-a)

sty·lis·tic [staɪ'lɪstɪk] ADJ stilistico(-a)

sty·lis·tics [staɪ'lɪstɪks] NSG stilistica

styl·ized ['staɪlaɪzd] ADJ stilizzato(-a)

sty·lus ['staɪləs] N (*pl* **styli**) (*of record player*) puntina; (*pen*) stilo

sty·mie ['staɪmɪ] VT (*fam*) ostacolare

styp·tic ['stɪptɪk] ADJ emostatico(-a); **styptic pencil** matita emostatica

Styro·foam® ['staɪrə,fəʊm] (*Am*) N polistirene
■ADJ (*cup*) di polistirene

Styx [stɪks] N (*Myth*): **the Styx** lo Stige

suave [swɑ:v] ADJ (*person, manners*) mellifluo(-a); (*question, suggestion*) insinuante

DID YOU KNOW ...?
suave is not translated by the Italian word *soave*

suave·ly ['swɑ:vlɪ] ADV (*see adj*) mellifluamente; in maniera insinuante

suav·ity ['swɑ:vɪtɪ], **suave·ness** ['swɑ:vnɪs] N (*see adj*) mellifluità; fare *m* insinuante

sub... [sʌb] PREF sub..., sotto...

sub [sʌb] N ABBR **1** = **submarine** **2** = **subscription**

sub·al·tern ['sʌbltən] N (*Mil*) subalterno

sub·atom·ic [,sʌbə'tɒmɪk] ADJ subatomico(-a)

sub·com·mit·tee ['sʌbkə,mɪtɪ] N sottocommissione *f*

sub·con·scious [ˌsʌb'kɒnʃəs] ADJ subcosciente
■ N: **the subconscious** il subcosciente, il subconscio
sub·con·scious·ly [ˌsʌb'kɒnʃəslɪ] ADV inconsciamente
sub·con·ti·nent [ˌsʌb'kɒntɪnənt] N: **the (Indian) subcontinent** il subcontinente (indiano)
sub·con·tract [*n* sʌb'kɒntrækt; *vb* ˌsʌbkən'trækt] N subappalto
■ VT subappaltare
sub·con·trac·tor [ˌsʌbkən'træktəʳ] N subappaltatore(-trice)
sub·cul·ture ['sʌbˌkʌltʃəʳ] N sottocultura
sub·di·rec·tory ['sʌbdɪˌrɛktərɪ] N (*Comput*) subdirectory *f inv*
sub·di·vide [ˌsʌbdɪ'vaɪd] VT suddividere
sub·di·vi·sion ['sʌbdɪˌvɪʒən] N suddivisione *f*
sub·due [səb'dju:] VT (*enemy*) sottomettere; (*children*) far star buono(-a); (*high spirits*) smorzare; (*passions etc*) controllare
sub·dued [səb'dju:d] ADJ (*person: downcast*) giù di morale; (*emotions*) contenuto(-a); (*voice, tone*) sommesso(-a); (*colours*) tenue; (*lighting*) soffuso(-a); **he's rather subdued these days** ultimamente non è allegro come al solito
sub·edit [ˌsʌb'ɛdɪt] VT (*book, article*) revisionare
sub·edi·tor [ˌsʌb'ɛdɪtəʳ] N redattore(-trice) aggiunto(-a)
sub·group ['sʌbˌgru:p] N sottogruppo
sub·head·ing ['sʌbˌhɛdɪŋ] N sottotitolo
sub·hu·man [ˌsʌb'hju:mən] ADJ subumano(-a)
◎ **sub·ject** [*n, adj* 'sʌbdʒɪkt; *vb* səb'dʒɛkt] N **1** (*topic: gen*) argomento, soggetto; (*Scol*) materia; **the subject of my project is the Internet** l'argomento della mia ricerca è Internet; **what's your favourite subject?** quale materia preferisci?; **let's keep to the subject** non divaghiamo; **let's drop the subject** lasciamo perdere; **(while we're) on the subject of money ...** a proposito di soldi...; **to change the subject** cambiare discorso **2** (*Gram*) soggetto **3** (*Pol: of country*) cittadino(-a); (*: of sovereign*) suddito(-a)
■ ADJ **1** **subject to** (*liable to: law, tax, disease, delays*) soggetto(-a) a; **subject to doing that** (*conditional upon*) a condizione di fare *or* che si faccia ciò; **subject to confirmation in writing** a condizione di ricevere conferma per iscritto; **these prices are subject to change without notice** questi prezzi sono suscettibili di modifiche senza preavviso; **subject to contract** (*Comm*) fino a stipulazione del contratto **2** (*people, nation*) assoggettato(-a), sottomesso(-a)
■ VT: **to subject sb to sth** sottoporre qn a qc; **to subject o.s. to ridicule/criticism** esporsi al ridicolo/ alle critiche; **she was subjected to severe criticism** è stata duramente criticata
subject heading N (*Library*) titolo
subject index N (*Library*) indice *m* per argomenti
sub·jec·tion [səb'dʒɛkʃən] N (*state*): **subjection (to)** sottomissione *f* (a), soggezione *f* (a); **to hold a people in subjection** tenere un popolo in servitù
sub·jec·tive [səb'dʒɛktɪv] ADJ soggettivo(-a)
sub·jec·tive·ly [səb'dʒɛktɪvlɪ] ADV soggettivamente
subject line N (*in email*) riga dove si specifica l'oggetto
subject matter N argomento
sub ju·di·ce [ˌsʌb'ju:dɪsɪ] ADJ (*Law*) sub iudice
sub·ju·gate ['sʌbdʒʊˌgeɪt] VT sottomettere, soggiogare
sub·junc·tive [səb'dʒʌŋktɪv] (*Gram*) ADJ congiuntivo(-a)
■ N congiuntivo; **in the subjunctive** al congiuntivo
sub·let [ˌsʌb'lɛt] VT, VI (*pt, pp* **sublet**) subaffittare
sub·lieu·ten·ant [ˌsʌblɛf'tɛnənt] N (*Naut*) sottotenente *m* di vascello
sub·li·mate ['sʌblɪˌmeɪt] VT (*Psych*) sublimare
sub·li·ma·tion [ˌsʌblɪ'meɪʃən] N (*Psych*) sublimazione *f*
sub·lime [sə'blaɪm] ADJ (*beauty, emotion, achievement*) sublime; (*indifference, contempt*) supremo(-a)
■ N sublime *m*; **from the sublime to the ridiculous** dal sublime al grottesco
■ VT (*Chem*) sublimare
sub·lime·ly [sə'blaɪmlɪ] ADV (*happy, beautiful*) immensamente; (*indifferent*) sommamente
sub·limi·nal [ˌsʌb'lɪmɪnl] ADJ subliminale
sub·limi·nal·ly [ˌsʌb'lɪmɪnəlɪ] ADV in modo subliminale
sub·machine gun [ˌsʌbmə'ʃi:nˌgʌn] N mitra *m inv*
sub·ma·rine ['sʌbməˌri:n] N sottomarino, sommergibile *m*
■ ADJ (*frm*) sottomarino(-a)
sub·merge [səb'mɜ:dʒ] VT (*flood*) sommergere; (*plunge*): **to submerge (in)** immergere (in); **the river burst its banks, submerging the village** il fiume ha rotto gli argini e ha sommerso il paese
■ VI (*submarine*) immergersi
sub·mer·sion [səb'mɜ:ʃən] N (*see vt*) sommersione *f*; immersione *f*
sub·mis·sion [səb'mɪʃən] N sottomissione *f*; (*to committee etc*) richiesta, domanda
sub·mis·sive [səb'mɪsɪv] ADJ sottomesso(-a), remissivo(-a)
sub·mis·sive·ly [səb'mɪsɪvlɪ] ADV in modo sottomesso, in modo remissivo
sub·mis·sive·ness [səb'mɪsɪvnɪs] N sottomissione *f*, remissività
sub·mit [səb'mɪt] VT (*proposal, claim*) presentare; **I submit that ...** propongo che...; **they have submitted a claim for a pay rise** hanno presentato una richiesta di aumento
■ VI (*give in*): **to submit to** (*pressure, threats*) cedere a; (*sb's will*) sottomettersi a; **we won't submit to their demands** non ci piegheremo alle loro richieste
sub·nor·mal [ˌsʌb'nɔ:məl] ADJ subnormale
sub·or·di·nate [*adj, n* sə'bɔ:dnɪt; *vb* sə'bɔ:dɪˌneɪt] ADJ (*rank, officer*) subalterno(-a); **subordinate clause** (*Gram*) proposizione *f* subordinata
■ N subalterno(-a), subordinato(-a)
■ VT: **to subordinate (to)** subordinare (a); **subordinating conjunction** (*Gram*) congiunzione *f* subordinativa
sub·or·di·na·tion [səˌbɔ:dɪ'neɪʃən] N subordinazione *f*
sub·orn [sə'bɔ:n] VT (*Law: witness*) subornare
sub·plot ['sʌbˌplɒt] N vicenda secondaria
sub·poe·na [səb'pi:nə] (*Law*) N citazione *f*, mandato di comparizione
■ VT citare in giudizio
sub-post office [sʌb'pəʊstˌɒfɪs] N ufficio postale secondario
sub·rou·tine ['sʌbru:ˌti:n] N (*Comput*) sottoprogramma *m*, subroutine *f inv*
sub·scribe [səb'skraɪb] VI: **to subscribe to** (*magazine etc*) abbonarsi a; (*fund*) sottoscrivere; (*opinion*) condividere, approvare; **to subscribe for** (*shares*) sottoscrivere; **thousands subscribed to the fund** migliaia di persone hanno contribuito alla raccolta di fondi; **to subscribe to a magazine** abbonarsi ad una rivista; **I don't subscribe to this view** non condivido questa opinione
■ VT (*money*) devolvere

Ss

sub·scrib·er [səbˈskraɪbəʳ] N (*to magazine, telephone*): **subscriber (to)** abbonato(-a) (a)
subscriber trunk dialling [-ˈdaɪəlɪŋ] N teleselezione *f*
sub·script [ˈsʌbˌskrɪpt] N (*Typ*) deponente *m*
sub·scrip·tion [səbˈskrɪpʃən] N (*to magazine etc*) abbonamento; (*membership fee*) quota d'iscrizione; (*for shares*) sottoscrizione *f*; **to take out a subscription to** abbonarsi a
sub·sec·tion [ˈsʌbˌsɛkʃən] N sottosezione *f*
◎**sub·se·quent** [ˈsʌbsɪkwənt] ADJ (*later*) successivo(-a); (*further*) ulteriore; **subsequent to** in seguito a; **subsequent events** avvenimenti successivi; **subsequent modifications** ulteriori modifiche
sub·se·quent·ly [ˈsʌbsɪkwəntlɪ] ADV successivamente, in seguito
sub·ser·vi·ence [səbˈsɜːvɪəns] N: **subservience (to)** sottomissione *f* (a)
sub·ser·vi·ent [səbˈsɜːvɪənt] ADJ: **subservient (to)** sottomesso(-a) (a)
sub·set [ˈsʌbˌsɛt] N (*Math*) sottoinsieme *m*
sub·side [səbˈsaɪd] VI (*flood*) calare, decrescere; (*road, land*) cedere, avvallarsi; (*wind, anger*) calmarsi, placarsi; **the violence is beginning to subside** la violenza sta cominciando a diminuire; **they are waiting for the water to subside** stanno aspettando che il livello dell'acqua cali; **at last the wind subsided** finalmente il vento si è calmato
sub·sid·ence [səbˈsaɪdəns] N (*of land etc*) cedimento, avvallamento; (*of waters etc*) abbassamento
sub·sidi·ari·ty [səbˌsɪdɪˈærɪtɪ] N (*Pol*) *principio del decentramento del potere*
sub·sidi·ary [səbˈsɪdɪərɪ] ADJ (*company*) consociato(-a); (*role etc*) secondario(-a); (*Brit Univ: subject*) complementare; **subsidiary cone** (*Geol*) cono vulcanico secondario
■ N (*Comm*) filiale *f*; (*Univ*) materia complementare
sub·si·dize [ˈsʌbsɪˌdaɪz] VT sovvenzionare
◎**sub·si·dy** [ˈsʌbsɪdɪ] N sovvenzione *f*, sussidio
sub·sist [səbˈsɪst] VI: **to subsist on sth** vivere di qc
sub·sist·ence [səbˈsɪstəns] N sopravvivenza; **means of subsistence** mezzi *mpl* di sussistenza
subsistence allowance N indennità *f inv* di trasferta
subsistence level N livello minimo di vita
subsistence wage N salario appena sufficiente per vivere
sub·soil [ˈsʌbˌsɔɪl] N sottosuolo
sub·son·ic [ˌsʌbˈsɒnɪk] ADJ subsonico(-a)
sub·spe·cies [ˈsʌbˌspiːʃiːz] N, PL INV sottospecie *f inv*
◎**sub·stance** [ˈsʌbstəns] N (*gen*) sostanza; **to lack substance** (*argument*) essere debole; (*accusation*) essere privo(-a) di fondamento; (*film, book*) essere scarso(-a) di contenuto; **a man of substance** un uomo benestante; **in substance** sostanzialmente, fondamentalmente
substance abuse N abuso di sostanze tossiche
sub·stand·ard [ˌsʌbˈstændəd] ADJ (*goods*) scadente; (*housing*) di qualità scadente
◎**sub·stan·tial** [səbˈstænʃəl] ADJ **1** (*considerable: amount, progress*) notevole, considerevole; (*: majority, proportion*) largo(-a), grande; (*: difference*) sostanziale; (*solid: building, table*) solido(-a); (*: meal*) sostanzioso(-a); (*wealthy: landowner, businessman*) ricco(-a); **a substantial sum** una somma notevole; **a substantial lunch** un pranzo sostanzioso; **a substantial structure** una struttura solida **2** (*frm: real*) reale
sub·stan·tial·ly [səbˈstænʃəlɪ] ADV **1** (*considerably*) notevolmente; **substantially bigger** molto più grande; **substantially different** notevolmente diverso(-a) **2** (*in essence*) sostanzialmente; **substantially correct** sostanzialmente corretto(-a) **3** (*solidly: built*) solidamente
sub·stan·ti·ate [səbˈstænʃɪˌeɪt] VT comprovare
sub·stan·tive [ˈsʌbstəntɪv] ADJ (*frm: issues, measures*) sostanziale; (*Gram*) sostantivo(-a)
■ N (*Gram*) sostantivo
◎**sub·sti·tute** [ˈsʌbstɪˌtjuːt] N (*person*) sostituto(-a); (*teacher*) supplente *m/f*; (*Sport*) riserva; (*thing*) surrogato; **coffee substitute** surrogato di caffè; **he's looking for a substitute** sta cercando un sostituto; **a substitute came on in the 71st minute** è entrata una riserva al 71° minuto; **there's no substitute for butter** non c'è niente di meglio del burro
■ VT: **to substitute sb/sth (for)** sostituire qn/qc (con *or* a); **they want to substitute gas for coal** vogliono sostituire il carbone con il gas
■ VI: **to substitute for sb** sostituire qn
sub·sti·tu·tion [ˌsʌbstɪˈtjuːʃən] N (*gen*) sostituzione *f*; (*in school*) supplenza
substitution reaction N (*Chem*) reazione *f* di sostituzione
sub·stra·tum [sʌbˈstrɑːtəm] N (*pl* **substrata** [sʌbˈstrɑːtə]) (*Geol, fig*) sostrato
sub·struc·ture [ˈsʌbˌstrʌktʃəʳ] N sottostruttura
sub·sume [səbˈsjuːm] VT: **to subsume within/under** (*frm*) includere in, inglobare in
sub·ten·ant [ˌsʌbˈtɛnənt] N subaffittuario(-a)
sub·tend [səbˈtɛnd] VT (*Geom*) sottendere
sub·ter·fuge [ˈsʌbtəfjuːdʒ] N sotterfugio
sub·ter·ra·nean [ˌsʌbtəˈreɪnɪən] ADJ sotterraneo(-a)
sub·ti·tle [ˈsʌbˌtaɪtl] N (*Cine*) sottotitolo
sub·tle [ˈsʌtl] ADJ (*gen*) sottile; (*flavour, perfume*) delicato(-a)
sub·tle·ty [ˈsʌtltɪ] N (*see adj*) sottigliezza; delicatezza
sub·tly [ˈsʌtlɪ] ADV (*see adj*) sottilmente; delicatamente
sub·to·tal [ˌsʌbˈtəʊtl] N totale *m* parziale
sub·tract [səbˈtrækt] VT sottrarre
sub·trac·tion [səbˈtrækʃən] N sottrazione *f*
sub·urb [ˈsʌbɜːb] N sobborgo; **a London suburb** un sobborgo di Londra; **in the suburbs** in periferia; **to live in the suburbs** vivere in periferia
sub·ur·ban [səˈbɜːbən] ADJ suburbano(-a), periferico(-a); **a suburban street** una via periferica; **a suburban shopping centre** un centro commerciale fuori città
sub·ur·ban·ite [səˈbɜːbəˌnaɪt] N abitante *m/f* dei sobborghi
sub·ur·bia [səˈbɜːbɪə] N periferia, sobborghi *mpl*
sub·ver·sion [səbˈvɜːʃən] N sovversione *f*
sub·ver·sive [səbˈvɜːsɪv] ADJ, N sovversivo(-a)
sub·vert [səbˈvɜːt] VT sovvertire
sub·way [ˈsʌbˌweɪ] N (*Brit: underpass*) sottopassaggio; (*Am: underground*) metropolitana
sub·zero [ˌsʌbˈzɪərəʊ] ADJ: **subzero temperatures** temperature *fpl* sotto zero
◎**suc·ceed** [səkˈsiːd] VI **1** (*be successful: gen*) riuscire, avere successo; **the plan did not succeed** il piano è fallito; **to succeed in life/business** avere successo nella vita/negli affari; **to succeed in doing sth** riuscire a fare qc; **they succeeded in persuading her** sono riusciti a persuaderla **2** (*follow*): **to succeed (to)** succedere (a)
■ VT (*monarch*) succedere a; **to succeed sb in a post** succedere a qn in un posto
suc·ceed·ing [səkˈsiːdɪŋ] ADJ (*following: in past*) successivo(-a), seguente; (*: in future*) futuro(-a);

succeeding generations generazioni *fpl* future; **in succeeding months** nei mesi successivi; **each succeeding year brought ...** ogni anno che passava recava...; **each succeeding year will bring further wealth** con ogni anno che passa aumenterà la ricchezza

◎**suc·cess** [sək'sɛs] N (*gen*) successo, riuscita; **she was a great success** ha avuto un grande successo; **without success** senza successo *or* risultato; **to make a success of sth** riuscire bene in qc; **to meet with success** avere successo

◎**suc·cess·ful** [sək'sɛsfʊl] ADJ (*person: in attempt*) che ha successo; (*: in life*) affermato(-a), di successo; (*attempt, plan, venture*) riuscito(-a), coronato(-a) da successo; (*play, film*) di successo; (*business*) prospero(-a); **to be successful in doing sth** riuscire a fare qc; **a successful lawyer** un avvocato affermato

suc·cess·ful·ly [sək'sɛsfəlɪ] ADV con successo

suc·ces·sion [sək'sɛʃən] N **1** (*series*) serie *f inv*; **in succession** di seguito; **in quick succession** in rapida successione; **a succession of jobs** una serie di lavori
2 (*to post etc*) successione *f*

suc·ces·sive [sək'sɛsɪv] ADJ (*days, months*) consecutivo(-a); (*generations*) successivo(-a); **on three successive days** per tre giorni consecutivi *or* di seguito; **each successive failure** ogni nuovo insuccesso; **he was the winner for a second successive year** ha vinto per il secondo anno consecutivo

suc·ces·sive·ly [sək'sɛsɪvlɪ] ADV successivamente

suc·ces·sor [sək'sɛsəʳ] N (*in office*) successore *m*; (*heir*) erede *m/f*

success story N successo

suc·cinct [sək'sɪŋkt] ADJ succinto(-a), breve

suc·cinct·ly [sək'sɪŋktlɪ] ADV succintamente

suc·cour, (*Am*) **suc·cor** ['sʌkəʳ] (*frm, liter*) N soccorso; **to provide succo(u)r to** prestare soccorso a
■ VT soccorrere, aiutare

suc·cu·lence ['sʌkjʊləns] N succulenza

suc·cu·lent ['sʌkjʊlənt] ADJ (*tasty*) succulento(-a)
■ N (*Bot*): **succulents** piante *fpl* grasse

suc·cumb [sə'kʌm] VI: **to succumb to** (*temptation, illness*) soccombere a; (*entreaties, charms*) cedere a

◎**such** [sʌtʃ] PREDETERMINER, DETERMINER
1 (*of this/that sort*) tale, del genere; **such a book** un tale libro, un libro del genere; **such books** tali libri, libri del genere; **such a thing** una cosa del genere; **I wouldn't dream of doing such a thing** non mi sognerei di fare una cosa del genere; **did you ever hear of such a thing?** hai mai sentito una cosa del genere?; **it was such a waste of time** era una tale perdita di tempo; **there's no such thing** non esiste; **there's no such thing as a unicorn** gli unicorni non esistono; **there's no such place in Italy** non c'è un posto del genere in Italia; **such was his answer** questa è stata la sua risposta; **such is life** così è la vita; **I said no such thing** non ho detto niente del genere; **in such cases** in casi del genere; **we had such a case last year** si è avuto un caso del genere l'anno scorso; **some such idea** un'idea del genere; **it was such as to/that** era tale da/che; **this is my car such as it is** questa è la mia macchina, se così si può chiamare
2 (*so much, so great*) tale, tanto(-a); **he's not such a fool as you think** non è così scemo come pensi; **I had such a fright** ho preso un tale spavento; **such courage** tanto coraggio; **I was in such a hurry** avevo una tale fretta; **I was in such a hurry that ...** avevo così tanta fretta che...; **such a lot of** talmente, così tanto(-a); **such a lot of work** così tanto lavoro; **making such a noise that** facendo un rumore tale che; **a noise such as to** un rumore tale da
3 (*so very*) talmente, così ; **such good food** cibo così buono; **such good books** libri così buoni; **such a clever girl** una ragazza così intelligente; **it's such a long time since we saw each other** è da tanto tempo che non ci vediamo; **such a long time ago** tanto tempo fa; **I haven't had such good tea for ages** erano secoli che non bevevo un tè così buono; **such a long trip** un viaggio così lungo; **such nice people** gente così simpatica
4 such as (*introducing examples*) come; **such a man as you** *or* **a man such as you** un uomo come te; **such writers as Updike** *or* **writers such as Updike** scrittori come Updike; **books such as these** libri come questi; **hot countries such as India** paesi caldi, come l'India; **such as?** per esempio?; **have you got such a thing as a torch?** hai una pila per caso?
■ PRON
1 (*this, that, those*): **such as wish to go** chi desidera andare; **but such is not the case** ma non è questo caso; **and such (like)** e così via; **I haven't many, but I'll give you such as I have** non ho molti, ma ti darò tutti quelli che ho
2 as such (*in that capacity*) come tale, in quanto tale; (*in itself*) di per sé; **and as such he was promoted** e come tale fu promosso; **there's no garden as such** non c'è un vero e proprio giardino; **he's not an expert as such, but ...** non è un vero e proprio esperto, però ...; **doctors as such are ...** i medici in quanto tali sono...; **the work as such is poorly paid** il lavoro di per sé non è pagato bene

such-and-such ['sʌtʃən,sʌtʃ] ADJ tale; **they live in such-and-such street** abitano nella tale strada; **such-and-such a place** il tale posto
■ N: **Mr such-and-such** il signor tal dei tali

such·like ['sʌtʃ,laɪk] (*fam*) ADJ simile, di tal genere; **sheep and suchlike animals** pecore *fpl* e animali *mpl* del genere
■ PRON: **and suchlike** e così via

suck [sʌk] VT (*gen*) succhiare; (*subj: baby*) poppare, succhiare; (*: pump, machine*) aspirare; **to suck one's thumb** succhiarsi il pollice; **to suck sth through a straw** bere qc con la cannuccia; **to suck an orange dry** succhiare tutto il succo di un'arancia; **to suck dry** (*fig: person: of money*) ripulire; (*: of energy*) esaurire
■ VI (*baby*) succhiare, poppare; **to suck at sth** succhiare qc
▸ **suck down** VT + ADV (*subj: current, mud*) inghiottire, risucchiare
▸ **suck in** VT + ADV (*subj: machine: dust, air etc*) aspirare; **to suck one's cheeks in** succhiarsi le guance
▸ **suck out** VT + ADV succhiare, far uscire succhiando
▸ **suck up** VT + ADV (*dust, liquid etc*) aspirare
■ VI + ADV (*fam*): **to suck up to sb** leccare i piedi a qn

suck·er ['sʌkəʳ] N (*fam: person*) babbeo(-a), citrullo(-a), gonzo(-a); (*Zool, Tech*) ventosa; (*Bot*) pollone *m*; (*Am: lollipop*) lecca lecca *m inv*; **he's a sucker for flattery** (*fam*) non sa resistere ai complimenti

suck·le ['sʌkl] VT allattare

su·crose ['su:krəʊz] N saccarosio

suc·tion ['sʌkʃən] N (*Tech*) aspirazione *f*

suction pump N pompa aspirante

Su·dan [su:'dɑ:n] N il Sudan

Su·da·nese [,su:də'ni:z] ADJ, N, PL INV sudanese (*m/f*)

Ss

◎**sud·den** ['sʌdn] ADJ improvviso(-a); **this is so sudden!** non me l'aspettavo!; **all of a sudden** all'improvviso, improvvisamente; **a sudden change** un cambiamento improvviso

sudden-death [ˌsʌdn'dɛθ], **sudden-death playoff** N **1** (*in football*) rigori *mpl* a oltranza; (*in American football*) tempo supplementare (*in cui vince la prima squadra che segna*) **2** (*Golf*): **sudden-death hole** *buca supplementare per decidere la vittoria*

sudden death N (*Sport: also:* **sudden-death play-off**) spareggio sudden death

◎**sud·den·ly** ['sʌdnlɪ] ADV improvvisamente, all'improvviso

sud·den·ness ['sʌdnnɪs] N: **the suddenness of his death/departure** la sua morte/partenza improvvisa

suds [sʌdz] NPL (*lather*) schiuma *fsg*; (*soapy water*) saponata *fsg*

sue [su:] VT: **to sue sb for libel/damages** *etc* citare qn per diffamazione/danni *etc*; **they're going to sue me** hanno intenzione di citarmi in giudizio
■VI: **to sue (for)** intentare causa (per); **to sue for divorce** intentare causa di divorzio

suede [sweɪd] N pelle *f* scamosciata; **a suede jacket** una giacca di pelle scamosciata
■ADJ scamosciato(-a)

suet ['sʊɪt] N grasso di rognone

Suez ['su:ɪz] N Suez *f*

Suez Canal N: **the Suez Canal** il canale di Suez

Suff. ABBR (*Brit*) = *Suffolk*

◎**suf·fer** ['sʌfəʳ] VT **1** (*hardship, hunger*) soffrire, patire; (*pain*) provare; (*undergo: loss, setback*) subire; **to suffer pangs of hunger** provare i morsi della fame; **we have suffered a serious blow** abbiamo subito un grosso colpo **2** (*tolerate: opposition, rudeness*) sopportare, tollerare; **she doesn't suffer fools gladly** non sopporta proprio gli stupidi
■VI (*physically*) soffrire; (*be adversely affected: town*) subire danni; (*: regiment*) subire perdite; **to suffer from** (*rheumatism, headaches, deafness*) soffrire di; (*malnutrition, the cold*) soffrire; (*a cold, influenza, bad memory*) avere; **I suffer from hay fever** soffro di raffreddore da fieno; **she suffers from a limp** zoppica; **she was suffering from shock** era sotto shock; **to suffer from the effects of alcohol/a fall** risentire degli effetti dell'alcol/di una caduta; **the house is suffering from neglect** la casa è in stato di abbandono; **your health will suffer** la tua salute ne risentirà; **to suffer for one's sins** scontare i propri peccati; **you'll suffer for it!** la pagherai!

suf·fer·ance ['sʌfərəns] N: **he was only there on sufferance** lì era più che altro sopportato

suf·fer·er ['sʌfərəʳ] N (*Med*): **sufferer (from)** malato(-a) (di); **diabetes sufferers** i diabetici

suf·fer·ing ['sʌfərɪŋ] N (*pain, grief*) sofferenza; (*hardship, deprivation*) privazione *f*

suf·fice [sə'faɪs] (*frm*) VI bastare, essere sufficiente
■VT: **suffice it to say ...** basti dire che...

suf·fi·cien·cy [sə'fɪʃənsɪ] N (*frm*) quantità sufficiente; **to have a sufficiency of paper** avere abbastanza carta

◎**suf·fi·cient** [sə'fɪʃənt] ADJ: **sufficient (for)** sufficiente (per); **that's sufficient** basta così ; **do you have sufficient money?** hai abbastanza soldi?; **a kilo will be sufficient** un chilo sarà sufficiente

suf·fi·cient·ly [sə'fɪʃəntlɪ] ADV sufficientemente, abbastanza; **sufficiently large** (*quantity*) sufficiente; (*number*) abbastanza grande; **she is sufficiently intelligent to understand** è abbastanza *or* sufficientemente intelligente per capire

suf·fix ['sʌfɪks] N suffisso

suf·fo·cate ['sʌfəˌkeɪt] VT, VI soffocare, asfissiare

suf·fo·cat·ing ['sʌfəˌkeɪtɪŋ] ADJ (*heat, atmosphere*) soffocante, opprimente

suf·fo·ca·tion [ˌsʌfə'keɪʃən] N soffocazione *f*, soffocamento; (*Med*) asfissia; **to die from suffocation** morire per asfissia

suf·frage ['sʌfrɪdʒ] N suffragio

suf·fra·gette [ˌsʌfrə'dʒɛt] N suffragetta
▷ www.cjbooks.demon.co.uk/suffrage.htm
▷ www.san.beck.org/GPJ19-Suffragettes.html

suf·fuse [sə'fju:z] VT (*frm*): **to suffuse (with)** (*colour*) tingere (di); **her face was suffused with joy** la gioia si dipingeva sul suo volto; **the room was suffused with light** nella stanza c'era una luce soffusa

◎**sug·ar** ['ʃʊgəʳ] N zucchero
■VT (*tea etc*) zuccherare; **to sugar the pill** (*fig*) indorare la pillola

sugar basin, sugar bowl N zuccheriera

sugar beet N barbabietola da zucchero

sugar cane N canna da zucchero

sugar-coated ['ʃʊgəˌkəʊtɪd] ADJ ricoperto(-a) di zucchero

sugar daddy [-'dædɪ] N (*fam*) vecchio amante *m* danaroso

sug·ared ['ʃʊgəd] ADJ: **sugared almonds** confetti *mpl* alla mandorla

sugar-free ['ʃʊgəˌfri:], **sug·ar·less** ['ʃʊgəlɪs] ADJ senza zucchero

sugar loaf N pan *m* di zucchero

sugar lump N zolletta di zucchero

sugar maple N acero canadese

sugar plantation N piantagione *f* di canne da zucchero

sugar refinery N raffineria di zucchero

sugar tongs NPL mollette *fpl* da zucchero

sug·ary ['ʃʊgərɪ] ADJ (*food etc*) zuccherato(-a), zuccherino(-a); (*fig: sentimental*) sdolcinato(-a), stucchevole

◎**sug·gest** [sə'dʒɛst] VT (*gen*) suggerire, proporre; (*evoke*) indicare, far pensare a; **to suggest doing sth** proporre *or* suggerire di fare qc; **it was you who suggested coming** sei stato tu a voler venire; **she suggested going out for a pizza** ha proposto di andare a mangiare la pizza; **he suggested (that) they should come too** ha proposto *or* suggerito che venissero anche loro; **I suggested they set off early** ho consigliato loro di partire presto; **this suggests that ...** questo fa pensare *or* indica che...; **what are you trying to suggest?** cosa stai cercando di insinuare?; **nothing suggests itself** non mi viene in mente niente; **what do you suggest I do?** cosa mi suggerisci di fare?

sug·gest·ible [sə'dʒɛstɪbəl] ADJ (*person*) suggestionabile, influenzabile

◎**sug·ges·tion** [sə'dʒɛstʃən] N **1** suggerimento, proposta; **an interesting suggestion** una proposta interessante; **to make suggestions** avanzare delle proposte; **if I may make** *or* **offer a suggestion** se mi è concesso avanzare una proposta; **my suggestion is that ...** propongo *or* suggerisco che...; **at sb's suggestion** su *or* dietro suggerimento di qn; **there's no suggestion of** non c'è niente che indichi *or* che faccia pensare a **2** (*trace*): **a suggestion of** un'idea di

sug·ges·tive [sə'dʒɛstɪv] ADJ **1** (*remark*) spinto(-a); (*look*) indecente **2** (*evocative*): **to be suggestive of** far pensare a, evocare; richiamare; **a style suggestive of Conrad** uno stile che richiama Conrad

sui·cid·al [ˌsʊɪˈsaɪdl] ADJ suicida; (*fig*) fatale, disastroso(-a); **I was feeling suicidal** volevo suicidarmi

◎ **sui·cide** [ˈsʊɪsaɪd] N **1** (*also fig*) suicidio; **to attempt suicide** tentare il suicidio; **to commit suicide** suicidarsi; **a case of attempted suicide** un caso di tentato suicidio **2** (*person*) suicida *m/f*

suicide attempt, suicide bid N tentato suicidio

suicide bomber N attentatore(-trice) suicida

suicide bombing N attentato suicida

suicide note N biglietto scritto prima di suicidarsi

suicide pact N patto suicida

◎ **suit** [suːt] N **1** (*for man*) abito; (*for woman*) tailleur *m inv*; (*for bathing*) costume *m*; (*astronaut's*) tuta; **a suit of armour** un'armatura **2** (*lawsuit*) causa; **to bring a suit against sb** intentare causa a qn **3** (*Cards*) colore *m*, seme *m*; **to follow suit** (*fig*) fare altrettanto
■ VT **1** (*adapt*): **to suit (to)** adattare (a); **to suit one's language to one's audience** usare un linguaggio adatto a chi ascolta; **to suit the action to the word** mettere in pratica le proprie parole; **to be suited to sth** (*suitable for*) essere adatto(-a) a qc; **they are well suited (to each other)** stanno bene insieme **2** (*be acceptable: time, day*) andare bene a; (: *food, climate*) fare per; (: *clothes, colour*) stare bene a; **what time would suit you?** a che ora ti andrebbe bene?; **that dress really suits you** quel vestito ti sta benissimo; **that suits me (down to the ground)** per me va benissimo; **it doesn't suit me to leave now** non mi va di partire ora; **the post suited her perfectly** il lavoro faceva proprio per lei **3** (*please*) contentare; **suit yourself whether you do it** *or* **not** se vuoi farlo fallo, se no lascia perdere; **suit yourself!** fa' come ti pare!

suit·abil·ity [ˌsuːtəˈbɪlɪtɪ] N (*for job*) idoneità; **I doubt the suitability of this book for children** dubito che sia un libro adatto ai bambini

◎ **suit·able** [ˈsuːtəbl] ADJ (*gen*) adatto(-a); **a suitable time** un'ora conveniente; **I haven't anything suitable to wear** non ho niente di adatto da mettermi; **the most suitable man for the job** l'uomo più adatto a questo lavoro; **we found somebody suitable** abbiamo trovato la persona adatta; **the film is not suitable for children** non è un film adatto ai bambini; **would tomorrow be suitable?** andrebbe bene domani?

suit·ably [ˈsuːtəblɪ] ADV (*dress*) in modo adatto; (*thank*) adeguatamente; **he was suitably impressed** ha giustamente ricevuto un'impressione favorevole; **to reply suitably** dare una risposta adeguata

suit·case [ˈsuːtˌkeɪs] N valigia

suite [swiːt] N (*of rooms*) appartamento; (: *in hotel*) suite *f inv*; (*Mus*) suite *f inv*; (*furniture*): **dining room suite** arredo *or* mobilia per la sala da pranzo; **a bathroom suite** i sanitari e gli arredi per il bagno; **a bedroom suite** una camera da letto; **a three-piece suite** un divano e due poltrone; **a suite at the Paris Hilton** una suite all'Hilton di Parigi

suit·ing [ˈsuːtɪŋ] N (*material*) tessuto per abiti da uomo

suit·or [ˈsuːtəʳ] N corteggiatore *m*, spasimante *m*

sul·fate [ˈsʌlfeɪt] N (*Am*) = **sulphate**

sul·fur *etc* [ˈsʌlfəʳ] (*Am*) = **sulphur** *etc*

sulk [sʌlk] VI tenere il broncio *or* il muso
■ N: **to have the sulks** tenere il broncio *or* il muso

sulki·ly [ˈsʌlkɪlɪ] ADV con aria imbronciata

sulki·ness [ˈsʌlkɪnɪs] N musoneria

sulky [ˈsʌlkɪ] ADJ (*comp* **-ier**, *superl* **-iest**) imbronciato(-a)

sul·len [ˈsʌlən] ADJ indisponente; (*sky*) cupo(-a); **to have a sullen face** avere il viso imbronciato

sul·len·ly [ˈsʌlənlɪ] ADV in modo indisponente

sul·len·ness [ˈsʌlənnɪs] N (*see adj*) musoneria, scontrosità; arroganza

sul·ly [ˈsʌlɪ] VT (*frm*) macchiare

sul·phate [ˈsʌlfeɪt] N solfato; **copper sulphate** solfato di rame

sul·phide [ˈsʌlfaɪd] N solfuro

sul·phite [ˈsʌlfaɪt] N solfito

sul·phona·mide [sʌlˈfɒnəˌmaɪd] N sulfamidico

sul·phur [ˈsʌlfəʳ] N zolfo

sulphur dioxide N anidride *f* solforosa, biossido di zolfo

sul·phu·ric [sʌlˈfjʊərɪk] ADJ: **sulphuric acid** acido solforico

sul·phur·ous [ˈsʌlfərəs] ADJ solforoso(-a); **sulphurous acid** acido solforoso

sul·tan [ˈsʌltən] N sultano

sul·tana [sʌlˈtɑːnə] N (*fruit*) uva sultanina *f inv*

sul·try [ˈsʌltrɪ] ADJ (*weather*) afoso(-a), opprimente; (*woman, character*) ardente, sensuale

◎ **sum** [sʌm] N (*piece of arithmetic*) somma, addizione *f*; (*amount of money*) somma; **a sum of money** una somma di denaro; **we do sums** facciamo le addizioni; **the sum of 6 and 4 is 10** 6 più 4 fa 10; **that is the sum (total) of his achievements** questo è tutto quello che ha fatto
► **sum up** VT + ADV (*review*) riassumere, ricapitolare; (*evaluate rapidly*) valutare, giudicare; **to sum up an argument** riassumere una discussione; **she quickly summed him up** capì subito che tipo era; **he summed up the situation quickly** valutò subito la situazione
■ VI + ADV riassumere; **to sum up ...** per riassumere..., riassumendo...

Su·ma·tra [sʊˈmɑːtrə] N Sumatra

sum·ma [ˈsʊmɑː] N summa

sum·mari·ly [ˈsʌmərɪlɪ] ADV sommariamente

sum·ma·rize [ˈsʌməˌraɪz] VT riassumere, riepilogare

sum·mary [ˈsʌmərɪ] N riassunto
■ ADJ (*dismissal, treatment, justice*) sommario(-a); (*perusal*) sbrigativo(-a)

sum·mat [ˈsʌmət] PRON (*Brit dial*) qualcosa

sum·ma·tion [sʌˈmeɪʃən] N (*frm: summary*) sommario; (: *total*) somma, totale *m*

◎ **sum·mer** [ˈsʌməʳ] N estate *f*; **in (the) summer** d'estate; **in the summer of 1995** nell'estate del 1995; **last/next summer** l'estate scorsa/prossima
■ ADJ (*gen*) estivo(-a), d'estate; **summer clothes** abiti estivi; **the summer holidays** le vacanze estive

summer camp N (*Am*) colonia estiva

summer·house [ˈsʌməˌhaʊs] N (*in garden*) padiglione *m*

summer lightning N temporale *m* estivo

summer school N corsi *mpl* estivi

summer solstice N solstizio d'estate

summer·time [ˈsʌməˌtaɪm] N (*season*) stagione *f* estiva, estate *f*

summer time N (*Brit: daylight saving time*) ora legale

sum·mery [ˈsʌmərɪ] ADJ estivo(-a)

summing-up [ˌsʌmɪŋˈʌp] N (*Law*) ricapitolazione *f* del processo (*fatta dal giudice alla giuria*)

◎ **sum·mit** [ˈsʌmɪt] N cima, vetta, sommità *f inv*; (*fig*) culmine *m*; (*Pol*) vertice *m*, summit *m inv*; **the NATO summit in Rome** il vertice della NATO a Roma; **after**

Ss

six hours we reached the summit dopo sei ore abbiamo raggiunto la cima
summit conference N incontro al vertice
sum·mon ['sʌmən] VT *(meeting)* convocare; *(aid, doctor, servant etc)* chiamare; *(Law)*: **to summon a witness** citare un testimone
▶ **summon up** VT + ADV *(courage, interest)* trovare; **to summon up all one's courage** farsi coraggio, armarsi di coraggio; **to summon up all one's strength** fare appello a tutte le proprie forze; **I couldn't summon up the courage to tell him** non ho trovato il coraggio di dirglielo; **I summoned up my courage** ho raccolto il coraggio
sum·mons ['sʌmənz] N *(pl* **-es***)* *(Law)* citazione *f*, mandato di comparizione; **to serve a summons on sb** notificare una citazione a qn
■VT citare (in giudizio)
sumo ['su:məʊ], **sumo wrestling** N sumo *m inv*
sump [sʌmp] N *(Aut)* coppa dell'olio, carter *m inv*
sump·tu·ous ['sʌmptjʊəs] ADJ sontuoso(-a)
sump·tu·ous·ly ['sʌmptjʊəslɪ] ADV sontuosamente
sump·tu·ous·ness ['sʌmptjʊəsnɪs] N sontuosità
Sun. ABBR (= **Sunday**) dom. (= *domenica*)
◎**sun** [sʌn] N sole *m*; **to get up with the sun** alzarsi allo spuntar del sole; **the sun is in my eyes** ho il sole negli occhi; **in the sun** al sole; **you've caught the sun!** come sei abbronzato!; **a place in the sun** *(also fig)* un posto al sole; **they have everything under the sun** hanno tutto ciò che possono desiderare; **there's nothing new under the sun** non c'è niente di nuovo sotto il sole
■VT: **to sun o.s.** godersi il sole
sun·bathe ['sʌn,beɪð] VI prendere il sole
sun·bather ['sʌn,beɪðə^r] N chi prende il sole
sun·bathing ['sʌn,beɪðɪŋ] N bagni *mpl* di sole; **to go sunbathing on the beach** andare a prendere il sole sulla spiaggia
sun·beam ['sʌn,bi:m] N raggio di sole
sun·bed ['sʌn,bɛd] N lettino solare
sun·belt ['sʌn,bɛlt] N: **the sunbelt** il sud, la zona più calda

SUNBELT

Gli Stati americani meridionali e sudoccidentali, dalla Carolina del Nord alla California, costituiscono la **Sunbelt**, così chiamata per il suo clima mite e soleggiato. Al nome si associa anche un rinnovato sviluppo economico, con aumento di popolazione e di potere politico. Gli stati settentrionali e nordoccidentali appartengono invece alla "Frostbelt", così chiamata per via dei lunghi inverni freddi, o "Rustbelt", per la presenza un tempo di stabilimenti industriali, ora perlopiù in declino.

sun·blind ['sʌn,blaɪnd] N tenda da sole
sun·block ['sʌn,blɒk] N crema a schermo totale
sun·burn ['sʌn,bɜ:n] N *(painful)* scottatura; *(tan)* abbronzatura
sun·burnt, **sun·burned** ['sʌn,bɜ:nt] ADJ *(tanned)* abbronzato(-a); *(painfully)* scottato(-a); **sunburnt shoulders** spalle scottate dal sole; **to get sunburnt** scottarsi
sun cream N crema solare
sun·dae ['sʌndeɪ] N coppa di gelato guarnita
Sun·day ['sʌndɪ] N domenica; **he'll never do it in a month of Sundays** non ci riuscirà mai e poi mai; *for usage see* **Tuesday**
Sunday best N abito della domenica
Sunday paper N giornale *m* della domenica

SUNDAY PAPERS

I **Sunday papers** sono i giornali che escono di domenica. Sono generalmente corredati da supplementi e riviste di argomento culturale, sportivo e di attualità e hanno un'alta tiratura.
▷ www.totaltravel.co.uk/library/britain/uk-newspapers/

Sunday school N ≈ scuola di catechismo
sun·deck ['sʌn,dɛk] N ponte *m* scoperto
sun·dial ['sʌn,daɪəl] N meridiana
sun·down ['sʌn,daʊn] N *(esp Am)* tramonto
sun-drenched ['sʌn,drɛntʃt] ADJ inondato(-a) dal sole
sun-dried ['sʌn,draɪd] ADJ essiccato(-a) al sole; **sun-dried tomatoes** pomodori *mpl* secchi
sun·dry ['sʌndrɪ] ADJ vari(e), diversi(e); **all and sundry** tutti quanti
■**sundries** NPL *(items)* varie *fpl*; *(Comm)* articoli *mpl* vari
sun·flower ['sʌn,flaʊə^r] N girasole *m*
sunflower oil N olio di semi di girasole
sunflower seeds NPL semi *mpl* di girasole
sung [sʌŋ] PP *of* **sing**
sun·glasses ['sʌn,glɑ:sɪz] NPL occhiali *mpl* da sole
sun·hat ['sʌn,hæt] N cappello *(per proteggersi dal sole)*
sunk [sʌŋk] PP *of* **sink**
sunk·en ['sʌŋkən] ADJ *(ship)* affondato(-a); *(eyes, cheeks)* infossato(-a); *(bath)* incassato(-a)
sun·lamp ['sʌn,læmp] N lampada a raggi UVA
sun·less ['sʌnlɪs] ADJ senza sole
sun·light ['sʌn,laɪt] N (luce *f* del) sole *m*; **in the sunlight** alla luce del sole
sun·lit ['sʌn,lɪt] ADJ illuminato(-a) dal sole
sun·ny ['sʌnɪ] ADJ *(comp* **-ier**, *superl* **-iest***)* **1** *(place, room etc)* assolato(-a), soleggiato(-a); *(day)* di sole; **it is sunny** c'è il sole; **the outlook is sunny** *(Met)* si prevede il sole **2** *(fig: person, disposition)* allegro(-a); *(: smile)* radioso(-a)
sun·rise ['sʌn,raɪz] N: **at sunrise** allo spuntar del sole; **before sunrise** prima dell'alba
sun·roof ['sʌn,ru:f] N *(on building)* tetto a terrazzo; *(Aut)* tettuccio apribile
sun·screen ['sʌn,skri:n] N *(protective ingredient)* filtro solare; *(cream, lotion)* crema *(or* lozione *f)* solare protettiva
sun·set ['sʌn,sɛt] N tramonto
sun·shade ['sʌn,ʃeɪd] N *(portable)* parasole *m inv*; *(for eyes)* visiera; *(in car)* aletta parasole; *(awning)* tenda da sole
sun·shine ['sʌn,ʃaɪn] N (luce *f* del) sole *m*; **in the sunshine** al sole; **hours of sunshine** *(Met)* ore *fpl* di sole; **six hours of sunshine** sei ore di sole; **she's a little ray of sunshine** *(iro)* è una dolce creatura
sun·specs ['sʌn,spɛks] NPL *(fam)* occhiali *mpl* da sole
sun·spot ['sʌn,spɒt] N *(Astron)* macchia solare
sun·stroke ['sʌn,strəʊk] N colpo di sole, insolazione *f*; **to get sunstroke** prendere un'insolazione
sun·suit ['sʌn,su:t] N prendisole *m inv*
sun·tan ['sʌn,tæn] N abbronzatura, tintarella; **her usual suntan** la sua solita abbronzatura
suntan cream N crema solare
suntan lotion N lozione *f* abbronzante
sun·tanned ['sʌn,tænd] ADJ abbronzato(-a)
suntan oil N olio solare

sun·trap ['sʌn,træp] N angolo molto assolato
sun umbrella N ombrellone *m*
sun·up ['sʌnʌp] N *(fam)* alba; **to work sunup to sundown** lavorare dall'alba al tramonto
◎ **su·per** ['su:pəʳ] ADJ *(fam)* fantastico(-a), splendido(-a); **we had a super time** ci siamo divertiti da morire
super... ['su:pəʳ] PREF super..., sovra..., iper...; **supersensitive** ipersensibile
supera·bun·dance ['su:pərə,bʌndəns] N sovrabbondanza
super·an·nu·at·ed [,su:pər'ænjʊ,eɪtɪd] *(frm)* ADJ *(old-fashioned)* démodé *inv*, passato(-a) di moda; *(antiquated)* antiquato(-a)
super·an·nua·tion [,su:pər,ænjʊ'eɪʃən] N *(pension)* pensione *f*; *(contribution)* contributi *mpl* pensionistici
◎ **su·perb** [su:'pɜ:b] ADJ *(quality)* superbo(-a); *(control, confidence)* magnifico(-a)
su·perb·ly [su:'pɜ:blɪ] ADV *(see adj)* superbamente; magnificamente
Super Bowl N *(American football)* super bowl *m inv*
super·bug ['su:pə,bʌg] N *(fam: Med)* batterio resistente agli antibiotici
super·charged ['su:pə,tʃɑ:dʒd] ADJ *(Aut)* sovralimentato(-a)
super·char·ger ['su:pə,tʃɑ:dʒəʳ] N compressore *m*
super·cili·ous [,su:pə'sɪlɪəs] ADJ *(frm)* altezzoso(-a), sprezzante
super·cili·ous·ly [,su:pə'sɪlɪəslɪ] ADV *(frm)* altezzosamente, sprezzantemente
super·cili·ous·ness [,su:pə'sɪlɪəsnɪs] N *(frm)* alterigia
super·con·duc·tiv·ity ['su:pə,kɒndʌk'tɪvɪtɪ] N superconduttività
super·con·duc·tor [,su:pəkɒn'dʌktəʳ] N superconduttore *m*
super·ego [,su:pər'i:gəʊ] N *(Psych)* super-ego *m inv*, super-io *m inv*
super·fi·cial [,su:pə'fɪʃəl] ADJ superficiale
super·fi·ci·al·ity [,su:pəfɪʃɪ'ælɪtɪ] N superficialità
super·fi·cial·ly [,su:pə'fɪʃəlɪ] ADV superficialmente
super·flu·ity [,su:pə'flʊɪtɪ] N sovrabbondanza
super·flu·ous [su'pɜ:flʊəs] ADJ superfluo(-a); **he felt rather superfluous** si sentì di troppo
super·flu·ous·ly [su'pɜ:flʊəslɪ] ADV inutilmente
super·glue ['su:pə,glu:] N colla a presa rapida
super·grass ['su:pə,grɑ:s] N pentito(-a)
super·high·way ['su:pə,haɪweɪ] N *(Am)* autostrada; **the information superhighway** l'autostrada telematica
super·hu·man [,su:pə'hju:mən] ADJ sovrumano(-a)
super·im·pose [,su:pərɪm'pəʊz] VT: **to superimpose (on)** sovrapporre (a)
super·in·tend [,su:pərɪn'tɛnd] VT *(work, shop, department)* dirigere, soprintendere; *(exam)* sorvegliare, vigilare; *(production)* controllare; *(counting of votes)* presiedere a
super·in·ten·dent [,su:pərɪn'tɛndənt] N soprintendente *m/f*, direttore(-trice); *(Police)* ≈ commissario (capo) di Pubblica Sicurezza
◎ **su·peri·or** [sʊ'pɪərɪəʳ] ADJ *(gen)*: **superior to** superiore a; *(Comm: goods, quality)* di prim'ordine, superiore; *(smug: person)* che fa il/la superiore; *(: smile, air)* di superiorità; *(: remark)* altezzoso(-a); **superior number** *(Typ)* esponente *m*; **superior technology** tecnologia di prim'ordine; **of superior quality** di qualità superiore; **he felt rather superior** si sentì importante
■ N *(in rank)* superiore *m/f*; **Mother Superior** *(Rel)* (madre *f*) superiora

su·peri·or·ity [sʊ,pɪərɪ'ɒrɪtɪ] N superiorità
superiority complex N *(fam)* complesso di superiorità
super·la·tive [su'pɜ:lətɪv] ADJ *(superb: quality, achievement)* eccellente; *(: indifference)* sommo(-a); *(Gram)* superlativo
■ N *(Gram)* superlativo; **to talk in superlatives** fare largo uso di superlativi nel parlare
super·la·tive·ly [su'pɜ:lətɪvlɪ] ADV *(good, intelligent)* estremamente; *(play, perform)* superlativamente; **to be superlatively fit** essere in ottima forma
super·man ['su:pə,mæn] N *(pl* **-men***)* superuomo
◎ **super·mar·ket** ['su:pə,mɑ:kɪt] N supermercato
super·mini ['su:pə,mɪnɪ] N utilitaria comoda
super·model ['su:pə,mɒdəl] N top model *m/f inv*
super·natu·ral [,su:pə'nætʃərəl] ADJ, N soprannaturale *(m)*
super·nova [,su:pə'nəʊvə] N supernova
super·nu·mer·ary [,su:pə'nju:mərərɪ] ADJ, N soprannumerario(-a)
super·pow·er ['su:pə,paʊəʳ] N *(Pol)* superpotenza
super·satu·rat·ed [,su:pə'sætʃə,reɪtɪd] ADJ *(solution)* soprassaturo(-a)
super·script ['su:pə,skrɪpt] N esponente *m*
super·sede [,su:pə'si:d] VT sostituire, soppiantare; **a superseded method** un metodo sorpassato
super·son·ic [,su:pə'sɒnɪk] ADJ supersonico(-a)
super·star ['su:pəstɑ:ʳ] N superstar *f inv*
super·state ['su:pə,steɪt] N *(Pol)* superpotenza
super·sti·tion [,su:pə'stɪʃən] N superstizione *f*
super·sti·tious [,su:pə'stɪʃəs] ADJ superstizioso(-a)
super·sti·tious·ly [,su:pə'stɪʃəslɪ] ADV superstiziosamente
super·store ['su:pə,stɔ:ʳ] N *(Brit)* ipermercato
super·struc·ture ['su:pə,strʌktʃəʳ] N sovrastruttura
super·tank·er ['su:pə,tæŋkəʳ] N superpetroliera
super·tax ['su:pə,tæks] N soprattassa
super·vise ['su:pə,vaɪz] VT *(person)* sorvegliare, vigilare; *(work, organization, research)* soprintendere a
super·vi·sion [,su:pə'vɪʒən] N *(of activity, process)* supervisione *f*; *(of person)* sorveglianza; **under medical supervision** sotto controllo medico; **they work under supervision** lavorano sotto sorveglianza
super·vi·sor ['su:pə,vaɪzəʳ] N sorvegliante *m/f*, soprintendente *m/f*, supervisore *m*; *(Univ)* relatore(-trice); *(in shop)* capocommesso(-a); **a supervisor in the factory** un sorvegliante della fabbrica; **he's a supervisor in a big store** è capocommesso in un grande magazzino
super·vi·sory ['su:pə,vaɪzərɪ] ADJ di sorveglianza, di vigilanza
super·woman ['su:pə,wʊmən] N superdonna
su·pine ['su:paɪn] ADJ supino(-a)
sup·per ['sʌpəʳ] N *(evening meal)* cena; *(late-night snack)* spuntino; **to have supper** cenare
sup·plant [sə'plɑ:nt] VT soppiantare
sup·ple ['sʌpl] ADJ *(comp* **-r**, *superl* **-st***)* elastico(-a), flessibile; *(person)* agile; **supple leather** morbido cuoio
sup·plement [*n* 'sʌplɪmənt; *vb* ,sʌplɪ'mɛnt] N *(also Press)* supplemento
■ VT *(diet etc)* integrare; *(income)* arrotondare; *(information)* completare
sup·plemen·ta·ry [,sʌplɪ'mɛntərɪ] ADJ supplementare
sup·ple·ness ['sʌplnɪs] N *(see adj)* elasticità, flessibilità; agilità
sup·pli·cant ['sʌplɪkənt] N *(frm)* supplice *m/f*
sup·pli·ca·tion [,sʌplɪ'keɪʃən] N *(frm)* supplica

Ss

supplier [sə'plaɪəʳ] N (*Comm*) fornitore(-trice)
◎**sup·ply¹** [sə'plaɪ] N (*delivery*) fornitura; (*stock*) provvista; (*Tech*) alimentazione *f*; **the electricity/water/gas supply** l'erogazione *f* di corrente/d'acqua/di gas; **to cut off the water supply** tagliare l'acqua; **a supply of paper** una provvista di carta; **the supply of fuel to the engine** l'afflusso di carburante al motore; **supply and demand** (*Econ*) domanda e offerta; **to be in short supply** scarseggiare, essere scarso(-a); **supplies** NPL (*food*) viveri *mpl*; (*Mil*) approvvigionamenti *mpl*, rifornimenti *mpl*; (: *food only*) sussistenza; **medical supplies** materiale *msg* sanitario; **office supplies** forniture *fpl* per ufficio
■VT (*goods, materials, information etc*) fornire; (*fill: need, want*) soddisfare; **to supply sth (with sth)** (*system, machine*) alimentare qc (con qc); **to supply sb (with sth)** (*with goods*) fornire a qn qc, rifornire qn di qc; (*Mil*) approvvigionare qn (di qc); **she supplied us with the necessary evidence** ci ha fornito le prove necessarie; **the centre supplied us with all the equipment** il centro ci ha fornito tutta l'attrezzatura; **most towns are supplied with electricity** quasi tutte le città sono dotate di elettricità; **who will supply their needs?** chi farà fronte ai loro bisogni?
■ADJ (*ship, train*) di rifornimento
sup·ply² ['sʌplɪ] ADV (*bend*) agilmente
supply teacher N (*Brit*) supplente *m/f*
◎**sup·port** [sə'pɔ:t] N (*gen*) sostegno, appoggio; (*object*) sostegno, supporto; **she was a great support to me** mi è stata di grande conforto; **moral support** aiuto morale; **he has no visible means of support** non è ben chiaro come si mantenga; **to speak in support of a candidate** parlare a favore di un candidato; **to lean on sb for support** (*also fig*) appoggiarsi a qn; **they stopped work in support (of)** hanno interrotto l'attività lavorativa per solidarietà (con); **our support comes from the workers** sono gli operai ad appoggiarci; **there's a great deal of support for his views** le sue opinioni sono ampiamente condivise
■VT (*gen*) sostenere, sorreggere; (*fig: person: emotionally*) sostenere; (: *financially*) mantenere; (: *proposal, project*) appoggiare; (: *Sport*) (: *team*) tifare per; (: *corroborate: evidence*) confermare, convalidare; **to support o.s.** (*financially*) mantenersi; **my friends have always supported me** i miei amici mi hanno sempre appoggiato; **what team do you support?** per quale squadra tifi?; **she had to support five children on her own** ha dovuto mantenere cinque figli da sola; **the pillars that support the ceiling** i pilastri che sostengono il soffitto; **all that is necessary to support life** tutto ciò che rende possibile l'esistenza di una forma di vita
◎**sup·port·er** [sə'pɔ:təʳ] N (*of proposal, project*) sostenitore(-trice); (*Pol etc*) sostenitore(-trice), fautore(-trice); (*Sport*) tifoso(-a); **a Liverpool supporter** un tifoso del Liverpool; **a supporter of the Labour Party** un simpatizzante del partito Laburista; **a major supporter of the tax reform plan** un importante sostenitore del piano di riforma fiscale
support group N gruppo di sostegno
sup·port·ing [sə'pɔ:tɪŋ] ADJ **1** (*Theatre, Cine: role, actor, actress*) non protagonista **2** (*wall*) sostegno
sup·port·ive [sə'pɔ:tɪv] ADJ **1** (*person*): **to be very supportive (towards sb)** dare il proprio appoggio (a qn); (*emotionally*) essere di grande conforto (per qn); **I have a supportive family/husband** la mia famiglia/mio marito mi appoggia **2** (*gesture, effort*) di aiuto
◎**sup·pose** [sə'pəʊz] VT **1** (*assume, believe*): **I suppose she'll come** suppongo che verrà; **I don't suppose she'll come** non credo che venga; **I suppose she won't come** penso che non verrà; **I suppose so/not** credo di sì /di no; **I don't suppose so** non credo; **I suppose he's late** suppongo che sia in ritardo; **you're going to accept, I suppose?** accetti, immagino?; **I don't suppose you could lend me £10?** *or* **I suppose you couldn't lend me £10?** non potresti per caso prestarmi dieci sterlina?; **he's supposed to be an expert** dicono che sia un esperto, passa per un esperto; **it's supposed to be ...** sembra che + *sub*; **it's supposed to be the best hotel in the city** sembra che sia il miglior albergo della città **2** (*assume as hypothesis*) supporre + *sub*, mettere + *sub*; **let us suppose that ...** supponiamo che..., mettiamo che...; **supposing you won the lottery ...** mettiamo che tu vinca alla lotteria...; **but just suppose he's right** ma supponi *or* metti che abbia ragione; **even supposing (that) it were true** anche nel caso (che) fosse vero; **always supposing (that) he comes** ammesso e non concesso che venga; **suppose** *or* **supposing it rains, what shall we do?** metti che piova, cosa facciamo?; **suppose she doesn't come?** e se non venisse? **3** (*in passive: ought*): **to be supposed to do sth** essere tenuto(-a) a fare qc; **he's supposed to ...** dovrebbe...; **he's supposed to leave on Sunday** dovrebbe partire domenica; **you're not supposed to smoke in the toilet** non è consentito fumare nel bagno; **you're not supposed to do that** non bisogna farlo **4** (*in imperative: I suggest*): **suppose you do it now?** e se lo facessi adesso?; **suppose we change the subject?** e se parlassimo d'altro? **5** (*presuppose*) presupporre
◎**sup·posed** [sə'pəʊzd] ADJ (*presumed*) presunto(-a); (*so-called*) cosiddetto(-a)
sup·pos·ed·ly [sə'pəʊzɪdlɪ] ADV (*presumably*) presumibilmente; (*seemingly*) apparentemente
sup·pos·ing [sə'pəʊzɪŋ] CONJ se, ammesso che + *sub*
sup·po·si·tion [ˌsʌpə'zɪʃən] N (*frm*) supposizione *f*, ipotesi *f inv*; **on the supposition that** partendo dal presupposto che + *sub*
sup·posi·tory [sə'pɒzɪtərɪ] N suppositorio
sup·press [sə'prɛs] VT (*emotion, revolt*) reprimere, soffocare; (*scandal*) mettere a tacere, soffocare; (*yawn, smile*) trattenere; (*publication*) sopprimere; (*news, the truth*) tacere; (*evidence*) occultare
sup·pres·sion [sə'prɛʃən] N (*of emotions etc*) repressione *f*; (*of scandal*) soffocamento; (*of truth*) il tacere; (*of evidence*) occultamento; (*of publication*) soppressione *f*
sup·pres·sor [sə'prɛsəʳ] N (*Elec*) soppressore *m*
sup·pu·rate ['sʌpjʊˌreɪt] VI suppurare
supra·na·tion·al [ˌsu:prə'næʃənl] ADJ sopranazionale
su·prema·cy [sʊ'prɛməsɪ] N supremazia
◎**su·preme** [sʊ'pri:m] ADJ (*in authority*) supremo(-a); (*very great*) sommo(-a), massimo(-a); **with supreme indifference** con somma indifferenza; **the supreme sacrifice** il sacrificio supremo; **to reign supreme** (*fig*) dominare
Supreme Court N (*Am*): **the Supreme Court** la corte suprema
su·preme·ly [sʊ'pri:mlɪ] ADV estremamente, sommamente
su·pre·mo [sʊ'pri:məʊ] N (*Brit fam*) grande capo
Supt ABBR (*Police*) = **superintendent**
sur·charge ['sɜ:ˌtʃɑ:dʒ] N (*gen*) supplemento, sovrapprezzo; (*tax*) soprattassa
■VT far pagare un sovrapprezzo (*or* una soprattassa)

surd [sɜːd] N (*Math*) espressione *f* irrazionale

◎**sure** [ʃʊəʳ] ADJ (*comp* **-r**, *superl* **-st**) (*gen*) sicuro(-a); (*definite, convinced*) sicuro(-a), certo(-a); **are you sure?** sei sicuro?; **it's sure to rain** pioverà di sicuro; **I'm sure it's going to rain** sono sicuro che pioverà; **I'm not sure how/why/when** non so bene come/perché/ quando + *sub*; **be sure to tell me if you see him** mi raccomando, dimmi se lo vedi; **to be sure of sth** essere sicuro(-a) di qc; **to be sure of o.s.** essere sicuro(-a) di sé; **to be sure of one's facts** essere sicuro(-a) dei fatti; **you can be sure of a good time there** puoi essere sicuro che ti divertirai; **to make sure of sth** assicurarsi di qc; **be** *or* **make sure you do it right** bada di farlo bene; **I'll find out for sure** vedrò di accertarmene; **I think I locked up, but I'll just make sure** credo di aver chiuso a chiave, ma voglio assicurarmene; **to make sure that** assicurarsi che; **I'm going to make sure the door's locked** voglio assicurarmi che la porta sia chiusa a chiave; **just to make sure** per sicurezza; **do you know for sure?** ne sei proprio sicuro?; **she'll leave, for sure** senza dubbio partirà; **I'm sure I don't know** *or* **I don't know, I'm sure** che vuoi che ne sappia io?; **he's a sure thing for president** ha la presidenza assicurata

■ADV: **is that O.K.? — sure!** va bene? — certo! *or* sicuro!; **that sure is pretty** *or* **that's sure pretty** (*Am*) è veramente *or* davvero carino; **sure enough!** (*of course*) sicuro!, senz'altro!; **sure enough** (*predictably*) infatti; **as sure as fate** ovviamente; **as sure as eggs is eggs** *or* **as sure as I'm standing here** e com'è vero Dio

sure-fire [ˈʃʊəˌfaɪəʳ] ADJ (*fam: winner, success*) sicuro(-a)

sure-footed [ʃʊəˈfʊtɪd] ADJ dal passo sicuro

◎**sure·ly** [ˈʃʊəlɪ] ADV (*certainly*) certamente, sicuramente; **surely we've met before?** ma non ci siamo già incontrati?; **surely you don't mean that!** non parlerai sul serio!; **surely you don't believe that?** non ci crederai davvero?; **surely not!** ma non è possibile!

sure·ness [ˈʃʊənɪs] N (*of aim, footing*) sicurezza; (*positiveness*) certezza

sure·ty [ˈʃʊərətɪ] N cauzione *f*; **to go** *or* **stand surety for sb** farsi garante per qn

surf [sɜːf] N (*waves*) cavalloni *mpl*; (*foam*) spuma; **to surf the Net** navigare in Internet

◎**sur·face** [ˈsɜːfɪs] N (*gen*) superficie *f*; (*of road*) piano stradale; **on the surface it seems that ...** (*fig*) superficialmente sembra che...; **we've only scratched the surface** (*fig: of argument, work*) abbiamo appena iniziato

■VT (*road*) asfaltare

■VI (*submarine etc*) risalire in superficie; (*fig: person: after absence*) farsi vivo(-a); (*: from bed*) emergere; **he surfaces in London occasionally** ogni tanto si fa vedere a Londra

■ADJ (*Mil, Naut*) di superficie

surface area N superficie *f*

surface mail N posta ordinaria

sur·face run·off [ˌsɜːfɪsˈrʌnɒf] N (*Geog*) acque *fpl* superficiali

surface tension N (*Phys*) tensione *f* di superficie

surface-to-air missile [ˌsɜːfɪstuˌɛəˈmɪsaɪl] N missile *m* terra aria *inv*

surface-to-surface [ˌsɜːfɪstəˈsɜːfɪs] ADJ (*Mil*) superficie-superficie *inv*

surf·board [ˈsɜːfˌbɔːd] N surf *m inv*

sur·feit [ˈsɜːfɪt] N (*frm*) sovrabbondanza; **a surfeit of** un surplus di

surf·er [ˈsɜːfəʳ] N surfista *m/f*

surf·ing [ˈsɜːfɪŋ], **surf·riding** [ˈsɜːfˌraɪdɪŋ] N surfing *m inv*, surf *m inv*; **to go surfing** fare surf

surge [sɜːdʒ] N (*of sea, sympathy*) ondata; (*of people*) marea; (*Elec*) sovratensione *f* transitoria; **a surge of anger** un impeto di rabbia; **a surge in inflation** un improvviso aumento dell'inflazione; **a surge of optimism** un'ondata di ottimismo

■VI (*water, people*) riversarsi; (*waves*) sollevarsi; (*Elec: power*) aumentare improvvisamente; **to surge into/ over sth** riversarsi in/su qc; **to surge forward** buttarsi avanti; **to surge round sb/sth** accalcarsi intorno a qn/qc; **the blood surged to her cheeks** il sangue le affluì al viso

sur·geon [ˈsɜːdʒən] N chirurgo

Surgeon General N (*Am*): **the Surgeon General** ≈ il ministro della Sanità

◎**sur·gery** [ˈsɜːdʒərɪ] N (*art*) chirurgia; (*operation*) intervento chirurgico; (*Brit Med: consulting room*) ambulatorio; (*: session*) visita ambulatoriale; (*Brit: of MP*) incontri *mpl* con gli elettori; **to undergo surgery** subire un intervento chirurgico

surgery hours NPL (*Brit*) orario *msg* di ambulatorio

sur·gi·cal [ˈsɜːdʒɪkəl] ADJ chirurgico(-a); **surgical cotton** cotone *m* idrofilo; **surgical dressing** medicazione *f*

sur·gi·cal·ly [ˈsɜːdʒɪkəlɪ] ADV chirurgicamente

surgical spirit N (*Brit*) alcol denaturato

surg·ing [ˈsɜːdʒɪŋ] ADJ (*crowd, waves*) impetuoso(-a)

sur·li·ness [ˈsɜːlɪnɪs] N scontrosità

sur·ly [ˈsɜːlɪ] ADJ (*comp* **-ier**, *superl* **-iest**) burbero(-a), scontroso(-a)

sur·mise [*n* ˈsɜːmaɪz *or* sɜːˈmaɪz; *vb* sɜːˈmaɪz] N congettura

■VT supporre, congetturare; **I surmised as much** me lo immaginavo

sur·mount [sɜːˈmaʊnt] VT (*difficulty*) sormontare

sur·mount·able [sɜːˈmaʊntəbl] ADJ sormontabile

sur·name [ˈsɜːˌneɪm] N cognome *m*

sur·pass [sɜːˈpɑːs] VT (*expectations, person*) superare; **it surpassed all his hopes** è andata meglio di quanto sperasse

sur·plice [ˈsɜːpləs] N (*Rel*) cotta

◎**sur·plus** [ˈsɜːpləs] N (*Fin, Comm*) surplus *m inv*; **to have a surplus of sth** avere qc in eccedenza; **labour surplus** eccedenza di manodopera; **trade surplus** surplus commerciale

■ADJ eccedente, d'avanzo; (*Fin, Comm*) di sovrappiù, in eccedenza; **surplus stock** merce *f* in sovrappiù; **it is surplus to our requirements** eccede i nostri bisogni

◎**sur·prise** [səˈpraɪz] N (*gen*) sorpresa; (*astonishment*) stupore *m*, sorpresa; **it came as quite a surprise to me** fu una grande sorpresa per me; **a look of surprise** uno sguardo di sorpresa; **much to my surprise** *or* **to my great surprise** con mia grande sorpresa; **to take by surprise** (*person*) cogliere di sorpresa; (*Mil: town, fort*) attaccare di sorpresa; **to give sb a surprise** fare una sorpresa a qn

■VT (*astonish*) sorprendere, stupire; (*catch unawares*) sorprendere, cogliere di sorpresa; **he surprised me into accepting** ho accettato perché colto alla sprovvista

■ADJ (*present, visit*) inaspettato(-a); (*attack*) di sorpresa

◎**surprised** ADJ: **to be surprised at** essere sorpreso(-a) di; **he was surprised to learn that ...** fu sorpreso di sapere che...; **I'm surprised at you!** mi meraviglio di te!; **I wouldn't be surprised if he accepts** non mi

Ss

sorprenderebbe se accettasse; **don't be surprised if he comes** non ti meravigliare se viene

◎**sur·pris·ing** [sə'praɪzɪŋ] ADJ sorprendente

sur·pris·ing·ly [sə'praɪzɪŋlɪ] ADV (*good, bad*) sorprendentemente; **(somewhat) surprisingly, he agreed** cosa (alquanto) sorprendente, ha accettato; **not surprisingly he refused** come c'era da aspettarsi ha rifiutato

sur·re·al [sə'rɪəl] ADJ (*unreal*) surreale; (*strange*) bizzarro(-a)

sur·re·al·ism [sə'rɪə,lɪzəm] N surrealismo ▷ www.artlex.com/ArtLex/s/surrealism.html

sur·re·al·ist [sə'rɪəlɪst] ADJ, N surrealista (*m/f*)

sur·re·al·is·tic [sə,rɪə'lɪstɪk] ADJ surreale; (*Art*) surrealistico(-a)

◎**sur·ren·der** [sə'rɛndəʳ] N resa, capitolazione *f*; **no surrender!** non ci arrendiamo!
■VT (*gen, Mil*): **to surrender (to)** consegnare (a); (*lease*) cedere; (*claim, right*) rinunciare a; (*hope*) abbandonare; (*insurance policy*) riscattare
■VI: **to surrender (to)** arrendersi (a)

surrender value N (*Insurance*) valore *m* di riscatto

sur·rep·ti·tious [,sʌrəp'tɪʃəs] ADJ furtivo(-a)

sur·rep·ti·tious·ly [,sʌrəp'tɪʃəslɪ] ADV furtivamente

sur·ro·gate ['sʌrəgɪt] N (*Brit: substitute*) surrogato
■ADJ surrogato(-a); **a surrogate son** un figlio sostitutivo

surrogate mother N madre *f* biologica

◎**sur·round** [sə'raʊnd] VT circondare; (*Mil*) accerchiare; **a town surrounded by hills** una città circondata da colline
■N bordo

sur·round·ing [sə'raʊndɪŋ] ADJ circostante; **the surrounding hills** le colline circostanti

sur·round·ings [sə'raʊndɪŋz] NPL (*of place*) dintorni *mpl*; (*environment*) ambiente *msg*; **in the surroundings** nei dintorni; **in beautiful surroundings** (*house, hotel*) in una bella posizione

sur·tax ['sɜː,tæks] N soprattassa

sur·ti·tles ['sɜː,taɪtlz] NPL sottotitoli *mpl* (*a teatro*)

sur·veil·lance [sɜː'veɪləns] N sorveglianza; **under surveillance** sotto sorveglianza

◎**sur·vey** [*n* 'sɜːveɪ; *vb* sɜː'veɪ] N **1** (*comprehensive view: of situation, developments*) quadro generale **2** (*inquiry, study*) indagine *f*, studio; **a survey of public opinion** un sondaggio d'opinione; **to carry out a survey of** fare un'indagine di; **they did a survey of a thousand students** è stata fatta un'indagine su un campione di mille studenti **3** (*Surveying: of building*) perizia; (*: of land*) rilevamento; (*: of country*) rilevamento topografico
■VT **1** (*look at*) guardare; (*: prospects, trends*) passare in rassegna; **they have surveyed a number of companies** hanno passato in rassegna diverse aziende **2** (*examine*) studiare, esaminare; **the book surveys events up to 1992** il libro esamina gli eventi fino al 1992; **he surveyed the room** ha esaminato la stanza **3** (*Surveying: building*) fare una perizia di; (*: land*) fare il rilevamento di; (*: country*) fare il rilevamento topografico di; **they have surveyed the area** hanno fatto un rilevamento della zona

sur·vey·ing [sə'veɪɪŋ] N (*of land*) agrimensura

sur·vey·or [sə'veɪəʳ] N (*of buildings*) perito; (*of land*) agrimensore *m*

survey ship N *nave utilizzata per rilevamenti idrografici*

◎**sur·viv·al** [sə'vaɪvəl] N (*act*) sopravvivenza; (*relic*) retaggio; **the survival of the fittest** (*Bio*) la selezione naturale; **in the business world it's a case of the survival of the fittest** nel mondo degli affari vige la legge della giungla

survival course N corso di sopravvivenza

survival kit N equipaggiamento di prima necessità

◎**sur·vive** [sə'vaɪv] VI (*gen*) sopravvivere; (*fig: in job etc*) durare; **you'll survive!** stai tranquillo che non morirai!
■VT sopravvivere a
▸ **survive on** VI + PREP sopravvivere con; **my salary's only just enough to survive on** col mio stipendio riesco a malapena a sopravvivere

sur·vi·vor [sə'vaɪvəʳ] N superstite *m/f*, sopravvissuto(-a); **there were no survivors** non ci sono stati superstiti

sus·cep·tibil·ity [sə,sɛptə'bɪlɪtɪ] N suscettibilità *f inv*; (*Med*) predisposizione *f*

sus·cep·tible [sə'sɛptəbl] ADJ **1** **to be susceptible to** (*infection, illness*) essere predisposto(-a) a, soggetto(-a) a; (*persuasion, flattery*) essere sensibile a; **young people are susceptible to adverts** la pubblicità fa facile presa sui giovani **2** (*impressionable*) (facilmente) impressionabile **3** **susceptible of change** (*frm*) suscettibile di cambiamenti

◎**sus·pect** [*adj, n* 'sʌspɛkt; *vb* sə'spɛkt] ADJ sospetto(-a)
■N persona sospetta
■VT (*person*): **to suspect (of)** sospettare (di); (*think likely*): **to suspect that** sospettare che + *sub*, supporre che + *sub*; **to suspect sb of a crime** sospettare qn di un delitto; **I suspect his motives** non mi convince; **I suspect that he is the author** immagino che sia lui l'autore; **he suspects nothing** non sospetta niente

sus·pect·ed [səs'pɛktɪd] ADJ presunto(-a); **to have a suspected fracture** avere una sospetta frattura

◎**sus·pend** [sə'spɛnd] VT (*gen*) sospendere; **it was suspended from the ceiling/between two posts** era appeso al soffitto/sospeso tra due pali; **he was suspended for cheating** è stato sospeso perché aveva imbrogliato

sus·pend·ed ani·ma·tion [sə,spɛndɪdænɪ'meɪʃən] N interruzione *f* delle funzioni vitali

sus·pend·ed sen·tence [sə,spɛndɪd'sɛntəns] N (*Law*) (condanna) condizionale *f*

sus·pend·er [sə'spɛndəʳ] N (*for stocking*) giarrettiera (di reggicalze); *see also* **suspenders**

suspender belt N (*Brit*) reggicalze *m inv*

sus·pend·ers [sə'spɛndəz] NPL (*Brit*) giarrettiere *fpl*; (*Am: braces*) bretelle *fpl*

sus·pense [sə'spɛns] N incertezza, apprensione *f*; (*in film, book*) suspense *f*; **we waited in suspense** attendevamo ansiosamente; **the suspense is killing me!** muoio dalla curiosità!; **the suspense was terrible** l'attesa era terribile; **a film with lots of suspense** un film ricco di suspense; **to keep sb in suspense** tenere qn in sospeso

suspense account N (*in ledger*) voce *f* in sospeso; (*Comm*) conto in sospeso

sus·pen·sion [sə'spɛnʃən] N (*gen, Aut*) sospensione *f*; (*of driving licence*) ritiro temporaneo

suspension bridge N ponte *m* sospeso

suspension points NPL (*Gram*) puntini *mpl* di sospensione

◎**sus·pi·cion** [sə'spɪʃən] N **1** (*suspicious belief*) sospetto; (*lack of trust*) diffidenza; **I had no suspicion that ...** non avevo il benché minimo sospetto che... + *sub*; **my suspicion is that ...** ho il sospetto che...+ *sub*; **arrested on suspicion of murder** arrestato(-a) per sospetto omicidio; **to be under suspicion** essere sospettato(-a);

above suspicion al di sopra di ogni sospetto; **I had my suspicions about him** non mi ha mai convinto troppo **2** (*hint*: *of danger, scandal*) segno; (: *of garlic*) punta

sus·pi·cious [səˈspɪʃəs] ADJ (*causing suspicion*) sospetto(-a); (*feeling suspicion*): **suspicious (of)** sospettoso(-a) (di), diffidente (di); **to be suspicious of** *or* **about sb/sth** nutrire dei sospetti nei riguardi di qn/qc; **that made him suspicious** questo lo ha insospettito; **a suspicious character** una tipo(-a) sospetto(-a); **suspicious behaviour** un comportamento sospetto; **he was suspicious at first** all'inizio era sospettoso

sus·pi·cious·ly [səˈspɪʃəslɪ] ADV (*look etc*) con sospetto; (*behave etc*) in modo sospetto; **it looks suspiciously like measles** ha tutta l'aria di essere morbillo

suss [sʌs] VT (*Brit fam*): **I've sussed it/him out** ho capito come stanno le cose/che tipo è

◎ **sus·tain** [səsˈteɪn] VT **1** (*weight*) sostenere, sopportare; (*body, life*) mantenere; (*Mus: note*) tenere; (*effort, role, pretence*) sostenere; **"objection sustained"** (*Am Law*) "obiezione accolta" **2** (*receive: damage, loss etc*) subire, soffrire

sus·tain·abil·ity N (*of resources*) sostenibilità; (*of policy, economy*) stabilità

sus·tain·able [səsˈteɪnəbl] ADJ **1** che può essere mantenuto(-a); (*Econ: rate, growth*) stabile; (*source, resource, energy*) rinnovabile; (*forest, timber*) che si può tagliare senza danneggiare l'ambiente; **sustainable development** sviluppo sostenibile

sus·tained [səsˈteɪnd] ADJ (*effort etc*) prolungato(-a)

sus·tain·ing [səsˈteɪnɪŋ] ADJ (*food*) nutriente

sus·te·nance [ˈsʌstɪnəns] N (*food*) nutrimento; (*livelihood*) mezzi *mpl* di sussistenza *or* di sostentamento; **there's not much sustenance in it** non è molto nutriente

su·ture [ˈsuːtʃəʳ] N (*Med*) sutura

SUV [ˌɛsjuːˈviː] N ABBR = **sports utility vehicle**

SW ABBR **1** (= **southwest(ern)**) SO (= *sud ovest*) **2** (*Radio*: = **short wave**) OC *fpl* (= *onde corte*)

swab [swɒb] N (*Med: for cleaning wound, for specimen*) tampone *m*
■ VT (*Naut: also:* **swab down**) redazzare

swad·dle [ˈswɒdl] VT (*in bandages*) fasciare, bendare; (*in blanket*) avvolgere; (*baby*) fasciare

swag [swæg] N (*fam*) malloppo

swag·ger [ˈswægəʳ] N andatura spavalda
■ VI pavoneggiarsi; **to swagger in** entrare pavoneggiandosi

swag·ger·ing [ˈswægərɪŋ] ADJ (*gait*) spavaldo(-a); (*gesture*) da fanfarone(-a); **a swaggering fellow** un fanfarone
■ N fanfaronate *fpl*

swal·low¹ [ˈswɒləʊ] N (*act*) deglutizione *f*; (*of food*) boccone *m*; (*of drink*) sorso
■ VT (*food, drink*) inghiottire, mandar giù, ingoiare; (*fig: suppress: anger, resentment*) inghiottire; (: *believe: story*) bere; **to swallow one's pride** mettere il proprio orgoglio sotto i piedi; **that's hard to swallow** è difficile crederci; **they swallowed it whole!** (*story*) se la sono bevuta in pieno!
■ VI inghiottire; (*fig*): **he swallowed hard and said ...** con l'emozione che gli serrava la gola ha detto...
► **swallow up** VT + ADV (*fig*) inghiottire; **they were soon swallowed up in the darkness** furono presto inghiottiti dalle tenebre; **I wished the ground would open and swallow me up** avrei voluto sprofondare

swal·low² [ˈswɒləʊ] N rondine *f*

swallow dive N (*Swimming*) tuffo ad angelo

swallow hole N (*Geol*) inghiottitoio

swam [swæm] PT *of* **swim**

swamp [swɒmp] N palude *f*, pantano
■ VT (*flood*) inondare, allagare; (: *boat etc*) sommergere; **to swamp (with)** (*fig*) sommergere (di)

swamp·land [ˈswɒmpˌlænd] N palude *f*, zona paludosa

swampy [ˈswɒmpɪ] ADJ paludoso(-a)

swan [swɒn] N cigno
■ VI (*fam*): **to swan around** fare la bella vita; **he swanned off to New York** se n'è andato bellamente a New York

swank [swæŋk] (*fam*) N **1** (*vanity, boastfulness*) ostentazione *f*; **he does it for swank** lo fa per mettersi in mostra **2** (*person*) spaccone(-a)
■ VI (*fam: show off*) mettersi in mostra; (: *talk boastfully*) fare lo(-a) spaccone(-a); **to swank about sth** vantarsi di qc

swanky [ˈswæŋkɪ] ADJ (*comp* **-ier**, *superl* **-iest**) (*fam: person*) pieno(-a) di sé; (: *car etc*) vistoso(-a)

swan's-down [ˈswɒnzˌdaʊn] N piumino (di cigno)

swan song N (*fig*) canto del cigno

swap [swɒp] N (*exchange*) scambio
■ VT (*cars, stamps etc*) scambiare; **to swap sth for sth else** scambiare qc con qualcos'altro; **he swapped the vouchers for tickets** ha scambiato i voucher con i biglietti; **to swap places with sb** cambiare di posto con qn
■ VI fare uno scambio; **do you want to swap?** vuoi fare scambio?
► **swap over, swap round** VT + ADV: **to swap sth over** *or* **round** cambiare di posto qc; **you can swap them over** li puoi cambiare di posto

SWAPO [ˈswɑːpəʊ] N ABBR = *South-West Africa People's Organization*

swarm¹ [swɔːm] N (*of bees, flying insects*) sciame *m*; (*of crawling insects*) schiera, esercito; (*fig: of tourists etc*) sciame *m*, frotta, stuolo; **swarm of ants** formicaio; **a swarm of people** una marea di gente; **in swarms** (*fig*) a frotte
■ VI (*bees*) sciamare; **to swarm about** (*crawling insects, people*) brulicare; **to swarm in/out** *etc* entrare/uscire *etc* a frotte; **to swarm with** (*people, insects*) brulicare di

swarm² [swɔːm] VI: **to swarm up a tree/rope** arrampicarsi su un albero/su per una corda

swarthi·ness [ˈswɔːðɪnɪs] N (*of person*) carnagione *f* scura; (*of complexion*) colore *m* scuro

swarthy [ˈswɔːðɪ] ADJ (*comp* **-ier**, *superl* **-iest**) (*person*) di carnagione scura; (*skin*) scuro(-a)

swash [swɒʃ] N (*sound*) sciabordio

swash·buck·ling [ˈswɒʃˌbʌklɪŋ] ADJ (*role, hero*) spericolato(-a); (*film, novel*) di cappa e spada

swas·ti·ka [ˈswɒstɪkə] N svastica, croce *f* uncinata

SWAT [swɒt] N ABBR (*Am*: = **Special Weapons and Tactics**) *corpo speciale di polizia*; **a SWAT team** ≈ un reparto di teste di cuoio

swat [swɒt] VT (*fly*) schiacciare
■ N (*Brit: also:* **fly swat**) acchiappamosche *m inv*

swathe¹ [sweɪð], **swath** [swɔːθ] N (*pl* **swathes** *or* **swaths** [swɔːðz]) (*of grass etc*) falciata

swathe² [sweɪð] VT: **to swathe in** (*bandages, blankets*) avvolgere in

swat·ter [ˈswɒtəʳ] N (*also:* **fly swatter**) acchiappamosche *m inv*

sway [sweɪ] N **1** (*movement: gen*) ondeggiamento; (*of*

Ss

boat) dondolio, rollio **2** (*rule, power*): **sway (over)** influenza (su); **to hold sway over sb** dominare qn
■ VI (*tree, hanging object*) ondeggiare; (*bridge, building, train*) oscillare; (*person*) barcollare; **the train swayed from side to side** il treno oscillava violentemente
■ VT **1** (*move*) far oscillare; **to sway one's hips** ancheggiare **2** (*influence*) influenzare; **these factors finally swayed me** questi fattori hanno finito per influenzarmi; **to be swayed by** essere influenzato(-a) da

Swa·zi·land ['swɑ:zɪ,lænd] N lo Swaziland

swear [swɛəʳ] (*pt* **swore**, *pp* **sworn**) VT (*gen*) giurare; **to swear an oath** prestare giuramento; **I swear it!** lo giuro!; **I swear (that) I did not steal it** giuro che non l'ho rubato, giuro di non averlo rubato; **to swear to do sth** promettere di fare qc; **I could have sworn that was Louise** avrei giurato che fosse Louise; **to swear sb to secrecy** far giurare a qn di mantenere il segreto
■ VI **1** (*solemnly: witness etc*) giurare; **to swear on the Bible** giurare sulla Bibbia; **to swear to the truth of sth** giurare che qc è vero; **I can't swear to it** non posso giurarlo; **I swear I didn't know** giuro che non lo sapevo; **he swore he wouldn't do it again** ha giurato che non l'avrebbe rifatto **2** (*use swearwords*): **to swear (at sb)** bestemmiare *or* imprecare (contro qn), dire parolacce (a qn); **he swore under his breath** ha imprecato sottovoce; **to swear like a trooper** bestemmiare come uno scaricatore di porto
▸ **swear by** VI + PREP (*fam*): **my mother swears by hot baths for backache** mia madre dice che non c'è rimedio migliore di un bagno caldo contro il mal di schiena
▸ **swear in** VT + ADV (*jury, witness, president*) prestare giuramento

swear·word ['swɛə,wɜ:d] N parolaccia; (*curse*) bestemmia

sweat [swɛt] N sudore *m*; **by the sweat of one's brow** con il sudore della fronte; **to get in** *or* **into a sweat about sth** (*fam*) farsi prendere dal panico per qc; **in a sweat** in un bagno di sudore; **to be in a cold sweat** (*also: fig*) avere i sudori freddi; **it was a real sweat!** è stata una faticaccia!; **no sweat!** (*fam*) non ci sono problemi!
■ VI (*person*) sudare; (*walls*) trasudare; (*fam: work hard*): **to sweat (over sth)** sudare (su qc); **to sweat like a pig** essere in un bagno di sudore, sudare sette camicie
■ VT: **to sweat blood** (*fig: work hard*) sudare sangue; (*: be anxious*) sudare freddo; **to sweat it out** (*fig fam*) armarsi di pazienza

sweat·band ['swɛt,bænd] N (*Sport*) fascia (elastica) (*per assorbire il sudore: da polso o da fronte*)

sweat·er ['swɛtəʳ] N maglione *m*

sweat gland N ghiandola sudoripara

sweat·ing ['swɛtɪŋ] N (*of person*) sudorazione *f*; (*of wall etc*) trasudazione *f*

sweat·shirt ['swɛtʃɜ:t] N felpa

sweat·shop ['swɛtʃɒp] N *azienda o fabbrica in cui i dipendenti sono sfruttati*

sweaty ['swɛtɪ] ADJ (*comp* **-ier**, *superl* **-iest**) (*gen*) sudato(-a), sudaticcio(-a); (*smell*) di sudore

Swede [swi:d] N svedese *m/f*

swede [swi:d] N (*Brit: vegetable*) rapa svedese

Swe·den ['swi:dn] N la Svezia

Swe·dish ['swi:dɪʃ] ADJ svedese
■ N (*language*) svedese *m*

◎ **sweep** [swi:p] (*vb: pt, pp* **swept**) N **1** (*of room*) scopata, spazzata; (*of chimney*) pulita **2** (*also:* **chimney sweep**) spazzacamino **3** (*range*) portata; (*movement: of arm*) ampio gesto; (*: of scythe, sword*) sciabolata; (*: of beam, searchlight*) fascio luminoso; (*curve: of road, hills etc*) curva; (*expanse: of countryside*) distesa; **a wide sweep of country** una vasta distesa di campi
■ VT **1** (*stairs, floor*) scopare, spazzare; (*chimney*) pulire; (*dust, snow*) spazzare; **she swept the floor** ha spazzato il pavimento; **to sweep (out) a room** scopare una stanza; **to sweep a problem under the carpet** (*fig*) accantonare un problema **2** (*move over: subj: waves, wind*) spazzare; (*: searchlight*) perlustrare; (*: disease*) dilagare in; (*: fashion, craze*) invadere; **to sweep the sea for mines** dragare il mare; **to sweep the horizon** (*with eyes, binoculars*) scrutare l'orizzonte; **to sweep the board** (*fig*) fare tabula rasa **3** (*remove with sweeping movement*) spazzar via; **to be swept overboard** essere spazzato(-a) fuori bordo; **the crowd swept him along** fu trascinato dalla folla; **he swept her off her feet** (*fig*) l'ha conquistata
■ VI **1** (*with broom*) scopare, spazzare **2** (*move*): **to sweep in/out/along** entrare/uscire/procedere maestosamente; **to sweep past sb** sfrecciare davanti a qn; **the hurricane swept through the city** l'uragano infuriava sulla città; **panic swept through the crowd** la folla fu assalita dal panico; **he swept past in a sports car** è passato sfrecciando alla guida di un'auto sportiva; **the mountains sweep down to the coast** le montagne digradano maestose fino al mare
▸ **sweep aside** VT + ADV spingere di lato; (*fig: objections*) scartare
▸ **sweep away** VT + ADV (*dust, rubbish*) spazzar via; (*subj: crowd, current*) trascinare via
▸ **sweep up** VI + ADV spazzare
■ VT + ADV (*leaves, rubbish*) raccogliere; (*pick up: books etc*) acchiappare

sweep·er ['swi:pəʳ] N **1** (*worker*) spazzino(-a) **2** (*machine*) spazzatrice *f* **3** (*Brit Ftbl*) libero

sweep·ing ['swi:pɪŋ] ADJ (*gesture*) ampio(-a); (*statement etc*) generico(-a); (*changes, reforms*) radicale, ampio(-a)

sweep·stake ['swi:p,steɪk] N lotteria (*spesso abbinata alle corse dei cavalli*)

◎ **sweet** [swi:t] ADJ (*comp* **-er**, *superl* **-est**) **1** (*taste*) dolce; **this coffee is too sweet** questo caffè è troppo dolce; **I love sweet things** adoro i dolci; **a sweet wine** un vino dolce **2** (*fresh, pleasant: smell, perfume, sound*) dolce; (*: breath*) fresco(-a); (*fig: success*) piacevole; (*: revenge*) dolce; **the sweet smell of success** il profumo del successo; **it was sweet to his ear** era musica per le sue orecchie **3** (*charming: person*) carino(-a), dolce; (*: smile, character*) dolce; (*: appearance, village, kitten*) grazioso(-a), carino(-a); **that's very sweet of you** è molto carino da parte tua; **what a sweet little dress!** che vestitino grazioso!; **he carried on in his own sweet way** (*iro*) ha continuato (a fare) come gli pareva
■ ADV: **to smell/taste sweet** avere un odore/sapore dolce
■ N (*Brit: toffee etc*) caramella; (*: dessert*) dolce *m*; **a bag of sweets** un sacchetto di caramelle; **are you going to have a sweet?** prendi il dolce?

sweet-and-sour [,swi:tənd'saʊəʳ] ADJ agrodolce; **sweet-and-sour pork** maiale in agrodolce

sweet·breads ['swi:t,brɛdz] NPL animelle *fpl*

sweet chestnut N (*Bot*) castagno

sweet corn N granturco dolce

sweet·en ['swi:tn] VT (*tea etc*) zuccherare; (*air*) profumare; (*fig: temper*) addolcire; (*: task*) rendere più piacevole; (*also*: **sweeten up**: *person*) ingraziarsi; (: *child*) tenere buono(-a)

sweet·en·er ['swi:tnəʳ] N (*Culin*) dolcificante *m*; (*fam*: *bribe*) zuccherino, contentino

sweet·en·ing ['swi:tnɪŋ] N (*substance*) dolcificante *m*

sweet·heart ['swi:t,hɑ:t] N innamorato(-a); **yes, sweetheart** sì , tesoro

sweetie ['swi:tɪ] N (*fam*: *toffee etc*) caramella; (: *person*) tesoro

sweet·ly ['swi:tlɪ] ADV (*gen*) dolcemente, con dolcezza; **the engine is running sweetly** il motore non dà problemi

sweet-natured [,swi:t'neɪtʃəd] ADJ di indole buona

sweet·ness ['swi:tnɪs] N (*gen*) dolcezza; (*of taste*) sapore *m* dolce; (*of breath*) freschezza; **now all is sweetness and light** adesso tutti sono felici e contenti

sweet nothings NPL: **to whisper sweet nothings in sb's ear** sussurrare paroline dolci a qn

sweet pea N pisello odoroso

sweet pepper N peperone *m*

sweet potato N patata americana *or* dolce

sweet shop N (*Brit*) negozio di dolciumi

sweet-smelling ['swi:t,smɛlɪŋ] ADJ profumato(-a)

sweet-tempered [,swi:t'tɛmpəd] ADJ: **to be sweet-tempered** avere un carattere *m* dolce

sweet tooth N: **to have a sweet tooth** avere un debole per i dolci, essere goloso(-a) di dolci

sweet william [-'wɪljəm] N (*flower*) garofano a mazzetti

swell [swɛl] (*vb*: *pt* **swelled**, *pp* **swollen**) N (*of sea*) mare *m* lungo

■ ADJ (*Am*: *fine, good*) eccezionale, favoloso(-a); **that's just swell** perfetto

■ VI (*ankle, eye etc*: *also*: **swell up**) gonfiarsi; (*sails*) prendere il vento; (*in size, number*) aumentare; (*sound, music*) diventare più forte; (*river etc*) ingrossarsi; **to swell with pride** gonfiarsi d'orgoglio; **the cheers swelled to a roar** gli applausi si tramutarono in un boato; **the numbers have swelled** i numeri sono aumentati; **my ankles swelled** mi si sono gonfiate le caviglie

■ VT (*numbers, sales etc*) far aumentare; (*sails*) gonfiare; (*river*) ingrossare

swell-headed [,swɛl'hɛdɪd] ADJ (*fam*) borioso(-a), pieno(-a) di sé

swell·ing ['swɛlɪŋ] N (*Med*) gonfiore *m*, tumefazione *f*

swel·ter ['swɛltəʳ] VI soffocare, morire di caldo

swel·ter·ing ['swɛltərɪŋ] ADJ soffocante, afoso(-a); **I'm sweltering** sto soffocando; **it was sweltering** faceva un caldo soffocante

swept [swɛpt] PT, PP *of* **sweep**

swerve [swɜ:v] N deviazione *f*; (*in car*) sterzata

■ VI deviare bruscamente; (*in car*) sterzare; (*in ship*) virare; (*boxer*) scartare; **nothing will make him swerve from his aims** niente lo distoglierà dai suoi propositi; **I swerved to avoid the cyclist** ho sterzato per evitare il ciclista

swift [swɪft] ADJ (*comp* **-er**, *superl* **-est**) (*movement*) rapido(-a), repentino(-a); (*runner*) veloce; (*reply, reaction*) pronto(-a)

■ N (*bird*) rondone *m*

swift·ly ['swɪftlɪ] ADV (*see adj*) rapidamente, repentinamente; velocemente; prontamente

swift·ness ['swɪftnɪs] N (*see adj*) rapidità, repentinità; velocità; prontezza

swig [swɪg] (*fam*) N (*drink*) sorsata; **he took a swig at his bottle** ha bevuto un lungo sorso dalla bottiglia

■ VT tracannare

swill [swɪl] N (*also pej*) broda

■ VT **1** (*clean*: *also*: **swill out**) risciacquare **2** (*fam*: *drink*: *beer etc*) tracannare

◎ **swim** [swɪm] (*vb*: *pt* **swam**, *pp* **swum**) N **1** nuotata; **it's a long swim back to the shore** è una bella nuotata fino alla spiaggia; **to go for a swim** andare a fare una nuotata; **let's go for a swim** andiamo a fare una nuotata; **to have a swim** fare una nuotata **2** (*fam*): **to be in the swim** essere al corrente

■ VT (*river etc*) attraversare a nuoto; (*distance*) nuotare per; **to swim the crawl** nuotare a crawl; **to swim a length** fare una vasca; **she can't swim a stroke** non sa nuotare

■ VI (*gen*) nuotare; (*as sport*) fare nuoto; **can you swim?** sai nuotare?; **I swam for an hour** ho nuotato per un'ora; **I've never swum in the sea** non ho mai nuotato nel mare; **to go swimming** andare a nuotare; **to swim across a river** attraversare un fiume a nuoto; **she swam across the river** ha attraversato il fiume a nuoto; **my head is swimming** (*fig*) mi gira la testa; **the meat was swimming in gravy** la carne galleggiava nel sugo; **eyes swimming with tears** occhi inondati di lacrime

swim bladder N (*Zool*) vescica natatoria

swim·mer ['swɪməʳ] N nuotatore(-trice)

swim·ming ['swɪmɪŋ] N nuoto; **swimming and cycling** il nuoto ed il ciclismo; **do you like swimming?** ti piace nuotare?

swimming baths NPL (*Brit*) piscina pubblica

swimming cap N cuffia

swimming costume N (*Brit*) costume *m* da bagno

swimming gala N gara di nuoto

swim·ming·ly ['swɪmɪŋlɪ] ADV (*smoothly*): **everything went swimmingly** tutto è andato liscio come l'olio

swimming pool N piscina

swimming trunks NPL calzoncini *mpl* da bagno

swim·suit ['swɪm,su:t] N costume *m* da bagno (*da donna*)

swin·dle ['swɪndl] N truffa

■ VT imbrogliare, truffare; **to swindle sb out of sth** estorcere qc a qn con l'inganno

swin·dler ['swɪndləʳ] N imbroglione(-a), truffatore(-trice)

swine [swaɪn] N **1** (*fig fam!*: *person*) porco (*fam!*); **you swine!** brutto porco! **2** (*pl inv*: *old*: *pig*) maiale *m*

◎ **swing** [swɪŋ] (*vb*: *pt, pp* **swung**) N

1 (*of pendulum, needle*) oscillazione *f*; (*distance*) arco; **to take a swing at sb** mollare un pugno a qn

2 (*seat for swinging*) altalena; **a slide and some swings** uno scivolo e alcune altalene; **to have a swing** andare sull'altalena; **it's swings and roundabouts** (*fig*) che ci vuoi fare, le cose a volte vanno bene, a volte vanno male

3 (*Pol*: *in attitudes, opinions, support*): **there was a swing towards/away from Labour** c'è stato un aumento/una diminuzione di voti per i Laburisti; **a sudden swing in public opinion** un improvviso cambiamento dell'opinione pubblica; **a swing to the left** una svolta a sinistra

4 (*Boxing, Golf*) swing *m inv*

5 (*rhythm*) ritmo; **to get into the swing of things** entrare nel pieno delle cose; **to be in full swing** essere in pieno corso; **the party went with a swing** la festa è stata una bomba

Ss

6 (*also:* **swing music**) swing *m*
7 a mood swing un cambiamento d'umore
■ VT
1 (*pendulum*) far oscillare; (*person on swing, in hammock*) dondolare, spingere; (*arms, legs*) dondolare, ciondolare; **to swing the door open** spalancare la porta
2 (*wield: axe, sword*) brandire, roteare; **he swung the case up onto his shoulder** si è messo la valigia sulla spalla; **he swung himself over the wall** si è lanciato al di là del muro; **she swung the car round** girò di colpo la macchina
3 (*influence: opinion, decision*) influenzare; **she managed to swing it so that we could all go** (*fam*) è riuscita a fare in modo che ci potessimo andare tutti; **what swung it for me was ...** ciò che mi ha fatto decidere è stato...
■ VI dondolare, oscillare; (*on swing, hammock*) dondolarsi; (*arms, legs*) ciondolare; **to swing to and fro** dondolare avanti e indietro; **a large key swung from his belt** dalla cintura gli dondolava una grossa chiave; **the door swung open** la porta si spalancò; **the door swung shut** la porta si chiuse sbattendo; **he'll swing for it** (*fam*) lo impiccheranno; **the road swings south** la strada prende la direzione sud; **he swung round** si voltò bruscamente; **the car swung into the square** la macchina svoltò bruscamente nella piazza; **to swing to the right** (*fig Pol*) svoltare a destra; **to swing into action** entrare in azione

swing bridge N ponte *m* girevole

swing door N porta a vento

swinge·ing ['swɪndʒɪŋ] ADJ (*cuts*) drastico(-a); (*attack, blow*) violento(-a); (*defeat, majority*) schiacciante; (*taxation*) forte; (*price increase*) enorme

swing·er ['swɪŋəʳ] N (*old*): **he's a swinger** (*sexually*) è un farfallone; (*socially*) è un festaiolo

swing·ing ['swɪŋɪŋ] ADJ (*step*) cadenzato(-a), ritmico(-a); (*rhythm, music*) trascinante; **swinging door** (*Am*) porta a vento

swing shift N (*Am*) turno serale

swing vote N (*Am*) voto dall'esito incerto

swing voter N (*Am: Pol*) elettore(-trice) indeciso(-a)

swing-wing ['swɪŋ,wɪŋ] ADJ (*Aer*) a geometria variabile

swipe [swaɪp] N: **to take a swipe at sb** dare uno schiaffo a qn
■ VT **1** (*hit: ball, person*) colpire; **he swiped the ball** ha colpito con forza la palla **2** (*fam: steal*) fregare, sgraffignare; **sb's swiped my stapler** qn mi ha fregato la cucitrice **3** (*Comput: card*) far passare nell'apposita macchinetta; **you get in by swiping a card** per entrare devi passare una scheda nell'apposita macchinetta
■ VI: **to swipe at sb/sth** tentare di colpire qn/qc

swipe card N scheda magnetica

swirl [swɜːl] N (*movement*) turbinio, turbine *m*, mulinello; (*of cream etc*) ricciolo
■ VI turbinare, far mulinello

swish [swɪʃ] N (*sound: of whip*) schiocco; (: *of skirts, grass*) fruscio
■ ADJ (*fam: smart*) all'ultimo grido, alla moda
■ VT (*whip*) schioccare; (*skirt*) far frusciare; (*tail*) agitare
■ VI (*whip*) schioccare; (*skirts, grass*) frusciare

Swiss [swɪs] ADJ svizzero(-a)
■ N, PL INV svizzero(-a); **the Swiss** gli svizzeri

Swiss cheese N formaggio svizzero

Swiss French ADJ svizzero(-a) francese

Swiss German ADJ svizzero(-a) tedesco(-a)

swiss roll N (*Culin*) *rotolo (di pan di Spagna) farcito di marmellata*

◎**switch** [swɪtʃ] N **1** (*Elec etc*) interruttore *m* **2** (*Rail: points*) scambio **3** (*change*) cambiamento, mutamento; (*exchange*) scambio; **a rapid switch of plan** un improvviso cambiamento di programma; **a policy switch** un cambiamento di politica **4** (*stick*) bacchetta; **riding switch** frustino
■ VT **1** (*change: plans, jobs*) cambiare; (: *allegiance*): **we switched partners** abbiamo cambiato partner; **to switch (to)** spostare (a); (: *conversation*) spostare (su)
2 (*exchange*) scambiarsi; (*transpose: also:* **switch round, switch over**) scambiare; (: *two objects*) invertire; **I switched hats with him** *or* **we switched hats** ci siamo scambiati i cappelli **3** (*TV, Radio: programme*) cambiare; **to switch the TV to another channel** cambiare canale; **to switch the radio to another programme** cambiare stazione; **to switch the heater to high** regolare la stufa al massimo **4** (*Rail*) deviare
■ VI (*also:* **switch over**) passare; **he switched to another topic** è passato a un altro argomento; **he has switched to Labour** è passato al partito laburista
▸ **switch back** VI + ADV (*gen*) ritornare; (*TV, Radio*): **to switch back to the other programme** rimettere l'altro programma, ritornare all'altro programma; **he switched back to being calm** è tornato alla calma
■ VT + ADV: **can you switch the heater back to "low"?** puoi rimettere la stufa al minimo?; **to switch the light back on/off** riaccendere/rispegnere la luce
▸ **switch off** VT + ADV (*Elec, TV, Aut*) spegnere
■ VI + ADV (*Elec, TV*) spegnersi da solo(-a); (*fig fam: not listen*) smettere di ascoltare
▸ **switch on** VT + ADV (*Elec, TV etc*) accendere; (*water supply*) aprire; (*machine, Aut*) mettere in moto, avviare; (: *ignition*) inserire; **to switch on the charm** diventare tutto(-a) gentile
■ VI + ADV (*heater, oven*) accendersi da solo(-a)

switch·back ['swɪtʃ,bæk] N (*Brit: roller coaster*) montagne *fpl* russe

switch·blade ['swɪtʃ,bleɪd] N (*also:* **switchblade knife**) coltello a scatto

switch·board ['swɪtʃ,bɔːd] N centralino

switchboard operator N centralinista *m/f*

switched-on [,swɪtʃt'ɒn] ADJ (*fam*) aggiornato(-a), alla moda

switch·over ['swɪtʃ,əʊvəʳ] N passaggio; **the switchover to the metric system** l'adozione *f* del sistema metrico decimale

Swit·zer·land ['swɪtsələnd] N la Svizzera

swiv·el ['swɪvl] N perno
■ VI (*also:* **swivel round**) girarsi

swol·len ['swəʊlən] PP *of* **swell**
■ ADJ (*ankle, finger, stomach*) gonfio(-a); (*river*) in piena; **my ankle is swollen** ho una caviglia gonfia; **her eyes were swollen with tears** aveva gli occhi gonfi di pianto; **you'll give him a swollen head** (*fig*) gli farai montare la testa

swollen-headed ['swəʊlən'hɛdɪd] ADJ (*Brit pej*) borioso(-a), pieno(-a) di sé

swoon [swuːn] (*old*) N svenimento
■ VI svenire; **to swoon over sb** (*fig*) morire dietro a qn

swoop [swuːp] N (*of bird etc*) picchiata; (*by police*): **swoop (on)** incursione *f* (in); **in one fell swoop** in un colpo solo
■ VI (*bird: also:* **swoop down**) scendere in picchiata; (*police*): **to swoop (on)** fare un'incursione (in); **the**

plane swooped low over the village l'aereo è sceso in picchiata sul villaggio; **the drug squad was about to swoop** la squadra antidroga stava par fare un'incursione

swop [swɒp] N, VT = **swap**

sword [sɔːd] N spada

sword dance N danza delle spade

sword·fish [ˈsɔːdˌfɪʃ] N pesce *m* spada *inv*

sword·play [ˈsɔːdˌpleɪ] N (*technique*) abilità nel maneggiare la spada; (*fighting*) combattimento con la spada

swords·man [ˈsɔːdzmən] N (*pl* **-men**) spadaccino

swords·man·ship [ˈsɔːdzmənʃɪp] N abilità con la spada

swore [swɔːʳ] PT *of* **swear**

sworn [swɔːn] PP *of* **swear**
■ ADJ (*enemy*) giurato(-a); (*friend*) per la pelle; (*ally*) fedele; (*testimony*) giurato(-a), fatto(-a) sotto giuramento

swot [swɒt] VT (*fam*) sgobbare su; **to swot up (on) one's maths** ripassare tutta la matematica
■ VI sgobbare; **to swot for an exam** sgobbare per un esame
■ N (*pej*) sgobbone(-a), secchione(-a)

swum [swʌm] PP *of* **swim**

swung [swʌŋ] PT, PP *of* **swing**

syca·more [ˈsɪkəmɔːʳ] N sicomoro

syco·phant [ˈsɪkəfənt] N adulatore(-trice)

syco·phan·tic [ˌsɪkəˈfæntɪk] ADJ (*frm*) ossequioso(-a), adulatore(-trice)

Syd·ney [ˈsɪdnɪ] N Sydney *f*
⊳ www.sydney.com.au

syl·lab·ic [sɪˈlæbɪk] ADJ sillabico(-a)

syl·la·ble [ˈsɪləbl] N sillaba

syl·la·bub [ˈsɪləˌbʌb] N (*Culin: dessert*) ≈ zabaione *m*

syl·la·bus [ˈsɪləbəs] N (*Scol, Univ*) programma *m*; **on the syllabus** in programma d'esame

syl·lo·gism [ˈsɪləˌdʒɪzəm] N sillogismo

sylph [sɪlf] N silfo

sylph·like [ˈsɪlfˌlaɪk] ADJ (*woman*) snella; (*figure*) da silfide

sym·bio·sis [ˌsɪmbɪˈəʊsɪs] N simbiosi *f inv*

sym·bi·ot·ic [ˌsɪmbɪˈɒtɪk] ADJ (*frm: relationship*) simbiotico(-a)

◎ **sym·bol** [ˈsɪmbəl] N simbolo

sym·bol·ic [sɪmˈbɒlɪk], **sym·boli·cal** [sɪmˈbɒlɪkəl] ADJ simbolico(-a); **to be symbolic of sth** simboleggiare qc

sym·boli·cal·ly [sɪmˈbɒlɪkəlɪ] ADV emblematicamente, simbolicamente

sym·bol·ism [ˈsɪmbəˌlɪzəm] N simbolismo

sym·boli·za·tion [ˌsɪmbəlaɪˈzeɪʃən] N simbolizzazione *f*

sym·bol·ize [ˈsɪmbəˌlaɪz] VT simboleggiare

sym·met·ri·cal [sɪˈmɛtrɪkəl] ADJ simmetrico(-a)

sym·met·ri·cal·ly [sɪˈmɛtrɪkəlɪ] ADV simmetricamente

sym·me·try [ˈsɪmɪtrɪ] N simmetria; **line symmetry** simmetria rispetto a una retta; **rotational symmetry** simmetria rotazionale

sym·pa·thet·ic [ˌsɪmpəˈθɛtɪk] ADJ (*showing pity*) compassionevole; (*kind, understanding*) comprensivo(-a); **they were sympathetic but could not help** sono stati molto comprensivi ma non hanno potuto aiutare; **I told my teacher and she was sympathetic** l'ho detto all'insegnante e lei è stata comprensiva; **to be sympathetic to a cause** (*well-disposed*) simpatizzare per una causa; **to be sympathetic towards** (*person*) essere comprensivo(-a) nei confronti di

> DID YOU KNOW ...?
> **sympathetic** is not translated by the Italian word *simpatico*

sym·pa·theti·cal·ly [ˌsɪmpəˈθɛtɪkəlɪ] ADV (*see adj*) in modo compassionevole; con comprensione

sym·pa·thize [ˈsɪmpəˌθaɪz] VI: **to sympathize (with sb)** (*feel pity*) partecipare al dolore (di qn); (*understand*) capire (qn); **I sympathize with you in your grief** ti sono molto vicino nel dolore; **I sympathize with what you say, but ...** capisco quello che vuoi dire, ma...

> DID YOU KNOW ...?
> **sympathize** is not translated by the Italian word *simpatizzare*

sym·pa·thiz·er [ˈsɪmpəˌθaɪzəʳ] N (*fig: esp Pol*): **sympathizer (with)** simpatizzante *m/f* (di)

◎ **sym·pa·thy** [ˈsɪmpəθɪ] N **1** (*pity, compassion*) compassione *f*; **you have my deepest sympathy** *or* **sympathies** hai tutta la mia comprensione; **you won't get any sympathy from me!** non venire a piangere da me!; **with our deepest sympathy** con le nostre più sincere condoglianze; **a letter of sympathy** una lettera di cordoglio **2** (*understanding*) comprensione *f*; (*fellow-feeling, agreement*) solidarietà; **I am in sympathy with your suggestions** mi trovo d'accordo con i tuoi suggerimenti; **to strike in sympathy with sb** scioperare per solidarietà con qn

> DID YOU KNOW ...?
> **sympathy** is not translated by the Italian word *simpatia*

sym·phon·ic [sɪmˈfɒnɪk] ADJ sinfonico(-a)

sym·pho·ny [ˈsɪmfənɪ] N sinfonia

symphony orchestra N orchestra sinfonica

sym·po·sium [sɪmˈpəʊzɪəm] N (*pl* **symposia**) simposio

◎ **symp·tom** [ˈsɪmptəm] N sintomo

symp·to·mat·ic [ˌsɪmptəˈmætɪk] ADJ: **symptomatic (of)** sintomatico(-a) (di)

syna·gogue [ˈsɪnəˌgɒg] N sinagoga

syn·apse [ˈsaɪnæps] N sinapsi *f*

sync [sɪŋk] N (*Tech*): **in/out of sync** in/fuori sincronia; **everything is out of sync** (*fig*) è tutto sballato(-a)

syn·chro·mesh [ˌsɪŋkrəʊˈmɛʃ] N cambio sincronizzato

syn·chro·ni·za·tion [ˌsɪŋkrənaɪˈzeɪʃən] N sincronizzazione *f*

syn·chro·nize [ˈsɪŋkrəˌnaɪz] VT sincronizzare
■ VI: **to synchronize with** essere in sincronia con

syn·chro·nized swim·ming [ˈsɪŋkrəˌnaɪzdˈswɪmɪŋ] N nuoto sincronizzato
⊳ www.fina.org

syn·cline [ˈsɪŋklaɪn] N sinclinale *f*

syn·co·pate [ˈsɪŋkəˌpeɪt] VT sincopare

syn·co·pa·tion [ˌsɪŋkəˈpeɪʃən] N (*Mus*) sincope *f*

syn·di·cate [*n* ˈsɪndɪkɪt; *vb* ˈsɪndɪˌkeɪt] N (*Comm etc*) sindacato; (*Press*) agenzia di stampa
■ VT (*Press*) vendere tramite agenzia di stampa

syn·di·cat·ed [ˈsɪndɪˌkeɪtɪd] ADJ (*Press: articles*) d'agenzia

syn·drome [ˈsɪndrəʊm] N sindrome *f*

syn·er·esis [sɪˈnɪərɪsɪs] N (*Gram*) crasi *f*

syn·od [ˈsɪnəd] N sinodo

syno·nym [ˈsɪnənɪm] N sinonimo

syn·ony·mous [sɪˈnɒnɪməs] ADJ: **synonymous (with)** sinonimo(-a) (di)

syn·ony·my [sɪˈnɒnəmɪ] N sinonimia

syn·op·sis [sɪˈnɒpsɪs] N (*pl* **synopses** [sɪˈnɒpsiːz]) (*of plot*) trama

Ss

syn·tac·tic [sɪn'tæktɪk], **syntactical** [sɪn'tæktɪk(əl)] ADJ sintattico(-a)
syn·tax ['sɪntæks] N sintassi *f inv*
synth [sɪnθ] N (*fam: Mus*) sintetizzatore *m*
syn·the·sis ['sɪnθəsɪs] N (*pl* **syntheses** ['sɪnθəsi:z]) sintesi *f inv*
syn·the·size ['sɪnθə,saɪz] VT sintetizzare
syn·the·siz·er ['sɪnθə,saɪzəʳ] N (*Mus*) sintetizzatore *m*
syn·thet·ic [sɪn'θɛtɪk] ADJ (*fabric etc*) sintetico(-a)
■ N prodotto sintetico; (*Textiles*) fibra sintetica
syphi·lis ['sɪfɪlɪs] N sifilide *f*
syphi·lit·ic [,sɪfɪ'lɪtɪk] ADJ, N sifilitico(-a)
sy·phon ['saɪfən] N, VB = **siphon**
Syria ['sɪrɪə] N la Siria
Syr·ian ['sɪrɪən] ADJ, N siriano(-a)
sy·ringe [sɪ'rɪndʒ] N siringa
■ VT (*Med*) siringare
syr·up ['sɪrəp] N sciroppo; **golden syrup** (*Brit*) melassa raffinata
syr·upy ['sɪrəpɪ] ADJ (*also fig*) sciropposo(-a)

◎**sys·tem** ['sɪstəm] N (*method*) sistema *m*; (*network*) rete *f*; (*Anat*) apparato; **it was quite a shock to his system** è stato uno shock per il suo organismo; **to get sth out of one's system** (*fig*) sfogarsi
sys·tem·at·ic [,sɪstə'mætɪk] ADJ sistematico(-a)
sys·tem·ati·cal·ly [,sɪstə'mætɪkəlɪ] ADV sistematicamente
sys·tema·ti·za·tion [,sɪstəmətaɪ'zeɪʃən] N sistematizzazione *f*
sys·tema·tize ['sɪstəmə,taɪz] VT sistematizzare
system disk N (*Comput*) disco di sistema
system operator N (*Comput*) operatore(-trice) di sistema
systems analysis N (*Comput*) analisi *f inv* dei sistemi
systems analyst N (*Comput*) sistemista
systems disk N (*Comput*) disco del sistema
systems engineer N (*Comput*) sistemista
systems software N (*Comput*) software *m inv* di sistema
sys·to·le ['sɪstəlɪ] N sistole *f*

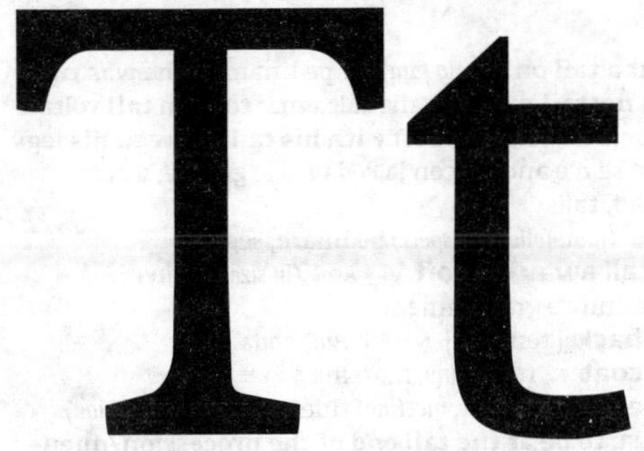

T, t [tiː] N (*letter*) T, t *m or f inv*; **T for Tommy** ≈ T come Taranto; **it fits you to a T** (*fam*) ti sta a pennello; **that's him to a T** (*fam*) è proprio lui

TA [ˌtiːˈeɪ] N ABBR (*Brit*) = **Territorial Army**

ta [tɑː] EXCL (*Brit fam*) grazie!

tab [tæb] N ABBR = **tabulator**
■ N (*label*) etichetta; (*flap on garment*) linguetta; (*Am fam: bill*) conto; **to keep tabs on sb/sth** (*fig fam*) tenere d'occhio qn/qc; **to pick up the tab** (*Am fam*) pagare il conto; **we can put it on your tab** possiamo metterlo sul suo conto

tab·by [ˈtæbɪ] N (*also:* **tabby cat**) (gatto(-a)) soriano(-a), gatto(-a) tigrato(-a)

tab·er·nac·le [ˈtæbəˌnækl] N tabernacolo

◎ **ta·ble** [ˈteɪbl] N **1** tavolo; (*for meals*) tavola; (*also:* **coffee table**) tavolino; **card table** tavolino da gioco; **to lay** *or* **set the table** apparecchiare *or* preparare la tavola; **to clear the table** sparecchiare; **at table** a tavola; **the entire table was in fits of laughter** l'intera tavolata moriva dalle risate; **to drink sb under the table** battere qn nel bere; **to turn the tables on sb** (*fig*) rovesciare la situazione a danno di qn **2** (*Math, Chem: illustration*) tavola; (*chart*) tabella; **table of contents** indice *m*; **league table** (*Ftbl, Rugby*) classifica
■ VT (*bill, motion: Brit: propose*) presentare; (*: Am: postpone*) rinviare

tab·leau [ˈtæbləʊ] N (*pl* **tableaux**) (*Theatre*) quadro vivente

table·cloth [ˈteɪblˌklɒθ] N tovaglia

table dancer N spogliarellista *f* (di lap dance)

table dancing N lap dance *f inv*

table d'hôte [ˌtɑːblˈdəʊt] N pasto a prezzo fisso
■ ADJ (*meal*) a prezzo fisso

table football N calcetto

table lamp N lampada da tavolo

table·land [ˈteɪblˌlænd] N tavolato, altopiano

table manners NPL maniere *fpl* a tavola

table·mat [ˈteɪblˌmæt] N tovaglietta

table napkin N tovagliolo

table salt N sale *m* fino *or* da tavola

table·spoon [ˈteɪblˌspuːn] N cucchiaio da portata *or* da tavola; (*also:* **tablespoonful**: *as measurement*) cucchiaiata; **a tablespoonful of sugar** un cucchiaio di zucchero

tab·let [ˈtæblɪt] N (*inscribed stone*) lapide *f*, targa; (*Med*) compressa; (*: for sucking*) pastiglia; (*for writing*) blocco; **tablet of soap** (*Brit*) saponetta

table talk N conversazione *f* a tavola

table tennis N tennis *m* da tavolo, ping-pong® *m*

table tennis player N giocatore(-trice) di ping-pong

table top N piano del tavolo

table·ware [ˈteɪblˌwɛəʳ] N servizi *mpl* da tavola

table wine N vino da tavola

tab·loid [ˈtæblɔɪd] N (*newspaper*) tabloid *m inv*

tabloid press N: **the tabloid press** i tabloid

TABLOID PRESS

Il termine **tabloid press** si riferisce ai quotidiani o ai settimanali popolari che, rispetto ai "quality papers", presentano le notizie in modo più sensazionalistico e meno approfondito e spesso hanno un formato ridotto. *Vedi anche* **quality papers**
▷ www.totaltravel.co.uk/library/britain/uk-newspapers/

ta·boo [təˈbuː] ADJ, N tabù (*m*) *inv*

tabu·lar [ˈtæbjʊləʳ] ADJ (*frm*) tabellare; **in tabular form** sotto forma di tabella

tabu·late [ˈtæbjʊˌleɪt] VT (*data, figures*) disporre in tabelle, tabulare

tabu·la·tion [ˌtæbjʊˈleɪʃən] N tabulazione *f*

tabu·la·tor [ˈtæbjʊˌleɪtəʳ] N tabulatore *m*

tacho·graph [ˈtækəˌgrɑːf] N tachigrafo

ta·chom·eter [tæˈkɒmɪtəʳ] N tachimetro

tac·it [ˈtæsɪt] ADJ tacito(-a)

tac·it·ly [ˈtæsɪtlɪ] ADV tacitamente

taci·turn [ˈtæsɪˌtɜːn] ADJ taciturno(-a)

taci·tur·nity [ˌtæsɪˈtɜːnɪtɪ] N l'essere taciturno, carattere *m* taciturno

Tacitus [ˈtæsɪtəs] N (*History, Literature*) Tacito

tack [tæk] N **1** (*nail*) bulletta; (*: for upholstery*) borchia; (*Am fam: also:* **thumbtack**) puntina da disegno; **a hammer and some tacks** un martello e dei chiodi;

to get down to brass tacks venire al sodo **2** (*Naut: course*) bordo; **to be on the port/starboard tack** avere le mura a sinistra/dritta; **to change tack** virare di bordo; (*fig*) cambiare linea di condotta; **to be on the right/wrong tack** (*fig*) essere sulla buona strada/ sulla strada sbagliata; **to try a different tack** (*fig*) prendere le cose per un altro verso **3** (*stitch*) punto d'imbastitura **4** (*for horse*) selleria, equipaggiamento
■ VT **1** (*nail*) imbullettare **2** (*Sewing*) imbastire; (*fig: add*): **to tack sth on to (the end of) sth** (*of letter, book*) aggiungere qc alla fine di qc; **I'll tack on a couple of paragraphs** aggiungerò un paio di paragrafi
■ VI (*Naut: change direction*) virare di bordo (in prua); (*go zigzag*) bordeggiare

tack·ing ['tækɪŋ] N **1** (*Sewing*) imbastitura **2** (*Naut*) virata

◎**tack·le** ['tækl] N **1** (*lifting gear*) paranco **2** (*equipment: esp for sport*) attrezzatura, equipaggiamento; **fishing tackle** attrezzatura da pesca **3** (*Ftbl*) contrasto; (*Rugby*) placcaggio
■ VT (*Ftbl*) contrastare; (*Rugby*) placcare; (*thief, intruder*) agguantare; (*fig: person, problem, job*) affrontare; **I'll tackle him about it at once** affronterò subito la cosa con lui

tack room N selleria

tacky ['tækɪ] ADJ (*comp* **-ier**, *superl* **-iest**) (*sticky*) appiccicoso(-a), appiccicaticcio(-a); (*: of paint, glue*) ancora bagnato(-a), non ancora asciutto(-a); (*fam: shabby*) scadente; (*: tasteless*) di cattivo gusto; **the paint was still tacky** la vernice era ancora appiccicaticcia; **a pair of tacky red sunglasses** un paio di occhialacci da sole rossi; **a tacky film** un filmaccio

taco ['tɑːkəʊ] N (*Culin*) sottile focaccia croccante di farina di mais, tipica della cucina messicana, che si mangia ripiena di carne e verdure

tact [tækt] N tatto

tact·ful ['tæktfʊl] ADJ (*person*) pieno(-a) di tatto; (*remark, reply*) discreto(-a); **to be tactful** avere tatto

tact·ful·ly ['tæktfəlɪ] ADV con tatto, con discrezione

◎**tac·tic** ['tæktɪk] N tattica; *see also* **tactics**

tac·ti·cal ['tæktɪkəl] ADJ tattico(-a)

tac·ti·cal·ly ['tæktɪkəlɪ] ADV tatticamente

tactical voting N voto tattico

tac·ti·cian [tæk'tɪʃən] N (*Mil, fig*) stratega *m/f*

tac·tics ['tæktɪks] N, NPL tattica; **strong-arm tactics** le maniere forti

tac·tile ['tæktaɪl] ADJ tattile

tact·less ['tæktlɪs] ADJ (*person*) privo(-a) di tatto, che manca di tatto; (*remark*) indelicato(-a)

tact·less·ly ['tæktlɪslɪ] ADV senza tatto

tad·pole ['tæd,pəʊl] N girino

taf·fe·ta ['tæfɪtə] N taffettà *m inv*

taf·fy ['tæfɪ] N (*Am*) caramella *f* mou *inv*

tag [tæg] N **1** (*label*) etichetta; (*metal point*) puntale *m*; **price/name tag** etichetta del prezzo/con il nome **2** (*game*) chiapparello
▸ **tag along** VI + ADV andare (*or* venire); **do you mind if I tag along?** ti dispiace se vengo anch'io?; **to tag along behind sb** andare (*or* venire) dietro a qn
▸ **tag on** VT + ADV: **to tag sth on (to the end of sth)** aggiungere qc (alla fine di qc)

ta·glia·tel·le [,tæljə'telɪ] NSG (*Culin*) tagliatelle *fpl*

tag line (*Am*) N (*of joke*) battuta; (*of advert*) slogan *m inv*

Ta·hi·ti [tɑː'hiːtɪ] N Tahiti *f*

t'ai chi [,taɪ'tʃiː] N, **t'ai chi ch'uan** [,taɪtʃiː'tʃwɑːn] N thai chi *m* (chuan)

◎**tail** [teɪl] N (*gen*) coda; (*of shirt*) estremità inferiore; **to put a tail on sb** (*fig fam*) far pedinare qn; **he was right on my tail** mi stava alle calcagna; **to turn tail** voltare la schiena; **he went off with his tail between his legs** (*fig*) se n'è andato con la coda fra le gambe; *see also* **head, tails**
■ VT (*fam: follow: suspect*) pedinare, seguire
▸ **tail away, tail off** VI + ADV (*in size, quality*) diminuire gradatamente

tail·back ['teɪl,bæk] N (*Brit Aut*) coda

tail coat N frac *m inv*, marsina

tail end N (*of party, meeting*) fine *f*; (*of train, procession*) coda; **to be at the tail end of the procession/queue** essere in coda alla processione/in fondo alla coda

tail flap N (*Aer*) timone *m* di profondità

tail·gate ['teɪl,geɪt] N (*Aut*) portellone *m* posteriore

tail light N (*Aut*) fanalino di coda; (*Rail*) luce *f* di coda

tai·lor ['teɪlə^r] N sarto; **tailor's dummy** manichino (da sarto); **tailor's (shop)** sartoria (da uomo)
■ VT (*suit*) confezionare; (*fig: to tailor sth (to)*) adattare qc (alle esigenze di)

tai·lored ['teɪləd] ADJ (*suit, dress*) attillato(-a)

tail·or·ing ['teɪlərɪŋ] N (*cut*) taglio

tailor-made [,teɪlə'meɪd] ADJ (*also fig*) fatto(-a) su misura; (*fig*): **it's tailor-made for you** è fatto apposta per te

tail·plane ['teɪl,pleɪn] N (*Aer*) stabilizzatore *m*

tails [teɪlz] N **1** SG (*of coin*) testa; **heads or tails** testa o croce **2** PL (*Dressmaking*) frac *m inv*, marsina; **to wear tails** essere in frac

tail·spin ['teɪl,spɪn] N (*Aer*) vite *f* di coda

tail·wind ['teɪl,wɪnd] N vento in coda

taint [teɪnt] N (*fig*) macchia; **the taint of madness** il marchio della pazzia
■ VT (*meat, food*) far avariare; (*fig: reputation*) infangare

taint·ed ['teɪntɪd] ADJ (*food*) avariato(-a), guasto(-a), andato(-a) a male; (*water, air*) contaminato(-a); (*fig: system*) inquinato(-a); (*: reputation*) infangato(-a)

Tai·wan [taɪ'wɑːn] N la Repubblica di Taiwan

Ta·jiki·stan [tɑː,dʒɪkɪ'stɑːn] N il Tagikistan

◎**take** [teɪk] (*vb: pt* **took**, *pp* **taken**) VT
1 (*gen*) prendere; (*remove, steal*) portar via; **let me take your coat** posso prenderti il cappotto?; **to take sb's hand** prendere qn per mano; **to take sb's arm** appoggiarsi al braccio di qn; **to take sb by the throat** afferrare qn alla gola; **he must be taken alive** dev'essere preso vivo; **to take the train** prendere il treno; **take the first on the left** prenda la prima a sinistra; **he hasn't taken any food for four days** non mangia nulla da quattro giorni; **to take notes** prendere appunti; **take 6 from 9** (*Math*) 9 meno 6; **he took £5 off the price** ha fatto uno sconto di 5 sterline; **to take a trick** (*Cards*) fare una presa; **"to be taken three times a day"** (*Med*) "da prendersi tre volte al dì"; **to take cold/fright** prendere freddo/paura; **to be taken ill** avere un malore; **I take size 8** porto la 42
2 (*bring, carry*) portare; (*accompany*) accompagnare; **I took the children with me** ho portato i bambini con me; **don't forget to take your camera** non scordarti di portare la macchina fotografica; **he goes to London every week, but he never takes me** va a Londra tutte le settimane ma non mi porta mai con sé; **to take for a walk** (*child, dog*) portare a fare una passeggiata
3 (*require: effort, courage*) volerci, occorrere; (*Gram*) prendere, reggere; **it takes about an hour** ci vuole circa un'ora; **it took me two hours to do it** *or* **I took**

two hours to do it mi ci sono volute due ore per farlo; **it won't take long** non ci vorrà molto tempo; **she's got what it takes to do the job** ha i requisiti necessari per quel lavoro; **it takes a brave man to do that** ci vuole del coraggio per farlo; **it takes a lot of time/courage** occorre *or* ci vuole molto tempo/coraggio; **it takes a lot of money to do that** ci vogliono un sacco di soldi per farlo; **that will take some explaining** non sarà facile da spiegare; **it takes some believing** bisogna fare uno sforzo per crederci
4 (*accept, receive*) accettare; (*obtain, win: prize*) vincere, ottenere; (*: 1st place*) conquistare; (*Comm: money*) incassare; **he didn't take my advice** non mi ha ascoltato; **how did he take the news?** come ha preso la notizia?; **please take a seat** prego, si sieda; **is this seat taken?** è occupato (questo posto)?; **do you take credit cards?** accettate carte di credito?; **it's worth taking a chance** vale la pena di correre il rischio; **it's £50, take it or leave it** sono 50 sterline, prendere o lasciare; **can you take it from here?** (*handing over task*) puoi andare avanti tu?; **you must take us as you find us** devi prenderci per quel che siamo
5 (*have room or capacity for: passengers*) contenere; (*support: subj: bridge*) avere una portata di; (*: chair*) tenere; **the hall will take 200 people** nel salone c'è posto per 200 persone; **the bus takes 60 passengers** l'autobus porta 60 persone; **it will take at least five litres** contiene almeno cinque litri
6 (*conduct: meeting*) condurre; (*: church service*) officiare; (*teach, study: course*) fare; (*exam, test*) fare, sostenere; **the professor is taking the French course himself** sarà il professore stesso a fare *or* tenere il corso di francese; **I only took Russian for one year** ho fatto russo solo per un anno; **have you taken your driving test yet?** hai già fatto l'esame di guida?; **I took the driving test** ho fatto *or* sostenuto l'esame di guida
7 (*understand, assume*) pensare; (*consider: case, example*) prendere; **how old do you take him to be?** quanti anni pensi che abbia?; **I took him for a doctor** l'ho preso per un dottore; **I took him to be foreign** l'ho preso per uno straniero; **I take it that ...** suppongo che...; **may I take it that ...?** allora posso star certo che...?; **take it from me!** credimi!; **take D.H. Lawrence, for example** prendete D.H. Lawrence, per esempio
8 (*put up with, tolerate: climate, alcohol*) sopportare; **she can't take the heat** non sopporta il caldo; **I can't take any more!** non ce la faccio più!; **I won't take no for an answer** non accetterò una risposta negativa *or* un rifiuto; **he can't take being criticized** non sopporta di essere criticato
9 (*negotiate: bend*) prendere; (*: fence*) saltare
10 (*attracted*): **to be taken with sb/sth** essere tutto(-a) preso(-a) da qn/qc; **I'm quite taken with the idea** l'idea non mi dispiace per niente
11 (*as function verb: see other element*): **to take a photograph** fare una fotografia; **to take a bath/ shower** fare un bagno/una doccia; **take your time!** calma!; **it took me by surprise** mi ha colto di sorpresa
■ VI (*dye, fire*) prendere; (*injection*) fare effetto; (*plant, cutting*) attecchire
■ N (*Cine*) ripresa
▸ **take after** VI + PREP assomigliare a; **she takes after her mother** assomiglia a sua madre
▸ **take against** VI + PREP prendere in antipatia
▸ **take along** VT + ADV portare
▸ **take apart** VT + ADV (*clock, machine*) smontare; (*fig fam: criticize*) demolire
▸ **take aside** VT + ADV prendere in disparte
▸ **take away** VI + ADV: **to take away from sth** danneggiare qc; **his bad temper took away from the pleasure of our party** ci ha guastato un po' la festa con il suo cattivo umore
■ VT + ADV
1 (*subtract*): **to take away (from)** sottrarre (da); **you need to take this amount away from the total** devi sottrarre questa cifra dal totale; **sixteen take away three** sedici meno tre
2 (*remove: person, thing, privilege*) togliere; (*carry away, lead away*) portar via; **they took away all his belongings** gli hanno portato via tutte le sue cose; **she was afraid her children would be taken away from her** temeva che le togliessero i bambini; **we took him away on holiday** l'abbiamo portato in vacanza; **pizzas to take away** pizze *fpl* da asporto
▸ **take back** VT + ADV
1 (*get back, reclaim*) riprendere; (*retract: statement, promise*) ritirare; **I take it all back!** ritiro tutto quello che ho detto!
2 (*return: book, goods, person*) riportare; **I took it back to the shop** l'ho riportato al negozio; **can you take him back home?** puoi riaccompagnarlo a casa?; **it takes me back to my childhood** (*fig*) mi ha fatto tornare alla mia infanzia
▸ **take down** VT + ADV
1 (*curtains, picture, vase from shelf*) tirare giù; **she took down a book from the top shelf** ha tirato giù un libro dall'ultimo scaffale
2 (*dismantle: scaffolding*) smontare; (*: building*) demolire; **he took down the bookcase** ha smontato la libreria
3 (*write down: notes, address*) prendere; (*: letter*) scrivere; **the policeman took down the details** il poliziotto ha preso nota dei particolari
▸ **take in** VT + ADV
1 (*bring in: object, harvest*) portare dentro; (*: person*) far entrare; (*: lodger*) prendere, ospitare; (*: orphan*) accogliere; (*: stray dog*) raccogliere
2 (*receive: money*) incassare; (*: laundry, sewing*) prendere a domicilio
3 (*Sewing*) stringere
4 (*include, cover*) coprire; (*prices*) includere, comprendere; **we took in Florence on the way** abbiamo visitato anche Firenze durante il viaggio
5 (*grasp, understand: meaning, complex subject*) capire; (*: situation*) rendersi conto di; (*: impressions, sights*) assimilare; (*: visually: surroundings, people, area*) prendere nota con uno sguardo; **I didn't really take it in** non avevo capito bene; **he took the situation in at a glance** ha afferrato subito la situazione
6 (*deceive, cheat*) imbrogliare, abbindolare; **they were taken in by his story** si sono lasciati abbindolare dalla sua storia; **to be taken in by appearances** farsi ingannare dalle apparenze
▸ **take off** VI + ADV
1 (*plane, passengers*) decollare; (*high jumper*) spiccare un salto; **the plane took off twenty minutes late** l'aereo ha decollato con venti minuti di ritardo
■ VT + ADV
1 (*remove: clothes*) togliere *or* togliersi; (*: price tag, lid, item from menu*) togliere; (*: leg, limb*) amputare; (*cancel: train*) sopprimere; **take your coat off** levati il cappotto
2 (*deduct: from bill, price*): **she took 50p off** ha fatto 50 penny di sconto

Tt

3 (*lead away*: *person, object*) portare; **she was taken off to the hospital** è stata portata all'ospedale; **to take o.s. off** andarsene
4 (*imitate*) imitare
■ VT + PREP
1 (*remove*: *clothes, price tag, lid*) togliere da; (: *item from menu*) cancellare da; (*cancel*: *train*) togliere da; **to take sb off sth** (*remove from duty, job*) allontanare qn da qc; **they took him off the Financial Page** (*journalist*) gli hanno tolto la pagina economica
2 (*deduct*: *from bill, price*): **he took 5% off the price for me** mi ha fatto uno sconto del 5% sul prezzo
▸ **take on** VI + ADV
1 (*old fam*: *become upset*) prendersela
2 (*song, fashion*) fare presa
■ VT + ADV
1 (*work*) accettare, intraprendere; (*responsibility*) prendersi, addossarsi; (*bet, challenger*) affrontare
2 (*worker*: *fig*: *qualities, form*) assumere; (*cargo, passengers*) caricare; **her face took on a wistful expression** sul suo volto si era dipinta un'espressione malinconica
▸ **take out** VT + ADV
1 (*bring, carry out*) portare fuori; **to take sb out to ...** portare qn a...; **he took her out to the theatre** l'ha portata a teatro; **can I take you out to lunch?** posso invitarti a pranzo fuori?; **he took the dog out for a walk** ha portato il cane a passeggio
2 (*extract*: *appendix, tooth*) togliere; (*remove*: *stain*) rimuovere, togliere; (*pull out*: *from pocket, drawer*): **to take sth out of sth** tirare fuori qc da qc, estrarre qc da qc; **he took a plate out of the cupboard** ha preso un piatto dalla credenza; **he opened his wallet and took out some money** ha aperto il portafoglio e ha tirato fuori dei soldi
3 (*insurance, patent, licence*) prendere, ottenere, procurarsi
4 **to take sb out of himself** far distrarre qn; **redecorating a house takes it out of you** è spossante ridipingere una casa; **don't take it out on me!** non prendertela con me!
▸ **take over** VI + ADV (*dictator, political party*) prendere il potere; **to take over from sb** prendere le consegne da qn, subentrare a qn; **I'll take over now** ti do il cambio
■ VT + ADV (*debts, business*) rilevare; (*company*) assumere il controllo di; **to take over from sb** subentrare a qn; **to take over sb's job** subentrare a qn nel lavoro; **they took over the company last year** hanno assunto il controllo della società l'anno scorso; **the tourists have taken over Florence** (*fig*) i turisti hanno preso d'assalto Firenze
▸ **take to** VI + PREP
1 (*develop liking for*: *person*) prendere in simpatia; (: *games, surroundings, activity*) prendere gusto a; **I just can't take to my friend's husband** il marito della mia amica non riesce proprio a piacermi; **she didn't take kindly to the idea** l'idea non le è piaciuta per niente
2 (*form habit of*): **to take to sth** darsi a qc; **to take to doing sth** prendere *or* cominciare a fare qc
3 (*escape to*) fuggire verso; **to take to one's bed** mettersi a letto
▸ **take up** VI + ADV: **to take up with sb** fare amicizia con qn; **she took up with bad company** si è messa a frequentare cattive compagnie
■ VT + ADV
1 (*raise, lift*) raccogliere; (: *subj*: *bus*) prendere; (: *carpet, floorboards*) sollevare; (: *road*) spaccare; (: *dress, hem*) accorciare
2 (*lead, carry upstairs*) portare su
3 (*continue*) riprendere
4 (*occupy*: *time, attention*) assorbire; (: *space*) occupare; **it will take up the whole of our Sunday** ci porterà via tutta la domenica; **he's very taken up with his work** è molto preso dal suo lavoro; **he's very taken up with her** non fa che pensare a lei
5 (*absorb*: *liquids*) assorbire
6 (*raise question of*: *matter, point*) affrontare
7 (*start*: *job, duties*) cominciare; (: *hobby, sport*): **to take up painting/golf/photography** cominciare a dipingere/giocare a golf/fare fotografie; **to take up a career as** intraprendere la carriera di
8 (*accept*: *offer, challenge*) accettare; **I'll take you up on your offer** accetto la tua offerta
9 (*adopt*: *cause, case, person*) appoggiare
▸ **take upon** VT + PREP: **to take sth upon o.s.** prendersi la responsabilità di qc; **to take it upon o.s. to do sth** prendersi la responsabilità di fare qc

take·away [ˈteɪkəˌweɪ] (*Brit*) N (*shop*) ≈ rosticceria (*meal*) piatto pronto (*da asporto*)
■ ADJ (*food*) da asporto, da portar via
take-home pay [ˈteɪkhəʊmˌpeɪ] N stipendio netto
tak·en [ˈteɪkən] PP *of* **take**
take·off [ˈteɪkˌɒf] N **1** (*Aer*) decollo; (*Horse-riding*) battuta **2** (*fam*: *imitation*) imitazione *f*
take·out [ˈteɪkˌaʊt] ADJ (*Am*) = **takeaway**
◎ **take·over** [ˈteɪkˌəʊvəʳ] N (*Comm*) assorbimento
takeover bid N offerta di assorbimento
tak·er [ˈteɪkəʳ] N: **drug-takers** drogati *mpl*; **at £100 he found few takers** per 100 sterline ha trovato pochi acquirenti; **his suggestion found no takers** la sua proposta non è stata accolta
take-up [ˈteɪkʌp] N *entità della domanda di un servizio cui si ha diritto*
tak·ing [ˈteɪkɪŋ] ADJ (*attractive*) accattivante
tak·ings [ˈteɪkɪŋz] NPL (*Fin*) introiti *mpl*, entrate *fpl*; (*at show*) incasso
talc [tælk], **tal·cum pow·der** [ˈtælkəmˌpaʊdəʳ] N talco
◎ **tale** [teɪl] N (*gen*) storia; (*story*) racconto; (*legend*) leggenda; (*pej*) fandonia; **to tell tales** (*inform*) fare la spia; (*lies*) dire bugie; **he told us the tale of his escape** ci ha raccontato la storia della sua fuga
◎ **tal·ent** [ˈtælənt] N **1** (*skill*) talento; **he's got a lot of talent** ha molto talento; **to have a talent for** essere portato(-a) per; **he has a talent for languages** è portato per le lingue, ha facilità nell'apprendere le lingue; **there isn't much musical talent in this town** non ci sono molti grandi talenti musicali in questa città; **there's not much talent about tonight** (*Brit fam*: *attractive people*) non c'è nessuno di decente in giro stasera **2** (*Bible*) talento
tal·ent·ed [ˈtæləntɪd] ADJ di talento; **she's a talented pianist** è una pianista di talento
talent scout N talent scout *m/f inv*
tal·is·man [ˈtælɪzmən] N talismano
◎ **talk** [tɔːk] N
1 (*conversation*) conversazione *f*; (*chat*) chiacchierata; (*speech*) discorso; (*interview*) discussione *f*; **talks** NPL (*Pol*) colloqui *mpl*; **to have a talk about** parlare di; **I had a talk with my Mum about it** ne ho parlato con mia mamma; **I must have a talk with you** devo parlarti
2 (*lecture*) conferenza; **to give a talk** tenere una

conferenza, fare un intervento; **she gave a talk on ancient Egypt** ha fatto un intervento sull'antico Egitto; **he will give us a talk on ...** ci parlerà di...; **to give a talk on the radio** parlare alla radio
3 *(gossip)* dicerie *fpl*, chiacchiere *fpl*; **the talk was all about the wedding** non si faceva che parlare del matrimonio; **there has been a lot of talk about him** si è molto parlato di lui; **she's the talk of the town** è sulla bocca di tutti; **it's just talk** sono solo chiacchiere
■ VI *(gen)* parlare; *(discuss)* discutere; *(chatter)* chiacchierare; **to talk about** parlare di; *(converse)* discorrere *or* conversare di; **what did you talk about?** di che cosa avete parlato?; **to talk to/with sb about** *or* **of sth** parlare a/con qn di qc; **to talk to o.s.** parlare da solo; **try to keep him talking** cerca di farlo parlare; **to get o.s. talked about** far parlare di sé; **it's all right for you to talk!** parli bene tu!; **look who's talking!** senti chi parla!, parli proprio tu!; **now you're talking!** questo sì che è parlare!; **he talks too much** *(talkative)* parla troppo; *(indiscreet)* non sa tenere la bocca chiusa; **they are talking of going to Sicily** pensano di andare in Sicilia; **who were you talking to?** con chi stavi parlando?; **he knows what he's talking about** lui sì che se ne intende; **talking of films, have you seen ...?** a proposito di film, hai visto...?
■ VT *(a language, slang)* parlare; **they were talking Arabic** parlavano arabo; **to talk business** parlare di affari; **to talk shop** parlare del lavoro *or* degli affari; **to talk nonsense** dire stupidaggini; **to talk sb into doing sth** persuadere *or* convincere qn a fare qc; **to talk sb out of doing sth** dissuadere qn dal fare qc
▶ **talk back** VI + ADV: **to talk back (to sb)** rispondere impertinentemente (a qn)
▶ **talk down** VI + ADV: **to talk down to sb** parlare a qn con condiscendenza
■ VT + ADV: **to talk a plane (*or* pilot) down** guidare l'atterraggio dalla torre di controllo
▶ **talk out** VT + ADV: **to talk things out** mettere le cose in chiaro discutendone
▶ **talk over** VT + ADV discutere; **to talk sth over with sb** discutere qc con qn; **I'll have to talk it over with my wife** devo parlarne con mia moglie
▶ **talk round** VT + ADV: **to talk sb round** convincere qn
■ VI + PREP *(subject, problem)* girare intorno a

talka·tive ['tɔːkətɪv] ADJ loquace, ciarliero(-a)

talked-of ['tɔːkt,ɒv] ADJ: **a much talked-of event** un avvenimento di cui si parla molto

talk·er ['tɔːkə^r] N parlatore(-trice); *(pej)* chiacchierone(-a)

talkie ['tɔːkɪ] N *(Cine: old fam)*: **with the advent of the talkie** con l'avvento del sonoro

talk·ing ['tɔːkɪŋ] ADJ *(doll, bird)* parlante
■ N parlare *m*; **I'll do the talking** parlo io; **she does all the talking** è lei che tiene in piedi la conversazione

talking book N audiolibro

talking point N argomento di conversazione

talking-to ['tɔːkɪŋ,tuː] N *(fam)*: **to give sb a good talking-to** fare una bella paternale a qn

talk show N *(Am: TV, Radio)* talk show *m inv*

◎ **tall** [tɔːl] ADJ *(comp* **-er**, *superl* **-est)** alto(-a); **to be two metres tall** essere alto due metri; **how tall are you?** quanto sei alto?; **I'm 6 feet tall** ≈ sono alto 1 metro 80; **that's a tall order!** è una bella pretesa!

tall·boy ['tɔːl,bɔɪ] N *(Brit)* cassettone *m* alto

tall·ness ['tɔːlnɪs] N altezza

tal·low ['tæləʊ] N sego

tall ship N grosso veliero

tall story N *(Brit)* storia incredibile

tal·ly ['tælɪ] N *(count)* conto, conteggio; *(running total)* totale *m*; *(score)* punteggio; **to keep a tally of sth** tener il conto di qc
■ VI: **to tally (with)** corrispondere (a)

Tal·mud ['tælmʊd] N Talmud *m*

tal·on ['tælən] N artiglio

DID YOU KNOW ...?
talon is not translated by the Italian word *tallone*

tama·rind ['tæmərɪnd] N tamarindo

tama·risk ['tæmərɪsk] N tamerice *f*, tamarisco

tam·bou·rine [,tæmbə'riːn] N tamburello

tame [teɪm] ADJ *(comp* **-r**, *superl* **-st)** *(animal)* addomesticato(-a); *(fig: person)* docile; *(: story, style)* scialbo(-a), insipido(-a); *(: book, performance)* banale; **tame monkeys** scimmie *fpl* addomesticate; **a tame report** una relazione scialba
■ VT *(wild creature)* addomesticare; *(lion, tiger, passion)* domare

tame·ly ['teɪmlɪ] ADV *(agree)* docilmente

Tam·il ['tæmɪl] ADJ tamil *inv*
■ N *(person)* tamil *m/f*; *(language)* tamil *m*

tam·ing ['teɪmɪŋ] N *(gen)* addomesticamento; **"The Taming of the Shrew"** "La Bisbetica Domata"

Tampax® ['tæmpæks] N, PL INV Tampax® *m inv*

tam·per ['tæmpə^r] VI: **to tamper with** manomettere; **someone had tampered with the brakes** qualcuno aveva manomesso i freni

tam·pon ['tæmpən] N tampone *m*

tan [tæn] N *(also:* **suntan)** abbronzatura; *(colour)* color *m* marrone chiaro; **to get a tan** abbronzarsi
■ ADJ marrone chiaro *inv*
■ VI abbronzarsi
■ VT *(person, skin)* abbronzare; *(leather)* conciare; **to tan sb's hide** *(fam)* darle a qn

tan·dem ['tændəm] N *(bicycle)* tandem *m inv*
■ ADV: **in tandem** in tandem

tan·doori [tæn'dʊərɪ] ADJ: **tandoori chicken** *(Culin)* *pollo speziato, cucinato in forno d'argilla, tipico della cucina indiana*

tang [tæŋ] N *(taste)* sapore *m* forte; *(smell)* odore *m* penetrante

tan·gent ['tændʒənt] N *(Geom)* tangente *f*; **to go off at a tangent** *(fig)* partire per la tangente

tan·gen·tial [,tæn'dʒenʃəl] ADJ *(frm)* marginale

tan·ge·rine [,tændʒə'riːn] N *specie di mandarino*

tan·gible ['tændʒəbl] ADJ *(proof, results)* tangibile; *(difference)* sostanziale; **tangible assets** patrimonio reale

tan·gibly ['tændʒəblɪ] ADV *(see adj)* in modo tangibile; sostanzialmente

Tan·gier [tæn'dʒɪə^r] N Tangeri *f*

tan·gle ['tæŋgl] N *(of wool, wire)* groviglio; *(in hair)* nodo; *(fig: muddle)* confusione *f*; **a tangle of wires** un groviglio di fili; **to get into a tangle** *(gen)* aggrovigliarsi; *(hair)* arruffarsi; *(person)* combinare un pasticcio; **we got into a tangle** ci siamo messi in un pasticcio
■ VT *(also:* **tangle up)** aggrovigliare; *(hair)* arruffare
■ VI aggrovigliarsi; *(hair)* ingarbugliarsi; **to tangle with sb** *(fig fam)* azzuffarsi con qn

tan·gled ['tæŋgəld] ADJ *(string, wires, hair)* aggrovigliato(-a); *(fig: situation, negotiations)* ingarbugliato(-a)

tan·go ['tæŋgəʊ] N tango

Tt

tangy ['tæŋɪ] ADJ (*comp* **-ier**, *superl* **-iest**) (*flavour, taste, smell*) aspro(-a)

◎**tank** [tæŋk] N **1** (*container: for gas, petrol*) serbatoio; (*: for rainwater*) cisterna; (*: for processing*) vasca; **fish tank** acquario; **fuel tank** serbatoio del carburante **2** (*Mil*) carro armato; **the army sent in its tanks** l'esercito ha inviato i carri armati

tank·ard ['tæŋkəd] N boccale *m* (con coperchio)

tanked-up [,tæŋkt'ʌp] ADJ (*Brit fam*): **to be tanked-up** essere sbronzo(-a)

tank·er ['tæŋkə^r] N (*ship: for oil*) petroliera; (*: for water*) nave *f* cisterna *inv*; (*aircraft*) aereocisterna; (*lorry*) autocisterna, autobotte *f*

tank·ful ['tæŋkfʊl] N: **a tankful of water** una cisterna (piena) d'acqua; **to pay for a tankful of petrol** (*for car*) pagare per un pieno (di benzina)

tank top N (*Brit*) pullover *m inv* senza maniche; (*Am*) canottiera

tanned [tænd] ADJ abbronzato(-a)

tan·ner ['tænə^r] N (*person*) conciatore(-trice)

tan·nery ['tænərɪ] N conceria

tan·nin ['tænɪn] N tannino

tan·ning ['tænɪŋ] N **1** (*by sun*) abbronzatura; (*of leather*) conciatura **2** (*fam: beating*) botte *fpl*

Tan·noy® ['tænɔɪ] N (*Brit*) altoparlante *m*; **over the Tannoy** con l'altoparlante

tan·ta·lize ['tæntə,laɪz] VT tormentare

tan·ta·liz·ing ['tæntə,laɪzɪŋ] ADJ (*food*) stuzzicante; (*idea, offer*) allettante

tan·ta·liz·ing·ly ['tæntə,laɪzɪŋlɪ] ADV in modo allettante; **we were tantalizingly close to victory** eravamo così vicino alla vittoria

tan·ta·mount ['tæntə,maʊnt] ADJ: **to be tantamount to** equivalere a; **tantamount to** equivalente a

tan·trum ['tæntrəm] N accesso di collera; **to have** *or* **throw a tantrum** fare le bizze *or* i capricci

Tan·za·nia [,tænzə'nɪə] N la Tanzania

Tan·za·nian [,tænzə'nɪən] ADJ, N tanzaniano(-a)

Taoiseach ['ti:ʃəx] N *Primo ministro della Repubblica d'Irlanda*

◎**tap¹** [tæp] N (*Brit: on sink*) rubinetto; **on tap** (*beer*) alla spina; (*fig: resources*) a disposizione; **the hot tap** il rubinetto dell'acqua calda
■VT (*barrel*) spillare; (*telephone*) mettere sotto controllo; (*telephone conversation*) intercettare; (*resources*) sfruttare, utilizzare

> DID YOU KNOW ...?
> **tap** is not translated by the Italian word *tappa*

tap² [tæp] N (*gentle blow*) colpetto; **there was a tap on the door** hanno bussato leggermente alla porta
■VT (*pat, knock*) picchiare leggermente su, dare un colpetto a; **I tapped him on the shoulder** gli ho dato un colpetto sulla spalla; **to tap one's foot** (*impatiently*) battere il piede; (*in time to music*) segnare il tempo con il piede; **to tap out a message in Morse** trasmettere un messaggio in Morse
■VI (*knock*) bussare; (*rain*) picchiettare

tap-dancer ['tæp,dɑ:nsə^r] N ballerino(-a) di tip tap

tap dancing N tip tap *m*
▷ www.tapdance.org/tap/referenc.htm

◎**tape** [teɪp] N (*gen, Sport: for recording*) nastro; (*also:* **magnetic tape**) nastro (magnetico); (*Sewing*) fettuccia; **on tape** (*song*) su nastro; **adhesive tape** nastro adesivo; **a tape of Oasis** una cassetta degli Oasis; **to break the tape** (*Sport*) tagliare la linea del traguardo
■VT (*record*) registrare (su nastro); **did you tape the film last night?** hai registrato il film di ieri sera?; (*also:* **tape up**) legare con un nastro; **I've got him taped** (*Brit fam*) ho capito il tipo

tape deck N piastra di registrazione

tape library N nastroteca

tape measure N metro a nastro

ta·per ['teɪpə^r] N (*waxed spill*) cerino; (*thin candle*) candelina
■VI (*also:* **taper off**) assottigliarsi; (*trousers*) restringersi

tape-record ['teɪprɪ,kɔ:d] VT registrare (su nastro)

tape recorder N registratore *m* (a nastro)

tape recording N registrazione *f*

ta·pered ['teɪpəd] ADJ (*trouser leg, stick*) affusolato(-a)

ta·per·ing ['teɪpərɪŋ] ADJ (*fingers*) affusolato(-a)

tap·es·try ['tæpɪstrɪ] N (*object*) arazzo, tappezzeria; (*art*) mezzo punto
▷ www.bayeuxtapestry.org.uk
▷ www.metmuseum.org/explore/Unicorn/unicorn_inside.htm

tape·worm ['teɪp,wɜ:m] N tenia, verme *m* solitario

tapio·ca [,tæpɪ'əʊkə] N tapioca

ta·pir ['teɪpə^r] N tapiro

tap·pet ['tæpɪt] N punteria

tap·root ['tæp,ru:t] N radice *f* principale

tap water N (*Brit*) acqua del rubinetto

tar [tɑ:^r] N catrame *m*; **low-/middle-tar cigarettes** sigarette a basso/medio contenuto di catrame
■VT (*road*) incatramare; **he's tarred with the same brush** (*fig*) è della stessa razza

ta·ran·tu·la [tə'ræntjʊlə] N tarantola

tar·dy ['tɑ:dɪ] ADJ (*comp* **-ier**, *superl* **-iest**) (*slow*) lento(-a); (*later than expected*) tardivo(-a), tardo(-a); (*Am: late: person*) in ritardo

tare [tɛə^r] N (*Comm*) tara

◎**tar·get** ['tɑ:gɪt] N (*gen: objective*) obiettivo; (*Mil, Archery*) bersaglio; (*fig*) obiettivo, bersaglio; **he achieved his target** ha raggiunto il suo obiettivo; **the bullet hit the target** il proiettile ha colpito il bersaglio; **she has been the target of criticism** è stata fatta oggetto *or* bersaglio di critiche; **the targets for production in 1990** gli obiettivi della produzione per il 1990; **to be on target** (*project*) essere nei tempi (di lavorazione)
■VT puntare su; **the company targets well-off childless couples** l'azienda punta sulle coppie benestanti senza figli

target area N (*Mil*) zona da colpire

target practice N (esercitazioni *fpl* di) tiro al bersaglio

tar·iff ['tærɪf] N (*price list*) tariffa; (*tax*) tariffa doganale, dazio

tariff barrier N barriera tariffaria

Tar·mac® ['tɑ:mæk] N (*Brit: on road*) macadam *m* al catrame; (*runway*): **the tarmac** la pista
■VT (*Brit*) macadamizzare con il catrame

tar·nish ['tɑ:nɪʃ] VT ossidare, annerire; (*fig: reputation*) infangare, macchiare; **the affair tarnished his reputation** la storia ha macchiato la sua reputazione
■VI ossidarsi, annerirsi; **it never rusts or tarnishes** non si arrugginisce né si annerisce

ta·rot ['tærəʊ] N tarocco

tarot cards NPL tarocchi *mpl*

tar·pau·lin [tɑ:'pɔ:lɪn] N (*waterproof cover*) (tela) incerata

tar·ra·gon ['tærəgən] N dragoncello

tar·ry¹ ['tærɪ] VI (*old, liter*) **1** (*linger*) trattenersi **2** (*delay*) tardare

tar·ry² ['tɑ:rɪ] ADJ (*road*) incatramato(-a); (*tar-stained*) macchiato(-a) di catrame

tart¹ [tɑːt] ADJ (*fruit, flavour*) aspro(-a), agro(-a); (*fig: remark*) caustico(-a)
▸ **tart up** VT + ADV (*Brit fam*) agghindare; **to tart o.s. up** *or* **get tarted up** farsi bello(-a); (*pej*) agghindarsi
tart² [tɑːt] N **1** (*Brit Culin: large*) crostata; (: *individual*) crostatina **2** (*fam offensive: woman*) puttana (*fam!*)
tar·tan ['tɑːtən] N tartan *m inv*, tessuto scozzese
■ ADJ di tessuto scozzese; **a tartan scarf** una sciarpa scozzese
tartan rug N coperta di tessuto scozzese
tar·tar¹ ['tɑːtər] N (*on teeth*) tartaro; **cream of tartar** cremortartaro
tar·tar² ['tɑːtər] N (*fig*) despota *m*
tartar sauce N salsa tartara
tart·ly ['tɑːtlɪ] ADV (*remark*) causticamente
tart·ness ['tɑːtnɪs] N (*of fruit*) asprezza, agro; (*of remark*) asprezza, causticità *f inv*
◎ **task** [tɑːsk] N compito; **a difficult task** un compito difficile; **to take sb to task (for sth)** richiamare qn all'ordine (per qc), rimproverare qn (per qc)
task·bar ['tɑːskˌbɑːr] N (*Comput*) barra delle applicazioni
◎ **task force** N (*Mil, Police*) unità *f inv* operativa, task force *f inv*
task·master ['tɑːskˌmɑːstər] N: **he's a hard taskmaster** è un vero tiranno
Tas·ma·nia [tæz'meɪnɪə] N la Tasmania
▹ www.parliament.tas.gov.au
▹ www.discovertasmania.com.au
tas·sel ['tæsəl] N nappa, fiocco
tas·selled ['tæsəld] ADJ guarnito(-a) di nappe
◎ **taste** [teɪst] N (*gen*) gusto; (*flavour*) sapore *m*, gusto; (*fig: glimpse, idea*) idea; **the soup had an odd taste** la minestra aveva un sapore un po' strano; **to have a taste of sth** assaggiare qc; **may I have a taste?** posso assaggiare?; **have a taste of everything!** assaggia un po' di tutto!; **to have a taste for sth** avere un'inclinazione per qc; **he acquired a taste for sports cars** gli è preso il gusto delle macchine sportive; **it's not to my taste** non è di mio gusto; **to be in bad** *or* **poor taste** essere di cattivo gusto; **a joke in bad taste** uno scherzo di cattivo gusto; **"sweeten to taste"** (*Culin*) "zuccherare a piacere"
■ VT **1** gustare; (*sample*) assaggiare; **would you like to taste it?** vuoi assaggiare?; **just taste this** assaggiane un pochino **2** (*notice flavour of*) sentire il sapore di; **you can taste the garlic (in it)** (ci) si sente il sapore dell'aglio **3** (*fig: experience*) assaporare; **once he had tasted power** una volta assaporato il gusto del potere
■ VI: **to taste of** (*fish, garlic*) sapere di, avere sapore di; **it tastes of fish** sa di pesce; **it tastes good/bad** ha un buon/cattivo sapore; **what does it taste like?** che sapore *or* gusto ha?; **rabbit tastes quite like chicken** il coniglio ha un gusto molto simile a quello del pollo

DID YOU KNOW ...?
taste is not translated by the Italian word *tasto*

taste bud N papilla gustativa
taste·ful ['teɪstfʊl] ADJ di (buon) gusto
taste·ful·ly ['teɪstfəlɪ] ADV con gusto
taste·less ['teɪstlɪs] ADJ (*food*) insipido(-a); (*decor, joke, remark*) di cattivo gusto
taste·less·ly ['teɪstlɪslɪ] ADV senza gusto
tast·er ['teɪstər] N assaggiatore(-trice)
tasty ['teɪstɪ] ADJ (*comp* **-ier**, *superl* **-iest**) (*food*) saporito(-a), gustoso(-a); (*dish, meal*) succulento(-a)
tat [tæt] N **1** (*Brit fam pej*) ciarpame *m* **2** *see* **tit³**
ta-ta ['tæ'tɑː] EXCL (*Brit fam: goodbye*) ciao!
Tate Britain [ˌteɪt'brɪtən] N Tate Britain *f*
Tate Modern [ˌteɪt'mɒdən] N Tate Modern *f*
▹ www.tate.org.uk
tat·tered ['tætəd] ADJ sbrindellato(-a)
tat·ters ['tætəz] NPL stracci *mpl*; **in tatters** a brandelli, sbrindellato(-a)
tat·tle ['tætl] VI spettegolare
■ N chiacchiere *fpl*, pettegolezzi *mpl*
tat·too¹ [tə'tuː] N (*on skin*) tatuaggio
■ VT tatuare
tat·too² [tə'tuː] N (*Mil: signal*) ritirata; (: *show*) parata militare
tat·too·ist [tæ'tuːɪst] N tatuatore(-trice)
tat·ty ['tætɪ] ADJ (*comp* **-ier**, *superl* **-iest**) (*Brit fam: shabby*) malandato(-a), malridotto(-a); (: *paint*) scrostato(-a)
taught [tɔːt] PT, PP *of* **teach**
taunt [tɔːnt] N scherno
■ VT: **to taunt sb (with)** schernire qn (per)
taunt·ing ['tɔːntɪŋ] ADJ beffardo(-a)
■ N frasi *fpl* di scherno
Tau·rus ['tɔːrəs] N (*Astron, Astrol*) Toro; **to be Taurus** essere del Toro; **I'm Taurus** sono del Toro
taut [tɔːt] ADJ (*comp* **-er**, *superl* **-est**) (*also fig*) teso(-a)
taut·en ['tɔːtən] VI tendersi
tau·to·logi·cal [ˌtɔːtə'lɒdʒɪkəl] ADJ tautologico(-a)
tau·tol·ogy [tɔː'tɒlədʒɪ] N tautologia
tav·ern ['tævən] N (*old*) taverna
taw·dry ['tɔːdrɪ] ADJ (*comp* **-ier**, *superl* **-iest**) pacchiano(-a)
taw·ny ['tɔːnɪ] ADJ (*comp* **-ier**, *superl* **-iest**) fulvo(-a)
tawny owl N allocco
◎ **tax** [tæks] N (*on income*) imposta, tasse *fpl* (*fam*); (*on goods, services*) tassa; **before/after tax** al lordo/netto delle imposte (*or* delle tasse); **free of tax** esente da imposte; esentasse *inv*; **a third of my wages goes in tax** un terzo del mio stipendio se ne va in tasse; **how much tax do you pay?** quanto paghi di tasse?; **to put a tax on sth** mettere una tassa su qc; **the tax on cigarettes** la tassa sulle sigarette; **nobody wants to pay more tax** nessuno vuole pagare più tasse
■ VT **1** (*Fin: people, salary, goods*) tassare; **tobacco and petrol are heavily taxed** le tasse sul tabacco e sulla benzina sono altissime **2** (*fig: resources*) gravare su; **to tax sb's patience** mettere alla prova la pazienza di qn **3** (*fig: accuse*): **to tax sb with sth/with doing sth** accusare qn di qc/di aver fatto qc
■ ADJ fiscale, delle tasse; **for tax purposes** per motivi fiscali
tax·able ['tæksəbl] ADJ imponibile
tax allowance N detrazione *f* d'imposta
taxa·tion [tæk'seɪʃən] N (*act*) tassazione *f*; (*taxes*) imposte *fpl*, tasse *fpl*; **this will mean higher taxation** questo significa tasse più alte; **system of taxation** sistema *m* fiscale
tax avoidance N elusione *f* fiscale
tax collector N esattore *m* delle imposte
tax credit N (*Fin*) detrazione *f* (fiscale)
tax-deductible [ˌtæksdɪ'dʌktɪbəl] ADJ detraibile dalle imposte
tax disc N (*Brit Aut*) ≈ bollo
tax evasion N evasione *f* fiscale
tax exemption N esenzione *f* fiscale
tax exile N *chi ripara all'estero per evadere le imposte*
tax-free [ˌtæks'friː] ADJ esente da imposte, esentasse *inv*
■ ADV senza pagare tasse

Tt

tax haven N paradiso fiscale
taxi ['tæksɪ] N taxi *m inv*
■VI (*Aer*) rullare
taxi·cab ['tæksɪ,kæb] N taxi *m inv*
taxi·der·mist ['tæksɪ,dɜːmɪst] N tassidermista *m/f*
taxi·der·my ['tæksɪ,dɜːmɪ] N tassidermia
taxi driver N tassista *m/f*
taxi·ing ['tæksɪɪŋ] N (*Aer*) rullaggio
taxi·meter ['tæksɪ,miːtəʳ] N tassametro
tax·ing ['tæksɪŋ] ADJ oneroso(-a)
tax inspector N ispettore *m* delle tasse
taxi rank N, (*Am*) **taxi stand** N posteggio dei taxi
taxi·way ['tæksɪ,weɪ] N (*Aer*) pista di rullaggio
tax·man ['tæks,mæn] N (*pl* **-men**) (*Brit fam*): **the taxman** il fisco
tax·ono·my [tæk'sɒnəmɪ] N tassonomia
tax·payer ['tæks,peɪəʳ] N contribuente *m/f*
tax rebate N rimborso fiscale
tax relief N sgravio fiscale
tax return N dichiarazione *f* dei redditi
tax shelter N *espediente legale per pagare meno tasse*
tax system N sistema *m* fiscale
tax year N anno fiscale
TB [,tiː'biː] N ABBR (= **tuberculosis**) TBC *f*
tbc, **TBC** [,tiːbiː'siː] ABBR (= **to be confirmed**) da confermarsi
T-bone steak [,tiːbəʊn'steɪk] N (*also:* **T-bone**) bistecca alla fiorentina
tbs. N ABBR = **tablespoonful**
T-cell ['tiː,sɛl] N (*Bio*) linfocita *m* T
TCP/IP ['tiːsiː,piː'aɪpiː] ABBR (*Comput:* = **transmission control protocol/Internet protocol**) TCP/IP *m*, protocollo per il controllo di trasmissione
TD [,tiː'diː] N ABBR (*Am*) **1** = **Treasury Department**; *see* **treasury** **2** (*Am Ftbl*) = **touchdown**
◎**tea** [tiː] N **1** (*beverage*) tè *m inv*; **I made a pot of tea** ho fatto un po' di tè; **would you like some tea?** vuoi del tè?; **a cup of tea** una tazza di tè; **tea with lemon** tè al limone; **it's just my cup of tea!** (*fig*) è proprio quello che fa per me! **2** (*Brit: main evening meal*) cena; (: *afternoon tea*) tè *m inv*; **we're having sausages and beans for tea** per cena abbiamo salsicce e fagioli; **we're invited to tea at the Browns'** siamo stati invitati per il tè dai Brown
■ADJ di tè, del tè
▷ www.tea.co.uk
▷ www.bramahmuseum.co.uk/tea/index.htm
tea bag N bustina di tè
tea break N (*Brit*) pausa sul lavoro (*per bere un tè, un caffè*)
tea caddy N barattolo per il tè
tea·cake ['tiː,keɪk] N (*Brit*) *panino dolce all'uvetta*
teacart ['tiː,kɑːt] N (*Am*) = **tea trolley**
◎**teach** [tiːtʃ] (*pt, pp* **taught**) VT insegnare; **I teach English** insegno inglese; **to teach sb sth** *or* **teach sth to sb** insegnare qc a qn; **to teach sb (how) to do sth** insegnare a qn come si fa qc; **I taught him (how) to write** gli ho insegnato a scrivere; **my sister taught me (how) to swim** mia sorella mi ha insegnato a nuotare; **it taught him a lesson** (*fig*) gli è servito da lezione; **that'll teach you!** così impari!; **I'll teach you to leave the gas on!** ti faccio vedere io cosa ti succede quando lasci il gas aperto!
■VI insegnare; **his wife teaches in our school** sua moglie insegna nella nostra scuola
◎**teach·er** ['tiːtʃəʳ] N (*gen*) insegnante *m/f*; (*in secondary school*) professore(-essa); (*in primary school*) maestro(-a); **French teacher** insegnante di francese
teacher's pet N (*fam pej*) beniamino dell'insegnante; **he's the teacher's pet** è il cocco della maestra
teacher training college N (*for primary schools*) ≈ istituto magistrale; (*for secondary schools*) *scuola universitaria per l'abilitazione all'insegnamento*
tea chest N cassa per il tè
teach-in ['tiːtʃ,ɪn] N seminario
◎**teach·ing** ['tiːtʃɪŋ] N (*gen*) insegnamento; **to go into teaching** fare l'insegnante; **she went into teaching 10 years ago** ha incominciato a insegnare 10 anni fa; **the teaching profession** l'insegnamento
▷ www.sosig.ac.uk/education/teaching_methods
▷ www.teachernet.gov.uk/
teaching aids NPL sussidi *mpl* didattici
teaching hospital N clinica universitaria
teaching practice N (*Brit*) *periodo di tirocinio per insegnanti*
teaching staff N (*Brit*) corpo insegnante *or* docente, insegnanti *mpl*
tea cloth N (*for dishes*) strofinaccio; (*Brit: for trolley, tray*) tovaglietta da tè
tea cosy N copriteiera *m inv*
tea·cup ['tiː,kʌp] N tazza da tè
tea dance N tè *m inv* danzante
teak [tiːk] N teak *m*
tea·kettle ['tiː,kɛtl] N (*Am*) bollitore *m*
teal [tiːl] N, PL INV alzavola
tea leaves NPL foglie *fpl* di tè
◎**team** [tiːm] N (*of people*) équipe *f inv*; (: *Sport*) squadra; (*of animals*) tiro; **home team** squadra di casa
▶ **team up** VI + ADV: **to team up (with)** mettersi insieme (a)
team games NPL giochi *mpl* di squadra
team-mate ['tiːm,meɪt] N compagno(-a) di squadra
team player N: **to be a team player** avere spirito di squadra
team spirit N (*cooperativeness*) spirito di collaborazione; (*Sport*) spirito di squadra
team·ster ['tiːmstəʳ] N (*Am*) camionista *m*
team teaching N team-teaching *m*
team·work ['tiːm,wɜːk] N lavoro d'équipe; (*Sport*) lavoro di squadra
tea party N tè *m inv* (*ricevimento*)
tea plate N piattino da frutta
tea·pot ['tiːpɒt] N teiera
◎**tear**[1] [tɛəʳ] (*vb: pt* **tore**, *pp* **torn**) N (*rip, hole*) strappo; **your shirt has a tear in it** hai uno strappo nella camicia, hai la camicia strappata; **there was a small tear in the sleeve** c'era un piccolo strappo sulla manica
■VT (*gen*) strappare; **torn by remorse** tormentato(-a) dal rimorso; **torn by war** (*fig*) devastato(-a) dalla guerra; **torn by his emotions** combattuto(-a); **he was torn between going and staying** era combattuto tra andare e restare; **to tear to pieces** *or* **to bits** *or* **to shreds** (*also fig*) fare a pezzi *or* a brandelli; **to tear a muscle** strapparsi un muscolo; **to tear a hole in** (*shirt*) fare un buco in; (*argument*) dimostrare che fa acqua; **to tear a letter** *or* **an envelope open** aprire una busta strappandola; **be careful or you'll tear the page** stai attento o strapperai la pagina; **he tore his jacket** gli si è strappata la giacca; **I've torn my jeans** mi si sono strappati i jeans; **that's torn it!** (*Brit fam*) sono fregato! (*or* siamo fregati! *etc*)
■VI (*be ripped*) strapparsi; (*subj: person, animal*): **to tear at**

sth strappare qc; **it won't tear, it's very strong** non si strappa, è molto resistente
▸ **tear along** VI + ADV (*rush*) correre all'impazzata
■ VI + PREP correre per
▸ **tear apart** VT + ADV (*also fig*) distruggere
▸ **tear away** VT + ADV: **to tear o.s. away (from sth)** (*fig*) staccarsi (da qc)
▸ **tear down** VT + ADV (*flag, poster*) tirare giù; (*building*) demolire
▸ **tear into** VI + PREP (*fam*): **to tear into sb** criticare ferocemente qn
▸ **tear loose** VT + ADV
1 **to tear o.s. loose** liberarsi (con uno strattone)
2 **to tear sth loose** strappare via qc
■ VI + ADV liberarsi (con uno strattone)
▸ **tear off** VT + ADV (*wrapping*) strappare; (*perforated section*) staccare; (*roof*) portare via
■ VT + PREP (*piece of material*) strappare da
▸ **tear out** VT + ADV (*sheet of paper, cheque*) staccare; **to tear one's hair out** strapparsi i capell
■ VI + ADV correre fuori
▸ **tear up** VT + ADV
1 (*also fig*) strappare; (*agreement*) annullare
2 (*plant, stake*) sradicare; (*sheet of paper*) strappare; **he tore the letter up** ha strappato la lettera

tear[2] [tɪəʳ] N lacrima; **a few tears** qualche lacrima; **to be close to tears** stare per piangere; **to burst into tears** scoppiare in lacrime; **to bring tears to sb's eyes** far venire le lacrime agli occhi a qn

tear·away ['tɛərə,weɪ] N (*Brit fam*) ragazzaccio

tear·drop ['tɪə,drɒp] N lacrima

tear·ful ['tɪəfʊl] ADJ (*face*) coperto(-a) di lacrime; (*voice*) piangente; (*person*) in lacrime; **she looked a bit tearful** sembrava che stesse per piangere

tear·ful·ly ['tɪəfəlɪ] ADV con le lacrime agli occhi

tear gas ['tɪə,gæs] N gas *m* lacrimogeno

tear·ing ['tɛərɪŋ] ADJ: **to be in a tearing hurry** avere una fretta terribile

tear-jerker ['tɪə,dʒɜ:kəʳ] N (*fam*): **the film/story is a real tear-jerker** è veramente un film/una storia strappalacrime

tea·room ['ti:,rʊm] N sala da tè

tear-stained ['tɪə,steɪnd] ADJ rigato(-a) di lacrime

tease [ti:z] N (*person*) burlone(-a)
■ VT (*playfully*) stuzzicare; (*: make fun of*) prendere in giro, canzonare; (*cruelly*) tormentare; **he's teasing you** ti sta prendendo in giro; **I was only teasing** ti stavo solo prendendo in giro; **stop teasing that poor animal!** smettila di tormentare quella povera bestia!
▸ **tease out** VT + ADV 1 (*tangle, knots*) sbrogliare; **to tease the tangles** *or* **knots out of one's hair** sbogliarsi i capelli 2 **to tease information out of sb** cavare delle informazioni a qn

tea·sel ['ti:zl] N (*Bot*) cardo dei lanaioli; (*Tech*) cardo

teas·er ['ti:zəʳ] N (*fam: problem*) rompicapo

tea service, tea set N servizio da tè

tea·shop ['ti:ʃɒp] N (*Brit*) sala da tè

tea·sing ['ti:zɪŋ] N burle *fpl*, beffe *fpl*
■ ADJ canzonatorio(-a)

Teas·maid® ['ti:z,meɪd] N *macchinetta per fare il tè*

tea·spoon ['ti:,spu:n] N (*also:* **teaspoonful:** *as measurement*) cucchiaino da tè; **a teaspoonful of sugar** un cucchiaino di zucchero

tea strainer N colino per il tè

teat [ti:t] N (*of bottle*) tettarella; (*of animal*) capezzolo

tea·time ['ti:,taɪm] N ora del tè; **at teatime** all'ora del tè; **teatime!** a tavola!

tea towel N (*Brit*) strofinaccio (per i piatti)

tea tray N vassoio da tè

tea trolley N (*Brit*) carrello da tè

tea urn N bollitore *m* per il tè

tech [tɛk] N ABBR 1 (*Brit fam*) = **technical college** 2 (*fam*) = **technology**

techie ['tɛkɪ] N (*fam*) patito(-a) della tecnologia

◎ **tech·ni·cal** ['tɛknɪkəl] ADJ (*process, word*) tecnico(-a); **this book is too technical for me** questo libro è troppo tecnico *or* specifico per me; **technical expert** tecnico specializzato; **technical offence** (*Law*) infrazione *f*

technical college N (*Brit*) ≈ istituto tecnico

tech·ni·cal·ity [,tɛknɪ'kælɪtɪ] N (*quality*) tecnicità *f inv*; (*detail*) dettaglio tecnico; **on a legal technicality** grazie a un cavillo legale; **I don't understand all the technicalities** non riesco a capire tutti i dettagli tecnici

tech·ni·cal·ly ['tɛknɪkəlɪ] ADV (*gen*) dal punto di vista tecnico; (*in theory*) tecnicamente, in teoria

technical support N (servizio di) assistenza tecnica

tech·ni·cian [tɛk'nɪʃən] N tecnico(-a)

Tech·ni·col·or® ['tɛknɪ,kʌləʳ] N Technicolor® *m*
■ ADJ (*fam*) in technicolor; **a Technicolor sunset** un tramonto in technicolor

◎ **tech·nique** [tɛk'ni:k] N tecnica

tech·no ['tɛknəʊ] N (*Mus*) techno *f inv*
▷ www.bbc.co.uk/dna/h2g2/A791336

tech·no·crat ['tɛknəʊ,kræt] N tecnocrate *m/f*

tech·no·logi·cal [,tɛknə'lɒdʒɪkəl] ADJ tecnologico(-a)

tech·nolo·gist [tɛk'nɒlədʒɪst] N tecnologo(-a)

◎ **tech·nol·ogy** [tɛk'nɒlədʒɪ] N tecnologia

techno·phobe ['tɛknəʊ,fəʊb] N refrattario(-a) alla tecnologia

tec·ton·ics [tɛk'tɒnɪks] NSG tettonica

ted·dy bear ['tɛdɪ,bɛəʳ] N (*also:* **teddy**) orsacchiotto

ted·dy boy ['tɛdɪ,bɔɪ] N (*Brit*) teddy boy *m inv*

te·di·ous ['ti:dɪəs] ADJ noioso(-a), tedioso(-a)

te·di·ous·ly ['ti:dɪəslɪ] ADV noiosamente; **tediously long** insopportabilmente lungo(-a)

te·di·ous·ness ['ti:dɪəsnɪs], **te·dium** ['ti:dɪəm] N noia, tedio

tee [ti:] N (*Golf*) tee *m inv*
▸ **tee off** VI + ADV (*Golf*) cominciare la partita

teem [ti:m] VI 1 brulicare, abbondare; **to teem with** brulicare di; **the area was teeming with tourists** la zona brulicava di turisti 2 **it's teeming (with rain)** piove a dirotto

teen·age ['ti:n,eɪdʒ] ADJ (*problems*) da adolescente; (*rebelliousness*) adolescenziale; (*fashions*) per teenager, per giovani; **teenage boy/girl** adolescente *m/f*; **she has two teenage daughters** ha due figlie adolescenti; **a teenage magazine** una rivista per ragazzi

◎ **teen·ager** ['ti:n,eɪdʒəʳ] N adolescente *m/f*, teenager *m/f inv*

teens [ti:nz] NPL: **he is still in his teens** è ancora un adolescente

tee·ny ['ti:nɪ] ADJ (*comp* **-ier**, *superl* **-iest**) (*fam*) piccolino(-a), piccino(-a)

tee-shirt ['ti:ʃɜ:t] N = **T-shirt**

tee·ter ['ti:təʳ] VI barcollare, vacillare; **to teeter on the edge** *or* **brink of** vacillare sull'orlo di

teeth [ti:θ] NPL *of* **tooth**

teethe [ti:ð] VI mettere i denti

teeth·ing ['ti:ðɪŋ] N dentizione *f*

teething ring N dentaruolo

teething troubles NPL (*fig*) difficoltà *fpl* iniziali

Tt

tee·to·tal ['ti:'təʊtl] ADJ astemio(-a)
tee·to·tal·ler, *(Am)* **tee·to·tal·er** ['ti:'təʊtləʳ] N *(person)* astemio(-a)
TEFL ['tɛfl] N ABBR = *Teaching of English as a Foreign Language*
Tef·lon® ['tɛflɒn] N Teflon® *m*
Te·he·ran [tɛə'rɑ:n] N Teheran *f*
tel. ABBR (= **telephone**) tel.
Tel Aviv ['tɛlə'vi:v] N Tel Aviv *f*
tel·co N (= **telecommunications company**) società *f inv* di telecomunicazioni
tele... ['tɛlɪ] PREF tele...
tele·cast ['tɛlɪ,kɑ:st] N trasmissione *f* televisiva
■VT, VI teletrasmettere
tele·com·mu·ni·ca·tions ['tɛlɪkə,mju:nɪ'keɪʃənz] NPL telecomunicazioni *fpl*
▷ www.itu.int/home
tele·com·mut·er ['tɛlɪkəm,ju:təʳ] N telelavoratore(-trice)
tele·com·mut·ing ['tɛlɪkə,mju:tɪŋ] N telelavoro
tele·con·fer·ence ['tɛlɪ,kɒnfərəns] N teleconferenza
tele·con·fer·en·cing ['tɛlɪ,kɒnfərənsɪŋ] N teleconferenze *fpl*; **teleconferencing facilities** dispositivi *mpl* per teleconferenza
tele·gram ['tɛlɪ,græm] N telegramma *m*
tele·graph ['tɛlɪ,grɑ:f] N *(apparatus)* telegrafo; *(message)* telegramma *m*; **by telegraph** via telegrafo
■VT trasmettere per telegrafo, telegrafare
tele·graph·ic [,tɛlɪ'græfɪk] ADJ telegrafico(-a)
te·leg·ra·phist [tɪ'lɛgrəfɪst] N telegrafista *m/f*
telegraph pole, telegraph post N *(Brit)* palo del telegrafo
telegraph wire N filo del telegrafo
te·leg·ra·phy [tɪ'lɛgrəfɪ] N telegrafia
Te·lema·chus [tə'lɛməkəs] N Telemaco
tele·mar·ket·ing ['tɛlɪ,mɑ:kɪtɪŋ] N vendita per telefono
te·lem·eter ['tɛlɪ,mi:təʳ] N telemetro
tele·ol·ogy [,tɛlɪ'ɒlədʒɪ] N teleologia
tele·path·ic [,tɛlɪ'pæθɪk] ADJ telepatico(-a)
te·lepa·thy [tɪ'lɛpəθɪ] N telepatia
◎**tele·phone** ['tɛlɪ,fəʊn] N telefono; **by telephone** telefonicamente; **to have a telephone** avere il telefono; **to be on the telephone** *(Brit: subscriber)* avere il telefono; *(be speaking)* essere al telefono; **I've just been on the telephone to my mother** ho appena parlato al telefono con mia madre
■VI telefonare
■VT *(person)* telefonare a; *(message)* telefonare
telephone banking N servizi *mpl* bancari per telefono
telephone box, *(Am)* **telephone booth** N cabina telefonica
telephone call N telefonata
telephone directory, telephone book N guida del telefono, elenco telefonico
telephone exchange N centralino (telefonico)
telephone kiosk N *(Brit)* cabina telefonica
telephone line N linea telefonica
telephone message N messaggio (telefonico)
telephone meter N contascatti *m inv*
telephone number N numero di telefono
telephone operator N centralinista *m/f*
telephone poll N *(Am)* sondaggio telefonico
telephone selling N *(Comm)* vendita per telefono
tele·phone tap·ping ['tɛlɪfəʊn,tæpɪŋ] N intercettazione *f* telefonica
tele·phon·ic [,tɛlɪ'fɒnɪk] ADJ telefonico(-a)
te·lepho·nist [tɪ'lɛfənɪst] N *(Brit)* telefonista *m/f*
te·leph·ony [tɪ'lɛfənɪ] N telefonia
tele·photo lens [,tɛlɪfəʊtəʊ'lɛnz] N teleobiettivo
tele·print·er ['tɛlɪ,prɪntəʳ] N telescrivente *f*
Tele·prompt·er® ['tɛlɪ,prɒmptəʳ] N *(Am)* gobbo
tele·sales ['tɛlɪ,seɪlz] N vendita per telefono
tele·scope ['tɛlɪ,skəʊp] N telescopio
■VI chiudersi a telescopio; *(fig: vehicles)* accartocciarsi
tele·scop·ic [,tɛlɪs'kɒpɪk] ADJ telescopico(-a); *(umbrella)* pieghevole
telescopic lens N *(Phot)* teleobiettivo
telescopic sight N *(on gun)* collimatore *m*
Tele·text® ['tɛlɪ,tɛkst] N *(system)* teletext *m inv*; *(in Italy)* televideo
tele·thon ['tɛlɪ,θɒn] N Telethon *m inv, maratona televisiva*
tele·type® ['tɛlɪ,taɪp] N *(Am)* = **teleprinter**
tele·van·gelist [,tɛlɪ'vændʒəlɪst] N telepredicatore(-trice)
tele·view·er ['tɛlɪ,vju:əʳ] N telespettatore(-trice)
tele·vise ['tɛlɪ,vaɪz] VT trasmettere per televisione, teletrasmettere
◎**tele·vi·sion** ['tɛlɪ,vɪʒən] N *(broadcasts, broadcasting industry)* televisione *f*; *(also:* **television set**) televisore *m*, televisione; **to watch television** guardare la televisione; **on television** alla televisione
■ADJ televisivo(-a)
▷ www.emmys.com
▷ www.cbc.ca
▷ www.sabc.co.za
▷ www.abc.net.au
▷ www.ctv.ca
▷ www.bafta.org
▷ www.bbc.co.uk
▷ www.pbs.org/
▷ http://tvnz.co.nz
television licence N *(Brit)* abbonamento alla televisione
television programme, *(Am)* **television program** N programma *m* televisivo
television set N televisore *m*, televisione *f*
tele·work·er ['tɛlɪ,wɜ:kəʳ] N telelavoratore(-trice)
tele·work·ing ['tɛlɪ,wɜ:kɪŋ] N telelavoro
tel·ex ['tɛlɛks] N telex *m inv*
■VI mandare un telex
■VT *(message)* trasmettere per telex; **to telex sb (about sth)** informare qn via telex (di qc)
◎**tell** [tɛl] *(pt, pp* **told**) VT
1 *(gen)* dire; *(story, adventure: relate)* raccontare; *(secret)* svelare; **to tell sb sth** dire qc a qn; **did you tell your mother?** l'hai detto a tua madre?; **I told him I was going on holiday** gli ho detto che andavo in vacanza; **to tell sb about sth** dire a qn di qc, raccontare qc a qn; **who told you?** chi te l'ha detto?; **I have been told that ...** mi è stato detto che...; **I am glad to tell you that ...** *(frm)* ho il piacere di comunicarle che...; **I cannot tell you how pleased I am** non so come esprimere la mia felicità; **so much happened that I can't begin to tell you** sono successe tante cose che non saprei da dove incominciare a raccontarti; **(I'll) tell you what ...** so io che cosa fare...; **I told you so!** *or* **didn't I tell you so?** te l'avevo (pur) detto!; **I was furious, I can tell you** ti dirò che ero furioso; **let me tell you** credimi; **you're telling me!** *(fam)* a me lo dici!, lo vieni a dire a me!; **don't tell me you can't do it!** non starmi a raccontare che non sei capace!; **tell me another!** *(fam)* raccontala giusta!; **to tell a story** raccontare una storia; **to tell lies** dire bugie; **to tell the time** leggere l'ora; **can you**

tell me the time? puoi dirmi l'ora?; **to tell the future/sb's fortune** predire il futuro/il futuro a qn
2 (*order, instruct*): **to tell sb to do sth** dire a qn di fare qc; **he told me to wait a moment** mi ha detto di aspettare un attimo; **do as you are told!** fai come ti si dice!; **he won't be told** non dà ascolto
3 (*indicate: subj: sign, dial*): **to tell sb sth** indicare qc a qn; **there was a sign telling us which way to go** c'era un cartello che ci indicava la strada
4 (*know, be sure of*) sapere; **how can you tell what he'll do?** come fai a prevedere cosa farà?; **there's no telling what may happen** non si può prevedere cosa succederà; **you can tell he's unhappy** si vede che è infelice
5 (*distinguish*): **to tell sth from** distinguere qc da; **to tell right from wrong** distinguere il bene dal male; **I couldn't tell them apart** non riuscivo a distinguerli; **I can't tell the difference between them** non riesco a distinguerli uno dall'altro
6 **400 all told** 400 in tutto
■ VI
1 (*talk*) parlare; (*fam: sneak, tell secrets*) fare la spia; **to tell (of)** parlare (di); **more than words can tell** più di quanto non riescano ad esprimere le parole; **that would be telling!** non te lo dico!
2 (*know, be certain*) sapere; **I can't tell** non saprei dire; **who can tell?** chi lo può dire?; **there is no telling** non si sa; **you never can tell** non si può mai dire
3 (*have effect*) farsi sentire, avere effetto; **to tell against sb** ritorcersi contro qn; **the strain is beginning to tell** la fatica incomincia a farsi sentire; **their lack of fitness began to tell** incominciavano a risentire della mancanza di forma
▸ **tell off** VT + ADV (*fam*): **to tell sb off (for sth/for doing sth)** sgridare qn (per qc/per aver fatto qc)
▸ **tell on** VI + PREP (*fam: inform against*) denunciare

tell·er ['tɛləʳ] N 1 (*of story*) narratore(-trice) 2 (*person: in bank*) cassiere(-a); (*: at election*) scrutatore(-trice)

tell·ing ['tɛlɪŋ] ADJ (*effective: blow*) efficace; (*significant: figures, remark, detail*) rivelatore(-trice)

telling-off ['tɛlɪŋ,ɒf] N (*fam*): **to give sb a telling-off** dare a qn una lavata di testa

tell·tale ['tɛl,teɪl] ADJ (*sign*) rivelatore(-trice)
■ N (*fam pej: person*) spione(-a), pettegolo(-a)

tel·lu·ric [tɛ'lʊərɪk] ADJ (*frm*) tellurico(-a)

tel·ly ['tɛlɪ] N ABBR (*Brit fam:* = **television**) tele *f inv*; **on the telly** alla tele

te·mer·ity [tɪ'mɛrɪtɪ] N (*frm*) audacia, temerarietà *f inv*

temp [tɛmp] (*Brit fam*) N ABBR (= **temporary**) lavoratore(-trice) interinale
■ VI avere un lavoro interinale

tem·per ['tɛmpəʳ] N (*nature*) temperamento, carattere *m*, indole *f*; (*mood*) umore *m*; (*fit of anger*) collera; **she has a sweet temper** è dolce per temperamento *or* di indole; **he's got a terrible temper** ha un pessimo carattere; **to be in a temper** essere in collera; **to be in a good/bad temper** essere di buon/cattivo umore; **to keep one's temper** restare calmo(-a); **to lose one's temper** perdere le staffe, andare in collera, arrabbiarsi; **I lost my temper** mi sono arrabbiato; **in a fit of temper** in un accesso d'ira; **to fly into a temper** andare su tutte le furie; **mind your temper!** *or* **temper, temper!** cerca di controllarti!, calma, calma!
■ VT (*moderate*) moderare; (*soften: metal*) temprare

tem·pera·ment ['tɛmpərəmənt] N (*nature*) temperamento, carattere *m*, indole *f*; (*moodiness*) umore *m* variabile

tem·pera·men·tal [,tɛmpərə'mɛntl] ADJ 1 (*moody: person*) capriccioso(-a); (*: fig: machine*) che fa i capricci; **the oven is temperamental** il forno fa i capricci
2 (*caused by one's nature*) innato(-a)

tem·per·ance ['tɛmpərəns] N (*frm: self-control*) moderazione *f*; (*in drinking*) temperanza nel bere; (*teetotalism*) astinenza dal bere

temperance hotel N albergo dove non si vendono alcolici

temperance society N lega antialcolica

tem·per·ate ['tɛmpərɪt] ADJ (*climate, zone*) temperato(-a); (*frm: language, response*) moderato(-a)

◎ **tem·pera·ture** ['tɛmprɪtʃəʳ] N temperatura; **the temperature was about 40 degrees** la temperatura era di circa 40 gradi; **to have** *or* **run a temperature** avere la febbre

tem·pered ['tɛmpəd] ADJ (*steel*) temprato(-a)

tem·per·ing ['tɛmpərɪŋ] N (*of metal*) tempera

tem·pest ['tɛmpɪst] N (*liter*) tempesta

tem·pes·tu·ous [tɛm'pɛstjʊəs] ADJ (*relationship, meeting*) burrascoso(-a)

tem·pi ['tɛmpi:] NPL *of* **tempo**

Tem·plar ['tɛmpləʳ] N (*Rel, History: also:* **Knight Templar**) templare *m*

template, (*Am*) **templet** ['tɛmplɪt] N sagoma

◎ **tem·ple** ['tɛmpl] N 1 (*Rel*) tempio 2 (*Anat*) tempia

tem·po ['tɛmpəʊ] N (*pl* **tempi** ['tɛmpi:]) (*Mus*) tempo; (*fig: of life*) ritmo; **the busy tempo of city life** il ritmo veloce della vita di città

tem·po·ral ['tɛmpərəl] ADJ temporale

tem·po·rari·ly ['tɛmpərərɪlɪ] ADV temporaneamente

◎ **tem·po·rary** ['tɛmpərərɪ] ADJ (*gen*) provvisorio(-a); (*powers, relief, improvement, job*) temporaneo(-a); (*worker*) avventizio(-a); **a temporary illness** una malattia passeggera; **temporary secretary** segretario(-a) temporaneo(-a) *or* straordinario(-a); **temporary teacher** supplente *m/f*

tem·po·rize ['tɛmpə,raɪz] VI (*delay deliberately*) temporeggiare; (*compromise*) adeguarsi, adattarsi (alle circostanze)

tempt [tɛmpt] VT (*person*) tentare; **to be tempted to do sth** essere tentato(-a) di fare qc; **I'm very tempted!** sono molto tentato(-a)!; **can I tempt you with another cake?** posso tentarti con un altro dolce?; **to tempt Providence** *or* **fate** sfidare il destino; **to tempt sb to do sth/into doing sth** indurre qn a fare qc

temp·ta·tion [tɛmp'teɪʃən] N tentazione *f*; **there is always a temptation to ...** si ha sempre la tentazione di...; **I couldn't resist the temptation** non sono riuscito a resistere alla tentazione

tempt·er ['tɛmptəʳ] N tentatore(-trice)

tempt·ing ['tɛmptɪŋ] ADJ (*offer*) allettante; (*food*) appetitoso(-a)

tempt·ing·ly ['tɛmptɪŋlɪ] ADV in modo allettante

tempt·ress ['tɛmptrɪs] N tentatrice *f*, seduttrice *f*

◎ **ten** [tɛn] ADJ dieci *inv*
■ N dieci *m inv*; **she's ten** ha dieci anni; **tens of thousands** decine di migliaia; **ten to one he'll be late** (*fam*) dieci a uno che arriva tardi; **they're ten a penny** (*fam*) ce ne sono a bizzeffe; *for usage see* **five**

ten·able ['tɛnəbl] ADJ sostenibile

te·na·cious [tɪ'neɪʃəs] ADJ tenace

te·na·cious·ly [tɪ'neɪʃəslɪ] ADV tenacemente

te·nac·ity [tɪ'næsɪtɪ] N tenacia

ten·an·cy ['tɛnənsɪ] N (*use of rented property*) locazione *f*, conduzione *f*; **to have a 5 year tenancy** avere un

Tt

contratto d'affitto di 5 anni; **during his tenancy** durante il periodo in cui abitava lì

ten·ant ['tɛnənt] N inquilino(-a)

◎**tend¹** [tɛnd] VI tendere; **to tend to do sth** tendere a fare qc; **that tends to be the case with young people** questa è la tendenza tra i giovani; **to tend to** *or* **towards sth** *(colour)* tendere a; *(characteristic)* propendere per qc

tend² [tɛnd] VT *(sick person)* prendersi cura di; *(cattle, machine)* badare a, occuparsi di

◎**ten·den·cy** ['tɛndənsɪ] N tendenza; **to have a tendency to do sth** avere la tendenza a fare qc

ten·den·tious [tɛn'dɛnʃəs] ADJ tendenzioso(-a)

ten·den·tious·ly [tɛn'dɛnʃəslɪ] ADV tendenziosamente

ten·der¹ ['tɛndəʳ] ADJ **1** tenero(-a); **to bid sb a tender farewell** salutare qn con tenerezza **2** *(sore: part of body)* sensibile, dolente; *(fig: subject)* delicato(-a); **my tummy felt tender** avevo la pancia dolorante; **tender to the touch** sensibile al tatto

ten·der² ['tɛndəʳ] N **1** *(Comm)* offerta; **to make a tender (for)** *or* **put in a tender (for)** fare un'offerta (per); **to put work out to tender** *(Brit)* dare lavoro in appalto **2** *(Fin)*: **to be legal tender** essere in corso legale

■VT presentare, offrire; **to tender one's resignation** *(frm)* rassegnare le proprie dimissioni

■VI *(Comm)*: **to tender (for)** fare un'offerta (per), concorrere a un appalto (per)

ten·der³ ['tɛndəʳ] N *(Rail, Naut)* tender *m inv*

tender-hearted [ˌtɛndə'hɑːtɪd] ADJ dal cuore tenero, sensibile

ten·der·ize ['tɛndəˌraɪz] VT *(Culin)* far intenerire

tender·loin ['tɛndəˌlɔɪn] N filetto di maiale

ten·der·ly ['tɛndəlɪ] ADV *(affectionately)* teneramente

ten·der·ness ['tɛndənɪs] N *(see adj)* tenerezza; sensibilità *f inv*

ten·don ['tɛndən] N tendine *m*

> **DID YOU KNOW ...?**
> **tendon** is not translated by the Italian word *tendone*

ten·dril ['tɛndrɪl] N viticcio

ten·ement ['tɛnɪmənt] N casamento

tenement block N isolato

Ten·erife [ˌtɛnə'riːf] N Tenerife *f*

ten·et ['tɛnət] N principio

ten·ner ['tɛnəʳ] N *(Brit fam)* (banconota da) dieci sterline *fpl*

Ten·nes·see [ˌtɛnɪ'siː] N Tennessee *m*
▷ www.state.tn.us/

◎**ten·nis** ['tɛnɪs] N tennis *m*

■ADJ da tennis

tennis ball N palla *or* pallina da tennis

tennis club N tennis club *m inv*

tennis court N campo da tennis

tennis elbow N *(Med)* gomito del tennista

tennis match N partita di tennis

tennis player N tennista *m/f*

tennis racket N racchetta da tennis

tennis shoes NPL scarpe *fpl* da tennis

ten·or ['tɛnəʳ] ADJ *(voice)* tenorile; *(part)* del tenore; *(instrument)* tenore *inv*

■N *(Mus, frm: of speech, discussion)* tenore *m*

ten·pin bowl·ing [ˌtɛnpɪn'bəʊlɪŋ] N *(Brit)* bowling *m*

tense¹ [tɛns] N *(Gram)* tempo; **in the present tense** al presente

tense² [tɛns] ADJ *(comp* **-r**, *superl* **-st**) teso(-a); **tense with fear** teso(-a) dalla paura

■VT *(tighten: muscles)* tendere

tensed up ['tɛnsd'ʌp] ADJ teso(-a)

tense·ly ['tɛnslɪ] ADV nervosamente

tense·ness ['tɛnsnɪs] N tensione *f*

◎**ten·sion** ['tɛnʃən] N tensione *f*

tent [tɛnt] N tenda

■ADJ da tenda

ten·ta·cle ['tɛntəkl] N tentacolo

ten·ta·tive ['tɛntətɪv] ADJ *(hesitant: person)* esitante, incerto(-a); *(provisional: conclusion, arrangement)* provvisorio(-a); **a tentative suggestion** un suggerimento incerto; **tentative plans** progetti *mpl* provvisori

ten·ta·tive·ly ['tɛntətɪvlɪ] ADV *(see adj)* con esitazione; provvisoriamente

tenter·hooks ['tɛntəˌhʊks] NPL: **to be on tenterhooks** essere sulle spine; **to keep sb on tenterhooks** tenere qn sulle spine

◎**tenth** [tɛnθ] ADJ decimo(-a); **the tenth floor** il decimo piano; **the tenth of August** il dieci agosto

■N *(in series)* decimo(-a); *(fraction)* decimo *m*; *for usage see* **fifth**

tent peg N picchetto (da tenda)

tent pole N palo da tenda, montante *m*

tenu·ous ['tɛnjʊəs] ADJ *(thread)* tenue; *(argument)* debole

ten·ure ['tɛnjʊəʳ] N *(of land)* possesso; *(of office)* incarico; **to have tenure** *(guaranteed employment)* essere di ruolo; **during his tenure as foreign minister** durante il suo incarico di primo ministro

tep·id ['tɛpɪd] ADJ *(also fig)* tiepido(-a)

te·qui·la [tɪ'kiːlə] N tequila

Ter. ABBR = Terrace

ter·cen·te·nary [ˌtɜːsɛn'tiːnərɪ] N terzo centenario

◎**term** [tɜːm] N **1** *(limit)* termine *m*; *(period)* periodo; **in the short term** a breve scadenza; **in the long term** a lungo andare; **a short-term solution** una soluzione a breve termine; **during his term of office** durante il suo incarico; **a 12 month term** un periodo di 12 mesi; **term of imprisonment** periodo di detenzione *or* prigionia; **to serve a 3-year term of imprisonment** scontare 3 anni di carcere **2** *(Scol)* trimestre *m*; *(Law)* sessione *f*; **the autumn/spring/summer term** il primo/secondo/terzo trimestre; **it's nearly the end of term** è quasi la fine del trimestre **3** *(word, expression)* termine *m*, vocabolo; **to tell sb sth in no uncertain terms** dire qc chiaro e tondo a qn, dire qc a qn senza mezzi termini; **in terms of ...** in termini di... **4 terms** NPL *(conditions)* condizioni *fpl*; *(Comm)* prezzi *mpl*, tariffe *fpl*; **terms of employment** condizioni di impiego; **terms of reference** termini *mpl* (stabiliti); **"easy terms"** *(Comm)* "facilitazioni di pagamento"; **reduced terms for pensioners** agevolazioni *fpl* per i pensionati; **on one's own terms** a modo proprio; **to come to terms with** *(person)* arrivare a un accordo con; *(problem)* affrontare, accettare; **he hasn't yet come to terms with his disability** non ha ancora accettato la propria invalidità; **not on any terms** a nessuna condizione **5 terms** NPL *(relations)*: **to be on good terms with** avere buoni rapporti con; essere in buoni rapporti con; **not to be on speaking terms with sb** non rivolgere la parola a qc

■VT *(name)* definire

term exams NPL esami *mpl* di fine trimestre
ter·mi·nal ['tɜ:mɪnəl] ADJ (*patient*) incurabile, terminale; (*disease*) letale; (*stages*) finale, terminale, conclusivo(-a)
■ N **1** (*Elec, Comput*) terminale *m* **2** (*of bus*) capolinea *m*; (*of train*) stazione *f* terminale; (*Aer depot: for oil, containers*) terminal *m inv*; **a computer terminal** un terminale; **an air terminal** un terminal
ter·mi·nal·ly ['tɜ:mɪnəlɪ] ADV: **the terminally ill** i malati terminali
ter·mi·nate ['tɜ:mɪˌneɪt] VT terminare, mettere fine a; (*contract*) rescindere
■ VI (*contract*) terminare, concludersi; (*train, bus*) finire; **to terminate in** finire in *or* con
ter·mi·na·tion [ˌtɜ:mɪ'neɪʃən] N fine *f*; (*of contract*) rescissione *f*; **termination of pregnancy** (*Brit Med*) interruzione *f* di gravidanza
ter·mi·nol·ogy [ˌtɜ:mɪ'nɒlədʒɪ] N terminologia
ter·mi·nus ['tɜ:mɪnəs] N (*pl* **termini** ['tɜ:mɪnaɪ]) (*of bus*) capolinea *m*; (*of train*) stazione *f* terminale; (*building: Rail*) stazione *f* di testa
ter·mite ['tɜ:maɪt] N termite *f*
term paper N (*Am Univ*) *saggio scritto da consegnare a fine trimestre*
term·time ['tɜ:mˌtaɪm] N: **in termtime** durante il trimestre
Terr., Ter. ABBR = **Terrace**
ter·race ['tɛrəs] N **1** (*patio, porch*) terrazza; **we were sitting on the terrace** eravamo seduti in terrazza **2** (*Brit: row of houses*) fila di case a schiera; **our house is in a terrace** abitiamo in una casa a schiera **3 the terraces** NPL (*Brit Sport*) le gradinate
ter·raced ['tɛrɪst] ADJ (*layered: hillside, garden*) terrazzato(-a), a terrazze; (*in a row: house, cottage*) a schiera; **a terraced house** una casa a schiera
ter·racing ['tɛrəsɪŋ] N (*Agr*) terrazzamento; (*Brit Sport*): **the terracing** le gradinate
ter·ra·cot·ta [ˌtɛrə'kɒtə] N terracotta
ter·rain [tə'reɪn] N terreno
ter·res·trial [tɪ'rɛstrɪəl] ADJ terrestre
◎ **ter·ri·ble** ['tɛrəbl] ADJ (*gen*) terribile, tremendo(-a); (*play, film*) orrendo(-a); (*performance, report*) pessimo(-a); (*weather*) bruttissimo(-a); **a terrible nightmare** un incubo terribile; **to be terrible at sth** essere un disastro in qc; **to feel terrible** sentirsi malissimo
ter·ri·bly ['tɛrəblɪ] ADV (*very*) tremendamente, terribilmente; (*very badly: play, sing*) malissimo; **I'm terribly sorry** mi spiace terribilmente; **he suffered terribly** ha sofferto moltissimo
ter·ri·er ['tɛrɪə^r] N terrier *m inv*
ter·rif·ic [tə'rɪfɪk] ADJ (*fam: very good: performance, book, news*) fantastico(-a), stupendo(-a), formidabile, eccezionale; (*extreme: heat, speed, noise, anxiety*) spaventoso(-a); (*: amount, scare*) enorme, impressionante; **that's terrific!** fantastico!; **you look terrific!** stai benissimo!; **a terrific amount** un'enorme quantità

> DID YOU KNOW ...?
> **terrific** is not translated by the Italian word *terrificante*

ter·ri·fy ['tɛrɪˌfaɪ] VT terrorizzare; **to be terrified** essere atterrito(-a); **to be terrified of** avere il terrore folle di; **to be terrified of** avere il terrore folle di
ter·ri·fy·ing ['tɛrɪˌfaɪɪŋ] ADJ terrificante
ter·ri·fy·ing·ly ['tɛrɪˌfaɪɪŋlɪ] ADV paurosamente, spaventosamente

ter·rine [tɛ'ri:n] N (*for pâté*) terrina
ter·ri·to·rial [ˌtɛrɪ'tɔ:rɪəl] ADJ territoriale
■ N: **Territorial** (*Brit: soldier*) soldato della milizia territoriale
Territorial Army N (*Brit*) Milizia Territoriale
territorial waters NPL acque *fpl* territoriali
◎ **ter·ri·tory** ['tɛrɪtərɪ] N territorio
ter·ror ['tɛrə^r] N (*fear*) terrore *m*; (*fam: child*) peste *f*; **to live in terror of sth** vivere nel terrore di qc; **she's a terror on the roads** al volante è un pericolo pubblico; **you little terror!** piccola peste!
terror attack N attentato terroristico
ter·ror·ism ['tɛrəˌrɪzəm] N terrorismo
◎ **ter·ror·ist** ['tɛrərɪst] ADJ, N terrorista (*m/f*); **a group of terrorists** un gruppo di terroristi; **a terrorist attack** un attentato terroristico
ter·ror·ize ['tɛrəˌraɪz] VT terrorizzare
terror-stricken ['tɛrəˌstrɪkən] ADJ terrorizzato(-a), atterrito(-a)
ter·ry ['tɛrɪ] N (*also:* **terry towelling**) (tessuto di) spugna
terse [tɜ:s] ADJ (*comp* **-r**, *superl* **-st**) (*style*) conciso(-a); (*reply*) laconico(-a)
terse·ly ['tɜ:slɪ] ADV (*see adj*) concisamente; laconicamente
terse·ness ['tɜ:snɪs] N (*see adj*) concisione *f*; laconicità *f inv*
ter·tiary ['tɜ:ʃərɪ] ADJ (*gen*) terziario(-a); **tertiary education** (*Brit*) educazione *f* superiore post-scolastica; **tertiary sector** (*Industry*) settore *m* terziario
Tery·lene® ['tɛrəˌli:n] N terital® *m*, terilene® *m*
TESL ['tɛsl] N ABBR = *Teaching of English as a Second Language*
TESSA ['tɛsə] N ABBR (*Brit:* = **Tax Exempt Special Savings Account**) *deposito a risparmio esente da tasse abolito nel 1999*
◎ **test** [tɛst] N (*trial, check*) prova; (*: of goods in factory*) controllo, collaudo; (*: of machinery*) collaudo; (*Med*) analisi *f inv*, esame *m*; (*Chem*) analisi; (*exam: of intelligence*) test *m inv*; (*: Scol: written*) compito in classe; (*: oral*) interrogazione *f*; (*Aut: also:* **driving test**) esame *m* di guida; **to do tests on sth** fare delle prove su qc; **they're going to do some more tests** devono fare altre analisi; **to have a blood test** fare le analisi del sangue; **we've got an English test tomorrow** abbiamo un compito in classe di inglese domani; **to put sth to the test** mettere qc alla prova; **it has stood the test of time** ha resistito alla prova del tempo; **nuclear tests** test *mpl inv* nucleari; **tests on animals** sperimentazione *f* sugli animali
■ VT (*gen*) provare, controllare; (*try, ascertain the worth of*) mettere alla prova; (*machine*) collaudare; (*Chem*) analizzare; (*blood, urine*) fare le analisi di; (*new drug*) sperimentare; (*Psych*) fare un test psicologico a; **to have one's eyes** *etc* **tested** farsi controllare la vista *etc*; **to test sb's patience** mettere alla prova la pazienza di qn; **to test sb in mathematics** esaminare *or* interrogare qn in matematica; **to test sb for sth** fare delle analisi a qn per qc; **to be tested for drugs** essere sottoposto(-a) all'antidoping; **to test sth for sth** analizzare qc alla ricerca di qc; **to test sth out** testare qc; **the drug was tested on rats** la medicina è stata sperimentata sui ratti; **test the water with your wrist** prova l'acqua con il polso; **he tested us on the new vocabulary** ci ha interrogato sui nuovi vocaboli
■ VI: **to test (for)** fare ricerche (per trovare); **to test**

Tt

positive for risultare positivo(-a) al test di; **testing, testing ...** (*Telec*) prova, prova...
■ ADJ di collaudo

tes·ta·ment [ˈtɛstəmənt] N testamento; **the Old/ New Testament** (*Rel*) il Vecchio/Nuovo Testamento

test ban N (*also:* **nuclear test ban**) divieto dei test nucleari

test bore N (*for oil*) sondaggio

test card N (TV) monoscopio

test case N (*Law, fig*) caso che costituisce un precedente

test drive N prova su strada

test-drive [ˈtɛst,draɪv] (*pt* **test-drove** [ˈtɛst,drəʊv]; *pp* **test-driven** [ˈtɛst,drɪvn]) VT provare su strada

tes·tes [ˈtɛsti:z] NPL *of* **testis**

test flight N (*Aer*) volo di prova *or* collaudo

tes·ti·cle [ˈtɛstɪkl] N testicolo

tes·ticu·lar [,tɛsˈtɪkjʊləʳ] ADJ (*Anat*) testicolare; **testicular cancer** cancro ai testicoli

tes·ti·fy [ˈtɛstɪ,faɪ] VI (*Law*) testimoniare, deporre; **to testify in favour** (*Brit*) *or* **favor** (*Am*) **of/against sb** testimoniare a favore di/contro qn; **they won't testify against him** non testimonieranno contro di lui; **to testify to sth** (*Law*) testimoniare qc; (*prove*) comprovare *or* dimostrare qc; (*be sign of*) essere una prova di qc; **the excavations testify to a high level of civilization** gli scavi testimoniano un alto grado di civilizzazione

testi·ly [ˈtɛstɪlɪ] ADV (*behave*) con impazienza; (*speak*) con irritazione, con un tono irritato

tes·ti·mo·nial [,tɛstɪˈməʊnɪəl] N **1** (*Brit: reference*) referenze *fpl*, benservito **2** (*gift*) tributo di riconoscimento, testimonianza di stima

tes·ti·mo·ny [ˈtɛstɪmənɪ] N (*Law*) testimonianza, deposizione *f*; **false testimony** falsa testimonianza

◎ **test·ing** [ˈtɛstɪŋ] ADJ (*difficult: time*) duro(-a)

testing ground N terreno di prova

tes·tis [ˈtɛstɪs] N (*pl* **testes**) (*frm*) testicolo

test marketing N lancio sperimentale sul mercato di un nuovo prodotto

test match N (*Cricket, Rugby*) partita internazionale

tes·tos·ter·one [tɛˈstɒstə,rəʊn] N testosterone *m*

test paper N (*Chem*) carta reattiva; (*Scol*) prova (scritta)

test pilot N pilota *m* collaudatore

test tube N (*Chem*) provetta

test-tube baby [,tɛsttju:bˈbeɪbɪ] N bambino(-a) in provetta

tes·ty [ˈtɛstɪ] ADJ (*comp* **-ier**, *superl* **-iest**) (*impatient: person*) irritabile; (: *remark*) stizzoso(-a)

teta·nus [ˈtɛtənəs] N tetano; **tetanus injection** antitetanica

tetchy [ˈtɛtʃɪ] ADJ (*comp* **-ier**, *superl* **-iest**) irritabile, irascibile

teth·er [ˈtɛðəʳ] N laccio; **to be at the end of one's tether** (*fig*) non poterne più
■ VT (*animal*) legare; **to be at the end of one's tether** non poterne più

Tex·as [ˈtɛksəs] N Texas *m*
▷ www.state.tx.us/

Tex-Mex [,tɛksˈmɛks] ADJ con influenze texane e messicane

◎ **text** [tɛkst] N **1** (*Telec*) sms *m inv*, messaggino **2** testo
■ VT mandare un sms *or* messaggino a; **I'll text you** ti manderò un sms

text·book [ˈtɛkst,bʊk] N libro di testo

text editor N (*Comput*) editor *m/f inv*

text file N (*Comput*) file *m inv* di testo

tex·tile [ˈtɛkstaɪl] ADJ tessile; **textile industry** industria tessile
■ N tessuto; **textiles** NPL (*industry*) industria tessile; (*materials*) tessuti *mpl*

text·ing [ˈtɛkstɪŋ] N, **text messaging** N invio di sms
▷ www.collins.co.uk/wordexchange/Sections/TextingWords.aspx?pg=113

text message N (*Telec*) sms *m inv*, messaggino

tex·tu·al [ˈtɛkstjʊəl] ADJ (*error, differences*) di testo; (*criticism*) testuale, basato(-a) sul testo

tex·ture [ˈtɛkstʃəʳ] N (*gen*) consistenza; (*of soil*) struttura; **I don't like the texture of this cheese** non mi piace la consistenza di questo formaggio; **the material has a rough texture** la stoffa è ruvida al tatto; **the smooth texture of her skin** la sua pelle liscia

TGIF [,ti:dʒi:aɪˈɛf] EXCL, ABBR (*fam:* = **thank God it's Friday**) finalmente è venerdì

TGWU [,ti:dʒi:dʌblju:ˈju:] N ABBR (*Brit:* = **Transport and General Workers' Union**) *sindacato degli operai dei trasporti e non specializzati*

Thai [taɪ] ADJ tailandese
■ N (*person*) tailandese *m/f*; (*language*) tailandese *m*

Thai·land [ˈtaɪ,lænd] N la Tailandia

tha·lido·mide® [θəˈlɪdəʊ,maɪd] N talidomide® *m*

Thames [tɛmz] N: **the Thames** il Tamigi

◎ **than** [ðæn; *weak form* ðən] CONJ che; (*with numerals, pronouns, proper names*) di; **you have more than me/ Mary/ten** ne hai più di me/Mary/dieci; **she's taller than me** è più alta di me; **I've got more CDs than tapes** ho più CD che cassette; **more than ever** più che mai; **she is older than you think** è più vecchia di quanto tu (non) creda; **it was a better play than we expected** la commedia è stata migliore di quanto (non) pensassimo; **they have more money than we have** hanno più soldi di noi; **it is better to phone than to write** è meglio telefonare che scrivere; **more/ less than 90** più/meno di 90; **more than once** più di una volta; **more often than not** il più delle volte; **I'd die rather than admit I'm wrong** piuttosto che ammettere di aver torto morirei; **no sooner did he leave than the phone rang** non appena uscì il telefono suonò; **you know her better than I do** la conosci meglio di me *or* di quanto non la conosca io

◎ **thank** [θæŋk] VT: **to thank sb (for sth/for doing sth)** ringraziare qn (per qc/per aver fatto qc); **don't forget to write and thank them** mi raccomando, scrivi per ringraziarli; **thank you (very much)** grazie (mille), tante grazie; **no thank you** no grazie; **to have only o.s. to thank for sth** dovere ringraziare se stesso per qc; **I have John to thank for getting me the job** devo ringraziare John per avermi trovato il lavoro; **I know who to thank!** (*iro*) so io chi devo ringraziare!; **thank heavens/God!** grazie al cielo/a Dio!; *see also* **thanks**

thank·ful [ˈθæŋkfʊl] ADJ: **thankful (to sb for sth)** grato(-a) *or* riconoscente (a qn per qc); **she was thankful for his support** gli era grata per il suo appoggio; **let us be thankful that it's over** ringraziamo il cielo che è tutto finito; **I'm thankful I've got a job** ringrazio il cielo di avere un lavoro; **thankful for/that ...** (*relieved*) sollevato(-a) da/dal fatto che...

thank·ful·ly [ˈθæŋkfəlɪ] ADV (*gratefully*) con riconoscenza; (*with relief*) con sollievo; **thankfully there were few victims** grazie al cielo ci sono state poche vittime

thank·less ['θæŋklɪs] ADJ (*unrewarding*: *task*) ingrato(-a); **a thankless task** un compito ingrato

thanks [θæŋks] NPL ringraziamenti *mpl*, grazie *m inv*; **thanks to** grazie a; **that's all the thanks I get!** bel ringraziamento!; **thanks to you ...** (*also iro*) grazie a te...; **it's all thanks to** (*also iro*) è tutto merito di; **it's small or no thanks to you that ...** non è certo per merito tuo se...; **thanks be to God** rendiamo grazie a Dio
■ EXCL grazie!; **(very) many thanks** grazie mille

thanks·giving ['θæŋks,gɪvɪŋ] N ringraziamento

Thanksgiving Day N (*Am*: *Thanksgiving*) giorno del ringraziamento

THANKSGIVING (DAY)

Negli Stati Uniti il quarto giovedì di novembre ricorre il **Thanksgiving (Day)**, festa nazionale che commemora il primo raccolto in terra americana ottenuto dai Padri Pellegrini, i primi coloni inglesi, nel 1621. È tradizione trascorrere la festa in famiglia (anche affrontando lunghi viaggi) con un pranzo a base di tacchino e tortino di zucca. *Vedi anche* **PILGRIM FATHERS**
▷ www.thanksgiving.org/2us.html

thank you ['θæŋk,ju:] N ringraziamento
■ ADJ: **a thankyou letter/card** una lettera/un biglietto di ringraziamento

◎**that** [ðæt; *weak form* ðət] **KEYWORD**
■ DEM ADJ
(*pl* **those**) quel (quell', quello) *m*, quella (quell') *f*; (*as opposed to "this"*) quello(-a) là; **that book** quel libro; **what about that cheque?** e quel famoso assegno?; **that wretched dog!** quel cagnaccio!; **that man** quell'uomo; **I only met her that once** l'ho incontrata solo quella volta; **that one over there** quello là; **it's not this picture but that one I like** non mi piace questo quadro ma quello là; **that crazy son of yours** quel pazzo di tuo figlio; **that woman** quella donna
■ DEM PRON (*pl* **those**) ciò; (*as opposed to "this"*) quello(-a); **after that** dopo; **and after that he left** dopodiché uscì ; **at that, she ...** al che lei...; **and they were late at that** e per di più erano in ritardo; **if it comes to that** se è per quello; **that's my house** quella è la mia casa; **I prefer this to that** preferisco questo a quello; **£5? — it must have cost more than that** 5 sterline? — dev'essere costato di più; **that is (to say), ...** cioè..., vale a dire...; **that's Joe** quello è Joe; **do it like that** fallo così ; **how do you like that?** (*iro*) niente male, ti pare?; **that's odd!** che strano!; **that's that!** punto e basta!; **you can't go and that's that!** non puoi andare e basta!; **that's true** è proprio vero; **what is that?** che cos'è quello?; **that's what he said** questo è ciò che ha detto; **who is that?** chi è quello?; **with that, she ...** con ciò lei...; **is that you?** sei tu?
■ DEM ADV così ; **he was that angry** (*fam*) tanto era arrabbiato; **cheer up, it isn't that bad** coraggio, non va poi così male; **that high** così alto(-a), alto(-a) così ; **it's about that high** è alto circa così ; **I didn't know he was that ill** non sapevo che fosse così malato; **that many** così tanti(-e); **that much** così tanto(-a); **this one isn't that much more difficult** questo non è poi tanto più difficile; **I can't work that much** non posso lavorare così tanto
■ REL PRON
1 che, il/la quale; (*indirect*) cui; **all (that) I have** tutto ciò che ho; **the box (that) I put it in** la scatola in cui l'ho messo; **the house (that) we're speaking of** la casa di cui stiamo parlando; **the man (that) I saw** l'uomo che ho visto; **the man (that) I gave it to** l'uomo (a) cui l'ho dato; **not that I know of** non che io sappia; **the people (that) I spoke to** le persone con cui *or* con le quali ho parlato
2 (*of time*: *when*) in cui; **on the day that he came** il giorno in cui *or* quando venne; **the evening/winter that** la sera/l'inverno in cui
■ CONJ che; **I believe that he exists** credo che esista; **not that I want to, of course** non che lo voglia, naturalmente; **oh that I could ...** oh se potessi...; **he said that ...** disse che...; **that he should behave like this is incredible** è incredibile che si sia comportato così ; **so that** *or* **that** affinché + *sub*, perché + *sub*

thatch [θætʃ] N (*on roof*) copertura di paglia (*or* frasche)
■ VT coprire con paglia (*or* frasche)

thatched [θætʃt] ADJ (*roof*) di paglia (*or* frasche); **a thatched cottage** un cottage con il tetto di paglia (*or* frasche)

Thatch·er·ism ['θætʃə,rɪzəm] N thatcherismo

thaw [θɔ:] N disgelo; (*fig*: *easing up*) distensione *f*
■ VT (*also*: **thaw out**: *food*) (fare) scongelare; **I forgot to thaw the chicken** ho dimenticato di scongelare il pollo
■ VI (*weather*) sgelare; (*ice*) sciogliersi; (*also*: **thaw out**: *frozen food, cold toes*) scongelarsi; (*fig*: *person*) aprirsi; (: *relations*) distendersi; **the ice began to thaw** il ghiaccio ha cominciato a sciogliersi; **it's thawing** sta sgelando

◎**the** [ði:; *weak form* ðə] **KEYWORD**
■ DEF ART
1 il (lo, l') *m*, la (l') *f*, i (gli) *mpl*, le *fpl*; **in this age of the computer ...** in quest'era di computer...; **she was the elder** era la maggiore delle due; **did you see the photographs?** hai visto le fotografie?; **to play the piano** suonare il piano; **if it is within the realms of the possible** se è umanamente possibile; **the rich and the poor** i ricchi e i poveri; **do you know the Smiths?** conosci gli Smith?; **could you pass me the sugar?** mi passi lo zucchero?; **it's on the table** è sulla tavola; **I haven't the time** non ho il tempo; **it was the year of the student riots** quello era l'anno delle manifestazioni studentesche
2 (*distributive*): **0.8 euros to the dollar** 0,8 euro per un dollaro; **eggs are usually sold by the dozen** di solito le uova si vendono alla dozzina; **this car does 30 miles to the gallon** ≈ questa macchina fa 11 chilometri con un litro; **paid by the hour** pagato(-a) a ore
3 (*emphatic*): **he's THE man for the job** è proprio l'uomo adatto al lavoro
4 (*in titles*): **Richard the Second** Riccardo secondo; **Ivan the Terrible** Ivan il terribile
■ ADV: **she looks all the better for it** adesso ha un aspetto molto più sano; **the more he works the more he earns** più lavora più guadagna; **(all) the more so because ...** soprattutto perché...; **the sooner the better** prima è, meglio è

◎**theatre**, (*Am*) **theater** ['θɪətə^r] N teatro; **to go to the theatre** andare a teatro; **operating theatre** sala

Tt

operatoria; **lecture theatre** auditorium *m inv*; **theatre of war** teatro di guerra
▷ www.theatrehistory.com/
▷ www.rsc.org.uk/
▷ www.nt-online.org
▷ www.stagework.org.uk
▷ www.shakespeares-globe.org/

theatre company, *(Am)* **theater company** N compagnia teatrale

theatre·goer, *(Am)* **theater·goer** [ˈθɪətəˌɡəʊəʳ] N habitué *m/f inv* del teatro, frequentatore(-trice) abituale di teatri

the·at·ri·cal [θɪˈætrɪkəl] ADJ *(also fig)* teatrale

Thebes [θi:bz] NSG Tebe *f*

thee [ði:] PRON *(old, poet)* ti

theft [θeft] N furto

◎ **their** [ðɛəʳ] POSS ADJ il/la loro, i/le loro *pl*; **their money** il loro denaro; **their parents** i loro genitori; **their house** la loro casa; **their girlfriends** le loro ragazze; **they took off their coats** si sono tolti il cappotto; **they washed their hair** si sono lavati i capelli; **someone has left their bag here** qualcuno ha lasciato qui la borsa

theirs [ðɛəz] POSS PRON il/la loro, i/le loro *pl*; **this car is theirs** questa macchina è loro; **is this car theirs?** è loro questa macchina?; **it's not our car, it's theirs** non è la nostra auto, è la loro; **a friend of theirs** un loro amico; **our garden is smaller than theirs** il nostro giardino è più piccolo del loro

the·ism [ˈθi:ɪzəm] N teismo

◎ **them** [ðɛm; *weak form* ðəm] PERS PRON PL **1** *(direct: unstressed)* li/le; (: *stressed: people*) loro; (: *things*) essi(-e); **I watched them** li ho guardati *or* le ho guardate; **he knows them** conosce loro; **if I were them** se io fossi in loro; **it's them!** eccoli!; **I'm looking for the tickets, have you seen them?** sto cercando i biglietti, li hai visti?; **where are the sweets, have you eaten them?** dove sono le caramelle? le hai mangiate? **2** *(indirect: people)* loro *(after verb)*, gli *(fam)*; (: *things*) essi(-e); **she gave them the money** ha dato loro i soldi, gli ha dato i soldi *(fam)* **3** *(after prep: people)* loro; (: *things*) essi(-e); **I'm thinking of them** penso a loro; **as for them** quanto a loro *(or* a questi); **it's for them** è per loro; **both of them** tutt'e due; **several of them** parecchi (di loro *or* di essi); **give me a few of them** dammene un po' *or* qualcuno; **I don't like either of them** non mi piace nessuno dei due; **none of them would do it** nessuno (di loro) lo voleva fare; **that was very good of them** è stato molto gentile da parte loro; **Sally came with them** Sally è venuta con loro

the·mat·ic [θɪˈmætɪk] ADJ *(frm: approach, treatment, arrangement)* per temi; *(Art, Mus, Literature, Ling)* tematico(-a)

◎ **theme** [θi:m] N *(of speech, argument)* tema *m*, argomento; *(Mus)* tema

theme park N parco a tema

theme pub N *(Brit)* pub *m inv* arredato a tema

theme song N *(of musical, film)* motivo conduttore; *(Am: signature tune)* sigla musicale

theme tune N tema *m* musicale

◎ **them·selves** [ðəmˈsɛlvz] PERS PRON PL *(reflexive)* si; *(emphatic)* loro stessi(-e); *(after prep)* se stessi(-e); **did they hurt themselves?** si sono fatti(-e) male?; **between themselves** tra (di) loro; **beginners like themselves** dei principianti come loro; **by themselves** da soli; **they did it (all) by themselves** hanno fatto tutto da soli; *see also* **oneself**

◎ **then** [ðɛn] ADV **1** *(at that time)* allora; **it was then that ...** fu allora che...; **there was no electricity then** allora non c'era l'elettricità; **before/since then** prima di/da allora; **until then** fino ad allora; **now and then** ogni tanto; **from then on** da allora in poi; **by then** allora; **then and there** all'istante **2** *(afterwards, next)* poi, dopo; **what happened then?** e poi cos'è successo?; **and then what?** e poi?, e allora?; **I get dressed, then I have breakfast** mi vesto e poi faccio colazione **3** *(in that case)* allora, dunque; **what do you want me to do then?** allora cosa vuoi che faccia?; **my pen's run out. – use a pencil then!** è finita la penna. – allora usa una matita!; **well then** dunque; **and** *or* **but then again** ma del resto; **I like it, but then I'm biased** mi piace, ma del resto non sono del tutto imparziale; **it would be awkward at work, and then there's the family** sarebbe difficile al lavoro, e poi c'è la famiglia
■ ADJ: **the then president** l'allora presidente *or* il presidente di allora

thence [ðɛns] ADV *(frm: from that place)* di lì *or* là; *(therefore)* quindi, perciò

thence·forth [ˈðɛnsˈfɔ:θ] ADV *(frm)* da allora in poi

theo·cen·tric [ˌθɪəˈsɛntrɪk] ADJ teocentrico(-a)

the·oc·ra·cy [θɪˈɒkrəsɪ] N *(Pol)* teocrazia

the·odo·lite [θɪˈɒdəˌlaɪt] N teodolite *m*

theo·lo·gian [θɪəˈləʊdʒɪən] N teologo(-a)

theo·logi·cal [θɪəˈlɒdʒɪkəl] ADJ teologico(-a)

theological virtues NPL virtù *fpl* teologali

the·ol·ogy [θɪˈɒlədʒɪ] N teologia

theo·rem [ˈθɪərəm] N *(Math)* teorema *m*

theo·ret·ical [θɪəˈrɛtɪkəl], **theoretic** [θɪəˈrɛtɪk] ADJ *(Science)* teoretico(-a); *(possibility)* teorico(-a)

theo·reti·cal·ly [θɪəˈrɛtɪkəlɪ] ADV in linea teorica; **theoretically possible** teoricamente possibile

theo·reti·cian [ˌθɪərɪˈtɪʃən] N teorico(-a)

theo·rist [ˈθɪərɪst] N teorico(-a)

theo·rize [ˈθɪəˌraɪz] VI: **to theorize (about)** teorizzare (su)

◎ **theo·ry** [ˈθɪərɪ] N *(statement, hypothesis)* teoria; **in theory** in teoria

thera·peu·tic [ˌθɛrəˈpju:tɪk] ADJ terapeutico(-a)

thera·peu·tics [ˌθɛrəˈpju:tɪks] NSG terapeutica

thera·pist [ˈθɛrəpɪst] N terapista *m/f*

◎ **thera·py** [ˈθɛrəpɪ] N terapia

◎ **there** [ðɛəʳ] KEYWORD
■ ADV
1 *(at that place)* lì *or* là; **he's not all there** *(fam)* gli manca un venerdì ; **back there** là dietro; **down there** laggiù; **to go there and back** andarci e ritornare; **in there** là dentro; **we left there** ce ne andammo; **on there** lassù; **over there** là; **put it there** mettilo lì *or* là; **we shall be there at 8** saremo lì alle 8; **we shall be there for sure** ci saremo di sicuro; **through there** di là; **he went there** ci è andato
2 *(to draw attention to sb/sth)*: **there he is!** eccolo (là)!; **mind out there!** attenzione!; **that man there** quell'uomo là; **there's the bus** ecco l'autobus; **there we differ** su questo non siamo d'accordo; **you there!** ehilà!; **there you are!** eccoti!; *(I told you so)* visto?; **there you are wrong** in questo hai torto; **there you go again** eccoti di nuovo
3 **there is** c'è; **there are** ci sono; **there has been ...** c'è stato...; **there is no wine left** non c'è più vino; **there might be time** forse c'è tempo; **there might**

be room forse c'è posto; **there was laughter at this** al che ci fu uno scoppio di risa; **there were 10 of them** erano in 10; **there will be 8 people for dinner tonight** ci saranno 8 persone a cena stasera
■ EXCL: **there, there, don't cry** su, su, non piangere

there·abouts [ˈðɛərəˌbaʊts] ADV (*place*) nei pressi, nei dintorni, da quelle parti; (*amount*) giù di lì , all'incirca; **ten pounds or thereabouts** dieci sterline o giù di lì

there·after [ˌðɛərˈɑːftəʳ] ADV (*past*) da allora in poi; (*future*) in seguito

there·by [ˌðɛəˈbaɪ] ADV con ciò

◎ **there·fore** [ˈðɛəˌfɔːʳ] ADV perciò, quindi; **it isn't therefore any better** per questo non è meglio

there·in [ˌðɛərˈɪn] ADV (*old, liter*) ivi; **and therein lies ...** ed in ciò sta la causa di...

there's [ðɛəz] ADV **1** = there is **2** = there has

there·upon [ˌðɛərʌˈpɒn] ADV (*at that point*) a quel punto; (*frm: on that subject*) in merito

therm [θɜːm] N ≈ 1.055 056 x 10^8 joule (*unità termica usata in Gran Bretagna*)

ther·mal [ˈθɜːməl] ADJ (*currents, spring*) termale; (*underwear*) termico(-a); (*paper*) termosensibile; **thermal baths** bagni *mpl* termali; **thermal underwear** biancheria termica

thermal power station N centrale *f* termoelettrica

thermal printer N stampante *f* termica

thermo... [ˈθɜːməʊ] PREF termo...

ther·mo·dy·nam·ic [ˌθɜːməʊdaɪˈnæmɪk] ADJ termodinamico(-a)

ther·mo·dy·nam·ics [ˌθɜːməʊdaɪˈnæmɪks] NSG termodinamica

ther·mom·eter [θəˈmɒmɪtəʳ] N termometro

ther·mo·nu·clear [ˌθɜːməʊˈnjuːklɪəʳ] ADJ termonucleare

ther·mo·plas·tic [ˌθɜːməʊˈplæstɪk] ADJ termoplastico(-a)

Ther·mos® [ˈθɜːməs] N (*also:* **Thermos flask** *or* **bottle**) thermos® *m inv*

ther·mo·set·ting [ˌθɜːməʊˈsɛtɪŋ] ADJ termoindurente

ther·mo·stat [ˈθɜːməˌstæt] N termostato

ther·mo·stat·ic [ˌθɜːməˈstætɪk] ADJ termostatico(-a)

thermostatic temperature control N termoregolazione *f*

the·sau·rus [θɪˈsɔːrəs] N dizionario dei sinonimi

◎ **these** [ðiːz] (*pl of* **this**) DEM ADJ questi(-e); (*as opposed to "those"*) questi(-e) (qui); **these shoes** queste scarpe; **I want these!** voglio questi!; **these ones (over here)** questi qui; **these ones are very interesting** questi qui sono molto interessanti; **how are you getting on these days?** come ti va di questi tempi?
■ DEM PRON questi(-e)

Theseus [ˈθiːsɪəs] N Teseo

the·sis [ˈθiːsɪs] N (*pl* **theses** [ˈθiːsiːz]) tesi *f inv*

◎ **they** [ðeɪ] PERS PRON PL **1** (*gen*) essi(-e); (*people only*) loro; **who are they?** chi sono loro?; **they have gone** sono partiti (*or* partite); **they were watching TV** stavano guardando la TV; **they're horrible** sono bruttissimi; **there they are** eccoli (*or* eccole) là; **THEY know nothing about it** LORO non ne sanno nulla **2** (*people in general*) si; **they say that ...** (*it is said that*) si dice che...

they'd [ðeɪd] **1** = they would **2** = they had

they'll [ðeɪl] **1** = they will **2** = they shall

they're [ðɛəʳ] = they are

they've [ðeɪv] = they have

◎ **thick** [θɪk] ADJ (*comp* **-er**, *superl* **-est**) **1** (*gen*) grosso(-a); (*wall, layer, line*) spesso(-a); (*hair*) folto(-a); (*soup, paint, smoke*) denso(-a); (*fog, vegetation*) fitto(-a); (*crowd*) compatto(-a); (*strong: accent*) marcato(-a); **it's 20 cm thick** ha uno spessore di 20 cm; **the furniture was thick with dust** sui mobili c'era la polvere di mesi; **the air was thick with exhaust fumes** l'aria era satura di gas di scarico; **the leaves were thick on the ground** sul terreno c'era una spessa coltre di foglie; **a thick accent** un forte accento; **they're thick as thieves** (*fig fam*) sono amici per la pelle **2** (*fam: stupid*) ottuso(-a), lento(-a); **he's a bit thick** è un po' tonto; **he's as thick as two short planks** (*Brit*) è proprio duro di comprendonio
■ ADV: **to spread sth thick** spalmare uno spesso strato di qc; **to cut sth thick** tagliare qc a fette grosse; **thick and fast** senza tregua; **to lay it on (a bit) thick** (*fig fam: exaggerate*) calcare un po' la mano
■ N: **in the thick of** (*activity, situation, event*) nel mezzo di; **in the thick of battle** nel mezzo della battaglia; **he likes to be in the thick of things** gli piace buttarsi nella mischia; **through thick and thin** nella buona e nella cattiva sorte

thick·en [ˈθɪkən] VT (*gen*) ispessire; (*sauce*) rendere più denso(-a)
■ VI (*gen*) ispessirsi; (*grow denser: forest, jungle*) infittirsi; **the plot thickens** (*fig*) il mistero s'infittisce, la trama si complica

thick·en·er [ˈθɪkənəʳ] N addensante *m*

thick·et [ˈθɪkɪt] N boscaglia

thick·headed [ˌθɪkˈhɛdɪd] ADJ (*fam*) ottuso(-a), tonto(-a)

thick-lipped [ˌθɪkˈlɪpt] ADJ dalle labbra grosse

thick·ly [ˈθɪklɪ] ADV (*spread*) a strati spessi; (*cut*) a fette grosse; (*populated*) densamente; **the snow fell thickly** la neve cadeva fitta fitta; **a thickly-wooded slope** un pendio molto boscoso

thick·ness [ˈθɪknɪs] N (*gen*) spessore *m*; (*of fog*) densità *f inv*; (*of hair*) foltezza

thickness gauge N spessimetro

thick·set [ˌθɪkˈsɛt] ADJ (*person*) tarchiato(-a), tozzo(-a)

thick-skinned [ˌθɪkˈskɪnd] ADJ (*fig: insensitive*) insensibile, coriaceo(-a)

thief [θiːf] N (*pl* **thieves** [θiːvz]) ladro(-a); **stop thief!** al ladro!

thieve [θiːv] VI rubare

thiev·ing [ˈθiːvɪŋ] ADJ ladro(-a); **you thieving scoundrel!** brutto ladruncolo!
■ N furti *mpl*

thigh [θaɪ] N coscia

thigh·bone [ˈθaɪˌbəʊn] N femore *m*

thim·ble [ˈθɪmbl] N ditale *m*

◎ **thin** [θɪn] ADJ (*comp* **-ner**, *superl* **-nest**) (*gen*) sottile; (*paper, glass*) fine; (*blanket, parcel, coat, fog*) leggero(-a); (*soup, paint, honey*) poco denso(-a); (*vegetation, hair, crowd*) rado(-a); (*population*) scarso(-a); (*person*) esile, magro(-a); (*crop, excuse, argument*) magro(-a); **a thin slice** una fettina sottile; **a thin soup** una minestra liquida; **at 20,000 metres the air is thin** a 20.000 metri l'aria è molto rarefatta; **the crowd seemed suddenly thinner** improvvisamente la folla sembrò essersi diradata; **she's very thin** è molto magra; **he's as thin as a rake** è magro come un chiodo; **to vanish into thin air** volatilizzarsi; **doctors are thin on the ground at the moment** i dottori scarseggiano in questo periodo
■ ADV: **to spread sth thin** spalmare uno strato sottile di qc; **to cut sth thin** tagliare qc a fette sottili

Tt

■VT (*also:* **thin down**: *sauce, paint*) diluire; (*also:* **thin out**: *trees, plants, hair*) sfoltire
■VI (*fog*) diradarsi; (*also:* **thin out**: *crowd*) disperdersi; **his hair is thinning** sta perdendo i capelli

thine [ðaɪn] POSS PRON (*old, poet*) il/la tuo(-a)

◎**thing** [θɪŋ] N
1 cosa; (*object*) oggetto; (*contraption*) aggeggio; **a thing of beauty** una bella cosa, un bell'oggetto; **things of value** oggetti di valore; **what's that thing?** cos'è quell'affare?; **what's that thing called?** come si chiama quel coso?; **the main thing is to keep calm** la cosa più importante è mantenere la calma; **the first thing to do is (to) check the facts** la prima cosa da fare è controllare i fatti; **the best thing would be to ...** la cosa migliore sarebbe di...; **for one thing** in primo luogo, tanto per cominciare; **what with one thing and another** tra una cosa e l'altra; **if it's not one thing it's the other** se non è una è l'altra; **it's neither one thing nor the other** non è né carne né pesce; **first thing (in the morning)** come *or* per prima cosa (di mattina); **last thing (at night)** come *or* per ultima cosa (di sera); **it's a good thing that he left** è stato un bene che se ne sia andato; **it was a close** *or* **near thing** ce l'ha fatta per un pelo; **to be just the thing for** essere proprio quello che ci vuole per; **it's the (very) thing** è proprio quello che ci vuole; **the thing is ...** il fatto è che...; **it's just one of those things** sono cose che capitano; **what a thing to say!** cosa dici mai!; **how are things (with you)?** come (ti) va?; **things are going badly** le cose vanno male; **things aren't what they used to be** non è più come una volta; **not a thing to say/to wear** niente da dire/ da mettersi; **I haven't done a thing about it yet** non ho ancora fatto niente; **he knows a thing or two** la sa lunga; **to make a mess of things** farla grossa, combinare un casino; **you did the right thing** (*fam*) hai fatto la cosa migliore; **to make a (big) thing out of sth** (*fam*) fare una tragedia di qc
2 things NPL (*belongings, clothes, equipment*) roba *sg*, cose *fpl*; **take your wet things off** togliti quella roba bagnata di dosso; **the tea things** le cose per il tè; **where shall I put my things?** dove metto le mie cose?; **take your things and go!** prendi la tua roba e vattene!
3 to do one's own thing (*fam*) fare quello che si vuole; **she's got a thing about mice** è terrorizzata dai topi; **he's got a thing about brunettes** ha un debole per le brune; **the latest thing in hats** l'ultimo grido in fatto di cappelli
4 (*creature*): **poor thing** poveretto(-a); **you poor thing!** poverino(-a)!; **what a sweet little thing!** che carino!

thingu·ma·bob ['θɪŋəmɪˌbɒb], **thinga·ma·jig** ['θɪŋəmɪˌdʒɪg], **thingum·my** ['θɪŋəmɪ] N (*fam*) coso, cosa

thingy ['θɪŋɪ] N (*fam: person, thing*) coso(-a)

◎**think** [θɪŋk] (*vb: pt, pp* **thought**) VI (*gen*): **to think of** *or* **about sth** pensare a qc; (*more carefully*) riflettere su qc; **to think of** *or* **about doing sth** pensare di fare qc; **to act without thinking** agire senza riflettere *or* pensare; **think before you reply** rifletti *or* pensa prima di rispondere; **think carefully** pensaci bene; **think again!** rifletti!, pensaci su!; **just think!** ma pensa un po'!; **let me think** fammi pensare; **let's think** pensiamoci un attimo; **to think twice before doing sth** pensare due volte prima di fare qc; **to think straight** concentrarsi; **to think aloud** pensare ad alta voce; **to think for o.s.** pensare con la propria testa; *see also* **think about, think of**
■VT
1 (*use one's brain, have ideas*) pensare; (*imagine*) pensare, immaginare; **I can't think what he can want** non riesco ad immaginare che cosa possa volere; **did you think to bring a corkscrew?** hai pensato di portare un cavatappi?; **I thought I might go swimming** ho pensato che potrei andare a nuotare; **think what you've done** pensa a ciò che hai fatto; **think what we could do** pensa che cosa potremmo fare; **to think evil thoughts** avere cattivi pensieri
2 (*believe, consider*): **to think (that ...)** pensare (che...), credere (che...); **we all thought him a fool** pensavamo tutti che fosse un cretino; **I don't think it likely** penso che sia improbabile; **who'd have thought it possible?** chi l'avrebbe mai pensato?; **I don't think it can be done** non penso che si possa fare; **I think (that) you're wrong** penso che tu abbia torto; **I thought as much** lo sapevo io; **I think/don't think so** penso *or* credo di sì /no; **I should think so too!** lo credo bene!; **what do you think?** che cosa ne pensi?; **who do you think you are?** ma chi credi di essere?; **what do you think I should do?** cosa pensi che dovrei fare?; **what do you think you're doing?** ma cosa stai facendo?; **anyone would have thought she was dying!** sembrava che stesse per morire!
■N: **to have a think about sth** riflettere su qc; **I'd like to have a think about it** vorrei pensarci su; **you've got another think coming!** (*fam*) ti sbagli!, hai capito male!

▸ **think about** VI + PREP (*remember*) pensare a; (*consider*) pensare di; **I'll think about it** ci penserò; **what are you thinking about?** a cosa stai pensando?; **have you thought about it?** ci hai pensato?; **what were you thinking about!** che cosa ti è saltato in mente!; *see also* **think** VT

▸ **think back** VI + ADV: **to think back (to)** ripensare (a), riandare con la mente (a)

▸ **think of** VI + PREP
1 (*remember: names*) ricordare; **you can't think of everything** non ci si può ricordare di tutto, non si può pensare a tutto; **I'll be thinking of you** ti penserò
2 (*consider, reckon*) pensare di; **to think of doing sth** pensare di fare qc; **I thought of going to Spain** pensavo di andare in Spagna; **he never thinks of other people's feelings** non si cura mai dei sentimenti degli altri; **think of the expense** pensa a quanto costa; **what do you think of him?** che cosa pensi di lui?; **what do you think of it?** che cosa ne pensi?; **I told him what I thought of him** gli ho detto ciò che pensavo di lui; **I wouldn't think of such a thing!** non mi sognerei mai di fare una cosa simile!; **to think highly of sb** stimare qn; **to think well of** avere una buona opinione di; **I didn't think much of it** non mi è piaciuto molto, non mi ha convinto
3 (*devise: plan*) escogitare; (: *solution*) trovare; **what will he think of next?** una ne fa e cento ne pensa!; *see also* **think** VT

▸ **think out** VT + ADV (*plan*) elaborare; (*solution*) trovare; **this needs thinking out** bisogna pensarci su

▸ **think over** VT + ADV: **to think sth over** riflettere su qc; **I'd like to think things over** vorrei pensarci su

▸ **think through** VT + ADV: **to think sth through** riflettere a fondo su qc

▸ **think up** VT + ADV (*idea, solution*) escogitare, ideare

think·able ['θɪŋkəbl] ADJ: **it isn't thinkable that ...** è impensabile che... + *sub*
think·er ['θɪŋkəʳ] N pensatore(-trice)
◎**think·ing** ['θɪŋkɪŋ] ADJ: **to any thinking person** a ogni persona ragionevole; **to put on one's thinking cap** (*fam*) mettersi a pensare, mettersi a ragionare
■ N pensiero; **to my (way of) thinking** a mio parere; **I've done some thinking about it** ci ho pensato un po' sopra
think tank N gruppo di esperti
thin-lipped [ˌθɪn'lɪpt] ADJ dalle labbra sottili; **he was thin-lipped with rage** stringeva i denti dalla rabbia
thin·ly ['θɪnlɪ] ADV (*spread*) in uno strato sottile; (*cut*) a fette sottili; (*scantily: dressed*) scarsamente; (*disguised*) malamente
thin·ner ['θɪnəʳ] COMP *of* **thin** ADJ
■ N solvente *m*
thin·ness ['θɪnnɪs] N (*gen*) sottigliezza; (*of person*) magrezza; (*of hair*) radezza; (*of soup*) eccessiva liquidità; (*of excuse*) debolezza
thin-skinned [ˌθɪn'skɪnd] ADJ (*fig: person*) permaloso(-a)
◎**third** [θɜːd] ADJ terzo(-a); **the third time** la terza volta; **the third of March** il tre marzo; **third time lucky!** questa è la volta buona!
■ N **1** (*in series*) terzo(-a); (*fraction*) terzo, terza parte *f*; **I came third** sono arrivato terzo; **a third of the population** un terzo della popolazione; *for usage see* **fifth** **2** (*Brit Scol: degree*) *laurea col minimo dei voti*
third ager [-eɪdʒəʳ] N persona nella terza età
third-class [ˌθɜːd'klɑːs] ADJ di terza classe
third degree N: **to give sb the third degree** (*fam: interrogation*) fare il terzo grado a qn
third-degree burns [ˌθɜːddɪgriː'bɜːnz] NPL ustioni *fpl* di terzo grado
third·ly ['θɜːdlɪ] ADV in terzo luogo, terzo
third party N (*Law*) terzo
third party insurance N (*Brit*) assicurazione *f* contro terzi
third person N (*Gram*) terza persona
third-rate [ˌθɜːd'reɪt] ADJ (di qualità) scadente, di terz'ordine
Third Way N: **the Third Way** (*Pol*) la terza via
◎**Third World** N: **the Third World** il Terzo Mondo
third-world [ˌθɜːd'wɜːld] ADJ del terzo mondo
thirst [θɜːst] N sete *f*; **thirst for knowledge** sete di conoscenza
■ VI: **to thirst for** (*fig*) essere assetato(-a) di
thirsty ['θɜːstɪ] ADJ (*comp* **-ier**, *superl* **-iest**) (*person*) assetato(-a), che ha sete; (*hum: work*) che fa venire sete; **to be thirsty** aver sete
◎**thir·teen** [ˌθɜː'tiːn] ADJ, N tredici (*m*) *inv*; **I'm thirteen** ho tredici anni; *for usage see* **five**
◎**thir·teenth** [ˌθɜː'tiːnθ] ADJ tredicesimo(-a); **the thirteenth floor** il tredicesimo piano; **the thirteenth of March** il tredici marzo
■ N (*in series*) tredicesimo(-a); (*fraction*) tredicesimo; *for usage see* **fifth**
◎**thir·ti·eth** ['θɜːtɪɪθ] ADJ trentesimo(-a)
■ N (*in series*) trentesimo(-a); (*fraction*) trentesimo; *for usage see* **fifth**
◎**thir·ty** ['θɜːtɪ] ADJ, N trenta (*m*) *inv*; *for usage see* **fifty**

this [ðɪs] **KEYWORD**
■ DEM ADJ (*pl* **these**) questo(-a); (*as opposed to "that"*) questo(-a) (qui); **this book** questo libro; **this man** quest'uomo; **this one here** questo qui; **it's not that picture but this one I like** non è quel quadro che mi piace, ma questo qui; **this time** questa volta; **this time next week** a quest'ora la settimana prossima; **this time last year** l'anno scorso in questo periodo; **this way** (*in this direction*) da questa parte; (*in this fashion*) così ; **this woman** questa donna
■ DEM PRON (*pl* **these**) questo(-a); (*as opposed to 'that'*) questo(-a) (qui); **what's all this I hear about you leaving?** mi hanno detto che te ne vai, è vero?; **this is April** è aprile; **this is Friday** è venerdì ; **do it like this** fallo così ; **it was like this** è successo *or* è andata così ; **this is Mr Brown** (*in introductions, in photo*) questo è il signor Brown; (*on telephone*) sono il signor Brown; **they were talking of this and that** stavano parlando del più e del meno; **I prefer this to that** preferisco questo a quello; **what is this?** che cos'è questo?; **this is what he said** questo è ciò che ha detto; **this is where I live** io abito qui; **who is this?** chi è questo?; **and with this he left** e con ciò se ne andò; **what with this and that I was busy all week** tra una cosa e l'altra non ho avuto un momento libero questa settimana; **where did you find this?** dove l'hai trovato?
■ DEM ADV: **this far** fino qui; **this high** alto(-a) così , così alto(-a); **it's about this high** è alto circa così

this·tle ['θɪsl] N cardo
thistle·down ['θɪslˌdaʊn] N pappo del cardo
thith·er ['ðɪðəʳ] ADV (*old, liter*) là, laggiù
tho' [ðəʊ] ABBR = **though**
thong [θɒŋ] N (*underwear*) perizoma *m*; (*Am: shoe*) infradito *m or f inv*, laccio *or* cinghia di cuoio
tho·rac·ic [θɔː'ræsɪk] ADJ (*Med*) toracico(-a)
thor·ax ['θɔːræks] N torace *m*
thorn [θɔːn] N spina; **you're a thorn in my side** *or* **flesh** (*fig*) sei la mia spina nel fianco *or* la mia croce
thorny ['θɔːnɪ] ADJ (*comp* **-ier**, *superl* **-iest**) irto(-a) di spine; (*fig: tricky*) spinoso(-a), scabroso(-a)
◎**thor·ough** ['θʌrə] ADJ (*work, worker*) preciso(-a), accurato(-a); (*search*) minuzioso(-a); (*examination, knowledge, research*) approfondito(-a); (*cleaning*) a fondo; (*complete: attr only: idiot, scoundrel*) vero(-a); **a thorough check** un controllo minuzioso; **she's very thorough** è molto meticolosa; **she has a thorough knowledge of the subject** ha una profonda conoscenza in materia; **he's a thorough rascal** è una canaglia matricolata, è un vero mascalzone
thorough·bred ['θʌrəˌbrɛd] ADJ, N (*horse*) purosangue (*m/f*) *inv*
thorough·fare ['θʌrəˌfɛəʳ] N strada transitabile; **"no thoroughfare"** (*Brit*) "divieto di transito"
thorough·going ['θʌrəˌgəʊɪŋ] ADJ (*examination, search*) accurato(-a), minuzioso(-a); (*analysis*) approfondito(-a); (*reform*) totale; **he's a thoroughgoing idiot** è un perfetto idiota
thor·ough·ly ['θʌrəlɪ] ADV **1** (*with vb: agree*) completamente; (*: understand*) perfettamente; (*: search, clean*) accuratamente, minuziosamente, a fondo; **she thoroughly agreed** fu completamente d'accordo; **I checked the car thoroughly** ho controllato la macchina meticolosamente; **mix the ingredients thoroughly** mescolare bene gli ingredienti; **I thoroughly enjoyed myself** mi sono divertito moltissimo **2** (*with adj: very*) assolutamente; **thoroughly clean** completamente pulito(-a); **a thoroughly unpleasant person** una persona assolutamente antipatica

Tt

thor·ough·ness ['θʌrənɪs] N precisione *f*

◎ **those** [ðəʊz] (*pl of* **that**) DEM ADJ quei (quegli) *mpl*, quelle *fpl*; (*as opposed to "these"*) quelli(-e) (là); **those days** quei giorni; **those pages** quelle pagine; **those students** quegli studenti; **those ones** quelli lì ; **pass me those books – those ones?** passami quei libri – quelli lì ?
■ DEM PRON quelli(-e); (*as opposed to 'these'*) quelli(-e) (là); **those of you who were here yesterday** quelli di voi che erano qua ieri; **those of us who fought in the war** noi che abbiamo combattuto la guerra; **I want those!** voglio quelli!

thou [ðaʊ] PRON (*old*) (*poet*) tu

◎ **though** [ðəʊ] CONJ benché + *sub*, sebbene + *sub*; **though it's raining ...** anche se piove...; **though it was raining** benché piovesse; **he's a nice person, though he's not very clever** è simpatico, anche se non è molto sveglio; **even though** anche se; **strange though it may appear** per quanto strano possa sembrare
■ ADV tuttavia, comunque; **it's not so easy, though** tuttavia non è così facile

◎ **thought** [θɔ:t] PT, PP *of* **think**
■ N (*reflection, mental activity*) pensiero; (*idea*) idea; (*opinion*) opinione *f*; (*intention*) intenzione *f*; **to be lost** *or* **deep in thought** essere assorto(-a) *or* perso(-a) nei propri pensieri; **after much thought** dopo molti ripensamenti; **I've just had a thought** mi è appena venuta un'idea; **that's a thought!** che bell'idea!; **I shudder at the very thought of it** rabbrividisco solo al pensiero; **to collect one's thoughts** raccogliere le proprie idee; **my thoughts were elsewhere** avevo la testa altrove; **with no thought for o.s.** senza pensare a se stesso; **to give sth some thought** prendere qc in considerazione, riflettere su qc; **it's the thought that counts** è il pensiero che conta; **it was a nice thought, thank you** è stato un pensiero carino, grazie

thought·ful ['θɔ:tfʊl] ADJ **1** (*pensive*) pensieroso(-a), pensoso(-a); (*serious: book*) ragionato(-a); (*: remark*) ponderato(-a) **2** (*considerate*) gentile, premuroso(-a); **she had a thoughtful expression on her face** aveva un'espressione pensierosa; **a thoughtful and caring man** un uomo premuroso ed attento; **how thoughtful of you!** che pensiero gentile!

thought·ful·ly ['θɔ:tfəlɪ] ADV **1** (*pensively*) con aria pensierosa; **he looked at me thoughtfully** mi ha guardato pensieroso **2** (*considerately*) gentilmente

thought·ful·ness ['θɔ:tfʊlnɪs] N (*pensiveness*) pensosità *f inv*, pensierosità *f inv*; (*kindness*) gentilezza

thought·less ['θɔ:tlɪs] ADJ (*person, remark, words*) sconsiderato(-a); (*behaviour*) scortese; **it was thoughtless of her to mention it** è stato poco delicato da parte sua parlarne; **thoughtless of the consequences** senza pensare alle conseguenze

thought·less·ly ['θɔ:tlɪslɪ] ADV (*see adj*) sconsideratamente; scortesemente

thought·less·ness ['θɔ:tlɪsnɪs] N (*of remark*) sconsideratezza; (*of behaviour*) negligenza, trascuratezza

thought-provoking ['θɔ:tprə,vəʊkɪŋ] ADJ che dà da pensare, stimolante

◎ **thou·sand** ['θaʊzənd] ADJ mille
■ N mille *m inv*; **one/two/five thousand** mille/duemila/cinquemila; **a thousand pounds** mille sterline; **a thousand and one/two** mille e uno/due; **about a thousand** circa un migliaio; **three thousand boys and five thousand girls** tremila ragazzi e cinquemila ragazze; **in their thousands** *or* **by the thousand** a migliaia; **thousands of** migliaia *fpl* di

thou·sandth ['θaʊzəndθ] ADJ millesimo(-a)
■ N (*in classification*) millesimo(-a); (*fraction*) millesimo

thrash [θræʃ] VT (*gen*) percuotere, picchiare; (*with whip*) frustare; (*with stick*) bastonare; (*Sport fam: defeat*) dare una batosta a, battere; **his father thrashed him** suo padre lo ha picchiato; **Liverpool will thrash them** il Liverpool li batterà
■ VI (*also:* **thrash about, thrash around**) agitarsi, dibattersi
▸ **thrash out** VT + ADV (*problem, difficulty: discuss*) sviscerare; (*: solve*) risolvere; (*plan*) mettere a punto con difficoltà; **a meeting to thrash out the problem** un incontro per sviscerare il problema

thrash·ing ['θræʃɪŋ] N: **to give sb a thrashing** (*beat*) picchiare qn di santa ragione; (*Sport fam: defeat*) dare una batosta a qn

thread [θrɛd] N **1** filo; **cotton/nylon thread** filo di cotone/di nailon; **to hang by a thread** (*fig*) essere appeso a un filo; **to lose the thread (of what one is saying)** perdere il filo (del discorso); **to pick up the thread again** (*fig*) riprendere il filo **2** (*of screw*) filettatura, filetto
■ VT (*needle, beads*) infilare; **to thread one's way through a crowd** infilarsi *or* farsi largo tra una folla; **to thread one's way between** infilarsi tra

thread·bare ['θrɛd,bɛə^r^] ADJ (*coat, blanket*) logoro(-a), consumato(-a), liso(-a); (*fig: argument*) trito(-a)

◎ **threat** [θrɛt] N minaccia; **to be a threat to sb/sth** costituire una minaccia per qn/qc; **to be under threat of** (*closure, extinction*) rischiare; (*exposure*) essere minacciato(-a) di

◎ **threat·en** ['θrɛtn] VT minacciare; **to threaten sb with sth** minacciare qn di qc; **to threaten to do sth** minacciare di fare qc
■ VI (*storm*) minacciare

◎ **threat·en·ing** ['θrɛtnɪŋ] ADJ minaccioso(-a)

threat·en·ing·ly ['θrɛtnɪŋlɪ] ADV minacciosamente

◎ **three** [θri:] ADJ tre *inv*; **she's three** ha tre anni
■ N tre *m inv*; **the best of three** (*Sport*) partita, rivincita e bella; *for usage see* **five**

three-D, **3-D** [,θri:'di:] ADJ (*also:* **three-dimensional**) tridimensionale
■ N: **to be in three-D** essere tridimensionale

three-dimensional [,θri:daɪ'mɛnʃənl] ADJ tridimensionale

three-legged [,θri:'lɛgɪd] ADJ (*table, stool*) a tre gambe

three-legged race N corsa a coppie (*con due gambe legate insieme*)

three-piece suit [,θri:pi:s'su:t] N completo (con gilè), tre pezzi *m inv*

three-piece suite [,θri:pi:s'swi:t] N *salotto comprendente un divano e due poltrone*

three-pin plug [,θri:,pɪn'plʌg] N spina a tre spinotti

three-ply [,θri:'plaɪ] ADJ (*wood*) a tre strati; (*wool*) a tre capi, a tre fili

three-point turn [,θri:pɔɪnt'tɜ:n] N (*Aut*) inversione a U (*eseguita in tre manovre*)

three-quarter [,θri:'kwɔ:tə^r^] N (*Rugby*) trequarti *m inv*

three-quarters [,θri:'kwɔ:təz] NPL tre quarti *mpl*; **three-quarters full** pieno per tre quarti

three Rs N: **the three Rs** leggere, scrivere e far di conto

three·some ['θri:səm] N (*people*) terzetto

three-wheeler [,θri:'wi:lə^r^] N (*car*) veicolo a tre ruote; (*tricycle*) triciclo

thresh [θrɛʃ] VT (*corn*) trebbiare

thresh·ing ma·chine ['θrɛʃɪŋməʃi:n] N trebbiatrice *f*, trebbia
thresh·old ['θrɛʃˌhəʊld] N (*also fig*) soglia; **to be on the threshold of** (*fig*) essere sulla soglia di
threshold agreement N (*Econ*) ≈ scala mobile
threshold population N (*Econ*) soglia di popolazione
threw [θru:] PT *of* throw
thrice [θraɪs] ADV (*frm, liter*) tre volte
thrift [θrɪft], **thrifti·ness** ['θrɪftɪnɪs] N parsimonia; **thrift is not one of his strong points** la parsimonia non è una delle sue qualità; **a life of hard work and thrift** una vita di duro lavoro e risparmio
thrift shop N *negozio che vende articoli a scopo di beneficenza*
thrifty ['θrɪftɪ] ADJ (*comp* **-ier**, *superl* **-iest**) parsimonioso(-a)
thrill [θrɪl] N (*of fear*) brivido; (*of pleasure, joy*) fremito; **it gave me a great thrill** è stata un'esperienza emozionante; **it was a great thrill to see my team win** che emozione vedere vincere la mia squadra!
■VT (*with fear*) far rabbrividire; (*with pleasure*) entusiasmare; (*audience*) elettrizzare; **I was thrilled to get your letter** la tua lettera mi ha fatto veramente piacere
■VI tremare; **to thrill at** *or* **to sth** fremere (di gioia) a qc
thrill·er ['θrɪlə^r] N thriller *m inv*
thrill·ing ['θrɪlɪŋ] ADJ (*book, play*) pieno(-a) di suspense; (*news, discovery*) entusiasmante; **a thrilling match** una partita entusiasmante
thrive [θraɪv] VI (*be healthy: person, animal*) crescere *or* svilupparsi bene; (*: plant*) crescere rigoglioso(-a); (*fig: business*) prosperare; **he thrives on it** gli fa bene, ne gode; **children thrive on milk** il latte è ottimo per i bambini; **lavender thrives in poor soil** la lavanda cresce rigogliosa nei terreni poveri; **she thrives on hard work** il lavoro le fa bene; **business is thriving** il commercio prospera
thriv·ing ['θraɪvɪŋ] ADJ (*industry, community*) fiorente
◎**throat** [θrəʊt] N gola; **to clear one's throat** schiarirsi la gola; **to have a sore throat** avere (il) mal di gola; **to stick in sb's throat** (*fig*) restare in gola a qn
throaty ['θrəʊtɪ] ADJ (*comp* **-ier**, *superl* **-iest**) (*voice*) roco(-a)
throb [θrɒb] N (*of heart*) palpito, battito; (*of pain*) fitta; (*of music*) battito; (*of engine*) vibrazione *f*; (*of drum*) rullio
■VI (*heart*) palpitare, battere forte; (*wound*) pulsare; (*engine*) vibrare; **my head is throbbing** mi martellano le tempie; **my arm is throbbing** ho delle fitte al braccio; **throbbing with life** (*fig: town*) pullulante di vita; **a throbbing pain** un dolore lancinante
throes [θrəʊz] NPL: **in the throes of** alle prese con; **in the throes of death** in agonia; **in the throes of war** dilaniato(-a) dalla guerra
throm·bo·sis [θrɒm'bəʊsɪs] N trombosi *f inv*; **coronary thrombosis** trombosi coronarica
throne [θrəʊn] N trono; **to ascend to the throne** salire al trono; **the heir to the throne** l'erede *m/f* al trono
throng [θrɒŋ] N moltitudine *f*
■VT affollare
■VI affollarsi
throt·tle ['θrɒtl] N (*on motorcycle*) (manopola del) gas; (*valve*) valvola a farfalla; (*on motorboats*) (manetta del) gas; **to open the throttle** dare gas; **to go at full throttle** andare a tutto gas
■VT (*strangle*) strangolare, strozzare
■VI: **to throttle back** *or* **down** togliere il gas

◎**through** [θru:] PREP
1 (*place*) attraverso; **to look through a telescope** guardare attraverso un telescopio; **to look through the window** (*look out*) guardare dalla finestra; (*look in*) guardare dentro; **to walk through the woods** camminare per *or* attraversare i boschi; **through the crowd** attraverso la folla; **he shot her through the head** le ha sparato in testa; **to go through** (*house, garden, wood*) attraversare; **to go through one's pockets** frugarsi le tasche; **to go through sb's papers** scartabellare le carte di qn
2 (*time, process*) per, durante; **all** *or* **right through the night** per tutta la notte; **he won't live through the night** non supererà la notte; **(from) Monday through Friday** (*Am*) da lunedì a venerdì ; **to go through a bad/good period** attraversare un brutto momento/periodo felice; **I am halfway through the book** sono a metà libro
3 (*owing to*) a causa di; (*by means of*) per, per mezzo di; (*thanks to*) grazie a; **through lack of resources** per mancanza di mezzi; **through the post** per posta; **he got the job through them** ha avuto quel posto grazie a loro; **it was through you that we were late** è colpa tua se siamo arrivati tardi; **I heard it through my sister** l'ho saputo da mia sorella; **I know him through my brother** lo conosco tramite mio fratello
■ADV
1 (*place*): **to let sb through** lasciar passare qn; **the soldiers didn't let us through** i soldati non ci hanno lasciato passare; **please go through into the dining room** prego, entrate in sala da pranzo; **to go through Birmingham** passare per Birmingham; **does this train go through to London?** va direttamente a Londra questo treno?; **the nail went right through** il chiodo è passato da parte a parte; **I am wet through** sono bagnato fino al midollo; **my coat is wet through** ho il cappotto inzuppato; **he is through to the finals** ce l'ha fatta a entrare in finale; **the wood has rotted through** il legno è completamente marcio
2 (*Brit Telec*): **to get through** ottenere la comunicazione; **to put sb through** passare la linea a qn; **to put sb through to sb** passare qn a qn; **you're through!** è in linea!
3 (*time, process*): **the party lasted right through until morning** la festa è andata avanti fino al mattino; **I read the book right through** ho letto il libro da cima a fondo
4 **through and through** fino in fondo
■ADJ
1 (*attr: traffic*) di passaggio; (*ticket, train, passage*) diretto(-a); **a through train** un treno diretto; **"no through road"** (*sign: Brit*) "strada senza uscita"; **"no through traffic"** (*sign: Am*) "divieto d'accesso"
2 (*finished*): **to be through** avere finito; **we'll be through at 7** avremo finito per le sette; **I'm through with my girlfriend** ho chiuso con la mia ragazza; **I'm not through with you yet** con te non ho ancora finito; **you're through!** sei finito!
◎**through·out** [θru:'aʊt] PREP **1** (*place*) in tutto(-a), dappertutto in; **throughout Italy** in tutta l'Italia
2 (*time, process*) per *or* durante tutto(-a); **throughout the year** per tutto l'anno; **throughout last summer** per tutta l'estate scorsa
■ADV **1** (*everywhere*) dappertutto; **the house is carpeted throughout** c'è la moquette dappertutto in casa **2** (*the whole time*) dal principio alla fine, sempre

Tt

through·put ['θru:ˌpʊt] N (*of goods, materials*) materiale *m* in lavorazione; (*Comput*) volume *m* di dati immessi
through·way, **thru·way** ['θru:ˌweɪ] N (*Am*) autostrada a pagamento
throve [θrəʊv] PT *of* **thrive**
◎ **throw** [θrəʊ] (*vb: pt* **threw**, *pp* **thrown**) N (*gen*) tiro; (*Sport*) lancio; (*in judo, wrestling*) atterramento
■ VT (*gen, fig*) lanciare, tirare, gettare; (*ball, javelin, hammer*) lanciare; (*dice*) gettare; (*horserider*) disarcionare, gettare a terra; (*judo opponent*) atterrare, mettere al tappeto; (*pottery*) tornire, formare al tornio; (*fig fam: disconcert*) sconcertare, disorientare; **to throw a ball 200 metres** lanciare una palla a duecento metri; **he threw the ball to me** mi ha lanciato la palla; **to throw a coat round one's shoulders** buttarsi un cappotto sulle spalle; **that really threw him** l'ha veramente sconcertato; **to throw a switch** (*Elec*) azionare una leva; **he was thrown from his horse** fu disarcionato; **to throw a party** dare una festa; **to throw open** (*doors, windows*) spalancare; (*house, gardens*) aprire al pubblico; (*competition, race*) aprire a tutti; **to throw o.s. off a cliff/into a river** gettarsi da una scogliera/in un fiume; **to throw o.s. at sb** (*rush at*) gettarsi *or* scagliarsi su qn; (*fig*) buttarsi su qn; **to throw o.s. into one's work** buttarsi a capofitto nel lavoro; **to throw o.s. at sb's feet** gettarsi ai piedi di qn; **to throw o.s. on sb's mercy** rimettersi alla pietà di qn
▸ **throw about**, **throw around** VT + ADV (*litter*) spargere; **to throw money about** *or* **around** sperperare il denaro; **to throw one's weight about** *or* **around** far pesare la propria presenza
▸ **throw away** VT + ADV (*rubbish, old things*) gettare *or* buttare via; (*chance, money, time*) sprecare, gettare *or* buttare via; **he threw it away** lo ha buttato via
▸ **throw back** VT + ADV
1 (*return: ball*) rinviare
2 (*head, hair*) buttare all'indietro; (*shoulders*) raddrizzare; **she was thrown back on her own resources** (*fig*) se l'è dovuta cavare da sola
▸ **throw down** VT + ADV (*object*) gettare giù; (*weapons*) deporre; **to throw o.s. down** gettarsi a terra; **to throw down the gauntlet** (*fig*) gettare il guanto
▸ **throw in** VT + ADV (*Sport: ball*) rimettere in gioco; (*add, include*) aggiungere; (*say casually: remark*) buttar lì
▸ **throw on** VT + ADV (*clothes*) buttarsi addosso; (*coal*) aggiungere
▸ **throw off** VT + ADV (*get rid of*) sbarazzarsi di, liberarsi di; (*escape: pursuers, dogs*) sbarazzarsi di, seminare
■ VT + PREP: **to throw sb off the trail** mettere qn fuori pista
▸ **throw out** VT + ADV
1 (*rubbish, person*) buttar fuori; (*fig: proposal*) respingere
2 (*offer: idea, suggestion*) lanciare
3 (*calculation, prediction*) far sballare
▸ **throw over** VT + ADV (*person*) piantare
▸ **throw together** VT + ADV (*clothes*) raccattare; (*meal*) raffazzonare; (*essay*) buttar giù; (*people*) fare incontrare
▸ **throw up** VI + ADV (*fam: vomit*) vomitare
■ VT + ADV (*ball*) lanciare in aria; **she threw up her hands in despair** ha alzato le braccia al cielo per la disperazione
throw·away ['θrəʊəˌweɪ] ADJ (*disposable: product*) da buttar via, usa e getta; (*casual: remark*) buttato(-a) lì
throw·back ['θrəʊˌbæk] N: **it's a throwback to** (*fig*) ciò risale a
throw·er ['θrəʊə^r] N lanciatore(-trice)
throw-in ['θrəʊˌɪn] N (*Ftbl*) rimessa in gioco
thrown [θrəʊn] PP *of* **throw**
thru [θru:] PREP, ADV (*Am*) = **through**
thrush[1] [θrʌʃ] N (*bird*) tordo
thrush[2] [θrʌʃ] N (*Med: esp in children*) mughetto; (*: Brit: in women*) candida
thrust [θrʌst] (*vb: pt, pp* **thrust**) N (*push*) spintone *m*; (*Aer, Space*) spinta; (*Mil: offensive*) attacco, offensiva; **forward thrust** spinta propulsiva; **it provides the thrust that makes the craft move** dà la spinta necessaria a far muovere l'apparecchio
■ VT (*push*) spingere con forza; (*push in: finger, stick, dagger*) conficcare; **they thrust him into a van** lo hanno spinto con forza su un furgone; **he thrust a book into my hands** mi ha cacciato un libro tra le mani; **she thrust her head out of the window** ha sporto la testa dalla finestra; **to thrust o.s. upon sb** (*fig*) imporre la propria presenza a qn; **they thrust the job on me** (*fig*) mi hanno costretto ad accettare il lavoro; **I thrust my way through the crowd** mi sono fatto largo tra la folla; **to thrust sb/sth aside** spingere qn/qc da una parte; **to thrust an idea aside** scartare un'idea
thrust·ing ['θrʌstɪŋ] ADJ (troppo) intraprendente
thru·way ['θru:ˌweɪ] N (*Am*) = **throughway**
Thucydides [θu:'sɪdɪˌdi:z] N (*History, Literature*) Tucidide *m*
thud [θʌd] N tonfo
■ VI: **to thud to the ground** cadere a terra con un tonfo; **to thud against the wall** colpire il muro con un tonfo
thug [θʌg] N teppista *m/f*, delinquente *m/f*
thug·gery ['θʌgərɪ] N brutalità *f inv*, violenza
thug·gish ['θʌgɪʃ] ADJ (*person*) violento(-a); (*behaviour*) violento(-a), da teppista
thumb [θʌm] N (*Anat*) pollice *m*; **to be under sb's thumb** (*fig*) essere succube di qn; **to be all thumbs** (*fig fam*) essere maldestro(-a); **to give sb/sth the thumbs up** (*fam: sign*) far segno di essere d'accordo con qn/qc; (*: approve*) dare l'okay a qn/qc; **to give sth the thumbs down** (*fam*) disapprovare *or* bocciare qc
■ VT (*book*) sfogliare; **to thumb a lift** *or* **a ride** (*fam*) fare l'autostop; **to thumb one's nose at sb** fare marameo a qn; **to thumb one's nose at sb/sth** (*fig fam*) beffarsi di qn/qc
■ VI: **to thumb through a book/magazine** sfogliare un libro/una rivista
thumb index N indice *m* a rubrica
thumb·nail ['θʌmneɪl] N unghia del pollice
thumbnail sketch N descrizione *f* breve
thumb·screw ['θʌmˌskru:] N (*instrument of torture*) *strumento di tortura con cui si schiacciano i pollici*; (*Tech*) vite *f* con testa ad alette
thumb·tack ['θʌmˌtæk] N (*Am*) puntina da disegno
thump [θʌmp] N (*blow*) forte colpo; (*noise of fall*) tonfo; **it came down with a thump** è caduto con un tonfo
■ VT (*hit hard: person*) picchiare; (*: door*) picchiare su; (*: table*) battere su
■ VI (*person: on door, table*) picchiare, battere; (*: move heavily*) camminare pesantemente; (*pound: heart*) battere forte
▸ **thump out** VT + ADV (*tune*) suonare pestando sui tasti
thump·ing ['θʌmpɪŋ] (*Brit fam*) ADJ: **a thumping headache** un mal di testa martellante
■ ADV: **it's a thumping great book** è un libro enorme

thun·der ['θʌndəʳ] N (*Met*) tuono; (*of hooves, traffic*) fragore *m*; **with a face like thunder** nero(-a) *or* scuro(-a) in volto
■VI (*Met, voice*) (*fig*) tuonare; **the guns thundered in the distance** i cannoni tuonavano in lontananza; **to thunder by** *or* **past** (*train*) passare rombando *or* con un rombo; **he thundered at him to stop** gli urlò di fermarsi

thunder·bolt ['θʌndə,bəʊlt] N fulmine *m*

thunder·clap ['θʌndə,klæp] N rombo di tuono

thunder·cloud ['θʌndə,klaʊd] N nube *f* temporalesca; (*fig*) nube minacciosa

thun·der·ing ['θʌndərɪŋ] ADJ **1 in a thundering rage/fury** in preda a una rabbia/furia tremenda; **in a thundering temper** d'umore collerico **2** (*Brit old fam: success, nuisance*) enorme
■ADV (*Brit old fam*): **thundering great** fenomenale

thun·der·ous ['θʌndərəs] ADJ (*applause*) fragoroso(-a)

thunder·storm ['θʌndə,stɔːm] N temporale *m*

thunder·struck ['θʌndə,strʌk] ADJ (*fig*) sbigottito(-a)

thun·dery ['θʌndərɪ] ADJ (*weather*) minaccioso(-a), da temporale, temporalesco(-a)

Thurs., Thur. ABBR (= **Thursday**) gio(v). (= *giovedì*)

Thurs·day ['θɜːzdɪ] N giovedì *m inv*; *for usage see* Tuesday

◎ **thus** [ðʌs] ADV (*frm: in this way*) così ; (*as a result*) perciò ; **they are thus better paid than other workers** sono quindi meglio pagati di altri impiegati; **it was not always thus** non è stato sempre così ; **thus far** fino ad ora

thwack [θwæk] N (*blow*) colpo; (*noise*) schiocco
■VT colpire

thwart [θwɔːt] VT ostacolare, contrastare

thy [ðaɪ] POSS ADJ (*old, poet*) il/la tuo(-a)

thyme [taɪm] N timo

thy·roid ['θaɪrɔɪd] N (*also:* **thyroid gland**) tiroide *f*

ti [tiː] N (*Mus*) si *m inv*

ti·ara [tɪ'ɑːrə] N (*woman's*) diadema *m*; (*of pope*) tiara

Ti·ber ['taɪbəʳ] N: **the Tiber** il Tevere

Ti·bet [tɪ'bɛt] N il Tibet

Ti·bet·an [tɪ'bɛtən] ADJ tibetano(-a)
■N (*person*) tibetano(-a); (*language*) tibetano

tibia ['tɪbɪə] N tibia

tic [tɪk] N (*Med*) tic *m inv*

tick¹ [tɪk] N **1** (*sound: of clock*) tic tac *m inv*; **the loud tick of the alarm clock** il forte ticchettio della sveglia **2** (*Brit fam: moment*) secondo, attimo; **in a tick** in un attimo; **I shan't be a tick** ci metto un secondo **3** (*Brit: mark*) segno, spunta; **to put a tick against sth** fare un segno a fianco di qc; **put a tick in the appropriate box** fare un segno sulla casella corrispondente
■VT spuntare, fare un segno su; **to tick the right answer** fare un segno sulla risposta giusta; *see also* tick off
■VI (*clock*) ticchettare, fare tic tac; **I can't understand what makes him tick** (*fig*) non riesco a capire come ragioni
▸ **tick away, tick by** VI + ADV (*hours, minutes*) scorrere
▸ **tick off** VT + ADV **1** (*Brit: from a list*) barrare; (*: fam: scold*) sgridare; **he ticked the names off the list** ha barrato i nomi dalla lista; **she ticked me off for being late** mi ha sgridato per il ritardo **2** (*Am fam: annoy*) seccare, infastidire
▸ **tick over** VI + ADV (*Brit: engine*) andare al minimo; (*: business, organization*) segnare il passo

tick² [tɪk] N (*Zool*) zecca

tick³ [tɪk] N (*Brit fam: credit*): **to buy sth on tick** comprare qc a credito

tick·er ['tɪkəʳ] N (*fam: watch*) orologio; (*: heart*) cuore *m*

ticker tape N nastro di telescrivente; (*Am: in parades*) stelle *fpl* filanti

◎ **tick·et** ['tɪkɪt] N (*gen*) biglietto; (*for library*) tessera; (*Comm: label on goods*) cartellino, etichetta; (*: from cash register*) scontrino; (*Am Pol*) lista dei candidati; **to get a (parking) ticket** (*Aut*) prendere una multa (per sosta vietata); **return ticket** (*Am*): **round-trip ticket** biglietto di andata e ritorno; **open/closed ticket** (*Aer*) biglietto aperto/chiuso; **admission is by ticket only** si ammettono solo le persone munite di biglietto; **the man inspecting the tickets** l'uomo che controlla i biglietti; **that's the ticket!** (*fig fam*) è quel che ci voleva!
■VT (*label: goods*) etichettare
■ADJ di biglietti

ticket agency N (*Theatre*) agenzia di vendita di biglietti

ticket collector N bigliettaio

ticket holder N persona munita di biglietto

ticket inspector N controllore *m*

ticket office N biglietteria

ticket tout N (*Brit*) bagarino

tick·ing¹ ['tɪkɪŋ] N (*of clock, watch*) ticchettio

tick·ing² ['tɪkɪŋ] N (*material*) tela da materassi

ticking-off [,tɪkɪŋ'ɒf] N (*Brit fam*): **to give sb a ticking-off** dare a qn una lavata di testa, sgridare qn

tick·le ['tɪkl] VT (*person*) fare il solletico a; (*fig: palate*) stuzzicare; (*: amuse*) divertire, far ridere; **it tickled his fancy** stuzzicava la sua fantasia; **to be tickled pink** (*fam*) andare in brodo di giuggiole
■VI: **it tickles** mi (*or* gli *etc*) fa il solletico
■N solletico; **to give sb a tickle** fare il solletico a qn

tick·ling ['tɪklɪŋ] N solletico
■ADJ (*sensation*) di solletico; (*cough*) che provoca una sensazione di irritazione in gola

tick·lish ['tɪklɪʃ], **tick·ly** ['tɪklɪ] ADJ (*fam: easily tickled: person*) che soffre il solletico; (*which tickles: blanket*) che provoca prurito; (*: cough*) che provoca una sensazione di irritazione in gola; (*fig: touchy: person*) permaloso(-a); (*: delicate: situation, problem*) delicato(-a); **to be ticklish** soffrire il solletico

tick·tock ['tɪk,tɒk] N tic tac *m inv*

tid·al ['taɪdl] ADJ (*flow*) di marea; (*river, estuary*) soggetto(-a) alla marea; **tidal range** escursione *f* di marea

tidal wave N onda di marea; (*fig: of protest, enthusiasm*) ondata

tid·bit ['tɪd,bɪt] N (*Am*) = titbit

tid·dler ['tɪdləʳ] N (*Brit fam: small fish*) pesciolino; (*: child*) bambinetto(-a)

tid·dly ['tɪdlɪ] ADJ (*comp* **-ier**, *superl* **-iest**) (*Brit fam: drunk*) brillo(-a)

tiddly·winks ['tɪdlɪ,wɪŋks] NSG gioco della pulce
▷ www.tiddlywinks.org
▷ www.etwa.org/

◎ **tide** [taɪd] N marea; (*fig: of emotion*) ondata; (*: of events*) corso; **the tide of public opinion** l'orientamento dell'opinione pubblica; **high/low tide** alta/bassa marea; **the tide has turned** la marea è cambiata; (*fig*) c'è stato un cambiamento (di tendenze); **to go with the tide** (*fig*) seguire la corrente; **to swim against the tide** (*fig*) andare controcorrente
■VT: **to tide sb over** *or* **through (until)** aiutare qn a tirare avanti (fino a); **can you lend me £10 to tide me**

Tt

over until Friday? mi puoi prestare 10 sterline per tirare avanti fino a venerdì ?

tide·mark ['taɪd,mɑ:k] N linea di marea

ti·di·ly ['taɪdɪlɪ] ADV in modo ordinato; **to arrange tidily** sistemare; **to dress tidily** vestirsi per benino

ti·di·ness ['taɪdɪnɪs] N ordine *m*

tid·ings ['taɪdɪŋz] NPL (*old*) notizie *fpl*

tidy ['taɪdɪ] ADJ (*comp* **-ier**, *superl* **-iest**) (*gen*) ordinato(-a), in ordine; (*hair, dress*) in ordine, curato(-a), a posto; (*room*) lindo(-a); (*work*) accurato(-a); (*drawing*) pulito(-a); (*person: in appearance*) curato(-a); (*: in character*) ordinato(-a); (*mind*) organizzato(-a); **a tidy sum** (*fam*) una bella sommetta

■ VT (*also:* **tidy up**: *room, toys*) mettere in ordine, riordinare; (*: one's hair*) ravviarsi; **go and tidy your room** vai a mettere in ordine la tua camera

▸ **tidy away** VT + ADV mettere via

▸ **tidy out** VT + ADV mettere in ordine

▸ **tidy up** VI + ADV fare ordine

■ VT + ADV = **tidy** VT; **to tidy o.s. up** rassettarsi

tidy-out ['taɪdɪ,aʊt], **tidy-up** ['taɪdɪ,ʌp] N: **to have a tidy-out (of)** (*fam*) dare una ripulita (a)

◎**tie** [taɪ] N

1 (*Brit: also:* **necktie**) cravatta; (*cord, ribbon, string*) legaccio; (*fig: bond*) legame *m*; **a red tie** una cravatta rossa; **black/white tie** (*on invitation*) smoking/abito di rigore; **the children are a tie** i bambini legano; **ties of friendship** legami d'amicizia; **family ties** legami familiari

2 (*Sport: draw*) pareggio; (*: match in series*) incontro; (*Pol*) parità *f inv* di voti; **the match ended in a tie** l'incontro è finito con un pareggio, la partita è finita in pareggio; **cup tie** (*Brit Sport: match*) incontro di coppa

3 (*Am Rail*) traversina

■ VT (*gen, fig*) legare; (*ribbon*) annodare; (*also:* **tie up**: *shoe*) allacciare, allacciarsi; **to tie sth in a bow** annodare qc; **to tie a knot (in sth)** fare un nodo (a qc); **to get tied in knots** (*also fig fam*) ingarbugliarsi; **to tie a necktie** fare il nodo a una cravatta; **my job ties me to London** il mio lavoro mi tiene a Londra; **his hands are tied** (*fig*) ha le mani legate

■ VI

1 (*dress, shoes*) allacciarsi

2 (*Sport: draw*) pareggiare; **they tied three-all** hanno pareggiato tre a tre

▸ **tie back** VT + ADV (*curtains*) fissare; **to tie back one's hair** farsi la coda (di cavallo)

▸ **tie down** VT + ADV assicurare, fissare con una corda; (*fig*): **to tie sb down to sth** costringere qn ad accettare qc; **to tie sb down to a promise/a price/a time** costringere qn a mantenere una promessa/ad accettare un prezzo/a venire a una certa ora; **to be tied down to sth** (*promise, date*) essere vincolato(-a) da qc; **to be tied down** (*restricted*) essere legato(-a) mani e piedi

▸ **tie in** VI + ADV: **to tie in (with)** (*correspond*) corrispondere (a); (*be connected*) avere legami (con)

■ VT + ADV: **to tie in (with)** (*meeting, visit*) far coincidere (con); (*findings*) far combaciare (con)

▸ **tie on** VT + ADV (*Brit: label*) attaccare

▸ **tie together** VT + ADV legare (insieme); **he tied the handles of the bag together** ha legato assieme i manici della borsa

▸ **tie up** VI + ADV (*Naut*) ormeggiare

■ VT + ADV (*person, parcel*) legare; (*boat*) ormeggiare; (*fig: capital*) impegnare; (*: business deal*) concludere; (*: connect*) ricollegare; **to be tied up (with sb/sth)** (*busy*) essere occupato(-a) *or* impegnato(-a) (con qn/a fare qc); **the traffic was tied up by the accident** il traffico è rimasto bloccato per l'incidente

tie-breaker ['taɪ,breɪkə^r], **tie-break** ['taɪ,breɪk] N (*Tennis*) tie-break *m inv*; (*in quiz*) spareggio

tie-in ['taɪ,ɪn] N (*Comm: link*) legame *m*

tie-on ['taɪ,ɒn] ADJ (*Brit: label*) volante

tie·pin ['taɪ,pɪn] N (*Brit*) fermacravatta *m inv*

tier [tɪə^r] N (*in theatre*) fila; (*in stadium*) gradinata; (*layer*) strato; (*of cake*) piano; **to arrange in tiers** disporre in file (*or* in strati); **tiers of seats** file di sedili; **a three-tier wedding cake** una torta nuziale a tre piani

tie rack N portacravatte *m inv*

Tier·ra del Fue·go [tɪ,ɛrədɛl'fweɪgəʊ] N Terra del Fuoco

tie tack N (*Am*) fermacravatta *m inv*

tie-up ['taɪ,ʌp] N (*connection*) legame *m*; (*Am*) ingorgo

tiff [tɪf] N battibecco; **a lovers' tiff** un battibecco tra innamorati

ti·ger ['taɪgə^r] N tigre *f*

◎**tight** [taɪt] ADJ 1 (*gen, clothes, budget, bend*) stretto(-a); (*rope*) teso(-a), tirato(-a); (*usu pred: firmly fixed, hard to move*) duro(-a); (*strict: control, discipline*) severo(-a), fermo(-a); (*Brit fam: mean*) tirchio(-a); **this dress is a bit tight** *or* **is a tight fit** questo vestito è un po' stretto; **tight jeans** jeans attillati; **to be in a tight spot** (*fig fam*) essere in una situazione difficile; **space is a bit tight** siamo un po' stretti; **money is a bit tight** siamo un po' a corto di denaro; **to keep a tight hold of sth** tenere qc stretto; **to keep a tight hold on the reins** (*fig*) tenere le redini in pugno; **under tight control** sotto stretto controllo 2 (*fam: drunk*) sbronzo(-a); **to get tight** sbronzarsi

■ ADV (*hold*) stretto(-a); (*close*) ermeticamente; (*grasp*) saldamente; (*squeeze*) fortemente; **to be packed tight** (*suitcase*) essere pieno(-a) zeppo(-a); (*people*) essere pigiati; **screw it up tight!** avvitalo stretto!; **pull the door tight!** chiudi bene la porta!; **to hold sb tight** tenere stretto(-a) qn; **everybody hold tight!** tenetevi stretti!; **the room was packed tight with people** la stanza era piena zeppa di persone; **to sleep tight** (*soundly*) dormire sodo

tight·en ['taɪtn] VT (*also:* **tighten up**: *gen*) stringere; (*: rope*) tendere; (*: regulation*) rendere più severo(-a); (*: control*) intensificare; **he tightened the rope** ha teso la corda; **to tighten one's grip** stringere la presa; **to tighten security** aumentare la sicurezza; **to tighten one's belt** (*fig*) tirare la cinghia

■ VI (*also:* **tighten up**) stringersi; (*rope*) tendersi; (*grasp*) farsi più stretto(-a)

▸ **tighten up** VI + ADV 1 = **tighten** VI 2 **to tighten up on sth** rendere qc più severo(-a)

■ VT + ADV = **tighten** VT

tight-fisted [,taɪt'fɪstɪd] ADJ (*fam*) avaro(-a), tirchio(-a)

tight-fitting [,taɪt'fɪtɪŋ] ADJ (*garment*) attillato(-a); (*lid*) ermetico(-a)

tight·knit [,taɪt'nɪt] ADJ (*family*) unito(-a); (*programme, schedule*) intenso(-a)

tight-lipped [,taɪt'lɪpt] ADJ: **to be tight-lipped** (*silent*) essere reticente; (*angry*) tenere le labbra serrate

tight·ly ['taɪtlɪ] ADV (*grasp*) bene, saldamente; **to hold sth tightly** tenere stretto qc; **she held his hand tightly** gli tenne stretta la mano; **tightly closed** ben chiuso(-a)

tight·ness ['taɪtnɪs] N (*of lid, screw*) resistenza; (*of discipline*) rigore *m*; (*of regulations*) rigidità *f inv*; **you should have seen the tightness of her trousers!**

avresti dovuto vedere com'erano stretti i suoi pantaloni!; **I can feel a tightness in my chest** ho un senso di oppressione al torace

tight·rope ['taɪt,rəʊp] N corda (da acrobata)

tightrope walker N funambolo(-a)

tights [taɪts] NPL (*Brit*) collant *m inv*

tight·wad ['taɪt,wɒd] N (*Am fam pej*) tirchione(-a)

ti·gress ['taɪgrɪs] N tigre *f* (femmina)

tile [taɪl] N (*on roof*) tegola; (*on floor, wall*) mattonella, piastrella; **roofs with red tiles** tetti con le tegole rosse; **black and white tiles** piastrelle bianche e nere; **a night on the tiles** (*Brit fam*) una notte brava

■ VT (*roof*) rivestire di tegole; (*floor, bathroom*) piastrellare

tiled [taɪld] ADJ (*floor, wall, bathroom*) a mattonelle, a piastrelle; (*roof*) rivestito(-a) di tegole; **a tiled roof** un tetto di tegole; **tiled walls** pareti *fpl* piastrellate

◎ **till, until**[1] [tɪl] PREP (*fam*): **I waited till ten o'clock** ho aspettato fino alle dieci; **not... till** non... prima di; **it won't be ready till next week** non sarà pronto prima della settimana prossima; **till now** finora; **till then** fino ad allora

till[2] [tɪl] N (*for money*) cassa, registratore *m* di cassa; **pay at the till** pagare alla cassa

till[3] [tɪl] VT (*land*) coltivare

till·er ['tɪlə^r] N (*Naut*) barra del timone

tilt [tɪlt] N **1** (*slope*) pendio; **to wear one's hat at a tilt** portare il cappello sulle ventitré **2** (*fam*): **(at) full tilt** a tutta velocità

■ VT inclinare, far pendere; **tilt it this way/the other way** inclinalo da questa/quella parte; **he tilted the mirror** ha inclinato lo specchio; **he tilted his chair back** ha inclinato la sedia indietro

■ VI inclinarsi, pendere; **to tilt to one side** inclinarsi da una parte; **the boat tilted dangerously** la barca si è inclinata pericolosamente; **he tilted back in his chair** si è inclinato indietro con la sedia

tilting train N treno a inclinazione variabile; ≈ pendolino®

tim·ber ['tɪmbə^r] N (*material*) legname *m*; (*trees*) alberi *mpl* da legname; **timber!** cade!

■ ADJ (*roof, cabin*) di legno

tim·bered ['tɪmbəd] ADJ (*house*) rivestito(-a) di legno

timber merchant N (*Brit*) commerciante *m/f* di legname

timber·yard ['tɪmbə,jɑ:d] N (*Brit*) deposito *m* legname *inv*

tim·bre ['tɪmbə^r] N timbro

◎ **time** [taɪm] N (*gen*)

1 tempo; **time and space** il tempo e lo spazio; **how time flies** come vola il tempo!; **only time will tell** si saprà solo col tempo; **time is on our side** il tempo è dalla nostra; **all in good time** senza fretta; **to have (the) time (to do sth)** avere il tempo (di fare qc); **I'm sorry, I haven't got time** scusa, non ho tempo; **to find the time for reading** trovare il tempo per leggere; **I've no time for them** (*too busy*) non ho tempo da perdere con loro; (*contemptuous*) non li posso soffrire; **I've no time for it** (*fig*) non ho tempo da perdere con cose del genere; **he lost no time in doing it** l'ha fatto subito senza perdere tempo; **it takes time to ...** ci vuole tempo per...; **to take one's time** prenderla con calma; **time is money** (*Proverb*) il tempo è denaro; **he'll do it in his own (good) time** (*without being hurried*) lo farà quando ha (un minuto di) tempo; **he'll do it in his own time** (*out of working hours*) lo farà nel suo tempo libero; **my time is my own** dispongo del mio tempo

2 (*period of time*) tempo; **a long time** molto tempo; **a long time ago** molto tempo fa; **a short time** poco tempo; **in a short time she will have left** fra poco sarà partita; **in a short time they were all gone** nel giro di poco tempo se ne erano andati tutti; **a short time after** poco tempo dopo; **for a time** per un po' di tempo; **have you been here all this time?** sei stato qui tutto questo tempo?; **for the time being** per il momento; **in no time** in un attimo; **it will be ready in no time** sarà pronto prestissimo; **in a week's time** fra una settimana

3 (*moment*) momento; (*period*) periodo; **any time** in qualsiasi momento; **come any time you like** vieni quando vuoi; **any time now** da un momento all'altro; **at that time** allora, a quel tempo; **at the present time** al momento, adesso; **at this time of the year** in questo periodo dell'anno; **(by) this time next year** in questo periodo l'anno prossimo; **by the time he arrived** quando è arrivato; **at the same time** (*simultaneously*) contemporaneamente; **but at the same time, I have to admit ...** tuttavia devo ammettere...; **at the same time as** nello stesso momento in cui; **at times** a volte; **at all times** in ogni momento, sempre; **from time to time** di tanto in tanto; **now is the time to go to Venice** questo è il periodo *or* momento giusto per andare a Venezia; **the time has come to leave** è arrivato il momento *or* l'ora di partire; **this is no time for jokes** non è il momento di scherzare; **this is neither the time nor the place to discuss it** non è né il luogo né il momento adatto per discuterne

4 (*by clock*) ora; **what time do you make it?** che ora fai?; **have you got the (right) time?** hai l'ora (esatta)?; **what's the time?** *or* **what time is it?** che ora è?, che ore sono?; **it was two o'clock, Italian time** erano le due, ora italiana; **what time do you get up?** a che ora ti alzi?; **in time** (*soon enough*) in tempo; (*after some time*) col tempo; **just in time** appena in tempo; **to arrive (just) in time for dinner** arrivare (appena) in tempo per cena; **on time** (*person*) puntuale; (*train*) in orario; **he never arrives on time** non è mai puntuale; **it's time for the news** (*on radio*) c'è il giornale radio; (*on television*) c'è il telegiornale; **time's up!** è (l')ora!; **to be 30 minutes behind/ahead of time** avere 30 minuti di ritardo/anticipo; **about time too!** era anche ora!; **it was about time you had a haircut** era proprio ora che ti tagliassi i capelli

5 (*era: often pl*) era; (*period*) periodo, epoca; **in modern times** nell'era moderna; **in Elizabethan times** nel periodo elisabettiano; **in my time** ai miei tempi; **during my time at HarperCollins** quando ero alla HarperCollins; **it was before my time** non ero ancora nata; **times were hard** erano tempi duri; **in times to come** nel tempo a venire; **to be ahead of one's time** precorrere i tempi; **to be behind the times** essere rimasto(-a) indietro

6 (*experience*): **to have a good time** divertirsi; **did you have a good time?** vi siete divertiti?; **to have a bad** *or* **rough time (of it)** passarsela male; **they had a hard time of it** è stata dura per loro

7 (*occasion*) volta; **three times** tre volte; **this/next time** questa/la prossima volta; **how many times?** quante volte?; **the last time I did it** l'ultima volta che l'ho fatto; **time after time** *or* **time and again** mille volte; **many's the time ...** più di una volta...; **I remember the time when ...** ricordo ancora quando...; **for weeks at a time** per settimane; **2 at a**

Tt

time 2 alla volta; **to carry 3 boxes at a time** portare 3 scatole per volta
8 (*Mus, Mil*) tempo; **to play/march in time** suonare/ marciare a tempo; **to keep time** andare a tempo; **to be out of time** essere *or* andare fuori tempo
9 (*Math*): **4 times 3 is 12** 4 per *or* volte 3 fa 12; **3 times as fast (as)** *or* **3 times faster (than)** 3 volte più veloce (di)
■ VT
1 (*schedule*) programmare; (*: measure duration of*) calcolare la durata di; (*choose time of: joke, request*): **to time sth well/badly** scegliere il momento più/meno opportuno per qc, fare qc al momento giusto/ sbagliato; **the footballer timed his shot perfectly** il giocatore ha calcolato il tiro alla perfezione; **the bomb was timed to explode 5 minutes later** la bomba era stata regolata in modo da esplodere 5 minuti più tardi
2 (*with stopwatch*) cronometrare; **to time an egg** controllare il tempo per la cottura di un uovo; **to time o.s.** prendere i propri tempi

time and motion expert N esperto nei tempi e nelle fasi di produzione
time and motion study N analisi *f inv* dei tempi e delle fasi di produzione
time bomb N bomba a orologeria
time capsule N capsula dal tempo (*che viene interrata per essere ritrovata in epoche successive*)
time·card ['taɪm,kɑ:d] N cartellino (di presenza)
time clock N (*Industry*) orologio marcatempo
time-consuming ['taɪmkən,sju:mɪŋ] ADJ che richiede molto tempo
time difference N differenza di fuso orario
time exposure N (*Phot*) posa lunga
time frame N tempi *mpl*
time-honoured, (*Am*) **time-honored** ['taɪm,ɒnəd] ADJ consacrato(-a) dal tempo
time·keeper ['taɪm,ki:pəʳ] N (*Sport*) cronometrista *m/f*; **he's a good timekeeper** è sempre puntuale; **my old watch is a good timekeeper** il mio vecchio orologio non perde un secondo
time lag N (*between events*) intervallo (di tempo); (*in travel*) differenza di fuso orario
time·less ['taɪmlɪs] ADJ (*frm: unchanging*) senza tempo; (*: unending*) eterno(-a), infinito(-a)
time limit N limite *m* di tempo; **to set a time limit** fissare un limite di tempo
time·line ['taɪm,laɪn] N (*length of time*) tempi *mpl*; (*dates*) tabella di successione cronologica
time·li·ness ['taɪmlɪnɪs] N (*see adj*) tempestività *f inv*; opportunità *f inv*
time·ly ['taɪmlɪ] ADJ tempestivo(-a); (*opportune*) opportuno(-a)
time off N tempo libero
time out N 1 (*Sport*) time out *m inv* 2 (*fam*): **to take time out** assentarsi termine (*da lavoro, attività*)
time·piece ['taɪm,pi:s] N (*old, frm*) orologio
tim·er ['taɪməʳ] N (*in kitchen*) contaminuti *m inv*; (*hourglass*) clessidra; (*Tech*) timer *m inv*, temporizzatore *m inv*
time-saving ['taɪm,seɪvɪŋ] ADJ che fa risparmiare tempo
time scale N tempi *mpl* d'esecuzione
time·server ['taɪm,sɜ:vəʳ] N (*pej*) 1 (*changing opinions*) voltagabbana *m/f inv* (*fig*) 2 (*in job*) imboscato(-a)
time-share ['taɪmʃɛəʳ] ADJ (*holiday home*) in multiproprietà
■ N (*property*) casa in multiproprietà; (*system*) multiproprietà *f inv*
time shar·ing ['taɪmʃɛərɪŋ] N 1 (*Comput*) time sharing *m inv*, ripartizione *f* del tempo 2 (*of property*) multiproprietà *f inv*
time sheet N foglio di presenza
time signal N segnale *m* orario
time signature N (*Mus*) indicazione *f* del tempo
time slot N (*TV, Radio*) fascia oraria
time switch N interruttore *m* a tempo
time·table ['taɪm,teɪbl] N (*for trains*) orario; (*programme of events*) programma *m*; **the train timetable** l'orario del treno; **History is one of the most important subjects on the timetable** Storia è una delle materie più importanti in programma
time warp N salto indietro nel tempo; **it's like going into** *or* **living in a time warp** è come fare un salto indietro nel tempo
time waster N (*person*) perditempo *m/f inv*; (*thing*) perdita di tempo
time·worn ['taɪm,wɔ:n] ADJ (*hackneyed: phrase, idea, excuse*) trito(-a) e ritrito(-a)
time zone N fuso orario
tim·id ['tɪmɪd] ADJ (*shy*) timido(-a); (*easily scared*) timoroso(-a), pauroso(-a)
ti·mid·ity [tɪ'mɪdɪtɪ] N timidezza
tim·id·ly ['tɪmɪdlɪ] ADV timidamente
tim·ing ['taɪmɪŋ] N (*of tennis player, cricketer*) coordinazione *f*; (*of musician*) tempismo; (*of comedian*) tempestività *f inv*; (*of demonstration, elections*) momento; (*of engine*) messa in fase; (*of race, industrial process*) cronometraggio; **that was good/bad timing** hai (*or* ha *etc*) scelto il momento opportuno/sbagliato; **that was perfect timing!** che tempismo!; **he arrived with perfect timing, just after she had left** arrivò, con tempismo perfetto, subito dopo che lei se n'era andata; **the timing of the announcement was carefully calculated** il momento in cui dare l'annuncio fu scelto con attenzione
timing device N (*on bomb*) timer *m inv*
tim·or·ous ['tɪmərəs] ADJ timoroso(-a)
tim·pa·ni ['tɪmpənɪ] NPL (*Mus*) timpani *mpl*
tim·pa·nist ['tɪmpənɪst] N timpanista *m/f*
tin [tɪn] N 1 (*metal*) stagno; (*also: tin plate*) latta
2 (*Brit: can*) barattolo *or* scatola (di latta); (*: for baking*) teglia; **a tin of paint** un barattolo di vernice; **a tin of beans** una scatola di fagioli; **a biscuit tin** una scatola per biscotti
■ VT (*Brit*) inscatolare
tin can N (*empty*) barattolo *or* scatola (di latta)
tin·der ['tɪndəʳ] N esca
tin·foil ['tɪn,fɔɪl] N (carta) stagnola
tinge [tɪndʒ] N (*of colour, fig*) punta, sfumatura; **her hair had a tinge of red in it** i suoi capelli avevano dei riflessi rossi
■ VT: **to be tinged with** avere una punta *or* sfumatura di
tin·gle ['tɪŋgl] N (*of skin*) formicolio; (*thrill*) fremito
■ VI (*cheeks, skin: from cold*) pungere, pizzicare; (*: from bad circulation*) formicolare; **my fingers are tingling** ho le dita informicolate; **my tongue is tingling** mi pizzica la lingua; **a tingling sensation** un formicolio; **to tingle with excitement** fremere dall'eccitazione
tin hat N (*fam*) elmetto
tink·er ['tɪŋkəʳ] N stagnino ambulante
► **tinker with** VI + PREP
► **tinker about with** VI + ADV + PREP (*play*) trastullarsi con; (*repair*) armeggiare intorno a, cercare di riparare; **he's always tinkering with his car** è

sempre lì ad armeggiare intorno alla macchina

tin·kle ['tɪŋkl] N **1** *(of bell)* tintinnio; *(Brit fam)*: **give me a tinkle** dammi un colpetto di telefono **2** *(fam: act of urinating)* pipì *fsg*
■VI *(bell)* tintinnare

tin·kling ['tɪŋklɪŋ] ADJ *(sound)* tintinnante, argentino(-a)
■N tintinnio

tin mine N miniera di stagno

tinned [tɪnd] ADJ *(Brit: food)* in scatola; **tinned peaches** pesche in scatola

tin·ni·tus [tɪ'naɪtəs] N *(Med)* ronzio auricolare

tin·ny ['tɪnɪ] ADJ *(comp* **-ier**, *superl* **-iest**) *(metallic: sound)* metallico(-a); *(pej: car, machine)* che sembra di latta

tin-opener ['tɪn,əʊpnəʳ] N *(Brit)* apriscatole *m inv*

Tin Pan Alley N *(fam)* il mondo della musica

tin·plate ['tɪn,pleɪt] N latta

tin·pot ['tɪn,pɒt] ADJ *(Brit fam: dictator, government)* da due soldi

tin·sel ['tɪnsəl] N decorazioni *fpl* natalizie *(argentate)*

tin soldier N soldatino di latta

tint [tɪnt] N *(gen)* sfumatura; *(colour)* tinta; *(for hair)* shampoo *m inv* colorante; **a delicate purple tint** una leggera sfumatura di viola
■VT *(hair)* fare uno shampoo colorante a

tint·ed ['tɪntɪd] ADJ *(hair)* tinto(-a); *(spectacles, glass)* colorato(-a); **tinted windows** *(Aut)* cristalli *mpl* fumé *inv*

tin whistle N *(Mus)* zufolo

◎**tiny** ['taɪnɪ] ADJ *(comp* **-ier**, *superl* **-iest**) minuscolo(-a)

◎**tip¹** [tɪp] N *(end)* punta; *(peak)* cima, vetta; *(of stick, umbrella: protective)* puntale *m*; **it's on the tip of my tongue** *(fig)* ce l'ho sulla punta della lingua; **it was just the tip of the iceberg** *(fig)* era solo la punta dell'iceberg
▶ **tip off** VT + ADV *(inform)* fare una soffiata a
▶ **tip up** VI + ADV ribaltarsi
■VT + ADV inclinare

tip² [tɪp] N **1** *(gratuity)* mancia **2** *(hint)* suggerimento; *(advice)* consiglio; *(: for horse race)* cavallo; **I'll give you a tip** ti darò un consiglio; **he didn't leave a tip** non ha lasciato la mancia; **a useful tip** un buon consiglio
■VT **1** *(porter, waiter)* dare la mancia a; **I tipped him £1** gli ho dato una mancia di 1 sterlina, gli ho dato 1 sterlina di mancia **2** *(predict: winner)* pronosticare; *(: horse)* dare vincente; **he is being tipped for the job** secondo i pronostici dovrebbe avere il posto

tip³ [tɪp] N *(Brit: for rubbish)* discarica, immondezzaio; *(: for coal waste)* discarica; **I took the old sofa to the tip** ho portato il vecchio divano in discarica; **this place is a complete tip!** che porcile!
■VT *(tilt)* inclinare; *(empty: also:* **tip out**) svuotare, scaricare; *(overturn: also:* **tip over**) rovesciare, capovolgere; **to tip sb off his seat** far cadere qn dalla sedia; **to tip away the dishwater** svuotare l'acqua dei piatti; **to tip back a chair** inclinare una sedia all'indietro; **he tipped out the contents of the box** ha rovesciato il contenuto della scatola; **she tipped the leftovers in the bin** ha vuotato gli avanzi nella pattumiera; **to tip over a glass of wine** rovesciare un bicchiere di vino; **to tip the balance** far pendere la bilancia da una parte
■VI *(incline)* pendere, essere inclinato(-a); *(also:* **tip over**) rovesciarsi

tip-off ['tɪp,ɒf] N *(information)* soffiata

tipped [tɪpt] ADJ *(Brit: cigarette)* col filtro; **steel-tipped** con la punta d'acciaio

tip·per ['tɪpəʳ] N *(truck)* autocarro a cassone ribaltabile

Tipp-Ex® ['tɪpɛks] N *(Brit)* liquido correttore

tip·ping ['tɪpɪŋ] N: **"no tipping"** "divieto di scarico"

tip·ple ['tɪpl] *(fam)* N drink *m inv* preferito; **to have a tipple** bere un bicchierino
■VI sbevazzare

tip·pler ['tɪpləʳ] N *(fam)* beone(-a)

tip·ster ['tɪpstəʳ] N *(Racing) chi vende informazioni sulle corse e altre manifestazioni oggetto di scommesse*

tip·sy ['tɪpsɪ] ADJ *(comp* **-ier**, *superl* **-iest**) brillo(-a)

tip·toe ['tɪp,təʊ] N: **to walk on tiptoe** camminare in punta dei piedi
■VI camminare in punta dei piedi

tip·top [,tɪp'tɒp] ADJ: **in tiptop condition** in ottime condizioni

TIR [,tiːaɪ'ɑːʳ] ABBR (= **transport internationaux routiers**) TIR *m inv*

ti·rade [taɪ'reɪd] N filippica

tire¹ ['taɪəʳ] VT *(exhaust)* stancare
■VI stancarsi; **he tires easily** si stanca facilmente; **to tire of sb/sth** stancarsi di qn/qc
▶ **tire out** VT + ADV sfinire, spossare; **the walk tired me out** la passeggiata mi ha sfinito

tire² ['taɪəʳ] *(Am)* = **tyre**

◎**tired** ['taɪəd] ADJ **1** stanco(-a); **to be/feel/look tired** essere/sentirsi/sembrare stanco(-a); **to be tired of sb/sth** essere stanco(-a) *or* stufo(-a) di qn/qc; **I'm tired of waiting** sono stufa di aspettare; **to get** *or* **grow tired of doing sth** stancarsi di fare qc **2** *(fig: cliché)* trito(-a) e ritrito(-a); *(fig: shabby)* consunto(-a)

tired·ly ['taɪədlɪ] ADV stancamente

tired·ness ['taɪədnɪs] N stanchezza

tire·less ['taɪəlɪs] ADJ instancabile

tire·less·ly ['taɪəlɪslɪ] ADV instancabilmente

tire·some ['taɪəsəm] ADJ *(job, person)* noioso(-a); *(situation)* seccante; **how tiresome!** che seccatura!

tir·ing ['taɪərɪŋ] ADJ faticoso(-a)

◎**tis·sue** ['tɪʃuː] N **1** *(thin paper)* velina; *(paper handkerchief)* fazzolettino di carta; **she blew her nose on a tissue** si è soffiata il naso con un fazzolettino di carta **2** *(Anat)* tessuto; **muscle tissue** tessuto muscolare **3** *(fig)*: **to weave a tissue of lies** ordire tutta una serie di menzogne

tissue paper N carta velina

tit¹ [tɪt] N *(bird: also:* **titmouse**) cincia

tit² [tɪt] N **1** *(fam: breast)* tetta **2** *(Brit fam)*: **to get on sb's tits** rompere le palle a qn *(fam)*; *(: person)* cretino(-a)

tit³ [tɪt] N: **to give tit for tat** rendere pan per focaccia

Ti·tan ['taɪtən] N Titano(-a)

ti·tan·ic [taɪ'tænɪk] ADJ titanico(-a)

ti·ta·nium [tɪ'teɪnɪəm] N titanio

tit·bit ['tɪt,bɪt] N, *(Am)* **tid·bit** ['tɪd,bɪt] N *(of food)* bocconcino, leccornia; *(fig: of news, information, gossip)* notizia ghiotta

titchy ['tɪtʃɪ] ADJ *(comp* **-ier**, *superl* **-iest**) *(Brit fam)* minuscolo(-a)

tithe [taɪð] N decima

tit·il·late ['tɪtɪ,leɪt] VT *(sexually)* titillare

titi·vate ['tɪtɪ,veɪt] VT agghindare

◎**ti·tle** ['taɪtl] N **1** *(gen)* titolo; **author and title** autore e titolo; **to hold a title** detenere un titolo **2** *(Law: right)*: **title (to)** diritto (a)

title bar N *(Comput)* barra del titolo

◎**ti·tled** ['taɪtld] ADJ *(person)* titolato(-a)

title deed N *(Law)* atto di proprietà

title holder N *(Sport)* detentore(-trice) del titolo

title page N frontespizio

Tt

title role N (*Theatre, Cine*) ruolo *or* parte *f* principale
title track N brano che dà il nome all'album
ti·tra·tion [taɪ'treɪʃən] N titolazione *f*
tit·ter ['tɪtə^r] N risatina nervosa
■VI ridere nervosamente, ridacchiare
tittle-tattle ['tɪtl,tætl] (*fam*) N pettegolezzi *mpl*, chiacchiere *fpl*
■VI pettegolare
titu·lar ['tɪtjʊlə^r] ADJ (*in name only*) nominale
tiz·zy ['tɪzɪ] N (*fam*): **to be in/get into a tizzy (about sth)** essere/mettersi in agitazione (per qc)
T-junction ['ti:,dʒʌŋkʃən] N (*Brit*) incrocio a T
TM [,ti:'ɛm] N ABBR **1** (= **transcendental meditation**) MT *f* **2** (*Comm*) = **trademark**
TN ABBR (*Am Post*) = **Tennessee**
TNT [,ti:ɛn'ti:] N ABBR (= trinitrotoluene) TNT *m*

◎**to** [tu:; *weak form* tə] PREP KEYWORD
1 (*direction: gen*) a; (: *towards*) verso; (: *to a country*) in; (: *to sb's house, office, shop*) da; **have you ever been to India?** sei mai stata in India?; **to go to the doctor's** andare dal dottore; **to go to France** andare in Francia; **to the left** a sinistra; **a letter to his wife** una lettera a sua moglie; **to go to Paris** andare a Parigi; **to go to Peter's** andare da Peter; **to go to Portugal** andare in Portogallo; **to the right** a destra; **the road to Edinburgh** la strada per Edimburgo; **to go to school** andare a scuola; **to go to the station** andare alla stazione
2 (*next to, with position*) a; **with one's back to the wall** con le spalle al muro; **the door is to the left (of)** la porta è a sinistra (di); **at right angles to sth** ad angolo retto con qc
3 (*as far as*) fino a; **to count to 10** contare fino a dieci; **to some extent** fino a un certo punto, in parte; **from here to London** da qui (fino) a Londra; **from 40 to 50 people** da 40 a 50 persone; **to be wet to the skin** essere bagnato(-a) fino al midollo
4 (*with expressions of time*) a; **it's twenty-five to 3** mancano venticinque minuti alle 3, sono le 2 e trentacinque
5 (*expressing indirect object*) a; **it belongs to him** gli appartiene, è suo; **to drink to sb** bere a qn *or* alla salute di qn; **to give sth to sb** dare qc a qn; **give it to me** dammelo; **the key to the front door** la chiave della porta d'ingresso; **to be kind to sb** essere gentile con qn; **a monument to the fallen** un monumento ai caduti; **the man I sold it to** *or* **it** l'uomo (a) cui l'ho venduto; **a solution to the problem** una soluzione al problema
6 (*in relation to*) (in confronto) a; **A is to B as C is to D** A sta a B come C sta a D; **30 miles to the gallon** ≈ 11 chilometri con un litro; **5 apples to the kilo** 5 mele in un chilo; **10 inhabitants to the square kilometre** 10 abitanti per chilometro quadrato; **that's nothing to what is to come** non è nulla in confronto a ciò che ancora deve venire; **superior to the others** superiore agli altri; **three goals to two** tre reti a due
7 (*about*): **that's all there is to it** questo è tutto, è tutto qui; **what do you say to this?** che cosa ne pensi?
8 (*according to*) secondo; **to the best of my recollection** per quanto mi ricordi io; **we danced to the music of ...** abbiamo ballato con la musica di...; **to my way of thinking** secondo il mio modo di pensare, a mio parere
9 (*purpose, result*): **to come to sb's aid** venire in aiuto a qn; **to sentence sb to death** condannare qn a morte; **to my great surprise** con mia grande sorpresa
■PARTICLE (*with verb*)
1 (*simple infinitive*): **to go/eat** andare/mangiare
2 (*following another verb*): **to start to cry** incominciare *or* mettersi a piangere; **to try to do** cercare di fare; **to want to do** voler fare
3 (*purpose, result*) per; **he did it to help you** l'ha fatto per aiutarti; **he came to see you** è venuto per vederti
4 (*with ellipsis of verb*): **you ought to** dovresti (farlo); **I don't want to** non voglio (farlo)
5 (*equivalent to relative clause*) da; **I have things to do** ho (delle cose) da fare; **he's not the sort to do that** non è il tipo da fare una cosa del genere; **now is the time to do it** è ora di farlo; **he has a lot to lose** rischia grosso; **he has nothing to lose** non ha nulla da perdere
6 (*after adjective etc*): **the first to go** il/la primo(-a) ad andarsene; **hard to believe** difficile da credere; **too old to ...** troppo vecchio(-a) per...; **ready to go** pronto(-a) a partire; **too young to ...** troppo giovane per...
■ADV
1 to go to and fro andare e tornare; **to pull/push the door to** (*closed*) accostare la porta
2 to come to (*recover consciousness*) riprendere conoscenza

toad [təʊd] N rospo
toad-in-the-hole [,təʊdɪnðə'həʊl] N (*Brit Culin*) *salsicce coperte di pastella e cotte nel forno*
toad·stool ['təʊd,stu:l] N fungo velenoso
toady ['təʊdɪ] (*pej*) N leccapiedi *m/f inv*
■VI: **to toady to sb** leccare i piedi a qn
toast [təʊst] N **1** (*bread*) pane *m* tostato; **a piece** *or* **slice of toast** una fetta di pane tostato *or* abbrustolito **2** (*drink, speech*) brindisi *m inv*; **to propose/drink a toast to sb** proporre (di fare)/fare un brindisi a qn; **the toast of the town/nation** (*fig*) il vanto della città/nazione
■VT **1** (*bread*) tostare, abbrustolire **2** (*drink to*) brindare a

DID YOU KNOW ...?
toast is not translated by the Italian word *toast*

toast·ed ['təʊstɪd] ADJ tostato(-a)
toast·er ['təʊstə^r] N tostapane *m inv*
toastie ['təʊstɪ] N (*Brit: Culin*) toast *m inv*; **a cheese and ham toastie** un toast con prosciutto e formaggio
toast·master ['təʊst,ma:stə^r] N direttore *m* dei brindisi
toast rack ['təʊst,ræk] N portatoast *m inv*
toasty ['təʊstɪ] N (*fam*) bello(-a) caldo(-a); **to feel toasty** sentirsi al calduccio
to·bac·co [tə'bækəʊ] N tabacco; **pipe tobacco** tabacco da pipa
to·bac·co·nist [tə'bækənɪst] N (*Brit*) tabaccaio(-a); **tobacconist's (shop)** tabaccheria
tobacco pouch N borsa per il tabacco
To·ba·go [tə'beɪgəʊ] N *see* **Trinidad**
to·bog·gan [tə'bɒgən] N toboga *m inv*, slittino; (*child's*) slitta, slittino
■VI andare in slittino
◎**to·day** [tə'deɪ] ADV oggi; (*these days*) al giorno d'oggi, oggigiorno; **a week from today** *or* **a week today** *or* **today week** (*Brit*) oggi a otto; **a fortnight today** (*Brit*) *or* (*Am*) **two weeks from today** quindici giorni a oggi; **what day is it today?** che giorno è oggi?; **what date is**

it today? quanti ne abbiamo oggi?; **today is the 4th of March** (oggi) è il 4 (di) marzo

■ N (*also fig*) oggi *m inv*; **writers of today** gli scrittori d'oggi; **today's paper** il giornale di oggi

tod·dle ['tɒdl] VI (*child*): **to toddle in/out** *etc* entrare/ uscire *etc* a passettini; (*fam: adult*): **he toddled off** se n'è andato camminando tranquillamente

tod·dler ['tɒdləʳ] N (*small child*) bambino(-a) che impara a camminare

tod·dy ['tɒdɪ] N: **hot toddy** grog *m inv*

to-do [tə'du:] N (*fam: fuss*): **to cause a to-do** fare delle storie

toe [təʊ] N (*Anat*) dito del piede; (*of shoe*) punta; **big toe** alluce *m*; **little toe** mignolino; **to keep sb on his toes** (*fig*) tenere qn sull'attenti

■ VT: **to toe the line** (*fig: conform*) conformarsi alle regole, stare in riga

toe·cap ['təʊ,kæp] N mascherina

toe·clip ['təʊ,klɪp] N (*Cycling*) puntapiedi *m inv*

TOEFL N ABBR = *Test(ing) of English as a Foreign Language*

toe·hold ['təʊ,həʊld] N punto d'appoggio

toe·nail ['təʊ,neɪl] N unghia del piede

toe·piece ['təʊ,pi:s] N (*Skiing*) puntale *m*

toe·rag ['təʊ,ræg] N (*Brit fam*) stronzetto(-a)

toff [tɒf] N (*Brit old fam*) gran signore(-a)

tof·fee ['tɒfɪ] N caramella *f* mou *inv*; **he can't sing for toffee** (*Brit fam*) come cantante non vale una cicca

toffee apple N (*Brit*) mela caramellata

toffee-nosed ['tɒfɪ,nəʊzd] ADJ (*Brit fam pej*) con la puzza sotto il naso

tofu ['təʊ,fu:] N tofu *m*; *caglio di latte di soia non fermentato*

toga ['təʊgə] N toga

◎ **to·geth·er** [tə'gɛðəʳ] ADV **1** (*gen*) insieme; **together with** insieme a; **all together** tutti insieme; **they were both in it together** (*pej*) vi erano implicati entrambi; **we're in this together** siamo nella stessa barca; **to bring the two sides together** far mettere d'accordo le due parti; **to gather together** radunarsi; **to put a meal together** mettere insieme un pranzo *or* una cena; **are they still together?** stanno ancora insieme? **2** (*simultaneously*) insieme, contemporaneamente, allo stesso tempo; (*continuously*) di seguito

to·geth·er·ness [tə'gɛðənɪs] N (*closeness*) intimità *f inv*; **family togetherness** intimità familiare

togged out ['tɒgd'aʊt] ADJ: **to be togged out in sth** essere abbigliato(-a) con qc; **to be togged out to do sth** essere abbigliato(-a) di tutto punto per fare qc

tog·gle ['tɒgl] N (*on coat*) olivetta

toggle switch N deviatore *m* a comando manuale; (*Comput*) tasto bistabile

Togo ['təʊgəʊ] N il Togo

togs [tɒgz] NPL (*fam: clothes*) vestiti *mpl*

toil [tɔɪl] N duro lavoro, fatica

■ VI lavorare sodo, faticare; **workers toiled for hours and hours** gli operai sgobbavano per ore ed ore; **to toil away at sth** lavorare duramente su qc; **to toil up a hill** arrancare su per una collina

toi·let ['tɔɪlɪt] N **1** (*Brit: lavatory*) gabinetto; **to go to the toilet** andare al gabinetto *or* al bagno; **she's in the toilet** è in gabinetto *or* in bagno; **where's the toilet?** dov'è la toilette? **2** (*old: dressing, washing*) toilette *f*; **she was at her toilet** si stava facendo la toilette

■ ADJ (*soap*) da toilette

toilet bag N (*Brit*) nécessaire *m inv* da toilette

toilet bowl N vaso *or* tazza del gabinetto

toilet paper N carta igienica

toi·let·ries ['tɔɪlɪtrɪz] NPL articoli *mpl* da toilette

toilet roll N (*Brit*) rotolo di carta igienica

toilet-train ['tɔɪlɪt,treɪn] VT: **to toilet-train a child** insegnare ad un bambino ad usare il vasino

toilet water N acqua di colonia

to-ing and fro-ing [,tu:ɪŋən'frəʊɪŋ] N (*pl* **to-ings and fro-ings**) (*Brit*) andirivieni *m inv*

to·ken ['təʊkən] N **1** (*Brit: voucher*) buono; **record token** buono *m* disco *inv*; **gift token** buono *m* omaggio *inv* **2** (*metal disc*) gettone *m* **3** (*sign, symbol*) segno; **by the same token** (*fig*) per lo stesso motivo; **as a token of our respect** come segno di rispetto

■ ADJ (*fee, strike*) simbolico(-a); (*resistance, gesture*) formale; **a token gesture** un gesto simbolico

to·ken·ism ['təʊkə,nɪzəm] N concessione *f* pro forma *inv*

To·kyo ['təʊkjəʊ] N Tokyo *f*

told [təʊld] PT, PP *of* **tell**

tol·er·able ['tɒlərəbl] ADJ **1** (*bearable*) sopportabile, tollerabile **2** (*fairly good*) passabile, discreto(-a); **the pain was tolerable** il dolore era sopportabile; **he got tolerable marks in English** ha ricevuto voti decenti in inglese

tol·er·ably ['tɒlərəblɪ] ADV (*good, comfortable*) abbastanza

tol·er·ance ['tɒlərəns] N (*of pain, hardship*) sopportazione *f*; (*of behaviour, Med, Tech*) tolleranza

tol·er·ant ['tɒlərənt] ADJ: **tolerant (of)** tollerante (nei confronti di)

tol·er·ant·ly ['tɒlərəntlɪ] ADV con tolleranza

tol·er·ate ['tɒlə,reɪt] VT (*gen, Med, Tech*) tollerare, sopportare

tol·era·tion [,tɒlə'reɪʃən] N tolleranza

toll¹ [təʊl] N **1** (*on road*) pedaggio **2** (*losses, casualties*): **the death toll on the roads** il numero di vittime sulle strade; **the severe winter has taken its toll on the crops** l'inverno rigido ha colpito duramente il raccolto

■ ADJ (*road, bridge*) a pedaggio

toll² [təʊl] VT, VI (*bell*) suonare lentamente e solennemente

■ N (*of bell*) rintocco

toll·bridge ['təʊl,brɪdʒ] N ponte *m* a pedaggio

toll call N (*Am Telec*) (telefonata) interurbana

toll-free [,təʊl'fri:] (*Am*) ADJ senza addebito, gratuito(-a); **toll-free number** ≈ numero verde

■ ADV gratuitamente

Tom [tɒm] N: **any Tom, Dick or Harry** chiunque, il primo venuto

tom [tɒm] N (*fam*) micio

to·ma·to [tə'mɑ:təʊ, *Am* tə'meɪtəʊ] N (*pl* **tomatoes**) pomodoro

■ ADJ (*juice, sauce*) di pomodoro

tomato paste N concentrato di pomodoro

tomb [tu:m] N tomba

tom·bo·la [tɒm'bəʊlə] N (*Brit*) tombola

tom·boy ['tɒm,bɔɪ] N: **she's a tomboy** è un maschiaccio

tomb·stone ['tu:m,stəʊn] N pietra tombale

tom·cat ['tɒm,kæt] N gatto maschio

tome [təʊm] N tomo; (*hum*) librone *m*

tom·fool·ery [,tɒm'fu:lərɪ] N sciocchezze *fpl*

tom·my gun ['tɒmɪ,gʌn] N (*fam*) fucile *m* mitragliatore

◎ **to·mor·row** [tə'mɒrəʊ] ADV (*also fig*) domani; **tomorrow morning** domani mattina; **a week from tomorrow** *or* **a week tomorrow** (*Brit*) domani a otto

■ N domani *m inv*; **tomorrow is Sunday** domani è

Tt

domenica; **the day after tomorrow** dopodomani; **tomorrow's paper** il giornale di domani; **tomorrow is another day** *(fig)* domani è un altro giorno

tom·tom ['tɒm,tɒm] N tamtam *m inv*

◎**ton** [tʌn] N *(weight)* tonnellata *(Brit =1016 kg; Am =907 kg)*; *(metric ton)* tonnellata; (*Naut*: *also*: **register ton**) tonnellata di stazza *(2.83 cu.m; 100 cu.ft)*; (: *also*: **displacement ton**) tonnellata inglese; **this suitcase weighs a ton** *(fam)* questa valigia pesa una tonnellata; **tons of sth** *(fam)* un mucchio *or* sacco di qc

to·nal ['təʊnl] ADJ tonale

◎**tone** [təʊn] N *(gen)* tono; *(of colour)* tonalità *f inv*; *(of musical instrument)* timbro; *(Telec)* segnale *m* acustico; **his tone of voice** il tono della sua voce; **leave a message after the tone** lasciate un messaggio dopo il segnale acustico; **dialling** *(Brit) or* **dial** *(Am)* **tone** *(Telec)* segnale *m* di libero; **to praise sb in ringing tones** *(fig)* portare qn alle stelle; **they were speaking in low tones** parlavano a voce bassa; **two tones of red** due tonalità di rosso; **to raise/lower the tone of sth** migliorare/abbassare il tono di qc

■VI (*also*: **tone in**: *colours*) intonarsi; **the curtains tone with the carpet** le tende si intonano con la moquette

▶ **tone down** VT + ADV *(moderate: colour, sound)* attenuare; *(fig: language, criticism)* moderare

▶ **tone up** VT + ADV *(muscles)* tonificare; **exercise tones the muscles** la ginnastica tonifica i muscoli

tone control N *(on radio, hi-fi)* tasto (per la regolazione) del tono

tone-deaf [,təʊn'dɛf] ADJ stonato(-a), completamente privo(-a) di orecchio (musicale)

tone·less ['təʊnlɪs] ADJ *(voce)* inespressivo(-a)

tone·less·ly ['təʊnlɪslɪ] ADV in modo inespressivo

ton·er ['təʊnəʳ] N *(for photocopier)* colorante *m* organico, toner *m inv*

Tonga Is·lands ['tɒŋgə,aɪləndz] NPL, **Tonga** N le (isole *fpl*) Tonga

tongs [tɒŋz] NPL *(for coal)* molle *fpl*, tenaglie *fpl*; *(for sugar, in laboratory)* pinza

tongue [tʌŋ] N **1** *(gen)* lingua; *(of shoe)* linguetta; *(of bell)* battaglio; **have you lost your tongue?** hai perso la lingua?; **hold your tongue!** chiudi quella bocca!; **to put out one's tongue (at sb)** mostrare la lingua (a qn); **to say sth tongue in cheek** *(fig)* dire qc ironicamente; **I can't get my tongue round it** *(fig)* non riesco a pronunziarlo **2** *(frm, liter: language)* lingua

tongue-tied ['tʌŋ,taɪd] ADJ *(fig)* muto(-a); **he was tongue-tied with embarrassment** l'imbarrazzo lo ha fatto ammutolire

tongue-twister ['tʌŋ,twɪstəʳ] N scioglilingua *m inv*

ton·ic ['tɒnɪk] N **1** *(Med)* ricostituente *m*; (*also*: **skin tonic**) tonico; **fresh air is the best tonic when you have a headache** l'aria fresca è il miglior rimedio per il mal di testa; **this will be a tonic to her** questo la tirerà su **2** (*also*: **tonic water**) acqua tonica; **a bottle of tonic** una bottiglia di acqua tonica **3** *(Mus)* nota tonica

■ADJ *(all senses)* tonico(-a); **tonic solfa** *(Mus)* solfeggio

◎**to·night** [tə'naɪt] ADV, N *(this evening)* questa sera, stasera; *(this night)* questa notte, stanotte; **are you going out tonight?** esci stasera?; **I'll see you tonight** ci vediamo stasera; **I'll sleep well tonight** stanotte dormirò bene; **tonight's TV programmes** *(Brit) or* **programs** *(Am)* i programmi della serata

ton·nage ['tʌnɪdʒ] N *(Naut)* tonnellaggio, stazza

tonne [tʌn] N *(Brit: metric ton)* tonnellata

ton·sil ['tɒnsl] N tonsilla; **to have one's tonsils out** farsi operare di tonsille

ton·sil·lec·to·my [,tɒnsɪ'lɛktəmɪ] N tonsillectomia

ton·sil·li·tis [,tɒnsɪ'laɪtɪs] N tonsillite *f*; **to have tonsillitis** avere la tonsillite

◎**too** [tu:] ADV **1** *(excessively)* troppo; **it's too sweet** è troppo dolce; **it's too sweet for me to drink** non lo bevo, è troppo dolce per me; **it's too heavy for me** è troppo pesante per me; **it's too heavy for me to lift** non riesco a sollevarlo, è troppo pesante per me; **the water's too hot** l'acqua è troppo calda; **it's too good to be true** è troppo bello per essere vero; **I'm not too sure about that** non ne sono troppo sicuro; **too much** troppo(-a); **too many** troppi(-e); **too bad!** *(unsympathetic)* tanto peggio!; *(expressing regret)* che peccato! **2** *(also)* anche; *(moreover)* per di più; **I went too** ci sono andato anch'io; **my sister came too** è venuta anche mia sorella; **I speak French and Japanese too** parlo il francese e (anche) il giapponese; **not only that, he's blind too!** non solo, ma è anche cieco!; **he's famous, intelligent and rich too** è famoso, intelligente e per di più anche ricco

took [tʊk] PT *of* **take**

◎**tool** [tu:l] N **1** *(gen, Tech)* attrezzo, utensile *m*, arnese *m*; **(set of) tools** (set *m inv* di) attrezzi; **the tools of one's trade** i ferri del mestiere **2** *(fig: person)* strumento; **he was a mere tool in their hands** non era che uno strumento *or* un fantoccio nelle loro mani

■VT lavorare con un attrezzo

tool·bag ['tu:l,bæg] N borsa degli attrezzi

tool·bar ['tu:l,bɑ:ʳ] N *(Comput)* barra degli strumenti

tool box N cassetta degli attrezzi

tooled [tu:ld] ADJ *(silver)* cesellato(-a); *(leather)* goffrato(-a)

tool kit N kit *m inv* di attrezzi

tool-maker ['tu:l,meɪkəʳ] N chi fabbrica attrezzi

tool·shed ['tu:l,ʃɛd] N capanno degli attrezzi

toot [tu:t] N colpo di clacson

■VT: **to toot one's horn** suonare il clacson

■VI suonare; *(with car horn)* suonare il clacson

◎**tooth** [tu:θ] N *(pl* **teeth**) *(Anat, Tech)* dente *m*; **to clean one's teeth** lavarsi i denti; **to have a tooth out** *or (Am)* **to have a tooth pulled** farsi togliere un dente; **to have a sweet tooth** essere ghiotto(-a) di dolci; **long in the tooth** *(fam: old)* vecchiotto(-a); **to be fed up to the (back) teeth with sb/sth** *(fam)* averne fin sopra i capelli di qn/qc; **to get one's teeth into** *(fig: work)* impegnarsi a fondo in; (: *subject*) immergersi in; **armed to the teeth** armato(-a) fino ai denti; **to fight tooth and nail** combattere con le unghie e con i denti; **it sets my teeth on edge** mi fa venire i brividi; **by the skin of one's teeth** per il rotto della cuffia; **in the teeth of great opposition** malgrado la forte opposizione

tooth·ache ['tu:θ,eɪk] N mal *m* di denti; **to have toothache** avere il mal di denti

tooth·brush ['tu:θ,brʌʃ] N spazzolino da denti

tooth·comb ['tu:θ,kəʊm] N: **to go through sth with a fine toothcomb** passare qc al setaccio

tooth fairy N: **the tooth fairy** *fatina che porta soldini in regalo a un bimbo quando perde un dente da latte*; ≈ topolino

tooth·less ['tu:θlɪs] ADJ sdentato(-a)

tooth·paste ['tu:θ,peɪst] N dentifricio

tooth·pick ['tu:θ,pɪk] N stuzzicadenti *m inv*

tooth powder N dentifricio in polvere

toothy ['tu:θɪ] ADJ *(comp* **-ier**, *superl* **-iest**) *(fam)* che ha una dentatura cavallina; **to give sb a toothy smile** fare a qn un sorriso a trentadue denti

toot·sie ['tʊtsɪ] N (*fam*) **1** (*toe*) ditino; (*foot*) piedino **2** (*Am old*) tesoro; (*woman*) bella ragazza; **hi, tootsie** ciao bella

◎ **top[1]** [tɒp] N

1 (*highest point: of mountain, page, ladder*) cima; (*: of list, table, queue*) testa; (*: of career*) apice *m*; **at the top of the hill** sulla cima della collina; **at the top of the stairs/page/street** in cima alle scale/alla pagina/alla strada; **at the top of the table** a capotavola; **to be top of the charts** essere in testa alla hit-parade; **Liverpool is at the top of the league** (*Sport*) il Liverpool è in testa alla classifica; **from top to bottom** (*fig*) da cima a fondo; **from top to toe** dalla testa ai piedi; **from the top** dall'alto; **from the top of the hill** dalla cima della collina; **on top** sopra; **on top of** in cima a, sopra; (*Brit: in addition to*) oltre a; **on top of the cupboard** sopra l'armadio; **to fall on top of sb** cadere addosso a qn; **he's going thin on top** (*fam*) sta incominciando a perdere i capelli; **to reach the top** (*fig: of career*) raggiungere l'apice; **the men at the top** (*fig*) quelli che sono al potere

2 (*surface*) superficie *f*; (*of box, cupboard, table*) sopra *m inv*, parte *f* superiore; (*roof: of car*) tetto; (*upper part: of bus*) piano superiore; **the top of the table needs wiping** bisogna pulire la superficie *or* il piano della tavola; **oil comes to the top** l'olio sale alla superficie; **seats on top!** (*Brit: in double-decker bus*) ci sono posti di sopra!; **the top of the milk** (*Brit*) la panna

3 (*Dressmaking: blouse*) camicia; (*: T-shirt*) maglietta; (*of pyjamas*) giacca; **a cotton top** una maglia di cotone; **a bikini top** il pezzo di sopra di un bikini

4 (*lid: of bottle*) tappo; (*: of box, jar*) coperchio; (*of pen*) tappo, cappuccio

5 (*also: top gear*): **to change into top** mettere la quarta (*or* quinta)

6 (*in phrases*): **on top of (all) that** per di più, inoltre; **there's a surcharge on top of that** in più c'è un sovrapprezzo; **it's just one thing on top of another** è una cosa dietro a un'altra; **to be/feel on top of the world** (*fam*) essere/sentirsi al settimo cielo; **to be/get on top of things** (*fig*) dominare/cominciare a dominare la situazione; **things are getting on top of me** (*fam*) mi sta precipitando tutto addosso; **to come out on top** (*fig*) uscire vincitore(-trice); **I can't tell you off the top of my head** a mente non te lo posso dire; **at the top of one's voice** (*fig*) a squarciagola; **over the top** (*Brit fam: behaviour*) eccessivo(-a); **to go over the top** (*Brit fam*) esagerare; **to be tops** essere il migliore

■ ADJ

1 (*highest: floor, step*) ultimo(-a); (*: shelf, drawer*) (ultimo(-a)) in alto; (*: price*) più alto(-a); (*: in rank*) primo(-a); **at top speed** a tutta velocità; **top gear** la marcia più alta, quarta (*or* quinta); **the top men in the party** i dirigenti del partito; **a top job** un posto di prestigio; **she's top dog at work** (*fig fam*) è il grande capo sul lavoro

2 (*best*) migliore; **to get top marks** (*Brit*) avere i voti migliori; **he always gets top marks in Italian** ha sempre degli ottimi voti in italiano; **to come top of the class** avere i voti più alti di tutta la classe, risultare il/la migliore della classe; **he came top in maths** *or* (*Am*) **math** ha avuto i voti migliori in matematica; **the top twenty** (*Mus*) i venti migliori dischi (della settimana); **to be on top form** (*fam*) sentirsi veramente in forma; **a top surgeon** un grande chirurgo

3 (*last: layer*) ultimo(-a); **the top coat (of paint)** l'ultima mano (di pittura); **she is in the top class at school** sta facendo l'ultimo anno di scuola

4 (*most important*) principale, più importante; **top model** top model *f inv*

■ ADV: **tops** al massimo; **it's worth £200 tops** vale al massimo 200 sterline

■ VT

1 sormontare; **a church topped by a steeple** una chiesa sovrastata da un campanile; **to top a cake with cream** coprire una torta di panna

2 (*be first in*) essere in testa a; **to top the bill** (*Theatre*) avere il primo posto sul cartellone

3 (*exceed*) superare; **and to top it all ...** (*fig*) e come se non bastasse...; **profits topped £50,000 last year** i profitti hanno superato le 50.000 sterline l'anno scorso

4 (*vegetables, fruit*) tagliare le punte a; **to top and tail fruit** tagliare le punte e i gambi alla frutta

▸ **top off** VT + ADV (*finish*): **to top off with** concludere con; **we topped off the dinner with a toast to the happy couple** abbiamo concluso il pranzo con un brindisi in onore della coppia felice

▸ **top up** VT + ADV riempire; **to top sb's glass up** riempire il bicchiere a qn, dare ancora da bere a qn; **to top up a battery** fare un rabbocco alla batteria

top[2] [tɒp] N (*toy*) trottola; **to sleep like a top** dormire come un ghiro

to·paz ['təʊpæz] N topazio

top-class [ˌtɒp'klɑːs] ADJ di prim'ordine

top·coat ['tɒpˌkəʊt] N (*old: overcoat*) soprabito

top-flight [ˌtɒp'flaɪt] ADJ di primaria importanza

top floor N ultimo piano

top hat N cilindro

top-heavy [ˌtɒp'hɛvɪ] ADJ (*structure*) con la parte superiore troppo pesante; **this company is top-heavy** (*fig*) ci sono troppi dirigenti in questa società

to·pi·ary ['təʊpɪərɪ] N arte *f* topiaria

top·ic ['tɒpɪk] N (*of conversation*) argomento; (*of essay*) soggetto; **the essay can be on any topic** per il tema si può scegliere un argomento qualunque

topi·cal ['tɒpɪkəl] ADJ d'attualità; **a highly topical question** un argomento di grande attualità

topi·cal·ity [ˌtɒpɪ'kælɪtɪ] N attualità *f inv*

top·knot ['tɒpnɒt] N crocchia

top·less ['tɒplɪs] ADJ (*bather*) a seno scoperto; **topless swimsuit** topless *m inv*

■ ADV (*sunbathe*) in topless; **to go topless** mettersi in topless

top-level [ˌtɒp'lɛvl] ADJ (*talks*) ad alto livello

top·most ['tɒpˌməʊst] ADJ il/la più alto(-a)

top-notch [ˌtɒp'nɒtʃ] ADJ (*fam: player, performer*) di razza; (*: school, car*) eccellente

to·pog·ra·pher [tə'pɒgrəfə^r] N topografo(-a)

to·pog·ra·phy [tə'pɒgrəfɪ] N topografia

to·pol·ogy [tə'pɒlədʒɪ] N topologia

to·pony·my [tə'pɒnɪmɪ] N toponimia

top·per ['tɒpə^r] N (*fam*) cilindro

top·ping ['tɒpɪŋ] N (*Culin*) guarnizione *f*

top·ple ['tɒpl] VT (*fig: overthrow*) far cadere, rovesciare; **strong winds toppled trees and electricity lines** forti venti hanno fatto cadere gli alberi e le linee elettriche

■ VI cadere, rovesciarsi; **he toppled backwards** cadde all'indietro

Tt

► **topple over** VI + ADV cadere
■ VI + PREP cadere da; **he toppled over a cliff** è caduto da una scogliera
top-ranking [ˌtɒpˈræŋkɪŋ] ADJ di massimo grado
top-secret [ˌtɒpˈsiːkrɪt] ADJ segretissimo(-a)
top-security [ˌtɒpsɪˈkjʊərɪtɪ] ADJ (*Brit*) di massima sicurezza
top·side [ˈtɒpˌsaɪd] N **1** (*Brit Culin*) girello **2** (*Naut*): **topsides** NPL opera morta
top·soil [ˈtɒpˌsɔɪl] N strato superficiale del terreno
top·spin [ˈtɒpˌspɪn] N (*Tennis*) effetto topspin
topsy-turvy [ˌtɒpsɪˈtɜːvɪ] ADJ, ADV sottosopra (*inv*)
top-up [ˈtɒpˌʌp] N (*Brit fam: refill*): **would you like a top-up?** vuoi che ti riempia la tazza (*or* il bicchiere *etc*)?
top-up fees [ˈtɒpʌpˌfiːz] NPL *somma aggiuntiva da pagare in seguito all'aumento delle tasse universitarie*
top-up loan N (*Brit*) prestito integrativo
To·rah [ˈtəʊrə] N: **the Torah** il Torà
torch [tɔːtʃ] N (*Brit: electric*) torcia elettrica, lampadina tascabile; (*flaming*) torcia, fiaccola; **to carry a torch for sb** (*fig*) essere innamorato(-a) cotto(-a) di qn
torch·light [ˈtɔːtʃˌlaɪt] N: **by torchlight** al lume di una fiaccola; **torchlight procession** fiaccolata
torch song N canzone *f* d'amore
tore [tɔːʳ] PT *of* **tear**[1]
torea·dor [ˈtɒrɪəˌdɔːʳ] N toreador *m inv*
tor·ment [*n* ˈtɔːment; *vb* tɔːˈmɛnt] N tormento, tortura; **to be in torment** (*also fig*) soffrire le pene dell'inferno
■ VT (*hurt*) tormentare; (*fig: annoy*) molestare, infastidire; **she was tormented by doubts** era tormentata *or* assillata dai dubbi
tor·men·tor [tɔːˈmɛntəʳ] N tormentatore(-trice)
torn [tɔːn] PP *of* **tear**[1]
tor·na·do [tɔːˈneɪdəʊ] N (*pl* **tornadoes**) tornado
tor·pe·do [tɔːˈpiːdəʊ] N (*pl* **torpedoes**) siluro
■ VT silurare
torpedo boat N motosilurante *f*
tor·pid [ˈtɔːpɪd] ADJ (*frm*) intorpidito(-a)
tor·por [ˈtɔːpəʳ] N (*frm*) torpore *m*
torque [tɔːk] N (*Phys*) coppia di torsione
torque wrench N chiave *f* torsiometrica *or* tarata
tor·rent [ˈtɒrənt] N (*also fig*) torrente *m*; **we got caught in a torrent of rain** una pioggia torrenziale ci ha sorpresi; **the rain came down in torrents** pioveva a dirotto; **a torrent of abuse** una sfilza di improperi
tor·ren·tial [tɒˈrɛnʃəl] ADJ torrenziale
tor·rid [ˈtɒrɪd] ADJ (*liter*) torrido(-a); (*fig*) denso(-a) di passione
tor·sion [ˈtɔːʃən] N torsione *f*
tor·so [ˈtɔːsəʊ] N (*Anat*) torso; (*Sculpture*) busto
tor·til·la [tɔːˈtiːə] N tortilla *f inv*
tortilla chip N sfogliatine *fpl* di mais
tor·toise [ˈtɔːtəs] N tartaruga
tortoise·shell [ˈtɔːtəsˌʃɛl] N guscio di tartaruga
■ ADJ di tartaruga
tor·tu·ous [ˈtɔːtjʊəs] ADJ tortuoso(-a)
tor·tu·ous·ly [ˈtɔːtjʊəslɪ] ADV contortamente
◎ **tor·ture** [ˈtɔːtʃəʳ] N tortura; **it was sheer torture!** (*fig*) è stata una vera tortura!
■ VT torturare; (*fig*) tormentare
tor·tur·er [ˈtɔːtʃərəʳ] N torturatore(-trice)
◎ **Tory** [ˈtɔːrɪ] ADJ tory *inv*, conservatore(-trice)
■ N tory *m/f inv*, conservatore(-trice); **the Tories** i conservatori
toss [tɒs] N **1** (*movement: of head*) scrollata; **to take a toss** (*from horse*) fare una caduta **2** (*of coin*) lancio; **to win/lose the toss** vincere/perdere a testa e croce; (*Sport*) vincere/perdere il sorteggio; **it's pointless to argue the toss** (*Brit fam*) è inutile stare a discutere; **I don't give a toss** (*Brit fam!*) non me ne frega un cazzo (*fam!*)
■ VT **1** (*repeatedly*) muovere bruscamente, scuotere; **the boat was tossed by the waves** l'imbarcazione era sballottata dalle onde **2** (*throw: ball*) lanciare, gettare; (*: head*) scuotere; (*subj: horse: head*) tirare su; (*: mane*) agitare; (*: rider*) disarcionare; (*subj*) (*: bull*) lanciare in aria; **to toss sth to sb** lanciare qc a qn; **she tossed me a can of beer** mi ha lanciato una lattina di birra; **to toss salad** mescolare l'insalata; **toss the salad in the dressing** mescola l'insalata con il condimento; **to toss a pancake** far saltare una crêpe; **to toss one's hair back** gettare indietro i capelli; **to toss a coin** lanciare in aria una moneta, fare a testa o croce; **I'll toss you for it** ce lo giochiamo a testa e croce
■ VI **1** (*also:* **toss about, toss around**) agitarsi; (*: boat*) rollare e beccheggiare; **to toss (in one's sleep)** *or* **toss and turn** (*in bed*) agitarsi nel sonno, girarsi e rigirarsi **2** (*also:* **toss up**) tirare a sorte, fare a testa e croce; **we tossed (up) for the last piece of cake** abbiamo fatto a testa e croce per l'ultima fetta di torta
► **toss off** VT + ADV **1** (*drink*) buttare giù; (*book, letter*) sfornare **2** (*Brit fam!: masturbate*) fare una sega a (*fam!*); **to toss o.s. off** farsi una sega (*fam!*)
■ VI + ADV (*Brit fam!*) (*masturbate*) farsi una sega (*fam!*)
toss·er [ˈtɒsəʳ] N (*Brit fam!*) testa di cazzo (*fam!*)
toss-up [ˈtɒsˌʌp] N (*fig fam*): **it was a toss-up who would get there first** avevano tutti le stesse probabilità di arrivare per primo
tot [tɒt] N **1** (*child*) bimbetto(-a), bimbo(-a); **a tiny tot** un bimbo piccolo **2** (*Brit: drink*) bicchierino; **a tot of rum** un bicchierino di rum
► **tot up** VT + ADV (*Brit: figures*) sommare
◎ **to·tal** [ˈtəʊtl] ADJ (*complete, utter*) totale, completo(-a); (*sum*) globale; **the total losses amount to ...** il totale delle perdite ammonta a...; **a total failure** un vero fiasco, un assoluto disastro; **he was in total ignorance of the fact that ...** non sapeva assolutamente che...
■ N totale *m*; **grand total** somma globale; **in total** in tutto
■ VT (*also:* **total up**: *add*) sommare; (*: amount to*) ammontare a
to·tali·tar·ian [ˌtəʊtælɪˈtɛərɪən] ADJ totalitario(-a)
to·tali·tari·an·ism [ˌtəʊtælɪˈtɛərɪəˌnɪzəm] N totalitarismo
to·tal·ity [təʊˈtælɪtɪ] N totalità *f inv*
to·tal·ly [ˈtəʊtəlɪ] ADV completamente
tote[1] [təʊt] N (*Brit fam: Racing*) totalizzatore *m*
tote[2] [təʊt] VT (*fam*) trascinare; **to tote a gun** portare con sé il fucile
tote bag N sporta
to·tem [ˈtəʊtəm] N totem *m inv*
to·tem pole N totem *m inv*
tot·ter [ˈtɒtəʳ] VI (*person*) camminare barcollando, barcollare; (*object, government*) vacillare; **to totter in/out** *etc* entrare/uscire *etc* barcollando
totty, tottie [ˈtɒtɪ] N (*Brit fam*) figa
tou·can [ˈtuːkən] N tucano
◎ **touch** [tʌtʃ] N
1 (*sense*) tatto; (*act of touching*) contatto; **rough to the touch** ruvido(-a) al tatto; **by touch** al tatto; **at the slightest touch** al minimo contatto; **the touch of her**

hand il tocco della sua mano; **a pianist with a delicate touch** un pianista dal tocco raffinato; **the personal touch** una nota personale, un tocco personale; **at the touch of a button** premendo un bottone; **it has a touch of genius** è quasi geniale; **to lose one's touch** (*fig*) perdere la mano; (*: with people*) perdere il proprio fascino; **to put the finishing touches to sth** dare gli ultimi ritocchi a qc
2 (*small amount: of milk*) goccio; (*: of colour, paint*) tocco; (*: of frost*) leggero strato; **a touch of irony** una punta *or* pizzico d'ironia; **to have a touch of flu** avere una leggera influenza
3 (*contact*) contatto; **to be in touch with sb** essere in contatto con qn; **to get in touch with sb** mettersi in contatto con qn; **I'll be in touch** mi farò sentire; **you can get in touch with me here** mi puoi rintracciare qui; **to keep in touch with sb** mantenere i rapporti con qn, tenersi in contatto con qn; **I'll keep in touch with Ann** mi terrò in contatto con Ann; **I haven't kept in touch with Hilary** non sono rimasta in contatto con Hilary; **keep in touch!** fatti vivo!; **to lose touch** (*friends*) perdersi di vista; **to lose touch with sb** perdere di vista qn; **to be out of touch with events** essere tagliato(-a) fuori
4 (*Brit: Ftbl, Rugby*): **the ball is in touch** la palla è fuori gioco
■ VT
1 (*gen*) toccare; (*brush lightly: fig: topic, problem*) sfiorare; **she touched his arm** gli ha toccato il braccio; **his hair touches his shoulders** i capelli gli sfiorano le spalle; **touch wood!** tocchiamo ferro!; **to touch sb for £5** (*fam*) chiedere 5 sterline in prestito a qn
2 (*neg phrases*): **don't touch that!** non toccare!; **I never touch gin** non tocco mai il gin; **you haven't touched your cheese** non hai neppure toccato il formaggio; **if you admit nothing, they can't touch you** (*fig*) se non confessi non ti possono toccare
3 (*move*) commuovere; (*affect*) riguardare; **I am touched by your offer** la tua offerta mi commuove; **she was touched by his gift** fu commossa dal suo regalo; **the story touched me deeply** la storia mi ha commosso profondamente; **it touches all our lives** riguarda tutti noi, ci tocca tutti
4 (*compare*) uguagliare; **nobody can touch them for quality** per quanto riguarda la qualità non li batte nessuno; **no artist in the country can touch him** non c'è artista nel paese che lo possa uguagliare
■ VI (*hands*) toccarsi; (*property, gardens*) confinare; **our hands touched** le nostre mani si sono sfiorate; **"do not touch"** "non toccare"
▸ **touch down** VT + ADV (*Rugby: score*): **to touch the ball down** segnare una meta
■ VI + ADV
1 (*on land*) atterrare; (*on sea*) ammarare; (*on moon*) allunare
2 (*Rugby: score*) segnare una meta
▸ **touch off** VT + ADV (*argument, riot*) provocare
▸ **touch on** VI + PREP (*topic, subject*) sfiorare, accennare a
▸ **touch up** VT + ADV
1 (*improve*) ritoccare
2 (*fam: sexually*) mettere le mani addosso a

touch-and-go [ˌtʌtʃən'gəʊ] ADJ incerto(-a); **it's touch-and-go whether ...** è incerto se...; **it was touch-and-go whether we'd go bankrupt** eravamo sull'orlo del fallimento; **it was touch-and-go with the sick man** il malato era tra la vita e la morte

touch·down ['tʌtʃˌdaʊn] N (*on land*) atterraggio; (*on sea*) ammaraggio; (*on moon*) allunaggio; (*Rugby*) meta

tou·ché [tuː'ʃeɪ] EXCL toccato!

touched [tʌtʃt] ADJ (*moved*) commosso(-a); (*fam: crazy*) tocco(-a), toccato(-a); **I was really touched** ero veramente commosso(-a)

touchi·ness ['tʌtʃɪnɪs] N permalosità *f inv*, suscettibilità *f inv*

touch·ing ['tʌtʃɪŋ] ADJ commovente

touch·ing·ly ['tʌtʃɪŋlɪ] ADV in modo toccante, in modo commovente

touch·line ['tʌtʃˌlaɪn] N (*Ftbl*) linea laterale; (*Rugby*) linea di touche

touch·pad ['tʌtʃpæd] N touchpad *m*

touch-screen ['tʌtʃˌskriːn] N (*Comput*) touch-screen *m inv*, schermo sensibile

touch-sensitive [ˌtʌtʃ'sɛnsɪtɪv] ADJ sensibile al tatto

touch·stone ['tʌtʃˌstəʊn] N pietra di paragone

touch-type ['tʌtʃˌtaɪp] VI dattilografare (*senza guardare i tasti*)

touchy ['tʌtʃɪ] ADJ (*comp* **-ier**, *superl* **-iest**) (*person*) permaloso(-a), suscettibile; (*subject*) delicato(-a); **he's touchy about his weight** è molto suscettibile quando si parla del suo peso

◎**tough** [tʌf] ADJ (*comp* **-er**, *superl* **-est**) **1** (*substance, fabric*) resistente, duro(-a); (*conditions, regulations*) duro(-a); (*meat*) duro(-a), tiglioso(-a); (*journey*) faticoso(-a), duro(-a); (*task, problem, situation*) difficile; (*fig: resistance*) tenace; (*: fight*) accanito(-a); **tough leather gloves** guanti *mpl* di pelle resistente; **the meat is tough** la carne è dura; **as tough as old boots** duro(-a) come una suola di scarpa; **it was tough, but I managed okay** è stata dura ma ce l'ho fatta; **tough opposition** opposizione tenace **2** (*person: hardy, resilient*) robusto(-a), resistente; (*: mentally strong*) resistente, tenace; (*: hard: in character*) inflessibile; (*: rough*) violento(-a), brutale; **they got tough with the workers** hanno adottato una politica inflessibile con i lavoratori; **he's a tough man to deal with** è un tipo difficile; **a tough guy** un duro; **he thinks he's a tough guy** crede di essere un duro; **he's a tough customer** (*fam*) è un osso duro **3** (*fam: unfortunate*): **but it was tough on the others** ma è stata una sfortuna per gli altri; **tough luck!** tanto peggio!; **if you can't get here on time, that's your tough luck!** (*unsympathetic*) se non ce la fai ad arrivare in orario, peggio per te!
■ N (*fam: gangster, lout*) delinquente *m/f*

tough·en ['tʌfn] VT (*also:* **toughten up**: *substance*) rinforzare, rendere più resistente; (*: metal*) indurire; (*: person*) rendere più forte

tough·ness ['tʌfnɪs] N (*see adj*) **1** resistenza; durezza; difficoltà *f inv*; accanimento **2** resistenza; tenacia; inflessibilità *f inv*; violenza

tou·pee ['tuːpeɪ] N toupet *m inv*, parrucchino

◎**tour** ['tʊəʳ] N (*gen*) giro; (*of building, exhibition, town*) visita; (*by performers, team*) tournée *f inv*; **package tour** viaggio organizzato; **a guided tour** una visita guidata; **a tour of the city** un giro della città; **a round the world tour** un giro del mondo; **to go on a tour of** (*region, country*) fare il giro di; (*museum, castle*) visitare; **to go on a walking/cycling tour of Tuscany** fare il giro della Toscana a piedi/in bicicletta; **on tour** (*Theatre*) in tournée; **to go on tour** andare in tournée, fare una tournée; **tour of inspection** giro d'ispezione
■ VT (*subj: tourists*) fare un giro di, fare un viaggio in; (*: performers, team*) fare una tournée in; **the Prime**

Tt

Minister is touring the country il primo ministro sta visitando il paese
■VI (*also:* **to go touring**) andare a fare un viaggio
tour de force ['tʊədə'fɔːs] N tour de force *m inv*
tour·ing ['tʊərɪŋ] N viaggi *mpl* turistici
touring company N (*Theatre*) compagnia in tournée
tour·ism ['tʊərɪzəm] N turismo
◎**tour·ist** ['tʊərɪst] N turista *m/f*; **there were lots of tourists** c'erano molti turisti
■ADJ (*attraction, season*) turistico(-a); **the tourist trade** il turismo
■ADV (*travel*) in classe turistica
tourist agency N agenzia di viaggi e turismo
tourist class N (*Aer*) classe *f* turistica
tourist information office N centro di informazioni turistiche
tourist office N ufficio del turismo
tour·isty ['tʊərɪstɪ] ADJ (*pej*) turistico(-a)
◎**tour·na·ment** ['tʊənəmənt] N torneo; **tennis tournament** torneo di tennis
tour·ni·quet ['tʊənɪˌkeɪ] N (*Med*) laccio emostatico, pinza emostatica
tour operator N (*Brit*) operatore *m* turistico
tou·sled ['taʊzld] ADJ (*hair*) arruffato(-a); (*bedclothes*) sottosopra *inv*
tout [taʊt] N (*for hotels*) procacciatore *m* di clienti; (*Brit: also:* **ticket tout**) bagarino; (*Racing*) portaquote *m inv*
■VI: **to tout for business** raccogliere ordinazioni; (*for hotels*) procacciare clienti
■VT: **to tout sth (around)** (*Brit*) cercare di (ri)vendere qc; **he is being touted as the greatest living singer** lo stanno facendo passare come il miglior cantante vivente
tow [təʊ] N rimorchio; **to give sb a tow** (*Aut*) rimorchiare qn; **to be on tow** essere a rimorchio; **"on tow"** *or* (*Am*) **"in tow"** "veicolo rimorchiato"; **he arrived with a friend in tow** (*fig, fam*) si è portato dietro un amico; **she had a child in tow** aveva un bimbo con sé
■VT (*boat, car, caravan*) rimorchiare; **he towed my car to the nearest garage** mi ha rimorchiato la macchina fino all'officina più vicina; **to tow a car away** portar via una macchina con il carro attrezzi
◎**to·wards** [tə'wɔːdz], **to·ward** [tə'wɔːd] PREP (*gen*) verso; (*of attitude*) nei confronti di, verso; (*of purpose*) per; **he came towards me** è venuto verso di me; **we walked towards the sea** ci siamo incamminati verso il mare; **the government is moving towards disaster** il governo si avvia al disastro; **towards noon/the end of the year** verso mezzogiorno/la fine dell'anno; **your attitude towards him** il tuo atteggiamento nei suoi confronti *or* verso di lui; **to feel friendly towards sb** provare un sentimento d'amicizia per qn; **to save towards sth** risparmiare per comprare qc; **half my salary goes towards paying the rent** metà del mio stipendio se ne va per l'affitto *or* in affitto; **he gave them £100,000 towards a house** ha dato loro centomila sterline per la casa
tow·bar ['təʊˌbɑː'] N barra di rimorchio
tow·boat ['təʊˌbəʊt] N rimorchiatore *m*
tow·el ['taʊəl] N (*also:* **hand towel**) asciugamano; (*also:* **bath towel**) telo da bagno; (*also:* **tea towel, dishtowel**) strofinaccio; **to throw in the towel** (*fig*) gettare la spugna
■VT: **to towel o.s. dry** asciugarsi con un asciugamano
tow·el·ling ['taʊəlɪŋ] N (*fabric*) (tessuto di) spugna
towel rail, towel rack N portasciugamano
◎**tow·er** ['taʊə'] N (*of castle, church*) torre *f*; **the towers of the castle** le torri del castello; **he was a tower of strength to me** mi ha dato un grande appoggio
■VI (*building, mountain*) innalzarsi; **to tower above** *or* **over sb/sth** sovrastare qn/qc
tower block N (*Brit*) palazzone *m*
tow·er·ing ['taʊərɪŋ] ADJ (*building, figure*) imponente, altissimo(-a); **in a towering rage** (*fig*) in preda a un violento accesso d'ira
Tower of London N: **the Tower of London** la Torre di Londra
▷ www.hrp.org.uk/webcode/tower_home.asp
tow·line ['təʊˌlaɪn] N (cavo da) rimorchio
◎**town** [taʊn] N città *f inv*; **to live in a town** vivere in città; **to be out of town** essere fuori città; **in (the) town** in città; **to go (in) to town** andare in città *or* in centro; **to go out on the town** (*fam*) uscire a far baldoria; **to go to town on sth** (*fig fam*) fare qc in grande
■ADJ (*centre*) della città; (*life*) di città; (*house*) in città
town centre N (*Brit*) centro (città)
town clerk N segretario comunale
town council N (*Brit*) consiglio comunale
town cri·er [ˌtaʊn'kraɪə'] N (*Brit*) banditore(-trice)
town hall N ≈ municipio
townie ['taənɪ] N (*Brit fam*) persona di città
town plan N pianta della città
town planner N (*Brit*) urbanista *m/f*
town planning N (*Brit: action*) pianificazione *f* urbana; (*: study*) urbanistica
town·ship ['taʊnʃɪp] N township *f inv*
towns·people ['taʊnzˌpiːpl] NPL cittadinanza, cittadini *mpl*
tow·path ['təʊˌpɑːθ] N alzaia
tow·rope ['təʊˌrəʊp] N (cavo da) rimorchio
tow truck N (*Am*) carro *m* attrezzi *inv*
tox·aemia, (*Am*) **tox·emia** [tɒk'siːmɪə] N tossiemia
tox·ic ['tɒksɪk] ADJ tossico(-a)
toxi·colo·gist [ˌtɒksɪ'kɒlədʒɪst] N tossicologo(-a)
toxi·col·ogy [ˌtɒksɪ'kɒlədʒɪ] N tossicologia
tox·in ['tɒksɪn] N tossina
◎**toy** [tɔɪ] N giocattolo
■ADJ (*railway, house*) in miniatura; (*gun*) giocattolo *inv*
▸ **toy with** VI + PREP **1** (*play with: object*) giocherellare con; (*: food*) trastullarsi con; (*: affections*) giocare con **2** (*consider: idea*) accarezzare
toy·box ['tɔɪˌbɒks] N baule *m* per i giocattoli
toy boy N (*Brit fam fig*) amante *m* bambino
toy car N automobilina, modellino
toy poodle N barboncino nano
toy·shop ['tɔɪˌʃɒp] N negozio di giocattoli
toy soldier N soldatino
◎**trace**[1] [treɪs] N (*sign*) traccia; **there was no trace of the robbers** non c'era traccia dei ladri; **there was no trace of it** non ne restava traccia; **to vanish without trace** sparire senza lasciar traccia; **I've lost all trace of them** ho completamente perso le loro tracce; **the postmortem revealed traces of poison in the blood** l'autopsia ha rivelato tracce di veleno nel sangue
■VT **1** (*draw*) tracciare; (*: with tracing paper*) ricalcare **2** (*follow*) seguire (le tracce di); (*find, locate*) rintracciare; **the police are trying to trace witnesses** la polizia sta cercando di rintracciare i testimoni; **I cannot trace any reference to the matter** non riesco a rintracciare alcun riferimento alla faccenda
▸ **trace back** VT + ADV: **they traced the weapon back to here** hanno stabilito che l'arma proviene da qui; **to**

trace one's roots trovare le proprie radici; **to trace back one's family to** risalire alle origini della propria famiglia fino a

trace² ['treɪs] N (*of harness*) tirella; **to kick over the traces** (*Brit fig*) sfuggire al controllo

trace element N oligoelemento

trac·ery ['treɪsərɪ] N (*of frost*) disegno

tra·chea [trə'kɪə] N (*Anat*) trachea

tra·cheal [trə'kɪəl] ADJ tracheale

trac·ing pa·per ['treɪsɪŋ,peɪpə^r] N carta da ricalco

◎**track** [træk] N **1** (*mark: of person, animal*) orma, traccia, impronta; (*: of vehicle*) solco; (*: of ship*) scia; **to be on sb's track** essere sulle tracce di qn; **they followed the tracks for miles** hanno seguito le tracce per miglia; **to follow in sb's tracks** (*also: fig*) seguire le orme di qn; **to keep track of** (*fig: person*) seguire le tracce di; (*: keep in touch with*) restare in contatto con; (*: event*) essere al corrente di; **to lose track of** (*fig: person*) perdere le tracce di; (*: lose contact with*) perdere di vista; (*: event*) non essere al corrente di; **to lose track of an argument** perdere il filo del discorso; **to make tracks (for)** (*fig fam*) avviarsi (a *or* verso) **2** (*path*) sentiero; (*: of comet, rocket*) traiettoria; (*: of suspect, animal*) pista, tracce *fpl*; **a mountain track** un sentiero di montagna; **to be on the right track** (*fig*) essere sulla buona strada; **to be on the wrong track** (*fig*) essere fuori strada; **to throw sb off the track** (*fig*) mettere qn fuori strada **3** (*Sport*) pista; **two laps of the track** due giri di pista **4** (*Rail*) binario, rotaie *fpl*; **a woman fell onto the tracks** una donna è caduta sui binari; **on the right/wrong side of the tracks** (*Am fam*) nei quartieri alti/poveri della città **5** (*Mus: on tape*) pista; **a 4-track tape** un nastro a 4 piste; **the first track on the record/tape** il primo pezzo del disco/nastro; **this is my favourite track** questo è il mio pezzo preferito **6** (*Comput*) pista

■VT (*person, animal*) seguire le tracce di

▸ **track down** VT + ADV (*locate: person*) snidare; (*: prey*) scovare; (*: sth lost*) rintracciare; **the police never tracked down the killer** la polizia non ha mai trovato l'assassino

track·ball ['træk,bɔ:l] N (*Comput*) mouse *m inv* integrato, trackball *f inv*

track·er dog ['trækə,dɒg] N (*Brit*) cane *m* poliziotto *inv*

track·er fund ['trækə,fʌnd] N (*Fin*) fondo indicizzato

track events NPL (*Sport*) gare *fpl* di atletica (*su pista*)

track·ing sta·tion ['trækɪŋ,steɪʃən] N (*Space*) osservatorio spaziale

track meet N (*Am*) meeting *m inv* di atletica

track race N prova su pista

track record N: **to have a good track record** (*fig*) avere un buon curriculum

track·suit ['træk,su:t] N tuta sportiva *or* da ginnastica

tract¹ [trækt] N **1** (*area*) distesa **2** (*Anat*): **respiratory tract** apparato respiratorio

tract² [trækt] N (*pamphlet*) trattatello, libretto, opuscolo

trac·table ['træktəbl] ADJ (*person*) accomodante; (*animal*) docile

tract house N (*Am*): **tract houses** casette *fpl* una uguale all'altra

trac·tion ['trækʃən] N trazione *f*

traction engine N trattrice *f*

trac·tor ['træktə^r] N trattore *m*

tractor·feed ['træktə,fi:d] N (*on printer*) trascinamento a trattore

◎**trade** [treɪd] N **1** (*commerce*) commercio; (*business*) affari *mpl*; **to do trade with sb** fare affari con qn, essere in rapporti commerciali con qn; **foreign trade** commercio estero; **free trade** il libero scambio; **to do a brisk** *or* **roaring trade** fare affari d'oro; **Department of Trade and Industry** (*Brit*) *or* **Department of Trade** (*Am*) ≈ Ministero del Commercio **2** (*industry*) industria, settore *m*; **he's in the cotton/building trade** è nell'industria cotoniera/edilizia; **the tourist trade** l'industria del turismo; **the arms trade** il commercio di armi; **the book trade** l'editoria **3** (*profession*) mestiere *m*; **to learn a trade** imparare un mestiere; **he's a butcher by trade** di mestiere fa il macellaio; **tailoring is a useful trade** quello del sarto è un mestiere utile; **to sell to the trade** vendere all'ingrosso

■VT (*fig: swap sth for sth*) barattare; **he traded his tennis racquet for a football** ha barattato la sua racchetta da tennis con un pallone; **I'd like to trade some cards** vorrei scambiare alcune figurine

■VI: **to trade with sb** fare affari con qn, intrattenere rapporti commerciali con qn; **they have traded with France for centuries** commerciano con la Francia da secoli

■ADJ (*association, route*) commerciale

▸ **trade in** VT + ADV (*old car*) cedere in permuta, dare dentro

■VI + PREP commerciare in

▸ **trade on** VI + PREP (*pej*) approfittare di, sfruttare

trade agreement N accordo commerciale

trade barrier N barriera commerciale

trade deficit N bilancio commerciale in deficit

Trade Descriptions Act N (*Brit*) legge *f* a tutela del consumatore

trade discount N sconto sul listino (*fatto al commerciante*)

trade fair N fiera campionaria

trade gap N = trade deficit

trade-in ['treɪd,ɪn] N **1 to take as a trade-in** accettare in permuta **2** (*car*) *macchina ceduta a parziale pagamento di una nuova*

trade-in price N prezzo di permuta

trade-in value N valore *m* di permuta

trade·mark ['treɪd,mɑ:k] N (*Comm*) marchio di fabbrica; (*fig*) marchio; **registered trademark** marchio registrato

trade mission N missione *f* commerciale

trade name N (*of product*) nome *m* depositato, marca; (*of a company*) ragione *f* sociale

trade-off ['treɪd,ɒf] N (*exchange*) scambio; (*balancing*) compromesso

trade press N stampa del settore commerciale

trade price N prezzo all'ingrosso

◎**trad·er** ['treɪdə^r] N commerciante *m/f*

trade reference N *referenze commerciali sulla solvibilità di un'azienda*

trade route N rotta commerciale

trade secret N segreto commerciale

trades·man ['treɪdzmən] N (*pl* **-men**) fornitore *m*; (*shopkeeper*) negoziante *m*; **tradesman's entrance** ingresso per i fornitori *or* di servizio

trade surplus N surplus *m inv* della bilancia commerciale

trade union, trades union (*Brit*) N sindacato

■ADJ (*official*) sindacale; **trade-union dues** quota di associazione al sindacato

▹ www.tuc.org.uk

▹ www.actu.asn.au

Tt

▷ www.union.org.nz
▷ www.clc-ctc.ca
▷ www.cosatu.org.za

trade un·ion·ism [ˌtreɪd'ju:njəˌnɪzəm], **trades un·ion·ism** [ˌtreɪdz'ju:njəˌnɪzəm] N (*Brit*) sindacalismo

trade unionist, trades unionist N (*Brit*) sindacalista *m/f*

trade wind N aliseo

trad·ing ['treɪdɪŋ] ADJ (*port, centre*) commerciale; (*nation*) che vive di commercio
■N commercio

trading estate N (*Brit*) zona industriale

trading post N stazione *f* commerciale

trading stamp N bollino premio

◎**tra·di·tion** [trə'dɪʃən] N tradizione *f*; **traditions** NPL tradizioni, usanze *fpl*

◎**tra·di·tion·al** [trə'dɪʃənl] ADJ tradizionale

tra·di·tion·al·ism [trə'dɪʃnəˌlɪzəm] N tradizionalismo

tra·di·tion·al·ist [trə'dɪʃnəlɪst] ADJ, N tradizionalista (*m/f*)

tra·di·tion·al·ly [trə'dɪʃnəlɪ] ADV per tradizione

tra·duce [trə'dju:s] VT (*frm*) calunniare, diffamare

◎**traf·fic** ['træfɪk] (*vb: pt, pp* **trafficked**) N traffico; **rail traffic** traffico ferroviario; **heavy traffic** traffico pesante; **the traffic is heavy during the rush hour** il traffico è molto intenso nelle ore di punta; **closed to heavy traffic** (*Aut*) divieto di transito per gli automezzi pesanti; **drug traffic** traffico di droga
■VI: **to traffic in** (*pej: liquor, drugs*) trafficare in
■ADJ (*Aut: regulations*) stradale

traffic calming [-'kɑ:mɪŋ] N *misure per rallentare il traffico cittadino*

traffic circle N (*Am*) isola rotatoria

traffic island N salvagente *m*, isola *f* spartitraffico *inv*

traffic jam N ingorgo (del traffico); **a 5-mile traffic jam** una coda di 5 miglia

traf·fick·er ['træfɪkə^r] N trafficante *m/f*

traffic lights NPL semaforo

traffic offence N (*Brit*) infrazione *f* al codice stradale

traffic sign N cartello stradale

traffic violation N (*Am*) = **traffic offence**

traffic warden N (*Brit*) ≈ vigile(-essa) (urbano(-a))

◎**trag·edy** ['trædʒɪdɪ] N (*gen, Theatre*) tragedia; **it is a tragedy that ...** è una vera disgrazia che...

trag·ic ['trædʒɪk] ADJ tragico(-a); **tragic actor** attore *m* tragico

tragi·cal·ly ['trædʒɪkəlɪ] ADV tragicamente

tragi·com·edy [ˌtrædʒɪ'kɒmɪdɪ] N tragicommedia

tragi·com·ic [ˌtrædʒɪ'kɒmɪk] ADJ tragicomico(-a)

◎**trail** [treɪl] N **1** (*of dust, smoke*) scia; **the hurricane left a trail of destruction** l'uragano non ha lasciato altro che distruzione dietro di sé **2** (*track*) orma; (*tracks*) pista, tracce *fpl*; **a trail of clues** una serie di indizi; **to be on sb's trail** essere sulle orme di qn, essere sulle tracce di qn **3** (*path*) sentiero; (*Skiing*) pista da fondo; **a forest trail** un sentiero nella foresta
■VT **1** (*drag*) trascinare, strascicare; **she trailed her fingers through the water** trascinava le dita nell'acqua; **don't trail your coat in the mud** non trascinare il cappotto nel fango; **don't trail mud into the house** non portare fango in casa **2** (*track: animal*) seguire le orme di; (*: person*) pedinare, seguire
■VI **1** (*object*) strisciare; (*plant*) arrampicarsi; (*dress*) strusciare; **to trail a plant over a wall** far attecchire una pianta al muro; **to trail by 2 goals** (*Sport*) essere in svantaggio di 2 goal; **Liverpool was trailing 3-1 at half time** il Liverpool era in svantaggio per 3 a 1 dopo il primo tempo **2** (*wearily: also:* **trail along**) trascinarsi
▶ **trail away, trail off** VI + ADV (*sound*) affievolirsi; (*interest, voice*) spegnersi a poco a poco
▶ **trail behind** VI + ADV essere al traino; **to trail behind sb** trascinarsi dietro a qn
▶ **trail off** VI + ADV = **trail away**

trail·blazer ['treɪlˌbleɪzə^r] N pioniere(-a)

trail·er ['treɪlə^r] N **1** (*Aut*) rimorchio; (*for horses*) van *m inv*; (*Am: caravan*) roulotte *f inv*; **a car and trailer** un'auto con rimorchio; **they live in a trailer** vivono in una roulotte **2** (*Cine*) trailer *m inv*

trailer park N (*Am*) campeggio per roulotte

trailer trash N (*Am fam*) baraccati *mpl*

trailer truck N (*Am*) autoarticolato

◎**train** [treɪn] N **1** (*Rail*) treno; **to go by train** andare in *or* col treno; **he went by train** ci è andato in treno; **to travel by train** viaggiare in treno; **in** *or* **on the train** in treno, sul treno; **to take the 3.00 train** prendere il treno delle 3; **to change trains** cambiare treno **2** (*line: of animals, vehicles*) fila; (*entourage*) seguito; (*of admirers*) codazzo **3** (*Brit: series*): **train of events** serie *f inv* di eventi; **my train of thought** il filo dei miei pensieri; **the earthquake brought great suffering in its train** il terremoto ha portato con sé disgrazie e sofferenze **4** (*of dress*) strascico, coda
■VT **1** (*instruct*) istruire; (*apprentice, doctor*) formare; (*Mil*) addestrare; (*sportsman*) allenare; (*mind, memory*) far esercitare; (*animal*) addestrare, ammaestrare; **to train sb to do sth** preparare qn a fare qc **2** **to train on** (*direct: gun*) puntare qc contro; (*: camera, telescope*) puntare (a *or* verso)
■VI **1** (*learn a skill*) fare pratica, fare tirocinio; **to train as** *or* **to be a lawyer** fare pratica come avvocato; **to train as a teacher** fare tirocinio come insegnante; **where did you train?** dove hai fatto pratica *or* tirocinio? **2** (*Sport*): **to train (for)** allenarsi (per); **to train for a race** allenarsi per una gara

train attendant N (*Am*) addetto(-a) ai vagoni letto

train·bearer ['treɪnˌbɛərə^r] N damigella; (*little boy*) paggio

trained [treɪnd] ADJ (*accountant, nurse*) diplomato(-a), qualificato(-a); (*teacher*) abilitato(-a) all'insegnamento; (*Sport: athlete, horse*) allenato(-a); (*animal*) addestrato(-a), ammaestrato(-a); **well-trained** (*child, dog*) ben educato(-a); **I've got him well-trained** (*hum*) l'ho addomesticato per bene; **highly trained workers** operai *mpl* altamente qualificati

trainee [treɪ'ni:] N (*gen: in trade*) apprendista *m/f*; (*for profession*) tirocinante *m/f*; **she's a management trainee** sta facendo tirocinio come dirigente
■ADJ: **to be a trainee teacher** fare il tirocinio come insegnante; **he's a trainee chef** sta facendo tirocinio come chef; **a trainee plumber** un apprendista idraulico

train·er ['treɪnə^r] N **1** (*Sport*) allenatore(-trice); (*of circus animals*) domatore(-trice); (*of dogs*) addestratore(-trice) **2** (*Brit: shoe*) scarpa da ginnastica; **a language trainer** un/un'insegnante di lingua

◎**train·ing** ['treɪnɪŋ] N (*in job*) pratica, tirocinio; (*for job*) formazione *f*; (*Mil*) addestramento; (*Sport*) allenamento; **to be in training** (*for race, event*) essere in allenamento; (*fit*) essere in forma; **to be out of training** essere fuori allenamento *or* forma; **he strained a muscle in training** si è fatto uno strappo durante l'allenamento
■ADJ (*scheme, centre: for job*) di formazione

professionale; (*Sport*) di allenamento
training college N istituto professionale
training course N corso di formazione professionale
training shoe N (*Brit*) scarpa da ginnastica
train service N collegamento ferroviario
train set N trenino elettrico
train·spot·ter ['treɪn,spɒtəʳ] N (*Brit*) *persona che per hobby osserva i treni che passano, ne annota il numero e cerca di "collezionarne" il più possibile*
trainspotting ['treɪn,spɒtɪŋ] N (*Brit*): **to go trainspotting** andare a osservare i treni
traipse [treɪps] VI (*fam*): **to traipse around** trascinarsi in giro; **to traipse around the shops** trascinarsi in giro per negozi
■ N: **a long traipse** una camminata sfiancante
trait [treɪt] N caratteristica, tratto
trai·tor ['treɪtəʳ] N traditore(-trice); **to turn traitor** passare al nemico
tra·jec·tory [trə'dʒɛktərɪ] N traiettoria
tram [træm], **tram·car** ['træm,kɑːʳ] N (*Brit*) tram *m inv*
▷ www.thetrams.co.uk/
tram·line ['træm,laɪn] N linea tranviaria
tram·lines ['træm,laɪnz] NPL (*Brit*) **1** rotaie *fpl* del tram **2** (*Tennis*) corridoio
tram·mel ['træməl] VT (*frm, liter*) intralciare
tram·mels ['træməls] NPL (*frm, liter*) legami *mpl*, vincoli *mpl*
tramp [træmp] N **1** (*sound of feet*) rumore *m* pesante (di passi) **2** (*long walk*) camminata; **to go for a tramp in the hills** andare a fare una camminata sui colli **3** (*person*) vagabondo(-a); **she's a tramp** (*fam pej*) è una sgualdrina
■ VT (*walk through: town, streets*) percorrere a piedi; **to tramp the streets looking for sth** battere le strade in cerca di qc
■ VI camminare con passo pesante; **the soldiers tramped past** i soldati sono passati marciando pesantemente; **he tramped up to the door** si è avvicinato con passi pesanti alla porta
tram·ple ['træmpl] VT: **to trample (underfoot)** (*crush*) calpestare; **to trample sth into the ground** calpestare qc
▶ **trample on** VI + PREP calpestare; **to trample on sb's feelings** (*fig*) calpestare i sentimenti di qn
tram·po·line ['træmpəlɪn] N trampolino
tram·way ['træmweɪ] N (*Brit*) tranvia
trance [trɑːns] N trance *f inv*; (*Med*) catalessi *f inv*; **to go into a trance** cadere in trance
tran·quil ['træŋkwɪl] ADJ tranquillo(-a)
tran·quil·lity, (*Am*) **tran·quil·ity** [træŋ'kwɪlɪtɪ] N tranquillità *f inv*
tran·quil·lize, (*Am*) **tran·quil·ize** ['træŋkwɪ,laɪz] VT (*Med*) calmare con un tranquillante
tran·quil·liz·er, (*Am*) **tran·quil·iz·er** ['træŋkwɪ,laɪzəʳ] N (*Med*) tranquillante *m*; **she's on tranquillizers** prende tranquillanti
trans... [trænz] PREF trans...
trans·act [træn'zækt] VT (*business*) trattare
◎ **trans·ac·tion** [træn'zækʃən] N (*business*) trattativa; (*in bank*) operazione *f*, transazione *f*; **transactions** NPL (*minutes*) atti *mpl*; **a commercial transaction** una transazione commerciale; **cash transaction** operazione in contanti
trans·at·lan·tic [,trænzət'læntɪk] ADJ transatlantico(-a)
trans·cend [træn'sɛnd] VT (*frm: go beyond*) trascendere, superare
trans·cend·ent [træn'sɛndənt] ADJ (*frm*) trascendente
tran·scen·den·tal [,trænsɛn'dɛntl] ADJ (*frm*) trascendentale
transcendental meditation N meditazione *f* trascendentale
tran·scribe [træn'skraɪb] VT trascrivere
tran·script ['trænskrɪpt] N trascrizione *f*
tran·scrip·tion [træn'skrɪpʃən] N trascrizione *f*
trans·duc·er [trænz'djuːsəʳ] N trasduttore *m*
tran·sect [træn'sɛkt] VT tagliare trasversalmente
tran·sept ['trænsɛpt] N (*Archit*) transetto
◎ **trans·fer** [*n* 'trænsfɜːʳ; *vb* træns'fɜːʳ] N **1** (*gen*) trasferimento; (*Pol: of power*) passaggio; (*Law*) cessione *f*; (*Ftbl*) cessione (*or* acquisto); **bank transfer** bonifico bancario; **by bank transfer** tramite trasferimento bancario; **they will be offered transfers to other locations** verrà loro proposto il trasferimento in altri posti; **the transfer of power** il passaggio di potere **2** (*picture, design: stick-on*) decalcomania, autoadesivo
■ VT **1** (*move*): **to transfer (from/to)** trasferire (da/a); (*Sport*): **to be transferred (from/to)** essere ceduto(-a) (da/a); **to transfer one's affections/ambitions to sb** trasferire i propri sentimenti/le proprie ambizioni su qn; **to transfer money from one account to another** trasferire il denaro da un conto su un altro; **to transfer sth to sb's name** mettere qc a nome di qn; **to make a transferred charge call** (*Brit*) fare una chiamata a carico del destinatario **2** (*picture, design*) decalcare
■ VI (*gen*) trasferirsi, passare; **she transferred from History to Classics** (*Univ*) è passata da Storia a Lettere Antiche
trans·fer·able [træns'fɜːrəbl] ADJ trasferibile; **not transferable** non cedibile, personale
trans·fer·ence ['trænsfərəns] N (*frm*) trasferimento; (*Psych*) transfert *m inv*
transfer list N (*Sport*) elenco dei giocatori che possono essere ceduti a un'altra squadra
trans·figu·ra·tion [,trænsfɪgə'reɪʃən] N (*liter, Rel*) trasfigurazione *f*
trans·fig·ure [træns'fɪgəʳ] VT (*liter*) trasfigurare
trans·fix [træns'fɪks] VT trafiggere; (*fig*): **transfixed with fear** paralizzato(-a) dalla paura
◎ **trans·form** [træns'fɔːm] VT trasformare
trans·for·ma·tion [,trænsfə'meɪʃən] N trasformazione *f*
trans·for·ma·tion·al [,trænsfə'meɪʃənl] ADJ (*Ling*) trasformazionale
trans·form·er [træns'fɔːməʳ] N (*Elec*) trasformatore *m*
trans·fu·sion [træns'fjuːʒən] N trasfusione *f*; **to give sb a blood transfusion** praticare una trasfusione di sangue a qn
trans·gen·der [træz'dʒɛndəʳ] N transgender *m/f inv*
■ ADJ = **transgendered**
transgendered [træs'dʒɛndəd] ADJ transgender *inv*
trans·genic [trænz'dʒɛnɪk] ADJ (*Bio*) transgenico(-a)
trans·gress [træns'grɛs] (*frm*) VI (*sin*) peccare
■ VT (*violate: moral law*) infrangere, trasgredire
trans·gres·sive [træns'grɛsɪv] ADJ trasgressivo(-a)
trans·gress·or [træns'grɛsəʳ] N (*frm*) trasgressore/ trasgreditrice
tran·ship [træn'ʃɪp] VT = **transship**
tran·si·ence ['trænzɪəns] N (*frm*) transitorietà
tran·si·ent ['trænzɪənt] ADJ transitorio(-a), fugace
tran·sis·tor [træn'zɪstəʳ] N (*Elec*) transistor *m inv*
tran·sis·tor·ized [træn'zɪstə,raɪzd] ADJ (*circuit*) transistorizzato(-a)

Tt

transistor radio N (radio *f inv* a) transistor *m inv*
trans·it ['trænzɪt] N transito; **in transit** in transito; **their luggage was lost in transit** il loro bagaglio è stato smarrito durante il trasferimento
transit camp N campo (di raccolta) profughi
◎ **tran·si·tion** [træn'zɪʃən] N transizione *f*, passaggio; **transition period** *or* **period of transition** periodo di transizione; **the transition to democracy** il passaggio alla democrazia
tran·si·tion·al [træn'zɪʃənl] ADJ (*period, government*) di transizione; (*measures*) transitorio(-a)
tran·si·tive ['trænzɪtɪv] ADJ (*Gram*) transitivo(-a)
transit lounge N (*Aer*) sala di transito
tran·si·tory ['trænzɪtərɪ] ADJ transitorio(-a)
transit passenger N passeggero in transito
Transit van ® N grosso furgone *m*, transporter *m inv*
transit visa N visto di transito
trans·lat·able [trænz'leɪtəbl] ADJ traducibile
trans·late [trænz'leɪt] VT: **to translate (from/into)** tradurre (da/in); **it is translated as** si traduce con
■ VI tradurre; **it won't translate** è intraducibile
trans·la·tion [trænz'leɪʃən] N (*of text*) traduzione *f*; (*Scol: as opposed to prose*) versione *f*; (*Geom*) traslazione *f*
trans·la·tor [trænz'leɪtə^r] N traduttore(-trice)
trans·lit·er·ate [trænz'lɪtə,reɪt] VT traslitterare
trans·lit·era·tion [,trænzlɪtə'reɪʃən] N traslitterazione *f*
trans·lu·cence [trænz'lu:sns] N traslucidità *f inv*
trans·lu·cent [trænz'lu:snt] ADJ traslucido(-a)
trans·mis·sion [trænz'mɪʃən] N (*Aut, TV, Radio*) trasmissione *f*
transmission cable N (*Aut*) flessibile *m* di trasmissione
transmission shaft N (*Aut*) albero di trasmissione
trans·mit [trænz'mɪt] VT (*illness, programme, message*) trasmettere
trans·mit·ter [trænz'mɪtə^r] N (*TV, Radio, Telec*) trasmettitore *m*
trans·mit·ting [trænz'mɪtɪŋ] ADJ (*TV, Radio, Telec*) trasmittente; **transmitting set** radiotrasmettitore *m*; **transmitting station** emittente *f*
trans·mute [trænz'mju:t] VT (*frm*): **to transmute (into)** tramutare (in)
tran·som ['trænsəm] N traversa
trans·par·en·cy [træns'pærənsɪ] N trasparenza; (*Phot*) diapositiva
trans·par·ent [træns'pærənt] ADJ trasparente; **a transparent lie** (*fig*) una menzogna palese
tran·spi·ra·tion [,trænspɪ'reɪʃən] N traspirazione *f*
tran·spire [træns'paɪə^r] VI **1** (*Bot, Physiology*) traspirare **2** (*frm: become known*): **it finally transpired that ...** alla fine si è venuto a sapere che... **3** (*incorrect use: happen*) succedere; **what transpired at the meeting?** cos'è successo all'incontro?
trans·plant [*vb* træns'plɑ:nt; *n* 'træns,plɑ:nt] VT (*also Med*) trapiantare
■ N (*Med*) trapianto; **to have a heart transplant** subire un trapianto cardiaco
◎ **trans·port** [*n* 'trænspɔ:t; *vb, adj* træns'pɔ:t] N **1** (*gen*) trasporto; (*vehicle*) mezzo di trasporto; **public transport** mezzi *mpl or* trasporti *mpl* pubblici; **rail transport** il trasporto ferroviario; **Department of Transport** (*Brit*) Ministero dei Trasporti; **have you got your own transport?** hai un tuo mezzo di trasporto?; **I haven't got any transport** non ho un mezzo **2** (*fig: of delight, rage*) trasporto; **to go into transports of joy** esultare dalla gioia
■ VT **1** trasportare; (*History: convicts*) deportare **2** (*fig*): **transported with delight** deliziato(-a); **transported with joy** estasiato(-a)
■ ADJ (*system, costs*) di trasporto
▷ http://europa.eu.int/comm/transport/index_en.html
trans·por·ta·tion [,trænspɔ:'teɪʃən] N **1** trasporto; (*vehicle*) mezzo di trasporto **2** (*History: of convicts*) deportazione *f*; **Department of Transportation** (*Am*) Ministero dei Trasporti
transport café N (*Brit*) trattoria per camionisti
trans·port·er [træns'pɔ:tə^r] N autotreno
trans·pose [træns'pəʊz] VT **1** (*frm: words*) trasporre **2** (*Mus*) trasportare
trans·po·si·tion [,trænspə'zɪʃən] N (*frm*) trasposizione *f*
trans·put·er [træns'pju:tə^r] N (*Comput*) trasputer *m inv*, *microchip molto veloce*
trans·sexu·al [trænz'sɛksjʊəl] N, ADJ transessuale (*m/f*) *inv*
trans·ship [træns'ʃɪp] VT trasbordare
tran·sub·stan·tia·tion ['trænsəb,stænʃɪ'eɪʃən] N (*Rel*) transustanziazione *f*
trans·ver·sal [trænz'vɜ:səl] (*Geom*) ADJ trasversale
■ N retta trasversale
trans·verse ['trænzvɜ:s] ADJ trasversale
trans·ves·tite [trænz'vɛstaɪt] N travestito(-a)
◎ **trap** [træp] N **1** (*snare, trick*) trappola; **to set** *or* **lay a trap (for sb)** tendere una trappola (a qn); **he was caught in his own trap** si è fregato con le sue stesse mani **2** (*fam: mouth*) boccaccia; **shut your trap!** (*fam*) chiudi quella boccaccia! **3** (*carriage*) calesse *m*
■ VT **1** prendere in trappola, intrappolare; **they trapped rabbits** catturavano conigli usando delle trappole; **to trap sb into saying sth** far raccontare qc a qn con un trucco **2** (*immobilize*) bloccare; (*: in wreckage*) intrappolare, bloccare; **to be trapped** rimanere intrappolato; **six people were trapped in the burning building** sei persone sono rimaste intrappolate nell'edificio in fiamme; **to trap one's finger in the door** chiudersi il dito nella porta; **to trap the ball** (*Ftbl*) stoppare la palla
trap door N botola
tra·peze [trə'pi:z] N (*circus*) trapezio
trapeze artist N trapezista *m/f*
tra·pezium [trə'pi:zɪəm] N (*Geom*) trapezio
trap·per ['træpə^r] N cacciatore *m* di animali da pelliccia
trap·pings ['træpɪŋz] NPL (*of public office*) bardatura, ornamenti *mpl*; (*fig: of success*) segni *mpl* esteriori; **the trappings of power** le manifestazioni esteriori del potere
Trap·pist ['træpɪst] ADJ trappista *m*
■ N trappista *m*
trash [træʃ] N (*Am: rubbish*) rifiuti *mpl*, spazzatura; (*pej: goods*) ciarpame *m*; (*fig: nonsense*) sciocchezze *fpl*, stupidaggini *fpl*; **I'll take out the trash** porto fuori la spazzatura; **the book is trash** il libro è una schifezza; **they're just trash** (*fam pej: people*) sono dei pezzenti
trash·can ['træʃ,kæn] N (*Am*) secchio della spazzatura
trashy ['træʃɪ] ADJ (*comp* **-ier**, *superl* **-iest**) (*fam: book, film*) scadente
trau·ma ['trɔ:mə] N trauma *m*
trau·mat·ic [trɔ:'mætɪk] ADJ (*Med*) traumatico(-a); (*Psych, fig*) traumatizzante, traumatico(-a)
◎ **trav·el** ['trævl] N il viaggiare, viaggi *mpl*; **travel is easier now** viaggiare è più facile al giorno d'oggi; **air**

travel is cheap these days viaggiare in aereo non costa molto di questi tempi; **when are you off on your travels?** quando parti per uno dei tuoi viaggi?; **if you meet him on your travels** (*fig*) se lo incontri in uno dei tuoi giri

■ VI **1** viaggiare; (*make a journey*) fare un viaggio; **to travel a country** percorrere un paese; **we shall be travelling in France** faremo un viaggio in Francia; **to travel round the world** fare un viaggio intorno al mondo, girare il mondo; **to travel by car** viaggiare in macchina; **I prefer to travel by train** preferisco viaggiare in treno; **they have travelled a lot** hanno viaggiato molto; **they have travelled a long way** sono venuti da lontano; **we travelled over 800 kilometres** abbiamo fatto più di ottocento chilometri; **to travel light** viaggiare con poco bagaglio; **this wine doesn't travel well** questo vino non resiste agli spostamenti **2** (*go at a speed*) viaggiare, andare; **it travels at 50 km/h** fa 50 km/h; **light travels at a speed of ...** la velocità della luce è di...; **news travels fast** le notizie si diffondono molto velocemente, le notizie volano **3** (*Tech: move*) spostarsi; **it travels along this wire** si sposta lungo questo filo **4** (*Comm*) fare il/la rappresentante (di commercio); **he travels in furs** fa il rappresentante di pellicce

■ VT (*road, distance*) percorrere, fare; **this is a much travelled road** questa è una strada di grande traffico

travel agency N agenzia (di) viaggi

travel agent N agente *m* di viaggio

trav·el·at·or ['trævə,leɪtə^r] N (*Brit*) tapis roulant *m inv*

travel brochure N dépliant *m inv* di viaggi

travel insurance N assicurazione *f* di viaggio

◎ **trav·el·ler**, (*Am*) **trav·el·er** ['trævlə^r] N (*gen*) viaggiatore(-trice); (*Comm*) commesso viaggiatore; (*Brit: gypsy*) zingaro(-a); **my fellow travellers** i miei compagni di viaggio

traveller's cheque, (*Am*) **traveler's check** N traveller's cheque *m inv*

trav·el·ling, (*Am*) **trav·el·ing** ['trævlɪŋ] ADJ (*circus, exhibition*) itinerante; (*expenses, allowance*) di viaggio; (*bag, rug, clock*) da viaggio

■ N viaggi *mpl*; **I love travelling** adoro viaggiare

travelling salesman, (*Am*) **traveling salesman** N commesso viaggiatore

trav·elogue ['trævəlɒg] N (*book*) diario di viaggio; (*film*) documentario di viaggio; (*talk*) conferenza su un viaggio

travel-sick ['trævl,sɪk] ADJ: **to get travel-sick** soffrire di mal d'auto

travel sickness N (*in car*) mal *m* d'auto; (*in plane*) mal d'aria; (*in boat*) mal di mare

trav·erse ['trævɜ:s] (*frm*) N (*line*) linea trasversale; (*crossbeam*) traversa; (*Mountaineering*) traversata

■ VT traversare, attraversare; (*Mountaineering*) traversare

■ VI (*Mountaineering*) fare una traversata

trav·es·ty ['trævɪstɪ] N parodia; **his trial was a travesty of justice** il suo processo è stato una farsa

trav·ol·at·or ['trævə,leɪtə^r] N (*Brit*) tapis roulant *m inv*

trawl [trɔ:l] N (*net*) rete *f* a strascico

■ VI: **to trawl (for sth)** pescare (qc) con rete a strascico

trawl·er ['trɔ:lə^r] N peschereccio (per la pesca a strascico)

trawl·ing ['trɔ:lɪŋ] N pesca a strascico

tray [treɪ] N (*for carrying*) vassoio; (*filing tray*) vassoio per la corrispondenza

treach·er·ous ['trɛtʃərəs] ADJ (*disloyal: person, act*) sleale; (*smile*) traditore(-trice); (*answer*) infido(-a); (*fig: surface, ground, tide*) pericoloso(-a); **a treacherous friend** un amico sleale; **treacherous intentions** intenzioni *fpl* disoneste; **road conditions today are treacherous** oggi il fondo stradale è pericoloso; **the treacherous waters of the Waikato River** le acque infide del fiume Waikato

treach·er·ous·ly ['trɛtʃərəslɪ] ADV (*act*) slealmente; (*speak*) con falsità; **the roads are treacherously icy** il fondo stradale è infido *or* pericoloso con questo ghiaccio

treach·ery ['trɛtʃərɪ] N slealtà *f inv*; **an act of treachery** un tradimento

trea·cle ['tri:kl] N (*Brit*) melassa

trea·cly ['tri:klɪ] ADJ (*substance*) sciropposo(-a); (*fig: voice*) melato(-a)

tread [trɛd] (*vb: pt* **trod**, *pp* **trodden**) N **1** (*footsteps*) passo; (*sound*) rumore *m* di passi; **to walk with (a) heavy tread** avere un'andatura pesante **2** (*of stair*) pedata; (*of tyre*) battistrada *m inv*

■ VT (*ground*) calpestare; (*path*) percorrere; (*grapes*) pigiare; **to tread water** tenersi a galla verticalmente (*muovendo solo le gambe*); **don't tread mud into the carpet** non infangare il tappeto; **he trod his cigarette end into the mud** ha schiacciato il mozzicone della sigaretta nel fango; **to tread a dangerous path** (*fig*) battere un sentiero pericoloso

■ VI (*walk*) camminare; **to tread on sth** calpestare qc; **he trod on a piece of glass** ha calpestato un pezzo di vetro; **to tread on sb's toes** (*also fig*) pestare i piedi a qn; **he trod on her foot** le ha pestato un piede; **we must tread very carefully** *or* **warily** dobbiamo muoverci con molta cautela

▸ **tread on** VI + PREP calpestare

trea·dle ['trɛdl] N pedale *m*

tread·mill ['trɛd,mɪl] N (*fig*): **to go back to the treadmill** tornare alla solita routine

tread pattern N (*of tyre*) disegno

treas. ABBR = **treasurer**

trea·son ['tri:zn] N tradimento

trea·son·able ['tri:zənəbl] ADJ proditorio(-a)

treas·ure ['trɛʒə^r] N (*no pl: gold, jewels*) tesori *mpl*; (*valuable object, fig: person*) tesoro; **our cleaner is a real treasure** la nostra donna delle pulizie è una vera rarità

■ VT (*value: friendship*) apprezzare molto, tenere in gran conto; (*keep: valuables*) custodire gelosamente; (*: memory*) fare tesoro di

treasure house N: **a treasure house of knowledge** (*fig*) un pozzo di scienza

treasure hunt N caccia al tesoro

treas·ur·er ['trɛʒərə^r] N tesoriere(-a)

treasure trove [-trəʊv] N *reperto archeologico di proprietà dello Stato*

◎ **treas·ury** ['trɛʒərɪ] N **1** tesoreria; **the Treasury** (*Brit*) *or* **the Treasury Department** (*Am*) ≈ il Ministero del Tesoro **2** (*fig*) pozzo

treasury bill N ≈ buono del tesoro

◎ **treat** [tri:t] N (*pleasure*) piacere *m*; (*present*) sorpresa, sorpresina; **it was a treat** mi (*or* ci *etc*) ha fatto veramente piacere; **as a birthday treat they took me to the theatre** come regalo di compleanno mi hanno portato a teatro; **to give sb a treat** fare una sorpresa a qn; **to have a treat in store** avere una sorpresa in serbo; **this is my treat** offro io; **to work a treat** funzionare a meraviglia

■ VT **1** (*gen, Tech*) trattare; **to treat sb like a child**

Tt

trattare qn come se fosse un bambino; **the hostages were well treated** gli ostaggi sono stati trattati bene **2** (*consider*) considerare; **to treat sth as a joke** considerare qc uno scherzo; **we treat all applications in the order in which we receive them** prendiamo in considerazione le domande nell'ordine in cui ci arrivano **3** (*give, buy for sb*): **to treat sb to sth** offrire qc a qn; **I'll treat you** offro io; **he treated himself to a new jacket** si è concesso il lusso di una giacca nuova **4** (*patient, illness*) curare; **he was treated with antibiotics/for bronchitis** è stato sottoposto a un trattamento di antibiotici/per la bronchite; **she was treated for a minor head wound** le hanno curato una ferita superficiale al capo

trea·tise ['tri:tɪz] N trattato

◎**treat·ment** ['tri:tmənt] N **1** trattamento; **to give sb preferential treatment** fare un trattamento di favore a qn; **we don't want any special treatment** non vogliamo un trattamento di favore; **he got good/bad treatment** è stato trattato bene/male; **our treatment of foreigners** il modo in cui trattiamo gli stranieri **2** (*Med: of illness*) cura; (*: of wound*) medicazione *f*; **to give sb medical treatment for sth** curare qc a qn; **to have treatment for sth** farsi curare qc; **an effective treatment for eczema** una cura efficace per l'eczema

◎**trea·ty** ['tri:tɪ] N trattato, patto; **to sell a house by private treaty** (*agreement*) vendere una casa con un accordo privato

tre·ble ['trɛbl] ADV (*3 times*) tre volte

■ADJ **1** triplo(-a), triplice; **he now earns treble what he did** guadagna il triplo rispetto a prima **2** (*Mus: voice, part*) da soprano; (*: note, instrument*) alto(-a)

■N **1** (*Mus*) soprano *m/f*; (*also:* **boy treble**) voce *f* bianca **2** (*Horse-riding*) doppia gabbia

■VT triplicare

■VI triplicarsi

treble clef N chiave *f* di violino

◎**tree** [tri:] N **1** (*Bot*) albero; (*fig*): **to be at the top of the tree** essere all'apice **2** (*also:* **shoetree**) tendiscarpe *m inv*

tree diagram N (*Math*) diagramma *m* ad albero

tree house N capanna costruita su un albero

tree line N limite *m* della vegetazione ad alto fusto

tree-lined ['tri:ˌlaɪnd] ADJ fiancheggiato(-a) da alberi

tree of heaven N albero del paradiso

tree·top ['tri:ˌtɒp] N cima di un albero

tree trunk N tronco d'albero

tre·foil ['trɛfɔɪl] N (*Bot*) trifoglio; (*Archit*) decorazione *f* a trifoglio

trek [trɛk] N (*hike*) spedizione *f*; (*fam: tiring walk*) camminata sfiancante; **a trek through the desert** una spedizione nel deserto

■VI (*hike*) fare una camminata lunga e faticosa; (*as holiday*) fare dell'escursionismo; (*fam*) trascinarsi; **they trekked through jungles** hanno fatto trekking nella giungla; **I trekked from shop to shop** mi sono trascinata da un negozio all'altro

trel·lis ['trɛlɪs] N graticcio; (*arched*) pergola

trem·ble ['trɛmbl] N (*of fear*) tremito; (*of passion, excitement*) fremito; **to be all of a tremble** (*fam*) tremare dalla testa ai piedi, tremare come una foglia

■VI tremare; (*machine*) vibrare; **to tremble with** tremare per; **to tremble at the thought of sth** tremare al pensiero di qc

trem·bling ['trɛmblɪŋ] ADJ tremante

■N tremore *m*, tremito

◎**tre·men·dous** [trə'mɛndəs] ADJ (*enormous: difference, pleasure*) enorme; (*dreadful: storm, blow*) tremendo(-a); (*: speed*) spaventoso(-a), folle; (*terrific: success*) strepitoso(-a); (*fam: excellent*) fantastico(-a), formidabile, meraviglioso(-a); **he was a tremendous person** era una persona fantastica

tre·men·dous·ly [trə'mɛndəslɪ] ADV incredibilmente; **he enjoyed it tremendously** gli è piaciuto da morire

trem·or ['trɛmə^r] N (*of fear, shock*) tremito, tremore *m*; (*of excitement*) fremito; (*also:* **earth tremor**) scossa di terremoto, scossa sismica; **it sent tremors down my spine** mi ha fatto venire i brividi

tremu·lous ['trɛmjʊləs] ADJ (*liter: trembling*) tremulo(-a); (*: timid*) timido(-a)

tremu·lous·ly ['trɛmjʊləslɪ] ADV (*liter: speak*) con voce tremula; (*: smile*) timidamente

trench [trɛntʃ] N (*gen*) fosso; (*Mil*) trincea

trench·ant ['trɛntʃənt] ADJ tagliente

trench coat N trench *m inv*

trench warfare N guerra di trincea

◎**trend** [trɛnd] N (*tendency*) tendenza; (*of events*) andamento, corso; (*of prices, coastline*) andamento; (*fashion*) moda; **the latest trend** l'ultima moda; **to set a trend** lanciare una moda; **to set the trend** essere all'avanguardia; **trend towards sth/away from sth** tendenza a qc/ad allontanarsi da qc; **there is a trend towards doing sth/away from doing sth** si tende a fare qc/a non fare qc; **there's a trend towards part-time employment** il lavoro part-time è sempre più diffuso

trend·set·ter ['trɛndˌsɛtə^r] N (*fam*) persona che detta la moda

trendy ['trɛndɪ] ADJ (*comp* **-ier**, *superl* **-iest**) (*Brit fam: person, idea*) à la page; (*: clothes, night club*) trendy

trepi·da·tion [ˌtrɛpɪ'deɪʃən] N (*frm*) trepidazione *f*

tres·pass ['trɛspəs] VI: **to trespass (on)** (*on land*) entrare abusivamente (in); (*fig: on time, hospitality*) abusare (di); **"no trespassing"** "proprietà privata", "vietato l'accesso"

■N (*on land*) transito abusivo

tres·pass·er ['trɛspəsə^r] N (*Bible, Law*) trasgressore *m*; **"trespassers will be prosecuted"** "vietato l'accesso – i trasgressori saranno puniti secondo i termini di legge"

tress [trɛs] N (*liter*) ciocca di capelli

tres·tle ['trɛsl] N cavalletto

trestle table N tavola su cavalletti

tri... [traɪ] PREF tri...

tri·age ['tri:ɑ:ʒ] N (*Med*) triage *m inv*; *immediata valutazione delle condizioni del ferito*

◎**tri·al** ['traɪəl] N **1** (*gen*) giudizio; (*proceedings*) processo; **trial by jury** processo penale con giuria; **to be on trial (for a crime)** essere sotto processo (per un reato); **to bring sb to trial (for a crime)** portare qn in giudizio (per un reato); **to go on trial** *or* **to stand trial** essere processato(-a); **to be sent for trial** essere rinviato(-a) a giudizio; **the witnesses at the trial** i testimoni del processo **2** (*test: gen*) prova; (*: of drugs*) sperimentazione *f*; (*: of machine*) collaudo; **trials** NPL (*Athletics*) prove *fpl* di qualificazione; (*Ftbl*) prova di selezione; **horse trials** concorso ippico; **a trial of strength** una prova di forza; **by trial and error** per tentativi; **to be on trial** (*drug*) essere in via di sperimentazione; (*machine*) essere al collaudo; **to give sb a trial** (*for job*) far fare una prova a qn **3** (*hardship*) prova, difficoltà *f inv*; (*worry*) cruccio; **it was a great trial** è stata una dura prova; **that child is a great trial to them** quel bambino è una continua

preoccupazione per loro; **the trials and tribulations of life** le tribolazioni della vita
■ ADJ (*flight, order, period*) di prova; **trial offer** offerta di lancio; **trial period** periodo di prova; **on a trial basis** in prova

trial balance N (*Comm*) bilancio di verifica

trial balloon N idea lanciata come banco di prova

trial run N periodo di prova

tri·an·gle ['traɪ,æŋgl] N (*Math, Mus*) triangolo

tri·an·gu·lar [traɪ'æŋgjʊləʳ] ADJ triangolare

tri·ath·lon [traɪ'æθlɒn] N triathlon *m inv*

trib·al ['traɪbəl] ADJ tribale; (*warfare*) fra tribù

trib·al·ism ['traɪbəlɪzəm] N (*Anthropology, Sociol*) organizzazione *f* tribale; (*pej*) tribalismo

tribe [traɪb] N tribù *f inv*

tribes·man ['traɪbzmən] N (*pl* **-men**) membro della tribù

tribu·la·tion [,trɪbjʊ'leɪʃən] N (*frm*) tribolazione *f*

tri·bu·nal [traɪ'bju:nl] N tribunale *m*; **tribunal of inquiry** commissione *f* d'inchiesta

tribu·tary ['trɪbjʊtərɪ] N (*river*) affluente *m*, tributario

trib·ute ['trɪbju:t] N tributo, omaggio; **to pay tribute to sb/sth** rendere omaggio a qn/qc; **floral tribute** omaggio floreale

trice [traɪs] N: **in a trice** (*Brit fam*) in un batter d'occhio, in un attimo

tri·ceps ['traɪsɛps] N, PL INV tricipite *m*

◎ **trick** [trɪk] N **1** (*joke, hoax*) scherzo, tiro; (*ruse, catch, special knack*) trucco; (*clever act*) stratagemma *m*; **to play a trick on sb** giocare un tiro a qn; **dirty** *or* **mean trick** scherzo di cattivo gusto; **there must be a trick in it** ci deve essere sotto qualche cosa; **he's up to his old tricks again** è tornato ai suoi vecchi trucchetti; **there's a trick to opening this door** c'è un trucco per aprire questa porta; **it's not easy, there's a trick to it** non è facile, c'è un trucco per farlo; **it's a trick of the light** è un effetto ottico; **he knows all the tricks of the trade** conosce tutti i trucchi del mestiere
2 (*habit*) mania; **he has a trick of turning up when least expected** ha il dono di spuntare quando uno meno se l'aspetta **3** (*Cards*) presa; (*also:* **conjuring trick**) gioco di prestigio; **that should do the trick** (*fam*) vedrai che funziona; **he doesn't miss a trick** (*fig*) non gliene scappa mai una
■ VT (*deceive*) ingannare, imbrogliare; (*swindle*) imbrogliare; **I've been tricked!** mi hanno imbrogliato!; **to trick sb into doing sth** convincere qn a fare qc con l'inganno; **to trick sb out of sth** fregare qc a qn

trick·ery ['trɪkərɪ] N inganno

trick·le ['trɪkl] N (*of liquid*) rivolo; (*in drops*) gocciolio; (*fig*): **we've had only a trickle of customers** abbiamo avuto solo pochi clienti; **there was a steady trickle of orders** gli ordini erano pochi ma regolari; **a trickle of water** un rivolo d'acqua
■ VI (*liquid*) gocciolare; (*ball*) rotolare lentamente; **tears trickled down her cheeks** le lacrime le scorrevano sulle guance; **to trickle in** (*orders, money*) arrivare a poco a poco; **to trickle in/out** (*people*) entrare/uscire alla spicciolata

trick photography N fotografia truccata

trick question N domanda *f* trabocchetto *inv*

trick·ster ['trɪkstəʳ] N imbroglione(-a)

tricky ['trɪkɪ] ADJ (*comp* **-ier**, *superl* **-iest**) (*situation, problem*) difficile; (*job, task*) delicato(-a); (*person: sly*) astuto(-a)

tri·col·our, (*Am*) **tri·col·or** ['trɪkələʳ] N tricolore *m*

tri·cy·cle ['traɪsɪkl] N triciclo

tried [traɪd] PT, PP *of* **try**
■ ADJ: **tried and tested** sperimentato(-a)

tri·er ['traɪəʳ] N: **to be a trier** essere perseverante

tri·fle ['traɪfl] N **1** (*unimportant thing*) cosa di poco valore, sciocchezza; **he worries about trifles** si preoccupa per niente; **he spends a lot on trifles** spende molto per delle sciocchezze; **it's a trifle difficult** è piuttosto difficile; **that seems a trifle ambitious** sembra un po' ambizioso; **a trifle long** un po' lungo(-a) **2** (*Brit Culin*) ≈ zuppa inglese; **trifle or ice cream?** zuppa inglese o gelato?
► **trifle with** VI + PREP prendere alla leggera; **he's not a person to be trifled with** non è una persona da prendere alla leggera; **to trifle with sb's affections** giocare con i sentimenti di qn

tri·fling ['traɪflɪŋ] ADJ insignificante

◎ **trig·ger** ['trɪgəʳ] N (*of gun, machine*) grilletto; **to pull the trigger** premere il grilletto
■ VT (*also:* **trigger off**: *event*) provocare, scatenare; **the incident which triggered the First World War** l'incidente che ha scatenato la prima guerra mondiale; **to trigger an alarm** far scattare l'allarme

trigger-happy ['trɪgə,hæpɪ] ADJ (*fam*) dalla pistola facile

trigo·no·met·ric [,trɪgənə'mɛtrɪk] ADJ trigonometrico(-a)

trigo·nom·etry [,trɪgə'nɒmɪtrɪ] N trigonometria

trike [traɪk] N (*fam*) triciclo

tri·lat·er·al [,traɪ'lætərəl] ADJ trilaterale

tril·by ['trɪlbɪ] N (*Brit: also:* **trilby hat**) cappello di feltro

trill [trɪl] N (*of bird, Mus*) trillo

tril·lion ['trɪljən] N **1** (*Am*) mille miliardi *mpl*; (*Brit*) trilione *m* **2** **trillions (of)** milioni *mpl* (di)

tril·ogy ['trɪlədʒɪ] N trilogia

trim [trɪm] ADJ (*comp* **-mer**, *superl* **-mest**) curato(-a), ordinato(-a); (*house, garden*) ben tenuto(-a); (*figure*) snello(-a)
■ N **1** **in good trim** (*car*) in buone condizioni; (*person*) in forma; **to keep in (good) trim** mantenersi in forma **2** (*haircut*) spuntata, regolata; **to have a trim** farsi spuntare i capelli **3** (*embellishment*) finiture *fpl*; (*decoration*) applicazioni *fpl*; (*on car*) guarnizioni *fpl*; **white with a black trim** bianco con una guarnizione nera; **car with grey interior trim** macchina con gli interni grigi
■ VT **1** (*cut: hedge, beard, edges*) regolare tagliando; (*: hair*) spuntare **2** **to trim (with)** (*decorate: Christmas tree*) decorare (con); **to trim sth with sth** (*edge*) mettere un bordo di qc a qc **3** (*Naut: sail*) orientare
► **trim off** VT + ADV tagliare via
■ VT + PREP: **to trim sth off sth** tagliare via qc da qc

tri·ma·ran ['traɪmə,ræn] N trimarano

trim·ming ['trɪmɪŋ] N (*edging*) bordura; **trimmings** NPL (*embellishments*) decorazioni *fpl*; (*extras*) accessori *mpl*; (*Culin*) guarnizione *f*; (*cuttings*) ritagli *mpl*; **turkey with all the trimmings** tacchino con contorno e tutto il resto

Trini·dad and To·ba·go [,trɪnɪdædəntə'beɪgəʊ] N Trinidad e Tobago *f*

Trini·ty ['trɪnɪtɪ] N: **the Trinity** la Trinità

Trinity Sunday N festa della santissima Trinità

trin·ket ['trɪŋkɪt] N (*piece of jewellery*) ciondolo; (*ornament*) ninnolo, gingillo

trio ['trɪəʊ] N trio

◎ **trip** [trɪp] N **1** viaggio; (*outing*) gita; (*excursion*) escursione *f*; **(away) on a trip** in viaggio; **to take a trip**

Tt

or **to go on a trip** fare un viaggio; **she does 3 trips to Milan a week** va a Milano 3 volte alla settimana; **I've made 2 trips to the shops already** sono già andata 2 volte a far la spesa; **have a good trip!** buon viaggio!; **a day trip** una gita di un giorno **2** *(Drugs slang)* trip *m inv*, viaggio **3** *(stumble)* passo falso
■ VI **1** *(stumble)* inciampare; **I tripped and fell** sono inciampato(-a) e caduto(-a) **2 to trip along** *or* **go tripping along** *(skip)* andare saltellando; *(move lightly)* camminare con passo leggero
■ VT = **trip up** VT + ADV
▸ **trip over** VI + ADV inciampare
■ VI + PREP inciampare in
▸ **trip up** VI + ADV inciampare; *(fig: make a mistake)* fare un passo falso
■ VT + ADV far inciampare, fare lo sgambetto a

tri·par·tite [ˌtraɪˈpɑːtaɪt] ADJ *(agreement)* tripartito(-a); *(talks)* a tre

tripe [traɪp] N *(Culin)* trippa; *(fam pej: rubbish)* sciocchezze *fpl*, fesserie *fpl*

tri·ple [ˈtrɪpl] ADJ triplo(-a)
■ ADV: **triple the distance/the speed** tre volte più lontano/più veloce
■ VT triplicare
■ VI triplicarsi

Triple Alliance N: **the Triple Alliance** la Triplice Alleanza

triple jump N salto triplo

tri·plets [ˈtrɪplɪts] NPL: **to have triplets** avere tre gemelli; **she's just had triplets** ha appena avuto tre gemelli *or* un parto trigemino

trip·li·cate [ˈtrɪplɪkɪt] N: **in triplicate** in triplice copia

tri·pod [ˈtraɪpɒd] N treppiede *m*

Tripo·li [ˈtrɪpəlɪ] N Tripoli *f*

trip·per [ˈtrɪpəʳ] N *(Brit)* gitante *m/f*

trip·tych [ˈtrɪptɪk] N trittico

trip·wire [ˈtrɪpˌwaɪəʳ] N *filo in tensione che fa scattare una trappola, un allarme ecc*

tri·syl·la·ble [ˌtraɪˈsɪləbl] N trisillabo

trite [traɪt] ADJ *(remark)* banale; *(story, idea)* trito(-a) e ritrito(-a)

Triton [ˈtraɪtən] N Tritone *m*

◎ **tri·umph** [ˈtraɪʌmf] N *(success)* successo; *(sense of triumph)* trionfo; *(victory)*: **triumph (over)** trionfo (su), vittoria (su); **in triumph** in trionfo
■ VI: **to triumph (over)** trionfare (su)

tri·um·phal [traɪˈʌmfəl] ADJ trionfale

tri·um·phant [traɪˈʌmfənt] ADJ *(jubilant)* trionfante; (: *homecoming*) trionfale; *(victorious)* vittorioso(-a)

tri·um·phant·ly [traɪˈʌmfəntlɪ] ADV *(march, carry)* in trionfo; *(announce)* con tono trionfante

tri·um·vi·rate [traɪˈʌmvɪrɪt] NSG OR PL *(frm)* triunvirato

trivia [ˈtrɪvɪə] NPL banalità *fpl*

triv·ial [ˈtrɪvɪəl] ADJ *(matter)* futile; *(excuse, comment)* banale; *(amount)* irrisorio(-a); *(mistake)* di poco conto

> DID YOU KNOW ...?
> **trivial** is not translated by the Italian word *triviale*

trivi·al·ity [ˌtrɪvɪˈælɪtɪ] N frivolezza; *(trivial detail)* futilità *f inv*

> DID YOU KNOW ...?
> **triviality** is not translated by the Italian word *trivialità*

trivi·al·ize [ˈtrɪvɪəˌlaɪz] VT sminuire

trod [trɒd] PT *of* **tread**

trod·den [ˈtrɒdn] PP *of* **tread**

trog·lo·dyte [ˈtrɒgləˌdaɪt] N *(frm)* troglodita *m/f*

troi·ka [ˈtrɔɪkə] N troica

Tro·jan [ˈtrəʊdʒən] ADJ, N troiano(-a)

Trojan horse N *(also Comput)* cavallo di Troia

troll [trəʊl] [trɒl] N troll *m inv*
■ VI *(fam)* vagare

trol·ley [ˈtrɒlɪ] N *(Brit: in station, supermarket) (also:* **tea trolley***)* carrello; (: *in hospital*) lettiga

trolley bus N filobus *m inv*

trol·lop [ˈtrɒləp] N *(old offensive)* sgualdrina

trom·bone [trɒmˈbəʊn] N trombone *m*

◎ **troop** [truːp] N *(gen, of scouts)* gruppo; *(Mil)* squadrone *m*; **troops** NPL *(Mil)* truppe *fpl*
■ VI *(walk)*: **to troop in/past/off** *etc* entrare/passare/andarsene *etc* in gruppo; **trooping the colour** *(Brit)* cerimonia del saluto alla bandiera

troop carrier N **1** *(plane)* aereo per il trasporto (di) truppe **2** *(Naut)* = **troopship**

troop·er [ˈtruːpəʳ] N *(Mil)* soldato di cavalleria; *(Am: policeman)* ≈ poliziotto *agente della polizia di uno stato*; **to swear like a trooper** bestemmiare come un turco

troop·ship [ˈtruːpʃɪp] N nave *f* per il trasporto (di) truppe

tro·phy [ˈtrəʊfɪ] N trofeo

trop·ic [ˈtrɒpɪk] N tropico; **the tropics** i tropici; **Tropic of Cancer/Capricorn** tropico del Cancro/Capricorno

tropi·cal [ˈtrɒpɪkəl] ADJ tropicale; **tropical rain forest** foresta pluviale equatoriale

trot [trɒt] N **1** *(pace)* trotto; **sitting/rising trot** *(Horse-riding)* trotto seduto/sollevato; **to break into a trot** *(horse, rider)* partire al trotto; *(person)* mettersi a camminare di buon passo; **to go for a trot** *(on horse)* andare a fare una trottata **2** *(Brit fam)*: **on the trot** di fila, uno(-a) dopo l'altro(-a); **three weeks on the trot** tre settimane di fila; **to be on the trot** *(fam)* essere sempre in movimento; **the baby keeps her on the trot** il bambino non le concede un attimo di tregua **3 the trots** *(fam: diarrhoea)* la cacarella
■ VI *(horse, rider)* andare al trotto, trottare; *(person)*: **to trot in/past** *etc* entrare/passare *etc* di corsa
▸ **trot out** VT + ADV *(excuse, reason)* tirar fuori; *(names, facts)* recitare di fila

trot·ter [ˈtrɒtəʳ] N **1** *(horse)* trottatore *m* **2** *(Culin)*: **pig's trotter** zampone *m*

◎ **trou·ble** [ˈtrʌbl] N **1** *(problems)* problemi *mpl*, difficoltà *fpl*; (: *as result of doing wrong*) guai *mpl*, pasticci *mpl*; (: *with sth mechanical*) noie *fpl*; *(unrest, fighting)* agitazione *f*, disordine *m*; **troubles** NPL disordini, conflitti *mpl*; **to have trouble doing sth** avere delle difficoltà a fare qc; **to be in trouble** *(having problems)* avere qualche problema *or* difficoltà; *(for doing wrong)* essere nei guai; **to get into trouble** cacciarsi nei guai; **to get sb into trouble** mettere *or* cacciare qn nei guai; **to help sb out of trouble** aiutare qn a tirarsi fuori dai guai; **what's the trouble?** cosa c'è che non va?; **the trouble is ...** c'è che..., il guaio è che...; **the trouble is, it's too expensive** il problema è che costa troppo; **don't go looking for trouble** non andare in cerca di guai; **the police are trying to prevent trouble** la polizia sta cercando di prevenire eventuali disordini; **engine trouble** noie al motore; **stomach trouble** disturbi *mpl* gastrici; **heart/back trouble** disturbi al cuore/di schiena **2** *(bother, effort)* sforzo; *(worry)* preoccupazione *f*; **it's no trouble** *(offering help)* non è un problema; **it's no trouble!** *(accepting thanks)* di niente!; **it's not worth the trouble** non vale la pena; **to go to (all) the trouble of doing sth** *or* **take**

the trouble to do sth darsi la pena di fare qc; **to take a lot of trouble over sth** mettere molto impegno in qc
■ VT **1** *(worry)* preoccupare; **my eyes have been troubling me** ho avuto dei disturbi agli occhi **2** *(bother, be nuisance to)* disturbare; **I'm sorry to trouble you** mi dispiace disturbarla; **I shan't trouble you with all the details** non starò ad annoiarla con tutti i particolari; **please don't trouble yourself** non si disturbi **3** *(+ infin: make the effort)*: **to trouble to do sth** darsi la pena di fare qc

trou·bled ['trʌbld] ADJ *(person, expression)* preoccupato(-a), inquieto(-a); *(period)* travagliato(-a); *(epoch, life)* agitato(-a), difficile

trouble-free [,trʌbl'fri:] ADJ *(life, car, trip)* senza problemi; *(area, factory)* tranquillo(-a); *(demonstration)* pacifico(-a)

trouble·maker ['trʌbl,meɪkə^r] N elemento disturbatore, agitatore(-trice)

trouble·shooter ['trʌbl,ʃu:tə^r] N *(Tech)* esperto(-a) *(chiamato in casi di emergenza)*; *(Pol)* mediatore(-trice); *(in conflict)* conciliatore *m*

trouble·shooting ['trʌbl,ʃu:tɪŋ] N risoluzione *f* dei problemi

trou·ble·some ['trʌblsəm] ADJ *(person)* molesto(-a), importuno(-a); *(headache)* fastidioso(-a); *(dispute, problem)* difficile, seccante; **a troublesome child** un bambino molesto

trouble spot N zona calda

trou·bling ['trʌblɪŋ] ADJ *(thought)* preoccupante; **these are troubling times** questi sono tempi difficili

trough [trɒf] N **1** *(also:* **feeding trough***)* mangiatoia, trogolo; *(also:* **drinking trough***)* abbeveratoio; *(channel)* canale *m* **2** *(between waves)* cavo; *(on graph)* punto più basso; *(Met)*: **trough of low pressure** area di bassa pressione, depressione *f*

trounce [traʊns] VT *(beat)* picchiare; *(defeat)* battere

troupe [tru:p] N *(Theatre)* compagnia, troupe *f inv*

trou·ser ['traʊzə^r] VT *(Brit fam)* intascare

trouser hanger N *(Brit)* reggipantaloni *m inv*

trouser press N *(Brit)* stiracalzoni *m inv*

trou·sers ['traʊzəz] NPL *(Brit)* pantaloni *mpl*, calzoni *mpl*; **short trousers** calzoncini *mpl*; **she wears the trousers** *(fig)* è lei che porta i calzoni

trouser suit N *(Brit)* completo *m* pantalone *inv*, tailleur *m inv* pantalone *inv*

trous·seau ['tru:səʊ] N corredo da sposa

trout [traʊt] N, PL INV trota
■ ADJ: **trout fishing** pesca della trota

trow·el ['traʊəl] N *(for garden)* paletta da giardiniere; *(builder's)* cazzuola

Troy [trɔɪ] N Troia

tru·an·cy ['trʊənsɪ] N *(Scol)* assenze *fpl* ingiustificate

tru·ant ['trʊənt] N *(Scol)*: **to play truant** marinare la scuola

truce [tru:s] N tregua; **to call a truce** dichiarare una tregua

DID YOU KNOW ...?
truce is not translated by the Italian word *truce*

◎**truck**[1] [trʌk] N **1** *(Brit: Rail: wagon)* carro *m* merci *inv (aperto)* **2** *(esp Am: lorry)* camion *m inv*, autocarro **3** *(for luggage)* carrello *m* portabagagli *inv*

truck[2] [trʌk] N: **to have no truck with sb** non volere avere a che fare con qn

truck driver N, *(Am)* **truck·er** ['trʌkə^r] N camionista *m/f*

truck·ing ['trʌkɪŋ] N *(Am)* autotrasporto, trasporto su gomma

trucking company N *(Am)* impresa di trasporti

truck·le ['trʌkəl] VI: **to truckle to sb** strisciare davanti a qn

truck·load ['trʌk,ləʊd] N carico *(di camion)*

trucu·lence ['trʌkjʊləns] N aggressività *f inv*, brutalità *f inv*

trucu·lent ['trʌkjʊlənt] ADJ aggressivo(-a), brutale

trucu·lent·ly ['trʌkjʊləntlɪ] ADV con aggressività, brutalmente

trudge [trʌdʒ] VI: **to trudge up/down/along** *etc* trascinarsi pesantemente su/giù/lungo *etc*; **to trudge round the town** girare la città in lungo e in largo

◎**true** [tru:] ADJ *(comp* **-r**, *superl* **-st***)* **1** *(not fiction: story)* vero(-a); *(accurate, correct: statement, description)* preciso(-a), esatto(-a), accurato(-a); *(: portrait, likeness)* fedele; **that can't be true!** non può essere vero!; **to come true** avverarsi; **I hope my dream will come true** spero che il mio sogno si avveri; **the same holds true of** *or* **for ...** lo stesso vale per...; **too true!** fin troppo vero!; **true, but ...** sì , ma... **2** *(real, genuine: emotion, interest)* sincero(-a), vero(-a); **true love** vero amore; **to behave like a true Englishman** comportarsi da vero inglese; **in the truest sense of the word** nel vero senso della parola **3** *(wall, beam)* a piombo; *(wheel)* centrato(-a) **4** *(faithful: friend)* fedele; **to be true to sb/sth** essere fedele a qn/qc; **to be true to one's word** tenere fede alla parola data; **true to life** verosimile; **to run true to type** essere fedele alla propria immagine
■ N: **to be out of true** *(wall, beam)* non essere a piombo; *(wheel)* non essere centrato(-a)

true-blue [,tru:'blu:] ADJ *(fam: loyal)* fedele, leale

true north N nord *m inv*

truf·fle ['trʌfl] N tartufo

tru·ism ['tru:ɪzəm] N verità *f inv* lapalissiana

◎**tru·ly** ['tru:lɪ] ADV *(genuinely: believe, love)* veramente, sinceramente; *(faithfully: serve, love, reflect)* fedelmente; *(emphatic: very)* veramente, davvero; **I truly never minded looking after Tom** sinceramente non mi è mai dispiaciuto occuparmi di Tom; **it was a truly remarkable victory** è stata veramente una vittoria straordinaria; **well and truly** per bene; **yours truly** *(in letter-writing)* distinti saluti

trump [trʌmp] N *(Cards)* atout *m inv*; **hearts are trumps** l'atout è di cuori; **to turn** *or* **come up trumps** *(fig)* fare miracoli
■ VT *(Cards)* tagliare, prendere con l'atout

trump card N atout *m inv*; *(fig)* asso nella manica

trumped-up [,trʌmpt'ʌp] ADJ *(charge)* inventato(-a), falso(-a)

trum·pet ['trʌmpɪt] N tromba; **a trumpet player** *(Jazz)* un(-a) trombettista
■ VI *(elephant)* barrire

trum·pet·er ['trʌmpɪtə^r] N suonatore *m* di tromba; *(Mil)* trombettiere *m*

trun·cate [trʌŋ'keɪt] VT *(report, speech)* tagliare

trun·cat·ed [trʌŋ'keɪtɪd] ADJ *(Geom)* tronco(-a)

trun·cheon ['trʌntʃən] N manganello, sfollagente *m inv*

trun·dle ['trʌndl] VT *(push, pull)*: **to trundle along** far rotolare (a fatica)
■ VI *(cart)* avanzare lentamente

trunk [trʌŋk] N *(of tree, person)* tronco; *(also:* **tree trunk***)* tronco d'albero; *(of elephant)* proboscide *f*; *(piece of luggage)* baule *m*; *(Am Aut: boot of car)* bagagliaio;

Tt

put it in the trunk mettilo nel portabagagli; *see also* trunks
trunk call N (*Brit: old Telec*) (telefonata) interurbana
trunk line N (*Rail, Telec*) linea principale
trunk road N (*Brit*) strada principale
trunks [trʌŋks] NPL: **(swimming** *or* **bathing) trunks** calzoncini *mpl* da bagno
truss [trʌs] VT (*also:* **truss up**) legare stretto; (*Culin*) legare
■ N (*Med*) cinto erniario
◎ **trust** [trʌst] N **1** **trust (in)** fiducia (in); **to put one's trust in sb** riporre la propria fiducia in qn; **to put one's trust in sth** riporre le proprie speranze in qc; **to be in a position of trust** ricoprire un incarico di fiducia; **you'll have to take it on trust** devi credermi sulla parola; **he betrayed my trust** ha tradito la mia fiducia **2** (*charge*): **to leave sth in sb's trust** affidare qc a qn *or* alle cure di qn **3** (*Law, Fin*) amministrazione *f* fiduciaria; **in trust** in amministrazione fiduciaria; **charitable trust** fondazione *f* benefica **4** (*Comm: also:* **trust company**) trust *m inv*
■ VT **1** (*have faith, confidence in*) avere fiducia in, fidarsi di; (*rely on*) fare affidamento su, contare su; **don't you trust me?** non ti fidi di me?; **trust me!** fidati di me!; **to trust sth to sb/trust sb with sth** (*entrust*) affidare qc a qn; **I wouldn't trust him an inch** non mi fiderei proprio di lui; **trust you!** (*fam*) ci avrei scommesso! **2** (*hope*): **to trust (that ...)** sperare (che...)
■ VI (*have faith*): **to trust in** credere in; **to trust to luck/fate** (*rely*) affidarsi alla fortuna/al destino
trusta·far·ian N (*Brit fam*) *rampollo di famiglia molto ricca che conduce uno stile di vita alternativo*
trust·ed [ˈtrʌstɪd] ADJ (*friend, adviser*) fidato(-a)
trus·tee [trʌsˈtiː] N (*Law*) amministratore(-trice) fiduciario(-a); (*of school, institution*) amministratore(-trice)
trust·ful [ˈtrʌstfʊl], **trust·ing** [ˈtrʌstɪŋ] ADJ fiducioso(-a)
trust·ful·ly [ˈtrʌstfəlɪ], **trust·ing·ly** [ˈtrʌstɪŋlɪ] ADV fiduciosamente, con fiducia
trust fund N fondo fiduciario
trust·worthi·ness [ˈtrʌstˌwɜːðɪnɪs] N (*of person*) affidabilità *f inv*; (*of statement*) attendibilità *f inv*
trust·worthy [ˈtrʌstˌwɜːðɪ] ADJ (*person*) fidato(-a), degno(-a) di fiducia; (*source of news*) attendibile
trusty [ˈtrʌstɪ] ADJ (*comp* **-ier**, *superl* **-iest**) (*hum*) fidato(-a)
◎ **truth** [truːθ] N verità *f inv*; **to tell the truth** dire la verità; **to tell (you) the truth** *or* **truth to tell** a dire il vero *or* la verità; **the truth of the matter is that ...** la verità è che...; **the truth hurts** la verità fa male; **there is some truth in what he says** c'è del vero in ciò che dice; **there isn't a word of truth in it** non c'è nulla di vero; **truth will out** la verità viene sempre a galla
truth drug N siero della verità
truth·ful [ˈtruːθfʊl] ADJ (*account*) veritiero(-a), esatto(-a); (*person*) sincero(-a)
truth·ful·ly [ˈtruːθfəlɪ] ADV sinceramente
truth·ful·ness [ˈtruːθfʊlnɪs] N (*of account*) veridicità *f inv*; (*of person*) sincerità *f inv*
truth serum N = truth drug
◎ **try** [traɪ] N **1** (*attempt*) tentativo, prova; **to give sth a try** provare qc; **why don't you give the exam a try?** perché non provi a fare l'esame?; **to have a try (at doing sth)** provare (a fare qc); **it's worth a try** vale la pena di tentare; **his third try** il suo terzo tentativo **2** (*Rugby*) meta
■ VT **1** (*usu + infin*): **to try to do sth** (*attempt*) provare a fare qc; (*seek*) cercare di fare qc; **to try one's (very) best** *or* **one's (very) hardest** mettercela tutta **2** (*sample, experiment with: method, car, food*) provare; **would you like to try some?** vuoi assaggiare?; **why not try him for the job?** perché non gli fai fare una prova?; **try pressing that switch** prova a schiacciare quell'interruttore **3** (*test: strength, vehicle, machine*) verificare, collaudare; (*tax, strain: patience, person*) mettere alla prova; (*: eyes*) affaticare; **to try one's hand at sth** (*fig*) cimentarsi in qc **4** (*Law*): **to try sb (for sth)** processare qn (per qc)
■ VI (*attempt*) provare; **I tried, but failed** ho tentato, ma non ci sono riuscito; **you must try harder** devi tentare ancora; **to try again** ritentare; **try again!** provaci ancora!
▸ **try for** VI + PREP mirare a
▸ **try on** VT + ADV **1** (*clothes, shoes*) provare **2** (*Brit fam*): **to try it on (with sb)** cercare di farla (a qn)
▸ **try out** VT + ADV (*test: sth new, different*) provare; (*employee*) far fare una prova a; **to try sth out on sb** far provare qc a qn
try·ing [ˈtraɪɪŋ] ADJ (*tiring: situation, time*) difficile, duro(-a); (*: day, experience*) logorante, pesante; (*tiresome: person*) noioso(-a), seccante; (*: child*) insopportabile; **to have a trying time** passare un periodo difficile
tryp·sin [ˈtrɪpsɪn] N tripsina
tsar [zɑːʳ] N zar *m inv*
tsa·ri·na [zɑːˈriːnə] N zarina
tsar·ist, tzar·ist, czar·ist [ˈzɑːrɪst] ADJ, N zarista (*m/f*)
tset·se fly [ˈtsɛtsɪˌflaɪ] N mosca *f* tse-tse *inv*
T-shirt [ˈtiːˌʃɜːt] N maglietta
T-square [ˈtiːˌskwɛəʳ] N riga a T
tsu·na·mi [tsʊˈnɑːmɪ] N tsunami *m inv*
TT [ˌtiːˈtiː] ADJ ABBR (*Brit fam*) = **teetotal**
■ ABBR (*Am Post*) = *Trust Territory*
tub [tʌb] N (*for washing clothes*) tinozza, mastello; (*for flowers*) vasca; (*for ice cream*) vaschetta; (*: individual*) coppetta; (*fam: also:* **bathtub**) vasca da bagno; **a tub of margarine** una vaschetta di margarina; **a hot tub** un bagno caldo
tuba [ˈtjuːbə] N tuba
tub·by [ˈtʌbɪ] ADJ (*comp* **-ier**, *superl* **-iest**) (*fam*) grassoccio(-a)
◎ **tube** [tjuːb] N **1** (*pipe*) tubo; (*of toothpaste, paint*) tubetto; (*Anat*) tuba; (*for tyre*) camera d'aria; **a cardboard tube** un tubo di cartone **2** (*Brit: London Underground*) metrò *m inv*, metropolitana **3** **the tube** (*Am fam: television*) la tele
■ ADJ (*Brit*) del metrò; **tube station** stazione *f* del metrò
tube·less [ˈtjuːblɪs] ADJ (*tyre*) senza camera d'aria
tu·ber [ˈtjuːbəʳ] N (*Bot*) tubero
tu·ber·cu·lar [tjʊˈbɜːkjʊləʳ] ADJ tubercolare
tu·ber·cu·lo·sis [tjʊˌbɜːkjʊˈləʊsɪs] N tubercolosi *f*
tub·ing [ˈtjuːbɪŋ] N tubi *mpl*, tubazione *f*; **a piece of tubing** un tubo
tubu·lar [ˈtjuːbjʊləʳ] ADJ tubolare
TUC [ˌtiːjuːˈsiː] N ABBR (*Brit:* = **Trades Union Congress**) confederazione *f* dei sindacati (britannici)
tuck [tʌk] N (*Sewing*) pince *f inv*, piega
■ VT (*put*) infilare, mettere, cacciare; **she tucked a blanket round him** lo ha avvolto in una coperta; **I tucked a note under her pillow** le ho infilato un biglietto sotto il cuscino
■ VI: **to tuck into a meal** (*Brit fam*) lanciarsi sul pasto
▸ **tuck away** VT + ADV (*put away*) riporre in un luogo

sicuro; (*hide*) nascondere; **she has her money safely tucked away** ha messo i soldi in un posto sicuro
▸ **tuck in** VI + ADV (*Brit fam: eat*) mangiare con grande appetito, abbuffarsi; **they all tucked into the huge breakfast** tutti hanno mangiato di gusto un'abbondante colazione; **tuck in!** abbuffati!
■ VT + ADV (*blankets*) rimboccare; (*shirt*) mettere dentro; **she tucked the blouse into her skirt** si è messa la camicia dentro la gonna; **to tuck sb in** rimboccare le coperte a qn; **I'll come and tuck you in** vengo a rimboccarti le coperte
▸ **tuck up** VT + ADV (*skirt, sleeves*) tirare su; **to tuck sb up** rimboccare le coperte a qn; **he tucked him up** gli ha rimboccato le coperte; **to be tucked up in bed** essere a letto con le coperte ben rimboccate

tuck box N (*Brit Scol: old*) scatola di dolciumi (*mandata da casa*)

tuck shop N (*Brit Scol: old*) negozio di pasticceria (*in o vicino ad una scuola*)

Tue., Tues. ABBR (= **Tuesday**) mar. (= *martedì*)

Tues·day ['tju:zdɪ] N martedì *m inv*; **(the date) today is Tuesday 23 March** oggi è martedì 23 marzo; **on Tuesday** martedì; **I saw her on Tuesday** l'ho vista martedì; **on Tuesdays** di *or* il martedì; **I go swimming on Tuesdays** vado in piscina il martedì; **every Tuesday** tutti i martedì; **every other Tuesday** ogni due martedì; **last/next Tuesday** martedì scorso/prossimo; **Tuesday next** martedì prossimo; **the following Tuesday** (*in past*) il martedì successivo; (*in future*) il martedì dopo; **the Tuesday before last** martedì di due settimane fa; **the Tuesday after next** non questo martedì ma il prossimo; **a week/fortnight** (*Brit*) **on Tuesday** *or* **Tuesday week/fortnight** (*Brit*) martedì fra una settimana/quindici giorni; **Tuesday morning/lunchtime/afternoon/evening** martedì mattina/all'ora di pranzo/pomeriggio/sera; **Tuesday night** martedì sera; (*overnight*) martedì notte; **the Tuesday film** (TV) il film del martedì; **Tuesday's newspaper** il giornale di martedì; **Shrove Tuesday** martedì grasso

tuft [tʌft] N (*of hair*) ciuffo, ciocca; (*of grass*) ciuffo

tug [tʌg] N **1** (*pull*) strattone *m*; **to give sth a (good) tug** dare uno strattone a qc **2** (*ship: also:* **tugboat**) rimorchiatore *m*
■ VT (*pull*) tirare con forza
■ VI: **to tug (at)** dare uno strattone (a)

tug-of-love [ˌtʌgəv'lʌv] N (*Brit fam*) contesa per la custodia dei figli; **tug-of-love children** *bambini coinvolti nella contesa per la custodia*

tug-of-war [ˌtʌgəv'wɔ:ʳ] N (*Sport*) tiro alla fune; (*fig*) braccio di ferro

tui·tion [tjʊ'ɪʃən] N (*Brit: lessons*) lezioni *fpl*; (*Am: fees*) tasse *fpl* scolastiche (*or* universitarie); **private tuition** lezioni private

tu·lip ['tju:lɪp] N tulipano

tulle [tju:l] N tulle *m*

tum·ble ['tʌmbl] N (*fall*) ruzzolone *m*, capitombolo; **to have a tumble** *or* **take a tumble** fare un ruzzolone *or* capitombolo
■ VI **1** (*fall*) ruzzolare, capitombolare, fare un capitombolo; (*somersault*) fare capriole; **to tumble downstairs** ruzzolare giù dalle scale; **he tumbled down the steps** ha fatto un capitombolo giù dalle scale **2** (*rush*): **to tumble into/out of bed** buttarsi a/cadere giù dal letto; **the children tumbled out of the room/the car** i bambini si sono precipitati fuori dalla stanza/dalla macchina **3** (*suddenly understand*): **to tumble to sth** (*Brit fam*) realizzare qc
■ VT far cadere
▸ **tumble over** VI + ADV ruzzolare

tumble·down ['tʌmblˌdaʊn] ADJ cadente, diroccato(-a)

tumble dryer N (*Brit*) asciugatrice *f*

tum·bler ['tʌmbləʳ] N (*glass*) bicchiere *m* (senza stelo)

tum·brel, tum·bril ['tʌmbrəl] N *carretta su cui si trasportavano i condannati alla ghigliottina durante la Rivoluzione francese*

tum·my ['tʌmɪ] N (*fam*) pancia

tummy·ache ['tʌmɪˌeɪk] N (*fam*) mal *m* di pancia

tumour, (*Am*) **tu·mor** ['tju:məʳ] N tumore *m*

tu·mult ['tju:mʌlt] N tumulto

tu·mul·tu·ous [tju:'mʌltjʊəs] ADJ tumultuoso(-a)

tuna ['tju:nə] N, PL INV (*also:* **tuna fish**) tonno

tun·dra ['tʌndrə] N tundra

◎ **tune** [tju:n] N **1** (*melody*) melodia, aria; **a familiar tune** una melodia familiare; **he gave us a tune** ci ha suonato qualcosa; **to change one's tune** (*fig*) cambiare tono; **to the tune of** (*fig: amount*) per la modesta somma di **2 in tune** (*instrument*) accordato(-a); (*person*) intonato(-a); **out of tune** (*instrument*) scordato(-a); (*person*) stonato(-a); **to sing in tune** cantare senza stonare; **to sing out of tune** stonare; **to play in tune** essere accordato(-a); **in tune with** (*fig*) in accordo con
■ VT (*Mus*) accordare; (*Aut: engine*) mettere a punto; (*Radio, TV*) regolare
■ VI (*Mus: also:* **tune up**) accordare lo strumento
▸ **tune in** VI + ADV (*Radio, TV*): **to tune in (to)** sintonizzarsi (su)

tune·ful ['tju:nfʊl] ADJ melodioso(-a)

tune·ful·ly ['tju:nfəlɪ] ADV melodiosamente

tune·less ['tju:nlɪs] ADJ poco melodioso(-a)

tune·less·ly ['tju:nlɪslɪ] ADV (*sing*) con voce stonata

tun·er ['tju:nəʳ] N **1** (*Radio: control*) sintonizzatore *m*, tuner *m inv* **2** (*also:* **piano tuner**) accordatore(-trice) di pianoforte

tuner amplifier N amplificatore *m* di sintonia

tung·sten ['tʌŋstən] N tungsteno

tu·nic ['tju:nɪk] N tunica

tun·ing ['tju:nɪŋ] N (*Mus*) accordatura; (*Aut*) messa a punto; (*Radio, TV*) sintonizzazione *f*

tuning fork N diapason *m inv*

Tu·nis ['tju:nɪs] N Tunisi *f*

Tu·ni·sia [tju:'nɪzɪə] N la Tunisia

Tu·ni·sian [tju:'nɪzɪən] ADJ, N tunisino(-a)

◎ **tun·nel** ['tʌnl] N (*gen*) galleria, tunnel *m inv*; (*Min*) galleria; **the Mont Blanc tunnel** il traforo del Monte Bianco
■ VT: **to tunnel one's way out** aprirsi un passaggio scavando; **to tunnel a passage** scavare un passaggio
■ VI scavare una galleria

tunnel vision N (*Med*) riduzione *f* del campo visivo; (*fig*) visuale *f* ristretta

tun·ny ['tʌnɪ] N (*Brit*) = **tuna**

tup·pence ['tʌpəns] N (*Brit fam*) = **twopence**

Tup·per·ware® ['tʌpəwɛəʳ] N ≈ frigoverre® *m inv*

tur·ban ['tɜ:bən] N turbante *m*

tur·bid ['tɜ:bɪd] ADJ (*liquid, fig: situation*) torbido(-a); (*smoke, fog*) denso(-a)

tur·bine ['tɜ:baɪn] N turbina

turbo ['tɜ:bəʊ] N turbo *m inv*

tur·bo... ['tɜ:bəʊ] PREF turbo...; **turbo(-charged) engine** motore *m* turbo *inv*

tur·bo·jet [ˌtɜ:bəʊ'dʒɛt] N turbogetto, turboreattore *m*

Tt

tur·bo·prop [ˌtɜːbəʊˈprɒp] N turboelica *m inv*
tur·bot [ˈtɜːbət] N, PL INV rombo gigante
tur·bu·lence [ˈtɜːbjʊləns] N turbolenza
tur·bu·lent [ˈtɜːbjʊlənt] ADJ turbolento(-a); *(sea)* agitato(-a)
turd [tɜːd] N *(fam!: faeces, person)* stronzo *(fam!)*
tu·reen [təˈriːn] N zuppiera
turf [tɜːf] N *(pl* **turfs** *or* **turves***)* *(grass)* tappeto erboso; *(one piece)* zolla erbosa; **the turf** *(horse racing)* l'ippica, le corse ippiche; *(racetrack)* l'ippodromo
■ VT *(also:* **turf over***)* ricoprire di zolle erbose
▸ **turf out** VT + ADV *(Brit fam)* buttar fuori
turf accountant N *(Brit)* allibratore *m*
turf war N guerra tra bande; *(fig)* guerra
tur·gid [ˈtɜːdʒɪd] ADJ *(liter: prose, speech)* ampolloso(-a), pomposo(-a)
Tu·rin [tjʊəˈrɪn] N Torino *f*
Turk [tɜːk] N turco(-a); **the Turks** i turchi
Tur·key [ˈtɜːkɪ] N la Turchia
tur·key [ˈtɜːkɪ] N tacchino
Turk·ish [ˈtɜːkɪʃ] ADJ turco(-a)
■ N *(language)* turco
Turkish bath N bagno turco
Turkish delight N *gelatine ricoperte di zucchero a velo*
tur·mer·ic [ˈtɜːmərɪk] N curcuma
tur·moil [ˈtɜːmɔɪl] N confusione *f*, tumulto; **to be in a turmoil** essere in uno stato di confusione
◎**turn** [tɜːn] N
1 *(rotation)* giro; **to give sth a turn** girare qc; **done to a turn** *(Culin)* cotto a puntino
2 *(change of direction: in road)* curva; **"no left turn"** "divieto di svolta a sinistra"; **to do a left turn** *(Aut)* girare a sinistra; **take the next left turn** prendi la prossima a sinistra; **a road full of twists and turns** una strada a zigzag *or* tutta a curve; **a sharp turn** una curva secca; **to take a turn in the park** fare un giro nel parco; **at the turn of the year/century** alla fine dell'anno/del secolo; **at every turn** *(fig)* a ogni piè sospinto; **things took a new turn** *(fig)* le cose hanno preso una nuova piega; **to take a turn for the better** *(situation, events)* volgere al meglio; *(patient, health)* migliorare; **to take a turn for the worse** *(situation, events)* volgere al peggio; *(patient, health)* peggiorare; **an odd turn of mind** una strana disposizione mentale; **turn of phrase** modo di esprimersi
3 *(Med)* attacco, crisi *f inv*; **he had a bad turn last night** la scorsa notte ha avuto una crisi *or* un peggioramento; **the news gave me quite a turn** *(fam)* la notizia mi ha fatto prendere un bello spavento
4 *(in series)* turno; **by turns** a turno; **in turn** a sua volta; **hot and cold by turns** ora caldo ora freddo; **and he, in turn, said ...** e lui, a sua volta, ha detto...; **they spoke in turn** hanno parlato a turno; **to take turns at (doing) sth** *or* **take it in turn(s) to do sth** fare qc a turno; **to take/wait/miss one's turn** fare/aspettare/saltare il proprio turno; **it's my turn** è il mio turno, tocca me; **whose turn is it?** a chi tocca?; **your turn will come** verrà anche il tuo momento; **to take turn and turn about** fare i turni; **to take turns at the wheel** fare i turni al volante; **to take a turn at the wheel** fare un turno al volante; **to speak out of turn** *(fig)* parlare a sproposito
5 *(performance)* numero; **to do a comedy turn** fare un numero comico
6 *(action)*: **to do sb a good turn** rendere un servizio a qn; **to do sb a bad turn** fare un brutto tiro a qn; **his good turn for the day** la sua buona azione quotidiana; **one good turn deserves another** una mano lava l'altra
■ VT
1 *(wheel, handle)* girare; *(: mechanically)* far girare; **turn the key in the lock** gira la chiave nella toppa
2 *(also:* **turn over***: record, mattress, steak)* girare, voltare, rivoltare; **to turn one's ankle** storcersi una caviglia; **it turns my stomach** mi fa rivoltare lo stomaco
3 *(direct: car, object)* voltare; *(: attention)* rivolgere; *(: gun, telescope)* puntare; **the fireman turned the hose on the building** il pompiere ha puntato l'idrante verso l'edificio; **to turn a gun on sb** puntare la pistola contro qn; **to turn one's back on sb** *(also fig)* voltare le spalle a qn; **to turn one's back on the past** tagliare i ponti col passato; **as soon as his back is turned** non appena volta le spalle; **power/success turned his head** il potere/il successo gli ha dato alla testa; **without turning a hair** senza battere ciglio; **to turn the other cheek** *(fig)* porgere l'altra guancia; **he turned his hand to cookery** si è dato alla cucina; **to turn the tables on sb** *(fig)* capovolgere la situazione a danno di qn; **they turned him against us** ce l'hanno messo contro
4 *(go past, round)* girare, voltare; **the car turned the corner** la macchina ha voltato l'angolo; **to have turned the corner** *(fig)* aver superato la fase critica; **he's turned 50** ha passato i 50; **it's turned four o'clock** sono le quattro passate
5 *(change)*: **to turn sb/sth into sth** trasformare qn/qc in qc; **to turn iron into gold** trasformare il ferro in oro; **to turn a book into a film** fare un film da un libro; **it turned him into a bitter man** lo ha reso un uomo pieno d'amarezza; **the shock turned her hair white** le sono venuti i capelli bianchi dallo shock; **the heat has turned the milk** il caldo ha fatto andare a male il latte
6 *(shape: wood, metal)* tornire; **to turn wood on a lathe** lavorare il legno con il tornio; **a well-turned phrase** un'espressione molto elegante; **a well-turned ankle** una caviglia ben tornita
■ VI
1 *(rotate)* girare; *(change direction: person)* girarsi, voltarsi; *(: vehicle)* girare, svoltare; *(: ship)* virare; *(: wind, tide, weather)* cambiare; *(reverse direction)* girarsi indietro; **my head is turning** *(fig)* mi gira la testa; **everything turns on his decision** *(fig)* tutto dipende dalla sua decisione; **to turn and go back** girare *or* girarsi e tornare indietro; **to turn left/right** *(Aut)* girare a sinistra/destra; **turn right at the lights** al semaforo gira a destra; **the car turned into a lane** la macchina ha svoltato in una stradina; **to wait for the weather to turn** aspettare che il tempo cambi; **he turned to me and smiled** si è girato verso di me e mi ha sorriso; **to turn to sb for help** rivolgersi a qn per un aiuto; **she has no-one to turn to** non ha nessuno cui potersi rivolgere; **he turned to politics** si è messo in politica, si è dato alla politica; **he turned to drink** si è dato al bere; **I don't know which way to turn** *(fig)* non so dove sbattere la testa; **the conversation turned to religion** la conversazione passò alla religione
2 *(become)* diventare; *(change)*: **to turn into sth** trasformarsi in qc, cambiare in qc; **the holiday turned into a nightmare** la vacanza si è trasformata in un incubo; **the milk has turned** il latte è andato a male; **to turn red** arrossire; **to turn nasty** diventare cattivo(-a); **when he's drunk he turns nasty** quando è ubriaco diventa cattivo; **he turned into a cynic** è

diventato cinico; **they turned communist** sono diventati comunisti; **a singer turned songwriter** un cantante divenuto autore

▸ **turn about, turn around** VI + ADV girarsi indietro

▸ **turn against** VI + PREP: **to turn against sb** mettersi contro qn

▸ **turn aside** VI + ADV girarsi *or* voltarsi dall'altra parte

▸ **turn away** VI + ADV girarsi *or* voltarsi dall'altra parte; **he turned away from the awful sight** ha distolto lo sguardo da quel tremendo spettacolo

■ VT + ADV

1 (*move: eyes*) distogliere; (*: head*) girare dall'altra parte; (*: gun*) spostare

2 (*reject: person*) mandar via; (*: business*) rifiutare

▸ **turn back** VI + ADV

1 (*on journey*) ritornare, tornare indietro; **we turned back** siamo tornati indietro

2 (*in book*) ritornare

■ VT + ADV

1 (*fold: bedclothes*) ripiegare

2 (*send back*) far tornare indietro; **to turn back the clock 20 years** ritornare indietro di 20 anni; **it's no use trying to turn the clock back** è inutile tornare sui propri passi

▸ **turn down** VT + ADV

1 (*fold: bedclothes, collar, page*) ripiegare

2 (*reduce: gas, heat, volume*) abbassare; **shall I turn the heating down?** abbasso il riscaldamento?

3 (*refuse: offer*) rifiutare; (*candidate*) scartare; **he turned down the offer** ha rifiutato l'offerta

▸ **turn in** VI + ADV

1 **to turn in (to)** girare (in); **she turned in at the house** ha girato per entrare nella casa

2 (*fam: go to bed*) andare a letto

■ VT + ADV

1 (*hand over*) consegnare; **to turn sb in** consegnare qn alla polizia

2 (*fold*) voltare in dentro

▸ **turn off** VI + ADV

1 (*from road*) girare, voltare

2 (*appliance, machine*) spegnersi

■ VT + ADV

1 (*light, radio, machine*) spegnere; (*tap*) chiudere; **I'll turn off the radio** spegnerò la radio; **you haven't turned off the tap** non hai chiuso il rubinetto

2 (*fam: person: also sexually*) fare schifo a

▸ **turn on** VI + ADV (*appliance*) accendersi

■ VT + ADV

1 (*light, radio, electricity*) accendere; (*tap*) aprire; (*engine*) avviare; **shall I turn on the light?** accendo la luce?; **she turned on the tap** ha aperto il rubinetto

2 (*fam: person: also sexually*) eccitare

▸ **turn out** VI + ADV

1 (*appear, attend: troops, doctor*) presentarsi; **to turn out for a meeting** presentarsi a un'assemblea

2 (*prove to be*) rivelarsi; **it turned out to be true/a mistake** è risultato essere vero/un errore; **things will turn out all right** andrà tutto bene; **how did the cake turn out?** come è venuta la torta?; **it turned out that ...** si è scoperto che...; **it turned out that she was right** è risultato che aveva ragione lei

■ VT + ADV

1 (*light, appliance, gas*) chiudere, spegnere

2 (*produce: goods*) produrre; (*: novel, good pupils*) creare; **to be well turned out** (*fig*) essere ben vestito(-a)

3 (*empty: pockets*) vuotare; (*tip out: cake*) capovolgere

4 (*clean out: room*) dare una bella pulita a

5 (*expel: tenant, employee*) mandar via

6 (*guard, police*) far uscire

▸ **turn over** VI + ADV

1 (*person*) girarsi; (*car*) capovolgersi; (*engine*) girare; **my stomach turned over** mi si è rivoltato lo stomaco; **she turned over onto her back** si è girata sulla schiena

2 (*in reading*) girare *or* voltare la pagina; (*in letter*): **please turn over** segue

■ VT + ADV

1 (*page, mattress, card*) girare; (*patient*) far girare; **to turn sth over in one's mind** riflettere a lungo *or* rimurginare su qualcosa

2 (*hand over: object, person*) consegnare

▸ **turn round** VI + ADV

1 (*person*) girarsi; (*vehicle*) girare

2 (*rotate*) girare; **to turn round and round** girare su se stesso(-a)

■ VT + ADV girare

▸ **turn up** VI + ADV

1 (*lost object*) saltar fuori; (*person*) arrivare, presentarsi; **something will turn up** salterà fuori qualcosa; **the painting turned up in an old house in Devon** il dipinto è saltato fuori in una vecchia casa nel Devon; **we waited but she didn't turn up** abbiamo aspettato ma non si è fatta vedere

2 (*point towards*) essere rivolto(-a) all'insù; **his nose turns up** ha il naso all'insù

■ VT + ADV

1 (*collar, sleeve, hem*) alzare, tirare su; **to turn up one's nose at sth** (*fig*) arricciare il naso davanti a qc

2 (*heat, gas, radio*) alzare; **can you turn up the volume?** puoi alzare il volume?

3 (*find*) scoprire

turn·about ['tɜːnəˌbaʊt], **turn·around** ['tɜːnəˌraʊnd] N (*fig*) voltafaccia *m inv*, dietrofront *m inv*

turn·coat ['tɜːnˌkəʊt] N voltagabbana *m/f inv*

◎ **turned-out** [ˌtɜːnd'aʊt] ADJ: **well** *or* **smartly turned-out** ben vestito(-a)

turned-up [ˌtɜːnd'ʌp] ADJ (*nose*) all'insù

turn·ing ['tɜːnɪŋ] N (*side road*) strada laterale; (*fork*) biforcazione *f*; (*bend*) curva; **the first turning on the right** la prima a destra; **we took the wrong turning** abbiamo sbagliato strada

turning circle, (*Am*) **turning radius** N diametro di sterzata

turning point N (*fig*) svolta decisiva; (*Math*) punto di ondulazione

tur·nip ['tɜːnɪp] N rapa

turn·off ['tɜːnˌɒf] N (*in road*) strada laterale

turn·out ['tɜːnˌaʊt] N 1 (*attendance*) presenza, affluenza; **there was a poor turnout** la partecipazione è stata molto scarsa 2 (*clean*) ripulita

turn·over ['tɜːnˌəʊvəʳ] N 1 (*Comm: amount of money*) giro d'affari; (*: of goods*) smercio; **an annual turnover of ten million pounds** un giro d'affari annuo di dieci milioni di sterline; **these goods have a rapid turnover** di questi prodotti c'è grande smercio; **there is a extremely high turnover in staff** c'è un ricambio molto rapido di personale 2 (*Culin*): **apple turnover** ≈ sfogliatella alle mele

turn·pike ['tɜːnˌpaɪk] N (*Am Aut*) autostrada (a pagamento)

turn·stile ['tɜːnˌstaɪl] N cancelletto girevole, tornella

turn·table ['tɜːnˌteɪbl] N (*of record player*) piatto; (*for trains*) piattaforma girevole

turn-up ['tɜːnˌʌp] N 1 (*Brit: of trousers*) risvolto 2 **that**

Tt

was a turn-up for the books (*Brit fam*) è stato un colpo di scena

tur·pen·tine ['tɜ:pən,taɪn] N trementina; **turpentine substitute** acquaragia

tur·pi·tude ['tɜ:pɪ,tju:d] N (*frm*) turpitudine *f*

turps [tɜ:ps] N ABBR (*Brit fam*) = **turpentine**

tur·quoise ['tɜ:kwɔɪz] N (*stone, colour*) turchese *m*
■ ADJ (*ring, earrings*) di turchesi; (*colour*) (color) turchese *inv*

tur·ret ['tʌrɪt] N torretta

tur·tle ['tɜ:tl] N testuggine *f*, tartaruga acquatica; **to turn turtle** (*boat*) scuffiare
■ ADJ (*soup*) di tartaruga

turtle·dove ['tɜ:tl,dʌv] N tortora

turtle·neck ['tɜ:tl,nɛk] N (*also:* **turtleneck sweater**) maglione *m* con il collo alto

Tus·can ['tʌskən] ADJ toscano(-a)
■ N (*person*) toscano(-a); (*dialect*) toscano

Tus·ca·ny ['tʌskənɪ] N la Toscana

tusk [tʌsk] N zanna

tus·sle ['tʌsl] N baruffa, mischia; **to have a tussle with** fare baruffa con; **a tussle with the goalie** uno scontro con il portiere; **a legal tussle** una battaglia legale
■ VI: **to tussle (with sb for sth)** far baruffa (con qn per qc)

tus·sock ['tʌsək] N ciuffo d'erba

tut [tʌt] (*also:* **tut-tut**) EXCL non si fa così!
■ VI *far schioccare la lingua in segno di disapprovazione*

tu·telage ['tju:tɪlɪdʒ] N (*frm*) tutela; **under sb's tutelage** sotto la tutela di qn

tu·tor ['tju:təʳ] N (*private teacher*) insegnante *m/f* privato(-a); (*living with family*) precettore *m*; (*Brit Univ*) docente *m/f* (*responsabile di un gruppo*)
■ VT: **to tutor sb in Italian** dare lezioni private d'italiano a qn

tu·to·rial [tju:'tɔ:rɪəl] N (*Univ*) seminario, esercitazione *f* (*di un gruppo limitato*)

tutu ['tu:tu:] N tutù *m inv*

tux [tʌks] N ABBR (*fam*) smoking *m inv*

tux·edo [tʌk'si:dəʊ] N (*Am*) smoking *m inv*

◎ **TV** [,ti:'vi:] N ABBR (= **television**) TV *f inv*, tivù *f inv*

TV dinner N *pasto veloce da mangiare davanti alla TV*

twad·dle ['twɒdl] N (*fam*) scemenze *fpl*

twain [tweɪn] NPL (*old, poet*): **the twain** i (*or* le) due; **and never the twain shall meet** e mai i (*or* le) due si incontreranno

twang [twæŋ] N (*of wire, bow*) suono acuto; (*of instrument*) suono vibrante; (*of voice*) accento nasale; **to speak with a twang** parlare con voce nasale
■ VT (*guitar*) pizzicare le corde di
■ VI vibrare

tweak [twi:k] N: **to give sb's nose/ear a tweak** dare un pizzicotto sul naso/una tirata d'orecchie a qn
■ VT (*nose*) pizzicare; (*ear, hair*) tirare

twee [twi:] ADJ (*Brit fam pej: person*) affettato(-a); (*: decor*) lezioso(-a)

tweed [twi:d] N (*cloth*) tweed *m*; **tweeds** NPL (*suit*) abito di tweed

tweet [twi:t] VI cinguettare

tweet·er ['twi:təʳ] N (*Stereo*) tweeter *m inv*

twee·zers ['twi:zəz] NPL pinzette *fpl*

◎ **twelfth** [twɛlfθ] ADJ dodicesimo(-a); **the twelfth floor** il dodicesimo piano; **the twelfth of August** il dodici agosto
■ N (*in series*) dodicesimo(-a); (*fraction*) dodicesimo; *for usage see* **fifth**

Twelfth Night N la notte dell'Epifania

◎ **twelve** [twɛlv] ADJ, N dodici (*m*) *inv*; **at twelve** alle dodici, a mezzogiorno; (*midnight*) a mezzanotte; **she's twelve** ha dodici anni; *for usage see* **five**

◎ **twen·ti·eth** ['twɛntɪɪθ] ADJ ventesimo(-a); **the twentieth floor** il ventesimo piano; **the twentieth of May** il venti maggio
■ N (*in series*) ventesimo(-a); (*fraction*) ventesimo; *for usage see* **fifth**

◎ **twen·ty** ['twɛntɪ] ADJ venti *inv*
■ N venti *m inv*; **he's twenty** ha vent'anni; *for usage see* **fifty**

twenty-first [,twɛntɪ'fɜ:st] N (*Brit fam: birthday*) il ventunesimo compleanno; (*: birthday party*): **I'm having my twenty-first on Saturday** sabato faccio una festa per il mio ventunesimo compleanno

twenty-four seven, 24-7 [,twɛntɪ,fɔ:'sɛvn] ADV (*fam*) tutti i giorni, 24 ore al giorno

twerp [twɜ:p] N (*fam*) idiota *m/f*

◎ **twice** [twaɪs] ADV due volte; **I tried twice** ho provato due volte; **twice as much** *or* **twice as many** il doppio, due volte tanto; **I have twice as many cigarettes as you** ho il doppio delle sigarette che hai tu; **there's twice as much wine here as beer** qui c'è vino in quantità due volte superiori alla birra; **twice a week** due volte alla settimana; **she is twice your age** ha il doppio dei tuoi anni; **twice as big** due volte più grande

twid·dle ['twɪdl] VT, VI: **to twiddle (with) sth** giocherellare con qc; **he was twiddling with the controls** stava giocherellando con i comandi; **to twiddle one's thumbs** (*fig*) girarsi i pollici

twig[1] [twɪg] N ramoscello

twig[2] [twɪg] VT, VI (*fam*) capire

twi·light ['twaɪ,laɪt] N (*evening, also fig*) crepuscolo; (*morning*) alba; **at twilight** al crepuscolo, all'alba; **in the twilight** nella penombra

twi·lit ['twaɪ,lɪt] ADJ **1** (*sky*) crepuscolare; (*place*) tetro(-a) **2** (*fig: shadowy*) nebuloso(-a)

twill [twɪl] N (*fabric*) twill *m*, spigato

◎ **twin** [twɪn] ADJ gemello(-a); **my twin brother** mio fratello gemello; **twin lead** (*Elec*) piattina
■ N gemello(-a)
■ VT: **to twin one town with another** fare il gemellaggio di una città con un'altra

twin-bedded [,twɪn'bɛdɪd] ADJ (*room*) a due letti

twin beds NPL letti *mpl* gemelli

twin-carburettor [,twɪnkɑ:bjʊ'rɛtəʳ] ADJ a doppio carburatore

twine [twaɪn] N cordicella, spago
■ VT intrecciare
■ VI (*plant*) attorcigliarsi

twin-engined [,twɪn'ɛndʒɪnd] ADJ a due motori; **twin-engined aircraft** bimotore *m*

twinge [twɪndʒ] N (*of pain*) fitta; **a twinge in my back** una fitta alla schiena; **a twinge of regret/sadness/conscience** una punta di rimpianto/tristezza/rimorso; **I've been having twinges of conscience** ho i rimorsi di coscienza

twin·kle ['twɪŋkl] N scintillio; **he had a twinkle in his eye** gli brillavano gli occhi
■ VI scintillare; (*eyes*) brillare

twin·kling ['twɪŋklɪŋ] N scintillio; **in the twinkling of an eye** in un batter d'occhio

twin room N (*also:* **twin-bedded room**) stanza a due letti

twin-set ['twɪn,sɛt] N (*Brit*) completo di golf e cardigan

twin town N città *f inv* gemellata
twirl [twɜ:l] N (*of body*) piroetta; (*in writing*) ghirigoro
■ VT (*also:* **twirl round**) far roteare; (: *knob*) far girare; (: *moustache*) arricciare
■ VI (*also:* **twirl round**) volteggiare, roteare
◎ **twist** [twɪst] N **1** (*in wire, flex*) piega; (*of tobacco*) treccia; (*of paper*) cartoccio; (*of lemon*) fettina **2** (*twisting action*) torsione *f*; **to give sth a twist** far girare qc; **to give one's ankle/wrist a twist** *or* **twist one's ankle/wrist** (*Med*) slogarsi la caviglia/il polso; **with a quick twist of the wrist** con un rapido movimento del polso **3** (*bend*) svolta, piega; (*fig: in story*) sviluppo imprevisto; **a road full of twists and turns** una strada a zigzag *or* tutta a curve; **the plot has an unexpected twist** la trama ha uno sviluppo inatteso; **to go round the twist** (*Brit fam*) ammattire, impazzire **4** **the twist** (*dance*) il twist; **to do the twist** ballare il twist
■ VT (*wrench out of shape*) far piegare, deformare; (*fig: sense, words*) travisare, distorcere; (*turn*) girare; (*unscrew*) svitare; (*weave: also:* **twist together**) intrecciare; (*roll around*) arrotolare; **you're twisting my words** stai travisando le mie parole; **she twisted her head sideways** ha girato la testa di lato; **to twist (round)** (*coil*) attorcigliare (intorno a); **his face was twisted with pain** il suo volto era contratto dal dolore; **to twist one's ankle/neck/wrist** (*Med*) slogarsi la caviglia/il collo/il polso; **to twist sb's arm** (*fig*) forzare qn
■ VI **1** (*rope*) attorcigliarsi; (*road*) snodarsi; **the road twisted and turned** la strada procedeva a zigzag **2** (*dance*) ballare il twist
▸ **twist off** VT + ADV svitare
▸ **twist round** VI + ADV (*person*) girarsi, voltarsi; (*thing*) arrotolarsi; (*road*) serpeggiare
■ VT + ADV (*words*) travisare
■ VT + PREP: **to twist sth round sth** mettere qc intorno a qc, avvolgere qc in qc; **to twist sb round one's little finger** (*fam*) rigirare qn
twist·ed ['twɪstɪd] ADJ (*wire, rope*) attorcigliato(-a); (*ankle, wrist*) slogato(-a); (*fig: logic, mind*) contorto(-a); **the twisted metal of the car** le lamiere contorte della macchina
twist·er ['twɪstə^r] N (*fam*) **1** (*cheat*) imbroglione(-a) **2** (*Am: tornado*) tornado
twist·ing ['twɪstɪŋ] ADJ (*path*) serpeggiante
■ N (*of body*) torsioni *fpl*; (*of meaning*) travisamento
twit [twɪt] N (*fam*) cretino(-a)
twitch [twɪtʃ] N (*slight pull*) tiratina; (*nervous*) tic *m inv*; **to give sth a twitch** dare una tiratina a qc
■ VI (*hands, face, muscles*) contrarsi; (*person: in particular situation*) agitarsi; (: *habitually*) avere un tic; (*tail, ears*) drizzarsi; (*nose*) muoversi
■ VT (*rope, sleeve*) tirare; **he twitched the letter out of her hand** le sfilò la lettera dalle mani; **the dog twitched its ears** il cane drizzò le orecchie; **the rabbit twitched its nose** il coniglio arricciò il naso
twitchy ['twɪtʃɪ] ADJ (*comp* **-ier**, *superl* **-iest**) (*fam*) nervosetto(-a)
twit·ter ['twɪtə^r] N (*of bird*) cinguettio; **to be all of a twitter** *or* **be in a twitter** (*fam*) essere in grande agitazione
■ VI (*bird*) cinguettare; (*person*) cicalare
◎ **two** [tu:] ADJ due *inv*
■ N due *m inv*; **she's two** ha due anni; **to break sth in two** spezzare qc in due; **two by two** *or* **in twos** a due a due; **to arrive in twos and threes** arrivare alla spicciolata; **to put two and two together** (*fig*) fare uno più uno, trarre le conclusioni; **that makes two of us** e così siamo in due; *for usage see* **five**
two-bit ['tu:,bɪt] ADJ (*esp Am fam pej*) da quattro soldi
two-dimensional [,tu:dɪ'mɛnʃənəl] ADJ **1** (*Geom*) bidimensionale **2** (*pej: superficial: characters*) senza spessore
two-door [,tu:'dɔ:^r] ADJ (*car*) a due porte
two-edged [,tu:'ɛdʒd] ADJ (*also fig*) a doppio taglio
two-faced [,tu:'feɪst] ADJ (*fig pej: person*) doppio(-a), falso(-a)
two·fer ['tu:fə^r] N (*fam*): **on a twofer** due al prezzo di uno
two·fold ['tu:,fəʊld] ADV: **to increase twofold** aumentare del doppio
■ ADJ (*increase*) doppio(-a); (*reply*) in due punti; **the purpose of the visit is twofold** lo scopo della nostra visita è duplice
two-handed [,tu:'hændɪd] ADJ (*Tennis*): **two-handed grip** impugnatura a due mani
two-horse ['tu:,hɔ:s] ADJ: **a two-horse race/contest** una gara con due possibili vincitori
two-legged [,tu:'lɛgd] ADJ a due gambe, bipede
two-party ['tu:,pɑ:tɪ] ADJ (*Pol*) bipartitico(-a)
two·pence ['tʌpəns] N (*Brit: amount*) due penny; (: *coin*) moneta da due penny
two-phase ['tu:,feɪz] ADJ (*Elec*) bifase
two-piece ['tu:,pi:s] ADJ a due pezzi
■ N (*also:* **two-piece suit**) due pezzi *m inv*; (*also:* **two-piece swimsuit**) (costume *m* da bagno a) due pezzi *m inv*
two-ply ['tu:,plaɪ] ADJ (*wool*) a due capi
two-seater [,tu:'si:tə^r] N (*car*) macchina a due posti; (*plane*) biposto
two·some ['tu:səm] N (*people*) coppia; **to go out in a twosome** uscire in coppia
two-stroke ['tu:,strəʊk] N (*engine*) due tempi *m inv*
■ ADJ a due tempi
two-time ['tu:,taɪm] VT (*fam*) fare le corna a
two-tone ['tu:,təʊn] ADJ (*colour*) bicolore
two-way ['tu:,weɪ] ADJ (*street*) a doppio senso; (*traffic*) a doppio senso di circolazione; **two-way radio** radio *f inv* ricetrasmittente
two-wheeler [,tu:'wi:lə^r] N bicicletta
TX ABBR (*Am Post*) = **Texas**
ty·coon [taɪ'ku:n] N: **(business) tycoon** magnate *m*
tym·pa·num ['tɪmpənəm] N (*Anat, Archit*) timpano
◎ **type** [taɪp] N **1** (*gen, Bio*) tipo; (*sort*) genere *m*, tipo; (*model*) modello; (*make: of tea, machine*) marca; **what type do you want?** che tipo vuole?; **what type of camera have you got?** che tipo di macchina fotografica hai?; **what type of person is he?** che tipo è?; **he's not my type** non è il mio tipo; **it's my type of film** è il mio genere di film; **he's a pleasant type** è un tipo piacevole **2** (*Typ: one letter*) carattere *m* (tipografico); (: *letters collectively*) caratteri (tipografici), tipi *mpl*; **in bold/italic type** in grassetto/corsivo
■ VT **1** (*also:* **type out**, **type up**: *letter*) battere (a macchina), dattilografare **2** (*disease*) classificare
■ VI dattilografare, battere a macchina
type·cast ['taɪp,kɑ:st] VT (*pt, pp* **typecast**) (*Cine, Theatre*) fare sempre fare la stessa parte a
type-cast ['taɪp,kɑ:st] ADJ (*actor*) a ruolo fisso
type·face ['taɪp,feɪs] N carattere *m* (tipografico)
type·script ['taɪp,skrɪpt] N dattiloscritto
type·set ['taɪp,sɛt] VT comporre
▹ www.historybuff.com/library/reftype.html
type·set·ter ['taɪp,sɛtə^r] N compositore *m*

Tt

type·set·ting ['taɪp,sɛtɪŋ] N composizione *f*
type·writ·er ['taɪp,raɪtəʳ] N macchina da scrivere
type·writ·ing ['taɪp,raɪtɪŋ] N dattilografia
type·writ·ten ['taɪp,rɪtn] ADJ dattiloscritto(-a), battuto(-a) a macchina
ty·phoid ['taɪfɔɪd] N febbre *f* tifoidea
ty·phoon [taɪ'fu:n] N tifone *m*
ty·phus ['taɪfəs] N tifo
◎**typi·cal** ['tɪpɪkəl] ADJ tipico(-a); **a typical case/ example** un caso/esempio tipico; **the typical Spaniard** il tipico spagnolo, lo spagnolo tipo; **(isn't that just) typical!** tipico!; **that's typical of her!** questo è tipico di lei!
typi·cal·ly ['tɪpɪkəlɪ] ADV tipicamente; **typically, he arrived home late** come al solito è arrivato a casa tardi
typi·fy ['tɪpɪ,faɪ] VT (*thing*) essere tipico(-a) di, caratterizzare; (*person*) impersonare
typ·ing ['taɪpɪŋ] N (*skill*) dattilografia; **have you finished that typing?** hai finito quelle cose che dovevi battere a macchina?
■ ADJ (*lesson*) di dattilografia; (*paper*) per macchina da scrivere
typing pool N ufficio *m* dattilografia *inv*
typ·ist ['taɪpɪst] N dattilografo(-a)
typo ['taɪpəʊ] N ABBR (*fam:* = **typographical error**) refuso
ty·pog·ra·pher [taɪ'pɒgrəfəʳ] N tipografo(-a)
ty·po·graph·ical [,taɪpə'græfɪkəl], **ty·po·graph·ic** [,taɪpə'græfɪk] ADJ tipografico(-a)
ty·pog·ra·phy [taɪ'pɒgrəfɪ] N tipografia
ty·pol·ogy [taɪ'pɒlədʒɪ] N tipologia
ty·ran·nical [tɪ'rænɪkəl], **ty·ran·nic** [tɪ'rænɪk] ADJ tirannico(-a)
ty·ran·ni·cal·ly [tɪ'rænɪkəlɪ] ADV tirannicamente
tyr·an·nize ['tɪrə,naɪz] VT tiranneggiare
■ VI: **to tyrannize over sb** tiranneggiare qn
tyr·an·ny ['tɪrənɪ] N tirannia
ty·rant ['taɪərənt] N tiranno
tyre, (*Am*) **tire** ['taɪəʳ] N (*Aut*) gomma, pneumatico
tyre gauge, (*Am*) **tire gauge** N manometro (per pneumatici)
tyre pressure, (*Am*) **tire pressure** N pressione *f* (dei pneumatici)
tyro, tiro ['taɪrəʊ] N (*Brit old frm*) principiante *m/f*
Ty·rol [tɪ'rəʊl] N: **the Tyrol** il Tirolo
Ty·ro·lean [,tɪrəʊ'li:ən], **Tyro·lese** [,tɪrə'li:z] ADJ, N tirolese (*m/f*)
Tyrrhenian Sea [tɪ,ri:nɪən'si:] N: **the Tyrrhenian Sea** il mar Tirreno
tzar [zɑ:ʳ] N = **tsar**
tzar·ist ['zɑ:rɪst] ADJ, N zarista *m/f*
tzet·ze fly ['tsɛtsɪ,flaɪ] N = **tsetse fly**

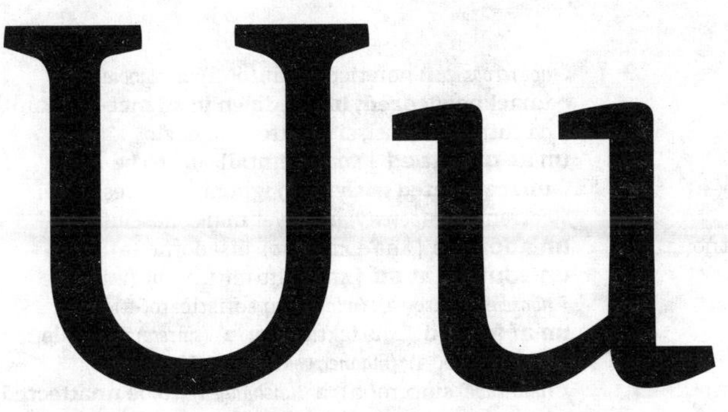

U, u [juː] N (*letter*) U, u *f or m inv*; **U for Uncle** ≈ U come Udine

U [juː] N ABBR (*Brit Cine*: = **universal**) per tutti

UAE [ˌjuːeɪ'iː] N ABBR (= **United Arab Emirates**) EAU (= *Emirati Arabi Uniti*)

UAW [ˌjuːeɪ'dʌbljuː] N ABBR (*Am*: = **United Automobile Workers**) *sindacato dei lavoratori del settore automobilistico*

UB40 [ˌjuːbiː'fɔːtɪ] N ABBR (*Brit*: = **unemployment benefit form 40**) *modulo per la richiesta del sussidio di disoccupazione*

U-bend ['juːˌbɛnd] N (*in pipe*) gomito

ubiqui·tous [juː'bɪkwɪtəs] ADJ (*frm*) onnipresente

ubiquity [juː'bɪkwɪtɪ] N (*frm*) onnipresenza, ubiquità

U-boat ['juːˌbəʊt] N sottomarino tedesco

UCAS ['juːkæs] N ABBR (*Brit*: = **Universities and Colleges Admissions Service**) *organo centrale di coordinamento per le ammissioni all'Università*
▷ www.ucas.co.uk

UDA [ˌjuːdiː'eɪ] N ABBR (*Brit*: = **Ulster Defence Association**) *organizzazione paramilitare protestante dell'Irlanda del Nord*

UDC [ˌjuːdiː'siː] N ABBR (*Brit*: = **Urban District Council**) *fino al 1974, consiglio amministrativo di distretto urbano*

ud·der ['ʌdəʳ] N mammella (*di animale*)

UDI [ˌjuːdiː'aɪ] ABBR (*Brit Pol*) = *unilateral declaration of independence*

UDR [ˌjuːdiː'ɑːʳ] N ABBR (*Brit*: = **Ulster Defence Regiment**) *reggimento dell'esercito britannico in Irlanda del Nord*

UEFA [juː'eɪfə] N ABBR (= **Union of European Football Associations**) UEFA *f*

UFO [ˌjuːɛf'əʊ] N ABBR (= **unidentified flying object**) ufo *m inv*

Ugan·da [juː'gændə] N Uganda

Ugan·dan [juː'gændən] ADJ, N ugandese (*m/f*)

UGC [ˌjuːdʒiː'siː] N ABBR (*Brit*: = **University Grants Committee**) *organo che autorizza sovvenzioni alle università*

ugh [ɜːh] EXCL puah!

ug·li·ness ['ʌglɪnɪs] N bruttezza

ugly ['ʌglɪ] ADJ (*comp* **-ier**, *superl* **-iest**) **1** (*not pretty*) brutto(-a); **as ugly as sin** brutto(-a) come la fame **2** (*nasty*: *situation, incident*) brutto(-a); (: *rumour*) inquietante; (: *mood, look*) minaccioso(-a); (: *crime, sight*) ripugnante; (: *vice*) osceno(-a); **an ugly customer** (*fam*) un brutto tipo

ugly duckling N brutto anatroccolo

UHF [ˌjuːeɪtʃ'ɛf] N ABBR (= **ultra-high frequency**) UHF *f*

UHT [ˌjuːeɪtʃ'tiː] ADJ ABBR (= *ultra-heat treated*): **UHT milk** latte *m* UHT *inv*

UK [juː'keɪ] N ABBR (= **United Kingdom**): **the UK** il Regno Unito

Ukraine [juː'kreɪn] N Ucraina

Ukrainian [juː'kreɪnɪən] ADJ ucraino(-a)
■ N ucraino(-a); (*language*) ucraino

ul·cer ['ʌlsəʳ] N (*gen*) ulcera, ulcerazione *f*; **(stomach) ulcer** ulcera gastrica, ulcera allo stomaco; **mouth ulcer** afta

ul·cer·at·ed ['ʌlsəˌreɪtɪd] ADJ ulcerato(-a)

ulna ['ʌlnə] N (*Anat*) ulna

Ul·ster ['ʌlstəʳ] N Ulster *m*

ul·te·ri·or [ʌl'tɪərɪəʳ] ADJ recondito(-a); **ulterior motive** secondo fine *m*

> DID YOU KNOW ...?
> **ulterior** is not translated by the Italian word ***ulteriore***

ul·ti·ma·ta [ˌʌltɪ'meɪtə] (*frm*) NPL *of* **ultimatum**

◎**ul·ti·mate** ['ʌltɪmɪt] ADJ **1** (*final*: *result, outcome*) finale; (: *conclusion*) definitivo(-a); (: *destination*) ultimo(-a) **2** (*greatest*: *insult*) massimo(-a); (: *authority*) supremo(-a), massimo(-a); **the ultimate deterrent** (*Mil*) il mezzo di dissuasione risolutivo; **the ultimate challenge** la sfida suprema **3** (*principle, cause*) fondamentale
■ N: **the ultimate in luxury** il non plus ultra del lusso

◎**ul·ti·mate·ly** ['ʌltɪmɪtlɪ] ADV (*in the end, eventually*) in fin dei conti, in definitiva; (*in the last analysis*) in ultima analisi; (*at last*) alla fine; **ultimately, it's your decision** in fin dei conti, la decisione è tua; **to be ultimately responsible for sth** dover rispondere per primi di qc

> DID YOU KNOW ...?
> **ultimately** is not translated by the Italian word ***ultimamente***

ul·ti·ma·tum [ˌʌltɪ'meɪtəm] N (*pl* **ultimatums** *or* **ultimata** [ˌʌltɪ'meɪtə]) (*Mil, fig*) ultimatum *m inv*; **to**

issue an ultimatum to dare l'ultimatum a
ultra... ['ʌltrə] PREF ultra...
ultra·con·ser·va·tive [ˌʌltrəkən'sɜːvətɪv] ADJ ultraconservatore(-trice), reazionario(-a)
ultra·ma·rine [ˌʌltrəmə'riːn] ADJ oltremarino(-a)
■ N oltremarino
ultra·mod·ern [ˌʌltrə'mɒdən] ADJ ultramoderno(-a)
ultra·sen·si·tive [ˌʌltrə'sɛnsɪtɪv] ADJ *(equipment)* ultrasensibile; *(skin, issue)* delicatissimo(-a)
ultra·son·ic [ˌʌltrə'sɒnɪk] ADJ ultrasonico(-a)
ultra·sound [ˌʌltrə'saʊnd] N *(Med)* ecografia
ultra·vio·let [ˌʌltrə'vaɪəlɪt] ADJ ultravioletto(-a)
Ulysses ['juːlɪˌsiːz] N Ulisse *m*
um·ber ['ʌmbə^r] *(frm)* N terra di Siena
■ ADJ color terra di Siena
um·bili·cal [ˌʌmbɪ'laɪkəl] ADJ ombelicale
umbilical cord N cordone *m* ombelicale
um·brage ['ʌmbrɪdʒ] N: **to take umbrage (at sth)** adombrarsi (a *or* per qc), risentirsi (di *or* per qc)
um·brel·la [ʌm'brɛlə] N ombrello; **under the umbrella of** *(fig)* sotto l'egida di; **an umbrella organization** *un'organizzazione a cui fanno capo diverse altre*
umbrella pine N pino domestico
umbrella stand N portaombrelli *m inv*
um·laut ['umlaʊt] N *(Ling)* umlaut *m inv*
um·pire ['ʌmpaɪə^r] N arbitro
■ VI arbitrare
■ VT arbitrare
ump·teen ['ʌmptiːn] ADJ *(fam)* non so quanti(-e), innumerevole; **umpteen times** centomila volte *fpl*, non so quante volte
ump·teenth ['ʌmptiːnθ] ADJ *(fam)* ennesimo(-a); **for the umpteenth time** per l'ennesima volta
UMW [ˌjuːɛm'dʌbljuː] N ABBR (= **United Mineworkers of America**) *sindacato dei minatori americani*
◎ **UN** [ˌjuː'ɛn] N ABBR = **United Nations; the UN** le Nazioni Unite, l'ONU *f*
un·abashed [ˌʌnə'bæʃt] ADJ imperterrito(-a)
un·abat·ed [ˌʌnə'beɪtɪd] ADJ *(energy, enthusiasm)* costante, inesauribile; **to be** *or* **continue unabated** *(storm, wind)* non accennare a diminuire; *(fighting)* senza tregua
◎ **un·able** [ʌn'eɪbl] ADJ: **to be unable to do sth** *(not to know how to)* non saper fare qc, non essere capace di fare qc; *(not to have it in one's power to)* non poter fare qc, essere nell'impossibilità di fare qc; **unfortunately, he was unable to come** purtroppo non è potuto venire
un·abridged [ˌʌnə'brɪdʒd] ADJ integrale
un·ac·cep·table [ˌʌnək'sɛptəbl] ADJ *(proposal, behaviour)* inaccettabile; *(price)* impossibile; **it's unacceptable that** è inammissibile che + *sub*
un·ac·com·pa·nied [ˌʌnə'kʌmpənɪd] ADJ *(child, person)* non accompagnato(-a); *(luggage)* incustodito(-a); *(singing, song)* senza accompagnamento; *(violin)* solo(-a)
un·ac·count·able [ˌʌnə'kaʊntəbl] ADJ *(inexplicable)* inspiegabile; *(not answerable)* non responsabile
un·ac·count·ably [ˌʌnə'kaʊntəblɪ] ADV *(inexplicably)* inesplicabilmente, inspiegabilmente
un·ac·count·ed [ˌʌnə'kaʊntɪd] ADJ: **unaccounted for** mancante; **two passengers are unaccounted for** due passeggeri mancano all'appello
un·ac·cus·tomed [ˌʌnə'kʌstəmd] ADJ **1** *(unused to)*: **to be unaccustomed to sth/to doing** non essere abituato(-a) a qc/a fare **2** *(unwonted)* insolito(-a); **with unaccustomed zeal** con insolito zelo
un·ac·knowl·edged [ˌʌnək'nɒlɪdʒd] ADJ **1** *(disregarded, not recognized)* non riconosciuto(-a) **2** *(ignored)*: **unacknowledged, he sat down in silence** ignorato da tutti i presenti, si sedette in silenzio
un·ac·quaint·ed [ˌʌnə'kweɪntɪd] ADJ: **to be unacquainted with** *(facts)* ignorare, non essere al corrente di; *(poverty)* non aver mai conosciuto
un·adorned [ˌʌnə'dɔːnd] ADJ disadorno(-a)
un·adul·ter·at·ed [ˌʌnə'dʌltəˌreɪtɪd] ADJ *(water, nonsense)* puro(-a); *(wine)* non sofisticato(-a)
un·af·fect·ed [ˌʌnə'fɛktɪd] ADJ **1** *(sincere)* naturale, spontaneo(-a); *(manner, voice)* non affettato(-a); *(gratitude)* sincero(-a) **2** *(unchanged)*: **to be unaffected by** non essere toccato(-a) da; **she was wholly unaffected by the news** la notizia non le ha fatto né caldo né freddo
un·af·fect·ed·ly [ˌʌnə'fɛktɪdlɪ] ADV senza affettazione
un·afraid [ˌʌnə'freɪd] ADJ: **to be unafraid** non aver paura
un·aid·ed [ʌn'eɪdɪd] ADV senza aiuto
■ ADJ: **by his own unaided efforts** con le sue sole forze, senza l'aiuto di nessuno
un·al·loyed [ˌʌnə'lɔɪd] ADJ *(liter: bliss, pleasure)* purissimo(-a)
un·al·ter·able [ʌn'ɒltərəbl] ADJ inalterabile
un·al·tered [ʌn'ɒltəd] ADJ inalterato(-a)
un·am·bigu·ous [ˌʌnæm'bɪgjʊəs] ADJ non ambiguo(-a), inequivocabile
un·am·bigu·ous·ly [ˌʌnæm'bɪgjʊəslɪ] ADV in modo chiaro, inequivocabilmente
un·am·bi·tious [ˌʌnæm'bɪʃəs] ADJ *(person)* poco ambizioso(-a); *(plan)* senza pretese
un-American [ʌnə'mɛrɪkən] ADJ *(anti-American)* antiamericano(-a); *(uncharacteristic of America)* poco americano(-a)
una·nim·ity [juːnə'nɪmɪtɪ] N unanimità
unani·mous [juː'nænɪməs] ADJ unanime
unani·mous·ly [juː'nænɪməslɪ] ADV all'unanimità
un·an·nounced [ˌʌnə'naʊnst] ADJ inatteso(-a)
■ ADV *(arrive)* senza preavviso
un·an·swer·able [ʌn'ɑːnsərəbl] ADJ *(case, argument)* irrefutabile; *(question)* senza risposta
un·an·swered [ʌn'ɑːnsəd] ADJ *(question, letter)* senza risposta; *(criticism)* non contestato(-a)
un·ap·peal·ing [ˌʌnə'piːlɪŋ] ADJ poco attraente
un·ap·pe·tiz·ing [ʌn'æpɪˌtaɪzɪŋ] ADJ poco appetitoso(-a)
un·ap·pre·cia·tive [ˌʌnə'priːʃɪətɪv] ADJ che non sa apprezzare; **an unappreciative audience** un pubblico indifferente
un·ap·proach·able [ˌʌnə'prəʊtʃəbl] ADJ *(person)* inavvicinabile, inabbordabile
un·ar·gu·able [ʌn'ɑːgjʊəbl] ADJ indiscutibile, incontestabile
un·ar·gu·ably [ʌn'ɑːgjʊəblɪ] ADV indiscutibilmente, incontestabilmente
un·armed [ʌn'ɑːmd] ADJ *(person)* disarmato(-a)
unarmed combat N lotta senz'armi
un·ashamed [ˌʌnə'ʃeɪmd] ADJ *(brazen)* sfrontato(-a), sfacciato(-a); **she was quite unashamed about it** non se ne vergognava minimamente
un·asham·ed·ly [ˌʌnə'ʃeɪmɪdlɪ] ADV sfacciatamente, sfrontatamente
un·asked [ʌn'ɑːskt] ADJ *(question)* non posto(-a), non formulato(-a)
■ ADV: **to do sth unasked** fare qc spontaneamente
un·as·sail·able [ˌʌnə'seɪləbl] ADJ *(fortress)* imprendibile; *(position, reputation)* inattaccabile

un·as·sist·ed [ˌʌnəˈsɪstɪd] ADJ, ADV senza nessun aiuto
un·as·sum·ing [ˌʌnəˈsjuːmɪŋ] ADJ modesto(-a), senza pretese
un·at·tached [ˌʌnəˈtætʃt] ADJ (*part*) staccato(-a); (*not married*) libero(-a), senza legami; (*independent*) indipendente, sciolto(-a)
un·at·tain·able [ˌʌnəˈteɪnəbl] ADJ irraggiungibile
un·at·tend·ed [ˌʌnəˈtɛndɪd] ADJ (*not looked after: luggage*) incustodito(-a); (*: patient, baby*) solo(-a), senza sorveglianza; **please do not leave your luggage unattended** si prega di non lasciare il bagaglio incustodito
un·at·trac·tive [ˌʌnəˈtræktɪv] ADJ (*person*) poco attraente; (*offer*) poco allettante; (*place*) privo(-a) di attrattiva
un·author·ized [ʌnˈɔːθəˌraɪzd] ADJ non autorizzato(-a)
un·avail·able [ˌʌnəˈveɪləbl] ADJ (*article, room, book*) non disponibile; (*person*) impegnato(-a)
un·avail·ing [ˌʌnəˈveɪlɪŋ] ADJ (*liter: effort*) vano(-a), inutile
un·avoid·able [ˌʌnəˈvɔɪdəbl] ADJ inevitabile
un·avoid·ably [ˌʌnəˈvɔɪdəblɪ] ADV (*detained*) per cause di forza maggiore
un·aware [ˌʌnəˈwɛəʳ] ADJ: **to be unaware of sth/that ...** non rendersi conto di *or* ignorare qc/che...; **she was unaware of the regulations** non era a conoscenza del regolamento
un·awares [ˌʌnəˈwɛəz] ADV: **to catch** *or* **take sb unawares** prendere qn alla sprovvista
un·bal·ance [ʌnˈbæləns] VT alterare l'equilibrio di
un·bal·anced [ˌʌnˈbælənst] ADJ non equilibrato(-a); (*mentally*) squilibrato(-a)
un·bear·able [ʌnˈbɛərəbl] ADJ insopportabile
un·bear·ably [ʌnˈbɛərəblɪ] ADV insopportabilmente
un·beat·able [ʌnˈbiːtəbl] ADJ imbattibile
un·beat·en [ˌʌnˈbiːtn] ADJ (*team, army*) imbattuto(-a); (*record*) insuperato(-a)
un·be·com·ing [ˌʌnbɪˈkʌmɪŋ] ADJ (*liter: unseemly: conduct, behaviour*) sconveniente; (*: unflattering: garment*) che non dona
un·be·known [ˌʌnbɪˈnəʊn], **un·be·knownst** [ˌʌnbɪˈnəʊnst] ADV (*old*): **unbeknown to** all'insaputa di; **unbeknown to me** a mia insaputa
un·be·lief [ˌʌnbɪˈliːf] N incredulità
un·be·liev·able [ˌʌnbɪˈliːvəbl] ADJ incredibile; **it's unbelievable that** è incredibile che + *sub*
un·be·liev·ably [ˌʌnbɪˈliːvəblɪ] ADV incredibilmente
un·be·liev·er [ˌʌnbɪˈliːvəʳ] N non credente *m/f*
un·be·liev·ing [ˌʌnbɪliːvɪŋ] ADJ incredulo(-a)
un·be·liev·ing·ly [ˌʌnbɪˈliːvɪŋlɪ] ADV con aria incredula; **he looked at me unbelievingly** mi ha guardato incredulo
un·bend [ʌnˈbɛnd] (*pt, pp* **unbent** [ˌʌnˈbɛnt]) VT (*pipe, wire*) raddrizzare
■ VI (*fig: person*) distendersi, rilassarsi
un·bend·ing [ʌnˈbɛndɪŋ] ADJ (*fig*) inflessibile, rigido(-a)
un·bi·ased, **unbiassed** [ʌnˈbaɪəst] ADJ obiettivo(-a), imparziale
un·bid·den [ʌnˈbɪdn] ADJ (*liter*): **he did it unbidden** lo ha fatto senza che nessuno glielo avesse chiesto; **he came in unbidden** è entrato senza essere stato invitato
un·blem·ished [ʌnˈblɛmɪʃt] ADJ senza macchia
un·blink·ing [ʌnˈblɪŋkɪŋ] ADJ (*person*) impassibile; **he looked at me with unblinking eyes** mi guardò senza batter ciglio
un·block [ʌnˈblɒk] VT (*pipe*) sbloccare
un·blush·ing [ʌnˈblʌʃɪŋ] ADJ inverecondo(-a)
un·bolt [ʌnˈbəʊlt] VT levare il catenaccio a
un·born [ʌnˈbɔːn] ADJ non ancora nato(-a); **the unborn child** il feto
un·bound·ed [ʌnˈbaʊndɪd] ADJ sconfinato(-a), senza limite
un·break·able [ʌnˈbreɪkəbl] ADJ infrangibile
un·bri·dled [ʌnˈbraɪdld] ADJ (*lust, ambition*) sfrenato(-a)
un·bro·ken [ʌnˈbrəʊkən] ADJ **1** (*intact*) intatto(-a), intero(-a); **his spirit remained unbroken** ha conservato un animo indomito **2** (*continuous: sleep, silence*) ininterrotto(-a); (*line of descent*) diretto(-a) **3** (*record*) insuperato(-a) **4** (*horse*) non domato(-a)
un·buck·le [ʌnˈbʌkl] VT slacciare
un·bur·den [ʌnˈbɜːdn] VT: **to unburden o.s. to sb** sfogarsi con qn
un·business·like [ʌnˈbɪznɪsˌlaɪk] ADJ (*shopkeeper*) che non ha il senso degli affari; (*transaction*) irregolare; (*fig: person*) poco efficiente
un·but·ton [ʌnˈbʌtn] VT sbottonare
uncalled-for [ˌʌnˈkɔːldfɔːʳ] ADJ (*remark*) fuori luogo *inv*; (*action*) ingiustificato(-a)
un·can·ni·ly [ʌnˈkænɪlɪ] ADV straordinariamente, incredibilmente
un·can·ny [ʌnˈkænɪ] ADJ (*comp* **-ier**, *superl* **-iest**) (*knack, resemblance*) sconcertante; (*sound, silence*) strano(-a), inquietante; **that's uncanny!** è strano!; **an uncanny resemblance** una rassomiglianza stupefacente
uncared-for [ˌʌnˈkɛədfɔːʳ] ADJ (*child, garden*) trascurato(-a); (*nails*) non curato(-a)
un·car·ing [ʌnˈkɛərɪŋ] ADJ indifferente, insensibile
un·ceas·ing [ʌnˈsiːsɪŋ] ADJ incessante
un·ceas·ing·ly [ʌnˈsiːsɪŋlɪ] ADV incessantemente, senza sosta
un·cer·emo·ni·ous [ˌʌnsɛrɪˈməʊnɪəs] ADJ (*abrupt, rude*) brusco(-a); **in unceremonious haste** in modo sbrigativo
un·cer·emo·ni·ous·ly [ˌʌnsɛrɪˈməʊnɪəslɪ] ADV senza tante cerimonie
un·cer·tain [ʌnˈsɜːtn] ADJ (*person, future, result*) incerto(-a); (*aims*) vago(-a); (*temper*) instabile; **the future is uncertain** l'avvenire è incerto; **I'm uncertain about what to do** sono incerto sul da farsi; **it is uncertain whether** non è sicuro se; **he is uncertain whether** non sa bene se; **in no uncertain terms** chiaro e tondo, senza mezzi termini
un·cer·tain·ly [ʌnˈsɜːtnlɪ] ADV (*say*) senza troppa convinzione, con aria incerta; (*move*) con passo incerto
un·cer·tain·ty [ʌnˈsɜːtntɪ] N (*of situation*) incertezza; (*confusion*) dubbi *mpl*; **the uncertainties of this life** le incognite della vita
un·chal·lenge·able [ʌnˈtʃælɪndʒəbl] ADJ incontestabile
un·chal·lenged [ˌʌnˈtʃælɪndʒd] ADJ (*gen, Law*) incontestato(-a); **to go unchallenged** non venire contestato(-a), non trovare opposizione; **to let a remark go unchallenged** lasciar passare un'osservazione senza replicare
un·changed [ˌʌnˈtʃeɪndʒd] ADJ (*plans, situation*) immutato(-a), invariato(-a); **he's completely unchanged** non è cambiato minimamente
un·chang·ing [ʌnˈtʃeɪndʒɪŋ] ADJ che resta immutato(-a)
un·char·ac·ter·is·tic [ʌnˌkærəktəˈrɪstɪk] ADJ (*generosity, behaviour*) insolito(-a); **that's uncharacteristic of him** non è (una cosa) da lui

Uu

un·chari·table [ʌn'tʃærɪtəbl] ADJ *(attitude)* poco generoso(-a), duro(-a); *(remark)* cattivo(-a)
un·chart·ed [ʌn'tʃɑ:tɪd] ADJ inesplorato(-a)
un·checked [ʌn'tʃɛkt] ADJ **1** *(unrestrained: anger)* incontrollato(-a); **to go unchecked** *(abuse, violence)* rimanere incontrollato(-a); *(virus, inflation)* dilagare; **to advance unchecked** *(army)* avanzare senza incontrare opposizione **2** *(not verified: facts)* non controllato(-a), non verificato(-a); *(typescript)* non corretto(-a)
un·chris·tian [ʌn'krɪstjən] ADJ poco cristiano(-a)
un·civ·il [ʌn'sɪvəl] ADJ scortese, maleducato(-a)
un·civi·lized [ʌn'sɪvɪˌlaɪzd] ADJ *(tribe, people)* selvaggio(-a); *(behaviour, conditions)* incivile, barbaro(-a)
un·claimed [ʌn'kleɪmd] ADJ *(prize, social security benefit)* non ritirato(-a); *(property)* non reclamato(-a)
un·clas·si·fied [ʌn'klæsɪˌfaɪd] ADJ **1** *(not secret: documents, information)* accessibile al pubblico **2** *(items, papers, road)* non classificato(-a); *(Brit: football results)* non classificato(-a) per campionato
◎ **un·cle** ['ʌŋkl] N zio
un·clean [ʌn'kli:n] ADJ sporco(-a); *(fig, Rel)* immondo(-a)
un·clear [ʌn'klɪə^r] ADJ non chiaro(-a); **I'm still unclear about what I'm supposed to do** non ho ancora ben capito cosa dovrei fare
Uncle Tom N *(pej) termine spregiativo usato per definire una persona di colore troppo servile con i bianchi*
un·climbed [ʌn'klaɪmd] ADJ *(mountain)* vergine
un·cloud·ed [ʌn'klaʊdɪd] ADJ senza nuvole; *(fig: mind, judgement)* lucido(-a); *(: happiness)* senza una nube
un·clut·tered [ˌʌn'klʌtəd] ADJ *(room)* privo(-a) di oggetti superflui; *(view)* non ostruito(-a)
un·coil [ʌn'kɔɪl] VT srotolare
■ VI srotolarsi
un·col·lect·ed [ˌʌnkə'lɛktɪd] ADJ *(luggage, prize)* non ritirato(-a); *(rubbish)* non portato(-a) via; *(tax)* non riscosso(-a)
un·combed [ʌn'kəʊmd] ADJ spettinato(-a)
un·com·fort·able [ʌn'kʌmfətəbl] ADJ **1** *(person, chair)* scomodo(-a); *(afternoon)* poco piacevole; *(situation)* sgradevole; **an uncomfortable position** una posizione scomoda; **to have an uncomfortable time** passare un brutto quarto d'ora; **to make life uncomfortable for sb** rendere la vita difficile a qn **2** *(uneasy, embarrassed)* a disagio, non a proprio agio; **to make sb feel uncomfortable** mettere qn a disagio; **the way he talks makes me feel uncomfortable** il modo in cui parla mi mette a disagio; **I had an uncomfortable feeling that ...** ho avuto la sgradevole sensazione che...
un·com·fort·ably [ʌn'kʌmfətəblɪ] ADV **1** *(sit)* scomodamente; *(dressed)* in modo poco pratico; *(hot)* eccessivamente **2** *(uneasily: say)* con voce inquieta; *(: think)* con inquietudine; **uncomfortably close** a una vicinanza preoccupante
un·com·mit·ted [ˌʌnkə'mɪtɪd] ADJ *(attitude, country)* neutrale; **to be uncommitted** *(person)* non essere impegnato(-a); **to remain uncommitted to** *(policy, party)* non dare la propria adesione a
un·com·mon [ʌn'kɒmən] ADJ **1** *(unusual)* insolito(-a); *(rare)* non comune, raro(-a); **an uncommon name** un nome insolito; **it's not uncommon that** non è raro che + *sub* **2** *(outstanding)* fuori dal comune
un·com·mon·ly [ʌn'kɒmənlɪ] ADV *(hot)* insolitamente; **not uncommonly** non di rado; **it was uncommonly kind of you** è stato squisito da parte sua; **to be uncommonly gifted** avere delle doti fuori del comune
un·com·mu·ni·ca·tive [ˌʌnkə'mju:nɪkətɪv] ADJ poco comunicativo(-a)
un·com·plain·ing [ˌʌnkəm'pleɪnɪŋ] ADJ che non si lamenta
un·com·plain·ing·ly [ˌʌnkəm'pleɪnɪŋlɪ] ADV senza lamentarsi
un·com·pli·cat·ed [ʌn'kɒmplɪˌkeɪtɪd] ADJ semplice, poco complicato(-a)
un·com·pli·men·ta·ry [ˌʌnkɒmplɪ'mɛntərɪ] ADJ poco gentile
un·com·pre·hend·ing [ʌnˌkɒmprɪ'hɛndɪŋ] ADJ *(baffled)* perplesso(-a)
un·com·pre·hend·ing·ly [ʌnˌkɒmprɪ'hɛndɪŋlɪ] ADV in modo perplesso
un·com·pro·mis·ing [ʌn'kɒmprəˌmaɪzɪŋ] ADJ *(honesty, dedication)* assoluto(-a); *(attitude)* intransigente
un·con·cealed [ˌʌnkən'si:ld] ADJ non dissimulato(-a)
un·con·cerned [ˌʌnkən'sɜ:nd] ADJ *(unworried)* tranquillo(-a); **she seemed unconcerned** sembrava tranquilla; **to be unconcerned about** non darsi pensiero di, non preoccuparsi di *or* per; **to be unconcerned by** essere indifferente a
un·con·cern·ed·ly [ˌʌnkən'sɜ:nɪdlɪ] ADV con indifferenza
un·con·di·tion·al [ˌʌnkən'dɪʃənl] ADJ *(surrender, refusal)* incondizionato(-a); *(freedom)* assoluto(-a)
un·con·di·tion·al·ly [ˌʌnkən'dɪʃnəlɪ] ADV incondizionatamente, senza condizioni
un·con·firmed [ˌʌnkən'fɜ:md] ADJ non confermato(-a)
un·con·gen·ial [ˌʌnkən'dʒi:nɪəl] ADJ *(person)* poco simpatico(-a); *(surroundings, work)* poco piacevole
un·con·nect·ed [ˌʌnkə'nɛktɪd] ADJ **1** *(unrelated)* senza connessione, senza rapporto; **to be unconnected with** essere estraneo(-a) a **2** *(incoherent)* sconnesso(-a)
un·con·scion·able [ʌn'kɒnʃənəbl] ADJ *(liter)* **1** *(excessive)* eccessivo(-a); **to be an unconscionable time doing sth** impiegare un tempo eccessivo a fare qc **2** *(unprincipled: liar)* spregiudicato(-a)
un·con·scious [ʌn'kɒnʃəs] ADJ **1** *(Med)* privo(-a) di sensi, svenuto(-a); **to fall unconscious** svenire, cadere (a terra) privo(-a) di sensi; **to knock sb unconscious** far perdere i sensi a qn con un colpo **2** *(unaware)*: **unconscious (of)** inconsapevole (di), ignaro(-a) (di) **3** *(unintentional: action, desire)* inconscio(-a)
■ N *(Psych)*: **the unconscious** l'inconscio
un·con·scious·ly [ʌn'kɒnʃəslɪ] ADV inconsciamente, senza rendersi conto
un·con·sti·tu·tion·al [ˌʌnkɒnstɪ'tju:ʃənl] ADJ *(frm)* anticostituzionale
un·con·sti·tu·tion·al·ity [ˌʌnkɒnstɪˌtju:ʃə'nælɪtɪ] N *(frm)* anticostituzionalità
un·con·sti·tu·tion·al·ly [ʌnˌkɒnstɪ'tju:ʃnəlɪ] ADV *(frm)* anticostituzionalmente
un·con·test·ed [ˌʌnkən'tɛstɪd] ADJ *(champion)* incontestato(-a); *(Pol: seat, election)* non disputato(-a)
un·con·trol·lable [ˌʌnkən'trəʊləbl] ADJ *(desire, epidemic)* incontrollabile; *(child)* indisciplinato(-a); *(laughter)* irrefrenabile; *(temper, reaction)* incontrollato(-a)
un·con·trol·lably [ˌʌnkən'trəʊləblɪ] ADV: **to laugh uncontrollably** ridere senza potersi fermare; **the car skidded uncontrollably** la macchina ha slittato e ne ho *(or hai etc)* perso il controllo
un·con·trolled [ˌʌnkən'trəʊld] ADJ *(laughter, weeping)*

irrefrenabile; (*child, dog*) scatenato(-a); (*inflation, price rises*) incontenibile
un·con·ven·tion·al [ˌʌnkənˈvɛnʃənl] ADJ poco convenzionale
un·con·vinced [ˌʌnkənˈvɪnst] ADJ: **to be** *or* **remain unconvinced** non essere convinto(-a)
un·con·vinc·ing [ˌʌnkənˈvɪnsɪŋ] ADJ non convincente, poco persuasivo(-a)
un·con·vinc·ing·ly [ˌʌnkənˈvɪnsɪŋlɪ] ADV in modo poco convincente
un·cooked [ʌnˈkʊkt] ADJ crudo(-a)
un·co·opera·tive [ˌʌnkəʊˈɒpərətɪv] ADJ restio(-a) a collaborare
un·co·ordi·nat·ed, unco-ordinated [ˌʌnkəʊˈɔːdɪˌneɪtɪd] ADJ (*person, movements, efforts*) scoordinato(-a)
un·cork [ʌnˈkɔːk] VT stappare
un·cor·robo·rat·ed [ˌʌnkəˈrɒbəˌreɪtɪd] ADJ (*evidence, confession*) non convalidato(-a)
un·count·able noun [ˌʌnkaʊntəblˈnaʊn] N (*Gram*) sostantivo non numerabile
un·cou·ple [ʌnˈkʌpl] VT sganciare
un·couth [ʌnˈkuːθ] ADJ (*old*) maleducato(-a), rozzo(-a), villano(-a)
un·cov·er [ʌnˈkʌvəʳ] VT **1** (*find out*) scoprire; (*: scandal*) portare alla luce **2** (*remove coverings of*) scoprire; (*: drain*) scoperchiare
un·criti·cal [ʌnˈkrɪtɪkəl] ADJ (*pej: reader, admirer*) poco critico(-a); (*: approach, attitude*) acritico(-a); **to be uncritical of** avere poco senso critico nei confronti di
un·crossed [ʌnˈkrɒst] ADJ (*cheque*) non sbarrato(-a)
un·crush·able [ʌnˈkrʌʃəbl] ADJ (*material*) ingualcibile
UNCTAD N ABBR (= **United Nations Conference on Trade and Development**) UNCTAD *f* (= *conferenza delle Nazioni Unite sul commercio e lo sviluppo*)
unc·tion [ˈʌŋkʃən] N: **extreme unction** (*Rel*) estrema unzione *f*
unc·tu·ous [ˈʌŋktjʊəs] ADJ (*liter*) untuoso(-a)
un·cul·ti·vat·ed [ʌnˈkʌltɪˌveɪtɪd] ADJ incolto(-a)
un·cul·tured [ʌnˈkʌltʃəd] ADJ (*person*) senza cultura, ignorante; (*mind*) poco raffinato(-a)
un·curl [ʌnˈkɜːl] VT (*gen*) srotolare; (*one's fingers*) distendere
un·dam·aged [ʌnˈdæmɪdʒd] ADJ (*goods*) in buono stato; (*fig: reputation*) intatto(-a)
un·dat·ed [ʌnˈdeɪtɪd] ADJ senza data
un·daunt·ed [ʌnˈdɔːntɪd] ADJ: **undaunted by** per nulla intimidito(-a) da; **to carry on undaunted** continuare imperterrito(-a)
un·de·cid·ed [ˌʌndɪˈsaɪdɪd] ADJ (*person*) indeciso(-a), incerto(-a); (*matter*) irrisolto(-a); **we are still undecided whether to go** siamo ancora indecisi se andare o meno
un·de·feat·ed [ˌʌndɪˈfiːtɪd] ADJ imbattuto(-a)
un·de·fined [ˌʌndɪˈfaɪnd] ADJ (*idea*) non ben definito(-a); (*number, quantity*) indefinito(-a); (*feeling*) vago(-a)
un·de·liv·ered [ˌʌndɪˈlɪvəd] ADJ non recapitato(-a); **if undelivered return to sender** in caso di mancato recapito rispedire al mittente
un·de·mand·ing [ʌndɪˈmændɪŋ] ADJ (*job, task, book, programme*) poco impegnativo(-a); (*person*) poco esigente
un·demo·crat·ic [ˌʌndɛməʊˈkrætɪk] ADJ antidemocratico(-a)
un·de·mon·stra·tive [ˌʌndɪˈmɒnstrətɪv] ADJ riservato(-a), poco espansivo(-a)
un·de·ni·able [ˌʌndɪˈnaɪəbl] ADJ innegabile, indiscutibile, fuori discussione
un·de·ni·ably [ˌʌndɪˈnaɪəblɪ] ADV innegabilmente, indiscutibilmente
◎ **un·der** [ˈʌndəʳ] PREP **1** (*beneath*) sotto; **under the table** sotto il tavolo; **from under the bed** da sotto il letto; **it's under there** sta lì sotto; **under water** sott'acqua; **the tunnel goes under the Channel** il tunnel passa sotto il Canale della Manica **2** (*less than*) meno di; (*: in rank, scale*) al di sotto di; **in under 2 hours** in meno di 2 ore; **people under 50 (years old)** gente al di sotto dei 50 (anni); **under 20 people** meno di 20 persone **3** (*fig: sb's leadership, sign of zodiac, letter in catalogue*) sotto; **under anaesthetic** sotto anestesia; **under discussion/repair/construction** in discussione/riparazione/costruzione; **to study under sb** studiare con qn *or* sotto la guida di qn; **under the circumstances** date le circostanze; **under the Romans** sotto i Romani; **under a false name** sotto falso nome; **he has 30 workers under him** ha 30 operai sotto di sé **4** (*according to*) secondo; **under the new law** secondo quanto previsto dalla nuova legge; **under British law they have done nothing wrong** in base alla legge britannica non hanno fatto nulla di male
■ ADV **1** (*beneath: position*) sotto; (*: direction*) sotto, di sotto; **to be under** (*under anaesthetic*) essere sotto anestesia **2** (*less*) al di sotto, meno; **girls of 14 and under** ragazze dai 14 anni in giù
under... [ˈʌndəʳ] PREF **1** (*in rank*) sotto..., aiuto; (*in age*): **the under-15s** i ragazzi al di sotto dei 15 anni; **undergardener** aiuto giardiniere *m* **2** (*insufficiently*) sotto...; **underprepared** poco preparato(-a); **undercooked** poco cotto(-a)
under·achieve [ˌʌndərəˈtʃiːv] VI non dare il meglio di sé
under·achiev·er [ˌʌndərəˈtʃiːvəʳ] N chi non dà il meglio di sé
under-age [ˌʌndərˈeɪdʒ] ADJ minorenne; **he's under-age** è minorenne
under·arm [ˈʌndərˌɑːm] ADV (*throw*) da sotto in su
■ ADJ (*temperature*) ascellare; (*deodorant*) per le ascelle; (*bowling*) da sotto in su; **underarm hair** i peli delle ascelle; **underarm serve** (*Tennis*) servizio dal basso verso l'alto
under·belly [ˈʌndəˌbelɪ] N (*Anat*) basso ventre *m*; (*fig*) punto debole; **the soft underbelly** il ventre molle
under·capi·tal·ized [ˌʌndəˈkæpɪtəˌlaɪzd] ADJ (*Fin*) carente di capitali
under·carriage [ˈʌndəˌkærɪdʒ] N (*Brit Aer*) carrello (d'atterraggio)
under·charge [ˌʌndəˈtʃɑːdʒ] VT far pagare di meno a
under·class [ˈʌndəˌklɑːs] N sottoproletariato
under·clothes [ˈʌndəˌkləʊðz] NPL biancheria *fsg* intima
under·coat [ˈʌndəˌkəʊt] N (*of paint*) mano *f* di fondo
under·cover [ˌʌndəˈkʌvəʳ] ADJ (*agent*) segreto(-a); (*meeting*) clandestino(-a); **an undercover agent** un agente segreto; **she was working undercover** agiva in incognito
under·cur·rent [ˈʌndəˌkʌrənt] N corrente *f* sottomarina; (*fig*) vena nascosta
under·cut [ˌʌndəˈkʌt] (*pt, pp* **undercut**) VT (*Comm*) vendere a minor prezzo di; **they were able to undercut their competitors** riuscivano ad avere prezzi inferiori rispetto ai concorrenti; **they plan to**

Uu

undercut fares on some routes introdurranno tariffe concorrenziali su alcune rotte

under·de·vel·oped [ˌʌndədɪˈvɛləpt] ADJ (*country*) sottosviluppato(-a); (*baby, muscles, photo*) non ben sviluppato(-a)

under·dog [ˈʌndəˌdɒg] N: **the underdog** (*in fight, contest*) il/la più debole; (*in society*) l'oppresso(-a); (*in family, organization*) l'ultima ruota del carro; **Inter were the underdogs on this occasion** in quest'occasione l'Inter era la squadra sfavorita

under·done [ˌʌndəˈdʌn] ADJ (*Culin: food*) poco cotto(-a); (*: steak*) al sangue

under·dressed [ˌʌndəˈdrɛst] ADJ non vestito(-a) in modo adeguato

under·em·ployed [ˌʌndərɪmˈplɔɪd] ADJ sottoccupato(-a)

under-employment [ˌʌndərɪmˈplɔɪmənt] N sottoccupazione *f*

under·es·ti·mate [ˌʌndərˈɛstɪˌmeɪt] VT sottovalutare

under·es·ti·ma·tion [ˌʌndərɛstɪˈmeɪʃən] N (*also:* **underestimate**) sottovalutazione *f*

under·ex·posed [ˌʌndərɪksˈpəʊzd] ADJ (*Phot*) sottoesposto(-a)

under·ex·po·sure [ˌʌndərɪkˈspəʊʒə^r] N (*Phot*) sottoesposizione *f*

under·fed [ˌʌndəˈfɛd] ADJ malnutrito(-a)

under·felt [ˈʌndəˌfɛlt] N *feltro su cui poggia la moquette*

under-financed [ˌʌndəˈfaɪnænst] ADJ senza fondi sufficienti

under·floor heat·ing [ˌʌndəflɔːˈhiːtɪŋ] N riscaldamento a pavimento

under·foot [ˌʌndəˈfʊt] ADV sotto i piedi, per terra; **to trample underfoot** (*also fig*) calpestare; **the children are always getting underfoot** i bambini sono sempre tra i piedi

under-funded [ˌʌndəˈfʌndɪd] ADJ insufficientemente sovvenzionato(-a)

under·gar·ment [ˈʌndəˌgɑːmənt] N indumento intimo

under·go [ˌʌndəˈgəʊ] (*pt* **underwent**, *pp* **undergone** [ˌʌndəˈgɒn]) VT sottoporsi a, subire; **to undergo changes** essere sottoposto(-a) a modifiche; **to undergo training** seguire un corso di formazione; **the car is undergoing repairs** la macchina è in riparazione

under·gradu·ate [ˌʌndəˈgrædjʊɪt] N (*also:* **undergrad**) studente(-essa) universitario(-a); **a group of undergraduates** un gruppo di studenti universitari
■ ADJ (*opinion, attitudes*) degli studenti; **undergraduate courses** corsi *mpl* di laurea

◎ **under·ground** [*adj* ˈʌndəˌgraʊnd; *adv* ˌʌndəˈgraʊnd] ADJ (*passage, cave, railway*) sotterraneo(-a); (*fig: political movement, press*) clandestino(-a); (*: Art, Cine*) underground *inv*; **an underground car park** un parcheggio sotterraneo
■ ADV sottoterra; (*fig*) clandestinamente; **moles live underground** le talpe vivono sottoterra; **to go underground** (*fig*) entrare in clandestinità
■ N **1** (*Brit Rail*): **the Underground** la metropolitana; **to go by underground** *or* **on the underground** andare in *or* con la metropolitana **2** (*Mil, Pol*): **the underground** il movimento clandestino, la resistenza; (*Art*) la controcultura, l'underground *m*

under·growth [ˈʌndəˌgrəʊθ] N sottobosco

under·hand [ˌʌndəˈhænd], **under·hand·ed** [ˌʌndəˈhændɪd] ADJ (*method*) equivoco(-a), poco pulito(-a); (*trick*) subdolo(-a), mancino(-a)

under·in·sured [ˌʌndərɪnˈʃʊəd] ADJ sottoassicurato(-a)

under·lay [ˈʌndəˌleɪ] N = **underfelt**

under·lie [ˌʌndəˈlaɪ] (*pt* **underlay** [ˌʌndəˈleɪ], *pp* **underlain** [ˌʌndəˈleɪn]) VT essere alla base di; **these objectives underlie his economic policy** questi obiettivi sono alla base della sua politica economica; **an underlying nervousness** un nervosismo di fondo; **the underlying cause** il motivo di fondo

under·line [ˌʌndəˈlaɪn] VT (*also fig*) sottolineare

under·ling [ˈʌndəlɪŋ] N (*pej*) galoppino, tirapiedi *m inv*

under·manned [ˌʌndəˈmænd] ADJ carente di personale

under·men·tioned [ˌʌndəˈmɛnʃənd] ADJ (riportato(-a)) qui sotto *or* qui di seguito

◎ **under·mine** [ˌʌndəˈmaɪn] VT (*fig*) minare; (*: authority*) pregiudicare

under·neath [ˌʌndəˈniːθ] PREP sotto, al di sotto di; **underneath the carpet** sotto la moquette
■ ADV sotto, di sotto; **I got out of the car and looked underneath** sono sceso dalla macchina e ho guardato sotto
■ N: **the underneath** la parte di sotto

under·nour·ished [ˌʌndəˈnʌrɪʃt] ADJ denutrito(-a)

under·nour·ish·ment [ˌʌndəˈnʌrɪʃmənt] N sottoalimentazione *f*, denutrizione *f*

under·paid [ˌʌndəˈpeɪd] PT, PP *of* **underpay**
■ ADJ mal pagato(-a), sottopagato(-a)

under·pants [ˈʌndəˌpænts] NPL (*Brit*) mutande *fpl* da uomo; (*Am*) mutande *fpl* da donna

under·pass [ˈʌndəˌpɑːs] N (*for cars*) sottopassaggio; (*for pedestrians*) sottopassaggio pedonale

under·pay [ˌʌndəˈpeɪ] (*pt, pp* **underpaid**) VT pagare male, sottopagare

under·pin [ˌʌndəˈpɪn] VT (*Archit*) puntellare; (*fig: argument, case*) corroborare

under·play [ˌʌndəˈpleɪ] VT minimizzare; **to underplay a role** (*Theatre*) recitare una parte con misura

under·popu·lat·ed [ˌʌndəˈpɒpjʊˌleɪtɪd] ADJ scarsamente popolato(-a), sottopopolato(-a)

under·price [ˌʌndəˈpraɪs] VT vendere sottoprezzo

under·priced [ˌʌndəˈpraɪst] ADJ (*product*) in vendita a un prezzo inferiore al dovuto

under·privi·leged [ˌʌndəˈprɪvɪlɪdʒd] ADJ svantaggiato(-a); **the underprivileged** i diseredati *mpl*

under·rate [ˌʌndəˈreɪt] VT sottovalutare

under·score [ˌʌndəˈskɔː^r] VT sottolineare

under·seal [ˈʌndəˌsiːl] VT (*Aut*) trattare con antiruggine

under·sec·re·tary [ˌʌndəˈsɛkrətrɪ] N sottosegretario

under·sell [ˌʌndəˈsɛl] (*pt, pp* **undersold**) VT (*competitors*) vendere a prezzi più bassi di; (*fig*) non valorizzare a sufficienza

under·sexed [ˌʌndəˈsɛkst] ADJ con scarsa libido

under·shirt [ˈʌndəˌʃɜːt] N (*Am*) maglietta, canottiera

under·shorts [ˈʌndəˌʃɔːts] NPL (*Am*) mutande *fpl* da uomo

under·side [ˈʌndəˌsaɪd] N parte *f* di sotto

under·signed [ˈʌndəˌsaɪnd] ADJ, N sottoscritto(-a); **I the undersigned** io sottoscritto

under·sized [ˌʌndəˈsaɪzd] ADJ (*pej*) troppo piccolo(-a)

under·skirt [ˈʌndəˌskɜːt] N sottogonna

under·sold [ˌʌndəˈsəʊld] PT, PP *of* **undersell**

under·spend [ˌʌndəˈspɛnd] VI spendere meno del previsto
■ VT: **to underspend a budget by sth** risparmiare qc sul budget

under·staffed [ˌʌndəˈstɑːft] ADJ a corto di personale

◎ **under·stand** [ˌʌndəˈstænd] (*pt, pp* **understood**) VT
1 (*gen*) capire; **to make o.s. understood** farsi capire; **do you understand?** capisci?; **I can't understand a word of it** non ci capisco un'acca; **I don't understand the question** non ho capito la domanda; **I don't understand why ...** non capisco perché...; **she understands children** capisce i bambini; **we understand one another** ci capiamo (tra di noi); **he doesn't understand how I feel** non mi capisce quello che provo; **I can understand his wanting to go** posso ben capire il suo desiderio di andarsene; **is that understood?** è chiaro?; **I wish it to be understood that ...** vorrei che fosse chiaro che...; **understood!** (*agreed*) intesi! 2 (*believe*) credere; **we understood we were to be paid** a quanto avevamo capito dovevamo essere pagati; **I understand you have been absent** mi risulta che lei è stato assente; **I understand you've heard about David** credo che tu abbia saputo di David; **it's understood that ...** resta inteso che...; **he let it be understood that he was leaving** ha dato a intendere che stava per partire; **she is understood to be ill** pare che stia poco bene
■ VI capire; **I quite understand** capisco benissimo, s'immagini; **she was, I understand, a Catholic** era, se non sbaglio, cattolica

under·stand·able [ˌʌndəˈstændəbl] ADJ comprensibile

under·stand·ably [ˌʌndəˈstændəblɪ] ADV comprensibilmente

◎ **under·stand·ing** [ˌʌndəˈstændɪŋ] ADJ (*person*) comprensivo(-a); (*smile*) indulgente
■ N 1 (*intelligence*) comprensione *f*; **his understanding of the situation is that ...** il modo in cui vede la situazione è che...; **it was my understanding that** quello che ho capito io era che + *sub*; **it is our understanding that they wanted to participate** crediamo che volessero partecipare; **a basic understanding of computing** una conoscenza di base dell'informatica 2 (*sympathy*) simpatia, comprensione *f*; **thank you for your patience and understanding** grazie della sua pazienza e comprensione 3 (*agreement*) accordo, intesa; **to come to an understanding with sb** giungere ad un accordo con qn; **there was an understanding between us** tra noi c'era un accordo; **on the understanding that he pays** a patto che *or* a condizione che paghi lui

under·state [ˌʌndəˈsteɪt] VT minimizzare, sminuire

under·state·ment [ˈʌndəˌsteɪtmənt] N understatement *m inv*; **that's an understatement!** a dir poco!

under·stood [ˌʌndəˈstʊd] PT, PP *of* **understand**
■ ADJ inteso(-a); (*implied*) sottinteso(-a)

under·study [ˈʌndəˌstʌdɪ] N (*Theatre*) doppio
■ VT sostituire

under·take [ˌʌndəˈteɪk] (*pt* **undertook**, *pp* **undertaken** [ˌʌndəˈteɪkən]) VT (*task*) intraprendere; (*responsibility*) assumersi; **to undertake a task** assumersi un compito; **to undertake to do sth** impegnarsi a fare qc

under·tak·er [ˈʌndəˌteɪkəʳ] N impresario di pompe funebri

under·tak·ing [ˌʌndəˈteɪkɪŋ] N 1 (*task*) impresa; **a massive undertaking** una grossa impresa; **it is quite an undertaking!** è una bella impresa! 2 (*promise*) promessa, assicurazione *f*; **to give an undertaking that ...** dare la propria parola che...

under·things [ˈʌndəˌθɪŋz] NPL (*fam*) biancheria *fsg* intima

under·tone [ˈʌndəˌtəʊn] N 1 (*low voice*) tono sommesso; **in an undertone** a mezza voce, sottovoce, a voce bassa 2: **undertones** NPL (*comic, religious*) sfumature *fpl*

under·took [ˌʌndəˈtʊk] PT *of* **undertake**

under·tow [ˈʌndəˌtəʊ] N (*of wave*) corrente *f* di risacca; (*undercurrent*) risucchio

under·used [ˌʌndəˈjuːzd] ADJ (*resources, facilities*) poco sfruttato(-a)

under·value [ˌʌndəˈvæljuː] VT (*person, contribution*) svalutare, sottovalutare; (*Comm, Fin*) deprezzare, svalutare

under·vest [ˈʌndəˌvɛst] N (*Brit*) maglietta intima

under·wa·ter [ˌʌndəˈwɔːtəʳ] ADJ (*swimming, photography*) subacqueo(-a); (*exploration*) sottomarino(-a); **underwater photography** fotografia subacquea
■ ADV sott'acqua; **this sequence was filmed underwater** questa scena è stata girata sott'acqua

under·way [ˌʌndəˈweɪ] ADJ: **to be underway** essere in corso

under·wear [ˈʌndəˌwɛəʳ] N biancheria intima

under·weight [ˌʌndəˈweɪt] ADJ (*person*) sottopeso *inv*; (*thing*) al di sotto del giusto peso

under·went [ˌʌndəˈwɛnt] PT *of* **undergo**

under·world [ˈʌndəˌwɜːld] N: **the underworld** (*criminal*) la malavita; (*hell*) gli inferi *mpl*

under·write [ˈʌndəˌraɪt] (*pt* **underwrote** [ˈʌndəˌrəʊt], *pp* **underwritten** [ˈʌndəˌrɪtn]) VT (*Fin*) sottoscrivere; (*Insurance*) assicurare

under·writ·er [ˈʌndəˌraɪtəʳ] N (*Insurance*) assicuratore(-trice); (*Fin*) sottoscrittore(-trice)

un·de·served [ˌʌndɪˈzɜːvd] ADJ immeritato(-a)

un·des·erved·ly [ˌʌndɪˈzɜːvɪdlɪ] ADV (*rewarded*) immeritatamente; (*punished*) ingiustamente

un·de·serv·ing [ˌʌndɪˈzɜːvɪŋ] ADJ: **to be undeserving of** non meritare, non essere degno(-a) di

un·de·sir·able [ˌʌndɪˈzaɪərəbl] ADJ (*effects*) indesiderato(-a); (*behaviour, habits, friendship*) discutibile; **it is undesirable for students to ...** gli studenti non devono...
■ N persona indesiderabile

un·de·tect·ed [ˌʌndɪˈtɛktɪd] ADJ: **to go undetected** passare inosservato(-a)

un·de·vel·oped [ˌʌndɪˈvɛləpt] ADJ (*land, resources*) non sfruttato(-a)

un·did [ʌnˈdɪd] PT *of* **undo**

un·dies [ˈʌndɪz] NPL (*fam*) biancheria *fsg* intima (*da donna*)

un·dig·ni·fied [ʌnˈdɪgnɪˌfaɪd] ADJ (*person*) senza dignità, poco dignitoso(-a); (*manner, action*) indecoroso(-a), sconveniente

un·di·lut·ed [ˌʌndaɪˈluːtɪd] ADJ (*concentrated*) non diluito(-a); (*fig: bliss, love*) totale, assoluto(-a)

un·dip·lo·matic [ˌʌndɪpləˈmætɪk] ADJ poco diplomatico(-a)

un·dis·cern·ing [ˌʌndɪˈsɜːnɪŋ] ADJ (*reader*) poco selettivo(-a); (*critic*) di scarso acume

un·dis·charged [ˌʌndɪsˈtʃɑːdʒd] ADJ (*debt*) non pagato(-a); (*bankrupt*) non riabilitato(-a)

un·dis·ci·plined [ʌnˈdɪsɪplɪnd] ADJ indisciplinato(-a)

un·dis·cov·ered [ˌʌndɪsˈkʌvəd] ADJ (*area*) inesplorato(-a); (*work of art*) ignoto(-a)

un·dis·crimi·nat·ing [ˌʌndɪsˈkrɪmɪˌneɪtɪŋ] ADJ (*choice*) indiscriminato(-a); (*person*) che non fa discriminazioni; (*taste*) non selettivo(-a)

Uu

un·dis·guised [ˌʌndɪsˈgaɪzd] ADJ (*dislike, amusement*) palese

un·dis·mayed [ˌʌndɪsˈmeɪd] ADJ (*liter*): **to be undismayed at** non lasciarsi impressionare da

un·dis·put·ed [ˌʌndɪsˈpju:tɪd] ADJ incontrastato(-a), indiscusso(-a)

un·dis·tin·guished [ˌʌndɪsˈtɪŋgwɪʃt] ADJ (*pej: person*) qualunque, mediocre; (*: career, design, performance*) mediocre; **an undistinguished poet** un poetucolo; **an undistinguished wine** un vino qualsiasi

un·dis·turbed [ˌʌndɪsˈtɜ:bd] ADJ **1** (*sleep*) tranquillo(-a); **to work undisturbed** lavorare in pace; **to leave sth undisturbed** lasciare qc così com'è **2** (*unworried*): **undisturbed (by)** indifferente (a); **the Prime Minister is undisturbed by rising inflation** l'aumento dell'inflazione non turba minimamente il primo ministro

un·di·vid·ed [ˌʌndɪˈvaɪdɪd] ADJ: **I want your undivided attention** esigo (da voi) la massima attenzione

undo [ʌnˈdu:] (*pt* **undid**, *pp* **undone**) VT **1** (*unfasten: button*) sbottonare; (*: shoelaces*) slacciare; (*: knot*) sciogliere; (*: parcel*) aprire; (*: knitting*) disfare; **she undid her coat** si è sbottonata il cappotto; **I can't undo the knot** non riesco a sciogliere il nodo **2** (*reverse: action, wrong*) riparare (a); (*spoil*) rovinare

un·do·ing [ʌnˈdu:ɪŋ] N rovina

un·done [ʌnˈdʌn] PP *of* undo

■ ADJ (*unfastened: button*) sbottonato(-a); **to come undone** slacciarsi; **to leave undone** (*shirt*) lasciare aperto(-a) *or* sbottonato(-a); (*job*) non fare, lasciare da fare

un·doubt·ed [ʌnˈdaʊtɪd] ADJ indubbio(-a)

un·doubt·ed·ly [ʌnˈdaʊtɪdlɪ] ADV indubbiamente, senza dubbio

un·dreamed [ʌnˈdri:md], **un·dreamt** [ʌnˈdrɛmt] ADJ: **undreamed of** mai sognato(-a)

un·dress [ʌnˈdrɛs] VT spogliare

■ VI (*also:* **get undressed**) spogliarsi, svestirsi

un·drink·able [ʌnˈdrɪŋkəbl] ADJ (*unpalatable*) imbevibile; (*polluted*) non potabile

un·due [ʌnˈdju:] ADJ eccessivo(-a)

un·du·lat·ing [ˈʌndjʊˌleɪtɪŋ] ADJ (*surface*) ondulato(-a); (*countryside*) collinoso(-a); (*sea*) ondeggiante

un·du·ly [ʌnˈdju:lɪ] ADV troppo, eccessivamente

un·dy·ing [ʌnˈdaɪɪŋ] ADJ (*liter: fame, glory*) imperituro(-a); (*: love*) eterno(-a)

un·earned [ʌnˈɜ:nd] ADJ (*praise, respect*) immeritato(-a)

unearned income N reddito non da lavoro

un·earth [ʌnˈɜ:θ] VT dissotterrare; (*fig: secret*) scoprire; (*: object*) scovare; (*: evidence*) portare alla luce; **they've unearthed some important documents** hanno scoperto alcuni documenti importanti

un·earth·ly [ʌnˈɜ:θlɪ] ADJ (*eerie: brightness*) innaturale; (*: noise, sound*) spettrale; **unearthly hour** (*fam*) ora impossibile

un·ease [ʌnˈi:z] N (*nervousness*) disagio; (*tension*) tensione *f*

un·easi·ly [ʌnˈi:zɪlɪ] ADV (*sleep*) male; (*glance, look*) con apprensione; **to be uneasily balanced** essere in equilibrio precario; **she glanced uneasily at him** gli lanciò uno sguardo inquieto

un·easi·ness [ʌnˈi:zɪnɪs] N disagio

un·easy [ʌnˈi:zɪ] ADJ (*person: worried*) inquieto(-a), preoccupato(-a), agitato(-a); (*: ill at ease*) a disagio; (*calm, peace*) precario(-a); (*night, sleep*) agitato(-a); (*silence*) imbarazzato(-a); **to feel uneasy about doing sth** non sentirsela di fare qc; **to feel uneasy about sth** essere preoccupato per qc; **to become uneasy about sb/sth** cominciare a preoccuparsi per qn/qc; **to have an uneasy conscience** non avere la coscienza a posto; **to have an uneasy feeling that ...** avere la spiacevole sensazione che...; **he looked uneasy** sembrava a disagio

un·eat·en [ʌnˈi:tn] ADJ (*breakfast, lunch*) non mangiato(-a); (*food, sandwiches*) avanzato(-a); **she left the steak uneaten** non ha nemmeno toccato la bistecca

un·eco·nom·ic [ˌʌni:kəˈnɒmɪk] ADJ (*wasteful: method, process*) antieconomico(-a); (*unprofitable*) poco redditizio(-a)

un·eco·nomi·cal [ˌʌni:kəˈnɒmɪkəl] ADJ (*car, machine*) poco economico(-a); (*use*) dispendioso(-a)

un·edu·cat·ed [ʌnˈɛdjʊˌkeɪtɪd] ADJ (*person*) senza istruzione, incolto(-a); (*speech*) popolare

un·emo·tion·al [ˌʌnɪˈməʊʃənl] ADJ (*person*) freddo(-a), impassibile; (*account*) distaccato(-a)

un·emo·tion·al·ly [ˌʌnɪˈməʊʃnəlɪ] ADV (*see adj*) impassibilmente; in modo distaccato

un·em·ploy·able [ˌʌnɪmˈplɔɪəbl] ADJ non adatto(-a) a nessun lavoro

un·em·ployed [ˌʌnɪmˈplɔɪd] ADJ disoccupato(-a), senza lavoro

■ NPL: **the unemployed** i disoccupati

◎ **un·em·ploy·ment** [ˌʌnɪmˈplɔɪmənt] N disoccupazione *f*

unemployment benefit, (*Am*) **unemployment compensation** N sussidio di disoccupazione

un·end·ing [ʌnˈɛndɪŋ] ADJ interminabile, senza fine

un·en·dur·able [ˌʌnɪnˈdjʊərəbl] ADJ (*frm*) insopportabile

un·en·ter·pris·ing [ʌnˈɛntəˌpraɪzɪŋ] ADJ poco intraprendente

un·en·thu·si·as·tic [ˌʌnɪnˌθu:zɪˈæstɪk] ADJ poco entusiasta

un·en·thu·si·as·ti·cal·ly [ˌʌnɪnˌθu:zɪˈæstɪkəlɪ] ADV senza entusiasmo

un·en·vi·able [ʌnˈɛnvɪəbl] ADJ poco invidiabile

un·equal [ʌnˈi:kwəl] ADJ (*length, objects*) disuguale; (*amounts*) diverso(-a); (*division of labour*) ineguale; **to be unequal to a task** (*frm*) non essere all'altezza di un compito

un·equalled, (*Am*) **un·equaled** [ʌnˈi:kwəld] ADJ senza pari, insuperato(-a)

un·equivo·cal [ˌʌnɪˈkwɪvəkəl] ADJ (*answer*) inequivocabile; (*person*) esplicito(-a), chiaro(-a)

un·equivo·cal·ly [ˌʌnɪˈkwɪvəkəlɪ] ADV inequivocabilmente

un·err·ing [ʌnˈɜ:rɪŋ] ADJ (*aim, taste, instinct*) infallibile

UNESCO [ju:ˈnɛskəʊ] N ABBR (= **United Nations Educational, Scientific, and Cultural Organization**) UNESCO *f*

un·ethi·cal [ʌnˈɛθɪkəl] ADJ (*methods*) moralmente inaccettabile; (*doctor's behaviour*) contrario(-a) all'etica professionale

un·even [ʌnˈi:vən] ADJ (*heartbeat, work, quality, performance*) irregolare; (*thickness*) ineguale; (*ground*) disuguale, accidentato(-a); **uneven distribution** distribuzione *f* poco uniforme; **an uneven surface** una superficie irregolare; **their performance has been uneven this season** il loro rendimento è stato discontinuo questa stagione

un·even·ly [ʌnˈi:vənlɪ] ADV (*distributed, spread*) in modo irregolare

un·even·ness [ʌnˈi:vənnɪs] N irregolarità

un·event·ful [ˌʌnɪˈvɛntfʊl] ADJ senza sorprese, tranquillo(-a)
un·ex·cep·tion·able [ˌʌnɪkˈsɛpʃnəbl] (*frm*) ADJ (*behaviour*) irreprensibile; (*style*) ineccepibile; (*speech*) inappuntabile
un·ex·cep·tion·al [ˌʌnɪkˈsɛpʃənl] ADJ che non ha niente d'eccezionale
un·ex·cit·ing [ˌʌnɪkˈsaɪtɪŋ] ADJ (*news*) poco emozionante; (*film, evening*) poco interessante; (*person*) scialbo(-a)
◎ **un·ex·pec·ted** [ˌʌnɪksˈpɛktɪd] ADJ inatteso(-a), imprevisto(-a)
un·ex·pect·ed·ly [ˌʌnɪksˈpɛktɪdlɪ] ADV (*happen*) inaspettatamente; (*die*) improvvisamente, inaspettatamente; (*arrive*) senza preavviso
un·ex·plained [ˌʌnɪksˈpleɪnd] ADJ inspiegato(-a)
un·ex·plod·ed [ˌʌnɪksˈpləʊdɪd] ADJ inesploso(-a)
un·ex·posed [ˌʌnɪksˈpəʊzd] ADJ (*film*) vergine
un·ex·pressed [ˌʌnɪksˈprɛst] ADJ inespresso(-a)
un·ex·pur·gat·ed [ʌnˈɛkspɜːˌgeɪtɪd] ADJ (*text, version*) integrale
un·fail·ing [ʌnˈfeɪlɪŋ] ADJ (*frm: remedy*) sicuro(-a), infallibile; (: *humour, supply, energy*) inesauribile; (: *zeal, courage*) senza riserve
un·fail·ing·ly [ʌnˈfeɪlɪŋlɪ] ADV immancabilmente, senza fallo
◎ **un·fair** [ʌnˈfɛəʳ] ADJ (*comp* **-er**, *superl* **-est**) (*person, decision, criticism*) ingiusto(-a); (*means, tactics*) sleale; (*competition*) scorretto(-a); **this is unfair!** è ingiusto!; **it's unfair that ...** non è giusto che... + *sub*; **to be unfair to sb** essere ingiusto(-a) verso qn; **unfair competition** concorrenza sleale
unfair dismissal N (*Industry*) licenziamento ingiustificato; licenziamento senza giusta causa
un·fair·ly [ʌnˈfɛəlɪ] ADV (*treat, criticize*) ingiustamente; (*play*) scorrettamente
un·fair·ness [ʌnˈfɛənɪs] N (*see adj*) ingiustizia; slealtà; scorrettezza
un·faith·ful [ʌnˈfeɪθfʊl] ADJ: **unfaithful (to sb)** infedele (a qn)
un·fa·mil·iar [ˌʌnfəˈmɪljəʳ] ADJ (*subject*) sconosciuto(-a); (*experience*) insolito(-a); (*surroundings*) estraneo(-a); **to be unfamiliar with sth** non essere pratico(-a) di qc, non avere familiarità con qc, avere scarsa familiarità con qc; **I heard an unfamiliar voice** ho sentito una voce sconosciuta
un·fash·ion·able [ʌnˈfæʃnəbl] ADJ (*clothes*) fuori moda; (*district*) non alla moda; **these trousers are unfashionable** questi pantaloni sono fuori moda *or* non vanno più
un·fas·ten [ʌnˈfɑːsn] VT (*buttons, seatbelt*) slacciare; (*scarf, rope*) sciogliere; (*gate*) aprire; **don't unfasten your seat belt** non slacciarti la cintura di sicurezza
un·fath·om·able [ʌnˈfæðəməbl] ADJ (*depths, mystery*) insondabile, imperscrutabile; (*person*) impenetrabile
un·fa·vour·able, (*Am*) **un·fa·vor·able** [ʌnˈfeɪvərəbl] ADJ (*circumstances, climate*) sfavorevole; (*report, impression*) negativo(-a)
un·fa·vour·ably, (*Am*) **un·fa·vor·ably** [ʌnˈfeɪvərəblɪ] ADV (*judge, see*) in senso sfavorevole; (*speak, review*) sfavorevolmente; **to look unfavourably upon** vedere di malocchio
un·feel·ing [ʌnˈfiːlɪŋ] ADJ insensibile, duro(-a)
un·femi·nine [ʌnˈfɛmɪnɪn] ADJ poco femminile
un·fet·tered [ʌnˈfɛtəd] ADJ: **unfettered (by)** senza restrizioni (da parte di)
un·fin·ished [ʌnˈfɪnɪʃt] ADJ (*task*) non finito(-a); (*letter*) da finire; (*business*) in sospeso; (*symphony*) incompiuto(-a); **I have some unfinished business to attend to** ho un affare in sospeso da regolare
un·fit [ʌnˈfɪt] ADJ (*unsuitable*): **unfit for** inadatto(-a) a; (*Sport: injured*) non in grado di giocare (*or* correre); (*out of training*) non in forma; **unfit for habitation** inabitabile; **to be unfit to do sth** non essere in grado di fare qc; **unfit for military service** inabile (al servizio militare); **to be unfit for work** non essere adatto(-a) al lavoro; **to be unfit to travel** non essere in grado di viaggiare; **to be unfit to hold office** non essere adatto all'incarico; **I'm really unfit at the moment** al momento sono proprio fuori forma
un·flag·ging [ʌnˈflægɪŋ] ADJ instancabile
un·flap·pable [ʌnˈflæpəbl] ADJ calmo(-a), composto(-a)
un·flat·ter·ing [ʌnˈflætərɪŋ] ADJ (*dress, hairstyle*) che non dona; (*portrait, light*) poco lusinghiero(-a)
un·flinch·ing [ʌnˈflɪntʃɪŋ] ADJ risoluto(-a), che non indietreggia
un·fo·cused, un·fo·cussed [ʌnˈfəʊkəst] ADJ (*camera*) non a fuoco; (*gaze, eyes*) perso(-a) nel vuoto; (*aims, desire*) vago(-a)
un·fold [ʌnˈfəʊld] VT (*newspaper, map, wings*) spiegare, aprire; (*arms*) distendere; (*fig: plan, idea*) esporre; (: *secret*) svelare; **she unfolded the map** ha aperto la cartina
■ VI (*flower*) schiudersi; (*fig: view*) spiegarsi; (: *story*) svolgersi
un·fore·see·able [ˌʌnfɔːˈsiːəbl] ADJ imprevedibile
un·fore·seen [ˌʌnfɔːˈsiːn] ADJ imprevisto(-a)
un·for·get·table [ˌʌnfəˈgɛtəbl] ADJ indimenticabile
un·for·giv·able [ˌʌnfəˈgɪvəbl] ADJ imperdonabile
un·for·giv·ably [ˌʌnfəˈgɪvəblɪ] ADV imperdonabilmente
un·for·giv·ing [ˌʌnfəˈgɪvɪŋ] ADJ implacabile, irremovibile
un·for·mat·ted [ʌnˈfɔːmætɪd] ADJ (*disk, text*) non formattato(-a)
un·formed [ʌnˈfɔːmd] ADJ (*clay*) informe, senza forma; (*character*) non ancora formato(-a); (*ideas*) non definito(-a)
un·for·tu·nate [ʌnˈfɔːtʃnɪt] ADJ (*deserving of pity*) povero(-a); (*unlucky*) sfortunato(-a); (*unsuitable, regrettable: event, remark*) infelice; (*habit*) deplorevole; **it is most unfortunate that he left** ci rincresce molto che se ne sia andato
■ N sfortunato(-a), sventurato(-a)
◎ **un·for·tu·nate·ly** [ʌnˈfɔːtʃnɪtlɪ] ADV purtroppo, sfortunatamente; **an unfortunately worded speech** un discorso infelice
un·found·ed [ʌnˈfaʊndɪd] ADJ infondato(-a), senza fondamento
un·freeze [ʌnˈfriːz] (*pt* **unfroze** [ʌnˈfrəʊz], *pp* **unfrozen** [ʌnˈfrəʊzn]) VT (*thaw*) sgelare; (*assets, bank account*) scongelare, sbloccare
un·fre·quent·ed [ʌnfrɪˈkwɛntɪd] ADJ poco frequentato(-a)
un·friend·ly [ʌnˈfrɛndlɪ] ADJ (*comp* **-ier**, *superl* **-iest**) (*person*): **unfriendly (to)** scostante (con), antipatico(-a) (con); (*attitude, reception*) ostile, poco amichevole; (*remark*) scortese; **the waiters are a bit unfriendly** i camerieri sono un po' antipatici
un·ful·filled [ˌʌnfʊlˈfɪld] ADJ **1** (*ambition*) non realizzato(-a); (*prophecy*) che non si è avverato(-a); (*desire*) insoddisfatto(-a); (*promise*) non mantenuto(-a); (*terms of contract*) non rispettato(-a) **2** (*person*) frustrato(-a)

Uu

un·furl [ʌn'fɜːl] VT (*flag, banner*) spiegare
un·fur·nished [ʌn'fɜːnɪʃt] ADJ non ammobiliato(-a)
un·gain·ly [ʌn'geɪnlɪ] ADJ sgraziato(-a), goffo(-a)
un·gen·er·ous [ʌn'dʒɛnərəs] ADJ (*frm: miserly, uncharitable*) poco generoso(-a)
un·get-at-able [ˌʌngɛt'ætəbl] ADJ (*fam*) inaccessibile
un·god·ly [ʌn'gɒdlɪ] ADJ (*person, language, action*) empio(-a); (*fam*): **at an ungodly hour** a un'ora allucinante; a un'ora impossibile
un·gov·ern·able [ʌn'gʌvənəbl] ADJ (*country*) ingovernabile; (*passion*) incontrollabile
un·gra·cious [ʌn'greɪʃəs] ADJ sgarbato(-a), scortese
un·gra·cious·ly [ʌn'greɪʃəslɪ] ADV sgarbatamente, scortesemente
un·gram·mati·cal [ˌʌngrə'mætɪkəl] ADJ sgrammaticato(-a), scorretto(-a)
un·grate·ful [ʌn'greɪtfʊl] ADJ ingrato(-a)
un·grate·ful·ly [ʌn'greɪtfəlɪ] ADV in modo ingrato, senza riconoscenza
un·grudg·ing [ʌn'grʌdʒɪŋ] ADJ (*help*) dato(-a) volentieri; (*praise*) sincero(-a)
un·guard·ed [ʌn'gɑːdɪd] ADJ **1** (*Mil*) indifeso(-a), sguarnito(-a) **2** (*fig: careless*) imprudente; **in an unguarded moment** in un momento di distrazione
un·ham·pered [ʌn'hæmpəd] ADJ: **unhampered by** libero(-a) da, non ostacolato(-a) da
un·hap·pi·ly [ʌn'hæpɪlɪ] ADV (*miserably*) tristemente, con aria infelice; (*unfortunately*) purtroppo, sfortunatamente; **she was unhappily married** non era felice con suo marito
un·hap·pi·ness [ʌn'hæpɪnɪs] N infelicità
◎ **un·hap·py** [ʌn'hæpɪ] ADJ (*comp* **-ier**, *superl* **-iest**) **1** (*sad*) infelice; **to look unhappy** avere l'aria triste; **he was very unhappy as a child** da bambino era molto infelice; **an unhappy state of affairs** una situazione spiacevole **2** (*not pleased*) scontento(-a); (*uneasy, worried*) preoccupato(-a), inquieto(-a); **unhappy with** (*arrangements*) insoddisfatto(-a) di; **to be unhappy about sth/doing sth** non essere contento(-a) di qc/di fare qc **3** (*unfortunate: remark, choice*) infelice; (: *coincidence*) sfortunato(-a)
un·harmed [ʌn'hɑːmd] ADJ (*person*) illeso(-a), sano(-a) e salvo(-a), incolume; (*thing*) intatto(-a)
UNHCR [juːɛneɪtʃsiː'ɑːʳ] N ABBR (= **United Nations High Commission for Refugees**) ACNUR *m* (= *Alto Commissariato delle Nazioni Unite per Rifugiati*)
un·healthy [ʌn'hɛlθɪ] ADJ (*comp* **-ier**, *superl* **-iest**) (*person*) cagionevole, poco sano(-a); (*climate, place, complexion*) malsano(-a); (*curiosity, interest*) morboso(-a); **an unhealthy girl** una ragazza cagionevole; **an unhealthy diet** una dieta poco sana; **an unhealthy climate** un clima insalubre
unheard-of [ʌn'hɜːdɒv] ADJ (*unprecedented*) inaudito(-a), senza precedenti; (*outrageous*) dell'altro mondo
un·heed·ed [ʌn'hiːdɪd] ADJ: **the warning went unheeded** l'avvertimento fu ignorato
un·help·ful [ʌn'hɛlpfʊl] ADJ (*person*) poco disponibile, di scarso aiuto; (*remark, advice*) di scarso aiuto
un·hesi·tat·ing [ʌn'hɛzɪˌteɪtɪŋ] ADJ (*reply, offer*) pronto(-a), immediato(-a); (*loyalty, faith*) che non vacilla; **she was unhesitating in her support** non ha esitato a darmi (*or* dargli *etc*) il suo appoggio
un·hesi·tat·ing·ly [ʌn'hɛzɪˌteɪtɪŋlɪ] ADV senza esitazione
un·hin·dered [ʌn'hɪndəd] ADJ (*progress*) senza ostacoli; (*movement*) senza impedimenti; **to be unhindered by moral scruples** agire senza farsi scrupoli
un·hinge [ʌn'hɪndʒ] VT (*door*) scardinare; (*fig: mind*) sconvolgere; (: *person*) far perdere la ragione a
un·hip [ˌʌn'hɪp] ADJ (*fam*) fuori moda
un·ho·ly [ʌn'həʊlɪ] ADJ profano(-a); **at an unholy hour** (*fam*) ad un'ora indecente; **an unholy alliance** una coalizione *f* paradossale
un·hook [ʌn'hʊk] VT (*remove: picture*) staccare; (: *trailer*) sganciare; (*undo: gate*) aprire; (: *dress*) slacciare
unhoped-for [ˌʌn'həʊptfɔːʳ] ADJ insperato(-a)
un·hur·ried [ʌn'hʌrɪd] ADJ (*person, steps*) tranquillo(-a); **after a little unhurried reflection** dopo averci pensato con calma
un·hur·ried·ly [ʌn'hʌrɪdlɪ] ADV senza fretta, con comodo
un·hurt [ʌn'hɜːt] ADJ incolume, illeso(-a)
un·hy·gien·ic [ˌʌnhaɪ'dʒiːnɪk] ADJ (*conditions*) non igienico(-a); (*surroundings*) insalubre
uni ['juːnɪ] N università; **he's at uni** è all'università
UNICEF ['juːnɪˌsɛf] N ABBR (= **United Nations International Children's Emergency Fund**) UNICEF *m or f*
uni·corn ['juːnɪˌkɔːn] N unicorno
un·iden·ti·fi·able [ˌʌnaɪdɛntɪ'faɪəbl] ADJ non identificabile
◎ **un·iden·ti·fied** [ˌʌnaɪ'dɛntɪˌfaɪd] ADJ non identificato(-a)
unidentified flying object N oggetto volante non identificato
uni·di·rec·tion·al [ˌjuːnɪdɪ'rɛkʃənl] ADJ unidirezionale
UNIDO ['juːnɪˌdəʊ] N ABBR (= **United Nations Industrial Development Organization**) UNIDO *f* (= *Organizzazione delle Nazioni Unite per lo sviluppo industriale*)
uni·fi·ca·tion [ˌjuːnɪfɪ'keɪʃən] N unificazione *f*
◎ **uni·form** ['juːnɪˌfɔːm] N (*Mil, school*) uniforme *f*, divisa; **in full uniform** in alta uniforme; **in uniform** in divisa; **out of uniform** in borghese; **school uniform** la divisa scolastica
■ ADJ (*colour, acceleration*) uniforme
uni·formed ['juːnɪˌfɔːmd] ADJ (*police*) in divisa
uni·form·ity [ˌjuːnɪ'fɔːmɪtɪ] N uniformità
uni·form·ly ['juːnɪˌfɔːmlɪ] ADV uniformemente
uni·fy ['juːnɪˌfaɪ] VT (*country*) unire; (*different parts, systems*) unificare
uni·lat·er·al [ˌjuːnɪ'lætərəl] ADJ unilaterale
uni·lat·er·al·ly [ˌjuːnɪ'lætərəlɪ] ADV unilateralmente
un·im·agi·nable [ˌʌnɪ'mædʒɪnəbl] ADJ inimmaginabile, inconcepibile
un·im·agi·na·tive [ˌʌnɪ'mædʒɪnətɪv] ADJ privo(-a) di fantasia
un·im·agi·na·tive·ly [ˌʌnɪ'mædʒɪnətɪvlɪ] ADV senza fantasia
un·im·paired [ˌʌnɪm'pɛəd] ADJ (*health, mental powers*) buono(-a) come prima; (*quality*) non danneggiato(-a)
un·im·peach·able [ˌʌnɪm'piːtʃəbl] ADJ (*honesty, character*) irreprensibile; (*conduct*) incensurabile; (*witness*) al di sopra di ogni sospetto
un·im·ped·ed [ˌʌnɪm'piːdɪd] ADJ (*development, access, growth*) senza impedimenti *or* costrizioni
■ ADV (*proceed, continue*) senza impacci
un·im·por·tant [ˌʌnɪm'pɔːtənt] ADJ (*matter*) senza importanza, di scarsa importanza; (*detail*) trascurabile
un·im·pressed [ˌʌnɪm'prɛst] ADJ (*unmoved*) niente affatto colpito(-a), indifferente; (*unconvinced*) niente affatto convinto(-a)
un·im·pres·sive [ˌʌnɪm'prɛsɪv] ADJ (*person, sight*) che lascia indifferente; (*amount*) insignificante;

(*achievement, result*) poco notevole; (*argument, performance*) poco convincente

un·in·formed [ˌʌnɪnˈfɔːmd] ADJ (*person*) non informato(-a), non al corrente; (*opinion, guess*) non fondato(-a) sulla conoscenza dei fatti

un·in·hab·it·able [ˌʌnɪnˈhæbɪtəbl] ADJ inabitabile

un·in·hab·it·ed [ˌʌnɪnˈhæbɪtɪd] ADJ (*house*) disabitato(-a); (*island*) deserto(-a)

un·in·hib·it·ed [ˌʌnɪnˈhɪbɪtɪd] ADJ (*person, behaviour*) disinibito(-a), senza inibizioni; (*emotion, laughter*) sfrenato(-a)

un·ini·ti·at·ed [ˈʌnɪnˈɪʃɪˌeɪtɪd] ADJ non iniziato(-a)
■ NPL: **the uninitiated** i profani

un·in·jured [ʌnˈɪndʒəd] ADJ (*person*) incolume; (*reputation*) salvo(-a)

un·in·spired [ˌʌnɪnˈspaɪəd] ADJ (*poem, performance*) privo(-a) d'ispirazione, piatto(-a); **he was uninspired by the essay topic** l'argomento del tema non l'ha ispirato

un·in·spir·ing [ˌʌnɪnˈspaɪərɪŋ] ADJ banale

un·in·stall [ˌʌnɪnˈstɔːl] VT (*Comput*) disinstallare

un·in·tel·li·gent [ˌʌnɪnˈtɛlɪdʒənt] ADJ poco intelligente

un·in·tel·li·gible [ˌʌnɪnˈtɛlɪdʒəbl] ADJ incomprensibile, inintelligibile

un·in·tend·ed [ˌʌnɪnˈtɛndɪd] ADJ non voluto(-a); **it was quite unintended** non l'ho (*or* l'ha *etc*) fatto apposta

un·in·ten·tion·al [ˌʌnɪnˈtɛnʃənl] ADJ involontario(-a)

un·in·ten·tion·al·ly [ˌʌnɪnˈtɛnʃnəlɪ] ADV senza volerlo, involontariamente

un·in·ter·est·ed [ʌnˈɪntrɪstɪd] ADJ (*person, attitude*) indifferente; **to be uninterested in politics** non interessarsi di politica

un·in·ter·est·ing [ʌnˈɪntrɪstɪŋ] ADJ (*person*) poco interessante; (*book, offer*) privo(-a) d'interesse

un·in·ter·rupt·ed [ˌʌnɪntəˈrʌptɪd] ADJ (*line, series*) ininterrotto(-a); (*work*) senza interruzioni; **to have an uninterrupted night's sleep** dormire una notte di filato

un·in·ter·rupt·ed·ly [ˌʌnɪntəˈrʌptɪdlɪ] ADV ininterrottamente

un·in·vit·ed [ˌʌnɪnˈvaɪtɪd] ADJ (*guest*) non invitato(-a); (*criticism, attention*) non richiesto(-a); **to arrive uninvited (at sb's house)** piovere in casa (a qn); **to help o.s. to sth uninvited** servirsi di qc senza chiedere il permesso

un·in·vit·ing [ˌʌnɪnˈvaɪtɪŋ] ADJ (*place, food*) poco invitante; (*offer*) poco allettante

Un·ion [ˈjuːnjən] N: **the Union** (*Am*) gli stati dell'Unione; (*Brit*) *unificazione della Gran Bretagna e dell'Irlanda del Nord dal 1920*

◎ **un·ion** [ˈjuːnjən] N **1** (*also:* **trade union**) sindacato; **do you belong to a union?** sei iscritto a un sindacato? **2** (*gen, also Pol*) unione *f*; **the union with England** l'unione con l'Inghilterra **3** (*club, society*) associazione *f*, circolo
■ ADJ (*leader, movement*) sindacale

union-bashing [ˈjuːnjənˌbæʃɪŋ] N (*Brit fam*) propaganda antisindacale

union card N tessera del sindacato

un·ion·ism [ˈjuːnjənɪzəm] N **1** (*Pol*) sindacalismo **2** (*Industry: also:* **trade unionism**) unionismo

Un·ion·ist [ˈjuːnjənɪst] N (*Pol: in Northern Ireland*) unionista *m/f*

un·ion·ist [ˈjuːnjənɪst] N = **trade unionist**

un·ion·ize [ˈjuːnjəˌnaɪz] VT sindacalizzare, organizzare in sindacato

Union Jack N *bandiera nazionale britannica*

Union of Soviet Socialist Republics N Unione *f* delle Repubbliche Socialiste Sovietiche

union shop N *stabilimento in cui tutti gli operai sono tenuti ad aderire ad un sindacato*

◎ **unique** [juːˈniːk] ADJ unico(-a); **to be unique to** essere esclusivo di

unique·ly [juːˈniːklɪ] ADV (*talented*) eccezionalmente; (*confined*) unicamente; **this is a uniquely western phenomenon** è un fenomeno limitato al mondo occidentale

unique·ness [juːˈniːknɪs] N singolarità, unicità

uni·sex [ˈjuːnɪˌsɛks] ADJ unisex *inv*

UNI·SON [ˈjuːnɪzn] N (*Brit*) *sindacato dei lavoratori di enti locali, servizio sanitario e altri settori*

uni·son [ˈjuːnɪzn] N: **in unison** (*Mus, fig*) all'unisono

◎ **unit** [ˈjuːnɪt] N **1** (*gen, Elec, Math, Mil*) unità *f inv*; **monetary/linguistic unit** unità monetaria/linguistica; **unit of length** unità di lunghezza; **unit of measurement** unità di misura **2** (*division, section*) reparto; (*of furniture*) elemento (componibile); (*team, squad*) squadra; **a kitchen unit** un elemento componibile della cucina; **production unit** reparto *m* produzione *inv*; **the basic social unit** il nucleo sociale di base; **research unit** (*personnel*) équipe *f inv*; (*building*) sede *f* di ricerca

unit cost N (*Industry*) costo unitario

unite [juːˈnaɪt] VT (*join: parts, pieces*) unire; (*unify: parts of country*) unificare; **they united their efforts** hanno unito i loro sforzi
■ VI (*join*) unirsi; (*companies*) fondersi; **to unite with sb/in doing** *or* **to do sth** unirsi a qn/per fare qc; **the two parties united** i due partiti si sono uniti

◎ **unit·ed** [juːˈnaɪtɪd] ADJ (*family, people*) unito(-a); (*effort*) unitario(-a); (*efforts*) comune, congiunto(-a)

United Arab Emirates NPL: **the United Arab Emirates** gli Emirati Arabi Uniti

◎ **United Kingdom** N: **the United Kingdom** il Regno Unito
▷ www.ukonline.gov.uk
▷ www.number-10.gov.uk

◎ **United Nations** N: **the United Nations** le Nazioni Unite, l'Organizzazione *f* delle Nazioni Unite
▷ www.unsystem.org

United States N: **the United States (of America)** gli Stati Uniti (d'America)
▷ www.whitehouse.gov/government
▷ www.usatourism.com
▷ www.tourstates.com/

unit price N (*Industry*) prezzo unitario

unit sales NPL numero di pezzi venduti

unit trust N (*Brit Fin*) fondo d'investimento

◎ **unity** [ˈjuːnɪtɪ] N (*in party, country*) unità; (*of members, individuals*) unione *f*; **in unity** in armonia, in pieno accordo

Univ. ABBR = **university**

uni·ver·sal [ˌjuːnɪˈvɜːsəl] ADJ (*phenomenon, disapproval*) generale; (*language, values*) universale; **a universal favourite** un(-a) gran favorito(-a)

universal joint, universal coupling N (*Tech*) giunto cardanico

uni·ver·sal·ly [ˌjuːnɪˈvɜːsəlɪ] ADV (*known*) universalmente; (*accepted*) all'unanimità

◎ **uni·verse** [ˈjuːnɪˌvɜːs] N: **the universe** l'universo

◎ **uni·ver·sity** [ˌjuːnɪˈvɜːsɪtɪ] N università *f inv*; **Oxford University** l'Università di Oxford; **to be at/go to university** essere/andare all'università

■ADJ (*student, professor, education*) universitario(-a)
▷ www.unesco.org/iau
▷ www.universitiesuk.ac.uk/
▷ www.clas.ufl.edu/CLAS/american-universities.html

university degree N (diploma *m* di) laurea

university year N anno accademico

un·just [ʌn'dʒʌst] ADJ ingiusto(-a); **to be unjust to sb** essere ingiusto(-a) con *or* verso qn

un·jus·ti·fi·able [ʌn'dʒʌstɪˌfaɪəbl] ADJ ingiustificabile

un·jus·ti·fi·ably [ʌn'dʒʌstɪˌfaɪəblɪ] ADV senza motivo

un·jus·ti·fied [ʌn'dʒʌstɪˌfaɪd] ADJ (*remark*) ingiustificato(-a), immotivato(-a); (*suspicion*) infondato(-a); (*Typ: text*) non giustificato(-a)

un·just·ly [ʌn'dʒʌstlɪ] ADV ingiustamente

un·kempt [ʌn'kɛmpt] ADJ (*hair*) scarmigliato(-a), spettinato(-a); (*appearance*) trasandato(-a)

un·kind [ʌn'kaɪnd] ADJ (*comp* **-er**, *superl* **-est**) (*person, remark*) poco gentile, scortese; (*: stronger*) villano(-a); (*fate, blow*) crudele; **the sun can be unkind to delicate skins** il sole può far male alle pelli delicate; **without wishing to be unkind, she's not the most interesting company** senza voler essere scortese, la sua compagnia non è delle più interessanti; **it's unkind of him to want my career to fail now** è crudele da parte sua volere che la mia carriera si interrompa adesso

un·kind·ly [ʌn'kaɪndlɪ] ADV (*speak*) in modo sgarbato; (*treat*) male; **don't take it unkindly if ...** non te la prendere se...

un·kind·ness [ʌn'kaɪndnɪs] N sgarbatezza; (*stronger*) cattiveria

un·know·able [ʌn'nəʊəbl] ADJ inconoscibile

un·know·ing [ʌn'nəʊɪŋ] ADJ inconsapevole, ignaro(-a)

un·know·ing·ly [ʌn'nəʊɪŋlɪ] ADV senza accorgersene, senza saperlo

◎**un·known** [ʌn'nəʊn] ADJ sconosciuto(-a), ignoto(-a); **the murderer is as yet unknown** ancora non si sa chi sia l'assassino; **it's unknown for her to get to work on time** quando mai è arrivata al lavoro in orario?; **unknown quantity** (*Math, fig*) incognita; **his intentions are unknown to me** non conosco le sue intenzioni; **a substance unknown to scientists** una sostanza ignota agli scienziati
■ADV: **unknown to me** a mia insaputa; **unknown to them he was nearby** era nelle vicinanze, a loro insaputa
■N **1** (*person*) sconosciuto(-a) **2** (*Math*) incognita; **the unknown** l'ignoto

Unknown Soldier, Unknown Warrior N: **the Unknown Soldier** il Milite Ignoto

un·lad·en [ʌn'leɪdn] ADJ (*ship, weight*) a vuoto

un·lady·like [ʌn'leɪdɪˌlaɪk] ADJ (*pej*) non da signora (perbene); **it's unladylike to swear** una vera signora non dice le parolacce

un·law·ful [ʌn'lɔːfʊl] ADJ illecito(-a), illegale

un·law·ful·ly [ʌn'lɔːfəlɪ] ADV illegalmente

un·lead·ed [ʌn'lɛdɪd] N (*also:* **unleaded petrol**) benzina senza piombo

un·leash [ʌn'liːʃ] VT (*dog*) sguinzagliare; (*fig*) scatenare

un·leav·ened [ʌn'lɛvnd] ADJ (*bread*) azzimo(-a), non lievitato(-a)

◎**un·less** [ʌn'lɛs] CONJ a meno che non + *sub*, se non + *indic*, a meno di + *infin*; **we won't get there on time unless we leave earlier** se non partiamo prima non arriveremo in tempo; **unless otherwise stated** salvo indicazione contraria; **unless I am mistaken** se non mi sbaglio

un·li·censed [ˌʌn'laɪsənst] ADJ (*vehicle*) senza bollo; (*Brit: hotel, restaurant*) senza licenza per la vendita di alcolici

◎**un·like** [ʌn'laɪk] ADJ diverso(-a), dissimile; **to be unlike sth** essere diverso(-a) da qc; **that photo is quite unlike her** quella foto non le somiglia affatto; **it's quite unlike him to do that** non è da lui fare una cosa simile
■PREP a differenza di, contrariamente a; **I, unlike others ...** diversamente dagli *or* a differenza degli altri, io...

un·like·li·hood [ʌn'laɪklɪhʊd], **un·like·li·ness** [ʌn'laɪklɪnɪs] N improbabilità

◎**un·like·ly** [ʌn'laɪklɪ] ADJ (*comp* **-ier**, *superl* **-iest**) (*happening*) improbabile; (*explanation*) inverosimile; **in the unlikely event that it does happen ...** dovesse succedere, cosa assai improbabile...; **it is unlikely that he will come** *or* **he is unlikely to come** è poco probabile che venga

un·lim·it·ed [ʌn'lɪmɪtɪd] ADJ (*time, power*) illimitato(-a); (*wealth*) smisurato(-a)

un·lined [ʌn'laɪnd] ADJ (*paper*) senza righe; (*garment*) senza fodera, sfoderato(-a)

un·list·ed [ʌn'lɪstɪd] ADJ (*item*) non elencato(-a); (*Stock Exchange: share*) non quotato(-a); (*Am Telec*): **unlisted number** numero fuori elenco

un·lit [ʌn'lɪt] ADJ (*lamp*) spento(-a); (*room*) senza luce; (*road*) non illuminato(-a)

un·load [ʌn'ləʊd] VT **1** scaricare **2** (*fam: get rid of*): **to unload onto sb** (*problem, children*) scaricare su qn
■VI scaricare

un·load·ing [ʌn'ləʊdɪŋ] N scarico

un·lock [ʌn'lɒk] VT aprire; **he unlocked the door of the car** ha aperto la portiera dell'auto; **she left the door unlocked** non ha chiuso la porta a chiave

unlooked-for [ˌʌn'lʊktfɔːʳ] ADJ inaspettato(-a), inatteso(-a)

un·loose [ʌn'luːs], **un·loos·en** [ʌn'luːsn] VT (*hair*) sciogliere; (*knot*) slegare, sciogliere

un·lov·able [ʌn'lʌvəbl] ADJ antipatico(-a)

un·loved [ʌn'lʌvd] ADJ non amato(-a); **to feel unloved** sentirsi non amato(-a)

un·lucki·ly [ʌn'lʌkɪlɪ] ADV purtroppo, sfortunatamente; **unluckily for her** per sua sfortuna

un·lucky [ʌn'lʌkɪ] ADJ (*comp* **-ier**, *superl* **-iest**) (*person, day*) sfortunato(-a); (*decision*) infausto(-a), infelice; (*number, object*) che porta sfortuna *or* male, di malaugurio; **she was unlucky enough to meet him** ha avuto la sfortuna di incontrarlo; **to be unlucky** (*person*) essere sfortunato(-a), non avere fortuna; (*number, thing*) portare sfortuna; **it's unlucky to walk under a ladder** porta sfortuna *or* male passare sotto una scala

un·made [ʌn'meɪd] ADJ (*bed*) disfatto(-a)

un·man·age·able [ʌn'mænɪdʒəbl] ADJ (*unwieldy: tool, vehicle*) poco maneggevole; (*: parcel, size*) ingombrante; (*uncontrollable: teenage child*) difficile; (*: hair*) ribelle; (*: situation*) difficile da gestire

un·manned [ˌʌn'mænd] ADJ (*spacecraft*) senza equipaggio

un·man·ner·ly [ʌn'mænəlɪ] ADJ maleducato(-a), scortese

un·marked [ʌn'mɑːkt] ADJ (*unstained*) pulito(-a), senza macchie; (*unblemished: face, body*) senza rughe; (*without marking: linen*) senza cifre; (*: banknote*) non segnato(-a); (*uncorrected: essay*) non corretto(-a); **unmarked police car** auto *f* civetta *inv*

un·mar·ried [ʌn'mærɪd] ADJ (*man*) celibe, non sposato;

(*woman*) nubile, non sposata; **unmarried couple** coppia non sposata
unmarried mother N ragazza *f* madre *inv*
un·mask [ʌn'mɑ:sk] VT (*fig*) smascherare
un·matched [ʌn'mætʃt] ADJ senza pari, impareggiabile
un·men·tion·able [ʌn'menʃnəbl] ADJ (*topic*) tabù *inv*; (*vice, disease*) innominabile; (*word*) irripetibile
un·mer·ci·ful [ʌn'mɜ:sɪfʊl] ADJ spietato(-a)
un·mer·ci·fully [ʌn'mɜ:sɪfəlɪ] ADV (*tease, bully*) senza pietà
un·mind·ful [ʌn'maɪndfʊl] ADJ: **to be unmindful of** (*frm*) essere incurante di
un·miss·able [ˌʌn'mɪsəbl] ADJ (*Brit fam*) imperdibile
un·mis·tak·able, un·mis·take·able [ˌʌnmɪs'teɪkəbl] ADJ (*person, sound*) inconfondibile; (*displeasure, meaning*) indubbio(-a), lampante; **his style was unmistakable** il suo stile era inconfondibile; **the similarities between the sisters are unmistakable** la somiglianza tra le due sorelle è indubbia
un·mis·tak·ably, un·mis·take·ably [ˌʌnmɪs'teɪkəblɪ] ADV senza timore di sbagliarsi, inconfondibilmente; **unmistakably clear** inequivocabilmente chiaro(-a)
un·miti·gat·ed [ʌn'mɪtɪˌgeɪtɪd] ADJ (*disaster, nonsense*) totale, completo(-a); (*criminal, scoundrel*) incallito(-a)
un·mo·ti·vat·ed [ʌn'məʊtɪˌveɪtɪd] ADJ immotivato(-a)
un·moved [ʌn'mu:vd] ADJ: **unmoved (by)** indifferente (a)
un·mu·si·cal [ʌn'mju:zɪkəl] ADJ (*sound*) disarmonico(-a); (*person*) che non ha orecchio
un·named [ʌn'neɪmd] ADJ (*fear, object*) senza nome; (*donor, author*) anonimo(-a)
un·natu·ral [ʌn'nætʃrəl] ADJ (*gen*) innaturale; (*affected*) affettato(-a); (*abnormal*) non normale; **genetic manipulation is unnatural** la manipolazione genetica è contro natura; **her back ached from lying in this unnatural position** le faceva male la schiena per la posizione innaturale in cui era sdraiata; **it's unnatural for him to behave like that** non è da lui comportarsi così
un·natu·ral·ly [ʌn'nætʃrəlɪ] ADV in modo innaturale; **the house was unnaturally silent** la casa era stranamente silenziosa; **not unnaturally she was worried** è comprensibile che fosse preoccupata
un·nec·es·sari·ly [ʌn'nɛsɪsərɪlɪ] ADV (*worry, suffer*) inutilmente; (*large, long, difficult*) eccessivamente
un·nec·es·sary [ʌn'nɛsɪsərɪ] ADJ (*superfluous*) non necessario(-a), superfluo(-a); (*useless*) inutile; **it was unnecessary to be rude!** non c'era bisogno di essere sgarbato!; **it's unnecessary for you to attend** non è necessario che tu intervenga
un·nerve [ʌn'nɜ:v] VT (*subj: accident*) sgomentare; (*: hostile attitude*) bloccare; (*experience*) far sentire disagio
unnerving [ʌn'nɜ:vɪŋ] ADJ inquietante
un·no·ticed [ʌn'nəʊtɪst] ADJ: **to go** *or* **pass unnoticed** passare inosservato(-a)
un·num·bered [ʌn'nʌmbəd] ADJ (*without a number: house*) senza numero, non numerato(-a); (*frm: innumerable*) innumerevole
UNO [ju:ɛn'əʊ] N ABBR (= **United Nations Organization**) ONU *f*
un·ob·jec·tion·able [ˌʌnəb'dʒɛkʃnəbl] ADJ (*person*) ammodo *inv*; (*conduct*) ineccepibile
un·ob·serv·ant [ˌʌnəb'zɜ:vənt] ADJ: **to be unobservant** non avere spirito di osservazione
un·ob·served [ˌʌnəb'zɜ:vd] ADJ inosservato(-a); **to go unobserved** passare inosservato(-a)
un·ob·struct·ed [ˌʌnəb'strʌktɪd] ADJ (*vision*) libero(-a); (*road*) sgombro(-a); (*pipe*) non ostruito(-a), non bloccato(-a); **an unobstructed view** un'ampia visuale
un·ob·tain·able [ˌʌnəb'teɪnəbl] ADJ (*food, materials*) introvabile; **this number is unobtainable** (*Telec*) è impossibile ottenere questo numero
un·ob·tru·sive [ˌʌnəb'tru:sɪv] ADJ discreto(-a)
un·ob·tru·sive·ly [ˌʌnəb'tru:sɪvlɪ] ADV (*discreetly*) con discrezione
un·oc·cu·pied [ʌn'ɒkjʊˌpaɪd] ADJ (*house*) vuoto(-a); (*seat, table, also Mil: zone*) libero(-a), non occupato(-a); (*person: not busy*) libero(-a), senza impegni
un·of·fi·cial [ˌʌnə'fɪʃəl] ADJ (*visit*) privato(-a), non ufficiale; (*unconfirmed: report, news*) ufficioso(-a); **in an unofficial capacity** in veste ufficiosa; **unofficial strike** sciopero non autorizzato; **unofficial figures** cifre ufficiose
un·of·fi·cial·ly [ˌʌnə'fɪʃəlɪ] ADV ufficiosamente
un·opened [ʌn'əʊpənd] ADJ (*letter*) chiuso(-a); (*present*) ancora incartato(-a); (*bottle, tin*) non aperto(-a)
un·op·posed [ˌʌnə'pəʊzd] ADJ (*enter, be elected*) senza incontrare opposizione; **the motion was unopposed by the committee** il comitato non si è opposto alla mozione
un·or·gan·ized [ʌn'ɔ:gəˌnaɪzd] ADJ (*person*) disorganizzato(-a); (*essay, life*) mal organizzato(-a)
un·origi·nal [ˌʌnə'rɪdʒɪnəl] ADJ poco originale, privo(-a) di originalità
un·ortho·dox [ʌn'ɔ:θəˌdɒks] ADJ poco ortodosso(-a)
un·os·ten·ta·tious [ˌʌnɒstən'teɪʃəs] ADJ modesto(-a), semplice
un·pack [ʌn'pæk] VT (*suitcases*) disfare; (*belongings*) sballare; **I unpacked my suitcase** ho disfatto la valigia; **I haven't unpacked my clothes yet** non ho ancora tolto i vestiti dalla valigia
■ VI disfare le valige *or* i bagagli; **I went to my room to unpack** sono andato in camera mia a disfare le valige
un·paid [ʌn'peɪd] ADJ (*bill, debt*) da pagare; (*holiday*) non pagato(-a); (*work*) non retribuito(-a)
un·pal·at·able [ʌn'pælətəbl] ADJ (*food*) immangiabile; (*drink*) imbevibile; (*fig: truth*) sgradevole
un·par·al·leled [ʌn'pærəˌlɛld] ADJ senza pari, impareggiabile
un·par·don·able [ʌn'pɑ:dnəbl] ADJ imperdonabile
un·par·lia·men·ta·ry [ˌʌnpɑ:lə'mɛntərɪ] ADJ (*Brit: language, behaviour*) non consono(-a) alla sede parlamentare
un·pat·ri·ot·ic [ˌʌnpætrɪ'ɒtɪk] ADJ (*person*) poco patriottico(-a); (*speech, attitude*) antipatriottico(-a)
un·per·turbed [ˌʌnpə'tɜ:bd] ADJ imperturbato(-a), imperterrito(-a); **unperturbed by sth** per nulla scosso(-a) da qc
un·pick [ʌn'pɪk] VT (*seam*) disfare; (*stitches*) togliere
un·pin [ʌn'pɪn] VT (*dress*) togliere gli spilli a; (*hair*) togliere le forcine a; (*notice*) staccare
un·planned [ʌn'plænd] ADJ (*visit*) imprevisto(-a); (*baby, pregnancy*) non previsto(-a)
un·pleas·ant [ʌn'plɛznt] ADJ (*smell, task*) sgradevole, spiacevole; (*person, remark*) antipatico(-a); (*day, experience*) brutto(-a); **to be unpleasant to sb** essere villano(-a) con qn; **an unpleasant situation** una situazione spiacevole; **an unpleasant smell** un odore sgradevole
un·pleas·ant·ly [ʌn'plɛzntlɪ] ADV in modo poco piacevole; **the room smelt unpleasantly of fish** c'era un odore sgradevole di pesce nella stanza; **it was unpleasantly close to the truth** era spiacevolmente

Uu

vicino al vero; **it's unpleasantly hot in here** qui dentro fa troppo caldo, per i miei gusti

un·pleas·ant·ness [ʌn'plɛzntnɪs] N (*bad feeling, quarrelling*) tensioni *fpl*; (*nastiness: of smell, event*) sgradevolezza; (*: of person*) antipatia

un·plug [ʌn'plʌg] VT staccare (la spina di); **she unplugs the TV before going to bed** stacca la presa della TV prima di andare a letto

un·pol·ished [ʌn'pɒlɪʃt] ADJ (*shoes, furniture*) non lucidato(-a); (*diamond*) grezzo(-a); (*manners, person*) rozzo(-a)

un·pol·lut·ed [ˌʌnpə'lu:tɪd] ADJ non inquinato(-a)

un·popu·lar [ʌn'pɒpjʊlə[r]] ADJ (*gen*) impopolare; **to be unpopular with sb** (*person, law*) non riscuotere l'approvazione di qn; **to make o.s. unpopular (with)** rendersi antipatico(-a) (a); (*subj: politician*) alienarsi le simpatie (di); **I'm unpopular with the boss at the moment** non sono nelle grazie del capo in questo momento; **he's unpopular with the rest of the class** è mal visto dal resto della classe

un·popu·lar·ity [ˌʌnpɒpjʊ'lærɪtɪ] N impopolarità

un·prec·edent·ed [ʌn'presɪdəntɪd] ADJ senza precedenti

un·pre·dict·able [ˌʌnprɪ'dɪktəbl] ADJ imprevedibile

un·preju·diced [ʌn'prɛdʒʊdɪst] ADJ (*not biased*) obiettivo(-a), imparziale; (*having no prejudices*) senza pregiudizi

un·pre·pared [ˌʌnprɪ'pɛəd] ADJ (*person*) impreparato(-a); (*speech*) improvvisato(-a); **it caught me unprepared** mi ha trovato impreparato; **he was unprepared for her reaction** la sua reazione lo colse alla sprovvista

un·pre·pos·sess·ing [ˌʌnpri:pə'zɛsɪŋ] ADJ poco attraente

un·pre·ten·tious [ˌʌnprɪ'tɛnʃəs] ADJ senza pretese

un·prin·ci·pled [ʌn'prɪnsɪpld] ADJ senza scrupoli

un·print·able [ʌn'prɪntəbl] ADJ non pubblicabile; (*fig: word, remark*) irripetibile

un·pro·duc·tive [ˌʌnprə'dʌktɪv] ADJ improduttivo(-a); (*discussion*) sterile

un·pro·fes·sion·al [ˌʌnprə'fɛʃənl] ADJ: **unprofessional conduct** scorrettezza professionale

un·prof·it·able [ʌn'prɒfɪtəbl] ADJ (*financially*) non redditizio(-a); (*: job, deal*) poco lucrativo(-a); (*fig*) infruttuoso(-a), poco produttivo(-a); **an unprofitable afternoon** un pomeriggio poco produttivo

UNPROFOR [ʌn'prəʊfɔ:[r]] N ABBR (= United Nations Protection Force) UNPROFOR *m*

un·prom·is·ing [ʌn'prɒmɪsɪŋ] ADJ poco promettente

un·pro·nounce·able [ˌʌnprə'naʊnsəbl] ADJ impronunciabile

un·pro·tect·ed [ˌʌnprə'tɛktɪd] ADJ (*town*) indifeso(-a); (*house*) esposto(-a), non riparato(-a); (*sex*) non protetto(-a)

un·prov·en [ˌʌn'pru:vən, ˌʌn'prəʊvən] ADJ non provato(-a), non dimostrato(-a)

un·pro·voked [ˌʌnprə'vəʊkt] ADJ (*attack*) non provocato(-a); (*unpleasant remark*) ingiustificato(-a)

un·pub·lished [ʌn'pʌblɪʃt] ADJ inedito(-a)

un·pun·ished [ʌn'pʌnɪʃt] ADJ: **to go unpunished** restare impunito(-a)

un·quali·fied [ʌn'kwɒlɪˌfaɪd] ADJ **1** (*worker*) non qualificato(-a); (*in professions*) non diplomato(-a), non abilitato(-a); (*applicant*) senza i requisiti necessari; **unqualified members of staff at the hospital** personale *m* non qualificato all'ospedale; **she was unqualified for the job** non era qualificata per il lavoro **2** (*absolute: assent, denial*) incondizionato(-a); (*: admiration*) senza riserve; (*: success, disaster*) completo(-a), assoluto(-a); **an unqualified success** un successo completo

un·ques·tion·able [ʌn'kwɛstʃənəbl] ADJ (*fact*) incontestabile, indiscutibile; (*honesty*) indiscusso(-a)

un·ques·tion·ably [ʌn'kwɛstʃənəblɪ] ADV indiscutibilmente

un·ques·tioned [ʌn'kwɛstʃənd] ADJ (*popularity, virtue*) indiscusso(-a); (*statement*) incontestato(-a)

un·ques·tion·ing [ʌn'kwɛstʃənɪŋ] ADJ (*obedience, acceptance*) cieco(-a)

un·rav·el [ʌn'rævəl] VT (*knitting*) disfare; (*wool*) dipanare, districare; (*threads*) sfilare, sbrogliare; (*fig: mystery*) risolvere; (*: plot*) venire a capo di
■VI (*knitting*) disfarsi; (*threads*) sbrogliarsi

un·read [ʌn'rɛd] ADJ non letto(-a); **a pile of unread magazines** una pila di riviste non lette; **I returned the book unread** ho restituito il libro senza leggerlo

un·read·able [ʌn'ri:dəbl] ADJ illeggibile

un·ready [ʌn'rɛdɪ] ADJ impreparato(-a)

un·real [ʌn'rɪəl] ADJ irreale; **an unreal situation** una situazione irreale; **unreal expectations** aspettative *fpl* esagerate; **it was unreal!** era incredibile!

un·re·al·is·tic [ˌʌnrɪə'lɪstɪk] ADJ (*idea*) illusorio(-a); (*estimate*) non realistico(-a); **you're being unrealistic if you think ...** ti fai delle illusioni se credi...

un·re·al·ity [ˌʌnrɪ'ælɪtɪ] N irrealtà

un·rea·son·able [ʌn'ri:znəbl] ADJ (*person, idea, behaviour*) irragionevole; (*price, time*) irragionevole, assurdo(-a); **it is unreasonable to expect that** è un po' troppo aspettarsi che + *sub*; **he makes unreasonable demands on me** pretende troppo da me; **he was most unreasonable about it** non ha voluto sentire ragioni; **her attitude was completely unreasonable** il suo atteggiamento era del tutto irragionevole

un·rea·son·ably [ʌn'ri:znəblɪ] ADV (*behave*) irragionevolmente; (*demand*) eccessivamente; **not unreasonably** a ragione

un·rea·son·ing [ʌn'ri:znɪŋ] ADJ irragionevole

un·rec·og·niz·able [ʌn'rɛkəgˌnaɪzəbl] ADJ irriconoscibile

un·rec·og·nized [ʌn'rɛkəgˌnaɪzd] ADJ (*talent, genius*) misconosciuto(-a); (*Pol: regime*) non riconosciuto(-a) ufficialmente; **he walked along the street unrecognized by passers-by** ha camminato per la strada senza che nessuno lo riconoscesse

un·re·cord·ed [ˌʌnrɪ'kɔ:dɪd] ADJ non documentato(-a), non registrato(-a)

un·re·fined [ˌʌnrɪ'faɪnd] ADJ (*petroleum*) greggio(-a); (*sugar*) non raffinato(-a); (*person, manners: coarse*) rozzo(-a)

un·re·hearsed [ˌʌnrɪ'hɜ:st] ADJ (*Theatre*) improvvisato(-a); (*spontaneous*) imprevisto(-a)

un·re·lat·ed [ˌʌnrɪ'leɪtɪd] ADJ: **unrelated (to)** (*unconnected*) senza nesso *or* rapporto (con); (*by family*) non imparentato(-a) (con), senza legami di parentela (con)

un·re·lent·ing [ˌʌnrɪ'lɛntɪŋ] ADJ (*rain, heat*) incessante; (*activity*) senza tregua; (*attack*) che non dà tregua; (*hatred*) irriducibile, implacabile; (*person*) spietato(-a)

un·re·li·abil·ity [ˌʌnrɪlaɪə'bɪlɪtɪ] N scarsa affidabilità

un·re·li·able [ˌʌnrɪ'laɪəbl] ADJ (*person*) su cui non si può contare *or* fare affidamento; (*source*) inattendibile; (*firm*) poco serio(-a); (*car, machine*) che non dà affidamento; **it's a nice car, but a bit unreliable** è una bella macchina, ma è un po' inaffidabile

un·re·lieved [,ʌnrɪ'li:vd] ADJ *(pain, gloom)* costante; *(anguish, depression)* totale; *(boredom)* mortale; *(monotony)* ininterrotto(-a); *(colour)* uniforme

un·re·mark·able [,ʌnrɪ'mɑ:kəbl] ADJ mediocre

un·re·mark·ed [ʌnrɪ'mɑ:kt] ADJ: **to go** *or* **remain unremarked** passare inosservato(-a)

un·re·mit·ting [,ʌnrɪ'mɪtɪŋ] *(frm)* ADJ *(activity)* senza sosta, incessante; *(efforts, demands)* costante; *(hatred)* irriducibile, implacabile

un·re·peat·able [,ʌnrɪ'pi:təbl] ADJ irripetibile

un·re·pent·ant [,ʌnrɪ'pɛntənt] ADJ *(sinner)* impenitente; *(believer, supporter)* irriducibile; **to be unrepentant about sth** non mostrare un'ombra di rimorso per qc

un·rep·re·senta·tive [,ʌnrɛprɪ'zɛntətɪv] ADJ *(untypical)* atipico(-a), poco rappresentativo(-a)

un·rep·re·sent·ed [ʌn,rɛprɪ'zɛntɪd] ADJ non rappresentato(-a)

un·re·quit·ed [,ʌnrɪ'kwaɪtɪd] ADJ *(liter: love)* non ricambiato(-a), non corrisposto(-a)

un·re·served [,ʌnrɪ'zɜ:vd] ADJ **1** *(seat)* non prenotato(-a), non riservato(-a) **2** *(approval, admiration)* senza riserve

un·re·serv·ed·ly [,ʌnrɪ'zɜ:vɪdlɪ] ADV *(without reservation)* senza riserve; *(frankly)* francamente

un·re·solved [,ʌnrɪ'zɒlvd] ADJ *(frm: difficulty, problem, issue)* irrisolto(-a)

un·re·spon·sive ['ʌnrɪs'pɒnsɪv] ADJ che non reagisce; **unresponsive to** insensibile a

un·rest [ʌn'rɛst] N *(disturbances)* agitazioni *fpl*

un·re·strained [,ʌnrɪ'streɪnd] ADJ sfrenato(-a)

un·re·strain·ed·ly [,ʌnrɪ'streɪnɪdlɪ] ADV sfrenatamente

un·re·strict·ed [,ʌnrɪ'strɪktɪd] ADJ senza una regolamentazione; *(power, time)* illimitato(-a); *(access, parking)* libero(-a)

un·re·ward·ed [,ʌnrɪ'wɔ:dɪd] ADJ non ricompensato(-a); **to go unrewarded** rimanere senza ricompensa

un·re·ward·ing [,ʌnrɪ'wɔ:dɪŋ] ADJ *(job)* ingrato(-a), senza soddisfazioni; *(: financially)* poco remunerativo(-a)

un·ripe [ʌn'raɪp] ADJ non maturo(-a)

un·ri·valled, *(Am)* **un·ri·valed** [ʌn'raɪvəld] ADJ senza pari; **to be unrivalled** non avere *or* non temere rivali

un·roll [ʌn'rəʊl] VT srotolare
■ VI srotolarsi

un·ro·man·tic [,ʌnrə'mæntɪk] ADJ poco romantico(-a)

un·ruf·fled [ʌn'rʌfld] ADJ *(person)* imperturbato(-a); *(hair)* a posto; *(water)* senza un'increspatura

un·ruled [ʌn'ru:ld] ADJ *(paper)* senza righe

un·ru·ly [ʌn'ru:lɪ] ADJ *(comp* **-ier**, *superl* **-iest**) *(behaviour)* indisciplinato(-a); *(child, mob)* turbolento(-a); *(hair)* ribelle

un·sad·dle [ʌn'sædl] VT *(horse)* dissellare; *(rider)* disarcionare

un·safe [ʌn'seɪf] ADJ *(machine, car, wiring)* pericoloso(-a); *(method)* poco sicuro(-a), rischioso(-a); **unsafe to drink** non potabile; **unsafe to eat** non commestibile; **to feel unsafe** non sentirsi sicuro(-a); **it's unsafe to go out alone at night** è pericoloso uscire da soli la sera

un·said [ʌn'sɛd] ADJ non detto(-a), taciuto(-a); **consider it unsaid** come non detto; **to leave sth unsaid** passare qc sotto silenzio; **it would have been better left unsaid** sarebbe stato meglio non dirlo; **much was left unsaid** molte cose sono rimaste non dette

un·sale·able, *(Am)* **un·sal·able** [ʌn'seɪləbl] ADJ invendibile

un·sat·is·fac·tory [,ʌnsætɪs'fæktərɪ] ADJ *(result)* poco soddisfacente; *(profits)* al di sotto delle aspettative; *(piece of work, hotel room)* che lascia a desiderare; *(on school report)* insufficiente

un·sat·is·fied [ʌn'sætɪs,faɪd] ADJ *(desire, need)* non appagato(-a); *(not fulfilled: person)* insoddisfatto(-a); *(not convinced)*: **unsatisfied (with)** poco convinto(-a) (di)

un·sat·is·fy·ing [ʌn'sætɪs,faɪɪŋ] ADJ *(result, work)* insoddisfacente, poco soddisfacente; *(meal)* che non soddisfa

un·satu·rat·ed [ʌn'sætʃə,reɪtɪd] ADJ *(fat)* insaturo(-a)

un·sa·voury, *(Am)* **un·sa·vory** [ʌn'seɪvərɪ] ADJ *(character, business, activity)* equivoco(-a), losco(-a); *(place, district, reputation)* poco raccomandabile; *(appearance)* sgradevole

un·scathed [ʌn'skeɪðd] ADJ senza un graffio, incolume; *(fig)* indenne

un·sched·uled [ʌn'ʃɛdju:ld, *Am* ʌn'skɛdju:ld] ADJ *(announcement, landing, stop)* non programmato(-a), imprevisto(-a)

un·sci·en·tif·ic [,ʌnsaɪən'tɪfɪk] ADJ poco scientifico(-a)

un·screw [ʌn'skru:] VT svitare
■ VI svitarsi

un·script·ed [ʌn'skrɪptɪd] ADJ *(Radio, TV)* improvvisato(-a)

un·scru·pu·lous [ʌn'skru:pjʊləs] ADJ *(person)* senza scrupoli, privo(-a) di scrupoli; *(means)* disonesto(-a)

un·scru·pu·lous·ly [ʌn'skru:pjʊləslɪ] ADV senza scrupoli

un·scru·pu·lous·ness [ʌn'skru:pjʊləsnɪs] N mancanza di scrupoli

un·sea·son·able [ʌn'si:znəbl] ADJ *(weather)* non tipico(-a) della stagione

un·sea·soned [ʌn'si:znd] ADJ *(food)* scondito(-a); *(timber)* non stagionato(-a); *(fig: inexperienced)* inesperto(-a)

un·seat [ʌn'si:t] VT *(rider)* disarcionare; *(fig: official)* spodestare; *(: Members of Parliament)* far perdere il seggio a

un·secured [,ʌnsɪ'kjʊəd] ADJ: **unsecured creditor** creditore *m* non privilegiato

un·seed·ed [ʌn'si:dɪd] ADJ *(Sport)* che non è una testa di serie

un·seem·ly [ʌn'si:mlɪ] ADJ *(pej)* sconveniente, indecoroso(-a)

un·seen [ʌn'si:n] ADJ *(person)* inosservato(-a); *(danger)* nascosto(-a); *(Scol: translation)* all'impronta
■ N *(Scol)* traduzione *f* all'impronta

un·self·con·scious [,ʌnsɛlf'kɒnʃəs] ADJ disinvolto(-a)

un·self·ish [ʌn'sɛlfɪʃ] ADJ *(person)* altruista; *(act)* disinteressato(-a)

un·self·ish·ly [ʌn'sɛlfɪʃlɪ] ADV con altruismo, generosamente

un·self·ish·ness [ʌn'sɛlfɪʃnɪs] N *(of person)* altruismo; *(of act)* generosità

un·ser·vice·able [ʌn'sɜ:vɪsəbl] ADJ inservibile

un·set·tle [ʌn'sɛtl] VT *(stomach, plans)* scombussolare; *(person)* disorientare

un·set·tled [ʌn'sɛtld] ADJ *(weather, market, situation)* instabile, variabile; *(person: restless)* irrequieto(-a); *(: itinerant)* nomade; *(frm: question, issue)* non risolto(-a); **to feel unsettled** sentirsi turbato(-a) *or* scombussolato(-a); **the staff were unsettled and**

Uu

demoralized il personale era turbato e demoralizzato; **unsettled weather** tempo instabile; **an unsettled dispute** una controversia irrisolta

un·set·tling [ʌn'sɛtlɪŋ] ADJ inquietante; **the news had an unsettling effect on me** la notizia mi ha scombussolato

un·shak·able, un·shake·able [ʌn'ʃeɪkəbl] ADJ irremovibile

un·shak·en [ʌn'ʃeɪkən] ADJ (*person*) nient'affatto scosso(-a), risoluto(-a); (*resolve*) saldo(-a) come prima

un·shav·en [ʌn'ʃeɪvn] ADJ non rasato(-a)

un·shock·able [ʌn'ʃɒkəbl] ADJ: **he is unshockable** niente lo scandalizza

un·shrink·able [ʌn'ʃrɪŋkəbl] ADJ irrestringibile

un·sight·ly [ʌn'saɪtlɪ] ADJ (*unattractive*) sgradevole a vedersi; (*ugly*) brutto(-a)

un·sink·able [ʌn'sɪŋkəbl] ADJ inaffondabile

un·skilled [ʌn'skɪld] ADJ (*worker, manpower*) non specializzato(-a); **an unskilled worker** un operaio non specializzato

un·so·ciable [ʌn'səʊʃəbl] ADJ (*pej: person*) poco socievole; **he's very unsociable** è un orso

un·so·cial [ʌn'səʊʃəl] ADJ: **unsocial hours** orario *msg* sconveniente

un·sold [ʌn'səʊld] ADJ invenduto(-a)

un·so·lic·it·ed [ˌʌnsə'lɪsɪtɪd] ADJ non richiesto(-a)

un·solved [ʌn'sɒlvd] ADJ non risolto(-a)

un·so·phis·ti·cat·ed [ˌʌnsə'fɪstɪˌkeɪtɪd] ADJ (*person, dress, habits*) semplice; (*machine*) primitivo(-a), rudimentale

un·sound [ʌn'saʊnd] ADJ (*health*) debole, cagionevole; (*in construction: floor, foundations*) malsicuro(-a); (*argument*) che non regge; (*opinion*) poco fondato(-a); (*policy, advice*) poco sensato(-a); (*judgment, investment*) poco sicuro(-a); (*business*) poco solido(-a); **of unsound mind** (*Law*) non in pieno possesso delle proprie facoltà mentali

un·spar·ing [ʌn'spɛərɪŋ] ADJ (*generous*): **to be unsparing of** *or* **in** non risparmiare; (*criticism*) spietato(-a)

un·spar·ing·ly [ʌn'spɛərɪŋlɪ] ADV (*generously*) generosamente; (*unmercifully*) spietatamente

un·speak·able [ʌn'spi:kəbl] ADJ (*behaviour, crime*) abominevole; (*pain, joy*) indicibile, indescrivibile

un·speak·ably [ʌn'spi:kəblɪ] ADV indicibilmente

un·speci·fied [ʌn'spɛsɪfaɪd] ADJ imprecisato(-a)

un·spoiled [ʌn'spɔɪld], **un·spoilt** [ʌn'spɔɪlt] ADJ (*countryside, beauty*) non deturpato(-a); (*child*) non viziato(-a); (*person*) genuino(-a)

un·spo·ken [ʌn'spəʊkən] ADJ (*words*) non detto(-a); (*thoughts*) non espresso(-a); (*agreement, approval*) tacito(-a)

un·sport·ing [ʌn'spɔ:tɪŋ] ADJ (*pej*) poco sportivo(-a)

un·sta·ble [ʌn'steɪbl] ADJ (*structure, situation, Chem, Phys*) instabile; (*person*) squilibrato(-a)

un·stamped [ʌn'stæmpt] ADJ (*letter*) non affrancato(-a)

un·steadi·ly [ˌʌn'stɛdɪlɪ] ADV in modo incerto

un·steady [ʌn'stɛdɪ] ADJ (*ladder, foothold*) instabile, malsicuro(-a); (*hand, voice*) tremante; (*economy*) vacillante; **to be unsteady on one's feet** non reggersi bene sulle gambe

un·stint·ing [ʌn'stɪntɪŋ] ADJ (*support*) incondizionato(-a); (*generosity*) illimitato(-a); (*praise*) senza riserve

un·stop·pable [ʌn'stɒpəbl] ADJ inarrestabile

un·stressed [ʌn'strɛst] ADJ (*syllable*) non accentato(-a)

un·stuck [ʌn'stʌk] ADJ: **to come unstuck** (*label*) staccarsi, scollarsi; (*fam: plan*) andare a monte, fallire; (*: person*) fare fiasco

un·sub·scribe [ˌʌnsəb'skraɪb] VI (*Comput*) disdire l'abbonamento

un·sub·stan·ti·at·ed [ˌʌnsəb'stænʃɪˌeɪtɪd] ADJ (*rumour, accusation*) infondato(-a)

un·suc·cess·ful [ˌʌnsək'sɛsfʊl] ADJ (*gen*) che non ha successo; (*writer*) fallito(-a); (*businessman*) di scarso successo; **to be unsuccessful** (*play, book, actor*) non avere successo; (*idea*) non avere fortuna; (*attempt, marriage, negotiation*) non riuscire, fallire; (*application*) avere esito negativo; **to be unsuccessful in an exam** non superare un esame; **to be unsuccessful in an attempt to do sth** fallire nel tentativo di fare qc; **an unsuccessful artist** un artista fallito

un·suc·cess·ful·ly [ˌʌnsək'sɛsfəlɪ] ADV senza successo

un·suit·able [ʌn'su:təbl] ADJ: **unsuitable (for)** (*clothes, colour*) non adatto(-a) (a), inadatto(-a) (a); (*moment*) inopportuno(-a) (a *or* per); **this film is unsuitable for children** non è un film adatto ai bambini; **unsuitable for children under 15** sconsigliabile ai minori di 15 anni; **he's unsuitable for the post** non è la persona adatta per quell'impiego; **the post is unsuitable for him** quel posto non fa per lui

un·suit·ed [ʌn'su:tɪd] ADJ: **to be unsuited for** *or* **to** non essere fatto(-a) per

un·sul·lied [ʌn'sʌlɪd] ADJ (*liter: reputation*) immacolato(-a)

un·sung [ʌn'sʌŋ] ADJ: **an unsung hero** un eroe misconosciuto

un·sup·port·ed [ˌʌnsə'pɔ:tɪd] ADJ (*claim*) senza fondamento; (*theory*) non dimostrato(-a); (*mother*) senza aiuti finanziari

un·sure [ʌn'ʃʊə^r] ADJ: **unsure of, unsure about** incerto(-a) su; **they are unsure about what to do** sono incerti(-e) su cosa fare; **to be unsure of o.s.** essere un*a* insicuro(-a)

un·sur·passed [ˌʌnsə'pɑ:st] ADJ insuperato(-a)

un·sus·pect·ed [ˌʌnsəs'pɛktɪd] ADJ insospettato(-a)

un·sus·pect·ing [ˌʌnsəs'pɛktɪŋ] ADJ (*gen*) che non sospetta nulla; (*public*) ignaro(-a)

un·sweet·ened [ʌn'swi:tnd] ADJ (*tea*) senza zucchero; (*fruit juice*) non zuccherato(-a)

un·swerv·ing [ʌn'swɜ:vɪŋ] ADJ (*loyalty, devotion*) ferreo(-a), incrollabile

un·sym·pa·thet·ic [ˌʌnsɪmpə'θɛtɪk] ADJ (*attitude*) poco incoraggiante; (*person: not understanding*) poco comprensivo(-a); (*: disagreeable*) antipatico(-a); (*response*) gelido(-a); **to be unsympathetic to a cause** non appoggiare una causa; **I explained, but he was unsympathetic** ho spiegato le mie ragioni, ma è stato poco comprensivo

un·sys·tem·at·ic [ˌʌnsɪstɪ'mætɪk] ADJ poco sistematico(-a)

un·tan·gle [ʌn'tæŋgl] VT (*knots, wool*) sbrogliare

un·tapped [ʌn'tæpt] ADJ (*resources*) non sfruttato(-a)

un·taxed [ʌn'tækst] ADJ (*goods*) esente da imposte; (*income*) non imponibile

un·teach·able [ʌn'ti:tʃəbl] ADJ (*person*) a cui è impossibile insegnare; (*subject*) impossibile da insegnare

un·ten·able [ʌn'tɛnəbl] ADJ (*position*) insostenibile

un·test·ed [ʌn'tɛstɪd] ADJ (*theory*) non sperimentato(-a); (*new product, method*) non collaudato(-a)

un·think·able [ʌn'θɪŋkəbl] ADJ impensabile, inconcepibile

un·think·ing [ʌn'θɪŋkɪŋ] ADJ (*remark*) sconsiderato(-a)
un·think·ing·ly [ʌn'θɪŋkɪŋlɪ] ADV senza pensare
un·ti·di·ly [ʌn'taɪdɪlɪ] ADV: **to dress untidily** non aver cura nel vestirsi; **to write/work untidily** scrivere/lavorare in modo disordinato
un·ti·di·ness [ʌn'taɪdɪnɪs] N (*of dress, person*) trascuratezza, sciatteria; (*of room*) disordine *m*
un·ti·dy [ʌn'taɪdɪ] ADJ (*comp* **-ier**, *superl* **-iest**) (*person, room, writing*) disordinato(-a)
un·tie [ʌn'taɪ] VT (*parcel*): **they are unsure about what to do** sono incerti su cosa fare; disfare; (*knot, shoelaces*) sciogliere; (*hands, person, dog*) slegare; **he couldn't untie the knots** non riusciva a sciogliere i nodi
◎ **un·til** [ʌn'tɪl] PREP fino a; (*after negative*) prima di; **until now** finora; **it's never been a problem until now** non è mai stato un problema, finora; **until then** fino ad allora; **until then I'd never been to Italy** fino ad allora non ero mai stato(-a) in Italia; **until such time as I decide otherwise** fino a quando non cambio idea; **from morning until night** dalla mattina alla sera; **until his arrival** fino al suo arrivo; **I waited until ten o'clock** ho aspettato fino alle dieci; **I didn't know anything about it until 10 minutes ago** non ne sapevo niente fino a 10 minuti fa; **it won't be ready until next week** non sarà pronto prima della settimana prossima
■ CONJ finché (non), fino a quando; **I won't see her until I return** non la vedrò fino al mio ritorno; **wait until I get back** aspetta finché torno; **he did nothing until I told him** non ha mosso un dito finché non gliel'ho detto; **we had a lovely view from here until they built the factory** qui si godeva une bella vista fino a quando non hanno costruito la fabbrica
un·time·ly [ʌn'taɪmlɪ] ADJ (*death, end*) prematuro(-a); (*remark*) fuori luogo, inopportuno(-a); **to come to an untimely end** (*person*) morire prematuramente; (*project*) naufragare anzitempo
un·tir·ing [ʌn'taɪərɪŋ] ADJ instancabile, indefesso(-a)
un·tir·ing·ly [ʌn'taɪərɪŋlɪ] ADV instancabilmente
un·tit·led [ˌʌn'taɪtld] ADJ senza titolo
un·told [ʌn'təʊld] ADJ (*loss, wealth*) incalcolabile; (*misery*) indicibile, indescrivibile; (*story, secret*) mai rivelato(-a); **untold damage** danni *mpl* incalcolabili
un·touch·able [ʌn'tʌtʃəbl] N (*in India*) paria *m inv*, intoccabile *m/f*
■ ADJ intoccabile
un·touched [ʌn'tʌtʃt] ADJ **1** (*unchanged*) così com'era; (*unaffected*) non toccato(-a); **she left her breakfast untouched** non ha nemmeno toccato la colazione; **untouched by human hand** manipolato(-a) a distanza **2** (*safe: person*) incolume; **the thieves left our cases untouched** i ladri non hanno toccato le nostre valigie **3** (*unmoved*): **untouched by her pleas** insensibile alle sue preghiere
un·to·ward [ˌʌntə'wɔ:d] ADJ (*frm*) increscioso(-a)
un·trace·able [ˌʌn'treɪsəbl] ADJ introvabile, irreperibile
un·trained [ʌn'treɪnd] ADJ (*worker, teacher*) privo(-a) di formazione professionale; (*troops*) privo(-a) di addestramento; **to the untrained eye/ear** ad un occhio inesperto/orrechio non esercitato
un·tram·melled, (*Am*) **un·tram·meled** [ʌn'træməld] ADJ (*liter*) senza vincoli
un·trans·lat·able [ˌʌntrænz'leɪtəbl] ADJ intraducibile
un·treat·ed [ʌn'tri:tɪd] ADJ (*illness, patient*) non curato(-a); (*sewage, water*) non depurato(-a); (*wood*) non trattato(-a)
un·tried [ʌn'traɪd] ADJ (*method*) non collaudato(-a); (*person*) non messo(-a) alla prova; (*Law: criminal*) non processato(-a); (*: case*) non portato(-a) in tribunale
un·trou·bled [ʌn'trʌbld] ADJ calmo(-a); **untroubled by the thought of** per niente preoccupato(-a) al pensiero di
un·true [ʌn'tru:] ADJ (*statement*) falso(-a), non vero(-a)
un·trust·wor·thy [ʌn'trʌst,wɜ:ðɪ] ADJ (*person*) di cui non ci si può fidare; (*source*) inattendibile, non degno(-a) di fede
un·truth [ʌn'tru:θ] N (*pl* **untruths** [ʌn'tru:ðz]) falsità *f inv*
un·truth·ful [ʌn'tru:θfʊl] ADJ falso(-a), menzognero(-a)
un·truth·ful·ly [ʌn'tru:θfəlɪ] ADV falsamente
un·us·able [ʌn'ju:zəbl] ADJ inservibile, inutilizzabile
un·used¹ [ʌn'ju:zd] ADJ (*new*) mai usato(-a), nuovo(-a); (*not made use of*) non usato(-a), non utilizzato(-a)
un·used² [ʌn'ju:st] ADJ: **to be unused to sth/to doing sth** non essere abituato(-a) a qc/a fare qc; **the company is unused to competition** l'azienda non è abituata ad avere concorrenti
◎ **un·usual** [ʌn'ju:ʒʊəl] ADJ (*uncommon*) insolito(-a); (*exceptional: event, talent*) non comune, raro(-a); **an unusual shape** una forma insolita; **it's unusual to get snow at this time of year** è raro che nevichi in questo periodo dell'anno; **it's unusual for him to be late** è strano che arrivi in ritardo; **that's unusual for her** che strano, non è da lei; **isn't it unusual!** che originale!
un·usu·al·ly [ʌn'ju:ʒʊəlɪ] ADV (*unaccustomedly*) insolitamente; (*exceptionally: tall, gifted*) eccezionalmente; **most unusually, she was late** fatto molto strano, era in ritardo
un·ut·ter·able [ʌn'ʌtərəbl] ADJ (*liter: joy, boredom*) indicibile
un·var·ied [ʌn'vɛərɪd] ADJ (*routine*) invariato(-a); (*diet*) monotono(-a)
un·var·nished [ʌn'vɑ:nɪʃt] ADJ (*wood*) non verniciato(-a); (*fig: truth*) nudo(-a) e crudo(-a); (*: account*) senza fronzoli
un·vary·ing [ʌn'vɛərɪɪŋ] ADJ immutabile
un·veil [ʌn'veɪl] VT (*plan*) svelare; (*monument*) scoprire, inaugurare
un·veil·ing [ʌn'veɪlɪŋ] N (*ceremony*) scoprimento
un·ven·ti·lat·ed [ʌn'ventɪˌleɪtɪd] ADJ non ventilato(-a)
un·voiced [ʌn'vɔɪst] ADJ (*consonant*) sordo(-a); (*opinion*) inespresso(-a)
un·waged [ʌn'weɪdʒd] (*Brit*) ADJ non retribuito(-a)
■ NPL: **the unwaged** i non salariati
un·want·ed [ʌn'wɒntɪd] ADJ (*person, effect*) non desiderato(-a); (*clothes*) smesso(-a); **to feel unwanted** sentirsi respinto(-a)
un·war·rant·ed [ʌn'wɒrəntɪd] ADJ ingiustificato(-a)
un·wary [ʌn'wɛərɪ] ADJ incauto(-a)
un·wa·ver·ing [ʌn'weɪvərɪŋ] ADJ (*support, faith*) incrollabile, fermo(-a)
un·wel·come [ʌn'welkəm] ADJ (*guest, news*) non gradito(-a); (*development*) sgradito(-a); **to feel unwelcome** sentire che la propria presenza non è gradita
un·well [ʌn'wel] ADJ indisposto(-a); **to feel unwell** non sentirsi bene; **he's unwell** è indisposto
un·whole·some [ʌn'həʊlsəm] ADJ (*food*) non genuino(-a); (*climate, smell*) malsano(-a); (*thoughts, influence*) cattivo(-a)
un·wieldy [ʌn'wi:ldɪ] ADJ poco maneggevole

Uu

un·will·ing [ʌn'wɪlɪŋ] ADJ riluttante; **to be unwilling to do sth** non essere disposto(-a) a fare qc, non voler fare qc; **he was unwilling to help me** non era disposto ad aiutarmi; **he was unwilling to admit he was wrong** non voleva ammettere di aver torto
un·will·ing·ly [ʌn'wɪlɪŋlɪ] ADV controvoglia, malvolentieri, di malavoglia
un·wind [ʌn'waɪnd] (*pt, pp* **unwound**) VT srotolare, svolgere; **he unwound the rope** ha srotolato la fune
■ VI srotolarsi; (*fam: relax*) distendersi, rilassarsi; **I need time to unwind** ho bisogno di tempo per rilassarmi
un·wise [ʌn'waɪz] ADJ (*decision, act*) avventato(-a); **it was unwise of you to do that** è stato imprudente da parte tua farlo
un·wise·ly [ʌn'waɪzlɪ] ADV imprudentemente; **she unwisely decided to take the job** ha deciso, poco saggiamente, di accettare il lavoro
un·wit·ting [ʌn'wɪtɪŋ] ADJ (*cause*) involontario(-a); (*victim*) inconsapevole; (*insult*) non intenzionale, non voluto(-a)
un·wit·ting·ly [ʌn'wɪtɪŋlɪ] ADV senza volerlo; **quite unwittingly** in tutta innocenza
un·wont·ed [ʌn'wəʊntɪd] ADJ (*frm*) inconsueto(-a)
un·work·able [ʌn'wɜːkəbl] ADJ (*plan*) inattuabile
un·world·ly [ʌn'wɜːldlɪ] ADJ poco materialista
un·wor·thy [ʌn'wɜːðɪ] ADJ (*undeserving*) non degno(-a); (*ignoble*) indegno(-a); **to be unworthy of sth/to do sth** non essere degno(-a) di qc/di fare qc
un·wound [ʌn'waʊnd] PT, PP *of* **unwind**
un·wrap [ʌn'ræp] VT (*present*) aprire, scartare; (*parcel*) disfare; **after lunch we unwrapped the presents** dopo pranzo abbiamo aperto i regali
un·writ·ten [ʌn'rɪtn] ADJ (*agreement*) tacito(-a); **it is an unwritten law that ...** la norma vuole che...
un·yield·ing [ʌn'jiːldɪŋ] ADJ (*person*) inflessibile; (*material*) rigido(-a), duro(-a)
un·zip [ʌn'zɪp] VT aprire (la chiusura lampo di); (*Comput*) dezippare, decomprimere

◎ **up** [ʌp] **KEYWORD**
■ ADV
1 (*upwards, higher*) su, in alto; **up above** su in alto, al di sopra; **to be up among the leaders** essere tra i primi; **he's been up and down all evening** non è stato fermo un momento, stasera; **to walk up and down** camminare su e giù; **to jump up and down** saltellare; **she's still a bit up and down** (*sick person*) ancora non si è ripresa del tutto; **my office is five floors up** il mio ufficio è al quinto piano; **to stop halfway up** fermarsi a metà salita; **a bit higher up** un po' più su *or* in alto; **up in the sky/mountains** su nel cielo/in montagna; **they've got the road up** la strada è interrotta; **"this side up"** "alto"; **the sun is up** è sorto il sole; **up there** lassù; **to throw sth up in the air** gettare qc in aria; **he goes up to Oxford next year** va a Oxford l'anno prossimo; **to be up with the leaders** essere tra i primi; **up with Leeds United!** viva il Leeds United!, forza Leeds United!
2 (*installed, built*): **to be up** (*building*) essere terminato(-a); (*tent*) essere piantato(-a); (*shutters*) essere sollevato(-a); (*wallpaper*) essere su; (*picture*) essere appeso(-a); (*notice*) essere esposto(-a)
3 (*out of bed*): **to be up** essersi alzato(-a); **to be up and about again** essere di nuovo in piedi; **to be up early** alzarsi presto; **to be up late** (*at night*) fare tardi
4 (*in price, value*): **to be up (by)** essere andato(-a) su (di); (*standard, level*): **to be up** essere salito(-a); **we are 3 goals up** abbiamo un vantaggio di 3 gol, vinciamo per 3 gol; **prices are up on last year** i prezzi sono più alti dell'anno scorso
5 (*finished*): **it's all up with her** (*fam*) per lei è finita; **the lease is up** il contratto d'affitto è scaduto; **his leave is up** il suo congedo è scaduto; **time's up** il tempo è scaduto; **when the year was up** finito l'anno
6 (*upwards*): **from £20 up** dalle 20 sterline in su
7 (*in or towards the north*) su; **he's up for the day** è qui per la giornata; **she's up from Birmingham** è arrivata da Birmingham; **up in Scotland** su in Scozia; **up North** su al Nord; **to live/go up North** vivere/andare su al Nord
8 (*Brit: knowledgeable*): **I'm not very well up on what's going on** non sono molto al corrente di ciò che sta succedendo; **he's well up in** *or* **on politics** è informatissimo sulla politica
9 (*fam: wrong*): **there's something up with him/with the TV** (lui)/la TV ha qualcosa che non va; **what's up?** cosa c'è che non va?; **what's up with him?** che ha?, che gli prende?
10 up to (*as far as*) fino a; **up to here** fin qui, fino a qui; **up to now** finora; **up to £100** fino a 100 sterline
11 what is he up to? (*fam pej: doing*) cosa sta combinando?; **he's up to no good** *or* **he's up to something** sta architettando qualcosa
12 up to (*equal to*) all'altezza di; **he is not up to it** non ne è capace; **I don't feel up to it** non me la sento; **the book isn't up to much** (*fam*) il libro non vale un granché
13 it's up to you to decide (*depends on*) sta *or* tocca a te decidere; **I'd go, but it's up to you** io ci andrei, ma dipende da te
14 to be up against opposition (*faced with*) trovarsi di fronte una forte opposizione; **you don't know what you're up against** non sai a cosa vai incontro; **he's really up against it** sta in un bell'impiccio
■ PREP: **to go up** (*stairs*) salire; (*hill*) salire su per; (*river*) risalire; **to travel up and down the country** viaggiare su e giù per il paese; **further up the page** più su nella stessa pagina; **halfway up the stairs** a metà scala; **it's up that road** è su per quella strada; **he went off up the road** se n'è andato su per la strada; **he pointed up the street** ha indicato in fondo alla strada; **to be up a tree** essere su un albero
■ N: **ups and downs** (*in life, career*) alti e bassi *mpl*; **the road is full of ups and downs** la strada è molto accidentata; **he's on the up and up** le cose gli vanno di bene in meglio
■ ADJ (*train, line*) per la città
■ VI (*fam*): **she upped and left** ha preso e se n'è andata; **he upped and punched him** gli ha mollato un pugno
■ VT (*fam: price*) alzare

up-and-coming [ˌʌpənd'kʌmɪŋ] ADJ promettente
up-and-down [ˌʌpən'daʊn] ADJ (*movement*) (in) su e giù; (*business, progress*) con molti alti e bassi
up-and-under [ˌʌpənd'ʌndəʳ] N (*Rugby*) calcio al volo
up·beat ['ʌpˌbiːt] N (*Mus*) tempo in levare; (*positive trend*) tendenza al rialzo
■ ADJ (*fam*) ottimistico(-a)
up·braid [ʌp'breɪd] VT (*frm*) rimproverare
up·bring·ing ['ʌpˌbrɪŋɪŋ] N educazione *f*
upcoming [ˌʌp'kʌmɪŋ] ADJ imminente, prossimo(-a)
up·country [ʌp'kʌntrɪ] ADV (*be*) all'interno; (*go*) verso l'interno

up·date [ʌp'deɪt] VT aggiornare

up·end [ʌp'ɛnd] VT (*box*) mettere in piedi; (*fig: system*) rovesciare

up-front [ˌʌp'frʌnt] (*fam*) ADJ franco(-a), aperto(-a); **up-front payment** pagamento immediato
■ADV (*pay*) in anticipo

up·grade [ʌp'greɪd] VT (*employee*) promuovere, avanzare di grado; (*job*) rivalutare; (*Comput*) far l'upgrade di; (*goods*) migliorare la qualità di; **universities cannot afford to upgrade laboratory facilities** le università non possono permettersi di modernizzare i laboratori; **I expect most Windows users will upgrade to Windows Longhorn** credo che gran parte degli utenti di Windows passeranno a Windows Longhorn; **travellers may want to upgrade from economy to business class** i viaggiatori potrebbero voler passare dalla classe economica alla classe business

up·heav·al [ʌp'hi:vəl] N (*disturbance*) scompiglio; (*Pol*) sconvolgimento; (*Geol*) sollevamento; **political upheaval** sconvolgimento politico

up·held [ʌp'hɛld] PT, PP *of* **uphold**

up·hill [ˌʌp'hɪl] ADV: **to go uphill** andare in salita, salire
■ADJ in salita, in su; (*fig: task, battle*) arduo(-a); **it was an uphill struggle** è stata dura; **uphill ski** sci *m inv* a monte; **it's uphill all the way** è tutta salita; (*fig*) è una continua lotta

up·hold [ʌp'həʊld] (*pt, pp* **upheld**) VT (*frm: law, principle*) difendere; (*: decision, verdict*) confermare

up·hol·ster [ʌp'həʊlstəʳ] VT (*cover*) tappezzare, ricoprire; (*pad*) imbottire; **to be well upholstered** (*fig hum*) essere bene in carne

up·hol·ster·er [ʌp'həʊlstərəʳ] N tappezziere(-a)

up·hol·stery [ʌp'həʊlstərɪ] N tappezzeria

up·keep ['ʌpˌki:p] N manutenzione *f*

up·lands ['ʌpləndz] NPL regioni *fpl* montagnose

up·lift [ʌp'lɪft] VT (*spiritually*) elevare, esaltare; (*materially*) sollevare, tirar su

up·load ['ʌpləʊd] VT (*Comput*) inviare, trasferire (*dal proprio computer ad un altro*)

up-market [ˌʌp'mɑ:kɪt] ADJ (*product*) che si rivolge ad una fascia di mercato superiore; (*restaurant*) elegante

◎**upon** [ə'pɒn] PREP = **on** PREP

◎**up·per** ['ʌpəʳ] ADJ **1** (*jaw, lip*) superiore; (*storey*) superiore, di sopra; **on the upper floor** al piano superiore; **the upper reaches of the Po** l'alto Po **2** (*in importance, rank*) superiore, più alto(-a), più elevato(-a); **the upper school** gli ultimi anni di scuola superiore; **the upper income bracket** la fascia di reddito più alto; **the upper middle class** l'alta borghesia
■N (*of shoe*) tomaia; **to be on one's uppers** (*fig fam*) non avere il becco d'un quattrino

Upper Chamber N (*Pol*): **the Upper Chamber** la Camera Alta

upper-class [ˌʌpə'klɑ:s] ADJ (*district*) signorile; (*people*) dell'alta borghesia; (*accent*) aristocratico(-a); (*attitude*) snob *inv*; **a wealthy upper-class family** una famiglia benestante dell'alta borghesia; **an upper-class accent** un accento aristocratico

upper classes NPL: **the upper classes** i ceti più elevati

upper crust N: **the upper crust** (*fam*) l'aristocrazia

upper·cut ['ʌpəˌkʌt] N (*Boxing*) uppercut *m inv*, montante *m*

upper hand N: **to have the upper hand** prendere il sopravvento

Upper House N: **the Upper House** (*in Britain*) la Camera Alta, la Camera dei Lords; (*in US etc*) il Senato

upper·most ['ʌpəˌməʊst] ADJ (*thought*) dominante; (*echelon*) più alto(-a), più elevato(-a); **it was uppermost in my mind** è stata la mia prima preoccupazione

Upper Volta N: **the Upper Volta** l'Alto Volta *m*

up·pish ['ʌpɪʃ] ADJ (*Brit fam*) con la puzza al *or* sotto il naso; **to get uppish** darsi importanza

up·pi·ty ['ʌpɪtɪ] (*fam*) ADJ **1** (*hard to control*): **to get uppity** alzare la cresta **2** = **uppish**

up·right ['ʌpˌraɪt] ADJ **1** (*posture*) ritto(-a), eretto(-a); (*post*) verticale **2** (*fig*) retto(-a), onesto(-a)
■ADV dritto(-a); **to stand upright** (*person*) stare dritto(-a); (*object*) essere in posizione verticale
■N **1** (*post*) supporto verticale; (*of door, window*) montante *m* **2** (*piano*) pianoforte *m* verticale *or* a mezza coda

up·ris·ing ['ʌpˌraɪzɪŋ] N rivolta, insurrezione *f*

up·roar ['ʌpˌrɔ:ʳ] N trambusto, clamore *m*; **the whole place was in uproar** c'era un gran baccano

up·roari·ous [ʌp'rɔ:rɪəs] ADJ (*group, meeting*) chiassoso(-a); (*laughter*) fragoroso(-a); (*welcome*) entusiastico(-a); (*very funny: joke, mistake*) esilarante

up·roari·ous·ly [ʌp'rɔ:rɪəslɪ] ADV (*see adj*) chiassosamente; fragorosamente; entusiasticamente; **he is uproariously funny** è (un tipo) spassosissimo

up·root [ʌp'ru:t] VT sradicare

◎**up·set** [*vb, adj* ʌp'sɛt; *n* 'ʌpˌsɛt] (*vb: pt, pp* **upset**) VT **1** (*container, contents*) rovesciare; (*boat*) capovolgere, rovesciare; (*fig: plan, schedule*) scombussolare **2** (*emotionally: disturb*) turbare; (*stronger*) sconvolgere; (*: offend*) offendere; (*: annoy*) contrariare, seccare; **to upset sb** turbare qn; **you'll only upset her if you mention it** riuscirai solo a turbarla menzionandolo; **don't upset yourself** non te la prendere **3** (*make ill: person*) far star male; (*: stomach*) scombussolare
■ADJ **1** (*emotionally: disturbed*) turbato(-a); (*stronger*) sconvolto(-a); (*: offended*) offeso(-a); (*: annoyed*) contrariato(-a), seccato(-a); **to get upset** (*distressed*) lasciarsi turbare *or* sconvolgere; (*offended*) offendersi; (*annoyed*) seccarsi; **don't get upset** non te la prendere; **she's still a bit upset** è ancora un po' turbata **2 I have an upset stomach** ho lo stomaco in disordine *or* scombussolato
■N **1** (*disturbance: in plans etc*) contrattempo, contrarietà *f inv*; (*emotional*) dispiacere *m*; **emotional upsets** disturbi emotivi **2 to have a stomach upset** (*Brit*) avere disturbi di stomaco; avere lo stomaco scombussolato

upset price N (*Am, Scot*) prezzo di riserva

up·set·ting [ʌp'sɛtɪŋ] ADJ (*distressing*) sconvolgente; (*disturbing*) scioccante

up·shot ['ʌpʃɒt] N (*result*) risultato; **the upshot of it all was that ...** la conclusione è stata che...; **the upshot is that we have unhappy employees** il risultato è che abbiamo dipendenti insoddisfatti

up·side down [ˌʌpsaɪd'daʊn] ADV (*person*) a testa in giù; (*object*) alla rovescia, sottosopra; **the painting was hung upside down** il quadro era appeso alla rovescia; **to turn upside down** capovolgere; (*mattress*) rivoltare; (*fig*) mettere sottosopra *or* a soqquadro
■ADJ (*person*) a testa in giù; (*object*) capovolto(-a); **the room was upside down** (*in disorder*) la stanza era tutta sottosopra *or* a soqquadro

up·stage [ˌʌp'steɪdʒ] VT: **to upstage sb** rubare la scena a qn

up·stairs [*adv, n* ˌʌp'stɛəz; *adj* 'ʌpstɛəz] ADV di sopra; **to**

Uu

go upstairs andare di sopra; **the people upstairs** quelli di sopra; **where's your coat? – it's upstairs** dov'è il tuo cappotto? – è di sopra; **he went upstairs to bed** è andato di sopra a coricarsi
■ N: **the upstairs** il piano di sopra
■ ADJ *(room)* al piano di sopra

up·stand·ing [ʌp'stændɪŋ] ADJ *(honourable)* retto(-a); *(strong)* aitante

up·start ['ʌpˌstɑ:t] N *(pej: in society)* parvenu *m inv*; *(in organization, hierarchy)* ultimo(-a) arrivato(-a) che si dà arie d'importanza

up·stream [ˌʌp'stri:m] ADV *(be)* a monte; *(swim)* controcorrente; **to swim upstream** nuotare controcorrente; **to sail upstream** risalire la corrente

up·surge ['ʌpˌsɜ:dʒ] N *(of enthusiasm)* ondata; *(of prices, inflation)* impennata, improvviso aumento

up·swing ['ʌpswɪŋ] N: **upswing (in sth)** ripresa (in qc)

up·take ['ʌpˌteɪk] N *(fam)*: **slow on the uptake** duro(-a) di comprendonio; **to be quick on the uptake** capire le cose al volo; *(number of people)* numero degli utilizzatori; *(of food, water etc)* consumo

up·thrust ['ʌpˌθrʌst] N *(gen, Phys)* spinta verso l'alto; *(Geol)* sollevamento

up·tight [ʌp'taɪt] ADJ *(fam)* teso(-a), nervoso(-a)

up-to-date [ˌʌptə'deɪt] ADJ *(figures, edition)* aggiornato(-a); *(person)* ben informato(-a), aggiornato(-a); *(ideas)* attuale, al passo coi tempi; *(clothes)* alla moda; **to bring sb up-to-date (on sth)** aggiornare qn (su qc)

up-to-the-minute [ˌʌptəðə'mɪnɪt] ADJ *(fashionable: dress, person)* all'ultimissima moda; (: *style*) attuale; *(latest: information)* dell'ultimo minuto

up·town [ˌʌp'taʊn] *(Am)* ADV *(walk, drive)* verso i quartieri residenziali; *(live)* in un quartiere residenziale
■ ADJ dei quartieri residenziali

up·turn ['ʌpˌtɜ:n] N *(fig: improvement)* ripresa; *(in value of currency)* rialzo; *(in luck)* svolta favorevole

up·turned [ʌp'tɜ:nd] ADJ *(box)* capovolto(-a), rovesciato(-a); *(nose)* all'insù

up·ward ['ʌpwəd] ADJ *(movement)* verso l'alto, in su; *(curve)* ascendente; **upward tendency** *(Fin)* tendenza al rialzo
■ ADV *(also:* **upwards)** 1 in su, verso l'alto; **to lie face upward** giacere supino(-a) 2 *(with numbers)*: **from the age of 13 upwards** dai 13 anni in su; **upwards of 500** 500 e più

upwardly-mobile [ˌʌpwədlɪ'məʊbaɪl] N: **to be upwardly-mobile** salire nella scala sociale

Ural Mountains [ˌjʊərəl'maʊntɪnz] NPL: **the Ural Mountains** *(also:* **the Urals)** gli Urali, i Monti Urali

ura·nium [jʊə'reɪnɪəm] N uranio

Ura·nus [jʊə'reɪnəs] N *(Myth, Astron)* Urano

◎ **ur·ban** ['ɜ:bən] ADJ urbano(-a); **urban sprawl** sviluppo urbanistico incontrollato, espansione *f* urbana tentacolare

ur·bane [ɜ:'beɪn] ADJ urbano(-a), civile

ur·bani·za·tion [ˌɜ:bənaɪ'zeɪʃən] N urbanizzazione *f*

urban legend, urban myth N leggenda metropolitana

ur·chin ['ɜ:tʃɪn] N monello(-a)

Urdu ['ɜ:du:] N urdu *m*

urea ['jʊərɪə] N urea

ureter [jʊə'ri:tə^r] N *(Anat)* uretere *m*

urethra [jʊə'ri:θrə] N *(Anat)* uretra

◎ **urge** [ɜ:dʒ] N impulso, stimolo, voglia; **to feel an urge to do sth** sentire l'impulso di fare qc
■ VT 1 *(try to persuade)* esortare; **to urge sb to do sth** esortare qn a fare qc; **they urged him to take action** lo hanno esortato ad agire; **he urged me to visit the Uffizi** mi ha raccomandato vivamente di visitare gli Uffizi; **he needed no urging** non si è fatto pregare 2 *(frm: advocate: measure)* fare pressioni per; (: *caution, acceptance*) raccomandare vivamente; **to urge that** insistere che + *sub*; **to urge sth on** *or* **upon sb** sottolineare a qn l'importanza di qc
▶ **urge on** VT + ADV *(also fig)* incitare, spronare

ur·gen·cy ['ɜ:dʒənsɪ] N *(of case, need)* urgenza; *(of tone of voice, pleas)* insistenza; **it is a matter of urgency** è una questione della massima urgenza

◎ **ur·gent** ['ɜ:dʒənt] ADJ 1 *(message, need)* urgente 2 *(earnest, persistent: plea)* pressante; (: *tone*) insistente, incalzante

ur·gent·ly ['ɜ:dʒəntlɪ] ADV *(see adj)* d'urgenza, urgentemente; in modo pressante, con insistenza

uri·nal [jʊ'raɪnl] N *(building)* vespasiano; *(vessel)* orinale *m*

uri·nary ['jʊərɪnərɪ] ADJ urinario(-a)

uri·nate ['jʊərɪˌneɪt] VI orinare

urine ['jʊərɪn] N orina

URL [ju:ɑ:r'ɛl] N ABBR *(Comput:* = **Uniform Resource Locator)** URL *m inv*, indirizzo Internet

urn [ɜ:n] N 1 *(vase)* urna 2 *(also:* **tea urn, coffee urn)** *capace contenitore provvisto di cannella per tè, caffè (specialmente nelle mense)*

Uru·guay ['jʊərəˌgwaɪ] N l'Uruguay *m*

Uru·guay·an [ˌjʊərə'gwaɪən] ADJ, N uruguaiano(-a)

US [ˌju:'ɛs] N ABBR (= **United States**): **the US** gli USA, gli Stati Uniti

◎ **us** [ʌs] PERS PRON PL 1 *(direct, indirect)* ci; *(stressed, after prep, in comparatives)* noi; **they saw us** ci hanno visto; **they're older than us** sono più vecchi di noi; **why don't you come with us?** perché non vieni con noi?; **we had some suitcases with us** avevamo con noi delle valigie; **let's go** andiamo; **us Scots** noialtri Scozzesi 2 *(fam: me)*: **give us a kiss** dammi un bacino

USA [ˌju:ɛs'eɪ] N ABBR 1 *(Geog:* = **United States of America)** USA *mpl* 2 *(Mil)* = *United States Army*

us·able ['ju:zəbl] ADJ utilizzabile, usabile

USAF [ˌju:ɛseɪ'ɛf] N ABBR = *United States Air Force*

us·age ['ju:zɪdʒ] N 1 *(Ling: use, way of using)* uso; **to be in common usage** essere nell'uso comune 2 *(custom)* usanza, uso 3 *(treatment, handling, use)* uso; *(of energy)* utilizzo; **it's had some rough usage** è stato un po' bistrattato

USB [ju:ɛs'bi:] N ABBR *(Comput:* = **Universal Serial Bus)** USB *m inv*; **USB port** porta *f* USB *inv*

USDAW ['ʌsˌdɔ:] N ABBR *(Brit:* = **Union of Shop, Distributive and Allied Workers)** *sindacato dei dipendenti di negozi, reti di distribuzione e simili*

◎ **use** [*n* ju:s; *vb* ju:z] N
1 *(gen)* uso, utilizzazione *f*, impiego; **a new use for old tyres** un nuovo modo di utilizzare vecchi copertoni; **directions for use** istruzioni *fpl* per l'uso; **for the use of the blind** ad uso dei non vedenti; **for use in case of emergency** da usarsi in caso di emergenza; **ready for use** pronto(-a) per l'uso; **to make use of sth** far uso di qc, utilizzare qc; **in use** in uso; **out of use** fuori uso; **is your old radio still in use?** funziona ancora la tua vecchia radio?; **to be in daily use** venire adoperato(-a) quotidianamente; **to be no longer in use** non essere più usato(-a); **it's gone** *or* **fallen out of use** non lo si usa più; **for one's own use** per uso personale; **fit for use** che si può ancora usare; **to make good use of sth**

or **put sth to good use** far buon uso di qc; **to find a use for sth** trovare il modo di utilizzare qc; **we have no further use for this** questo non ci serve più
2 (*usefulness*): **to be of use** essere utile, servire; **it's (of) no use** non serve, è inutile; **it's no use!** niente da fare!; **it's no use discussing it further** non serve a niente continuare a discuterne; **it's no use shouting, she's deaf** è inutile gridare, è sorda; **what's the use of all this?** a che serve tutto ciò?; **she's no use as a teacher** non vale niente come insegnante
3 (*ability or right to use*): **to lose the use of one's legs** perdere l'uso delle gambe; **I've got the use of the car this evening** stasera posso prendere la macchina
■ VT
1 (*gen*) usare; **to use force** usare la forza; **"to be used only in emergencies"** "da usare solo in caso d'emergenza"; **to use sth as a hammer** usare qc come martello; **what's this used for?** a che serve?; **I could use a drink** (*fam*) non mi dispiacerebbe bere qualcosa; **this room could use some paint** (*fam*) una passata di vernice non farebbe male a questa stanza; **use your head** *or* **brains!** usa la testa *or* il cervello!; **use your eyes!** apri gli occhi!
2 (*make use of, exploit: influence*) servirsi di, adoperare; (: *opportunity*) sfruttare, approfittare di; **to use drugs** fare uso di droghe
3 (*use up, consume*) consumare; (*finish*) finire; (*supplies*) usare, utilizzare
4 (*old liter: treat*) trattare
■ AUX VB: **I used to go there every day** ci andavo ogni giorno, ero solito(-a) andarci ogni giorno; **I used to live in London** ho abitato a Londra; **she used to do it** era solita farlo, lo faceva (una volta); **I didn't use to like maths when I was at school** la matematica non mi piaceva quando andavo a scuola; **things are not what they used to be** non è più come una volta
▸ **use up** VT + ADV (*strength*) usare; (*left-overs*) utilizzare; (*supplies*) dare fondo a; (*petrol, paper, money*) finire; **we've used up all the paint** abbiamo finito la vernice

◎ **used**[1] [ju:zd] ADJ (*secondhand: clothing*) usato(-a); (: *car*) di seconda mano, d'occasione, usato(-a); (*dirty: glass, napkin*) (già) usato(-a)

used[2] [ju:st] ADJ: **to be used to sth** essere abituato(-a) a qc; **don't worry, I'm used to it** non preoccuparti, ci sono abituato(-a); **to be used to doing sth** essere abituato(-a) a *or* avere l'abitudine di fare qc; **he wasn't used to driving on the right** non era abituato(-a) a guidare sulla destra; **to get used to** abituarsi a, fare l'abitudine a

◎ **use·ful** ['ju:sfʊl] ADJ 1 (*gen*) utile; **he's a useful man to know** è una conoscenza utile; **that's a useful thing to know** buono a sapersi; **it is very useful to be able to drive** saper guidare è molto utile; **to make o.s. useful** rendersi utile; **to come in useful** fare comodo, tornare utile 2 (*fam: capable: player*) bravino(-a); **he is useful with a gun** sa maneggiare il fucile

use·ful·ly ['ju:sfəlɪ] ADV utilmente

use·ful·ness ['ju:sfʊlnɪs] N utilità

use·less ['ju:slɪs] ADJ 1 (*no good: remedy*) inefficace; (: *advice*) inutile; (*unusable: object*) inservibile; **he's useless as a forward** come centravanti non vale niente; **I'm useless at tennis!** a tennis sono un impedito!; **you are useless!** sei un inetto! 2 (*pointless*) inutile; **it's useless arguing with him** non serve a niente *or* è inutile discutere con lui

Use·net ['ju:znɛt] N (*Comput*) Usenet *m or f*

◎ **user** ['ju:zəʳ] N (*of public service, dictionary*) utente *m/f*; (*of petrol, gas*) consumatore(-trice); **car users** automobilisti *mpl*; **library users** lettori *mpl*; **drug users** drogati *mpl*

user-friendly [ˌju:zə'frɛndlɪ] ADJ (*machine, Comput*) di facile uso

user group N gruppo *m* utenti *inv*

user interface N (*Comput*) interfaccia *f* utente *inv*

user·name ['ju:zəˌneɪm] N (*Comput*) nome *m* utente *inv*

U-shaped ['ju:ʃeɪpt] ADJ ad U

ush·er ['ʌʃəʳ] N (*Law*) usciere *m*; (*in theatre, cinema*) maschera; (*at wedding*) *valletto che accompagna gli ospiti ai loro posti*
■ VT: **to usher sb in** far entrare qn; **it ushered in a new era** (*fig*) ha inaugurato una nuova era

ush·er·ette [ˌʌʃə'rɛt] N (*in cinema*) mascherina

USIA [ˌju:ɛsaɪ'eɪ] N ABBR = *United States Information Agency*

USM [ˌju:ɛs'ɛm] N ABBR = *United States Mint; United States Mail*

USN [ˌju:ɛs'ɛn] N ABBR = *United States Navy*

USP [ˌju:ɛs'pi:] N ABBR (= **unique selling point**) caratteristica che favorisce la vendita del prodotto

USPHS [ˌju:ɛspi:eɪtʃ'ɛs] N ABBR = *United States Public Health Service*

USPO [ˌju:ɛspi:'əʊ] N ABBR = *United States Post Office*

USS [ˌju:ɛs'ɛs] ABBR = *United States Ship (or Steamer)*

USSR [ˌju:ɛsɛs'ɑ:ʳ] N ABBR (= **Union of Soviet Socialist Republics**) URSS *f*

usu. ABBR = **usually**

◎ **usu·al** ['ju:ʒʊəl] ADJ (*gen*) solito(-a); **as usual** come al solito, come d'abitudine; **more than usual** più del solito; **at the usual time** alla solita ora; **earlier than usual** prima del solito; **as is usual on these occasions** come vuole la tradizione; **as is usual with this type of housing** come sempre in questo genere di alloggi; **he's not his usual self** di solito non è così ; **he'll soon be his usual self again** tornerà presto ad essere quello di sempre; **"business as usual"** "l'ufficio (*or* il negozio *etc*) è aperto al pubblico"; **it's not usual for her to be late** non è sua abitudine arrivare in ritardo
■ N: **the usual, please!** (*fam: drink*) il solito, per favore!

Uu

◎ **usu·al·ly** ['ju:ʒʊəlɪ] ADV di solito; **to be more than usually careful** fare ancora più attenzione del solito

usu·rer ['ju:ʒərəʳ] N (*old*) usuraio(-a)

usurp [ju:'zɜ:p] VT usurpare

usurp·er [ju:'zɜ:pəʳ] N usurpatore(-trice)

usu·ry ['ju:ʒʊrɪ] N (*frm old*) usura

UT ABBR (*Am Post*) = **Utah**

Utah ['ju:tɔ:] N Utah *m*
▹ www.utah.gov/main/index

uten·sil [ju:'tɛnsl] N utensile *m*

uter·us ['ju:tərəs] N utero

utili·tar·ian [ˌju:tɪlɪ'tɛərɪən] ADJ 1 (*Philosophy*) utilitarista, utilitaristico(-a) 2 (*furniture*) funzionale

util·ity [ju:'tɪlɪtɪ] N (*usefulness*) utilità; (*also:* **public utility**) servizio pubblico; **privatized utilities** servizi pubblici privatizzati; **of great utility** di grande utilità

utility room N *locale adibito alla stiratura dei panni ecc*

uti·li·za·tion [ˌju:tɪlaɪ'zeɪʃən] N utilizzazione *f*

uti·lize ['ju:tɪˌlaɪz] VT (*frm: facilities, resources*) utilizzare; (: *talent, opportunity*) sfruttare

ut·most ['ʌtˌməʊst] ADJ 1 (*greatest: simplicity, caution*) massimo(-a); (: *danger*) estremo(-a); **with the utmost speed** a tutta velocità; **of the utmost importance** della massima importanza; **it is of the utmost**

importance that è estremamente importante che + *sub* **2** (*furthest: limits*) estremo(-a)
■ N: **to do one's utmost (to do sth)** fare tutto il possibile (per fare qc); **to the utmost of one's ability** al limite delle proprie capacità

uto·pia [ju:ˈtəʊpɪə] N utopia

uto·pian [ju:ˈtəʊpɪən] ADJ utopico(-a)

ut·ter¹ [ˈʌtəʳ] ADJ (*disaster, silence*) totale, assoluto(-a); (*madness*) puro(-a); (*fool*) perfetto(-a); **that's utter nonsense** sono tutte sciocchezze

ut·ter² [ˈʌtəʳ] VT (*groan, sigh*) emettere; (*cry, insult*) lanciare; (*word*) pronunciare, proferire; **she never uttered a word** non ha fiatato

ut·ter·ance [ˈʌtərəns] N (*remark, statement*) parole *fpl*; (*expression*) espressione *f*

ut·ter·ly [ˈʌtəlɪ] ADV completamente, del tutto

utter·most [ˈʌtəˌməʊst] = **utmost**

U-turn [ˈju:ˌtɜ:n] N inversione *f* a U; (*fig*) voltafaccia *m inv*, cambiamento di rotta, dietro-front *m inv*; **I braked and did a U-turn** ho frenato e fatto un'inversione a U; **a humiliating U-turn** un umiliante voltafaccia

Uzbekistan [ˌʊzbɛkɪˈstɑ:n] N l'Uzbekistan *m*

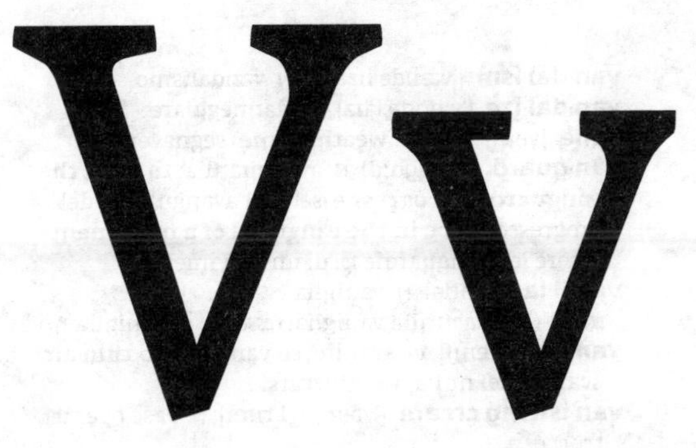

V, v [vi:] N (*letter*) V, v *f or m inv*; **V for Victor** ≈ V come Venezia

V ABBR (= **volt**) V

v. ABBR **1** (= **verse**) v. **2** (= **vide**) v. (= *vedi*) **3** = **versus**

VA [ˌvi:ˈeɪ] ABBR (*Am Post*) = **Virginia**

vac [væk] N ABBR (*Brit fam*) = **vacation**

va·can·cy [ˈveɪkənsɪ] N **1** (*job*) posto (vacante); **have you any vacancies?** avete bisogno di personale?; **there were no vacancies** non c'erano posti vacanti; **they have vacancies for programmers** cercano programmatori; **"vacancy for a secretary"** "segretaria cercasi" **2** (*in boarding house etc*) stanza libera; **"no vacancies"** "completo" **3** (*emptiness*) vuoto

DID YOU KNOW ...?
vacancy is not translated by the Italian word *vacanza*

va·cant [ˈveɪkənt] ADJ **1** (*seat, room*) libero(-a); (*property, house*) vuoto(-a), libero(-a); (*post*) vacante; **vacant lot** terreno non occupato; (*for sale*) terreno in vendita **2** (*look, expression*) vuoto(-a), vacuo(-a), assente

va·cant·ly [ˈveɪkəntlɪ] ADV con sguardo assente; **to gaze vacantly into space** guardare nel vuoto

va·cate [vəˈkeɪt] VT (*house, seat, room*) lasciare libero(-a); (*post*) lasciare, dare le dimissioni da

va·ca·tion [vəˈkeɪʃən] N (*esp Am*) vacanza, ferie *fpl*; (*Univ*) vacanze *fpl*; **on vacation** in vacanza, in ferie; **to take a vacation** prendere una vacanza, prendere le ferie
■VI (*Am*) andare in vacanza; **he vacations in Jamaica** va in vacanza in Giamaica

vacation course N corso estivo

vac·ci·nate [ˈvæksɪˌneɪt] VT vaccinare

vac·ci·na·tion [ˌvæksɪˈneɪʃən] N vaccinazione *f*

vac·cine [ˈvæksi:n] N vaccino; **polio vaccine** vaccino antipolio

vac·il·late [ˈvæsɪˌleɪt] VI (*frm*): **to vacillate (between)** oscillare (tra)

vacu·ous [ˈvækjʊəs] ADJ (*look, expression*) vacuo(-a); (*comment*) stupido(-a), insulso(-a)

vacuum [ˈvækjʊm] N (*also fig*) vuoto; **in a vacuum** (*fig*) in assoluto isolamento; **their departure has left a vacuum** la loro partenza ha lasciato un vuoto
■VT passare l'aspirapolvere in; **to vacuum the lounge** passare l'aspirapolvere nel salotto
■VI passare l'aspirapolvere; **I've already vacuumed** ho già passato l'aspirapolvere

vacuum cleaner N aspirapolvere *m inv*

vacuum flask, (*Am*) **vacuum bottle** N termos *m inv*

vacuum-packed [ˈvækjʊmˌpækt] ADJ confezionato(-a) sottovuoto *inv*

vade me·cum [ˌvɑ:dɪˈmeɪkʊm] N (*liter*) vademecum *m inv*

vaga·bond [ˈvægəˌbɒnd] N vagabondo(-a), barbone(-a)

va·gary [ˈveɪgərɪ] N (*usu pl*) capriccio

va·gi·na [vəˈdʒaɪnə] N vagina

vagi·nal [vəˈdʒaɪnəl] ADJ vaginale

va·gran·cy [ˈveɪgrənsɪ] N vagabondaggio

va·grant [ˈveɪgrənt] N vagabondo(-a), barbone(-a)

vague [veɪg] ADJ (*comp* **-r**, *superl* **-st**) (*gen*) vago(-a); (*directions, description*) impreciso(-a), confuso(-a); (*indistinct: memory*) sfocato(-a); (*person: absent-minded*) distratto(-a); **I have a vague idea that ...** ho la vaga impressione che...; **I haven't the vaguest idea** non ho la minima *or* più pallida idea; **the vague outline of a ship** la sagoma indistinta *or* confusa di una nave; **a vague look** uno sguardo assente *or* vuoto

vague·ly [ˈveɪglɪ] ADV vagamente

vague·ness [ˈveɪgnɪs] N (*of outline*) indeterminatezza; (*of meaning*) vaghezza; (*of person*) distrazione *f*

vain [veɪn] ADJ (*comp* **-er**, *superl* **-est**) **1** (*attempt, hope*) vano(-a), inutile; **in vain** invano, inutilmente; **all our efforts were in vain** tutti i nostri sforzi sono stati inutili **2** (*person*) vanitoso(-a); **he's terribly vain** è terribilmente vanitoso

vain·ly [ˈveɪnlɪ] ADV (*see adj*) invano; vanitosamente

val·ance [ˈvæləns] N volant *m inv*, balza

val·edic·tion [ˌvælɪˈdɪkʃən] N (*frm*) discorso di commiato

val·edic·tory [ˌvælɪˈdɪktərɪ] ADJ (*frm*) di commiato

va·len·cy [ˈveɪlənsɪ], **va·lence** (*Am*) [ˈveɪləns] N (*Chem*) valenza

val·en·tine [ˈvælənˌtaɪn] N (*card*) *biglietto di auguri per San Valentino*; (*sweetheart*) innamorato(-a)

Valentine's Day [ˈvæləntaɪnzdeɪ] N San Valentino

va·lerian [və'lɛərɪən] N valeriana
val·et ['vælei] N cameriere *m* personale
valet parking N servizio di parcheggio (*offerto da albergo ecc ai clienti*)
valet service N (*for car*) servizio completo di lavaggio; (*for clothes*) servizio di lavanderia
val·iant ['væljənt] ADJ (*liter*) coraggioso(-a), valoroso(-a); **a valiant knight** un prode cavaliere
val·iant·ly ['væljəntlɪ] ADV (*liter*) coraggiosamente
val·id ['vælɪd] ADJ (*ticket, document, excuse*) valido(-a); (*claim, objection*) giustificato(-a)
vali·date ['vælɪ,deɪt] VT (*contract, document*) convalidare; (*argument, claim*) comprovare
va·lid·ity [və'lɪdɪtɪ] N (*of document*) validità; (*of argument*) fondatezza, validità
va·lise [və'li:z] N (*old*) borsa da viaggio
Va·lium® ['vælɪəm] N Valium® *m inv*
Val·kyrie [væl'kɪərɪ] N valchiria
◎**val·ley** ['vælɪ] N valle *f*
val·or·ous ['vælərəs] ADJ (*liter*) valoroso(-a)
val·our ['vælə^r], (*Am*) **val·or** N (*liter*) valore *m* (*coraggio*)
◎**valu·able** ['væljʊəbl] ADJ (*contribution, time*) prezioso(-a); (*painting, object*) di valore, costoso(-a); **valuable help** un aiuto prezioso; **a valuable painting** un quadro di valore
valuables ['væljʊəblz] NPL preziosi *mpl*, oggetti *mpl* di valore
valua·tion [,væljʊ'eɪʃən] N (*of monetary worth*) valutazione *f*; (*of quality*) valutazione, stima; **what is your valuation of him?** che opinione ti sei fatto di lui?
◎**value** ['vælju:] N **1** (*worth*) valore *m*; (*usefulness*) utilità; **to lose (in) value** (*currency*) svalutarsi; (*property*) perdere (di) valore; **to gain (in) value** (*currency*) guadagnare; (*property*) aumentare di valore; **of no value** di nessun valore, senza valore; **to be of great value to sb** avere molta importanza per qn; **it has been of no value to him** non gli è servito a nulla; **you get good value (for money) in that shop** si compra bene in quel negozio; **this dress is good value (for money)** questo abito ha un buon prezzo **2**: **values** NPL (*principles*) valori *mpl*
■VT (*financially*) valutare, stimare; (*friendship, independence etc*) tenere a, apprezzare; **we're going to get the house valued** abbiamo intenzione di far valutare la casa; **it is valued at £80** è valutato 80 sterline; **it's not something I value very much** non è una cosa cui do molto valore
value add·ed tax [,væljʊædɪd'tæks] N (*Brit*) imposta sul valore aggiunto
val·ued ['vælju:d] ADJ (*appreciated*) stimato(-a), apprezzato(-a), tenuto(-a) in grande considerazione
value judgment N giudizio di valore
value·less ['væljʊlɪs] ADJ privo(-a) di valore
valu·er ['væljʊə^r] N stimatore(-trice)
valve [vælv] N (*all senses*) valvola
vam·pire ['væmpaɪə^r] N vampiro
vampire bat N (*Zool*) vampiro
◎**van¹** [væn] N (*Aut: small*) furgoncino; (: *for furniture*) furgone *m*; (*Rail*) vagone *m*
van² [væn] N ABBR = **vanguard**
va·na·dium [və'neɪdɪəm] N vanadio
Van·cou·ver [v[ae]n'ku:və^r] N Vancouver *f*
▷ http://vancouver.ca/
V and A [,vi:ənd'eɪ] N ABBR (*Brit*) = *Victoria and Albert Museum*
van·dal ['vændəl] N vandalo
van·dal·ism ['vændə,lɪzəm] N vandalismo
van·dal·ize ['vændə,laɪz] VT danneggiare
vane [veɪn] N (*also:* **weathervane**) segnavento
van·guard ['væn,gɑ:d] N avanguardia; **to be in the vanguard of progress** essere all'avanguardia del progresso; **to be in the vanguard of a movement** essere le avanguardie *fpl* di un movimento
va·nil·la [və'nɪlə] N vaniglia
■ADJ (*ice cream*) alla vaniglia; (*essence*) di vaniglia
van·ish ['vænɪʃ] VI svanire; **to vanish into thin air** svanire nel nulla, volatilizzarsi
van·ish·ing cream ['vænɪʃɪŋ,kri:m] N base *f* per il trucco
van·ish·ing point ['vænɪʃɪŋ,pɔɪnt] N punto di fuga
van·ity ['vænɪtɪ] N vanità *f inv*
vanity case N beauty case *m inv*
vanity mirror N (*Aut*) specchietto di cortesia
vanity unit N *elemento da bagno con lavandino incorporato*
van·quish ['væŋkwɪʃ] VT (*liter*) sconfiggere
van·tage ['vɑ:ntɪdʒ] N (*also:* **advantage**: *Tennis*) vantaggio
vantage point N punto d'osservazione (favorevole)
vap·id ['væpɪd] ADJ (*liter*) scipito(-a), scialbo(-a)
va·por·ize ['veɪpə,raɪz] VT vaporizzare
■VI vaporizzarsi
va·pour ['veɪpə^r], (*Am*) **va·por** N vapore *m*
vapour trail N (*Aer*) scia
vari·abil·ity [,vɛərɪə'bɪlɪtɪ] N variabilità
vari·able ['vɛərɪəbl] ADJ (*output, performance*) non costante; (*weather, wind*) variabile; (*mood*) mutevole
■N (*Math*) variabile *f*
vari·ance ['vɛərɪəns] N **1** **to be at variance (with sb over sth)** essere in disaccordo (con qn per qc); **to be at variance (with sth)** (*facts, statements*) essere in contraddizione (con qc) **2** (*Math*) varianza
vari·ant ['vɛərɪənt] N variante *f*
■ADJ diverso(-a)
vari·ation [,vɛərɪ'eɪʃən] N (*of amount, quality, also Mus*) variazione *f*; (*in opinion*) cambiamento
vari·cose veins [,værɪkəʊs'veɪnz] NPL varici *fpl*, vene *fpl* varicose
var·ied ['vɛərɪd] ADJ (*types, sizes, qualities*) vario(-a), diverso(-a); (*life*) movimentato(-a); (*diet*) diversificato(-a)
varie·gat·ed ['vɛərɪ,geɪtɪd] ADJ variegato(-a)
◎**va·ri·ety** [və'raɪətɪ] N (*type*) varietà *f inv*, tipo; (*range, diversity*) molteplicità, varietà; **in a wide** *or* **large variety of colours** in una vasta gamma di colori; **for a variety of reasons** per una serie di motivi; **for variety** per variare
variety artist N artista *m/f* di varietà
variety show N spettacolo di varietà
◎**vari·ous** ['vɛərɪəs] ADJ (*several*) diverso(-a), vario(-a); (*different*) diverso(-a), differente; **at various times** (*different*) in momenti diversi *or* differenti; **various times** (*several*) diverse *or* varie volte; **we visited various villages in the area** abbiamo visitato vari paesini della zona; **we went our various ways home** ognuno è tornato a casa per la sua strada
vari·ous·ly ['vɛərɪəslɪ] ADV in modo vario, variamente
var·nish ['vɑ:nɪʃ] N (*for wood*) vernice *f* trasparente; (*for nails*) smalto; **a tin of varnish** un barattolo di vernice
■VT (*wood*) verniciare; (*nails*) smaltare; **to varnish one's nails** smaltarsi le unghie, mettersi lo smalto sulle unghie
▸ **varnish over** VT + ADV: **to varnish over sth** (*event, fact*) mascherare qc

◎ **vary** ['vɛərɪ] VT variare
■ VI **1** *(change)*: **to vary (with** *or* **according to)** variare (con *or* a seconda di) **2** *(deviate)*: **to vary (from)** discostarsi (da); **the temperature/her mood varies** la temperatura/il suo umore è variabile; **these items vary in price** questi articoli si differenziano per il prezzo

vary·ing ['vɛərɪɪŋ] ADJ variabile, che varia; **with varying degrees of success** con più o meno successo

vas·cu·lar ['væskjʊlə^r] ADJ *(system)* vascolare; **vascular bundle** *(Bot)* fascio vascolare

vase [vɑːz, *Am* veɪz] N vaso

vas·ec·to·my [væ'sɛktəmɪ] N vasectomia

Vas·eline® ['væsɪ,liːn] N vaselina®

vaso·con·stric·tor [,veɪzəʊkən'strɪktə^r] N vasocostrittore *m*

vaso·di·la·tor [,veɪzəʊdaɪ'leɪtə^r] N vasodilatatore *m*

◎ **vast** [vɑːst] ADJ *(comp* **-er**, *superl* **-est)** *(territory, expanse)* vasto(-a); *(sum, amount)* ingente; *(difference, improvement)* enorme; **at vast expense** con enorme dispendio di capitale

vast·ly ['vɑːstlɪ] ADV *(grateful, rich)* enormemente; **vastly superior to** di gran lunga superiore a; **he's vastly mistaken if ...** sbaglia di grosso se...; **a vastly overrated player** un giocatore incredibilmente sopravvalutato

vast·ness ['vɑːstnɪs] N *(of territory)* vastità, immensità; **the vastness of his wealth** la vastità delle sue ricchezze

◎ **VAT** ['viːeɪtiː, væt] N ABBR *(Brit:* = **value added tax)** IVA *f*

vat [væt] N *(for wine, dye)* tino

Vati·can ['vætɪkən] N: **the Vatican** il Vaticano

Vatican council N concilio vaticano

vat·man ['vætmən] N *(Brit fam)*: **the vatman** *(inspector)* l'ispettore *m* dell'IVA; *(Inland Revenue)* il fisco

vau·de·ville ['vəʊdəvɪl] N *(esp Am)* vaudeville *m*

vault[1] [vɔːlt] N *(Archit)* volta; *(of bank)* caveau *m inv*; *(tomb)* cripta, tomba; **family vault** cappella di famiglia, tomba di famiglia

vault[2] [vɔːlt] VT, VI: **to vault (over) sth** saltare qc con un balzo

vault·ed ['vɔːltɪd] ADJ a volta

vaunt·ed ['vɔːntɪd] ADJ: **much vaunted** tanto celebrato(-a)

VC [,viː'siː] N ABBR **1** *(Brit:* = **Victoria Cross)** *medaglia al valore* **2** = **vice-chairman**

VCR [,viːsiː'ɑː^r] N ABBR = **video cassette recorder**

VD [,viː'diː] N ABBR = **venereal disease**

VDU [,viːdiː'juː] N ABBR = **visual display unit**

veal [viːl] N (carne *f* di) vitello

vec·tor ['vɛktə^r] N *(Math, Phys, Bio)* vettore *m*

veer [vɪə^r] VI *(ship, car)* virare; *(wind)* girare; **wind veering westerly at times** vento con tendenza a provenire da occidente; **the plane veered off the runway** l'aereo ha sterzato uscendo di pista; **the country has veered to the left** il paese ha fatto una svolta a sinistra; **the conversation veered round to politics** la conversazione si è spostata sulla politica

veg [vɛdʒ] N ABBR *(Brit fam)* = **vegetable(s)**

ve·gan ['viːgən] N vegetaliano(-a), vegano(-a)

veg·eburg·er, veg·gie·burg·er ['vɛdʒɪ,bɜːgə^r] N hamburger *m inv* vegetariano

◎ **veg·eta·ble** ['vɛdʒɪtəbl] N **1** verdura; **vegetables** NPL *(in restaurant)* ≈ contorno *msg* (di verdure); **would you like some vegetables?** desidera un contorno di verdure?; *(at home)* vuoi un po' di verdura? **2** *(generic term: plant)* vegetale *m*
■ ADJ *(oil, wax)* vegetale; *(soup)* di verdura; **vegetable soup** minestra di verdura

vegetable garden N orto

vegetable knife N coltello per pelare le verdure

vegetable marrow N *(Am)* zucca

vegetable rack N carrello *m inv* portaverdure

veg·etar·ian [,vɛdʒɪ'tɛərɪən] ADJ, N vegetariano(-a)
▷ www.vegsoc.org

veg·etari·an·ism [,vɛdʒɪ'tɛərɪə,nɪzəm] N vegetarianismo

veg·etate ['vɛdʒɪ,teɪt] VI vegetare

veg·eta·tion [,vɛdʒɪ'teɪʃən] N vegetazione *f*

veg·eta·tive ['vɛdʒɪtətɪv] ADJ *(also Bot)* vegetativo(-a)

veg·gie ['vɛdʒɪ] N, ADJ *(fam)* vegetariano(-a)

veg·gie·burg·er ['vɛdʒɪ,bɜːgə^r] N = **vegeburger**

ve·he·mence ['viːɪməns] N veemenza

ve·he·ment ['viːɪmənt] ADJ *(speech, passions)* veemente, violento(-a); *(attack)* vigoroso(-a); *(dislike, hatred)* profondo(-a); **there was vehement opposition** ci fu una dura opposizione

ve·he·ment·ly ['viːɪməntlɪ] ADV con veemenza

◎ **ve·hi·cle** ['viːɪkl] N veicolo; *(fig)* mezzo

ve·hicu·lar [vɪ'hɪkjʊlə^r] ADJ *(frm)*: **"no vehicular traffic"** "chiuso al traffico di veicoli"

veil [veɪl] N velo; **a black veil** un velo nero; **to take the veil** *(Rel)* prendere il velo; **under a veil of secrecy** protetto(-a) da una cortina di segretezza
■ VT velare, coprire con un velo; **the town was veiled in mist** la città era avvolta dalla nebbia

veiled [veɪld] ADJ *(also fig)* velato(-a)

vein [veɪn] N *(in body, stone, also fig)* vena; *(Bot: on leaf)* nervatura; **in melancholy vein** d'umore *m* malinconico; **in a different vein** in un tenore *m* diverso; **to reply in similar vein** rispondere a tono

veined [veɪnd] ADJ *(hand)* venoso(-a); *(leaf)* nervoso(-a)

Vel·cro® ['vɛlkrəʊ] N velcro®

veld, veldt [vɛlt] N: **the veld** l'altopiano sudafricano

vel·lum ['vɛləm] N *(writing paper)* pergamena

ve·loc·ity [vɪ'lɒsɪtɪ] N velocità *f inv*

ve·lour(s) [və'lʊə^r] N velours *m inv*

vel·vet ['vɛlvɪt] N velluto
■ ADJ *(skirt, curtain)* di velluto

vel·vet·een [,vɛlvɪ'tiːn] N vellutino

vel·vety ['vɛlvɪtɪ] ADJ vellutato(-a)

ve·nal ['viːnl] ADJ *(frm)* venale

ve·nal·ity [viː'nælɪtɪ] N *(frm)* venalità

ven·det·ta [vɛn'dɛtə] N vendetta, faida

vend·ing ma·chine ['vɛndɪŋməʃiːn] N distributore *m* automatico

ven·dor ['vɛndɔː^r] N venditore(-trice); **street vendor** venditore ambulante

ve·neer [və'nɪə^r] N impiallacciatura; *(fig)* parvenza, vernice *f*

ven·er·able ['vɛnərəbl] ADJ venerabile; *(old man, appearance)* venerando(-a)

ven·er·ate ['vɛnə,reɪt] VT *(frm)* venerare

ven·era·tion [,vɛnə'reɪʃən] N venerazione *f*

ve·nereal [vɪ'nɪərɪəl] ADJ venereo(-a)

venereal disease N malattia venerea

Ve·netian [vɪ'niːʃən] ADJ, N veneziano(-a)

Venetian blind N veneziana

Venetian glass N vetro di Murano

Ven·ezue·la [,vɛnɪ'zweɪlə] N Venezuela *m*

Ven·ezue·lan [,vɛnɪ'zweɪlən] ADJ, N venezuelano(-a)

venge·ance ['vɛndʒəns] N vendetta; **to take vengeance on sb** vendicarsi di qn; **to seek vengeance on** cercare di vendicarsi di; **with a vengeance** *(fig)* a

Vv

più non posso, sul serio; **it started to rain again with a vengeance** ricominciò a piovere sul serio

venge·ful ['vɛndʒfʊl] ADJ (*liter*) vendicativo(-a)

ve·nial ['viːnɪəl] ADJ (*Rel, frm: sin*) veniale

Ven·ice ['vɛnɪs] N Venezia

veni·son ['vɛnɪsən] N carne *f* di cervo

ven·om ['vɛnəm] N (*also fig*) veleno

ven·om·ous ['vɛnəməs] ADJ (*also fig*) velenoso(-a)

vent [vɛnt] N (*Tech: airhole*) presa d'aria; (*of jacket*) spacco; **to give vent to one's anger** sfogare la propria rabbia; **to give vent to one's feelings** dare sfogo ai propri sentimenti

■ VT: **to vent one's anger (on sb/sth)** scaricare *or* sfogare la propria rabbia (su qn/qc)

DID YOU KNOW ...?
vent is not translated by the Italian word *vento*

ven·ti·late ['vɛntɪˌleɪt] VT ventilare, arieggiare

ven·ti·la·tion [ˌventɪ'leɪʃən] N aerazione *f*, ventilazione *f*

ventilation shaft N condotto di aerazione

ven·ti·la·tor ['vɛntɪˌleɪtə^r] N ventilatore *m*

ven·tri·cle ['vɛntrɪkəl] N (*Anat*) ventricolo

ven·trilo·quism [vɛn'trɪləˌkwɪzəm] N ventriloquio

ven·trilo·quist [vɛn'trɪləkwɪst] N ventriloquo(-a)

◎**ven·ture** ['vɛntʃə^r] N impresa; **a business venture** un'iniziativa commerciale; **a new venture in publishing** una nuova iniziativa editoriale; **this new venture** questa nuova impresa; **joint venture** joint venture *f inv*

■ VT (*money, reputation, life*) rischiare; (*opinion, guess*) azzardare; **to venture to do sth** azzardarsi a fare qc; **if I may venture an opinion** se posso azzardare *or* arrischiare un parere; **nothing ventured, nothing gained** chi non risica non rosica

■ VI: **to venture on sth** avventurarsi in qc; **to venture out (of doors)** arrischiarsi ad uscire (di casa), azzardarsi ad uscire (di casa)

venture capital N (*Fin*) capitale *m* a rischio

venture capitalist N (*Fin*) *chi presta capitali a rischio*

◎**venue** ['vɛnjuː] N luogo (designato) (*per concerto, incontro sportivo, convegno*)

Venus ['viːnəs] N (*Astron, Myth*) Venere *f*

ve·rac·ity [və'ræsɪtɪ] N (*frm*) veridicità

ve·ran·da, ve·ran·dah [və'rændə] N veranda

verb [vɜːb] N verbo

ver·bal ['vɜːbəl] ADJ verbale

ver·bal·ize ['vɜːbəlaɪz] VT (*feelings, emotions, ideas*) esprimere, tradurre in parole

■ VI esprimersi

ver·bal·ly ['vɜːbəlɪ] ADV a voce, verbalmente

ver·ba·tim [vɜː'beɪtɪm] ADV, ADJ parola per parola

ver·bi·age ['vɜːbɪɪdʒ] N (*frm pej*) verbalismo

ver·bose [vɜː'bəʊs] ADJ verboso(-a), prolisso(-a)

ver·bose·ly [vɜː'bəʊslɪ] ADV verbosamente

ver·bos·ity [vɜː'bɒsɪtɪ] N verbosità

ver·dant ['vɜːdənt] ADJ (*liter*) verdeggiante

◎**ver·dict** ['vɜːdɪkt] N (*Law*) verdetto, sentenza; (*opinion*) giudizio, parere *m*; **verdict of guilty/not guilty** verdetto di colpevolezza/non colpevolezza; **his verdict on the wine was unfavourable** ha dato un giudizio sfavorevole sul vino

ver·di·gris ['vɜːdɪgrɪs] N verderame *m*

verge [vɜːdʒ] N (*of road*) bordo, margine *m*; (*fig*) orlo; **"soft verges"** (*Brit*) "banchina cedevole"; **to be on the verge of** (*disaster*) essere sull'orlo di; (*a discovery*) essere alle soglie di; **she was on the verge of tears** stava quasi per piangere, era lì lì per piangere; **a car parked on the verge of the road** una macchina parcheggiata sul bordo della strada; **a company on the verge of bankruptcy** una società sull'orlo del fallimento; **to be on the verge of doing sth** essere sul punto di fare qc

► **verge on** VI + PREP rasentare

ver·ger ['vɜːdʒə^r] N (*Rel*) sagrestano

veri·fi·able ['vɛrɪˌfaɪəbl] ADJ verificabile

veri·fi·ca·tion [ˌvɛrɪfɪ'keɪʃən] N verifica, accertamento

veri·fy ['vɛrɪˌfaɪ] VT (*check*) verificare, controllare; (*confirm the truth of*) confermare

veri·si·mili·tude [ˌvɛrɪsɪ'mɪlɪˌtjuːd] N (*frm*) verosimiglianza

veri·table ['vɛrɪtəbl] ADJ vero(-a)

ver·mil·ion [və'mɪljən] ADJ vermiglio(-a)

■ N vermiglio

ver·min ['vɜːmɪn] NPL animali *mpl* nocivi; (*fig pej*) parassiti *mpl*

ver·mi·nous ['vɜːmɪnəs] ADJ infestato(-a) dai parassiti

Ver·mont [vɜː'mɒnt] N Vermont *m*

▷ www.vermont.gov/

ver·mouth ['vɜːməθ] N vermut *m inv*

ver·nacu·lar [və'nækjʊlə^r] N vernacolo

■ ADJ vernacolare

ver·ni·er ['vɜːnɪə^r] N (*Tech: rule*) verniero

ve·roni·ca [və'rɒnɪkə] N (*Bot*) veronica

ver·ru·ca [və'ruːkə] N verruca

ver·sa·tile ['vɜːsəˌtaɪl] ADJ (*person*) versatile; (*machine, tool*) multiusi *inv*

ver·sa·til·ity [ˌvɜːsə'tɪlɪtɪ] N (*of person*) versatilità

verse [vɜːs] N **1** (*of poem*) verso; (*: stanza*) strofa; (*of Bible*) versetto; **the last verse** l'ultimo verso **2** (*no pl: poetry*) poesia, versi *mpl*; **in verse** in versi

versed [vɜːst] ADJ: **to be well versed in sth** essere molto versato(-a) in qc

◎**ver·sion** ['vɜːʃən] N versione *f*

ver·sus ['vɜːsəs] PREP (*Law, Sport, gen*) contro

ver·te·bra ['vɜːtɪbrə] N (*pl* **vertebrae** ['vɜːtɪbriː]) vertebra

ver·te·bral ['vɜːtɪbrəl] ADJ vertebrale

ver·te·brate ['vɜːtɪbrɪt] ADJ vertebrato(-a)

■ N vertebrato

ver·tex ['vɜːtɛks] N (*pl* **vertices** ['vɜːtɪsiːz]) vertice *m*

ver·ti·cal ['vɜːtɪkəl] ADJ (*gen*) verticale, perpendicolare; (*cliff*) a picco; **vertical takeoff** (*Aer*) decollo verticale

■ N verticale *f*

vertical integration N integrazione *f* verticale

ver·ti·cal·ly ['vɜːtɪkəlɪ] ADV verticalmente

ver·tigi·nous [vɜː'tɪdʒɪnəs] ADJ (*frm: cliff, descent, view*) che dà le vertigini

ver·ti·go ['vɜːtɪgəʊ] N vertigine *f*; **to suffer from vertigo** soffrire di vertigini; **I get vertigo** mi vengono le vertigini

verve [vɜːv] N (*of person*) verve *f*, brio; (*of painting, writing*) vivacità

◎**very** ['vɛrɪ] ADV **1** (*extremely*) molto, tanto; **very happy** molto felice, felicissimo(-a); **it's very cold** fa molto freddo; **very well** molto bene; **very little** molto poco; **very much** molto, tanto; (*stronger*) moltissimo, tantissimo; **very much younger** molto più giovane; **are you tired? — (yes,) very** sei stanco? — (sì ,) tanto; **he's so very poor** è poverissimo **2** (*absolutely*): **the very first** il/la primissimo(-a), proprio il/la primo(-a); **the very last** l'ultimissimo(-a), proprio l'ultimo(-a); **the very latest design** l'ultimissimo modello; **they are the very best of friends** sono grandissimi amici;

to wish sb the very best of luck augurare a qn ogni fortuna; **at the very most** al massimo; **at the very least** come minimo, almeno; **at the very latest** al più tardi; **he won't come until 9 o'clock, at the very earliest** non arriverà prima delle 9, al più presto; **the very same hat** lo stesso identico cappello; **it's my very own** è proprio mio
■ ADJ **1** *(precise)* stesso(-a); **that very day** quello stesso giorno; **his very words** le sue stesse parole; **her very words were ...** le sue parole testuali furono...; **he's the very man we want** è proprio l'uomo che cercavamo; **the very book which** proprio il libro che; **the very thing!** proprio quel che ci vuole!; **at that very moment** proprio in quel momento; **the very next day** proprio il giorno dopo **2** *(mere)* solo(-a); **the very thought (of it) alarms me** il solo pensiero mi spaventa, sono spaventato solo al pensiero; **the very idea!** neanche per sogno! **3** *(extreme)*: **at the very bottom/top** proprio in fondo/in cima; **at the very end** proprio alla fine; **to the very end** fino alla fine; **in the very depths of the jungle** nel cuore della giungla

very high frequency N *(Radio)* altissima frequenza

ves·pers ['vɛspəz] NPL *(Rel)* vespro

◎ **ves·sel** ['vɛsl] N *(ship)* vascello, nave *f*; *(container)* recipiente *m*; *(Anat)* vaso; **fishing vessel** nave da pesca; **blood vessel** vaso sanguigno

vest[1] [vɛst] N *(Brit: with sleeves)* maglia intima; *(: sleeveless)* canottiera; *(Am: waistcoat)* panciotto, gilè *m inv*; **thermal vest** canottiera termica; **bullet-proof vest** giubbotto *m* antiproiettile *inv*

> DID YOU KNOW ...?
> **vest** is not translated by the Italian word *veste*

vest[2] [vɛst] VT *(frm)*: **to vest sb with sth** investire qn di qc; **to vest powers/authority in sb** conferire poteri/autorità a qn

vest·ed in·te·rest [ˌvɛstɪd'ɪntrɪst] N: **to have a vested interest in doing sth** avere un interesse personale nel fare qc; **vested interests** NPL *(Comm)* diritti *mpl* acquisiti

ves·ti·bule ['vɛstɪbjuːl] N atrio, vestibolo

ves·tige ['vɛstɪdʒ] N vestigio; **the last vestiges of** le ultime vestigia di

ves·tig·ial [vɛ'stɪdʒɪəl] ADJ **1** *(Bio: organ)* vestigiale, rudimentale **2** *(frm: remaining)*: **vestigial traces of** tracce residue di

vest·ment ['vɛstmənt] N *(Rel)* paramento liturgico

vest pocket N *(Am)* taschino

ves·try ['vɛstrɪ] N sagrestia

Ve·su·vi·us [vɪ'suːvɪəs] N Vesuvio

vet[1] [vɛt] N *(esp Brit)* veterinario
■ VT *(text)* rivedere; *(person, application)* esaminare minuziosamente; **to vet sb for a job** informarsi su qn prima di offrirgli un posto

vet[2] [vɛt] N ABBR *(esp Am)* = **veteran**

◎ **vet·er·an** ['vɛtərən] ADJ: **veteran soldier** veterano; **a veteran teacher** un(-a) veterano(-a) dell'insegnamento; **she's a veteran campaigner for ...** lotta da sempre per...
■ N *(also:* **war veteran***)* reduce *m*

veteran car N *(Brit)* auto *f inv* d'epoca *(anteriore al 1919)*

vet·eri·nar·ian [ˌvɛtərɪ'nɛərɪən] N *(Am)* = **veterinary surgeon**

vet·eri·nary ['vɛtərɪnərɪ] ADJ veterinario(-a)

veterinary surgeon N *(Brit)* veterinario

veto ['viːtəʊ] N *(pl* **vetoes***)* veto; **to use** *or* **exercise one's veto** esercitare il proprio diritto di veto; **to put a veto on** (op)porre il veto a
■ VT (op)porre il veto a

vet·ting ['vɛtɪŋ] N *(also:* **positive vetting**: *Brit) indagine per accertare l'idoneità di un aspirante ad una carica ufficiale*

vex [vɛks] VT irritare, contrariare

vexa·tion [vɛk'seɪʃən] N *(state)* irritazione *f*; *(problem)* contrarietà *f inv*, cruccio

vexa·tious [vɛk'seɪʃəs], **vex·ing** ['vɛksɪŋ] ADJ irritante, fastidioso(-a)

vexed [vɛkst] ADJ **1** irritato(-a); **to be/get vexed (with sb about sth)** essere irritato(-a)/irritarsi (con qn per qc) **2** *(question)* controverso(-a), dibattuto(-a)

vex·ing ['vɛksɪŋ] ADJ **1** *(annoying)* = **vexatious** **2** *(puzzling)* sconcertante

VG [ˌviː'dʒiː] ABBR *(Brit Scol:* = **very good***)* ottimo

VHF [ˌviːeɪtʃ'ɛf] N ABBR (= **very high frequency**) VHF *f*

VI ABBR *(Am Post)* = *Virgin Islands*

◎ **via** ['vaɪə] PREP *(by way of: place)* via; *(: person)* attraverso, tramite; *(by means of)* tramite, attraverso, per mezzo di; **we went to Rome via London** siamo andati a Roma passando per Londra; **they can send their work via email** possono mandare il loro lavoro tramite posta elettronica; **via satellite** via satellite

vi·abil·ity [ˌvaɪə'bɪlɪtɪ] N attuabilità

vi·able ['vaɪəbl] ADJ *(proposal)* attuabile, fattibile; *(foetus)* in grado di sopravvivere; **a viable alternative** un'alternativa possibile; **the foetus was not viable** il feto non era in grado di sopravvivere

via·duct ['vaɪəˌdʌkt] N viadotto

Viagra® [vaɪ'ægrə] N *(Med)* Viagra *m inv*

vial ['vaɪəl] N fiala

vibes [vaɪbz] NPL ABBR *(fam)* **1** *(vibrations)* atmosfera; **I got good vibes** l'impressione è stata buona **2** *(Mus)* = **vibraphone**

vi·bran·cy ['vaɪbrənsɪ] N vitalità

vi·brant ['vaɪbrənt] ADJ *(sound)* vibrante; *(colour)* vivace, vivo(-a); **to be vibrant with life** sprizzare vita da tutti i pori

vi·bra·phone ['vaɪbrəˌfəʊn] N vibrafono

vi·brate [vaɪ'breɪt] VI: **to vibrate (with)** *(quiver)* vibrare (per); *(resound)* risuonare (di); *(footsteps)* risuonare

vi·bra·tion [vaɪ'breɪʃən] N vibrazione *f*

vi·bra·tor [vaɪ'breɪtə^r] N *(for massage)* vibromassaggiatore *m* (elettrico); *(sex toy)* vibratore *m*

vic·ar ['vɪkə^r] N *(Church of England)* pastore *m*; *(Roman Catholic)* vicario

vic·ar·age ['vɪkərɪdʒ] N canonica *(anglicana)*

vi·cari·ous [vɪ'kɛərɪəs] ADJ: **to get vicarious pleasure out of sth** trarre piacere indirettamente da qc

vice- [vaɪs] PREF vice...

◎ **vice**[1] [vaɪs] N vizio; **vices and virtues** vizi e virtù

vice[2] [vaɪs] N *(tool)* morsa; **held in a vice** stretto (-a) in una morsa

vice-chairman [ˌvaɪs'tʃɛəmən] N *(pl* **-men***)* vicepresidente *m*

vice-chancellor [ˌvaɪs'tʃɑːnsələ^r] N *(Brit Univ)* rettore *m (eletto, non onorario)*

vice-consul [ˌvaɪs'kɒnsəl] N viceconsole *m*

vice-presidency [ˌvaɪs'prɛzɪdənsɪ] N vicepresidenza

vice-president [ˌvaɪs'prɛzɪdənt] N vicepresidente *m*

vice·roy ['vaɪsrɔɪ] N viceré *m inv*

vice squad N (squadra del) buon costume *f*

vice ver·sa [ˌvaɪsɪ'vɜːsə] ADV viceversa

vi·cin·ity [vɪ'sɪnɪtɪ] N vicinanze *fpl*

vi·cious ['vɪʃəs] ADJ *(attack)* brutale; *(blow, kick)* dato(-a) con cattiveria, violento(-a); *(animal)* cattivo(-a); *(remark,*

criticism) crudele; (*glare*) malevolo(-a), d'odio; (*tongue*) velenoso(-a); **a vicious habit** un vizio
vicious circle N circolo vizioso
vi·cious·ly ['vɪʃəslɪ] ADV (*fight*) ferocemente; (*hit*) con cattiveria; (*speak*) malignamente; (*glare*) con odio, velenosamente
vi·cious·ness ['vɪʃəsnɪs] N (*of behaviour*) brutalità, ferocia; (*of remark, criticism*) cattiveria, malignità
vi·cis·si·tudes [vɪ'sɪsɪtju:dz] NPL (*frm*) vicissitudini *fpl*
◎**vic·tim** ['vɪktɪm] N vittima; **to be the victim of** essere la vittima di; **he was the victim of a mugging** è stato vittima di un'aggressione; **to fall victim to** (*fig: desire, sb's charms*) essere vittima di
vic·timi·za·tion [ˌvɪktɪmaɪ'zeɪʃən] N persecuzione *f*; **to be the subject of victimization by sb** essere oggetto di persecuzione da parte di qn
◎**vic·tim·ize** ['vɪktɪˌmaɪz] VT perseguitare
victim support N: **victim support scheme** *programma di sostegno delle vittime di un crimine*
vic·tor ['vɪktə^r] N (*in sport, battle*) vincitore(-trice)
Vic·to·ria [vɪk'tɔ:rɪə] N Victoria
▷ www.vic.gov.au
▷ www.victoria-australia.worldweb.com
Vic·to·rian [vɪk'tɔ:rɪən] ADJ, N vittoriano(-a)
Vic·to·ri·ana [vɪkˌtɔ:rɪ'ɑ:nə] NPL *oggetti d'antiquariato dell'epoca vittoriana*
vic·to·ri·ous [vɪk'tɔ:rɪəs] ADJ (*gen*) vittorioso(-a); (*shout*) di vittoria, trionfante
◎**vic·to·ry** ['vɪktərɪ] N vittoria; **to win a victory over sb** riportare una vittoria su qn
vict·uals ['vɪtlz] NPL (*old*) vettovaglie *fpl*
vi·cu·ña [vɪ'kju:njə] N vigogna
vide ['vaɪdɪ] IMPERS VB vedi
◎**video** ['vɪdɪəʊ] N (*fam*) video *m inv*; **it's out on video** è uscito su videocassetta; **she lent me a video** mi ha prestato una videocassetta; **have you got a video?** hai il videoregistratore?
■ VT registrare; **I'll video the programme** registrerò il programma
video camera N videocamera
video cassette N videocassetta
video (cassette) recorder N videoregistratore *m*
video conference N videoconferenza
video conferencing [-'kɒnfərənsɪŋ] N videoconferenza; **video conferencing facilities** dispositivi *mpl* per videoconferenza
video diary N *film amatoriale fatto con la videocamera*
video·disk ['vɪdɪəʊˌdɪsk] N videodisco
video game N videogioco
video nasty N (*fam*) horror-film *m inv* (*a sfondo pornografico*)
video·phone ['vɪdɪəʊˌfəʊn] N videotelefono
video recorder N videoregistratore *m*
video recording N videoregistrazione *f*
video shop N videonoleggio
video·tape ['vɪdɪəʊˌteɪp] VT registrare su videocassetta
video tape N videocassetta
video wall N maxischermo (*composto da più pannelli*)
vie [vaɪ] VI: **to vie (with sb) for sth** competere (con qn) per qc; **to vie with one another for sth** contendersi qc; **nationalist politicians vying for power** politici nazionalisti che si contendono il potere
Vi·en·na [vɪ'ɛnə] N Vienna
Vi·et·nam, **Viet Nam** [ˌvjɛt'næm] N Vietnam *m*
Vi·et·nam·ese [ˌvjɛtnə'mi:z] ADJ vietnamita *inv*
■ N (*person*) vietnamita *m/f*; (*language*) vietnamita *m*
◎**view** [vju:] N **1** (*sight*) vista; (*panorama*) veduta; **there's an amazing view** c'è una vista fantastica; **a splendid view of the river** una splendida veduta del fiume; **50 views of Venice** 50 vedute di Venezia; **you'll get a better view from here** da qui vedrai meglio; **back/front view of the house** la casa vista da dietro/davanti; **to be in** *or* **within view (of sth)** essere in vista (di qc); **the house is within view of the sea** la casa ha la vista sul mare; **to come into** *or* **within view** arrivare in vista; **the city suddenly came into view** la città apparve all'improvviso; **in full view of sb** sotto gli occhi di qn; **hidden from view** nascosto(-a) alla vista; **on view** (*house*) in visione; (*exhibit*) in esposizione; **an overall view of the situation** (*survey*) una visione globale della situazione **2** (*opinion*) punto di vista, opinione *f*; **in my view** a mio parere, a mio avviso; **to take** *or* **hold the view that ...** essere dell'opinione che...; **to take a dim** *or* **poor view of sth** accogliere male qc; **they have similar views on this matter** hanno punti di vista simili sull'argomento **3** (*consideration*): **in view of the fact that ...** visto che..., considerato che...; **in view of this, ...** visto ciò... **4** (*intention*): **to have in view** avere in mente; **to keep sth in view** non perdere qc di vista; **with this in view** a questo scopo; **with a view to doing sth** con l'intenzione di fare qc
■ VT (*house*) vedere; (*television*) guardare; (*situation*) considerare; **how do you view this development?** come consideri questo sviluppo?; **how does the government view it?** che cosa ne pensa il governo?
View·data® ['vju:ˌdeɪtə] N (*Brit*) *sistema di televideo*
◎**view·er** ['vju:ə^r] N **1** (TV) telespettatore(-trice) **2** (*for slides*) visore *m*
view·finder ['vju:ˌfaɪndə^r] N (*Phot*) mirino
view·point ['vju:ˌpɔɪnt] N (*on hill*) posizione *f*; (*fig*) punto di vista
vig·il ['vɪdʒɪl] N veglia; **to keep vigil** vegliare; **a prayer vigil** una veglia di preghiera
vigi·lance ['vɪdʒɪləns] N vigilanza
vigi·lant ['vɪdʒɪlənt] ADJ vigile
vigi·lan·te [ˌvɪdʒɪ'læntɪ] N vigilante *m/f* (*privato cittadino*)
vi·gnette [vɪ'njɛt] N (*description*) quadretto; (*illustration in book*) illustrazione *f*; (*Art, Phot*) ritratto a mezzo busto su sfondo sfumato
vig·or·ous ['vɪgərəs] ADJ (*handshake, speech, protest*) vigoroso(-a), energico(-a); (*character*) vitale; (*plant*) forte
vig·or·ous·ly ['vɪgərəslɪ] ADV (*move, grow*) con vigore; (*speak, protest*) vigorosamente
vig·our, (*Am*) **vig·or** ['vɪgə^r] N vigore *m*
Vi·king ['vaɪkɪŋ] ADJ, N vichingo(-a)
▷ www.jorvik-viking-centre.co.uk/
▷ www.pbs.org/wgbh/nova/vikings
▷ www.bbc.co.uk/schools/vikings/beliefs/index.shtml
vile [vaɪl] ADJ (*horrible*) orrendo(-a); (*very bad: temper*) pessimo(-a); (*: smell*) disgustoso(-a); **what a vile trick!** che scherzo meschino!; **a vile habit** un vizio detestabile
vili·fi·ca·tion [ˌvɪlɪfɪ'keɪʃən] N (*frm*) diffamazione *f*
vili·fy ['vɪlɪˌfaɪ] VT (*frm*) diffamare
vil·la ['vɪlə] N villa
◎**vil·lage** ['vɪlɪdʒ] N paese *m*, villaggio
■ ADJ (*of a village, villages*) di paese; (*local*) del paese; **a village inn** una locanda di paese; **the village inn** la locanda del paese; **the village idiot** lo scemo del villaggio
village green N *spazio verde al centro del paese*

vil·lag·er ['vɪlɪdʒəʳ] N abitante *m/f* di paese, paesano(-a)
vil·lain ['vɪlən] N mascalzone *m*; (*hum: rascal*) briccone(-a); (*scoundrel*) canaglia; (*in novel, film*) cattivo; (*fam: criminal*) delinquente *m*

> DID YOU KNOW ...?
> **villain** is not translated by the Italian word ***villano***

vil·lain·ous ['vɪlənəs] ADJ scellerato(-a), infame
vil·lainy ['vɪlənɪ] N scelleratezza
vim [vɪm] N (*fam*) energia
vinai·grette [ˌvɪneɪ'grɛt] N vinaigrette *f inv*
vin·di·cate ['vɪndɪˌkeɪt] VT (*assertion, claim*) provare la fondatezza di, confermare; **he was finally vindicated** fu alla fine provato che aveva ragione

> DID YOU KNOW ...?
> **vindicate** is not translated by the Italian word ***vendicare***

vin·di·ca·tion [ˌvɪndɪ'keɪʃən] N giustificazione *f*; **in vindication of** a conferma di
vin·dic·tive [vɪn'dɪktɪv] ADJ vendicativo(-a); **to feel vindictive towards sb** volersi vendicare di qn
vin·dic·tive·ly [vɪn'dɪktɪvlɪ] ADV vendicativamente
vine [vaɪn] N (*grapevine*) vite *f*; (*climbing plant*) rampicante *m*

> DID YOU KNOW ...?
> **vine** is not translated by the Italian word ***vino***

vin·egar ['vɪnɪgəʳ] N aceto
vin·egary ['vɪnɪgərɪ] ADJ (*wine, taste, smell*) che sa d'aceto; (*person*) acido(-a)
vine·grower ['vaɪnˌgrəʊəʳ] N viticoltore *m*
vine-growing ['vaɪnˌgrəʊɪŋ] ADJ viticolo(-a)
■ N viticoltura
vine·yard ['vɪnjəd] N vigna, vigneto
vin·tage ['vɪntɪdʒ] N (*harvest*) vendemmia; (*season*) periodo della vendemmia; (*year*) annata; **what vintage is this wine?** di che annata è questo vino?; **the 1980 vintage** il vino del 1980; **a good vintage** una buona annata
vintage car N auto *f inv* d'epoca
vintage comedy N commedia classica
vintage wine N vino d'annata
vintage year N: **it has been a vintage year for plays** è stata una buona annata per il teatro
vint·ner ['vɪntnəʳ] N (*retailer*) vinaio(-a); (*wholesaler*) commerciante *m/f* di vini
vi·nyl ['vaɪnɪl] N vinile *m*; (*record*) disco di vinile
vio·la¹ [vɪ'əʊlə] N (*Mus*) viola
vio·la² [vɪ'əʊlə] N (*Bot*) viola
◎ **vio·late** ['vaɪəˌleɪt] VT violare
vio·la·tion [ˌvaɪə'leɪʃən] N violazione *f*; **in violation of sth** in contravvenzione *f inv* a qc
◎ **vio·lence** ['vaɪələns] N violenza; (*Pol*) incidenti *mpl* violenti; **outbreaks of violence** episodi di violenza; **acts of violence** atti di violenza; **robbery with violence** rapina a mano armata; **sex and violence** violenza e sesso; **to do violence to sth** (*fig*) fare violenza a qc
◎ **vio·lent** ['vaɪələnt] ADJ (*gen*) violento(-a); **to die a violent death** morire di morte violenta; **a violent temper** un temperamento violento; **to be in a violent temper** essere furioso(-a); **a violent dislike of sb/sth** una violenta avversione per qn/qc; **by violent means** con l'uso della forza
vio·lent·ly ['vaɪələntlɪ] ADV (*attack, react*) in modo violento, violentemente; (*severely: sick, angry*) terribilmente; **to fall violently in love with sb** innamorarsi follemente di qn
vio·let ['vaɪəlɪt] N (*Bot*) violetta; (*colour*) violetto
■ ADJ violetto(-a)
vio·lin [ˌvaɪə'lɪn] N violino
■ ADJ (*case, concerto*) per violino
vio·lin·ist [ˌvaɪə'lɪnɪst] N violinista *m/f*
VIP [ˌviːaɪ'piː] N ABBR (= **very important person**) VIP *m/f inv*
vi·per ['vaɪpəʳ] N (*Zool, also fig*) vipera
vi·ra·go [vɪ'rɑːgəʊ] N (*frm pej*) virago *f*
vi·ral ['vaɪərəl] ADJ virale; (*advertising, marketing*) fatto(-a) da utenti Internet tramite la distribuzione di videoclip
Virgil ['vɜːdʒɪl] N Virgilio
vir·gin ['vɜːdʒɪn] N vergine *f*; **she/he is a virgin** lei/lui è vergine; **the Virgin** (*Mary*) la Beata Vergine
■ ADJ (*fig: forest, soil*) vergine; **virgin snow** neve fresca
vir·gin·al ['vɜːdʒɪnəl] ADJ **1** (*chaste*) verginale **2** (*pristine*) immacolato(-a)
■ N (*Mus*) spinetta
Vir·ginia [və'dʒɪnjə] N Virginia
▷ www.virginia.gov/cmsportal/
Vir·ginia creep·er [vəˌdʒɪnjə'kriːpəʳ] N vite *f* del Canada
vir·gin·ity [vɜː'dʒɪnɪtɪ] N verginità
Vir·go ['vɜːgəʊ] N (*Astron, Astrol*) Vergine *f*; **to be Virgo** essere della Vergine; **I'm Virgo** sono della Vergine
vir·ile ['vɪraɪl] ADJ virile
vi·ril·ity [vɪ'rɪlɪtɪ] N virilità
vir·tual ['vɜːtjʊəl] ADJ effettivo(-a), vero(-a); (*Comput, Phys*) virtuale; **the virtual leader** il capo all'atto pratico; **the strike led to the virtual closure of the dock** lo sciopero ha praticamente portato alla chiusura del porto; **it was a virtual defeat** di fatto è stata una sconfitta; **it's a virtual impossibility** è praticamente impossibile; **it's a virtual certainty** è praticamente una certezza
◎ **vir·tu·al·ly** ['vɜːtjʊəlɪ] ADV (*in effect*) di fatto; (*to all intents and purposes*) praticamente; **she virtually runs the business** di fatto è lei che gestisce l'azienda; **it is virtually impossible to do anything** è praticamente impossibile fare qualcosa

> DID YOU KNOW ...?
> **virtually** is not translated by the Italian word ***virtualmente***

virtual memory N (*Comput*) memoria virtuale
virtual reality N (*Comput*) realtà *f* virtuale
vir·tue ['vɜːtjuː] N (*goodness*) virtù *f inv*; (*advantage*) pregio, vantaggio; **it has the virtue of simplicity** *or* **of being simple** ha il pregio di essere semplice; **its other great virtue is its quality** l'altro pregio è la qualità; **I see no virtue in doing that** non vedo nessun vantaggio nel farlo; **to make a virtue of necessity** fare di necessità virtù; **by virtue of** in virtù di, grazie a; **vices and virtues** vizi e virtù
vir·tu·os·ity [ˌvɜːtjʊ'ɒsɪtɪ] N virtuosismo
vir·tuo·so [ˌvɜːtjʊ'əʊzəʊ] N virtuoso(-a)
vir·tu·ous ['vɜːtjʊəs] ADJ virtuoso(-a)
viru·lence ['vɪrʊləns] N (*frm*) virulenza
viru·lent ['vɪrʊlənt] ADJ (*frm*) virulento(-a)
◎ **vi·rus** ['vaɪərəs] N virus *m inv*
visa ['viːzə] N visto
vis-à-vis [ˌviːzə'viː] PREP rispetto a, in confronto a, nei riguardi di
vis·cer·al ['vɪsərəl] ADJ (*liter*) viscerale
vis·cose ['vɪskəʊs] N viscosa

Vv

vis·cos·ity [vɪs'kɒsɪtɪ] N viscosità
vis·count ['vaɪkaʊnt] N visconte *m*
vis·cous ['vɪskəs] ADJ viscoso(-a)
vise [vaɪs] N (*Am*) = **vice²**
vis·ibil·ity [ˌvɪzɪ'bɪlɪtɪ] N visibilità
◎**vis·ible** ['vɪzəbl] ADJ **1** visibile; **visible to the naked eye** che si può vedere ad occhio nudo, visibile ad occhio nudo; **to become visible** apparire **2** (*obvious*) evidente; **visible exports/imports** esportazioni *fpl*/importazioni *fpl* visibili; **a visible effort** uno sforzo palese
vis·ibly ['vɪzəblɪ] ADV visibilmente
Visi·goth ['vɪzɪˌgɒθ] N Visigoto
◎**vi·sion** ['vɪʒən] N **1** (*eyesight*) vista, capacità visiva; **loss of vision** la perdita della vista **2** (*imagination, foresight, apparition*) visione *f*; **a man of vision** un uomo lungimirante *or* che vede lontano; **my vision of the future** la mia visione del futuro; **his vision of society** la sua visione della società; **to see visions** avere le visioni; **to have a vision of** immaginare; **I had visions of having to walk home** già mi vedevo dover andare a casa a piedi
vi·sion·ary ['vɪʒənərɪ] N visionario(-a)
■ ADJ lungimirante; (*dreamlike*) irreale
vision defect N difetto della vista
◎**vis·it** ['vɪzɪt] N visita; (*stay*) soggiorno; **to go on a visit to** (*person*) andare in visita da; (*place*) andare a visitare; **to pay a visit to** (*person*) fare una visita a; (*place*) andare a visitare; **on a private/official visit** in visita privata/ufficiale
■ VT **1** (*person*) andare a trovare; (*frm*) andare in visita da; (*place: go and see*) visitare; (*: inspect*) ispezionare; **I visited my grandmother last week** sono andato(-a) a trovare mia nonna la settimana scorsa; **we'd like to visit the castle** ci piacerebbe visitare il castello **2** (*stay with: person*) essere ospite di
▶ **visit with** VI + PREP (*Am*) chiacchierare con
vis·ita·tion [ˌvɪsɪ'teɪʃən] N **1** (*frm: by official*) visita; (*: by bishop*) visita pastorale **2** (*hum*): **a visitation (from sb)** una visita inopportuna (da parte di qn) **3** (*Rel*): **the Visitation of the Blessed Virgin Mary** la Visitazione della Beata Vergine **4** (*frm: calamity*) punizione *f* divina
vis·it·ing ['vɪzɪtɪŋ] ADJ (*speaker, professor, team*) ospite
visiting card N biglietto da visita
visiting hours NPL orario *msg* delle visite
◎**visi·tor** ['vɪzɪtəʳ] N (*guest*) ospite *m/f*; (*tourist*) turista *m/f*; (*in hospital, at zoo, exhibition*) visitatore(-trice); **important visitors** visitatori importanti; **visitors to the town** i visitatori della città; **to have a visitor** avere una visita; **you've got a visitor** (*in hospital, at home*) c'è una visita per te
visitors' book N (*in hotel*) registro dei clienti; (*in museum*) registro dei visitatori
vi·sor ['vaɪzəʳ] N (*on helmet*) visiera; (*Aut*) aletta parasole
VISTA ['vɪstə] N ABBR (= **Volunteers in Service to America**) *volontariato in zone depresse degli Stati Uniti*
vis·ta ['vɪstə] N (*view*) vista; (*fig*) prospettiva
vis·ual ['vɪzjʊəl] ADJ visivo(-a)
visual aid N sussidio visivo
visual arts NPL: **the visual arts** le arti figurative
visual display unit N (*Comput*) videoterminale *m*
visu·al·ize ['vɪzjʊəˌlaɪz] VT (*imagine*) immaginare, immaginarsi; (*foresee*) prevedere; **to visualize sb doing sth** immaginare qn che fa qc
visu·al·ly ['vɪzjʊəlɪ] ADV: **visually handicapped** (*blind*) non vedente; (*visually impaired*) videoleso(-a); **visually the film was good** sul piano dell'immagine il film era buono; **visually appealing** piacevole a vedersi
◎**vi·tal** ['vaɪtl] ADJ **1** (*gen*) vitale; (*error*) fatale; **of vital importance (to sb/sth)** di vitale importanza (per qn/qc); **it is vital that** è essenziale che; **it's vital to sterilize the equipment** è essenziale sterilizzare l'attrezzatura; **vital information** informazioni *fpl* d'importanza vitale **2** (*lively*) pieno(-a) di vitalità
vi·tal·ity [vaɪ'tælɪtɪ] N vitalità; **his performance lacked vitality** la sua esecuzione mancava di brio
vi·tal·ly ['vaɪtəlɪ] ADV: **vitally important** di vitale importanza; **vitally urgent** estremamente urgente
vital signs NPL segni *mpl* vitali
vital statistics NPL (*of population*) statistica *fsg* demografica; (*fam: woman's*) misure *fpl*
◎**vita·min** ['vɪtəmɪn] N vitamina; **with added vitamins** vitaminizzato(-a)
vitamin deficiency N carenza vitaminica, avitaminosi *f*
vitamin tablet N (confetto di) vitamina
vi·ti·ate ['vɪʃɪˌeɪt] VT (*frm: all senses*) viziare
vit·re·ous ['vɪtrɪəs] ADJ (*china, enamel*) vetrificato(-a); (*rock*) vetroso(-a)
vit·ri·fy ['vɪtrɪˌfaɪ] VT vetrificare
vit·ri·ol ['vɪtrɪɒl] N (*Chem*) vetriolo; (*fig*) veleno
vit·ri·ol·ic [ˌvɪtrɪ'ɒlɪk] ADJ (*fig*) al vetriolo
vi·tu·pera·tive [vɪ'tju:pərətɪv] ADJ (*frm: person*) offensivo(-a); (*: speech*) ingiurioso(-a)
viva ['vaɪvə] N (*also:* **viva voce**) (esame *m*) orale *m*
vi·va·cious [vɪ'veɪʃəs] ADJ vivace, pieno(-a) di brio
vi·vac·ity [vɪ'væsɪtɪ] N vivacità
viv·id ['vɪvɪd] ADJ (*colour*) vivo(-a), vivido(-a); (*dream, recollection, expression on face*) chiaro(-a); (*description, memory*) vivido(-a); **to have a vivid imagination** avere una fervida immaginazione
viv·id·ly ['vɪvɪdlɪ] ADV (*describe*) in modo vivido; (*remember*) chiaramente; **so vividly described** descritto(-a) così vividamente; **I remember it vividly** lo ricordo chiaramente
viv·id·ness ['vɪvɪdnɪs] N (*of colour, description*) vivacità; (*of impression, recollection*) chiarezza
vivi·sec·tion [ˌvɪvɪ'sɛkʃən] N vivisezione *f*
vix·en ['vɪksn] N volpe *f* femmina; (*pej: woman*) vipera
viz ABBR (= **videlicet:** *namely*) cioè
vi·zier [vɪ'zɪəʳ] N visir *m inv*
VLF [ˌvi:ɛl'ɛf] N ABBR (= **very low frequency**) VLF (= *bassissima frequenza*)
v-mail ['vi:ˌmeɪl] N (*Comput*) voicemail *m or f inv*, messaggeria vocale
V-neck ['vi:ˌnɛk] N maglione *m* con scollo a V
V-necked [ˌvi:'nɛkt] ADJ con scollo a V
VOA [ˌvi:əʊ'eɪ] N ABBR (= **Voice of America**) voce *f* dell'America (*alla radio*)
vo·cabu·lary [vəʊ'kæbjʊlərɪ] N (*gen*) vocabolario; (*in textbook*) vocabolario, dizionario; **we have to learn all the new vocabulary** dobbiamo imparare tutti i vocaboli nuovi
vo·cal ['vəʊkəl] ADJ **1** (*gen*) vocale **2** (*fig: vociferous*) pronto(-a) a esprimere la propria opinione
vocal chords NPL corde *fpl* vocali
vo·cal·ic [vəʊ'kælɪk] ADJ vocalico(-a)
vo·cal·ist ['vəʊkəlɪst] N cantante *m/f* (*in un gruppo*)
vo·cal·ize ['vəʊkəˌlaɪz] VT (*Ling*) vocalizzare; (*frm: opinions etc*) esprimere, dar voce a
vo·cals ['vəʊkəlz] NPL: **lead vocals** voce *fsg* solista; **backing vocals** accompagnamento vocale
vo·ca·tion [vəʊ'keɪʃən] N vocazione *f*; **to have a**

vocation for teaching avere la vocazione dell'insegnamento
vo·ca·tion·al [vəʊ'keɪʃənl] ADJ (*training*) professionale
vocational guidance N orientamento professionale
voca·tive ['vɒkətɪv] ADJ vocativo(-a)
■ N vocativo
vo·cif·er·ous [vəʊ'sɪfərəs] ADJ rumoroso(-a)
vod·ka ['vɒdkə] N vodka *f inv*
▷ www.ginvodka.org
vogue [vəʊg] N (*fashion*) moda; (*popularity*) voga; **to be in vogue, be the vogue** essere di moda, essere in voga
◎ **voice** [vɔɪs] N (*gen, Gram*) voce *f*; **to lose one's voice** perdere la voce; **she is in fine voice again** ha riacquistato la sua bella voce; **in a loud/soft voice** a voce alta/bassa; **at the top of one's voice** a tutta voce, con quanta voce si ha in gola *or* in corpo; **with one voice** all'unisono; **to have a voice in the matter** aver voce in capitolo; **to give voice to** esprimere; **I heard voices** sentivo delle voci
■ VT (*feelings, opinions*) esprimere
voice-activated [,vɔɪs'æktɪveɪtəd] ADJ che si attiva con la voce
voice·less ['vɔɪslɪs] ADJ (*Ling*) sordo(-a); (*mute*) muto(-a)
voice·mail ['vɔɪs,meɪl] N = **v-mail**
voice-over ['vɔɪs,əʊvəʳ] N (*TV, Cine*) voce *f* fuori campo *inv*
void [vɔɪd] ADJ (*frm: Law*) nullo(-a); (*empty*) vuoto(-a); **void of** privo(-a) di; **to make** *or* **render a contract void** invalidare un contratto
■ N vuoto; **to fill the void** colmare il vuoto
voile [vɔɪl] N voile *m*
VoIP N ABBR (*Comput*: = **voice-over Internet protocol**) *protocollo che consente di telefonare tramite Internet*
◎ **vol.** ABBR (= **volume**) vol.
vola·tile ['vɒlə,taɪl] ADJ (*Chem*) volatile; (*fig: situation*) esplosivo(-a); (*: character*) volubile
vola·til·ity [,vɒlə'tɪlɪtɪ] N **1** (*market, situation*) instabilità *f* **2** (*person, temper*) volubilità *f* **3** (*Chem: of liquid, chemicals, substance*) volatilità *f*
vol-au-vent ['vɒlə,vɒŋ] N vol-au-vent *m inv*
vol·can·ic [vɒl'kænɪk] ADJ vulcanico(-a)
vol·ca·no [vɒl'keɪnəʊ] N (*pl* **volcanoes**) vulcano
vole [vəʊl] N: **field vole** topo campagnolo comune; **water vole** arvicola
vo·li·tion [və'lɪʃən] N: **of one's own volition** di propria volontà
vol·ley ['vɒlɪ] N (*of shots, stones, insults*) raffica, scarica; (*of gunfire*) salva; (*Tennis*) volée *f inv*, volata
volley·ball ['vɒlɪ,bɔ:l] N pallavolo *f*
▷ www.volleyball.org
▷ www.volleyballengland.org/
▷ www.volleyball.ca/
▷ www.usavolleyball.org/
volt [vəʊlt] N volt *m inv*
volt·age ['vəʊltɪdʒ] N tensione *f*, voltaggio; **high/low voltage** alta/bassa tensione
voltage regulator N regolatore *m* di tensione
volte ['vɒltɪ] N (*Horse-riding*) volta
volte-face ['vɒlt'fɑ:s] N voltafaccia *m inv*
volt·me·ter ['vəʊlt,mi:təʳ] N voltimetro
vol·uble ['vɒljʊbl] ADJ loquace

DID YOU KNOW ...?
voluble is not translated by the Italian word ***volubile***

◎ **vol·ume** ['vɒlju:m] N **1** (*book*) volume *m*; **volume one/two** volume primo/secondo **2** (*size, sound*) volume *m*; (*of tank*) capacità *f inv*; **he turned down the volume** ha abbassato il volume; **the volume of sales** il volume delle vendite **3** **to speak volumes** (*express a great deal*) dire tutto; **his expression spoke volumes** la sua espressione lasciava capire tutto; **it speaks volumes for his charm** la dice lunga sul suo fascino
volume control N (*Radio, TV*) regolatore *m or* manopola del volume
volume discount N (*Comm*) vantaggio sul volume di vendita
volu·met·ric [,vɒljʊ'mɛtrɪk] ADJ volumetrico(-a)
vo·lu·mi·nous [və'lu:mɪnəs] ADJ voluminoso(-a); (*writer*) prolifico(-a); (*notes*) abbondante
vol·un·tari·ly ['vɒləntərɪlɪ] ADV spontaneamente, volontariamente
◎ **vol·un·tary** ['vɒləntərɪ] ADJ (*statement, confession*) spontaneo(-a); (*attendance*) facoltativo(-a); (*unpaid: contribution, work, worker*) volontario(-a); **attendance is voluntary** la frequenza è facoltativa; **to do voluntary work** fare volontariato; **voluntary contributions** contributi *mpl* volontari
voluntary liquidation N (*Comm*) liquidazione *f* volontaria
◎ **vol·un·teer** [,vɒlən'tɪəʳ] N (*Mil, gen*) volontario(-a)
■ VT (*one's help, services, suggestion*) offrire spontaneamente; (*information*) fornire; **no-one volunteered an answer** nessuno si è offerto di rispondere; **he rarely volunteers his opinion** è raro che esprima la propria opinione spontaneamente
■ VI (*for a task*) offrirsi come volontario(-a), offrirsi spontaneamente; (*Mil*) arruolarsi volontario(-a); **to volunteer to do sth** offrirsi spontaneamente di fare qc, offrirsi volontario(-a) per fare qc
■ ADJ (*forces, helpers*) volontario(-a); (*corps*) di volontari
vo·lup·tu·ous [və'lʌptjʊəs] ADJ (*pleasure, sensation*) voluttuoso(-a); (*lips, figure*) sensuale
vo·lup·tu·ous·ness [və'lʌptjʊəsnɪs] N voluttuosità, sensualità
vom·it ['vɒmɪt] N vomito
■ VT, VI vomitare
vom·it·ing ['vɒmɪtɪŋ] N vomito
voo·doo ['vu:du:] N vudù *m*
vo·ra·cious [və'reɪʃəs] (*liter*) ADJ (*appetite*) smisurato(-a); (*reader*) avido(-a)
vo·ra·cious·ly [və'reɪʃəslɪ] ADV (*eat*) voracemente; (*read*) avidamente
vo·rac·ity [vɒ'ræsɪtɪ] N voracità
vor·tex ['vɔ:tɛks] N (*pl* **vortices** ['vɔ:tɪsi:z]) (*frm: whirl*) vortice *m*; (*fig*) turbine *m*
◎ **vote** [vəʊt] N voto; (*ballot, election*) votazione *f*; **vote for/against** voto a favore/contrario; **to put sth to the vote, take a vote on sth** mettere qc ai voti; **to have the vote** avere diritto di voto; **as the 1997 vote showed** com'è risultato dalle votazioni del 1997; **the Labour vote has decreased** il partito laburista ha perso voti; **they won by two votes** hanno vinto per due voti; **now let's take a vote** passiamo ora alla votazione
■ VT (*gen*) votare; (*sum of money*) votare a favore di; **the bill was voted through parliament** la proposta di legge è stata approvata dal parlamento; **he was voted secretary** è stato eletto segretario; **to vote a proposal down** respingere una proposta
■ VI: **to vote (for sb/sth)** votare (per qn/qc); **to vote on sth** mettere qc ai voti; **to vote Labour/Conservative** votare laburista/conservatore; **to vote to do sth** scegliere di fare qc; **to vote against/in favour of sth** votare a favore di/contro qc; **I vote we turn back** (*fam*) io propongo di tornare indietro

▸ **vote down** VT + ADV bocciare ai voti
▸ **vote in** VT + ADV eleggere
▸ **vote out** VT + ADV: **to vote sb out** votare a sfavore della rielezione di qn
vote of confidence N (*Pol*) voto di fiducia
vote of no confidence N (*Pol*) voto di sfiducia; **to pass a vote of no confidence** dare il voto di sfiducia
vote of thanks N discorso di ringraziamento
◎ **vot·er** ['vəʊtəʳ] N elettore(-trice)
vot·ing ['vəʊtɪŋ] N votazione *f*, voto
voting booth N cabina elettorale
voting paper N (*Brit*) scheda elettorale
voting right N (*of shareholder*) diritto di voto
vo·tive ['vəʊtɪv] ADJ (*offering*) votivo(-a)
vouch [vaʊtʃ] VI: **to vouch for sth** garantire qc; **to vouch for sb** garantire per qn
vouch·er ['vaʊtʃəʳ] N buono, tagliando, coupon *m inv*; **travel voucher** voucher *m inv*; **a gift voucher** un buono acquisto
vouch·safe [ˌvaʊtʃ'seɪf] VT (*liter, frm*): **to vouchsafe sth (to sb)** (*reply, help*) accordare qc (a qn); (*peace*) garantire qc (a qn)
vow [vaʊ] N voto; **to take** *or* **make a vow to do sth** fare voto di fare qc; **to take one's vows** (*Rel*) prendere i voti ■ VT (*obedience, allegiance*) giurare; **to vow to do sth/that** giurare di fare qc/che
vow·el ['vaʊəl] N vocale *f*
vowel sound N suono vocalico
voy·age ['vɔɪɪdʒ] N viaggio per mare; **the voyage out/back** il viaggio di andata/di ritorno
voy·ag·er ['vɔɪədʒəʳ] N viaggiatore(-trice)
vo·yeur [vwɑː'jɜːʳ] N guardone(-a), voyeur *m inv*
vo·yeur·ism [vwɑː'jɜːrɪzəm] N voyeurismo
VP [ˌviː'piː] N ABBR (= **vice-president**) VP
vs ABBR = **versus**
V-sign ['viːˌsaɪn] N: **to give (sb) the V-sign** (*for victory*) fare il segno di vittoria; (*Brit: as insult*) ≈ fare le corna
VSO [ˌviːes'əʊ] N ABBR (*Brit*: = **Voluntary Service Overseas**) *servizio volontario nei paesi in via di sviluppo*
VT ABBR (*Am Post*) = **Vermont**
Vulcan ['vʌlkən] N Vulcano
vul·cani·za·tion [ˌvʌlkənaɪ'zeɪʃən] N vulcanizzazione *f*
vul·can·ize ['vʌlkəˌnaɪz] VT vulcanizzare
vul·gar ['vʌlgəʳ] ADJ (*gen, pej*) volgare
vulgar fraction N (*Math*) frazione *f* ordinaria
vul·gar·ity [vʌl'gærɪtɪ] N volgarità
vulgar Latin N latino volgare
Vul·gate ['vʌlgeɪt] N (*Bible*): **the Vulgate** la Vulgata
vul·ner·abil·ity [ˌvʌlnərə'bɪlɪtɪ] N vulnerabilità
◎ **vul·ner·able** ['vʌlnərəbl] ADJ (*person*) vulnerabile; (*position*) esposto(-a)
vul·ture ['vʌltʃəʳ] N avvoltoio

Ww

W, w ['dʌblju:] N (*letter*) W, w *f or m inv*; **W for William** ≈ W come Washington
W ABBR **1** (= West) O **2** (*Elec:* = watt) W
WA ABBR **1** (*Am Post*) = Washington **2** (*Australia Post*) = Western Australia
wacky, whacky ['wækɪ] ADJ (*comp* **-ier**, *superl* **-iest**) (*fam*) pazzoide
wad [wɒd] N (*of cloth*) tampone *m*; (*of chewing gum, putty*) pallina; (*of cotton wool*) batuffolo; (*of papers, banknotes*) fascio; **a wad of banknotes** una mazzetta di banconote
wad·ding ['wɒdɪŋ] N imbottitura
wad·dle ['wɒdl] VI camminare come una papera; **to waddle in/out** *etc* entrare/uscire *etc* camminando come una papera
wade [weɪd] VI: **to wade through** (*water, mud*) camminare in; (*long grass, corn*) farsi strada attraverso; (*fig: book*) leggere con fatica; **to wade ashore** raggiungere a piedi la riva; **to wade into sb** (*fig*) scagliarsi su qn; **he waded in and helped us** (*fig*) si rimboccò le maniche e ci aiutò
■ VT (*river*) guadare
wad·er ['weɪdəʳ] N (*bird*) trampoliere *m*; (*boot*) stivale *m* da pesca
wadi ['wɒdɪ] N uadi *m inv*
wa·fer ['weɪfəʳ] N (*Culin, Elec*) wafer *m inv*; (*with ice cream*) cialda; (*Rel*) ostia
wafer-thin [ˌweɪfə'θɪn] ADJ sottilissimo(-a)
waf·fle ['wɒfl] N (*Culin*) cialda; (*fam: talk*) chiacchiere *fpl*, ciance *fpl*
■ VI (*fam: also:* **waffle on**) cianciare, chiacchierare; (*in exam, essay*) chiacchierare molto e dire poco
waffle iron N stampo per cialde
waft [wɑ:ft] VT (*sound, scent*) portare
■ VI diffondersi
wag¹ [wæg] N: **with a wag of its tail** dimenando la coda
■ VT: **the dog wagged its tail** il cane scodinzolò; **he wagged his head** scosse la testa; **to wag one's finger at sb** fare un cenno di rimprovero a qn scuotendo il dito
■ VI (*tail*) dimenarsi; **that'll set the tongues wagging** (*fig*) farà scatenare le malelingue; **his tongue never stops wagging** (*fig*) non sta mai zitto
wag² [wæg] N (*joker*) burlone(-a)
◎ **wage** [weɪdʒ] N (*often pl*) paga; **a day's wages** un giorno di paga; **she gets a good wage** è pagata bene; **minimum wage** minimo salariale; **a low wage** una paga bassa; **he collected his wages** ha ritirato la paga
■ VT (*campaign*) intraprendere; **to wage war** fare la guerra
■ ADJ (*demand, negotiations*) salariale
wage claim N rivendicazione *f* salariale
waged [weɪdʒd] ADJ remunerato(-a)
wage differential N differenziali *mpl* salariali
wage earn·er ['weɪdʒˌ3:nəʳ] N salariato(-a); **the family wage earner** il sostegno economico della famiglia
wage freeze N blocco dei salari
wage packet N (*Brit*) busta *f* paga *inv*
wa·ger ['weɪdʒəʳ] N: **wager (on)** scommessa (su)
■ VT (*sum of money*): **to wager (on)** puntare (su), scommettere (su); **to wager that ...** scommettere che...
wage rise N aumento di stipendio
wages clerk N contabile *m/f*
wag·gle ['wægl] N: **with a waggle of her hips** ancheggiando; **with a waggle of its tail** scodinzolando
■ VT (*tail*) dimenare, agitare; **to waggle one's hips** ancheggiare
■ VI dimenarsi, agitarsi
wag·on, wag·gon ['wægən] N (*horse-drawn*) carro; (*truck*) camion *m inv*; (*Rail*) vagone *m* merci *inv*; (*trolley*) carrello; **a horse and wagon** un carro trainato da un cavallo; **he's on the wagon again!** (*fam*) ha nuovamente smesso di bere!
wag·on·er, wag·gon·er ['wægənəʳ] N carrettiere *m*
wagon·load, wag·gon·load ['wægənˌləʊd] N (*on train*) carico; (*on cart*) carrettata
wagon train N (*Am History*) carovana di carri
wag·tail ['wægˌteɪl] N (*Zool*) ballerina; **grey wagtail** ballerina gialla
waif [weɪf] N bambino(-a) abbandonato(-a); (*slight*

person) creatura gracile; **waifs and strays** trovatelli *mpl*

wail [weɪl] N (*of suffering*) gemito; (*of baby*) vagito; (*of siren*) urlo; (*of wind*) ululato; **a wail of protest** un urlo di protesta
■ VI (*see n*) gemere; vagire; urlare; ululare

wail·ing ['weɪlɪŋ] N (*of suffering*) gemito; (*of baby*) vagito; (*of siren*) urlo; (*of wind*) ululato

wain·scot·ing, **wain·scot·ting** ['weɪnskətɪŋ] N perlinatura

waist [weɪst] N (*Anat, of dress*) vita; (*fig: narrow part: of violin*) strozzatura; **he put his arm round her waist** le ha messo un braccio attorno alla vita; **stripped to the waist** nudo(-a) fino alla cintura, a torso nudo; **to be up to one's waist in mud** essere nel fango fino alla vita

waist·band ['weɪstˌbænd] N cintura

waist·coat ['weɪsˌkəʊt] N panciotto, gilè *m inv*

waist-deep [ˌweɪst'di:p] ADV fino alla cintura, fino alla vita
■ ADJ alto(-a) fino alla cintura, alto(-a) fino alla vita

waist·ed ['weɪstɪd] ADJ (*dress*) segnato(-a) in vita; **high-/low-waisted** a vita alta/bassa

waist·line ['weɪstˌlaɪn] N vita; **to watch one's waistline** badare alla linea

waist measurement, waist size N punto *m or* giro *m* vita *inv*

◎ **wait** [weɪt] N: **wait (for)** attesa (di); **to have a long wait** aspettare a lungo; **a 2-hour wait** un'attesa di 2 ore; **to lie in wait (for sb)** tendere un agguato (a qn)
■ VT **1** (*turn, chance*) aspettare, attendere **2** (*Am: delay: dinner etc*) ritardare
■ VI **1** **to wait (for sb/sth)** aspettare (qn/qc); **how long have you been waiting?** da quanto tempo aspetti?; **I'll wait for you** ti aspetto; **wait for me!** aspettami!; **to wait for sb to do sth** aspettare che qn faccia qc; **wait a moment!** (aspetta) un momento!; **wait and see!** aspetta e vedrai!; **we'll have to wait and see** dobbiamo vedere come vanno le cose; **just you wait!** ti faccio vedere io!; **just you wait till your father comes home!** vedrai quando torna tuo padre!; **wait till you're older** aspetta di essere cresciuto(-a); **to keep sb waiting** far aspettare qn; **they kept us waiting for hours** ci hanno fatto aspettare per ore; **"repairs while you wait"** "riparazioni lampo"; **I can't wait for the holidays** non vedo l'ora che arrivino le vacanze; **I can't wait to see his face** non vedo l'ora di vedere che faccia farà; **I can hardly wait!** non vedo l'ora!; **that was worth waiting for** valeva la pena aspettare tanto **2** (*as servant*): **to wait at table** servire a tavola
▸ **wait about**, **wait around** VI + ADV restare ad aspettare
▸ **wait behind** VI + ADV trattenersi
▸ **wait in** VI + ADV restare a casa ad aspettare
▸ **wait on** VI + PREP servire; **to wait on sb hand and foot** servire qn in tutto e per tutto
▸ **wait up** VI + ADV restare alzato(-a) (ad aspettare); **don't wait up for me** non rimanere alzato ad aspettarmi
▸ **wait upon** VI + PREP (*old: visit*) presentare i propri rispetti a

wait·er ['weɪtəʳ] N cameriere *m*

wait·ing ['weɪtɪŋ] N attesa; (*Brit Aut*): **"no waiting"** "divieto di sosta"

waiting game N: **to play a waiting game** temporeggiare

waiting list N lista d'attesa

waiting room N sala d'attesa *or* d'aspetto

wait·ress ['weɪtrɪs] N cameriera

waive [weɪv] VT (*claim*) rinunciare a; (*rule, age limit*) non tener conto di

waiv·er ['weɪvəʳ] N rinuncia

wake¹ [weɪk] N (*of ship*) scia; **in the wake of** sulla scia di; **to follow in sb's wake** (*fig*) camminare dietro a qn; **it left a trail of destruction in its wake** ha lasciato dietro di sé una scia di distruzione

wake² [weɪk] N (*over corpse*) veglia funebre

◎ **wake³** [weɪk] (*pt* **woke** *or* **waked**, *pp* **woken** *or* **waked**)
VI (*also:* **wake up**) svegliarsi, destarsi; **wake up!** (*also fig*) svegliati!; **there's enough noise to wake the dead!** c'è un baccano del diavolo!; **to wake up to sth** (*fig*) rendersi conto di qc
■ VT (*also:* **wake up**) svegliare; (*memories, desires*) risvegliare; **to wake sb (up) to sth** (*fig*) aprire gli occhi a qn su qc; **to wake one's ideas up** (*fam*) darsi una mossa

wake·ful ['weɪkfʊl] ADJ (*person, night*) insonne

wak·en ['weɪkən] VT, VI = **wake³**

wake-up call ['weɪkʌpˌkɔ:l] N (*in hotel*) sveglia telefonica; (*fig*) avvertimento

wak·ing ['weɪkɪŋ] ADJ: **in my waking hours** quando sono sveglio(-a)

Wales [weɪlz] N Galles *m*; **the Prince of Wales** il Principe di Galles
▹ www.wales.gov.uk/
▹ www.visitwales.com

◎ **walk** [wɔ:k] N
1 (*stroll, ramble*) passeggiata; (*path, place to walk*) percorso, sentiero; **to take sb/one's dog for a walk** portare qn/il cane a spasso; **to go for a walk** (*short*) fare quattro passi *or* un giretto; (*long*) fare una passeggiata; **we went for a walk** abbiamo fatto una passeggiata; **it's only a 10-minute walk from here** ci vogliono solo 10 minuti a piedi da qui; **there's a nice walk by the river** c'è una bella passeggiata lungo il fiume; **from all walks of life** (*fig*) con ogni tipo di esperienza
2 (*gait*) passo, andatura, camminata; **at a walk** (*of person, horse*) al passo; **he has an odd sort of walk** ha una camminata tutta particolare
■ VT
1 (*distance*) percorrere a piedi; **we walked 40 kilometres yesterday** ieri abbiamo percorso 40 chilometri a piedi; **to walk the streets** vagare per le strade; (*prostitute*) battere il marciapiede; **you can walk it in a few minutes** puoi arrivarci a piedi in pochi minuti; **he walked it** (*fig*) è stato uno scherzo per lui
2 (*cause to walk: invalid*) aiutare a camminare; (*lead: dog*) portare a spasso *or* fuori; (*: horse*) portare; **I'll walk you home** ti accompagno a casa; **to walk sb into the ground** *or* **off their feet** far stancare qn a furia di camminare
■ VI (*gen*) camminare; (*for pleasure, exercise*) passeggiare; (*not drive or ride*) andare a piedi; **are you walking or going by bus?** ci vai a piedi o in autobus?; **they walked in silence for a while** hanno camminato in silenzio per un po'; **to walk in one's sleep** camminare nel sonno; (*habitually*) essere sonnambulo(-a); **can your little boy walk yet?** tuo figlio sa già camminare?; **walk a little with me** accompagnami per un pezzo; **to walk up and down (the room)** camminare su e giù (per la stanza); **we had to walk** siamo dovuti andare a piedi; **to walk home** andare a casa a piedi; **we were out walking in the hills** stavamo passeggiando in collina; **to walk into sth** (*bump into*) andare a sbattere

contro qc; (*fig: fall into: trap*) cadere in qc
▸ **walk about, walk around** VI + ADV camminare; **I've been walking about all afternoon** sono stato in giro tutto il pomeriggio
■ VI + PREP: **to walk about the room** camminare per la stanza; **to walk about the town** gironzolare per la città
▸ **walk across** VI + PREP attraversare
▸ **walk away** VI + ADV allontanarsi (a piedi), andare via; (*fig: unhurt*) uscire illeso(-a); **to walk away with sth** (*fig: win easily*) vincere facilmente qc
▸ **walk away from** VI + ADV + PREP
1 (*pej: job, marriage, relationship*) mollare, piantare
2 **to walk away from an accident** uscire incolume da un incidente
▸ **walk in** VI + ADV entrare
▸ **walk off** VI + ADV = **walk away**
■ VT + ADV (*lunch*) smaltire; (*headache*) far passare camminando
▸ **walk off with** VI + ADV + PREP (*fam*): **to walk off with sth** (*steal*) andarsene con qc; (*win: prize, bargain*) assicurarsi qc con facilità
▸ **walk on** VI + ADV (*go on walking*) continuare a camminare; (*Theatre*) fare la comparsa
▸ **walk out** VI + ADV (*go out*) uscire; (*as protest*) uscire in segno di protesta; (*strike*) scendere in sciopero; **to walk out of a meeting** abbandonare una riunione in segno di protesta; **he walked out of the meeting in protest** ha abbandonato la riunione in segno di protesta; **to walk out on sb** abbandonare qn; **he walked out on his wife and family** ha abbandonato la moglie e la famiglia
▸ **walk over** VI + PREP (*defeat*) schiacciare; **to walk all over sb** (*dominate*) mettere i piedi in testa a qn
▸ **walk up** VI + ADV (*approach*): **to walk up (to)** avvicinarsi (a); **walk up, walk up!** (*at fair*) avanti!

walk·about ['wɔ:kə,baʊt] N: **to go (on a) walkabout** *avere incontri informali col pubblico durante una visita ufficiale*

walk·er ['wɔ:kəʳ] N (*person*) camminatore(-trice); (*for babies*) girello; **he's a good walker** gli piace camminare; **he's a slow walker** ha il passo lento

walkie-talkie [,wɔ:kɪ'tɔ:kɪ] N walkie-talkie *m inv*

walk-in ['wɔ:k,ɪn] ADJ: **walk-in cupboard** stanzino

walk·ing ['wɔ:kɪŋ] N camminare *m*; **to do a lot of walking** camminare molto; **I did some walking in the Alps last summer** ho fatto escursionismo sulle Alpi l'estate scorsa
■ ADJ: **it's within walking distance** ci si arriva a piedi; **he's a walking encyclopaedia** è un'enciclopedia ambulante; **the walking wounded** i feriti in grado di camminare; **walking boots** pedule *fpl*; **walking tour** (*of a city*) giro a piedi; **a walking tour of the hills** una lunga gita a piedi sulle colline

walking holiday N vacanza fatta di lunghe camminate

walking shoes NPL scarpe *fpl* da passeggio

walking stick N bastone *m* da passeggio

Walk·man® ['wɔ:kmən] N walkman® *m inv*

walk-on ['wɔ:k,ɒn] ADJ (*Theatre: part*) da comparsa

walk·out ['wɔ:k,aʊt] N (*from conference*) abbandono; (*strike*) sciopero selvaggio *or* a sorpresa; **to stage a walkout** (*from conference*) ritirarsi in segno di protesta; (*from work*) scendere in sciopero

walk·over ['wɔ:k,əʊvəʳ] N (*Sport*) vittoria facile; **the exam was a walkover** l'esame è stato una vera passeggiata

walk-up ['wɔ:k,ʌp] N (*Am*) casa senza ascensore

walk·way ['wɔ:k,weɪ] N passaggio pedonale

◎ **wall** [wɔ:l] N (*internal, of tunnel, cave*) muro, parete *f*; (*outside*) muro; (*Anat*) parete; (*of tyre*) fianco; (*fig: of smoke*) cortina; **the Berlin Wall** il muro di Berlino; **the Great Wall of China** la Grande Muraglia Cinese; **the city walls** le mura della città; **it drives me up the wall** (*fam*) mi fa uscire dai gangheri; **to go to the wall** (*fig: firm*) andare a rotoli *or* in rovina; **walls have ears** (*fam*) anche i muri hanno orecchi
■ ADJ (*clock*) a muro
▸ **wall in** VT + ADV (*garden etc*) circondare con un muro
▸ **wall off** VT + ADV (*area of land*) recingere con un muro
▸ **wall up** VT + ADV (*entrance etc*) murare

wal·la·by ['wɒləbɪ] N wallaby *m inv*

wall bars NPL (*Sport*) spalliera *fsg*

wall cupboard N pensile *m*

walled [wɔ:ld] ADJ (*city*) fortificato(-a); (*house, garden*) cinto(-a) da mura

wal·let ['wɒlɪt] N portafoglio

wall·flower ['wɔ:l,flaʊəʳ] N violaciocca (gialla); (*fig*): **to be a wallflower** fare (da) tappezzeria

wall hanging N tappezzeria

wall light N applique *f inv*

wall map N carta murale

Wal·loon [wɒ'lu:n] ADJ vallone
■ N (*person*) vallone *m/f*; (*language*) vallone *m*

wal·lop ['wɒləp] (*fam*) N (*blow*) cazzotto; (*sound*): **with a wallop** con un tonfo
■ VT (*fam: person*) suonarle a; **to wallop the table** battere il pugno sul tavolo

wal·lop·ing ['wɒləpɪŋ] (*fam*) N: **to give sb a walloping** suonarle a qn
■ ADJ (*also:* **walloping great**) enorme

wal·low ['wɒləʊ] VI: **to wallow (in)** (*in water, mud*) rotolarsi (in); (*in bath*) sguazzare (in); **to wallow in one's grief** crogiolarsi nel proprio dolore; **to wallow in luxury** nuotare nell'oro

wall·paper ['wɔ:l,peɪpəʳ] N carta da parati, tappezzeria; (*Comput*) sfondo

◎ **Wall Street** N Wall Street *f*

wall-to-wall [,wɔ:ltə'wɔ:l] ADJ: **wall-to-wall carpeting** moquette *f*

wal·ly ['wɒlɪ] N (*fam*) scemo(-a)

wal·nut ['wɔ:l,nʌt] N (*nut*) noce *f*; (*tree, wood*) noce *m*
■ ADJ (*furniture*) di noce; (*cake*) di noci

wal·rus ['wɔ:lrəs] N tricheco

waltz [wɔ:lts] N valzer *m inv*
■ VI ballare il valzer; **to waltz in/out** *etc* (*confidently*) entrare/uscire *etc* con fare sicuro; (*cheekily*) entrare/uscire *etc* con fare spavaldo

wan [wɒn] ADJ (*gen*) pallido(-a); (*look, person*) triste

wand [wɒnd] N (*also:* **magic wand**) bacchetta magica; (*of usher*) mazza

wan·der ['wɒndəʳ] N: **to go for a wander around the shops/the town** fare un giro per i negozi/in città
■ VI (*person*) gironzolare, girare senza meta; (*river, road*) serpeggiare; (*stray: from path*) allontanarsi; (*: thoughts, eyes*) vagare; **to wander around** gironzolare; **I just wandered around for a while** ho gironzolato per un po'; **to wander back/out** *etc* tornare indietro/uscire *etc* con calma; **don't go wandering off** non allontanarti; **to wander from** *or* **off the point** divagare; **to let one's mind** *or* **attention wander** distrarsi
■ VT (*streets, hills*) girovagare per; **to wander the world** girare il mondo

Ww

wan·der·er ['wɒndərə^r] N giramondo *m/f inv*
wan·der·ing ['wɒndərɪŋ] ADJ (*tribe*) nomade; (*minstrel, actor*) girovago(-a); (*path, river*) tortuoso(-a); (*mind*) distratto(-a)
■ **wanderings** NPL peregrinazioni *fpl*, vagabondaggi *mpl*
wandering Jew N **1** (*Bot*) miseria **2** **the Wandering Jew** l'ebreo errante
wan·der·lust ['wɒndə,lʌst] N sete *f* di viaggi
wane [weɪn] VI (*moon*) calare; (*fig*) declinare, scemare
■ N: **to be on the wane** = **to wane**
wan·gle ['wæŋgl] (*fam*) N astuzia
■ VT (*job, ticket*) rimediare *or* procurare (con l'astuzia); (*days off*) ottenere (con l'astuzia); **he wangled his way in** è riuscito ad entrare con un sotterfugio
wan·gler ['wæŋglə^r] N (*fam*) furbacchione(-a)
wan·gling ['wæŋglɪŋ] N (*fam*) astuzia
wan·ing ['weɪnɪŋ] ADJ (*moon*) calante; (*fig: power, influence, strength*) in declino
wank [wæŋk] VI (*fam!*) farsi una sega (*fam!*)
wank·er ['wæŋkə^r] N (*fam!*) testa di cazzo (*fam!*), coglione (*fam!*)
wan·ly ['wɒnlɪ] ADV tristemente
wan·na·be ['wɒnəbi:] N (*fam*) *persona che vorrebbe essere famosa*; **an Elvis wannabe** un imitatore di Elvis
◎ **want** [wɒnt] N
1 (*lack*): **want (of)** mancanza (di); **for want of** per mancanza di; **for want of anything better to do** non avendo nulla di meglio da fare; **it wasn't for want of trying** non si può dire che non ci abbia (*or* abbiamo *etc*) provato
2 (*poverty*) miseria, povertà; **to be in want** essere in miseria
3 (*need*) bisogno; **to be in want of sth** avere bisogno di qc; **it fills a long-felt want** soddisfa un bisogno che si sentiva da tempo
4 (*requirements*): **wants** NPL esigenze *fpl*; **my wants are few** ho poche esigenze
■ VT
1 (*gen*) volere; (*wish, desire*) volere, desiderare; **to want to do sth** voler fare qc; **what do you want to do tomorrow?** che cosa vuoi fare domani?; **to want sb to do sth** volere che qn faccia qc; **I want you to tell me** voglio che tu mi dica; **I want it done now** voglio che sia fatto subito; **what do you want with me?** cosa vuoi da me?; **you've got him where you want him** (*fig*) ce l'hai in pugno; **you don't want much!** (*iro*) ti accontenti di poco!; **do you want some cake?** vuoi un po' di torta?; **she wants £5,000 for the car** vuole *or* chiede 5.000 sterline per la macchina; **I don't want you interfering!** non voglio che tu ti intrometta!; **I know when I'm not wanted** so quando non mi si vuole; **you're wanted on the phone** ti vogliono al telefono; **I don't want to** non ne ho voglia; **"cook wanted"** "cercasi cuoco"; **he is wanted for murder** è ricercato per omicidio; **to want sb** (*sexually*) desiderare qn
2 (*need, require: subj: person*) avere bisogno di; (*: task*) richiedere; (*ought*) dovere; **you want to see a doctor** dovresti andare dal dottore; **that's the last thing I want!** (*fam*) è l'ultima cosa che vorrei!; **it's just what we wanted!** (*fam*) è proprio quello che ci voleva!; **you want a screwdriver to do that** ti ci vuole un cacciavite per farlo; **it only wanted the parents to come in ...** bastava solo che i genitori entrassero...; **you want your head seeing to** tu hai bisogno di uno psicanalista; **the window wants cleaning** la finestra ha bisogno di una pulita
■ VI (*lack*): **to want (for)** mancare (di); **she doesn't want for friends** gli amici non le mancano; **they want for nothing** a loro non manca nulla
▸ **want out** VI + ADV (*fam*) volerne uscire
want ads NPL (*Am*) annunci *mpl* economici
want·ing ['wɒntɪŋ] ADJ: **to be wanting (in)** mancare (di); **humour is completely wanting in his work** la sua opera manca totalmente di senso dell'umorismo; **he is wanting in confidence** non è abbastanza sicuro di sé; **he was tried and found wanting** lo hanno messo alla prova e non è risultato all'altezza
wan·ton ['wɒntən] ADJ (*wilful*) gratuito(-a), ingiustificato(-a); (*shameless: woman*) scostumato(-a)
wan·ton·ly ['wɒntənlɪ] ADV (*see adj*) gratuitamente, ingiustificatamente; in modo scostumato
WAP [wæp] N ABBR (= **Wireless Application Protocol**) WAP *m*; **WAP phone** telefono WAP
◎ **war** [wɔ:^r] N guerra; (*fig*): **war (on** *or* **against)** lotta (contro); **to be at/go to war (with)** essere/entrare in guerra (con); **to make war (on)** fare guerra (a); **a war of words** una guerra verbale; **to have been in the wars** (*fig hum*) essere malridotto(-a); **the war against organized crime** la lotta contro la criminalità organizzata
■ VI: **to war (with)** guerreggiare (con), far guerra (a)
■ ADJ (*wound, crime, bride*) di guerra
war·ble ['wɔ:bl] N (*of bird*) trillo
■ VI (*bird*) trillare; (*person*) gorgheggiare
war·bler ['wɔ:blə^r] N uccello canoro; **reed warbler** cannaiola comune; **sedge warbler** forapaglie *m inv* comune; **willow warbler** luì *m inv* grosso
war·bling ['wɔ:blɪŋ] N (*of bird*) trillo, gorgheggio
war correspondent N corrispondente *m/f* di guerra
war cry N grido di guerra
ward [wɔ:d] N **1** (*in hospital*) corsia, reparto **2** (*Law*) pupillo(-a); **ward of court** minore *m/f* sotto tutela (giudiziaria) **3** (*Pol*) collegio (elettorale)
▸ **ward off** VT + ADV (*blow, attack*) parare, schivare; (*attacker*) respingere; (*danger, depression*) scongiurare
war dance N danza di guerra
war·den ['wɔ:dn] N (*of institution*) direttore(-trice); (*of park, game reserve*) guardiano(-a)
war·der ['wɔ:də^r] N guardia carceraria
war·dress ['wɔ:drɪs] N guardia carceraria (*donna*)
ward·robe ['wɔ:drəʊb] N (*cupboard*) guardaroba *m inv*, armadio; (*clothes*) guardaroba; (*Theatre*) costumi *mpl*
wardrobe mistress N costumista
ward·room ['wɔ:d,rʊm] N (*Naut*) quadrato (di poppa)
ware·house ['wɛə,haʊs] N deposito, magazzino
ware·house·man ['wɛə,haʊsmən] N (*pl* **-men**) magazziniere *m*
ware·hous·ing ['wɛə,haʊzɪŋ] N magazzinaggio
wares [wɛəz] NPL merci *fpl*
war·fare ['wɔ:,fɛə^r] N (*fighting*) guerra, lotta; (*technique*) arte *f* bellica
war footing N: **on a war footing** sul piede di guerra
war game N war game *m inv*
war·head ['wɔ:,hɛd] N (*Mil*) testata
war·horse ['wɔ:,hɔ:s] N (*fig*): **old warhorse** veterano
wari·ly ['wɛərɪlɪ] ADV cautamente, con prudenza
wari·ness ['wɛərɪnɪs] N cautela, prudenza
war·like ['wɔ:,laɪk] ADJ battagliero(-a), bellicoso(-a)
◎ **warm** [wɔ:m] ADJ (*comp* **-er**, *superl* **-est**) **1** (*gen*) caldo(-a); **I'm warm** *or* **I feel warm** ho caldo; **I'm too warm** ho troppo caldo; **it's warm today** oggi fa caldo; **it's warm in here** fa caldo qui; **it's warm work** è un

lavoro che ti fa sudare; **warm water** acqua calda; **come and get warm** vieni a scaldarti; **keep yourself warm!** non prendere freddo!; **it keeps me warm** mi tiene caldo; **to keep sth warm** tenere qc in caldo; **am I getting warm?** (*fig: in game*) fuocherello? **2** (*fig: colour*) caldo(-a); (*: thanks, congratulations, apologies*) sentito(-a); (*: welcome, applause*) caloroso(-a); (*: person, greeting*) cordiale; (*: heart*) d'oro; (*: supporter*) convinto(-a); **with my warmest thanks** con i miei più sentiti ringraziamenti; **a warm welcome** una calorosa accoglienza

■ VT (*gen*) scaldare; **to warm o.s. by the fire** scaldarsi vicino al fuoco; **she warmed her hands by the fire** si è scaldata le mani vicino al fuoco; **it warmed my heart** mi ha fatto tanto piacere

■ VI (*food, water*) scaldarsi; **he warmed to his subject** si appassionò all'argomento; **I** *or* **my heart warmed to him** mi è entrato in simpatia

▸ **warm up** VI + ADV (*person*) scaldarsi, scaldarsi i muscoli; (*fig: party*) animarsi; **spend the first five minutes warming up** innanzitutto, fai cinque minuti di riscaldamento

■ VT + ADV (*food*) scaldare, riscaldare; (*engine*) scaldare; (*fig: party, audience*) animare; **I'll warm up some lasagne for you** ti riscaldo delle lasagne

warm-blooded [ˌwɔːmˈblʌdɪd] ADJ (*animal*) a sangue caldo

warm-down [ˈwɔːmdaʊn] N (*Sport*) esercizi *mpl* di defaticamento

war memorial N monumento ai caduti

warm front N (*Met*) fronte *m* caldo

warm-hearted [ˌwɔːmˈhɑːtɪd] ADJ cordiale, affettuoso(-a)

warm·ing pan [ˈwɔːmɪŋˌpæn] N scaldaletto

warm·ly [ˈwɔːmlɪ] ADV (*recommend*) caldamente; (*welcome, thank, applaud*) calorosamente; **to dress warmly** portare indumenti pesanti

war·monger [ˈwɔːˌmʌŋgəʳ] N guerrafondaio

war·monger·ing [ˈwɔːˌmʌŋgərɪŋ] N bellicismo

warmth [wɔːmθ] N calore *m*; (*fig*) calore, calorosità

warm-up [ˈwɔːmˌʌp] N (*Sport*) riscaldamento

◎ **warn** [wɔːn] VT: **to warn (of** *or* **about)** avvertire (di), avvisare (di); **to warn sb not to do sth** *or* **against doing sth** avvertire qn di non fare qc; **you have been warned!** sei avvisato!; **well, I warned you!** be', ti avevo avvertito!; **to warn sb off** *or* **against sth** mettere qn in guardia contro qc

◎ **warn·ing** [ˈwɔːnɪŋ] N (*gen*) avvertimento, ammonimento; (*by police, judge*) diffida; (*advance notice*): **warning (of)** preavviso (di); **to give sb a warning that** avvertire qn che; **to give sb due/a few days' warning** avvertire qn a tempo debito/con qualche giorno di anticipo; **without (any) warning** senza preavviso; **let this be a warning to you!** che ti serva da ammonimento!; **gale warning** (*Met*) avviso di burrasca

warning device N dispositivo d'allarme

warning light N spia luminosa

warning shot N: **to fire a warning shot** sparare (in aria) un colpo di avvertimento

warning triangle N (*Aut*) triangolo

warp [wɔːp] N (*in weaving*) ordito; (*of wood*) curvatura, deformazione *f*

■ VT (*wood*) deformare, curvare; (*fig: mind, personality, judgment*) influenzare negativamente

■ VI (*wood*) deformarsi, curvarsi

warp·age [ˈwɔːpɪdʒ] N (*Textiles*) orditura

war paint N pitture *fpl* di guerra (*dei pellirosse*)

war·path [ˈwɔːˌpɑːθ] N: **to be on the warpath** (*fig*) essere sul sentiero di guerra

warped [wɔːpt] ADJ (*wood*) curvo(-a); (*fig: character, sense of humour etc*) contorto(-a)

war·plane [ˈwɔːˌpleɪn] N aereo militare

war·rant [ˈwɒrənt] N **1** (*Law: to arrest*) mandato di cattura; (*: to search*) mandato di perquisizione; (*for travel etc*) buono; **there is a warrant out for his arrest** è stato emesso un mandato di cattura nei suoi confronti **2** (*justification*) giustificazione *f*

■ VT **1** (*justify, merit*) giustificare; **nothing warrants such an assumption** nulla giustifica questa ipotesi **2** (*guarantee*) garantire; **I'll warrant you he'll be back soon** ti assicuro *or* garantisco che sarà di ritorno presto

war·rant·ed [ˈwɒrəntɪd] ADJ (*action, remark*) giustificato(-a); (*Comm: goods*) garantito(-a)

warrant officer N (*Mil*) sottufficiale *m*

war·ran·ty [ˈwɒrəntɪ] N (*Comm*) garanzia; **under warranty** in garanzia

war·ren [ˈwɒrən] N (*also:* **rabbit warren**) tana; (*fig*) alveare *m*; **a warren of little streets** un dedalo di stradine

war·ring [ˈwɔːrɪŋ] ADJ (*interests etc*) opposto(-a), in lotta; (*nations*) in guerra

war·ri·or [ˈwɒrɪəʳ] N guerriero(-a)

War·saw [ˈwɔːsɔː] N Varsavia

Warsaw Pact N: **the Warsaw Pact** il patto di Varsavia

war·ship [ˈwɔːʃɪp] N nave *f* da guerra

wart [wɔːt] N (*Med*) porro, verruca

wart·hog [ˈwɔːtˌhɒg] N facocero

war·time [ˈwɔːˌtaɪm] N: **in wartime** in tempo di guerra

■ ADJ (*regulations, rationing etc*) di guerra

wary [ˈwɛərɪ] ADJ (*comp* **-ier**, *superl* **-iest**) (*gen*) prudente; (*manner*) cauto(-a); **to be wary (of)** essere diffidente (di), diffidare (di); **to keep a wary eye on sth** tenere d'occhio qc; **to be wary about** *or* **of doing sth** andare cauto(-a) nel fare qc, esitare a fare qc

was [wɒz] 1ST, 3RD PERS SG PT *of* **be**

◎ **wash** [wɒʃ] N **1** (*act of washing*) lavata; **to have a wash** darsi una lavata, lavarsi; **to give sth a wash** dare una lavata a qc, lavare qc; **it needs a wash** ha bisogno di essere lavato; **to be in the wash** essere a lavare; **your jeans are in the wash** i tuoi jeans sono a lavare; **it ran in the wash** si è stinto nel lavaggio; **it'll all come out in the wash** (*fig: work out*) tutto si sistemerà **2** (*of ship*) scia **3** (*Art*) lavatura

■ VT **1** (*gen*) lavare; **to wash o.s.** lavarsi; **to wash one's hands/hair** lavarsi le mani/i capelli; **he washed his hands** si è lavato le mani; **have you washed your hair?** ti sei lavata i capelli?; **to wash one's hands of sth** (*fig*) lavarsene le mani (di qc); **I'll wash the dishes** lavo io i piatti **2** (*lap: sea, waves*) bagnare, lambire; **an island washed by a blue sea** un'isola bagnata da un mare azzurro **3** (*sweep, carry: sea*) portare, trascinare; **he was washed overboard** fu trascinato in mare dalle onde

■ VI **1** (*have a wash*) lavarsi; (*do the washing*) fare il bucato; **man-made fabrics usually wash well** di solito i tessuti sintetici si lavano facilmente; **I'll wash if you'll wipe** (*dishes*) io lavo i piatti se tu li asciughi; **that excuse won't wash!** (*fam*) quella scusa non regge! **2** (*sea*): **to wash against sth** frangersi contro qc; **to wash over sth** infrangersi su qc

▸ **wash away** VT + ADV (*mark*) togliere lavando; (*subj: river etc*) trascinare via; (*fig: sins etc*) cancellare

Ww

▸ **wash down** VT + ADV (*walls, car*) lavare; (*pill, food*) mandar giù (*con acqua etc*)
▸ **wash off** VI + ADV andare via con il lavaggio
■VT + ADV (*dirt*) togliere (lavando)
▸ **wash out** VT + ADV (*stain*) togliere (lavando); (*bottle, paintbrush*) sciacquare
▸ **wash through** VT + ADV dare una lavata a
▸ **wash up** VI + ADV (*Brit: do dishes*) lavare i piatti; (*Am: have a wash*) darsi una lavata, lavarsi
■VT + ADV **1** (*Brit: dishes*) lavare, rigovernare **2** (*subj: sea etc*) portare, trascinare **3** **to be all washed up** (*fig: fam*) essere finito(-a)

wash·able ['wɒʃəbl] ADJ lavabile
wash·basin ['wɒʃ,beɪsn], **wash·bowl** ['wɒʃbəʊl] N lavabo, lavandino
wash·cloth ['wɒʃ,klɒθ] N (*Am*) pezzuola (per lavarsi)
wash·day ['wɒʃ,deɪ] N giorno di bucato
washed-out ['wɒʃt'aʊt] ADJ (*faded: colour*) slavato(-a), sbiadito(-a); (*tired: person*) sfinito(-a), distrutto(-a); *see also* **wash out**
wash·er ['wɒʃə[r]] N **1** (*Tech*) rondella; **a rubber washer** una guarnizione di gomma **2** (*washing machine*) lavatrice *f*; **your shirt's in the washer** la tua camicia è in lavatrice
wash-hand basin ['wɒʃhænd,beɪsn] N (*Brit old*) lavabo, lavandino
wash house N lavanderia
wash·ing ['wɒʃɪŋ] N **1** (*act*) lavaggio; (: *of clothes*) bucato; **to do the washing** fare il bucato **2** (*clothes themselves*) bucato; **dirty washing** biancheria da lavare
washing line N (*Brit*) corda del bucato
washing machine N lavatrice *f*
washing powder N (*Brit*) detersivo in polvere per bucato
washing soda N soda
Wash·ing·ton ['wɒʃɪŋtən] N Washington *f*
▹ www.about.dc.gov
▹ www.washington.org
▹ www.dcpages.com/Tourism
▹ http://access.wa.gov/
washing-up [,wɒʃɪŋ'ʌp] N (*dishes*) piatti *mpl* sporchi; **to do the washing-up** lavare i piatti, rigovernare
washing-up bowl N catino, bacinella
washing-up liquid N (*Brit*) detersivo liquido per i piatti
wash leather N pelle *f* di daino
wash-out ['wɒʃ,aʊt] N (*fam: plan, party, person*) disastro
wash·room ['wɒʃ,rʊm] N bagno, gabinetto
wash·stand ['wɒʃ,stænd] N lavamano *m inv*
wash·tub ['wɒʃ,tʌb] N tinozza per il bucato
wasn't ['wɒznt] = **was not**
WASP, **Wasp** N ABBR (*Am:* = **White Anglo-Saxon Protestant**) WASP *m* (= *bianco/a protestante anglosassone*)
wasp [wɒsp] N vespa; **wasp's nest** nido di vespe
wasp·ish ['wɒspɪʃ] ADJ (*character*) litigioso(-a); (*comment*) pungente
wasp·ish·ly ['wɒspɪʃlɪ] ADV (*comment*) astiosamente
Wassermann ['wæsəmən] N (*Med*): **Wassermann test** (reazione *f*) wassermann *f inv*
wast·age ['weɪstɪdʒ] N (*gen*) spreco; (*of time, Comm: through pilfering*) perdita; (*in manufacturing*) scarti *mpl*; (*amount wasted*) scarto; **natural wastage** normale diminuzione *f* del personale
◎**waste** [weɪst] ADJ (*material*) di scarto; (*food*) avanzato(-a); (*land, ground: in city*) abbandonato(-a), desolato(-a); (: *in country*) incolto(-a); **to lay waste** devastare
■N **1** (*gen*) spreco; (*of time*) perdita; **it's such a waste!** è un tale spreco!; **it's a waste of money** è uno spreco di denaro; **it's a waste of effort** è fatica sprecata; **it's a waste of breath** è fiato sprecato; **it's a waste of time doing that** è tempo sprecato; **to go to waste** andare sprecato(-a) **2** (*waste material: industrial, chemical etc*) scorie *fpl*; (*rubbish*) spazzatura, immondizia, rifiuti *mpl*; **nuclear waste** scorie *mpl* radioattive **3** (*land: often pl*) distesa desolata; **desert waste** landa desertica
■VT (*gen*) sprecare; (*time, opportunity*) perdere, sprecare; **to waste time** perdere tempo; **there's no time to waste** non c'è tempo da perdere; **you didn't waste much time finding a replacement!** (*iro*) non hai perso tempo a rimpiazzarmi!; **I don't like wasting money** non mi piace sprecare i soldi; **he's wasted in that job** è sprecato in quel lavoro; **sarcasm is wasted on him** non afferra il sarcasmo; **to waste one's breath** sprecare (il) fiato; **waste not, want not** (*Proverb*) chi risparmia guadagna
▸ **waste away** VI + ADV deperire, consumarsi
waste·basket ['weɪst,bɑːskɪt] N (*Am*) = **wastepaper basket**
waste·bin ['weɪst,bɪn] N (*basket*) cestino per la cartaccia; (*in kitchen*) pattumiera
wast·ed ['weɪstɪd] ADJ **1** (*efforts*) sprecato(-a), inutile **2** (*face: from disease, starvation*) scarno(-a); (*limbs: from disease*) atrofizzato(-a)
waste disposal N smaltimento dei rifiuti
waste disposal unit N tritarifiuti *m inv*
waste·ful ['weɪstfʊl] ADJ (*person*) sprecone(-a); (*process*) dispendioso(-a); **to be wasteful with** *or* **of sth** sprecare qc
waste·ful·ly ['weɪstfəlɪ] ADV: **to spend wastefully** fare degli sprechi nello spendere; **to use sth wastefully** non utilizzare al meglio qc
waste·ful·ness ['weɪstfʊlnɪs] N (*of person*) prodigalità; (*of process*) spreco, dispendio
waste ground N (*Brit*) terreno incolto *or* abbandonato
waste·land ['weɪst,lænd] N terra desolata
waste·paper ['weɪst,peɪpə[r]] N cartaccia
wastepaper basket N cestino per la cartaccia
waste pipe N tubo di scarico
waste products N (*Industry*) materiali *mpl* di scarto; (*from body*) materiali *mpl* di rifiuto
wast·er ['weɪstə[r]] N (*good-for-nothing*) perdigiorno *m/f*; (*spendthrift*) sprecone(-a)
wast·ing ['weɪstɪŋ] ADJ: **wasting disease** deperimento organico
wast·rel ['weɪstrəl] N (*layabout*) perdigiorno *m/f*; (*spendthrift*) spendaccione(-a), sprecone(-a)
watch[1] [wɒtʃ] N (*also:* **wrist watch**) orologio (da polso); **it's 10 o'clock by my watch** il mio orologio fa le 10; **he was wearing an expensive watch** portava un orologio costoso
◎**watch**[2] [wɒtʃ] N
1 (*act of watching*) sorveglianza; **to be on the watch for** (*danger, person*) stare in guardia contro; (*vehicle*) stare all'erta per l'arrivo di; (*bargain*) essere a caccia di; **to keep watch over** (*prisoner*) sorvegliare; (*patient*) vigilare; **to keep a close watch on sb/sth** sorvegliare da vicino qn/qc; **to keep watch for sb/sth** stare all'erta per qn/qc
2 (*period of duty*) guardia; (*Naut*) quarto; (*sentry*) sentinella; **officer of the watch** (*Naut*) ufficiale *m* di quarto; **to be on watch** (*Naut*) essere di guardia; **I had the first watch** feci il primo turno di guardia

■ VT
1 (*guard*: *gen*) tener d'occhio
2 (*observe*: *gen*) guardare; (*subj*: *police*) tenere d'occhio, sorvegliare; (*monitor*: *case*) seguire; **to watch sb do(ing) sth** osservare qn mentre fa qc; **you can't do that! — just you watch (me)!** non puoi farlo! — e come no, sta' a vedere!; **to watch one's chance** aspettare il momento propizio; **to watch the time** controllare l'ora; **a new actor to be watched** un nuovo attore molto promettente *or* da seguire; **I was watching TV** stavo guardando la TV; **the police were watching the house** la polizia sorvegliava la casa
3 (*be careful with*) stare attento(-a) a; **to watch one's language** moderare i termini, badare a come si parla; **watch it!** attento!; **watch how you drive/what you're doing** fai attenzione a come guidi/quel che fai; **she watches the calories** sta attenta alle calorie; **watch your head** attento alla testa; **we shall have to watch our spending** dovremo limitare le spese; **to watch the clock** (*fig*) tenere d'occhio l'orologio; **to watch sb's interests** badare agli interessi di qn
■ VI (*observe*) guardare; (*keep guard*) fare *or* montare la guardia; (*pay attention*) stare attento(-a); (*at bedside*) vegliare; **to watch for sb/sth** aspettare qn/qc; **the doctors are watching for any deterioration in his condition** i medici lo tengono sotto osservazione nell'eventualità che le sue condizioni peggiorino
▸ **watch out** VI + ADV fare attenzione *f*, stare attento(-a); **to watch out for** (*keep watch*) fare attenzione a; (*be on the alert*) stare attento(-a) a; **watch out!** (*also threatening*) attento!, occhio!
▸ **watch over** VI + PREP sorvegliare

watch·band ['wɒtʃ,bænd] N (*Am*) cinturino dell'orologio
watch chain N catena dell'orologio
watch·dog ['wɒtʃ,dɒg] N cane *m* da guardia; (*fig*) sorvegliante *m/f*
■ ADJ di controllo; **a government watchdog committee** un comitato statale di controllo
watch·er ['wɒtʃəʳ] N (*observer*) osservatore(-trice); (*spectator*) spettatore(-trice)
watch·ful ['wɒtʃfʊl] ADJ: **to be watchful for sth** stare attento a qc; **to keep a watchful eye on sb** guardare con occhio vigile qn; **under the watchful eye of** sotto lo sguardo vigile di
watch·ful·ness ['wɒtʃfʊlnɪs] N attenzione *f*, vigilanza
watch·maker ['wɒtʃ,meɪkəʳ] N orologiaio(-a)
watch·making ['wɒtʃ,meɪkɪŋ] N orologeria (*arte*)
watch·man ['wɒtʃmən] N (*pl* **-men**) guardiano; **night watchman** guardiano notturno
watch·strap ['wɒtʃ,stræp] N cinturino dell'orologio
watch·tower ['wɒtʃ,taʊəʳ] N torre *f* di guardia
watch·word ['wɒtʃ,wɜːd] N parola d'ordine
◎ **wa·ter** ['wɔːtəʳ] N (*gen*) acqua; **fresh/salt water** acqua dolce/salata; **"hot and cold water in all rooms"** "acqua corrente calda e fredda in tutte le camere"; **a glass of water** un bicchiere d'acqua; **I'd like a drink of water** vorrei un bicchier d'acqua; **the High Street is under water** la strada principale è inondata; **to turn on the water** aprire il rubinetto dell'acqua; **to spend money like water** spendere e spandere, avere le mani bucate; **a lot of water has flowed under the bridge since then** (*fig*) da allora è passata molta acqua sotto i ponti; **that theory won't hold water** (*fig*) quella teoria fa acqua; **to pour cold water on sth** (*fig*) mostrarsi poco entusiasta di qc; **it's like water off a duck's back** (*fig*) è come parlare al muro; **the waters of the Tiber** le acque del Tevere; **British waters** acque *fpl* (territoriali) britanniche; **to take the waters** fare la cura delle acque (termali); **the waters** (*in pregnancy*) le acque; **to pass water** orinare; **water on the brain** (*Med*) idrocefalia; **water on the knee** (*Med*) sinovite *f*
■ VT (*garden, plant*) annaffiare; (*horses, cattle*) abbeverare; (*wine*) annacquare
■ VI (*eyes*) lacrimare; **to make sb's mouth water** far venire l'acquolina in bocca a qn; **my mouth is watering** ho l'acquolina in bocca
■ ADJ (*pressure, supply*) dell'acqua; (*purifier, power*) idrico(-a)
▸ **water down** VT + ADV (*milk, wine*) diluire; (*fig*: *claim*) moderare, attenuare; (: *report, article*) edulcorare

water bed N materasso ad acqua
water biscuit N cracker *m inv*
water blister N vescica
water·borne ['wɔːtə,bɔːn] ADJ (*disease*) trasmesso(-a) con l'acqua
water bottle N (*for drinking*) borraccia; (*for heat*) borsa dell'acqua calda
water buffalo N bufalo indiano
water cannon N idrante *m*
water chestnut N castagna d'acqua
water closet N (*Brit*: *frm*) water closet *m inv*
water·colour, (*Am*) **water·color** ['wɔːtə,kʌləʳ] N (*picture*) acquerello; (*paints*): **watercolours** NPL acquerelli *mpl*
water-cooled ['wɔːtə,kuːld] ADJ raffreddato(-a) ad acqua
water cooler N distributore *f* d'acqua fresca; **water-cooler TV** i programmi televisivi più chiacchierati
water·course ['wɔːtə,kɔːs] N corso d'acqua
water·cress ['wɔːtə,krɛs] N crescione *m*
wa·ter di·vin·er ['wɔːtədɪ,vaɪnəʳ] N rabdomante *m/f*
wa·tered ['wɔːtəd] ADJ (*silk*) damascato(-a)
water·fall ['wɔːtə,fɔːl] N cascata
water·fowl ['wɔːtə,faʊl] N, PL INV uccello acquatico
water·front ['wɔːtə,frʌnt] N (*seafront*) lungomare *m*; (*at docks*) banchina, fronte *m* del porto
water gauge N indicatore *m* del livello dell'acqua
water heater N scaldabagno, scaldaacqua *m inv*
water hole N pozza d'acqua
water ice N (*Brit Culin*) sorbetto
wa·ter·ing ['wɔːtərɪŋ] N (*of plants*) annaffiatura; (*of field, region*) irrigazione *f*; (*of animals*) abbeveraggio
watering can N annaffiatoio
watering hole N 1 = **water hole** 2 (*hum*) bar *m inv*
water jump N (*Horse-riding*) riviera
water level N livello dell'acqua; (*of flood*) livello delle acque
water lily N ninfea
water·line ['wɔːtə,laɪn] N (*Naut*) linea di galleggiamento
water·logged ['wɔːtə,lɒgd] ADJ (*ground etc*) impregnato(-a) *or* imbevuto(-a) d'acqua; (*fields, football pitch*) allagato(-a); (*shoes*) inzuppato(-a)
Wa·ter·loo [,wɔːtə'luː] N: **to meet one's Waterloo** (*fig*) subire una disfatta
water main N conduttura dell'acqua
water·mark ['wɔːtə,mɑːk] N (*in paper*) filigrana; (*left by tide*) segno della marea
water meadow N acquitrino
water·melon ['wɔːtə,mɛlən] N anguria, cocomero
water mill N mulino ad acqua
water pistol N pistola ad acqua

Ww

water polo N pallanuoto *f*
▷ www.fina.org
water·proof ['wɔ:tə,pru:f] ADJ impermeabile
■ N impermeabile *m*
■ VT impermeabilizzare
water·proof·ing ['wɔ:tə,pru:fɪŋ] N impermeabilizzazione *f*
water rat N topo d'acqua
water rate N canone *m* per la fornitura dell'acqua
water-repellent ['wɔ:tərɪ,pɛlənt] ADJ idrorepellente
water-resistant ['wɔ:tərɪ,zɪstənt] ADJ *(fabric)* impermeabile; *(sun lotion)* resistente all'acqua
water·shed ['wɔ:tə∫ɛd] N *(Geog, also fig)* spartiacque *m inv*; *(Brit: TV)* inizio della seconda serata *(ora dopo la quale i ragazzi in genere non guardano più la televisione)*
water·side ['wɔ:tə,saɪd] N lungomare
■ ADJ sul lungomare
water-ski ['wɔ:tə,ski:] VI praticare lo sci d'acqua *or* acquatico
water-skiing ['wɔ:tə,ski:ɪŋ] N sci *m* d'acqua *or* acquatico
water softener N addolcitore *m* d'acqua; *(substance)* anti-calcare *m*
water-soluble [,wɔ:tə'sɒljʊbl] ADJ idrosolubile, solubile in acqua
water·spout ['wɔ:tə,spaʊt] N *(pipe, channel)* pluviale *m*; *(Met)* tromba d'acqua
water table N livello idrostatico
water tank N serbatoio *or* cisterna d'acqua
water·tight ['wɔ:tə,taɪt] ADJ *(compartment, seal)* stagno(-a); *(fig: excuse, argument)* inattaccabile; **the roof is not watertight** il tetto non è a tenuta stagna
water torture N tortura della goccia (d'acqua)
water tower N serbatoio a torre
water vapour N vapore *m* acqueo
water·way ['wɔ:tə,weɪ] N corso d'acqua navigabile
water·wheel ['wɔ:tə,wi:l] N ruota idraulica
water wings NPL braccioli *mpl* salvagente
water·works ['wɔ:tə,wɜ:ks] NSG *(place)* impianto idrico; *(fig fam)*
■ NPL: **to turn on the waterworks** piangere come una fontana; **to have trouble with one's waterworks** avere dei problemi alla vescica
wa·tery ['wɔ:tərɪ] ADJ *(tea, soup)* acquoso(-a); *(coffee)* lungo(-a); *(pale: sun, colour)* slavato(-a), pallido(-a); *(eyes)* umido(-a); **to go to a watery grave** perire tra i flutti
watt [wɒt] N watt *m inv*
watt·age ['wɒtɪdʒ] N potenza in watt
wat·tle ['wɒtl] N **1** *(woven sticks)* graticcio **2** *(on turkey)* bargiglio
wattle and daub N: **houses of wattle and daub** case di paglia e fango
◎**wave** [weɪv] N **1** *(gen, Phys, Radio)* onda; *(in hair, on surface)* ondulazione *f*; *(fig: of enthusiasm, strikes etc)* ondata; **in waves** a ondate; **short/medium/long wave** *(Radio)* onde *fpl* corte/medie/lunghe; **the new wave** *(Cine)* la nouvelle vague; *(Mus)* la new wave; **he was knocked over by a big wave** è stato travolto da una grossa onda **2** *(greeting)* cenno di saluto; *(signal)* gesto, cenno; **to give sb a wave** salutare qn con la mano; **with a wave of his hand** con un cenno della mano; **a friendly wave** un cenno amichevole
■ VT **1** *(brandish: flag, banner, handkerchief)* sventolare; *(: stick, umbrella)* agitare; *(beckon, motion)* far segno a; **he waved the ticket under my nose** mi sventolò il biglietto sotto il naso; **to wave sb goodbye** *or* **wave goodbye to sb** salutare qn con la mano; **she waved a greeting to the crowd** salutò la folla con un cenno della mano; **he waved us over to the best table** ci indicò con la mano il tavolo migliore **2** *(hair)* ondulare
■ VI **1** *(person)* gesticolare; **to wave to** *or* **at sb** fare un cenno a qn; **he waved at me** mi ha fatto un cenno con la mano **2** *(flag, branches etc)* ondeggiare, sventolare **3** *(hair)* essere mosso(-a) *or* ondulato(-a)
► **wave about, wave around** VT + ADV *(object)* agitare; **to wave one's arms about** *(in talking)* gesticolare
► **wave aside, wave away** VT + ADV *(person)*: **to wave sb aside** fare cenno a qn di spostarsi; *(fig: suggestion, objection)* respingere, rifiutare
► **wave down** VT + ADV: **to wave sb/a car down** far segno a qn/a un'auto di fermarsi
► **wave off** VT + ADV: **to wave sb off** salutare qn
► **wave on** VT + ADV *(subj: policeman)* fare segno di avanzare a
wave·band ['weɪv,bænd] N *(Radio)* gamma di lunghezza d'onda
wave·length ['weɪv,lɛŋθ] N *(Phys, Radio)* lunghezza d'onda; **we're not on the same wavelength** *(fig)* non siamo sulla stessa lunghezza d'onda
wa·ver ['weɪvə^r] VI *(flame, needle etc)* oscillare; *(voice)* tremare; *(fig: hesitate)*: **to waver (between)** tentennare, titubare; **she's beginning to waver** comincia a vacillare
wa·ver·ing ['weɪvərɪŋ] ADJ *(flame)* tremolante; *(needle)* oscillante; *(voice)* tremulo(-a); *(voters, support)* tentennante
■ N *(of flame)* tremolio; *(of needle)* oscillazione *f*; *(of voice)* tremito; *(fig: hesitation)* tentennamento, titubanza
wavy ['weɪvɪ] ADJ *(comp* **-ier**, *superl* **-iest**) *(hair, surface)* ondulato(-a); *(line)* ondeggiante, sinuoso(-a); **a wavy line** una linea ondulata; **wavy hair** i capelli mossi
wax[1] [wæks] N cera; *(for skis)* sciolina; *(in ear)* cerume *m*
■ ADJ di cera
■ VT *(furniture, car)* dare la cera a; *(skis)* sciolinare
wax[2] [wæks] VI *(moon)* crescere; **to wax enthusiastic** diventare entusiasta; **to wax eloquent about sth** diventare infervorato(-a) nel parlare di qc
wax·en ['wæksən] ADJ *(of wax)* di cera; *(fig: pale)* cereo(-a)
wax paper, waxed paper N carta oleata
wax·wing ['wæks,wɪŋ] N beccofrusone *m*
wax·work ['wæks,wɜ:k] N *(model)* statua di cera
wax·works ['wæks,wɜ:ks] NSG OR PL museo delle cere
waxy ['wæksɪ] ADJ *(comp* **-ier**, *superl* **-iest**) *(fig: complexion)* cereo(-a)
◎**way** [weɪ] N
1 *(road, lane)* strada; *(path, access)* passaggio; *(in street names)* via; **private/public way** strada privata/pubblica; **the way across the fields** il sentiero attraverso i campi; **the Appian Way** la via Appia; **across** *or* **over the way** di fronte
2 *(route)* strada; **the Way of the Cross** *(Rel)* la via crucis; **to ask one's way to the station** chiedere la strada per la stazione; **can you tell me the way to the station?** mi sa indicare la strada per la stazione?; **the way back** la via del ritorno; **we came a back way** siamo arrivati per strade secondarie; **she went by way of Birmingham** è andata passando per Birmingham; **to go the wrong way** andare dalla parte sbagliata; **to lose one's way** perdere la strada, perdersi; **the way in** l'entrata, l'ingresso; **the way out** l'uscita; **to find one's way into a building** riuscire a entrare in un

edificio; **don't bother, I'll find my own way out** non si scomodi, troverò l'uscita; **to find a way out of a problem** trovare una via d'uscita a un problema; **to take the easy way out** scegliere la soluzione più facile; **on the way** (*en route*) per strada; (*expected*) in arrivo; **on the way to work** andando a lavorare; **you pass it on your way home** ci passi davanti andando a casa; **he lost it on the way to school** lo ha perso andando a scuola; **he's on his way to becoming an alcoholic** è sulla strada dell'alcolismo; **to be on one's way** essere in cammino *or* sulla strada; **economic recovery is on the way** siamo sulla strada della ripresa economica; **I'm on my way** sto arrivando; **he's on his way** sta arrivando; **it's time we were on our way** è ora di andare; **all the way (here/home)** per tutta la strada (venendo qui/andando a casa); **I'm with you all the way** (*fig fam*) sono assolutamente d'accordo con te; **to make one's (own) way home** andare a casa (da solo(-a)); **I know my way about town** sono pratico della città; **I don't know the way** non so la strada; **to lead the way** fare strada; (*fig*) essere all'avanguardia; **I don't want to take you out of your way** non voglio farti deviare; **the village is rather out of the way** il villaggio è abbastanza fuori mano; **that's nothing out of the way these days** non è nulla di eccezionale al giorno d'oggi; **to go out of one's way to help sb** farsi in quattro per aiutare qn; **can you see your way (clear) to helping me tomorrow?** pensi di potermi aiutare domani?; **to go one's own way** (*fig*) fare di testa propria; **to make one's way in the world** farsi strada nel mondo; **he worked his way up in the company** si è fatto strada nella ditta; **the company isn't paying its way** la ditta non rende più; **he put me in the way of some good contracts** mi ha procurato dei buoni contratti

3 (*space sb wants to go through*) strada; **to be** *or* **get in the** *or* **sb's way** essere d'intralcio *or* d'impiccio a qn; **am I in your way?** (*of sb watching sth*) ti tolgo la visuale?; **to stand in sb's way** intralciare il passaggio a qn; (*fig*) essere d'ostacolo a qn; **"give way"** (*Brit Aut*) "dare la precedenza"; **to stand in the way of progress** ostacolare il progresso; **to get out of the** *or* **sb's way** lasciare passare qn; **get out of the way!** togliti di mezzo!; **to keep out of sb's way** evitare qn, stare alla larga da qn; **to move sth out of the way** togliere di torno qc; **as soon as I've got this essay out of the way** appena mi sono liberato di questo tema; **keep those matches out of his way** tieni lontano da lui quei fiammiferi; **to push/elbow one's way through the crowd** farsi strada a spinte/gomitate tra la folla; **he lied his way out of it** se l'è cavata mentendo; **he crawled/limped his way to the gate** andò a carponi/zoppicando verso il cancello; **to make way (for sb/sth)** far strada (a qn/qc); (*fig*) lasciare il posto *or* fare largo (a qn/qc); **to leave the way open for further talks** lasciare aperta la possibilità di ulteriori colloqui

4 (*direction*) direzione *f*, parte *f*; **which way? — this way** da che parte? — da questa (parte), in quale direzione? — per di qua; **come this way** vieni da questa parte; **this way for ...** da questa parte per...; **which way did he go?** da che parte è andato?; **which way do we go from here?** da che parte dobbiamo andare da qui?; (*fig*) cosa facciamo adesso?; **are you going my way?** fai la strada che faccio io?; **the supermarket is this way** il supermercato è da questa parte; **everything is going my way** (*fig*) mi sta andando tutto liscio; **this way and that** di qua e di là; **down our way** dalle nostre parti; **she didn't know which way to look** non sapeva da che parte guardare; **put it the right way up** (*Brit*) mettilo in piedi dalla parte giusta; **to be the wrong way round** essere al contrario; **to look the other way** (*fig*) guardare dall'altra parte; **to be in a fair way to doing sth** essere sulla strada giusta per fare qc; **to split sth three ways** dividere qc in tre

5 (*indicating distance, motion, progress*): **to come a long way** (*also fig*) fare molta strada; **it's a long way** è lontano; **it's a long way away** è molto lontano da qui; **a little way along the road** un po' più avanti lungo la strada; **she'll go a long way** (*fig*) farà molta strada; **we've come a long way since those days** abbiamo fatto molta strada da allora; **it should go a long way towards convincing him** dovrebbe contribuire molto a convincerlo; **to be under way** (*work, project*) essere in corso; **to get under way** avviarsi; **the job is now well under way** il lavoro ora è ben avviato

6 (*means*) mezzo, modo; (*manner*) modo; **a way of life** uno stile di vita; **the British way of life** lo stile di vita britannico; **there are ways and means** il modo per farlo si trova; **we'll find a way of doing it** troveremo un modo per farlo; **the only way of doing it** l'unico modo per farlo; **there are no two ways about it** non ci sono dubbi; **he has his own way of doing it** ha un modo tutto suo per farlo; **she looked at me in a strange way** mi ha guardato in modo strano; **I'll do it (in) my own way** lo farò a modo mio; **they've had it all their own way too long** hanno fatto per troppo tempo a modo loro; **to get one's own way** aver la vinta; **I will help in every way possible** aiuterò in tutti i modi possibili; **he helped in a small way** ha aiutato un pochino; **in no way** *or* **not in any way** per nulla; **no way!** (*fam*) neanche per sogno!; **there's no way I'll do it** non lo farò per nessun motivo al mondo; **do it this way** fallo in questo modo *or* così ; **in this way** così , in questo modo; **it was this way ...** è stato così ...; **(in) one way or another** in un modo o nell'altro; **in a way** in un certo senso; **in some ways** in un certo senso, sotto certi aspetti; **in many ways** per molti versi; **to my way of thinking** a mio modo di vedere; **either way I can't help you** non ti posso aiutare in nessun caso; **to go on in the same old way** continuare nel modo di sempre; **the way things are** come stanno le cose; **in the ordinary way (of things)** normalmente

7 (*habit*) abitudine *f*; (*manner*) modo di fare; **the ways of the Spaniards** i costumi degli Spagnoli; **foreign ways** abitudini *fpl* forestiere; **he has his little ways** ha le sue piccole abitudini; **it's not my way** non è mia abitudine fare così ; **he has a way with people** ci sa fare con la gente; **he has a way with him** ci sa fare; **to get into/out of the way of doing sth** prendere/perdere l'abitudine di fare qc

8 (*state*): **things are in a bad way** le cose si mettono male; **he's in a bad way** è ridotto male; **to be in the family way** (*fam*) aspettare un bambino

9 (*with "by"*): **by the way** a proposito; **but that's just by the way** ma questo è tra parentesi; **by way of a warning** come avvertimento; **she's by way of being an artist** è una specie di artista

■ ADV (*fam*): **it happened way back** è successo molto tempo fa; **way back in 1900** nel lontano 1900; **it's way out in Nevada** è nel lontano Nevada; **he was way out in his estimate** la sua valutazione era decisamente errata

way·bill ['weɪˌbɪl] N (*Comm*) bolla di accompagnamento

Ww

way·farer ['weɪ,fɛərəʳ] N (*old*) viandante *m/f*
way·faring ['weɪ,fɛərɪŋ] ADJ (*old: man, gipsy*) vagabondo(-a)
■ N vagabondaggi *mpl*
way·lay [weɪ'leɪ] (*pt, pp* **waylaid**) VT (*old*) intercettare; **I got waylaid** (*fig*) ho avuto un contrattempo
way-out [,weɪ'aʊt] ADJ (*fam*) eccentrico(-a)
way·side ['weɪ,saɪd] N bordo della strada; **along the wayside** *or* **by the wayside** sul ciglio della strada; **to fall by the wayside** (*fig*) perdersi lungo la strada
■ ADJ (*flowers, café*) sul bordo della strada
way station N (*Am Rail*) stazione *f* secondaria; (*fig*) tappa
way·ward ['weɪwəd] ADJ (*self-willed*) ribelle, capriccioso(-a)
WC [,dʌblju:'si:] N ABBR (*Brit:* = **water closet**) WC *m inv*
WCC [,dʌblju:si:'si:] N ABBR (= **World Council of Churches**) *Consiglio ecumenico delle Chiese*
◎**we** [wi:] PERS PRON PL noi; **we understand** abbiamo capito; (*stressed*) noi sì che abbiamo capito; **here we are** eccoci; **we Italians** noi *or* noialtri italiani; **as we say in Florence ...** come si dice a Firenze...; **we all make mistakes** tutti possiamo sbagliare; **we aren't so lucky** noi non siamo così fortunati; **we'll arrive tomorrow** arriveremo domani
◎**weak** [wi:k] ADJ (*comp* **-er**, *superl* **-est**) (*gen*) debole; (*tea, coffee*) leggero(-a); (*health*) precario(-a); (*excuse, effort*) inefficace; **to grow weak(er)** = **to weaken** VI; **a weak chin** un mento sfuggente; **to have weak eyes** *or* **eyesight** avere la vista debole; **to have a weak heart** soffrire di cuore; **her French is weak** *or* **she is weak at French** è scarsa in francese; **weak in the head** (*fam*) tocco(-a); toccato(-a); **to go weak at the knees** (*with excitement, hunger etc*) avere le gambe che fanno giacomo giacomo; **the weak link in the chain** l'anello debole della catena; **weak verb** verbo debole
◎**weak·en** ['wi:kən] VT (*gen*) indebolire; (*grip*) allentare; (*influence*) diminuire; (*solution, mixture*) diluire; **this fact weakens your case** questo fatto sminuisce il tuo argomento; **the recession weakened many firms** la recessione ha indebolito molte aziende
■ VI (*gen*) indebolirsi; (*grip*) allentarsi; (*influence*) diminuire; (*give way*) cedere; **we must not weaken now** non dobbiamo cedere proprio ora; **her resolve did not weaken** la sua determinazione non si è indebolita
weak·en·ing ['wi:kənɪŋ] N (*gen*) indebolimento; (*of grip*) allentamento; (*of influence*) diminuzione *f*
weak-kneed [,wi:k'ni:d] ADJ (*fig*) debole, codardo(-a)
weak·ling ['wi:klɪŋ] N (*physically*) mingherlino(-a); (*morally*) smidollato(-a)
weak·ly ['wi:klɪ] ADJ deboluccio(-a), gracile
■ ADV debolmente
weak-minded [,wi:k'maɪndɪd] ADJ debole di carattere
weak·ness ['wi:knɪs] N debolezza; **chocolate is one of my weaknesses** il cioccolato è una delle mie passioni; **to have a weakness for sth** avere un debole per qc
weak-willed [,wi:k'wɪld] ADJ debole
weal [wi:l] N (*welt*) piaga
◎**wealth** [wɛlθ] N (*money, resources*) ricchezza, ricchezze *fpl*; (*fig: abundance*): **wealth and fame** ricchezza e fama; **wealth (of)** dovizia *or* abbondanza (di)
wealth tax N imposta sul patrimonio
wealthy ['wɛlθɪ] ADJ (*comp* **-ier**, *superl* **-iest**) ricco(-a)
wean [wi:n] VT (*baby*) svezzare; **to wean sb (away) from alcohol** far perdere a qn il vizio del bere
◎**weap·on** ['wɛpən] N arma; **weapons of mass destruction** armi di distruzione di massa
weap·on·ize ['wɛpənaɪz] VT usare nella fabbricazione di armi
wea·pon·ry ['wɛpənrɪ] N armamenti *mpl*
weapons-grade ['wɛpənz,greɪd] ADJ per la fabbricazione di armi
◎**wear** [wɛəʳ] (*vb: pt* **wore**, *pp* **worn**) N
1 (*use*) uso; **shoes for everyday wear** scarpe da mettere tutti i giorni; **there's still a lot of wear in these** (*shoes, carpets, tyres*) sono ancora in buono stato; **I've had a lot of wear out of this jacket** porto questa giacca da anni; **to stand up to a lot of wear** durare a lungo
2 (*deterioration through use*) logoramento, logorio; **wear and tear** usura; **fair wear and tear** (*Comm*) normale usura; **the wear on the engine** l'usura del motore; **she looks the worse for wear** (*old, exhausted*) sembra sciupata; (*hung-over*) ha l'aria distrutta
3 (*clothing*) abbigliamento; **children's wear** confezioni *fpl* per bambini; **sports/baby wear** abbigliamento sportivo/per neonati; **summer wear** abiti *mpl* estivi; **evening wear** abiti *npl* da sera
■ VT
1 (*spectacles, necklace, beard*) portare; (*clothes*) portare, indossare; (*look, smile*) avere; **to wear make-up** truccarsi; **she wasn't wearing any make-up** non era truccata; **she wore her blue dress** portava il vestito blu; **she was wearing a black coat** portava un cappotto nero; **he wore black trousers and a T-shirt** portava pantaloni neri e una maglietta; **this is the first time I've worn these shoes** è la prima volta che metto queste scarpe; **I have nothing to wear to the dinner** non ho niente da mettermi per la cena; **to wear one's hair long** portare i capelli lunghi; **he wore a big smile** sfoderò un gran sorriso
2 (*damage through use*) consumare, logorare; **I always manage to wear my jumpers at the elbow** i miei maglioni sono sempre consumati nei gomiti; **they have worn a path across the lawn** hanno formato un sentiero nel prato a forza di camminarci sopra; **to wear a hole in sth** bucare qc a furia di usarlo(-a); **the rocks had been worn smooth** le rocce erano state levigate dal tempo
3 (*fam: believe, tolerate*) bere; **he won't wear that** questa non la beve
■ VI
1 (*last*) durare; **she has worn well** porta bene i suoi anni; **that theory has worn well** quella teoria è ancora valida
2 (*become worn: shoes, inscription etc*) consumarsi; (*: rocks*) levigarsi; **the stone steps are beginning to wear** gli scalini di pietra cominciano a consumarsi; **the edges have worn smooth** gli spigoli si sono smussati; **that excuse is wearing a bit thin** quella scusa non regge più
► **wear away** VT + ADV (*rock, pattern etc*) consumare
■ VI + ADV consumarsi
► **wear down** VT + ADV (*heel, tyre tread etc*) consumare; (*fig: opposition etc*) fiaccare; (*: strength*) esaurire; **to wear down sb's patience** far perdere la pazienza a qn
■ VI + ADV (*heels, tyre tread*) consumarsi
► **wear off** VI + ADV (*plating, paint etc*) consumarsi; (*pain, excitement etc*) diminuire; (*anaesthetic*) perdere efficacia; **after a while the novelty wore off** dopo un po' non era più una novità; **the feeling soon wore off** presto la sensazione svanì

▸ **wear on** VI + ADV avanzare, passare; **as the evening wore on** nel corso della serata

▸ **wear out** VT + ADV consumare, logorare; (*fig: exhaust*) stancare; (*: patience*) far perdere; **he wore out his shoes wandering round the city** ha consumato le scarpe gironzolando per la città; **don't wear yourself out!** non stancarti troppo!; **to be worn out** essere consumato(-a); (*fig: person*) essere estenuato(-a) *or* distrutto(-a)

■ VI + ADV (*shoes, carpet etc*) consumarsi; **his strength wore out** era spossato; **her patience wore out** ha perso la pazienza

▸ **wear through** VT + ADV consumare

■ VI + ADV consumarsi

wear·able ['wɛərəbl] ADJ indossabile

wear·er ['wɛərə^r] N: **the wearers of the blue coats** quelli che portano il cappotto blu; **will the wearer of the red jacket come forward?** si prega la persona che indossa la giacca rossa di venire avanti

wea·ri·ly ['wɪərɪlɪ] ADV stancamente

wea·ri·ness ['wɪərɪnɪs] N stanchezza

wear·ing ['wɛərɪŋ] ADJ (*tiring*) stancante, logorante

wea·ri·some ['wɪərɪsəm] ADJ (*tiring*) estenuante; (*boring*) noioso(-a)

wea·ry ['wɪərɪ] ADJ (*comp* **-ier**, *superl* **-iest**) (*tired*) stanco(-a), affaticato(-a); (*dispirited*) stanco(-a), abbattuto(-a); (*tiring: wait, day*) estenuante; **to be weary of sb/sth** essere stanco(-a) di qn/qc; **five weary miles** cinque lunghe miglia

■ VT stancare

■ VI: **to weary of sb/sth** stancarsi di qn/qc

wea·sel ['wi:zl] N (*Zool*) donnola

◎ **weath·er** ['wɛðə^r] N tempo; **in this weather** con questo tempo; **what's the weather like?** che tempo fa?; **it gets left outside in all weathers** rimane fuori con qualsiasi tempo; **to be under the weather** (*fig: ill*) sentirsi poco bene; **to make heavy weather of sth** far sembrare qc più difficile di quello che sia

■ VT **1** (*wood*) stagionare **2 to weather the storm** (*ship*) resistere alla tempesta; (*fig*) superare le difficoltà

■ VI (*rocks*) logorarsi; (*wood*) stagionare

■ ADJ (*bureau, ship, chart, station*) meteorologico(-a)

weather-beaten ['wɛðə,bi:tn] ADJ (*rocks, building*) logorato(-a) dalle intemperie; (*person, skin*) segnato(-a) dal tempo

weather·board ['wɛðə,bɔ:d] N tavola di copertura

weather·boarding ['wɛðə,bɔ:dɪŋ] N rivestimento con tavole di copertura

weather-bound ['wɛðə,baund] ADJ bloccato(-a) dalle intemperie

weather·cock ['wɛðə,kɒk] N banderuola

weath·ered ['wɛðəd] ADJ (*skin, rocks*) segnato(-a) dalle intemperie; (*wood*) stagionato(-a)

weather eye N: **to keep a weather eye on sth** (*fig*) tener d'occhio qc

weather forecast N previsioni *fpl* del tempo

weather forecaster N meteorologo(-a)

weath·er·ing ['wɛðərɪŋ] N (*of rocks*) degradazione *f* meteorica

weather·man ['wɛðə,mæn] N (*pl* **-men**) meteorologo

weather·proof ['wɛðə,pru:f] ADJ (*garment*) impermeabile

weather report N bollettino meteorologico

weather situation N condizioni *fpl* meteorologiche

weather·vane ['wɛðə,veɪn] N = **weathercock**

weave [wi:v] (*pp: pt* **wove**, *pp* **woven**) N trama

■ VT (*threads, basket*) intrecciare; (*fabric*) tessere; **I wove this rug myself** ho tessuto io stesso questo tappeto; **he wove these details into the story** ha intrecciato nella storia questi dettagli; **he wove a story round these experiences** ha intessuto una storia attorno a queste esperienze

■ VI (*pt, pp* **weaved**) tessere; (*fig: move in and out*) zigzagare; **to weave in and out of the traffic** zigzagare nel traffico

weav·er ['wi:və^r] N tessitore(-trice)

weav·ing ['wi:vɪŋ] N tessitura

Web [wɛb] N: **the Web** (*Comput*) il Web, la Rete

web [wɛb] N (*of spider*) ragnatela, tela; (*between toes*) membrana interdigitale; (*fig*) insieme *m*; **it was a web of lies** era un castello di menzogne

webbed [wɛbd] ADJ: **webbed foot** piede *m* palmato

web·bing ['wɛbɪŋ] N (*on chair*) cinghie *fpl*

web browser N (*Comput*) browser *m inv*

web·cam ['wɛb,kæm] N (*Comput*) webcam *f inv*

web·cast ['wɛb,kɑ:st] N (*Comput*) trasmissione *f* diffusa in Internet

web·chat ['wɛb,tʃæt] N (*Comput*) chat *f inv* in Internet

web-footed [,wɛb'fʊtɪd] ADJ palmipede, dai piedi palmati

web·log ['wɛb,lɒg] N (*Comput*) blog *m inv*

web·master ['wɛbm,ɑ:stə^r] N (*Comput*) webmaster *m inv*; *gestore di un sito Internet*

web page N (*Comput*) pagina *f* web *inv*

web ring N (*Comput*) serie *f* di siti Internet collegati tra loro

web search N (*Comput*) ricerca in Internet

web·site ['wɛbsaɪt] N (*Comput*) sito Internet

web·stream·ing ['wɛb,stri:mɪŋ] N (*Comput*) *sistema di trasmissione diretta di materiale video o audio in Internet*

web·zine ['wɛb,zi:n] N (*Comput*) rivista elettronica

Wed. ABBR (= Wednesday) mer(c). (= *mercoledì*)

we'd [wi:d] = **we had, we would**

wed [wɛd] VT sposare; **to be wedded to one's job/an idea** essere consacrato(-a) al proprio lavoro/a un'idea

■ VI sposarsi

■ N: **the newly-weds** gli sposi novelli

wed·ded ['wɛdɪd] ADJ (*wife, husband*) legittimo(-a); (*bliss, life*) coniugale

◎ **wed·ding** ['wɛdɪŋ] N matrimonio, nozze *fpl*; **silver/golden** *etc* **wedding** nozze *fpl* d'argento/d'oro *etc*; **to have a church wedding** sposarsi in chiesa

■ ADJ (*cake, dress, reception*) nuziale

wedding anniversary N anniversario di matrimonio

wedding breakfast N (*old*) pranzo nuziale

wedding day N giorno delle nozze *or* del matrimonio

wedding dress N abito da sposa

wedding invitation N partecipazione *f* di nozze

wedding night N prima notte di nozze

wedding present N regalo di nozze

wedding ring N fede *f*, vera

wedge [wɛdʒ] N (*under door*) zeppa; (*for splitting sth*) cuneo; (*piece: of cheese, cake*) fetta; **it's the thin end of the wedge** (*fig*) è l'inizio della fine; **to drive a wedge between two people** intaccare il rapporto tra due persone

■ VT mettere una zeppa sotto *or* in; **to wedge a door open** tenere aperta una porta con un fermo; **the car was wedged between two lorries** la macchina era incastrata tra due camion

wedge-heeled shoes [,wɛdʒhi:ld'ʃu:z] NPL scarpe *fpl* con la zeppa

wedge-shaped ['wɛdʒʃeɪpt] ADJ a forma di cuneo

Ww

wed·lock ['wɛdlɒk] N (*old*) vincolo matrimoniale
Wednes·day ['wɛnzdɪ] N mercoledì *m inv*; *for usage see* Tuesday
wee [wiː] ADJ (*comp* **-er**, *superl* **-est**) (*Scot fam*) piccolo(-a); **a wee bit** uno zinzino
weed [wiːd] N (*plant*) erbaccia; (*weak person*) tipo(-a) allampanato(-a); **the garden's full of weeds** il giardino è pieno di erbacce
■ VT (*flower bed*) diserbare
■ VI strappare le erbacce
▸ **weed out** VT + ADV (*fig*) eliminare
weed·ing ['wiːdɪŋ] N diserbatura
weed-killer ['wiːdˌkɪləʳ] N diserbante *m*, erbicida *m*
weedy ['wiːdɪ] ADJ (*comp* **-ier**, *superl* **-iest**) (*fam: person*) allampanato(-a)
◎ **week** [wiːk] N settimana; **once/twice a week** una volta/due volte alla settimana; **this week** questa settimana; **next/last week** la settimana prossima/scorsa; **in the middle of the week** a metà settimana; **in a week's time** tra una settimana; **a week today** oggi a otto, una settimana a oggi; **2 weeks ago** 2 settimane fa; **in 2 weeks' time** fra 2 settimane, fra 15 giorni; **Tuesday week** *or* **a week on Tuesday** martedì a otto; **to take 3 weeks' holiday** prendere 3 settimane di ferie; **the week ending January 3rd** ≈ la prima settimana di gennaio; **a 35-hour week** una settimana lavorativa di 35 ore; **week in, week out** *or* **week after week** settimana dopo settimana; **every other week** una settimana sì e una no, a settimane alterne; **to knock sb into the middle of next week** (*fam*) darle di santa ragione a qn
week·day ['wiːkˌdeɪ] N giorno feriale; (*Comm*) giornata lavorativa; **on weekdays** durante la settimana, nei giorni feriali
◎ **week·end** [ˌwiːk'ɛnd] N week-end *m inv*, fine settimana *m or f inv*; **a long weekend** un fine settimana lungo (*che include il venerdì o il lunedì*); **at the weekend** durante il fine settimana; **at weekends** al weekend *or* fine settimana; **last weekend** l'altro fine settimana; **to go away for the weekend** andare via per il weekend *or* il fine settimana
■ ADJ (*cottage*) per il fine settimana; (*visit*) di fine settimana
weekend case N borsa da viaggio
◎ **week·ly** ['wiːklɪ] ADJ settimanale
■ ADV settimanalmente, ogni settimana; **£45 weekly** 45 sterline alla settimana
■ N (*magazine*) settimanale *m*
week·night ['wiːkˌnaɪt] N serata infrasettimanale
wee·ny, **wee·ney** ['wiːnɪ], **ween·sie** (*Am*) ['wiːnzɪ] ADJ (*comp* **-ier**, *superl* **-iest**) (*fam*) minimo(-a); **a weeny bit more** ancora un pochino
weep [wiːp] (*vb: pt, pp* **wept**) VT (*tears*) versare, piangere
■ VI piangere; (*Med: wound etc*) essudare; **to weep for sb** piangere per qn; **to weep bitterly** piangere amaramente; **I could have wept!** mi sarei messo a piangere!; **she wept for hours** pianse per ore
■ N: **to have a good weep** farsi un bel pianto
weep·ing ['wiːpɪŋ] N pianto
weeping willow N salice *m* piangente
weepy ['wiːpɪ] ADJ piagnucoloso(-a)
■ N (*fam: film*) film *m* strappalacrime *inv*
wee·vil ['wiːvl] N (*Zool*) tonchio
wee·wee ['wiːwiː] (*fam*) N pipì *f inv*
■ VI fare la pipì
weft [wɛft] N (*Textiles*) trama
◎ **weigh** [weɪ] VT **1** (*also fig*) pesare; **how much do you weigh?** quanto pesi?; **to weigh o.s.** pesarsi; **it weighs a ton** (*also fig*) pesa una tonnellata; **to weigh sth in one's hand** soppesare qc; **to weigh sth in one's mind** soppesare mentalmente qc; **to weigh the pros and cons** valutare i pro e i contro **2** **to weigh anchor** (*Naut*) salpare, levare l'ancora
■ VI (*fig: be a worry*): **to weigh on sb** pesare su qn; **to weigh against sb** giocare a sfavore di qn; **to weigh with sb** avere importanza *or* contare per qn; **it weighs on her mind** la preoccupa; **that didn't weigh with him** quello per lui non aveva importanza
▸ **weigh down** VT + ADV (*branches*) piegare; (*person: with worry*) opprimere; **to be weighed down by sth** curvarsi sotto il peso di qc; **to be weighed down with sorrows** essere oppresso(-a) dai dispiaceri
▸ **weigh in** VI + ADV (*Sport*) pesarsi (prima di una gara); **he weighed in at 60 kilos** al controllo del peso era 60 chili
▸ **weigh out** VT + ADV (*goods*) pesare
▸ **weigh up** VT + ADV (*alternatives, situation*) pesare, valutare
weigh·bridge ['weɪˌbrɪdʒ] N bascula
weigh-in ['weɪˌɪn] N (*Sport*) pesata
weigh·ing ['weɪɪŋ] N pesatura
weighing machine N bilancia *f* pesapersone *inv*
◎ **weight** [weɪt] N **1** (*gen, fig*) peso; **the weight of the load** il peso del carico; **sold by weight** venduto(-a) a peso; **it** (*or* **he** *etc*) **is worth its** (*or* **his** *etc*) **weight in gold** vale tanto oro quanto pesa; **to put on/lose weight** ingrassare/dimagrire; **to carry weight** (*fig*) avere peso; **these are arguments of some weight** questi sono argomenti di un certo peso; **that's a weight off my mind** mi sono tolto un peso; **they won by sheer weight of numbers** hanno vinto solo per superiorità numerica; **to chuck** *or* **throw one's weight about** (*fam*) fare il/la prepotente; **he doesn't pull his weight** non lavora quanto dovrebbe **2** (*for scales etc*) peso; **weights and measures** pesi e misure
■ VT (*also:* **weight down**) mettere dei pesi su
weight belt N (*Diving*) cintura dei pesi
weight·ed ['weɪtɪd] ADJ: **to be weighted in favour of/against** essere nettamente a favore di/contro
weight·ing ['weɪtɪŋ] N indennità *f inv* speciale (*per carovita etc*)
weight·less ['weɪtlɪs] ADJ senza peso
weight·less·ness ['weɪtlɪsnɪs] N assenza di peso
weight·lifter ['weɪtˌlɪftəʳ] N pesista *m/f*
weight·lifting ['weɪtˌlɪftɪŋ] N sollevamento pesi, pesistica
weight training N: **to do weight training** allenarsi con i pesi; fare pesi
weighty ['weɪtɪ] ADJ (*comp* **-ier**, *superl* **-iest**) (*fig: problems, duties, considerations*) importante
weir [wɪəʳ] N sbarramento
weird [wɪəd] ADJ (*comp* **-er**, *superl* **-est**) strano(-a), bizzarro(-a)
weird·ly ['wɪədlɪ] ADV stranamente
weird·ness ['wɪədnɪs] N stranezza
weir·do ['wɪədəʊ] N (*fam*) tipo(-a) allucinante
welch [wɛlʃ] VI = **welsh**
◎ **wel·come** ['wɛlkəm] ADJ (*gen*) gradito(-a); **welcome!** benvenuto(-a)!; **welcome to Britain!** benvenuti in Gran Bretagna!; **to be welcome** (*person*) essere il/la benvenuto(-a); **welcome back!** bentornato(-a)!; **you will always be welcome here** qui sarai sempre il benvenuto; **to make sb welcome** accogliere bene qn; **you're welcome** (*after thanks*) prego; **thank you! –**

you're welcome! grazie! – di niente!; **you're welcome to try** prova pure; **you're welcome to (borrow) it** prendilo pure; **it's a welcome change** è un piacevole cambiamento

■ N accoglienza, benvenuto; **a cold/warm welcome** un'accoglienza fredda/calorosa; **a welcome speech** un discorso di benvenuto; **to bid sb welcome** dare il benvenuto a qn; **the crowd gave him an enthusiastic welcome** la folla lo accolse con entusiasmo; **what sort of a welcome will this product get?** che accoglienza avrà questo prodotto?

■ VT accogliere, ricevere; (*also:* **bid welcome**) dare il benvenuto a; (*fig: change, suggestion, development*) rallegrarsi di; (: *criticism*) accettare di buon grado; **everyone was there to welcome me** erano tutti lì ad accogliermi; **I'd welcome your help** gradirei il tuo aiuto; **we welcome this step** siamo lieti di questa iniziativa; **he didn't welcome the suggestion** non ha gradito il suggerimento

wel·com·ing ['wɛlkəmɪŋ] ADJ accogliente

weld [wɛld] VT saldare

■ N saldatura

weld·en ['wɛldən] (*Skiing*) N serpentina

■ VI fare la serpentina

weld·er ['wɛldəʳ] N (*person*) saldatore *m*

weld·ing ['wɛldɪŋ] N saldatura

welding torch N cannello per saldatura

◎ **wel·fare** ['wɛl,fɛəʳ] N **1** (*gen*) bene *m*; (*comfort*) benessere *m*; **the nation's welfare** il bene della nazione; **spiritual welfare** benessere spirituale; **to look after sb's welfare** preoccuparsi di qn; **child welfare** protezione *f* dell'infanzia; **they're concerned for your welfare** si preoccupano del tuo benessere

2 (*social aid etc*) assistenza sociale; **to be on welfare** vivere con il sussidio statale; **they were living off welfare** vivevano del sussidio statale; **some states are cutting welfare** alcuni stati stanno tagliando sulla previdenza sociale

■ ADJ (*aid, organization*) di assistenza sociale

welfare centre N centro di assistenza sociale

welfare state N: **the welfare state** lo stato sociale

welfare work N assistenza sociale

welfare worker N assistente *m/f* sociale

we'll [wi:l] = we will, we shall

well- [wɛl] PREF bene

well¹ [wɛl] N (*for water etc*) pozzo; (*of stairs*) tromba; (*of lift*) gabbia

■ VI (*tears, emotions*) sgorgare

► **well up** VI + ADV (*tears, emotions*) sgorgare

◎ **well²** [wɛl] (*comp* **better**, *superl* **best**) ADV

1 (*gen*) bene; **very well** benissimo; **she plays the flute very well** suona molto bene il flauto; **you did that really well** l'hai fatto proprio bene; **he did as well as he could** ha fatto come meglio poteva; **to do well (in sth)** andare bene (in qc); **she's doing really well at school** va molto bene a scuola; **to be doing well** stare bene; **the patient is doing well** il paziente si sta rimettendo; **you did well to come** hai fatto bene a venire; **he did well to come tenth** anche arrivare decimo è stato per lui un buon risultato; **well done!** ben fatto!, bravo(-a)!; **to think well of sb** avere una buona opinione di qn; **to be well in with sb** essere in buoni rapporti con qn; **to do well by sb** trattare bene qn; **it was well worth it** ne valeva certo la pena; **you're well out of it** è un bene che tu ne sia uscito; **well and truly** completamente; **well over a thousand** molto *or* ben più di mille; **all** *or* **only too well** anche troppo bene; **and well I know it!** è proprio vero!; **he's well away** (*fam: drunk*) è completamente andato

2 (*probably, reasonably*): **we might just as well have ...** tanto valeva...; **she cried, as well she might** piangeva a buon diritto; **one might well ask why ...** ci si potrebbe ben chiedere perché...; **you may well ask!** buona domanda!; **you might as well tell me** potresti anche dirmelo; **I might** *or* **may as well come** quasi quasi vengo; **I couldn't very well leave** non potevo andarmene così

3 as well (*in addition*) anche; **she sings, as well as playing the piano** oltre a suonare il piano, canta; **X as well as Y** sia X che Y; **we worked hard, but we had some fun as well** abbiamo lavorato sodo, ma ci siamo anche divertiti; **we went to Verona as well as Venice** siamo stati a Venezia e anche a Verona

■ ADJ

1 (*healthy*): **to be well** stare bene; **I'm not very well at the moment** non sto molto bene in questo periodo; **get well soon!** guarisci presto!; **I don't feel well** non mi sento bene

2 (*acceptable, satisfactory*) buono(-a); **all is not well** non va tutto bene; **that's all very well, but ...** va benissimo, ma..., d'accordo, ma...; **well and good** bene; **it would be as well to ask** sarebbe bene chiedere; **it's just as well we asked** abbiamo fatto bene a chiedere

■ EXCL (*gen*) bene; (*resignation, hesitation*) be'; **well, as I was saying ...** dunque, come stavo dicendo...; **well, well, well!** ma guarda un po'!; **very well then** va bene, molto bene; **very well, if that's the way you want it** (*unenthusiastic*) va bene, se questo è quello che vuoi; **well I never!** ma no!, ma non mi dire!; **well there you are then!** ecco, hai visto!; **it's enormous! Well, quite big anyway** è gigantesco! Be', diciamo molto grande; **well? What's wrong?** allora? Cosa c'è che non va?

■ N: **to wish sb well** augurare ogni bene a qn; (*in exam, new job*) augurare a qn di riuscire

well-advised [,wɛləd'vaɪzd] ADJ (*action, decision*) saggio(-a)

well-appointed [,wɛlə'pɔɪntɪd] ADJ (*flat, hotel etc*) ben attrezzato(-a), ben equipaggiato(-a)

well-balanced [,wɛl'bælənst] ADJ equilibrato(-a)

well-behaved [,wɛlbɪ'heɪvd] ADJ (*child*) che si comporta bene, beneducato(-a)

well-being [,wɛl'bi:ɪŋ] N benessere *m*

well-bred [,wɛl'brɛd] ADJ educato(-a), beneducato(-a)

well-brought-up [,wɛlbrɔ:t'ʌp] ADJ ben educato(-a)

well-built [,wɛl'bɪlt] ADJ (*person*) ben fatto(-a); (*house*) ben costruito(-a)

well-chosen [,wɛl'tʃəʊzn] ADJ (*remarks, words*) ben scelto(-a), appropriato(-a)

well-connected [,wɛlkə'nɛktɪd] ADJ: **to be well-connected** avere amicizie influenti

well-developed [,wɛldɪ'vɛləpt] ADJ ben sviluppato(-a)

well-disposed [,wɛldɪ'spəʊzd] ADJ: **well-disposed to(wards)** bendisposto(-a) verso

well-dressed [,wɛl'drɛst] ADJ ben vestito(-a), vestito(-a) bene

well-earned [,wɛl'ɜ:nd] ADJ (*rest*) meritato(-a)

well-educated [,wɛl'ɛdjʊ,keɪtɪd] ADJ colto(-a), istruito(-a)

well-endowed [,wɛlɪn'daʊd] ADJ (*also fig*) ben dotato(-a)

well-fed [,wɛl'fɛd] ADJ ben nutrito(-a)

well-founded [,wɛl'faʊndɪd] ADJ fondato(-a)

well-groomed [,wɛl'gru:md] ADJ (*person*) curato(-a)

Ww

(nel vestire); (*horse*) ben strigliato(-a); (*dog*) ben tenuto(-a)

well-grounded [ˌwɛl'graʊndɪd] ADJ ben fondato(-a)

well-heeled [ˌwɛl'hiːld] ADJ (*fam: wealthy*) agiato(-a), facoltoso(-a)

well-hung [ˌwɛl'hʌŋ] ADJ (*hum*) ben dotato(-a)

wel·lies ['wɛlɪz] NPL (*fam*) = **wellingtons**

well-informed [ˌwɛlɪn'fɔːmd] ADJ (*knowledgeable*) informato(-a); (*having knowledge of*) ben informato(-a)

Wel·ling·ton ['wɛlɪŋtən] N (*city*) Wellington *f*
 ▷ www.wellingtonnz.com

wel·ling·tons ['wɛlɪŋtəns] NPL (*also:* **wellington boots**) stivali *mpl* di gomma

well-intentioned [ˌwɛlɪn'tɛnʃənd] ADJ benintenzionato(-a)

well-judged [ˌwɛl'dʒʌdʒd] ADJ (*aim, shot*) ben calcolato(-a); (*remark*) ben ponderato(-a); (*estimate*) giusto(-a)

well-kept [ˌwɛl'kɛpt] ADJ (*house, grounds*) ben tenuto(-a); (*secret*) ben custodito(-a); (*hair, hands*) ben curato(-a)

◎**well-known** [ˌwɛl'nəʊn] ADJ noto(-a), famoso(-a); **a well-known film star** un famoso divo del cinema

well-liked [ˌwɛl'laɪkt] ADJ (*person*) benvoluto(-a); (*film, book*) di successo, gradito(-a)

well-lined [ˌwɛl'laɪnd] ADJ (*fam*): **to have well-lined pockets** avere il portafoglio ben fornito; **to have a well-lined stomach** avere la pancia piena

well-made [ˌwɛl'meɪd] ADJ ben fatto(-a)

well-mannered [ˌwɛl'mænəd] ADJ (*person*) beneducato(-a); (*remark*) cortese

well-meaning [ˌwɛl'miːnɪŋ] ADJ (*person*) spinto(-a) da buone intenzioni

well-meant [ˌwɛl'mɛnt] ADJ (*remark, act*) dettato(-a) dalle migliori intenzioni

well·ness ['wɛlnɪs] N benessere *m*; **wellness clinic** centro *m* benessere *inv*

well-nigh [ˌwɛl'naɪ] ADV: **well-nigh impossible** quasi impossibile

well-off [ˌwɛl'ɒf] ADJ (*rich*) benestante, danaroso(-a); **you're well-off without him** puoi fare tranquillamente a meno di lui; **you don't know when you're well-off** non sai quanto sei fortunato
 ■ NPL: **the well-off** i benestanti; *see also* **better-off**

well-oiled [ˌwɛl'ɔɪld] ADJ (*fam: drunk*) sbronzo(-a)

well-preserved [ˌwɛlprɪ'zɜːvd] ADJ (*person*): **to be well-preserved** portare bene i propri anni

well-read [ˌwɛl'rɛd] ADJ colto(-a)

well-spent [ˌwɛl'spɛnt] ADJ (*money*) ben speso(-a); **that was time well-spent** non è stata una perdita di tempo

well-spoken [ˌwɛl'spəʊkən] ADJ che parla bene

well-stacked [ˌwɛl'stækt] ADJ (*fam: woman*) ben carrozzata

well-stocked [ˌwɛl'stɒkt] ADJ (*shop, larder*) ben fornito(-a); (*river*) pescoso(-a)

well-thought-of [ˌwɛl'θɔːtɒv] ADJ rispettato(-a); (*person*) benvoluto(-a)

well-thought-out ['wɛlˌθɔːt'aʊt] ADJ (*plan*) ben ponderato(-a)

well-thumbed [ˌwɛl'θʌmd] ADJ (*book, magazine*) consumato(-a) dall'uso

well-timed [ˌwɛl'taɪmd] ADJ opportuno(-a), tempestivo(-a)

well-to-do [ˌwɛltə'duː] ADJ abbiente, benestante

well-tried [ˌwɛl'traɪd] ADJ sperimentato(-a)

well-wisher ['wɛlˌwɪʃəʳ] N ammiratore(-trice); **letters from well-wishers** lettere *fpl* di incoraggiamento

well-woman clinic [wɛl'wʊmənˌklɪnɪk] N ≈ consultorio (familiare)

well-worn [ˌwɛl'wɔːn] ADJ (*path*) molto battuto(-a); (*carpet, clothes*) logoro(-a), liso(-a); (*fig: phrase*) trito(-a) e ritrito(-a)

Welsh [wɛlʃ] ADJ gallese; **Welsh Assembly** (*Pol*) *organo legislativo autonomo gallese*
 ■ N **1**: **the Welsh** NPL i gallesi **2** (*language*) gallese *m*

welsh [wɛlʃ] VI (*fam*): **to welsh on** (*promise*) venir meno a; (*debt*) non pagare

Welsh dresser N *credenza con alzata a ripiani*

Welsh·man ['wɛlʃmən] N (*pl* **-men**) gallese *m*

Welsh rabbit, Welsh rarebit N crostino al formaggio

Welsh·woman ['wɛlʃˌwʊmən] N (*pl* **-women**) gallese *f*

welt [wɛlt] N (*bruise*) livido

wel·ter ['wɛltəʳ] N massa, mucchio

wel·ter·weight ['wɛltəˌweɪt] N peso welter *m inv*

wench [wɛntʃ] N (*old, liter*) ragazzotta; **a serving wench** una servetta
 ■ VI (*old*) andare a donne

wend [wɛnd] VT (*frm*): **to wend one's way home** incamminarsi verso casa

went [wɛnt] PT *of* **go**

wept [wɛpt] PT, PP *of* **weep**

we're [wɪəʳ] = **we are**

were [wɜːʳ] 2ND PERS SG, PL PT *of* **be**

weren't [wɜːnt] = **were not**

were·wolf ['wɪəˌwʊlf] N (*pl* **-wolves**) licantropo, lupo mannaro (*fam*)

◎**west** [wɛst] N ovest *m*, ponente *m*, occidente *m*; **the wind is in** *or* **from the west** il vento viene da ovest *or* da ponente *or* da occidente; **(to the) west of** a ovest di; **Stroud is west of Oxford** Stroud è a ovest di Oxford; **in the west** a ovest; **in the west of** nella parte occidentale di; **the West** (*Pol*) l'Occidente *m*
 ■ ADJ (*gen*) ovest *inv*; (*part, coast*) occidentale; (*wind*) di ponente; **the west coast** la costa occidentale
 ■ ADV verso ovest; **to sail west** navigare verso ovest; **a house facing west** una casa esposta a ovest; **we were travelling west** andavamo verso ovest

west·bound ['wɛstˌbaʊnd] ADJ (*traffic*) diretto(-a) a ovest; (*carriageway*) ovest *inv*

West Country N: **the West Country** il sud-ovest dell'Inghilterra

west·er·ly ['wɛstəlɪ] ADJ (*wind*) di ponente; **westerly wind** vento di ponente; **in a westerly direction** verso ovest

◎**west·ern** ['wɛstən] ADJ (*also Pol*) occidentale, dell'ovest; **in Western France/Europe** nella Francia/nell'Europa occidentale; **the western coast of Scotland** la costa occidentale della Scozia
 ■ N (*film*) western *m inv*; (*novel*) romanzo *m* western *inv*

Western Australia N Australia occidentale
 ▷ www.wa.gov.au
 ▷ www.westernaustralia.net

Western Cape N Capo occidentale
 ▷ www.capegateway.gov.za/
 ▷ www.capetourism.org

west·ern·er ['wɛstənəʳ] N occidentale *m/f*

west·erni·za·tion [ˌwɛstənaɪ'zeɪʃən] N occidentalizzazione *f*

west·ern·ize ['wɛstəˌnaɪz] VT occidentalizzare

west·ern·ized ['wɛstəˌnaɪzd] ADJ occidentalizzato(-a)

west·ern·most ['wɛstənˌməʊst] ADJ il/la più occidentale; **the westernmost stretches of the desert** le distese più occidentali del deserto

West German ADJ, N tedesco(-a) occidentale
West Germany N Germania Occidentale
West Indian ADJ delle Indie Occidentali; **the West Indian team** la squadra caraibica; **the West Indian community** la comunità caraibica
■ N abitante *m/f* (*or* originario(-a)) delle Indie Occidentali
West Indies NPL: **the West Indies** le Indie Occidentali
West·min·ster ['wɛst,mɪnstəʳ] N il parlamento (britannico)
West Virginia N West Virginia *m*
▷ www.wv.gov/
west·ward ['wɛstwəd] ADJ (*direction*) ovest *inv*
■ ADV (*also:* **westwards**) a ovest, verso ovest
◎ **wet** [wɛt] ADJ (*comp* **-ter**, *superl* **-test**) **1** bagnato(-a); (*damp*) umido(-a); (*soaked*) fradicio(-a); (*paint, varnish, ink*) fresco(-a); **in wet clothes** coi vestiti bagnati; **to get wet** bagnarsi; **to be wet through** *or* **wet to the skin** essere fradicio(-a) fino alle ossa; **dripping wet** gocciolante; **he's still wet behind the ears** (*fig*) ha ancora il latte alla bocca **2** (*rainy*) piovoso(-a); **a wet day** una giornata piovosa; **wet weather** tempo piovoso; **it was wet all week** è piovuto tutta la settimana **3** (*fam pej: person*) smidollato(-a)
■ N **1** (*moisture*) umidità; (*rain*) pioggia; **it got left out in the wet** l'hanno lasciato fuori sotto la pioggia **2** (*fam pej: person*) smidollato(-a)
■ VT bagnare; **to wet the bed** bagnare il letto; **to wet one's pants** *or* **o.s.** farsela addosso
wet blanket N (*fig*) guastafeste *m/f inv*; **what a wet blanket you are!** (*fam*) che pesante che sei!
wet·ness ['wɛtnɪs] N umidità
wet nurse N balia
wet suit N muta (*da subacqueo*)
we've [wi:v] = **we have**
whack [wæk] N **1** (*blow*) (forte) colpo **2** (*fam: attempt*): **to have a whack at sth/at doing sth** provare qc/a fare qc, tentare qc/di fare qc **3** (*fam: share*) parte *f*, fetta **4** (*fam*): **to take a whack at sb** sputtanare pubblicamente qn **5** (*of money*) parte *f*; **to pay full whack for sth** pagare in pieno qc **6** **out of whack** sballato(-a)
■ VT (*person*) dare un ceffone a; (*ball*) colpire con forza; (*fam: defeat*) dare una batosta a
whacked [wækt] ADJ (*fam: exhausted*) sfinito(-a), stremato(-a)
whack·ing ['wækɪŋ] ADJ (*fam: also:* **whacking great**) enorme
■ N (*spanking*) sculacciata; (*fig*) batosta
whacky ['wækɪ] = **wacky**
whale [weɪl] N (*Zool*) balena; **we had a whale of a time** (*fam*) ci siamo divertiti da matti
whale·bone ['weɪl,bəʊn] N (*in corset*) stecca di balena
whale oil N olio di balena
whal·er ['weɪləʳ] N (*person*) baleniere *m*; (*ship*) baleniera
whal·ing ['weɪlɪŋ] N caccia alla balena
whaling fleet N flotta baleniera
whaling industry N industria baleniera
whaling ship, whaling vessel N (nave *f*) baleniera
wham [wæm] EXCL (*fam*) bang
wharf [wɔ:f] N (*pl* **wharfs** *or* **wharves** [wɔ:vz]) banchina
wharf·age ['wɔ:fɪdʒ] N diritti *mpl* di ormeggio

◎ **what** [wɒt] KEYWORD
■ ADJ che, quale; **to what extent?** fino a che punto?; **buy what food you like** compra il cibo che vuoi; **what a fool I was!** che sciocco sono stato!; **what good would that do?** a che può servire?; **what little I had** il poco che avevo; **what a mess!** che disordine!; **what a nuisance!** che seccatura!; **for what reason?** per quale motivo?; **what time is it?** che ore sono?; **in what way did it strike you as odd?** in che cosa esattamente ti è sembrato strano?
■ PRON
1 (*interrogative*) che cosa, cosa, che; **what were you talking about?** di cosa stavate parlando?; **what is his address?** qual è il suo indirizzo?; **he asked me what she had said** mi ha chiesto che cosa avesse detto lei; **what is it (*or* he *etc*) called?** come si chiama?; **what will it cost?** quanto sarà? *or* costerà?; **what are you doing?** che *or* (che) cosa fai?; **what are you doing that for?** perché lo fai?; **what is that tool for?** a che *or* a cosa serve quello strumento?; **what's happening?** che *or* (che) cosa succede?; **it's WHAT?** come?, cosa?; **I don't know what to do** non so cosa fare; **what's the weather like?** che tempo fa?; **what's in there?** cosa c'è lì dentro?; **what is it now?** che c'è ora?; **tell me what you're thinking about** dimmi a cosa stai pensando; **tell us what you're laughing at** dicci perché stai ridendo; **what is the Italian for "book"?** come si dice "book" in italiano?; **what do you want now?** che cosa vuoi adesso?; **I wonder what he'll do now** mi chiedo cosa farà adesso
2 (*relative*) ciò che, quello che; **I saw what you did** ho visto quello che hai fatto; **is that what happened?** è andata così ?; **it's just what I wanted** è proprio ciò che volevo; **I know what, let's go to the cinema** sai cosa facciamo? – andiamo al cinema; **say what you like** di' quello che vuoi; **she's not what she was** non è più quella di una volta; **I tell you what, why not come back later?** sai cosa ti dico? perché non torniamo più tardi?; **what I want is a cup of tea** ciò che voglio adesso è una tazza di tè; **I saw what was on the table** ho visto quello che c'era sul tavolo; **he knows what's what** (*fam*) sa come stanno le cose; **I'll show her what's what!** le farò vedere io!
3 **what about me?** e io?; **what about doing ...?** cosa ne diresti di fare...; **what about a drink?** beviamo qualcosa?; **what about going to the cinema?** e se andassimo al cinema?; **... and what have you** (*fam*) ...e roba del genere; **you know John — yes, what about him?** conosci John — sì , perché?; **what about it?** (*what do you think*) cosa ne pensi?; **what about that money you owe me?** e quei soldi che mi devi?; **and what's more** e per di più; **...and what not** (*fam*) ... e così via; **so what** e allora?; **what with one thing and another** tra una cosa e l'altra
■ EXCL (*disbelieving*) cosa?!, come?!; **what, no coffee!** come, non c'è caffè?!

what-d'ye-call-her ['wɒtdtʃə'kɔ:ləʳ], **what's-her-name** ['wɒtsəneɪm] N (*fam*) cosa... come si chiama
what-d'ye-call-him ['wɒtdtʃə'kɔ:lɪm], **whats-his-name** ['wɒtsɪzneɪm] N (*fam*) coso(-a)
what-d'ye-call it ['wɒtdtʃə'kɔ:l,ɪt], **what·sit** ['wɒtsɪt], **what's-its-name** ['wɒtsɪtsneɪm] N (*fam*) coso, aggeggio
◎ **what·ev·er** [wɒt'ɛvəʳ] PRON **1** (*anything that*) (tutto) ciò che, (tutto) quello che; (*no matter what*) qualsiasi *or* qualunque cosa + *sub*; **do whatever you want** fa' quello *or* ciò che vuoi; **do whatever is necessary** fai qualunque cosa sia necessaria, fai tutto quello che è

Ww

necessario; **whatever happens** qualsiasi *or* qualunque cosa succeda; **whatever it costs** costi quel che costi; **or whatever they're called** o come caspita si chiamano **2** (*emphatic*): **whatever do you mean?** cosa vorresti dire?; **whatever did you do that for?** perché mai l'hai fatto?

■ ADJ, ADV (*any*): **whatever book you choose** qualsiasi *or* qualunque libro tu scelga; (*all*): **give me whatever money you've got** dammi i soldi che hai; **nothing whatever** proprio niente; **it's no use whatever** non serve proprio a nulla; **for whatever reason** per qualunque ragione; **no reason whatever** *or* **whatsoever** nessuna ragione al mondo; **there was no reason whatever for the attack** non c'era nessuna ragione al mondo per attaccare

what·so·ev·er [ˌwɒtsəʊˈɛvəʳ] = whatever

wheat [wiːt] N grano, frumento

wheat·ear [ˈwiːtˌɪəʳ] N (*Zool*) culbianco

wheat·en [ˈwiːtn] ADJ di frumento, di grano

wheat·germ [ˈwiːtˌdʒɜːm] N germe *m* di grano

wheat·meal [ˈwiːtˌmiːl] N *tipo di farina integrale di frumento*

whee·dle [ˈwiːdl] VT: **to wheedle sb into doing sth** convincere qn a fare qc con lusinghe; **to wheedle sth out of sb** (*favour etc*) ottenere qc da qn con lusinghe; (*secret, name*) farsi dire qc da qn con lusinghe

whee·dling [ˈwiːdlɪŋ] ADJ (*voice, tone*) suadente

■ N lusinghe *fpl*

◎ **wheel** [wiːl] N (*gen*) ruota; (*also:* **steering wheel**) volante *m*; (*Naut*) timone *m*; (*also:* **potter's wheel**) tornio da vasaio; (*also:* **spinning wheel**) filatoio; **at the wheel** (*Aut*) al volante; (*Naut*) al timone; **the front wheel** la ruota anteriore; **this car is a four-wheel drive** questa è una macchina a quattro ruote motrici; **to take the wheel** prendere il volante; (*Naut*) prendere il timone; **the wheel of fortune** la ruota della fortuna; **the wheels of government** gli ingranaggi dello stato; **there are wheels within wheels** (*fig*) è più complesso di quello che sembra; **to put one's shoulder to the wheel** (*fig*) darci dentro; **the wheel has come** *or* **turned full circle** (*fig*) la fortuna è girata

■ VT (*push: bicycle, pram etc*) spingere; **we wheeled it over to the window** l'abbiamo spinto verso la finestra

■ VI (*birds*) roteare; **to wheel left** (*Mil*) fare una conversione a sinistra; **to wheel round** (*person*) girarsi sui tacchi, voltarsi; **to wheel and deal** (*fam*) trafficare

wheel·bar·row [ˈwiːlˌbærəʊ] N carriola

wheel·base [ˈwiːlˌbeɪs] N (*Aut*) interasse *m*, passo

wheel·chair [ˈwiːlˌtʃɛəʳ] N sedia a rotelle

wheel clamp N (*Brit*) ceppo bloccaruota

wheeled [wiːld] ADJ a ruote; **a three-wheeled car** un'auto a tre ruote

wheeler-dealer [ˈwiːləˌdiːləʳ] N trafficone(-a)

wheel·house [ˈwiːlˌhaʊs] N (*Naut*) timoneria

wheelie bin [ˈwɪːlɪˌbɪn] N cassonetto (*con le ruote*)

wheel·ing [ˈwiːlɪŋ] N: **wheeling and dealing** traffici *mpl*

wheel·wright [ˈwiːlˌraɪt] N carradore *m*

wheeze [wiːz] VI ansimare

■ N respiro affannoso

wheezy [ˈwiːzɪ] ADJ (*comp* **-ier**, *superl* **-iest**) (*person*) chi respira con affanno; (*breath*) sibilante

whelk [wɛlk] N (*Zool*) buccino

whelp [wɛlp] N cucciolo

◎ **when** [wɛn] KEYWORD

■ ADV quando; **when did it happen?** quando è successo?; **I know when it happened** lo so io quando è successo; **say when!** (*pouring drinks*) dimmi (quando) basta; **since when do you like Indian food?** da quando (in qua) ti piace la cucina indiana?

■ CONJ

1 (*at, during or after the time that*) quando; **when I came in** quando sono entrato; **be careful when you cross the road** *or* **when crossing the road** stai attento quando attraversi la strada; **even when** anche quando; **when it's finished, it will measure ...** quando sarà finito misurerà...; **when you've read it** quando l'hai *or* avrai letto; **why walk when you can take a bus?** perché camminare se puoi andare in autobus?

2 (*the time that*): **she told me about when she was in Milan** mi parlò di quando era a Milano; **that was when I needed you** era allora che avevo bisogno di te; **that's when the train arrives** il treno arriva a quell'ora

3 (*relative: in, on or at which*) in cui; **on the day when** il giorno in cui; **one day when it was raining** un giorno che pioveva; **at the very moment when ...** proprio quando...; **during the time when she lived abroad** nel periodo in cui viveva all'estero; **in the winter when ...** nell'inverno in cui...

4 (*whereas, although*) mentre, sebbene; **you call the policy rigid, when in fact it is very flexible** la definisci rigida, mentre in realtà è una politica molto flessibile

whence [wɛns] ADV (*liter: from where*) da dove

◎ **when·ever** [wɛnˈɛvəʳ] CONJ **1** (*rel: at whatever time*) quando, in qualsiasi momento + *sub*; (*every time that*) quando, ogni volta che; **come whenever you like** vieni quando vuoi; **leave whenever it suits you** parti quando ti fa comodo *or* in qualsiasi momento ti faccia comodo; **I go whenever I can** ci vado quando posso; **whenever you see one of those, stop** fermati quando ne vedi uno **2** (*in questions*): **whenever did I say that?** quando mai l'ho detto?

■ ADV: **tomorrow or whenever** domani o in un altro momento; **... last month, or whenever it was ...** lo scorso mese, o non ricordo quando; **last week or whenever** la settimana scorsa o non so più quando

◎ **where** [wɛəʳ] ADV dove; **where are you from?** di dove sei?; **where am I?** dove sono?; **where do you live?** dove abiti?; **where are you going (to)?** dove stai andando?; **where have you come from?** da dove sei venuto?; **did he tell you where he was going?** ti ha detto dove andava?; **where should we be if ...?** dove saremmo se...?

■ CONJ **1** (*gen*) dove; **there's a cinema where the butcher's used to be** dove una volta c'era la macelleria ora c'è un cinema; **where possible** quando è possibile, se possibile; **from where I'm standing it looks fine** da dove sono, mi sembra vada bene; **so that's where they've got to!** ecco dove erano finiti!; **this is where we found it** è qui che l'abbiamo trovato; **that's where we got to in the last lesson** è qui che siamo arrivati nell'ultima lezione; **that's just where you're wrong!** è proprio lì che ti sbagli!; **sometimes a teacher will be listened to, where a parent might not** qualche volta si è più disposti ad ascoltare un insegnante che un genitore **2** (*rel: in, on, at which*) dove, in (*or* da, su *etc*) cui; **the town where we come from** la città da cui veniamo; **the house where I was**

born la casa in cui sono nato; **the hill where the heather grows** la collina dove *or* su cui cresce l'erica

where·abouts ['wɛərə,bauts] ADV dove; **whereabouts did you say you lived?** da che parte hai detto che abiti?

■ NPL: **to know sb's whereabouts** sapere dove si trova qn; **his current whereabouts are unknown** non si sa dove si trovi attualmente

◎ **where·as** [wɛər'æz] CONJ (*while on the other hand*) mentre; (*Law*) considerato che

where·by [wɛə'baɪ] ADV (*frm*) per cui

where·fore ['wɛə,fɔː] N *see* **why** N

where·in [wɛər'ɪn] ADV (*frm*) dove

where·upon [,wɛərə'pɒn] ADV (*frm*) al che, dopo di che

wher·ever [wɛər'ɛvəʳ] CONJ dovunque + *sub*; **wherever you go I'll go too** dovunque tu vada andrò anch'io; **some people have a good time wherever they are** alcune persone si divertono dovunque siano; **wherever they went they were cheered** venivano acclamati dovunque andassero; **Udine, wherever that is** un posto che non so dove sia ma che si chiama Udine; **sit wherever you like** siediti dove vuoi

■ ADV **1 in Naples, Florence, or wherever** a Napoli, Firenze o in qualche altro posto **2** (*in questions*) dove; **wherever did he put it?** dove (mai) l'ha messo?

where·with·al ['wɛəwɪð,ɔːl] N: **the wherewithal (to do sth)** i mezzi *mpl* (per fare qc)

whet [wɛt] VT (*tool*) affilare; (*appetite, curiosity*) stuzzicare

◎ **wheth·er** ['wɛðəʳ] CONJ (*if*) se; (*no matter whether*) che + *sub*; **whether you want to or not** che tu voglia o no; **whether it's sunny or not** che ci sia il sole o no; **I am not certain whether he'll come (or not)** non so con certezza se verrà (o no), non sono sicuro che venga; **whether they come or not** che vengano o meno; **I don't know whether you know ...** non so se lo sai...; **I doubt whether that's true** dubito che sia vero; **I don't know whether to accept or not** non so se accettare o no; **it's doubtful whether** è poco probabile che

whet·stone ['wɛt,stəun] N cote *f*

whew [hwjuː] EXCL uuh!

whey [weɪ] N siero

◎ **which** [wɪtʃ] KEYWORD

■ ADJ

1 (*interrogative*) quale; **which book do you want?** quale libro vuoi?; **she didn't say which books she wanted** non ha detto quali libri voleva; **which books are yours?** quali sono i tuoi libri?; **tell me which one you want** dimmi quale vuoi; **which one of you?** chi di voi?; **which one/ones do you want?** quale/quali vuoi?; **which way did she go?** da che parte è andata?

2 in which case nel qual caso; **he lived in Italy for a year, during which time ...** ha vissuto in Italia per un anno, periodo in cui...; **by which time** e a quel punto

■ PRON

1 (*interrogative: the one or ones that*) quale; **I know which I'd rather have** io lo so quale preferirei; **I don't mind which** non mi importa quale; **which of these are yours?** quali di questi sono tuoi?; **which of your sisters?** quale delle tue sorelle?; **which of you?** chi di voi?; **which do you want?** quale vuoi?; **I can't tell which is which** non riesco a distinguere l'uno dall'altro

2 (*relative: that*) che; (*indirect*) cui, il/la quale; **the book about which** il libro del quale *or* di cui; **after which** dopo di che; **the apple (which) you ate** la mela che hai mangiato; **the apple which is on the table** la mela che è sul tavolo; **the hotel at which we stayed** l'albergo in cui abbiamo soggiornato; **from which one can deduce ...** dal che si può dedurre...; **he said he was there, which is true** ha detto che c'era, il che è vero; **the meeting (which) we attended** la riunione a cui abbiamo partecipato; **the chair on which** la sedia sulla quale *or* su cui; **you're late, which reminds me ...** sei in ritardo, il che mi fa venire in mente...; **it rained a lot, which upset her** ha piovuto tanto e ciò l'ha irritata

which·ever [wɪtʃ'ɛvəʳ] ADJ (*that one which*) quello(-a) che; (*no matter which*) qualsiasi + *sub*, qualunque + *sub*; **take whichever one you prefer** prendi quello che preferisci; **take whichever book you prefer** prendi il libro che preferisci; **whichever book you take** qualsiasi libro tu prenda; **you can choose whichever system you want** puoi scegliere il sistema che vuoi; **whichever system you have there are difficulties** qualsiasi sistema tu abbia ci sono delle difficoltà; **whichever way you ...** in qualunque modo tu...; **whichever way you look at it** da qualunque punto di vista lo si consideri

■ PRON (*the one which*) quello(-a) che; (*no matter which one*) qualsiasi + *sub*, qualunque + *sub*; **whichever of the methods you choose** qualsiasi *or* qualunque metodo tu scelga; **choose whichever you like** scegli quello che ti piace

whiff [wɪf] N (*of gas, sth unpleasant*) zaffata; (*of sea air, perfume*) odore *m*; **to catch a whiff of sth** sentire l'odore di qc; **a few whiffs of this could knock you out** se annusi un po' di questo svieni

◎ **while** [waɪl] N **1 a while** un po' (di tempo); **for a little while** per un po'; **for a long while** per un bel po', a lungo; **after a while** dopo un po'; **for a while** per un po', per un certo periodo; **I lived in London for a while** ho abitato a Londra per un po'; **in a while** tra poco; **once in a while** ogni tanto, una volta ogni tanto; **it will be a good while before he gets here** gli ci vorrà un bel po' (di tempo) per arrivare qui; **a little while ago** poco fa; **he was here a while ago** era qui poco fa; **in between whiles** nel frattempo; **quite a while** diverso tempo; **I haven't seen him for quite a while** è da diverso tempo che non lo vedo; **all the while** tutto il tempo **2 we'll make it worth your while** faremo in modo che non ti penta; **it might be worth your while to ...** forse ti converrebbe...

■ CONJ **1** (*during the time that*) mentre; (*as long as*) finché, mentre; **while this was happening** mentre avveniva questo; **she fell asleep while reading** si addormentò mentre stava leggendo; **it won't happen while I'm here** non accadrà finché sono qui io; **you hold the torch while I look inside** tieni la pila mentre io guardo dentro **2** (*although*) benché + *sub*, sebbene + *sub*, anche se; **while I agree with what you have said** benché sia d'accordo *or* anche se sono d'accordo con ciò che hai detto; **while this may seem expensive, it's worth it** anche se può sembrare costoso, vale la spesa **3** (*whereas*) mentre; **I enjoy sport, while he prefers reading** a me piace lo sport, mentre lui preferisce la lettura; **Isobel is very dynamic, while Kay is more laid-back** Isobel è molto attiva mentre Kay è più tranquilla

▸ **while away** VT + ADV (*time, hours*) far passare

Ww

while-you-wait [ˌwaɪlju:ˈweɪt] ADJ: **"while-you-wait shoe repairs"** "riparazioni lampo" *(di scarpe)*
◎**whilst** [waɪlst] CONJ = **while** CONJ
whim [wɪm] N capriccio; **a passing whim** una passione momentanea; **as the whim takes me** come mi gira
whim·per [ˈwɪmpəʳ] N *(of person)* gemito; (: *whine)* piagnucolio; *(of dog)* mugolio
■VI *(see n)* gemere; piagnucolare; mugolare
whim·per·ing [ˈwɪmpərɪŋ] N *(of person)* gemiti *mpl*, piagnucolio; *(of dog)* mugolio
■ADJ *(see n)* gemente, piagnucoloso(-a); mugolante
whim·si·cal [ˈwɪmzɪkəl] ADJ *(person)* particolare; *(look)* curioso(-a); *(idea, story)* fantasioso(-a); **a whimsical smile** uno strano sorrisetto
whim·si·cal·ly [ˈwɪmzɪkəlɪ] ADV *(describe)* in modo fantastico; *(smile, look)* curiosamente
whin [wɪn] N *(Bot)* ginestrone *m*
whin·chat [ˈwɪnˌtʃæt] N *(Zool)* staccino
whine [waɪn] N *(of dog)* guaito; *(of child)* piagnucolio; *(of engine)* sibilo; *(of bullet)* fischio
■VI *(dog)* guaire; *(child)* piagnucolare; *(engine)* sibilare; *(bullet)* fischiare; *(fig fam: complain)* piagnucolare, lamentarsi; **don't come whining to me about it** non venire a piangere da me
whinge [wɪndʒ] VI: **whinge about** *(fam pej)*: **to whinge (about)** frignare (per), lamentarsi (di)
whin·ing [ˈwaɪnɪŋ] N *(of dog)* guaito; *(of child)* piagnucolio; *(of engine)* sibilo; *(fam: complaining)* lamentele *fpl*
■ADJ *(dog)* che guaisce; *(child)* piagnucoloso(-a); *(engine)* sibilante
whin·ny [ˈwɪnɪ] VI nitrire
■N nitrito
◎**whip** [wɪp] N **1** frusta; *(also:* **riding whip)** frustino **2** *(Parliament: person)* capogruppo; **three-line whip** ordine *m* tassativo di votare **3** *(Culin)* mousse *f inv*
■VT **1** frustare, fustigare; *(Culin: cream etc)* montare; **whip the cream** montare la panna; **whip the egg whites** sbattere gli albumi **2** *(fam: move quickly)*: **he whipped the book off the table** tolse rapidamente il libro dal tavolo; **they whipped her into hospital** la portarono d'urgenza all'ospedale; **he whipped a gun out of his pocket** estrasse fulmineamente una pistola dalla tasca; **the car whipped round the corner** la macchina svoltò l'angolo a gran velocità
■VI: **to whip along/away** *etc* fare una corsa; **she whipped round when she heard me** si voltò di scatto quando mi sentì
▶ **whip up** VT + ADV *(cream)* montare, sbattere; *(fam: meal)* improvvisare; (: *stir up: support, feeling)* suscitare

WHIP

Nel Parlamento britannico i **whips** sono parlamentari incaricati di mantenere la disciplina tra i deputati del loro partito durante le votazioni e di verificare la loro presenza in aula.

▷ www.publicwhip.org.uk/

whip hand N: **to have the whip hand (over sb)** avere il predominio (su qn)
whip·lash [ˈwɪpˌlæʃ] N *(blow from whip)* frustata; *(Med: also:* **whiplash injury)** colpo di frusta
whipped cream [ˌwɪptˈkri:m] N panna montata
whip·per·snap·per [ˈwɪpəˌsnæpəʳ] N *(also:* **young whippersnapper)** piccolo(-a) impertinente
whip·pet [ˈwɪpɪt] N piccolo levriero inglese
whip·ping [ˈwɪpɪŋ] N: **to give sb a whipping** dare delle frustate *fpl* a qn
whipping boy N *(fig)* capro espiatorio
whipping cream N panna da montare
whip-round [ˈwɪpˌraʊnd] N *(Brit fam)* colletta; **to have a whip-round for sb** fare una colletta per qn
whip·stitch [ˈwɪpˌstɪtʃ] N sopraggitto
whirl [wɜ:l] N *(spin)* vortice *m*, turbinio; *(of dust, water etc)* turbine *m*; *(of cream)* ricciolo; **my head is in a whirl** mi gira la testa; **the social whirl** il vortice della vita mondana; **let's give it a whirl** *(fam)* facciamo un tentativo
■VT *(also:* **whirl round**: *dance partner)* far roteare, far volteggiare; **the wind whirled the leaves** il vento ha sollevato le foglie in un vortice; **he whirled us round the town** ci ha fatto visitare la città a tutta velocità *or* in un baleno; **he whirled us off to the theatre** ci trascinò con sé al teatro
■VI *(also:* **whirl round**: *wheel, merry-go-round)* girare; (: *dancers)* volteggiare; (: *leaves, dust)* sollevarsi in un vortice; **the countryside whirled past us** la campagna sfrecciava accanto a noi; **the dancers whirled past us** i danzatori passarono accanto a noi volteggiando; **my head was whirling** mi girava la testa
whirl·pool [ˈwɜ:lˌpu:l] N mulinello, vortice *m*
whirl·wind [ˈwɜ:lˌwɪnd] N tromba d'aria, turbine *m*
■ADJ *(romance etc)* travolgente
whirr, **whir** [wɜ:ʳ] N *(of insect wings, machine)* ronzio
■VI ronzare
whisk [wɪsk] N *(Culin: also:* **hand whisk)** frusta, frullino a mano; (: *also:* **electric whisk)** frullino elettrico; **with a whisk of its tail** con un colpo di coda
■VT **1** *(Culin)* frullare, sbattere; (: *egg whites)* montare a neve; **whisk the yolks with the sugar** sbattere i tuorli e lo zucchero **2** **whisk the eggs into the mixture** incorporare le uova all'impasto mescolando energicamente; **he was whisked away in a police car** è stato trascinato via in una macchina della polizia; **the horse whisked the flies away with its tail** il cavallo scacciava le mosche con la coda; **the waiter whisked the dishes away** il cameriere tolse in fretta i piatti; **they whisked him off to a meeting** lo trascinarono di gran fretta a una riunione
whisk·ers [ˈwɪskəz] NPL *(also:* **side whiskers)** basette *fpl*; *(beard)* barba; *(moustache, of animal)* baffi *mpl*
whis·ky, *(Am)* **whis·key** [ˈwɪskɪ] N whisky *m inv*; **a whisky and soda** un whisky e soda
▷ www.scotchwhisky.net
◎**whis·per** [ˈwɪspəʳ] N **1** *(gen)* sussurro, bisbiglio; *(of leaves)* fruscio, stormire *m*; **to speak in a whisper** bisbigliare **2** *(rumour)* voce *f*
■VT bisbigliare, sussurrare; **to whisper sth to sb** bisbigliare qc a qn
■VI *(gen)* bisbigliare; *(leaves)* frusciare, stormire; **to whisper to sb** bisbigliare a qn
whis·per·ing [ˈwɪspərɪŋ] N bisbiglio; *(of leaves)* fruscio; **there's been a lot of whispering about her** sono corse parecchie voci sul suo conto
whispering campaign N campagna diffamatoria
whispering gallery N galleria acustica
whist [wɪst] N whist *m*
whist drive N torneo di whist
whis·tle [ˈwɪsl] N *(sound)* fischio; *(instrument)*

fischietto; **the referee blew his whistle** l'arbitro fischiò; **the police searched him, but he was as clean as a whistle** la polizia lo ha perquisito ma lui era pulito; **the handle broke off as clean as a whistle** il manico si è staccato di netto; **to blow the whistle on** (*inform on*) fare una soffiata su
■ VT: **to whistle a tune** fischiettare un motivetto
■ VI (*gen*) fischiare; (*in low tone*) fischiettare; **he whistled for a taxi** fischiò per fermare un taxi; **the referee whistled for a foul** l'arbitro fischiò un fallo; **the bullet whistled past my ear** la pallottola mi fischiò vicino all'orecchio; **he's whistling in the dark** (*fig*) lo fa (*or* dice) per darsi coraggio; **he can whistle for it!** (*fig fam*) se lo può sognare!
▸ **whistle up** VT + ADV (*taxi, dog*) fare un fischio a

whistle-blower ['wɪsl,bləʊəʳ] N *persona che scopre e denuncia gli illeciti dell'azienda per cui lavora*

whistle-blowing ['wɪsl,bləʊɪŋ] N *denuncia degli illeciti dell'azienda per cui si lavora*

whistle-stop ['wɪsl,stɒp] ADJ: **whistle-stop tour** (*Pol*) visita *f* lampo *inv* (*in una città nel corso di una campagna elettorale*)

Whit [wɪt] (*fam*) N Pentecoste *f*
■ ADJ (*holiday, weekend*) di Pentecoste

whit [wɪt] N: **not a whit** neanche un po'; **not a whit of truth** neanche un briciolo di verità; **the place hasn't changed a whit** il posto non è cambiato affatto *or* per nulla

◎ **white** [waɪt] ADJ (*comp* **-er**, *superl* **-est**) (*gen*) bianco(-a), candido(-a); **to turn** *or* **go white** (*person*) sbiancare; (*hair*) diventare bianco(-a); **a white man** un bianco; **white people** i bianchi; **a white Christmas** un Natale con la neve; **the great white hope** (*fig*) la promessa numero uno; **to be as white as a sheet** essere bianco(-a) come un cencio; **as white as snow** niveo(-a), bianco *or* candido come la neve; **white with fear** pallido(-a) dalla paura; **it washes the clothes whiter than white** lava più bianco del bianco; **he's got white hair** ha i capelli bianchi
■ N **1** (*colour, of eyes*) bianco; (*of egg*) bianco, albume *m*; **the whites** (*washing*) i capi bianchi; **tennis whites** completo *msg* da tennis; **dressed in white** vestito(-a) di bianco; **her dress was a dazzling white** il suo abito era di un bianco abbagliante **2** (*person*) bianco(-a)

white·bait ['waɪt,beɪt] N bianchetti *mpl*

white·beam ['waɪt,bi:m] N sorbo comune

white bread N pane *m* bianco

white coffee N (*Brit*) caffè *m inv* con latte

white-collar ['waɪt,kɒləʳ] ADJ: **white-collar job** lavoro impiegatizio

white-collar worker N impiegato(-a), colletto bianco

white elephant N (*fam*) cattedrale *f* nel deserto

white-faced [,waɪt'feɪst] ADJ pallido(-a), bianco(-a)

white flag N bandiera bianca

white goods NPL (*appliances*) elettrodomestici *mpl*; (*linen*) biancheria *fsg* per la casa

white-haired [,waɪt'hɛəd] ADJ canuto(-a), dai capelli bianchi

◎ **White·hall** ['waɪt,hɔ:l] N (*street*) *strada londinese dove hanno sede i ministeri del governo inglese*; (*British Government*) il governo inglese

white horse N (*on wave*) cresta di spuma (dell'onda)

white-hot [,waɪt'hɒt] ADJ (*metal*) incandescente

◎ **White House** N (*Am*): **the White House** la Casa Bianca

WHITE HOUSE

La **White House** è la residenza ufficiale del presidente degli Stati Uniti e ha sede a Washington DC. Spesso il termine viene usato per indicare l'esecutivo del governo statunitense.
▹ www.whitehouse.gov/

white knight N (*Fin*) *persona o società che fa un'offerta ed evita che un'azienda in difficoltà venga rilevata da un'altra*

white-knuckle ['waɪt,nʌkl] ADJ spericolato(-a)

white lead N biacca

white lie N bugia pietosa, bugia innocua

white meat N carni *fpl* bianche

whit·en ['waɪtn] VT (*shoes*) dare il bianchetto a

white·ness ['waɪtnɪs] N (*gen*) bianco; (*of skin*) candore *m*; (*pallor*) biancore *m*

whit·en·ing ['waɪtnɪŋ] N (*substance*) bianchetto

white noise N (*Radio, TV*) sibilo (per interferenza)

White·out® ['waɪt,aʊt] N bianchetto

white·out ['waɪt,aʊt] N (*Met*): **there is a whiteout** tutto è coperto di neve

white paper N (*Pol*) ≈ libro bianco

white pepper N pepe *m* bianco

white sale N fiera del bianco

white sauce N besciamella

white spirit N acquaragia (sintetica)

white·thorn ['waɪt,θɔ:n] N biancospino

white·wash ['waɪt,wɒʃ] N (bianco di) calce *f*
■ VT (*wall*) imbiancare (con la calce); (*fig: person, sb's faults*) coprire; (*: motives*) dissimulare; (*: event, episode*) sminuire

white-water rafting [,waɪtwɔ:tə'rɑ:ftɪŋ] N (*Sport*) rafting *m*

white wedding N matrimonio in bianco

white wine N vino bianco

whith·er ['wɪðəʳ] ADV (*liter*) dove

whit·ing ['waɪtɪŋ] N INV (*fish*) merlango

whit·ish ['waɪtɪʃ] ADJ biancastro(-a), bianchiccio(-a)

whit·low ['wɪtləʊ] N patereccio

Whit Monday N lunedì *m inv* di Pentecoste

Whit·sun ['wɪtsən] N (*also:* **Whitsuntide**) Pentecoste *f*; (*week*) settimana di Pentecoste

Whit Sunday N Pentecoste *f*

whit·tle ['wɪtl] VT (*wood*) intagliare
▸ **whittle away** VT + ADV (*fig*) ridurre
▸ **whittle down** VT + ADV (*fig*) ridurre, tagliare

whiz, whizz [wɪz] VI (*motorbike, sledge etc*) sfrecciare; (*bullet*) sibilare; **to whiz through the air** sfrecciare; **cars were whizzing past** le macchine passavano sfrecciando

whiz kid N (*fam*) mago(-a)

WHO [,dʌblju:eɪtʃ'əʊ] N ABBR (= **World Health Organization**) OMS *f* (= *Organizzazione Mondiale della Sanità*)

◎ **who** [hu:] PRON **KEYWORD**
1 (*si può anche usare al posto di "whom" nella lingua parlata: interrogative*) chi; **who should it be but Graham!** chi poteva essere se non Graham!; **who's the book by?** chi è l'autore del libro?; **who are you looking for?** chi stai cercando?; **who is it?** chi è?; **I know who it was** io so chi è stato; **who's there?** chi è?; **who does she think she is?** (*fam*) chi si crede di essere?; **you'll soon find out who's who** presto li conoscerai
2 (*relative*) che; **my cousin who lives in New York** mio

Ww

cugino che vive a New York; **those who can swim** quelli che sanno nuotare, chi sa nuotare

whoa [wəʊ] EXCL (*also:* **whoa there**) altolà!
who'd [hu:d] = **who would, who had**
who·dun·it, whodunnit [hu:'dʌnɪt] N (*fam*) (romanzo) giallo
who·ever [hu:'ɛvəʳ] PRON **1** (*the person that, anyone that*) chiunque + *sub*, chi; (*no matter who*) chiunque + *sub*; **whoever said that was an idiot** chiunque l'abbia detto *or* chi l'ha detto è un idiota; **whoever finds it** chiunque lo trovi; **ask whoever you like** chiedi a chiunque; **invite whoever you like** invita chi vuoi; **it won't be easy, whoever does it** non sarà facile, chiunque lo faccia; **whoever she marries** chiunque lei sposi **2** (*in questions*) chi (mai); **whoever told you that?** chi (mai) te l'ha detto?
◎**whole** [həʊl] ADJ **1** (*entire*: + *sg n*) intero(-a), tutto(-a); (: + *pl n*) intero(-a); **with my whole heart** con tutto il mio cuore; **a whole lot of things** una gran quantità di cose, moltissime cose; **a whole lot of people** moltissima gente; **a whole lot better** molto meglio; **the whole lot** tutto; **the whole lot (of them)** tutti(-e); **3 whole days** 3 giorni interi; **the whole day** tutto il giorno, il giorno intero; **the whole afternoon** tutto il pomeriggio; **I read the whole book** ho letto tutto il libro *or* il libro per intero; **the whole world** tutto il mondo, il mondo intero; **the whole class** la classe intera; **a whole box of chocolates** un'intera scatola di cioccolatini; **whole villages were destroyed** interi paesi furono distrutti; **is that the whole truth?** è tutta la verità?; **but the whole purpose** *or* **point was to ...** ma lo scopo era proprio di... **2** (*intact, unbroken*) intero(-a); (: *series, set*) completo(-a); **to swallow sth whole** mandar giù qc intero(-a); (*fig*): **he swallowed it whole** l'ha bevuta tutta; **to our surprise he came back whole** con nostra sorpresa tornò sano e salvo
■ N **1** (*all*): **the whole of the film** tutto il film, il film intero; **the whole of the sum** la somma intera, l'intera somma; **the whole of the time** tutto il tempo; **the whole of August** tutto agosto; **the whole of Italy** tutta l'Italia, l'Italia intera; **the whole of Wales was affected** tutto il Galles è stato colpito; **the whole of the town** la città intera, tutta la città; **as a whole** nell'insieme, nel suo insieme; **on the whole** nel complesso **2** (*entire unit*) tutto; **they make a whole** formano un tutto; **two halves make a whole** due metà fanno un intero
whole·food ['həʊl,fu:d] N: **wholefoods** alimenti *mpl* integrali
■ ADJ: **wholefood diet** dieta a base di prodotti integrali
whole·hearted [,həʊl'hɑ:tɪd] ADJ (*approval, agreement*) incondizionato(-a), totale; (*thanks, congratulations*) sentito(-a), sincero(-a); **to be wholehearted in sth** fare qc di tutto cuore
whole·hearted·ly [,həʊl'hɑ:tɪdlɪ] ADV (*approve, agree*) incondizionatamente; (*thank, congratulate*) sentitamente, di tutto cuore; (*do, work, play*) con impegno, mettendoci l'anima
whole·meal ['həʊl,mi:l] ADJ (*Brit*: *flour, bread*) integrale; **wholemeal bread** pane *m* integrale
whole milk N latte *m* intero
whole note N (*Am Mus*) semibreve *f*
whole number N numero intero
whole·sale ['həʊlseɪl] ADJ (*prices, trade*) all'ingrosso; (*fig*: *slaughter, destruction*) in massa, totale; (*acceptance*) in blocco; (*modification*) su vasta scala; **wholesale prices** prezzi *mpl* all'ingrosso; **wholesale destruction** distruzione *f* su vasta scala; **his work came in for wholesale criticism** il suo lavoro è stato criticato in blocco
■ ADV (*see adj*) all'ingrosso; in massa; in blocco; su vasta scala
■ N commercio *or* vendita all'ingrosso
whole·sal·er ['həʊl,seɪləʳ] N grossista *m/f*
whole·some ['həʊlsəm] ADJ (*gen*) sano(-a); (*climate*) salubre
whole·wheat ['həʊl,wi:t] ADJ (*Am*) = **wholemeal**
who'll [hu:l] = **who will**
whol·ly ['həʊlɪ] ADV completamente, del tutto
wholly-owned subsidiary [,həʊlɪəʊndsəb'sɪdɪərɪ] N società interamente controllata

◎**whom** [hu:m] **KEYWORD**
PRON
1 (*spesso sostituito da "who" nella lingua parlata*: *interrogative*) chi; **from whom did you receive it?** da chi l'hai ricevuto?; **whom did you see?** chi hai visto?
2 (*relative*: *direct object*) che, *prep* + il/la quale; (: *indirect*) cui; **the man whom I saw** l'uomo che ho visto; **three policemen, none of whom wore a helmet** tre poliziotti, nessuno dei quali portava il casco; **those to whom I spoke** le persone con le quali ho parlato; **the lady with whom I was talking** la signora con cui stavo parlando

whoop [hu:p] N grido
■ VI gridare; (*Med*: *when coughing*) tossire in modo convulso
■ VT: **to whoop it up** (*fam*) fare baldoria
whoo·pee [wʊ'pi:] EXCL urrà!, evviva!
■ N: **to make whoopee** (*fam*) fare baldoria
whoop·ing cough ['hu:pɪŋ,kɒf] N pertosse *f*, tosse *f* asinina (*or* canina *or* cavallina)
whoops [wu:ps] EXCL (*also*: **whoops-a-daisy**: *avoiding fall etc*) ops!
whoosh [wuʃ] N: **it came out with a whoosh** (*sauce, water*) è uscito(-a) di getto; (*air*) è uscito(-a) con un sibilo
whop·per ['wɒpəʳ] N (*fam*: *large thing*) cosa enorme; (: *lie*) balla
whop·ping ['wɒpɪŋ] ADJ (*fam*: *also*: **whopping great**) enorme
whore [hɔ:ʳ] N (*pej*) puttana
whore·house ['hɔ:,haʊs] N (*old*) bordello
whorl [wɜ:l] N (*of shell*) voluta
who's [hu:z] = **who is, who has**

◎**whose** [hu:z] **KEYWORD**
■ POSS PRON di chi; **whose is this?** di chi è questo?; **I know whose it is** io lo so di chi è
■ POSS ADJ
1 (*interrogative*) di chi; **whose daughter are you?** di chi sei figlia?; **whose fault was it?** di chi era la colpa?; **whose hat is this?** di chi è questo cappello?; **whose pencil have you taken?** di chi è la matita che hai preso?
2 (*relative*) il/la cui; **the girl whose sister you were speaking to** la ragazza alla cui sorella stavi parlando; **the man whose wife I was talking to** l'uomo alla cui moglie stavo parlando; **the man whose son you rescued** l'uomo di cui hai salvato il figlio; **those whose passports I have** quelli di cui ho il passaporto;

the woman whose car was stolen la donna la cui macchina è stata rubata

Who's Who N chi è *m inv*

who've [hu:v] = who have

◎ **why** [waɪ] ADV, CONJ perché; **why is he always late?** perché è sempre in ritardo?; **I wonder why he said that** mi chiedo perché l'abbia detto; **why not do it now?** perché non farlo adesso?; **why did you do it?** perché l'hai fatto?; **why don't you come too?** perché non vieni anche tu?; **the reason why** il motivo per cui; **there's no reason why** non c'è motivo per cui + *sub*; **why (ever) not?** perché no?; **so that's why he did it!** ecco perché l'ha fatto!

■ EXCL (*surprise*) guarda guarda!, ma guarda un po'!; (*remonstrating*) ma via!; (*explaining*) ebbene!; **why, it's you!** guarda guarda, *or* ah sei tu!; **why, it's obvious!** ma via, è ovvio!

■ N: **the whys and (the) wherefores** le ragioni *or* i motivi; **the why and the how** il perché e il percome

WI N ABBR (*Brit*: = **Women's Institute**) *circolo femminile*

■ ABBR **1** (*Geog*) = **West Indies** **2** (*Am Post*) = **Wisconsin**

wick [wɪk] N stoppino, lucignolo

wick·ed ['wɪkɪd] ADJ (*person, remark, smile*) cattivo(-a), malvagio(-a); (*: mischievous*) malizioso(-a); (*satire*) sferzante; (*system, policy*) iniquo(-a); (*fam: price, weather etc*) allucinante; **she has a wicked temper** ha un caratteraccio; **that was a wicked thing to do** è stata una cattiveria; **a wicked blow** un brutto colpo; **a wicked sense of humour** un senso dell'umorismo un po' malizioso

wick·ed·ly ['wɪkɪdlɪ] ADV (*remark, smile, behave*) perfidamente, con cattiveria; (*roguishly*) maliziosamente; **wickedly expensive** terribilmente costoso; **a wickedly humorous play** una commedia maliziosamente spiritosa

wick·ed·ness ['wɪkɪdnɪs] N (*see adj*) cattiveria, malvagità; malizia; iniquità

wick·er ['wɪkə[r]] N vimini *mpl*

■ ADJ di vimini

wicker·work ['wɪkə,wɜ:k] N oggetti *mpl* di vimini

◎ **wick·et** ['wɪkɪt] (*Cricket*) N porta

wicket keeper N (*Cricket*) ≈ portiere *m*

◎ **wide** [waɪd] ADJ (*comp* **-er**, *superl* **-est**) (*gen*) largo(-a); (*publicity, margin*) ampio(-a); (*ocean, desert, region*) vasto(-a); (*fig: considerable: variety, choice*) grande, ampio(-a), vasto(-a); **it is 3 metres wide** è largo 3 metri; **his wide knowledge of the subject** la sua vasta conoscenza dell'argomento; **in the whole wide world** nel mondo intero, in tutto il mondo; **a wide road** una strada larga; **a wide choice of hotels** un'ampia scelta di alberghi; **the wide screen** il grande schermo

■ ADV (*aim, fall*) lontano dal bersaglio; **set wide apart** (*houses, eyes*) ben distanziato(-a); (*legs*) divaricato(-a); **to be wide open** (*door*) essere spalancato(-a); **to open wide** spalancare; **to shoot wide** tirare a vuoto *or* fuori bersaglio; **the ball went wide** la palla ha mancato il bersaglio; **to be wide open to criticism/attack** essere esposto(-a) alle critiche/agli attacchi

wide-angle lens [,waɪdæŋgl'lenz] N grandangolare *m*

wide-awake [,waɪdə'weɪk] ADJ completamente sveglio(-a); (*fig*) sveglio(-a)

wide boy N (*Brit fam*) truffatore *m*

wide-eyed [,waɪd'aɪd] ADJ con gli occhi spalancati

wide·ly ['waɪdlɪ] ADV (*distributed, scattered*) ampiamente, largamente; (*read etc*) molto; (*travel*) in lungo e in largo; (*differing*) molto, profondamente; (*popularly, by many people*) generalmente; **widely used** di largo uso; **to be widely read** (*author*) essere molto letto(-a); (*reader*) essere molto colto(-a); **it is widely believed that** è una credenza diffusa che; **widely-held opinions** opinioni molto diffuse; **to be widely spaced** (*houses, trees*) essere molto distanziati(-e); **it's widely available** è facilmente reperibile

wid·en ['waɪdn] VT (*also fig*) ampliare, allargare; **they're widening the road** stanno allargando la strada

■ VI (*also:* **widen out**) ampliarsi

wide·ness ['waɪdnɪs] N (*see adj*) larghezza; vastità; ampiezza

wide open ADJ (*door*) spalancato(-a); (*defences*) vulnerabile; (*outcome*) aperto(-a); **the door was wide open** la porta era spalancata

wide-ranging [,waɪd'reɪndʒɪŋ] ADJ (*survey, report*) vasto(-a); (*interests*) svariato(-a)

wide·screen ['waɪdskri:n] ADJ (*television*) a schermo panoramico

◎ **wide·spread** ['waɪd,sprɛd] ADJ (*disease, belief*) molto diffuso(-a); **there is widespread fear that ...** c'è una paura diffusa che...

widg·eon ['wɪdʒən] = **wigeon**

wid·ow ['wɪdəʊ] N vedova; **to be left a widow** restare vedova; **she is a golf widow** (*hum*) è una vedova del gioco del golf; **widow's peak** attaccatura dei capelli a forma di V (sulla fronte)

■ VT: **to be widowed** restare vedovo(-a)

wid·owed ['wɪdəʊd] ADJ (che è rimasto(-a)) vedovo(-a); **his widowed mother** sua madre (rimasta) vedova

wid·ow·er ['wɪdəʊə[r]] N vedovo

wid·ow·hood ['wɪdəʊhʊd] N vedovanza

width [wɪdθ] N (*see adj*) larghezza; ampiezza; (*of fabric*) altezza; **it's 7 metres in width** è largo 7 metri

width·ways ['wɪdθ,weɪz], **width·wise** ['wɪdθ,waɪz] ADV trasversalmente

wield [wi:ld] VT (*sword, axe*) maneggiare; (*: brandish*) brandire; (*power, influence*) esercitare

◎ **wife** [waɪf] N (*pl* **wives**) moglie *f*; **the wife** (*fam*) la padrona; **it's just an old wives' tale** è solo una superstizione

wife·ly ['waɪflɪ] ADJ coniugale, di moglie

wife-swapping ['waɪf,swɒpɪŋ] N scambio delle mogli

wig [wɪg] N parrucca

wig·eon ['wɪdʒən] N (*Zool*) fischione *m*

wig·ging ['wɪgɪŋ] N (*Brit fam old*) lavata di capo

wig·gle ['wɪgl] N: **with a wiggle of her hips** ancheggiando

■ VT (*fingers, loose tooth*) muovere; **to wiggle one's hips** ancheggiare

■ VI (*person*) dimenarsi, agitarsi; (*worm*) agitarsi, muoversi; (*tooth, loose screw*) tentennare

wig·gly ['wɪglɪ] ADJ (*line*) ondulato(-a), sinuoso(-a)

wig·wam ['wɪg,wæm] N wigwam *m inv*

◎ **wild** [waɪld] ADJ (*comp* **-er**, *superl* **-est**) **1** (*not domesticated: animal, plant*) selvatico(-a); (*horse*) brado(-a); (*countryside*) selvaggio(-a); **a wild animal** un animale selvatico; **in its wild state** allo stato selvatico; **to grow wild** (*plant*) crescere incolto(-a); **wild horses wouldn't make me tell you** (*fig*) non riuscirai a cavarmelo neanche con la forza; **to sow one's wild oats** (*fig*) correre la cavallina **2** (*rough: wind, weather*) violento(-a); (*sea, night*) tempestoso(-a) **3** (*unrestrained, disorderly: child*) turbolento(-a); (*appearance, look*) selvaggio(-a); (*eyes*) sbarrato(-a); (*hair*) incolto(-a); **to lead a wild life** fare una vita sregolata; **to run wild**

Ww

(*children*) scatenarsi **4** (*fam: angry*) fuori di sé; **to go wild** infuriarsi; **wild with indignation** fuori di sé dall'indignazione; **it makes me wild** mi manda su tutte le furie **5** (*fam: enthusiastic*): **to be wild about** andare pazzo(-a) per; **to be wild with joy** essere fuori di sé dalla gioia; **I'm not wild about the idea** non è che l'idea mi faccia impazzire; **to go wild (with)** non stare più in sé (da); **the audience went wild** la folla andò in delirio **6** (*rash, extravagant: idea*) folle; (*: laughter*) sguaiato(-a); (*erratic: shot, guess*) azzardato(-a); **it's a wild exaggeration** è una grossa esagerazione; **you've let your imagination run wild** hai lavorato troppo di fantasia

■ N: **the wild** la natura; **to live out in the wilds** (*hum*) vivere a casa del diavolo

wild card N (*Comput*) carattere *m* jolly *inv*; m inv (*fig*) incognita; (*Sport*) *permesso di partecipazione a una gara accordato a un giocatore che non si è qualificato*

wild·cat ['waɪld,kæt] N gatto(-a) selvatico(-a)

wildcat strike N sciopero (a gatto) selvaggio

wild cherry N (*tree*) ciliegio dolce; (*fruit*) ciliegia dolce

wil·de·beest ['wɪldɪ,bi:st] N gnu *m inv*

wil·der·ness ['wɪldənɪs] N (*gen*) deserto; (*neglected garden*) giungla; **the garden was a wilderness** il giardino era una giungla

wild·fire ['waɪld,faɪəʳ] N: **to spread like wildfire** diffondersi a macchia d'olio

wild·fowl ['waɪld,faʊl] NPL selvaggina *fsg* di penna

wild goat N capra selvatica

wild-goose chase [,waɪld'gu:s,tʃeɪs] N (*fig*): **to be on a wild-goose chase** seguire una pista falsa

wild·life ['waɪld,laɪf] N natura, flora e fauna

■ ADJ (*sanctuary, reserve*) naturale

wild·ly ['waɪldlɪ] ADV (*gen*) violentemente; (*behave*) in modo sfrenato; (*talk*) fervorosamente; (*rush around*) come un(-a) pazzo(-a); (*exaggerate*) largamente; (*applaud, cheer*) freneticamente; **to guess wildly** tirare a indovinare; **wildly happy/enthusiastic** terribilmente felice/entusiasta; **her heart was beating wildly** il cuore le batteva forte

wild·ness ['waɪldnɪs] N (*gen*) violenza; (*of countryside, scenery*) aspetto selvaggio; (*of the weather*) avversità; **the wildness of his appearance** il suo aspetto selvaggio; **the wildness of her imagination** la sua fervida immaginazione

Wild West N: **the Wild West** il far West

wiles [waɪlz] NPL astuzie *fpl*

wil·ful, (*Am*) **will·ful** ['wɪlfʊl] ADJ (*deliberate: act*) intenzionale, premeditato(-a); (*self-willed*) testardo(-a), ostinato(-a)

wil·ful·ly, (*Am*) **will·ful·ly** ['wɪlfəlɪ] ADV (*see adj*) intenzionalmente, premeditatamente; testardamente

wil·ful·ness ['wɪlfʊlnɪs] N testardaggine *f*

◎ **will¹** [wɪl] KEYWORD

(*pt* **would**)

■ MODAL AUX VB

1 (*forming future tense*): **will you be there?** ci sarai?; **he will come** verrà; **will you do it? — yes, I will/no, I won't** lo farai? — sì (lo farò)/no (non lo farò); **I will finish it tomorrow** lo finirò domani; **I will have finished it by tomorrow** lo finirò entro domani; **you won't lose it, will you?** non lo perderai, vero?

2 (*in conjectures*): **he will** *or* **he'll be there by now** dovrebbe essere arrivato ormai; **that will be the postman** sarà il postino

3 (*in commands, requests, offers*): **will you be quiet!** vuoi fare silenzio?; **will you come?** vieni?; **won't you come with us?** non vuoi venire con noi?; **will you have a cup of tea?** vorresti una tazza di tè?; **will you help me?** mi puoi aiutare?; **I won't go — oh yes you will, my lad!** non ci andrò — oh sì che ci andrai, ragazzo mio!; **I will not** *or* **won't put up with it!** non intendo tollerarlo!; **will you sit down** (*politely*) prego, si accomodi; (*angrily*) vuoi metterti seduto!

4 (*expressing habits, persistence, capability*): **the car will do 100 mph** la macchina fa 100 miglia all'ora; **accidents will happen** gli incidenti possono capitare; **he will often sit there for hours** spesso rimane seduto lì per ore; **the car won't start** la macchina non parte; **he WILL fidget!** e continua a muoversi!

■ VI (*wish*) volere; **(just) as you will!** come vuoi!; **say what you will** di' quello che vuoi

will² [wɪl] N **1** volontà; **to have a will of one's own** avere una volontà indipendente; **to do sth of one's own free will** fare qc di propria volontà; **the will to win/live** la voglia di vincere/vivere; **against sb's will** contro la volontà *or* il volere di qn; **at will** a volontà; **to work with a will** lavorare di buona lena; **with the best will in the world** con tutta la più buona volontà del mondo; **where there's a will there's a way** volere è potere; **a strong will** una forte volontà **2** (*testament*) testamento; **the last will and testament of** le ultime volontà di; **to make a will** fare testamento; **he made a will** ha fatto testamento

■ VT **1** (*urge on by willpower*): **to will sb to do sth** pregare (tra sé) perché qn faccia qc; **he willed himself to stay awake** si costrinse a restare sveglio; **he willed himself to go on** andò avanti con un grande sforzo di volontà **2** (*leave in one's will*): **to will sth to sb** lasciare qc a qn in eredità

wil·lie, **wil·ly** ['wɪlɪ] N (*Brit fam*) pisello (*fig*)

wil·lies ['wɪlɪz] NPL (*fam*): **it gives me the willies** mi fa venire i brividi

◎ **will·ing** ['wɪlɪŋ] ADJ **1** (*obedience, help*) spontaneo(-a); (*helper, worker*) volenteroso(-a); **a willing pupil** un alunno volenteroso; **he's very willing** è pieno di buona volontà; **there were plenty of willing hands** erano tutti disposti a dare una mano **2** **to be willing (to do sth)** essere disposto(-a) (a fare qc); **he wasn't very willing to help me** non aveva una gran voglia di aiutarmi; **God willing** se Dio vuole

■ N: **to show willing** mostrarsi disponibile

will·ing·ly ['wɪlɪŋlɪ] ADV volentieri

will·ing·ness ['wɪlɪŋnɪs] N disponibilità, buona volontà; **I don't doubt her willingness** non metto in dubbio la sua buona volontà

will-o'-the-wisp [,wɪləðə'wɪsp] N (*also fig*) fuoco fatuo

wil·low ['wɪləʊ] N (*also:* **willow tree**) salice *m*; **white willow** salice bianco

wil·low·herb ['wɪləʊ,hɜ:b] N epilobio

willow pattern N motivo cinese (*in blu su ceramica bianca*)

wil·lowy ['wɪləʊɪ] ADJ slanciato(-a)

will·power ['wɪl,paʊəʳ] N forza di volontà

wil·ly ['wɪlɪ] = willie

willy-nilly [,wɪlɪ'nɪlɪ] ADV volente o nolente

wilt [wɪlt] VI (*flower*) appassire; (*fig: person*) crollare; (*: effort, enthusiasm*) diminuire

Wilts [wɪlts] ABBR (*Brit*) = *Wiltshire*

wily ['waɪlɪ] ADJ (*comp* **-ier**, *superl* **-iest**) astuto(-a), furbo(-a); **he's a wily old devil** *or* **bird** *or* **fox** (*fam*) è una vecchia volpe, è un furbo matricolato *or* di tre cotte

wimp [wɪmp] N (*fam*) pappamolle *m/f*
wim·ple ['wɪmpl] N soggolo
◎ **win** [wɪn] (*vb: pt, pp* **won**) N (*in sports etc*) vittoria; **their fifth win in a row** la quinta vittoria consecutiva
■ VT (*battle, race, cup, prize*) vincere; (*victory*) conquistare, aggiudicarsi; (*sympathy, popularity, support, friendship*) conquistare, ottenere; (*person*) accattivarsi, conquistare; (*contract*) aggiudicarsi; **I won £20 from him** gli ho vinto 20 sterline; **to win sb's favour/heart** conquistare il favore/cuore di qn; **she won it at tennis** l'ha vinto a tennis; **it won him first prize** gli ha valso il primo premio; **did you win?** hai vinto?; **he won a gold medal** ha vinto una medaglia d'oro; **to win the lottery** vincere alla lotteria; **he won the support of the poor** si è conquistato il sostegno dei poveri; **to win a victory** aggiudicarsi una vittoria; **to win the day** (*Mil, fig*) avere il sopravvento
■ VI vincere; **O.K., you win** (*fam*) va bene, ti do ragione
▸ **win back** VT + ADV riconquistare
▸ **win over**, **win round** VT + ADV convincere; **we won him over to our point of view** l'abbiamo convinto ad accettare il nostro punto di vista
▸ **win out**, **win through** VI + ADV uscirne vittorioso(-a)
wince [wɪns] N: **to give a wince** rabbrividire; (*grimace*) smorfia
■ VI rabbrividire; (*grimace*) fare una smorfia (*di dolore*); **he winced at the thought** rabbrividì al pensiero
win·cey·ette [ˌwɪnsɪ'ɛt] N cotone *m* felpato
winch [wɪntʃ] N argano, verricello
■ VT: **to winch up/down** sollevare/abbassare con un argano
◎ **wind**[1] [wɪnd] N **1** vento; **high** *or* **strong wind** vento forte; **the wind is in the west** il vento viene da ponente; **into** *or* **against the wind** controvento; **to go like the wind** filare come il vento; **to run before the wind** (*Naut*) andare con il vento in poppa; **there's something in the wind** (*fig*) c'è qualcosa nell'aria; **to get wind of sth** venire a sapere qc; **to get** *or* **have the wind up** (*fam*) agitarsi; **to take the wind out of sb's sails** smontare qn, spegnere l'entusiasmo di qn; **to sail close to the wind** (*fig*) spingere le cose troppo in là; (*act almost illegally*) rasentare l'illegalità; (*risk causing offence*) rischiare di offendere; **to throw caution to the winds** gettare la prudenza alle ortiche **2** (*flatulence*) flatulenza; **to break wind** fare aria; (*fam*): **to bring up wind** (*baby*) fare il ruttino **3** (*breath*) respiro, fiato; **to get one's wind back** *or* **one's second wind** riprendere fiato; **to be short of wind** essere senza fiato **4** (*Mus*): **the wind(s)** i fiati *mpl*
■ VT: **to wind sb** (*with punch etc*) mozzare il fiato a qn; **to wind a baby** far fare il ruttino a un bambino
wind[2] [waɪnd] (*pt, pp* **wound**) VT **1** (*roll, coil*) avvolgere, arrotolare; **he wound the rope round a tree** ha avvolto la fune attorno a un albero; **to wind sth into a ball** aggomitolare qc **2** (*clock, watch, toy*) caricare
■ VI (*also:* **wind its way**: *river, path*) serpeggiare; (*procession*) snodarsi
▸ **wind back** VT + ADV (*tape*) riavvolgere
▸ **wind down** VT + ADV (*car window*) abbassare; (*fig: production, business*) diminuire
■ VI + ADV rilassarsi, distendersi
▸ **wind forward** VT + ADV (*tape*) mandare avanti
▸ **wind in** VT + ADV (*fishing line*) riavvolgere
▸ **wind on** VT + ADV (*film, tape*) far avanzare
▸ **wind up** VT + ADV **1** (*car window*) alzare; (*clock, toy*) caricare; **to wind sb up** (*fig fam: annoy*) far venire i nervi a *or* innervosire qn; (*: kid, trick*) prendere in giro qn **2** (*close: meeting, debate*) concludere, chiudere; (*: company*) chiudere; **the company will be wound up** la società verrà chiusa
■ VI + ADV (*meeting, debate*) concludersi; (*fam: end up*) finire; **we wound up in Rome** siamo finiti a Roma; **he'll wind up in jail** finirà in prigione
wind·bag ['wɪndˌbæg] N (*fam: person*) trombone *m*
wind·blown ['wɪndˌbləʊn] ADJ (*hair, trees*) agitato(-a) dal vento; (*hills, balconies etc*) battuto(-a) dal vento
wind·break ['wɪndˌbreɪk] N frangivento
Wind·breaker® ['wɪndˌbreɪkə^r] N (*Am*) = **windcheater**
wind·cheater ['wɪndˌtʃiːtə^r] N giacca a vento
wind·er ['waɪndə^r] N (*Brit: on watch*) corona di carica; (*Aut: also:* **window winder**) manovella *f* alzacristalli *inv*
wind erosion N erosione *f* del vento
wind·fall ['wɪndˌfɔːl] N (*apple etc*) frutto fatto cadere dal vento; (*fig*) colpo di fortuna
wind farm N centrale *f* eolica
wind gauge N anemometro
wind·ing ['waɪndɪŋ] ADJ (*road, path*) serpeggiante, tortuoso(-a); (*staircase*) a chiocciola
wind instrument N (*Mus*) strumento a fiato
wind·lass ['wɪndləs] N argano, verricello
wind·less ['wɪndlɪs] ADJ senza vento
wind·mill ['wɪndˌmɪl] N mulino a vento
◎ **win·dow** ['wɪndəʊ] N (*gen, Comput*) finestra; (*of car, train*) finestrino; (*also:* **window pane**) vetro; (*also:* **stained glass window**) vetrata; (*also:* **shop window**) vetrina; (*of booking office etc*) sportello; (*in envelope*) finestrella; **to break a window** rompere un vetro; **a broken window** un vetro rotto; **to clean the windows** pulire i vetri; **to look out of the window** guardare fuori della finestra; **"do not lean out of the window"** "vietato sporgersi dal finestrino"; **the kitchen window** la finestra della cucina; **he wound down the window** ha abbassato il finestrino
window box N cassetta per i fiori (*da tenere sul davanzale*)
window cleaner N lavavetri *m/f*
window dresser N (*Comm*) vetrinista *m/f*
window dressing N (*Comm*) vetrinistica; (*fig*) fumo negli occhi
window envelope N busta a finestra
window frame N telaio di finestra
window ledge N davanzale *m*
window pane N vetro
window sash N telaio di finestra
window seat N (*in house*) *panchetta fissa vicino alla finestra*; (*in train etc*) posto vicino al finestrino
window-shopping ['wɪndəʊˌʃɒpɪŋ] N: **to go window-shopping** andare a vedere le vetrine
window·sill ['wɪndəʊˌsɪl] N davanzale *m*
wind·pipe ['wɪndˌpaɪp] N (*Anat*) trachea
wind power N energia eolica
wind·proof ['wɪndˌpruːf] ADJ a prova di vento
wind·screen ['wɪndskriːn], **wind·shield** (*Am*) ['wɪndʃiːld] N parabrezza *m inv*
windscreen washer N lavacristallo
windscreen wiper N tergicristallo
wind·sock ['wɪndˌsɒk] N manica a vento
Wind·sor Castle [ˌwɪnzə'kɑːsl] N castello di Windsor
▹ www.royal.gov.uk/
wind·surfer ['wɪndˌsɜːfə^r] N (*person*) windsurfista *m/f*; (*board*) windsurf *m inv*
wind·surfing ['wɪndˌsɜːfɪŋ] N windsurf *m inv* (*l'attività*); **to go windsurfing** fare del windsurf

Ww

wind·swept ['wɪnd,swɛpt] ADJ (*landscape*) ventoso(-a); (*square*) spazzato(-a) dal vento; (*person*) scompigliato(-a) per il vento
wind tunnel ['wɪnd,tʌnəl] N galleria aerodinamica *or* del vento
wind·ward ['wɪndwəd] (*Naut*) ADJ, ADV sopravvento *inv*
■ N lato sopravvento; **to windward** sopravvento
windy ['wɪndɪ] ADJ (*comp* **-ier**, *superl* **-iest**)
1 ventoso(-a); **it's windy** c'è vento; **a windy day** una giornata ventosa **2** (*fam old*: *afraid, nervous*): **windy (about)** teso(-a) (per), nervoso(-a) (per)
◎**wine** [waɪn] N vino; **a glass of wine** un bicchiere di vino; **white/red wine** vino bianco/rosso
■ VT: **to wine and dine sb** offrire un ottimo pranzo a qn
■ ADJ (*bottle*) da vino; (*vinegar*) di vino
▷ www.upenn.edu/museum/Wine/wineintro.html
wine bar N enoteca (*per degustazione*)
wine cellar N cantina
wine cooler N secchiello del ghiaccio (*per vino o champagne*)
wine·glass ['waɪn,glɑːs] N bicchiere *m* da vino
wine list N lista *or* carta dei vini
wine merchant N commerciante *m* di vini
wine·press ['waɪn,prɛs] N torchio
wine·skin ['waɪn,skɪn] N otre *m*
wine tast·ing ['waɪn,teɪstɪŋ] N degustazione *f* di vini
wine waiter N sommelier *m inv*
◎**wing** [wɪŋ] N **1** (*gen, also Sport, Archit, Pol*) ala; (*Brit Aut*) fiancata; **to take sb under one's wing** prendere qn sotto le proprie ali; **the left wing of the Conservative Party** la sinistra del Partito Conservatore **2**: **the wings** NPL (*Theatre*) le quinte
winged [wɪŋd] ADJ alato(-a)
wing·er ['wɪŋəʳ] N (*Sport*) ala
wing·less ['wɪŋlɪs] ADJ (*insect etc*) privo(-a) di ali
wing mirror N (*Brit*) specchietto laterale esterno
wing nut N galletto
wing·span ['wɪŋ,spæn], **wing·spread** ['wɪŋ,sprɛd] N apertura alare, apertura d'ali
wing tip N punta dell'ala
wink [wɪŋk] N (*blink*) strizzata d'occhi; (*meaningful*) occhiolino, strizzatina d'occhi; **to give sb a wink** ammiccare *or* fare l'occhiolino a qn; **in a wink** in un batter d'occhio; **I didn't sleep a wink** non ho chiuso occhio
■ VI (*meaningfully*): **to wink (at sb)** fare l'occhiolino (a qn), ammiccare (a qn); (*blink*) strizzare gli occhi; (*light, star etc*) baluginare
wink·ing ['wɪŋkɪŋ] ADJ (*light, star*) baluginante
■ N: **it's as easy as winking** è un gioco da bambini
win·kle ['wɪŋkl] N litorina
■ VT: **to winkle a secret out of sb** carpire un segreto a qn
◎**win·ner** ['wɪnəʳ] N (*gen*) vincitore(-trice); **to pick a winner** (*horse*) scegliere il cavallo vincente; (*gen*) fare un affare; **it's a winner!** (*fam*) è un successone!; (*likely to be a success*) è un successo garantito!
◎**win·ning** ['wɪnɪŋ] ADJ **1** (*gen*) vincente; (*hit, shot, goal*) decisivo(-a); **the winning team** la squadra vincitrice; **the winning goal** il gol della vittoria **2** (*charming*) affascinante; **a winning smile** un sorriso accattivante; *see also* **winnings**
winning post N traguardo
win·nings ['wɪnɪŋz] NPL vincita *fsg*
win·now ['wɪnəʊ] VT (*grain*) vagliare, mondare

win·some ['wɪnsəm] ADJ accattivante
◎**win·ter** ['wɪntəʳ] N inverno; **in winter** d'inverno, in inverno; **the winter of 1981** l'inverno del 1981; **it's winter** è inverno; **last winter** lo scorso inverno
■ ADJ (*clothes, weather, day*) invernale, d'inverno
winter cherry N alchechengi *m inv*
winter sports NPL sport *mpl* invernali
winter·time ['wɪntə,taɪm] N inverno, stagione *f* invernale
win·try, **win·tery** ['wɪntrɪ] ADJ invernale; (*fig*: *look*) freddo(-a)
win-win [,wɪn'wɪn] ADJ: **a win-win situation** una situazione vantaggiosa per tutti
◎**wipe** [waɪp] N pulita, passata; **to give sth a wipe** dare una pulita *or* una passata a qc
■ VT (*gen*) pulire; (*blackboard, tape*: *Comput*) cancellare; **to wipe one's eyes** asciugarsi gli occhi; **to wipe one's nose** soffiarsi il naso; **to wipe one's feet** *or* **shoes** pulirsi i piedi; **to wipe one's bottom** pulirsi il sedere; **to wipe the dishes** asciugare i piatti; **to wipe sth dry** asciugare qc; **to wipe the floor with sb** (*fig fam*) schiacciare qn
▸ **wipe away** VT + ADV (*marks*) togliere; (*tears*) asciugare
▸ **wipe down** VT + ADV pulire
▸ **wipe off** VT + ADV cancellare; (*stains*) togliere (strofinando)
▸ **wipe out** VT + ADV **1** (*erase*: *writing, memory*) cancellare; (: *debt*) liquidare **2** (*destroy*: *town, race, enemy*) annientare
▸ **wipe up** VI + ADV (*dry dishes*) asciugare i piatti
■ VT + ADV asciugare
wip·er ['waɪpəʳ] N (*Aut*) tergicristallo; **intermittent wiper** tergicristallo (a funzionamento) intermittente
wiper arm N braccio del tergicristallo
◎**wire** ['waɪəʳ] N **1** filo di ferro; (*Elec*) filo (elettrico); **copper wire** filo di rame; **the telephone wire** il filo del telefono; **to get one's wires crossed** (*fam*) fraintendere **2** (*telegram*) telegramma *m*; **to the wire** fino all'ultimo momento
■ VT **1** (*Elec*: *house*) fare l'impianto elettrico di; (*circuit*) installare; (: *also*: **wire up**: *two pieces of equipment*) collegare, allacciare; **to wire a room for sound** installare un impianto di sonorizzazione in una stanza **2** (*Telec*) telegrafare **3** **to wire sth to sth** (*tie*) attaccare qc a qc con un filo
wire brush N spazzola metallica
wire cutters NPL tronchese *msg or fsg*
wired [waɪəd] ADJ **1** (*clothing, material*) rinforzato(-a) (con filo metallico) **2** (*place*: *fitted with alarm*) collegato(-a) ad un sistema di allarme; (: *bugged*) avere dei microfoni nascosti
wireless ['waɪəlɪs] (*old*) N (*Brit*) radio *f*; (*also*: **wireless set**) (apparecchio *m*) radio *f inv*; **on the wireless** per radio; **by wireless** via radio
■ ADJ (*station, programme*) radiofonico(-a); (*technology*) wireless *inv*, senza fili
Wireless Application Protocol N (*Comput*) WAP *m*
wireless operator N operatore *m* radio *inv*
wire netting N rete *f* metallica
wire·pulling ['waɪə,pʊlɪŋ] N (*esp Am fam*) maneggi *mpl*, intrighi *mpl*
wire service N (*Am*) = **news agency**
wire-tapping ['waɪə,tæpɪŋ] N intercettazione *f* telefonica
wire wool N lana d'acciaio
wir·ing ['waɪərɪŋ] N (*Elec*) impianto elettrico

wiry ['waɪərɪ] ADJ (*comp* **-ier**, *superl* **-iest**) (*person*) asciutto(-a) e muscoloso(-a); (*hair*) ispido(-a)

Wis·con·sin [wɪs'kɒnsɪn] N Wisconsin *m*
▷ www.wisconsin.gov/

wis·dom ['wɪzdəm] N (*of person*) saggezza; (*of remark, action*) opportunità; **words of great wisdom** parole di grande saggezza; **I have doubts about the wisdom of his decision** ho dubbi sull'opportunità della sua decisione

wisdom tooth N dente *m* del giudizio

◎**wise**[1] [waɪz] ADJ (*comp* **-r**, *superl* **-st**) (*gen, person*) saggio(-a); (: *learned*) sapiente; (*prudent: advice, remark*) prudente; **a wise man** un saggio; **the Three Wise Men** i Re Magi; **to be wise after the event** giudicare con il senno di poi; **it was wise of you not to do that** sei stato saggio a non farlo; **I'm none the wiser** ne so quanto prima; **it would be wiser to stay at home** sarebbe più sensato rimanere a casa; **to get wise to sb/sth** (*fam*) aprire gli occhi su qn/qc; **to put sb wise to sb/sth** (*fam*) mettere qn al corrente di qn/qc
▶ **wise up** VI + ADV (*esp Am fam*): **to wise up to** aprire gli occhi su; **wise up!** svegliati!

wise[2] [waɪz] N (*old*): **in no wise** affatto, in nessun modo; **in this wise** in tal guisa
■ ADV ENDING: **workwise** per quel che riguarda il lavoro; **how are we foodwise?** come stiamo a cibo?

wise·crack ['waɪz,kræk] N (*fam*) battuta, spiritosaggine *f*

wise guy N (*fam*) sapientone(-a), furbone(-a)

wise·ly ['waɪzlɪ] ADV (*decide*) saggiamente; (*nod, smile*) con aria saggia

◎**wish** [wɪʃ] N **1** (*desire*) desiderio; (*specific desire*) richiesta; **I had no wish to upset you** non avevo nessuna intenzione di farti star male; **to go against sb's wishes** andare contro il volere di qn; **I'll grant you three wishes** ti concedo di esprimere tre desideri; **you shall have your wish** realizzerai il tuo desiderio; **to make a wish** esprimere un desiderio; **make a wish** esprimi un desiderio; **she had no wish for conversation** non aveva alcuna voglia di conversare
2 best wishes (*in greetings*) tanti auguri; (*in letter*) cordiali saluti; **give her my best wishes** le porga i miei più cordiali saluti; **with best wishes** con i migliori auguri; **"with best wishes, Kathy"** "cari saluti, Kathy"
■ VT **1** (*want*) volere, desiderare; **to wish sb to do sth** volere che qn faccia qc; **to wish to do sth** voler fare qc; **I wish to make a complaint** voglio fare reclamo; **I wish he'd shut up** (*fam*) magari chiudesse il becco; **I wish I'd gone too** vorrei esserci andato anch'io; **I wish you were here!** come vorrei che tu fossi qui!; **I wish I could!** mi piacerebbe!, magari! **2** (*foist*): **to wish sb on sb** appioppare *or* affibbiare qn a qn; **to wish sth on sb** rifilare qc a qn **3** (*bid, express*) augurare; **to wish sb goodbye** dire arrivederci a qn; **to wish sb good luck/a happy Christmas/a happy birthday** augurare a qn buona fortuna/buon Natale/buon compleanno; **to wish sb well** augurare ogni bene a qn; **to wish sb ill** voler del male a qn
■ VI: **to wish for sth** desiderare qc; **she has everything she could wish for** ha tutto ciò che desidera; **what more could you wish for?** cosa vuoi di più?

wish·bone ['wɪʃ,bəʊn] N (*of turkey, chicken etc*) forcella

wish·ful ['wɪʃfʊl] ADJ: **it's just wishful thinking** è solo un'illusione

wishy-washy ['wɪʃɪ,wɒʃɪ] ADJ (*fam: colour*) slavato(-a); (: *person, argument, ideas*) insulso(-a)

wisp [wɪsp] N (*of straw, smoke*) filo; (*of hair*) ciuffetto

wispy ['wɪspɪ] ADJ (*hair*) fine, sottile; (*clouds*) vaporoso(-a)

wis·te·ria [wɪs'tɪərɪə] N glicine *m*

wist·ful ['wɪstfʊl] ADJ (*look, smile*) pieno(-a) di rammarico; (: *nostalgic*) nostalgico(-a)

wist·ful·ly ['wɪstfəlɪ] ADV (*see adj*) con rammarico; nostalgicamente

wit [wɪt] N **1** (*understanding: gen pl*) intelligenza; **native wit** buon senso; **to be at one's wits' end** avere esaurito tutte le risorse, non sapere più che fare; **I'm at my wits' end!** non so più cos'altro fare!; **to have** *or* **keep one's wits about one** avere presenza di spirito; **use your wits!** usa il cervello!; **to live by one's wits** vivere di espedienti; **to collect one's wits** rimettersi in sesto; **to be frightened** *or* **scared out of one's wits** essere spaventato(-a) a morte **2** (*humour, wittiness*) spirito, arguzia; **he was known for his intelligence and wit** era conosciuto per la sua intelligenza e il suo spirito **3** (*person*) persona arguta, bello spirito
4 (*namely*): **to wit** cioè

witch [wɪtʃ] N strega

witch·craft ['wɪtʃ,krɑːft] N stregoneria

witch doctor N stregone *m*

witch hazel, **wych-hazel** ['wɪtʃ,heɪzl] N (*Bot*) amamelide *f*; (*astringent*) tonico astringente a base di amamelide

witch-hunt ['wɪtʃ,hʌnt] N caccia alle streghe

◎**with** [wɪð, wɪθ] PREP **KEYWORD**
1 (*gen*) con; **she mixed the sugar with the eggs** mischiò lo zucchero con le uova; **she stayed with friends** è stata a casa di amici; **to stay overnight with friends** passare la notte da amici; **I was with him** ero con lui; **he had no money with him** non aveva denaro con sé; **to be with it** (*fam: up-to-date*) essere à la page; **to rise with the sun** alzarsi all'alba; **she just wasn't with us** (*fig*) era completamente assente; **I'm with you** (*fig: I understand*) ti seguo
2 (*descriptive*) con; **the fellow with the big beard** il tipo con la *or* dalla barba folta; **the man with the grey hat** l'uomo dal *or* con il cappello grigio; **a room with a view** una camera con vista (sul mare *etc*)
3 (*manner, means, cause*) con; **red with anger** rosso(-a) dalla *or* per la rabbia; **to cut wood with an axe** tagliare la legna con l'ascia; **to shake with fear** tremare di paura; **she's gone down with flu** ha preso l'influenza; **in bed with measles** a letto con il morbillo; **white with snow** bianco(-a) a causa della neve; **covered with snow** coperto(-a) di neve; **to walk with a stick** camminare con l'aiuto di un bastone; **with tears in her eyes** con le lacrime agli occhi; **with that, he left** con ciò se ne andò; **with time** col tempo
4 (*concerning, in the case of*): **she's good with children** ci sa fare con i bambini; **you must be patient with her** devi avere pazienza con lei; **how are things with you?** (*fam*) come te la passi?; **the trouble with Harry is that ...** il guaio con Harry è che...
5 (*in proportion*) a seconda di; **it varies with the time of year** varia a seconda della stagione
6 (*in spite of*) nonostante; **with all his faults I still like him** nonostante i suoi difetti mi piace ancora

◎**with·draw** [wɪθ'drɔː] (*pt* **withdrew**, *pp* **withdrawn**) VT: **to withdraw (from)** (*gen*) ritirare (da); (*money from bank*) prelevare (da); **they withdrew all their savings**

Ww

hanno prelevato tutti i loro risparmi; **he withdrew his remarks** ha ritirato quanto aveva detto
■ VI: **to withdraw from** (*gen*) ritirarsi da; (*move away*) allontanarsi da; **to withdraw in sb's favour** ritirarsi a favore di qn; **to withdraw to a new position** (*Mil*) arretrare su una nuova posizione; **to withdraw into o.s.** chiudersi in se stesso(-a); **the troops withdrew** la truppe si sono ritirate

◎ **with·draw·al** [wɪθ'drɔ:əl] N (*gen*) ritiro; (*of money*) prelievo; (*of army*) ritiro; (*Med*) sindrome *f* da astinenza; **the withdrawal of their savings** il prelievo dei loro risparmi; **the withdrawal of the troops** la ritirata delle truppe

withdrawal symptoms NPL crisi *fsg* di astinenza

with·drawn [wɪθ'drɔ:n] PP *of* **withdraw**
■ ADJ chiuso(-a) in se stesso(-a)

with·drew [wɪθ'dru:] PT *of* **withdraw**

with·er ['wɪðə[r]] VT far appassire
■ VI (*plant*) appassire; (*limb*) atrofizzarsi; (*fig: love, passion*) spegnersi; (*: beauty*) sfiorire

with·ered ['wɪðəd] ADJ (*plant*) appassito(-a), vizzo(-a); (*skin*) avvizzito(-a); (*limb*) atrofizzato(-a); **a withered old woman** una vecchietta grinzosa

with·er·ing ['wɪðərɪŋ] ADJ (*tone, look, remark*) raggelante

with·ers ['wɪðəz] NPL garrese *msg* (*di cavallo*)

with·hold [wɪð'həʊld] (*pt, pp* **withheld**) VT (*money from pay etc*) trattenere; (*truth, news*) nascondere; (*refuse: consent*) non concedere, negare; **to withhold from** (*permission*) rifiutare a; (*information*) nascondere a; **I'm withholding my rent until the roof is repaired** non pagherò l'affitto finché il tetto non sarà stato riparato

◎ **with·in** [wɪð'ɪn] PREP **1** (*inside*) dentro; **a voice within me said ...** una vocina dentro di me disse...; **within herself** dentro di sé; **to be within the law** restare nei limiti della legalità; **to live within one's income** vivere secondo i propri mezzi; **within sight of** in vista di; **within easy reach** a portata di mano; vicino(-a); **the shops are within easy reach** i negozi sono vicini; **communication within the organization** la comunicazione all'interno dell'organizzazione
2 (*less than*): **we were within 100 metres of the summit** eravamo a meno di 100 metri dalla vetta; **within a mile of** entro un miglio da; **within ten kilometres** a meno di dieci chilometri; **within a year of her death** meno di un anno prima della (*or* dopo la) sua morte; **correct to within a millimetre** preciso(-a) al millimetro; **within an hour** entro un'ora; **within an hour from now** da qui a un'ora; **within the week** entro questa settimana; **he returned within the week** è tornato prima della fine della settimana
■ ADV: **"car for sale – apply within"** "auto in vendita – rivolgersi all'interno"

◎ **with·out** [wɪð'aʊt] PREP senza; **without speaking** senza parlare; **he did it without telling me** l'ha fatto senza dirmelo; **he came without a coat/any money** è venuto senza cappotto/soldi; **without a coat or hat** senza cappotto né cappello; **the bus left without me** l'autobus è partito senza di me; **he is without friends** non ha amici; **to be quite without shame** non avere un minimo di pudore; **without anybody knowing** senza che nessuno lo sappia; **to go** *or* **do without sth** fare a meno di qc

with-profits ['wɪθ,prɒfɪts] ADJ (*Fin*) indicizzato(-a)

with·stand [wɪθ'stænd] (*pt, pp* **withstood** [wɪθ'stud]) VT resistere a

wit·less ['wɪtlɪs] ADJ (*pej*) stupido(-a); **to scare sb witless** spaventare qn a morte; **to be scared witless** essere spaventato(-a) a morte

◎ **wit·ness** ['wɪtnɪs] N **1** (*person*) testimone *m/f*; **witness for the prosecution/defence** testimone a carico/discarico; **to call sb as a witness** chiamare qn a testimoniare; **there were no witnesses** non c'erano testimoni **2** (*evidence*) testimonianza; **to bear witness to sth** (*subj: person*) testimoniare qc; (*: thing, result*) provare qc
■ VT **1** (*event, crime*) essere testimone di; (*change, improvement*) constatare **2** (*attest by signature: document*) autenticare
■ VI (*testify*) testimoniare; **to witness to sth/having seen sth** testimoniare qc/di aver visto qc

witness box, (*Am*) **witness stand** N banco dei testimoni

wit·ti·cism ['wɪtɪ,sɪzəm] N arguzia

wit·ti·ly ['wɪtɪlɪ] ADV argutamente

wit·ting·ly ['wɪtɪŋlɪ] ADV (*frm*) deliberatamente, intenzionalmente

wit·ty ['wɪtɪ] ADJ (*comp* **-ier**, *superl* **-iest**) arguto(-a), spiritoso(-a)

wives [waɪvz] NPL *of* **wife**

wiz·ard ['wɪzəd] N mago, stregone *m*; (*fig*) mago; **he's a financial wizard** è un mago della finanza; **he's a wizard at maths** è un genio matematico

wiz·ard·ry ['wɪzədrɪ] N magia

wiz·ened ['wɪznd] ADJ raggrinzito(-a)

wk ABBR = **week**

WMD [,dʌblju:ɛm'di:] N ABBR = **weapon of mass destruction**

WO [,dʌblju:'əʊ] N ABBR = **warrant officer**

wob·ble ['wɒbl] N: **to have a wobble** (*chair*) traballare; **she had a wobble in her voice** le tremava la voce
■ VI (*table, chair, wheel, cyclist*) traballare; (*dancer, acrobat*) vacillare; (*compass needle*) oscillare; (*hand, voice*) tremare

wob·bly ['wɒblɪ] ADJ (*comp* **-ier**, *superl* **-iest**) (*hand, voice*) tremante; (*table, chair*) traballante; (*object about to fall*) che oscilla pericolosamente; (*wheel*) che ha troppo gioco; **to feel wobbly** (*person*) sentirsi debole

wodge [wɒdʒ] N (*Brit fam*): **a wodge of** un grosso pezzo di

woe [wəʊ] N (*liter, hum*) dolore *m*; **woe is me!** me tapino(-a)!; **woe betide him who ...** guai a chi...; **a tale of woe** una triste storia

woe·be·gone ['wəʊbɪ,gɒn] ADJ triste

woe·ful ['wəʊfʊl] ADJ (*sad*) triste; (*deplorable*) deplorevole, vergognoso(-a)

woe·ful·ly ['wəʊfəlɪ] ADV (*sadly: sigh, say etc*) tristemente; (*deplorably: inadequate etc*) deplorabilmente

wog [wɒg] N (*offensive*) *termine offensivo riferito a persona di colore*

wok [wɒk] N wok *m inv*; *padella concava usata nella cucina cinese*

woke [wəʊk] PT *of* **wake**[1]

wok·en ['wəʊkən] PP *of* **wake**[1]

wold [wəʊld] N altopiano

wolf [wʊlf] N (*pl* **wolves** [wʊlvz]) **1** lupo; (*fig*): **a wolf in sheep's clothing** un lupo in veste di agnello; **to keep the wolf from the door** sbarcare il lunario; **to cry wolf** gridare al lupo **2** (*fig fam: womanizer*) mandrillo, drago
■ VT (*also:* **wolf down**) divorare

wolf·hound ['wʊlf,haʊnd] N cane *m* lupo

wolf·ish ['wʊlfɪʃ] ADJ (*features, appetite*) da lupo; (*fig: grin, ideas*) feroce

wolf whistle N: **he gave her a wolf whistle** le ha fischiato dietro
wol·ver·ine ['wʊlvəˌri:n] N ghiottone *m*
wolves [wʊlvz] NPL *of* **wolf**
◎**wom·an** ['wʊmən] N (*pl* **women**) donna; **a man and two women** un uomo e due donne; **young woman** giovane donna; **come along, young woman!** su, signorina!; **I have a woman who comes in to do the cleaning** ho una donna che viene a fare le pulizie; **woman of the world** donna di mondo; **the little woman** (*hum: wife*) la mogliettina; **the woman in his life** la donna della sua vita; **women's page** (*Press*) rubrica femminile
woman doctor N dottoressa
woman driver N guidatrice *f*
woman friend N amica
woman-hater ['wʊmənˌheɪtəʳ] N misogino
wom·an·hood ['wʊmənˌhʊd] N femminilità; **to reach womanhood** diventare donna
wom·an·ize ['wʊmənaɪz] VI correre dietro alle donne
wom·an·iz·er ['wʊmənaɪzəʳ] N donnaiolo
wom·an·iz·ing ['wʊmənaɪzɪŋ] N avventure *fpl* con le donne
wom·an·kind ['wʊmənˌkaɪnd] N (*frm*) le donne
wom·an·like ['wʊmənˌlaɪk] ADJ (*features*) femminile; (*behaviour*) da donna
wom·an·li·ness ['wʊmənlɪnɪs] N femminilità
wom·an·ly ['wʊmənlɪ] ADJ femminile; **womanly behaviour** comportamento da donna
woman teacher N insegnante *f*
womb [wu:m] N (*Anat*) grembo
wom·bat ['wɒmbæt] N vombato orsino
wom·en ['wɪmɪn] NPL *of* **woman**
women·folk ['wɪmɪnˌfəʊk] NPL donne *fpl*
wom·en's lib·ber [ˌwɪmɪnz'lɪbəʳ] N (*fam*) femminista
Women's Liberation ['wɪmɪnsˌlɪbə'reɪʃən] N (*also:* Women's Lib) Movimento per la Liberazione della Donna
women's movement N: **the women's movement** il movimento per la liberazione della donna
won [wʌn] PT, PP *of* **win**
◎**won·der** ['wʌndəʳ] N **1** (*feeling*) meraviglia, stupore *m*; **in wonder** con stupore; **lost in wonder** stupefatto(-a) **2** (*object or cause of wonder*) miracolo, portento; **the wonders of science** i miracoli della scienza; **the Seven Wonders of the World** le sette meraviglie del mondo; **it is no** *or* **little** *or* **small wonder that he left** c'è poco *or* non c'è da meravigliarsi che sia partito; **the wonder of it was that ...** la cosa incredibile *or* sorprendente era che...; **to do** *or* **work wonders** fare miracoli; **no wonder!** non mi meraviglio!; **no wonder he got upset** non mi stupisce che si sia arrabbiato
■VT chiedersi, domandarsi; **I wonder whether** *or* **if ...** mi chiedo se...; **I wonder why she said that** mi chiedo perché l'abbia detto; **I was wondering if you could give me a lift** mi chiedevo se potessi darmi un passaggio; **I wonder where/how/when** mi chiedo dove/come/quando
■VI **1** (*ask o.s., speculate*): **to wonder about** pensare di; **I was wondering about going out for dinner** pensavo di andare fuori a cena, magari; **does she know about it? — I wonder** lo sa? — è quello che mi chiedo anch'io **2** (*be surprised*) stupirsi, meravigliarsi; **we all wonder you're still alive** ci meravigliamo tutti che tu sia ancora vivo; **to wonder at sth** stupirsi di qc
◎**won·der·ful** ['wʌndəfʊl] ADJ meraviglioso(-a), stupendo(-a)
won·der·ful·ly ['wʌndəfəlɪ] ADV (*with adjective*) meravigliosamente; (*with verb*) a meraviglia
won·der·ing ['wʌndərɪŋ] ADJ stupito(-a), stupefatto(-a)
wonder·land ['wʌndəˌlænd] N paese *m* delle meraviglie
won·der·ment ['wʌndəmənt] N stupore *m*, meraviglia
won·ky ['wɒŋkɪ] ADJ (*comp* **-ier**, *superl* **-iest**) (*Brit fam: chair, table*) traballante; **to go wonky** (*TV picture, machine*) fare i capricci
won't [wəʊnt] PT, PT = **will not**
wont [wəʊnt] N: **as is his/her wont** com'è solito(-a) fare
woo [wu:] VT corteggiare; (*fig: voters, audience*) cercare di conquistare
◎**wood** [wʊd] N **1** (*material*) legno; (*timber*) legname *m*; **touch wood!**, (*Am*) **knock on wood!** tocca ferro!; **aged in the wood** invecchiato(-a) in botti di legno; **it's made of wood** è di legno **2** (*forest*) bosco; **woods** NPL boschi *mpl*; **we're not out of the wood yet** (*fig*) non ne siamo ancora usciti completamente; **he can't see the wood for the trees** (*fig*) si perde nei dettagli; **we went for a walk in the wood** siamo andati a passeggiare nel bosco **3** (*Golf*) mazza di legno; (*Bowls*) boccia
■ADJ **1** (*made of wood*) di legno **2** (*living etc in a wood*) di bosco, silvestre
wood anemone N anemone *m* dei boschi
wood·bine ['wʊdˌbaɪn] N (*honeysuckle*) caprifoglio
wood·carving ['wʊdˌkɑ:vɪŋ] N scultura in legno
wood·chuck ['wʊdˌtʃʌk] N marmotta americana
wood·cock ['wʊdˌkɒk] N beccaccia
wood·craft ['wʊdˌkrɑ:ft] N conoscenza dei boschi
wood·cut ['wʊdˌkʌt] N incisione *f* su legno
wood·cut·ter ['wʊdˌkʌtəʳ] N taglialegna *m inv*
wood·ed ['wʊdɪd] ADJ coperto(-a) di boschi, boscoso(-a); **thickly/sparsely wooded** a bosco fitto/rado
◎**wood·en** ['wʊdn] ADJ **1** (*made of wood*) di legno; **a wooden chair** una sedia di legno **2** (*fig: movements, manner*) impacciato(-a), rigido(-a); (*: face, stare*) inespressivo(-a); (*: personality*) goffo(-a); **to give a wooden performance** (*actor*) recitare in maniera impacciata
wood engraving N (*Art*) incisione *f* su legno
wood·land ['wʊdlənd] N zona boscosa
■ADJ di bosco, silvestre
wood·louse ['wʊdˌlaʊs] N (*Zool*) onisco
wood·pecker ['wʊdˌpɛkəʳ] N picchio
wood pigeon N colombaccio
wood·pile ['wʊdˌpaɪl] N catasta di legna
wood pulp N pasta di legno
wood shavings NPL trucioli *mpl* di legno
wood·shed ['wʊdˌʃɛd] N legnaia
woods·man ['wʊdzmən] N (*pl* **-men**) (*lumberjack*) taglialegna *m inv*; (*forester*) guardaboschi *m inv*
wood·wind ['wʊdˌwɪnd] NPL (*Mus*): **the woodwind** i legni *mpl*
wood·work ['wʊdˌwɜ:k] N **1** (*craft, subject*) falegnameria **2** (*wooden parts of room*) parti *fpl* in legno
wood·worm ['wʊdˌwɜ:m] N tarlo; **to have woodworm** essere tarlato(-a)
woody ['wʊdɪ] ADJ (*stem, plant etc*) ligneo(-a)
woof[1] [wʊf] N (*of dog*) bau bau *m*
■VI abbaiare; **woof, woof!** bau bau!
woof[2] [wʊf] N (*Textiles*) trama

Ww

woof·er ['wʊfə[r]] N woofer *m inv*

wool [wʊl] N lana; **all wool** *or* **pure wool** pura lana; **pure new wool** pura lana vergine; **knitting wool** lana per lavorare a maglia; **a ball of wool** un gomitolo di lana; **to pull the wool over sb's eyes** *(fam)* gettare fumo negli occhi a qn

■ ADJ *(dress)* di lana; *(shop)* di lane, di filati; *(trade, industry)* della lana

wool·gather·ing ['wʊl,gæðərɪŋ] N *(fig)*: **to be woolgathering** avere la testa fra le nuvole

wool·len, *(Am)* **wool·en** ['wʊlən] ADJ *(cloth, dress)* di lana; *(industry)* della lana

■ **woollens** NPL indumenti *mpl* di lana

wool·ly, *(Am)* **wooly** ['wʊlɪ] ADJ *(comp* **-ier**, *superl* **-iest**) *(jumper etc)* di lana; *(fig: clouds)* come batuffoli; (: *ideas*) confuso(-a), vago(-a); (: *essay, book*) sul vago

■ N *(fam)* indumento di lana

woozy ['wu:zɪ] ADJ *(comp* **-ier**, *superl* **-iest**) *(fam)* stordito(-a), intontito(-a)

◎ **word** [wɜ:d] N

1 *(gen)* parola; **what's the word for "pen" in Italian?** come si dice "pen" in italiano?; **what does this word mean?** cosa vuol dire questa parola?; **the word "ginseng" is Chinese** la parola "ginseng" è cinese; **words** NPL *(of song)* parole *fpl*, testo; **in the words of Dante** come disse Dante; **word for word** parola per parola, testualmente; **words per minute** parole al minuto; **to put sth into words** esprimere qc a parole; **silly isn't the word for it!** sciocco non è la parola esatta!; **words fail me** non ho parole; **in a word** in una parola; **in other words** in altre parole, in altri termini; **not in so many words** non esplicitamente; **those were her very words** quelle furono le sue testuali parole; **the last word in** l'ultima novità in fatto di; **to have the last word** avere l'ultima parola; **to give sb a word of warning** dare a qn un piccolo avvertimento; **I can't get a word out of him** non riesco a cavargli una parola di bocca; **by word of mouth** con il passaparola; **to take the words out of sb's mouth** rubare le parole di bocca a qn; **don't put words into my mouth!** non mettermi parole in bocca!; **to have a word with sb** fare un discorsetto a qn; **could I have a word with you?** posso parlarti un attimo?; **to put in a (good) word for sb** mettere una buona parola per qn; **without a word** senza una parola; **don't say** *or* **breathe a word about it** non farne parola; **to have words with sb** *(quarrel with)* venire a parole con qn

2 *(news)* notizia, notizie *fpl*; **is there any word from Peter yet?** non ci sono ancora notizie da parte di Peter?; **word came from headquarters that ...** il quartiere generale ci ha fatto sapere che...; **to bring/send word of sth to sb** portare/dare la notizia di qc a qn; **to leave word (with sb, for sb) that ...** lasciare detto (a qn) che...; **word of command** ordine *m*; **to give the word to do sth** dare l'ordine di fare qc

3 *(promise)* parola; **word of honour** parola d'onore; **he is a man of his word** è un uomo di parola; **to be as good as one's word** *or* **keep one's word** essere di parola, tenere fede alla parola data; **to break one's word** mancare di parola; **to give sb one's word (that ...)** dare a qn la propria parola (che...); **I've only got your word for it** devo fidarmi di quello che dici tu; **to take sb at his word** prendere qn in parola; **I'll take your word for it** ti credo sulla parola

4 *(gospel)*: **the Word** il Verbo, la parola di Dio; **to preach the Word** predicare la buona novella

■ VT *(document, protest)* formulare

word-blind ['wɜ:d,blaɪnd] ADJ dislessico(-a)

word blindness N dislessia

word·book ['wɜ:d,bʊk] N vocabolario

word game N gioco con le parole

wordi·ness ['wɜ:dɪnɪs] N verbosità

word·ing ['wɜ:dɪŋ] N *(of contract, document)* formulazione *f*; **to change the wording** formulare diversamente

word list N lemmario

word order N ordine *m* delle parole

word-perfect [,wɜ:d'pɜ:fɪkt] ADJ *(speech etc)* imparato(-a) a memoria; **to be word-perfect** *(actor)* sapere a memoria la parte

word·play ['wɜ:d,pleɪ] N gioco di parole

word processing N word processing *m inv*

word processor N *(machine)* word processor *m inv*

word wrap N *(Comput)* ritorno a margine automatico

wordy ['wɜ:dɪ] ADJ *(comp* **-ier**, *superl* **-iest**) verboso(-a), prolisso(-a)

wore [wɔ:[r]] PT *of* **wear**

◎ **work** [wɜ:k] N

1 *(gen)* lavoro; **it's hard work** è un lavoro duro; **to be at work (on sth)** lavorare (a qc); **men at work** lavori in corso; **it's all in a day's work** è una cosa di ordinaria amministrazione; **to get on with one's work** continuare il proprio lavoro; **the forces at work** gli elementi che influiscono; **work on the new school has begun** sono cominciati i lavori per la nuova scuola; **a good piece of work** un buon lavoro; **to set sb to work doing sth** mettere qn a fare qc; **to set to work (on)** *or* **start work (on)** mettersi al lavoro (a); **I'm trying to get some work done** sto cercando di lavorare; **to make short** *or* **quick work of** *(sth)* sbrigare in fretta; *(fig fam: sb)* sistemare subito

2 *(employment, job)* lavoro; **to go to work** andare al lavoro; **he's at work today** oggi è al lavoro; **to look for work** cercare lavoro; **she's looking for work** sta cercando lavoro; **to be out of work** essere disoccupato(-a); **to be in work** avere un lavoro; **to put** *or* **throw sb out of work** licenziare qn; **to be off work** essere in congedo; **he's off work this week** questa settimana non lavora; **he hasn't done a day's work in his life** non ha mai lavorato in vita sua; **they have little work experience** hanno poca esperienza lavorativa

3 *(product: of writer, musician, scholar)* opera; **his life's work** il lavoro di tutta la sua vita; **he sells a lot of his work** vende molti dei suoi lavori; **good works** opere *fpl* buone; **work of art/reference** opera d'arte/di consultazione; **the works of Dickens** le opere di Dickens; **he's a nasty piece of work** *(fig)* è un tipaccio; *see also* **works**

■ VT

1 *(students, employees)* far lavorare; **to work sb hard** far lavorare molto qn; **to work o.s. to death** ammazzarsi di lavoro

2 *(operate)* azionare; **can you work the photocopier?** sai usare la fotocopiatrice?; **I can't work the video** non riesco a far funzionare il videoregistratore; **it is worked by electricity** va a corrente

3 *(miracle)* fare; *(change)* operare; **to work wonders** fare miracoli; **she managed to work her promotion** è riuscita a garantirsi la promozione; **they worked it so that she could come** *(fam)* hanno fatto in modo che potesse venire; **to work sth into a speech** far scivolare

qc in un discorso; **to work one's passage on a ship** pagarsi il viaggio su una nave lavorando (*a bordo della stessa*); **to work one's way through college** lavorare per pagarsi gli studi; **to work one's way along sth** avanzare lentamente lungo qc; **to work one's hands free** riuscire a liberarsi le mani; **to work sth loose** far smollare qc; **to work one's way through a book** leggersi pazientemente un libro; **he worked his way up from the factory floor** ha cominciato come umile operaio; **to work one's way up to the top of a company** farsi strada fino al vertice di una società; **to work o.s. into a rage** andare in bestia

4 (*shape: metal, dough, clay, wood*) lavorare; (*exploit: mine*) sfruttare; (*: land*) coltivare; (*Sewing: design*) ricamare; **worked by hand** lavorato(-a) a mano

■ VI

1 lavorare; **to work towards/for sth** lavorare in vista di/per qc; **to work hard** lavorare sodo; **they are working hard** lavorano sodo; **to work at** *or* **on sth** (*essay, project*) lavorare su qc; **she works in a shop** lavora in un negozio; **she's working at her desk** sta lavorando alla scrivania; **to work to rule** (*Industry*) fare uno sciopero bianco; **to work like a Trojan** lavorare come un*a* pazzo(-a)

2 (*machine, plan, brain*) funzionare; (*drug, medicine*) fare effetto; **to get sth working** far funzionare qc; **it works off the mains** funziona a corrente; **the heating isn't working** il riscaldamento non funziona; **my plan worked perfectly** il mio piano ha funzionato a meraviglia; **it works both ways** (*fig*) funziona nei due sensi

3 (*mouth, face, jaws*) contrarsi; **her mouth worked in her sleep** le si muoveva la bocca nel sonno

4 (*move gradually*) muoversi pian piano; **to work loose** (*screw*) allentarsi; **he worked slowly along the cliff** avanzava lentamente lungo la scogliera; **to work round to a question** formulare una domanda dopo averci girato intorno

▶ **work in** VI + ADV (*arrangement*) inserirsi

■ VT + ADV (*reference*) inserire, infilare

▶ **work off** VT + ADV (*fat*) eliminare; (*annoyance, tension*) sfogare; (*debt*) pagare lavorando

▶ **work on** VI + PREP

1 (*task, novel*) lavorare a; **he's working on the car** sta facendo dei lavori alla macchina; **the police are working on the case** la polizia sta facendo indagini sul caso

2 (*principle, assumption*) basarsi su; **we've no clues to work on** non abbiamo indizi su cui basarci; **we're working on the principle that ...** partiamo dal presupposto che... *+ sub*

3 (*persuade, influence*): **to work on sb** lavorarsi qn

▶ **work out** VI + ADV

1 (*problem*) risolversi

2 (*amount to*): **the cost worked out at £50** il costo ammontava a 50 sterline; **it works out at £100** fa 100 sterline

3 (*succeed: plan, marriage*) riuscire, funzionare; **I hope it all works out for you** spero che ti vada tutto bene; **things aren't working out as planned** le cose non stanno andando come previsto

4 (*Sport*) allenarsi; **I work out twice a week** faccio ginnastica due volte alla settimana

■ VT + ADV

1 (*problem, calculation*) risolvere; **I can't work out the percentage** non riesco a calcolare la percentuale; **things will work themselves out** tutto si sistemerà; **I just couldn't work it out** non riuscivo proprio a capire

2 (*devise: plan, details*) mettere a punto

3 (*understand: behaviour*) capire

4 (*exhaust: resources*) esaurire

▶ **work over** VT + ADV (*fam*) pestare

▶ **work up** VT + ADV

1 (*develop: trade*) sviluppare; **to work up an appetite** farsi venire appetito; **to work up enthusiasm for sth** entusiasmarsi per qc

2 to work sb up into a temper/fury far arrabbiare/ infuriare qn

▶ **work up to** VI + ADV + PREP (*point, climax*) preparare il terreno a

work·able ['wɜːkəbl] ADJ (*plan*) fattibile; (*solution*) realizzabile; (*land*) coltivabile; (*mine*) sfruttabile

worka·day ['wɜːkəˌdeɪ] ADJ niente di speciale

worka·hol·ic [ˌwɜːkə'hɒlɪk] N stacanovista *m/f*, maniaco(-a) del lavoro

work·bag ['wɜːkˌbæg] N borsa da lavoro

work basket N cestino da lavoro

work·bench ['wɜːkˌbentʃ] N banco da lavoro

work·book ['wɜːkˌbʊk] N quaderno per esercizi

work·box ['wɜːkˌbɒks] N (*for sewing*) cofanetto da lavoro

work·day ['wɜːkˌdeɪ] N (*Am*) giorno lavorativo *or* feriale

worked up [ˌwɜːkt'ʌp] ADJ: **to get worked up** andare su tutte le furie; **don't get all worked up!** non agitarti tanto!

◎ **work·er** ['wɜːkəʳ] N (*gen, Agr*) lavoratore(-trice); (*esp Industry*) operaio(-a); **a good worker** un bravo lavoratore; **he's a poor worker** non lavora bene; **a factory worker** un operaio; **office worker** impiegato(-a); **management and workers** il padronato e i lavoratori

worker-priest [ˌwɜːkə'priːst] N prete *m* operaio

work·fare ['wɜːkˌfɛəʳ] N *programma che prevede la frequenza a corsi di formazione per ricevere il sussidio di disoccupazione*

work force N forza *f* lavoro *inv*

work·horse ['wɜːkˌhɔːs] N cavallo da lavoro; (*fig: person*) lavoratore(-trice) indefesso(-a)

work·house ['wɜːkˌhaʊs] N (*Brit History*) ospizio (*in cui i ricoverati lavoravano*)

work-in ['wɜːkˌɪn] N (*Brit*) *forma di protesta in cui gli operai occupano e continuano a lavorare in una fabbrica o azienda minacciata di chiusura*

◎ **work·ing** ['wɜːkɪŋ] ADJ (*day*) feriale; (*week*) lavorativo(-a); (*tools, conditions, lunch*) di lavoro; (*clothes*) da lavoro; (*mother*) che lavora; (*partner*) attivo(-a); **an 8-hour working day** una giornata lavorativa di 8 ore; **working knowledge** conoscenza pratica; **in working order** funzionante; *see also* **workings**

working capital N (*Comm*) capitale *m* d'esercizio

working class N classe *f* operaia *or* lavoratrice

working-class [ˌwɜːkɪŋ'klɑːs] ADJ: **to be working-class** appartenere alla classe operaia; **to come from a working-class background** venire da una famiglia di operai; **I'm working-class** vengo da una famiglia operaia; **a working-class family** una famiglia operaia

working group N gruppo di lavoro

working man N lavoratore *m*, operaio

working men's club N circolo aziendale

working model N modello operativo

working party N (*Brit*) commissione *f* d'inchiesta

work·ings ['wɜːkɪŋz] NPL **1** (*way sth works*)

Ww

funzionamento *msg*; **the workings of his mind** i meccanismi della sua mente **2** (*of quarry*) scavi *mpl*

work-in-progress [ˌwɜːkɪnˈprəʊɡrɛs] (*Comm*) N (*value*) valore *m* del manufatto in lavorazione

work·load [ˈwɜːkˌləʊd] N carico di lavoro

work·man [ˈwɜːkmən] N (*pl* **-men**) operaio

work·man·like [ˈwɜːkmənˌlaɪk] ADJ (*attitude*) professionale; (*work*) ben fatto(-a)

work·man·ship [ˈwɜːkmənʃɪp] N (*of worker*) abilità professionale; (*of thing*) fattura

work·mate [ˈwɜːkˌmeɪt] N collega *m/f* di lavoro

work·out [ˈwɜːkˌaʊt] N (*Sport*) allenamento

work permit N permesso di lavoro

work·room [ˈwɜːkˌrʊm] N laboratorio

works [wɜːks] N (*Brit*) **1** NPL (*of machine, clock*) meccanismo; (*Admin*) opere *fpl*; (*Mil*) opere, fortificazioni *fpl*; **road works** lavori stradali; **to give sb the works** (*fam: treat harshly*) dare una strigliata a qn **2** PL INV (*factory etc*) fabbrica, stabilimento; **works outing** gita aziendale

works council N consiglio aziendale

work sharing [-ʃɛərɪŋ] N *divisione di un posto di lavoro tra due o più persone con relativa divisione di stipendio*

work sheet N scheda; (*Comput*) foglio col programma di lavoro

work·shop [ˈwɜːkʃɒp] N officina; (*fig*): **a music workshop** un seminario di musica; **a drama workshop** un laboratorio teatrale

work·shy [ˈwɜːkʃaɪ] ADJ pigro(-a), indolente

work·space [ˈwɜːkˌspeɪs] N spazio di lavoro

work station N stazione *f* di lavoro

work study N studio di organizzazione del lavoro

work surface N piano di lavoro

work·top [ˈwɜːkˌtɒp] N piano di lavoro

work-to-rule [ˌwɜːktəˈruːl] N (*Brit*) sciopero bianco

◎ **world** [wɜːld] N **1** (*gen*) mondo; **in the world** al mondo; **all over the world** in tutto il mondo; **to be on top of the world** essere al settimo cielo; **it's a small world!** com'è piccolo il mondo!; **alone in the world** solo(-a) al mondo; **it's not the end of the world!** (*fam*) non è la fine del mondo!; **to live in a world of one's own** vivere in un mondo tutto proprio; **the business world** il mondo degli affari; **the world we live in** il mondo in cui viviamo; **to come** *or* **go down** *or* **go up** *or* **rise in the world** scendere/salire nella scala sociale; **to come into the world** venire al mondo; **the next world** l'aldilà *m inv*; **to have the best of both worlds** avere un doppio vantaggio; **it's out of this world!** (*fam*) è la fine del mondo!; **he's not long for this world** non gli rimane molto da vivere **2** (*phrases*): **I wouldn't do it for the world** *or* **for anything in the world** non lo farei per niente al mondo; **what in the world is he doing?** che caspita sta facendo?; **to think the world of sb** pensare un gran bene di qn; **there's a world of difference between ...** c'è un abisso tra...; **to do sb a world of good** fare un gran bene a qn; **the world and his wife** un miliardo di persone; **they're worlds apart** non hanno niente in comune; **she looked for all the world as if she was dead** sembrava proprio che fosse morta; **the world's worst cook** la cuoca peggiore che possa esistere

■ ADJ (*tour, power*) mondiale; (*record*) del mondo, mondiale

world champion N campione(-essa) mondiale

world-class [ˈwɜːldˈklɑːs] ADJ (*sportsman, player*) di livello internazionale

World Cup N (*Ftbl*): **the World Cup** il campionato mondiale *or* i mondiali *mpl* di calcio

World Fair N (*Comm*): **the World Fair** la fiera mondiale

world-famous [ˌwɜːldˈfeɪməs] ADJ di fama mondiale

World Health Organization N: **the World Health Organization** l'Organizzazione *f* Mondiale della Sanità

world leader N (*of state*) capo di stato; (*person, company*) leader *m/f* mondiale; (*product*) prodotto leader sul mercato

world·ly [ˈwɜːldlɪ] ADJ (*comp* **-ier**, *superl* **-iest**) (*matters, person*) mondano(-a); (*attitude, pleasures*) materiale

worldly-wise [ˌwɜːldlɪˈwaɪz] ADJ di mondo

world music N musica etnica, world music *f inv*

▷ www.africanmusic.org

▷ www.ceolas.org/ceolas.html

▷ www.sbgmusic.com/html/teacher/reference/cultures.html

World Series N (*Am Baseball*): **the World Series** torneo di spareggio al termine del campionato di baseball

World Trade Organization N Organizzazione *f* Mondiale del Commercio

World War I N la prima guerra mondiale

▷ www.worldwar1.com

▷ www.firstworldwar.com

World War II N la seconda guerra mondiale

▷ www.ibiblio.org/pha

▷ www.war-experience.org/

world-weary [ˈwɜːldˈwɪərɪ] ADJ stanco(-a) della vita

◎ **worldwide** [ˌwɜːldˈwaɪd] ADJ mondiale, universale; **his books have sold 200 million copies worldwide** i suoi libri hanno venduto 200 milioni di copie nel mondo

World Wide Web N: **the World Wide Web** (*Comput*) il Web

worm [wɜːm] N (*Zool: also person: pej*) verme *m*; **to have worms** (*Med*) avere i vermi; **the worm will turn** (*Proverb*) anche la pazienza ha un limite; **a can of worms** (*fam*) un vespaio; **you worm!** (*fam*) verme!; (*Comput*) baco

■ VT **1 to worm one's way through a crowd** insinuarsi tra la folla; **to worm one's way into a group** infiltrarsi in un gruppo; **to worm one's way into sb's confidence** riuscire a conquistare la fiducia di qn **2 to worm a secret out of sb** carpire un segreto a qn

worm·cast [ˈwɜːmˌkɑːst] N *mucchietto di terra scavata da un verme*

worm-eaten [ˈwɜːmˌiːtn] ADJ (*apple*) bacato(-a); (*wood*) tarlato(-a)

worm·wood [ˈwɜːmˌwʊd] N (*Bot*) assenzio

wormy [ˈwɜːmɪ] ADJ (*comp* **-ier**, *superl* **-iest**) (*fruit*) bacato(-a); (*furniture*) tarlato(-a)

worn [wɔːn] PP *of* **wear**

■ ADJ (*carpet, tyre*) consumato(-a), logoro(-a); (*person*) stanco(-a), sfinito(-a); **the carpet is a bit worn** la moquette è un po' consumata

worn-out [ˌwɔːnˈaʊt] ADJ (*thing*) consunto(-a), logoro(-a); (*person*) sfinito(-a); **worn-out shoes** scarpe logore; **I'm worn out!** sono sfinito!

◎ **wor·ried** [ˈwʌrɪd] ADJ preoccupato(-a); **to be worried about sth** essere preoccupato per qc; **I was worried about my job** ero preoccupato per il mio lavoro; **to be**

worried sick (*fam*) essere preoccupatissimo(-a); **to be worried to death about sth/sb** (*fam*) essere molto ansioso(-a) per qc/qn; **to look worried** avere l'aria preoccupata

wor·ried·ly ['wʌrɪdlɪ] ADV (*say, look about etc*) ansiosamente

wor·rier ['wʌrɪəʳ] N ansioso(-a)

wor·ri·some ['wʌrɪsəm] ADJ **1** (*causing worry*) preoccupante **2** (*worried*) ansioso(-a)

◎ **wor·ry** ['wʌrɪ] N preoccupazione *f*; **what's your worry?** cosa ti preoccupa?; **to cause sb a lot of worry** creare un sacco di preoccupazioni a qn; **that's the least of my worries** questa è l'ultima cosa di cui mi preoccupo

■ VT **1** (*cause concern*) preoccupare; **to worry o.s. sick (about** *or* **over sth)** preoccuparsi da morire (per qc); **don't worry yourself** *or* **your head about it** non fartene un pensiero **2** (*bother*) disturbare, importunare **3** (*subj: dog: bone*) azzannare; (*: sheep*) inseguire e attaccare

■ VI: **to worry about** *or* **over sth/sb** preoccuparsi di qc/ per qn; **don't worry!** non preoccuparti!

▸ **worry at** VI + PREP **1** (*gnaw*) rosicchiare **2** (*try to deal with*): **to worry at sth** scervellarsi su qc

wor·ry·ing ['wʌrɪɪŋ] ADJ (*problem*) preoccupante; **it's a worrying time for her** è un brutto momento per lei; **she's not the worrying kind** non è il tipo che si preoccupa

◎ **worse** [wɜːs] ADJ (*comp of* **bad**) peggiore; **worse than** peggio *or* peggiore di; **the situation is worse than we expected** la situazione è peggiore di quanto ci aspettassimo; **it was even worse than mine** era anche peggiore del mio; **it's worse than ever** è peggio che mai; **it could have been worse!** poteva andare peggio!; **he was the worse for drink** (*fam*) aveva un po' bevuto; **he is none the worse for it** non ha avuto brutte conseguenze; **to get worse** *or* **grow worse** peggiorare; **it gets worse and worse** va peggiorando (sempre di più); **in March the weather will get worse** in marzo il tempo peggiorerà; **so much the worse for you!** tanto peggio per te!; **I've got to work this weekend, worse luck** devo lavorare questo fine settimana, sfortunatamente

■ ADV (*comp of* **badly**) peggio; **I'm feeling worse** mi sento peggio; **she's behaving worse than ever** si comporta peggio che mai; **I don't think any the worse of you** non per questo ti stimo meno; **I won't think any the worse of you (for having done)** non ti stimerò di meno (per aver fatto); **you might do worse than (to) marry him** sposare lui non è il male peggiore

■ N peggio; **a change for the worse** un cambiamento in peggio, un peggioramento; **worse followed** a questo seguì il peggio; **there is worse to come** il peggio deve ancora venire

wors·en ['wɜːsn] VT (*health, situation*) peggiorare; (*chances*) diminuire

■ VI peggiorare

worse off ADJ più povero(-a); (*fig*): **you'll be worse off this way** così sarà peggio per te; **he is now worse off than before** ora è in condizioni economiche peggiori di prima

wor·ship ['wɜːʃɪp] N **1** (*adoration*) adorazione *f*, culto; (*also:* **organized worship**) culto; **place of worship** (*Rel*) luogo di culto **2** (*Brit: in titles*): **Your Worship** (*to judge*) Vostro Onore; (*to mayor*) signor sindaco

■ VT adorare, venerare; **she worships her children** (*fig*) adora i suoi bambini; **he worships the ground she treads on** bacia la terra su cui lei cammina

■ VI (*Rel*) assistere alle funzioni

wor·ship·per ['wɜːʃɪpəʳ] N adoratore(-trice); (*in church*) fedele *m/f*, devoto(-a)

◎ **worst** [wɜːst] ADJ (*superl of* **bad**) il/la peggiore; **it was the worst possible time** era il momento peggiore *or* meno opportuno; **the worst film of the three** il peggiore fra i tre film; **the worst pupil in the school** il peggior alunno della scuola; **my worst enemy** il mio peggior nemico; **one of his worst efforts** una delle sue prove peggiori

■ ADV (*superl of* **badly**) peggio; **he sings worst of all** canta peggio di tutti; **to come off worst** (*in fight, argument*) avere la peggio

■ N peggio *m or f*; (*of crisis, storm*) culmine *m*; **at (the) worst** alla peggio, per male che vada; **the worst of it is that ...** il peggio è che...; **the worst is yet to come** il peggio deve ancora venire; **if the worst comes to the worst** nel peggiore dei casi; **to get the worst of an argument** avere la peggio in una discussione; **he brings out the worst in me** risveglia in me gli istinti peggiori; **we're over** *or* **past the worst of it now** il peggio è passato, ora; **do your worst!** sono pronto al peggio!

worst-case [ˌwɜːst'keɪs] ADJ: **the worst-case scenario** la peggiore delle ipotesi

wor·sted ['wʊstɪd] N (*cloth*) pettinato; **wool worsted** lana pettinata

◎ **worth** [wɜːθ] ADJ: **to be worth** valere; **how much is it worth?** quanto vale?; **it's worth £5** vale 5 sterline; **it's worth a great deal/a lot of money** vale molto/un sacco di soldi; **it's worth a great deal to me** (*sentimentally*) ha un gran valore per me; **he is worth his weight in gold** vale tanto oro quanto pesa; **I'll tell you this for what it's worth** ti dico questo, per quello che può valere; **what's it worth to you?** che valore ha per te?; **to run for all one is worth** correre a gambe levate; **it hardly seemed worth mentioning** non mi sembrava abbastanza importante da parlarne; **it's well worth the effort/expense** vale lo sforzo/la spesa; **it's not worth the paper it's written on** non vale nemmeno la carta su cui è scritto; **it's worth it** ne vale la pena; **is it worth it?** ne vale la pena?; **it's not worth it** *or* **it's not worth the trouble** non ne vale la pena; **it's more than my life is worth** non oserei mai; **is it worth doing?** vale la pena di farlo?

■ N valore *m*; **50 pence worth of apples** 50 pence di mele; **he had no chance to show his true worth** non ebbe occasione di mostrare quanto valeva

worth·less ['wɜːθlɪs] ADJ (*effort, action, attempt*) inutile; (*assurance, guarantee, object*) senza valore, di nessun valore; **a worthless individual** un individuo spregevole

worth·while [ˌwɜːθ'waɪl] ADJ (*gen*) che vale la pena; (*book, film*) che merita; (*life, work, activity*) utile; (*contribution*) valido(-a); (*cause*) lodevole; **a worthwhile trip** un viaggio che vale la pena di fare; **a worthwhile book** un libro che vale la pena leggere; **to be worthwhile** valere la pena; **it might be worthwhile to take out insurance** potrebbe valere la pena stipulare un'assicurazione

wor·thy ['wɜːðɪ] ADJ (*comp* **-ier**, *superl* **-iest**) (*gen*) degno(-a); (*cause, aim, motive*) lodevole; **a worthy cause** una degna causa; **worthy of** degno di; **worthy of note** *or* **mention** degno di nota

■ N (*hum*) personalità *f inv*

Ww

◎**would** [wʊd] KEYWORD
MODAL AUX VB (*conditional of* **will**)
1 (*conditional tense*): **she would come** verrebbe; **if you asked him he would do it** se tu glielo chiedessi lo farebbe; **he would have come** sarebbe venuto; **if you had asked him he would have done it** se tu gliel'avessi chiesto l'avrebbe fatto; **you'd think she had enough to worry about** si direbbe che abbia già abbastanza preoccupazioni
2 (*in indirect speech*): **I said I would do it** ho detto che l'avrei fatto
3 (*emphatic*): **you WOULD be the one to forget!** è proprio da te dimenticartelo!; **it WOULD have to snow today!** doveva proprio nevicare oggi!; **you WOULD say that, wouldn't you!** e ti pareva! sapevo che avresti detto così !
4 (*insistence*): **she wouldn't behave** ha continuato a comportarsi male; **I told her not to but she would do it** le avevo detto di non farlo ma lei l'ha voluto fare a tutti i costi
5 (*conjecture*): **what would this be?** questo cosa sarebbe?; **it would have been about midnight** sarà stato verso mezzanotte; **it would seem so** sembrerebbe proprio di sì
6 (*wish*): **what would you have me do?** cosa desideri che faccia?; **would (that) it were not so!** (*old liter*) magari non fosse così !
7 (*in offers, invitations, requests*): **would you ask him to come in?** lo faccia entrare per cortesia; **would you care for some tea?** gradiresti del tè?; **would you close the door, please** chiuda la porta per favore; **would you like a biscuit?** gradisce un biscotto?
8 (*habit*): **he would go there on Mondays** ci andava il lunedì ; **he would paint it each year** era solito dipingerlo ogni anno

would-be ['wʊd,bi:] ADJ: **a would-be poet/politician** un aspirante poeta/politico
wouldn't ['wʊdnt] = would not
◎**wound**[1] [wu:nd] N ferita; **leg/bullet wound** ferita alla gamba/di proiettile
■VT (*also fig*) ferire
wound[2] [waʊnd] PT, PP *of* **wind**[2]
wound·ed ['wu:ndɪd] ADJ (*also fig*) ferito(-a); **a wounded man** un ferito
■NPL: **the wounded** i feriti
wound·ing ['wu:ndɪŋ] ADJ (*blow, remark*) che lascia il segno
wound up [,waʊnd'ʌp] ADJ teso(-a)
wove [wəʊv] PT *of* **weave**
wo·ven ['wəʊvən] PP *of* **weave**
wow [waʊ] EXCL (*fam*) wow!
WP [,dʌblju:'pi:] ABBR (*Brit fam*: = **weather permitting**) tempo permettendo
■N ABBR = word processing, word processor
WPC [,dʌblju:pi:'si:] N (*Brit*: = **woman police constable**) donna *f* poliziotto *inv*, agente *f* di polizia femminile
wpm ABBR = words per minute; *see* word
WRAC [,dʌblju:ɑ:reɪ'si:] N ABBR (*Brit*: = **Women's Royal Army Corps**) *ausiliarie dell'esercito*
WRAF [,dʌblju:ɑ:reɪ'ɛf] N ABBR (*Brit*: = **Women's Royal Air Force**) *ausiliarie dell'aeronautica militare*
wraith [reɪθ] N spettro
wran·gle ['ræŋgl] N litigio, alterco
■VI: **to wrangle (about *or* over)** litigare (su)
◎**wrap** [ræp] N (*shawl*) scialle *m*; (*housecoat*) vestaglia; (*rug*) coperta; (*cape*) mantellina; **still under wraps** (*fig*: *plan, scheme*) ancora segreto(-a)
■VT (*also*: **wrap up**) avvolgere, incartare; **the scheme is wrapped in secrecy** il piano è avvolto nel mistero
▶ **wrap up** VT + ADV **1** (*gen*) avvolgere; (*parcel*) incartare; (*child*) coprire bene; **she's wrapping her Christmas presents** sta incartando i regali di Natale; **she wrapped it up a bit, but what she meant was ...** ci ha girato un po' intorno, ma intendeva dire che...
2 (*fam*: *finalize*) concludere; **I think that (just) about wraps it up** direi che questo è tutto ciò che c'è da dire
3 to be wrapped up in sb/sth essere completamente preso(-a) da qn/qc; **she's wrapped up in herself** non pensa che a se stessa
■VI + ADV **1** (*dress warmly*) coprirsi (bene) **2** (*fam*: *be quiet*): **wrap up!** chiudi il becco!
wrap·over ['ræp,əʊvəʳ] ADJ (*skirt*) a portafoglio
wrap·per ['ræpəʳ] N (*on chocolate*) carta; (*postal*) fascetta; (*of book*) foderina, copertina
wrap·ping ['ræpɪŋ] N (*for chocolate, parcel*) carta
wrapping paper N (*brown*) carta da pacchi; (*for gift*) carta da regali
wrath [rɒθ] N (*liter*) ira, collera
wreak [ri:k] VT (*destruction, havoc*) portare, causare; **to wreak vengeance on** vendicarsi su
wreath [ri:θ] N (*pl* **wreaths** [ri:ðz]) (*of flowers*) ghirlanda; (*at funeral*) corona; (*of smoke*) anello; (*mist*) corona
wreathed [ri:ðd] ADJ: **a face wreathed in smiles** un volto raggiante; **wreathed in mist** avvolto(-a) nella nebbia
wreck [rɛk] N (*of ship, scheme etc*) naufragio; (*ship itself*) relitto; (*fig*: *old car etc*) rottame *m*; (: *building*) rudere *m*; **that car is a wreck!** quella macchina è un rottame!; **to be a complete wreck** essere distrutto(-a); **I'm a wreck** *or* **I feel a wreck** sono distrutto
■VT (*gen*) distruggere, rovinare; (*ship*) far naufragare; (*train*) far deragliare; (*house*) demolire; (*health*) rovinare; **to be wrecked** (*Naut*) fare naufragio; **the explosion wrecked the whole house** l'esplosione ha completamente distrutto la casa; **the trip was wrecked by bad weather** il brutto tempo ha rovinato la gita
wreck·age ['rɛkɪdʒ] N (*of ship*) relitto; (*of car etc*) rottami *mpl*; (*of building*) macerie *fpl*; **the wreckage of the coach** i rottami della corriera; **the wreckage of the building** le macerie dell'edificio
wreck·er ['rɛkəʳ] N (*Naut*: *salvager*) addetto al ricupero di relitti; (*Am*: *breaker, salvager*) demolitore *m*; (: *breakdown van*) carro *m* attrezzi *inv*
WREN [rɛn] N ABBR (*Brit*) *membro del WRNS*
wren [rɛn] N scricciolo
wrench [rɛntʃ] N **1** (*tug*) strattone *m*; **to give sth a wrench** dare uno strattone a qc **2** (*tool*) chiave *f*; **a screwdriver and a wrench** un cacciavite e una chiave
3 (*fig*) strazio; **it'll be a wrench to leave after all these years** sarà uno strazio partire dopo tutti questi anni
■VT **1 to wrench sth (away) from *or* off sb** strappare qc a qn; **they wrenched the suitcase from his hand** gli hanno strappato di mano la valigia; **he wrenched it out of my hands** me lo ha strappato di mano; **she wrenched herself free** si liberò con uno strattone; **to wrench a door open** aprire bruscamente una porta
2 (*Med*) slogare, storcere
wrest [rɛst] VT: **to wrest sth from sb** strappare qc a qn

wres·tle ['rɛsl] N: **to have a wrestle with sb** fare la lotta con qn
■ VI **1** lottare, fare la lotta; (*Sport*) praticare la lotta libera **2** (*fig*): **to wrestle with** (*one's conscience, device, machine*) lottare con; (*temptation, sins*) lottare contro; **they are currently wrestling with the problem of vandalism** attualmente stanno lottando contro il problema del vandalismo
■ VT: **to wrestle sb to the ground** mettere qn a terra; **the policemen wrestled him to the ground** i poliziotti lo hanno messo a terra
wres·tler ['rɛsləʳ] N (*Sport*) lottatore(-trice)
wres·tling ['rɛslɪŋ] N (*Sport*) lotta libera; (*also:* **all-in wrestling**: *Brit*) catch *m*
wrestling match N incontro di lotta libera
wretch [rɛtʃ] N disgraziato(-a), sciagurato(-a); **little wretch!** (*often hum*) birbante!
wretch·ed ['rɛtʃɪd] ADJ **1** (*house, conditions*) misero(-a), disgraziato(-a); (*life*) gramo(-a); (*pittance*) misero(-a); (*unhappy, depressed*) infelice, triste; **I feel wretched** (*fam: ill*) sto malissimo; **the outlook for these wretched people is grim** le prospettive per questi disgraziati sono ben tristi **2** (*fam: very bad: weather, behaviour*) pessimo(-a), atroce; (*holiday*) orrendo(-a), orribile; (*results*) pessimo(-a); (*child*) pestifero(-a); **I feel wretched about it** (*fam: conscience-stricken*) mi sento un verme; **what wretched luck!** (*fam*) che scalogna!; **where's that wretched dog?** (*fam*) dov'è quel maledetto cane?; **I've got to do the wretched thing again** (*fam*) devo rifare 'sta maledetta cosa
wretch·ed·ly ['rɛtʃɪdlɪ] ADV (*live*) miseramente; (*say, weep*) tristemente; (*pay*) male; (*treat, behave, perform*) in modo atroce
wretch·ed·ness ['rɛtʃɪdnɪs] N (*of life, conditions, pay*) miseria; (*unhappiness*) infelicità; (*of behaviour, weather*) meschinità
wrick, rick [rɪk] VT: **to wrick one's ankle** slogarsi la caviglia; **to wrick one's neck** farsi uno strappo (muscolare) al collo
wrig·gle ['rɪgl] VT (*toes, fingers*) muovere; **to wriggle one's way through** (*tunnel*) attraversare strisciando; (*undergrowth*) strisciare in
■ VI (*also:* **wriggle about** *or* **around**) agitarsi, dimenarsi; (*fish: on hook*) contorcersi; **to wriggle along/down** avanzare/scendere strisciando; **to wriggle free** liberarsi contorcendosi; **to wriggle through a hole** contorcersi per passare attraverso un buco; **he managed to wriggle out of it** (*fig*) se l'è cavata con un espediente
■ N contorsione *f*
wrig·gly ['rɪglɪ] ADJ (*comp* **-ier**, *superl* **-iest**) che si dimena
wring [rɪŋ] (*pt, pp* **wrung**) VT **1** (*also:* **wring out**: *wet clothes*) strizzare **2** (*twist*) torcere; **I'll wring your neck!** (*fam*) ti torco il collo!; **she wrung my hand** mi strinse forte la mano; **to wring one's hands** (*fig: in distress*) torcersi le mani; **to wring sb's heart** (*fig*) stringere il cuore a qn **3** (*also:* **wring out**: *confession, truth, money*) estorcere
wring·er ['rɪŋəʳ] N strizzatoio (manuale)
wring·ing ['rɪŋɪŋ] ADJ (*also:* **wringing wet**) bagnato(-a) fradicio(-a)
wrin·kle ['rɪŋkl] N (*on face, skin*) ruga; (*in stockings, paper etc*) grinza
■ VT (*fabric*) stropicciare; (*nose*) arricciare; (*flat surface, skin*) corrugare, raggrinzire
■ VI (*see vt*) stropicciarsi; arricciarsi; corrugarsi, raggrinzirsi
wrin·kled ['rɪŋkld], **wrin·kly** ['rɪŋklɪ] ADJ (*fabric, paper*) stropicciato(-a); (*nose*) arricciato(-a); (*surface*) corrugato(-a), increspato(-a); (*skin*) rugoso(-a), pieno(-a) di rughe; **his suit was wrinkled** il suo vestito era stropicciato
wrist [rɪst] N polso
wrist·band ['rɪst,bænd] N (*of shirt*) polsino; (*of watch*) cinturino
wrist loop N (*Mountaineering*) dragona
wrist·watch ['rɪst,wɒtʃ] N orologio da polso
writ [rɪt] N (*Law*) mandato; **to issue a writ against sb** *or* **serve a writ on sb** notificare un mandato di comparizione a qn
◎ **write** [raɪt] (*pt* **wrote**, *pp* **written**) VT scrivere; (*list*) compilare; (*certificate*) redigere; **she wrote that she'd arrive soon** scrisse che sarebbe arrivata presto; **to write sb a letter** scrivere una lettera a qn; **he wrote me a letter last week** mi ha scritto una lettera la settimana scorsa; **I was writing a letter** stavo scrivendo una lettera; **have you written the letter?** hai scritto la lettera?; **he's just written another novel** ha appena scritto un altro romanzo; **how is his name written?** come si scrive il suo nome?; **she wrote three pages** ha scritto tre pagine; **his guilt was written all over his face** gli si leggeva in faccia che era colpevole
■ VI scrivere; **to write to sb** scrivere a qn; **it's nothing to write home about** (*fam*) non è niente di speciale; **I'll write for the catalogue** scriverò per farmi mandare il catalogo; **to write for a paper** scrivere per un giornale
▸ **write away** VI + ADV: **to write away for** (*information*) richiedere per posta; (*goods*) ordinare per posta
▸ **write back** VI + ADV rispondere (*con una lettera*)
▸ **write down** VT + ADV (*make a note of*) segnare, annotare; (*put in writing*) mettere per iscritto; **I wrote down the address** ho annotato l'indirizzo; **can you write it down for me, please?** me lo può scrivere, per favore?
▸ **write in** VT + ADV inserire
■ VI + ADV scrivere; **to write in for sth** scrivere per richiedere qc
▸ **write into** VT + PREP includere in, scrivere in
▸ **write off** VI + ADV = **write away**
■ VT + ADV (*debt*) estinguere; (*scheme*) porre un termine a; (*smash up: car*) distruggere; **to write off a debt** estinguere un debito; **to write off a car** rottamare una macchina; **he was written off as useless** (*fig*) fu deciso che era un incompetente punto e basta
▸ **write out** VT + ADV (*gen*) scrivere; (*list, form*) compilare; (*cheque*) fare; (*copy: essay*) ricopiare
▸ **write up** VT + ADV (*notes, diary*) aggiornare; (*write report on: developments etc*) mettere per iscritto; **she wrote the play up in the Glasgow Herald** ha scritto una recensione della commedia sul Glasgow Herald
write-off ['raɪt,ɒf] N (*Comm*) perdita; (*fig: car etc*) rottame *m*; **the car is a write-off** la macchina è ridotta ad un rottame
write-protect [,raɪtprə'tɛkt] VT (*Comput*) proteggere contro scrittura
write-protected [,raɪtprə'tɛktɪd] ADJ (*Comput*) protetto(-a) da scrittura
◎ **writ·er** ['raɪtəʳ] N (*of letter, report*) autore(-trice); (*as profession*) scrittore(-trice); **to be a good/poor writer**

Ww

scrivere/non scrivere bene; **he's a thriller writer** è un autore di gialli; **he's a writer of novels** è un romanziere; **writer's cramp** crampo dello scrivano

write-up ['raɪt,ʌp] N (*review*) recensione *f*

writhe [raɪð] VI contorcersi; **to writhe with embarrassment** morire di vergogna

◎**writ·ing** ['raɪtɪŋ] N (*art*) scrivere *m*; (*sth written*) scritto; (*handwriting*) scrittura; **writings** NPL (*author's works*) opera *fsg*; **in writing** per iscritto; **to put sth in writing** mettere qc per iscritto; **in my own writing** scritto di mio pugno; **I can't read your writing** non riesco a leggere la tua scrittura; **Aubrey's biographical writings** gli scritti biografici di Aubrey; **writing is my profession** faccio lo scrittore di professione; **writing is just a hobby with me** scrivere è solo un hobby per me; **the writing on the wall** (*fig*) il presagio della rovina; **there's writing on the wall** c'è una scritta sul muro

writing case N nécessaire *m inv* per la corrispondenza

writing desk N scrivania

writing pad N (*for letters*) blocco di carta da lettere; (*for notes*) bloc notes *m inv*

writing paper N carta da lettere

writing table N scrittoio

◎**writ·ten** ['rɪtn] PP *of* **write**

■ ADJ scritto(-a)

written word N: **the written word** la parola scritta

WRNS [,dʌblju:ɑ:rɛn'ɛs] N ABBR (*Brit:* = **Women's Royal Naval Service**) *ausiliarie della marina militare*

◎**wrong** [rɒŋ] ADJ

1 (*morally*) sbagliato(-a), riprovevole; (*unfair*) ingiusto(-a), sbagliato(-a); (*wicked*) cattivo(-a); **it's wrong to steal, stealing is wrong** non si deve rubare; **lying is wrong** non si dicono le bugie; **you were wrong to do that** hai sbagliato a fare così ; **what's wrong with a drink now and again?** che c'è di male nel bere un bicchierino ogni tanto?

2 (*incorrect*) sbagliato(-a), errato(-a); **to be wrong** (*answer*) essere sbagliato(-a); (*in doing, saying*) avere torto, sbagliarsi; **I was wrong in thinking that ...** avevo torto a pensare che...; **you are wrong about that** ti sbagli; **the information they gave us was wrong** le informazioni che ci hanno dato erano sbagliate; **the wrong answer** la risposta sbagliata; **you've got the wrong number** ha sbagliato numero

3 (*improper, not sought, not wanted*) sbagliato(-a), inadatto(-a); **to say/do the wrong thing** dire/fare qc che non va

4 (*amiss*): **is anything** *or* **something wrong?** c'è qualcosa che non va?; **what's wrong (with you)?** che cos'hai?, cosa c'è che non va?; **what's wrong with her?** cos'ha?; **there's nothing wrong** va tutto bene; **sth must be wrong** dev'esserci qc che non va; **there is something wrong with my lights** le luci non funzionano bene; **what's wrong with your arm?** cos'hai al braccio?; **what's wrong with the car?** cos'ha la macchina che non va?; **to be wrong in the head** (*fam*) essere un po' tocco(-a)

■ ADV (*spell, pronounce*) in modo sbagliato, erroneamente; **to do sth wrong** sbagliare; **you've done it wrong** hai sbagliato; **you're doing it all wrong** stai sbagliando tutto; **you did wrong to do it** hai fatto male agendo così ; **to get sth wrong** sbagliare qc; **don't get me wrong** (*fam*) non fraintendermi; **to go wrong** (*on route*) sbagliare strada; (*in calculation*) sbagliarsi, commettere un errore; (*morally*) prendere una cattiva strada; (*plan etc*) andare male, fallire; **the robbery went wrong and they got caught** la rapina è andata male e li hanno presi; **something went wrong with the brakes** è successo qualcosa ai freni; **you can't go wrong** non puoi sbagliarti; **you won't go far wrong if you follow his advice** non rischi più di tanto a seguire il suo consiglio

■ N

1 (*evil*) male *m*; **to do wrong** far (del) male; **he can do no wrong in her eyes** ai suoi occhi lui è perfetto

2 (*unjust act*) torto; **to do sb a wrong** fare un torto a qn; **to be in the wrong** avere torto; **to put sb in the wrong** mettere qn dalla parte del torto; **to right a wrong** riparare a un torto; **to suffer a wrong** subire un torto

■ VT fare (un) torto a

wrong·doer ['rɒŋ,du:əʳ] N malfattore(-trice)

wrong·doing ['rɒŋ,du:ɪŋ] N malefatta, misfatto

wrong-foot ['rɒŋ,fʊt] VT (*Ftbl, also fig*) prendere in contropiede

wrong·ful ['rɒŋfʊl] ADJ (*unjust: accusation*) ingiusto(-a); (*unlawful: arrest, imprisonment*) illegale, illecito(-a); **wrongful dismissal** licenziamento ingiustificato

wrong·ful·ly ['rɒŋfəlɪ] ADV (*see adj*) ingiustamente; illegalmente

wrong-headed [,rɒŋ'hɛdɪd] ADJ (*stubborn*) ostinato(-a); (*mistaken*) sbagliato(-a)

wrong·ly ['rɒŋlɪ] ADV (*answer, do, count*) erroneamente; (*treat*) ingiustamente; (*accuse, dismiss*) a torto

wrong number N: **you have the wrong number** (*Telec*) ha sbagliato numero

wrong side N (*of cloth*) rovescio

wrote [rəʊt] PT *of* **write**

wrought [rɔ:t] (*old, liter*) **1** PT, PP *of* **wreak 2 great changes have been wrought** sono avvenuti dei grandi cambiamenti

■ ADJ (*silver*) lavorato(-a); (*iron*) battuto(-a)

wrought-iron [,rɔ:t'aɪən] ADJ di ferro battuto

wrought-up [,rɔ:t'ʌp] ADJ: **to be wrought-up** essere teso(-a)

wrung [rʌŋ] PT, PP *of* **wring**

WRVS [,dʌblju:ɑ:rvi:'ɛs] N ABBR (*Brit:* = **Women's Royal Voluntary Service**) *ausiliarie al servizio della collettività*

wry [raɪ] ADJ beffardo(-a); **to make a wry face** fare una smorfia

wry·ly ['raɪlɪ] ADV beffardamente

wt. ABBR = **weight**

WTO [,dʌblju:ti:'əʊ] N ABBR OMC (= *Organizzazione Mondiale del Commercio*)

▷ www.wto.org

wuss [wʊs] N (*fam*) codardo(-a), vigliacco(-a)

WV ABBR (*Am Post*) = **West Virginia**

WWW [,dʌblju:,dʌblju:'dʌblju:] N ABBR (*Comput:* = **World Wide Web**) WWW *m*

WY ABBR (*Am Post*) = **Wyoming**

Wyo·ming [waɪ'əʊmɪŋ] N Wyoming *m*

▷ http://wyoming.gov/

WYSIWYG ABBR (*Comput:* = **what you see is what you get**) *quello che vedi sullo schermo è quello che ottieni in stampa*

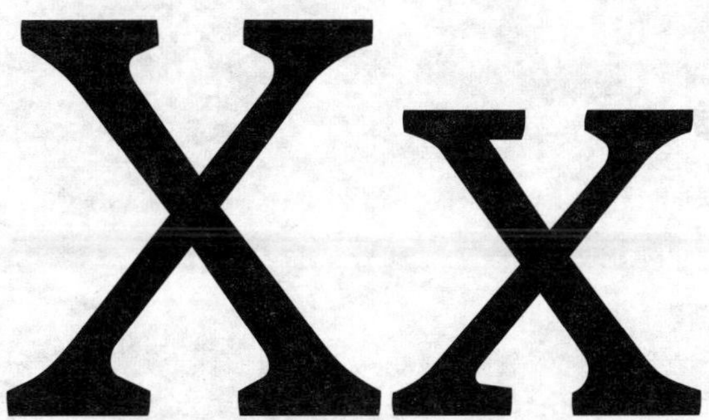

X, x [ɛks] N (*letter, Math*) X, x *f or m inv*; **X for Xmas** ≈ X come Xeres; **if you have x dollars a year** se hai x dollari all'anno; **x marks the spot** il punto è segnato con una croce
X-certificate [ˌɛksəˈtɪfɪkət] ADJ (*Brit Cine*) vietato ai minori di 18 anni (*secondo un sistema di censura non più in uso*)
X-chromosome [ˌɛksˈkrəʊməsəʊm] N cromosoma *m* X
xen·on [ˈzɛnɒn] N (*Chem*) xeno
xeno·phobe [ˈzɛnəˌfəʊb] N (*frm*) xenofobo(-a)
xeno·pho·bia [ˌzɛnəˈfəʊbɪə] N (*frm*) xenofobia
xeno·phobic [ˌzɛnəˈfəʊbɪk] ADJ (*frm*) xenofobo(-a), xenofobico(-a)
Xenophon [ˈzɛnəfən] N Senofonte *m*
Xer·ox® [ˈzɪərɒks] VT fotocopiare
■ N (*also:* **Xerox machine**) fotocopiatrice *f*; (*photocopy*) fotocopia
Xerxes [ˈzɜːksiːz] N Serse *m*
XL [ˌɛksˈɛl] ABBR (= **extra large**) XL *f inv*
Xmas [ˈɛksməs, ˈkrɪsməs] N ABBR = **Christmas**
X-rated [ˌɛksˈreɪtɪd] ADJ (*Am: film*) ≈ vietato ai minori di 18 anni
X-ray [ˈɛksˌreɪ] N (*ray*) raggio X; (*photograph*) radiografia; **x-rays** raggi X; **to have an X-ray** farsi fare una radiografia
■ VT radiografare; **they X-rayed my arm** mi hanno fatto una radiografia al braccio
■ ADJ (*examination*) radiografico(-a)
X-ray picture N lastra
xy·lem [ˈzaɪləm] N (*Bot*) xilema *m*
xy·lo·phone [ˈzaɪləˌfəʊn] N xilofono

Yy

Y, y [waɪ] N (*letter*) Y, y *f or m inv*; **Y for Yellow**, (*Am*) **Y for Yoke** ≈ Y come Yacht

◎ **yacht** [jɒt] N yacht *m inv*, panfilo da diporto

yacht club N yacht club *m inv*, circolo nautico

yacht·ing ['jɒtɪŋ] N yachting *m*, navigazione *f* da diporto

yachts·man ['jɒtsmən] N (*pl* **-men**) yachtsman *m inv*

yachts·woman ['jɒts,wʊmən] N (*pl* **-women**) yachtswoman *f inv*

yak[1] [jæk] N (*Zool*) yak *m inv*

yak[2] [jæk] (*fam*) VI cicalare, cianciare
■ N cicaleccio

yam [jæm] N (*plant, tuber*) igname *m*; (*sweet potato*) patata dolce

Yank [jæŋk], **Yan·kee** ['jæŋkɪ] (*fam often pej*) N yankee *m/f inv*
■ ADJ yankee *inv*

yank [jæŋk] N strattone *m*
■ VT tirare, dare uno strattone a; **to yank a nail out** strappare via un chiodo; **she yanked open the drawer** aprì il cassetto con uno strattone

yap [jæp] (*of dog*) N guaito
■ VI (*dog*) guaire

yap·ping ['jæpɪŋ] ADJ (*dog*) che guaisce
■ N guaiti *mpl*

Yard [jɑːd] N (*Brit fam*): **the Yard** Scotland Yard *m inv*

◎ **yard**[1] [jɑːd] N **1** (*measure*) iarda (*91,44 cm*), yard *f inv*; **to sell sth by the yard** ≈ vendere qc al metro; **yards of** (*fig*) chilometri di **2** (*Naut*) pennone *m*

yard[2] [jɑːd] N (*courtyard, farmyard*) cortile *m*; (*Am: garden*) giardino; (*worksite*) cantiere *m*; (*for storage*) deposito; **builder's yard** deposito di materiale da costruzione; **back yard** (*Brit*) cortile sul retro; (*Am*) giardino sul retro

yard·age ['jɑːdɪdʒ] N ≈ metraggio

yard·arm ['jɑːdɑːm] N (*Naut*) varea

yard·stick ['jɑːdstɪk] N (*fig*) metro, criterio

yarn [jɑːn] N **1** (*wool, thread*) filato **2** (*tale*) storia, racconto; **to spin sb a yarn** raccontare a qn una grossa balla

yash·mak ['jæʃmæk] N velo (*indossato dalle donne musulmane*)

yawn [jɔːn] N sbadiglio; **to give a yawn** fare uno sbadiglio
■ VI sbadigliare; (*fig: hole, chasm*) aprirsi; **"yes", she yawned** "sì ", disse con uno sbadiglio
■ VT: **to yawn one's head off** non riuscire a smettere di sbadigliare

yawn·ing ['jɔːnɪŋ] ADJ (*fig: gap, abyss*) spalancato(-a)

Y-chromosome ['waɪ,krəʊməsəʊm] N cromosoma *m* Y

yd(s). ABBR *of* **yard(s)**

ye[1] [jiː] PRON (*old*) = **you** (*pl*)

ye[2] [jiː] DEF ART (*old: on shop signs*) = **the**

yea [jeɪ] (*old*) ADV (*yes*) sì
■ N: **to count the yeas and the nays** (*votes*) contare i sì e i no

◎ **yeah** [jɛə] ADV (*fam*) sì

◎ **year** [jɪə'] N **1** (*gen*) anno; **this year** quest'anno; **every year** tutti gli anni, ogni anno; **all (the) year round** (per) tutto l'anno; **year in, year out** anno dopo anno; **year by year** *or* **from year to year** col passar degli anni; **years and years ago** tanti anni fa; **from one year to the next** da un anno all'altro; **three times a year** tre volte all'anno; **in the year 1869** nell'anno 1869, nel 1869; **in the year of grace** nell'anno di grazia; **last year** l'anno scorso; **next year** (*looking to future*) l'anno prossimo *or* venturo; **the next year** (*in past time*) l'anno seguente *or* successivo; **he got 10 years** (*in prison*) si è beccato 10 anni; **it takes years** ci vogliono anni; **I met him a year last January** a gennaio fa un anno che l'ho conosciuto; **a year tomorrow** domani tra un anno; **I haven't seen her for years** non la vedo da anni, sono anni che non la vedo; **over the years** con gli anni; **to be fifteen years old** avere quindici anni; **an eight-year-old child** un bambino di otto anni; **she's three years old** ha tre anni; **she's in her fiftieth year** compierà cinquant'anni; **it's taken years off her** l'ha ringiovanita; **a** *or* **per year** all'anno **2** (*Scol, Univ*) anno; **he's in the second year** è al secondo anno; **he was in my year at university** frequentavamo lo stesso anno di università **3** (*of wine*) annata **4** (*age*): **old/young for one's years** vecchio/giovane per i suoi anni *or* per la sua età; **from her earliest years** fin dall'infanzia, fin dalla più tenera età; **he's getting on in years** ha i suoi anni ormai

year·book ['jɪəˌbʊk] N annuario

year·ling ['jɪəlɪŋ] N *(racehorse)* yearling *m inv*

year·long [jɪə'lɒŋ] ADJ di un anno

year·ly ['jɪəlɪ] ADJ annuale; **twice-yearly** semestrale
■ ADV annualmente; **three times yearly** tre volte all'anno

yearn [jɜːn] VI: **to yearn for sb/sth** desiderare ardentemente qn/qc; **to yearn to do sth** struggersi dal desiderio di fare qc

yearn·ing ['jɜːnɪŋ] ADJ *(desire)* intenso(-a); *(look, tone)* desideroso(-a), bramoso(-a)
■ N: **yearning (for)** desiderio struggente (di)

yearn·ing·ly ['jɜːnɪŋlɪ] ADV con smania, con desiderio

year-round [jɪə'raʊnd] ADJ che dura tutto l'anno; **a year-round swimming pool** una piscina aperta tutto l'anno

yeast [jiːst] N lievito; **dried yeast** lievito disidratato *(or* in polvere)

yeasty ['jiːstɪ] ADJ *(comp* **-ier**, *superl* **-iest**) *(smell, flavour)* di lievito

yell [jɛl] N urlo; **to give a yell** *or* **let out a yell** lanciare un urlo; **a yell of laughter** una fragorosa risata
■ VI urlare
■ VT *(order, name)* urlare

yell·ing ['jɛlɪŋ] ADJ urlante
■ N urla *fpl*

◎ **yel·low** ['jɛləʊ] ADJ *(comp* **-er**, *superl* **-est**) **1** *(colour)* giallo(-a); **to go** *or* **turn yellow** *(person)* diventare giallo(-a); *(leaf, paper)* ingiallire **2** *(fam pej: cowardly)* fifone(-a)
■ N *(colour)* giallo; *(of an egg)* rosso
■ VI ingiallire

yellow card N *(Sport)* cartellino giallo

yellow fever N febbre *f* gialla

yellow·hammer ['jɛləʊˌhæməʳ] N *(Zool)* zigolo giallo

yel·low·ish ['jɛləʊɪʃ] ADJ giallastro(-a), giallognolo(-a)

Yellow Pages ® NPL *(Telec)*: **the Yellow Pages** le pagine gialle®

Yellow Sea N: **the Yellow Sea** il mar Giallo

yelp [jɛlp] N *(of dog)* guaito; *(of person)* strillo
■ VI *(see n)* guaire, strillare

yelp·ing ['jɛlpɪŋ] ADJ *(dog)* che guaisce
■ N guaiti *mpl*

Yem·en ['jɛmən] N Yemen *m*

Yem·eni ['jɛmənɪ] ADJ, N yemenita *(m/f)*

◎ **yen**[1] [jɛn] N *(currency)* yen *m inv*

yen[2] [jɛn] N *(fam)*: **to have a yen to do sth** avere una gran voglia di fare qc

yeo·man ['jəʊmən] N *(pl* **-men**) *(Brit old)* piccolo proprietario terriero

Yeoman of the Guard N Guardiano della Torre di Londra

yep [jɛp] ADV *(fam)* = yes

yer [jəʳ] *(fam)* = you; your

◎ **yes** [jɛs] ADV sì ; **to say yes (to)** dire di sì (a); **do you like it? – yes** ti piace? – sì ; **don't you want any? — yes (I do)!** non ne vuoi? — ma sì !; **yes yes, but what if it doesn't?** sì , va bene, ma se non lo fa?
■ N sì *m inv*

yes man N *(pej)* yes-man *m inv*

◎ **yes·ter·day** ['jɛstəˌdeɪ] ADV ieri; **yesterday morning/evening** ieri mattina/sera; **the day before yesterday** l'altro ieri; **a week yesterday** *(past)* una settimana fa, ieri; **late yesterday** ieri in serata; **it rained all (day) yesterday** ieri è piovuto tutto il giorno; **the great men of yesterday** i grandi uomini del passato
■ N ieri *m inv*

yes·ter·year ['jɛstəˌjɪəʳ] N *(old, liter)* il tempo andato

◎ **yet** [jɛt] ADV **1** *(already, up to now, so far)* già; *(now, by now)* ancora; **I wonder if he's come yet** mi chiedo se non sia già arrivato; **not yet** non ancora; **he hasn't come yet** non è ancora arrivato; **it is not finished yet** non è ancora finito; **have you told your parents yet?** lo hai già detto ai tuoi genitori?; **I needn't go (just) yet** non è ancora il momento di andare; **don't go (just) yet** non andare già via; **this is his best film yet** finora questo è il suo film migliore; **as yet** per ora, finora; **there's no news as yet** per ora non ci sono notizie
2 *(still)* ancora; **he may come yet** *or* **he may yet come** può ancora arrivare; **that question is yet to be decided** quella questione è ancora da decidere; **a settlement might yet be possible** è ancora possibile trovare un accordo; **I'll do it yet!** prima o poi ce la farò!
3 *(in addition, even)*: **yet again** di nuovo; **yet another/more** ancora un altro/più; **yet once more** ancora una volta; **a few days yet** ancora qualche giorno **4** *(frm)*: **nor yet** tanto meno; **I do not like him, nor yet his sister** lui non mi piace, e tanto meno sua sorella
■ CONJ ma, tuttavia; **and yet** eppure, tuttavia; **it was funny, yet sad at the same time** era buffo e triste nel contempo; **and yet I enjoyed it** e tuttavia mi è piaciuto

yeti ['jɛtɪ] N yeti *m inv*

yew [juː] N *(also:* **yew tree**) tasso

Y-fronts® ['waɪˌfrʌnts] NPL mutande *fpl* da uomo *(con apertura davanti)*

YHA [ˌwaɪeɪtʃ'eɪ] N ABBR *(Brit:* = **Youth Hostels Association**) associazione degli ostelli della gioventù

Yid·dish ['jɪdɪʃ] ADJ, N yiddish *(m) inv*

◎ **yield** [jiːld] N *(of land, mine)* resa; *(of investment)* rendita; *(of crops)* raccolto; **a yield of 5%** un profitto del 5%
■ VT **1** *(produce: harvest, dividend)* fruttare; *(: results)* fornire, produrre; *(: information, opportunity)* fornire
2 *(surrender)* cedere
■ VI *(surrender)*: **to yield (to)** cedere (a), arrendersi (a); *(break, collapse)* cedere; *(Am Aut)* dare la precedenza; **to yield to temptation** cedere alla tentazione
▸ **yield up** VT + ADV *(liter: secret)* svelare, rivelare

yield·ing ['jiːldɪŋ] ADJ *(person)* arrendevole; *(ground, surface)* cedevole

yip·pee [jɪ'piː] EXCL *(fam)* hurrà!

YMCA [ˌwaɪɛmsiː'eɪ] N ABBR (= **Young Men's Christian Association**) YMCA *f*

yo [jəʊ] EXCL *(fam)* ehi, ciao

yob ['jɒb], **yob·bo** ['jɒbəʊ] N *(Brit fam)* teppista *m/f*

yo·del ['jəʊdl] VI fare lo jodel
■ N jodel *m inv*

yoga ['jəʊgə] N yoga *m inv*

yo·ghurt, yo·ghourt, yo·gurt ['jɒgət] N yogurt *m inv*

yoke [jəʊk] N **1** *(of oxen, also fig)* giogo; **under the yoke of** *(fig)* sotto il giogo di **2** *(on dress)* sprone *m*
■ VT *(also:* **yoke together**: *oxen)* aggiogare

yo·kel ['jəʊkəl] *(pej)* N zotico(-a), villano(-a)

yolk [jəʊk] N tuorlo, rosso (d'uovo)

yomp [jɒmp] VI *(Brit Mil fam)* percorrere un terreno accidentato

yon·der ['jɒndəʳ] ADV *(old)*: **(over) yonder** laggiù, là

yonks [jɒŋks] ADV *(Brit fam)*: **I haven't seen her for yonks** è un secolo che non la vedo

Yorks [yɔːks] ABBR *(Brit)* = Yorkshire

Yy

York·shire pud·ding ['jɔ:kʃə'pʊdɪŋ] N *tipo di bignè salato, cotto in forno, che accompagna il tradizionale arrosto della domenica in Gran Bretagna*

Yo·semi·te [jəʊ'sɛmətɪ] N parco di Yosemite ▷ www.nps.gov/yose/

◎ **you** [ju:] KEYWORD
PERS PRON **1** (*subject: singular*) tu; (: *plural*) voi; (: *singular: polite form*) lei; (: *plural: very formal*) loro; **you and I will go** tu ed io andiamo; **you angel!** sei un angelo!; **you are very kind** è molto gentile da parte tua (*or* sua *etc*); **here you are!** eccoti!; **that dress just isn't you** quel vestito proprio non ti si addice; **you Italians** voi *or* voialtri italiani; **if I was** *or* **were you** se fossi in te (*or* lei *etc*)
2 (*see* **1**) (*object: direct*) ti; la; vi; loro (*after verb*); (: *indirect*) ti; le; vi; loro (*after verb*); **I'll phone you later** ti chiamo più tardi/la chiamerò più tardi/vi chiamerò più tardi/li chiamerò più tardi; **I'll see you tomorrow** ci vediamo domani; **I gave it to you** te l'ho dato; gliel'ho dato; ve l'ho dato; l'ho dato loro
3 (*see* **1**) (*stressed, after preposition, in comparisons*) te; lei; voi; loro; **it's for you** è per te (*or* lei *etc*); **she's younger than you** è più giovane di te (*or* lei *etc*); **I told YOU to do it** ho detto a TE (*or* LEI *etc*) di farlo
4 (*impersonal: one*) si; **you can't do that!** non si fanno queste cose!; **fresh air does you good** l'aria fresca fa bene; **you know who/what** sappiamo chi/cosa; **you never can tell** non si sa mai; **you never know** non si sa mai

you'd [ju:d] = you would, you had

you'll [ju:l] = you will, you shall

◎ **young** [jʌŋ] ADJ (*comp* **-er**, *superl* **-est**) (*gen*) giovane; (*vegetables*) novello(-a); (*offender*) minorenne; **a young man** un giovanotto; **a young lady** una signorina; **young people** i giovani; **young children** bambini piccoli; **they have a young family** hanno dei bambini piccoli; **in my young days** quand'ero giovane; **you're too young** sei troppo giovane; **she's not so young as she was** non è più tanto giovane; **younger** più giovane; **he's younger than me** è più giovane di me; **my younger brother** il mio fratello minore; **the younger son** il figlio minore; **he is two years younger than her** ha due anni meno di lei; **if I were 15 years younger** se avessi 15 anni di meno; **my youngest brother** il mio fratello minore; **the youngest** (*masculine*) il più giovane; **the youngest** *or* **he's the youngest** è il più giovane; **the youngest** (*feminine*) la più giovane; **she's the youngest in the class** è la più giovane della classe; **she is the youngest competitor** è la concorrente più giovane; **you're only young once** si è giovani una volta sola; **she's young at heart** è giovane di spirito; **he looks young for his age** sembra più giovane di quanto sia in realtà; **the night is young** la notte è appena cominciata; **to grow** *or* **get younger** ringiovanire; **the younger generation** la nuova generazione
■ NPL (*of animals*) piccoli *mpl*, prole *fsg*; **the young** (*young people*) i giovani

young gun N giovane *m/f* emergente

young·ish ['jʌŋɪʃ] ADJ abbastanza giovane

◎ **young·ster** ['jʌŋstə^r] N (*child*) bambino(-a); (*young person*) giovane *m/f*

◎ **your** [jʊə^r] POSS ADJ **1** SG il/la tuo(-a); PL i/le tuoi/tue; (*sg: polite form*) il/la suo(-a); PL i/le suoi/sue; PL il/la vostro(-a); PL i/le vostri(-e); (*sg: polite: very formal*) il/la loro; (: *pl*) i/le loro; **your house** la tua (*or* sua *etc*) casa; **your brother** tuo (*or* suo *etc*) fratello; **your address** il tuo indirizzo; **your pen** la tua penna; **your parents** i tuoi genitori; **your father** tuo padre; **your mother** tua madre; **children, give these letters to your parents** ragazzi, date queste lettere ai vostri genitori; **your ticket, madam** il suo biglietto, signora; **wash your hands** lavati le mani; **remember to take your umbrella, sir** non dimentichi di prendere l'ombrello **2** (*impersonal: one's*): **it's bad for your health** danneggia la salute; **your average Italian** l'italiano medio

you're [jʊə^r] = you are

◎ **yours** [jʊəz] POSS PRON, SG il/la tuo(-a); PL i/le tuoi/tue; PL il/la vostro(-a); PL i/le vostri(-e); (*sg: polite form*) il/la suo(-a); (: *pl*) i/le suoi/sue; (*pl: very formal*) il/la loro; PL i/le loro; **yours is red, mine is green** il tuo (*or* suo *etc*) è rosso, il mio è verde; **this is yours** questo è il tuo (*or* suo *etc*); **a friend of yours** un tuo (*or* suo *etc*) amico; **my garden is smaller than yours** il mio giardino è più piccolo del tuo; **that bag's not mine, it's yours** questa borsa non è la mia, è la tua; **is this bag yours?** è tua questa borsa?; **our parents and yours** i nostri genitori e i vostri; **is that car yours, sir?** è sua quella macchina, signore?; **yours faithfully/sincerely** (*in letters*) distinti/cordiali saluti; **what's yours?** (*fam: drink*) tu che prendi?

◎ **your·self** [jə'sɛlf] PERS PRON (*pl* **yourselves** [jə'sɛlvz]) **1** (*reflexive: sg*) ti; (: *pl*) vi; (*sg: polite*) si; (*pl: very formal*) si; **have you hurt yourself?** ti sei (*or* si è) fatto male?; **have you hurt yourselves?** vi siete (*or* si sono) fatti male?; **did you enjoy yourself, sir?** si è divertito, signore? **2** (*emphatic: sg*) tu stesso(-a); (: *pl*) voi stessi(-e); (*sg: polite*) lei stesso(-a); (*pl: very formal*) loro stessi(-e); **you yourself told me** me l'hai detto proprio tu, tu stesso me l'hai detto; **a beginner like yourself** un principiante come te; **an important person like yourself** una persona importante come lei **3** (*after prep*) te, te stesso(-a); (: *polite*) lei, lei stesso(-a); (: *pl*) voi, voi stessi(-e); (: *very formal*) loro, loro stessi(-e); **(all) by yourself** (tutto) da solo; **do you like travelling by yourself?** ti piace viaggiare da solo? **4** (*impersonal: reflexive*) si; (: *emphatic*) se stessi; (: *after prep*) sé, se stessi; *see also* **oneself**

◎ **youth** [ju:θ] N **1** giovinezza, gioventù *f*; **in early youth** nella prima giovinezza; **in my youth** da giovane, quando ero giovane **2** (*pl* **youths** [ju:ðz]) (*boy*) ragazzo, giovane *m* **3** PL (*young people*) giovani *mpl*; **the youth of today** i giovani di oggi

youth club N circolo giovanile

youth·ful ['ju:θfʊl] ADJ (*air, figure, manner*) giovanile; (*mistakes*) di gioventù

youth·ful·ness ['ju:θfʊlnɪs] N giovinezza; **youthfulness of appearance** aspetto giovanile

youth hostel N ostello della gioventù

youth leader N animatore(-trice) (di circolo giovanile)

youth movement N movimento giovanile

you've [ju:v] = you have

yowl [jaʊl] N (*of dog, person*) latrato; (*of cat*) miagolio
■ VI (*see n*) latrare; miagolare

yo-yo ['jəʊjəʊ] N yo-yo *m inv*

yr ABBR = year

Y-shaped ['waɪʃeɪpt] ADJ a forma di ipsilon

YT [,waɪ'ti:] ABBR (*Canada*) = *Yukon Territory*

yucky, yuk·ky ['jʌkɪ] ADJ (*fam*) schifoso(-a)

Yu·go·slav [ju:gəʊ'slɑ:v] ADJ, N jugoslavo(-a)
Yu·go·sla·via [ju:gəʊ'slɑ:vɪə] N Jugoslavia; **the former Yugoslavia** l'ex Jugoslavia; **in the former Yugoslavia** nell'ex Jugoslavia
Yu·go·sla·vian [ju:gəʊ'slɑ:vɪən] ADJ, N jugoslavo(-a)
yuk [jʌk] EXCL (*fam*) puh!, puah!
yuk·ky ['jʌkɪ] ADJ = **yucky**
Yu·kon ['ju:kɒn] N Yukon *m*
▹ www.gov.yk.ca
yule [ju:l] N = **Yuletide**
yule log N (*cake*) tronchetto di Natale; (*piece of wood*) *ceppo nel caminetto a Natale*
Yule·tide ['ju:l,taɪd] N (*old*) periodo natalizio
yum·my ['jʌmɪ] ADJ (*comp* **-ier**, *superl* **-iest**) (*fam: food*) delizioso(-a), squisito(-a)
yum-yum [jʌm'jʌm] EXCL gnam gnam!
yup·pie ['jʌpɪ] N yuppie *m/f inv*
YWCA [,waɪdʌblju:si:'eɪ] N ABBR (= **Young Women's Christian Association**) *organizzazione che mette a disposizione ostelli per donne*

Z, z [zɛd, *Am* zi:] N (*letter*) Z, z *f or m inv*; **Z for Zebra** ≈ Z come Zara

Z ABBR (*atomic number*) Z

Za·ire [zɑ:ˈi:əʳ] N lo Zaire *m*

Zam·bia [ˈzæmbɪə] N lo Zambia *m*

Zam·bian [ˈzæmbɪən] ADJ, N zambiano(-a)

zany [ˈzeɪnɪ] ADJ (*comp* **-ier**, *superl* **-iest**) (*fam*) pazzoide, un po' pazzo(-a)

zap [zæp] VT (*fam: destroy*) far fuori; (*Comput*) cancellare; (*TV*) fare zapping; **I zapped the file** ho cancellato il file; **a plan to zap their missiles** un piano per distruggere i loro missili

zap·per [ˈzæpəʳ] N (*fam*) telecomando

zeal [zi:l] N (*fervour*) zelo; (*enthusiasm*) entusiasmo; **zeal for** ansia di

zeal·ot [ˈzɛlət] N zelota *m/f*

zeal·ous [ˈzɛləs] ADJ (*supporter, believer, worker*) zelante

zeal·ous·ly [ˈzɛləslɪ] ADV (*support*) con zelo, in modo zelante

zeb·ra [ˈzi:brə] N zebra

zebra crossing N (*Brit*) strisce *fpl* (pedonali), zebre *fpl*

zed [zɛd], **zee** (*Am*) [zi:] N (*letter name*) zeta *m or f inv*

Zen [zɛn] N Zen *m inv*

zen·ith [ˈzɛnɪθ] N (*liter: of civilization*) culmine *m*; (*of career*) apice *m*; (*Astron*) zenit *m inv*

zeph·yr [ˈzɛfəʳ] N (*liter*) zefiro

zep·pe·lin [ˈzɛpəlɪn] N zeppelin *m inv*

◎ **zero** [ˈzɪərəʊ] N zero; **5° below zero** 5° sotto zero
■ADJ (*altitude, gravity*) zero *inv*; (*fam: interest, hope*) nullo(-a)
▸ **zero in on** VI + ADV + PREP (*target*) essere puntato(-a) su; (*problem, subject*) concentrarsi su

zero-emission [ˌzɪərəʊɪˈmɪʃən] ADJ a emissioni zero

zero hour N ora zero

zero option N (*Pol*) opzione *f* zero

zero-rated [ˌzɪərəʊˈreɪtɪd] ADJ (*Brit Comm*) ad aliquota zero

zero tolerance N tolleranza zero

zest [zɛst] N **1** (*enthusiasm*): **zest (for)** gusto (per), entusiasmo (per); (*fig: spice*) sapore *m*; **zest for living** *or* **life** gioia di vivere **2** (*Culin: of orange, lemon*) buccia

zest·ful [ˈzɛstfʊl] ADJ entusiasta

Zeus [zju:s] N Zeus *m*

zib·et [ˈzɪbɪt] N zibetto

zig·zag [ˈzɪɡˌzæɡ] N zigzag *m inv*
■VI zigzagare; **to zigzag across/down/up** attraversare/scendere/salire a zigzag
■ADJ a zigzag

Zim·ba·bwe [zɪmˈbɑ:bwɪ] N lo Zimbabwe

Zim·ba·bwean [zɪmˈbɑ:bwɪən] ADJ dello Zimbabwe

Zim·mer® [ˈzɪməʳ] N (*also:* **Zimmer frame**: *Brit*) deambulatore *m*

zinc [zɪŋk] N zinco
■ADJ di zinco

zine [zi:n] N (*fam*) fanzine *f inv*; *rivista per appassionati*

zing [zɪŋ] N (*fam*) verve *f inv*

Zi·on·ism [ˈzaɪəˌnɪzəm] N sionismo

Zi·on·ist [ˈzaɪənɪst] ADJ sionistico(-a)
■N sionista *m/f*

zip [zɪp] N **1** (*Brit: zip fastener*) cerniera (lampo), zip *m inv*; **the zip's stuck** la cerniera lampo è inceppata **2** (*fam: energy*) energia, forza; **put a bit of zip into it** mettici un po' di entusiasmo
■VT: **to zip up** chiudere la cerniera di; **zipped pockets** (*with zips*) tasche con cerniera; (*zipped up*) tasche con la cerniera chiusa; **he zipped the bag open/closed** ha aperto/chiuso la cerniera della borsa; (*Comput*) zippare
■VI: **to zip past** sfrecciare davanti; **a sports car zipped past me** una macchina sportiva mi è sfrecciata davanti; **to zip along to the shops** fare una corsa per comprare qc

zip code N (*Am Post*) codice *m* di avviamento postale

zip file N (*Comput*) file *m inv* zippato

zip·per [ˈzɪpəʳ] N (*Am*) = **zip** N **1**

zip·py [ˈzɪpɪ] ADJ (*fam*) scattante

zir·con [ˈzɜ:kən] N zircone *m*

zit [zɪt] N brufolo

zith·er [ˈzɪðəʳ] N cetra

zo·di·ac [ˈzəʊdɪæk] N zodiaco

zom·bie [ˈzɒmbɪ] N zombie *m/f inv*; **like a zombie** come uno zombie, come un morto che cammina

zon·al [ˈzəʊnl] ADJ zonale

◎ **zone** [zəʊn] N zona; **danger zone** zona pericolosa; **war zone** zona di guerra

■VT zonizzare
zon·ing ['zəʊnɪŋ] N zonizzazione *f*
zonked [zɒŋkt] ADJ (*fam: exhausted*) distrutto(-a)
zoo [zu:] N zoo *m inv*, giardino zoologico
zoo keeper N guardiano di zoo
zoo·logi·cal [ˌzəʊə'lɒdʒɪkəl] ADJ zoologico(-a)
zoological garden N (*frm*) giardino zoologico
zo·olo·gist [zəʊ'ɒlədʒɪst] N zoologo(-a)
zo·ol·ogy [zəʊ'ɒlədʒɪ] N zoologia
▷ www.academicinfo.net/zoo.html
zoom [zu:m] N (*sound*) rombo
■VI (*go fast*): **to zoom off** sfrecciare via; **the police car zoomed by very close to him** la macchina della polizia gli è sfrecciata accanto
▸ **zoom in** VI + ADV (*Phot, Cine*): **to zoom in (on sb/sth)** zumare (su qn/qc)
▸ **zoom out** VI + ADV allargare l'immagine
zoom lens N zoom *m inv*
zoo·tech·nics [ˌzəʊə'tɛknɪks] NSG zootecnia
zuc·chi·ni [zu:'ki:nɪ] N, PL INV (*Am*) zucchina; **potatoes and zucchini** patate e zucchine
Zulu ['zu:lu:] ADJ, N zulù (*m/f*) *inv*
Zü·rich ['zjʊərɪk] N Zurigo *f*

Zz

Lingua e Funzioni
Language in Use

Lingua e Funzioni

Indice

Sezione inglese-italiano

Language in Use

Contents

Italian-English section

Introduzione

Uno dei principali obiettivi di chi impara una lingua straniera è quello di riuscire a esprimersi in quella lingua in modo naturale, corretto e adeguato alla situazione. Il dizionario bilingue è uno strumento prezioso e, se fatto bene, consente di trovare le traduzioni per tutte le parole che ci servono a costruire frasi e periodi in una lingua che non è la nostra. Va detto però che, come sostengono numerosi docenti ed esperti, il passaggio, di necessità "frazionato", dalla propria lingua all'espressione in una lingua straniera può portare a distorcerne significati e costruzioni, con risultati non del tutto soddisfacenti.

Per questo motivo abbiamo voluto creare una sezione supplementare che proponiamo come uno strumento complementare al dizionario bilingue.

Abbiamo identificato quelle che riteniamo funzioni importanti dell'espressione linguistica e raccolto centinaia di esempi che abbiamo tradotto e raggruppato a seconda della funzione espressa. In particolare ci siamo voluti soffermare su concetti quali l'obbligo, la possibilità e il permesso che, per l'uso dei verbi modali inglesi, risultano particolarmente ostici dal punto di vista sintattico e lessicale. Ogni funzione, comunque, presenta problemi intrinseci legati al contesto, alle convenzioni linguistiche e al destinatario del messaggio.

La sezione comprende non solo esempi di conversazione tratti da contesti reali, ancora una volta utilizzando i corpora elettronici di lingua a nostra disposizione, ma anche esempi di lettere commerciali, lettere personali, domande di impiego, curriculum vitae e poi partecipazioni di nozze, inviti a battesimo e così via.

Particolarmente approfondito è il capitolo sulla dissertazione, con esempi articolati ed esaustivi che illustrano come strutturare, sviluppare e concludere un argomento, e dove le traduzioni, di necessità meno letterali di quanto debbano essere in un dizionario, fanno luce sui complessi meccanismi di corrispondenza tra le due lingue.

Quando è stato ritenuto utile, le frasi sono state fatte precedere da titoletti quali *formale*, *informale*, *in modo più diretto*, *meno diretto* e così via, che ne specificano il registro linguistico e l'ambito d'uso, indicazioni preziose e spesso cruciali per la corretta espressione nella lingua straniera.

Introduction

One of the chief aims of foreign language learners is to be able to express themselves naturally and correctly, and in a way which is appropriate to the particular situation. A bilingual dictionary is an invaluable tool, providing translations for all the words needed to construct sentences in the other language. The fact remains, however - and teachers and experts in the field frequently point this out - that putting one's ideas into another language can be a frustrating process, resulting in clumsy constructions and a distorted version of what one wants to say.

It is for this reason that we have added a further resource, to be used alongside the dictionary itself.

We have identified various key functions that language can perform. Hundreds of examples, with translations, have been grouped according to the function they perform. Particular attention has been paid to such concepts as obligation, possibility and permission, which are expressed very differently in Italian. All functions, however, present their own problems, depending on the particular context, the particular person addressed, and linguistic conventions.

As well as examples of spoken language, this section also contains useful examples of private and business letters, job applications and CVs, and email, together with announcements of engagements, marriages and deaths, and invitations.

There is a particularly detailed section on essay writing, where you will find extended examples demonstrating techniques for structuring, developing, and concluding a reasoned argument. The translations here are inevitably less literal than they are in a dictionary, and serve to illustrate that an utterance in one language cannot always be adequately rendered by a word-for-word translation.

Where appropriate the examples are graded according to whether they are neutral or emphatic, or according to register, under such headings as *formal, informal, more directly, less directly*, and so on, thus providing an indispensable tool to help learners express themselves appropriately in the foreign language.

1 Suggerimenti

1.1 Per dare suggerimenti

You might like to think it over before giving me your decision.	*forse preferiresti...*
You could help me clear out my office, **if you don't mind.**	*potresti... se non ti dispiace*
We could stop off in Venice for a day or two, **if you like.**	*potremmo... se vuoi...*
I've got an idea – **let's organize** a surprise birthday party for Megan!	*... organizziamo...*
If you've no objection(s), I'll speak to them personally.	*se non hai obiezioni...*
If I were you, I'd be very careful.	*se fossi in te...*
I would recommend (that) you discuss it with him first.	*ti suggerisco di...*
It would be in your interest to have a word with the owner first.	*forse ti converrebbe...*
Go and see Pompeii – **it's a must!**	*non devi assolutamente perderla*

► *In modo diretto*

I suggest that you go to bed and try to sleep.	*ti consiglio di...*
I'd like to suggest that you seriously consider taking a long holiday.	*ti consiglierei di...*
We propose that half the fee be paid in advance, and half on completion.	*proponiamo che...*
I cannot put it too strongly: **you really must** see a doctor.	*... devi assolutamente...*

► *In modo meno diretto*

Say you were to approach the problem from a different angle.	*mettiamo che...*
In these circumstances, **it might be better to** wait.	*...forse sarebbe meglio...*
It might be a good thing *o* **a good idea** to warn her about this.	*forse sarebbe il caso di...*
Perhaps it would be as well to change the locks.	*forse faremmo bene a...*
Perhaps you should take up a sport.	*forse dovresti...*
Might I be allowed to offer a little advice? – talk it over with a solicitor before you go any further.	*mi permette di darle un suggerimento?*
May I suggest that you install bigger windows?	*se mi è concesso di dare un suggerimento...*

► *Facendo una domanda*

How do you fancy a holiday in Australia?	*che ne diresti di...*
I was thinking of going for a drink later. **How about it?**	*... che ne dici?*
What would you say to a trip up to town next week?	*che ne diresti di...*
Would you like to stay in Paris for a couple of nights?	*ti piacerebbe...*
What if you try ignoring her and see if that stops her complaining?	*e se...*
What you need is a change of scene. **Why not** go on a cruise?	*... perché non...*
Suppose *o* **Supposing** you left the kids with me for a few days?	*e se...*
How would you feel about taking calcium supplements?	*che ne pensi di...*
Have you ever thought of starting up a magazine of your own?	*hai mai pensato di...*

1.2 Per chiedere un suggerimento a qualcuno

Have you any idea how I should go about it to get the best results?	*hai idea di come dovrei...*
I've no idea what to call our new puppy; **have you any suggestions?**	*... cosa suggerisci?*
I can only afford to buy one of them: **which do you suggest?**	*... quale mi consigli?*
I wonder if you could suggest where we might go for a few days?	*potresti suggerirmi...*
I'm a bit doubtful about where to start.	*non so bene*

2 Consigli

2.1 Per chiedere un consiglio

What would you do **if you were me?**	*... al mio posto...*
Would a pear tree grow here? If not, **what would you recommend?**	*... cosa mi consiglia?*
Do you think I ought to tell the truth?	*pensi che dovrei...*
What would you advise me to do in the circumstances?	*cosa mi consiglieresti di fare...*
Would you advise me to seek promotion with this firm or apply for another job?	*mi consiglierebbe di...*

2.2 Per dare un consiglio

► *In modo indiretto*

It might be wise *o* **sensible** *o* **a good idea to** consult a specialist. *forse sarebbe opportuno...*
It might be better to think it over before taking any decisions. *forse sarebbe meglio...*
You'd be as well to state your position at the outset. *faresti bene a...*
You'd be ill-advised to have any dealings with this firm. *sarebbe un errore...*
It would certainly be advisable to book a table. *è senz'altro consigliabile...*
Do be sure to read the small print before you sign anything. *ti raccomando di...*
Try to avoid upset**ting** her; she'll only make your life a misery. *cerca di evitare di...*

► *In modo diretto*

If you ask me you'd better take some extra cash. *secondo me, dovresti...*
If you want my advice, you should steer well clear of them. *se vuoi un consiglio, dovresti...*
If you want my opinion, I'd go by air to save time. *se vuoi sapere come la penso, io al posto tuo...*

Whatever you do, don't drink the local schnapps. *ma soprattutto non...*
In your shoes *o* **If I were you,** I'd be thinking about moving on. *se fossi in te...*
Take my advice and don't rush into anything. *segui il mio consiglio...*
I'd be very careful not to commit myself at this stage. *starei molto attento a non...*
I think you ought to *o* **should** seek professional advice. *penso che dovresti...*
My advice would be to have nothing to do with them. *ti consiglierei di...*
I would advise you to pay up promptly. *ti consiglierei di...*
I would advise against call**ing** the police unless he threatens you. *ti sconsiglio di...*
I would strongly advise you to reconsider this decision. *le consiglio caldamente di...*
I would urge you to reconsider selling the property. *le raccomando vivamente di...*

2.3 Per dare un avvertimento

It's none of my business but **I don't think you should** get involved. *io non penso che dovresti...*
A word of caution: watch what you say to him. *un consiglio...*
I should warn you that he's not an easy customer to deal with. *ti avverto che...*
Take care not to lose the vaccination certificate. *fai attenzione a non...*
Watch you don't trip over your shoelaces. *bada di non...*
Make sure that *o* **Mind that** *o* **See that you don't** say anything they might find offensive. *bada bene di non...*
I'd think twice about sharing a flat with him. *ci penserei su due volte prima di...*

You risk a long delay in Amsterdam **if** you come back by that route. *rischi... se...*

---

3 Offerte

I would be delighted to help out, if I may. *sarei ben felice di...*
It would give me great pleasure to show you round the city. *mi farebbe molto piacere...*
We would like to offer you the post of Sales Director. *siamo lieti di offrirle...*
Do let me know if I can help in any way. *mi faccia sapere se posso...*
If we can be of any further assistance, **please do not hesitate to** contact us. *se possiamo... non esitate a...*

► *Usando una domanda diretta*

Say we were to offer you a 5% rise, how would that sound? *mettiamo che...*
Could I give you a hand with your luggage? *posso...*
Shall I do the photocopies for you? *vuoi che...*
Is there anything I can do to help? *posso far qualcosa per...*
May *o* **Can I offer you** a drink? *posso offrirti...*
Would you like me to find out more about it for you? *vuoi che...*
You will let me show you around Glasgow, won't you? *mi permetterà di...*

4 Richieste

Please would you drop by on your way home and pick up your papers.	*per piacere potresti...*
Would you mind looking after Hannah for a couple of hours ?	*ti dispiacerebbe...*
Could I ask you to watch out for anything suspicious?	*posso chiederti di...*

► *In comunicazioni scritte*

I should be grateful if you could confirm whether it would be possible to increase my credit limit to £5000.	*Le sarei grato se potesse...*
We would ask you not to use the telephone for long-distance calls.	*siete pregati di non...*
You are requested to park at the rear of the building.	*siete pregati di...*
We look forward to receiv**ing** confirmation of your order within 14 days.	*restiamo in attesa di...*
Kindly inform us if you require alternative arrangements to be made.	*vogliate gentilmente farci sapere se...*

► *In modo più indiretto*

I would rather you didn't breathe a word to anyone about this.	*preferirei che tu non...*
I would appreciate it if you could let me have copies.	*ti sarei grato se potessi...*
I wonder whether you could help me?	*per caso potresti...*
I hope you don't mind if I borrow your exercise bike?	*spero non ti dispiaccia se...*
It would be very helpful *o* **useful if you could** have everything ready beforehand.	*ci sarebbe di grande aiuto se poteste...*
If it's not too much trouble, would you pop my suit into the dry cleaner's on your way past?	*se non ti è di troppo disturbo, potresti...*
You won't forget to lock up before you leave, will you?	*non dimenticarti di...*

5 Paragoni

The streets are narrow **compared with** English ones.	*paragonate a...*
The bomb used to blow the car up was small **in** *o* **by comparison with** those often used nowadays.	*in confronto a...*
If you compare the facilities we have here **with** those in other towns, you soon realize how lucky we are.	*se si paragonano... a...*
It is interesting to note the **similarities and the differences between** the two approaches.	*... le somiglianze e le differenze fra...*
In contrast to the opulence of the Kirov, the Northern Ballet Theatre is a modest company.	*in confronto a...*
Only 30% of females died **as opposed to** 57% of the males.	*... a differenza di...*
Unlike other loan repayments, those to the IMF cannot simply be rescheduled.	*a differenza di...*
Whereas burglars often used to make off only with video recorders, they now also tend to empty the fridge.	*mentre...*
What differentiates these wines **from** a good champagne is their price.	*quello che differenzia... da...*

► *Per dire che qualcosa è migliore*

Orwell was, indeed, **far superior to** him intellectually.	*... di gran lunga superiore a...*
I think high-speed trains **have the edge over** aircraft .	*sono superiori a...*
Michaela was altogether **in a class of her own.**	*... in una categoria a parte*

► *Per dire che qualcosa è peggiore*

Matthew's piano playing **is not a patch on** his sister's.	*... non regge il confronto con...*
My old chair **was nowhere near as** comfortable as my new one.	*... era ben lontana dall'essere così...*
The parliamentary opposition **is no match for** the government.	*... non è in grado di tenere testa a ...*
Commercially-made ice-cream **is far inferior to** the home-made variety.	*... è di gran lunga inferiore a...*
The truth was that **he was never in the same class as** his friend.	*... non è mai stato allo stesso livello di...*

He doesn't rate anything **that doesn't measure up to** Shakespeare. *... che non regga il confronto con ...*

Her charms **don't bear comparison with** Marlene's sultry sex appeal. *... non sono paragonabili a...*

They're far bigger and stronger than us – **we can't compete with** them. *non possiamo competere con...*

► *Per paragonare cose simili*

The new computerized system costs **much the same as** a more conventional one. *... praticamente quanto...*

When it comes to performance, **there's not much to choose between** them. *... non c'è molta differenza fra...*

The impact was **equivalent to** 250 hydrogen bombs exploding. *... equivalente a...*

In Kleinian analysis, the psychoanalyst's role **corresponds to** that of mother. *... corrisponde a...*

The immune system **can be likened to** *o* **compared to** a complicated electronic network. *... può essere paragonato a...*

It's swings and roundabouts – what you win in one round, you lose in another. *a conti fatti il risultato non cambia...*

► *Per paragonare cose dissimili*

You cannot compare a small local library **with** a large city one. *... non si può paragonare... a*

There's no comparison between the sort of photos I take **and** those a professional could give you. *non c'è paragone fra... e...*

We might be twins, but **we have nothing in common.** *...non abbiamo niente in comune...*

The modern army **bears little resemblence to** the army of 1940. *... assomiglia ben poco a...*

6 Opinioni

6.1 Per chiedere l'opinione di qualcuno

What do you think of the new Managing Director? *cosa ne pensi di...*

What is your opinion on women's rights? *qual è la tua opinione su...*

What are your thoughts on the way forward? *hai qualche idea su...*

What is your attitude to people who say there is no such thing? *cosa ne pensi di...*

What are your own feelings about the way the case was handled? *cosa ne pensi di ...*

How do you see the next stage develop**ing**? *come prevedi che...*

I would value your opinion on how best to set this all up. *mi piacerebbe avere la tua opinione su...*

6.2 Per esprimere la propria opinione

In my opinion, eight years as President is quite enough for anyone *a mio avviso...*

I don't see it as my duty to take sides. *secondo me...*

I feel that politicians sometimes lose their sense of proportion. *ho la sensazione che...*

It seems to me that the successful designer leads the public. *mi sembra che...*

I am under the impression that he is essentially a man of peace. *ho l'impressione che...*

I am of the opinion that the rules should be looked at and refined. *sono dell'opinione che...*

I'm convinced that we all need a new vision of the future. *sono convinto che...*

I daresay there are so many names that you get them mixed up. *..., immagino*

We're prepared to prosecute the company, which **to my mind** has committed a criminal offence. *secondo il mio parere...*

From my point of view activities like these should not be illegal. *dal mio punto di vista...*

As far as I'm concerned, Barnes had it coming to him. *secondo me...*

If you ask me, there's something a bit strange going on. *se vuoi sapere cosa ne penso...*

6.3 Per rispondere senza esprimere un'opinione

Would I say she had been a help? **It depends** what you mean by help. *... dipende da...*

It could be seen as a triumph, but **it depends on your point of view.** *...è una questione di punti di vista*

It's hard to say whether she has benefited from the treatment or not. *è difficile dire se...*

I'm not in a position to comment on whether the director's accusations are well-founded. — *non mi è possibile fare commenti su...*

I'd prefer not to comment on operational decisions. — *preferiri non esprimere un giudizio su...*

I'd rather not commit myself at this stage. — *preferirei non impegnarmi*

I don't have any strong feelings about it. — *non ho alcuna preferenza su...*

This isn't something I've given much thought to. — *... su cui abbia riflettuto seriamente*

I know nothing about fine wine. — *non so nulla di...*

7 Gusti e preferenze

7.1 Per chiedere a qualcuno cosa preferisca

Would you like to visit the castle while you are here? — *ti piacerebbe...*

How would you feel about Simon join**ing** us? — *cosa ne diresti se...*

What do you like doing **best** when you're on holiday? — *cosa ti piace fare più di tutto...*

What's your favourite film? — *qual è il tuo... favorito?*

What's your favourite way to relax at the end of a hectic day? — *tu cosa fai per...*

Which of the two proposed options **do you prefer?** — *quale... preferisci?*

7.2 Per parlare di ciò che piace

I'm very keen on gardening. — *mi piace moltissimo...*

I'm very fond of white geraniums and blue petunias. — *mi piacciono particolarmente...*

There's nothing I like more than a quiet night in with a good book. — *niente mi piace di più che...*

I have a weakness for rich chocolate gateaux. — *ho un debole per...*

I've always had a soft spot for Dublin. — *ho sempre avuto un debole per...*

7.3 Per parlare di ciò che non piace

Acting **isn't really my thing** – I'm better at singing. — *... non è il mio forte...*

Some people might find it funny but **it's not my kind of** humour. — *... non è il mio tipo di...*

Pubs and clubs **are not my cup of tea.** — *... non sono esattamente il mio genere*

Sitting for hours on motorways **is not my idea of fun.** — *non trovo per niente divertente...*

The idea of walking home at 11 o'clock at night **doesn't appeal to me.** — *... non mi sorride affatto*

I've gone off the idea of cycling round Holland. — *ho abbandonato l'idea di...*

I can't stand *o* **can't bear** the thought of seeing him. — *non sopporto l'idea di...*

I'm not keen on seafood. — *non vado pazza per...*

What I hate most is waiting in queues for buses. — *la cosa che odio di più...*

There's nothing I dislike more than going to work in the dark. — *non c'è niente che io odi di più...*

I find it intolerable that people like him should be so powerful. — *trovo intollerabile che...*

7.4 Per dire cosa si preferisce

I'd prefer not to *o* **I'd rather not** talk about it just now. — *preferirei non...*

I'd rather you gave me your comments in writing. — *preferirei che tu...*

I like the blue curtains **better than** the red ones. — *mi piacciono di più di...*

I'd prefer red wine **to** white wine. — *preferirei... piuttosto che...*

7.5 Per dire che qualcosa ci è indifferente

It makes no odds whether you have a million pounds or nothing, we won't judge you on your wealth. — *non cambia nulla se...*

I really don't care what you say as long as you tell her something. — *non m'interessa che cosa...*

It's all the same to me whether he comes or not. — *per me è uguale se...*

I don't mind at all – let's do whatever is easiest. — *per me non fa differenza...*

It doesn't matter which method you choose to us. — *non ha importanza quale...*

I don't feel strongly about the issue of privatization. — *non ho grandi convinzioni riguardo a...*

8 Intenzioni e desideri

8.1 Per chiedere a qualcuno cosa intenda fare

Will you take the job? *hai intenzione di...*
What flight **do you intend** to take? *... intendi...*
What do you propose to do with the money? *cosa conti di fare...*
What did you have in mind for the rest of the programme? *cosa avevi in mente per...*
Have you anyone in mind for the job? *hai qualcuno in mente per...*

8.2 Per esprimere le proprie intenzioni

We're toying with the idea of releasing a compilation album. *stiamo meditando di...*
I'm thinking of retiring next year. *sto pensando di...*
I'm hoping to go and see her when I'm in Paris. *spero di...*
I studied history **with a view to** becoming a politician. *... per ...*
We bought the land **in order to** farm it. *... per...*
We plan to move *o* **We are planning on** moving next year. *contiamo di...*
Our aim *o* **Our object in** buying the company **is to** provide work for the villagers. *il nostro obiettivo...è di...*

► *In modo più convinto*

I am going to sell the car as soon as possible. *ho l'intenzione di...*
I intend to put the house on the market. *ho l'intenzione di...*
I have made up my mind to *o* **I have decided to** go to Japan. *ho deciso di...*
I went to Rome **with the intention of** visiting her, but she had left. *... con l'idea di...*
We have every intention of winning a sixth successive championship. *abbiamo tutta l'intenzione di...*
I have set my sights on recapturing the title. *miro a...*
My overriding ambition is to get into politics. *il mio più grande desiderio è di...*
I resolved to do everything in my power to help you. *ho deciso di...*

8.3 Per dire che cosa non si ha intenzione di fare

I don't mean to offend you but I think you're wrong. *non voglio...*
I have no intention of accepting the post. *non ho alcuna intenzione di...*
We are not thinking of taking on more staff. *non stiamo pensando di...*

8.4 Per dire cosa ci piacerebbe fare

I'd like to see the Sistine Chapel some day. *mi piacerebbe...*
I want to work abroad when I leave college. *voglio...*
We want her to be an architect when she grows up. *vogliamo che lei...*
I'm keen to develop the business. *ci tengo a...*

► *Con più entusiasmo*

I'm dying to go to Australia but I can't afford it. *muoio dalla voglia di...*
My ambition is to become an opera singer. *la mia massima aspirazione è...*
I insist on speaking to the manager. *insisto a volere...*

8.5 Per dire quello che non si vuole fare

I would prefer not to *o* **I would rather not** have to speak to her. *preferirei non...*
I wouldn't want to have to change my plans just because of her. *non vorrei...*
I don't want to *o* **I have no wish to** *o* **I have no desire to** take the credit for something I didn't do. *non voglio ...*
I refuse to be patronized by the likes of her. *mi rifiuto di...*

9 Permesso

9.1 Per chiedere l'autorizzazione a fare qualcosa

Can I *o* **Could I** borrow your car this afternoon? *posso...*
Are we allowed to say what we're up to or is it top secret at the moment? *siamo autorizzati a...*

Would it be all right if I arrived on Monday instead of Tuesday? *andrebbe bene se...*

We leave tomorrow. **Is that all right by you?** *... ti va bene?*

Do you mind if I come to the meeting next week? *ti dispiace se...*

Would you let me come into partnership with you? *mi permettete di...*

Would you have any objection to sailing at once? *avresti delle obiezioni a...*

With your permission, I'd like to ask some questions. *se mi permette, mi piacerebbe...*

► *In modo più indiretto*

Is there any chance of borrowing your boat while we're at the lake? *c'è qualche speranza di...*

I wonder if I could possibly use your telephone? *potrei forse...*

Might I be permitted to suggest the following ideas? *posso permettermi di...*

9.2 Come concedere il permesso

You can have anything you want. *puoi...*

It's all right by me if you want to skip the Cathedral visit. *non ho problemi se...*

You have my permission to be absent for that week. *vi autorizzo a...*

I've nothing against her going there with us. *non ho nulla in contrario a...*

The Crown **was agreeable to** having the case called on March 23. *... ha acconsentito a...*

I do not mind if my letter is forwarded to the person concerned. *non ho niente in contrario se...*

► *In modo più deciso*

If you need to keep your secret, **of course you must** keep it. *... devi ovviamente...*

By all means charge a reasonable consultation fee. *non esitate a...*

I have no objection at all to your quoting me in your article. *non ho assolutamente niente in contrario a...*

We would be delighted to have you. *saremmo felicissimi di...*

9.3 Per negare il permesso

You can't *o* **you mustn't** go anywhere near the research lab. *non potete...*

I don't want you to see that man again. *non voglio che tu...*

I'd rather you didn't give them my name. *preferirei che tu non...*

You're not allowed to leave the ship until relieved. *non siete autorizzati a...*

I've been forbidden alcohol **by** my doctor. *.. mi è stato proibito...da...*

I couldn't possibly allow you to pay for all this. *non posso assolutamente lasciarti...*

You must not enter the premises without the owners' authority. *non è permesso...*

We cannot allow the marriage to take place. *non possiamo permettere che...*

► *In modo formale*

I absolutely forbid you to take part in any further search. *le proibisco assolutamente di...*

You are forbidden to contact my children. *le è proibito...*

Smoking **is strictly forbidden** at all times. *... è assolutamente vietato...*

It **is strictly forbidden to** carry weapons in this country. *è fatto assoluto divieto di...*

---

10 Obbligo

10.1 Per dire che si è obbligati a fare qualcosa

You need to be very good, **no two ways about it.** *... devi assolutamente*

You've got to *o* **You have to** be back before midnight. *devi...*

You need to *o* **You must** have an address in Prague before you can apply for the job. *devi...*

I have no choice: this is how **I must** live and I cannot do otherwise. *devo...*

He was forced to ask his family for a loan. *fu obbligato a...*

A degree **is indispensable** for future entrants to the profession. *... è indispensabile...*

It is essential to know what the career options are before choosing a course of study. *è essenziale...*

Wearing a seatbelt **is a requirement of the law.** *... è obbligatorio per legge*

Wearing the kilt **is compulsory for** all those taking part. — *... è obbligatorio per...*
We have no alternative but to fight. — *non abbiamo altra scelta che...*
Three passport photos **are required.** — *sono necessarie...*

10.2 Per sapere se si ha l'obbligo di fare qualcosa

Do I have to *o* **Have I got to** be home by midnight? — *devo...*
Is it necessary to go into so much detail? — *è necessario...*
Ought I to tell my colleagues? — *dovrei...*
Should I call the police? — *dovrei...*
Am I meant to *o* **Am I expected to** *o* **Am I supposed to** fill in this bit of the form? — *devo...*

10.3 Per dire che non si è obbligati a fare qualcosa

You don't have to *o* **You needn't** go there if you don't want to. — *non sei obbligato a...*
You are not obliged to *o* **You are under no obligation to** invite him. — *non sei obbligato a...*
It is not necessary to *o* **it is not compulsory to** *o* **obligatory to** have a letter of acceptance. — *non è indispensabile...*
The Council **does not expect you to** pay all of your bill at once. — *... non esige che ...*

10.4 Per dire che è proibito fare qualcosa

On no account must you be persuaded to give up the cause. — *in nessun caso devi...*
You are not allowed to sit the exam more than three times. — *non si può...*
Smoking **is not allowed** in the dining room. — *non è permesso...*
You mustn't show this document to any unauthorized person. — *non devi...*
You're not supposed to *o* **meant to** use this room unless you are a club member. — *non siete autorizzati a...*

► *In modo più formale*

It is forbidden to bring the camera into the gallery. — *è proibito ...*
Smoking **is forbidden** *o* **is not permitted** in the dining room. — *... è vietato...*

---

11 Accordo

11.1 Per dire che si è d'accordo

I fully agree with you *o* **I totally agree with you** on this point. — *sono assolutamente d'accordo con te...*
We are in complete agreement on this. — *siamo completamente d'accordo*
I entirely take your point about the extra vehicles needed. — *condivido pienamente la tua opinione in merito a...*
I think **we see completely eye to eye** on this issue. — *... la vediamo esattamente allo stesso modo*
I feel that **his comments are quite correct.** — *... le sue osservazioni siano esatte*
We talked it over and **we are both of the same mind.** — *... siamo dello stesso avviso*
You're quite right in pointing at distribution as the main problem. — *hai ragione a...*
We have been thinking along the same lines. — *la pensiamo allo stesso modo*
We share your views on the proposed expansion of the site. — *condividiamo il vostro punto di vista...*
My own experience certainly **bears out** *o* **confirms** what you say. — *... è confermato dalla mia esperienza personale*
I have to concede that the results are quite eye-catching. — *devo dare atto che...*
I agree up to a point. — *sono d'accordo fino ad un certo punto*

► *In modo informale*

Go for a drink instead of working late? **Sounds good to me!** — *... buona idea!*
That's a lovely idea. — *ma che magnifica idea!*
I'm all for encouraging a youth section in video clubs such as ours. — *ci sto a...*
I couldn't agree with you more. — *sono perfettamente d'accordo con te*

► *In modo più formale*

Our conclusions are entirely consistent with your findings. — *le nostre conclusioni confermano in pieno...*

Independent statistics **corroborate** those of your researcher. — *... corroborano...*

11.2 Per esprimere l'accordo con quanto proposto

This certainly **seems the right way to go about it.** — *... sembra il modo giusto di procedere*

We certainly welcome this development. — *guardiamo con favore a...*

► *In modo più informale*

It's a great idea, I like the sound of that. — *è un'ottima idea*

I'll go along with his proposal. — *sono d'accordo con...*

► *In modo più formale*

This solution **is most acceptable** to us. — *... ci trova d'accordo*

The proposed scheme **meets with our approval.** — *... ha la nostra approvazione*

This is a proposal which **deserves our wholehearted support.** — *...merita tutto il nostro sostegno*

We assent to *o* **We give our assent to** your plan to develop the site. — *diamo il nostro assenso a...*

11.3 Per dire che si è d'accordo con quanto chiesto

Of course **I'll be happy to** organize it for you. — *sarò lieto di...*

I'll do as you suggest and send him the documents. — *seguirò il vostro consiglio...*

There's no problem about getting tickets for him. — *non è un problema...*

► *In modo più formale*

Reputable builders **will not object to** this reasonable request. — *... non faranno obiezioni a...*

We should be delighted to cooperate with you in this enterprise. — *saremmo lieti di...*

An army statement said **it would comply with** the ceasefire. — *... rispetterà...*

---

12 Dissenso

12.1 Per esprimere dissenso

There must be some mistake – **it can't possibly** cost as much as that. — *... non è possibile che...*

You're wrong in thinking that I haven't understood. — *sbagli a credere che...*

Surveys **do not bear out** Mrs Fraser's assumption . — *... non comprovano...*

I cannot agree with you on this. — *non posso essere d'accordo con te...*

We cannot accept the view that the lack of research and development explains the decline of Britain. — *non condividiamo affatto l'opinione secondo la quale...*

We must agree to differ on this one. — *rassegniamoci al fatto che le nostre idee divergono*

I entirely reject his contentions. — *respingo assolutamente*

I totally disagree with the previous two callers. — *non sono per niente d'accordo con...*

This is your view of the events: **it is certainly not mine.** — *... non è certamente la mia*

Surely you can't believe that he'd do such a thing. — *ovviamente non crederai che...*

12.2 Per dire che non si è d'accordo con quanto proposto

I'm dead against this idea. — *sono assolutamente contrario a ...*

Right idea, wrong approach. — *l'idea è buona, la tattica è sbagliata*

I will not hear of such a thing. — *non voglio neanche sentir parlare di...*

It is not feasible to change the schedule at this late stage. — *non è possibile...*

This is **not a viable alternative.** — *... non è fattibile*

► *Con minore decisione*

I'm not too keen on this idea. — *non mi piace tanto...*
I don't think much of this idea. — *non mi piace tanto...*
This doesn't seem to be the right way of dealing with the problem. — *non mi sembra il modo giusto di...*
I regret that I am not in a position to accept your kind offer. — *sono desolato di non poter...*

12.3 Per dire che non si intende fare qualcosa

I'm sorry but **I just can't** do it. — *... mi è semplicemente impossibile*
I cannot in all conscience leave those kids in that atmosphere. — *in tutta coscienza non posso...*

► *Con maggiore decisione*

This is quite out of the question for the time being. — *è fuori discussione...*
I wouldn't dream of doing a thing like that. — *non mi sognerei neanche di...*
I refuse point blank to have anything to do with this affair. — *mi rifiuto categoricamente di...*

► *... e in modo formale*

I'm afraid I must refuse. — *mi dispiace ma devo rifiutare*
I cannot possibly comply with this request. — *non posso assolutamente soddisfare...*
In view of the timescale, **I must reluctantly decline to** take part. — *... mi trovo purtroppo costretto a declinare dal...*

---

13 Approvazione

13.1 Come approvare un'affermazione

I couldn't have put it better myself. — *io stesso non avrei saputo esprimerlo meglio*
We must oppose terrorism, whatever its source. **Hear, hear!** — *... bravo!*

13.2 Come approvare una proposta

It's just the job! — *è proprio quello che ci vuole!*
This is just the sort of thing I wanted. — *è esattamente quello che volevo*
This is exactly what I had in mind. — *è proprio ciò che avevo in mente*
Thank you for sending the draft agenda: **I like the look of it very much.** — *... mi pare vada benissimo*
We are all very enthusiastic about his latest set of proposals. — *abbiamo accolto con entusiasmo*
I shall certainly give it my backing. — *darò sicuramente il mio appoggio*
Any game which is as enjoyable as this **meets with my approval.** — *... incontra tutta la mia approvazione*
Skinner's plan **deserves our total support** . — *... merita tutto il nostro sostegno*
We recognize the merits of this scheme. — *riconosciamo i vantaggi di...*
We view your proposal to extend the site **favourably.** — *consideriamo favorevolmente...*
The project **is worthy of our attention.** — *... merita la nostra attenzione...*

13.3 Come approvare un'idea

You're quite right to wait before making such an important decision. — *hai perfettamente ragione a...*
I'd certainly go along with that! — *sono completamente d'accordo!*
I'm very much in favour of that sort of thing. — *sono completamente favorevole a...*
What an excellent idea! — *che magnifica idea!*

---

14 Disapprovazione

This doesn't seem to be the right way of going about it. — *non sembra il modo migliore di...*
I don't think much of what this government has done so far. — *non ho una grande opinione di...*
I can't say I'm pleased about what has happened. — *non posso dire di essere soddisfatto di...*

inglese – italiano

The police **took a dim view of** her attempt to help her son break out of jail. — *... non ha visto di buon occhio...*

We have a low *o* **poor opinion of** opportunists like him. — *non abbiamo gran rispetto per...*

They **should not have** refused to give her the money. — *non avrebbero dovuto...*

► *Più direttamente*

I'm fed up with having to wait so long for payments to be made. — *sono stufo di...*

I've had (just) about enough of this whole supermodel thing. — *comincio ad averne abbastanza di...*

I can't bear *o* **stand** people who smoke in restaurants. — *non sopporto...*

How dare he say that! — *come osa...*

He was quite wrong to repeat what I said about her. — *ha fatto male a...*

We are opposed to all forms of professional malpractice. — *siamo contrari a...*

We condemn any intervention which could damage race relations. — *condanniamo...*

I must object to the tag "soft porn actress". — *non posso accettare...*

I strongly disapprove of such behaviour. — *disapprovo totalmente...*

15 Scuse

15.1 Come scusarsi

I'm really sorry, Steve, but we won't be able to come on Saturday. — *mi dispiace molto...*

I'm sorry that your time has been wasted. — *mi dispiace che...*

I am sorry to have to say this to you but you're no good. — *mi dispiace dovere...*

Apologies if I wasn't very good company last night. — *scusa se...*

I must apologize for what happened. — *vi prego di accettare le mie scuse per...*

I owe you an apology. — *ti devo delle scuse...*

Do forgive me for being a little abrupt. — *vogliate scusarmi se...*

Please forgive me for behaving so badly. — *vi prego di perdonarmi se...*

Please accept our apologies. — *vi preghiamo di accettare le nostre scuse...*

15.2 Ammettendo di essere responsabili

I admit I overreacted, but someone needed to speak out against her. — *ammetto di...*

I have no excuse for what happened. — *non ho scusanti per...*

It is my fault that our marriage is on the rocks. — *è colpa mia se...*

The government **is not entirely to blame** for the crisis. — *... non è il solo responsabile ...*

I should never have let him rush out of the house in anger. — *non avrei mai dovuto...*

Oh, but **if only I hadn't** lost the keys. — *... se solo non avessi...*

I hate to admit that **I made a stupid mistake.** — *... ho fatto uno stupido errore*

My mistake was to arrive wearing a jacket and polo-neck jumper. — *ho commesso l'errore di...*

15.3 Per dire che si è dispiaciuti

I'm very upset about her decision. — *... mi addolora molto...*

I feel awful but I couldn't let him make a fool of himself. — *mi spiace moltissimo...*

I'm afraid I can't help you very much. — *purtroppo non posso...*

It is a pity that my profession profits from others' misfortunes. — *è triste che...*

It is unfortunate that the matter has come to a head just now. — *è un peccato che...*

We **very much regret that** we have been unable to agree. — *... siamo estremamente dispiaciuti di...*

The accused **bitterly regrets** this incident and it won't happen again. — *... è terribilmente dispiaciuto di...*

We regret to inform you that the post of Editor has now been filled. — *ci dispiace doverla informare che...*

15.4 Declinando la propria responsabilità

I didn't do it on purpose, it just happened. — *non l'ho fatto apposta...*

Sorry, Nanna. **I didn't mean to** upset you. — *...non intendevo...*

Sorry about not coming to the meeting. **I was under the** — *..mi era sembrato di capire che...*

impression that it was just for managers.

We are simply trying to protect the interests of local householders. — *stiamo semplicemente tentando di...*

I know this hurts you but **I had no choice**. I had to put David's life above all else. — *... non ho avuto scelta...*

We were obliged to accept their conditions. — *siamo stati obbligati a...*

Under the circumstances **we have no alternative but to** accept. — *... non possiamo far altro che*

I had nothing to do with the placing of any advertisement. — *... non ho avuto niente a che fare con...*

16 Certezza, probabilità, possibilità e capacità

16.1 Certezza

She was bound to discover that you and I had talked. — *era inevitabile che...*

I'm sure *o* **certain (that)** he'll keep his word. — *sono certo che...*

I'm positive *o* **convinced (that)** it was your mother I saw. — *sono sicuro che...*

We now know for certain *o* **for sure that** the exam papers were seen by several students before the day of the exam. — *sappiamo per certo che...*

I made sure *o* **certain that** no one was listening to our conversation. — *mi sono assicurato che...*

From all the evidence **it is clear that** they were planning to sell up. — *...è chiaro che...*

It is undeniable that racial tensions in Britain have been increasing. — *è innegabile che...*

There is no doubt that the talks will be long and difficult. — *non c'è alcun dubbio che...*

Her pedigree **is beyond dispute** *o* **question**. — *...non è in discussione...*

You have my absolute assurance that this is the case. — *lei ha la mia più totale assicurazione che...*

I can assure you that I had nothing to do with it. — *posso assicurarle che...*

Make no mistake about it – I will return when I have proof. — *non ti illudere...*

16.2 Probabilità

There is a good *o* **strong chance that** they will agree to the deal. — *ci sono buone probabilità che...*

It seems highly likely that it was Bert who told Peter. — *sembra molto probabile che...*

The chances *o* **the odds are that** he will play safe in the short term. — *c'è da scommettere che...*

The probability is that your investment will be worth more in two years' time. — *è molto probabile che...*

The child's hearing will, **in all probability,** be severely affected. — *...con ogni probabilità...*

You will **very probably** be met at the airport by one of our men. — *molto probabilmente...*

It is quite likely that you will get withdrawal symptoms at first. — *è molto probabile che...*

The likelihood is that the mood of mistrust and recrimination will intensify. — *ci sono molte probabilità che...*

The person indicted is, **in all likelihood,** going to be guilty as charged. — *...con ogni probabilità...*

There is reason to believe that the books were stolen from the library. — *c'è motivo di ritenere che...*

The cheque **should** reach you by Saturday. — *...dovrebbe...*

It wouldn't surprise me if he was working for the Americans. — *non mi sorprenderei se...*

16.3 Possibilità

The situation **could** change from day to day. — *...potrebbe...*

Britain **could perhaps** play a more positive role in developing policy. — *...forse potrebbe...*

I venture to suggest (that) a lot of it is to do with his ambitions. — *mi azzarderei a suggerire che...*

It is possible that psychological factors play some unknown role in the healing process. — *è possibile che...*

It is conceivable that the economy is already in recession. — *è plausibile che...*

It may be that the whole battle will have to be fought over again. — *può accadere che...*

It may be (the case) that they got your name from the voters' roll. — *può darsi che...*

There is a small chance that your body could reject the implants. — *c'è una piccola possibilità che...*

16.4 Per dire quello che si è capaci di fare

Our Design and Print Service **can** supply envelopes. *...può...*
Applicants must **be able to** use a computer. *...essere in grado di...*
He is qualified to teach physics. *è abilitato a...*

---

17 Incertezza, improbabilità, impossibilità e incapacità

17.1 Incertezza

I doubt if *o* **It is doubtful whether** he knows where it came from. *dubito che...*
I have my doubts about replacing donations with taxpayers' cash. *ho i miei dubbi riguardo a...*
It isn't known for sure *o* **It isn't certain** where she is. *non si sa con certezza...*
No one can say for sure how any child will develop. *nessuno può dire con certezza...*
I'm not convinced that you can teach people who don't want to learn. *non sono convinto che...*
We are still in the dark about where the letter came from. *brancoliamo ancora nel buio per quel che riguarda...*
How long this muddle can last **is anyone's guess**. *...non è facile da indovinare*
It is touch and go whether base rates will have to go up. *...c'è il rischio che...*
I'm wondering if I should offer to help? *mi chiedo se...*

17.2 Improbabilità

You have **probably not** yet seen the document I am referring to. *probabilmente non...*
It is highly improbable that there will be a challenge for the party leadership in the near future. *è molto improbabile che...*
It is very doubtful whether the expedition will reach the summit. *è molto improbabile che...*
It was hardly to be expected that democratization would be easy. *c'era poco da aspettarsi che...*

17.3 Impossibilità

There can be no changes in the schedule. *non sono ammissibili...*
People said prices would inevitably rise; **this cannot be the case**. *...non può essere così*
I couldn't possibly invite George and not his partner. *non posso assolutamente...*
The report **rules out any possibility of** exceptions. *...esclude ogni possibilità di...*
There is no question of us getting this finished on time. *è semplicemente impossibile che...*
There is not (even) the remotest chance that *o* **There is absolutely no chance that** he will succeed. *non c'è (nemmeno) la minima possibilità che...*
The idea of trying to govern twelve nations from one centre **is unthinkable**. *...è inconcepibile*
Since we had over 500 applicants, **it would be quite impossible to** interview them all. *...sarebbe davvero impossibile...*

17.4 Incapacità

I can't drive, I'm afraid. *non so...*
I don't know how to use a computer. *non so come...*
The army **has been unable to** suppress the political violence. *...non è stato in grado di...*
The congress had shown itself **incapable of** real reform. *...incapace di...*
His fellow-directors **were not up** to running the business. *...non erano all'altezza di...*
We hoped the sales team would be able to think up new marketing strategies, but they **were** unfortunately **not equal to the task**. *...non erano pari al compito*
I'm afraid the task **proved** (to be) **beyond his capabilities**. *...si è rivelato superiore alle sue capacità*
I'd like to leave him but I feel that such a step **is beyond me**. *...mi sia impossibile*
He simply couldn't cope with the stresses of family life. *semplicemente non ce la faceva più a reggere...*
I'm not in a position to say how much truth there is in the reports. *non sono in grado di...*
It is quite impossible for me to describe the horror of the scene. *è semplicemente impossibile per me...*

inglese – italiano

18 Spiegazioni

18.1 Spiegare la ragione di qualcosa

He was sacked **for the simple reason that** he just wasn't up to it any more.	*...per la semplice ragione che...*
The reason that we admire her is that she knows what she is doing.	*la ragione per cui...*
He said he could not be more specific **for** security **reasons**.	*...per ragioni di...*
They could be facing debts this year, **largely because of** rising costs.	*...in gran parte a causa di...*
The organization seeks to prohibit unequal treatment of persons **on account of** their gender.	*...per via di...*
This practice was discontinued **as a result of** pressure from the government.	*...come risultato di...*
They are facing higher costs **owing to** rising inflation.	*...dovuti a...*
The full effects will be delayed **due to** factors beyond our control.	*...a causa di...*
Thanks to their generosity, the charity can afford to buy new equipment.	*grazie a...*
He shot to fame **on the strength of** a letter he had written to the papers.	*...grazie a...*
This is an impossibility **in view of** their geographical location.	*...considerando...*
The police have put considerable pressure on the Government to toughen its stance **in the light of** recent events.	*...alla luce di...*
In the face of this continued disagreement, the parties have asked for the polling to be postponed.	*di fronte a...*
Babies have died **for want of** *o* **for lack of** proper medical attention	*...per mancanza di...*
The warder was freed unharmed **in exchange for** the release of a colleague.	*...in cambio di...*
The court had ordered his release, **on the grounds that** he had already been acquitted of most of the charges against him.	*...per il motivo che...*
I am absolutely in favour of civil disobedience **on** moral **grounds**.	*...per motivi...*
It is unclear why they initiated this week's attack, **given that** negotiations were underway.	*...dato che...*
Seeing that he had a police escort, the only time he could have switched containers was on the way to the airport.	*visto che...*
As he had been up since 4 a.m., he was doubtless very tired.	*dato che...*
I'm always on a diet, **since** I put on weight easily.	*...dal momento che...*
I cannot accept this decision. **So** I confirm it is my intention to appeal to a higher authority	*...perciò...*
What the Party said was taken to be right, **therefore** anyone who disagreed must be wrong.	*...quindi...*
The thing is that once you've retired there's no going back.	*il fatto è che...*

18.2 Spiegare la causa di qualcosa

The serious dangers to your health **caused by** *o* **brought about by** cigarettes are now better understood.	*...causati da...*
When the picture was published recently, **it gave rise to** *o* **led to** speculation that the three were still alive and being held captive.	*...ha dato origine a...*
This lack of recognition **was at the root of** the dispute.	*...era alla radice di...*
This unrest **dates from** colonial times.	*...ha la sua origine in...*
The custom **goes back to** pre-Christian days.	*...risale a...*

ingiese – italiano

19 Come redigere una domanda di lavoro

11 North Street
Barnton
BN7 2BT

19th August 2005

The Personnel Director
J. M. Kenyon Ltd.
Firebrick House
Clifton
MC45 6RB

Dear Sir or Madam

With reference to your advertisement in today's *Guardian*, I wish to apply for the post of Personnel Officer.

I enclose my curriculum vitae. Please do not hesitate to contact me if you require any further details.

Yours faithfully
Rosalind Williamson
Rosalind Williamson

CURRICULUM VITAE

Name: Rosalind Anna WILLIAMSON
Address: 11 North Street, Barnton, BN7 2BT, England
Telephone: Barnton (0294) 476230
Date of Birth: 6.5.80
Marital Status: Single
Nationality: British
Qualifications: B.A. 2nd class Honours degree in Italian with French
University of Newby, England (June 2001)
A-levels: Italian (A), French (B), English (A) (1998)
GCSEs in 9 subjects. (1996)
Present Post: Assistant Personnel Officer, Metal Company plc, Barnton (since January 2003)
Previous Employment: Nov. 2001 – Jan. 2002 Personnel trainee, Metal Company plc
Skills, interests and Experience: fluent Italian & French; adequate German; some Russian; car owner and driver (clean licence); riding & sailing
Referees:
Ms. Alice Bluegown, Personnel Manager, Metal Company plc, Barnton NB4 3KL
Dr. I.O. Sono, Department of Italian, University of Newby, Newby, SR13 2RR

19.1 Come iniziare la lettera

In reply to your advertisement for a Trainee Manager in today's Guardian, I would be grateful if you would send me further details of the post.	*in riferimento al vostro annuncio...*
I wish to apply for the post of bilingual correspondent, as advertised in this week's Euronews.	*vorrei sottoporre la mia candidatura per il posto di...*
I am writing to ask if there is any possibility of work in your company.	*vi sarei grato se voleste farmi sapere se ci sono possibilità di impiego...*
I would like to work in Britain in my summer vacation.	*mi piacerebbe lavorare...*

19.2 Come presentare le precedenti esperienze di lavoro

I have three **years' experience** of office work/this kind of work.	*ho... anni di esperienza ...*
I am familiar with computers.	*ho una buona conoscenza di...*
As well as speaking fluent English, **I have a working knowledge of** German.	*...oltre a parlare correntemente... ho una buona conoscenza del...*
I am currently working in this field/a related field.	*attualmente lavoro...*
As you will see from my CV, I have worked abroad before.	*come risulta dal mio curriculum...*
Although I have no experience of this type of work **I have** had other jobs and can supply references.	*sebbene non abbia precedente esperienza di... ho tuttavia...*
My current salary is ... per annum and I have four weeks' paid leave.	*la mia remunerazione attuale è di...*

19.3 Per spiegare le proprie motivazioni

I would like to make better use of my languages.	*mi piacerebbe sfruttare meglio...*
I am keen to work in public relations.	*desidero inserirmi nel campo di...*

19.4 Come concludere la lettera

I will be available from the end of April.	*sono disponibile a partire da...*
I am available for interview at any time.	*mi tengo a vostra disposizione per un eventuale colloquio*
Please do not hesitate to contact me for further information.	*non esitate a contattarmi...*
Please do not contact my current employers.	*vi sarei estremamente riconoscente se evitaste di contattare il mio attuale datore di lavoro*
I enclose a stamped addressed envelope/an international reply coupon.	*accludo...*

19.5 Per accettare o rifiutare un'offerta di lavoro

Thank you for your letter of 20 March. **I will be pleased to attend for interview** at your Manchester office on Thursday 7 April at 10 am.	*... sarò felice di incontrarLa per un colloquio...*
I would like to confirm my acceptance of the post of Marketing Executive.	*desidero communicar Le che sono lieto di accettare...*
I would be delighted to accept this post. However, would it be possible to postpone my starting date until 8 May?	*sono ben felice di accettare il posto offertomi. Tuttavia...*
I would be glad to accept your offer, however, the salary stated is somewhat lower than what I had hoped for.	*in linea di massima sono felice di accettare la Sua offerta, tuttavia...*
Having given your offer careful thought, **I regret that I am unable to accept.**	*... sono spiacente di non poter accettare*

inglese – italiano

Flowers To Go
117 Rollesby Road
Beccles
NR6 9DL
Tel: 0161 654 3171
email: FTG@Flowers.co.uk

Ms Sharon McNeil
41 Courthill Street
Beccles
NR14 8TR

18 January 2005

Dear Ms McNeil

Special Offer! 5% discount on orders received in January!

Thank you for your recent enquiry. We can deliver fresh flowers anywhere in the country at very reasonable prices. Our bouquets come beautifully wrapped, with satin ribbons, attractive foil backing, a sachet of plant food and, of course, your own personalized message. For that special occasion, we can even deliver arrangements with a musical greeting, the ideal surprise gift for birthdays, weddings or Christmas!

Whatever the occasion, you will find just what you need to make it special in our latest brochure, which I have pleasure in enclosing, along with our current price list. All prices include delivery within the UK.

A discount of 5% will apply on all orders received before the end of January.

We look forward to heading from you.

Yours sincerely

Daisy Duckworth

Daisy Duckworth
Promotions Assistant

SMITH & JONES LTD

Quality Rainwear

Block 39, New Industrial Estate, Newtown SV7 3 QS

Tel.: 01277 321388

email: SJR@rainwear.co.uk

To: J Brown
Fax: 01325 528596

From: Ian Mackintosh
Fax: 01277 321390

Date: 4/8/2005

Subject: Children's rainwear

No. pages (incl this one): 1

Dear Mr Brown

Thank you for your enquiry. We have posted our latest catalogue to you, and would draw your attention particularly to our SUNFLOWER range. We are prepared to offer the usual discount on these items, and we look forward to receiving your order.

Yours sincerely

Ian Mackintosh

If you have any difficulties receiving this message, please phone Jill Gage on 01277 333456

20 Corrispondenza Commerciale

20.1 Come richiedere informazioni e come rispondere

We see from your advertisement you are offering cut-price holidays, **and would be grateful if you would send us** details.
abbiamo appreso da... e vi saremmo grati se poteste inviarci...

I read about the Society in the NCT newsletter and would be interested to learn more. **Please send me details** of membership.
ho letto di... e vi sarei grata se poteste inviarmi informazioni più precise circa...

In response to your enquiry of 8 March, **we have pleasure in enclosing** full details on our holidays, **together with** our price list.
a seguito della Sua lettera del... siamo lieti di accludere...insieme a...

Thank you for your enquiry about the Society for Wildlife Protection. **I enclose** a leaflet explaining our beliefs. **Should you wish** to join, a membership form is also enclosed.
La ringraziamo della Sua richiesta di informazioni circa... accludo... nel caso in cui Lei voglia...

20.2 Ordinazioni e come rispondere

We would like to place an order for the following items.
desideriamo ordinare...

Please find enclosed our order no. 3011 for ...
alla presente si acclude l'ordinativo n...

The enclosed order is based on your current price list.
l'ordinativo accluso...

I wish to order a can of "Buzz off!" wasp repellent **and enclose a cheque for** £3.50.
vorrei ordinare... e accludo un assegno di...

Thank you for your order of 3 May, which will be dispatched within 30 days.
La ringraziamo del Suo ordinativo in data...

We acknowledge receipt of your order no. 3570 and advise that the goods will be dispatched within 7 working days.
con la presente accusiamo ricevuta del Suo ordinativo n....

We regret that the goods are temporarily out of stock.
siamo desolati di comunicarLe che le merci sono momentaneamente esaurite

20.3 Consegne

Our delivery time is 60 days from receipt of order.
i nostri tempi di consegna sono di...

Please allow 28 days **for delivery.**
la consegna è prevista entro...

We await confirmation of your order.
attendiamo conferma del Suo ordinativo

We confirm that the goods were dispatched on 4 September.
Le diamo conferma che la merce è stata spedita in data...

We cannot accept responsibility for goods damaged in transit.
decliniamo qualsiasi responsabilità per quanto riguarda...

20.4 Reclami

We have not yet received the items ordered on 6 May.
non abbiamo ancora ricevuto...

Unfortunately, the goods were damaged in transit.
purtroppo...

The goods received differ significantly from the description in your catalogue.
gli articoli ricevuti non corrispondono alla descrizione che appare nel vostro catalogo

If the goods do not arrive by 20 May, **we will cancel our order.**
...ci troveremo costretti ad annullare l'ordinazione

20.5 Pagamento

The total amount payable/outstanding is ...
la cifra da regolare ammonta a...

We would be grateful if you would pay immediately.
Le saremmo grati se volesse saldare il conto...

Please send payment by return.
vogliate farci pervenire il saldo a stretto giro di posta

The balance **is due within** 14 working days of receipt of goods.
...è dovuto entro...

We enclose a cheque for... **as payment for invoice no.** L/58.	*...a saldo della vostra fattura n....*
We must point out an error in your account and **would be grateful if you would adjust your invoice** accordingly.	*...vi saremmo riconoscenti se voleste rettificare la vostra fattura...*
The mistake was due to an accounting error, and **we enclose a credit note for** the sum involved.	*...La preghiamo di accettare un buono di credito per...*
Thank you for your cheque for ... in settlement of our invoice. We look forward to doing business with you in the near future.	*La ringraziamo dell'assegno dell'ammontare di...*

inglese – italiano

11 South Street
BARCOMBE
BN7 2BT

14th March 2005

Dear Betty

It seems such a long time since we last met and caught up with each other's news. However, I'm writing to say that Peter and I plan to take our holiday this summer in the Lake District, and we'll be in your area some time during the morning of Friday, July 23rd. Will you be home then? Perhaps we could call in? It would be lovely to see you and Alan again and to get news of Janie and Mark. Do let me know whether that day is convenient. We would expect to arrive at your place around 11am or so, and hope very much to see you then.

With love from

Susan

65 Middlewich Street
ADDENBOROUGH
AG3 9LL

23rd January 2005

James Nash
Nash Knives Ltd.,
25 Townhead St.
HARLEY
SG16 4BD

Dear Mr. Nash

Some years ago I bought a SHARPCUTTER penknife from you, and it has been an invaluable tool. Unfortunately, however, I have now lost it, and wonder if you still stock this range? If so, I would be grateful if you would let me have details of the various types of knife you make, and their prices.

Yours sincerely

Thomas Armitage

Thomas Armitage

21 Corrispondenza generale

21.1 Come iniziare una lettera

► *Per scrivere a qualcuno che si conosce*

Thank you *o* **Thanks for your letter** which arrived yesterday. — *grazie della lettera...*

It was good *o* **nice** *o* **lovely to hear from you.** — *mi ha fatto molto piacere ricevere tue notizie*

I'm sorry I haven't written for so long, and hope you'll forgive me; I've had a lot of work recently and ... — *mi dispiace di non aver scritto prima...*

This is a difficult letter for me to write. — *non è facile per me scrivere questa lettera...*

► *Per scrivere a un'organizzazione*

I am writing to ask whether you have in stock a book entitled ... — *le scrivo per chiederle se...*

Please send me... I enclose a cheque for ... — *la prego di inviarmi...*

When I left last week, I think I may have left a red coat. **Would you be so kind as to let me know whether** it has been found? — *... sarebbe così gentile da farmi sapere se...*

I would like to know whether you still have any vacancies. — *... gradirei sapere se...*

21.2 Come concludere una lettera (prima dei saluti) a un conoscente

Helen joins me in sending very best wishes to you all. — *Helen si unisce a me nell'inviarvi...*

Susie sends her regards. — *Susie vi invia i suoi saluti*

Please remember me to your partner – I hope she is well. — *porgi i miei più cari saluti a...*

If there is anything else I can do, **please don't hesitate to get in touch** again. — *...non esitate a contattarmi...*

I look forward to hearing from you. — *attendo con impazienza la vostra lettera*

► *A un amico*

Say hello to Martin for me. — *dì ciao a Martin da parte mia*

Give my warmest regards to Vincent. — *cari saluti a Vincent*

Carmela asks me to give you her best wishes. — *Carmela mi incarica di trasmettervi i suoi saluti*

Hoping to hear from you before too long. — *sperando di ricevere presto tue notizie*

► *A un amico intimo*

Rhona **sends her love**/Ray **sends his love.** — *...ti abbraccia*

Give my love to Daniel and Laura, and tell them how much I miss them. — *un abbraccio a...*

Jodie and Carla **send you a big hug.** — *un abbraccio forte forte da...*

21.3 Per organizzare un viaggio

► *Come chiedere informazioni e prenotare*

Please send me details of your prices. — *le sarei grato se potesse inviarmi...*

I would like to book bed-and-breakfast accommodation with you. — *vorrei prenotare...*

► *Per confermare o annullare una prenotazione*

Please consider this a firm booking and hold the room until I arrive, however late in the evening. — *la prego di voler confermare la mia prenotazione*

Please confirm the following by fax: one single room with shower for the nights of 20–23 November 2005. — *le sarei grato se volesse confermare via fax ...*

We expect to arrive in the early evening. — *contiamo di arrivare...*

I am afraid I must ask you to alter my booking from 25 August to 3 September. — *purtoppo mi trovo costretto a chiederle di cambiare la mia prenotazione da...*

I am afraid (that) I must cancel the booking made with you for the week beginning 5 September. — *...mi trovo costretto a disdire la prenotazione...*

inglese – italiano

22 Ringraziamenti

Just a line to say thanks for the lovely book which arrived today.	*solo due righe per ringraziare del...*
I can't thank you enough for finding my watch.	*non so come ringraziarti di...*
(Would you) please thank him from me.	*per favore ringrazialo da parte mia*
We greatly appreciated your support.	*abbiamo apprezzato molto...*
Your advice and understanding **were much appreciated.**	*vi sono molto riconoscente per...*
I am writing to thank you *o* **to say thank you for** allowing me to quote your experience in my article on multiple births.	*le scrivo per ringraziarla di...*
Please accept our sincere thanks for all your help and support.	*i nostri più sentiti ringraziamenti per...*
A big thank you to everyone involved in the show this year.	*tanti ringraziamenti a...*
We would like to express our appreciation to the University of Durham Research Committee for providing a grant.	*desideriamo esprimere la nostra riconoscenza a...*
► ***A un gruppo***	
Thank you on behalf of the Operatic Society **for** all your support.	*sentiti ringraziamenti da parte di... per....*
We send our heartfelt thanks to you both.	*inviamo i nostri più vivi ringraziamenti a entrambi...*

23 Auguri

I hope you have a lovely holiday.	*spero che passiate...*
With love and best wishes for your wedding anniversary.	*con i più sinceri auguri di...*
(Do) give my best wishes to your mother **for** a happy and healthy retirement.	*trasmetti i miei più sinceri auguri a... per...*
Len **joins me in sending you our very best wishes for** your future career.	*... si unisce a me nel trasmettervi i nostri più cari auguri per...*
► ***Per Natale***	
Merry Christmas and a happy New Year.	*Buon Natale e Felice Anno Nuovo*
With season's greetings and very best wishes from ...	*auguri di Buone Feste da...*
May I send you all our very best wishes for 2006.	*i nostri migliori auguri a voi tutti per un felice...*
► ***Per un compleanno***	
All our love and best wishes on your 21st **birthday.**	*tanti cari auguri per il tuo... compleanno*
Wishing you a happy birthday for next Wednesday.	*ti auguro di trascorrere un felice compleanno mercoledì prossimo...*
I am writing to wish you **many happy returns (of the day).**	*...cento di questi giorni*
► ***Per una pronta guarigione***	
Sorry (to hear) you're ill – **get well soon!**	*...guarisci presto!*
I was very sorry to learn that you were ill, and **send you my best wishes for a speedy recovery.**	*... le invio i miei più sinceri auguri di pronta guarigione*
► ***Per augurare buona fortuna***	
Good luck in your driving test. I hope things go well for you.	*in bocca al lupo per...*
Sorry to hear you didn't get the job – **better luck next time!**	*... spero che tu sia più fortunato la prossima volta!*
We all wish you the best of luck in your new job.	*ti facciamo i nostri migliori auguri...*
► ***Per congratularsi con qualcuno di persona***	
You're doing a great job! **Good for you!** Keep it up!	*...bravo!...*
You've finished the job already? **Well done!**	*...bravo!*
Congratulations! When is the baby due?	*...congratulazioni!*
We all send you our love and congratulations on such an excellent result.	*le nostre più sentite congratulazioni per...*

24 Partecipazioni, inviti e risposte

24.1 Partecipazioni

► *Come annunciare una nascita e come rispondere*

Julie Archer **gave birth to** a 6lb 5oz **baby son**, Andrew, last Monday. **Mother and baby are doing well.**
...annuncia la nascita del piccolo... Sia la mamma che il bimbo stanno bene

Ian and Zoë Pitt **are delighted to announce the birth of a daughter**, Laura, on 1st May 2005, at Minehead Hospital.
...sono lieti di annunciare la nascita della piccola...

On 1st December, 2004, **to** Paul and Diane Kelly (née Smith) **a son**, John Alexander, a brother for Helen.
...annunciano la nascita del piccolo...

Congratulations on the birth of your son.
...sentite congratulazioni per la nascita di...

We were delighted to hear about the birth of Stephanie, and send our very best wishes to all of you.
abbiamo ricevuto con gioia l'annuncio della nascita di...

► *Come annunciare il fidanzamento e come rispondere*

I'm sure you'll be pleased to hear that Jim and I **got engaged** yesterday.
sono sicura che sarai felice di sapere che... ci siamo fidanzati...

It is with much pleasure that the engagement is announced between Michael, younger son of Mr and Mrs Perkins, York, and Jennifer, only daughter of Dr and Mrs Campbell, Hucknall.
siamo lieti di annunciare il fidanzamento fra ...

Congratulations to you both on your engagement, and very best wishes for a long and happy life together.
felicitazioni a entrambi in occasione del vostro fidanzamento

I was delighted to hear of your engagement, and wish you both all the best for your future together.
ho appreso con grande gioia del vostro fidanzamento...

► *Come annunciare il matrimonio e come rispondere*

● **Ad amici e parenti**

Helen and James **have decided to get married** on the 4th June.
...hanno deciso di sposarsi...

I'm getting married in June, to a lovely man named Mark Beattie.
mi sposerò...

Mr and Mrs William Morris **are delighted to announce the marriage of** their daughter Sarah to Mr. Jack Bond.
...sono lieti di annunciare il matrimonio di...

Congratulations on your marriage, and best wishes to you both.
congratulazioni in occasione del vostro matrimonio e tantissimi auguri a entrambi...

We were delighted to hear about your daughter's marriage to Iain, and wish them both well for their future life together.
abbiamo appreso con grande gioia del matrimonio di vostra figlia con...

► *Come annunciare un lutto e come rispondere*

My husband **died suddenly** in March.
...è improvvisamente mancato

It is with great sadness that I have to tell you that Joe's father **passed away** three weeks ago.
è con grande tristezza che devo comunicarti che... è mancato...

► *Sul giornale*

Suddenly (*o* **Peacefully**), at home, on Sunday 3 July, 2005, Alan, aged 77 years, **beloved husband** of May and **loving father** of Jo.
è improvvisamente venuto a mancare (o si è spento serenamente)... ne danno il triste annuncio la moglie... e il figlio...

My husband and I **were greatly saddened to learn of the passing of** Dr Smith, and send (*o* offer) you and your family our most sincere condolences.
abbiamo appreso con profondo dolore della scomparsa di...

► *Per comunicare che si è cambiato indirizzo*

We are moving house next week. **Our new address** as of 4th May 2005 **will be ...**
il nostro nuovo indirizzo... sarà...

24.2 Inviti

► *Inviti ufficiali e come rispondere*

Mr and Mrs James Waller **request the pleasure of your company at the marriage of** their daughter Mary to Mr Richard Hanbury. — *hanno il piacere di invitarLa al matrimonio di…*

We thank you for your kind invitation to the marriage of your daughter Annabel on 20th November, **and have much pleasure in accepting.** — *vi ringraziamo infinitamente del vostro gentile invito a… al quale saremo onorati di partecipare*

We regret that we are unable to accept your invitation to the marriage of your daughter on 6th May. — *siamo spiacenti di non poter accettare il vostro invito a…*

► *Inviti vari*

We are giving a dinner party next Saturday **and would be delighted if you and your partner could come.** — *saremmo felici se lei e suo marito (o sua moglie) poteste venire alla cena che si terrà…*

I am planning a party for my nephew – **hope you'll be able to make it** — *ho in programma una festa… e spero che possiate venire*

I'm having a party next week for my 18th – **come along and bring a friend.** — *farò una festa… vieni e porta qualcuno*

► *Inviti a teatro, cena ecc. e come rispondere*

Why don't you come down for the weekend? — *perché non venite a trovarci…*

Would you and Gordon **like to come** to dinner next Saturday? — *perché tu e… non venite…*

Would you be free for lunch next Tuesday? — *sei libera per…*

Perhaps we could meet for coffee some time next week? — *che ne dici di…*

Yes, I'd love to meet up with you tomorrow. — *sarei contentissima di…*

It was good of you to invite me, I've been longing to do something like this for ages. — *è stato molto gentile da parte tua invitarmi…*

► *Come scusarsi di non poter intervenire*

I wish I could come, but unfortunately I have something else on. — *vorrei tanto poter venire, ma purtroppo…*

It was very kind of you to invite me to your dinner party next Saturday. **Unfortunately I will not be able to accept.** — *…sfortunatamente non posso accettare*

► *Per dire che non si è sicuri*

I'm not sure what I'm doing that night, but I'll let you know later. — *non sono sicura di…*

It all depends on whether I can get a sitter for Rosie at short notice. — *dipende tutto se…*

25 La Dissertazione

25.1 La struttura in generale

► *Per introdurre un concetto*

In modo impersonale

It is often said *o* **asserted** *o* **claimed that** America has traded higher inequality for faster growth. — *si afferma da più parti che…*

It is a cliché to say that American accents are infinitely more glamorous than their British counterparts. — *è un luogo comune dire che…*

It is undeniably true that Gormley helped to turn his union members into far more sophisticated workers. — *è innegabile che…*

It is a well-known fact that in this age of technology, it is computer screens which are responsible for many illnesses. — *è un fatto ben noto che…*

It is sometimes forgotten that much Christian doctrine comes from Judaism. — *talvolta si dimentica che…*

It would be naïve to suppose that in a radically changing world these 50-year-old arrangements can survive. — *sarebbe da ingenui credere che…*

It would hardly be an exaggeration to say that their friendship with Britten was among the most creative in the composer's life. — *si potrebbe dire, senza timore di esagerare, che…*

inglese – italiano

It is hard to open a newspaper nowadays without reading that TV is going to destroy reading.
al giorno d'oggi non si può aprire un giornale senza leggere che...

It is important to try to understand some of the systems and processes invloved in order to create a healthier body.
prima di tutto, è importante cercare di capire...

It is in the nature of sociological theory to make broad generalizations about such things as the evolution of society.
è nella natura stessa di...

It is often the case that early interests lead on to a career.
si verifica spesso che...

In modo soggettivo

By way of introduction, let me summarize the background.
per iniziare, permettetemi di...

I would like to start with a sweeping statement which can be easily challenged.
comincerei con...

Before going specifically into the issue of criminal law, **I wish first to summarize** how Gewirth derives his principles of morality and justice.
prima di addentrarmi nei dettagli della questione di...vorrei esporre a grandi linee...

Let us look at what self-respect in your job actually means.
esaminiamo...

We commonly think of people **as** isolated individuals but, in fact, few of us ever spend much time alone.
solitamente pensiamo a... come...

What we are mainly concerned with here is the conflict between what the hero says, and what he actually does.
il nostro interesse primario qui si concentra su...

We live in a world in which the word "equality" is liberally bandied about.
viviamo in un mondo in cui...

► ***Per esporre un concetto o un problema***

The concept of controlling insects by genetic means isn't new.
l'idea di...

The idea of getting rich without effort has universal appeal.
l'idea di...

The question of whether Hamlet was really insane has long occupied critics.
... la questione di...

One of the most striking aspects of this issue is the way (in which) it arouses strong emotions.
uno degli aspetti più interessanti di questo problema è...

There are a number of issues on which they openly disagree.
c'è tutta una serie di questioni...

► ***Come introdurre delle generalizzazioni***

People who work outside the home **tend to believe that** parenting is an easy option.
coloro che... sono portati a credere che...

Many gardeners **have a tendency to** treat plants like humans.
hanno la tendenza a...

Viewed psychologically, it seems **we all have the propensity for** such traits.
...tutti abbiamo una propensione per...

For the majority of people, literature is a subject which is studied at school but which has no relevance to life as they know it.
per la grande maggioranza della gente...

For most of us, housework is a necessary but boring task.
per la maggior parte di noi...

History provides **numerous examples** *o* **instances of** misguided national heroes who did more harm than good in the long run.
...numerosi esempi di...

► ***Per mettere a fuoco un particolare aspetto***

The impact of these theories on the social sciences, and economics **in particular**, was extremely significant.
...in particolare...

One particular issue raised was, if he had been old enough to be hanged when he was convicted, what would have happened?
un problema particolare...

A more specific point relates to using this insight as a way of challenging our hidden assumptions about reality.
un aspetto più specifico...

25.2 Per presentare un argomento

In apertura

First of all, let us consider the advantages of urban life.
cominciamo con l'esaminare...

Let us begin with an examination of this question.
iniziamo con un esame di...

The first thing that needs to be said is that the author is presenting a one-sided view.
per prima cosa va detto che...

What should be established at the very outset is that we are dealing here with a practical issue rather than a philosophical one. — *la prima constatazione che si impone è che ...*

► ***Per dire di cosa si vuole/non si vuole parlare***

In the next section, I will pursue the question of whether the expansion of the prison system can be explained by this theory. — *nella prossima sezione svilupperò ...*

I will then deal with the question of whether or not the requirements are compatible with criminal procedure. — *tratterò quindi il problema di...*

We shall see how the subtle level of consciousness is the basis for the spiritual level. — *...vedremo come...*

I will confine myself to a few points. — *mi limiterò a...*

We will not concern ourselves here with these issues. — *in questa sede non ci occuperemo di...*

Let us now look at the development of human rights. — *esaminiamo ora...*

It is beyond the scope of this book to discuss every aspect of this large problem ... — *...va al di là degli obiettivi di...*

► ***La presentazione del problema***

The main issue under discussion is how the party should re-define itself. — *il problema principale in discussione è...*

A second, related problem is that business ethics has mostly concerned itself with grand theorizing. — *un secondo problema, strettamente connesso al primo, è...*

The basic issue at stake is this: is research to be judged by its value in generating new ideas? — *questo è il problema fondamentale che ci si pone...*

An important aspect of Milton's imagery is the play of light and shade — *un aspetto importante di...*

It is worth mentioning here that when this was first translated, the opening reference to Heidegger was entirely deleted. — *vale la pena ricordare qui che...*

Finally, there is the argument that watching too much television may stunt a child's imagination. — *infine, c'è chi sostiene che...*

► ***Per analizzare più da vicino i fatti citati***

In their joint statement the two presidents use tough language but **is there any real substance in** what's been agreed? — *...c'è qualcosa di concreto in...*

This is a question which **merits close(r) examination.** — *...merita un (più) attento esame*

This raises once again the question of whether a government's right to secrecy should override the public's right to know. — *...ciò solleva ancora una volta la questione circa...*

This poses the question of whether these measures are really helping the people they were intended to help. — *ci si chiede quindi se...*

► ***Analisi dei problemi***

It is interesting to consider why this scheme has been so successful. — *è interessante esaminare perché...*

On the question of whether civil disobedience is likely to help end the war, Chomsky is deliberately diffident. — *in merito alla questione se...*

We are often faced with the choice between our sense of duty **and** our own personal inclinations. — *siamo spesso costretti a operare una scelta fra... e*

When we speak of realism in music, **we do not at all have in mind** the illustrative bases of music. — *quando parliamo di... non pensiamo affatto a...*

It is reasonable to assume that most of us are to some extent contaminated by environmental poisons. — *si può presumere con una certa sicurezza che...*

► ***Come motivare una teoria***

An argument in support of this approach **is that** it produces ... — *a favore di... c'è da dire che...*

In support of his theory, Dr Gold notes that most oil contains higher-than-atmospheric concentrations of helium-3. — *a sostegno della sua teoria...*

This is the most telling argument in favour of an extension of the right to vote. — *questo è l'argomento più convincente a favore di...*

The second reason for advocating this course of action **is that** it benefits the community at large. — *la seconda ragione per sostenere la validità di... è che...*

The third, more fundamental, reason for looking to the future **is that** even the angriest investors realize they need a successful market. — *il terzo e più importante motivo, per... è che...*

25.3 Come presentare la tesi opposta

► *Come confutare una tesi*

In fact, the idea of there being a rupture between a so-called old criminology and an emergent new criminology **is misleading.** — *in realtà l'idea che… è fuorviante*

In order to argue this, **I will show that** Wyeth's **position is**, in actual fact, **untenable.** — *dimostrerò come il punto di vista di… sia indifendibile*

It is claimed, however, that the strict Leboyer method is not essential for a less traumatic birth experience. — *tuttavia si afferma…*

This need not mean that we are destined to suffer for ever. **Indeed, the opposite may be true.** — *questo non vuol dire necessariamente che… può essere vero l'esatto contrario*

Many observers, though, **find it difficult to share his opinion that** it could mean the end of the Tamil Tigers. — *…non condividono la sua opinione che…*

On the other hand, there are more important factors that should be taken into consideration. — *d'altro canto…*

The judgement **may well be true but** the evidence given to sustain it is unlikely to convince the sceptical. — *portrebbe essere giusto, ma…*

Reform **is all very well, but** it is pointless if the rules are not enforced. — *va bene, ma…*

The case against the use of drugs in sport rests primarily on the argument that … **This argument is weak, for two reasons.** — *…questa tesi ha due punti deboli*

According to one theory, the ancestors of vampire bats were fruit-eating bats. But **this idea does not hold water.** — *…questo ragionamento fa acqua da tutte le parti*

Their claim to be a separate race **does not stand up to** historical scrutiny. — *…non regge a…*

The trouble with this idea is not that it is wrong, **but rather that** it is uninformative. — *il problema riguardo a questa idea non è che… ma piuttosto che…*

The difficulty with this view is that he bases the principle on a false premise. — *il punto debole di questa tesi è che…*

But removing healthy ovaries **is entirely unjustified in my opinion.** — *…secondo me è totalmente ingiustificato*

► *Come proporre un'alternativa*

Another approach may be to develop substances capable of blocking the effects of the insect's immune system. — *un altro approccio potrebbe essere quello di…*

However, the other side of the coin is the fact that an improved self-image really can lead to prosperity. — *comunque, l'altro aspetto della questione…*

It is more accurate to speak of a plurality of new criminologies rather than of a single new criminology. — *sarebbe più preciso parlare di…*

Paradoxical as it may seem, computer models of mind can be positively humanizing. — *per quanto possa sembrare paradossale…*

25.4 Per introdurre la sintesi

► *Come valutare i pro e i contro*

How can we reconcile these two opposing viewpoints? — *come è possibile conciliare…*

On balance, making money honestly is more profitable than making it dishonestly. — *tutto sommato…*

Since such vitamins are more expensive, **one has to weigh up the pros and cons.** — *…si devono soppesare i pro e i contro*

We need to look at the pros and cons of their theory. — *dobbiamo considerare i pro e i contro di…*

The benefits of partnership in a giant trading market will almost certainly **outweigh the disadvantages.** — *i vantaggi di… superano gli svantaggi*

The two perspectives are not mutually exclusive. — *i due punti di vista non sono inconciliabili*

► *Come optare per una tesi*

Dr Meaden's theory **is the most convincing explanation.** — *…è la spiegazione più convincente*

The truth *o* **fact of the matter is that** in a free society you can't turn every home into a fortress. — *la verità è che...*

But **the truth is that** Father Christmas has a rather mixed origin. — *...la verità è che...*

Although this sounds dangerous, **in actual fact** it is quite safe. — *...in realtà...*

When all is said and done, it must be acknowledged that a purely theoretical approach to social issues is sterile. — *a conti fatti dobbiamo riconoscere che...*

► ***Per ricapitolare***

In this chapter, **I have demonstrated** *o* **shown that** the Cuban alternative has been undergoing considerable transformations. — *...ho dimostrato che...*

The overall picture shows that prison sentences were relatively frequent, but not particularly severe. — *il quadro d'insieme mostra che...*

To recap *o* **To sum up then, (we may conclude that)** there are in effect two possible solutions to this problem. — *ricapitolando, (si può concludere che)...*

To sum up this chapter I will offer two examples ... — *riassumendo questo capitolo...*

To summarize, we have seen that industry was hit after the war by a deteriorating international competitive position. — *in breve...*

Habermas's argument, **in a nutshell**, is as follows. — *...in poche parole...*

But **the key to the whole argument is** a single extraordinary paragraph. — *...il punto focale di tutta la questione è...*

To round off this section on slugs, gardeners may be interested to hear that there are three species of slugs in Britain. — *per terminare questa sezione...*

► ***Per concludere***

From all this it follows that it is impossible to extend those kinds of security measures to all potential targets of terrorism. — *da tutto ciò consegue che...*

This, of course, **leads to the logical conclusion that** those who actually produce do have a claim to the results of their efforts. — *ci porta logicamente a concludere che...*

There is only one logical conclusion we can reach, which is that we ask our customers what they want. — *c'è una sola conclusione logica...*

The inescapable conclusion is that the criminal justice system does not simply reflect the reality of crime; it helps to create it. — *non ci resta altro che concludere che...*

We must conclude that there is no solution to the problem of defining crime. — *si deve concludere che...*

In conclusion, because interpersonal relationships are so complex, there can be no easy way of preventing conflict. — *per concludere...*

The upshot of all this, is that treatment is unlikely to be available. — *come risultato si ha che...*

So it would appear that butter is not significantly associated with heart disease after all. — *sembrerebbe dunque che...*

This only goes to show that a good man is hard to find. — *questa è la prova che...*

The lesson to be learned from this **is that** you cannot hope to please everyone all of the time. — *l'insegnamento che si può trarre... è che...*

At the end of the day, the only way the drug problem will be beaten is when people are encouraged not to take them. — *in fin dei conti...*

Ultimately, then, while we may have some sympathy for these criminals, we must do our utmost to protect society from them. — *in definitiva, quindi...*

25.5 Come strutturare un paragrafo

► ***Per aggiungere ulteriori informazioni***

In addition, the author does not really empathize with his hero. — *inoltre...*

This award-winning writer, **in addition to** being a critic, biographer and poet, has written 26 crime novels. — *...oltre a*

But this is only part of the picture. **Added to this** are fears that a major price increase would cause riots. — *...oltre a ciò...*

An added complication is that the characters are not aware of their relationship to one another. — *un'altra...*

The question also arises as to how this idea can be put into practice. — *si pone inoltre la questione di...*

Politicians, **as well as** academics, tend to feel strongly about it. *... così come...*
But, **over and above that**, each list contains names and addresses. *...oltre a ciò...*
Furthermore, ozone is, like carbon dioxide, a greenhouse gas. *inoltre*

► ***Per fare dei paragoni***

Compared with the heroine, Alison is an insipid character. *paragonata a...*
In comparison with the Czech Republic, the culture of Bulgaria is less westernized. *se la si paragona con...*
This is a high percentage for the English Midlands but low **by comparison with** some other parts of Britain. *in confronto a...*
On the one hand, there is no longer a Warsaw Pact threat. **On the other (hand)**, the changes could have negative side-effects. *da un lato... dall'altro*
Similarly, a good historian is not obsessed by dates. *analogamente...*
There can only be one total at the bottom of a column of figures and **likewise** only one solution to any problem. *...ugualmente...*
What others say of us will translate into reality. **Equally**, what we affirm as true of ourselves will likewise come true. *...allo stesso modo...*
There will not be a change in the way we are regarded by our partners, and, **by the same token**, the way we regard them. *...per la stessa ragione*
There is a fundamental difference between adequate nutrient intake and optimum nutrient intake. *c'è una fondamentale differenza fra...*

► ***Per collegare vari punti***

Firstly, I would like to outline the benefits of the system. *prima di tutto...*
We are concerned **first and foremost** with the practical applications. *...in primo luogo...*
In order to understand the conflict, **it is first of all necessary** to know something of the history of the area. *per capire... è necessario prima di tutto...*
Secondly, it might be simpler to develop chemical weapons. *in secondo luogo...*
In the first/second place, the objectives were contradictory. *in primo, secondo luogo...*

► ***Per esprimere un punto di vista personale***

In my opinion they areunderestimating the scale of the epidemic. *a mio parere...*
My personal opinion is that the argument lacks depth. *sono del parere che...*
Speaking personally, I cannot understand the argument. *...parlando a titolo personale...*
Personally, I think that no one can appreciate ethnicity more than black or African people themselves. *personalmente...*
For my part, I cannot agree with the leadership on this question. *da parte mia...*
My own view is that economic factors determine the outcome. *trovo che...*
In my view, it only perpetuates the very problem that it sets out to address. *secondo me...*
Although the author argues the case for patriotism, **I feel that** he does not do it with any great personal conviction. *...penso che...*
I believe that there can be no quick fix for our problems. *credo che...*
It seems to me that what we have is a political problem that needs to be solved at a political level. *mi sembra che...*
I would maintain that we have made a significant effort. *desidero precisare che...*

► ***Per introdurre il punto di vista di qualcun altro***

He maintains that intelligence is conditioned by upbringing. *sostiene che...*
Bukharin **asserts that** all great revolutions are accompanied by destructive internal conflict. *...sostiene che...*
It **states that** some form of deterrent will be needed. *...afferma che...*
What he is saying is that the time of the old, highy structured political party is over. *ciò che sostiene è che...*
His admirers **would have us believe that** watching this film is more like going to church than having a night at the pictures. *...vorrebbero farci credere che...*
According to the report, poverty fosters violence. *secondo...*

► *Per introdurre un esempio*

To take another example many thousands of sick people have been condemned to a life of sickness and pain because ... — *...prendendo un altro esempio...*

Let us consider, **for example** *o* **for instance**, the problems faced by immigrants arriving in a strange country. — *...per esempio...*

His meteoric rise **is the most striking example yet** of voters' disillusionment with the record of the previous government. — *...è l'esempio più lampante di...*

The case of Henry Howey Robson **serves to illustrate** the courage exhibited by young men in the face of battle. — *...serve a illustrare...*

Just consider, **by way of illustration**, the difference in amounts accumulated if interest is paid gross rather than net. — *...come esempio...*

A case in point is the decision to ban contact with the public. — *un esempio tipico è...*

Take the case of the soldier returning from war. — *prendiamo il caso di...*

As the Prime Minister **remarked** recently, the Channel Tunnel had greatly benefited the whole of the European Community. — *come... ha osservato...*

25.6 I meccanismi di un dibattito

► *Per esprimere una supposizione*

That could be interpreted as trying to gain an unconstitutional political advantage. — *...potrebbe essere interpretato...*

The sales figure was higher than expected and **could be taken to mean that** inflationary pressures remain strong. — *...farebbe supporre che...*

In such circumstances, **it might well be prudent** to diversify. — *...sarebbe senza dubbio più prudente...*

These substances do not remain effective for long. **This is possibly because** they work against the insects' instinct to feed. — *...è possibile che ciò avvenga perché...*

It is not beyond the bounds of possibility that it may succeed. — *...non è impossibile che...*

Mr Fraser's assertion **leads one to suppose** that he is in full agreement with Catholic teaching as regards marriage. — *...ci porta a supporre che...*

It is probably the case that all long heavy ships are vulnerable. — *...probabilmente si può dire che...*

After hearing nothing from the taxman for so long, most people **might reasonably assume that** their tax affairs were in order. — *...è giustamente portata a credere che...*

One could be forgiven for thinking that because the substances are chemicals they'd be easy to study. — *è comprensibile che si pensi che...*

I venture to suggest that very often when people like him talk about love, they actually mean lust. — *...mi permetto di avanzare l'ipotesi che...*

► *Per esprimere una certezza*

It is clear that any risk to the human foetus is very low. — *è chiaro che...*

He is **indisputably** a fine orator. — *...indiscutibilmente*

British universities are **undeniably** good, but they are not turning out enough top scientists. — *...innegabilmente...*

There can be no doubt that the Earth's dramatic cooling which destroyed the environment and life style of these creatures. — *non c'è dubbio alcuno che...*

It is undoubtedly true that over the years there has been a much greater emphasis on safer sex. — *è senza dubbio vero che...*

As we all know, adultery is far from uncommon. — *come tutti ben sappiamo...*

One thing is certain: the party is far from united. — *una cosa è certa...*

► *Per esprimere un dubbio*

It is doubtful whether, in the present repressive climate, anyone would be brave or foolish enough to demonstrate publicly. — *ci sono forti dubbi che...*

It remains to be seen whether they will try to intervene. — *rimane da vedere se...*

I have a few reservations about the book. — *ho delle riserve su...*

It is by no means certain that they will make up their minds today. — *non è affatto certo che...*

It is questionable whether media coverage of terrorist organizations actually affects terrorism. — *non si sa se...*

The crisis **puts a question mark** against the Prime Minister's stated commitment to intervention. — *...rimette in questione...*

Both these claims **are true up to a point** and they need to be made. But they are limited in their significance. — *...sono vere fino a un certo punto...*

► ***Per esprimere che si è d'accordo (vedi anche 11. Accordo)***

I agree wholeheartedly with the opinion that smacking should be outlawed. — *sono completamente d'accordo con...*

One must acknowledge that this will make change more painful. — *si deve prendere atto che...*

It cannot be denied that there are similarities between them. — *è innegabile che...*

Courtney – **rightly in my view** – is strongly critical of the snobbery and élitism that is all too evident in these circles. — *...giustamente, a mio avviso*

Preaching was considered an important activity, **and rightly so** in a country with a high illiteracy rate. — *...a buon diritto...*

You may dispute his right to tell people how to live their lives, **but it is hard to disagree with** his picture of modern society. — *...ma è difficile non essere d'accordo con...*

► ***Per esprimere il dissenso (vedi anche 12. Dissenso)***

I must disagree with the article on criminality: it is dangerous to suggest that to be a criminal one must look like a criminal. — *non sono d'accordo con...*

I find it hard to believe that there is no link at all. — *mi riesce difficile credere che...*

The strength of their feelings **is scarcely credible.** — *...è poco credibile*

Her claim to have been the first to discover the phenomenon **lacks credibility.** — *...non è credibile*

Nevertheless, **I remain unconvinced by** Milton. — *...non mi ha affatto convinto*

Many do not believe that water contains anything remotely dangerous. Sadly, **this is far from the truth.** — *...si è molto lontani dalla verità*

To say that everyone requires the same amount of a vitamin is as stupid as saying we all have blonde hair. **It simply isn't true.** — *...semplicemente non è vero*

His remarks **were** not only highly offensive to black and other ethnic minorities but **totally inaccurate.** — *...sono stati... completamente errati*

Stomach ulcers are often associated with good living. **(But) in reality** there is no evidence to support this theory. — *... (ma) in realtà...*

This version of an economy **does not stand up to close scrutiny.** — *...non regge a un più attento esame*

► ***Per enfatizzare***

Nowadays, **there is clearly** less stigma attached to unmarried mothers. — *...chiaramente c'è...*

Once again **the facts speak for themselves.** — *...i fatti parlano da sé*

Few will argue with the principle that a fund should be set up. — *quasi nessuno metterebbe in discussione la necessità di...*

Hyams **supports this claim** by looking at sentences produced by young children learning German. — *...corrobora questa affermazione...*

The most important thing is to reach agreement from all sides. — *la cosa più importante è...*

Perhaps **the most important aspect of** cognition is the ability to manipulate symbols. — *...l'aspetto più importante di...*

► ***Per mettere in evidenza un concetto***

It would be impossible to exaggerate the importance of these two volumes for anyone with a serious interest in the subject. — *non si può sottolineare abbastanza l'importanza di...*

The symbolic importance of Jerusalem for both Palestinians and Jews **is almost impossible to overemphasize.** — *è praticamente impossibile esagerare...*

It is important to be clear that Jesus does not identify himself with Yahweh. — *è importante chiarire che...*

It is significant that Mandalay seems to have become the central focus in this debate. — *è significativo che...*

It should not be forgotten that many of those now in exile were close to the centre of power until only one year ago. — *non dobbiamo dimenticare che...*

It should be stressed that there is only one way that pet owners could possibly contract such a condition from their pets. *va sottolineato che...*

There is a very important point here and that is that the accused claims that he was with Ms Martins all evening. *c'è da sottolineare un aspetto molto importante qui ed è che...*

At the beginning of his book Mr Stone **makes a telling point.** *...fa un'osservazione significativa...*

In order to focus attention on Hobson's distinctive contributions to macroeconomics, these wider issues are neglected here. *poiché si vuole attirare l'attenzione su...*

These statements **are interesting in that** they illustrate different views. *...sono interessanti in quanto...*

26 Al telefono

26.1 Per ottenere un numero

You'll have to look up the number in the phone book. *deve cercare il numero sull'elenco telefonico*

You should get the number from International Directory Enquiries. *può avere il numero tramite il servizio informazioni internazionali*

Can you give me the number of Europost, 54 Broad Street, Newham? *mi può dare il numero di...*

The number's not in the book. *il numero non è sull'elenco*

They're ex-directory (*Brit*) / **They're unlisted** (*Am*). *il numero non compare sull'elenco*

What is the code for Exeter? *qual è il prefisso di...*

Can I dial direct to Colombia? *posso telefonare direttamente in...*

You omit the "0" when dialling the UK from Italy. *deve omettere lo "0" iniziale quando chiama...*

How do I make an outside call? / What do I dial for an outside line? *che numero devo fare per ottenere la linea esterna?*

26.2 Diversi tipi di telefonate

It's a local call. *è una chiamata urbana*

It's a long distance call from Manchester. *è una chiamata interurbana da...*

I want to make an international call. *vorrei fare una telefonata internazionale*

I want to make a reverse charges call to a London number (*Brit*) / **I want to call** a London number **collect** (*Am*). *vorrei fare una telefonata a carico del destinatario a...*

What do I dial to get the speaking clock? *che numero devo fare per l'ora esatta?*

I'd like an alarm call for 7.30 tomorrow morning. *vorrei la sveglia telefonica alle...*

What number do I dial to get room service? *che numero devo fare per il servizio in camera?*

26.3 Risponde l'operatore

Which number, please? *che numero desidera?*

Which town, please? *di quale città?*

Where are you calling from? *da dove chiama?*

Would you repeat the number, please? *può ripetere il numero, per favore?*

You can dial the number direct. *può chiamare questo numero direttamente*

Replace the receiver and dial again. *riagganci il ricevitore e componga di nuovo il numero*

There's a Mr Sandy Campbell **calling you from** Canberra **and wishes you to pay for the call. Will you accept it?** *c'è una telefonata a suo carico dal signor... accetta la chiamata?*

(*Directory Enquiries*) **There's no listing under that name.** *non c'è nessun abbonato con questo nome*

There's no reply from 45 77 57 84. *il... non risponde*

I'll try to reconnect you. *provo a passarle di nuovo la comunicazione*

Hold the line, caller. *attenda in linea, prego*

Shall I put you through? *le passo la comunicazione?*

I'm trying it for you now.	*sto provando il numero*
It's ringing / Ringing for you now.	*sta suonando*
The line is engaged (*Brit*) **/ The line is busy** (*Am*)	*la linea è occupata*

26.4 Risponde l'abbonato

Could I have extension 516? / Can you give me extension 516?	*mi può passare l'interno 516, per favore?*
Is that Mr Lambert**'s phone?**	*è il numero del signor...?*
Could I speak to Mr Swinton**, please? / I'd like to speak to Mr** Swinton**, please. / Is Mr** Swinton **there?**	*potrei parlare con il signor... per favore?*
Could you put me through to Dr Henderson**, please?**	*mi può passare il dottor..., per cortesia?*
Who's speaking?	*chi parla?*
I'll try again later.	*richiamerò più tardi*
I'll call back in half an hour.	*richiamerò tra una mezz'ora*
Could I leave my number for her to call me back?	*potrei lasciare il mio numero per farmi richiamare?*
Can I leave a message, please?	*posso lasciare un messaggio, per favore?*
I'm ringing from a callbox (*Brit*) **/ I'm calling from a pay phone** (*Am*).	*sto telefonando da una cabina telefonica*
I'm phoning from England.	*sto telefonando da...*
Would you ask him to ring me when he gets back?	*potrebbe chiedergli di chiamarmi quando rientra?*
Could you tell her I called?	*potrebbe dirle che ho chiamato?*

26.5 Risponde il centralino/la centralinista

Queen's Hotel, **can I help you?**	*pronto,... desidera?*
Who's calling, please?	*chi parla, per cortesia?*
Who shall I say is calling?	*può dirmi il suo nome ?*
Do you know his extension number?	*sa il numero dell'interno?*
I'm putting you through now.	*le passo la comunicazione*
I'm putting you through now to Mrs Thomas.	*le passo la signora...*
I've got Miss Martin **on the line for you.**	*c'è una telefonata in linea per lei da...*
Dr Craig **is on the other line.**	*il dottor... è sull'altra linea*
Please hold / Could you hold the line, please?	*rimanga in linea, per favore*
Sorry to keep you waiting.	*mi scusi per l'attesa*
There's no reply.	*non risponde*
You're through to our Sales Department.	*è in linea con...*

26.6 Per rispondere al telefono

Hello, this is Anne **speaking.**	*Pronto, sono...*
(*Is that Anne?*) **Speaking.**	*sono io*
Would you like to leave a message?	*vuole lasciare un messaggio?*
Can I take a message for him?	*vuole lasciargli un messaggio?*

26.7 In caso di difficoltà

I can't get through (at all).	*non riesco a prendere la linea*
The number is not ringing.	*non mi dà nessun segnale*
I'm getting "number unobtainable".	*mi dà il segnale di numero non raggiungibile*
Their phone is out of order.	*il loro apparecchio è fuori servizio*
We were cut off.	*è caduta la linea*
I must have dialled the wrong number.	*devo aver fatto un numero sbagliato*
I've called them several times with no reply.	*li ho chiamati diverse volte ma non ho avuto risposta*

I got the wrong extension.	*mi hanno passato l'interno sbagliato*
This is a very bad line.	*la linea è molto disturbata*
Sorry we are unable to connect your call.	*siamo spiacenti di non essere in grado di passarle la comunicazione*

26.8 Messaggi registrati

This is a recorded message.	*questo è un messaggio registrato*
Please speak after the tone (Brit) **/after the beep** (Am).	*per favore parlate dopo il segnale acustico*
Please press the hash key (Brit) **number sign** (Am) **after the beep.**	*premere il tasto cancelletto dopo il segnale acustico*
Press the star (*) key twice.	*prema due volte il tasto asterisco*
The following options are available from the main menu.	*è possibile scegliere tra le seguenti opzioni del menu principale*
If you would like to speak to a Customer Services advisor, **please press one.**	*se desidera parlare con…, prema uno*
Please replace the handset and try again.	*per favore riagganci e componga di nuovo il numero*
The number you are calling knows you are waiting.	*l'avviso di chiamata è stato inoltrato*
The number you are calling is engaged (Brit) **/busy** (Am). **Please try again later.**	*il numero dell'utente desiderato è occupato. La preghiamo di riprovare più tardi*
The number you have dialled has been changed. Please redial using the area code/number 0208.	*il numero dell'utente desiderato è cambiato. Per favore componga di nuovo il numero con il prefisso…*
The number you have dialled no longer exists.	*il numero selezionato è inesistente*
Your call is in a queue and will be answered shortly.	*i nostri operatori sono tutti momentaneamente occupati. La preghiamo di restare in linea per non perdere la priorità acquisita*
The number you have dialled has not been recognized. Please check and call again.	*il numero selezionato è inesistente. La preghiamo di voler verificare il numero*
This number has now been changed. Please ring 465322.	*il numero da lei chiamato è cambiato. Il nuovo numero è il…*

26.9 Telefono cellulare

The mobile you have dialled is switched off.	*il telefono della persona chiamata potrebbe essere spento o non raggiungibile*
Your airtime balance is …	*il suo credito residuo è di …*
There is no reception.	*qui non c'è campo.*
My battery needs recharging.	*ho la batteria del cellulare scarica*
The phone line is breaking up.	*la linea è molto disturbata*
My battery is low.	*la mia batteria è quasi scarica*
I can't get a signal here.	*non riesco a prendere il segnale qui*
I haven't got any credit on my phone.	*non ho più credito sul cellulare*

26.10 SMS

	INGLESE	ITALIANO
@	at	chiocciola
2	too	anche
2day	today	oggi
2moro	tomorrow	domani
2nite	tonight	stasera
2u	to you	a te, a voi
4	for	per
afaic	as far as I'm concerned	per quanto mi riguarda
afaik	as far as I know	per quel che so
atb	all the best	saluti
b	be	essere
bbl	be back later	torno più tardi
bbs	be back soon	torno presto
bcnu	be seeing you	ci vediamo
brb	be right back	torno subito
btw	by the way	a proposito
bykt	but you knew that	ma lo sapevi già
cid	consider it done	consideralo già fatto
coz	because	perché
cu	see you	ci vediamo
cul8r	see you later	ci vediamo più tardi
cw2cu	can't wait to see you	non vedo l'ora di vederti
ez	easy	facile
fwiw	for what it's worth	per quel che vale
fyi	for your information	a titolo d'informazione
gal	get a life	ma non hai altro a cui pensare?
gbtm	get back to me	fammi sapere
gr8	great	grande
gtg	got to go	devo andare
h8	hate	odiare
hth	hope this helps	spero che serva
iac	in any case	in ogni caso
iccl	I couldn't care less	non me ne potrebbe importare di meno
idk	I don't know	non so
iluvu	I love you	ti amo
imho	in my humble opinion	secondo il mio modesto parere
iou	I owe you	ti devo
iykwim	if you know what I mean	se sai cosa intendo
kit	keep in touch	fatti vivo/a
l8	late	tardi
l8er	later	più tardi

inglese – italiano

	INGLESE	ITALIANO
lol	laughing out loud/lots of love	ridere ad alta voce/baci
lv	love	amore
m8	mate	amico
mob	mobile	cellulare
msg	message	messaggio
myob	mind your own business	fatti gli affari tuoi
ne	any	qualche/alcun etc
njoy	enjoy	buon divertimento
no1	no one	nessuno
np	no problem	non c'è problema
oic	oh I see	ah, capisco
ott	over the top	esagerato/a
pcm	please call me	chiamami per favore
plz	please	per favore
r	are	sei, siamo, siete, sono
rn	right now	adesso
ruok	are you OK?	stai bene?
sum1	someone	qualcuno
thx	thanks	grazie
ti2go	time to go	è ora di andare
tmb	text me back	rispondimi per sms
ttyl	talk to you later	ci sentiamo più tardi
txt	text	sms
txt me	text me	mandami un sms
u	you	tu, voi
v	very	molto
wan2	want to	volere
wbs	write back soon	rispondi presto
wiv	with	con
wknd	weekend	fine settimana
wud	what are you doing?	cosa stai facendo?
x	kiss	bacio
xlnt	excellent	eccellente
y	why	perché
yr	your	tuo, vostro

27 Posta elettronica

Mandare un messaggio

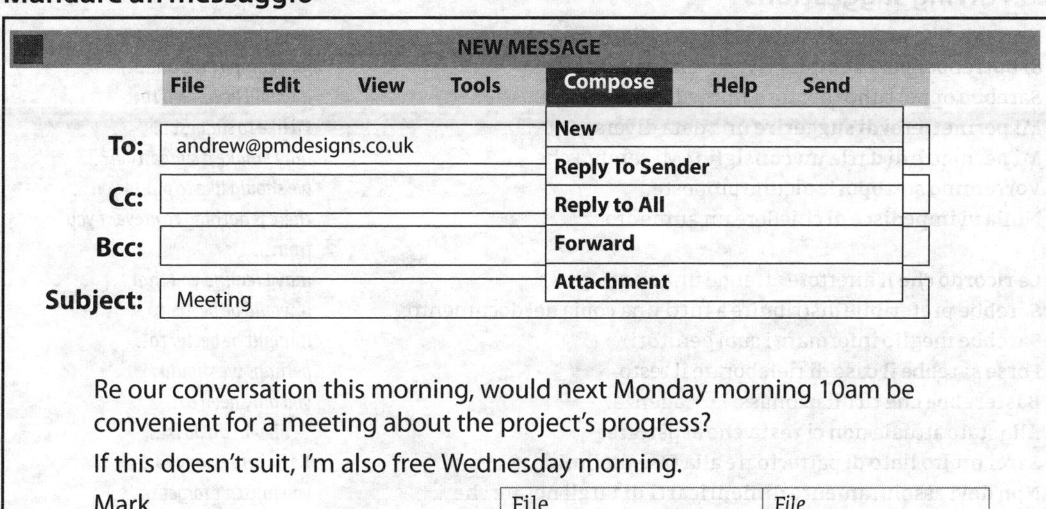

Re our conversation this morning, would next Monday morning 10am be convenient for a meeting about the project's progress?

If this doesn't suit, I'm also free Wednesday morning.

Mark

File	*File*
Edit	*Modifica*
View	*Visualizza*
Tools	*Strumenti*
Compose	*Messaggio*
Help	*Help*
Send	*Invia*
New	*Nuovo*
Reply to sender	*Rispondi al mittente*

Ricevere un messaggio

MEETING

File Edit View Tools Reply Help

From: andrew collins (andrew@pmdesigns.co.uk)

Sent: 30 November 2005 08.30

To: mark.gordon@typo.co.uk

Subject: Meeting

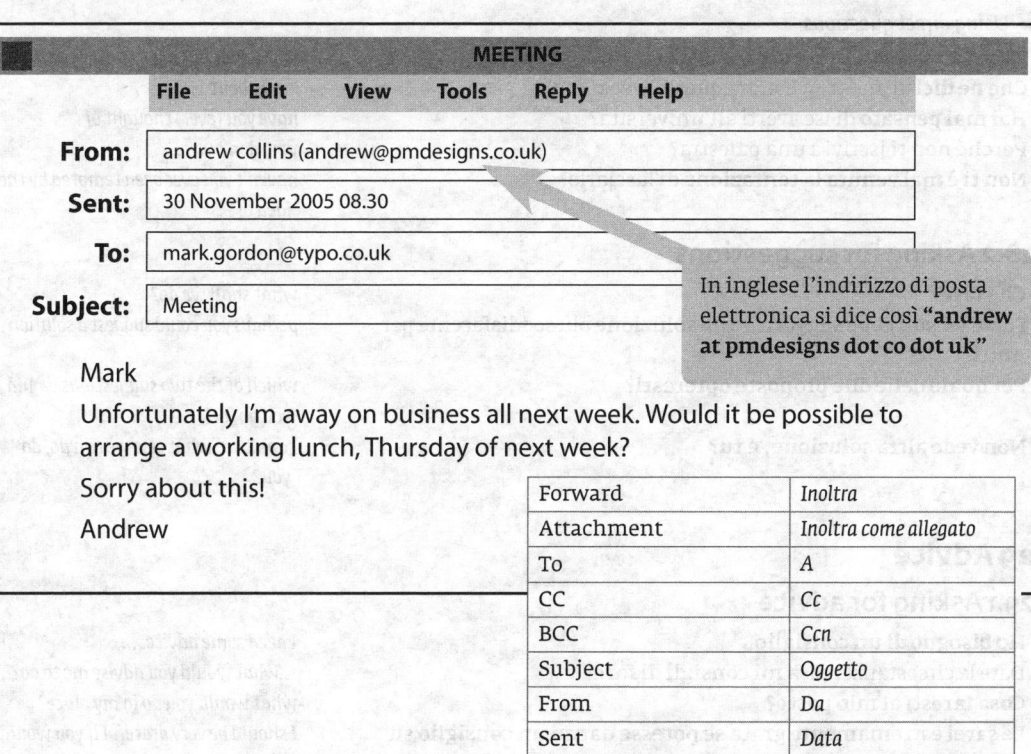

In inglese l'indirizzo di posta elettronica si dice così **"andrew at pmdesigns dot co dot uk"**

Mark

Unfortunately I'm away on business all next week. Would it be possible to arrange a working lunch, Thursday of next week?

Sorry about this!

Andrew

Forward	*Inoltra*
Attachment	*Inoltra come allegato*
To	*A*
CC	*Cc*
BCC	*Ccn*
Subject	*Oggetto*
From	*Da*
Sent	*Data*
Received	*Ricevuto*

28 Suggestions

28.1 Giving suggestions

Non sarebbe una cattiva idea chiedergli un parere. — *it might not be a bad idea to ...*
Si potrebbe, per esempio, rivedere la prima parte. — *for example, we could ...*
Sarebbe opportuno inviargli immediatamente il dossier. — *it would be as well to ...*
Mi permetterei di suggerire una data diversa. — *I'd like to suggest ...*
Mi permette di darle un consiglio? Mi sembra che ... — *may I make a suggestion? ...*
Vorremmo sottoporle alcune proposte. — *we should like to put to you ...*
Nulla vi impedisce di chiedere un aumento. — *there is nothing to prevent you from ...*
Le ricordo che il direttore attende una sua risposta. — *may I remind you that ...*
Sarebbe preferibile distribuire a tutti una copia del documento. — *it would be better to ...*
Sarebbe meglio informare i suoi genitori. — *it might be better to ...*
Forse sarebbe il caso di rielaborare il testo. — *perhaps we should ...*
Basterebbe che tu dilazionassi la scadenza. — *you only need to ...*
Allo stato attuale **non ci resta che** aspettare. — *... all we can do is ...*
Sarei molto lieto di partecipare alla fase preliminare. — *I'd be very happy to ...*
Non devi assolutamente dimenticarti di fargli notare che ... — *you mustn't forget to ...*
Si potrebbe adottare un altro metodo. — *we could ...*
Potresti andarci domani. — *you could ...*
Faresti meglio ad andare in vacanza a settembre. — *you'd be better off going ...*
È urgentissimo e **dovresti** cercare di finirlo per domani. — *... you ought to ...*
Se fossi in te *or* **Al tuo posto** *or* **Personalmente** non ci andrei. — *if I were you ...*
A mio avviso non dovresti rifiutare. — *in my view ...*
Ti consiglio di prendere le dovute precauzioni. — *I advise you to ...*
Se lei è d'accordo la richiamo domani. — *if you agree ...*
Propongo di parlargliene immediatamente. — *I suggest that ...*
Ti consiglierei di prenderti una lunga vacanza. — *I'd advise you to ...*

► *Using direct questions*

E se andassimo a cena fuori stasera? — *what about going ...*
Che ne dici di andare a Londra questo week-end? — *how about ...*
Hai mai pensato di iscriverti all'università? — *have you (ever) thought of ...*
Perché non ti iscrivi a una palestra? — *why don't you ...*
Non ti è mai venuta la tentazione di lasciarlo? — *haven't you ever been tempted by the idea of ...*

28.2 Asking for suggestions

Che fare? — *what shall we do?*
Forse lei potrebbe suggerire una soluzione più soddisfacente per tutti — *perhaps you could suggest a solution ...*
Per quale delle due proposte opteresti? — *which of the two suggestions would you go for?*
Non vedo altra soluzione, e tu? — *I don't see what else we can do, do you?*

29 Advice

29.1 Asking for advice

Ho bisogno di un consiglio. — *I need some advice: ...*
Date le circostanze, **cosa mi consigli di fare?** — *...what would you advise me to do?*
Cosa faresti al mio posto? — *what would you do in my place?*
Le sarei estremamente grata se potesse darmi un consiglio su come ... — *I should be very grateful if you would advise me as to ...*

English – Italian

29.2 Giving advice

Personalmente trovo che dovresti insistere. — *personally, I think you should ...*
Se vuoi il mio consiglio, interrompi questa relazione. — *my advice would be to ...*
Se mi permetti di darti un consiglio faresti meglio a non andarci. — *if I can give you some advice, you'd do better ...*
Ti raccomando la massima discrezione. — *please keep this absolutely confidential*
Ti sconsiglio vivamente di prendere il treno. — *I (strongly) advise you not to ...*
Al tuo posto *or* **Se fossi in te,** me ne andrei immediatamente. — *if I were you ...*
A mio avviso, dovresti rivolgerti a uno specialista. — *in my opinion, you should ...*
Mi permetta di suggerirle Oslo quale sede migliore per ... — *may I suggest ...*
Si sconsiglia un uso eccessivo di antibiotici. — *it is inadvisable to ...*
Sarebbe opportuno ottenere prima di tutto la sua autorizzazione. — *it would be wise to ...*
Prenditi una vacanza, **è la cosa migliore che tu possa fare.** — *... it's the best thing you could do*
Sbagli a non pretendere di essere pagato per le ore extra. — *you'd be wrong not to ...*
Hai avuto torto a fidarti di lui. — *you were wrong to ...*
Sarebbe una buona idea anticipare l'incontro. — *it might be a good idea to ...*

► *More tentatively*

Non vedo perché tu non debba dirglielo. — *there is no reason why you shouldn't ...*
Hai mai pensato ad un corso di informatica? — *have you ever thought of ...*
Forse potreste spiegarglielo di persona. — *perhaps you could ...*
Mi domando se non sarebbe meglio aspettare qualche giorno. — *I wonder if it wouldn't be ...*
Non sarebbe mica una cattiva idea comprarne due dozzine — *it wouldn't at all be a bad idea to ...*

29.3 Warning someone about something

Sarebbe opportuno spedirgliene una copia, così non se ne dimentica. — *you'd be as well to ... so that ...*
Diffidate di tutti quelli senza una tessera di riconoscimento. — *beware of ...*
Sarebbe pura follia mettersi in viaggio il 15 di agosto. — *it would be madness to ...*
L'avverto che se il vestito non sarà pronto, non salderò il conto. — *I warn you that ...*
Correte il rischio di perdere tutti i vostri risparmi. — *you are running the risk of ...*
Ti troverai nei guai se non inizi subito a studiare. — *you'll be in trouble if ...*
Un consiglio: smettila di fare commenti saccenti. — *a word of warning: ...*
Ti avverto che comincio ad averne abbastanza delle tue continue assenze. — *I warn you that ...*
E non venirti poi a lamentare che non sei stato selezionato! — *don't come to me complaining that ...*

30 Offers

Mi chiedo se non sarebbe meglio se lo facessi io. — *I wonder if it wouldn't be better ...*
Se lo desidera, potremmo venire con lei. — *we could ... if you like ...*
Se vuole, le posso mandare un'altra segretaria. — *I can ..., if you like ...*
Mi permetta almeno di pagare le spese del telefono! — *at least let me ...*
Andrò **volentieri** a tener compagnia alla nonna. — *I'll gladly ...*
Siamo lieti di offrirle il posto di segretaria. — *we should like to offer you ...*
Non esiti a chiedermi ulteriori spiegazioni, se necessario. — *don't hesitate to ask me ...*
Provvederò io a farla avvisare in tempo. — *I'll see to it that ...*
Sono pronto ad occuparmi io di tutto. — *I'm ready to ...*
Sono lieto di mettermi a sua completa disposizione. — *I would be happy to ...*

► *Using questions*

Mi permette di accompagnarla a visitare il reparto vendite? — *may I ...*
Posso aiutarti a finirlo? — *can I ...*
Vuole che l'aiuti ad archiviare le pratiche? — *would you like me to ...*
Perché non lascia a noi l'intera organizzazione del viaggio? — *why not leave ... to us ...*
Vuole che prenoti io l'hotel? — *would you like me to ...*

English – Italian

E se venissi io a far da baby-sitter domani sera? — *shall I come and ...*
Cosa ne dite se ci andassi io? — *what would you say if ...*
Che ne direste di organizzare una cena per gli ex allievi? — *how about ...*

31 Requests

Può, per cortesia, mandare un'auto ad attendermi all'aeroporto? — *could you ...*
Le spiacerebbe occuparsi lei delle prenotazioni? — *would you mind ...*
Vorrei sapere se la banca è aperta il sabato mattina. — *I'd like to ...*
Conto su di lei affinché l'assegno venga spedito in tempo. — *I'm counting on you to ...*
Preferirei che non ne facesse parola. — *I would rather you ...*
Le spiace fare una fotocopia? — *would you mind ...*
Potrebbe gentilmente spedirmene due copie? — *would you kindly ...*
Siete tenuti a presentare il bilancio prima del 12. — *you are requested to ...*
Può, per cortesia, comunicarmi la data della sua partenza? — *would you kindly ...*
Mi sarebbe di enorme aiuto se potesse sostituirmi. — *it would be really helpful if ...*

► ***More formally***

Sarebbe così gentile da confermarmi la data e l'ora del suo arrivo? — *would you please be kind enough to ...*
Mi trovo costretto a ribadirle che si deve rivolgere al direttore in persona. — *I must insist that ...*
Vi saremmo grati se poteste regolare immediatamente la fattura. — *we would be very grateful if you would ...*

32 Comparisons

Rispetto ai supermercati, i negozi rionali sono spesso più cari. — *in comparison with ...*
Paragonata a Londra, Roma è decisamente più piccola. — *if you compare it with ...*
È stato spesso paragonato al nostro Pasolini. — *he has often been compared to ...*
In rapporto, è meno caro in agosto. — *comparatively speaking ...*
Quest'articolo è **molto più** interessante **di** quello che ho letto ieri. — *... (much) more ... than ...*
Le vendite sono aumentate considerevolmente **rispetto all'**anno scorso. — *... in comparison with ...*
È diventato **sempre più** difficile/**sempre meno** facile affittare un alloggio in centro a prezzi accessibili. — *... more and more ... / ...less and less ...*
La casa nuova è **molto simile** all'altra, **ma più piccola.** — *... is very like ... but smaller*
Ricorda vagamente un tempio greco. — *it is somewhat reminiscent of ...*
I loro due stili **non si assomigliano affatto.** — *... are not at all alike*
I romanzi sono entrambi storici, ma **le somiglianze finiscono qui.** — *... there the likeness ends*
La casa ha il giardino, **mentre tutte le altre** hanno un cortiletto. — *... whereas all the others ...*
Sono molto simili, ma l'aaltro appartamento ha un bagno più grande. — *they are very similar, but ...*
Quello che lo distingue dagli altri scrittori neorealisti è ... — *what distinguishes him from ...*

► ***Comparing favourably***

Questo vino è **nettamente superiore all'altro.** — *... far superior to ...*
Non c'è confronto: lui è molto più simpatico. — *there is no comparison: ...*

► ***Comparing unfavourably***

Il film è **molto meno interessante del** libro da cui è stato tratto. — *... is far less interesting than ...*
La qualità di questo tessuto è **decisamente inferiore.** — *... is certainly inferior*
L'ultimo romanzo **non regge al** *or* **il confronto** con i precedenti. — *... doesn't bear comparison with ...*
La qualità della sua produzione poetica è **di gran lunga inferiore a** quella dei romanzi. — *...is not nearly as good as ...*

► ***Comparing similar things***

Le due case **sono molto simili.** — *... are very similar ...*
Corrisponde a 6 intere settimane di lavoro. — *it is the equivalent of ...*
Non vedo alcuna differenza fra i due metodi. — *I cannot see any difference between ...*
Il valore degli immobili è crollato e **lo stesso vale** per i terreni. — *... the same is true of ...*

English – Italian

▶ *Comparing dissimilar things*

Non c'è assolutamente confronto fra i due candidati.	*there is simply no comparison between ...*
È certamente **difficile stabilire un confronto fra** i due.	*it is ...difficult to draw a comparison between ...*
Non è proprio possibile paragonare due opere così diverse.	*one just cannot compare ...*

33 Opinions

33.1 Asking for somebody's opinion

Vorrei la tua opinione a proposito di ...	*I'd like your opinion on ...*
Che ne pensi del suo comportamento?	*what do you think of ...*
Mi puoi dire qual è la tua opinione in proposito?	*can you give me your opinion ...*
A vostro avviso *or* **Secondo voi** sarebbe meglio dare più libertà ai giovani?	*in your opinion ...*
Qual è la vostra opinione sulle TV private?	*what is your attitude to ...*
Mi piacerebbe sapere cosa ne pensate del programma del festival.	*I'd like to know what you think of ...*
Sarei lieto di avere la vostra opinione sulla scelta dei materiali.	*I'd be glad to have your opinion ...*

33.2 Expressing your opinion

Penso/Credo di aver seguito alla lettera le tue istruzioni.	*I think that ...*
Presumo/Suppongo/Immagino che tu sappia già di cosa si tratta.	*I presume that ...*
Credo che la loro proposta sia stata accolta favorevolmente.	*I believe that ...*
A mio avviso si può fare di meglio.	*in my view ...*
Secondo me non la si doveva lasciare da sola in casa.	*in my opinion ...*
A mio parere il governo dovrebbe intervenire immediatamente.	*my own view is that ...*
Da quanto vedo non si può rimediare in altro modo.	*as far as I can see ...*
Ho l'impressione che i suoi genitori lo trascurino un po'.	*I have the impression that ...*
Ripensandoci, mi sembra meglio non rispondere.	*on second thoughts, we'd better ...*
Sono persuaso che finiranno per mettersi d'accordo.	*I'm sure that ...*
Sono convinto che questa sia l'unica soluzione possibile.	*it is my belief that ...*
Ho la sensazione che stia per andarsene.	*I've got a feeling that ...*
Devo dire che i risultati mi paiono proprio scadenti.	*I must say that ...*
Ho paura che sia ormai troppo tardi.	*I fear it may be ...*
Se volete la mia opinione, non ne vale la pena.	*if you want my opinion ...*
Non posso fare a meno di pensare che l'abbia fatto apposta.	*I can't help thinking that ...*
Con tutto il rispetto, mi sembra che questa non sia una soluzione soddisfacente.	*with all due respect, I feel that ...*

33.3 Replying without giving an opinion

È difficile dire quali saranno le reazioni del pubblico.	*it is difficult to tell ...*
Preferirei non pronunciarmi su una questione così delicata.	*I'd rather not commit myself ...*
È difficile dare un giudizio definitivo.	*it is difficult to give a final opinion*
Devo ammettere di **non avere alcuna idea** in proposito.	*... I have no particular views ...*
Non ci ho mai riflettuto seriamente.	*I've never really thought about it*
Non sta a me fare delle critiche.	*it's not for me to ...*
Tutto dipende da quello che si intende con ...	*it all depends on what you mean by ...*

34 Likes, dislikes and preferences

34.1 Asking people what they like

Ti piacerebbe ricominciare a giocare a tennis?	*would you like to ...*
Ti piace lavorare con lui?	*do you like ...*
Quale ti piace di più: il piano o il violino?	*which do you prefer ...*

English – Italian

34.2 Saying what you like

Il concerto **mi è piaciuto moltissimo.** *I enjoyed ... very much*
Occuparmi del giardino **mi dà grandissima soddisfazione.** *I really enjoy ...*
Mi piace che la gente sia puntuale. *I like people to ...*
... **ma più di tutto preferisco** trascorrere una serata tranquilla con pochi amici. *... but what I like better than anything else is ...*

34.3 Saying what you dislike

Se c'è una cosa che odio è aspettare l'autobus sotto la pioggia. *if there's one thing I hate, it's ...*
Odio a morte quelli che si danno troppe arie. *I really hate ...*
Il suo comportamento **non mi piace per niente.** *I don't like ... at all*
Trovo molto difficile parlare in pubblico. *I find it hard to ...*
Non sopporto proprio chi arriva costantemente in ritardo. *I just can't bear ...*
Mi è stato subito antipatico. *I took an instant dislike to him*
Non è niente di speciale, non so perché tutti ne vadano matti. *it's nothing special ...*

34.4 Saying what you prefer

Preferisco le pesche **alle** albicocche. *I prefer ... to ...*
Leggere è probabilmente il mio passatempo **preferito.** *... favourite ...*
Preferirei se partissi immediatamente. *I'd rather you ...*
Se non c'è in rosso nella mia taglia, **piuttosto prendo** quello blu. *... I'll have ... instead*
Sarebbe meglio comprare un tavolo rotondo. *It would be better to ...*
Per me venerdì **andrebbe meglio.** *... would suit me better*
Preferirei che non pronunciassi il suo nome in mia presenza. *I'd rather you didn't ...*
Hanno una spiccata predilezione per il teatro giapponese. *they have a marked preference for ...*

34.5 Expressing indifference

Che tu venga *or* **no per me è** *or* **fa lo stesso.** *... I really don't mind whether you come or not*
A dir la verità, **non ho alcuna preferenza.** *... I have no particular preference.*
Fai come vuoi: a me piacciono entrambe. *you choose: ...*
Non ha la minima importanza. *it's of no importance whatsoever*
È un genere che **mi lascia totalmente indifferente.** *... doesn't interest me in the slightest*

35 Intentions and desires

35.1 Asking what someone intends or wants

Che cosa conti/pensi di fare?/Cosa intendi fare? *what do you intend to do?*
Ci farebbe molto piacere conoscere le vostre intenzioni. *it would be good to know what your intentions are*
Perché non ti iscrivi a un corso di danza classica? *why don't you ...*
Cosa speri di ottenere comportandoti così? *what are you hoping to ...*
Vogliamo sapere cosa i nostri clienti si aspettano di trovare nei supermercati. *we want to know what our customers expect to find ...*

35.2 Talking about intentions

Ho intenzione di sostituire tutte le piastrelle in cucina. *I'm going to ...*
Avevo in mente di andare a un concerto. *what I wanted to do was to ...*
Aveva programmato di andare ad almeno due delle conferenze. *he had planned to ...*
Avevo intenzione di parlargliene, ma poi non l'ho fatto. *I was going to speak to him about it ...*
L'avevo preso in prestito **con l'intenzione di** fare delle fotocopie, ma poi non ho avuto tempo. *... intending to ...*
Progettavo di ristrutturare il fienile. *I was planning to ...*

English – Italian

► *With more determination*

Voglio dimagrire di almeno quattro chili. — *I want to ...*

Desidero farvelo pervenire immediatamente. — *I want ...*

Ho deciso di invitare tutto il parentado per Natale. — *I have decided to ...*

È fermamente deciso a fare il giro del mondo. — *he is determined to ...*

Voglio che tutti ne **siano** a conoscenza. — *I want everyone to be ...*

Non se ne parla neanche di vendere la macchina. — *there is no question of ...*

Sono assolutamente contrario a concedere ulteriori dilazioni. — *I am dead against ...*

► *More enthusiastically*

Muoio dalla voglia di vederlo. — *I'm dying to ...*

Desidero ardentemente andarci, ma non posso permettermelo. — *I'd really love to ...*

35.3 Saying what you would like

Vorrei due biglietti per domani sera, ma temo che sia tutto esaurito. — *I'd like (to have) ...*

Vorrei andare al cinema. — *I'd like to ...*

Avrei voluto congratularmi di persona. — *I should have liked to ...*

Se solo avessi avuto un po' più di tempo! — *if only I had ...*

C'è da sperare che tutto vada secondo i piani. — *it is to be hoped that ...*

Sarebbe auspicabile che intervenissero tutti i membri. — *it is to be hoped that ...*

Soprattutto **mi auguro che** si trovi una rapida soluzione. — *... my hope is that ...*

35.4 Saying what you don't want to do

Preferirei non doverglielo dire io. — *I'd rather not have to ...*

Non voglio dover cambiare i miei piani solo per lei. — *I don't want to have to ...*

Mi rifiuto di subire le sue continue prepotenze. — *I refuse ...*

Non ho la minima *or* **alcuna intenzione di** consultarlo. — *I have no intention of ...*

---

36 Permission

36.1 Asking for permission

Potrei essere trasferito a un altro dipartimento? — *could I ...*

Spero non la secchi troppo inserire questi piccoli cambiamenti. — *I hope it won't be too much bother to ...*

Se non crea troppi problemi, mi piacerebbe partecipare a questa fase. — *I'd like to ... if it's no trouble*

Mi permette di usare il suo computer, per un attimo? — *would you allow me to ...*

Sarebbe così gentile da prestarmi il suo programma? — *would you be kind enough to ...*

È permesso *or* **Si possono** fare telefonate personali? — *are you allowed to ...*

Sarebbe mica possibile avere una stanza più grande? — *would it be at all possible to ...*

36.2 Giving permission

Se volete **potete** comprarne uno nuovo. — *... you may o can ...*

Vi do il mio permesso di uscire due ore prima. — *I give you my permission to ...*

Ma certamente, fate come vi pare più opportuno. — *by all means, do ...*

Vi autorizzo ben volentieri a parlargliene. — *I certainly authorise you to ...*

36.3 Having permission

Mi ha detto che, se avessi voluto, avrei potuto assentarmi un'ora o due. — *he said I could ... if I wanted to*

Sono autorizzato a firmare gli assegni in sua vece. — *I am authorised to ...*

Gli lasciano bere il caffè anche se ha solo 3 anni. — *they let him ...*

Solo i genitori **possono** firmare le giustificazioni. — *... can ...*

In questo tipo di calcolo **è tollerato un errore del 3%.** — *...3% error is allowable*

36.4 Refusing permission

Non potete iscrivervi a più di cinque corsi. — *you can't ...*

Non vi permetto di spedirgli questa foto. — *I will not allow you to ...*

Preferirei che non ci andaste. — *I'd rather you didn't ...*

English – Italian

Mi oppongo assolutamente ad ogni cambiamento nel testo.	*I absolutely refuse to allow you to ...*
Mi è stato proibito di fumare.	*I have been forbidden to ...*
Il dottore mi ha proibito tutti i grassi.	*my doctor has banned ...*
Mi dispiace doverla deludere, ma la sua proposta è stata respinta.	*I'm sorry to have to disappoint you ...*
Le proibisco categoricamente di contattare la concorrenza.	*I absolutely forbid you to ...*
È contro il regolamento consultare il catalogo generale.	*it is against the rules to ...*
È assolutamente vietato l'uso del telefono.	*... is strictly prohibited*
Non vi è consentito utilizzare la mensa.	*you are not allowed to ...*

37 Obligation

37.1 Saying what someone must do

Devi assolutamente mostrarti più tollerante.	*you really must ...*
Tutti i prestiti**devono essere** autorizzati dal direttore.	*... must be ...*
È mio dovere informarvi che l'ufficio sarà chiuso per inventario.	*I have to ...*
Dovete assolutamente presentargli le vostre scuse.	*you absolutely must ...*
Non si può accedere all'Università **senza** un titolo di scuola superiore.	*you cannot ... without ...*
Lo sciopero mi costringe a rimandare la partenza di un giorno.	*the strike means I have to ...*
Dovete trovarvi un avvocato.	*you have got to ...*
Si è visto costretto a chiedere l'intervento del direttore.	*he found himself forced to ...*
Si è sentito obbligato a dare le dimissioni.	*he felt he had to ...*
È obbligatorio versare l'intera somma entro la fine dell'anno.	*the whole sum is payable ...*
Non ne avevo alcuna intenzione, ma **sono stato costretto**.	*... I was made to*
Mi trovo costretto, ancora una volta, **a** chiedere un prestito.	*I find myself forced to ...*
È indispensabile segnalare *or* **È indispensabile che** segnaliate l'incidente entro 24 ore.	*it is essential to ...*
Per ottenere questo documento **ci si deve** rivolgere al Consolato.	*in order to ... you have to ...*
Mi è stato dato l'incarico di organizzare il corso.	*I have been given the task of ...*

37.2 Enquiring if one is obliged to do something

È indispensabile *or* **Dobbiamo** *or* **Si deve avere l'invito?**	*is it necessary to ...*
Devo proprio andarci oggi?	*do I really have to ...*

37.3 Saying what someone is not obliged to do

Non c'è bisogno di prenotare così in anticipo.	*there is no need to ...*
Nessuno vi obbliga *or* **Non siete obbligati a** mangiare in mensa.	*you don't have to ...*
Non voglio mica costringervi a dirmi di che si tratta!	*I have no desire to force you to ...*
Non è obbligatorio essere muniti di un documento di identità.	*it is not necessary to ...*
Non è necessario *or* **indispensabile** confermare la prenotazione.	*it is not necessary to ...*
Non vale la pena tradurre tutto il capitolo.	*it isn't worth ...*
È inutile chiedergli un parere.	*there is no point in ...*
Non siete tenuti a dirgli di che si tratta.	*you don't have to ...*

37.4 Saying what someone must not do

Non si può sostenere l'esame più di tre volte.	*one is not allowed to ...*
È vietato parcheggiare davanti alla Questura.	*it is forbidden to ...*
Non bisogna impedire ai bambini di farsi degli amici.	*one must not ...*
Non puoi assentarti per più di due mesi.	*you cannot ...*
Non si può richiedere la carta d'identità **se non si** risiede nel Comune.	*you cannot ... unless you ...*
Non ti permetto di usare questo linguaggio con me.	*I will not allow you to ...*
Non possiamo tollerare un tale comportamento in classe.	*we cannot allow ...*
Mi raccomando, non parlargliene.	*whatever you do, don't ...*
Ti proibisco *or* **Non ti permetto di** andarci da solo.	*I forbid you to ...*
È vietato usare il flash.	*It is forbidden to use ...*
È vietato fumare in sala.	*smoking is forbidden ...*

38 Agreement

38.1 Agreeing with a statement

Siamo dello stesso avviso su questo punto./ **Condividiamo la vostra posizione su** questo punto. — *we agree with you on ...*

Sono pienamente d'accordo con te. — *I entirely agree with ...*

Come te, sono dell'avviso che si dovrebbe insistere. — *like you, I believe that ...*

Hai perfettamente ragione a voler chiarire la faccenda. — *you are quite right to ...*

Come hai fatto notare, **è vero che** non sono state vagliate tutte le possibilità. — *... it is true that ...*

Devo ammettere che non è uno stupido. — *I admit that ...*

Sono d'accordo con te **che** la situazione è molto delicata. — *I agree ... that ...*

Capisco *or* **Comprendo fin troppo bene** le sue incertezze. — *I fully understand ...*

Senza dubbio hai ragione quando dici che è più facile, ma ... — *you are probably right when you say ...*

38.2 Agreeing to a proposal

Sono d'accordo sul fatto che dovreste cercare di parlargli. — *I agree that you should ...*

Siamo d'accordo a modificare il regolamento. — *we agree to ...*

Sono d'accordo con quello che voi avete proposto. — *I agree with what ...*

A grandi linee accetto le vostre proposte. — *I am broadly in agreement with ...*

Siamo d'accordo a concedervi una dilazione. — *we agree to ...*

Penso che tu abbia ragione ad indicare il mese di settembre come il più adatto. — *I think you are right to ...*

Ho saputo che ti sei ritirato e **non posso che darti ragione.** — *... I can only feel you did right*

D'accordo, ne discuteremo di persona. — *all right ...*

▶ *More informally*

Che ne dici di andare a prendere un aperitivo? **Buona idea!** — *... sounds good to me!*

È una magnifica idea! — *It's a great idea!*

Due settimane in montagna? **Mi sembra una buona idea.** — *... I'd go for that*

▶ *More formally*

Il progetto **incontra la nostra più completa approvazione.** — *... meets with our entire approval*

Farò del mio meglio per adeguarmi alle esigenze del resto del team. — *I'll do my best to ...*

Sono lieto di darle tutto il mio sostegno in questa impresa. — *I am happy to give you my full support ...*

Non mancherò di appoggiare la vostra proposta. — *I shall certainly support ...*

Accettiamo la vostra proposta. — *we accept ...*

38.3 Agreeing to a request

Come richiesto, lascerò libero l'appartamento il 31 maggio. — *as you asked me to ...*

Vi assicuro che **seguirò le vostre istruzioni alla lettera**. — *... I shall follow your instructions to the letter*

Non mancherò di seguire i vostri consigli nella preparazione del programma. — *I shall certainly follow your advice about ...*

Abbiamo preso nota dei vostri suggerimenti. — *we have noted ...*

Mi va benissimo incontrarci alle 5. — *it suits me perfectly ...*

Sarò felicissimo di mettermi a vostra completa disposizione. — *I shall be delighted to ...*

39 Disagreement

39.1 Disagreeing with what someone has said

È sbagliato dire che non si è impegnato a fondo. — *it is wrong to say ...*

Non è vero che mi hai visto al ristorante, non ci sono mai stato. — *it isn't true that ...*

Non sono d'accordo con te. — *I don't agree with you*

Sbagli se credi che sia stata io. — *you are wrong ...*

La differenza è minima, **ma si è pur sempre trattato di un errore.** — *... but there has still been a mistake*

Hai torto *or* **Sbagli a** credere che l'abbia fatto apposta. — *you are wrong to ...*

English – Italian

Penso che tu abbia fatto male a dirglielo. — *I think you were wrong to ...*
Non condivido il vostro punto di vista. — *I don't share your opinion*
Mi è impossibile accettare il vostro punto di vista. — *I cannot accept ...*
Nego categoricamente di aver fatto pressione su di lui. — *I categorically deny ...*
Non capisco come possiate andare in vacanza date le circostanze. — *I can't understand how ...*
Non voglio offenderti, ma **io la vedo in modo totalmente diverso.** — *I see things quite differently*
Mi dispiace contraddirti *or* **doverti contraddire, ma** l'ho visto coi miei occhi. — *I am sorry to have to contradict you, but ...*

39.2 Disagreeing with what someone proposes

In questa fase è **impossibile apportare dei cambiamenti.** — *it's impossible to ...*
Non sono d'accordo che si debba annullare la riunione. — *I don't agree we should ...*
Ci opponiamo con fermezza all'apertura di un altro supermercato. — *we are totally opposed to ...*
Mi rifiuto di andarci. — *I refuse to ...*
Se sta pensando di dare le dimissioni sappia che **porrò il veto.** — *... I shall veto it*
Temo di non poter accettare la vostra proposta. — *I'm afraid I can't accept ...*
È stato molto gentile da parte vostra offrire di aiutarmi, ma **credo di potercela fare** da sola. — *... I think I can manage ...*
Siamo molto dispiaciuti di non poter accettare la vostra gentile offerta. — *we are very sorry we cannot accept your kind offer*

39.3 Refusing a request

Mi è veramente impossibile *or* **Non posso proprio farlo** prima di martedì. — *I cannot possibly do it ...*
Sfortunatamente non posso fissare un appuntamento per lunedì. — *unfortunately I cannot ...*
Mi è difficile al momento svolgere questo lavoro. — *it is difficult for me to ...*
Ci dispiace non poter mandare avanti il progetto. — *we are sorry we cannot go ahead with ...*
Siamo spiacenti di informarvi che non potremo applicare i soliti termini di consegna. — *we regret to have to inform you that we cannot ...*

► ***More assertively***

È fuori questione che debba essere io ad occuparmene. — *it is out of the question for me to ...*
Mi rifiuto assolutamente di lavorare in queste condizioni. — *I totally refuse to ...*
Non accetterò mai di lavorare con lui. — *I will never agree to ...*

---

40 Approval

Sono totalmente d'accordo con te. — *I couldn't agree with you more*
Non avrei potuto esprimermi meglio. — *I couldn't have put it better myself*
Dobbiamo opporci al terrorismo! **Bravo!** — *... hear, hear!*
Condivido pienamente la sua posizione. — *I fully endorse ...*
Questa è un'idea eccellente! — *what an excellent idea!*
Siamo favorevoli a introdurre dei cambiamenti. — *we are in favour of ...*
Hai fatto bene ad andarci subito. — *you did right to ...*
Penso che tu abbia ragione *or* **che tu non abbia torto a** chiedergli una spiegazione. — *I think you are right to ...*
Trovo che faccia bene ad approfondire la sua cultura generale. — *I approve of his ...*
Ho apprezzato moltissimo la vostra gentile offerta. — *I greatly appreciated ...*
Mi è piaciuta moltissimo la coreografia. — *I liked ... very much*

► ***More formally***

L'autore ha voluto **giustamente sottolineare** l'importanza del periodo. — *... rightly emphasizes ...*
Approviamo senza riserve tutte le vostre iniziative. — *we unreservedly approve ...*
Accogliamo l'iniziativa **con grande entusiasmo.** — *we welcome wholeheartedly ...*
Quello che è stato detto finora **ci ha fatto un'impressione molto favorevole.** — *we are very favourably impressed by ...*
L'iniziativa **ha tutto il nostro appoggio.** — *we declare our full support for ...*

English – Italian

41 Disapproval

Do la colpa a te. — *I blame you*

Non avrebbe dovuto iniziare così presto. — *he shouldn't have ...*

Avresti piuttosto dovuto suggerirgli di partire prima. — *you would have done better to ...*

Penso che abbia avuto torto a fare così. — *I think he was wrong to ...*

È un'idea **che disapprovo totalmente.** — *... which I am profoundly unhappy about*

È veramente deplorevole che ci sia stato tanto ritardo. — *it is most unfortunate that ...*

Non posso fare a meno di esprimere il mio disappunto circa la mancanza di servizi. — *I feel compelled to express my disappointment ...*

Non sono disposto a tollerare *or* **Non ammetto** un altro ritardo. — *I cannot tolerate ...*

Non riesco a capire come si sia potuto ignorare il problema. — *I can't understand how ...*

Sono decisamente contrario alla vivisezione. — *I am totally against ...*

Con quale diritto si sono permessi di apportare delle modifiche senza la mia autorizzazione? — *what right did they have to ...*

42 Certainty, probability, possibility and capability

42.1 Expressing certainty

Sono certo che non è in casa. — *I'm sure ...*

È ovvio che la pubblicità condiziona le nostre scelte. — *it is obvious that ...*

Salta agli occhi che non è gente del posto ... si capisce dai vestiti. — *it's patently obvious that ...*

Sono sicura che questa è la sua data di nascita. — *I'm sure that ...*

Siamo convinti che rubino le macchine per venderle. — *we are convinced that ...*

È chiaro che questo sarà il principale argomento di conversazione. — *it is clear that ...*

È naturale che ci sia sempre qualcuno pronto a crederci. — *of course ...*

La data di inizio **sarà quasi certamente** la prima domenica di marzo. — *...will almost certainly be ...*

Si sa per certo che i sequestratori erano non più di tre. — *we know for certain that ...*

Senza (alcun) dubbio questa vittoria è un grande stimolo per la squadra. — *without a doubt ...*

Non c'è il minimo dubbio che le condizioni di vita erano disumane. — *there can't be the slightest doubt that ...*

È innegabile che certe melodie evochino suggestioni particolari. — *it is undeniable that ...*

42.2 Expressing probability

Qui in questo quartiere **è facile che** ti aggrediscano. — *... you are quite likely to be ...*

Vedrai che tutto si risolverà nel migliore dei modi. — *you'll see how ...*

Probabilmente ha subito qualche ritardo lungo il percorso. — *... probably ...*

Deve essersi dimenticato della sua promessa. — *he must have ...*

La cosa più probabile è che non fosse questa la sua vera intenzione. — *... probably ...*

(Molto) probabilmente si tratta di un falso allarme. — *... (very) probably ...*

Sembra che la banca abbia l'intenzione di alzare il tasso di interesse. — *it seems that ...*

Non ci sarebbe da meravigliarsi se alla fin fine fossero gli animali a correre maggiori rischi — *it wouldn't be surprising if ...*

Non mi sorprenderebbe se fosse il corridore francese a vincere la tappa. — *I shouldn't be surprised if ...*

Secondo l'ufficio meteorologico, **ci sono molte probabilità che** si verifichino nuove eruzioni. — *it is very likely that ...*

Ha ancore molte *or* **buone probabilità di** vincere la corsa. — *he still has a good chance of ...*

Tutto fa supporre *or* **sembra indicare che** i divorzi continueranno ad aumentare. — *all the indications are that ...*

42.3 Expressing possibility

Può darsi che decida di rinviare tutto. — *I may ...*

Chissà che non si debba rientrare prima del previsto. — *perhaps ...*

Forse i nostri sospetti sono infondati. — *perhaps ...*

English – Italian

Esiste sempre la possibilità che i prezzi aumentino.	*there's always the possibility that ...*
C' è la possibilità che gli alluvionati abbiano bevuto acqua inquinata.	*it is possible that ...*
È possibile pensare che l'errore sia stato fatto di proposito.	*it is possible that ...*

42.4 Expressing capability

Sai scrivere a macchina?	*can you ...*
Sai usare il nuovo programma?	*do you know how to ...*
Parlo il francese **e capisco** lo spagnolo.	*I can speak ... I can understand ...*
Posso investire fino a trentamila euro in questo progetto.	*I can ...*
Si richiedono **conoscenze di base di** meccanica.	*... a basic knowledge of ...*
Il ragazzo **ha attitudine per** la fisica e la matematica.	*... has an aptitude for ...*
L'essere umano **ha la capacità di** raziocinio.	*... has the capacity for ...*

43 Doubt, improbability, impossibility and incapability

43.1 Expressing doubt

Non so se sia il caso di discutere di questo argomento proprio ora.	*I don't know whether ...*
Non sono sicuro di quali siano le sue condizioni.	*I'm not sure what ... are*
Non è chiaro chi uscirà più danneggiato da questa situazione.	*it isn't clear who ...*
Non sono certo che lo sciopero serva a qualcosa.	*I'm not sure that ...*
Mi chiedo se valga davvero la pena lavorare fuori casa.	*I wonder whether ...*
Non sono (pienamente) convinto che la sua proposta sia valida.	*I'm not (entirely) convinced that ...*
Dubito che ci sarà un'altra offerta simile a questa.	*I doubt whether ...*
Rimangono ancora dei dubbi sulle circostanze del furto.	*doubts still remain about ...*
Vedremo poi se convenga o meno.	*we shall see in due course whether ...*
Non si sa con certezza se sia una malattia ereditaria.	*no one knows for certain whether ...*

43.2 Expressing improbability

È difficile che l'atleta partecipi al campionato il prossimo anno.	*... is unlikely to ...*
Dubito molto che il cambiamento possa apportare un miglioramento.	*I very much doubt whether ...*
Non pare che farà bel tempo.	*it doesn't look as if ...*
Mi meraviglierebbe *or* **sorprenderebbe (molto)** se la frutta conservasse intatta la sua qualità.	*I should be (very) surprised if ...*
È (molto) poco probabile che l'aumento delle multe si traduca in una diminuzione delle infrazioni.	*... is (very) unlikely to ...*
È (molto/abbastanza) improbabile che si verifichi un incidente.	*... is (very/pretty) unlikely to ...*
Chi perde il posto di lavoro **ha sempre meno probabilità di** trovarne un altro.	*... has less and less chance of ...*

43.3 Expressing impossibility

No, non ero a Parigi. **Magari!**	*chance would be a fine thing!*
A quest'ora **non può essere** il postino.	*...it can't be ...*
Non è possibile che si tratti della stessa persona.	*it can't be ...*
È assolutamente impossibile che l'albero cresca n queste condizioni.	*... can't possibly ...*
Mi è (materialmente) impossibile salutare tutti di persona.	*it would be (physically) impossible for me to ...*
La strada del negoziato **ha scarse possibilità di** successo.	*has very little chance of ...*
Non c'è la minima possibilità che i sindacati giungano a un accordo con il governo.	*there isn't the slightest chance of ...*
Mi è impossibile telefonarle questa mattina.	*I can't ...*

43.4 Expressing incapability

Non vedo niente da qui.	*I can't see anything ...*
Non so come spiegare quello che ho visto.	*I can't explain ...*
Si riusciva a stento a respirare, tanta era la folla.	*one could hardly ...*

Certi studenti **non si sentono in grado di** competere con i coetanei.	*... feel incapable of ...*
Questo ragazzo **non è adatto a** questo lavoro.	*... is no good at ...*
Manca delle attitudini necessarie per una missione di questa portata.	*he hasn't the necessary aptitude for ...*
Molto spesso la polizia **si trova impossibilitata ad** agire.	*... find themselves unable to ...*

44 Explanations

44.1 Emphasizing the reason for something

Affrettammo il passo **perché si** era messo a piovere.	*... because ...*
Siccome tardavi ad arrivare, abbiamo deciso di andarcene.	*as ...*
Le piante sono marcite **per** la pioggia eccessiva.	*... due to ...*
Possiede 10.000 azioni **grazie ai** risparmi di tutta una vita.	*... thanks to ...*
Con tutta la neve che ha fatto non arriva la posta.	*what with ...*
È che siamo abituati a mangiare a quest'ora.	*it's just that ...*
Ha avuto molta sfortuna. **Per questo** mi fa tanta pena.	*that's why ...*
Il fenomeno **ha a che fare con** le nuove forme di convivenza civile.	*... has a great deal to do with ...*
Non voleva fiori **per paura che** le scatenassero un attacco allergico.	*... for fear that ...*
Non è la religione **la causa di** questa guerra.	*... is not the cause of ...*
Visto che l'incendio aveva prodotto una densa nuvola di fumo, si è deciso di far evacuare la zona.	*seeing that ...*

► ***More formally***

Il problema è grave, **dato che** il consumo supera la produzione.	*... given that ...*
L'evacuazione dell'edificio si è rivelata difficoltosa **a causa del**l'impraticabilità di una delle uscite d'emergenza	*... because of ...*
Per ragioni di sicurezza parcheggiamo la macchina lontano da casa.	*for safety reasons ...*
A seguito della crisi economica, le vendite si sono ridotte in modo considerevole.	*as a result of ...*
Date le avverse condizioni meteorologiche, ci vediamo costretti a rinviare la cerimonia.	*owing to ...*
I problemi di degrado dell'area **sono dovuti a** una cattiva gestione da parte del comune.	*... are due to ...*
La scarsità di piogge **ha provocato** una grave siccità al sud.	*... has caused ...*
In base a questa teoria, l'evoluzione **è il risultato di** un'interazione tra le mutazioni e la selezione.	*... is a result of ...*
La diminuzione della competitività **deriva principalmente dagli** elevati costi di produzione.	*... is mainly due to ...*
La forza di questa poesia **sta nel**la sua straordinaria musicalità.	*... lies in ...*
L'esplosione, **provocata da** una bomba, ha causato un alto numero di feriti.	*... which was caused by ...*
Personalmente, **l'attribuisco ad** un errore del guidatore.	*... I attribute it to ...*

44.2 Emphasizing the result of something

Non volevo uscire a stomaco vuoto, **così** mi sono fatto un panino.	*... so ...*
Mi piace **tanto** il lavoro che faccio **che** non ho voglia di cambiare.	*... so much that ...*
Sono usciti di buon'ora, **cosicché** quando lui è arrivato ha trovato la casa vuota.	*... so that ...*
Il ricordo della guerra lo segnò **a tal punto che** non si fidò più di nessuno.	*... in such a way that ...*
Non producono anticorpi **e pertanto** non possono immunizzarsi contro virus e parassiti.	*... and therefore ...*

English – Italian

45 Apologies

45.1 Apologizing

Scusa se non ti ho chiamato ieri. *I'm sorry I ...*
Mi scuso di non averle potuto telefonare la settimana scorsa. *I am sorry I ...*
Vi prego di scusarmi di non essermi messo in contatto prima. *please accept my apologies for ...*
La prego di scusarmi per non averglielo chiesto prima. *do forgive me for ...*
Imperdonabile da parte mia! *it's unforgivable of me!*
Mi dispiace moltissimo, ma non posso venire venerdì prossimo. *I am very sorry but ...*
Sfortunatamente mi è impossibile accettare l'invito. *unfortunately I cannot ...*
È colpa mia: mi sono completamente dimenticata di spedirgliela. *it is my fault ...*

► *More formally*

Non posso far altro che rinnovarle le mie scuse. *I can only say once again how sorry I am*
Ci teniamo a porgerle le nostre scuse per quanto è avvenuto. *we must apologize for ...*
Vi prego di scusare il ritardo con cui vi rispondo. *I must ask you to forgive ...*
Siamo desolati di non poter pubblicare il suo articolo. *we are very sorry not to ...*
Siamo profondamente dispiaciuti degli inconvenienti causati. *we greatly regret ...*
Siamo veramente rammaricati per questo increscioso malinteso. *we are very sorry about ...*
Mi dispiace informarla che purtroppo la sua domanda è stata respinta. *I must regretfully inform you that ...*
Mi rincresce di non poter presenziare al seminario. *I regret that I cannot ...*

45.2 Admitting responsibility

Riconosco di aver sbagliato a dargli il tuo numero di telefono. *I realize I was wrong ...*
Non è arrivato **per un errore da parte nostra.** *... because of a mistake on our part*
Sono io il responsabile di questo malinteso. *I am to blame for ...*
Ammetto *or* **Riconosco di** essere stato tentato molte volte di dirglielo. *I admit that I ...*
Mi assumo la responsabilità di quanto avvenuto. *I accept full responsibility for ...*

45.3 Expressing regret

Solo ora mi rendo conto che **non avrei mai dovuto dirglielo.** *I should never have ...*
Se solo non mi avesse vista! *if only ...*
Sono sicuro che comprenderete i motivi della mia scelta. *I am sure you will understand ...*
Purtroppo me ne sono completamente dimenticato. *unfortunately ...*
Non avevo intenzione di andarmene, ma ho dovuto farlo. *I didn't mean to ...*
So bene che non è la soluzione migliore, ma **ho dovuto** prendere una decisione lì per lì. *I had to ...*
Ho creduto di far bene ad avvertirlo, ma non è servito a niente. *I thought I was doing the right thing ...*
Non ho potuto far altrimenti *or* **nient'altro.** *I couldn't do anything else*

45.4 Disclaiming responsibility

Ti giuro che **non l'ho fatto apposta!** *... I didn't do it on purpose*
Spero che tu mi creda quando ti dico che **ho dovuto accettare.** *... I had no choice but to ...*
Ti assicuro che **io non c'entro** *or* **non ho niente a che fare con la faccenda.** *... is nothing to do with me*

English – Italian

PAOLA ROSSOTTI
VIA SANTO STEFANO 45
ROMA

C.O.G.E.A.T SpA
Ufficio Personale
Via Dante 88
Milano

Roma, 14 ottobre 2005

Con riferimento all'annuncio apparso su "Il Commercio e l'Industria" del 12 ottobre gradirei venisse presa in considerazione la mia candidatura per il posto di segretaria personale del Direttore Amministrativo presso la Vostra società.

Alla presente allego copia del mio Curriculum Vitae dove troverete le informazioni relative ai titoli di studio conseguiti e alla mia precedente esperienza lavorativa.

In attesa di un cortese riscontro da parte Vostra, porgo i miei più distinti saluti.

Paola Rossotti

Paola Rossotti

CURRICULUM VITAE

Nome: Silvana

Cognome: MARCONINI

Luogo e data di nascita: Torino, 3 marzo 1975

Domicilo attuale: via San Francesco 28, Torino

Numero telefonico: 011-75 36 83

Curiculum scolastico: Maturità conseguita nel luglio 1993 presso il liceo classico Gioberti con la votazione finale di 60/60
Dal 1993 al 1997 frequenta la facoltà di Scienze dell'Informazione presso l'Università di Torino e consegue la laurea in data 6 aprile 1998 con la votazione finale di 110 e lode

Corsi postuniversitari: Master in Business Administration (MBA) conseguito presso la London Business School nel 2000

Impiego attuale: Dal 2002 al 2004 lavora presso la società L.O.G.I. a Torino in qualità di EDP manager – coordina un'èquipe di 10 persone; è responsabile di tutto il settore informatico

Motivazione per il cambio di lavoro: Desidera arricchire la propria professionalità con lavori sempre più stimolanti

Precedenti esperienze lavorative

Dal 1998 al 1999: Programmatore presso la società Fornasetti in un'èquipe di 6 persone

Dal 1999 al 2002: Analista programmatore presso la società Inteltel in qualità di responsabile dei DSS

Referenze:

dott. Zanda
Via Cristoforo Colombo 39
Torino
Tel: 011-68 12 04

dott. Cena
Viale Bruno Buozzi 19
Torino
Tel: 011-87 11 93

English – Italian

46.1 Starting your letter

In riferimento all'annuncio apparso oggi su "La Settimana" vi sarei grato se poteste fornirmi maggiori dettagli.	*in reply to your advertisement ...*
Vi sarei estremamente grato se voleste considerare il mio nominativo in relazione all'annuncio apparso ieri su "il Corriere della Sera".	*I wish to apply ...*
È mio vivo desiderio lavorare in Italia e vi sarei estremamente riconoscente se poteste farmi sapere se ci sono possibilità d'impiego.	*I would very much like to work in ...*

46.2 Detailing your experience

Ho tre **anni di esperienza quale** segretaria.	*I have ...years' experience of working as a ...*
Parlo l'inglese correntemente, ho una buona conoscenza del tedesco e qualche conoscenza di svedese.	*as well as speaking fluent English, I have a working knowledge of German and a reading knowledge of Swedish.*
Sebbene non abbia esperienza in questo settore, **ho** tuttavia lavorato a progetti abbastanza simili ...	*although I do not have experience in ..., I have ...*
Attulamente il mio stipendio annuo è di € ...	*my current salary is ...*

46.3 Giving your reasons for applying

Quest'offerta mi interessa moltissimo poiché **sono ansiosa di inserirmi nel** campo dell'editoria.	*... I am keen to work in ...*
È mia intenzione lavorare in Italia **per migliorare la conoscenza** della lingua.	*... to improve my knowledge ...*

46.4 Closing the letter

Sono disponibile a partire dalla fine di aprile.	*I will be available from ...*
Mi tengo a vostra disposizione per un eventuale colloquio.	*I am available for ...*
Non esiti a contattarmi se desidera ulteriori informazioni.	*do not hesitate to contact me ...*

46.5 Accepting and refusing

Vi ringrazio della Vostra del 19 marzo e **sarò lieta di incontrarla per un colloquio** il 12 ottobre alle ore 15.	*... I will be pleased to attend for interview ...*
Dopo attenta considerazione, **sono spiacente di doverle comunicare che non possiamo accettare** la sua offerta.	*...I regret that I am unable to accept ...*
Sarei felice di accettare la sua offerta, tuttavia non mi è possibile iniziare prima del 10 maggio.	*I would be glad to accept your offer, however ...*

46.6 Asking for and giving a reference

Mi è stato richiesto di includere due referenze nella mia domanda e **vi sarei estremamente riconoscente se mi autorizzaste a fare il vostro nominativo.**	*... I would be very grateful if you would permit me to give your name*
La signorina Grazia Conti ha presentato domanda come receptionist presso il nostro hotel e ha fornito il vostro nominativo come referenza. **Vi saremmo perciò estremamente grati se poteste farci pervenire la vostra valutazione sul suo operato.**	*... we would be most grateful if you would give us your assessment of her*
La vostra risposta verrà trattata con la massima riservatezza.	*your reply will be treated in the strictest confidence*
Il signor Conti ha lavorato presso la nostra ditta per 11 anni, durante i quali **si è sempre dimostrato un impiegato modello, completamente affidabile e dotato di un notevole senso di responsabilità.**	*... he has always been a model employee – reliable at all times and extremely responsible*

English – Italian

47 Commercial correspondence

L'Arte Orafa
Gioielli antichi e moderni
Via S. Francesco 18, 10104 Vercelli

Ref/1200/Ma
Oggetto: invio documentazione

La Pulce
Piazza 4 Novembre, 26
Cuneo

26 gennaio 2005

Spett. Ditta,
vi ringraziamo della vostra in data 20 ottobre contenente la richiesta di informazioni sui nostri articoli. Siamo lieti di inviarvi il catalogo completo e il listino prezzi. Cogliamo l'occasione per segnalarvi la nuova serie natalizia al momento oggetto di una vantaggiosa offerta di lancio.

Restiamo a vostra completa disposizione per ulteriori informazioni e vi preghiamo di accettare i nostri più distinti saluti.

Il direttore commerciale

Paolo Morelli

dott. Paolo Morelli
Allegato n. 1:
documentazione completa

Il Lampadario
Via Milano 14, 44031 Pavia

A: Marta Pollini
Fax: 0382-234698

Da: Carlo Marini
Fax: 01-528439

Data: 15 luglio 2005

Oggetto: Ordine art. 235

Numero di pagina inclusa questa: 1

Gentile sig. Marini

La ringrazio della Sua lettera del 21 maggio.

Devo purtroppo confermarLe che l'articolo da Lei richiesto è attualmente esaurito. Mi permetto di inviarLe il nostro nuovo catalogo augurandomi che Lei possa trovare tra i nuovi modelli un articolo di Suo gradimento.

Colgo l'occasione per invitarLa a visitare la mostra dei nuovi articoli che si terrà presso il nostro negozio di via Milano in data 21 giugno 2005.

RingraziandoLa nuovamente per il suo interesse.

Distinti saluti

Marta Pollini

In caso di problemi nella ricezione dal fax, contattare Gianna Bianci al numero 0382-365987

English – Italian

47.1 Enquiries and replies

Vi saremmo grati se poteste inviarci un catalogo dei vostri articoli, inclusivo del listino prezzi, di eventuali offerte di sconto e dei tempi di consegna. — *we would be grateful if you would send us ...*

A seguito della vostra richiesta accludiamo il catalogo dei nostri articoli **e** il listino prezzi, valido fino al 31 marzo. — *in response to your enquiry, we have pleasure in enclosing ... together with ...*

Vi ringraziamo della vostra richiesta di informazioni del 16 giugno e siamo lieti di potervi offrire le seguenti condizioni: ... — *thank you for your enquiry of ...*

Questa offerta è **valida solo se ci farete pervenire una conferma prima del** 31 gennaio prossimo. — *... subject to your firm acceptance by ...*

47.2 Orders and replies

Vogliate inviarci immediatamente i seguenti articoli nelle taglie e quantità sottoelencate ... — *please send us ...*

Questo ordinativo è basato sul vostro listino prezzi del 30 giugno. — *the enclosed order ...*

Vi ringraziamo del vostro ordinativo in data 16 maggio a cui daremo seguito il più presto possibile. — *thank you for your order of ...*

Ci occorreranno circa 3 settimane per dar seguito al vostro ordinativo. — *please allow 3 weeks for ...*

47.3 Deliveries

I nostri tempi di consegna sono di due mesi dalla data di ricevimento dell'ordinativo. — *our delivery time is ...*

Siamo in attesa di vostre istruzioni sulla consegna. — *we await your instructions ...*

La merce vi è stata spedita per ferrovia **il** 4 luglio. — *the goods were despatched ... on ...*

47.4 Complaining

Non abbiamo ancora ricevuto gli articoli di cui al nostro ordine del 26 agosto. — *we have not yet received ...*

Siamo costretti a segnalarvi un errore nel lotto ricevuto in data 3 febbraio. — *we wish to draw your attention to an error ...*

Purtroppo le merci sono state danneggiate durante il trasporto. — *unfortunately ...*

47.5 Payment

Alla presente accludiamo la fattura n. 64321. — *we enclose ...*

Il totale ammonta a ... — *the total amount payable is ...*

Abbiamo provveduto al pagamento con un bonifico presso il vostro conto corrente n. ... — *we have arranged for payment with a credit transfer to your current account no.*

48 General correspondence

48.1 Standard formulae

► *Used when the person is not personally known to you*

OPENING

Egregio Signore,
Gentile Signora,
Gentile Signora/Egregio Signor Paolozzi,

CLOSING

Distinti saluti

► *Used for acquaintances and friends*

Fairly informal: "tu" form could be used

OPENING

Caro Patrizio,
Cara Silvia,
Cari Claudio e Paola,

CLOSING

(Cari) saluti
Cordialmente

English - Italian

Torino, 10 dicembre 2005

Carissimi Carlo e Francesca,

sono secoli non ci si vede e cosi ho pensato di scrivervi per sentire cosa ne pensavate di venire da noi per qualche giorno. Abbiamo un sacco di cose da raccontarci e si potrebbe anche approfittare dell'occasione per fare un po' i turisti. Siccome le vacanze di Natale si stanno avvicinando che ne direste dei giorni fra S. Stefano e Capodanno? Fateci sapere qualcosa al più presto.

Non preoccupatevi per i bambini: naturalmente saranno i benvenuti!

Nella speranza di rivedervi presto, vi inviamo i nostri più affettuosi saluti.

Elena e Piercarlo

CARLA BOINOTTI
Via San Carlo 18
10100 Torino

Torino, 16 agosto 2005

Spett. Ditta,

qualche anno fa ho acqistato presso il vostro negozio un servizio da caffè in porcellana di Limoges, modello "Trianon".

Ho purtroppo rotto due tazzine e poiché vorrei sostituirle gradirei sapere se il modello è ancora in produzione. In caso di risposta affermativa, gradirei ricevere il vostro listino prezzi insieme alle modalità di consegna.

Ringraziandovi in anticipo, invio distinti saluti.

Carla Boinotti

Carla Boinotti

Standard formulae

► ***Used for close friends and family***

OPENING

Caro Franco,
Carissima zia Carla,
Mio caro Giovanni,
Mia cara Ingrid
Carissimi nonni,

CLOSING

Ti abbraccio affettuosamente
Tante belle cose a tutti
Bacioni
Un abbraccio
A presto

English – Italian

Standard formulae

► *Writing to a firm*

Spett....,

► *To a person in an important position*

OPENING

Al Magnifico Rettore dell'Università di Torino,

Al Chiarissimo professore...

Sua eccellenza, onorevole...

CLOSING

Gradisca i sensi della più viva stima

Con rispettosa cordialità

48.2 Starting a letter

► *Writing to someone you know*

Sono stata molto contenta di ricevere tue notizie. — *it was lovely to hear from you*

Non ci sentiamo da così tanto tempo che mi sento proprio in dovere di scrivervi almeno due righe per ... — *it's such a long time since we were in touch that I felt I had to write a few lines just to ...*

► *Writing to an organization*

Vi sarei estremamente riconoscente se poteste controllare ... — *I would be most grateful if you could ...*

Vi prego di inviarmi ... Accludo un assegno dell'ammontare di € .... — *Please send me ...*

Credo di aver dimenticato un impermeabile beige nella stanza del vostro hotel e **vi sarei estremamente grata se poteste controllare** se è stato rinvenuto. — *... would you kindly let me know if ...*

Sono molto interessata ai vostri corsi estivi e **vorrei sapere se** vi sono ancora dei posti per ... — *... I would like to know whether ...*

48.3 Ending a letter

► *To an acquaintance*

Cari saluti anche da Pietro. — *Pietro joins me in sending ...*

I miei più cordiali saluti anche a Marco. — *give my kindest regards to Marco*

Giovanna vi abbraccia. — *Giovanna sends her love*

E mi raccomando, scrivimi se posso esserti d'aiuto. — *don't hesitate to get in touch ...*

► *To a friend*

Caterina mi ha detto di salutarti. — *Caterina asks me to give you her best wishes*

Saluta Sandra da parte mia. — *say hello to Sandra for me*

Scrivimi quando hai un po' di tempo libero. — *do write ...*

E non dimenticarti di **mandarci tue notizie** ogni tanto. — *do let us have your news ...*

Attendo con impazienza la tua risposta. — *hoping to hear from you soon*

► *To a close friend*

Abbraccia Mariella da parte mia e dille che sento la sua mancanza. — *give my love to ...*

Un caro abbraccio a tutte e due da Maria. — *Maria sends her love to you both*

48.4 Travel plans

► *Enquiring about and booking accommodation*

Vi sarei grato se poteste inviarmi il vostro tariffario. — *please send me ...*

Vorrei prenotare una camera con prima colazione. — *I would like to book bed-and-breakfast accommodation with you*

Vorrei prenotare una (camera) matrimoniale *or* **doppia per me e mia moglie e una a due letti per i bambini.** — *I wish to book a double room for my wife and myself and a twin room for our chidren ...*

► *Confirming and cancelling a booking*

Vogliate confermare per cortesia la disponibilità di una camera singola con doccia per una settimana a partire dal 24 giugno. — *please let me know if you have ...*

Vi prego di comunicarmi l'ammontare della caparra necessaria per la prenotazione. — *would you please let me know what deposit you require on this booking*

English – Italian

Vi prego di confermare la mia prenotazione. — *please consider this a firm booking ...*

Purtroppo sono costretto a chiedervi di cambiare la prenotazione dal 25 agosto al 3 settembre. — *I am afraid I must ask you to alter my booking ...*

Per ragioni indipendenti dalla mia volontà **sono costretto ad annullare la prenotazione.** — *I am afraid (that) I have to cancel the booking ...*

Vorrei prenotare una piazzola per un camper e una tenda (due adulti e due bambini) dal 15 giugno al 7 luglio incluso. — *I wish to reserve a site for a camper van and a tent ...*

49 Thanks

Un grazie ad entrambi per il vostro gentile pensiero. — *thank you both for your kind thought*

Scrivo per ringraziarvi di tutto cuore dei magnifici fiori. — *I am writing to thank you most warmly for ...*

Non so come ringraziarvi per il vostro aiuto ... — *I don't know how to thank you for ...*

È stato veramente gentile da parte vostra scriverci. — *it was really very kind of you to ...*

Ringrazialo da parte mia per quello che ha fatto. — *give him my thanks for ...*

Vi ringrazio di avermi fatto pervenire il nuovo indirizzo. — *thank you for letting me have ...*

Grazie per avermi aiutato a correggere la tesi. — *thank you for ...*

► *On behalf of a group*

A nome dell'intero comitato ci tengo **ad esprimere la nostra gratitudine per il sostegno fornitoci.** — *I am writing on behalf of ...to express our gratitude to you for ...*

► *To a group*

Vi prego di trasmettere i miei sentiti ringraziamenti ai vostri colleghi. — *please give my warmest thanks to your colleagues*

Vi prego di accettare i nostri più vivi ringraziamenti per il vostro contributo. — *I would ask you to accept our most sincere thanks for ...*

50 Best wishes

► *For any occasion*

I migliori auguri di ... da ... — *with all good wishes for ... from ...*

Cari auguri di ... — *with love and best wishes for ...*

Vogliate accettare i nostri più cordiali auguri per ... — *please accept our best wishes for ...*

► *Season's Greetings*

Buon Natale e Felice Anno Nuovo da ... — *Merry Christmas and Happy New year from ...*

Auguri di Buone Feste da ... — *Season's greetings from ...*

► *Birthday greetings*

Buon compleanno da ... — *Happy Birthday from ...*

Tanti auguri di buon compleanno. — *best wishes for a happy birthday*

I nostri più sinceri auguri in occasione dei tuoi 18 anni. — *our very best wishes on your 18th birthday*

Cento di questi giorni! — *many happy returns (of the day)*

► *Get well wishes*

I miei più sentiti auguri di pronta guarigione. — *very best wishes for a speedy recovery*

► *Wishing someone success*

Le auguro tutto il successo che giustamente merita nella sua nuova carriera. — *I wish you every success in your new career*

► *Congratulations*

Verbally

Congratulazioni! — *Congratulations!*

Bravo! — *Well done!*

In writing

Mi felicito *or* **Mi congratulo** con lei **per** i brillanti risultati conseguiti. — *congratulations on ...*

Le invio le mie più sentite congratulazioni per la sua promozione. — *allow me to congratulate you on ...*

English – Italian

51 Announcements, invitations and replies

51.1 Announcements

► ***Announcing a birth and responding***

Paolo e Giovanna Carlotti **sono lieti di annunciare la nascita della piccola** Francesca.

... are happy to announce the birth of ...

Dario **annuncia assieme a mamma e papà la nascita del fratellino** Carlo.

... joins Mummy and Daddy in announcing the birth of his little brother ...

Abbiamo ricevuto con immensa gioia l'annuncio della nascita del piccolo Fulvio. Congratulazioni e auguri!

we are delighted to learn of the birth of ...

► ***Announcing an engagement and responding***

Speranza e Fulvio Carretta **annunciano il fidanzamento della loro figlia** *Carolina con Aldo Benotti*.

... are happpy to announce the engagement of ...

Abbiamo appreso con immensa gioia del vostro fidanzamento e vi inviamo i nostri più sinceri auguri.

we were delighted to hear of your engagement and send you our warmest good wishes

► ***Announcing a wedding***

Paolo Rossi e Laura Torasso **annunciano il loro matrimonio che verrà celebrato** il giorno 3 maggio alle ore 11 nella chiesa di San Giovanni. Paolo Rossi, via del Carmelo 18 – Laura Torasso, vicolo Sant'Antonio 1.

... are happy to announce their marriage, which will take place ...

► ***Announcing a death and responding***

È mancato all'affetto dei suoi cari Carlo Bonuzzi. **Ne danno il triste annuncio** la moglie Marisa con le adorate figlie Paola e Luisa. **I funerali si svolgeranno** nella parrocchia di Santa Maria in Santena venerdì 6 dicembre alle ore 10. **La salma verrà tumulata nella tomba di famiglia a Chieri.**

the death is announced of ... he leaves ... ... the funeral will take place ... burial will be in the family tomb ...

Con immenso dolore diamo il triste annuncio che la nostra cara mamma ci ha lasciate il 3 dicembre dopo una breve malattia.

we announce with deep sorrow the death of our beloved mother on 3 December after a short illness

Irene e Cesare Fava **partecipano al vostro profondo dolore e vi porgono le loro più sentite condoglianze.**

... join with you in your grief and offer their most sincere condolences

È con profondo dolore che apprendiamo della morte del vostro caro papà. Ci stringiamo a voi con affetto in quest'ora dolorosa.

we were greatly saddened to learn of the death of your dear father. We send you our warmest love and sympathy in your loss

► ***Announcing a change of address***

Vi prego di voler prender nota che **il nostro nuovo indirizzo a partire dal** 3 novembre **sarà il seguente: ...**

... our new address ... will be ...

51.2 Invitations

► ***Invitation to a wedding and replies***

Paolo e Chiara **riceveranno amici e parenti alle ore 13 presso l'hotel** Rex, via Fortezza 18, Torino - R.S.V.P.

... request the pleasure of your company afterwards at ... (on card inside wedding invitation)

Ci congratuliamo con voi per la felice notizia e saremo lieti di partecipare alla cerimonia.

congratulations on your good news – we have great pleasure in accepting your invitation to the wedding

Ci congratuliamo con voi per la felice notizia ma **purtroppo a causa di improrogabili impegni non potremo partecipare alla cerimonia.**

... to our great regret a previous engagement makes it impossible for us to accept your invitation to the wedding

Sincere felicitazioni.

warmest congratulations

Con i nostri più sinceri auguri.
with our very best wishes

Carissimi auguri di ogni felicità alla cara Francesca in occasione del suo matrimonio.
best wishes for every happiness to dear Francesca on the occasion of her marriage

► *Formal invitations and replies*

L'arch. Elvino Rossi **ha l'onore di invitarLa** il 6 dicembre alle ore 18 **al** cocktail che si terrà in occasione della presentazione del volume "Architettura: nuovi itinerari"
...has pleasure in inviting you to ...

I signori Dossi **saranno onorati di averla quale ospite** mercoledì 18 dicembre alle ore 20.
...request the pleasure of your company on ...

Vi ringrazio del cortese invito a presenziare al lancio della vostra nuova collana al quale **sarò onoratissimo di intervenire/ma purtroppo non potrò intervenire** a causa di impegni precedenti.
thanks ... and accepts with pleasure/but regrets that she cannot accept

► *Informal invitations and replies*

Michela e Giovanni **verranno a cena** da noi venerdì e **saremmo felicissimi se anche voi poteste partecipare.**
... are coming to dinner ... and we would be delighted if you could join us

Che ne diresti di passare la giornata a Santa Margherita?
would you like to spend the day ...

Quando sarete di passaggio a Torino dateci un colpo di telefono: **sarebbe bello ritrovarsi per una cena.**
when you are in ... it would be lovely if we could have dinner together

Abbiamo in programma di trascorre il mese di luglio a Cortina **e saremmo felicissimi di ospitarvi** per qualche giorno.
we plan to spend July ... and would be delighted if you could join us ...

Un grazie per il vostro gentile invito: verrò sicuramente!
thank you for your very kind invitation I'm looking forward very much to being with you

Pensavamo di trascorrere la settimana delle vacanze pasquali a Porretta Terme **e vi telefoneremo per organizzare un incontro.**
we are thinking of spending Easter week ... and we'll give you a ring to arrange a meeting

Ci ha fatto un enorme piacere ricevere il vostro invito a trascorrere qualche giorno da voi e **contiamo di raggiungervi per il fine settimana del** 31 luglio.
we were so pleased to have your invitation ... we hope to come for the weekend of ...

Purtroppo non potrò partecipare martedì prossimo alla vostra serata a causa di precedenti ed inderorogabili impegni.
unfortunately a previous engagement makes it impossible for me to accept your invitation for next Tuesday

Mi piacerebbe moltissimo venire da voi per un fine settimana, ma purtroppo nelle date da voi indicate sono già impegnata.
I'd love to spend a weekend with you but unfortunately I can't manage any of the dates you suggest

Purtroppo non potrò liberarmi prima della fine di dicembre: **che ne direste di spostare ad allora il nostro incontro?**
unfortunately I won't be free until ... shall we put off our meeting until then?

52 Essay writing

52.1 The broad outline of the essay

► *Introductory remarks*

Al giorno d'oggi molti concordano nel sostenere **che** la disoccupazione minaccia la struttura stessa della società; **sta di fatto** che talune misure implicano a loro volta dei cambiamenti fondamentali, **tali da farci domandare se** il rimedio non sia peggiore del male.
it is generally agreed today that ... however ...imply ...this leads us to wonder whether ...

"L'automobile, un lusso indispensabile". Ecco **un'affermazione che sentiamo spesso** a proposito della moderna società dei consumi.
... we often hear this said ...

Ancora una volta si tratta di sapere se valga la pena sacrificarsi.
once more the question arises ...

Non passa una settimana senza che si legga un articolo sul problema della disoccupazione: **a volte** per sottolineare il ruolo dell'imprenditoria privata, **altre** per criticare quello della scuola. — *hardly a week goes by without ... sometimes ... sometimes ...*

Queste posizioni così contradditorie mettono ancora una volta in discussione il ruolo della famiglia. — *this clash of opinions calls once again into question ...*

Un problema ricorrente al giorno d'oggi è quello del risanamento del debito pubblico. — *one recurring problem today is ...*

Non si può negare il fatto che la televisione abbia influenzato profondamente la nostra percezione della vita politica. — *it cannot be denied that ...*

Sarebbe da ingenui credere che i politici agiscano sempre disinteressatamente. — *it would be naïve to believe that ...*

Viviamo in un mondo in cui la pace è costantemente minacciata. — *we live in a world where ...*

Non si può aprire un giornale senza trovare l'ennesimo episodio di violenza. — *it is impossible to open a newspaper without finding some new example of ...*

52.2 Developing the argument

Prendiamo come punto di partenza l'attuale ruolo del governo. — *let us begin with ...*

Sarà utile esaminare il modo in cui l'autore ha definito i suoi personaggi. — *it would be useful to consider ...*

Secondo l'autore la vita di provincia soffoca lo sviluppo culturale del personaggio ed **egli ritorna più volte su questo concetto.** — *the author would have us believe that ... he repeatedly returns to this idea*

Se cerchiamo di analizzare le cause dell'insoddisfazione degli insegnanti, **per prima cosa dobbiamo riconoscere** le loro difficotà oggettive. — *if we set out to analyse ... we must first acknowledge ...*

Un tale atteggiamento merita di essere analizzato più da vicino. — *such an attitude deserves closer examination ...*

L'aspetto più significativo consiste nella totale mancanza di coerenza. — *the most significant feature is ...*

Questa affermazione può sembrare azzardata, ma **solleva nondimeno una questione essenziale**, quella del rapporto fra arte e morale. — *this assertion ... it however raises a fundamental question ...*

52.3 The other side of the argument

Dopo aver analizzato il contenuto, **passiamo ora ad esaminare** lo stile. — *... let us now consider ...*

Poiché la mancanza di vegetazione riguarda un'area limitata, **dobbiamo cercare altri fattori che** possano aver contribuito a creare tale squilibrio. — *... we need to look for other factors which ...*

L'autore ha un bell'insistere sull'importanza della relazione fra l'eroina e il maestro: non riesce tuttavia a essere pienamente convincente. — *despite the author's efforts to stress ...*

È necessario a questo punto affrontare la questione della censura televisiva. — *we must now consider ...*

Passiamo ora ad analizzare i personaggi. — *now we come to ...*

Ed è **questa una ragione sufficiente per** invocare il ritorno della pena di morte? — *is this really a good enough reason for ...*

Passiamo ora ad un altro aspetto del problema, vale a dire ... — *let us now turn our attention to ...*

Avendo stabilito che l'eroe non è spinto dal desiderio di vendetta, **esaminiamo ora più da vicino** la scena in cui si trova in presenza del padre. — *... let us take a closer look at ...*

Sarebbe interessante scoprire se si riscontra lo stesso fenomeno anche in altri paesi. — *it would be interesting to see whether ...*

Ci si può accostare al problema da un'angolatura completamente diversa e considerare la portata politica di queste misure. — *the problem could also be approached from another angle, by ...*

Secondo l'autore la forma è più importante del contenuto, **ma naturalmente si può ugualmente affermare l'esatto contrario.** — *for the author ... but of course one may equally well hold the opposite to be true*

English – Italian

Siamo dunque autorizzati ad affermare che i difensori dei diritti degli animali siano diventati i profeti di una nuova moralità? — *is it then reasonable to claim that ...*

C'è un secondo aspetto che non può essere trascurato ed è il modo in cui i più giovani reagiscono al problema. — *there is a second consideration which cannot be ignored, namely the way ...*

52.4 The balanced view

Dopo un'attenta analisi dobbiamo comunque far notare che è la rapidità dei cambiamenti che potrebbe essere il fattore più importante. — *when everything has been taken into account, it must nonetheless be pointed out that ...*

Si deve comunque riconoscere che un intervento del governo è a questo punto indispensabile. — *it must however be recognized that ...*

Dobbiamo tener conto anche di un terzo fattore. — *we must allow for a third factor*

Infine ci si deve domandare se l'interesse dell'opera non risieda invece nello studio della struttura sociale. — *finally we must ask ourselves if ...*

La posizione dell'autore **è più complessa** di quanto non appaia a prima vista. — *... is more complex ...*

Dovremmo forse spingerci oltre e chiederci se il risvolto psicologico non sia il tema centrale del testo. — *we should perhaps go further and ask whether ...*

► ***In conclusion***

Alla fine di questa complessa analisi che **cosa si può concludere?** — *... what conclusions may be drawn?*

Gli incidenti **a cui abbiamo accennato precedentemente dimostrano chiaramente che** i regolamenti non sono stati rispettati. — *... which have been discussed earlier prove that ...*

Sembrerebbe dunque che nel suo romanzo l'autore non sia interessato al contesto sociale. — *it would seem clear that ...*

Come valutare le attività di questi primi mesi del nuovo governo? — *... how should we assess the performance of ...*

In definitiva il nostro più grande problema è la mancanza di immaginazione. — *all in all ...*

Sembra che l'opinione pubblica sia sempre più cosciente del rischio nucleare. — *it would appear then that ...*

Questi dunque sono i principali mezzi espressivi utilizzati dall'autore. — *these then are ...*

52.5 Constructing a paragraph

► ***Ordering various elements within it***

Si possono citare vari argomenti a questo proposito. — *several arguments could be mentioned ...*

Chi sono i poveri al giorno d'oggi? Be', **da un lato** ci sono quelli che nascono poveri, **dall'altro** quelli che lo diventano. — *on the one hand ... and on the other ...*

I primi hanno analizzato gli aspetti sociali, **i secondi** si sono fatti carico delle implicazioni economiche. — *the first ...the second ...*

Ciò è dovuto essenzialmente a tre fattori: il primo ... — *this is basically due to three factors: first ...*

La scuola è oggetto di critiche continue **così come** l'assistenza sanitaria. — *... as is ...*

Prima di affrontare la questione dello stile, **vorrei soffermarmi brevemente sulla** scelta delle metafore. — *let us look briefly at ...*

Senza entrare troppo nei dettagli, *or* **Senza soffermarmi troppo sui dettagli ci terrei** a sottolineare l'importanza del suo intervento. — *without going into too much detail, we should ...*

Come vedremo in seguito più dettagliatamente, sono soprattutto i personaggi secondari a far progredire l'azione. — *as we shall see in greater detail later ...*

Si riprende qui un'idea già esposta in precedenza. — *here we touch again on an idea dealt with earlier*

Ritorneremo ancora su questo punto, tuttavia vogliamo già qui segnalare la totale assenza di emozioni in questo passaggio. — *we shall return to this later, but ...*

Ma per ritornare all'argomento che più ci sta a cuore *or* **interessa, ...** — *but to return to the topic which interests us most, ...*

► ***Adding elements***

In più c'è da dire che il progetto è straordinariamente ben congegnato. *moreover ...*

Inoltre, vogliamo far notare che gli operai sono stati sottopagati. *we must also remember that ...*

Esamineremo le origini del problema e **anche** alcune possibili soluzioni. *... as well as ...*

Si devono includere anche le persone anziane nella statistica? **Oppure** si devono escludere i giovani? **O ancora** si deve analizzare un campione più ampio? *or ... or finally ...*

Varie categorie sono state completamente ignorate, e in **particolare** le segretarie e le centraliniste. *... in particular ...*

Dal partito comunista **all**'estrema destra, **tutti si sono trovati d'accordo** nel condannare questo ennesimo atto di terrorismo. *from ... to ... all are agreed ...*

Medici, chirurghi, anestesisti, infermieri: **tutti sono** ugualmente indispensabili. *doctors, surgeons ... they are all ...*

A questo si deve aggiungere una notevole attenzione ai dettagli. *added to that, ...*

Per quanto concerne l'inquinamento chimico dobbiamo riconoscere che si tratta di un problema gravissimo. *as far as ... is concerned ...*

E per quanto riguarda le trasmissioni destinate ai giovanissimi, non sempre la qualità viene al primo posto. *as for the ...*

► ***Introducing one's own point of view***

A mio avviso *or* **Secondo me** or questo è il miglior capitolo del libro. *in my view ...*

Per quanto mi riguarda *or* **Da parte mia** non c'è stato alcun ripensamento. *as far as I am concerned ...*

Personalmente, quello che mi ha colpito di più è stata la reazione del giudice. *personally, what I found most striking was ...*

Se mi è permesso di esprimere un'opinione in proposito, mi sembra che l'autore si sia avventurato su un terreno minato. *if I may be permitted to give my opinion ...*

Sono dell'opinione che la televisione abbia un effetto nefasto sulla formazione dei bambini. *I maintain that ...*

L'autore afferma, **a pieno titolo secondo me**, che questi sono atteggiamenti disfattisti. *... and rightly, in my opinion ...*

► ***Introducing someone else's point of view***

Secondo l'autore il principale motivo del crimine è la gelosia. *according to the author ...*

Come viene spesso sottolineato dagli esperti, l'importante è inventare nuove soluzioni. *as the experts often stress ...*

Dice/Afferma/Crede/Dichiara che questo sistema presenterà numerosi problemi in futuro. *he says/thinks/believes/declares that*

L'autore ci ricorda/ci segnala la necessità di apportare dei cambiamenti. *the author draws our attention to/reminds us/points out ...*

Insiste sul fatto che sono state le rivalità intestine a indebolire l'organizzazione. *he emphasizes (the fact) that*

Gli esperti **sostengono che** ... è possibile imparare le lingue senza alcuno sforzo. *... claim that ...*

Secondo la versione ufficiale dei fatti, gli arrestati sarebbero solo qualche decina. *according to the official version of the facts ...*

► ***Introducing an example***

Prendiamo il caso dell'utilizzo delle armi chimiche. *consider the case of ...*

Basta citare ad esempio i documentari a sfondo educativo. *one need only mention ...*

Uno degli esempi più eclatanti si trova nel terzo capitolo. *one of the most striking examples ...*

In questo caso, ad esempio, mille operai rischiano di perdere il posto. *in this case, for example, ...*

► ***Introducing a quotation or source***

Stando agli autori della relazione, "l'importante non è sfamare l'Africa, ma partecipare al suo rimboschimento." *according to ...*

Conclude/Dichiara/Osserva La Fontaine, "Il più forte ha sempre ragione". — *... concludes ...*

Come ha fatto notare il presidente, "la crescita economica dipende dagli Investimenti." — *as the president has pointed out ...*

Il Foscolo **scrive:..** — *... writes: ...*

... riprende l'idea (di) ... — *... takes up the same theme ...*

A dirla con ... — *in the words of ...*

In un articolo pubblicato recentemente in " ..." troviamo la seguente affermazione **a firma di ...** — *in a recent article in ... (written) by ...*

52.6 The mechanics of the argument

► *Stating facts*

È vero che i lavori sono cominciati. — *it is true that ...*

Si constata *or* **Si osserva** un notevole miglioramento. — *... is noticeable*

È *or* **Si tratta di** una questione semplicissima. — *it is a ...*

Il nuovo programma è **stato fatto oggetto di** violentissime critiche. — *... has been the object of ...*

Non dobbiamo perdere di vista i fatti: l'inquinamento del Reno è aumentato e ... — *we must not lose sight of the facts: ...*

Man mano che ci si inoltra nella lettura dell'opera si aprono nuove prospettive. — *as one reads on, new perspectives open up*

L'autore racconta delle numerose superstizioni concernenti piante e animali. — *the author details ...*

► *Making a supposition*

È probabile che la loro reazione possa essere violenta. — *it is probable that ...*

Viene qui citata la possibilità di un nuovo vertice. — *the possibility of ... is mentioned here*

Ci potrebbe essere un'altra spiegazione. — *there could be ...*

Supponiamo che il clima subisca una drastica mutazione ... — *let us suppose that ...*

Il rifiuto **fa pensare** *or* **lascia pensare che** i fondi necessari non siano a rrivati in tempo. — *... leads one to think that ...*

Questo spiegherebbe l'abbassamento delle temperature in febbraio. — *this would explain ...*

Si presuppone che l'autore fosse a conoscenza dei fatti. — *one may assume that ...*

► *Expressing a certainty*

È chiaro *or* **evidente che questa scoperta costituisce un gran passo avanti.** — *it is clear that ...*

Il suo secondo romanzo è **senza dubbio** il migliore. — *... is indisputably or undeniably ...*

Tutto fa credere *or* **pensare che** vincerà lei. — *everything leads one to the conclusion that ...*

Senza dubbio ha del talento. — *there can be no doubt that ...*

Tutti sono d'accordo nel criticare i suoi metodi. — *everyone agrees in criticising ...*

È chiaro che gli avvenimenti hanno preso una brutta piega. — *it is clear that ...*

Come tutti sanno la camomilla è un rimedio sicuro contro l'insonnia. — *as everyone knows ...*

► *Indicating doubt or uncertainty*

Sembra che abbia cercato di contattarli. — *it would seem that ...*

È possibile *or* **Può essere** *or* **Può darsi che** non se ne sia accorto. — *it is possible that ...*

Forse alla gente piacerà di più questo tipo di trasmissione. — *perhaps people will prefer ...*

Sarebbe forse preferibile risparmiare più elettricità. — *it might be preferable to ...*

Potrebbe trattarsi di *or* **essere** un nuovo virus. — *it could be ...*

Questo potrebbe spiegare il ritardo della reazione. — *this could explain ...*

Questo rimette in dubbio la validità delle statistiche. — *this again calls into question ...*

È difficile credere che sia stata presa una tale decisione. — *it is difficult to believe that ...*

► *Conceding a point*

Sebbene i personaggi siano descritti con cura, mancano di autenticità. — *although ...*

Lo stile è interessante **seppure** appesantito da un uso eccessivo di figure retoriche. — *... albeit ...*

English – Italian

Fino ad un certo punto hanno ragione, però ... *they are right up to a point, but ...*

Sono d'accordo con l'autore su molti punti, tuttavia ho ancora qualche riserva. *I agree with the author on many points, but ...*

Ovviamente *or* **Sicuramente** la riduzione della velocità limiterà il numero degli incidenti, **ma** si creeranno altri problemi. *of course ... but ...*

Per quanto grande sia la sua bravura di regista, resta tuttavia il fatto che la storia è decisamente poco plausibile. *no matter how talented he is ...*

Non si può negare che l'introduzione dei robot abbia ridotto i costi. *it cannot be denied that ...*

Senza dubbio la pubblicità aumenta le vendite, ma costa anche parecchio. *... undoubtedly ...*

Pur ammettendo *or* **riconoscendo** che i nuovi quartieri sono serviti ad alloggiare migliaia di senzatetto, **ci si deve render conto che** le condizioni di vita sono spesso intollerabili. *while recognizing ...one must also accept that ...*

Senza dubbio la solitudine è uno dei mali della società moderna, **ma** sono spesso gli individui stessi a crearne le condizioni. *undeniably ...but ...*

► ***Emphasizing particular points***

Per sottolineare la complessità del problema l'autore si addentra nella descrizione dei risvolti sociali. *in order to emphasize ...*

Sarà bene precisare che si tratta di un metodo ancora largamente usato. *we should make it quite clear that ...*

Non dimentichiamoci che le donne vivono nel complesso più a lungo degli uomini. *let us not forget that ...*

È quest'incidente **che** ha iniziato la rivolta. *it was this ...which ...*

Se non se n'è ancora occupata è **per indifferenza e non per mancanza di tempo.** *it is lack of interest rather than lack of time that has prevented her from ...*

Non solo si è opposto alla riduzione del budget, **ma** ha chiesto ulteriori finanziamenti. *not only did he ...but ...*

Questo non significa che il libro sia poco valido, ma **piuttosto** che l'autore è ancora immaturo. *this does not mean that ..., but rather ...*

L'ambizione, **ecco che cosa** lo distingue dagli altri. *... that is what ...*

Lungi dal trasformarci in deficienti, la televisione ci informa e diverte. *far from turning us into ...*

La disoccupazione sta aumentando e **il fenomeno è aggravato dall'**inerzia governativa. *... the problem is made worse by ...*

Ci sono numerose inesattezze, **ma la cosa più grave è che** l'intera cronologia è errata. *... but the worst thing is that ...*

È una legge ingiusta, **oggi più che mai**, con l'evoluzione che c'è stata nella protezione dei diritti del malato. *... now more than ever that ...*

► ***Moderating a statement***

Senza voler criticare i suoi metodi, ho l'impressione che avrebbe potuto scegliere una soluzione più economica. *without wishing to criticize ...*

L'autore ha ragione **nel complesso**, ma .... *... by and large ...*

Sarebbe bene chiarire insieme alcuni punti. *here it might be a good idea to clarify certain points*

Senza voler dare troppa importanza ai dettagli, occorre tuttavia una revisione. *without laying too much emphasis on details ...*

Sarebbe ingiusto rimproverargli la sua inesperienza. *it would be unfair to ...*

Sarebbe di cattivo gusto chiedergli i particolari. *it would be churlish to ...*

► ***Indicating agreement***

Molti lo trovano orribile **e, in effetti,** *or* **effettivamente,** è un pugno in un occhio. *... and indeed ...*

Si deve ammettere che ci sono stati dei miglioramenti. *one must admit that ...*

La spiegazione che ci ha dato è **pienamente convincente** *or* **ci ha pienamente convinti.** *... is wholly convincing*

Non possiamo far altro che inchinarci di fronte alla sua rettitudine. *we can only pay tribute to his integrity*

English - Italian

Come suggerito dall'autore *or* **Come suggerisce l'autore**, si dovrebbero proseguire le ricerche. — *as the author suggests ...*

Effettivamente **tutto sembrerebbe far pensare ad** un incidente. — *everything would seem to point to ...*

È evidente *or* **chiaro che** si tratta di un metodo efficace. — *it is clear that ...*

► ***Indicating disagreement***

È impossibile accettare il suo punto di vista. — *it is impossible to accept ...*

È un suggerimento che non merita neanche di essere preso in esame. — *it is a suggestion which doesn't merit a moment's consideration*

Gli abitanti hanno **protestato contro** la costruzione del ponte. — *... protested against ...*

Questi fatti sono in contraddizione con la versione ufficiale. — *these facts contradict ...*

Sono costretto **ad esprimere qualche riserva/a sollevare delle obiezioni.** — *... to express some reservations/raise some objections*

È una tesi discutibile. — *this is a questionable view*

L'autore commette un grave errore inducendoci a pensare che sia stato raggiunto un accordo. — *the author makes a grave mistake in ...*

Non condivido il punto di vista dell'autore. — *I do not share the author's point of view*

Anche se ha ragione su questo punto, sta di fatto che ... — *even if he is right ...*

► ***Indicating approval***

Non è difficile capire come un simile atteggiamento abbia trovato molti consensi. — *one can well understand how ...*

Effettivamente la soluzione migliore sarebbe restaurarlo. — *the best solution would certainly be to ...*

Basta leggere le prime righe per essere immediatamente trasportati nella Venezia del '700. — *you have only to read the opening lines to be ...*

Hanno avuto ragione ad includere nello studio anche i minorenni. — *they were right to ...*

L'autore **sottolinea a ragione** *or* **giustamente** questo punto. — *... rightly emphasizes ...*

Era ora che qualcuno prendesse le difese degli anziani. — *it was certainly high time that ...*

Finalmente un'opera che tratta dei problemi delle lavoratrici part-time. — *at last, a work which deals with ...*

► ***Indicating disapproval***

È un peccato che l'autore non sia presente. — *it is a pity that ...*

Sarebbe un peccato se un'opera di tale portata non venisse tradotta. — *it would be a pity if ...*

Sfortunatamente è un'opera di limitatissimo interesse. — *unfortunately ...*

Sorprende la rapidità con cui le riforme sono state applicate. — *one may well be surprised at ...*

È difficile immaginare come gli allievi ne possano beneficiare. — *it is difficult to see how ...*

Tutti **hanno criticato** aspramente il progetto di una nuova autostrada. — *... have condemned ...*

Si accusa il governo *or* **Si rimprovera al governo di** non aver agito in tempo. — *there are complaints that the government ...*

► ***Making a correction***

In realtà non è di questo che sto parlando. — *in (actual) fact ...*

Sei molto lontano dalla verità: in realtà ... — *you are very far from the truth: in fact ...*

Ad un'analisi più attenta le sue critiche **non sembrano per niente giustificate.** — *on closer examination ...do not seem to be at all justified*

Sono critiche senza alcun fondamento. — *these criticisms are quite without foundation*

► ***Indicating the reason for something***

È dovuto ad un malinteso. — *this arises from ...*

Questo è il motivo per cui ci è impossibile terminare in tempo. — *it is for this reason that ...*

Non ci si può basare su queste cifre, **visto che** i dati di partenza sono così approssimativi. — *... given that ...*

Se è stato accettato è **certamente perché** hanno fatto delle pressioni. — *... it is undoubtedly because ...*

Questo spiega *or* **spiegherebbe** il calo delle vendite in febbraio. — *this would explain ...*

L'autore **lascia intendere che** il vero motivo sia un altro. — *... suggests that ...*

English – Italian

► *Setting out the consequences of something*

La decisione **ha avuto conseguenze disastrose.** — *... had fatal consequences*

Si può dunque concludere *or* **dedurre che** l'autore non sia completamente d'accordo con un tale concetto di autorità. — *one is led to the conclusion that ...*

Era molto scontento delle condizioni e **questo è il motivo per cui** si è licenziato. — *... this is why ...*

Ed ecco perché la famiglia occupa una posizione centrale nel suo romanzo. — *and that is why ...*

La sospensione del servizio **avrà come conseguenza** un aumento del traffico automobilistico. — *... will result in ...*

I posti verranno ridotti di un terzo, **il che implica** il licenziamento di tre impiegati. — *... which means ...*

Il personaggio principale non appare in questo capitolo, **con il risultato che** le figure secondarie occupano una posizione primaria. — *... and as a consequence ...*

Si è rifiutato di dare una spiegazione, il **che sembra confermare la sua colpevolezza.** — *... which seems to confirm his guilt*

► *Contrasting or comparing*

Alcuni dicono che la produzione di energia è essenziale per lo sviluppo, **altri sostengono** il contrario. — *some say ... others declare ...*

Mentre alcuni sono certi del declino dei servizi sociali, **altri,** al contrario, sbandierano i risultati positivi recentemente conseguiti. — *while some people ... others ...*

È molto meglio del suo rivale. — *he is far better than ...*

Questa, **in confronto al** suo primo romanzo, è un'opera molto più raffinata. — *... compared with ...*

Fra questi due libri **non c'è confronto.** — *... there is no comparison*

53 The telephone

53.1 Getting a number

Vorrei il 46 57 86, per favore. (quarantasei cinquantasette ottantasei or quattro sei cinque sette otto sei) — *could you get me ..., please*

Deve cercare il numero sull'elenco telefonico. — *you'll have to look up the number in the phone book*

Può avere il numero tramite il servizio informazioni internazionali. — *you should get the number from International Directory Enquiries*

Mi può passare il servizio informazioni, per favore? — *could you put me through to ...*

Vorrei il numero della ditta Decapex, via Manzoni 20, Vercelli. — *can you give me the number of ...*

Il numero non è sull'elenco. — *the number is not in the book*

Qual è il prefisso di Livorno? — *what is the code for ...*

Posso telefonare in Colombia **direttamente** *or* **senza passare per il centralino?** — *can I dial direct to ...*

Se chiama l'Inghilterra **dall'Italia deve omettere lo "0" iniziale.** — *you leave off the "0" when dialling ... from ...*

Cosa devo fare per ottenere la linea esterna? — *how do I make an outside call?*

53.2 Different types of calls

È una telefonata *or* **chiamata urbana.** — *it's a local call*

È una telefonata *or* **chiamata interurbana da Foggia.** — *it's a long distance call from ...*

Vorrei fare una telefonata a carico del destinatario. — *I want to make a reverse charges call to ...*

Vorrei telefonare pagando con la carta di credito. — *I'd like to pay for the call by credit card*

English – Italian

Qual è il numero per avere l'ora esatta? — *what do I dial to get the speaking clock?*

Vorrei la sveglia telefonica alle 7.30 domani mattina. — *I'd like an alarm call for …*

53.3 The operator speaks

Che numero desidera? — *which number, please?*

Da dove chiama? — *where are you calling from?*

Mi ripete il numero, per favore? — *would you repeat the number, please?*

Può chiamare questo numero direttamente. — *you can dial the number direct*

Riagganci il ricevitore e componga di nuovo il numero. — *replace the receiver and dial again*

C'è una telefonata a suo carico dal signor Baresi **da** Amsterdam. **Accetta la chiamata?** — *there's a Mr …. from … who wishes you to pay for the call. Will you accept it?*

Prego, **è in linea.** — *…you are connected*

(Servizio Informazioni) **Non c'è nessun abbonato con questo nome.** — *there's no listing under that name*

Il 45 77 57 84 **non risponde.** — *there's no reply from …*

Provo a ridarle la linea. — *I'll try to reconnect you*

Attenda in linea, prego. — *hold the line, caller.*

Al momento tutte le linee per la Francia sono occupate. Riprovi più tardi. — *all lines to … are engaged. Please try later*

È un telefono a scheda. — *it's a card phone*

Sto cercando di darle la linea. — *I'm trying it for you now*

La linea è occupata. — *the line is engaged (Brit)/ the line is busy (Am)*

53.4 When your number answers

Mi può passare l'interno 516, per favore? — *could I have extension …*

Parla il signor Lamberti? — *is this …?*

Vorrei parlare con il signor Matta, **per favore.** /**C'è** il signor Matta, **per favore?** — *could I speak to …, please?*

Mi può passare il dottor Asselle, per cortesia? — *could you put me through to …*

Chi parla? — *who's speaking?*

Richiamerò più tardi. — *I'll try again later*

Potrei lasciare il numero per farmi richiamare? — *could I leave my number for her to call me back?*

Sto telefonando *or* **chiamando da una cabina (telefonica).** — *I'm ringing from a callbox (Brit)/ … from a pay station (Am)*

Sto telefonando *or* **chiamando dall'Inghilterra.** — *I'm phoning from …*

Potrebbe chiedergli di chiamarmi quando rientra? — *would you ask him to ring me when he gets back?*

53.5 The switchboard operator speaks

Pronto, Hotel Rex, **desidera?** — *… can I help you?*

Chi parla, per cortesia? — *who is calling, please?*

Può dirmi il suo nome? — *who shall I say is calling?*

Sa il numero dell'interno? — *do you know his extension number?*

Glielo passo. — *I'm connecting you now*

Le passo la signora Marelli. — *I'm putting you through to …*

C'è la signorina Martini **in linea.** — *I've got … on the line*

Il dottor Cassini **è sull'altra linea.** — *…is on the other line*

Rimanga in linea, per favore. — *could you hold the line, please?*

Non risponde nessuno. — *there's no reply*

English – Italian

53.6 Answering the telephone

Pronto, sono Anna.	*hello, this is ... (speaking)*
(Anna?) **Sì, sono io.**	*...speaking*
Vuole lasciare un messaggio?	*would you like to leave a message?*
Resti in linea.	*hold the line, please*
Metta giù e la richiamo io.	*hang up and I'll call you back*
Questo è un messaggio registrato.	*this is a recorded message*
Lasciate un messaggio dopo il segnale acustico.	*please leave a message after the tone (Brit)/beep (Am)*

53.7 In case of difficulty

Non riesco a prendere la linea.	*I can't get through*
Non mi dà nessun segnale.	*the number is not ringing*
Mi dà il messaggio "il numero selezionato è inesistente".	*I'm getting "number unobtainable"*
Il loro apparecchio è fuori servizio.	*their phone is out of order*
È caduta la linea.	*we were cut off*
Devo aver sbagliato numero.	*I must have dialled the wrong number*
C'è un'interferenza sulla linea.	*we've got a crossed line*
Li ho chiamati diverse volte ma non ho avuto risposta.	*I've called them several times with no reply*
Mi ha dato un numero sbagliato.	*I got the wrong number*
La linea è molto disturbata.	*this is a very bad line*

53.8 Recorded messages

Informazione gratuita. **Il numero selezionato è inesistente.**	*the number you have dialled has not been recognized*
La preghiamo di consultare l'elenco abbonati.	*Please look up the new number in the phone book*
L'utente da lei chiamato ha cambiato numero. Attenda in linea senza riagganciare poiché stiamo inoltrando automaticamente la sua chiamata al nuovo numero 45 63 02.	*this number has now been changed. Please hold the line while we try to connect you to the new number...*

53.9 Mobile phones

Il cliente da lei chiamato non è al momento raggiungibile. La preghiamo di richiamare più tardi.	*the person you are calling is not available. Please try later.*
L'utente da lei chiamato potrebbe avere il cellulare spento.	*the phone you are calling may be switched off.*
Il suo credito residuo è di ...	*your airtime balance is ...*
Qui non c'è campo.	*there is no reception*
Ho la batteria del cellulare scarica.	*my battery needs recharging*

53.10 Texting

	ITALIANO	ENGLISH
+o-	più o meno	more or less
1	uno/a	un/uno/una
1000TA	mille volte ti amo	I love you to bits
3no	treno	train
6	sei	you are
Al7Cie	al settimo cielo	in seventh heaven
Am	amore	love
AmXSe	amore per sempre	love for ever
B8	botto	blow
Ba	bacio	kiss
Ba&Ab	baci e abbracci	hugs and kisses
BaA	baci appassionati	passionate kisses
BACI8	baciotto	little kiss
bn	bene	well
C6?	ci sei?	are you there?
cm	come	how
cmq	comunque	anyway
cn	con	with
cpt	capito	I see
Cre	cretino/a	idiot
cs?	cosa?	what
cs	cosa	thing
c ved	ci vediamo	see you soon
D6?	dove sei?	where are you?
disp	dispiace	sorry
Dom	domani, domanda	tomorrow, question
dv	dove	where
ETAT	e ti amo tanto	and I love you so much
ILY	I love you	I love you
int	interessante	interesting
K6?	chi sei?	who are you?
ke	che	that
ke cs...?	che cosa...?	what?
KiCa6	chi cavolo sei?	who the hell are you?
m	me	me
MiDi	mi dispiace	(I'm) sorry
msg	messaggio	message
nn	non	no
NN	nessuno	no one
NP	no problem	no problem
Og	oggi	today
PS	post-scriptum	PS
QCN	qualcuno	someone
QCS	qualcosa	something
qnd	quando	when

	ITALIANO	ENGLISH
r8	rotto/a	broken
RiS	rispondi subito	text me back quickly
risp	rispondi	text me back
RiSS	rispondimi subitissimo	text me back at once
S8	sotto	under(neath)
SC8DT	sono cotto/a di te	I'm crazy about you
sn	sono	I am
SRE	essere	to be
SS$	sono senza soldi	I haven't got any money
t	tu	you
TAT	ti amo tanto	I love you loads
TATXS	ti amerò per sempre	I'll love you for ever
TNT	tanto	a lot, loads
Tod	ti odio	I hate you
tps	ti penso sempre	I think about you all the time
TT	tutto, tutta, tutti, tutte	all, every
TVB	ti voglio bene	I love you
TVTB	ti voglio tanto bene	I love you loads
WE	week-end	weekend
X'	perché	why/because
XF	per favore	please
xké	perché	why/because
XM	per me	for me
xò	però	but

English – Italian

54 Email

Sending a message

NUOVO MESSAGGIO

File **Modifica** **Visualizza** **Strumenti** **Messaggio** **Help** **Invia**

Nuovo
Rispondi al mittente
Rispondi a tutti
Inoltra
Inoltra come allegato

A: g.mari@videx.it
Cc: s.boni.@videx.it
Ccn:
Oggetto: Riunione

Sarebbe il caso di incontrarci per discutere della questione della ristrutturazione dell'ufficio e dell'assunzione di una nuova impresa di pulizie.

Penso che potrebbe andar bene lunedì prossimo. Pensateci e datemi una risposta.

Un saluto.

Pietro

File	*File*
Modifica	*Edit*
Visualizza	*View*
Strumenti	*Tools*
Messaggio	*Compose*
Help	*Help*
Invia	*Send*
Nuovo	*New*
Rispondi al mittente	*Reply to sender*

Receiving a message

RIUNIONE

File **Modifica** **Visualizza** **Strumenti** **Rispondi** **Help**

Da: Gloria Mari (g.mari@videx.it)
Data: 26/9/2005
A: p.sierra@videx.it
Cc: s.boni.@videx.it
Oggetto: Re: Riunione

In Italian, when telling someone your email address, you say: **"g punto mari chiocciola videx punto it"**

A me sembra che lunedì possa andare. Propongo di incontrarci la mattina sul presto; per esempio alle nove nella sala riunioni. Aspetto una risposta.

Un saluto.

Gloria

Inoltra	*Forward*
Inoltra come allegato	*Attachment*
A	*To*
Cc	*CC*
Ccn	*BCC*
Oggetto	*Subject*
Da	*From*
Data	*Date*
Ricevuto	*Received*

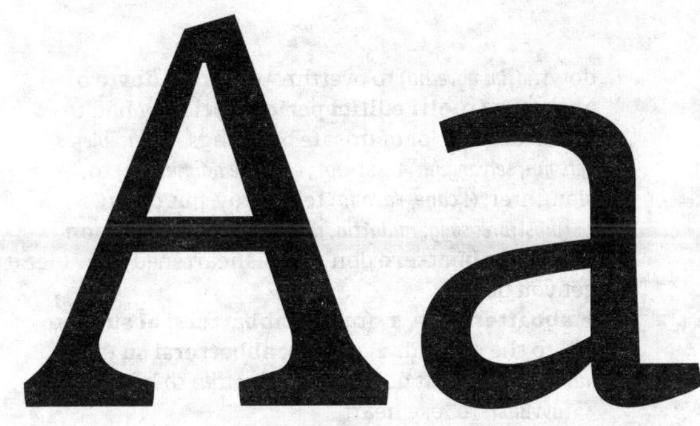

A, a [a] SF O M INV (*lettera*) A, a; **A come Ancona** ≈ A for Andrew (*Brit*), ≈ A for Able (*Am*); **dalla a alla zeta** from A to Z

A [a] ABBR **1** = **autostrada; sull'A1** ≈ on the M1 (*Brit*) **2** (= **altezza**) h **3** (= **area**) A

a [a] PAROLA CHIAVE

PREP (*a+il*=al, *a+lo*=allo, *a+l'*=all', *a+la*=alla, *a+i*=ai, *a+gli*=agli, *a+le*=alle)

1 (*complemento di termine*) to (*spesso omesso*); **dare qc a qn** to give sth to sb, give sb sth; **ho dato un giocattolo a Sandro** I gave Sandro a toy, I gave a toy to Sandro

2 (*stato in luogo: posizione*) at; (*: in*) in; (*: su*) on; **abitare a Milano/al terzo piano** to live in Milan/on the third floor; **è a 10 chilometri da qui** it's 10 kilometres from here; **essere a scuola/a casa/al cinema** to be at school/at home/at the cinema; **lavora alle poste/alle ferrovie** he works at the Post Office/for the railway; **alla radio** on the radio; **alla televisione** on television

3 (*moto a luogo*) to; **andare a casa/a Roma/al mare** to go home/to Rome/to the seaside

4 (*tempo*) at; (*epoca, stagione*) in; (*fino a*) to, till, until; **alle 3** at 3 o'clock; **all'alba** at dawn; **a 18 anni si diventa maggiorenni** at 18 you come of age; **dalle 3 alle 5** from 3 to *o* till 5 (o'clock); **a domani!** see you tomorrow!; **tornerà a giorni** he'll be back in a few days; **a lunedì!** see you on Monday!; **a maggio** in May; **a mezzanotte** at midnight; **tornerà a minuti** he'll be back in a few minutes; **a Natale** at Christmas; **a primavera** in spring

5 (*mezzo, modo*): **andare a cavallo** to go on horseback; **bistecca ai ferri** grilled steak; **bistecca alla fiorentina** T-bone steak; **fatto a mano** made by hand, handmade; **scrivere qc a matita** to write sth in pencil *o* with a pencil; **alla milanese** Milanese-style, in the Milanese fashion; **una barca a motore** a motorboat; **andare a piedi** to go on foot; **gonna a pieghe** pleated skirt; **pasta al pomodoro** pasta with *o* in tomato sauce; **gonna a righe** striped skirt; **entrare a uno a uno** to come in one by one

6 (*rapporto*) by, per; (*con prezzi*) at; **essere pagato a giornata** to be paid by the day; **vendere qc a 6 euro il chilo** to sell sth at 6 euros a *o* per kilo; **prendo 2000 euro al mese** I get 2000 euros a *o* per month; **viaggiare a 100 km all'ora** to travel at 100 km an *o* per hour; **essere pagato a ore** to be paid by the hour

7 (*scopo, fine*) for, to; **restare a cena** to stay for *o* to dinner

AA SIGLA = *Alto Adige*

AAST [a'a'ɛsse'ti] SIGLA F = *Azienda Autonoma di Soggiorno e Turismo*

AA.VV. ABBR = *autori vari*

ab. ABBR = **abitante**

abaco, chi ['abako] SM (*Archit, Mat*) abacus

abate [a'bate] SM abbot

abat-jour [aba'ʒur] SM INV bedside lamp

abbacchiato, a [abbak'kjato] AGG (*fam*) down, depressed; **ha un'aria abbacchiata** he's looking a bit down

abbacinare [abbatʃi'nare] VT to dazzle

abbacinato, a [abbatʃi'nato] AGG dazzled, blinded

abbagliante [abbaʎ'ʎante] AGG dazzling; **fare uso dei fari abbaglianti** to have one's headlights on full (*Brit*) *o* high (*Am*) beam

■ SM, GEN PL (*Aut*): **accendere gli abbaglianti** to put one's headlights on full (*Brit*) *o* high (*Am*) beam

abbagliare [abbaʎ'ʎare] VT (*anche fig*) to dazzle; (*illudere*) to delude; **non lasciarti abbagliare** don't let yourself be taken in

abbaglio, gli [ab'baʎʎo] SM blunder; **prendere un abbaglio** to blunder, make a blunder

abbaiare [abba'jare] VI: **abbaiare (a)** to bark (at); (*fig: gridare rabbiosamente*) to bawl (at)

abbaino [abba'ino] SM (*finestra*) dormer window; (*soffitta*) attic room

abbandonare [abbando'nare] VT **1** (*gen*) to abandon; (*famiglia, paese*) to abandon, desert; **abbandonare qn a se stesso** to leave sb to his (*o* her) own devices; **i suoi genitori lo hanno abbandonato quando era piccolo** his parents abandoned him when he was little; **il coraggio lo abbandonò** his courage deserted him; **abbandonare la nave** (*anche fig*) to abandon ship; **abbandonare il campo** (*Mil, fig*) to retreat

2 (*trascurare*: *casa, lavoro*) to neglect 3 (*rinunciare a*) to give up; (: *studi, progetto, speranza*) to abandon, give up; **abbandonare la gara** to withdraw from the race; **hanno abbandonato tutte le speranze** they gave up all hope 4 (*lasciare andare*: *redini*) to slacken; **abbandonò la testa sul cuscino** he let his head fall back on the pillow
▸ **abbandonarsi** VR to let o.s. go; **si abbandonò sul divano** he sank onto the couch; **abbandonarsi a qc** (*ricordi, passioni*) to give o.s. up to sth; **abbandonarsi a qn** (*affidarsi*) to put o.s. in sb's hands

abbandonato, a [abbando'nato] AGG 1 (*casa*) deserted; (*miniera*) disused 2 (*trascurato*: *terreno, podere*) neglected 3 (*bambino*) abandoned

abbandono [abban'dono] SM 1 (*di famiglia, paese*) desertion, abandonment; **abbandono del tetto coniugale** (*Dir*) desertion 2 (*trascuratezza*) neglect; **in abbandono** (*edificio, giardino*) neglected; **lasciare qc in stato di abbandono** to neglect sth 3 (*rinuncia*: *di progetto*) abandonment, dropping, giving up 4 (*Sport*) withdrawal; **vincere per abbandono dell'avversario** to win by default 5 (*rilassamento, cedimento*) abandon; **momenti di abbandono** moments of abandon

abbarbicarsi [abbarbi'karsi] VIP: **abbarbicarsi (a)** (*anche fig*) to cling (to)

abbassamento [abbassa'mento] SM lowering; (*di pressione, livello dell'acqua*) fall; (*di prezzi*) reduction; **abbassamento di temperatura** drop in temperature

abbassare [abbas'sare] VT 1 to lower; (*leva*) to press down; (*finestrino della macchina*) to wind down; (*finestrino del treno, tapparella*) to pull down; **abbassare le armi** (*Mil*) to lay down one's arms; **abbassò la testa per la vergogna** he hung his head in shame; **abbassare la guardia** (*Sport, fig*) to drop one's guard 2 (*volume, radio, TV*) to turn down; (*voce*) to lower; **ti dispiace abbassare il volume?** would you mind turning down the volume? 3 (*diminuire*: *prezzi*) to reduce, bring down 4 (*luce*) to dim; (*fari*) to dip (*Brit*), dim (*Am*) 5 (*Geom*: *perpendicolare*) to drop
▸ **abbassarsi** VR (*chinarsi*) to bend down, stoop; (: *per evitare*) to duck; (*fig*: *umiliarsi*) to demean o.s.; **abbassarsi a fare qc** to lower o.s. to do sth
▸ **abbassarsi** VIP 1 (*temperatura, prezzi*) to drop, fall; (*marea*) to go out, fall; (*livello*) to go down; (*sipario*) to fall 2 (*peggiorare*: *vista*) to deteriorate

abbasso [ab'basso] ESCL: **abbasso il re!** down with the king!; **abbasso l'Inter!** down with Inter!

abbastanza [abbas'tantsa] AVV 1 (*a sufficienza*) enough; **non mangia abbastanza** he doesn't eat enough; **non avevo studiato abbastanza** I hadn't studied enough; **non ho abbastanza tempo/denaro** I don't have *o* haven't got enough *o* sufficient time/money; **hai trovato una casa abbastanza grande per la tua famiglia?** have you found a big enough house for your family?; **non ho abbastanza soldi per comprarlo** I don't have enough money to buy it; **averne abbastanza di qn/qc** to have had enough of sb/sth, be fed up with sb/sth 2 (*alquanto*) quite, rather, fairly; **un vino abbastanza dolce** quite a sweet wine, a fairly sweet wine; **è abbastanza alto** he's quite tall; **vanno abbastanza d'accordo** they get on O.K; **l'esame era abbastanza difficile** the exam was quite difficult; **ti piace il film? — sì, abbastanza** are you enjoying the film? — yes, quite *o* it's o.k.

abbattere [ab'battere] VT 1 (*edificio, muro, ostacolo*) to knock down; (*albero*) to fell, cut down; (*sogg*: *vento*) to bring down; (*aereo*) to shoot down; (*porta*) to break down; (*fig*: *governo*) to overthrow; **hanno dovuto abbattere molti edifici pericolanti** they had to knock down a lot of unsafe buildings 2 (*uccidere*: *persona, selvaggina*) to shoot; (: *bestie da macello*) to slaughter; (: *cane, cavallo*) to destroy, put down 3 (*prostrare*: *sogg*: *malattia, disgrazia*) to lay low; **non lasciarti abbattere** don't be disheartened, don't let it get you down
▸ **abbattersi** VIP 1 (*cadere*): **abbattersi al suolo** to fall to the ground 2 (*colpire*): **abbattersi su** (*sogg*: *maltempo*) to beat down on; (: *disgrazia*) to hit, strike 3 (*avvilirsi*) to lose heart

abbattimento [abbatti'mento] SM 1 (*di albero*) felling; (*di muro*) knocking down; (*di casa*) demolition; (*di aereo*) shooting down (*Brit*), downing (*Am*); (*di animali*: *a caccia*) shooting; (: *al macello*) slaughter 2 (*prostrazione*: *fisica*) exhaustion; (: *morale*) despondency

abbattuto, a [abbat'tuto] AGG despondent, depressed; **mi è sembrato un po' abbattuto** he seemed a bit depressed

abbazia [abbat'tsia] SF abbey; **l'abbazia di Westminster** Westminster Abbey

abbecedario, ri [abbetʃe'darjo] SM ABC book

abbellimento [abbelli'mento] SM 1 (*ornamento*) embellishment 2 (*Mus*) embellishment, grace note

abbellire [abbel'lire] VT to make (more) attractive; (*racconto*) to embellish
▸ **abbellirsi** VIP to become more attractive

abbeveraggio, gi [abbeve'raddʒo] SM (*di animali*) watering

abbeverare [abbeve'rare] VT to water
▸ **abbeverarsi** VR to drink

abbeverata [abbeve'rata] SF (*atto*) watering; (*luogo*) watering place

abbeveratoio, oi [abbevera'tojo] SM drinking trough

abbi, abbia, abbiamo, abbiano, abbiate VB *vedi* **avere**

abbiccì [abbit'tʃi] SM INV (*alfabeto*) ABC, alphabet; (*fig*) ABC, rudiments *pl*; (*abbecedario, sillabario*) ABC book; **l'abbiccì del fai da te** the abc of do-it-yourself

abbiente [ab'bjɛnte] AGG well-to-do, well-off; **una famiglia abbiente** a well-off family; **gli abbienti** SMPL the well-to-do; **gli abbienti e i non abbienti** the haves and the have-nots

abbietto *ecc* [ab'bjɛtto] AGG = **abietto** *ecc*

abbiezione [abbjet'tsjone] SF = **abiezione**

abbigliamento [abbiʎʎa'mento] SM (*modo di vestire*) clothes *pl*; (*vestiario*) clothing; **abbigliamento maschile/femminile** menswear/ladieswear; **capo di abbigliamento** article of clothing; **industria dell'abbigliamento** clothing industry, fashion business; **spende molto per l'abbigliamento** he spends a lot on clothes

abbigliare [abbiʎ'ʎare] VT (*aiutare a vestire*) to dress; (*agghindare*) to dress up
▸ **abbigliarsi** VR to dress

abbinamento [abbina'mento] SM (*vedi vb*) combination; linking; matching

abbinare [abbi'nare] VT: **abbinare (con *o* a)** (*gen*) to combine (with); (*nomi*) to link (with); (*colori ecc*) to match (with), to go (with); **ha una camicia da abbinare a questi pantaloni?** have you got a shirt to go with these trousers?

abbinata [abbi'nata] SF = **accoppiata**

abbindolamento [abbindola'mento] SM (*fig*) trick

abbindolare [abbindo'lare] VT (*fig*) to trick, take in, cheat; **si è fatto abbindolare** he was done

abbiocco, chi [ab'bjɔkko] SM: **far venire l'abbiocco a qn** *(pranzo, cibo pesante)* to make sb sleepy

abbisognare [abbizoɲ'ɲare] VI **1** *(aus* **essere***)* *(essere necessario)*: **chiedi ciò che ti abbisogna** ask for what you need; **mi abbisogna il tuo aiuto** I need your help **2** *(aus* **avere***)* *(aver bisogno)*: **abbisognare di** to need; **abbisognare di denaro/di consigli** to need (some) money/advice

abboccamento [abbokka'mento] SM **1** *(colloquio)* preliminary meeting **2** *(Tecn: di tubi)* connection

abboccare [abbok'kare] VI *(aus* **avere***)* *(pesce)* to bite; *(fig: farsi raggirare)* to swallow the bait; **abboccare all'amo** *(anche fig)* to rise to the bait
■ VT *(Tecn: tubi, condutture)* to connect, join (up)

abboccato, a [abbok'kato] AGG *(vino)* medium sweet

abboffarsi *ecc* [abbof'farsi] = **abbuffarsi** *ecc*

abbonamento [abbona'mento] SM **1 abbonamento (a)** *(rivista)* subscription (to); *(teatro, trasporti)* season ticket (for); **l'abbonamento ad una rivista** a magazine subscription; **abbonamento settimanale/ mensile** *(a teatro, trasporti)* weekly/monthly ticket; **fare l'abbonamento (a qc)** to take out a subscription (to sth), buy a season ticket (for sth); **in abbonamento** for subscribers only, for season ticket holders only **2** *(al telefono)* rental; **abbonamento alla televisione** television licence

abbonare[1] [abbo'nare] VT *(cifra)* to deduct; *(fig: perdonare)* to forgive

abbonare[2] [abbo'nare] VT: **abbonare qn (a qc)** *(rivista)* to take out a subscription for sb (to sth); *(teatro, trasporti)* to buy sb a season ticket (for sth); *(televisione ecc)* to get *o* buy a licence (for sth) for sb
▶ **abbonarsi** VR: **abbonarsi (a)** *(rivista)* to subscribe (to); *(teatro, trasporti)* to buy a season ticket (for); **abbonarsi al telefono** to have a telephone installed *o* put in; **abbonarsi alla televisione** to get *o* buy a television licence

abbonato, a [abbo'nato] AGG: **essere abbonato** *(a rivista)* to be a subscriber; *(a teatro, trasporti)* to be a season ticket holder; *(alla televisione ecc)* to be a licence holder; *(fig: abituato)*: **viene a cena da noi ogni settimana: ormai c'è abbonato!** he comes to our house for dinner every week: it's part of his routine!
■ SM/F *(vedi abbonare[2])* subscriber; season ticket holder; licence holder; **abbonato al telefono** telephone subscriber; **elenco abbonati** telephone directory

abbondante [abbon'dante] AGG **1** *(gen)* abundant, plentiful; *(misure)* generous; *(nevicata)* heavy; **un'abbondante colazione** a big breakfast; **in quel ristorante le porzioni sono più abbondanti** the portions are bigger in that restaurant **2** *(abito: troppo grande)* too big, on the large side; *(: ampio)* loose-fitting

abbondantemente [abbondante'mente] AVV: **ha piovuto abbondantemente** it rained heavily; **abbiamo mangiato abbondantemente** we had plenty to eat; **ci hanno rifornito abbondantemente di carta** they gave us an ample supply of paper

abbondanza [abbon'dantsa] SF **1** *(gran quantità)* abundance; **in abbondanza** plenty; **ne ho in abbondanza** I've got plenty; **dovresti mangiare frutta e verdura in abbondanza** you should eat plenty of fruit and vegetables; **ci sono pere in abbondanza** there are plenty of pears, there is an abundance of pears **2** *(ricchezza)* plenty; **vivere nell'abbondanza** to live in plenty

abbondare [abbon'dare] VI **1** *(aus* **essere***)* to abound, be plentiful **2** *(aus* **avere***)* **abbondare di** to be full of, abound in; **abbondare in** *o* **di cortesie** to be extremely polite

abbordabile [abbor'dabile] AGG *(persona)* approachable; *(prezzo)* affordable

abbordare [abbor'dare] VT **1** *(Naut)* to go alongside; *(: nave nemica)* to board **2** *(curva, salita)* to take **3** *(persona)* to accost; *(questione, argomento)* to tackle

abbottonare [abbotto'nare] VT to button (up), do up; **abbottonarsi il cappotto** to button (up) one's coat
▶ **abbottonarsi** VR *(fig fam: diventare riservato)* to clam up

abbottonato, a [abbotto'nato] AGG *(camicia ecc)* buttoned (up); *(fig)* buttoned up

abbottonatura [abbottona'tura] SF buttons *pl*; **questo cappotto ha l'abbottonatura da uomo/da donna** this coat buttons on the man's/woman's side

abbozzare [abbot'tsare] VT **1** *(scultura)* to rough-hew; *(disegno)* to sketch, outline; *(romanzo)* to sketch out **2** *(fig: idea, progetto)* to outline; *(: contratto)* to draft; **abbozzare un sorriso** to give a faint smile *o* a hint of a smile; **abbozzare un saluto** *(con la mano)* to half wave; *(con un cenno del capo)* to half nod

abbozzo [ab'bɔttso] SM **1** *(di scultura, disegno)* sketch, outline; *(di libro)* rough outline **2** *(di progetto)* outline; *(di contratto)* draft; *(fig: accenno)* hint; **un abbozzo di sorriso** the ghost of a smile

abbracciare [abbrat'tʃare] VT **1** *(persona)* to embrace, hug; **ti abbraccio** *(in una lettera)* lots of love **2** *(professione)* to take up; *(fede)* to embrace **3** *(includere)* to include; **abbracciare qc con lo sguardo** to take sth in at a glance; **la sua opera abbraccia due secoli di storia** his work covers two hundred years of history
▶ **abbracciarsi** VR *(uso reciproco)* to hug *o* embrace (one another)

abbraccio, ci [ab'brattʃo] SM embrace, hug; **ci siamo salutati con un abbraccio** we hugged and said goodbye; **un abbraccio** *(in lettera, cartolina)* love; **un abbraccio, Francesca** (lots of) love, Francesca

abbrancare [abbran'kare] VT to grasp, seize; **abbrancare per il colletto qn** to seize hold of sb by the collar
▶ **abbrancarsi** VR: **abbrancarsi a qc** to grab hold of sth

abbreviare [abbre'vjare] VT *(gen)* to shorten; *(parola)* to abbreviate, shorten

abbreviazione [abbrevjat'tsjone] SF *(vedi vb)* shortening; abbreviation

abbrivio, vi [ab'brivjo] SM *(Naut)* headway; **prendere l'abbrivio** *(fig: iniziare)* to get under way; **abbrivio residuo** residual thrust

abbronzante [abbron'dzante] AGG *(prodotto)* suntan *attr*, sun *attr*
■ SM *(crema)* suntan cream; *(olio)* suntan oil

abbronzare [abbron'dzare] VT *(pelle)* to tan; *(metalli)* to bronze
▶ **abbronzarsi** VIP to get a tan; **stare ad abbronzarsi** to sunbathe

abbronzato, a [abbron'dzato] AGG (sun)tanned; **è abbronzatissima** she's very tanned

abbronzatura [abbrondza'tura] SF (sun)tan

abbrustolire [abbrusto'lire] VT *(pane)* to toast; *(semi, caffè)* to roast
▶ **abbrustolirsi** VIP: **abbrustolirsi al sole** *(fig)* to soak up the sun

abbrutimento [abbruti'mento] SM degradation

abbrutire [abbru'tire] VT *(degradare)* to degrade; **essere**

Aa

abbrutito dall'alcol to be ruined by drink; **la guerra abbrutisce l'uomo** war brutalizes people
▶ **abbrutirse** VIP to be degraded, be brutalized
abbuffarsi [abbuf'farsi] VR (*fam*): **abbuffarsi (di qc)** to stuff o.s. (with sth)
abbuffata [abbuf'fata] SF (*fam*) nosh-up, blow-out; (*fig*) binge; **farsi un'abbuffata** to stuff o.s.
abbuiare [abbu'jare] VB IMPERS (*aus* **essere**) to get dark
▶ **abbuiarsi** VIP (*farsi buio*) to grow dark; (*fig: espressione, volto*) to darken
abbuonare [abbwo'nare] VT = **abbonare'**
abbuono [ab'bwɔno] SM **1** (*Comm*) discount **2** (*Ippica*) handicap
abdicare [abdi'kare] VI **1** (*al trono*): **abdicare (a)** to abdicate (from); (*rinunciare*): **abdicare a** to renounce, give up; **abdicare a una carica** to give up a position **2** (*venir meno a: responsabilità, dovere*) to abdicate
abdicatario, ria, ri, rie [abdika'tarjo] AGG abdicating
abdicazione [abdikat'tsjone] SF abdication
Abele [a'bele] SM Abel
aberrante [aber'rante] AGG aberrant
aberrazione [aberrat'tsjone] SF aberration
abetaia [abe'taja] SF fir wood
abete [a'bete] SM (*albero*) fir (tree); (*legno*) fir; **abete bianco** silver fir; **abete rosso** spruce
abiettamente [abjetta'mente] AVV despicably
abietto, a [a'bjɛtto] AGG (*spregevole: persona, azione*) despicable, vile; (*squallido: condizioni*) abject, appalling
abiezione [abjet'tsjone] SF (*vedi agg*) vileness; abjectness
abigeato [abidʒe'ato] SM (*Dir*) rustling
abile ['abile] AGG **1** (*capace*) skilful, able; **essere abile in qc** to be good at sth; **è molto abile nel suo lavoro** he's very good at his job; **un abile chirurgo/artigiano** a skilful surgeon/craftsman **2** (*accorto*) clever; (*astuto*) shrewd; **un'abile mossa** a good *o* clever move; **un abile uomo d'affari** a shrewd businessman **3** (*idoneo*): **abile (a qc/a fare qc)** fit (for sth/to do sth); **abile al servizio militare** fit for military service
abilità [abili'ta] SF INV **1** (*capacità*) ability; (*destrezza*) skill; **questo lavoro richiede una grande abilità** this work requires great skill; **abilità nel fare qc** ability to do sth; **una grande abilità nella guida** great skill in driving **2** (*accortezza*) cleverness; (*astuzia*) shrewdness
abilitante [abili'tante] AGG qualifying; **corsi abilitanti** (*Scol*) ≈ teacher training *sg*
abilitare [abili'tare] VT: **abilitare qn a qc/a fare qc** to qualify sb for sth/to do sth; **è stato abilitato all'insegnamento** he has qualified as a teacher
abilitato, a [abili'tato] AGG **1** (*qualificato*) qualified **2** (*Telec*) which has an outside line
■ SM/F qualified person; **solo gli abilitati possono partecipare** only those with the required qualifications may take part
abilitazione [abilitat'tsjone] SF qualification; **esame di abilitazione** qualifying exam; **conseguire l'abilitazione** to qualify
abilmente [abil'mente] AVV (*vedi agg*) skilfully; cleverly
abissale [abis'sale] AGG abysmal; (*fig: senza limiti: ignoranza*) profound; **Mario è di un'ignoranza abissale!** Mario is a total ignoramus!
abissino, a [abis'sino] AGG, SM/F Abyssinian
abisso [a'bisso] SM (*anche fig*) abyss, gulf; **gli abissi marini** the depths of the sea; **tra noi c'è un abisso** we are poles apart; **essere sull'orlo dell'abisso** to be on the brink of ruin; **è un abisso di ignoranza** he is utterly ignorant
abitabile [abi'tabile] AGG habitable
abitabilità [abitabili'ta] SF INV: **licenza** *o* **autorizzazione di abitabilità** *document stating that a property is fit for habitation*
abitacolo [abi'takolo] SM (*di aereo*) cockpit; (*di macchina*) inside; (*di camion*) (driver's) cab
abitante [abi'tante] SM/F (*di città, paese*) inhabitant; (*di casa*) occupant
abitare [abi'tare] VI (*aus* **avere**) **abitare in, a** to live (in); **abitare in campagna/a Roma/all'estero** to live in the country/in Rome/abroad; **dove abiti?** where do you live?; **abito a Firenze** I live in Florence; **abito qui da sei anni** I've been living here for six years; **abita al numero 10** she lives at number 10; **abitano al sesto piano** they live on the sixth floor
■ VT (*casa*) to live in, dwell in (*letter*); (*luogo*) to inhabit
abitato, a [abi'tato] AGG (*casa, appartamento*) occupied, inhabited
■ SM (*anche:* **centro abitato**) built-up area
abitazione [abitat'tsjone] SF (*casa*) house, residence (*frm*)
abito ['abito] SM **1** (*da donna*) dress; (*da uomo*) suit; **in abito da cerimonia** in formal dress; **"è gradito l'abito scuro"** "dress formal"; **in abito da sera** in evening dress; **abito da sposa** wedding dress **2** (*vestiti*): **abiti** SMPL clothes, dress *no pl*; **abiti civili** civilian clothes *pl*, civvies *pl* (*fam*) **3** (*disposizione*): **abito mentale** way of thinking **4** (*Rel*) habit; **l'abito non fa il monaco** (*Proverbio*) you can't tell a book by its cover, you can't judge by appearances
abituale [abitu'ale] AGG usual; (*cliente, frequentatore*) regular
abitualmente [abitual'mente] AVV usually, normally
abituare [abitu'are] VT: **abituare qn (a qc/a fare qc)** to accustom sb to sth/to doing sth, get sb used to sth/to doing sth
▶ **abituarsi** VR: **abituarsi a qc/a fare qc** to get used to *o* accustomed to sth/to doing sth, accustom o.s. to sth/to doing sth (*frm*); **adesso mi ci sono abituato** I'm used to it now
abitudinario, ria, ri, rie [abitudi'narjo] AGG: **essere abitudinario** to be set in one's ways; **è un po' abitudinario** he's rather set in his ways
■ SM/F creature of habit
abitudine [abi'tudine] SF habit; **aver l'abitudine di fare qc** to be in the habit of doing sth; **prendere/perdere l'abitudine di fare qc** to get into/out of the habit of doing sth; **per abitudine** from *o* out of habit; **come d'abitudine** as usual; **d'abitudine** usually; **buona** *o* **bella/cattiva** *o* **brutta abitudine** good/bad habit; **ci ho fatto l'abitudine** I've got used to it
abiura [a'bjura] SF (*Rel*) abjuration
abiurare [abju'rare] VT (*Rel*) to abjure; (*principi*) to renounce
ablativo [abla'tivo] SM, AGG ablative
abluzione [ablut'tsjone] SF (*Rel*) ablution
abnegazione [abnegat'tsjone] SF (self-)abnegation, self-denial; **con abnegazione** selflessly
abnorme [ab'nɔrme] AGG (*enorme*) extraordinary; (*anormale*) abnormal
abolire [abo'lire] VT to abolish; (*Dir*) to repeal; **abbiamo abolito lo zucchero dalla nostra dieta** we have eliminated sugar from our diet; **abolire una legge/tassa** to abolish a law/tax

abolizione [abolit'tsjone] SF abolition
abomaso [abo'mazo] SM (*Zool*) abomasum
abominevole [abomi'nevole] AGG abominable
aborigeno, a [abo'ridʒeno] AGG aboriginal
■SM/F aboriginal, aborigine; **aborigeno australiano** Aborigine
aborrire [abor'rire] VT to abhor, loathe
abortire [abor'tire] VI **1** (*aus* **avere**) (*Med*) to abort; (: *accidentalmente*) to have a miscarriage, miscarry; (: *volontariamente*) to have an abortion **2** (*aus* **essere**) (*fig: progetto ecc*) to fail, come to nothing, miscarry (*frm*); (*Inform*) to abort
abortista, i, e [abor'tista] AGG pro-choice, pro-abortion
■SM/F pro-choicer
aborto [a'bɔrto] SM **1** (*provocato*) abortion; (*spontaneo*) miscarriage; **aborto clandestino** backstreet abortion **2** (*feto*) aborted foetus; (*fig*) freak; **è un aborto di quadro** (*fig*) it's a ghastly painting
abracadabra [abraka'dabra] SM INV abracadabra
Abramo [a'bramo] SM Abraham
abrasione [abra'zjone] SF abrasion
abrasivo, a [abra'zivo] AGG, SM abrasive
abrogare [abro'gare] VT (*legge*) to repeal, abrogate (*frm*)
abrogazione [abrogat'tsjone] SF repeal, abrogation (*frm*)
abruzzese [abrut'tsese] AGG of *o* from the Abruzzi
■SM/F inhabitant *o* native of the Abruzzi
Abruzzo [a'bruttso] SM: **l'Abruzzo** the Abruzzi
ABS [abi'ɛsse] SIGLA M (= **Anti-Blockier System**) ABS (= *anti-lock braking system*)
abside ['abside] SF apse
Abu Dhabi [abu'dabi] SF Abu Dhabi
abulia [abu'lia] SF (*Psic*) abulia; (*fig*) lethargy
abulico, a, ci, che [a'buliko] AGG (*vedi sf*) abulic; lethargic
abusare [abu'zare] VI (*aus* **avere**) **abusare di qc** (*fare uso eccessivo: di pazienza, cortesia*) to take advantage of; (: *di alcol, stupefacenti*) to abuse; (*fare uso indebito: di potere, autorità, fiducia*) to abuse; **abusare di qn** to abuse sb; **non vorrei abusare della tua gentilezza** I don't want to take advantage of your kindness
abusivamente [abuziva'mente] AVV without authorization, unlawfully, illegally; **occupare abusivamente una casa** to squat
abusivismo [abuzi'vizmo] SM (*anche:* **abusivismo edilizio**) unlawful building, building without planning permission (*Brit*)
abusivo, a [abu'zivo] AGG unauthorized; **edilizia abusiva** unauthorized building; **occupante abusivo** (*di una casa*) squatter; **taxi abusivo** unlicensed taxi

> **LO SAPEVI...?**
> **abusivo** non si traduce mai con la parola inglese *abusive*

abuso [a'buzo] SM **1** (*uso eccessivo*) excessive use; (*uso improprio*) abuse, misuse; **fare abuso di** (*stupefacenti, medicine*) to abuse; **abuso di potere** abuse of power; **abuso di medicinali** drug abuse **2** (*violenza*) abuse; **abusi sessuali sui minori** child abuse
A.C. ABBR = assegno circolare; *vedi* assegno
a.C. ABBR (= **avanti Cristo**) BC; **il primo secolo a.C.** the first century BC
acacia, cie [a'katʃa] SF acacia
acaro ['akaro] SM (*Zool*) mite; **acaro della scabbia** itch mite
acca ['akka] SF letter H; **non capire un'acca** not to understand a thing; **non sai un'acca di latino** you don't know a thing about Latin
accadde *ecc* VB *vedi* **accadere**
accademia [akka'dɛmja] SF (*scuola: d'arte, militare*) academy; (*società*) learned society; **accademia d'arte drammatica** drama school; **accademia di Belle Arti** art school; **accademia militare** military academy; **Accademia della Crusca** *national academy for the study and preservation of the Italian language*
▷ www.accademiadellacrusca.it/
accademicamente [akkademika'mente] AVV (*vedi agg*) academically; academically, pedantically
accademico, a, ci, che [akka'dɛmiko] AGG academic; (*fig: pedante*) academic, pedantic; **anno accademico** academic year
■SM/F academician
accademismo [akkade'mizmo] SM academicism
accadere [akka'dere] VB IRREG (*aus* **essere**)
■VI to happen, occur; **mi è accaduto di incontrarlo** I happened to meet him; **è accaduto l'anno scorso** it happened last year
■VB IMPERS to happen; **accadde che...** it happened that ...
accaduto [akka'duto] SM event; **raccontare l'accaduto** to describe what happened; **in seguito all'accaduto** following what happened
accalappiacani [akkalappja'kani] SM INV dog-catcher
accalappiare [akkalap'pjare] VT (*animali*) to catch; (*fig: persona*) to trick, dupe
accalcare [akkal'kare] VT
▶ **accalcarsi** VIP to crowd, throng; **i tifosi accalcavano lo stadio** *or* **i tifosi si accalcavano nello stadio** the fans crowded *o* thronged the stadium
accaldarsi [akkal'darsi] VIP to get hot
accaldato, a [akkal'dato] AGG hot; **era tutto accaldato dopo la corsa** he was boiling hot after the race
accalorarsi [akkalo'rarsi] VR (*infervorarsi*) to become worked up, get excited
accampamento [akkampa'mento] SM (*Mil, di zingari ecc*) camp, encampment; **togliere/porre l'accampamento** to strike/pitch camp
accampare [akkam'pare] VT **1** (*Mil*) to encamp **2** (*fig: diritti*) to assert; (: *pretese*) to advance; **accampare scuse** to make excuses
▶ **accamparsi** VR (*Mil*) to pitch camp; (*fare campeggio*) to camp; (*sistemarsi alla meglio*) to bed down
accanimento [akkani'mento] SM (*odio, furia*) fury; (*tenacia*) tenacity, perseverance; **con accanimento** (*furiosamente*) furiously; (*tenacemente*) assiduously; **lavorare con accanimento** to work extremely hard; **accanimento terapeutico** *medical treatment that uselessly prolongs the life of a terminally ill patient*
accanirsi [akka'nirsi] VIP **1** (*infierire*): **accanirsi (contro)** to rage (against) **2** (*ostinarsi*): **accanirsi a** *o* **nel fare qc** to persist in doing sth; **accanirsi nello studio** to study very hard; **è inutile che ti accanisci a fare domande** there's no point going on and on asking questions
accanitamente [akkanita'mente] AVV (*vedi agg*) fiercely; assiduously
accanito, a [akka'nito] AGG (*odio*) fierce; (*lavoratore*) assiduous; (*giocatore*) inveterate; (*tifoso, sostenitore*) keen; **fumatore accanito** chain smoker
accanto [ak'kanto] AVV nearby, near; **abito qui accanto** (*di fianco*) I live next door; (*vicino*) I live near here; **la casa accanto** the house next door; **accanto a**

Aa

PREP next to, beside; **accanto alla porta** by the door; **la tua camera è accanto alla mia** your room's next to mine; **siediti accanto a me** sit next to me

accantonamento[1] [akkantona'mento] SM (*di progetto, idea*) shelving

accantonamento[2] [akkantona'mento] SM (*Mil*) quartering

accantonare [akkanto'nare] VT (*progetto, idea, problema*) to shelve; (*argomento*) to leave aside; (*denaro, viveri*) to put aside, set aside; **abbiamo deciso di accantonare il progetto per il momento** we decided to shelve the project for the moment; **sono riusciti ad accantonare una bella somma** they managed to set aside a considerable sum of money

accaparramento [akkaparra'mento] SM (*Comm*) buying up

accaparrare [akkapar'rare] VT **1** (*Comm*) to buy up **2** (*assicurare con caparra*) to pay a deposit on, secure (by deposit) **3** **accaparrarsi qc** (*simpatia, voti*) to secure sth (for o.s.); **accaparrarsi il mercato** to corner the market; **accaparrarsi il posto migliore** to grab the best seat

accapigliarsi [akkapiʎ'ʎarsi] VR (*uso reciproco*) to come to blows; (*fig*) to squabble

accappatoio, oi [akkappa'tojo] SM (*da bagno*) bathrobe; (*da spiaggia*) beach robe

accapponare [akkappo'nare] VI (*aus* **essere**), **accapponarsi** VIP: **mi si è accapponata la pelle** I came out in goosepimples *o* gooseflesh; **uno spettacolo da far accapponare la pelle** a sight to make your flesh creep

accarezzare [akkaret'tsare] VT **1** to caress; (*in modo spinto*) to fondle; (*animali, capelli*) to stroke; **accarezzarsi il mento** to stroke one's chin; **stava accarezzando il gatto** he was stroking the cat **2** (*fig: idea,progetto*) to toy with

accartocciare [akkartot'tʃare] VT (*carta*) to roll up, screw up
▶ **accartocciarsi** VIP (*foglie*) to curl up

accartocciato, a [akkartot'tʃato] AGG (*vedi vb*) rolled up; curled up

accasarsi [akka'sarsi] VR (*sposarsi*) to get married; (*metter su casa*) to set up house

accasciarsi [akkaʃ'ʃarsi] VIP to collapse; (*fig: deprimersi*) to lose heart; **accasciarsi su una sedia** to collapse into a chair; **si è accasciata al suolo all'improvviso** she suddenly collapsed onto the ground

accatastare [akkatas'tare] VT to stack, pile

accattonaggio [akkatto'naddʒo] SM begging

accattone, a [akkat'tone] SM/F beggar

accavallare [akkaval'lare] VT: **accavallare le gambe** to cross one's legs
▶ **accavallarsi** VIP (*sovrapporsi: muscolo, nervo*): **mi si è accavallato un tendine** I've pulled a tendon; (*fig: avvenimenti*) to overlap; (*addensarsi: pensieri, nubi*) to gather

accecante [attʃe'kante] AGG (*abbagliante*) blinding, dazzling

accecare [attʃe'kare] VT to blind; (*abbagliare*) to dazzle
▶ **accecarsi** VIP to become *o* go blind

accedere [at'tʃɛdere] VI IRREG: **accedere a** **1** (*aus* **essere**) (*luogo*) to enter; (*scuola: essere ammesso*) to enter, be admitted to **2** (*aus* **avere**) (*avere accesso a: notizia, fonte*) to gain access to **3** (*acconsentire: richiesta*) to accede to

accelerare [attʃele'rare] VI (*aus* **avere**) to accelerate, speed up
■ VT to speed up; **accelerare il passo** to quicken one's pace

accelerato, a [attʃele'rato] AGG (*rapido*) quick, rapid; **tempo/ritmo accelerato** fast tempo/rhythm
■ SM (*treno: ant*) local train, stopping train

acceleratore [attʃelera'tore] SM (*Aut*) accelerator

accelerazione [attʃelerat'tsjone] SF acceleration

accendere [at'tʃɛndere] VB IRREG
■ VT **1** (*fiammifero, candela, sigaretta, fuoco*) to light; **accendere il camino** to light the fire; **abbiamo acceso le candeline** we lit the candles; **mi fa accendere?** do you have a light? **2** (*radio, TV, luce, lampada*) to switch *o* turn on; (*gas*) to light; (*Aut: motore*) to switch on; **accendi il computer/il telefonino** switch on the computer/the phone **3** (*fig: speranza, desiderio*) to arouse **4** (*Fin: conto*) to open; (*: ipoteca*) to raise; **accendere un debito** to take out a loan
▶ **accendersi** VIP **1** (*fuoco*) to start; (*legna secca*) to catch fire; (*riscaldamento, luce, TV*) to come on **2** (*fig: di sentimenti*): **accendersi di gioia** (*occhi, volto*) to light up with joy; **accendersi in volto** (*per la vergogna*) to go red **3** (*fig: disputa*) to flare up

accendigas [attʃendi'gas] SM INV gas lighter (*for cooker ecc*)

accendino [attʃen'dino] SM (cigarette) lighter; **accendino a gas/elettronico** gas/electronic lighter

accendisigari [attʃendi'sigari] SM INV (cigarette) lighter

accennare [attʃen'nare] VT **1** (*indicare*) to indicate, point out; **le accennai la porta** I showed her the door **2** (*abbozzare*): **accennare un saluto** (*con la mano*) to make as if to wave; (*col capo*) to half nod; **accennare un sorriso** to half smile **3** (*citare*) to mention; **mi ha accennato qualcosa a proposito del suo progetto** he mentioned something to me about his project **4** (*canzone, melodia: al piano*) to pick out; (*: canticchiando*) to hum
■ VI (*aus* **avere**) **1** (*far cenno*): **mi accennò di star zitto** he signalled to me to keep quiet **2** (*far atto di*): **accennare a fare qc** to show signs of doing sth; **accennò ad alzarsi, ma poi si trattenne** he made as if to get up but then stopped; **accenna a piovere** it looks as if it's going to rain **3** **accennare a** (*menzionare*) to mention; (*alludere a*) to hint at; **ha accennato al fatto che vuole partire** he mentioned that he wants to leave

accenno [at'tʃenno] SM (*menzione, allusione, abbozzo*) hint; (*segno premonitore*) sign; **fare accenno a qc** to mention sth; **non ha fatto accenno all'accaduto** he made no mention of what had happened; **con un accenno di sorriso** with a hint of a smile

accensione [attʃen'sjone] SF **1** (*Aut*) ignition **2** (*di fiammifero, candela, sigaretta, fuoco*) lighting **3** (*di radio, TV, luce, lampada*) switching *o* turning on; (*di gas*) lighting, turning on **4** (*Fin: di conto*) opening; (*: di ipoteca*) raising; (*: di debito*) contracting

accentare [attʃen'tare] VT (*scrivendo*) to put an accent on; (*parlando*) to stress; **gli articoli non sono accentati** there is no (written) accent on the articles

accentazione [attʃentat'tsjone] SF (*vedi vb*) marking with an accent; stressing

accento [at'tʃɛnto] SM **1** (*pronuncia*) accent; **parla con un accento straniero** he speaks with a foreign accent **2** (*Fonetica*) accent, stress; (*fig*) stress, emphasis; **l'accento cade sulla penultima sillaba** the stress is on the penultimate syllable; **mettere l'accento su qc** (*fig*) to stress sth **3** (*segno grafico*) accent; **accento**

Aa

grave/acuto/circonflesso grave/acute/circumflex accent; **si scrive con l'accento sulla "u"** it's spelled with an accent on the "u" **4** (*inflessione*) tone (of voice); **un breve accento di tristezza** a slight note of sadness

accentramento [attʃentra'mento] SM (*Amm*) centralization

accentrare [attʃen'trare] VT (*potere ecc*) to centralize; (*fig: interesse, sguardi*) to attract, draw

accentratore, trice [attʃentra'tore] AGG (*persona*) unwilling to delegate; **politica accentratrice** policy of centralization; **governo accentratore** centralizing government

accentuare [attʃentu'are] VT **1** (*mettere in rilievo*) to emphasize, accentuate **2** (*sillaba, parola*) to stress, emphasize

▶ **accentuarsi** VIP (*tendenza*) to become more marked *o* pronounced *o* noticeable; (*crisi*) to become worse

accerchiare [attʃer'kjare] VT to encircle, surround; **accerchiarono il castello** they surrounded the castle

accertamento [attʃerta'mento] SM (*verifica*) check; (: *Fisco*) assessment; (*Dir*) investigation; **essere in corso di accertamento** to be under investigation; **è stato ricoverato per ulteriori accertamenti** he's been admitted to hospital for further tests; **accertamento d'imposta** tax assessment

accertare [attʃer'tare] VT **1** (*verificare*) to verify, check **2** (*Fisco: reddito*) to assess

▶ **accertarsi** VR: **accertarsi di qc/che** to make sure of sth/that, ascertain sth/that

acceso, a [at'tʃeso] PP *di* **accendere**

■ AGG **1** (*fuoco, lampada*) lit; (*luce, televisore, gas*) on; (*Fin*) open; **c'era la luce accesa** the light was on; **aveva in mano una candela accesa** he was holding a lighted candle **2** (*intenso: colore*) bright, vivid; (*infervorato: discussione, parole*) heated; **acceso di** (*ira, entusiasmo ecc*) burning with

accessibile [attʃes'sibile] AGG (*luogo*) accessible; (*persona*) approachable; (*prezzo*) affordable; **accessibile a tutti** (*prezzo, articolo*) within everyone's means, affordable; (*concetto, materia*) within the reach of everyone; **la zona è facilmente accessibile in macchina** the area is easily accessible by car

accessibilità [attʃessibili'ta] SF accessibility; **data l'accessibilità del prezzo...** given that the price is reasonable ...

accesso [at'tʃɛsso] SM **1** (*gen, Inform*) access; **vietato l'accesso** no entry, no admittance; **di facile accesso** (*luogo*) (easily) accessible; **avere accesso a** to have access to; **nessuno aveva accesso all'edificio** nobody had access to the building; **dare accesso a** (*sogg: porta, scala*) to lead to; (: *corso*) to lead to, open the door to; (: *qualifica*) to open the door to; **tempo di accesso** (*Inform*) access time; **accesso casuale** random access; **accesso sequenziale** sequential access; **accesso seriale** serial access **2** (*impulso violento: di rabbia, gelosia, Med: di tosse*) fit; (: *di febbre*) attack, bout

accessoriato, a [attʃesso'rjato] AGG (*Aut*) (fitted) with accessories

accessorio, ria, ri, rie [attʃes'sɔrjo] AGG secondary, of secondary importance

■ SM (*Aut, Moda ecc*) accessory

accessorista, i [attʃesso'rista] SM (*Aut*) car-accessory dealer

accetta [at'tʃetta] SF hatchet; **fatto con l'accetta** (*fig: lavoro ecc*) clumsily done; **tagliato con l'accetta** (*dal carattere grossolano*) uncouth; (*dai lineamenti marcati*) craggy

accettabile [attʃet'tabile] AGG acceptable

accettare [attʃet'tare] VT (*gen, Comm*) to accept; (*proposta*) to agree to, accept; **ha accettato l'invito** she accepted the invitation; **accettare di fare qc** to agree to do sth; **accettare qn come socio** to accept sb as a member

accettazione [attʃettat'tsjone] SF **1** (*gen*) acceptance; **accettazione bancaria** bank acceptance **2** (*di albergo, ospedale ecc*) reception; **accettazione bagagli** (*Aer*) check-in (desk)

accetto, a [at'tʃɛtto] AGG: **bene/male accetto** welcome/unwelcome; **ben accetto a tutti** (*persona*) well-liked by everybody

accezione [attʃet'tsjone] SF meaning, sense

acchiappamosche [akkjappa'moske] SM INV (fly) swatter

acchiappare [akkjap'pare] VT (*prendere, catturare*) to catch; (*afferrare*) to seize; **l'ho rincorso ma non sono riuscito ad acchiapparlo** I ran after him but couldn't catch him

acchito [ak'kito] SM: **di primo acchito** at first

acciaccato, a [attʃak'kato] AGG **1** (*persona*) full of aches and pains **2** (*abito, cappello*) crushed; (*macchina*) battered

acciacco, chi [at'tʃakko] SM ailment; **acciacchi** SMPL aches and pains

acciaieria [attʃaje'ria] SF steelworks *sg*

acciaio, ai [at'tʃajo] SM steel; **d'acciaio** (*trave*) steel *attr*, of steel; (*fig: uomo, nervi*) of steel; **acciaio al carbonio** carbon steel; **acciaio inossidabile** stainless steel

accidentale [attʃiden'tale] AGG accidental; **in circostanze accidentali** accidentally

accidentalità [attʃidentali'ta] SF fortuity, chance nature

accidentalmente [attʃidental'mente] AVV (*per caso*) by chance; (*non deliberatamente*) accidentally, by accident

accidentato, a [attʃiden'tato] AGG (*terreno*) uneven, rough; (*strada*) bumpy, uneven

accidente [attʃi'dɛnte] SM **1** (*gen, Filosofia*) accident; (*disgrazia*) mishap **2** (*fam: colpo apoplettico*) stroke; (: *fig*) fit, shock; **quando ho visto il conto mi è venuto un accidente!** I had a fit when I saw the bill!; **mandare un accidente a qn** to curse sb **3** (*fig: niente*): **non vale un accidente** it's not worth a damn; **non capisco un accidente** it's as clear as mud to me

accidenti [attʃi'dɛnti] ESCL (*fam: per rabbia*) damn (it)!; (: *per meraviglia*) good heavens!; **accidenti a lui!** damn him!; **ma che accidenti vuole?** what on earth does he want?; **accidenti, che bella moto!** wow, what a great bike!

accidia [at'tʃidja] SF sloth; (*Rel*) accidie

accigliato, a [attʃiʎ'ʎato] AGG frowning

accingersi [at'tʃindʒersi] VR IRREG: **accingersi a fare** to be all set to do; **mi accingevo ad andare a letto** I was about to go to bed

accinto, a [at'tʃinto] PP *di* **accingersi**

acciottolato [attʃotto'lato] SM cobblestones *pl*

acciuffare [attʃuf'fare] VT to seize, catch

acciuga, ghe [at'tʃuga] SF anchovy; **magro come un'acciuga** as thin as a rake; **stretti come acciughe** packed like sardines

acclamare [akkla'mare] VT **1** (*applaudire*) to cheer, applaud **2** (*eleggere*) to acclaim

■ VI (*aus* **avere**) **acclamare a** to cheer, applaud

Aa

acclamazione [akklamat'tsjone] SF *(vedi vb)* applause; acclamation

acclimatare [akklima'tare] VT to acclimatize
▸ **acclimatarsi** VR to become acclimatized

acclimatazione [akklimatat'tsjone] SF acclimatization

accludere [ak'kludere] VT IRREG: **accludere (a)** to enclose (with); **accludo una copia di...** I enclose a copy of ...

accluso, a [ak'kluzo] PP *di* **accludere**
■ AGG enclosed; **qui accluso troverete...** please find enclosed ...

accoccolarsi [akkokko'larsi] VR to crouch (down)

accodarsi [akko'darsi] VR to follow, tag along (behind)

accogliente [akkoʎ'ʎɛnte] AGG *(atmosfera)* welcoming, friendly; *(stanza)* pleasant, cosy

accoglienza [akkoʎ'ʎɛntsa] SF welcome, reception; **fare una buona accoglienza a qn** to welcome sb; **fare una cattiva accoglienza a qn** to give sb a cool reception

accogliere [ak'kɔʎʎere] VT IRREG **1** *(persona: ricevere)* to receive; (: *calorosamente)* to welcome; *(sogg: sala, stadio)* to accommodate, hold; **mi ha accolto a braccia aperte** she welcomed me with open arms; **questa sala può accogliere 600 persone** this hall can hold *o* accommodate 600 people **2** *(notizia)* to receive **3** *(richiesta)* to agree to, accept

accoglimento [akkoʎʎi'mento] SM *(di proposta)* acceptance; *(di richiesta)* granting

accolgo *ecc* [ak'kɔlgo] VB *vedi* **accogliere**

accollare [akkol'lare] VT *(fig)*: **accollare qc a qn** *(spesa, responsabilità, obbligo)* to force sth on sb; **accollarsi qc** to take sth upon o.s., shoulder sth

accollato, a [akkol'lato] AGG *(vestito)* high-necked; *(scarpa)* ankle-high

accolsi *ecc* [ak'kɔlsi] VB *vedi* **accogliere**

accolta [ak'kɔlta] SF *(letter)* assembly, gathering; *(pegg)* bunch

accoltellamento [akkoltella'mento] SM stabbing, knifing

accoltellare [akkoltel'lare] VT to knife, stab; **l'hanno accoltellato in una rissa** he was stabbed in a fight
▸ **accoltellarsi** VR *(uso reciproco)* to attack each other with knives

accolto, a [ak'kɔlto] PP *di* **accogliere**

accomandante [akkoman'dante] AGG *(Dir)*: **socio accomandante** limited partner

accomandatario, ria, ri, rie [akkomanda'tarjo] AGG *(Dir)*: **socio accomandatario** active partner

accomandita [akko'mandita] SF *(Dir)*: **(società in) accomandita** limited partnership

accomiatare [akkomja'tare] VT to dismiss
▸ **accomiatarsi** VR: **accomiatarsi (da)** to take one's leave (of), say goodbye (to)

accomodamento [akkomoda'mento] SM *(accordo)* arrangement, agreement; **trovare un accomodamento** to come to an agreement

> **LO SAPEVI...?**
> **accomodamento** non si traduce mai con la parola inglese ***accommodation***

accomodante [akkomo'dante] AGG accommodating

accomodare [akkomo'dare] VT **1** *(riparare)* to fix, repair, mend **2** *(sistemare)* to arrange; (: *fig: questione, lite)* to settle
▸ **accomodarsi** VIP: **le cose col tempo si accomoderanno** things will get sorted out in time
▸ **accomodarsi** VR **1** *(sedersi)* to sit down; **si accomodi!** *(venga avanti)* come in!; *(mi segua)* this way please!; *(si sieda)* please take a seat! **2** *(uso reciproco: accordarsi)*: **accomodarsi (con qn su qc)** to come to an agreement (with sb on sth)

> **LO SAPEVI...?**
> **accomodare** non si traduce mai con la parola inglese ***accommodate***

accompagnamento [akkompaɲɲa'mento] SM **1** *(Mus)* accompaniment; **senza accompagnamento** unaccompanied **2** *(Comm)*: **lettera di accompagnamento** accompanying letter **3** *(Dir)*: **indennità di accompagnamento** attendance allowance

accompagnare [akkompaɲ'ɲare] VT **1** *(gen)* to accompany, come *o* go with; *(Mus)* to accompany; **accompagnare qn a casa** to see sb home; **ti accompagno** I'll come with you; **ti accompagno io all'aeroporto** I'll take you to the airport; **mi ha accompagnato a casa in macchina** she took me home in her car; **accompagnare qn alla porta** to show sb out; **accompagnare qn al piano** to accompany sb on the piano; **accompagnare un regalo con un biglietto** to put in *o* send a card with a present **2** *(fig: seguire)* to follow; **accompagnare qn con lo sguardo** to follow sb with one's eyes; **accompagnare la porta** to close the door gently; **accompagnare il colpo** *(Tennis)* to follow through
▸ **accompagnarsi** VIP *(armonizzarsi)* to go well together; **accompagnarsi a** *(colori)* to go with, match; *(cibi)* to go with;
▸ **accompagnarsi** VR *(frequentare)*: **accompagnarsi a qn** to associate with sb

accompagnatore, trice [akkompaɲɲa'tore] SM/F **1** companion, escort; **il suo accompagnatore** her escort **2** *(Mus)* accompanist **3** *(Sport)* team manager; **accompagnatore turistico** courier

accomunare [akkomu'nare] VT **1** *(persone)* to unite, join; **molti interessi ci accomunano** we have many interests in common; **non voglio che mi si accomuni a lui** I don't want to be associated with him **2** *(ricchezze, idee)* to pool, share

acconciatura [akkontʃa'tura] SF *(pettinatura)* hairstyle; *(ornamento)* headdress

accondiscendente [akkondiʃʃen'dɛnte] AGG affable

accondiscendere [akkondiʃ'ʃendere] VI IRREG *(aus* **avere**) **accondiscendere a** to agree to, consent to

accondisceso, a [akkondiʃ'ʃeso] PP *di* **accondiscendere**

acconsentire [akkonsen'tire] VI *(aus* **avere**) **acconsentire (a)** to agree (to), consent (to); **ha acconsentito a darci le informazioni in suo possesso** he agreed to give us the information he had; **chi tace acconsente** *(Proverbio)* silence means consent

accontentare [akkonten'tare] VT to satisfy; **cercare di accontentare tutti** to try to please everybody; **è molto difficile da accontentare** she's very difficult to please
▸ **accontentarsi** VIP: **accontentarsi (di)** to content o.s. (with); **mi dovrò accontentare di vederlo in TV** I'll have to make do with seeing it on TV; *(essere soddisfatto)* to be content (with), be satisfied (with); **accontentarsi di poco** to be easily pleased; **chi si accontenta gode** *(Proverbio)* well pleased is well served

acconto [ak'konto] SM *(sullo stipendio)* advance; *(caparra)* deposit, down payment; **versare una somma in acconto** to pay a sum of money as a deposit; **ho**

versato un acconto per il viaggio I've paid a deposit for the trip; **acconto di dividendo** *(Fin)* interim dividend

accoppiamento [akkoppja'mento] SM *(vedi vb)* pairing off; mating; coupling, connecting (up)

accoppiare [akkop'pjare] VT **1** *(persone, cose)* to pair off; **essere ben accoppiati** to be well matched, go well together **2** *(animali)* to mate **3** *(Tecn)* to couple, connect (up)
▶ **accoppiarsi** VR *(animali)* to mate; *(persone: formare una coppia)* to pair off

accoppiata [akkop'pjata] SF *(Ippica, anche fig)* each-way bet; **un'accoppiata vincente** a winning combination

accoppiatore [akkoppja'tore] SM *(Tecn)* coupler; **accoppiatore acustico** *(Inform)* acoustic coupler

accoramento [akkora'mento] SM distress; **nel vedere il suo accoramento fui commosso** when I saw how heartbroken he was I was filled with pity

accoratamente [akkorata'mente] AVV heartbrokenly

accorato, a [akko'rato] AGG heartfelt

accorciare [akkor'tʃare] VT to shorten; **far accorciare una gonna** to have a skirt shortened; **devo accorciare questi jeans** I need to shorten these jeans
▶ **accorciarsi** VIP to grow *o* get shorter; **le giornate si stanno accorciando** the days are getting shorter

accorciata [akkor'tʃata] SF: **dare un'accorciata a** *(gonna, tenda)* to shorten; *(capelli, frangia)* to trim

accordare [akkor'dare] VT **1** *(concedere)*: **accordare qc a qn** to grant sb sth *o* sth to sb **2** *(Mus)* to tune **3** *(Gramm)*: **accordare qc (con qc)** to make sth agree (with sth)
▶ **accordarsi** VR *(uso reciproco: mettersi d'accordo)* **accordarsi (con qn su *o* per qc)** to agree (on sth with sb)
▶ **accordarsi** VIP *(intonarsi: sogg: colore)*: **accordarsi (con qc)** to match (sth)

accordata [akkor'data] SF *(Mus)*: **dare un'accordata a** to tune up

accordatore, trice [akkorda'tore] SM/F piano tuner

accordatura [akkorda'tura] SF *(Mus)* tuning

accordo [ak'kɔrdo] SM **1** *(gen, Gramm)* agreement; *(armonia)* harmony; **andare d'accordo (con qn)** to get on well (with sb); **vanno d'accordo** they get on well together; **non vado d'accordo con i miei** I don't get on well with my parents; **essere d'accordo** to agree, be in agreement; **su questo siamo tutti d'accordo** we all agree on this; **mettersi d'accordo (con qn)** to agree *o* come to an agreement (with sb); **mettersi d'accordo per fare qc** to arrange to do sth; **ci siamo messi d'accordo per andare al cinema** we arranged to go to the cinema; **rimanere d'accordo** to agree; **siamo rimasti d'accordo che sarebbe venuto a prendermi** we agreed that he'd come and pick me up; **d'accordo!** agreed!, all right!, O.K.! *(fam)*; **sono d'accordissimo** I quite agree; **decidere di comune accordo di fare qc** to make a joint decision to do sth; **prendere accordi con** to reach an agreement with; **stringere un accordo** to reach an agreement **2** *(Mus)* chord; **conosci gli accordi di quella canzone?** can you play that song?
■ **accordo commerciale** trade agreement; **accordo di esclusiva** exclusive agency agreement; **Accordo generale sulle tariffe doganali ed il commercio** General Agreement on Tariffs and Trade

accorgersi [ak'kɔrdʒersi] VIP IRREG: **accorgersi di** *(notare)* to notice; *(capire)* to realize; **accorgersi che** to notice (*o* realize) that; **non si sono accorti di niente** they didn't notice anything; **si è accorto del furto solo il giorno dopo** he only noticed it had been stolen the next day; **mi sono accorto subito che qualcosa non andava** I immediately realized something was wrong

accorgimento [akkordʒi'mento] SM **1** *(espediente)* trick, device **2** *(astuzia)* shrewdness *no pl*

accorrere [ak'korrere] VI IRREG *(aus* **essere***)* **accorrere (a)** to rush up (to), hurry (to), run up (to); **la gente accorreva da tutte le direzioni** people came running from all directions; **accorrere in aiuto di qn** to rush to sb's aid

accorsi [ak'korsi] VB **1** *vedi* **accorgersi** **2** *vedi* **accorrere**

accorso, a [ak'korso] PP *di* **accorrere**

accortamente [akkorta'mente] AVV *(con avvedutezza)* wisely, sensibly; *(con astuzia)* shrewdly

accortezza [akkor'tettsa] SF *(avvedutezza)* good sense; *(astuzia)* shrewdness

accorto, a [ak'kɔrto] PP *di* **accorgersi**
■ AGG shrewd, alert; **stare accorto** to be on one's guard

accostamento [akkosta'mento] SM *(di colori ecc)* combination

accostare [akkos'tare] VT **1** **accostare qc a qc** *(mettere vicino: oggetto)* to move sth near sth; (: *colori, stili)* to match sth with sth; *(appoggiare: scala)* to lean sth against sth; **accosta la sedia al tavolo** move your chair nearer the table; **ha accostato la tazza alle labbra** he put the cup to his lips **2** *(avvicinare: persona)* to approach, come up to **3** *(socchiudere: persiane)* to half-close; (: *porta)* to push (*o* pull) to; **lasciare la porta accostata** to leave the door ajar; **ha accostato le imposte** he half-closed the shutters
■ VI *(aus* **avere***)* **1** **accostare (a)** *(Aut)* to draw up (at); *(Naut)* to come alongside; **accosti per favore!** pull in, please! **2** *(Naut: modificare la rotta)* to alter course
▶ **accostarsi** VR **1** *(andare o venire vicino)* **accostarsi (a)** to approach, go (*o* come) nearer; **accostarsi a qc/qn** *(Aut)* to draw up at sth/next to sb; *(Naut)* to come alongside **2** *(fig: abbracciare: fede, religione)* **accostarsi (a)** to turn to; (: *idee politiche)* to come to agree with **3** *(somigliare)* **accostarsi (a)** to be like, resemble

account [ə'kaʊnt] SM INV *(Inform: codice)* ISP account number; **account utente** user account; **account Internet** Internet account

accovacciarsi [akkovat'tʃarsi] VR to crouch (down)

accozzaglia [akkot'tsaʎʎa] SF *(pegg: di persone)* odd assortment; (: *di oggetti, colori, idee)* jumble, hotchpotch

accrebbi *ecc* [ak'krebbi] VB *vedi* **accrescere**

accreditare [akkredi'tare] VT **1** *(Comm, Fin)*: **accreditare qc a *o* a favore di qn** to credit sb with sth; **accreditare su un conto** to credit to an account **2** *(convalidare)* to confirm; (: *voce)* to substantiate; (: *notizia)* to confirm the truth of **3** *(diplomatico)* to accredit
▶ **accreditarsi** VIP *(teoria ecc)* to gain ground *o* credence

accreditato, a AGG *(diplomatico, giornalista)* accredited; *(notizie)* confirmed

accredito [ak'kredito] SM *(Comm, Fin: atto)* crediting; (: *effetto)* credit

accrescere [ak'kreʃʃere] VB IRREG
■ VT to increase
▶ **accrescersi** VIP to grow, increase

Aa

accrescimento [akkreʃʃi'mento] SM increase, growth
accrescitivo, a [akkreʃʃi'tivo] AGG, SM (*Gramm*) augmentative
accresciuto, a [akkreʃʃuto] PP *di* **accrescere**
accucciarsi [akkut'tʃarsi] VR (*cane*) to lie down; (*persona*) to crouch down
accudire [akku'dire] VI (*aus* **avere**) **accudire a** to attend to
■ VT to look after
acculturarsi [akkultu'rarsi] VIP (*Sociol*) to integrate, become integrated
acculturazione [akkulturat'tsjone] SF (*Sociol*) acculturation, integration
accumulare [akkumu'lare] VT (*gen*) to accumulate; (*energia*) to store; **il treno ha accumulato un ritardo di 3 ore** the train is running 3 hours late; **accumulare degli arretrati** to have backpay due *o* owing
▶ **accumularsi** VIP to accumulate; (*Fin*) to accrue
accumulatore [akkumula'tore] SM (*Elettr*) accumulator, (storage) battery
accumulazione [akkumulat'tsjone] SF (*vedi vb*) accumulation; storage
accumulo [ak'kumulo] SM accumulation
accuratamente [akkurata'mente] AVV carefully, thoroughly
accuratezza [akkura'tettsa] SF (*precisione*) accuracy; (*diligenza*) care, thoroughness
accurato, a [akku'rato] AGG (*preciso*) accurate; (*diligente*) careful, thorough; **una descrizione accurata** a detailed description; **un lavoro accurato** a careful piece of work
accusa [ak'kuza] SF (*gen*) accusation; (*Dir*) charge; **fare** *o* **muovere un'accusa a qn** to make an accusation against sb; **l'accusa** *or* **la pubblica accusa** (*Dir*) the prosecution; **mettere qn sotto accusa** (*Dir*) to indict sb; **in stato di accusa** (*Dir*) committed for trial
accusabile [akku'zabile] AGG (*Dir*) chargeable
accusare [akku'zare] VT **1** (*incolpare*): **accusare qn di (fare) qc** to accuse sb of (doing) sth; **mi ha accusato di avergli rotto lo stereo** he accused me of breaking his stereo; **accusare qn/qc di qc** (*biasimare*) to blame sb/sth for sth; **accusare qn di qc** (*Dir*) to charge sb with sth **2** (*sentire: dolore*) to feel; (*mostrare*): **accusare la fatica** to show signs of exhaustion; **ha accusato il colpo** (*fig*) you could see that he had felt the blow **3** (*Comm*): **accusare ricevuta (di)** to acknowledge receipt (of)
accusativo [akkuza'tivo] AGG, SM (*Gramm*) accusative
accusato, a [akku'zato] SM/F accused
accusatore, trice [akkuza'tore] AGG accusing
■ SM/F accuser; (*Dir*) prosecutor
acerbo, a [a'tʃɛrbo] AGG (*non maturo: frutto*) unripe; (*: fig: bellezza*) adolescent; (*: persona*) very young
acero ['atʃero] SM maple; **acero campestre** field maple
acerrimamente [atʃerrima'mente] AVV very fiercely
acerrimo, a [a'tʃɛrrimo] AGG bitter
acetato [atʃe'tato] SM acetate
acetilene [atʃeti'lɛne] SM acetylene, ethyne
aceto [a'tʃeto] SM vinegar; **sotto aceto** pickled; **mettere sotto aceto** to pickle; **aceto balsamico** balsamic vinegar
acetone [atʃe'tone] SM (*Chim*) acetone; (*per unghie*) nail varnish remover
acetosa [atʃe'tosa] SF (*Bot*) sorrel
acetosella [atʃeto'sɛlla] SF (*Bot*) wood sorrel
Achille [a'kille] SM Achilles
ACI ['atʃi] SIGLA M (= **Automobile Club d'Italia**) ≈ AA (*Brit*), ≈ AAA (*Am*)
acidamente [atʃida'mente] AVV (*rispondere*) acidly, tartly
acidificare [atʃidifi'kare] VT, VI (*aus* **essere**) to acidify
acidificazione [atʃidifikat'tsjone] SF acidification
acidità [atʃidi'ta] SF INV (*vedi agg*) acidity, sourness, tartness; **acidità (di stomaco)** heartburn
acido, a ['atʃido] AGG (*anche fig*) acid, sour, tart; (*Chim*) acid; **latte acido** sour milk; **giallo/verde acido** acid yellow/green
■ SM acid; **sapere di acido** to taste sour
■ **acido acetico** acetic acid; **acido acetilsalicilico** acetylsalicylic acid; **acido cloridrico** hydrogen chloride; **acido lisergico** lysergic acid; **acido muriatico** hydrochloric acid; **acido solfidrico** hydrogen sulphide; **acido solforoso** sulphurous acid
acidulo, a [a'tʃidulo] AGG slightly sour, slightly acid
acino ['atʃino] SM: **acino (d'uva)** grape
aclassista, i, e [aklas'sista] AGG (*Pol*) classless
ACLI ['akli] SIGLA FPL (= **Associazioni Cristiane dei Lavoratori Italiani**) *Catholic Association of Italian Workers*
acme ['akme] SF acme, peak; (*Med*) crisis
acne ['akne] SF (*anche:* **acne giovanile**) acne
ACNUR ['aknur] SIGLA M (= **Alto Commissariato delle Nazioni Unite per i Rifugiati**) UNHCR (= *United Nations High Commission for Refugees*)
acqua ['akkwa] SF **1** (*gen*) water; (*pioggia*) rain; **le acque** SFPL (*Med*) the waters; **mi dai un bicchiere d'acqua, per favore?** could I have a glass of water please?; **prendere l'acqua** to get caught in the rain, get wet; **far la cura delle acque** to go to a spa **2** (*fraseologia*): **acqua, acqua!** (*in giochi*) you're cold!; **acqua in bocca!** mum's the word!; **(all')acqua e sapone** (*faccia, ragazza: senza trucco*) without makeup; (*: semplice*) natural; **buttare acqua sul fuoco** to pour oil on troubled waters; **è sempre stata un'acqua cheta** she has always seemed a quiet one; **fare acqua (da tutte le parti)** (*situazione, posizione*) to be shaky; **la sua versione dei fatti fa acqua da tutte le parti** his version of what happened won't hold water; **essere con** *o* **avere l'acqua alla gola** to be snowed under; **tirare acqua al proprio mulino** to feather one's own nest; **è acqua passata** that's (ancient) history; **è passata molta acqua sotto i ponti** a lot of water has flowed under the bridge; **trovarsi** *o* **navigare in cattive acque** to be in deep water
■ **acqua di calce** limewater; **acqua di colonia** eau de Cologne, cologne; **acqua corrente** running water; **acqua distillata** distilled water; **acqua dolce** fresh water; **acqua gassata** fizzy water; **acqua di mare** sea water; **acqua minerale** mineral water; **acqua ossigenata** hydrogen peroxide; **acqua pesante** (*Fis*) heavy water; **acqua piovana** rain water; **acqua potabile** drinking water; **acqua ragia** = **acquaragia**; **acqua di rose** rose water; **all'acqua di rose** mild; **acqua del rubinetto** tap water; **acqua salata** salt water; **acqua santa** = **acquasanta**; **acqua sorgiva** *o* **di sorgente** spring water; **acqua tonica** tonic water; **acque superficiali** (*Geog*) surface runoff *sg*; **acque territoriali** territorial waters *pl*
acquaforte [akkwa'fɔrte] SF (*pl* **acqueforti**) etching
acquaio, ai [ak'kwajo] SM (kitchen) sink
acquamarina [akkwama'rina] SF (*pietra, colore*) aquamarine
acquapark [akkwa'park] SM INV water park
acquaplano SM aquaplane

acquaragia [akkwa'radʒa] SF turpentine
acquarello [akkwa'rello] SM = acquerello
acquario, ri [ak'kwarjo] SM **1** (*vasca per pesci, edificio*) aquarium **2** (*Astrol*): **Acquario** Aquarius; **essere dell'Acquario** to be Aquarius *o* (an) Aquarian
acquartierare [akkwartje'rare] VT
▶ **acquartierarsi** VR (*Mil*) to quarter
acquasanta [akkwa'santa] SF holy water
acquasantiera [akkwasan'tjɛra] SF holy water font
acquascooter [akkwas'kuter] SM INV Jet Ski®
acquatico, a, ci, che [ak'kwatiko] AGG aquatic; (*sport, sci*) water *attr*; **sport acquatici** water sports; **uccello acquatico** waterfowl
acquattarsi [akkwat'tarsi] VR to crouch (down)
acquavite [akkwa'vite] SF (*pl* **acquaviti** *o* **acqueviti**) spirit
acquazzone [akkwat'tsone] SM downpour
acquedotto [akkwe'dotto] SM (*conduttura*) aqueduct; (*intero sistema*) water system; **un acquedotto romano** a Roman aqueduct
acqueo, a ['akkweo] AGG: **vapore acqueo** water vapour (*Brit*) *o* vapor (*Am*); **umore acqueo** aqueous humour (*Brit*) *o* humor (*Am*)
acquerellista, i, e [akkwerel'lista] SM/F watercolourist (*Brit*) *o* watercolorist (*Am*)
acquerello [akkwe'rɛllo] SM (*tecnica*) watercolours (*Brit*), watercolors (*Am*); (*opera*) watercolour (*Brit*), watercolor (*Am*)
acquerugiola [akkwe'rudʒola] SF drizzle
acquiescente [akkwjeʃ'ʃɛnte] AGG acquiescent
acquiescenza [akkwjeʃ'ʃɛntsa] SF acquiescence
acquietare [akkwje'tare] VT (*dolore*) to ease; (*desiderio, fame*) to appease
▶ **acquietarsi** VIP to calm down
acquifero, a [ak'kwifero] AGG (*Geol*) aquiferous, water-bearing; **falda acquifera** aquifer
acquirente [akkwi'rɛnte] SM/F buyer
acquisire [akkwi'zire] VT (*diritto, proprietà*) to acquire; (*qualità, cognizione*) to acquire, gain
acquisitivo, a [akkwizi'tivo] AGG (*Dir*): **contratto acquisitivo** purchase contract
acquisito, a [akkwi'zito] AGG acquired; **diritto acquisito** acquired right
acquisizione [akkwizit'tsjone] SF acquisition
acquistare [akkwis'tare] VT **1** (*casa, mobili*) to buy, purchase; (*beni, diritti*) to acquire; **acquistare a rate** to buy on hire purchase; **acquistare in contanti** to buy for cash **2** (*fig: esperienza, pratica ecc*) to gain; **acquistare importanza** to become important; **acquistare terreno** to gain ground
■ VI (*aus* **avere**) to improve; **acquistare in bellezza** to become more beautiful; **ha acquistato in salute** his health has improved
acquisto [ak'kwisto] SM purchase; **andare a fare acquisti** to go shopping; **fare molti acquisti** to buy a lot of things; **fare un buon/cattivo acquisto** (*anche fig*) to get a good/bad buy; **ecco il nostro ultimo acquisto** (*persona*) here is our latest recruit; **campagna acquisti** (*Sport*) transfer season; **potere d'acquisto** (*Econ*) buying power; **acquisto d'impulso** impulse buying; **acquisto rateale** instalment purchase, hire purchase (*Brit*)
acquitrino [akkwi'trino] SM bog, marsh
acquitrinoso, a [akkwitri'noso] AGG boggy, marshy
acquolina [akkwo'lina] SF: **far venire l'acquolina in bocca a qn** to make sb's mouth water; **solo a vederlo ti fa venire l'acquolina in bocca!** it makes your mouth water just to look at it!; **ho l'acquolina in bocca** *or* **mi viene l'acquolina in bocca** my mouth is watering
acquoso, a [ak'kwoso] AGG watery; **soluzione acquosa** aqueous solution
acre ['akre] AGG (*sapore, odore*) acrid, pungent; (*fig: polemica*) bitter; (*: critica*) harsh, biting
acredine [a'krɛdine] SF (*fig*) bitterness
acrilico, a, ci, che [a'kriliko] AGG, SM acrylic
acrimonia [akri'mɔnja] SF acrimony
acritico, a, ci, che [a'kritiko] AGG uncritical
acrobata, i, e [a'krɔbata] SM/F acrobat
acrobatica [akro'batika] SF acrobatics *sg*
acrobaticamente [akrobatika'mente] AVV acrobatically
acrobatico, a, ci, che [akro'batiko] AGG (*ginnastica*) acrobatic; (*Aer*) aerobatic
acrobazia [akrobat'tsia] SF **1** (*ginnica*) acrobatic feat; **fare acrobazie** (*anche fig*) to perform acrobatics **2** (*aerea*) aerobatic feat; **acrobazie aeree** aerobatics
acronimo [a'krɔnimo] SM acronym
acropoli [a'krɔpoli] SF INV: **l'Acropoli** the Acropolis
acuire [aku'ire] VT to sharpen; (*desiderio*) to increase
▶ **acuirsi** VIP (*gen*) to increase; (*crisi, dissidio*) to worsen
aculeo [a'kuleo] SM (*di riccio, istrice, pianta*) prickle; (*di vespa, ape*) sting
acume [a'kume] SM perspicacity; **con grande acume** with great shrewdness; **non ci vuole tanto acume per capire che...** you don't need to be a genius to realize that ...
acuminato, a [akumi'nato] AGG sharp
acustica [a'kustika] SF (*scienza*) acoustics *sg*; (*di ambiente*) acoustics *pl*; **la sala ha un'ottima acustica** the hall has excellent acoustics
acusticamente [akustika'mente] AVV acoustically
acustico, a, ci, che [a'kustiko] AGG acoustic; **apparecchio acustico** hearing aid; **chitarra acustica** acoustic guitar; **cornetto acustico** ear trumpet
acutamente [akuta'mente] AVV (*osservare, rilevare*) acutely, sharply
acutezza [aku'tettsa] SF (*vedi agg*) acuteness; keenness; intensity; sharpness; shrillness; (*Mus*) high pitch
acutizzare [akutid'dzare] VT to intensify
▶ **acutizzarsi** VIP (*crisi, malattia*) to become worse, worsen
acuto, a [a'kuto] AGG **1** (*Mat, Med, Gramm*) acute; (*vista, udito, senso dell'umorismo*) keen; (*desiderio, fastidio, sofferenza*) intense; (*mente, osservazione, dolore*) sharp, acute; **ho sentito un dolore acuto al braccio** I felt a sharp pain in my arm **2** (*suono, voce*) shrill, high-pitched, piercing; (*Mus*) high
■ SM (*Mus*) high note
AD ABBR (= Anno Domini) AD
ad [ad] PREP (*davanti a vocale*) = **a**
adagiare [ada'dʒare] VT to lay *o* set down carefully
▶ **adagiarsi** VR (*mettersi comodo*) to make o.s. comfortable; (*sdraiarsi*) to lie down, stretch out; **si è adagiato (nell'ozio)** (*fig*) he just sat back (in this situation)
adagio[1] [a'dadʒo] AVV (*lentamente*) slowly; (*con cura*) with care, gently; **vacci adagio con la birra!** go easy on the beer!; **adagio!** easy does it!; **adagio adagio** gradually
adagio[2]**, gi** [a'dadʒo] SM **1** (*Mus*) adagio **2** (*proverbio*) adage, saying

Aa

adamitico, a, ci, che [ada'mitiko] AGG: **in costume adamitico** in one's birthday suit
Adamo [a'damo] SM Adam
adattabile [adat'tabile] AGG (*persona*) adaptable
adattabilità [adattabili'ta] SF adaptability
adattamento [adatta'mento] SM (*Bio, Med, di romanzo*) adaptation; (*di stanza, edificio*) conversion; **avere spirito di adattamento** to be adaptable
adattare [adat'tare] VT (*gen*): **adattare qc (a)** to adapt sth (to); (*camera*) to convert sth (into); **si era fatta adattare il cappotto della madre** she had her mother's coat altered to fit her
▶ **adattarsi** VR **1** (*adeguarsi*) **adattarsi (a)** (*ambiente, situazione, tempi*) to adapt (to); **si adatta facilmente** she adapts easily, she's very adaptable; **si sta adattando alla situazione** she is adapting to the situation **2** (*accontentarsi*) **adattarsi a qc/a fare qc** to make the best of sth/of doing sth; **dobbiamo adattarci** we'll have to make the best of it;
▶ **adattarsi** VIP (*addirsi*) **adattarsi a** to be suitable for
adattatore [adatta'tore] SM (*Elettr*) adapter, adaptor
adatto, a [a'datto] AGG: **adatto (a)** (*giusto*) right (for); (*appropriato*) suitable (for); **è la persona più adatta per** *o* **a fare questo lavoro** he is the most suitable person for this job *o* to do this job; **non è il momento adatto** it's not the right moment; **un vestito adatto all'occasione** a suitable dress for the occasion
addebitare [addebi'tare] VT: **addebitare qc a qn** to charge sth to sb; **mi hanno addebitato un'interurbana** they charged a long-distance call to me; (*fig: incolpare*) to blame sb for sth; **addebitare qc in conto a qn** (*Comm*) to debit sb's account with sth
addebito [ad'debito] SM **1** (*Comm*) debit **2** (*imputazione*) blame; **muovere (un) addebito di qc a qn** to accuse sb of sth
addenda [ad'dɛnda] SMPL addenda
addendo [ad'dɛndo] SM (*Mat*) addend
addensamento [addensa'mento] SM (*vedi vb*) thickening; gathering
addensante [adden'sante] SM (*Chim*) thickener
addensare [adden'sare] VT to thicken
▶ **addensarsi** VIP (*nebbia*) to get thicker; (*nuvole, folla*) to gather; (*salsa, sugo*) to thicken
addentare [adden'tare] VT to bite into; **ha addentato il panino** he bit into the roll
addentrarsi [adden'trarsi] VIP: **addentrarsi in** (*posto*) to penetrate, go into; (*fig: problema*) to go (deeply) into; **si sono addentrati nel bosco** they went deep into the wood
addentro [ad'dentro] AVV (*fig*): **essere (molto) addentro a** *o* **in qc** to be well up on sth, be well-versed in sth
addestrabile [addes'trabile] AGG that can be trained
addestramento [addestra'mento] SM (*gen*) training; (*Mil*) drill; (*Equitazione: specialità*) dressage; **il corso di addestramento dura un mese** the training course lasts a month; **addestramento professionale** vocational training
addestrare [addes'trare] VT: **addestrare qn/qc a** *o* **per qc** to train sb/sth for sth; **quel cane è stato addestrato alla guardia** that dog has been trained as a watchdog
▶ **addestrarsi** VR: **addestrarsi (a** *o* **in qc)** to train (in sth), practise (*Brit*) *o* practice (*Am*) sth
addetto, a [ad'detto] PP *di* **addirsi**
■ AGG: **addetto a** (*persona*) employed on, in charge of; (*oggetto*) intended for
■ SM/F **1 l'addetto alla manutenzione** the maintenance man; **gli addetti ai lavori** authorized personnel *sg*; (*fig*) those in the know; **"vietato l'ingresso ai non addetti ai lavori"** "authorized personnel only"; **addetti alle pulizie** cleaning staff; **addetto stampa** press officer; **addetto al telex** telex operator **2** (*Diplomazia*) attaché; **addetto commerciale** commercial attaché; **addetto militare** military attaché

> **LO SAPEVI...?**
> **addetto** non si traduce mai con la parola inglese ***addict***

addì [ad'di] AVV (*Amm*): **addì 31 luglio 2004** on (the) 31st (of) July 2004, on July 31st 2004
addiaccio [ad'djattʃo] SM: **all'addiaccio** (*Mil*) without shelter; **dormire all'addiaccio** to sleep in the open
addietro [ad'djɛtro] AVV (*letter: nel passato, prima*) before, ago; **l'aveva conosciuto anni addietro** she'd met him years before
addio [ad'dio] ESCL goodbye, farewell (*old*); **dire addio a qn/qc** (*anche fig*) to say goodbye to sb/sth; **se arrivano i bambini, addio pace!** if the children turn up, that'll be the end of our peace and quiet!
■ SM goodbye, farewell; **serata d'addio** (*Teatro*) farewell performance; **addio al celibato** stag night; **addio al nubilato** hen night *o* party
addirittura [addirit'tura] AVV (*perfino*) even; **gli hanno addirittura proibito di uscire di casa** they've even forbidden him to leave the house; **il suo comportamento è addirittura ridicolo** his behaviour is downright ridiculous; **addirittura?!** really!; **gli hanno proibito di uscire di casa – addirittura?!** they've forbidden him to leave the house – really?!
addirsi [ad'dirsi] VIP IRREG E DIF: **addirsi a** to suit, be suitable for; **questo comportamento non si addice a un padre di famiglia** such behaviour doesn't suit a man with a family
Addis Abeba [ad'dis a'beba] SF Addis Ababa
additare [addi'tare] VT to point out; (*fig*) to expose
additivo, a [addi'tivo] AGG, SM additive
addivenire VI IRREG (*aus* **essere**) **addivenire a** to come to
addizionale [addittsjo'nale] AGG additional
■ SF (*anche:* **imposta addizionale**) surtax
addizionare [addittsjo'nare] VT (*Mat*) to add (up); **addizionare qc a qc** to add sth to sth
addizionatrice [addittsjona'tritʃe] SF adding machine
addizione [addit'tsjone] SF (*Mat, Chim*) addition; **fare un'addizione** to do a sum

> **LO SAPEVI...?**
> **addizione** non si traduce mai con la parola inglese ***addiction***

addobbare [addob'bare] VT **1** (*chiesa, sala, vetrina*) to decorate; **addobbare a festa** to deck out **2** (*scherz: persona*) to put on one's glad rags
▶ **addobbarsi** VR (*scherz*) to dress up
addobbo [ad'dɔbbo] SM decoration; **addobbi natalizi** Christmas decorations
addolcire [addol'tʃire] VT **1** (*caffè, bevanda*) to sweeten **2** (*fig: mitigare: brutta notizia, carattere*) to soften; (*: calmare*) to soothe, calm **3** (*Tecn: acqua*) to soften; (*: acciaio*) to temper
▶ **addolcirsi** VIP (*fig: carattere, persona*) to mellow, soften
addolcitore [addoltʃi'tore] SM water softener (*device*)

addolorare [addolo'rare] VT to grieve, sadden; **la notizia mi ha addolorato molto** I was very sad to hear the news; **mi ha addolorato molto sapere che...** I was very sad to hear that ...
▶ **addolorarsi** VIP: **addolorarsi (per)** to be saddened (by)
Addolorata SF (*Rel*): **l'Addolorata** Our Lady of Sorrows
addolorato, a [addolo'rato] AGG upset, distressed
addome [ad'dɔme] SM abdomen
addomesticabile [addomesti'kabile] AGG which can be tamed; **poco addomesticabile** difficult to tame
addomesticamento [addomestika'mento] SM taming
addomesticare [addomesti'kare] VT (*anche fig*) to tame; **è riuscita ad addomesticare il marito** she's managed to make her husband more civilized
addomesticato, a [addomesti'kato] AGG tame
addominale [addomi'nale] AGG abdominal; **un dolore addominale** an abdominal pain
■ **addominali** SMPL (*muscoli*) stomach muscles; (*esercizi*) sit-ups; **fare un po' di addominali** to do sit-ups
addormentare [addormen'tare] VT (*anche fig*): **(far) addormentare** to send to sleep
▶ **addormentarsi** VIP to go to sleep, fall asleep; **non voleva addormentarsi** he didn't want to go to sleep; **mi sono addormentato davanti alla TV** I fell asleep in front of the TV; **mi si è addormentato un piede** my foot has gone to sleep
addormentato, a [addormen'tato] AGG sleeping, asleep; (*fig: tardo*) stupid, dopey; **un bambino addormentato** a sleeping baby; **ero ancora mezzo addormentato** I was still half asleep
addossare [addos'sare] VT **1** (*appoggiare*): **addossare qc a qc** to lean sth against sth **2** (*attribuire*): **addossare la colpa/la responsabilità di qc a qn** to lay the blame/the responsibility for sth on sb; **si addossò la colpa** he took the blame
▶ **addossarsi** VR (*appoggiarsi*) **addossarsi a** to stand against; **stava addossato al muro** he was leaning against the wall; **si sono addossati gli uni agli altri** they crowded together
addosso [ad'dɔsso] AVV (*sulla persona*) on; **avere addosso** to wear; **aveva addosso un vecchio impermeabile** she was wearing an old raincoat; **mettersi addosso il cappotto** to put one's coat on; **addosso non ho molti soldi** I don't have much money on me; **ho una tale sfortuna addosso** I've had such a run of bad luck; **farsela addosso** to wet o.s.; **addosso a** PREP (*sopra*) on; (*molto vicino*) right next to; **uno addosso all'altro** on top of each other; **gli ombrelloni sono praticamente uno addosso all'altro** the beach umbrellas are practically on top of each other; **andare (o venire) addosso a** (*Aut: altra macchina*) to run into; (*: pedone*) to run over; **cadere addosso a qn** to fall on top of sb; **mettere gli occhi addosso a qn/qc** to take quite a fancy to sb/sth; **mettere le mani addosso a qn** (*picchiare*) to hit sb, lay hands on sb; (*catturare*) to seize sb; (*molestare*) to touch sb up; **dare addosso a qn** (*fig*) to attack sb; **il mio capo mi sta addosso** my boss is breathing down my neck
addotto, a [ad'dotto] PP *di* **addurre**
adduco *ecc* [ad'duko] VB *vedi* **addurre**
addurre [ad'durre] VT IRREG **1** (*Dir: fatti, prove, ragioni*) to produce **2** (*citare: esempi, scuse, argomenti, fatti*) to advance, put forward
addussi *ecc* [ad'dussi] VB *vedi* **addurre**
Ade ['ade] SM Hades
adeguamento [adegwa'mento] SM adjustment
adeguare [ade'gware] VT: **adeguare qc (a)** (*stipendio*) to adjust sth (to); (*produzione, struttura*) to bring into line (with)
▶ **adeguarsi** VR (*conformarsi*) **adeguarsi (a)** to adapt (to)
adeguatamente [adegwata'mente] AVV (*pagare*) adequately, properly; (*rispondere*) satisfactorily; (*comportarsi*) properly
adeguatezza [adegwa'tettsa] SF (*vedi agg*) adequacy; suitability; fairness
adeguato, a [ade'gwato] AGG: **adeguato (a)** (*proporzionato*) adequate (to); (*adatto*) suitable (for); (*equo*) fair; **una preparazione adeguata** proper preparation; **un compenso adeguato** fair payment; **uno stipendio adeguato al mio titolo di studio** a salary appropriate to my qualifications
adempiere [a'dempjere] VT, VI (*aus* **avere**) **adempiere (a)** (*promessa*) to carry out, fulfil (*Brit*), fulfill (*Am*); (*ordine*) to carry out; **adempiere al proprio dovere** to do one's duty
adempimento [adempi'mento] SM (*di dovere, ordine*) carrying out; (*di promessa*) fulfilment (*Brit*), fulfillment (*Am*); **nell'adempimento del proprio dovere** in the performance of one's duty
adempire [adem'pire] VT = **adempiere**
Aden ['aden] SF Aden; **il golfo di Aden** the Gulf of Aden
adenoidi [ade'nɔidi] SFPL adenoids
adenoma, i [ade'nɔma] SM adenoma
adepto, a [a'dɛpto] SM/F disciple, follower
aderente [ade'rɛnte] AGG **1** (*abiti*) tight-fitting **2** (*fig: fedele*): **una traduzione aderente al testo originale** a translation faithful to the original
■ SM/F: **aderente (a)** follower (of), supporter (of)
aderenza [ade'rɛntsa] SF **1** (*gen, Med*) adhesion; (*Aut: di ruota*) grip **2** (*fig: conoscenze*): **aderenze** SFPL connections, contacts
aderire [ade'rire] VI (*aus* **avere**) **aderire (a)** **1** (*stare attaccato*) to adhere (to), stick (to); **aderire alla strada** (*Aut*) to grip the road **2** (*partito*) to join; (*idea*) to support **3** (*richiesta*) to agree to
adescamento [adeska'mento] SM (*Dir*) soliciting; (*lusinga*) enticement
adescare [ades'kare] VT **1** (*Dir*) to solicit; (*attirare*) to lure, entice **2** (*Tecn: pompa*) to prime
adesione [ade'zjone] SF **1** (*iscrizione: a partito*) joining; (*assenso*) agreement, acceptance; (*appoggio*) support; **dare/rifiutare la propria adesione ad un'iniziativa** to give one's support to/to refuse to support a proposal **2** (*Fis*) adhesion
adesività [adezivi'ta] SF adhesiveness
adesivo, a [ade'zivo] AGG adhesive; **nastro adesivo** sticky tape
■ SM **1** (*sostanza*) adhesive **2** (*anche*: **autoadesivo**) sticker; **faccio collezione di adesivi** I collect stickers
adesso [a'dɛsso] AVV (*ora*) now; (*poco fa*) just now; (*fra poco*) any moment now; **adesso non posso, sto studiando** I can't do it now, I'm studying; **e me lo dici adesso?** now you tell me!; **da adesso in poi** from now on; **per adesso** for the moment, for now
ad hoc [a'dɔk] AVV, AGG INV ad hoc
ad honorem [ado'nɔrem] AGG INV: **laurea ad honorem** honorary degree
adiacente [adja'tʃɛnte] AGG adjacent, adjoining;

Aa

adiacente a adjacent to
adiacenze [adja'tʃɛntse] SFPL vicinity *sg*, environs
adibire [adi'bire] VT: **adibire qc a** to use sth as; **questo edificio è adibito a deposito merci** this building is used as a goods depot; **la stanza era stata adibita a studio** the room had been used as a study
Adige ['adidʒe] SM: **l'Adige** the Adige
adipe ['adipe] SM (adipose) fat
adiposità [adiposi'ta] SF adiposity
adiposo, a [adi'poso] AGG (*Anat*) adipose
adirarsi [adi'rarsi] VIP: **adirarsi (con qn per qc)** to get angry (with sb over sth); **si è adirato moltissimo** he got very angry
adirato, a [adi'rato] AGG angry
adire [a'dire] VT (*Dir*): **adire le vie legali** to institute *o* commence legal proceedings; **adire un'eredità** to take legal possession of an inheritance
adito ['adito] SM: **dare adito a** (*sospetti*) to give rise to
adocchiare [adok'kjare] VT (*scorgere*) to catch sight of; (*desiderare*) to have one's eye on
adolescente [adoleʃ'ʃɛnte] AGG adolescent
■SM/F adolescent, teenager
adolescenza [adoleʃ'ʃɛntsa] SF adolescence
adolescenziale [adoleʃʃen'tsjale] AGG of adolescence
adombrare [adom'brare] VT (*fig*: *celare*) to veil, conceal
▶ **adombrarsi** VIP (*cavallo*) to shy; (*persona*: *offendersi*) to be offended; (: *insospettirsi*) to grow suspicious
Adone [a'done] SM Adonis; **un adone** (*fig*) an Adonis
adoperare [adope'rare] VT to use
▶ **adoperarsi** VR: **adoperarsi (per *o* per fare qc)** to make every effort (to do sth), strive (to do sth); **adoperarsi in favore di qn** to do one's best for sb
adorabile [ado'rabile] AGG adorable
adorabilmente [adorabil'mente] AVV adorably
adorare [ado'rare] VT (*gen*) to adore; (*Rel*) to adore, worship; **adoro le ciliegie!** I love cherries!
adorazione [adorat'tsjone] SF (*gen*) adoration; (*Rel*) worship, adoration
adornare [ador'nare] VT (*anche fig*): **adornare (di *o* con)** to adorn (with)
▶ **adornarsi** VR: **adornarsi (di *o* con)** to adorn o.s. (with)
adorno, a [a'dorno] AGG: **adorno (di)** adorned (with)
adottare [adot'tare] VT (*gen*) to adopt; (*libro di testo*) to choose, select; (*decisione, provvedimenti*) to pass; **è stato adottato** he was adopted; **dovremo adottare una soluzione diversa** we'll have to find another solution
adottivo, a [adot'tivo] AGG (*genitori*) adoptive; (*figlio, patria*) adopted
adozione [adot'tsjone] SF (*vedi vb*) adoption; selection; **si rende necessaria l'adozione di misure di sicurezza** security measures will have to be adopted; **adozione a distanza** child sponsorship
adrenalina [adrena'lina] SF adrenaline, epinephrine (*Am*)
adrenalinico, a, ci, che [adrena'liniko] AGG (*fig*: *vivace, eccitato*) charged-up
adriatico, a, ci, che [adri'atiko] AGG Adriatic
■SM: **l'Adriatico** the Adriatic
ADSL [adiɛsse'ɛlle] SIGLA M (*Inform*) ADSL (= *Asymmetric Digital Subscriber Line*)
adulare [adu'lare] VT to flatter
adulatore, trice [adula'tore] SM/F flatterer
adulatorio, ria, ri, rie [adula'tɔrjo] AGG flattering
adulazione [adulat'tsjone] SF flattery
adulterare [adulte'rare] VT to adulterate; (*fig*: *informazione*) to distort
adulterio, ri [adul'tɛrjo] SM adultery
adultero, a [a'dultero] AGG adulterous
■SM/F adulterer/adulteress
adulto, a [a'dulto] AGG adult; (*fig*) mature
■SM/F adult, grown-up
adunanza [adu'nantsa] SF meeting, assembly
adunare [adu'nare] VT
▶ **adunarsi** VIP to assemble, gather
adunata [adu'nata] SF (*Mil*) muster, parade
adunco, a, chi, che [a'dunko] AGG hooked
ADUSBEF [adus'bef] SIGLA M (= **Associazione Difesa Utenti Servizi Bancari e Finanziari**) *association that protects consumers from abuses by financial institutions*
aerare [ae'rare] VT (*arieggiare*) to ventilate; **"aerare il locale prima di soggiornarvi"** "ventilate the room before use"
aerazione [aerat'tsjone] SF **1** ventilation **2** (*Tecn*) aeration
aereo, a [a'ɛreo] AGG **1** (*gen, Aer, Posta*) air *attr*; (*navigazione, fotografia*) aerial; (*linea elettrica*) overhead *attr*; **traffico aereo** air traffic; **per via aerea** by airmail **2** (*Bot*: *radice*) aerial
■SM (*anche*: **aeroplano**) plane; **l'aereo era in ritardo** the plane was late; **viaggiare in aereo** to fly; **mi piace viaggiare in aereo** I like flying; **aereo da caccia** fighter (plane); **aereo da guerra** warplane; **aereo di linea** airliner; **aereo a reazione** jet (plane); **aereo da trasporto merci** cargo plane; **aereo da turismo** light aircraft *inv*
aerobica [ae'rɔbika] SF aerobics *sg*; **faccio aerobica due volte alla settimana** I do aerobics twice a week
aerobio, bi [ae'rɔbjo] SM aerobe
aerobus ['aerobus] SM INV airbus
aerodinamica [aerodi'namika] SF aerodynamics *sg*
aerodinamico, a, ci, che [aerodi'namiko] AGG (*Fis*) aerodynamic; (*affusolato*) streamlined
aerofagia [aerofa'dʒia] SF aerophagia
aerofotografia [aerofotogra'fia] SF aerial photography
aerogramma, i [aero'gramma] SM aerogramme, air letter
aeromobile [aero'mɔbile] SM aircraft *inv*, airliner
aeromodellismo [aeromodel'lizmo] SM aircraft modelling
aeromodello [aeromo'dɛllo] SM model aircraft
aeronauta, i [aero'nauta] SM pilot
aeronautica [aero'nautika] SF (*scienza*) aeronautics *sg*; **aeronautica civile** civil aviation; **aeronautica militare** air force
aeronautico, a, ci, che [aero'nautiko] AGG aeronautical
aeronavale [aerona'vale] AGG (*forze, manovre*) air and sea *attr*
aeroplano [aero'plano] SM (aero)plane (*Brit*), (air)plane (*Am*)
aeroporto [aero'pɔrto] SM airport; **ci vediamo in aeroporto** I'll meet you at the airport; **l'aeroporto di Heathrow** Heathrow Airport
aeroportuale [aeroportu'ale] AGG airport *attr*
aerorimessa [aerori'messa] SF hangar
aeroscalo [aeros'kalo] SM airstrip
aerosol [aero'sɔl] SM INV aerosol
aerospaziale [aerospat'tsjale] AGG aerospace
aerostatico, a, ci, che [aeros'tatiko] AGG aerostatic; **pallone aerostatico** air balloon
aerostato [ae'rɔstato] SM aerostat
aerostazione [aerostat'tsjone] SF airport (buildings)

aerotaxi [aero'taksi] SM INV air taxi
aerovia [aero'via] SF airway
AF SIGLA (= **alta frequenza**) HF
■ ABBR (*Amm*): = **assegni familiari**
afa ['afa] SF closeness; **c'è un'afa terribile** it's terribly close
afasia [afa'zia] N (*Med*) aphasia
affabile [af'fabile] AGG friendly
affabilità [affabili'ta] SF affability
affabilmente [affabil'mente] AVV affably
affaccendarsi [affattʃen'darsi] VR: **affaccendarsi a fare qc** to be busy doing sth, bustle about doing sth; **si affaccendava intorno ai fornelli** she was busy at the stove
affaccendato, a [affattʃen'dato] AGG busy; **sono molto affaccendato** I'm very busy
affacciarsi [affat'tʃarsi] VR (*sporgersi*): **affacciarsi (a)** to appear (at); **affacciarsi alla finestra** to appear at the window; **affacciarsi alla vita** (*bambino*) to come into the world; **un dubbio gli si affacciò alla mente** a sudden doubt came into his mind
■ VIP (*guardare*): **affacciarsi su** *or* **il balcone si affaccia sulla piazza** the balcony looks (out) onto the square
affamato, a [affa'mato] AGG starving, hungry; **affamato d'affetto** starved of affection
affannare [affan'nare] VT to leave breathless
▶ **affannarsi** VR (*preoccuparsi*) **affannarsi (per)** to worry (about), get worked up (about); (*sforzarsi*) **affannarsi a fare qc** to do one's utmost to do sth, hurry *o* race to do sth; **è inutile che ti affanni a trovar scuse** don't waste your breath looking for excuses
affanno [af'fanno] SM **1** breathlessness; **ho fatto le scale a piedi e mi è venuto l'affanno** I got out of breath going up the stairs, I was panting after walking up the stairs **2** (*preoccupazione*) worry
affannosamente [affannosa'mente] AVV (*respirare*) with difficulty; (*freneticamente*) anxiously
affannoso, a [affan'noso] AGG (*respiro*) laboured; (*fig*: *ricerca*: *di oggetto, regalo*) frantic; (: *della verità*) painstaking
affare [af'fare] SM **1** (*faccenda*) matter, affair; (*Dir*) case; **è stato un brutto affare** it was a nasty business; **questo non è affar tuo** this is none of your business; **sono affari miei** that's my business; **fatti gli affari tuoi!** mind your own business!; **affare di cuore** love affair; **affare di Stato** (*Pol, anche fig*) affair of state **2** (*Comm*: *transazione*) piece of business, (business) deal; (*occasione*) bargain; **affare fatto!** done!, it's a deal!; **concludere un affare** to conclude a (business) deal; **hai fatto un (buon) affare** you got a bargain; **a quel prezzo è proprio un affare** it's a real bargain at that price **3** (*fam*: *coso*) thing; **come funziona quest'affare?** how does this thing work? **4 affari** SMPL (*gen, Pol*) affairs; (*commercio*) business *sg*; **come vanno gli affari?** how's business?; **un viaggio d'affari** a business trip; **è qui per affari** he's here on business; **uomo d'affari** businessman; **ministro degli Affari Esteri** Foreign Secretary (*Brit*), Secretary of State (*Am*); **affari esteri** (*Pol*) external affairs
affarista, i, e [affa'rista] SM/F shrewd businessman/businesswoman; (*pegg*) profiteer, unscrupulous businessman/businesswoman
affascinante [affaʃʃi'nante] AGG (*uomo, donna*) terribly attractive; (*argomento, libro*) fascinating
affascinare [affaʃʃi'nare] VT (*ammaliare*) to bewitch, enchant; (*sedurre*) to charm, fascinate; **il racconto mi ha affascinato** I was charmed by the story
affastellare [affastel'lare] VT (*rami*) to tie up in bundles
affaticamento [affatika'mento] SM tiredness
affaticare [affati'kare] VT to tire; **la salita mi ha affaticato molto** the climb tired me out
▶ **affaticarsi** VR (*stancarsi*) to get tired; **non voglio affaticarmi troppo** I don't want to get too tired; **affaticarsi a fare qc** to tire o.s. out doing sth
affaticato, a [affati'kato] AGG tired
affatto [af'fatto] AVV (*interamente*) completely; **non...affatto** not ... at all; **non mi piace affatto** I don't like it at all; **non sei affatto divertente** you're not at all funny; **niente affatto!** not at all!
affermare [affer'mare] VT (*dichiarare*) to declare; (*diritti*) to assert; **afferma di essere innocente** he maintains that he is innocent; **ha affermato di averlo visto** she said she'd seen him; **affermò col capo** he nodded in agreement
▶ **affermarsi** VR (*imporsi*) to make o.s. *o* one's name known; **si è affermato come avvocato** he made his name as a lawyer
affermativamente [affermativa'mente] AVV in the affirmative, affirmatively
affermativo, a [afferma'tivo] AGG affirmative; **dare una risposta affermativa** to say yes
affermato, a [affer'mato] AGG established, well-known
affermazione [affermat'tsjone] SF **1** (*dichiarazione*) statement; (*di diritti, verità*) assertion **2** (*successo*) achievement; **una grande affermazione degli azzurri** a great triumph for the Italian team
afferrare [affer'rare] VT (*prendere*) to seize, grasp; (*fig*: *idea*) to grasp, get; **l'hanno afferrato per un braccio** they grabbed him by the arm; **afferrare un'occasione** to seize an opportunity; **afferrare un concetto** to get an idea; **afferri il concetto?** do you get the idea?; **non ho afferrato quello che hai detto** (*sentito*) I didn't get *o* catch what you said; (*capito*) I didn't understand what you said; **scusa, non ho afferrato il tuo nome** sorry, I didn't catch your name
▶ **afferrarsi** VR: **afferrarsi a** to cling to
Aff. Est. ABBR = Affari Esteri
affettare[1] [affet'tare] VT (*tagliare a fette*) to slice
affettare[2] [affet'tare] VT (*ostentare*) to affect
affettato[1]**, a** [affet'tato] AGG sliced
■ SM (sliced) cold meat (*ham ecc*)
affettato[2]**, a** [affet'tato] AGG (*lezioso*) affected
affettatrice [affetta'tritʃe] SF meat slicer
affettazione [affettat'tsjone] SF affectation
affettivamente [affettiva'mente] AVV: **essere affettivamente legato a** (*città, oggetto*) to be (sentimentally) attached to
affettivo, a [affet'tivo] AGG (*vita*) emotional; **la sfera affettiva** the area of feelings and emotions; **la vita affettiva** personal relationships; **avere un valore affettivo** to have sentimental value; **una collanina con un valore puramente affettivo** a little necklace with only sentimental value
affetto[1] [af'fɛtto] SM **1** (*sentimento*) affection; **trova difficile dimostrare il suo affetto** he finds it difficult to show affection; **con affetto** (*nelle lettere*) with love, affectionately yours **2** (*persona, cosa*) object of affection; **gli affetti familiari** one's nearest and dearest
affetto[2]**, a** [af'fɛtto] AGG: **essere affetto da** to suffer from
affettuosamente [affettuosa'mente] AVV

Aa

affectionately; **(ti saluto) affettuosamente, Roberta** (*nelle lettere*) love Roberta

affettuosità [affettuosi'ta] SF INV **1** affection **2 affettuosità** SFPL (*manifestazioni*) demonstrations of affection

affettuoso, a [affettu'oso] AGG affectionate; **il mio gatto è molto affettuoso** my cat's very affectionate; **un saluto** *o* **un abbraccio affettuoso, Roberta** (*nelle lettere*) love Roberta

affezionarsi [affettsjo'narsi] VIP: **affezionarsi a** to get *o* grow fond of; **mi sono molto affezionata a lei** I got very fond of her

affezionatamente [affettsjonata'mente] AVV affectionately

affezionato, a [affettsjo'nato] AGG **1 affezionato a** fond of; (*attaccato*) attached to; **sono molto affezionato a mia zia** I'm very fond of my aunt **2** (*abituale*: *cliente*) regular

affezione [affet'tsjone] SF **1** (*Med*) ailment, disorder **2** (*affetto*) affection

affiancare [affjan'kare] VT **1** (*mettere a fianco*: *due oggetti*) to place side by side; **affiancare qc a qc** (*un oggetto a un altro*) to put sth beside *o* next to sth **2** (*Mil*) to flank **3** (*fig*: *sostenere*) to support
▶ **affiancarsi** VR: **affiancarsi a qn** to stand beside sb

affiatamento [affjata'mento] SM team spirit; **c'è molto affiatamento fra di loro** (*giocatori, colleghi*) they make a good team

affiatarsi [affja'tarsi] VR (*colleghi*) to work well together; (*giocatori*) to play well together

affiatato, a [affja'tato] AGG: **essere affiatati** to get on; **formano una squadra affiatata** they make a good team; **una coppia molto affiatata** a very close couple

affibbiare [affib'bjare] VT **1** (*appioppare*): **affibbiare qc a qn** (*soprannome, colpa*) to pin sth on sb; (*compito sgradevole*) to saddle sb with sth; **affibbiare uno schiaffo a qn** to slap sb in the face **2** (*allacciare*) to buckle, do up

affidabile [affi'dabile] AGG (*persona, fonte d'informazioni*) reliable; **una macchina affidabile** a reliable car

affidabilità [affidabili'ta] SF reliability

affidamento [affida'mento] SM **1** (*fiducia*) trust, confidence; (*garanzia*) assurance; **dare affidamento** to seem reliable; **fare affidamento su qn/qc** to rely *o* count on sb/sth; **sai che puoi fare affidamento su di me** you know you can rely on me; **non si può fare affidamento sui mezzi pubblici!** you can't rely on public transport!; **quel tipo lì non mi dà nessun affidamento** I don't trust that chap at all **2** (*Dir*: *di bambino*) fostering; **avere/dare in affidamento** to foster; **bambini in affidamento** foster children

affidare [affi'dare] VT: **affidare qn/qc a qn** to entrust sb/sth to sb; **affidare un incarico a qn** to entrust sb with a task
▶ **affidarsi** VR: **affidarsi a** to place one's trust in; **mi affido alla tua discrezione** I rely on your discretion

affidatario, a, ri, rie AGG foster *attr*

affievolire [affjevo'lire] VT (*forze*) to weaken; (*suoni*) to make faint
▶ **affievolirsi** VIP (*suoni*) to grow faint; (*passione, affetto*) to fade, grow less

affiggere [af'fiddʒere] VT IRREG to stick up

affilacoltelli [affilakol'tɛlli] SM INV knife-sharpener

affilare [affi'lare] VT to sharpen
▶ **affilarsi** VIP (*viso, naso*) to get thinner

affilato, a [affi'lato] AGG (*gen*) sharp; (*volto, naso*) thin; **attento, quel coltello è molto affilato** be careful, that knife's very sharp!

affiliare [affi'ljare] VT (*aggregare*) to affiliate
▶ **affiliarsi** VR: **affiliarsi (a qc)** to join (sth), become a member (of sth)

affiliato, a [affi'ljato] SM/F (*membro*) affiliated member

affiliazione [affiljat'tsjone] SF affiliation

affinare [affi'nare] VT (*Tecn, fig*: *gusto*) to refine; (: *ingegno*) to sharpen

affinché [affin'ke] CONG (+ *congiunt*) in order that, so that

affine [af'fine] AGG similar
■ SM/F **1** (*di coniuge*) in-law **2** (*prodotto dello stesso tipo*) similar product; **sapone e affini** soap and allied products

affinità [affini'ta] SF INV affinity

affioramento [affjora'mento] SM **1** (*Naut*) surfacing **2** (*Geol*) outcrop

affiorare [affjo'rare] VI (*aus* **essere**) **1** (*venire in superficie*) to appear on the surface; **affiorare alla** *o* **in superficie** to come to the surface; **affiorare da** to emerge from **2** (*fig*: *indizi*) to come to light

affissi *ecc* [af'fissi] VB *vedi* **affiggere**

affissione [affis'sjone] SF billposting; **"divieto di affissione"** "stick no bills"

affisso, a [af'fisso] PP *di* **affiggere**
■ SM **1** (*avviso*) notice; (*manifesto*) poster, bill **2** (*Gramm*) affix

affittacamere [affitta'kamere] SM/F INV landlord/landlady; **fare l'affittacamere** to take in lodgers

affittare [affit'tare] VT **1** (*dare in affitto*: *casa*) to rent (out), let; (: *macchina*) to hire (out) (*Brit*), rent (out); **"affittasi"** "to let"; **hanno affittato la casa a degli studenti** they've rented the house to students **2** (*prendere in affitto*: *casa*) to rent; (: *macchina*) to hire (*Brit*), rent; **ho affittato una casa al mare** I rented a house at the seaside

affitto [af'fitto] SM **1** (*vedi vb*) renting; hiring; **dare in affitto** to rent (out), let; to hire (out); **prendere in affitto** to rent; to hire; **contratto d'affitto** lease **2** (*prezzo*) rent; **quant'è l'affitto?** how much is the rent?

affittuario, ri [affittu'arjo] SM tenant

affliggere [af'fliddʒere] VB IRREG
■ VT **1** (*sogg*: *malattia*) to trouble; (: *notizia*) to grieve, distress; (: *persona*: *con lamentele*) to torment; **i dolori reumatici la affliggono da tempo** she has been troubled with rheumatics for years; **la malattia che lo affligge** the illness he suffers from; **continua ad affliggermi con quella vecchia storia** he's for ever boring me to death with that old story;
▶ **affliggersi** VIP: **affliggersi (per)** (*preoccuparsi*) to worry (over); **non affliggerti per simili sciocchezze** don't worry over such silly things

afflissi *ecc* [af'flissi] VB *vedi* **affliggere**

afflitto, a [af'flitto] PP *di* **affliggere**
■ AGG: **aver l'aria afflitta** to look miserable
■ SM/F: **gli afflitti** SMPL the afflicted

afflizione [afflit'tsjone] SF distress, torment

afflosciarsi [afflo∫'∫arsi] VIP **1** (*perdere tensione*: *vela, tenda*) to become limp; (: *pelle*) to become flabby, sag; (*sgonfiarsi*: *palloncino*) to go down **2** (*accasciarsi*: *persona*) to collapse, go limp

affluente [afflu'ɛnte] SM (*Geog*) tributary

affluenza [afflu'ɛntsa] SF (*di persone, merci*) influx; (*di liquidi*) flow; (*degli elettori*) turnout

LO SAPEVI...?
affluenza non si traduce mai con la parola inglese *affluence*

affluire [afflu'ire] VI (*aus* **essere**) **1** (*liquidi*) to flow **2** (*persone, merci*) to pour in; **affluire in** to pour into
afflusso [af'flusso] SM (*di gente, prodotti*) influx; (*di liquidi*) flow
affogare [affo'gare] VI (*aus* **essere**) (*anche fig*) to drown; **per poco non affogavo** I nearly drowned; **affogare in un bicchier d'acqua** to be unable to cope with the slightest difficulty
■ VT (*gen, fig*) to drown; **affogare i dispiaceri nell'alcol** to drown one's sorrows in drink;
▶ **affogarsi** VR to drown o.s.
affogato, a [affo'gato] AGG **1** drowned; **è morta affogata** she drowned **2** (*Culin: uova*) poached
■ SM: **un affogato al caffè** coffee with ice cream
affollamento [affolla'mento] SM **1** crowding **2** (*folla*) crowd
affollare [affol'lare] VT (*gen, fig*) to crowd
▶ **affollarsi** VIP (*gen, fig*) to crowd; **affollarsi intorno a qn/qc** to crowd around sb/sth
affollato, a [affol'lato] AGG: **affollato (di)** crowded (with); **la spiaggia era affollatissima** the beach was very crowded
affondamento [affonda'mento] SM (*di nave*) sinking; (*di àncora*) dropping
affondare [affon'dare] VT **1** (*mandare a fondo: nave*) to sink; (: *àncora*) to drop **2** (*immergere*): **affondare in qc** to sink into sth; **affondare le mani in tasca** to plunge one's hands into one's pockets
■ VI (*aus* **essere**) **1** (*andare a fondo*) to sink; **la nave è affondata rapidamente** the ship sank quickly **2** (*penetrare*): **affondare in qc** to sink into sth; **sono affondato nella neve fino al ginocchio** I sank up to my knees in the snow
affondata [affon'data] SF (*Aer*) dive
affondo [af'fondo] SM (*Scherma, Ginnastica*) lunge; **fare un affondo** to lunge
affossamento [affossa'mento] SM (*avvallamento*) hollow
affossare [affos'sare] VT (*respingere: proposta, progetto*) to ditch
affrancare [affran'kare] VT **1** (*con francobolli*) to stamp; **ricorda di affrancare la lettera prima di imbucarla** remember to put a stamp on the letter before you post it; **affrancare (a macchina)** to frank (*Brit*), meter (*Am*) **2** (*liberare: schiavo, popolo*) to liberate, free; (*beni, proprietà*) to redeem
▶ **affrancarsi** VR (*da schiavitù, passione, debiti*) to free o.s.
affrancatrice [affranka'tritʃe] SF franking machine (*Brit*), postage meter (*Am*)
affrancatura [affranka'tura] SF (*valore*) postage; (*operazione*) stamping, franking (*Brit*), metering (*Am*); **affrancatura a carico del destinatario** postage paid (*Brit*), post-paid (*Am*)
affranto, a [af'franto] AGG (*dallo sconforto, dal dolore*): **affranto (da)** overcome (with)
affresco, schi [af'fresko] SM fresco
affrettare [affret'tare] VT (*lavoro, operazione*) to speed up; (*partenza*) to bring forward; **affrettare il passo** to quicken one's pace
▶ **affrettarsi** VR (*sbrigarsi*) to hurry up; **affrettati o perderai il treno** hurry up, or you'll miss the train; **affrettarsi a fare qc** to hurry *o* hasten to do sth
affrettatamente [affrettata'mente] AVV hurriedly, hastily, in a hurry
affrettato, a [affret'tato] AGG **1** (*veloce: passo, ritmo*) quick, fast **2** (*frettoloso: decisione*) hurried, hasty; (: *lavoro*) rushed
affrontare [affron'tare] VT (*nemico, pericolo*) to face, confront; (*situazione*) to face up to; (*questione*) to deal with, tackle; (*Equitazione: ostacolo*) to negotiate; **affrontare una spesa** to meet an expense; **prima o poi dovrai affrontare il problema** sooner or later you'll have to face up to the problem; **è un argomento difficile da affrontare** it's a difficult thing to talk about; **affrontano domani la prova decisiva per il campionato** tomorrow they face the decider for the championship
▶ **affrontarsi** VR (*uso reciproco: scontrarsi*) to confront each other
affronto [af'fronto] SM affront; **fare un affronto a qn** to insult sb
affumicare [affumi'kare] VT **1** (*riempire di fumo*) to fill with smoke **2** (*annerire*) to blacken with smoke **3** (*alimenti*) to smoke
affumicato, a [affumi'kato] AGG (*salmone, prosciutto*) smoked; (*lenti*) tinted
affusolare [affuso'lare] VT to taper
affusolato, a [affuso'lato] AGG tapering
afgano, a; afghano, a [af'gano] AGG, SM/F Afghan
Afghanistan [af'ganistan] SM Afghanistan
a.f.m. ABBR (*Comm:* = **a fine mese**) e.o.m. (= *end of month*)
afono, a ['afono] AGG voiceless
aforisma, i [afo'rizma] SM aphorism
afosità [afosi'ta] SF closeness
afoso, a [a'foso] AGG close; **oggi è una giornata afosa** it's muggy today
Africa ['afrika] SF Africa; **vengono dall'Africa** they come from Africa
africano, a [afri'kano] AGG, SM/F African
afrikaans [afri'ka:ns] SM INV (*lingua*) Afrikaans
afrikander [æfri'kændə] SM/F INV Afrikaner
afroamericano, a AGG Afro-American
afroasiatico, a, ci, che [afroa'zjatiko] AGG Afro-Asian
afrodisiaco, a, ci, che [afrodi'ziako] AGG, SM aphrodisiac
Afrodite [afro'dite] SF Aphrodite
afta ['afta] SF (*Med*) aphtha
AG SIGLA = *Agrigento*
Agamennone [aga'mennone] SM Agamemnon
agar-agar ['agar'agar] SM INV agar-agar
agata ['agata] SF agate
agave ['agave] SF (*Bot*) agave
agenda [a'dʒɛnda] SF **1** (*taccuino*) diary; **l'ho segnato sull'agenda** I noted it in my diary; **agenda elettronica** personal organizer; **agenda tascabile** pocket diary; **agenda da tavolo** desk diary **2** (*in una riunione*) agenda
agente [a'dʒɛnte] SM **1** (*Polizia*) policeman, police officer **2** (*incaricato*) agent, representative **3** (*Chim, Med, Meteor*) agent; **resistente agli agenti atmosferici** weather-resistant; **agente assicurativo** insurance agent
■ **agente di cambio** stockbroker; **agente di custodia** prison officer; **agente immobiliare** estate agent (*Brit*), realtor (*Am*); **agente marittimo** shipping agent; **agente di polizia** *o* **di Pubblica Sicurezza** police officer; **agente provocatore** agent provocateur; **agente segreto** secret agent; **agente teatrale** theatrical agent; **agente di vendita** sales agent

Aa

agenzia [adʒen'tsia] SF **1** (*impresa*) agency **2** (*succursale*) branch office
■ **agenzia di collocamento** employment agency; **agenzia immobiliare** estate agent's (office) (*Brit*), real estate office (*Am*); **agenzia d'informazioni** news agency; **Agenzia Internazionale per l'Energia Atomica** International Atomic Energy Agency; **agenzia matrimoniale** marriage bureau; **agenzia pubblicitaria** advertising agency; **agenzia di stampa** press agency
▷ www.ansa.it/
▷ www.agi.it/
▷ www.asca.it/
agenzia di viaggi travel agency

AGESCI [a'dʒeʃʃi] SIGLA F = **Associazione Guide e Scouts Cattolici Italiani**

agevolare [adʒevo'lare] VT **1** (*facilitare*: *compito, operazione*): **agevolare qc (a qn)** to make sth easier (for sb), facilitate sth (for sb) **2** (*aiutare*): **agevolare qn (in qc)** to help sb (with sth); **ho cercato di agevolarlo in ogni modo** I tried to help him in every way possible

agevolazione [adʒevolat'tsjone] SF (*facilitazione economica*): **concedere delle agevolazioni** to give special terms; **agevolazione di pagamento** payment on easy terms; **agevolazioni creditizie** credit facilities; **agevolazioni fiscali** tax relief

agevole [a'dʒevole] AGG (*salita, compito*) easy; (*strada*) smooth; **gli ha reso più agevole il compito** it made things easier for him

agevolmente [adʒevol'mente] AVV easily

agganciare [aggan'tʃare] VT (*unire con un gancio*) to hook; (*ricevitore del telefono*) to hang up; (*Ferr*: *vagone, vettura*) to couple; (*fig*: *ragazza*) to pick up

aggancio, ci [ag'gantʃo] SM **1** (*Tecn*) coupling **2** (*fig*: *conoscenza*) contact

aggeggio, gi [ad'dʒeddʒo] SM (*fam*) thingy; **a cosa serve quest'aggeggio?** what's this thing for?

aggettivale [addʒetti'vale] AGG adjectival

aggettivato, a [addʒetti'vato] AGG: **sostantivo aggettivato** noun used as an adjective

aggettivazione [addʒettivat'tsjone] SF adjectival use

aggettivo [addʒet'tivo] SM adjective

agghiacciante [aggjat'tʃante] AGG chilling

agghiacciare [aggjat'tʃare] VT: **agghiacciare qn** *or* **agghiacciare il sangue a qn** to make sb's blood run cold
▶ **agghiacciarsi** VIP: **mi si è agghiacciato il sangue** my blood ran cold

agghindarsi [aggin'darsi] VR to dress o.s. up

agghindato, a [aggin'dato] AGG dressed up

aggio, gi ['addʒo] SM (*Fin*) premium

aggiogare [addʒo'gare] VT (*buoi*) to yoke; (*popolo*) to subjugate

aggiornamento [addʒorna'mento] SM (*vedi vb*) updating; revision; postponement, adjournment; **corso di aggiornamento** refresher course

aggiornare [addʒor'nare] VT **1** (*testo*) to update; (: *rivedere*) to revise; (*persona*) to bring up-to-date; **mi piace tenermi aggiornato (su ciò che succede)** I like to keep up to date with what's happening; **tienimi aggiornato!** keep me posted!; **"Aggiorna"** (*Inform*) "Refresh" **2** (*rimandare*): **aggiornare (a)** to postpone (till), put off (till); (: *Dir*) to adjourn (till); **la seduta è stata aggiornata a lunedì** the session has been postponed until Monday
▶ **aggiornarsi** VR: **aggiornarsi (su qc)** to bring (*o* keep) o.s. up to date (about sth)

aggiornato, a [addʒor'nato] AGG up-to-date; **un orario aggiornato** an up-to-date timetable; **tenersi aggiornato su qc** to keep up to date with sth; **mi tengo aggiornato sulle novità discografiche** I keep up to date with the new releases

aggiotaggio, gi [addʒo'taddʒo] SM (*Econ*) rigging the market

aggirare [addʒi'rare] VT (*andare intorno a*) to go round; **aggirare un ostacolo/problema** (*fig*) to get round an obstacle/problem
▶ **aggirarsi** VIP **1** **aggirarsi in** *o* **per** (*girare qua e là*) to go about, wander about; (: *tipo sospetto*) to hang about; **l'ho visto che si aggirava da queste parti** I've seen him wandering about this area **2** (*approssimarsi*) to be around; **il prezzo s'aggira sul milione** the price is around the million mark

aggiudicare [addʒudi'kare] VT (*premio, merito*): **aggiudicare qc a qn** to award sb sth, award sth to sb; (*all'asta*) to knock sth down to sb; **aggiudicato!** (*all'asta*) gone!; **si è aggiudicato il primo posto** he won first place

aggiungere [ad'dʒundʒere] VB IRREG
■ VT to add; **aggiungi ancora un po' di latte** add a bit more milk
▶ **aggiungersi** VIP: **aggiungersi a** to add to

aggiunsi *ecc* [ad'dʒunsi] VB *vedi* **aggiungere**

aggiunta [ad'dʒunta] SF addition; **in aggiunta...** what's more ...

aggiunto, a [ad'dʒunto] PP *di* **aggiungere**
■ AGG (*Amm*: *aiuto*) assistant *attr*; (: *sostituto*) stand-in; **sindaco aggiunto** deputy mayor
■ SM (*Amm*) assistant

aggiustare [addʒus'tare] VT **1** (*riparare*) to repair, mend; **mi ha aggiustato la bicicletta** he mended my bike for me **2** (*adattare*: *vestito*) to alter; (*regolare*: *tiro, mira*) to adjust; **si è aggiustato la cravatta** he straightened his tie; **gli aggiustò un manrovescio** he gave him a backhander **3** (*fig*: *sistemare*: *lite, conti*) to settle; **ti aggiusto io!** I'll fix you!
▶ **aggiustarsi** VR **1** (*uso reciproco*: *accordarsi*) to come to an agreement; (*per soldi*) to settle (up) **2** (*arrangiarsi*): **mi aggiusterò sul divano** the sofa will be fine

agglomerato [agglome'rato] SM **1** (*di rocce*) agglomerate, conglomerate; **agglomerato urbano** built-up area **2** (*Tecn*) agglomeration; **agglomerato di legno** chipboard

aggomitolare [aggomito'lare] VT to wind

aggradare [aggra'dare] VI DIF (*letter*): **se vi aggrada** if you so desire *o* wish

aggrapparsi [aggrap'parsi] VR (*anche fig*) **aggrapparsi (a)** to hold (onto); **si è aggrappato alla ringhiera** he held onto the banister; **aggrappati a me!** hold onto me!

aggravamento [aggrava'mento] SM worsening; **c'è stato un aggravamento** there has been a turn for the worse

aggravante [aggra'vante] (*Dir*) AGG aggravating
■ SF aggravating circumstance

aggravare [aggra'vare] VT (*peggiorare*) to worsen; (*accrescere*) to increase; **la pioggia ha aggravato ulteriormente la situazione** the rain has made the situation even worse
▶ **aggravarsi** VIP (*situazione, malato*) to get worse

aggravato, a [aggra'vato] AGG (*Dir*) aggravated

aggravio, vi [ag'gravjo] SM: **aggravio fiscale** tax increase

aggraziatamente [aggrattsjata'mente] AVV (*muoversi*) gracefully

aggraziato, a [aggrat'tsjato] AGG (*movimenti*) graceful; (*lineamenti*) pretty; (*modi*) gracious

aggredire [aggre'dire] VT to attack; **è stato aggredito mentre tornava in albergo** he was attacked as he was going back to his hotel

aggregare [aggre'gare] VT: **aggregare qn a qc** to include sb in sth; (*a un club*) to admit sb to sth
▶ **aggregarsi** VR: **aggregarsi (a)** to join; (*a un club*) to become a member of
▶ **aggregarsi** VIP (*Geol, Bio*) to aggregate

aggregato, a [aggre'gato] AGG (*associato*) associated; **socio aggregato** associate member; **aggregato a un reparto** attached to a section
■ SM (*gen, Bot, Geol*) aggregate; **aggregato urbano** built-up area

aggregazione [aggregat'tsjone] SF (*gen, Fis, Chim*) aggregation

aggressione [aggres'sjone] SF **1** (*contro una persona*) attack, assault; **subire un'aggressione** to be attacked; **aggressione a mano armata** armed assault **2** (*Mil, Pol: contro un paese*) aggression; **patto di non aggressione** non-aggression pact **3** (*fig: a volto, capelli, monumento*) attack

aggressivamente [aggressiva'mente] AVV aggressively

aggressività [aggressivi'ta] SF aggressiveness

aggressivo, a [aggres'sivo] AGG (*anche fig*) aggressive

aggressore [aggres'sore] SM (*persona*) attacker; (*Pol*) aggressor
■ AGG (*stato, esercito*) aggressor *attr*

aggrottare [aggrot'tare] VT: **aggrottare le sopracciglia/la fronte** to frown

aggrovigliare [aggroviʎ'ʎare] VT (*fili, matassa*) to (en)tangle; **aggrovigliare la matassa** (*fig*) to complicate things
▶ **aggrovigliarsi** VIP to become tangled; (*fig*) to become complicated

agguantare [aggwan'tare] VT to catch (hold of), seize

agguato [ag'gwato] SM **1** (*insidia*) trap; **tendere un agguato a qn** to set a trap for sb; **cadere in un agguato** to fall into a trap **2** (*appostamento*) ambush; **stare** *o* **essere in agguato** to lie in ambush

agguerrito, a [aggwer'rito] AGG (*sostenitore, nemico*) fierce

aghiforme [agi'forme] AGG needle-shaped

agiatamente [adʒata'mente] AVV (*vivere*) comfortably

agiatezza [adʒa'tettsa] SF prosperity; **vivere nell'agiatezza** to live in comfort

agiato, a [a'dʒato] AGG (*vita, condizione*) comfortable, easy; (*persona, famiglia*) well-off, well-to-do

agibile [a'dʒibile] AGG (*luogo pubblico*) conforming to required standards; **la strada non è agibile** the road is impassable

agibilità SF (*di locale, luogo pubblico*) conformity to standards

agile ['adʒile] AGG agile, nimble

agilità [adʒili'ta] SF agility, nimbleness

agilmente [adʒil'mente] AVV with agility, nimbly

agio, gi ['adʒo] SM **1** ease, comfort; **sentirsi/trovarsi a proprio agio** to feel/be at ease; **mi sono sentito subito a mio agio** I immediately felt at ease; **mettere qn a proprio agio** to put sb at their ease; **ha fatto del suo meglio per mettermi a mio agio** he did his best to put me at my ease; **mettersi a proprio agio** to make o.s. at home *o* comfortable **2** (*opportunità*): **dare agio a qn di fare qc** to give sb the chance of doing sth **3 agi** SMPL comforts; **vivere negli agi** to live in comfort

agire [a'dʒire] VI **1** (*gen*) to act; (*comportarsi*) to behave; **bisogna agire immediatamente** we must act *o* take action at once; **agisce senza riflettere** he acts without thinking; **ha agito male verso i colleghi** he behaved badly towards his colleagues; **non mi piace il suo modo di agire** I don't like the way he goes about things; **agire su qn/qc** to act on sb/sth **2** (*esercitare un'azione*) to work, function; **la leva agisce sul cambio** the lever operates the gear; **una medicina che agisce rapidamente** a medicine which acts *o* takes effect quickly **3** (*Dir*): **agire contro qn** to take (legal) action against sb, start proceedings against sb

AGIS ['adʒis] SIGLA F (= **Associazione Generale Italiana dello Spettacolo**) Italian Association for the Performing Arts

agitare [adʒi'tare] VT **1** (*liquido, bottiglia*) to shake; (*mano, fazzoletto*) to wave; **"agitare prima dell'uso"** "shake well before use"; **il vento agitava i rami** the wind was shaking the branches **2** (*fig: incitare*) to incite; (*: turbare*) to trouble, disturb
▶ **agitarsi** VIP **1** (*rami*) to sway; (*bambino*) to fidget; (*mare*) to get rough; (*dubbio, pensiero*) to stir; (*folla*) to become restless; **agitarsi nel sonno** to toss and turn in one's sleep **2** (*turbarsi*) to get worked up, get upset; (*eccitarsi*) to get excited; **non è il caso di agitarsi tanto** there's no need to get so worked up **3** (*Pol*) to agitate

agitato, a [adʒi'tato] AGG **1** (*malato*) restless; (*bambino*) fidgety; (*mare*) rough **2** (*persona: turbato*) worried, upset; (*: eccitato*) excited

agitatore, trice [adʒita'tore] SM/F (*Pol*) agitator

agitazione [adʒitat'tsjone] SF **1** (*inquietudine*) agitation; **essere in uno stato di agitazione** to be worked up; **mettersi in agitazione** to get worked up; **mettere in agitazione qn** to upset *o* distress sb **2** (*Pol*) agitation, unrest; **entrare in agitazione** to take industrial action

agit-prop ['adʒit'prɔp] SM/F INV agitprop

agli ['aʎʎi] PREP + ART *vedi* **a**

aglio, gli ['aʎʎo] SM garlic; **uno spicchio d'aglio** a clove of garlic

agnellino [aɲɲel'lino] SM **1** (*piccolo*) baby lamb **2** (*pelliccia*): **agnellino di Persia** Persian Lamb **3** (*fig: persona*): **è (buono come) un agnellino** he's (as quiet as) a lamb

agnello [aɲ'ɲɛllo] SM lamb; **agnello arrosto** roast lamb; **Agnello di Dio** (*Rel*) Lamb of God

agnosticismo [aɲɲosti'tʃismo] SM agnosticism

agnostico, a, ci, che [aɲ'ɲɔstiko] AGG, SM/F agnostic

ago, aghi ['ago] SM (*gen*) needle; (*della bilancia*) pointer; **lavoro ad ago** needlework; **è come cercare un ago in un pagliaio** it's like looking for a needle in a haystack; **ago da calza** knitting needle; **ago magnetico** magnetic needle

agonia [ago'nia] SF **1** (*Med*) death throes *pl*; **entrare in agonia** to be close to death; **è stata una lunga agonia** it was a slow death **2** (*fig*) agony

agonismo SM competitiveness

agonisticamente [agonistika'mente] AVV competitively

agonistico, a, ci, che [ago'nistiko] AGG (*Sport fig*) competitive

agonizzante [agonid'dzante] AGG dying

agonizzare [agonid'dzare] VI (*aus* **avere**) (*malato*) to be dying; (*fig: civiltà*) to decline

agopuntura [agopun'tura] SF acupuncture

Aa

agopunturista, i, e [agopuntu'rista] SM/F acupuncturist
agorafobia [agorafo'bia] SF agoraphobia
agorafobo, a [ago'rafobo] AGG agoraphobic
agostiniano, a [agosti'njano] AGG, SM/F (*Rel*) Augustinian
agosto [a'gosto] SM August; *per fraseologia vedi* **luglio**
agraria [a'grarja] SF agriculture
▹ www.agraria.org/
▹ www.inea.it/
agrario, ria, ri, rie [a'grarjo] AGG (*scuola, scienza*) agricultural; (*leggi*) agrarian; **scienze agrarie** agricultural science; **riforma agraria** land reform
■ SM landowner
▹ www.agraria.org/
▹ www.inea.it/
agricolo, a [a'grikolo] AGG (*gen*) agricultural; (*lavoratori, prodotti, macchine*) farm *attr*; (*popolazione*) farming; **terreno agricolo** agricultural land
agricoltore [agrikol'tore] SM farmer; **fa l'agricoltore** he's a farmer
agricoltura [agrikol'tura] SF agriculture; **agricoltura biologica** organic farming; **agricoltura intensiva** intensive farming
agrifoglio, gli [agri'fɔʎʎo] SM holly
agrigentino, a [agridʒen'tino] AGG of *o* from Agrigento
■ SM/F inhabitant *o* native of Agrigento
agrimensore [agrimen'sore] SM land surveyor
agrimensura SF land surveying
agrimonia [agri'mɔnja] SF agrimony
agriturismo [agritu'rizmo] SM farm holidays *pl*
agrituristico, a, ci, che [agritu'ristiko] AGG farm holiday *attr*
agro, a ['agro] AGG bitter, sharp
agroalimentare [agroalimen'tare] AGG (*settore, industria*) food and agriculture *attr*
agrodolce [agro'doltʃe] AGG (*sapore*) bittersweet; (*salsa*) sweet and sour
■ SM (*Culin*) sweet-and-sour sauce; **in agrodolce** sweet and sour; **maiale in agrodolce** sweet and sour pork
agronomia [agrono'mia] SF agronomy
agronomo, a [a'grɔnomo] SM/F agronomist
agrostide [a'grɔstide] SF bent (grass)
agrume [a'grume] SM (*spesso al pl: pianta*) citrus; (: *frutto*) citrus fruit
agrumeto [agru'meto] SM citrus grove
aguzzare [agut'tsare] VT to sharpen; **aguzzare la vista** *o* **gli occhi** to strain to see; **aguzzare le orecchie** to prick up one's ears; **aguzzare l'ingegno** to sharpen one's wits; **il bisogno aguzza l'ingegno** (*Proverbio*) necessity is the mother of invention
aguzzino, a [agud'dzino] SM/F jailer; (*fig*) tyrant
aguzzo, a [a'guttso] AGG sharp
ah [a] ESCL ah!, oh!; **ah si?** really?
ahi ['ai] ESCL (*dolore*) ouch!
ahimè [ai'mɛ] ESCL (*spec letter*) alas!
AI ABBR (= **Aeronautica Italiana**) Italian Air Force
ai ['ai] PREP + ART *vedi* **a**
Aia ['aja] SF: **L'Aia** The Hague
aia ['aja] SF (*cortile*) farmyard; (*per battere il grano*) threshing floor
Aiace [a'jatʃe] SM Ajax
AIDDA [a'idda] SIGLA F (= **Associazione Imprenditrici Donne Dirigenti d'Azienda**) *association of women entrepreneurs and managers*
AIDO ['aido] SIGLA F = *Associazione Italiana Donatori Organi*
AIDS ['aidz *o* aidi'ɛsse] SIGLA M O F AIDS; **ha l'AIDS** he's got AIDS
AIE ['aiɛ] SIGLA F (= **Associazione Italiana degli Editori**) *publishers' association*
AIEA [a'jɛa] SIGLA F (= **Agenzia Internazionale per l'Energia Atomica**) IAEA
AIED ['ajɛd] SIGLA F (= **Associazione Italiana Educazione Demografica**) ≈ FPA (= *Family Planning Association*)
aiola [a'jɔla] SF = **aiuola**
airbag ['ɛəbæg] SM INV airbag; **airbag laterali** side airbags; **airbag lato guida/passeggero** driver/passenger airbag
AIRC [airk] SIGLA F = *Associazione Italiana per la Ricerca sul Cancro*
airone [ai'rone] SM heron; **airone bianco** great white egret
air-terminal ['ɛəˌtə:minl] SM INV air terminal
aitante [ai'tante] AGG robust
aiuola [a'jwɔla] SF flower bed; **"non calpestare le aiuole"** "keep off the flower beds"; **aiuola spartitraffico** (*Aut*) traffic island
aiutante [aju'tante] SM/F **1** (*nel lavoro*) assistant; **fare da aiutante a qn** to be sb's assistant **2** (*Mil*) adjutant; **aiutante di campo** aide-de-camp **3** (*Naut*) master-at-arms; **aiutante di bandiera** flag lieutenant
aiutare [aju'tare] VT to help; (*assistere*) to assist; **ha detto che ci avrebbe aiutati** he said he would help us; **aiutare qn (a fare qc)** to help sb (to do sth); **mi puoi aiutare a compilare questo modulo?** can you help me to fill in this form?; **aiutare la digestione** to aid (the) digestion
▶ **aiutarsi** VR **1** to help o.s.; **aiutati, che Dio ti aiuta** God helps those who help themselves **2** (*uso reciproco*) to help one another
aiuto [a'juto] SM **1** (*soccorso*) help, assistance, aid; **mi serve il tuo aiuto** I need your help; **prestare** *o* **dare aiuto a qn** to help sb; **venire in aiuto di qn** to help sb, come to sb's assistance *o* aid; **essere di aiuto (a qn)** (*persona*) to be a help (to sb); (*cosa*) to be useful (to sb); **se posso esserti d'aiuto...** if I can be of help to you ...; **mi è stata di grande aiuto** she has been a great help to me; **grazie per la guida, mi è stata di grande aiuto** thanks for the guidebook, it was very useful; **chiedere aiuto a qn** to ask sb for help; **correre in aiuto di qn** to rush to sb's assistance; **gridare aiuto** to shout for help; **c'è qualcuno che grida aiuto** there's somebody shouting for help; **aiuti** SMPL (*viveri, finanziamenti ecc.*) aid *sg*; **aiuti umanitari** humanitarian aid **2** (*aiutante, assistente*) assistant; **aiuto contabile** junior accountant; **aiuto giardiniere** under gardener; **aiuto regista** assistant director
■ ESCL help!
aizzare [ait'tsare] VT **1** (*cani*): **aizzare contro qn** to set on sb **2** (*folla*) to incite; (*contendenti*) to urge on
AL SIGLA = *Alessandria*
al [al] PREP + ART *vedi* **a**
a.l. ABBR = **anno luce**
ala ['ala] SF (*pl* **ali**) (*gen*) wing; (*di cappello*) brim; (*di mulino*) sail; **ala destra/sinistra** (*Sport*) right/left wing(er); **fare ala** to make way; **avere le ali ai piedi** to have wings; **prendere qn sotto la propria ala protettrice** to take sb under one's wing; **spiegare le ali** (*fig*) to spread one's wings; **tarpare le ali a qn** to clip sb's wings
Alabama [ala'bama] SM Alabama
alabastro [ala'bastro] SM alabaster; **una lampada di**

alabastro an alabaster lamp
alacre ['alakre] AGG (*persona*) eager; (*mente, fantasia*) lively
alacremente [alakre'mente] AVV promptly
alacrità [alakri'ta] SF promptness, speed
alamaro [ala'maro] SM (*abbottonatura*) frog; **alamari** SMPL frogging *sg*
alambicco, chi [alam'bikko] SM still (*Chim*)
alano [a'lano] SM Great Dane
alare[1] [a'lare] AGG wing *attr*
alare[2] [a'lare] SM (*di camino*) firedog, andiron
Alaska [a'laska] SF Alaska
alato, a [a'lato] AGG winged
alba ['alba] SF dawn; **all'alba** at dawn, at daybreak; **alzarsi all'alba** to get up at dawn; **spunta l'alba** dawn is breaking
albanese [alba'nese] AGG, SM/F, SM Albanian
Albania [alba'nia] SF Albania; **viene dall'Albania** he comes from Albania
albatro ['albatro] SM, **albatros** ['albatros] SM INV albatross
albeggiare [albed'dʒare] VB IMPERS (*aus* **essere**) to dawn; **comincia ad albeggiare** day is dawning; **albeggiava quando arrivò a casa** day was breaking when he arrived home
alberato, a [albe'rato] AGG (*viale, piazza*) lined with trees, tree-lined
alberatura [albera'tura] SF (*Naut*) masts *pl*
albergare [alber'gare] VT (*letter: sentimenti*) to harbour ■VI (*aus* **avere**) (*letter*) to dwell
albergatore, trice [alberga'tore] SM/F (*proprietario*) hotel owner, hotelier; (*gestore*) hotel manager/manageress
alberghiero, a [alber'gjɛro] AGG (*settore, industria*) hotel *attr*; **scuola alberghiera** catering college; **faccio la scuola alberghiera** I'm at catering college
albergo, ghi [al'bɛrgo] SM hotel; **ho dormito in albergo** I spent the night in a hotel; **albergo diurno** *public toilets with washing and shaving facilities ecc*
albero ['albero] SM **1** (*pianta*) tree; **albero da frutto** fruit tree; **albero genealogico** family tree; **albero di mele** apple tree; **albero di Natale** Christmas tree **2** (*Naut*) mast; **albero maestro** mainmast **3** (*Tecn*) shaft; **albero a camme** *o* **della distribuzione** camshaft; **albero motore** *o* **a gomiti** crankshaft; **albero di trasmissione** transmission shaft
albicocca, che [albi'kɔkka] SF apricot; **marmellata di albicocche** apricot jam
albicocco, chi [albi'kɔkko] SM apricot tree
albino, a [al'bino] AGG, SM/F (*Bio*) albino
albo ['albo] SM (*registro professionale*) register; (*Amm: bacheca*) notice board; (*fascicolo illustrato*) album; **radiare dall'albo** to strike off
albori [al'bori] SMPL (*letter*) dawn *sg*
album ['album] SM INV (*libro, disco*) album; **hai sentito il suo ultimo album?** have you heard her latest album?; **album per francobolli/fotografie** stamp/photo album; **album da disegno** sketch book
albume [al'bume] SM egg white, albumen (*termine tecn*)
albumina [albu'mina] SF albumin
alcali ['alkali] SM INV alkali
alcalino, a [alka'lino] AGG alkaline
alcantara [alkan'tara] SM artificial suede
alce ['altʃe] SM elk, moose
alcelafo [al'tʃɛlafo] SM hartebeest
alchechengi [alke'kɛndʒi] SM INV winter cherry
alchimia [alki'mia] SF alchemy
alchimista, i, e [alki'mista] SM/F alchemist
alchino [al'kino] SM alkyne
alcol ['alkol] SM INV (*gen, Chim*) alcohol; **alcol denaturato** methylated spirits *pl* (*Brit*), wood alcohol (*Am*); **alcol etilico** ethyl alcohol, ethanol; **alcol metilico** methyl alcohol
alcolicità [alkolitʃi'ta] SF alcoholic strength
alcolico, a, ci, che [al'kɔliko] AGG alcoholic; **è alcolico?** is it alcoholic?
■SM alcohol; **non bevo alcolici** I don't drink; **non vendono alcolici** they don't sell alcoholic drinks
alcolimetro SM Breathalyzer®
alcolismo [alko'lizmo] SM alcoholism
alcolista, i, e [alko'lista] SM/F alcoholic
alcolizzato, a [alkolid'dzato] AGG, SM/F alcoholic
alcoltest [alkol'tɛst] SM INV Breathalyzer®
alcool *ecc* ['alkool] SM INV = **alcol** *ecc*
alcova [al'kɔva] SF alcove
alcuno, a [al'kuno] AGG (*dav sm:* alcun + *consonante, vocale,* alcuno + *s impura, gn, pn, ps, x, z; dav sf:* alcuna + *consonante,* alcun' + *vocale*) **1** (*nessuno*): **non... alcuno** no, not any; **non c'è alcuna fretta** there's no hurry, there isn't any hurry; **senza alcun riguardo** without any consideration **2 alcuni(e)** some, a few; **sono uscito con alcuni amici** I went out with some friends
■**alcuni(e)** PRON PL some, a few; **ne ho prese alcune** I took some
aldilà [aldi'la] SM: **l'aldilà** the next life, the after-life
aleatorio, ria, ri, rie [alea'tɔrjo] AGG (*incerto*) uncertain
aleggiare [aled'dʒare] VI (*aus* **avere**) (*fig: profumo, sospetto*) to be in the air
alesatura [aleza'tura] SF boring
Alessandria [ales'sandria] SF Alessandria; **Alessandria d'Egitto** Alexandria
alessandrino, a [alessan'drino] AGG of *o* from Alessandria
■SM/F inhabitant *o* native of Alessandria
alessia [ales'sia] SF alexia (*Med*), word blindness
aletta [a'letta] SF (*Tecn, Zool*) fin; (*Aer*) tab
alettone [alet'tone] SM (*Aer*) aileron; (*Aut*) spoiler
Aleutine [aleu'tine] SFPL: **le isole Aleutine** the Aleutian Islands
alfa ['alfa] AGG INV, SM O F INV alpha
alfabeticamente [alfabetika'mente] AVV alphabetically, in alphabetical order
alfabetico, a, ci, che [alfa'bɛtiko] AGG alphabetical; **in ordine alfabetico** in alphabetical order
alfabetizzare [alfabetid'dzare] VT (*popolazione*) to make literate
alfabetizzazione [alfabetiddzat'tsjone] SF (*leggere e scrivere*) literacy; **corso di alfabetizzazione informatica** introductory computing course
alfabeto [alfa'bɛto] SM alphabet; **alfabeto fonetico** phonetic alphabet; **alfabeto Morse** Morse code
alfanumerico, a, ci, che [alfanu'mɛriko] AGG alphanumeric
alfiere [al'fjɛre] SM (*Mil*) standard-bearer; (*Scacchi*) bishop
alfine [al'fine] AVV finally, in the end
alga, ghe ['alga] SF strand of seaweed, alga (*Bot*); **alghe** SFPL seaweed *sg*, algae (*Bot*)
algebra ['aldʒebra] SF algebra; **questo per me è algebra** (*fig*) this is Greek to me
Algeri [al'dʒeri] SF Algiers

Aa

Algeria [aldʒe'ria] SF Algeria; **viene dall'Algeria** he comes from Algeria
algerino, a [aldʒe'rino] AGG, SM/F Algerian; **è algerina** she's Algerian
algoritmico, a;, ci;, che [algo'ritmiko] AGG algorithmic
algoritmo [algo'ritmo] SM algorithm
ALI ['ali] SIGLA F (= **Associazione Librai Italiani**) *booksellers' association*
aliante [ali'ante] SM (*Aer*) glider
alias ['aljas] AVV alias
alibi ['alibi] SM INV alibi; **aveva un alibi di ferro** he had a cast-iron alibi
alice [a'litʃe] SF anchovy
alienante [alje'nante] AGG alienating
alienare [alje'nare] VT (*gen*) to alienate; (*Dir: trasferire*) to transfer; **alienarsi un amico** to alienate a friend
▶ **alienarsi** VR: **alienarsi (da)** to cut o.s. off (from)
alienato, a [alje'nato] AGG (*gen*) alienated; (*Dir*) transferred; (*pazzo*) insane
■ SM/F lunatic, insane person
alienazione [aljenat'tsjone] SF (*gen*) alienation; (*Dir*) transfer; **alienazione mentale** (*Psic*) insanity
alieno, a [a'ljɛno] AGG: **alieno (da)** opposed (to), averse (to)
■ SM/F alien
alimentare[1] [alimen'tare] AGG food *attr*; **generi alimentari** foodstuffs; **regime alimentare** diet
alimentare[2] [alimen'tare] VT **1** (*Tecn*) to feed, supply; (*: stufa*) to add fuel to; (*: caldaia*) to stoke; (*: fuoco*) to stoke up **2** (*fig: tener vivo*) to keep alive **3** (*nutrire*) to nourish, feed
▶ **alimentarsi** VR: **alimentarsi di** to live *o* feed on
alimentari [alimen'tari] SMPL foodstuffs
■ SM (*anche:* **negozio di alimentari**) grocer's shop; **c'è un (negozio di) alimentari qui vicino?** is there a grocer's near here?
alimentarista, i, e [alimenta'rista] SM/F dietician
alimentatore [alimenta'tore] SM **1** (*Tecn, Elettr*) feeder **2** (*operaio*) stoker
alimentazione [alimentat'tsjone] SF **1** (*nutrizione*) nutrition; (*cibi*) diet; **alimentazione equilibrata/priva di grassi** balanced/low fat diet **2** (*Tecn*) feeding; (*: di caldaia*) stoking **3** (*Inform: di carta*) feed; **alimentazione a fogli singoli** sheet feed; **alimentazione a modulo continuo** stream feed
alimento [ali'mento] SM **1** (*cibo*) food; **contenitore per alimenti** food container **2** (*Dir*): **alimenti** SMPL alimony; **pagare gli alimenti** to pay alimony

> **LO SAPEVI...?**
> **alimento** non si traduce mai con la parola inglese ***ailment***

aliquota [a'likwota] SF **1** (*Mat*) aliquot **2** (*Fin*) rate; **aliquota d'imposta** (*Fisco*) tax rate; **aliquota minima** (*Fisco*) basic rate
aliscafo [alis'kafo] SM hydrofoil
aliseo [ali'zɛo] SM (*Geog*) trade wind
alitare [ali'tare] VI (*aus* **avere**) (*persona*) to breathe; (*vento*) to blow gently
alito ['alito] SM (*anche fig*) breath; **avere l'alito cattivo** to have bad breath; **non c'è un alito di vento** there isn't a breath of wind
all' [all] PREP + ART *vedi* **a**
all. ABBR (= **allegato**) enc.
alla ['alla] PREP + ART *vedi* **a**
allacciamento [allattʃa'mento] SM (*Tecn*) connection; **allacciamento all'elettricità** connection to the power supply; **far fare l'allacciamento dell'acqua/del gas** to have the water/gas connected
allacciare [allat'tʃare] VT **1** (*cintura, mantello, cerniera*) to fasten, do up; (*scarpe*) to lace (up), tie; **allacciare** *o* **allacciarsi la cintura di sicurezza** to fasten one's seat belt; **allacciarsi il cappotto** to fasten one's coat; **allacciare due funi** to join two ropes together; **allacciati le scarpe** lace up your shoes **2** (*Tecn: luce, gas, telefono*) to connect; (*due località*) to link; **il telefono non è ancora allacciato** the phone hasn't been connected yet **3** (*fig: rapporti*) to start
allacciatura [allattʃa'tura] SF fastening
allagamento [allaga'mento] SM (*atto*) flooding *no pl*; (*effetto*) flood
allagare [alla'gare] VT to flood; **la pioggia aveva allagato le strade** the rain had flooded the roads
▶ **allagarsi** VIP to flood, be flooded; **si è allagato lo scantinato** the basement is flooded
allampanato, a [allampa'nato] AGG lanky
allargare [allar'gare] VT **1** (*passaggio*) to widen; (*buco*) to enlarge; (*vestito*) to let out; (*scarpe nuove*) to break in; (*fig: orizzonti*) to widen, broaden; **stanno allargando la strada** they're widening the road **2** (*aprire: braccia*) to open
▶ **allargarsi** VI (*aus* **avere**) (*Aut*): **allargare in curva** to take a bend wide
▶ **allargarsi** VIP (*gen*) to widen; (*scarpe, pantaloni*) to lose its shape; (*espandersi: problema, fenomeno*) to spread; **si sentì allargare il cuore** he felt his heart swell
allarmante [allar'mante] AGG alarming, very worrying
allarmare [allar'mare] VT to alarm; **non volevo allarmarti** I didn't want to alarm you
▶ **allarmarsi** VIP to become alarmed
allarme [al'larme] SM (*gen*) alarm; **dare l'allarme** to give *o* sound the alarm; **essere in allarme per qc** to be alarmed about sth; **mettere qn in allarme** to alarm sb; **i ladri hanno fatto scattare l'allarme** the burglars set off the alarm; **era solo un falso allarme** it was just a false alarm; **allarme aereo** air-raid warning; **allarme rosso** red alert
allarmismo [allar'mizmo] SM scaremongering
allarmista, i, e [allar'mista] SM/F alarmist, scaremonger
allarmisticamente [allarmistika'mente] AVV in an alarmist way
allarmistico, a, ci, che [allar'mistiko] AGG alarmist
allascare [allas'kare] VT (*Naut: vela*) to slacken
allattamento [allatta'mento] SM (*vedi vb*) (breast-)feeding; suckling; **allattamento artificiale** bottle-feeding; **allattamento naturale** breast-feeding
allattare [allat'tare] VT (*sogg: donna*) to (breast-)feed; (*: animale*) to suckle; **allattare artificialmente** to bottle-feed
alle ['alle] PREP + ART *vedi* **a**
alleanza [alle'antsa] SF alliance; **Alleanza Democratica** (*Pol*) *moderate centre-left party*; **Alleanza Nazionale** (*Pol*) *party on the far right*
alleare [alle'are] VT to unite
▶ **allearsi** VR to form an alliance; **allearsi a** *o* **con qn/qc** to become allied with sb/sth; **l'Italia e la Germania si allearono contro la Francia** Italy and Germany joined forces against France
alleato, a [alle'ato] AGG allied
■ SM/F ally
■ **gli Alleati** SMPL the Allies
alleg. ABBR (= **allegato**) encl.

allegare [alle'gare] VT **1** (*in lettera*): **allegare (a)** to enclose (with); **alleghiamo alla presente una fotocopia** we enclose herewith a photocopy; **allego una copia di...** I enclose a copy of ... **2** (*in e-mail*) to attach; **hai dimenticato di allegare il file!** you forgot to attach the file! **3** (*gen, Dir: addurre*) to adduce, put forward **4** (*denti*) to set on edge

allegato, a [alle'gato] AGG enclosed
■ SM (*in e-mail*) attachment; (*in lettera*) enclosure; **l'allegato può contenere un virus** the attachment may contain a virus; **in allegato Vi inviamo...** (*in e-mail*) please find attached ...; (*in lettera*) please find enclosed ...

alleggerimento [alleddʒeri'mento] SM (*gen*) lightening; (*di sofferenza, coscienza*) easing; (*di tasse*) reduction

alleggerire [alleddʒe'rire] VT **1** (*rendere più leggero*) to lighten, make lighter; (*fig: responsabilità*) to lighten; (: *sofferenza*) to relieve, lessen, alleviate; (: *lavoro, tasse*) to reduce; (: *coscienza*) to ease; **lo hanno alleggerito del portafoglio** (*scherz*) he's had his wallet pinched **2** (*Sci*) to unweight

allegoria [allego'ria] SF allegory

allegoricamente [allegorika'mente] AVV allegorically

allegorico, a, ci, che [alle'gɔriko] AGG allegorical

allegramente [allegra'mente] AVV (*gen*) cheerfully; (*arredato*) brightly

allegria [alle'gria] SF cheerfulness, gaiety; **mettere allegria a qn** to cheer sb up; **su, un po' di allegria!** come on, cheer up!; **tutte queste luci colorate fanno allegria** all these coloured lights make things more cheerful *o* brighten the place up

allegro, a [al'legro] AGG **1** (*persona*) cheerful; (*colore*) bright; (*musica*) lively; **è un tipo sempre allegro** he's always cheerful; **c'è poco da stare allegri** things are pretty grim, there's not much to be cheerful about **2** (*un po' brillo*) merry, tipsy
■ SM (*Mus*) allegro

allele [al'lɛle] SM (*Bio*) allele

alleluia [alle'luja] SM INV, ESCL hallelujah

allenamento [allena'mento] SM training; **si è fatto male al braccio durante l'allenamento** he hurt his arm during training; **essere fuori allenamento** (*anche fig*) to be out of practice

allenare [alle'nare] VT to train; **ha allenato la squadra per due anni** he trained the team for two years
▶ **allenarsi** VR to train; **ci alleniamo ogni giovedì** we train every Thursday

allenatore, trice [allena'tore] SM/F trainer, coach; **l'allenatore della nazionale italiana** the Italian national coach

allentamento [allenta'mento] SM (*fig*) relaxing

allentare [allen'tare] VT **1** (*nodo, cintura, vite*) to loosen; **allentare le redini** (*anche fig*) to slacken the reins; **allentare il passo** to slacken one's pace **2** (*diminuire: disciplina*) to relax
▶ **allentarsi** VIP (*nodo, stringhe*) to loosen, become loose; (*ingranaggio, vite*) to loosen, work loose

allergia, gie [aller'dʒia] SF allergy

allergico, a, ci, che [al'lɛrdʒiko] AGG: **allergico (a)** allergic (to); **sono allergico alle fragole** I'm allergic to strawberries

allertare VT to alert

allestimento [allesti'mento] SM preparation, setting up; **in allestimento** in preparation

allestire [alles'tire] VT **1** (*spettacolo, mostra, fiera*) to organize, stage; (*vetrina*) to dress; (*cena*) to prepare; **hanno allestito la mostra in fretta e furia** they organized the exhibition in a mad rush **2** (*esercito, nave*) to equip

allettante [allet'tante] AGG attractive; **una prospettiva allettante** an attractive prospect

allettare [allet'tare] VT to attract, entice; **l'idea non mi alletta** the idea doesn't appeal to me

allevamento [alleva'mento] SM **1** (*di animali*) breeding, rearing; **pollo d'allevamento** battery hen **2** (*luogo*) (stock) farm; (: *per cavalli*) stud farm; (: *per cani*) kennels *pl*

allevare [alle'vare] VT (*animali*) to breed, rear; (*bambini*) to bring up; **allevato male** (*bambino*) badly brought up

allevatore, trice [alleva'tore] SM/F breeder

alleviare [alle'vjare] VT (*pene, stanchezza*) to alleviate, relieve

allibire [alli'bire] VI (*aus* **essere**) (*dallo stupore*) to be appalled; (*dalla paura*) to go white

allibito, a [alli'bito] AGG (*vedi vi*) appalled; white; **rimanere allibito** to be appalled

allibratore [allibra'tore] SM bookmaker

allietare [allje'tare] VT to delight, gladden
▶ **allietarsi** VIP to be delighted, rejoice

allievo, a [al'ljɛvo] SM/F pupil, student; **è uno dei miei migliori allievi** he's one of my best pupils; **allievo ufficiale** (*Mil*) cadet

alligatore [alliga'tore] SM alligator

allineamento [allinea'mento] SM alignment

allineare [alline'are] VT (*persone, cose*) to line up; (*Tip*) to align; (*Mil*) to draw up in lines; (*fig: economia, salari*) to adjust; **ci ha allineati in fondo alla palestra** he lined us up at the back of the gym
▶ **allinearsi** VR (*anche Mil*) to line up; **allinearsi a** *o* **con** (*conformarsi*) to go along with

allineato, a [alline'ato] AGG aligned, in line; **testo allineato/non allineato** justified/unjustified text; **paesi non allineati** (*Pol*) non-aligned countries

allo ['allo] PREP + ART *vedi* **a**

allocare [allo'kare] VT to allocate

allocco, a, chi, che [al'lɔkko] SM (*Zool*) tawny owl
■ SM/F fool

allocuzione [allokut'tsjone] SF address

allodola [al'lɔdola] SF (sky)lark

alloggiare [allod'dʒare] VI (*aus* **avere**) **alloggiare (in)** to stay (at); **alloggia al Ritz** he's staying at the Ritz; **ho alloggiato presso una famiglia scozzese** I stayed with a Scottish family
■ VT to accommodate, put up

alloggio, gi [al'lɔddʒo] SM **1** (*abitazione provvisoria*) accommodation (*Brit*), accommodations (*Am*); **l'alloggio è compreso nel prezzo** accommodation is included in the price; **vitto e alloggio** board and lodging **2** (*appartamento*) flat (*Brit*), apartment (*Am*); **la crisi degli alloggi** the housing problem; **cercare alloggio** to look for somewhere to live

allontanamento [allontana'mento] SM (*gen*) separation; (*affettivo*) estrangement; (*di funzionario*) removal; (*di studente*) exclusion, expulsion; **c'è stato un graduale allontanamento fra i due paesi** relations between two countries have grown cooler

allontanare [allonta'nare] VT **1** (*persona*) to take away; (*oggetto*) to move away, take away; (*fig: affetti, amici*) to alienate; **allontanare una poltrona dal fuoco** to move an armchair away from the fire; **la polizia fece allontanare i passanti** the police moved

Aa

on the bystanders; **la maestra ha allontanato Maria da Roberto** the teacher has separated Maria and Roberto **2** (*mandare via*) to send away, send off; (*licenziare*) to dismiss **3** (*fig: pericolo*) to avert; (*: sospetti*) to divert
▶ **allontanarsi** VR: **allontanarsi (da)** to go away (from); to move away (from); (*fig: possibilità*) to grow more remote; **c'eravamo allontanati troppo** we had wandered too far; **allontanati dall'orlo, è pericoloso** move away from the edge, it's dangerous; **allontanarsi da qn** to wander away from sb; (*fig*) to grow away from sb

allora [al'lora] AVV **1** (*in quel momento*) then, at that moment; (*a quel tempo*) then, in those days, at that time; **proprio allora ha squillato il telefono** just at that moment the phone rang; **è stato allora che ho capito che tipo era** it was then that I realized what kind of person he was; **allora non lo sapevo** I didn't know about it then; **da allora non l'ho più visto** I haven't seen him since then; **da allora in poi** since then, from then on; **allora aveva ancora i capelli lunghi** at that time she still had long hair; **la gente di allora** people then *o* in those days **2** (*in questo caso*) then, in that case, so; (*dunque*) well then, so; **hai paura? – allora dillo!** are you frightened? – (well) then, say so!; **allora, che facciamo stasera?** so, what are we going to do this evening?; **allora? Com'è andata?** so, how did it go?; **allora vieni?** well (then), are you coming?; **e allora?** (*che fare?*) what now?; (*e con ciò?*) so what?

allorché [allor'ke] CONG (*letter*) when, as soon as

alloro [al'lɔro] SM laurel; **una foglia d'alloro** a bay leaf; **riposare** *o* **dormire sugli allori** to rest on one's laurels

allotropo [al'lɔtropo] SM allotrope

alluce ['allutʃe] SM big toe

allucinante [allutʃi'nante] AGG (*scena, spettacolo*) awful, terrifying; (*fam: incredibile*) amazing

allucinare [allutʃi'nare] VT (*abbagliare*) to dazzle; (*dare allucinazioni*) to cause to hallucinate; (*fig: impressionare fortemente*) to shock

allucinato, a [allutʃi'nato] AGG (*persona*) suffering from hallucinations; (*: fig*) shocked; (*sguardo*) staring
■ SM/F: **sguardo da allucinato** staring eyes

allucinazione [allutʃinat'tsjone] SF hallucination; **avere le allucinazioni** (*anche fig*) to hallucinate

allucinogeno, a [allutʃi'nɔdʒeno] AGG hallucinogenic, mind-expanding
■ SM hallucinogen

alludere [al'ludere] VI IRREG (*aus* **avere**) **alludere a** to allude to, hint at; **a cosa alludevi?** what were you referring to?

alluminio [allu'minjo] SM aluminium (*Brit*), aluminum (*Am*)

allunaggio, gi [allu'naddʒo] SM moon landing

allunare [allu'nare] VI (*aus* **essere**) to land on the moon

allungabile [allun'gabile] AGG extendable

allungare [allun'gare] VT **1** (*rendere più lungo*) to lengthen; **basterebbe allungare un po' la gonna** the skirt just needs lengthening a bit; **allungare il passo** to hurry up; **allungare la strada** to take the long way round **2** (*tendere*) to stretch out; **allungare le gambe** to stretch one's legs; **non c'era posto per allungare le gambe** there was no room to stretch your legs; **allungare le orecchie/il collo** to strain one's ears/crane one's neck; **allungare le mani** (*rubare*) to pick pockets; (*picchiare*) to become violent; **non allungare le mani sulla mia ragazza** keep your hands off my girlfriend **3** (*fam: dare*) to pass, hand; **mi allunghi il sale per favore?** could you pass me the salt please?; **gli allungò uno schiaffo** he gave him a slap **4** (*diluire*) to dilute, water down
▶ **allungarsi** VIP (*diventare più lungo*) to grow *o* get longer; (*: ombre*) to lengthen; (*: pianta*) to grow taller; (*: vestito, maglione*) to stretch; **le giornate si stanno allungando** the days are getting longer;
▶ **allungarsi** VR (*stendersi*) to stretch out

allungato, a [allun'gato] AGG (*Equitazione*): **passo/trotto allungato** extended walk/trot

allusi *ecc* [al'luzi] VB *vedi* **alludere**

allusione [allu'zjone] SF: **allusione (a)** allusion (to), hint (at); **un'allusione velata** a veiled hint

allusivamente [alluziva'mente] AVV allusively

allusivo, a [allu'zivo] AGG allusive

alluso, a [al'luzo] PP *di* **alludere**

alluvionale [alluvjo'nale] AGG alluvial; **materiale alluvionale** alluvium

alluvionato, a [alluvjo'nato] AGG (*regione, città*) flooded
■ SM/F flood victim

alluvione [allu'vjone] SF flood; **l'alluvione ha causato molti danni** the flood caused a lot of damage

almanacco, chi [alma'nakko] SM almanac

almeno [al'meno] AVV at least; **potevi almeno telefonare, no?** you could at least have phoned, couldn't you?; **dammene almeno uno!** at least give me one!; **ci saranno state almeno tremila persone** there must have been at least three thousand people
■ CONG: **(se) almeno** if only; **(se) almeno piovesse!** if only it would rain!; **se almeno sapessi dov'è!** if only I knew where it was!

alogeno, a [a'lɔdʒeno] AGG (*luce, lampada*) halogen *attr*
■ SF (*lampada*) halogen lamp
■ SM (*Chim*) halogen

alone [a'lone] SM (*di sole, luna*) halo; (*di fiamma, lampada*) glow; (*di macchia*) ring; **un alone di mistero** an aura *o* air of mystery

alpaca ['alpaka] SM INV alpaca

alpe ['alpe] SF (*letter: montagna*) alp; (*pascolo*) mountain pasture

alpeggio, gi [al'peddʒo] SM mountain pasture

alpestre [al'pɛstre] AGG (*delle Alpi*) alpine; (*montuoso*) mountainous

Alpi ['alpi] SFPL: **le Alpi** the Alps

alpinismo [alpi'nizmo] SM mountaineering, climbing
▷ www.cai.it/

alpinista, i, e [alpi'nista] SM/F mountaineer, climber

alpino, a [al'pino] AGG (*montano*) alpine, mountain *attr*; (*delle Alpi*) Alpine; **il paesaggio alpino** the Alpine scenery
■ SM (*Mil*): **gli alpini** *Italian Alpine troops*

alquanto, a [al'kwanto] AGG INDEF a certain amount of, some; **alquanti(e)** quite a few, several
■ PRON INDEF PL: **alquanti(e)** quite a few, several
■ AVV rather, somewhat

Alsazia [al'sattsja] SF Alsace

alsaziano, a [alsat'tsjano] AGG, SM/F, SM Alsatian

alt [alt] ESCL halt!, stop!
■ SM: **dare l'alt** to call a halt

altalena [alta'lena] SF (*a funi*) swing; (*a bilico, anche fig*) seesaw; **un'altalena di fortuna e disgrazie** a series of ups and downs

altamente [alta'mente] AVV (*specializzato, qualificato*)

highly; *(seccato, scocciato)* extremely; **me ne frego altamente** I don't give a damn
altare [al'tare] SM altar; **altare maggiore** high altar
altarino SM *(scherz)*: **scoprire gli altarini** to reveal one's guilty secrets
alteramente [altera'mente] AVV proudly
alterare [alte'rare] VT **1** *(fatti, verità)* to distort; *(registro)* to falsify; *(qualità, colore)* to affect, impair; *(alimenti)* to adulterate **2** *(piani)* to alter, change; *(persona)* to irritate
▶ **alterarsi** VIP **1** *(alimenti)* to go bad *o* off; *(vino)* to spoil **2** *(irritarsi)* to get angry, lose one's temper
alterazione [alterat'tsjone] SF *(vedi vt)* distortion; falsification; impairment; adulteration; alteration, change; **alterazione del polso** change in the pulse rate
altercare [alter'kare] VI *(aus* **avere***)* to argue, quarrel
alterco, chi [al'tɛrko] SM row, altercation
alter ego [alte'rɛgo] SM INV alter ego
alternamente [alterna'mente] AVV alternately
alternanza [alter'nantsa] SF alternation; *(Agr)* rotation
alternare [alter'nare] VT *(avvicendare)*: **alternare qc a** *o* **con qc** to alternate sth with sth; *(Agr)* to rotate
▶ **alternarsi** VR: **alternarsi (a** *o* **con)** to alternate (with)
alternatamente [alternata'mente] AVV = **alternamente**
alternativa [alterna'tiva] SF alternative; **non abbiamo alternative** we have no alternative; **in alternativa** as an alternative
alternativo, a [alterna'tivo] AGG *(energia, medicina ecc)* alternative
alternato, a [alter'nato] AGG alternate; *(Elettr)* alternating; **passo alternato** *(Sci)* classic striding
alternatore [alterna'tore] SM alternator
alterno, a [al'tɛrno] AGG *(gen)* alternate; *(mutevole: fortuna, vicenda)* changing; **a giorni alterni** every other day, on alternate days; **circolazione a targhe alterne** *(Aut)* *vedi* **circolazione**
altero, a [al'tɛro] AGG proud
altezza [al'tettsa] SF **1** *(di edificio, persona)* height; *(quota)* height, altitude; *(di suono)* pitch; *(di acqua, pozzo)* depth; *(di tessuto)* width; *(fig: d'animo)* greatness; **è di altezza media** she's of medium height; **avere un'altezza di...** to be ... high; **ha un'altezza di cinque centimetri** it's five centimetres high; **altezza sul mare** height above sea level; **da un'altezza di 2.000 metri** from a height of 2,000 metres; **essere all'altezza di una situazione** *(fig)* to be equal to a situation; **non sono all'altezza** *(fig)* I'm not up to it **2** *(Geom)* perpendicular height; *(: linea)* perpendicular; *(Astron)* elevation, altitude **3** *(prossimità)*: **all'altezza di** near; **l'albergo è all'altezza di piazza Verdi** the hotel is near Piazza Verdi; **all'altezza di Capo Horn** off Cape Horn **4** *(titolo)* highness; **Sua Altezza** Your Highness
altezzosamente [altettsosa'mente] AVV haughtily, arrogantly
altezzosità [altettsosi'ta] SF haughtiness, arrogance
altezzoso, a [altet'tsoso] AGG haughty, arrogant
alticcio, cia, ci, ce [al'tittʃo] AGG tipsy
altimetro [al'timetro] SM altimeter
altipiano [alti'pjano] SM = **altopiano**
altisonante [altiso'nante] AGG high-sounding, pompous
Altissimo [al'tissimo] SM: **l'Altissimo** the Most High
altitudine [alti'tudine] SF altitude

alto, a ['alto] AGG
1 *(gen)* high, tall; **un edificio alto** a tall building; **un muro alto 10 metri** a wall 10 metres high; **quanto sei alto?** how tall are you?; **è alto 1 metro e 80** ≈ he's 6 foot (tall); **Marisa è più alta di me** Marisa's taller than me; **Matteo è il più alto della famiglia** Matteo is the tallest in the family; **andare a testa alta** *(fig)* to carry one's head high; **aveva la febbre alta** she had a high temperature; **salto in alto** high jump
2 *(suono: elevato)* high(-pitched); *(: forte)* loud; **ad alta voce** out loud, aloud; **l'ha detto a voce alta perché sentissero tutti** she said it in a loud voice so that everybody would hear; **abbassa un po', è troppo alto** turn it down a bit, it's too loud; **ad alto rischio** high-risk
3 *(fig: elevato: carica, dignitario)* high; *(: sentimenti, pensieri)* lofty, noble; **avere un'alta opinione di sé** to have a high opinion of o.s.
4 *(profondo: acqua)* deep; **in quel punto l'acqua è molto alta** the water's very deep there; **essere ancora in alto mare** *(fig)* to still have a long way to go; **a notte alta** in the dead of night
5 *(Geog)*: **l'alta Italia** Northern Italy; **l'alto Po** the upper reaches of the Po
6 *(largo: tessuto)* wide
■ SM *(parte superiore)* top (part); **in alto** up; **mani in alto!** hands up!; **guardare in alto** to look up; **là in alto** up there; **dall'alto** *(fig)* from on high; **dall'alto di** from the top of; **dall'alto della torre si vede tutta la città** from the top of the tower you can see the whole city; **dall'alto in** *o* **al basso** up and down; **guardare dall'alto in basso qn** *(fig)* to look down on sb; **alti e bassi** ups and downs; **la sua carriera ha avuto alti e bassi** his career has had its ups and downs
■ AVV *(volare)* high; **"alto"** *(su casse di imballaggio)* "this side up"
■ **alta definizione** high definition; **alta fedeltà** high fidelity, hi-fi; **alta moda** haute couture; **alta pressione** *(Meteor)* high pressure; **alta società** high society; **alta stagione** high *o* peak season; **alta velocità** *(Ferr)* high speed rail system; **alto comando** *(Mil)* high command; **alto commissario** high commissioner; **l'Alto Medioevo** the Early Middle Ages
altoatesino, a [altoate'zino] AGG of *o* from the Alto Adige
■ SM/F inhabitant *o* native of the Alto Adige
altoforno [alto'forno] SM blast furnace
altolà [alto'la] ESCL *(Mil)* halt!
■ SM INV: **gli hanno dato l'altolà** they ordered him to stop
altolocato, a [altolo'kato] AGG of high rank, highly placed; **amicizie altolocate** friends in high places
altoparlante [altopar'lante] SM (loud)speaker
altopiano [alto'pjano] SM *(pl* **altipiani***)* upland plain, plateau; **altopiano basaltico** lava plateau
altresì [altre'si] AVV *(letter)* also
altrettanto, a [altret'tanto] AGG as much; **altrettanti(e)** as many; **ho altrettanta fiducia in te** I have as much *o* the same confidence in you
■ PRON as much; **altrettanti(e)** as many; **domani dovrò comprarne altrettanto** I'll have to buy as much *o* the same tomorrow; **sono 2 mesi che cerco lavoro, e temo che ne passeranno altrettanti prima di trovarlo** I have been looking for work for 2 months now, and I'm afraid it'll be as long again before I find any; **se n'è andato ed io ho fatto altrettanto** he left

Aa

and so did I *o* and I followed suit; **tanti auguri! — grazie, altrettanto** all the best! — thank you, the same to you
■ AVV equally; **lui è altrettanto bravo** he is equally clever, he is just as clever

altri ['altri] PRON PERS SG *(qualcun altro)* someone else; (: *in frasi negative*) anyone else; **né tu né altri potrete convincermi** neither you nor anyone else is going to persuade me; **non si tocca la roba d'altri** you shouldn't touch other people's things

altrimenti [altri'menti] AVV **1** *(in caso contrario)* otherwise, or else; **sbrigati, altrimenti arriveremo in ritardo** hurry up or we'll be late **2** *(in modo diverso)* differently; **non posso fare altrimenti** I can't do otherwise

altro, a ['altro] PAROLA CHIAVE
■ AGG INDEF
1 *(diverso)* other, different; **questa è un'altra cosa** that's another *o* a different thing; **erano altri tempi** things were different then
2 *(supplementare)* other; **prendi un altro cioccolatino** have another chocolate; **gli altri allievi usciranno più tardi** the other pupils *o* the rest of the pupils will come out later
3 *(opposto)* other; **dall'altra parte della strada** on the other *o* opposite side of the street; **d'altra parte** on the other hand
4 *(nel tempo)*: **domani l'altro** the day after tomorrow; **l'altro giorno** the other day; **l'altro ieri** the day before yesterday; **quest'altro mese** next month
5 chi/dove/chiunque altro who/where/anybody else; **noi altri** = noialtri; **voi altri** = voialtri
■ PRON INDEF
1 *(persona, cosa diversa o supplementare)*: **un altro/ un'altra** another (one); **altri(e)** others; *(persone)* others, other people; **prendine un altro** take another one; **se non lo fai tu lo farà un altro** if you don't do it someone else will; **da un giorno all'altro** *(improvvisamente)* from one day to the next; *(presto)* any day now; **aiutarsi l'un l'altro** to help one another *o* each other
2 *(opposizione)*: **l'altro(a)** the other (one); **gli altri/ le altre** the others; **l'uno e l'altro** both (of them); **o l'uno o l'altro** either (of them); **né l'uno né l'altro** neither (of them); **non questo, l'altro** not this one, the other one
3 *(sostantivato: solo maschile)* something else; *(in espressioni interrogative)* anything else; **non faccio altro che studiare** I do nothing but study, all I do is study; **non ho altro da dire** I have nothing else to say, I don't have anything else to say; **desidera altro?** (would you like) anything else?; **gli dirò questo ed altro!** I'll tell him this and more besides!; **ci mancherebbe altro!** that's all we need!; **più che altro** above all; **se non altro** at least; **tra l'altro** among other things; **sei contento? — tutt'altro!** are you pleased? — far from it! *o* anything but!; **ci vuole altro per spaventarmi!** it takes a lot more (than this) to frighten me!

altroché [altro'ke] ESCL certainly!, and how!
altronde [al'tronde] AVV: **d'altronde** on the other hand
altrove [al'trove] AVV elsewhere, somewhere else
altrui [al'trui] AGG INV other people's, others'; **la roba altrui** other people's things *pl*
altruismo [altru'izmo] SM altruism
altruista, i, e [altru'ista] AGG altruistic
■ SM/F altruist
altruisticamente [altruistika'mente] AVV altruistically
altruistico, a, ci, che [altru'istiko] AGG altruistic
altura [al'tura] SF **1** *(rialto)* height, high ground **2** *(Naut)*: **d'altura** deep-sea
alunno, a [a'lunno] SM/F pupil
alveare [alve'are] SM (bee)hive
alveo ['alveo] SM riverbed
alveolo [al'vɛolo] SM alveolus
alzabandiera [altsaban'djɛra] SM INV *(Mil)*: **l'alzabandiera** the raising of the flag
alzacristallo [altsakris'tallo] SM *(Aut)* window winder *(Brit)*, window roller *(Am)*; **alzacristalli elettrici** electric windows
alzare [al'tsare] VT **1** *(gen)* to raise; *(peso)* to lift; **è troppo pesante, non riesco nemmeno ad alzarla** it's too heavy, I can't even lift it; **alzare gli occhi** *o* **lo sguardo** to raise one's eyes; **lo sciopero fece alzare i prezzi** the strike caused an increase in prices **2** *(issare: bandiera, vela)* to hoist **3** *(costruire)* to build, erect **4** *(fraseologia)*: **alzare le carte** to cut the cards; **non ha alzato un dito per aiutarmi** he didn't lift a finger to help me; **alzare il gomito** to drink too much; **alzare le mani su qn** to lay hands on sb; **alzare le spalle** to shrug one's shoulders; **alzare i tacchi** to take to one's heels; **alzare la voce** *(per farsi sentire)* to speak up; *(per intimidire, in collera)* to raise one's voice
▶ **alzarsi** VR *(persona)* to rise, get up; **a che ora ti alzi la mattina?** what time do you get up in the morning?; **si è alzato e se n'è andato** he got up and went away; **alzarsi (in piedi)** to stand up, get to one's feet; **alzarsi da tavola** to get up from the table; **alzarsi col piede sbagliato** to get out of bed on the wrong side;
▶ **alzarsi** VIP **1** *(sorgere: sole, luna)* to rise; (: *vento*) to rise, get up **2** *(aumentare: temperatura)* to rise; *(fiamma)* to leap up
alzata [al'tsata] SF **1** *(vedi vb)* raising; lifting; **un'alzata di spalle** a shrug; **un'alzata d'ingegno** a flash of genius; **votare per alzata di mano** to vote by show of hands **2** *(di mobile)* upper part, top **3** *(per dolci)* cakestand
alzato, a [al'tsato] AGG *(braccio)* raised; *(persona: in piedi)* up; **rimanere/stare alzato (tutta la notte)** to stay up (all night)
■ SM *(Archit)* elevation
alzavola [al'tsavola] SF teal
Alzheimer [al'tsaimer] SM *(anche:* **morbo di Alzheimer***)* Alzheimer's (disease)
AM [a'ɛmme] SIGLA F (= **Aeronautica Militare**) ≈ RAF
amabile [a'mabile] AGG **1** *(persona, conversazione)* pleasant, amiable **2** *(vino)* sweet
amabilità [amabili'ta] SF INV pleasantness, amiability
amabilmente [amabil'mente] AVV pleasantly, amiably
amaca, che [a'maka] SF hammock
amalgama, i [a'malgama] SM *(Chim)* amalgam; *(fig)* amalgam, mixture
amalgamare [amalga'mare] VT to amalgamate, combine; *(impastare)* to mix
▶ **amalgamarsi** VIP *(sostanze)* to amalgamate, combine; *(Culin)* to mix; *(fig: gruppo, squadra)* to become unified
amante [a'mante] AGG *(appassionato)*: **amante di** fond

of, keen on; **è amante del jazz** he's keen on jazz
■ SM/F lover; (*extraconiugale: uomo*) lover; (*: donna*) lover, mistress; **sono amanti da anni** they've been lovers for years

amaramente [amara'mente] AVV bitterly

amaranto [ama'ranto] SM (*Bot*) love-lies-bleeding
■ AGG INV: **color amaranto** reddish purple

amare [a'mare] VT (*provare affetto*) to love; (*: amante, marito, moglie*) to love, be in love with; (*amico, musica, sport*) to be fond of, love; **ti amo** I love you; **mi ami?** do you love me?; **noi amiamo la musica classica** we love *o* enjoy *o* are fond of classical music; **amare fare qc** to like *o* love doing *o* to do sth; **farsi amare da qn** to win sb's love
▶ **amarsi** VR (*uso reciproco*) to be in love, love each other; **si amano** they love each other

amareggiare [amared'dʒare] VT to embitter; **amareggiarsi la vita** to make one's life a misery
▶ **amareggiarsi** VR to get upset

amareggiato, a [amared'dʒato] AGG embittered

amarena [ama'rɛna] SF (sour) black cherry

amaretto [ama'retto] SM (*biscotto*) amaretto biscuit; (*liquore*) amaretto liqueur

amarezza [ama'rettsa] SF bitterness; **le amarezze della vita** life's disappointments

amarico, a [a'mariko] AGG Amharic
■ SM/F (*abitante*) Amhara
■ SM (*lingua*) Amharic

amaro, a [a'maro] AGG (*sapore, fig*) bitter; (*caffè*) without sugar; (*spiacevole*) unpleasant, bitter; (*triste*) unhappy; (*doloroso*) painful; **avere la bocca amara** to have a bitter taste in one's mouth
■ SM **1** (*liquore*) bitters *pl* **2** (*gusto*) bitter taste; (*fig: tristezza, dolore*) bitterness; **mi ha lasciato l'amaro in bocca** it left a bitter taste in my mouth
▷ www.amariamari.com/

amarognolo, a [ama'roɲɲolo] AGG slightly bitter

amato, a [a'mato] AGG beloved, loved, dear
■ SM/F loved one

amatore, trice [ama'tore] SM/F **1** (*amante*) lover **2** (*appassionato*) lover; (*intenditore: di vini ecc*) connoisseur; **pezzo da amatore** collector's item **3** (*dilettante*) amateur

amazzone [a'maddzone] SF **1** (*Mitol*) Amazon; **il Rio delle Amazzoni** (*Geog*) the (river) Amazon **2** (*cavallerizza*) horsewoman; (*abito*) riding habit; **cavalcare all'amazzone** to ride sidesaddle

Amazzonia [amad'dzɔnja] SF Amazonia

amazzoniano, a [amaddzo'njano] AGG Amazonian

amazzonico, a, ci, che [amad'dzɔniko] AGG (*gen*) Amazonian; (*giungla, bacino*) Amazon *attr*

ambasceria [ambaʃʃe'ria] SF embassy

ambasciata [ambaʃ'ʃata] SF embassy; (*messaggio*) message; **l'ambasciata britannica** the British Embassy
▷ www.esteri.it/

ambasciatore, trice [ambaʃʃa'tore] SM/F ambassador; **ambasciator non porta pena!** don't take it out on me (*o* him *ecc*)!

ambedue [ambe'due] AGG INV both; **ambedue i ragazzi** both boys
■ PRON INV both

ambidestro, a [ambi'dɛstro] AGG ambidextrous

ambientale [ambjen'tale] AGG (*temperatura*) ambient *attr*; (*problemi, tutela*) environmental

ambientalismo [ambjenta'lizmo] SM environmentalism

ambientalista, i, e [ambjenta'lista] AGG environmental
■ SM/F environmentalist

ambientamento SM (*in luogo, lavoro*): **periodo di ambientamento** settling-in period

ambientare [ambjen'tare] VT (*film, racconto*) to set; **il film è ambientato nella Chicago degli anni venti** the film is set in Chicago in the twenties
▶ **ambientarsi** VR to get used to one's surroundings, settle down; **ti stai ambientando nella nuova scuola?** are you settling into your new school?

ambientazione [ambjentat'tsjone] SF (*di film, racconto*) setting

ambiente [am'bjɛnte] SM **1** environment; **la difesa dell'ambiente** the protection of the environment; **negli ambienti politici** in political circles **2** (*stanza*) room
■ AGG INV: **temperatura ambiente** room temperature
▷ www.minambiente.it
▷ www.fondoambiente.it/

ambiguamente [ambigua'mente] AVV ambiguously

ambiguità [ambigui'ta] SF INV ambiguity

ambiguo, a [am'biguo] AGG ambiguous; (*persona*) shady; **una risposta ambigua** an ambiguous answer

ambio ['ambjo] SM (*Equitazione*) amble

ambire [am'bire] VT, VI (*aus* **avere**) **ambire a** to aspire to; **un premio molto ambito** a much sought-after prize

ambito ['ambito] SM area; (*tecnico, specialistico*) field; (*fig: cerchia*) sphere, circle

ambivalente [ambiva'lɛnte] AGG (*termini*) with two possible interpretations

ambivalenza [ambiva'lɛntsa] SF ambivalence

ambizione [ambit'tsjone] SF ambition; **la mia ambizione è fare il giornalista** my ambition is to be a journalist

ambizioso, a [ambit'tsjoso] AGG ambitious

ambo ['ambo] AGG (*pl m* **ambo** *o* **ambi**, *pl f* **ambo** *o* **ambe**) both; **da ambo** *o* **ambe le parti** from *o* on both sides
■ SM (*al gioco*) double

ambosessi [ambo'sɛssi] AGG INV of either sex, male or female

ambra ['ambra] SF amber; **ambra grigia** ambergris

ambrosia [am'brɔzja] SF ambrosia

ambulante [ambu'lante] AGG travelling, itinerant; (*biblioteca*) mobile; **un venditore ambulante** a travelling salesman; **sei un'enciclopedia ambulante!** you're a walking encyclopaedia!
■ SM pedlar

ambulanza [ambu'lantsa] SF (*veicolo*) ambulance; (*Mil*) field hospital; **devo chiamare l'ambulanza?** shall I call an ambulance?

ambulatoriale [ambulato'rjale] AGG (*Med*) outpatients *attr*; **intervento ambulatoriale** operation in a doctor's surgery; **visita ambulatoriale** visit to the doctor's surgery (*Brit*) *o* office (*Am*)

ambulatorio, ri [ambula'tɔrjo] SM (*di medico*) surgery (*Brit*), doctor's office (*Am*); (*di ospedale*) outpatients' department; **a che ora apre l'ambulatorio?** what time does the surgery open?

AMDI ['amdi] SIGLA F = *Associazione Medici Dentisti Italiani*

AME ['ame] SIGLA M = *Accordo Monetario Europeo*

ameba [a'mɛba] SF amoeba (*Brit*), ameba (*Am*)

amebiasi [ame'biazi] SF (*Med*) amoebiasis

amen ['amen] ESCL (*Rel*) amen; **e allora amen!** (*fam*) alright, alright

■SM: **in un amen** in the twinkling of an eye
amenità [ameni'ta] SF INV **1** (*di luogo, pensieri*) pleasantness *no pl* **2** (*facezia*) pleasantry
ameno, a [a'mɛno] AGG **1** (*luogo, lettura, pensieri*) pleasant, agreeable **2** (*faceto*: *tipo, discorso*) droll, amusing
America [a'mɛrika] SF America; **l'America latina** Latin America; **l'America meridionale** South America; **l'America settentrionale** North America; **vengono dall'America** they come from America
americanata [amerika'nata] SF (*pegg*): **le Olimpiadi sono state una vera americanata** the Olympics were a typical American extravaganza; **gli piacciono le americanate** he likes everything that's typically American
americanismo [amerika'nizmo] SM (*espressione*) Americanism; (*ammirazione*) love of America
americanizzare [amerikanid'dzare] VT to Americanize
▶ **americanizzarsi** VIP to become Americanized
americano, a [ameri'kano] AGG American; **confronto all'americana** identity parade; **servizio all'americana** table mats
■SM/F American
ametista [ame'tista] SF amethyst
amfetamina [anfeta'mina] SF amphetamine
amianto [a'mjanto] SM asbestos
amichevole [ami'kevole] AGG (*anche Sport*) friendly; **potresti avere un atteggiamento un po' più amichevole** you could be a bit friendlier; **in via amichevole** amicably
■SF (*Sport*) friendly match
amichevolmente [amikevol'mente] AVV in a friendly way
amicizia [ami'tʃittsja] SF **1** (*rapporto*) friendship; **ci tengo molto alla sua amicizia** her friendship is very important to me; **fare amicizia con qn** to make friends with sb; **abbiamo fatto subito amicizia** we immediately became friends; **un'affettuosa amicizia** (*euf*: *relazione sentimentale*) a close friendship
2 amicizie SFPL (*amici*) friends; **ha molte amicizie influenti** she has a lot of influential friends *o* friends in high places
amico, a, ci, che [a'miko] AGG friendly
■SM/F **1** friend; **la mia migliore amica** my best friend; **ha molti amici** she's got a lot of friends; **amico del cuore** best friend; **amico d'infanzia** childhood friend; **amico intimo** close friend; **Michela e le sue amiche** Michela and her (girl)friends; **siamo molto amici** we're good friends; **sono amici per la pelle** they're great pals; **è un mio amico** he's a friend of mine; **un mio amico avvocato** a lawyer friend of mine; **farsi qn amico** to make friends with sb; **senza amici** friendless **2** (*euf*: *amante*) friend, man friend/lady friend **3** (*appassionato*) lover, enthusiast; **amico degli animali** animal lover; **club degli amici della musica** music club
amido ['amido] SM starch
amilasi [ami'lazi] SF amylase
amletico, a, ci, che [am'lɛtiko] AGG: **dubbio amletico** paralyzing doubt
ammaccare [ammak'kare] VT (*auto, pentola, cappello*) to dent; (*frutta, parte del corpo*) to bruise
▶ **ammaccarsi** VIP (*vedi vt*) to get dented; bruise
ammaccatura [ammakka'tura] SF (*segno*: *su auto ecc*) dent; (: *su parte del corpo*) bruise; **c'è un'ammaccatura sullo sportello** there's a dent in the door
ammaestrare [ammaes'trare] VT (*addestrare*) to teach; (: *animali*) to train; (: *scherz fig*: *persona*) tame; **orso/cavallo ammaestrato** performing bear/horse
ammainabandiera [ammainaban'djɛra] SM INV (*Mil*): **l'ammainabandiera** the lowering of the flag
ammainare [ammai'nare] VT (*vela, bandiera*) to lower, haul down
ammalarsi [amma'larsi] VIP to fall *o* become ill; **mi sono ammalato e non sono potuto partire** I got ill and couldn't go
ammalato, a [amma'lato] AGG ill, unwell, sick; **metà della classe era ammalata** half the class was ill
■SM/F sick person; (*paziente*) patient
ammaliare [amma'ljare] VT (*con sortilegio*) to bewitch; (*fig*) to bewitch, enchant, charm
ammaliatore, trice [ammalja'tore] SM/F (*uomo*) charmer; (*donna*) enchantress
■AGG bewitching, charming
ammanco, chi [am'manko] SM (*Amm, Econ*) deficit; **c'è stato un ammanco di cassa di 300 euro** the till was 300 euros short
ammanettare [ammanet'tare] VT to handcuff
ammanicato, a [ammani'kato], **ammanigliato, a** [ammaniʎ'ʎato] AGG (*fam*) well-connected, with friends in high places
ammansire [amman'sire] VT (*animale*) to tame; (*fig*: *persona*) to calm (down)
ammantarsi [amman'tarsi] VR (*persona*) to wrap o.s.; (: *fig*): **ammantarsi di virtù** to pretend virtue
■VIP: **ammantarsi di** (*prato*: *di fiori*) to be carpeted with; (*cielo*: *di stelle*) to be studded with
ammantato, a [amman'tato] AGG: **ammantato di neve** with a mantle of snow
ammaraggio, gi [amma'raddʒo] SM (*vedi vb*) (sea) landing; splashdown
ammarare [amma'rare] VI (*aus* **essere**) (*aereo*) to make a sea landing; (*astronave*) to splash down
ammassare [ammas'sare] VT (*cose, fig*: *ricchezze*) to pile up, accumulate, amass; (*persone*) to pack
▶ **ammassarsi** VIP (*cose*) to pile up, accumulate; (*persone*) to crowd; **la gente si era ammassata sull'autobus** people were crammed together on the bus
ammasso [am'masso] SM (*cumulo*) pile, heap; (*Econ*) stockpile; **portare all'ammasso** (*grano, olio*) to stockpile
ammattire [ammat'tire] VI (*aus* **essere**) (*anche fig*) to go mad, be driven mad
ammazzacaffè SM INV (*fam*) *brandy etc after a meal*
ammazzare [ammat'tsare] VT (*uccidere*) to kill; (*fig*: *affaticare*) to exhaust, wear out; **ammazzare il tempo** to kill time
▶ **ammazzarsi** VR (*uso reciproco*) to kill each other; (*suicidarsi*) to kill o.s, commit suicide; **ammazzarsi di lavoro** to kill o.s. with work, work o.s. to death;
▶ **ammazzarsi** VIP (*rimanere ucciso*) to die, be killed
ammenda [am'mɛnda] SF **1** (*Dir, Sport*) fine **2** (*riparazione*): **fare ammenda di qc** to make amends for sth
ammesso, a [am'messo] PP *di* **ammettere**
ammettere [am'mettere] VT IRREG **1** (*far entrare*: *visitatore*) to admit, let in, allow in; (*accettare*: *nuovo socio, studente*) to admit; **ammettere qn ad un club** to admit sb to a club; **essere ammesso agli esami orali** to be admitted to *o* to be allowed to do the oral exams
2 (*riconoscere*: *colpa, errore, fatto*) to admit, acknowledge; **ha ammesso di avere torto** she admitted she was

wrong **3** (*supporre*) to suppose, assume; **ammettiamo che sia vero** let us suppose *o* assume that it's true; **ammettiamo che venga...** suppose he comes ...; **ammesso (e non concesso) che...** (just) assuming that ... **4** (*tollerare*: *scuse, comportamento*) to accept; (*permettere*) to allow; **non ammetto che si bestemmi** I will not tolerate swearing; **non ammetto scuse** I won't accept any excuses

ammezzato [ammed'dzato] SM (*anche*: **piano** ammezzato) mezzanine, entresol

ammiccare [ammik'kare] VI (*aus* **avere**) **ammiccare (a)** to wink (at)

amministrare [amminis'trare] VT **1** (*ditta*) to manage, run; (*patrimonio*) to administer; (*stato*) to run, govern **2** (*Rel, Dir*) to administer

amministrativamente [amministrativa'mente] AVV administratively

amministrativo, a [amministra'tivo] AGG administrative

amministratore [amministra'tore] SM (*Amm*) administrator; (*di stabile*) manager of flats; **amministratore aggiunto** associate director; **amministratore di condominio** house manager; **amministratore delegato** managing director, chief executive; **amministratore fiduciario** trustee; **amministratore unico** sole director

amministrazione [amministrat'tsjone] SF (*vedi vb*) management, running; administration; government; **consiglio d'amministrazione** board of directors; **amministrazione controllata** temporary receivership; **amministrazione fiduciaria** trusteeship; **amministrazione locale** local government; **amministrazione pubblica** public administration, ≈ civil service **amministrazione straordinaria** *control by a government-appointed administrator*

amminoacido [ammino'atʃido] SM amino acid

ammiraglia [ammi'raʎʎa] SF (*nave*) flagship

ammiragliato [ammiraʎ'ʎato] SM (*ufficio*) admiralship; (*consesso, sede*) admiralty

ammiraglio, gli [ammi'raʎʎo] SM admiral

ammirare [ammi'rare] VT to admire; **ci siamo fermati ad ammirare il paesaggio** we stopped to admire the view; **lo ammiro** I admire him

ammiratore, trice [ammira'tore] SM/F admirer

ammirazione [ammirat'tsjone] SF admiration

ammirevole [ammi'revole] AGG admirable

ammirevolmente [ammirevol'mente] AVV admirably

ammisi *ecc* [am'mizi] VB *vedi* **ammettere**

ammissibile [ammis'sibile] AGG (*comportamento*) acceptable; (*Dir*: *testimonianza*) admissible

ammissione [ammis'sjone] SF **1** (*a club*) admission, entry; (*a scuola*) entrance, acceptance; **esame d'ammissione** entrance exam **2** (*di colpa, errore*) admission

Amm.ne ABBR = **amministrazione**

ammobiliare [ammobi'ljare] VT to furnish

ammobiliato, a [ammobi'ljato] AGG (*camera, appartamento*) furnished

ammodernare [ammoder'nare] VT to modernize

ammodo, a modo [am'mɔdo] AVV (*per bene*) well, properly
■ AGG INV respectable, nice

ammogliare [ammoʎ'ʎare] VT to find a wife for
▶ **ammogliarsi** VR to marry, take a wife (*old*)

ammollo [am'mɔllo] SM soaking; **mettere/lasciare i panni in ammollo** to leave the clothes to soak

ammoniaca [ammo'niaka] SF ammonia

ammoniacato, a [ammonia'kato] AGG containing ammonia
■ SM ammoniate

ammonimento [ammoni'mento] SM (*rimprovero*) reprimand, admonishment; (*lezione*) lesson, warning

ammonio, ni [am'mɔnjo] SM ammonium; **idrossido di ammonio** ammonium hydroxide
■ AGG INV: **ione ammonio** ammonium ion

ammonire [ammo'nire] VT **1** (*rimproverare*) to admonish, reprimand; (*avvertire*) to warn; **è stato ammonito dall'insegnante** he was reprimanded by the teacher **2** (*Dir*) to caution; (*Calcio*) to book; **è stato ammonito dall'arbitro** he was booked by the referee

ammonitivo, a [ammoni'tivo] AGG warning

ammonito, a [ammo'nito] SM/F (*gen*) person who has been warned; (*Calcio*) booked player

ammonizione [ammonit'tsjone] SF **1** (*monito*) warning; (*rimprovero*) reprimand **2** (*Dir*) caution; (*Calcio*) booking

ammontare [ammon'tare] VI (*aus* **essere**) **ammontare a** to amount to, add up to; **a quanto ammonta il totale?** what does the total come to?
■ SM (*somma*) (total) amount

ammonticchiare [ammontik'kjare] VT to pile up, heap up

ammorbare [ammor'bare] VT **1** (*diffondere malattia*) to infect **2** (*sogg*: *odore*) to foul; **un tanfo tremendo ammorbava l'aria** a terrible stench poisoned the air

ammorbidente [ammorbi'dɛnte] SM fabric softener

ammorbidire [ammorbi'dire] VT to soften
▶ **ammorbidirsi** VIP to soften; **ammorbidirsi con l'età** (*fig*) to mellow with age

ammortamento [ammorta'mento] SM (*Fin*: *estinzione di debito*) redemption, amortization; (: *in bilancio*) depreciation; **ammortamento fiscale** capital allowance

ammortare [ammor'tare] VT (*Fin*: *debito*) to pay off, redeem; (: *spese d'impianto*) to write off

ammortizzamento [ammortiddza'mento] SM **1** (*Fin*): = ammortamento) **2** (*Aut*) cushioning

ammortizzare [ammortid'dzare] VT **1** (*Fin*: *debito*) to pay off, redeem; (: *spese d'impianto*) to write off **2** (*Aut, Tecn*: *attutire*) to cushion, absorb

ammortizzatore [ammortiddza'tore] SM (*Aut, Tecn*) shock absorber; **ammortizzatori sociali** *measures to cushion the effects of unemployment*

Amm.re ABBR = **amministratore**

ammucchiare [ammuk'kjare] VT (*disporre in mucchio*) to heap, pile up; (: *denaro*) to pile up, accumulate; **ha ammucchiato le sue cose in un angolo** she piled up her things in a corner
▶ **ammucchiarsi** VIP (*cose*) to pile up, accumulate; (*persone*) to crowd

ammuffire [ammuf'fire] VI (*aus* **essere**) to go *o* grow mouldy (*Brit*) *o* moldy (*Am*); (*fig*: *persona*) to moulder, languish; **il pane è ammuffito** the bread's gone mouldy

ammuffito, a [ammuf'fito] AGG mouldy; (*fig*) fossilized

ammutinamento [ammutina'mento] SM mutiny

ammutinarsi [ammuti'narsi] VIP to mutiny

ammutinato, a [ammuti'nato] AGG mutinous
■ SM mutineer

ammutolire [ammuto'lire] VI (*aus* **essere**) to be struck dumb

amnesia [amne'zia] SF amnesia

Aa

amnio, ni ['amnjo] SM amnion
amniocentesi [amnjo'tʃentezi] SF INV (*Med*) amniocentesis
amniotico, a, ci, che [am'njɔtiko] AGG amniotic; **liquido amniotico** amniotic fluid
amnistia [amnis'tia] SF amnesty
amnistiare [amnis'tjare] VT to amnesty, grant an amnesty to
amo ['amo] SM (*Pesca*) (fish) hook; (*fig*) bait; **l'abbiamo preso all'amo** (*fig*) he's swallowed the bait; **gettare l'amo** to cast one's line; (*fig*) to lay bait
amorale [amo'rale] AGG amoral
amoralità [amorali'ta] SF amorality
amore [a'more] SM **1** (*affetto*) love, affection; (*sessuale*) love; **una canzone d'amore** a love song; **il suo amore per lui/per le piante** her love for him/of plants; **fare qc con amore** to do sth with loving care; **fare l'amore** *o* **all'amore (con qn)** to make love (with sb); **mi ha raccontato tutto dei suoi amori** he told me all about his love affairs **2** (*persona*) love; **vieni, amore** come here, darling *o* love; **il tuo bambino è un amore** your baby is a darling **3** (*fraseologia*): **per amore di** for the sake of; **per l'amor del cielo!** for heaven's sake!; **per l'amor di Dio!** for God's sake!; **per amore o per forza** willy-nilly; **andare d'amore e d'accordo con qn** to get on like a house on fire with sb; **che amore di vestito!** what a lovely dress!; **amore libero** free love; **amore di sé** egoism, selfishness; **amor proprio** self-esteem, pride
amoreggiamento [amoreddʒa'mento] SM flirting
amoreggiare [amored'dʒare] VI (*aus* **avere**) to flirt
amorevole [amo'revole] AGG loving, affectionate
amorfo, a [a'mɔrfo] AGG amorphous; (*fig*: *persona*) colourless; **ma come sei amorfo!** how apathetic you are!
amorino [amo'rino] SM cupid
amorosamente [amorosa'mente] AVV lovingly
amoroso, a [amo'roso] AGG (*affettuoso*) loving, affectionate; (*d'amore*: *sguardo*) amorous; (: *poesia, lettera*) love *attr*; **uno sguardo amoroso** an amorous look; **una relazione amorosa** an affair
■ SM/F (*fam*) sweetheart
amperaggio, gi [ampe'raddʒo] SM amperage
ampere [ɑ̃'pɛr] SM INV (*Elettr*) amp(ère)
amperometro [ampe'rɔmetro] SM ammeter
ampiamente [ampja'mente] AVV (*trattare, discutere*) fully
ampiezza [am'pjettsa] SF **1** (*di sala*) (large) size; (*di gonna*) fullness; (*fig*: *di fenomeno*) scale; **ampiezza di vedute** broad-mindedness **2** (*Fis*) amplitude, range; (*Geom*) size; (*Mus*) range
ampio, pia, pi, pie ['ampjo] AGG **1** (*vasto*: *spazio, sala*) spacious; (: *strada, corridoio*) wide, broad; **di ampio respiro** (*fig*: *ricerca, articolo*) wide-ranging; **di ampie vedute** broad-minded **2** (*largo*: *vestito*) loose; **una gonna ampia** a full skirt **3** (*abbondante*: *garanzie*) ample
amplesso [am'plɛsso] SM (*sessuale*) intercourse
ampliamento [amplia'mento] SM (*di strada*) widening; (*di aeroporto*) expansion; (*fig*) broadening
ampliare [ampli'are] VT (*allargare*) to widen; (*fig*: *discorso*) to enlarge (up)on; (: *raggio di azione*) to widen; **ampliare le proprie conoscenze** to broaden one's knowledge; **vorrei ampliare la cucina** I'd like to make the kitchen bigger
▶ **ampliarsi** VIP to grow, increase
amplificare [amplifi'kare] VT (*suono*) to amplify; (*fig*: *sensazione*) to increase; (: *pregi*) to extol
amplificatore [amplifika'tore] SM (*Tecn, Mus*) amplifier
amplificazione [amplifikat'tsjone] SF amplification
ampolla [am'polla] SF **1** (*per olio, aceto*) cruet **2** (*Chim*) round-bottom flask
ampollina [ampol'lina] SF (*Rel*) ampulla
ampollosamente [ampollosa'mente] AVV bombastically
ampollosità [ampollosi'ta] SF INV bombast
ampolloso, a [ampol'loso] AGG bombastic
amputare [ampu'tare] VT (*Med*) to amputate; (*fig*: *testo, scritto*) to cut
amputazione [amputat'tsjone] SF amputation
Amsterdam ['amsterdam] SF Amsterdam
amuleto [amu'lɛto] SM lucky charm
AN [a'ɛnne] SIGLA = *Ancona*
■ SIGLA F (*Pol*: = **Alleanza Nazionale**) National Alliance; *Italian right-wing party*
ANA ['ana] SIGLA F (= **Associazione Nazionale Alpini**) *Italian association of alpine soldiers*
ANAAO [a'nao] SIGLA F (= **Associazione Nazionale Aiuti e Assistenti Ospedalieri**) *national union of Italian hospital doctors*
anabbagliante [anabbaʎ'ʎante] (*Aut*) AGG dipped (*Brit*), dimmed (*Am*)
■ SM dipped (*Brit*) *o* dimmed (*Am*) headlight
anabolismo [anabo'lizmo] SM anabolism
anabolizzante [anabolid'dzante] SM anabolic steroid
■ AGG (*sostanza*) anabolic
anaconda [ana'kɔnda] SM INV anaconda
anacronismo [anakro'nizmo] SM anachronism
anacronisticamente [anakronistika'mente] AVV anachronistically
anacronistico, a, ci, che [anakro'nistiko] AGG anachronistic
anaerobico, a, ci, che [anae'rɔbico] AGG anaerobic
anaerobio, bi [anae'rɔbjo] SM anaerobe
anafilattico, a, ci, che [anafi'lattiko] AGG (*Med*): **shock anafilattico** toxic shock syndrome
anagrafe [a'nagrafe] SF (*Amm*: *registro*) register of births, marriages and deaths; (: *ufficio*) registry *o* register office (*Brit*), office of vital statistics (*Am*); **anagrafe tributaria** *central tax records*
anagraficamente [anagrafika'mente] AVV according to public records
anagrafico, a, ci, che [ana'grafiko] AGG (*Amm*): **dati anagrafici** personal data *o* records; **luogo di residenza anagrafica** place of residence
anagramma, i [ana'gramma] SM anagram
analcolico, a, ci, che [anal'kɔliko] AGG non-alcoholic; **bevanda analcolica** non-alcoholic drink; **bibita analcolica** soft drink; **birra analcolica** alcohol-free beer
■ SM non-alcoholic aperitif
anale [a'nale] AGG anal
analfabeta, i, e [analfa'bɛta] AGG, SM/F illiterate
analfabetismo [analfabe'tizmo] SM illiteracy
analgesico [anal'dʒɛziko] SM painkiller, analgesic
analisi [a'nalizi] SF INV **1** (*gen*) analysis; (*di orina, sangue*) test; **analisi del sangue** blood test; **all'analisi dei fatti** on examining the facts; **in ultima analisi** all in all, in the final analysis; **sono in analisi da 5 anni** (*Psic*) I've been in analysis for the past 5 years; **analisi dei costi** cost analysis; **analisi di mercato** market analysis; **analisi dei sistemi** systems analysis; **analisi delle vendite** sales analysis **2** (*Gramm*): **analisi**

grammaticale parsing; **analisi logica** sentence analysis

analista, i, e [ana'lista] SM/F (*Chim, Med, Inform*) analyst; (*Psic*) (psycho)analyst; **analista finanziario** financial analyst; **analista di sistemi** systems analyst

analiticamente [analitika'mente] AVV analytically

analitico, a, ci, che [ana'litiko] AGG analytic(al); **indice analitico** index

analizzare [analid'dzare] VT (*gen*) to analyse (*Brit*), analyze (*Am*); (*sangue, orina*) to test, analyse; (*Gramm: frase*) to parse; (*poesia, testo*) to give a commentary on

anallergico, a, ci, che [anal'lɛrdʒiko] AGG (*Med*) hypoallergenic

analogamente [analoga'mente] AVV similarly, in a similar way

analogia, gie [analo'dʒia] SF analogy; **per analogia (con)** by analogy (with)

analogicamente [analodʒika'mente] AVV analogically, by analogy

analogico, a, ci, che [ana'lɔdʒiko] AGG analogical; (*calcolatore, orologio*) analog(ue)

analogo, a, ghi, ghe [a'nalogo] AGG: **analogo (a)** analogous (to), similar (to)

ananas ['ananas] SM INV pineapple

anarchia [anar'kia] SF anarchy

anarchico, a, ci, che [a'narkiko] AGG anarchistic; (*disordinato*) anarchic(al); **un poeta anarchico** an anarchist poet
■ SM/F anarchist; **gli anarchici** the anarchists

anarchismo SM anarchism

anarco-insurrezionalista, i, e [a'narko-insurretsjona'lista], **anarchico-insurrezionalista, i, e** AGG anarcho-insurrectionalist

ANAS ['anas] SIGLA F (= **Azienda Nazionale Autonoma delle Strade**) *national roads department*

anatema, i [ana'tɛma] SM (*Rel*) anathema; **scagliare** *o* **gettare l'anatema contro** to anathematize

anatomia [anato'mia] SF (*gen*) anatomy; (*analisi*) analysis

anatomicamente [anatomika'mente] AVV anatomically

anatomico, a, ci, che [ana'tɔmiko] AGG anatomical; **sedile anatomico** contoured *o* anatomical seat

anatomizzare [anatomid'dzare] VT to anatomize

anatra ['anatra] SF duck; **anatra all'arancia** duck with orange sauce; **anatra selvatica** mallard

anatroccolo [ana'trɔkkolo] SM duckling

ANCA ['anka] SIGLA F (= **Associazione Nazionale Cooperative Agricole**) ≈ NFU (= *National Farmers Union*)

anca, che ['anka] SF (*di persona*) hip; (*di animale*) haunch

ANCC [a'ɛnnetʃi'tʃi] SIGLA F = *Associazione Nazionale Carabinieri*

ANCE ['antʃe] SIGLA F (= **Associazione Nazionale Costruttori Edili**) *national association of builders*

ancestrale [antʃes'trale] AGG ancestral

anche ['anke] CONG **1** (*pure*) also, too; **e va anche a Roma** and he's going to Rome too, and he's also going to Rome; **parla inglese e anche italiano** he speaks English and Italian too *o* as well; **vengo anch'io!** I'm coming too!; **sono stanchissimo! – anch'io!** I'm really tired! – me too!; **gli ho parlato ieri — anch'io** I spoke to him yesterday — so did I; **anche oggi non potrò venire** I won't be able to come today either; **potrebbe anche cambiare idea, ma...** he may change his mind, but ...; **avresti anche potuto avvertirmi** you could have let me know **2** (*perfino*) even; **lo saprebbe fare anche un bambino** even a child could do it; **anche se** (*ipotesi*) even if; (*nonostante*) although; **anche se dovesse piovere** even if it rained; **me lo ricordo anche se avevo solo sei anni** I remember it, although I was only six; **anche volendo, non finiremmo in tempo** however much we wanted to, we wouldn't finish in time

ancheggiare [anked'dʒare] VI (*aus* **avere**) to wiggle (one's hips)

anchilosato, a [ankilo'zato] AGG stiff

ANCI ['antʃi] SIGLA F (= **Associazione Nazionale dei Comuni Italiani**) *national confederation of local authorities*

ancia, ce ['antʃa] SF (*Mus*) reed

anconetano, a [ankone'tano] AGG of *o* from Ancona
■ SM/F inhabitant *o* native of Ancona

ancora[1] ['ankora] SF (*Naut, fig*) anchor; **gettare/levare l'ancora** to cast/weigh anchor; **ancora galleggiante** sea anchor; **ancora di salvezza** (*fig*) last hope

ancora[2] ['ankora] AVV **1** (*tuttora*) still; **è ancora innamorato di lei** he's still in love with her; **ancora oggi** still today; **stava ancora dormendo** he was still asleep **2** (*di nuovo*) again; **ancora tu!** (not) you again!; **sei andato ancora a Parigi da allora?** have you been back to Paris since then? **3** **non ancora** not yet; **è pronto? – no, non ancora** is it ready? – no, not yet; **il direttore non è ancora qui** the manager isn't here yet **4** (*più*) (some) more; **ancora un po'** a little more; **vuoi ancora zucchero?** would you like some more sugar?; **mi dai ancora un po' di gelato?** could I have a bit more ice-cream?; **vorrei ancora latte** I'd like more milk; **ne vorrei ancora** I'd like some more; **prendi ancora un biscotto** have another biscuit; **ci sono ancora caramelle?** are there any sweets left?; **cosa vuoi ancora?** what else do you want?; **ancora per una settimana** for another week, for one week more; **ancora una volta** once more, once again; **ancora un po' e finivamo in acqua** we almost ended up in the water
■ CONG (*nei comparativi*) even, still; **ancora di più/meno** even more/less; **ancora meglio/peggio** even *o* still better/worse; **ancora altrettanto** as much again; **oggi fa ancora più freddo** it's even colder today

ancoraggio, gi [anko'raddʒo] SM anchorage; **tassa d'ancoraggio** anchorage dues *pl*

ancorare [anko'rare] VT
▶ **ancorarsi** VR (*anche fig*) to anchor

ANCR [ankr] SIGLA F (= **Associazione Nazionale Combattenti e Reduci**) *servicemen's and ex-servicemen's association*

Andalusia [andalu'zia] SF Andalusia

andaluso, a [anda'luzo] AGG, SM/F Andalusian

andamento [anda'mento] SM (*di malattia*) course; (*della Borsa, del mercato*) trend; (*del lavoro*) progress

andante [an'dante] SM (*Mus*) andante
■ AGG (*corrente*) current; (*di poco pregio*) cheap, second-rate

andare [an'dare] **PAROLA CHIAVE**
■ VI IRREG (*aus* **essere**)
1 (*gen*) to go; **andare in bicicletta** to cycle; **andare a casa** to go home; **andare a cavallo** to ride; **dove va (messa) questa vite?** where does this screw go?; **andare a letto** to go to bed; **andare lontano** (*anche fig*) to go far; **andare in macchina** to drive; **andare a male** to go bad; **andare per i 50** (*età*) to be getting on for 50; **andare in città a piedi** to walk to town; **andare a Roma** to go to Rome; **andrò all'università l'anno**

Aa

prossimo I'm going to university next year; **vado e vengo** I'll be back in a minute; **andare e venire** to come and go
2 *(essere)*: **se non vado errato** if I'm not mistaken; **va fatto entro oggi** it's got to be done today; **andare fiero di qc/qn** to be proud of sth/sb; **ne va della nostra vita** our lives are at stake; **vado pazzo per la pizza** I'm crazy about pizza, I adore pizza; **la situazione va peggiorando** the situation is getting worse; **andare perduto** to go missing; **non va trascurato il fatto che...** we shouldn't forget *o* overlook the fact that ...; **va sempre vestita di rosso** she always wears red
3 *(salute, situazione)*: **come va? — bene grazie** how are you? — fine thanks; **va bene** *(d'accordo)* all right, O.K *(fam)*; **ti è andata bene** you got away with it; **andare di bene in meglio** to get better and better; **com'è andata?** how did it go?; **come va (la salute)? — va bene** how are you? — I'm fine; **come va la scuola?** how's school?; **come vai a scuola?** how are you getting on at school?
4 *(funzionare)* to work; **la macchina va a benzina** the car runs on petrol; **non riesco a far andare la macchina** I can't start the car; **la lavatrice non va** the washing machine won't work
5 **andare a qn** *(calzare: scarpe, vestito)* to fit sb; *(essere gradito)*: **quest'idea non mi va** I don't like this idea; **questi jeans non mi vanno più** these jeans don't fit me any more; **ti va il cioccolato?** do you like chocolate?; **ti va di andare al cinema?** do you feel like going to the cinema?; **ti va (bene) se ci vediamo alle 5?** is it ok if we meet at 5?
6 *(essere venduto)* to sell; *(essere di moda)* to be fashionable; **un modello che va molto** a style that sells well
7 *(+ infinito)*: **andare a pescare** to go fishing; **andare a prendere qc/qn** to go and get sth/sb; **andare a sciare** to go skiing; **andare a vestirsi** to go and get dressed
8 *(fraseologia)*: **va là che ti conosco bene** come off it, I know you too well; **vai a quel paese!** *(fam)* get lost!; **vada per una birra** ok, I'll have a beer; **chi va piano va sano e va lontano** *(Proverbio)* more haste less speed; **va da sé** *(è naturale)* it goes without saying; **per questa volta vada** let's say no more about it this time; **andiamo!** let's go!; *(coraggio!)* come on!
9 **andarsene** to go away; **me ne vado** I'm off, I'm going; **se ne sono andati** they've gone
10 *(+ avverbio, preposizione) vedi* **fuori, via** *ecc*
■ SM: **a lungo andare** in time, in the long run; **con l'andar del tempo** with the passing of time; **racconta storie a tutto andare** she's forever talking rubbish; **andare e venire** coming and going

andata [an'data] SF *(viaggio)* outward journey; **all'andata c'era brutto tempo** on the outward journey there was bad weather; **all'andata ci ho messo due ore** it took me two hours to get there; **biglietto di sola andata** single *(Brit) o* one-way ticket; **biglietto di andata e ritorno** return *(Brit) o* round-trip *(Am)* ticket; **partita/girone di andata** *(Sport)* first leg/ first half of the season
andatura [anda'tura] SF **1** *(modo di camminare)* gait, walk **2** *(Sport)* pace; **imporre l'andatura** to set the pace **3** *(Naut)* tack
andazzo [an'dattso] SM *(pegg)*: **con** *o* **di questo andazzo, finiremo male** the way things are going, we'll end up in a mess; **le cose hanno preso un brutto andazzo** things have taken a turn for the worse
Ande ['ande] SFPL: **le Ande** the Andes
andino, a [an'dino] AGG Andean
andirivieni [andiri'vjɛni] SM INV coming and going
Andorra [an'dɔrra] SF Andorra
andrò *ecc* [an'drɔ] VB *vedi* **andare**
androceo [andro'tʃɛo] SM *(Bot)* androecium
androginia [androdʒi'nia] SF androgyny
androgino, a [an'drɔdʒino] AGG androgynous
■ SM hermaphrodite, androgyne
andrologia [androlo'dʒia] SF *(Med)* andrology, study of men's diseases
andrologo, a; **, gi**; **, ghe** [an'drɔlogo] SM/F *(Med)* andrologist, specialist in men's diseases
Andromaca [an'drɔmaka] SF Andromache
Andromeda [an'drɔmeda] SF Andromeda
androne [an'drone] SM entrance hall
aneddoto [a'nɛddoto] SM anecdote
anelare [ane'lare] VI *(aus* **avere***)* **anelare a qc/a fare qc** to long *o* yearn for sth/to do sth
anelito [a'nɛlito] SM *(letter)*: **anelito (di)** longing (for), yearning (for)
anellidi [a'nɛllidi] SMPL *(Zool)* annelids
anello [a'nɛllo] SM *(gen, fig)* ring; *(di catena)* link; **un anello d'oro** a gold ring; **ad anello** ring-shaped; **anello di fidanzamento/nuziale** engagement/ wedding ring; **anello di congiunzione/mancante** *(fig)* connecting/missing link
anemia [ane'mia] SF anaemia *(Brit)*, anemia *(Am)*; **anemia falciforme** sickle-cell anaemia
anemico, a, ci, che [a'nɛmiko] AGG anaemic *(Brit)*, anemic *(Am)*
■ SM/F an(a)emic person
anemometro [ane'mɔmetro] SM wind gauge
anemone [a'nɛmone] SM anemone; **anemone di bosco** wood anemone; **anemone di mare** sea anemone
anestesia [aneste'zia] SF anaesthesia *(Brit)*, anesthesia *(Am)*; **fare l'anestesia a qn** to give sb an anaesthetic; **sotto anestesia** under anaesthetic, under anaesthesia; **anestesia locale** local anaesthetic; **anestesia totale** general anaesthetic
anestesista, i, e [aneste'zista] SM/F anaesthetist *(Brit)*, anesthetist *(Am)*
anestetico, a, ci, che [anes'tɛtiko] AGG, SM anaesthetic *(Brit)*, anesthetic *(Am)*
anestetizzare [anestetid'dzare] VT to anaesthetize *(Brit)*, anesthetize *(Am)*
anfetamina [anfeta'mina] SF amphetamine
anfetaminico, a, ci, che [anfeta'miniko] AGG *(fig)* hyper *(fam)*
anfibio, bia, bi, bie [an'fibjo] AGG amphibious
■ SM **1** *(Zool)* amphibian; *(veicolo)* amphibious
2 **anfibi** SMPL *(scarpe)* heavy-duty boots
anfiteatro [anfite'atro] SM amphitheatre *(Brit)*, amphitheater *(Am)*
anfitrione [anfitri'one] SM *(letter)* host
anfora ['anfora] SF amphora
anfotero, a [an'fɔtero] AGG *(Chim)* amphoteric
anfratto [an'fratto] SM cleft
angariare [anga'rjare] VT to vex
angelica [an'dʒɛlika] SF *(Bot)* angelica
angelicamente [andʒelika'mente] AVV like an angel, angelically
angelico, a, ci, che [an'dʒɛliko] AGG angelic(al)
angelo ['andʒelo] SM angel; **fabbricante d'angeli** *(euf)* backstreet abortionist; **angelo custode** guardian angel

Angelus ['andʒelus] SM (*Rel*) Angelus
angheria [ange'ria] SF vexation
angina [an'dʒina] SF (*tonsillite*) tonsillitis; **angina pectoris** angina (pectoris)
angioino, a [andʒo'ino] AGG, SM/F Angevin
angioma, i [an'dʒɔma] SM (*Med*) angioma
angioplastica, che [andʒo'plastika] SF (*Med*) angioplasty
anglicanesimo [anglika'nezimo] SM anglicanism
anglicano, a [angli'kano] AGG, SM/F Anglican
anglicismo [angli'tʃizmo] SM anglicism
anglicizzare [anglitʃid'dzare] VT to anglicize ▶ **anglicizzarsi** VR to become anglicized
anglista, i, e [an'glista] SM/F anglicist
anglofilo, a [an'glɔfilo] AGG anglophilic, anglophile ■SM/F anglophile
anglosassone [anglo'sassone] AGG, SM/F Anglo-Saxon
Angola [an'gɔla] SF Angola
angolano, a [ango'lano] AGG, SM/F Angolan
angolare[1] [ango'lare] AGG (*gen, Geom*) angular; **mobile angolare** corner unit; **pietra angolare** (*Archit, fig*) cornerstone
angolare[2] [ango'lare] VT (*Calcio, Tennis, Cine*) to angle
angolazione [angolat'tsjone] SF (*Fot, Cine, TV, fig*) angle; **visto da questa angolazione** seen from this angle
angolo ['angolo] SM **1** (*di stanza, tavolo, strada, bocca*) corner; **fare angolo con** (*strada*) to run into; **sull'** *o* **all'angolo della strada** on *o* at the corner of the street; **è la casa all'angolo con via Garibaldi** it's the house on the corner of Via Garibaldi; **faccio un salto al negozio all'angolo** I'm just popping out to the corner shop; **dietro l'angolo** (*anche fig*) round the corner; **il cinema è proprio dietro l'angolo** the cinema's just round the corner; **abito in via Cairoli angolo via Bersaglio** I live on the corner of via Cairoli and via Bersaglio; **ho scoperto degli angoli di Londra che non conoscevo** I've discovered some out-of-the-way bits of London I never knew before; **starsene in un angolo** to stay all by one's self; **non startene sempre in un angolo, vieni con noi** don't stay on your own all the time, come with us; **angolo cottura** (*di appartamento*) kitchen area **2** (*Geom*) angle; **angolo retto/acuto/ottuso** right/acute/obtuse angle
angoloso, a [ango'loso] AGG (*oggetto*) angular; (*volto, corpo*) angular, bony
angora ['angora] SF: **lana d'angora** angora
angoscia [an'gɔʃʃa] SF (*gen, Psic*) anguish *no pl*
angosciare [angoʃ'ʃare] VT to cause anguish to; **la scena mi ha angosciato** I was very upset by what I saw; **il pensiero della morte mi angoscia** the thought of dying terrifies me ▶ **angosciarsi** VIP: **angosciarsi (per)** (*preoccuparsi*) to become anxious (about); (*provare angoscia*) to get upset (about *o* over)
angosciatamente [angoʃʃata'mente] AVV with anguish
angosciato, a [angoʃ'ʃato] AGG upset, distressed
angosciosamente [angoʃʃosa'mente] AVV with anguish
angoscioso, a [angoʃ'ʃoso] AGG (*scena, situazione*) distressing, harrowing; (*attesa*) agonizing
anguilla [an'gwilla] SF eel
anguria [an'gurja] SF watermelon
angustia [an'gustja] SF (*letter*) **1** (*di spazio*) lack of space **2** (*povertà*) poverty, want; **vive in angustia** he lives in straitened circumstances **3** (*ansia*) anguish, distress
angustiare [angus'tjare] VT to torment, distress ▶ **angustiarsi** VIP: **angustiarsi (per)** to become distressed (about)
angusto, a [an'gusto] AGG (*stanza, letto*) narrow; (*fig: pensiero*) mean, petty; (*: mente*) narrow
anice ['anitʃe] SM **1** (*Bot: pianta*) anise; (*: frutto*) aniseed; **una caramella all'anice** an aniseed sweet **2** (*liquore*) anisette
anidride [ani'dride] SF (*Chim*) **anidride carbonica** carbon dioxide; **anidride solforosa** sulphur dioxide
anidro, a ['anidro] AGG anhydrous
anilina [ani'lina] SF aniline
anima ['anima] SF **1** (*gen*) soul; **volere un bene dell'anima a qn** to be extremely fond of sb; **con tutta l'anima** with all one's heart; **mettere l'anima in qc/nel fare qc** to put one's heart into sth/into doing sth; **vendere l'anima (al diavolo)** to sell one's soul (to the devil); **anima e corpo** body and soul, wholeheartedly; **rompere l'anima a qn** to drive sb mad; **mi hai rotto l'anima** I've had enough of you; **il nonno buon'anima...** Grandfather, God rest his soul ...; **la buon'anima di Mario** (*defunto*) the dear departed Mario **2** (*persona*) soul; (*abitante*) inhabitant; **il paese conta 1000 anime** the town has 1000 inhabitants; **un'anima in pena** (*anche fig*) a tormented soul; **anima gemella** soul mate; **l'anima della festa** the life and soul of the party; **non c'era neanche un'anima** there wasn't a soul; **non c'era anima viva** there wasn't a living soul
animale [ani'male] SM (*gen, fig*) animal ■AGG animal; **grasso animale** animal fat
animalesco, a, schi, sche [anima'lesko] AGG (*gesto, atteggiamento*) animal-like
animalismo [anima'lizmo] SM animal rights movement
animalista, i, e [anima'lista] AGG animal rights *attr*; **il movimento animalista** the animal rights movement ■SM/F animal rights activist
animare [ani'mare] VT **1** (*dare vita a*) to animate; (*serata, conversazione*) to liven up, enliven; **la gioia le animava il volto** her face shone with joy **2** (*sogg: sentimento*) to drive, impel; **era animato dal desiderio di libertà** he was driven by the desire for freedom **3** (*incoraggiare: persona, commercio*) to encourage ▶ **animarsi** VIP (*persona, oggetto, strada*) to come to life; (*festa*) to liven up, become animated; (*scaldarsi: conversazione, persona*) to become animated
animatamente [animata'mente] AVV (*parlare*) animatedly
animato, a [ani'mato] AGG **1** (*vivace: strada*) lively, busy; (*: conversazione*) lively, animated **2** (*vivo*) animate
animatore, trice [anima'tore] AGG (*principio*) guiding; (*forza*) driving ■SM/F (*turistico, di festa, gruppo*) organizer; (*di spettacolo*) compère; (*Cine*) animator; **è sempre lui l'animatore della festa** he's always the life and soul of the party
animazione [animat'tsjone] SF (*eccitazione*) excitement; (*vivacità*) liveliness; (*di città, strada*) bustle; (*Cine*) animation; **animazione teatrale** amateur dramatics
animismo [ani'mizmo] SM animism
animo ['animo] SM **1** (*mente*) mind; (*disposizione*) character, disposition; **stato d'animo** state of mind; **avere in animo di fare qc** to have a mind to do sth, intend to do sth; **mettersi l'animo in pace** to set

Aa

one's mind at rest; **fare qc di buon/mal animo** to do sth willingly/unwillingly **2** *(coraggio)* courage; **perdersi d'animo** to lose heart; **fare animo a qn** to cheer sb up; **farsi animo** to pluck up courage; **fatti animo!** *or* **animo!** cheer up!

animosamente [animosa'mente] AVV with animosity

animosità [animosi'ta] SF animosity

anione [a'njone] SM anion

anisetta [ani'zetta] SF anisette

ANITA [a'nita] SIGLA F = *Associazione Naturista Italiana*

anitra ['anitra] SF = **anatra**

Ankara ['ankara] SF Ankara

ANM [a'ɛnne'ɛmme] SIGLA F (= **Associazione Nazionale dei Magistrati**) *national association of magistrates*

ANMI [a'ɛnne'ɛmme'i] SIGLA F (= **Associazione Nazionale Marinai d'Italia**) *national association of seamen*

ANMIG ['anmig] SIGLA F (= **Associazione Nazionale Mutilati e Invalidi di Guerra**) *national association for disabled ex-servicemen*

annacquare [annak'kware] VT to dilute; *(vino)* to water down

annacquato, a [annak'kwato] AGG *(vedi vt)* watered down; diluted

annaffiare [annaf'fjare] VT *(fiori, piante)* to water

annaffiatoio, oi [annaffja'tojo] SM watering can

annali [an'nali] SMPL annals

annaspare [annas'pare] VI *(aus* **avere***)* *(nell'acqua)* to flounder; *(fig: nel buio, nell'incertezza)* to grope

annata [an'nata] SF *(gen)* year; *(di vino)* vintage, year; *(importo annuo)* annual amount; **è stata una buona annata** it was a good year; **vino di annata** vintage wine

annebbiare [anneb'bjare] VT *(gen, fig)* to cloud
▶ **annebbiarsi** VIP to become foggy; *(vista)* to become blurred

annegamento [annega'mento] SM drowning; **è morto per annegamento** he drowned

annegare [anne'gare] VI *(aus* **essere***)* to drown; **non sapeva nuotare ed è annegato** he couldn't swim and drowned
■ VT to drown; **annegare i dispiaceri nel vino** to drown one's sorrows;
▶ **annegarsi** VR to drown o.s.

annegato, a [anne'gato] SM/F drowned man/woman

annerire [anne'rire] VT to blacken
■ VI *(aus* **essere***)*, **annerirsi** VIP to go *o* become black

annessione [annes'sjone] SF *(Pol)* annexation

annesso, a [an'nɛsso] PP *di* **annettere**
■ AGG *(attaccato: gen)* attached; *(: Pol)* annexed
■ SMPL: **fra annessi e connessi...** what with one thing and another ...; **...e tutti gli annessi e connessi** ... and so on and so forth; **mi occupo del nuovo progetto con tutti gli annessi e connessi** I'm working on the new project and everything relating to it

annettere [an'nɛttere] VT IRREG *(Pol)* to annexe *(Brit)*, annex *(Am)*; *(accludere)* to attach

Annibale [an'nibale] SM Hannibal

annichilire [anniki'lire], **annichilare** [anniki'lare] VT to annihilate; *(fig)* to devastate

annidarsi [anni'darsi] VR *(uccello)* to nest; *(fig: persona)* to hide
■ VIP *(paura, dubbio, invidia)* to take root

annientamento [annjenta'mento] SM annihilation, destruction

annientare [annjen'tare] VT to annihilate, destroy

anniversario, ri [anniver'sarjo] SM anniversary; **è il loro anniversario di matrimonio** it's their wedding anniversary

anno ['anno] SM **1** year; **l'anno scorso** last year; **l'anno prossimo** next year; **anno per** *o* **dopo anno** year after year; **è aperto tutto l'anno** it's open all year round; **uno studente del primo anno** a first year student; **gli anni venti** the twenties; **gli anni novanta** the nineties; **un anno di affitto** a year's rent; **sono anni che non ti vedo** it's been ages since I last saw you, I haven't seen you for ages *o* years; **correva l'anno di grazia ...** it was in the year of grace ...; **Buon Anno!** Happy New Year!; **gli anni di piombo** *the Seventies in Italy, a time of terrorist outrages* **2** *(età)*: **quanti anni hai?** — **ho 40 anni** how old are you? — I'm 40; **quando compi gli anni?** when is your birthday?; **una ragazza di vent'anni** a girl of twenty; **un bambino di 6 anni** a 6-year-old child; **porta bene gli anni** she doesn't look her age; **porta male gli anni** she looks older than she is
■ **anno accademico** academic year; **anno bisestile** leap year; **anno commerciale** business year; **anno finanziario** financial year; **anno giudiziario** legal year; **anno luce** *(Astron)* light year; **anno sabbatico** sabbatical year; **anno santo** *(Rel)* holy year

annodare [anno'dare] VT *(lacci)* to tie; *(cravatta)* to knot, tie; *(fune, corda)* to knot; *(due corde)* to knot *o* tie together; **annodarsi la cravatta** to tie *o* knot one's tie
▶ **annodarsi** VIP to become *o* get knotted *o* tangled

annoiare [anno'jare] *(tediare)* to bore; **scusa, ti sto annoiando?** sorry, am I boring you?
▶ **annoiarsi** VIP to get bored; **a stare a casa mi annoio** I get bored staying at home; **annoiarsi di qc/di fare qc** to be bored with sth/with doing sth

> **LO SAPEVI...?**
> **annoiare** non si traduce mai con la parola inglese *annoy*

annoiato, a [anno'jato] AGG bored

> **LO SAPEVI...?**
> **annoiato** non si traduce mai con la parola inglese *annoyed*

annonario, ria, ri, rie [anno'narjo] AGG: **tessera annonaria** ration book

annoso, a [an'noso] AGG *(questione, problema)* age-old

annotare [anno'tare] VT **1** *(scrivere)* to note, note down *(Brit)*, take down **2** *(commentare: testo)* to annotate

annotazione [annotat'tsjone] SF **1** *(appunto)* note **2** *(di testo)* annotation

annottare [annot'tare] VB IMPERS *(aus* **essere***)* **annotta** night is falling

annoverare [annove'rare] VT to number

annuale [annu'ale] AGG *(gen)* annual, yearly; *(pianta)* annual

annualmente [annual'mente] AVV annually, yearly

annuario, ri [annu'arjo] SM *(gen)* annual publication; *(di scuola ecc)* yearbook

annuire [annu'ire] VI *(aus* **avere***)* *(assentire: anche:* **annuire col capo***)* to nod

annullamento [annulla'mento] SM *(vedi vb)* cancellation; annulment; quashing; destruction

annullare [annul'lare] VT **1** *(francobollo, ordine, contratto)* to cancel; *(Dir: testamento, matrimonio)* to annul; *(: sentenza)* to quash; *(partita, risultati)* to declare void; **hanno annullato il viaggio** they cancelled the trip **2** *(distruggere)* to destroy

▶ **annullarsi** VR: **annullarsi (a vicenda)** to cancel each other out
annullo [an'nullo] SM (*Amm*) cancelling
annunciare [annun'tʃare] VT (*gen*) to announce; (*predire*) to foretell; (*essere segno di*) to be a sign of; **annunciare una brutta notizia a qn** to break bad news to sb; **il barometro annuncia pioggia** the barometer is indicating rain; **entrò senza farsi annunciare** he came in unannounced
annunciato, a [annun'tʃato] AGG (*tragedia, catastrofe*) that has been predicted
annunciatore, trice [annuntʃa'tore] SM/F (*Radio, TV*) announcer
Annunciazione [annuntʃat'tsjone] SF (*Rel*): **l'Annunciazione** the Annunciation
annuncio, ci [an'nuntʃo] SM (*gen*) announcement; (*presagio*) sign; **hanno dato l'annuncio ieri** they made the announcement yesterday; **mettere un annuncio sul giornale** to place *o* put an advert(isement) in the newspaper; **annunci economici** classified ad(vertisement)s, small ads; **annunci mortuari** (*colonna*) death announcements; **annuncio pubblicitario** advertisement
annuo, a ['annuo] AGG annual, yearly
annusare [annu'sare] VT (*anche fig*) to smell; (*cane*) to smell, sniff; **il cane mi ha annusato le mani** the dog sniffed my hands; **annusare tabacco** to take snuff
annuvolamento [annuvola'mento] SM clouding (over)
annuvolare [annuvo'lare] VT to cloud
▶ **annuvolarsi** VIP to become cloudy, cloud over
ano ['ano] SM anus
anodizzare [anodid'dzare] VT to anodize
anodo ['anodo] SM anode
anomalia [anoma'lia] SF (*gen*) anomaly; (*Med*) abnormality; **anomalia di funzionamento** (*Tecn*) technical fault
anomalo, a [a'nɔmalo] AGG anomalous
anonima [a'nonima] SF: **l'Anonima sequestri** *kidnapping gang*
anonimamente [anonima'mente] AVV anonymously
anonimato [anoni'mato] SM anonymity; **conservare l'anonimato** to remain anonymous
anonimo, a [a'nɔnimo] AGG anonymous; **una telefonata anonima** an anonymous phone call; **un tipo anonimo** (*banale*) a colourless (*Brit*) *o* colorless (*Am*) character
■ SM/F (*persona*) unknown person; (*pittore, autore ecc*) anonymous painter (*o* writer *ecc*)
anoressante [anores'sante] SM appetite suppressant
anoressia [anores'sia] SF anorexia; **anoressia nervosa** anorexia nervosa
anoressico, a, ci, che [ano'rɛssiko] AGG anorexic
anormale [anor'male] AGG abnormal
■ SM/F mentally retarded person, subnormal person
anormalità [anormali'ta] SF INV abnormality
ANPA SIGLA F (= **Agenzia Nazionale di Protezione Ambientale**) EPA
ANSA ['ansa] SIGLA F (= **Agenzia Nazionale Stampa Associata**) *national press agency*
▷ www.ansa.it/
ansa ['ansa] SF (*curva*) loop, bend; (*di vaso*) handle; (*Anat*) loop
ansante [an'sante] AGG out of breath, panting
ansia ['ansja] SF anxiety; **stare *o* essere in ansia (per qn/qc)** to be anxious (about sb/sth); **con ansia** anxiously
ansietà [ansje'ta] SF INV anxiety
ansimare [ansi'mare] VI (*aus* **avere**) to pant, gasp for breath; (*respirare pesantemente*) to breathe heavily
ansiosamente [ansjosa'mente] AVV (*gen*) anxiously; (*con desiderio*) eagerly
ansioso, a [an'sjoso] AGG (*agitato*) anxious; (*desideroso*): **ansioso di fare qc** anxious *o* eager to do sth
anta ['anta] SF (*di armadio*) door; (*di finestra*) shutter
antagonismo [antago'nizmo] SM antagonism
antagonista, i, e [antago'nista] SM/F antagonist
■ AGG antagonistic
antagonistico, a, ci, che [antago'nistiko] AGG antagonistic
antartico, a, ci, che [an'tartiko] AGG Antarctic
■ SM: **l'Antartico** the Antarctic
Antartide [an'tartide] SF Antarctica
ante... ['ante] PREF pre..., ante...
antebellico, a, ci, che [ante'bɛlliko] AGG prewar *attr*
antecedente [antetʃe'dɛnte] AGG previous, preceding
■ SM **1** (*Gramm, Filosofia*) antecedent **2** (*antefatto*): **gli antecedenti** previous history *sg*
antefatto [ante'fatto] SM prior event; **gli antefatti dell'incidente** the events leading up to the accident, what happened before the accident
anteguerra [ante'gwɛrra] SM prewar period; **dell'anteguerra** prewar
■ AGG INV prewar; (*scherz*) ancient
ante litteram ['ante 'litteram] AGG INV ahead of one's time
antenato [ante'nato] SM ancestor, forefather
antenna [an'tenna] SF (*Zool*) antenna, feeler; (*Radio, TV*) aerial; **bisogna regolare l'antenna** the aerial needs adjusting; **(d)rizzare le antenne** (*fig*) to prick up one's ears; **antenna parabolica** (satellite) dish
anteporre [ante'porre] VT IRREG: **anteporre qc a qc** to place *o* put sth before sth
anteposto, a [ante'posto] PP *di* **anteporre**
anteprima [ante'prima] SF (*Teatro, Cine*) preview; **presentare qc in anteprima** to preview sth; **comunichiamo in anteprima la notizia di...** we are bringing you advance news of ...; **anteprima di stampa** (*Inform*) print preview
antera [an'tɛra] SF (*Bot*) anther
anteriore [ante'rjore] AGG **1** (*tempo*) previous, preceding **2** (*spazio*) front *attr*; **lo sportello anteriore** the front door; **zampe anteriori** forelegs
anteriormente [anterjor'mente] AVV **1** (*prima*) previously, before, earlier; **anteriormente a** prior to **2** (*davanti*) in front
antesignano [antesiɲ'ɲano] SM forerunner; (*Storia*) standard-bearer
anti... ['anti] PREF **1** (*contro*) anti... **2** (*prima*) ante...
antiaderente [antiade'rɛnte] AGG non-stick
antiaereo, a [antia'ɛreo] AGG anti-aircraft *attr*
antiallergico, a, ci, che [antial'lɛrdʒiko] AGG, SM hypoallergenic
antiatomico, a, ci, che [antia'tɔmiko] AGG anti-nuclear; **rifugio antiatomico** fallout shelter
antibatterico, a; , ci; , che [antibat'tɛriko] AGG, SM antibacterial
antibiotico, a, ci, che [antibi'ɔtiko] AGG, SM antibiotic
antibloccaggio [antiblok'kaddʒo] AGG INV (*Aut*): **sistema antibloccaggio** anti-lock brake
anticaglia [anti'kaʎʎa] SF piece of old junk; **anticaglie** SFPL old junk; **negozio di anticaglie** junk shop

Aa

anticalcare [antikal'kare] AGG (*prodotto, detersivo*) anti-limescale
■ SM limescale remover
anticamente [antika'mente] AVV formerly
anticamera [anti'kamera] SF (*ingresso*) hall; (*sala d'attesa*) antechamber, anteroom; **fare anticamera** to be kept waiting; **non mi passerebbe neanche per l'anticamera del cervello** it wouldn't even cross my mind
anticarie [anti'karje] AGG INV which fights tooth decay
anticarro [anti'karro] AGG INV antitank
antichità [antiki'ta] SF INV **1** antiquity; **nell'antichità** in ancient times **2** **antichità** SFPL antiques; **negozio di antichità** antique shop
anticiclone [antitʃi'klone] SM anticyclone
anticiclonico, a, ci, che [antitʃi'klɔniko] AGG anticyclonic; **zona anticiclonica** anticyclone area
anticima [anti'tʃima] SF (*Alpinismo*) foresummit, subsidiary summit
anticipare [antitʃi'pare] VT **1** (*spostare prima nel tempo*) to bring forward; **anticipare un incontro di 3 giorni** to bring a meeting forward 3 days; **anticipare i tempi** (*accelerare*) to speed things up; (*precorrere*) to be ahead of one's time **2** (*precedere: reazione, risposta*) to anticipate; **anticipare qn nel fare qc** to do sth before sb; **mi ha anticipato** he did it before me; **anticipare la palla/l'avversario** (*Sport*) to keep ahead of the ball/one's opponent **3** (*sorpresa, notizia*) to reveal **4** (*pagare*) to pay in advance; (*prestare*) to lend; **puoi anticiparmi un po' di soldi?** can you lend me some money?
■ VI (*aus* **avere**) to come early, arrive early; **anticipare di un'ora** to come *o* arrive an hour earlier
anticipatamente [antitʃipata'mente] AVV (*arrivare*) earlier than expected; (*pagare*) in advance
anticipato, a [antitʃi'pato] AGG (*prima del previsto*) early; **pagamento anticipato** payment in advance; **pensionamento anticipato** early retirement
anticipazione [antitʃipat'tsjone] SF **1** (*spostamento*) bringing forward **2** (*di notizia*) anticipation; (*: pronostico*) forecast; **vi diamo delle anticipazioni sui risultati** we have advance news for you on the results; **è difficile fare delle anticipazioni sull'esito della partita** it's difficult to predict the result of the match **3** (*di denaro*) advance; **anticipazione bancaria** bank loan
anticipo [an'titʃipo] SM (*gen, Fin*) advance; **con due giorni di anticipo** two days in advance; **con mezz'ora di anticipo** half an hour early; **in anticipo** early; **sei in anticipo** you're early; **arrivare in anticipo** to arrive early *o* ahead of time; **avvertire qn in anticipo** to warn sb in advance *o* beforehand; **pagare in anticipo** to pay in advance; **gli ho dato un anticipo sullo stipendio** I gave him an advance on his salary; **con un sensibile anticipo** well in advance
anticlan [anti'klan] AGG INV (*magistrato, processo*) anti-mafia
anticlericale [antikleri'kale] AGG, SM/F anticlerical
antico, a, chi, che [an'tiko] AGG **1** (*vecchio: mobile, quadro*) antique; (*: manoscritto*) ancient; **abitano in un'antica villa di campagna** they live in an old house in the country; **un mobile antico** an antique; **all'antica** old-fashioned; **un uomo all'antica** an old-fashioned man **2** (*dell'antichità*) ancient; **gli antichi Romani** the ancient Romans; **nei tempi antichi** in ancient times
■ **gli antichi** SMPL the ancients

anticoagulante [antikoagu'lante] AGG, SM anticoagulant
anticoncezionale [antikontʃettsjo'nale] AGG, SM contraceptive
anticonformismo [antikonfor'mizmo] SM unconventionality
anticonformista, i, e [antikonfor'mista] AGG unconventional
■ SM/F unconventional person
anticonformistico, a, ci, che [antikonfor'mistiko] AGG nonconformist
anticongelante [antikondʒe'lante] AGG, SM antifreeze
anticongiunturale [antikondʒuntu'rale] AGG (*Econ*): **misure anticongiunturali** measures to remedy the economic situation; **soluzione anticongiunturale** solution to the (unfavourable) economic situation
anticorpo [anti'kɔrpo] SM antibody
anticostituzionale [antikostituttsjo'nale] AGG unconstitutional
anticostituzionalità [anticostituttsjonali'ta] SF INV unconstitutionality
anticostituzionalmente [anticostituttsjonal'mente] AVV unconstitutionally
anticristo [anti'kristo] SM Antichrist
anticrittogamico, a, ci, che [antikritto'gamiko] AGG fungicidal
■ SM fungicide
antidemocratico, a, ci, che [antidemo'kratiko] AGG undemocratic
antidepressivo, a [antidepres'sivo] AGG, SM antidepressant
antidiluviano, a [antidilu'vjano] AGG (*fig: antiquato*) ancient, antediluvian
antidivo, a [anti'divo] SM/F: **essere un antidivo** to rebel against the star system
antidolorifico, ci [antidolo'rifiko] SM painkiller
antidoping [anti'dɔpin(g)] AGG INV drug testing; **legge antidoping** drug testing regulations; **test antidoping** drug *o* drugs (*Brit*) test
■ SM INV drug *o* drugs (*Brit*) test; **risultare positivo all'antidoping** to fail a drug test
antidorcade [anti'dɔrkade] SF (*Zool*) springbok
antidoto [an'tidoto] SM antidote
antidroga [anti'drɔga] AGG INV anti-drugs *attr*
antieconomico, a, ci, che [antieko'nɔmiko] AGG uneconomic(al)
antiemorragico, a, ci, che [antiemor'radʒiko] AGG, SM haemostatic
antieroe [antie'rɔe] SM antihero
antiestetico, a, ci, che [anties'tɛtiko] AGG unsightly
antietà [antie'ta] AGG INV (*farmaco*) anti-ageing
antifascismo [antifaʃ'ʃizmo] SM antifascism
antifascista, i, e [antifaʃ'ʃista] AGG, SM/F antifascist
antifecondativo, a [antifekonda'tivo] AGG contraceptive
antifona [an'tifona] SF (*Mus, Rel*) antiphon; **capire l'antifona** (*fig*) to take the hint; **ha capito l'antifona e se n'è andato** he took the hint and left
antiforfora [anti'forfora] AGG INV anti-dandruff
antifurto [anti'furto] AGG INV, SM INV alarm
antigas AGG INV: **maschera antigas** gas mask
antigelo [anti'dʒɛlo] AGG INV antifreeze *attr*
■ SM INV (*per motore*) antifreeze; (*per cristalli*) de-icer
antigene [an'tidʒene] SM (*Bio*) antigen
antigienico, a, ci, che [anti'dʒɛniko] AGG unhygienic
antiglobal [anti'global] AGG INV antiglobalization *attr*

antiglobalizzazione [antiglobaliddzat'tsjone] AGG INV (*movimento*) anti-globalization *attr*
Antigone [an'tigone] SF Antigone
Antille [an'tille] SFPL: **le Antille** the Antilles
antilope [an'tilope] SF antelope
antimafia [anti'mafja] AGG INV anti-Mafia *attr*
antimateria [antima'tɛrja] SF antimatter
antimilitarismo [antimilita'rizmo] SM antimilitarism
antimilitarista, i, e [antimilita'rista] AGG, SM/F antimilitarist
antimilitaristico, a, ci, che [antimilita'ristiko] AGG antimilitarist
antimonio [anti'mɔnjo] SM antimony
antincendio [antin'tʃɛndjo] AGG INV fire *attr*; **scala antincendio** fire escape
antinebbia [anti'nebbja] SM INV (*Aut*: *anche*: **faro antinebbia**) fog light
antinevralgico, a, ci, che [antine'vraldʒiko] AGG painkilling
■ SM painkiller
antinfiammatorio, a [antinfjamma'tɔrjo] AGG, SM anti-inflammatory
antinfluenzale [antinfluen'tsale] AGG anti-flu *attr*
■ SM flu remedy
antintrusione [antintru'zjone] AGG INV: **barre antintrusione** (*Aut*) side impact bars
antiorario, ria, ri, rie [antio'rarjo] AGG anticlockwise (*Brit*), counterclockwise (*Am*); **in senso antiorario** in an anticlockwise *o* counterclockwise direction
antipanico [anti'paniko] AGG INV (*porta*) emergency *attr*
antipastiera [antipas'tjɛra] SF hors d'oeuvre tray
antipasto [anti'pasto] SM hors d'oeuvre, starter
antipatia [antipa'tia] SF antipathy, dislike; **avere antipatia per** not to like; **ho una certa antipatia per i viaggi in pullman** I don't really like travelling by coach; **prendere in antipatia** to take a dislike to; **l'ha preso subito in antipatia** she took an instant dislike to him
antipatico, a, ci, che [anti'patiko] AGG unpleasant, disagreeable; **un tipo antipatico** an unpleasant person
■ SM/F unpleasant person; (*rompiscatole*) nuisance
antipiega [anti'pjɛga] AGG INV (*tessuto, vestito*) crease-resistant, non-crease
antipiretico, a, ci, che [antipi'rɛtiko] AGG, SM antipyretic
antiplacca [anti'plakka] AGG INV (*dentifricio*) anti-plaque
antipodi [an'tipodi] SMPL: **gli antipodi** the antipodes; **essere agli antipodi** (*fig*) to be poles apart
antipolio [anti'pɔljo] SF INV (*anche*: **vaccino antipolio**) polio vaccine
antiproiettile [antipro'jɛttile] AGG INV bulletproof
antipulci [anti'pultʃi] AGG INV flea *attr*; **collare antipulci** flea collar
antiquariato [antikwa'rjato] SM (*cose antiche*) antiques *pl*; (*Comm*) antique trade; **negozio di antiquariato** antique shop; **un pezzo d'antiquariato** an antique
antiquario, ri [anti'kwarjo] SM antique dealer; **fa l'antiquario** he's an antique dealer; **negozio di antiquario** antique shop
antiquato, a [anti'kwato] AGG antiquated, old-fashioned
antiriciclaggio [antiritʃi'kladdʒo] AGG INV (*attività, legge*) anti-laundering
antiriflesso [antiri'flesso] AGG INV (*schermo, lenti*) non-glare *attr*
antiruggine [anti'ruddʒine] AGG INV anti-rust *attr*
■ SM INV rust preventer
antirughe [anti'ruge] AGG INV (*crema, prodotto*) anti-wrinkle
■ SM INV anti-wrinkle cream
antisdrucciolevole [antizdruttʃo'levole] AGG non-slip
antisdrucciolo [antiz'druttʃolo] AGG INV non-slip
antisemita, i, e [antise'mita] AGG anti-semitic
■ SM/F anti-semite
antisemitismo [antisemi'tizmo] SM anti-semitism
antisettico, a, ci, che [anti'sɛttiko] AGG, SM antiseptic
antisfondamento [antisfonda'mento] AGG INV toughened
antisismico, a, ci, che [antista'miniko] AGG (*costruzione, edificio*) earthquake-proof; (*criteri, norme*) anti-earthquake
antisommossa [antisom'mɔssa] AGG INV riot *attr*; **in assetto (*o* tenuta) antisommossa** in riot gear; **reparto antisommossa** riot police *o* squad
antispastico, a, ci, che [antis'pastiko] AGG, SM antispasmodic
antistaminico, a, ci, che [antista'miniko] AGG, SM antihistamine
antistante [antis'tante] AGG opposite
antitartaro [anti'tartaro] AGG INV anti-tartar
antiterrorismo [antiterro'rizmo] SM antiterrorism, anti-terrorist measures *pl*
■ AGG INV antiterrorist *attr*
antiterrorista, i, e [antiterro'rista] AGG antiterrorist *attr*
antiterroristico, a, ci, che [antiterro'ristiko] AGG antiterrorist
antitesi [an'titezi] SF INV antithesis
antitetanico, a, ci, che [antite'taniko] AGG (*siero, iniezione*) tetanus *attr*
■ SF: **l'antitetanica** tetanus injection *o* jab (*fam*)
antitetico, a, ci, che [anti'tɛtiko] AGG antithetical
antitraspirante [antitraspi'rante] AGG (*deodorante*) antiperspirant
antitruffa [anti'truffa] AGG INV (*legge, indagine*) fraud *attr*; (*verifica, metodo*) anti-fraud *attr*
antitrust [anti'trast] AGG INV (*legge*) antitrust
antitumorale [antitumo'rale] AGG (anti-)cancer *attr*
■ SM (anti-)cancer drug
antiuomo [anti'wɔmo] AGG INV: **mina antiuomo** anti-personnel mine
antiusura [antiu'zura] AGG INV (*legge*) against loan-sharking; (*prodotto*) that prevents wear and tear
antivaioloso, a [antivajo'lozo] AGG smallpox *attr*; **vaccinazione antivaiolosa** smallpox vaccination
antivento [anti'vɛnto] AGG INV (*giubbotto*) windproof
antivigilia [antivi'dʒilja] SF: **l'antivigilia di Natale/Capodanno** the day before Christmas Eve/New Year's Eve
antivipera [anti'vipera] AGG INV: **siero antivipera** remedy for snake bites
antivirus [anti'virus] SM INV (*Inform*) antivirus software *no pl*
antologia, gie [antolo'dʒia] SF anthology
antologico, a, ci, che [anto'lɔdʒiko] AGG anthological
antonomasia [antono'mazja] SF antonomasia; **per antonomasia** par excellence

Aa

antrace [an'tratʃe] SM anthrax
antracite [antra'tʃite] SF anthracite
antro ['antro] SM cave, cavern
antropofago, a, gi, ghe [antro'pɔfago] AGG cannibal *attr*
■SM cannibal
antropologia [antropolo'dʒia] SF anthropology; **antropologia criminale** criminology
antropologico, a, ci, che [antropo'lɔdʒiko] AGG anthropological
antropologo, a, gi, ghe [antro'pɔlogo] SM/F anthropologist
antropomorfo, a [antropo'mɔrfo] AGG anthropomorphic
anulare [anu'lare] AGG ring *attr*; **raccordo anulare** (*Aut*) ring road
■SM (*Anat*) ring finger
Anversa [an'versa] SF Antwerp
anzi ['antsi] AVV **1** (*avversativo*) on the contrary; **non mi dispiace, anzi sono contento** I don't mind, in fact I'm glad **2** (*rafforzativo*) or rather, or better still
anzianità [antsjani'ta] SF INV (*età avanzata*) old age; (*Amm*) seniority; **anzianità di servizio** length of service
anziano, a [an'tsjano] AGG (*vecchio*) elderly, old; (*socio*) senior; **è tuo nonno quel signore anziano?** is that old gentleman your grandfather?
■SM/F senior citizen (*euf*), old person; (*di associazione*) senior member; **un anziano** an old man; **un'anziana** an old woman; **gli anziani** the elderly

> **LO SAPEVI...?**
> **anziano** non si traduce mai con la parola inglese *ancient*

anziché [antsi'ke] CONG rather than; **preferisco telefonare anziché scrivere** I prefer to phone rather than write; **ho comprato quello giallo anziché quello rosso** I bought the yellow one rather than the red one; **quest'anno andiamo al mare anziché in montagna** this year we're going to the seaside instead of to the mountains
anzitempo [antsi'tɛmpo] AVV (*in anticipo*) early; **morire anzitempo** to die before one's time
anzitutto [antsi'tutto] AVV first of all
AO SIGLA = *Aosta*
aoristo [ao'risto] SM (*Gramm*) aorist
aorta [a'ɔrta] SF aorta
aostano, a [aos'tano] AGG of *o* from Aosta
■SM/F inhabitant *o* native of Aosta
AP SIGLA = *Ascoli Piceno*
apartheid [a'partheit] SM INV (*Pol*) apartheid
apartitico, a, ci, che [apar'titiko] AGG (*Pol*) non-party *attr*
apatia [apa'tia] SF apathy
apaticamente [apatika'mente] AVV apathetically
apatico, a, ci, che [a'patiko] AGG apathetic
a.p.c. ABBR = **a pronta cassa**; *vedi* **pronto**
ape ['ape] SF bee; **ape regina** queen bee

> **LO SAPEVI...?**
> **ape** non si traduce mai con la parola inglese *ape*

aperitivo [aperi'tivo] SM aperitif; **prendiamo un aperitivo?** shall we have an aperitif?
apertamente [aperta'mente] AVV openly; **ne abbiamo parlato apertamente** we talked about it frankly
aperto, a [a'pɛrto] PP *di* **aprire**
■AGG (*gen, fig*) open; (*rubinetto*) on, running; (*gas*) on; **hai lasciato la porta aperta** you've left the door open; **lasciare la macchina aperta** to leave the car unlocked; **di mentalità aperta** open-minded; **i miei sono molto aperti** my parents are very open-minded; **a cuore aperto** (*intervento*) open heart *attr*; (*fig*) frankly, sincerely; **a bocca aperta** open-mouthed; **rimanere a bocca aperta** (*fig*) to be taken aback; **sognare ad occhi aperti** to daydream; **all'aria aperta** in the open air
■SM: **all'aperto** outdoors; (*cinema, piscina*) open-air *attr*; (*giochi, vacanze*) outdoor *attr*; **abbiamo dormito all'aperto** we slept outdoors
apertura [aper'tura] SF **1** (*gen, Carte*) opening; (*Pol*) opening up; (*Fot*) aperture; **orario di apertura** opening times; **in apertura di** at the beginning of; **movimento di apertura** (*Tennis*) backswing; **apertura di credito** (*Comm*) granting of credit **2** (*ampiezza*) width, spread; **apertura alare** wing span; **apertura mentale** open-mindedness
API ['api] SIGLA F = *Associazione Piccole e Medie Industrie*
apice ['apitʃe] SM peak, summit; (*fig*) height, peak; **essere all'apice del successo** to be at the height *o* peak of one's success
apicoltore, trice [apikol'tore] SM/F beekeeper
apicoltura [apikol'tura] SF beekeeping
apnea [ap'nɛa] SF: **immergersi in apnea** to dive without breathing apparatus
apocalisse [apoka'lisse] SF (*Rel*): **l'Apocalisse** (the book of) Revelation, the Apocalypse; (*fig*) apocalypse
apocalittico, a, ci, che [apoka'littiko] AGG apocalyptic
apocrifo, a [a'pɔkrifo] AGG apocryphal
apogeo [apo'dʒɛo] SM (*Astron*) apogee; (*fig: culmine*) zenith, apogee
apolide [a'pɔlide] (*Pol*) AGG stateless
■SM/F stateless person
apolitico, a, ci, che [apo'litiko] AGG (*neutrale*) non-political; (*indifferente*) apolitical
Apollo [a'pɔllo] SM Apollo
apologia, gie [apolo'dʒia] SF (*frm*) apologia; **fare l'apologia di** to extol the virtues of; **accusare qn di apologia di reato** (*Dir*) to accuse sb of attempting to defend criminal acts
apoplessia [apoples'sia] SF (*Med*) apoplexy
apoplettico, a, ci, che [apo'plɛttiko] AGG apoplectic; **colpo apoplettico** apoplectic fit
apostata, i, e [a'pɔstata] SM/F apostate
a posteriori [a poste'rjɔri] AGG INV after the event (*dopo sostantivo*)
■AVV looking back
apostolato [aposto'lato] SM (*Rel*) apostolate; **fare opera di apostolato** (*anche fig*) to spread the word
apostolico, a, ci, che [apos'tɔliko] AGG apostolic
apostolo [a'pɔstolo] SM apostle
apostrofare[1] [apostro'fare] VT (*parola*) to write with an apostrophe
apostrofare[2] [apostro'fare] VT (*persona*) to address indignantly
apostrofo [a'pɔstrofo] SM (*segno*) apostrophe
apoteosi [apote'ɔzi] SF INV apotheosis
app. ABBR (= **appendice**) app.
appagamento [appaga'mento] SM (*vedi vb*) satisfaction; fulfilment
appagare [appa'gare] VT (*gen*) to satisfy; (*desiderio*) to fulfil; (*fame*) to satisfy; (*sete*) to quench
▶ **appagarsi** VR: **appagarsi di** to be satisfied with
appagato, a [appa'gato] AGG satisfied

appaiare [appa'jare] VT (*oggetti*) to pair; (*animali*) to match, couple

appaio *ecc* [ap'pajo] VB *vedi* **apparire**

Appalachi [appa'laki] SMPL: **i Monti Appalachi** the Appalachian Mountains

appallottolare [appallotto'lare] VT (*carta, foglio*) to screw into a ball
▶ **appallottolarsi** VR (*gatto*) to roll up into a ball

appaltare [appal'tare] VT (*dare in appalto*) to put out to contract; (*prendere in appalto*) to undertake on contract

appaltatore, trice [appalta'tore] SM contractor
■ AGG contracting

appalto [ap'palto] SM contract; **dare in appalto** to put out to contract; **prendere in appalto** to take on a contract for; **gara di appalto** invitation to tender

appannaggio, gi [appan'naddʒo] SM (*Pol: compenso*) annuity; (*fig*) prerogative

appannare [appan'nare] VT (*vetro*) to steam up, mist up; (*metallo*) to tarnish; (*vista*) to blur
▶ **appannarsi** VIP (*vedi vt*) to steam up, mist up; to tarnish; (*vista: offuscarsi*) to blur; (*: affievolirsi*) to grow dim

apparato [appa'rato] SM **1** (*impianto*) equipment, machinery; **apparato burocratico** bureaucratic machinery; **apparato scenico** (*Teatro*) set **2** (*Anat, Bio*) apparatus; **apparato circolatorio** circulatory system **3** (*sfoggio*) display, pomp

apparecchiare [apparek'kjare] VT: **apparecchiare (la tavola)** to set *o* lay the table; **ti aiuto ad apparecchiare?** shall I help you to set the table?

apparecchiatura [apparekkja'tura] SF (*Tecn: impianto*) equipment *no pl*; (*: macchina*) machine, device

apparecchio, chi [appa'rekkjo] SM **1** (*gen*) instrument, device, piece of equipment; **un complicato apparecchio elettronico** a complex electronic device; **apparecchio acustico** hearing aid; **apparecchio telefonico** telephone **2** (*per denti*) brace; **porta l'apparecchio** he wears a brace **3** (*Radio, TV*) set **4** (*Aer*) aircraft *inv*

apparente [appa'rɛnte] AGG apparent

apparentemente [apparente'mente] AVV apparently

apparenza [appa'rɛntsa] SF **1** (*aspetto*) appearance; **l'apparenza inganna** appearances can be deceptive; **in** *o* **all'apparenza** to all appearances, seemingly **2 apparenze** SFPL (*convenienze sociali*) appearances; **badare alle apparenze** to care about appearances; **salvare le apparenze** to keep up appearances; **giudicare dalle apparenze** to judge by appearances

apparire [appa'rire] VI IRREG (*aus* **essere**) **1** (*mostrarsi*) to appear; **apparire in sogno** to appear in a dream; **l'uomo gli apparve davanti all'improvviso** the man suddenly appeared in front of *o* before him **2** (*essere evidente*): **apparire (chiaro)** to seem clear; **dalle indagini è apparso chiaro il suo coinvolgimento** the enquiries clearly demonstrate his involvement **3** (*sembrare*) to seem, appear; **appare che...** it appears *o* turns out that ...; **apparve sorpreso di vedermi** he seemed surprised to see me

appariscente [appariʃ'ʃɛnte] AGG (*vestito*) showy; (*colore*) gaudy, garish; (*bellezza*) striking

apparizione [apparit'tsjone] SF (*comparsa*) appearance; (*fantasma*) apparition

apparso, a [ap'parso] PP *di* **apparire**

appartamento [apparta'mento] SM flat (*Brit*), apartment (*Am*); **un appartamento ammobiliato** a furnished flat

appartarsi [appar'tarsi] VR to withdraw

appartato, a [appar'tato] AGG (*luogo*) secluded

appartenente [apparte'nɛnte] AGG: **appartenente a** belonging to
■ SM/F: **appartenente (a)** member (of); **un appartenente al partito comunista** a member of the communist party

appartenenza [apparte'nɛntsa] SF: **appartenenza (a)** (*gen*) belonging (to); (*a un partito, club*) membership (of)

appartenere [apparte'nere] VI IRREG (*aus* **essere** *o* **avere**) **appartenere a 1** (*chiesa, fede*) to belong to; (*club, partito*) to be a member of **2** (*essere di proprietà*) to belong to; **mi appartiene di diritto** it belongs to me by right; **questa collana apparteneva a mia nonna** this necklace belonged to my grandma; **a chi appartiene questo libro?** who does this book belong to?

apparvi *ecc* [ap'parvi] VB *vedi* **apparire**

appassimento [appassi'mento] SM withering

appassionante [appassjo'nante] AGG thrilling, exciting

appassionare [appassjo'nare] VT to grip, fascinate; **il romanzo mi ha appassionato molto** the novel really gripped me
▶ **appassionarsi** VIP: **appassionarsi a qc** to develop a passion for sth, get very interested in sth

appassionatamente [appassjonata'mente] AVV (*amare, credere*) passionately; (*lavorare*) enthusiastically

appassionato, a [appassjo'nato] AGG **1** (*entusiasta*): **essere appassionato di qc** to love sth; **è appassionato di musica jazz** he loves jazz **2** (*passionale*) passionate
■ SM/F enthusiast

appassire [appas'sire] VI (*aus* **essere**) (*pianta*) to wither; (*fig: bellezza, speranze*) to fade

appellare [appel'lare] VI (*aus* **avere**) (*Dir*): **appellare (contro)** to appeal (against)
▶ **appellarsi** VIP **1 appellarsi a** (*rivolgersi*) to appeal to; **mi appello alla vostra generosità** I appeal to your generosity **2** (*Dir*) **appellarsi contro** to appeal against; **si è appellato contro la sentenza** he appealed against the sentence

appellativo [appella'tivo] SM name

appello [ap'pɛllo] SM **1** (*chiamata per nome*) roll-call; **fare l'appello** (*Scol*) to call the register; (*Mil*) to call the roll **2** (*Univ: sessione d'esame*) exam session **3** (*Dir*) appeal; **corte d'appello** court of appeal **4** (*invocazione*) appeal; **fare appello a** (*anche fig*) to call upon, appeal to

appena [ap'pena] AVV (*a stento*) hardly, scarcely; (*solamente, da poco*) just; **ci si vede appena** you can hardly see; **se n'è appena andato** he's just left; **sono appena le 9** it's only just 9 o'clock; **l'indirizzo era appena leggibile** the address was only just legible; **sarà alto appena appena un metro e 80** he is certainly no more than 6 foot tall; **un po' di latte? – grazie, appena un goccio** milk? – yes please, just a drop; **appena in tempo** just in time
■ CONG as soon as; **l'ho riconosciuto appena l'ho visto** I recognized him as soon as I saw him; **appena possibile** as soon as possible; **ha detto che sarebbe venuto appena possibile** he said he'd come as soon as possible; **(non) appena (furono) arrivati...** as soon as they had arrived ...; **appena...che** *o* **quando** no sooner ... than; **era appena tornato quando è dovuto ripartire** no sooner *o* scarcely had he returned than he had to leave again; **non appena ho finito, vado** I'll leave the moment I've finished

appendere [ap'pɛndere] VB IRREG

Aa

■VT: **appendere (a)** to hang (on *o* up); **dove posso appendere il cappotto?** where can I hang my coat?;
▶ **appendersi** VR: **appendersi a qc** to hang on to sth

appendiabiti [appendi'abiti] SM INV hook, peg; (*mobile*) hall stand (*Brit*), hall tree (*Am*)

appendice [appen'ditʃe] SF (*Anat, di libro*) appendix; **romanzo d'appendice** popular serial (*formerly appearing in newspapers*)

appendicite [appendi'tʃite] SF appendicitis; **ha un'appendicite acuta** he's got acute appendicitis

appendino [appen'dino] SM (coat) hook

Appennini [appen'nini] SMPL: **gli Appennini** the Apennines

appenninico, a, ci, che [appen'niniko] AGG Apennine

appesantire [appesan'tire] VT (*anche fig*) to weigh down; (*atmosfera*) to make strained; **i soldati erano appesantiti dall'armatura** the soldiers were weighed down by the armour; **quella torta mi ha appesantito lo stomaco** that cake is sitting on my stomach
▶ **appesantirsi** VIP (*gen*) to grow heavier; (*ingrassare*) to put on weight; (*fig: atmosfera, situazione*) to become strained

appeso, a [ap'peso] PP *di* **appendere**

appestare [appes'tare] VT (*Med*) to infect with plague; (: *contagiare*) to infect; (*aria, stanza*) to make stink; **il fumo delle sigarette ha appestato la stanza** the cigarette smoke made the room stink

appestato, a [appes'tato] AGG (*Med*) infected with the plague; (: *contagioso*) infected; (*aria*) stinking

appetibile [appe'tibile] AGG (*cibo*) appetizing; (*lavoro, ragazza*) attractive

appetibilità [appetibili'ta] SF (*vedi agg*) appetizing nature; attractiveness

appetito [appe'tito] SM **1** (*gen*) appetite; **la camminata mi ha messo appetito** the walk has given me an appetite; **avere appetito** to have an appetite; **non ho appetito** I'm not hungry; **perdere l'appetito** to lose one's appetite; **buon appetito!** enjoy your meal! (*said by waiter*), bon appétit! (*said by fellow diner*); **stuzzicare l'appetito** (*anche fig*) to whet one's appetite **2** (*istinti*): **appetiti** SMPL instincts; **soddisfare/frenare i propri appetiti** satisfy/curb one's instincts *o* appetite

appetitoso, a [appeti'toso] AGG (*cibo*) appetizing; (*fig*) attractive, desirable

appezzamento [appettsa'mento] SM (*anche:* **appezzamento di terreno**) plot, piece of ground

appianabile [appja'nabile] AGG resolvable, soluble

appianamento [appjana'mento] SM (*vedi vt*) levelling; settlement; ironing out

appianare [appja'nare] VT (*terreno*) to flatten, level; (*fig: contesa, lite*) to settle; (*difficoltà*) to iron out, smooth away
▶ **appianarsi** VIP (*divergenze*) to be ironed out

appiattire [appjat'tire] VT to flatten; (*fig: rendere monotono*) to make dull, make boring
▶ **appiattirsi** VR (*farsi piatto: persona, animale*) to flatten o.s.; **si appiattì al** *o* **contro il muro** he flattened himself against the wall; **appiattirsi al suolo** to lie flat on the ground;
▶ **appiattirsi** VIP (*diventare piatto: oggetto*) to become flatter; (*fig*) to become dull

appiccare [appik'kare] VT: **appiccare il fuoco a qc** to set fire to sth, set sth on fire

appiccicare [appittʃi'kare] VT: **appiccicare (a** *o* **su)** to stick (on); **appiccicare un soprannome a qn** (*fig: appioppare*) to pin a nickname on sb; **questa colla non appiccica bene** this glue doesn't stick very well
▶ **appiccicarsi** VR: **appiccicarsi (a)** to stick (to); (*fig: persona*) to cling (to)

appiccicaticcio, cia, ci, ce [apittʃika'tittʃo] AGG sticky

appiccicoso, a [apittʃi'koso] AGG sticky; (*fig: persona*): **essere appiccicoso** to cling like a leech

appiedato, a [appje'dato] AGG: **rimanere appiedato** to be left without means of transport

appieno [ap'pjɛno] AVV fully

appigliarsi [appiʎ'ʎarsi] VR: **appigliarsi a** to grasp, seize (hold of), take hold of; (*fig: scusa, pretesto*) to cling to; **non appigliarti a quella scusa** don't try that as an excuse

appiglio, gli [ap'piʎʎo] SM (hand)hold; (*fig: pretesto*) pretext, excuse

appiombo [ap'pjombo] SM perpendicularity; (*di muro*) plumb
■AVV (*anche:* **a piombo**) perpendicularly

appioppare [appjop'pare] VT: **appioppare qc a qn** (*nomignolo*) to pin sth on sb; (*compito difficile*) to saddle sb with sth; **gli ha appioppato un pugno sul muso** he punched him in the face

appisolarsi [appizo'larsi] VIP to doze off; **mi ero appisolato un attimo** I dozed off for a moment

applaudire [applau'dire] VI (*aus* **avere**) **applaudire (a)** to applaud, clap; (*fig*) to applaud; **applaudivano tutti** everybody was clapping
■VT (*anche fig*) to applaud

applaudito, a [applau'dito] AGG famous, celebrated

applauso [ap'plauzo] SM applause *no pl*; **hanno ricevuto molti applausi** they got a lot of applause; **un applauso** a round of applause

applicabile [appli'kabile] AGG: **applicabile (a)** applicable (to)

applicabilità [applikabili'ta] SF applicability

applicare [appli'kare] VT (*gen*) to apply; (*cucire*) to sew on; **applicare la mente a qc** to apply one's mind to sth; **(fare) applicare una legge/un regolamento** to enforce a law/a regulation; **applicare una tassa** to impose a tax
▶ **applicarsi** VR: **applicarsi (a** *o* **in)** to apply o.s. (to)

applicativo [applika'tivo] AGG (*Inform*): **programma applicativo** application

applicato, a [appli'kato] AGG (*arte, scienze*) applied
■SM/F (*Amm*) clerk

applicatore [applika'tore] SM applicator

applicazione [applikat'tsjone] SF **1** (*gen*) application; (*di legge, norma*) enforcement **2** (*su stoffa*) appliqué **3** (*Inform: programma*) application

applique [a'plik] SF INV wall light

appoggiare [appod'dʒare] VT **1** (*posare*): **appoggiare qc su qc** to put sth (down) on sth, lay sth (down) on sth; **puoi appoggiare il pacco sul tavolo** you can put the parcel on the table **2** (*mettere contro*): **appoggiare qc a qc** to lean *o* rest sth against sth; **appoggia la scala al muro** lean the ladder against the wall **3** (*sostenere: idea, candidato*) to support, back
■VI (*aus* **avere**) **appoggiare su** to rest on
▶ **appoggiarsi** VR: **appoggiarsi a** *o* **su** (*reggersi*) to lean against; (*fig*) to rely on *o* upon; **si è dovuto appoggiare al muro per sostenersi** he had to lean against the wall for support

appoggiatesta [appoddʒa'tɛsta] SM INV headrest

appoggiato, a [appod'dʒato] AGG (*Ling*): **consonante appoggiata** consonant joined with another

appoggio, gi [ap'pɔddʒo] SM (*gen, fig*) support;

(*Alpinismo*) press hold; **ho bisogno di tutto il vostro appoggio** I need all your support; **appoggio morale** moral support; **ho un appoggio importante al ministero** I have an important contact in the ministry

appollaiarsi [appolla'jarsi] VR (*anche fig*) to perch; **se ne stava appollaiato sullo sgabello** he was perched on the stool

appongo *ecc* [ap'pongo] VB *vedi* **apporre**

apporre [ap'porre] VT IRREG (*firma*) to append; (*sigillo, nome*) to affix

apportare [appor'tare] VT (*novità, cambiamento*) to bring (about); **apportare (delle) modifiche a** to modify

apporto [ap'pɔrto] SM (*gen, Fin*) contribution; **dare il proprio apporto a qc** to make one's contribution to sth

apposi *ecc* [ap'posi] VB *vedi* **apporre**

appositamente [appozita'mente] AVV (*apposta*) on purpose; (*specialmente*) specially

appositivo, a [appozi'tivo] AGG (*Gramm*) appositional

apposito, a [ap'pɔzito] AGG (*adatto*) appropriate, proper; (*fatto appositamente*) special; **i rifiuti vanno gettati negli appositi cestini** rubbish should be put in the bins provided

apposizione [appozit'tsjone] SF (*Gramm*) apposition

apposta [ap'pɔsta] AVV (*intenzionalmente*) on purpose, intentionally, deliberately; (*proprio*) specially; **scusa, non l'ho fatto apposta** I'm sorry, I didn't do it on purpose; **neanche a farlo apposta,...** by sheer coincidence, ...; **sono venuto apposta per (vedere) te** I came here specially for you/to see you

appostamento [apposta'mento] SM (*agguato*) ambush; (*Mil*) post

appostare [appos'tare] VT (*Mil*) to post, station
▶ **appostarsi** VR to lie in wait

apposto, a [ap'posto] PP *di* **apporre**

apprendere [ap'prɛndere] VT IRREG (*imparare*) to learn; (*venire a sapere*) to learn, find out; **hai appreso la notizia?** have you heard the news?

> **LO SAPEVI...?**
> **apprendere** non si traduce mai con la parola inglese *apprehend*

apprendimento [apprendi'mento] SM learning

apprendista, i, e [appren'dista] SM/F apprentice

apprendistato [apprendis'tato] SM apprenticeship; **fare l'apprendistato** to serve one's apprenticeship

apprensione [appren'sjone] SF apprehension; **essere in uno stato di apprensione** to be anxious; **non stare in apprensione** don't worry

apprensivamente [apprensiva'mente] AVV apprehensively, anxiously

apprensivo, a [appren'sivo] AGG apprehensive, anxious

appreso, a [ap'preso] PP *di* **apprendere**

appresso [ap'prɛsso] AVV (*vicino*) nearby, close up; (*con sé*) with me (*o* you ecc); (*dietro*) behind me (*o* you ecc); **me lo porto sempre appresso** I always carry it with me; **stammi appresso** stay *o* keep close to me
■ PREP: **appresso a** near, close to; **andare appresso a qn** to go after sb, follow sb
■ AGG INV (*dopo*): **il giorno appresso** the next day, the day after

apprestare [appres'tare] VT to prepare, get ready
▶ **apprestarsi** VR: **apprestarsi a fare qc** to prepare *o* get ready to do sth

appretto [ap'prɛtto] SM starch

apprezzabile [appret'tsabile] AGG (*notevole*) noteworthy, significant; (*percepibile*) appreciable; **è un'opera apprezzabile da tutti** it is a work which everybody can enjoy

apprezzamento [apprettsa'mento] SM
1 appreciation **2** (*commento*) comment; **fare apprezzamenti su** to make comments about, pass comment on

apprezzare [appret'tsare] VT to appreciate

approccio, ci [ap'prɔttʃo] SM approach

approdare [appro'dare] VI (*aus* **essere** *o* **avere**) (*Naut*) to land; **approdare a** (*fig*) to arrive at; **non approderà a nulla** (*piano, progetto*) it won't come to anything; (*persona*) he won't achieve anything

approdo [ap'prɔdo] SM (*Naut: l'approdare*) landing; (*luogo*) landing place

approfittare [approfit'tare] VI (*aus* **avere**)
approfittare di (*persona, situazione ecc*) to take advantage of, make the most of; **dovresti approfittare dell'occasione** you should make the most of the opportunity; **approfittiamo della bella giornata e andiamo al parco!** let's make the most of the weather and go to the park!; **approfittane!** make the most of it!; **approfittarsi di qn** to take advantage of sb

> **LO SAPEVI...?**
> **approfittare** non si traduce mai con la parola inglese *profit*

approfondimento [approfondi'mento] SM deepening; **per l'approfondimento di questo argomento si consulti...** for a thorough examination of this subject consult ...

approfondire [approfon'dire] VT (*fossa*) to deepen, make deeper; (*fig: conoscenza*) to deepen, increase; (*argomento*) to go into, study in depth; **approfondire un problema** to go into a problem in more depth; **vorrei approfondire la materia** I'd like to study the subject in depth
▶ **approfondirsi** VIP (*gen, fig*) to deepen

approfonditamente [approfondita'mente] AVV thoroughly

approfondito, a [approfon'dito] AGG (*esame, studio, conoscenza*) thorough, detailed; **un'analisi approfondita** a thorough analysis

approntare [appron'tare] VT to prepare, get ready

appropriarsi [appro'prjarsi] VIP: **appropriarsi di qc** to appropriate sth; **si è appropriato del mio motorino** he took my moped; **appropriarsi indebitamente di** to embezzle

appropriato, a [appro'prjato] AGG appropriate, suitable

appropriazione [approprjat'tsjone] SF appropriation; **appropriazione indebita** (*Dir*) embezzlement, misappropriation

approssimare [approssi'mare] VT (*cifra*): **approssimare per eccesso/per difetto** to round up/down
▶ **approssimarsi** VR (*frm*) to approach, draw near

approssimativamente [approssimativa'mente] AVV roughly, approximately

approssimativo, a [approssima'tivo] AGG (*calcolo*) rough, approximate; (*numero*) approximate; **è solo un calcolo approssimativo** it's only a rough estimate; **è stato molto approssimativo nel darmi informazioni** the information he gave me was very vague

approssimazione [approssimat'tsjone] SF

Aa

approximation; **per approssimazione** approximately, roughly

approvabile [appro'vabile] AGG that can be approved

approvare [appro'vare] VT **1** (*comportamento, decisione, azione*) to approve of; **non approvo ciò che hai fatto** I don't approve of what you've done **2** (*candidato, legge*) to pass; (*mozione*) to approve; **hanno approvato il progetto** they approved the project

approvazione [approvat'tsjone] SF (*vedi vb*) approval; passing

approvvigionamento [approvvidʒona'mento] SM **1** (*atto*) supplying **2** (*provviste*): **approvvigionamenti** SMPL supplies

approvvigionare [approvvidʒo'nare] VT: **approvvigionare (di)** to supply (with)

▶ **approvvigionarsi** VR (*fare provviste*) **approvvigionarsi (di)** to stock up (with)

appuntamento [appunta'mento] SM (*d'affari, dal medico*) appointment; (*amoroso*) date; **darsi appuntamento** to arrange to meet (one another); **ci siamo dati appuntamento alle otto davanti al cinema** we arranged to meet at eight in front of the cinema; **il medico mi ha dato un appuntamento per mercoledì** the doctor gave me an appointment for Wednesday; **venerdì ho un appuntamento dal dentista** I've got a dental appointment on Friday; **stasera ho appuntamento con il mio ragazzo** I've got a date with my boyfriend tonight; **appuntamento al buio** blind date

appuntare[1] [appun'tare] VT **1** (*fissare: con spillo: foglio ecc*) to pin (on); (*: due cose tra loro*) to pin (together); (*: piega dei pantaloni ecc*) to pin **2** (*puntare: dito*) to point; (*: sguardo*) to fix, rivet

▶ **appuntarsi** VIP (*interesse, attenzione*) **appuntarsi su** to be focussed on

> **LO SAPEVI...?**
> **appuntare** non si traduce mai con la parola inglese *appoint*

appuntare[2] [appun'tare] VT (*annotare*) to note down, take note of

appuntato [appun'tato] SM (*Carabinieri*) corporal

appuntino [appun'tino] AVV (*anche:* **a puntino**) perfectly; **cotto appuntino** cooked to perfection

appuntire [appun'tire] VT to sharpen

appuntito, a [appun'tito] AGG (*lama, lancia*) pointed; (*matita*) sharp

appunto[1] [ap'punto] SM **1** (*nota*) note; **prendere appunti** to take notes; **non avevo preso appunti** I hadn't taken notes **2** (*rimprovero*) reproach; **fare/muovere un appunto a qn** to find fault with sb

appunto[2] [ap'punto] AVV (*precisamente, proprio*) exactly, just; **dicevo appunto ieri** I was just saying yesterday; **si parlava (per l')appunto di questo** we were talking about that very thing; **stavo appunto per chiederti di venire** I was (actually) just going to ask you to come; **per l'appunto!** *or* **appunto!** exactly!

appurare [appu'rare] VT (*verificare*) to check, verify; (*: verità*) to ascertain

▶ **appurarsi** VR: **appurarsi di qc/che** to make sure of sth/that, check sth/that

apribottiglie [apribot'tiʎʎe] SM INV bottle-opener

aprile [a'prile] SM April; **pesce d'aprile!** April Fool!; **aprile dolce dormire** (*Proverbio*) April slumbers; *per fraseologia vedi* **luglio**

a priori [a pri'ɔri] AVV, AGG a priori

aprioristicamente [aprioristika'mente] AVV a priori

aprioristico, a, ci, che [aprio'ristiko] AGG a priori

apripista [apri'pista] SM/F INV (*Sci*) trailmaker

aprire [a'prire] VB IRREG

■ VT **1** (*gen*) to open; (*porta chiusa a chiave*) to unlock; (*camicia*) to undo, unfasten; (*ali, anche fig*) to spread; **va' ad aprire (la porta)** go and open *o* answer the door; **posso aprire la finestra?** can I open the window?; **dai, non apri i regali?** come on, aren't you going to open your presents?; **non ha aperto bocca** he didn't say a word, he didn't open his mouth; **tutto ciò mi ha aperto gli occhi** all that was an eye-opener to me; **apri bene gli orecchi** listen carefully; **aprirsi un varco tra la folla** to cut one's way through the crowd **2** (*acqua, rubinetto*) to turn on; (*gas*) to turn on, switch on; **non riesco ad aprire il rubinetto** I can't turn the tap on **3** (*istituire: negozio, club, conto*) to open; (*inchiesta*) to open, set up; (*strada*) to build; **aprire bottega** to open shop **4** (*dare inizio: anno, stagione*) to start, open; (*lista*) to head; (*processione*) to lead; **aprire (il gioco)** (*Carte*) to open play; **aprire il fuoco** to open fire; **aprire le ostilità** (*Mil*) to begin hostilities; **aprire una sessione** (*Inform*) to log on **5** (*Dir: testamento*) to read

■ VI (*aus* **avere**) to open; **a che ora apre la banca?** what time does the bank open?; **la banca apre alle otto** the bank opens at eight;

▶ **aprirsi** VIP **1** (*gen*) to open; (*fiore*) to open (up); **la finestra si apre sulla piazza** the window looks onto the square; **la porta dev'essersi aperta** the door must have come open; **quest'abito si apre sul davanti** this dress opens at the front; **la vita che le si apre davanti** the life which is opening in front of *o* before her; **mi si aprì davanti la vista del mare** the sea appeared before me; **davanti a quella scena le si è aperto il cuore** (*commuoversi*) she was moved by the scene before her; (*rallegrarsi*) the scene gladdened her heart; **apriti cielo!** heaven forbid!; (*cominciare*) to start, open

▶ **aprirsi** VR (*confidarsi*) **aprirsi (con qn)** to open one's heart (to sb), confide (in sb)

apriscatole [apris'katole] SM INV tin (*Brit*) *o* can opener

APT [api'ti] SIGLA F (= **Azienda di Promozione Turistica**) tourist board

AQ SIGLA = *L'Aquila*

aquagym [akkwa'dʒim] SF aquarobics

aquaplaning ['aekwəpleiniŋ] SM INV (*Aut*): **andare** *o* **entrare in aquaplaning** to aquaplane

aquario, ri [a'kwarjo] SM = **acquario**

aquila ['akwila] SF eagle; **sei un'aquila!** (*anche iro*) you're a genius!; **aquila reale** golden eagle

aquilano, a [akwi'lano] AGG of *o* from L'Aquila

■ SM/F inhabitant *o* native of L'Aquila

aquilegia, gie [akwi'lɛdʒa] SF (*Bot*) columbine, aquilegia

aquilino, a [akwi'lino] AGG aquiline; **naso aquilino** aquiline nose

aquilone [akwi'lone] SM **1** (*giocattolo*) kite; **facciamo volare l'aquilone!** let's fly the kite! **2** (*vento*) north wind

AR SIGLA = *Arezzo*

A/R ABBR (= **andata e ritorno**) return

Ara ['ara] SF (*Zool: pappagallo*) macaw

ara[1] ['ara] SF (*letter: altare*) altar

ara[2] ['ara] SF (*unità di misura*) are (= *one hundred square metres*)

arabesco, schi [ara'besko] SM arabesque

Arabia Saudita [a'rabja sau'dita] SF Saudi Arabia; **vengono dall'Arabia Saudita** they come from Saudi Arabia

arabico, a, ci, che [a'rabiko] AGG Arabic; **il deserto arabico** the Arabian desert; **la penisola arabica** the Arabian peninsula
arabile [a'rabile] AGG arable
arabo, a ['arabo] AGG *(popolo, paesi)* Arab; *(lingua, arte)* Arabic, Arab; **numeri arabi** Arabic numerals
■ SM/F *(persona)* Arab
■ SM *(lingua)* Arabic; **parlano l'arabo** they speak Arabic; **questo per me è arabo** *(fig)* it's all Greek to me, it sounds like double Dutch to me *(Brit)*; **ma parlo arabo?** *(fig)* don't you understand English?
arachide [a'rakide] SF peanut, groundnut; **olio di semi di arachide** peanut oil
Aragona [ara'gona] SF Aragon
aragosta [ara'gosta] SF lobster
■ AGG INV: **color aragosta** bright orange
araldica [a'raldika] SF heraldry
araldo [a'raldo] SM herald
aramaico, a, ci, che [ara'maiko] AGG, SM Aramaic
ARAN ['aran] SIGLA F (= **Agenzia per la Rappresentanza Negoziale della Pubblica amministrazione**) *body that represents public sector workers in pay negotiations*
aranceto [aran'tʃeto] SM orange grove
arancia, ce [a'rantʃa] SF orange; **arancia amara** Seville orange; **succo d'arancia** orange juice
aranciata [aran'tʃata] SF orangeade; **aranciata amara** bitter orange (drink)
arancio, ci [a'rantʃo] SM orange tree; *(colore)* orange; **fiori di arancio** orange blossom *sg*
■ AGG INV *(colore)* orange
arancione [aran'tʃone] AGG INV, SM bright orange; **una maglietta arancione** an orange T-shirt
■ SM/F *(fam)*: **gli arancioni** the Hare Krishna people
arare [a'rare] VT to plough *(Brit)*, plow *(Am)*
■ VI *(aus* **avere***)* *(Naut: ancora)* to drag
aratore [ara'tore] SM ploughman *(Brit)*, plowman *(Am)*
aratro [a'ratro] SM plough *(Brit)*, plow *(Am)*
aratura [ara'tura] SF ploughing *(Brit)*, plowing *(Am)*
araucaria [arau'karja] SF *(Bot)* monkey puzzle (tree)
arazzo [a'rattso] SM tapestry
arbitraggio, gi [arbi'traddʒo] SM **1** *(Sport)* refereeing; (: *Tennis, Cricket)* umpiring **2** *(Dir)* arbitration **3** *(Fin)* arbitrage
arbitraggista, i, e [arbitrad'dʒista] SM/F *(Fin)* arbitrage(u)r
arbitrare [arbi'trare] VT *(Sport)* to referee; (: *Tennis, Cricket)* to umpire; *(Dir)* to arbitrate
arbitrariamente [arbitrarja'mente] AVV arbitrarily
arbitrario, ria, rie [arbi'trarjo] AGG arbitrary
arbitrato [arbi'trato] SM *(Sport, Dir)* arbitration
arbitrio, rii [ar'bitrjo] SM **1** *(capacità, potere)* will; *(atto)* arbitrary act; **libero arbitrio** free will; **prendersi l'arbitrio di fare qc** to take the liberty of doing sth **2** *(sopruso)*: **commettere un arbitrio** to act unlawfully
arbitro ['arbitro] SM **1** *(Sport)* referee; (: *Cricket, Tennis)* umpire **2** *(di contese)* arbitrator; *(fig)*: **un arbitro di eleganza** an arbiter of fashion
arboreo, a [ar'bɔreo] AGG: **piante arboree** trees; **fusto arboreo** woody stem
arboscello [arboʃʃello] SM sapling
arbustivo, a [arbus'tivo] AGG shrub-like
arbusto [ar'busto] SM shrub
arca ['arka] SF ark; **l'Arca di Noè** Noah's Ark
arcade ['arkade] SM/F Arcadian
Arcadia [ar'kadja] SF Arcadia
arcadico, a, ci, che [ar'kadiko] AGG Arcadian
arcaico, a, ci, che [ar'kaiko] AGG archaic
arcaismo [arka'izmo] SM archaism
arcangelo [ar'kandʒelo] SM archangel
arcano, a [ar'kano] AGG arcane
■ SM mystery
arcata [ar'kata] SF *(Anat)* arch
Arch. ABBR = **architetto**
archeggio, gi [ar'keddʒo] SM *(Mus)* bowing
archeologia [arkeolo'dʒia] SF arch(a)eology; **è laureata in archeologia** she's got a degree in archaeology
▷ www.archeologia.beniculturali.it/
archeologico, a, ci, che [arkeo'lɔdʒiko] AGG arch(a)eological
archeologo, a, gi, ghe [arke'ɔlogo] SM/F arch(a)eologist
archetipo [ar'kɛtipo] SM archetype
archetto [ar'ketto] SM *(Mus)* bow
archibugio, gi [arki'budʒo] SM *(Storia)* arquebus
Archimede [arki'mɛde] SM Archimedes
architettare [arkitet'tare] VT *(ideare)* to devise; *(macchinare)* to plan, concoct
architetto [arki'tetto] SM architect; **sua madre fa l'architetto** his mother is an architect
architettonicamente [arkitettonika'mente] AVV architecturally
architettonico, a, ci, che [arkitet'tɔniko] AGG architectural
architettura [arkitet'tura] SF architecture; **studia architettura** he's studying architecture; **architettura del paesaggio** landscaping
architrave [arki'trave] SM architrave
archiviare [arki'vjare] VT *(documenti)* to file; *(Dir)* to dismiss; **archiviare un caso** to dismiss a case; **per questa volta archiviamo la faccenda** *(passiamoci sopra)* let's forget about it this time
archiviazione [arkivjat'tsjone] SF *(vedi vb)* filing; dismissal
archivio, vi [ar'kivjo] SM *(insieme di documenti, luogo)* archives *pl*; *(mobile)* filing cabinet; *(Inform)* archive
archivista, i, e [arki'vista] SM/F *(Amm)* archivist; *(in ufficio)* filing clerk
ARCI ['artʃi] SIGLA F = *Associazione Ricreativa Culturale Italiana*
arciduca, chi [artʃi'duka] SM archduke
arciere [ar'tʃɛre] SM archer
arcigno, a [ar'tʃiɲɲo] AGG *(espressione)* frowning, grim; *(persona)* severe
arcione [ar'tʃone] SM saddlebow; **montare in arcione** to get into the saddle
Arcip. ABBR = **arcipelago**
arcipelago, ghi [artʃi'pɛlago] SM archipelago
arciprete [artʃi'prɛte] SM archpriest
arcivescovado [artʃivesko'vado] SM *(sede)* archbishop's palace
arcivescovile [artʃivesko'vile] AGG of an archbishop *(o* archbishops); **palazzo arcivescovile** archbishop's palace
arcivescovo [artʃi'veskovo] SM archbishop
arco, chi ['arko] SM **1** *(arma, Mus)* bow; **arco e frecce** bow and arrows; **strumento ad arco** string(ed) instrument; **archi** SMPL *(Mus)* strings **2** *(Geom)* arc; *(Archit, forma)* arch; **ad arco** arched; **arco costituzionale** *parties formulating Italy's post-war constitution*; **arco trionfale** triumphal arch **3** *(lasso di tempo)* space; **nell'arco di 3 settimane** within the space of 3 weeks;

la somma verrà pagata in un arco di 6 mesi the sum will be paid over a period of 6 months

arcobaleno [arkoba'leno] SM rainbow

arcolaio, ai [arko'lajo] SM wool-winder, skein-winder

arcuare [arku'are] VT (*schiena*) to arch; (*bastone*) to bend

arcuato, a [arku'ato] AGG (*gen*) curved, bent; (*sopracciglia*) arched; **dalle gambe arcuate** bow-legged

ardente [ar'dɛnte] AGG (*sole, fuoco*) blazing, burning; (*sguardo*) passionate; (*ammiratore*) ardent; (*passione*) ardent, burning; (*preghiera, desiderio*) fervent

ardentemente [ardente'mente] AVV (*desiderare, sperare*) fervently, passionately

ardere ['ardere] VB IRREG
■ VT (*anche fig*) to burn; **legna da ardere** firewood
■ VI (*aus* **essere**) to burn; **ardere di passione/dalla curiosità** to burn with passion/curiosity; **ardere d'amore** to burn with love

ardesia [ar'dɛzja] SF (*minerale*) slate; (*colore*) slate-grey

ardimento [ardi'mento] SM daring

ardimentoso, a [ardimen'toso] AGG daring, bold

ardire [ar'dire] VI DIF (*aus* **avere**) **ardire (di) fare qc** to dare (to) do sth
■ SM (*audacia*) daring, boldness; (*impudenza*) impudence

arditamente [ardita'mente] AVV (*vedi agg*) bravely; daringly; impertinently

ardito, a [ar'dito] AGG (*coraggioso*) brave, daring; (*temerario*) daring; (*impertinente*) impertinent, bold; **impresa ardita** risky undertaking; **scollatura ardita** daring neckline

ardore [ar'dore] SM (*calore intenso*) (blazing) heat; (*fig: passione*) ardour; (*: fervore*) fervour, eagerness

arduo, a ['arduo] AGG (*impresa*) arduous, difficult; (*problema*) difficult; (*salita*) steep

area ['area] SF **1** (*gen, Geom*) area; **nell'area dei partiti di sinistra** among the parties of the left **2** (*Edil*) land, ground; **un'area di 25 chilometri quadrati** an area of 25 square kilometres; **area di attesa** (*Aer*) holding position; **area convocazione gruppi** (*Aer*) meeting point; **area edificabile** building land; **area di meta** (*Rugby*) in-goal area; **area della porta** (*Calcio*) goal area; **area di rigore** (*Calcio*) penalty area; **area di servizio** (*Aut*) service area

arena [a'rɛna] SF **1** (*gen, fig*) arena; (*per corride*) bullring **2** (*letter: sabbia*) sand

arenaria [are'narja] SF sandstone

arenario, ria, ri, rie [are'narjo] AGG (*rocce, pietra*) sandstone *attr*

arenarsi [are'narsi] VIP (*Naut*) to run aground; (*fig: trattative*) to come to a standstill; **la mia pratica si è arenata** my file is gathering dust

arenicola [are'nikola] SF (*Bot*) lugworm

arenile [are'nile] SM strand

areola [a'rɛola] SF (*Anat*) areola

areoplano [areo'plano] SM = **aeroplano**

aretino, a [are'tino] AGG of *o* from Arezzo
■ SM/F inhabitant *o* native of Arezzo

argano ['argano] SM winch; (*Naut*) capstan

argentare [ardʒen'tare] VT to silver-plate

argentato, a [ardʒen'tato] AGG silver-plated; (*colore*) silver, silvery; (*capelli*) silver(-grey)

argenteo, a [ar'dʒɛnteo] AGG silver, silvery

argenteria [ardʒente'ria] SF (*oggetti*) silverware, silver; (*fabbrica*) silverware factory

argentiere [ardʒen'tjɛre] SM silversmith

Argentina [ardʒen'tina] SF Argentina; **vengono dall'Argentina** they come from Argentina

argentina [ardʒen'tina] SF (*maglietta*) crewneck sweater

argentino[1]**, a** [ardʒen'tino] AGG (*voce*) silvery

argentino[2]**, a** [ardʒen'tino] SM/F, AGG (*dell'Argentina*) Argentinian

argento [ar'dʒɛnto] SM **1** silver; **un anello d'argento** a silver ring; **piatto d'argento** silver dish; **capelli d'argento** silver(-grey) hair; **avere l'argento vivo addosso** (*fig*) to be fidgety; **argento dorato** silver gilt; **argento vivo** (*Chim*) quicksilver **2 argenti** SMPL (*argenteria*) silverware *sg*, silver *sg*

argilla [ar'dʒilla] SF clay; **un vaso d'argilla** a clay pot

argilloso, a [ardʒil'loso] AGG (*contenente argilla*) clayey; (*simile ad argilla*) clay-like

arginare [ardʒi'nare] VT (*fiume, acque*) to embank; (*: con diga*) to dyke up; (*fig: inflazione, corruzione*) to check; (*: spese*) to limit; **arginare la piena** to stem the flow of water; **arginare l'avanzata nemica** to check the enemy advance

argine ['ardʒine] SM (*di fiume*) embankment, bank; **rompere gli argini** to break the banks; **porre un argine a** (*fig*) to check, hold back

argo ['argo] SM (*Chim*) argon

argomentare [argomen'tare] VI (*aus* **avere**) **argomentare (su** *o* **di qc)** to argue (about sth)

argomentazione [argomentat'tsjone] SF argument

argomento [argo'mento] SM **1** (*tema*) subject; **argomento di conversazione** topic of conversation; **qual è l'argomento del film/del libro?** what is the film/book about?; **cambiare argomento** to change the subject; **visto che siamo entrati in argomento...** since we're on the subject ...; **tornare sull'argomento** to bring the matter up again **2** (*argomentazione*) argument; **addurre/confutare un argomento** to put forward/refute an argument

argonauta, i [argo'nauta] SM Argonaut

arguire [argu'ire] VT to deduce, infer

argutamente [arguta'mente] AVV (*con spirito*) wittily; (*con prontezza*) quick-wittedly

arguto, a [ar'guto] AGG (*battuta, conversazione*) witty; (*persona*) quick-witted; (*sguardo*) sharp, keen

arguzia [ar'guttsja] SF (*spirito*) wit; (*battuta*) witty remark

aria[1] ['arja] SF **1** (*gen*) air; **aria di mare/montagna** sea/mountain air; **all'aria (aperta)** in the open (air); **vivere all'aria aperta** to live an outdoor life; **mettere le lenzuola all'aria** to air the sheets; **cambiare l'aria in una stanza** to air a room; **è meglio cambiare aria** (*fig fam: andarsene*) we'd better make ourselves scarce; **esco a prendere una boccata d'aria** I'm going out for a breath of (fresh) air; **manca l'aria** it's stuffy; **un po' d'aria fresca** a bit of fresh air; **che aria tira?** (*fig: atmosfera*) what's the atmosphere like?; **c'è aria di burrasca** (*anche fig*) there's a storm brewing; **vivere** *o* **campare d'aria** to live on thin air; **aria!** (*fam: vattene*) out of the way!, move!; **aria compressa** compressed air; **aria condizionata** air conditioning **2 andare all'aria** (*piano, progetto*) to come to nothing; **buttare** *o* **mandare all'aria** (*progetto, piano*) to ruin, upset; **buttare all'aria qc** (*mettere a soqquadro*) to turn sth upside-down; **discorsi a mezz'aria** vague remarks; **ha la testa per aria** he's got his head in the clouds; **lasciare tutto per aria** (*in disordine*) to leave everything in a mess; **sta sempre con la pancia all'aria** he's always lazing about

aria[2] ['arja] SF **1** (*espressione, aspetto*) look, air; (*modi*) manner, air; **avere l'aria allegra** to look happy; **avere**

l'aria stanca to look tired; **hai l'aria così stanca oggi** you look so tired today; **quel ragazzo ha l'aria intelligente** that boy looks *o* seems intelligent; **ha l'aria della persona onesta** he looks (like) *o* seems (to be) an honest person; **ha l'aria di voler piovere** it looks like *o* as if it's going to rain; **ha un'aria di famiglia** there is a family likeness; **cos'è quell'aria da funerale?** what are you looking so gloomy about?
2 arie SFPL airs (and graces); **darsi delle arie** to put on airs; **si dà un sacco di arie** he thinks he's so important!

aria[3] ['arja] SF (*Mus: di opera*) aria; (*: di canzonetta*) tune
Ariadne [a'rjadne] SF Ariadne
arianesimo [arja'nezimo] SM Arianism
ariano[1], **a** [a'rjano] AGG, SM/F (*Rel: eretico*) Arian
ariano[2], **a** [a'rjano] AGG, SM/F (*Nazismo, Ling*) Aryan
aridamente [arida'mente] AVV (*fig*) insensitively
aridità [aridi'ta] SF aridity, dryness; (*fig*) lack of feeling
arido, a ['arido] AGG (*suolo, regione*) arid; (*clima*) dry; (*fig: persona*) insensitive; **cuore arido** heart of stone
arieggiare [arjed'dʒare] VT **1** (*stanza, abiti*) to air **2** (*imitare*) to imitate
ariete [a'rjɛte] SM **1** (*Zool*) ram **2** (*Astrol*): **Ariete** Aries; **essere dell'Ariete** to be Aries **3** (*Storia, Mil*) battering ram
arietta [a'rjetta] SF (*brezza*) breeze; (*Mus*) arietta
aringa, ghe [a'ringa] SF herring; **aringa affumicata** smoked herring, kipper; **aringa marinata** pickled herring
arioso, a [a'rjoso] AGG (*ambiente, stanza*) airy; (*Mus*) ariose
arista ['arista] SF (*Culin*) chine of pork for roasting
aristocraticamente [aristokratika'mente] AVV aristocratically
aristocratico, a, ci, che [aristo'kratiko] AGG (*gen, fig*) aristocratic
■SM/F aristocrat
aristocrazia [aristokrat'tsia] SF aristocracy
Aristofane [ari'stɔfane] SM Aristophanes
Aristotele [ari'stɔtele] SM Aristotle
aristotelico, a, ci, che [aristo'tɛliko] AGG Aristotelian
aritmetica [arit'mɛtika] SF arithmetic
aritmetico, a, ci, che [arit'mɛtiko] AGG arithmetical
aritmia [arit'mia] SF (*anche:* **aritmia cardiaca**) arrhythmia
Arizona [ari'dzona] SF Arizona
Arkansas [ar'kansas] SM Arkansas
arlecchino [arlek'kino] SM (*Teatro*) harlequin
arma, i ['arma] SF **1** (*anche fig*) weapon; **un'arma pericolosa** a dangerous weapon; **battersi all'arma bianca** to fight with blades; **all'armi!** to arms!; **passare qn per le armi** to execute sb; **arma a doppio taglio** (*fig*) double-edged weapon; **combattere ad armi pari** (*anche fig*) to fight on equal terms; **deporre le armi** (*anche fig*) to lay down one's arms; **essere alle prime armi** (*fig*) to be a novice, have just started; **come batterista sono ancora alle prime armi** I've just started playing the drums; **prendere armi e bagagli e partire** (*fig*) to pack up and go; **traffico d'armi** arms trafficking; **arma da fuoco** firearm; **armi atomiche** atomic weapons; **armi biologiche** biological weapons; **armi convenzionali/non convenzionali** conventional/unconventional weapons; **armi di distruzione di massa** weapons of mass destruction **2** (*corpo dell'esercito*) arm, force; (*dei carabinieri*) force **3** (*servizio militare*): **essere sotto le armi** to be in the army *o* in the forces; **andare sotto le armi** to join the army *o* forces; **chiamare alle armi** to call up (*Brit*), draft (*Am*)
armadietto [arma'djɛtto] SM (*dei medicinali*) medicine cabinet *o* cupboard; (*in cucina*) (kitchen) cupboard; (*per abiti*) locker
armadillo [arma'dillo] SM armadillo
armadio, di [ar'madjo] SM (*gen*) cupboard, closet (*Am*); (*per abiti*) wardrobe; **armadio a muro** built-in cupboard
armaiolo [arma'jɔlo] SM **1** (*fabbricante*) armourer; (*: di armi da fuoco*) gunsmith **2** (*venditore*) arms dealer
armamentario, ri [armamen'tarjo] SM (*attrezzatura*) equipment, tools *pl*; (*scherz*) paraphernalia
armamento [arma'mento] SM **1** (*armi: di soldato*) arms *pl*, weapons *pl*; (*: di nazione*): **armamenti** SMPL arms, armaments; **la corsa agli armamenti** the arms race; **società di armamenti** shipowning company **2** (*azione: di nazione*) armament; (*Naut*) fitting out, equipping; (*: provvedere di uomini*) manning
armare [ar'mare] VT **1** (*persona, nazione, fortezza*) to arm; (*arma da fuoco*) to cock **2** (*Naut*) to equip, fit out; (*: di uomini*) to man **3** (*Edil*) to prop up, shore up
▶ **armarsi** VR (*Mil*) to take up arms; **armarsi di** (*anche fig*) to arm o.s. (with)
armata [ar'mata] SF (*esercito*) army; (*flotta*) fleet; **corpo d'armata** army corps *pl o sg*
armato, a [ar'mato] AGG **1 armato (di)** (*anche fig*) armed (with); **era armato di coltello** he was armed with a knife; **armato fino ai denti** armed to the teeth; **sono partiti armati di tutto punto** they set off equipped for anything; **rapina a mano armata** armed robbery **2** (*Tecn: cemento, volta*) reinforced
■SM (*soldato*) soldier
armatore, trice [arma'tore] AGG shipping *attr*
■SM shipowner
armatura [arma'tura] SF **1** (*corazza*) (suit of) armour *no pl* (*Brit*), armor *no pl* (*Am*) **2** (*struttura di sostegno*) framework; (*impalcatura*) scaffolding **3** (*Elettr: di cavo*) sheath; (*: di condensatore*) plate
armeggiare [armed'dʒare] VI (*aus* **avere**) (*affaccendarsi*): **armeggiare (intorno a qc)** to mess about (with sth)
Armenia [ar'mɛnja] SF Armenia
armeno, a [ar'mɛno] AGG, SM/F, SM Armenian
armento [ar'mento] SM herd
armeria [arme'ria] SF (*deposito*) armoury (*Brit*), armory (*Am*); (*negozio*) gun shop; (*collezione*) collection of arms
armistizio, zi [armis'tittsjo] SM armistice
armonia [armo'nia] SF (*concordia, Mus*) harmony; (*conformità*) agreement; **vivere in armonia con qn** to live in harmony with sb, get on very well with sb
armonica, che [ar'mɔnika] SF **1** (*anche:* **armonica a bocca**) harmonica, mouth organ; **suono l'armonica** I play the harmonica **2** (*Mus, Fis*) harmonic; **armoniche superiori** overtones
armonico, a, ci, che [ar'mɔniko] AGG **1** (*Mus*) harmonic; **cassa armonica** sound box **2** (*ben proporzionato*) harmonious
armoniosamente [armonjosa'mente] AVV harmoniously
armonioso, a [armo'njoso] AGG (*voce*) melodious; (*suono*) harmonious; (*lingua*) musical; (*movimenti*) graceful; (*corpo*) well-proportioned
armonizzare [armonid'dzare] VT (*Mus, leggi*) to harmonize; (*fig: colori*) to match
■VI (*aus* **avere**) **armonizzare (con)** to harmonize (with); to match

Aa

armonizzazione [armoniddzat'tsjone] SF (*di leggi*) harmonization
arnese [ar'nese] SM **1** (*strumento, utensile*) tool, implement; **arnesi da giardino/falegname** gardening/carpenter's tools **2** (*oggetto qualsiasi*) gadget, thing **3** **essere male in arnese** (*vestito male*) to be poorly *o* badly dressed; (*di salute malferma*) to be in poor health; (*di condizioni economiche*) to be hard up
arnia ['arnja] SF (bee)hive
aroma, i [a'rɔma] SM **1** (*odore*) aroma **2** (*erbe*): **aromi** SMPL herbs (and spices); **aromi naturali/artificiali** natural/artificial flavouring *sg* (*Brit*) *o* flavoring *sg* (*Am*)
aromaterapeuta, i, e [aromatera'pɛuta] SM/F aromatherapist
aromaterapia [aromatera'pia] SF aromatherapy
aromaticità [aromatitʃi'ta] SF INV aromatic quality
aromatico, a, ci, che [aro'matiko] AGG aromatic; (*cibo*) spicy; **erbe aromatiche** herbs
aromatizzare [aromatid'dzare] VT flavour (*Brit*), flavor (*Am*)
arpa ['arpa] SF harp
arpeggiare [arped'dʒare] VI (*aus* **avere**) (*suonare l'arpa*) to play the harp; (*fare arpeggi*) to play arpeggios
arpeggio, gi [ar'peddʒo] SM arpeggio
arpia [ar'pia] SF (*Mitol*) Harpy; (*fig*) harpy
arpionare [arpjo'nare] VT to harpoon
arpione [ar'pjone] SM (*Pesca*) harpoon; (*uncino, Alpinismo*) hook; (*cardine*) hinge
arrabattarsi [arrabat'tarsi] VIP: **arrabattarsi per fare qc** to do all one can to do sth, strive to do sth
arrabbiare [arrab'bjare] VI (*aus* **essere**) **1** (*cane*) to be affected with rabies **2** (*persona*): **far arrabbiare qn** to make sb angry; **mi ha fatto veramente arrabbiare** he really made me angry
▶ **arrabbiarsi** VIP to get angry, fly into a rage; **non ti arrabbiare!** don't get angry!; **arrabbiarsi per qc** to get angry about sth
arrabbiato, a [arrab'bjato] AGG **1** (*cane*) rabid, with rabies **2** (*persona*) angry; **era molto arrabbiato** he was very angry; **è più arrabbiato di lei** he's angrier than she is; **Gianni era il più arrabbiato di tutti** Gianni was the angriest of all; **un giocatore arrabbiato** (*fig: entusiasta*) a keen player
arrabbiatura [arrabbja'tura] SF: **prendersi un'arrabbiatura (per qc)** to become furious (over sth)
arraffare [arraf'fare] VT to snatch, seize; (*rubare*) to pinch
arrampicarsi [arrampi'karsi] VIP to climb (up); **arrampicarsi sul tetto** to climb (up) onto the roof; **arrampicarsi sugli specchi** *o* **sui vetri** (*fig*) to clutch at straws
arrampicata [arrampi'kata] SF climb; **arrampicata libera** free climbing
arrampicatore, trice [arrampika'tore] SM/F (*gen, Sport*) climber; **arrampicatore sociale** (*fig*) social climber
arrancare [arran'kare] VI (*aus* **avere**) to limp, hobble; (*fig*) to struggle along
arrangiamento [arrandʒa'mento] SM (*Mus*) arrangement
arrangiare [arran'dʒare] VT (*gen, Mus*) to arrange; **abbiamo arrangiato un pranzo alla bell'e meglio** we've rustled up some lunch; **ti arrangio io!** (*fam*) I'll fix you!, I'll sort you out!
▶ **arrangiarsi** VIP (*cavarsela*) to get by *o* along, manage; **con l'arte di arrangiarsi si risolve tutto** with a bit of ingenuity you can sort anything out; **arrangiati un po' tu!** (*fam*) sort it out for yourself!
arrangiatore, trice [arrandʒa'tore] SM/F (*Mus*) arranger
arrapante [arra'pante] AGG (*fam: sessualmente eccitante*) sexually arousing
arrapare [arra'pare] (*fam*) VT (*eccitare sessualmente*) to make randy (*Brit*), make horny
▶ **arraparsi** VR to get randy (*Brit*), get horny
arrapato, a [arra'pato] AGG (*fam*) randy (*Brit*), horny
arrecare [arre'kare] VT (*causare*) to cause; **arrecare danni/disturbo** to do damage/cause trouble
arredamento [arreda'mento] SM **1** (*azione*) furnishing; (*mobilia*) furniture **2** (*arte*) interior design
arredare [arre'dare] VT to furnish
arredatore, trice [arreda'tore] SM/F interior designer
arredo [ar'rɛdo] SM furnishings *pl*; **per l'arredo della vostra casa...** to furnish your home ...; **arredi sacri** religious ornaments; **arredo urbano** street furniture
arrembaggio, gi [arrem'baddʒo] SM (*Naut*) boarding; **si buttarono all'arrembaggio dei posti migliori** (*fig*) there was a mad scramble for the best seats
arrendersi [ar'rɛndersi] VIP IRREG (*persona*): **arrendersi (a)** (*polizia, nemico*) to give o.s. up (to), surrender (to); **si sono arresi alla polizia** they surrendered to the police; **arrendersi all'evidenza (dei fatti)** to accept *o* yield to the evidence; **non ce la faccio, mi arrendo** I can't do it, I give up
arrendevole [arren'devole] AGG (*persona*) yielding, compliant
arrendevolezza [arrendevo'lettsa] SF compliancy
arrendevolmente [arrendevol'mente] AVV compliantly
arreso, a [ar'reso] PP *di* **arrendersi**
arrestare [arres'tare] VT (*Dir*) to arrest; (*fermare*) to stop, halt; **i rapinatori sono stati arrestati ieri** the robbers were arrested yesterday
▶ **arrestarsi** VR to stop
arrestato, a [arres'tato] SM/F person under arrest
arresto [ar'rɛsto] SM **1** (*Dir*) arrest; **mandato d'arresto** warrant of arrest *o* arrest warrant; **essere in stato di arresto** to be under arrest; **la dichiaro in arresto** I'm putting you under arrest; **essere/mettere agli arresti** (*Mil*) to be/place under arrest; **arresti domiciliari** house arrest **2** (*azione*) stopping; (*sosta, pausa*) interruption; (*Comm: nella produzione*) stoppage; **aspettate l'arresto del treno** wait until the train stops *o* comes to a stop; **segnale d'arresto** stop sign; **il gioco ha avuto una battuta d'arresto** the game was interrupted; **le discussioni fra i due partiti subirono un arresto** discussions between the two parties came to a standstill; **arresto cardiaco** (*Med*) cardiac arrest
arretramento [arretra'mento] SM (*gen*) moving back; (*Mil: in battaglia*) falling back
arretrare [arre'trare] VI (*aus* **essere**) to move back, withdraw; **arretrare davanti** *o* **di fronte a qc** (*fig*) to shrink from sth
■ VT to move back
arretratezza [arretra'tettsa] SF backwardness
arretrato, a [arre'trato] AGG **1** (*paese, zona*) backward; **un paese arretrato** a backward country **2** (*numero di giornale, pagamento, interesse*) back *attr*; **numero arretrato** back number; **ho un sacco di lavoro arretrato da finire** I've got a huge backlog of work to finish
■ SM **1** **essere in arretrato con qc** to be behind with

sth **2 arretrati** SMPL arrears; **gli arretrati dello stipendio** back pay *sg*

arricchimento [arrikki'mento] SM (*anche fig*) enrichment

arricchire [arrik'kire] VT to make rich; **arricchire qc di** *o* **con qc** (*fig*) to enrich sth with sth
▶ **arricchirsi** VIP (*persona*) to grow *o* become *o* get rich; (*collezione*) **arricchirsi di** to be enriched with

arricchito, a [arrik'kito] SM/F nouveau riche

arricciaburro [arrittʃa'burro] SM INV butter curler

arricciacapelli [arrittʃaka'pelli] SM INV curling tongs *pl*

arricciare [arrit'tʃare] VT (*capelli, baffi*) to curl; **arricciare il naso** (*fig*) to turn up one's nose
▶ **arricciarsi** VIP to become curly

arridere [ar'ridere] VI IRREG (*aus* **avere**) (*fortuna, successo*): **arridere a qn** to smile on sb

arringa [ar'ringa] SF (*gen*) (formal) address; (*Dir*) address by counsel

arringare [arrin'gare] VT to address

arrischiare [arris'kjare] VT (*parola, giudizio*) to venture, hazard
▶ **arrischiarsi** VR: **arrischiarsi (a fare qc)** to venture (to do sth), dare (to do sth)

arrischiato, a [arris'kjato] AGG (*pericoloso*: *impresa, speculazione*) risky; (*avventato*: *giudizio, ipotesi*) rash

arriso, a [ar'riso] PP *di* **arridere**

arrivare [arri'vare] VI (*aus* **essere**)
1 (*essere a destinazione*) to arrive; (*avvicinarsi*) to come; (*raggiungere*): **arrivare a** to reach, arrive at, get to; **arrivare in orario** to arrive on time; **arrivare in ritardo** to arrive late; **arrivare a casa** to arrive *o* get *o* reach home; **arrivare a Roma/in Italia** to arrive in Rome/in Italy; **sono arrivato a Londra alle sette** I arrived in London at seven; **a che ora arrivi a scuola?** what time do you arrive at school?; **mi è arrivato un pacco dall'Italia** a parcel has arrived for me from Italy, I've had a parcel from Italy; **come si arriva al castello?** how do you get to the castle?; **arrivare a destinazione** to arrive at *o* reach one's destination; **arrivare ad una conclusione** to reach a conclusion; **arrivare allo scopo** to reach one's goal; **arrivare al potere** to come to power; **arrivare primo** (*in un luogo*) to be the first to arrive; (*in classifica*) to come (in) first; **non credevo arrivasse a tanto** *o* **a quel punto** I didn't think he'd go that far; **arrivo!** (I'm) coming!; **siamo arrivati** we're here; **per fare arrivare la corrente alla macchina** in order to connect the machine up to the electricity supply; **l'acqua mi arrivava alle ginocchia** the water came up to my knees; **la notizia è arrivata fino a lui** the news (even) reached him; **non ci arrivo** (*a prendere qc*) I can't reach it; (*a capire qc*) I can't understand it, I don't get it; **è arrivato il momento di...** the time has come to ...; **a questo siamo arrivati!** so this is what we've come to!; **il suo stipendio non arriva a 1000 euro** his salary is less than 1000 euros; **dove ti arriva la gonna?** how long is the skirt on you?; **se non la smetti ti arriva uno schiaffo** (*fam*) if you don't stop it *o* leave off you'll get a smack; **chi tardi arriva male alloggia** (*Proverbio*) the early bird catches the worm
2 (*riuscire*): **arrivare a fare qc** to manage to do sth, succeed in doing sth; **non arriverò mai a capirlo** I'll never understand him; **non arriverà a niente** he'll never get anywhere, he'll never achieve anything; **non ci arrivo da solo** I can't do it on my own

arrivato, a [arri'vato] AGG **1** (*persona di successo*) successful **2 ben arrivato!** welcome!
■ SM/F **1** (*persona di successo*): **essere un arrivato** to have made it **2 nuovo arrivato** newcomer; **l'ultimo arrivato** the last to arrive

arrivederci [arrive'dertʃi] ESCL goodbye!; **arrivederci, signora Cooper!** goodbye, Mrs Cooper!; **arrivederci a domani!** see you tomorrow!

arrivederla [arrive'derla] ESCL goodbye!

arrivismo [arri'vizmo] SM social climbing

arrivista, i, e [arri'vista] SM/F social climber

arrivistico, a, ci, che [arri'vistiko] AGG: **avere manie arrivistiche** to be pushy

arrivo [ar'rivo] SM **1** arrival; **al mio arrivo** on my arrival; **telefonami al tuo arrivo in Italia** phone me when you arrive in *o* get to Italy; **essere in arrivo** to be arriving; **il treno proveniente da Roma è in arrivo sul binario 1** the train from Rome is arriving *o* coming in at platform 1; **arrivi e partenze** arrivals and departures **2** (*Sport*) finish, finishing line **3** (*Comm*): **questi sono gli ultimi arrivi** these have just come in; **ci sono nuovi arrivi?** has anything new come in?

arroccare [arrok'kare] VT (*Scacchi*) to castle
▶ **arroccarsi** VR: **arroccarsi in qc** (*fig*) to shelter behind sth

arrogante [arro'gante] AGG arrogant

arrogantemente [arrogante'mente] AVV arrogantly

arroganza [arro'gantsa] SF arrogance

arrogare [arro'gare] VT: **arrogarsi il diritto di fare qc** to assume the right to do sth; **arrogarsi il merito di qc** to claim credit for sth

arrossamento [arrossa'mento] SM reddening

arrossare [arros'sare] VT (*occhi, pelle*) to redden, make red
▶ **arrossarsi** VIP to go *o* turn red

arrossire [arros'sire] VI (*aus* **essere**) **arrossire (di, per)** (*vergogna, imbarazzo*) to blush (with); (*piacere*) to flush (with); **è arrossito per l'imbarazzo** he went red with embarrassment; **arrossire fino alle orecchie** to go *o* turn bright red, blush to the roots of one's hair

arrostimento [arrosti'mento] SM (*vedi vb*) roasting; grilling

arrostire [arros'tire] VT (*al forno*) to roast; (*ai ferri, alla griglia*) to grill; **sotto un sole che arrostiva** under a blazing sun
▶ **arrostirsi** VIP: **arrostirsi al sole** to soak up *o* roast in the sun

arrosto [ar'rɔsto] AGG INV (*vedi vb*) roast; grilled; **pollo arrosto** roast chicken
■ SM roast; **arrosto arrotolato** stuffed rolled veal; **arrosto di manzo** roast beef
■ AVV: **fare** *o* **cuocere arrosto** (*vedi vb*) to roast; to grill; **pollo da fare arrosto** roasting chicken

arrotare [arro'tare] VT **1** (*lame, coltelli*) to sharpen; (*denti*) to grind **2 arrotare la erre** to roll one's r's **3** (*investire con un veicolo*) to run over

arrotino [arro'tino] SM knife-grinder

arrotolare [arroto'lare] VT (*stoffa, sigaretta*) to roll; (*carta*) to roll up

arrotondare [arroton'dare] VT (*cifra*) to round up; (*per difetto*) to round down; (*forma, oggetto*) to (make) round; (*fig*: *stipendio*) to supplement; **fa dei lavoretti extra per arrotondare lo stipendio** he does part-time jobs to supplement his salary

arrotondato, a [arroton'dato] AGG rounded

arrovellare [arrovel'lare] VT: **arrovellarsi il cervello** to rack one's brains

Aa

▶ **arrovellarsi** VR: **arrovellarsi (per qc)** to rack one's brains (about sth)
arroventare [arroven'tare] VT to make red hot
▶ **arroventarsi** VIP to become red hot
arroventato, a [arroven'tato] AGG red-hot
arruffare [arruf'fare] VT to ruffle; (*fili*) to tangle
▶ **arruffarsi** VIP to become tousled
arruffato, a [arruf'fato] AGG (*capelli, pelo*) tousled, ruffled; (*piume*) ruffled
arruffianare [arruffja'nare] (*fam*) VT: **arruffianarsi qn** to lick *o* suck up to sb
■ VIP: **arruffianarsi con qn** to lick *o* suck up to sb
arrugginire [arruddʒi'nire] VI (*aus* **essere**) to rust, get rusty
■ VT to rust
▶ **arrugginirsi** VIP (*metallo*) to rust, get rusty; (*fig: atleta, memoria*) to become rusty
arrugginito, a [arruddʒi'nito] AGG (*anche fig*) rusty; **un lucchetto arrugginito** a rusty padlock
arruolamento [arrwola'mento] SM enlistment
arruolare [arrwo'lare] VT to enlist
▶ **arruolarsi** VR to enlist; **arruolarsi volontario** to join up, enlist
arsenale [arse'nale] SM (*cantiere navale*) dockyard; (*di armi*) arsenal; **si è portato dietro un arsenale** he had everything but the kitchen sink with him, he brought everything but the kitchen sink
arsenico [ar'sɛniko] SM arsenic
arsi *ecc* ['arsi] VB *vedi* **ardere**
arso, a ['arso] PP *di* **ardere**
■ AGG (*bruciato*) burnt; (*arido*) dry
arsura [ar'sura] SF **1** (*siccità*) drought; (*sete*) thirst **2** (*calore: del sole*) burning heat; (*: di febbre*) burning
art. ABBR (= articolo) art.
arte ['arte] SF **1** (*gen*) art; (*abilità*) skill; (*mestiere, attività*) craft; **galleria d'arte** art gallery; **opera d'arte** work of art; **con arte** skilfully; **a regola d'arte** (*fig*) perfectly; **avere l'arte di fare qc** to have the knack of doing sth; **senz'arte né parte** penniless and jobless; **arti figurative** visual arts **2** (*Storia*) guild; **l'arte della lana** the woollen guild; **arti e mestieri** arts and crafts; **arti marziali** martial art
artefatto, a [arte'fatto] AGG (*stile, modi*) artificial
artefice [ar'tefitʃe] SM/F (*autore*) author; **il sommo artefice** (*Dio*) the supreme Architect
Artemide [ar'tɛmide] SF Artemis
arteria [ar'tɛrja] SF (*Anat, fig*) artery
arteriosclerosi [arterjoskle'rɔzi] SF arteriosclerosis (*Med*), hardening of the arteries
arteriosclerotico, a, ci, che [arterjoskle'rɔtiko] AGG (*Med*) suffering from hardening of the arteries; (*fig scherz*) senile
arterioso, a [arte'rjoso] AGG (*Anat*) arterial
artesiano, a [arte'zjano] AGG: **pozzo artesiano** artesian well
artico, a, ci, che ['artiko] AGG Arctic; **il Circolo polare artico** the Arctic Circle; **l'Oceano artico** the Arctic Ocean
■ SM: **l'Artico** the Arctic
articolare[1] [artiko'lare] AGG (*Anat*) articular, of the joints
articolare[2] [artiko'lare] VT **1** (*muovere: giunture*) to move **2** (*pronunciare: parole*) to articulate **3** (*suddividere: discorso, periodo*) to split (up), divide; **ha articolato bene la sua relazione** his presentation was well organized
▶ **articolarsi** VIP (*discorso, progetto*): **articolarsi in** to be divided into
articolato, a [artiko'lato] AGG **1** (*snodato*) articulated **2** (*linguaggio*) articulate; **un ragionamento ben articolato** a clear and well developed argument **3** (*Gramm*): **preposizione articolata** preposition combined with the definite article
articolazione [artikolat'tsjone] SF **1** (*Anat, Tecn*) joint; **ha dolori alle articolazioni** her joints ache **2** (*di voce, concetto*) articulation
articolo [ar'tikolo] SM **1** (*Gramm*) article; **articolo determinativo/indeterminativo** definite/ indefinite article **2** (*di giornale, legge, regolamento*) article; **abbiamo letto un articolo sull'effetto serra** we read an article about the greenhouse effect; **articolo di fede** (*Rel*) article of faith; **articolo di fondo** (*Stampa*) editorial, leader, leading article **3** (*Comm*) item, article; **quel suo amico è un bell'articolo** (*fig*) that friend of his is a real character; **negozio di articoli sportivi** sports shop; **articoli di cancelleria** stationery; **articoli casalinghi** kitchenware; **articoli di lusso** luxury goods; **articoli di marca** branded *o* brand-name goods; **articoli da regalo** gifts; **articolo civetta** loss leader
Artide ['artide] SM: **l'Artide** the Arctic
artificiale [artifi'tʃale] AGG (*gen*) artificial; (*allegria*) forced, unnatural
artificialmente [artifitʃal'mente] AVV (*vedi agg*) artificially; unnaturally
artificiere [artifi'tʃɛre] SM (*Mil*) artificer; (*: per disinnescare bombe*) bomb disposal expert
artificio, ci [arti'fitʃo] SM (*espediente*) trick; (*ricerca di effetto*) artificiality; **fuochi d'artificio** fireworks
artificioso, a [artifi'tʃoso] AGG (*comportamento*) unnatural; (*argomento*) forced
artigianale [artidʒa'nale] AGG craft *attr*; **laboratorio artigianale** workshop; **lavoro artigianale** craftsmanship; **è un pezzo artigianale** it was made by a craftsman; **produzione artigianale** production by craftsmen
artigianalmente [artidʒanal'mente] AVV by craftsmen
artigianato [artidʒa'nato] SM **1** (*arte*) craft; **corso di artigianato** arts and crafts course; **fiera dell'artigianato** craft fair **2** (*prodotti*) arts and crafts *pl*; **un negozio di artigianato locale** a shop selling local crafts **3** (*categoria*) artisans *pl*, craftsmen *pl*
artigiano, a [arti'dʒano] AGG craft *attr*
■ SM/F craftsman/craftswoman; (*idraulico, elettricista*) engineer
artigliere [artiʎ'ʎɛre] SM artilleryman
artiglieria [artiʎʎe'ria] SF artillery; **tiro di artiglieria** artillery fire
artiglio, gli [ar'tiʎʎo] SM (*di felini*) claw; (*di rapaci*) talon; **sfoderare gli artigli** (*fig*) to show one's claws; **cadere negli artigli di qn** (*fig*) to fall into sb's clutches
artista, i, e [ar'tista] SM/F (*pittore, scultore ecc*) artist; (*di spettacolo, circo*) artiste; **è un artista** he's an artist; **un lavoro da artista** (*fig*) a professional piece of work; **artista di varietà** variety artist
artisticamente [artistika'mente] AVV artistically
artistico, a, ci, che [ar'tistiko] AGG artistic; **non ho nessuna inclinazione artistica** I'm not at all artistic; **liceo artistico** secondary school specializing in art
arto ['arto] SM limb
artrite [ar'trite] SF arthritis
artritico, a, ci, che [ar'tritiko] AGG, SM/F arthritic
artropodi [ar'trɔpodi] SMPL arthropods *pl*
artroscopia [artrosko'pia] SF arthroscope

artrosi [ar'trɔzi] SF INV osteoarthritis
Artù [ar'tu] SM: **re Artù** King Arthur
arvicola [ar'vikola] SF (*Zool*) water vole
arzigogolare [ardzigogo'lare] VI (*aus* **avere**) (*fantasticare*) to daydream; (*cavillare*) to quibble
arzigogolato, a [ardzigogo'lato] AGG tortuous
arzigogolo [ardzi'gɔgolo] SM tortuous expression
arzillo, a [ar'dzillo] AGG lively, sprightly
Asburgo [az'burgo] SM INV: **gli Asburgo** the House of Hapsburg, the Hapsburgs
asce ['aʃʃe] SFPL *di* **ascia**
ascella [aʃ'ʃɛlla] SF (*Anat*) armpit
ascellare [aʃʃel'lare] AGG underarm *attr*
ascendente [aʃʃen'dɛnte] AGG (*moto, piano*) ascending, upward; (*Mus: scala*) ascending
■ SM **1** (*influenza*): **ascendente (su)** ascendancy (over) **2** (*Astrol*) ascendant **3** (*antenato*) ancestor
ascendenza [aʃʃen'dɛntsa] SF ancestry
ascendere [aʃ'ʃendere] VI IRREG (*aus* **essere**) (*frm*): **ascendere al trono** to ascend the throne; **ascendere a grandi onori** to rise to great honours
ascensionale [aʃʃensjo'nale] AGG (*forza, moto*) upward; **velocità ascensionale** (*Aer*) rate of climb
ascensione [aʃʃen'sjone] SF **1** (*Alpinismo*) ascent, climb; (*Aer*) ascent **2** (*Rel*): **l'Ascensione** the Ascension **3** **(isola dell')Ascensione** Ascension Island
ascensore [aʃʃen'sore] SM lift (*Brit*), elevator (*Am*); **l'ascensore è guasto** the lift's out of order
ascesa [aʃ'ʃesa] SF (*gen*) ascent, climb; (*fig: al trono*) accession; (*: al potere, successo*) rise
ascesi [aʃ'ʃɛzi] SF asceticism
asceso, a [aʃ'ʃeso] PP *di* **ascendere**
ascesso [aʃ'ʃɛsso] SM abscess
asceta, i [aʃ'ʃɛta] SM/F ascetic
ascetico, a, ci, che [aʃ'ʃɛtiko] AGG ascetic(al)
ascetismo [aʃʃe'tizmo] SM asceticism
ascia, sce ['aʃʃa] SF axe; (*più piccola*) hatchet
ascissa [aʃ'ʃissa] SF (*Mat*) x-axis
asciugacapelli [aʃʃugaka'pelli] SM INV hair dryer
asciugamano [aʃʃuga'mano] SM towel; **asciugamano da bagno** bath towel
asciugare [aʃʃu'gare] VT (*gen*) to dry; (*sudore*) to wipe; **asciugare i piatti** to wipe *o* dry the dishes; **asciugarsi le mani/le lacrime** to dry one's hands/one's eyes; **asciugati i capelli** dry your hair
▶ **asciugarsi** VIP (*panni*) to dry; **la maglietta si è asciugata in fretta** the T-shirt soon got dry; **asciugarsi al sole** to dry in the sun;
▶ **asciugarsi** VR (*persona*) to dry o.s.; **asciugarsi al sole** to dry off in the sun
asciugatoio, oi [aʃʃuga'tojo] SM = **essiccatoio**
asciugatrice [aʃʃuga'tritʃe] SF spin-dryer; **asciugatrice a centrifuga** tumble dryer
asciuttezza [aʃʃut'tettsa] SF (*vedi agg*) dryness; leanness; curtness
asciutto, a [aʃ'ʃutto] AGG (*gen, fig*) dry; (*magro: viso, corpo ecc*) lean; (*brusco: risposta*) curt; **è asciutta la maglietta?** is the T-shirt dry?; **rimanere** *o* **restare a bocca asciutta** (*fig*) to be disappointed
■ SM: **tenere all'asciutto** to keep in a dry place; **rimanere** *o* **restare all'asciutto** (*fig*) to be broke; **sono rimasto all'asciutto, puoi prestarmi 50 euro?** I haven't got a bean, can you lend me 50 euros?
ascolano, a [asko'lano] AGG of *o* from Ascoli
■ SM/F inhabitant *o* native of Ascoli
ascoltare [askol'tare] VT (*persona, musica, radio, discorso ecc*) to listen to; **mi stai ascoltando?** are you listening to me?; **ascoltare qn parlare/cantare** to listen to sb talk/sing; **ascoltare qn con un orecchio solo** to half listen to sb; **ascoltare il consiglio di qn** to listen to *o* heed sb's advice; **ascoltare la messa/una lezione** to attend Mass/a class; **ascoltare un testimone** (*Dir*) to hear a witness
ascoltatore, trice [askolta'tore] SM/F listener
ascolto [as'kolto] SM **1** (*Radio*) reception; (*gen, programma*): **essere** *o* **stare in ascolto (di qc)** to be listening (to sth); **mettersi in ascolto (di qc)** to listen (to sth); **indice di ascolto** (*TV, Radio*) audience rating **2** (*attenzione*): **dare** *o* **prestare ascolto a qn/ai consigli di qn** to listen to *o* heed sb/sb's advice; **non presterai ascolto a queste chiacchiere** you won't take any notice of *o* you won't listen to these rumours, will you?
ASCOM ['askom] SIGLA F (= **Associazione Commercianti**) *association of merchants and shopkeepers*
ascorbico, a, ci, che [as'kɔrbiko] AGG: **acido ascorbico** ascorbic acid
ascritto, a [as'kritto] PP *di* **ascrivere**
ascrivere [as'krivere] VT IRREG **1** (*attribuire*): **ascrivere qc a qn** to attribute sth to sb; **ascrivere qc a merito di qn** to give sb credit for sth **2** (*annoverare*): **ascrivere (tra)** to number (among)
asessuale [asessu'ale] AGG (*Bio*) asexual
asessuato, a [asessu'ato] AGG asexual
asettico, a, ci, che [a'sɛttiko] AGG aseptic
asfaltare [asfal'tare] VT to asphalt
asfalto [as'falto] SM asphalt
asfissia [asfis'sia] SF asphyxia, asphyxiation
asfissiante [asfis'sjante] AGG (*gas*) asphyxiant, asphyxiating; (*fig: calore, ambiente*) stifling, suffocating; (*: persona*) tiresome
asfissiare [asfis'sjare] VT to asphyxiate, suffocate; (*fig: opprimere*) to stifle; (*fig: infastidire*) to get on sb's nerves; **asfissiare (con il gas)** to gas; **è morto asfissiato** he died of suffocation; **la sta asfissiando con la sua gelosia** he's stifling her with his jealousy
■ VI (*aus* **essere**) to suffocate, asphyxiate
▶ **asfissiarsi** VR to suffocate o.s.; **asfissiarsi col gas** to gas o.s.
Asia ['azja] SF Asia; **vengono dall'Asia** they come from Asia
asiatico, a, ci, che [a'zjatiko] AGG Asian, Asiatic
■ SM/F Asian, Asiatic
■ SF (*Med*) Asian flu
asilo [a'zilo] SM **1** **asilo (infantile)** nursery (school); **Paolo va all'asilo** Paolo goes to nursery school; **asilo nido** day nursery (*for children aged 0 to 3*), crèche **2** (*rifugio*) shelter, refuge; (*Pol*) asylum; **diritto di asilo** right of asylum; **dare/chiedere asilo** to grant/seek political asylum
asimmetria [asimme'tria] SF asymmetry
asimmetricamente [asimmetrika'mente] AVV asymmetrically
asimmetrico, a, ci, che [asim'mɛtriko] AGG asymmetric(al)
asina ['asina] SF she-ass
asinello [asi'nɛllo] SM (little) donkey
asinino, a [asi'nino] AGG: **tosse asinina** whooping cough
asino ['asino] SM (*Zool*) donkey, ass; (*fig*) fool, ass; (*: scolaro*) dunce; **a dorso d'asino** on the back of a donkey; **qui casca l'asino!** there's the rub!

Aa

ASL [azl] SIGLA F (= **Azienda Sanitaria Locale**) local health centre
asma ['azma] SF asthma
asmatico, a, ci, che [az'matiko] AGG, SM/F asthmatic
asociale [aso'tʃale] AGG antisocial; (*chiuso*) unsociable ■SM/F unsociable person
asocialità [asotʃali'ta] SF antisocial behaviour
asola ['azola] SF buttonhole
asparago, gi [as'parago] SM asparagus *no pl*; **gli asparagi sono buoni** asparagus is nice; **un mazzo di asparagi** a bunch of asparagus
aspergere [as'pɛrdʒere] VT IRREG: **aspergere (di** *o* **con)** to sprinkle (with)
asperità [asperi'ta] SF INV (*di terreno, roccia*) roughness *no pl*, ruggedness *no pl*; (*fig*) harshness *no pl*; **le asperità della vita** the trials of life
aspersi *ecc* [as'pɛrsi] VB *vedi* **aspergere**
aspersione [asper'sjone] SF (*anche Rel*) sprinkling
asperso, a [as'pɛrso] PP *di* **aspergere**
aspersorio, ri [asper'sɔrjo] SM aspersorium
aspettare [aspet'tare] VT **1** (*attendere*) to wait for, await (*frm*); **è un'ora che aspetto** I've been waiting for an hour; **aspettiamo che arrivi** let's wait for him to come; **aspetta un po'** wait a second *o* moment, hold on; **aspetta un attimo!** wait a minute!; **aspetta a giudicare!** wait and see!; **aspettare la fine** (*di film ecc*) to wait until the end; **aspettare conferma** (*Comm*) to await confirmation; **sto aspettando una telefonata importante** I'm expecting an important phone call; **aspettare un bambino** (*essere incinta*) to be expecting (a baby); **mia sorella aspetta un bambino** my sister's expecting a baby; **aspettare qn** to wait for sb; **è mezz'ora che ti aspetto** I've been waiting for you for half an hour; **sto aspettando un'amica** I'm waiting for a friend; **aspettami, vengo anch'io!** wait for me, I'm coming too!; **fare aspettare qn** to keep sb waiting; **mi ha fatto aspettare un'ora** he kept me waiting for an hour; **farsi aspettare** to keep people waiting; **aspetta e spera!** that'll be the day!; **chi la fa, l'aspetti!** (*Proverbio*) it'll all come home to roost **2** (*essere in serbo: notizia, evento ecc*) to be in store for, lie ahead of; **non sapeva che cosa lo aspettasse** he didn't know what was in store for him *o* lay ahead of him **3 aspettarsi qc** to expect sth; **non mi aspettavo che partisse** I didn't expect him to leave; **era meglio di quanto mi aspettassi** it was better than I expected; **quando meno te l'aspetti** when you least expect it; **me l'aspettavo!** I thought as much!
aspettativa [aspetta'tiva] SF **1** (*previsione, speranza*) expectation; **contro ogni mia aspettativa** against all my expectations; **inferiore/superiore all'aspettativa** worse/better than expected; **corrispondere alle/deludere le aspettative di qn** to come up to/fall short of sb's expectations; **superare ogni aspettativa** to exceed *o* go beyond all expectations; **aspettativa di vita** life expectancy **2** (*Amm*): **chiedere l'aspettativa** to ask for *o* put in for leave; **essere/mettersi in aspettativa** to be on/take leave (of absence)
aspetto [as'pɛtto] SM **1** (*apparenza*) appearance, look; **cura molto il suo aspetto** he takes great care of his appearance; **un uomo di bell'aspetto** a good-looking man; **all'aspetto** *o* **a giudicare dall'aspetto, pare una persona onesta** as far as we can tell, he seems an honest person; **avere l'aspetto di** to look like **2** (*di questione ecc*) aspect, side; **un aspetto positivo** a positive aspect; **sotto un certo aspetto** in some ways

aspic [as'pik] SM INV: **aspic di pollo** chicken in aspic
aspide ['aspide] SM asp
aspidistra [aspi'distra] SF (*Bot*) aspidistra
aspirante [aspi'rante] AGG **1** (*Tecn*) suction *attr* **2** (*artista*) aspiring; **un aspirante attore** an aspiring actor
■SM/F (*a un titolo*) aspirant; (*candidato*) candidate
aspirapolvere [aspira'polvere] SM INV vacuum cleaner, hoover®; **passare l'aspirapolvere** to vacuum, hoover
aspirare [aspi'rare] VT **1** (*fumo*) to inhale; (*aria, profumo*) to breathe in **2** (*Tecn*) to suck (up) **3** (*Fonetica*) to aspirate
■VI (*aus* **avere**) (*anelare*): **aspirare a qc/a fare qc** to aspire to sth/to do sth
aspiratore [aspira'tore] SM (*di aria, gas*) extractor fan; (*di liquidi*) aspirator, extractor
aspirazione [aspirat'tsjone] SF **1** (*Tecn*) suction **2** (*anelito*) aspiration; (*ambizione*) ambition **3** (*Fonetica*) aspiration
aspirina® [aspi'rina] SF aspirin; **prendi due aspirine** take two aspirins
asportare [aspor'tare] VT to take away; (*Med*) to remove
asportazione [asportat'tsjone] SF (*anche Med*) removal
asporto SM: **da asporto** (*gelato, pizza*) take-away
aspramente [aspra'mente] AVV (*rimproverare*) harshly
asprezza [as'prettsa] SF INV (*vedi agg*) sourness; sharpness; pungency; rugged nature; severity; harshness, roughness; strictness
asprigno, a [as'priɲɲo] AGG rather sour
aspro, a ['aspro] AGG **1** (*agrumi*) sour; (*vino*) sharp; (*odore*) pungent, acrid; (*paesaggio*) rugged; (*clima*) severe, harsh; **questo pompelmo è molto aspro** this grapefruit is very sour **2** (*fig: voce, giudizio*) harsh, rough; (*: disciplina, regime*) strict **3** (*Fonetica*): **"s" aspra** unvoiced "s"
Ass. ABBR **1** = **assicurazione 2** = **assicurata 3** = **assegno**
assaggiare [assad'dʒare] VT (*pietanza, bevanda*) to taste, try; **vuoi assaggiare?** would you like to taste it?; **fammi assaggiare** let me have a taste; **gli hanno fatto assaggiare la frusta** (*fig*) they gave him a taste of the whip
assaggiatore, trice [assaddʒa'tore] SM/F taster
assaggini [assad'dʒini] SMPL (*Culin*) *selection of first courses*
assaggio, gi [as'saddʒo] SM (*prova, degustazione*) tasting, sampling; (*piccola quantità*) taste; (*campione*) sample
assai [as'sai] AVV (*molto*) a lot, much; (*: con agg*) very; **è assai più giovane di me** she is very much *o* a lot younger than me; **sono assai contento del risultato** I'm very pleased with the result; **m'importa assai di lui!** what do I care about him!
assalgo *ecc* [as'salgo] VB *vedi* **assalire**
assalire [assa'lire] VT IRREG to attack, assail; (*fig*) to assail; **fu assalito dai malviventi** he was attacked by thugs; **assalire a parole** to attack verbally
assalitore, trice [assali'tore] SM/F attacker, assailant
assaltare [assal'tare] VT (*Mil*) to storm; (*banca*) to raid; (*treno, diligenza*) to hold up
assalto [as'salto] SM **1** (*Mil*) attack, assault; **truppe d'assalto** assault troops; **d'assalto** (*fig: editoria, giornalista ecc*) aggressive **2** (*rapina*) raid; **prendere d'assalto** (*fig: negozio, treno*) to storm; (*: personalità*) to besiege

assaporare [assapo'rare] VT (*anche fig*) to savour (*Brit*), savor (*Am*)
assassinare [assassi'nare] VT (*gen*) to murder; (*Pol*) to assassinate
assassinio, nii [assas'sinjo] SM murder; (*politico*) assassination
assassino, a [assas'sino] SM/F murderer; (*Pol*) assassin
■ AGG (*mania, tendenza*) murderous; (*seducente: sguardo, occhiata*) seductive
assatanato, a [assata'nato] AGG (*fam: eccitato*) randy
asse[1] ['asse] SF (*di legno*) board; **asse di equilibrio** (*Ginnastica*) beam; **asse del gabinetto** lavatory seat; **asse da stiro** ironing board
asse[2] ['asse] SM (*Geom*) axis; (*Tecn*) axle; **l'asse terrestre** the earth's axis; **l'asse Roma-Berlino** (*alleanza*) the Rome-Berlin axis
assecondare [assekon'dare] VT: **assecondare qn (in qc)** to go along with sb (in sth); **assecondare i desideri di qn** to go along with sb's wishes; **assecondare i capricci di qn** to give in to sb's whims
assediante [asse'djante] SM/F besieger
assediare [asse'djare] VT (*anche fig*) to besiege
assediato, a [asse'djato] AGG (*anche fig*) besieged
■ **gli assediati** SMPL people under siege
assedio, di [as'sɛdjo] SM (*anche fig*) siege; **porre in stato di assedio** to lay siege to; **cingere d'assedio** to besiege
assegnamento [asseɲɲa'mento] SM: **fare assegnamento su** to rely on
assegnare [asseɲ'ɲare] VT: **assegnare (a)** (*gen*) to assign (to); (*premio, borsa di studio*) to award (to); (*somma*) to allocate (to), allot (to)
assegnatario, ria, ri, rie [asseɲɲa'tarjo] SM/F (*Dir*) assignee; **l'assegnatario del premio** the person awarded the prize
assegnazione [asseɲɲat'tsjone] SF (*di casa, somma*) allocation; (*di carica*) assignment; (*di premio, borsa di studio*) awarding
assegno [as'seɲɲo] SM **1** (*Comm*): **contro assegno** cash on delivery **2** (*somma integrativa*): **assegni familiari** ≈ child benefit *sg*; **assegno di studio** ≈ study grant **3** (*Fin*): **assegno (bancario)** cheque (*Brit*), check (*Am*); **un assegno per** *o* **di 500 euro** a cheque for 500 euros; **ha pagato con un assegno** he paid by cheque; **assegno in bianco** blank cheque; **assegno circolare** bank draft; **"assegno non trasferibile"** "account payee only"; **assegno post-datato** post-dated cheque; **assegno sbarrato** crossed cheque; **assegno a vuoto** dud cheque
assemblaggio, gi [assem'bladdʒo] SM (*Industria*) assembly; (*Inform*) assembling
assemblare [assem'blare] VT (*Industria, Inform, anche fig*) to assemble
assemblatore [assembla'tore] SM assembly worker
■ AGG (*Inform*): **programma assemblatore** assembler
assemblea [assem'blɛa] SF (*gen*) assembly; (*raduno, adunanza*) meeting **assemblea generale** general meeting
assembleare [assemble'are] AGG (*decisione, riunione*) of the meeting, of the assembly
assembramento [assembra'mento] SM (public) gathering; **divieto di assembramento** ban on public meetings
assembrarsi [assem'brarsi] VIP to gather
assennatamente [assennata'mente] AVV sensibly, wisely
assennatezza [assenna'tettsa] SF good sense, wisdom
assennato, a [assen'nato] AGG sensible, wise
assenso [as'sɛnso] SM approval, assent; (*Dir*) consent; **dare/negare il proprio assenso** give/not give *o* withhold one's consent
assentarsi [assen'tarsi] VIP (*gen*) to go out; **il direttore dovrà assentarsi per un paio di giorni** the manager will be away for a couple of days; **si assenta spesso dal lavoro** he is frequently absent from work
assente [as'sɛnte] AGG **1** **assente (da)** (*gen*) away (from); (*malato, studente*) absent (from); **il direttore è momentaneamente assente** the manager is out at the moment; **oggi sono assenti due scolari** two pupils are absent today **2** (*espressione, sguardo*) vacant, faraway; **avere lo sguardo assente** to look miles away
■ SM/F absentee; **quanti assenti ci sono oggi?** how many people are absent today?; **non sparlare degli assenti** you shouldn't talk behind people's backs; **il grande assente alla riunione** the most notable absentee at the meeting
assenteismo [assente'izmo] SM absenteeism
assenteista, i, e [assente'ista] SM/F (*dal lavoro*) absentee; **è un assenteista** he is often absent
assentire [assen'tire] VI (*aus* **avere**) **assentire (a)** to agree (to), assent (to)
assenza [as'sɛntsa] SF absence; **in assenza di** in the absence of; **in mia assenza** in my absence; **non ho fatto nessuna assenza a scuola/in ufficio** I haven't missed a day at school/at the office; **quanto durerà la sua assenza?** how long will he be away for?
assenzio, zi [as'sɛntsjo] SM **1** (*Bot*) wormwood **2** (*liquore*) absinthe
asserire [asse'rire] VT to maintain, assert; **ha asserito di avere ragione** he maintained (that) he was right
asserragliarsi [asserraʎ'ʎarsi] VR: **asserragliarsi (in)** to barricade o.s. (in)
assertore, trice [asser'tore] SM/F supporter, upholder
asservimento [asservi'mento] SM (*azione*) enslavement; (*stato, anche fig*): **asservimento (a)** slavery (to); subservience (to)
asservire [asser'vire] VT to enslave; (*fig: animo, passioni*) to subdue
▶ **asservirsi** VR: **asservirsi (a)** to submit (to)
asserzione [asser'tsjone] SF assertion
assessorato [assesso'rato] SM (*carica*) councillorship; **assessorato alla cultura** *local authority arts and entertainment department*
assessore [asses'sore] SM councillor
assestamento [assesta'mento] SM (*gen, Geol, Edil*) settlement; **essere in via di assestamento** (*terreno*) to be settling; **la situazione è in via di assestamento** things are settling down
assestare [asses'tare] VT (*gen, Geol*) to settle; **assestare un colpo a qn** to deal sb a blow; **assestare la mira** to adjust one's aim
▶ **assestarsi** VIP (*situazione ecc*) to settle down; (*terreno*) to settle
assestato, a [asses'tato] AGG: **un colpo ben assestato** a well-aimed blow
assetato, a [asse'tato] AGG thirsty; **assetato di** (*fig*) thirsting for; **assetato di potere** greedy for power; **assetato di sangue** bloodthirsty
assetto [as'sɛtto] SM **1** (*ordine*) order, arrangement; **dare un assetto nuovo a qc** to (re)arrange sth; **in assetto di guerra** ready for war; **in assetto antisommossa** in riot gear **2** (*Aer, Naut*) trim; (*Aut*)

Aa

balance; (*Equitazione*) seat; **assetto delle ruote** (*Aut*) (wheel) alignment; **assetto territoriale** country planning

assiale [as'sjale] AGG axial

assicurare [assiku'rare] VT **1** (*Assicurazione: vita, casa*) to insure; (*lettera, pacco*) to register; **la macchina non era assicurata contro il furto** the car wasn't insured against theft **2** (*garantire*) assure; **assicurare l'avvenire ai figli** to secure the children's future; **assicurarsi qc** to secure *o* ensure sth for o.s.; **assicurarsi un lavoro** to get a job for o.s; **assicurare qn alla giustizia** (*arrestare*) to arrest sb **3** (*per tranquillizzare*): **assicurare qn che** to assure sb that; **mi ha assicurato che sarebbe venuto** he assured me that he'd come; **te l'assicuro!** I assure you! **4** (*fermare, legare*): **assicurare (a)** to secure (to); (*Alpinismo*) to belay
▶ **assicurarsi** VR **1** (*Assicurazione*) **assicurarsi (contro qc)** to insure o.s. (against sth) **2** (*accertarsi*) **assicurarsi di/che** to make sure of/that; **assicurati che la porta sia ben chiusa** make sure the door's closed properly **3** (*legarsi*) **assicurarsi (a)** to fasten o.s. (to), tie o.s. (to)

assicurata [assiku'rata] SF registered letter

assicurativo, a [assikura'tivo] AGG insurance *attr*

assicurato, a [assiku'rato] AGG insured
■ SM/F policy holder

assicuratore, trice [assikura'tore] AGG insurance *attr*; **società assicuratrice** insurance company
■ SM/F insurance agent

assicurazione [assikurat'tsjone] SF **1** (*conferma, garanzia*) assurance **2** (*contratto*) insurance (policy); **fare un'assicurazione** to take out insurance; **assicurazione contro furti** theft insurance; **assicurazione contro incendi** fire insurance; **assicurazione contro terzi** third party insurance; **assicurazione multi-rischio** comprehensive insurance; **assicurazione sulla vita** life insurance **3** (*Alpinismo*) belaying

assideramento [assidera'mento] SM (*Med*) exposure

assiderare [asside'rare] VT to freeze; **questo freddo mi sta assiderando** (*fig*) I'm chilled to the bone
▶ **assiderarsi** VIP to freeze

assiderato, a [asside'rato] AGG frozen; **morire assiderato** to die of exposure

assiduamente [assidua'mente] AVV (*vedi agg*) assiduously; regularly

assiduità [assidui'ta] SF (*vedi agg*) assiduity; regularity; **assiduità alle lezioni** (*Scol*) regular attendance at classes; **viene a trovarmi con assiduità** he comes to see me frequently

assiduo, a [as'siduo] AGG (*cure, studio, applicazione*) assiduous; (*visitatore, lettore*) regular

assieme [as'sjɛme] AVV (*insieme*) together
■ PREP: **assieme a** (together) with

assillante [assil'lante] AGG (*dubbio, pensiero*) nagging; (*creditore*) pestering

assillare [assil'lare] VT (*sogg: dubbio, pensiero, persona*) to nag at; (: *creditore*) to hound; **continua ad assillarmi con i suoi problemi** he keeps pestering me with his problems

assillo [as'sillo] SM **1** (*pensiero tormentoso*) nagging worry, worrying thought; **aver l'assillo di qc** to be constantly worrying about sth **2** (*Zool*) horsefly, gadfly

assimilabile [assimi'labile] AGG (*sostanza*) easily assimilated; (: *cibo*) digestible

assimilare [assimi'lare] VT (*anche fig*) to assimilate

assimilazione [assimilat'tsjone] SF assimilation

assiolo [assi'ɔlo] SM horned owl

assioma [as'sjɔma] SM axiom

assiomatico, a, ci, che [assjo'matiko] AGG axiomatic

assise [as'size] SFPL (*Dir*): **la Corte d'Assise** ≈ the crown court (*Brit*)

assistente [assis'tɛnte] SM/F (*gen*) assistant; **il direttore ha chiamato una sua assistente** the manager called one of his assistants; **assistente ai lavori** supervisor; **assistente dell'arbitro** (*Calcio*) assistant referee; **assistente di polizia** inspector; **assistente sanitario** health worker; **assistente sociale** social worker; **assistente universitario** ≈ (assistant) lecturer **assistente di volo** (*Aer*) flight attendant

assistenza [assis'tɛntsa] SF (*aiuto*) assistance; **dare** *o* **prestare assistenza a qn** to assist sb, give assistance to sb; **fare opera di assistenza** to help out; **assistenza legale** legal aid; **assistenza ospedaliera** free hospital treatment; **assistenza sanitaria** health service; **assistenza sociale** social security; **assistenza tecnica** after-sales service; **assistenza a terra** (*Aer*) ground handling

assistenziale [assisten'tsjale] AGG (*ente, organizzazione*) welfare *attr*; (*opera*) charitable

assistenzialismo [assistentsja'lizmo] SM (*pegg*) excessive state aid

assistere [as'sistere] VB IRREG
■ VI (*aus* **avere**) **assistere a** (*essere presente*) to be present at, attend; (*incidente, scena*) to witness; (*spettacolo*) to watch; (*sorvegliare*: *lavori, esami*) to supervise
■ VT (*aiutare*) to assist; (*malato*) to look after; (: *curare*) to treat; **assiste la madre ammalata** she's looking after her sick mother

assistito, a [assis'tito] PP *di* **assistere**
■ SM/F (*di medico*) patient; (*di avvocato, ente assistenziale*) client
■ AGG assisted; **fecondazione assistita** assisted conception; **traduzione assistita** assisted translation

ASSITALIA [assi'talja] SIGLA FSG (= **Assicurazioni d'Italia**) Association of Italian Insurers

asso ['asso] SM **1** (*carta, dado*) ace; **asso di picche/cuori** *ecc* ace of spades/hearts *ecc*; **avere un** *o* **l'asso nella manica** (*fig*) to have an ace up one's sleeve; **piantare qn in asso** to leave sb in the lurch **2** (*campione*) ace; **asso del volante** ace driver

ASSOBANCARIA [assoban'karja] SIGLA F (= **Associazione Bancaria italiana**) Italian Banking Association

associare [asso'tʃare] VT **1** (*idee, parole, fatti*): **associare (a)** to associate (with); **il suo nome è stato associato alla Mafia** his name has been linked with the Mafia **2** **associare qn a** (*ad un circolo*) to make sb a member of; (*ad una ditta*) to take sb into partnership in; **associare qn alle carceri** to take sb to prison
▶ **associarsi** VR **1** **associarsi con qn** (*in una ditta*) to enter into partnership with sb **2** **associarsi a** (*circolo*) to join, become a member of; (*dolori, gioie, lutto*) to share in

associativo, a [assotʃa'tivo] AGG **1** (*Mat*) associative **2** **quota associativa** (*a club ecc*) enrolment fee

associato, a [asso'tʃato] AGG **1** **professore associato** ≈ senior lecturer (*Brit*), ≈ associate professor (*Am*) **2** (*di associazione*) associate
■ SM/F (*socio*) member

associazione [assotʃat'tsjone] SF **1** (*gen, Pol, Sport ecc*) association; **associazione a** *o* **per delinquere** (*Dir*) criminal association; **associazione di categoria** trade association; **Associazione Europea di Libero Scambio**

European Free Trade Association; **associazione in partecipazione** (*Comm*) joint venture **2** (*di idee*) association; **per associazione di idee** by association of ideas

assodare [asso'dare] VT **1** (*accertare: fatti, verità*) to ascertain **2** (*muro, posizione*) to strengthen
▶ **assodarsi** VIP (*sostanza*) to harden

assodato, a [asso'dato] AGG well-founded

assoggettamento [assoddʒetta'mento] SM subjection

assoggettare [assoddʒet'tare] VT (*persone*) to subjugate; (*fig: passioni, istinti*) to curb
▶ **assoggettarsi** VR: **assoggettarsi a** to submit to; (*adattarsi*) to adapt to

assolato, a [asso'lato] AGG sunny

assoldare [assol'dare] VT (*sicario*) to hire; (*spia*) to recruit

assolo [as'solo] SM (*Mus*) solo

assolsi *ecc* [as'sɔlsi] VB *vedi* **assolvere**

assolto, a [as'sɔlto] PP *di* **assolvere**

assolutamente [assoluta'mente] AVV absolutely; **è assolutamente incredibile** it's absolutely incredible; **devo assolutamente andare** I've simply got to go; **assolutamente no** certainly not

assolutismo [assolu'tizmo] SM absolutism

assoluto, a [asso'luto] AGG (*gen, Pol, Gramm*) absolute; **in caso di assoluta necessità** if absolutely essential; **è in assoluto il più bravo** he is without doubt *o* altogether the best
■ SM (*Filosofia*): **l'assoluto** the absolute

assoluzione [assolut'tsjone] SF (*Rel*) absolution; (*Dir*) acquittal; **dare l'assoluzione a qn** to give sb absolution; **concedere l'assoluzione a qn** to acquit sb

assolvere [as'sɔlvere] VT IRREG **1** **assolvere qn (da)** (*Rel*) to absolve sb (from); (*Dir*) to acquit sb (of); **è stato assolto dall'accusa di omicidio** he was acquitted of murder **2** (*adempiere: mansioni, compiti*) to carry out, perform; **assolvere il proprio dovere** to perform one's duty

assomigliare [assomiʎ'ʎare] VI (*aus* **essere** *o* **avere**) **assomigliare a** (*nell'aspetto*) to resemble, look like; (*nel carattere*) to be like
▶ **assomigliarsi** VR (*uso reciproco*) to be alike, resemble each other; **si assomigliano come due gocce d'acqua** they are as like as two peas (in a pod)

assommare [assom'mare] VT to combine
■ VI (*aus* **essere**) (*ammontare*): **assommare a** to amount to, come to

assonanza [asso'nantsa] SF assonance

assone [as'sone] SM (*Anat*) axon

assonnato, a [asson'nato] AGG sleepy; **hai l'aria assonnata** you look sleepy

assonometria [assonome'tria] SF (*Mat*) axonometry

assopimento [assopi'mento] SM doziness, sleepiness

assopire [asso'pire] VT **1** **far assopire** to make drowsy **2** (*dolore*) to soothe
▶ **assopirsi** VIP to doze off

assorbente [assor'bɛnte] AGG absorbent; **carta assorbente** blotting paper
■ SM: **assorbente (igienico)** sanitary towel; **assorbente interno** tampon

LO SAPEVI...?
assorbente non si traduce mai con la parola inglese ***absorbing***

assorbimento [assorbi'mento] SM (*Chim, Fis*) absorption; (*Bot*) uptake

assorbire [assor'bire] VT (*liquidi*) to absorb, soak up; (*suono*) to absorb; (*tempo, attenzione*) to take up, occupy; (*cultura, influenza*) to assimilate, absorb

assordante [assor'dante] AGG (*rumore, musica*) deafening

assordare [assor'dare] VT to deafen; **abbassa il volume, mi stai assordando!** turn down the volume, you're deafening me!

assortimento [assorti'mento] SM assortment, variety

assortire [assor'tire] VT (*combinare*) to combine; (: *colori*) to match; (*disporre*) to arrange

assortito, a [assor'tito] AGG **1** (*combinato: persone, cose, colori*): **bene/male assortito** well/badly matched **2** (*antipasti, cioccolatini*) assorted; **una scatola di cioccolatini assortiti** a box of assorted chocolates

assorto, a [as'sɔrto] AGG: **essere assorto in qc** to be engrossed in sth

assottigliare [assottiʎ'ʎare] VT **1** (*affilare*) to sharpen **2** (*ridurre: spessore*) to make thinner, thin (down); (: *provviste*) to reduce; (: *caviglie*) to slim; (: *girovita*) to reduce, slim down
▶ **assottigliarsi** VIP (*provviste*) to dwindle; (*caviglie, girovita*) to slim down

assuefare [assue'fare] VB IRREG
■ VT: **assuefare a** to get used to, accustom to
▶ **assuefarsi** VR: **assuefarsi a** to become *o* get accustomed *o* used to; (*droga*) to become addicted to

assuefatto, a [assue'fatto] PP *di* **assuefare**

assuefazione [assuefat'tsjone] SF (*Med*) addiction; **questo medicinale non dà assuefazione** this drug is not habit-forming

assumere [as'sumere] VT IRREG **1** (*impiegato*) to take on, engage, employ; **l'azienda assumerà due operai** the company is going to take on two workers; **essere assunto** to get a job; **è stata assunta come programmatrice** she's got a job as a programmer **2** (*atteggiamento, espressione*) to assume, put on; (*comando, potere*) to assume, take over; (*incarico*) to take up; **assumersi il compito di fare qc** to take on the job of doing sth; **si è assunto ogni responsabilità** he's taken responsibility for everything; **assumere informazioni su qn/qc** to make enquiries about sb/sth **3** (*supporre*) to assume; **assumendo (come ipotesi) che...** assuming that ... **4** (*droga*) to take **5** (*innalzare a dignità*) to raise

assunsi *ecc* [as'sunsi] VB *vedi* **assumere**

assunto, a [as'sunto] PP *di* **assumere**
■ SM (*Filosofia*) proposition

assunzione [assun'tsjone] SF **1** (*di impiegati*) employment, engagement; **ci sono state poche assunzioni** few people have been taken on; **il problema delle assunzioni** the employment problem **2** (*Rel*): **l'Assunzione** the Assumption

assurdamente [assurda'mente] AVV absurdly

assurdità [assurdi'ta] SF INV absurdity; **l'assurdità della situazione** the absurdity of the situation; **che assurdità!** how absurd!; **dire delle assurdità** to talk nonsense

assurdo, a [as'surdo] AGG absurd; **che idea assurda!** what a ridiculous idea!; **è assurdo!** it's ridiculous!

asta ['asta] SF **1** (*palo*) pole; **salto con l'asta** pole vault; **bandiera a mezz'asta** flag at half-mast **2** (*di occhiali*) arm (*Brit*), stem (*Am*); (*di compasso, bilancia*) arm; (*Sci: di skilift*) bar **3** (*Comm*) auction; **mettere all'asta** to put up for auction; **vendere all'asta** to auction off; **vendita all'asta** auction sale; **asta fallimentare** bankruptcy sale **4** (*nella scrittura*) stroke

astante [as'tante] SM/F bystander
astanteria [astante'ria] SF casualty department
astemio, mia, mi, mie [as'tɛmjo] AGG teetotal
■ SM/F teetotaller

LO SAPEVI...?
astemio non si traduce mai con la parola inglese *abstemious*

astenersi [aste'nersi] VR IRREG: **astenersi (dal fare qc/da qc)** to abstain *o* refrain (from doing sth/from sth); **astenersi dal dire** to refrain from saying; **astenersi dal bere/dal fumo** to keep off drink/cigarettes; **astenersi (dal voto)** (*Pol*) to abstain
astensione [asten'sjone] SF abstention
astensionismo [astensjo'nizmo] SM (*Pol*) abstention
astensionista, i, e [astensjo'nista] SM/F (*Pol*) abstentionist
asterisco, schi [aste'risko] SM asterisk (*di telefono, computer*) star key
asteroide [aste'rɔide] SM asteroid
astice ['astitʃe] SM lobster
astigiano, a [asti'dʒano] AGG of *o* from Asti
■ SM/F inhabitant *o* native of Asti
astigmatico, a, ci, che [astig'matiko] AGG astigmatic
■ SM/F person suffering from astigmatism
astigmatismo [astigma'tizmo] SM astigmatism
astina [as'tina] SF (*dell'olio*) dipstick
astinenza [asti'nɛntsa] SF abstinence; **fare astinenza (da)** (*Rel*) to abstain (from); **essere in crisi di astinenza** (*di droga*) to suffer from withdrawal symptoms
astio ['astjo] SM: **astio (contro)** rancour (against), resentment (towards); **portare astio a qn** to bear sb a grudge
astiosamente [astjosa'mente] AVV resentfully
astiosità [astjosi'ta] SF INV rancour, resentment
astioso, a [as'tjoso] AGG resentful
astore [as'tore] SM (*Zool*) goshawk
astrakan ['astrakan] SM INV astrakhan
astrale [as'trale] AGG astral; **influsso astrale** (*Astrol*) influence of the planets
astrarre [as'trarre] VB IRREG
■ VT: **astrarre (da)** to abstract (from)
▶ **astrarsi** VR: **astrarsi da** to cut o.s. off from
astrattamente [astratta'mente] AVV in the abstract
astrattezza [astrat'tettsa] SF abstract nature
astrattismo [astrat'tizmo] SM (*Arte*) abstract art
astratto, a [as'tratto] PP *di* **astrarre**
■ AGG, SM abstract; **in astratto** in the abstract
astrazione [astrat'tsjone] SF abstraction
astringente [astrin'dʒɛnte] AGG, SM astringent
astro ['astro] SM (*Astron, fig*) star; (*Bot*) aster; **un astro nascente del cinema italiano** a rising star of Italian cinema
astrofisica [astro'fizika] SF astrophysics *sg*
astrologia [astrolo'dʒia] SF astrology
astrologico, a, ci, che [astro'lɔdʒiko] AGG astrological
astrologo, a, gi, ghe [as'trɔlogo] SM/F astrologer
astronauta, i, e [astro'nauta] SM/F astronaut
astronautica [astro'nautika] SF astronautics *sg*
astronautico, a, ci, che [astro'nautiko] AGG astronautical
astronave [astro'nave] SF spaceship
astronomia [astrono'mia] SF astronomy
astronomico, a, ci, che [astro'nɔmiko] AGG (*anche fig*) astronomic(al); **prezzi astronomici** astronomical prices
astronomo, a [as'trɔnomo] SM/F astronomer

astruso, a [as'truzo] AGG (*discorso, ragionamento*) abstruse
astuccio, ci [as'tuttʃo] SM (*per gioielli*) box, case; (*per compasso, matite*) case; **un astuccio portapenne** a pencil case
astutamente [astuta'mente] AVV astutely, shrewdly
astuto, a [as'tuto] AGG astute, shrewd, cunning; **un astuto uomo d'affari** a shrewd businessman; **astuto come una volpe** cunning as a fox
astuzia [as'tuttsja] SF (*qualità*) astuteness, shrewdness, cunning; (*azione*) trick
AT SIGLA = *Asti*
■ ABBR (= **alta tensione**) HT
ATA ['ata] SIGLA F (= **Associazione Turistica Albergatori**) *Italian association of hoteliers*
atavico, a, ci, che [a'taviko] AGG primitive, atavistic (*frm*)
atavismo [ata'vizmo] SM atavism
ateismo [ate'izmo] SM atheism
ateistico, a, ci, che [ate'istiko] AGG atheistic
atelier [atə'lje] SM INV (*sartoria*) fashion house; (*studio*) studio; (*laboratorio*) workshop
atemporale [atempo'rale] AGG atemporal
Atena [a'tena] SF Athena
Atene [a'tene] SF Athens; **quest'estate andremo ad Atene** we're going to Athens this summer; **abita ad Atene** she lives in Athens
ateneo [ate'nɛo] SM university
ateniese [ate'njese] AGG, SM/F Athenian
ateo, a ['ateo] AGG atheistic; **essere ateo** to be an atheist
■ SM/F atheist
atipico, a, ci, che [a'tipiko] AGG atypical; (*lavoro, lavoratore*) not permanent
Atlante [a'tlante] SM (*Mitol*) Atlas; **la catena di Atlante** the Atlas Mountains *pl*
atlante [a'tlante] SM (*libro, Anat*) atlas
atlantico, a, ci, che [a'tlantiko] AGG Atlantic
■ SM: **l'(Oceano) Atlantico** the Atlantic (Ocean)
atleta, i, e [a'tlɛta] SM/F athlete
atletica [a'tlɛtika] SF athletics *sg*; **guardo sempre l'atletica in TV** I always watch the athletics on TV; **atletica leggera** track and field events *pl*; **atletica pesante** weightlifting and wrestling
▷ www.fidal.it/
▷ www.atleticaleggera.com/home.htm
atleticamente [atletika'mente] AVV athletically
atletico, a, ci, che [a'tlɛtiko] AGG athletic
ATM [ati'ɛmme] SIGLA F (= **Azienda Trasporti Municipali**) *municipal transport corporation*
atmosfera [atmos'fɛra] SF (*anche fig*) atmosphere; **c'era una bella atmosfera** there was a nice atmosphere; **atmosfera controllata** protective atmosphere
atmosferico, a, ci, che [atmos'fɛriko] AGG atmospheric
atollo [a'tɔllo] SM atoll
atomico, a, ci, che [a'tɔmiko] AGG atomic; (*nucleare*) nuclear; **numero atomico** atomic number; **bomba atomica** atom bomb; **guerra atomica** nuclear war
atomistica [ato'mistika] SF (*Chim*) atomic theory
atomistico, ci [ato'mistiko] SM (*Filosofia*) atomist
atomizzatore [atomiddza'tore] SM (*di acqua, lacca*) spray; (*di profumo*) atomizer
atomo ['atomo] SM atom
atono, a ['atono] AGG (*Fonetica*) unstressed
atrio, ri ['atrjo] SM (*di albergo*) entrance hall, lobby; (*di*

stazione, aeroporto) concourse; *(Storia, Anat)* atrium

atroce [a'trotʃe] AGG *(delitto)* atrocious; *(sofferenza, destino)* terrible, dreadful; *(dolore)* excruciating; *(tempo)* ghastly, dreadful; **un mal di testa atroce** a terrible headache; **fa un freddo atroce** it's dreadfully cold; **in modo atroce** dreadfully; **ho l'atroce dubbio che...** I have the horrible feeling that ...

atrocemente [atrotʃe'mente] AVV *(soffrire)* atrociously; *(seviziato, ucciso)* savagely

atrocità [atrotʃi'ta] SF INV *(caratteristica)* atrocity, atrociousness; *(azione)* atrocity

atrofia [atro'fia] SF atrophy

atrofico, a, ci, che [a'trɔfiko] AGG atrophic

atrofizzare [atrofid'dzare] VT
▶ **atrofizzarsi** VIP to atrophy

attaccabottoni [attakkabot'toni] SM/F INV *(fam)*: **è un tremendo attaccabottoni** he'll latch onto anyone

attaccabrighe [attakka'brige] SM/F INV quarrelsome person

attaccamento [attakka'mento] SM *(a tradizioni ecc)* attachment; *(a persona, famiglia)* affection; **il suo attaccamento alla madre** his affection for his mother

attaccante [attak'kante] SM/F *(Calcio)* forward; **gioca da attaccante** he's a forward

attaccapanni [attakka'panni] SM INV *(su parete)* hook, peg; *(mobile)* hall stand

attaccare [attak'kare] VT **1** *(far aderire)* to attach; *(incollare: manifesto)* to stick up; *(: francobollo)* to stick (on); *(cucire)* to sew (on); *(legare)* to tie (up); *(appendere: quadro)* to hang (up); **devo attaccare due bottoni** I've got to sew two buttons on; **non so dove attaccare questo poster** I don't know where to stick this poster **2** *(Mil, Sport, fig)* to attack **3** *(cominciare: discorso, lite)* to start, begin; **attaccare discorso con qn** to start a conversation with sb **4** *(contagiare, anche fig)* to affect; **ha attaccato il morbillo a sua cugina** he's given his cousin the measles; **non vorrei attaccarti il raffreddore** I wouldn't want to give you my cold
■ VI *(aus* **avere***)* **1** *(incollare)* to stick **2** *(aver successo)*: **la nuova moda non attacca** the new fashion isn't catching on; **con me non attacca!** it doesn't work with me!, that won't work with me! **3** *(cominciare)* to start, begin; **attaccare a suonare** to strike up; **quando attacca a cantare non la smette più** once she starts singing she never stops; **ha attaccato con una delle sue lamentele** *o* **a lamentarsi** he started whingeing;
▶ **attaccarsi** VIP **1**: **attaccarsi (a)** *(appiccicarsi)* to stick (to); *(aggrapparsi: anche fig)* to cling (to); **le pagine si sono attaccate** the pages have stuck together; **attaccati alla corda!** hold on tight to the rope!; **è inutile che ti attacchi a dei pretesti** there's no point (in) making excuses; **attaccarsi alla bottiglia** *(fig)* to take to the bottle; **il sugo si è attaccato** the sauce has stuck **2** *(affezionarsi)*: **attaccarsi a** to become attached to **3** *(trasmettersi per contagio)* to be contagious

attaccaticcio, cia, ci, ce [attakka'tittʃo] SM: **sapere d'attaccaticcio** to taste burnt
■ AGG sticky; **è una persona attaccaticcia** *(fig)* he *(o* she) is a very clingy person

attaccatura [attakka'tura] SF *(di manica)* join; **attaccatura dei capelli** hairline

attaccatutto® [attakka'tutto] SM INV superglue

attacchinaggio [attakki'naddʒo] SM billposting *no pl*

attacchino, a [attak'kino] SM/F billposter

attacco, chi [at'takko] SM **1** *(Mil, Sport, anche fig)* attack; *(giocatori)* forward line, forwards *pl*; *(Alpinismo)* start; **giocare in attacco** to play an attacking game **2** *(Med)* fit; **un attacco di tosse** a coughing fit; **un attacco epilettico** an epileptic fit; **un attacco d'asma** an asthma attack **3** *(Sci)* binding; **attacchi di sicurezza** safety bindings **4** *(Tecn)* connection; *(Elettr)* socket

attaché [ata'ʃe] SM INV *(Amm)* attaché

attanagliare [attanaʎ'ʎare] VT *(anche fig)* to grip; **attanagliato dalla paura** gripped by fear

attardarsi [attar'darsi] VIP to linger; **attardarsi a fare qc** *(fermarsi)* to stop to do sth; *(stare più a lungo)* to stay behind to do sth; **dev'essersi attardato in ufficio** he must have stayed on *o* behind at the office

attecchire [attek'kire] VI *(aus* **avere***)* *(pianta)* to take root; *(fig)* to catch on

atteggiamento [atteddʒa'mento] SM *(disposizione mentale)* attitude; *(aria)* air; *(del corpo)* pose; **non mi piace il suo atteggiamento** I don't like his attitude; **atteggiamento dimesso** unassuming attitude; **perché hai avuto quell'atteggiamento strano quando l'abbiamo incontrato?** why did you act so strangely when we met him?; **è tutto un atteggiamento il suo** it's all an act with him

atteggiare [atted'dʒare] VT: **atteggiare il viso a compassione** to assume a sympathetic expression
▶ **atteggiarsi** VR: **atteggiarsi ad artista** to play *o* act the artist

attempato, a [attem'pato] AGG elderly

attendarsi [atten'darsi] VIP to camp, pitch one's tent

attendente [atten'dɛnte] SM *(Mil)* orderly, batman

attendere [at'tɛndere] VB IRREG
■ VT *(aspettare)* to wait for, await *(frm)*; **cosa sta attendendo?** what are you waiting for?; **attendo l'arrivo di mio fratello** I'm waiting for my brother to arrive; **attenda in linea** hold the line, please
■ VI *(aus* **avere***)* **attendere a** *(dedicarsi)* to attend to

attendibile [atten'dibile] AGG *(scusa, storia)* credible; *(fonte, testimone, notizia)* reliable; *(persona)* trustworthy

attendibilità [attendibili'ta] SF *(vedi agg)* credibility; reliability; trustworthiness

attenersi [atte'nersi] VR IRREG: **attenersi a** *(istruzioni, regolamento)* to keep to, stick to

attentamente [attenta'mente] AVV *(con attenzione)* attentively; *(con cura)* carefully

attentare [atten'tare] VI *(aus* **avere***)* **attentare a** *(libertà, diritti)* to attack; **attentare alla vita di qn** to make an attempt on sb's life

attentato [atten'tato] SM *(a libertà, onore)* attack; *(contro persona)* assassination attempt; **un attentato terroristico** a terrorist attack; **un attentato suicida** suicide bombing, a suicide attack; **commettere un attentato contro qn** *o* **alla vita di qn** to make an attempt on sb's life

attentatore, trice [attenta'tore] SM/F attacker

attenti [at'tɛnti] ESCL *(Mil)* attention!
■ SM: **mettersi/stare sull'attenti** to come to/stand at attention

attento, a [at'tɛnto] AGG **1** *(che presta attenzione)* attentive; **avere lo sguardo attento** to watch attentively **2** *(avviso di pericolo)*: **attento!** (be) careful!, look *o* watch out!; **attenti al cane** beware of the dog; **attento alle dita!** mind your fingers!; **stai attento!** *(non distrarti)* pay attention!; *(stai in guardia)* be careful!; **stai attento quando attraversi la strada** be careful when you cross the road **3** *(accurato: esame, ricerca)* careful, thorough

attenuante [attenu'ante] *(Dir)* AGG: **circostanze**

Aa

attenuanti extenuating circumstances
▪SF extenuating *o* mitigating circumstance; **concedere le attenuanti (generiche/specifiche)** to make allowances for the (general/particular) extenuating circumstances

attenuare [attenu'are] VT (*dolore*) to ease, alleviate; (*rumore*) to reduce, deaden; (*colpo*) to soften; (*Dir*: *colpa*) to mitigate
▶ **attenuarsi** VIP to ease, abate

attenuazione [attenuat'tsjone] SF (*vedi vb*) easing, alleviation; reduction; softening; mitigation

attenzione [atten'tsjone] ESCL watch out!, (be) careful!
▪SF **1** (*gen*) attention; (*cura*) care; **gli piace essere al centro dell'attenzione** he likes to be the centre of attention; **cerca di richiamare l'attenzione del cameriere** try and attract the waiter's attention; **con attenzione** (*ascoltare*) carefully, attentively; (*esaminare*) carefully, closely; **attenzione al gradino** mind the step; **fare** *o* **prestare attenzione** (*stare in guardia*) to be careful; (*ascoltare, guardare*) to pay attention; **alla cortese attenzione di** (*Comm*) for the attention of **2 attenzioni** SFPL (*gentilezze*) attentions; **avere mille attenzioni per qn** *or* **coprire qn di attenzioni** to lavish attentions on sb

atterraggio, gi [atter'raddʒo] SM landing; **all'atterraggio** on landing; **essere in fase di atterraggio** to be coming in to land; **atterraggio di fortuna** emergency landing

atterrare [atter'rare] VI (*aus* **avere** *o* **essere**) (*aereo, persona*) to land; **l'aereo ha appena atterrato** the plane has just landed
▪VT (*avversario*) to floor, bring down

atterrire [atter'rire] VB DIF
▪VT to terrify
▶ **atterrirsi** VIP to become terrified

atterrito, a [atter'rito] AGG terrified

attesa [at'tesa] SF wait; **dopo una lunga attesa** after a long wait; **lista d'attesa** waiting list; **sala d'attesa** waiting room; **l'attesa durò a lungo** it was a long wait; **essere in attesa di qc** to be waiting for sth; **è in attesa del terzo figlio** she is expecting her third baby; **in attesa di una vostra risposta** (*Comm*) awaiting your reply; **restiamo in attesa di Vostre ulteriori notizie** (*Comm*) we look forward to hearing (further) from you

attesi *ecc* [at'tesi] VB *vedi* **attendere**

atteso, a [at'teso] PP *di* **attendere**
▪AGG long-awaited

attestare [attes'tare] VT: **attestare qc/che** to testify to sth/(to the fact) that

attestato [attes'tato] SM (*certificato*) certificate; **quest'attestato certifica che** this document testifies to the fact that

attestazione [attestat'tsjone] SF (*certificato*) certificate; (*dichiarazione*) statement

Attica ['attika] SF Attica

attico¹, a, ci, che ['attiko] AGG (*Storia*) Attic

attico², ci ['attiko] SM (*soffitta*) attic; (*di lusso*) penthouse

attiguità [attigui'ta] SF adjacency

attiguo, a [at'tiguo] AGG (*contiguo*) adjoining; (*adiacente*) adjacent; **il suo appartamento è attiguo al nostro** his flat is next to ours

Attila ['attila] SM Attila

attillato, a [attil'lato] AGG (*vestito*) skin-tight, close-fitting

attimo ['attimo] SM moment; **aspetta un attimo** wait a minute; **un attimo, per favore** just a moment, please; **un attimo di pazienza!** wait a moment!; **fra un attimo** in a minute *o* moment; **un attimo fa** a moment ago; **ci metto un attimo** I'll just be a minute; **torno tra un attimo** I'll be back in a minute; **in un attimo** in a moment; **attimo per attimo** moment by moment

attinente [atti'nɛnte] AGG: **attinente a** relating to, concerning

attinenza [atti'nɛntsa] SF connection

attingere [at'tindʒere] VT IRREG: **attingere a** *o* **da** (*acqua*) to draw from; (*denaro, risorse*) to draw on, obtain from; **attingere informazioni a una fonte sicura** to obtain information from a reliable source

attinia [at'tinja] SF (*Bot*) actinia

attinto, a [at'tinto] PP *di* **attingere**

attirare [atti'rare] VT (*attenzione, persona*) to attract; **l'ha fatto per attirare la sua attenzione** he did it to attract her attention; **l'idea mi attira** the idea appeals to me; **attirarsi delle critiche** to incur criticism

> **LO SAPEVI...?**
> **attirare** non si traduce mai con la parola inglese *attire*

attitudinale [attitudi'nale] AGG: **test attitudinale** aptitude test

attitudine [atti'tudine] SF (*disposizione*) aptitude; **avere attitudine per qc** to have a flair for sth

> **LO SAPEVI...?**
> **attitudine** non si traduce mai con la parola inglese *attitude*

attivamente [attiva'mente] AVV actively; **partecipare attivamente a qc** to play an active part in sth

attivare [atti'vare] VT (*motore, azienda*) to start; (*dispositivo, mina*) to activate; **attivare la circolazione** (*Med*) to stimulate the circulation

attivismo [atti'vizmo] SM activism

attivista, i, e [atti'vista] SM/F activist

attivistico, a, ci, che [atti'vistiko] AGG activist

attività [attivi'ta] SF INV **1** (*gen*) activity; **mi piacciono le attività all'aria aperta** I like outdoor activities; **essere/entrare in attività** to be/become active **2** (*Comm*: *azienda*) business; **le attività e passività di un'azienda** the assets and liabilities of a business; **attività liquide** liquid assets

attivo, a [at'tivo] AGG (*gen, Gramm*) active; (*Comm*) profit-making; **bilancio attivo** credit balance; **un'azienda attiva** a going concern; **popolazione attiva** working population
▪SM (*Comm*) assets *pl*; **in attivo** in credit; **chiudere in attivo** to show a profit; **avere qc al proprio attivo** (*fig*) to have sth to one's credit

attizzare [attit'tsare] VT (*fuoco*) to poke (up); (*fig*: *passioni, odi*) to stir up

attizzatoio, oi [attittsa'tojo] SM poker

atto¹ ['atto] SM **1** (*azione, gesto*) action, deed, act; **atti di sabotaggio** acts of sabotage; **atto eroico** heroic feat; **essere in atto** to be under way; **cogliere** *o* **sorprendere qn nell'atto di fare qc** to catch sb in the act of doing sth; **all'atto pratico** in practice; **mettere in atto qc** to put into action *o* practice; **fare (l')atto di fare qc** to make as if to do sth; **atti osceni (in luogo pubblico)** (*Dir*) indecent exposure (*o* obscene behaviour) **2** (*dimostrazione*): **atto di fede/affetto** *ecc* act of faith/friendship *ecc*; **dare atto a qn di qc** to give sb credit for sth; **prendere atto di qc** to take note of sth **3** (*Dir: documento*) document; (*del parlamento*) act; (*notarile*) deed; **atti** SMPL (*di congresso ecc*) proceedings; (*di processo*) records; **mettere agli atti** to put on record; **atto di morte** death certificate; **atto di nascita** birth certificate; **atto di proprietà** title deed; **atto pubblico** official document; **atto di vendita** bill of sale **4** (*Teatro*) act; **durante il secondo atto** during the second act; **una commedia in 3 atti** a three-act play; **atto unico** one-act play

atto², a ['atto] AGG: **atto a** fit for, capable of; **atto alle armi** fit for military service; **atto a proseguire gli studi** capable of going on with one's studies

attonito, a [at'tɔnito] AGG astonished, amazed, dumbfounded

attorcigliare [attortʃiʎ'ʎare] VT to twist
▶ **attorcigliarsi** VIP **1** to twist; **le funi si sono attorcigliate** the cords have got twisted;
▶ **attorcigliarsi** VR (*serpente*) to coil

attore, trice [at'tore] SM/F actor/actress; (*Dir*) plaintiff; **un attore famoso** a famous actor

attorniare [attor'njare] VT (*circondare*) to surround
▶ **attorniarsi** VR: **attorniarsi di** to surround o.s. with

attorno [at'torno] AVV around; **è entrato e si è guardato attorno** he came in and looked around *o* about him; **tutt'attorno** all around; **d'attorno** = di torno
■ PREP: **attorno a** around, round; **stare attorno a qn** to hang round sb; **attorno al fuoco** around *o* round the fire; **seduti attorno al fuoco abbiamo cantato fino all'alba** we sat round the fire and sang until dawn

attraccare [attrak'kare] VT, VI (*aus* **essere** *o* **avere**) (*Naut*) to dock, berth

attracco, chi [at'trakko] SM (*Naut: manovra*) docking, berthing; (*: luogo*) berth

attrae *ecc* [at'trae] VB *vedi* **attrarre**

attraente [attra'ɛnte] AGG (*gen*) attractive; **dai modi attraenti** charming; **una prospettiva ben poco attraente** not a particularly attractive *o* exciting prospect

attraggo *ecc* [at'traggo] VB *vedi* **attrarre**

attrarre [at'trarre] VT IRREG (*anche fig*) to attract; **l'ha fatto per attrarre la sua attenzione** he did it to attract her attention; **l'idea non mi attrae per niente** the idea doesn't appeal to me at all; **l'attrasse a sé** he drew her into his arms

attrassi *ecc* [at'trassi] VB *vedi* **attrarre**

attrattiva [attrat'tiva] SF **1** (*fascino*) attraction, charm; **esercitare una grande** *o* **forte attrattiva su qn** to hold a great attraction for sb; **dotato di grande attrattiva** charming **2** (*cosa attraente*): **attrattive** SFPL attractions; **una località che offre molte attrattive per i giovani** a town with a lot to offer to young people

attratto, a [at'tratto] PP *di* **attrarre**

attraversamento [attraversa'mento] SM crossing; **attraversamento pedonale** pedestrian crossing

attraversare [attraver'sare] VT (*strada, fiume, ponte*) to cross; (*bosco, città, periodo*) to go through; (*sogg: fiume*) to run through; **attraversare la strada di corsa** to rush across the road; **stai attento quando attraversi la strada** be careful when you cross the road; **attraversare il fiume a nuoto** to swim across the river; **attraversare il ponte correndo** to run across the bridge; **il fiume attraversa la città** the river passes through the town; **la pallottola gli ha attraversato il braccio** the bullet went straight through his arm; **attraversare un brutto periodo** to go through a bad patch; **sta attraversando un periodo difficile** she's going through a difficult time

attraverso [attra'vɛrso] PREP **1** (*gen*) through; **abbiamo camminato attraverso i campi** we walked through the fields; **sono entrati attraverso la finestra** they got in through the window; **ha ottenuto il lavoro attraverso suo zio** he got the job through his uncle **2** (*da una parte all'altra*) across; **ha nuotato attraverso il fiume** he swam across the river **3** (*di tempo*) over, through; **attraverso i secoli** over *o* through the centuries

attrazione [attrat'tsjone] SF **1** (*gen, Fis*) attraction; **esercitare una grande attrazione su qc** to hold a great attraction for sb; **provare attrazione per qn** to feel attracted to sb; **uno spettacolo di grande attrazione** a very entertaining show **2** (*di circo, luna park*) attraction

attrezzare [attret'tsare] VT (*gen*) to equip; (*nave*) to rig

attrezzato, a [attret'tsato] AGG (*laboratorio, studio*) having the necessary equipment, fully equipped; **ben attrezzato** well-equipped; **una palestra ben attrezzata** a well-equipped gym

attrezzatura [attrettsa'tura] SF equipment *no pl*; (*di nave*) rigging; **attrezzature sportive** sports facilities; **attrezzature per uffici** office equipment

attrezzista, i, e [attret'tsista] SM/F (*Atletica*) gymnast; (*Teatro*) propman, property man

attrezzistica [attret'tsistika] SF gymnastics *sg*

attrezzistico, a, ci, che [attret'tsistiko] AGG: **ginnastica attrezzistica** gymnastics *sg*

attrezzo [at'trettso] SM tool, implement; **attrezzi da giardinaggio** gardening tools; **carro attrezzi** breakdown truck; **gli attrezzi** SMPL (*Atletica*) the apparatus *sg*

attribuibile [attribu'ibile] AGG: **attribuibile a** attributable to

attribuire [attribu'ire] VT: **attribuire qc a qn** (*gen*) to attribute sth to sb; (*premio*) to give *o* award sth to sb; **non attribuirmi colpe che non ho** don't blame me for things I didn't do; **va attribuito a lui il merito di tale successo** he should be given the credit for this success; **attribuirsi il merito di qc** to take the credit for sth; **il dipinto è stato attribuito a Picasso** the painting has been attributed to Picasso

attributo [attri'buto] SM (*gen, Gramm*) attribute; **gli attributi maschili** (*scherz*) the male attributes

attribuzione [attribut'tsjone] SF (*vedi vb*) attribution; awarding

attrice [at'tritʃe] SF actress; **un'attrice famosa** a famous actress

attrito [at'trito] SM (*anche fig*) friction

attuabile [attu'abile] AGG feasible

attuabilità [attuabili'ta] SF feasibility

attuale [attu'ale] AGG (*presente*) present; (*di attualità*) topical; (*che è in atto*) current; **al momento attuale** at the present moment; **l'attuale proprietario** the present owner; **lo stato attuale dell'economia** the present state of the economy; **l'attuale situazione politica** the current political situation; **le leggi attuali** the current legislation; **un problema attuale** a current problem; **il suo attuale ragazzo** her current boyfriend; **è un filosofo ancora attuale** his philosophy is still relevant today; **il marrone è molto attuale** (*di moda*) brown is very fashionable

LO SAPEVI...?
attuale non si traduce mai con la parola inglese *actual*

Aa

attualità [attuali'ta] SF INV **1** (*di argomento*) topicality; **un problema di grande attualità** a very topical question; **argomento d'attualità** topical subject **2** (*avvenimenti*) current affairs *pl*; **un programma di attualità** a current affairs programme; **notizie d'attualità** the news *sg*; **settimanale d'attualità** (weekly) news magazine

> **LO SAPEVI...?**
> **attualità** non si traduce mai con la parola inglese ***actuality***

attualizzare [attualid'dzare] VT to focus attention on
attualmente [attual'mente] AVV at the moment, at present; **attualmente sono in tournée in America** they're on tour in America at the moment

> **LO SAPEVI...?**
> **attualmente** non si traduce mai con la parola inglese ***actually***

attuare [attu'are] VT to carry out
▶ **attuarsi** VIP to be realized
attuativo, a [attwa'tivo] AGG (*provvedimento, aspetto*) implementational
attuazione [attuat'tsjone] SF carrying out; **di facile/difficile attuazione** easy/difficult to carry out; **l'attuazione del progetto sembra impossibile** it seems an impossible plan to carry out
attutimento [attuti'mento] SM (*di suono*) deadening; (*di colpo, caduta*) cushioning
attutire [attu'tire] VT (*colpo, caduta*) to cushion; (*suono*) to deaden; (*dolore*) to ease, reduce
▶ **attutirsi** VIP (*suono*) to die down; (*dolore*) to ease
AU ABBR = **allievo ufficiale**
audace [au'datʃe] AGG **1** (*coraggioso*: *persona*) daring, audacious; (: *impresa*) daring, bold **2** (*ipotesi*) daring; (*proposta*) suggestive; (*provocante*: *scollatura*) daring; (*sfacciato*) impudent, bold
audacemente [audatʃe'mente] AVV daringly
audacia [au'datʃa] SF (*vedi agg*) daring, audacity; boldness; impudence; **tutti hanno notato l'audacia del suo vestito** everyone noticed her daring dress
audio ['audjo] SM INV (*TV, Radio, Cine*) sound; **il video funziona ma l'audio no** there's a picture but no sound
audiocassetta [audjokas'setta] SF (audio) cassette
audioleso, a [audjo'lezo] SM/F person who is hard of hearing
audiolibro [au'djolibro] SM talking book
audiovisivo, a [audjovi'zivo] AGG audiovisual; **sussidi audiovisivi** audiovisual aids
Auditel ['auditel] SIGLA F (= **Audience Televisiva**) ≈ JICTAR (= *Joint Industry Committee for Television Advertising Research*)
auditorio, ri [audi'tɔrjo], **auditorium** [audi'tɔrjum] SM auditorium
audizione [audit'tsjone] SF hearing; (*Mus*) audition
auge ['audʒe] SF: **essere in auge** to be at the top
augurale [augu'rale] AGG: **messaggio augurale** greeting
augurare [augu'rare] VT (*buon viaggio, buonanotte ecc*) to wish; **ti auguro Buon Natale** I wish you a Merry Christmas; **gli augurò di guarire presto** he wished him a speedy recovery; **augurarsi qc/che succeda qc** to hope for sth/that sth will happen; **me lo auguro** I hope so; **mi auguro di no/sì** I hope not/so; **mi auguro che tu guarisca presto** I hope you get well soon
augurio, ri [au'gurjo] SM **1** greeting; **auguri di Natale/Pasqua** Christmas/Easter greetings; **biglietto di auguri** greetings card; **fare gli auguri a qn** to give sb one's best wishes, wish sb all the best; **tanti auguri!** best wishes!, all the best!; (*di compleanno*) happy birthday!; (*buona fortuna*) good luck!; **auguri di pronta guarigione!** get well soon! **2** (*presagio*): **essere di cattivo/di buon augurio** to be ominous/a good omen
augusto, a [au'gusto] AGG (*letter*) august
aula ['aula] SF (*di scuola*) classroom; (*di università*) lecture room *o* theatre; (*di tribunale*) courtroom; (*di Parlamento ecc*) chamber; **silenzio in aula!** (*Dir*) silence in court!; **aula bunker** *high security court for Mafia trials*; **aula magna** main hall
aulicamente [aulika'mente] AVV (*scrivere*) in a highly stylized way
aulico, a, ci, che ['auliko] AGG (*tono*) dignified; (*stile*) refined
aumentare [aumen'tare] VT (*prezzo*) to increase, put up; (*stipendi*) to increase, raise; **gli hanno aumentato l'affitto** his rent's gone up
■ VI (*aus* **essere**) (*gen*) to increase; (*prezzi*) to go up, rise, increase; (*livello*) to rise; (*qualità*) to improve; **il prezzo della benzina è aumentato** the price of petrol has gone up; **aumentare di peso** (*persona*) to put on weight; **la produzione è aumentata del 50%** production has increased by 50%; **la disoccupazione è aumentata del 10%** unemployment's gone up by 10%
aumento [au'mento] SM: **aumento (di)** increase (in), rise (in); **un imprevisto aumento delle nascite** an unexpected rise in the birth rate; **c'è stato un aumento del 5% sul prezzo** there's been a 5% increase in the price; **aumento di stipendio** pay rise; **ottenere un aumento (di stipendio)** to get a (pay) rise; **essere in aumento** (*gen*) to be rising, be going up; (*qualità*) to be improving; **i prezzi sono in aumento** prices are rising
au pair [o'pɛr] SF INV au pair (girl)
aura ['aura] SF (*Med, fig*) aura; (*letter*: *venticello*) light breeze
aureo, a ['aureo] AGG (*di oro*) gold *attr*; (*fig*: *colore, periodo*) golden
aureola [au'rɛola] SF (*Rel, Astron*) halo
auricolare [auriko'lare] AGG auricular, ear *attr*; **padiglione auricolare** external ear
■ SM (*Radio*) earphone
aurifero, a [au'rifero] AGG gold *attr*
aurora [au'rɔra] SF (*anche fig*) dawn
auscultare [auskul'tare] VT (*Med*) to auscultate
ausiliare [auzi'ljare] AGG, SM (*gen, Gramm*) auxiliary
ausiliaria [auzi'ljarja] SF (*Mil*) *member of Women's Army Auxiliary Corps*
ausiliario, ria, ri, rie [auzi'ljarjo] AGG, SM/F auxiliary
ausilio [au'ziljo] SM aid; **con l'ausilio di** with the aid of
auspicabile [auspi'kabile] AGG desirable; **è auspicabile che** it is to be hoped that
auspicare [auspi'kare] VT to hope for; **ci si auspica che** it is hoped that
auspicio, ci [aus'pitʃo] SM **1** (*presagio*) omen; **essere di buon auspicio** to be a good omen, augur well **2** (*aiuto, protezione*) auspices *pl*; **sotto gli auspici di** under the auspices of
austeramente [austera'mente] AVV austerely; **vivere austeramente** to lead an austere life
austerità [austeri'ta] SF (*gen, Econ*) austerity
austerity [ɔs'teriti] SF INV (*Econ*) austerity
austero, a [aus'tero] AGG (*persona, vita*) austere; (*disciplina*) strict

Australasia [austra'lazja] SF Australasia
australe [aus'trale] AGG southern
Australia [aus'tralja] SF Australia; **ti è piaciuta l'Australia?** did you like Australia?; **quest'estate andremo in Australia** we're going to Australia this summer
australiano, a [austra'ljano] AGG, SM/F Australian
Austria ['austria] SF Austria; **ti è piaciuta l'Austria?** did you like Austria?; **quest'estate andremo in Austria** we're going to Austria this summer
austriaco, a, ci, che [aus'triako] AGG, SM/F Austrian
austroungarico, a, ci, che [austroun'gariko] AGG Austro-Hungarian
autarchia [autar'kia] SF (*Econ*) autarky; (*Pol*) autarchy
autarchico, a, ci, che [au'tarkiko] AGG (*sistema*) self-sufficient, autarkic; (*prodotto*) home *attr*, home-produced
aut aut ['aut 'aut] SM INV ultimatum; **dare un aut aut** to give *o* issue *o* deliver an ultimatum
autentica, che [au'tɛntika] SF authentication
autenticamente [autentika'mente] AVV authentically, genuinely
autenticare [autenti'kare] VT to authenticate
autenticazione [autentikat'tsjone] SF authentication
autenticità [autentitʃi'ta] SF authenticity
autentico, a, ci, che [au'tɛntiko] AGG (*quadro, firma*) authentic, genuine; (*notizia, sentimento, fatto*) true; **la firma è autentica** the signature is genuine; **è un autentico cretino** he's an absolute fool
autismo [au'tizmo] SM (*Psic*) autism; **essere affetto da autismo** to be autistic
autista, i, e [au'tista] SM/F driver; (*personale*) chauffeur; **fa l'autista di autobus** he's a bus driver; **auto con autista** chauffeur-driven car
autistico, a [au'tistiko] AGG (*Psic*) autistic
auto ['auto] SF INV (motor) car, automobile (*Am*); **verremo in auto** we'll come by car; **auto blu** official car; **auto da corsa** racing car (*Brit*); race car (*Am*)
auto... ['auto] PREF **1** self-, auto... **2** (*Aut*) car *attr*
autoabbronzante [autoabbron'dzante] AGG self-tanning
■ SM self-tanning cream
autoadesivo, a [autoade'zivo] AGG self-adhesive
■ SM sticker
autoaiuto [autoa'juto] SM self-help; **un gruppo di autoaiuto** a self-help group
autoambulanza [autoambu'lantsa] SF ambulance
autoanalisi SF (*Psic*) self-analysis
autoarticolato [autoartiko'lato] SM articulated lorry (*Brit*), semi (trailer) (*Am*)
autoassicurazione [autoassikurat'tsjone] SF (*Dir*) self-insurance; (*Alpinismo*) self belay, self-belaying system
autoavvolgente [autoavvol'dʒɛnte] AGG: **tendina autoavvolgente** roller blind; **cintura di sicurezza autoavvolgente** (*Aut*) inertia-reel seat-belt
autobiografia [autobiogra'fia] SF autobiography
autobiografico, a, ci, che [autobio'grafiko] AGG autobiographic(al); **un romanzo autobiografico** an autobiographical novel
autoblinda [auto'blinda] SF INV armoured (*Brit*) *o* armored (*Am*) car
autobomba [auto'bomba] SF INV car carrying a bomb; **l'autobomba si trovava a pochi metri** the car bomb was a few metres away
autobotte [auto'botte] SF tanker
autobus ['autobus] SM INV bus; **vado a scuola in autobus** I go to school by bus; **autobus a due piani** double-decker bus
autocandidarsi [autokandi'darsi] VR: **autocandidarsi (a)** (*a carica*) to put oneself forward (for), apply (for); (*a elezione*) to stand (in)
autocandidatura [autokandida'tura] SF (*a carica*) application; (*a elezione*) candidature
autocarro [auto'karro] SM lorry (*Brit*), truck
autocertificazione [autotʃertifikat'tsjone] SF self-declaration
autocisterna [autotʃis'tɛrna] SF tanker
autoclave [auto'klave] SF autoclave
autocolonna [autoko'lonna] SF convoy
autocombustione [autokombus'tjone] SF spontaneous combustion
autocommiserazione [autokommizerat'tsjone] SF self-pity
autocompiacimento [autokompjatʃi'mento] SM self-satisfaction
autocontrollo [autokon'trɔllo] SM self-control
autoconvincersi [autokon'vintʃersi] VR to persuade oneself
autoconvincimento [autokonvintʃi'mento] SM self-persuasion
autocopiante AGG: **carta autocopiante** carbonless paper
autocrate [au'tɔkrate] SM autocrat
autocratico, a, ci, che [auto'kratiko] AGG autocratic
autocrazia [autokrat'tsia] SF autocracy
autocritica, che [auto'kritika] SF self-criticism
autocritico, a, ci, che [auto'kritiko] AGG self-critical
autoctono, a [au'tɔktono] AGG, SM/F native
autodemolizione [autodemolit'tsjone] SF breaker's yard (*Brit*), junk yard (*Am*)
autodenunciarsi [autodenun'tʃarsi] VR to criticize oneself
autodeterminazione [autodeterminat'tsjone] SF self-determination; **l'autodeterminazione dei popoli** self-determination of peoples
autodiagnostica [autodiaɲ'ɲɔstika] SF fault diagnosis
autodidatta, i, e [autodi'datta] SM/F self-taught person, autodidact (*frm*); **è un autodidatta** he is self-taught
autodidattico, a, ci, che [autodi'dattiko] AGG teach-yourself *attr*
autodifesa [autodi'fesa] SF self-defence
autodisciplina [autodiʃʃi'plina] SF self-discipline
autodistruttività [autodistruttivi'ta] SF self-destructiveness
autodistruttivo, a [autodistrut'tivo] AGG (*persona, comportamento*) self-destructive
autodromo [au'tɔdromo] SM motor racing track
autoescludersi [autoes'kludersi] VR to exclude oneself, rule oneself out
autoesclusione [autoesklu'zjone] SF self-exclusion
autoferrotranviario, ria, ri, rie [autoferrotran'vjarjo] AGG public transport *attr*
autofilotranviario, ria, ri, rie [autofilotran'vjarjo] AGG bus, trolley and tram *attr*
autofocus [auto'fɔkus] AGG INV (*Fot*) autofocus
autofurgone [autofur'gone] SM van
autogeno, a [au'tɔdʒeno] AGG **1** **saldatura autogena**

Aa

welding **2 training autogeno** autogenic training, autogenics

autogestione [autodʒes'tjone] SF worker management

autogestito, a [autodʒes'tito] AGG *(fabbrica)* under worker management

autogol [auto'gɔl] SM INV *(Calcio, anche fig)* own goal; **ha fatto autogol** he scored an own goal

autogonfiabile [autogon'fjabile] AGG self-inflating

autogoverno [autogo'vɛrno] SM self-government

autografo, a [au'tɔgrafo] AGG, SM autograph; **mi ha fatto l'autografo!** he gave me his autograph!

autogrill [auto'gril] SM INV motorway café *(Brit)*, roadside restaurant *(Am)*

autoimmune [autoim'mune] AGG autoimmune

autoimmunità [autoimmuni'ta] SF autoimmunity

autoinstallante [autoinstal'lante] AGG *(programma)* self-installing

autoinvitarsi [autoinvi'tarsi] VR to invite oneself

autoironia [autoiro'nia] SF self-mockery

autoironico, a; , ci; , che [autoi'rɔniko] AGG self-mocking

autolavaggio, gi [autola'vaddʒo] SM *(Aut)* car wash; **autolavaggio automatico** (automatic) car wash

autolesionismo [autolezjo'nizmo] SM self-destruction; *(fisicamente)* self-mutilation

autolesionista, i, e [autolezjo'nista] AGG self-destructive

autolettiga, ghe [autolet'tiga] SF ambulance

autolettura [autolet'tura] SF customer reading

autolinea [auto'linea] SF bus service

automa, i [au'tɔma] SM *(anche fig)* automaton

automaticamente [automatika'mente] AVV automatically

automatico, a, ci, che [auto'matiko] AGG automatic; **porte a chiusura automatica** automatic doors; **selezione automatica** *(Telec)* direct dialling, subscriber trunk dialling

■ SM *(bottone)* press stud, snap fastener

■ SF: **(pistola) automatica** automatic (pistol)

automatismo [automa'tizmo] SM *(Tecn: metodo)* automation; (: *congegno*) mechanism; *(Psic)* automatism

automatizzare [automatid'dzare] VT to automate

automazione [automat'tsjone] SF automation; **automazione delle procedure d'ufficio** office automation

automedicazione [automedikat'tjone] SF: **medicinale di automedicazione** self-medication

automezzo [auto'mɛddzo] SM motor vehicle

automobile [auto'mɔbile] SF (motor) car, automobile *(Am)*; **viaggiare in automobile** to travel by car

▷ www.aci.it/

▷ www.museoauto.it/

automobilina [automobi'lina] SF (toy) car

automobilismo [automobi'lizmo] SM *(gen)* motoring; *(Sport)* motor racing

automobilista, i, e [automobi'lista] SM/F motorist

automobilistico, a, ci, che [automobi'listiko] AGG *(industria, assicurazione, incidente)* car *attr*, automobile *attr (Am)*; *(sport)* motor *attr*

automotrice [automo'tritʃe] SF railcar

autonoleggio, gi [autono'leddʒo] SM car hire *(Brit)*, car rental; **c'è un autonoleggio da queste parti?** is there a car hire place near here?

autonomamente [autonoma'mente] AVV independently, autonomously

autonomia [autono'mia] SF *(Pol)* autonomy; *(fig: di idee, comportamento)* independence; *(Tecn: di macchine, motori)* range; **autonomia di volo** *(Aer)* flight range

autonomista, i, e [autono'mista] AGG, SM/F *(Pol)* autonomist

autonomo, a [au'tɔnomo] AGG *(Pol)* autonomous; *(sindacato, pensiero)* independent; **lavoro autonomo** self-employment

■ **autonomi** SMPL *independent trade union members*

autoparcheggio, gi [autopar'keddʒo] SM car park *(Brit)*, parking lot *(Am)*

autoparco, chi [auto'parko] SM *(insieme di automezzi)* transport fleet; *(parcheggio)* car park *(Brit)*, parking lot *(Am)*

autopilota, i [autopi'lɔta] SM *(Aer)* autopilot

autopista [auto'pista] SF fairground race track

autopompa [auto'pompa] SF fire engine

autopsia [autop'sia] SF autopsy, post-mortem (examination)

autopubblica, che [auto'pubblika] SF taxi

autopulente [autopu'lɛnte] AGG *(forno)* self-cleaning

autopullman [auto'pulman] SM INV *(di linea)* bus; *(per gite turistiche)* coach

autoradio [auto'radjo] SF INV *(apparecchio)* car radio; *(autoveicolo)* radio car; **gli hanno rotto il finestrino per rubare l'autoradio** they broke the window to steal his car radio

autoraduno [autora'duno] SM *(Sport)* motor racing meeting

autore, trice [au'tore] SM/F *(gen, scrittore)* author; *(di pittura)* painter; *(di scultura)* sculptor; *(di musica)* composer; **l'autore del delitto/del furto** the person who committed the crime/the robbery; **quadro d'autore** painting by a famous artist; **diritti d'autore** copyright *sg*; *(compenso)* royalties

autoreferenziale [autoreferen'tsjale] AGG self-referential

autoreggente [autored'dʒɛnte] AGG: **calze autoreggenti** hold-up stockings, hold-ups

autoregolamentazione [autoregolamentat'tsjone] SF self-regulation

autorespiratore [autorespira'tore] SM *(sub)* breathing apparatus; **autorespiratore ad aria** aqualung; **autorespiratore ad ossigeno** oxygen re-breather

autoreverse [autore'vɛrs] SM INV autoreverse

autorevole [auto'revole] AGG *(giudizio)* authoritative; *(fonte)* reliable; *(influente: persona)* influential

autorevolezza [autorevo'lettsa] SF authority

autorevolmente [autorevol'mente] AVV authoritatively, with authority

autoricambio [autori'kambjo] SM car part, auto part; **negozio di autoricambi** shop selling car *o* auto parts

autoricaricabile [autorikari'kabile] AGG: **scheda autoricaricabile** top-up card

autorilevazione [autorilevat'tsjone] SF *(Inform)*: **autorilevazione di errori** automatic error detection

autorimessa [autori'messa] SF garage

autorità [autori'ta] SF INV **1** *(potere)* authority; **agire d'autorità** to act with authority, have the authority to act; **esercitare la propria autorità su qn** to exercise one's authority over sb **2** *(Amm: governo, ente)*: **l'autorità** *or* **le autorità** the authorities *pl*; **le autorità competenti** the relevant authorities; **erano presenti tutte le autorità** all the public services were represented **3** *(esperto)* authority, expert; **è una vera**

autorità in questo campo he's a real expert in this field **4** *(prestigio)* repute
autoritariamente [autoritarja'mente] AVV in an authoritarian way
autoritario, ria, ri, rie [autori'tarjo] AGG *(sistema, persona)* authoritarian
autoritarismo [autorita'rizmo] SM authoritarianism
autoritratto [autori'tratto] SM self-portrait
autorizzare [autorid'dzare] VT to give permission for, authorize; **autorizzare qn a fare qc** to give sb permission to do sth; **mi hanno autorizzato ad aprire la corrispondenza** I was given permission to open correspondence; **"vietato l'accesso al personale non autorizzato"** "authorized personnel only"
autorizzazione [autoriddzat'tsjone] SF *(permesso)* authorization, permission; *(documento)* permit; **autorizzazione a procedere** *(Dir)* authorization to proceed
autosalone [autosa'lone] SM car showroom
autoscatto [autos'katto] SM *(Fot)* self-timer
autoscontro [autos'kontro] SM dodgem car *(Brit)*, bumper car *(Am)*
autoscuola [autos'kwɔla] SF driving school
autosnodato [autozno'dato] SM articulated vehicle
autosospendersi [autosos'pɛndere] VR to resign temporarily; from public office
autostazione [autostat'tsjone] SF *(Aut)* service station; *(di corriere)* bus station
autostima [auto'stima] SF self-esteem
autostop [autos'tɔp] SM hitchhiking; **fare l'autostop** to hitchhike; **è andato a Parigi in** *o* **con l'autostop** he hitchhiked to Paris
autostoppista, i, e [autostop'pista] SM/F hitchhiker; **abbiamo dato un passaggio ad un autostoppista** we gave a hitchhiker a lift
autostrada [autos'trada] SF motorway *(Brit)*, highway *(Am)*; **autostrada informatica** information (super)highway
autostradale [autostra'dale] AGG motorway *attr*
autosufficiente [autosuffi'tʃɛnte] AGG self-sufficient
autosufficienza [autosuffi'tʃɛntsa] SF self-sufficiency
autosuggestionarsi [autosuddʒestjo'narsi] VR to get o.s. into a state
autosuggestione [autosuddʒes'tjone] SF *(Psic)* autosuggestion
autotassazione [autotassat'tsjone] SF *tax system where people assess themselves*
autotrasportatore [autotrasporta'tore] SM road haulier
autotrasporto [autotras'pɔrto] SM *(di persone)* road transport; *(di merci)* road haulage
autotreno [auto'trɛno] SM lorry with trailer *(Brit)*, trailer truck *(Am)*
autovaccino [autovat'tʃino] SM autogenous vaccine
autoveicolo [autove'ikolo] SM motor vehicle
autovelox [auto'vɛloks] ® SM INV speed camera
autovettura [autovet'tura] SF (motor) car
autunnale [autun'nale] AGG *(di autunno)* autumn *attr*, fall *attr (Am)*; *(da autunno)* autumnal
autunno [au'tunno] SM autumn, fall *(Am)*; **in autunno** in autumn; **l'autunno della vita** the autumn of life *o* one's years
AV SIGLA = *Avellino*
a/v ABBR *(Comm)* = **a vista**; *vedi* **vista**
avallare [aval'lare] VT *(Fin)* to guarantee; *(sostenere)* to back; *(confermare)* to confirm
avallo [a'vallo] SM *(Fin)* guarantee
avambraccio, ci [avam'brattʃo] SM forearm
avamposto [avam'posto] SM *(Mil)* outpost
Avana [a'vana] SF Havana
avana [a'vana] SM INV *(sigaro)* Havana (cigar); *(colore)* tobacco brown
■ AGG *(colore)* tobacco-brown, tobacco-coloured
avance [a'vɑ̃s] SF *(pl* **avances)** **fare delle avances a qn** to make advances to sb
avanguardia [avan'gwardja] SF **1** *(Mil, fig)* vanguard; **essere all'avanguardia** to be in the vanguard **2** *(Arte)* avant-garde; **d'avanguardia** avant-garde *attr*
avanguardismo [avangwar'dizmo] SM avant-garde trend
avanguardista, i, e [avangwar'dista] SM/F avant-garde artist
avanscoperta [avansko'perta] SF *(Mil)* reconnaissance; **andare in avanscoperta** to reconnoitre
avanspettacolo [avanspet'takolo] SM *(Teatro)* curtain raiser
avanti [a'vanti] AVV **1** *(moto: andare, venire)* forward; **fare un passo avanti** to take a step forward; **ho fatto un passo avanti** I took a step forward; **farsi avanti** to come forward; **avanti e indietro** backwards and forwards, to and fro; **essere avanti negli studi** *(a scuola)* to be well ahead in one's studies; **essere avanti di 5 punti** *(Sport ecc)* to be ahead *o* be leading by 5 points; **tirare avanti** *(fig)* to get by, survive; **in avanti** forward; **spostalo un po' in avanti** move it forward a bit; **piegarsi in avanti** to bend forward; **più avanti** further on **2** *(tempo: prima)* before; **l'anno avanti** the year before **3** *(tempo: posteriore a)*: **d'ora in avanti** from now on; **più avanti** later; **essere avanti con gli** *o* **negli anni** to be well on in years; **il mio orologio è** *o* **va avanti** my watch is fast; **mettere avanti l'orologio** to put the clock forward; **bisogna mettere l'orologio avanti di un'ora** you have to put the clock forward an hour; **guardare avanti** to look ahead **4** **andare avanti** to go forward; *(continuare)* to go on, carry on; *(fig: fare progressi)* to get on; *(: sopravvivere)* to get by; **non aspettatemi, andate avanti!** don't wait for me, go on (ahead)!; **non possiamo andare avanti così** we can't carry *o* go on like this; **la mia tesi sta andando avanti** my thesis is coming on **5** **mandare avanti la famiglia** to provide for one's family; **mandare avanti un'azienda** to run a business **6** **avanti!** *(entra)* come in!; *(non fare così)* come on!; **avanti! si accomodi!** come (o go) in and sit down!; **avanti il prossimo!** next please!; **avanti, assaggialo!** go on, taste it!; **avanti, march!** forward, march!; **avanti tutta!** *(Naut)* full speed ahead!
■ PREP: **avanti a** *(luogo)* before, in front of; *(tempo)* before; **avanti Cristo** before Christ; **nel 55 avanti Cristo** in 55 BC
■ SM INV *(Sport)* forward
avantielenco [avantie'lɛnko] SM *general information section of the phone book*
avantreno [avan'trɛno] SM *(Aut)* front chassis
avanzamento [avantsa'mento] SM *(gen)* advance; *(progresso)* progress; *(promozione di grado)* promotion
avanzare¹ [avan'tsare] VT *(proposta ecc)* to put forward; *(spostare in avanti: oggetto)* to move forward; **avanzare qn di grado** to promote sb
■ VI *(aus* **essere** *o* **avere)** *(procedere)* to advance, move forward; *(stagioni)* approach; *(fig: nello studio ecc)* to

Aa

make progress; **avanzare negli anni** to grow older, get on; **con l'avanzare degli anni** with the passing of time; **avanzare di grado** to be promoted

avanzare² [avan'tsare] VI (*aus* **essere**) **1** (*essere d'avanzo*) to be left over, remain; **è avanzato del pane da ieri** there is some bread left over from yesterday; **non m'avanza molto tempo** I haven't (got) much time left; **basta e avanza** that's more than enough **2** (*Mat*): **sette diviso tre fa due e avanza uno** seven divided by three is two remainder one
■ VT: **avanzare qc (da qn)** (*essere creditore*) to be owed sth by sb; **avanzo dieci euro da te** you owe me ten euros

avanzata [avan'tsata] SF (*Mil*) advance

avanzato, a [avan'tsato] AGG (*teoria, tecnica*) advanced; **essere in età avanzata** to be of an advanced age; **a primavera avanzata** late on in *o* in late spring; **a un'ora avanzata della notte** late at night

avanzo [a'vantso] SM **1** (*gen, Mat*) remainder; (*di stoffa*) remnant; (*di carta*) scrap; **avanzo di galera** (*fig*) jailbird; **avanzi** SMPL (*di cibo*) leftovers **2** (*sovrappiù*): **averne d'avanzo (di qc)** to have more than enough (of sth); **ce n'è d'avanzo** there is more than enough **3** (*Comm*) surplus; (*eccedenza di bilancio*) profit carried forward

> **LO SAPEVI...?**
> **avanzo** non si traduce mai con la parola inglese ***advance***

avaramente [avara'mente] AVV meanly, stingily

avaria [ava'ria] SF (*guasto meccanico*) breakdown, failure; (*danneggiamento*) damage; **motore in avaria** engine out of action; **subire un'avaria all'elica** to suffer *o* have a damaged propeller

avariare [ava'rjare] VT to damage
▶ **avariarsi** VIP (*cibo*) to go off, go bad

avariato, a [ava'rjato] AGG (*cibo*) off; (*merce*) damaged

avarizia [ava'rittsja] SF (*peccato*) avarice; (*tirchieria*) meanness, stinginess; **crepi l'avarizia!** hang the expense!

avaro, a [a'varo] AGG **1** (*tirchio*) mean, stingy, tight-fisted; **è più avara di lui** she's stingier than him **2** **avaro di** (*complimenti, parole*) sparing (with)
■ SM/F miser

avellinese [avelli'nese] AGG of *o* from Avellino
■ SM/F inhabitant *o* native of Avellino

avemaria [avema'ria] SF INV (*preghiera*) Hail Mary, Ave Maria; (*suono delle campane*) Angelus

avena [a'vena] SF oats *pl*

avere [a'vere] VB IRREG **PAROLA CHIAVE**
■ VT
1 (*gen*) to have; (*ricevere, ottenere*) to get; (*indossare*) to wear, have on; **avere da bere** to have something to drink; **avere da mangiare** to have something to eat; **non ha soldi** he has no money, he doesn't have any money, he hasn't got any money; **ho le mani sporche** my hands are dirty; **aveva le mani che gli tremavano** his hands were shaking
2 (*età, forma, colore*) to be; **quanti anni hai?** how old are you?; **ho vent'anni** I am twenty (years old); **ha 2 anni più di me** he's two years older than me; **aveva la mia stessa età** he was the same age as me; **avere fame** to be hungry; **avere paura** to be afraid
3 (*tempo*): **ne hai ancora per molto?** have you got much longer to go?; **ne avremo ancora per due giorni prima di arrivare a Londra** we've got another two days to go before we get to London; **quanti ne abbiamo oggi?** what's the date today?
4 (*fraseologia*): **averne fin sopra i capelli** (*fam*) to be fed up to the teeth; **ce l'hai con me?** are you angry with me?; **cos'hai?** what's wrong *o* what's the matter (with you)?; **avere qc da fare** to have sth to do; **ho ancora due lettere da scrivere** I have to *o* must write another two letters, I've still got two letters to write; **non hai che da dirglielo** you only have to tell him; **non hai da preoccuparti per me** you don't have to *o* needn't worry about me; **ma cos'hai da lamentarti?** what have you got to complain about?; **questo non ha niente a che vedere** *o* **fare con me** that's got nothing to do with me
■ VB AUS (*con participio passato*): **lo hai/avevi sentito?** have/had you heard from him?; **l'ho incontrata ieri** I met her yesterday; **quando l'avrò visto, ti dirò** when I've seen him, I'll let you know
■ VB IMPERS: **si è avuto un risultato imprevisto** there was a surprising result; **ieri si è avuto un abbassamento di temperatura** there was a drop in temperature yesterday
■ SM
1 **il dare e l'avere** (*Fin*) debits and credits *pl*
2 (*ricchezze*): **gli averi** SMPL wealth *sg*, fortune *sg*

averla [a'verla] SF (*Zool*) red-backed shrike

aviatore, trice [avja'tore] SM/F pilot, aviator

aviatorio, ria, ri, rie [avja'tɔrjo] AGG air *attr*, aviation *attr*

aviazione [avjat'tsjone] SF aviation; **aviazione civile** civil aviation; **aviazione militare** air force
▷ www.enac-italia.it/index.htm

avicoltura [avikol'tura] SF (*di pollame*) poultry farming; (*di uccelli*) bird breeding

avidamente [avida'mente] AVV (*gen*) greedily; (*leggere*) avidly

avidità [avidi'ta] SF: **avidità (di)** (*denaro ecc*) greed (for); (*gloria*) thirst (for)

avido, a ['avido] AGG: **avido (di)** (*pegg*) greedy (for); (*fig: di conoscenza*) eager (for)

aviere [a'vjɛre] SM (*Mil*) airman

aviogetto [avjo'dʒɛtto] SM jet

aviorimessa [avjori'messa] SF hangar

aviotrasportato, a [avjotraspor'tato] AGG (*truppe*) airborne

AVIS ['avis] SIGLA F (= **Associazione Volontari Italiani del Sangue**) Italian Blood Donors' Association

avitaminosi [avitami'nɔzi] SF vitamin deficiency

avo ['avo] SM (*antenato*) ancestor; (*letter: nonno*) grandfather; **i miei avi** my forebears; **i nostri avi** our ancestors

avocado [avo'kado] SM INV (*albero*) avocado; (*frutto*) avocado (pear)

avorio, ri [a'vɔrjo] SM ivory; **torre d'avorio** (*fig*) ivory tower

avulso, a [a'vulso] AGG: **parole avulse dal contesto** words taken out of context; **avulso dalla società** (*fig*) cut off from society

avuto PP *di* **avere**

Avv. ABBR = **Avvocato**

avvalersi [avva'lersi] VIP: **avvalersi di** to avail o.s. of

avvallamento [avvalla'mento] SM (*Geol*) depression, sinking *no pl*; (*di strada ecc*) subsidence

avvalorare [avvalo'rare] VT (*comprovare*) to confirm; **avvalorare una tesi** to confirm a theory

avvampare [avvam'pare] VI (*aus* **essere**) (*fuoco*) to flare up; (*fig: cielo, nuvole*) to become red; (: *arrossire*) to blush; **avvampare per la collera** to flare up with anger

avvantaggiare [avvantad'dʒare] VT (*favorire*) to favour (*Brit*), favor (*Am*)
▶ **avvantaggiarsi** VR **1** (*acquistare vantaggio*) to gain an advantage *o* get ahead; **avvantaggiarsi negli affari** to get ahead in business; **avvantaggiarsi nella carriera/nello studio** to get ahead in one's career/in one's studies; **avvantaggiarsi di qualche metro/minuto** to gain a few metres/minutes; **avvantaggiarsi su qn** to get ahead of sb **2** (*avvalersi*): **avvantaggiarsi di** to take advantage of

avvedersi [avve'dersi] VIP IRREG: **avvedersi di qn/qc** to notice sb/sth

avvedutamente [avveduta'mente] AVV (*vedi agg*) prudently; astutely

avvedutezza [avvedu'tettsa] SF (*vedi agg*) prudence; astuteness

avveduto, a [avve'duto] AGG (*accorto*) prudent; (*scaltro*) astute

avvelenamento [avvelena'mento] SM poisoning

avvelenare [avvele'nare] VT to poison; **avvelenare l'esistenza a qn** to make sb's life a misery; **è inutile avvelenarsi il sangue per così poco** there's no point in making yourself miserable over nothing
▶ **avvelenarsi** VR to poison o.s.

avvelenatore, trice [avvelena'tore] SM/F poisoner

avvenente [avve'nɛnte] AGG attractive

avvenenza [avve'nɛntsa] SF attractiveness

avvengo *ecc* [av'vɛngo] VB *vedi* **avvenire**

avvenimento [avveni'mento] SM event; **i principali avvenimenti sportivi** the main sporting events

avvenire [avve'nire] VI IRREG (*aus* **essere**) to happen, occur
■ AGG INV future *attr*
■ SM (*gen*) future; (*carriera*) future, prospects *pl*; **fa progetti per l'avvenire** she's making plans for the future; **in avvenire** in the future

avveniristico, a, ci, che [avveni'ristiko] AGG futuristic

avvenni *ecc* [av'venni] VB *vedi* **avvenire**

avventare [avven'tare] VT (*scagliare*): **gli avventò contro il cane** he set the dog on him
▶ **avventarsi** VR (*scagliarsi*): **avventarsi su** *o* **contro qn/qc** to hurl o.s. at sb/sth

avventatamente [avventata'mente] AVV rashly

avventatezza [avventa'tettsa] SF rashness

avventato, a [avven'tato] AGG (*giudizio*) rash; **è stata una decisione avventata** it was a rash decision

avventiziato [avventit'tsjato] SM (*di impiegato*) temporary employment; (*di operaio*) casual labour *o* work

avventizio, zia, zi, zie [avven'tittsjo] AGG (*impiegato*) temporary; (*guadagno*) casual
■ SM temporary clerk

avvento [av'vɛnto] SM **1** (*venuta*) coming, advent; **avvento al trono** accession to the throne **2** (*Rel*): **l'Avvento** Advent

avventore [avven'tore] SM customer

avventura [avven'tura] SF (*gen*) adventure; (*vicenda amorosa*) (love) affair; **è la vacanza ideale per chi ama l'avventura** it's an ideal holiday for anyone who likes adventure; **ha avuto un'avventura con una donna sposata** he had an affair with a married woman; **avere spirito d'avventura** to be adventurous

avventurarsi [avventu'rarsi] VR: **avventurarsi (in qc)** to venture (into sth)

avventuriero, a [avventu'rjɛro] SM/F adventurer/tress

avventurosamente [avventurosa'mente] AVV adventurously; **vivere avventurosamente** to lead an adventurous life

avventuroso, a [avventu'roso] AGG adventurous

avvenuto, a [avve'nuto] PP *di* **avvenire**

avverarsi [avve'rarsi] VIP to come true; **il suo sogno si è avverato** her dream came true

avverbiale [avver'bjale] AGG adverbial

avverbialmente [avverbjal'mente] AVV adverbially

avverbio, bi [av'vɛrbjo] SM adverb

avverrà *ecc* [avver'ra] VB *vedi* **avvenire**

avversare [avver'sare] VT to oppose

avversario, ria, ri, rie [avver'sarjo] AGG opposing; **la squadra avversaria** the opposing team
■ SM/F (*Sport*) opponent; (*Pol*) adversary, opponent; **ha battuto l'avversario** he beat his opponent

avversione [avver'sjone] SF: **avversione (per)** loathing (for), aversion (to); **nutrire un'avversione per** to harbour a dislike for

avversità [avversi'ta] SF INV adversity; **le avversità della vita** life's tribulations

avverso, a [av'vɛrso] AGG (*forze, sorte*) adverse, hostile; (*tempo*) unfavourable (*Brit*), unfavorable (*Am*), adverse; (*persona*: *contrario*): **avverso a** against

avvertenza [avver'tɛntsa] SF **1** (*avviso*) warning; **avvertenza ai lettori** (*prefazione*) foreword **2** (*cautela*) care *no pl* **3** (*per l'uso*): **avvertenze** SFPL instructions

avvertibile [avver'tibile] AGG (*suono, movimento*) perceptible

avvertimento [avverti'mento] SM warning

> **LO SAPEVI...?**
> **avvertimento** non si traduce mai con la parola inglese ***advertisement***

avvertire [avver'tire] VT **1** (*informare*): **avvertire (di)** to inform (of), let know (of); **avvertimi prima di partire** let me know when you're leaving; **avresti anche potuto avvertirmi** you could have told me; **se mi avessi avvertito sarei arrivato prima** if you'd told me I'd have come sooner **2** (*ammonire*) to warn; **ti avevo avvertito!** I warned you! **3** (*percepire*: *suono*) to perceive, hear; (*sentire*: *dolore*) to feel

avvezzo, a [av'vettso] AGG: **avvezzo a** accustomed to, used to

avviamento [avvia'mento] SM **1** (*gen, atto*) starting; (*: effetto*) start **2** (*insegnamento preparatorio*: *ad una carriera*) training; (*: ad uno studio*) introduction **3** (*Meccanica*: *messa in moto*) starting; **avviamento a freddo** cold start; **motorino d'avviamento** starter (motor) **4** (*Comm*) goodwill

avviare [avvi'are] VT **1** (*indirizzare*: *a studi, mestiere*) to lead, direct **2** (*mettere in moto*) to start (up); **avviare con la manovella** (*Aut*) to crank, give a crank start to **3** (*iniziare*: *attività, impresa*) to start up, set up; (*: trattative*) to set in motion; (*: discussione*) to get going; (*: lavoro a maglia*) to cast on
▶ **avviarsi** VIP (*incamminarsi*) **avviarsi (a** *o* **verso qc)** to set out *o* off (for sth); (*fig*: *essere sul punto di*): **avviarsi a fare qc** to be about to do sth, be on the point of doing sth; **avviati, poi ti raggiungo** you go on ahead and I'll catch you up; **l'estate si avvia alla fine** summer is drawing to an end

avviato, a [avvi'ato] AGG (*attività, negozio*) thriving; **"vendesi attività ben avviata"** "profitable business for sale"
■ SM/F person who has found his (*o* her) first job

Aa

avvicendamento [avvitʃenda'mento] SM (*gen*) alternation; (*Agr*: *delle colture*) rotation; **c'è molto avvicendamento di personale** there is a high turnover of staff

avvicendare [avvitʃen'dare] VT to alternate
▸ **avvicendarsi** VR (*uso reciproco*) to alternate; **si avvicendano in cucina** they take it in turns in the kitchen

avvicinabile [avvitʃi'nabile] AGG (*fig*: *persona*) approachable

avvicinamento [avvitʃina'mento] SM (*Mil, Aer*) approach; **ha ottenuto un avvicinamento** (*soldato*) he has been posted nearer home; (*in un lavoro*) he has been given a transfer nearer home; **l'avvicinamento dei due paesi** the rapprochement between the two countries

avvicinare [avvitʃi'nare] VT **1** (*mettere vicino*): **avvicinare (a)** to bring near (to); **avvicina la sedia al tavolo** bring the chair nearer to the table, draw the chair up to the table; **dovrò avvicinare il tavolo alla finestra** I'll have to move the table closer to the window; **il dolore li ha avvicinati** (*fig*) their sorrow has brought them closer together **2** (*farsi vicino a*: *persona*) to approach; **lo avvicinò per strada e si presentò** she came up to him in the street and introduced herself
▸ **avvicinarsi** VIP **1** (*andare vicino*) **avvicinarsi (a)** to approach, go (*o* come) up to; **il treno si avvicinava alla stazione** the train was approaching the station; **avvicinati!** come here!, come closer!; **mi ha fatto cenno di avvicinarmi** he beckoned to me to come closer; **mi si avvicinò un mendicante** a beggar came up to me **2** (*essere imminente*: *stagione, periodo*) to draw near **3** (*somigliare*) **avvicinarsi (a)** to be similar (to), be close (to)

avvilente [avvi'lɛnte] AGG (*umiliante*) humiliating; (*scoraggiante*) discouraging, disheartening

avvilimento [avvili'mento] SM (*vedi vb*) humiliation; discouragement

avvilire [avvi'lire] VT (*mortificare*) to humiliate; (*scoraggiare*) to dishearten, discourage; (*degradare*) to degrade
▸ **avvilirsi** VIP to lose heart, become discouraged

avvilito, a [avvi'lito] AGG (*scoraggiato*) disheartened, discouraged; (*depresso*) depressed

avviluppare [avvilup'pare] VT **1** (*avvolgere*): **avviluppare (in)** to wrap up (in); (*sogg*: *nebbia*) to envelop **2** (*ingarbugliare*) to entangle
▸ **avvilupparsi** VR (*avvolgersi*) **avvilupparsi in qc** to wrap o.s. up in sth
▸ **avvilupparsi** VIP (*aggrovigliarsi*) to get entangled *o* tangled up

avvinazzato, a [avvinat'tsato] AGG drunken
■ SM/F drunkard

avvincente [avvin'tʃɛnte] AGG (*spettacolo, lettura*) enthralling

avvincere [av'vintʃere] VT IRREG (*sogg*: *spettacolo, lettura*) to enthral, fascinate

avvinghiare [avvin'gjare] VT to clutch, clasp
▸ **avvinghiarsi** VR: **avvinghiarsi a** to cling to; **gli si avvinghiò al collo** she threw her arms round his neck

avvinsi *ecc* [av'vinsi] VB *vedi* **avvincere**

avvinto, a [av'vinto] PP *di* **avvincere**

avvio, vii [av'vio] SM start, beginning; **dare l'avvio a qc** to start sth off; **prendere l'avvio** to get going, get under way; **"Avvio"** (*in computer*) "Start"

avvisaglia [avvi'zaʎʎa] SF: **le prime avvisaglie** (*sintomo*: *di temporale ecc*) the first signs; (: *di malattia*) the first signs, the first symptoms

avvisare [avvi'zare] VT **1** (*informare*) to inform, notify **2** (*mettere in guardia*) to warn; **uomo avvisato, mezzo salvato** (*Proverbio*) forewarned is forearmed

avvisatore [avviza'tore] SM (*apparecchio d'allarme*) alarm; **avvisatore acustico** horn; **avvisatore d'incendio** fire alarm

avviso [av'vizo] SM **1** (*comunicazione*: *al pubblico*) notice; **hai letto l'avviso in bacheca?** have you read the notice on the board?; **dare l'avviso a qn di qc** to give sb notice of sth; **fino a nuovo avviso** until further notice; **avviso di chiamata** (*servizio*) call waiting; (*segnale*) call waiting signal **2** (*documento di notificazione*) notice; **avviso di garanzia** notification (*of impending investigation and of the right to name a defence lawyer*); **avviso di sfratto** eviction order **3** (*Comm*): **avviso di consegna** consignment note; **avviso di pagamento** payment advice; **avviso di spedizione** delivery note **4** (*consiglio, avvertimento*) warning; **dare un avviso a qn** to warn sb; **mettere qn sull'avviso** to put sb on their guard **5** (*opinione*) opinion; **a mio avviso** in my opinion; **a mio avviso è una montatura pubblicitaria** in my opinion it's a publicity stunt **6** (*inserzione pubblicitaria*) advertisement, ad

> **LO SAPEVI...?**
> **avviso** non si traduce mai con la parola inglese ***advice***

avvistamento [avvista'mento] SM sighting

avvistare [avvis'tare] VT to sight

avvitare [avvi'tare] VT (*vite*) to screw in (*o* down); (*fissare con viti*) to screw; (*lampadina*) to screw in
▸ **avvitarsi** VR (*vite, lampadina*) to screw in; (*Aer*) to spin, go into a spin

avvizzimento [avvittsi'mento] SM withering

avvizzire [avvit'tsire] VI (*aus* **essere**), **avvizzirsi** VIP to wither, shrivel

avvizzito, a [avvit'tsito] AGG withered, shrivelled

avvocatessa [avvoka'tessa] SF (*fam*) (female) lawyer

avvocato [avvo'kato] SM **1** (*gen*) lawyer; (*in corti inferiori*) solicitor; (*in corti superiori*) barrister (*Brit*), attorney(-at-law) (*Am*); **suo padre fa l'avvocato** his father's a lawyer; **consultare il proprio avvocato** to consult one's lawyer; **avvocato di parte civile/difensore** counsel for the plaintiff/the defence **2** (*fig*) advocate, defender; **avvocato delle cause perse** defender of lost causes; **avvocato del diavolo** devil's advocate; **fare l'avvocato del diavolo** to play devil's advocate

avvocatura [avvoka'tura] SF **1** (*professione*) legal profession; **esercitare l'avvocatura** to practise law **2** (*insieme degli avvocati*): **l'avvocatura** the Bar

avvolgere [av'vɔldʒere] VB IRREG
■ VT **1** (*bambino, oggetto*) to wrap (up); (*arrotolare*: *tappeto*) to roll up; (: *bobina*) to wind up; **puoi avvolgere la scatola con questa carta** you can wrap the box in this paper; **avvolto dalla nebbia** enveloped in fog; **avvolto dal mistero/silenzio** shrouded in mystery/silence **2** **avvolgere qc intorno a qc** to wind sth round sth
▸ **avvolgersi** VR to wrap o.s. up; **si è avvolto nella coperta** he wrapped himself up in the blanket

avvolgibile [avvol'dʒibile] AGG roll-up *attr*, roller *attr*
■ SM (roller) blind (*Brit*), window shade (*Am*)

avvolgimento [avvoldʒi'mento] SM (*Elettr*) winding

avvolsi *ecc* [av'vɔlsi] VB *vedi* **avvolgere**

avvolto, a [av'vɔlto] PP *di* **avvolgere**

avvoltoio, oi [avvol'tojo] SM (*gen, fig*) vulture

avvoltolare [avvolto'lare] VT to roll up
▶ **avvoltolarsi** VR (*rotolarsi*: *nel fango*) to roll (around)
ayatollah [ajatol'la] SM INV ayatollah
ayurvedico, a, ci, che [ajur'vɛdiko] AGG Ayurvedic
azalea [addza'lɛa] SF azalea
Azerbaigian [addzɛrbai'dʒan] SM Azerbaijan
azerbaigiano, a [addzɛrbai'dʒano] AGG Azerbaijani
■ SM/F Azerbaijani
■ SM (*lingua*) Azerbaijani
azero [ad'dʒɛro] AGG, SM/F Azeri
azienda [ad'dzjɛnda] SF (*gen*) company, business, firm, concern; **azienda agricola** commercial farm; **azienda (autonoma) di soggiorno e turismo** tourist board; **azienda avicola** poultry farm; **azienda a partecipazione statale** *company in which the state has a controlling interest*; **azienda pubblica** state (run) company; **Azienda sanitaria locale** local health centre
aziendale [addzjen'dale] AGG company *attr*; **la nostra politica aziendale** our company policy; **gestione aziendale** business management; **mensa aziendale** company canteen; **organizzazione aziendale** business administration
azimut ['addzimut] SM INV (*Astron*) azimuth
azionabile [attsjo'nabile] AGG (*macchina ecc*) that can be operated; **la macchina è azionabile tramite l'uso di questa leva** the machine is operated by this lever
azionare [attsjo'nare] VT to activate
azionario, ria, ri, rie [attsjo'narjo] AGG share *attr*; **mercato azionario** stock market; **capitale azionario** share capital
azione[1] [at'tsjone] SF **1** (*l'agire*) action; **entrare in azione** (*piano*) to come into operation; **passare all'azione** to take action; (*Mil*) to go into action **2** (*atto*) action, act; **buona/cattiva azione** good/bad deed **3** (*effetto*) action; **l'azione dei gas tossici** the action of toxic gases **4** (*Teatro, Sport*) action; (*trama*) plot; **film d'azione** action movie **5** (*Dir*: *processo*) (law)suit, action
azione[2] [at'tsjone] SF (*Fin*: *titolo*) share (*Brit*), stock (*Am*); **azioni ordinarie** ordinary shares; **azioni preferenziali** preference shares (*Brit*), preferred stock *sg* (*Am*)
azionista, i, e [attsjo'nista] SM/F shareholder
azoto [ad'dzɔto] SM nitrogen
AZT [adzeta'ti] SIGLA M (= **azidotimidina**) AZT (= *azidothymidine*)

azteco, a, chi, che [as'tɛko] AGG, SM/F Aztec
azzannare [attsan'nare] VT to maul, bite
azzardare [addzar'dare] VT (*domanda, ipotesi*) to hazard, venture; (*uso assoluto*) to take a risk
▶ **azzardarsi** VIP: **azzardarsi a fare qc** to dare (to) do sth
azzardato, a [addzar'dato] AGG (*ipotesi, risposta*) rash; (*impresa*) risky; **non voglio dare un parere azzardato, ma...** I don't want to be hasty *o* rash, but ...
azzardo [ad'dzardo] SM risk; **gioco d'azzardo** gambling; **gli piace giocare d'azzardo** (*anche fig*) he likes gambling
azzeccare [attsek'kare] VT (*bersaglio*) to hit, strike; (*indovinare*: *risposta, pronostico*) to guess; **ha azzeccato il pronostico al totocalcio** he had a win on the pools; **non ne azzecca mai una** he never gets anything right; **che ci azzecca?** (*fam*) what's that got to do with it?
azzeramento [addzera'mento] SM (*Inform*) reset
azzerare [addze'rare] VT **1** (*Mat, Fis*) to make equal to zero, reduce to zero **2** (*Tecn*: *strumento*) to (re)set to zero; (*Inform*) to reset
azzimato, a [addzi'mato] AGG dressed up, spruced up
azzimo, a ['addzimo] AGG (*non lievitato*: *pane*) unleavened
■ SM unleavened bread
azzittire [attsit'tire] VT: **azzittire qn** to silence sb, shut sb up
■ VI (*aus* **essere**) to fall *o* become silent
azzoppare [attsop'pare] VT to lame, make lame
▶ **azzopparsi** VIP to become lame
Azzorre [ad'dzɔrre] SFPL: **le Azzorre** the Azores
azzuffarsi [attsuf'farsi] VIP (*gen*) to come to blows; (*bambini*) to squabble; **s'azzuffa sempre col fratello** she's always fighting with her brother
azzurrato, a [addzur'rato] AGG (*Aut*: *cristalli*) tinted; (*lenti*) (blue-)tinted
azzurrino, a [addzur'rino] AGG light blue, pale blue
azzurro, a [ad'dzurro] AGG **1** (*colore*) blue, azure; **occhi azzurri** blue eyes; **il principe azzurro** Prince Charming **2** (*Sport*: *della nazionale italiana*) of the Italian team **3** (*Pol*) *relating to the political party Forza Italia*
■ SM **1** (*colore*) blue, azure **2** (*Sport*: *atleta*) member of the Italian team; **gli azzurri** SMPL the Italian team
azzurrognolo, a [addzur'roɲɲolo] AGG bluish

B, b [bi] SF O M INV (*lettera*) B, b; **B come Bologna** ≈ B for Benjamin (*Brit*), ≈ B for Baker (*Am*)
BA SIGLA = *Bari*
babà [ba'ba] SM INV: **babà (al rum)** rum baba
babau [ba'bau] SM INV ogre, bogey man
babbeo [bab'bɛo] SM fool, idiot
babbione, a [bab'bjɔne] AGG, SM/F idiot
babbo ['babbo] SM (*fam*) dad, daddy; **è un regalino per il mio babbo** it's a little present for my dad; **Babbo Natale** Father Christmas, Santa Claus
babbuccia, ce [bab'buttʃa] SF (Turkish) slipper; (*per neonati*) bootee
babbuino [babbu'ino] SM baboon
Babele [ba'bɛle] SF **1** (*confusione*) chaos, confusion **2** (*Bibbia*) Babel; **la torre di Babele** the tower of Babel
babilonese [babilo'nese] AGG, SM/F Babylonian
Babilonia [babi'lɔnja] SF Babylon
babordo [ba'bordo] SM (*Naut*) port side; **a babordo** to port
baby ['bebi] SM/F INV (*neonato*) (newborn) baby, infant; (*fam: piccola dose di whisky*) tot, shot
■ AGG INV: **pensione baby** *pension paid to someone who has worked for only a short time, usually 15-20 years*; **pensionato baby** *person who retires with a pension after only 15-20 years' employment*
baby-doll ['beibi dɔl] SM INV baby-dolls *pl*
babysitter ['beɪbɪsitəʳ] SM/F INV baby-sitter
bacato, a [ba'kato] AGG (*frutto*) worm-eaten, maggoty; (*fig: mente*) diseased; (*: persona*) corrupt
bacca, che ['bakka] SF berry
baccalà [bakka'la] SM INV (*pesce*) dried salted cod; (*fig: persona sciocca*) dummy; **secco come un baccalà** (*magro*) as thin as a rake
baccano [bak'kano] SM row, din; **fare baccano** to make a row *o* din; **smettetela di fare baccano!** stop making this racket!
baccello [bat'tʃɛllo] SM pod
bacchetta [bak'ketta] SF (*bastoncino*) rod, stick; (*di tamburo*) drumstick; (*di direttore d'orchestra*) baton; (*per mangiare alla cinese*) chopstick; **comandare a bacchetta** to rule with a rod of iron; **bacchetta magica** magic wand
bacchettata [bakket'tata] SF: **dare una bacchettata a qn** to hit sb with a stick
bacchiare [bak'kjare] VT to knock down (*fruit, nuts*)
Bacco ['bakko] SM Bacchus
bacheca, che [ba'kɛka] SF **1** (*per affissione*) notice board (*Brit*), bulletin board (*Am*); **appendilo in bacheca** put it on the notice board; **bacheca elettronica** (*Inform*) bulletin board **2** (*mobile*) showcase, display case
bachelite [bake'lite] SF bakelite®
bachicoltura [bakikol'tura] SF breeding of silkworms
baciamano [batʃa'mano] SM: **fare il baciamano a qn** to kiss sb's hand
baciare [ba'tʃare] VT to kiss; **lo baciò sulla guancia** she kissed him on the cheek, she kissed his cheek; **le sponde baciate dal sole** the sun-kissed shores
▶ **baciarsi** VR (*uso reciproco*) to kiss (each other *o* one another); **ci siamo baciati** we kissed
bacillare [batʃil'lare] AGG bacterial
bacillo [ba'tʃillo] SM bacillus, germ
bacinella [batʃi'nɛlla] SF (*gen: recipiente*) bowl; (*per lavarsi*) basin; **una bacinella di plastica** a plastic bowl
bacino [ba'tʃino] SM **1** (*Anat*) pelvis; **sollevate il bacino** raise your pelvis **2** (*Ceog*) basin **3** (*Geol*) field, bed; **bacino carbonifero** coalfield; **bacino petrolifero** oilfield **4** (*Naut*) dock; **bacino di carenaggio** dry dock; **bacino galleggiante** floating dock
bacio, ci ['batʃo] SM **1** kiss; **dare un bacio a qn** to give sb a kiss; **coprire qn di baci** to smother sb with kisses; **dare il bacio della buonanotte a qn** to kiss sb goodnight; **tanti baci** (*fine di lettera*) love and kisses, lots of love; **un bacio sulla guancia** a kiss on the cheek **2** (*gusto di gelato*) chocolate and hazelnut
backup [be'kap] SM INV (*Inform*) backup
baco, chi ['bako] SM (*gen: verme*) worm, maggot; (*larva*) grub; (*Inform*) bug; **questa mela ha il baco** there's a worm in this apple; **baco da seta** silkworm
bacucco, a, chi, che [ba'kukko] AGG senile; **è un vecchio bacucco** he's an old fool
bada ['bada] SF: **tenere qn a bada** (*tener d'occhio*) to keep an eye on sb; (*tenere a distanza*) to hold sb at bay
badante [ba'dante] SM/F care worker

badare [ba'dare] VI (*aus* **avere**) **badare a** **1** (*occuparsi di*: *negozio, casa*) to look after, mind; (: *bambino, malato*) to take care of, look after; (: *cliente*) to attend to; **bada agli affari tuoi!** *or* **bada ai fatti tuoi!** mind your own business! **2** (*fare attenzione*) to pay attention to, mind; **nessuno gli ha badato** nobody paid any attention to him; **bada (a te)!** watch out!; **bada a non cadere** mind *o* be careful you don't fall **3** (*preoccuparsi*) to care about; **non bada a ciò che dice la gente** he doesn't care what people say; **è un tipo che non bada a spese** he doesn't mind how much he spends

badessa [ba'dessa] SF (*Rel*) abbess

badia [ba'dia] SF abbey

badile [ba'dile] SM shovel

baffo ['baffo] SM **1** **baffi** SMPL (*di persona*) moustache *sg*; (*di animale*) whiskers; **un pranzo da leccarsi i baffi** a mouth-watering meal; **ridere sotto i baffi** to laugh up one's sleeve; **di quello che mi ha detto me ne faccio un baffo** (*fam*) I don't give *o* care a damn about what he said **2** (*sgorbio, sbavatura*) smear, smudge

baffuto, a [baf'futo] AGG (*persona*) with a moustache

bagagliaio, ai [bagaʎ'ʎajo] SM **1** (*di auto*) boot (*Brit*), trunk (*Am*); (*di treno*) luggage van (*Brit*), baggage car (*Am*); (*di aereo*) hold; **puoi mettere la valigia nel bagagliaio** you can put your case in the boot **2** (*deposito bagagli*) left-luggage office

bagaglio, gli [ba'gaʎʎo] SM luggage *no pl*, baggage *no pl*; **hai molti bagagli?** have you got a lot of luggage?; **ho lasciato i miei bagagli all'albergo** I left my luggage at the hotel; **dove si ritirano i bagagli?** where's the baggage reclaim?; **fare/disfare i bagagli** to pack/unpack; **hai già fatto i bagagli?** have you packed?; **ho preso armi e bagagli e me ne sono andato** I packed up and left; **un bagaglio culturale** a store of knowledge; **bagaglio appresso** accompanied luggage; **bagaglio consentito** free luggage allowance; **bagaglio in eccesso** excess luggage; **bagaglio a mano** hand luggage

bagarino [baga'rino] SM ticket tout

bagarre [ba'gar] SF INV **1** (*Ciclismo*): **fare bagarre** to jostle **2** (*baruffa*) row

bagascia, sce [ba'gaʃʃa] SF (*fam!*) whore

bagattella [bagat'tɛlla] SF **1** (*inezia*) trifle, trifling matter **2** (*Mus*) bagatelle

baggianata [baddʒa'nata] SF foolish action; **dire baggianate** to talk nonsense

Baghdad [bag'dad] SF Baghdad

bagliore [baʎ'ʎore] SM (*di fuoco*) glow; (*di fari*) glare; (*di lampi*) flash; **un bagliore di speranza** a gleam *o* ray of hope

bagnante [baɲ'ɲante] SM/F bather

bagnare [baɲ'ɲare] VT **1** (*gen*) to wet; (*inzuppare*) to soak; (*labbra*) to moisten; (*annaffiare*) to water; **bagnarsi le labbra** to moisten one's lips; **le lacrime bagnavano il suo viso** her face was bathed in tears; **hai bagnato le piante?** did you water the plants?; **non voglio bagnarmi le scarpe** I don't want to get my shoes wet **2** (*sogg*: *fiume*) to flow through; (: *mare*) to wash, bathe; **il Mediterraneo bagna Genova** Genoa stands on the Mediterranean coast **3** (*fam*: *festeggiare bevendo*) to drink to, toast; **abbiamo bagnato la sua promozione** we celebrated his promotion
▶ **bagnarsi** VR (*fare il bagno*) to bathe; **il bambino si è bagnato** the baby has wet himself;
▶ **bagnarsi** VIP (*prendere acqua*) to get wet; (*inzupparsi*) to get soaked, get drenched; **ci siamo bagnati anche se avevamo l'ombrello** we got soaked even though we had an umbrella

bagnasciuga [baɲɲaʃ'ʃuga] SM INV (*battigia*) water's edge

bagnata [baɲ'ɲata] SF: **dare una bagnata a** (*pianta*) to water; (*stoffa*) to sprinkle with water

bagnato, a [baɲ'ɲato] AGG wet; **ho i capelli bagnati** my hair's wet; **bagnato di lacrime** bathed in tears; **bagnato di sudore** (*viso, fronte*) bathed in sweat; (*camicia*) soaked with sweat; **bagnato fino alle ossa** soaked to the skin; **bagnato fradicio** wet through, drenched; **sei bagnato fradicio!** you're soaking wet!; **essere bagnato come un pulcino** to be like a drowned rat, be sopping wet; **sembrare un pulcino bagnato** to look a pathetic sight
■ SM wet surface; **piove sempre sul bagnato** (*fig*) it never rains but it pours

bagnino, a [baɲ'ɲino] SM/F lifeguard; (*in piscina*) swimming pool attendant; **fa il bagnino** he's a lifeguard

bagno ['baɲɲo] SM **1** (*gen, Chim, Fot*) bath; (*in piscina*) swim; (*al mare*) swim, bathe; **fare il bagno** (*nella vasca*) to have a bath; (*in piscina*) to go swimming; (*al mare*) to go swimming *o* bathing; **preferisci il bagno o la doccia?** which do you prefer, a bath or a shower?; **fare il bagno a qn** to give sb a bath; **mettere qc a bagno** to leave sth to soak; **vasca da bagno** bath, bathtub **2** (*locale*: *anche*: **stanza da bagno**) bathroom; **qui c'è il bagno e lì la camera da letto** the bathroom's here, and the bedroom's there; **scusi, dov'è il bagno?** where's the toilet *o* loo, please? (*Brit*), where's the bathroom, please? (*Am*) **3** (*stabilimento balneare*) private beach
■ **bagni di mare** sea bathing *sg*; **bagni pubblici** public baths; **bagno di fango** mud bath; **bagno di folla** (*fig*) adulation of the crowd; **bagno di sabbia** sand bath; **bagno di sangue** (*fig*) blood bath; **bagno turco** Turkish bath

Bb

bagnomaria [baɲɲoma'ria] SM INV: **cuocere a bagnomaria** to cook in a bain marie (*Brit*), to cook in a double boiler (*Am*)

bagnoschiuma [baɲɲo'skjuma] SM INV bubble bath

Bahama [ba'hama] SFPL: **le Bahama** the Bahamas

Bahrein [ba'rein] SM Bahrain *o* Bahrein

baia ['baja] SF (*Geog*) bay

baiadera [baja'dɛra] AGG INV (*tessuto*) bayadere

baio, aia, ai, aie ['bajo] AGG (*cavallo*) bay

baionetta [bajo'netta] SF bayonet; **innesto a baionetta** bayonet fitting

baionettata [bajonet'tata] SF (*colpo*) bayonet thrust; (*ferita*) bayonet wound

baita ['baita] SF mountain hut

balalaica, che [bala'laika] SF balalaika

balaustra [bala'ustra], **balaustrata** [balaus'trata] SF balustrade

balbettare [balbet'tare] VT (*gen*) to stammer (out); (*sogg*: *bambino*) to babble; **balbettare delle scuse** to mumble an excuse
■ VI (*aus* **avere**) (*vedi vt*) to stammer; to babble

balbettio, ii [balbet'tio] SM (*vedi vb*) stammering; babbling

balbuzie [bal'buttsje] SF INV stammer; **essere affetto da balbuzie** to have a stammer

balbuziente [balbut'tsjɛnte] AGG stammering; **essere balbuziente** to stammer
■ SM/F stammerer

Balcani [bal'kani] SMPL: **i Balcani** the Balkans

balcanico, a, ci, che [bal'kaniko] AGG Balkan
balconata [balko'nata] SF (*Archit*) balcony; (*galleria*) gallery
balconcino [balkon'tʃino] SM: **reggiseno a balconcino** push-up bra
balcone [bal'kone] SM balcony; **il balcone dà sul giardino** the balcony looks onto the garden
baldacchino [baldak'kino] SM canopy; **letto a baldacchino** four-poster (bed)
baldanza [bal'dantsa] SF (*sicurezza*) self-confidence; (*spavalderia*) audacity, boldness
baldanzosamente [baldantsosa'mente] AVV (*vedi sf*) self-confidently; boldly
baldanzoso, a [baldan'tsoso] AGG (*vedi sf*) self-confident; audacious, bold
baldo, a ['baldo] AGG bold
baldoria [bal'dɔrja] SF merrymaking, revelry; **fare baldoria** to have a good time
baldracca, che [bal'drakka] SF (*fam!*) whore
Baleari [bale'ari] SFPL: **le (isole) Baleari** the Balearic Islands
balena [ba'lena] SF (*Zool*) whale; (*fig pegg*) barrel of lard; **caccia alla balena** whaling; **olio di balena** whale oil; **balena bianca** white whale (*used in reference to the former Christian Democrat Party*)
balenare [bale'nare] VI (*aus* **essere**) (*gen*) to flash; **mi è balenata un'idea** an idea flashed into *o* through my mind; **l'ira balenò nel suo sguardo** his eyes flashed with rage
baleniera [bale'njɛra] SF (*per la caccia*) whaler, whaling ship
baleno [ba'leno] SM flash of lightning; **in un baleno** in a flash
balera [ba'lɛra] SF (*locale*) dance hall; (*pista*) dance floor
balestra [ba'lɛstra] SF **1** (*arma*) crossbow **2** (*Tecn*) leaf spring
balestruccio, ci [bales'truttʃo] SM house martin
balia[1] ['balja] SF (*anche fig*) wet-nurse; **balia asciutta** nanny
balia[2] [ba'lia] SF (*potere assoluto*): **essere in balia di** to be at the mercy of; **la nave era in balia delle onde** the ship was at the mercy of the waves; **essere lasciato in balia di se stesso** to be left to one's own devices
balilla [ba'lilla] SM INV (*Storia*) *member of Fascist youth group*
balistica [ba'listika] SF ballistics *sg*
balistico, a, ci, che [ba'listiko] AGG ballistic; **perito balistico** ballistics expert
balla ['balla] SF **1** (*quantità*) bale **2** (*fam: fandonia*) rubbish *no pl*; **raccontare una balla a qn** to tell sb a lie; **un sacco di balle** a pack of lies, a load of rubbish
ballabile [bal'labile] SM (*Mus*) dance number, dance tune
ballare [bal'lare] VI (*aus* **avere**) **1** to dance; **abbiamo ballato tutta la sera** we danced all night; **andare a ballare** to go dancing; **andiamo a ballare?** shall we go dancing?; **ballare come un orso** to dance like an elephant **2** (*traballare: mobile*) to wobble; **le onde facevano ballare la nave** the waves tossed the ship about; **abbiamo ballato in volo** we had a bumpy flight; **quella giacca gli balla addosso** he's lost in that jacket
■ VT to dance; **ballare il valzer** to (dance the) waltz
ballata [bal'lata] SF ballad
ballatoio, oi [balla'tojo] SM (*balcone*) gallery, walkway
ballerina [balle'rina] SF **1** (female) dancer; **prima ballerina** prima ballerina; **ballerina classica** ballerina, ballet dancer; **voleva fare la ballerina** she wanted to be a dancer; **ballerina di rivista** chorus girl **2** (*scarpa*) pump **3** (*uccello*) wagtail; **ballerina gialla** grey wagtail
ballerino [balle'rino] SM (male) dancer; (*classico*) ballet dancer; **un ottimo ballerino** a very good dancer
balletto [bal'letto] SM **1** (*spettacolo*) ballet; (*Mus*) ballet music **2** (*corpo di ballo*) dance troupe; (: *classico*) corps de ballet
ballo ['ballo] SM (*danza, festa*) dance, ball; (*giro di danza*) dance; **un ballo sudamericano** a Latin American dance; **fare un ballo** to have a dance; **essere in ballo** (*fig*) to be at stake; **tirare in ballo qn** (*fig*) to involve sb; **tirare in ballo qc** to bring sth up, raise sth; **entrare in ballo** (*fig: persona*) to become *o* get involved; (: *cosa*) to come into the picture, become a factor; **ballo liscio** ballroom dancing; **ballo in maschera** *o* **mascherato** fancy-dress ball
ballottaggio, gi [ballot'taddʒo] SM (*Pol*) second ballot
balneare [balne'are] AGG bathing *attr*; **località balneare** seaside town; **la stagione balneare** the summer season; **governo balneare** (*Pol*) caretaker government
baloccare [balok'kare] VT (*trastullare*) to keep amused
▶ **baloccarsi** VR (*perder tempo*) to fritter (one's) time away
balocco, chi [ba'lɔkko] SM toy, plaything
balordaggine [balor'daddʒine] SF (*vedi agg*) stupidity, foolishness; unreliability; peculiarity; **non dire balordaggini!** don't talk nonsense!
balordamente [balorda'mente] AVV (*vedi agg*) stupidly, foolishly; unreliably; oddly, peculiarly
balordo, a [ba'lordo] AGG (*sciocco*) stupid, silly, foolish; (*di poco affidamento*) unreliable; (*strampalato*) odd, peculiar
■ SM/F (*sciocco*) fool, stupid person; (*tipo strampalato*) odd sort
balsamico, a, ci, che [bal'samiko] AGG (*aria, brezza*) balmy; **pomata balsamica** balsam
balsamo ['balsamo] SM (*lenimento*) balsam, balm; (*fig*) balm; **balsamo (per capelli)** (hair) conditioner
baltico, a, ci, che ['baltiko] AGG Baltic
■ SM: **il (mar) Baltico** the Baltic (Sea)
baluardo [balu'ardo] SM (*bastione*) bulwark, rampart; (*fig*) bulwark
baluginare [baludʒi'nare] VI (*aus* **essere**) to flicker; **gli baluginò il sospetto che...** suddenly the suspicion came into his mind that ...
balza ['baltsa] SF **1** (*di stoffa*) frill **2** (*rupe*) crag **3** (*di cavallo*) white sock
balzana [bal'tsana] SF (*di cavallo*) sock
balzano, a [bal'tsano] AGG (*persona, idea*) queer, odd; **è un cervello balzano** he's a queer fish
balzare [bal'tsare] VI (*aus* **essere**) to leap, jump; **balzare in piedi** to leap *o* jump to one's feet; **balzare giù dal letto/dalla sedia** to leap *o* jump out of bed/up from one's chair; **balzare in macchina/a cavallo** to jump into a car/onto a horse; **il cuore le balzò in gola per la gioia/paura** her heart leapt with joy/fear; **la verità balza agli occhi** the truth is obvious; **gli balzò in mente che...** it came to him that ...
balzo[1] ['baltso] SM (*salto*) leap, jump; (*di palla*) bounce; **fare un balzo** to jump; **fare un balzo in avanti** to leap forward; **un balzo in avanti** (*fig*) a great leap forward; **prendere la palla al balzo** (*fig*) to seize one's opportunity
balzo[2] ['baltso] SM (*di rupe*) crag, cliff

bambagia, gie [bam'badʒa] SF *(ovatta)* cottonwool *(Brit)*, absorbent cotton *(Am)*; *(cascame)* cotton waste; **tenere qn nella bambagia** *(fig)* to mollycoddle sb
bambinaia [bambi'naja] SF nursemaid
bambino, a [bam'bino] SM/F *(gen)* child, (little) boy/girl; *(neonato)* baby; **quando ero bambino** when I was a child; **chi è quel bambino?** who's that little boy?; **aspetta un bambino** she's expecting a baby; **c'erano dei bambini che giocavano nel parco** there were some children playing in the park; **lo saprebbe fare anche un bambino!** a child could do it!; **fare il bambino** to behave childishly; **è un bambino!** he's really childish!
■ AGG: **una scienza ancora bambina** a science still in its infancy
bamboccio, ci [bam'bɔttʃo] SM *(bambino)* bouncing child; *(pupazzo)* rag doll; *(fig)* big baby
bambola ['bambola] SF *(giocattolo)* doll, dolly; *(fig: donna)* doll
bambolotto [bambo'lɔtto] SM male doll
bambù [bam'bu] SM INV bamboo; **di bambù** bamboo
banale [ba'nale] AGG *(gen)* banal, commonplace; *(idea, scusa)* trite; *(incidente)* trivial, minor; *(persona)* ordinary; *(vita)* humdrum, dull; **è solo un banale raffreddore** it's just a common *o* garden cold, it's just an ordinary cold; **si è trattato di un banale incidente** it was a minor accident; **la trama del libro era un po' banale** the plot of the book was rather banal
banalità [banali'ta] SF INV **1** *(vedi agg)* banality; triteness; triviality; ordinariness; dullness **2** *(parole)* truism, trite remark; **dire una banalità** to make a trite remark
banalmente [banal'mente] AVV in a banal way, without originality
banana [ba'nana] SF banana; **banana split** banana split
banano [ba'nano] SM banana tree
banca, che ['banka] SF *(istituto, edificio)* bank; **in banca** in the bank; **andare in banca** to go to the bank; **devo andare in banca** I need to go to the bank; **avere un conto in banca** to have a bank account; **banca dati** *(Inform)* data bank; **banca del sangue** blood bank; **banca del tempo** local exchange and trading system, LETS
▷ www.bancaditalia.it/
▷ www.abi.it/
bancarella [banka'rɛlla] SF stall; **l'ho comprato in una bancarella al mercato** I bought it from a stall in the market
bancario, ria, ri, rie [ban'karjo] AGG bank *attr*, banking; **il settore bancario** the banking sector; **prestito bancario** bank loan; **assegno bancario** (bank) cheque
■ SM/F bank employee
bancarotta [banka'rotta] SF *(Fin)* bankruptcy; *(fig)* failure; **andare in bancarotta** *or* **fare bancarotta** to go bankrupt
bancarottiere, a [bankarot'tjɛre] SM/F bankrupt
banchettare [banket'tare] VI *(aus* **avere***)* to banquet, feast
banchetto [ban'ketto] SM banquet; **fare un banchetto (a base di qc)** to feast (on sth)
banchiere [ban'kjɛre] SM *(Fin, nei giochi)* banker
banchina [ban'kina] SF **1** *(di porto)* quay, wharf **2** *(di stazione)* platform **3** *(per pedoni)* footway; *(per ciclisti)* cycle path; **banchina cedevole** *(Aut)* soft verge *(Brit)* *o* shoulder *(Am)*; **banchina spartitraffico** *(Aut)* central reservation *(Brit)*, median (strip) *(Am)*
banchisa [ban'kiza] SF pack ice
banco, chi ['banko] SM **1** *(sedile)* seat, bench; (: *in Parlamento*) bench; **banco di chiesa** pew; **banco degli imputati** *(Dir)* dock; **banco di scuola** desk; **banco dei testimoni** witness box *(Brit)* *o* stand *(Am)* **2** *(di negozio)* counter; *(di mercato)* stall; **medicinali da banco** over-the-counter medicines; **sotto banco** *(fig)* under the counter; **banco del Lotto** lottery-ticket office **3** *(di officina)* (work)bench; **banco di prova** test bed; *(fig)* testing ground **4** *(Fin)* bank; **tenere il banco** *(nei giochi)* to be (the) banker; **tener banco** *(fig)* to monopolize the conversation **5** *(Meteor)* bank, patch; **banco di nebbia** fog bank **6** *(Geol: strato)* layer; (: *di coralli*) reef; **banco di ghiaccio** ice floe; **banco di sabbia** sandbank **7** *(di pesci)* shoal
bancogiro [banko'dʒiro] SM credit transfer
Bancomat® ['bankomat] SM INV automated banking; *(tessera)* cash card
banconota [banko'nɔta] SF banknote; **una banconota da cento euro** a hundred euro note
banda[1] ['banda] SF *(di suonatori)* band; *(di ladri, guerriglieri)* band, gang; *(di amici)* gang, group; **suona nella banda del paese** she plays in the village band; **una banda di rapinatori** a gang of robbers
banda[2] ['banda] SF **1** *(di stoffa)* band, strip; *(di metallo)* band, strip; *(di carta)* strip; *(di calcolatore)* tape; **banda larga** *(Inform)* broadband; **banda perforata** *(Inform)* punch tape; **banda stretta** *(Inform)* narrowband **2** *(Fis, Radio)* band
bandana [ban'dana] SF bandanna
banderuola [bande'rwɔla] SF *(Meteor)* weathercock, weathervane; **essere una banderuola** *(fig)* to be fickle
bandiera [ban'djɛra] SF flag; **alzare bandiera bianca** to show the white flag; **la bandiera italiana** the Italian flag; **battere bandiera italiana** *(nave)* to fly the Italian flag; **cambiare bandiera** *(fig)* to change sides; **bandiera ombra** *o* **di comodo** flag of convenience
bandierina [bandje'rina] SF *(Naut)* pennant; *(Calcio)*: **tiro dalla bandierina** corner
bandire [ban'dire] VT **1** *(annunciare)* to announce, proclaim; **bandire un concorso** to announce a competition *(for posts in large organizations)* **2** *(porre al bando: prodotto)* to ban; (: *sentimenti*) to banish; (: *complimenti, ciance*) to dispense with; (: *persona*) to exile; **l'hanno bandito dall'ordine degli avvocati** he has been struck off
bandita [ban'dita] SF reserve
banditismo [bandi'tizmo] SM banditry
bandito [ban'dito] SM bandit, outlaw; *(fig: persona senza scrupoli)* rogue
banditore [bandi'tore] SM **1** *(Storia)* town crier **2** *(di aste)* auctioneer
bando ['bando] SM **1** *(annuncio)* (public) announcement, (public) notice; **bando di concorso** announcement of a public examination **2** *(esilio)* exile; **mettere al bando qn** to exile sb; *(fig)* to freeze sb out; **bando alle ciance!** that's enough talk!
bandolo ['bandolo] SM *(di matassa)* end; **trovare il bandolo della matassa** *(fig)* to find the key to the problem
bang [bæŋ] SM INV: **bang sonico** sonic boom
Bangkok [ban'kɔk] SF Bangkok
Bangladesh [bangla'dɛʃ] SM Bangladesh
banjo ['bændʒou] SM INV banjo
baobab [bao'bab] SM INV baobab, monkey bread tree

Bb

BAR [bar] SIGLA M (= **Battaglione Addestramento Reclute**) *battalion for the training of recruits*
bar [bar] SM INV (*locale*) bar (*serving coffee, alcoholic drinks, snacks ecc*); (*mobile*) cocktail cabinet
bara ['bara] SF coffin
baracca, che [ba'rakka] SF hut; (*pegg*) hovel; (*fam pegg: oggetto*) piece of junk; **mandare avanti la baracca** to keep things going; **come va la baracca?** how are you managing?; **piantare baracca e burattini** to throw everything up
baraccato, a [barak'kato] SM/F *person living in temporary camp or shanty town*
baracchino [barak'kino] SM **1** (*chiosco*) stall **2** (*apparecchio*) CB radio
baraccone [barak'kone] SM booth, stall; **baracconi** SMPL (*parco dei divertimenti*) funfair *sg*; **fenomeno da baraccone** circus freak
baraccopoli [barak'kɔpoli] SF INV shanty town
baraonda [bara'onda] SF (*confusione*) chaos; (*movimento di gente*) hubbub, bustle
barare [ba'rare] VI (*aus* **avere**) to cheat; **hai barato!** you cheated!
baratro ['baratro] SM (*anche fig*) abyss
barattare [barat'tare] VT: **barattare qc con qc** (*merce*) to barter sth for sth; (*francobolli, dischi*) to swap sth for sth (*Brit*), to trade sth for sth (*Am*)
baratto [ba'ratto] SM (*Comm*) barter; (*scambio*) exchange; **fare un baratto con qn** to swap with sb (*Brit*), to trade with sb (*Am*)
barattolo [ba'rattolo] SM (*di vetro*) jar; (*di latta*) tin, can; (*di plastica*) pot
barba ['barba] SF **1** beard; **ha la barba** he's got a beard; **farsi la barba** to shave; **una barba di 3 giorni** 3 days' growth; **farsi crescere la barba** to grow a beard; **farla in barba a qn** (*fig*) to fool sb; **servire qn di barba e capelli** (*fig*) to teach sb a lesson; **che barba!** (*persona, libro*) what a bore! **2** (*Bot*) (fine) root
barbabietola [barba'bjɛtola] SF beetroot (*Brit*), beet (*Am*); **barbabietola da zucchero** sugar beet
Barbados [bar'bados] SF Barbados *sg*
barbagianni [barba'dʒanni] SM INV barn owl
barbaramente [barbara'mente] AVV (*uccidere*) savagely; (*saccheggiare*) barbarously
barbarico, a, ci, che [bar'bariko] AGG (*invasione*) barbarian; (*usanze, metodi*) barbaric
barbarie [bar'barje] SF INV (*condizione*) barbarism; (*crudeltà*) barbarity
barbaro, a ['barbaro] AGG (*popolo*) barbarian; (*comportamento, crimine*) barbaric, barbarous; (*stile, gusto*) appalling
■ SM barbarian; **i Barbari** SMPL the Barbarians
barbecue ['ba:bikju:] SM INV barbecue
barbiere [bar'bjɛre] SM barber; **fa il barbiere** he's a barber; **devo andare dal barbiere** I need a haircut
barbiturico, a, ci, che [barbi'turiko] AGG barbituric
■ SM barbiturate
barboncino [barbon'tʃino] SM poodle
barbone[1] [bar'bone] SM (*anche:* **cane barbone**) (French) poodle
barbone[2], a SM/F (*vagabondo*) tramp, vagrant
barboso, a [bar'boso] AGG boring
barbuto, a [bar'buto] AGG bearded
barca[1], che ['barka] SF boat; **andare in barca** (*a vela*) to go sailing; (*a remi*) to go boating; **si è comprato una barca** he's bought himself a boat; **barca a motore** motorboat; **barca a remi** rowing boat (*Brit*), rowboat (*Am*); **barca a vela** sailing boat (*Brit*), sailboat (*Am*)
barca[2] ['barka] SF (*fig: quantità*): **una barca di** heaps of, tons of; **ha una barca di soldi** she's got loads of money
barcaiolo [barka'jɔlo] SM boatman
barcamenarsi [barkame'narsi] VIP (*nel lavoro*) to get by
Barcellona [bartʃel'lona] SF Barcelona
barcollamento [barkolla'mento] SM staggering
barcollare [barkol'lare] VI (*aus* **avere**) to stagger; **ha barcollato ed è caduto** he staggered and fell
barcone [bar'kone] SM (*quadrangolare*) scow; (*per costruzione di ponti*) pontoon
bardare [bar'dare] VT (*cavallo*) to harness; (*fig: persona*) to dress up
► **bardarsi** VR to dress up
bardatura [barda'tura] SF (*di cavallo*) harness; (*fig*) finery
bardo ['bardo] SM bard
bardotto [bar'dɔtto] SM (*Zool*) hinny
barella [ba'rɛlla] SF (*per malati*) stretcher; **l'hanno portato via in barella** he was carried away on a stretcher
barelliere [barel'ljɛre] SM stretcher bearer
Barents ['barents] SM: **il mare di Barents** the Barents Sea
barese [ba'rese] AGG of *o* from Bari
■ SM/F inhabitant *o* native of Bari
bargiglio, gli [bar'dʒiʎʎo] SM wattle
baricentro [bari'tʃɛntro] SM centre (*Brit*) *o* center (*Am*) of gravity
barile [ba'rile] SM (*gen*) barrel; (*di vino*) cask, barrel
bario ['barjo] SM barium
barista, i, e [ba'rista] SM/F (*cameriere*) barman/barmaid; (*proprietario*) bar owner; **fa la barista** she works in a bar

> **LO SAPEVI...?**
> **barista** non si traduce mai con la parola inglese ***barrister***

baritonale [barito'nale] AGG baritone *attr*
baritono [ba'ritono] SM baritone
barlume [bar'lume] SM (faint) light; (*fig: di speranza, idea*) glimmer
baro ['baro] SM (*Carte*) cardsharp
barocco, a, chi, che [ba'rɔkko] AGG, SM baroque
barometro [ba'rɔmetro] SM barometer
baronale [baro'nale] AGG baronial
barone [ba'rone] SM baron; **i baroni della medicina** (*fig pegg*) the big shots in the medical profession
baronessa [baro'nessa] SF baroness
baronetto [baro'netto] SM baronet
barra ['barra] SF **1** (*gen*) bar; (*di legno, metallo*) rod, bar; **barra delle applicazioni** (*Inform*) taskbar; **barra di rimorchio** (*Aut*) tow bar; **barra di scorrimento** (*Inform*) scroll bar; **barra spaziatrice** space-bar; **barra stabilizzatrice** (*Aut*) anti-roll bar; **barra degli strumenti** (*Inform*) toolbar; **barre laterali** *o* **antintrusione** (*Aut*) side impact bars **2** (*Naut*) helm; (*: piccola*) tiller **3** (*segno tipografico*) slash; **barra inversa** backslash
barracano [barra'kano] SM barracan
barracuda [barra'kuda] SM INV barracuda
barrage [ba'raʒ] SM INV (*Equitazione*) jump-off
barrare [bar'rare] VT to bar; **barrate la risposta esatta** tick the right answer
barricare [barri'kare] VT to barricade
► **barricarsi** VR: **barricarsi in/dietro** to barricade o.s. in/behind; **barricarsi in camera** to shut o.s. up in one's room

barricata [barri'kata] SF barricade; **essere dall'altra parte della barricata** (*fig*) to be on the other side of the fence
barricato, a [barri'kato] AGG (*vino*) aged in oak barrels
barriera [bar'rjɛra] SF (*gen, fig, Fis*) barrier; (*corallina*) reef; (*Calcio*) wall; (*Equitazione: ostacolo*) pole; **la Grande Barriera Corallina** the Great Barrier Reef; **barriera doganale** trade *o* tariff barrier; **la barriera del suono** the sound barrier; **le barriere architettoniche** physical obstacles (*preventing access to buildings by the disabled*)
barrique [bar'rik] SM INV oak barrel
barrire [bar'rire] VI (*aus* **avere**) to trumpet
barrito [bar'rito] SM trumpeting
barroccio, ci [bar'rɔttʃo] SM cart
baruffa [ba'ruffa] SF quarrel, row; **fare baruffa** to quarrel, have a row
barzelletta [bardzel'letta] SF joke, funny story; **raccontare una barzelletta** to tell a joke; **mi ha raccontato una barzelletta molto divertente** he told me a very funny joke
basalto [ba'zalto] SM basalt
basamento [baza'mento] SM (*parte inferiore, piedistallo*) base; (*Tecn*) bed, base plate

> **LO SAPEVI...?**
> **basamento** non si traduce mai con la parola inglese *basement*

basare [ba'zare] VT: **basare (su)** (*argomento*) to base (on), found (on); (*edificio*) to build on; **il film è basato su un fatto realmente accaduto** the film is based on a true story
▶ **basarsi** VR: **basarsi su** (*sogg: argomento, fatti, prove*) to be based on, be founded on; (*: persona*) to base o.s. on, base one's arguments on; (*: edificio*) to be built on; **mi baso sulle esperienze precedenti** I'm going on past experience
basco, a, schi, sche ['basko] AGG Basque
■ SM/F Basque
■ SM **1** (*lingua*) Basque **2** (*berretto*) beret
bascula ['baskula], **basculla** [bas'kulla] SF weighing machine, weighbridge
basculante [basku'lante] AGG (*bussola, tavolo*) self-stabilizing
base ['baze] SF **1** (*gen, Mil, Chim, Mat*) base; **la base della lampada** the lamp base; **la base del partito** (*Pol*) the rank and file of the party **2** (*fig: fondamento*) basis; (*: di problema, idea*) origin, root; **base di partenza** starting point **3 basi** SFPL (*fondamento*) basis *sg*, foundation *sg*; **gettare le basi per qc** to lay the basis *o* foundations for sth; **avere buone basi** (*Scol*) to have a sound educational background **4** (*fraseologia*): **prodotto a base di carne** meat-based product; **liquore a base di caffè** coffee liqueur; **essere alla base di qc** to be at the basis of; (*di problema*) to be at the root of; **la fiducia stava alla base della nostra amicizia** trust was the basis of our friendship; **servire da** *o* **come base a** (*punto di partenza*) to act as the basis for; **di base** basic; **il suo stipendio di base è piuttosto basso** her basic salary is quite low; **regole di base** basic rules; **in base a** (*notizie, informazioni*) according to; **in base a ciò...** on that basis ...; **in base a questo depliant ci sono tre alberghi** according to this brochure there are three hotels; **sulla base di** on the basis of
■ AGG INV (*prezzo, problema, stipendio*) basic
baseball ['bezbol] SM INV baseball
▷ www.baseball-softball.it/
basetta [ba'zetta] SF side whisker, sideburn
BASIC ['beisik] SIGLA M (*Inform*) BASIC
basico, a, ci, che ['baziko] AGG (*Chim*) basic
basilare [bazi'lare] AGG basic, fundamental
Basilea [basi'lɛa] SF Basle
basilica, che [ba'zilika] SF basilica
basilico [ba'ziliko] SM (*Bot*) (sweet) basil
basito, a [ba'zito] AGG: **rimanere basito** to be astounded
basket ['basket] SM INV (*sport*) basketball; **gioco a basket** I play basketball
bassa ['bassa] SF lowlands *pl*
bassamente [bassa'mente] AVV (*in modo vile*) meanly
bassezza [bas'settsa] SF (*d'animo, di sentimenti*) baseness; (*azione*) base action
bassista, i; , e [bas'sista] SM/F bass player
basso, a ['basso] AGG **1** (*gen*) low; (*persona*) short; (*suono*) soft, low; (*: profondo*) deep; **il volume è troppo basso** the sound's too low; **parlare a voce bassa** to speak in a low voice; **è basso e grasso** he's short and fat; **Simona è più bassa di me** Simona is shorter than me; **i rami bassi** the lower *o* bottom branches; **a occhi bassi** with lowered eyes; **l'ho avuto a basso prezzo** I got it cheap; **c'è bassa marea** it's low tide, the tide is out; **in quel punto l'acqua è bassa** the water's shallow there; **in bassa stagione** in the low season **2** (*inferiore: qualità*) poor, inferior; (*abietto: azione, istinto*) base, mean **3** (*Geog*): **il basso Po** the lower Po; **i Paesi Bassi** the Netherlands **4** (*Storia: tardo*) late; **il basso Medioevo** the late Middle Ages; **basso latino** low Latin
■ AVV (*volare, mirare*) low; (*parlare*) softly, in a low voice
■ SM **1** (*parte inferiore*) bottom, lower part; (*: di pagina*) foot, bottom; **in basso** at the bottom; **io sono quella in basso a destra nella foto** I'm the one in the bottom right of the photo; **è là in basso** it's down there; **più in basso** lower down; **mettilo un po' più in basso** put it a bit lower down; **scendere da basso** to go downstairs; **cadere in basso** (*fig*) to come down in the world **2** (*Mus*) bass; **suonare il basso** to play bass (guitar)
bassofondo [basso'fondo] SM (*pl* **bassifondi**) shallows *pl*; **i bassifondi (della città)** (*quartieri emarginati*) the seediest parts of the town
bassopiano [basso'pjano] SM (*pl* **bassopiani** *o* **bassipiani**) low-lying plain
bassorilievo [bassori'ljɛvo] SM (*pl* **bassorilievi**) bas-relief
bassotto, a [bas'sɔtto] AGG squat
■ SM (*cane*) dachshund
bastante [bas'tante] AGG sufficient
bastardaggine [bastar'daddʒine] SF (*pegg*) meanness, rottenness
bastardo, a [bas'tardo] AGG bastard *attr*; (*animale*) crossbred; (*pianta*) hybrid; **cane bastardo** mongrel
■ SM/F (*figlio, anche insulto*) bastard; **bastardo!** (*fam*) (you) bastard!
■ SM (*cane*) mongrel
bastare [bas'tare] VI (*aus* **essere**) **1** to be enough, be sufficient; **questa pasta non basta per cinque persone** this pasta isn't enough for five people; **bastare a qn** to be enough for sb; **mi bastano 10 euro per oggi** 10 euro will do me *o* will be sufficient (for me) for today; **75 euro ti bastano per 2 giorni** 75 euro will last you 2 days; **fatti bastare questi soldi!** mind you make this money last!; **bastare a se stesso** to be self-sufficient **2** (*fraseologia*): **basta!** that's enough!, stop it!, that will do!; **punto e basta!** and that's that!; **basta con queste scuse** enough of these excuses; **dimmi basta** (*versando da bere*) say when!; **basta così?**

Bb

(*al bar ecc*) will that be all?; **basta così, grazie** that's enough, thank you; (*nei negozi*) that's all, thank you; **basta e avanza** that's more than enough
■ VB IMPERS: **basta chiedere** *o* **che chieda a un vigile** you have only to *o* need only ask a policeman; **basta rivolgersi all'ufficio competente** you just have to contact the relevant department; **non basta volerlo, bisogna sapere come fare** it's not enough to want to, you have to know how to; **e come se non bastasse...** and as if that wasn't enough ...; **basti dire che...** suffice it to say that ...; **basta un niente per farla arrabbiare** the slightest thing will get her annoyed, it only takes the slightest thing to annoy her; **quanto basta** as much as is necessary; **basta che** (*purché*) provided (that); **basta che tu lo chieda** you only have to ask

bastian [bas'tjan] SM: **bastian contrario** awkward customer

bastimento [basti'mento] SM ship, vessel

bastione [bas'tjone] SM bastion

basto ['basto] SM pack saddle

bastonare [basto'nare] VT to beat, thrash; **avere l'aria di un cane bastonato** to look crestfallen

bastonata [basto'nata] SF blow (*with a stick*); **prendere qn a bastonate** to give sb a beating; **l'hanno ucciso a bastonate** they beat him to death

bastoncello [baston'tʃɛllo] SM (*Anat*) retinal rod

bastoncino [baston'tʃino] SM (*piccolo bastone*) small stick; (*Tecn*) rod; (*Sci*) ski pole; **bastoncini di pesce** (*Culin*) fish fingers (*Brit*), fish sticks (*Am*)

bastone [bas'tone] SM **1** (*gen*) stick; (*Rel*) staff; **l'ha picchiato con un bastone** he hit him with a stick; **mettere i bastoni fra le ruote a qn** (*fig*) to put a spoke in sb's wheel; **bastone da passeggio** walking stick **2** **bastoni** SMPL (*Carte*) *suit in Neapolitan pack of cards*

batacchio, chi [ba'takkjo] SM (*di campana*) clapper; (*di porta*) (door-)knocker

batida [ba'tida] SM INV (*drink*) batida

batiscafo [batis'kafo] SM bathyscaph

batista [ba'tista] SF (*tessuto*) batiste

batosta [ba'tɔsta] SF (*colpo, smacco*) blow; (*Sport: sconfitta*) beating

battage [ba'taʒ] SM INV: **battage promozionale** *o* **pubblicitario** hype

battaglia [bat'taʎʎa] SF (*Mil*) battle; (*fig*) fight

battagliero, a [battaʎ'ʎɛro] AGG (*esercito, popolo*) warlike; (*fig: spirito, persona*) aggressive

battaglio, gli [bat'taʎʎo] SM (*di campana*) clapper; (*di porta*) (door-)knocker

battaglione [battaʎ'ʎone] SM battalion

battelliere [battel'ljɛre] SM boatman

battello [bat'tɛllo] SM (*gen*) boat; (*canotto*) dinghy; **battello pneumatico** rubber dinghy; **battello di salvataggio** lifeboat

battente [bat'tɛnte] SM **1** (*di finestra*) shutter; (*di porta*) *one side of a double door*; **porta a due battenti** double door; **chiudere i battenti** (*fig*) to shut up shop **2** (*per bussare*) (door-)knocker **3** (*di orologio*) hammer

battere ['battere] VT **1** (*percuotere: persona*) to beat, strike, hit; (*: panni, tappeti*) to beat; (*: ferro*) to hammer; (*: grano*) to thresh; **battere il ferro finché è caldo** (*fig*) to strike while the iron is hot; **batté un pugno sul tavolo** he beat his fist on the table; **battersi il petto** to beat one's breast; (*fig*) to repent; **battere (a macchina)** to type; **battere il tempo** *or* **battere il ritmo** (*Mus*) to beat time **2** (*avversario*) to beat, defeat; (*concorrenza, record*) to beat; **in matematica nessuno lo batte** there's no one to beat him at maths; **li abbiamo battuti due a zero** we beat them two nil; **ha battuto il record mondiale** she's beaten the world record **3** (*urtare: parte del corpo*) to hit; **ha battuto il mento sul gradino** he hit his chin on the step; **batteva i denti per il freddo** his teeth were chattering with the cold; **battere i piedi** to stamp one's feet; **battere i tacchi** to click one's heels; **battere le mani** to clap one's hands **4** (*sbattere: ali*) to beat; **senza battere ciglio** without batting an eyelid; **in un batter d'occhio** in the twinkling of an eye **5** (*rintoccare: le ore*) to strike; **il pendolo batteva le 8** the grandfather clock was striking 8 o'clock **6** (*Culin*) to beat **7** (*Sport: palla*) to hit; **battere un rigore** (*Calcio*) to take a penalty **8** (*percorrere: campagna, paese*) to scour, comb; (*Caccia*) to beat; **battere (il marciapiede)** (*esercitare la prostituzione*) to be on the game **9** **battersela** to run off **10** (*Fin*): **battere moneta** to mint coin
■ VI (*aus* **avere**) **1** (*cuore, polso*) to beat; (*pioggia, sole*): **gli batteva forte il cuore** his heart was beating fast; **battere (su)** to beat down (on); **la pioggia batteva sui vetri** the rain beat *o* lashed against the window panes; **battere in testa** (*Aut*) to knock **2** (*insistere*): **battere su** to insist on; **battere su un argomento** to harp on a topic **3** (*bussare*): **battere (a)** to knock (at) **4** **battere in ritirata** to beat a retreat, fall back
▶ **battersi** VIP (*lottare*) to fight; (*: fig*) to fight, battle; **battersi all'ultimo sangue** to fight to the last

batteria [batte'ria] SF **1** (*Elettr, Mil, Agr*) battery; **la batteria è scarica** the battery's flat; **batteria da cucina** pots and pans *pl* **2** (*Sport*) heat **3** (*Mus*): **la batteria** the drums *pl*; **suona la batteria** he plays the drums

battericida, i [batteri'tʃida] SM germicide

batterico, a, ci, che [bat'tɛriko] AGG bacterial

batterio, ri [bat'tɛrjo] SM bacterium; **batteri patogeni** bacteria which cause disease

batteriologia [batterjolo'dʒia] SF bacteriology

batteriologico, a, ci, che [batterjo'lɔdʒiko] AGG bacteriological; **guerra batteriologica** germ *o* biological warfare

batteriologo, gi [batte'rjɔlogo] SM bacteriologist

batterista, i, e [batte'rista] SM/F drummer

battesimale [battezi'male] AGG baptismal

battesimo [bat'tezimo] SM **1** (*sacramento*) baptism; (*rito*) christening, baptism; **nome di battesimo** Christian name; **tenere qn a battesimo** to be godfather (*o* godmother) to sb **2** (*cerimonia inaugurale: di nave*) christening; **battesimo dell'aria** first flight; **battesimo del fuoco** baptism of fire

battezzare [batted'dzare] VT **1** (*Rel*) to baptize, christen; (*nave*) to christen **2** (*chiamare*) to call, name, christen; (*fig: dare un soprannome*) to nickname

battibaleno [battiba'leno] SM: **in un battibaleno** in a flash

battibecco, chi [batti'bekko] SM squabble

batticarne [batti'karne] SM INV steak hammer

batticuore [batti'kwɔre] SM palpitations *pl*; **avevo il batticuore** (*fig*) my heart was thumping

battigia, gie [bat'tidʒa] SF water's edge

battimano [batti'mano] SM applause *no pl*, clapping *no pl*

battipanni [batti'panni] SM INV carpet beater

battiscopa [battis'kopa] SM INV skirting (board)

battista, i, e [bat'tista] AGG, SM/F Baptist; **San Giovanni Battista** Saint John the Baptist

battistero [battis'tɛro] SM baptist(e)ry
battistrada [battis'trada] SM INV **1** *(di pneumatico)* tread **2** *(Sport)* pacemaker; **fare da battistrada** *(in una gara)* to set the pace, make the running; **fare da battistrada a qn** *(fig)* to prepare the way for sb
battitappeto [battitap'peto] SM INV upright vacuum cleaner; **passare il battitappeto** to vacuum, hoover
battito ['battito] SM *(pulsazione)* beat, throb; **battito della pioggia/dell'orologio** drumming of the rain/ ticking of the clock; **battito cardiaco** heartbeat
battitore [batti'tore] SM **1** *(Cricket)* batsman; *(Baseball)* batter **2** *(Caccia)* beater
battitura [batti'tura] SF **1** *(anche:* **battitura a macchina***)* typing **2** *(del grano)* threshing
battuta [bat'tuta] SF **1** *(Teatro)* cue; *(osservazione)* remark; *(spiritosaggine)* witty remark; **fare una battuta** to crack a joke, make a witty remark; **aver la battuta pronta** *(fig)* to have a ready answer; **ma dai, era solo una battuta** come on, it was only a joke; **non ho perso una battuta della loro conversazione** I didn't miss a word of what they were saying; **è ancora alle prime battute** *(progetto, commedia)* it's just started **2** *(di caccia)* beat, beating; *(di polizia)*: **fare una battuta in una zona** to scour *o* comb an area **3** *(Tennis)* service; **alla battuta Federer** Federer is now serving **4** *(Mus)* bar; **battuta d'arresto** *o* **d'aspetto** bar rest; **gli affari hanno subito una battuta d'arresto** it's a slack period for business **5** *(di macchina da scrivere)* key stroke
battuto [bat'tuto] SM *(Culin)* mirepoix
batuffolo [ba'tuffolo] SM wad; **un batuffolo di cotone** a wad of cotton wool
bau bau ['bau 'bau] ESCL woof woof!, bow wow!
baud [bod] SM INV *(Telec)* baud
baule [ba'ule] SM *(valigia)* trunk; *(Aut)* boot *(Brit)*, trunk *(Am)*
bauxite [bauk'site] SF bauxite
bava ['bava] SF *(di persona, bambino)* dribble; *(di animale)* slaver, slobber; *(di cane idrofobo)* foam; *(di lumaca)* slime; *(di baco da seta)* silk filament; **aver la bava alla bocca** *(anche fig)* to be foaming at the mouth; **non c'era nemmeno una bava di vento** there wasn't a breath of wind
bavaglino [bavaʎ'ʎino] SM bib
bavaglio, gli [ba'vaʎʎo] SM gag; **mettere il bavaglio a qn/qc** *(anche fig)* to gag sb/sth; **si è liberato del bavaglio** he got the gag off
bavarese [bava'rese] AGG, SM/F Bavarian
■ SF *(Culin)* bavarois
bavero ['bavero] SM collar
Baviera [ba'vjɛra] SF Bavaria
bavoso, a [ba'voso] AGG dribbling
bazar [bad'dzar] SM INV bazaar
bazooka [bə'zu:kə] SM INV bazooka
bazzecola [bad'dzɛkola] SF (mere) trifle
bazzicare [battsi'kare] VT *(persona)* to hang about with; *(posto)* to hang about *o* around
■ VI *(aus* **avere***)* **bazzicare con qn** to hang about with sb; **bazzicare in un posto** to hang about *o* around a place
BCE [bitʃi'e] SIGLA F (= **Banca Centrale Europea**) ECB (= *European Central Bank*)
beach volley [bitʃvollei] SF beach volleyball
▷ www.beachvolley.it/
bearsi [be'arsi] VIP: **bearsi di qc/a fare qc** to delight in sth/in doing sth; **bearsi alla vista di** to feast one's eyes on
beatamente [beata'mente] AVV blissfully; **vivere beatamente** to lead a life of bliss
beatificare [beatifi'kare] VT *(Rel)* to beatify
beatitudine [beati'tudine] SF *(Rel)* beatitude; *(felicità)* bliss
beato, a [be'ato] AGG *(Rel)* blessed; *(felice)* blissfully happy; **una vita beata** a life of bliss; **beata ignoranza** blissful ignorance; **beato lui!** lucky him!, how lucky he is!; **beato chi ti vede!** *(fam)* long time no see!
beauty-case ['bju:ti'keis] SM INV vanity bag *o* case *o* box
bebè [be'bɛ] SM INV baby
beccaccia, ce [bek'kattʃa] SF woodcock; **beccaccia di mare** oystercatcher
beccaccino [bekkat'tʃino] SM snipe
beccare [bek'kare] VT **1** *(sogg: uccello)* to peck (at) **2** *(fam: cogliere sul fatto)* to nab, catch; **l'hanno beccato a rubare in un negozio** they caught him shoplifting; **non mi becchi più!** you won't catch me out like that again! **3** *(fam: beccarsi)* to get; **beccarsi un raffreddore** to catch a cold
▶ **beccarsi** VR *(uso reciproco: uccelli)* to peck (at) one another; (: *fig: litigare)* to squabble
beccata [bek'kata] SF peck
beccheggiare [bekked'dʒare] VI *(aus* **avere***)* *(Aer, Naut)* to pitch
beccheggio, gi [bek'keddʒo] SM *(Aer, Naut)* pitching
beccherò *ecc* [bekke'rɔ] VB *vedi* **beccare**
becchime [bek'kime] SM birdseed
becchino [bek'kino] SM gravedigger
becco¹, chi ['bekko] SM **1** *(di uccello)* beak, bill; **non ho il becco di un quattrino** *(fam)* I'm broke **2** *(fam: bocca)* mouth; **chiudi il becco!** shut your mouth!, shut your trap!; **mettere il becco in qc** to poke one's nose into sth; **tu non mettere becco!** you keep out of this! **3** *(bruciatore)* burner; **becco Bunsen** Bunsen burner **4** *(di caffettiera)* spout
becco², chi ['bekko] SM *(Zool)* billy-goat; *(fig fam)* cuckold
beccofrusone [bekkofru'zone] SM waxwing
beccuccio, ci [bek'kuttʃo] SM *(di ampolla, bricco)* lip; *(di teiera)* spout
beduino, a [bedu'ino] AGG, SM/F Bedouin
Befana [be'fana] SF **1** *(festività) national holiday (Jan 6, feast of the Epiphany)* **2** *(personaggio) kind old woman who, according to legend, comes down the chimney* **3** *(donna brutta)* old hag, old witch

BEFANA

Marking the end of the traditional 12 days of Christmas on 6 January, the **Befana**, or the feast of the Epiphany, is a national holiday in Italy. It is named after the old woman who, legend has it, comes down the chimney the night before, bringing gifts to children who have been good during the year and leaving lumps of coal for those who have not.

beffa ['bɛffa] SF: **farsi beffa** *o* **beffe di qn** to make a fool of sb; **farsi beffa** *o* **beffe di qc** to make fun of sth; **ma questa è una beffa!** this is some kind of sick joke!
beffardamente [beffarda'mente] AVV mockingly
beffardo, a [bef'fardo] AGG mocking
beffare [bef'fare] VT to make a fool of, mock
▶ **beffarsi** VIP: **beffarsi di** to scoff at
beffeggiare [beffed'dʒare] VT to laugh at, mock

Bb

bega, ghe ['bɛga] SF (*litigio*) quarrel, dispute; (*problema*): **non voglio beghe** I don't want any trouble
begli ['bɛʎʎi] AGG *vedi* **bello**
begonia [be'gɔnja] SF begonia
beh [bɛ] ESCL well!
bei ['bɛi] AGG *vedi* **bello**
beige [bɛʒ] AGG INV beige; **una gonna beige** a beige skirt
Beirut [bei'rut] SF Beirut
bel[1] [bɛl] AGG *vedi* **bello**
bel[2] [bɛl] SM INV (*Fis*) bel
belare [be'lare] VI (*aus* **avere**) (*Zool, fig*) to bleat
belato [be'lato] SM bleating
belga, gi, ghe ['bɛlga] AGG, SM/F Belgian
Belgio ['bɛldʒo] SM Belgium; **andremo in Belgio quest'estate** we're going to Belgium this summer; **mi è piaciuto molto il Belgio** I really liked Belgium
Belgrado [bel'grado] SF Belgrade
bella ['bɛlla] SF **1** beauty, belle; (*innamorata*) sweetheart; **la Bella addormentata nel bosco** Sleeping Beauty **2** (*anche:* **bella copia**) fair copy **3** (*Sport, Carte*) deciding match
belladonna [bella'dɔnna] SF (*Bot*) deadly nightshade
bellamente [bella'mente] AVV (*gentilmente*) nicely; (*comodamente*) comfortably, at one's ease
belletto [bel'letto] SM (*ant*) rouge
bellezza [bel'lettsa] SF **1** (*qualità*) beauty; (*: di donna*) beauty, loveliness; (*: di uomo*) handsomeness; **una donna di eccezionale bellezza** an exceptionally beautiful woman; **un istituto di bellezza** a beauty salon; **chiudere** *o* **finire qc in bellezza** to finish sth with a flourish; **e per finire in bellezza...** (*iro*) and to round it all off perfectly ...; **che bellezza!** fantastic! **2** (*persona, cosa*) beauty; **ciao bellezza!** hello gorgeous!; **le bellezze di Roma** the beauties *o* sights of Rome; **questo vestito è una bellezza** this dress is really lovely **3** (*quantità*): **ho pagato la bellezza di trecento euro** I paid three hundred euros, no less; **ha impiegato la bellezza di 2 anni a finirlo** he took a good 2 years to finish it
bellico, a, ci, che ['bɛlliko] AGG war *attr*; **macchina bellica** war machine; **industria bellica** arms industry; **materiale bellico** military material
bellicosamente [bellikosa'mente] AVV belligerently
bellicosità [bellikosi'ta] SF belligerence
bellicoso, a [belli'koso] AGG (*popolo, nazione*) warlike; (*fig: persona*) quarrelsome
belligerante [bellidʒe'rante] AGG belligerent
belligeranza [bellidʒe'rantsa] SF belligerence
bellimbusto [bellim'busto] SM dandy

bello, a ['bɛllo] PAROLA CHIAVE

■ AGG (*davanti sm* bel + *consonante*, bell' + *vocale*, bello + *s impura, gn, pn, ps, x, y, z, pl* bei + *consonante*, begli + *s impura ecc o vocale*)

1 (*oggetto, donna, paesaggio*) beautiful, lovely; (*uomo*) handsome, good-looking; **le Belle Arti** fine arts; **che bello!** how lovely!; **è una gran bella donna** she's a very good-looking woman; **belle maniere** elegant manners; **il bel mondo** high society; **una bella pettinatura** a nice hairstyle

2 (*tempo*) fine, beautiful, lovely; **fa bello** the weather's lovely *o* beautiful; **è una bella giornata** it's a lovely *o* beautiful day; **fa bel tempo** it's lovely weather

3 (*quantità*) considerable; **una bella cifra** a considerable sum of money; **ha avuto un bel coraggio** he was very brave; (*iro*) he had a nerve; **ce n'è rimasto un bel pezzo** there's still a good bit left

4 (*buono*) good, fine; **una bella azione** a good deed; **fare una bella dormita** to have a nice long sleep; **una bella idea** a good *o* nice idea; **un bel lavoro** a good job; **un bel pensiero** a kind thought; **una bella tazza di tè** a nice cup of tea

5 (*rafforzativo*): **è una truffa bella e buona!** it's a real con!; **è bell'e fatto** it's done now; **sei un bel matto** you're absolutely crazy; **nel bel mezzo di** right in the middle of; **non mi ha dato un bel niente** he gave me absolutely nothing

6 (*fraseologia*): **dirne delle belle** to tell some whoppers; **farne delle belle** to get up to mischief; **farsi (più) bello** to get better looking; **è andata a farsi bella** she's gone to make herself beautiful; **farsi bello di qc** (*vantarsi*) to show off about sth; **alla bell'e meglio** somehow or other; **oh bella!** *or* **è bella!** (*iro*) that's nice!; **fare la bella vita** to lead an easy life

■ SM

1 **il bello** the beautiful, beauty; **amare il bello** to love beauty *o* beautiful things; **il bello è che...** the best bit about it is that ...; **adesso viene il bello** (*iro*) now comes the best bit; **che fai di bello stasera?** what are you doing this evening?; **proprio sul più bello** at that very moment

2 (*tempo*): **si sta mettendo al bello** the weather is clearing up

■ SM/F (*fidanzato*) sweetheart

bellunese [bellu'nese] AGG of *o* from Belluno
■ SM/F inhabitant *o* native of Belluno
belva ['belva] SF wild beast *o* animal; **essere una belva** (*fig*) to be an animal
belvedere [belve'dere] SM INV panoramic viewpoint
bemolle [be'mɔlle] SM INV (*Mus*) flat
benché [ben'ke] CONG although, though
benda ['bɛnda] SF (*Med*) bandage; (*per gli occhi*) blindfold; **avere gli occhi coperti da una benda** to be blindfolded; **avere la benda agli occhi** (*fig*) to be blind
bendaggio, gi [ben'daddʒo] SM (*atto*) bandaging; (*effetto*) bandage
bendare [ben'dare] VT (*ferita*) to bandage; (*occhi*) to blindfold; **mi ha bendato la mano** he bandaged my hand; **l'hanno bendato e imbavagliato** he was blindfolded and gagged
bendisposto, a [bendis'posto] AGG: **essere bendisposto verso qn/qc** to be well-disposed towards sb/sth

bene ['bɛne] PAROLA CHIAVE

■ AVV

1 (*gen*) well; (*funzionare*) properly, well; **faresti bene a studiare** you'd do well *o* you'd be well advised to study; **hai fatto bene** you did the right thing; **ben fatto!** well done!; **guida bene** he drives well, he's a good driver; **parla bene l'italiano** he speaks Italian well, he speaks good Italian; **parlare bene di qn** to speak well of sb; **gente per bene** respectable people; **sto poco bene** I'm not very well; **ha preso bene la notizia** he took the news well; **se ben ricordo** *or* **bene** if I remember correctly; **sto bene** I'm fine; **va bene** all right, okay

2 (*con attenzione, completamente*): **ascoltami bene** listen to me carefully; **ben bene** thoroughly; **ho legato il pacco ben bene** I've tied the parcel securely; **hai capito bene?** do you understand?; **chiudi bene la**

porta close the door properly; **per bene** thoroughly; **ho sistemato le cose per bene** I've sorted things out properly

3 (*molto*: + *aggettivo*) very; (: + *comparativo, avverbio*) (very) much; **ben contento** very pleased; **è ben difficile** it's very difficult; **ben più caro** much more expensive; **ben più lungo** much longer

4 (*rafforzativo*: *appunto*): **lo credo bene** I'm not surprised; **te l'avevo ben detto io che...** I DID tell you that ..., I certainly did tell you that ...; **sai bene che non dovresti uscire** you know perfectly well you shouldn't go out; **come tu ben sai** as you well know; **lo so ben io** *or* **fin troppo bene** I know only too well; **lo spero bene** I certainly hope so

5 (*addirittura, non meno di*) at least; **hai fatto ben 7 errori** you've made at least 7 mistakes; **sono ben 3 giorni che non la vedo** I haven't seen her for at least 3 days

6 (*in esclamazioni*): **ho finito — bene!** I've finished — good!; **bene, allora possiamo partire** right then, we can go; **bene, puoi continuare da solo** all right, you can continue on your own; **bene bene!** good (good)!

7 (*fraseologia*): **né bene né male** so-so; **di bene in meglio** better and better; **tutto è bene quel che finisce bene** all's well that ends well

■ AGG INV: **la gente bene** (*ricca, snob*) well-to-do people; **la Roma bene** the Roman bourgeois

■ SM

1 good; **far del bene** to do good; **fare del bene a qn** to do sb a good turn; **fare bene a** (*salute*) to be good for; **quella vacanza ti ha fatto bene** that holiday has done you good; **a fin di bene** for a good reason; **sul tavolo c'era ogni ben di Dio** there were all sorts of good things on the table; **l'ho fatto per il suo bene** I did it for his own good; **è stato un bene** it was a good thing; **volere un bene dell'anima a qn** to love sb very much; **vuole molto bene a suo padre** he loves his father very much, he's very fond of his father

2 beni SMPL (*proprietà, anche Dir*) possessions, property *sg*; (*Econ*) goods; **beni ambientali** the environment *sg*; **beni di consumo** consumer goods; **beni culturali** cultural heritage *sg*

▷ www.fondoambiente.it/

▷ www.beniculturali.it/

beni (di) rifugio *safe assets bought during periods of inflation*; **beni immobili** property *sg* (*Brit*), real estate *sg* (*Am*); **beni mobili** personal *o* movable property *sg*; **beni patrimoniali** fixed assets; **beni privati** private property *sg*; **beni pubblici** public property *sg*

benedettino, a [benedet'tino] AGG, SM/F Benedictine

benedetto, a [bene'detto] PP *di* **benedire**

■ AGG blessed; (*santo*) holy; **acqua benedetta** holy water; **Dio benedetto!** Good Lord!

benedire [bene'dire] VT IRREG (*persona*) to bless; (*chiesa*) to consecrate; **che Dio ti benedica!** God bless you!; **l'ho mandato a farsi benedire** (*fig*) I told him to go to hell

benedizione [benedit'tsjone] SF (*atto*) blessing; (*funzione*) benediction; **dare la propria benedizione a qn** to bless sb

beneducato, a [benedu'kato] AGG well-mannered, polite

benefattore, trice [benefat'tore] SM/F benefactor/ benefactress

beneficenza [benefi'tʃɛntsa] SF charity; **fare opere di beneficenza** to do charity work; **istituto di beneficenza** charitable organization; **festa di beneficenza** charity event; **concerto di beneficenza** charity concert

beneficiare [benefi'tʃare] VI (*aus* **avere**) **beneficiare di** to benefit by, benefit from; **beneficiare di una borsa di studio** to be awarded a scholarship

beneficiario, ria, ri, rie [benefi'tʃarjo] AGG, SM/F (*Dir*) beneficiary

beneficio, ci [bene'fitʃo] SM benefit; **trarre beneficio da** to benefit from *o* by; **il beneficio del dubbio** the benefit of the doubt; **con beneficio d'inventario** (*fig*) with reservations; **trarre beneficio da** to benefit from

benefico, a, ci, che [be'nefiko] AGG (*gen*) beneficial; (*persona*) charitable; **un effetto benefico** a beneficial effect; **un'associazione benefica** a charitable organization

Benelux ['bɛneluks] SM: **il Benelux** the Benelux countries, Benelux

benemerenza [beneme'rɛntsa] SF merit; **attestato di benemerenza** certificate of merit

benemerito, a [bene'merito] AGG meritorious

beneplacito [bene'platʃito] SM (*approvazione*) approval; (*permesso*) permission

benessere [be'nɛssere] SM, SOLO SG (*salute*) well-being; (*agiatezza*) comfort

benestante [benes'tante] AGG well-to-do, well-off; **una famiglia benestante** a well-off family; **viene da una famiglia più benestante della mia** his family is better off than mine

■ SM/F: **essere un benestante** to be well-off

■ **i benestanti** SMPL the well-off

benestare [benes'tare] SM INV approval

beneventano, a [beneven'tano] AGG of *o* from Benevento

■ SM/F inhabitant *o* native of Benevento

benevolente [benevo'lɛnte] AGG (*letter*) benevolent

benevolenza [benevo'lɛntsa] SF benevolence; **trattare qn con benevolenza** to treat sb kindly

benevolmente [benevol'mente] AVV kindly, benevolently

benevolo, a [be'nɛvolo] AGG benevolent

benfatto, a [ben'fatto] AGG (*lavoro*) good; (*mobile*) well made; (*pietanza*) well cooked; **una ragazza benfatta** a girl with a good figure

Bengala [ben'gala] SM Bengal

bengala [ben'gala] SM INV Bengal light

bengalese [benga'lese] AGG, SM/F Bengali

■ SM (*lingua*) Bengali

bengodi [ben'gɔdi] SM land of plenty

beniamino, a [benja'mino] SM/F favourite (*Brit*), favorite (*Am*); **è il beniamino della maestra** he's the teacher's pet

benignamente [beniɲɲa'mente] AVV kindly

benignità [beniɲɲi'ta] SF (*cortesia*) kindness; **trattare con benignità** to treat kindly

benigno, a [be'niɲɲo] AGG (*gen, Med*) benign; (*sguardo, sorriso*) kindly, kind; (*critica*) favourable (*Brit*), favorable (*Am*); **tumore benigno** benign tumour

benintenzionato, a [benintentsjo'nato] AGG well-meaning; **in fondo era benintenzionato** after all he meant well

beninteso [benin'teso] AVV (*certamente*) of course, certainly

■ **beninteso che** CONG provided that

benpensante [benpen'sante] SM/F conformist

benservito [benser'vito] SM reference; **dare il**

Bb

benservito a qn (*sul lavoro*) to give sb the sack, fire sb; (*fig*) to send sb packing

bensì [ben'si] CONG (*ma*) but (rather); (*anzi*) on the contrary

benvenuto, a [benve'nuto] AGG welcome; **benvenuti a Roma!** welcome to Rome!
■ SM/F: **essere il(la) benvenuto(a)** to be welcome
■ SM welcome; **dare il benvenuto a qn** to welcome sb

benvisto, a [ben'visto] AGG: **essere benvisto (da)** to be well thought of (by)

benvolere [benvo'lere] VT DIF: **farsi benvolere da tutti** to win everybody's affection; **prendere a benvolere qn/qc** to take a liking to sb/sth

benvoluto, a [benvo'luto] AGG loved, well liked

benzina [ben'dzina] SF petrol (*Brit*), gas(oline) (*Am*); **rimanere senza benzina** to run out of petrol *o* gas; **siamo rimasti senza benzina** we ran out of petrol; **fare benzina** to get petrol *o* gas; **benzina normale** 3-star petrol (*Brit*), normal grade gasoline (*Am*); **benzina super** 4-star petrol (*Brit*), premium gasoline (*Am*); **benzina verde** *o* **senza piombo** unleaded petrol *o* gas, lead-free petrol *o* gas

benzinaio, aia, ai, aie [bendzi'najo] SM/F (*persona*) petrol (*Brit*) *o* gas (*Am*) pump attendant
■ SM (*posto*) petrol station

benzodiazepina [bendzodjadze'pina] SF (*Med*) benzodiazepene

beone, a [be'one] SM heavy drinker

bequadro [be'kwadro] SM INV (*Mus*) natural

bere ['bere] VT IRREG (*gen*) to drink; (*fig: assorbire*) to soak up; **vuoi bere qc?** would you like sth to drink?; **bere un bicchiere di vino/un caffè** to have a glass of wine/a (cup of) coffee; **chi porta da bere?** who's going to bring the drinks?; **ti offro** *o* **ti pago da bere** I'll buy you a drink; **bere qc tutto d'un fiato** to down sth in one gulp; **bevi un po' d'acqua** have a drink of water; **sono le preoccupazioni a farlo bere** his problems have made him turn to drink; **bere come una spugna** to drink like a fish; **bere per dimenticare** to drown one's sorrows (in drink); **bere alla salute di qn** to drink to sb's health; **il motore beve la benzina** the engine is heavy on petrol; **bere le parole di qn** to drink in sb's words; **questa volta non me la dai a bere!** I won't be taken in this time!; **questa non la bevo** I'm not buying that
■ SM drink; **si è dato al bere** he has turned to drink

bergamasco, a, schi, sche [berga'masko] AGG of *o* from Bergamo
■ SM/F inhabitant *o* native of Bergamo

bergamotto [berga'mɔtto] SM bergamot

berillio [be'rilljo] SM (*Chim*) beryllium

Bering ['berɛ̃ŋ] SM: **il mar di Bering** the Bering Sea

berlina[1] [ber'lina] SF: **mettere alla berlina** (*fig*) to hold up to ridicule

berlina[2] [ber'lina] SF (*Aut*) saloon (car) (*Brit*), sedan (*Am*)

berlinese [berli'nese] AGG Berlin *attr*, of *o* from Berlin
■ SM/F Berliner

Berlino [ber'lino] SF Berlin; **nella vecchia Berlino est...** in former East Berlin...

Bermuda [ber'muda] SFPL: **le Bermuda** Bermuda *sg*

bermuda [ber'muda] SMPL (*calzoni*) Bermuda shorts; **un paio di bermuda** a pair of Bermuda shorts

Berna ['bɛrna] SF Bern

bernoccolo [ber'nɔkkolo] SM bump; **ho un bernoccolo in fronte** I've got a bump on my forehead; **avere il bernoccolo di qc** (*fig: disposizione*) to have a bent *o* flair for sth

berretta [ber'retta] SF cap; **berretta da prete** biretta

berretto [ber'retto] SM cap; **berretto da baseball** baseball cap; **berretto con visiera** peaked cap

berrò *ecc* [ber'rɔ] VB *vedi* **bere**

bersagliare [bersaʎ'ʎare] VT (*colpire ripetutamente*) to bombard; **bersagliare di pugni** to rain blows on; **bersagliare di domande** to bombard with questions; **è bersagliato dalla sfortuna** he's dogged by ill fortune

bersagliere [bersaʎ'ʎɛre] SM *member of rifle regiment in Italian army*

bersaglio, gli [ber'saʎʎo] SM target; (*fig*) target, butt; **colpire il bersaglio** to hit the target; (*fig*) to reach one's target; **ha mancato il bersaglio** he missed the target; **era il bersaglio di tutti i loro scherzi** he was the butt of all their jokes

bertuccia, ce [ber'tuttʃa] SF Barbary ape

besciamella [beʃʃa'mɛlla] SF béchamel sauce

bestemmia [bes'temmja] SF (*gen*) curse; (*Rel*) blasphemy; **dire una bestemmia** to swear; (*Rel*) to blaspheme

bestemmiare [bestem'mjare] VT (*gen*) to curse, swear; (*Rel*) to blaspheme; **non l'ho mai sentito bestemmiare** I've never heard him swear; **bestemmiare come un turco** to swear like a trooper

bestemmiatore, trice [bestemmja'tore] SM/F (*gen*) swearer; (*Rel*) blasphemer

bestia ['bestja] SF (*anche fig*) beast, animal; **non voglio bestie in casa!** I don't want animals in the house!; **andare in bestia** to fly into a rage; **lavorare come una bestia** to work like a dog; **mi guardavano come se fossi una bestia rara** they looked at me as if I came from another planet; **bestia!** (*sciocco*) you stupid fool!; **bestia feroce** wild beast *o* animal; **bestia da macello** animal for slaughter; **bestia da soma** beast of burden; **bestia da tiro** draught animal

bestiale [bes'tjale] AGG (*gen*) brutal; (*passione, istinto*) animal *attr*; (*fam: terribile*) beastly, terrible; **ha fatto un freddo bestiale** it's been terribly cold; **fa un caldo bestiale** it's absolutely boiling, it's terribly hot; **ho una fame bestiale** I could eat a horse

bestialità [bestjali'ta] SF INV **1** (*qualità*) brutality; (*perversione sessuale*) bestiality **2 dire/fare una bestialità dopo l'altra** to say/do one idiotic thing after another

bestialmente [bestjal'mente] AVV brutishly, like an animal

bestiame [bes'tjame] SM livestock; (*bovino*) cattle *pl*

bestiola [bes'tjɔla] SF (small) animal

betabloccante [betablok'kante] AGG: **farmaco betabloccante** (*Med*) beta-blocker

Betlemme [bet'lɛmme] SF Bethlehem

betoniera [beto'njɛra] SF cement mixer

bettola ['bettola] SF tavern; (*pegg*) dive; **contegno da bettola** coarse behaviour

betulla [be'tulla] SF birch; **betulla argentata** *o* **bianca** silver birch

bevanda [be'vanda] SF drink, beverage (*frm*); **bevanda alcolica/non alcolica** alcoholic/soft drink

beveraggio, gi [beve'raddʒo] SM (*per animali*) bran mash; (*pozione*) potion; **beveraggi** SMPL (*bevande*) drinks

beverone [beve'rone] SM (*per animali*) bran mash
bevibile [be'vibile] AGG drinkable
bevitore, trice [bevi'tore] SM/F drinker; **un gran bevitore** a heavy drinker
bevo *ecc* ['bevo] VB *vedi* **bere**
bevuta [be'vuta] SF drink; **fare una (bella) bevuta** to have a booze-up (*fam*)
bevuto, a [be'vuto] PP *di* **bere**
bevvi *ecc* ['bevvi] VB *vedi* **bere**
BG SIGLA = *Bergamo*
BI [bi] SIGLA F = *Banca d'Italia*
■ SIGLA = *Biella*
biacca, che ['bjakka] SF (*anche:* **biacca di piombo**) white lead
biada ['bjada] SF fodder
biadesivo, a [biade'zivo] AGG: **nastro biadesivo** double-sided sticky tape
Biancaneve [bjanka'neve] SF Snow White
biancheggiare [bjanked'dʒare] VI (*aus* **avere**) to look white
biancheria [bjanke'ria] SF (*per casa*) linen; **biancheria da donna** ladies' underwear, lingerie; **biancheria intima** underwear
bianchetto [bjan'ketto] SM **1** (*per scarpe*) whitener; **dare il bianchetto alle scarpe** to whiten one's shoes **2** (*correttore*) whiteout, Tippex®
bianchezza [bjan'kettsa] SF whiteness
bianchiccio, cia, ci, ce [bjan'kittʃo] AGG whitish, off-white; (*persona*) pale
bianco, a, chi, che ['bjanko] AGG **1** (*gen*) white; **essere bianco come un cencio** to be as white as a sheet; **avere i capelli bianchi** to have white hair, be white-haired; **ha i capelli bianchi** she's got white hair; **far venire i capelli bianchi a qn** (*fig*) to make sb's hair turn white; **notte bianca** *o* **in bianco** sleepless night **2** (*pagina*) blank; **votare scheda bianca** to return a blank voting slip **3** (*Mus*): **voce bianca** treble (voice)
■ SM **1** (*colore*) white; (*intonaco*) whitewash; (*vino*) white wine; **vestire di bianco** to dress in white; **in bianco e nero** (*TV, Fot*) black and white; **passare una notte in bianco** to have a sleepless night; **andare in bianco** (*non riuscire*) to fail; (*fam: in amore*) to fail to score **2** (*non scritto*): **un assegno in bianco** a blank cheque; **lasciare in bianco** to leave blank **3** (*Culin*): **bianco d'uovo** egg-white; **pesce/carne in bianco** boiled fish/meat; **mangiare in bianco** to be on a light *o* bland diet
■ SM/F (*persona*) white man/white woman
biancosegno [bjanko'seɲɲo] SM (*Dir*) signature to a blank document
biancospino [bjankos'pino] SM hawthorn
biascicare [bjaʃʃi'kare] VT to mumble
biasimare [bjazi'mare] VT (*persona*) to blame; (*condotta, azione*) to disapprove of, censure; **non posso biasimarti** I don't blame you
biasimevole [bjazi'mevole] AGG blameworthy
biasimo ['bjazimo] SM (*vedi vt*) blame; disapproval, censure; **degno di biasimo** blameworthy
Bibbia ['bibbja] SF Bible
biberon [bibe'rɔn] SM INV (baby's) bottle, feeding bottle
bibita ['bibita] SF drink; **vendono gelati e bibite** they sell ice cream and drinks; **bibita analcolica** soft drink
biblico, a, ci, che ['bibliko] AGG biblical
bibliografia [bibljogra'fia] SF bibliography
bibliografico, a, ci, che [bibljo'grafiko] AGG bibliographical
bibliografo, a [bibli'ɔgrafo] SM/F bibliographer
biblioteca, che [bibljo'tɛka] SF (*edificio*) library; (*mobile*) bookcase
▷ www.internetculturale.it/
bibliotecario, ria, ri, rie [bibljote'karjo] SM/F librarian
biblioteconomia [bibljotekono'mia] SF librarianship
bicamerale [bikame'rale] AGG (*sistema*) bicameral *attr*
■ SF (*anche:* **commissione bicamerale**) *parliamentary commission consisting of members of both houses*
bicarbonato [bikarbo'nato] SM: **bicarbonato (di sodio)** bicarbonate (of soda)
bicchierata [bikkje'rata] SF (*bevuta*) drink
bicchiere [bik'kjɛre] SM glass; **bicchiere di vino** glass of wine; **bere un bicchiere** to have a drink; **è (facile) come bere un bicchier d'acqua** it's as easy as pie; **bicchiere a calice** goblet; **bicchiere di carta** paper cup; **bicchiere graduato** measuring jug; **bicchiere da vino** wine glass
bicefalo, a [bi'tʃɛfalo] AGG two-headed
bici ['bitʃi] SF INV (*fam*) bike
bicicletta [bitʃi'kletta] SF bicycle, bike; **andare in bicicletta** to cycle, to ride a bike; **sai andare in bicicletta?** can you ride a bike?; **ci andai in bicicletta** I went there on my bike; **bicicletta da corsa** racing cycle
▷ www.fiab-onlus.it/
bicilindrico, a, ci, che [bitʃi'lindriko] AGG (*Tecn*) two-cylinder *attr*
bicipite [bi'tʃipite] AGG **1** (*Anat*): **(muscolo) bicipite** biceps *sg o pl* **2** (*che ha due teste*) two-headed
■ SM biceps *sg o pl*
bicocca, che [bi'kɔkka] SF hovel
bicolore [biko'lore] AGG two-tone; **governo bicolore** (*Pol*) two-party government
bicromato [bikro'mato] SM dichromate
bicromia [bikro'mia] SF (*procedimento*) two-colour printing; (*illustrazione*) two-colour print
bidè, bidet [bi'dɛ] SM INV bidet
bidello, a [bi'dɛllo] SM/F (*di scuola*) janitor; (*di università*) porter
bidimensionale [bidimensjo'nale] AGG two-dimensional
bidirezionale [bidirettsjo'nale] AGG bidirectional
bidonare [bido'nare] VT (*fam: imbrogliare*) to cheat, swindle; (*: piantare in asso*) to let down
bidonata [bido'nata] SF (*fam: imbroglio*) swindle; (*: delusione*) let-down; **fare** *o* **tirare una bidonata a qn** (*imbrogliare*) to cheat *o* do sb; (*deludere*) to let sb down
bidone [bi'done] SM **1** (*recipiente*) drum; (*più piccolo*) can; **bidone da latte** churn; **bidone per la spazzatura** *o* **dei rifiuti** *o* **dell'immondizia** dustbin **2** = **bidonata**
bidonville [bidɔ̃'vil] SF INV shanty town
biecamente [bjeka'mente] AVV sinisterly, in a sinister way
bieco, a, chi, che ['bjɛko] AGG sinister
biella ['bjɛlla] SF (*Tecn*) connecting rod
biellese [bjel'lese] AGG of *o* from Biella
■ SM/F inhabitant *o* native of Biella
Bielorussia [bjelo'russja] SF Belarus, Belorussia
bielorusso, a AGG, SM/F Belarussian, Belorussian
biennale [bien'nale] AGG (*che dura 2 anni*) two-year *attr*; (*che avviene ogni 2 anni*) two-yearly, biennial; **la mostra è biennale** the exhibition is held every two years
■ SF: **la Biennale di Venezia** *the Venice Arts Festival*

Bb

BIENNALE

Dating back to 1895, the **Biennale di Venezia** is an international festival of the contemporary arts. It takes place every two years in the "Giardini Pubblici". The various countries taking part each put on exhibitions in their own pavilions. There is a section dedicated to the work of young artists, as well as a special exhibition organized around a specific theme for that year.
▷ www.labiennale.org/

biennalmente [biennal'mente] AVV (*vedi agg*) every two years; biennially
biennio, ni [bi'ɛnnjo] SM **1** period of two years; **nel prossimo biennio** over the next two years **2** (*Univ*) two-year foundation course
bierre [bi'ɛrre] SM/F *member of the Red Brigades*
bietola ['bjɛtola] SF (*Bot*) chard; (*fam: barbabietola*) beet
bifamiliare [bifami'ljare] AGG (*villa, casetta*) semi-detached
■ SF semi-detached house
bifase [bi'faze] AGG (*Elettr*) two-phase *attr*
bifocale [bifo'kale] AGG bifocal
bifolco, a, chi, che [bi'folko] SM/F (*pegg*) bumpkin, yokel
bifora ['bifora] SF (*Archit*) mullioned window
biforcarsi [bifor'karsi] VIP (*fiume, strada*) to divide, fork; (*Ferr*) to branch
biforcazione [biforkat'tsjone] SF (*di fiume, strada*) fork; (*Ferr*) junction
biforcuto, a [bifor'kuto] AGG (*anche fig*) forked; **lingua biforcuta** forked tongue
bifronte [bi'fronte] AGG (*anche fig*) two-faced
big [big] SM INV (*dello spettacolo*) star; (*dell'industria*) big noise, big shot
bigamia [biga'mia] SF bigamy
bigamo, a ['bigamo] AGG bigamous
■ SM/F bigamist
bighellonare [bigello'nare] VI (*aus* **avere**) to loaf about
bighellone, a [bigel'lone] SM/F loafer
bigio, gia, gi, ge *o* gie ['bidʒo] AGG dull grey
bigiotteria [bidʒotte'ria] SF (*gioielli*) costume jewellery (*Brit*) *o* jewelry (*Am*); (*negozio*) shop selling costume jewel(le)ry
biglia ['biʎʎa] SF = **bilia**
bigliardo [biʎ'ʎardo] SM = **biliardo**
bigliettaio, aia, ai, aie [biʎʎet'tajo] SM/F (*in treno*) ticket inspector; (*in autobus*) conductor/conductress; (*in cinema, teatro*) box-office attendant
bigliettazione [biʎʎettat'tsjone] SF: **bigliettazione automatica** (*su autobus*) automatic ticketing system
biglietteria [biʎʎette'ria] SF (*gen*) ticket office; (*di teatro*) box office; (*per prenotazioni*) booking office
biglietto [biʎ'ʎetto] SM **1** (*per viaggio, entrata*) ticket; **fare/comprare il biglietto** to get/buy one's ticket; **hai fatto il biglietto?** have you bought a ticket?; **biglietto di andata e ritorno** return (ticket) (*Brit*), round-trip ticket (*Am*); **biglietto aperto** (*Aer*) open ticket; **biglietto chiuso** (*Aer*) closed ticket; **biglietto omaggio** complimentary ticket; **biglietto di (sola) andata** single (ticket) (*Brit*), one-way ticket (*Am*) **2** (*banconota*): **biglietto (di banca)** banknote, note, bill (*Am*); **un biglietto da 10 euro** a 10 euro note **3** (*nota*) note; (*cartoncino*) card; **mi ha mandato un biglietto per il compleanno** he sent me a card for my birthday; **biglietto d'auguri** greetings card; **biglietto da visita** visiting card

BIGLIETTI

Bus, tram and underground tickets can be bought in tobacconists' and newsagents' shops and must be stamped in the special machines on entering the bus, tram or underground station. You can often buy a book of ten tickets. Rail tickets on the other hand can be purchased at station ticket offices and travel agencies, and must be stamped before departure using the special yellow machines in the stations.
▷ www.trenitalia.it/

bignè [biɲ'ɲɛ] SM INV cream puff
bigodino [bigo'dino] SM roller
bigoncia, ce [bi'gontʃa] SF wooden tub
bigotteria [bigotte'ria] SF pharisaism
bigotto, a [bi'gɔtto] AGG pharisaic
■ SM/F pharisee
bijou [bi'ʒu] SM INV (*gioiello*) piece of costume jewellery; (*fig*) jewel, gem
bikini [bi'kini] SM INV bikini
bilancia, ce [bi'lantʃa] SF **1** (*gen*) scales *pl*; (*a due piatti*) pair of scales; (*di precisione*) balance; (*bascula*) weighing machine; **mettere qc sulla bilancia** to weigh sth; (*fig*) to weigh sth up; **hai una bilancia?** have you got any scales? **2** (*Astrol: Bilancia*) Libra; **essere della Bilancia** to be Libra **3** (*Econ*): **bilancia commerciale/dei pagamenti** balance of trade/payments **4** (*Pesca*) drop-net
bilanciare [bilan'tʃare] VT **1** (*tenere in equilibrio*) to balance; **bilanciare il carico** to spread the load evenly **2** (*Comm*) to balance; **bilanciare le uscite e le entrate** to balance expenditure and revenue; **le uscite bilanciano le entrate** expenditure and revenue balance out **3** (*fig: valutare*) to weigh up
▶ **bilanciarsi** VR **1** (*uso reciproco: equipararsi*) to be equal **2** (*stare in equilibrio*) to balance (o.s.)
bilanciato, a [bilan'tʃato] AGG balanced
bilanciere [bilan'tʃɛre] SM (*di orologio*) balance wheel; (*di motore*) compensator; (*per sollevamento pesi*) bar
bilancino [bilan'tʃino] SM (*bilancia*) balance; (*sci nautico*) ski rope handle; **dobbiamo pesare la questione col bilancino** we must weigh up the problem very carefully
bilancio, ci [bi'lantʃo] SM (*Comm: cifre*) balance; (: *documento*) balance sheet; **fare il bilancio** *or* **chiudere il bilancio** to draw up the balance sheet; **far quadrare il bilancio** to balance the books; **chiudere il bilancio in attivo/passivo** to make a profit/loss; **fare il bilancio della situazione** (*fig*) to assess the situation; **bilancio consolidato** consolidated balance; **bilancio consuntivo** final balance; **bilancio preventivo** budget; **bilancio mensile/settimanale** monthly/weekly balance; **bilancio dello stato** budget; **bilancio di verifica** trial balance
bilaterale [bilate'rale] AGG bilateral
bilateralmente [bilateral'mente] AVV bilaterally
bile ['bile] SF (*Med*) bile; (*fig: rabbia*) anger, rage; **era verde dalla bile** he was white with rage
bilia ['bilja] SF **1** (*di vetro*) marble; **giocare a bilie** to play marbles **2** (*da biliardo: pallina*) billiard ball; (: *buca*) (billiard) pocket
biliardino [biljar'dino] SM (small) billiard table; (*elettrico*) pinball

biliardo [bi'ljardo] SM pool; (*tavolo*) pool table; **giocare a biliardo** to play pool; **sai giocare a biliardo?** can you play pool?; **sala da biliardo** poolroom
▷ www.fibis.it/

biliare [bi'ljare] AGG (*Med*) biliary; **calcolo biliare** gallstone

bilico ['biliko] SM: **essere** *o* **stare in bilico** to be balanced; (*fig*) to be undecided; **essere in bilico tra la vita e la morte** to be suspended between life and death; **tenere qn in bilico** to keep sb in suspense

bilingue [bi'lingwe] AGG bilingual

bilinguismo [bilin'gwizmo] SM bilingualism

bilione [bi'ljone] SM (*mille milioni*) thousand million, billion (*Am*); (*milione di milioni*) billion (*Brit*), trillion (*Am*)

bilioso, a [bi'ljoso] AGG (*fig*) bad-tempered

bilocale [bilo'kale] SM two-room flat (*Brit*) *o* apartment (*Am*)

bimbo, a ['bimbo] SM/F (*bambino*) child, little boy/girl; (*bebè*) baby

bimensile [bimen'sile] AGG twice-monthly, fortnightly (*Brit*)

bimestrale [bimes'trale] AGG (*che dura 2 mesi*) two-month *attr*; (*che avviene ogni 2 mesi*) two-monthly, bimonthly; **pagamento bimestrale** payment every 2 months; **rivista bimestrale** bimonthly magazine

bimestralmente [bimestral'mente] AVV every two months

bimestre [bi'mɛstre] SM two-month period; **ogni bimestre** every two months

bimetallico, a, ci, che [bime'talliko] AGG bimetallic

bimotore [bimo'tore] AGG twin-engined
■ SM (*aereo*) twin-engined plane

binario[1], ria, ri, rie [bi'narjo] AGG (*Astron, Chim, Mat, Mus*) binary

binario[2], ri [bi'narjo] SM (*rotaie*) (railway) track *o* line; (*piattaforma*) platform; **uscire dai binari** to come off the rails; (*fig*) to go off the rails; **camminava lungo il binario** he was walking along the track; **da quale binario parte il treno per Cambridge?** which platform does the Cambridge train go from?; **binario morto** dead-end track; **siamo su un binario morto** (*fig*) we're not going to get anywhere; **binario unico/doppio** single/double track

binocolo [bi'nɔkolo] SM (*gen*) binoculars *pl*; (*da teatro*) opera glasses *pl*; **guardava gli uccelli con il binocolo** she was looking at the birds through binoculars; **binocolo prismatico** prism binoculars

binoculare [binoku'lare] AGG binocular

binomio, mia, mi, mie [bi'nɔmjo] AGG binomial
■ SM **1** (*Mat*) binomial **2** (*fig: due persone*): **il binomio Laurel e Hardy** the Laurel and Hardy duo

bio... ['bio] PREF bio...

bioagricolo, a [bioa'grikolo] AGG organic

bioagricoltura [bioagrikol'tura] SF organic farming

bioarchitettura [bioarkitet'tura] SF environmentally friendly architecture, eco-friendly architecture

biochimica [bio'kimika] SF biochemistry

biochimico, a, ci, che [bio'kimiko] AGG biochemical
■ SM/F biochemist

biocompatibile [biokompa'tibile] AGG environmentally friendly, eco-friendly

biocompatibilità [biokompatibili'ta] SF eco-friendliness

biodegradabile [biodegra'dabile] AGG biodegradable

biodegradabilità [biodegradabili'ta] SF biodegradability

biodinamica [biodi'namika] SF biodynamics

biodinamico, a; , ci; , che [biodi'namiko] AGG biodynamic

biodiversità [biodiversi'ta] SF INV biodiversity
▷ www.biodiversita.info/
▷ www.abc-onlus.org/

bioetica [bio'ɛtika] SF bioethics *sg*

bioetico, a, ci, che [bio'ɛtiko] AGG bioethical

biofabbrica [bio'fabbrika] SF factory producing biological control agents

biofisica [bio'fizika] SF biophysics *sg*

biofisico, a, ci, che [bio'fiziko] AGG biophysical
■ SM/F biophysicist

biogenetica [biodʒe'nɛtika] SF biogenesis

biogenetico, a; , ci; , che [biodʒe'nɛtiko] AGG biogenic

biografia [biogra'fia] SF biography

biografico, a, ci, che [bio'grafiko] AGG biographical

biografo, a [bi'ɔgrafo] SM/F biographer

bioingegneria [bioindʒeɲɲe'ria] SF bioengineering

biologia [biolo'dʒia] SF biology

biologico, a, ci, che [bio'lɔdʒiko] AGG (*scienze, fenomeni ecc*) biological; (*agricoltura, prodotti*) organic; **guerra biologica** biological warfare

biologo, a, gi, ghe [bi'ɔlogo] SM/F biologist; **è biologa** she's a biologist

biondeggiare [bjonded'dʒare] VI (*aus* **avere**) (*letter: messi*) to be golden

biondiccio, cia, ci, ce [bjon'dittʃo] AGG fairish, blondish

biondo, a ['bjondo] AGG (*capelli*) fair, blond; (*persona*) fair, fair-haired; **biondo cenere/platino** ash/platinum blond
■ SM (*colore*) blond; (*uomo*) fair-haired man
■ SF (*donna*) blonde

bionica [bi'ɔnika] SF bionics *sg*

bionico, a, ci, che [bi'ɔniko] AGG bionic

biopsia [bio'psia] SF biopsy

bioritmo [bio'ritmo] SM biorhythm

bios [bi'os] SM INV (*Inform*) BIOS

biosfera [bios'fɛra] SF biosphere

biotech [bio'tɛk] SM INV, AGG biotech

biotecnologia [bioteknolo'dʒia] SF biotechnology

biotecnologico, a; , ci; , che [biotekno'lodʒiko] AGG biotechnological

bioterrorismo [bioterro'rizmo] SM bioterrorism

bioterrorista, i; , e [bioterro'rista] SM/F bioterrorist

bipartitico, a, ci, che [bipar'titiko] AGG (*Pol*) two-party *attr*

bipartitismo [biparti'tizmo] SM (*Pol*) two-party system

bipartito, a [bipar'tito] (*Pol*) AGG two-party *attr*
■ SM two-party alliance

bipede ['bipede] AGG, SM biped

biplano [bi'plano] SM biplane

bipolare [bipo'lare] AGG bipolar

bipolarismo [bipola'rizmo] SM *a situation in which the political parties in a country form themselves into two opposing blocks*

bipolarista, i; , e [bipola'rista] AGG (*Pol*) bipolar

biposto [bi'posto] AGG INV two-seater *attr*

birba ['birba] SF rascal, rogue

birbante [bir'bante] SM rascal, rogue

birbanteria [birbante'ria] SF (*qualità*) mischievousness; (*azione*) mischievous trick

birbonata [birbo'nata] SF naughty trick

birbone, a [bir'bone] AGG (*bambino*) naughty; **fare un tiro birbone a qn** to play a naughty trick on sb
■ SM/F (*bambino*) little rascal

Bb

bireattore [bireat'tore] SM twin-engined jet
birichinata [biriki'nata] SF prank, practical joke
birichino, a [biri'kino] AGG (*bambino*) mischievous, impish; (*adulto*) sly; **sguardo birichino** sly look
■ SM/F (*bambino*) little rascal, scamp
birillo [bi'rillo] SM skittle (*Brit*), pin (*Am*); **birilli** SMPL (*gioco*) skittles *sg*
Birmania [bir'manja] SF Burma
birmano, a [bir'mano] AGG, SM/F Burmese
■ SM (*lingua*) Burmese
biro® ['biro] SF INV biro®
birra ['birra] SF (*gen*) beer, ale; **fabbrica di birra** brewery; **a tutta birra** (*fig: veloce*) at top speed, flat out; **birra in bottiglia** bottled beer; **birra chiara** lager; **birra scura** stout; **birra alla spina** draught beer
▷ www.birreonline.net
birraio, ai [bir'rajo] SM (*fabbricante*) brewer
birreria [birre'ria] SF (*locale*) ≈ bierkeller (*fabbrica*) brewery
bis [bis] ESCL encore!
■ SM INV encore; **chiedere il bis** (*Teatro*) to call for an encore; (*fig: a tavola*) to ask for a second helping; **fare il bis di** to have some more; **facciamo il bis di gelato?** shall we have some more ice cream?
■ AGG INV (*treno, autobus*) relief *attr* (*Brit*), additional; (*numero*): **12 bis** 12a
bisaccia, ce [bi'zattʃa] SF knapsack
Bisanzio [bi'zantsjo] SF Byzantium
bisavolo, a [bi'zavolo], **bisavo, a** [bi'zavo] SM/F great-grandfather *m*, great-grandmother *f*
■ **bisavoli** SMPL (*antenati*) forefathers
bisbeticamente [bizbetika'mente] AVV ill-temperedly, crabbily
bisbetico, a, ci, che [biz'bɛtiko] AGG ill-tempered, crabby
bisbigliare [bizbiʎ'ʎare] VT, VI (*aus* **avere**) (*anche fig*) to whisper; **mi ha bisbigliato qc all'orecchio** he whispered sth in my ear
bisbiglio[1], **glii** [bizbiʎ'ʎio] SM (*anche fig*) whisper
bisbiglio[2], **gli** [biz'biʎʎo] SM (*anche fig*) whispering
bisboccia, ce [biz'bɔttʃa] SF binge, spree; **fare bisboccia** to go on a binge
bisca, sche ['biska] SF gambling den
Biscaglia [bis'kaʎʎa] SF: **il golfo di Biscaglia** the Bay of Biscay
biscazziere [biskat'tsjɛre] SM *manager (o owner) of a gambling den*
bischero ['biskero] SM **1** (*fam: toscano*) fool, idiot **2** (*Mus*) peg
biscia, sce ['biʃʃa] SF grass snake; **biscia d'acqua** water snake
biscottato, a [biskot'tato] AGG crisp; **fette biscottate** rusks
biscottiera [biskot'tjɛra] SF biscuit barrel; (*di latta*) biscuit tin
biscottificio, ci [biskotti'fitʃo] SM biscuit factory
biscotto [bis'kɔtto] SM biscuit
biscuit [bis'kɥt] SM INV (*anche:* **porcellana di biscuit**) biscuit
bisdrucciolo, a [biz'druttʃolo] AGG (*Gramm*) *with the stress on the fourth-last syllable*
bisecare [bise'kare] VT (*Mat*) to bisect
bisessuale [bisessu'ale] AGG, SM/F bisexual
bisessualità [bisessuali'ta] SF INV bisexuality
bisestile [bizes'tile] AGG: **anno bisestile** leap year
bisettimanale [bisettima'nale] AGG twice-weekly
bisettore, trice [biset'tore] AGG bisecting
■ SF bisector
bisex [bi'sɛks] AGG INV, SM/F INV (*fam*) bi (*fam*), bisexual
bisezione [biset'tsjone] SF (*Geom*) bisection
bisillabo, a [bi'sillabo] AGG disyllabic
■ SM disyllable
bislacco, a, chi, che [biz'lakko] AGG odd, weird; **è una testa bislacca** he's an odd fellow
bislungo, a, ghi, ghe [biz'lungo] AGG oblong
bismuto [biz'muto] SM (*Chim*) bismuth
bisnipote [bizni'pote] SM/F (*di nonni*) great-grandchild, great-grandson/granddaughter; (*di zii*) great-nephew/niece
bisnonno, a [biz'nɔnno] SM/F great-grandfather/grandmother; **i miei bisnonni** my great-grandparents
bisognare [bizoɲ'ɲare] VB IMPERS: **bisogna partire** we must leave, we've got to leave, we'll have to leave; **bisogna parlargli** we'll (*o* I'll) have to talk to him; **bisogna arrivare un'ora prima per il check-in** you have to get there an hour earlier to check in; **bisogna prenotare?** is it necessary to book?; **bisogna che arriviate in tempo** you must *o* you'll have to arrive on time; **bisognerebbe che si decidesse** he should make up his mind; **bisognerebbe telefonargli** we should phone him; **non bisogna lamentarsi sempre** one *o* you shouldn't complain all the time; **bisogna vedere!** (*dipende*) I'll (*o* you'll *ecc*) have to see how things go!; **bisogna proprio dire che...** it has to be said that ...
■ VI (*aus* **essere**) (*aver bisogno*) to need, want; **cosa le bisogna?** (*ant: in negozio*) can I help you?
bisognevole [bizoɲ'ɲevole] AGG (*letter*): **bisognevole di** in need of
bisogno [bi'zoɲɲo] SM **1** (*necessità*) need, necessity; **aver bisogno di** to need, be in need of; **hai bisogno di qc?** do you need anything?; **aver bisogno di fare qc** to need to do sth; **ho bisogno di cambiare dei soldi** I need to change some money; **sentire il bisogno di qc/di fare qc** to feel the need for sth/to do sth; **c'è bisogno di te qui** we need you here; **non c'è bisogno che venga anche tu** there's no need for you to come too; **non c'è bisogno di gridare** there's no need to shout; **in caso di bisogno** if need be, if necessary; **nel momento del bisogno** in one's hour of need **2** (*povertà*) poverty, need; **trovarsi nel bisogno** to be in want **3** (*euf: necessità corporali*): **fare i bisogni** (*persona*) to go to the toilet; (*animale*) to do its business
bisognoso, a [bizoɲ'ɲoso] AGG **1** (*che ha bisogno*): **bisognoso di** in need of, needing; **essere bisognoso di qc** to need sth **2** (*povero*) poor, needy; **le famiglie più bisognose** the poorest families
bisonte [bi'zonte] SM (*Zool*) bison
bisso ['bisso] SM (*tessuto*) fine linen
bistecca, che [bis'tekka] SF steak; **bistecca al sangue/ai ferri** rare/grilled steak
bistecchiera [bistek'kjɛra] SF gridiron
bisticciare [bistit'tʃare] VI (*aus* **avere**), **bisticciarsi** VR (*uso reciproco*) to bicker, squabble, quarrel; **bisticciano sempre** they're always quarrelling
bisticcio, ci [bis'tittʃo] SM **1** (*litigio*) quarrel, squabble **2** (*gioco di parole*) pun, play on words
bistrattare [bistrat'tare] VT to maltreat
bistro ['bistro] SM bistre
bistrò [bis'trɔ] **bistrot** [bis'tro] SM INV (*locale*) bistro
bisturi ['bisturi] SM INV (*Med*) scalpel
bisunto, a [bi'zunto] AGG (*unto*) very greasy; **un cappotto unto e bisunto** a filthy, greasy coat

bit [bit] SM INV *(Inform)* bit
bitorzolo [bi'tortsolo] SM *(sulla testa)* bump; *(sul corpo)* lump
bitorzoluto, a [bitortso'luto] AGG *(albero)* gnarled, knotted; *(faccia)* warty
bitta ['bitta] SF *(Naut: sulla banchina)* bollard; *(: sulla nave)* bitt
bitter ['bitter] SM INV bitters *pl*
bitumare [bitu'mare] VT to bituminize
bitume [bi'tume] SM bitumen
bituminoso, a [bitumi'noso] AGG bituminous
bivaccare [bivak'kare] VI *(aus* **avere***)* *(Mil)* to bivouac; *(fig)* to bed down
bivacco, chi [bi'vakko] SM bivouac
bivio, vi ['bivjo] SM *(di una strada)* fork, junction; **al bivio prendi la strada che va a destra** go right at the junction; **trovarsi davanti a un bivio** *(fig)* to be at a crossroads
bizantino, a [biddzan'tino] AGG Byzantine; *(fig: pedante)* pedantic; **questioni bizantine** convoluted questions
bizza ['biddza] SF tantrum; **fare le bizze** to throw a tantrum; **la macchina fa le bizze oggi** the car is playing up today
bizzarramente [biddzarra'mente] AVV oddly, strangely
bizzarria [biddzar'ria] SF **1** *(qualità)* eccentricity, weirdness **2** *(azione)* whim, caprice; *(cosa)* oddity
bizzarro, a [bid'dzarro] AGG **1** *(strano, eccentrico)* odd, queer, eccentric **2** *(focoso: cavallo)* frisky
bizzeffe [bid'dzɛffe] AVV: **a bizzeffe** in abundance, in plenty, galore; **avere soldi a bizzeffe** to be rolling in money
bizzosamente [biddzosa'mente] AVV *(vedi agg)* irritably; capriciously
bizzoso, a [bid'dzoso] AGG **1** *(irascibile)* irritable, quick-tempered; *(capriccioso)* capricious, self-willed **2** *(ombroso: cavallo)* frisky
BL SIGLA = *Belluno*
blandamente [blanda'mente] AVV mildly
blandire [blan'dire] VT *(alleviare)* to soothe; *(lusingare)* to flatter
blando, a ['blando] AGG *(medicina, rimedio)* mild, gentle; *(liquore)* weak; *(sapore, cibo)* bland; *(punizione)* light, mild
blasfemo, a [blas'fɛmo] AGG blasphemous
■ SM/F blasphemer
blasone [bla'zone] SM coat of arms, escutcheon
blaterare [blate'rare] VI *(aus* **avere***)* to blether
■ VT to blether about; **ma cosa vai blaterando?** what are you blethering about?
blatta ['blatta] SF cockroach
blazer ['bleizə] SM INV blazer
blindare [blin'dare] VT *(veicolo)* to armour; *(porta)* to reinforce
blindata [blin'data] SF *(macchina)* armoured car *o* limousine
blindato, a [blin'dato] AGG armoured *(Brit)*, armored *(Am)*; **camera blindata** strongroom; **mezzo blindato** armoured vehicle; **porta blindata** reinforced door; **vetro blindato** bulletproof glass; **condurre una vita blindata** *(fig)* to live surrounded by maximum security
blister ['blister] SM INV blister pack
blitz [blits] SM INV *(Mil)* blitz; *(di polizia)* swoop, raid
bloccare [blok'kare] VT **1** *(ostruire: strada)* to block (up); *(fermare: assegno, pallone, persona)* to stop; *(: comandi, meccanismo)* to jam; *(: merci)* to stop, hold up; *(: negoziati)* to block, hold up; *(: prezzi, affitti)* to freeze; **la strada è bloccata da una frana** the road is blocked by a landslide; **la neve ha bloccato molti paesi** the snow has cut off many villages, many villages are snow-bound; **la polizia ha bloccato le vie d'accesso alla città** the police have blocked off the roads leading to the city; **ha bloccato la macchina** he braked suddenly, he slammed on the brakes; **blocca la sicura** put on the safety catch; **rimanere bloccato** to be stuck; **sono rimasto bloccato in un ingorgo/nell'ascensore** I was stuck in a traffic jam/in the lift **2** *(Mil)* to blockade **3** *(Inform)* to block
▶ **bloccarsi** VIP *(motore)* to stall; *(freni, porta)* to jam, stick; *(ascensore)* to get stuck, stop; **si è bloccato nel bel mezzo del discorso** he suddenly stopped in the middle of what he was saying; **ho frenato ma la macchina non si è bloccata** I braked, but the car didn't stop
bloccaruota [blokka'rwɔta] AGG INV: **ceppi bloccaruota** wheel clamps *(Brit)*, Denver boot *(Am)*
bloccasterzo [blokkas'tertso] SM *(Aut)* steering lock
bloccherò *ecc* [blokke'rɔ] VB *vedi* **bloccare**
blocchetto [blok'ketto] SM notebook; *(di biglietti)* book; **un blocchetto di biglietti per l'autobus** a book of tickets for the bus; **blocchetto delle ricevute** receipt book
blocchista, i [blok'kista] SM *(Comm)* wholesale dealer
blocco[1], chi ['blɔkko] SM **1** *(gen)* block; **in blocco** *(Comm)* in bulk; **considerare/condannare qc in blocco** *(fig)* to take/condemn sth as a whole; **blocchi di partenza** *(Sport)* starting blocks **2** *(per appunti)* notebook; *(di carta da lettere)* (writing) pad **3** *(Pol)* bloc, coalition; **l'ex blocco orientale** the former Eastern bloc **4** *(Aut)*: **blocco cilindri** cylinder block; **blocco motore** engine block
blocco[2], chi ['blɔkko] SM **1** *(Mil)* blockade; **posto di blocco** *(sul confine)* frontier post; *(di polizia: anche:* **blocco stradale***)* road block **2** *(Comm)* freeze; **blocco degli affitti** rent freeze; **blocco dei salari** wage freeze **3** *(Med)*: **blocco cardiaco** cardiac arrest; **blocco mentale** mental block; **blocco renale** kidney failure
bloc-notes [blɔk'nɔt] SM INV notebook, notepad
blu [blu] AGG INV, SM INV dark blue; **blu scuro** navy (blue); **blu elettrico** electric blue
bluastro, a [blu'astro] AGG bluish
blue jeans [bludʒi:nz] SMPL (blue) jeans
blues [blu:z] SM INV *(Mus)* blues *pl*
bluette [bly'ɛt] AGG INV, SM INV bright blue
bluff [blœf] SM INV *(anche fig)* bluff; **un bluff pubblicitario** a publicity stunt
bluffare [bluf'fare] VI *(aus* **avere***)* *(anche fig)* to bluff
bluffatore, trice [bluffa'tore] SM/F bluffer
blusa ['bluza] SF *(camicetta)* blouse; *(per pittore)* smock; *(per operaio)* overall
blusante [blu'zante] AGG loose-fitting
blusotto [blu'zɔtto] SM jerkin
BN SIGLA = *Benevento*
BO SIGLA = *Bologna*
boa[1] ['bɔa] SM INV **1** *(serpente)* boa (constrictor) **2** *(sciarpa)* feather boa
boa[2] ['bɔa] SF *(Naut)* buoy
boato [bo'ato] SM *(di esplosione)* noise; *(di folla)* roar; *(di tuono)* rumble; **boato sonico** sonic boom
boat people [bot'pipol] SMPL boat people
bob [bɔb] SM INV bobsleigh
bobbista, i, e [bob'bista] SM/F *(Sport)* bobsledder, bobsleigh rider

Bb

bobina [bo'bina] SF **1** (*Elettr*) coil; **bobina d'accensione** (*Aut*) ignition coil **2** (*di film*) reel; (*di pellicola*) spool **3** (*di cotone*) reel, bobbin, spool
BOC [bok] SIGLA M INV (= Buono Ordinario del Comune) *local government bond*
bocca, che ['bokka] SF **1** (*gen*) mouth; **per bocca** orally; **rimanere a bocca asciutta** to have nothing to eat; (*fig*) to be disappointed; **rimanere a bocca aperta** (*fig*) to be taken aback; **non ha aperto bocca** (*parlare*) he didn't open his mouth; **vuoi chiudere la bocca?** (*star zitto*) will you shut up?; **essere sulla bocca di tutti** (*persona, notizia*) to be the talk of the town; **essere di bocca buona** to eat anything; (*fig*) to be easily satisfied; **fare la bocca a qc** to acquire a taste for sth; **non voglio metter bocca in questa storia** I don't want to interfere; **mi hai tolto la parola di bocca** you took the words out of my mouth; **in bocca al lupo!** good luck!; **respirazione bocca a bocca** mouth-to-mouth resuscitation, kiss of life (*fam*) **2** (*di fiume, recipiente*) mouth; **bocca d'acqua** hydrant **3** (*Bot*): **bocca di leone** snapdragon
boccaccia, ce [bok'kattʃa] SF **1** (*smorfia*): **fare le boccacce** to pull faces **2** (*persona maldicente*) foul-mouthed person
boccaglio, gli [bok'kaʎʎo] SM (*Tecn*) nozzle; (*di respiratore*) mouthpiece
boccale[1] [bok'kale] AGG (*Anat*) oral
boccale[2] [bok'kale] SM (*recipiente*) jug; (*per bere*) mug; **boccale da birra** beer mug, tankard
boccaporto [bokka'pɔrto] SM (*Naut*) hatch
boccascena [bokkaʃ'ʃɛna] SM INV proscenium
boccata [bok'kata] SF mouthful; (*di fumo*) puff; **prendere una boccata d'aria** to go out for a breath of (fresh) air
boccetta [bot'tʃetta] SF phial, small bottle
boccheggiante [bokked'dʒante] AGG **1** (*che boccheggia*) gasping (for breath) **2** (*morente*) at one's last gasp
boccheggiare [bokked'dʒare] VI (*aus* **avere**) to gasp
bocchetta [bok'ketta] SF **1** (*di strumento musicale*) mouthpiece; (*di tasca da pasticciere*) nozzle **2** (*di serratura*) plate **3** **bocchetta stradale** drain cover
bocchettone [bokket'tone] SM (*Tecn*) (pipe) union
bocchino [bok'kino] SM (*di pipa, strumento musicale*) mouthpiece; (*per sigarette*) cigarette holder
boccia, ce ['bɔttʃa] SF **1** (*palla di legno, metallo*) bowl; **il gioco delle bocce** bowls *sg*; **giocare a bocce** to play bowls **2** (*bottiglia*) bottle; (*: da vino*) carafe
bocciare [bot'tʃare] VT **1** (*respingere*) to reject; (*: agli esami*) to fail; **essere bocciato agli esami** to fail one's exams; **andava male in tutte le materie ed è stato bocciato** he did badly in all subjects and was kept down **2** (*alle bocce*) to hit
bocciatura [bottʃa'tura] SF (*agli esami*) failure
boccino [bot'tʃino] SM (*Bocce*) jack
boccio, ci ['bɔttʃo] SM bud; **in boccio** (*albero, pianta*) in bud
bocciodromo [bot'tʃɔdromo] SM bowling ground
bocciolo [bot'tʃɔlo] SM bud; **bocciolo di rosa** rosebud
boccola ['bokkola] SF (*fibbia*) buckle
boccolo ['bokkolo] SM curl
bocconcino [bokkon'tʃino] SM (*pietanza deliziosa*) delicacy
boccone [bok'kone] SM (*quantità di cibo*) mouthful; **un boccone di pane** a mouthful of bread; **mangiare un boccone** to have a bite to eat; **finire tutto in un boccone** to gulp everything down at once; **inghiottire un boccone amaro** (*fig*) to swallow a bitter pill; **boccone del prete** (*Culin*) parson's nose
bocconi [bok'koni] AVV face downwards; **cadere bocconi** to fall flat on one's face
body ['bɔdi] SM INV (*intimo*) body stocking; (*per danza, ginnastica*) leotard
Boemia [bo'ɛmja] SF Bohemia
boemo, a [bo'ɛmo] AGG, SM/F Bohemian
boero, a [bo'ɛro] AGG, SM/F Boer
bofonchiare [bofon'kjare] VI (*aus* **avere**) to grumble
Bogotà [bogo'ta] SF Bogotà
bohemien [boe'mjɛ̃] AGG INV, SM/F INV bohemian
boia ['bɔja] SM INV **1** (*carnefice*) executioner; (*: in impiccagione*) hangman; (*fig: mascalzone*) rogue, scoundrel **2** (*in escl: fam*): **boia d'una miseria!, boia d'un mondo ladro!** damn!, blast!
■ AGG INV (*fam*): **fa un freddo boia** it's cold as hell
boiata [bo'jata] SF (*fam: robaccia*) rubbish; **quel film era una boiata** that film was (a load of) rubbish; **non dire boiate!** (*sciocchezze*) don't talk rubbish!
boicottaggio, gi [boikot'taddʒo] SM boycott; (*fig*) sabotage
boicottare [boikot'tare] VT (*Econ, fig: persona*) to boycott; (*: piani*) to sabotage
boiler ['bɔilə] SM INV water heater
bolentino [bolen'tino] SM (*Pesca*) fishing line
bolero [bo'lɛro] SM bolero
bolgia, ge ['bɔldʒa] SF (*fig*): **c'era una tale bolgia al cinema** the cinema was absolutely mobbed
bolide ['bɔlide] SM **1** (*Astron*) meteor; **come un bolide** like a flash, at top speed; **entrare/uscire come un bolide** to charge in/out **2** (*auto da corsa*) racing car (*Brit*), race car (*Am*)
bolina [bo'lina] SF (*Naut*): **di bolina** close-hauled, on the wind
Bolivia [bo'livja] SF Bolivia
boliviano, a [boli'vjano] AGG, SM/F Bolivian
bolla[1] ['bolla] SF bubble; (*Med*) blister; **fare le bolle di sapone** to blow bubbles; **finire in una bolla di sapone** (*fig*) to come to nothing; **bolla speculativa** speculative bubble
bolla[2] ['bolla] SF **1** (*Comm*) bill, receipt; **bolla di accompagnamento** waybill; **bolla di consegna** delivery note **2** (*Rel*): **bolla papale** papal bull
bollare [bol'lare] VT (*timbrare*) to stamp; (*sigillare*) to seal; (*fig*) to brand; **bollato a vita** (*fig*) branded for life; **carta bollata** official stamped paper
bollatrice [bolla'tritʃe] SF stamping machine
bollente [bol'lɛnte] AGG (*che bolle*) boiling; (*caldissimo*) boiling (hot); **cuocere in acqua bollente** cook in boiling water; **la minestra è bollente!** the soup is boiling hot!; **calmare i bollenti spiriti** to calm down
bolletta [bol'letta] SF **1** (*conto: del gas, telefono*) bill; **bolletta della luce** electricity bill **2** (*ricevuta*) receipt; **bolletta di carico** bill of lading; **bolletta di consegna** delivery note; **bolletta doganale** clearance certificate; **bolletta di trasporto aereo** air waybill **3** (*fam: senza soldi*): **essere in bolletta** to be broke, be hard up
bollettario, ri [bollet'tarjo] SM duplicate receipt pad
bollettino [bollet'tino] SM **1** (*comunicato, periodico*) bulletin; **bollettino meteorologico** weather report **2** (*Comm: dei prezzi, cambi*) list; (*: modulo*) form; **bollettino di ordinazione** order form; **bollettino di spedizione** consignment note
bollicina [bolli'tʃina] SF bubble; **acqua con le bollicine** fizzy water

bollilatte [bolli'latte] SM INV milk pan
bollino [bol'lino] SM coupon; **bollino blu** (*di alimenti*) *blue sticker guaranteeing quality*; (*per auto, moto*) *blue sticker indicating that emissions are within the permitted levels*
bollire [bol'lire] VT to boil; **fare bollire** (*acqua*) to boil, bring to the boil; (*biberon*) to sterilize; (*panni*) to boil
■ VI (*aus* **avere**) to boil, be boiling; **l'acqua bolle** the water's boiling; **qui dentro si bolle (dal caldo)** it's boiling (hot) in here; **qualcosa bolle in pentola** (*fig*) there's something brewing
bollito, a [bol'lito] AGG boiled
■ SM (*Culin*) ≈ boiled beef
bollitore [bolli'tore] SM **1** (*per acqua*) kettle; (*per latte*) milk pan **2** (*Tecn*) boiler
bollitura [bolli'tura] SF **1** (*azione*) boiling **2** (*acqua*) cooking liquid
bollo ['bollo] SM (*timbro*) stamp; (*sigillo*) seal; (*su bestiame*) brand; **carta da bollo** official stamped paper; **marca da bollo** revenue stamp; **tassa di bollo** stamp duty; **bollo di circolazione** (*Aut*) road tax; **bollo per patente** driving licence tax; **bollo postale** postmark
bollore [bol'lore] SM: **dare un bollore a qc** to bring sth to the boil (*Brit*) *o* a boil (*Am*); **i bollori della gioventù** (*fig*) youthful enthusiasm *sg*; **ti sono passati i bollori?** have you calmed down?
bolo ['bɔlo] SM (*alimentare*) bolus; (*di ruminante*) cud
Bologna [bo'loɲɲa] SF Bologna
bolognese [boloɲ'ɲese] AGG Bolognese, of *o* from Bologna; **spaghetti alla bolognese** spaghetti bolognese
■ SM/F inhabitant *o* native of Bologna
bolsaggine [bol'saddʒine] SF (*di cavallo*) heaves *sg*, broken wind
bolscevico, a, chi, che [bolʃe'viko] AGG, SM/F Bolshevik
bolscevismo [bolʃe'vizmo] SM Bolshevism
bolso, a ['bolso] AGG (*cavallo*) broken-winded
bolzanino, a [boltza'nino] AGG of *o* from Bolzano
■ SM/F inhabitant *o* native of Bolzano
boma ['bɔma] SM INV (*Naut*) boom
bomba ['bomba] SF bomb; (*Calcio: tiro violento*) drive; **è scoppiata una bomba alla stazione** a bomb went off at the station; **la notizia fu una bomba** the news came as a bombshell; **sei stato una bomba!** you were tremendous!; **guarda che bomba!** (*donna, macchina*) what a beauty!; **tornare a bomba** (*al punto*) to get back to the point; **bomba atomica** atom bomb; **bomba chimica** chemical weapon; **bomba a mano** hand grenade; **bomba N** Neutron bomb; **bomba ad orologeria** time bomb; **bomba umana** suicide bomber
bombarda [bom'barda] SF **1** (*arma: antica*) bombard; (*: moderna*) mortar **2** (*Mus*) bombardon
bombardamento [bombarda'mento] SM (*vedi vb*) bombardment; bombing; shelling; **un bombardamento aereo** an air raid; **è rimasto ucciso durante il bombardamento aereo** he was killed in the bombing; **bombardamento a tappeto** saturation bombing
bombardare [bombar'dare] VT (*gen, Fis*) to bombard; (*con bombe*) to bomb; (*con cannone*) to shell; **bombardare di domande/lettere** to bombard with questions/letters
bombardiere [bombar'djɛre] SM (*aereo*) bomber; (*persona*) bombardier
bombarolo, a [bomba'rɔlo] SM/F terrorist bomber
bombato, a [bom'bato] AGG (*cappello, scatola*) rounded
bombé [bø'be] AGG INV rounded
bombetta [bom'betta] SF bowler (hat) (*Brit*), derby (*Am*); **la classica bombetta inglese** the famous English bowler hat
bombola ['bombola] SF cylinder; **bombola del gas** gas cylinder; **bombola d'insetticida** fly spray; **bombola di ossigeno** oxygen cylinder
bomboletta [bombol'etta] SF spray can
bomboniera [bombo'njɛra] SF box of sweets (*as souvenir at weddings, first communions*)
bonaccia [bo'nattʃa] SF (*Naut*) dead calm; (*fig*) lull; **il mare è in bonaccia** the sea is dead calm
bonaccione, a [bonat'tʃone] AGG good-natured, easy-going
■ SM/F good-natured sort
bonariamente [bonarja'mente] AVV (*vedi agg*) good-naturedly; kindly
bonarietà [bonarje'ta] SF (*vedi agg*) good nature, affability; kindliness
bonario, ria, ri, rie [bo'narjo] AGG (*persona*) good-natured, affable; (*modi, aspetto*) kindly
bonifica, che [bo'nifika], **bonificazione** [bonifikat'tsjone] SF (*operazione*) reclamation; (*terreno*) reclaimed land; **opere di bonifica** land reclamation works
bonificabile [bonifi'kabile] AGG reclaimable
bonificare [bonifi'kare] VT **1** (*terreno*) to reclaim; (*Mil*) to clear of mines **2** (*Comm*) to give a discount to
bonifico, ci [bo'nifiko] SM (*Comm: riduzione, abbuono*) discount; (*Banca*) credit transfer
Bonn [bɔn] SF Bonn
bonsai ['bonsai] SM INV (*tecnica, pianta*) bonsai
bontà [bon'ta] SF (*gen*) goodness, kindness; (*di prodotti*) quality; **bontà d'animo** *o* **di cuore** goodness of heart; **bontà sua!** (*iro*) how kind of him!; **abbia la bontà di ascoltarmi!** will you please listen to me?
bonus malus ['bɔnus'malus] SM INV (*Assicurazioni*) insurance with no-claims bonus
bonzo ['bondzo] SM Buddhist monk, bonze
book [buk] SM INV (*di modella, fotografo*) portfolio
bookmark ['bukmark] SM INV (*Inform*) bookmark
borace [bo'ratʃe] SM borax
borbonico, a, ci, che [bor'bɔniko] AGG Bourbon; (*pegg*) backward, out of date
■ SM/F Bourbon
borbottamento [borbotta'mento] SM (*vedi vb*) muttering; moaning, grumbling; rumbling
borbottare [borbot'tare] VT (*pronunciare confusamente*) to mutter
■ VI (*aus* **avere**) to mutter; (*lamentarsi*) to moan, grumble; (*tuono, stomaco*) to rumble
borbottio, tii [borbot'tio] SM (*vedi vb*) muttering; moaning, grumbling; rumbling
borchia ['bɔrkja] SF (*di abiti, cinture, borse*) stud; (*Tecn*) boss; (*da tappezziere*) upholsterer's nail
bordare [bor'dare] VT **1** (*fare il bordo a*) to hem, edge; **un vestito bordato di rosso** a dress with a red border **2** (*Naut: vele*) to spread
bordata [bor'data] SF **1** (*di cannoni, anche fig*) broadside **2** (*Naut*) tack
bordatura [borda'tura] SF (*di abiti, tende*) border, edge
bordeaux [bɔr'do] SM INV (*colore*) burgundy, maroon; (*vino*) Bordeaux
bordello [bor'dɛllo] SM brothel; **fare bordello** (*fam!*) to kick up a hell of a row; **questa stanza è un bordello** (*fam!*) this room's a shambles
bordo ['bordo] SM **1** (*orlo*) edge; (*guarnizione*) border; (*di cratere, ruota*) rim; **il bordo del tavolo/letto** the edge of

Bb

the table/bed; **sul bordo della strada** at the roadside; **eravamo seduti sul bordo della piscina** we were sitting on the edge of the pool; **è nero, con un bordo rosso** it's black, with a red border; **a bordo campo** (*Calcio*) on the touchline **2** (*Naut: fiancata di nave*) ship's side; **virare di bordo** (*anche fig*) to change course; **fuori bordo** overboard; **a bordo di** (*nave, aereo*) aboard, on board; **era a bordo di una macchina rossa** he was in a red car; **c'erano cento passeggeri a bordo dell'aereo** there were a hundred passengers on board the plane; **salire a bordo (di qc)** (*aereo, nave*) to go on board (sth), board (sth); (*macchina*) to get in(to sth); **siamo saliti a bordo dell'aereo** we got on the plane; **persona d'alto bordo** (*fig*) VIP; **prostituta d'alto bordo** high-class prostitute

bordura [bor'dura] SF (*di abiti, aiuole*) border; (*di pietanze*) garnish

boreale [bore'ale] AGG northern; **aurora boreale** northern lights *pl*, aurora borealis

borgata [bor'gata] SF (*in campagna*) hamlet; (*a Roma*) working-class suburb

borghese [bor'gese] AGG **1** (*gen*) middle-class; (*pegg*) bourgeois; **una famiglia borghese** a middle-class family **2** **essere in (abito) borghese** to be in civilian clothes *o* in civvies; **poliziotto in borghese** plainclothes policeman
■ SM/F (*vedi agg*) middle-class person; bourgeois; **piccolo borghese** (*pegg*) petty bourgeois

borghesemente [borgese'mente] AVV in a middle class fashion; (*pegg*) in a bourgeois way

borghesia [borge'zia] SF bourgeoisie, middle classes *pl*; **alta/piccola borghesia** upper/lower middle classes *pl*

borgo, ghi ['borgo] SM (*paese*) village; (*quartiere cittadino*) district; (*sobborgo*) suburb

Borgogna [bor'goɲɲa] SF Burgundy

borgomastro [borgo'mastro] SM burgomaster

boria ['bɔrja] SF conceit, arrogance

boriosamente [borjosa'mente] AVV conceitedly, arrogantly

borioso, a [bo'rjoso] AGG conceited, arrogant

borlotto [bor'lɔtto] SM kidney bean

Borneo ['bɔrneo] SM Borneo

boro ['bɔro] SM (*Chim*) boron

borotalco® [boro'talko] SM talcum powder

borraccia, ce [bor'rattʃa] SF (*per soldati, cowboy*) water-bottle, flask

borraccina [borrat'tʃina] SF (*Bot*) moss

borragine [bor'radʒine] SF borage

Borsa ['borsa] SF (*Fin*): **la Borsa (valori)** the Stock Exchange; **giocare in Borsa** to speculate on the Stock Exchange; **Borsa merci** commodity exchange
▷ www.borsaitalia.it/it/mercati/homepage/
▷ www.piazzaffari.org/
▷ www.ilsole24ore.com/

borsa ['borsa] SF (*gen*) bag; (*borsetta*) handbag (*Brit*), purse (*Am*); (*Ciclismo*) pannier; **ho una valigia e una borsa** I've got one case and one bag; **o la borsa o la vita!** your money or your life!; **aver le borse sotto gli occhi** to have bags under one's eyes
■ **borsa dell'acqua calda** hot water bottle; **borsa del ghiaccio** ice bag; **borsa portalavoro** knitting bag; **borsa del postino** mailbag; **borsa della spesa** shopping bag; **borsa di studio** (*per studente bisognoso*) (student's) grant; (*per studente meritevole e bisognoso*) scholarship; **borsa del tabacco** tobacco pouch; **borsa degli utensili** toolbag; **borsa da viaggio** travelling bag

borsaiolo, a [borsa'jɔlo] SM/F pickpocket

borsanera [borsa'nera] SF black market

borseggiare [borsed'dʒare] VT: **mi hanno borseggiato!** I've been robbed!, I've had my pocket picked!; **mi hanno borseggiato del portafoglio** my wallet has been stolen

borseggiatore, trice [borseddʒa'tore] SM/F pickpocket

borseggio, gi [bor'seddʒo] SM pickpocketing

borsellino [borsel'lino] SM purse

borsello [bor'sɛllo], **borsetto** [bor'setto] SM handbag (*for man*)

borsetta [bor'setta] SF handbag; **borsetta da sera** evening bag

borsista, i, e [bor'sista] SM/F **1** (*di borsa di studio*) grant holder **2** (*Borsa*) speculator

borsistico, a, ci, che [bor'sistiko] AGG Stock-Exchange *attr*, on the Stock Exchange

boscaglia [bos'kaʎʎa] SF brush

boscaiolo [boska'jɔlo], **boscaiuolo** [boska'jwɔlo] SM (*legnaiuolo*) woodcutter, lumberjack (*Am*); (*guardiano*) forester

boschereccio, cia, ci, ce [boske'rettʃo] AGG woodland *attr*

boschetto [bos'ketto] SM copse, grove

boschivo, a [bos'kivo] AGG (*terreno*) wooded, woody; (*flora, vegetazione*) woodland *attr*

bosco, schi ['bɔsko] SM wood; **un bosco di querce** an oak wood; **una passeggiata nel bosco** a walk in the woods

boscosità [boskosi'ta] SF density of woodland

boscoso, a [bos'koso] AGG wooded

bosniaco, a, ci, che [boz'niako] AGG, SM/F Bosnian

Bosnia-Erzegovina ['bɔznja erdze'govina] SF Bosnia-Herzegovina

boss [bɔs] SM INV boss

bosso ['bɔsso] SM (*pianta*) box; (*legno*) boxwood

bossolo ['bɔssolo] SM cartridge case

Bot, bot [bɔt] SIGLA M INV = **buono ordinario del Tesoro**

botanica [bo'tanika] SF botany

botanico, a, ci, che [bo'taniko] AGG botanic(al); **orto** *o* **giardino botanico** botanical gardens *pl*
■ SM/F botanist

botola ['bɔtola] SF trap door

Bot-people [bot 'pipol] SMPL *investors who only invest in BOT (short term Italian Treasury bonds) because they do not trust other forms of investment*

Botswana [bots'wana] SM Botswana

botta ['bɔtta] SF **1** (*percossa*) blow; (*fig: colpo, danno*) blow, shock; **gli menò una botta in testa** he struck him a blow on the head; **dare (un sacco di) botte a qn** to give sb a good thrashing; **prendere una botta** to be hit; **ha preso una botta sulla testa** he was hit on the head; **fare a botte** to fight **2** (*Scherma*) thrust; **botta e risposta** (*fig*) cut and thrust

bottaio, ai [bot'tajo] SM cooper

bottarga [bot'targa] SF *roe of grey mullet or tuna, pressed and salted*

botte ['botte] SF barrel, cask; **volta a botte** (*Archit*) barrel vault; **volere la botte piena e la moglie ubriaca** (*Proverbio*) to want to have one's cake and eat it; **essere in una botte di ferro** (*fig*) to be (as) safe as houses

bottega, ghe [bot'tega] SF (*negozio*) shop; (*laboratorio*) workshop; **aprire/mettere su bottega** to open/set up shop; **chiudere bottega** to shut up shop; (*fig*) to give up; **stare a bottega (da qn)** to serve one's apprenticeship (with sb); **avere la bottega aperta** (*fam*) to have one's flies undone; **le Botteghe Oscure** (*Pol*) *headquarters of P.D.S.*

bottegaio, aia, ai, aie [botte'gajo] SM/F shopkeeper

botteghino [botte'gino] SM (*Teatro, Cine*) box office; (*del lotto*) lottery office

bottiglia [bot'tiʎʎa] SF bottle; **bottiglia di vino** bottle of wine; **una bottiglia da 1 litro** a litre bottle; **in bottiglia** bottled; **birra in bottiglia** bottled beer; **vino in bottiglia** bottled wine; **bottiglia Molotov** Molotov cocktail; **bottiglia da vino** wine bottle
■ AGG INV: **verde bottiglia** bottle green

bottiglieria [bottiʎʎe'ria] SF (*negozio*) wine shop; (*deposito*) wine cellar

bottiglione [bottiʎ'ʎone] SM large bottle

bottino[1] [bot'tino] SM (*di guerra*) booty; (*di rapina, furto*) loot; **fare bottino di qc** to make off with sth

bottino[2] [bot'tino] SM (*pozzonero*) cesspool, cesspit

botto ['bɔtto] SM (*di mortaretti*) thud; (*spari*) rattle; **abbiamo sentito un gran botto** we heard a loud bang; **di botto** (*fam*) suddenly; **si è fermato di botto** he stopped suddenly; **in un botto** (*fam*) in a flash

bottone [bot'tone] SM **1** (*di giacca, radio*) button; **premere** *o* **spingere un bottone** to press a button; **stanza dei bottoni** control room; (*fig*) nerve centre; **attaccare un bottone** (*alla camicia*) to sew on a button; **attaccare un bottone a qn** (*fig: trattenere*) to buttonhole sb; **attaccare bottone con qn** (*fig: conversare*) to strike up a conversation with sb; **bottone automatico** press stud **2** (*Bot*) bud; **botton d'oro** buttercup

bottoniera [botto'njɛra] SF (*Tecn*) control panel

bottonificio, ci [bottoni'fitʃo] SM button factory

botulino [botu'lino] AGG: **bacillo botulino** botulinus

botulismo [botu'lizmo] SM botulism

bouclé [bu'kle] AGG INV bouclé

boule [bul] SF INV hot water bottle

bouquet [bu'kɛ] SM INV (*di fiori, del vino*) bouquet

boutique [bu'tik] SF INV boutique

bovaro [bo'varo] SM herdsman

bove ['bɔve] SM = **bue**

bovino, a [bo'vino] AGG bovine; (*allevamento*) cattle *attr*; **carne bovina** beef; **occhi bovini** (*fig*) protruding eyes
■ **bovini** SMPL cattle

bowling ['bouliŋ] SM INV (*gioco*) (tenpin) bowling; (*luogo*) bowling alley

box [bɔks] SM INV (*per cavalli*) horsebox; (*per macchina*) lock-up, garage; (*per macchina da corsa*) pit; (*per bambini*) playpen; **metti la macchina nel box** put the car in the garage; **tuo fratello è nel box** your brother is in his playpen; **box doccia** shower cubicle

> **LO SAPEVI...?**
> **box** non si traduce mai con la parola inglese *box*

boxare [bok'sare] VI (*aus* **avere**) to box

boxe [bɔks] SF INV boxing; **un incontro di boxe** a boxing match

boxer ['bɔkser] SM INV (*cane*) boxer
■ SMPL (*mutande*): **un paio di boxer** a pair of boxer shorts

boxeur [bɔk'sœr] SM INV (*pugile*) boxer

boy ['bɔi] SM INV (*ballerino di rivista*) dancer; (*in albergo*) bellboy

bozza[1] ['bɔttsa] SF (*fam: bernoccolo*) bump

bozza[2] ['bɔttsa] SF (*di lettera, contratto, romanzo*) draft; (*Tip: di stampa*) proof; **rivedere** *o* **correggere le bozze** to proofread; **prima/seconda/terza bozza** first/revised proof; **bozza in colonna** galley proof; **bozza impaginata** page proof

bozzettista, i, e [bottset'tista] SM/F (*di pubblicità*) commercial artist; (*scrittore*) sketch writer

bozzetto [bot'tsetto] SM (*disegno*) sketch; (*modello*) scale model

bozzo ['bɔttso] SM bump

bozzolo ['bɔttsolo] SM cocoon; **uscire dal bozzolo** (*fig*) to come out of one's shell; **chiudersi nel proprio bozzolo** (*fig*) to withdraw into one's shell

BR [bi'ɛrre] SIGLA FPL = **Brigate Rosse**
■ SIGLA = *Brindisi*

braca, che ['braka] SF **1** **brache** SFPL (*fam: pantaloni*) trousers, pants (*Am*); (*: mutandoni*) drawers; **calare** *o* **calarsi le brache** (*fig fam*) to chicken out
2 (*allacciatura: per operai*) (safety) harness

braccare [brak'kare] VT (*anche fig*) to hunt

braccetto [brat'tʃetto] AVV: **a braccetto** arm in arm; **prendere qn a braccetto** to take sb by the arm; **tenersi a braccetto** to be arm in arm; **si tenevano a braccetto** they were arm in arm

braccherò *ecc* [brakke'rɔ] VB *vedi* **braccare**

bracciale [brat'tʃale] SM (*ornamento*) bracelet; (*distintivo*) armband; **bracciali** (*per nuotare*) armbands

braccialetto [brattʃa'letto] SM bracelet, bangle; **un braccialetto d'argento** a silver bracelet; **braccialetto elettronico** electronic tag

bracciante [brat'tʃante] SM/F (day) labourer

bracciata [brat'tʃata] SF **1** (*quantità*) armful; **a bracciate** by the armful **2** (*nel nuoto*) stroke

braccio ['brattʃo] SM **1** (*pl f* **braccia**) (*Anat*) arm; **mi fa male il braccio** my arm hurts; **tenere/prendere in braccio** to hold/take in one's arms; **dare** *o* **offrire il braccio a qn** to give sb one's arm; **camminare sotto braccio** to walk arm in arm; **è il suo braccio destro** (*fig*) he's his right-hand man; **braccio di ferro** (*anche fig*) trial of strength; **alzare le braccia al cielo** to throw up one's arms; **a braccia** (*sollevare, portare*) with one's own hands; **a braccia aperte** with open arms; **incrociare le braccia** to fold one's arms; (*fig*) to down tools; **gettare le braccia al collo a qn** to throw one's arms round sb's neck; **mi sono cascate le braccia** (*fig*) I could have wept; **avere buone braccia** to be big and strong **2** (*pl f* **braccia**) (*Naut: unità di misura*) fathom
3 (*pl m* **bracci**) (*di croce, gru, fiume, grammofono*) arm; (*di edificio*) wing; **braccio di mare** sound; **braccio della morte** death row

bracciolo [brat'tʃɔlo] SM arm

bracco, chi ['brakko] SM hound

bracconiere [brakko'njɛre] SM poacher

brace ['bratʃe] SF embers *pl*; **alla brace** barbecued; **pollo alla brace** barbecued chicken

> **LO SAPEVI...?**
> **brace** non si traduce mai con la parola inglese *brace*

braciere [bra'tʃɛre] SM brazier

braciola [bra'tʃɔla] SF (*con osso*) chop; (*senza osso*) steak; **una braciola di maiale** a pork chop

bradipo ['bradipo] SM (*Zool*) sloth

brado, a ['brado] AGG (*animale*) wild; **allo stato brado** in the wild *o* natural state

braille [braj] AGG INV, SM INV braille

brama ['brama] SF: **brama (di/di fare)** longing (for/to do), yearning (for/to do)

bramare [bra'mare] VT: **bramare (qc/di fare qc)** to

Bb

long (for sth/to do sth), yearn (for sth/to do sth)

bramire [bra'mire] VI (*aus* **avere**) (*cervo*) to bell; (*orso*) to roar

bramito [bra'mito] SM (*di cervo*) bell; (*di orso*) roar

bramosamente [bramosa'mente] AVV (*guardare*) longingly, yearningly

bramosia [bramo'sia] SF: **bramosia (di)** longing (for), yearning (for)

bramoso, a [bra'moso] AGG (*sguardo*) longing; **essere bramoso di qc** to long *o* yearn for sth

branca, che ['branka] SF **1** (*settore, ramo*) branch; **una branca della medicina** a branch of medicine **2** (*fig: artigli*) **branche** SFPL (*di vizio*) grip; (*di usuraio*) clutches

branchia ['brankja] SF (*Zool*) gill

branchiale [bran'kjale] AGG branchial

branco, chi ['branko] SM (*di uccelli, pecore*) flock; (*di cani, lupi*) pack; (*di balene, delfini*) school; (*fig pegg: di persone*) gang, pack; **entrare nel branco** (*fig*) to go with the crowd

brancolare [branko'lare] VI (*aus* **avere**) to grope, feel one's way; **brancolare nel buio** (*fig*) to grope in the dark

branda ['branda] SF (*da campo, per militari*) camp bed, folding bed; (*per marinai*) hammock; **giù dalle brande!** everybody up!

brandello [bran'dɛllo] SM scrap, shred; **a brandelli** in tatters, in rags; **fare a brandelli** to tear to shreds

brandina [bran'dina] SF camp bed (*Brit*), cot (*Am*)

brandire [bran'dire] VT to brandish

brano ['brano] SM (*gen*) piece; (*di libro*) passage; **un brano di musica classica** a piece of classical music; **abbiamo letto un brano da "I Promessi Sposi"** we read a passage from "I Promessi Sposi"; **fare a brani** (*fig*) to tear to pieces

branzino [bran'tsino] SM sea-bass

brasare [bra'zare] VT **1** (*Culin*) to braise **2** (*Tecn*) to braze

brasato, a [bra'zato] AGG (*Culin*) braised
■ SM braised beef

Brasile [bra'zile] SM Brazil; **andremo in Brasile quest'estate** we're going to Brazil this summer; **mi è piaciuto molto il Brasile** I really liked Brazil

Brasilia [bra'zilja] SF Brasilia

brasiliano, a [brazi'ljano] AGG, SM/F Brazilian

bravata [bra'vata] SF (*azione spavalda*) act of bravado; (*millanterie*): **bravate** SFPL bravado *sg*

bravo, a ['bravo] AGG **1** (*abile*) good, clever, skilful, capable; **essere bravo in qc/a fare qc** to be good at sth/at doing sth; **sono abbastanza bravo in inglese** I'm quite good at English; **un bravo insegnante/medico** a good teacher/doctor; **essere bravo a scuola** to do well at school; **il più bravo** the best; **è il più bravo della classe** he's the best in the class; **bravo!** well done!; **bravi!** (*in chiusura di spettacolo*) bravo! **2** (*buono*) good; (*onesto*) honest; **è un brav'uomo** he's a decent chap; **sono brave persone** they're good people; **fai il bravo** be good; **su da bravo!** (*fam*) there's a good boy! **3** (*coraggioso*) brave **4** (*rafforzativo*): **mi sono fatto le mie brave 8 ore di lavoro** I put in a full 8 hours' work; **si beve il suo bravo mezzo litro ogni giorno** he drinks his pint every day

bravura [bra'vura] SF cleverness, skill; **pezzo di bravura** (*Mus*) bravura piece

breccia[1], ce ['brettʃa] SF breach; (*Geol*) breccia; **essere sulla breccia** (*fig*) to be going strong; **fare breccia nell'animo** *o* **nel cuore di qn** to find the way to sb's heart

breccia[2], ce ['brettʃa] SF, **brecciame** [bret'tʃame] SM road metal

brefotrofio, fi [brefo'trɔfjo] SM orphanage (*for abandoned children*)

Brema ['brɛma] SF Bremen

bresaola [bre'zaola] SF (*Culin*) *kind of dried salted beef*

bresciano, a [breʃʃano] AGG of *o* from Brescia
■ SM/F inhabitant *o* native of Brescia

Bretagna [bre'taɲɲa] SF Brittany; **Gran Bretagna** Great Britain

bretella [bre'tɛlla] SF **1** (*di sottoveste, reggiseno*) strap; **bretelle** (*di calzoni*) braces **2** (*raccordo stradale*) motorway link road; (*Aer*) exit runway

bretone ['brɛtone] AGG, SM/F Breton

breve ['brɛve] AGG (*gen*) brief, short; (*vita, strada*) short; **una breve visita** a short visit; **tra breve** shortly; **a breve distanza** near, not far; **sarò breve** I'll be brief; **per farla breve** to cut a long story short; **in breve** in short; **a breve** (*Comm*) short-term
■ SF **1** (*Mus*) breve **2** (*vocale*) short vowel; (*sillaba*) short syllable

brevemente [breve'mente] AVV briefly

brevettabile [brevet'tabile] AGG patentable

brevettare [brevet'tare] VT to patent

brevettato, a [brevet'tato] AGG patented; (*scherz*) tried and tested

brevetto [bre'vetto] SM **1** (*d'invenzione*) patent; **Ufficio Brevetti** Patent Office **2** (*patente*): **brevetto di pilota** pilot's licence (*Brit*) *o* license (*Am*)

breviario, ri [bre'vjarjo] SM (*Rel*) breviary; (*compendio*) compendium

brevi manu ['brɛvi 'manu] AVV: **consegnare qc brevi manu a qn** to hand sth directly to sb

brevità [brevi'ta] SF brevity

brezza ['breddza] SF breeze; **brezza di terra/mare** land/sea breeze

bric-à-brac ['brika'brak] SM INV bric-à-brac

bricco, chi ['brikko] SM jug; **bricco del caffè** coffeepot; **bricco del latte** milk jug

bricconata [brikko'nata] SF mischievous trick

briccone [brik'kone] SM/F rascal, rogue

briciola ['britʃola] SF (*di pane*) crumb; (*frammento*) scrap; **non ha lasciato che le briciole** (*anche fig*) he only left the scraps; **ridurre in briciole** (*biscotto*) to crumble up; (*fig: persona*) to take to pieces

briciolo ['britʃolo] SM bit; (*fig: di buon senso, verità*) grain; **non ha un briciolo di cervello** she hasn't got a bit of sense

bricolage [briko'laʒ] SM INV do-it-yourself; **negozio/rivista di bricolage** do-it-yourself shop/magazine

bridge [bridʒ] SM INV bridge

briga, ghe ['briga] SF **1** (*cura, fastidio*) bother, trouble; **darsi** *o* **prendersi la briga di fare qc** to take the trouble to do sth; **si è preso la briga di telefonare a tutti** he took the trouble to phone everybody **2** (*lite*): **attaccar briga** to start a quarrel

brigadiere [briga'djɛre] SM (*dei Carabinieri, Finanza*) ≈ sergeant

brigantaggio, gi [brigan'taddʒo] SM brigandage; (*organizzazione*) brigands *pl*

brigante [bri'gante] SM brigand, bandit; (*fig: bambino*) rascal

brigantino [brigan'tino] SM (*Naut*) brig, brigantine

brigata [bri'gata] SF **1** (*gruppo*) group; (*comitiva*) party; **un'allegra brigata di amici** a lively bunch of friends

2 (*Mil*) brigade; **generale di brigata** brigadier (*Brit*), brigadier general (*Am*); **le Brigate Rosse** (*Pol*) the Red Brigades
brigatismo [briga'tizmo] SM *phenomenon of the Red Brigades*
brigatista, i, e [briga'tista] SM/F (*Pol*) *member of the Red Brigades*
briglia ['briʎʎa] SF (*di cavallo*) rein, bridle; (*per bambino*) rein; **a briglia sciolta** at full gallop; (*fig*) at full speed; **allentare/tirare la briglia** (*anche fig*) to slacken/ tighten the reins
brik® [brik] SM INV carton
brillante [bril'lante] AGG **1** (*luce, raggi, colori*) bright; (*: più intenso*) brilliant; (*che luccica*) shining; (*: occhi*) sparkling; **una camicia verde brillante** a bright green shirt **2** (*successo, carriera, studioso*) brilliant; (*conversazione*) brilliant, sparkling; **è una persona brillante** he has a sparkling wit
■ SM (*diamante*) diamond; (*anello*) diamond ring; **un anello con brillante** a diamond ring
brillantemente [brillante'mente] AVV (*superare un esame, conversare*) brilliantly
brillantina [brillan'tina] SF brilliantine
brillare[1] [bril'lare] VT (*riso*) to husk
brillare[2] [bril'lare] VI (*aus* **avere**) **1** (*sole*) to shine; (*stelle*) to shine, twinkle; (*occhi*) to shine, sparkle; (*diamante*) to sparkle; **le stelle brillano in cielo** the stars are shining in the sky; **gli occhi le brillavano di gioia** her eyes sparkled *o* shone with joy; **brilla per la sua bellezza/intelligenza** she is outstandingly beautiful/intelligent; **brillare per la propria assenza** to be conspicuous by one's absence **2** (*mina*) to go off, explode
■ VT (*mina*) to set off
brillo, a ['brillo] AGG (*fam*) tipsy, merry; **era un po' brillo** he was a bit tipsy
brina ['brina] SF (hoar)frost; **c'è ancora la brina sui campi** there's still frost on the fields
brinare [bri'nare] VB IMPERS (*aus* **essere**) **stanotte è brinato** there was a frost last night
brinata [bri'nata] SF (hoar)frost
brindare [brin'dare] VI (*aus* **avere**) to make a toast; **brindare a qn/qc** to drink to *o* toast sb/sth; **brindare alla salute di qn** to drink sb's health; **brindiamo alla macchina nuova!** let's drink to the new car!
brindello [brin'dɛllo] SM = **brandello**
brindisi ['brindizi] SM INV toast; **fare un brindisi (a qn/qc)** to drink a toast (to sb/sth); **facciamo un brindisi!** let's drink a toast!
brindisino, a [brindi'zino] AGG of *o* from Brindisi
■ SM/F inhabitant *o* native of Brindisi
brio ['brio] SM, SOLO SG liveliness; **essere pieno di brio** to be very lively *o* full of life
brioche [bri'ɔʃ] SF INV brioche
briosamente [briosa'mente] AVV with spirit, in a lively manner
brioso, a [bri'oso] AGG lively
briscola ['briskola] SF (*gioco di carte*) *type of card game*; (*seme vincente*) trump(s); (*carta*) trump card
britannico, a, ci, che [bri'tanniko] AGG British; **le isole britanniche** the British Isles
■ SM/F British person, Briton
■ **i britannici** SMPL the British
brivido ['brivido] SM (*di freddo*) shiver; (*di ribrezzo*) shudder; (*di piacere*) thrill; **avere i brividi** (*anche fig*) to have the shivers; **ho i brividi** I've got the shivers; **far venire i brividi a qn** (*fig*) to give sb the shivers; **racconti del brivido** suspense stories
brizzolato, a [brittso'lato] AGG greying; (*persona*) grey-haired; **capelli brizzolati** greying hair
brocca, che ['brɔkka] SF jug
broccato [brok'kato] SM brocade
broccolo ['brɔkkolo] SM (*Bot, Culin*) broccoli *no pl*
broda ['brɔda] SF (*pegg*) dishwater
brodaglia [bro'daʎʎa] SF (*pegg*) dishwater
brodetto [bro'detto] SM (*brodo leggero*) light broth; **brodetto alla marinara** *sort of bouillabaisse*
brodo ['brɔdo] SM broth; (*per cucinare*) stock; **riso/pasta in brodo** rice/noodle soup; **dadi da brodo** stock cubes; **tutto fa brodo** (*fig*) every little helps; **lasciare (cuocere) qn nel suo brodo** (*fig*) to let sb stew (in his own juice); **brodo di manzo** beef tea; **brodo di pollo** chicken soup; **brodo ristretto** consommé
brogliaccio, ci [broʎ'ʎattʃo] SM (*Amm*) daybook
broglio, gli ['brɔʎʎo] SM: **broglio elettorale** gerrymandering
bromo ['brɔmo] SM (*Chim*) bromine
bromuro [bro'muro] SM bromide
bronchiale [bron'kjale] AGG bronchial
bronchiolo [bron'kiolo] SM bronchiole
bronchite [bron'kite] SF bronchitis
broncio, ci ['brontʃo] SM sulky expression; (*malumore*) sulkiness; **avere** *o* **tenere il broncio** to sulk; **gli tiene il broncio** he's not speaking to him
bronco, chi ['bronko] SM bronchial tube
broncopolmonite [bronkopolmo'nite] SF bronchial pneumonia
brontolare [bronto'lare] VT to mutter, mumble
■ VI (*aus* **avere**) (*mormorare*) to mutter, mumble; (*protestare*) to grumble; **non fa altro che brontolare** he's always grumbling; **mi brontola lo stomaco** my stomach is rumbling
brontolio, lii [bronto'lio] SM (*vedi vb*) muttering, mumbling; grumbling; rumbling
brontolone, a [bronto'lone] AGG grumbling
■ SM/F grumbler
brontosauro [bronto'sauro] SM brontosaurus
bronzare [bron'dzare] VT (*rivestire*) to bronze; (*brunire*) to burnish
bronzatura [brondza'tura] SF (*vedi vb*) bronzing; burnishing
bronzeo, a ['brondzeo] AGG (*di bronzo*) bronze; (*color bronzo*) bronze(-coloured)
bronzetto [bron'dzetto] SM bronze statuette
bronzina [bron'dzina] SF (*Tecn*) bush
bronzo ['brondzo] SM (*metallo, oggetto*) bronze; **ha vinto la medaglia di bronzo** she won the bronze medal; **che faccia di bronzo!** what (brazen) cheek!
bross. ABBR = **in brossura**; *vedi* **brossura**
brossura [bros'sura] SF: **in brossura** (*libro*) paperback
browser ['brauzer] SM INV (*Inform*) browser
brucare [bru'kare] VT to browse on, nibble at
brucherà *ecc* [bruke'ra] VB *vedi* **brucare**
bruciacchiare [brutʃak'kjare] VT to singe, scorch
▶ **bruciacchiarsi** VIP to get singed *o* scorched
bruciapelo [brutʃa'pelo] AVV: **a bruciapelo** point-blank; **sparare a bruciapelo** to fire at point-blank range
bruciare [bru'tʃare] VT **1** (*gen*) to burn; (*edificio*) to burn down; (*stoffa: stirando*) to scorch; (*Med: verruca*) to cauterize; **oh no, ho bruciato la torta!** oh no, I've burnt the cake!; **mi sono bruciata un dito** I've burnt my finger; **bruciato dal sole** (*terreno*) sun-scorched; (*volto*) sunburnt; (*: ustionato*) burnt by the sun

Bb

2 (*fraseologia*): **bruciare gli avversari** (*Sport, fig*) to leave the rest of the field behind; **bruciare le cervella a qn** to blow sb's brains out; **bruciare le tappe** *o* **i tempi** (*Sport, fig*) to shoot ahead; **bruciarsi le ali** (*fig*) to burn one's fingers; **bruciarsi la carriera** to ruin one's career
■ VI (*aus* **essere**) **1** (*gen*) to burn; (*edificio, bosco*) to be on fire **2** (*essere molto caldo*) to be burning (hot); (: *sole*) to be scorching, be burning; **bruciare di febbre** to run a high temperature **3** (*produrre bruciore*): **gli occhi mi bruciano** my eyes are smarting *o* stinging; **il viso mi brucia** my face is burning; **mi brucia molto questa offesa** that insult really rankles;
▶ **bruciarsi** VR, VIP (*persona*) to burn o.s.; **mi sono bruciata!** I've burnt myself!; **si è bruciato l'arrosto** the joint is burnt; **si è bruciata una lampadina** a bulb has blown

bruciato, a [bru'tʃato] AGG burnt; **gioventù bruciata** Beat Generation
■ SM: **odore di bruciato** (smell of) burning; **sento odore di bruciato** I can smell burning; **questa zuppa sa di bruciato** this soup tastes burnt

bruciatore [brutʃa'tore] SM (*Tecn*) burner

bruciatura [brutʃa'tura] SF **1** (*atto*) burning *no pl* **2** (*parte bruciata*) burn; (*scottatura*) scald; **una bruciatura di primo grado** a first-degree burn

bruciore [bru'tʃore] SM burning *o* smarting sensation; **provocare bruciore** to sting

bruco, chi ['bruko] SM (*Zool*) grub; (: *di farfalla*) caterpillar

brufolo ['brufolo] SM pimple, spot

brufoloso, a [brufo'loso] AGG pimply, spotty

brughiera [bru'gjɛra] SF moor, heath

brugo, ghi ['brugo] SM (*Bot*) heather

brûlé [bry'le] AGG INV: **vin brûlé** mulled wine

brulicante [bruli'kante] AGG: **brulicante di** (*anche fig*) swarming with, teeming with

brulicare [bruli'kare] VI (*aus* **avere**) to swarm; **il mercato brulicava di gente** the market was heaving with people

brulichio, chii [bruli'kio] SM swarming

brullo, a ['brullo] AGG bare

bruma ['bruma] SF mist, haze

brunch [brantʃ] SM INV brunch

brunire [bru'nire] VT (*metallo*: *levigare*) to burnish, polish

brunitura [bruni'tura] SF burnishing, polishing

bruno, a ['bruno] AGG (*capelli*) brown, dark; (*carnagione*) dark; (*persona*) dark(-haired); **è bruno** he's got dark hair
■ SM/F dark-haired person

brusca, sche ['bruska] SF scrubbing brush; (*per cavalli*) horse brush

bruscamente [bruska'mente] AVV (*frenare, fermarsi*) suddenly; (*rispondere, reagire*) sharply

bruschetta [brus'ketta] SF *slice of toasted bread seasoned with oil and garlic*

bruschezza [brus'kettsa] SF brusqueness, abruptness

brusco, a, schi, sche ['brusko] AGG (*movimento*) abrupt, sudden; (*modi, persona*) abrupt, brusque; **ha fatto una brusca frenata** he braked suddenly; **è stato un po' brusco con me** he was a bit abrupt with me

bruscolo ['bruskolo] SM speck

brusio, sii [bru'zio] SM hubbub, buzz; **il brusio degli insetti** the buzzing of the insects

brutale [bru'tale] AGG rough, brutal; **per dirla in modo brutale** to put it bluntly

brutalità [brutali'ta] SF INV brutality

brutalizzare [brutalid'dzare] VT to brutalize

brutalmente [brutal'mente] AVV brutally

Bruto ['bruto] SM Brutus

bruto, a ['bruto] AGG brute; **forza bruta** brute force *o* strength
■ SM (*uomo violento*) brute

brutta ['brutta] SF rough copy, first draft

bruttezza [brut'tettsa] SF ugliness

brutto, a ['brutto] AGG **1** (*persona, vestito, casa*) ugly; **è proprio brutto!** he's really ugly!; **è il posto più brutto che abbia mai visto** it's the ugliest place I've ever seen; **brutto come la fame** as ugly as sin
2 (*cattivo*: *gen*) bad; (: *ferita, malattia, strada, affare*) nasty; (: *carattere*) unpleasant, nasty; **ho un brutto raffreddore** I've got a bad cold; **ho fatto un brutto sogno** I had a bad dream; **ho preso un brutto voto in matematica** I got a bad mark in maths; **ha fatto brutto (tempo) ieri** yesterday the weather was bad; **che brutta giornata!** what a horrible day!; **brutto cattivo!** you naughty boy!; **brutto stupido!** you stupid clown!; **avere un brutto male** (*euf*) to have cancer; **passare un brutto momento** to go through a difficult period; **passare un brutto quarto d'ora** to have a nasty time of it; **vedersela brutta** (*per un attimo*) to have a nasty moment; (*per un periodo*) to have a bad time of it; **brutta copia** rough copy
■ SM **1** **il brutto** the ugly; **è il brutto della famiglia** he's the ugly member of the family; **il brutto è che...** the problem *o* unfortunate thing is that ...; **stiamo andando verso il brutto** (*Meteor*) the weather is taking a turn for the worse
■ AVV: **guardare qn di brutto** to give sb a nasty look; **picchiare qn di brutto** to give sb a bad *o* nasty beating; **sta lavorando di brutto** he's working furiously

bruttura [brut'tura] SF (*oggetto*) ugly thing

Bruxelles [bry'sɛl] SF Brussels; **vivo a Bruxelles** I live in Brussels

BS SIGLA = *Brescia*

BSE [bi'ɛsse'e] SIGLA F BSE (= *Bovine Spongiform Encephalopathy*)

BT [bi'ti] ABBR (= **bassa tensione**) LT
■ SIGLA M = **buono del Tesoro**

btg ABBR = **battaglione**

BTP [biti'pi] SIGLA M INV = **buono del Tesoro poliennale**

bubbone [bub'bone] SM swelling

bubbonico, a, ci, che [bub'bɔniko] AGG: **peste bubbonica** bubonic plague

buca, che ['buka] SF (*gen, Golf*) hole; (*più profondo*) pit; (*di biliardo*) pocket; (*avvallamento*) hollow; **la strada è piena di buche** the road is full of holes; **mi ha dato buca** (*fam*) she didn't turn up; **buca delle lettere** (*per imbucare*) post box; (*in portone*) letterbox; **buca del suggeritore** (*Teatro*) prompter's box

bucaneve [buka'neve] SM INV snowdrop

bucaniere [buka'njɛre] SM buccaneer

bucare [bu'kare] VT (*forare*) to make a hole (*o* holes) in; (: *biglietto*) to punch; (: *gomma*) to puncture; (*pungere*) to pierce; **ho bucato (una gomma)** I've got a puncture; **abbiamo bucato e siamo arrivati in ritardo** we had a puncture and arrived late; **avere le mani bucate** (*fig*) to be a spendthrift
▶ **bucarsi** VR (*pungersi*) to prick o.s.
▶ **bucarsi** VIP (*forarsi*: *gomma, palla*) to puncture; (*fam*: *drogarsi*) to mainline; **si è bucata una gomma** I've got a puncture

Bucarest ['bukarest] SF Bucharest
bucato [bu'kato] SM washing; **fare il bucato** to do the washing; **stirare il bucato** to do the ironing; **lenzuola di bucato** freshly-laundered sheets
buccia, ce ['buttʃa] SF **1** *(di verdura, frutta: gen)* skin; *(: di agrumi, patate)* skin, peel; *(: di piselli)* pod; **una buccia di banana** a banana skin; **aggiungi un po' di buccia di limone grattugiata** add some grated lemon rind **2** *(di salumi)* skin; *(di formaggio)* rind **3** *(corteccia)* bark
bucherellare [bukerel'lare] VT to riddle with holes
bucherellato, a [bukerel'lato] AGG riddled (with holes)
bucherò *ecc* [buke'rɔ] VB *vedi* **bucare**
buco, chi ['buko] SM *(gen)* hole; *(omissione)* gap; *(orifizio, apertura)* aperture; **c'è un buco nella tasca** there's a hole in the pocket; **il buco della serratura** keyhole; **fare un buco nell'acqua** to fail, draw a blank; **farsi un buco** *(fam: drogarsi)* to have a fix; **buco nero** *(anche fig)* black hole
bucolicamente [bukolika'mente] AVV bucolically, pastorally
bucolico, a, ci, che [bu'kɔliko] AGG bucolic, pastoral
Budapest ['budapest] SF Budapest
Budda ['budda] SM INV Buddha
buddismo [bud'dizmo] SM Buddhism
buddista, i, e [bud'dista] AGG, SM/F Buddhist
buddistico, a, ci, che [bud'distiko] AGG Buddhist
budello [bu'dɛllo] SM **1** *(pl f* **budella***) (intestino)* bowel, intestine, gut **2** *(materiale)* gut **3** *(vicolo)* alley
budget ['bʌdʒit] SM INV budget; **budget pubblicitario** advertising budget
budgetario, ria, ri, rie [buddʒe'tarjo] AGG budgetary
budino [bu'dino] SM pudding; **budino al cioccolato** chocolate pudding
bue ['bue] SM *(pl* **buoi***)* **1** *(Zool)* ox; **bue marino** dugong; **bue muschiato** musk ox; **bue selvatico** bison **2** *(Culin)* beef; **carne di bue** beef
Buenos Aires [bwenos 'aires] SF Buenos Aires
bufala ['bufala] SF *(fam)* **1** *(errore)* howler; *(notizia non vera)* unfounded story **2** **quel film è una bufala** that film is utter rubbish
bufalo, a ['bufalo] SM buffalo; **bufalo indiano** water buffalo
bufera [bu'fɛra] SF *(anche fig)* storm
buffamente [buffa'mente] AVV in a funny way
buffet [by'fɛ] SM INV **1** *(mobile)* sideboard **2** *(bar)* buffet, refreshment bar
buffetteria [buffette'ria] SF buffet service
buffetto [buf'fetto] SM flick
buffo, a ['buffo] AGG *(ridicolo)* funny, comical; *(divertente)* funny, amusing; *(strano)* funny, odd; *(Teatro)* comic; **pensa a qc di più buffo** think of sth funnier; **è la cosa più buffa che abbia mai sentito** it's the funniest thing I've ever heard
buffonata [buffo'nata] SF *(azione)* prank, jest; *(parola)* jest; **fare buffonate** *(anche fig)* to clown about; **dire buffonate** to joke; *(fig)* to talk rubbish
buffone [buf'fone] SM *(anche fig)* clown, buffoon; *(pegg)* joker; **fare il buffone** *(fig)* to play the fool, clown about; **buffone di corte** court jester
buffoneria [buffone'ria] SF buffoonery
buffonesco, a, schi, sche [buffo'nesko] AGG clownish, comical
buggerare [buddʒe'rare] VT *(fam)* to swindle, cheat
bugia[1], gie [bu'dʒia] SF *(menzogna)* lie; **dire** *o* **raccontare bugie** to tell lies; **non dico mai le bugie** I never tell lies; **bugia pietosa** white lie; **le bugie hanno le gambe corte** *(Proverbio)* truth will out
bugia[2], gie [bu'dʒia] SF *(candeliere)* candleholder
bugiardo, a [bu'dʒardo] AGG lying, deceitful; **essere bugiardo** to be a liar
■ SM/F liar; **mi ha dato del bugiardo** he called me a liar; **bugiardo patologico** compulsive liar
bugigattolo [budʒi'gattolo] SM *(ripostiglio)* boxroom; *(pegg)* poky little room
bugliolo [buʎ'ʎɔlo] SM *(Naut)* (ship's) bucket
bugna ['buɲɲa] SF *(Archit)* boss; *(Naut)* clew cringle
buio, a, i *o* **ii, e** ['bujo] AGG *(oscuro)* dark; *(tetro, triste)* gloomy, dismal; **un vicolo buio** a dark alley
■ SM dark, darkness; **al buio** in the dark; **si sta facendo buio** *(imbrunisce)* it is growing *o* getting dark; **ha paura del buio** she's afraid of the dark; **buio pesto** pitch-dark, pitch-black
bulbo ['bulbo] SM **1** *(gen, Bot)* bulb **2** **bulbo oculare** eyeball **3** *(Naut)* ballast
Bulgaria [bulga'ria] SF Bulgaria
bulgaro, a ['bulgaro] AGG, SM/F Bulgarian; **i Bulgari** Bulgarians
■ SM *(lingua)* Bulgarian
bulimia [buli'mia] SF bulimia
bulimico, a, ci, che [bu'limiko] AGG, SM/F bulimic
bulino [bu'lino] SM *(Tecn)* burin, graver; **lavorare a bulino** to engrave
bulldozer ['buldouzə] SM INV bulldozer
bulletta [bul'letta] SF tack, stud
bullismo [bul'lizmo] SM bullying
bullo ['bullo] SM *(persona)* tough; **fare il bullo** to act tough

LO SAPEVI...?
bullo non si traduce mai con la parola inglese ***bull***

bullonare [bullo'nare] VT *(Tecn)* to bolt
bullone [bul'lone] SM bolt
bum [bum] ESCL *(scoppio)* boom!, bang!
■ SM INV bang; **fare bum** to bang
bungalow ['bʌngəlou] SM INV *(casa)* bungalow; *(per vacanze)* holiday chalet
bunker ['bunker] SM INV *(Mil)* bunker
buoi ['bwɔji] SMPL *di* **bue**
buonafede [bwona'fede] SF good faith; **in buonafede** in good faith
buonanima [bwo'nanima] SF: **mio nonno buonanima...** *or* **la buonanima di mio nonno** my grandfather, God rest his soul ...
buonanotte [bwona'nɔtte] ESCL good night!
■ SF: **dare la buonanotte a qn** to say good night to sb
buonasera [bwona'sera] ESCL *(anche:* **buona sera***)* good evening!
■ SF: **dare la buonasera a qn** to wish sb good evening; **signorina buonasera** *(TV)* female TV announcer
buoncostume [bwonkos'tume] SM public morality
■ SF: **la (squadra del) buoncostume** *(Polizia)* the vice squad
buondì [bwon'di] ESCL hello!
buongiorno [bwon'dʒorno] ESCL good morning *(o* afternoon)!
■ SM: **dare il buongiorno a qn** to wish sb good morning
buongrado [bwon'grado] AVV: **di buongrado** willingly
buongustaio, aia, ai, aie [bwongus'tajo] SM/F gourmet
buongusto [bwɔn'gusto] SM (good) taste; **abbi il buongusto di non farti più vedere** I hope you'll have

Bb

the decency not to show your face again

buonismo [bwo'nizmo] SM do-goodery

buonista, i; , e [bwo'nista] AGG do-gooding

buono[1], a ['bwɔno] PAROLA CHIAVE

■AGG (*comp* **migliore**) (*superl* **ottimo** (*davanti sm:* buon + *consonante, vocale,* buono + *s impura, gn, pn, ps, x, z; davanti sf:* buona + *consonante,* buon' + *vocale*)) (*gen*) good; (*prodotto*) good (quality); (*odore, ambiente, atmosfera*) good, nice, pleasant; (*posizione, ditta, impresa*) sound; **essere in buona compagnia** to be in good company; **essere di buona famiglia** to come from a good family; **avere un buon odore** to smell good *o* nice; **più buono** better; **avere un buon sapore** to taste good *o* nice; **buon senso** = buonsenso **buona società** polite society; **stai buono!** behave!; **tenere buono qn** (*bambino*) to keep sb quiet; (*fig: persona influente*) to keep sb sweet

2 (*generoso: persona, azione*) good, kind, kindly; **una persona di buon cuore** a good-hearted person; **essere buono come il pane** to have a heart of gold; **è una buona ragazza** she's a good-hearted girl

3 (*abile, idoneo*): **essere buono a nulla** to be no good *o* use at anything; *vedi anche* **sm/f quest'acqua non è buona da bersi** this water isn't safe to drink; **buono da buttar via** fit for the dustbin; **mi sembra buono per questo lavoro** he seems suitable for the job

4 (*utile, vantaggioso*): **a buon mercato** cheap; **buono a sapersi** that's good to know; **è stata una buona scelta** it was a good choice

5 (*giusto, valido*) correct, right; (: *motivo*) valid; **ad ogni buon conto** in any case; **a buon diritto** rightfully; **al momento buono** at the right moment

6 (*utilizzabile*) usable; (: *biglietto, passaporto*) valid; **è ancora buona questa vernice?** is this paint still okay *o* usable?; **non è più buono** (*latte*) it's off; (*pane*) it's stale

7 (*con valore intensivo*) good; **peserà dieci chili buoni** it must weigh a good ten kilos; **di buon mattino** early in the morning; **ci vuole un mesetto buono** it takes a good month *o* a month at least; **un buon numero** a good *o* large number; **deciditi una buona volta!** make up your mind once and for all!

8 (*auguri*): **buon appetito!** enjoy your meal!; **buon compleanno!** happy birthday!; **tante buone cose!** all the best!; **buon divertimento!** have a nice time!; **buona fortuna!** good luck!; **buon giorno!** (*in mattinata*) good morning!; (*di pomeriggio*) good afternoon!; **buon Natale!** happy Christmas!; **buona notte!** good night!; **buona permanenza!** enjoy your stay!; **buon riposo!** sleep well!; **buona sera!** good evening!; **buon viaggio!** have a good trip!

9 (*fraseologia*): **fare qc alla buona** to do sth simply *o* in a simple way; **stasera mi vesto alla buona** I'm not getting dressed up this evening; **è un tipo alla buona** he's an easy-going sort; **accetterà con le buone o con le cattive** he'll have to agree whether he wants to or not; **l'ho fatto di buon grado** I did it willingly; **che Dio ce la mandi buona!** here's hoping!; **essere in buone mani** to be in good hands; **con le buone maniere** in a kind *o* friendly way; **mettere una buona parola per qn** to put in a good word for sb; **essere a buon punto** to be well advanced; **siamo a buon punto con il pranzo** dinner's nearly ready; **questa sì che è buona!** that's a good one!; **mi dica, buon uomo** tell me, my good man; **fare buon viso a cattivo gioco** to put a brave face on things

■SM/F (*persona*) good *o* upright person; **i buoni e i cattivi** (*in film*) the goodies and the baddies; **un buono a nulla** a good-for-nothing

■SM, SOLO SG (*bontà*) goodness, good; **di buono c'è che...** the good thing about it is that ...; **essere un poco di buono** to be a nasty piece of work; **è una poco di buono** she's a slut

buono[2] ['bwɔno] SM **1** (*Comm*) coupon, voucher **2** (*Fin*) bill, bond; **buono d'acquisto** credit note, credit slip; **buono benzina** petrol coupon; **buono di cassa** cash voucher; **buono di consegna** delivery note; **buono fruttifero** interest-bearing bond; **buono d'imbarco** shipping note; **buono d'imposta** *special credit instrument for tax-relief purposes*; **buono mensa** canteen voucher; **buono pasto** meal ticket; **buono (ordinario) del Tesoro** short-term treasury bond, treasury bill; **buono postale fruttifero** interest-bearing bond (*issued by Italian Post Office*); **buono sconto** coupon; **buono del Tesoro poliennale** (*Econ*) long-term treasury bond

buonora [bwo'nora] SF (*anche:* **buon'ora**): **di buonora** early; **alla buonora** finally, at last

buonsenso [bwon'sɛnso] SM, SOLO SG common sense; **non ha un briciolo di buonsenso** she hasn't a bit of common sense

buontempone, a [bwontem'pone] SM/F jovial person

buonumore [bwonu'more] SM (*anche:* **buon umore**): **essere di buonumore** to be in a good mood; **oggi sono di buonumore** I'm in a good mood today

buonuomo [bwo'nwɔmo] SM = **buon uomo**

buonuscita [bwonuʃʃita] SF **1** (*Industria*) golden handshake **2** (*di affitti*) *sum paid for the relinquishing of tenancy rights*

burattinaio, ai [buratti'najo] SM puppeteer, puppet master

burattino [burat'tino] SM (*anche fig*) puppet

▷ www.buma.it/

burberamente [burbera'mente] AVV grumpily, gruffly

burbero, a ['burbero] AGG surly, gruff

■SM/F surly person, gruff person; **un burbero benefico** a rough diamond

bureau [by'ro] SM INV (*mobile*) writing desk, bureau

buretta [bu'retta] SF (*Chim*) burette

burino, a [bu'rino] SM/F (*romanesco*) country bumpkin

burla ['burla] SF prank, trick; **per burla** for fun, for a joke

burlare [bur'lare] VT to make fun of

▶ **burlarsi** VIP: **burlarsi di** = **vt**

burlescamente [burleska'mente] AVV (*per burla*) in jest; (*in chiave burlesca*) as a burlesque

burlesco, a, schi, sche [bur'lesko] AGG (*tono, voce*) jesting; (*stile*) burlesque

burlone, a [bur'lone] SM/F joker

burocrate [bu'rɔkrate] SM (*anche pegg*) bureaucrat

burocraticamente [burokratika'mente] AVV bureaucratically

burocratico, a, ci, che [buro'kratiko] AGG bureaucratic; **lungaggini burocratiche** red tape

burocratismo [burokra'tizmo] SM bureaucratic attitude

burocratizzare [burokratid'dzare] VT to bureaucratize

burocrazia [burokrat'tsia] SF bureaucracy

burqa, burka ['burka] SM INV burka

burrasca, sche [bur'raska] SF (*anche fig*) storm; **c'è** *o* **tira aria di burrasca** (*anche fig*) there's a storm brewing *o* in the air; **mare in burrasca** stormy sea; **c'è**

burrasca in famiglia there's trouble at home
burrascosamente [burraskosa'mente] AVV stormily
burrascoso, a [burras'koso] AGG (*anche fig*) stormy
burrificio, ci [burri'fitʃo] SM creamery
burro ['burro] SM butter; **pane e burro** bread and butter; **pasta/riso al burro** buttered pasta/rice; **uovo al burro** egg fried in butter; **questa bistecca è un burro** (*tenero*) this steak melts in your mouth; **avere le mani di burro** (*fig*) to be butter-fingered; **burro di cacao** cocoa butter; (*per labbra*) lip salve
burrone [bur'rone] SM ravine, gorge
burroso, a [bur'roso] AGG buttery
buscare [bus'kare] VT (*anche:* **buscarsi**: *raffreddore, schiaffo*) to get; **buscarle** to catch it, get a good hiding; (*essere battuto*) to get a drubbing
buscherò *ecc* [buske'rɔ] VB *vedi* **buscare**
busillis [bu'zillis] SM INV: **qui sta il busillis** there's the rub
bussare [bus'sare] VI (*aus* **avere**) **1** to knock; **bussare alla porta** to knock at the door; **ho bussato alla porta** I knocked at the door; **stanno bussando** there's somebody at the door **2** (*Carte*) *to knock on the table to induce partner to play his highest card*
bussola ['bussola] SF **1** (*strumento nautico*) compass; **bussola giroscopica/magnetica** gyro/magnetic compass; **perdere la bussola** (*fig*) to lose one's head, lose one's bearings **2** (*porta*) revolving door **3** (*cassetta sigillata*) collection box
bussolotto [busso'lɔtto] SM (*per dadi*) dice-shaker
busta ['busta] SF **1** (*da lettera*) envelope; **in busta aperta/chiusa** in an unsealed/sealed envelope; **busta a finestra** window envelope; **busta paga** pay packet; (*listino*) pay slip **2** (*astuccio: di occhiali*) case; **busta portatrucco** make-up bag
bustarella [busta'rella] SF bribe, backhander; **dare una bustarella a qn** to slip sb a backhander; **lo scandalo delle bustarelle** the bribes scandal
bustina [bus'tina] SF **1** (*piccola busta*) envelope **2** (*di cibi, farmaci*) sachet; **una bustina di zucchero** a sachet of sugar; **bustina di tè** tea bag **3** (*Mil*) forage cap
bustino [bus'tino] SM corselet(te)
busto ['busto] SM **1** (*Anat, Scultura*) bust; **a mezzo busto** (*fotografia, ritratto*) half-length; **stare a busto eretto** to stand up straight; **piegate il busto in avanti** bend your trunk forward **2** (*indumento*) corset
butano [bu'tano] SM butane
buttafuori [butta'fwɔri] SM INV bouncer
buttare [but'tare] VT
1 (*gettare*) to throw; **ha buttato il cappotto sul letto** he threw his coat onto the bed; **buttare fuori qn** to throw sb out; **buttare qc addosso a qn** to throw sth at sb; **buttare qc a qn** to throw sth to sb; **buttare qc per terra** to throw sth on the ground; **buttare la pasta/il riso** (*Culin*) to put pasta/rice into boiling water; **hai già buttato la pasta?** have you put the pasta in?; **buttarsi il cappotto sulle spalle** to throw one's coat round one's shoulders; **buttarsi qc dietro le spalle** to throw sth over one's shoulder; (*fig: passato*) to put sth behind one
2 (*anche:* **buttare via**: *nella spazzatura*) to throw away, discard; (*sprecare: soldi, tempo*) to waste; **era rotto e l'ho buttato via** it was broken and I threw it away; **non è un tipo da buttar via** he's not bad looking
3 **buttare giù** (*scritto*) to jot down, scribble down; (*cibo, boccone*) to gulp down; (*edificio*) to pull down, knock down; (*governo*) to bring down; **buttare giù un muro** to knock down a wall; **buttare giù due righe** to scribble a couple of lines; **buttare giù qn** (*deprimere*) to get sb down
4 (*fraseologia*): **buttare la colpa addosso a qn** to lay the blame on sb; **buttare a mare** (*fig: soldi, occasione*) to throw away; **buttare i soldi dalla finestra** to throw money down the drain; **ho buttato là una frase** I mentioned it in passing; **gli ha buttato in faccia tutto il suo disprezzo** she told him to his face how much she despised him; **mi ha buttato in faccia tutta la verità** he flung the truth at me
■ VI (*aus* **avere**) (*fam: apparire*): **la faccenda butta male** things are looking bad
▶ **buttarsi** VR (*saltare*) to jump; **buttiamoci!** (*saltiamo*) let's jump!; (*rischiamo*) let's have a go!; **buttarsi in acqua** to jump into the water; **buttarsi dalla finestra** to jump out of the window; **buttarsi su** *o* **addosso a qn** to launch o.s. at sb; **buttarsi nelle braccia di qn** to throw o.s. into sb's arms; **buttarsi in ginocchio** to throw o.s. down on one's knees; **buttarsi (anima e corpo) in qc** to throw o.s. (wholeheartedly) into sth; **buttarsi giù** (*stendersi*) to lie down; (*stimarsi poco*) to have a low opinion of o.s.; (*scoraggiarsi*) to get depressed *o* miserable; **buttarsi nella mischia** (*anche fig*) to throw o.s. into the fray; **buttarsi sulla preda** (*anche fig*) to pounce on one's prey
buttata [but'tata] SF (*Bot*) sprouting
butterare [butte'rare] VT to pock-mark
butterato, a [butte'rato] AGG pock-marked, pitted
buzzo ['buddzo] SM: **di buzzo buono** (*con impegno*) with a will
buzzurro, a [bud'dzurro] SM/F (*pegg*) boor
bypassare [baipas'sare] VT (*strada*) to bypass; (*fig: ostacolo*) to bypass, to circumvent
byte ['bait] SM INV (*Inform*) byte
BZ SIGLA = Bolzano

C, c [tʃi] SF O M INV (*lettera*) C, c; **C come Como** ≈ C for Charlie
C [tʃi] ABBR **1** (*Geog*) = **capo** **2** (= **Celsius, centigrado**) C **3** (= **conto**) a/c
■ SIGLA M (*Inform*) C
CA SIGLA = *Cagliari*
c.a. ABBR **1** (*Elettr:* = **corrente alternata**) AC **2** (*Comm*) = *corrente anno*
ca. ABBR (= **circa**) ca (= *circa*)
CAB [kab] SIGLA M (= **Codice di Avviamento Bancario**) sort code
cab. ABBR = **cablogramma**
cabala ['kabala] SF (*intrigo*) cabal
cabaret [kaba'rɛ] SM INV cabaret
cabina [ka'bina] SF (*di nave*) cabin; (*di ascensore*) cage; (*di funivia*) car; (*in spiaggia*) beach hut; (*in piscina*) cubicle; **una cabina di seconda classe** a second-class cabin
■ **cabina di blocco** *o* **di manovra** (*Ferr*) signal box; **cabina elettorale** polling booth; **cabina elettrica** substation; **cabina di guida** driver's cab; **cabina passeggeri** (*Aer*) passenger cabin *o* compartment; **cabina di pilotaggio** (*Aer: gen*) cockpit; (*: in aereo di linea*) flight deck; **cabina di proiezione** (*Cine*) projection booth; **cabina di prova** changing room (*in shop*); **cabina di regia** control room (*Radio, TV*); **cabina telefonica** telephone booth *o* box, callbox
cabinato, a [kabi'nato] AGG (*Naut*) with a cabin
■ SM cabin cruiser
cabinovia [kabino'via] SF two-seater cablecar
cablaggio, gi [ka'bladdʒo] SM wiring
cablare [ka'blare] VT to cable
cablatura [kabla'tura] SF = **cablaggio**
cablografia [kablogra'fia] SF cable telegraphy
cablogramma, i [kablo'gramma] SM cable(gram)
cabotaggio, gi [kabo'taddʒo] SM **1** (*Naut*) coastal navigation; **nave da cabotaggio** tramp, coaster **2 di piccolo cabotaggio** (*fig: di poco conto: attività*) small-scale
cabotare [kabo'tare] VI (*aus* **avere**) to ply along the coast
cabrare [ka'brare] VI (*aus* **avere**) (*Aer*) to nose up
cabrata [ka'brata] SF (*Aer*) nose-up
cabriolet [kabrio'lɛ] SM INV (*auto*) convertible
cacao [ka'kao] SM INV (*albero*) cacao; (*polvere*) cocoa
cacare [ka'kare] (*fam!*) VI (*aus* **avere**), VT to shit (*fam!*); **cacare (qn/qc)** (*essere interessato*) to give a shit *o* toss (about sb/sth); **mi piace molto ma lui non mi caca** I like him a lot but he doesn't give a shit *o* toss about me; **cacarsi sotto** *o* **addosso** (*fig: avere paura*) to shit o.s. (*fam!*); **va' a cacare!** piss off! (*fam!*)
cacarella [kaka'rɛlla] SF (*fam: dissenteria*) runs *pl*; **far venire la cacarella a qn** (*fig fam*) to scare the shit out of sb (*fam!*)
cacata [ka'kata] SF (*fig fam!: cosa brutta, mal fatta*) shit (*fam!*)
cacatoa [kaka'tɔa], **cacatua** [kaka'tua] SM INV cockatoo
cacca ['kakka] SF (*fam: anche fig*) shit (*fam!*); **fare la cacca** (*linguaggio infantile*) to have a poo; **dover fare la cacca** to have to have a poo
caccia¹ ['kattʃa] SF **1** hunting; (*con fucile*) shooting, hunting; **sono contro la caccia** I'm against hunting; **andare a caccia** to go hunting; **la domenica vanno a caccia** they go hunting on Sundays; **andare a caccia di leoni** to go lion-hunting; **battuta di caccia** hunting party **2** (*anche:* **stagione di caccia**) hunting (*o* shooting) season **3** (*cacciagione*) game **4** (*fig: inseguimento, ricerca*) chase; **dare la caccia a qn** to give chase to sb; **la polizia gli dava la caccia** the police was going after him; **essere a caccia di notizie/libri** to be on the lookout for news/books; **essere a caccia di un impiego/una casa** to be job-hunting *o* house-hunting; **essere a caccia di uomini/soldi** to be after men/money; **andare a caccia di guai** to go looking for trouble
■ **caccia al cervo** deer hunting, deerstalking; **caccia grossa** big game hunting; **caccia alle streghe** witch-hunt; **caccia subacquea** harpoon fishing; **caccia al tesoro** treasure hunt; **caccia all'uomo** manhunt
▷ www.fidc.it/
caccia² ['kattʃa] SM INV (*aereo*) fighter; (*nave*) destroyer
cacciabombardiere [kattʃabombar'djɛre] SM fighter-bomber
cacciagione [kattʃa'dʒone] SF game

cacciare [kat'tʃare] VT **1** (*Sport*) to hunt; (*con fucile*) to shoot, hunt; **ha imparato a cacciare e a pescare da bambino** he learned to hunt and fish as a child **2** (*mandar via: persona*): **cacciare qn di casa/dal paese/dalla scuola** to throw sb out of the house/the country/school; (*: nemico*) to drive away; (*: tristezza, malinconia, dubbio*) to chase away; **se continua così, lo cacceranno dalla squadra** if he goes on like this, they'll throw him out of the team **3** (*fam: mettere*): **cacciare qn in prigione** to throw sb into prison; **cacciarsi qc in testa** (*cappello*) to pull sth on; (*idea*) to get sth into one's head; **dove hai cacciato quel libro?** where have you put that book? **4** (*fam: emettere*): **cacciare un grido** to let out a cry *o* yell **5** (*fam: estrarre*): **cacciare fuori** to pull out; **cacciare fuori un coltello** to pull out a knife; **cacciare fuori la lingua** to stick out one's tongue; **caccia fuori i soldi!** pay up!, cough up!
▶ **cacciarsi** VR **1** (*fam: nascondersi*) to hide o.s.; **ma dove si sarà cacciato?** where can he (*o* it) have got to? **2** (*fam: mettersi*): **cacciarsi nei guai** *o* **in un bel pasticcio** to get into a lot of trouble; **si caccia sempre nei guai** she's always getting into trouble

cacciata [kat'tʃata] SF: **la cacciata dell'invasore** the driving out of the invader

cacciatora [kattʃa'tora] SF **1** (*giacca*) hunting jacket **2** (*Culin*): **pollo** *ecc* **alla cacciatora** chicken *ecc* chasseur

cacciatore [kattʃa'tore] SM hunter; **cacciatore di dote** fortune-hunter; **cacciatore di frodo** poacher; **cacciatore di teste** (*anche fig*) headhunter

cacciatorpediniere [kattʃatorpedi'njɛre] SM destroyer

cacciavite [kattʃa'vite] SM INV screwdriver; **cacciavite cercafase** mains tester; **cacciavite a croce** *o* **a stella** Philips® screwdriver

cacciucco [kat'tʃukko] SM *spiced fish soup*

cachemire [kaʃmir] SM INV cashmere

cachet [ka'ʃɛ] SM INV **1** (*Med: compressa*) tablet; (*: capsula*) capsule **2** (*compenso*) fee **3** (*colorante per capelli*) rinse

cachi[1] ['kaki] SM INV (*albero, frutto*) persimmon

cachi[2] ['kaki] AGG INV, SM khaki

cacio, ci ['katʃo] SM cheese; **venire** *o* **cadere come il cacio sui maccheroni** (*fig*) to turn up at the right moment

cacofonia [kakofo'nia] SF cacophony

cacofonico, a, ci, che [kako'fɔniko] AGG cacophonous

cactus ['kaktus] SM INV cactus

cadauno, a [kada'uno] AGG, PRON INDEF each

cadavere [ka'davere] SM corpse, (dead) body; **sembrare un cadavere ambulante** to look like death warmed up

cadaverico, a, ci, che [kada'vɛriko] AGG (*fig*) deathly pale; **rigidità cadaverica** rigor mortis

caddi *ecc* ['kaddi] VB *vedi* **cadere**

cadente [ka'dɛnte] AGG falling; (*fig: edificio*) tumbledown; (*: persona*) decrepit; **stella cadente** falling *o* shooting star

cadenza [ka'dɛntsa] SF (*gen*) cadence; (*ritmo*) rhythm; (*inflessione*) intonation; (*Mus*) cadenza; **a cadenza regolare** at regular intervals

cadenzare [kaden'tsare] VT to mark the rhythm of; **marciare con passo cadenzato** to march in time

cadere [ka'dere] VI IRREG (*aus* **essere**) **1** (*persona, oggetto*) to fall; (*tetto*) to fall in; (*aereo*) to crash; **ho inciampato e sono caduta** I tripped and fell; **cadere dalla bicicletta/da un albero/dalle scale** to fall off one's bicycle/from a tree/down the stairs; **è caduto dalla bicicletta** he fell off his bike; **sono caduto dal letto** I fell out of bed; **cadere bocconi** to fall flat on one's face; **cadere in ginocchio** to fall on(to) one's knees; **cadere lungo disteso** to fall flat on one's back; **cadere in piedi** (*anche fig*) to land on one's feet; **cadere ai piedi di qn** to fall at sb's feet; **cadere dal sonno** to be falling asleep on one's feet; **cadere a terra** to fall down, fall to the ground; **far cadere** (*urtando*) to knock over *o* down; (*dall'alto*) to drop; **cadere dalle nuvole** (*fig*) to be taken aback; **quando gliel'ho detto è caduto dalle nuvole** when I told him about it he was very surprised; **la conversazione cadde su Garibaldi** the conversation came round to Garibaldi; **mi è caduto lo sguardo su una vecchia foto** my eye fell upon an old photo; **ti è caduta la sciarpa** you've dropped your scarf; **questi pantaloni cadono bene** these trousers hang well **2** (*staccarsi: denti, capelli*) to fall out; (*: foglie*) to fall **3** (*scendere: pioggia, neve*) to fall, come down; (*: notte, stella*) to fall **4** (*cessare: vento*) to drop; **è caduta la linea** I (*o* you *ecc*) have been cut off **5** (*data*) to fall; **quest'anno il mio compleanno cade di martedì** my birthday falls on a Tuesday this year **6** (*venire a trovarsi*): **cadere ammalato** to fall ill; **cadere in disgrazia** to fall into disgrace; **cadere in errore** to make a mistake; **cadere in trappola** fall into a trap; **cadere in miseria/oblio** to sink into poverty/oblivion **7** (*soldato, fortezza, governo*) to fall; **far cadere il governo** to bring down the government **8** **lasciar cadere** (*oggetto, fig: discorso, proposta*) to drop; (*frase, parola*) to slip in; **si lasciò cadere sulla poltrona** he dropped *o* fell into the armchair

cadetto, a [ka'detto] AGG **1** younger; **ramo cadetto** cadet branch **2** (*Sport*) junior *attr*
■ SM (*gen, Mil*) cadet; (*Sport*) junior

cadmio ['kadmjo] SM cadmium

cadrò *ecc* [ka'drɔ] VB *vedi* **cadere**

caducità [kadutʃi'ta] SF transience

caduco, a, chi, che [ka'duko] AGG **1** (*fig letter*) short-lived, fleeting **2** (*Bot*) deciduous

caduta [ka'duta] SF (*gen, Rel*) fall; **ha fatto una brutta caduta** he had a nasty fall; **la caduta dei capelli** hair loss
■ **caduta libera** (*Fis*) free fall; **caduta massi** falling rocks; **caduta del sistema** (*Inform*) system failure; **caduta di tensione** (*Elettr*) voltage drop

caduto, a [ka'duto] PP *di* **cadere**
■ AGG (*morto*) dead
■ SM dead soldier; **monumento ai caduti** war memorial

caffè [kaf'fɛ] SM INV (*bevanda*) coffee; (*bar*) café; **si sono incontrati in un caffè** they met in a café; **un gelato al caffè** a coffee ice cream; **caffè corretto** coffee with a shot of spirits; **caffè decaffeinato** decaffeinated coffee; **caffè espresso** espresso coffee; **caffè in grani** coffee beans; **caffè lungo** weak black coffee; **caffè macchiato** coffee with a dash of milk; **caffè macinato** ground coffee; **caffè d'orzo** barley coffee; **caffè ristretto** strong black coffee; **caffè solubile** instant coffee

caffeario, ria, ri, rie [kaffe'arjo] AGG coffee *attr*

caffeina [kaffe'ina] SF caffeine

caffellatte [kaffel'latte] SM INV white coffee

caffettano [kaffet'tano] SM kaftan

caffetteria [kaffette'ria] SF coffee shop, coffee bar

Cc

caffettiera [kaffet'tjɛra] SF (*per fare il caffè*) coffee-maker; (*per servire il caffè*) coffeepot
cafonaggine [kafo'naddʒine] SF boorishness
cafone, a [ka'fone] SM/F (*persona*) boor, ill-mannered person; **comportarsi da cafone** to be ill-mannered
■ AGG (*persona, comportamento, risposta*) boorish, ill-mannered
cagare [ka'gare] VI = **cacare**
cagionare [kadʒo'nare] VT to cause, be the cause of
cagione [ka'dʒone] SF cause
cagionevole [kadʒo'nevole] AGG (*salute*) delicate, weak
cagliare [kaʎ'ʎare] VI (*aus* **essere**)
■ VT to curdle
cagliaritano, a [kaʎʎari'tano] AGG of *o* from Cagliari
■ SM/F inhabitant *o* native of Cagliari
cagliata [kaʎ'ʎata] SF curd
cagliatura [kaʎʎa'tura] SF curdling
caglio, gli ['kaʎʎo] SM rennet
cagna ['kaɲɲa] SF (*Zool*) bitch
cagnara [kaɲ'ɲara] SF uproar; **far cagnara** to make a din
cagnesco [kaɲ'ɲesko] AGG: **guardare qn in cagnesco** to scowl at sb
CAI ['kai] SIGLA M = *Club Alpino Italiano*
caimano [kai'mano] SM cayman
Caino [ka'ino] SM Cain
Cairo ['kairo] SF Cairo
cala ['kala] SF **1** (*baia*) bay **2** (*Naut*) hold
calabrese [kala'brese] AGG, SM/F Calabrian
calabrone [kala'brone] SM hornet
calafatare [kalafa'tare] VT (*Naut*) to caulk
calamaio, ai [kala'majo] SM inkpot, inkwell
calamaro [kala'maro] SM squid; **calamari alla griglia** grilled squid
calamita [kala'mita] SF (*anche fig*) magnet
calamità [kalami'ta] SF INV disaster, calamity; **è una calamità naturale** (*fig*) he's a walking disaster; **calamità naturale** natural disaster
calamitare [kalami'tare] VT (*anche fig*) to magnetize
calamitato, a [kalami'tato] AGG (*ago della bussola*) magnetic
calamo ['kalamo] SM (*Zool, penna*) quill
calandra [ka'landra] SF (*macchina*) calender; (*Aut*) radiator grill
calante [ka'lante] AGG falling; **sole calante** setting sun; **luna calante** waning moon
calare [ka'lare] VT (*gen*) to lower; (*Maglia*) to decrease; (*ancora*) to drop, lower; (*perpendicolare*) to drop; (*fam: ecstasy*) to drop; **calare il sipario** to lower the curtain
■ VI (*aus* **essere**) **1** (*gen*) to come down, fall; (*sole*) to set, go down; (*notte, silenzio*) to fall **2** (*diminuire: vento, febbre*) to drop; (*: temperatura, prezzo*) to drop, fall; (*: suono*) to die away; **la popolazione è calata del dieci per cento** the population has decreased by ten percent; **il prezzo della benzina è calato** the price of petrol has fallen; **la temperatura è calata improvvisamente** the temperature suddenly dropped; **calare di peso** to lose weight; **sono calato (di) 3 chili** I've lost 3 kilos; **cala!** (*non esagerare*) come off it! **3** (*invadere*): **calare (su)** to descend (on)
▶ **calarsi** VR **1** (*discendere*) to lower o.s.; **calarsi da una finestra/in un crepaccio** to lower o.s. from a window/into a crevasse **2** **calarsi nella parte** (*Teatro*): **si è calato bene nella parte** he has really got into the part; **si è calato un po' troppo nella parte del giovane dirigente** (*fig*) he goes a bit too far in playing the young executive
■ SM: **al calar del sole** at sunset; **al calar della luna** when the moon goes down
calata [ka'lata] SF (*invasione*) invasion
calca ['kalka] SF throng, press
calcagno [kal'kaɲɲo] SM (*pl* **calcagna** (*negli usi figurati*)) (*Anat, di scarpa*) heel; **aveva la polizia alle calcagna** the police were hot on his heels; **il mio capo mi sta sempre alle calcagna** my boss is never off my back
calcare[1] [kal'kare] VT **1** (*premere*) to press down; (*: coi piedi*) to tread, press down; **calcarsi il cappello sugli occhi** to pull one's hat down over one's eyes; **le scene** (*fig*) to be on the stage; **calcare le orme di qn** (*fig*) to follow in sb's footsteps; **calcare la mano** (*fig*) to overdo it, exaggerate **2** (*mettere in rilievo*) to stress; **calcare le parole** to accentuate each syllable
calcare[2] [kal'kare] SM limestone; (*incrostazione*) (lime)scale
calcareo, a [kal'kareo] AGG limestone *attr*
calce[1] ['kaltʃe] SF lime; **calce spenta** slaked lime; **calce viva** quicklime
calce[2] ['kaltʃe] SM (*Amm*): **in calce a** at the foot of; **"firma in calce"** "please sign below"
calcedonio [kaltʃe'dɔnjo] SM chalcedony
calcestruzzo [kaltʃes'truttso] SM concrete
calcetto [kal'tʃetto] SM (*calcio-balilla*) table football; (*calcio a cinque*) five-a-side (football)
calcherò *ecc* [kalke'rɔ] VB *vedi* **calcare**
calciare [kal'tʃare] VI (*aus* **avere**)
■ VT to kick
calciatore [kaltʃa'tore] SM (*Calcio*) (football) player, footballer; (*Rugby*) kicker
calcificarsi [kaltʃifi'karsi] VIP to calcify
calcificazione [kaltʃifikat'tsjone] SF calcification
calcina [kal'tʃina] SF (lime) mortar
calcinaccio, ci [kaltʃi'nattʃo] SM flake of plaster; **un mucchio di calcinacci** a pile of rubble
calcio[1], ci ['kaltʃo] SM **1** (*pedata: anche Sport*) kick; **dare un calcio a qn** to give sb a kick, kick sb; **mi ha dato un calcio** he gave me a kick **2** (*sport*) football, soccer; **giochi a calcio?** do you play football?; **una partita di calcio** a football match; **squadra di calcio** football team **3** (*di pistola, fucile*) butt
■ **calcio d'angolo** corner (kick); **calcio d'inizio** kick-off; **calcio di prima** (*Calcio*) *direct free kick*; **calcio di punizione** free kick; **calcio di rigore** penalty kick; **calcio di rimessa** (*Calcio*) goal kick; **calcio di rinvio** (*Rugby*) drop-out; **calcio di seconda** (*Calcio*) indirect free kick
▷ www.figc.it/
calcio[2] ['kaltʃo] SM (*Chim*) calcium
calcio-balilla ['kaltʃo ba'lilla] SM INV table football
calcio-mercato ['kaltʃo mer'kato] SM football market
▷ www.calciomercato.com/index.php
calcisticamente [kaltʃistika'mente] AVV from a footballing point of view, as regards football
calcistico, a, ci, che [kal'tʃistiko] AGG football *attr*
calco, chi ['kalko] SM (*Scultura*) cast, mould (*Brit*), mold (*Am*), casting, moulding (*Brit*), molding (*Am*); (*di disegno*) tracing; (*Ling*) calque, loan translation
calcografia [kalkogra'fia] SF (*incisione, arte*) copper engraving
calcolare [kalko'lare] VT (*fare il conto di*) to calculate, work out; (*considerare*) to reckon on, take into account; (*ponderare*) to weigh (up); **hai calcolato quanto viene a testa?** have you worked out how much it comes to each?; **calcolo che sarò di ritorno fra 5 giorni** I

reckon I'll be back in 5 days' time; **calcolare i pro e i contro** to weigh up the pros and cons

calcolatore, trice [kalkola'tore] AGG (*fig*) calculating
■SM computer
■SF (*anche:* **macchina calcolatrice**) calculator
■SM/F (*persona*) calculating person

calcolo ['kalkolo] SM **1** (*anche Mat*) calculation; **fare il calcolo di qc** to work sth out; **ho fatto il calcolo di quanto gli dovevo** I worked out how much I owed him; **ho fatto un rapido calcolo** I did a quick calculation; **fare i propri calcoli** (*fig*) to weigh up the pros and cons; **per calcolo** out of self-interest; **a un calcolo approssimativo** at a rough estimate; **calcolo differenziale** differential calculus; **calcolo infinitesimale** infinitesimal calculus; **calcolo integrale** integral calculus **2** (*Med*) stone, calculus (*termine tecn*); **calcolo renale** (*Med*) stone in the kidneys

caldaia [kal'daja] SF boiler

caldamente [kalda'mente] AVV (*fig: con cordialità*) warmly; (: *con fervore*) fervently

caldarrosta [kaldar'rɔsta] SF roast chestnut

caldeggiare [kalded'dʒare] VT to support

calderone [kalde'rone] SM cauldron; (*fig*) hotchpotch; **mettere tutto nello stesso calderone** (*fig*) to treat everything in the same way

caldo, a ['kaldo] AGG (*gen, fig*) warm; (*molto caldo*) hot; (*appassionato*) keen; (*cordiale: persona, accoglienza*) warm, friendly, cordial; **l'acqua calda** hot water; **la minestra è troppo calda** the soup's too hot; **il tuo cappotto è più caldo del mio** your coat is warmer than mine; **è il mese più caldo** it's the hottest month; **una bella coperta calda** a nice warm blanket; **batti il ferro finché è caldo** strike while the iron is hot; **piangere a calde lacrime** to weep bitterly; **essere una testa calda** to be hot-headed
■SM heat; **non sopporto il caldo** I can't stand the heat; **fa caldo** it's warm; (*molto caldo*) it's hot; **fa caldo qui, non trovi?** it's hot here, isn't it?; **col caldo che fa…** in this heat …; **ho caldo** I'm warm; (*molto caldo*) I'm hot; **ti tengo in caldo la minestra** I'm keeping your soup hot for you; **non mi fa né caldo né freddo** I couldn't care less; **quel ragazzo non mi fa né caldo né freddo** I'm indifferent to that boy; **a caldo** (*fig*) in the heat of the moment

LO SAPEVI...?
caldo non si traduce mai con *cold*

caleidoscopico, a, ci, che AGG kaleidoscopic

caleidoscopio, pi [kaleidos'kɔpjo] SM kaleidoscope

calendario, ri [kalen'darjo] SM calendar; **calendario degli incontri** (*Calcio*) fixtures list

calende [ka'lɛnde] SFPL calends; **rimandare qc alle calende greche** to put sth off indefinitely

calesse [ka'lɛsse] SM (*carrozza*) gig

calibrare [kali'brare] VT (*Tecn*) to calibrate; (*fig: misurare attentamente*) to gauge

calibrato, a [kali'brato] AGG (*Tecn*) calibrated; (*fig: discorso, giudizio*) balanced; **abiti a taglie calibrate** (*Sartoria*) outsize clothes

calibratura [kalibra'tura] SF calibration

calibro ['kalibro] SM (*di arma*) calibre, bore; (*strumento*) callipers *pl*; (*fig*) calibre; **di grosso calibro** (*fig*) prominent; **un personaggio di grosso calibro** a prominent figure

calice[1] ['kalitʃe] SM (*Bot*) calyx

calice[2] ['kalitʃe] SM (*coppa*) goblet; (*bicchiere*) stem glass; (*Rel*) chalice

califfo [ka'liffo] SM (*Storia*) caliph

California [kali'fɔrnja] SF California; **vengono dalla California** they come from California

californiano, a [kalifor'njano] AGG, SM/F Californian

caligine [ka'lidʒine] SF (*nebbia*) fog; (: *mista a fumo*) smog

caliginoso, a [kalidʒi'noso] AGG (*nebbioso*) foggy

Caligola [ka'ligola] SM Caligula

call centre [kol'sɛnter] SM INV call centre (*Brit*) *o* center (*Am*)

calle ['kalle] SF narrow street (*in Venice*)

callifugo, ghi [kal'lifugo] SM (*pomata*) anti-corn cream; (*cerotto*) corn plaster

calligrafia [kalligra'fia] SF (*scrittura*) handwriting; (*arte*) calligraphy; **non capisco la sua calligrafia** I can't read her writing

calligrafico, a, ci, che [kalli'grafiko] AGG (*vedi sf*) handwriting *attr*; calligraphic

Calliope [kal'liope] SF Calliope

callista, i, e [kal'lista] SM/F chiropodist

callo ['kallo] SM callus; (*sui piedi*) corn; **pestare i calli a qn** (*fig*) to tread on sb's toes; **fare il callo a qc** to get used to sth; **callo osseo** callus

calloso, a [kal'loso] AGG (*mano*) callous

calma ['kalma] SF (*vedi agg*) quietness, peacefulness; stillness; calm; (*tranquillità*) peace (and quiet), quietness; **finalmente un po' di calma** a bit of peace at last; **con calma** (*senza fretta*) slowly; **fai con calma** take your time; **mare in calma** calm sea; **calma!** steady on!; **calma, non spingete!** steady on, don't push!; **calma e sangue freddo!** keep cool *o* calm!; **è un giorno di calma nel negozio** it's a quiet day in the shop

calmante [kal'mante] AGG relaxing
■SM (*Med: analgesico*) painkiller; (: *sedativo*) tranquillizer, sedative

calmare [kal'mare] VT (*gen*) to calm; (*persona*) to calm (down); (*dolore*) to soothe; **ho cercato di calmarlo** I tried to calm him down; **non riusciva a calmare i dolori** he couldn't relieve the pain
▶ **calmarsi** VIP (*mare, persona*) to calm down, grow calm; (*dolore*) to ease; (*febbre, rabbia*) to subside; (*vento*) to abate; **calmati e dimmi tutto** calm down and tell me everything

calmierare [kalmje'rare] VT (*Comm: prezzi*) to control

calmiere [kal'mjɛre] SM (*Comm*): **calmiere dei prezzi** price control(s)

calmo, a ['kalmo] AGG (*atmosfera*) quiet, peaceful; (*aria, cielo*) still; (*persona, mare*) calm; **il mare è calmo, oggi** the sea's calm today; **stare calmo** to keep calm; **state calmi, non c'è pericolo** keep calm, there's no danger

calo ['kalo] SM: **calo (di)** (*gen*) fall (in), drop (in); (*di prezzi*) fall (in); (*di peso*) loss (of); (*di volume*) shrinkage; **un forte calo delle vendite** a big drop in sales; **un calo di prezzi** a fall in prices; **calo di peso** weight loss; **la sua popolarità ha subito un grosso calo** his popularity has fallen sharply

calore [ka'lore] SM (*gen*) warmth; (*intenso, Fis*) heat; (*fig: entusiasmo*) fervour; **accogliere qn con calore** to welcome sb warmly; **essere in calore** (*animale*) to be on heat

caloria [kalo'ria] SF calorie

calorico, a, ci, che [ka'lɔriko] AGG calorific

calorifero [kalo'rifero] SM radiator

calorifico, a, ci, che [kalo'rifiko] AGG calorific, heat producing

calorosamente [kalorosa'mente] AVV (*con cordialità*) warmly; (*con entusiasmo*) fervently

Cc

calorosità [kalorosi'ta] SF (*vedi agg*) warmth; heartiness
caloroso, a [kalo'roso] AGG (*persona, accoglienza*) warm; (*applauso*) hearty, enthusiastic; **un'accoglienza calorosa** a warm welcome; **è un tipo caloroso** he doesn't feel the cold
caloscia, sce [ka'lɔʃʃa] SF galosh
calotta [ka'lɔtta] SF (*di cappello*) crown
■ **calotta cranica** (*Anat*) skullcap; **calotta glaciale** (*Geog*) icecap; **calotta polare** (*Geog*) polar icecap; **calotta sferica** (*Mat*) segment of a sphere; **calotta dello spinterogeno** (*Aut*) distributor cap
calpestare [kalpes'tare] VT to tread on, trample on; **"vietato calpestare l'erba"** "keep off the grass"; **calpestare i diritti di qn** to encroach on sb's rights; **non farti calpestare** (*fig*) don't let people walk all over you
calpestio, tii [kalpes'tio] SM (*di piedi*) tread, treading; (: *rumore*) stamping
calumet [kaly'mɛ] SM INV (*anche:* **calumet della pace**) peace pipe
calunnia [ka'lunnja] SF slander; **spargere calunnie sul conto di qn** to spread slander about sb
calunniare [kalun'njare] VT to slander
calunniatore, trice [kalunnja'tore] AGG slanderous
■ SM/F slanderer
calunniosamente [kalunnjosa'mente] AVV slanderously
calunnioso, a [kalun'njoso] AGG slanderous
Calvario [kal'varjo] SM (*Rel*) Calvary; (*fig*) ordeal, trial; **da allora la sua vita è stata un calvario** her life since then has been one of suffering
calvinismo [kalvi'nizmo] SM Calvinism
calvinista, i, e [kalvi'nista] AGG, SM/F Calvinist
calvizie [kal'vittsje] SF baldness
calvo, a ['kalvo] AGG bald
■ SM bald man
calza ['kaltsa] SF (*da uomo*) sock; (*da donna: con reggicalze*) stocking; **una calza bucata** a sock with a hole in it; **fare la calza** to knit; **calze** (*calzini, calzettoni*) socks; (*collant*) tights; (*con reggicalze*) stockings; **calze elastiche** support stockings (*o* tights); **calze di nailon** nylons, (nylon) stockings (*o* tights)
calzamaglia [kaltsa'maʎʎa] SF tights *pl*; (*per danza, ginnastica*) leotard; **una calzamaglia** a pair of tights; **una calzamaglia di lana** a pair of woollen tights
calzante [kal'tsante] AGG (*fig*) appropriate, fitting
■ SM shoehorn
calzare [kal'tsare] VT (*scarpe, guanti: portare*) to wear; (: *mettere*) to put on
■ VI (*aus* **avere**, *nel senso fig* **essere**) to fit; **calzare a pennello** to fit like a glove; **questa descrizione gli calza a pennello** that describes him to a T
calzascarpe [kaltsas'karpe] SM INV shoehorn
calzatura [kaltsa'tura] SF footwear; **negozio di calzature** shoeshop
calzaturiero, a [kaltsatu'rjɛro] AGG shoe *attr*
calzaturificio, ci [kaltsaturi'fitʃo] SM shoe factory
calzetta [kal'tsetta] SF ankle sock; **una mezza calzetta** (*fig*) a nobody
calzettone [kaltset'tone] SM knee-length sock; **un paio di calzettoni** a pair of knee socks
calzificio, ci [kaltsi'fitʃo] SM hosiery factory
calzino [kal'tsino] SM (short) sock; **un paio di calzini** a pair of socks
calzolaio, ai [kaltso'lajo] SM (*che ripara*) cobbler; (*che fabbrica*) shoemaker; **mio padre fa il calzolaio** my father's a cobbler
calzoleria [kaltsole'ria] SF (*negozio*) shoe shop; (*arte*) shoemaking
calzoncini [kaltson'tʃini] SMPL shorts; **calzoncini da bagno** (swimming) trunks
calzone [kal'tsone] SM **1 calzone destro/sinistro** right/left trouser leg **2 calzoni** SMPL trousers (*Brit*), pants (*Am*); **portare i calzoni** (*anche fig*) to wear the trousers; **calzoni alla cavallerizza** jodhpurs; **calzoni corti** shorts; **calzoni alla zuava** knickerbockers **3** (*Culin*) calzone (*savoury turnover made with pizza dough*)
camaleonte [kamale'onte] SM (*Zool, fig*) chameleon
camaleontismo [kamaleon'tizmo] SM (*Pol*) opportunism
cambiadischi [kambja'diski] SM INV (*anche:* **cambiadischi automatico**) record changer
cambiale [kam'bjale] SF (*Comm*) bill (of exchange); (: *pagherò cambiario*) promissory note; **firmare cambiali per qc** to pay sth up in instalments; **cambiale di comodo** *o* **favore** accommodation bill
cambiamento [kambja'mento] SM change; **un cambiamento di orario** a change in the timetable
cambiare [kam'bjare] VT **1** (*gen*) to change; (*modificare*) to alter; **cambiare (l')aria in una stanza** to air a room; **vado in montagna per cambiare aria** I'm going to the mountains for a change of air; **è ora di cambiare aria** (*andarsene*) it's time to move on; **cambiare casa** to move (house); **ha cambiato casa il mese scorso** she moved house last month; **cambiare indirizzo** to change address; **cambiare treno** to change trains; **cambiare marcia** (*Aut*) to change gear; **cambiamo argomento** let's change the subject; **cambiare idea** to change one's mind; **scusi, ho cambiato idea, prendo quell'altro** sorry, I've changed my mind, I'll have that one; **cambiare le carte in tavola** (*fig*) to change one's tune **2** (*barattare*): **cambiare (qc con qn/qc per qc)** to exchange (sth with sb/sth for sth); **ho cambiato la mia macchina con quella del mio amico** I exchanged cars with my friend; **se non va bene me lo cambia?** if it's not right will you change it? **3** (*valuta*) to change; **mi puoi cambiare 100 euro?** can you change 100 euros for me?; **vorrei cambiare questi euro in sterline** I'd like to change these euros into pounds
■ VI (*aus* **essere**) (*variare*) to change, alter; **ultimamente è molto cambiato** he's changed a lot recently;
▶ **cambiarsi** VIP (*modificarsi*) to change
▶ **cambiarsi** VR: **cambiarsi (d'abito)** to get changed, change (one's clothes); **devo andare a casa a cambiarmi** I've got to go home and get changed
cambiario, ria, ri, rie [kam'bjarjo] AGG (*Fin*) exchange *attr*
cambiavalute [kambjava'lute] SM INV exchange office
cambio, bi ['kambjo] SM **1** (*gen*) change; (*modifica*) alteration, change; **dare il cambio a qn** to take over from sb, relieve sb; **se sei stanco ti do il cambio** if you're tired I'll take over from you; **fare il** *o* **un cambio** to change (over); **facciamo a cambio** let's change over *o* swap; **effettuare il cambio di campo** (*Sport*) to change ends; **in cambio di** in exchange for; **mi ha dato un CD in cambio del pallone** he gave me a CD in exchange for the football; **ho portato solo un cambio d'abito** I've only brought one change of clothes; **il cambio della guardia** the changing of the guard

2 (*Fin*) exchange; (*anche:* **tasso di cambio**) rate of exchange; **agenzia di cambio** bureau de change; **cambio a termine** forward exchange **3** (*Aut, Ciclismo*) gears *pl*; **cambio di marcia** gear change; **macchina con il cambio automatico** automatic (car)

cambista, i [kam'bista] SM (foreign-)exchange agent

Cambital ['kambital] SIGLA M = *Ufficio italiano dei cambi*

Cambogia [kam'bodʒa] SF Cambodia

cambogiano, a [kambo'dʒano] AGG, SM/F Cambodian

cambusa [kam'buza] SF pantry (*on ship*)

camelia [ka'mɛlja] SF camellia

camera ['kamera] SF **1** (*gen*) room; (*anche:* **camera da letto**) bedroom; (*mobili*) bedroom suite; **una camera grande** a large room; **è rimasto in camera sua tutto il pomeriggio** he stayed in his bedroom the whole afternoon **2** (*Pol*) Chamber, House; **le Camere** ≈ (the Houses of) Parliament (*Brit*), Congress (*Am*)
■ **camera ardente** chapel of rest; **camera d'aria** (*di pneumatico*) inner tube; (*di pallone*) bladder; **camera blindata** strongroom; **camera a bolle** (*Fis*) bubble chamber; **camera di combustione** combustion chamber; **Camera di commercio** Chamber of Commerce
⊳ www.camcom.it/
⊳ www.britchamitaly.com/index-it.asp
⊳ www.amcham.it/italian/home.asp
camera di decompressione decompression chamber; **Camera dei Deputati** Chamber of Deputies, ≈ House of Commons (*Brit*), ≈ House of Representatives (*Am*) **camera a due letti** twin-bedded room; **camera a gas** gas chamber; **camera del lavoro** trades union centre (*Brit*), labor union centre (*Am*); **camera matrimoniale** double room; **camera a nube** (*Fis*) cloud chamber; **camera oscura** (*Fot*) darkroom; **camera da pranzo** dining room; **camera singola** single room

LO SAPEVI...?
camera non si traduce mai con la parola inglese *camera*

CAMERA
The **Camera dei deputati** is the lower house of the Italian Parliament and is presided over by the "Presidente della Camera" who is chosen by the "deputati". Elections to the Chamber are normally held every 5 years. Since the electoral reform of 1993 members have been voted in via a system which combines a first-past-the-post element with proportional representation. *Vedi* **Parlamento**
⊳ www.camera.it/

cameraman ['kæmərəmən] SM INV (*TV*) cameraman

camerata[1] [kame'rata] SF (*dormitorio*) dormitory

camerata[2] [kame'rata] SM/F comrade (*of right-wing group*)

cameratesco, a, schi, sche [kamera'tesko] AGG: **spirito cameratesco** sense of comradeship

cameratismo [kamera'tizmo] SM comradeship

cameretta [kame'retta] SF (*piccola camera*) small bedroom; (*su piano stradale*) manhole

cameriera [kame'rjɛra] SF (*domestica*) maid; (*che serve a tavola*) waitress; (*che fa le camere*) chambermaid

cameriere [kame'rjɛre] SM (*domestico*) (man)servant; (*di ristorante*) waiter; **fa il cameriere** he's a waiter; **scusi, cameriere!** excuse me!

camerino [kame'rino] SM (*Teatro*) dressing room

cameristico, a, ci, che [kame'ristiko] AGG chamber-music *attr*

Camerun ['kamerun] SM Cameroon

camice ['kamitʃe] SM (*di medico, tecnico*) white coat; (*di chirurgo*) gown; (*di sacerdote*) alb

camiceria [kamitʃe'ria] SF (*fabbrica*) shirt factory; (*negozio*) shirt shop (*Brit*), shirt store (*Am*)

camicetta [kami'tʃetta] SF blouse

camicia, cie [ka'mitʃa] SF **1** (*da uomo*) shirt; (*da donna*) blouse; **nascere con la camicia** (*fig*) to be born with a silver spoon in one's mouth; **sudare sette camicie** (*fig*) to have a hell of a time **2** (*Tecn: involucro*) jacket
■ **camicia di forza** straitjacket; **camicia nera** (*fascista*) Blackshirt; **camicia da notte** (*da donna*) nightdress; (*da uomo*) nightshirt; **camicia verde** *supporter of Lega Nord*

camiciaio, aia, ai, aie [kami'tʃajo] SM/F (*sarto*) shirtmaker; (*che vende camicie*) shirtseller

camiciola [kami'tʃɔla] SF vest

camiciotto [kami'tʃɔtto] SM (*camicia sportiva*) casual shirt; (*per operai*) smock

caminetto [kami'netto] SM hearth, fireplace

camino [ka'mino] SM **1** (*focolare*) fireplace, hearth; **accendere il camino** to light the fire **2** (*comignolo, ciminiera, di vulcano*) chimney

camion ['kamjon] SM INV lorry (*Brit*), truck (*Am*)

camionabile [kamjo'nabile] AGG for heavy vehicles
■ SF road for heavy vehicles

camioncino [kamjon'tʃino] SM van

camionetta [kamjo'netta] SF jeep

camionista, i [kamjo'nista] SM/F lorry driver (*Brit*), truck driver (*Am*); **mio padre fa il camionista** my father's a lorry driver

camma ['kamma] SF cam; **albero a camme** camshaft

cammello [kam'mello] SM (*Zool, colore*) camel; (*stoffa*) camel hair

cammeo [kam'mɛo] SM cameo

camminare [kammi'nare] VI (*aus* **avere**) **1** (*gen*) to walk; **non sono abituato a camminare tanto** I'm not used to walking so much; **camminare a carponi** *o* **a quattro zampe** to go on all fours, crawl; **camminare a grandi passi** to stride (along); **camminare a testa alta** (*fig*) to walk with one's head held high; **con questo traffico non si cammina** you can't move with all this traffic; **cammina cammina, siamo arrivati** after a long walk, we arrived; **cammina!** (*spicciati*) come on!; (*levati di torno*) go away! **2** (*funzionare*) to work, go; **il mio orologio non cammina più** my watch has stopped

camminata [kammi'nata] SF walk; **fare una camminata** to go for a walk

camminatore, trice [kammina'tore] SM/F walker

cammino [kam'mino] SM (*viaggio*) walk; (*sentiero*) path; (*itinerario, direzione, tragitto*) way; **un'ora di cammino** an hour's walk; **lungo il cammino** along the way; **mettersi in cammino** to set *o* start off; **riprendere il cammino** to continue on one's way; **cammin facendo** on the way; **il cammino della virtù** (*fig*) the path of virtue

camomilla [kamo'milla] SF (*Bot*) camomile; (*infuso*) camomile tea

camorra [ka'mɔrra] SF Camorra; (*fig*) racket

camorrista, i, e [kamor'rista] SM/F member of the Camorra; (*fig*) racketeer

camorristico, a, ci, che [kamor'ristiko] AGG Camorra *attr*, of the Camorra

camoscio, sci [ka'mɔʃʃo] SM (*Zool, pelle*) chamois; **scarpe di camoscio** suede shoes

Cc

campagna [kam'paɲɲa] SF **1** (*gen*) country, countryside; (*paesaggio*) countryside; **vivere/abitare in campagna** to live in the country; **andare in campagna** to go to the country; **siamo andati in campagna a passeggiare** we went for a walk in the country; **la campagna inglese è proprio bella** the English countryside is really beautiful **2** (*terra coltivata*) land **3** (*Pol, Comm, Mil*) campaign; **fare una campagna** to campaign; **campagna acquisti** (*Calcio*) *negotiations between football clubs to buy and sell players*; **campagna promozionale vendite** sales campaign; **campagna pubblicitaria** publicity campaign

campagnolo, a [kampaɲ'ɲɔlo] AGG country *attr*
■ SM/F countryman/woman
■ SF (*Aut*) cross-country vehicle

campale [kam'pale] AGG (*Mil*) field *attr*; **una giornata campale** (*fig*) a hectic *o* hard day

campana [kam'pana] SF bell; **suonare le campane a martello/a morte** to sound the alarm bell/death knell; **sordo come una campana** as deaf as a doorpost; **sentire l'altra campana** (*fig*) to hear the other side of the story; **campana (per la raccolta del vetro)** bottle bank; **campana pneumatica** diving bell; **campana di vetro** bell jar; **tenere qn sotto una campana di vetro** (*fig*) to wrap sb up in cotton wool

campanaccio, ci [kampa'nattʃo] SM (*di mucca*) cowbell; (*di capra*) goatbell

campanaro [kampa'naro] SM bell-ringer

campanella [kampa'nɛlla] SF **1** (*a scuola*) (school) bell **2** (*di tenda*) curtain ring **3** (*Bot*) campanula; **campanella scozzese** harebell

campanello [kampa'nɛllo] SM (*di porta, bicicletta, da tavola*) bell; **hai suonato il campanello?** have you rung the bell?; **campanello d'allarme** (*anche fig*) alarm bell

campanile [kampa'nile] SM bell tower, belfry

campanilismo [kampani'lizmo] SM parochialism

campanilista, i, e [kampani'lista] AGG parochial
■ SM/F parochial (-minded) person

campanilisticamente [kampanilistika'mente] AVV parochially

campanilistico, a, ci, che [kampani'listiko] AGG parochial

campano, a [kam'pano] AGG of *o* from Campania

campanula [kam'panula] SF (*Bot*) bellflower; (*: genere*) campanula

campare [kam'pare] VI (*aus* **essere**) (*vivere*) to live; (*tirare avanti*) to get by, manage; **campare d'aria** (*fig*) to live on air; **campare alla giornata, tirare a campare** to live from day to day

campata [kam'pata] SF (*Archit, Elettr*) span

campato, a [kam'pato] AGG: **campato in aria** (*ragionamento ecc*) unsound, unfounded

campeggiamento [kampeddʒa'mento] SM (*Mil*) encampment

campeggiare [kamped'dʒare] VI (*aus* **avere**) **1** (*gen, Mil*) to camp **2** (*risaltare*) to stand out

campeggiatore, trice [kampeddʒa'tore] SM/F camper

campeggio, gi [kam'peddʒo] SM (*luogo*) camp site; (*attività*) camping; **c'è un campeggio qui vicino?** is there a camp site near here?; **nel campeggio** on the camp site; **andare in campeggio** to go camping; **quest'estate andremo in campeggio** we're going camping this summer; **"vietato il campeggio"** "no camping"

camper ['kæmpəʳ] SM INV motor caravan (*Brit*), motor home (*Am*)

camperista, i, e [kampe'rista] SM/F *someone who has a camper van*

campestre [kam'pɛstre] AGG country *attr*, rural; **corsa campestre** cross-country race

campetto [kam'petto] SM (*Sport*) small playing field; (*Sci*) nursery slope

Campidoglio [kampi'dɔʎʎo] SM: **il Campidoglio** the Capitol

CAMPIDOGLIO

The **Campidoglio**, one of the Seven Hills of Rome, has been inhabited since the Bronze Age and was at the centre of political life in the city during the Middle Ages. Its square, designed by Michelangelo, houses the Palazzo Senatorio together with the "palazzi" of the Museo Capitolino and the Museo dei Conservatori. The Palazzo Senatorio is currently the home of the "Comune di Roma".

▷ www.romecity.it/Campidoglio.htm

camping ['kæmpiŋ] SM INV camp site

LO SAPEVI...?
camping non si traduce mai con la parola inglese *camping*

campionamento [kampjona'mento] SM sampling

campionare [kampjo'nare] VT (*Statistica, Mus*) to sample

campionario, ria, ri, rie [kampjo'narjo] SM (*Comm*) collection of samples
■ AGG: **fiera campionaria** trade fair

campionato [kampjo'nato] SM championship; **il campionato di calcio** the Premiership, the Premier League (*Brit*); **il campionato di serie A** (*di calcio*) the Italian Premier League

campionatura [kampjona'tura] SF (*Statistica: azione*) sampling; (*: campioni*) range of samples, collection of samples; (*Mus*) sampling

campione¹, essa [kam'pjone] SM/F (*Sport*) champion; **campione di tennis/del mondo** tennis/world champion; **il campione del mondo di sci** the world skiing champion; **sei un campione in matematica** (*fig*) you're brilliant at mathematics

campione² [kam'pjone] AGG INV **1** (*Sport: squadra, pugile*) champion *attr* **2** (*Statistica: test, analisi, indagine*) sample *attr*
■ SM (*Comm, Statistica*) sample; **vendita su campione** sale on sample
■ **campione casuale** (*Statistica*) random sample; **campione gratuito** free sample; **campione di misura** (*Fis*) standard measure; **campione senza valore** sample only

campo ['kampo] SM **1** (*gen, Agr, Fis*) field; **campo di grano** cornfield; **la vita dei campi** life in the country, country life; **fiori di campo** wild flowers; **nel suo campo è uno dei migliori** he's one of the best in his field; **a tutto campo** (*Sport*) attacking and defending; (*fig: colloqui, inchiesta*) open-ended **2** (*di calcio*) field, pitch; (*da golf*) course; (*da tennis*) court; (*da cricket*) pitch; **campo ostacoli** (*Equitazione*) jumping arena; **campo in terra battuta** (*Tennis*) clay court **3** (*Mil*) field, battlefield; (*: accampamento*) camp; **abbandonare il campo** (*anche fig*) to leave the field; **scendere in campo** (*anche fig*) to enter the field, join the fray **4** (*pittura*) background; (*Araldica*) field
■ **campo da aviazione** airfield; **campo base** (*Alpinismo*) base camp; **campo di battaglia** battlefield; **campo**

carbonifero coalfield; **campo di concentramento** concentration camp; **campo di forze** (*Fis*) force field; **campo giochi** play area; **campo lungo** (*Cine, TV, Fot*) long shot; **campo nomadi** travellers' camp; **campo petrolifero** oilfield; **campo profughi** refugee camp; **campo sportivo** sports ground; **campo di visibilità** range of visibility; **campo visivo** field of vision

campobassano, a [kampobas'sano] AGG of *o* from Campobasso
■ SM/F inhabitant *o* native of Campobasso

camposanto [kampo'santo] SM (*pl* **campisanti**) cemetery

camuffamento [kamuffa'mento] SM disguise

camuffare [kamuf'fare] VT: **camuffare (da)** to disguise (as)
▶ **camuffarsi** VR: **camuffarsi (da)** to disguise o.s. (as)

camuso, a [ka'muzo] AGG (*naso*) snub; (*persona*) snub-nosed

Can. ABBR = canale

Cana ['kana] SF Cana

Canada [kana'da] SM: **il Canada** Canada; **andremo in Canada quest'estate** we're going to Canada this summer; **mi è piaciuto molto il Canada** I really liked Canada

canadese [kana'dese] AGG, SM/F Canadian
■ SF (*anche:* **tenda canadese**) ridge tent

canaglia [ka'naʎʎa] SF (*persona*) scoundrel, rogue; **stato canaglia** rogue state

canalare [kana'lare] AGG: **cura canalare** root canal treatment

canale [ka'nale] SM (*gen, Elettr, TV, fig*) channel; (*artificiale*) canal; (*condotto*) conduit; (*Anat*) duct, canal; (*Alpinismo*) gully; **su che canale è il film?** which channel is the film on?; **canale di bonifica** *o* **di drenaggio** drainage canal; **i canali di Venezia** the canals of Venice; **il canale di Panama** the Panama Canal; **il Canal Grande** the Grand Canal; **il canale della Manica** the English Channel

canalizzare [kanalid'dzare] VT to canalize, channel

canalizzato, a [kanalid'dzato] AGG: **traffico canalizzato** directed traffic

canalizzazione [kanaliddzat'tsjone] SF canalization

canalone [kana'lone] SM (*Geol*) gorge

canapa ['kanapa] SF (*Bot, tessuto*) hemp; **canapa indiana** (*Bot*) Indian hemp; (*droga*) cannabis

canapè [kana'pɛ] SM INV (*divano*) settee, couch; (*Culin*) canapé

canapo ['kanapo] SM (*Naut*) hawser

Canarie [ka'narje] SFPL: **le (isole) Canarie** the Canary Islands, the Canaries

canarino [kana'rino] SM canary

canasta [ka'nasta] SF canasta

Canberra [kan'bɛrra] SF Canberra

cancan [kan'kan] SM INV (*ballo*) cancan; (*fig: confusione*) din, row; (*: scandalo*) fuss

cancellabile [kantʃel'labile] AGG erasable

cancellare [kantʃel'lare] VT **1** (*con gomma*) to erase, rub out; (*con penna*) to cross out, score out **2** (*fig: ricordo*) erase; (*volo, treno, appuntamento*) to cancel; **cancellare la lavagna** to clean the blackboard; **cancellare qn dalla faccia della terra** to wipe sb off the face of the earth
▶ **cancellarsi** VIP (*ricordo*) to fade

cancellata [kantʃel'lata] SF railing(s *pl*)

cancellatura [kantʃella'tura] SF (*con gomma*) erasure; (*con penna*) crossing out

cancellazione [kantʃellat'tsjone] SF (*Dir, Comm*) cancellation; **cancellazione del debito pubblico** cancellation of the public debt

cancelleria [kantʃelle'ria] SF **1** (*materiale per scrivere*) stationery **2** (*Dir, Amm*) chancery

cancelletto [kantʃel'letto] SM (*tasto*) hash (*Brit*), pound sign (*Am*); **cancelletto di partenza** (*Sport*) starting gate

cancellierato [kantʃellje'rato] SM (*Amm*) chancellery

cancelliere [kantʃel'ljɛre] SM **1** (*di tribunale*) clerk of the court **2** (*Pol*) chancellor; **Cancelliere dello Scacchiere** Chancellor of the Exchequer (*Brit*)

cancello [kan'tʃɛllo] SM gate

cancerizzarsi [kantʃerid'dzarsi] VIP to become cancerous

cancerizzazione [kantʃeriddzat'tsjone] SF cancerization

cancerogeno, a [kantʃe'rɔdʒeno] AGG carcinogenic
■ SM carcinogen

canceroso, a [kantʃe'roso] AGG (*Med*) cancerous
■ SM/F cancer patient

cancrena [kan'krɛna] SF (*Med*) gangrene; (*fig: corruzione*) corruption; **andare in cancrena** to become gangrenous

cancro ['kankro] SM **1** (*Med, fig*) cancer; (*Bot*) canker; **cancro ai polmoni** lung cancer **2** (*Astron, Astrol*): **Cancro** Cancer; **essere del Cancro** to be Cancer

candeggiante [kanded'dʒante] SM bleach
■ AGG bleaching *attr*

candeggiare [kanded'dʒare] VT to bleach

candeggina [kanded'dʒina] SF bleach

candeggio, gi [kan'deddʒo] SM bleaching; **fare il candeggio (di qc)** to bleach (sth)

candela [kan'dela] SF **1** candle; **a lume di candela** by candlelight; **tenere la candela** (*fig*) to play gooseberry (*Brit*), be a third wheel (*Am*) **2** (*Aut*) spark(ing) plug; **3** (*Elettr*): **una lampadina da 100 candele** a 100 watt bulb

candelabro [kande'labro] SM candelabra *inv*

candeletta [kande'letta] SF (*Med*) pessary

candeliere [kande'ljɛre] SM **1** candlestick **2** (*Naut*) stanchion

> **LO SAPEVI...?**
> **candeliere** non si traduce mai con *chandelier*

Candelora [kande'lɔra] SF: **la Candelora** Candlemas

candelotto [kande'lɔtto] SM candle; **candelotto di dinamite** stick of dynamite; **candelotto fumogeno** smoke-bomb; **candelotto lacrimogeno** tear gas grenade

candidamente [kandida'mente] AVV (*vedi agg 2*) ingenuously, naïvely; candidly, frankly; innocently

candidare [kandi'dare] VT to present as candidate
▶ **candidarsi** VR: **candidarsi (per** *o* **a)** (*Pol*) to stand (*Brit*) *o* run (*Am*) as candidate (for)

candidato, a [kandi'dato] SM/F: **candidato (a)** (*a una carica*) candidate (for); (*a un lavoro*) applicant (for)

candidatura [kandida'tura] SF (*a una carica*) candidature; (*a un lavoro*) application; **presentare la propria candidatura alle elezioni** to stand (*Brit*) *o* run (*Am*) for election

candido, a ['kandido] AGG **1** (*bianco*) (pure) white; **bianco candido** pure white; **candido come la neve** (as) white as snow **2** (*fig: ingenuo*) ingenuous, naïve; (*: sincero*) candid, frank; (*: innocente*) pure, innocent

candito, a [kan'dito] AGG candied
■ **canditi** SMPL candied fruit *sg*

candore [kan'dore] SM (*vedi agg*) brilliant white;

Cc

ingenuousness, naïvety; candour (*Brit*), candor (*Am*), frankness; purity, innocence

cane ['kane] SM (*Zool*) dog; (*di pistola*) cock, hammer; **qui si mangia da cani** the food is rotten here; **che vita da cani!** it's a dog's life!; **questo lavoro è fatto da cani** this job is a real botch-up; **quell'attore è un cane** he's a rotten actor; **fa un freddo cane** it's bitterly cold; **non c'era un cane** there wasn't a soul; **essere solo come un cane** to be all on one's own; **essere come cane e gatto** to fight like cat and dog
■ **cane barbone** (French) poodle; **cane da caccia** hunting dog; **cane per ciechi** guide dog (*Brit*), seeing eye dog (*Am*); **cane da guardia** watchdog, guard dog; **cane lupo** alsatian (dog) (*Brit*), German shepherd (dog) (*Am*); **cane delle praterie** prairie dog; **cane da punta** pointer; **cane randagio** stray dog; **cane di razza** pedigree dog; **cane da salotto** lap dog; **cane da slitta** husky

> **LO SAPEVI...?**
> **cane** non si traduce mai con la parola inglese *cane*

canestro [ka'nɛstro] SM (*gen, Sport*) basket; **centrare il canestro** *o* **fare (un) canestro** (*Sport*) to shoot a basket

canfora ['kanfora] SF camphor

canforato, a [kanfo'rato] AGG camphorated

cangiante [kan'dʒante] AGG iridescent; **seta cangiante** shot silk

canguro [kan'guro] SM kangaroo

canicola [ka'nikola] SF scorching heat

canile [ka'nile] SM kennel; (*di allevamento*) kennels *pl*; **canile municipale** dog pound

canino, a [ka'nino] AGG **1** (*razza*) canine; (*mostra*) dog *attr*; **tosse canina** whooping cough; **rosa canina** dog rose **2** (*dente*) canine
■ SM (*dente*) canine, eyetooth

canizie [ka'nittsje] SF (*letter: chioma bianca*) white hair

canna ['kanna] SF **1** (*Bot*) reed; **canna da zucchero** sugar cane **2** (*bastone*) stick, cane; **canna da pesca** (fishing) rod **3** (*di fucile*) barrel; (*di organo*) pipe; (*di bicicletta*) crossbar; **canna fumaria** chimney flue **4** (*Droga: gergo*) joint

cannaiola [kanna'jɔla] SF (*uccello*) reed warbler

cannare [kan'nare] VT, VI (*fam: sbagliare*) to screw up

cannella[1] [kan'nɛlla] SF (*di conduttura, botte*) tap

cannella[2] [kan'nɛlla] SF (*Bot, Culin*) cinnamon

cannello [kan'nɛllo] SM (*forato*) tube; (*Chim*) pipette; (*non forato*) stick; (*Tecn*) blowpipe

cannelloni [kannel'loni] SMPL (*Culin*) cannelloni *sg*; **i cannelloni sono buoni** the cannelloni is good

canneto [kan'neto] SM bed of reeds

cannetta [kan'netta] SF (*da passeggio*) walking stick

cannibale [kan'nibale] SM/F cannibal

cannibalesco, a, schi, sche [kanniba'lesko] AGG cannibalistic

cannibalismo [kanniba'lizmo] SM cannibalism

cannocchiale [kannok'kjale] SM telescope

cannolo [kan'nɔlo] SM (*Culin*) cream horn; **cannolo alla siciliana** *pastry horn filled with cream cheese, candied fruit and chocolate*

cannonata [kanno'nata] SF cannon shot; **cannonata a salve** gun salute; **è una vera cannonata!** (*fig*) it's (*o* he's *ecc*) fantastic

cannoncino [kannon'tʃino] SM **1** (*Mil*) light gun **2** (*di abito*) box pleat **3** (*Culin*) cream horn

cannone [kan'none] SM **1** (*arma*) gun; (*Storia*) cannon; (*fig: chi eccelle*) ace; **donna cannone** (*in circo*) fat lady **2** (*tubo*) pipe, tube **3** (*di abito*) box pleat **4** (*Sci*): **cannone per innevamento artificiale** snow cannon

cannoneggiare [kannoned'dʒare] VT to shell

cannoniera [kanno'njɛra] SF (*Naut*) gunboat; (*di fortificazione*) embrasure

cannoniere [kanno'njɛre] SM **1** (*Naut*) gunner **2** (*Calcio*) goal scorer

cannuccia, ce [kan'nuttʃa] SF (drinking) straw

canoa [ka'nɔa] SF canoe; **andare in canoa** to go canoeing

canoismo [kano'izmo] SM canoeing

canoista, i, e [kano'ista] SM/F canoeist

cañon [ka'ɲon] SM INV canyon

canone ['kanone] SM **1** **canoni** SMPL (*criteri*) canons, rules; (*di comportamento*) norm **2** (*pagamento periodico*) rent, fee; **legge dell'equo canone** fair rent act; **canone d'abbonamento alla TV** TV licence fee (*Brit*); **canone d'affitto** rent; **canone agricolo** land rent **3** (*Rel, Mus*) canon

canonica [ka'nɔnika] SF presbytery

canonico, a, ci, che [ka'nɔniko] (*Rel*) AGG canonical; **diritto canonico** canon law
■ SM canon

canonizzare [kanonid'dzare] VT to canonize

canonizzazione [kanoniddzat'tsjone] SF canonization

canorità [kanori'ta] SF INV melodiousness

canoro, a [ka'nɔro] AGG: **uccello canoro** songbird

canotta [ka'nɔtta] SF = **canottiera**

canottaggio, gi [kanot'taddʒo] SM rowing; **circolo di canottaggio** rowing club; **gara di canottaggio** boat race

canottiera [kanot'tjɛra] SF vest (*Brit*), undershirt (*Am*)

canotto [ka'nɔtto] SM dinghy; **canotto pneumatico** rubber dinghy; **canotto di salvataggio** lifeboat

canovaccio, ci [kano'vattʃo] SM **1** (*tela*) canvas; (*per lavare i piatti*) dishcloth; (*per asciugare i piatti*) tea towel (*Brit*), dish towel (*Am*); (*per pulire*) duster **2** (*Teatro: trama*) plot

cantante [kan'tante] SM/F singer; **fare il cantante** to be a singer; **cantante lirico** *o* **d'opera** opera singer

cantare [kan'tare] VI (*aus* **avere**) (*gen, uccelli*) to sing; (*gallo*) to crow; **ha cantato per tutta la sera** he sang all evening; **cantare da tenore/da soprano** to be a tenor/soprano; **fare cantare qn** (*fig*) to make sb talk; **i complici hanno cantato** (*fam*) his accomplices talked
■ VT (*Mus*) to sing; (*Poesia: anche:* **cantare in versi**) to sing of; **cantare messa** to sing mass; **cantare vittoria** to crow

cantastorie [kantas'tɔrje] SM/F INV story-teller

cantata [kan'tata] SF singsong; (*Mus*) cantata

cantautore, trice [kantau'tore] SM/F singer-songwriter

canterellare [kanterel'lare] VT, VI (*aus* **avere**) to sing to o.s.; (*a bocca chiusa*) to hum

canticchiare [kantik'kjare] VT, VI (*aus* **avere**) sing to o.s.; (*a bocca chiusa*) to hum

cantico, ci ['kantiko] SM canticle

cantiere [kan'tjɛre] SM **1** (*anche:* **cantiere navale**) shipyard **2** (*anche:* **cantiere edile**) building site

cantieristico, a, ci, che [kantje'ristiko] AGG: **industria cantieristica** shipbuilding industry

cantilena [kanti'lɛna] SF (*filastrocca*) lullaby; (*intonazione*) singsong; (*fig: lamentela*) whining

cantilenare [kantile'nare] VT to speak in a singsong voice

cantina [kan'tina] SF (*locale*) cellar; **è in cantina** it's in the cellar; **cantina sociale** cooperative winegrowers' association

LO SAPEVI...?
cantina non si traduce mai con *canteen*

canto[1] ['kanto] SM (*il cantare, arte*) singing; (*canzone*) song; (*Poesia*) lyric poem; (*: capitolo*) canto; **lezioni di canto** singing lessons; **il canto dell'usignolo** (*il cantare*) the singing of the nightingale; (*melodia*) the song of the nightingale; **al canto del gallo** at cockcrow; **il canto del cigno** (*fig*) swan song; **canto gregoriano** Gregorian chant; **canto di Natale** (Christmas) carol

canto[2] ['kanto] SM: **da un canto... d'altro canto** on the one hand ... on the other hand; **da un canto ti capisco** in a way I understand you; **dal canto mio** (*per ciò che mi riguarda*) for my part, as for me, as far as I'm concerned

cantonata [kanto'nata] SF (*di edificio*) corner; **prendere una cantonata** (*fig*) to blunder

cantone[1] [kan'tone] SM (*angolo*) corner; **in un cantone** (*fig: in disparte*) in a corner

cantone[2] [kan'tone] SM (*Pol, Amm*) canton

cantoniera [kanto'njɛra] AGG: **(casa) cantoniera** road inspector's house

Canton Ticino N Ticino

cantore, a [kan'tore] SM/F (*Rel*) singer; (*poeta*) poet

cantoria [kanto'ria] SF (*luogo, persone*) choir

cantuccio, ci [kan'tuttʃo] SM corner, nook

canuto, a [ka'nuto] AGG (*persona*) white-haired; (*barba, capelli*) white

canzonare [kantso'nare] VT to tease, make fun of

canzonatore, trice [kantsona'tore] AGG teasing
■ SM/F teaser, tease

canzonatorio, ria, ri, rie [kantsona'tɔrjo] AGG teasing

canzonatura [kantsona'tura] SF teasing; (*beffa*) joke

canzone [kan'tsone] SF (*Mus*) song; (*poesia*) canzone; **è sempre la stessa canzone** (*fig*) it's always the same old story; **canzone di gesta** (*poema epico*) chanson de geste
▷ www.interviu.it/canzone.htm

canzonetta [kantso'netta] SF popular song

canzonettista, i, e [kantsonet'tista] SM/F (cabaret) singer

canzoniere [kantso'njɛre] SM (*Mus*) song book; (*Letteratura*) collection of poems

caolino [kao'lino] SM kaolin

caos ['kaos] SM INV (*anche fig*) chaos

caoticamente [kaotika'mente] AVV chaotically

caotico, a, ci, che [ka'ɔtiko] AGG chaotic

CAP [kap] SIGLA M = **codice di avviamento postale**

Cap. ABBR (= **capitano**) Capt. (= *captain*)

cap. ABBR (= **capitolo**) ch.

capace [ka'patʃe] AGG **1** (*capiente*) large, capacious; **una stanza capace** a large room; **questa borsa è poco capace** this bag doesn't hold much **2** (*in grado, dotato*) able, capable; **un insegnante molto capace** a very able teacher; **capace di fare qc** able to do sth, capable of doing sth; **sei capace di farlo da solo?** can you *o* are you able to do it on your own?; **sei capace di nuotare?** can you swim?; **non è stata capace di farlo** she couldn't do it; **è capace di tutto** he's capable of anything; **capace d'intendere e di volere** (*Dir*) in full possession of one's faculties; **è capace di venire nonostante tutto** he's quite likely to come in spite of everything

capacità [kapatʃi'ta] SF INV **1** (*capienza*) capacity; **misure di capacità** measures of capacity **2** (*abilità*) ability, capability; **ha la capacità di trarre il meglio dagli altri** he has the ability to bring out the best in others; **è un compito superiore alle sue capacità** it's a task beyond his capabilities **3** (*Dir, Fis*) capacity; **capacità giuridica** legal capacity **4 capacità produttiva** (*di impresa*) production capacity

capacitarsi [kapatʃi'tarsi] VIP: **capacitarsi (di qc)** to comprehend

capanna [ka'panna] SF hut

capannello [kapan'nello] SM knot (of people)

capanno [ka'panno] SM (*di cacciatori*) hide; (*da spiaggia*) bathing hut; (*degli attrezzi*) tool shed

capannone [kapan'none] SM (*gen*) shed; (*Agr*) barn; (*Aer*) hangar

caparbiamente [kaparbja'mente] AVV stubbornly, obstinately

caparbietà [kaparbje'ta] SF stubbornness, obstinacy

caparbio, bia, bi, bie [ka'parbjo] AGG stubborn, obstinate

caparra [ka'parra] SF deposit, down payment

capatina [kapa'tina] SF: **fare una capatina da qn/in centro** to pop in on sb/into town

capeggiare [kaped'dʒare] VT (*rivolta*) to head, lead

capello [ka'pello] SM (*uno*) hair; (*capigliatura*): **capelli** SMPL hair *sg*; **c'è un capello nella minestra** there's a hair in the soup; **mi lavo i capelli ogni giorno** I wash my hair every day; **ho i capelli ancora bagnati** my hair is still wet; **ha i capelli ricci** she's got curly hair; **avere i capelli bianchi** to have white hair; **dai capelli scuri** dark-haired; **capelli d'angelo** (*Culin*) *long thin pasta*; **avere un diavolo per capello** to be in a foul temper; **averne fin sopra i capelli di qc/qn** to be fed up to the (back) teeth with sth/sb; **mettersi le mani nei capelli** (*fig*) to be in despair; **prendersi per i capelli** (*fig*) to come to blows; **strapparsi i capelli** (*fig*) to tear one's hair out; **mi ci hanno tirato per i capelli** (*fig*) they dragged me into it; **tirato per i capelli** (*spiegazione*) far-fetched

capellone, a [kapel'lone] SM/F hippie

capelluto, a [kapel'luto] AGG: **il cuoio capelluto** the scalp

capelvenere [kapel'vɛnere] SM (*Bot*) maidenhair

capestro [ka'pɛstro] SM (*di forca*) noose; (*per animali*) halter

capezzale [kapet'tsale] SM bolster; (*fig*) bedside; **accorrere al capezzale di qn** to rush to sb's bedside

capezzolo [ka'pettsolo] SM nipple

capidoglio, gli [kapi'dɔʎʎo] SM = **capodoglio**

capiente [ka'pjɛnte] AGG capacious

capienza [ka'pjɛntsa] SF capacity

capigliatura [kapiʎʎa'tura] SF hair, head of hair

capillare [kapil'lare] AGG (*Anat, Fis*) capillary; (*fig: analisi, ricerca*) detailed
■ SM (*Anat: anche*: **vaso capillare**) capillary

capillarità [kapillari'ta] SF (*Fis*) capillarity; (*fig*) comprehensiveness

capinera [kapi'nera] SF (*uccello*) blackcap

capire [ka'pire] VT to understand; **si capisce che...** it is clear that ...; **si capisce!** (*certamente!*) of course!, certainly!; **capisco** I see, I understand; **va bene, capisco** ok, I understand; **fammi capire...** let's get this straight ...; **capisci, è un problema di soldi** you see, it's a problem of money; **non ho capito una parola** I didn't understand a word; **non ho capito, puoi ripetere?** I don't understand, could you say it again?; **bisogna capirla, poverina** you've got to try

Cc

and understand her, poor thing; **capire al volo** to catch on straight away; **capire male** to misunderstand; **farsi capire** to make o.s. understood; **capirai!** (*sai che sforzo!*) big deal!
▶ **capirsi** VR (*uso reciproco*) to understand each other *o* one another

capitale [kapi'tale] AGG **1** (*mortale*): **pena capitale** capital punishment; **sentenza capitale** death sentence; **i sette peccati capitali** the seven deadly sins **2** (*fondamentale*) main *attr*, chief *attr*; **d'importanza capitale** of capital *o* the utmost importance
■ SF (*Amm*) capital (city); (*fig: centro*) centre
■ SM (*Fin, Econ*) capital; **ho speso un capitale per quella macchina** (*fig*) I've spent a fortune on that car; **capitale azionario** equity capital, share capital; **capitale d'esercizio** working capital; **capitale fisso** capital assets *pl*, fixed capital; **capitale immobile** real estate; **capitale liquido** cash assets *pl*; **capitale mobile** movables *pl*; **capitale nominale** authorized capital; **capitale di rischio** risk capital; **capitale sociale** (*di società*) authorized capital; (*di club*) funds *pl*; **capitale di ventura** venture capital, risk capital

capitalismo [kapita'lizmo] SM capitalism

capitalista, i, e [kapita'lista] AGG, SM/F capitalist

capitalisticamente [kapitalistika'mente] AVV in a capitalist way

capitalistico, a, ci, che [kapita'listiko] AGG capitalist

capitalizzare [kapitalid'dzare] VT to capitalize

capitalizzazione [kapitaliddzat'tsjone] SF capitalization

capitanare [kapita'nare] VT to lead; (*Calcio*) to captain

capitaneria [kapitane'ria] SF: **capitaneria (di porto)** port authorities *pl*

capitano [kapi'tano] SM (*Mil, Naut, Sport*) captain; (*Aer: di squadriglia*) flight lieutenant (*Brit*), captain (*Am*); **capitano di industria** captain of industry; **capitano di lungo corso** master mariner; **capitano di ventura** (*Storia*) mercenary leader

capitare [kapi'tare] VI (*aus* **essere**) **1** (*giungere casualmente*) to arrive, find o.s.; (*presentarsi: cosa*) to turn up, present itself; **capitare a proposito/bene/male** to turn up at the right moment/at a good time/at a bad time; **siamo capitati nella zona più pericolosa della città** we found ourselves in the most dangerous area of the city **2** (*accadere*) to happen; **se ti capita di vederlo** if you happen to see him; **mi è capitato un guaio** I had a spot of trouble; **non mi è mai capitato** it's never happened to me; **sono cose che capitano** these things happen
■ VB IMPERS (*aus* **essere**) to happen; **capita spesso di incontrarci** *o* **che ci incontriamo** we often bump into one another

capitello [kapi'tɛllo] SM (*Archit*) capital

capitolare [kapito'lare] VI (*aus* **avere**) (*Mil*) to capitulate, surrender; (*fig*) to give in

capitolato [kapito'lato] SM (*Dir*) terms *pl*, specifications *pl*

capitolazione [kapitolat'tsjone] SF (*Mil, fig*) capitulation

capitolino, a [kapito'lino] AGG Capitoline

capitolo [ka'pitolo] SM **1** (*di testo, Rel*) chapter; **non ho voce in capitolo** (*fig*) I have no say in the matter **2** (*di bilancio*) item

capitombolare [kapitombo'lare] VI (*aus* **essere**) to tumble, fall headlong

capitombolo [kapi'tombolo] SM tumble, headlong fall; **fare un capitombolo** to take a tumble

capitone [kapi'tone] SM (*Zool*) large (female) eel

capo ['kapo] SM **1** (*Anat*) head; **a capo chino/alto** with one's head bowed/held high; **da capo a piedi** from head to foot; **era coperto di fango da capo a piedi** he was covered in mud from head to foot; **mal di capo** headache; **rompersi il capo** (*fig*) to rack one's brains; **fra capo e collo** (*all'improvviso*) out of the blue **2** (*di fabbrica, ufficio*) head, boss; (*di tribù*) chief; **il mio capo è molto esigente** my boss is very demanding; (*di partito, movimento*) leader; **essere a capo di qc** to head sth, be at the head of sth; **capo del personale** personnel manager; **capo di stato** head of state **3** (*oggetto*) item, article; **un capo di biancheria (intima)/vestiario** an item of underwear/clothing; **capo di bestiame** head *inv* of cattle **4** (*estremità: di tavolo, scale*) head, top; (*: di filo*) end; **era seduto all'altro capo del tavolo** he was sitting at the other end of the table; **da un capo all'altro** from one end to the other; **in capo a** (*tempo*) within; (*luogo*) at the top of; **andare in capo al mondo per qn** (*fig*) to go to the ends of the earth for sb; **da capo** all over again; **ricominciare da capo** to start all over again; **ha sbagliato e ha dovuto ricominciare da capo** he made a mistake and had to start all over again; **a capo** new paragraph; **andare a capo** to start a new paragraph; **"punto a capo"** "full stop – new paragraph"; **fare un discorso senza né capo né coda** to talk nonsense; **un discorso senza né capo né coda** a senseless *o* meaningless speech **5** (*di corda, lana*) ply; **lana a 3 capi** 3-ply wool **6** (*Geog*) cape; **Capo di Buona Speranza** Cape of Good Hope; **Capo Horn** Cape Horn **7** (*Dir*): **capo d'accusa** charge
■ AGG INV (*giardiniere, sorvegliante*) head *attr*; **redattore capo** chief editor

capobanda [kapo'banda] SM (*pl* **capibanda**) (*Mus*) bandmaster; (*di malviventi, fig*) gang leader

capobarca [kapo'barka] SM (*pl* **capibarca**) skipper

capocannoniere [kapokanno'njɛre] SM (*pl* **capicannonieri**) (*Calcio*) leading goal scorer; (*Naut*) head gunner

capocchia [ka'pɔkkja] SF head; **capocchia di spillo** pin head

capoccia [ka'pɔttʃa] SM INV (*di lavoranti*) overseer; (*pegg: capobanda*) boss

capoccione [kapot'tʃone] SM (*persona intelligente*) brainbox; (*fig pegg: persona importante*) bigwig

capocellula [kapo'tʃellula] SM/F (*pl m* **capicellula**, *pl f* **capocellula**) (*Pol*) leader of a cell

capoclasse [kapo'klasse] SM/F (*pl m* **capiclasse**, *pl f* **capoclasse**) (*Scol*) ≈ form captain (*Brit*), ≈ class president (*Am*)

capocomico, a, ci, che [kapo'kɔmiko] SM/F leader of a theatre company

capocordata [kapokor'data] SM/F (*pl m* **capicordata**, *pl f* **capocordata**) (*Alpinismo*) leader (of a roped party)

capocronista [kapokro'nista] SM/F (*pl m* **capicronisti**, *pl f* **capocroniste**) news editor

capocuoco, a [kapo'kwɔko] SM/F (*pl m* **capocuochi** *o* **capicuochi**, *pl f* **capocuoche**) head cook *o* chef

Capodanno [kapo'danno] SM New Year; **il veglione di Capodanno** New Year's Eve party

capodivisione [kapodivi'zjone] SM/F (*pl m* **capidivisione**, *pl f* **capodivisione**) (*Amm*) head of department

capodoglio, gli [kapo'dɔʎʎo] SM sperm whale

capofabbrica [kapo'fabbrika] SM/F (*pl m* **capifabbrica**, *pl f* **capofabbrica**) (factory) supervisor
capofamiglia [kapofa'miʎʎa] SM/F (*pl m* **capifamiglia**, *pl f* **capofamiglia**) head of the family
capofila [kapo'fila] SM/F (*pl m* **capifila**, *pl f* **capofila**) leader; **a capofila** at the head of the queue (*Brit*) *o* line (*Am*)
capofitto [kapo'fitto] **a capofitto** AVV headlong, headfirst; **gettarsi a capofitto in qc** (*fig*) to rush headlong into sth
capogabinetto [kapogabi'netto] SM/F (*pl m* **capigabinetto**, *pl f* **capogabinetto**) ≈ parliamentary private secretary (*Brit*)
capogiro [kapo'dʒiro] SM dizziness *no pl*; **aver un capogiro** to have a dizzy spell; **ho avuto un capogiro** I felt dizzy; **far venire il capogiro a qn** to make sb dizzy; **da capogiro** (*fig*) astonishing, staggering
capogruppo [kapo'gruppo] SM/F (*pl m* **capigruppo**, *pl f* **capogruppo**) group leader
capolavoro [kapola'voro] SM (*anche fig*) masterpiece
capolinea [kapo'linea] SM (*pl* **capilinea**) terminus; (*fig*) the end of the line
capolino [kapo'lino] SM: **far capolino** to peep out (*o* in *ecc*)
capolista [kapo'lista] SM/F (*pl m* **capilista**, *pl f* **capolista**) (*Pol*) *top candidate on electoral list*
■ SF (*Sport*) top team
capoluogo [kapo'lwɔgo] SM (*pl* **capoluoghi** *o* **capiluoghi**) **capoluogo (di provincia)** ≈ county town (*Brit*), county seat (*Am*), administrative centre (*Brit*) *o* center (*Am*)
capomastro [kapo'mastro] SM (*pl* **capomastri** *o* **capimastri**) master builder
capopartito [kapopar'tito] SM/F (*pl m* **capipartito**, *pl f* **capopartito**) party leader
capopattuglia [kapopat'tuʎʎa] SM (*pl* **capipattuglia**) patrol leader
caporale [kapo'rale] SM (*Mil*) lance corporal (*Brit*), private first class (*Am*)
caporalesco, a, schi, sche [kapora'lesko] AGG (*pegg*) bossy
caporalmaggiore [kaporalmad'dʒore] SM (*Mil*) corporal
caporedattore, trice [kaporedat'tore] SM/F (*pl m* **capiredattori**, *pl f* **caporedattrici**) editor in chief
caporeparto [kapore'parto] SM/F (*pl m* **capireparto**, *pl f* **caporeparto**) (*di operai*) foreman; (*di ufficio*) head of department; (*di negozio*) floor-manager
caporione [kapo'rjone] SM gang leader; (*istigatore*) ringleader
caposala [kapo'sala] SM/F (*pl m* **capisala**, *pl f* **caposala**) (*in ospedale*) head nurse; (: *donna*) ward sister
caposaldo [kapo'saldo] SM (*pl* **capisaldi**) (*Mil*) stronghold; (*Topografia*) datum point; (*fig: fondamento*) cornerstone, basis
caposcalo [kapos'kalo] SM/F (*pl m* **capiscalo**, *pl f* **caposcalo**) (*di linea aerea*) airline manager
caposcuola [kapo'skwɔla] SM/F (*pl m* **capiscuola**, *pl f* **caposcuola**) (*Arte, Mus, Letteratura*) founder
caposervizio [kaposer'vittsjo] SM/F (*pl m* **capiservizio**, *pl f* **caposervizio**) departmental *o* section head; **caposervizio della redazione sportiva** Sports editor
caposezione [kaposet'tsjone] SM/F (*pl m* **capisezione**, *pl f* **caposezione**) section *o* departmental head
caposquadra [kapos'kwadra] SM/F (*pl m* **capisquadra**, *pl f* **caposquadra**) (*di operai*) foreman, ganger; (*Mil*) squad leader; (*Sport*) team captain
caposquadriglia [kaposkwa'driʎʎa] SM (*pl* **capisquadriglia**) (*Aer, Naut*) squadron leader (*Brit*), major (*Am*)
capostazione [kapostat'tsjone] SM/F (*pl m* **capistazione**, *pl f* **capostazione**) (*Ferr*) station master
capostipite [kapos'tipite] SM/F (*pl* **capostipiti**) progenitor; (*fig*) earliest example
capotasto [kapo'tasto] SM (*Mus*) capo
capotavola [kapo'tavola] SM/F (*pl m* **capitavola**, *pl f* **capotavola**) (*persona*) head of the table; **sedere a capotavola** to sit at the head of the table
capote [ka'pɔt] SF INV (*Aut*) hood (*Brit*), top
capotreno [kapo'treno] SM/F (*pl m* **capitreno** *o* **capotreni**, *pl f* **capotreno**) (*Ferr*) guard (*Brit*), conductor (*Am*)
capotribù [kapotri'bu] SM/F (*pl m* **capitribù**, *pl f* **capotribù**) chief
capottare [kapot'tare] VI = **cappottare**
capoturno [kapo'turno] SM/F (*pl m* **capiturno**, *pl f* **capoturno**) shift supervisor
capoufficio [kapouf'fitʃo] SM/F (*pl m* **capiufficio**, *pl f* **capoufficio**) head clerk
Capo Verde ['kapo 'verde] SM: **il Capo Verde** Cape Verde
capoverso [kapo'vɛrso] SM **1** (*di verso, periodo*) first line; (*Tip*) indent; (*paragrafo*) paragraph **2** (*Dir: comma*) section
capovolgere [kapo'vɔldʒere] VB IRREG
■ VT (*gen*) to turn upside down; (*barca*) to capsize, overturn; (*macchina*) to overturn; (*fig: situazione, posizione*) to reverse, change completely
▶ **capovolgersi** VIP (*gen*) to overturn; (*barca*) to capsize; (*fig*) to be reversed
capovolgimento [kapovoldʒi'mento] SM (*fig*) reversal, complete change
capovolto, a [kapo'vɔlto] PP *di* **capovolgere**
■ AGG upside down; (*barca*) capsized
cappa[1] ['kappa] SF **1** (*mantello*) cloak, cape; **film/romanzo di cappa e spada** swashbuckler; **sentirsi sotto una cappa di piombo** to feel oppressed **2** (*del camino*) hood; (*Industria*) chimney; **cappa aspirante** (*per cucina*) extractor hood **3** (*Naut*): **mettersi in cappa** to heave to
cappa[2] ['kappa] SM O F INV (*lettera*) K, k
cappella [kap'pɛlla] SF (*Rel*) chapel; (: *cantori*) choir
cappellaio, aia, ai, aie [kappel'lajo] SM/F hatter
cappellano [kappel'lano] SM chaplain; **cappellano militare** army chaplain
cappelleria [kappelle'ria] SF hat shop
cappelletti [kappel'letti] SMPL *type of ring-shaped ravioli filled with meat*
cappelliera [kappel'ljɛra] SF hat box
cappello [kap'pɛllo] SM hat; (*di fungo*) cap; **cappello di paglia** straw hat; **levarsi/togliersi il cappello** to raise/take off one's hat; **ti faccio tanto di cappello!** (*fig*) I take my hat off to you!; **cappello a bombetta** bowler (hat) (*Brit*), derby (*Am*); **cappello a cilindro** top hat
cappero ['kappero] SM (*Bot, Culin*) caper; **capperi!** (*fam*) gosh!
cappio, pi ['kappjo] SM (*nodo*) slip-knot; (*capestro*) noose
cappone [kap'pone] SM capon
cappottare [kappot'tare] VI (*aus* **avere**) (*Aut*) to overturn; **la macchina ha cappottato in curva** the car overturned on the bend

Cc

cappotto¹ [kap'pɔtto] SM (over)coat; **m'infilo il cappotto e sono pronta** I'll put my coat on and I'll be ready

cappotto² [kap'pɔtto] SM: **dare** *o* **fare cappotto** (*nei giochi*) to win the grand slam

cappuccino¹ [kapput'tʃino] AGG, SM (*Rel*) Capuchin

cappuccino² [kapput'tʃino] SM (*caffè*) cappuccino

cappuccio, ci [kap'puttʃo] SM **1** (*copricapo*) hood; (*di frate*) cowl; (*di biro*) cap; **una felpa col cappuccio** a sweatshirt with a hood **2** (*fam*) = **cappuccino²**

capra ['kapra] SF **1** (*Zool*) (she-)goat, nanny-goat (*fam*); **formaggio di capra** goat cheese **2** (*Tecn*) trestle

capraio, aia, ai, aie [ka'prajo] SM/F goatherd

caprese [ka'prese] AGG from *o* of Capri
■ SM/F inhabitant *o* native of Capri

capretto [ka'pretto] SM kid

Capri ['kapri] SF Capri

capriata [kapri'ata] SF (*Edil*) truss

capriccio, ci [ka'prittʃo] SM **1** (*gen*) whim, caprice; (*di bambino*) tantrum; **è solo un capriccio** it's just a whim; **levarsi** *o* **togliersi il capriccio** to indulge one's whim; **fare i capricci** to be awkward, be naughty; **fare un capriccio** to throw a tantrum; **capricci della moda** whims of fashion; **capriccio della natura** freak of nature; **capriccio della sorte** quirk of fate **2** (*Mus*) capriccio

capricciosamente [kaprittʃosa'mente] AVV (*vedi agg*) capriciously, naughtily

capriccioso, a [kaprit'tʃoso] AGG (*donna*) capricious; (*bambino*) naughty; (*tempo*) changeable; **un bambino capriccioso** a naughty boy; **insalata capricciosa** (*Culin*) *mixed salad with mayonnaise*

Capricorno [kapri'kɔrno] SM Capricorn; **essere del Capricorno** (*Astrol*) to be Capricorn; **sono del Capricorno** I'm Capricorn

caprifoglio, gli [kapri'fɔʎʎo] SM honeysuckle

caprimulgo, gi [kapri'mulgo] SM (*uccello*) nightjar

caprino, a [ka'prino] AGG goat *attr*
■ SM (*formaggio*) goat cheese

capriola [kapri'ɔla] SF (*salto*) somersault; (*Danza*) cabriole; (*Equitazione*) capriole; **fare una capriola** to turn a somersault; **sai fare le capriole?** can you do somersaults?; **fare le capriole per la gioia** to be jumping for joy

capriolo [kapri'ɔlo] SM roe deer; (*maschio*) roebuck

capro ['kapro] SM (he-)goat, billy-goat (*fam*); **capro espiatorio** (*fig*) scapegoat

caprone [ka'prone] SM (he-)goat, billy-goat (*fam*)

capsula ['kapsula] SF (*di medicinali, spaziale, Anat*) capsule; (*di dente*) crown; (*di arma, bottiglia*) cap

captare [kap'tare] VT (*segnale radio*) to pick up; (*pensiero*) to read; **captare lo sguardo di qn** to catch sb's eye

capziosamente [kaptsjosa'mente] AVV speciously

capziosità [kaptsjosi'ta] SF speciousness

capzioso, a [kap'tsjoso] AGG specious

CAR [kar] SIGLA M = *Centro Addestramento Reclute*

carabattole [kara'battole] SFPL odds and ends

carabina [kara'bina] SF rifle

carabiniere [karabi'njɛre] SM carabiniere

CARABINIERI

Originally part of the armed forces, the **Carabinieri** are police who now have civil as well as military duties, such as maintaining public order. They include paratroop units and mounted divisions and report to either the Minister of the Interior or the Minister of Defence, depending on the function they are performing.

> www.carabinieri.it/

> www.romacivica.net/anc/

Caracas [ka'rakas] SF Caracas

caracollare [karakol'lare] VI (*aus* **avere**) (*Equitazione*) to caracole

caraffa [ka'raffa] SF carafe

Caraibi [ka'raibi] SMPL: **i Caraibi** the Caribbean *sg*; **andrò ai Caraibi quest'estate** I'm going to the Caribbean this summer; **il mar dei Caraibi** the Caribbean (Sea)

caraibico, a, ci, che [kara'ibiko] AGG Caribbean

carambola [ka'rambola] SF (*Biliardo*) cannon

caramella [kara'mɛlla] SF (*dolciume*) sweet; (*monocolo*) monocle; **vuoi una caramella?** would you like a sweet?; **una caramella alla menta** a mint

caramellare [karamel'lare] VT (*zucchero*) to caramelize; (*stampo, arance*) to coat with caramel

caramellato, a [karamel'lato] AGG caramelized; **mela caramellata** toffee apple

caramello [kara'mɛllo] SM caramel

caramente [kara'mente] AVV affectionately

carato [ka'rato] SM **1** (*di oro, diamante*) carat **2** (*Naut*) *twenty-fourth part of the ownership of a ship*

carattere [ka'rattere] SM **1** (*gen*) character, nature; **avere un buon/brutto carattere** to be good-/ill-natured, be good-/bad-tempered; **aver carattere** to have character; **mancare di/avere poco carattere** to lack character, have no backbone; **informazione di carattere tecnico/confidenziale** information of a technical/confidential nature; **essere in carattere con qc** (*intonarsi*) to be in harmony with sth; **incompatibilità di carattere** personality clash **2** ■ SPESSO PL (*caratteristica*) characteristic, feature, trait; **caratteri sessuali** sexual characteristics **3** (*Tip*) character, letter; **in carattere corsivo/neretto** *o* **grassetto** in italic/bold type; **carattere jolly** (*Inform*) wild card

caratteriale [karatte'rjale] AGG (*studio, indagine*) character *attr*; (*disturbi*) emotional

caratterino [karatte'rino] SM difficult nature *o* character

caratterista, i, e [karatte'rista] SM/F character actor/actress

caratteristica, che [karatte'ristika] SF characteristic, feature

caratteristicamente [karatteristika'mente] AVV characteristically, typically

caratteristico, a, ci, che [karatte'ristiko] AGG (*tipico*) typical, characteristic; (*distintivo*) distinctive; **il sapore caratteristico del caviale** the distinctive taste of caviar; **un elemento caratteristico dell'architettura locale** a distinctive feature of the local architecture; **un ristorante caratteristico** a traditional restaurant; **segni caratteristici** (*su passaporto*) distinguishing marks

caratterizzare [karatterid'dzare] VT (*essere tipico*) to characterize, be typical *o* characteristic of; (*descrivere*) distinguish

caratterizzazione [karatteriddzat'tsjone] SF characterization

caravanserraglio, gli [karavanser'raʎʎo] SM caravanserai

caravella [kara'vɛlla] SF (*nave*) caravel

carboidrato [karboi'drato] SM carbohydrate

carbonaia [karbo'naja] SF *(catasta di legna)* charcoal pit; *(locale)* coal cellar
carbonaio, ai [karbo'najo] SM *(chi fa carbone)* charcoal-burner; *(commerciante)* coalman, coal merchant
carbonaro [karbo'naro] SM *(Storia)* member of the Carbonari society
carbonato [karbo'nato] SM carbonate; **carbonato acido** hydrogen carbonate
carbonchio, chi [kar'bonkjo] SM *(Med, Veterinaria)* anthrax; *(Bot)* smut
carboncino [karbon'tʃino] SM *(bastoncino)* charcoal crayon; *(disegno)* charcoal drawing
carbone [kar'bone] SM coal; (*anche*: **carbone dolce** *o* **di legna**) charcoal; *(di lampada ad arco)* carbon; **essere** *o* **stare sui carboni ardenti** to be like a cat on hot bricks *(Brit)* *o* on a hot tin roof *(Am)*; **carbone bianco** hydroelectric power; **carbone fossile** (pit) coal
carbonella [karbo'nɛlla] SF charcoal slack
carboneria [karbone'ria] SF *(Storia)* secret society of the Carbonari
carbonico, a, ci, che [kar'boniko] AGG carbonic
carbonifero, a [karbo'nifero] AGG carboniferous, coal *attr*
carbonio [kar'bɔnjo] SM *(Chim)* carbon
carbonizzare [karbonid'dzare] VT *(legna)* to carbonize; (: *parzialmente*) to char; **morire carbonizzato** to be burned to death; **hanno trovato i resti carbonizzati della vittima** they found the charred remains of the victim
carburante [karbu'rante] AGG combustible
■ SM (motor) fuel; **siamo rimasti senza carburante** we've ran out of fuel
carburare [karbu'rare] VI *(aus* **avere***)* **carburare bene/male** *(Aut)* to be well/badly tuned; **oggi non carburo** *(fig: persona)* I'm half asleep today, my brain's not working today
carburatore [karbura'tore] SM carburettor *(Brit)*, carburetor *(Am)*
carburazione [karburat'tsjone] SF carburation
carburo [kar'buro] SM carbide
carcassa [kar'kassa] SF **1** *(di animale)* carcass; *(fig pegg: macchina)* (old) wreck **2** *(struttura portante)* framework, frame; (: *di nave*) hulk **3** *(Aut: pneumatico)* carcass; **pneumatico a carcassa radiale/diagonale** radial/ cross-ply tyre *(Brit)* *o* tire *(Am)*
carcerario, ria, ri, rie [kartʃe'rarjo] AGG prison *attr*
carcerato, a [kartʃe'rato] SM/F prisoner
carcerazione [kartʃerat'tsjone] SF imprisonment
carcere ['kartʃere] SM *(pl f* **carceri***)* *(edificio)* prison, jail; *(pena)* imprisonment; **sono evasi dal carcere** they escaped from prison; **essere/mettere in carcere** to be in/send to prison *o* jail; **gli hanno dato dieci anni di carcere** he was sent to prison for ten years; **condannato a due anni di carcere** sentenced to two years' imprisonment; **carcere di massima sicurezza** top-security prison
carceriere, a [kartʃe'rjɛre] SM/F *(anche fig)* jailer
carcinoma [kartʃi'nɔma] SM carcinoma
carciofo [kar'tʃɔfo] SM artichoke
cardamomo [karda'mɔmo] SM cardamom
cardanico, a, ci, che [kar'daniko] AGG: **giunto cardanico** universal joint
cardano [kar'dano] SM: **trasmissione a cardano** shaft drive
cardare [kar'dare] VT to card
cardellino [kardel'lino] SM goldfinch
cardiaco, a, ci, che [kar'diako] AGG cardiac, heart *attr*; **attacco cardiaco** heart attack
cardigan ['kardigan] SM INV cardigan
cardinalato [kardina'lato] SM cardinalship, cardinalate
cardinale [kardi'nale] AGG cardinal
■ SM *(Rel)* cardinal
cardinalizio, zia, zi, zie [kardina'littsjo] AGG *(titolo, cappello)* of a cardinal
cardine ['kardine] SM *(di porta, finestra)* hinge; *(fig: fondamento)* cornerstone, foundation
cardiochirurgia [kardjokirur'dʒia] SF heart surgery
cardiochirurgo, ghi *o* **gi** [kardjoki'rurgo] SM heart surgeon
cardiologia [kardjolo'dʒia] SF cardiology
cardiologo, a, gi [kar'djɔlogo] SM/F heart specialist, cardiologist
cardiopalmo [kardjo'palmo] SM palpitation
cardiopatico, a, ci, che [kardjo'patiko] AGG suffering from a heart complaint
■ SM/F person suffering from a heart complaint
cardo ['kardo] SM *(Bot)* thistle; *(commestibile)* cardoon
carena [ka'rɛna] SF *(Naut)* keel
carenare [kare'nare] VT *(Naut)* to careen; *(veicolo)* to streamline
carente [ka'rɛnte] AGG: **carente di** lacking in
carenza [ka'rɛntsa] SF shortage, lack, scarcity; *(Med)* deficiency; **carenza vitaminica** vitamin deficiency
carestia [kares'tia] SF famine; *(fig: penuria)* scarcity, lack, dearth; **migliaia di persone rischiano di morire a causa della carestia** thousands of people may die as a result of the famine
carezza [ka'rettsa] SF caress; **dare** *o* **fare una carezza a** *(persona)* to caress; *(animale)* to stroke, pat
carezzare [karet'tsare] VT = **accarezzare**
carezzevole [karet'tsevole] AGG sweet, endearing
carezzevolmente [karettsevol'mente] AVV endearingly
cargo, ghi ['kargo] SM *(nave)* cargo boat, freighter; *(aereo)* freighter
cariare [ka'rjare] VT to decay; **lo zucchero caria i denti** sugar decays teeth
▶ **cariarsi** VIP *(denti)* to decay
cariatide [ka'rjatide] SF caryatid
cariato, a [ka'rjato] AGG *(dente)* decayed, bad
carica, che ['karika] SF **1** *(ufficio, funzione)* position, office; **ricoprire** *o* **rivestire una carica** to hold a position; **in carica** in office; **il presidente in carica** the president in office; **rimanere in carica per...** to hold office for...; **il Presidente è rimasto in carica per cinque anni** the President held office for five years; **entrare/essere in carica** to come into/be in office; **uscire di carica** to leave office; **carica onorifica** honorary appointment **2** *(di orologio)* winding; **è finita la carica** it's wound down; **dare la carica all'orologio** to wind up the clock **3** *(di arma, missile)* charge **4** *(attacco: Mil, di animali)* charge; **tornare alla carica** *(fig)* to insist, persist; **entrare a passo di carica** to charge in **5** *(fig: energia)* drive; **dare la carica a qn** to give sb strength, encourage sb; **ha una forte carica di simpatia** he's very likeable
caricabatteria [karikabatte'ria] SM INV *(Aut)* battery charger; *(di telefonino)* charger
caricare [kari'kare] VT **1** *(gen)* to load; *(fig: esagerare)* to exaggerate; *(tinta)* to deepen **2** **caricare su/in** *(merci*

Cc

ecc) to load on/into; **caricare in macchina** (*passeggero*) to give a lift to; (*valigie*) to put into the car **3** (*sovraccaricare*): **caricare di** (*merci ecc*) to overload with; (*fig: di lavoro, responsabilità*) to overload with, to overburden with **4** (*orologio*) to wind up; (*batteria, accumulatore*) to charge; (*fucile, macchina fotografica*) to load; (*pipa, stufa*) to fill; (*caldaia, altoforno*) to stoke; **avevo dimenticato di caricare la sveglia** I'd forgotten to wind the alarm clock; **come si carica questa macchina fotografica?** how do you load the film in this camera?; **caricare un programma** (*Inform*) to load a program; **hai caricato il programma?** have you loaded the program? **5** (*attaccare: Mil*) to charge; (: *Sport*) to tackle; **la polizia ha caricato i dimostranti** the police charged the demonstrators

▸ **caricarsi** VR **1** **caricarsi di** to overburden *o* overload o.s. with; (*fig: di responsabilità, impegni*) to overburden o.s. with **2** (*concentrarsi*) **caricarsi per una gara** to gear o.s. up for a race

caricato, a [kari'kato] AGG (*affettato*) affected

caricatore [karika'tore] SM **1** (*di armi*) magazine; (*Fot*) cartridge **2** (*operaio*) loader

■ AGG: **piano caricatore** loading platform

caricatura [karika'tura] SF caricature; **fare la caricatura di qn** to do a caricature of sb

caricaturale [karikatu'rale] AGG ridiculous, grotesque

caricaturista, i, e [karikatu'rista] SM/F caricaturist

carico, a, chi, che ['kariko] AGG **1** (*veicolo*): **carico (di)** loaded *o* laden (with), full (of); (*persona*): **carico di** laden with; **è tornato carico di pacchi e pacchetti** he came back loaded with parcels; **un camion carico di mattoni** a lorry with a load of bricks; **carico di debiti** up to one's ears in debt; **carico di lavoro** weighed down with work **2** (*forte: colore*) strong, deep; (: *caffè, tè*) strong **3** (*caricato: orologio*) wound up; (: *fucile, macchina fotografica*) loaded; (: *pipa*) full; (: *batteria*) charged; (*bomba*) live; **il fucile era carico** the gun was loaded

■ SM **1** (*il caricare*) loading; **fare il carico** to load; **operazioni di carico** loading operations **2** (*materiale caricato*) load; (: *su nave*) freight, cargo; (*Comm*) shipment; **trasportava un carico di arance** it was carrying a load of oranges; **a pieno carico** with a full load; **capacità di carico** cargo capacity; **carico utile** pay load **3** (*Elettr*) charge **4** (*Econ*): **essere a carico di qn** (*onere, spese ecc*) to be charged to sb, be payable by sb; (*persona*) to be dependent on sb, be supported by sb; **a carico del cliente** at the customer's expense; **ha dei familiari a carico?** do you have any dependants? **5** (*Dir*) charge; **ha carichi pendenti?** do you have any charges pending?; **essere a carico di qn** (*accusa, prova*) to be against sb; **testimone a carico** witness for the prosecution **6** (*fig: peso*) burden, weight; **farsi carico di** (*problema, responsabilità*) to take on; **carico di lavoro** (*di ditta, reparto*) workload; **carico fiscale** tax burden

Cariddi [ka'riddi] SF Charybdis

carie ['karje] SF (*Med*) decay; (*Bot*) rot; **ho una carie** I've got a hole in one of my teeth

carillon [kari'jõ] SM INV musical box

carino, a [ka'rino] AGG (*gen*) nice; (*ragazza, bambino*) pretty, lovely; (*ragazzo*) good-looking; **carina questa maglietta!** that's a nice T-shirt!; **ha una casa molto carina** she's got a very nice house; **è carino tuo fratello** your brother's nice-looking; **essere carino con qn** to be nice to sb; **sono stati molto carini con me** they were very nice to me; **è stato molto carino da parte tua** that was really nice *o* kind of you

carisma [ka'rizma] SM charisma

carismatico, a, ci, che [kariz'matiko] AGG charismatic

carissimo, a [ka'rissimo] AGG (*molto caro*) very dear; (*molto costoso*) very expensive; **Carissimo Paolo** (*nelle lettere*) Dearest Paul

carità [kari'ta] SF INV (*gen, Rel*) charity; **chiedere la carità (a qn)** to beg for charity (from sb); (*fig*) to come begging (to sb); **c'era uno che chiedeva la carità fuori dalla chiesa** there was a man begging outside the church; **fare la carità a** to give (something) to; **vivere di carità** to live on charity; **per carità!** (*figurarsi*) you've got to be joking!; (*per favore*) please!; (*non ti disturbare!*) please don't bother!; (*non è un disturbo*) not at all!, it's no trouble at all!; (*neanche per sogno*) good heavens, no!; **uscire con lui? Per carità!** go out with him? You're joking!; **fammi la carità di star zitto** please be so kind as to keep quiet

caritatevole [karita'tevole] AGG charitable

caritatevolmente [karitatevol'mente] AVV charitably

carlinga, ghe [kar'linga] SF fuselage

Carlo Magno ['karlo 'maɲɲo] SM Charlemagne

carlona [kar'lona] SF: **alla carlona** carelessly, roughly

carme ['karme] SM solemn poem

carmelitano, a [karmeli'tano] AGG, SM/F Carmelite

carminio [kar'minjo] SM (*colorante*) carmine

■ AGG INV carmine, crimson

carnagione [karna'dʒone] SF complexion; **ha la carnagione chiara** she's got a fair complexion

carnaio, ai [kar'najo] SM (*ammasso di cadaveri*) charnel house; (*fig: luogo affollato*): **è un carnaio** it's swarming with people

carnale [kar'nale] AGG **1** (*sessuale: desiderio, conoscenza*) carnal; **violenza carnale** rape **2** (*consanguineo: fratello, sorella*) full *attr*, blood *attr*

carnalità [karnali'ta] SF carnality

carnalmente [karnal'mente] AVV (*gen*) carnally; **unirsi carnalmente** to have (sexual) intercourse

carne ['karne] SF **1** (*gen, fig*) flesh; **in carne e ossa** in the flesh, in person; **era proprio lui, in carne e ossa!** it was really him, in the flesh!; **carne da macello** (*fig*) cannon fodder; **color carne** flesh coloured; **carne viva** raw flesh; **essere (bene) in carne** to be well padded, be plump; **è carne della mia carne** he's my own flesh and blood **2** (*Culin*) meat; **preferisci la carne o il pesce?** which do you prefer, meat or fish?; **non essere né carne né pesce** (*fig*) to be neither fish nor fowl; **mettere troppa carne al fuoco** (*fig*) to have too many irons in the fire; **carne arrosto/ai ferri** roast/grilled meat; **carne bianca** (*di pollo, agnello, coniglio*) white meat; **carne bovina** *o* **di manzo** beef; **carne di cavallo** *o* **equina** horseflesh, horse meat; **carne suina** *o* **di maiale** pork; **carne ovina** *o* **di pecora** mutton; **carne rossa** (*di manzo o maiale*) red meat; **carne in scatola** tinned (*Brit*) *o* canned (*Am*) meat; **carne tritata** mince (*Brit*), hamburger meat (*Am*), minced (*Brit*) *o* ground (*Am*) meat; **carne di vitello** veal

carnefice [kar'nefitʃe] SM (*boia*) executioner; (*nell'impiccagione*) hangman; (*fig*) torturer

carneficina [karnefi'tʃina] SF carnage; (*fig*) disaster; **fare una carneficina** to carry out a massacre

carnevale [karne'vale] SM *carnival period*; **il carnevale di Venezia** the Venice Carnival

CARNEVALE

Carnevale is the name given to the period between Epiphany (6 January) and the beginning of Lent, when people throw parties, put on processions with spectacular floats, build bonfires in the "piazze" and dress up infabulous costumes and masks. Building to a peak just before Lent, **Carnevale** culminates in the festivities of Martedì grasso (Shrove Tuesday). The most famous are the **Carnevale di Viareggio** with its parade of allegorical floats and the **Carnevale di Venezia** with open-air shows and balls in the city's squares.

▷ www.carnevale.venezia.it/
▷ www.viareggio.ilcarnevale.com/

carnevalesco, a, schi, sche [karneva'lesko] AGG carnival *attr*

carniere [kar'njɛre] SM game bag

carnivoro, a [kar'nivoro] AGG carnivorous
■ SM carnivore

carnosità [karnosi'ta] SF fleshiness; (*di labbra*) fullness

carnoso, a [kar'noso] AGG (*gen*) fleshy; (*pianta, frutto, radice*) pulpy; (*labbra*) full

caro, a ['karo] AGG **1** (*amato*): **caro (a)** dear (to); (: *ricordo*) fond; **mi è tanto caro** it (*o* he) is very dear to me; **Caro Paolo** (*nelle lettere*) Dear Paul; **tanti cari saluti** best wishes; **cara signora!** my dear lady!; **se ti è cara la vita** if you value your life; **tener caro il ricordo di qn/qc** to cherish the memory of sb/sth **2** (*costoso*) dear, expensive; **a caro prezzo** at a high price; **vendere cara la pelle** to sell one's life dear
■ SM/F: **mio caro, mia cara** my dear; **i miei cari** my dear ones
■ AVV (*costare, pagare*) a lot, a great deal; **questo insulto ti costerà caro** you'll pay dearly for that insult; **lo pagherai caro** you'll pay a lot for it

caro-affitto [karo af'fitto] SM rent increases *pl*

caro-benzina [karo ben'dzina] SM increases *pl* in the price of petrol

carogna [ka'roɲɲa] SF carrion *inv*; (*fam: persona vile*) swine *inv*; **sei una carogna!** you're a pig!

carognata [karoɲ'ɲata] SF (*fam*) rotten trick; **fare una carognata a qn** to play a rotten trick on sb

Caronte [ka'ronte] SM Charon

carosello [karo'zɛllo] SM (*giostra*) merry-go-round, carousel (*Am*); (*movimento vorticoso: di automobili, idee*) whirl; **all'uscita dello stadio si sono formati dei caroselli** outside the stadium there was a whirl of cars

carota [ka'rɔta] SF **1** carrot **2** (*Mineralogia*) core

carotide [ka'rɔtide] SF carotid

carovana [karo'vana] SF (*gen*) caravan; (*convoglio*) convoy

carovaniero, a [karova'njɛro] AGG caravan *attr*; **strada carovaniera** caravan route

carovita [karo'vita] SM INV high cost of living; (*indennità*) cost of living allowance

carpa ['karpa] SF (*pesce*) carp

carpaccio [kar'pattʃo] SM *thin slices of raw meat or fish served with olive oil or with a sauce*

Carpazi [kar'pattsi] SMPL: **i Carpazi** the Carpathian Mountains, the Carpathians

carpello [kar'pɛllo] SM (*Bot*) carpel

carpenteria [karpente'ria] SF carpentry

carpentiere [karpen'tjɛre] SM carpenter

carpino ['karpino] SM (*albero*) hornbeam

carpione [kar'pjone] SM (*Culin*): **pesce in carpione** soused fish

carpire [kar'pire] VT: **carpire qc a qn** (*denaro*) to get sth out of sb; **carpire un segreto/un'informazione a qn** to worm a secret/information out of sb

carpo ['karpo] SM (*Anat*) wrist joint, carpus (*termine tecn*)

carponi [kar'poni] AVV on all fours, on one's hands and knees; **mettersi/stare a carponi** to get down/be on all fours

carrabile [kar'rabile] AGG suitable for vehicles; **"passo carrabile"** "keep clear"

carraio, aia, ai, aie [kar'rajo] AGG carriage *attr*; **passo carraio** driveway

carrarese [karra'rese] AGG of *o* from Carrara
■ SM/F inhabitant *o* native of Carrara

carré [kar're] SM INV **1** (*Culin: lombata*) loin **2** (*taglio di capelli*) bob
■ AGG INV: **pan carré** toasting loaf

carreggiabile [karred'dʒabile] SF (*anche*: **strada carreggiabile**) road open to light traffic

carreggiata [karred'dʒata] SF (*Aut*) carriageway (*Brit*), roadway; **strada a due carreggiate** dual carriageway (*Brit*), divided highway (*Am*); **tenersi in carreggiata** (*fig*) to keep to the right path; **rimettersi in carreggiata** (*fig: recuperare*) to catch up

carrellare [karrel'lare] VI (*aus* **avere**) (*Cine, TV*) to track

carrellata [karrel'lata] SF (*Cine, TV: tecnica*) tracking; (: *scena*) tracking shot; **carrellata di successi** medley of hits; **una carrellata su...** a brief look at ...

carrellista, i [karrel'lista] SM/F (*Cine, TV*) dolly operator

carrello [kar'rɛllo] SM (*gen, Ferr*) trolley; (*di teleferica*) car; (*Aer*) undercarriage; (*di macchina da scrivere*) carriage; (*Cine, TV*) dolly; **carrello elevatore** fork-lift truck; **carrello portaverdure** vegetable rack; **carrello portavivande** (food) trolley

carretta [kar'retta] SF (*piccolo carro*) cart; (*pegg: veicolo*) old wreck; **tirare la carretta** (*fig*) to plod along; **carretta del mare** *old and unsafe boat, generally used to carry illegal immigrants*

carrettata [karret'tata] SF cartload

carrettiere [karret'tjɛre] SM carter; **usa un linguaggio da carrettiere** he talks like a navvy

carretto [kar'retto] SM handcart; **carretto a mano** wheelbarrow

carriera [kar'rjɛra] SF career; **fare carriera** to get on (in one's job), to have a successful career; **non è facile far carriera per una donna con figli** it's not easy for a woman with children to have a career; **farà sicuramente carriera** he'll get on; **una brillante carriera universitaria** a brilliant university career; **prospettive di carriera** career prospects; **ufficiale di carriera** (*Mil*) regular officer; **di** *o* **a gran carriera** (*fig*) at full speed

carrierista, i, e [karrje'rista] SM/F careerist

carrieristico, a, ci, che [karrje'ristiko] AGG career *attr*

carriola [karri'ɔla] SF wheelbarrow

carrista, i [kar'rista] SM (*Mil: guidatore*) tank driver; (: *soldato*) tank soldier

carro ['karro] SM **1** cart, wagon; (*per carnevale*) float; **mettere il carro davanti ai buoi** (*fig*) to put the cart before the horse **2** (*Astron*): **il Gran/Piccolo Carro** the Great/Little Bear
■ **carro armato** (*Mil*) tank; **carro attrezzi** (*Aut*) breakdown van (*Brit*), tow truck (*Am*); **carro bestiame** (*Ferr*) animal wagon; **carro funebre** hearse; **carro merci**

Cc

(*Ferr*) goods wagon (*Brit*), freight car (*Am*)
carroccio [kar'rɔttʃo] SM (*Pol*): **il Carroccio** *symbol of Lega Nord*
carrozza [kar'rɔttsa] SF (*gen, Ferr*) carriage, coach; **(signori) in carrozza!** all aboard!; **carrozza belvedere** observation car; **carrozza letto** sleeper (*Brit*), Pullman® (*Am*); **carrozza ristorante** dining *o* restaurant car
carrozzabile [karrot'tsabile] AGG: **(strada) carrozzabile** road open to vehicles
carrozzato, a [karrot'tsato] AGG **1** (*Aut*): **macchina carrozzata da Bertone** car designed by Bertone **2** (*fam: donna*) well-stacked
carrozzella [karrot'tsɛlla] SF (*per bambini*) pram (*Brit*), baby carriage (*Am*); (*per invalidi*) wheelchair
carrozzeria [karrottse'ria] SF **1** (*Aut: rivestimento*) bodywork, body, coachwork (*Brit*); **carrozzeria portante** chassis **2** (*Aut: officina*) body shop
carrozziere [karrot'tsjɛre] SM (*Aut: progettista*) car designer; (*: meccanico*) panel beater (*Brit*), auto bodyworker (*Am*)
carrozzina [karrot'tsina] SF pram (*Brit*), baby carriage (*Am*)
carrozzino [karrot'tsino] SM (*di motocicletta*) side-car
carrozzone [karrot'tsone] SM (*di circo, zingari*) caravan (*Brit*), wagon (*Am*)
carruba [kar'ruba] SF (*frutta*) carob
carrubo [kar'rubo] SM (*albero*) carob (tree)
carrucola [kar'rukola] SF pulley
carta ['karta] SF
1 (*gen*) paper; (*statuto*) charter; **un foglio di carta** a sheet of paper; **sulla carta** (*in teoria*) on paper
2 (*da gioco*) card; **dare le carte** to deal the cards; **giocare una carta** to play a card; **giocare l'ultima carta** (*anche fig*) to play one's last card; **a carte scoperte** (*anche fig*) cards on the table; **mettere le carte in tavola** to lay one's cards on the table; **cambiare le carte in tavola** (*fig*) to shift one's ground; **fare le carte a qn** (*Cartomanzia*) to tell sb's fortune using cards
3 (*documenti*): **carte** SFPL papers, documents; **devo fare tutte le carte per il passaporto** I've got to sort out all the documents and forms for the passport application; **fare carte false** (*fig*) to go to great lengths; **avrebbe fatto carte false pur di ottenere quel posto** he would have gone to any lengths to get that job
4 (*al ristorante*) menu; **alla carta** à la carte
■ **carta di alluminio** aluminium (*Brit*) *o* aluminum (*Am*) foil; **carta assegni** bank card; **carta assorbente** blotting paper; **carta automobilistica** road map; **carta bianca**: **dare carta bianca a qn** to give sb carte blanche; **carta da bollo** *o* **bollata** *o* **legale** (*Amm*) official stamped paper; **carta di credito** credit card; **carta di credito telefonica** phone card (*for calls that are charged to the phone bill*); **carta da cucina** kitchen roll *o* paper *o* towel (*Brit*), paper towel (*Am*); **carta da disegno** drawing paper; **carta geografica** map; **carta di giornale** newsprint; **carta d'identità** identity card; **carta igienica** toilet paper; **carta d'imbarco** boarding card; **carta intelligente** smart card; **carta da lettere** writing paper; **carta libera** *o* **semplice** (*Amm*) unstamped paper; **carta lucida** tracing paper; **carta millimetrata** graph paper; **carta moschicida** fly-paper; **carta nautica** (nautical) chart; **carta oleata** waxed *o* wax paper (*spec Am*); **carta da pacchi** *o* **da imballaggio** wrapping paper, brown paper; **carta paraffinata** *o* **vegetale** (*Culin*) greaseproof paper (*Brit*); **carta da parati** wallpaper; **carta per prelievi automatici** cash card; **carta da regalo** (gift) wrapping paper; **carta stagnola** tinfoil (*Brit*); **carta stradale** *o* **automobilistica** road map; **carta velina** tissue paper; **carta verde** (*Aut*) green card (*Brit*); **carta vetrata** glasspaper, sandpaper; **carta dei vini** wine list; **carta da visita** visiting card; **(color) carta da zucchero** mid blue; **carte da gioco** playing cards
cartacarbone [kartakar'bone] SF carbon paper
cartaccia, ce [kar'tattʃa] SF waste paper
cartaceo, a, cei, cee [kar'tatʃeo] AGG paper *attr*
Cartagine [kar'tadʒine] SF Carthage
cartaginese [kartadʒi'nese] AGG, SM/F Carthaginian
cartamodello [kartamo'dɛllo] SM (*Cucito*) paper pattern
cartamoneta [kartamo'neta] SF paper money
cartapecora [karta'pɛkora] SF parchment, vellum
cartapesta [karta'pesta] SF papier-mâché; **di cartapesta** papier-mâché *attr*; (*fig*) weak; **eroe di cartapesta** tin god
cartario, ria, ri, rie [kar'tarjo] AGG paper *attr*
cartastraccia, ce [kartas'trattʃa] SF waste paper
cartavetrare [kartave'trare] VT (*legno, metallo*) to sand (down)
carteggio, gi [kar'teddʒo] SM correspondence
cartella [kar'tɛlla] SF **1** (*custodia: di cartoncino*) folder; (*borsa: di professionista*) briefcase; (*: di scolaro*) schoolbag, satchel; (*pratica, incartamento*) file, dossier; (*Inform*) folder; **cartella trasparente** transparent folder **2** (*Tip*) page **3** (*Lotteria*) lottery ticket; (*Tombola*) tombola card **4** **cartella clinica** (*Med*) case sheet
cartellino [kartel'lino] SM (*del prezzo*) price label, price tag; (*scheda*) card; **timbrare il cartellino** (*all'entrata*) to clock in *o* on; (*all'uscita*) to clock out *o* off; **cartellino giallo/rosso** (*Calcio*) yellow/red card; **cartellino di presenza** *o* **orario** clock card, timecard
cartellista, i [kartel'lista] SM (*Econ, Pol*) member of a cartel
cartello[1] [kar'tɛllo] SM (*avviso*) notice, sign; (*stradale*) sign, signpost; (*di dimostranti, pubblicitario*) placard, poster; (*di negozio*) sign; **cosa indica quel cartello?** what does that sign say?; **sul cartello c'era scritto "tutto esaurito"** the sign said "sold out"
cartello[2] [kar'tɛllo] SM (*Econ, Pol*) cartel
cartellone [kartel'lone] SM (*pubblicitario*) placard, (advertising) poster; (*Teatro*) bill, playbill; (*Cine*) poster; (*di tombola*) scoring frame, board; **tenere il cartellone** (*Teatro*) to have a long run
cartellonista, i, e [kartello'nista] SM/F poster designer
cartellonistica [kartello'nistika] SF poster designing
carter ['karter] SM INV (*di bicicletta, moto*) chain guard; (*Aut*) oil sump
cartesiano, a [karte'zjano] AGG Cartesian
cartiera [kar'tjɛra] SF paper mill
cartiglio, gli [kar'tiʎʎo] SM scroll
cartilagine [karti'ladʒine] SF cartilage
cartina [kar'tina] SF **1** (*Geog*) map **2** (*di sigarette*) cigarette paper; (*piccolo involto*) packet
cartoccio, ci [kar'tɔttʃo] SM **1** (*involucro*) cornet; **cuocere al cartoccio** (*Culin*) to bake in tinfoil *o* aluminium (*Brit*) *o* aluminum (*Am*); **patate al cartoccio** ≈ jacket potatoes (*Brit*) **2** (*Mil*) powder charge
cartografia [kartogra'fia] SF cartography
cartografo, a [kar'tɔgrafo] SM/F cartographer

cartolaio, aia, ai, aie [karto'lajo] SM/F stationer
cartolarizzare [kartolarid'dzare] VT *to convert credits of banks, companies and public bodies into shares that can be bought and sold*
cartolarizzazione [kartolarid'dzatsjone] SF *the conversion of credits of banks, companies and public bodies into shares that can be bought and sold*
cartoleria [kartole'ria] SF stationer's (shop); **lo trovi in cartoleria** you'll get it at a stationer's
cartolina [karto'lina] SF postcard; **mandami una cartolina** send me a postcard; **cartolina di auguri** greetings card; **cartolina illustrata** picture postcard; **cartolina postale** stamped postcard; **cartolina precetto** *o* **rosa** (*Mil*) call-up papers *pl* (*Brit*), draft card (*Am*)
cartomante [karto'mante] SM/F fortune-teller (*using cards*)
cartomanzia [kartoman'tsia] SF fortune-telling (*using cards*)
cartonato, a [karto'nato] AGG (*carta, busta*) stiffened; **copertina cartonata** hard cover
cartoncino [karton'tʃino] SM (*materiale*) thin cardboard; (*biglietto*) card
cartone [kar'tone] SM **1** (*materiale*) cardboard; **una scatola di cartone** a cardboard box **2** (*Arte*) cartoon; **cartone animato** (*Cine*) cartoon; **i cartoni animati di Tom e Jerry** Tom and Jerry cartoons **3** (*imballaggio*) large cardboard box; (*scatola: del latte, dell'aranciata*) carton; **un cartone di latte** a carton of milk
cartongesso [karton'dʒɛsso] SM plasterboard
cartonificio, ci [kartoni'fitʃo] SM cardboard mill
cartonista, i, e [karto'nista] SM/F (*Cine*) cartoonist
cartuccia, ce [kar'tuttʃa] SF (*di arma*) cartridge; (*di penna*) refill, cartridge; **mezza cartuccia** (*fig: persona da poco*) good-for-nothing; **cartuccia a salve** blank (cartridge)
cartucciera [kartut'tʃɛra] SF cartridge belt
carving ['karvin(g)] SM (*Sci*) carving
casa ['kasa] SF
1 (*edificio*) house; **una bella casa grande** a nice big house; **casa a quattro piani** four-storey(ed) (*Brit*) *o* four-storied (*Am*) house; **casa di campagna** (*grande*) house in the country; (*piccola*) country cottage; **casa di mattoni** brick house; **case a schiera** terraced (*Brit*) *o* row (*Am*) houses; **hanno una bella casa** they have a nice flat; **la Casa Bianca** (*Pol*) the White House
2 (*abitazione*) home; **essere/stare a** *o* **in casa** to be/stay at home; **sono stato in casa tutta la sera** I was at home all evening; **eravamo a casa mia** we were at my house; **non è a casa** she isn't at home; **sarò a casa tra un'ora** I'll be home in an hour; **tornare a casa** to come/go back home; **è tornato a casa tardi** he got home late; **andare a casa** to go home; **vado a casa mia/tua** I'm going home/to your house; **c'è nessuno in casa?** is anybody in?; **vieni a casa nostra?** are you coming to our house *o* place?; **uscire di casa** to leave home; **dove sta di casa?** where does he live?; **non sa dove stia di casa la cortesia** he doesn't know the meaning of courtesy; **essere di casa** to be like one of the family; **è una ragazza tutta casa e chiesa** she is a home-loving, church-going girl; **fatto in casa** home-made; **pane fatto in casa** home-made bread; **fai come se fossi a casa tua** make yourself at home; **abitare a casa del diavolo** to live in the back of beyond; **"tanti saluti a casa"** "best wishes to all the family"
3 (*casato, stirpe*) house, family; **casa d'Asburgo** House of Hapsburg
4 (*ditta*) firm, company
■ **casa di correzione** ≈ community home (*Brit*), ≈ reform school (*Am*); reformatory (*Am*); **casa di cura** nursing home; **casa discografica** record company; **casa editrice** publishing house; **casa famiglia** (*per bambini, anziani*) (care) home; (*per malati di mente, ex-tossicodipendenti*) halfway house; **Casa delle Libertà** House of Liberties; *centre-right coalition*; **casa madre** head office; **casa di moda** fashion house; **casa popolare** ≈ council house *o* flat (*Brit*), ≈ public housing unit (*Am*) **casa di riposo** (old people's) home, care home; **casa dello studente** hall of residence (*Brit*), dormitory (*Am*); **casa di tolleranza** *o* **d'appuntamenti** brothel
Casablanca [kasa'blanka] SF Casablanca
casacca, che [ka'zakka] SF (*Mil*) coat; (*giacca*) jacket; (*di fantino*) blouse
casaccio [ka'zattʃo] SM: **a casaccio** (*per caso*) at random; (*senza cura*) any old how; (*senza riflettere*) off the top of one's head
casale [ka'sale] SM (*gruppo di case*) hamlet; (*casolare*) farmhouse
casalinga, ghe [kasa'linga] SF housewife; **fa la casalinga** she's a housewife
casalingo, a, ghi, ghe [kasa'lingo] AGG **1** (*occupazione, lavoro*) domestic, household *attr* **2** (*fatto in casa*) home-made; (*semplice*) homely; (*amante della casa*) home-loving; **cucina casalinga** (plain) home cooking;
■ SMPL (*oggetti*): **casalinghi** household articles
casamento [kasa'mento] SM block (of flats) (*Brit*), apartment building *o* house (*Am*)
casata [ka'sata] SF family, (family) lineage
casato [ka'sato] SM family name; **è di nobile casato** he's of noble birth
casba ['kazba] SF kasbah
Casc. ABBR = **cascata**
cascame [kas'kame] SM (*Tessile*) waste
cascamorto [kaska'mɔrto] SM love-sick Romeo; **fare il cascamorto** to play the love-sick Romeo; **non fare il cascamorto con me** there's no point in chasing after me
cascante [kas'kante] AGG drooping, droopy; **avere le guance/le spalle cascanti** to be heavy-jowled/round-shouldered
cascare [kas'kare] VI (*aus* **essere**) to fall; **far cascare qc** to drop sth; **cascare per terra** to fall to the ground, fall down; **è cascato dal letto** he fell out of bed; **cascare dalla fame** to be faint with hunger; **cascare dal sonno** to be falling asleep on one's feet; **cascare dalle nuvole** (*fig*) to be taken aback; **cascare bene/male** (*fig*) to land lucky/unlucky; **cascarci** to fall for it; **gli ho detto che tu eri partito e lui c'è cascato** I told him you had left and he fell for it; **caschi il mondo** no matter what; **non cascherà il mondo se...** it won't be the end of the world if ...
cascata [kas'kata] SF (*di acqua*) waterfall, cascade; (*fig: di capelli*) cascade; **sono le cascate più alte del mondo** they're the biggest waterfalls in the world; **cascata di ghiaccio** icefall; **le cascate del Niagara** the Niagara Falls; **le cascate Vittoria** the Victoria Falls
cascatore, trice [kaska'tore] SM/F (*Cine*) stuntman/stuntwoman
cascherò *ecc* [kaske'rɔ] VB *vedi* **cascare**
caschetto [kas'ketto] SM (*pettinatura*) pageboy
cascina [kaʃ'ʃina] SF farmstead
cascinale [kaʃʃi'nale] SM (*casolare*) farmhouse; (*cascina*) farmstead

Cc

casco, schi ['kasko] SM **1** (*Mil, Sport*) helmet; (*da motociclista*) crash helmet; (*da parrucchiere*) (hair-)dryer; **i caschi blu** UN troops, the Blue Helmets **2** (*di banane*) bunch

caseario, ria, ri, rie [kaze'arjo] AGG dairy *attr*

caseggiato [kased'dʒato] SM (*edificio*) large block of flats (*Brit*), large apartment building (*Am*) *o* house; (*gruppo di case*) group of houses

caseificio, ci [kazei'fitʃo] SM creamery

caseina [kaze'ina] SF casein

casella [ka'sɛlla] SF (*quadretto*) box; (*di scacchiera*) square; (*di mobile, schedario*) pigeonhole; **casella postale** post office box; **casella di posta elettronica** mailbox; **casella di ricezione** (*Inform*) stacker

casellante [kasel'lante] SM (*Ferr*) signalman; (: *al passaggio livello*) level-crossing keeper; (*su autostrada*) toll collector

casellario, ri [kasel'larjo] SM (*mobile*) filing cabinet; (*raccolta di pratiche*) files *pl*; **casellario giudiziale** *o* **giudiziario** court records *pl*; **casellario penale** police files *pl*

casello [ka'sɛllo] SM (*Ferr*) signal box (*Brit*), signal tower (*Am*); (*di autostrada*) tollgate

casereccio, cia, ci, ce [kase'rettʃo] AGG home-made

caserma [ka'sɛrma] SF barracks *pl*; **caserma dei vigili del fuoco** fire station

casermone [kaser'mone] SM (*pegg*) barracks *pl*

casertano, a [kaser'tano] AGG of *o* from Caserta ■ SM/F inhabitant *o* native of Caserta

casetta [ka'setta] SF (*piccola casa*) small house; (*tenda*) family tent

casinista, i, e [kasi'nista] SM/F muddler

casino [ka'sino] SM **1** (*fam: bordello*) brothel **2** (*fig fam: rumore*) row, racket; (: *disordine*) mess; (: *guaio*) trouble; **ha fatto un casino** he made an awful row; he messed everything up; **cos'è questo casino?** what's this bloody racket?; **in camera mia c'è un gran casino** my bedroom is in a hell of a mess; **in questo periodo ho tanti casini** I've got loads of problems at the moment; **mettere qn nei casini** put sb in a hell of a mess **3** (*fam: grande quantità*) loads; **mi piace un casino** I really like it; **un casino di** loads of; **c'era un casino di gente** there were loads of people; **c'era un casino di macchine** there was a hell of a lot of traffic **4** **casino di caccia** hunting lodge

casinò [kazi'nɔ] SM INV casino

casistica [ka'zistika] SF record of cases; **secondo la casistica degli incidenti stradali** according to road accident data

caso ['kazo] SM

1 (*fatalità, destino*) chance; **è un puro caso** it's sheer chance; **il caso ha voluto che...** by chance ...; **non è un caso** it's no coincidence; **si dà il caso che...** it so happens that ...; **guarda caso** strangely enough; **a caso** at random; **ho aperto il libro a caso** I opened the book at random

2 (*fatto, Gramm, Med, Dir*) case; **per lui è un caso di coscienza** he is in a moral dilemma; **questi sono i casi della vita!** that's life!; **caso limite** borderline case

3 (*bisogno*): **fare al caso di qn** to be just what sb needs; **fa al caso mio** it's just what I need; **non è il caso che tu te la prenda** there's no need for you to be upset; **non è il caso di arrabbiarsi!** there's no point getting angry!; **non mi sembra il caso di insistere** I wouldn't insist on that; **è il caso che ce ne andiamo** we'd better go; **forse sarebbe il caso di andarcene** perhaps we'd better go

4 (*possibilità, evenienza*) possibility, event; **i casi sono due** there are two possibilities; **in ogni caso** in any case; **in ogni caso non ci perdi niente** in any case you've got nothing to lose; **in caso contrario** otherwise; **in tal caso** *or* **in quel caso** in that case; **be', in tal caso dovremo rimandare la partenza** well, in that case we'll have to put off our departure; **in caso di necessità** *o* **bisogno** in case of need; **al caso** if need be, should the opportunity arise; **per caso** by chance, by accident; **l'ho incontrato per caso** I met him by chance; **nel caso che...** in case ...; **ti do il mio numero di telefono, nel caso che tu venga a Roma** I'll give you my phone number, in case you come to Rome; **caso mai** if by chance; **caso mai non possiate venire...** if (by chance) you can't come ...; **dovrei essere lì alle 5, caso mai aspetta** I should be there for 5; if (by any chance) I'm not, wait; **fare** *o* **porre** *o* **mettere il caso che...** to suppose that ...; **mettiamo il caso che** supposing; **mettiamo il caso che ti inviti: accetteresti?** supposing he invited you, would you go?; **a seconda dei casi** depending on the circumstances; **nel migliore dei casi** at best; **nel peggiore dei casi** at worst

5 (*attenzione*): **far caso a qn/qc** to pay attention to sb/sth; **hai fatto caso al suo cappello?** did you notice his hat?; **non ci ho fatto caso** I didn't notice; **non farci caso** don't pay any attention

casolare [kaso'lare] SM cottage

casomai [kazo'mai] CONG = **caso mai**

casotto [ka'sɔtto] SM **1** (*di sentinella*) sentry box; (*di guardiano*) shelter; (*in spiaggia*) bathing hut, bathing cabin **2** (*fam*) = **casino 1, 2**

Caspio ['kaspjo] SM: **il mar Caspio** the Caspian Sea

caspita ['kaspita] ESCL (*di sorpresa*) good heavens!; (*di impazienza*) for goodness' sake!

cassa ['kassa] SF **1** (*gen, Tip, di orologio*) case; (*gabbia*) crate; (*mobile*) chest; (*scatola*) box; **ho comprato una cassa di birra** I bought a case of beer **2** (*Comm: macchina*) cash register; (: *sportello*) cash desk; (: *in supermercato*) checkout (counter); **"si prega di pagare alla cassa"** "please pay at the desk"; **"cassa"** "pay here"; **registratore di cassa** till; **piccola cassa** petty cash; **battere cassa** (*fig*) to come looking for money **3** (*ente finanziario*) fund **4** (*istituto bancario*) bank ■ **cassa acustica** (*Mus*) speaker; **cassa d'aria** (*Naut*) airlock; **cassa armonica** (*Mus*) soundbox; **cassa automatica prelievi** cashpoint (*Am*), cash dispenser (*Brit*), automatic telling machine (*Brit*); **cassa comune** kitty; **cassa continua** night safe (*Brit*), night depository (*Am*); **cassa del fucile** rifle stock; **cassa da imballaggio** packing case; **cassa integrazione** *system whereby the state pays part of the salaries of employees of a company that is in difficulty for a certain period of time*; **mettere in cassa integrazione** ≈ to lay off **Cassa del Mezzogiorno** *development fund for the South of Italy, now abolished*; **cassa da morto** coffin; **cassa mutua** *o* **malattia** health insurance scheme; **cassa di risonanza** (*Fis*) resonance chamber; (*fig*) platform; **cassa di risparmio** savings bank; **cassa rurale e artigiana** credit institution (*for farmers and craftsmen*); **cassa toracica** (*Anat*) chest

cassaforte [kassa'fɔrte] SF (*pl* **casseforti**) safe; **hanno forzato la cassaforte** they forced open the safe

Cassandra [kas'sandra] SF (*Mitol, fig*) Cassandra

cassapanca, che [kassa'panka] SF settle

cassare [kas'sare] VT (*Dir: annullare*) to annul, repeal

cassata [kas'sata] SF (*gelato*) tutti-frutti

cassazione [kassat'tsjone] SF (*Dir*) cassation
casseruola [kasse'rwɔla] SF saucepan; **pollo in casseruola** chicken casserole
cassetta [kas'setta] SF **1** (*gen*) box; (*musicassetta*) cassette; **una cassetta di mele** a box of apples; **ce l'ho sia su CD che su cassetta** I've got it on CD and on cassette; **pane a** *o* **in cassetta** toasting loaf; **cassetta degli arnesi** toolbox; **cassetta delle lettere** letterbox; **cassetta di sicurezza** strongbox **2** (*Cine, Teatro: incasso*) box-office takings *pl*; **far cassetta** to be a box-office success; **film di cassetta** (*commerciale*) box-office draw
cassettiera [kasset'tjɛra] SF chest of drawers
cassetto [kas'setto] SM drawer; **è nel primo cassetto** it's in the top drawer
cassettone [kasset'tone] SM (*mobile*) chest of drawers; **soffitto a cassettoni** (*Archit*) panelled ceiling
cassia ['kassja] SF cassia
cassiere, a [kas'sjɛre] SM/F cashier; (*in supermercato*) check-out assistant (*Brit*), check-out clerk (*Am*); **cassiere di banca** bank teller
cassintegrato, a [kassinte'grato] SM/F *worker who has been laid off and receives money from the state*
Cassio ['kassjo] SM Cassius
cassone [kas'sone] SM (*cassa*) large case, large chest
cassonetto [kasso'netto] SM (*per rifiuti*) wheelie-bin
Cast. ABBR = **castello**
cast [ka:st] SM INV (*Cine*) cast
casta ['kasta] SF caste
castagna [kas'taɲɲa] SF chestnut; **prendere qn in castagna** (*fig*) to catch sb in the act; **castagna d'acqua** water chestnut
castagnaccio, ci [kastaɲ'ɲattʃo] SM chestnut cake
castagno [kas'taɲɲo] SM (*albero*) chestnut (tree); (*legno*) chestnut; **castagno comune** *o* **dolce** sweet chestnut
castagnola [kastaɲ'ɲɔla] SF (*petardo*) firecrack
castamente [kasta'mente] AVV chastely
castano, a [kas'tano] AGG (*capelli*) chestnut (brown); (*occhi*) brown; (*persona*) brown-haired; **ha gli occhi e i capelli castani** she's got brown eyes and brown hair
castellano, a [kastel'lano] SM/F lord/lady of the manor
castello [kas'tɛllo] SM **1** castle; **castello di carte** house of cards; **castello di sabbia** sand castle; **fare castelli in aria** to build castles in the air; **letti a castello** bunk-beds **2** (*Naut*): **castello di poppa** quarter-deck; **castello di prua** fo'c'sle **3** (*Tecn*) scaffolding
castigare [kasti'gare] VT to punish, chastise
castigatamente [kastigata'mente] AVV (*vestirsi*) demurely
castigatezza [kastiga'tettsa] SF (*irreprensibilità*) faultlessness
castigato, a [kasti'gato] AGG (*casto, modesto*) pure, chaste; (*abbigliamento*) demure; (*emendato: prosa, versione*) expurgated, amended
Castiglia [kas'tiʎʎa] SF Castille
castigliano, a [kastiʎ'ʎano] AGG, SM/F Castilian
castigo, ghi [kas'tigo] SM punishment; **per castigo** as a punishment; **mettere/essere in castigo** to punish/be punished; **sono in castigo e non posso uscire** I'm being punished and I'm not allowed to go out; **castigo di Dio** (*fig*) scourge
castità [kasti'ta] SF chastity
casto, a ['kasto] AGG chaste, pure
Castore ['kastore] SM (*Mitol, Astron*) Castor
castorino [kasto'rino] SM coypu; **pelliccia di castorino** nutria fur
castoro [kas'tɔro] SM beaver
castrante [kas'trante] AGG frustrating
castrare [kas'trare] VT (*gen*) to castrate; (*cavallo*) to geld; (*gatto*) to neuter, doctor (*Brit*), fix (*Am*); (*fig: iniziativa*) to frustrate
castrato, a [kas'trato] AGG (*vedi vb*) castrated; gelded; neutered
■ SM (*agnello*) wether; (*Culin*) mutton
castrazione [kastrat'tsjone] SF castration
castronaggine [kastro'naddʒine] SF (*fam*) stupidity
castrone [kas'trone] SM gelding
castroneria [kastrone'ria] SF (*fam*): **dire castronerie** to talk rubbish
casual ['kæʒuəl] AGG INV (*abito, moda*) casual
■ SM INV (*abbigliamento*) casual wear
casuale [kazu'ale] AGG chance *attr*, fortuitous
casualità [kazuali'ta] SF chance nature

LO SAPEVI...?
casualità non si traduce mai con ***casualty***

casupola [ka'supola] SF simple little cottage
casus belli ['kazus'bɛlli] SM INV (*Pol, fig*) casus belli
catabolismo [katabo'lizmo] SM catabolism
cataclisma, i [kata'klizma] SM cataclysm; (*fig*) catastrophe; **sembra che ci sia stato un cataclisma qui** this place looks as though a bomb has hit it
catacomba [kata'komba] SF catacomb
catafalco, chi [kata'falko] SM catafalque
catafascio [kata'faʃʃo] SM: **mandare a catafascio** to wreck; **andare a catafascio** to go to rack and ruin
catalessi [kata'lɛssi] SF INV (*Med*) catalepsy; **entrare** *o* **cadere in catalessi** to have a cataleptic fit; (*fig*) to go into a trance
catalisi [ka'talizi] SF INV catalysis
catalitico, a, ci, che [kata'litiko] AGG: **marmitta catalitica** catalytic converter
catalizzare [katalid'dzare] VT (*anche fig*) to act as a catalyst (up)on
catalizzato, a [katalid'dzato] AGG (*Aut*) fitted with a catalytic converter
catalizzatore [kataliddza'tore] SM (*Aut*) catalytic converter; (*Chim, fig*) catalyst
catalogare [katalo'gare] VT to catalogue, list
Catalogna [kata'loɲɲa] SF Catalonia
catalogo [ka'talogo] SM catalogue
catamarano [katama'rano] SM catamaran
catanese [kata'nese] AGG of *o* from Catania
■ SM/F inhabitant *o* native of Catania
catanzarese [katandza'rese] AGG of *o* from Catanzaro
■ SM/F inhabitant *o* native of Catanzaro
catapecchia [kata'pekkja] SF hovel
cataplasma, i [kata'plazma] SM (*Med*) poultice
catapulta [kata'pulta] SF catapult
catapultare [katapul'tare] VT to catapult
► **catapultarsi** VR to catapult
cataratta [kata'ratta] SF = **cateratta**
catarifrangente [katarifran'dʒɛnte] AGG reflecting
■ SM reflector
catarro [ka'tarro] SM catarrh
catarsi [ka'tarsi] SF INV catharsis
catasta [ka'tasta] SF pile, stack
catastale [katas'tale] AGG (*Amm*): **ufficio catastale** land registry (office); **rilievo catastale** cadastral survey
catasto [ka'tasto] SM (*Amm: inventario*) land register, cadaster; (*anche:* **ufficio del catasto**) land registry (office)

Cc

catastrofe [ka'tastrofe] SF catastrophe, disaster
catastroficamente [katastrofika'mente] AVV catastrophically
catastrofico, a, ci, che [katas'trɔfiko] AGG *(evento)* catastrophic, disastrous; *(persona, previsione)* pessimistic
catechesi [kate'kɛzi] SF INV catechesis
catechismo [kate'kizmo] SM catechism
catechista, i, e [kate'kista] SM/F catechist
catechistico, a, ci, che [kate'kistiko] AGG catechistic
catechizzare [katekid'dzare] VT *(Rel)* to catechize; *(fig)* to indoctrinate
catecumeno [kate'kumeno] SM catechumen
categoria [katego'ria] SF *(gen)* category; *(di albergo)* class; **di terza categoria** *(albergo, locale, anche pegg)* third-class
categoricamente [kategorika'mente] AVV categorically
categorico, a, ci, che [kate'gɔriko] AGG *(gen)* categorical; *(rifiuto)* categorical, flat
catena [ka'tena] SF *(gen, di negozi)* chain; *(di montagne)* range, chain; *(fig: legame)* bond, chain; **reazione a catena** *(anche fig)* chain reaction; **susseguirsi a catena** to happen in quick succession; **tenere un cane alla catena** to keep a dog on a chain; **catena alimentare** food chain; **catena di montaggio** *(Tecn)* assembly line; **catena di Sant'Antonio** chain letter; **catena umana** human chain; **catene da neve** *(Aut)* snow chains
catenaccio, ci [kate'nattʃo] SM bolt; **chiudere con il catenaccio** to bolt; **fare catenaccio** *(Calcio)* to play defensively
catenella [kate'nɛlla] SF *(ornamento)* chain; *(di orologio)* watch chain; *(di porta)* door chain; **punto catenella** *(in ricamo, maglia)* chain stitch
cateratta [kate'ratta] SF **1** *(Med, Geog)* cataract **2** *(saracinesca)* sluice(gate)
catering ['katerin(g)] SM catering; **servizio catering** catering service
caterva [ka'tɛrva] SF *(di cose)* loads *pl*, heaps *pl*; *(di persone)* horde
catetere [kate'tɛre] SM *(Med)* catheter
cateto [ka'tɛto] SM *(Geom)* cathetus; **in un triangolo rettangolo l'ipotenusa è uguale alla somma dei cateti** in a right-angled triangle the length of the hypotenuse equals the sum of the other two sides
Catilina [kati'lina] SM Catiline
catinella [kati'nɛlla] SF basin; **piovere a catinelle** to rain cats and dogs
catino [ka'tino] SM basin
catione [ka'tjone] SM cation
catodico, a, ci, che [ka'tɔdiko] AGG cathode *attr*; **tubo a raggi catodici** cathode-ray tube
catodo ['katodo] SM cathode
Catone [ka'tone] SM Cato
catorcio, ci [ka'tɔrtʃo] SM *(pegg)* old wreck
catramare [katra'mare] VT to tar
catrame [ka'trame] SM tar
cattedra ['kattedra] SF **1** *(mobile)* (teacher's) desk; **cattedra episcopale** bishop's throne; **salire** *o* **montare in cattedra** *(fig)* to pontificate **2** *(incarico: Scol)* teaching post; *(: Univ)* chair, professorship
cattedrale [katte'drale] SF cathedral
cattedraticamente [kattedratika'mente] AVV *(pegg)* pedantically
cattedratico, a, ci, che [katte'dratiko] AGG *(insegnamento)* university *attr*; *(pegg)* pedantic
■ SM/F professor

cattivello, a [katti'vɛllo] AGG naughty
cattiveria [katti'vɛrja] SF **1** *(qualità)* wickedness, nastiness; *(: di bambino)* naughtiness; **lo ha fatto per pura cattiveria** he did it out of sheer spite **2** *(azione)* nasty *o* wicked action; **fare una cattiveria** to do something nasty *o* wicked; *(bambino)* to be naughty **3** *(discorso)*: **dire una cattiveria** to say sth spiteful
cattività [kattivi'ta] SF *(di animali)* captivity
cattivo, a [kat'tivo] AGG **1** *(persona, azione)* bad, wicked; *(bambino: birichino)* naughty, bad; **un bambino cattivo** a naughty boy; **brutto cattivo!** you naughty boy!; **quel ragazzo è un cattivo soggetto** that boy's a bit of a rascal; **farsi cattivo sangue** to worry, get in a state; **farsi un cattivo nome** to earn a bad reputation for o.s., earn o.s. a bad reputation **2** *(di qualità, gen)* bad; *(odore, sapore)* bad, nasty; *(cibo guasto)* off; *(insegnante, salute)* bad, poor; *(mare)* rough; **è sempre di cattivo umore** he's always in a bad mood; **ha un cattivo odore** it's got a nasty smell; **con le buone o con le cattive (maniere)** by hook or by crook
■ SM/F bad *o* wicked person; *(nei film)* villain; **fa sempre la parte del cattivo** he always plays the villain; **fare il cattivo** *(bambino)* to be naughty; **i cattivi** *(nei film)* the baddies *(Brit)*, the bad guys *(Am)*; **e quindi i cattivi sono finiti in prigione** and so the baddies ended up in prison
cattocomunista, i, e AGG combining Catholic and Communist ideas
■ SM/F Catholic-communist
cattolicamente [kattolika'mente] AVV according to the Catholic faith
cattolicesimo [kattoli'tʃezimo] SM Catholicism
▷ www.vatican.va/phome_it.htm
cattolico, a, ci, che [kat'tɔliko] AGG, SM/F (Roman) Catholic
cattura [kat'tura] SF capture; **ordine di cattura** *(Dir)* warrant of *o* for arrest
catturare [kattu'rare] VT *(gen, fig: attenzione)* to capture, catch
Catullo [ka'tullo] SM Catullus
caucasico, a, ci, che [kau'kaziko] AGG, SM/F Caucasian
Caucaso ['kaukazo] SM: **il Caucaso** the Caucasus
caucciù [kaut'tʃu] SM INV India rubber
causa ['kauza] SF **1** *(motivo, ragione)* cause, reason; *(ideale)* cause; **quella è stata la causa principale** that was the main cause; **essere causa di qc** to be the cause of sth, be the reason for sth; **a causa di** because of; **l'aeroporto è chiuso a causa della nebbia** the airport is closed because of the fog; **per causa sua** because of him; **causa persa** *(anche fig)* lost cause; **far causa comune** to make common cause; **giusta causa** true and just cause **2** *(Dir)* case, lawsuit, action; **intentare** *o* **fare** *o* **muovere causa a qn** to sue sb; **mi ha fatto causa** he sued me; **perorare una causa** to plead a case; **parte in causa** litigant; **tu non sei parte in causa in tutto ciò** all this doesn't concern you; **rimettere qc in causa** *(fig)* to bring sth up again **3** *(Gramm)*: **complemento di causa** complement of cause
causale [kau'zale] AGG *(rapporto, nesso, Gramm)* causal
■ SF cause, reason; **causale di versamento** *(Amm)* description of payment
causalità [kauzali'ta] SF causality
causare [kau'zare] VT to cause; **potrebbe causare dei problemi** it might cause problems
causticamente [kaustika'mente] AVV caustically

caustico, a, ci, che ['kaustiko] AGG (*Chim, fig*) caustic
cautamente [kauta'mente] AVV cautiously, carefully
cautela [kau'tɛla] SF **1** (*prudenza*) caution, prudence; **"maneggiare con cautela"** "handle with care" **2** (*precauzione*) precaution
cautelare[1] [kaute'lare] AGG precautionary
cautelare[2] [kaute'lare] VT to protect
▶ **cautelarsi** VR: **cautelarsi (da *o* contro)** to take precautions (against)
cautelativo, a [kautela'tivo] AGG (*misura*) precautionary
cauterizzare [kauterid'dzare] VT (*Med*) to cauterize
cauto, a ['kauto] AGG prudent, cautious; **andare cauto** (*fig*) to tread carefully
cauzionare [kauttsjo'nare] VT to guarantee
cauzione [kaut'tsjone] SF **1** (*Dir: deposito*) security, guarantee; (: *per libertà provvisoria*) bail; **rilasciare dietro cauzione** to release on bail **2** (*somma*) caution money
cav. ABBR = **cavaliere**
cava ['kava] SF quarry (*Geol*)

LO SAPEVI...?
cava non si traduce mai con *cave*

cavalcare [kaval'kare] VT (*sogg: persona: cavallo*) to ride; (: *muro*) to sit astride; (*sogg: ponte*) to span
■ VI (*aus* **avere**) (*andare a cavallo*) to ride; **sai cavalcare?** can you ride?; **andare a cavalcare** to go riding
cavalcata [kaval'kata] SF ride; **fare una cavalcata** to go for a ride; **abbiamo fatto una cavalcata nel bosco** we went for a ride in the woods
cavalcatura [kavalka'tura] SF mount
cavalcavia [kavalka'via] SM INV flyover (*Brit*), overpass (*Am*); (*sopra ferrovia*) railway bridge
cavalcioni [kaval'tʃoni] **a cavalcioni (di)** AVV astride; **era seduto a cavalcioni del muretto** he was sitting astride the wall
cavaliere [kava'ljɛre] SM **1** rider, horseman; (*Mil*) cavalryman, trooper **2** (*accompagnatore*) escort; (*nel ballo*) partner; (*gentiluomo*) gentleman **3** (*titolo, Storia*) knight; **l'hanno fatto cavaliere del lavoro** he has been knighted for services to industry
cavalla [ka'valla] SF mare
cavalleggero [kavalled'dʒɛro] SM light cavalryman
cavallerescamente [kavallereska'mente] AVV chivalrously
cavalleresco, a, schi, sche [kavalle'resko] AGG knightly; (*fig: comportamento*) chivalrous, noble; **poema cavalleresco** poem of chivalry
cavalleria [kavalle'ria] SF **1** (*Mil*) cavalry **2** (*Storia, fig: lealtà, cortesia*) chivalry
cavallerizza [kavalle'rittsa] SF (*maneggio*) riding school; **alla cavallerizza** (*abbigliamento, stivali*) riding *attr*
cavallerizzo, a [kavalle'rittso] SM/F (*nel circo*) circus rider; (*maestro di equitazione*) riding instructor
cavalletta [kaval'letta] SF (*Zool*) grasshopper; (: *dannosa*) locust
cavalletto [kaval'letto] SM (*supporto*) trestle; (*da pittore*) easel; (*Fot*) tripod
cavallina [kaval'lina] SF **1** (*Zool*) filly **2** (*gioco*) leapfrog **3** (*attrezzo ginnico*) (vaulting) horse; **correre la cavallina** (*fig*) to sow one's wild oats
cavallino, a [kaval'lino] AGG (*fig: volto, risata*) horsy
cavallo [ka'vallo] SM **1** horse; **ti piacciono i cavalli?** do you like horses?; **a cavallo** on horseback; **a cavallo di** (*sedia, moto, bici*) astride, straddling; **andare a cavallo** to go on horseback, ride; **sai andare a cavallo?** can you ride?; **essere a cavallo** to ride; **siamo a cavallo** (*fig*) we've made it; **montare a/scendere da cavallo** to mount/dismount; **denti da cavallo** horsy teeth; **da cavallo** (*fig: dose*) drastic; (: *febbre*) raging; **a cavallo tra** halfway between; **vivere a cavallo tra due periodi** to straddle two periods; **a caval donato non si guarda in bocca** (*Proverbio*) don't look a gift horse in the mouth **2** (*dei pantaloni*) crotch; (*Scacchi*) knight; (*attrezzo ginnico*) (vaulting) horse **3** (*anche:* **cavallo vapore**) horsepower
■ **cavallo di battaglia** (*Teatro*) tour de force; (*fig*) hobby-horse; **cavallo da corsa** racehorse; **cavallo a dondolo** rocking horse; **cavallo di Frisia** (*Mil*) cheval-de-frise; **cavallo purosangue** *o* **di razza** thoroughbred; **cavallo da sella** saddle horse; **cavallo da soma** packhorse; **cavallo vincente** (*lit*) winning horse; (*fig: persona*) (surefire) winner
cavallona SF (*donna*) tall ungainly girl
cavallone [kaval'lone] SM (*onda*) breaker
cavalluccio, ci [kaval'luttʃo] SM: **cavalluccio marino** sea horse
cavapietre [kava'pjɛtre] SM INV quarryman
cavare [ka'vare] VT **1** (*gen*) to take out, draw out; (*marmo*) to extract; (*dente*) to pull, extract; (*informazioni, soldi*) to obtain, get; **cavare gli occhi a qn** (*anche fig*) to scratch sb's eyes out; **me l'hai cavato di bocca** you took the words out of my mouth; **non gli ho cavato una parola (di bocca)** I couldn't get a word out of him **2 cavarsi** (*capriccio, voglia*) to satisfy; (*fame*) to satisfy, appease; (*sete*) to quench, slake; (*giacca, scarpe*) to take off; **cavarsi il pane di bocca** (*fig*) to make sacrifices **3 cavarsela** (*farcela*) to manage, get on all right; (*da impiccio*) to find a way out; **come te la cavi?** how are things?; **cavarsela (a buon mercato)** to come off lightly, get away with it; **se l'è cavata bene** (*in un processo*) he got off lightly; (*in un esame*) he did quite well; **se l'è cavata con qualche graffio** she came out of it with only a few scratches
cavastivali [kavasti'vali] SM INV bootjack
cavatappi [kava'tappi], **cavaturaccioli** [kavatu'rattʃoli] SM INV corkscrew
cavatorsoli [kava'torsoli] SM INV apple corer
caveau [ka'vo] SM INV vault
cavedano [ka'vedano] SM (*pesce*) chub
caverna [ka'vɛrna] SF cave, cavern; **uomo delle caverne** caveman
cavernicolo, a [kaver'nikolo] SM/F cave-dweller
cavernoso, a [kaver'noso] AGG (*voce*) deep
cavetto [ka'vetto] SM (*Elettr*) lead
cavezza [ka'vettsa] SF halter
cavia ['kavja] SF (*anche fig*) guinea pig; **fare da cavia** (*fig*) to act as a guinea pig
caviale [ka'vjale] SM caviar
cavicchio, chi [ka'vikkjo] SM (*Tecn*) wooden pin; (*Agr*) dibble
caviglia [ka'viʎʎa] SF (*Anat*) ankle; (*cavicchio*) pin, peg
cavigliera [kaviʎ'ʎɛra] SF (*fascia elastica*) ankle bandage
cavillare [kavil'lare] VI (*aus* **avere**) to quibble, split hairs
cavillo [ka'villo] SM quibble
cavillosamente [kavillosa'mente] AVV: **discutere cavillosamente su qc** to quibble over sth
cavilloso, a [kavil'loso] AGG quibbling, hairsplitting
cavità [kavi'ta] SF INV hollow; (*Anat*) cavity; **cavità sotterranea** underground cave

Cc

cavo¹, a ['kavo] AGG hollow
■ SM (*Anat*) cavity
cavo² ['kavo] SM (*gen, Tecn, Telec*) cable; (*Naut*) rope; **televisione via cavo** cable television; **cavo di traino** (*Aut*) tow rope
cavolata [kavo'lata] SF (*fam*) stupid thing, foolish thing; **dire cavolate** to talk rubbish *o* nonsense; **fare cavolate** to do stupid things
cavolfiore [kavol'fjore] SM cauliflower
cavolino [kavo'lino] SM: **cavolino di Bruxelles** Brussels sprout
cavolo ['kavolo] SM **1** (*Bot*) cabbage; **una minestra di cavolo** cabbage soup; **cavolo cappuccio** spring cabbage; **cavolo da foraggio** kale; **questo c'entra come il cavolo a merenda** that's completely beside the point **2** (*fam: euf per cazzo*): **non fa un cavolo dalla mattina alla sera** he doesn't do a damn thing from morning till night; **non m'importa un cavolo** I don't give a damn; **che cavolo vuoi?** what the heck do you want?; **cavolo!** (*imprecazione*) damn!; (*di ammirazione*) wow!; **ci presterà la macchina? — sì, col cavolo!** will she lend us the car? — fat chance!
cazzata [kat'tsata] SF (*fam!: stupidaggine*) stupid thing, something stupid; **dire cazzate** to talk crap (*fam!*); **ha fatto un'altra delle sue cazzate!** he's boobed again!, he's ballsed things up again; **quel film è una vera cazzata** that film is a load of crap (*fam!*)
cazzeggiare [kattzed'dʒare] VI (*aus* **avere**) (*fam*) to piss around *o* about
cazziare [kats'sjare] VT (*fam: rimproverare*) to have a go at (*Brit*), to bawl out (*Am*)
cazziatone [kattsja'tone] SM (*fam: rimprovero*) bollocking (*Brit*); **fare a qn un cazziatone** to give sb a bollocking
cazzo ['kattso] SM **1** (*fam!: pene*) prick (*fam!*) **2** (*fig fam!*): **non gliene importa un cazzo** he doesn't give a shit (*fam!*) *o* fuck (*fam!*) about it; **che cazzo vuoi?** what the fuck (*fam!*) do you want?; **non ha fatto un cazzo oggi** he's been pissing about (*fam!*) all day today; **fatti i cazzi tuoi** mind your own fucking (*fam!*) business; **cazzo!** fuck! (*fam!*); **testa di cazzo** dickhead (*fam!*), prick (*fam!*); **che film del cazzo!** what a crap (*fam!*) film!; **grazie al cazzo!** thanks for nothing!; **stare sul cazzo a qn** to get up sb's nose
cazzotto [kat'tsɔtto] SM punch; **tirare un cazzotto** to throw a punch; **fare a cazzotti** to have a punch-up (*Brit*)
cazzuola [kat'tswɔla], **cazzola** [kat'tsɔla] SF trowel
CB SIGLA = *Campobasso*
■ SIGLA M INV (= **Citizens' Band**) CB radio
CC ABBR = *Carabinieri*
C.C. ABBR = **codice civile**
cc ABBR (= **centimetro cubo**) cc
c.c. ABBR **1** (= **conto corrente**) c/a, a/c **2** (*Elettr:* = **corrente continua**) DC
c/c ABBR (= **conto corrente**) c/a, a/c
CCD [tʃitʃi'di] SIGLA M (*Pol:* = **Centro Cristiano Democratico**) Christian Democratic Centre (*Italian political party of the centre*)
CCI SIGLA F (= **Camera di Commercio Internazionale**) ICC (= *International Chamber of Commerce*)
CCIAA ABBR = *Camera di Commercio, Industria, Artigianato e Agricoltura*
CCT [tʃitʃi'ti] SIGLA M = **certificato di credito del Tesoro**
CD [tʃi'di] SM INV (= **compact disc**) CD; (*lettore*) CD player
■ ABBR (= **Corpo Diplomatico**) CD
cd. ABBR = **cosiddetto**
C.d.A. [tʃidi'a] SIGLA M = **consiglio d'amministrazione**; *vedi* **consiglio**
c.d.d. ABBR (= **come dovevasi dimostrare**) QED (= *quod erat demonstrandum*)
C.d.F. [tʃidi'ɛffe] SIGLA M = **consiglio di fabbrica**; *vedi* **consiglio**
C.d.L. [tʃidi'ɛlle] SIGLA F = **Casa delle Libertà**; *vedi* **casa**
C.d.R. [tʃidi'ɛrre] SIGLA M = **comitato di redazione**; *vedi* **comitato**
CD-ROM [tʃidi'rɔm] SM INV (= **Compact Disc Read Only Memory**) CD-Rom
C.D.U. [tʃidi'u] SIGLA M (= **Cristiano Democratici Uniti**) United Christian Democrats (*Italian centre-right political party*)
CE SIGLA = *Caserta*
■ [tʃi'e] SIGLA F **1** = **Consiglio d'Europa** **2** = **Comunità Europea**
ce [tʃe] PRON, AVV *vedi* **ci**
CECA [tʃe'ka] SIGLA F (= **Comunità Europea del Carbone e dell'Acciaio**) ECSC (= *European Coal and Steel Community*)
cecchino [tʃek'kino] SM sniper; (*Pol*) *member of parliament who votes against his own party*
cece ['tʃetʃe] SM chickpea, garbanzo (*Am*)
Cecenia [tʃe'tʃɛnja] SF Chechnya
ceceno, a [tʃe'tʃɛno] AGG, SM/F Chechen
cecità [tʃetʃi'ta] SF blindness; **cecità da neve** snow blindness
ceco, a, chi, che ['tʃɛko] AGG, SM/F Czech; **la Repubblica ceca** the Czech Republic
■ SM (*lingua*) Czech
Cecoslovacchia [tʃekozlo'vakkja] SF Czechoslovakia
cecoslovacco, a, chi, che [tʃekozlo'vakko] AGG, SM/F Czechoslovakian
CED [tʃed] SIGLA M = **centro elaborazione dati**
cedenze [tʃe'dɛntse] SFPL (*Fin: di azioni, titoli*) drop *sg* in value
cedere ['tʃɛdere] VT **1** (*concedere*): **cedere qc (a qn)** to give sth up (to sb); (*eredità, diritto*) to transfer sth (to sb), make sth over (to sb); **cedere il posto a qn** (*in autobus*) to give sb one's seat; **le ho ceduto il posto** I gave her my seat; **cedere il passo (a qn)** to let (sb) pass in front; **cedere il passo a qc** (*fig*) to give way to sth; **cedere la parola (a qn)** to hand over (to sb) **2** (*Comm: vendere*) to sell; **"cedo"** *or* **"cedesi"** "for sale"
■ VI (*aus* **avere**) **1** (*crollare: persona*) to give in; (*: terreno*) to give way, subside; (*: muro*) to collapse, fall down; **la sedia a sdraio ha ceduto sotto il suo peso** the deckchair collapsed under his weight; **il suo cuore ha ceduto** his heart couldn't take the strain; **ha insistito tanto che alla fine ho ceduto** she was so insistent that in the end I gave in **2** (*soccombere*): **cedere a** to give way to, to surrender to, yield to, give in to **3** (*deformarsi: tessuto, scarpe*) to give
cedevole [tʃe'devole] AGG (*materiale*) supple, pliable, yielding; (*terreno*) soft
cedibilità [tʃedibili'ta] SF (*Comm*) transferability
cediglia [tʃe'diʎʎa] SF cedilla
cedimento [tʃedi'mento] SM (*di terreno*) sinking, subsiding; **ha avuto un cedimento** (*terreno*) it has subsided; (*fig: persona*) he broke down
cedola ['tʃɛdola] SF (*Comm, Fin*) coupon, voucher; (*di assegno*) counterfoil
cedrata [tʃe'drata] SF citron juice
cedro¹ ['tʃedro] SM (*frutto, albero*) citron

cedro² ['tʃedro] SM (*legno, albero*) cedar; **cedro bianco** Lawson's cypress; **cedro del Libano** cedar of Lebanon
cedrone [tʃe'drone] AGG INV: **gallo cedrone** capercaillie
ceduo, a ['tʃɛduo] AGG: **bosco ceduo** copse, coppice
CEE ['tʃee] SIGLA F (= **Comunità Economica Europea**) EEC (= *European Economic Community*)
cefalea [tʃefa'lɛa] SF (*Med*) headache
cefalo ['tʃɛfalo] SM grey mullet (*Brit*), mullet (*Am*)
ceffo ['tʃɛffo] SM (*pegg*) ugly mug
ceffone [tʃef'fone] SM slap, smack; **dare un ceffone a qn** to slap sb
CEI ['tʃei] SIGLA F (= **Conferenza Episcopale Italiana**) *Italian Bishops' Conference*
ceko, a ['tʃɛko] AGG, SM/F, SM = **ceco**
celare [tʃe'lare] VT to conceal; **celare qc alla vista di qn** to conceal sth from sb
▶ **celarsi** VR (*nascondersi*) to hide, conceal o.s.; (*stare nascosto*) to be hidden, be concealed
celeberrimo, a [tʃele'bɛrrimo] AGG SUPERL *di* **celebre**
celebrante [tʃele'brante] SM (*Rel*) celebrant
celebrare [tʃele'brare] VT (*messa, matrimonio, festa*) to celebrate; (*cerimonia*) to hold; **celebrare le lodi di qn/qc** to sing the praises of sb/sth
celebrato, a [tʃele'brato] AGG famous, well-known, celebrated
celebrazione [tʃelebrat'tsjone] SF celebration
celebre ['tʃɛlebre] AGG famous, celebrated
celebrità [tʃelebri'ta] SF INV (*fama, notorietà*) fame; (*persona*) celebrity; **arrivare alla celebrità** to become famous; **raggiungere la celebrità** to rise to fame
celere ['tʃɛlere] AGG quick, fast, swift; (*Scol, Univ: corso*) crash *attr*
■ SF (*Polizia*) riot police
celerità [tʃeleri'ta] SF quickness, speed
celeste [tʃe'lɛste] AGG **1** (*colore*) pale blue, sky-blue; **una gonna celeste** a pale blue skirt; **ha gli occhi celesti** she's got blue eyes **2** (*di cielo*) celestial; (*divino*) heavenly, celestial; **la volta celeste** the vault *o* canopy of heaven
■ SM (*colore*) pale blue, sky blue
celestiale [tʃeles'tjale] AGG heavenly, celestial
celestialmente [tʃelestjal'mente] AVV (*fig*) divinely
celia ['tʃɛlja] SF joke; **per celia** as a joke, in jest
celibato [tʃeli'bato] SM celibacy; **addio al celibato** stag night
celibe ['tʃɛlibe] AGG single, unmarried; (*prete*) celibate
■ SM single *o* unmarried man, bachelor
celidonia [tʃeli'dɔnja] SF (*pianta*) celandine
cella ['tʃɛlla] SF cell; **cella a combustione** (*Fis*) fuel cell; **cella frigorifera** cold store; **cella di isolamento**: **essere in cella di isolamento** to be in solitary confinement; **cella di rigore** punishment cell; **cella a secco** (*Chim*) dry cell
cellofanare [tʃellofa'nare] VT to wrap in cellophane
cellophane® [sɛlɔ'fan] SM cellophane®
cellula ['tʃɛllula] SF (*in ogni senso*) cell; **cellula nervosa** neuron, nerve cell; **cellula uovo** ovum
cellulare [tʃellu'lare] AGG cellular; **differenziazione/divisione cellulare** (*Bio*) cell differentiation/division; **segregazione cellulare** (*Dir*) solitary confinement
■ SM (*furgone*) police van; (*telefono*) cellphone
cellulite [tʃellu'lite] SF cellulitis; **una crema contro la cellulite** an anti-cellulite cream
celluloide [tʃellu'lɔide] SF celluloid
cellulosa [tʃellu'losa] SF cellulose
celta ['tʃɛlta] SM/F Celt
celtico, a, ci, che ['tʃɛltiko] AGG, SM Celtic
cembalo ['tʃembalo] SM (*Mus*) harpsichord
cementare [tʃemen'tare] VT (*anche fig*) to cement
cemento [tʃe'mento] SM cement; **cemento armato** reinforced concrete
cena ['tʃena] SF dinner; (*leggera*) supper; **invitare qn a cena** to invite sb to dinner; **mi hanno invitato a cena** they've invited me to dinner; **vieni a cena da noi?** would you like to come and have dinner with us?; **andare fuori a cena** to go out for dinner; **ti telefono all'ora di cena** I'll phone you at dinner time; **l'Ultima Cena** (*Rel*) the Last Supper
cenacolo [tʃe'nakolo] SM (*circolo*) coterie, circle; (*Rel, dipinto*) (the) Last Supper
cenare [tʃe'nare] VI (*aus* **avere**) to have dinner, dine; **hai cenato?** have you had dinner?
cenciaiolo, a [tʃentʃa'jɔlo] SM/F rag-merchant
cencio, ci ['tʃentʃo] SM (*straccio*) rag; (: *per pulire*) cloth; (: *per spolverare*) duster; **vestito di cenci** dressed in rags; **essere ridotto a un cencio** to feel washed out; **essere bianco come un cencio** to be as white as a sheet
cencioso, a [tʃen'tʃoso] AGG (*persona*) (dressed) in rags; (*indumento*) tattered
cenere ['tʃenere] SF ash, ashes *pl*; (*di carbone, legno*) cinders *pl*; (*di defunto*): **ceneri** SFPL ashes; **biondo cenere** ash blonde
Cenerentola [tʃene'rɛntola] SF (*anche fig*) Cinderella
cenno ['tʃenno] SM **1** (*segno*) sign, signal; (: *con la testa*) nod; (: *con gli occhi*) wink; (: *con la mano*) gesture; (: *di saluto*) wave; **capirsi/parlare a cenni** to understand each other/speak with gestures; **cenno d'intesa** sign of agreement; **fare cenno di sì/no** to nod (one's head)/shake one's head; **mi fece un cenno di saluto con la mano/con la testa** he waved/nodded to me; **far cenno di no** (*con il dito*) to wag one's finger; **far cenno a qn** to gesture to sb; **mi ha fatto cenno di avvicinarmi** he beckoned to me to come forward
2 (*breve esposizione*) mention, short account; (*allusione*) hint; **fare cenno a qn/qc** to mention sb/sth; **cenni di storia dell'arte** an outline of the history of art
3 (*indizio*) sign; **al primo cenno di pioggia** at the first sign of rain
cenone [tʃe'none] SM: **cenone di Capodanno** New Year's Eve dinner
cenotafio, fi [tʃeno'tafjo] SM cenotaph
censimento [tʃensi'mento] SM census; **fare il censimento** to take a census
▷ www.istat.it/
▷ http://censimenti.istat.it/
censire [tʃen'sire] VT: **censire qc** to take a census of sth
CENSIS ['tʃɛnsis] SIGLA M (= **Centro Studi Investimenti Sociali**) *independent institute carrying out research on social conditions in Italy*
censo ['tʃɛnso] SM (*Storia*) census; (*ricchezza*) wealth
censore [tʃen'sore] SM (*anche Storia*) censor; (*fig: critico*) critic
censura [tʃen'sura] SF (*Psic, Cine, Stampa: controllo*) censorship; (*ufficio*) board of censors, censor's office; (*fig, Pol, Rel*) censure
censurare [tʃensu'rare] VT (*Psic, Cine, Stampa*) to censor; (*fig, Pol, Rel*) to censure
cent. ABBR = **centesimo**
centauro [tʃen'tauro] SM (*Mitol*) centaur; (*fig*) motorcycle rider
centellinare [tʃentelli'nare] VT to sip; (*fig*) to savour (*Brit*), savor (*Am*)
centenario, ria, ri, rie [tʃente'narjo] AGG **1** (*che ha*

Cc

cento anni) hundred-year-old; **un edificio centenario** a (one) hundred-year-old building **2** (*che ricorre ogni cento anni*) centennial *attr*, centenary *attr*
■SM/F (*persona*) centenarian
■SM (*anniversario*) centenary, centennial (*Am*)

centennale [tʃenten'nale] AGG centennial *attr*; **tradizione centennale** age-old tradition

centerbe [tʃen'tɛrbe] SM INV *liqueur from the Abruzzi made with herbs*

centesimale [tʃentezi'male] AGG hundredth

centesimo, a [tʃen'tɛzimo] AGG hundredth
■SM (*centesima parte*) hundredth; (*moneta*: *di dollaro, euro*) cent; **costa ottanta centesimi** it costs eighty cents; **pochi centesimi di secondo** it's not worth a penny (*Brit*) *o* a red cent (*Am*); **essere senza un centesimo** to be penniless, a few hundredths of a second; **non vale un centesimo**

centigrado, a [tʃen'tigrado] AGG centigrade; **20 gradi centigradi** 20 degrees centigrade

centilitro [tʃen'tilitro] SM centilitre (*Brit*), centiliter (*Am*)

centimetro [tʃen'timetro] SM **1** (*misura*) centimetre (*Brit*), centimeter (*Am*); **lungo venti centimetri** twenty centimetres long **2** (*nastro*) measuring tape (*in centimetres*)

centinaio [tʃenti'najo] SM (*pl(f)* **centinaia**) hundred; **un centinaio di** about a hundred; **un centinaio di persone** about a hundred people, a hundred or so people; **centinaia** hundreds; **ci sono stato centinaia di volte** I've been there hundreds of times; **diverse centinaia di sterline** several hundred pounds; **a centinaia** (*merce*: *vendere*) by the hundred; (*persone*: *venire*) in (their) hundreds

centinodia [tʃenti'nɔdja] SF (*pianta*) knotgrass

cento ['tʃɛnto] AGG INV a hundred, one hundred; **centouno** one *o* a hundred and one; **seicento** six hundred; **cento di questi giorni!** many happy returns (of the day)!
■SM INV a hundred, one hundred; **per cento** per cent; **cinque per cento** five per cent; **al cento per cento** a hundred per cent; **ne sono sicuro al cento per cento** I'm a hundred per cent sure; **cento di questi giorni!** many happy returns!; *per fraseologia vedi* **cinque**

centodieci [tʃento'djɛtʃi] AGG, SM INV one hundred and ten; **laurearsi con centodieci e lode** (*Univ*) ≈ to graduate with first-class honours (*Brit*), ≈ to graduate summa cum laude (*Am*)

centometrista, i, e [tʃentome'trista] SM/F one hundred metres runner *o* swimmer

centomila [tʃento'mila] AGG INV a *o* one hundred thousand; **te l'ho detto centomila volte** (*fig*) I've told you a thousand times

centone [tʃen'tone] SM **1** (*fam*: *centomila lire*) *one hundred thousand lire note* **2** (*Letteratura*) cento

centrafricano, a [tʃentrafri'kano] AGG of the Central African Republic; **la Repubblica Centrafricana** the Central African Republic

centrale [tʃen'trale] AGG (*gen*) central; (*stazione, ufficio*) main; **dov'è la stazione centrale?** where's the main station?; **l'albergo è molto centrale** the hotel is very central; **sede centrale** head office; **la sede centrale è a Roma** the head office is in Rome
■SF (*sede principale*) head office; **centrale elettrica** power station *o* plant (*Am*); **centrale del latte** dairy; **centrale nucleare** nuclear power station *o* plant (*Am*); **centrale di polizia** police headquarters *pl*; **centrale telefonica** (telephone) exchange; **centrale termoelettrica** thermal power station *o* plant (*Am*)

centralina [tʃentra'lina] SF (*elettrica, telefonica*) junction box

centralinista, i, e [tʃentrali'nista] SM/F (*Telec*) operator; (*in ditta, albergo*) switchboard operator

centralino [tʃentra'lino] SM (*Telec*) (telephone) exchange; (*di ditta, albergo*) switchboard

centralismo SM centralism

centralità [tʃentrali'ta] SF (*gen*) centrality; (*Pol*) centre

centralizzare [tʃentralid'dzare] VT to centralize

centralizzazione [tʃentraliddzat'tsjone] SF centralization

centrare [tʃen'trare] VT (*gen*) to hit the centre (*Brit*) *o* center (*Am*) of; (*Sport, Tecn*) to centre; (*bersaglio*) to hit in the centre; **centrare (in pieno)** (*freccette*) to score a bull's eye; **centrare una risposta** to get the right answer; **hai centrato il problema** you've hit the nail on the head

centrato, a [tʃen'trato] AGG (*colpo, pugno*): **ben centrato** well-aimed

centrattacco, chi [tʃentrat'takko] SM, **centravanti** [tʃentra'vanti] SM INV centre forward

centrifuga, ghe [tʃen'trifuga] SF (*Tecn*) centrifuge; (*di lavatrice*) spin-dryer; **centrifuga lunga/corta** long/short spin; **centrifuga elettrica** juice extractor; **centrifuga scolaverdure** (*Culin*) salad spinner

centrifugare [tʃentrifu'gare] VT (*Tecn*) to centrifuge; (*biancheria*) to spin-dry; (*Culin*: *verdura, frutta*) to extract the juice from

centrifugo, a, ghi, ghe [tʃen'trifugo] AGG: **forza centrifuga** centrifugal force

centrino [tʃen'trino] SM doily

centripeto, a [tʃen'tripeto] AGG: **forza centripeta** centripetal force

centrista, i, e [tʃen'trista] AGG (*Pol*) centrist, centre *attr*

centro ['tʃɛntro] SM (*gen*) centre (*Brit*), center (*Am*); (*di città*) (town *o* city) centre; (*di bersaglio*) bull's eye; **al centro della piazza c'è una fontana** there's a fountain in the centre of the square; **siamo andati in centro a fare spese** we went into the town centre to do some shopping; **abiti in centro o in periferia?** do you live in the town centre or in the suburbs?; **fare centro** to hit the bull's eye; (*Calcio*) to score; (*fig*) to hit the nail on the head
■**centri vitali** (*anche fig*) vital organs; **centro di accoglienza** reception centre; **centro balneare** seaside resort; **centro benessere** wellness centre; **centro commerciale** shopping centre *o* mall (*Am*); (*città*) commercial centre; **centro di costo** cost centre; **centro elaborazione dati** data-processing unit; **centro nervoso** (*Anat*) nerve centre; **centro ospedaliero** hospital complex; **centro di ricerche** research centre; **centro sociale** community centre; **centro sportivo** sports centre; **centro storico** old town

centrocampista, i; , e [tʃentrokam'pista] SM/F (*Calcio*) midfielder

centrocampo [tʃentro'kampo] SM (*Sport*) midfield

centrodestra [tʃentro'dɛstra] SM (*Pol*) centre right

centrodestro [tʃentro'dɛstro] SM (*Calcio*) inside right

centromediano [tʃentrome'djano] SM (*Calcio*) centre half

centrosinistra [tʃentrosi'nistra] SM (*Pol*) centre left

centrosinistro [tʃentrosi'nistro] SM (*Calcio*) inside left

centrotavola [tʃentro'tavola] SM (*pl* **centritavola**) centrepiece

centroterzino [tʃentroter'tsino] SM (*Calcio*) central defender

centuplicare [tʃentupli'kare] VT to increase a hundred times, increase a hundredfold
centuplo, a ['tʃɛntuplo] AGG a hundred times as much
■ SM: **il centuplo di 2** a hundred times 2
centurione [tʃentu'rjone] SM centurion
ceppo ['tʃeppo] SM **1** (*di albero*) (tree) stump; (*fig: genealogico*) stock **2** (*ciocco*) log; (*per decapitazione*) (chopping) block **3** (*di aratro, ancora*) stock; (*Tecn*) brake shoe **4 ceppi** SMPL (*di prigioniero*) shackles, fetters
cera ['tʃera] SF **1** (*sostanza*) wax; **cera per pavimenti** floor polish; **dare la cera (a qc)** to polish (sth); **museo delle cere** waxworks *sg*; **cera d'api** beeswax **2** (*fig: aspetto*): **avere una bella/brutta cera** to look well/ill
ceralacca [tʃera'lakka] SF sealing wax
ceramica [tʃe'ramika] SF **1** (*materiale*) baked clay, ceramic; (*Arte*) ceramics *sg*; **una tazza di ceramica** a china cup **2 ceramiche** SFPL pottery
▹ www.racine.ra.it/micfaenza/index.htm
▹ www.ceramicaraku.com
ceramista, i, e [tʃera'mista] SM/F ceramist, ceramic artist
cerato, a [tʃe'rato] AGG waxed, wax *attr*; **tela cerata** oilskin
■ SM oilcloth
■ SF (*indumento*) oilskins *pl*
Cerbero ['tʃɛrbero] SM Cerberus
cerbiatto [tʃer'bjatto] SM (*animale*) fawn
cerbottana [tʃerbot'tana] SF (*arma*) blowpipe; (*giocattolo*) peashooter
cerca ['tʃerka] SF: **andare/essere in cerca di** to go/be looking for, go/be in search of
cercafase [tʃerka'faze] SM INV mains tester
cercafughe [tʃerka'fuge] SM INV leak detector
cercapersone [tʃerkaper'sone] SM INV pager, bleeper (*Brit*), beeper (*Am*)
cercare [tʃer'kare] VT (*gen*) to look for, search for; (*fama, gloria*) to seek; **le ho cercate dappertutto** I've looked for them everywhere; **l'hai cercato sul dizionario?** have you looked it up in the dictionary?; **cercare lavoro/casa** to look for work/a house; **stai cercando lavoro?** are you looking for a job?; **cercare moglie/marito** to be looking for a wife/husband; **cercare qn con gli occhi** to look round for sb; **cercare le parole** to search for words; **cercare guai** to be looking for trouble; **cercare fortuna** to seek one's fortune
■ VI (*aus* **avere**) **cercare di fare qc** to try to do sth; **cerca di non far tardi** try not to be late; **ho cercato di spiegargli il motivo** I tried to explain the reason to him
cercatore, trice [tʃerka'tore] SM/F searcher, seeker; **cercatore d'oro** gold digger
cercherò *ecc* [tʃerke'rɔ] VB *vedi* **cercare**
cerchia ['tʃerkja] SF (*anche fig*) circle; **cerchia di mura** city walls
cerchiare [tʃer'kjare] VT (*botte*) to hoop
cerchiato, a [tʃer'kjato] AGG: **occhiali cerchiati d'osso** horn-rimmed spectacles; **hai gli occhi cerchiati** you've got dark rings under your eyes
cerchietto [tʃer'kjetto] SM **1** (*per capelli*) hairband; **cerchietto d'oro** (*anello*) gold band **2** (*gioco*): **cerchietti** SMPL *game between 2 players in which each tries to throw a hoop over the other's stick*
cerchio, chi ['tʃerkjo] SM (*gen, Geom, di persone*) circle; (*di ruota*) rim; (*giocattolo, di botte*) hoop; **mettersi in cerchio** to stand in a circle; **eravamo seduti in cerchio** we were sitting in a circle; **dare un colpo al cerchio e uno alla botte** (*fig*) to keep two things going at the same time; **avere un cerchio alla testa** (*fig: mal di testa*) to have a headache; **cerchi in lega leggera** (*Aut*) light-alloy wheels
cerchione [tʃer'kjone] SM (wheel)rim
cereale [tʃere'ale] AGG, SM cereal
cerebrale [tʃere'brale] AGG cerebral
cerebralmente [tʃerebral'mente] AVV in a cerebral way
cerebroleso, a [tʃerebro'lezo] SM/F person suffering from brain damage
cereo, a ['tʃɛreo] AGG (*volto*) wan, waxen
Cerere ['tʃɛrere] SF Ceres
ceretta [tʃe'retta] SF (*per depilazione*) depilatory wax; **ceretta a caldo/freddo** hot/cold (depilatory) wax
cerfoglio, gli [tʃer'fɔʎʎo] SM chervil; **cerfoglio selvatico** cow parsley
cerimonia [tʃeri'mɔnja] SF **1** ceremony; (*Rel*) service **2 cerimonie** SFPL ceremony *sg*; **fare cerimonie** to stand on ceremony; **senza tante cerimonie** (*senza formalità*) informally; (*bruscamente*) unceremoniously, without so much as a by-your-leave
cerimoniale [tʃerimo'njale] SM (*regole*) ritual, custom, etiquette; (*libro*) book of etiquette, ceremonial; **cerimoniale di corte** court etiquette
cerimoniere [tʃerimo'njɛre] SM master of ceremonies
cerimoniosamente [tʃerimonjosa'mente] AVV ceremoniously
cerimonioso, a [tʃerimo'njoso] AGG ceremonious, formal
cerino [tʃe'rino] SM (*fiammifero*) wax match; (*stoppino*) taper; **una scatola di cerini** a box of wax matches
CERN [tʃern] SIGLA M (= **Consiglio Europeo per la Ricerca Nucleare**) CERN
cernia ['tʃɛrnja] SF (*anche*: **cernia gigante**) groper; (*anche*: **cernia di fondo**) stone bass
cerniera [tʃer'njɛra] SF (*di porte, finestre*) hinge; (*di abito: anche*: **cerniera lampo**) zip (fastener) (*Brit*), zipper (*Am*); (*di bracciale*) clasp
cernita ['tʃɛrnita] SF selection; **fare una cernita di** to select
cero ['tʃero] SM (church) candle
cerone [tʃe'rone] SM (*trucco*) greasepaint
cerotto [tʃe'rɔtto] SM (*Med*) (sticking) plaster (*Brit*), Bandaid® (*Am*)
cerro ['tʃɛrro] SM (*albero*) Turkey oak
certamente [tʃerta'mente] AVV certainly, surely
certezza [tʃer'tettsa] SF certainty; **avere la certezza che...** to be certain *o* sure that ...; **sapere con certezza che...** to know for sure that ...
certificare [tʃertifi'kare] VT to certify
certificato [tʃertifi'kato] SM certificate; **certificato azionario** share certificate; **certificato di credito del Tesoro** government bond, treasury bill (*Am*); **certificato di matrimonio** marriage certificate; **certificato medico** doctor's certificate, medical certificate; **certificato di nascita** birth certificate
certificazione [tʃertifikat'tsjone] SF **1** (*di documento*) certification **2 certificazione di bilancio** (*Econ*) external audit
certo, a ['tʃɛrto] AGG **1** (*dopo sostantivo: indubbio: gen*) certain; (*: prova*) positive, definite; **è cosa certa** it's quite certain, there's no doubt about it; **è un sintomo certo di malattia** it's a sure sign of illness **2** (*sicuro*) certain, sure; **essere certo di qc/di fare qc** to be sure *o* certain of sth/of doing sth; **sono certo che verrà** I'm

Cc

sure she'll come; **ne sono più che certo** I'm absolutely sure of it; **non sono certo di poter venire** I'm not sure I can come

■ AGG INDEF *(prima del sostantivo)* **1** certain; **devo sbrigare una certa faccenda** there is a certain matter I must attend to; **un certo signor Bonanno** a (certain) Mr Bonanno; **c'è un certo Stefano che ti cerca** someone called Stefano is looking for you; **in un certo senso** in a way, in a certain sense; **in certi casi** in some *o* certain cases; **un certo non so che** an indefinable something; **fino ad un certo punto** up to a point **2** *(con valore intensivo)* some; **certe volte** sometimes; **certe volte non ti capisco proprio!** sometimes I just don't understand you!; **avere una certa età** to be getting on; **di una certa età** past one's prime, not so young; **un fatto di una certa importanza** a fact of some importance; **certi giorni l'ufficio apre più tardi** some days the office opens later; **certa gente non è mai contenta** some people are never satisfied; **non vado a vedere certi film** I don't watch such bad films; **in quel locale c'erano certe facce!** there were some really unpleasant faces in that place!; **ho visto certe borse oggi – le avrei comprate tutte** I saw some terrific handbags today – I could have bought the lot

■ PRON INDEF PL: **certi/e** *(persone)* some (people); *(cose)* some

■ AVV certainly; *(senz'altro)* of course; **certo che sì/no** certainly/certainly not; **posso portare un amico? – ma certo!** may I bring a friend? – yes, of course!; **certo che puoi!** of course you can!; **sì certo** yes indeed; **no certo** certainly not

■ SM: **di certo** certainly

certosino [tʃerto'zino] SM Carthusian monk; *(liquore)* chartreuse; **è un lavoro da certosino** it's a pernickety job

certuni [tʃer'tuni] PRON PL INDEF some (people)

cerume [tʃe'rume] SM (ear) wax

cerva ['tʃɛrva] SF female (deer), doe

cervella [tʃer'vɛlla] SFPL *(Culin)* brains *pl*

cervelletto [tʃervel'letto] SM cerebellum

cervello [tʃer'vɛllo] SM **1** *(Anat)* *(pl f* **cervella***)* brain, brains; **far saltare le cervella a qn** to blow sb's brains out **2** *(fig: intelligenza)*: **avere molto cervello** to be very clever; **ha poco cervello** he's not very bright; **avere il cervello fino** to be sharp-witted; **avere il cervello di una gallina** to be brainless *o* peabrained; **dovevi avere abbastanza cervello da evitarlo** you should have had enough sense to avoid it; **gli ha dato di volta il cervello** he's gone off his head; **cervello elettronico** computer **3** *(persona)* mind; **è lui il cervello della banda?** is he the brains behind the operation?; **fuga dei cervelli** brain drain.

cervelloticamente [tʃervellotika'mente] AVV bizarrely, oddly

cervellotico, a, ci, che [tʃervel'lɔtiko] AGG bizarre, odd

cervicale [tʃervi'kale] AGG cervical

cervice [tʃer'vitʃe] SF cervix

Cervino [tʃer'vino] SM Matterhorn

cervo ['tʃɛrvo] SM **1** *(mammifero)* deer; (: *maschio)* stag; (: *femmina)* doe; **carne di cervo** venison **2** *(insetto)*: **cervo volante** stag beetle

Cesare ['tʃezare] SM Caesar

cesareo, a [tʃe'zareo] AGG *(anche Med)* Caesarean *(Brit)*, Cesarean *(Am)*; **parto cesareo** Caesarean (section)

cesellare [tʃezel'lare] VT to chisel; *(incidere)* to engrave

cesellatore, trice [tʃezella'tore] SM/F engraver

cesellatura [tʃezella'tura] SF *(lavoro)* chiselling; *(Arte)* engraving

cesello [tʃe'zɛllo] SM *(strumento)* chisel; *(Arte)* engraving

CESIS [tʃezis] SIGLA M (= **Comitato Esecutivo per i Servizi di Informazione e di Sicurezza**) *committee on intelligence and security matters, reporting to the Prime Minister*

cesoie [tʃe'zoje] SFPL shears

cespite ['tʃɛspite] SM (source of) income

cespo ['tʃespo] SM tuft

cespuglio, gli [tʃes'puʎʎo] SM bush

cespuglioso, a [tʃespuʎ'ʎoso] AGG *(anche fig)* bushy

cessare [tʃes'sare] VI **1** *(aus* **essere***)* *(aver termine: pioggia, vento, rumore)* to stop **2** *(aus* **avere***)* *(smettere)*: **cessare di fare qc** to stop doing sth; **non ha ancora cessato di piovere** it hasn't stopped raining yet

■ VT to stop, put an end to; *(produzione)* to discontinue; **cessare il fuoco** *(Mil)* to cease fire; **"cessato allarme"** "all clear"

cessate il fuoco [tʃes'sateil'fwoko] SM INV ceasefire

cessazione [tʃessat'tsjone] SF cessation; *(interruzione)* suspension

cessione [tʃes'sjone] SF transfer

cesso ['tʃɛsso] SM *(fam: gabinetto)* bog *(Brit)*, john *(Am)*; (: *pegg: luogo)* dive; **quel film era proprio un cesso** that film was a load of shit *(fam!)*

cesta ['tʃesta] SF (large) basket

cestello [tʃes'tɛllo] SM *(per bottiglie)* crate; *(di lavatrice)* drum

cestinare [tʃesti'nare] VT to throw away; *(fig: proposta)* to turn down; (: *romanzo)* to reject

cestino [tʃes'tino] SM basket; *(per la carta straccia)* wastepaper basket; **un cestino di fragole** a punnet of strawberries; **cestino da lavoro** *(Cucito)* work basket, sewing basket; **cestino dei rifiuti** litter bin *(Brit)*, trashcan *(Am)*; **cestino da viaggio** packed lunch *o* dinner *(for train travellers)*; **cestino di vimini** wicker basket

cesto ['tʃesto] SM *(gen, Sport)* basket

cesura [tʃe'zura] SF caesura

cetaceo [tʃe'tatʃeo] SM sea mammal

ceto ['tʃɛto] SM (social) class

cetra ['tʃetra] SF zither

cetriolino [tʃetrio'lino] SM gherkin

cetriolo [tʃetri'ɔlo] SM cucumber

CFC [tʃieffe'tʃi] SIGLA MPL (= **clorofluorocarburi**) CFC

cfr., cf. ABBR (= **confronta**) cf.

CFS [tʃieffe'ɛsse] SIGLA M (= **Corpo Forestale dello Stato**) *body responsible for the planting and management of forests*

cg ABBR (= **centigrammo**) cg

CGIL [tʃidʒi'ɛlle] SIGLA F (= **Confederazione Generale Italiana del Lavoro**) *trades union organization*

CH SIGLA = *Chieti*

chalet [ʃa'lɛ] SM INV chalet

champagne [ʃɑ̃'paɲ] SM INV champagne

chance [ʃɑ̃s] SF INV chance

charlotte [ʃar'lɔt] SF INV *(Culin)* charlotte

charme [ʃarm] SM charm

charter ['tʃa:tə] AGG INV *(volo)* charter *attr*; *(aereo)* chartered

■ SM INV *(aereo)* chartered plane

chassis [ʃa'si] SM INV chassis

chat line [tʃæt 'laɪn] SF INV *(sito)* chat room

chattare [tʃat'tare] VI *(aus* **avere***)* to chat (online)

che [ke] PAROLA CHIAVE

■ PRON

1 (*relativo: persona: soggetto*) who; (: *oggetto*) whom, that; (: *cosa, animale*) which, that (*spesso omesso*); **l'uomo che sta parlando** the man who is speaking; **la ragazza che hai visto** the girl whom you saw; **i bambini che vedi nel cortile** the children whom *o* that you see in the yard; **il giorno che...** the day (that) ...; **la sera che ti ho visto** the evening I saw you; **il libro che è sul tavolo** the book which *o* that is on the table

2 (*la qual cosa*) which; **dovrei ottenere il massimo dei voti, il che è improbabile** I would have to get top marks, which is unlikely

3 (*indefinito*): **quell'uomo ha un che di losco** there's something suspicious about that man; **un certo non so che** an indefinable something; **quel film non era un gran che** that film was nothing special; **quella ragazza ha un non so che di affascinante** there's something fascinating about that girl

4 (*interrogativo*) what; **che (cosa) fai?** what are you doing?; **di che (cosa) hai bisogno?** what do you need?; **non so che dire** I don't know what to say; **ma che dite!** what are you saying!

■ AGG

1 (*interrogativo*) what; (: *di numero limitato*) which; **che giorno è oggi?** what day is it today?; **che vestito ti vuoi mettere?** what (*o* which) dress do you want to put on?; **di che attore stai parlando?** which actor are you talking about?

2

■ ESCL what; **che bel vestito!** what a lovely dress!; **che buono!** how delicious!; **guarda in che stato sei ridotto!** look at the mess you're in!

■ CONG

1 (*con proposizioni subordinate*) that (*talvolta omesso*); **ero così felice che corsi a dirlo a tutti** I was so happy (that) I ran off to tell everyone; **nasconditi qui che non ti veda nessuno** hide here, so nobody can see you; **so che tu c'eri** I know (that) you were there; **voglio che tu venga** I want you to come

2 (*temporale*): **mi sono svegliato che era ancora buio** it was still dark when I woke up; **sono anni che non lo vedo** I haven't seen him for *o* in years, it's years since I saw him; **era appena uscita di casa che suonò il telefono** she had no sooner gone out than *o* she had hardly gone out when the telephone rang; **arrivai che eri già partito** you had already left when I arrived

3 (*in frasi imperative, in concessive*): **che venga pure!** let him come by all means!; **che sia benedetto!** may God bless him!

4 **non che sia stupido** not that he's stupid; **non è che non mi interessi la commedia, è che sono stanco e vorrei andare a letto** it's not that the play doesn't interest me, it's just that I'm tired and I'd like to go to bed; **che tu venga o no, noi partiamo lo stesso** we're leaving whether you come or not

5 (*comparativo: con più, meno*) than; **è più furbo che intelligente** he's more cunning than intelligent; *vedi anche* **non, più, meno, così** *ecc*

chef [ʃɛf] SM INV chef

chela ['kɛla] SF nipper

chemin de fer [ʃə'mɛ̃d'fɛr] SM INV (*Carte*) chemin de fer

chemioterapia [kemjotera'pia] SF chemotherapy

chemiotropismo [kemjotro'pizmo] SM chemotropism

chemisier [ʃəmi'zje] SM INV shirtwaister (*Brit*), shirtwaist (*Am*)

chepì [ke'pi] SM INV kepi

chèque [ʃɛk] SM INV cheque (*Brit*), check (*Am*)

cheratina [kera'tina] SF keratin

cherosene [kero'zɛne] SM paraffin (*Brit*), kerosene (*Am*)

cherubino [keru'bino] SM (*anche fig*) cherub

chetare [ke'tare] VT to hush, silence
▶ **chetarsi** VIP to quieten down, fall silent

chetichella [keti'kɛlla] AVV: **alla chetichella** unobtrusively, stealthily; **andarsene alla chetichella** to slip away

cheto, a ['keto] AGG quiet, silent

chetone [ke'tone] SM (*Chim*) ketone

chi [ki] PRON PAROLA CHIAVE

1 (*interrogativo: soggetto*) who; (: *oggetto*) who, whom; **non sapevo a chi rivolgermi** I didn't know who to ask; **con chi desidera parlare?** who do you wish to speak to (*Brit*) *o* with (*Am*)?; **con chi parli?** who are you talking to?, to whom are you talking?; **di chi è questo libro?** whose book is this?, whose is this book?; **di chi stai parlando?** who are you talking about?; **dimmi chi ti piace di più tra loro** tell me which of them you like best; **ha telefonato non so chi per te** somebody or other phoned up for you; **chi l'ha visto?** who saw him?; **chi viene di voi?** which of you is coming?; **chi hai visto?** who *o* whom did you see?

2 (*relativo*) whoever, anyone who; **lo racconterò a chi so io** I know who I'll tell about it; **lo riferirò a chi di dovere** I'll pass it on to the relevant person; **esco con chi mi pare** I'll go out with whoever I like; **so io di chi parlo** I'm naming no names; **invita chi vuoi** invite whoever *o* anyone you like; **chi arriva prima vince** whoever gets there first wins

3 (*indefinito*): **chi... chi...** some ... some ..., some ...others ...; **i bambini hanno avuto i regali: chi dolci, chi giocattoli e così via** the children have had their presents: some got sweets, others toys and so on; **chi dice una cosa, chi un'altra** some say one thing, some another

4 (*fraseologia*): **ride bene chi ride ultimo** (*Proverbio*) he who laughs last laughs longest (*Brit*) *o* best (*Am*); **si salvi chi può** every man for himself; **chi si somiglia si piglia** (*Proverbio*) birds of a feather flock together; **chi va piano va sano e va lontano** (*Proverbio*) more haste less speed

chiacchiera ['kjakkjera] SF 1 **chiacchiere** SFPL (*conversazione*) chatter *sg*; (*pettegolezzi*) gossip *sg*, talk *sg*; **fare due** *o* **quattro chiacchiere** to have a chat; **perdersi in chiacchiere** to waste time talking

3 (*loquacità*) talkativeness; **con la sua chiacchiera convincerebbe chiunque** with his gift of the gab he could persuade anyone

chiacchierare [kjakkje'rare] VI (*aus* **avere**) to chat; (*discorrere futilmente*) to chatter; (*spettegolare*) to gossip; **ci siamo fermati a chiacchierare sotto casa sua** we stopped to chat outside her house; **una relazione molto chiacchierata** a much talked about relationship

chiacchierata [kjakkje'rata] SF chat; **farsi una chiacchierata** to have a chat

chiacchierio, rii [kjakkje'rio] SM chattering

chiacchierone, a [kjakkje'rone] SM/F chatterbox; (*pegg*) gossip

Cc

■AGG talkative, chatty; (*pegg*) gossipy
chiamare [kja'mare] VT **1** (*persona*) to call; (*nome*) to call out; (*per telefono*) to call, phone; **chiamare qn per nome** to call *o* address sb by his (*o* her) name; **chiamare qn a gran voce** to call out loudly to sb; **chiamare qn da parte** to take sb aside; **chiamare (qn in) aiuto** to call (sb) for help; **mandare a chiamare qn** to send for sb, call sb in; **mi sono fatto chiamare presto stamattina** (*svegliare*) I asked to be called early this morning; **hanno chiamato la polizia** they called the police; **l'ho chiamato ma non mi ha sentito** I called to him but he didn't hear me; **ha chiamato Loredana** Loredana phoned; **chiamare il 113** to call the police; **chiamare il 118** to call an ambulance **2** (*dare un nome*) to call, name; (*soprannominare*) to (nick)name, call; **e chiamala sfortuna!** and you call that bad luck! **3** (*Mil*): **chiamare alle armi** to call up **4** (*Dir*): **chiamare qn in giudizio** *o* **in causa** to summons sb; **non mi chiamare in causa!** (*fig*) don't bring me into it!
▶ **chiamarsi** VIP: **come ti chiami? — mi chiamo Michela** what's your name? *o* what are you called? — my name is Michela *o* I'm called Michela; **questo è quello che si chiama un buon affare** that's what you call a bargain; **questa si chiama fortuna!** that's what I call luck!
chiamata [kja'mata] SF (*gen*) call; (*Dir*) summons; **fare una chiamata** (*Telec*) to make a (phone) call; **chiamata alle armi** (*Mil*) call-up (*Brit*), draft (*Am*); **chiamata urbana** local call; **chiamata alle urne** (*Pol*) election
chiappa ['kjappa] SF (*fam: natica*) cheek; **chiappe** SFPL backside *sg*; **alza le chiappe!** get up off your backside!
chiara ['kjara] SF (*fam*) egg white
chiaramente [kjara'mente] AVV (*in modo chiaro*) clearly; (*francamente*) frankly; **chiaramente, potremmo farlo così** obviously, we could do it this way
chiarezza [kja'rettsa] SF (*anche fig*) clearness, clarity
chiarificare [kjarifi'kare] VT (*anche fig*) to clarify, make clear
chiarificatore, trice [kjarifika'tore] AGG clarifying, explanatory; **avere un incontro chiarificatore** to have a meeting to clarify matters
chiarificazione [kjarifikat'tsjone] SF clarification *no pl*, explanation
chiarimento [kjari'mento] SM clarification *no pl*, explanation
chiarire [kja'rire] VT (*gen*) to clarify, make clear, explain; (*mistero, dubbio*) to clear up; **vorrei chiarire alcuni punti** I'd like to get some points clear; **alla fine il mistero è stato chiarito** in the end the mystery was solved; **chiarire le idee a qn** to clarify things for sb; **ti chiarisco io le idee!** I'll sort you out!
chiaro, a ['kjaro] AGG **1** (*di colore: mobili, vestiti*) light-coloured; (*colore*) light; (*capelli, carnagione*) fair; **pantaloni verde chiaro** light green trousers; **ha i capelli chiari** she's got fair hair **2** (*limpido: anche fig*) clear; (*luminoso*) bright; **si sta facendo chiaro** it's getting light, the day is dawning; **un no chiaro e tondo** a very definite no; **sarò chiaro** I'll come to the point; **sia chiara una cosa** let's get one thing straight **3** (*evidente, ovvio*) obvious, clear; **è chiaro!** it's blatantly obvious; **non voglio averci niente a che fare, è chiaro?** I want nothing to do with it, is that clear?; **era chiaro che non se l'aspettava** he clearly wasn't expecting it
■SM **1** (*colore*): **vestirsi di chiaro** to wear light colours *o* light-coloured clothes **2** (*luce, luminosità*) day, daylight; **fare chiaro** to get light; **fa chiaro alle 7** it gets light at 7 o'clock; **chiaro di luna** moonlight; **mettere in chiaro qc** (*fig*) to clear sth up; **trasmissione in chiaro** (*TV*) uncoded broadcast
■AVV (*parlare, vedere*) clearly; **parliamoci chiaro** let's be frank
chiarore [kja'rore] SM (diffuse) light; **col chiarore della luna** in the moonlight
chiaroscuro [kjaros'kuro] SM (*Pittura*) chiaroscuro
chiaroveggente [kjaroved'dʒɛnte] AGG, SM/F clairvoyant
chiaroveggenza [kjaroved'dʒɛntsa] SF clairvoyance
chiasso ['kjasso] SM din, uproar; **cos'è tutto questo chiasso?** what's all this noise?; **far chiasso** to make a din; (*fig*) to make a fuss; (*scalpore*) to cause a stir; **smettetela di fare chiasso!** be quiet!
chiassosamente [kjassosa'mente] AVV (*vedi agg*) noisily; gaudily
chiassoso, a [kjas'soso] AGG (*rumoroso*) noisy, rowdy; (*vistoso: colori*) showy, gaudy
chiatta ['kjatta] SF barge
chiavare [kja'vare] VT, VI (*aus* **avere**) (*fam!*) to screw (*fam!*)
chiavata [kja'vata] SF (*fam!*) screw (*fam!*)
chiave ['kjave] SF **1** (*gen, fig*) key; **ho perso le chiavi di casa** I've lost my house keys; **chiudere a chiave** to lock; **mi raccomando, chiudi a chiave la porta** make sure you lock the door; **tenere sotto chiave** (*anche fig*) to keep under lock and key; **prezzo chiavi in mano** (*di macchina*) on-the-road price (*Brit*), sticker price (*Am*); (*di casa*) price with immediate entry *o* possession; **in chiave politica** in political terms; **rifare qc in chiave moderna** to produce a modern version of sth; **la chiave di lettura di questo brano...** the key to an understanding of this passage ...; **chiave di basso/di violino** (*Mus*) bass/treble clef; **chiave d'accensione** (*Aut*) ignition key **2** (*Tecn*) spanner (*Brit*), wrench (*Am*); **chiave a brugola** Allen key; **chiave a bussola** socket wrench; **chiave a croce** spider; **chiave fissa** spanner (*Brit*), wrench (*Am*); **chiave a forcella** fork spanner (*Brit*) *o* wrench (*Am*); **chiave inglese** monkey wrench; **chiave a rullino** adjustable spanner (*Brit*) *o* wrench (*Am*); **chiave torsiometrica** *o* **tarata** torque wrench **3** (*Archit*): **chiave di volta** (*anche fig*) keystone
■AGG INV key *attr*
chiavetta [kja'vetta] SF (*Tecn*) key; (*di orologio*) winder; **la chiavetta d'accensione** the ignition key
chiavistello [kjavis'tɛllo] SM bolt
chiazza ['kjattsa] SF stain, splash; **una chiazza rossa sul vestito** a red mark on her dress; **chiazza di petrolio** oil slick
chiazzare [kjat'tsare] VT to stain, splash
chic [ʃik] AGG INV chic, elegant
chicane [ʃi'kan] SF INV (*Aut*) chicane
chicchessia [kikkes'sia] PRON INDEF anyone, anybody
chicchirichì [kikkiri'ki] ESCL, SM INV cock-a-doodle-doo
chicco, chi ['kikko] SM (*di cereale, riso*) grain; (*di caffè*) bean; (*d'uva*) grape; (*di rosario*) bead; (*di grandine*) hailstone
chiedere ['kjɛdere] VB IRREG
■VT **1** (*per sapere*) to ask; (*per avere*) to ask for; (*: intervista*) to ask for, request; (*: intervento, volontari*) to call for; **chiedere qc a qn** to ask sb for sth, ask sb sth; **chiedi a Lidia come si chiama il suo cane** ask Lidia what her dog's called; **mi ha chiesto l'ora** he asked

me the time; **ho chiesto il conto al cameriere** I asked the waiter for the bill; **mi ha chiesto degli spiccioli** he asked me for some change; **chiedi dov'è l'albergo** ask where the hotel is; **chiedersi (se)** to wonder (whether); **mi chiedo cosa stia facendo** I wonder what she's doing; **chiedere scusa a qn** to apologize to sb; **ho chiesto scusa a Marco** I apologized to Marco; **chiedo scusa!** I'm sorry!; **chiedere a qn di fare qc** *o* **che faccia qc** to ask sb to do sth; **chiedi a Giulia di spostarsi un po'** ask Giulia to move over a bit; **chiedere il permesso di fare qc** to ask permission to do sth; **chiedere notizie di qn** to inquire *o* ask after sb; **mi ha chiesto del mio viaggio** he asked me about my trip; **ci chiede di partire** he wants us *o* is asking us to go **2** *(fraseologia)*: **chiedere il divorzio** to ask for a divorce; **chiedere l'elemosina** to beg; **chiedere giustizia** to demand justice; **chiedere l'impossibile** to ask (for) the impossible; **chiedere la mano di qn** to ask for sb's hand in marriage; **chiedere la pace** to sue for peace; **non chiedo altro** that's all I want; **non chiedo altro che partire con te** all I want is to leave with you

■ VI *(aus* **avere***)* **chiedere di qn** *(salute)* to ask about *o* after sb; *(al telefono)* to ask for sb, want sb; *(per vederlo)* to ask for sb; **tutti i miei amici chiedono di te** all my friends are asking after you; **c'è un certo Andrea che chiede di te** someone called Andrea is looking for you; **il padrone chiede di te** the boss wants to see you

chierica ['kjerika] SF *(Rel)* tonsure; *(fig)* bald patch
chierichetto [kjeri'ketto] SM altar boy
chierico, ci ['kjeriko] SM *(Rel)* cleric; (: *seminarista)* seminarist
chiesa ['kjɛza] SF church; **va in chiesa ogni domenica** he goes to church every Sunday; **Chiesa anglicana** Church of England; **Chiesa cattolica** (Roman) Catholic Church; **essere di chiesa** to be a churchgoer
chiesi *ecc* ['kjɛzi] VB *vedi* **chiedere**
chiesto, a ['kjɛsto] PP *di* **chiedere**
chiffon [ʃi'fɔ̃] SM INV chiffon
Chigi ['kidʒi] SM: **palazzo Chigi** *(Pol) offices of the Italian Prime Minister*
chiglia ['kiʎʎa] SF keel
chignon [ʃi'ɲɔ̃] SM INV chignon
chihuahua SM INV chihuahua
chilo ['kilo] SM kilo; **quarantacinque chili** forty five kilos; **mezzo chilo di ciliegie** half a kilo of cherries
■ PREF: **chilo-** kilo ...
chilogrammo [kilo'grammo] SM kilogram(me)
chilohertz SM INV kilohertz
chilometraggio, gi [kilome'traddʒo] SM *(Aut)* ≈ mileage
chilometrico, a, ci, che [kilo'mɛtriko] AGG kilometric; *(fig)* endless
chilometro [ki'lɔmetro] SM kilometre *(Brit)*, kilometer *(Am)*; **cinquanta chilometri all'ora** ≈ thirty miles per hour; **abbiamo camminato per dei chilometri** ≈ we walked for miles
chilowatt ['kilovat] SM INV kilowatt
chilowattora [kilovat'tora] SM INV kilowatt hour
chimera [ki'mɛra] SF chimera
chimica ['kimika] SF chemistry; **la professoressa di chimica** the chemistry teacher
chimicamente [kimika'mente] AVV chemically
chimico, a, ci, che ['kimiko] AGG chemical; **sostanza chimica** chemical
■ SM/F chemist; **fa il chimico** he's a chemist
chimono [ki'mɔno] SM INV kimono

china[1] ['kina] SF *(pendio)* slope, descent; *(salita)* incline; **risalire la china** *(fig)* to be on the road to recovery
china[2] ['kina] SF *(albero)* cinchona; *(liquore) drink made with alcohol and cinchona bark*
china[3] ['kina] SF *(inchiostro)* Indian ink
chinare [ki'nare] VT to lower, bend; **chinare il capo** *(anche fig)* to bow one's head
▶ **chinarsi** VR to stoop, bend (over)
chincaglieria [kinkaʎʎe'ria] SF **1** *(negozio)* fancy-goods shop **2** **chincaglierie** SFPL *(cianfrusaglie)* fancy goods, knick-knacks
chinino [ki'nino] SM quinine
chino, a ['kino] AGG: **a capo chino, a testa china** head bent *o* bowed
chinotto [ki'nɔtto] SM *(bevanda) type of bitter orange drink*
chintz [tʃints] SM INV chintz
chioccia, ce ['kjɔttʃa] SF broody hen
chioccio, cia, ci, ce ['kjɔttʃo] AGG *(voce)* clucking
chiocciola ['kjɔttʃola] SF *(Zool)* snail; *(di indirizzo e-mail)* at; **scala a chiocciola** spiral staircase
chiodato, a [kjo'dato] AGG *(scarpe, bastone)* spiked; **pneumatici chiodati** snow tyres *(Brit)* *o* tires *(Am)*
chiodino [kjo'dino] SM **1** *(piccolo chiodo)* tack, small nail **2** *(fungo)* honey fungus
chiodo ['kjɔdo] SM **1** *(Tecn)* nail; (: *per lamiere)* rivet; *(da scarpone)* hobnail; *(Alpinismo)* piton; *(di scarpe da calcio)* stud; *(di scarpe da atleta, pneumatico)* spike; **chiodo a espansione** expansion bolt; **chiodo da ghiaccio** *(Alpinismo)* ice piton **2** *(Culin)*: **chiodo di garofano** clove **3** *(fraseologia)*: **roba da chiodi!** it's unbelievable!; **chiodo scaccia chiodo** *(Proverbio)* one problem drives away another; **chiodo fisso** fixation; **per lui è diventato un chiodo fisso** it's become a fixation with him
chioma ['kjɔma] SF *(capelli)* head of hair; *(di cavallo)* mane; *(di albero)* foliage; *(di cometa)* tail
chiomato, a [kjo'mato] AGG *(letter: frondoso: albero)* leafy; (: *con pennacchio: elmo)* plumed
chiosa ['kjɔza] SF gloss, note
chiosare [kjo'zare] VT to gloss, annotate
chiosco, schi ['kjɔsko] SM kiosk, stall
chiostro ['kjɔstro] SM cloister
chiromante [kiro'mante] SM/F palmist; *(indovino)* fortune-teller
chiromanzia [kiroman'tsia] SF *(vedi sm/f)* palmistry; fortune-telling
chiropratico, a, ci, che [kiro'pratiko] SM/F chiropractor
chiroterapia [kirotera'pia] SF chiropractic
chirurgia [kirur'dʒia] SF surgery; **chirurgia estetica** *o* **plastica** plastic surgery; **specialista in chirurgia plastica** plastic surgeon
chirurgicamente [kirurdʒika'mente] AVV surgically; **intervenire chirurgicamente** to operate
chirurgico, a, ci, che [ki'rurdʒiko] AGG *(Med, anche fig)* surgical
chirurgo, ghi *o* **gi** [ki'rurgo] SM surgeon; **fa il chirurgo** he's a surgeon
chissà [kis'sa] AVV: **chissà!** who knows!, I wonder!; **chissà chi/come** goodness knows who/how; **chissà che non riesca** you never know, he might succeed; **chissà se verrà alla festa** I wonder if he'll come to the party; **chissà chi glielʼha detto** I wonder who told him
chitarra [ki'tarra] SF guitar; **suona la chitarra** he plays the guitar; **una chitarra elettrica** an electric guitar

Cc

chitarrista, i, e [kitar'rista] SM/F guitarist, guitar player

chiudere ['kjudere] VB IRREG

■VT **1** to close, shut; *(pugno, lista, caso)* to close; *(busta, lettera)* to seal; *(giacca, camicia)* to do up, fasten; *(gas, rubinetto)* to turn off; **chiudere a chiave** to lock; **sei sicuro di aver chiuso a chiave?** are you sure you locked it?; **chiudere col catenaccio** to bolt; **sta sempre chiusa in casa** she never goes out; **chiudere la porta in faccia a qn** *(anche fig)* to slam the door in sb's face; **chiudere un occhio su** to turn a blind eye to; **chiudere gli occhi davanti a** *(fig)* to close one's eyes to; **chiudersi le dita nella porta** to catch one's fingers in the door; **non ho chiuso occhio tutta la notte** I didn't sleep a wink all night; **chiudi la bocca!** *o* **il becco!** *(fam)* shut up!; **chiudi la finestra, per favore** close the window please; **ricordati di chiudere il gas** remember to turn off the gas; **chiudi bene il rubinetto** turn the tap off properly; **chiuditi la camicia** do up your shirt **2** *(strada)* to block off; *(frontiera)* to close; *(aeroporto, negozio, scuola)* to close (down), shut (down); *(definitivamente: fabbrica)* to close down, shut down; **il centro è stato chiuso al traffico** the town centre is closed to traffic **3** *(recingere)* to enclose **4** *(terminare)* to end; **con lui ho chiuso** I've finished with him

■VI *(aus* **avere***)* *(scuola, negozio)* to close, shut; (: *definitivamente*) to close down, shut down; **a che ora chiude il negozio?** what time does the shop close?; **la fabbrica ha chiuso due anni fa** the factory closed two years ago;

▶ **chiudersi** VIP *(porta, ombrello)* to close, shut; *(fiore, ferita)* to close up; *(periodo lungo, vacanze)* to finish; **la porta si è chiusa** the door closed;

▶ **chiudersi** VR: **chiudersi in casa** to shut o.s. up in the house; **chiudersi in se stesso** to withdraw into o.s.

chiunque [ki'unkwe] PRON REL whoever, anyone who; **chiunque sia** whoever it is; **chiunque chiami, di' che non ci sono** if anyone phones, tell them I'm not in; **chiunque sia, fallo entrare** whoever that is, let them in; **di chiunque sia la colpa, nessuno la passerà liscia** I don't care who is to blame, nobody's going to get away with it; **chiunque lo abbia fatto...** whoever did it ...

■PRON INDEF anyone, anybody; **chiunque ti direbbe che hai torto** ask anybody and they'd tell you you're wrong; **potrebbe farlo chiunque** anyone could do it; **puoi chiederlo a chiunque** you can ask anybody; **attacca discorso con chiunque** she'll talk to anyone; **chiunque altro** anyone else, anybody else; **posso farlo meglio di chiunque altro** I can do it better than anyone else

chiurlo ['kjurlo] SM *(uccello)* curlew

chiusa ['kjusa] SF **1** *(terreno circondato)* enclosure **2** *(sbarramento fluviale)* sluice; (: *per navigazione*) lock **3** *(di discorso)* conclusion, ending

chiusi *ecc* ['kjusi] VB *vedi* **chiudere**

chiuso, a ['kjuso] PP *di* **chiudere**

■AGG **1** *(porta)* shut, closed; (: *a chiave*) locked; *(senza uscita: strada, corridoio)* blocked off; *(rubinetto)* off; **"chiuso"** *(negozio ecc)* "closed"; **"chiuso al pubblico"** "no admittance to the public"; **una finestra chiusa** a closed window; **la porta era chiusa** the door was shut; **la banca è chiusa per sciopero** the bank is closed because of a strike; **a occhi chiusi** with one's eyes closed; **lo saprei fare ad occhi chiusi** I could do it with my eyes closed; **sono rimasto chiuso fuori** I was locked out; **chiuso a chiave** locked; **ho il naso chiuso** I've got a blocked-up nose **2** *(persona)* uncommunicative, introverted; *(mente)* narrow; *(ambiente, club)* exclusive; **un ragazzo molto chiuso** a very introverted boy **3** *(concluso: discussione, seduta)* finished; (: *iscrizione, lista*) closed

■SM: **stare al chiuso** *(fig)* to be shut up; **odore di chiuso** musty smell

chiusura [kju'sura] SF **1** *(fine)* end; *(Comm: definitiva)* closing down; **chiusura anticipata** early closing; **orario di chiusura** closing time; **termine di chiusura** closing date; **discorso di chiusura** closing speech **2** *(di porta, cassaforte)* lock; *(di vestito)* fastening, fastener; **chiusura centralizzata (delle porte)** *(Aut)* central locking (device); **chiusura ermetica** hermetic seal; **a chiusura ermetica** airtight; **un recipiente a chiusura ermetica** an airtight container; **chiusura lampo** zip (fastener) *(Brit)*, zipper *(Am)*; **chiusura di sicurezza** safety lock; **chiusura sicurezza bambini** *(Aut)* child-proof lock **3** *(Pol)*: **chiusura verso la destra/sinistra** refusal to collaborate with the right/ left

choc [ʃɔk] SM INV, AGG INV shock

C.I. ABBR = **carta d'identità**; *vedi* **carta**

ci [tʃi] *(dav lo la, li, le, ne diventa* ce*)* PRON PERS **1** *(ogg diretto)* us; **ci hanno visto** they saw us; **ascoltaci** listen to us; **ci chiamava** he was calling to us **2** *(complemento di termine)* (to) us; **ci dai da mangiare?** will you give us something to eat?; **ce l'hanno dato** they gave it to us; **ci dissero di tornare più tardi** they told us to come back later; **ci sembrava una buona idea** it seemed a good idea to us; **ci ha sorriso** he smiled at us **3** *(con verbi riflessivi, pronominali, reciproci)*: **ci siamo divertiti** we enjoyed ourselves; **ci siamo annoiati** we got bored; **ci vediamo più tardi!** see you later!; **ci amiamo** we love each other; **ci siamo preparati** we prepared ourselves; **ci siamo stancati** we got tired; **ci siamo lavati i denti** we brushed our teeth

■PRON DIMOSTR *(di ciò, su ciò, in ciò ecc)* about (*o* on *o* of) it; **non so che farci** I don't know what to do about it; **che c'entro io?** what have I got to do with it?; **cosa c'entra?** what's that got to do with it?; **ci puoi giurare, ci puoi scommettere** you can bet on it; **ci puoi contare** you can depend on it; **ci penserò** I'll think about it; **non ci credo** I don't believe it

■AVV **1** *(qui)* here; *(lì)* there; **qui non ci ritorno più** I'm not coming back here again; **son qui e ci resto** here I am and here I stay; **ci andiamo?** shall we go there?; **ci andrò domani** I'll go tomorrow; **ci sei mai stato?** have you ever been there?; **ci sei?** *(sei pronto)* are you ready?; *(hai capito)* do you follow?; **non ci si sta tutti, non ci stiamo tutti** we won't all fit in **2** **c'è** there is; **ci sono** there are; **non c'era nessuno** there was nobody there; **c'è nessuno in casa?** is (there) anybody in?; **c'era una volta...** once upon a time ... **3** *(con verbi di moto)*: **ci passa sopra un ponte** a bridge passes over it; **non ci passa più nessuno per di qua** nobody comes this way anymore; *vedi* **mancare**; **stare**; **volere** *ecc*

CIA ['tʃia] SIGLA F (= **Central Intelligence Agency**) CIA

C.ia ABBR (= **compagnia**) Co.

ciabatta [tʃa'batta] SF slipper; **trattare qn come una ciabatta** to treat sb like dirt

ciabattare [tʃabat'tare] VI *(aus* **avere***)* to shuffle about (in one's slippers)

ciabattino [tʃabat'tino] SM cobbler

ciac [tʃak] ESCL (*camminando sul fango ecc*) squelch!; **ciac, si gira!** action!
■ SM (*Cine*) clapper board
Ciad [tʃad] SM Chad
cialda ['tʃalda] SF wafer
cialtrone, a [tʃal'trone] SM/F rascal, scoundrel
ciambella [tʃam'bɛlla] SF **1** (*Culin*) *ring-shaped cake*; **non tutte le ciambelle riescono col buco** (*Proverbio*) things can't be expected to turn out right every time **2** (*oggetto: gen*) ring; (: *cuscino*) round cushion; (: *salvagente*) rubber ring; **a ciambella** ring-shaped
ciambellano [tʃambel'lano] SM chamberlain
ciancia, ce ['tʃantʃa] SF gossip *no pl*, tittle-tattle *no pl*
cianciare [tʃan'tʃare] VI (*aus* **avere**) to gossip, tittle-tattle
ciancicare [tʃantʃi'kare] VT (*parole*) to mumble; (*cibo*) to chew slowly; (*vestito*) to crush
cianfrusaglia [tʃanfru'zaʎʎa] SF knick-knack; **cianfrusaglie** SFPL bits and pieces
cianotico, a, ci, che [tʃa'nɔtiko] AGG cyanotic
cianuro [tʃa'nuro] SM cyanide
ciao ['tʃao] ESCL (*all'arrivo*) hello!, hi!; (*alla partenza*) bye(-bye)!
ciarlare [tʃar'lare] VI (*aus* **avere**) to chatter; (*pegg*) to gossip
ciarlatano [tʃarla'tano] SM (*pegg: gen*) charlatan; (: *medico*) quack
ciarliero, a [tʃar'ljɛro] AGG chatty, talkative
ciarpame [tʃar'pame] SM rubbish, junk
ciascuno, a [tʃas'kuno] AGG (*dav sm:* ciascun + *consonante, vocale,* ciascuno + *s impura, gn, pn, ps, x, z; dav sf:* ciascuna + *consonante,* ciascun' + *vocale*) (*con valore distributivo*) every, each; (*ogni*) every; **ciascun ragazzo** every *o* each boy; **ciascun uomo nasce libero** every man is born free; **ciascun candidato deve presentare un tema** each candidate has to submit an essay
■ PRON INDEF (*con valore distributivo*) each (one); **ciascuno di** each (one) *o* every one of; **ciascuno di noi avrà la sua parte** each of us will have his share; **ci ha dato 20 euro (per) ciascuno** he gave each of us 20 euros; **ne avevamo uno per ciascuno** we had one each; **costano cinquanta euro ciascuno** they cost fifty euros each
cibare [tʃi'bare] VT to feed
► **cibarsi** VR: **cibarsi di** (*anche fig*) to live on
cibarie [tʃi'barje] SFPL foodstuffs, provisions
cibernauta, i; , e [tʃiber'nauta] SM/F = **cybernauta**
cibernetica [tʃiber'nɛtika] SF cybernetics *sg*
ciberspazio [tʃiber'spattsjo] SM = **cyberspazio**
cibo ['tʃibo] SM food; **cibi precotti** ready-cooked food; **son 2 giorni che non tocca cibo** he hasn't eaten for 2 days
ciborio, ri [tʃi'bɔrjo] SM (*Rel*) ciborium
cicala [tʃi'kala] SF (*Zool*) cicada; **cicala di mare** squilla
cicalare [tʃika'lare] VI (*aus* **avere**) to chatter (away), jabber (away)
cicaleccio, ci [tʃika'lettʃo] SM (*di persone*) chatter, chattering; (*di uccelli*) chirping
cicalino [tʃika'lino] SM (*cercapersone*) pager (*Brit*), bleeper (*Am*)
cicalio, lii [tʃika'lio] SM chatter, chattering
cicatrice [tʃika'tritʃe] SF (*anche fig*) scar
cicatrizzante [tʃikatrid'dzante] AGG healing
■ SM healing substance
cicatrizzare [tʃikatrid'dzare] VT, VI (*aus* **avere**) to heal
► **cicatrizzarsi** VIP to form a scar, heal (up)
cicca, che ['tʃikka] SF **1** (*mozzicone: di sigaretta*) cigarette end, stub; (: *di sigaro*) cigar butt; **non vale una cicca** (*fig*) it's not worth tuppence (*Brit*) *o* a red cent (*Am*), it's worthless **2** (*fam: sigaretta*) fag
cicchetto [tʃik'ketto] SM **1** (*bicchierino*) drop, nip; **andiamo a farci un cicchetto** let's go for a drink **2** (*rimprovero*) telling-off, ticking-off (*Brit*)
ciccia ['tʃittʃa] SF (*fam: grasso umano*) fat, flab; (: *carne*) meat; **avere troppa ciccia** to be on the plump side
ciccione, a [tʃit'tʃone] SM/F (*fam*) fatty
Cicerone [tʃitʃe'rone] SM (*Storia*) Cicero
cicerone [tʃitʃe'rone] SM (*guida turistica*) guide; **fare da cicerone a qn** to show sb around
cicisbeo [tʃitʃiz'bɛo] SM (*Storia*) gallant; (*damerino*) dandy
ciclabile [tʃi'klabile] AGG suitable for cycling, cycle *attr*; **una pista ciclabile** a cycle track
ciclamino [tʃikla'mino] SM cyclamen
ciclicamente [tʃiklika'mente] AVV cyclically
ciclicità [tʃiklitʃi'ta] SF cyclic nature
ciclico, a, ci, che ['tʃikliko] AGG cyclical
ciclismo [tʃi'klizmo] SM cycling; **un campione di ciclismo** a cycling champion
▷ www.federciclismo.it/
ciclista, i, e [tʃi'klista] SM/F cyclist; **un ciclista professionista** a professional cyclist
ciclistico, a, ci, che [tʃi'klistiko] AGG cycle *attr*
ciclo ['tʃiklo] SM (*gen, Chim, Fis*) cycle; (*di lezioni, conferenze*) series, course; **la malattia deve fare il suo ciclo** the illness must run its course; **un ciclo di film di fantascienza** a series of sci-fi films; **ciclo dell'azoto** nitrogen cycle; **ciclo biologico** life history; **ciclo del carbonio** carbon cycle
ciclocross [tʃiklo'krɔs] SM INV cyclocross
cicloescursionismo [tʃikloeskursjo'nizmo] SM cycling trips *pl*
ciclomotore [tʃiklomo'tore] SM moped
ciclone [tʃi'klone] SM cyclone; (*fig*) whirlwind
ciclonico, a, ci, che [tʃi'klɔniko] AGG cyclonic
Ciclope [tʃi'klɔpe] SM (*Mitol*) Cyclops *sg*
ciclopico, a, ci, che [tʃi'klɔpiko] AGG (*fig*) gigantic, huge
ciclopista [tʃiklo'pista] SF cycle path, cycle track
ciclostilare [tʃiklosti'lare] VT to cyclostyle (*Brit*), mimeograph (*Am*), duplicate
ciclostilato [tʃiklosti'lato] SM duplicate (copy)
ciclostile [tʃiklos'tile] SM **1** (*macchina*) cyclostyle (*Brit*), Mimeograph® (*Am*), duplicator **2** (*foglio*) duplicate copy
ciclotrone [tʃiklo'trone] SM cyclotron
cicloturismo [tʃiklotu'rizmo] SM cycling holidays *pl*
cicogna [tʃi'koɲɲa] SF **1** (*uccello*) stork **2** (*autotreno*) trailer lorry *o* truck
cicoria [tʃi'kɔrja] SF chicory
cicuta [tʃi'kuta] SF hemlock
CIDA ['tʃida] SIGLA F = *Confederazione Italiana Dirigenti d'Azienda*
ciecamente [tʃɛka'mente] AVV (*anche fig*) blindly
cieco[1], a, chi, che ['tʃɛko] AGG (*anche fig*) blind; **essere cieco da un occhio** to be blind in one eye; **il mio cane è cieco da un occhio** my dog's blind in one eye; **alla cieca** (*anche fig*) blindly; **andare alla cieca** to grope along; **cieco come una talpa** as blind as a bat; **essere cieco d'amore** to be blinded by love; **vicolo cieco** (*anche fig*) blind alley
■ SM/F blind man/woman; **i ciechi** the blind
cieco[2] ['tʃɛko] SM (*Anat*) caecum (*Brit*), cecum (*Am*)

Cc

ciellino, a [tʃiel'lino] SM/F (*Pol*) member of CL movement

cielo ['tʃɛlo] SM **1** sky; (*letter*) heavens *pl*; **un cielo azzurro** a blue sky; **miniera a cielo aperto** opencast mine; **toccare il cielo con un dito** to walk on air; **essere al settimo cielo** to be in seventh heaven; **volare nel cielo italiano** (*Aer*) to fly in Italian airspace **2** (*Rel*) heaven; **il regno dei cieli** the kingdom of heaven; **santo cielo!** good heavens!; **per amor del cielo!** for heaven's sake!; **voglia il cielo che torni presto** I hope to heaven (that) he comes back soon

cifra ['tʃifra] SF **1** (*numero*) figure, numeral; **un numero di 5 cifre** a five-figure number; **scrivere un numero in cifre** to write a number in figures; **fare cifra tonda** to make a round figure; **una cifra** (*fam: molto*) loads; **di questi ne abbiamo venduti una cifra** we've sold loads of these; **ci siamo divertiti una cifra** we had a brilliant time **2** (*somma di denaro*) figure, sum; **è una cifra astronomica** it's an astronomical figure; **mi è costato una cifra** (*fam*) it cost me a fortune; **l'ha pagato una bella cifra** he paid a lot for it **3 cifre** SFPL (*monogramma*) initials, monogram *sg* **4** (*codice*) code, cipher

cifrare [tʃi'frare] VT **1** (*messaggio*) to (put into) code, encode, cipher **2** (*lenzuola, camicie*) to embroider initials *o* a monogram on

cifrario, ri [tʃi'frarjo] SM code book

cifrato, a [tʃi'frato] AGG **1** (*codice*) coded, ciphered **2** (*lenzuola, camicie*) monogrammed

ciglio, gli ['tʃiʎʎo] SM **1** (*pl f* **ciglia**) (eye)lash; **ciglia finte** false eyelashes; **non ha battuto ciglio** (*fig*) he didn't bat an eyelid **2** (*di strada, fossato*) edge, side; **sul ciglio della strada** at the edge of the road

cigno ['tʃiɲɲo] SM swan

cigolante [tʃigo'lante] AGG (*vedi vb*) squeaking, creaking

cigolare [tʃigo'lare] VI (*aus* **avere**) (*porta*) to squeak, creak; (*ruota*) to squeak; (*parquet*) to creak

cigolio, lii [tʃigo'lio] SM (*vedi vb*) squeaking; creaking

CIIS ['tʃiis] SIGLA M (= **Comitato Interparlamentare per l'Informazione e la Sicurezza**) *all-party committee on intelligence and security*

Cile ['tʃile] SM Chile; **viene dal Cile** he comes from Chile

cilecca [tʃi'lekka] SF: **far cilecca** (*fucile*) to misfire; (*fig*) to fail; **le ginocchia mi hanno fatto cilecca** my knees gave way

cileno, a [tʃi'lɛno] AGG, SM/F Chilean

ciliare [tʃi'ljare] AGG (*Anat*) ciliary

cilicio, ci [tʃi'litʃo] SM hair shirt

ciliegia, gie *o* **ge** [tʃi'ljɛdʒa] SF cherry; **marmellata di ciliegie** cherry jam

ciliegina [tʃiljɛ'dʒina] SF glacé cherry; **la ciliegina sulla torta** (*fig*) the icing *o* cherry on the cake

ciliegino [tʃilje'dʒino] SM (*pomodorino*) cherry tomato

ciliegio, gi [tʃi'ljɛdʒo] SM (*albero*) cherry (tree); (*legno*) cherry (wood); **ciliegio dolce** wild cherry

cilindrata [tʃilin'drata] SF (*Aut*) (cubic) capacity; **macchina di grossa/piccola cilindrata** a big-engined/small-engined car; **qual è la cilindrata della tua auto?** what's the engine capacity of your car?

cilindrico, a, ci, che [tʃi'lindriko] AGG cylindrical

cilindro [tʃi'lindro] SM (*gen, Tecn, Geom*) cylinder; (*di macchina da scrivere*) roller; (*cappello*) top hat

CIM [tʃim] SIGLA M (= **Centro d'Igiene Mentale**) *mental health centre*

cima ['tʃima] SF **1** (*gen*) top; (*estremità*) end; (*di montagna*) top, summit, peak; **sulla cima del monte** on the top of the mountain; **si è posato sulla cima dell'albero** it landed on the top of the tree; **conquistare una cima** (*Alpinismo*) to conquer a peak; **in cima a** (*lista, classifica*) at the top of; (*montagna*) at the top of, on the summit of; **sono in cima alla classifica** they're at the top of the league; **da cima a fondo** from top to bottom; **leggere qc da cima a fondo** to read sth from beginning to end; **hanno perquisito la casa da cima a fondo** they searched the house from top to bottom **2** (*persona*) genius; **essere una cima** to be a genius; **non è una cima, ma se la cava** he's not a genius, but he does OK; **è una cima in matematica** he's a genius at maths **3** (*Naut*) rope, cable **4** (*Bot*) top, head

cimare [tʃi'mare] VT (*albero*) to pollard; (*tessuto*) to trim

cimasa [tʃi'maza] SF moulding

cimelio, li [tʃi'mɛljo] SM relic

cimentare [tʃimen'tare] VT (*pazienza, persona*) to try, to put to the test

▸ **cimentarsi** VR: **cimentarsi in qc** to undertake (the challenge of) sth; (*atleta, concorrente*) to try one's hand at sth; **cimentarsi con qn** to compete with sb

cimento [tʃi'mento] SM (*prova rischiosa*) trial

cimice ['tʃimitʃe] SF **1** (*Zool*) (bed)bug **2** (*radiotrasmittente*) bug

cimiero [tʃi'mjɛro] SM crest; (*fig: elmo*) helmet

ciminiera [tʃimi'njɛra] SF (*di fabbrica*) chimney (stack); (*di nave*) funnel

cimitero [tʃimi'tɛro] SM cemetery, graveyard; **cimitero di automobili** scrapyard; **questo posto è un cimitero!** (*fig*) this place is like a morgue!

cimosa [tʃi'mosa] SF (*Tessitura*) selvage

cimurro [tʃi'murro] SM distemper

Cina ['tʃina] SF China; **andremo in Cina a Pasqua** we're going to China at Easter; **mi è piaciuta molto la Cina** I really liked China

cinabro [tʃi'nabro] SM cinnabar

cincia, ce ['tʃintʃa] SF (*uccello*) tit; **cincia mora** coal tit

cinciallegra [tʃintʃal'legra] SF (*uccello*) great tit

cinciarella [tʃintʃa'rɛlla] SF (*uccello*) bluetit

cincillà [tʃintʃil'la] SM INV chinchilla

cincin, cin cin [tʃin'tʃin] ESCL cheers!

Cincinnato [tʃintʃin'nato] SM (*Storia*) Cincinnatus

cincischiare [tʃintʃis'kjare] VI (*aus* **avere**) (*perder tempo*) to mess about, fiddle about

cine ['tʃine] SM INV (*fam*) cinema; **andare al cine** to go to the cinema

cineamatore [tʃineama'tore] SM amateur film-maker (*Brit*) *o* moviemaker (*Am*)

cineasta, i, e [tʃine'asta] SM/F **1** person in the film (*Brit*) *o* movie (*Am*) industry; **è un cineasta** he's in films **2** film-maker (*Brit*), moviemaker (*Am*)

cinecamera [tʃine'kamera] SF cine camera

Cinecittà [tʃinetʃit'ta] SF *film studios on the outskirts of Rome*

▹ www.cinecitta.com/

▹ www.cinecittastudios.it/

cineclub [tʃine'klub] SM INV film club

cineforum [tʃine'fɔrum] SM INV cinema discussion

cinegiornale [tʃinedʒor'nale] SM newsreel

cinema ['tʃinema] SM INV cinema; **andare al cinema** to go to the cinema *o* movies (*Am*); **andiamo al cinema?** shall we go to the cinema?; **cosa danno al cinema stasera?** what's on at the cinema tonight?; **fare del cinema** to be in the film business;

industria/divo del cinema film industry/star; **cinema muto** silent films
▷ www.luce.it/istitutoluce/index.htm
▷ www.cinematografo.it/

cinema d'essai [sine'ma dɛ'sɛ] SM INV avant-garde cinema, experimental cinema

cinemascope ['sinməskoup] SM INV Cinemascope®

cinematica [tʃine'matika] SF (*Fis*) kinematics *sg*

cinematico, a, ci, che [tʃine'matiko] AGG kinematic

cinematografare [tʃinematogra'fare] VT to film

cinematografia [tʃinematogra'fia] SF (*arte, tecnica*) cinematography; (*industria*) film-making (*Brit*) *o* moviemaking (*Am*) industry, cinema

cinematograficamente [tʃinematografika'mente] AVV cinematographically; **realizzare cinematograficamente** to make into a film (*Brit*) *o* movie (*Am*)

cinematografico, a, ci, che [tʃinemato'grafiko] AGG **1** (*attore, critica, festival*) film (*Brit*) *attr*, movie (*Am*) *attr*; **casa cinematografica** film studio, film company; **festival cinematografico** film festival; **regista cinematografico** film director; **sala cinematografica** cinema; **successo cinematografico** box-office success **2** (*fig: stile*) cinematographic

cinematografo [tʃinema'tɔgrafo] SM (*locale*) cinema (*Brit*), movie theatre (*Am*); (*arte*) cinema, films *pl* (*Brit*), movies *pl* (*Am*)

cinepresa [tʃine'presa] SF cine camera

cinerario, ria, ri, rie [tʃine'rarjo] AGG: **urna cineraria** funeral urn

cinereo, a [tʃi'nɛreo] AGG (*colore*) ash-grey; (*pallido*) pale, ashen

cinescopio, pi [tʃines'kɔpjo] SM (*TV*) cathode-ray tube

cinese [tʃi'nese] AGG Chinese
■ SM/F Chinese man/woman; **i Cinesi** the Chinese
■ SM (*lingua*) Chinese; **parla cinese** she speaks Chinese

cineseria [tʃinese'ria] SF chinoiserie

cineteca, che [tʃine'tɛka] SF (*collezione*) film collection, film library; (*locale*) film library

cinetica [tʃi'nɛtika] SF kinetics *sg*

cinetico, a, ci, che [tʃi'nɛtiko] AGG kinetic

cingere ['tʃindʒere] VT IRREG **1** (*circondare*) to surround, encircle; **cingere una città di mura** to surround a city with walls; **cingere d'assedio** to besiege, lay siege to **2** (*avvolgere*): **le cinse la vita con le braccia** he put his arms round her waist; **cingersi la vita con una corda** to tie a rope round one's waist; **cingersi la testa con fiori** to wreath one's head with flowers

cinghia ['tʃingja] SF (*cintura*) belt, strap; (*di portabagagli, zaino*) strap; (*Tecn*) belt; (*Equitazione*) girth; **tirare la cinghia** (*fig*) to tighten one's belt; **cinghia di trasmissione** drive belt; **cinghia del ventilatore** fan belt

cinghiale [tʃin'gjale] SM (*animale*) wild boar; (*pelle*) pigskin

cinghiata [tʃin'gjata] SF: **prendere qn a cinghiate** to give sb a leathering

cingolato, a [tʃingo'lato] AGG (*veicolo*) caterpillar *attr*

cingolo ['tʃingolo] SM (*di veicoli*) caterpillar

cinguettare [tʃingwet'tare] VI (*aus* **avere**) (*uccelli*) to twitter; (*bambini*) to chatter

cinguettio, tii [tʃingwet'tio] SM (*vedi vb*) twittering; chattering

cinicamente [tʃinika'mente] AVV cynically

cinico, a, ci, che ['tʃiniko] AGG cynical
■ SM/F cynic

ciniglia [tʃi'niʎʎa] SF chenille

cinismo [tʃi'nizmo] SM cynicism

cinofilo, a [tʃi'nɔfilo] SM/F dog lover

cinquanta [tʃin'kwanta] AGG INV, SM INV fifty; **ha cinquant'anni** he is fifty; **gli anni cinquanta** the Fifties, the 50s; **cinquantuno** fifty-one

cinquantenario, ri [tʃinkwante'narjo] SM fiftieth anniversary

cinquantenne [tʃinkwan'tɛnne] AGG fifty-year-old; **un signore cinquantenne** a man of fifty, a fifty-year-old man
■ SM/F fifty-year-old man/woman; (*sulla cinquantina*) man/woman in his/her fifties

cinquantennio, ni [tʃinkwan'tɛnnjo] SM (period of) fifty years

cinquantesimo, a [tʃinkwan'tɛzimo] AGG, SM/F, SM fiftieth

cinquantina [tʃinkwan'tina] SF **1 una cinquantina (di)** about fifty, fifty or so; **eravamo una cinquantina** there were about fifty of us **2** (*età*): **avere una cinquantina d'anni** *or* **essere sulla cinquantina** (*persona*) to be about fifty, be in one's fifties; **avere una cinquantina d'anni** (*mobile, casa*) to be about fifty years old

cinque ['tʃinkwe] AGG INV five; **paragrafo/pagina/capitolo cinque** paragraph/page/chapter five; **i cinque settimi della cifra** five-sevenths of the amount; **abito in Via Cavour, numero cinque** I live at number five Via Cavour; **un bambino di cinque anni** a child of five; **ha cinque anni** he is five; **un biglietto da cinque sterline** a five-pound note; **siamo in cinque** there are five of us; **sono le due meno cinque** it's five to two; **sono arrivati alle cinque** they arrived at five o'clock; **le cinque di sera** five o'clock in the evening; **cinque volte su dieci** five times out of ten; **mettersi in fila per cinque** to form rows of five
■ SM INV five; **due più tre fa cinque** two plus three make five; **il cinque nel dieci ci sta due volte** five goes into ten twice; **uno sconto del cinque per cento** a five percent discount; **abito in Via Cavour cinque** I live at 5 Via Cavour; **il cinque dicembre 1988** the fifth of December 1988; **arrivare il cinque ottobre** to arrive on October 5th; **prendere un cinque** (*Scol*) to get five out of ten; **il cinque di fiori** (*Carte*) the five of clubs

cinquecentesco, a, schi, sche [tʃinkwetʃen'tesko] AGG sixteenth-century

cinquecento [tʃinkwe'tʃɛnto] AGG INV five hundred; **cinquecento sterline** five hundred pounds
■ SM INV five hundred; **il Cinquecento** (*secolo*) the sixteenth century
■ SF INV (*Aut*) Fiat 500

cinquemila [tʃinkwe'mila] AGG INV, SM INV five thousand

cinquina [tʃin'kwina] SF (*Lotto, Tombola*) set of five winning numbers

cinsi *ecc* ['tʃinsi] VB *vedi* **cingere**

cinta ['tʃinta] SF (*anche:* **cinta muraria**) city walls *pl*; **muro di cinta** (*di giardino*) surrounding wall

cintare [tʃin'tare] VT to enclose

cinto, a ['tʃinto] PP *di* **cingere**
■ SM: **cinto erniario** truss

cintola ['tʃintola] SF (*cintura*) belt; (*vita*) waist

cintura [tʃin'tura] SF **1** belt; **una cintura di pelle** a leather belt; **cintura dei pesi** (*di subacqueo*) weight belt; **cintura di salvataggio** lifebelt (*Brit*), life preserver (*Am*); **cintura di sicurezza** (*Aut, Aer*) safety *o* seat belt;

Cc

allacciare la cintura (di sicurezza) to fasten one's safety *o* seat belt **2** (*vita*) waist **3** (*Urbanistica*) **cintura industriale** industrial belt; **cintura verde** green belt

cinturare [tʃintu'rare] VT (*Calcio*) to grab around the waist; (*Lotta*) to hold in a waist lock

cinturato, a [tʃintu'rato] AGG (*pneumatico*) radial(-ply) ■SM radial tyre (*Brit*) *o* tire (*Am*)

cinturino [tʃintu'rino] SM strap; **cinturino dell'orologio** watch strap

cinturone [tʃintu'rone] SM gun belt

CIO ['tʃio] SIGLA M (= **Comitato olimpico internazionale**) IOC (= *International Olympic Committee*)

ciò [tʃɔ] PRON DIMOSTR **1** (*questa cosa*) this; (*quella cosa*) that; **ciò è vero** this (*o* that) is true; **ciò significa che...** this means that ...; **di ciò parleremo più tardi** we'll talk about this (*o* that) later; **con tutto ciò** for all that, in spite of everything; **da ciò deduco che...** from this I deduce that ...; **e con ciò me ne vado!** and now I'm off!; **e con ciò ha concluso il suo discorso** and with that he finished his speech; **e con ciò?** so what?; **oltre a ciò** besides that, furthermore; **nonostante ciò** *or* **ciò nonostante** nevertheless, in spite of that; **aveva la febbre e ciò nonostante è uscito** he had a temperature, but went out anyway; **detto ciò...** having said that ... **2 ciò che** what; **ciò che voglio dirti è importante** what I want to tell you is important; **gli sarò sempre grato per ciò che ha fatto** I'll always be grateful to him for what he's done; **l'hanno sgridato per ciò che ha fatto** he got told off for what he did; **è questo tutto ciò che hai fatto?** is this all (that) you've done?

ciocca, che ['tʃɔkka] SF (*di capelli*) lock; **perde i capelli a ciocche** her hair is coming out in handfuls

ciocco, chi ['tʃɔkko] SM log

cioccolata [tʃokko'lata] SF chocolate; **una tavoletta di cioccolata** a bar of chocolate; **una (tazza di) cioccolata calda** a (cup of) hot chocolate

cioccolatino [tʃokkola'tino] SM chocolate; **una scatola di cioccolatini** a box of chocolates

cioccolato [tʃokko'lato] SM chocolate; **cioccolato al latte/fondente** milk/plain chocolate

cioè [tʃo'ɛ] AVV that is (to say); **vengo tra poco — cioè?** I'll come soon — what do you mean by soon?; **partirò il tredici, cioè domenica prossima** I'm leaving on the thirteenth, that's next Sunday; **questo è il mio, cioè no, il tuo!** this is mine, or rather, I mean yours!

ciondolare [tʃondo'lare] VI (*aus* **avere**) to dangle; (*fig: bighellonare*) to hang around, loaf (about); **l'ubriaco camminava ciondolando** the drunk swayed from side to side as he walked ■VT (*far dondolare*) to dangle, swing

ciondolo ['tʃondolo] SM pendant; **ciondolo portafortuna** good-luck charm

ciondoloni [tʃondo'loni] AVV: **con le braccia/gambe ciondoloni** with arms/legs dangling

ciononostante [tʃononos'tante] AVV nonetheless, nevertheless

ciospo ['tʃɔspo] SM (*fam!: brutta ragazza*) dog, minger

ciotola ['tʃɔtola] SF bowl

ciottolo ['tʃɔttolo] SM (*di fiume*) pebble; (*di strada*) cobble(stone)

CIP [tʃip] SIGLA M = **Comitato Interministeriale dei Prezzi**

cip [tʃip] SM INV (*Poker*) stake

CIPE ['tʃipe] SIGLA M = **Comitato Interministeriale per la Programmazione Economica**

CIPI ['tʃipi] SIGLA M = **Comitato Interministeriale di coordinamento per la Politica Industriale**

cipiglio [tʃi'piʎʎo] SM frown

cipolla [tʃi'polla] SF **1** onion; (*di tulipano*) bulb; **mangiare pane e cipolla** (*fig*) to live on bread and dripping **2** (*Med*) bunion **3** (*scherz: orologio*) timepiece

cipollina [tʃipol'lina] SF (baby) onion; **cipolline sottaceto** pickled onions; **cipolline sottolio** baby onions in oil

cippo ['tʃippo] SM (*celebrativo*) memorial stone; (*di confine*) boundary stone

cipresso [tʃi'prɛsso] SM cypress

cipria ['tʃiprja] SF (face) powder; **cipria compatta/in polvere** solid/loose powder

cipriota, i, e [tʃipri'ɔta] AGG Cypriot; **la questione cipriota** the Cyprus question ■SM/F Cypriot

Cipro ['tʃipro] SM Cyprus

circa ['tʃirka] PREP: **circa (a)** regarding, concerning, about; **circa gli accordi presi in precedenza** with reference to previous agreements; **non mi ha detto niente circa i suoi progetti** he didn't tell me anything about his plans ■AVV (*quasi*) about, approximately, roughly; **costerà circa venti sterline** it'll cost about twenty pounds; **erano circa le 3 quando è partita** *or* **è partita alle 3 circa** she left at about 3; **mancano 20 minuti circa all'arrivo del treno** the train is due in about 20 minutes; **a mezzogiorno circa** (at) about midday

Circe ['tʃirtʃe] SF (*Mitol*) Circe

circo, chi ['tʃirko] SM **1** (*Storia romana*) circus; **circo (equestre)** (*spettacolo*) circus; **il circo bianco** *world cup skiers and their entourages* **2** (*Geog*) cirque, corrie
▷ www.circo.it/

circolante [tʃirko'lante] AGG circulating

circolare[1] [tʃirko'lare] VI (*aus* **avere** *e* **essere**) (*gen, Anat, Econ*) to circulate; (*persone*) to go about; (*notizie, idee*) to circulate, go about; **circolare!** move along!; **circolare in città diventa sempre più difficile** (*Aut*) driving in town is getting more and more difficult; **i camion non possono circolare di domenica** lorries are not allowed on the roads on Sundays; **circola voce che...** there is a rumour going about that ...; **far circolare qc** to pass sth round; **Luca ne ha fatto circolare una copia in classe** Luca passed a copy round the class

circolare[2] [tʃirko'lare] AGG circular; **assegno circolare** banker's draft; **un movimento circolare** a circular movement ■SF **1** (*Amm*) circular (letter); **ha inviato una circolare** he's sent out a circular **2** (*linea di autobus*) circle line

circolatorio, ria, ri, rie [tʃirkola'tɔrjo] AGG circulatory

circolazione [tʃirkolat'tsjone] SF (*di sangue, aria, moneta*) circulation; (*di merci, veicoli*) movement; **mettere in circolazione** (*moneta*) to put into circulation; (*fig: voce, notizie*) to spread, put about; **togliere dalla circolazione** (*moneta*) to withdraw from circulation; (*fig: persona*) to remove; **tassa di circolazione** (*Aut*) road tax; **libretto di circolazione** (*Aut*) registration document (*Brit*), registration (*Am*); **circolazione monetaria** money in circulation; **circolazione stradale** (*Aut*) traffic; **circolazione a targhe alterne** *antipollution measure*

CIRCOLAZIONE A TARGHE ALTERNE

Circolazione a targhe alterne was introduced by some town councils to combat the increase in traffic and pollution in town centres. It stipulates that on days with an even date, only cars whose number plate ends in an even number or a zero may be on the road; on days with an odd date, only cars with odd registration numbers may be used. Public holidays are generally, but not always, exempt.

circolo ['tʃirkolo] SM **1** (*gen, Geog, Mat*) circle; **entrare in circolo** (*Med*) to enter the bloodstream; **circolo vizioso** vicious circle **2** (*club*) club; **circolo giovanile** youth club; **circolo letterario** literary circle *o* society; **circolo ufficiali** officers' club
circoncidere [tʃirkon'tʃidere] VT IRREG to circumcize
circoncisione [tʃirkontʃi'zjone] SF circumcision
circonciso, a [tʃirkon'tʃizo] PP *di* **circoncidere**
circondare [tʃirkon'dare] VT (*gen*) to surround; (*racchiudere*) to encircle; (: *con uno steccato*) to enclose; **la polizia aveva circondato il palazzo** the police had surrounded the building; **circondare qn di cure** to give sb the best of attention; **circondare qn di attenzioni** to be very attentive towards sb; **è sempre stato circondato d'affetto** he has always been surrounded by affection
▶ **circondarsi** VR: **circondarsi di** to surround o.s. with
circondariale [tʃirkonda'rjale] AGG: **casa circondariale di pena** district prison
circondario, ri [tʃirkon'darjo] SM **1** (*Dir*) administrative district **2** (*zona circostante*) neighbourhood (*Brit*), neighborhood (*Am*)
circonferenza [tʃirkonfe'rɛntsa] SF circumference; **circonferenza fianchi/vita** hip/waist measurement
circonflessione [tʃirkonfles'sjone] SF curving, bending
circonflesso, a [tʃirkon'flɛsso] PP *di* **circonflettere**
■ AGG: **accento circonflesso** circumflex accent
circonflettere [tʃirkon'flɛttere] VT IRREG to curve, bend
circonlocuzione [tʃirkonlokut'tsjone] SF circumlocution
circonvallazione [tʃirkonvallat'tsjone] SF ring road (*Brit*), beltway (*Am*); (*per evitare una città*) by-pass
circoscritto, a [tʃirkos'kritto] PP *di* **circoscrivere**
■ AGG (*zona*) limited; (*fenomeno, contagio*) localized
circoscrivere [tʃirkos'krivere] VT IRREG (*Geom*) to circumscribe; (*zona*) to mark out; (*incendio, contagio*) to contain, confine; (*fig: problema, concetto*) to define, describe
circoscrizionale [tʃirkoskrittsjo'nale] AGG area *attr*, district *attr*
circoscrizione [tʃirkoskrit'tsjone] SF (*Amm*) district, area; **circoscrizione elettorale** constituency
circospetto, a [tʃirkos'pɛtto] AGG circumspect, cautious; **un'occhiata circospetta** a cautious look; **con fare circospetto** with a suspicious air
circospezione [tʃirkospet'tsjone] SF circumspection, prudence, caution
circostante [tʃirkos'tante] AGG (*territorio*) surrounding, neighbouring (*Brit*), neighboring (*Am*); (*persone*) in the vicinity
circostanza [tʃirkos'tantsa] SF (*occasione*) occasion; (*situazione*): **circostanze** SFPL circumstances; **in questa circostanza** on this occasion; **date le circostanze** in view of *o* under the circumstances; **date le circostanze, è stato un buon risultato** In the circumstances, it was a good result; **circostanze aggravanti/attenuanti** (*Dir*) aggravating/mitigating circumstances; **parole di circostanza** words suited to the occasion
circostanziare [tʃirkostan'tsjare] VT (*evento, fatto*) to give a detailed account of
circostanziatamente [tʃirkostantsjata'mente] AVV in detail
circostanziato, a [tʃirkoskan'tsjato] AGG detailed
circuire [tʃirku'ire] VT (*fig*) to fool, take in
circuito [tʃir'kuito] SM **1** (*Elettr*) circuit; **andare in** *o* **fare corto circuito** to short-circuit; **circuito chiuso/integrato** closed/integrated circuit; **televisione a circuito chiuso** closed-circuit television **2** (*Aut*) track, circuit; **circuito di attesa** (*Aer*) holding pattern; **circuito di gara** racing track; **circuito di prova** test circuit **3** (*sale cinematografiche*) circuit
circumnavigare [tʃirkumnavi'gare] VT to circumnavigate
circumnavigazione [tʃirkumnavigat'tsjone] SF circumnavigation
cireneo [tʃire'nɛo] SM: **il Cireneo** Simon of Cyrene
cirillico, a, ci, che [tʃi'rilliko] AGG Cyrillic
Ciro ['tʃiro] SM (*Storia*) Cyrus
cirro ['tʃirro] SM (*Meteor*) cirrus
cirrocumulo [tʃirro'kumulo] SM cirrocumulus
cirrosi [tʃir'rɔzi] SF (*Med*) cirrhosis; **cirrosi epatica** cirrhosis (of the liver)
CISAL ['tʃizal] SIGLA F (= **Confederazione Italiana Sindacati Autonomi dei Lavoratori**) *trades union organization*
cisalpino, a [tʃizal'pino] AGG cisalpine
CISL [tʃizl] SIGLA F (= **Confederazione Italiana Sindacati Lavoratori**) *trades union organization*
CISNAL ['tʃiznal] SIGLA F (= **Confederazione Italiana Sindacati Nazionali dei Lavoratori**) *trades union organization*
cisposo, a [tʃis'poso] AGG: **avere gli occhi cisposi** to be bleary-eyed
ciste ['tʃiste] SF = **cisti**
cistercense [tʃister'tʃɛnse] AGG, SM Cistercian
cisterna [tʃis'tɛrna] SF tank, cistern
■ AGG INV: **nave cisterna** (*per petrolio*) tanker; (*per acqua*) water-supply ship; **camion cisterna** tanker (lorry)
cisti ['tʃisti] SF INV cyst
cistifellea [tʃisti'fɛllea] SF (*Anat*) gall bladder
cistite [tʃis'tite] SF cystitis
CIT [tʃit] SIGLA F = *Compagnia Italiana Turismo*
cit. ABBR (= **citato, citata**) cit.
citare [tʃi'tare] VT **1** (*Dir*) to summon; (: *testimone*) to subpoena; **citare qn per danni** to sue sb for damages **2** (*passo, testo, autore*) to cite; **citare qn/qc a modello** *o* **ad esempio** to cite sb/sth as an example
citazione [tʃitat'tsjone] SF **1** (*Dir: vedi vb*) summons *sg*; subpoena **2** (*di testo*) quotation, citation **3** (*menzione*) citation; **citazione all'ordine del giorno** (*Mil*) mention in dispatches
citofonare [tʃitɔfo'nare] VI (*aus* **avere**) to call on the entry phone
citofono [tʃi'tɔfono] SM (*di appartamento*) entry phone; (*in uffici*) intercom
citologia [tʃitolo'dʒia] SF cytology
citologico, a, ci, che [tʃito'lɔdʒiko] AGG: **esame citologico** *test for detection of cancerous cells*
citologo, gi [tʃi'tɔlogo] SM cytologist
citoplasma, i [tʃito'plazma] SM cytoplasm
citrato [tʃi'trato] SM citrate; (*anche:* **citrato di magnesia effervescente**) ≈ milk of magnesia
citrico, a, ci, che ['tʃitriko] AGG citric
citrullo, a [tʃi'trullo] SM/F (*fam*) half-wit
città [tʃit'ta] SF INV **1** (*gen*) town; (*grande*) city; **la mia**

Cc

città my home town; **Firenze è una bella città** Florence is a beautiful city; **ti faccio visitare la città** I'll show you round the town; **abitare in città** to live in town *o* in the city; **abiti in città o in campagna?** do you live in town or in the country?; **andare in città** to go to *o* into town; **vita di città** town *o* city life; **la città vecchia/nuova** the old/new (part of) town; **Città del Capo** Cape Town; **città di mare/di provincia** seaside/ provincial town; **la Città Santa** (*Gerusalemme*) the Holy City; **città dormitorio** dormitory town; **città giardino** garden city; **città mercato** shopping centre *o* mall (*Am*); **città satellite** satellite town; **città degli studi** *o* **universitaria** university campus

cittadella [tʃitta'dɛlla] SF citadel, stronghold

cittadinanza [tʃittadi'nantsa] SF **1** (*città, popolazione*) town, citizens *pl*, inhabitants *pl* of a town *o* city; **tutta la città** the whole town **2** (*Dir*) citizenship; **avere/ prendere la cittadinanza britannica** to have/take British citizenship; **ha la cittadinanza britannica** he has British citizenship

cittadino, a [tʃitta'dino] AGG (*vie, popolazione, vita*) town *attr*, city *attr*

■ SM/F (*abitante di città*) city *o* town dweller; (*di uno Stato*) citizen; **privato cittadino** private citizen; **cittadino britannico** British subject *o* citizen

city bike [siti'baik] SF INV city bike

city car [siti'kar] SF INV city car

city manager [citi'manadʒer] SM INV city manager (*administrator appointed by a city council to manage the city's affairs*)

ciuccio, ci ['tʃiuttʃo] SM (*fam*) comforter, dummy (*Brit*), pacifier (*Am*)

ciuco, a, chi, che ['tʃuko] SM/F ass; (*fig: persona*) ass, fool

ciuffo ['tʃuffo] SM (*gen*) tuft; (*di prezzemolo*) bunch; (*di capelli*): **porta il ciuffo di lato** she wears her fringe to the side

ciuffolotto [tʃuffo'lɔtto] SM bullfinch

ciulare [tʃu'lare] VT (*fam!: fare sesso*) to shag (*fam!*); (: *imbrogliare*) to rip off; (: *rubare*) to steal

ciurma ['tʃurma] SF (*di nave*) crew

ciurmaglia [tʃur'maʎʎa] SF mob, rabble

civetta [tʃi'vetta] SF **1** owl; **civetta notturna** little owl **2** (*fig: donna*) flirt, coquette; **fare la civetta con qn** to flirt with sb

■ AGG INV: **auto/nave civetta** decoy car/ship

civettare [tʃivet'tare] VI (*aus* **avere**) **civettare (con qn)** to flirt (with sb)

civetteria [tʃivette'ria] SF flirtatiousness, coquetry

civettuolo, a [tʃivet'twɔlo] AGG flirtatious, coquettish; **un cappellino civettuolo** a pert little hat

civicamente [tʃivika'mente] AVV (*con civismo*) public-spiritedly

civico, a, ci, che ['tʃiviko] AGG **1** (*museo*) town *attr*, municipal; **centro civico** civic centre; **guardia civica** (town) policeman; **museo civico** town museum **2** (*dovere*) civic; **senso civico** public spirit; **educazione civica** civics *sg*

civile [tʃi'vile] AGG **1** civil; **Diritto Civile** Civil Law; **diritti civili** civil rights; **convivenza civile** life in society; **società civile** civil society; **stato civile** marital status **2** (*non militare*) civilian; **abiti civili** civilian clothes **3** (*civilizzato*) civilized; (*educato*) polite, civil; **un paese civile** a civilized country

■ SM private citizen, civilian

civilista, i, e [tʃivi'lista] SM/F (*avvocato*) civil lawyer; (*studioso*) expert in civil law

civilizzare [tʃivilid'dzare] VT (*paese, popolo*) to civilize ▶ **civilizzarsi** VR (*fig*) to become civilized, become more refined

civilizzato, a [tʃivilid'dzato] AGG civilized

civilizzatore, trice [tʃiviliddza'tore] AGG civilizing

■ SM/F civilizer

civilizzazione [tʃiviliddzat'tsjone] SF civilization

civilmente [tʃivil'mente] AVV (*vedi agg 3*) in a civilized way; politely, civilly

civiltà [tʃivil'ta] SF INV **1** (*civilizzazione*) civilization; **una società con un alto grado di civiltà** a highly civilized society **2** (*gentilezza, educazione*) courtesy, civility; **con civiltà** in a civilized manner

civismo [tʃi'vizmo] SM civic-mindedness, public spirit

CL [tʃi'ɛlle] SIGLA F (*Pol:* = **Comunione e Liberazione**) *Catholic youth movement*

■ SIGLA = *Caltanissetta*

cl ABBR (= **centilitro**) cl

clacson ['klakson] SM INV (*Aut*) horn, hooter (*Brit*); **suonare il clacson** to sound the horn

clamore [kla'more] SM (*frastuono*) din, uproar, clamour (*Brit*), clamor (*Am*); (*fig: scalpore*) outcry; **suscitare** *o* **destare clamore** to cause a sensation

clamorosamente [klamorosa'mente] AVV (*gen*) sensationally; **essere clamorosamente sconfitto** to be resoundingly defeated

clamoroso, a [klamo'roso] AGG (*sconfitta*) resounding; (*applausi*) noisy; (*fig: notizia, processo*) sensational

> **LO SAPEVI...?**
> **clamoroso** non si traduce mai con *clamorous*

clan [klan] SM INV clan; (*fig: gruppo*) team; (: *mafioso*) gang, clan

clandestinamente [klandestina'mente] AVV (*riunirsi, sposarsi*) secretly; **viaggiare clandestinamente** (*in aereo, nave*) to stow away; **importare clandestinamente** (*gen*) to import illegally; (*di contrabbando*) to smuggle

clandestinità [klandestini'ta] SF INV (*di attività*) secret nature; **vivere nella clandestinità** to live in hiding; (*ricercato politico*) to live underground

clandestino, a [klandes'tino] AGG (*illecito*) illicit; (*segreto: matrimonio, incontro*) clandestine, secret; (: *movimento, radio*) underground *attr*

■ SM/F (*anche:* **immigrato clandestino**) illegal immigrant; (*anche:* **passeggero clandestino**) stowaway

claque [klak] SF INV claque

clarinetto [klari'netto] SM clarinet

clarinista, i, e [klari'nista] SM/F clarinet player, clarinettist

clarino [kla'rino] SM clarinet

clarissa [kla'rissa] SF (*Rel*) Poor Clare

classe ['klasse] SF **1** (*gen, fig*) class; **lotta di classe** class struggle; **classe di leva 1958** (*Mil*) class of 1958; **viaggiare in prima/seconda classe** to travel first/ second class; **un albergo di prima classe** a first-class hotel; **classe turistica** (*Aer*) economy class; **una donna di (gran) classe** a woman with class **2** (*Scol*) class; (: *aula*) classroom; **compagno di classe** schoolmate; **un mio compagno di classe** a boy in my class; **che classe fai quest'anno?** what class are you in this year?; **siamo rimasti in classe durante l'intervallo** we stayed in the classroom during the break

classicamente [klassika'mente] AVV classically

classicheggiante [klassiked'dʒante] AGG in the

classical style
classicismo [klassi'tʃizmo] SM classicism
classicista, i, e [klassi'tʃista] SM/F classicist
classicità [klassitʃi'ta] SF **1** (*di opera artistica, letteraria*) classical nature **2** (*mondo greco, latino*) classical antiquity
classico, a, ci, che ['klassiko] AGG **1** (*arte, letteratura, civiltà*) classical; **studi classici** classical studies; **danza classica** ballet dancing; **musica classica** classical music; **non mi piace la musica classica** I don't like classical music **2** (*moda, esempio*) classic; **un film classico** a classic film; **classico!** that's typical!
■ SM **1** (*autore antico*) classical author; (*opera famosa*) classic; **un classico del cinema francese** a classic of the French cinema **2** (*anche:* **liceo classico**) *secondary school with emphasis on the humanities*
classifica, che [klas'sifika] SF (*di gara sportiva*) placings *pl*; (*di concorso, esame*) list; (*di dischi*) charts *pl*; **essere primo in classifica** to be placed first, come first; (*disco*) to be number one (in the charts); (*squadra*) to be top of the league; **classifica finale** final results *pl*; **classifica generale** overall placings *pl*; **classifica del campionato** (*Calcio*) league table
classificare [klassifi'kare] VT (*catalogare*) to classify; (*candidato, compito*) to grade
▶ **classificarsi** VIP (*Sport*) to be placed; **classificarsi primo/secondo** to be placed first/second; **si è classificata prima** she was placed first
classificatore [klassifika'tore] SM (*cartella*) loose-leaf file; (*mobile*) filing cabinet
classificazione [klassifikat'tsjone] SF (*vedi vt*) classification; grading
classismo [klas'sizmo] SM class consciousness
classista, i, e [klas'sista] AGG class-conscious
■ SM/F class-conscious person
classistico, a, ci, che [klas'sistiko] AGG (*politica*) class *attr*
claudicante [klaudi'kante] AGG (*zoppo*) lame; (*fig: prosa*) halting
claunesco, a, schi, sche [klau'nesko] AGG (*aspetto, espressione*) clownish
clausola ['klauzola] SF clause
claustrofobia [klaustrofo'bia] SF claustrophobia; **soffrire di claustrofobia** to suffer from claustrophobia
claustrofobico, a, ci, che [klaustrofo'biko] AGG claustrophobic
clausura [klau'zura] SF (*Rel*): **monaca di clausura** nun belonging to an enclosed order; **fare una vita di clausura** (*fig*) to lead a cloistered life
clava ['klava] SF (*arma primitiva*) club; (*attrezzo da ginnastica*) Indian club
clavicembalista, i, e [klavitʃemba'lista] SM/F harpsichord player, harpsichordist
clavicembalo [klavi'tʃembalo] SM harpsichord
clavicola [kla'vikola] SF collarbone, clavicle (*termine tecn*); **si è fratturato la clavicola** he broke his collarbone
clavicordo [klavi'kɔrdo] SM clavichord
clemente [kle'mɛnte] AGG (*persona*) merciful; (*tempo, stagione*) mild
clementina [klemen'tina] SF clementine
clemenza [kle'mɛntsa] SF (*di persona*) mercy, clemency; (*di tempo, stagione*) mildness
Cleopatra [kleo'patra] SF Cleopatra
cleptomane [klep'tɔmane] SM/F kleptomaniac
cleptomania [kleptoma'nia] SF kleptomania
clergyman ['kləːdʒimən] SM INV clergyman's suit
clericale [kleri'kale] AGG clerical; **potere clericale** power of the clergy
■ SM/F clericalist, supporter of the power of the clergy
clero ['klɛro] SM clergy
clessidra [kles'sidra] SF (*a sabbia*) hourglass; (*ad acqua*) water clock
cliccare [klik'kare] VI (*aus* **avere**) (*Inform*): **cliccare su** to click on
cliché [kli'ʃe] SM INV (*Tip*) plate; (*fig*) cliché
client ['clajent] SM INV (*Inform*) client
cliente [kli'ɛnte] SM/F (*gen*) customer; (*di albergo*) guest; (*di professionista*) client; **il negozio era pieno di clienti** the shop was full of customers; **cliente abituale/occasionale** regular/occasional customer; **sono un cliente fisso di quel bar** I'm a regular at that bar
clientela [klien'tɛla] SF (*di negozio*) customers *pl*; (*di professionista*) clients *pl*; (*di sartoria*) clientele
clientelare [kliente'lare] AGG = **clientelistico**
clientelismo [kliente'lizmo] SM: **clientelismo politico** political nepotism
clientelistico, a, ci, che [kliente'listiko] AGG: **favoritismo clientelistico** political nepotism
clima, i ['klima] SM climate; (*fig*) atmosphere; **c'è un clima piuttosto teso** there's a rather tense atmosphere
■ ABBR (*Aut: climatizzatore*) air con
climaterio [klima'tɛrjo] SM climacteric
climatico, a, ci, che [kli'matiko] AGG climatic; **stazione climatica** health resort
climatizzatore [klimatiddza'tɔre] SM (*Aut*) air conditioner; **una macchina con il climatizzatore** a car with air conditioning
climatizzazione [klimatiddzat'tsjone] SF air conditioning
clinica, che ['klinika] SF **1** (*Med: disciplina*): **clinica medica/chirurgica** clinical medicine/surgery **2** (*settore d'ospedale*) clinic; (*casa di cura*) clinic, nursing home
clinicamente [klinika'mente] AVV clinically
clinico, a, ci, che ['kliniko] AGG (*medico, esame*) clinical; **quadro clinico** case history; **avere l'occhio clinico** (*fig*) to have an expert eye
■ SM (*medico*) clinician; (*docente*) professor of clinical medicine
Clio ['klio] SF Clio
clip [klip] SF INV (*per foglio*) paper clip; (*di orecchino, abito*) clip; **orecchini a clip** clip-on earrings
clistere [klis'tɛre] SM (*Med*) enema; (*: apparecchio*) enema (syringe)
clitoride [kli'tɔride] SM O F (*Anat*) clitoris
cloaca, che [klo'aka] SF **1** (*fogna*) sewer; (*pozzo nero*) cesspool, cesspit **2** (*Anat*) cloaca
cloche [klɔʃ] SF INV (*Aer*) control stick, joystick; **cambio a cloche** (*Aut*) (floor-mounted) gear lever (*Brit*) *o* stick (*Brit*) *o* shaft (*Am*); **cappello a cloche** cloche hat
clonare [klo'nare] VT (*Bio, fig*) to clone
clonazione [klonat'tsjone] SF (*Bio, fig*) cloning
clone ['klone] SM clone
cloridrico, a, ci, che [klo'ridriko] AGG hydrochloric
cloro ['klɔro] SM chlorine
clorofilla [kloro'filla] SF chlorophyll (*Brit*), chlorophyl (*Am*)
clorofilliano, a [klorofil'ljano] AGG (*Bot*): **fotosintesi clorofilliana** photosynthesis
cloroformio [kloro'fɔrmjo] SM chloroform

Cc

cloroformizzare [kloroformid'dzare] VT to chloroform
clorosi [klo'rɔzi] SF INV (*Med, Bot*) chlorosis
cloruro [klo'ruro] SM chloride; **cloruro di sodio** sodium chloride
clou [klu] SM INV: **il clou della serata** the highlight of the evening
club [klub] SM INV club
cm ABBR (= **centimetro**) cm
c.m. ABBR (= **corrente mese**) inst
CN SIGLA = *Cuneo*
c/n ABBR = *conto nuovo*
CNEL [knel] SIGLA M (= **Consiglio Nazionale dell'Economia e del Lavoro**) *body that advises the government and parliament on work-related issues*
CNEN [knen] SIGLA M (= **Comitato Nazionale per l'Energia Nucleare**) ≈ AEA (*Brit*), AEC (*Am*)
CNR [tʃi'ɛnne'ɛrre] SIGLA M (= **Consiglio Nazionale delle Ricerche**) *science research council*
CO SIGLA = *Como*
Co. ABBR (= **compagnia**) Co.
c/o ABBR (= **care of**) c/o
coabitare [koabi'tare] VI (*aus* **avere**) to live in the same flat (*Brit*) *o* apartment (*Am*) *o* house
coabitazione [koabitat'tsjone] SF living in the same flat (*Brit*) *o* apartment (*Am*) *o* house
coadiutore, trice [koadju'tore] SM/F assistant
coadiuvante [koadju'vante] AGG (*farmaco*) adjuvant
coadiuvare [koadju'vare] VT: **coadiuvare qn in qc** to cooperate with sb on sth
coagulante [koagu'lante] AGG coagulative
■SM coagulant
coagulare [koagu'lare] VT
▶ **coagularsi** VIP (*sangue*) to coagulate, clot; (*latte*) to curdle
coagulazione [koagulat'tsjone] SF (*vedi vb*) coagulation, clotting; curdling
coagulo [ko'agulo] SM (*di sangue*) clot; (*di latte*) curd
coalizione [koalit'tsjone] SF coalition; **governo di coalizione** coalition government
coalizzare [koalid'dzare] VT to unite in a coalition
▶ **coalizzarsi** VR (*uso reciproco*) to form a coalition
coartare [koar'tare] VT (*letter*): **coartare qn a fare qc** to coerce sb into doing sth
coatto, a [ko'atto] AGG (*Dir*) compulsory, forced; **condannare al domicilio coatto** to place under house arrest
coautore, trice [koau'tore] SM/F co-author
cobalto [ko'balto] SM cobalt
cobaltoterapia [kobaltotera'pia] SF (*Med*) cobalt treatment, cobalt therapy
COBAS ['kɔbas] SIGLA MPL (= **Comitati di base**) *independent trades unions*
⊳ www.cobas-scuola.org/
COBOL ['kɔbol] SIGLA M (*Inform*) COBOL (= *Common Business Oriented Language*)
cobra ['kɔbra] SM INV cobra
coca[1] ['kɔka] SF (*Bot*) coca
coca[2] ['kɔka] SF **1** (*bevanda*) Coke® **2** (*fam: cocaina*) coke
Coca cola® ['kɔka'kɔla] SF Coca Cola®
cocaina [koka'ina] SF cocaine
cocainismo [kokai'nizmo] SM cocaine addiction
cocainomane [kokai'nɔmane] SM/F cocaine addict; **è un cocainomane** he's a cocaine addict
cocca, che ['kɔkka] SF (*di freccia*) (arrow) notch
coccarda [kok'karda] SF cockade
cocchiere [kok'kjɛre] SM coachman
cocchio, chi ['kɔkkjo] SM (*carrozza*) coach; (*biga*) chariot
coccige [kot'tʃidʒe] SM (*Anat*) coccyx
coccinella [kottʃi'nɛlla] SF ladybird (*Brit*), ladybug (*Am*)
cocciniglia [kottʃi'niʎʎa] SF (*Zool*) cochineal; **rosso di cocciniglia** cochineal
coccio, ci ['kɔttʃo] SM **1** earthenware; **un vaso di coccio** an earthenware pot **2** (*frammento*) fragment (of pottery), potsherd; **chi rompe paga e i cocci sono suoi** (*Proverbio*) any damage must be paid for
cocciutaggine [kottʃu'taddʒine] SF stubbornness, pig-headedness
cocciuto, a [kot'tʃuto] AGG stubborn, pig-headed
cocco[1], chi ['kɔkko] SM coconut palm; **noce di cocco** coconut; **latte di cocco** coconut milk; **gelato al cocco** coconut ice cream
cocco[2], chi ['kɔkko] SM (*batterio*) coccus
cocco[3], a, chi, che ['kɔkko] SM/F (*fam*) love, darling; **è il cocco della mamma** he's mummy's darling
coccodrillo [kokko'drillo] SM crocodile; **lacrime di coccodrillo** (*fig*) crocodile tears
coccolare [kokko'lare] VT to cuddle
▶ **coccolarsi** VR (*uso reciproco*) to cuddle
cocente [ko'tʃɛnte] AGG (*sole*) burning, scorching; (*fig: dolore*) burning; (*: rimorso*) bitter
cocker ['kɔkə] SM INV cocker (spaniel)
cocktail ['kɔkteil] SM INV (*bevanda*) cocktail; (*festa*) cocktail party
coclea ['kɔklea] SF (*Anat*) cochlea
cococò [koko'kɔ] SM/F INV (= **collaborazione coordinata continuativa**) *employee on short term contract and without employment rights such as paid holiday*
cocomero [ko'komero] SM watermelon
cocotte [ko'kɔt] SF INV (*Culin*) cast-iron casserole
cocuzzolo [ko'kuttsolo] SM (*di montagna*) summit, top; (*della testa*) crown, top (of the head)
cod. ABBR = **codice**
coda ['koda] SF **1** tail; (*di abiti*) train; **coda di cavallo** (*acconciatura*) ponytail; **ha la coda di cavallo** she's got a ponytail; **vettura/fanale di coda** rear coach/light; **in coda a** (*veicolo, treno*) at the rear of; (*processione*) at the tail end of; **con la coda fra le gambe** (*fig*) with one's tail between one's legs; **avere la coda di paglia** (*fig*) to have a guilty conscience; **guardare con la coda dell'occhio** to look out of the corner of one's eye; **mi guardava con la coda dell'occhio** she was looking at me out of the corner of her eye; **incastro a coda di rondine** dovetail joint **2** (*fila*) queue (*Brit*), line (*Am*); **fare la coda, mettersi in coda** to join the queue, queue (up) (*Brit*), line up (*Am*); **prendi il vassoio e mettiti in coda** take a tray and join the queue; **la coda si fa da questa parte** queue this side **3** (*Culin*): **coda di rospo** frogfish tail
codardamente [kodarda'mente] AVV like a coward, in a cowardly way
codardia [kodar'dia] SF cowardice
codardo, a [ko'dardo] AGG cowardly
■SM/F coward
codazzo [ko'dattso] SM throng
codecisione [kodetʃi'zjone] SF joint decision
codesto, a [ko'desto] AGG, PRON DIMOSTR (*letter, toscano*) this, that
codibugnolo [kodi'buɲɲolo] SM (*uccello*) long-tailed tit
codice ['kɔditʃe] SM **1** code; **messaggio in codice**

message in code, coded message **2** (*manoscritto antico*) codex
■ **codice di avviamento postale** postcode (*Brit*), zip code (*Am*); **codice a barre** bar code; **codice di carattere** (*Inform*) character code; **codice civile** civil code; **codice fiscale** tax code; **codice genetico** genetic code; **codice macchina** (*Inform*) machine code; **codice penale** penal code; **codice postale** postcode; **sai qual è il codice postale?** do you know what the postcode is?; **codice professionale** code of practice; **codice segreto** (*di tessera magnetica*) PIN (number); **codice della strada** highway code (*Brit*)

codicillo [kodi'tʃillo] SM codicil

codifica [ko'difika] SF codification; (*Inform: di programma*) coding

codificare [kodifi'kare] VT (*Dir*) to codify; (*informazioni, segreti, dati*) to encode

codificazione [kodifikat'tsjone] SF (*vedi vb*) codification; encoding

codino[1] [ko'dino] SM (*di capelli*) pigtail; **ha il codino** he's got a ponytail

codino[2], a [ko'dino] AGG reactionary
■ SM/F (*fig: persona*) reactionary

coeditore [koedi'tore] SM co-publisher

coedizione [koedit'tsjone] SF co-edition

coefficiente [koeffi'tʃɛnte] SM coefficient; **coefficiente di resistenza** drag coefficient *o* factor

coercibile [koer'tʃibile] AGG coercible; (*Fis*) compressible

coercibilità [koertʃibili'ta] SF (*vedi agg*) coercibility; compressibility

coercitivo, a [koertʃi'tivo] AGG coercive

coercizione [koertʃit'tsjone] SF coercion

coerente [koe'rɛnte] AGG (*Geol*) coherent; (*fig: pensiero, azione*) consistent, coherent

coerentemente [koerente'mente] AVV (*fig*) consistently

coerenza [koe'rɛntsa] SF (*vedi agg*) coherence; consistency

coesione [koe'zjone] SF cohesion

coesistente [koezis'tɛnte] AGG coexistent

coesistenza [koezis'tɛntsa] SF coexistence

coesistere [koe'zistere] VI IRREG (*aus* **essere**) to coexist

coesistito, a [koezis'tito] PP *di* **coesistere**

coesivo, a [koe'sivo] AGG cohesive

coetaneo, a [koe'taneo] AGG (of) the same age; **essere coetaneo di qn** to be the same age as sb; **ma allora siamo coetanei!** so we're the same age!
■ SM/F contemporary; **preferisco la compagnia dei miei coetanei** I prefer the company of people my own age

coevo, a [ko'ɛvo] AGG contemporary

cofanetto [kofa'netto] SM casket; **cofanetto dei gioielli** jewel case; **cofanetto da lavoro** workbox; **cofanetto regalo** gift box

cofano ['kɔfano] SM **1** coffer **2** (*Aut*) bonnet (*Brit*), hood (*Am*)

coffa ['kɔffa] SF (*Naut*) top

cofinanziamento [kofinantsja'mento] SM co-financing

cogitabondo, a [kodʒita'bondo] AGG (*letter*) thoughtful, deep in thought

cogli ['koʎʎi] PREP + ART *vedi* **con**

cogliere ['kɔʎʎere] VT IRREG **1** (*fiori, frutta*) to pick, gather; **ho colto una mela dall'albero** I picked an apple off the tree **2** (*fig: afferrare*) to grasp, seize, take; **cogliere il significato di qc** to grasp the meaning of sth; **cogliere l'occasione** *o* **l'opportunità (per fare)** to take the opportunity (to do); **ha colto l'occasione buona** he chose the right moment; **cogliere nel segno** (*fig*) to hit the nail on the head **3** (*sorprendere*) to catch, surprise; **cogliere sul fatto** *o* **in flagrante/alla sprovvista** to catch red-handed/unprepared; **l'ho colto sul fatto** I caught him red-handed; **cogliere qn in fallo** to catch sb out

coglionaggine [koʎʎo'naddʒine] SF (*fam!*) (bloody) stupidity

coglionata [koʎʎo'nata], **coglioneria** ['koʎʎone'ria] SF (*fam!*): **dire una coglionata** to talk a load of balls (*fam!*)

coglione, a [koʎ'ʎone] SM (*fam!: testicolo*): **coglioni** SMPL balls (*fam!*); **rompere i coglioni a qn** to get on sb's tits (*Brit fam!*)
■ SM/F (*fam!: persona sciocca*) dickhead (*fam!*)

cognac [kɔ'ɲak] SM INV cognac

cognato, a [koɲ'ɲato] SM/F brother-/sister-in-law

cognitivismo [koɲɲiti'vizmo] SM cognitivism

cognitivo, a [koɲɲi'tivo] AGG cognitive

cognizione [koɲɲit'tsjone] SF (*conoscenza*) knowledge; (*Dir*) cognizance; (*Filosofia*) cognition; **con cognizione di causa** with full knowledge of the facts

cognome [koɲ'ɲome] SM surname; **come ti chiami di cognome?** what's your surname?

COGNOME

Most married women keep their maiden name, but often use their husband's surname as well. Children take the surname of the first parent to recognize them officially. If both parents do this at the same time, then the child takes the father's surname.

coi ['koi] PREP + ART *vedi* **con**

coibentare [koiben'tare] VT to insulate

coibentazione [koibentat'tsjone] SF insulation

coibente [koi'bɛnte] AGG insulating

coincidenza [kointʃi'dɛntsa] SF **1** coincidence; **che coincidenza, vado anch'io a Bologna** what a coincidence, I'm going to Bologna too **2** (*Ferr, Aer, di autobus*) connection; **ho perso la coincidenza** I missed my connection

coincidere [koin'tʃidere] VI IRREG (*aus* **avere**) to coincide

coinciso, a [koin'tʃizo] PP *di* **coincidere**

coinquilino [koinkwi'lino] SM (*in condominio*) fellow tenant; (*in appartamento*) flatmate (*Brit*), roommate (*Am*)

cointeressato, a [kointeres'sato] SM/F (*Comm*) associate

cointeressenza [kointeres'sɛntsa] SF (*Comm*): **avere una cointeressenza in qc** to own shares in sth; **cointeressenza dei lavoratori** profit-sharing

cointestare [kointes'tare] VT: **cointestare qc** to put sth in joint names

cointestatario, a [kointesta'tarjo] SM/F (*di casa, auto*) joint owner; (*di conto bancario*) joint account holder

cointestazione [kointestat'tsjone] SF joint ownership

coinvolgere [koin'vɔldʒere] VT IRREG to involve, implicate; **coinvolgere qn in qc** to involve sb in sth; **non mi coinvolgere in questa storia** don't involve me in this business

coinvolgimento [koinvoldzi'mento] SM involvement

coinvolsi *ecc* VB *vedi* **coinvolgere**

Cc

coinvolto, a [koin'vɔlto] PP *di* **coinvolgere**
coito ['kɔito] SM coitus; **coito interrotto** coitus interruptus
coke ['kouk] SM INV: **(carbone) coke** coke
Col. ABBR (= **colonnello**) Col.
col [kol] PREP + ART *vedi* **con**
colà [ko'la] AVV there
colabrodo [kola'brɔdo] SM INV colander, strainer
colapasta [kola'pasta] SM INV colander
colare [ko'lare] VT **1** *(liquido)* to strain; *(pasta)* drain; **hai colato la pasta?** have you drained the pasta? **2** *(metalli)* to cast; *(oro fuso)* to pour
■ VI *(aus* **essere***)* **1** *(cadere a gocce)* to drip; *(cera, formaggio)* to run; **il sudore gli colava dalla fronte** sweat dripped from his brow; **mi cola il naso** my nose is running; **mi cola il sangue dal naso** my nose is bleeding **2** *(perdere: botte)* to leak **3** *(nave)*: **colare a picco** to sink straight to the bottom
colata [ko'lata] SF *(di metallo fuso)* casting; *(di lava)* flow
colazione [kolat'tsjone] SF *(anche:* **prima colazione***)* breakfast; *(anche:* **seconda colazione***)* lunch; **cosa mangi a colazione?** what do you have for breakfast?; **fare colazione** to have breakfast *o* lunch; **colazione all'inglese** English *o* full breakfast; **colazione di lavoro** working lunch
colbacco, chi [kol'bakko] SM *(Mil)* busby; *(da donna, uomo)* fur hat
COLDIRETTI [koldi'rɛtti] SIGLA F (= **Confederazione nazionale coltivatori diretti**) *federation of Italian farmers*
colecisti [kole'tʃisti] SF INV *(Anat)* gall bladder
colei [ko'lɛi] PRON DIMOSTR *(sogg)* she; *(complemento)* her; **colei che** the woman who, the one who
coleotteri [kole'ɔtteri] SMPL coleoptera *pl*
colera [ko'lɛra] SM INV cholera
colesterolo [koleste'rɔlo] SM cholesterol
colf [kɔlf] SF INV home help
colgo *ecc* ['kɔlgo] VB *vedi* **cogliere**
colibrì [koli'bri] SM INV hummingbird
colica ['kɔlika] SF *(Med)* colic
colino [ko'lino] SM strainer; **colino per il tè** tea strainer
colite [ko'lite] SF *(Med)* colitis
colla¹ ['kɔlla] SF glue; **un tubetto di colla** a tube of glue; **colla di farina** paste; **colla di pesce** fish glue, isinglass
colla² ['kolla] PREP + ART *vedi* **con**
collaborare [kollabo'rare] VI *(aus* **avere***)* *(lavorare insieme)* to cooperate; *(Pol)* to collaborate; **collaborare a** *(progetto)* to contribute to, collaborate on; **ho collaborato ad un progetto molto interessante** I worked on a very interesting project; **collaborare ad un giornale** to contribute to a newspaper; **collaborare con la polizia** to help the police with their enquiries; **tu e Luca dovete cercare di collaborare** you and Luca must try to work together
collaboratore, trice [kollabora'tore] SM/F *(vedi vb)* contributor; collaborator; **tutti i nostri collaboratori** all the members of our team; **è uno dei nostri collaboratori più validi** he's one of our best people; **stiamo cercando due collaboratori per questo progetto** we're looking for two people to work on this project; **collaboratore di un giornale** contributor to a newspaper; **collaboratrice domestica/familiare** home help; **collaboratore esterno** freelance, freelancer; **collaboratore di giustizia** = **pentito**
collaborazione [kollaborat'tsjone] SF *(vedi vb)* cooperation; collaboration; contribution; **in collaborazione con** in collaboration with
collaborazionismo [kollaborattsjo'nizmo] SM *(Pol)* collaboration
collaborazionista, i, e [kollaborattsjo'nista] SM/F collaborationist
collage [kɔ'laʒ] SM INV collage
collagene [kolla'dʒɛne] SM collagen
collana [kol'lana] SF **1** necklace; **collana di fiori** garland of flowers **2** *(raccolta di libri, scritti)* collection, series *sg*
collant [kɔ'lɑ̃] SM INV tights *pl*; **un paio di collant** a pair of tights
collante [kol'lante] SM *(colla)* glue, adhesive; *(fig)* glue
collare [kol'lare] SM collar
collarino [kolla'rino] SM *(Rel)* clerical collar
collasso [kol'lasso] SM *(Med)* collapse; **avere un collasso** to collapse; **ha avuto un collasso mentre giocava a pallone** he collapsed while playing football; **un collasso cardiaco** heart failure
collaterale [kollate'rale] AGG collateral; **effetti collaterali** side effects
collaudare [kollau'dare] VT to test, try out
collaudatore, trice [kollauda'tore] SM/F tester; **collaudatore di aeroplani/automobili** test pilot/driver
collaudo [kol'laudo] SM *(azione)* testing *no pl*; *(prova)* test; **fare il collaudo di qc** to test sth; **volo/giro di collaudo** test flight/run
collazionare [kollattsjo'nare] VT to collate
collazione [kollat'tsjone] SF collation
colle¹ ['kɔlle] SM *(collina)* hill; *(valico)* pass
colle² ['kolle] PREP + ART *vedi* **con**
collega, ghi, ghe [kol'lɛga] SM/F colleague; **un suo collega** a colleague of hers
collegamento [kollega'mento] SM **1** *(gen, fig: legame)* connection **2** *(Mil)* liaison; **ufficiale di collegamento** liaison officer **3** *(Radio)* link(-up); **siamo ora in collegamento con...** we are now linked to ... **4** *(Inform)* link; **collegamento ipertestuale** hyperlink
collegare [kolle'gare] VT to connect, join, link; *(città, zone)* to join, link; *(Elettr)* to connect (up); **devi collegare la stampante al computer** you have to connect the printer to the computer; **l'autostrada collega Bologna a Firenze** the motorway links Bologna and Florence
▶ **collegarsi** VIP to join, meet; *(Radio, TV)* to link up; **collegarsi a** to connect to; **collegarsi con** *(Telec)* to get through to
collegiale [kolle'dʒale] AGG *(riunione, decisione)* collective; *(Scol)* boarding school *attr*
■ SM/F boarder; *(fig: persona timida e inesperta)* schoolboy/schoolgirl
collegialità [kolledʒali'ta] SF **1** collegial nature; *(di decisione)* joint nature **2** *(Rel)* collegiality
collegialmente [kolledʒal'mente] AVV *(decidere)* as a body
collegio, gi [kol'lɛdʒo] SM **1** *(ordine di professionisti, Rel)* college **2** *(convitto)* boarding school; **collegio militare** military college **3** *(Amm)*: **collegio elettorale** constituency
collera ['kɔllera] SF anger; **andare in collera** to get angry; **essere in collera con qn** to be angry with sb
collerico, a, ci, che [kol'lɛriko] AGG *(persona)* quick-tempered, irascible; *(parole)* angry; *(temperamento)* choleric
colletta [kol'lɛtta] SF collection; **abbiamo fatto una**

colletta per comprarle un regalo we had a collection to buy her a present
collettivamente [kollettiva'mente] AVV collectively
collettivismo [kolletti'vizmo] SM collectivism
collettività [kollettivi'ta] SF community
collettivizzare [kollettivid'dzare] VT to collectivize
collettivo, a [kollet'tivo] AGG (*benessere, bisogno, interesse*) common, general; (*responsabilità*) collective; (*impresa*) group *attr*; **fenomeno collettivo** popular phenomenon; **nome collettivo** (*Gramm*) collective noun; **società in nome collettivo** (*Comm*) partnership ■SM (*Pol*) collective
colletto [kol'letto] SM (*di vestito, Bot: di albero*) collar; (*di dente*) neck; **colletti bianchi** (*fig*) white-collar workers
collettore [kollet'tore] SM (*Aut*) manifold; **collettore di aspirazione** inlet manifold; **collettore di scarico** exhaust manifold
collezionare [kollettsjo'nare] VT to collect; **colleziono cartoline da tutto il mondo** I collect postcards from all over the world
collezione [kollet'tsjone] SF (*gen*) collection; **una collezione di francobolli** a stamp collection; **fare collezione di** (*francobolli*) to collect
collezionismo [kollettsjo'nizmo] SM collecting
collezionista, i, e [kollettsjo'nista] SM/F collector; **un collezionista di francobolli** a stamp collector
collier [kɔ'lje] SM INV necklace
collimare [kolli'mare] VI (*aus* **avere**) **collimare (con)** (*idee*) to coincide (with), agree (with)
collimatore [kollima'tore] SM (*gen*) telescopic sight; (*Ottica*) collimator
collimazione [kollimat'tsjone] SF (*Ottica*) collimation; (*fig: di idee*) coincidence
collina [kol'lina] SF hill; (*zona*) hills; **una città di collina** a town in the hills, a hill town
collinare [kolli'nare] AGG hill *attr*
collinoso, a [kolli'noso] AGG hilly
collirio, ri [kol'lirjo] SM eyedrops *pl*; **vorrei un collirio** I'd like some eyedrops
collisione [kolli'zjone] SF (*di veicoli*) collision; (*fig*) clash, conflict; **entrare in collisione con qc** to collide with sth
collo[1] ['kɔllo] SM neck; (*di abito*) neck, collar; **a collo alto** (*maglione*) high-necked; **portare qc al collo** to wear sth round one's neck; **buttare le braccia al collo di qn** *or* **portava un foulard al collo** she had a scarf round her neck, to throw one's arms round sb; **fino al collo** (*anche fig*) up to one's neck; **essere nei guai fino al collo** to be in deep trouble; **è nei guai fino al collo** he's up to his neck in it; **collo del piede** instep
collo[2] ['kɔllo] SM (*pacco*) parcel, package; (*bagaglio*) piece of luggage
collo[3] ['kollo] PREP + ART *vedi* **con**
collocamento [kolloka'mento] SM (*impiego*) employment; (*disposizione*) placing, arrangement; **agenzia di collocamento** employment agency; **ufficio di collocamento** ≈ Jobcentre (*Brit*), state *o* federal employment agency (*Am*); **collocamento a riposo** retirement
collocare [kollo'kare] VT **1** (*porre: libri, mobili*) to place, position; (*: cavi*) to lay; **questo libro va collocato fra le sue opere migliori** this book ranks among his best works **2** (*trovare un impiego a qn*) to place, find a job for; **collocare qn a riposo** to pension sb off, retire sb **3** (*Comm: merce*) to place, find a market for
collocazione [kollokat'tsjone] SF **1** (*gen*) placing, positioning; **l'opera va considerata nella sua collocazione storica** the work has to be considered within its historical setting **2** (*in biblioteca*) classification
colloidale [kolloi'dale] AGG colloidal
colloquiale [kollo'kwjale] AGG (*gen*) colloquial; (*tono*) informal
colloquialmente [kollokwjal'mente] AVV colloquially
colloquiare [kollo'kwjare] VI (*aus* **avere**) to talk, converse
colloquio, qui [kol'lɔkwjo] SM **1** (*conversazione*) talk, conversation; (*ufficiale, per un lavoro*) interview; **domani ha un colloquio di lavoro** she's got a job interview tomorrow; **concedere un colloquio a qn** to grant sb an interview; **avviare un colloquio con qn** (*Pol*) to start talks with sb **2** (*Univ*) preliminary oral exam
colloso, a [kol'loso] AGG sticky
collottola [kol'lɔttola] SF nape of the neck; **afferrare qn per la collottola** to grab sb by the scruff of the neck
collusione [kollu'zjone] SF (*Dir*) collusion
collutorio, ri [kollu'tɔrjo] SM mouthwash
colluttazione [kolluttat'tsjone] SF scuffle
colma ['kolma] SF (*di fiume*) high-water level
colmare [kol'mare] VT: **colmare (di)** (*riempire*) to fill (to the brim) (with); (*fig*) to fill (with); **colmare una lacuna** (*fig*) to fill a gap; **colmare un divario** (*fig*) to bridge a gap; **colmare qn di** to shower sb with; **colmare qn di gentilezze** to overwhelm sb with kindness
colmo[1]**, a** ['kolmo] AGG: **colmo (di)** full (of)
colmo[2] ['kolmo] SM (*punto più alto*) summit, top; (*fig*): **il colmo della maleducazione** the height of bad manners; **essere al colmo della disperazione** to be in the depths of despair; **essere al colmo dell'ira** to be in a towering rage; **e per colmo di sfortuna…** and to cap it all …; **è il colmo!** that beats everything!; **questo è il colmo!** this is ridiculous!
colomba [ko'lomba] SF dove; **colomba dal collare** collared dove; **colomba pasquale** (*Culin*) *dove-shaped Easter cake*
colombaccio, ci [kolom'battʃo] SM wood pigeon, ringdove
colombaia [kolom'baja] SF dovecote; (*piccionaia*) pigeon coop
Colombia [ko'lombja] SF Colombia
colombiano, a [kolom'bjano] AGG, SM/F Colombian
Colombo [ko'lombo] SM: **Cristoforo Colombo** Christopher Columbus
colombo [ko'lombo] SM (*Zool*) pigeon; (*fig fam*): **colombi** SMPL lovebirds
colon ['kɔlon] SM INV (*Anat*) colon
Colonia [ko'lɔnja] SF Cologne
colonia[1] [ko'lɔnja] SF (*gen*) colony; (*per bambini*) holiday camp; **era una colonia britannica** it was a British colony; **colonia marina** seaside holiday camp
colonia[2] [ko'lɔnja] SF (*anche:* **acqua di colonia**) (eau de) cologne
coloniale [kolo'njale] AGG colonial ■SM/F colonist, settler
colonialismo [kolonja'lizmo] SM colonialism
colonialista, i, e [kolonja'lista] AGG, SM/F colonialist
colonialistico, a, ci, che [kolonja'listiko] AGG colonialist
colonico, a, ci, che [ko'lɔniko] AGG: **casa colonica** farmhouse
colonizzare [kolonid'dzare] VT to colonize

Cc

colonizzatore, trice [koloniddza'tore] AGG colonizing
■SM/F colonizer
colonizzazione [koloniddzat'tsjone] SF colonization
colonna [ko'lonna] SF (*gen*) column; **le colonne di un tempio** the columns of a temple; **le colonne di Ercole** (*Geog*) the Pillars of Hercules; **in colonna** in a column; **stare in colonna** (*Aut*) to be caught in a tailback (*Brit*) *o* backup (*Am*); **una colonna di 10 chilometri** (*Aut*) a 10-kilometre tailback; **colonna sonora** (*Cine*) sound track; **colonna vertebrale** spine, spinal column
colonnato [kolon'nato] SM colonnade
colonnello [kolon'nɛllo] SM colonel
colono [ko'lɔno] SM **1** (*contadino*) (tenant) farmer
2 (*abitante di una colonia*) colonist, settler
Colorado [kolo'rado] SM Colorado
colorante [koio'rante] AGG colouring (*Brit*), coloring (*Am*)
■SM colorant; (*alimentare*) colo(u)ring
colorare [kolo'rare] VT to colour (*Brit*), color (*Am*); (*disegno*) to colo(u)r in
▶ **colorarsi** VIP: **il cielo si colorava di rosso** the sky was turning red
colorato, a [kolo'rato] AGG coloured (*Brit*), colored (*Am*); **una camicia colorata** a coloured shirt; **una maglietta molto colorata** a brightly coloured T-shirt
colorazione [kolorat'tsjone] SF (*atto*) colouring (*Brit*), coloring (*Am*); (*colore*) colour (*Brit*), color (*Am*), colo(u)ring; **colorazione politica** political sympathies *pl*
colore [ko'lore] SM **1** (*gen, fig*) colour (*Brit*), color (*Am*); (*pittura*) paint; (*Carte*) suit; **di che colore è?** what colo(u)r is it?; **di (un) colore chiaro/scuro** light-/dark-colo(u)red; **un cappotto color ruggine** a rust-coloured coat; **color fragola** strawberry-colo(u)red; **senza** *o* **privo di colore** (*fig*) colo(u)rless; **di colore** colo(u)red; **una ragazza di colore** a black girl; **gente di colore** black people, people of colo(u)r; **cambiare colore** (*anche fig*) to change colo(u)r; **a colori** (*film, TV, foto*) colo(u)r *attr*, in colo(u)r; **TV a colori** colour TV; **colori a olio/a tempera** oil/tempera paints
2 (*fraseologia*): **riprendere colore** (*fig*) to get one's colo(u)r back; **diventare di tutti i colori** to turn scarlet; **è diventato di tutti i colori per l'imbarazzo** he went red with embarrassment; **dirne di tutti i colori a qn** to hurl insults at sb; **farne di tutti i colori** to get up to all sorts of tricks *o* mischief; **in gita ne abbiamo fatte di tutti i colori** on the trip we got up to all sorts of things; **passarne di tutti i colori** to go through all sorts of problems
colorificio, ci [kolori'fitʃo] SM dye factory
colorire [kolo'rire] VT (*colorare*) to colour (*Brit*), color (*Am*); (*fig*) to enliven, embellish
colorito, a [kolo'rito] AGG (*guance, viso*) rosy, pink; (*racconto, linguaggio*) colourful (*Brit*), colorful (*Am*); **sei più colorito oggi** you've got more colo(u)r in your cheeks today
■SM (*carnagione*) complexion
coloro [ko'loro] PRON DIMOSTR PL (*sogg*) they; (*complemento*) them; **coloro che** those who; *vedi anche* colui
colossale [kolos'sale] AGG colossal, huge, enormous
colosso [ko'lɔsso] SM (*statua*) colossus; (*fig*) giant, colossus; **è un colosso!** (*fisicamente*) he's enormous!
colpa ['kolpa] SF (*responsabilità*) fault; (*colpevolezza*) guilt; (*biasimo*) blame; (*morale*) sin; **di chi è la colpa?** whose fault is it?; **è colpa mia** it's my fault; **per colpa di** because of, thanks to; **per colpa sua** because of him, thanks to him; **l'incidente è successo per colpa sua** the accident was his fault; **per colpa sua non possiamo uscire** it's his fault we can't go out; **essere in colpa** to be at fault; **sentirsi in colpa** to feel guilty; **se non ci vado mi sento in colpa** if I don't go I feel guilty; **senso di colpa** sense of guilt; **confessare le proprie colpe** to admit one's faults; **dare la colpa di qc a qn** to blame sb for sth; **non dare la colpa a me!** don't blame me!; **addossarsi la colpa di qc** to take the blame for sth; **si è addossato lui la colpa** he took the blame
colpaccio [kol'pattʃo] SM: **che colpaccio!** what a result!
colpevole [kol'pevole] AGG guilty; **dichiarare qn colpevole (di qc)** to find sb guilty (of sth); **dichiararsi colpevole** to plead guilty; **colpevole di omicidio** guilty of murder
■SM/F culprit; **non hanno trovato il colpevole** they haven't found the culprit
colpevolezza [kolpevo'lettsa] SF guilt
colpevolizzare [kolpevolid'dzare] VT: **colpevolizzare qn** to make sb feel guilty
colpevolmente [kolpevol'mente] AVV guiltily
colpire [kol'pire] VT (*anche fig*) to hit, strike; (*toccare*) to affect; **è stata colpita alla testa** she was hit *o* struck on the head; **colpire qn con un pugno** to punch sb; **lo ha colpito con un pugno** he punched him; **colpire qn a morte** to strike sb dead; **il nuovo provvedimento colpirà gli spacciatori** the new measure will hit drug pushers; **colpire nel segno** (*fig*) to hit the nail on the head, be spot on (*Brit*); **rimanere colpito da qc** to be amazed *o* struck by sth; **sono rimasto colpito dalla sua reazione** I was shocked by his reaction; **la sua bellezza mi ha colpito** I was struck by her beauty; **qual è la cosa che ti ha colpito di più?** what's the thing that struck you most?; **colpire l'immaginazione** to catch the imagination; **un'epidemia che colpisce le persone anziane** an epidemic which affects old people; **le regioni colpite dal maltempo** the regions affected by the bad weather; **colpito dalla paralisi/dalla sfortuna** stricken with paralysis/by misfortune; **è stato colpito da ordine di cattura** there is a warrant out for his arrest
colpo ['kolpo] SM
1 (*aggressivo*) blow; (*urto*) knock; (*fig: affettivo*) blow, shock; **colpo basso** blow below the belt; **colpo mortale** mortal blow; **colpo di spada** sword blow; **colpo di remo** oar stroke; **dare un colpo a qn** to hit sb; **un colpo in testa** a blow on the head; **dare un colpo in testa a qn** to hit sb over the head; **gli ha dato un colpo in testa** he hit him on the head; **prendere un colpo in** *o* **alla testa** to bump one's head; **prendere qn a colpi di bastone** to set about sb with a stick; **darsi un colpo di pettine** to run a comb through one's hair; **è stato un brutto colpo per lui** it came as a hard blow to him; **un colpo di coda** (*di cavallo*) a flick of the tail; **con un colpo d'ala l'uccello si è librato in volo** with a flap of its wings the bird took flight
2 (*di arma da fuoco*) shot; **hanno sparato 10 colpi di cannone** they fired 10 cannon shots; **mi restano solo 2 colpi** I've only got 2 rounds left; **abbiamo sentito dei colpi** we heard shots; **sparare un colpo** to fire; **ha sparato dei colpi in aria** he fired into the air
3 (*Med*) stroke; **colpo (apoplettico)** (apopleptic) fit; **ti venisse un colpo!** (*fam*) drop dead!; **mi hai fatto venire un colpo!** what a fright you gave me!; **colpo**

d'aria chill; **ho preso un colpo d'aria** I've caught a chill; **colpo di calore** heat stroke; **colpo di frusta** *o* **della strega** whiplash; **colpo di sole** sunstroke; **colpo di tosse** fit of coughing
4 (*Pugilato*) punch; (*Scherma*) hit; **colpo basso** (*Pugilato, fig*) blow *o* punch below the belt
5 (*furto*) raid; **fare un colpo** to carry out a raid; **hanno preso gli autori di quel colpo in banca** they caught those responsible for the bank job *o* raid; **tentare il colpo** (*fig*) to have a go; **ho fatto un buon colpo** I pulled it off
6 (*fraseologia*): **al primo colpo** at the first attempt; **di colpo** *or* **tutto d'un colpo** suddenly; **si è fermato di colpo** he stopped suddenly; **far colpo** to cause a sensation; **hai fatto colpo sulla mia amica!** you were a hit with my friend!; **sul colpo** instantly; **è morto sul colpo** he died instantly; **sono andato in quel negozio a colpo sicuro** I went into that shop knowing I would find what I wanted; **il motore perde colpi** (*Aut*) the engine is misfiring
■ **colpi di sole** (*nei capelli*) highlights; **colpo d'approccio** (*Tennis*) approach shot; **colpo di fortuna** stroke of (good) luck; **colpo di fulmine** love at first sight; **è stato un colpo di fulmine** it was love at first sight; **colpo giornalistico** newspaper coup; **colpo gobbo** smart move; (*al gioco*) lucky strike; **colpo di grazia** (*fig*) coup de grâce; **colpo di mano** (*Mil*) surprise attack; (*fig*) surprise action; **colpo d'occhio**: **a colpo d'occhio** at a glance; **avere colpo d'occhio** to have a good eye; **colpo di rimbalzo** (*Tennis*) ground stroke; **colpo di scena** (*Teatro*) coup de théâtre; (*fig*) dramatic turn of events; **colpo di Stato** coup (d'état); **colpo di telefono** phone call; **dare un colpo di telefono a qn** to give sb a ring; **ti do un colpo di telefono domani sera** I'll give you a ring tomorrow evening; **colpo di testa** (*Calcio*) header (*Brit*); (*fig*) (sudden) impulse *o* whim; **colpo di vento** gust (of wind)

colposo, a [kol'poso] AGG: **omicidio colposo** manslaughter

colsi *ecc* ['kɔlsi] VB *vedi* **cogliere**

coltellata [koltel'lata] SF (*colpo*) stab; (*ferita*) knife *o* stab wound; **dare una coltellata a qn** to stab sb

coltelleria [koltelle'ria] SF (*assortimento*) set of knives; (*fabbrica*) cutlery works *sg*; (*negozio*) cutler's (shop)

coltelliera [koltel'ljɛra] SF knife box

coltello [kol'tɛllo] SM knife; **avere il coltello dalla parte del manico** to have the whip hand; **c'era una nebbia che si tagliava con il coltello** the fog was so thick you could have cut it with a knife; **coltello da cucina** kitchen knife; **coltello a serramanico** flick knife, clasp knife

coltivabile [kolti'vabile] AGG (*pianta, varietà*) fit for cultivation; (*terreno*) cultivable, cultivatable

coltivabilità [koltivabili'ta] SF cultivability

coltivare [kolti'vare] VT (*terreno, fig: amicizia*) to cultivate; (*piante*) to grow, cultivate; **coltivavano pomodori** they grew tomatoes; **coltivare un campo a grano** to plant a field with corn; **coltivare la mente** to cultivate one's mind

coltivatore, trice [koltiva'tore] SM grower, farmer; **coltivatore diretto** small independent farmer

coltivazione [koltivat'tsjone] SF growing, cultivation; **la coltivazione del mais** maize growing; **coltivazione intensiva** intensive farming

coltivo, a [kol'tivo] AGG (*terreno*) cultivated, under cultivation

colto[1], a ['kolto] AGG (*istruito*) cultured, well-educated; **una persona molto colta** a very well-educated person

colto[2], a ['kɔlto] PP *di* **cogliere**

coltre ['koltre] SF (*anche fig*) blanket

coltura [kol'tura] SF **1** cultivation; **coltura alternata** crop rotation **2** (*Bio*) culture; **coltura batterica** bacterial culture

colui [ko'lui] PRON DIMOSTR (*sogg*) he; (*complemento*) him; **colui che** the man who, the one who; **colui che parla** the one *o* the man *o* the person who is speaking

colza ['kɔltsa] SF (*Bot*) rape

com. ABBR = **comunale; commissione**

coma ['kɔma] SM INV coma; **essere in coma** to be in a coma; (*fig*) to be dead tired; **oggi sono in coma!** I'm half dead today!; **entrare in coma** to go into a coma; **è entrato in coma** he's gone into a coma

comandamento [komanda'mento] SM commandment

comandante [koman'dante] SM (*Mil*) commander, commandant; (*di reggimento*) commanding officer; (*Aer, Naut*) captain; **comandante del porto** harbour master; **comandante in seconda** second-in-command

comandare [koman'dare] VT **1** (*ordinare*) to order, command; (*essere al comando di*) to command, be in charge of; **comandare a qn di fare qc** to order sb to do sth; **comandare a bacchetta** to rule with a rod of iron **2** (*azionare*) to operate, control; **comandare a distanza** to operate by remote control
■ VI (*aus* **avere**) to be in charge, be in command; **qui comando io!** I'm in charge here!; **è lei che comanda in casa** she's the boss in the house

comando [ko'mando] SM **1** (*ordine*) command, order; (: *Inform*) command; **ubbidire a un comando** to obey an order **2** (*autorità, sede*) command; **essere al comando (di)** to be in command *o* in charge (of); (*Sport: di classifica*) to be at the top (of); (: *di gara*) to be in the lead (in); **assumere il comando di** to assume command of; (*Sport*) to take the lead in; **comando generale** general headquarters *pl* **3** (*Tecn*) control; **doppi comandi** dual controls; **comandi manuali** hand controls; **comando a distanza** remote control

comare [ko'mare] SF (*madrina*) godmother; (*donna pettegola*) gossip; **le allegre comari di Windsor** the Merry Wives of Windsor

comasco, a, schi, sche [ko'masko] AGG of *o* from Como
■ SM/F inhabitant *o* native of Como

comatoso, a [koma'toso] AGG comatose

combaciare [komba'tʃare] VI (*aus* **avere**) to fit together; (*fig: coincidere*) to agree, coincide, correspond; **i due pezzi combaciano perfettamente** the two pieces fit together perfectly; **le tue idee non combaciano con le mie** your ideas are different from mine

combattente [kombat'tɛnte] AGG fighting, combatant
■ SM fighter, combatant; **ex-combattente** ex-serviceman

combattere [kom'battere] VT to fight; (*fig: teoria, malattia*) to combat, fight (against); **hanno sempre combattuto contro l'ingiustizia** they've always fought against injustice
■ VI (*aus* **avere**) to fight

combattimento [kombatti'mento] SM (*Mil*) battle, fight, fighting *no pl*; (*Pugilato*) match; **mettere fuori combattimento** to knock out; **combattimento (a) corpo a corpo** hand-to-hand combat; **combattimento di galli** cockfighting

Cc

combattività [kombattivi'ta] SF fighting spirit

combattivo, a [kombat'tivo] AGG pugnacious

combattuto, a [kombat'tuto] AGG **1** (*incerto: persona*) uncertain, undecided; **combattuto tra due possibilità** torn between two possibilities **2** (*gara, partita*) hard-fought

combinare [kombi'nare] VT **1** (*mettere insieme*) to combine **2** (*organizzare: incontro*) to arrange; (*concludere: affare*) to conclude; **che cosa stai combinando?** what are you up to?; **che cosa hai combinato?** what have you gone and done?; **ci hai combinato un bel guaio!** you've got us into a nice mess!; **oggi non ho combinato nulla** I haven't got anything done today
■ VI (*aus* **avere**) (*corrispondere*): **combinare (con)** to correspond (with)
▸ **combinarsi** VR (*fam: conciarsi*): **ma come ti sei combinato?** what on earth have you got on?, what on earth have you done to yourself?
▸ **combinarsi** VIP (*Chim*) to combine

combinata [kombi'nata] SF (*Sci*) combination

combinazione [kombinat'tsjone] SF **1** (*accostamento, unione*) combination **2** (*caso fortuito*) chance, coincidence; **per combinazione** by chance; **per combinazione era lì anche lui** by chance he was there too; **(guarda) che combinazione!** what a coincidence! **3** (*di cassaforte*) combination

combriccola [kom'brikkola] SF (*gruppo di amici*) party; (*banda*) gang

comburente [kombu'rɛnte] SM (*Chim*) combustive agent

combustibile [kombus'tibile] AGG combustible
■ SM fuel

combustibilità [kombustibili'ta] SF combustibility

combustione [kombus'tjone] SF combustion; **a lenta combustione** slow-burning

combutta [kom'butta] SF: **essere in combutta** to be in league *o* in cahoots; **fare combutta con qn** to be in league *o* in cahoots with sb

come ['kome] PAROLA CHIAVE

■ AVV

1 (*alla maniera di, nel modo che*) as, like (*davanti a sostantivo, pronome*); **com'è vero Dio** as God is my witness; **bianco come la neve** (as) white as snow; **veste come suo padre** he dresses like his father; **a scuola come a casa** both at school and at home, at school as well as at home; **ci vuole uno come lui** we need somebody like him; **è come parlare al muro** it's like talking to the wall; **non hanno accettato il progetto: come dire che siamo fregati** they didn't accept the plan: which means we've had it

2 (*in quale modo: interrogativo, esclamativo*) how; **come mai?** how come?; **come mai non sei partito?** whyever didn't you leave?; **non hanno accettato il mio assegno — come mai?** they didn't accept my cheque — whyever not?; **vieni? — come no!** are you coming? — of course!; **come stai?** how are you?; **come glielo dico?** how will I tell him?; **non so come dirglielo** I don't know how to tell him; **come?** *or* **come dici?** pardon? (*Brit*), sorry?, excuse me? (*Am*), what did you say?; **com'è il tuo amico?** what's your friend like?; **com'è che non hai telefonato?** how come you didn't phone?

3 (*il modo in cui*): **mi piace come scrive** I like the way he writes, I like his style of writing; **ecco come è successo** this is how it happened; **attento a come parli!** mind your tongue!

4 (*in qualità di*) as; **ti parlo come amico** I'm speaking to you as a friend; **come presidente, dirò che...** speaking as your president I must say that ...; **lo hanno scelto come rappresentante** they've chosen him as their representative

5 (*quanto*): **come è brutto!** how ugly he (*o* it) is!; **come mi dispiace!** I'm terribly sorry!

6 **A come Ancona** ≈ A for Andrew; **come non detto** let's forget it; **oggi come oggi** at the present time; **ora come ora** right now; *vedi anche* **così**, **tanto**

■ CONG

1 (*in quale modo*): **mi scrisse come si era rotto un braccio** he wrote to tell me about how he had broken an arm; **mi ha spiegato come l'ha conosciuto** he told me how he met him; **dovevi vedere come lo picchiava** you should have seen the way he was hitting him

2 (*quanto*) how; **sai come sia sensibile** you know how sensitive he is

3 (*correlativo*) as; (*con comparativi di maggioranza*) than; **si comporta come ha sempre fatto** he behaves as he has always done; **è meglio/peggio di come mi aspettavo** it is better/worse than I expected

4 (*appena che, quando*) as soon as; **come arrivò si mise a lavorare** as soon as he arrived he set to work, no sooner had he arrived than he set to work; **come se n'è andato, tutti sono scoppiati a ridere** as soon as he left, everyone burst out laughing

5 **come (se)** as if, as though; **la trattano come (se) fosse la loro schiava** they treat her like a slave *o* as if she were their slave

6 (*in proposizioni incidentali*) as; **come puoi constatare** as you can see; **come sai** as you know

■ SM INV: **il come e il perché** the whys and the wherefores; **non so dirti il come e il quando di tutta questa faccenda** I couldn't tell you how and when all this happened

COMECON ['kɔmekon] SIGLA M (= **Consiglio di mutua assistenza economica**) COMECON

comedone [kome'done] SM blackhead

cometa [ko'meta] SF comet

comica, che ['kɔmika] SF *short slapstick silent film*

comicamente [komika'mente] AVV comically, funnily

comicità [komitʃi'ta] SF (*di libro, film, attore*) comic quality; (*di situazione*) funny side

comico, a, ci, che ['kɔmiko] AGG (*gen, buffo*) comic(al); (*Teatro*) comic; **una scena comica** a funny scene
■ SM **1** (*comicità*) comic spirit, comedy; **il comico è che...** the funny thing is that ... **2** (*attore*) comedian, comic actor; **è un comico famoso** he's a well-known comedian

comignolo [ko'miɲɲolo] SM chimney (top)

cominciare [komin'tʃare] VT to start, begin; **hai cominciato il libro che ti ho prestato?** have you started the book I lent you?; **cominciare a fare/col fare** to begin to do/by doing; **ha cominciato a ridere** she started to laugh; **ha cominciato a piangere** she started crying
■ VI (*aus* **essere**) to start, begin; **una parola che comincia per J** a word beginning with J; **il film comincia con un'esplosione** the film starts with an explosion; **tanto per cominciare** to start with; **tanto per cominciare non sappiamo se funzionerà** in the first place we don't know if it'll work; **a cominciare**

da domani starting (from) tomorrow; **cominciamo bene!** (*iro*) we're off to a fine start!

comitato [komi'tato] SM committee, board; **far parte di un comitato** to be on a committee; **comitato direttivo** steering committee; **comitato di gestione** works council; **Comitato Interministeriale per la Programmazione Economica** interdepartmental committee for economic planning; **Comitato Interministeriale di coordinamento per la Politica Industriale** interdepartmental committee for industrial development; **Comitato Interministeriale dei Prezzi** interdepartmental committee on prices; **comitato di redazione** committee of journalists (*meeting to decide on something, for example whether to strike*)

comitiva [komi'tiva] SF group, party; **viaggiare in comitiva** to travel in *o* as a group; **una comitiva di turisti** a group of tourists; **sconto per comitive** group discount

comizio, zi [ko'mittsjo] SM rally; **comizio elettorale** election rally

comma, i ['kɔmma] SM (*Dir*) subsection

commando [kom'mando] SM INV commando unit

commedia [kom'mɛdja] SF **1** (*Teatro*) play; (: *comica*) comedy; **commedia musicale** musical; **la Divina Commedia** the Divine Comedy **2** (*finzione*) sham, play-acting *no pl*; **è tutta una commedia** it's just play-acting; **fare la commedia** to play-act; **commedia dell'arte** commedia dell'arte; **commedia all'italiana** *Italian satirical film comedies made in the 1950s and 1960s*

▷ www.italica.rai.it/cinema/commedia/

commediante [komme'djante] SM/F comedian/comedienne; (*pegg*) third-rate actor/actress; (*fig: ipocrita*) sham

commediografo, a [komme'djɔgrafo] SM/F (*autore*) comedy writer

commemorabile [kommemo'rabile] AGG commemorable

commemorare [kommemo'rare] VT to commemorate

commemorativo, a [kommemora'tivo] AGG commemorative, memorial

commemorazione [kommemorat'tsjone] SF commemoration

commendatore [kommenda'tore] SM *official title awarded for services to one's country*

commensale [kommen'sale] SM/F table companion

commensurabile [kommensu'rabile] AGG (*Mat*) commensurable

commensurabilità [kommensurabili'ta] SF (*Mat*) commensurability

commentare [kommen'tare] VT (*dare un giudizio su: fatto, avvenimento*) to comment on; (*Radio, TV*) to give a commentary on; (*annotare*) to annotate; **qualcuno vuole commentare quello che ho detto?** does anyone want to comment on what I've been saying?

commentatore, trice [kommenta'tore] SM/F (*Radio, TV*) commentator; (*di testo*) annotator

commento [kom'mento] SM (*osservazione*) comment; (*letterario, Radio, TV*) commentary; **fare un commento su qn/qc** to comment on sb/sth; **fare il commento di una partita** to give the commentary on a match; **senza fare commenti** without passing comment; **è meglio che io non faccia commenti** it is better if I don't say anything; **commento musicale** (*Cine*) background music

commerciabile [kommer'tʃabile] AGG marketable, saleable

commerciabilità [kommertʃabili'ta] SF marketability, saleability

commerciale [kommer'tʃale] AGG (*gen*) commercial; (*corrispondenza*) business *attr*, commercial; (*fiera, bilancio*) trade *attr*; (*pegg: film*) commercial; **le attività industriali e commerciali** industrial and commercial activities; **un'attività commerciale** a business; **avere rapporti commerciali con** to trade with; **interrompere i rapporti commerciali con** to interrupt trade with

commercialista, i, e [kommertʃa'lista] SM/F (*laureato*) graduate in economics and commerce; (*consulente*) business consultant; (: *fiscale, per contabilità*) accountant

▷ www.portalecommercialista.it/

commercializzabile [kommertʃalid'dzabile] AGG marketable

commercializzare [kommertʃalid'dzare] VT (*prodotto*) to market; (*pegg: arte*) to commercialize

commercializzazione [kommertʃaliddzat'tsjone] SF marketing

commercialmente [kommertʃal'mente] AVV commercially

commerciante [kommer'tʃante] SM/F trader, dealer; (*negoziante*) shopkeeper, tradesman; **i commercianti del centro** the shopkeepers in the town centre; **commerciante di legname** timber merchant; **commerciante all'ingrosso** wholesaler; **commerciante in proprio** sole trader

commerciare [kommer'tʃare] VI (*aus* **avere**) **commerciare in** to deal *o* trade in; **commerciare con qn** to do business with sb

■ VT to deal *o* trade in

commercio, ci [kom'mɛrtʃo] SM (*vendita, affari*) trade, commerce; **il commercio della lana** the wool trade; **essere in commercio** (*prodotto*) to be in the shops, be on the market *o* on sale; **mettere in commercio** to put on the market; **essere nel commercio** (*persona*) to be in business; **economia e commercio** economics and business studies; **commercio elettronico** e-commerce, e-business; **commercio equo e solidale** fair trade; **commercio all'ingrosso** wholesale trade; **commercio al minuto** retail trade

commessa [kom'messa] SF (*ordinazione*) order

commesso, a [kom'messo] PP *di* **commettere**

■ SM/F (*addetto alla vendita*) shop assistant (*Brit*), sales clerk (*Am*); **fa la commessa** she's a shop assistant; **commesso viaggiatore** travelling salesman

■ SM (*impiegato*) clerk; **commesso di banca** bank clerk

commestibile [kommes'tibile] AGG edible; **commestibili** SMPL foodstuffs

commestibilità [kommestibili'ta] SF edibility

commettere [kom'mettere] VT IRREG **1** (*errore*) to make; (*delitto, peccato*) to commit **2** (*ordinare*) to commission, order

commiato [kom'mjato] SM leave-taking; **prendere commiato da qn** to take one's leave of sb

commilitone [kommili'tone] SM fellow soldier, comrade-in-arms

comminare [kommi'nare] VT (*Dir*) to make provision for

commiserare [kommize'rare] VT to commiserate with, sympathize with

commiserazione [kommizerat'tsjone] SF commiseration; **sorriso di commiserazione** (*anche pegg*) pitying smile

Cc

commisi *ecc* [kom'mizi] VB *vedi* **commettere**
commissariamento [kommissarja'mento] SM temporary receivership
commissariare [kommissa'rjare] VT to put under temporary receivership
commissariato [kommissa'rjato] SM **1** (*di polizia*) police station **2** (*carica*) commissionership; (*sede*) commissioner's office
commissario, ri [kommis'sarjo] SM **1** (*funzionario*): **commissario (di Pubblica Sicurezza)** ≈ (police) superintendent (*Brit*), (police) captain (*Am*); **alto commissario** high commissioner; **commissario di bordo** (*Naut*) purser; (*Aer*) chief steward, purser; **commissario d'esame** member of an examining board **2** (*Sport*) steward; **commissario di gara** race official; **commissario tecnico (della Nazionale)** national team manager
commissionare [kommissjo'nare] VT to order, place an order for
commissionario, ri [kommissjo'narjo] SM (*Comm, Fin*) agent, broker
commissione [kommis'sjone] SF **1** (*incarico*) errand; **fare una commissione** to go on an errand; **devo fare delle commissioni** I have some shopping to do **2** (*Comm: ordinazione*) order; (*: percentuale*) commission; **fatto su commissione** made to order; **vendere su commissione** to sell on commission; **ha una commissione sulle vendite** he gets commission on sales; **commissioni bancarie** bank charges **3** (*comitato*) committee, board; **commissione d'esame** examining board; **Commissione Europea** European Commission
▷ http://europa.eu.int/comm/index_it.htm
commissione d'inchiesta committee of enquiry; **commissione parlamentare** parliamentary (*Brit*) *o* Congressional (*Am*) commission; **commissione permanente** standing committee
commisurare [kommizu'rare] VT: **commisurare (a)** to adapt (to); **bisogna commisurare la retribuzione alle ore di lavoro** payment must be in proportion to the number of hours worked
commisurato, a [kommizu'rato] AGG: **commisurato a** in proportion to
committente [kommit'tɛnte] SM/F (*Comm*) purchaser, customer
commosso, a [kom'mɔsso] PP *di* **commuovere**
■ AGG moved, touched; **essere commosso fino alle lacrime** to be moved to tears
commovente [kommo'vɛnte] AGG moving, touching; **una storia commovente** a moving story
commozione [kommot'tsjone] SF **1** (*emozione*) emotion, deep feeling; **non riusciva a nascondere la commozione** he couldn't hide his emotion; **si è messa a piangere per la commozione** she got emotional and started to cry **2** (*Med*): **commozione cerebrale** concussion
commuovere [kom'mwɔvere] VB IRREG
■ VT to move, touch, affect; **mi hai commosso** I'm touched *o* moved;
▶ **commuoversi** VIP to be moved; get emotional; **si è commossa** she got emotional
commutare [kommu'tare] VT **1** (*Dir: pena*) to commute **2** (*Elettr*) to switch *o* change over, commutate (*termine tecn*)
commutatore [kommuta'tore] SM (*Elettr*) commutator
commutazione [kommutat'tsjone] SF (*Dir, Elettr*) commutation; **commutazione di pacchetto** (*Inform*) packet switching
comò [ko'mɔ] SM INV chest of drawers, bureau (*Am*)
comodamente [komoda'mente] AVV (*in modo comodo*) comfortably; (*senza sforzo*) easily
comodino [komo'dino] SM bedside table
comodità [komodi'ta] SF INV **1** (*vedi agg*) convenience; handiness; comfort; **la comodità di abitare in centro** the convenience of living in the town centre; **ho la comodità di avere la fermata sotto casa** conveniently for me, the stop is outside my house **2** **le comodità della vita moderna** modern conveniences

LO SAPEVI...?
comodità non si traduce mai con *commodity*

comodo, a ['kɔmodo] AGG (*conveniente*) convenient; (*pratico*) handy; (*utile*) useful; (*confortevole*) comfortable; (*facile*) easy; **una poltrona comoda** a comfortable chair; **gli piace la vita comoda** he likes an easy life; **stia comodo!** don't bother to get up!; **stai comodo lì?** are you comfortable there?; **è comodo dare la colpa agli altri** it's easy to blame other people; **sarebbe più comodo incontrarci in centro** it would be more convenient to meet in the town centre
■ SM: **con comodo** at one's convenience *o* leisure; **fai con comodo** take your time; **fare il proprio comodo** to please o.s., do as one pleases; **amare il proprio comodo** to like one's comforts; **far comodo** to be a help; **quei soldi mi hanno fatto comodo** that money came in handy; **una macchina mi farebbe comodo** a car would do me nicely, a car would be very handy; **una soluzione di comodo** a convenient arrangement
compact disc ['kəmpakt 'disk] SM INV compact disc
compaesano, a [kompae'zano] SM/F (*dello stesso paese*) fellow countryman/woman; (*della stessa città*) person from the same town; **è un mio compaesano** he comes from the same town *o* country as I do
compagine [kom'padʒine] SF **1** (*Pol*): **la compagine del partito** the party en bloc; **la compagine dello Stato** the government as a whole **2** (*squadra*) team
compagnia [kompaɲ'ɲia] SF **1** company; **fare compagnia a qn** to keep sb company; **quand'era malato andavo a fargli compagnia** when he was ill I used to go and keep him company; **essere di compagnia** to be sociable; **è un tipo di compagnia** he's a sociable kind of person; **dama di compagnia** lady-in-waiting **2** (*gruppo di persone*) group, party; (*Mil, Comm, Teatro*) company; **compagnia aerea** airline; **compagnia di bandiera** (*aerea*) national airline; **lavora in una compagnia di assicurazioni** he works for an insurance company; **frequentare cattive compagnie** to keep bad company; **...e compagnia bella** (*e gli altri*) ... and co.; (*eccetera, eccetera*) ... and so on
compagno, a [kom'paɲɲo] SM/F (*gen*) companion; (*nel gioco*) partner; (*della vita*) life companion; (*Pol*) comrade; **compagno di classe** classmate; **i miei compagni di classe** my classmates; **un mio compagno di classe** a boy in my class; **compagno di giochi** playmate; **compagno di lavoro** workmate; **compagno di scuola** schoolfriend; **è una mia compagna di scuola** she's one of my schoolfriends; **compagno di squadra** team-mate; **compagno di sventura** companion in misfortune; **compagno di viaggio** fellow traveller
compaio *ecc* [kom'pajo] VB *vedi* **comparire**
companatico [kompa'natiko] SM: **pane e companatico** ≈ bread and dripping

comparare [kompa'rare] VT to compare
comparativamente [komparativa'mente] AVV comparatively
comparativo, a [kompara'tivo] AGG, SM comparative
comparato, a [kompa'rato] AGG comparative
comparazione [komparat'tsjone] SF comparison
compare [kom'pare] SM *(padrino)* godfather; *(complice)* accomplice; *(fam: amico)* old pal, old mate
comparire [kompa'rire] VI IRREG *(aus* **essere***)* *(presentarsi)* to appear; *(uscire: libro, giornale)* to come out; **comparire in giudizio** *(Dir)* to appear before the court
comparizione [komparit'tsjone] SF *(Dir)* appearance; **mandato di comparizione** summons *sg*
comparsa [kom'parsa] SF **1** *(apparizione)* appearance; **fare la propria comparsa** to put in an appearance; **nessuno si aspettava la sua comparsa** no one expected him to turn up **2** *(persona: Cine)* extra; (: *Teatro)* walk-on
comparso, a [kom'parso] PP *di* **comparire**
compartecipare [kompartetʃi'pare] VI *(aus* **avere***)* *(Comm)*: **compartecipare a** to have a share in; **compartecipare agli utili** to share in the profits
compartecipazione [kompartetʃipat'tsjone] SF *(divisione con altri)* sharing; *(quota)* share; **compartecipazione agli utili** profit-sharing; **in compartecipazione** jointly
compartecipe [kompar'tetʃipe] AGG: **essere compartecipe agli utili** to share in the profits
compartimentale [kompartimen'tale] AGG district *attr*
compartimentazione [kompartimentat'tsjone] SF compartmentation, division into compartments
compartimento [komparti'mento] SM **1** *(Amm: circoscrizione)* district **2** *(Naut)*: **compartimento stagno** watertight compartment
comparvi *ecc* [kom'parvi] VB *vedi* **comparire**
compassatamente [kompassata'mente] AVV imperturbably
compassato, a [kompas'sato] AGG *(persona)* composed; **freddo e compassato** cool and collected
compassione [kompas'sjone] SF compassion, pity; **provare** *o* **sentire compassione per qn** *or* **avere compassione di qn** to pity sb, feel sorry for sb; **fare compassione** to arouse pity; **mi ha fatto compassione vederli ridotti così** I was sorry to see them in such a state; **ha perso tutti gli amici e mi fa proprio compassione** he's lost all his friends, and I feel really sorry for him
compassionevole [kompassjo'nevole] AGG *(che sente compassione)* compassionate; *(che suscita compassione)* pitiful, pathetic
compassionevolmente [kompassjonevol'mente] AVV *(vedi agg)* compassionately; pitifully, pathetically
compasso [kom'passo] SM (pair of) compasses *pl*; **compasso per spessori** callipers *pl*
compatibile [kompa'tibile] AGG **1** *(conciliabile, Inform)* compatible **2** *(scusabile)* understandable, excusable
compatibilità [kompatibili'ta] SF *(gen, Inform)* compatibility
compatibilmente [kompatibil'mente] AVV: **compatibilmente con i miei impegni** depending on my commitments
compatimento [kompati'mento] SM: **con aria di compatimento** with a condescending air
compatire [kompa'tire] VT *(aver compassione di)* to feel sorry for, sympathize with; *(scusare)* to make allowances for; **bisogna compatirlo, poveretto** *(iro)* you've got to make allowances for him, poor thing
compatriota, i, e [kompatri'ɔta] SM/F fellow countryman/woman, compatriot
compatta [kom'patta] SF *(auto)* (small) hatchback
compattezza [kompat'tettsa] SF *(solidità)* compactness; *(fig: unità)* solidarity
compatto, a [kom'patto] AGG *(roccia)* solid; *(folla)* dense; *(partito)* united; *(gruppo)* close-knit
compendio, di [kom'pɛndjo] SM compendium, outline
compensare [kompen'sare] VT **1** *(lavoro)* to pay for; *(danno)* to give compensation for; **è stato compensato per il danno ricevuto** he has received compensation for the damage **2** *(bilanciare)* to compensate for, make up for; **le perdite dell'anno scorso saranno compensate dagli utili di quest'anno** this year's profits will compensate for last year's losses
▶ **compensarsi** VR *(uso reciproco)* to balance each other out
compensato [kompen'sato] SM *(anche:* **legno compensato***)* plywood
compensazione [kompensat'tsjone] SF compensation
compenso [kom'pɛnso] SM *(retribuzione)* remuneration, payment; *(onorario)* fee; *(ricompensa)* reward, compensation; **in compenso** *(d'altra parte)* on the other hand; **è brutto, ma in compenso è molto simpatico** he's not handsome, but he's very nice; **ha un lavoro noiosissimo. In compenso è pagato molto bene** his job is very boring – the plus side is that it's very well paid
compera ['kompera] SF: **fare le compere** to do the shopping
comperare [kompe'rare] VT = **comprare**
competente [kompe'tɛnte] AGG *(gen, Dir)* competent; *(capace)* qualified; **è lui il competente in materia** he's the expert; **rivolgersi all'ufficio competente** to apply to the office concerned
competentemente [kompetente'mente] AVV competently
competenza [kompe'tɛntsa] SF **1** *(capacità)* competence, expertise; *(Dir: autorità)* jurisdiction; **non ho competenza in materia** I'm not an expert on that; **è di competenza del tribunale di Milano** it comes under the jurisdiction of the Milan courts; **l'argomento non è di mia competenza** I am not qualified to speak on that subject; **questo lavoro non è di mia competenza** that's not my job; **definire le competenze** to establish responsibilities **2** *(onorario)*: **competenze** SFPL fees
competere [kom'pɛtere] VI DIF **1** *(gareggiare)* to compete, vie **2** *(Dir)*: **competere a** to lie with, come under the jurisdiction of, lie within the competence of; *(spettare: compito)* to lie with; (: *denaro)* to be due to; **non mi compete** it's not my responsibility; **avrai ciò che ti compete** you'll have what is due to you
competitivamente [kompetitiva'mente] AVV competitively
competitività [kompetitivi'ta] SF competitiveness
competitivo, a [kompeti'tivo] AGG competitive
competitore, trice [kompeti'tore] SM/F competitor
competizione [kompetit'tsjone] SF competition, contest; **spirito di competizione** competitive spirit; **auto da competizione** racing car
compiacente [kompja'tʃɛnte] AGG obliging, courteous; *(pegg)* accommodating
compiacenza [kompja'tʃɛntsa] SF courtesy; **abbiate**

Cc

la compiacenza di aspettarmi please be so good as to wait for me

compiacere [kompja'tʃere] VB IRREG
■VI (*aus* **avere**) **compiacere a** to gratify, please
■VT to please, make happy
▶ **compiacersi** VIP (*provare soddisfazione*): **compiacersi di** *o* **per qc** to be delighted at sth, be pleased with sth; (*rallegrarsi*): **compiacersi con qn per qc** to congratulate sb for *o* on sth

compiacimento [kompjatʃi'mento] SM satisfaction

compiaciuto, a [kompja'tʃuto] PP *di* **compiacere**

compiacqui *ecc* VB *vedi* **compiacere**

compiangere [kom'pjandʒere] VT IRREG to feel sorry for, sympathize with

compiansi *ecc* VB *vedi* **compiangere**

compianto, a [kom'pjanto] PP *di* **compiangere**
■AGG: **il compianto presidente** the late lamented president
■SM mourning, grief

compiere ['kompjere] VT (*adempiere*) to carry out, fulfil (*Brit*), fulfill (*Am*); (*finire*) to finish, complete; **compiere gli anni** to have one's birthday; **quando compi gli anni?** when is your birthday?; **quanti anni compi?** how old will you be?; **ha compiuto 18 anni il mese scorso** he turned 18 last month; **compiere il proprio dovere** to carry out one's duty; **compiere una buona azione** to do a good deed
▶ **compiersi** VIP **1** (*giungere a termine*) to end **2** (*avverarsi: speranze*) to be fulfilled; (*: profezie*) to come true

compieta [kom'pjɛta] SF (*Rel*) compline

compilare [kompi'lare] VT (*gen*) to compile; (*modulo*) to complete, fill in, fill out (*Am*); **compilare il modulo in stampatello** fill in the form in block letters

compilatore, trice [kompila'tore] SM/F compiler

compilazione [kompilat'tsjone] SF (*vedi vb*) compilation; completion

compimento [kompi'mento] SM (*termine, conclusione*) completion, fulfilment (*Brit*), fulfillment (*Am*); **portare a compimento qc** to conclude sth, bring sth to a conclusion

compire *ecc* VB = **compiere**

compitare [kompi'tare] VT to spell out

compitezza [kompi'tettsa] SF politeness, courtesy

compito¹, a [kom'pito] AGG well-mannered, polite

compito² ['kompito] SM **1** (*incarico*) job, task, duty; (*dovere*) duty; **a me è toccato il compito di portare le bibite** it was my job to bring the drinks **2** (*Scol: a casa*) piece of homework; (*: in classe*) class test; **domani c'è il compito in classe di matematica** we've got a maths test tomorrow; **fare i compiti** to do one's homework; **non posso, devo fare i compiti** I can't, I've got to do my homework

compiutamente [kompjuta'mente] AVV completely

compiutezza [kompju'tettsa] SF (*completezza*) completeness; (*perfezione*) perfection

compiuto, a [kom'pjuto] AGG: **a 20 anni compiuti** at 20 years of age, at age 20; **ho dieci anni compiuti** I'm ten; **un fatto compiuto** a fait accompli

compleanno [komple'anno] SM birthday; **buon compleanno!** happy birthday!

complementare [komplemen'tare] AGG (*gen, Geom*) complementary; (*materia di studio, esame*) subsidiary

complementarità [komplementari'ta] SF complementarity

complemento [komple'mento] SM **1** (*Gramm*) complement; **complemento oggetto** *o* **diretto/indiretto** direct/indirect object **2** (*Mil*) reserve (troops *pl*); **di complemento** reserve *attr*

complessato, a [komples'sato] AGG, SM/F: **essere (un) complessato** to be full of complexes

complessità [komplessi'ta] SF complexity

complessivamente [komplessiva'mente] AVV (*nell'insieme*) on the whole, in all; (*in tutto*) altogether

complessivo, a [komples'sivo] AGG (*ammontare, prezzo, spesa*) total; (*voti*) overall; **visione complessiva** overview

complesso, a [kom'plɛsso] AGG complex, complicated; **un problema complesso** a complex problem; **numeri complessi** complex numbers; **proposizione complessa** compound sentence
■SM **1** (*insieme*) whole; (*di leggi*) body; (*organizzazione, posto*) complex; **nel** *o* **in complesso** by and large, generally speaking, on the whole; **nel complesso mi è piaciuto abbastanza** on the whole I quite liked it; **è stato un complesso di cose a farmi cambiare idea** it was a combination of things that made me change my mind; **il complesso delle manifestazioni culturali avverrà in luglio** the vast majority of cultural events will take place in July; **complesso industriale** industrial complex; **complesso vitaminico** multi-vitamin **2** (*Psic*) complex; **ha il complesso del naso grosso** she's got a complex about the size of her nose; **complesso d'inferiorità** inferiority complex **3** (*Mus*) band, ensemble; (*: di musica leggera*) group; **suona in un complesso** he plays in a band

completamente [kompleta'mente] AVV completely

completamento [kompleta'mento] SM completion

completare [komple'tare] VT to complete, finish

completezza [komple'tettsa] SF completeness

completo, a [kom'plɛto] AGG (*gen*) complete; (*resoconto, elenco*) full, complete; (*fiasco, fallimento*) complete, utter; **è stato un disastro completo!** it was a complete disaster!; **computer completo di stampante** computer complete with printer
■SM (*abito*) suit; (*di lenzuola*) set; **completo di lenzuola singole/matrimoniali** set of sheets for a single/double bed; **portava un completo grigio** he was wearing a grey suit; **completo da sci** ski suit; **essere al completo** (*albergo*) to be full; (*teatro*) to be sold out

complicare [kompli'kare] VT to complicate; **non per complicarti la vita, ma...** not that I want to make life difficult for you, but ...
▶ **complicarsi** VIP to become complicated

complicazione [komplikat'tsjone] SF complication; **salvo complicazioni** unless any difficulties arise; (*Med*) unless there are any complications

complice ['kɔmplitʃe] SM/F accomplice

complicità [komplitʃi'ta] SF INV complicity; **un sorriso/uno sguardo di complicità** a knowing smile/look

complimentarsi [komplimen'tarsi] VIP: **complimentarsi con qn per qc** to congratulate sb on sth

complimento [kompli'mento] SM **1** (*lode*) compliment; **fare un complimento a qn** to compliment sb, pay sb a compliment **2** **complimenti** SMPL (*congratulazioni*) congratulations; **le faccio i miei complimenti per...** may I congratulate you on ...; **complimenti!** congratulations!; **complimenti per la promozione!** congratulations on your promotion!; **complimenti, parli molto bene l'italiano!** you speak very good

Italian!; **complimenti, che bella casa!** your house is lovely! **3 complimenti**
■SMPL (*cerimonie*) ceremony *sg*; **fa sempre tanti complimenti** he always stands on ceremony; **senza complimenti!** (*offrendo qualcosa*) help yourself!; **non fare complimenti** *o* **senza complimenti, se ti fa piacere resta con noi** feel free to stay with us if you'd like to; **senza tanti complimenti ha preso la mia macchina e se n'è andato** without so much as a by your leave he took my car and off he went

complimentoso, a [komplimen'toso] AGG ceremonious

complottare [komplot'tare] VI (*aus* **avere**) to plot, conspire

complotto [kom'plɔtto] SM plot, conspiracy

compone *ecc* [kom'pone] VB *vedi* **comporre**

componente [kompo'nɛnte] AGG component
■SM/F (*persona*) member
■SM (*Elettr*) component, part; (*Chim*) component
■SF (*fig*: *elemento*) element; **c'era in lui una componente di sadismo** there was an element of sadism in his character

compongo *ecc* [kom'pongo] VB *vedi* **comporre**

componibile [kompo'nibile] AGG (*mobili, cucina*) fitted

componimento [komponi'mento] SM **1** (*gen, Mus*) composition; (*Letteratura*) work, writing **2** (*Dir*) settlement

comporre [kom'porre] VB IRREG
■VT **1** (*creare*: *musica, poesia*) to compose; **ha composto la colonna sonora** he composed the soundtrack; **essere composto da** to be composed of, consist of; **la casa è composta da tre stanze** the house consists of three rooms **2** (*mettere in ordine*) to arrange **3** (*Telec*) to dial; **alzare il ricevitore e comporre il numero** lift the receiver and dial the number **4** (*Tip*) to set **5** (*Dir*: *vertenza*) to settle
▶ **comporsi** VIP: **comporsi di** to consist of, be composed of

comportamentale [komportamen'tale] AGG behavioural (*Brit*), behavioral (*Am*)

comportamentismo [komportamen'tizmo] SM (*Psic*) behaviourism (*Brit*), behaviorism (*Am*)

comportamentista, i, e [komportamen'tista] SM/F behaviourist (*Brit*), behaviorist (*Am*)

comportamento [komporta'mento] SM (*umano, animale*) behaviour (*Brit*), behavior (*Am*); (*di prodotto*) performance; **non capisco il suo comportamento** I don't understand her behaviour

comportare [kompor'tare] VT (*richiedere*) to call for, require; (*implicare*) to imply, involve, entail; **ciò comporta una spesa ingente** it involves a huge financial outlay
▶ **comportarsi** VIP to behave; **comportati bene!** behave!; **non ci si comporta così** that's no way to behave; **comportarsi da vigliacco** to behave like a coward

composi *ecc* [kom'pozi] VB *vedi* **comporre**

composito, a [kom'pɔzito] AGG composite

compositore, trice [kompozi'tore] SM/F (*Mus*) composer
■SM (*Tip*) compositor, typesetter
■SF (*Tip*) typesetting machine

composizione [kompozit'tsjone] SF **1** (*gen, Chim, Mus*) composition **2** (*Tip*) typesetting, composition **3** (*Dir*) settlement

compossesso [kompos'sɛsso] SM (*Dir*) joint possession

compost ['kompost] SM INV compost

composta [kom'posta] SF (*Culin*) stewed fruit, compote

compostaggio [kompos'taddʒo] SM composting

compostamente [komposta'mente] AVV composedly; **stai seduto compostamente!** sit properly!

compostezza [kompos'tettsa] SF (*vedi agg*) composure; decorum

composto, a [kom'posto] PP *di* **comporre**
■AGG **1** (*Gramm*) compound *attr*; (*Mat*) composite; (*formato da più elementi*) compound *attr* **2** (*atteggiamento*) composed; (*persona*: *decoroso*) dignified; **stai seduto composto** sit properly
■SM (*Chim*) compound; (*Culin*) mixture; (*Agr*) compost

comprare [kom'prare] VT **1** to buy; **cosa hai comprato?** what did you buy?; **comprare qc a qn** to buy sth for sb, buy sb sth; **ho comprato un regalino per mia sorella** I bought a little present for my sister; **comprare qc a occhi chiusi** *o* **a scatola chiusa** to buy sth with complete confidence **2** (*corrompere*: *giudice, testimone*) to bribe; (*voti*) to buy; **comprare il silenzio di qn** to bribe sb to keep quiet, buy sb's silence

compratore, trice [kompra'tore] SM/F buyer, purchaser

compravendita [kompra'vendita] SF (*Comm*) (contract of) sale; **un atto di compravendita** a deed of sale

comprendere [kom'prɛndere] VT IRREG **1** (*includere*) to include; (*contenere*) to comprise, consist of **2** (*capire*) to understand

comprendonio [kompren'donjo] SM: **essere duro di comprendonio** to be slow on the uptake

comprensibile [kompren'sibile] AGG understandable

comprensibilmente [komprensibil'mente] AVV (*in modo giustificabile*) understandably; (*con chiarezza*) clearly, comprehensibly

comprensione [kompren'sjone] SF understanding

comprensivamente [komprensiva'mente] AVV **1** (*così da includere*) inclusively **2** (*con tolleranza*) understandingly

comprensivo, a [kompren'sivo] AGG **1** (*Comm*): **comprensivo (di)** (*prezzo*) inclusive (of) **2** (*tollerante*) understanding; **è molto comprensivo** he's very understanding

> **LO SAPEVI...?**
> **comprensivo** non si traduce mai con *comprehensive*

comprensorio, ri [kompren'sɔrjo] SM (*Amm*: *territorio*) district

compreso, a [kom'preso] PP *di* **comprendere**
■AGG (*incluso*) inclusive, included; **tutto compreso** all inclusive, all-in (*Brit*); **la vacanza, tutto compreso, costa mille euro** the holiday costs one thousand euros, all-inclusive; **dall'8 al 22 compreso** from the 8th to the 22nd inclusive; **aperto tutta la settimana domenica compresa** open all week including Sunday

compressa [kom'prɛssa] SF (*Med*: *pastiglia*) tablet; (: *garza*) compress

compressione [kompres'sjone] SF compression

compresso, a [kom'prɛsso] PP *di* **comprimere**
■AGG compressed, pressed

compressore [kompres'sore] SM **1** compressor **2** (*anche*: **rullo compressore**) steamroller

comprimario, ria, ri, rie [kompri'marjo] SM/F (*Teatro*) supporting actor/actress

comprimere [kom'primere] VT IRREG to compress, press; (*file*) to compress

Cc

compromesso, a [kompro'messo] PP *di* compromettere
■ SM (*accordo*) compromise; (*Dir*) arbitration agreement; **arrivare a un compromesso** to reach a compromise; **soluzione di compromesso** compromise solution; **vive di compromessi** his life is a series of compromises

compromettente [kompromet'tɛnte] AGG compromising

compromettere [kompro'mettere] VB IRREG
■ VT (*reputazione*) to compromise, jeopardize; (*libertà, avvenire, risultato*) to jeopardize; **compromettersi la reputazione** to compromise *o* jeopardize one's reputation;
▶ **compromettersi** VR to compromise o.s.

comproprietà [komproprje'ta] SF (*Dir*) joint ownership

comproprietario, ria, ri, rie [komproprje'tarjo] SM/F (*Dir*) joint owner

comprova [kom'prɔva] SF: **a comprova di** as proof of

comprovabile [kompro'vabile] AGG provable, demonstrable

comprovare [kompro'vare] VT to prove, confirm

compuntamente [kompunta'mente] AVV contritely

compunto, a [kom'punto] AGG (*contrito*) contrite; **con fare compunto** (*iro*) with a solemn air

compunzione [kompun'tsjone] SF (*vedi agg*) contrition; solemnity

computabile [kompu'tabile] AGG calculable

computare [kompu'tare] VT to calculate, estimate

computer [kəm'pju:tər] SM INV computer; **lavora molto col computer** he works a lot on the computer; **computer di bordo** (*Aut*) trip computer

computerizzare [kompjuterid'dzare] VT to computerize

computerizzato, a [kompjuterid'dzato] AGG computerized

computerizzazione [kompjuteriddzat'tsjone] SF computerization

computisteria [komputiste'ria] SF (*Comm*) book-keeping, accounting

computo ['kɔmputo] SM (*calcolo*) counting, calculation; **fare il computo di** to count

comunale [komu'nale] AGG (*del comune*) town *attr*, municipal; **è un impiegato comunale** he works for the local council; **consiglio/palazzo comunale** town council/hall

comunanza [komu'nantsa] SF: **comunanza di interessi** community of interests

comune[1] [ko'mune] AGG **1** (*gen, Gramm*) common; (*diffuso*) common, widespread; (*consueto*) everyday; **è un problema molto comune** it's a very common *o* widespread problem; **di intelligenza non comune** of exceptional intelligence; **un nostro comune amico** a mutual friend of ours; **il bene comune** the common good; **di comune accordo** by common consent; **di uso comune** in common use; **un luogo comune** a commonplace; **cassa comune** kitty; **fare cassa comune** to pool one's money; **mal comune, mezzo gaudio** a trouble shared is a trouble halved
2 (*ordinario*) ordinary; (*di livello medio*) average; **la gente comune** ordinary folk
■ SM **1** (*di più persone*): **avere qc in comune** to have sth in common, share sth; **non abbiamo niente in comune** we haven't got anything in common; **abbiamo un amico in comune** we've got a mutual friend; **avere il bagno in comune** to share a bathroom, have a communal bathroom; **mettere le provviste in comune** to pool *o* share one's provisions **2 fuori del comune** out of the ordinary

comune[2] [ko'mune] SM (*Amm: sede*) town hall; (*: autorità*) town council; **lavora per il comune** she works for the council; **devi andare al comune per richiedere il certificato** you have to go to the town hall to get the certificate; **l'età dei Comuni** (*Storia*) the age of the city states; **la Camera dei Comuni** *or* **i Comuni** (*Brit Pol*) the House of Commons, the Commons

COMUNE

The **Comune** is the smallest autonomous political and administrative unit. It keeps records of births, marriages and deaths and has the power to levy taxes and vet proposals for public works and town planning. It is run by a "Giunta comunale", which is elected by the "Consiglio Comunale". The **Comune** is headed by the "sindaco" (mayor) who since 1993 has been elected directly by the citizens.
▷ www.comuni-italiani.it/
▷ www.anci.it/anci.cfm

comune[3] [ko'mune] SF (*comunità, anche Storia*) commune

comunella [komu'nɛlla] SF: **fare comunella** to band together

comunemente [komune'mente] AVV (*gen*) commonly; (*normalmente*) normally

comunicabile [komuni'kabile] AGG communicable

comunicabilità [komunikabili'ta] SF communicability

comunicando, a [komuni'kando] SM/F (*Rel*) communicant

comunicante [komuni'kante] AGG communicating

comunicare [komuni'kare] VT **1** (*trasmettere*) to communicate; **comunicare una notizia a qn** to give sb a piece of news; **comunicare qc a qn** to inform sb of sth **2** (*Rel*) to administer communion to
■ VI (*aus* **avere**) (*stanze, persone*) to communicate; **questa porta comunica con l'esterno** this door leads outside;
▶ **comunicarsi** VIP **1** (*propagarsi*) to spread **2** (*Rel*) to receive communion

comunicativa [komunika'tiva] SF communicativeness; **ha molta comunicativa** she is very communicative

comunicativo, a [komunika'tivo] AGG communicative

comunicato [komuni'kato] SM communiqué; **comunicato stampa** press release

comunicazione [komunikat'tsjone] SF **1** (*collegamento*) communication; **porta di comunicazione** communicating door; **essere in comunicazione (con)** (*Anat, Tecn*) to be connected (with); **mettersi in comunicazione con qn** to contact sb; **vie di comunicazione** means of communication; **le comunicazioni ferroviarie/stradali/telefoniche sono interrotte** rail/road/telephone communications have broken down; **non c'è più comunicazione tra loro** there's no longer any communication between them **2** (*Telec*) call; **passare la comunicazione a qn** to put sb through; **le passo la comunicazione** I'll put the call through to you; **ottenere la comunicazione** to get through; **non**

riesco ad avere la comunicazione I can't get through; **si è interrotta la comunicazione** we've been cut off **3** (*messaggio*) message, communication; (*annuncio*) announcement; **ho una comunicazione urgente per lei** I have an urgent message for you; **salvo comunicazioni contrarie da parte Vostra** unless we hear from you to the contrary

comunione [komu'njone] SF (*Rel*, *fig*) communion; **fare la comunione** to receive communion; **prima comunione** first communion; **fare la prima comunione** to make one's first communion; **comunione dei beni** (*Dir*: *tra coniugi*) joint ownership of property

comunismo [komu'nizmo] SM communism

comunista, i, e [komu'nista] AGG, SM/F communist

comunità [komuni'ta] SF INV community; **c'è una grossa comunità britannica in Toscana** there's a big British community in Tuscany; **Comunità (Economica) Europea** European (Economic) Community; **comunità terapeutica** therapeutic community (*rehabilitation centre run by voluntary organization for people with drug, alcohol etc dependency*)

comunitario, ria, ri, rie [komuni'tarjo] AGG community *attr*

comunque [ko'munkwe] AVV (*in ogni modo*) anyhow, anyway, in any case; **devi farlo comunque** you'll have to do it anyway; **accetterà comunque** he'll accept in any case; **i miei non vogliono, ma ci vado comunque** my parents don't want me to, but I'm going anyway; **e comunque al biglietto ci penso io** and as for the ticket I'll see to that
■ CONG **1** (*in qualunque modo*) however, no matter how; **comunque vada** whatever happens; **comunque vada, sono contento che sia finita** however it turns out, I'm glad it's over; **comunque sia** however that may be **2** (*tuttavia*) however, nevertheless; **comunque potevi avvertirmi** however *o* nevertheless you could have let me know, you could have let me know though

con [kon] PREP (*può fondersi con l'articolo determinativo: con + il* = col, *con + lo* = collo, *con + l'* = coll', *con + la* = colla, *con + i* = coi, *con + gli* = cogli, *con + le* = colle)
1 (*gen*) with; **ci andrò con lei** I'll go with her; **con chi sei stato?** who were you with?; **con chi era il film?** who was in the film?; **riso col burro** rice with butter; **un ragazzo con gli occhi azzurri** a boy with blue eyes, a blue-eyed boy; **è a letto con la febbre** he's in bed with a temperature
2 (*complemento di relazione*) with; (*nei confronti di*) with, towards; **sono in contatto con loro** I am in touch with them; **è sposata con uno scozzese** she's married to a Scot; **si è sposata con uno scozzese** she married a Scot, she got married to a Scot; **hai parlato con lui?** have you spoken to him?; **essere gentile con qn** to be kind to sb; **è gentile con tutti** she's nice to everybody; **è brava con i bambini** she's good with children; **confrontare qc con qc** to compare sth with *o* to sth; **sono tutti con lui** (*dalla sua parte*) they are all on his side, they are all behind him
3 (*per mezzo di*) with; (: *aereo, macchina*) by; **scrivere con la penna** to write with a pen; **prendilo con le mani** pick it up with your hands; **condisci l'insalata con l'olio** dress the salad with oil; **arrivare col treno/l'aereo/con la macchina** to arrive by train/by plane/by car; **lo hanno fatto venire con una scusa** they used a pretext to get him to come, they got him to come by means of a pretext
4 (*complemento di modo o maniera*) with; **con pazienza** with patience, patiently; **con la forza** by force; **con molta attenzione** with great attention, very attentively; **con mia grande sorpresa/mio grande stupore** to my great surprise/astonishment; **lo accolse con un sorriso** she greeted him with a smile
5 (*complemento di causa*): **con questo freddo non potremo partire** we can't leave in this cold weather; **con tutti i debiti che ha...** with all his debts ..., given all his debts ...; **con il 1° di ottobre** as of October 1st; **con l'autunno cadono le foglie** with the coming of autumn the leaves fall from the trees
6 (*nonostante*): **con tutti i suoi difetti...** in spite of all his faults ...; **con tutto ciò** in spite of that, for all that; **con tutto che era arrabbiato** even though he was angry, in spite of the fact that he was angry
7 (*con l'infinito*): **se vuoi dimagrire, comincia col mangiare meno** if you want to lose weight, start by eating less; **finì col dirgli che aveva ragione lei** he ended up saying she was right; **con l'insistere tanto l'hai fatto arrabbiare** you've annoyed him with your pestering; **col passar del tempo** with the passing of time, in the course of time; **col sorgere del sole** with the dawn
8 **e con ciò se n'è andato** and with that he left; **e con questo?** so what?; **come va con la tua gamba?** how's your leg?; **come va con Alberto?** how are you getting on with Alberto?

conato [ko'nato] SM: **conato di vomito** retching; **avere un conato di vomito** to retch

conca, che ['konka] SF (*Geog*) valley, basin

concatenare [konkate'nare] VT to link up, connect
▶ **concatenarsi** VR (*uso reciproco*) to be connected

concatenato, a [konkate'nato] AGG (*eventi*) connected; (*Geol*) interlocking

concatenazione [konkatenat'tsjone] SF connection, link

concavo, a ['kɔnkavo] AGG concave

concedente [kontʃe'dɛnte] SM/F (*Dir*) conveyor

concedere [kon'tʃedere] VB IRREG
■ VT **1** (*permettere*): **concedere a qn di fare qc** to allow sb to do sth; (*dare*): **concedere qc a qn** to grant sb sth; **gli concesse di uscire** he gave him permission to go out; **concedere un prestito** to grant a loan; **mi hanno concesso un prestito** they gave me a loan; **mi concedi un minuto d'attenzione** may I have your attention? **2** (*ammettere*): **concedere (che)** to concede (that) **3** **concedersi qc/di fare qc** (*permettersi*) to allow o.s. sth/to do sth; to treat o.s. to sth; **concedersi il lusso di andare in vacanza** to allow o.s. the luxury of a holiday; **si è concesso una bella macchina** he treated himself to a nice car;
▶ **concedersi** VR: **concedersi a qc** (*donna*: *sessualmente*) to give o.s. to sb

concentramento [kontʃentra'mento] SM concentration

concentrare [kontʃen'trare] VT to concentrate; **concentrare l'attenzione su qc** to focus one's attention on sth
▶ **concentrarsi** VR: **concentrarsi (in)** (*raccogliere l'attenzione*) to concentrate (on); (*adunarsi*) to assemble (in)

concentrato, a [kontʃen'trato] SM concentrate; **concentrato di pomodoro** tomato purée

concentrazione [kontʃentrat'tsjone] SF (*gen*) concentration; **concentrazione orizzontale/verticale** (*Econ*) horizontal/vertical integration

Cc

concentricità [kontʃentritʃi'ta] SF (*Geom*) concentricity
concentrico, a, ci, che [kon'tʃɛntriko] AGG (*Geom*) concentric
concepibile [kontʃe'pibile] AGG conceivable
concepimento [kontʃepi'mento] SM conception
concepire [kontʃe'pire] VT **1** (*bambino*) to conceive **2** (*idea*) to conceive; (*progetto*) to devise, conceive; (*metodo, piano*) to devise; **un elettrodomestico concepito per vari usi** an electrical appliance devised for various purposes **3** (*immaginare*) to imagine, understand, conceive (of); **non riesco a concepire una cosa simile** I just can't imagine such a thing
conceria [kontʃe'ria] SF tannery
concernere [kon'tʃɛrnere] VT DIF to concern, regard; **per quanto mi concerne** as far as I'm concerned
concertare [kontʃer'tare] VT (*ordire: piano*) to devise, plan; (*Mus: spartito*) to harmonize; (*: sinfonia*) to rehearse
concertazione [kontʃertat'tjone] SF *agreement through consultation between government and representatives of workers and employers*
concertino [kontʃer'tino] SM concertino
concertista, i, e [kontʃer'tista] SM/F concert performer
concertistico, a, ci, che [kontʃer'tistiko] AGG concert *attr*
concerto [kon'tʃɛrto] SM (*Mus*) concert; (*: componimento*) concerto; **sala per concerti** concert hall
concessi *ecc* [kon'tʃɛssi] VB *vedi* **concedere**
concessionaria [kontʃessjo'narja] SF (*Comm: ditta*) authorized dealer *o* agency
concessionario, ria, ri, rie [kontʃessjo'narjo] AGG concessionary
■ SM (*Comm*) agent, dealer; **concessionario esclusivo (di)** sole agent (for)
concessione [kontʃes'sjone] SF concession
concessiva [kontʃes'siva] SF (*Gramm*) concessive clause
concessivo, a [kontʃes'sivo] AGG concessive
concesso, a [kon'tʃɛsso] PP *di* **concedere**
concettismo [kontʃet'tizmo] SM (*Arte*) conceptism; (*fig: di scrittore*) use of conceits, ≈ euphuism
concettistico, a, ci, che [kontʃet'tistiko] AGG (*fig: stile*) marked by the use of conceits, ≈ euphuistic
concetto [kon'tʃɛtto] SM (*nozione*) concept; (*opinione*) opinion; **non ho afferrato bene il concetto** I haven't quite got the idea; **farsi un concetto di** to form an opinion of; **è un impiegato di concetto** ≈ he's a white-collar worker; **lascialo in pace, sta facendo un lavoro di concetto** (*iro*) leave him alone, he's concentrating
concettoso, a [kontʃet'toso] AGG full of conceits
concettuale [kontʃettu'ale] AGG conceptual
concezione [kontʃet'tsjone] SF **1** (*idea*) view, idea; **che concezione hai della vita?** how do you see life?, what is your view of life? **2** (*ideazione*) conception
conchiglia [kon'kiʎʎa] SF (*Zool*) shell; (*Culin*) pasta shell
concia ['kontʃa] SF (*vedi vt 1*) tanning; curing
conciare [kon'tʃare] VT **1** (*pelli*) to tan; (*tabacco*) to cure **2** (*maltrattare: scarpe, libri*) to treat badly; (*: persona*) to ill-treat; **guarda come hai conciato quei libri** look at the mess you've made of those books; **ti hanno conciato male** *o* **per le feste!** they've really beaten you up!
▶ **conciarsi** VR (*ridursi male*) to get into a mess; (*vestirsi male*): **ma guarda come si è conciata!** what on earth has she got on?
conciatore [kontʃa'tore] SM (*vedi vt 1*) tanner; curer
conciatura [kontʃa'tura] SF (*vedi vt 1*) tanning; curing
conciliabile [kontʃi'ljabile] AGG compatible
conciliabilità [kontʃiljabili'ta] SF compatibility
conciliabolo [kontʃi'ljabolo] SM secret meeting
conciliante [kontʃi'ljante] AGG conciliatory
conciliare[1] [kontʃi'ljare] VT **1** (*mettere d'accordo*) to reconcile; **conciliare una contravvenzione** to settle a fine on the spot **2** (*favorire: sonno*) to be conducive to, induce; **concilia il sonno** it helps you sleep **3** **conciliarsi qc** (*stima, simpatia*) to gain *o* win sth (for o.s.)
▶ **conciliarsi** VIP: **lo studio non si concilia con il mio lavoro** I can't combine studying with my job
conciliare[2] [kontʃi'ljare] AGG council *attr*
conciliazione [kontʃiljat'tsjone] SF (*accordo*) reconciliation; (*Dir*) settlement; **la Conciliazione** (*Storia*) the Lateran Pact
concilio, lii [kon'tʃiljo] SM **1** (*Rel*) council **2** (*riunione*) conference, meeting
concimare [kontʃi'mare] VT to fertilize; (*con letame*) to manure
concime [kon'tʃime] SM (*chimico*) fertilizer; (*letame*) manure
concione [kon'tʃone] SF: **tenere una concione** (*iro*) to speechify
concisione [kontʃi'zjone] SF concision, conciseness
conciso, a [kon'tʃizo] AGG concise, succinct
concistoro [kontʃis'tɔro] SM (*Rel*) consistory
concitatamente [kontʃitata'mente] AVV excitedly
concitato, a [kontʃi'tato] AGG excited, agitated
concitazione [kontʃitat'tsjone] SF excitement, agitation
concittadino, a [kontʃitta'dino] SM/F fellow citizen
conclave [kon'klave] SM (*Rel*) conclave
concludente [konklu'dɛnte] AGG (*argomentazione*) conclusive, convincing; (*persona*): **poco concludente** inefficient
concludere [kon'kludere] VB IRREG
■ VT **1** (*affare, trattato*) to conclude; (*discorso*) to finish, end, conclude, bring to an end; (*operare positivamente*) to achieve; **non ho concluso nulla oggi** I haven't achieved anything today; **per concludere...** and to conclude ...; **cerchiamo di concludere** let's try to come to a conclusion **2** (*dedurre*): **concludere che** to conclude that, come to the conclusion that; **cosa possiamo concludere dalla discussione?** what can we conclude from the debate?;
▶ **concludersi** VIP (*finire*) to end, conclude, come to an end
conclusionale [konkluzjo'nale] AGG (*Dir*): **comparsa conclusionale** summing up, summation
conclusione [konklu'zjone] SF (*gen*) conclusion; (*di discorso*) close, end; (*risultato*) result; **trarre una conclusione** to draw a conclusion; (*Calcio*) shot on goal; **in conclusione** in conclusion
conclusivo, a [konklu'zivo] AGG (*finale*) final, closing, conclusive
concluso, a [kon'kluzo] PP *di* **concludere**
concomitante [konkomi'tante] AGG concomitant
concomitanza [konkomi'tantsa] SF (*di circostanze, fatti*) combination
concordabile [konkor'dabile] AGG (*prezzo*) negotiable
concordante [konkor'dante] AGG (*testimonianze, Gramm*): **essere concordanti** to agree

concordanza [konkor'dantsa] SF (*anche Gramm*) agreement; (*elenco*): **concordanze** SFPL concordances

concordare [konkor'dare] VT (*fissare*: *prezzo*) to agree on; (*Gramm*) to make agree; **concordare una tregua** to agree to a truce
■ VI (*aus* **avere**) (*essere d'accordo*) to agree, coincide; (: *testimonianze*) to agree, tally

concordato [konkor'dato] SM (*patto*) agreement; (*Rel*) concordat

concorde [kon'kɔrde] AGG (*d'accordo*) in agreement; (*simultaneo*) simultaneous; **concordi nel condannarlo** unanimous in their condemnation of him

concordemente [konkorde'mente] AVV by mutual consent

concordia [kon'kɔrdia] SF concord, harmony

concorrente [konkor'rɛnte] AGG **1** (*Geom*) concurrent **2** (*Comm*) competing *attr*
■ SM/F (*Comm, Sport*) competitor; (*a un concorso di bellezza*) contestant

concorrenza [konkor'rɛntsa] SF competition; **le due ditte si fanno una concorrenza spietata** the two firms are in fierce competition with each other, there is fierce competition between the two firms; **non temono la concorrenza** they are unbeatable; **a prezzi di concorrenza** at competitive prices; **concorrenza sleale** unfair competition

concorrenziale [konkorren'tsjale] AGG competitive

concorrere [kon'korrere] VI IRREG (*aus* **avere**) **1 concorrere (a)** (*contribuire*: *a guarigione, spesa*) to contribute (to); (*partecipare*: *a un'impresa*) to take part (in); **concorri alla gara di domani?** are you taking part in the competition tomorrow? **2** (*competere*): **concorrere (a)** to compete (for); (*a una cattedra*) to apply (for) **3 concorrere (in)** (*Mat*) to converge *o* meet (in)

concorso, a [kon'korso] PP *di* **concorrere**
■ SM **1** (*gen*) competition; (*esame*) competitive examination; **partecipanti fuori concorso** non-competitors; **concorso di bellezza** beauty contest; **concorso ippico** showjumping event; **concorso a premi** competition; **ha partecipato ad un concorso a premi e ha vinto** she went in for a competition and won; **concorso per titoli** competitive examination for qualified candidates **2** (*partecipazione*): **concorso (a)** contribution (to); **concorso di colpa** (*Dir*) contributory negligence; **concorso in reato** (*Dir*) complicity in a crime **3** (*affluenza*) gathering; **concorso di circostanze** combination of circumstances

concretamente [konkreta'mente] AVV concretely

concretare [konkre'tare] VT (*attuare*) to put into practice
▶ **concretarsi** VIP (*attuarsi*) to materialize, be realized

concretezza [konkre'tettsa] SF concreteness

concretizzare [konkretid'dzare] VT = **concretare**

concreto, a [kon'krɛto] AGG (*gen*) concrete; (*vantaggi*) positive; **una prova concreta** concrete evidence
■ SM: **in concreto** in reality; **ma cosa fa in concreto?** what's he actually doing?; **fare qualcosa di concreto** to get something concrete done

concubina [konku'bina] SF concubine

concubinato [konkubi'nato] SM concubinage

concubino, a [konku'bino] SM/F: **sono concubini** (*scherz*) they are living together

concupire [konku'pire] VT to lust after

concupiscente [konkupiʃ'ʃɛnte] AGG (*letter*) concupiscent

concupiscenza [konkupiʃ'ʃɛntsa] SF lust, concupiscence

concussione [konkus'sjone] SF (*Dir*) extortion

> **LO SAPEVI...?**
> **concussione** non si traduce mai con *concussion*

condanna [kon'danna] SF **1** (*Dir*: *sentenza*) sentence; **scontare una condanna** to serve a sentence; **ha già avuto due condanne per furto** he has two previous convictions for theft; **condanna a morte** death sentence **2** (*disapprovazione*) condemnation

condannabile [kondan'nabile] AGG (*biasimevole*) open to censure

condannare [kondan'nare] VT **1** (*Dir*): **condannare (a)** to sentence (to); **condannare qn a 5 anni di prigione** to sentence sb to 5 years' imprisonment; **l'hanno condannato a cinque anni di prigione** he's been sentenced to five years in prison; **condannare qn per** to convict sb of; **condannare qn per rapina a mano armata** to convict sb *o* find sb guilty of armed robbery; **li hanno condannati per rapina a mano armata** they were convicted of armed robbery; **è condannato al letto** he is confined to bed **2** (*disapprovare*) to condemn, censure; **non me la sento di condannarlo** I don't condemn him

condannato, a [kondan'nato] SM/F prisoner, convict

condensa [kon'dɛnsa] SF condensation

condensare [konden'sare] VT
▶ **condensarsi** VIP to condense

condensato, a [konden'sato] AGG (*denso*) condensed; (*riassunto*) summarized; **latte condensato** condensed milk
■ SM (*di bugie, errori*) heap

condensatore [kondensa'tore] SM condenser, capacitor

condensazione [kondensat'tsjone] SF condensation

condimento [kondi'mento] SM (*di insalata*) dressing; (*di carne*) seasoning; (*salsa*) sauce

condire [kon'dire] VT (*cibo*) to season, flavour; (*insalata*) to dress; (*fig*) to spice, season; **una salsa per condire la pasta** a sauce for pasta; **hai condito la pasta?** have you mixed the sauce with the pasta?

condirettore, trice [kondiret'tore] SM/F (*gen*) joint manager/manageress; (*di giornale*) co-editor

condiscendente [kondiʃʃen'dɛnte] AGG (*indulgente*) obliging; (*arrendevole*) compliant

condiscendenza [kondiʃʃen'dɛntsa] SF (*disponibilità*) obligingness; (*arrendevolezza*) compliance

condiscendere [kondiʃ'ʃendere] VI IRREG (*aus* **avere**) **condiscendere a** to agree to

condiscepolo, a [kondiʃ'ʃepolo] SM/F fellow disciple

condisceso, a [kondiʃ'ʃeso] PP *di* **condiscendere**

condividere [kondi'videre] VT IRREG to share; **condivide l'appartamento con il fratello** he shares the flat with his brother; **condividere l'opinione di qn** to agree with sb; **non condivido le tue opinioni** I don't agree with you

condiviso, a [kondi'vizo] PP *di* **condividere**

condizionale [kondittsjo'nale] AGG (*Gramm*) conditional
■ SM (*Gramm*) conditional (mood)
■ SF **1** (*Gramm*) conditional clause **2** (*Dir*) suspended sentence

condizionamento [kondittsjona'mento] SM conditioning; **condizionamento d'aria** air conditioning

condizionare [kondittsjo'nare] VT (*gen, Psic*) to condition

condizionatamente [kondittsjonata'mente] AVV conditionally

Cc

condizionato, a [kondittsjo'nato] AGG conditioned; **ad aria condizionata** air-conditioned
condizionatore [kondittsjona'tore] SM: **condizionatore (d'aria)** air conditioner
condizione [kondit'tsjone] SF **1** (*stato*) condition; **in buone condizioni** in good condition; **la macchina è ancora in buone condizioni** the car is still in good condition; **in condizioni pessime** in a very bad state, in poor condition; **condizioni di salute** state of health; **migliorare le proprie condizioni finanziarie** to improve one's financial position; **non sei in condizione di guidare** you're not in a fit state to drive; **condizioni di lavoro** working conditions **2** (*situazione*) situation; **essere** *o* **trovarsi in condizione di fare qc** to be in a position to do sth; **mettere qn in condizione di fare qc** to make it possible for sb to do sth; **mi trovo in una condizione assurda** I'm in an absurd situation **3** (*di patto*) condition; (*di contratto*) condition, term; (*di pagamento*) term, condition; **porre una condizione** to lay down *o* make a condition; **ad un'unica condizione** on one condition; **lo farò ad una sola condizione** I'll do it on one condition; **non lo farò a nessuna condizione** on no account will I do it; **a condizione che** on condition that, provided that; **condizioni a convenirsi** terms to be arranged; **condizioni di vendita** sales terms
condoglianze [kondoʎ'ʎantse] SFPL condolences; **fare le proprie condoglianze a qn** to offer one's sympathy *o* condolences to sb
condominiale [kondomi'njale] AGG: **riunione condominiale** residents' meeting; **spese condominiali** common charges
condominio, nii [kondo'minjo] SM (*Dir*) condominium, joint ownership; (*edificio*) jointly-owned block of flats (*Brit*), condominium (*Am*)
condomino [kon'domino] SM joint owner
condonare [kondo'nare] VT (*Dir*) to remit
condono [kon'dono] SM (*Dir*) remission; **condono edilizio** *conditional amnesty for work done without planning permission*; **condono fiscale** *conditional amnesty for people evading tax*; **condono tombale** tax amnesty (*for all past offences*)
condor ['kɔndor] SM INV condor
condotta [kon'dotta] SF **1** (*comportamento*) conduct, behaviour (*Brit*), behavior (*Am*); (*di un affare ecc*) handling; **tenere una buona/cattiva condotta** to behave well/badly **2** (*Amm: di medico*) *country medical practice controlled by a local authority* **3** (*Tecn: tubature*) piping
condottiero [kondot'tjɛro] SM (mercenary) leader; (*Storia*) condottiere
condotto, a PP *di* **condurre**
■AGG: **medico condotto** local authority doctor (*in a country district*)
■SM **1** (*Anat*) duct; **condotto uditivo** auditory canal **2** (*Tecn: di liquido*) pipe, conduit; (: *di aria*) duct
conducente [kondu'tʃɛnte] SM/F driver; **il conducente dell'autobus** the bus driver
conducibilità [kondutʃibili'ta] SF = **conduttività**
conduco *ecc* [kon'duko] VB *vedi* **condurre**
condurre [kon'durre] VB IRREG
■VT **1** (*persona: accompagnare*) to take; (: *guidare*) to lead; **condurre qn a casa** (*a piedi*) to walk sb home; (*in macchina*) to drive *o* take sb home; **mi ha condotto a casa** he took me home; **condurre qn per mano** to take sb by the hand; **condurre alla vittoria** to lead to victory; **condurre in salvo qn** to lead sb to safety; **condurre qn alla follia** to drive sb mad; **questo ci conduce a pensare che...** this leads us to think that ... **2** (*azienda, affari*) to run, manage; (*trattative*) to hold, conduct; (*orchestra*) to conduct; **condurre (la gara)** (*Sport*) to lead, be in the lead; **condurre a termine** to conclude **3** (*automobile*) to drive; (*aereo*) to pilot; (*barca*) to steer **4** (*trasportare: acqua, gas*) to convey **5** (*Fis*) to conduct
▶ **condursi** VR to behave, conduct o.s.
condussi *ecc* [kon'dussi] VB *vedi* **condurre**
conduttività [konduttivi'ta] SF (*Fis*) conductivity
conduttivo, a [kondut'tivo] AGG (*Fis*) conductive
conduttore, trice [kondut'tore] AGG: **filo conduttore** (*fig*) thread; **motivo conduttore** leitmotiv
■SM **1** (*Fis*) conductor **2** (*di mezzi pubblici*) driver
conduttura [kondut'tura] SF (*gen*) pipe; (*di acqua, gas*) main
conduzione [kondut'tsjone] SF **1** (*di affari, ditta*) management; **a conduzione familiare** (*ditta*) family-run **2** (*Dir: locazione*) lease **3** (*Fis*) conduction
confabulare [konfabu'lare] VI (*aus* **avere**) to confab
confabulazione [konfabulat'tsjone] SF confab
confacente [konfa'tʃɛnte] AGG: **confacente a qn/qc** suitable for sb/sth; **clima confacente alla salute** healthy climate
CONFAGRICOLTURA [konfagrikol'tura] SIGLA F (= **Confederazione generale dell'agricoltura italiana**) *confederation of Italian farmers*
⊳ www.confagricoltura.it/
CONFAPI [kon'fabi] SIGLA F = *Confederazione italiana della piccola e media industria*
confarsi [kon'farsi] VIP (*essere adatto*): **confarsi a qn/qc** to be suitable for sb/sth, suit sb/sth; **questo modo di parlare non ti si confà** it doesn't become you to speak like that; **questo clima non mi si confà** this climate isn't good for me; **il lavoro non gli si confà** (*scherz*) work doesn't agree with him!
CONFARTIGIANATO [konfartidʒa'nato] SIGLA F = *Confederazione generale dell'artigianato italiano*
⊳ www.confartigianato.it/Default.jsp
CONFCOMMERCIO [konfkom'mɛrtʃo] SIGLA F = *Confederazione Generale del Commercio*
⊳ www.confcommercio.it/
confederale [konfede'rale] AGG confederal
confederarsi [konfede'rarsi] VR to form a confederation
confederativo, a [konfedera'tivo] AGG confederal, confederative
confederato, a [konfede'rato] AGG, SM/F confederate
confederazione [konfederat'tsjone] SF confederacy, confederation; **confederazione imprenditoriale** employers' association
conferenza [konfe'rɛntsa] SF **1** (*discorso*) lecture; **fare** *o* **tenere una conferenza su qc** to give a lecture on sth, lecture on sth; **terrà una conferenza nell'aula magna** he's going to give a lecture in the main hall; **sala conferenze** lecture theatre **2** (*Pol, Amm: riunione*) conference; **una conferenza sull'inquinamento atmosferico** a conference on air pollution; **conferenza stampa** press conference; **conferenza al vertice** summit conference
conferenziere, a [konferen'tsjɛre] SM/F lecturer, speaker
conferimento [konferi'mento] SM conferring, awarding
conferire [konfe'rire] VT: **conferire (a)** (*premio, titolo, incarico*) to confer (on); (*tono, aria*) to give (to)

■VI (*aus* **avere**) **1** (*avere un colloquio*) to confer **2** (*contribuire, giovare*): **conferire a qn/qc** to be good for sb/sth

conferma [kon'ferma] SF confirmation; **dare conferma** to confirm; **a conferma di** in confirmation of

confermare [konfer'mare] VT to confirm; **l'eccezione conferma la regola** the exception proves the rule; **devo confermare la prenotazione** I've got to confirm the booking; **ha confermato che verrà** he's confirmed that he's coming; **si è confermato campione** he has confirmed his position as champion

CONFESERCENTI [konfezer'tʃenti] SIGLA F = *Confederazione degli esercenti attività commerciali e turistiche*
⊳ www.confesercenti.it/

confessabile [konfes'sabile] AGG which can be disclosed

confessare [konfes'sare] VT (*gen*) to confess, admit; (*Rel*) to confess; **ti confesso che...** I must confess that...; **confesso di essere stupito** I must admit I'm amazed; **l'omicida ha confessato** the murderer confessed
▶ **confessarsi** VR **1** (*Rel*): **(andare a) confessarsi** to go to confession **2** **confessarsi colpevole** to admit one's guilt

confessionale [konfessjo'nale] AGG confessional
■SM (*Rel*) confessional (box)

confessione [konfes'sjone] SF **1** (*gen, Rel*) confession **2** (*fede*) denomination

confesso, a [kon'fɛsso] AGG: **essere reo confesso** to have pleaded guilty

confessore [konfes'sore] SM (*Rel*) confessor

confettiera [konfet'tjɛra] SF sweet (*Brit*) *o* candy (*Am*) box, bonbonnière

confetto [kon'fɛtto] SM **1** (*dolciume*) sugared almond; **a quando i confetti?** when are we going to be hearing wedding bells? **2** (*pillola*) pill

confettura [konfet'tura] SF (*gen*) jam; (*di arance*) marmalade

confezionare [konfettsjo'nare] VT **1** (*pacco, merce: involgere*) to wrap up; (*: per vendita*) to package **2** (*articoli di abbigliamento*) to make (up)

confezionato, a [konfettsjo'nato] AGG (*gelato, pollo*) prepacked; (*abiti*) ready-made; **confezionato a mano** hand-made; **confezionato su misura** made to measure

confezione [konfet'tsjone] SF **1** (*gen*) making, preparation; (*di abiti da uomo*) tailoring; (*di abiti da donna*) dressmaking **2** (*imballaggio*) packaging; **una confezione di caramelle** a packet of sweets; **confezione natalizia** Christmas pack; **confezione regalo** gift pack; **fare una confezione regalo** to giftwrap; **mi può fare una confezione regalo?** can you giftwrap it for me?; **confezione risparmio** economy size; **confezione da viaggio** travel pack; **confezioni per signora** ladies' wear *no pl*; **confezioni da uomo** menswear *no pl*

conficcare [konfik'kare] VT: **conficcare in** (*chiodo, punta*) to hammer into, drive into, stick into; (*unghie*) to stick into, dig into; **mi si è conficcata una spina nel dito** a thorn stuck into my finger
▶ **conficcarsi** VIP to stick

confidare [konfi'dare] VT: **confidare qc a qn** to confide sth to sb; **ti voglio confidare un segreto** I want to tell you a secret
■VI (*aus* **avere**) **confidare in** (*persona, capacità ecc*) to have confidence in; **confido nella tua discrezione** I am relying on your discretion; **confido in una buona riuscita** I am confident of a successful outcome;
▶ **confidarsi** VR: **confidarsi con qn** to confide in sb; **aveva bisogno di confidarsi con qualcuno** she needed to confide in somebody

confidente [konfi'dɛnte] AGG confiding, trusting
■SM/F (*persona amica*) confidant/confidante; (*informatore*) informer; **è un confidente della polizia** he is a police informer

confidenza [konfi'dɛntsa] SF **1** (*familiarità*) intimacy, familiarity; **essere in confidenza** *o* **avere confidenza con qn** to be on friendly terms with sb; **prendersi (troppe) confidenze** to take liberties **2** (*rivelazione*) confidence; **fare una confidenza a qn** to confide something to sb; **dire qc in confidenza a qn** to tell sb sth in confidence **3** (*dimestichezza*): **prendere confidenza col proprio lavoro** to become more confident about one's work

confidenziale [konfiden'tsjale] AGG (*lettera, informazione*) confidential; (*maniere, parole*) familiar; **in via confidenziale** confidentially

configurare [konfigu'rare] VT (*Inform*) to set
▶ **configurarsi** VIP (*fig*) to take shape

configurazione [konfigurat'tsjone] SF (*gen*) shape, configuration; (*Astron, Geog*) configuration; (*Inform*) setting

confinante [konfi'nante] AGG neighbouring (*Brit*), neighboring (*Am*)

confinare [konfi'nare] VI (*aus* **avere**) **confinare con** (*anche fig*) to border on; **l'Italia confina ad ovest con la Francia** Italy has a border with France to the west
■VT **1** (*relegare*): **confinare qn in** to confine sb to; **la malattia l'ha confinata in casa** her illness confined her to the house **2** (*Pol*) to intern
▶ **confinarsi** VR (*isolarsi*) **confinarsi in** to shut o.s. up in

confinato, a [konfi'nato] AGG interned
■SM/F internee

CONFINDUSTRIA [konfin'dustrja] SIGLA F (= **Confederazione Generale dell'Industria**) ≈ CBI (*Brit*)
⊳ www.confindustria.it/

confine [kon'fine] SM (*di territorio, nazione*) border, frontier; (*di proprietà*) boundary; **abbiamo passato il confine** we crossed the border; **territorio di confine** border zone; **senza confine** (*fig*) boundless; **i confini della scienza** the frontiers of science

confino [kon'fino] SM (*Pol*) internment; **mandare al confino qn** to send sb into internal exile

confisca [kon'fiska] SF confiscation

confiscare [konfis'kare] VT to confiscate

confiteor [kon'fiteor] SM INV Confiteor

conflagrazione [konflagrat'tsjone] SF (*incendio*) conflagration; (*fig: guerra*) sudden outbreak of hostilities

conflitto [kon'flitto] SM (*gen, Mil*) conflict; (*fig: contrasto*) clash, conflict; **essere in conflitto con qc** to clash with sth; **essere in conflitto con qn** to be at loggerheads with sb; **conflitto d'interessi** conflict of interests

conflittuale [konflittu'ale] AGG: **rapporto conflittuale** relationship based on conflict

conflittualità [konflittuali'ta] SF INV conflicts *pl*

confluenza [konflu'ɛntsa] SF (*di fiumi, fig*) confluence; (*di strade*) junction

confluire [konflu'ire] VI (*aus* **essere** *e* **avere**) (*fiumi*) to meet, flow into each other; (*strade*) to meet; (*fig: idee,*

Cc

persone) to meet, come together
confondere [kon'fondere] VB IRREG
■VT **1** (*mischiare*) to mix up, confuse; **confondere le idee a qn** to mix sb up, confuse sb; **tutti questi discorsi mi confondono le idee** all this talk is getting me confused; **confondere le carte in tavola** (*fig*) to confuse the issue **2** (*scambiare*): **confondere qc con qc** to confuse sth with sth; **confondo sempre i due fratelli** I always get the two brothers mixed up; **non starai confondendo i nomi?** you're not mixing up the names, are you?; **ho confuso le date** I mixed up the dates **3** (*turbare*) to confuse; (*imbarazzare*) to embarrass; (*disorientare*: *nemico, avversario*) to trick
▶ **confondersi** VIP **1** (*colori, sagoma*) to merge; (*ricordi*) to become confused; (*persona*): **confondersi tra la folla** to mingle with the crowd **2** (*sbagliarsi*) to be mistaken, get mixed up; **no, scusa, mi sono confuso: era ieri** no, sorry, I've got mixed up: it was yesterday **3** (*turbarsi*) to become confused
conformare [konfor'mare] VT: **conformare (a)** (*adeguare*) to adapt (to)
▶ **conformarsi** VR: **conformarsi (a)** to conform (to)
conformazione [konformat'tsjone] SF conformation
conforme [kon'forme] AGG: **conforme a** (*simile*) similar to; (*corrispondente*) in keeping with
conformemente [konforme'mente] AVV accordingly; **conformemente a** in accordance with, according to
conformismo [konfor'mizmo] SM conformity
conformista [konfor'mista] SM/F (*gen*) conformist
conformità [konformi'ta] SF conformity; **in conformità a** in conformity with
confortante [konfor'tante] AGG comforting
confortare [konfor'tare] VT **1** (*consolare*) to comfort, console; **mi conforta sapere...** I'm glad to know ... **2** (*tesi, accusa*) to strengthen, support
confortevole [konfor'tevole] AGG (*comodo*) comfortable; (*confortante*) comforting
conforto [kon'fɔrto] SM **1** (*consolazione, sollievo*) comfort, consolation; **i conforti (religiosi)** the last sacraments **2** (*conferma*) support; **a conforto di qc** in support of sth
confratello [konfra'tɛllo] SM (*Rel*) brother
confraternita [konfra'tɛrnita] SF brotherhood
confrontabile [konfron'tabile] AGG comparable
confrontare [konfron'tare] VT (*paragonare*) to compare; **abbiamo confrontato le nostre scuole** we compared our schools
▶ **confrontarsi** VR (*scontrarsi*) to have a confrontation

> **LO SAPEVI...?**
> **confrontare** non si traduce mai con *confront*

confronto [kon'fronto] SM **1** (*paragone*) comparison; (*Dir, Mil, Pol*) confrontation; **a confronto di** *o* **in confronto a** compared with *o* to, in comparison with *o* to; **mettere a confronto** to compare; (*Dir*) to confront; **fare un confronto fra due cose** to compare two things; **non c'è confronto!** there's no comparison!; **senza confronti** beyond comparison; **reggere al confronto con** to stand comparison with; **confronto all'americana** (*Dir*) identity parade **2** (*di testi*) collation **3 nei miei (*o* tuoi *ecc*) confronti** towards me (*o* you *ecc*); **non ho risentimento nei suoi confronti** I don't feel any resentment towards him
confucianesimo [konfutʃa'nezimo] SM Confucianism
confusamente [konfuza'mente] AVV (*distinguere, vedere*) vaguely; (*capire*) in a confused way, vaguely; (*parlare*) confusedly; (: *timidamente*) in an embarrassed way
confusi *ecc* [kon'fuzi] VB *vedi* **confondere**
confusionale [konfuzjo'nale] AGG: **stato confusionale** (*Med*) confused state
confusionario, ria, ri, rie [konfuzjo'narjo] AGG muddle-headed
■SM/F muddle-headed person
confusione [konfu'zjone] SF (*disordine, errore*) confusion; (*chiasso*) racket, noise; (*imbarazzo*) embarrassment; **c'è stata confusione tra i due nomi** there's been a mix-up over the two names, the two names have been confused; **ha approfittato della confusione per scappare** he took advantage of the confusion to escape; **che confusione!** what a mess!; **far confusione** (*disordine*) to make a mess; (*chiasso*) to make a racket; (*confondere*) to confuse things; **essere in uno stato di confusione mentale** to be confused in one's mind
confuso, a [kon'fuzo] PP *di* **confondere**
■AGG (*gen*) confused; (*discorso, stile*) muddled; (*persona*: *turbato*) embarrassed; (*immagine, ricordo*) hazy; **sono un po' confuso** I'm a bit confused; **la situazione è ancora confusa** the situation is still confused
confutare [konfu'tare] VT to confute, refute
confutazione [konfutat'tsjone] SF confutation, refutation
congedando [kondʒe'dando] SM (*Mil*) serviceman about to be discharged
congedare [kondʒe'dare] VT (*gen*) to dismiss; (*Mil*: *soldati*) to demobilize; (*licenziare*) to sack; **congedare per invalidità** to invalid out
▶ **congedarsi** VR: **congedarsi (da)** to take one's leave (of); (*soldato*) to be demobilized (from)
congedo [kon'dʒɛdo] SM **1** (*permesso, Mil*) leave; **andare in congedo** to go on leave; **chiedere un congedo per motivi di salute** to apply for sick leave; **congedo assoluto** (*Mil*) discharge; **congedo parentale** parental leave **2** (*commiato*): **prendere congedo da qn** to take one's leave of sb **3** (*Teatro*: *finale*) finale; (*Poesia*: *coda*) envoy
congegnare [kondʒeɲ'ɲare] VT (*motore*) to construct, put together; (*fig*: *trama, scherzo*) to devise
congegno [kon'dʒeɲɲo] SM (*dispositivo*) device; (*meccanismo*) mechanism
congelamento [kondʒela'mento] SM (*gen*) freezing; (*Med*) frostbite; **congelamento dei prezzi** (*Econ*) price freeze; **congelamento salariale** wage freeze
congelare [kondʒe'lare] VT (*gen, Econ*) to freeze
▶ **congelarsi** VIP to freeze

> **LO SAPEVI...?**
> **congelare** non si traduce mai con *congeal*

congelato, a [kondʒe'lato] AGG (*gen, Econ*) frozen; **sono congelato!** I'm frozen!
congelatore [kondʒela'tore] AGG freezer *attr*
■SM (*macchina*) deepfreeze, freezer
congelazione [kondʒelat'tsjone] SF = **congelamento**
congeniale [kondʒe'njale] AGG congenial
congenialità [kondʒenjali'ta] SF congeniality
congenito, a [kon'dʒɛnito] AGG congenital
congerie [kon'dʒɛrje] SF INV (*di oggetti*) heap; (*di idee*) muddle, jumble
congestionare [konʒestjo'nare] VT (*Med, strada*) to congest; **essere congestionato** (*persona, viso*) to be flushed; (*zona*: *per traffico*) to be congested
congestione [kondʒes'tjone] SF congestion
congettura [kondʒet'tura] SF conjecture,

supposition; **fare mille congetture** to let one's imagination run riot

congetturare [kondʒettu'rare] VT to conjecture

congiungere [kon'dʒundʒere] VB IRREG
■ VT (*gen*) to join (together); (*punti*) to join, connect; (*luoghi*) to link, connect; **il ponte congiunge l'isoletta alla terraferma** the bridge links the island to the mainland;
▶ **congiungersi** VIP (*gen*) to join (together); (*Mil*) to join forces; **congiungersi in matrimonio** to be joined in matrimony

congiungimento [kondʒundʒi'mento] SM (*di punti*) joining, connecting, linking; (*di luoghi*) connecting; **mettere in atto un congiungimento** (*Mil*) to join forces

congiuntivite [kondʒunti'vite] SF (*Med*) conjunctivitis; **ha la congiuntivite** she's got conjunctivitis

congiuntivo, a [kondʒun'tivo] AGG, SM (*Gramm*) subjunctive

congiunto, a [kon'dʒunto] PP *di* **congiungere**
■ AGG (*mani*) clasped, joined; (*azione, sforzo*) joint
■ SM/F (*parente*) relative

congiuntura [kondʒun'tura] SF **1** (*punto di contatto*) join, junction; (*Anat*) joint **2** (*circostanza*) juncture, circumstance; (*opportunità*) occasion; **in questa congiuntura** at this juncture **3** (*Econ*) economic situation; **superare la (bassa) congiuntura** to overcome the economic crisis

congiunturale [kondʒuntu'rale] AGG of the economic situation; **crisi congiunturale** economic crisis

congiunzione [kondʒun'tsjone] SF (*gen*) join; (*Anat*) joint; (*di due linee ferroviarie*) junction; (*Astron, Gramm*) conjunction

congiura [kon'dʒura] SF (*anche fig*) conspiracy, plot

congiurare [kondʒu'rare] VI (*aus* **avere**) **congiurare (ai danni di** *o* **contro qn)** to conspire (against sb), plot (against sb); **tutto sembra congiurare contro di me** everything seems to be conspiring against me

LO SAPEVI...?
congiurare non si traduce mai con *conjure*

congiurato, a [kondʒu'rato] SM/F conspirator

conglobare [konglo'bare] VT to merge

conglomerare [konglome'rare] VT (*gen*) to amass

conglomerato [konglome'rato] SM (*gen*) conglomeration; (*Geol*) conglomerate; (*Edil*) concrete

Congo ['kɔngo] SM (*paese, fiume*) the Congo

congolese [kongo'lese] AGG, SM/F Congolese *inv*

congratularsi [kongratu'larsi] VIP: **congratularsi con qn (per qc)** to congratulate sb (on sth)

congratulazioni [kongratulat'tsjoni] SFPL congratulations; **congratulazioni per la promozione!** congratulations on your promotion!; **fare le (proprie) congratulazioni a qn per qc** to congratulate sb on sth

congrega, ghe [kon'grɛga] SF gang, band, bunch

congregazionalismo [kongregattsjona'lizmo] SM Congregationalism

congregazione [kongregat'tsjone] SF congregation

congressista, i, e [kongres'sista] SM/F participant at a congress

congresso [kon'grɛsso] SM congress; **sala (dei) congressi** conference hall; **il congresso del partito socialista** the Socialist Party conference

congressuale [kongressu'ale] AGG congressional

congruamente [kongrua'mente] AVV (*pagare, rimunerare*) fairly, suitably

congruente [kongru'ɛnte] AGG congruent

congruenza [kongru'ɛntsa] SF coherence

congruo, a ['kɔngruo] AGG (*prezzo, compenso*) adequate, fair; (*ragionamento*) coherent, consistent

conguagliare [kongwaʎ'ʎare] VT (*Comm*) to balance; (*stipendio*) to adjust

conguaglio, gli [kon'gwaʎʎo] SM **1** (*vedi vb*) balancing; adjusting **2** (*somma di denaro*) balance

CONI ['koni] SIGLA M = *Comitato Olimpico Nazionale Italiano*

coniare [ko'njare] VT (*monete*) to mint; (*medaglie*) to strike; (*fig: parole nuove*) to coin

coniazione [konjat'tsjone] SF (*vedi vb*) minting; striking; coining

conico, a, ci, che ['kɔniko] AGG conic(al), cone-shaped

conifera [ko'nifera] SF conifer

coniglia [ko'niʎʎa] SF (doe) rabbit

conigliera [koniʎ'ʎɛra] SF (*gabbia*) rabbit hutch; (*più grande*) rabbit run

coniglietta [koniʎ'ʎetta] SF (*fam*) bunny girl

coniglietto [koniʎ'ʎetto] SM bunny

coniglio, gli [ko'niʎʎo] SM (*Zool*) rabbit; (*maschio*) buck; **pelliccia di coniglio** rabbit fur; **sei un coniglio!** (*fig*) you're chicken!

conio, nii ['kɔnjo] SM **1** (*punzone*) minting die **2** (*impronta*) stamp; **moneta di nuovo conio** newly-minted coin **3** (*invenzione*) coining; **parole di nuovo conio** newly-coined words

coniugale [konju'gale] AGG (*amore, diritti*) conjugal; (*vita*) married, conjugal

coniugare [konju'gare] VT **1** (*Gramm*) to conjugate **2** (*far coesistere*) to combine; **coniugare lo sviluppo industriale con il rispetto dell'ambiente** to combine industrial development with respect for the environment

coniugato, a [konju'gato] AGG (*Amm*) married

coniugazione [konjugat'tsjone] SF (*Gramm*) conjugation

coniuge ['kɔnjudʒe] SM/F spouse; **i doveri di un coniuge** the duties of a spouse; **i coniugi** the couple, the husband and wife; **una coppia di coniugi** a married couple; **i coniugi Bianchi** Mr and Mrs Bianchi

connaturale [konnatu'rale] AGG: **connaturale a qn/qc** natural to sb/sth

connaturarsi [konnatu'rarsi] VIP (*abitudine, vizio*): **connaturarsi in qn** to become second nature to sb

connaturato, a [konnatu'rato] AGG inborn

connazionale [konnattsjo'nale] AGG of the same country
■ SM/F compatriot, fellow-countryman/woman

Connecticut [kon'nektikat] SM Connecticut

connessione [konnes'sjone] SF connection; (*Inform: a Internet*) connection; **connessione di idee** association of ideas; **connessione remota** (*Inform*) remote connection

connesso, a [kon'nɛsso] PP *di* **connettere**
■ AGG connected

connettere [kon'nɛttere] VT IRREG **1** (*uso assoluto: ragionare*) to think straight; **la mattina non riesco a connettere** I can't think straight in the morning **2** **connettere (a)** (*gen, fig*) to connect (with), link (to); (*Elettr*) to connect (with); **non avevo connesso i due fatti** I hadn't connected the two facts

connettivo, a [konnet'tivo] AGG: **tessuto connettivo** connective tissue

connettore [konnet'tore] SM (*Elettr*) connector

Cc

connivente [konni'vɛnte] AGG: **essere connivente (in qc con qn)** to connive (at sth with sb)
connivenza [konni'vɛntsa] SF (*Dir*) connivance
connotare [konno'tare] VT to connote
connotati [konno'tati] SMPL distinguishing marks; **dare i connotati di qn** to give a description of sb; **rispondere ai connotati** to fit the description; **cambiare i connotati a qn** (*fam*) to beat sb up
connotativo, a [konnota'tivo] AGG connotative
connotazione [konnotat'tsjone] SF connotation
connubio, bi [kon'nubjo] SM (*matrimonio*) marriage; (*fig*) union
cono ['kɔno] SM (*in tutti i sensi*) cone; **un cono al cioccolato** a chocolate cone; **cono gelato** ice-cream cone
conobbi *ecc* [ko'nobbi] VB *vedi* **conoscere**
conoide [ko'nɔide] SM (*Geom*) conoid
conoscente [konoʃ'ʃɛnte] SM/F acquaintance; **una mia conoscente** an acquaintance of mine
conoscenza [konoʃ'ʃɛntsa] SF **1** (*sapere, nozione*) knowledge *no pl*; (*Filosofia*) cognition; **essere a conoscenza di qc** to know sth; **venire a conoscenza di qc** to get to know sth, learn of sth; **portare qn a conoscenza di qc** to inform sb of sth; **la polizia è venuta a conoscenza del fatto che...** it has come to the knowledge of the police that ...; **le mie conoscenze in questo campo** my knowledge in this field; **per vostra conoscenza** for your information; **prendere conoscenza di qc** (*Dir, Amm*) to take cognizance of sth; **conoscenza tecnica** know-how **2** (*amicizia, persona*) acquaintance; **fare la conoscenza di qn** to make sb's acquaintance; **lieto di fare la sua conoscenza** pleased to meet you; **ha ottenuto il lavoro grazie alle sue conoscenze** she got the job because of her contacts **3** (*sensi, coscienza*) consciousness; **perdere/riprendere conoscenza** to lose/regain consciousness
conoscere [ko'noʃʃere] VB IRREG
■ VT **1** (*gen*) to know; (*persona, avvenimento*) to be acquainted with, know; (*testo, abitudine*) to be familiar with, know; (*posto, ristorante*) to know of; **conoscere qn di vista** to know sb by sight; **lo conosco solo di vista** I only know him by sight; **l'ha conosciuto all'università** she met him at university; **conosci i motori?** do you know anything about engines?; **non conosco bene la città** I don't know the town well; **conosco la canzone** (*fig*) I've heard it all before; **conosce il fatto suo** he knows what he's talking about; **non conosce il mondo** he isn't very worldly-wise **2** (*successo*) to enjoy, have; (*privazioni*) to know, experience; **conoscere tempi difficili** to go through hard times **3** **far conoscere qn/qc** to make sb/sth known; **ti farò conoscere mio marito** I'll introduce you to my husband; **mi ha fatto conoscere la musica classica** he introduced me to classical music; **farsi conoscere** (*fig*) to make a name for o.s. **4** (*riconoscere*): **conoscere qn dalla voce** to recognize sb by his voice
▶ **conoscersi** VR **1** (*se stessi*) to know o.s. **2** (*uso reciproco*) to know each other; (*: incontrarsi*) to meet; **si sono conosciuti un anno fa** they (first) met a year ago; **ci siamo conosciuti in vacanza** we met on holiday; **da quanto vi conoscete?** how long have you known one another?; **ci conosciamo da poco tempo** we haven't known each other long
conoscitivo, a [konoʃʃi'tivo] AGG cognitive
conoscitore, trice [konoʃʃi'tore] SM/F connoisseur
conosciuto, a [konoʃ'ʃuto] PP *di* **conoscere**
■ AGG (*universo*) known; (*attore, autore, artista*) well-known; **un attore conosciuto** a well-known actor; **conosciuto in tutto il mondo** well-known throughout the world, world-famous
conquista [kon'kwista] SF (*anche fig*) conquest; **partire alla conquista di qc** to set out to conquer sth; **le conquiste della scienza** the achievements of science
conquistare [konkwis'tare] VT (*territorio, fortezza*) to conquer; (*felicità, successo, ricchezza*) to gain; (*simpatia, fiducia*) to win, gain; (*cuore*) to win over; **si è conquistato la simpatia di tutti** he's made himself popular with everybody
conquistatore, trice [konkwista'tore] AGG (*esercito, truppe*) conquering
■ SM (*in guerra*) conqueror; (*seduttore*) lady-killer
cons. ABBR = **consiglio**
consacrare [konsa'krare] VT **1** (*Rel*) to consecrate; (*: sacerdote*) to ordain; (*: re*) to anoint; (*abitudine, tradizione, uso*) to establish **2** (*vita, tempo, sforzi*): **consacrare (a)** to dedicate (to), devote (to)
▶ **consacrarsi** VR (*dedicarsi*): **consacrarsi a qn/qc** to dedicate o.s. to sb/sth
consacrazione [konsakrat'tsjone] SF (*Rel: vedi vb*) consecration; ordination; anointing
consanguineità [konsangwinei'ta] SF consanguinity, blood relationship
consanguineo, a [konsan'gwineo] AGG related by blood
■ SM/F blood relation
consapevole [konsa'pevole] AGG: **consapevole di qc** aware *o* conscious of sth; **rendere qn consapevole di qc** to make sb aware of sth
consapevolezza [konsapevo'lettsa] SF awareness, consciousness; **acquistare consapevolezza di qc** to become aware *o* conscious of sth
consapevolmente [konsapevol'mente] AVV consciously; **l'ha fatto consapevolmente** he was fully aware of what he was doing
consciamente [konʃa'mente] AVV consciously; **non l'ha fatto consciamente** he didn't know what he was doing
conscio, a, sci, sce ['kɔnʃo] AGG: **conscio (di)** aware (of), conscious (of); **è conscio dei suoi limiti** he is aware of *o* knows his limitations
■ SM (*Psic*): **il conscio** the conscious
consecutiva [konseku'tiva] SF (*Gramm*) consecutive clause
consecutivo, a [konseku'tivo] AGG (*Gramm, senza interruzione*) consecutive; (*successivo: giorno*) following, next; **per tre giorni consecutivi** for three consecutive days; **consecutivo a** following upon
consegna [kon'seɲɲa] SF **1** (*Comm: il consegnare*) delivery; (*: merce consegnata*) consignment; **la consegna è garantita in giornata** same-day delivery is guaranteed; **alla consegna** on delivery; **si può pagare alla consegna** you can pay on delivery; **pagamento alla consegna** cash on delivery; **consegna in contrassegno** cash on delivery; **consegna a domicilio** home delivery; **consegna sollecita** prompt delivery **2** (*custodia*) care; **prendere in consegna qn** (*bambino*) to take sb into one's care; (*prigioniero*) to take custody of sb; **prendere qc in consegna** to take sth into safekeeping; **dare qc in consegna a qn** to give sth to sb for safekeeping, entrust sth to sb **3** (*Mil: ordine*) orders *pl*; (*: punizione*) confinement to barracks; **un soldato fedele alla consegna** a soldier who obeys

orders; **passare le consegne a qn** to hand over to sb

consegnare [konseɲ'ɲare] VT **1 consegnare qc (a qn)** (*lettera, pacco, merce*) to deliver sth (to sb); (*lavoro finito*) to hand sth in (to sb), submit sth (to sb); **mi hanno consegnato il pacco stamattina** the parcel was delivered this morning; **il meccanico non mi ha ancora consegnato la macchina** I haven't had the car back from the mechanic yet; **consegnare qn alla polizia** to hand sb over to the police **2** (*Mil: soldato*) to confine to barracks

consegnatario, ria, ri, rie [konseɲɲa'tarjo] SM/F consignee

consegnato [konseɲ'ɲato] SM (*Mil*) soldier confined to barracks

conseguente [konse'gwɛnte] AGG consequent

conseguentemente [konsegwente'mente] AVV (*come conseguenza*) consequently; (*comportarsi*) consistently

conseguenza [konse'gwɛntsa] SF consequence; **di** *o* **per conseguenza** consequently; **senza lasciare conseguenze** without having any effect; **pagare le conseguenze** to pay the consequences; **non aveva pensato alle conseguenze** he hadn't thought of the consequences

conseguibile [konse'gwibile] AGG achievable, attainable

conseguimento [konsegwi'mento] SM (*di scopo, risultato*) achievement, attainment; **al conseguimento della laurea** on graduation

conseguire [konse'gwire] VT (*scopo*) to achieve, attain; (*vittoria*) to gain; **conseguire la laurea** to graduate, obtain one's degree
■ VI (*aus essere*) (*derivare*): **ne consegue che...** it follows that ...

consenso [kon'sɛnso] SM (*permesso*) consent; (*approvazione*) approval; **dare/negare il proprio consenso a qc** to give/refuse one's consent to sth; **per consenso unanime** unanimously; **consenso informato** informed consent

consensuale [konsensu'ale] AGG (*Dir*) by mutual consent

consensualmente [konsenswal'mente] AVV: **separarsi consensualmente** to separate by mutual consent

consentire [konsen'tire] VI (*aus avere*) **consentire a qc/a fare qc** to agree *o* consent to sth/to do sth
■ VT: **consentire a qn qc/di fare qc** to allow *o* permit sb sth/to do sth; **è un lavoro che non consente distrazioni** you can't afford to be distracted in this kind of job; **mi si consenta di ringraziare...** I would like to thank ...

consenziente [konsen'tsjɛnte] AGG (*gen, Dir*) consenting

consequenziale [konsekwen'tsjale] AGG consequential

conserto, a [kon'sɛrto] AGG: **a braccia conserte** with one's arms folded

conserva [kon'sɛrva] SF: **mettere cibi in conserva** to preserve food; **conserva di frutta** jam, preserve; **conserva di pomodoro** tomato purée; **conserve alimentari** tinned (*Brit*) *o* canned (*Am*) *o* bottled foods

conservante [konser'vante] SM (*per alimenti*) preservative

conservare [konser'vare] VT **1** (*gen*) to keep; (*andatura, velocità*) to maintain; **lo conservo in una scatola** I keep it in a box; **conservare la calma** to keep calm; **conservare il proprio sangue freddo** (*fig*) to keep one's head; **conservo sempre un buon ricordo di lui** I still have fond memories of him **2** (*monumenti*) to preserve **3** (*Culin*) to preserve; (: *in frigo*) to keep; **conservare le cipolline sott'aceto** to pickle onions; **conservare i pomodori in bottiglia** to bottle tomatoes
▶ **conservarsi** VIP (*cibo*) to keep; **si conserva bene per alcune settimane** it keeps well for several weeks; **conservarsi in buona salute** to keep healthy; **si conserva bene** (*persona*) he (*o* she) is well-preserved

conservatore, trice [konserva'tore] AGG (*gen, Pol*) conservative; **il partito Conservatore** the Conservative Party
■ SM/F **1** (*di museo*) curator; (*di biblioteca*) librarian; (*di archivio*) keeper **2** (*Pol*) Conservative

conservatorio, ri [konserva'tɔrjo] SM (*di musica*) conservatory; **studio al conservatorio** I'm at music school

conservatorismo [konservato'rizmo] SM (*Pol*) conservatism

conservazione [konservat'tsjone] SF **1** (*di cibi, monumenti*) preservation; **in buono stato di conservazione** well-preserved; **istinto di conservazione** instinct of self-preservation; **a lunga conservazione** (*latte, panna*) long-life *attr* **2** (*di energia, dell'ambiente naturale*) conservation

conserviero, a [konser'vjɛro] AGG: **industria conserviera** canning industry

consesso [kon'sɛsso] SM (*assemblea*) assembly; (*riunione*) meeting

considerabile [konside'rabile] AGG worthy of consideration

considerare [konside'rare] VT **1** (*gen*) to consider, regard; **considerato che...** considering that ...; **giochi bene, considerato che hai cominciato da poco** you play well, considering that you only started recently; **tutto considerato** all things considered; **tutto considerato non è male** it's not bad, all things considered; **ti considero un amico** I think of you as *o* consider you a friend; **bisogna considerare i pro e i contro** you have to consider the pros and cons; **considerare un onore fare qc** to consider it an honour to do sth **2** (*stimare*): **considerare molto qn** to think highly of sb **3** (*Dir: contemplare*): **la legge non considera questo caso** the law does not provide for this case
▶ **considerarsi** VR: **considerarsi un genio** to consider o.s. a genius; **si considerano amici** they consider themselves friends; **puoi considerarti fortunato!** you can think yourself lucky!; **si considera il migliore** he thinks he's the best

consideratamente [konsiderata'mente] AVV cautiously, carefully

considerato, a [konside'rato] AGG **1** (*stimato*) highly thought of, esteemed **2** (*prudente*) cautious, careful

considerazione [konsiderat'tsjone] SF **1** (*esame, riflessione*) consideration; **agire senza considerazione** to act rashly; **voglio che tu agisca con considerazione** I'd like you to think carefully about what you're doing; **meritare considerazione** to be worthy of consideration; **prendere qn/qc in considerazione** to take sb/sth into consideration **2** (*stima*) esteem, regard; **godere di molta considerazione** to be very highly thought of; **avere (una grande) considerazione per qn** to think highly of sb **3** (*pensiero, osservazione*) observation

considerevole [konside'revole] AGG considerable

Cc

considerevolmente [konsiderevol'mente] AVV considerably

consigliabile [konsiʎ'ʎabile] AGG advisable

consigliare [konsiʎ'ʎare] VT **1** (*raccomandare: ristorante, film, prudenza*): **consigliare (a qn)** to recommend (to sb); **che cosa mi consigli?** what do you recommend?; **ti consiglio la pizza** I'd recommend the pizza **2** (*suggerire*): **consigliare a qn di fare qc** to advise sb to do sth; **si consiglia ai passeggeri di...** passengers are advised to ...; **gli ha consigliato di andarsene prima possibile** she advised him to leave as soon as possible; **ti consiglierei di sbrigarti** I'd advise you to get a move on; **ti consiglio di non accettare l'invito** I advise you not to accept the invitation
▶ **consigliarsi** VIP: **consigliarsi con qn** to ask sb's advice, ask sb for advice; **consigliarsi col proprio avvocato** to consult one's lawyer

consigliere, a [konsiʎ'ʎɛre] SM/F (*gen*) adviser; (*Pol, Amm*) councillor, council member; **consigliere d'amministrazione** (*Comm*) board member; **consigliere comunale** town councillor; **consigliere delegato** (*Comm*) managing director

consiglio, gli [kon'siʎʎo] SM **1** advice *no pl*; **un consiglio** some advice, a piece of advice; **mi ha chiesto un consiglio** she asked me for advice; **ti do due consigli...** I'll give you two bits of advice...; **un consiglio da amico** a friendly piece of advice; **seguire il consiglio** *o* **i consigli di qn** to take sb's advice; **ho seguito i tuoi consigli** I followed your advice **2** (*assemblea*) council; **hanno fatto un consiglio di famiglia** they held a family conference; **consiglio d'amministrazione** board of directors; board; **consiglio comunale** town council (*headed by the sindaco (mayor): it elects the giunta comunale, which is responsible for running a comune*); **Consiglio d'Europa** European Council
▷ www.coe.int/
consiglio di fabbrica works council; **Consiglio dei Ministri**: **il Consiglio dei Ministri** *the Italian Cabinet*; **Consiglio di Sicurezza** Security Council; **Consiglio di stato** *advisory body to the Italian government on administrative matters and their legal implications*; **Consiglio superiore della magistratura** *magistrates' governing body*

CONSIGLI

The **Consiglio dei Ministri**, the Italian Cabinet, is headed by the "Presidente del Consiglio", the Prime Minister, who is the leader of the Government. The **Consiglio superiore della Magistratura**, the magistrates' governing body, ensures their autonomy and independence as enshrined in the Constitution. Chaired by the "Presidente della Repubblica", it mainly deals with appointments and transfers, and can take disciplinary action as required. Of the 30 magistrates elected to the **Consiglio** for a period of four years, 20 are chosen by their fellow magistrates and 10 by Parliament. The "Presidente della Repubblica" and the "Vicepresidente" are ex officio members.
▷ www.palazzochigi.it/

consiliare [konsi'ljare] AGG (*decisione, assemblea*) council *attr*; (*: direzionale*) board *attr*

consimile [kon'simile] AGG similar

consistente [konsis'tɛnte] AGG (*tessuto*) solid; (*fig: prova, testimonianza*) sound; (*somma*) sizeable

LO SAPEVI...?
consistente non si traduce mai con *consistent*

consistenza [konsis'tɛntsa] SF **1** (*di impasto*) consistency; (*di stoffa*) texture **2** (*di sospetti, voci, ragionamenti*): **senza consistenza** ill-founded, groundless; **acquistare consistenza** to gain substance **3** (*Comm*): **consistenza di cassa** cash in hand; **consistenza di magazzino** stock in hand; **consistenza patrimoniale** financial solidity

consistere [kon'sistere] VI IRREG (*aus* **essere**) (*essere composto di*): **consistere di qc** to consist of sth, be made up of sth; (*fondarsi, risiedere in*): **consistere in qc/nel fare qc** to consist in sth/in doing sth; **in che consiste il tuo lavoro?** what does your job entail?

consistito, a [konsis'tito] PP *di* **consistere**

CONSOB ['kɔnsob] SIGLA F (= **Commissione nazionale per le società e la borsa**) *regulatory body for the Italian Stock Exchange*
▷ www.consob.it/

consociarsi [konso'tʃarsi] VR to go into partnership

consociativismo [konsotʃati'vismo] SM (*Pol*) pact-building

consociativo, a [konsotʃa'tivo] AGG (*Pol: democrazia*) based on pacts

consociato, a [konso'tʃato] AGG associated
■ SM/F associate
■ SF associated company

consociazione [konsotʃat'tsjone] SF (*lega*) association

consocio, cia, ci, cie [kon'sɔtʃo] SM/F associate, partner

consolante [konso'lante] AGG consoling, comforting

consolare[1] [konso'lare] VT (*confortare*) to console, comfort; (*rallegrare*) to cheer up; **ho cercato di consolarla un po'** I tried to cheer her up a bit; **se ti può consolare...** if it is of any consolation *o* comfort to you ...
▶ **consolarsi** VIP (*trovare conforto*) to console o.s., be comforted; (*rallegrarsi*) to cheer up; **la vedova si è consolata presto** the widow got over her loss quickly; **il bambino si è consolato vedendo le caramelle** the child cheered up when he saw the sweets

consolare[2] [konso'lare] AGG consular

consolato [konso'lato] SM (*officio*) consulate; (*carica*) consulship; **il consolato italiano** the Italian consulate
▷ www.esteri.it/ita/2_11_6.asp

consolatore, trice [konsola'tore] AGG consoling, comforting

consolazione [konsolat'tsjone] SF **1** comfort, consolation; **l'unica consolazione è che...** the only consolation is that...; **sei la mia unica consolazione** you're my one consolation; **premio di consolazione** consolation prize **2** (*piacere*): **è una consolazione vederlo di nuovo in salute** it's a pleasure *o* joy to see him well again

console ['kɔnsole] SM consul

consolidamento [konsolida'mento] SM consolidation, strengthening; (*Econ*) funding operations *pl*

consolidare [konsoli'dare] VT (*anche fig*) to consolidate, strengthen, reinforce; **consolidare le proprie posizioni** (*Mil*) to consolidate one's position
▶ **consolidarsi** VIP (*Geol*) to consolidate; (*fig: patrimonio, posizione*) to become more stable; **la società si è consolidata** the company has consolidated its position

consolidato, a [konsoli'dato] AGG consolidated; **è**

un'amicizia ormai consolidata it's a firm friendship; **debito consolidato** (*Econ*) funded debt

consolidazione [konsolidat'tsjone] SF consolidation, strengthening

consolle [kon'sɔlle] SF INV console; **consolle di comando** control panel

consommé [kõsɔ'me] SM INV consommé

consonante [konso'nante] SF consonant

consonantico, a, ci, che [konso'nantiko] AGG consonantal

consonanza [konso'nantsa] SF consonance

consono, a ['kɔnsono] AGG: **consono a** consistent with, consonant with

consorella [konso'rɛlla] AGG F sister *attr*

consorte [kon'sɔrte] SM/F (*coniuge*) consort
■ AGG: **principe consorte** prince consort

consorteria [konsorte'ria] SF clique

consorziale [konsor'tsjale] AGG consortium *attr*

consorziarsi [konsor'tsjarsi] VR to form a consortium

consorzio, zi [kon'sɔrtsjo] SM consortium; **consorzio agrario** farmers' cooperative; **consorzio di garanzia** (*Comm*) underwriting syndicate

constare [kon'stare] VI (*aus* **essere**) (*essere composto*): **constare di** to consist of, be composed of, be made up of
■ VB IMPERS (*essere noto*): **mi consta che...** I know that ...; **a quanto mi consta** as far as I know

constatare [konsta'tare] VT DIF **1** (*notare*) to notice, note, observe; **come può constatare** as you can see; **non faccio che constatare** I'm merely making an observation **2** (*verificare*) to establish, verify; (*decesso*) to certify

constatazione [konstatat'tsjone] SF observation; **fare una constatazione** to make an observation; **constatazione amichevole** (*in incidenti stradali*) *jointly-agreed statement for insurance purposes*

consuetamente [konsueta'mente] AVV usually, normally

consueto, a [konsu'ɛto] AGG usual, habitual; **il suo consueto buonumore** his usual good humour
■ SM: **come di consueto** as usual; **più/meno del consueto** more/less than usual

consuetudinario, ria, ri, rie [konsuetudi'narjo] AGG (*abituale*) usual, habitual; **diritto consuetudinario** (*Dir*) common law
■ SM/F (*persona: abitudinario*) creature of habit, lover of routine

consuetudine [konsue'tudine] SF **1** (*abitudine*) habit; (*tradizione*) custom; **è sua consuetudine alzarsi prestissimo** he usually gets up very early, he is in the habit of getting up very early; **secondo la consuetudine** according to custom **2** (*Dir*) common law

consulente [konsu'lɛnte] AGG consulting
■ SM/F (*tecnico, amministrativo*) consultant; **consulente aziendale** management consultant; **consulente legale** legal adviser

consulenza [konsu'lɛntsa] SF (*prestazione professionale*) consultancy; (*consigli*) advice; **chiedere una consulenza** to ask for professional advice; **contratto di consulenza** consultancy agreement; **ufficio di consulenza fiscale** tax consultancy office; **consulenza legale** legal advice; **consulenza medica** medical advice; **consulenza tecnica** technical consultancy *o* advice

consulta [kon'sulta] SF (*riunione*) meeting
⊳ www.giurcost.org/index.php

consultare [konsul'tare] VT (*medico, esperto*) to consult, seek the advice of; (*dizionario*) to look up, consult
▶ **consultarsi** VR (*scambiarsi pareri: uso reciproco*) to confer, consult each other
▶ **consultarsi** VIP (*chiedere consiglio*) **consultarsi con qn** to consult (with) sb, seek the advice of sb

consultazione [konsultat'tsjone] SF consultation; (*Pol*) **consultazioni** SFPL talks, consultations; **dopo lunga consultazione** after much consultation; **libro di consultazione** reference book; **consultazione popolare** referendum

consultivo, a [konsul'tivo] AGG consultative

consulto [kon'sulto] SM (*Med*) consultation

consultorio, ri [konsul'tɔrjo] SM: **consultorio familiare** family planning clinic; **consultorio pediatrico** children's clinic

consumare [konsu'mare] VT **1** (*logorare: scarpe, vestiti*) to wear out; **ho consumato la suola delle scarpe** I've worn the soles of my shoes out **2** (*cibo*) to consume; (*sogg: malattia, passione*) to consume, devour; **desidera consumare i pasti in camera?** (*in albergo*) would you like to have your meals brought up to your room? **3** (*usare: acqua, luce, benzina*) to use; (*finire*) to use up; **quanto consuma questa macchina?** what sort of mileage does this car do?; **la mia moto consuma molto** my motorbike uses a lot of petrol (*Brit*) *o* gas (*Am*) **4** (*Dir: matrimonio*) to consummate
▶ **consumarsi** VIP (*vestiario*) to wear (out); (*candela*) to burn down; (*penna, pennarello*) to run dry; (*persona: per malattia*) to waste away; **consumarsi (di)** to be consumed (with)

consumato, a [konsu'mato] AGG **1** (*vestiti, scarpe, tappeto*) worn **2** (*persona: esperto*) accomplished

consumatore, trice [konsuma'tore] SM/F (*Comm*) consumer

consumazione [konsumat'tsjone] SF **1** (*al bar: bibita*) drink; (*: spuntino*) snack **2** (*Dir: del matrimonio*) consummation

consumismo [konsu'mizmo] SM consumerism

consumista, i, e [konsu'mista] SM/F consumerist

consumistico, a, ci, che [konsu'mistiko] AGG consumer *attr*

consumo [kon'sumo] SM **1** (*gen*) consumption, use; **consumo di benzina** petrol (*Brit*) *o* gas (*Am*) consumption; **fare largo consumo di qc** to use sth heavily; **per mio uso e consumo** for my personal use **2** (*Econ*): **generi** *o* **beni di consumo** consumer goods; **beni di largo consumo** basic commodities; **imposta di consumo** tax on consumer goods; **la società dei consumi** the consumer society

consuntivo, a [konsun'tivo] AGG (*Econ: bilancio*) final
■ SM (*Econ*) final balance; **fare un consuntivo (della situazione)** (*fig*) to take stock (of the situation)

consunto, a [kon'sunto] AGG (*abiti*) worn out, shabby; (*volto*) wasted

consunzione [konsun'tsjone] SF (*Med*) consumption

consuocero, a [kon'swɔtʃero] SM/F son-in-law's *o* daughter-in-law's father/mother

conta ['konta] SF (*nei giochi*): **fare la conta** to see who is going to be 'it'

contabile [kon'tabile] AGG (*Comm*) book-keeping *attr*, accounts *attr*, accounting *attr*; **la situazione contabile** the accounting situation; **i libri contabili** the accounts
■ SM/F book-keeper, accountant

contabilità [kontabili'ta] SF INV (*attività, tecnica*) accounting, accountancy; (*insieme dei libri*) books *pl*,

Cc

accounts *pl*; **tenere la contabilità** to keep the accounts; **(ufficio) contabilità** accounts department; **contabilità finanziaria** financial accounting; **contabilità di gestione** management accounting

contachilometri [kontaki'lɔmetri] SM INV ≈ mileometer (*Brit*), odometer (*Am*)

contadinesco, a, schi, sche [kontadi'nesko] AGG (*campagnolo*) country *attr*; (*pegg*) coarse, oafish

contadino, a [konta'dino] AGG (*di campagna*) country *attr*; (*rurale*) peasant *attr*; **la rivolta contadina** the peasant revolt
■SM/F **1** countryman/woman; (*bracciante*) farm worker; **mio zio è contadino** my uncle works on the land **2** (*Storia, pegg*) peasant
■SM (*fattore*) tenant farmer

contagiare [konta'dʒare] VT (*anche fig*) to infect

contagio, gi [kon'tadʒo] SM **1** infection; (*per contatto diretto*) contagion; **il vaiolo si prende per contagio** smallpox is contracted by touch **2** (*malattia*) disease; (*epidemia*) epidemic

contagiosamente [kontadʒosa'mente] AVV (*vedi agg*) infectiously; contagiously

contagioso, a [konta'dʒoso] AGG (*gen*) infectious; (*per contatto*) contagious; (*fig: riso, allegria*) infectious, contagious; **una malattia contagiosa** an infectious disease; **non preoccuparti, non è contagioso** don't worry, it's not catching

contagiri [konta'dʒiri] SM INV (*Aut*) rev counter

contagocce [konta'gottʃe] SM INV dropper; **mi dà i soldi con il contagocce** he counts every penny he gives me

container [kən'teinə] SM INV container

contaminare [kontami'nare] VT (*gen*) to contaminate; (*buon nome*) to tarnish; (*testo*) to corrupt

contaminazione [kontaminat'tsjone] SF contamination

contaminuti [kontami'nuti] SM INV timer

contante [kon'tante] AGG: **denaro contante** cash
■**contanti** SMPL cash *sg*; **pagare in contanti** to pay cash

contare [kon'tare] VT **1** (*calcolare, enumerare*) to count; **li ho contati, sono quindici** I've counted them, there are fifteen; **le telefonate non si contavano più** I (*o* you *ecc*) couldn't keep count of the telephone calls; **ha sempre i minuti contati** he never has a spare moment; **ha i giorni contati** *or* **ha le ore contate** his days are numbered; **ho i soldi contati** I haven't a penny to spare; **amici così si contano sulla punta delle dita** you can count the number of friends like that on the fingers of one hand **2** (*considerare*) to include, count (in), consider; **senza contare** (*senza includere*) not counting; (*senza parlare di*) not to mention; **eravamo in dieci, senza contare i professori** there were ten of us, not counting the teachers; **contare di fare qc** to intend to do sth, to think of; **contavamo di partire nel pomeriggio** we were thinking of leaving in the afternoon; **conto di essere lì per mezzogiorno** I think I'll be there by midday **3** (*fam: raccontare*) to tell; **contarle grosse** to tell tall stories
■VI (*aus* **avere**) **1** (*calcolare*) to count; **contare fino a 100** to count to 100; **conta fino a cinquanta e poi vieni a cercarci** count to fifty and then come and look for us **2** (*fare assegnamento*): **contare su qn/qc** to count on sb/sth, rely on sb/sth; **sai che puoi contare su di me** you know you can count on me; **puoi contarci** you can count on it **3** (*avere importanza*) to count, matter, be of importance; **la gente che conta** the people who matter; **alla sua festa c'era tutta la Milano che conta** everybody who is anybody in Milan was at her party

contascatti [kontas'katti] SM INV telephone meter

contatore [konta'tore] SM counter; (*della luce*) meter; **contatore del gas** gas meter

contattare [kontat'tare] VT to contact

contatto [kon'tatto] SM **1** (*gen*) contact; **essere/venire a contatto con qc** to be in/come into contact with sth; **a contatto con l'aria** in contact with (the) air; **non sopporto la lana a contatto con la pelle** I can't wear wool next to my skin; **mettere qc a contatto con qc** to put sth against sth; **essere in contatto con qn** to be in touch with sb; **prendere contatto con qn** to get in touch *o* contact with sb; **mantenere i contatti (con qn)** to maintain contact (with sb), keep in touch (with sb); **mettersi in contatto con qn** to contact sb; **devo mettermi in contatto con John** I must contact John; **mantenersi in contatto** to keep in touch; **ci siamo mantenuti in contatto** we've kept in touch; **il loro contatto negli Stati Uniti era Chris** their contact in the United States was Chris **2** (*Elettr, Radio*) contact; **aprire/chiudere il contatto** (*Elettr*) to make/break contact; **fare contatto** (*Elettr: fili*) to touch; **stabilire il contatto** (*Radio*) to make contact

conte ['konte] SM (*in Europa*) count; (*in Gran Bretagna*) earl

contea [kon'tɛa] SF **1** (*Storia: in Europa*) count; (*: in Gran Bretagna*) earldom **2** (*Amm: nei paesi anglosassoni*) county

conteggiare [konted'dʒare] VT (*fare il conto di*) to work out; (*addebitare*) to charge (for), put on the bill

conteggio, gi [kon'teddʒo] SM **1** (*gen*) reckoning, calculation; **fare il conteggio di** to calculate **2 conteggio alla rovescia** countdown **3** (*Pugilato*) count

contegno [kon'teɲɲo] SM (*comportamento*) behaviour (*Brit*), behavior (*Am*); (*atteggiamento*) attitude; **avere** *o* **tenere un contegno esemplare** to behave perfectly; **ha assunto un contegno poco simpatico nei nostri confronti** he assumed a rather unpleasant attitude towards us; **darsi un contegno** (*ostentare disinvoltura*) to act nonchalant; (*ricomporsi*) to pull o.s. together

contegnosamente [konteɲɲosa'mente] AVV in a dignified way

contegnoso, a [konteɲ'ɲoso] AGG (*dignitoso*) dignified; (*riservato*) reserved

contemplare [kontem'plare] VT (*paesaggio*) to gaze at; (*possibilità*) to contemplate; (*Dir: considerare*) to provide for, make provision for

contemplativamente [kontemplativa'mente] AVV: **vivere contemplativamente** to lead a contemplative life

contemplativo, a [kontempla'tivo] AGG contemplative

contemplazione [kontemplat'tsjone] SF contemplation

contempo [kon'tɛmpo] SM: **nel contempo** meanwhile, in the meantime

contemporaneamente [kontemporanea'mente] AVV at the same time, simultaneously, contemporaneously; **sono arrivati contemporaneamente** they arrived at the same time; **contemporaneamente a** at the same time as

contemporaneo, a [kontempo'raneo] AGG: **contemporaneo (di** *o* **a)** contemporary (with); **la sua partenza fu contemporanea al mio arrivo** his

departure coincided with my arrival; **l'arte contemporanea** contemporary *o* modern art
■SM/F contemporary

contendente [konten'dɛnte] AGG contending
■SM/F *(avversario)* opponent, adversary; *(per un titolo)* contestant

contendere [kon'tɛndere] VB IRREG
■VT *(contestare)*: **contendere qc a qn** to contend with *o* be in competition with sb for sth; **si contendono il titolo** they are competing for the title; **si contendevano l'affetto della madre** they were vying with each other for their mother's affection
■VI *(aus* **avere***)* *(disputare, litigare)* to quarrel; *(competere)* to compete; **contendere per qc** to quarrel over *o* about sth

contenere [konte'nere] VB IRREG
■VT **1** *(racchiudere)* to contain; (: *sogg: recipienti, locali pubblici)* to hold; (: *cinema, veicoli)* to hold, seat; **questo succo non contiene zucchero** this juice does not contain sugar; **lo stadio può contenere centomila spettatori** the stadium can hold a hundred thousand spectators **2** *(frenare: entusiasmo, sentimenti, epidemia)* to contain; (: *truppe, avanzata nemica)* to hold in check
▶ **contenersi** VR to contain o.s

contenimento [konteni'mento] SM *(di fluidi)* containing, holding; *(di prezzi, spesa pubblica)* control

contenitore [konteni'tore] SM container; **un contenitore di plastica** a plastic container

contentabile [konten'tabile] AGG: **essere difficilmente contentabile** to be hard *o* difficult to please

contentare [konten'tare] VT to please; *(soddisfare)* to satisfy
▶ **contentarsi** VIP: **contentarsi (di)** to content o.s. (with); **si contenta di poco** he is easily satisfied; **chi si contenta gode** *(Proverbio)* a contented mind is a perpetual feast

contentezza [konten'tettsa] SF *(felicità)* happiness; *(soddisfazione)* contentment

contentino [konten'tino] SM sop

contento, a [kon'tɛnto] AGG *(lieto)* happy, glad; *(soddisfatto)* satisfied, pleased; **contento di** *(auto, persona)* pleased with; *(promozione, cambiamento)* happy *o* pleased about; **sono contento di vederti** I'm glad to see you; **sono contento di averti ritrovato** I'm happy to have met up with you again; **e non contento di ciò...** and not content with that ...; **far contento qn** to make sb happy; **sono andato per far contenta la mamma** I went to make my mum happy; **sono contento così** *(mi basta)* I've got enough; **sei contento adesso?** are you happy now?; **sono contenta che ti piaccia** I'm glad you like it; **oggi sono più contento** I'm happier today

contenuto, a [konte'nuto] AGG *(ira, entusiasmo)* restrained, suppressed; *(forza)* contained
■SM *(di cassa, valigia)* contents *pl*; *(di libro, film, discorso)* content; **ha rovesciato sul tavolo il contenuto della borsa** he tipped the contents of the bag out onto the table

contenzioso, a [konten'tsjoso] AGG *(Dir)* contentious
■SM *(Amm: ufficio)* legal department

conterraneo, a [konter'raneo] SM/F fellow countryman/woman

contesa [kon'tesa] SF *(litigio, contrasto)* quarrel, argument; *(Dir)* dispute

conteso, a [kon'teso] PP *di* **contendere**
■AGG *(premio, carica)* sought after

contessa [kon'tessa] SF countess

contessina [kontes'sina] SF *(in Europa)* daughter of a count; *(in Gran Bretagna)* daughter of an earl

contestabile [kontes'tabile] AGG questionable, disputable

contestare [kontes'tare] VT **1** *(criticare)* to question, protest against; **contestare il sistema** to protest against the system **2** *(disputare)* to dispute, contest; **contestare a qn il diritto di fare qc** to contest sb's right to do sth **3** *(Dir: notificare)* to notify; **contestare un reato a qn** to charge sb with a crime; **contestare una contravvenzione a qn** to issue sb with a fine

contestatario, ria, ri, rie [kontesta'tarjo] AGG, SM/F = contestatore

contestatore, trice [kontesta'tore] AGG anti-establishment
■SM/F protester

contestazione [kontestat'tsjone] SF **1** *(Pol)* anti-establishment activity; **la contestazione studentesca del '68** the student protests of '68 **2** *(Dir: disputa)* dispute; **in caso di contestazione** if there are any objections **3** *(Dir: notifica)* notification; **si proceda alla contestazione delle accuse** please read out the charges

contesto [kon'tɛsto] SM context; **visto nel contesto** seen in context

LO SAPEVI...?
contesto non si traduce mai con *contest*

contestuale [kontestu'ale] AGG *(gen)* contextual; *(Dir)* contemporary

contestualmente [kontestual'mente] AVV *(contemporaneamente)* at the same time

contiguità [kontigui'ta] SF proximity

contiguo, a [kon'tiguo] AGG *(camere, case)* adjoining, adjacent; **essere contiguo a** to be adjacent *o* next to

continentale [kontinen'tale] AGG continental; **l'Europa continentale** *(Geog)* continental Europe; *(per gli inglesi)* the Continent

continentalità [kontinentali'ta] SF *(di clima)* continental nature, continentality

continente[1] [konti'nɛnte] SM *(gen)* continent; *(terraferma)* mainland

continente[2] [konti'nɛnte] AGG moderate; **essere continente nel bere/mangiare** to drink/eat in moderation

continenza [konti'nɛntsa] SF continence

contingentare [kontindʒen'tare] VT *(Econ)* to place a quota on, fix a quota on

contingente [kontin'dʒɛnte] AGG contingent
■SM **1** *(gen, Mil, Filosofia)* contingent; **contingente di leva** draft *(Am)*; *group of soldiers called up for military service* **2** *(Comm)* quota

contingenza [kontin'dʒɛntsa] SF **1** *(gen)* contingency; *(circostanza)* circumstance **2** *(anche:* **indennità di contingenza***)* cost-of-living allowance

continuamente [kontinua'mente] AVV *(senza interruzione)* continuously, nonstop; *(ripetutamente)* continually; **perché vieni continuamente a disturbarmi?** why do you keep coming and bothering me?; **è piovuto continuamente** it rained nonstop; **cambia idea continuamente** she keeps changing her mind

continuare [kontinu'are] VT *(studi, progetto)* to continue (with), carry on with, go on with; *(viaggio)* to continue; *(tradizione)* to continue, carry on; **continuò la lettura** he went on reading
■VI *(riferito a persona: aus avere; riferito a cosa: aus avere o*

Cc

essere) to continue, go on; **continui pure** do go on; **per oggi basta, continueremo domani** that's enough for today, we'll carry on tomorrow; **continuano le trattative** negotiations are continuing; **continuare a fare qc** to go on *o* keep on *o* continue doing sth; **ha continuato a dormire nonostante il chiasso** she went on sleeping despite the noise; **continuava a credere in lei** he continued to believe in her; **continuò per la sua strada** he continued on his way; **la strada continua fino al bosco** the road carries on *o* continues as far as the wood; **se continua così...** if it (*o* he *o* she) goes on like this ...; **se i dolori continuano...** if the pain persists ...; **"continua"** (*di romanzi a puntate*) "to be continued"; **"continua a pagina 9"** "continued on page 9"; (*aus* **essere** *e* **avere**)
■ VB IMPERS: **continua a nevicare/a fare freddo** it's still snowing/cold

continuativamente [kontinuativa'mente] AVV uninterruptedly

continuativo, a [kontinua'tivo] AGG (*occupazione*) permanent; (*periodo*) consecutive

continuatore, trice [kontinua'tore] SM/F: **essere continuatore di** (*tradizione*) to continue, carry on

continuazione [kontinuat'tsjone] SF continuation; **la continuazione di un romanzo** the sequel to a novel; **in continuazione** continuously

continuità [kontinui'ta] SF continuity

continuo, a [kon'tinuo] AGG (*ininterrotto*) continuous; (*che si ripete*) continual; (*Elettr: corrente*) direct; **sono stufa delle sue lamentele continue** I'm fed up with her constant complaints; **c'è un continuo viavai di gente** there are people constantly coming and going; **di continuo** continually; **piove di continuo da tre giorni** it's been raining nonstop for three days

contitolare [kontito'lare] SM/F co-owner

conto ['konto] SM

1 (*calcolo*) calculation; **fare di conto** to count; **ho fatto un rapido conto** I did a quick calculation

2 (*Banca, Comm*) account; (*fattura: di ristorante, albergo*) bill; (*: di prestazione*) account, bill; **il conto, per favore** could I have the bill, please?; **pagare** *o* **saldare il conto** to pay the bill; **fare i conti** to do the accounts; **dobbiamo fare il conto delle spese** we must work out the expenses; **far bene/male i propri conti** (*anche fig*) to get one's sums right/wrong; **non aveva fatto i conti con possibili imprevisti** he hadn't allowed for anything unexpected happening; **fare i conti senza l'oste** to forget the most important thing; **fare i conti con qn** to settle one's account with sb; **farò i conti con te più tardi!** I'll sort you out later!; **avere un conto in sospeso (con qn)** to have an outstanding account (with sb); (*fig*) to have a score to settle (with sb); **fare i conti in tasca a qn** to pry into sb's financial affairs

3 (*stima, considerazione*): **di poco/nessun conto** of little/no importance; **tener conto di qn/qc** to take sb/sth into consideration *o* account; **non avevo tenuto conto del fuso orario** I hadn't allowed for the time difference; **tenere qc da conto** to take great care of sth

4 (*fraseologia*): **a conti fatti, in fin dei conti** all things considered, when all is said and done; **be', in fin dei conti non ha tutti i torti** well, after all, he's quite right; **ad ogni buon conto** in any case; **per conto mio** (*a mio avviso*) in my opinion, as far as I'm concerned; (*a nome mio*) on my behalf; (*da solo*) on my own; **per conto mio la faccenda è un po' strana** in my opinion it's all rather strange; **voglio starmene per conto mio** I want to be on my own; **ci vado per conto mio** I'm going on my own; **per conto di** on behalf of; **telefono per conto di Sara** I'm phoning on behalf of Sara; **sul conto di** about; **girano strane voci sul conto di Luca** I've heard some strange things about Luca; **mi hanno detto strane cose sul suo conto** I've heard some strange things about him; **fare conto che...** (*supporre*) to suppose that ...; **fare conto su qn/qc** to rely *o* depend *o* count on sb/sth; **chiedere conto di qc a qn** to ask sb to give an account *o* explanation of sth; **rendere conto a qn di qc** to be accountable to sb for sth; **rendersi conto di qc/che...** to realize sth/that; **non si era reso conto che c'ero anch'io** he hadn't realized I was there too; **non ti rendi conto delle conseguenze!** you don't realize what will happen!; **essere alla resa dei conti ...** to come to the day of reckoning
■ **conto in banca** *o* **bancario** bank account; **conto capitale** capital account; **conto cassa** cash account; **conto cifrato** numbered account; **conto corrente** current account (*Brit*), checking account (*Am*); **conto corrente postale** ≈ National Girobank payment, post office account; **conto in partecipazione** joint account; **conto passivo** account payable; **conto profitti e perdite** profit and loss account; **conto alla rovescia** countdown; **conto scoperto** overdrawn account; **avere il conto scoperto** to be overdrawn; **conto valutario** foreign currency account

contorcere [kon'tɔrtʃere] VB IRREG
■ VT to twist; (*viso*) to contort
► **contorcersi** VR: **contorcersi dal dolore** to writhe with pain; **contorcersi dalle risa** to double up with laughter

contorcimento [kontortʃi'mento] SM = **contorsione**

contornare [kontor'nare] VT (*gen, fig*) to surround; (*ornare*) to decorate, trim
► **contornarsi** VR: **contornarsi di** to surround o.s. with

contorno [kon'torno] SM **1** (*linea esterna*) outline, contour; (*ornamento*) border; **fare da contorno a** to surround **2** (*Culin*) vegetables *pl*; **non prendo il contorno** I don't want any vegetables; **cosa prendi come contorno?** what would you like to go with it?; **arrosto con contorno di piselli** roast meat served with peas

contorsione [kontor'sjone] SF contortion

contorsionismo [kontorsjo'nizmo] SM contortionism

contorsionista, i, e [kontorsjo'nista] SM/F contortionist

contortamente [kontorta'mente] AVV (*fig: ragionare*) tortuously

contorto, a [kon'tɔrto] PP *di* **contorcere**
■ AGG twisted; (*fig: ragionamento, stile*) tortuous

contrabbandare [kontrabban'dare] VT to smuggle

contrabbandiere, a [kontrabban'djɛre] SM/F smuggler

contrabbando [kontrab'bando] SM smuggling, contraband; **fare il contrabbando** to smuggle; **di contrabbando** contraband, smuggled; **sigarette di contrabbando** contraband cigarettes; **merce di contrabbando** contraband *no pl*, smuggled goods *pl*; **contrabbando di droga** drug smuggling

contrabbasso [kontrab'basso] SM (*Mus*) (double) bass

contraccambiare [kontrakkam'bjare] VT (*favore, auguri*) to return; (*gentilezza*) to repay; **vorrei**

contraccambiare I'd like to show my appreciation
contraccettivo, a [kontrattʃet'tivo] AGG, SM contraceptive
contraccolpo [kontrak'kolpo] SM (*gen*) rebound; (*di arma da fuoco*) recoil; (*fig*) repercussion
contraccusa [kontrak'kuza] SF (*Dir*) countercharge
contrada [kon'trada] SF (*letter: paese*) land; (*quartiere*) quarter, district; (*via*) street
contraddetto, a [kontrad'detto] PP *di* **contraddire**
contraddire [kontrad'dire] VB IRREG
■ VT to contradict; **mi contraddice sempre** he's always contradicting me;
▶ **contraddirsi** VR to contradict o.s.; (*uso reciproco: persone*) to contradict each other; (*: testimonianze*) to be contradictory
contraddistinguere [kontraddis'tingwere] VB IRREG
■ VT (*merce*) to mark; (*fig: atteggiamento, persona*) to distinguish
▶ **contraddistinguersi** VIP: **l'opera si contraddistingue per rigore scientifico** the work stands out because of its scientific accuracy
contraddistinto, a [kontraddis'tinto] PP *di* contraddistinguere
contraddittorietà [kontraddittorje'ta] SF contradictory nature
contraddittorio, ria, ri, rie [kontraddit'tɔrjo] AGG (*affermazione, testimonianza, personaggio*) contradictory; (*comportamento*) inconsistent; (*sentimenti*) conflicting
■ SM (*Dir: di testimoni*) cross-examination; (*Pol: dibattito*) debate
contraddizione [kontraddit'tsjone] SF contradiction; **cadere in contraddizione** to contradict o.s.; **essere in contraddizione** (*tesi, affermazioni*) to contradict one another; **essere in contraddizione con** to contradict; **spirito di contraddizione** argumentativeness
contrae *ecc* [kon'trae] VB *vedi* **contrarre**
contraente [kontra'ɛnte] AGG (*Dir: parte*) contracting
■ SM/F contracting party, contractor
contraerea [kontra'ɛrea] SF (*Mil*) anti-aircraft artillery
contraereo, a [kontra'ɛreo] AGG (*Mil*) anti-aircraft *attr*
contraffare [kontraf'fare] VT IRREG (*firma*) to forge; (*banconota*) to forge, counterfeit; (*voce*) to disguise; (*cibo, vino*) to adulterate
contraffatto, a [kontraf'fatto] PP *di* **contraffare**
■ AGG (*firma*) forged; (*banconota*) forged, counterfeit; (*voce*) disguised; (*cibo, vino*) adulterated
contraffattore, trice [kontraffat'tore] SM/F (*di firme*) forger; (*di monete*) forger, counterfeiter
contraffazione [kontraffat'tsjone] SF **1** (*vedi vb*) forging *no pl*, forgery; counterfeiting; disguising *no pl*; adulteration **2** (*esemplare contraffatto*) forgery
contrafforte [kontraf'fɔrte] SM **1** (*Archit*) buttress **2** (*Geog*) spur
contraggo *ecc* [kon'traggo] VB *vedi* **contrarre**
contralto [kon'tralto] SM (*Mus*) contralto; (*: voce maschile*) alto
contrammiraglio, gli [kontrammi'raʎʎo] SM rear admiral
contrappello [kontrap'pɛllo] SM (*Mil*) second roll call
contrappesare [kontrappe'sare] VT to counterbalance; (*fig: decisione*) to weigh up
▶ **contrappesarsi** VR (*uso reciproco*) to counterbalance each other
contrappeso [kontrap'peso] SM counterbalance, counterweight
contrapporre [kontrap'porre] VB IRREG
■ VT **1** (*opporre*): **contrapporre qc a qc** to counter sth with sth; **contrapporre un rifiuto ad una richiesta** to counter a request with a refusal; **contrapporre un ostacolo a qc** to set an obstacle in the way of sth **2** (*paragonare*): **contrapporre qc (a qc)** to compare sth (with sth)
▶ **contrapporsi** VR: **contrapporsi a qc** to contrast with sth, be opposed to sth; **i loro punti di vista si contrappongono** they hold opposing points of view
contrapposizione [kontrappozit'tsjone] SF (*opposizione*) juxtaposition; (*confronto*) comparison; (*contrasto*) contrast; **due interpretazioni in contrapposizione** two conflicting interpretations
contrapposto, a [kontrap'posto] PP *di* **contrapporre**
■ AGG (*argomenti, concetti*) contrasting; (*posizioni*) opposing
contrappunto [kontrap'punto] SM counterpoint
contrariamente [kontrarja'mente] AVV: **contrariamente a** contrary to; **contrariamente al solito** just for once; **contrariamente al solito non ha ottenuto un buon risultato** unusually for him he wasn't successful
contrariare [kontra'rjare] VT (*ostacolare: persona*) to oppose; (*: piani*) to thwart; (*irritare*) to annoy
contrariato, a [kontra'rjato] AGG annoyed
contrarietà [kontrarje'ta] SF INV (*avversità*) adversity, misfortune; (*fastidio*) trouble; (*avversione*) aversion
contrario, ria, ri, rie [kon'trarjo] AGG (*gen*) opposite; (*sfavorevole*) unfavourable (*Brit*), unfavorable (*Am*); (*avverso: sorte*) adverse; (*: venti*) contrary; **essere contrario a qc** (*persona*) to be against sth; **sono contrario alla vivisezione** I'm against vivisection; **sono contrario a questo tuo modo di comportarti** I disapprove of the way you're behaving; **è contrario ai miei principi** it's against my principles; **in caso contrario** otherwise; **in direzione contraria** in the opposite direction
■ SM opposite; **al contrario** on the contrary; **al contrario di** contrary to; **al contrario di quanto si crede, è piuttosto grande** contrary to what people think, it's quite big; **avere qualcosa in contrario** to have some objection; **io avrei qualcosa in contrario** I have an objection; **non ho niente in contrario** I've no objection; **se qualcuno ha qualcosa in contrario lo dica subito** if anyone has an objection they should say so at once; **è esattamente il contrario** it's quite the opposite *o* reverse; **fa tutto il contrario di quello che dice** he does the complete opposite of what he says
contrarre [kon'trarre] VB IRREG
■ VT **1** (*muscoli, volto*) to tense; **contrarre un muscolo** to contract a muscle **2** (*malattia, debito, prestito*) to contract; (*abitudine, vizio*) to pick up; (*accordo, patto*) to enter into; **contrarre una malattia** to contract an illness; **contrarre matrimonio** to marry;
▶ **contrarsi** VIP (*gen, Gramm*) to contract
contrassegnare [kontrasseɲ'ɲare] VT to mark
contrassegnato, a [kontrasseɲ'ɲato] AGG marked; **contrassegnato da un'etichetta** labelled
contrassegno [kontras'seɲɲo] SM (distinguishing) mark
■ AVV (*Comm*): **spedire in contrassegno** to send COD
contrassi *ecc* [kon'trassi] VB *vedi* **contrarre**
contrastante [kontras'tante] AGG contrasting
contrastare [kontras'tare] VT (*avanzata, piano*) to hinder; (*desiderio, diritto*) to dispute, contest; **una vittoria contrastata** a hard-fought victory

Cc

■VI (*aus* **avere**) (*discordare*): **contrastare (con)** to clash (with), contrast (with); **questi colori contrastano fra di loro** these colours clash
contrastivo, a [kontras'tivo] AGG (*Ling*) contrastive
contrasto [kon'trasto] SM **1** (*gen, TV, Fot*) contrast; **per contrasto** in contrast **2** (*conflitto*) conflict; (*disputa, litigio*) quarrel, dispute; **un contrasto di opinioni** a difference of opinion; **essere in/venire a contrasto con qn** to be in/get into a disagreement with sb
contrattabile [kontrat'tabile] AGG negotiable
contrattaccare [kontrattak'kare] VT to counterattack
contrattacco [kontrat'takko] SM counterattack; **passare al contrattacco** (*fig*) to fight back
contrattare [kontrat'tare] VT (*uso assoluto: trattare*) to negotiate; (: *mercanteggiare*) to bargain; (*terreno, merce*) to bargain over, negotiate the price of; **contrattare il prezzo** to negotiate the price
contrattazione [kontrattat'tsjone] SF (*trattativa*) negotiation; **dopo lunghe contrattazioni ho spuntato un buon prezzo** after much bargaining I managed to get a good price
contrattempo [kontrat'tɛmpo] SM hitch; **per una serie di contrattempi** because of a series of difficulties; **sono arrivato in ritardo per un contrattempo** there was a problem, and I arrived late
contrattile [kon'trattile] AGG contractile
contratto, a [kon'tratto] PP *di* **contrarre**
■AGG (*volto, mani*) tense; (*muscoli*) tense, contracted; (*Gramm*) contracted
■SM contract; **il contratto sarà firmato domani** the contract will be signed tomorrow; **contratto di acquisto** purchase agreement; **contratto di affitto** lease; **contratto collettivo di lavoro** collective agreement; **contratto di lavoro** contract of employment; **contratto di locazione** lease; **contratto a termine** forward contract
contrattuale [kontrattu'ale] AGG contractual; **forza contrattuale** (*di sindacato*) bargaining power
contrattualmente [kontrattual'mente] AVV contractually; **è stato deciso contrattualmente che...** it has been decided in the contract that ...
contravvenire [kontravve'nire] VI IRREG (*aus* **avere**) **contravvenire a** (*legge, regolamento*) to contravene; (*obbligo*) to fail to meet
contravventore, trice [kontravven'tore] SM/F offender
contravvenuto, a [kontravve'nuto] PP *di* contravvenire
contravvenzione [kontravven'tsjone] SF **1** (*Aut: multa*) fine; **elevare una contravvenzione a qn** to fine sb **2** (*trasgressione*): **contravvenzione (a)** contravention (of)
contrazione [kontrat'tsjone] SF (*gen, Med, Gramm*) contraction; **contrazione (di)** (*di prezzi, vendite*) decrease (in), fall (in)
contribuente [kontribu'ɛnte] SM/F (*Fisco*) taxpayer
contribuire [kontribu'ire] VI (*aus* **avere**) **contribuire a qc** to contribute to sth; **abbiamo contribuito tutti alla spesa** we all contributed to the cost; **contribuire a fare qc** to help do sth; **tutto ciò ha contribuito a peggiorare la situazione** all this has made things worse
contributivo, a [kontribu'tivo] AGG contributory
contributo [kontri'buto] SM **1** (*gen*) contribution; **dare il proprio contributo a qc** to make one's contribution to sth **2 contributi** SMPL (*tasse*) charges, tax; (*sovvenzioni*) subsidy, contribution; **contributi previdenziali** ≈ national insurance (*Brit*) *o* welfare (*Am*) contributions **contributi sindacali** trade (*Brit*) *o* labor (*Am*) union dues
contribuzione [kontribut'tsjone] SF contribution
contrito, a [kon'trito] AGG contrite, penitent; **con aria contrita** penitently
contrizione [kontrit'tsjone] SF contrition
contro ['kontro] PREP **1** (*gen*) against; **non ho niente contro di lui** I've nothing against him; **sono tutti contro di me** they are all against me; **lottare contro qn/qc** to fight against sb/sth; **la lotta contro la droga** the fight against drugs; **è contro il divorzio** he's against *o* opposed to divorce; **il Milan contro la Juventus** Milan versus *o* against Juventus; **pastiglie contro la tosse** throat lozenges; **un ottimo rimedio contro l'influenza** an excellent treatment for flu **2** (*contatto, direzione*) against; **si appoggiò contro la porta** he leaned against the door; **ho sbattuto contro la porta** I bumped into the door; **si è schiantato contro un albero** it crashed into a tree; **puntò la pistola contro di me** he pointed his gun at me; **spararono contro la polizia** they shot at the police **3** (*Comm: in cambio di*): **contro pagamento/ricevuta** on payment/receipt **4** (*contrariamente a*): **contro ogni mia aspettativa** contrary to my expectations **5 contro corrente, contro luce, contro voglia** *ecc vedi* **controcorrente, controluce, controvoglia** *ecc*
■AVV against; **votare contro** to vote against; **hanno votato contro** they voted against it; **dar contro a qn** to contradict sb; **per contro** on the other hand
■SM INV con; **il pro e il contro** the pros and cons
■PREF counter...
controanalisi [kontroa'nalizi] SF INV (*per doping*) further test
controbattere [kontro'battere] VT (*ribattere*) to answer back; (*confutare*) to refute
controbilanciare [kontrobilan'tʃare] VT (*gen, fig*) to counterbalance
controcampo [kontro'kampo] SM (*Cine*) reverse shot
controcorrente [kontrokor'rɛnte] AVV: **nuotare controcorrente** (*in un fiume*) to swim upstream; (*nel mare*) to swim against the tide; **andare controcorrente** (*fig*) to swim against the tide
controcultura [kontrokul'tura] SF counterculture
controcurva [kontro'kurva] SF (*Sci*) counter-turn
controdado [kontro'dado] SM locknut
controfagotto [kontrofa'gɔtto] SM (*Mus*) double bassoon
controfax [kontro'faks] SM INV reply to a fax
controffensiva [kontroffen'siva] SF (*Mil, fig*) counteroffensive
controfigura [kontrofi'gura] SF (*Cine*) stuntman/woman, double; **essere la controfigura di qn** to play sb's double
controfiletto [kontrofi'letto] SM sirloin
controfinestra [kontrofi'nɛstra] SF: **mettere le controfinestre** to have double glazing installed
controfirma [kontro'firma] SF countersignature
controfirmare [kontrofir'mare] VT to countersign
controindicazione [kontroindikat'tsjone] SF contraindication
controinterrogare [kontrointerro'gare] VT (*Dir*) to cross-examine
controinterrogatorio, ri [kontrointerroga'tɔrjo] SM cross-examination
controllare [kontrol'lare] VT **1** (*verificare: gen*) to

check; (: *biglietto*) to inspect, check; **controlla che la porta sia ben chiusa** check that the door is shut properly; **mi hanno controllato il passaporto** my passport was checked **2** (*sorvegliare*) to watch, keep a close watch on; (: *ufficio, impiegato*) to supervise **3** (*tenere a freno, dominare: anche Mil, Calcio*) to control
▶ **controllarsi** VR to control o.s.; **non riuscivo a controllarmi** I couldn't control myself

controllata [kontrol'lata] SF **1** (*gen*) check; **dare una controllata a qc** to check sth over **2** (*Comm: società*) associated company

controllato, a [kontrol'lato] AGG (*persona: non impulsivo*) self-controlled, self-possessed; (*reazioni*) controlled

controllo [kon'trɔllo] SM **1** (*verifica: gen*) check; (: *di biglietti*) inspection; **fare un controllo di** to check sth, to inspect sth; **visita di controllo** (*Med*) checkup **2** (*sorveglianza*) supervision; **telefono sotto controllo** tapped telephone; **base di controllo** (*Aer*) ground control **3** (*padronanza, regolamentazione*) control; **sotto controllo** under control; **la situazione è sotto controllo** the situation is under control; **esercitare il controllo su qc** to have control over sth; **perdere il controllo (di qc)** (*di macchina, situazione*) to lose control (of sth); **ha perso il controllo della macchina** he lost control of the car; **ha perso il controllo (di sé)** he lost control (of himself), he lost his self-control
■ **controllo bagagli** baggage *o* luggage check; **controllo dei costi** cost control; **controllo doganale** customs inspection; **controllo di gestione** management control; **controllo delle nascite** birth control; **controllo passaporti** passport control; **controllo dei prezzi** price control; **controllo qualità** quality control; **controllo di sicurezza** (*in aeroporto*) security check; **controllo del traffico aereo** air-traffic control

controllore [kontrol'lore] SM (*di autobus, treno*) (ticket) inspector; (*doganale*) customs officer; **controllore di volo** air-traffic controller

controluce [kontro'lutʃe] SF INV (*Fot*) backlit shot
■ AVV: **(in) controluce** against the light; (*fotografare*) into the light; **guardala controluce** look at it against the light

contromano [kontro'mano] AVV: **guidare contromano** to drive on the wrong side of the road; (*in un senso unico*) to drive the wrong way up a one-way street

contromarca, che [kontro'marka] SF pass-out (ticket)

contromarcia [kontro'martʃa] SF (*Mil*) countermarch

contromisura [kontromi'zura] SF countermeasure

controparte [kontro'parte] SF (*Dir*) opposing party

contropartita [kontropar'tita] SF (*fig: compenso*): **come contropartita** in return

contropedale [kontrope'dale] SM pedal brake

contropelo [kontro'pelo] AVV (*di stoffa*) against the nap; **radersi contropelo** to shave against the growth; **accarezzare un gatto contropelo** to stroke a cat the wrong way
■ SM: **fare il contropelo** to shave against the growth

contropiede [kontro'pjɛde] SM (*Sport*): **azione di contropiede** sudden counter-attack; **prendere qn in contropiede** to wrong-foot sb; (*fig*) to catch sb off his (*o* her) guard

controproducente [kontroprodu'tʃɛnte] AGG counterproductive

controproposta [kontropro'posta] SF counterproposal

controprova [kontro'prɔva] SF (*di esperimento, conti*) countercheck

contrordine [kon'trordine] SM counter-order; **salvo contrordine** unless I (*o* you *ecc*) hear to the contrary

Controriforma [kontrori'forma] SF (*Storia*) Counter-Reformation

controrivoluzionario, a [kontrorivoluttsjo'narjo] AGG, SM/F counter-revolutionary

controrivoluzione [kontrorivolut'tsjone] SF counter-revolution

controsenso [kontro'sɛnso] SM (*contraddizione*) contradiction in terms; (*assurdità*) nonsense

controsoffitto [kontrosof'fitto] SM false ceiling

controspionaggio, gi [kontrospio'naddʒo] SM counterespionage

controsterzare [kontroster'tsare] VI (*aus* **avere**) (*Aut*) to steer the other way

controtendenza [kontroten'dɛntsa] SF: **essere in controtendenza** to go against the prevailing trend

controvalore [kontrova'lore] SM equivalent (value)

controvento [kontro'vɛnto] AVV against the wind; **navigare controvento** to sail to windward

controversia [kontro'vɛrsja] SF (*gen*) controversy; (*Dir*) dispute; **ha suscitato molte controversie** it provoked a great deal of controversy; **controversia sindacale** industrial dispute

controverso, a [kontro'vɛrso] AGG controversial

controvoglia [kontro'vɔʎʎa] AVV: **(di) controvoglia** reluctantly, unwillingly; **l'ho mangiato controvoglia** I ate it, though I didn't want to; **è andato alla festa controvoglia** he went to the party, though he didn't want to

contumace [kontu'matʃe] AGG (*Dir*): **rendersi contumace** to default, fail to appear in court
■ SM/F (*Dir*) defaulter

contumacia [kontu'matʃa] SF (*Dir*) default; **processare qn in contumacia** to try sb in his (*o* her) absence; **giudizio in contumacia** judgment by default

contumaciale [kontuma'tʃale] AGG (*Dir: processo*) by default; (*Med: ospedale*) quarantine *attr*

contundente [kontun'dɛnte] AGG: **corpo contundente** blunt instrument

conturbante [kontur'bante] AGG (*sguardo, bellezza*) perturbing, thrilling

conturbare [kontur'bare] VT to perturb, thrill

contusione [kontu'zjone] SF (*Med*) bruise

contuso, a [kon'tuzo] AGG bruised
■ SM/F (*in incidente*) person suffering from cuts and bruises; **numerosi i contusi negli scontri con la polizia** the number of people slightly hurt in the clashes with the police was high

conurbazione [konurbat'tsjone] SF conurbation

convalescente [konvaleʃʃɛnte] AGG, SM/F convalescent

convalescenza [konvaleʃʃɛntsa] SF convalescence; **essere in convalescenza** to be convalescing; **ha fatto una convalescenza di 3 mesi** he spent 3 months convalescing

convalida [kon'valida] SF (*vedi vb*) validation; stamping; confirmation

convalidare [konvali'dare] VT (*Amm*) to validate; (*biglietto*) to stamp; (*Dir, fig: dubbi, sospetti*) to confirm

convegno [kon'veɲɲo] SM (*incontro*) meeting; (*riunione ufficiale*) convention, conference, congress; **darsi convegno** (*appuntamento*) to arrange to meet

convenevoli [konve'nevoli] SMPL courtesies,

Cc

civilities; **scambiarsi i convenevoli** to exchange the usual courtesies

conveniente [konve'njɛnte] AGG **1** (*adatto, opportuno*): **conveniente (a)** suitable (for), fitting (for) **2** (*vantaggioso: prezzo*) cheap; (: *affare*) profitable

convenientemente [konvenjente'mente] AVV (*opportunamente*) suitably; (*vantaggiosamente*) profitably

convenienza [konve'njɛntsa] SF **1** (*l'essere vantaggioso di: prezzo*) cheapness; (: *affare*) advantage, profit; **non vedo la convenienza di trovarci a Milano** I don't think Milan is the most convenient place to meet; **fare qc per convenienza** to do sth out of self-interest; **non c'è convenienza a vendere adesso** there's no advantage in selling at the moment; **la convenienza di abitare in centro** the advantage of living in the centre; **matrimonio di convenienza** marriage of convenience **2** (*decoro*) propriety; **andare oltre i limiti della convenienza** to go beyond the pale **3** (*norme sociali*): **le convenienze** SFPL the proprieties, social conventions

convenire [konve'nire] VB IRREG
■ VT to agree upon; **come convenuto** as agreed; **resta convenuto che...** it is agreed that ...; **in data da convenire** on a date to be agreed
■ VI (*aus* **essere**) **1** (*aus* **avere**) (*essere d'accordo*): **convenire (su qc/che...)** to agree (upon sth/that ...); **devi convenire che hai torto** you must admit you are in the wrong; **ne convengo** I agree **2** (*essere meno caro*) to be cheap **3** (*riunirsi*) to gather, assemble **4** **convenire a qn** (*essere vantaggioso*) to be worthwhile for sb; (*essere consigliabile*) to be advisable for sb; **questo affare non mi conviene** this transaction isn't worth my while; **ti conviene accettare** you would be well advised to accept; **non gli conviene fare il furbo** he'd better not try to get clever; **se vuoi evitare il traffico ti conviene partire presto** if you want to avoid the traffic you'd better leave early
■ VB IMPERS (*aus* **essere**) **conviene fare così** it is advisable to do this; **conviene andarsene** we'd better go, we should go; **comprare al supermercato conviene sempre** it's always cheaper to shop at the supermarket; **converrebbe rimandare la gita** we'd better put off the trip;
▶ **convenirsi** VIP: **convenirsi a** to suit, befit; **come si conviene ad una signorina** as befits a young lady

conventicola [konven'tikola] SF (*cricca*) clique

convento [kon'vɛnto] SM (*di suore*) convent; (*di frati*) monastery; **entrare in convento** (*suora*) to enter a convent; **accontentiamoci di quel che passa il convento** let's make the best of things

conventuale [konventu'ale] AGG of a convent

convenuto, a [konve'nuto] PP *di* **convenire**
■ AGG (*ora, luogo, prezzo*) agreed
■ SM **1** (*cosa pattuita*) agreement; **secondo il convenuto** as agreed **2** (*Dir*) defendant **3** (*i presenti*): **i convenuti** SMPL those present

convenzionale [konventsjo'nale] AGG (*gen*) conventional

convenzionalmente [konventsjonal'mente] AVV conventionally, in a conventional way

convenzionato, a [konventsjo'nato] AGG (*ospedale, clinica*) providing free health care, ≈ National Health Service *attr* (*Brit*)

convenzione [konven'tsjone] SF **1** (*Dir, Pol*) agreement **2** (*assunto generale, tradizione*) convention; (*tacito accordo*) understanding; **le convenzioni (sociali)** social conventions **3** (*Pol, Dir: convegno*) convention

convergente [konver'dʒɛnte] AGG convergent

convergenza [konver'dʒɛntsa] SF convergence; (*Aut*) toe-in

convergere [kon'vɛrdʒere] VI IRREG E DIF (*aus* **essere**) **convergere (su)** (*gen, Mat*) to converge (on); (*interesse*) to centre (on)

conversa [kon'vɛrsa] SF (*Rel*) lay sister

conversare [konver'sare] VI (*aus* **avere**) to talk, to have a conversation

conversazione [konversat'tsjone] SF conversation; **fare conversazione** (*chiacchierare*) to chat, have a chat

conversione [konver'sjone] SF (*gen*): **conversione (a/in)** conversion (to/into); **conversione a U** (*Aut*) U-turn

converso, a [kon'vɛrso] PP *di* **convergere**; **per converso** AVV conversely

convertibile [konver'tibile] AGG: **convertibile (in)** convertible (into)
■ SF (*Aut*) convertible

convertibilità [konvertibili'ta] SF convertibility

convertire [konver'tire] VT (*gen, Inform*) to convert; (*persuadere*): **convertire qn (a qc)** to convert sb (to sth); **convertire qc in qc** to convert sth into sth
▶ **convertirsi** VR: **convertirsi (a qc)** to be converted (to sth); **si è convertito al buddismo** he has become a Buddhist;
▶ **convertirsi** VIP: **l'amore si convertì in odio** love turned to hate

convertito, a [konver'tito] AGG converted
■ SM/F convert

convertitore [konverti'tore] SM (*Elettr*) converter; **convertitore di coppia** (*Aut*) torque converter

convessità [konvessi'ta] SF INV convexity

convesso, a [kon'vɛsso] AGG convex

convettore [konvet'tore] SM convector

convezione [konvet'tsjone] SF convection

convincente [konvin'tʃɛnte] AGG convincing; **una spiegazione convincente** a convincing explanation

convincere [kon'vintʃere] VB IRREG
■ VT to convince; **va bene, mi hai convinto** ok, you've convinced me; **convincere qn di qc** to convince sb of sth; **convincere qn a fare qc** to persuade sb to do sth, talk sb into doing sth; **mi ha convinto a comprarlo** she persuaded me to buy it;
▶ **convincersi** VR: **convincersi di qc/che...** to convince o.s. of sth/that ...

convincimento [konvintʃi'mento] SM conviction, belief

convinto, a [kon'vinto] PP *di* **convincere**
■ AGG convinced; **in tono convinto** with conviction

convinzione [konvin'tsjone] SF conviction, firm belief; **fare opera di convinzione su qn** to try to convince sb

convissuto [konvis'suto] PP *di* **convivere**

convitato, a [konvi'tato] SM/F guest

convitto [kon'vitto] SM boarding school

convivente [konvi'vɛnte] SM/F (*partner*) partner; (*compagno di appartamento*) flatmate (*Brit*), roommate (*Am*)

convivenza [konvi'vɛntsa] SF living together; (*Dir*) cohabitation; **la convivenza con quell'uomo non dev'esser facile** it can't be easy living with that man

convivere [kon'vivere] VI IRREG (*aus* **avere**) to live together; (*Dir*) to cohabit; **convivere con qn** to live with sb

conviviale [konvi'vjale] AGG convivial

convocare [konvo'kare] VT (*riunione*) to convene, call; (*parlamento*) to convene; (*persona subordinata*) to summon, send for; **convocare una riunione** to call a meeting; **tutti i genitori sono stati convocati** all parents have been asked to attend; **il giocatore è stato convocato in nazionale** the player has been chosen to play for the national team

convocazione [konvokat'tsjone] SF **1** (*atto: vedi vb*) convening; summoning; **lettera di convocazione** (letter of) notification to appear *o* attend **2** (*riunione*) meeting, summons *sg*

convogliare [konvoʎ'ʎare] VT **1** (*dirigere*) to direct, send; (: *acque*) to channel; (: *fig: energie*): **convogliare su** to channel into **2** (*trasportare*) to carry, transport, convey

convoglio, gli [kon'vɔʎʎo] SM **1** (*Naut, Mil*) convoy; **convoglio (ferroviario)** train **2** (*corteo funebre*) funeral procession

convolare [konvo'lare] VI (*aus* **essere**) **convolare a (giuste) nozze** (*scherz*) to tie the knot

convolvolo [kon'vɔlvolo] SM bindweed

convulsamente [konvulsa'mente] AVV convulsively

convulsione [konvul'sjone] SF (*Med*) convulsion; (*di riso*) fit

convulsivo, a [konvul'sivo] AGG convulsive

convulso, a [kon'vulso] AGG (*gen*) convulsive; (*pianto*) uncontrollable, violent; (*fig: stile, parlare*) jerky; (: *attività, ritmo*) feverish

cookie ['kuki] SM INV (*Inform*) cookie

Coop. [ko'op] ABBR F = **cooperativa**

cooperare [koope'rare] VI (*aus* **avere**) **cooperare (a qc/a fare qc)** to cooperate (in sth/to do sth); **le autorità francesi e britanniche stanno cooperando** the French and British authorities are working together; **cooperare ad un progetto** to work together on a project

cooperativa [koopera'tiva] SF cooperative; **cooperativa edilizia** building cooperative (*selling houses to its members*)

cooperativo, a [koopera'tivo] AGG cooperative

cooperatore, trice [koopera'tore] SM/F (*collaboratore*) collaborator; (*socio di cooperativa*) cooperative member

cooperazione [kooperat'tsjone] SF cooperation

coordinamento [koordina'mento] SM coordination

coordinare [koordi'nare] VT to coordinate

coordinata [koordi'nata] SF (*Ling, Mat, Geog*) coordinate; **coordinate chilometriche est/nord** (*Cartografia*) eastings/northings

coordinato, a [koordi'nato] AGG (*Mat, Ling*) coordinate; (*movimenti*) coordinated; (*abbigliamento, arredamento*): **coordinati** SMPL coordinates

coordinatore, trice [koordina'tore] SM/F coordinator

coordinazione [koordinat'tsjone] SF coordination

coorte [ko'ɔrte] SF (*Storia*) cohort

Copenaghen [kope'nagen] SF Copenhagen

coperchio, chi [ko'pɛrkjo] SM cover; (*di pentola*) lid

Copernico [ko'pɛrniko] SM Copernicus

coperta [ko'pɛrta] SF **1** (*di lana*) blanket; (*da viaggio*) rug; **una bella coperta calda** a nice warm blanket; **stare sotto le coperte** to be in bed; **coperta elettrica** electric blanket **2** (*Naut*) deck; **tutti in coperta!** all hands on deck!

copertamente [koperta'mente] AVV covertly, secretly

copertina [koper'tina] SF (*di libro, rivista*) cover; (: *sovraccoperta*) jacket; **la sua faccia è sulla copertina di questa settimana** her picture is on this week's cover; **in copertina** on the cover; **ragazza copertina** cover girl

coperto, a [ko'pɛrto] PP *di* **coprire**

■AGG (*gen, Assicurazione*) covered; (*luogo: riparato*) sheltered; (*piscina, campo da tennis*) indoor *attr*; (*cielo*) overcast; **essere ben coperto** to be wearing warm clothes; **sei ben coperto?** are you wearing warm clothes?; **tieni il bambino ben coperto** keep the child well wrapped up; **coperto di** covered with; **libri coperti di polvere** books covered with dust; **una parete coperta di poster** a wall covered with posters; **una piscina coperta** an indoor pool; **il cielo è coperto** the sky is overcast

■SM **1 al coperto** under cover, indoors; **in caso di pioggia la festa si svolgerà al coperto** if it rains, the party will be held indoors; **mettersi al coperto** to take shelter; **essere al coperto** (*fig*) to be safe **2** (*posto a tavola*) place; **ho messo 12 coperti** I've set the table for 12; **(prezzo del) coperto** (*al ristorante*) cover charge; **il coperto è compreso nel conto** the cover charge is included in the bill

copertone [koper'tone] SM **1** (*Aut*) tyre (*Brit*), tire (*Am*) **2** (*telone impermeabile*) tarpaulin

copertura [koper'tura] SF **1** (*gen: atto*) covering; (*Edil*) roofing; **attività di copertura** cover-up; **materiali da copertura** roofing (materials) **2** (*Econ, Comm, Assicurazione*) cover; **copertura assicurativa** insurance cover **3** (*Sport*): **fare un gioco di copertura** to play a defensive game **4** (*Mil*) cover

copia ['kɔpja] SF (*gen*) copy; (*Fot*) print; **non è l'originale, è una copia** it's not the original, it's a copy; **brutta/bella copia** rough/final copy; **essere l'esatta copia di qn/qc** to be the spitting image of sb/sth; **hanno venduto un milione di copie dell'album** a million copies of the album have been sold; **vorrei due copie di ciascuna foto** I'd like two prints of each photo; **copia carbone** carbon copy; **copia conforme** (*Dir*) certified copy; **copia omaggio** presentation copy

Cc

copiacommissione [kopjakommis'sjone] SM INV order book

copiare [ko'pjare] VT to copy; (*Inform*) to back up, copy; **copiare (qc da qn)** (*in compito a scuola*) to copy (sth from sb); **non dovete copiare** you mustn't copy

copiativo, a [kopja'tivo] AGG: **carta copiativa** carbon paper; **inchiostro copiativo** indelible ink; **matita copiativa** indelible pencil

copiatrice [kopja'tritʃe] SF copier, copying machine

copiatura [kopja'tura] SF copying

copiglia [ko'piʎʎa] SF (*Tecn*) cotter (pin)

copilota, i [kopi'lɔta] SM/F copilot

copione [ko'pjone] SM (*Cine, Teatro*) script; **come da** *o* **secondo copione** according to plan, as planned

copiosamente [kopjosa'mente] AVV copiously

copioso, a [ko'pjoso] AGG copious

copisteria [kopiste'ria] SF copy bureau

coppa¹ ['kɔppa] SF **1** (*gen*) cup; (*Sport*) trophy, cup; (*per gelato, frutta*) bowl; (*per spumante*) champagne glass; (*Rel*) chalice; **coppa di gelato** (*in confezione*) tub of ice cream; **prendi un cono o una coppa?** are you going to have a cone or a tub?; **una coppa di champagne** a glass of champagne; **la nostra squadra ha vinto la coppa** our team won the cup; **coppa dell'olio** (*Aut*) oil sump (*Brit*) *o* pan (*Am*); **coppa della ruota** (*Aut*) hubcap **2** (*Carte*): **coppe** SFPL *suit in Neapolitan pack of cards*

coppa² ['kɔppa] SF (*Culin*) large pork sausage

coppia ['kɔppja] SF (*di persone*) couple; (*di animali, Sport*) pair; **sono una bella coppia** they're a nice-looking couple; **fare una bella coppia** to make a nice couple; **una coppia di sposi** a married couple; **una coppia di canarini** a pair of canaries; **a coppie** *or* **in coppia** in pairs; **gara a coppie** competition for pairs; **coppia di forze** (*Fis*) torque

coppola ['kɔppola] SF peaked cap

copra ['kɔpra] SF copra

coprente [ko'prɛnte] AGG (*colore, cosmetico*) covering; (*calze*) opaque

copricapo [kopri'kapo] SM headgear *no pl*; (*cappello*) hat

copricostume [koprikos'tume] SM beach robe

copridivano [kopridi'vano] SM INV throw

coprifuoco, chi [kopri'fwɔko] SM curfew

copriletto [kopri'lɛtto] SM INV bedspread

coprimaterasso [koprimate'rasso] SM mattress cover

coprimozzo [kopri'mɔddzo] SM hubcap

copripiumino [kopripju'mino] SM INV duvet cover

coprire [ko'prire] VB IRREG

■VT (*gen*) to cover; (*occupare: carica, posto*) to hold; (*persona: proteggere: anche fig*) to cover, shield; (*fig: suono*) to drown; (*: segreto, sentimenti*) to conceal; **copri bene il bambino** wrap the child up well; **coprire di** *o* **con** (*gen*) to cover with; **era coperto di lividi** he was bruised all over *o* covered in bruises; **ho coperto la bici con un telo di plastica** I covered the bike with a plastic sheet; **coprire qn di insulti/di doni** to shower insults/gifts on sb; **coprire qn di ridicolo** to cover sb with ridicule; **coprire qn di baci** to smother sb with kisses; **coprire (le spalle a) qn** (*in una sparatoria*) to cover sb; **coprire un rischio** (*Econ, Assicurazione*) to cover a risk; **coprire le spese** to break even; **coprire un percorso in un'ora** to cover a distance in one hour;

▶ **coprirsi** VR (*persona*) to wrap (o.s.) up; (*: Assicurazione*): **coprirsi contro** to insure o.s. against; **coprirsi di gloria/di ridicolo** to cover o.s. with glory/with ridicule;

▶ **coprirsi** VIP (*cielo*) to cloud over; (*rivestirsi*): **coprirsi di** (*muffa, macchie*) to be covered in

coprisedile [koprise'dile] SM (*per auto*) seat cover

coprisella [kopri'sɛlla] SM INV saddle cover

coproduzione [koprodut'tsjone] SF (*Cine*) co-production

copula ['kɔpula] SF (*Gramm*) copula; (*congiunzione*) conjunction

copulativo, a [kopula'tivo] AGG copulative

copulazione [kopulat'tsjone] SF copulation

copyright ['kɔpirait] SM INV copyright

coque [kɔk] SF INV: **uovo alla coque** (soft-)boiled egg

coraggio [ko'raddʒo] SM **1** courage, bravery; **aver coraggio** to be courageous, be brave; **avere il coraggio di fare qc** to be brave enough to do sth; **ha avuto il coraggio di dire la verità** he was brave enough to tell the truth; **non ho avuto il coraggio di chiederglielo** I hadn't the nerve to ask him; **avere il coraggio delle proprie azioni** to have the courage of one's convictions; **ha dimostrato molto coraggio** she showed great courage; **dimostrare coraggio in battaglia** to show courage *o* bravery in battle; **aver un coraggio da leone** to be as brave as a lion; **farsi coraggio** to pluck up courage; **si è fatto coraggio e le ha chiesto di uscire con lui** he plucked up courage and asked her to go out with him; **fare coraggio a qn** to cheer sb up; **coraggio!** (*forza!*) come on!; (*animo!*) cheer up!; **coraggio, siamo quasi arrivati!** come on, we're nearly there! **2** (*sfacciataggine*) nerve; **hai un bel coraggio!** you've got a nerve!

coraggiosamente [koraddʒosa'mente] AVV bravely, courageously

coraggioso, a [korad'dʒoso] AGG brave, courageous

corale [ko'rale] AGG (*Mus*) choral; (*adesione, consenso*) unanimous

corallino, a [koral'lino] AGG coral *attr*

corallo [ko'rallo] SM coral; **il mar dei Coralli** the Coral Sea

coralmente [koral'mente] AVV (*rispondere, approvare*) unanimously

Corano [ko'rano] SM: **il Corano** the Koran

corazza [ko'rattsa] SF (*Storia*) cuirass; (*Mil*) armo(u)r(-plate); (*Sport*) protective clothing; (*di animali*) carapace, shell; **corazza di indifferenza** hard shell of indifference

corazzare [korat'tsare] VT to armour

▶ **corazzarsi** VR (*proteggersi*) **corazzarsi contro qc** to protect o.s. from sth

corazzata [korat'tsata] SF battleship

corazzato, a [korat'tsato] AGG (*Mil*) armo(u)red; **essere corazzato contro le avversità** to be hardened *o* proof against adversities

corazziere [korat'tsjɛre] SM (*Storia*) cuirassier; (*guardia presidenziale*) *carabiniere of the President's guard*

corbelleria [korbelle'ria] SF (*parola*) stupid remark; (*azione*) foolish action; **non dire corbellerie!** don't talk nonsense!, don't be so silly!

corda ['kɔrda] SF **1** (*fune*) rope; (*Pugilato*): **le corde** the ropes; **una corda per saltare** a skipping rope; **saltare la corda** to skip (*Brit*), jump rope (*Am*); **di corda** (*suole*) rope *attr*; **scarpe di corda** espadrilles **2** (*di violino, arco, racchetta*) string; **strumenti a corda** stringed instruments **3** (*Anat*): **corde vocali** vocal cords; **corda dorsale** (*Zool*) spinal chord **4** (*Geom*) chord **5** (*fraseologia*): **dare corda a qn** to let sb have his (*o* her) way; **dare la corda a un orologio** to wind a clock; **mettersi la corda al collo** (*fig*) to put one's head in the noose; **tenere sulla corda qn** to keep sb on tenterhooks; **essere giù di corda** to feel down; **oggi sono un po' giù di corda** I'm feeling a bit down today; **tagliare la corda** to sneak off, slip away; **tendere** *o* **tirare troppo la corda** (*fig*) to push one's luck

cordame [kor'dame] SM ropes *pl*; (*Naut*) rigging

cordata [kor'data] SF (*Alpinismo*) roped party; (*fig: Pol*) network; *alliance system in financial and business world*; **in cordata** roped together

cordiale [kor'djale] AGG (*accoglienza*) warm, cordial; (*persona*) warm; **una persona molto cordiale** a very friendly person; **è la ragazza più cordiale che abbia mai conosciuto** she's the friendliest girl I've ever met; **cordiali saluti** (*in lettere*) best regards; **c'è una cordiale antipatia tra noi** we cordially dislike one another

■SM (*bevanda*) cordial

cordialità [kordjali'ta] SF **1** warmth, cordiality **2** (*saluti*): **cordialità** SFPL best wishes

cordialmente [kordjal'mente] AVV warmly, cordially

cordigliera [kordiʎ'ʎɛra] SF cordillera

cordiglio, gli [kor'diʎʎo] SM (*di frate, monaca*) (knotted) cord; (*di sacerdote*) priest's girdle

cordless ['kordles] SM INV, AGG INV (*anche:* **telefono cordless**) cordless phone

cordoglio [kor'dɔʎʎo] SM grief, sorrow; (*lutto*) mourning; **esprimere il proprio cordoglio a qn** to offer sb one's sympathy *o* condolences

cordone [kor'done] SM (*gen*) cord; (*di telefono*) cord, flex; (*di borsa*) string; (*linea: di poliziotti, soldati*) cordon; **cordone litoraneo** (*Geog*) offshore bar; **cordone ombelicale** (*Anat*) umbilical cord; **cordone sanitario** quarantine line, cordon sanitaire

Corea [ko'rεa] SF Korea; **la Corea del Nord/Sud** North/South Korea
corea [ko'rεa] SF (*Med*) chorea
coreano, a [kore'ano] AGG, SM/F Korean
coreografia [koreogra'fia] SF choreography
coreograficamente [koreografika'mente] AVV choreographically
coreografico, a, ci, che [koreo'grafiko] AGG choreographic
coreografo, a [kore'ɔgrafo] SM/F choreographer
coriaceo, a [ko'rjatʃeo] AGG (*Bot, Zool*) coriaceous; (*fig*) tough
coriandolo [ko'rjandolo] SM **1** (*per carnevale*): **coriandoli** SMPL confetti *sg* **2** (*Bot*) coriander
coricare [kori'kare] VT (*persona: a letto*) to put to bed; (: *a terra, su divano*) to put down, lay down; (*bottiglia*) to rest, lay
▶ **coricarsi** VR (*andare a letto*) to go to bed; (*riposarsi*) to lie down
coricherò *ecc* VB *vedi* **coricare**
Corinto [ko'rinto] SF Corinth
corinzio, zia, zi, zie [ko'rintsjo] AGG (*Arte*) Corinthian; **ordine/capitello corinzio** Corinthian order/capital
corista, i, e [ko'rista] SM/F (*Rel*) choir member, chorister; (*Teatro*) member of the chorus; **i coristi** (*Teatro*) the chorus
■ SM tuning fork
cormorano [kormo'rano] SM cormorant
corna ['kɔrna] SFPL *vedi* **corno**
cornacchia [kor'nakkja] SF crow; **cornacchia grigia** hooded crow; **cornacchia nera** carrion crow
cornalina [korna'lina] SF carnelian, cornelian
cornamusa [korna'muza] SF bagpipes *pl*
cornata [kor'nata] SF butt; **dare una cornata a qn** to butt sb; (*infilzare*) to gore sb
cornea ['kɔrnea] SF (*Anat*) cornea
corneo, a ['kɔrneo] AGG horny
corner ['kɔrner] SM INV (*Calcio*) corner (kick); **salvarsi in corner** (*fig: in gara, esame*) to get through by the skin of one's teeth; **mi son salvato in corner** (*in situazione imbarazzante*) I just managed to wriggle out of it
cornetta [kor'netta] SF (*Mus*) cornet; (*di telefono*) receiver; **sollevare la cornetta e comporre il numero** lift the receiver and dial the number; **riattaccare la cornetta** to hang up
cornetto [kor'netto] SM **1** (*Culin: brioche*) croissant; (: *gelato*) cone, cornet (*Brit*); (: *fagiolino*) runner bean (*Brit*), string bean (*Am*) **2** (*amuleto*) horn-shaped talisman **3** **cornetto acustico** ear trumpet
cornice [kor'nitʃe] SF (*gen*) frame; (*Archit, Sci*) cornice; (*Geog*) ledge; (*fig*) background, setting; **una cornice d'argento** a silver frame; **fare da cornice a** (*fig*) to frame
corniciaio, ai [korni'tʃajo] SM picture framer
corniciatura [kornitʃa'tura] SF framing
cornicione [korni'tʃone] SM (*di edificio*) ledge; (: *Archit*) cornice
cornificare [kornifi'kare] VT (*fam: marito, moglie*) to cheat on
corno ['kɔrno] SM (*pl m* **corni**) (*Mus*) horn; **corno da caccia** hunting horn; **corno inglese** (*Mus*) English horn, cor anglais
■ SM, NO PL **1** (*materiale*) horn; **di corno** (*bottone, manico*) horn *attr* **2** (*fam*): **un corno!** not on your life!; **felice? — un corno!** happy? — anything but!; **non me ne importa un corno!** I don't give a damn!; **non è vero un corno!** that's rubbish! **3** (*Geog*): **il Corno d'Africa** Horn of Africa; **i paesi del Corno d'Africa** Somaliland
■ SM (*pl f* **corna**) **1** (*Zool: di toro, lumaca*) horn; (: *di cervo*) antler **2** (*fam*): **fare le corna** (*per scaramanzia*) to keep one's fingers crossed; **fare le corna a qn** (*a marito, moglie*) to cheat on sb; **dire peste e corna di qn** to call sb every name under the sun; **rompersi le corna** to burn one's fingers

LO SAPEVI...?
corno non si traduce mai con *corn*

Cornovaglia [korno'vaʎʎa] SF Cornwall; **andremo in Cornovaglia a Pasqua** we're going to Cornwall at Easter; **mi è piaciuta molto la Cornovaglia** I really liked Cornwall
cornuto, a [kor'nuto] AGG **1** (*con corna*) horned **2** (*fam: tradito*) cheated on; **arbitro cornuto!** bloody ref!
■ SM/F (*fam*) cheated-on husband/wife; **cornuto!** (*fam!*) bastard! (*fam!*)
coro ['kɔro] SM (*gen, fig*) chorus; (*Rel: cantori, luogo*) choir; **canta in un coro** he sings in a choir; **un coro di proteste** a chorus of protests; **in coro** in chorus; **tutti in coro** all together
coroide [ko'rɔide] SF (*Anat*) choroid
corolla [ko'rɔlla] SF (*Bot*) corolla
corollario, ri [korol'larjo] SM corollary
corona [ko'rona] SF **1** (*di re*) crown; (*di nobile*) coronet; **cingere la corona** to assume the crown; **fare corona intorno a qn** (*fig*) to form a circle round sb **2** (*di fiori*) wreath; **corona d'alloro** laurel wreath; **corona funebre** *o* **mortuaria** funeral wreath; **corona del rosario** rosary, rosary beads *pl*; **corona di spine** crown of thorns **3** (*di dente*) crown **4** (*Geom*): **corona circolare** outer circle
coronamento [korona'mento] SM **1** (*di impresa*) completion; (*di carriera*) crowning achievement; **il coronamento dei propri sogni** the fulfilment of one's dreams **2** (*Edil*) crown; (*Naut*) taffrail
coronare [koro'nare] VT **1** (*cingere*): **coronare (di)** (*anche fig*) to crown (with) **2** (*realizzare: impresa*) to bring to a successful conclusion; **coronare i propri sogni** to fulfil one's dreams; **uno sforzo coronato dal successo** an effort crowned with success
coronaria [koro'narja] SF coronary artery
coronario, ria, ri, rie [koro'narjo] AGG coronary
corpetto [kor'petto] SM (*da donna*) bodice; (*da uomo*) waistcoat
corpo ['kɔrpo] SM (*gen, Chim, fig*) body; (*cadavere*) corpse, (dead) body; (*di opere*) corpus; **corpo liquido/gassoso** liquid/gaseous substance; **non ho niente in corpo da stamattina** I haven't eaten anything since this morning; **darsi anima e corpo a** to give o.s. heart and soul to; **(a) corpo a corpo** *agg* hand-to-hand; **andare di corpo** to empty one's bowels; **dare corpo a qc** to give substance to sth; **prendere corpo** (*idea, progetto*) to take shape; **a corpo morto** (*fig*) like a dead weight, heavily; **lo colpì con tutta la forza che aveva in corpo** she hit him with all her strength; **l'incendio ha divorato l'intero corpo dell'edificio** the fire destroyed the entire building; **l'intero corpo delle opere di Leopardi** the entire works of Leopardi; **esercizi a corpo libero** floor exercises
■ **corpo d'armata** army corps *sg*; **corpo di ballo** corps de ballet; **corpo dei carabinieri** ≈ police force **corpo celeste** heavenly body; **corpo a corpo** (*lotta*) hand-to-hand fight; **corpo diplomatico** diplomatic corps *sg*; **corpo elettorale** electorate; **corpo estraneo** foreign body; **corpo di guardia** (*soldati*) guard; (*locale*) guardroom; **corpo insegnante** teachers *pl*, teaching

Cc

staff; **corpo dei pompieri** fire brigade; **corpo del reato** material evidence; **corpo di spedizione** (*Mil*) task force

corporale [korpo'rale] AGG (*bisogni*) bodily; (*punizione*) corporal
■SM (*Rel*) corporal

corporativismo [korporati'vizmo] SM corporatism

corporativistico, a, ci, che [korporati'vistiko] AGG corporatist

corporativo, a [korpora'tivo] AGG corporate

corporatura [korpora'tura] SF build, physique; **di corporatura media** of medium build

corporazione [korporat'tsjone] SF professional body, corporation; (*Storia*) guild

corporeo, a [kor'pɔreo] AGG bodily, physical

corposo, a [kor'poso] AGG (*vino*) full-bodied

corpulento, a [korpu'lɛnto] AGG stout, corpulent

corpulenza [korpu'lɛntsa] SF stoutness, corpulence

corpuscolo [kor'puskolo] SM corpuscle

Corpus Domini ['kɔrpus'domini] SM (*Rel: festa*) Corpus Christi

corredare [korre'dare] VT: **corredare di** (*apparecchio, laboratorio*) to provide *o* furnish *o* equip with; **un elettrodomestico corredato di vari accessori** an electrical appliance complete with various accessories; **domanda corredata dai seguenti documenti** application accompanied by the following documents
▶ **corredarsi** VR: **corredarsi di** to equip o.s. with

corredo [kor'rɛdo] SM (*di attrezzi*) kit; (*da sposa*) trousseau

correggere [kor'rɛddʒere] VB IRREG
■VT (*gen*) to correct; (*compiti*) to correct, mark (*Brit*), grade (*Am*); (*Tip*) to proofread; (*fig: abuso*) to remedy; **deve ancora correggere i compiti di ieri** she hasn't marked yesterday's homework yet; **...correggimi se sbaglio** ... if I'm not mistaken; **correggere il caffè con la grappa** to lace one's coffee with grappa;
▶ **correggersi** VR to correct o.s.

corregionale [korredʒo'nale] AGG: **sono corregionali** they come from the same area
■SM/F: **è un mio corregionale** he comes from the same area as me

correlativo, a [korrela'tivo] AGG correlative

correlatore, trice [korrela'tore] SM/F (*Univ: di tesi*) assistant supervisor

correlazione [korrelat'tsjone] SF (*gen*) correlation; **correlazione dei tempi** (*Gramm*) sequence of tenses

corrente [kor'rɛnte] AGG **1** (*acqua del rubinetto*) running; **acqua corrente** running water **2** (*uso, anno*) current; (*moneta*) valid; **è opinione corrente che...** it is commonly believed that ...; **la vostra lettera del 5 corrente mese** (*in lettere commerciali*) in your letter of the 5th of this month, in your letter of the 5th inst. (*Brit frm*) **3** (*ordinario: merce*) ordinary; **articoli di qualità corrente** average-quality products
4 (*quotidiano: spese, affari*) everyday
■SM: **essere al corrente di** (*notizia*) to know about; (*scoperte scientifiche*) to be well-informed about; **tenere qn al corrente** to keep sb informed; **mettere qn al corrente (di)** to inform sb (of); **mi ha messo al corrente degli ultimi sviluppi** she told me about the latest developments
■SF (*Elettr, di acque*) current; (*di aria*) airstream, current of air; (*spiffero*) draught (*Brit*), draft (*Am*); (*di opinioni*) trend; **c'è corrente qui dentro** there's a draught in here; **tagliare la corrente** (*Elettr*) to cut off the power; **è andata via la corrente** (*Elettr*) the electricity's gone off; **presa di corrente** socket; **una corrente di simpatia** a wave of sympathy; **la corrente l'ha trascinato al largo** the current carried him out to sea; **andare contro corrente** (*anche fig*) to swim against the stream; **seguire la corrente** (*fig*) to follow the trend; **corrente alternata** alternating current; **corrente continua** direct current; **la Corrente del Golfo** the Gulf Stream; **corrente di risacca** (*Geog*) undertow

correntemente [korrente'mente] AVV (*comunemente*) commonly; **parlare una lingua correntemente** to speak a language fluently; **parla correntemente il francese** she speaks French fluently

correntista, i, e [korren'tista] SM/F (*Fin*) (current (*Brit*) *o* checking (*Am*)) account holder

correo, a ['kɔrreo] SM/F (*Dir*) accomplice

correre ['korrere] VB IRREG
■VI (*quando si esprime o sottindende una meta*) (*aus* **essere**) (*senza una meta e nel senso Sport*) (*aus* **avere**) (*gen*) to run; (*affrettarsi*) to hurry; (*precipitarsi*) to rush; (*Sport*) to race, run; (*diffondersi: notizie*) to go round; **abbiamo corso come pazzi per non perdere il treno** we ran like mad to catch the train; **sono corso subito fuori** I immediately rushed outside; **oggi ho corso un'ora** I went running for an hour today; **corre troppo in macchina** he drives too fast; **non correre!** (*anche fig*) not so fast!; **correre dietro a qn** (*anche fig*) to run after sb; **ci corre!** (*c'è una differenza*) there's a big difference!; **correva l'anno 1265** it was the year 1265; **corre voce che...** it is rumoured that ...; **il tempo corre** time is getting on
■VT (*gen*) to run; (*pericolo*) to face; (*Sport*) to run; (*: gara*) to compete in; **correre i 100 metri** to run in the 100 metres; **correre i 100 metri a tempo di record** to run the 100 metres in record time; **correre un rischio** to run a risk; **non voglio correre il rischio di non trovare posto** I don't want to risk not getting a seat

corresponsabile [korrespon'sabile] AGG jointly responsible; (*Dir*) jointly liable
■SM/F person jointly responsible; (*Dir: civile*) person jointly liable; (*: penale*) accomplice

corresponsabilità [korresponsabili'ta] SF (*vedi agg*) joint responsibility; joint liability

corresponsione [korrespon'sjone] SF payment

coressi *ecc* [kor'rɛssi] VB *vedi* **correggere**

correttamente [korretta'mente] AVV (*gen*) correctly; (*comportarsi*) properly; (*: nello sport*) fairly

correttezza [korret'tettsa] SF (*di comportamento*) correctness; (*Sport*) fair play; **è questione di correttezza** it's a question of propriety *o* good manners

correttivo, a [korret'tivo] AGG corrective

corretto, a [kor'rɛtto] PP *di* **correggere**
■AGG (*gen*) correct; (*comportamento*) proper, correct; **caffè corretto al cognac** coffee with a shot of cognac; **la risposta corretta** the correct answer

correttore, trice [korret'tore] SM/F: **correttore di bozze** proofreader
■SM **1 (liquido) correttore** correction *o* correcting fluid, Tipp-Ex® (*Brit*), White Out® (*Am*) **2** (*cosmetico*) blemish cover; **correttore ortografico** (*Inform*) spellchecker

correzione [korret'tsjone] SF **1** (*gen*) correction; (*di compiti*) marking (*Brit*), grading (*Am*); (*miglioramento*) improvement; **correzione di bozze** proofreading; **correzione ortografica** (*Inform: atto*) spelling check;

(: *processo*) spellchecking **2** (*castigo*): **casa di correzione** ≈ community home (*Brit*), ≈ reform school (*Am*), reformatory (*Am*)

corrida [kor'rida] SF bullfight

corridoio, oi [korri'dojo] SM (*gen*) corridor, passage; (*laterale: di aereo, treno*) corridor; (*centrale: di aereo, pullman*) aisle; (*Tennis*) alley; **manovre di corridoio** (*Pol*) lobbying *sg*; **corridoio aereo** air corridor

corridore [korri'dore] SM (*Sport*) runner; (: *su veicolo*) racer

corriera [kor'rjɛra] SF bus, coach (*Brit*)

corriere [kor'rjɛre] SM **1** (*gen*) messenger; (*Mil, diplomatico*) courier; (*spedizioniere*) carrier **2** (*Zool*): **corriere grosso** ringed plover

corrimano [korri'mano] SM handrail

corrispettivo [korrispet'tivo] SM amount due; **versare a qn il corrispettivo di una prestazione** to pay sb the amount due for his (*o* her) services

corrispondente [korrispon'dɛnte] AGG corresponding ■ SM/F (*gen, Stampa, TV*) correspondent

corrispondenza [korrispon'dɛntsa] SF **1** (*conformità*) correspondence; (*fig: connection*) relation; **non c'è corrispondenza tra le due versioni** the two versions do not correspond **2** (*posta: atto di scrivere*) correspondence; (*insieme di lettere*) mail; **evadere la corrispondenza** to deal with one's correspondence; **corrispondenza in arrivo/partenza** incoming/ outgoing mail; **corso per corrispondenza** correspondence course; **vendita per corrispondenza** mail-order shopping **3** (*Mat*) relation

corrispondere [korris'pondere] VB IRREG ■ VT **1** (*pagare*) to pay **2** (*ricambiare: amore*) to return ■ VI (*aus* **avere**) **1** (*equivalere*): **corrispondere (a)** to correspond (to); **quello che ha detto non corrisponde a verità** what he said doesn't fit the facts; **a ciascun numero corrisponde una lettera** each number corresponds to a letter **2** (*per lettera*): **corrispondere con** to correspond with

corrisposto, a [korris'posto] PP *di* **corrispondere** ■ AGG (*affetto, sentimento*) reciprocated

corroborante [korrobo'rante] AGG fortifying, stimulating; **clima corroborante** bracing climate ■ SM (*liquore*) pick-me-up

corroborare [korrobo'rare] VT (*rinvigorire*) to invigorate, strengthen, fortify; (*fig: ipotesi*) to corroborate, bear out

corrodere [kor'rodere] VB IRREG ■ VT (*metalli, fig*) to corrode; (*legno*) to eat into; **la carie corrode i denti** teeth are eaten away by decay ▶ **corrodersi** VIP to corrode; (*roccia*) to erode, wear away

corrompere [kor'rompere] VB IRREG ■ VT (*gen, fig*) to corrupt; (*testimone, giudice*) to bribe, corrupt; (*linguaggio*) to debase ▶ **corrompersi** VIP (*costumi*) to become corrupt

corrosione [korro'zjone] SF corrosion

corrosivamente [korroziva'mente] AVV corrosively

corrosività [korrozivi'ta] SF corrosiveness

corrosivo, a [korro'sivo] AGG, SM corrosive

corroso, a [kor'roso] PP *di* **corrodere**

corrottamente [korrotta'mente] AVV corruptly

corrotto, a [kor'rotto] PP *di* **corrompere** ■ AGG corrupt

corrucciarsi [korrut'tʃarsi] VIP to become upset; **si corrucciò in viso** his face took on a worried expression

corrucciato, a [korrut'tʃato] AGG (*volto, sguardo*) worried

corrugare [korru'gare] VT: **corrugare la fronte** *o* **le sopracciglia** to frown, knit one's brows

corruppi *ecc* [kor'ruppi] VB *vedi* **corrompere**

corruttela [korrut'tɛla] SF (*letter*) corruption, depravity

corruttibile [korrut'tibile] AGG corruptible

corruttibilità [korruttibili'ta] SF corruptibility

corruttore, trice [korrut'tore] SM/F corrupter; (*con denaro*) briber

corruzione [korrut'tsjone] SF corruption; (*con denaro*) bribery; **corruzione di minorenne** (*Dir*) corruption of a minor

corsa ['korsa] SF **1** (*azione*) running *no pl*; **andare** *o* **essere di corsa** to be in a hurry; **andarsene/arrivare di corsa** to rush off/in; **fare qc di corsa** to do sth quickly; **ho fatto i compiti di corsa e sono uscito** I did my homework quickly and went out; **ho mangiato di corsa un panino e sono uscito** I had a quick sandwich and went out; **ho dovuto fare una corsa** I had to dash; **"vietato scendere dal treno in corsa"** "do not alight from the train while it is in motion"; **abbiamo preso i cappotti e via di corsa** we grabbed our coats and off we went; **faccio una corsa e torno!** I'll be straight back!; **è una corsa contro il tempo** it's a race against time; **corsa all'oro** gold rush **2** (*Sport: gara*) race; (: *disciplina*) racing *no pl*; (: *atletica*) running *no pl*; **da corsa** (*auto, moto*) racing; **auto da corsa** racing car; **cavallo da corsa** racehorse; **fare una corsa** to run a race; **va spesso alle corse** he often goes to the races; **corsa automobilistica/ciclistica** motor/cycle racing; **corsa con i sacchi** sack race; **corsa campestre** cross-country race; **corsa ad ostacoli** (*Ippica*) steeplechase; (*Atletica*) hurdles *sg*; **corsa piana** *o* **in piano** (*Ippica*) flat race; **corsa a siepi** (*Ippica*) hurdle race **3** (*di autobus, taxi*) trip, journey; **a che ora c'è l'ultima corsa?** when is the last bus?; **quanto costa la corsa?** what's the fare? **4** (*Fis: di pendolo*) movement; (: *di pistone*) stroke **5** (*Naut, Mil*): **guerra di corsa** privateering

corsaro, a [kor'saro] AGG: **nave corsara** privateer ■ SM privateer, corsair

corsetteria [korsette'ria] SF corsetry

corsetto [kor'setto] SM corset

corsi *ecc* ['korsi] VB *vedi* **correre**

corsia [kor'sia] SF **1** (*gen*) gangway, passage; (*Aut, Sport*) lane; **autostrada a 4 corsie** 4-lane motorway (*Brit*) *o* freeway (*Am*); **corsia di accelerazione** (*Aut*) acceleration lane; **corsia di decelerazione** (*Aut*) deceleration lane; **corsia di emergenza** (*Aut*) hard shoulder (*Brit*), shoulder (*Am*); **corsia preferenziale** ≈ bus lane (*fig*) fast track; **corsia di sorpasso** (*Aut*) overtaking lane, fast lane **2** (*in ospedale*) ward; **è ricoverato in corsia** he's a patient in the ward

Corsica ['korsika] SF Corsica

corsivo, a [kor'sivo] AGG (*scrittura*) cursive; (*Tip*) italic ■ SM **1** cursive (writing); (*Tip*) italics *pl* **2** (*Stampa*) brief article of comment (*in italics*)

corso[1], a ['korso] PP *di* **correre**

corso[2], a ['kɔrso] AGG, SM/F Corsican

corso[3] ['korso] SM **1** (*fluire: di acqua, tempo*) course; **corso d'acqua** (*naturale*) river, stream; (*artificiale*) waterway; **discendere il corso del Nilo** to go down the Nile; **dare corso a** to start; **dar libero corso a** to give free expression to; **in corso** (*lavori*) in progress, under way; (*anno, mese*) current; **in corso di riparazione** in the process of being repaired; **nel corso di** during; **nel corso del tempo** in the course of time; **il nuovo corso del partito laburista** the new

Cc

direction of the Labour Party **2** (*Scol, Univ*) course; **un corso d'inglese** an English course; **seguire un corso serale** to go to an evening class; **tenere un corso su** to give a course on; **primo anno di corso** first year; **studente fuori corso** *undergraduate who has not completed course in due time*; **corso di aggiornamento** refresher course **3** (*strada cittadina*) main street; (*nei nomi di strada*) avenue; **ha un negozio sul corso** she's got a shop in the main street **4** (*Fin: di moneta*) circulation; (*: di titoli, valori*) rate, price; **aver corso legale** to be legal tender; **una banconota fuori corso** a banknote no longer legal tender

corte ['korte] SF **1** (*seguito del re*) court **2** (*attenzioni, gentilezze*): **fare la corte a qn** (*per amore*) to court sb; (*per interesse*) to butter sb up **3** (*Dir*) court; **Corte d'Appello** court of appeal; **Corte d'Assise** (*in Inghilterra e Galles*) ≈ crown court (*in Scozia*) ≈ high court **Corte di Cassazione** court of cassation; *the highest judicial authority*; **Corte dei Conti** *audit court*; **Corte Costituzionale** *special court dealing with constitutional and ministerial matters*
▷ www.giurcost.org/
corte marziale court-martial **4** (*cortile*) (court)yard

CORTI

The **Corte d'Appello** hears appeals against sentences passed by courts in both civil and criminal cases and can modify sentences where necessary. The **Corte d'Assise** tries serious crimes such as manslaughter and murder; its judges include both legal professionals and members of the public. Similar in structure, the **Corte d'Assise d'Appello** hears appeals imposed by these two courts. The **Corte di Cassazione** is the highest judicial authority and ensures that the law is correctly applied by the other courts; it may call for a re-trial if required. The **Corte dei Conti** ensures the Government's compliance with the law and the Constitution. Reporting directly to Parliament, it oversees the financial aspects of the state budget. The politically independent **Corte Costituzionale** decides whether laws comply with the principles of the Constitution, and has the power to impeach the "Presidente della Repubblica"
▷ www.cortecostituzionale.it/
▷ www.cortedicassazione.it/
▷ www.corteconti.it/

corteccia, ce [kor'tettʃa] SF (*di albero*) bark; (*Anat*) cortex
corteggiamento [korteddʒa'mento] SM courtship
corteggiare [korted'dʒare] VT to court, woo
corteggiatore [korteddʒa'tore] SM suitor
corteo [kor'tɛo] SM procession; **i dimostranti hanno sfilato in corteo** the demonstrators marched past; **corteo funebre** funeral cortège
cortese [kor'teze] AGG courteous; (*Letteratura*) courtly
cortesemente [korteze'mente] AVV courteously; **la preghiamo cortesemente di…** (*in lettera*) we should be most grateful if you would …
cortesia [korte'zia] SF (*qualità*) courtesy; (*atto*) favour; **fare una cortesia a qn** to do sb a favour; **mi faresti una cortesia?** would you do me a favour?; **fammi la cortesia di star zitto!** do me a favour and shut up!; **fammi una cortesia, spegni quella radio** would you please turn off that radio; **per cortesia, dov'è…?** excuse me, please, where is …?; **per cortesia, dov'è il bagno?** excuse me, where's the toilet?
cortigiano, a [korti'dʒano] SM/F courtier
■ SF (*euf: prostituta*) courtesan
cortile [kor'tile] SM (*di edificio: all'interno*) (court)yard; (*: davanti*) forecourt; (*: all'esterno, dietro*) yard; (*di cascina*) farmyard
cortina [kor'tina] SF curtain, drape (*Am*); (*anche fig*) screen; **una cortina di fumo/nebbia** a wall of smoke/mist; **la cortina di ferro** the Iron Curtain; **una cortina di silenzio** a wall of silence
cortisone [korti'zone] SM cortisone
corto, a ['korto] AGG (*tutti i sensi*) short; **maniche corte** short sleeves; **questi pantaloni sono troppo corti** these trousers are too short; **la settimana corta** the 5-day week; **la strada più corta** (*anche fig*) the quickest way; **avere la vista corta** (*anche fig*) to be short-sighted; **essere** *o* **rimanere a corto di qc** to be short of sth; **sono a corto di soldi** I'm short of money; **essere a corto di parole** to be at a loss for words
■ AVV: **tagliare corto** to come straight to the point

LO SAPEVI...?
corto non si traduce mai con *curt*

■ SM (*Cine*) short
cortocircuito [kortotʃir'kuito] SM short-circuit
cortometraggio, gi [kortome'traddʒo] SM (*Cine*) short (feature film)
corvé [kor've] SF INV (*Mil*) fatigue duty; **sabato siamo di corvé** (*scherz*) we are on chores on Saturday
corvetta [kor'vetta] SF corvette
corvino, a [kor'vino] AGG: **capelli corvini** jet-black hair
corvo ['kɔrvo] SM (*anche:* **corvo imperiale**) raven; **corvo comune** *o* **nero** rook
cosa ['kɔsa] SF **1** (*gen*) thing; **ogni cosa** *or* **tutte le cose** everything; **il terremoto ha distrutto ogni cosa** the earthquake destroyed everything; **qualche cosa** something; **c'è qualche altra cosa da discutere** there's something else to discuss; **vuole qualche cosa da mangiare?** would you like something to eat?; **nessuna cosa** nothing; **è una cosa da poco** it's nothing; **devo dirti una cosa** I've got something to tell you; **come prima cosa** first of all; **facciamo le cose per bene** let's do things properly; **la cosa migliore sarebbe partire di mattina** the best thing would be to leave in the morning; **tante belle cose!** all the best! **2** (*situazione, fatto*) it, things *pl*; **la cosa non è chiara** it isn't clear, things aren't clear; **ti voglio spiegare la cosa** let me explain things to you; **è successa una cosa strana** something strange has happened; **sono cose da ragazzi** that's kids for you; **ormai è cosa fatta!** (*positivo*) it's in the bag!; (*negativo*) it's done now!; **a cose fatte** when all is said and done, when it's all over; **le cose stanno così** this is how things stand; **sono cose che capitano!** these things happen! **3** (*preoccupazione, problema*) matter, affair, business *no pl*; **brutta cosa!** it's a nasty business *o* matter!; **la cosa non mi riguarda** the matter doesn't concern me; **è tutt'altra cosa** that's quite another matter; **eh no, non è la stessa cosa!** excuse me, but that's not the same thing!
■ PRON INTERROG: **(che) cosa?** what?; **(che) cos'è?** what is it?; **a cosa pensi?** what are you thinking about?; **cosa stai facendo?** what are you doing?; **che cosa ha detto?** what did he say?; **cosa?!** what?!; *vedi anche* **che**
cosacco, chi [ko'zakko] SM Cossack
Cosa Nostra [koza 'nɔstra] SF Cosa Nostra

cosare [ko'sare] VT (*fam*): **hai cosato la macchina?** have you thingummy'd the car?
cosca, sche ['kɔska] SF (*di mafiosi*) clan
coscia, sce ['kɔʃʃa] SF (*Anat*) thigh; (*Culin*: *di pollo*) leg; **una coscia di pollo** a chicken leg; **una coscia d'agnello** a leg of lamb
cosciente [koʃ'ʃɛnte] AGG (*gen, Med*) conscious; (*consapevole*): **cosciente di** conscious *o* aware of
coscientemente [koʃʃente'mente] AVV consciously
coscienza [koʃ'ʃɛntsa] SF **1** (*morale*) conscience; **aver qc sulla coscienza** to have sth on one's conscience; **avere la coscienza a posto/sporca** to have a good *o* clear/bad *o* guilty conscience; **in (tutta) coscienza** in all conscience *o* honesty **2** (*sensi*) consciousness; **perdere/riacquistare coscienza** to lose/regain consciousness **3** (*psicologica*) awareness; **avere coscienza di/che...** to be aware *o* conscious of/that ...; **prendere coscienza di qc** to become aware of sth, realize sth; **coscienza politica** political awareness **4** (*serietà*) conscientiousness; **coscienza professionale** conscientiousness; **persona di coscienza** honest *o* conscientious person
coscienziosamente [koʃʃentsjosa'mente] AVV conscientiously
coscienziosità [koʃʃentsjosi'ta] SF conscientiousness
coscienzioso, a [koʃʃen'tsjoso] AGG conscientious
cosciotto [koʃ'ʃɔtto] SM (*Culin*) leg
coscritto [kos'kritto] SM (*Mil*) conscript
coscrizione [koskrit'tsjone] SF (*Mil*) conscription
cosecante [kose'kante] SF (*Mat*) cosecant
coseno [ko'seno] SM (*Mat*) cosine
cosentino, a [kozen'tino] AGG of *o* from Cosenza
■ SM/F inhabitant *o* native of Cosenza
così [ko'si] AVV **1** (*in tal modo*) so; (*in questo modo*) (in) this way, like this, like that; **devi ripiegarlo così** you have to fold it like this; **se lo tiri così lo rompi** if you pull it like that you'll break it; **ho detto così** that's what I said; **ha detto così: "sei bugiardo"** this is what he said: "you're a liar"; **non ho detto così** I didn't say that; **se fosse così** if this were the case; **le cose stanno così** this is how things stand; **vorrei una scatola larga così e lunga così** (*accompagnato da gesti*) I'd like a box this *o* so wide and this *o* so long; **non scriverlo così, ma così!** don't write it like that, write it like this!; **e così feci anch'io** and I did likewise; **basta così!** that's enough! **2** (*talmente*) so; **fa così bello oggi** it's such a lovely day, the weather's so lovely today; **una persona così gentile** such a kind person; **è così simpatica!** she's so nice!; **è così lontano** it's so far away; **non sono così stupido!** I'm not that stupid!; **così... che...** so ... that ...; **era così stanco che è andato subito a letto** he was so tired that he went to bed immediately **3** **così... come** as ... as; **non è così onesto come credi** he's not as *o* so honest as you think; **se si comporta così come ha sempre fatto...** if he goes on behaving like this ...; **me lo dia così com'è** give it to me as it is **4** **per così dire** so to speak, so to say; **e così via** and so on; **è così o non è così?** isn't that so?; **così così** so so; **com'era il concerto? – così così** what was the concert like? – so-so; **e così?** well?
■ AGG INV (*tale*): **non ho mai visto un film così** I've never seen such a film; **non ho mai conosciuto una persona così** I've never met such a person, I've never met a person like that; **i tipi così mi danno ai nervi** people like that get on my nerves
■ CONG (*perciò*) so, therefore; **pioveva, così sono rimasto a casa** it was raining so I stayed at home
cosicché [kosik'ke] CONG so (that)
cosiddetto, a [kosid'detto] AGG so-called
cosmesi [koz'mɛzi] SF INV (*scienza*) cosmetics *sg*; (*prodotti*) cosmetics *pl*; (*trattamento*) beauty treatment
cosmetico, a, ci, che [koz'metiko] AGG, SM cosmetic
cosmico, a, ci, che ['kɔzmiko] AGG cosmic
cosmo ['kɔzmo] SM (*universo*) cosmos; (*spazio*) outer space
cosmologia [kozmolo'dʒia] SF cosmology
cosmonauta, i, e [kozmo'nauta] SM/F cosmonaut
cosmonave [kozmo'nave] SF spaceship
cosmopolita, i, e [kozmopo'lita] AGG, SM/F (*anche fig*) cosmopolitan
cosmopolitico, a, ci, che [kozmopo'litiko] AGG cosmopolitan
cosmopolitismo [kozmopoli'tizmo] SM cosmopolitanism
coso ['kɔso] SM (*fam*: *oggetto*) thing, thingummy; (: *aggeggio*) contraption; (: *persona*) what's his name, thingummy
cospargere [kos'pardʒere] VT IRREG: **cospargere di** to sprinkle with
cosparso, a [kos'parzo] PP *di* **cospargere**
cospetto [kos'pɛtto] SM (*presenza*): **in** *o* **al cospetto di** in the presence of, in front of; **giurare al cospetto di Dio** to swear before God
cospicuamente [kospikua'mente] AVV: **remunerato cospicuamente** generously paid
cospicuità [kospikui'ta] SF vast quantity; **la cospicuità delle sue risorse** his considerable resources
cospicuo, a [kos'pikuo] AGG considerable, large
cospirare [kospi'rare] VI (*aus* **avere**) (*gen*) to conspire, plot; (*fig*: *circostanze*) to conspire
cospiratore, trice [kospira'tore] SM/F plotter, conspirator; **con fare da cospiratore** with a conspiratorial air
cospirazione [kospirat'tsjone] SF (*anche fig*) plot, conspiracy
cossi *ecc* ['kɔssi] VB *vedi* **cuocere**
Cost. ABBR = **costituzione**
costa ['kɔsta] SF **1** (*litorale*) coast; (*spiaggia*) shore; (*tra terra e mare*) coastline; **una città sulla costa** a town on the coast; **navigare sotto costa** to hug the coast; **la Costa d'Avorio** the Ivory Coast; **la Costa Azzurra** the French Riviera **2** (*di montagna*) slope; **a mezza costa** halfway up (*o* down) the slope **3** (*nervatura*: *di nave, Bot*) rib; (: *di tessuto*) ribbing *no pl*; (*dorso*: *di libro*) spine; **punto a coste** (*Maglia*) rib (stitch); **velluto a coste** corduroy
costà [kos'ta] AVV (*letter*) there
costante [kos'tante] AGG (*gen, Mat*) constant; (*persona*) steadfast
■ SF (*Mat*) constant; **è una costante della letteratura del '900** it is a standard feature of 20th century literature
costantemente [kostante'mente] AVV constantly
costanza [kos'tantsa] SF (*gen*) constancy; (*fig*: *fermezza*) constancy, steadfastness; **il Lago di Costanza** Lake Constance
costare [kos'tare] VI (*aus* **essere**) (*anche fig*) to cost; **quanto costa quell'anello?** how much does that ring cost?; **quanto t'è costato?** how much did it cost you?; **è costato trenta euro** it cost thirty euros; **costare caro** to be expensive, cost a lot; **mangiare fuori tutte le sere costa caro** eating out every evening is expensive; **costare poco** to be cheap; **cosa vuoi che ti**

Cc

costi I am not asking much of you; **costare un occhio della testa** to cost a fortune; **costi quel che costi** no matter what; **gli è costato la vita** it cost him his life

Costa Rica ['kɔsta 'rika] SF Costa Rica

costaricano, a [kostari'kano] AGG, SM/F Costa Rican

costata [kos'tata] SF (*Culin: di manzo*) large chop

costato [kos'tato] SM (*Anat*) ribs *pl*

costeggiare [kosted'dʒare] VT (*Naut*) to hug, skirt; (*sogg: persona*) to walk (*o* drive *ecc*) alongside; (*: strada*) to run alongside

costei [kos'tɛi] PRON DIMOSTR (*sogg*) she; (*complemento*) her; (*pegg*) this woman

costellare [kostel'lare] VT: **costellare (di)** to stud (with); **il prato era costellato di margherite** the field was studded with daisies

costellazione [kostellat'tsjone] SF constellation

costernare [koster'nare] VT to dismay, fill with consternation

costernato, a [koster'nato] AGG dismayed

costernazione [kosternat'tsjone] SF dismay, consternation

costì [kos'ti] AVV (*letter*) here

costiera [kos'tjɛra] SF (stretch of) coast; (*strada*) coast road

costiero, a [kos'tjɛro] AGG coastal, coast *attr*; **nave costiera** coaster

costina [kos'tina] SF: **costine di maiale** spareribs

costipato, a [kosti'pato] AGG (*stitico*) constipated; (*raffreddato*): **essere costipato** to have a bad cold

costipazione [kostipat'tsjone] SF (*vedi agg*) constipation; bad cold

costituente [kostitu'ɛnte] AGG (*gen, Chim, Pol*) constituent *attr*

■ SM (*Chim*) constituent

■ SF: **la Costituente** *or* **l'Assemblea costituente** the Constituent Assembly

costituire [kostitu'ire] VT **1** (*fondare: società, comitato, governo*) to set up, form; (*accumulare: patrimonio, raccolta*) to build up, put together; **hanno costituito un nuovo gruppo** they've formed a new group **2** (*formare: sogg: elementi, parti*) to constitute, make up **3** (*essere, rappresentare*) to be, constitute; **costituisce un vero problema!** it's a real problem!; **il fatto non costituisce reato** (*Dir*) this is not a crime **4** (*Dir: nominare*) to appoint; **costituire qn presidente/erede** to appoint sb chairman/one's heir

▶ **costituirsi** VR **1** (*organizzarsi*) **costituirsi in società** to form a company; **costituirsi in regione autonoma** to become an independent region **2** (*ricercato*) **costituirsi (alla polizia)** to give o.s. up (to the police) **3** (*Dir*): **costituirsi parte civile** *to associate in an action with the public prosecutor for damages*

costitutivo, a [kostitu'tivo] AGG constituent, component; **atto costitutivo** (*Dir: di società*) memorandum of association

costituzionale [kostituttsjo'nale] AGG constitutional

costituzionalismo [kostituttsjona'lizmo] SM constitutionalism

costituzionalità [kostituttsjonali'ta] SF constitutionality

costituzionalmente [kostituttsjonal'mente] AVV constitutionally

costituzione [kostitut'tsjone] SF **1** (*formazione*) setting-up, establishment; (*struttura*) composition, make-up; (*Med*) constitution; **certificato di sana e robusta costituzione** certificate of good health **2** (*Dir*) constitution

COSTITUZIONE

The foundation of the Italian Republic as a result of the referendum of June 2nd 1946 was followed by the creation of the "Constituent Assembly", which drew up and approved the text of the Italian Constitution. The Constitution came into force on 1st January 1948 and consists of an introduction setting out the general principles, a section on the rights and duties of citizens and a section on the organization of the state.

▷ www.quirinale.it/costituzione/costituzione.htm

costo ['kɔsto] SM (*anche fig*) cost; **il costo della vacanza** the cost of the holiday; **determinazione dei costi** costing; **sotto costo** for less than cost price; **a ogni** *o* **qualunque costo** *or* **a tutti i costi** at all costs; **dev'essere evitato a tutti i costi** it must be avoided at all costs; **l'ha voluto portare a tutti i costi** he was determined to bring it, no matter what; **non vuol cedere a nessun costo** there's no way he'll give in, he won't give in no matter what

■ **costi di esercizio** running costs; **costi fissi** fixed costs; **costi di gestione** operating costs; **costi d'impianto** set-up costs; **costi indiretti** indirect costs; **costi di produzione** production costs; **costo, assicurazione e nolo** cost, insurance and freight; **costo del denaro** cost of money; **costo del lavoro** cost of labour; **costo e nolo** cost and freight; **costo della vita** cost of living

costola ['kɔstola] SF (*Anat, Bot, Archit*) rib; **mi sono rotto una costola** I broke a rib; **è magrissimo, gli si contano le costole** he's so thin you can see his ribs; **se lo prendo gli rompo le costole!** if I catch him I'll break every bone in his body!; **ha la polizia alle costole** the police are hard on his heels

costoletta [kosto'letta] SF (*Culin*) cutlet

costolone [kosto'lone] SM (*Archit*) rib

costoro [kos'toro] PRON DIMOSTR PL (*sogg*) they; (*complemento*) them; (*pegg*) these people

costosamente [kostosa'mente] AVV expensively

costoso, a [kos'toso] AGG costly, expensive; **un albergo costoso** an expensive hotel

costretto, a [kos'tretto] PP *di* **costringere**

costringere [kos'trindʒere] VT IRREG: **costringere qn (a fare qc)** to force *o* compel sb (to do sth); **mi ci hanno costretto con la forza** they forced me to do it; **mi ha costretto a dire la verità** she made me tell the truth; **la paralisi lo costringe a una sedia a rotelle** the paralysis confines him to a wheelchair; **è stato costretto a ritirarsi dalla gara** he had to withdraw from the competition; **vedersi costretto a fare qc** to find o.s. forced *o* compelled to do sth

costrittivo, a [kostrit'tivo] AGG coercive

costrittore [kostrit'tore] AGG: **muscolo costrittore** constrictor

costrizione [kostrit'tsjone] SF **1** (*obbligo*) compulsion; **è legato da costrizione morale** he is morally obliged **2** (*violenza*) coercion, duress

costruire [kostru'ire] VT IRREG (*gen*) to build, construct; (*fig: teoria, frasi, fortuna*) to construct, build up; **qui costruiranno il nuovo stadio** they're going to build the new stadium here; **in questa città non si costruisce più da anni** there's been no building work done in this town for years; **questo verbo si costruisce con il congiuntivo** this verb takes the subjunctive; **costruire sulla sabbia** (*fig*) to build on sand

LO SAPEVI...?
costruire non si traduce mai con *construe*

costruttivo, a [kostrut'tivo] AGG (*Edil*) building *attr*; (*fig*) constructive; **schema costruttivo** (*Tecn*) design, plan; **tecnica costruttiva** (*Edil*) building techniques *pl*; (*Ingegneria*) assembly techniques *pl*

costrutto [kos'trutto] SM (*Gramm*) construction

costruttore, trice [kostrut'tore] AGG building *attr*
■ SM (*fabbricante*) manufacturer; (*Edil*) builder

costruzione [kostrut'tsjone] SF **1** (*fabbricazione*) building, construction; (*struttura: anche Tecn, Gramm*) construction; **la costruzione del ponte è durata sette anni** it took seven years to build the bridge; **di recente costruzione** of recent construction, recently built; **in (via di) costruzione** under construction; **essere in costruzione** to be under construction; **l'autostrada è in costruzione** the motorway is under construction; **materiali/legno da costruzione** building materials/timber; **scienza delle costruzioni** construction theory; **le costruzioni** (*gioco*) building blocks **2** (*edificio*) building; **una costruzione in vetro e acciaio** a building made of glass and steel

costui [kos'tui] PRON DIMOSTR (*sogg*) he; (*complemento*) him; (*pegg*) this fellow, this man; **si può sapere chi è costui?** (*pegg*) just who is that fellow?

costume [kos'tume] SM **1** (*gen*) custom; (*abitudine*) habit; **usi e costumi di una popolazione** habits and customs of a people; **di facili costumi** of loose morals, of easy virtue; **il buon costume** public morality **2** (*indumento*) costume; **costume nazionale** national costume *o* dress; **costume da bagno** (*da donna*) bathing *o* swimming costume (*Brit*), swimsuit; (*da uomo*) bathing *o* swimming trunks *pl*

costumista, i, e [kostu'mista] SM/F (*Cine, Teatro, TV*) costume maker, costume designer

cotangente [kotan'dʒɛnte] SF (*Mat*) cotangent

cote ['kote] SF whetstone

cotechino [kote'kino] SM (*Culin*) pork sausage

cotenna [ko'tenna] SF bacon rind

cotiledone [koti'lɛdone] SM cotyledon

cotillon [kɔti'jɔ̃] SM INV (*piccolo omaggio*) favour

cotogna [ko'toɲɲa] SF (*anche:* **mela cotogna**) quince

cotognata [kotoɲ'ɲata] SF quince jelly

cotogno [ko'toɲɲo] SM quince (tree)

cotoletta [koto'letta] SF (*di maiale, montone*) chop; (*di vitello, agnello*) cutlet

cotonare [koto'nare] VT (*capelli*) to backcomb

cotonato [koto'nato] SM (*tessuto: di cotone*) cotton fabric; (*: misto*) cotton mix
■ AGG (*capelli*) backcombed

cotonatura [kotona'tura] SF (*di capelli*) backcombing

cotone [ko'tone] SM **1** (*gen*) cotton; **di cotone** cotton *attr*; **una maglietta di cotone** a cotton T-shirt; **cotone mercerizzato** mercerised cotton; **cotone pettinato** brushed cotton; **cotone da rammendo** darning thread **2** (*anche:* **cotone idrofilo**) cotton wool (*Brit*), cotton (*Am*); **batuffolo di cotone** wad of cotton wool (*Brit*) *o* cotton (*Am*)

cotoniero, a [koto'njɛro] AGG cotton *attr*

cotonificio, ci [kotoni'fitʃo] SM cotton mill

cotta¹ ['kɔtta] SF (*fam*): **prendersi una cotta (per qn)** to get a crush (on sb)

cotta² ['kɔtta] SF **1** (*Rel*) surplice **2** (*Storia*): **cotta d'arme** surcoat; **cotta di maglia** chain mail

cottimista, i, e [kotti'mista] SM/F pieceworker

cottimo ['kɔttimo] SM (*anche:* **lavoro a cottimo**) piecework; **lavorare a cottimo** to do piecework

cotto, a ['kɔtto] PP *di* **cuocere**
■ AGG (*Culin*) cooked; **cotta o cruda?** cooked or raw?; **sono cotti gli spaghetti?** is the spaghetti done?; **mele cotte** stewed apples; **ben cotto** well cooked; (*carne*) well done; **poco cotto** underdone; **troppo cotto** overdone; **cotto a puntino** cooked to perfection; **essere cotto (di qn)** (*fig fam*) to have a crush (on sb); **è proprio cotto!** he's smitten!, he's head-over-heels in love; **essere cotto (di sonno/stanchezza)** (*fam*) to be done in; **dirne di cotte e di crude a qn** to call sb every name under the sun; **farne di cotte e di crude** to get up to all kinds of mischief
■ SM brickwork; **mattone di cotto** fired brick; **pavimento in cotto** tile floor

cotton fioc® ['kɔtton'fiɔk] SM INV cotton bud

cottura [kot'tura] SF (*Culin, gen*) cooking; (*: in forno*) baking; (*: di arrosto*) roasting; (*: in umido*) stewing; **cottura a fuoco lento** simmering

coupé [ku'pe] SM INV (*Aut*) coupé

couperose [kupəroz] SF INV blotches *pl* (*on the face*)

coupon [ku'pɔ̃] SM INV coupon

court-bouillon ['kuətbu:jɒn] SM INV court-bouillon

cous cous [kus'kus] SM couscous

cova ['kova] SF (*di uccello: atto, periodo*) brooding; **fare la cova** to brood, sit

covalente [kova'lɛnte] AGG covalent; **legame covalente** covalent bond

covare [ko'vare] VI (*aus* **avere**) (*fuoco, fig: odio, rancore*) to smoulder (*Brit*), smolder (*Am*); **qui gatta ci cova** there's something fishy about this
■ VT **1** (*sogg: uccello: uova*) to sit on; (*uso assoluto*) to sit on its eggs **2** (*fig: malattia*) to be sickening for; (*: odio, rancore*) to nurse; **sta covando un raffreddore** he is sickening for a cold; **covare odio verso qn** to nurse hatred for sb

covata [ko'vata] SF (*anche fig*) brood

covo ['kovo] SM den, lair; **un covo di terroristi** a terrorist base; **quel bar è un covo di spacciatori** that bar is a haunt for drug pushers

covone [ko'vone] SM sheaf

coyote [ko'jote] SM INV coyote

cozza ['kɔttsa] SF mussel; (*fig: brutta ragazza*) dog, minger; **spaghetti con le cozze** spaghetti with mussels

cozzare [kot'tsare] VI (*aus* **avere**) (*animali: con le corna*) to butt; (*veicoli*) to collide; (*fig: caratteri, idee*) to clash; **cozzare contro** to collide with; **cozzare contro un muro** to crash into a wall
■ VT (*fig*): **cozzare il capo contro il muro** to bang one's head against a brick wall

cozzo ['kɔttso] SM (*di corna*) butt; (*di veicoli*) crash, collision; (*fig: di idee*) clash

C.P. ABBR **1** (= **cartolina postale**) pc **2** (= **casella postale**) P.O. box **3** (*Naut*): = **capitaneria (di porto)** **4** (*Dir*): = **codice penale**)

CPS [tʃipi'ɛsse] SIGLA M (*Inform*) cps (= *characters per second*)

CPU [tʃipi'u] SIGLA F (*Inform*) CPU (= *central processing unit*)

CR SIGLA = *Cremona*

crac [krak] SM INV **1** (*rumore*) crack **2** (*rovina: economica*) crash

craccare [krak'kare] VT (*Inform*) to crack

Cc

crack [krak] SM INV (*droga*) crack
cracking ['krækiŋ] SM (*Chim*) cracking
Cracovia [kra'kɔvja] SF Cracow
CRAL [kral] SIGLA M (= **Circolo Ricreativo Aziendale Lavoratori**) *employees' recreational facility*
crampo ['krampo] SM cramp; **avere un crampo alla gamba** to have cramp in one's leg; **ho un crampo alla gamba** I've got cramp in my leg; **avere i crampi allo stomaco** to have stomach cramps; **ho i crampi allo stomaco dalla fame** I've got hunger pangs
cranico, a, ci, che ['kraniko] AGG cranial
cranio, ni ['kranjo] SM **1** skull; (*Anat*) cranium; **avere il cranio duro** (*fig*) to be pig-headed; **fa trentamila lire a cranio** (*fam*) it's thirty thousand lire a head **2** (*genio*): **essere un cranio (in qc)** to be a genius (at sth)
crash test [kraʃ 'tɛst] SM INV crash test
crasi ['krazi] SF INV (*Gramm*) syneresis, crasis
cratere [kra'tɛre] SM crater
crauti ['krauti] SMPL sauerkraut *sg*
cravatta [kra'vatta] SF tie; **fare il nodo alla cravatta** to tie one's tie; **cravatta a farfalla** bow tie
cravattino [kravat'tino] SM bow tie
crawl [krɔːl] SM INV crawl; **nuotare a crawl** to do the crawl
creanza [kre'antsa] SF (good) manners *pl*; **per buona creanza** out of politeness
creare [kre'are] VT (*gen*) to create; (*eleggere*) to make, appoint; (*fondare*) to set up; **creare un precedente** to create a precedent; **creare un problema a qn** to create a problem for sb; **mi ha creato un sacco di problemi** it's caused me a lot of problems; **crearsi una clientela** to build up a clientele; **ha creato un personaggio molto divertente** he created a very funny character; **la notizia ha creato il panico** the news caused panic
creatina [krea'tina] SF creatin(e)
creativamente [kreativa'mente] AVV creatively
creatività [kreativi'ta] SF INV creativity
creativo, a [krea'tivo] AGG creative
creato [kre'ato] SM: **il creato** the Creation
creatore, trice [krea'tore] AGG creative
■ SM/F creator; (*fondatore*) founder; **un creatore di alta moda** fashion designer; **il Creatore** (*Dio*) the Creator; **andare al Creatore** to go to meet one's maker
creatura [krea'tura] SF creature; (*bimbo*) baby, infant; **povera creatura!** poor thing!; **le mie creature** my babies
creazione [kreat'tsjone] SF (*gen*) creation; (*fondazione*) foundation, establishment
crebbi *ecc* VB *vedi* **crescere**
credente [kre'dɛnte] SM/F (*Rel*) believer
credenza¹ [kre'dɛntsa] SF (*fede, opinione*) belief
credenza² [kre'dɛntsa] SF (*armadio*) sideboard
credenziale [kreden'tsjale] AGG: **lettere credenziali** credentials
■ **credenziali** SFPL (*anche fig*) credentials
credere ['kredere] VT **1** to believe; **lo** *o* **ci credo** I believe it; **come puoi credere una cosa simile?** how can you believe such a thing?; **lo credo bene!** I should think so too! **2** (*pensare*) to believe, think; **ti credevo meno ingenuo** I didn't think you were so naive; **lo credo onesto** I believe him to be honest; **ti credevo morto** I thought you were dead; **credo che sia stato lui (a farlo)** I think it was him, I think he did it; **credo che arrivi domani** I think he's arriving tomorrow; **credeva di aver perso le chiavi** she thought she had lost her keys; **credo di sì/no** I think/don't think so; **voleva farmi credere che...** he wanted me to think that ...; **voleva darmi a credere che non la conosceva** he tried to convince me that he didn't know her **3** (*ritenere opportuno*): **fai quello che credi** *o* **come credi** do as you please; **ha creduto bene di mollare tutto** he thought it best to let everything go
■ VI (*aus* **avere**) to believe; **credere a qn/qc** to believe sb/sth; **non ti credo** I don't believe you; **non dirmi che credi ai fantasmi!** don't tell me you believe in ghosts!; **come puoi credere a una cosa simile?** how can you believe such a thing?; **non posso crederci!** I can't believe it!; **credere in qn/qc** to believe in sb/sth; **credere in Dio** to believe in God; **ti credo sulla parola** I'll take your word for it; **gli credo poco** I have little faith in him; **non credeva ai suoi occhi/alle sue orecchie** he could not believe his eyes/ears; **credevo a uno scherzo** I thought it was a joke; **si è creduto ad una truffa** it looked like a swindle;
▶ **credersi** VR: **si crede furbo** he thinks he's smart; **chi ti credi di essere!** who do you think you are!
credibile [kre'dibile] AGG credible, believable
credibilità [kredibili'ta] SF credibility
credibilmente [kredibil'mente] AVV credibly
creditizio, zia, zi, zie [kredi'tittsjo] AGG credit *attr*
credito ['kredito] SM **1** (*Fin*) credit; **comprare/vendere a credito** to buy/sell on credit *o* easy terms; **"non si fa credito"** "no credit", "cash terms only"; **essere in credito** to be owed money; (*Banca*) to be in credit; **credito agevolato** easy credit terms; **credito formativo** (*Scol*) *a system that gives students credit for extra work done*; *vedi anche* **debito formativo credito d'imposta** tax credit **2** (*credibilità*) credit; **acquistare credito** (*teoria, partito*) to gain acceptance; **dare credito a qc** to give credit to sth; **non puoi dar credito alla sua parola** you can't trust him; **trovare credito presso qn** to win sb's trust
creditore, trice [kredi'tore] AGG, SM/F creditor
credo ['krɛdo] SM INV (*Rel, fig*) creed; **credo politico** political credo
credulità [kreduli'ta] SF credulity, gullibility
credulo, a [kre'dulo] AGG credulous
credulone, a [kredu'lone] SM/F gullible person
crema ['krɛma] SF (*Culin*) cream; (: *con uova, zucchero ecc*) custard; (*cosmetico, fig*) cream; **un gelato alla crema** a vanilla ice; **una pasta con la crema** a cake with a custard filling
■ **crema da barba** shaving cream; **crema di bellezza** beauty cream; **crema di cacao** (*liquore*) crème de cacao; **crema al cioccolato** chocolate custard; **crema idratante** moisturizing cream; **crema pasticciera** confectioner's custard; **crema di riso** rice custard; **crema solare** sun cream
cremagliera [kremaʎ'ʎɛra] SF rack; **ferrovia a cremagliera** rack railway
cremare [kre'mare] VT to cremate
crematorio, ria, ri, rie [krema'tɔrjo] AGG crematory
■ SM crematorium
cremazione [kremat'tsjone] SF cremation
cremisi ['krɛmizi] AGG INV, SM INV crimson
Cremlino [krem'lino] SM: **il Cremlino** the Kremlin
cremlinologia [kremlinolo'dʒia] SF Kremlinology
cremlinologo, gi [kremli'nɔlogo] SM Kremlinologist
cremonese [kremo'nese] AGG of *o* from Cremona
■ SM/F inhabitant *o* native of Cremona
cremortartaro [kremor'tartaro] SM cream of tartar
cremoso, a [kre'moso] AGG creamy

cren [krɛn] SM (*Bot*) horseradish; (*salsa*) horseradish sauce
crepa ['krɛpa] SF crack
crepaccio, ci [kre'pattʃo] SM (*nella roccia*) large crack, fissure; (*nel ghiaccio*) crevasse
crepacuore [krepa'kwɔre] SM: **morire di crepacuore** to die of a broken heart
crepapelle [krepa'pɛlle] AVV: **ridere a crepapelle** to split one's sides laughing; **mangiare a crepapelle** to eat till one bursts
crepare [kre'pare] VI (*aus* **essere**) (*fam: morire*) to kick the bucket, snuff it (*Brit*); **crepare dal ridere** *o* **dalle risa** to kill o.s. laughing, split one's sides laughing; **crepare dall'invidia** to be green with envy
▶ **creparsi** VIP (*spaccarsi*) to crack
crêpe [krɛp] SF INV (*Culin*) pancake; **una crêpe al cioccolato** a chocolate pancake
crepitare [krepi'tare] VI (*aus* **avere**) (*fuoco*) to crackle; (*pioggia*) to patter; (*foglie*) to rustle
crepitio, tii [krepi'tio] SM (*vedi vb*) crackling; pattering; rustling
crepuscolare [krepusko'lare] AGG twilight *attr*; **luce crepuscolare** twilight
crepuscolo [kre'puskolo] SM (*anche fig*) twilight, dusk; **al crepuscolo** at twilight
crescendo [kreʃ'ʃɛndo] SM (*Mus, anche fig*) crescendo; **suonare in crescendo** to play a crescendo; **la sua carriera è stata un crescendo di successi** his career has gone from strength to strength
crescente [kreʃ'ʃɛnte] AGG (*gen*) growing, increasing; (*luna*) waxing; **luna crescente** waxing moon
crescere ['kreʃʃere] VB IRREG
■ VI (*aus* **essere**) **1** (*gen*) to grow; (*persona: diventare adulto*) to grow up; (*: diventare più alto*) to grow taller; **il bambino/l'albero è cresciuto** the child/tree has grown; **com'è cresciuto tuo fratello!** hasn't your brother grown!; **i suoi capelli non crescono molto** her hair doesn't grow very fast; **sono cresciuto in Sardegna** I grew up in Sardinia; **farsi crescere la barba/i capelli** to grow a beard/one's hair; **si sta facendo crescere i capelli** she's growing her hair **2** (*aumentare: rumore, prezzo, numero*) to increase; (*: città, quartiere*) to expand; (*: luna*) to wax; **la popolazione mondiale cresce velocemente** the world's population is increasing rapidly; **i prezzi crescono ogni giorno** prices are going up daily; **la città è cresciuta a vista d'occhio** the city has grown before our very eyes
■ VT (*fam: coltivare*) to grow; (*: allevare: figli*) to raise
crescione [kreʃ'ʃone] SM watercress; **crescione inglese** *o* **degli orti** garden cress
crescita ['kreʃʃita] SF: **crescita (di)** growth (in); **crescita zero** zero growth
cresciuto, a [kreʃ'ʃuto] PP *di* **crescere**
cresima ['krɛzima] SF (*Rel*) confirmation; **fare la cresima** to be confirmed
cresimare [krezi'mare] (*Rel*) VT to confirm
▶ **cresimarsi** VIP to be confirmed
Creso ['krɛzo] SM Croesus
crespella [kres'pɛlla] SF (stuffed) pancake
crespo, a ['krespo] AGG (*capelli*) frizzy; (*tessuto*) puckered; **ha i capelli crespi** she's got frizzy hair
■ SM (*tessuto*) crêpe
cresta ['kresta] SF (*gen*) crest; (*di uccello*) crest; (*di pollo*) comb; (*di montagna*) ridge; **alzare la cresta** (*fig*) to become cocky; **abbassare la cresta** (*fig*) to climb down; **far abbassare la cresta a qn** to take sb down a peg or two; **far la cresta sulla spesa** to keep some of the shopping money for o.s.; **essere sulla cresta dell'onda** to be riding high; **cresta di gallo** (*Bot*) cockscomb; (*Med fam*) condyloma
Creta ['kreta] SF Crete
creta ['kreta] SF (*argilla*) clay
cretese [kre'tese] AGG, SM/F Cretan
cretinata [kreti'nata] SF (*fam*): **dire/fare una cretinata** to say/do something stupid; **non dire cretinate!** don't talk rubbish!
cretineria [kretine'ria] SF stupidity
cretinismo [kreti'nizmo] SM (*Med*) cretinism
cretino, a [kre'tino] AGG (*Med*) cretinous; (*pegg*) cretinous, moronic; **ma come sei cretina!** you're so stupid!
■ SM/F (*vedi agg*) cretin; cretin, moron; **quel cretino mi ha quasi investito** that idiot nearly ran me over
CRI [kri] SIGLA F = *Croce Rossa Italiana*
cric[1] [krik] SM INV (*rumore*) creak
cric[2] [krik] SM INV (*martinetto*) jack
cricca, che ['krikka] SF clique
criceto [kri'tʃɛto] SM hamster
criminale [krimi'nale] AGG criminal
■ SM/F criminal; **criminale di guerra** war criminal
criminalità [kriminali'ta] SF **1** criminal nature **2** (*delinquenza*) crime; **la criminalità organizzata** organized crime
criminalizzare [kriminalid'dzare] VT to criminalize
CRIMINALPOL [kriminal'pɔl] SIGLA F = *polizia criminale*
crimine ['krimine] SM (*anche fig*) crime; **crimini di guerra** war crimes
criminologia [kriminolo'dʒia] SF criminology
criminosamente [kriminosa'mente] AVV criminally
criminosità [kriminosi'ta] SF criminality
criminoso, a [krimi'noso] AGG criminal
crinale [kri'nale] SM ridge, crest
crine ['krine] SM horsehair; **di crine** horsehair *attr*; **crine vegetale** vegetable fibre
criniera [kri'njɛra] SF (*di animale*) mane
crinolina [krino'lina] SF crinoline
criochirurgia [kriokirur'dʒia] SF cryosurgery
criolite [krio'lite] SF cryolite
cripta ['kripta] SF crypt
criptare [krip'tare] VT (*TV*) to encrypt
criptato, a [krip'tato] AGG (*programma, messaggio*) encrypted
criptico, a, ci, che ['kriptiko] AGG cryptic
crisalide [kri'zalide] SF chrysalis
crisantemo [krizan'tɛmo] SM chrysanthemum
crisi ['krizi] SF INV **1** (*gen, Pol, Econ*) crisis; **il paese sta uscendo dalla crisi (economica)** the country is emerging from the (economic) crisis; **essere in crisi** (*partito, impresa*) to be in a state of crisis; (*persona*) to be upset; **in questo periodo sono in crisi** I've got a lot of problems at the moment; **mettere qn in crisi** to put sb in a difficult position; **la crisi degli alloggi** the housing crisis; **crisi energetica** energy crisis **2** (*Med*) attack; (*di epilessia*) fit; **crisi da astinenza** withdrawal symptoms *pl*; **crisi di nervi** fit of hysterics, attack of nerves; **crisi di pianto** fit of tears
crisma ['krizma] SF (*Rel*) chrism; **un matrimonio con tutti i crismi** a proper wedding
cristalleria [kristalle'ria] SF (*fabbrica*) crystal glassworks *sg*; (*oggetti*) crystalware
cristallino, a [kristal'lino] AGG (*Mineralogia*) crystalline; (*fig: suono, acque*) crystal clear

Cc

■SM (*Anat*) crystalline lens
cristallizzare [kristallid'dzare] VI (*aus* **essere**), **cristallizzarsi** VIP to crystallize; (*fig*) to become fossilized
■VT (*gen*) to crystallize, turn into crystals; **zucchero cristallizzato** granulated sugar
cristallizzazione [kristalliddzat'tsjone] SF crystallization
cristallo [kris'tallo] SM crystal; (*di finestra*) pane (of glass); **un bicchiere di cristallo** a crystal glass; **a cristalli liquidi** (*schermo, display*) liquid crystal; **cristallo liquido** liquidcrystal; **cristallo di rocca** rock crystal
cristalloterapia [kristallotera'pia] SF crystal therapy
cristianamente [kristjana'mente] AVV like a Christian, in a Christian way
cristianesimo [kristja'nezimo] SM Christianity
cristiania [kris'tjania] SM INV (*Sci*) Christy, Christie
cristianità [kristjani'ta] SF (*condizione*) Christianity; (*popoli, territorio*) Christendom
cristianizzare [kristjanid'dzare] VT to convert to Christianity
cristiano, a [kris'tjano] AGG Christian
■SM/F (*anche fig*) Christian; **un povero cristiano** (*fig*) a poor soul *o* beggar; **non c'era un cristiano per le strade** there wasn't a soul on the streets; **comportarsi da cristiano** (*fig*) to behave in a civilized manner
cristo ['kristo] SM **1** **Cristo** Christ; **nell'anno 54 avanti/dopo Cristo** in 54 B.C./A.D; **(un) povero cristo** (a) poor beggar **2** (*immagine, oggetto*) figure of Christ
criterio, ri [kri'tɛrjo] SM **1** (*norma*) criterion, rule; **con criterio approssimativo** approximately **2** (*buon senso*) (common) sense; **dovresti avere più criterio** you should have more sense; **è una persona di poco criterio** he doesn't have much common sense
critica ['kritika] SF **1** (*biasimo*) criticism; **una critica costruttiva** constructive criticism **2** **la critica** (*attività*) criticism; (*i critici*) critics *pl*; (*opera, studio*) appreciation, critique; (*recensione*) review; **fare la critica di** (*libro, film*) to review; **una critica sul film** a review of the film
criticabile [kriti'kabile] AGG open to criticism
criticamente [kritika'mente] AVV critically
criticare [kriti'kare] VT (*biasimare*) to criticize, find fault with; (*giudicare*: *opera*) to give a critique of; **ha sempre qualcosa da criticare** she always finds something to criticize
critico, a, ci, che ['kritiko] AGG critical; **aver spirito critico** to have a critical mind; **al momento critico** at the critical moment; **età critica** (*gen*) difficult age; (*menopausa*) change of life
■SM (*gen*) critic; (*recensore*) reviewer; **critico cinematografico** film critic; **critico letterario** literary critic
criticone, a [kriti'kone] SM/F faultfinder; **sei il solito criticone!** you're always finding fault!
crittogramma [kritto'gramma] SM (*testo in cifre*) cryptograph; (*Enigmistica*) cryptogram
crivellare [krivel'lare] VT: **crivellare (di)** to riddle (with)
crivello [kri'vɛllo] SM riddle
croato, a [kro'ato] AGG, SM/F Croatian, Croat
Croazia [kro'attsja] SF: **la Croazia** Croatia; **ti è piaciuta la Croazia?** did you like Croatia?; **andrò in Croazia quest'estate** I'm going to Croatia this summer
croccante [krok'kante] AGG crisp, crunchy; **un biscotto croccante** a crisp biscuit; **un panino croccante** a crusty roll
■SM (*Culin*) almond crunch
crocchetta [krok'ketta] SF (*Culin*) croquette
crocchia ['krɔkkja] SF chignon, bun
crocchio, chi ['krɔkkjo] SM (*di persone*) small group, cluster
croce ['krotʃe] SF (*gen*) cross; **farsi il segno della croce** to make the sign of the cross, cross o.s.; **Cristo in croce** *o* **sulla croce** Christ on the cross; **in croce** (*di traverso*) crosswise; (*fig*) on tenterhooks; **mettere in croce** (*anche fig*: *criticare*) to crucify; (*tormentare*) to nag to death; **facciamoci una croce sopra** let's forget about it; **quella malattia è la sua croce** that illness is her cross in life; **ognuno ha la sua croce da portare** we each have our cross to bear; **punto croce** (*Maglia*) cross stitch; **croce greca** Greek cross; **croce latina** Latin cross; **Croce di Malta** Maltese cross; **croce uncinata** swastika; **la Croce Rossa** the Red Cross; **chiama la Croce Rossa!** (*uso improprio*) call an ambulance!
crocefiggere *ecc* = **crocifiggere** *ecc*
crocerossina [krotʃeros'sina] SF Red Cross nurse
crocetta [kro'tʃetta] SF (*Naut*) crosstree
crocevia [krotʃe'via] SM INV crossroads *sg*
crochet [krɔ'ʃɛ] SM INV **1** (*arnese*) crochet hook **2** (*lavoro*) crochet
crociata [kro'tʃata] SF (*anche fig*) crusade
crociato, a [kro'tʃato] AGG cross-shaped; **parole crociate** crossword puzzle *sg*
■SM (*anche fig*) crusader
crocicchio, chi [kro'tʃikkjo] SM crossroads *sg*
crociera [kro'tʃɛra] SF **1** (*viaggio*) cruise; **velocità di crociera** (*Aut, Aer, Naut*) cruising speed; **altezza di crociera** (*Aer*) cruising height; **andare in crociera** *or* **fare una crociera** to go on a cruise; **sono andati in crociera nel Mediterraneo** they went on a Mediterranean cruise **2** (*Archit*) transept; **volta a crociera** cross vault
crociere [kro'tʃɛre] SM (*Zool*) crossbill
crocifiggere [krotʃi'fiddʒere] VT IRREG (*anche fig*) to crucify
crocifissione [krotʃifis'sjone] SF (*anche fig*) crucifixion
crocifisso, a [krotʃi'fisso] PP *di* **crocifiggere**
■SM crucifix
croco, chi ['krɔko] SM crocus
crogiolarsi [krodʒo'larsi] VIP **1** (*scaldarsi*): **crogiolarsi al sole** to bask in the sun **2** (*bearsi*): **crogiolarsi nelle illusioni** to harbour (*Brit*) *o* harbor (*Am*) illusions
crogiolo [kro'dʒɔlo], **crogiuolo** [kro'dʒwɔlo] SM (*Chim, Metallurgia*) crucible; (*Vetreria*) pot; (*fig*: *di popoli*) melting pot
crollare [krol'lare] VI (*aus* **essere**) (*gen, fig*) to collapse; (*tetto*) to cave in; (*prezzi, titoli*) to slump; **il ponte è crollato** the bridge collapsed; **si lasciò crollare sul letto** he collapsed onto the bed; **dopo 2 giorni di interrogatorio è crollato** he broke down after 2 days of interrogation
crollo ['krɔllo] SM (*anche fig*) collapse; (*Fin*) slump, sudden fall; **avere un crollo** (*fisico*) to collapse; (*psichico*) to have a breakdown; **crollo in Borsa** slump in prices on the Stock Exchange; **il crollo del '29** the Wall Street Crash
croma ['krɔma] SF (*Mus*) quaver (*Brit*), eighth note (*Am*)
cromare [kro'mare] VT to chromium-plate

cromatico, a, ci, che [kro'matiko] AGG chromatic; **sfumature cromatiche** shades of colour
cromatismo [kroma'tizmo] SM (*Ottica*) chromatism; (*Mus*) chromaticism
cromato, a [kro'mato] AGG chromium-plated
cromatografia [kromatogra'fia] SF chromatography
cromatura [kroma'tura] SF chromium plating
cromo ['krɔmo] SM (*Chim*) chromium
■ AGG INV: **giallo cromo** chrome yellow
cromosoma, i [kromo'sɔma] SM chromosome
cromoterapia [kromotera'pia] SF colour therapy
cronaca, che ['krɔnaka] SF **1** (*Storia*) chronicle **2** (*di giornale*) news *sg*; (*resoconto: sportivo*) commentary; (*: di viaggio*) coverage; **fatto** *o* **episodio di cronaca** news item; **cronaca mondana** *o* **rosa** gossip column; **cronaca nera** crime news *sg*; (*rubrica*) crime column
cronicizzarsi [kronitʃid'dzarsi] VIP to become chronic
cronico, a, ci, che ['krɔniko] AGG (*anche fig*) chronic
■ SM (*Med*) chronic invalid
cronista, i, e [kro'nista] SM/F (*Stampa*) columnist; (*Radio, TV*) commentator; (*storico*) chronicler
cronistoria [kronis'tɔrja] SF chronicle; (*fig*) blow-by-blow account
Crono ['krɔno] SM Cronus
cronografo [kro'nɔgrafo] SM chronograph
cronologia [kronolo'dʒia] SF chronology; **"Cronologia"** (*Inform*) "History"
cronologicamente [kronolodʒika'mente] AVV chronologically
cronologico, a, ci, che [krono'lɔdʒiko] AGG chronological
cronometraggio, gi [kronome'traddʒo] SM (precision) timing
cronometrare [kronome'trare] VT to time
cronometrico, a, ci, che [krono'mɛtriko] AGG chronometric(al); (*fig: puntualità*) perfect
cronometrista, i, e [kronome'trista] SM/F timekeeper
cronometro [kro'nɔmetro] SM chronometer; (*a scatto*) stopwatch
cross [krɔs] SM INV (*Sport: motocross*) motocross; (*Pugilato, Calcio*) cross; **moto da cross** rally bike
crossare [kros'sare] VI (*aus* **avere**) (*Calcio*) to cross
crosta ['krɔsta] SF (*di formaggio, pane*) crust; (*Med*) scab; (*Zool*) shell; (*di ghiaccio*) layer; (*fig pegg: quadro*) daub; **crosta lattea** (*Anat*) cradle cap; **crosta terrestre** earth's crust
crostaceo [kros'tatʃeo] SM (*Zool*) shellfish *no pl*
crostata [kros'tata] SF (*Culin*) tart; **una crostata di albicocche** an apricot tart
crostino [kros'tino] SM (*da brodo*) croûton; (*da antipasto*) canapé
crotalo ['krɔtalo] SM (*Zool*) rattlesnake
croton ['krɔton] SM INV (*Bot*) croton
crotoniate [kroto'njate] AGG of *o* from Crotone
■ SM/F inhabitant *o* native of Crotone
croupier [kru'pje] SM INV croupier
crucciare [krut'tʃare] VT to torment, worry
▶ **crucciarsi** VIP: **crucciarsi per** to torment o.s. over
crucciato, a [krut'tʃato] AGG worried
cruccio, ci ['kruttʃo] SM torment, worry
cruciale [kru'tʃale] AGG crucial
cruciverba [krutʃi'vɛrba] SM INV crossword (puzzle)
crudamente [kruda'mente] AVV (*descrivere, esprimersi*) bluntly
crudele [kru'dɛle] AGG (*anche fig*) cruel; **non essere così crudele!** don't be so cruel!
crudelmente [krudel'mente] AVV cruelly
crudeltà [krudel'ta] SF INV (*anche fig*) cruelty
crudezza [kru'dettsa] SF (*di linguaggio*) bluntness
crudo, a ['krudo] AGG **1** (*Culin, Tecn*) raw; **mangia carne cruda** he eats raw meat; **la bistecca è un po' cruda** the steak is underdone **2** (*fig: descrizione, linguaggio*) blunt; **cruda realtà** harsh reality

> **LO SAPEVI...?**
> **crudo** non si traduce mai con *crude*

cruento, a [kru'ɛnto] AGG bloody
cruiser ['kru:zə] SM INV cruiser
crumiro, a [kru'miro] SM/F (*pegg*) scab, blackleg (*Brit*)
cruna ['kruna] SF eye (of a needle)
crusca ['kruska] SF bran
cruscotto [krus'kɔtto] SM (*Aut*) dashboard
CS SIGLA = *Cosenza*
■ ABBR **1** (*Mil*): = *comando supremo* **2** (*Aut*) = **codice della strada**
c.s. ABBR = **come sopra**; *vedi sopra*
CSI [tʃi'ɛsse'tʃi] SIGLA F (= **Comunità di stati indipendenti**) CIS
CSM, Csm [tʃi'ɛsse'ɛmme] SIGLA M (= **Consiglio Superiore della Magistratura**) *magistrates' internal board of supervisors*
CT SIGLA = *Catania*
■ ABBR = **commissario tecnico**
CTF [tʃiti'ɛffe] SIGLA F (= **Chimica e Tecnologia Farmaceutica**) *degree course in pharmaceutical chemistry and technology*
Cuba ['kuba] SF Cuba
cubano, a [ku'bano] AGG, SM/F Cuban
cubatura [kuba'tura] SF cubic capacity
cubetto [ku'betto] SM (small) cube; **cubetto di ghiaccio** ice cube
cubico, a, ci, che ['kubiko] AGG (*gen*) cubic; **radice cubica** cube root
cubismo [ku'bizmo] SM cubism
cubista, i; , e [ku'bista] AGG (*pittore, quadro etc*) Cubist
■ SM/F (*in discoteca*) platform dancer; *dancer who performs on raised platform in a club*
cubito ['kubito] SM (*Anat*) ulna
cubo ['kubo] AGG cubic
■ SM **1** (*gen*) cube; **elevare al cubo** (*Mat*) to cube **2** (*in discoteca*) *platform*
cuccagna [kuk'kaɲɲa] SF abundance, plenty; **paese della cuccagna** land of plenty; **è finita la cuccagna!** the party's over!; **albero della cuccagna** greasy pole (*fig*)
cuccare [kuk'kare] VT (*fam*) **1** (*beccare*) to catch; **l'ho cuccato che frugava nella mia borsa** I caught him going through my bag **2** (*rubare*) to pinch; **mi hanno cuccato il portafoglio** my wallet has been pinched **3** (*sopportare*): **ho dovuto cuccarmela tutta la sera** I had to put up with her all evening
cuccetta [kut'tʃetta] SF (*di treno*) couchette; (*di nave*) berth
cucchiaiata [kukkja'jata] SF spoonful, tablespoonful
cucchiaino [kukkja'ino] SM coffee spoon, ≈ teaspoon (*contenuto*) ≈ teaspoonful (*Pesca*) spinner; **due cucchiaini di zucchero** two teaspoons of sugar
cucchiaio, ai [kuk'kjajo] SM (*gen*) spoon; (*da tavola*) tablespoon; (*cucchiaiata*) spoonful; tablespoonful; **forchetta, coltello e cucchiaio** fork, knife and spoon; **aggiungere un cucchiaio di farina** add a spoonful of flour; **ha mangiato qualche cucchiaio di minestra** she ate a few spoonfuls of soup; **cucchiaio da portata** serving spoon

Cc

cucchiaione [kukkja'jone] SM (*Culin*) basting spoon
cuccia, ce ['kuttʃa] SF (*di cane: letto*) dog's basket; (*: canile*) kennel; **a cuccia!** *or* **fai la cuccia!** down (boy)!
cucciolata [kuttʃo'lata] SF litter; **era il più piccolo della cucciolata** it was the smallest of the litter
cucciolo ['kuttʃolo] SM (*gen*) cub; (*di cane*) pup, puppy; (*fig: persona*): **vieni qua, cucciolo!** come here, pet!
cucina [ku'tʃina] SF (*locale*) kitchen; (*arte culinaria*) cooking, cookery; (*cibo*) cooking, food; (*elettrodomestico*) cooker; **una cucina spaziosa** a big kitchen; **mi piace la cucina greca** I like Greek cooking; **è molto brava in cucina** she's very good at cooking; **da cucina** (*utensile*) kitchen *attr*; **di cucina** (*libro, lezione*) cookery *attr*; **cucina da campo** primus stove; **cucina componibile** fitted kitchen; **cucina economica** kitchen range; **cucina a gas** gas cooker
cucinare [kutʃi'nare] VT to cook; **oggi cucino io!** I'll cook today!; **chi ha cucinato?** who did the cooking?
cuciniere, a [kutʃi'njɛre] SM/F cook
cucinino [kutʃi'nino] SM kitchenette
cucire [ku'tʃire] VT (*gen*) to sew; (*vestito, Med: ferita*) to sew up; (*libro, cuoio*) to stitch; **non so cucire** I can't sew; **cucire a macchina** to machine-sew; **macchina da cucire** sewing machine; **cucire la bocca a qn** (*fig*) to shut sb up
cucito, a [ku'tʃito] AGG (*vedi vb*) sewn; stitched; **cucito a mano** hand-sewn; **stare cucito addosso a qn** (*fig: persona*) to cling to sb
■ SM sewing
cucitrice [kutʃi'tritʃe] SF (*per fogli*) stapler; (*Tip: per libri*) stitching machine
cucitura [kutʃi'tura] SF (*di stoffa, cuoio, libro*) stitching; (*costura*) seam
cucù [ku'ku] SM INV **1** (*Zool: cuculo*) cuckoo **2** (*verso del cuculo*): **far cucù** to go boo; **cucù, eccomi qua!** peek-a-boo!; **orologio a cucù** cuckoo clock
cuculo [ku'kulo] SM cuckoo
CUF [kuf] SIGLA F (= **Commissione Unica del Farmaco**) ≈ FDA (*Am*) (= *Food and Drug Administration*) ≈ CSM (*Brit*) (= *Committee for the Safety of Medicines*)
cuffia ['kuffja] SF bonnet, cap; (*da infermiera*) cap; (*per ascoltare*) headphones *pl*, headset; (*Tecn*) casing; (*Bot*) root cap; **cuffia da bagno** (*da piscina*) bathing cap; (*da doccia*) shower cap
cugino, a [ku'dʒino] SM/F cousin
cui ['kui] PRON REL **1** (*nei complementi indiretti: riferito a persona*) whom; (*: riferito a oggetto, animale*) which; **la persona (a) cui si riferiva** the person he referred to *o* to whom he referred; **le ragazze di cui ti ho parlato** the girls I spoke to you about *o* about whom I spoke to you; **il libro di cui parlavo** the book I was talking about *o* about which I was talking; **il motivo per cui non insisto** the reason I'm not insisting; **il motivo per cui non sono venuto** the reason why I didn't come; **il quartiere in cui abito** the area *o* district where I live; **l'anno in cui prese la laurea** the year he took his degree, the year when *o* in which he took his degree; **il ponte su cui camminavamo** the bridge we were walking on **2** (*come genitivo possessivo: riferito a persona*) whose; (*: riferito a oggetto, animale*) of which, whose; **il signore la cui figlia ho incontrato ieri** the gentleman whose daughter I met yesterday; **la persona di cui ti ho dato il numero di telefono ieri** the person whose telephone number I gave you yesterday; **un'attrice il cui nome mi sfugge** an actress whose name I can't remember **3** **per cui** (*perciò*) therefore, so; **io non c'ero, per cui non chiedere a me** I wasn't there, so don't ask me
culaccio, ci [ku'lattʃo] SM (*Culin*) rump
culbianco, chi [kul'bjanko] SM (*Zool*) wheatear
culinaria [kuli'narja] SF cuisine, cookery
culinario, ria, ri, rie [kuli'narjo] AGG culinary
culla ['kulla] SF (*anche fig*) cradle; **fin dalla culla** from the cradle, since I was (*o* you were *ecc*) a baby
cullare [kul'lare] VT (*bambino*) to rock; (*fig: idea, speranza*) to cherish
▶ **cullarsi** VR (*gen*) to sway; **cullarsi in vane speranze** to cherish fond hopes; **cullarsi nel dolce far niente** to sit back and relax
culminante [kulmi'nante] AGG: **posizione culminante** (*Astron*) highest point; **punto** *o* **momento culminante** (*fig*) climax
culminare [kulmi'nare] VI (*aus* **essere**) **culminare (in)** (*Astron*) to reach its highest point (at); **culminare in** *o* **con** (*fig*) to culminate in
culminazione [kulminat'tsjone] SF (*Astron*) culmination
culmine ['kulmine] SM (*di torre, monte*) summit, top; (*fig*): **ero al culmine della felicità** my happiness knew no bounds; **essere al culmine del successo** to be at the peak of one's success; **era al culmine del successo** he was at the peak of his success
culo ['kulo] SM (*fam!*) **1** (*sedere*) arse (*Brit fam!*), ass (*Am fam!*); **alza il culo!** get off your arse!; **prendere qn per il culo** to take the piss out of sb (*Brit fam!*); **essere culo e camicia con qc** to be really close to sb **2** (*fortuna*): **aver culo** to be lucky; **che culo!** lucky bastard! (*fam!*)
culottes [ky'lɔt] SFPL French knickers
culto ['kulto] SM (*religione*) religion; (*adorazione*) worship, adoration; (*venerazione: anche fig*) cult; **culto della personalità** personality cult; **culto degli eroi** hero worship; **avere il culto della propria persona** to be vain about one's personal appearance
cultore, trice [kul'tore] SM/F: **essere un cultore di** to have a keen interest in
cultura [kul'tura] SF (*gen*) culture; (*conoscenza*) learning, knowledge, education; **di cultura** (*persona*) cultured; (*istituto*) cultural, of culture; **la cultura occidentale** western culture; **avere una certa cultura** to be educated; **una donna di grande cultura** a well-educated woman; **una persona di scarsa cultura** a person without much education; **cultura generale** general knowledge; **una domanda di cultura generale** a general knowledge question; **cultura di massa** mass culture
culturale [kultu'rale] AGG cultural; **una serie di manifestazioni culturali** a series of cultural events; **scambi culturali** cultural exchanges
culturalmente [kultural'mente] AVV culturally
culturismo [kultu'rizmo] SM body-building
culturista, i, e [kultu'rista] SM/F body-builder
cumino [ku'mino] SM cumin
cumulare [kumu'lare] VT (*gen*) to accumulate, amass; (*Amm: impieghi*) to hold concurrently
cumulativamente [kumulativa'mente] AVV (*pagare*) in one go
cumulativo, a [kumula'tivo] AGG (*gen*) cumulative; (*prezzo*) (all-)inclusive; (*biglietto*) group *attr*; **un biglietto cumulativo** a group ticket
cumulo ['kumulo] SM **1** (*mucchio*) heap, pile; **cumulo delle pene** (*Dir*) consecutive sentences; **cumulo dei redditi** (*Fisco*) combined incomes **2** (*Meteor*) cumulus
cumulonembo [kumulo'nembo] SM cumulonimbus
cuneese [kune'ese] AGG of *o* from Cuneo

■SM/F inhabitant *o* native of Cuneo
cuneiforme [kunei'forme] AGG, SM cuneiform
cuneo ['kuneo] SM wedge
cunetta [ku'netta] SF **1** (*di strada*) dip; **pieno di cunette** bumpy **2** (*scolo: nelle strade di città*) gutter; (*: di campagna*) ditch
cunicolo [ku'nikolo] SM (*galleria*) tunnel; (*di miniera*) pit, shaft; (*di talpa*) hole
cuocere ['kwɔtʃere] VB IRREG
■VT **1** (*gen*): **(far) cuocere** to cook; **cuocere al forno** (*pane*) to bake; (*arrosto*) to roast; **cuocere in umido/a vapore/in padella** to stew/steam/fry; **da cuocere** (*frutta*) cooking *attr* **2** (*mattoni*) to fire
■VI (*aus* **essere**) to cook
▶ **cuocersi** VIP (*cibo*) to cook
cuoco, a, chi, che ['kwɔko] SM/F cook; (*di ristorante*) chef
cuoiame [kwo'jame] SM leather goods *pl*
cuoio, oi ['kwɔjo] SM **1** (*pelle di animale*) leather; (*prima della concia*) hide; **in** *o* **di cuoio** leather *attr*; **scarpe di cuoio** leather shoes **2** (*Anat*): **il cuoio capelluto** the scalp
■**cuoia** SFPL: **tirare le cuoia** (*fam*) to kick the bucket
cuore ['kwɔre] SM **1** (*Anat, fig: cosa centrale*) heart; **la ginnastica fa bene al cuore** exercise is good for your heart; **un'operazione al cuore** a heart operation; **a cuore** heart-shaped; **una scatola a forma di cuore** a heart-shaped box; **nel cuore della città/della notte/della mischia** in the heart of the city/middle of the night/midst of the fight; **intervento a cuore aperto** open-heart operation **2** (*fig: animo*): **aver buon cuore** to be kind-hearted; **una persona di buon cuore** a kind-hearted soul; **parlare col cuore in mano** to speak frankly; **col cuore in gola** with one's heart in one's mouth; **senza cuore** heartless; **aprire il proprio cuore a qn** to open one's heart to sb; **non ho il cuore di dirglielo** I haven't the heart to tell him; **il cuore mi dice che...** I feel in my heart that ...; **avere un cuore da leone** to be brave-hearted; **mettiti il cuore in pace, non tornerà mai più** you'll have to accept that he'll never come back; **avere la morte nel cuore** to be sick at heart; **nel profondo del cuore** in one's heart of hearts; **ringraziare di cuore** to thank sincerely; **un grazie di cuore** heartfelt thanks; **ho a cuore il successo del progetto** the success of the project matters to me; **mi sta molto a cuore** it's very important to me; **mi si stringeva il cuore** *or* **mi piangeva il cuore** my heart ached; **mi piange il cuore a vedere questo spreco** I hate to see such waste; **toccare il cuore a qn** to move sb; **club dei cuori solitari** lonely hearts club **3** (*Carte*): **cuori** SMPL hearts
cupamente [kupa'mente] AVV (*pensierosamente*) gloomily, morosely; (*fig: descrivere*) gloomily, bleakly
cupidamente [kupida'mente] AVV (*vedi agg*) greedily; lustfully
cupidigia [kupi'didʒa] SF greed, covetousness
Cupido [ku'pido] SM Cupid; **cupido** (*Arte*) cupid
cupido, a ['kupido] AGG (*bramoso*) greedy; (*lascivo*) lustful
cupo, a ['kupo] AGG (*caverna, notte*) pitch-black; (*voce, abisso*) deep; (*colore, cielo*) dark; (*suono*) dull; (*fig: carattere*) sullen, morose
cupola ['kupola] SF (*di chiesa, osservatorio*) dome; (*più piccola*) cupola; (*fig: della Mafia*) Mafia high command; **a cupola** dome-shaped
cura ['kura] SF **1** care; **avere** *o* **prendersi cura di qn/qc** to look after sb/sth; **abbi cura di fare come ti ho detto** be sure to do exactly as I've told you, take care to do exactly as I've told you; **abbi cura di te** take care of yourself, look after yourself; **si dedica completamente alla cura dell'azienda** he devotes all his time to running the company; **questa pianta ha bisogno di molte cure** this plant needs a lot of attention; **a cura di** (*Stampa*) edited by; **trasmissione a cura di** (*TV, Radio*) programme produced by **2** (*accuratezza*) care, accuracy; **con cura** carefully; **"maneggiare con cura"** "handle with care"; **senza cura** carelessly; **se lo facessi con un po' più di cura...** if you took a bit more care over it ... **3** (*Med: trattamento*) (course of) treatment; **fare una cura** to follow a course of treatment; **sto facendo una cura contro l'acne** I'm having treatment for my acne; **è in cura presso il dott. Bianchi** she's one of Dr Bianchi's patients; **è stato in cura presso i migliori medici** he has received treatment from the best doctors; **le hanno dato una cura a base di ormoni** they prescribed a course of hormone treatment for her; **non hanno ancora trovato una cura** they haven't found a cure yet; **cura dimagrante** diet; **cura del sonno** sleep therapy
curabile [ku'rabile] AGG curable
curante [ku'rante] AGG: **medico curante** doctor (in charge of a patient)
curapipe [kura'pipe] SM INV pipe cleaner
curare [ku'rare] VT **1** (*Med*) to treat; (*: guarire*) to cure; **gli curarono la pertosse** they treated him for whooping cough; **farsi curare da qn per qc** to be treated by sb for sth; **devi curare** *o* **curarti questo raffreddore** you must see about that cold **2** (*occuparsi di*) to look after; (*: azienda*) to run, look after; (*: libro*) to edit; **curare l'edizione di un'antologia** to be the editor of an anthology
▶ **curarsi** VR **1** (*gen*) to take care of o.s., look after o.s.; (*Med*) to follow a course of treatment; **si sta curando con delle vitamine** he's taking vitamins **2** (*esteticamente*) to take trouble over one's appearance
▶ **curarsi di** VIP (*occuparsi di*) to look after; (*preoccuparsi di*) to bother about
curaro [ku'raro] SM curare
curatela [kura'tɛla] SF (*Dir*) guardianship
curativo, a [kura'tivo] AGG curative
curato [ku'rato] SM (*Rel*) parish priest; (*: protestante*) vicar, minister
curatore, trice [kura'tore] SM/F **1** (*Dir: guardian*) (*: di testamento*) administrator; **curatore fallimentare** (official) receiver **2** (*di antologia*) editor
curdo, a ['kurdo] AGG, SM (*lingua*) Kurdish
■SM/F Kurd
curia ['kurja] SF **1** (*Rel*): **la Curia (Romana)** the (Roman) Curia; **curia vescovile** diocesan administration **2** (*Dir*) local lawyers' association; **curia notarile** notaries' association *o* guild
curiosaggine [kurjo'saddʒine] SF nosiness
curiosamente [kurjosa'mente] AVV (*con curiosità*) curiously; (*insolitamente*) strangely, oddly
curiosare [kurjo'sare] VI (*aus* **avere**) (*aggirarsi*) to look round, wander round; **curiosare nei negozi** to look round *o* wander around the shops; **curiosare tra vecchi giornali** to browse through old newspapers; **curiosare nelle faccende altrui** to poke one's nose into other people's affairs
curiosità [kurjosi'ta] SF INV **1** (*gen*) curiosity; (*pegg*) curiosity, inquisitiveness; **provare curiosità per** to be

Cc

curious about; **siamo andati per curiosità** we went out of curiosity; **per curiosità, quanto l'hai pagato?** as a matter of interest, how much did you pay for it? **2** (*cosa rara*) curio, curiosity

curioso, a [ku'rjoso] AGG (*gen*) curious; (*che vuol sapere*) inquiring; (*pegg*) curious, inquisitive; (*strano*) odd, strange, curious; **un fatto/tipo curioso** an odd thing/ person; **essere curioso di qc/di sapere qc** to be curious about sth/to know sth
■ SM/F busybody, nosy parker (*Brit fam*); **una folla di curiosi** a crowd of onlookers
■ SM: **il curioso è che...** the funny *o* curious thing is that ...

curriculum [kur'rikulum] SM INV: **curriculum (vitae)** curriculum vitae, CV

curry ['kʌri] SM INV curry; **riso al curry** curried rice; **pollo al curry** chicken curry, curried chicken

cursore [kur'sore] SM (*su strumento di misura, videoterminale*) cursor; (*su radio*) slider

curva ['kurva] SF **1** (*gen, Mat, Tecn*) curve; (*traiettoria*) trajectory; **una bionda tutta curve** (*fam*) a curvaceous blonde **2** (*di strada, fiume*) bend; **prendere una curva** (*Aut*) to take a bend; **sorpassare in curva** to overtake on a bend; **curva a gomito** hairpin bend; **curva stretta** sharp bend **3** (*Geog*) contour; **curva di livello** contour line **4** (*Sci*) turn; **curva a sci uniti** parallel turn; **curva a spazzaneve** snow-plough turn, basic turn **5** (*Calcio*) *curved area behind the goal where the hard-core fans go*

curvare [kur'vare] VT to bend
■ VI (*aus* **avere**) **1** (*strada*) to bend; **curvare a sinistra/destra** to bend to the left/right **2** (*veicolo*) to take a bend; **curvare a sinistra/destra** to follow the road to the left/right;
▶ **curvarsi** VR (*chinarsi*) to bend down
▶ **curvarsi** VIP (*legno*) to warp; (*persona*) **curvarsi con la vecchiaia** to become bent with age

curvatura [kurva'tura] SF (*gen, Mat*) curvature; (*di strada*) camber; **curvatura alla spina dorsale** (*Med*) curvature of the spine

curvilineo, a [kurvi'lineo] AGG (*gen, Mat*) curvilinear
■ SM (*strumento*) drawing stencil

curvo, a ['kurvo] AGG (*gen*) curved; (*piegato*) bent; **camminare curvo** to walk with a stoop; **stare curvo** to slouch; **non stare curvo!** don't slouch!; **una linea curva** a curved line

CUS [kus] SIGLA M = *Centro Universitario Sportivo*

cuscinetto [kuʃʃi'netto] SM **1** (*per timbri*) pad; (*puntaspilli*) pincushion; (*Tecn*) bearing; **cuscinetto a sfere** ball bearing **2** (*fam: deposito adiposo*) spare tyre (*Brit*) *o* tire (*Am*)
■ AGG INV: **stato cuscinetto** (*fig*) buffer state

cuscino [kuʃ'ʃino] SM (*gen*) cushion; (*guanciale*) pillow; **cuscino di fiori** wreath

cuscus [kus'kus] SM INV couscous

cuspide ['kuspide] SF (*Mat, Astron, Astrol*) cusp; (*Archit*) spire

custode [kus'tɔde] SM/F (*di museo*) keeper, custodian; (*di parco*) warden; (*di casa*) concierge; (*di fabbrica, carcere*) guard

custodia [kus'tɔdja] SF **1** care; **avere qc in custodia** to look after sth; **dare qc in custodia a qn** to entrust sth to sb's care **2** (*Dir*) custody; **affidare a qn la custodia di** to give sb custody of; **agente di custodia** prison warder; **custodia delle carceri** prison security; **custodia cautelare** remand (*Brit*) **3** (*astuccio*) case, holder

custodire [kusto'dire] VT (*conservare*) to keep; (*fare la guardia: casa, carcere*) to guard; **i gioielli sono custoditi in cassaforte** the jewels are kept in a safe

cutaneo, a [ku'taneo] AGG skin *attr*

cute ['kute] SF (*Anat*) skin

cuticola [ku'tikola] SF cuticle

cutrettola [ku'trettola] SF (*uccello*) wagtail

CV ABBR (= **cavallo vapore**) h.p.

c.v.d. ABBR (= **come volevasi dimostrare**) QED (= *quod erat demonstrandum*)

c.vo ABBR = **corsivo**

cybercaffè [tʃiberkaf'fɔ] SM INV cybercafe

cybernauta, i, e [tʃiber'nauta] SM/F cybernaut

cyberspazio [tʃiber'spattsjo] SM cyberspace

cyclette® [si'klɛt] SF INV exercise bike

D, d [di] SF O M INV (*lettera*) D, d; **D come Domodossola** ≈ D for David (*Brit*), ≈ D for Dog (*Am*)

D [di] ABBR **1** (= destra) R **2** (*Ferr*): = diretto

da [da] PAROLA CHIAVE

PREP (*da + il*= dal, *da + lo*= dallo, *da + l'*= dall', *da + la*= dalla, *da + i*= dai, *da + gli*= dagli, *da + le*= dalle)

1 (*agente, mezzo*) by; **fare qc da sé** to do sth (for) o.s.; **dipinto da un grande artista** painted by a great artist; **riconoscere qn dal passo** to recognize sb by his (*o* her) step

2 (*causa*): **tremare dal freddo** to shiver with cold; **morire dallo spavento** to die of fright

3 (*provenienza, distanza, separazione*) from; (: *fuori di*) out of; (: *giù da*) off; **a 3 km da Roma** 3 km(s)from Rome; **arrivare da Milano** to arrive from Milan; **da dove vieni?** where do you come from?; **l'aereo parte da Gatwick** the plane departs from Gatwick; **scendere dal treno** to get off the train; **staccarsi da qn** to leave *o* part from sb; **toglitelo dalla testa** get it out of your head; **uscire dalla scuola** to come out of school

4 (*stato in luogo*) at; (: *presso*) at, with; **abita da quelle parti** he lives somewhere round there, he lives in that area; **ti aspetto dal macellaio** I'll wait for you at the butcher's; **sono da Pietro** I'm at Pietro's (house); **vive da un amico** he's living at a friend's *o* with a friend

5 (*moto a luogo*) to; (*moto per luogo*) through; **questo treno passa da Genova** this train goes through Genoa; **è uscito dalla finestra** he went out through *o* by (way of) the window; **vado da Pietro/dal giornalaio** I'm going to Pietro's (house)/to the newsagent's

6 (*tempo: durata*) for; (: *a partire da: nel passato*) since; (: *nel futuro*) from; **da allora** since then; **vivo qui da un anno** I've been living here for a year; **è a Londra da martedì** he has been in London since Tuesday; **da oggi in poi** from today onwards; **d'ora in poi** *o* **in avanti** from now on; **da quando sei qui** since you have been here; **sono qui dalle sei** I've been here since six o'clock

7 (*qualità, caratteristica*): **una ragazza dai capelli biondi** a fair-haired girl; a girl with fair hair; **un vestito da 300 euro** a 300-euro dress; **un ragazzo dagli occhi azzurri** a blue-eyed boy; a boy with blue eyes; **sordo da un orecchio** deaf in one ear; **è una cosa da poco** it's nothing special

8 (*modo*) like; **trattare qn da amico** to treat sb like *o* as a friend; **non è da lui** it's not like him; **comportarsi da uomo** to behave like a man; **è da vigliacchi fare così** that's a spineless way to behave

9 (*predicativo*) as; **da bambino piangevo molto** I cried a lot as a child *o* when I was a child; **da giovane** as a young man (*o* woman); **fare da guida** to act as a guide; **fare da maestro** to act as a teacher; **fare da padre a** to be a father to; **da studente** as a student

10 (*fine, scopo*): **cavallo da corsa** racehorse; **macchina da corsa** racing car; **vino da pasto** table wine; **abito da sera** evening dress

11 (*seguito da infinito: consecutivo*) that (*spesso omesso*); (: *finale*) to; **casa da affittare** house to let; **qualcosa da bere** something to drink; **qualcosa da mangiare** something to eat; **ero così stanco da non stare più in piedi** I was so tired (that) I couldn't stand; **casa da vendere** house for sale

12 da... a... from ... to ...; **contare da 1 a 10** to count from 1 to 10; **dalle 3 alle 5** from 3 to *o* till 5 (o'clock); **c'erano dalle 30 alle 40 persone** there were between 30 and 40 people there; **è cambiato dall'oggi al domani** he changed overnight

dà [da] VB *vedi* **dare**

dabbasso [dab'basso] AVV = **da basso**; *vedi* **basso**

dabbenaggine [dabbe'naddʒine] SF (*pegg*) simple-mindedness, credulity

dabbene [dab'bɛne] AGG INV honest, decent

Dacca ['dakka] SF Dacca

daccapo [dak'kapo] AVV = **da capo**; *vedi* **capo ricominciare daccapo** to start all over again

dacché [dak'ke] CONG (*letter*) since

dacia, cie ['datʃa] SF dacha

dado ['dado] SM (*nel gioco*) dice *pl inv*; (*Culin*) stock cube (*Brit*), bouillon cube (*Am*); (*Tecn*) (screw) nut; (*Archit*) dado; **giocare a dadi** to play dice; **tagliare a dadi** (*Culin*) to dice; **il dado è tratto** (*fig*) the die is cast

daffare [daf'fare] SM INV work; **avere un gran daffare**

to be very busy; **darsi daffare perché si faccia qc** to work hard to get sth done

dagherrotipo [dager'rɔtipo] SM daguerreotype

dagli ['daʎʎi], **dai** [dai] PREP + ART *vedi* **da**

daino ['daino] SM (*maschio*) (fallow) deer *pl inv*; (*femmina*) female fallow deer *pl inv*, doe; **pelle di daino** buckskin, chamois leather

Dakar [da'kar] SF Dakar

dal[1] [dal] PREP + ART *vedi* **da**

dal[2] ABBR (= **decalitro**) dal

dalia ['dalja] SF dahlia

dall' [dall], **dalla** ['dalla], **dalle** ['dalle], **dallo** ['dallo] PREP + ART *vedi* **da**

dalmata, i ['dalmata] SM (*cane*) Dalmatian

dalmatica, che [dal'matika] SF (*Rel*) dalmatic

daltonico, a, ci, che [dal'tɔniko] AGG colour-blind (*Brit*), colorblind (*Am*)
■ SM/F colo(u)r-blind person

daltonismo [dalto'nizmo] SM colo(u)r blindness

dam ABBR (= **decametro**) dam

dama ['dama] SF **1** lady; (*nei balli*) partner; **dama di compagnia** lady's companion; **dama di corte** lady-in-waiting **2** (*gioco*) draughts *sg* (*Brit*), checkers *sg* (*Am*); **giocare a dama** to play draughts; **far dama** to crown a draughtsman
▷ www.fid.it/

damascare [damas'kare] VT to damask

damaschino [damas'kino] SM (*tessuto*) damask cloth

Damasco [da'masko] SF Damascus

damasco, schi [da'masko] SM damask

damigella [dami'dʒɛlla] SF (*Storia*) damsel; **damigella d'onore** (*di sposa*) bridesmaid

damigiana [dami'dʒana] SF demijohn

dammeno [dam'meno] AGG INV: **per non essere dammeno di qn** so as not to be outdone by sb; **è un grande imbroglione e sua moglie non è dammeno** he's an out-and-out crook and so is his wife

DAMS [dams] SIGLA M (= **Discipline delle Arti, della Musica, dello Spettacolo**) *faculty of the performing arts*

danaro [da'naro] SM = **denaro**

danaroso, a [dana'roso] AGG wealthy

dancing ['da:nsiŋ] SM INV dance hall

danese [da'nese] AGG Danish
■ SM/F Dane; **i danesi** the Danes
■ SM **1** (*lingua*) Danish; **parli danese?** do you speak Danish? **2** (*cane*) Great Dane

Daniele [dan'jɛle] SM Daniel

Danimarca [dani'marka] SF Denmark; **ti è piaciuta la Danimarca?** did you like Denmark?; **andrò in Danimarca quest'estate** I'm going to Denmark this summer

dannare [dan'nare] VT (*Rel*) to damn; **far dannare qn** (*fig*) to drive sb mad; **dannarsi l'anima per qc** (*affannarsi*) to work o.s. to death for sth
▶ **dannarsi** VR (*affannarsi*) **dannarsi per fare qc** to wear o.s. out doing sth

dannato, a [dan'nato] AGG damned; **quella dannata macchina!** (*fam*) that damned car!
■ **i dannati** SMPL the damned

dannazione [dannat'tsjone] SF damnation
■ ESCL: **dannazione!** damn!

danneggiare [danned'dʒare] VT (*gen*) to damage; (*rovinare*) to spoil; (*fig: persona*) to harm; **la parte danneggiata** (*Dir*) the injured party

danno[1] ['danno] SM (*gen*) damage; (*a persona*) harm, injury; **arrecare danno a qc** to damage sth; **arrecare danno a qn** to harm sb, do sb harm; **il maltempo ha provocato ingenti danni** the bad weather caused serious damage; **ho provocato un piccolo danno alla macchina** I damaged the car slightly; **fare danni** to do damage; **la grandine ha fatto molti danni** the hail did a lot of damage; **senza fare danni** without doing any damage; **il danno ormai è fatto** the damage has been done; **a danno di qn** to sb's detriment; **non c'è stato nessun danno alle persone** nobody was hurt; **in caso di perdita o danno** in case of loss or damage; **chiedere/risarcire i danni** to sue for/pay damages; **due milioni di risarcimento danni** two million in damages

danno[2] ['danno] VB *vedi* **dare**

dannosamente [dannosa'mente] AVV harmfully

dannosità [dannosi'ta] SF harmfulness

dannoso, a [dan'noso] AGG: **dannoso (a** *o* **per)** harmful (to), bad (for); **una sostanza dannosa** a harmful substance; **il fumo è dannoso alla salute** smoking damages your health

dantesco, a, schi, sche [dan'tesko] AGG Dantesque; **l'opera dantesca** Dante's work

dantista, i, e [dan'tista] SM/F Dante scholar

Danubio [da'nubjo] SM: **il Danubio** the Danube

danza ['dantsa] SF: **la danza** dancing; **una danza** a dance; **fare danza** to study dancing; **scuola/maestro di danza** dancing school/master; **danza classica** ballet dancing; **danza di guerra** war dance; **danza tribale** tribal dance

danzante [dan'tsante] AGG dancing; **serata danzante** dance

danzare [dan'tsare] VT, VI (*aus* **avere**) to dance

danzatore, trice [dantsa'tore] SM/F dancer

dappertutto [dapper'tutto] AVV everywhere

dappocaggine [dappo'kaddʒine] SF ineptitude

dappoco [dap'pɔko] AGG INV (*anche:* **da poco**: *inetto*) inept; (*insignificante*) insignificant, negligible

dapprima [dap'prima] AVV at first

Dardanelli [darda'nelli] SMPL: **i Dardanelli** the Dardanelles

dardo ['dardo] SM dart, arrow

dare ['dare] VB IRREG
■ VT
1 (*gen*) to give; (*premio, borsa di studio*) to give, award; **dare qc a qn** to give sb sth, give sth to sb; **gli ho dato un libro** I gave him a book; **gli ho dato la cartina** I gave the map to him; **dammelo** give it to me; **dare qc da fare a qn** to give sb sth to do; **dare da mangiare/bere a qn** to give sb sth to eat/drink; **dare uno schiaffo/un calcio a qn** to give sb a slap/kick, slap/kick sb; **mi dai la macchina?** can I have the car?; **dare a qn il permesso di fare qc** to give sb permission to do sth; **gli hanno dato ordine di sparare** they gave him the order to fire; **questo trucco ti dà un'aria volgare** that make-up makes you look common; **ha dato sedicimila euro per la macchina** he paid sixteen thousand euros for the car; **gli hanno dato 5 anni** (*di prigione*) they gave him 5 years; **quanti anni mi dai?** how old do you think I am?; **queste scene mi danno il voltastomaco** these scenes make me feel sick; **dare del cretino a qn** to call sb a fool; **dare la vita per qc** to give (up) one's life for sth; **dare tutto se stesso a qn/qc** to give one's all to sb/sth; **darsi una pettinata** to give one's hair a comb
2 (*organizzare*: *festa, banchetto*) to hold, give; (: *spettacolo*) to perform, put on; (: *film*) to show; **danno ancora quel film?** is that film still showing?
3 (*produrre*: *frutti, soldi*) to yield, produce; (: *calore*) to give

off; (: *suono*) to make; **gli investimenti hanno dato il 10% di interesse** the investments yielded 10% interest; **gli ha dato un figlio** she bore him a son
4 dare qc per certo to be sure of sth; **dare qn per disperso** to report sb missing; **dare qn per morto** to give sb up for dead; **dare qc/qn per perso** to give sth/ sb up for lost; **dare qc per scontato** to take sth for granted; **dare ad intendere a qn che...** to lead sb to believe that ...; **ciò mi dà da pensare** (*insospettire*) that gives me food for thought; (*preoccupare*) that worries me; **non è dato a tutti di essere intelligenti** not everyone is blessed with intelligence; **dar via** to give away
■VI (*aus* **avere**)
1 (*finestra, casa: guardare*): **dare su** to overlook, give onto, look (out) onto; **la mia finestra dà sul giardino** my window looks onto the garden; **il giardino dà sulla strada** the garden faces onto the road
2 (*colore: tendere*): **dare su** to tend towards; **un colore che dà sul verde** a greenish colour
▶ **darsi** VR: **darsi a** (*musica, politica*) to devote o.s. to; **darsi al bere/al gioco** to take to drink/to gambling; **darsi alla bella vita** to have a good time; **darsi ammalato** to report sick; **darsi prigioniero** to surrender; **darsi per vinto** to give in; **darsi da fare per fare qc** to go to a lot of bother to do sth; **devi darti da fare** you'll have to get busy; **coraggio, diamoci da fare!** come on, let's get on with it!;
▶ **darsi** VIP
1 può darsi maybe, perhaps; **può darsi che venga** he may come, perhaps he will come; **si dà il caso che...** it so happens that ...
2 darsela a gambe to take to one's heels
■SM (*Fin*): **il dare e l'avere** debits and credits *pl*

LO SAPEVI...?
dare non si traduce mai con la parola inglese *dare*

Dar-es-Salaam [daresa'lam] SF Dar-es-Salaam
dark [dark] AGG INV (*moda, musica*) Goth
darsena ['darsena] SF (*Naut*) dock
data ['data] SF date; **che data è oggi?** what's today's date?; **in data da destinarsi** on a date still to be announced; **lettera in data 4 febbraio** letter dated the 4th February; **in data odierna** as of today; **senza data** undated; **amicizia di lunga** *o* **vecchia data** long-standing friendship; **data di emissione** date of issue; **data di nascita** date of birth; **data di scadenza** expiry date
datare [da'tare] VT to date; **non datato** undated
■VI: **datare da** to date back to, date from; **a datare da oggi** dating from today
datario, ri [da'tarjo] SM (*timbro*) date stamp; (*di orologio*) (universal) calendar
datato, a [da'tato] AGG (*film, romanzo*) dated
datazione [datat'tsjone] SF (*Archeol, Geol*) dating
dativo [da'tivo] SM (*Gramm*) dative
dato, a ['dato] AGG **1** (*certo*): **in quel dato giorno** on that particular day; **in dati casi** in certain cases
2 (*stabilito*): **entro quel dato giorno** by that particular day; **in un dato periodo** at a given time
3 (*considerato*): **data la situazione** given *o* considering *o* in view of the situation; **dato che...** given that ...
■SM (*Mat, Sci*) datum; **dati** SMPL data *pl inv*; **è un dato di fatto** it's a fact; **dati sensibili** sense data
datore, trice [da'tore] SM/F: **datore di lavoro** employer
dattero ['dattero] SM **1** (*Bot: albero*) date palm; (: *frutto*) date **2** (*Zool*): **dattero di mare** date mussel
dattilografare [dattilogra'fare] VT to type
dattilografia [dattilogra'fia] SF typing
dattilografo, a [datti'lɔgrafo] SM/F typist; **fa la dattilografa** she's a typist
dattiloscritto, a [dattilos'kritto] AGG typewritten
■SM typescript
dattiloscrivere [dattilos'krivere] VT to type
dattorno [dat'torno] AVV = **di torno**; *vedi* **torno**
davanti [da'vanti] AVV in front; (*all'inizio di: gruppo*) at the front; (*dirimpetto*) opposite; **posso andare davanti?** (*in macchina*) can I go *o* sit in front?; **davanti c'era un bel giardino** at the front there was a nice garden
■**davanti a** PREP **1** (*posizione: gen*) in front of; (: *dirimpetto a*) opposite; (*distanza*) ahead of; **ogni mattina passo davanti a casa tua** every morning I go past your house; **camminava davanti a me** he was walking ahead of *o* in front of me; **era seduto davanti a me** (*più in là*) he was sitting in front of me; (*faccia a faccia*) he was sitting opposite *o* facing me; **era seduto davanti a me al cinema** he was sitting in front of me at the cinema; **la casa davanti alla mia** the house opposite mine; **la mia casa è davanti al municipio** my house is opposite *o* faces the town hall **2** (*al cospetto di*) before, in front of; **comparire davanti al giudice** to appear before the judge; **davanti a Dio** before God; **davanti al pericolo** in the face of danger
■AGG INV front *attr*; **le file davanti sono occupate** the front rows are taken; **le zampe davanti** the front *o* fore paws
■SM INV front
davanzale [davan'tsale] SM (window)sill
davanzo [da'vantso] AVV = **d'avanzo**; *vedi* **avanzo**
Davide ['davide] SM David
davvero [dav'vero] AVV really; **è successo davvero** it really happened; **dico davvero** I mean it
dazebao [daddze'bao] SM INV political poster
daziario, ria, ri, rie [dat'tsjarjo] AGG excise *attr*
dazio, zi ['dattsjo] SM (*somma*) duty, tax; (*luogo*) customs *pl*; **dazio doganale** customs duty; **dazio d'importazione** import duty
dB ABBR (= decibel) dB, db
DC [di'tʃi] SIGLA F (= **Democrazia Cristiana**) *former political party of the centre*
d.C. ABBR (= **dopo Cristo**) A.D.
DD ABBR (*Ferr*) = **direttissimo**
D.D.L. [didi'ɛlle] SIGLA M = **Disegno di Legge**; *vedi* **disegno**
DDT [didi'ti] SIGLA M (= **dicloro-difenil-tricloroetano**) D.D.T.
dea ['dɛa] SF (*anche fig*) goddess
debbo *ecc* ['dɛbbo] VB *vedi* **dovere**
debellare [debel'lare] VT to overcome
debilitante [debili'tante] AGG debilitating
debilitare [debili'tare] VT to debilitate
▶ **debilitarsi** VIP to become debilitated
debilitazione [debilitat'tsjone] SF debilitation
debitamente [debita'mente] AVV (*vedi agg*) duly; properly
debito[1], a ['debito] AGG (*dovuto*) due; (*appropriato*) proper; **a tempo debito** at the right *o* appropriate time; **ogni cosa a tempo debito** I'll (*o* we'll) think about it when the time comes, everything in due time
debito[2] ['debito] SM **1** (*anche fig*) debt; **ha molti debiti** he's got a lot of debts; **far debiti** to get into debt; **essere/sentirsi in debito verso qn** to be/feel

Dd

indebted to sb; **debito formativo** (*Scol*) *a system that allows a student who has not reached a sufficient standard in a subject to move up to the next year, and make up the insufficiency at a later date*; *vedi anche* **credito formativo** **2** (*Comm*) debit; **debito consolidato** consolidated debt; **debito formativo** failure to achieve the required standard; **debito d'imposta** tax liability; **debito pubblico** national debt

debitore, trice [debi'tore] SM/F debtor; **ti sono debitore** (*anche fig*) I'm in your debt; **ti sono debitore di un favore** I owe you a favour

debole ['debole] AGG (*gen*) weak, feeble; (*luce*) dim, faint; (*speranza, lamento, suono*) faint; (*polso*) faint, weak; (*argomentazioni*) weak, poor; **mi sento debole** I feel weak; **essere debole di vista** to have weak *o* poor eyesight; **essere debole di stomaco** to have a delicate stomach; **essere debole in matematica** to be bad at mathematics; **è troppo debole con lei** he's too soft with her; **un debole suono** a faint sound; **una luce debole** a dim light
■ SM/F (*persona*) weakling; **i deboli** the weak
■ SM weakness; **ha un debole per la cioccolata** he's got a weakness for chocolate; **ha un debole per me** she's got a soft spot for me

debolezza [debo'lettsa] SF (*anche fig*) weakness

debolmente [debol'mente] AVV (*vedi agg*) weakly; dimly; faintly

debosciato, a [deboʃ'ʃato] AGG debauched
■ SM/F debauchee

debugger [di:bʌge[r]] SM INV (*Inform*) debugger

debugging [di:dʌgiŋ] SM INV (*Inform*) debugging

debuttante [debut'tante] SM/F (*gen*) beginner, novice; (*Teatro*) *actor o actress at the beginning of his (o her) career*; **ballo delle debuttanti** debutantes' ball

debuttare [debut'tare] VI (*aus* **avere**) to make one's debut

debutto [de'butto] SM (*anche fig*) debut; **fare il proprio debutto** (*anche fig*) to make one's debut

decade ['dɛkade] SF period of ten days

decadente [deka'dɛnte] AGG, SM/F (*gen, Arte*) decadent

decadentismo [dekaden'tizmo] SM (*Arte*) Decadence

decadentista, i, e [dekaden'tista] SM/F (*Arte*) Decadent

decadenza [deka'dɛntsa] SF **1** (*processo*) decline; (*stato*) decadence; **una civiltà in decadenza** a civilisation in decline **2** (*Dir*) loss, forfeiture

decadere [deka'dere] VI IRREG (*aus* **essere**) **1** (*costumi*) to fall into decline **2** (*scadere*) to lapse

decadimento [dekadi'mento] SM (*Fis*) decay

decaduto, a [deka'duto] AGG (*nobile*) impoverished; (*norma*) no longer in force

decaedro [deka'ɛdro] SM (*Mat*) decahedron

decaffeinato, a [dekaffei'nato] AGG decaffeinated; **caffè decaffeinato** decaffeinated coffee
■ SM decaffeinated coffee, decaff (*fam*); **un decaffeinato** a decaff

decalcificare [dekaltʃifi'kare] VT (*Med*) to decalcify

decalcificazione [dekaltʃifikat'tsjone] SF (*Med, Geol*) decalcification

decalcomania [dekalkoma'nia] SF (*figura*) transfer (*of design, drawing*)

decalitro [de'kalitro] SM decalitre (*Brit*), decaliter (*Am*), ten litres

decalogo, ghi [de'kalogo] SM (*Rel*) Decalogue; (*fig*) rulebook

decametro [de'kametro] SM decametre (*Brit*), decameter (*Am*), ten metres

decano [de'kano] SM (*Rel*) dean; (*fig*) doyen

decantare[1] [dekan'tare] VT (*virtù, bravura*) to hymn; (*persona*) to sing the praises of

decantare[2] [dekan'tare] (*Chim*) VT to leave to settle
■ VI to settle

decantazione [dekantat'tsjone] SF (*Chim*) settling

decapitare [dekapi'tare] VT (*gen*) to decapitate; (*per pena capitale*) to behead

decapitazione [dekapitat'tsjone] SF (*vedi vb*) decapitation; beheading

decappottabile [dekappot'tabile] AGG, SF (*Aut*) convertible; **una macchina decappottabile** a convertible

decathlon, **decatlon** ['dɛkatlon] SM INV (*Sport*) decathlon

decedere [de'tʃɛdere] VI (*aus* **essere**) (*frm*) to die

deceduto, a [detʃe'duto] AGG deceased

decelerare [detʃele'rare] VT, VI (*aus* **avere**) to decelerate, slow down

decelerazione [detʃelerat'tsjone] SF deceleration

decennale [detʃen'nale] AGG (*che dura 10 anni*) ten-year *attr*; (*che ricorre ogni 10 anni*) ten-yearly, every ten years
■ SM (*ricorrenza*) tenth anniversary

decenne [de'tʃɛnne] AGG: **un bambino decenne** a ten-year-old child, a child of ten

decennio, ni [de'tʃɛnnjo] SM decade

decente [de'tʃɛnte] AGG (*decoroso: abiti*) decent, respectable; (*contegno*) proper; (*accettabile*) satisfactory, decent

decentemente [detʃente'mente] AVV decently; **cerca di fare questo lavoro decentemente** try and do this job properly, try and make a decent job of this

decentramento [detʃentra'mento] SM, **decentralizzazione** [detʃentraliddzat'tsjone] SF decentralization

decentrare [detʃen'trare], **decentralizzare** [detʃentralid'dzare] VT to decentralize

decentrato, a [detʃen'trato] AGG (*amministrazione*) decentralized; **ufficio decentrato** (*del comune*) local office

decenza [de'tʃɛntsa] SF decency, propriety

decesso [de'tʃɛsso] SM (*frm*) death; **atto di decesso** death certificate

decibel [detʃi'bɛl] SM INV decibel

decidere [de'tʃidere] VB IRREG
■ VT **1** (*stabilire*): **decidere qc** to decide on sth; **decidere una data/un'ora** to agree on a date/time, fix a date/time; **decidere che** to decide that; **decidere di fare qc/di non fare qc** to decide to do sth/against doing sth; **ho deciso di non andarci** I decided not to go; **sta a lui decidere** it's up to him to decide; **ha deciso il nostro futuro** it determined our future **2** (*risolvere: disputa*) to settle, resolve; **decidere una lite** (*Dir*) to settle a dispute
■ VI (*aus* **avere**) (*persona*) to decide, make up one's mind; **hai deciso?** have you decided?; **è venuto il momento di decidere** it's time to decide *o* make a decision; **non so decidere tra questi modelli** I can't decide which of these models to choose; **fu quel fatto a decidere del mio futuro** that was what decided *o* determined my future;
▶ **decidersi** VIP (*persona*) to come to *o* make a decision; **non so decidermi** I can't decide; **decidersi a fare** to make up one's mind to do; **finalmente si è deciso a parlare** he finally made up his mind to talk

deciduo, a [de'tʃiduo] AGG deciduous

deciframento [detʃifra'mento] SM *(di calligrafia)* deciphering
decifrare [detʃi'frare] VT *(codice)* to decode, decipher; *(calligrafia)* to decipher, make out; *(enigma)* to find the key to; *(fig: intenzioni, atteggiamento)* to work out
decilitro [de'tʃilitro] SM decilitre *(Brit)*, deciliter *(Am)*
decimale [detʃi'male] AGG, SM decimal
decimare [detʃi'mare] VT *(anche fig)* to decimate
decimazione [detʃimat'tsjone] SF *(anche fig)* decimation
decimetro [de'tʃimetro] SM decimetre *(Brit)*, decimeter *(Am)*
decimo, a ['dɛtʃimo] AGG tenth
■ SM **1** *(Mat)* tenth **2** *(Med)*: **avere dieci decimi di vista** to have twenty-twenty vision
■ SM/F *(in ordine, graduatoria)*: **il decimo da sinistra** the tenth from the left; *per fraseologia vedi* **quinto**
decina [de'tʃina] SF **1** *(Mat)*: **la colonna delle decine** the tens column **2** *(circa 10)* about ten, ≈ about a dozen; **una decina di macchine** ≈ about a dozen cars; **decine di lettere** ≈ dozens of letters, ≈ letters by the dozen *vedi anche* **cinquantina**
decisamente [detʃiza'mente] AVV definitely, decidedly
decisi *ecc* [de'tʃizi] VB *vedi* **decidere**
decisionale [detʃizjo'nale] AGG decision-making *attr*
decisione [detʃi'zjone] SF **1** *(scelta, Dir)* decision; **prendere una decisione** to take *o* make a decision; **ho preso una decisione** I've made a decision
2 *(risolutezza)* decisiveness; **con decisione** decisively, resolutely; **agire con decisione** to act decisively
decisionismo [detʃizjo'nizmo] SM decisiveness *(especially in politics)*
decisionista, i; , e [detʃizjo'nista] SM/F decisive person *(especially in politics)*
decisivamente [detʃiziva'mente] AVV decisively
decisivo, a [detʃi'zivo] AGG *(gen)* decisive; *(fattore)* deciding; **il suo voto è stato decisivo** his vote was decisive
deciso, a [de'tʃizo] PP *di* **decidere**
■ AGG **1** *(persona, carattere)* determined; *(tono)* firm, resolute; **essere deciso a fare qc** to be determined to do sth; **essere deciso a tutto** to be ready to do anything; **sei proprio deciso?** are you quite sure?; **entrò con passo deciso** he marched in resolutely
2 *(netto: colpo)* clean **3** *(definitivo)*: **non c'è ancora niente di deciso** nothing has been decided yet
declamare [dekla'mare] VT, VI *(aus* **avere***)* to declaim
declamatorio, ria, ri, rie [deklama'tɔrjo] AGG declamatory
declassare [deklas'sare] VT to downgrade; **1ª declassata** *(Ferr) first-class carriage which may be used by second-class passengers*
declinabile [dekli'nabile] AGG *(Gramm)* declinable
declinare [dekli'nare] VI *(aus* **avere***)* *(pendio)* to slope down; *(fig: popolarità)* to decline
■ VT **1** *(Gramm)* to decline **2** *(rifiutare: invito, offerta)* to decline, turn down; **ho declinato l'offerta** I turned down the offer; **declinare ogni responsabilità** to disclaim all responsibility **3 declinare le proprie generalità** *(frm)* to give one's particulars
declinazione [deklinat'tsjone] SF **1** *(Gramm)* declension **2** *(Fis, Astron)* declination
declino [de'klino] SM decline; **in declino** declining, on the decline
declivio, vi [de'klivjo] SM (downward) slope
decodificare [dekodifi'kare] VT to decode
decodificatore [dekodifika'tore] SM decoder
decodificazione [dekodifikat'tsjone] SF decoding
decollare [dekol'lare] VI *(aus* **avere***)* *(anche fig)* to take off; **l'aereo è decollato alle otto** the plane took off at eight o'clock
décolleté [dekolə'te] AGG INV *(abito)* low-necked, low-cut; **scarpa décolleté** court shoe
■ SM INV *(di abito)* low neckline; *(di donna)* cleavage
decollo [de'kɔllo] SM *(Aer, fig)* take-off; **al decollo** on take-off; **in fase di decollo** during take-off; **decollo verticale** vertical take-off
decolorante [dekolo'rante] AGG *(Chim)* decolorizing *o* decolouring; *(per capelli)* bleaching
■ SM *(vedi agg)* decolorizing *o* decolouring agent; bleach
decolorare [dekolo'rare] VT *(vedi agg)* to decolorize *o* decolour; to bleach
decolorazione [dekolorat'tsjone] SF *(vedi agg)* decolorizing *o* decolouring; bleaching
decomporre [dekom'porre] VB IRREG, VT
▶ **decomporsi** VIP to decompose
decomposizione [dekompozit'tsjone] SF decomposition; **un cadavere in decomposizione** a decomposing corpse
decomposto, a [dekom'posto] PP *di* **decomporre**
decompressimetro [dekompres'simetro] SM *(nuoto subacqueo)* decompression gauge
decompressione [dekompres'sjone] SF decompression; **fare la decompressione** to decompress
decomprimere [dekom'primere] VT *(file)* to decompress
deconcentrare [dekontʃen'trare] VT: **far deconcentrare qn** to make sb lose their concentration
▶ **deconcentrarsi** VR to lose one's concentration
deconcentrato, a [dekontʃen'trato] AGG distracted
decongelare [dekondʒe'lare] VT to defrost
decongestionamento [dekondʒestjona'mento] SM relieving of congestion
decongestionante [dekondʒestjo'nante] SM decongestant
decongestionare [dekondʒestjo'nare] VT *(Med, traffico)* to relieve congestion in
decorare [deko'rare] VT *(ornare, anche Mil)* to decorate; **decorare qn al valor militare** to decorate sb for bravery
decorativo, a [dekora'tivo] AGG decorative
decoratore, trice [dekora'tore] SM/F **1** (interior) decorator **2** *(Teatro)* set designer
decorazione [dekorat'tsjone] SF *(ornamento, medaglia)* decoration
decoro [de'kɔro] SM *(decenza)* decorum; *(dignità)* dignity; **vestirsi con decoro** to be properly dressed
decoroso, a [deko'roso] AGG *(contegno, abito)* dignified, decorous; *(fig: stipendio)* decent
decorrenza [dekor'rɛntsa] SF: **con decorrenza da** (as) from
decorrere [de'korrere] VI IRREG *(aus* **essere***)*
1 decorrere da to have effect from, run from; **a decorrere da** (as) from, starting from **2** *(trascorrere)* to pass, elapse *(frm)*; **è decorso un anno dalla sua morte** a year has passed *o* elapsed since he died
decorso, a [de'korso] PP *di* **decorrere**
■ SM *(di malattia)* course
decotto [de'kɔtto] SM *(Farmacologia)* decoction
decrebbi *ecc* [de'krebbi] VB *vedi* **decrescere**
decrepito, a [de'krɛpito] AGG *(vecchio)* decrepit; *(fig)* obsolete

Dd

decrescere [de'kreʃʃere] VI IRREG *(aus* **essere***)* *(gen)* to decrease, diminish; *(prezzi, febbre)* to go down; *(piena)* to subside; *(luna)* to wane; *(marea)* to ebb
decresciuto, a [dekreʃ'ʃuto] PP *di* **decrescere**
decretare [dekre'tare] VT *(Dir)* to decree; *(stabilire)* to order; **decretare lo stato d'emergenza** to declare a state of emergency; **decretare la nomina di qn** to nominate sb for appointment
decreto [de'kreto] SM decree; **decreto legge** ≈ decree with the force of law **decreto di sfratto** eviction order
decubito [de'kubito] SM *(Med)*: **piaghe da decubito** bedsores
decuplicare [dekupli'kare] VT to increase tenfold
decuplo, a ['dɛkuplo] AGG tenfold
■ SM: **guadagno il decuplo di prima** I earn ten times more than I used to
decurtare [dekur'tare] VT *(debito, somma)* to reduce
decurtazione [dekurtat'tsjone] SF reduction
Dedalo ['dɛdalo] SM Daedalus
dedalo ['dɛdalo] SM maze, labyrinth
dedica, che ['dɛdika] SF dedication
dedicare [dedi'kare] VT *(gen, Rel)* to dedicate; *(energie, sforzi)* to devote; **le ha dedicato una canzone** he dedicated a song to her; **ha dedicato la sua vita alla scienza** he devoted his life to science
▶ **dedicarsi** VR: **dedicarsi a** *(votarsi)* to devote o.s. to; **mi dedicherò alla musica** I'm going to devote myself to music; **dedicarsi alla casa** *(occuparsene)* to look after the house; **dedicarsi anima e corpo a** to give o.s. up body and soul to
dedicatorio, ria, ri, rie [dedika'tɔrjo] AGG dedicatory
dedicherò *ecc* [dedike'rɔ] VB *vedi* **dedicare**
dedito, a ['dɛdito] AGG: **dedito a** *(studio)* dedicated *o* devoted to; *(vizio)* addicted to; **essere dedito allo studio** to be a very keen student; **essere dedito al bere** to be a heavy drinker; **essere dedito al gioco** to be a gambler
dedizione [dedit'tsjone] SF dedication, devotion
dedotto, a [de'dotto] PP *di* **dedurre**
deducibile [dedu'tʃibile] AGG **1** *(per deduzione)* which can be deduced, deducible **2** *(detraibile)* deductible; **spese deducibili (dalle tasse)** (tax-)deductible expenses
deduco *ecc* [de'duco] VB *vedi* **dedurre**
dedurre [de'durre] VT IRREG **1** *(capire, concludere)* to deduce, infer; **ne deduco che...** I deduce from this that...; **dal suo comportamento ho dedotto che era stanco** I realized from the way he was behaving that he was tired **2** *(togliere)*: **dedurre (da)** to deduct (from); **l'IVA va dedotta alla fine** VAT is deducted at the end
dedussi *ecc* [de'dussi] VB *vedi* **dedurre**
deduttivamente [deduttiva'mente] AVV by deduction, deductively
deduttivo, a [dedut'tivo] AGG deductive
deduzione [dedut'tsjone] SF *(in tutti i sensi)* deduction
défaillance [defa'jɑ̃s] SF INV *(Sport: crisi)* collapse; **avere un attimo di défaillance** *(debolezza)* to have a moment of weakness
defalcare [defal'kare] VT to deduct
defaticamento [defatika'mento] SM *(Sport: anche:* **esercizi di defaticamento***)* warming-down
defecare [defe'kare] VI *(aus* **avere***)* to defecate
■ VT *(Chim)* to refine
defenestrare [defenes'trare] VT *(fig)* to remove from office; *(in senso proprio)* to throw out of the window
defenestrazione [defenestrat'tsjone] SF *(fig: azione)* removal from office, dismissal
deferente [defe'rɛnte] AGG **1** *(persona)* deferential **2** *(Anat: dotto, canale)* deferent
deferenza [defe'rɛntsa] SF deference
deferire [defe'rire] VT: **deferire qc a** *(Dir)* to refer sth to
defezionare [defettsjo'nare] VI *(aus* **avere***)* to defect; *(Mil)* to desert
defezione [defet'tsjone] SF *(vedi vb)* defection; desertion
defibrillatore [defibrilla'tɔre] SM *(Med)* defibrillator
deficiente [defi'tʃɛnte] AGG **1** *(fam pegg: sciocco)* half-witted, half-wit **2** *(mancante)*: **deficiente di** deficient in
■ SM/F mentally handicapped person; *(fam pegg: sciocco)* idiot
deficienza [defi'tʃɛntsa] SF *(gen)* deficiency; *(carenza)* shortage; *(fig: lacuna)* weakness
deficit ['dɛfitʃit] SM INV deficit
deficitario, ria, ri, rie [defitʃi'tarjo] AGG *(Fin)* in deficit; **bilancio deficitario** deficit; **a causa della gestione deficitaria dello scorso anno...** due to last year's deficit ...
defilarsi [defi'larsi] VR *(svignarsela)* to slip away, slip off
défilé [defi'le] SM INV fashion show
definire [defi'nire] VT **1** *(descrivere)* to define; **il suo comportamento si può definire irresponsabile** his behaviour can be described as irresponsible **2** *(risolvere: vertenza)* to settle; **dobbiamo definire la questione al più presto** we must settle this matter as soon as possible **3** *(determinare)* to define
definitamente [definita'mente] AVV clearly
definitiva [defini'tiva] SF: **in definitiva** *(dopotutto)* in the end; *(tutto sommato)* all in all
definitivamente [definitiva'mente] AVV *(decidere)* once and for all, definitively; *(stabilirsi)* for good, permanently; *(lasciarsi)* for good; *(assumere)* on a permanent basis, permanently
definitivo, a [defini'tivo] AGG *(gen)* final, definitive; *(chiusura, vittoria, edizione)* definitive
definito, a [defi'nito] AGG *(gen)* definite; **ben definito** clear, clear cut
definizione [definit'tsjone] SF *(gen)* definition; *(di disputa, vertenza)* settlement; *(di tempi, obiettivi)* establishment; **ad alta definizione** *(Fot, TV)* high definition
deflagrare [defla'grare] VI *(aus* **avere***)* *(anche fig)* to explode
deflagrazione [deflagrat'tsjone] SF explosion
deflazionare [deflattsjo'nare] VT *(Econ)* to deflate
deflazione [deflat'tsjone] SF *(Econ)* deflation
deflazionistico, a; **, ci**; **, che** [deflattsjo'nistiko] AGG deflationary
deflettore [deflet'tore] SM *(Aut)* quarterlight *(Brit)*, deflector *(Am)*
deflorare VT deflower
deflorazione [deflorat'tsjone] SF deflowering, defloration
defluire [deflu'ire] VI *(aus***essere***)***defluire da***(liquido)*to flow away from; *(folla)* to stream
deflusso [de'flusso] SM *(anche fig)* flow; *(di marea)* ebb
defogliante [defoʎ'ʎante] SM defoliant
deforestare [defores'tare] VT to deforest
deforestazione [deforestat'tsjone] SF deforestation
deformabile [defor'mabile] AGG *(gen, Fis)* deformable
deformante [defor'mante] AGG *(Med)* deforming; *(specchio)* distorting
deformare [defor'mare] VT *(oggetto)* to put out of

shape; (*legno*) to warp; (*corpo*) to deform; (*fig: immagine, visione, verità, fatto*) to distort
▶ **deformarsi** VIP (*vedi vt*) to lose its shape; to warp; to become deformed; (*fig: immagine*) to become distorted
deformazione [deformat'tsjone] SF (*Med*) deformation; **questa è deformazione professionale!** that's how you get when you do this job!
deforme [de'forme] AGG (*mani, piedi, corpo*) misshapen; (*volto*) disfigured; (*fig: brutto, sgradevole*) hideous
deformità [deformi'ta] SF INV (*Med*) deformity
deframmentare [deframmen'tare] VT (*Inform*) to defragment
deframmentazione [deframmentat'tsjone] SF (*Inform*) defragmentation
defraudare [defrau'dare] VT: **defraudare qn di qc** to cheat *o* swindle sb out of sth, defraud sb of sth
defunto, a [de'funto] AGG dead, late *attr*; **il defunto presidente** the late president
■ SM/F deceased person; **il defunto** the deceased; **i defunti** the dead; **commemorazione dei defunti** (*ricorrenza*) All Souls' Day
degenerare [dedʒene'rare] VI (*aus* **avere**) **degenerare (in)** to degenerate (into)
degenerativo, a AGG degenerative
degenerato, a [dedʒene'rato] AGG, SM/F degenerate
degenerazione [dedʒenerat'tsjone] SF degeneration, degeneracy
degenere [de'dʒɛnere] AGG degenerate
degente [de'dʒɛnte] SM/F (*di ospedale*) in-patient
degenza [de'dʒɛntsa] SF confinement in *o* to bed; **degenza ospedaliera** period in hospital
degli ['deʎʎi] PREP + ART *vedi* **di**
deglutire [deglu'tire] VT to swallow
deglutizione [deglutit'tsjone] SF swallowing
degnamente [deɲɲa'mente] AVV worthily
degnare [deɲ'ɲare] VT: **non mi ha degnato di uno sguardo** he didn't so much as look at me; **non mi ha degnato di una risposta** he didn't deign to answer me
▶ **degnarsi** VIP: **degnarsi di fare qc** to deign *o* condescend to do sth; **vedo che ti sei degnato!** (*iro*) how gracious of you!
degno, a ['deɲɲo] AGG (*gen*) worthy; (*dignitoso*) dignified; **degno di** worthy of; **degno di fiducia** trustworthy; **degno di fede** (*persona, testimonianza*) reliable; **degno di lode** praiseworthy; **non è degno di te** (*persona*) he is not worthy of you; **fare una cosa del genere non è degno di te** it's unworthy of you to do a thing like that; **non è degno di essere chiamato padre** he is not fit to be called a father; **il suo degno figlio** (*anche iro*) his good *o* worthy son
degradante [degra'dante] AGG degrading
degradare [degra'dare] VT (*Mil*) to demote; (*fig: persona*) to degrade
▶ **degradarsi** VR to degrade o.s., demean o.s.
degradazione [degradat'tsjone] SF (*vedi vt*) demotion; degradation
degrado [de'grado] SM: **degrado urbano** urban decay
degustare [degus'tare] VT to sample, taste
degustazione [degustat'tsjone] SF **1** (*azione*) tasting, sampling **2** (*negozio*): **degustazione di vini** specialist wine bar; **degustazione di caffè** specialist coffee shop
dei ['dei] PREP + ART *vedi* **di**
deificare [deifi'kare] VT to deify
deiscente [deiʃ'ʃɛnte] AGG (*Bot*) dehiscent
del [del] PREP + ART *vedi* **di**
delatore, trice [dela'tore] SM/F (police) informer
Delaware ['deləwɛə] SM Delaware
delazione [delat'tsjone] SF informing
delega, ghe ['dɛlega] SF **1** (*di autorità, poteri*) delegation **2** (*procura*) proxy; **per delega** by proxy; **per delega notarile** ≈ through a solicitor (*Brit*) *o* lawyer
delegare [dele'gare] VT to delegate; **delegare qn a fare qc** to delegate sb to do sth; (*Dir*) to empower *o* authorise sb to do sth
delegato, a [dele'gato] AGG: **amministratore delegato, consigliere delegato** managing director
■ SM/F delegate
delegazione [delegat'tsjone] SF delegation
delegherò *ecc* [delege'rɔ] VB *vedi* **delegare**
deleterio, ria, ri, rie [dele'tɛrjo] AGG (*effetto*) deleterious; (*sostanza*) noxious
delfino[1] [del'fino] SM (*Zool*) dolphin; **nuotare a delfino** (*Sport*) ≈ to do the butterfly (stroke)
delfino[2] [del'fino] SM (*Storia*) dauphin; (*fig: successore*) probable successor
Delhi ['deli] SF Delhi
delibera [de'libera] SF decision; (*del Parlamento*) resolution
deliberare [delibe'rare] VT: **deliberare qc** to come to a decision on sth; **deliberare di fare qc** to decide to do sth
■ VI (*aus* **avere**) (*Dir*): **deliberare su qc** to rule on sth
deliberatamente [deliberata'mente] AVV deliberately, on purpose
deliberato, a [delibe'rato] AGG (*intenzionale*) deliberate
deliberazione [deliberat'tsjone] SF = **delibera**
delicatamente [delikata'mente] AVV (*toccare*) delicately; (*accarezzare, appoggiare*) gently
delicatezza [delika'tettsa] SF (*vedi agg*) delicacy; softness, paleness; lightness; gentleness; frailty; fragility; thoughtfulness, considerateness, tactfulness
delicato, a [deli'kato] AGG **1** (*gen*) delicate; (*tessuto*) delicate, fine; (*colore*) delicate, soft, pale; (*profumo*) delicate, light; (*carezza*) gentle, soft; (*salute*) delicate, frail; (*meccanismo*) delicate, fragile; **è delicato di stomaco** he has a delicate stomach **2** (*che richiede tatto*) delicate; (*che dimostra tatto*) thoughtful, considerate, tactful
delimitare [delimi'tare] VT (*anche fig*) to delimit (*frm*)
delimitazione [delimitat'tsjone] SF delimitation (*frm*)
delineare [deline'are] VT (*anche fig*) to outline
▶ **delinearsi** VIP to be outlined; (*fig: situazione*) to take shape; **si sta delineando un periodo difficile** there are hard times ahead
delinquente [delin'kwɛnte] SM/F delinquent, criminal; (*fig: mascalzone*) scoundrel, wretch; **la polizia ha arrestato il delinquente** the police arrested the criminal; **delinquente abituale** (*Dir*) persistent offender
delinquenza [delin'kwɛntsa] SF delinquency, criminality; **un aumento della delinquenza** an increase in crime; **delinquenza minorile** juvenile delinquency; **delinquenza organizzata** organized crime
deliquio, qui [de'likwjo] SM (*frm*) swoon; **cadere in deliquio** to swoon
delirante [deli'rante] AGG (*Med*) delirious; (*fig: folla*) frenzied; (*: discorso, mente*) insane
delirare [deli'rare] VI (*aus* **avere**) (*Med*) to be delirious; (*fig*) to rave
delirio, ri [de'lirjo] SM (*Med*) delirium; **in delirio** (*Med*) delirious; **andare in delirio per qc** to go wild about

sth; **mandare in delirio** to send into a frenzy; **la folla in delirio** the frenzied crowd

delirium tremens [de'lirjum'trɛmens] SM INV (*Med*) delirium tremens

delitto [de'litto] SM (*misfatto, anche fig*) crime; (*Dir*) crime, offence; **ha commesso un terribile delitto** he committed a terrible crime

delittuoso, a [delittu'oso] AGG criminal

delizia [de'littsja] SF delight; **con mia grande delizia** to my great delight; **che delizia!** how delightful!

deliziare [delit'tsjare] VT to delight
▶ **deliziarsi** VIP: **deliziarsi di qc/a fare qc** to take delight in sth/in doing sth

deliziosamente [delittsjosa'mente] AVV (*vedi agg*) delightfully; deliciously

delizioso, a [delit'tsjoso] AGG (*gen*) delightful; (*sapore, odore, cibo*) delicious

della ['della], **delle** ['delle], **dello** ['dello] PREP + ART *vedi* di

delta ['dɛlta] SM INV (*Geog*) delta
■ SM O F INV **1** (*in alfabeto greco*) delta **2** (*Aer*): **ala a delta** delta wing

deltaplanista, i, e [deltapla'nista] SM/F hang-glider (*person*)

deltaplano [delta'plano] SM hang-glider; **volo col deltaplano** hang-gliding; **andare in deltaplano** to hang-glide

delucidazione [delutʃidat'tsjone] SF clarification *no pl*; **vorrei delle delucidazioni in merito** I would like some more details on that

deludente [delu'dɛnte] AGG disappointing; **un film un po' deludente** a rather disappointing film

deludere [de'ludere] VT IRREG to disappoint; **mi hai molto deluso** you've really disappointed me; **il suo ultimo film mi ha deluso** his last film was disappointing

> **LO SAPEVI...?**
> **deludere** non si traduce mai con la parola inglese *delude*

delusi *ecc* [de'luzi] VB *vedi* **deludere**

delusione [delu'zjone] SF disappointment; **è stata una delusione** it was a disappointment; **che delusione!** what a disappointment!; **dare una delusione a qn** to disappoint sb; **avere una delusione amorosa** to be disappointed in love

> **LO SAPEVI...?**
> **delusione** non si traduce mai con la parola inglese *delusion*

deluso, a [de'luzo] PP *di* **deludere**
■ AGG disappointed; **sono deluso del voto che ho preso** I'm disappointed with the mark I got

demagogia [demago'dʒia] SF demagogy

demagogico, a, ci, che [dema'gɔdʒiko] AGG (*politica, iniziativa*) popularity-seeking

demagogo, ghi [dema'gɔgo] SM demagogue

demandare [deman'dare] VT (*Amm*) to transfer

demaniale [dema'njale] AGG state *attr*

demanio, ni [de'manjo] SM (*Amm*) state property; (: *ufficio*) state property office

demarcare [demar'kare] VT to demarcate

demarcazione [demarkat'tsjone] SF demarcation; **linea di demarcazione** demarcation line

demente [de'mɛnte] SM/F (*anche fig*) lunatic
■ AGG (*Med*) demented, mentally deranged; (*fam*) crazy, mad

demenza [de'mɛntsa] SF (*anche fig*) madness, insanity; **demenza senile** (*Med*) senile dementia

demenziale [demen'tsjale] AGG insane; (*comicità*) surreal, off-the-wall

demerito [de'mɛrito] SM demerit; **ciò torna a tuo demerito** that reflects badly on you

demistificare [demistifi'kare] VT (*mito*) to demystify, to debunk (*fam*)

demi-volée [demivo'le] SF INV (*Tennis*) half volley

demmo ['demmo] VB *vedi* **dare**

demo ['dɛmo] SM INV demo

democraticamente [demokratika'mente] AVV democratically

democraticità [demokratitʃi'ta] SF democratic nature

democratico, a, ci, che [demo'kratiko] AGG democratic
■ SM/F democrat; **Democratici di sinistra** (*Pol*) Democrats of the Left (*Italian left-wing party*)

democratizzare [demokratid'dzare] VT to democratize

democrazia [demokrat'tsia] SF democracy; **le democrazie occidentali** the western democracies; **la Democrazia Cristiana** the Christian Democrat Party

democristiano, a [demokris'tjano] AGG, SM/F Christian Democrat

Democrito [de'mɔkrito] SM Democritus

démodé [demɔ'de] AGG INV old-fashioned, out-of-date

demografia [demogra'fia] SF demography
▷ www.irpps.cnr.it/

demograficamente [demografika'mente] AVV demographically

demografico, a, ci, che [demo'grafiko] AGG demographic; **incremento demografico** increase in population

demolire [demo'lire] VT (*casa, oggetto, teoria*) to demolish; (*persona*: *criticare*) to tear to pieces

demolitore, trice [demoli'tore] AGG (*anche fig*) destructive
■ SM (*operaio*) demolition worker

demolizione [demolit'tsjone] SF (*anche fig*) demolition

demone ['dɛmone] SM demon

demoniaco, a, ci, che [demo'niako] AGG demoniac(al); (*fig: diabolico*) fiendish, diabolic

demonico, a, ci, che [de'mɔniko] AGG, SM (*letter*) demonic

demonio, ni [de'mɔnjo] SM demon, devil; (*fig: genio*) genius; **il Demonio** the Devil; **quel ragazzino è un demonio** that child is a little devil

demonizzare [demonid'dzare] VT to make a monster of

demonizzazione [demoniddzat'tsjone] SF demonizing, demonization

demoralizzare [demoralid'dzare] VT to demoralize
▶ **demoralizzarsi** VIP to become demoralized; **non demoralizzarti** don't let it get you down

demoralizzato, a [demoralid'dzato] AGG demoralized

demoralizzazione [demoraliddzat'tsjone] SF demoralization

demordere [de'mɔrdere] VI IRREG (*aus* **avere**) to give up; **non demordere (da)** to refuse to give up

demoscopia [demosko'pia] SF analysis of public opinion

demoscopico, a, ci, che [demos'kɔpiko] AGG: **indagine demoscopica** opinion poll

Demostene [de'mɔstene] SM Demosthenes

demotivare [demoti'vare] VT: **demotivare qn** to take away sb's motivation

demotivato, a [demoti'vato] AGG demotivated, lacking motivation
denaro [de'naro] SM **1** money; **denaro contante** *o* **liquido** cash; **non ho molto denaro con me** I haven't got much money with me **2** *(misura di fibre tessili)* denier **3 denari** SMPL *(Carte) suit in Neapolitan pack of cards*
denaturato, a [denatu'rato] AGG: **alcol denaturato** methylated spirits, denatured alcohol *(Am)*
denaturazione [denaturat'tsjone] SF denaturation
denazionalizzare [denattsjonalid'dzare] VT *(industria)* to denationalize
denazionalizzazione [denattsjonaliddzat'tsjone] SF denationalization
dendrite [den'drite] SF *(Anat)* dendrite
denigrare [deni'grare] VT to denigrate, run down
denigratorio, ria, ri, rie [denigra'tɔrjo] AGG disparaging, denigrating
denigrazione [denigrat'tsjone] SF denigration
denitrificazione [denitrifikat'tsjone] SF *(Chim)* denitrification
denominare [denomi'nare] VT to name
denominatore [denomina'tore] SM *(Mat)* denominator; **denominatore comune** *(anche fig)* common denominator
denominazione [denominat'tsjone] SF *(gen)* name, designation *(frm)*; *(classificazione)* denomination; **denominazione di origine controllata** *mark guaranteeing the quality and origin of a wine*
denotare [deno'tare] VT to indicate, denote
densamente [densa'mente] AVV densely
densità [densi'ta] SF *(gen, Fis)* density; *(di nebbia)* thickness, denseness; *(di vernice)* thickness; *(di folla)* denseness; **ad alta/bassa densità di popolazione** densely/sparsely populated; **ad alta densità di manodopera** labour-intensive; **a doppia/alta densità** *(Inform)* double-/high-density
denso, a ['denso] AGG *(gen)* dense, thick; *(vernice, fumo, minestra)* thick; **una minestra densa** a thick soup; **una frase densa di significato** a phrase charged with meaning
dentale [den'tale] AGG dental
dentario, ria, ri, rie [den'tarjo] AGG dental
dentaruolo [denta'rwɔlo] SM teething ring
dentata [den'tata] SF *(morso)* bite; *(segno)* toothmark
dentato, a [den'tato] AGG *(Tecn)* toothed; *(Bot)* dentate
dentatura [denta'tura] SF **1** set of teeth, teeth *pl* **2** *(Tecn: di ruota)* serration
dente ['dente] SM **1** *(Anat)* tooth; **denti sporgenti** buck teeth; **mettere i denti** to teethe; **mal di denti** toothache; **avere mal di denti** to have toothache; **lavarsi i denti** to clean *o* brush one's teeth; **mi lavo i denti dopo ogni pasto** I clean my teeth after every meal; **dente del giudizio** wisdom tooth; **dente da latte** milk tooth **2** *(di sega, pettine)* tooth; *(di ingranaggio)* cog; *(di forchetta, tridente)* prong **3** *(Geog)* jagged peak **4** *(Bot)*: **dente di leone** dandelion **5** *(fraseologia)*: **al dente** *(Culin)* al dente; **avere il dente avvelenato contro** *o* **con qn** to bear sb a grudge; **via il dente, via il dolore** once it's over I'll *(o* you'll *ecc)* feel better; **mettere qc sotto i denti** to have a bite to eat; **mostrare i denti** to show one's teeth; **parlare a denti stretti** to speak unwillingly; **stringere i denti** to grit one's teeth

LO SAPEVI...?
dente non si traduce mai con la parola inglese *dent*

dentellare [dentel'lare] VT *(gen)* to indent, notch; *(lama)* to serrate; *(stoffa)* to pink
dentellato, a [dentel'lato] AGG *(gen)* indented, notched; *(francobollo)* perforated; *(foglia)* serrated; *(Geog: cresta)* jagged; *(pizzo)* scalloped
dentellatura [dentella'tura] SF *(gen)* indentation; *(di francobollo)* perforation; *(di cresta)* jagged outline; *(di pizzo)* scalloping
dentice ['dɛntitʃe] SM *(Zool)* sea bream
dentiera [den'tjɛra] SF **1** *(Med)* dentures *pl*, (set of) false teeth *pl (fam)*; **porta la dentiera** she's got false teeth **2** *(Tecn)* rack
dentifricio, cia, ci, cie [denti'fritʃo] SM toothpaste; **dentifricio al fluoro** fluoride toothpaste
■ AGG: **pasta dentifricia** toothpaste
dentista, i, e [den'tista] SM/F dentist; **fa la dentista** she's a dentist
dentistico, a, ci, che [den'tistiko] AGG *(gabinetto, studio)* dentist's; **studi dentistici** dentistry *sg*
dentizione [dentit'tsjone] SF dentition
dentro ['dentro] AVV **1** *(all'interno)* inside; *(in casa)* indoors; **qui/là dentro** in here/there; **andare dentro** to go inside *(o* indoors); **vai dentro** go inside; **non va dentro** it won't go in (here); **vieni dentro** come inside *o* in; **col freddo che c'era, dentro si stava bene** with the cold weather we were better off indoors; **hai visto dentro?** have you seen inside?; **cioccolatini con dentro le nocciole** chocolates with hazelnut centres; **piegato in dentro** folded over; **o dentro o fuori!** either come in or go out!; **darci dentro** *(fig fam)* to slog away, work hard **2** *(fam: in carcere)* inside; **l'hanno messo dentro** they've put him away *o* inside; **è dentro da un anno** he's been inside for a year **3** *(fig: nell'intimo)* inwardly; **sentire qc dentro** to feel sth deep down inside o.s.; **tenere tutto dentro** to keep everything bottled up (inside o.s.)
■ PREP: **dentro (a)** in; **dentro l'armadio** in the cupboard; **dentro le mura/i confini** within the walls/frontiers; **è dentro a quel cassetto** it's in that drawer; **è dentro alla politica/agli affari** he's involved in politics/business; **dentro di me pensai...** I thought to myself ...; **ci sono dentro fino al collo** *(fig)* I'm in it up to my neck
■ SM inside
denuclearizzare VT to denuclearize
denuclearizzato, a [denuklearid'dzato] AGG *(comune, zona)* denuclearized, nuclear-free
denudare [denu'dare] VT *(persona)* to strip; *(parte del corpo)* to bare
▶ **denudarsi** VR to strip
denudazione [denudat'tsjone] SF *(Geol)* denudation
denuncia, ce *o* **cie** [de'nuntʃa], **denunzia** [de'nuntsja] SF **1** *(Dir)*: **sporgere denuncia contro qn** to report sb to the police **2** *(dichiarazione)* notification; **denuncia delle nascite** registration of births; **denuncia dei redditi** income tax return
denunciare [denun'tʃare], **denunziare** [denun'tsjare] VT **1** *(Dir)*: **denunciare qn/qc (alla polizia)** to report sb/sth (to the police); **lo ha denunciato alla polizia** he reported him to the police **2** *(dichiarare: nascite, redditi)* to declare; *(accusare pubblicamente)* to denounce; *(rivelare)* to expose; **ha denunciato la corruzione all'interno del partito** he exposed the corruption within the party
denutrito, a [denu'trito] AGG undernourished
denutrizione [denutrit'tsjone] SF malnutrition
deodorante [deodo'rante] AGG, SM deodorant

Dd

deodorare [deodo'rare] VT to deodorize
deontologia [deontolo'dʒia] SF: **deontologia professionale** professional code of conduct
depauperare [depaupe'rare] VT (*frm*) to impoverish
depenalizzazione [depenaliddzat'tsjone] SF decriminalization
dépendance [depɑ̃'dɑ̃s] SF INV outbuilding
deperibile [depe'ribile] AGG perishable; **merce deperibile** perishables *pl*, perishable goods *pl*
deperibilità [deperibili'ta] SF INV perishability
deperimento [deperi'mento] SM (*di persona*) wasting away; (*di merci*) deterioration; **il loro deperimento è dovuto a denutrizione** they are in a serious state because of malnutrition
deperire [depe'rire] VI (*aus* **essere**) (*persona*) to waste away; (*pianta*) to wilt; **ti trovo un po' deperito** you look rather run-down to me
depilare [depi'lare] VT to depilate; **depilarsi le sopracciglia** to pluck one's eyebrows; **depilarsi le gambe** (*con rasoio*) to shave one's legs; (*con ceretta*) to wax one's legs
depilatorio, ria, ri, rie [depila'tɔrjo] AGG hair-removing *attr*, depilatory; **crema depilatoria** hair-removing cream
■ SM (*sostanza*) hair-remover, depilatory
depilazione [depilat'tsjone] SF depilation, hair-removal
depistaggio, gi [depis'taddʒo] SM: **un tentativo di depistaggio delle indagini** an attempt to throw the inquiry off the track
depistare [depis'tare] VT (*polizia, autorità*) to set on the wrong track
dépliant [depli'ɑ̃] SM INV leaflet; (*opuscolo*) brochure
deplorare [deplo'rare] VT (*biasimare*) to deplore; (*perdita*) to lament
deplorazione [deplorat'tsjone] SF censure, disapproval
deplorevole [deplo'revole], **deplorabile** [deplo'rabile] AGG deplorable
deplorevolmente [deplorevol'mente], **deplorabilmente** [deplorabil'mente] AVV deplorably
depone *ecc* [de'pone] VB *vedi* **deporre**
deponente [depo'nɛnte] SM (*Gramm*) deponent
depongo *ecc* [de'pongo] VB *vedi* **deporre**
deporre [de'porre] VB IRREG
■ VT **1** (*gen: valigia*) to put down; (*fig: abbandonare: orgoglio, vecchio rancore*) to put aside, forget; **deporre le armi** (*Mil*) to lay down arms **2** (*rimuovere: persona*) to remove; (*: re*) to depose; **lo deposero dalla carica** they removed him from office **3** (*sogg: uccello*): **deporre le uova** to lay eggs **4** (*Dir*): **deporre il vero** to tell the truth; **deporre il falso** to give false evidence
■ VI (*aus* **avere**) (*Dir*) to testify
deportare [depor'tare] VT to deport
deportato, a [depor'tato] AGG deported
■ SM/F deportee
deportazione [deportat'tsjone] SF deportation
deposi *ecc* [de'posi] VB *vedi* **deporre**
depositante [depozi'tante] SM/F (*Comm*) depositor
depositare [depozi'tare] VT **1** (*gen: oggetto*) to put down, lay down; (*merci*) to store; **depositare qc per terra** to put sth down; **ha depositato qui tutti i libri e se n'è andato** he dumped all his books here and left **2** (*Banca*) to deposit; **depositare una somma in banca** to pay a sum of money into the bank **3** (*sogg: fiume, vino*) to deposit
■ VI (*aus* **avere**) (*liquido*) to leave some sediment
▶ **depositarsi** VIP (*sabbia, polvere*) to settle
depositario, ria, ri, rie [depozi'tarjo] SM/F (*gen*) depository; (*fig: confidente*) repository; (*: custode: di verità, tradizioni*) custodian
deposito [de'pɔzito] SM **1** (*atto*): **il deposito della merce ci è costato molto** storing the goods cost us a lot; **il deposito dei bagagli è gratuito** there is no charge for left luggage **2** (*di liquidi*) sediment, deposit; (*di acqua calcarea*) fur, (lime) scale; **deposito alluvionale** drift **3** (*Fin*) deposit; **fare** *o* **eseguire un deposito** to put down *o* pay a deposit; **denaro in deposito** money on deposit; **deposito bancario** bank deposit; **deposito cauzionale** deposit **4** (*magazzino*) warehouse; (*Mil, di autobus*) depot; **lasciare in deposito** (*merce*) to store; **deposito bagagli** left-luggage office; **deposito di munizioni** ammunition dump
deposizione [depozit'tsjone] SF **1** (*gen, Dir*) deposition; (*da una carica*) removal; **fare una falsa deposizione** to perjure o.s. **2** (*Arte, Rel*): **la Deposizione** the Deposition
deposto, a [de'posto] PP *di* **deporre**
depravare [depra'vare] VT to corrupt, pervert
depravato, a [depra'vato] AGG depraved
■ SM/F degenerate
depravazione [depravat'tsjone] SF depravity
deprecabile [depre'kabile] AGG deplorable
deprecare [depre'kare] VT to deplore, deprecate
depredare [depre'dare] VT to plunder, loot; **depredare qn di qc** to rob sb of sth
depressione [depres'sjone] SF (*in tutti i sensi*) depression; **area** *o* **zona di depressione** (*Meteor*) area of low pressure; **essere in uno stato di depressione** (*Med*) to be depressed, be in a state of depression
depressivo, a [depres'sivo] AGG depressive; **in uno stato depressivo** in a depressed state, in a state of depression
depresso, a [de'presso] PP *di* **deprimere**
■ AGG depressed; **zona depressa** (*Econ*) depressed area
deprezzamento [deprettsa'mento] SM: **deprezzamento (di)** depreciation (of)
deprezzare [depret'tsare] VT to bring down the value of
▶ **deprezzarsi** VIP to depreciate
deprimente [depri'mɛnte] AGG depressing; **una storia deprimente** a depressing story
deprimere [de'primere] VB IRREG
■ VT to depress
▶ **deprimersi** VIP to become depressed
depurare [depu'rare] VT (*liquido*) to purify; (*sangue*) to cleanse
▶ **depurarsi** VIP (*liquido*) to be purified; (*corpo*) to be cleansed
depurativo, a [depura'tivo] AGG, SM depurative
depuratore, trice [depura'tore] AGG purifying
■ SM: **depuratore d'acqua** water purifier; **depuratore di gas** scrubber
depurazione [depurat'tsjone] SF purification; **impianto di depurazione** purification plant
deputare [depu'tare] VT (*incaricare*): **deputare qn a fare qc** to delegate sb to do sth
deputato, a [depu'tato] SM/F **1** (*Pol*) deputy, ≈ member of Parliament (*Brit*), ≈ representative (*Am*), ≈ Congressman/Congresswoman (*Am*) **2** (*Amm*) delegate, representative
deputazione [deputat'tsjone] SF (*gruppo*) deputation, delegation
deragliamento [deraʎʎa'mento] SM derailment

deragliare [deraʎ'ʎare] VI (*aus* **avere**) to be derailed, go off the rails; **far deragliare un treno** to derail a train
dérapage [dera'paʒ] SM INV (*di veicolo, Aer*) skid; (*Sci*) sideslipping
derapare [dera'pare] VI (*aus* **avere**) (*veicolo, Aer*) to skid; (*Sci*) to sideslip
derapata [dera'pata] SF (*vedi vb*) skid; sideslip; **fare una derapata** (*di veicolo*) to skid, go into a skid; (*sugli sci*) to sideslip
derattizzazione [derattiddzat'tsjone] SF rodent control
derby ['dɛrbi] SM INV (*Calcio*) local derby (*Brit*)
deregolamentare [deregolamen'tare] VT to deregulate
deregolamentato, a [deregolamen'tato] AGG deregulated
deregolamentazione [deregolamentat'tsjone] SF deregulation
derelitto, a [dere'litto] AGG abandoned; (*casa*) derelict, abandoned
■ SM/F destitute person; **i derelitti** the destitute
deretano [dere'tano] SM (*fam*) backside
deridere [de'ridere] VT IRREG to mock, deride
derisi *ecc* [de'risi] VB *vedi* **deridere**
derisione [deri'zjone] SF mockery, derision
deriso, a [de'rizo] PP *di* **deridere**
derisorio, ria, ri, rie [deri'zɔrjo] AGG (*gesto, tono*) mocking
deriva [de'riva] SF **1** (*Aer, Naut*) drift; **andare alla deriva** (*anche fig*) to drift; **la deriva dei continenti** (*Geol*) continental drift **2** (*dispositivo: Aer*) fin; (*: Naut*) centreboard (*Brit*), centerboard (*Am*) **3** (*Naut: barca*) dinghy
derivare [deri'vare] VI (*aus* **essere**) **derivare da** to derive from; (*corso d'acqua*) to spring from; **questa parola deriva dal francese** this word is of French derivation; **da quella decisione non sono derivati altro che guai** nothing but trouble has come out of that decision
■ VT **1** (*Chim, Gramm, Mat*) to derive; **"gas" deriva dalla parola greca "chaos"** "gas" derives from the Greek word "chaos"; **da ciò ha derivato che...** hence he concluded that ... **2** (*corso d'acqua*) to divert
derivata [deri'vata] SF (*Mat*) derivative
derivato, a [deri'vato] AGG derived
■ SM (*Chim, Gramm*) derivative; (*prodotto*) by-product
derivazione [derivat'tsjone] SF (*gen*) derivation; (*di acque*) diversion; (*Elettr*) shunt; (*Telec*) extension (*in house*)
dermatite [derma'tite] SF dermatitis
dermatologia [dermatolo'dʒia] SF dermatology
dermatologico, a, ci, che [dermato'lɔdʒiko] AGG dermatological
dermatologo, a, gi, ghe [derma'tɔlogo] SM/F dermatologist
dermatosi [derma'tɔzi] SF INV dermatosis
dermoprotettivo, a [dermoprotet'tivo] AGG (*crema, trattamento*) protecting the skin
deroga, ghe ['dɛroga] SF (special) dispensation; **in deroga a** as a (special) dispensation to; **è una norma che non ammette deroghe** there can be no exceptions to this rule
derogare [dero'gare] VI (*aus* **avere**) (*Dir*): **derogare a** to repeal in part
derrate [der'rate] SFPL: **derrate alimentari** foodstuffs
derubare [deru'bare] VT: **derubare qn di qc** to rob sb of sth; **lo hanno picchiato e derubato** he was attacked and robbed; **mi hanno derubato del portafoglio** I had my wallet stolen
derubato, a [deru'bato] SM/F victim of a theft
deruralizzazione [deruraliddzat'tsjone] SF rural depopulation
desalatore [desala'tore] SM = **dissalatore**
desalinizzare [desalinid'dzare] VT = **dissalare**
desalinizzazione [desalinizzat'tsjone] SF = **dissalazione**
descrittivo, a [deskrit'tivo] AGG descriptive
descritto, a [des'kritto] PP *di* **descrivere**
descrivere [des'krivere] VT IRREG (*in tutti i sensi*) to describe; **descrivere qc a qn** to describe sth to sb; **mi ha descritto ciò che aveva trovato** he described to me what he had found
descrivibile [deskri'vibile] AGG: **facilmente descrivibile** easy to describe; **non è descrivibile** it's indescribable
descrizione [deskrit'tsjone] SF description; **fare una descrizione** to give a description
desensibilizzare [desensibilid'dzare] VT (*Med, fig*) to desensitize
desertico, a, ci, che [de'zɛrtiko] AGG desert *attr*
desertificare [dezertifi'kare] VT to turn into a desert
desertificazione [dezertifikat'tsjone] SF desertification
deserto, a [de'zɛrto] AGG deserted; **le strade erano deserte** the streets were deserted; **isola deserta** desert island
■ SM desert
déshabillé [dezabi'je] SM INV: **essere in déshabillé** to be half-dressed; **sono ancora in déshabillé** I'm not dressed yet
desiderabile [deside'rabile] AGG desirable
desiderare [deside'rare] VT **1** (*volere*) to want, wish for; **desiderare (di) fare qc** to want *o* wish to do sth; **desidererei andarmene** I would like to leave; **desidero che lei venga domani** I'd like you to come tomorrow; **desiderava migliorare il suo inglese** he wanted to improve his English; **desidero parlarvi subito** I'd like to speak to you immediately; **desidera?** (*in bar*) what would you like?; (*in negozio, ufficio*) can I help you?; **sei desiderato al telefono** you're wanted on the phone; **farsi desiderare** (*fare il prezioso*) to play hard to get; (*farsi aspettare*) to take one's time; **lascia molto a desiderare** it leaves a lot to be desired; **la casa lascia un po' a desiderare** the house is not ideal **2** (*sessualmente*) to desire
desiderio, ri [desi'dɛrjo] SM (*gen*) wish; (*più intenso, carnale*) desire; **sentì il desiderio di andarsene** he felt a desire to leave; **esprimi un desiderio!** make a wish!
desideroso, a [deside'roso] AGG: **desideroso di** longing *o* eager for
designare [desiɲ'ɲare] VT (*persona*) to designate, appoint; (*data, ora*) to fix; **la vittima designata** the intended victim
designazione [desiɲɲat'tsjone] SF designation, appointment
desinare [dezi'nare] (*toscano*) VI (*aus* **avere**) to dine, have dinner
■ SM dinner
desinenza [dezi'nɛntsa] SF (*Gramm*) ending, inflexion
desistenza [dezis'tɛntsa] SF (*Pol*): **patto di desistenza** *agreement by a political party to withdraw its candidate(s) in order to maximise the chances of candidate(s) from a party with which it is allied*

Dd

desistere [de'sistere] VI IRREG (*aus* **avere**) **desistere (da qc/dal fare qc)** to give up (sth/doing sth), desist from (doing sth) (*frm*)
desistito, a [desis'tito] PP *di* **desistere**
desktop ['dɛsktop] SM INV desktop
desolante [dezo'lante] AGG distressing
desolatamente [dezolata'mente] AVV desolately
desolato, a [dezo'lato] AGG (*paesaggio*) desolate; (*persona: sconsolato*) distressed; **essere desolato (per qc)** (*spiacente*) to be terribly sorry (about sth); **sono desolato!** I'm terribly sorry!
desolazione [dezolat'tsjone] SF desolation
despota, i ['dɛspota] SM despot
dessert [de'sɛr] SM INV dessert; **da dessert** dessert *attr*
dessi *ecc* ['dessi] VB *vedi* **dare**
destabilizzante [destabilid'dzante] AGG destabilizing
destabilizzare [destabilid'dzare] VT to destabilize
destare [des'tare] VT (*svegliare*) to wake (up); (*fig: dubbio, sospetti, pietà*) to arouse; (*: curiosità, invidia*) to arouse, to awaken; **destare la preoccupazione/la sorpresa di qn** to cause sb concern/surprise; **non destare il can che dorme** (*Proverbio*) let sleeping dogs lie
▶ **destarsi** VIP to wake up
deste *ecc* ['deste] VB *vedi* **dare**
destinare [desti'nare] VT **1** (*designare*): **destinare qc a qn** to intend *o* mean sth for sb; **era destinato a morir giovane** he was destined *o* fated to die young; **la sorte che gli è stata destinata** the fate that was in store for him; **libri destinati ai bambini** books (written) for children **2** (*devolvere*): **destinare una somma all'acquisto di qc** to intend to use *o* earmark a sum to buy sth; **i fondi saranno destinati alla ricerca** the money will be used for research **3** (*assegnare*) to appoint, assign; **è destinato alla nuova filiale** he's been appointed to the new branch **4** (*indirizzare*) to address; **sai dov'è destinata la lettera?** do you know where the letter is going? **5** (*decidere*): **destinare un giorno a qc/a fare qc** to set aside a day for sth/to do sth; **in data da destinarsi** at some future date, at a date to be decided
destinatario, ria, ri, rie [destina'tarjo] SM/F (*di lettera*) addressee; (*di merce*) consignee; (*di mandato*) payee
destinazione [destinat'tsjone] SF destination; (*scopo*) purpose; **giungere a destinazione** to reach one's destination; **sono giunti a destinazione** they reached their destination
destino [des'tino] SM (*sorte*) fate, destiny; (*futuro*) destiny; **il mio destino** my destiny; **era destino che accadesse** it was fated *o* destined to happen
destituire [destitu'ire] VT (*funzionario*) to dismiss, remove
destituzione [destitut'tsjone] SF dismissal, removal

> **LO SAPEVI...?**
> **destituzione** non si traduce mai con la parola inglese *destitution*

desto, a ['desto] AGG (wide) awake; **tener desto l'interesse del pubblico** to hold the public's attention; **sogno o son desto?** am I dreaming?
destra ['dɛstra] SF **1** (*mano*) right hand; **scrivo con la destra** I write with my right hand **2** (*parte*) right, right-hand side; **a destra** (*stato in luogo*) on the right; (*moto a luogo*) to the right; **a destra di** to the right of; **sulla destra, nella foto...** on the right of the photograph ...; **corsia di destra** right-hand lane; **guida a destra** right-hand drive; **tenere la destra** to keep to the right; **voltare a destra** to turn right; **spostarsi verso destra** to move to the right **3** (*Pol*): **la destra** the right; **di destra** right-wing; **un partito di destra** a right-wing party
destreggiarsi [destred'dʒarsi] VIP to manoeuvre (*Brit*), maneuver (*Am*)
destrezza [des'trettsa] SF skill, dexterity
destriero [des'trjɛro] SM steed; (*da battaglia*) warhorse, charger
destrismo [des'trizmo] SM **1** (*Med*) right-handedness **2** (*Pol*) right-wing tendencies
destro, a ['dɛstro] AGG **1** (*mano, braccio*) right; (*lato*) right-hand **2** (*persona: abile*) adroit, skilful (*Brit*), skillful (*Am*)
■ SM (*Boxe*) right
destrorso, a [des'trɔrso] AGG (*moto*) clockwise; (*Pol: scherz*) rightist
■ SM/F (*Pol: scherz*) rightist
destrosio [des'trɔzjo] SM dextrose
desueto, a [desu'ɛto] AGG (*letter: parola, uso*) obsolete
desumere [de'sumere] VT IRREG (*dedurre*) to infer, deduce; (*trarre: informazioni*) to obtain; **desumo da ciò che te ne vuoi andare** I gather from this that you want to leave
desunto, a [de'sunto] PP *di* **desumere**
detassare [detas'sare] VT to remove the duty (*o* tax) from
detective [di'tektiv] SM INV (*anche:* **detective privato**) private detective
detenere [dete'nere] VT IRREG (*incarico, primato*) to hold; (*proprietà*) to have, possess; (*prigioniero*) to detain, hold
detengo *ecc* [de'tɛngo] VB *vedi* **detenere**
detenni *ecc* [de'tenni] VB *vedi* **detenere**
detentivo, a [deten'tivo] AGG: **pena detentiva** prison sentence
detentore, trice [deten'tore] SM/F (*di titolo, primato*) holder
detenuto, a [dete'nuto] SM/F prisoner
detenzione [deten'tsjone] SF **1** (*di titolo, primato*) holding; (*di armi, stupefacenti*) possession **2** (*Dir*) detention
detergente [deter'dʒɛnte] AGG (*gen*) detergent; (*crema, latte*) cleansing *attr*; **latte detergente** cleansing milk
■ SM (*detersivo*) detergent; (*cosmetico*) cleanser
detergere [de'tɛrdʒere] VT IRREG (*gen*) to clean; (*pelle, viso*) to cleanse; (*sudore*) to wipe (away)
deteriorabile [deterjo'rabile] AGG (*gen*) liable to deteriorate; (*cibi*) perishable
deterioramento [deterjora'mento] SM: **deterioramento (di)** deterioration (in)
deteriorare [deterjo'rare] VT (*macchinari, merce*) to damage, cause to deteriorate; (*alimenti*) to spoil, cause to go bad
▶ **deteriorarsi** VIP (*vedi vt*) to deteriorate; to go bad
deteriore [dete'rjore] AGG (*merce*) second-rate; (*significato*) pejorative
determinante [determi'nante] AGG decisive, determining
determinare [determi'nare] VT (*gen*) to determine; (*causare*) to bring about, cause
determinativo, a [determina'tivo] AGG determining; **articolo determinativo** (*Gramm*) definite article
determinato, a [determi'nato] AGG **1** (*gen*) certain; (*particolare*) specific; **in determinate circostanze** in certain circumstances **2** (*risoluto*) determined, resolute; **è molto determinato** he's very determined
determinazione [determinat'tsjone] SF (*atto*)

determining; (*decisione*) decision; (*risolutezza*) determination; **determinazione dei costi** (*Econ*) costing

determinismo [determi'nizmo] SM determinism

determinista, i, e [determi'nista] SM/F determinist

deterrente [deter'rɛnte] AGG, SM deterrent

deterrò *ecc* [deter'rɔ] VB *vedi* **detenere**

detersivo [deter'sivo] SM (*gen*) detergent; (*per bucato*) washing powder (*Brit*), soap powder; **un detersivo neutro** a mild detergent; **detersivo per bucato a mano** hand-washing powder/liquid; **detersivo per lavatrice** detergent for use in washing machines; **detersivo per i pavimenti** floor cleaner; **detersivo per i piatti** washing-up liquid

deterso, a [de'tɛrso] PP *di* **detergere**

detestabile [detes'tabile] AGG (*carattere, abitudine*) detestable, odious; (*tempo, cibo*) dreadful, appalling

detestabilmente [detestabil'mente] AVV detestably

detestare [detes'tare] VT to detest, hate, loathe; **lo detesto!** I detest him!; **detesto mentire** I hate lying

detiene *ecc* [de'tjɛne] VB *vedi* **detenere**

detonante [deto'nante] AGG detonating, explosive
■ SM explosive

detonare [deto'nare] VI (*aus* **avere**) to detonate, explode

detonatore [detona'tore] SM detonator

detonazione [detonat'tsjone] SF (*di esplosivo*) detonation, explosion; (*di arma*) bang; (*di motore*) knocking, pinking (*Brit*)

detrae *ecc* [de'trae] VB *vedi* **detrarre**

detraggo *ecc* [de'traggo] VB *vedi* **detrarre**

detrarre [de'trarre] VT IRREG: **detrarre (da)** to deduct (from), take away (from)

detrassi *ecc* [de'trassi] VB *vedi* **detrarre**

detratto, a [de'tratto] PP *di* **detrarre**

detrazione [detrat'tsjone] SF deduction; **detrazione d'imposta** tax allowance

detrimento [detri'mento] SM: **a detrimento di** to the detriment of

detrito [de'trito] SM (*Geol*) detritus; (*: fluviale*) silt, alluvium

detronizzare [detronid'dzare] VT (*anche fig*) to dethrone

detta ['detta] SF: **a detta di** according to; **a detta sua** according to him (*o* her)

dettagliante [dettaʎ'ʎante] SM/F (*Comm*) retailer, retail dealer

dettagliare [dettaʎ'ʎare] VT (*racconto, descrizione*) to detail, give full details of

dettagliatamente [dettaʎʎata'mente] AVV in detail

dettaglio, gli [det'taʎʎo] SM **1** detail; **in dettaglio** in detail; **entrare** *o* **scendere nei dettagli** to go into details *o* particulars **2** (*Comm*): **al dettaglio** (*prezzo, vendita*) retail; **prezzo al dettaglio** retail price; **vendere al dettaglio** to (sell) retail

dettame [det'tame] SM dictate

dettare [det'tare] VT (*lettera, condizioni*) to dictate; **dettare legge** (*fig*) to lay down the law; **fa' come ti detta il cuore** follow your heart

dettato [det'tato] SM dictation

dettatura [detta'tura] SF dictation; **scrivere qc sotto dettatura** to take sth down from dictation; **l'ha scritto sotto dettatura** it was dictated to him

detto, a ['detto] PP *di* **dire**
■ AGG **1** (*Amm, Comm: suddetto*) above-mentioned, aforementioned; **detti prodotti vi saranno consegnati in settimana** the above-mentioned products will be delivered to you by the end of the week; **nel detto giorno** on that day **2** (*soprannominato*) called, known as **3** (*fraseologia*): **detto fatto** no sooner said than done; **è presto detto!** it's easier said than done!; **come non detto** let's forget it
■ SM (*motto*) saying; **un detto cinese** a Chinese saying

deturpare [detur'pare] VT (*anche fig*) to disfigure; (*moralmente*) to sully

deturpazione [deturpat'tsjone] SF disfigurement

deumidificatore [deumidifika'tore] SM dehumidifier

deuterio, ri [deu'tɛrjo] SM (*Chim*) deuterium

Deuteronomio [deutero'nɔmjo] SM (*Bibbia*) Deuteronomy

devastante [devas'tante] AGG (*anche fig*) devastating

devastare [devas'tare] VT to devastate; (*fig: sogg: malattia*) to ravage

devastatore, trice [devasta'tore] AGG destructive

devastazione [devastat'tsjone] SF devastation, destruction

deviante [devi'ante] AGG deviant

deviare [devi'are] VI (*aus* **avere**) (*veicolo*): **deviare (da)** to turn off (from); (*pallone*) to deflect; **il viale devia dal corso principale** the avenue leads off the main road; **deviare dalla retta via** to go astray
■ VT (*traffico, fiume, conversazione*) to divert; (*proiettile, colpo, pallone*) to deflect; **il traffico è stato deviato** the traffic has been diverted; **deviare qn dalla retta via** to lead sb astray

deviato, a [devi'ato] AGG (*fig: organizzazione*) corrupt, bent (*fam*)

deviatore [devia'tore] SM (*Ferr: persona*) signalman

deviazione [deviat'tsjone] SF (*gen*) deviation; (*Aut*) diversion; **fare una deviazione** to make a detour; **deviazione della colonna vertebrale** curvature of the spine

devitalizzare [devitalid'dzare] VT (*dente, nervo*) to devitalize, kill

devitalizzazione [devitaliddzat'tsjone] SF devitalization

devo *ecc* ['devo] VB *vedi* **dovere**

devolution [devo'luʃʃon] SF INV = **devoluzione 2**

devoluto, a [devo'luto] PP *di* **devolvere**

devoluzione [devolut'tsjone] **1** SF (*di beni*) transfer **2** (*Pol*) devolution

devolvere [de'vɔlvere] VT IRREG (*somma*) to transfer; **devolvere qc in beneficenza** to give sth to charity

devotamente [devota'mente] AVV devoutly

devoto, a [de'vɔto] AGG (*Rel*) devout, pious; (*affezionato*) devoted
■ SM/F devout person; **i devoti** (*i fedeli*) the faithful

devozione [devot'tsjone] SF (*Rel*) devoutness; (*affetto, dedizione*) devotion; **avere una devozione per qn** to worship sb; **dire/fare le devozioni** (*Rel: preghiere*) to say/make one's devotions

dg ABBR (= **decigrammo**) dg

di [di] PAROLA CHIAVE
(*di + il* = del, *di + lo* = dello, *di + l'* = dell', *di + la* = della, *di + i* = dei, *di + gli* = degli, *di + le* = delle)
■ PREP
1 (*possesso*) of; (*composto da, scritto da*) by; **la macchina del mio amico/dei miei amici** my friend's/friends' car; **la figlia dell'amica di mia madre** the daughter of my mother's friend, my mother's friend's daughter; **una commedia di Goldoni** a play by Goldoni; **l'ultimo libro di Umberto Eco** Umberto

Dd

Eco's latest book, the latest book by Umberto Eco
2 (*specificazione, denominazione*) of; **il sindaco di Milano** the mayor of Milan; **il mese di marzo** the month of March; **la vita di campagna** country life; **tavolo di cucina** kitchen table; **sala di lettura** reading-room; **il direttore dell'azienda** the manager of the company; **il professore d'inglese** the English teacher, the teacher of English; **il nome di Maria** the name Mary
3 (*materiale*): **fatto di legno** made of wood; **una casa di mattoni** a brick house, a house made of brick(s); **un'orologio d'oro** a gold watch; **un sacchetto di plastica** a plastic bag
4 (*provenienza*) from, out of; (*posizione*) in, on; **uscire di casa** to come out of *o* leave the house; **i negozi di Milano** the Milan shops, the shops in Milan; **i vicini del piano di sopra** the upstairs neighbours, the people who live on the floor above us; **sono di Roma** I am *o* come from Rome
5 (*tempo*): **di domenica** on Sundays; **d'estate** in (the) summer; **di giorno** by day; during the day; **di mattina** in the morning; **di notte** by night; at night; in the night; **di sera** in the evening
6 (*misura*): **un bimbo di 2 anni** a 2-year-old child, a child of two; **un viaggio di 100 chilometri** a 100-kilometre journey; **un chilo di farina** a kilo of flour; **un viaggio di 2 giorni** a 2-day journey; **un milione di lire** a million lire; **una stanza di 2 metri per 3** a room measuring 2 metres by 3; **un gioiello di valore** a valuable piece of jewellery; **un bicchiere di vino** a glass of wine
7 (*mezzo, modo, causa*): **vestirsi di bianco** to dress in white; **fermarsi di botto** to stop dead *o* suddenly; **rispondere di brutto** to answer brusquely; **è debole di cuore** he has a weak heart; **urlare di dolore** to scream with pain; **ridere di gusto** to laugh heartily; **morire di cancro** to die of cancer; **spalmare di burro** to spread with butter; **sporcare qc di sugo** to get sauce on sth
8 (*argomento*) about, of; **discutere del tempo** to talk about the weather; **trattato di medicina** medical treatise; **parlare di qc** to talk about sth; **libro di storia** history book
9 (*abbondanza, privazione*): **pieno di** full of; **povero di carbone** poor in coal; **privo di** lacking in; **ricco di risorse naturali** rich in natural resources
10 (*paragone nei comparativi*) than; (*paragone nei superlativi*) of; **il migliore della classe** the best in the class; **è meglio di me** he's better than me; **è il migliore di tutti** he is the best of all; **il migliore dei suoi libri** his best book, the best of his books; **il migliore della città** the best in the city
11 (*seguito da infinito*): **sa di aver sbagliato** he knows (that) he did the wrong thing; **credo di capire** I think (that) I understand; **ti chiedo di dirmi la verità** I beg you to tell me the truth; **è degno di esser ricordato** it's worth remembering; **tentò di scappare** he tried to escape
■ ART PARTITIVO (*affermativo*) some; (*negativo*) any; (*interrogativo*) any, some; **vuoi dei biscotti?** would you like some biscuits?, do you want any biscuits?; **non ho dei libri** I haven't any books, I have no books; **non vedo niente di meglio** I can't see anything better; **c'erano delle persone che non conoscevo** there were some people I didn't know; **ho dei soldi** I've got some money; **non c'è nulla di strano** there's nothing odd about it; **c'è del vero in quello che dici** there's some truth in what you say; **vuoi del vino?** would you like some wine?, do you want any wine?

dì [di] SM (*letter*) day; **buon dì!** good day (to you)!; **a dì** = **addì**
DIA ['dia] SIGLA F = *Direzione Investigativa Antimafia*
diabete [dia'bɛte] SM diabetes *sg*
diabetico, a, ci, che [dia'bɛtiko] AGG, SM/F diabetic
diabolicamente [djabolika'mente] AVV diabolically
diabolico, a, ci, che [dja'bɔliko] AGG (*anche fig*) diabolical
diaconato [diako'nato] SM diaconate
diacono [di'akono] SM (*Rel*) deacon
diadema, i [dia'dɛma] SM (*di sovrano*) diadem; (*di donna*) tiara
diafano, a [di'afano] AGG diaphanous; (*fig*: *mani, volto*) transparent
diaframma, i [dia'framma] SM (*Anat, Fot*) diaphragm; (*contraccettivo*) diaphragm, Dutch cap; (*schermo*) screen
diagnosi [di'aɲɲozi] SF INV (*anche fig*) diagnosis *sg*; **diagnosi prenatale** prenatal diagnosis
diagnostica [diaɲ'ɲɔstika] SF diagnostics *sg*
diagnosticamente [diaɲɲostika'mente] AVV diagnostically
diagnosticare [diaɲɲosti'kare] VT (*anche fig*) to diagnose
diagnostico, a, ci, che [diaɲ'ɲɔstiko] AGG diagnostic; **aiuti diagnostici** (*Inform*) debugging aids
■ SM diagnostician
diagonale [diago'nale] AGG (*motivo, disegno*) diagonal; **in linea diagonale** diagonally; **tessuto diagonale** twill; **tiro diagonale** (*Calcio*) cross
■ SF diagonal; **in diagonale** diagonally
■ SM **1** (*tessuto*) twill **2** (*Calcio*) cross; (*Tennis*) crosscourt shot; **diagonale incrociato** (*Tennis*) return crosscourt shot
diagonalmente [diagonal'mente] AVV diagonally
diagramma, i [dia'gramma] SM (*gen, Mat*) diagram; (*grafico*) chart, graph; **diagramma a barre** bar chart; **diagramma di flusso** flow chart; **diagramma a torta** pie chart
dialettale [dialet'tale] AGG dialectal; **poesia dialettale** poetry in dialect
dialettalmente [dialettal'mente] AVV in dialect
dialettica [dia'lɛttika] SF dialectic; **ha una dialettica travolgente** he's highly articulate
dialetticamente [dialettika'mente] AVV dialectically
dialettico, a, ci, che [dia'lɛttiko] AGG dialectic
dialetto [dia'lɛtto] SM dialect

DIALETTO

The official language of Italy is Italian, but there are many and very diverse dialects. Most Italian dialects belong to one of five main groups: Gallo-Italic, Venetian, Tuscan, Central and Southern.

dialisi [di'alizi] SF INV (*Chim, Med*) dialysis *sg*
dialogante [dialo'gante] AGG: **unità dialogante** (*Inform*) interactive terminal
dialogare [dialo'gare] VI (*aus* **avere**) **dialogare (con)** to have a dialogue (*Brit*) *o* dialog (*Am*) (with); (*conversare*) to converse (with)
■ VT (*scena*) to write the dialogue (*Brit*) *o* dialog (*Am*) for
dialogico, a, ci, che [dia'lɔdʒiko] AGG dialogue (*Brit*) *attr*, dialog (*Am*) *attr*
dialogo, ghi [di'alogo] SM dialogue (*Brit*), dialog (*Am*); **tra noi non c'è più dialogo** we don't talk anymore
diamante [dia'mante] SM **1** (*gen*) diamond; (*di*

diamante) diamond *attr*; **un anello con diamante** a diamond ring; **nozze di diamante** diamond wedding anniversary **2** (*Naut*: *di ancora*) crown

diametralmente [diametral'mente] AVV diametrically

diametro [di'ametro] SM diameter

diamine ['djamine] ESCL: **che diamine?** what on earth?

Diana ['djana] SF Diana

diapason [di'apazon] SM INV (*Mus*: *strumento*) tuning fork; (: *tono*) diapason

diapositiva [diapozi'tiva] SF slide, transparency

diaria [di'arja] SF daily (expense) allowance

diario, ri [di'arjo] SM (*gen*) diary, journal; **tenere un diario** to keep a diary; **diario di bordo** (*Naut*) log(book); **diario di classe** (*Scol*) class register; **diario degli esami** (*Scol*) exam timetable; **diario scolastico** homework diary

diarrea [diar'rɛa] SF diarrhoea (*Brit*), diarrhea (*Am*)

diaspora [di'aspora] SF (*Storia*) Diaspora

diastole [di'astole] SF (*Anat*) diastole

diatriba [di'atriba] SF diatribe

diavoleria [djavole'ria] SF **1** (*azione*) act *o* piece of mischief **2** (*aggeggio*) weird contraption

diavoletto[1]**, a** [djavo'letto] SM/F (*fig*: *bambino*) little devil, imp

diavoletto[2] SM (*bigodino*) hair-curler

diavolo ['djavolo] SM **1** devil; **povero diavolo!** poor devil!; **è un buon diavolo** he's a good sort; **avere un diavolo per capello** to be in a foul temper; **avere il diavolo in corpo** (*bambino*) to have the devil in one; (*adulto*) to be fidgety; **avere una fame/un freddo del diavolo** to be ravenously hungry/frozen stiff; **mandare qn al diavolo** (*fam*) to tell sb to go to hell; **l'ho mandato al diavolo** I told him to go to hell; **va al diavolo!** (*fam*) go to hell!; **fare il diavolo a quattro** to kick up a fuss **2** **diavolo!** for goodness' sake!; **che diavolo vuoi?** what the hell do you want?; **dove diavolo è finito?** where the hell has it (*o* he) got to? **3** (*Zool*): **diavolo orsino** Tasmanian devil

dibattere [di'battere] VT (*argomento*) to debate, discuss
▶ **dibattersi** VR (*anche fig*) to struggle, wrestle; **dibattersi tra mille difficoltà** to have to contend with a host of difficulties; **dibattersi nel dubbio** to be racked by indecision

dibattimento [dibatti'mento] SM (*dibattito*) debate, discussion; (*Dir*) hearing

dibattito [di'battito] SM (*gen*) debate, discussion; (*in parlamento*) debate

diboscare [dibos'kare] VT (*zona, montagna*) to deforest

dicastero [dikas'tɛro] SM ministry

dice *ecc* VB *vedi* **dire**

dicembre [di'tʃembre] SM December; *per fraseologia vedi* **luglio**

dicembrino, a [ditʃem'brino] AGG December *attr*

diceria [ditʃe'ria] SF rumour (*Brit*), rumor (*Am*), piece of gossip; **sono solo dicerie** it's just gossip

dichiarare [dikja'rare] VT (*gen*) to declare; (*annunciare*) to announce; **dichiarare guerra (a)** to declare war (on); **dichiarare qn colpevole** to declare sb guilty; **si dichiara che...** it is hereby declared that ...; **il portavoce ha dichiarato che...** the spokesman said that ...; **vi dichiaro marito e moglie** I pronounce you man and wife; **articoli da dichiarare** (*Dogana*) goods to declare; **nulla da dichiarare** (*Dogana*) nothing to declare
▶ **dichiararsi** VR **1** to declare o.s.; **dichiararsi soddisfatto** to declare o.s. satisfied; **dichiararsi a favore di/contro** to declare o.s. *o* come out in favour of/against; **dichiararsi colpevole/non colpevole** to plead guilty/not guilty; **dichiararsi vinto** to acknowledge defeat **2** (*innamorato*) to declare one's love

dichiaratamente [dikjarata'mente] AVV openly

dichiarato, a [dikja'rato] AGG (*nemico, ateo*) avowed; (*cocainomane, anarchico*) self-confessed

dichiarazione [dikjarat'tsjone] SF (*proclamazione*) declaration; (*discorso, commento*) statement; **ha rilasciato una dichiarazione alla polizia** he made a statement to the police; **dichiarazione (d'amore)** declaration of love; **le ha fatto una dichiarazione d'amore** he told her he loved her; **dichiarazione doganale** customs declaration; **dichiarazione di guerra** declaration of war; **dichiarazione d'indipendenza** declaration of independence; **dichiarazione dei redditi** statement of income; (*modulo*) tax return

diciannove [ditʃan'nɔve] AGG INV, SM INV nineteen; *per fraseologia vedi* **cinque**

diciannovenne [ditʃanno'vɛnne] AGG, SM/F nineteen-year-old; *per fraseologia vedi* **cinquantenne**

diciannovesimo, a [ditʃanno'vɛzimo] AGG, SM/F nineteenth; *per fraseologia vedi* **quinto**

diciassette [ditʃas'sɛtte] AGG INV, SM INV seventeen; *per fraseologia vedi* **cinque**

diciassettenne [ditʃasset'tɛnne] AGG, SM/F seventeen-year-old; *per fraseologia vedi* **cinquantenne**

diciassettesimo, a [ditʃasset'tɛzimo] AGG, SM/F seventeenth; *per fraseologia vedi* **quinto**

diciottenne [ditʃot'tɛnne] AGG, SM/F eighteen-year-old; *per fraseologia vedi* **cinquantenne**

diciottesimo, a [ditʃot'tɛzimo] AGG, SM/F eighteenth; *per fraseologia vedi* **quinto**

diciotto [di'tʃɔtto] AGG INV eighteen
■ SM INV eighteen; (*Univ*) *minimum (pass) mark awarded in Italian universities for any individual exam*; *per fraseologia vedi* **cinque**

dicitore, trice [ditʃi'tore] SM/F (*frm*) speaker

dicitura [ditʃi'tura] SF wording, words *pl*

dico *ecc* ['diko] VB *vedi* **dire**

dicotiledone [dikoti'lɛdone] AGG (*Bot*) dicotyledon

dicotomia [dikoto'mia] SF dichotomy

didascalia [didaska'lia] SF (*di illustrazione*) caption; (*Teatro*) stage directions *pl*; (*Cine*) subtitle; (: *in film muto*) title

didascalico, a, ci, che [didas'kaliko] AGG didactic

didattica [di'dattika] SF (*scienza*) didactics *sg*; (*metodologia*) teaching methodology

didatticamente [didattika'mente] AVV didactically

didattico, a, ci, che [di'dattiko] AGG (*gen*) didactic; (*programma, metodo*) teaching; (*centro, libro*) educational

didentro [di'dentro] SM INV (*gen*) inside; (*di casa, auto*) interior; **dal didentro** from inside

didietro [di'djɛtro] SM INV (*di casa*) rear, back; (*euf*) bottom; **dal didietro** from behind

Didone [di'done] SF Dido

dieci ['djɛtʃi] AGG INV ten
■ SM INV ten; **dare un dieci a qn** (*voto*) to give sb ten out of ten; *per fraseologia vedi* **cinque**

diecimila [djetʃi'mila] AGG INV, SM INV ten thousand

diecina [dje'tʃina] SF = **decina**

diedi *ecc* ['djɛdi] VB *vedi* **dare**

diedro [di'ɛdro] SM (*Geom*: *anche*: **angolo diedro**) dihedral (angle), dihedron

dielettrico, ci [die'lɛttriko] SM, AGG (*Fis*) dielectric
dieresi [di'ɛrezi] SF INV dieresis *sg*
diesel ['di:zəl] AGG INV, SM INV (*motore, automobile*) diesel; **motore diesel** diesel engine; **macchina diesel** diesel car
diesse [di'ɛsse] SM/F INV = **diessino**
diessino, a; (*Pol*) [dies'sino] AGG of (*o* belonging to) the Democrats of the Left (*Italian left-wing party*)
■ SM/F *member (o supporter) of Democrats of the Left*
dieta ['djɛta] SF **1** diet; **essere** *o* **stare a dieta** to be on a diet; **mettersi a dieta** to diet, go on a diet; **rompere la dieta** to break one's diet **2** (*Storia*) diet, Diet
dietetica [die'tɛtika] SF dietetics *sg*
dieteticamente [dietetika'mente] AVV dietetically
dietetico, a, ci, che [die'tɛtiko] AGG diet *attr*
dietologo, a, gi, ghe [dje'tɔlogo] SM/F dietician
dietro ['djɛtro] AVV behind; (*in fondo: di gruppo, stanza*) at the back; **qua/là dietro** behind here/there; **dev'essere qua dietro** it must be behind here; **abita qua dietro** he lives round the corner; **2 file dietro** 2 rows (further) back; **vestito che si abbottona dietro** dress which buttons at the back; **non guardar dietro** don't look back; **guarda se arriva qualcuno (da) dietro** look and see if anyone is coming up behind us; **ti metti tu dietro?** (*in macchina*) are you going to go in the back?; **essere seduto dietro** (*in macchina*) to be sitting in the back; (*in autobus*) to be sitting at the back; **la firma è dietro** the signature is on the back; **attacca il foglio dietro** attach the sheet to the back; **passa dietro!** go round the back!; **di dietro** (*gen*) back; (*entrare, stare*) at the back; **la porta di dietro** the back door; **zampe di dietro** hind legs; **il sedile di dietro** the back seat; **da dietro** (*assalire*) from behind, from the rear; **da dietro non ti ho riconosciuto** I didn't recognize you from the back
■ PREP
1 (*anche:* **dietro a**: *posizione*) behind; **era dietro alla scrivania** he was behind his desk; **dietro la casa/il banco** behind the house/the counter; **dietro la porta** behind the door; **dietro l'angolo** round the corner; **dietro di** *o* **a lui/lei** behind him/her; **sono seduti dietro di me** they're sitting behind me; **guarda cosa c'è scritto dietro il foglio** look what is written on the other side of the page; **camminare uno dietro l'altro** to walk one behind the other *o* in single file; **andare dietro a** (*anche fig*) to follow; **stare dietro a qn** (*sorvegliare*) to keep an eye on sb; (*corteggiare*) to hang around sb; **portarsi dietro qn/qc** to bring sb/sth with one, bring sb/sth along; **gli hanno riso/parlato dietro** they laughed at/talked about him behind his back
2 (*anche:* **dietro a**: *dopo*) after; **uno dietro l'altro** (*dopo*) one after the other; (*in fila*) one behind the other; **sono arrivati uno dietro l'altro** they arrived one after the other
3 (*Amm, Comm*): **dietro pagamento/consegna** on payment/delivery; **dietro ricevuta di pagamento** on receipt of payment; **dietro richiesta** (*orale*) on demand, upon request; (*scritta*) on application
■ SM INV (*di foglio, quadro, giacca*) back; (*di casa*) back, rear; (*di pantaloni*) seat
■ AGG INV (*vedi sm*): **la parte dietro** the back; the rear; the seat; **le file dietro** the back rows
dietro front ['djɛtro 'front] ESCL about turn! (*Brit*), about face! (*Am*)
■ SM INV (*Mil*) about-turn, about-face; (*fig*) volte-face, about-turn, about-face; **fare dietro front** (*Mil, fig*) to about-turn, about-face; (*tornare indietro*) to turn (a)round; **dietro front da fermo** (*Sci*) kick turn
difatti [di'fatti] CONG in fact, as a matter of fact
difendere [di'fɛndere] VB IRREG
■ VT (*gen, Dir: proteggere*) to defend; (*: opinioni*) to defend, stand up for, uphold; (*: dal freddo*) to protect; **difendere gli interessi di qn** to look after sb's interests; **sapersi difendere** to know how to look after o.s.;
▶ **difendersi** VR **1** (*proteggersi*) **difendersi (da/contro)** to defend o.s. (from/against); **difendersi dal freddo** to protect o.s. from the cold **2** (*cavarsela*) to get by; **in matematica mi difendo** I get by at maths
difensiva [difen'siva] SF: **sulla difensiva** (*anche fig*) on the defensive
difensivo, a [difen'sivo] AGG defensive
difensore [difen'sore] SM/F (*gen*) defender; (*di moralità*) upholder; (*Dir*) counsel for the defence
■ AGG: **avvocato difensore** defence counsel, defense lawyer (*Am*), counsel for the defence (*Brit*) *o* defense (*Am*)
difesa [di'fesa] SF (*gen, Mil, Dir, Sport*) defence (*Brit*), defense (*Am*); **senza difese** defenceless; **per legittima difesa** in self-defence; **prendere le difese di qn** to defend sb, take sb's part; **la parola alla difesa** (*Dir*) the defence may speak; **giocare in difesa** (*Sport*) to play in defence; **Ministro/Ministero della Difesa** Minister/ Ministry of Defence; **la difesa dell'ambiente** protection of the environment
difesi *ecc* [di'fesi] VB *vedi* **difendere**
difeso, a [di'feso] PP *di* **difendere**
difettare [difet'tare] VI (*aus* **avere**) **1** (*essere difettoso*) to be defective **2** (*mancare*): **difettare di** to be lacking in, lack
difettivo, a [difet'tivo] AGG (*Gramm*) defective
difetto [di'fɛtto] SM **1** (*imperfezione: di fabbricazione*) fault, flaw, defect; (*: morale*) fault, failing, defect; (*: fisico*) defect; **ha molti difetti** he has many faults; **è senza difetti** (*persona*) he has no faults; **l'arroganza è il suo difetto** pride is his failing; **difetto di pronuncia** speech defect **2** (*mancanza*): **difetto di** lack of; **se la memoria non mi fa difetto** if my memory serves me well
difettosamente [difettosa'mente] AVV defectively
difettosità [difettosi'ta] SF faultiness, defective nature
difettoso, a [difet'toso] AGG defective, faulty, imperfect
diffamare [diffa'mare] VT (*a parole*) to slander; (*per iscritto*) to libel
diffamatore, trice [diffama'tore] SM/F (*vedi vb*) slanderer; libeller, libelist
diffamatorio, ria, ri, rie [diffama'tɔrjo] AGG (*vedi vb*) slanderous; libellous (*Brit*), libelous (*Am*)
diffamazione [diffamat'tsjone] SF (*vedi vb*) slander; libel
differente [diffe'rɛnte] AGG: **differente (da)** different (from)
differentemente [differente'mente] AVV differently, in a different way
differenza [diffe'rɛntsa] SF **1** (*diversità*): **non c'è alcuna differenza** there's no difference; **differenza (di)** difference (in); **differenza di età** age difference, difference in age; **una differenza di prezzo** a difference in price; **non fare differenza (tra)** to make no distinction (between); **a differenza di** unlike; **a differenza del calcio qui il rugby non è molto diffuso** unlike football, rugby isn't very popular here;

con la differenza che... with the difference that ...; **non fa differenza che venga o meno** it makes no difference whether he comes or not **2** (*Mat*) difference; **differenza di potenziale** (*Mat, Fis*) potential difference

differenziale [differen'tsjale] AGG differential
■ SM (*Aut, Mat*) differential

differenziare [differen'tsjare] VT to differentiate
▶ **differenziarsi** VIP (*essere differente*) to be different, differ; (*diventare differente*) to become different

differenziazione [differentsjat'tsjone] SF differentiation

differimento [differi'mento] SM deferment, postponement

differire [diffe'rire] VT to defer, postpone, put off; **differire qc di un mese** to postpone *o* defer sth for a month
■ VI (*aus* **essere**) (*essere differente*): **differire (da/in)** to differ (from/in), be different (from/in); **differire per grandezza** to differ *o* be different in size

differita [diffe'rita] SF: **in differita** (*trasmettere*) prerecorded

difficile [dif'fitʃile] AGG **1** (*problema, lavoro, periodo*) difficult; (*situazione*) difficult, awkward; **un esercizio difficile** a difficult exercise; **difficile da fare** difficult *o* hard to do; **sta attraversando momenti difficili** he's going through a difficult period; **non farla tanto difficile** don't make it more difficult than it is **2** (*persona: intrattabile*) difficult, awkward; (*: nei gusti*) fussy; **suo marito ha un carattere difficile** her husband is hard to get on with, her husband is an awkward character; **difficile da accontentare** hard to please; **essere difficile nel mangiare** to be fussy about one's food **3** (*improbabile*) unlikely; **è difficile che venga** he's unlikely to come
■ SM/F: **fare il (la) difficile** to be difficult, be awkward
■ SM difficulty, difficult part; **il difficile è finire in tempo** the difficulty lies in finishing in time, the problem is getting finished in time; **ora che il difficile è fatto...** now that the difficult part has been done ...

difficilmente [diffitʃil'mente] AVV **1** (*con difficoltà*) with difficulty **2** (*con scarsa probabilità*): **difficilmente verrà** he's unlikely to come; **verrai? — difficilmente** will you come? — probably not

difficoltà [diffikol'ta] SF INV difficulty; **non arrenderti alla prima difficoltà** don't give up at the first difficulty; **difficoltà finanziarie** financial difficulties; **trovare difficoltà a fare qc** to find it difficult to do sth; **fare delle difficoltà** to make difficulties, raise objections; **trovarsi in difficoltà** to have problems

difficoltoso, a [diffikol'toso] AGG (*compito*) difficult, hard; (*persona*) difficult, hard to please; **digestione difficoltosa** poor digestion

diffida [dif'fida] SF (*Dir*) notice, warning

diffidare [diffi'dare] VI (*aus* **avere**) (*sospettare*): **diffidare di** to distrust, be suspicious *o* distrustful of; **diffida di lui** don't trust him
■ VT (*Dir*): **diffidare qn dal fare qc** to warn sb not to do sth, caution sb against doing sth

diffidente [diffi'dɛnte] AGG: **diffidente (nei confronti di)** distrustful (of), suspicious (of); **è diffidente nei miei confronti** he's suspicious of me

> **LO SAPEVI...?**
> **diffidente** non si traduce mai con la parola inglese ***diffident***

diffidenza [diffi'dɛntsa] SF distrust, suspicion; **con diffidenza** suspiciously

> **LO SAPEVI...?**
> **diffidenza** non si traduce mai con la parola inglese ***diffidence***

diffondere [dif'fondere] VB IRREG
■ VT (*luce, calore*) to give out, spread, diffuse (*frm*); (*malattia, idea, notizie, scritto*) to spread, circulate; **la notizia è stata diffusa per radio** the news was broadcast *o* given out on the radio;
▶ **diffondersi** VIP (*anche fig*) to spread

diffrazione [diffrat'tsjone] SF (*Fis*) diffraction

diffusamente [diffuza'mente] AVV (*trattare*) at length

diffusi *ecc* [dif'fuzi] VB *vedi* **diffondere**

diffusione [diffu'zjone] SF (*gen*) diffusion; (*di giornale*) circulation; (*di cultura, religione, malattia*) spread; (*Fis*) scattering

diffuso, a [dif'fuzo] PP *di* **diffondere**
■ AGG **1** (*notizia, malattia*) widespread; **un'usanza diffusa** a common custom; **è opinione diffusa che...** it's widely held that ... **2** (*Fis*) diffuse; **luce diffusa** diffused light

diffusore [diffu'zore] SM (*Tecn*) diffuser

difilato [difi'lato] AVV (*subito*) straightaway, straight away; (*direttamente*) straight, directly; **ho lavorato per 8 ore difilato** I worked 8 hours without a break

difterite [difte'rite] SF (*Med*) diphtheria

diga, ghe ['diga] SF (*sbarramento*) dam, dyke (*against flooding*); (*: portuale*) breakwater

digerente [didʒe'rɛnte] AGG digestive

digeribile [didʒe'ribile] AGG digestible

digeribilità [didʒeribili'ta] SF INV digestibility

digerire [didʒe'rire] VT (*cibo, fig: nozioni*) to digest; (*: insulto*) to stomach, put up with; **ci vogliono otto ore per digerire** it takes eight hours to digest; **non ho digerito bene** i've got indigestion

digestione [didʒes'tjone] SF digestion

digestivo, a [didʒes'tivo] AGG digestive
■ SM (after-dinner) liqueur

Digione [di'dʒone] SF Dijon

digitale [didʒi'tale] AGG (*Anat, Tecn*) digital; **impronta digitale** fingerprint; **orologio digitale** digital watch; **radio/TV digitale** digital radio/TV
■ SF (*Bot*) foxglove
■ SM (*settore*) digital sector; **digitale terrestre** digital terrestrial

digitalizzare [didʒitalid'dzare] VT (*Inform*) to digitize

digitalizzazione [didʒitaliddzat'tjone] SF (*Inform*) digitization

digitare [didʒi'tare] VT (*dati*) to key (in)

digiunare [didʒu'nare] VI (*aus* **avere**) (*gen, Rel*) to fast; **digiunare per protesta** to go on hunger strike

digiuno, a [di'dʒuno] SM fast, fasting; **alcune diete prevedono il digiuno** some diets involve fasting; **a digiuno** on an empty stomach; **sono a digiuno** I haven't eaten; **stare a digiuno** to fast; **è una medicina da prendersi a digiuno** this medicine should be taken before meals
■ AGG: **digiuno di** (*fig: cognizioni*) ignorant of; **sono completamente digiuno di informatica** I haven't a clue about computers, I don't know anything about computers

dignità [diɲɲi'ta] SF dignity

dignitario, ri [diɲɲi'tarjo] SM dignitary

dignitosamente [diɲɲitosa'mente] AVV in a dignified way, with dignity

Dd

dignitoso, a [diɲɲi'toso] AGG (*contegno, abito*) dignified; (*fig: stipendio*) decent
DIGOS ['digos] SIGLA F (= **Divisione Investigazioni Generali e Operazioni Speciali**) *police department dealing with political security*; ≈ Special Branch
digradare [digra'dare] VI (*pendio*) to slope, decline
digressione [digres'sjone] SF digression
digrignare [digriɲ'ɲare] VT: **digrignare i denti** (*animale*) to bare its teeth; (*persona*) to grind one's teeth
digrossare [digros'sare] VT (*tronco*) to trim; (*pietra, marmo*) to rough-hew
dilagare [dila'gare] VI (*aus* **essere**) to overflow, flood; (*fig: corruzione*) to spread, be rampant; (*: malattia*) to spread
dilaniare [dila'njare] VT to tear to pieces; **era dilaniato dal rimorso** (*fig*) he was overwhelmed by remorse
dilapidare [dilapi'dare] VT to squander
dilapidatore, trice [dilapida'tore] SM/F squanderer
dilatare [dila'tare] VT (*pupille*) to dilate; (*stomaco*) to dilate, cause to expand; (*gas, metallo*) to cause to expand; (*tubo, buco*) to enlarge; (*passaggio, cavità*) to open (up)
▶ **dilatarsi** VIP (*vedi vt*) to dilate; to expand; to become enlarged; to open up
dilatazione [dilatat'tsjone] SF (*Anat*) dilation; (*di gas, metallo*) expansion
dilazionabile [dilattsjo'nabile] AGG deferrable
dilazionare [dilattsjo'nare] VT to defer, delay
dilazione [dilat'tsjone] SF deferment
dileggiare [diled'dʒare] VT to mock, scoff at, deride
dileggio, gi [di'leddʒo] SM mockery, scoffing, derision; **per dileggio** in derision *o* mockery
dileguare [dile'gware] VT to dispel, disperse; **il vento ha dileguato le nubi** the wind has dispersed the clouds
▶ **dileguarsi** VIP (*nebbia*) to disperse; (*fig: dubbio, persona*) to vanish, disappear
dilemma, i [di'lɛmma] SM dilemma
dilettante [dilet'tante] AGG amateur *attr*; (*pegg*) amateur *attr*, dilettante *attr*; **un fotografo dilettante** an amateur photographer
■ SM/F (*vedi agg*) amateur; dilettante
dilettantismo [dilettan'tizmo] SM (*pegg*) amateurishness; (*Sport*) amateurism
dilettantistico, a, ci, che [dilettan'tistiko] AGG (*pegg*) amateurish; (*Sport*) amateur *attr*
dilettare [dilet'tare] VT **1** (*dar piacere*) to delight, please, give pleasure to; **mi dilettava l'idea di partire** the thought of going away was a delight **2** (*intrattenere*) to amuse, entertain
▶ **dilettarsi** VIP: **dilettarsi a fare qc** to delight *o* take pleasure in doing sth, enjoy doing sth; **dilettarsi di qc** to have sth as a hobby; **si diletta di pittura** painting is a hobby of his
dilettevole [dilet'tevole] AGG delightful
diletto¹, a [di'lɛtto] AGG beloved
■ SM/F beloved, loved one
diletto² [di'lɛtto] SM delight, pleasure; **trarre diletto da** to take pleasure *o* delight in; **per diletto** for pleasure
diligente [dili'dʒɛnte] AGG (*scrupoloso*) diligent, hard-working, assiduous; (*accurato*) careful, accurate; **un alunno diligente** a hard-working student
diligentemente [dilidʒente'mente] AVV (*vedi agg*) diligently, assiduously; carefully
diligenza¹ [dili'dʒɛntsa] SF (*qualità*) diligence
diligenza² [dili'dʒɛntsa] SF (*carrozza*) stagecoach
diliscare [dilis'kare] VT (*pesce*) to bone
diluire [dilu'ire] VT (*gen: liquidi*) to dilute; (*vernice*) to thin (down); (*polverina, medicina*) to dissolve
diluizione [diluit'tsjone] SF (*vedi vb*) dilution; thinning; dissolving
dilungarsi [dilun'garsi] VIP to talk at length; **dilungarsi in una descrizione** to go into a detailed description
diluviare [dilu'vjare] VB IMPERS (*aus* **essere** *o* **avere**) to pour (down), rain hard; **sta diluviando** it's pouring
diluvio, vi [di'luvjo] SM (*pioggia*) downpour, deluge; (*fig: di insulti*) torrent; **ieri c'è stato un diluvio** there was torrential rain yesterday; **il diluvio universale** the Flood
dimagrante [dima'grante] AGG slimming *attr*; **fare una cura dimagrante** to go on a (slimming) diet
dimagrimento [dimagri'mento] SM loss of weight
dimagrire [dima'grire] VI (*aus* **essere**) to become thin, lose weight, get thinner; **è dimagrita** she's lost weight; **è dimagrito di 5 kg** he has lost 5 kg
dimenare [dime'nare] VT (*braccia*) to wave (about); (*coda*) to wag; (*corpo, testa*) to shake; (*sedere*) to wiggle
▶ **dimenarsi** VR (*agitarsi: nel letto*) to toss (about), toss and turn; (*: per liberarsi, ballando*) to fling o.s. about; (*gesticolare*) to gesticulate wildly
dimensionale [dimensjo'nale] AGG dimensional
dimensione [dimen'sjone] SF **1** (*Mat, Filosofia, Fis*) dimension, size; **a 3 dimensioni** 3-dimensional **2** (*misura*): **dimensioni** SFPL dimensions, measurements, size *sg*; **di quali dimensioni è la stanza?** what are the dimensions *o* measurements of the room?, what size is the room?, what does the room measure?; **di piccole dimensioni** small; **di grandi dimensioni** large **3** (*fig*): **ricondurre qc alle giuste dimensioni** to get sth back in perspective; **considerare un discorso nella sua dimensione politica** to look at a speech in terms of its political significance; **di dimensioni allarmanti** of alarming proportions
dimenticanza [dimenti'kantsa] SF (*svista*) oversight; **è stata una dimenticanza** it was an oversight
dimenticare [dimenti'kare] VT (*gen*) to forget; (*preoccupazioni*) to forget (about); (*omettere*) to leave out; **dimenticare di fare qc** to forget to do sth; **dimenticare** *o* **dimenticarsi qc** to forget sth; **ho dimenticato il tuo numero di telefono** I've forgotten your phone number; **ho dimenticato l'ombrello in ufficio** I left my umbrella at the office
▶ **dimenticarsi** VIP: **dimenticarsi di qc/di fare qc** to forget (about) sth/to do sth; **non me ne dimenticherò** I won't forget
dimenticatoio [dimentika'tojo] SM (*scherz*): **cadere/mettere nel dimenticatoio** to sink into/consign to oblivion
dimentico, a, chi, che [di'mentiko] AGG: **dimentico di** (*che non ricorda*) forgetful of; (*incurante*) oblivious of, unmindful of
dimero ['dimero] SM (*Chim*) dimer
dimessamente [dimessa'mente] AVV (*vestire, vivere*) modestly, simply
dimesso, a [di'messo] PP *di* **dimettere**
■ AGG modest, unassuming, humble; **in abiti dimessi** simply dressed; **con voce dimessa** humbly
dimestichezza [dimesti'kettsa] SF (*familiarità*) familiarity; **avere dimestichezza con qc** to be familiar with sth

dimettere [di'mettere] VB IRREG
► **dimettersi** VT (*da ospedale*) to discharge; (*da carcere*) to release; (*da carica*) to dismiss; **far dimettere qn** to have sb dismissed;
■ VR: **dimettersi (da)** to resign, hand *o* give in one's notice; **si è dimesso ieri** he resigned yesterday
dimezzare [dimed'dzare] VT to cut in half, halve
diminuendo [diminu'ɛndo] SM (*Mus*) diminuendo
diminuire [diminu'ire] VT (*gen*) to reduce, decrease, diminish; (*prezzi*) to bring down, reduce; **la ditta ha deciso di diminuire i prezzi** the company has decided to cut its prices; **dobbiamo diminuire le spese del venti per cento** we must cut spending by twenty percent
■ VI (*aus* **essere**) (*gen*) to diminish, to decrease; (*vento, rumore*) to die down, die away; (*prezzo, valore, pressione*) to go down, fall, decrease; **la popolazione è diminuita del dieci per cento** the population has decreased by ten percent; **il prezzo della carne è diminuito** the price of meat has fallen; **diminuire d'intensità** to decrease in intensity, subside; **diminuire di volume** (*massa*) to be reduced in volume; **diminuire di peso** (*persona*) to lose weight; (*Fis*) to be reduced in weight
diminutivo, a [diminu'tivo] AGG, SM diminutive
diminuzione [diminut'tsjone] SF reduction; (*calo*) decrease; (: *di temperatura, pressione*) fall; **in diminuzione** on the decrease; **temperature in diminuzione** drop in temperatures; **essere in diminuzione** to be dropping; **la temperatura è in diminuzione** the temperature is dropping; **diminuzione della produttività** fall in productivity; **diminuzione di peso** loss of weight
dimisi *ecc* [di'mizi] VB *vedi* **dimettere**
dimissionare [dimissjo'nare] VT (*Amm*) to dismiss
dimissionario, ria, ri, rie [dimissjo'narjo] AGG outgoing
dimissioni [dimis'sjoni] SFPL resignation *sg*; **dare** *o* **rassegnare le dimissioni** to give/hand in *o* tender one's resignation, resign; **ha dato le dimissioni** he handed in his resignation
dimora [di'mɔra] SF (*abitazione*) residence; **senza fissa dimora** of no fixed address *o* abode; **estrema dimora** (*euf*) last resting place
dimorare [dimo'rare] VI (*aus* **avere**) (*anche fig: sentimenti*) to dwell
dimostrabile [dimos'trabile] AGG demonstrable
dimostrante [dimos'trante] SM/F (*Pol*) demonstrator
dimostrare [dimos'trare] VT **1** (*verità, funzionamento*) to demonstrate, show; (*colpevolezza, teorema, tesi*) to prove, demonstrate; **ciò dimostra che hai ragione** this proves *o* shows you are right **2** (*simpatia, affetto, interesse*) to show, display; **non dimostra la sua età** he doesn't look his age **3** (*Pol*) to demonstrate
► **dimostrarsi** VR **1** (*rivelarsi*) to prove to be; **si è dimostrato coraggioso** he showed courage; **si è dimostrato esatto** it turned out to be correct **2** (*apparire*) **dimostrarsi entusiasta/interessato** to show one's enthusiasm/interest
dimostrativo, a [dimostra'tivo] AGG (*gen, Gramm*) demonstrative; **azione dimostrativa** (*Mil*) demonstration
dimostratore, trice [dimostra'tore] SM/F (*Comm*) demonstrator
dimostrazione [dimostrat'tsjone] SF **1** demonstration, proof; **una dimostrazione d'affetto** a show of affection; **una chiara dimostrazione di inefficienza** (*prova*) clear proof of inefficiency **2** (*manifestazione, Mat*) demonstration; **una dimostrazione studentesca** a student demonstration
dina ['dina] SF (*Fis*) dyne
dinamica [di'namika] SF (*gen, Fis*) dynamics *sg*
dinamicamente [dinamika'mente] AVV dynamically
dinamicità [dinamitʃi'ta] SF dynamism
dinamico, a, ci, che [di'namiko] AGG (*fig: persona, vita*) dynamic, dynamical; (*Fis, Mus*) dynamic
dinamismo [dina'mizmo] SM dynamism
dinamitardo, a [dinami'tardo] AGG: **attentato dinamitardo** dynamite attack
■ SM/F dynamiter
dinamite [dina'mite] SF dynamite
dinamo ['dinamo] SF INV dynamo
dinamometro [dina'mɔmetro] SM dynamometer
dinanzi [di'nantsi] AVV ahead; **dinanzi a** PREP (*di fronte*) in front of; (*al cospetto*) in the presence of, before; **si presentò dinanzi a me** he appeared before me; **dinanzi ad una tale situazione...** faced with such a situation ...
dinastia [dinas'tia] SF dynasty
dinastico, a, ci, che [di'nastiko] AGG dynastic(al)
dingo, ghi ['dingo] SM dingo
diniego, ghi [di'njɛgo] SM (*rifiuto*) refusal; (*negazione*) denial; **ha opposto un netto diniego** he refused point-blank; **scuotere la testa in segno di diniego** to shake one's head
dinoccolato, a [dinokko'lato] AGG lanky; **andatura dinoccolata** slouching walk
dinosauro [dino'sauro] SM dinosaur
dintorni [din'torni] SMPL outskirts; **nei dintorni** nearby; **abita nei dintorni** she lives nearby; **nei dintorni di** in the vicinity *o* neighbourhood of; **un paese nei dintorni di Milano** a village outside Milan; **Palermo e dintorni** Palermo and the surrounding area
dintorno [din'torno] AVV (a)round, (round)about
dio, dei ['dio] SM **1** (*Mitol, fig*) god; **gli dei** the gods; **si crede un dio** he thinks he's wonderful; **canta come un dio** he sings divinely **2** (*Rel*): **Dio** God; **credi in Dio?** do you believe in God?; **Dio padre** God the Father; **un senza Dio** a godless person; **il buon Dio** the good Lord **3** (*fraseologia*): **Dio mio!** my goodness!, my God!; **Dio buono** *o* **santo!** for God's sake!; **per Dio!** by God!; **grazie a Dio!** *o* **Dio sia lodato** *o* **ringraziato!** thank God!; **com'è vero Dio** as God is my witness; **Dio sa quando finirà** God knows when it's going to come to an end; **viene giù che Dio la manda** it's raining cats and dogs, it's pouring with rain; **come Dio volle arrivammo** somehow or other we got there; **se Dio vuole...** God willing ...; **(che) Dio ce la mandi buona** let's hope for the best; **Dio ce ne scampi e liberi** God forbid
diocesi [di'ɔtʃezi] SF INV diocese
Diocleziano [dioklet'tsjano] SM Diocletian
diodo ['diodo] SM diode
Diogene [di'ɔdʒene] SM Diogenes
dionea [dio'nɛa] SF (*Bot*) Venus's-flytrap, Venus flytrap
Dioniso [di'ɔniso] SM Dionysus
diossina [dios'sina] SF dioxin
diottria [diot'tria] SF (*Fis*) dioptre (*Brit*), diopter (*Am*)
dipanare [dipa'nare] VT (*matassa*) to wind (up *o* into a ball); (*fig: questione*) to sort out, disentangle
dipartimentale [dipartimen'tale] AGG (*Amm*) departmental

Dd

dipartimento [diparti'mento] SM (*gen, Univ*) department
dipartita [dipar'tita] SF (*euf: decesso*) passing (away)
dipendente [dipen'dɛnte] AGG **1 personale dipendente** employees *pl* **2** (*gen*): **dipendente da** (*alcol, droga*) addicted to; **è completamente dipendente da sua madre** he's completely dependent on his mother
■ SM/F employee; **dipendenti** PL employees, staff *sg o pl*, personnel *pl*; **un dipendente della ditta** an employee of the firm
■ SF (*Gramm: anche:* **proposizione dipendente**) subordinate *o* dependent clause
dipendenza [dipen'dɛntsa] SF **1** dependency; (*economica*) dependence; (*da droga*) addiction; **un farmaco che provoca dipendenza** an addictive drug **2 alle dipendenze di** employed by; **ha 10 persone alle sue dipendenze** (*datore di lavoro*) he employs 10 people; (*caporeparto*) he has 10 people under him
dipendere [di'pɛndere] VI IRREG (*aus* **essere**) **dipendere da 1** (*gen*) to depend on; **dipende!** it depends!; **dipende solo da te** it depends entirely on you, it's entirely up to you; **andiamo? – Non lo so. Dipende da Mario** are we going? – I don't know. It depends on Mario; **non voglio più dipendere dai miei genitori** I don't want to be dependent on my parents any longer; **la sua risposta è dipesa dal fatto che era nervosa** she answered that way because she was irritated **2** (*impiegato, filiale*) to be answerable to; **la ditta dipendeva da una compagnia americana** the firm was controlled by an American company **3** (*essere mantenuto, soggetto*) to depend (up)on, be dependent on **4** (*Gramm*) to be subordinate (to)
dipesi *ecc* [di'pesi] VB *vedi* **dipendere**
dipeso, a [di'peso] PP *di* **dipendere**
dipingere [di'pindʒere] VB IRREG
■ VT (*gen, Arte*) to paint; (*fig*) to describe, depict
▶ **dipingersi** VIP (*tingersi*) **il cielo si dipinse di rosso** the sky turned red; **gli si dipinse sul viso la delusione** (*fig*) his face expressed *o* clearly showed his disappointment
dipinsi *ecc* [di'pinsi] VB *vedi* **dipingere**
dipinto, a [di'pinto] PP *di* **dipingere**
■ SM (*quadro*) painting
diploma, i [di'plɔma] SM diploma, certificate; **diploma di laurea** degree (certificate); **diploma di maturità** A level certificate (*Brit*), (high-school) graduation diploma (*Am*)
diplomare [diplo'mare] VT to award a diploma to, graduate (*Am*)
▶ **diplomarsi** VIP to obtain a diploma, graduate (*Am*)
diplomaticamente [diplomatika'mente] AVV diplomatically
diplomatico, a, ci, che [diplo'matiko] AGG diplomatic; **cerca di essere diplomatico** try to be diplomatic; **rompere le relazioni diplomatiche** to break off diplomatic relations
■ SM (*anche fig*) diplomat
diplomato, a [diplo'mato] AGG qualified
■ SM/F qualified person, holder of a diploma, graduate (*Am*)
diplomazia [diplomat'tsia] SF (*anche fig*) diplomacy; (*corpo diplomatico*) diplomatic corps *sg*; **entrare in diplomazia** to enter *o* join the diplomatic service
dipolo [di'pɔlo] SM (*Fis*) dipole; **antenna a dipolo** (*Radiotecnica*) dipole aerial
diportista, i, e [dipor'tista] SM/F pleasure-boat owner
diporto [di'pɔrto] SM: **imbarcazione da diporto** pleasure craft *inv*
diradare [dira'dare] VT (*vegetazione*) to thin (out); (*nebbia, gas*) to clear, dissipate; **diradare le visite** to call less frequently
■ VI (*aus* **essere**), **diradarsi** VIP (*vegetazione*) to thin out; (*folla*) to disperse; (*nebbia*) to clear (up); (*visite*) to become less frequent
diramare [dira'mare] VT (*comunicato, ordine*) to issue; (*notizia*) to circulate; **diramare gli inviti** (*spedire*) to send out invitations
▶ **diramarsi** VIP **1** (*sentiero, strada*) to branch off; (*vene*) to spread; (*fusti*) to branch **2** (*diffondersi*) **la notizia si è diramata** the news spread
diramazione [diramat'tsjone] SF **1** (*diffusione: di ordine*) issuing; (*: di notizia*) circulation **2** (*biforcazione*) fork **3** (*ramificazione*) branch

dire ['dire] PAROLA CHIAVE
■ VT IRREG
1 (*gen*) to say; **dire qc a qn** to say sth to sb, tell sb sth; **disse che accettava** he said he would accept; **dicono** *o* **si dice che...** (*impersonale*) they say that ..., it is said that ...; **dicono** *o* **si dice che siano ricchissimi** they are said to be very rich, people say they are very rich; **come dicono gli inglesi** as the English say; **come si dice in inglese?** how do you say it in English?; **come si dice 'penna' in inglese?** what is the English for 'penna'?; **lascialo dire** (*esprimersi*) let him have his say; (*ignoralo*) just ignore him, don't take any notice of him; **non disse una parola** he didn't say *o* utter a word; **dice sempre quello che pensa** he always says what he thinks; **di' liberamente ciò che pensi** feel free to say what you think; **dicano pure quello che vogliono!** let them say what they like!; **sa quello che dice** he knows what he's talking about; **Roberta... — sì, dimmi** Roberta ... — yes, what is it?; **dire di sì/no** to say yes/no; **"non ci vado" – disse** "I'm not going" – he said; **dica?** (*in negozio*) what can I do for you?
2 (*raccontare, riferire, indicare*) to tell; **dire a qn qc** to tell sb sth; **dire a qn di fare qc** to tell sb to do sth; **mi si dice che...** I am told that ...; **può dirmi da che parte devo andare?** can you tell me which way to go?; **mi ha detto tutto** he told me everything
3 (*significare*) to mean; **ti dice niente questo nome?** does this name mean anything to you?, does this name ring a bell?; **quel libro non mi ha detto niente** that book didn't appeal to me; **come sarebbe a dire?** what do you mean?
4 (*recitare*) to say, recite; **dire a memoria** to recite by heart; **dire (la) Messa** to say Mass; **dire le preghiere** to say one's prayers
5 (*pensare*) to think; **chi l'avrebbe mai detto!** who would have thought it!; **cosa** *o* **che ne dici di questa musica?** what do you think of this music?; **che ne diresti di andarcene?** let's make a move, shall we?; **si direbbe che non menta** (*impersonale*) you would think he was telling the truth
6 (*ammettere*) to say, admit; **devi dire che ha ragione** you must admit that he's right
7 far dire qc a qn to make sb say sth; **non me lo farò dire due volte** I won't need to be asked twice; **gliel' ho fatto dire dalla segretaria** I had his secretary tell him about it, I got his secretary to tell him about it; **mandare a dire qc a qn** (*riferire*) to let sb know sth
8 dirsi to say to o.s.; (*definirsi*) to call o.s., claim to be; (*uso reciproco*) to say to each other; **"coraggio" – si disse**

"come on" – he said to himself; **si dicono esperti** they claim to be experts; **si dissero addio** they said goodbye (to each other); **si son detti qualcosa all'orecchio** they whispered something to one another
9 *(fraseologia)*: **per così dire** so to speak; **sono stanco — e a me lo dici?!** I'm tired — me too!; **non c'è che dire** there's no doubt about it; **avere** *o* **a che dire con qn** to have words with sb; **e chi mi dice che è vero?** and who's to say that's true?; **dimmi con chi vai e ti dirò chi sei** *(Proverbio)* you can tell what somebody is like by the company they keep; **trovare da dire su qc/qn** to find fault with sth/sb; **l'idea mi stuzzica, non dico di no** the idea is tempting, I don't deny it; **non ti dico la scena!** you can't imagine the scene!; **per così dire** so to speak; **lo conosco per sentito dire** I've heard about him; **a dir poco** to say the least; **dico sul serio** I'm serious; **il che è tutto dire** need I say more?; **a dire il vero...** to tell the truth ...
■ SM: **tra il dire e il fare c'è di mezzo il mare** *(Proverbio)* it's easier said than done; **è un bel dire il suo** what he says is all very well

directory [di'rɛktori] SF INV *(Inform)* directory
diressi *ecc* [di'rɛssi] VB *vedi* **dirigere**
diretta [di'rɛtta] SF: **in diretta** *(trasmettere)* live; **un incontro di calcio in diretta** a live football match
direttamente [diretta'mente] AVV *(immediatamente)* directly, straight; *(personalmente)* directly; *(senza intermediari)* direct, straight; **andiamo direttamente a casa** let's go straight home; **non mi riguarda direttamente** it doesn't directly concern me; **parla direttamente col preside** speak to the headmaster direct
direttissima [diret'tissima] SF *(Dir)*: **processo per direttissima** summary trial
direttissimo [diret'tissimo] SM *(Ferr)* fast (through) train
direttiva [diret'tiva] SF directive, instruction; **seguire le direttive del partito** to stick to the party line
direttivo, a [diret'tivo] AGG *(Pol, Amm)* executive; *(Comm)* managerial, executive
■ SM leadership, leaders *pl*
diretto, a [di'rɛtto] PP *di* **dirigere**
■ AGG *(gen, Gramm)* direct; **la strada più diretta** the most direct route; **è il suo diretto superiore** he's his immediate superior; **c'è una diretta dipendenza tra i due fatti** the two events are directly connected
■ SM **1** *(Ferr: anche:* **treno diretto***)* through train **2** *(Boxe)* jab
direttore [diret'tore] SM *(gen)* director; *(responsabile: di banca, fabbrica)* manager; **direttore artistico** *(Teatro, Mus)* artistic director; **direttore di carcere** prison governor *(Brit) o* warden *(Am)*; **direttore didattico** (primary school) headmaster *(Brit)*, (elementary school) principal *(Am)*; **direttore di macchina** *(Naut)* chief engineer; **direttore d'orchestra** conductor; **direttore del personale** personnel manager; **direttore di produzione** *(Cine)* producer; *(Industria)* production manager; **direttore responsabile** *(Stampa)* editor (in chief); **direttore sportivo** team manager; **direttore tecnico** *(Sport)* trainer, coach
direttrice[1] [diret'tritʃe] SF *(vedi sm)* director; manager; **direttrice didattica** (primary school) headmistress *(Brit)*, (elementary school) principal *(Am)*
direttrice[2] [diret'tritʃe] SF **1** *(Geom)* directrix **2** *(fig: di partito)* policy, line

direzionale [direttsjo'nale] AGG directional
direzione [diret'tsjone] SF **1** *(senso: anche fig)* direction; **è nella direzione opposta** it's in the opposite direction; **in direzione di** towards, in the direction of; **in che direzione vai?** which way are you going?; **prendere la direzione giusta/sbagliata** to go the right/wrong way; **sbagliare direzione** to go the wrong way **2** *(conduzione: gen)* running; *(: di società)* management; *(: di giornale)* editorship; *(: di partito)* leadership; **assumere la direzione delle operazioni** to take charge of operations **3** **la direzione** *(direttori)* the management; *(ufficio)* director's *(o* manager's *o* editor's *o* headmaster's *ecc)* office
dirigente [diri'dʒɛnte] AGG managerial; **classe dirigente** ruling class
■ SM/F executive
dirigenza [diri'dʒɛntsa] SF *(di ditta)* management; *(di partito)* leadership
dirigenziale [diridʒen'tsjale] AGG managerial
dirigere [di'ridʒere] VB IRREG
■ VT **1** *(condurre)* to run; *(ditta)* to manage; *(giornale)* to edit; *(partito, inchiesta)* to lead; *(operazioni, traffico)* to direct; *(orchestra)* to conduct; **dirigere il traffico** to direct the traffic; **dirigere i lavori** to be in charge of the work **2** *(arma)*: **dirigere verso** *o* **contro** to point at; **dirigere contro** *(critiche)* to direct at, aim at; **dirigere l'attenzione su qc/qn** to turn one's attention to sth/sb; **dirigere i propri passi verso** to make one's way towards; **dirigere lo sguardo verso** to look towards; **a chi era diretta quell'osservazione?** who was that remark intended for?; **era diretto verso casa** he was heading home; **dove sei diretto?** where are you heading?; **il treno era diretto a Pavia** the train was en route for Pavia; **eravamo diretti a nord** we were heading north; **mi hanno diretto qui** they sent me here **3** *(pacco, lettera)* to address
▶ **dirigersi** VR *(prendere una direzione)* **dirigersi a** *o* **verso** *(luogo)* to make one's way towards, make *o* head for; **si è diretto verso la porta** he made for the door; **dirigersi verso** *(persona)* to come/go towards; **l'aereo si dirigeva a nord** the plane was on its way *o* flying north; **si diresse a** *o* **verso casa** he headed home, he set off home; **dove si è diretto?** which way did he go?
dirigibile [diri'dʒibile] SM airship
dirimpetto [dirim'pɛtto] AVV opposite; **vivono qui dirimpetto** they live opposite; **dirimpetto a** PREP opposite; **era seduto dirimpetto a me** he was sitting opposite me; **la tua casa è dirimpetto alla mia** your house is opposite mine
■ AGG INV opposite; **la casa dirimpetto** the house opposite
diritto[1], a [di'ritto] AGG **1** *(strada, palo, linea)* straight; *(persona: eretto)* erect, upright; *(fig: onesto)* upright, honest, straight; **stare su diritto** to stand up straight; **una strada diritta** a straight road **2** *(Maglia)*: **punto diritto** plain (stitch)
■ AVV straight, directly; **verrò diritto al punto** I'll come straight to the point; **vai sempre diritto fino al semaforo** keep straight on till you get to the traffic lights; **è andato diritto dal direttore** he went straight to the manager
■ SM **1** *(di vestito)* right side **2** *(Tennis)* forehand **3** *(Maglia)* plain stitch, knit stitch
diritto[2] [di'ritto] SM **1** *(prerogativa)* right; **ti spetta di diritto** it is yours by right; **a buon diritto** quite rightly; **avere il diritto di fare qc** to have the right to do sth; **aver diritto a qc** to be entitled to sth; **ho il**

Dd

diritto di sapere I have a right to know; **diritto d'asilo** right of asylum; **diritto di voto** (*elettore*) right to vote; (*azionista*) voting right **2** (*Dir*): **il diritto** (the) law; **studia diritto** he's studying law **3 diritti** SMPL (*tasse*) fees, dues; **"tutti i diritti sono riservati"** "all rights reserved"; **diritti d'autore** (*compenso*) royalties, copyright *sg*; **diritti di magazzinaggio** demurrage *sg*; **diritti di segreteria** administrative charges
dirittura [dirit'tura] SF **1** (*Sport*): **dirittura (d'arrivo)** (home *o* final) straight **2** (*fig: rettitudine*) rectitude
diroccato, a [dirok'kato] AGG (*semidistrutto*) in ruins; (*cadente*) dilapidated, tumbledown
dirompente [dirom'pɛnte] AGG (*anche fig*) explosive; **bomba dirompente** fragmentation bomb
dirottamente [dirotta'mente] AVV: **piangere dirottamente** to cry one's heart out; **pioveva dirottamente** it was raining very heavily, it was pouring (with rain)
dirottamento [dirotta'mento] SM: **dirottamento (aereo)** hijacking, hijack
dirottare [dirot'tare] VT (*aereo: sotto minaccia*) to hijack; (*traffico*) to divert; (*nave, aereo*) to change the course of
■ VI (*aus* **avere**) (*Naut*) to change course
dirottatore, trice [dirotta'tore] SM/F hijacker
dirotto, a [di'rotto] AGG: **scoppiare in un pianto dirotto** to burst into tears; **piove a dirotto** it's pouring (with rain), it's raining cats and dogs
dirozzare [dirod'dzare] VT (*pietra, marmo*) to rough-hew; (*fig: stile, maniere*) to polish, refine; (*: persona*) to smooth the rough edges off
dirupo [di'rupo] SM precipice, crag
diruttore [dirut'tore] SM (*Aer*) spoiler
disabile [di'zabile] SM/F disabled person
■ AGG disabled
disabitato, a [dizabi'tato] AGG uninhabited
disabituare [dizabitu'are] VT: **disabituare qn a qc/a fare qc** to break sb of a habit/the habit of doing sth
▶ **disabituarsi** VIP: **disabituarsi a qc/a fare qc** to get out of the habit of sth/of doing sth
disaccordo [dizak'kɔrdo] SM **1** disagreement; **essere in disaccordo** to disagree **2** (*Mus*) discord
disadattamento [dizadatta'mento] SM maladjustment
disadattato, a [dizadat'tato] AGG maladjusted
■ SM/F maladjusted person, misfit
disadorno, a [diza'dorno] AGG plain, unadorned
disaffezione [dizaffet'tsjone] SF disaffection
disagevole [diza'dʒevole] AGG (*scomodo*) uncomfortable; (*difficile*) difficult
disagevolmente [dizadʒevol'mente] AVV uncomfortably
disagiatamente [dizadʒata'mente] AVV (*vivere*) in hardship, in poverty
disagiato, a [diza'dʒato] AGG (*povero*) poor, needy; **vivere in condizioni disagiate** to live in poverty
disagio, gi [di'zadʒo] SM **1** (*scomodità*) discomfort; (*difficoltà*) difficulty **2** (*imbarazzo*) awkwardness; **essere** *o* **trovarsi a disagio** to be ill-at-ease *o* uncomfortable; **mettere qn a disagio** to make sb feel ill-at-ease *o* uncomfortable; **sentirsi a disagio** to feel ill at ease
disalberare [dizalbe'rare] VT (*Naut*) to dismast
disamina [di'zamina] SF close examination; **sottoporre a disamina** to put under close scrutiny
disamorarsi [dizamo'rarsi] VIP: **disamorarsi di** (*persona*) to fall out of love with, cease to love; (*studio, lavoro*) to lose interest in
disappannare [dizappan'nare] VT to demist
disappetenza [dizappe'tɛntsa] SF lack of appetite
disapprovare [dizappro'vare] VT: **disapprovare (qc)** to disapprove (of sth); **disapprovano il mio comportamento** they disapprove of my behaviour
disapprovazione [dizapprovat'tsjone] SF disapproval; **un'occhiata di disapprovazione** a disapproving glance; **con aria di disapprovazione** disapprovingly
disappunto [dizap'punto] SM (*delusione*) disappointment; (*fastidio*) annoyance; **con mio disappunto** to my disappointment (*o* annoyance)
disarcionare [dizartʃo'nare] VT to unseat
disarmante [dizar'mante] AGG (*sorriso*) disarming; (*calma*) soothing; **con fare disarmante** disarmingly
disarmare [dizar'mare] VT (*Mil, fig*) to disarm; (*Naut*) to lay up
■ VI (*aus* **avere**) (*Mil*) to disarm; (*fig*) to surrender, give in
disarmo [di'zarmo] SM (*Mil*) disarmament; (*di nave*) laying up
disarmonia [dizarmo'nia] SF disharmony
disarticolare [dizartiko'lare] VT to dislocate
disarticolato, a [dizartiko'lato] AGG (*suoni, discorso*) disjointed
disastrato, a [dizas'trato] AGG devastated; **zona disastrata** disaster area
■ SM/F (*di alluvione, terremoto*) victim
disastro [di'zastro] SM (*anche fig*) disaster; **è il più grande disastro aereo mai avvenuto** it's the worst air disaster ever; **i disastri dovuti alla grandine** the damage caused by the hailstorm; **quel cameriere è un disastro!** that waiter is awful!
disastrosamente [dizastrosa'mente] AVV disastrously
disastroso, a [dizas'troso] AGG (*gen*) disastrous; **effetti disastrosi** disastrous effects; **in condizioni disastrose** in a terrible *o* appalling state
disattento, a [dizat'tɛnto] AGG careless, inattentive
disattenzione [dizatten'tsjone] SF carelessness, lack of attention; **un errore di disattenzione** a careless mistake
disattivare [dizatti'vare] VT (*bomba*) to de-activate, defuse; (*Inform*) to deactivate
disavanzo [diza'vantso] SM (*Econ*) deficit
disavventura [dizavven'tura] SF misadventure, mishap
disbrigo, ghi [diz'brigo] SM: **disbrigo (di)** (*corrispondenza, pratiche*) dealing (with)
discapito [dis'kapito] SM: **a discapito di** to the detriment of; **lo fai a tuo discapito** if you do this it will be to your disadvantage
discarica, che [dis'karika] SF (*di rifiuti*) rubbish tip *o* dump
discendente [diʃʃen'dɛnte] AGG descending
■ SM/F descendant
discendenza [diʃʃen'dɛntsa] SF **1** (*origine*) descent, lineage; **di nobile/umile discendenza** of noble/humble descent **2** (*discendenti*) descendants *pl*
discendere [diʃʃendere] VB IRREG
■ VI (*aus* **essere**) **1** (*scendere*) to come (*o* go) down, descend; **discendere da** (*treno*) to get off; (*macchina*) to get out of; (*tetto*) to get down from; **discendere da cavallo** to dismount, get off one's horse; **le tenebre discesero sulla città** darkness descended on the town **2** (*provenire*): **discendere da** to be descended from, come from

■VT (*scale*) to come (*o* go) down, descend
discepolo, a [diʃʃepolo] SM/F (*Rel*) disciple; (*seguace*) follower, disciple; (*scolaro*) pupil
discernere [diʃʃɛrnere] VT DIF (*distinguere*: *anche fig*) to discern; **discernere il bene dal male** to distinguish good from evil
discernimento [diʃʃerni'mento] SM discernment
discesa [diʃʃesa] SF **1** (*atto*) descent; **la discesa dei barbari** the barbarian invasion; **fare una discesa in corda doppia** (*Alpinismo*) to abseil; **discesa libera** (*Sci*) downhill (race) **2** (*pendio*) slope, downhill stretch; **una discesa ripida** a steep slope; **in discesa** downhill *attr*; **da casa nostra al paese la strada è in discesa** it's downhill from our house to the village
discesista, i, e [diʃʃe'sista] SM/F (*Sci*) downhill skier
disceso, a [diʃʃeso] PP *di* **discendere**
dischetto [dis'ketto] SM **1** (*Inform*) diskette, floppy disk **2** (*Calcio*) penalty spot
dischiudere [dis'kjudere] VT IRREG (*aprire*) to open; (*fig*: *rivelare*) to disclose, reveal
dischiusi *ecc* [dis'kjusi] VB *vedi* **dischiudere**
dischiuso, a [dis'kjuso] PP *di* **dischiudere**
discinto, a [diʃʃinto] AGG half-undressed
disciogliere [diʃʃɔʎʎere] VB IRREG
■VT **1** (*sciogliere*: *medicina*) to dissolve; (*liquefare*) to melt
▶ **disciogliersi** VIP (*vedi vt*) to dissolve; to melt
disciolto, a [diʃʃɔlto] PP *di* **disciogliere**
disciplina [diʃʃi'plina] SF (*regola*) discipline; (*materia*) discipline, subject
disciplinare[1] [diʃʃipli'nare] VT to discipline
disciplinare[2] [diʃʃipli'nare] AGG (*provvedimento*) disciplinary
disciplinatamente [diʃʃiplinata'mente] AVV in a disciplined way
disciplinato, a [diʃʃipli'nato] AGG disciplined
disc-jockey ['disk 'dʒɔki] SM/F INV disc jockey
disco, schi ['disko] SM **1** (*gen, Anat*) disc (*Brit*), disk (*Am*); (*Inform*) disk; (*Sport*) discus; **il lancio del disco** the discus; **chi ha vinto il lancio del disco?** who won the discus? **2** (*Mus*) record, disc; **uno dei miei dischi preferiti** one of my favourite records; **cambia disco!** (*fam*) change the subject!; **disco magnetico** (*Inform*) magnetic disk; **disco orario** (*Aut*) parking disc; **disco rigido** *o* **fisso** (*Inform*) hard *o* fixed disk; **disco volante** flying saucer
discobar [disko'bar] SM INV club
discofilo, a [dis'kɔfilo] SM/F record collector
discografia [diskogra'fia] SF **1** (*tecnica*) recording, record-making **2** (*industria*) record industry **3** (*elenco*) discography
discografico, a, ci, che [disko'grafiko] AGG record *attr*, recording *attr*; **casa discografica** record(ing) company
■SM record producer
discoide [dis'kɔide] AGG disc-shaped
discolo, a ['diskolo] AGG (*bambino*) undisciplined, unruly
■SM/F rascal
discolpa [dis'kolpa] SF defence, excuse; **a discolpa di qn** in sb's defence
discolpare [diskol'pare] VT: **discolpare qn** to prove sb's innocence, clear sb (of blame)
▶ **discolparsi** VR to clear o.s., prove one's innocence; (*giustificarsi*) to excuse o.s.
disconoscere [disko'noʃʃere] VT IRREG (*meriti*) to ignore, disregard; **disconoscere la paternità di un figlio** (*Dir*) to deny paternity

disconosciuto, a [diskonoʃʃuto] PP *di* **disconoscere**
discontinuamente [diskontinua'mente] AVV sporadically
discontinuità [diskontinui'ta] SF INV (*vedi agg*) discontinuity; irregularity
discontinuo, a [diskon'tinuo] AGG (*linea*) discontinuous, broken; (*rendimento, stile*) irregular, erratic; (*interesse*): **essere discontinuo nel lavoro** to lack application
discordante [diskor'dante] AGG (*gen, suoni*) discordant; (*testimonianze, opinioni*) conflicting; (*colori*) clashing
discordanza [diskor'dantsa] SF (*gen*) discordance, dissonance; (*Mus*) discord; **discordanza di opinioni** difference of opinion; **ci sono discordanze tra le due versioni** the two versions conflict
discordare [diskor'dare] VI (*aus* **avere**) **1 discordare (da)** (*opinioni*) to conflict (with) **2** (*stonare*: *suono, colore*) to clash (with)
discorde [dis'kɔrde] AGG conflicting; **essere di parere discorde** to be of a different opinion
discordia [dis'kɔrdja] SF discord, dissension; **essere in discordia con** to be at variance with
discorrere [dis'korrere] VI IRREG (*aus* **avere**) **discorrere (di)** to talk (about), chat (about)
discorsività [diskorsivi'ta] SF (*di stile*) conversational nature
discorsivo, a [diskor'sivo] AGG (*stile*) conversational, colloquial
discorso [dis'korso] PP *di* **discorrere**
■SM **1** (*gen*) speech; **fare un discorso** (*in pubblico*) to make a speech; **gli ho fatto un bel discorso ieri** (*iro*) I gave him a piece of my mind yesterday; **cambiare discorso** to change the subject; **è un altro discorso** that's another matter; **non son discorsi da fare!** what sort of attitude is that? **2** (*Ling*): **analisi del discorso** discourse analysis; **discorso diretto/indiretto** direct/indirect *o* reported speech
discostare [diskos'tare] VT (*letter*) to move away
▶ **discostarsi** VR, VIP (*anche fig*) **discostarsi da** to move away from
discosto, a [dis'kɔsto] AGG (*letter*): **discosto da** remote from; **tenersi discosto da** to stay away from
■AVV at a distance, at some distance, far away
discoteca, che [disko'tɛka] SF **1** (*sala da ballo*) disco, club; **una discoteca alla moda** a popular club; **vado in discoteca di sabato** I go clubbing on Saturdays **2** (*raccolta*) record library **3** (*negozio*) record shop
discount [dis'kaunt] SM INV (*supermercato*) *cut-price supermarket*
discredito [dis'kredito] SM discredit, disrepute; **gettare il discredito su** to bring discredit on; **cadere in discredito** to fall into disrepute; **tornare a discredito di qn** to redound to sb's discredit (*frm*)
discrepanza [diskre'pantsa] SF discrepancy
discretamente [diskreta'mente] AVV (*con discrezione*) discreetly, tactfully; (*sufficientemente*) fairly
discreto, a [dis'kreto] AGG **1** (*abbastanza buono*) reasonable, fair; **un voto discreto** a reasonable mark **2** (*non forte*: *tinta, trucco*) subtle **3** (*persona*: *riservato*) discreet; **è una persona molto discreta** he's very discreet; **fu discreto da parte sua andarsene** it was tactful of him to leave
discrezionale [diskrettsjo'nale] AGG discretionary
discrezione [diskret'tsjone] SF **1** (*riservatezza*) discretion; **ti prego la massima discrezione** I'm relying on your absolute discretion **2** (*arbitrio*): **a propria discrezione** at one's own discretion

Dd

3 (*discernimento*): **l'età della discrezione** the age of discretion
discriminante [diskrimi'nante] AGG (*fattore, elemento*) decisive
■ SF (*Dir*) extenuating circumstance
■ SM (*Mat*) discriminant
discriminare [diskrimi'nare] VT to discriminate
discriminazione [diskriminat'tsjone] SF discrimination; **la discriminazione razziale** racial discrimination
discussi *ecc* [dis'kussi] VB *vedi* **discutere**
discussione [diskus'sjone] SF (*gen*) discussion; (*lite*) argument; **fare una discussione** to have a discussion; **avere una discussione** to have an argument; **abbiamo avuto una discussione** we had an argument; **ho avuto una discussione col capo** (*lite*) I had words with my boss; **mettere in discussione** to bring into question; **questo è fuori discussione** this is out of the question; **la sua onestà è fuori discussione** his honesty is beyond question; **fila a letto, senza discussioni!** go to bed and don't argue!
discusso, a [dis'kusso] PP *di* **discutere**
■ AGG controversial
discutere [dis'kutere] VB IRREG
■ VT (*dibattere*) to discuss, debate; (*contestare*) to question, dispute; **è da discutere** (*se ne parlerà ancora*) it remains to be discussed; (*è in dubbio*) it's questionable; **discutere una proposta di legge** to debate a (parliamentary) bill; **discutere la tesi (di laurea)** to present *o* submit one's (degree) thesis
■ VI (*aus* **avere**) **1** (*conversare*): **discutere (di)** to talk (about), to discuss; **discutono spesso di politica** they often discuss politics **2** (*litigare*) to argue; **non voglio mettermi a discutere con te** I don't want to argue with you; **mi ha ubbidito senza discutere** he obeyed me without question
discutibile [disku'tibile] AGG questionable
discutibilità [diskutibili'ta] SF questionable nature
discutibilmente [diskutibil'mente] AVV questionably
disdegnare [dizdeɲ'ɲare] VT to disdain, to scorn
disdegno [diz'deɲɲo] SM disdain, contempt, scorn
disdegnosamente [dizdeɲɲosa'mente] AVV disdainfully, scornfully, contemptuously
disdegnoso, a [dizdeɲ'ɲoso] AGG (*letter*) disdainful, scornful, contemptuous
disdetta [diz'detta] SF **1** **dare la disdetta di** (*contratto, viaggio, appuntamento*) to cancel; **dare la disdetta di un contratto d'affitto** (*locatario*) to give notice; (*locatore*) to give notice (to quit) **2** (*sfortuna*): **per disdetta** unfortunately; **che disdetta!** hard luck!
disdetto, a [dis'detto] PP *di* **disdire**
disdicevole [dizdi'tʃevole] AGG improper, unseemly
disdicevolmente [dizditʃevol'mente] AVV in an unseemly fashion
disdire [diz'dire] VT IRREG (*prenotazione, appuntamento*) to cancel; **disdire un contratto d'affitto** (*locatario*) to give notice; (*locatore*) to give notice (to quit)
diseducare [dizedu'kare] VT to have a negative influence on
disegnare [diseɲ'ɲare] VT **1** (*gen*) to draw; (*a contorno*) to outline; (*fig: descrivere*) to describe, portray; **mio fratello sta disegnando** my brother is drawing **2** (*progettare: mobile, casa*) to design; **disegna mobili** he designs furniture
disegnatore, trice [diseɲɲa'tore] SM/F (*tecnico*) draughtsman/draughtswoman; (*progettista*) designer
disegno [di'seɲɲo] SM **1** drawing; (*schizzo*) sketch; **un bel disegno** a beautiful drawing; **disegno a matita** pencil drawing; **disegno dal vero** from life drawing **2** (*su carta, stoffa*) design, pattern; **un disegno a fiori** a floral design **3** (*fig: schema*) outline, plan; (: *progetto*) plan, project; **disegno di legge** (*Dir*) bill
disequazione [dizekwat'tsjone] SF (*Mat*) inequality
diserbante [dizer'bante] AGG herbicidal
■ SM herbicide, weed-killer
diserbare [dizer'bare] VT to weed
diserbo [di'zɛrbo] SM weeding
diseredare [dizere'dare] VT to disinherit
diseredato, a [dizere'dato] AGG disinherited; (*fig*) deprived
■ SM/F disinherited person; (*fig*) deprived person
disertare [dizer'tare] VT to desert, abandon, leave; **ieri ho disertato la riunione** yesterday I gave the meeting a miss
■ VI (*aus* **avere**) (*Mil, fig*): **disertare (da qc)** to desert (sth)
disertore [dizer'tore] SM (*Mil, fig*) deserter
diserzione [dizer'tsjone] SF (*Mil, fig*) desertion
disfacimento [disfatʃi'mento] SM (*di cadavere*) decay; (*fig: di istituzione, impero, società*) decline, decay; **in disfacimento** in decay
disfare [dis'fare] VB IRREG
■ VT **1** (*gen*) to undo; (*nodo*) to untie, undo; (*sciogliere*) to melt; (*meccanismo*) to take to pieces; **disfare il letto** to strip the bed; **disfare le valigie** to unpack (one's cases); **ha disfatto la valigia** he's unpacked; **ha disfatto il pacco** he undid the parcel **2** (*distruggere*) to destroy
▶ **disfarsi** VR: **disfarsi di** (*liberarsi*) to get rid of; **ce ne siamo disfatti** we got rid of it;
▶ **disfarsi** VIP **1** (*nodo, pacco*) to come undone; (*neve*) to melt **2** (*andare a pezzi*) to fall to pieces
disfatta [dis'fatta] SF (*anche fig*) (utter) defeat
disfattismo [disfat'tizmo] SM defeatism
disfattista, i, e [disfat'tista] SM/F defeatist
disfatto, a [dis'fatto] PP *di* **disfare**
■ AGG (*gen*) undone, untied; (*letto*) unmade
disfida [dis'fida] SF (*letter, sfida*) challenge; (*duello*) duel
disfunzione [disfun'tsjone] SF (*Med*) dysfunction; **disfunzione cardiaca** heart trouble
disgelare [dizdʒe'lare] VT, VI (*aus* **essere**), VB IMPERS, **disgelarsi** VIP to thaw
disgelo [diz'dʒɛlo] SM thaw
disgiungere [diz'dʒundʒere] VT IRREG to separate
disgiuntivo, a [dizdʒun'tivo] AGG (*Gramm*) disjunctive
disgiunto, a [dis'dʒunto] PP *di* **disgiungere**
disgrazia [diz'grattsja] SF **1** (*sventura*) bad luck, misfortune; **per disgrazia** unfortunately **2** (*incidente*) accident; (*calamità*) disaster; **è successa una disgrazia** something terrible has happened **3** (*sfavore*) disgrace; **cadere in disgrazia** to fall into disgrace
disgraziatamente [dizgrattsjata'mente] AVV unfortunately
disgraziato, a [dizgrat'tsjato] AGG (*persona: povero*) poor, wretched; (: *sfortunato*) unfortunate, unlucky; (: *pegg: sciagurato*) good-for-nothing; (*periodo, attività, impresa*) ill-fated
■ SM/F (*povero*) poor wretch; (*sciagurato*) rascal, rogue, scoundrel
disgregamento [dizgrega'mento] SM disintegration; (*fig*) break-up

disgregare [dizgre'gare] VT to cause to disintegrate, break up; (*fig: partito, famiglia*) to break up
▶ **disgregarsi** VIP to disintegrate, break up; (*fig*) to break up

disgregazione [dizgregat'tsjone] SF disintegration; (*fig*) break-up

disguido [diz'gwido] SM hitch; **disguido postale** error in postal delivery

disgustare [dizgus'tare] VT to disgust, sicken, make sick
▶ **disgustarsi** VIP: **disgustarsi di** to be disgusted by, be sickened by

disgusto [diz'gusto] SM (*anche fig*) disgust

disgustosamente [dizgustosa'mente] AVV disgustingly

disgustoso, a [dizgus'toso] AGG disgusting

disidratante [dizidra'tante] AGG dehydrating
■SM (*Chim*) dehydrating agent

disidratare [dizidra'tare] VT to dehydrate

disidratato, a [dizidra'tato] AGG dehydrated

disidratazione [dizidratat'tsjone] SF dehydration

disilludere [dizil'ludere] VB IRREG
■VT to disillusion, disenchant
▶ **disilludersi** VIP to be disillusioned, be disenchanted

disillusione [dizillu'zjone] SF disillusion, disenchantment

disilluso, a [dizil'luzo] PP *di* **disilludere**
■AGG disillusioned, disenchanted
■SM/F disillusioned *o* disenchanted person

disimballare [dizimbal'lare] VT (*merci*) to unpack

disimparare [dizimpa'rare] VT to forget; **ho disimparato il francese** I've forgotten my French

disimpegnare [dizimpeɲ'ɲare] VT **1** (*persona: da obblighi*): **disimpegnare da** to release (from); (*àncora*) to clear **2** (*oggetto in pegno*) to redeem, get out of pawn
▶ **disimpegnarsi** VR: **disimpegnarsi da** (*obblighi*) to release o.s. from, free o.s. from

disincagliare [dizinkaʎ'ʎare] VT (*barca*) to refloat
▶ **disincagliarsi** VIP to get afloat again

disincantare [dizinkan'tare] VT to disenchant

disincantato, a [dizinkan'tato] AGG disenchanted, disillusioned

disincentivare [dizintʃenti'vare] VT to discourage

disincrostare [dizinkros'tare] VT to descale

disinfestante [dizinfes'tante] AGG disinfesting
■SM pesticide

disinfestare [dizinfes'tare] VT to disinfest

disinfestazione [dizinfestat'tsjone] SF disinfestation

disinfettante [dizinfet'tante] AGG, SM disinfectant

disinfettare [dizinfet'tare] VT to disinfect

disinfezione [dizinfet'tsjone] SF disinfection

disinformazione [dizinformat'tsjone] SF misinformation

disingannare [dizingan'nare] VT to disillusion

disinganno [dizin'ganno] SM disillusion

disinibito, a [dizini'bito] AGG uninhibited

disinnescare [dizinnes'kare] VT to defuse

disinnestare [disinnes'tare] VT (*marcia*) to disengage

disinquinare [dizinkwi'nare] VT to free from pollution

disinserire [dizinse'rire] VT (*Elettr*) to disconnect

disinstallare [dizinstal'lare] VT (*programma*) to uninstall, to remove

disinstallazione [dizinstallat'tsjone] SF removal

disintasare [dizinta'sare] VT (*tubo*) to unblock, clear

disintegrare [dizinte'grare] VT (*gen*) to cause to disintegrate; (*edificio*) to shatter; (*fig: opposizione, avversari*) to annihilate
▶ **disintegrarsi** VIP (*anche fig*) to disintegrate

disintegrazione [dizintegrat'tsjone] SF disintegration

disinteressare [dizinteres'sare] VT: **disinteressare qn a qc** to cause sb to lose interest in sth
▶ **disinteressarsi** VIP: **disinteressarsi di** to take no interest in

disinteressatamente [dizinteressata'mente] AVV disinterestedly

disinteressato, a [dizinteres'sato] AGG disinterested

disinteresse [dizinte'resse] SM **1** (*indifferenza*) disinterest, indifference **2** (*generosità*) disinterestedness, unselfishness

disintossicante [dizintossi'kante] AGG detoxifying; **una cura disintossicante** a detox

disintossicare [dizintossi'kare] VT to detoxify; (*alcolizzato, drogato*) to treat for alcoholism (*o* drug addiction); **disintossicare l'organismo** to clear out one's system
▶ **disintossicarsi** VR to clear out one's system; (*alcolizzato, drogato*) to be treated for alcoholism (*o* drug addiction)

disintossicazione [dizintossikat'tsjone] SF (*vedi vb*) detoxification; treatment for alcoholism (*o* drug addiction)

disinvoltamente [dizinvolta'mente] AVV (*vedi agg*) confidently; casually

disinvolto, a [dizin'vɔlto] AGG (*sicuro*) confident; (*spigliato*) casual, nonchalant, free and easy; **con fare disinvolto** nonchalantly; **ha un modo di fare molto disinvolto** she's got a very relaxed manner

disinvoltura [dizinvol'tura] SF (*vedi agg*) confidence; casualness, nonchalance, ease; **con disinvoltura** with ease, easily

dislessia [dizles'sia] SF dyslexia

dislessico, a, ci, che [dis'lɛssiko] AGG, SM/F dyslexic

dislivello [dizli'vɛllo] SM difference in height; (*fig*) gap

dislocamento [dizloka'mento] SM (*Naut*) displacement

dislocare [dizlo'kare] VT **1** (*Mil, Amm*) to post **2** (*Naut*) to displace

dislocazione [dizlokat'tsjone] SF **1** (*di truppe*) stationing **2** (*Med*) dislocation

dismesso, a [diz'messo] AGG (*strada*) unadopted (*Brit*)

dismisura [dizmi'sura] SF: **a dismisura** excessively

disobbedire *ecc* [dizobbe'dire] = **disubbidire** *ecc*

disobbligare [dizobbli'gare] VT: **disobbligare (da)** to free *o* release from an obligation
▶ **disobbligarsi** VR (*sdebitarsi*) **disobbligarsi con qn per qc** to repay sb for sth

disoccupato, a [dizokku'pato] AGG unemployed, out of work; **è ancora disoccupato** he's still unemployed
■SM/F unemployed person; **i disoccupati** the unemployed, people out of work

disoccupazione [dizokkupat'tsjone] SF unemployment; **la disoccupazione è in aumento** unemployment is rising

disonestà [dizones'ta] SF INV dishonesty; **è una disonestà** it's dishonest

disonestamente [dizonesta'mente] AVV dishonestly

disonesto, a [dizo'nɛsto] AGG dishonest
■SM/F dishonest person

disonorare [dizono'rare] VT (*nome, famiglia*) to disgrace, bring disgrace upon, to dishonour (*Brit*), dishonor (*Am*)

Dd

▶ **disonorarsi** VR to bring disgrace on o.s., bring dishono(u)r on o.s.
disonorato, a [dizono'rato] AGG (*famiglia*) dishono(u)red, disgraced
disonore [dizo'nore] SM disgrace, dishonour (*Brit*), dishonor (*Am*); **essere il disonore della propria famiglia** to be a disgrace to one's family
disonorevole [dizono'revole] AGG dishono(u)rable
disonorevolmente [dizonorevol'mente] AVV dishono(u)rably
disopra [di'sopra] AVV = **di sopra**; *vedi* **sopra**
■SM INV top, upper part
disordinare [dizordi'nare] VT to mess up, disarrange; (*Mil*) to throw into disorder
disordinatamente [dizordinata'mente] AVV (*alla rinfusa*) untidily; (*senza chiarezza*) incoherently; (*sregolatamente*) uncontrollably, immoderately
disordinato, a [dizordi'nato] AGG (*persona*) untidy, disorderly; (*compito*) untidy; (*fuga, vita*) disorderly; **un ragazzo disordinato** an untidy boy; **disordinato nel lavoro** disorganized in one's work
disordine [di'zordine] SM **1** (*confusione*) untidiness, disorder; **non sopporto il disordine** I can't stand mess; **che disordine!** what a mess!; **essere/mettere in disordine** to be/make untidy; **ho i capelli in disordine** my hair is in a mess; **disordine mentale** mental confusion **2 disordini** SMPL (*Pol*) disorder *sg*; (*tumulti*) disturbances, riots; **i disordini della settimana scorsa** the disturbances of last week
disorganicamente [dizorganika'mente] AVV piecemeal
disorganico, a, ci, che [dizor'ganiko] AGG incoherent, disorganized
disorganizzare [dizorganid'dzare] VT to disorganize
disorganizzato, a [dizorganid'dzato] AGG disorganized
disorganizzazione [dizorganiddzat'tsjone] SF disorganization
disorientamento [dizorjenta'mento] SM (*fig*) disorientation
disorientare [dizorjen'tare] VT (*anche fig*) to disorientate, disorient
▶ **disorientarsi** VIP (*anche fig*) to lose one's bearings, become disorientated
disorientato, a [dizorjen'tato] AGG disorientated, disoriented
disossare [dizos'sare] VT (*Culin*) to bone
disotto [di'sotto] AVV = **di sotto**; *vedi* **sotto**
■SM INV bottom, underside
dispaccio, ci [dis'pattʃo] SM dispatch, despatch
disparato, a [dispa'rato] AGG disparate; **le cose più disparate** the most oddly assorted things
dispari ['dispari] AGG INV (*numero*) odd, uneven; (*Mil: forze*) unequal; **numeri dispari** odd numbers
disparità [dispari'ta] SF INV: **disparità (di)** (*disuguaglianza*) disparity (in); (*divergenza*) difference (in)
disparte [dis'parte] **in disparte** AVV (*da lato*) aside, apart; **mettere qc in disparte** to put *o* set sth aside; **stare** *o* **starsene** *o* **tenersi in disparte** to stand apart; (*fig*) to keep to o.s., hold *o* keep o.s. aloof; **se ne stava in disparte** he was by himself
dispendio, di [dis'pɛndjo] SM (*di denaro, energie*) expenditure; (: *spreco*) waste
dispendiosamente [dispendjosa'mente] AVV extravagantly
dispendioso, a [dispen'djoso] AGG (*tenore di vita*) extravagant; (*impresa, viaggio*) expensive
dispensa [dis'pɛnsa] SF **1** (*fascicolo*) instalment; (*Univ*) duplicated lecture notes *pl*, handout **2** (*esenzione*): **dispensa (da)** exemption (from); (*Rel*) dispensation (from) **3** (*locale*) larder, pantry; (*mobile*) sideboard
dispensare [dispen'sare] VT **1** (*esonerare*): **dispensare qn da/dal fare qc** to exempt sb from/from doing sth **2** (*elemosine, favori*) to distribute, hand out
▶ **dispensarsi** VR: **dispensarsi dal fare qc** to get out of *o* avoid doing sth
dispenser [dɪs'pɛnsəʳ] SM INV dispenser
disperante [dispe'rante] AGG desperate
disperare [dispe'rare] VI (*aus* **avere**) **disperare (di)** to despair (of); **disperare di fare qc** to despair of doing sth
▶ **disperarsi** VIP to despair; **non disperarti in quel modo!** don't get so upset!; **far disperare qn** to drive sb mad
disperata [dispe'rata] **alla disperata** AVV recklessly
disperatamente [disperata'mente] AVV desperately
disperato, a [dispe'rato] AGG (*persona*) in despair; (*caso*) hopeless; (*tentativo, gesto*) desperate; **grido disperato** cry of despair; **è un caso disperato** he is a hopeless case; **un gesto disperato** a desperate gesture; **ho un disperato bisogno di soldi** I desperately need money
■SM/F **1** (*fam: spiantato*): **è un povero disperato** he's a no-hoper **2 lavorare come un disperato** to work furiously *o* like mad
disperazione [disperat'tsjone] SF despair; **per disperazione** in desperation; **in preda alla disperazione** overcome by despair; **quel bambino è la mia disperazione** that child drives me mad
disperdere [dis'pɛrdere] VB IRREG
■VT (*folla*) to disperse; (*nemico*) to scatter; (*fig: energia, sostanze*) to waste, squander; **la polizia ha disperso la folla** the police dispersed the crowd; **"non disperdere nell'ambiente"** (*vetro, lattine*) ≈ "please recycle" (*pile, batterie*) ≈ "please dispose of carefully"
▶ **disperdersi** VIP (*folla*) to disperse; (*nemico*) to scatter; (*energia, sostanze*) to be wasted; (*calore*) to be lost
dispersione [disper'sjone] SF (*vedi vb*) scattering, dispersal; waste; (*Chim, Fis*) dispersion; **dispersione di calore** heat loss
dispersivamente [dispersiva'mente] AVV in a disorganized way
dispersività [dispersivi'ta] SF lack of organization
dispersivo, a [disper'sivo] AGG (*lavoro*) disorganized
disperso, a [dis'pɛrso] PP *di* **disperdere**
■AGG (*sparpagliato*) scattered, dispersed; (*smarrito: persona*) missing
■SM/F missing person; (*Mil*) missing soldier
dispetto [dis'pɛtto] SM **1** (*molestia*) piece of spite; **fare un dispetto a qn** to play a nasty *o* spiteful trick on sb, to tease sb; **smettila di fargli dispetti** stop teasing him; **a dispetto di** in spite of, despite; **per dispetto** out of spite **2** (*stizza*) vexation; **con suo grande dispetto** much to his annoyance
dispettosamente [dispettosa'mente] AVV spitefully
dispettoso, a [dispet'toso] AGG spiteful
dispiacere [dispja'tʃere] SM **1** (*rammarico*) regret, sorrow; (*dolore*) grief; **con mio grande dispiacere** much to my regret; **con grande dispiacere vi annuncio...** I regret to announce ...; **impazzire dal dispiacere** to go mad with grief **2** (*disappunto*) disappointment; **non puoi dare questo dispiacere a tua madre** you can't upset your mother in this way **3 dispiaceri** SMPL (*preoccupazioni*) worries, troubles; **il**

figlio le ha dato molti dispiaceri her son has given her a lot of trouble
■ VI IRREG (*aus* **essere**) **dispiacere a** **1** (*causare dolore*) to upset; (*causare disagio, noia*) to displease; **ciò che hai fatto è dispiaciuto ai tuoi** your parents are upset (*o* displeased) at your behaviour, you have upset your parents by what you have done; **mi dispiace** I'm sorry; **non posso venire, mi dispiace** I'm sorry I can't come **2** (*risultare sgradito*): **ti dispiace se fumo?** do you mind if I smoke?; **se non le dispiace...** if you don't mind ...; **ti dispiace prestarmelo?** would you mind lending it to me?; **l'idea non mi dispiace** I don't dislike the idea;
▶ **dispiacersi** VIP **dispiacersi (per** *o* **di qc)** to regret (sth)

dispiaciuto, a [dispja'tʃuto] PP *di* **dispiacere**
■ AGG sorry

displuvio, vi [dis'pluvjo] SM **1** (*Geog*) watershed **2** (*di tetto*) ridge

dispone *ecc* [dis'pone] VB *vedi* **disporre**

dispongo *ecc* [dis'pongo] VB *vedi* **disporre**

disponibile [dispo'nibile] AGG (*posto, merce*) available; (*persona: solerte, gentile*) helpful; **è disponibile in molti colori** it's available in many colours; **sei disponibile stasera?** are you free this evening?; **è sempre molto disponibile** he's always willing to help

disponibilità [disponibili'ta] SF INV **1** (*gen*) availability; (*solerzia, gentilezza*) helpfulness **2** (*Fin*): **disponibilità** SFPL available funds, resources

disporre [dis'porre] VB IRREG
■ VT **1** (*mettere*) to place, put; (*sistemare*) to arrange; (*preparare*) to prepare, make ready **2** (*ordinare*) to order; **la legge dispone che...** the law lays down that ...; **ha disposto che nessuno se ne andasse** he gave orders that no-one should leave
■ VI (*aus* **avere**) **1** (*decidere*) to decide; **abbiamo disposto diversamente** we have decided otherwise, we have made other arrangements **2** **disporre di** to have, have at one's disposal; **lo stadio dispone di 50.000 posti** the stadium holds 50,000 people;
▶ **disporsi** VR **1** (*posizione*) to put o.s., place o.s., arrange o.s.; **disporsi in fila** to line up; **disporsi in cerchio** to form a circle **2** (*prepararsi*) **disporsi a fare qc** to prepare o.s. *o* get ready to do sth; **disporsi all'attacco** to prepare for an attack

disposi *ecc* [dis'posi] VB *vedi* **disporre**

dispositivo [dispozi'tivo] SM **1** (*meccanismo*) device; **dispositivo di controllo** *o* **di comando** control device; **dispositivo di sicurezza** (*gen*) safety device; (*di arma da fuoco*) safety catch **2** (*Mil: posizione*) order; **dispositivo di marcia** marching order **3** (*Dir*) pronouncement

disposizione [disposit'tsjone] SF **1** (*sistemazione: di mobili*) arrangement; (*: di locali*) layout; (*Sport: di squadra*) positioning; **la disposizione dei mobili** the arrangement of the furniture; **ha cambiato la disposizione dei mobili** he rearranged the furniture **2** (*ordine*) order; (*: Dir*) provision; **disposizioni** (*preparativi, misure*) measures; **dare disposizione** *o* **disposizioni a qn affinché faccia qc** to give orders to sb to do sth; **ho dato disposizioni precise** I gave precise orders; **per disposizione di legge** by law; **le sue ultime disposizioni furono...** his last instructions were ...; **disposizione testamentaria** provisions of a will; **disposizioni di sicurezza** safety measures **3** **a disposizione** at one's disposal; **avere a disposizione** to have available *o* at one's disposal; **abbiamo a disposizione cinque computer nuovi** we've got five new computers at our disposal; **sono a tua disposizione** I am at your disposal; **resti a disposizione della polizia** be prepared to assist the police with their enquiries **4** **disposizione d'animo** mood, frame of mind **5** (*tendenza*) bent

disposto, a [dis'posto] PP *di* **disporre**
■ AGG (*incline*): **disposto a fare** disposed *o* prepared to do; **non sono disposta ad aiutarti se non mi paghi** I'm not prepared to help you if you don't pay me; **essere ben/mal disposto verso qn** to be well-/ill-disposed towards sb
■ SM (*Dir*) provision

dispoticamente [dispotika'mente] AVV (*vedi agg*) despotically; tyrannically

dispotico, a, ci, che [dis'potiko] AGG despotic; (*fig*) tyrannical, overbearing

dispotismo [dispo'tizmo] SM despotism; (*fig*) tyranny

dispregiativo, a [dispredʒa'tivo] AGG disparaging; (*Ling*) pejorative

dispregio, gi [dis'prɛdʒo] SM disparagement

disprezzabile [dispret'tsabile] AGG contemptible, despicable; **una somma non disprezzabile** a not inconsiderable sum of money

disprezzare [dispret'tsare] VT (*gen*) to scorn, to despise; (*persona*) to look down on

disprezzo [dis'prɛttso] SM scorn, contempt; **mi ha guardato con disprezzo** he looked at me with contempt; **ha agito con disprezzo del pericolo** he acted with a total disregard for the danger involved

disputa ['disputa] SF **1** (*dibattito*) discussion **2** (*lite*) argument, dispute

disputare [dispu'tare] VI (*aus* **avere**) **disputare di** (*dibattere*) to discuss
■ VT **1** (*gara*) to take part in; (*partita*) to play; **quando si disputerà la gara?** when will the competition take place? **2** (*contrastare*) to contest, dispute; **gli hanno disputato il diritto di farlo** they disputed his right to do it **3** **disputarsi qc** to compete for sth, fight for sth; **disputarsi il pallone** to fight for the ball

Dd

disquisire [diskwi'zire] VI to discourse on

disquisizione [diskwizit'tsjone] SF detailed analysis; **è inutile stare a fare disquisizioni sul perché** there's no point discussing all the ins and outs of it

dissacrante [dissa'krante] AGG debunking

dissacrare [dissa'krare] VT to debunk

dissalare [dissa'lare] VT (*acqua di mare*) to desalinate

dissalatore [dissala'tore] SM desalination plant

dissalazione [dissalat'tsjone] SF desalination

dissanguamento [dissangwa'mento] SM (*Med*) loss of blood

dissanguare [dissan'gware] VT (*fig: persona*) to bleed white *o* dry; **morire dissanguato** to bleed to death
▶ **dissanguarsi** VIP (*Med*) to lose blood; (*fig*) to ruin o.s.

dissapore [dissa'pore] SM slight disagreement

disse *ecc* VB *vedi* **dire**

dissecare [disse'kare] VT to dissect

disseccare [dissek'kare] VT
▶ **disseccarsi** VIP to dry up

dissellare [dissel'lare] VT to unsaddle

disseminare [dissemi'nare] VT to scatter, spread; (*fig: malcontento*) to breed

disseminazione [disseminat'tsjone] SF (*Bot*) dispersal

dissennatezza [dissenna'tettsa] SF foolishness

dissennato, a [dissen'nato] AGG (*persona*) foolish; (*idea*) senseless

dissenso [dis'sɛnso] SM (*protesta*) dissent;

(*disapprovazione*) disapproval; **scrittori del dissenso** dissident writers

dissenteria [dissente'ria] SF dysentery

dissentire [dissen'tire] VI (*aus* **avere**) to dissent; **dissentire da qn su qc** to disagree with sb on sth

dissenziente [dissen'tsjɛnte] AGG dissenting ■SM/F dissenter

disseppellire [disseppel'lire] VT (*esumare*: *cadavere*) to disinter, exhume; (*dissotterrare*: *anche fig*) to dig up, unearth

dissertare [disser'tare] VI (*aus* **avere**) **dissertare di** *o* **su** (*parlare*) to speak on; (*scrivere*) to write on

dissertazione [dissertat'tsjone] SF dissertation

disservizio, zi [disser'vittsjo] SM inefficiency; **i disservizi delle ferrovie** the inefficiency of the railways

dissestare [disses'tare] VT (*anche fig*) to upset, disturb; **dissestare il bilancio** to unbalance the budget

dissestato, a [disses'tato] AGG (*fondo stradale*) uneven; (*economia, finanze*) shaky; **"strada dissestata"** (*per lavori in corso*) "road up" (*Brit*), "road out" (*Am*)

dissesto [dis'sɛsto] SM (*Fin, Econ*) disorder; **dissesto finanziario** serious financial difficulties; **in dissesto** in disorder; **dissesto idrogeologico** hydrogeological disturbance (*which could lead to natural disasters*)

dissetante [disse'tante] AGG refreshing, thirst-quenching; **una bevanda dissetante** a refreshing drink

dissetare [disse'tare] VT (*persona*) to quench the thirst of; (*animale*) to water, give water to
▶ **dissetarsi** VR to quench one's thirst

dissezione [disset'tsjone] SF dissection

dissi *ecc* VB *vedi* **dire**

dissidente [dissi'dɛnte] AGG, SM/F dissident

dissidenza [dissi'dɛntsa] SF dissidence

dissidio, di [dis'sidjo] SM disagreement; **dissidio di opinioni** difference of opinion

dissimile [dis'simile] AGG: **dissimile (da)** different (from), dissimilar (to)

dissimulare [dissimu'lare] VT (*nascondere*) to hide, conceal; (*mentire*) to dissemble (*frm*); **non sa dissimulare** he's not good at pretending

dissimulatore, trice [dissimula'tore] SM/F dissembler

dissimulazione [dissimulat'tsjone] SF (*vedi vb*) concealment; dissembling

dissipare [dissi'pare] VT **1** (*disperdere*: *nubi, nebbia*) to disperse; (*fig*: *dubbi, timori*) to dispel **2** (*sprecare*) to squander
▶ **dissiparsi** VIP (*nubi*) to disperse; (*nebbia*) to clear, lift; (*dubbi, timori*) to vanish, disappear

dissipatamente [dissipata'mente] AVV dissolutely

dissipatezza [dissipa'tettsa] SF dissipation

dissipato, a [dissi'pato] AGG dissolute, dissipated

dissipatore, trice [dissipa'tore] SM/F squanderer

dissipazione [dissipat'tsjone] SF **1** (*sperpero*) squandering, waste **2** (*dissipatezza*) dissipation

dissociare [disso'tʃare] VT to dissociate
▶ **dissociarsi** VR: **dissociarsi da** to dissociate o.s. from

dissociativo, a [dissotʃa'tivo] AGG dissociative

dissociato, a [disso'tʃato] AGG (*terrorista*) who disowns his (*or* her) criminal past

dissociazione [dissotʃat'tsjone] SF dissociation

dissodamento [dissoda'mento] SM (*Agr*) tillage

dissodare [disso'dare] VT (*Agr*) to till, turn over

dissolto, a [dis'sɔlto] PP *di* **dissolvere**

dissolutamente [dissoluta'mente] AVV dissolutely

dissolutezza [dissolu'tettsa] SF dissoluteness; **vivere nella dissolutezza** to lead a dissolute life

dissolutivo, a [dissolu'tivo] AGG (*forza*) divisive; **processo dissolutivo** (*anche fig*) process of dissolution

dissoluto, a [disso'luto] AGG dissolute, licentious ■SM/F dissolute person

dissoluzione [dissolut'tsjone] SF dissolution

dissolvenza [dissol'vɛntsa] SF (*Cine*) fade-out

dissolvere [dis'sɔlvere] VB IRREG
■VT (*sostanza*) to dissolve; (*nebbia*) to disperse, dispel, clear (away); (*neve*) to melt; (*fig*: *dubbio*) to dispel
▶ **dissolversi** VIP (*vedi vt*) to dissolve; to disperse, dispel, clear (away); to melt; to be dispelled

dissonante [disso'nante] AGG (*suono*) dissonant, discordant

dissonanza [disso'nantsa] SF (*di suoni*) dissonance, discord; (*fig*: *di opinioni*) clash

dissotterrare [dissotter'rare] VT (*cadavere*) to disinter, exhume; (*tesori, rovine*) to dig up, unearth; (*fig*: *sentimenti, odio*) to bring up again, resurrect

dissuadere [dissua'dere] VT IRREG to dissuade; **dissuadere qn da qc/da fare qc** to dissuade sb from sth/from doing sth

dissuasione [dissua'zjone] SF dissuasion

dissuasivo, a [dissua'zivo] AGG dissuasive

dissuaso, a [dissu'azo] PP *di* **dissuadere**

distaccamento [distakka'mento] SM (*Mil*) detachment

distaccare [distak'kare] VT **1 distaccare (da)** (*persona*) to separate (from), take away (from); (*etichetta, francobollo*) to remove, take off; (*vagone, ricevuta*) to detach (from); **distaccare lo sguardo da qn** to look away from sb **2** (*Amm*: *dipendente*) to transfer; (*Mil*: *reparto*) to detach **3** (*Sport*) to outdistance, leave behind; **li distaccò di 20 metri** he outdistanced them by 20 metres
▶ **distaccarsi** VIP **1** (*bottone, etichetta*) **distaccarsi (da qc)** to come off (sth) **2 distaccarsi (da)** (*persona, famiglia*: *gradualmente*) to grow away (from); (: *nettamente*) to leave; (*mondo*) to become detached (from) **3** (*distinguersi*) to stand out (from)

distaccato, a [distak'kato] AGG detached

distacco, chi [dis'takko] SM **1** (*separazione*) detachment; (: *fig*) parting; **il distacco fu molto doloroso** it was very painful to part; **il distacco dalla famiglia è spesso difficile** leaving home is often difficult **2** (*indifferenza*) coldness; **con distacco** coldly; **mi guardava con distacco** he looked at me coldly **3** (*Sport*): **vincere con un distacco di 100m** to win by a 100m

distante [dis'tante] AGG **1** (*luogo*): **essere distante (da)** to be a long way (from); **la casa è molto distante dal centro** the house is a long way (away) from the (town) centre; **è distante da qui?** is it far from here?, is it a long way from here?; **non è distante** it's not far **2** (*tempo*): **essere distante nel tempo** to be in the distant past; **sono distanti gli anni in cui…** it's a long time since … **3** (*fig*: *persona, atteggiamento*) distant
■AVV far away, a long way away; **non si vede da così distante** you can't see it from this distance *o* from so far away; **non abitano distante** they don't live far away

distanza [dis'tantsa] SF **1** (*gen*) distance; **abito ad una certa distanza dal centro** I live a fair distance *o* quite a distance from the (town) centre; **qual è la distanza tra Glasgow ed Edimburgo?** how far is it from Glasgow to Edinburgh?, how far is Glasgow from Edinburgh?; **le 2 barche erano a 3 metri di distanza** the 2 boats were 3 metres apart; **era a 2 metri di distanza** she was 2 metres away; **a poca distanza da qui** not far from here; **comando a distanza** remote control; **distanza focale** focal length; **distanza di sicurezza** (*Aut*) braking distance; **distanza di tiro** (*Mil*) range; **distanza di visibilità** (*Aer, Naut*) visibility **2** (*tempo*): **a distanza di 2 giorni** 2 days later; **sono nati a qualche anno di distanza** they were born within a few years of one another **3** (*Sport*) distance; **gara su media/lunga distanza** middle-/long-distance race **4** (*fraseologia*): **prendere le distanze da qc/qn** to dissociate o.s. from sth/sb; **tenere** *o* **mantenere le distanze** to keep one's distance; **tenere qn a distanza** to keep sb at arm's length

distanziare [distan'tsjare] VT **1** (*oggetti*) to place at intervals; (*piante*) to space out **2** **distanziare qn** (*Sport*) to leave sb behind, outdistance sb; (*superare*) to outstrip, surpass

distare [dis'tare] VI DIF: **distare (da)** to be a long way (from); **dista molto da qui?** is it far (away) from here?; **non dista molto** it's not far (away); **quanto dista?** how far is it?; **distiamo pochi chilometri da Roma** we are only a few kilometres (away) from Rome

distendere [dis'tendere] VB IRREG
■VT (*braccia, gambe*) to stretch (out); (*muscoli*) to relax; (*tovaglia*) to spread; (*bucato*) to hang out; **non c'era posto per distendere le gambe** there was no room to stretch your legs; **fecero distendere il ferito sul letto** they laid the injured man on the bed; **distendere i nervi** to relax; **è ottimo per distendere i nervi** it's just the thing to help you relax;
▶ **distendersi** VR (*persona*) to lie down, stretch out; (*fig: rilassarsi*) to relax
▶ **distendersi** VIP (*estendersi*) **i prati si distendevano a perdita d'occhio** the fields stretched out as far as the eye could see

distensione [disten'sjone] SF (*Pol*) détente; (*rilassamento*) relaxation; (*estensione*) stretching

distensivo, a [disten'sivo] AGG (*gen*) relaxing, restful; (*Pol*) conciliatory

distesa [dis'tesa] SF **1** expanse, stretch; **la distesa del mare** the expanse of the sea **2** **le campane suonavano a distesa** the bells pealed out

distesamente [distesa'mente] AVV in detail

disteso, a [dis'teso] PP *di* **distendere**
■AGG (*allungato: persona, gamba*) stretched out; (*rilassato: persona, atmosfera*) relaxed; **essere disteso** to be lying; **era distesa sul letto** she was lying on the bed; **se ne stava disteso sul letto** he was stretched out on the bed; **cadere lungo disteso** to fall flat on one's face; **avere un volto disteso** to look relaxed

distillare [distil'lare] VT to distil; **acqua distillata** distilled water

distillato [distil'lato] SM distillate

distillazione [distillat'tsjone] SF distillation

distilleria [distille'ria] SF distillery

distinguere [dis'tingwere] VB IRREG
■VT **1** (*differenziare*) to distinguish, single out; **distinguere tra** to tell the difference between; **non li distinguo tra loro** I can't tell the difference between them; **distinguere il vero dal falso** to tell truth from falsehood; **la sua energia lo distingue dagli altri** his energy distinguishes him *o* sets him apart from the others **2** (*percepire*) to distinguish, discern; **era troppo buio per distinguere la sua faccia** it was too dark to see *o* make out his (*o* her) face; **non riesco a distinguere il numero dell'autobus** I can't see the number of the bus **3** (*contrassegnare: con etichetta*) to mark, indicate **4** (*frm: dividere*) to divide, separate
▶ **distinguersi** VIP **1** (*essere riconoscibile*) to be distinguished **2** (*emergere*) to stand out, be conspicuous, distinguish o.s.; **un whisky che si distingue per il suo aroma** a whisky with a distinctive bouquet; **si è sempre distinta per la sua eleganza** her elegance always makes her stand out from the crowd

distinguo [dis'tingwo] SM INV distinction

distinta [dis'tinta] SF (*Comm*) note; (*elenco*) list; **distinta di pagamento** receipt; **distinta di versamento** paying-in slip

distintamente [distinta'mente] AVV (*con chiarezza*) distinctly, clearly; (*separatamente*) individually

distintivo, a [distin'tivo] SM badge
■AGG distinguishing

distinto, a [dis'tinto] PP *di* **distinguere**
■AGG **1** (*differente*) different, distinct; **due materie distinte** two distinct subjects **2** (*chiaro*) distinct, clear **3** (*elegante, dignitoso: signore*) distinguished; (*: modi*) refined; **un signore dall'aspetto distinto** a distinguished-looking man; **modi distinti** excellent manners; **distinti saluti** (*in lettera*) yours faithfully *o* truly

distinzione [distin'tsjone] SF **1** (*gen*) distinction; **non faccio distinzioni** (*tra persone*) I don't discriminate; (*tra cose*) it's all one *o* the same to me; **senza distinzione di razza/religione...** without distinction of race/religion ... **2** (*signorilità*) distinction, refinement **3** (*onore*) honour, distinction

distogliere [dis'tɔʎʎere] VT IRREG **1** (*allontanare*) to remove, take away; **distogliere lo sguardo** to look away **2** (*distrarre*) to distract; **cerca di distoglierla mentre portiamo via la torta** try and distract her while we take the cake away **3** (*fig: dissuadere*) to dissuade, deter; **distogliere qn da qc** to dissuade sb from sth

distolto, a [dis'tɔlto] PP *di* **distogliere**

distorcere [dis'tɔrtʃere] VB IRREG
■VT **1** (*contorcere*) to twist; (*fig: verità, versione dei fatti*) to twist, distort; **distorcersi una caviglia** to sprain one's ankle **2** (*Fis, Ottica*) to distort
▶ **distorcersi** VR (*contorcersi*) to twist

distorsione [distor'sjone] SF **1** (*Med*) sprain **2** (*Fis, Ottica*) distortion

distorto, a [dis'tɔrto] PP *di* **distorcere**
■AGG (*Fis, Ottica, fig*) distorted

distrarre [dis'trarre] VB IRREG
■VT (*distogliere*) to distract, divert; (*divertire*) to amuse, entertain; **non distrarlo dal lavoro** don't distract him from his work; **distrarre lo sguardo** to look away;
▶ **distrarsi** VR (*non fare attenzione*) to let one's mind wander; (*svagarsi*) to take one's mind off things; **ho bisogno di distrarmi un po'** I need to take my mind off things; **si distrae spesso durante le lezioni** his mind often wanders during lessons; **non distrarti!** pay attention!

distrattamente [distratta'mente] AVV absent-mindedly, without thinking

distratto, a [dis'tratto] PP *di* **distrarre**
■AGG (*persona*) absent-minded; (*pegg*) inattentive; **è molto distratto** he's very absent-minded; **scusa, ero distratta** I'm sorry, I wasn't paying attention

Dd

distrazione [distrat'tsjone] SF **1** (*caratteristica*) absent-mindedness; (*disattenzione*) carelessness; **errori di distrazione** slips of the pen, careless mistakes; **mi scusi, è stato un attimo di distrazione** I'm sorry, I wasn't thinking **2** (*divertimento*) distraction, amusement, entertainment

distretto [dis'tretto] SM (*circoscrizione*) district; **distretto militare** recruiting office

distrettuale [distrettu'ale] AGG district *attr*

distribuire [distribu'ire] VT **1** (*dare: gen*) to distribute; (*posta*) to deliver; (*lavoro, mansioni: assegnare*) to allocate, assign; (*: ripartire*) to share out; (*carte*) to deal (out); **distribuisci i quaderni** hand out the exercise books **2** (*disporre*) to arrange; (*Mil*) to deploy

distributivo, a [distribu'tivo] AGG distributive

distributore, trice [distribu'tore] SM (*apparecchio*) dispenser; (*Aut, Elettr*) distributor; (*di sigarette, bibite*) vending machine, slot machine; (*di biglietti*) ticket machine; **distributore (di benzina)** (*pompa*) petrol (*Brit*) *o* gas (*Am*) pump; (*stazione*) petrol (*Brit*) *o* gas (*Am*) station
■ SM/F distributor

distribuzione [distribut'tsjone] SF **1** (*vedi vb*) distribution; delivery; allocation, assignment; sharing out, dealing; arrangement; deployment **2** (*Comm, Tecn*) distribution; **regolare la distribuzione** (*Aut*) to set the timing

districare [distri'kare] VT (*sbrogliare*) to unravel, to disentangle; (*fig: chiarire*) to unravel, sort out
► **districarsi** VR **1** (*tirarsi fuori*) **districarsi da** to extricate o.s. from **2** (*fig: cavarsela*) to manage, get by

distrofia [distro'fia] SF (*Med*) dystrophy; **distrofia muscolare** muscular dystrophy

distruggere [dis'truddʒere] VT IRREG (*gen*) to destroy; (*popolazione*) to wipe out; (*fig: speranze*) to ruin, destroy; (*: persona*) to shatter

distruttibile [distrut'tibile] AGG destructible

distruttivo, a [distrut'tivo] AGG destructive

distrutto, a [dis'trutto] PP *di* **distruggere**
■ AGG (*fig*): **sono distrutto!** (*stanco*) I'm exhausted *o* knackered (*fam*)!; (*dal dolore*) I'm devastated!

distruttore, trice [distrut'tore] AGG destructive
■ SM/F destroyer
■ SM: **distruttore di documenti** shredder

distruzione [distrut'tsjone] SF destruction

disturbare [distur'bare] VT (*importunare*) to disturb, trouble, bother; (*portar scompiglio*) to disturb, interrupt; **disturbo?** am I disturbing you?; **non vorrei disturbare** I don't want to be a nuisance; **"non disturbare"** "do not disturb"; **la disturba se fumo? — non mi disturba affatto** do you mind if I smoke? — no, I don't mind at all
► **disturbarsi** VR to bother, to put o.s. out; **stia comodo, non si disturbi** please don't get up; **non doveva disturbarsi!** you shouldn't have gone to all that trouble!; **grazie del regalo, ma non dovevi disturbarti!** thank you for the present, but you shouldn't have!

disturbo [dis'turbo] SM **1** (*incomodo*) trouble, bother, inconvenience; **non è affatto un disturbo** it's no trouble at all; **ci scusiamo per il disturbo** we apologize for any inconvenience; **prendersi il disturbo di fare qc** to take the trouble to do sth; **disturbo della quiete pubblica** (*Dir*) breach of the peace **2** (*Med*) (slight) problem, ailment; **disturbi di stomaco** stomach trouble *sg* **3** (*Radio, TV*): **disturbi** SMPL noise *sg*, interference *sg*, static *sg*

disubbidiente [dizubbi'djɛnte] AGG disobedient

disubbidienza [dizubbi'djɛntsa] SF disobedience; **disubbidienza civile** civil disobedience

disubbidire [dizubbi'dire] VI (*aus* **avere**) **disubbidire (a qn)** to disobey (sb); **mi ha disubbidito** he disobeyed me; **disubbidire alla legge** to break the law

disuguaglianza [dizugwaʎ'ʎantsa] SF inequality

disuguale [dizu'gwale] AGG **1** (*gen: differente*) different; (*grandezze, altezze*) unequal **2** (*non uniforme: superficie*) uneven, irregular

disumanamente [dizumana'mente] AVV (*senza umanità*) inhumanly, cruelly; (*atrocemente*) terribly

disumanità [dizumani'ta] SF INV inhumanity

disumano, a [dizu'mano] AGG inhuman; **un grido disumano** a terrible cry

disunione [dizu'njone] SF (*separazione*) disunity

disunire [dizu'nire] VT (*separare*) to take apart, separate; (*fig: disgregare*) to divide, disunite
► **disunirsi** VIP (*oggetti*) to come apart; (*elementi*) separate

disunito, a [dizu'nito] AGG disunited, divided

disuso [di'zuzo] SM disuse; **cadere in disuso** to fall into disuse

disvalore [dizva'lore] SM (*Econ*) non-value

dita ['dita] SFPL *di* **dito**

ditale [di'tale] SM (*per cucire*) thimble; (*per ferita*) fingerstall

ditata [di'tata] SF (*colpo*) jab (with one's finger), poke; (*segno*) fingermark

dito ['dito] SM (*pl(f)* **dita**) **1** (*di mano, guanto*) finger; **dito del piede** toe; **mettersi le dita nel naso** to pick one's nose **2** (*misura*): **per me solo un dito di vino** just a drop of wine for me; **accorciare una gonna di un dito** to shorten a skirt by an inch **3** (*fraseologia*): **avere sulla punta delle dita** (*materia*) to have at one's fingertips; **si possono contare sulle dita di una mano** you can count them on the fingers of one hand; **un pranzetto da leccarsi le dita** a scrumptious meal; **mettere il dito sulla piaga** (*fig*) to touch a sore spot; **non ha mosso un dito (per aiutarmi)** he didn't lift a finger (to help me); **ormai è segnato a dito** everyone knows about him now

ditta ['ditta] SF firm, business; **Spett. Ditta F.lli Gobi** (*su busta*) Messrs Gobi; (*su lettera*) Dear Sirs; **usa la macchina della ditta** he has the use of a company car; **son due giorni che non viene in ditta** he hasn't been into the office for the past two days

dittafono® [dit'tafono] SM Dictaphone®

dittatore [ditta'tore] SM dictator; **fare il dittatore** to be bossy

dittatoriale [dittato'rjale] AGG dictatorial

dittatorio, ria, ri, rie [ditta'tɔrjo] AGG dictatorial

dittatura [ditta'tura] SF dictatorship

dittongo, ghi [dit'tɔngo] SM diphthong

diuresi [diu'rɛzi] SF INV (*Med*) diuresis

diuretico, a, ci, che [diu'rɛtiko] AGG, SM (*Med*) diuretic

diurnista, i, e [diur'nista] SM/F *temporary employee paid by the day*

diurno, a [di'urno] AGG day *attr*, daytime *attr*; **ore diurne** daytime *sg*; **spettacolo diurno** matinée; **albergo diurno** *public toilets with washing and shaving facilities*

diva ['diva] SF *vedi* **divo**

divagare [diva'gare] VI (*aus* **avere**) to digress; **divagare dal tema** to stray *o* wander from the point

divagazione [divagat'tsjone] SF digression

divampare [divam'pare] VI (*aus* **essere**) (*incendio*) to flare up, break out, blaze up; (*fig: rivolta*) to break out; (*: passione*) to blaze

divano [di'vano] SM sofa, settee; (*senza schienale*) divan; **sul divano** on the sofa; **divano letto** bed settee, sofa bed

divaricare [divari'kare] VT to open (wide); **a gambe divaricate** with his (*o* her) legs wide apart

divario, ri [di'varjo] SM (*differenza*) difference; **divario tecnologico** technological gap

divengo *ecc* [di'vɛngo] VB *vedi* **divenire**

divenire [dive'nire] VI IRREG (*aus* **essere**) to become
■ SM (*Filosofia*) becoming

divenni *ecc* [di'venni] VB *vedi* **divenire**

diventare [diven'tare] VI (*aus* **essere**) (*gen*) to become; **diventare famoso/medico** to become famous/a doctor; **è diventato famoso** he became famous; **diventare vecchio** to grow old; **la situazione è diventata pericolosa** the situation has become dangerous; **le foglie sono diventate gialle** the leaves have turned yellow; **il latte è diventato acido** the milk has gone sour; **la maglietta è diventata rosa dopo il lavaggio** the T-shirt went pink in the wash; **è diventato rosso in faccia** he turned *o* grew red in the face; **come sei diventato grande!** how tall you've got!; **ora che sei diventato grande** now that you're grown up; **mangia la minestra, non farla diventare fredda** eat your soup, don't let it go *o* get cold; **c'è da diventare matti** it's enough to drive you mad

divenuto, a [dive'nuto] PP *di* **divenire**

diverbio, bi [di'vɛrbjo] SM dispute, quarrel, altercation (*frm*)

divergente [diver'dʒɛnte] AGG divergent

divergenza [diver'dʒɛntsa] SF divergence; **divergenza d'opinioni** difference of opinion

divergere [di'vɛrdʒere] VI DIF (*Mat*) to diverge, be divergent; (*fig: opinioni*) to differ, diverge

diverrò *ecc* [diver'rɔ] VB *vedi* **divenire**

diversamente [diversa'mente] AVV **1** (*in modo differente*) differently; **diversamente da quanto stabilito** contrary to what had been decided **2** (*altrimenti*) otherwise

diversificare [diversifi'kare] VT (*gen*) to vary; (*Comm: prodotti*) to diversify
▶ **diversificarsi** VIP: **diversificarsi (per)** to differ (in)

diversificazione [diversifikat'tsjone] SF **1** (*il diversificare*) diversification **2** (*diversità*) difference

diversione [diver'sjone] SF (*anche Mil*) diversion

diversità [diversi'ta] SF INV (*differenza*) difference; (*varietà*) variety, diversity

diversivo, a [diver'sivo] AGG diversionary; **fare un'azione diversiva** to create a diversion
■ SM (*divertimento*) diversion, distraction

diverso, a [di'vɛrso] AGG (*differente*): **diverso (da)** different (from); **è diverso da me** he's different from me; **secondo me è diverso** I don't see it like that
■ AGG INDEF: **diversi(e)** PL (*alcuni, parecchi*) several; **diversi amici** several friends; **diversi mesi fa** some *o* several months ago; **gliel'ho detto diverse volte** I told him several times; **c'era diversa gente** there were quite a few people; **diverse persone me l'hanno detto** several *o* various people told me that ■ PRON INDEF: **diversi(e)** PL several; (*persone*) several (people); **diversi dicono che...** various people say that ...; **ne ho presi diversi** (*libri, bicchieri*) I took several (of them)
■ SM/F (*euf: handicappato*) handicapped person; (*: omosessuale*) homosexual

divertente [diver'tɛnte] AGG (*piacevole*) amusing, entertaining; (*comico*) funny, amusing; **una barzelletta divertente** a funny joke; **Mario è molto divertente** Mario is very funny; **era molto divertente** it was great *o* good fun

divertimento [diverti'mento] SM **1** (*passatempo*) pastime; (*piacere*) amusement, pleasure, entertainment; **per divertimento** for fun; **fare qc per divertimento** to do sth for fun; **buon divertimento!** enjoy yourself!, have a good time!; **bel divertimento!** (*iro*) that sounds like fun! **2** (*Mus*) divertimento, divertissement

divertire [diver'tire] VT to amuse, entertain; **mi ha divertito molto la sua storia** I was very amused by her story; **far divertire qn** to amuse sb
▶ **divertirsi** VR to enjoy o.s., amuse o.s., have fun; **divertiti!** have a good time!; **ti sei divertito alla festa?** did you have a good time at the party?; **divertirsi a fare qc** to enjoy doing sth; **divertirsi alle spalle di qn** to have a laugh at sb's expense

divertito, a [diver'tito] AGG amused

divetta [di'vetta] SF starlet

divezzare [divet'tsare] VT (*anche fig*): **divezzare (da)** to wean (from)

dividendo [divi'dɛndo] SM (*Fin, Mat*) dividend

dividere [di'videre] VB IRREG
■ VT **1** (*gen, Mat*) to divide; (*compito, risorse*) to share out; (*dolce*) to divide (up); **dividere in 5 parti/per 5** to divide *o* split into 5 parts/in 5; **dividere 100 per 2** to divide 100 by 2; **su questo argomento gli studiosi sono divisi** scholars are divided on this matter; **si stavano picchiando e hanno dovuto dividerli** they were fighting and had to be separated; **niente potrà dividerci** nothing can come between us; **si sono divisi il bottino** they split *o* divided the loot between them; **abbiamo diviso i soldi** we shared out the money; **è diviso dalla moglie** he's separated from his wife **2** (*condividere*) to share; **non ho niente da dividere con te** I have nothing in common with you;
▶ **dividersi** VR **1** **si divide tra casa e lavoro** he divides his time between home and work **2** (*uso reciproco: persone*) to separate, part; (*: coppia*) to separate
▶ **dividersi** VIP (*scindersi*): **dividersi (in)** to divide (into), split up (into); (*ramificarsi*) to fork; **il libro si divide in 5 capitoli** the book is divided into 5 chapters; **a questo punto le nostre strade si dividono** we must now go our separate ways

divieto [di'vjɛto] SM prohibition; **"divieto di accesso"** "no entry"; **"divieto di caccia"** "no hunting"; **"divieto di parcheggio"** "no parking"; **"divieto di sosta"** "no waiting"; **"divieto di transito"** "no thoroughfare"

divinamente [divina'mente] AVV (*gen*) divinely (*ant*), beautifully; (*come rafforzativo*) extremely

divinatorio, ria, ri, rie [divina'tɔrjo] AGG: **arte divinatoria** divination

divinazione [divinat'tsjone] SF divination

divincolarsi [divinko'larsi] VR to wriggle (free), struggle (free); **cercava di divincolarsi** he was struggling to free himself

divinità [divini'ta] SF INV divinity

divinizzare [divinid'dzare] VT to deify

divino, a [di'vino] AGG (*gen*) divine; (*fig fam*) divine, heavenly

divisa¹ [di'viza] SF (*uniforme*) uniform; **un ufficiale in divisa** a uniformed officer

Dd

divisa² [di'viza] SF (*Fin*) (foreign) currency
divisi *ecc* [di'vizi] VB *vedi* **dividere**
divisibile [divi'zibile] AGG divisible
divisionale [divizjo'nale] AGG (*Mil: comandante*) divisional; (*: raggruppamento*) in divisions
divisione [divi'zjone] SF (*gen*) division; **divisione del lavoro** division of labour; **divisione in sillabe** syllable division; (*a fine riga*) hyphenation
divismo [di'vizmo] SM (*esibizionismo*) prima donna behaviour; (*fanatismo di massa*) hero worship
diviso, a [di'vizo] PP *di* **dividere**
divisore [divi'zore] SM (*Mat*) divisor; **massimo comun divisore** highest common denominator
divisorio, ria, ri, rie [divi'zɔrjo] AGG (*siepe, muro esterno*) dividing; (*muro interno*) dividing, partition *attr*
■ SM (*in una stanza*) partition
divo, a ['divo] SM/F star; **un divo del cinema** a film star; **come una diva** like a prima donna
divorare [divo'rare] VT (*fig: cibo, libro*) to devour; (*: patrimonio*) to squander; (*sogg: passione, malattia, fuoco*) to consume, devour; **divorare qn con gli occhi** to devour sb with one's eyes; **divorare qc con gli occhi** to eye sth greedily; **questa macchina divora i chilometri** ≈ this car eats up the miles
▶ **divorarsi** VIP: **divorarsi da** (*rabbia, odio*) to be consumed *o* eaten up with
divoratore, trice [divora'tore] AGG (*passione*) consuming; (*febbre*) burning
■ SM/F: **è un divoratore di carne** he's a great meat eater; **una divoratrice di uomini** (*fig*) a man-eater; **un divoratore di libri** (*fig*) an avid reader, a bookworm
divorziare [divor'tsjare] VI (*aus* **avere**) to get divorced; **hanno divorziato** they got divorced; **divorziare dalla moglie/dal marito** to divorce one's wife/husband
divorziato, a [divor'tsjato] AGG divorced
■ SM/F divorcé(e)
divorzio, zi [di'vɔrtsjo] SM divorce
divorzista, i, e [divor'tsista] SM/F **1** supporter of divorce **2** (*avvocato*) divorce lawyer
divulgare [divul'gare] VT **1** (*segreto*) to divulge, disclose **2** (*rendere accessibile: teoria, scienza*) to popularize
▶ **divulgarsi** VIP (*notizia, dottrina*) to spread
divulgativo, a [divulga'tivo] AGG popular
divulgatore, trice [divulga'tore] SM/F popularizer
divulgazione [divulgat'tsjone] SF (*vedi vb*) disclosure; popularization; spread
dizionario, ri [dittsjo'narjo] SM dictionary; **un dizionario di inglese** an English dictionary
dizione [dit'tsjone] SF **1** (*modo di parlare*) diction, delivery; (*recitazione*) recitation; (*pronuncia*) pronunciation; **corso di dizione** elocution classes *pl* **2** (*locuzione*) idiom, expression
DJ [di'dʒei] SIGLA M/F DJ (= *disc jockey*)
Djakarta [dʒa'karta] SF Djakarta
D.L. [di'ɛlle] SIGLA M = **decreto legge**; *vedi* **decreto**
dl ABBR (= **decilitro**) dl
dm ABBR (= **decimetro**) dm
DNA [di'ɛnne'a] SIGLA M (= **acido deossiribonucleico**) DNA
■ SIGLA F = *Direzione Nazionale Antimafia*
do [dɔ] SM INV (*Mus*) C; (*: solfeggiando la scala*) do(h)
dobbiamo [dob'bjamo] VB *vedi* **dovere**
doberman ['do:bərman] SM INV Doberman (pinscher)
DOC, doc [dɔk] ABBR = **denominazione di origine controllata**
■ AGG INV: **vini doc** quality wines; **un fiorentino doc** a Florentine born and bred
doc. ABBR = **documento**
doccia, ce ['dottʃa] SF **1** (*impianto*) shower; **fare la doccia** to have a shower; **doccia fredda** (*fig*) slap in the face **2** (*grondaia*) gutter
docciaschiuma [dottʃas'kjuma] SM INV shower gel
docente [do'tʃɛnte] AGG teaching; **personale non docente** non-teaching staff
■ SM/F (*di università*) lecturer (*Brit*), professor (*Am*)
docenza [do'tʃɛntsa] SF (*Univ*): **ottenere la libera docenza** to become a lecturer
DOCG [dɔtʃi'dʒi] ABBR (= **denominazione di origine controllata e garantita**) *label guaranteeing the quality and origin of a wine*
docile ['dɔtʃile] AGG (*persona*) docile, meek; (*cavallo*) docile, well-behaved; **capelli docili al pettine** manageable hair
docilità [dotʃili'ta] SF (*vedi agg*) docility; meekness
docilmente [dotʃil'mente] AVV (*vedi agg*) docilely; meekly
documentabile [dokumen'tabile] AGG which can be documented
documentare [dokumen'tare] VT to document
▶ **documentarsi** VR: **documentarsi (su)** to gather information *o* material (about)
documentario, ria, ri, rie [dokumen'tarjo] AGG documentary
■ SM documentary (film)
documentazione [dokumentat'tsjone] SF documentation
documento [doku'mento] SM **1** (*gen*) document; **documento di identità** proof of identity; **ha un documento (d'identità)?** do you have any identification?; **documenti** papers; **documenti prego!** may I see your papers, please?; **è andato a ritirare i documenti** he went to pick up the papers **2** (*storico*) historical document; **i dolmen sono un importante documento della preistoria** dolmen provide important evidence on the prehistoric period
Dodecanneso [dodekan'nɛzo] SM: **le isole del Dodecanneso** the Dodecanese Islands
dodicenne [dodi'tʃɛnne] AGG, SM/F twelve-year-old; *per fraseologia vedi* **cinquantenne**
dodicesimo, a [dodi'tʃɛzimo] AGG, SM/F twelfth; *per fraseologia vedi* **quinto**
dodici ['doditʃi] AGG INV, SM INV twelve; *per fraseologia vedi* **cinque**
doga, ghe ['dɔga] SF stave
dogana [do'gana] SF customs *pl*; (*tassa*) (customs) duty; **passare la dogana** to go through customs; **pagare la dogana su qc** to pay duty on sth
doganale [doga'nale] AGG customs *attr*
doganiere [doga'njɛre] SM customs officer
doge ['dɔdʒe] SM doge
doglie ['dɔʎʎe] SFPL (*Med*) labour *sg* (*Brit*), labor *sg* (*Am*); **avere le doglie** to be in labour
dogma, i ['dɔgma] SM dogma
dogmaticamente [dogmatika'mente] AVV dogmatically
dogmatico, a, ci, che [dog'matiko] AGG dogmatic
■ SM/F dogmatic person
dolce ['doltʃe] AGG **1** (*zuccherato, piacevole*) sweet; (*formaggio, clima*) mild; (*modi, carattere*) gentle, mild; (*suono, voce, colore*) soft; (*ricordo*) pleasant; (*pendio*) gentle; (*decollo*) smooth; (*legno, carbone*) soft; **un formaggio dolce** a mild cheese; **è molto dolce con me** he's very

sweet to me; **cerca di essere più dolce con tua madre** try to be nicer to your mother; **il caffè mi piace dolce** I like my coffee sweet; **nutriva la dolce speranza di rivederlo** she cherished the hope of seeing him again; **il dolce far niente** sweet idleness; **la dolce vita** the good life; **la dolce morte** euthanasia **2** (*Fonetica*) soft
■SM **1** **preferire il dolce al salato** to prefer sweet things to savoury foods **2** (*Culin*: *portata*) sweet, dessert; (: *torta*) cake; **hai ordinato il dolce?** have you ordered a dessert?; **mi piacciono i dolci** I like sweet things

dolceamaro, a, ri, re [doltʃea'maro] AGG bittersweet

dolcemente [doltʃe'mente] AVV (*sorridere, cantare*) sweetly; (*parlare*) softly; (*baciare, trattare*) gently; **il pendio digradava dolcemente verso il mare** the land sloped gently down towards the sea

dolcevita [doltʃe'vita] SF (*anche*: **maglione (a) dolcevita**) rollneck (sweater)

dolcezza [dol'tʃettsa] SF (*vedi agg* 1) sweetness; mildness; gentleness; softness; pleasantness; smoothness; **parlare con dolcezza** to speak gently

dolciario, ria, ri, rie [dol'tʃarjo] AGG confectionery *attr*

dolciastro, a [dol'tʃastro] AGG (*sapore*) sweetish; (: *stucchevole*) sickly sweet; (*fig*: *tono*) ingratiating

dolcificante [doltʃifi'kante] AGG sweetening
■SM sweetener

dolcificare [doltʃifi'kare] VT to sweeten

dolciumi [dol'tʃumi] SMPL sweets, confectionery *sg*

dolente [do'lente] AGG **1** (*addolorato*: *espressione*) sorrowful, doleful, sad; **essere dolente per qc** to be very sorry about sth, regret sth profoundly
2 (*dolorante*: *braccio, gamba*) sore, painful; (: *dente, testa*) aching

dolere [do'lere] VB IRREG
■VI (*aus* **essere**) (*dente*) to ache; (*gamba, schiena*) to hurt, ache; **mi duole la testa** my head is aching, I've got a headache;
▶ **dolersi** VIP **1** **dolersi di** (*errore, cattiva azione*) to regret; (*peccato*) to repent of **2** (*protestare*) to complain

dolgo *ecc* ['dɔlgo] VB *vedi* **dolere**

dollaro ['dɔllaro] SM dollar

dolmen ['dɔlmen] SM INV dolmen

dolo ['dɔlo] SM **1** (*Dir*) malice **2** (*letter*: *frode*) fraud, deceit

Dolomiti [dolo'miti] SFPL: **le Dolomiti** the Dolomites

dolomitico, a, ci, che [dolo'mitiko] AGG (*Geol*) dolomite, dolomitic; (*delle Dolomiti*) of (*o* from) the Dolomites

dolorante [dolo'rante] AGG aching, sore; **sono ancora dolorante** I'm still aching

dolore [do'lore] SM (*fisico*) pain; (*morale*) distress, sorrow, grief; **un dolore acuto** a sharp pain; **avere un dolore a** (*braccio, dito*) to have a pain in; **ho un dolore al braccio** I've got a pain in my arm; **ha dei dolori di testa** he gets headaches; **morire di dolore** to die of grief; **se lo scoprono sono dolori!** if they find out there'll be trouble!; **è con grande dolore che annunciamo la scomparsa di...** with great sorrow we announce the death of ...

dolorosamente [dolorosa'mente] AVV (*con dolore*) painfully; (*con angoscia*) with anguish

doloroso, a [dolo'roso] AGG (*operazione*) painful; (*situazione*) distressing; (*notizia*) sad; **è un'operazione dolorosa** it's a painful operation; **una notizia dolorosa** a sad piece of news

dolosamente [dolosa'mente] AVV (*Dir*) maliciously

doloso, a [do'loso] AGG (*Dir*) malicious; **incendio doloso** arson

dolsi *ecc* ['dɔlsi] VB *vedi* **dolere**

dom. ABBR (= **domenica**) Sun.

domanda [do'manda] SF **1** (*interrogazione*) question; **fare una domanda a qn** to ask sb a question; **ti ha fatto molte domande?** did he ask you a lot of questions? **2** **domanda (di)** (*richiesta*) request (for); (: *d'impiego, iscrizione*) application (for); **hai spedito la domanda?** have you sent off your application?; **fare domanda d'impiego** to apply for a job; **presentare una domanda** to send in an application; **fare domanda all'autorità giudiziaria** to apply to the courts; **far regolare domanda (di qc)** to apply through the proper channels (for sth) **3** (*Econ*): **la domanda** demand; **la domanda e l'offerta** supply and demand

domandare [doman'dare] VT **1** (*per sapere*: *ora, nome, indirizzo*) to ask; **domandare qc a qn** to ask sb sth; **mi ha domandato l'ora** he asked me the time; **mi ha domandato se volevo andare alla festa** he asked me if I wanted to go to the party **2** (*per ottenere*: *informazione, consiglio, aiuto*) to ask for; **domandare qc a qn** to ask sb for sth; **domandare il permesso di** *o* **per fare qc** to ask permission to do sth; **domandare scusa a qn** to beg sb's pardon, say sorry to sb; **domandare un favore a qn** to ask sb a favour, ask a favour of sb; **domandare la parola** to ask leave *o* permission to speak **3** **domandarsi** to wonder, ask o.s.; **mi domando dove possa essere** I wonder where it can be; **mi domando e dico perché devo rimanere qua?** why on earth have I got to stay here?
■VI (*aus* **avere**) **domandare di qn** (*chiedere come sta*) to ask after sb; **mi ha domandato di te** she asked after you; (*voler vedere o parlare a*) to ask for sb; **c'è un signore che domanda di te** (*al telefono*) there's a gentleman asking to speak to you; (*voler vedere*) there's a gentleman asking to speak to *o* see you

LO SAPEVI...?
domandare non si traduce mai con la parola inglese *demand*

domani [do'mani] AVV tomorrow; **domani mattina** tomorrow morning; **domani stesso** tomorrow; **domani l'altro** the day after tomorrow; **domani a mezzogiorno** at midday tomorrow; **domani (a) otto** tomorrow week, a week tomorrow; **domani è sabato** tomorrow's Saturday; **a domani!** see you tomorrow!; **credi che ci presterà la macchina? — sì, domani!** (*fam iro*) do you think he'll lend us the car? — fat chance!
■SM INV **1** (*il giorno dopo*) next day, the next *o* following day **2** **il domani** (*il futuro*) the future; **un domani** some day; **chi sa cosa ci riserva il domani** who knows what the future holds

domare [do'mare] VT (*belva*) to tame; (*cavallo*) to break in; (*fig*: *popolo, rivolta*) to subdue; (: *incendio*) to bring under control; (: *passione*) to master, control

domatore, trice [doma'tore] SM/F (*gen*) tamer; **domatore di cavalli** horsebreaker; **domatore di leoni** lion tamer

domattina [domat'tina] AVV tomorrow morning

domenica, che [do'menika] SF Sunday; **ha messo il vestito della domenica** he is dressed in his Sunday best; **domenica delle Palme** Palm Sunday; **domenica di Pasqua** Easter Sunday; *per fraseologia vedi* **martedì**

domenicale [domeni'kale] AGG Sunday *attr*

domenicano, a [domeni'kano] AGG, SM/F (*Rel*) Dominican

domestico, a, ci, che [do'mɛstiko] AGG (*lavori*) domestic, household *attr*; (*vita*) domestic, family *attr*; (*animale: addomesticato*) domestic, domesticated; **lavori domestici** housework; **animale domestico** (*di compagnia*) pet; **le pareti domestiche** one's own four walls
■ SM/F (domestic) servant; **domestica a ore** cleaning woman

domiciliare [domitʃi'ljare] AGG domiciliary; **essere agli arresti domiciliari** to be under house arrest; **fare una perquisizione domiciliare** to carry out a house search; **visita domiciliare** (*di medico*) home visit
■ VT: **domiciliare una bolletta** to set up a direct debit
▶ **domiciliarsi** VR to take up residence

domiciliato, a [domitʃi'ljato] AGG: **domiciliato (a)** resident (in), domiciled (in)

domiciliazione [domitʃiljat'tsjone] SF (*di bolletta*) setting up of a direct debit

domicilio, li [domi'tʃiljo] SM (*gen*) residence; (*Dir*) domicile; (*indirizzo*) address, place of residence (*frm*); **qual è il suo domicilio?** where is your place of residence?; **cambiare domicilio** to change one's address; **visita a domicilio** (*di medico*) house call; **"recapito a domicilio"** "deliveries"; **violazione di domicilio** (*Dir*) breaking and entering

dominante [domi'nante] AGG (*colore, nota, anche Bio*) dominant; (*opinione*) prevailing; (*idea*) main *attr*, chief *attr*; (*posizione*) dominating *attr*; (*classe, partito*) ruling *attr*
■ SF (*Mus*) dominant

dominare [domi'nare] VT (*gen*) to dominate; (*governare*) to rule; (*situazione*) to control; (*passioni, sentimenti*) to master; **la fortezza domina la pianura** the fortress has a commanding position overlooking the plain; **dominare i mari** to rule the seas *o* waves; **è dominato dal padre** he is dominated by his father; **da lassù si domina uno stupendo panorama** there is a wonderful view from up there
■ VI (*aus* **avere**) **1** (*regnare*): **dominare (su)** to reign (over) **2** (*primeggiare*): **dominare su tutti per intelligenza** to excel everyone in intelligence
▶ **dominarsi** VR (*controllarsi*) to control o.s.

dominatore, trice [domina'tore] AGG ruling *attr*
■ SM/F ruler

dominazione [dominat'tsjone] SF domination

dominicano, a [domini'kano] AGG, SM/F Dominican; **la Repubblica Dominicana** the Dominican Republic

dominio, ni [do'minjo] SM **1** (*Pol: supremazia*) dominion; (*: potere*) power; **esercitare il dominio su** to exercise power over; **domini coloniali** colonies; **il dominio indiscusso di un artista** an artist's undisputed pre-eminence; **essere di dominio pubblico** (*notizia*) to be common knowledge **2** (*controllo: gen*) control; (*: delle passioni, di una materia*) mastery; **dominio di sé** self-control

domino ['dɔmino] SM INV (*gioco*) dominoes *sg*
■ AGG: **effetto domino** domino effect

don [dɔn] SM (*sacerdote*) Father; (*titolo spagnolo o meridionale*) Don

donare [do'nare] VT (*gen*) to give; (*organo*) to donate; **mi ha donato un libro** he gave me a book; **donare il sangue** to give blood; **donare qc a qn** to give sb sth; **donare tutto se stesso a qn** to devote o.s. entirely to sb; **donare la vita per** to give one's life for
■ VI (*aus* **avere**) (*abito, colore*): **donare a** to suit, become; **quel vestito ti dona** that dress suits you

donatore, trice [dona'tore] SM/F (*gen*) giver; (*Med*) donor; **donatore di organi** organ donor; **donatore di sangue** blood donor

donazione [donat'tsjone] SF donation; **atto di donazione** (*Dir*) deed of gift

donde ['donde] AVV (*letter*) whence

dondolare [dondo'lare] VT (*sedia*) to rock; (*ciondolare: corda, gambe*) to dangle
■ VI (*aus* **avere**) (*barca*) to rock, sway; (*altalena*) to sway; (*corda, lampadario*) to swing (to and fro)
▶ **dondolarsi** VR (*su sedia*) to rock (backwards and forwards); (*su altalena*) to swing (backwards and forwards)

dondolio, lii [dondo'lio] SM (gentle) rocking

dondolo ['dondolo] SM: **cavallo/sedia a dondolo** rocking horse/chair

dongiovanni [dondʒo'vanni] SM INV Don Juan, lady-killer

donna ['dɔnna] SF **1** woman; **ho visto due donne giovani** I saw two young women; **da donna** (*abito*) woman's, lady's; **figlio di buona donna!** (*fam*) son of a bitch!; **donna di casa** housewife; **donna a ore** daily (help); **donna delle pulizie** cleaning lady, cleaner; **donna di servizio** maid; **donna di strada** prostitute, streetwalker **2** (*titolo*) Donna **3** (*Carte*) queen

donnaiolo [donna'jɔlo] SM womanizer

donnola ['dɔnnola] SF weasel

dono ['dono] SM **1** (*regalo*) gift, present; (*donazione*) donation; **fare un dono a qn** to give sb a present; **portare qc in dono a qn** to bring sth as a gift *o* present for sb **2** (*dote*) gift, talent; **un dono di natura** a natural gift *o* talent; **il dono della parola** the gift of speech

dopante [do'pante] AGG: **sostanza dopante** banned *o* prohibited substance

dopare [do'pare] VT to dope
▶ **doparsi** VR to take a banned *o* prohibited substance

doping ['dɔpin(g)] SM doping

dopo ['dopo] AVV **1** (*in seguito*) afterwards, after; (*poi*) then; (*più tardi*) later; **il giorno dopo** the next *o* following day; **un anno dopo** a year later; **è successo un anno dopo** it happened a year later; **parecchio/poco (tempo) dopo** long/not long after(wards); **prima studia, dopo usciremo** get your (school) work done first then we'll go out; **prima pensa e dopo parla** think before you speak; **è accaduto 2 mesi dopo** it happened 2 months later; **ci vediamo dopo** see you later; **ho rimandato tutto a dopo** I've postponed everything till later **2** (*oltre*) after, next; **ecco la chiesa – la mia casa è subito dopo** there's the church – my house is just past it; **non questa strada, quella dopo** not this street but the next one
■ PREP (*gen*) after; **dopo un anno** after a year, a year later; **dopo le vacanze** after the holidays; **rimandare qc a dopo Natale** to postpone sth till after Christmas; **è arrivato dopo cena/di me** he arrived after supper/me; **non l'ho più sentito dopo la sua partenza** I haven't heard from him since he left; **uno dopo l'altro** one after the other; **è subito dopo la chiesa** it's just past the church; **la Cina del dopo Mao** post-Mao China; **dopo tutto** = **dopotutto**
■ CONG (*temporale*): **dopo mangiato va a dormire** after eating *o* after a meal he has a sleep; **dopo aver mangiato è uscito** after having something to eat *o* after eating he went out; **dopo che è partito** after he left; **dopo tutto ciò che gli ho detto** after all I said to him; **dopo che** = **dopoché**

dopobarba [dopo'barba] SM INV after-shave
dopoché [dopo'ke] CONG after, when
dopodiché [dopodi'ke] AVV after which
dopodomani [dopodo'mani] AVV, SM the day after tomorrow; **ci vediamo dopodomani** see you the day after tomorrow
dopoguerra [dopo'gwɛrra] SM INV post-war period, postwar years *pl*
dopolavoro [dopola'voro] SM recreational club
dopopranzo [dopo'prandzo] SM INV afternoon
■ AVV: **studierò dopopranzo** I'm going to study after lunch *o* this afternoon
doposci [dopoʃʃi] SM INV: **i doposci** (*stivali*) après-ski boots
doposcuola [dopos'kwɔla] SM INV *supervised study and recreation after school hours*
doposole [dopo'sole] SM INV, AGG aftersun
dopotutto [dopo'tutto] AVV after all
doppiaggio, gi [dop'pjaddʒo] SM (*Cine*) dubbing
▷ www.artemotore.com/doppiaggio.html
doppiamente [doppja'mente] AVV **1** doubly **2** (*con falsità*): **ha agito doppiamente** he acted deceitfully
doppiare¹ [dop'pjare] VT (*Cine*) to dub
doppiare² [dop'pjare] VT **1** (*Naut*) to round **2** (*Sport*) to lap
doppiatore, trice [doppja'tore] SM/F dubber
doppietta [dop'pjetta] SF **1** (*fucile*) double-barrelled (*Brit*) *o* double-barreled (*Am*) shotgun; (*sparo*) shot from both barrels **2** (*Calcio*) double; (*Boxe*) one-two **3** (*Aut*) double-declutch (*Brit*), double-clutch (*Am*)
doppiezza [dop'pjettsa] SF (*fig: di persona*) duplicity
doppio, pia, pi, pie ['doppjo] AGG (*gen*) double; (*vantaggio*) double, twofold; (*fig: persona*) deceitful; **battere una lettera in doppia copia** to type a letter with a carbon copy; **chiudere a doppia mandata** to double-lock; **un utensile a doppio uso** a dual-purpose utensil; **fare il doppio gioco** (*fig*) to play a double game; **doppio senso** double entendre; **frase a doppio senso** sentence with a double meaning; **strada a doppio senso di circolazione** two-way street; **un doppio whisky** a double whisky; **doppi vetri** double-glazing; **fare doppio clic su** (*Inform*) to double-click on; **doppio fallo** (*Tennis*) double fault
■ SM **1 pagare il doppio** to pay twice as much *o* double the amount; **10 è il doppio di 5** 10 is twice *o* two times 5 **2** (*Tennis*) doubles (match); **facciamo un doppio** let's have a game of doubles; **doppio misto** mixed doubles **3** (*attore*) understudy
■ AVV double; **vedere** *o* **vederci doppio** to see double
doppiofondo [doppjo'fondo] SM (*di valigia*) false bottom; (*Naut*) double hull
doppione [dop'pjone] SM duplicate (copy)
doppiopetto [doppjo'pɛtto] SM INV double-breasted jacket
doppista, i, e [dop'pista] SM/F (*Tennis*) doubles player
dorare [do'rare] VT (*oggetto*) to gild; (*metallo*) to gold-plate; (*Culin: arrosto*) to brown; **dorare la pillola** (*fig*) to sugar the pill
dorato, a [do'rato] AGG (*oggetto*) gilt, gilded; (*abbronzatura, giallo*) golden
doratura [dora'tura] SF **1** (*vedi vb*) gilding; gold-plating; browning **2** (*ornamento*) gilt, decoration
dorifora [do'rifora] SF (*Zool*) Colorado beetle
dormicchiare [dormik'kjare] VI (*aus* **avere**) to doze
dormiente [dor'mjɛnte] AGG sleeping; **cellula dormiente** sleeper cell
■ SM/F sleeper
dormiglione, a [dormiʎ'ʎone] SM/F sleepyhead; **sveglia, dormiglione!** wake up, sleepyhead!
dormire [dor'mire] VI (*aus* **avere**) **1** to sleep; (*essere addormentato*) to be asleep, be sleeping; **sta dormendo** she's sleeping; **andare a dormire** to go to bed; **vado a dormire** I'm going to bed; **abbiamo dormito a Bologna** we spent the night in Bologna; **il caffè non mi fa dormire** coffee keeps me awake; **sono pensieri che non mi fanno dormire** I'm losing sleep thinking about all this; **i campi dormono sotto la neve** (*fig*) the fields slumber under the snow **2** (*fraseologia*): **dormire come un ghiro** to sleep like a log; **dormire della grossa** to sleep soundly, be dead to the world; **dormire con gli occhi aperti** to sleep with one eye open; **dormire in piedi** (*essere stanco*) to be asleep on one's feet; (*essere imbambolato*) to be half asleep; **dormire tranquillo** *o* **tra due guanciali** (*senza preoccupazioni*) to rest easy; **è meglio dormirci sopra** you'd (*o* we'd *ecc*) better sleep on it
■ VT: **dormire sonni tranquilli/agitati** to have a good/bad night's sleep, sleep well/badly; **dormire il sonno del giusto** to sleep the sleep of the just; **dormire il sonno eterno** to sleep the sleep of the dead
dormita [dor'mita] SF sleep; **fare una bella dormita** to have a good sleep
dormitorio, ri [dormi'tɔrjo] SM (*gen*) dormitory; **dormitorio pubblico** night shelter (*run by local authority*)
■ AGG INV: **città dormitorio** dormitory town, commuter town
dormiveglia [dormi'veʎʎa] SM INV: **essere nel dormiveglia** to be half-asleep, be drowsy; **nel dormiveglia ha sentito un rumore** he was half-asleep when he heard a noise
dorrò *ecc* [dor'rɔ] VB *vedi* **dolere**
dorsale [dor'sale] AGG **1** (*Anat*) dorsal, back *attr*; **spina dorsale** backbone, spine **2** (*Sport*): **nuoto dorsale** backstroke; **salto dorsale** Fosbury flop
■ SF (*catena montuosa*) ridge
■ SM (*di sedia*) back
dorsalmente [dorsal'mente] AVV dorsally
dorsista, i, e [dor'sista] SM/F (*Nuoto*) backstroke swimmer
dorso ['dɔrso] SM **1** (*gen*) back; (*di libro*) spine; (*di monte*) ridge, crest; **a dorso di cavallo** on horseback; **sdraiati sul dorso** lie on your back **2** (*Nuoto*) backstroke; **nuotare a dorso** to do the backstroke
DOS [didi'ɛsse] SIGLA M DOS (= *Disk Operating System*)
dosaggio, gi [do'zaddʒo] SM (*atto*) measuring out; (*dose*) dosage (*frm*); **sbagliare il dosaggio** to get the amount wrong
dosare [do'zare] VT (*ingredienti*) to measure out; (*Med*) to dose; (*fig: forze, risorse*) to husband; **saper dosare le proprie forze** to know how much effort to make
dosatore [doza'tore] SM (*apparecchio*) dispenser; (*su bottiglia*) optic® (*Brit*); (*recipiente*) measuring cap
dose ['dɔze] SF (*Med*) dose; (*di farina, zucchero*) amount, quantity; (*di whisky, vodka*) measure; **ha avuto la sua dose di preoccupazioni** he's had his fair share of worries; **ci vuole una buona dose di coraggio** it takes a lot of courage
dossale [dos'sale] SM (*di altare*) reredos
dossier [do'sje] SM INV dossier, file
dosso ['dɔsso] SM **1** (*rilievo*) rise; (: *di strada*) bump **2 levarsi i vestiti di dosso** to take one's clothes off; **levarsi un peso di dosso** (*fig*) to take a weight off one's mind
dotare [do'tare] VT: **dotare di** (*attrezzature*) to equip

with, provide *o* supply with; (*fig: qualità*) to endow with

dotato, a [do'tato] AGG **1** (*ricco di doti*) gifted, talented; **un bambino molto dotato** a highly gifted *o* talented child **2** **dotato di** (*attrezzature*) equipped with; (*bellezza, intelligenza*) endowed with; **le vetture sono dotate di sofisticati strumenti di sicurezza** the cars are equipped with sophisticated safety devices

dotazione [dotat'tsjone] SF **1** (*gen, Mil, Naut*) equipment; **dare qc in dotazione a qn** to issue sb with sth, issue sth to sb; **avere in dotazione una somma** to have a sum at one's disposal; **i macchinari in dotazione alla fabbrica** the machinery in use in the factory **2** (*rendita*) endowment

dote ['dɔte] SF (*di sposa*) dowry; (*Fin*) endowment; (*fig*) gift, talent; **portare qc in dote** to bring a dowry of sth; **avere doti naturali per** to have a natural talent for

Dott. ABBR (= dottore) Dr

dotto[1], a ['dɔtto] AGG (*persona*) erudite, learned; (*citazione*) learned; **lingue dotte** classical languages
■ SM/F scholar

dotto[2] ['dotto] SM (*Anat*) duct

dottorale [dotto'rale] AGG doctoral; (*iro: tono*) pedantic

dottorato [dotto'rato] SM ≈ PhD **dottorato di ricerca** doctorate
▷ www.dottorato.it/

dottore, essa [dot'tore] SM/F **1** (*medico*) doctor; **andare dal dottore** to go to the doctor **2** (*laureato*) graduate; **dottore in lettere** ≈ Bachelor of Arts **3** (*studioso*) scholar

DOTTORE

In Italy anyone who has a university degree in any subject can be addressed with the title of "dottore"; so someone who is called "dottore" is not necessarily a medical doctor.

dottrina [dot'trina] SF (*Filosofia, Rel*) doctrine; (*cultura*) learning, erudition

dottrinale [dottri'nale] AGG doctrinal

dottrinario, ria, ri, rie [dottri'narjo] AGG doctrinaire
■ SM/F doctrinarian

Dott.ssa ABBR (= dottoressa) Dr

double face [dubl'fas] AGG INV reversible

dove ['dove] AVV (*gen*) where; (*in cui*) where, in which; (*dovunque*) wherever; **dove vivi?** where do you live?; **di dove sei?** where are you from?, where do you come from?; **non so da dove iniziare** I don't know where to begin; **da dove è entrato?** where did he get in?; **la città dove abito** the city where *o* in which I live; **da dove abito vedo...** from where I live I can see ...; **per** *o* **da dove sei passato?** which way did you go?; **siediti dove vuoi** sit wherever you like; **ti do una mano fin dove posso** I'll help you as much as I can; **(fin) dove è arrivato con il programma?** (*insegnante*) how far has he got with the syllabus?
■ CONG (*letter: allorquando*): **e dove non vi piacesse fate come volete** and if you are not happy about it do what you like
■ SM where; **gente arrivava da ogni dove** people were arriving from all over; **per ogni dove** everywhere

dovere [do'vere] PAROLA CHIAVE
■ VT IRREG (*soldi, riconoscenza*) to owe; **gli devo il mio successo** I owe my success to him, I have him to thank for my success; **devo tutto ai miei genitori** I owe everything to my parents; **crede che tutto gli sia dovuto** he thinks he has a god-given right to everything
■ VB AUS (*nei tempi composti prende l'ausiliare del verbo che accompagna*)
1 (*obbligo*) to have to; **come si deve** (*bene*) properly; (*meritatamente*) properly, as he (*o she ecc*) deserves; **è una persona come si deve** he is a very decent person; **non avrebbe dovuto esserne informata che il giorno dopo** she was not supposed to hear about it until the following day; **non devi fare rumore** you mustn't *o* you're not to make a noise; **avrebbe dovuto farlo** he should have *o* ought to have done it; **lui deve farlo** he has (got) to do it, he must do it; **devo farlo subito?** do I have to *o* have I got to do it immediately?; **ha dovuto pagare** he had to pay; **è dovuto partire** he had to leave; **devo partire domani** I'm leaving tomorrow; (*purtroppo*) I've got to leave tomorrow; **non devi zuccherarlo** (*non è necessario*) there's no need to add sugar
2 (*fatalità*): **doveva accadere** it was bound to happen; **lo farò, dovessi morire** I'll do it if it kills me; **tutti dobbiamo morire** we all have to die
3 (*previsione*): **deve arrivare alle 10** he should *o* is due to arrive at 10; **sembra che le cose si debbano sistemare** things seem to be sorting themselves out
4 (*probabilità*): **deve essere difficile farlo** it must be difficult to do; **non deve essere uno stupido** he can't be stupid; **dev'essere tardi** it must be late; **devono essere le 4** it must be 4 o'clock; **devo averlo fatto** I must have done it
■ SM (*obbligo*) duty; **a dovere** (*bene*) properly; (*debitamente*) as he (*o she ecc*) deserves; **rivolgersi a chi di dovere** to apply to the appropriate authority *o* person; **fare il proprio dovere di elettore** to do one's duty as a voter; **farsi un dovere di qc** to make sth one's duty; **avere il senso del dovere** to have a sense of duty

doverosamente [doverosa'mente] AVV duly

doveroso, a [dove'roso] AGG (*ubbidienza*) dutiful; (*rispetto*) (right and) proper, due; **è doveroso avvertirlo** we (*o you ecc*) ought to warn him; **mi sembrava doveroso aiutarlo** I thought I ought to help him

dovizia [do'vittsja] SF abundance; **descrivere qc con dovizia di particolari** to give a very detailed description of sth

dovrò *ecc* [do'vrɔ] VB *vedi* **dovere**

dovunque [do'vunkwe] AVV **1** (*in qualsiasi luogo*) wherever; **dovunque vada** wherever I go; **dovunque tu sia** wherever you are; **ti troverò dovunque tu vada** I'll find you wherever you go **2** (*dappertutto*) everywhere; **si trovano dovunque** they can be found everywhere; **l'ho cercato dovunque** I've looked for it everywhere; **c'erano libri un po' dovunque** there were books all over the place

dovutamente [dovuta'mente] AVV (*debitamente: redigere, compilare*) correctly; (*: rimproverare*) as he (*o she ecc*) deserves

dovuto, a [do'vuto] AGG (*denaro*) owing, owed; (*rispetto*) due; **essere dovuto a** to be due to; **il ritardo è dovuto al maltempo** the delay is due to the bad weather; **è dovuto al temporale** it's due to the storm, it's because of the storm; **nel modo dovuto** in the proper way, properly
■ SM due; **mi hanno pagato più del dovuto** they paid me more than what I was owed; **ho lavorato più del**

dovuto I worked more than I actually had to
Down ['daun] AGG INV: **bambino Down** Down's (syndrome) child
■SM/F INV person with Down's (syndrome)
dozzina [dod'dzina] SF dozen; **c'erano persone/libri a dozzine** there were dozens of people/books; **una dozzina di uova** a dozen eggs; **di** *o* **da dozzina** (*scrittore, spettacolo*) second-rate
dozzinale [doddzi'nale] AGG (*prodotto*) cheap, shoddy; (*persona*) second-rate
D.P.R. [dipi'ɛrre] SIGLA M (= **Decreto del Presidente della Repubblica**) Presidential Decree
draga, ghe ['draga] SF dredger
dragaggio, gi [dra'gaddʒo] SM dredging; **dragaggio di mine** minesweeping
dragare [dra'gare] VT to dredge; **dragare il mare** (*per mine*) to sweep the sea (*for mines*)
dragherò *ecc* [drage'rɔ] VB *vedi* **dragare**
drago, ghi ['drago] SM dragon; **in inglese è un drago** (*fig fam*) he's a genius at English
dragoncello [dragon'tʃɛllo] SM tarragon
dramma, i ['dramma] SM **1** (*Teatro*) drama **2** (*fig: vicenda tragica*) drama, tragedy; **fare un dramma di qc** to make a drama out of sth
drammaticamente [drammatika'mente] AVV dramatically
drammaticità [drammatitʃi'ta] SF **1** (*Teatro*) dramatic force **2** (*fig: di situazione*) drama
drammatico, a, ci, che [dram'matiko] AGG **1** (*Teatro*): **arte drammatica** drama; **scuola d'arte drammatica** drama school; **autore drammatico** dramatist **2** (*situazione*) terrible **3** (*emotivo*) dramatic
drammatizzare [drammatid'dzare] VT to dramatize
drammaturgia [drammatur'dʒia] SF drama
drammaturgo, a, ghi, ghe [dramma'turgo] SM/F dramatist, playwright
drappeggiare [drapped'dʒare] VT to drape
▶ **drappeggiarsi** VR to drape o.s.
drappeggio, gi [drap'peddʒo] SM (*tessuto*) drapery; (*di abito*) folds
drappello [drap'pɛllo] SM (*Mil*) squad, platoon; (*gruppo*) group
drappo ['drappo] SM cloth
drasticamente [drastika'mente] AVV drastically
drastico, a, ci, che ['drastiko] AGG drastic
drenaggio, gi [dre'naddʒo] SM drainage
drenare [dre'nare] VT to drain
Dresda ['drɛsda] SF Dresden
dressage [drɛ'saʒ] SM INV (*Equitazione*) dressage
dribblare [drib'blare] (*Calcio*) VI (*aus* **avere**) to dribble (the ball)
■VT (*avversario*) to avoid, dodge
dribbling ['dribliŋ] SM INV (*Calcio*) dribbling
dritta ['dritta] SF (*destra*) right, right hand (side); (*Naut*) starboard; **a dritta e a manca** (*fig*) on all sides, right, left and centre; **dare una dritta a qn** (*fam: informazione*) to give sb a few (useful) tips
dritto, a ['dritto] AGG **1** = **diritto 1** **2** (*fam: scaltro*) sharp, crafty
■SM = **diritto 1**
■SM/F (*fam: furbo*): **è un dritto** he's a crafty *o* sly one
■AVV = **diritto 1**
drittofilo [dritto'filo] SM INV (*di tessuto*) grain; **tagliare in drittofilo** to cut on the grain
driver ['draiver] SM INV (*Inform*) driver
drizzare [drit'tsare] VT (*palo, quadro*) to straighten; (*innalzare: antenna, muro*) to erect; (*volgere: sguardo, occhi*) to turn, direct; **drizzare le orecchie** to prick up one's ears
▶ **drizzarsi** VR: **drizzarsi in piedi** to rise to one's feet, stand up; **drizzarsi a sedere** to sit up
droga, ghe ['drɔga] SF **1** (*stupefacente*) drug; **la droga** drugs *pl*; **spacciare droga** to peddle drugs; **fare uso di droga** to take *o* be on drugs; **droghe leggere** soft drugs; **droghe pesanti** hard drugs **2** (*spezia*) spice
drogare [dro'gare] VT **1** (*persona, animale*) to drug, dope; **questa bevanda è drogata** this drink has been doped **2** (*Culin*) to season, spice
▶ **drogarsi** VR to take drugs, be on drugs
drogato, a [dro'gato] SM/F drug addict
drogheria [droge'ria] SF ≈ grocer's (shop) (*Brit*), ≈ grocery (store) (*Am*)
drogherò *ecc* [droge'rɔ] VB *vedi* **drogare**
droghiere, a [dro'gjɛre] SM/F ≈ grocer
dromedario, ri [drome'darjo] SM dromedary
DS [di'ɛsse] SIGLA MPL (= **Democratici di Sinistra**) Democrats of the Left (*Italian left-wing party*)
DT ABBR = **direttore tecnico**
dual band [dual 'bɛnd] AGG (*telefonino*) dual band
duale [du'ale] AGG, SM (*Gramm*) dual
dualismo [dua'lizmo] SM (*Filosofia*) dualism; (*fig: contrasto*) conflict
dualista, i, e [dua'lista] SM/F dualist
dubbio, bia, bi, bie ['dubbjo] SM (*incertezza*) doubt; **mettere in dubbio** (*affermazione, buona fede*) to doubt, question; (*esito, successo*) to put in doubt; **ha messo in dubbio la mia onestà** he questioned my honesty; **avere il dubbio che** to suspect (that), be afraid that; **ho il dubbio che sia stato lui** I suspect that it was him; **ho i miei dubbi in proposito** I have my doubts about it; **essere in dubbio** (*risultato*) to be doubtful *o* uncertain; **sono in dubbio se partire o no** I don't know whether to go or not; **essere in dubbio fra** to hesitate between; **nutrire seri dubbi su qc** to have grave doubts about sth; **senza dubbio** doubtless, no doubt, undoubtedly; **è senza dubbio uno dei suoi quadri più belli** it's undoubtedly one of his finest paintings; **senza alcun dubbio** without a doubt; **esprimere un dubbio su** to express (one's) doubts about
■AGG **1** (*incerto: gen*) doubtful; (*: avvenire*) uncertain **2** (*equivoco, discutibile: qualità, gusto*) dubious, questionable; **uno scherzo di dubbio gusto** a joke in poor taste; **di dubbia provenienza** of dubious origin
dubbiosamente [dubbjosa'mente] AVV (*vedi agg*) hesitantly, uncertainly; in a puzzled way
dubbioso, a [dub'bjoso] AGG **1** (*esitante*) hesitant, uncertain; (*perplesso: persona*) uncertain; (*: sguardo, aria*) puzzled; **essere dubbioso su qc** to be uncertain about sth, question the truth of sth **2** (*incerto: esito*) uncertain, doubtful
dubitare [dubi'tare] VI (*aus* **avere**) **1** **dubitare di** (*onestà*) to doubt, have (one's) doubts as to; (*autenticità*) to question; (*riuscita*) to be doubtful of; **nessuno dubita della tua onestà** nobody doubts your honesty **2** (*ritenere improbabile*): **dubito che venga** I doubt if *o* whether he'll come; **pensi che telefonerà? – dubito** do you think he'll phone? – I doubt it; **non dubito che verrà** I have no doubt that he'll come, I'm sure he'll come **3** (*diffidare*): **dubitare di sé** to be unsure of o.s.; **dubitare di qn** to mistrust sb
Dublino [du'blino] SF Dublin; **vive a Dublino** he lives in Dublin
duca, chi ['duka] SM duke

ducale [du'kale] AGG ducal
ducato¹ [du'kato] SM (*titolo*) dukedom; (*territorio*) duchy, dukedom
ducato² [du'kato] SM (*moneta*) ducat
duce ['dutʃe] SM (*Storia*) (Roman) commander; (: *del fascismo*) Duce
duchessa [du'kessa] SF duchess
due ['due] AGG INV **1** two; **due bambini** two children; **due volte** twice; **l'ho fatto due volte** I did it twice; **a due a due** two at a time, two by two **2** (*fig: pochi*) a couple, a few; **dire due parole** to say a few words; **vorrei dire due parole** I'd like to say a few words; **starò via due o tre giorni** I'll be away for two or three days; **ci metto due minuti** it'll only take me a couple of minutes
■ SM INV two; *per fraseologia vedi* **cinque**
due alberi ['due'alberi] SM INV (*Naut*) two-master
duecentesco, a, schi, sche [duetʃen'tesko] AGG thirteenth-century
duecento [due'tʃɛnto] AGG INV two hundred
■ SM INV two hundred; **il Duecento** (*secolo*) the thirteenth century
duellante [duel'lante] SM duellist
duellare [duel'lare] VI (*aus* **avere**) to fight a duel
duello [du'ɛllo] SM duel; **sfidare a duello** to challenge to a duel
duemila [due'mila] AGG INV two thousand
■ SM INV two thousand; **il duemila** the year two thousand
duepezzi, due pezzi [due'pɛttsi] SM INV (*da bagno*) bikini, two-piece swimsuit; (*abito*) two-piece (suit)
duetto [du'etto] SM (*Mus*) duet
dulcis in fundo ['dultʃis in'fundo] AVV to cap it all
duna ['duna] SF dune
dune buggy ['dju:n'bʌgi] SM INV beach buggy
dunque ['dunkwe] CONG (*perciò*) therefore, so; (*allora*) well (now), well (then); **fallo dunque!** do it then!; **ho sbagliato, dunque è giusto che paghi** I made a mistake, so it's fair I should pay; **dunque, come dicevo...** well, as I was saying...
■ SM INV: **venire al dunque** to come to the point
duo ['duo] SM INV (*Mus*) duet; (*Teatro, Cine, fig*) duo; **formano un duo ben assortito** they're a well-matched pair *o* couple
duodeno [duo'dɛno] SM (*Anat*) duodenum
duole *ecc* ['dwɔle] VB *vedi* **dolere**
duomo¹ ['dwɔmo] SM cathedral
duomo² ['dwɔmo] SM (*Tecn*) dome
duplex ['dupleks] SM INV (*Telec*) party line
duplicare [dupli'kare] VT to duplicate
duplicato [dupli'kato] SM duplicate
duplicatore [duplika'tore] SM duplicator
duplicazione [duplikat'tsjone] SF duplication
duplice ['duplitʃe] AGG (*gen*) double, twofold; (*incarico, scopo*) dual; **in duplice copia** in duplicate; **il problema ha un duplice aspetto** the problem is twofold
duplicità [duplitʃi'ta] SF (*fig*) duplicity

duralluminio [durallu'minjo] SM Duralumin®
duramente [dura'mente] AVV harshly, severely
durante [du'rante] PREP (*nel corso di*) during, in the course of; (*per tutta la durata di*) throughout, for; **durante la notte** during the night; **durante l'intera giornata** throughout the day, for the entire day; **vita natural durante** for life
durare [du'rare] VI (*aus* **essere** *o* **avere**) (*gen*) to last; **la festa durò tutta la notte** the party went on all night; **lo stipendio ti deve durare tutto il mese** your salary will have to last you the month; **così non può durare!** this can't go on any longer!; **questa storia dura da un pezzo** this business has been going on for some time; **le batterie non sono durate a lungo** the batteries didn't last long; **durare in carica** to remain in office
■ VT: **durare fatica a fare qc** to have a hard job doing sth, have difficulty in doing sth
durata [du'rata] SF (*gen*) duration, length; (*di prodotto, pianta*) life; **per tutta la durata di** throughout; **di breve durata** (*vacanza*) short; (*felicità*) short-lived; **di lunga durata** long-lasting; **durata della vita** life span; **durata media della vita** (*Statistica*) life expectancy
duraturo, a [dura'turo] AGG (*ricordo, fama*) enduring; (*pace*) lasting
durevole [du'revole] AGG (*materiale*) durable; **beni durevoli** (*Econ*) durable goods
durezza [du'rettsa] SF (*gen, di acque*) hardness; (*di metallo*) strength; (*di spazzola*) stiffness; (*di voce*) harshness; (*fig: severità*) severity; (: *rigidità*) rigidity, severity; (: *ostinazione*) stubbornness
duro, a ['duro] AGG **1** (*resistente: gen*) hard; (: *serratura*) stiff; (: *carne*) tough; **duro d'orecchi** (*sordo*) hard of hearing; **duro di comprendonio** *o* **di testa** slow-witted; **avere la pelle dura** (*fig: persona*) to be tough; **pane duro** stale bread; **il materasso è troppo duro per me** the mattress is too hard for me; **l'insegnamento è un lavoro duro** teaching is hard work **2** (*fig: severo: persona*) harsh, hard; (: *disciplina*) harsh, strict; (: *atteggiamento*) harsh, unbending; (: *inverno*) hard; **duro di cuore** hard-hearted; **non essere troppo duro con lui** don't be too hard on him **3** (*ostinato*) stubborn, obstinate **4** (*faticoso*) hard; **l'insegnamento è un lavoro duro** teaching is hard work
■ SM **1** (*durezza*) hardness; (*parte dura*) hard part; **dormire sul duro** to sleep on a hard bed **2** (*fig: difficoltà*) hard part; **il duro deve ancora venire** the hard part is still to come
■ SM/F (*persona*) tough one; **fare il duro** to act tough
■ AVV: **tener duro** (*resistere*) to stand firm, hold out
durone [du'rone] SM (*callo*) hard skin
duttile ['duttile] AGG (*sostanza*) malleable; (*fig: carattere*) flexible; (: *stile*) adaptable
duvet [dyve] SM INV down jacket
dvd, DVD [divu'di] SM INV (*disco*) DVD; (*lettore*) DVD player

Dd

Ee

E, e [e] SF O M INV (*lettera*) E, e; **E come Empoli** ≈ E for Edward (*Brit*), ≈ E for Easy (*Am*)

E ABBR (= **Est**) E

e [e] CONG (*spesso ed dav a vocale*) **1** and; **io e te** me and you; **Davide ed un suo amico** David and a friend of his; **un metro e novanta** one metre ninety; **ho speso 3 euro e settanta centesimi** I spent 3 euros seventy cents; **ho pagato quattro sterline e cinquanta** I paid four pounds fifty; **tutt'e tre** all three of them; **tutt'e due** both (of them); **è bell'e fatto** it's well and truly finished; **mi piace molto, e a te?** I like it a lot, what about you?; **io non ci vado, e tu?** I'm not going, how about you? **2** (*avversativo*) but; (*eppure*) and yet; **lo credevo onesto e non lo è** I thought he was honest but he isn't; **sapeva di sbagliare e l'ha fatto ugualmente** he knew it was a mistake but he did it all the same **3** (*ebbene*) well, well then; **e deciditi dunque!** well make up your mind then!; **e smettila!** stop it!

è [ɛ] VB *vedi* **essere**

EA ABBR = **ente autonomo**; *vedi* **ente**

EAD ABBR (= **elaborazione automatica dei dati**) A.D.P.

ebanista, i [eba'nista] SM cabinet-maker

ebanisteria [ebaniste'ria] SF cabinet-making

ebano ['ɛbano] SM ebony

ebbene [eb'bɛne] CONG well (then)

ebbi *ecc* ['ɛbbi] VB *vedi* **avere**

ebbrezza [eb'brettsa] SF intoxication, inebriation; **in stato di ebbrezza** inebriated; (*ubriaco*) intoxicated; (*autista*) under the influence of drink; **l'ebbrezza del successo** the exhilaration of success

ebbro, a ['ɛbbro] AGG intoxicated, inebriated; **ebbro di gioia** drunk with joy

ebdomadario, ria, ri, rie [ebdoma'darjo] AGG, SM weekly

Ebe ['ebe] SF Hebe

ebetaggine [ebe'taddʒine] SF (*letter*) obtuseness

ebete ['ɛbete] AGG slow-witted, moronic (*fam*)
■ SM/F half-wit, moron (*fam*)

ebetismo [ebe'tizmo] SM feeble mindedness

ebola ['ɛbola] SM (*virus*) ebola

ebollizione [ebollit'tsjone] SF boiling; **in ebollizione** boiling; **portare ad ebollizione** to bring to the boil; **punto di ebollizione** boiling point

ebraico, a, ci, che [e'braiko] AGG Jewish; (*scritture*) Hebrew; (*tradizione*) Hebraic
■ SM (*lingua*) Hebrew

ebraismo [ebra'izmo] SM (*Rel, Storia*) Judaism; (*lingua*) Hebraism

ebraista, i, e [ebra'ista] SM/F Hebraist

ebreo, a [e'brɛo] AGG Jewish; **è ebreo** he's Jewish
■ SM/F Jewish man/woman; (*Storia*) Jew/Jewess; **gli ebrei** the Jews; **l'Ebreo errante** the Wandering Jew

Ebridi ['ɛbridi] SFPL: **le (isole) Ebridi** the Hebrides

eburneo, a [e'burneo] AGG (*letter: di avorio, anche fig*) ivory *attr*

E/C ABBR = **estratto conto**

EC ABBR = **Eurocity**

ecatombe [eka'tombe] SF (*fig: strage*) slaughter, massacre

ecc. ABBR (= **eccetera**) etc.; **vendono libri, dischi, magliette, poster ecc** they sell books, records, T-shirts, posters etc

eccedente [ettʃe'dɛnte] SM excess

eccedenza [ettʃe'dɛntsa] SF excess; **un'eccedenza di peso** some excess weight; **bagaglio in eccedenza** excess baggage

eccedere [et'tʃɛdere] VT (*competenza, aspettative*) to exceed; (*limiti*) to overstep
■ VI (*aus* **avere**) to go too far; **eccedere nel mangiare** to eat too much; **eccedere nel bere** to drink to excess

eccellente [ettʃel'lɛnte] AGG excellent; (*cadavere, arresto*) of a prominent person

eccellentemente [ettʃellente'mente] AVV excellently

eccellentissimo, a [ettʃellen'tissimo] AGG (*titolo onorifico*) most excellent

eccellenza [ettʃel'lɛntsa] SF **1** excellence; **per eccellenza** par excellence **2** (*titolo*): **Sua Eccellenza** His Excellency

eccellere [et'tʃɛllere] VI IRREG (*aus* **avere** *o* **essere**) **eccellere (in)** to excel (at); **eccellere in tutto** to excel at everything; **eccellere su tutti** to surpass everyone

eccelsamente [ettʃelsa'mente] AVV sublimely

eccelso, a [et'tʃɛlso] PP *di* **eccellere**

■ AGG (*cima*) lofty; (*fig*) towering, lofty
■ SM: **l'Eccelso** (*Rel*) the Almighty

eccentricamente [ettʃentrika'mente] AVV eccentrically

eccentricità [ettʃentritʃi'ta] SF INV eccentricity

eccentrico, a, ci, che [et'tʃɛntriko] AGG (*persona, Mat*) eccentric; **suo zio è un po' eccentrico** his uncle's a bit eccentric; **si veste in modo eccentrico** she wears unusual clothes
■ SM (*Tecn*) cam

eccepibile [ettʃe'pibile] AGG (*argomento, decisione*) questionable

eccepire [ettʃe'pire] VT: **eccepire che** to object that; **non avere niente da eccepire** to have no objections

eccessivamente [ettʃessiva'mente] AVV excessively

eccessivo, a [ettʃes'sivo] AGG excessive; **proibirgli di uscire mi sembra un po' eccessivo** I think it's a bit excessive to forbid him to go out

eccesso [et'tʃɛsso] SM excess; **gentile fino all'eccesso** kind to a fault; **arrotondare una cifra per eccesso** to round up a figure; **dare in eccessi** to fly off the handle, fly into a rage; **devo smaltire il peso in eccesso** I must lose some excess weight; **eccesso di velocità** (*Aut*) speeding; **ha preso una multa per eccesso di velocità** she was fined for speeding; **eccesso di zelo** excess of zeal; **peccare per eccesso di zelo** to be overzealous

eccetera [et'tʃɛtera] AVV et cetera, and so on; **...eccetera eccetera** ... and so on and so forth

eccetto [et'tʃɛtto] PREP except; **tutti eccetto lui** everybody except him
■ CONG: **eccetto che** (*tranne che*) except; **eccetto che (non) piova...** unless it rains ...

eccettuare [ettʃettu'are] VT: **se si eccettua...** apart from ..., other than ...; **eccettuati i presenti** present company excepted

eccezionale [ettʃettsjo'nale] AGG exceptional; **in via del tutto eccezionale** in this one instance, exceptionally; **è un film eccezionale** it's a really good film; **in circostanze eccezionali** in exceptional circumstances

eccezionalità [ettʃettsjonali'ta] SF INV exceptional nature

eccezionalmente [ettʃettsjonal'mente] AVV exceptionally

eccezione [ettʃet'tsjone] SF **1** exception; **d'eccezione** (*provvedimento*) exceptional, special; (*ospite*) special; **a eccezione** *o* **con l'eccezione di** with the exception of, except for; **l'eccezione che conferma la regola** the exception which proves the rule; **fare un'eccezione alla regola** to make an exception to the rule; **mi dispiace, non posso fare eccezioni** I'm sorry, I can't make exceptions; **va bene, ma lui è un'eccezione** okay, but he's an exception **2** (*Dir: obiezione*) objection

ecchimosi [ek'kimozi] SF INV bruise

eccidio, di [et'tʃidjo] SM massacre

eccipiente [ettʃi'pjɛnte] SM (*Med*) excipient

eccitabile [ettʃi'tabile] AGG excitable

eccitabiltà [ettʃitabili'ta] SF INV excitability

eccitamento [ettʃita'mento] SM (*gen*) stimulation; (*incitamento*) incitement

eccitante [ettʃi'tante] AGG (*gen*) exciting; (*sostanza*) stimulating
■ SM stimulant

eccitare [ettʃi'tare] VT **1** (*persona: sessualmente*) to arouse; (*curiosità, interesse*) to arouse, excite; (*sensi, fantasia*) to stir; (*folla*) to incite **2** (*agitare*) to excite; **il caffè eccita** coffee acts as a stimulant
▶ **eccitarsi** VIP (*sessualmente*) to become aroused; (*entusiasmarsi*) to get excited; (*innervosirsi*) to get worked up

eccitato, a [ettʃi'tato] AGG (*sessualmente*) aroused; (*emozionato*) excited; (*innervosito*) worked up

eccitazione [ettʃitat'tsjone] SF (*gen*) excitement; (*del sistema nervoso*) stimulation; (*Elettr*) excitation

ecclesiale [ekkle'zjale] AGG church *attr*

ecclesiastico, a, ci, che [ekkle'zjastiko] AGG (*ufficio*) ecclesiastical; (*gerarchia, beni*) ecclesiastical, church *attr*; (*abito*) clerical
■ SM ecclesiastic

ecco ['ɛkko] AVV: **ecco qui/là** here/there it is; **ecco i nostri amici** here are our friends; **ecco il treno** here comes *o* here's the train; **ecco! (prendi)** here you are!; **eccomi** here I am; **eccone due** here are two (of them); **ecco perché** that's why; **ah, ecco perché non è venuto!** so that's why he didn't come!; **ed ecco che sul più bello...** and just at that moment ...; **ecco fatto** there, that's that done, there we are

eccome [ek'kome] AVV rather; **ti piace? — eccome!** do you like it? — I certainly do!; **era difficile? – eccome!** was it difficult? – yes it was!; **ti sei divertito? – eccome!** did you enjoy yourself? – yes I did!; **lo so eccome!** don't I know it!

ECG SIGLA M (= **elettrocardiogramma**) ECG

echeggiare [eked'dʒare] VI (*aus* **essere** *o* **avere**) to echo; **echeggiare di** to echo *o* resound with

echinococco, chi [ekino'kɔkko] SM (*Zool*) echinococcus

echinodermi [ekino'dɛrmi] SMPL (*Zool*) echinoderms

eclatante [ekla'tante] AGG (*notizia*) extraordinary; (*esempio*) striking

eclettico, a, ci, che [e'klɛttiko] AGG, SM/F eclectic

eclettismo [eklet'tizmo] SM eclecticism

eclissare [eklis'sare] VT (*anche fig*) to eclipse
▶ **eclissarsi** VIP (*persona: scherz*) to disappear

eclissi [e'klissi] SF INV eclipse

eco ['ɛko] SM O F (*pl m* **echi**) echo; **fare eco a qc/qn** to echo sth/sb; **suscitò** *o* **ebbe una vasta eco** it caused a considerable stir

ecocardiogramma, i [ekocardjo'gramma] SM (*Med*) echocardiogram

ecocompatibile [ekokompa'tibile] AGG eco-friendly

ecocompatibilità [ekokompatibili'ta] SF eco-friendliness

ecografia [ekogra'fia] SF (*Med*) ultrasound, echography; **ho fatto un'ecografia** I had a scan

ecografico, a, ci, che [eko'grafiko] AGG (*Med*) ultrasound *attr*

ecografo [e'kɔgrafo] SM (*Med*) (ultrasound) scanner

ecologia [ekolo'dʒia] SF ecology; **i problemi dell'ecologia** environmental issues
▷ www.minambiente.it/Sito/home.asp

ecologicamente [ekolodʒika'mente] AVV ecologically; (*sicuro, dannoso*) environmentally

ecologico, a, ci, che [eko'lɔdʒiko] AGG ecological; (*detersivo, vernice ecc*) environmentally friendly, eco-friendly; **un detersivo ecologico** an environmentally friendly detergent; **una catastrofe ecologica** an ecological disaster; **pelliccia ecologica** fake fur

ecologista, i, e [ekolo'dʒista] SM/F ecologist; (*ambientalista*) environmentalist
■ AGG (*movimento*) ecology *attr*; (*gruppo, attivista*) environmental

ecologo, a, gi, ghe [e'kɔlogo] SM/F ecologist

e-commerce [i'kɔmers] SM e-commerce
ecomostro [eko'mostro] SM *ugly and environmentally damaging building*
economato [ekono'mato] SM (*Scol, Univ*) bursar's office
econometria [ekonome'tria] SF econometrics *sg*
econometro [eko'nɔmetro] SM (*Aut*) trip computer
economia [ekono'mia] SF **1** (*scienza*) economics *sg*; (*di paese, nazione*) economy; **l'economia è in crisi** the economy is in crisis; **studia economia** he's studying economics; **economia aziendale** business management; **economia domestica** home economics *sg*; **economia di mercato** market economy; **economia e commercio** (*Univ*) business studies
▷ www.sdabocconi.it/
economia pianificata planned economy; **economia politica** (*Univ*) political economy; **economia di scala** economy of scale; **economia sommersa** black (*Brit*) *o* underground (*Am*) economy **2** (*impiego razionale*) economy; (*risparmio*) saving; **dobbiamo fare economia** we must economize *o* make economies; **vivere in economia** to live frugally; **lavori in economia** (*nei cantieri edili*) building work involving direct labour
▷ www.mef.gov.it/
▷ www.ilsole24ore.com/
economicamente [ekonomika'mente] AVV economically
economico, a, ci, che [eko'nɔmiko] AGG (*Econ*) economic; (*che costa poco*) inexpensive; (*che fa risparmiare*) economical; **un albergo economico** an inexpensive hotel; **più economico** cheaper; **è più economico viaggiare in pullman** it's cheaper to travel by coach; **crisi economica** economic crisis; **viaggiare in classe economica** to travel economy class; **edizione economica** low price edition
economista, i, e [ekono'mista] SM/F economist
economizzare [ekonomid'dzare] VT (*soldi, forze*) to save
■ VI (*aus* **avere**) **economizzare (su)** to economize (on), cut down (on)
economizzatore [ekonomiddza'tore] SM (*Tecn*) fuel-saving device
economo, a [e'kɔnomo] AGG thrifty
■ SM/F (*Amm*) bursar
ecoscandaglio, gli [ekoskan'daʎʎo] SM echo sounder
ecosistema, i [ekosis'tɛma] SM ecosystem
ecotassa [eko'tassa] SF green tax
ecoterrorismo [ekoterro'rizmo] SM ecoterrorism
ecoterrorista, i; , e [ekoterro'rista] SM/F ecoterrorist
ecoturismo [ekotu'rizmo] SM ecotourism
écru [e'kry] AGG INV (*tessuto*) raw; (*colore*) ecru, natural-coloured; **lino écru** unbleached linen; **seta écru** raw silk
ecstasy [eks'tazi] SF INV Ecstasy
ectoplasma, i [ekto'plazma] SM ectoplasm
ECU, ecu ['ɛku] SIGLA M O F INV ECU, ecu (= *European Currency Unit*)
Ecuador [ekwa'dɔr] SM Ecuador
ecumenico, a, ci, che [eku'mɛniko] AGG ecumenical
ecumenismo [ekume'nizmo] SM ecumenicalism
eczema, i [ek'dzɛma] SM eczema
Ed. ABBR = **editore**
ed [ed] CONG *vedi* **e**
ed. ABBR = **edizione**
edema, i [e'dɛma] SM oedema; **edema polmonare** pulmonary oedema
Eden ['ɛden] SM Eden
edera ['edera] SF ivy
edicola [e'dikola] SF newspaper kiosk *o* stand, newsstand (*Am*)
edicolante [ediko'lante] SM/F newspaper-seller
edificante [edifi'kante] AGG edifying; **è uno spettacolo poco edificante** it isn't a very edifying spectacle
edificare [edifi'kare] VT **1** (*casa*) to build; (*teoria*) to construct; (*azienda*) to set up **2** (*indurre al bene*) to edify
edificazione [edifikat'tsjone] SF **1** building **2** (*morale*) edification
edificio, ci [edi'fitʃo] SM (*costruzione*) building; (*struttura: sociale*) structure; (: *filosofico, critico*) framework
edile [e'dile] AGG building *attr*, construction *attr*; **un cantiere edile** a building site; **un operaio edile** a construction worker
■ SM construction worker
edilizia [edi'littsja] SF building (trade)
edilizio, zia, zi, zie [edi'littsjo] AGG building *attr*
Edimburgo [edim'burgo] SF Edinburgh; **abita ad Edimburgo** she lives in Edinburgh; **domani andremo a Edimburgo** we're going to Edinburgh tomorrow
Edipo [e'dipo] SM Oedipus; **complesso di Edipo** Oedipus complex
editare [edi'tare] VT (*Inform*) to edit
edito, a ['ɛdito] AGG published
editore, trice [edi'tore] AGG publishing *attr*
■ SM/F (*imprenditore*) publisher; (*chi cura la pubblicazione*) editor
editoria [edito'ria] SF publishing; **editoria elettronica** electronic publishing
▷ www.aie.it/
▷ www.siae.it/
editoriale [edito'rjale] AGG publishing *attr*; **l'industria editoriale** the publishing industry
■ SM (*articolo di fondo*) leader, editorial
editorialista, i, e [editorja'lista] SM/F leader writer
editto [e'ditto] SM edict
edizione [edit'tsjone] SF **1** (*di libro, giornale*) edition; **la seconda edizione del libro** the second edition of the book; **edizione economica** paperback; **si trova anche in edizione economica** it's also available in paperback; **edizione a tiratura limitata** limited edition **2** **la quarantesima edizione della Fiera di Milano** the fortieth Milan Trade Fair
edonismo [edo'nizmo] SM hedonism
edonista, i, e [edo'nista] SM/F hedonist
edonistico, a, ci, che [edo'nistiko] AGG hedonistic
edotto, a [e'dɔtto] AGG informed; **rendere qn edotto su qc** to inform sb about sth
edredone [edre'done] SM (*Zool*) eider (duck)
educanda [edu'kanda] SF boarder (*girl*)
educare [edu'kare] VT (*gen, fig: gusto*) to educate; (*allevare*) to bring up; **educare qn a rispettare qc** to bring sb up to respect sth
educatamente [edukata'mente] AVV politely
educativo, a [eduka'tivo] AGG educational
educato, a [edu'kato] AGG (*gen*) polite; (*bambino*) well-behaved, well-mannered; **è un ragazzo molto educato** he's a very polite boy; **non è educato fare così** it's not good manners *o* polite *o* nice to do that; **non è educato fissare la gente** it's rude to stare at people

LO SAPEVI...?
educato non si traduce mai con la parola inglese *educated*

Ee

educatore, trice [eduka'tore] SM/F educator; (*pedagogista*) educationalist
educazione [edukat'tsjone] SF **1** (*comportamento*) (good) manners *pl*; **per educazione** out of politeness; **buona/cattiva educazione** good/bad manners; **questa è pura mancanza d'educazione!** this is sheer bad manners!; **ma che razza di educazione!** how rude! **2** (*formazione*) education; (*familiare*) upbringing; **un'educazione umanistica** a classical education; **ha avuto un'educazione molto severa** he had a very strict upbringing; **educazione fisica** physical education *o* training
▷ www.istruzione.it/
educherò *ecc* [eduke'rɔ] VB *vedi* **educare**
EE SIGLA (= **Escursionista Estero**) *letters that appear on the number plates of cars bought by foreigners in Italy*
EED [ee'di] SIGLA F (= **elaborazione elettronica dei dati**) EDP
EEG [ee'dʒi] SIGLA M (= **elettroencefalogramma**) EEG
efebo [e'fɛbo] SM (*Storia*) ephebe; (*fig*) youth
efelide [e'fɛlide] SF freckle
efemera [e'fɛmera] SF (*Zool*) mayfly
effemeride [effe'mɛride] SF (*Astron*) ephemeris
effeminatezza [effemina'tettsa] SF effeminacy
effeminato, a [effemi'nato] AGG effeminate
efferatezza [effera'tettsa] SF brutality
efferato, a [effe'rato] AGG brutal, savage
effervescente [effervеʃ'ʃɛnte] AGG (*gen*) effervescent; (*fig: persona, personalità*) bubbly; **bibita effervescente** fizzy drink; **digestivo effervescente** liver salts
effervescenza [efferveʃ'ʃɛntsa] SF effervescence
effettivamente [effettiva'mente] AVV (*in effetti*) in fact; (*a dire il vero*) really, actually

> **LO SAPEVI...?**
> **effettivamente** non si traduce mai con la parola inglese ***effectively***

effettivo, a [effet'tivo] AGG **1** (*vero e proprio*) real **2** (*impiegato, professore*) permanent; (*Mil*) regular
■ SM **1** (*Amm*): **effettivi** SMPL permanent staff; (*Mil*) strength **2** (*di patrimonio*) sum total

> **LO SAPEVI...?**
> **effettivo** non si traduce mai con la parola inglese ***effective***

effetto[1] [ef'fɛtto] SM **1** (*risultato*) effect; **avere** *o* **produrre un effetto (su)** to have *o* produce an effect (on); **l'effetto voluto** the desired effect; **far effetto** (*medicina*) to take effect, (start to) work; **la pastiglia farà effetto tra una mezz'ora** you'll feel the effect of the pill in about half an hour; **sotto l'effetto dell'alcool** under the influence of alcohol; **in effetti** in fact; **in effetti non ha tutti i torti** in fact she's quite right; **a questo** *o* **tale effetto** to this end; **l'effetto voluto** the desired effect; **la legge ha effetto retroattivo** the law is retroactive **2** (*fig: impressione*) effect, impression; **ebbe l'effetto di una bomba** it had a shattering effect; **fare effetto su qn** to make an impression on sb; **il sangue mi fa effetto** I can't take the sight of blood; **mi fa un effetto strano pensare che...** it gives me a strange feeling to think that ...; **che effetto fa?** what's it like?; **cercare l'effetto** to try to impress; **effetti speciali** (*Cine*) special effects; **un film ricco di effetti speciali** a film with lots of special effects; **effetto cocktail** (*Med*) cocktail effect; **effetto neve** (*TV*) snow; **effetto serra** (*Meteor*) greenhouse effect **3** (*Sport: di palla*) spin; **colpire d'effetto una palla** to put a spin on a ball **4** (*Comm: cambiale*) bill
effetto[2] [ef'fɛtto] SM, SPEC PL **effetti personali** personal effects, personal belongings
effettore [effet'tore] SM (*Anat*) effector
effettuare [effettu'are] VT (*gen*) to make; (*controllo, volontà altrui*) to carry out; **effettuare una fermata** (*treni, bus*) to stop
► **effettuarsi** VIP to take place
efficace [effi'katʃe] AGG (*provvedimento, rimedio*) effective; **un rimedio efficace contro il raffreddore** an effective remedy for colds
efficacemente [effikatʃe'mente] AVV effectively
efficacia [effi'katʃa] SF effectiveness
efficiente [effi'tʃɛnte] AGG (*persona, macchina*) efficient; (*misura*) effective; **un impiegato efficiente** an efficient worker
efficientemente [effitʃente'mente] AVV efficiently
efficientismo [effitʃen'tizmo] SM (show of) hyper-efficiency
efficienza [effi'tʃɛntsa] SF efficiency
effigiare [effi'dʒare] VT to represent, portray
effigie, gi [ef'fidʒe] SF effigy; (*ritratto*) portrait
effimero, a [ef'fimero] AGG (*gen*) ephemeral, fleeting; (*speranza, gloria*) short-lived
efflorescenza [effloreʃ'ʃɛntsa] SF (*Chim, Geol*) efflorescence
effluvio, vi [ef'fluvjo] SM (*anche iro*) scent, perfume
effusione [effu'zjone] SF **1** (*gen*) effusion; **effusione lavica** (*Geol*) lava flow **2** **con effusione** (*salutare, abbracciare*) warmly
e.g. ABBR (= **exempli gratia**) e.g.
egemone [e'dʒɛmone] AGG (*stato*) hegemonic
egemonia [edʒemo'nia] SF hegemony
Egeo [e'dʒɛo] SM: **l'Egeo, il mar Egeo** the Aegean (Sea)
egida ['ɛdʒida] SF: **sotto l'egida di** under the aegis of
Egitto [e'dʒitto] SM Egypt; **andremo in Egitto questa primavera** we're going to Egypt this spring; **mi è piaciuto molto l'Egitto** I really liked Egypt
egiziano, a [edʒit'tsjano] AGG Egyptian
■ SM/F Egyptian
■ SM (*lingua*) Ancient Egyptian
egizio, zia, zi, zie [e'dʒittsjo] AGG, SM/F Ancient Egyptian
egli ['eʎʎi] PRON PERS (*poco usato*) he; **egli stesso** he himself
ego ['ɛgo] SM INV (*Psic*) ego
egocentrico, a, ci, che [ego'tʃɛntriko] AGG egocentric, self-centred (*Brit*), self-centered (*Am*)
■ SM/F self-centred (*Brit*) *o* self-centered (*Am*) person
egocentrismo [egotʃen'trizmo] SM egocentricity
egoismo [ego'izmo] SM selfishness; (*Psic*) egoism
egoista, i, e [ego'ista] AGG selfish; (*Psic*) egoistic; **penso di essere stato molto egoista** I think I've been very selfish; **sei egoista!** you're selfish!
■ SM/F selfish person; (*Psic*) egoist; **è un grande egoista** he's a very selfish person
egoisticamente [egoistika'mente] AVV selfishly; (*Psic*) egoistically
egoistico, a, ci, che [ego'istiko] AGG selfish; (*Psic*) egoistic
egotismo [ego'tizmo] SM egotism
egotista, i, e [ego'tista] AGG egotistic
■ SM/F egotist
Egr., **egr.** ABBR = **Egregio**
egregio, gia, gi, gie [e'grɛdʒo] AGG distinguished; **Egregio Signore** (*nelle lettere*) Dear Sir

eguaglianza *ecc* [egwaʎ'ʎantsa] = **uguaglianza** *ecc*
egualitario, ria, ri, rie [egwali'tarjo] AGG, SM/F egalitarian
egualitarismo [egwalita'rizmo] SM egalitarianism
EI ABBR = *Esercito Italiano*
eiaculazione [ejakulat'tsjone] SF *(Fisiologia)* ejaculation; **eiaculazione precoce** premature ejaculation
eiettabile [ejet'tabile] AGG: **seggiolino eiettabile** ejector seat
elaborare [elabo'rare] VT *(proposta)* to elaborate, develop; *(concetto, idea)* to work out; *(dati)* to process
elaborato, a [elabo'rato] AGG elaborate; **motore elaborato** *(Aut)* souped-up engine
elaboratore [elabora'tore] SM *(Inform)*: **elaboratore elettronico** computer
elaborazione [elaborat'tsjone] SF *(gen)* elaboration; *(di concetto, idea)* working out; *(Inform)* **elaborazione (automatica) dei dati** (automatic) data processing; **elaborazione a blocchi** batch processing; **elaborazione conversazionale** interactive computing; **elaborazione elettronica dei dati** electronic data processing; **elaborazione testi** word processing
elargire [elar'dʒire] VT to give (generously)
elargizione [elardʒit'tsjone] SF donation
elasticamente [elastika'mente] AVV elastically
elasticità [elastitʃi'ta] SF *(vedi agg)* elasticity; spring; flexibility; laxness
elasticizzato, a [elastitʃid'dzato] AGG *(tessuto)* stretch *attr*; **tessuto elasticizzato** stretch material
elastico, a, ci, che [e'lastiko] AGG *(materiale)* elastic; *(fig: andatura)* springy; (: *mente, vedute, misure)* flexible; (: *principi morali)* lax
■ SM *(per cucito: nastro)* elastic *no pl*; *(di gomma)* elastic band, rubber band
e-learning [i'lɜnɪŋ] SM INV e-learning
elefante [ele'fante] SM elephant
elefantesco, a, schi, sche [elefan'tesko] AGG elephantine
elegante [ele'gante] AGG elegant, smart; **una giacca elegante** a smart jacket; **è sempre elegante** she's always smart
elegantemente [elegante'mente] AVV elegantly; *(vestirsi)* elegantly, smartly
eleganza [ele'gantsa] SF elegance; *(nel vestirsi)* elegance, smartness
eleggere [e'lɛddʒere] VT IRREG: **eleggere (a)** to elect (to); **hanno eletto il nuovo presidente** they've elected the new president
elegia, gie [ele'dʒia] SF elegy
elementare [elemen'tare] AGG *(gen)* elementary; *(rozzo, rudimentale)* rudimentary; *(principi, nozioni)* basic; *(Chim)* elemental; **alcune nozioni elementari di informatica** some basic knowledge of computing; **scuola elementare** primary *(Brit)* o grade *(Am)* school; **la prima elementare** the first year of primary *(Brit)* o grade *(Am)* school; **la seconda elementare** the second year at primary school *(Brit)* o grade *(Am)* school
■ **le elementari** SFPL primary *(Brit)* o grade *(Am)* school *sg*
elemento [ele'mento] SM *(gen, Chim)* element; *(di meccanismo)* part, component; *(di pila)* cell; *(di cucina componibile)* unit; **un elemento chimico** a chemical element; **elementi di algebra** basic algebra; **la furia degli elementi** the fury of the elements; **non è stato scoperto nessun nuovo elemento** no new facts have come to light; **è il migliore elemento della squadra** he's the best player in the team; **essere nel proprio elemento** to be in one's element; **elementi in parallelo/in serie** *(Fis)* parallel/series elements
elemosina [ele'mɔzina] SF charity, alms *pl (ant)*; **chiedere l'elemosina** to beg; **per strada tanti chiedevano l'elemosina** there were a lot of people begging in the street; **dare qc in elemosina** to give sth to charity; **cassetta delle elemosine** *(in chiesa)* alms box; **non ho bisogno della tua elemosina** *(fig)* I don't need your charity
elemosinare [elemozi'nare] VT to beg for
■ VI *(aus* **avere)** to beg
Elena ['ɛlena] SF Helen
elencare [elen'kare] VT to list
elencherò *ecc* [elenke'rɔ] VB *vedi* **elencare**
elenco, chi [e'lɛnko] SM list; **fare un elenco di** *(scritto)* to make a list of, list; *(orale)* to list; **c'è un elenco di ostelli della gioventù** there's a list of youth hostels; **elenco telefonico** telephone directory *o* phone book; **l'ho cercato sull'elenco telefonico** I looked him up in the phone book
elessi *ecc* [e'lɛssi] VB *vedi* **eleggere**
elettivo, a [elet'tivo] AGG *(carica)* elective
eletto, a [e'lɛtto] PP *di* **eleggere**
■ AGG *(Pol)* elected; *(pubblico)* select; **il popolo eletto** the chosen people
■ SM **1** *(Pol)* elected member **2** *(Rel)*: **gli eletti** SMPL the elect, the chosen
elettorale [eletto'rale] AGG electoral, election *attr*; **campagna elettorale** election campaign; **sistema elettorale** electoral system
elettorato [eletto'rato] SM: **elettorato (attivo)** electorate
elettore, trice [elet'tore] SM/F voter
Elettra [e'lɛttra] SF Electra
elettrauto [elet'trauto] SM INV *(Aut: officina)* workshop for electrical repairs; (: *tecnico)* electrician
elettricamente [elettrika'mente] AVV electrically
elettricista, i [elettri'tʃista] SM electrician; **fa l'elettricista** he's an electrician
elettricità [elettritʃi'ta] SF electricity; **c'è elettricità nell'aria** *(fig)* the atmosphere is electric
elettrico, a, ci, che [e'lɛttriko] AGG *(gen)* electric; *(impianto, corrente)* electric(al); **un filo elettrico** an electric wire; **tariffe elettriche** electricity charges; **blu elettrico** electric blue
■ SM *(operaio)* electricity worker, power worker
elettrificare [elettrifi'kare] VT *(linea ferroviaria)* to electrify
elettrificazione [elettrifikat'tsjone] SF electrification
elettrizzante [elettrid'dzante] AGG *(fig)* electrifying
elettrizzare [elettrid'dzare] VT to charge (with electricity); *(fig: pubblico, atmosfera)* to electrify
▶ **elettrizzarsi** VIP to become charged with electricity; *(fig: persona)* to be electrified, be thrilled
elettrizzato, a [elettrid'dzato] AGG charged with electricity; *(fig)* electrified, thrilled
elettrizzazione [elettriddzat'tsjone] SF electrification; *(Fis)* charging
elettro... [e'lɛttro] PREF electro...
elettrocalamita [elettrokala'mita] SF electromagnet
elettrocardiogramma, i [elettrokardjo'gramma] SM electrocardiogram
elettrochimica [elettro'kimika] SF electrochemistry
elettrochimico, a, ci, che [elettro'kimiko] AGG electrochemical

elettrodinamica [elettrodi'namika] SF electrodynamics *sg*
elettrodo [e'lɛttrodo] SM electrode
elettrodomestico, a, ci, che [elettrodo'mɛstiko] AGG: **(apparecchio) elettrodomestico** domestic (electrical) appliance
elettroencefalogramma, i [elettroentʃefalo'gramma] SM electroencephalogram, EEG
elettroesecuzione [elettroezekut'tsjone] SF electrocution
elettrogeno, a [elet'trɔdʒeno] AGG: **gruppo elettrogeno** generator
elettrolisi [elet'trɔlizi] SF electrolysis
elettrolita, i [elet'trɔlita] SM electrolyte
elettromagnete [elettromaɲ'ɲete] SM electromagnet
elettromagnetico, a, ci, che [elettromaɲ'ɲɛtiko] AGG electromagnetic
elettromagnetismo [elettromaɲɲe'tizmo] SM electromagnetism
elettromeccanico, a, ci, che [elettromek'kaniko] AGG electromechanical
elettromotore, trice [elettromo'tore] AGG: **forza elettromotrice** electromotive force
elettromotrice [elettromo'tritʃe] SF electric train
elettrone [elet'trone] SM electron
elettronegatività [elettronegativi'ta] SF INV electronegativity
elettronica [elet'trɔnika] SF electronics *sg*
elettronicamente [elettronika'mente] AVV electronically; **elaborato elettronicamente** computerized
elettronico, a, ci, che [elet'trɔniko] AGG (*gen*) electronic; (*carica, microscopio*) electron *attr*; **musica elettronica** electronic music; **posta elettronica** e-mail; **ingegneria elettronica** electronic engineering
elettroscopio, pi [elettros'kɔpjo] SM electroscope
elettroshock [elettroʃ'ʃɔk] SM INV electroconvulsive therapy, (electro)shock treatment
elettrostatica [elettros'tatika] SF electrostatics *sg*
elettrostatico, a, ci, che [elettros'tatiko] AGG electrostatic
elettrotecnica [elettro'tɛknika] SF electrotechnology
elettrotecnico, a, ci, che [elettro'tɛkniko] AGG electrotechnical
■SM electrical engineer
elettrovalente [elettrova'lɛnte] AGG (*Chim, Fis*) electrovalent
elevare [ele'vare] VT **1** (*alzare: muro*) to put up; (*sguardo, occhi*) to raise, lift; (*tenore di vita*) to raise; **elevare un edificio di un piano** to add a floor to a building; **elevare qn al rango di** to raise *o* elevate sb to the rank of; **elevare al trono** to raise to the throne **2** (*Mat*) to raise; **elevare un numero al quadrato** to square a number **3** (*Amm*): **elevare una contravvenzione a qn** to fine sb
▶ **elevarsi** VIP, VR (*gen*) to rise; **elevarsi (con lo spirito)** (*fig*) to be uplifted
elevatezza [eleva'tettsa] SF (*altezza*) elevation; (*di animo, pensiero*) loftiness
elevato, a [ele'vato] AGG (*gen*) high; (*cime*) high, lofty; (*fig: stile, sentimenti*) lofty; **poco elevato** not very high
elevatore [eleva'tore] SM elevator
elevazione [elevat'tsjone] SF (*gen, Mat*) raising; (*di terreno*) elevation; (*Sport*) lift; **l'Elevazione** (*Rel*) the Elevation
elezione [elet'tsjone] SF **1** (*Pol, Amm*) election; **indire le elezioni** to hold an election; **giorno delle elezioni** election day; **elezioni amministrative** ≈ local council election **elezioni anticipate** early election (*held before end of fixed term of legislature*); **elezioni politiche** general election **2** (*scelta*) choice; **patria d'elezione** adopted country
elfo ['ɛlfo] SM elf
eliambulanza [eliambu'lantsa] SF air ambulance
elica, che ['ɛlika] SF (*Aer, Naut*) propeller, screw; (*Mat*) helix
elicoidale [elikoi'dale] AGG helicoidal
elicottero [eli'kɔttero] SM helicopter
elidere [e'lidere] VB IRREG
■VT (*Fonetica*) to elide
▶ **elidersi** VR (*uso reciproco*) to cancel each other out, neutralize each other
eliminacode [elimina'kode] SM INV ticket machine (*issues numbered tickets for customers in a shop, office etc.*)
eliminare [elimi'nare] VT (*anche fig*) to eliminate; **la nostra squadra è stata eliminata alle semifinali** our team was eliminated in the semi-final
eliminatorio, ria, ri, rie [elimina'tɔrjo] AGG (*prova, gara*) eliminatory
■SF (*Sport*) heat, eliminating round
eliminazione [eliminat'tsjone] SF elimination; **per eliminazione** by a process of elimination
Elio ['ɛljo] SM (*Mitol*) Helios
elio ['ɛljo] SM (*Chim*) helium
eliocentrico, a, ci, che [eljo'tʃɛntriko] AGG heliocentric
eliporto [eli'pɔrto] SM heliport
ELISA [e'liza] SIGLA M (*Med*) ELISA (= *Enzyme-linked immunosorbent assay*)
elisabettiano, a [elizabet'tjano] AGG Elizabethan
elisione [eli'zjone] SF (*Fonetica*) elision
elisir [eli'zir] SM INV elixir; **elisir di lunga vita** elixir of life
eliso, a [e'lizo] PP *di* **elidere**
elisoccorso [elisok'korso] SM (*servizio*) air ambulance
elitario, ria, ri, rie [eli'tarjo] AGG elitist
élite [e'lit] SF INV élite
ella ['ella] PRON PERS (*letter*) she; **ella stessa** she herself
Ellade ['ɛllade] SF Hellas
ellenico, a, ci, che [el'lɛniko] AGG Hellenic
ellepì [elle'pi] SM INV LP
ellisse [el'lisse] SF (*Geom*) ellipse
ellissi [el'lissi] SF INV (*Gramm*) ellipsis; (*Geom*) = **ellisse**
ellittico, a, ci, che [el'littiko] AGG (*Geom, Gramm*) elliptic(al)
elmetto [el'metto] SM helmet
elmo ['elmo] SM helmet
elogiare [elo'dʒare] VT to praise, laud (*frm*)
elogiativo, a [elodʒa'tivo] AGG laudatory
elogio, gi [e'lɔdʒo] SM **1** praise; **fare l'elogio di qn/qc** to praise sb/sth, speak highly of sb/sth **2** (*ufficiale*) eulogy; **elogio funebre** funeral oration
eloquente [elo'kwɛnte] AGG eloquent; **un discorso eloquente** an eloquent speech; **questi dati sono eloquenti** these facts speak for themselves
eloquentemente [elokwente'mente] AVV eloquently
eloquenza [elo'kwɛntsa] SF eloquence
eloquio, qui [e'lɔkwjo] SM (*letter*) discourse
elsa ['elsa] SF hilt
El Salvador ['el salva'dɔr] SM El Salvador
elucubrare [eluku'brare] VT (*anche iro*) to ponder (on *o*

over); **che cosa stai elucubrando?** what are you dreaming up now?

elucubrazioni [elukubrat'tsjoni] SFPL (*anche iro*) cogitations, ponderings

eludere [e'ludere] VT IRREG (*gen*) to evade, elude; (*sorveglianza, nemico*) to evade, dodge

elusi *ecc* [e'luzi] VB *vedi* **eludere**

elusione [elu'zjone] SF: **elusione fiscale** tax avoidance

elusivamente [eluziva'mente] AVV (*rispondere*) evasively

elusivo, a [elu'zivo] AGG (*risposta, parole*) evasive

eluso, a [e'luzo] PP *di* **eludere**

elvetico, a, ci, che [el'vetiko] AGG Swiss

emaciato, a [ema'tʃato] AGG emaciated

e-mail, email [i'meil] SF INV (*messaggio, sistema*) email
■ AGG INV (*indirizzo*) email

emanare [ema'nare] VT **1** (*odore, calore*) to give off *o* out; (*raggi*) to emit; (*fascino*) to radiate **2** (*emettere: legge*) to promulgate; (*: ordine, circolare*) to issue
■ VI (*aus* **essere**) **emanare da** to emanate from

emanazione [emanat'tsjone] SF **1** (*di raggi, calore*) emission; (*di odori*) exhalation **2** (*di legge*) promulgation; (*di ordine, circolare*) issuing

emancipare [emantʃi'pare] VT to emancipate
▶ **emanciparsi** VR to become liberated *o* emancipated

emancipato, a [emantʃi'pato] AGG emancipated

emancipazione [emantʃipat'tsjone] SF emancipation

emarginare [emardʒi'nare] VT (*socialmente*) to marginalize

emarginato, a [emardʒi'nato] SM/F marginalized person, disadvantaged person

emarginazione [emardʒinat'tsjone] SF marginalization

ematologia [ematolo'dʒia] SF (*Med*) haematology (*Brit*), hematology (*Am*)

ematoma, i [ema'tɔma] SM bruise; (*termine tecn*) haematoma (*Brit*), hematoma (*Am*)

embargo, ghi [em'bargo] SM embargo

emblema, i [em'blɛma] SM emblem

emblematicamente [emblematika'mente] AVV (*vedi agg*) emblematically; symbolically

emblematico, a, ci, che [emble'matiko] AGG emblematic; (*atteggiamento, parole*) symbolic

embolia [embo'lia] SF embolism

embrionale [embrio'nale] AGG embryonic, embryo *attr*; **sacco embrionale** embryo sac; **allo stadio embrionale** (*progetto, piano*) at the embryo stage

embrione [embri'one] SM embryo

emendamento [emenda'mento] SM (*Dir*) amendment; (*di scritto*) emendation

emendare [emen'dare] VT (*legge*) to amend; (*testo*) to emend

emergente [emer'dʒɛnte] AGG emerging; **paesi emergenti** developing countries

emergenza [emer'dʒɛntsa] SF emergency; **in caso di emergenza** in case of an emergency; **in caso di emergenza chiama questo numero** in case of emergency call this number; **stato di emergenza** state of emergency; **è un'emergenza** it's an emergency

LO SAPEVI...?
emergenza non si traduce mai con la parola inglese *emergence*

EMERGENZA

The emergency services in Italy have separate telephone numbers. They are: 112 for the "carabinieri", 113 for the police, 115 for the fire service, 116 for the breakdown service and 118 for the ambulance service.
▷ www.paginebianche.it/numeriutili.html

emergere [e'mɛrdʒere] VI IRREG (*aus* **essere**) (*sommergibile*) to surface; (*fig: verità, fatti*) to emerge; (*: persona: distinguersi*) to stand out

emerito, a [e'mɛrito] AGG (*insigne*) distinguished; **professore emerito** professor emeritus; **è un emerito cretino!** he's a complete idiot!

emersi *ecc* [e'mɛrsi] VB *vedi* **emergere**

emersione [emer'sjone] SF (*sottomarino*): **navigare in emersione** to sail on the surface; **pronto all'emersione** ready to surface; **emersione (dal sommerso)** regularization (of illegal working)

emerso, a [e'mɛrso] PP *di* **emergere**
■ AGG (*Geog*): **le terre emerse** the world's land surface

emesso, a [e'messo] PP *di* **emettere**

emetico, a, ci, che [e'mɛtiko] AGG, SM emetic

emettere [e'mettere] VT IRREG **1** (*Fis*) to emit; (*luce*) to give out; (*calore, odore*) to give off; (*suono, fischio*) to give, let out; (*Radio*) to transmit; (*Inform*) to output; **emettere un grido di dolore** to give a cry of pain; **emettere un gemito** to groan, utter a groan **2** (*Fin: titoli, assegno*) to issue; (*: moneta*) to put into circulation, issue **3** (*pronunciare: giudizio*) to express, voice; (*Dir: ordine, mandato di cattura*) to issue; **emettere una sentenza** to pass sentence

emiciclo [emi'tʃiklo] SM semicircle, hemicycle; (*della Camera dei deputati*) floor

emicrania [emi'kranja] SF migraine; **aveva l'emicrania** he had a migraine

emigrante [emi'grante] AGG, SM/F emigrant

emigrare [emi'grare] VI (*aus* **essere**) **emigrare (in)** (*persona*) to emigrate (to); (*animale: migrare*) to migrate (to); **erano emigrati in Germania** they had emigrated to Germany

emigrato, a [emi'grato] AGG emigrant
■ SM/F emigrant; (*Storia*) émigré

emigrazione [emigrat'tsjone] SF (*vedi vb*) emigration; migration; **emigrazione di capitali** flight of capital

emiliano, a [emi'ljano] AGG of *o* from Emilia
■ SM/F inhabitant *o* native of Emilia

eminente [emi'nɛnte] AGG (*posizione*) high, lofty; (*scienziato ecc*) eminent, distinguished

eminentemente [eminente'mente] AVV (*principalmente*) mainly, principally

eminentissimo [eminen'tissimo] SM (*in lettere*) His Eminence; (*nel rivolgersi personalmente*) Your Eminence

eminenza [emi'nɛntsa] SF **1** (*titolo: di cardinale*): **Eminenza** Eminence; **eminenza grigia** (*fig*) éminence grise **2** (*qualità*) distinction, eminence

emirato [emi'rato] SM emirate; **gli Emirati Arabi Uniti** the United Arab Emirates

emiro [e'miro] SM emir

emisfero [emis'fɛro] SM (*gen*) hemisphere; **emisfero australe/boreale** southern/northern hemisphere

emisi *ecc* [e'mizi] VB *vedi* **emettere**

emissario, ri [emis'sarjo] SM **1** (*Geog*) outflowing river **2** (*inviato*) emissary

emissione [emis'sjone] SF (*di suoni, onde, calore,*

Ee

radiazioni) emission; (*di energia*) output; (*di francobolli, titoli, assegni*) issue

emittente [emit'tɛnte] AGG (*Radio, TV*) transmitting, broadcasting; (*banca*) issuing
■ SF (*stazione*) transmitting station, broadcasting station; **emittente privata** independent station; **un'emittente radiofonica locale** a local radio station

emivita [emi'vita] SF half-life

emoderivato [emoderi'vato] SM blood product

emofilia [emofi'lia] SF haemophilia (*Brit*), hemophilia (*Am*)

emofiliaco, a, ci, che [emofi'liako] AGG, SM/F haemophiliac (*Brit*), hemophiliac (*Am*)

emoglobina [emoglo'bina] SF haemoglobin (*Brit*), hemoglobin (*Am*)

emolisi [emo'lizi] SF (*Bio*) haemolysis

emolliente [emol'ljɛnte] AGG (*crema, preparato*) soothing

emorragia, gie [emorra'dʒia] SF haemorrhage (*Brit*), hemorrhage (*Am*); **emorragia interna** internal bleeding

emorroidi [emor'rɔidi] SFPL haemorrhoids (*Brit*), hemorrhoids (*Am*), piles

emostatico, a, ci, che [emos'tatiko] AGG haemostatic (*Brit*), hemostatic (*Am*); **laccio emostatico** tourniquet; **matita emostatica** styptic pencil

emoticon [e'motikon] SF INV emoticon

emotivamente [emotiva'mente] AVV emotionally

emotività [emotivi'ta] SF INV emotional nature

emotivo, a [emo'tivo] AGG emotional; **è molto emotiva** she's very emotional

emotrasfuso, a [emotras'fuzo] SM/F person who has received a blood transfusion

emozionale [emottsjo'nale] AGG emotional

emozionante [emottsjo'nante] AGG (*che appassiona*) thrilling, exciting; (*che commuove*) moving; **è stata un'avventura emozionante** it was an exciting adventure

emozionare [emottsjo'nare] VT (*appassionare*) to thrill, excite; (*commuovere*) to move
▶ **emozionarsi** VIP (*vedi vt*) to get excited; to be moved; **emozionarsi facilmente** to be excitable; to be easily moved

emozionato, a [emotsjo'nato] AGG (*commosso*) moved; (*agitato*) nervous; **scusami sono un po' emozionato** sorry, I feel a bit overwhelmed; **ero troppo emozionato per fare un discorso** I was too emotional to make a speech; **era molto emozionato all'esame** he was very nervous during the exam

emozione [emot'tsjone] SF emotion; **a caccia di emozioni** in search of excitement; **le tremava la voce per l'emozione** her voice trembled with emotion

empatia [empa'tia] SF empathy

Empedocle [em'pɛdokle] SM Empedocles

empiamente [empja'mente] AVV (*Rel*) impiously, blasphemously; (*crudelmente*) cruelly

empietà [empje'ta] SF INV (*Rel*) impiety; (*crudeltà*) cruelty; (*azione crudele*) cruel deed

empio, pia, pi, pie ['empjo] AGG (*Rel*) impious; (*crudele*) cruel

empiricamente [empirika'mente] AVV empirically

empirico, a, ci, che [em'piriko] AGG empirical

empirismo [empi'rizmo] SM empiricism

emporio, ri [em'pɔrjo] SM emporium, general store

Ems ABBR EMS (= *Enhanced Messaging Service*)

emù [e'mu] SM INV emu

emulare [emu'lare] VT to emulate

emulazione [emulat'tsjone] SF emulation

emulo, a ['ɛmulo] SM/F imitator

emulsionare [emulsjo'nare] VT to emulsify

emulsione [emul'sjone] SF emulsion

EN SIGLA = *Enna*

enalotto [ena'lɔtto] SM ≈ National Lottery

enciclica, che [en'tʃiklika] SF (*Rel*) encyclical

enciclopedia [entʃiklope'dia] SF encyclopaedia (*Brit*), encyclopedia (*Am*)

enciclopedico, a, ci, che [entʃiklo'pɛdiko] AGG encyclopaedic (*Brit*), encyclopedic (*Am*)

enclave [ɑ̃'klav] SF INV enclave

enclitico, a, ci, che [en'klitiko] AGG (*Gramm*) enclitic; **particella enclitica** enclitic particle

encomiabile [enko'mjabile] AGG commendable, praiseworthy

encomiabilmente [enkomjabil'mente] AVV admirably, in a praiseworthy manner

encomiare [enko'mjare] VT to commend, praise

encomio, mi [en'kɔmjo] SM commendation; **encomio solenne** (*Mil*) mention in dispatches

endemico, a, ci, che [en'dɛmiko] AGG endemic

endocrino, a [en'dɔkrino] AGG endocrine

endogeno, a [en'dɔdʒeno] AGG **1** (*gen, Bio, Med*) endogenous **2** (*Geol*): **fenomeni endogeni** internal processes; **rocce endogene** endogenous rocks

endorfina [endor'fina] SF endorphin

endoscheletro [endos'kɛletro] SM (*Anat*) endoskeleton

endoscopia [endosko'pia] SF (*Med*) endoscopy

endotermico, a, ci, che [endo'tɛrmiko] AGG endothermic

endovena [endo'vena] SF (*Med*) intravenous injection
■ AVV: **iniettare qc endovena** to inject sth intravenously

endovenoso, a [endove'noso] AGG (*Med*) intravenous; **per via endovenosa** intravenously
■ SF intravenous injection

ENEA [e'nɛa] SIGLA M (= **Ente per le Nuove tecnologie, l'Energia e l'Ambiente**) *national agency for research into new technology, energy and the environment*

Enea [e'nɛa] SM (*Storia*) Aeneas

ENEL ['enel] SIGLA M (= **Ente Nazionale per l'Energia Elettrica**) *national electricity board*

energetico, a, ci, che [ener'dʒɛtiko] AGG (*risorse, crisi*) energy *attr*; (*sostanza, alimento*) energy-giving

energia, gie [ener'dʒia] SF **1** (*vigore*) energy, strength, vigour (*Brit*), vigor (*Am*); **avere molta energia** to be very energetic; **avere poca energia** to lack energy, have little energy; **dedicare tutte le proprie energie a qc** to devote all one's energies to sth; **come fai ad essere così pieno di energia?** how do you manage to be so full of energy? **2** (*Fis*) energy; (*Tecn*) power; **liberare energia** to release energy; **consumo di energia** power consumption; **energia alternativa**: **fonti di energia alternativa** sources of alternative energy; **energia nucleare** nuclear energy; **energia termica** heat energy

energicamente [enerdʒika'mente] AVV energetically, vigorously

energico, a, ci, che [e'nɛrdʒiko] AGG (*persona*) energetic, vigorous; (*resistenza, rifiuto*) forceful, vigorous; (*cura*) potent, powerful; (*provvedimenti*) drastic

energumeno [ener'gumeno] SM (*scherz*) brute

enfasi ['ɛnfazi] SF INV emphasis; (*pegg*) pomposity; **con enfasi** emphatically; (*pegg*) pompously; **porre l'enfasi su** to stress, place the emphasis on, emphasize

enfaticamente [enfatika'mente] AVV emphatically; **sottolineare enfaticamente il fatto che...** to lay great stress on the fact that ...

enfatico, a, ci, che [en'fatiko] AGG (*tono, discorso*) emphatic; (: *pegg*) pompous

enfatizzare [enfatid'dzare] VT to emphasize, stress

enfisema, i [enfi'zɛma] SM (*Med*) emphysema; **enfisema polmonare** pulmonary emphysema

ENI ['ɛni] SIGLA M = *Ente Nazionale Idrocarburi*

enigma, i [e'nigma] SM (*mistero*) enigma, riddle; (*gioco*) puzzle, riddle; **quell'uomo è un enigma** that man is an enigma; **il suo comportamento rimane un enigma** his behaviour is inexplicable

enigmaticamente [enigmatika'mente] AVV enigmatically

enigmatico, a, ci, che [enig'matiko] AGG enigmatic

enigmistica [enig'mistika] SF: **essere un appassionato di enigmistica** to be very keen on doing puzzles; **rivista di enigmistica** puzzles magazine

ENIT ['enit] SIGLA M (= **Ente Nazionale Italiano per il Turismo**) *Italian tourist board*

ennese [en'nese] AGG of *o* from Enna
■ SM/F inhabitant *o* native of Enna

ennesimo, a [en'nɛzimo] AGG (*Mat, fam*) nth; **all'ennesima potenza** to the nth power *o* degree; **per l'ennesima volta** for the umpteenth time

enologia [enolo'dʒia] SF oenology (*Brit*), enology (*Am*)

enologico, a, ci, che [eno'lɔdziko] AGG oenological (*Brit*), enological (*Am*); **l'industria enologica** the wine industry

enologo, a, gi [e'nɔlogo] SM/F oenologist (*Brit*), enologist (*Am*), wine expert

enorme [e'norme] AGG (*gen*) enormous, huge; (*distesa, riserva*) vast, enormous; (*pazienza, forza*) tremendous, enormous; **è un negozio enorme** it's a huge shop; **ha avuto un enorme successo** it was a huge success

enormemente [enorme'mente] AVV enormously, tremendously; **ci siamo divertiti enormemente** we enjoyed ourselves tremendously *o* hugely; **ciò mi ha deluso enormemente** I was greatly *o* tremendously disappointed by it

enormità [enormi'ta] SF INV **1** (*di peso, somma*) hugeness; (*di distesa*) vastness; (*di richiesta*) enormity; (*di prezzo*) unreasonableness **2** (*stupidaggine*) blunder, howler; **non dire enormità!** don't talk nonsense!; **l'ho pagato un'enormità** I paid a fortune for it

enoteca, che [eno'tɛka] SF (*per vendita*) wine shop, ≈ off-licence (*per degustazione*) wine bar

ENPA ['ɛnpa] SIGLA M (= **Ente Nazionale Protezione Animali**) ≈ RSPCA (*Brit*), ≈ SPCA (*Am*)

ENPAS ['ɛnpas] SIGLA M (= **Ente Nazionale Previdenza e Assistenza Dipendenti Statali**) *welfare organization for State employees*

ensemble [ã'sãbl] SM INV (*Mus*) ensemble

entalpia [ental'pia] SF (*Fis*) enthalpy

ente ['ɛnte] SM **1** (*Amm*) body, corporation, board; **ente autonomo** ≈ local board; **ente locale** ≈ local authority (*Brit*), local government (*Am*); **ente pubblico** public body; **ente di ricerca** research organization **2** (*Filosofia*) being

enterite [ente'rite] SF (*Med*) enteritis

entità [enti'ta] SF INV **1** (*di perdita, danni, investimenti*) extent; (*di popolazione*) size; **di scarsa/una certa entità** (*avvenimento, incidente*) of slight/some importance **2** (*Filosofia*) entity

entomologia [entomolo'dʒia] SF (*Zool*) entomology

entourage [ãtu'raʒ] SM INV entourage

entraî neuse [ãtrɛ'nø:z] SF INV night-club hostess

entrambi, e [en'trambi] AGG, PRON both; **entrambi i ragazzi** both boys, both of the boys; **entrambe le sorelle** both sisters, both of the sisters; **vennero entrambi** they both came, both of them came; **mi piacciono entrambi** I like them both, I like both of them; **si può parcheggiare su entrambi i lati della strada** you can park on both sides of the street

entrante [en'trante] AGG (*prossimo: mese, anno*) next, coming

entrare [en'trare] PAROLA CHIAVE

VI (*aus* **essere**)

1 to go (*o* come) in, enter; (*con la macchina*) to drive in; **entri pure!** do come in!; **"si prega di bussare prima di entrare"** "knock before entering"; **entrare dalla finestra** to get in by the window; **entrare in automobile** to get into the car; **non entrare in acqua subito dopo aver mangiato!** don't go into the water when you've just eaten!; **mi è entrato qualcosa nell'occhio** I've got something in my eye

2 (*soldi, prodotti*) to enter, come in; (*contenuto*) to go in; (: *adattarsi*) to fit in; **il regalo non entra nella scatola** the present won't go *o* fit into the box; **queste scarpe non mi entrano** I can't get into these shoes; **entra acqua dal tetto** there's water coming in through the roof; **la matematica non mi entra proprio in testa** I just can't get the hang of maths, I just can't get maths to sink in

3 **far entrare** (*visitatore, cliente*) to show in; (*animale*) to let in; (*oggetto*) to fit in; (*merce: d'importazione*) to bring in; (: *di contrabbando*) to smuggle in; **far entrare qn in banca** (*come impiegato*) to get sb a job in a bank; **far entrare qn in un club** (*ammettere*) to let sb into a club; **non riesco a fargli entrare in testa che ce la può fare** I can't get him to understand that he can do it; **gli hanno fatto entrare in testa la trigonometria** they've managed to teach him trigonometry

4 **entrare in** (*club, partito*) to join, become a member of; (*professione*) to go into; **entrare in affari** to go into business; **entrare nei vent'anni di età** to turn twenty; **entrare in argomento** to get onto the subject; **entrare in ballo** to come into play; **entrare in carica** to take up office; **entrare in commercio con qn** to go into business with sb; **entrare in convalescenza** to begin one's convalescence; **entrare in convento** to enter a convent; **entrare in discussione con qn** to enter into discussions with sb; **entrare in gioco** to come into play; **entrare in guerra** (*all'inizio*) to go to war; (*a conflitto iniziato*) to come into the war; **entrare nella professione legale** to go into the law; **entrare al servizio di qn** to enter sb's service; **entrare in società con qn** to go into partnership with sb; **entrare nella storia** to go down in history; **entrare in vigore** (*legge*) to come into force *o* effect

5 **entrarci** to have to do with; **quello che dici non c'entra (niente)** what you say has nothing to do with it; **tu non c'entri in questa faccenda** this is none of your business; **io non c'entro** it's got nothing to do with me

entrata [en'trata] SF **1** (*ingresso: di persona*) entry, entrance; (: *di merci, veicoli*) entry; **alla sua entrata** as he entered; **alla sua entrata in scena** (*Teatro*) on his entrance; (*fig*) when he came on to the scene; **all'entrata in guerra degli Stati Uniti** when the

Ee

United States came into the war; **dopo la sua entrata in carica** after he took office; **con l'entrata in vigore dei nuovi provvedimenti...** once the new measures come into effect ... **2** (*accesso*) admission; **"entrata libera"** "admission free"; **biglietto di entrata** (entrance) ticket **3** (*porta*) entrance; (*vestibolo*) entrance (hall); **l'entrata principale è sulla via laterale** the main entrance is in the side street; **entrata degli artisti** (*Teatro*) stage door; **entrata di servizio** service *o* tradesmen's entrance **4 entrate** SFPL (*Econ*) income *sg*; (*Comm*) takings, receipts; **entrate e uscite** income and expenditure; **entrate tributarie** tax revenue *sg*

entratura [entra'tura] SF (*conoscenza*) contact

entrecôte [ɑ̃trə'kot] SF INV (*Culin*) entrecôte, rib steak

entro ['entro] PREP within; **entro un mese** within a month; **avremo i risultati entro un mese** we'll have the results within a month; **entro domani** by tomorrow; **entro febbraio** by the end of February; **entro quattro anni** within four years; **devo pagare entro il dodici febbraio** I've got to pay by the twelfth of February; **entro e non oltre il 25 aprile** no later than 25th April

entrobordo [entro'bordo] (*Naut*) AGG INV inboard ■ SM INV (*motore*) inboard motor; (*motoscafo*) boat with an inboard engine

entropia [entro'pia] SF (*Fis*) entropy

entroterra [entro'terra] SM INV hinterland; **l'entroterra australiano** the (Australian) outback

entusiasmante [entuzjaz'mante] AGG exciting

entusiasmare [entuzjaz'mare] VT to fill with enthusiasm, excite
▶ **entusiasmarsi** VIP: **entusiasmarsi per qc** to be enthusiastic about *o* over sth

entusiasmo [entu'zjazmo] SM enthusiasm; **all'inizio era pieno di entusiasmo** at the start he was full of enthusiasm

entusiasta, i, e [entu'zjasta] AGG: **entusiasta (di)** enthusiastic (about *o* over); **sono entusiasta dell'idea** I'm enthusiastic about the idea; **non sono entusiasta dei risultati** I'm not too happy about the results; **non era troppo entusiasta, ma ha accettato** he wasn't exactly delighted, but he agreed
■ SM/F enthusiast

entusiasticamente [entuzjastika'mente] AVV enthusiastically

entusiastico, a, ci, che [entu'zjastiko] AGG enthusiastic

enucleare [enukle'are] VT (*frm: problema*) to clarify

enumerare [enume'rare] VT to enumerate, list

enumerazione [enumerat'tsjone] SF enumeration

enunciare [enun'tʃare] VT (*pensiero*) to express; (*fatti*) to state; (*teorema, teoria*) to set out

enzima, i [en'dzima] SM enzyme

eolico, a, ci, che [e'ɔliko] AGG (*Geog*) aeolian

epatico, a, ci, che [e'patiko] AGG hepatic; **cirrosi epatica** cirrhosis of the liver

epatite [epa'tite] SF hepatitis; **epatite virale** viral hepatitis

epatta [e'patta] SF (*Astron*) epact

epica ['ɛpika] SF epic (poetry)

epicentro [epi'tʃɛntro] SM epicentre

epico, a, ci, che ['ɛpiko] AGG (*anche fig*) epic

epicureo, a [epiku'rɛo] AGG, SM/F epicurean

Epicuro [epi'kuro] SM Epicurus

epidemia [epide'mia] SF epidemic; **un'epidemia di influenza** a flu epidemic

epidemicamente [epidemika'mente] AVV: **diffondersi epidemicamente** (*anche fig*) to spread like wildfire

epidemico, a, ci, che [epi'dɛmiko] AGG epidemic

epidermico, a, ci, che [epi'dɛrmiko] AGG (*Anat*) skin *attr*; (*fig: interesse, impressione*) superficial

epidermide [epi'dɛrmide] SF (*Anat*) skin, epidermis

epidurale [epidu'rale] SF (*Med*) epidural

Epifania [epifa'nia] SF Epiphany

epiglottide [epi'glɔttide] SF (*Med*) epiglottis

epigono [e'pigono] SM imitator

epigrafe [e'pigrafe] SF epigraph; (*su libro*) dedication

epigrafico, a, ci, che [epi'grafiko] AGG epigraphic; (*fig: stile*) concise

epigramma, i [epi'gramma] SM epigram

epigrammatica [epigram'matika] SF epigrammatic poetry

epigrammatico, a, ci, che [epigram'matiko] AGG epigrammatic

epilatore [epila'tɔre] SM epilator

epilessia [epiles'sia] SF epilepsy

epilettico, a, ci, che [epi'lɛttiko] AGG, SM/F epileptic; **una crisi epilettica** an epileptic fit

epilobio, bi [epi'lɔbjo] SM (*Bot*) willowherb

epilogo, ghi [e'pilogo] SM epilogue; (*fig*) conclusion

episcopale [episko'pale] AGG episcopal

episcopato [episko'pato] SM episcopacy

episodicamente [epizodika'mente] AVV occasionally

episodico, a, ci, che [epi'zɔdiko] AGG (*romanzo, narrazione*) episodic; (*fig: occasionale*) occasional

episodio, di [epi'zɔdjo] SM episode; **sceneggiato a episodi** serial; **un episodio imbarazzante della sua vita** an embarrassing episode in her life; **un grave episodio di intolleranza razziale** a serious instance of racism

epistola [e'pistola] SF epistle

epistolare [episto'lare] AGG epistolary; **essere in rapporto** *o* **relazione epistolare con qn** to correspond *o* be in correspondence with sb

epistolario, ri [episto'larjo] SM letters *pl*

epitaffio, fi [epi'taffjo] SM epitaph

epitelio, li [epi'tɛljo] SM (*Anat*) epithelium

epiteto [e'piteto] SM (*Gramm*) attribute; (*fig*) epithet; **un epiteto irripetibile** an unrepeatable insult

epoca, che ['ɛpoka] SF (*gen*) time; (*periodo storico*) age, era, epoch; (*Geol*) age; **all'epoca di** at the time of; **in epoca bizantina** in the Byzantine era; **viviamo in un'epoca difficile** we live in difficult times *o* in a difficult age; **a quell'epoca** at that time; **a quell'epoca mi trovavo a Londra** at that time I was in London; **mobili d'epoca** period furniture; **fare epoca** (*scandalo*) to cause a stir; (*cantante, moda*) to mark a new era; **lo sbarco sulla luna ha fatto epoca** the moon landing was an epoch-making event

epopea [epo'pɛa] SF (*anche fig*) epic

eppure [ep'pure] CONG and yet, nevertheless; **sembra impossibile, eppure è vero!** it seems impossible, and yet it's true!; **non è venuto all'appuntamento, eppure aveva promesso** he didn't come to the meeting, though he'd promised he would

EPT [epi'ti] SIGLA M (= **Ente Provinciale per il Turismo**) *local tourist bureau*

epurare [epu'rare] VT (*Pol*) to purge

epurazione [epurat'tsjone] SF purge; **epurazione etnica** ethnic cleansing

equalizzatore [ekwaliddza'tore] SM (*Elettr*) equalizer

equamente [ekwa'mente] AVV equitably, fairly

equanime [e'kwanime] AGG (*imparziale*) impartial
equanimità [ekwanimi'ta] SF INV (*imparzialità*) impartiality
equatore [ekwa'tore] SM equator
equatoriale [ekwato'rjale] AGG equatorial; **clima equatoriale** equatorial climate
equazione [ekwat'tsjone] SF equation
equestre [e'kwɛstre] AGG equestrian; **circo equestre** circus; **una statua equestre** an equestrian statue
equidistante [ekwidis'tante] AGG equidistant
equilatero [ekwi'latero] AGG equilateral
equilibrare [ekwili'brare] VT (*gen*) to balance; (*controbilanciare*) to counterbalance; **equilibrare qc con qc** to balance sth against sth (else)
▶ **equilibrarsi** VR (*uso reciproco: forze ecc*) to counterbalance each other
equilibratamente [ekwilibrata'mente] AVV (*giudicare, decidere*) sensibly, judiciously
equilibrato, a [ekwili'brato] AGG (*carico, giudizio, dieta, alimentazione*) balanced; (*persona*) well-balanced
equilibratura [ekwilibra'tura] SF (*Aut*) balancing
equilibrio, ri [ekwi'librjo] SM (*gen*) balance, equilibrium; (*armonia*) harmony; **perdere l'equilibrio** to lose one's balance; **ha perso l'equilibrio ed è caduto** he lost his balance and fell; **stare in equilibrio su** (*persona*) to balance on; (*oggetto*) to be balanced on; **equilibrio mentale** (mental) equilibrium *o* stability; **equilibrio economico** economic stability; **equilibrio politico** balance of power; **è una persona priva di equilibrio** he is not a well-balanced person, he is rather unstable
equilibrismo [ekwili'brizmo] SM tightrope walking; (*fig*) juggling; (*Pol*) balancing act
equilibrista, i, e [ekwili'brista] SM/F tightrope walker
equino, a [e'kwino] AGG horse *attr*, equine; **carne equina** horsemeat; **una razza equina** a breed of horses
equinozio, zi [ekwi'nɔttsjo] SM equinox
equipaggiamento [ekwipaddʒa'mento] SM **1** (*operazione: di nave*) equipping, fitting out; (*: di spedizione, esercito*) equipping, kitting out (*fam*) **2** (*attrezzatura*) equipment, gear; **equipaggiamento da sci/da sub** skiing/diving equipment
equipaggiare [ekwipad'dʒare] VT (*nave, esercito, spedizione*) to equip; (*per uno sport*) to kit out
▶ **equipaggiarsi** VR to equip o.s.
equipaggio, gi [ekwi'paddʒo] SM (*gen, Naut*) crew; (*Aer*) (air)crew; **l'equipaggio dell'aereo** the cabin crew
equiparabile [ekwipa'rabile] AGG comparable
equiparare [ekwipa'rare] VT (*Amm: stipendi, gradi*) to make equal, level
equiparazione [ekwiparat'tsjone] SF levelling
équipe [e'kip] SF INV (*gen, Sport*) team; **lavorare in équipe** to work as a team; **lavoro d'équipe** teamwork
equipollente [ekwipol'lɛnte] AGG equivalent
equità [ekwi'ta] SF INV equity, fairness
equitazione [ekwitat'tsjone] SF (horse-)riding; **c'è una scuola di equitazione qua vicino** there's a riding school near here
equivalente [ekwiva'lɛnte] AGG: **equivalente (a)** equivalent (to)
■ SM equivalent
equivalenza [ekwiva'lɛntsa] SF equivalence
equivalere [ekwiva'lere] VB IRREG
■ VI (*aus* **essere** *o* **avere**) **equivalere a** (*valore*) to be equivalent to; (*affermazione*) to be tantamount to; **equivale a dire che...** that is the same as saying that ...;
▶ **equivalersi** VR (*uso reciproco: forze*) to counterbalance each other; (*: soluzioni*) to amount to the same thing
equivalso, a [ekwi'valso] PP *di* **equivalere**
equivocare [ekwivo'kare] VI (*aus* **avere**) (*capire male*): **equivocare (su qc)** to misunderstand (sth)
equivoco, a, ci, che [e'kwivoko] AGG (*risposta, discorso*) equivocal, ambiguous; (*persona*) shady; (*locale*) disreputable
■ SM (*malinteso*) misunderstanding; **dar luogo a un equivoco** to cause a misunderstanding; **cadere in un equivoco** to misunderstand; **è stato tutto un equivoco** it was all a misunderstanding; **ci dev'essere stato un equivoco** there must have been some misunderstanding; **a scanso di equivoci** (so as) to avoid any misunderstanding, so that it will be perfectly clear
equo, a ['ɛkwo] AGG (*gen*) equitable, fair; **un equo compenso** a fair *o* adequate reward
Era ['ɛra] SF (*Mitol*) Hera
era ['ɛra] SF (*gen*) era; (*Geol*) period; **l'era cristiana** the Christian era; **l'era glaciale** the ice age; **l'era spaziale** the space age
era *ecc* ['ɛra] VB *vedi* **essere**
erariale [era'rjale] AGG: **ufficio erariale** ≈ tax office; **spese erariali** public expenditure *sg*; **imposte erariali** revenue taxes
erario, ri [e'rarjo] SM: **l'erario** ≈ the Treasury
ERASMUS [e'razmus] SIGLA M ERASMUS (= *European (Community) Action Scheme for the Mobility of University Students*)
erba ['ɛrba] SF grass; (*Culin, Med*) herb; (*fam: marijuana*) grass, pot; **in erba** (*fig: pittore, scultore*) budding; **fare di ogni erba un fascio** (*fig*) to lump everything (*o* everybody) together; **eravamo sdraiati sull'erba** we were lying on the grass; **erba cipollina** chives *pl*; **erba medica** lucerne; **erbe aromatiche** herbs
erbaccia, ce [er'battʃa] SF weed
erbaceo, a [er'batʃeo] AGG herbaceous
erbario, ri [er'barjo] SM (*raccolta*) herbarium; (*libro*) herbal
erbette [er'bette] SFPL beet tops
erbicida, i, e [erbi'tʃida] AGG herbicidal
■ SM weed-killer
erbivendolo, a [erbi'vendolo] SM/F greengrocer
erbivoro, a [er'bivoro] AGG herbivorous
■ SM/F herbivore
erborista, i, e [erbo'rista] SM/F herbalist
erboristeria [erboriste'ria] SF (*scienza*) herbalism; (*negozio*) herbalist's (shop)
erboso, a [er'boso] AGG grassy; **tappeto erboso** lawn
Ercole ['ɛrkole] SM (*Mit*) Hercules
erculeo, a [er'kuleo] AGG (*anche fig*) Herculean
erede [e'rɛde] SM/F heir/heiress; **erede di qc** heir to sth; **erede al trono** heir to the throne; **erede legittimo** heir-at-law; **nominare qn proprio erede** to make sb one's heir; **lei è l'unica erede** she's the only heir
eredità [eredi'ta] SF INV **1** (*Dir*) inheritance; (*fig*) heritage; **lasciare qc in eredità a qn** to leave *o* bequeath sth to sb; **suo padre gli ha lasciato in eredità una bella casa** his father left him a beautiful house; **ricevere qc in eredità** to inherit sth; **aveva paura di perdere l'eredità** he was afraid of losing his inheritance **2** (*Bio*) heredity
ereditare [eredi'tare] VT to inherit; **ereditare qc da**

Ee

qn to inherit sth from sb; **ha ereditato la casa del nonno** she inherited her grandfather's house
ereditarietà [ereditarje'ta] SF INV heredity
ereditario, ria, ri, rie [eredi'tarjo] AGG hereditary; **una malattia ereditaria** a hereditary disease
ereditiera [eredi'tjɛra] SF heiress
eremita, i [ere'mita] SM hermit
eremitaggio, gi [eremi'taddʒo] SM hermitage
eremo ['ɛremo] SM hermitage; (*fig*) retreat
eresia [ere'zia] SF (*Rel, fig*) heresy; **dire eresie** (*fig*) to talk nonsense
eressi *ecc* [e'rɛssi] VB *vedi* **erigere**
ereticamente [eretika'mente] AVV heretically
eretico, a, ci, che [e'rɛtiko] AGG heretical
■SM/F heretic
eretto, a [e'rɛtto] PP *di* **erigere**
■AGG (*capo, busto*) erect, upright
erezione [eret'tsjone] SF **1** (*Fisiologia*) erection **2** (*costruzione: di monumento*) raising; (*: di palazzo, chiesa*) building
ergastolano, a [ergasto'lano] SM/F prisoner serving a life sentence, lifer (*fam*)
ergastolo [er'gastolo] SM (*pena*) life imprisonment; (*luogo di pena*) prison (*for those serving life sentence*); **condannato all'ergastolo** given a life sentence; **gli hanno dato tre ergastoli** he was given three life sentences
ergonomia [ergono'mia] SF ergonomics *sg*, biotechnology (*Am*)
ergonomico, a, ci, che [ergo'nɔmiko] AGG ergonomic(al)
ergoterapia [ergotera'pia] SF occupational therapy
erica, che ['ɛrika] SF heather
erigere [e'ridʒere] VB IRREG
■VT (*monumento*) to erect, raise; (*fig: fondare*) to found
▶ **erigersi** VR (*fig: costituirsi*): **erigersi a giudice/difensore (di)** to set o.s. up as a judge/a defender (of)
eritema, i [eri'tɛma] SM (*Med*) inflammation, erythema (*termine tecn*); **eritema solare** sunburn
Eritrea [eri'trɛa] SF Eritrea
eritrocita, i [eritro'tʃita] SM (*Anat*) erythrocyte
ermafrodito, a [ermafro'dito] AGG, SM hermaphrodite
ermellino [ermel'lino] SM (*animale: d'inverno*) ermine; (*: d'estate*) stoat; (*pelliccia*) ermine
ermeticamente [ermetika'mente] AVV hermetically; (*fig*) impenetrably
ermetico, a, ci, che [er'mɛtiko] AGG **1** (*contenitore*) airtight; (*fig: sguardo, volto*) inscrutable, impenetrable; **a chiusura ermetica** hermetically sealed **2** (*Letteratura*) hermetic
ermetismo [erme'tizmo] SM (*Letteratura*) Hermeticism
ernia ['ɛrnja] SF (*Med*) hernia; **ernia del disco** slipped disc
ero *ecc* ['ɛro] VB *vedi* **essere**
Erode [e'rɔde] SM Herod
erodere [e'rodere] VT IRREG to erode
Erodoto [e'rɔdoto] SM Herodotus
eroe [e'rɔe] SM hero
erogare [ero'gare] VT (*gas, luce*) to supply; (*somma*) to distribute
erogatore [eroga'tore] SM supply valve
erogazione [erogat'tsjone] SF (*vedi vb*) supply; distribution
erogeno, a [e'rɔdʒeno] AGG erogenous; **zona erogena** erogenous zone
eroicamente [eroika'mente] AVV heroically
eroico, a, ci, che [e'rɔiko] AGG heroic
eroicomico, a, ci, che [eroi'kɔmiko] AGG mock-heroic
eroina¹ [ero'ina] SF (*donna*) heroine; **l'eroina del romanzo** the heroine of the novel
eroina² [ero'ina] SF (*droga*) heroin; **l'eroina è una droga pesante** heroin is a hard drug
eroinomane [eroi'nɔmane] SM/F heroin addict
eroinomania [eroinoma'nia] SF heroin addiction
eroismo [ero'izmo] SM heroism
erompere [e'rompere] VI IRREG: **erompere (da)** (*lava, folla*) to erupt (from); **erompere in un pianto dirotto** to burst into tears
eros ['ɛros] SM INV Eros
erosione [ero'zjone] SF erosion; **erosione fiscale** tax avoidance
erosivo, a [ero'zivo] AGG erosive
eroso, a [e'roso] PP *di* **erodere**
eroticamente [erotika'mente] AVV erotically
erotico, a, ci, che [e'rɔtiko] AGG erotic
erotismo [ero'tizmo] SM eroticism
erotomane [ero'tɔmane] SM erotomaniac; (*scherz*) sex maniac
erotto [e'rotto] PP *di* **erompere**
erpete ['ɛrpete] SM (*Med*) herpes *sg*
erpice ['ɛrpitʃe] SM (*Agr*) harrow
errabondo, a [erra'bondo] AGG (*letter*) wandering
errante [er'rante] AGG (*letter*) wandering; **cavaliere errante** knight errant
errare [er'rare] VI (*aus* **avere**) **1** (*letter: vagare*): **errare (per)** to wander (about), roam (about); **errare con la fantasia** (*fig*) to let one's imagination wander **2** (*frm: sbagliare*) to be mistaken, make a mistake; **se non erro...** if I'm not mistaken ...
errata corrige [er'rata 'kɔrridʒe] SM INV erratum, corrigendum
erratamente [errata'mente] AVV (*vedi agg*) wrongly; mistakenly
errato, a [er'rato] AGG (*calcolo*) wrong, incorrect; (*idea, interpretazione*) mistaken, erroneous; **se non vado errato** if I am not mistaken
erroneamente [erronea'mente] AVV erroneously, mistakenly
erroneo, a [er'rɔneo] AGG erroneous, mistaken
errore [er'rore] SM mistake, error; **fare un errore** to make a mistake; **non ho fatto neanche un errore** I didn't make a single mistake; **per errore** by mistake; **salvo errori** (*scritto*) errors excepted; (*nel parlare*) if I am not mistaken; **salvo errori ed omissioni** errors and omissions excepted; **è stato un errore di gioventù** it was a youthful error; **errore di calcolo** (*anche fig*) miscalculation; **errore giudiziario** miscarriage of justice; **errore di giudizio** *o* **di valutazione** error of judgment; **errore di ortografia** spelling mistake; **errore di stampa** printing error, misprint
ERSA ['ɛrsa] SIGLA M = *Ente Regionale di Sviluppo Agricolo*
erta ['erta] SF **1** (*salita*) steep slope **2** **stare all'erta** (*vigilare*) to be on the alert
erto, a ['erto] AGG (*letter*) (very) steep
erudire [eru'dire] VT (*frm, scherz*) to teach, educate
eruditamente [erudita'mente] AVV eruditely
erudito, a [eru'dito] AGG (*persona*) learned, erudite; (*opera*) scholarly, learned
■SM/F scholar
erudizione [erudit'tsjone] SF erudition
eruttare [erut'tare] VT (*lava*) to spew (out)
eruttivo, a [erut'tivo] AGG eruptive; **roccia eruttiva** igneous rock

eruzione [erut'tsjone] SF (*Geol*) eruption; (*Med*) rash; **eruzione cutanea** rash

ES ABBR **1** (= **elettroshock**) ECT **2** = **Eurostar**

es. ABBR (= **esempio**) e.g.

ESA SIGLA M (= **European Space Agency**) ESA

esacerbare [ezatʃer'bare] VT to exacerbate

esacerbato, a [ezatʃer'bato] AGG embittered

esagerare [ezadʒe'rare] VI (*aus* **avere**) (*gen*) to exaggerate; (*eccedere*) to go too far; **non esagerare!** don't exaggerate!; **esagerare con le pretese** to demand too much, expect too much; **esagerare con la prudenza** to be overcautious; **senza esagerare** without exaggeration; **non ti sembra di esagerare un po'?** don't you think that's a bit of an exaggeration?; **esagerare nel bere/nel mangiare** to drink/eat too much; **ha esagerato un po' nel bere** he had a bit too much to drink
■ VT to exaggerate

esageratamente [ezadʒerata'mente] AVV excessively

esagerato, a [ezadʒe'rato] AGG (*notizia, proporzioni*) exaggerated; (*curiosità, pignoleria*) excessive; (*prezzo*) exorbitant; **sarebbe esagerato dire che...** it would be an exaggeration to say that ...
■ SM/F: **sei il solito esagerato** you're exaggerating as usual

esagerazione [ezadʒerat'tsjone] SF exaggeration; **costare un'esagerazione** to cost the earth; **che esagerazione!** what nonsense!

esagitato, a [ezadʒi'tato] AGG (*persona, animo*) agitated

esagonale [ezago'nale] AGG hexagonal

esagono [e'zagono] SM hexagon

esalare [eza'lare] VT (*odori*) to give off; **esalare l'ultimo respiro** to breathe one's last
■ VI (*aus* **essere**) **esalare (da)** to emanate (from)

esalazione [ezalat'tsjone] SF (*emissione*) exhalation; (*odore*) fumes *pl*

esaltante [ezal'tante] AGG exciting

esaltare [ezal'tare] VT **1** (*lodare: pregi, virtù*) to extol **2** (*eccitare: immaginazione*) to fire; (*: folla*) to excite, stir
▶ **esaltarsi** VR: **esaltarsi (per qc)** to grow excited (about sth)

esaltato, a [ezal'tato] AGG (*giovane, mente*) overexcited
■ SM/F fanatic

esaltazione [ezaltat'tsjone] SF **1** (*elogio*) extolling **2** (*mistica*) exaltation

esame [e'zame] SM **1** (*gen*) examination, exam; **essere all'esame** to be under examination; **prendere in esame** to examine, consider; **fare un esame di coscienza** to examine one's conscience; **dopo un attento esame della situazione** after careful study *o* consideration of the situation **2** (*Scol*) exam, examination; **dare** *o* **sostenere un esame** to sit (*Brit*) *o* take an exam; **non ho passato l'esame** I didn't pass the exam; **quando saprai il risultato degli esami?** when will you get your exam results?; **esame di guida** driving test **3** (*Med*) examination, test; **farsi fare degli esami** to have some tests done *o* carried out; **gli faranno degli esami** he's having some tests done; **esame del sangue** blood test; **esame della vista** eye test

esaminando, a [ezami'nando] SM/F examinee

esaminare [ezami'nare] VT **1** (*gen*) to examine; (*proposta, elementi*) to consider, examine **2** (*oggetto*) to examine, study **3** (*candidati*) to interview; (*Scol*) to examine

esaminatore, trice [ezamina'tore] AGG examining *attr*
■ SM/F examiner

esangue [e'zangwe] AGG (*pallido*) pale, wan; (*privo di vigore*) lifeless

esanime [e'zanime] AGG lifeless

esasperare [ezaspe'rare] VT (*persona*) to exasperate; (*situazione*) to exacerbate
▶ **esasperarsi** VIP to become exasperated

esasperato, a [ezaspe'rato] AGG exasperated

esasperazione [ezasperat'tsjone] SF exasperation

esattamente [ezatta'mente] AVV exactly; **è esattamente quello che intendevo** it's exactly what I meant

esattezza [ezat'tettsa] SF **1** (*correttezza: di calcolo, affermazione*) accuracy; **per l'esattezza** to be precise; **con esattezza** exactly; **rispondere con esattezza** (*in modo corretto*) to answer correctly, give a *o* the correct answer; (*in modo preciso*) to give a detailed answer **2** (*accuratezza: di persona*) precision

esatto, a [e'zatto] PP *di* **esigere**
■ AGG **1** (*corretto: calcolo, risposta*) correct, right; (*ora*) exact, right; (*dimensioni, quantità*) exact, precise; (*prezzo, peso*) exact; **sono le tre esatte** it's exactly three o'clock; **è l'esatto contrario** it's the exact opposite *o* it's just the opposite; **esatto!** exactly!; **allora, hai deciso di partire? — esatto!** so, you've decided to leave? — that's right!; **non mi ricordo le parole esatte** I can't remember the exact words; **ha dato la risposta esatta** he gave the correct answer **2** (*accurato: resoconto, descrizione*) accurate; (*: impiegato*) careful; **le scienze esatte** the exact sciences

esattore, trice [ezat'tore] SM/F: **esattore delle tasse** tax collector; **esattore del gas/della luce** gas/electricity man

esattoria [ezatto'ria] SF: **esattoria comunale** council tax office (*Brit*), assessor's office (*Am*)

Ee

esaudibile [ezau'dibile] AGG (*desiderio, richiesta*) which can be granted

esaudire [ezau'dire] VT (*desiderio, richiesta*) to grant, fulfil (*Brit*), fulfill (*Am*); (*preghiera*) to answer, grant

esauribile [ezau'ribile] AGG exhaustible

esauriente [ezau'rjɛnte] AGG (*gen*) exhaustive; (*risposta*) complete

esaurientemente [ezaurjente'mente] AVV exhaustively

esaurimento [ezauri'mento] SM (*gen*) exhaustion; **svendita (fino) ad esaurimento della merce** clearance sale; **esaurimento nervoso** nervous breakdown

esaurire [ezau'rire] VT **1** (*consumare: scorte, risorse*) to exhaust, use up; (*: pozzo, miniera*) to exhaust; (*: carburante*) to use up; (*: forze, energie*) to expend, use up; **vorrei una borsa di paglia — mi spiace, le abbiamo esaurite** I'd like a straw bag — I'm sorry we've sold out of them; **l'aereo aveva esaurito il carburante** the plane had run out of fuel **2** (*portare a termine: indagine*) to conclude; (*: argomento*) to exhaust **3** (*persona*) to exhaust, wear out
▶ **esaurirsi** VR (*persona*) to exhaust o.s., wear o.s. out
▶ **esaurirsi** VIP (*provviste*) to run out; (*fondi*) to run out, dry up; (*ispirazione*) to dry up

esaurito, a [ezau'rito] AGG (*gen*) exhausted; (*esausto: persona*) run-down *attr*; (*merci*) sold out; (*libro: non più stampato*) out of print; **tutto esaurito** sold out; **i biglietti erano tutti esauriti** all the tickets were sold out; **registrare il tutto esaurito** (*teatro*) to have a full house; **essere esaurito** (*persona*) to be worn out; **sono un po' esaurito** I'm a bit run-down

esausto, a [e'zausto] AGG (*spossato*) exhausted, worn out; **sono esausta!** I'm exhausted!

esautorare [ezauto'rare] VT (*dirigente, funzionario*) to deprive of authority; (*parlamento, istituzione*) to reduce the authority of

esazione [ezat'tsjone] SF collection (of taxes)

esborso [ez'borso] SM (*Amm*) disbursement

esca ['eska] SF (*anche fig*) bait; **mettere l'esca all'amo** to bait the hook

escalation [eskə'leiʃən] SF INV (*Mil*) escalation; **un'escalation di violenza** a rising spiral of violence

escamotage [ɛskamɔ'taʒ] SM INV subterfuge

escandescenza [eskandeʃʃɛntsa] SF: **dare in escandescenze** to fly into a rage

escatologia [eskatolo'dʒia] SF (*Rel*) eschatology

escavatore, trice [eskava'tore] AGG excavating
■ SM/F (*macchina*) excavator

escavazione [eskavat'tsjone] SF excavation

esce *ecc* ['ɛʃʃe] VB *vedi* **uscire**

Eschilo ['ɛskilo] SM Aeschylus

eschimese [eski'mese] AGG, SM/F, SM Eskimo

esci *ecc* ['ɛʃʃi] VB *vedi* **uscire**

escl. ABBR (= **escluso**) excl.

esclamare [eskla'mare] VI (*aus* **avere**) to exclaim, cry out

esclamativo, a [esklama'tivo] AGG: **punto esclamativo** exclamation mark

esclamazione [esklamat'tsjone] SF exclamation

escludere [es'kludere] VT IRREG **1** (*estromettere*): **escludere qn (da)** to exclude sb (from); **fu escluso dall'elenco** his name was left off the list; **è stato escluso dalla gara** he was excluded from the competition **2** (*ritenere o rendere impossibile*) to rule out, exclude; **escludo che si tratti di omicidio** I think we can rule out murder; **la polizia ha escluso la tesi del suicidio** the police ruled out *o* excluded the possibility of suicide; **una teoria esclude l'altra** one theory excludes another; **vieni domani? — lo escludo!** *o* **è escluso!** are you coming tomorrow? — it's out of the question!

esclusi *ecc* [es'kluzi] VB *vedi* **escludere**

esclusione [esklu'zjone] SF exclusion; **a esclusione di** *o* **fatta esclusione per** except (for), apart from; **senza esclusione (alcuna)** without exception; **senza esclusione di colpi** (*fig*) with no holds barred; **procedere per esclusione** to follow a process of elimination; **esclusione sociale** social exclusion

esclusiva [esklu'ziva] SF **1** (*Comm*): **avere l'esclusiva di qc** to be the sole agent for sth; **avere l'esclusiva di vendita** to have the exclusive *o* sole selling rights **2** (*Stampa*) exclusive; **intervista in esclusiva** exclusive interview

esclusivamente [eskluziva'mente] AVV exclusively, solely; **non è una professione esclusivamente femminile** it's not an exclusively female profession; **la colpa è esclusivamente tua** the fault is entirely yours

esclusivismo [eskluzi'vizmo] SM intransigence; (*Pol, Econ*) preferential treatment

esclusivista, i, e [eskluzi'vista] SM/F **1** intransigent person **2** (*Comm*) sole agent

esclusivo, a [esklu'zivo] AGG exclusive; **un ristorante esclusivo** an exclusive restaurant

escluso, a [es'kluzo] PP *di* **escludere**
■ AGG: **nessuno escluso** without exception; **è escluso che venga** there is no question of his coming; **non è escluso che lo si faccia** the possibility can't be ruled out, we (*o* they) might do it; **tutti lo sapevano, escluso me** everybody knew about it, except me; **costa cinquecento sterline, escluso l'albergo** it costs five hundred pounds, not including the hotel; **IVA esclusa** excluding VAT, exclusive of VAT

esco *ecc* ['ɛsko] VB *vedi* **uscire**

escogitare [eskodʒi'tare] VT to devise, think up

escono ['ɛskono] VB *vedi* **uscire**

escoriare [esko'rjare] VT to graze
► **escoriarsi** VR to graze o.s.

escoriazione [eskorjat'tsjone] SF abrasion, graze

escrementi [eskre'menti] SMPL excrement *sg*, faeces *pl*

escrescenza [eskreʃʃɛntsa] SF (*Bio*) excrescence

escrezione [eskret'tsjone] SF excretion

escudo [es'kudo] SM (*pl* **escudos**) escudo

escursione [eskur'sjone] SF **1** (*gita*) excursion, trip; (: *a piedi*) hike, walk; **escursione in montagna** hillwalking **2** (*Meteor*): **escursione termica** temperature range

escursionista, i, e [eskursjo'nista] SM/F (*gitante*) (day) tripper; (: *a piedi*) hiker, walker

esecrabile [eze'krabile] AGG execrable, abominable

esecrabilmente [ezekrabil'mente] AVV abominably

esecrando, a [eze'krando] AGG (*letter*) abhorrent, abominable

esecrare [eze'krare] VT to abhor, loathe; (*persona*) to loathe

esecutivo, a [ezeku'tivo] AGG executive; **(potere) esecutivo** executive power
■ SM (*comitato*) executive committee

esecutore, trice [ezeku'tore] SM/F **1** (*Dir*): **esecutore (testamentario)** executor/executrix; **l'esecutore del progetto** the person who realized the project **2** (*Mus*) performer

esecuzione [ezekut'tsjone] SF **1** (*di lavoro, ordini, piano*) execution, carrying out; (*Mus*) performance; **mettere in esecuzione** *o* **dare esecuzione a** (*progetto, ordine*) to carry out; **è responsabile dell'esecuzione dei lavori** he's responsible for carrying out the work **2** (*Dir*) execution; **esecuzione capitale** execution

esegesi [eze'dʒɛzi] SF exegesis

esegeta, i, e [eze'dʒɛta] SM/F commentator

eseguibile [eze'gwibile] SM (*Inform*) executable

eseguire [eze'gwire] VT (*lavoro, ordini, piano*) to carry out, execute; (*Mus: sinfonia, pezzo*) to perform, execute; **ha fatto eseguire dei lavori** he had some work done; **eseguire un pagamento** to make a payment; **eseguire un programma** (*Inform*) to run a program; **"Esegui"** "Run"; **stava solo eseguendo gli ordini** he was only carrying out orders; **ha eseguito un valzer di Chopin** she performed a waltz by Chopin

esempio, pi [e'zɛmpjo] SM example; **ad** *o* **per esempio** for example *o* instance; **citare come** *o* **ad esempio** to quote as an example; **dare il buon/cattivo esempio** to set a good/bad example; **essere un esempio di virtù** to be a paragon of virtue; **fare un esempio** to give an example; **fammi un esempio** give me an example; **prendere (l')esempio da qn** to follow sb's example; **che ti serva d'esempio!** let that be a lesson to you!; **un esempio per tutti noi** an example to us all

esemplare[1] [ezem'plare] AGG (*vita, punizione*) exemplary; (*allievo*) model *attr*; **dare una punizione esemplare a qn** to make an example of sb

esemplare[2] [ezem'plare] SM (*Bot, Zool, Geol*) specimen; (*di francobollo, moneta*) example; (*di libro*) copy; **un esemplare rarissimo** a very rare specimen

esemplarmente [ezemplar'mente] AVV in an exemplary way
esemplificare [ezemplifi'kare] VT to illustrate
esemplificativo, a [ezemplifika'tivo] AGG illustrative
esemplificazione [ezemplifikat'tsjone] SF *(atto)* exemplification; *(esempio)* example
esentare [ezen'tare] VT: **esentare qn/qc (da qc)** to exempt sb/sth (from sth)
esentasse [ezen'tasse] AGG INV tax-free
esente [e'zɛnte] AGG: **esente da** *(dispensato da)* exempt from; **esente da dazio** duty-free; **esente da tasse** *o* **imposte** untaxed; **anche lui non è esente da difetti** even he has his failings
esenzione [ezen'tsjone] SF: **esenzione (da)** exemption (from); **esenzione fiscale** tax exemption
esequie [e'zɛkwje] SFPL funeral rites, obsequies
esercente [ezer'tʃɛnte] SM/F *(gestore)* trader, owner of a business
esercitare [ezertʃi'tare] VT **1** *(professione)* to practise *(Brit)*, practice *(Am)*; *(diritto)* to exercise; **esercitare (su)** *(controllo, influenza)* to exert (over); *(pressione)* to exert (on); *(autorità, potere)* to exercise (over); **esercitare il proprio controllo su qn** to exert control over sb; **quel medico non esercita più** that doctor is no longer in practice **2** *(corpo, mente, voce)* to train, exercise
▶ **esercitarsi** VR *(sportivo)* to train; *(musicista)* to practise; **esercitarsi nella guida** to practise one's driving; **esercitarsi a fare qc** to practise doing sth; **esercitarsi in palestra** to train in the gym
esercitazione [ezertʃitat'tsjone] SF **1** *(Univ: di materie scientifiche)* practical (class); *(: di lingue)* language class **2** *(Mil)*: **esercitazione navale/militare** naval/military exercise; **esercitazioni di tiro** target practice *sg*
esercito [e'zɛrtʃito] SM *(Mil)* army; *(fig: di persone)* host
esercizio, zi [ezer'tʃittsjo] SM **1** *(compito, movimento)* exercise; **abbiamo fatto un esercizio di matematica** we did a maths exercise; **essere fuori esercizio** to be out of practice; **fare (molto) esercizio** *(pratica)* to practise *(Brit)* *o* practice *(Am)* a lot; *(movimento)* to take a lot of exercise; **questi esercizi sviluppano gli addominali** these exercises develop the abdominal muscles **2** *(di professione, culto)* practice; *(di diritto)* exercising; *(di funzioni)* exercise; **nell'esercizio delle proprie funzioni** in the execution of one's duties **3** *(Comm, Amm: gestione)* running, management; *(: azienda gestita)* business, concern; **costi d'esercizio** overheads; **quella ditta è in esercizio da pochi mesi** that firm has only been in business for a few months; **aprire un esercizio** to set up a business, open a shop *(o* bar *o* restaurant *ecc)*; **pubblico esercizio** commercial concern; **licenza d'esercizio** licence to trade **4** *(Fin: anche:* **esercizio finanziario***)* financial year; **il bilancio dell'esercizio 2005** the budget for the 2005 financial year
esfoliante [esfo'ljante] SM exfoliator
esfoliazione [esfoljat'tsjone] SF *(Med)* exfoliation
esibire [ezi'bire] VT *(bravura, capacità)* to exhibit, display; *(documenti)* to produce, present
▶ **esibirsi** VR *(attore, artista)* to perform; *(fig)* to show off
esibizione [ezibit'tsjone] SF **1** *(spettacolo)* performance, show **2** *(sfoggio)* exhibition, showing off **3** *(di documento)* presentation
esibizionismo [ezibittsjo'nizmo] SM **1** *(mettersi in mostra)* exhibitionism **2** *(Psic)* exhibitionism; *(Dir)* indecent exposure
esibizionista, i, e [ezibittsjo'nista] SM/F exhibitionist; *(Psic)* exhibitionist, flasher *(Brit fam)*
esigente [ezi'dʒɛnte] AGG demanding; **un cliente molto esigente** a very demanding customer; **è esigente nel mangiare** he's particular about his food
esigenza [ezi'dʒɛntsa] SF requirement, need; **avere troppe esigenze** to be too demanding; **andare incontro alle esigenze del mercato** *o* **dei consumatori** to meet the demands of the market *o* of consumers; **sentire l'esigenza di qc/di fare qc** to feel the need for sth/to do sth
esigere [e'zidʒere] VT IRREG **1** *(pretendere)* to demand; *(comportare, richiedere)* to require, call for; **esigere qc da qn** to demand sth from *o* of sb; **il proprietario esige il pagamento immediato** the owner is demanding immediate payment; **esigere che qn faccia qc** to expect sb to do sth; **esige il rispetto di tutti** he demands everybody's respect; **è un lavoro che esige molta concentrazione** it's a job which demands a lot of concentration; **esigere troppo da se stessi** to expect too much of oneself **2** *(riscuotere: debito)* to collect
esigibile [ezi'dʒibile] AGG *(assegno, somma)* payable
esiguità [ezigui'ta] SF INV *(di patrimonio, compenso)* meagreness; *(di risorse)* scarcity
esiguo, a [e'ziguo] AGG *(numero, quantità)* small, tiny; *(patrimonio, compenso)* meagre; *(risorse)* scanty
esilarante [ezila'rante] AGG hilarious; **gas esilarante** laughing gas
esile ['ɛzile] AGG *(persona)* slender, slim; *(stelo)* thin; *(voce)* faint; **un esile filo di speranza** a faint ray of hope, a glimmer of hope
esiliare [ezi'ljare] VT *(Pol)* to exile; *(fig)* to banish
▶ **esiliarsi** VR *(Pol)* to go into exile
esiliato, a [ezi'ljato] AGG exiled
■ SM/F exile
esilio, li [e'ziljo] SM exile; **vive in esilio da diversi anni** he's been living in exile for several years; **mandare in esilio** to exile
esilità [ezili'ta] SF INV *(vedi agg)* slenderness, slimness; thinness; faintness
esilmente [ezil'mente] AVV *(debolmente)* faintly, feebly
esimere [e'zimere] VT: **esimere qn da qc** to exempt sb from sth
▶ **esimersi** VR: **esimersi da qc/dal fare qc** to get out of sth/doing sth
esimio, mia, mi, mie [e'zimjo] AGG distinguished, eminent; **un esimio cretino** *(iro)* a prize idiot
Esiodo [e'ziodo] SM Hesiod
esistente [ezis'tɛnte] AGG *(gen)* existing; **tuttora esistente** *(persona)* still alive *o* living; *(casa)* which still stands
esistenza [ezis'tɛntsa] SF *(gen)* existence; *(vita)* life, existence
esistenziale [ezisten'tsjale] AGG existential
esistenzialismo [ezistentsja'lizmo] SM existentialism
esistenzialista, i, e [ezistentsja'lista] AGG, SM/F existentialist
esistenzialistico, a, ci, che [ezistentsja'listiko] AGG existentialist
esistere [e'zistere] VI IRREG *(aus* **essere***)* *(gen)* to exist; **esistono ancora dubbi in merito** there are still some doubts about it; **questo modello esiste in due colori** this model comes *o* is available in two colours; **Babbo**

Ee

Natale non esiste Santa Claus doesn't exist; **non esiste!** (*fam*) no way!
esistito, a [ezis'tito] PP *di* **esistere**
esitante [ezi'tante] AGG hesitant, faltering
esitare [ezi'tare] VI (*aus* **avere**) to hesitate; **esitava a prendere una decisione** he was reluctant to take a decision; **esitava tra il sì e il no** he wasn't sure whether to say yes or no; **esitò a rispondere** he hesitated before answering; **senza esitare** without (any) hesitation
esitazione [ezitat'tsjone] SF hesitation; **dopo molte esitazioni** after much hesitation; **senza esitazioni** unhesitatingly, without (any) hesitation
esito ['ɛzito] SM result, outcome; **avere buon esito** to be successful; **le analisi hanno avuto esito negativo** the results of the tests were negative; **l'esito degli esami** the exam results
esiziale [ezit'tsjale] AGG (*frm*) fatal, disastrous
eskimo ['ɛskimo] SM (*giaccone*) parka
esodo ['ɛzodo] SM exodus; **l'esodo di Ferragosto** ≈ the August bank holiday exodus; **l'esodo dei capitali all'estero** the outflow of funds into overseas investments; **l'Esodo** (*Bibbia*) the Exodus
esofago, gi [e'zɔfago] SM oesophagus (*Brit*), esophagus (*Am*)
esogeno, a [e'zɔdʒeno] AGG (*Med, Geog, Geol*) external; **fenomeni esogeni** external processes
esonerare [ezone'rare] VT: **esonerare da** (*servizio militare*) to exempt from; (*lezioni*) to excuse from
esonero [e'zɔnero] SM exemption
Esopo [e'zɔpo] SM Aesop
esorbitante [ezorbi'tante] AGG exorbitant, excessive
esorbitare [ezorbi'tare] VI (*aus* **avere**) **esorbitare da** to go beyond
esorcismo [ezor'tʃizmo] SM exorcism
esorcista, i [ezor'tʃista] SM exorcist
esorcizzare [ezortʃid'dzare] VT (*anche fig*) to exorcize
esordiente [ezor'djɛnte] AGG: **un attore/calciatore esordiente** an actor/footballer making his professional debut
■ SM/F (*attore, giocatore*) newcomer
esordio, di [e'zɔrdjo] SM debut, first appearance; **un'attrice al suo esordio come regista** an actress making her directorial debut; **questo è il suo esordio in nazionale** this is his debut in the national team; **la sua carriera è ancora agli esordi** his career is just beginning
esordire [ezor'dire] VI (*aus* **avere**) (*Cine, Teatro, Mus, Sport*) to make one's debut; (*fig*) to start out, begin (one's career); **esordì giovanissima** she made her debut when she was very young; **esordì dicendo che...** he began by saying (that) ...
esortare [ezor'tare] VT to exhort, urge; **esortare qn a fare qc** to urge sb to do sth; **lo esortai a partire al più presto** I urged him to leave as soon as possible
esortativo, a [ezorta'tivo] AGG exhortatory
esortazione [ezortat'tsjone] SF exhortation
esosità [ezozi'ta] SF INV (*vedi agg*) exorbitance; greed
esoso, a [e'zɔzo] AGG **1** (*prezzo*) exorbitant **2** (*persona: avido*) grasping
esoterico, a, ci, che [ezo'tɛriko] AGG esoteric
esotermico, a, ci, che [ezo'tɛrmiko] AGG (*Chim*) exothermic
esoticamente [ezotika'mente] AVV exotically
esotico, a, ci, che [e'zɔtiko] AGG exotic; **frutta esotica** exotic fruit
esotismo [ezo'tizmo] SM exoticism
espadrilles [ɛspa'drij] SFPL espadrilles
espandere [es'pandere] VT IRREG (*gen*) to expand; (*confini*) to extend; (*influenza*) to extend, widen
▶ **espandersi** VIP to expand; (*influenza*) to spread
espandibile [espan'dibile] AGG (*Inform: memoria*) expandable
espansione [espan'sjone] SF (*estensione*) expansion; **in espansione** (*economia*) booming; (*universo*) expanding; **a espansione** (*Tecn: motori*) expansion *attr*
espansionismo [espansjo'nizmo] SM expansionism
espansionistico, a, ci, che [espansjo'nistiko] AGG expansionist
espansività [espansivi'ta] SF INV expansiveness
espansivo, a [espan'sivo] AGG (*persona*) expansive, communicative; **poco espansivo** reserved, not very forthcoming
espanso, a [es'panso] PP *di* **espandere**
espatriare [espa'trjare] VI (*aus* **essere**) to leave the country
espatrio, ri [es'patrjo] SM expatriation; **permesso di espatrio** authorization to leave the country
espediente [espe'djɛnte] SM expedient; **cercare un espediente per trarsi d'impaccio** to try and find a way out of a difficult situation; **vivere di espedienti** to live by *o* on one's wits
espellere [es'pɛllere] VT IRREG **1** **espellere (da)** (*da partito, associazione, scuola*) to expel (from); (*da paese*) to deport (from); **l'hanno espulso dalla scuola** he was expelled from the school; **espellere (dal campo)** (*Sport*) to send off (the field); **tutt'e due i calciatori sono stati espulsi** both players were sent off **2** (*gas*) to discharge; (*cartucce usate*) to eject
esperanto [espe'ranto] SM Esperanto
Esperidi [es'pɛridi] SFPL Hesperides
esperienza [espe'rjɛntsa] SF **1** experience; **senza esperienza** inexperienced; **avere molta esperienza di/in** to have a lot of experience of/in; **parlare/sapere per esperienza** to speak/know from experience; **fare** *o* **acquisire esperienza** to gain experience; **ha dieci anni di esperienza nell'insegnamento** he has ten years' teaching experience; **è stata un'esperienza molto utile** it was a very useful experience; **esperienze di lavoro** work experience **2** (*scientifico*) experiment
esperimento [esperi'mento] SM experiment; **a titolo di esperimento** by way of experiment; **sottoporre qc ad esperimento** to carry out an experiment on sth; **fare un esperimento** to carry out *o* do an experiment; **esperimenti nucleari** nuclear tests; **esperimenti sugli animali** animal experiments
espertamente [esperta'mente] AVV expertly
esperto, a [es'pɛrto] AGG **1** (*competente*) expert; (*operaio*) skilled **2** (*che ha esperienza*) experienced; **è abbastanza esperto nella guida** he is a fairly experienced driver
■ SM/F expert; **è un esperto di botanica** he is an expert on botany; **un esperto di computer** a computer expert
espettorare [espetto'rare] VT (*Med*) to expectorate
espiantare [espjan'tare] VT (*organo*) to transplant
espianto [es'pjanto] SM (*Med*) removal
espiare [espi'are] VT to expiate, atone for
espiatorio, ria, ri, rie [espia'tɔrjo] AGG expiatory
espiazione [espiat'tsjone] SF: **espiazione (di)** expiation (of), atonement (for)
espirare [espi'rare] VT, VI (*aus* **avere**) to breathe out, exhale

espirazione [espirat'tsjone] SF breathing out, exhalation
espletamento [espleta'mento] SM (*Amm*) carrying out; **l'espletamento delle pratiche richiede due mesi** the completion of all formalities will require two months
espletare [esple'tare] VT (*Amm*) to carry out
esplicare [espli'kare] VT (*incarico, attività*) to carry out, perform
esplicativo, a [esplika'tivo] AGG explanatory
esplicazione [esplikat'tsjone] SF (*di incarico, attività*) carrying out, performance
esplicitamente [esplitʃita'mente] AVV explicitly
esplicito, a [es'plitʃito] AGG explicit; **proposizione esplicita** (*Gramm*) sentence (*containing finite verb*)
esplodere [es'plɔdere] VI IRREG (*aus* **essere**) (*anche fig*) to explode; (*bomba*) to explode, blow up; **far esplodere una bomba** to explode a bomb; **esplodere per la rabbia** to explode with anger; **esplodere in una risata** to burst out laughing; **è esplosa l'estate** summer has arrived with a bang; **l'ordigno è esploso uccidendo tre persone** the bomb exploded, killing three people
■ VT: **esplodere un colpo contro qn** to fire a shot at sb
esplorare [esplo'rare] VT **1** (*gen, fig*) to explore; **appena arrivati siamo usciti ad esplorare la città** as soon as we arrived we went out to explore the town **2** (*Mil*) to reconnoitre
esplorativo, a [esplora'tivo] AGG exploratory
esploratore, trice [esplora'tore] SM/F explorer; **giovani esploratori** (boy) scouts
■ SM (*militare*) scout; (: *nave*) scout (ship)
esplorazione [esplorat'tsjone] SF exploration; (*Mil*) reconnaissance; **mandare qn in esplorazione** to send sb to scout ahead
esplosione [esplo'zjone] SF (*gen, fig: di moda, crisi*) explosion; (: *di rabbia, gioia*) outburst; **esplosione demografica** population explosion; **l'esplosione ha distrutto il palazzo** the explosion destroyed the building
esplosivo, a [esplo'zivo] AGG, SM explosive; **una notizia esplosiva** a bombshell
esploso, a [es'plɔzo] PP *di* **esplodere**
■ AGG (*disegno*) exploded
■ SM exploded view
esponente [espo'nɛnte] SM/F (*rappresentante*) exponent, representative
■ SM (*Mat*) exponent
esponenziale [esponen'tsjale] AGG (*Mat*) exponential
espongo [es'pongo], **esponi** *ecc* [es'poni] VB *vedi* esporre
esporre [es'porre] VB IRREG
■ VT **1** (*esibire: merce*) to put on display, display; (: *quadri*) to exhibit, show; (: *avviso*) to put up; (: *bandiera*) to put out, raise; **esposto al pubblico** on display to the public; **ha esposto la merce in vetrina** he displayed the goods in the window; **espone i suoi quadri in una galleria d'arte** he's showing his paintings in an art gallery **2** (*spiegare*) to explain; (*argomento, teoria*) to put forward, expound; (*fatti, ragionamenti*) to set out; (*dubbi, riserve*) to express; **esporre a voce/per iscritto** to explain verbally/in writing; **ha esposto i fatti con grande chiarezza** she explained the facts very clearly **3** (*mettere in pericolo*): **esporre qn al pericolo** to expose sb to danger; **esporre il fianco a critiche** to lay o.s. open to criticism **4** (*alla luce, all'aria, anche Fot*) to expose
▶ **esporsi** VR: **esporsi a** (*sole, pericolo*) to expose o.s. to; (*critiche*) to lay o.s. open to; **stai attento a non esporti troppo** (*compromettersi*) be careful about sticking your neck out
esportare [espor'tare] VT to export
esportatore, trice [esporta'tore] AGG exporting *attr*
■ SM/F exporter
esportazione [esportat'tsjone] SF (*azione*) exportation, export; (*di prodotti*) exports *pl*; **di esportazione** (*agenzia, permesso*) export *attr*; **prodotti per l'esportazione** export goods
espose *ecc* [es'pose] VB *vedi* **esporre**
esposimetro [espo'zimetro] SM (*Fot*) exposure meter, light meter
espositore, trice [espozi'tore] AGG exhibiting
■ SM/F exhibitor
esposizione [espozit'tsjone] SF **1** (*di merce*) display; (*di fatti, ragioni: narrazione*) exposition; (: *spiegazione*) explanation **2** (*fiera, mostra*) exhibition, show **3** (*posizione di casa*) aspect; **casa con esposizione a nord** house facing north, north-facing house **4** (*Fot, al sole*) exposure; **tempo di esposizione** (*Fot*) shutter speed
esposto, a [es'posto] PP *di* **esporre**
■ AGG **1** (*edificio*): **esposto a nord** facing north, north-facing; **la casa è esposta a nord** the house faces north **2** (*Med: frattura*) compound *attr* **3** (*Alpinismo: passaggio, via*) exposed
■ SM (*Amm*) statement, account; (: *petizione*) petition; **fare un esposto a qn** to submit a report to sb, give sb a report
espressamente [espressa'mente] AVV (*esplicitamente*) expressly, explicitly; (*appositamente*) especially
espressione [espres'sjone] SF (*gen, Mat*) expression; **libertà di espressione** freedom of expression; **ha usato un'espressione volgare** he used a coarse expression; **avere un'espressione stupita** to look surprised
espressionismo [espressjo'nizmo] SM expressionism
espressionista, i, e [espressjo'nista] AGG, SM/F expressionist
espressività [espressivi'ta] SF INV expressiveness
espressivo, a [espres'sivo] AGG expressive; **silenzio espressivo** eloquent silence
espresso[1], a [es'prɛsso] PP *di* **esprimere**
espresso[2], a [es'prɛsso] AGG (*desiderio, treno*) express; (*caffè*) espresso; **un caffè espresso** an espresso
■ SM (*lettera*) express letter; (*treno*) express; (*caffè*) espresso (coffee); **un espresso e un cappuccino, per favore** an espresso and a cappuccino, please; **abbiamo preso l'espresso per Roma** we took the express train to Rome
esprimere [es'primere] VB IRREG
■ VT to express; (*opinione*) to voice, express; **ognuno è libero di esprimere il proprio parere** everybody's free to express their own opinion; **esprimere un desiderio** to make a wish; **dai, esprimi un desiderio!** go on, make a wish!;
▶ **esprimersi** VIP to express o.s.; **trovo difficile esprimermi in inglese** I find it difficult to express myself in English; **esprimersi a gesti** to use sign language
esprimibile [espri'mibile] AGG expressible
espropriare [espro'prjare] VT (*terreni, edifici*) to place a compulsory purchase order on; **l'hanno espropriato dei suoi beni** they dispossessed him of his property, they expropriated his property

espropriazione [espropjat'tsjone] SF, **esproprio, pri** [es'prɔprjo] SM expropriation; **espropriazione per pubblica utilità** compulsory purchase
espugnare [espuɲ'ɲare] VT to take by force, storm
espulsi *ecc* [es'pulsi] VB *vedi* **espellere**
espulsione [espul'sjone] SF (*da partito, scuola ecc*) expulsion; (*da paese*) deportation; (*dal campo di gioco*) sending off
espulso, a [es'pulso] PP *di* **espellere**
essa ['essa] PRON F (*fpl* **esse**) *vedi* **esso**
essenza [es'sɛntsa] SF **1** (*di argomento*) gist, essence; (*Filosofia*) essence **2** (*estratto: di piante*) (essential) oil, essence; (: *alimentare*) essence
essenziale [essen'tsjale] AGG: **essenziale (a)** essential (to *o* for); (*stile, linguaggio*) simple; **olio essenziale** essential oil; **requisiti essenziali** prerequisites
■ SM: **l'essenziale** (*l'importante*) the main *o* most important thing; (*oggetti necessari*) the (basic) essentials *pl*; (*punti principali*) the essentials *pl*; **riduciamo il discorso all'essenziale** let's restrict our discussion to the basic *o* essential points; **l'essenziale è che venga** the main *o* important thing is that he should come; **l'essenziale è che tu sia arrivato sano e salvo** the main thing is that you got here safe and sound
essenzialmente [essentsjal'mente] AVV essentially, basically

essere ['ɛssere] (*aus* **essere**) PAROLA CHIAVE
■ VI
1 (*copulativo*) to be; **chi è quel tipo? — è Giovanni** who is that (guy)? — it's Giovanni; **è giovane/malato** he is young/ill; **siamo in dieci a volerci andare** there are ten of us wanting to go *o* who want to go; **è (un) professore** he is a teacher; **non è vero** that's not true
2 (*trovarsi*) to be; (*vivere*) to live; **essere in piedi** to be standing; **sono qui da tre ore** I've been here for three hours; **è a Roma dal 1990** he's been (living) in Rome since 1990; **è a tavola** he is eating
3 (*diventare*) to be; **quando sarai calmo** when you calm down; **quando sarai grande** when you grow up *o* are grown up; **quando sarai medico** when you are a doctor
4 (*esistere*) to be; **essere o non essere** to be or not to be; **sia la luce – e la luce fu** let there be light – and there was light; **è il miglior meccanico che ci sia** he is the best mechanic there is
5 (*provenire*): **è di Genova** he is *o* comes from Genoa
6 (*appartenenza*): **di chi è questo libro? — è mio** whose book is this? — it's mine; **non potrò essere dei vostri quest'estate** I won't be able to join you this summer
7 (*data*): **è il 12 giugno** it is June 12th; **era il 1962** it was 1962; **erano gli anni Sessanta** it was the Sixties
8 (*ora*): **che ora è?** *o* **che ore sono? — sono le due** what's the time? *o* what time is it? — it's two o'clock; **saranno state le cinque** it must have been five o'clock
9 (*+ da + infinito*): **è da fare subito** it should be done *o* needs to be done *o* is to be done immediately; **è da spedire stasera** it has (got) to be sent tonight
■ VB AUS
1 (*tempi composti: attivo*): **è arrivato?** has he arrived?; **è arrivato ieri?** did he arrive yesterday?; **è andato in Inghilterra** he has gone to England; **è stato in Inghilterra** he has been to England; **sono cresciuto in Italia** I grew up in Italy
2 (*tempi composti: passivo*): **è stato fabbricato in India** it was made in India; **è stato investito da un'auto** he was run over by a car
3 (*tempi composti: riflessivo*): **si sono vestiti** they dressed, they got dressed; (: *reciproco*): **si sono baciati** they kissed; **non si sono visti** they didn't see each other
■ VB IMPERS
1 **è che non mi piace** the fact is I don't like it; **che ne sarà della macchina?** what will happen to the car?; **sarà come dici tu** you may be right; **come sarebbe a dire?** what do you mean?; **come se niente fosse** as if nothing had happened; **è da tre ore che ti aspetto** I've been waiting for you for three hours; **non è da te** it's not like you; **sia detto fra noi** between you and me; **è Pasqua** it's Easter; **è possibile che venga** he may come; **può essere** perhaps; **sarà quel che sarà** what will be will be; **sia quel che sia, io me ne vado** whatever happens I'm off; **è tardi** it's late
2 (*costare*): **sono 200 euro** that's 200 euros, that comes to 200 euros; **quant'è?** how much is it?; **quant'è in tutto?** how much does that come to?
3 **esserci: c'è** there is, **ci sono** there are; **non c'è altro da dire** there's nothing else to be said *o* there's nothing more one can say; **che (cosa) c'è?** what's wrong *o* the matter?; **che c'è di nuovo?** what's new?; **ci sono 60 chilometri** it's 60 kilometres; **cosa c'è** what's wrong *o* the matter?; **c'è da strapparsi i capelli** it's enough to drive you up the wall; **ce n'è per tutti** there's enough for everybody; **quanti invitati ci saranno?** how many guests will there be?; **quanto c'è da qui a Edimburgo?** how far is it from here to Edinburgh?; **c'era una volta...** once upon a time there was ...; *vedi anche* **ci**
■ SM being; **essere umano** human being; **gli esseri viventi** the living *pl*

essi ['essi] PRON MPL *vedi* **esso**
essiccare [essik'kare] VT (*gen*) to dry; (*legname*) to season; (*bacino, palude*) to drain
► **essiccarsi** VIP (*fiume, pozzo*) to dry up; (*vernice*) to dry (out)
essiccatoio, oi [essikka'tojo] SM (*Industria tessile*) dryer; (*per grano, mais*) drying warehouse; (*per pelli*) drying room
essiccatore [essikka'tore] SM (*Chim*) desiccator
essiccazione [essikkat'tsjone] SF drying (process); (*Chim*) desiccation
esso, a ['esso] PRON PERS (NEUTRO) it; (*riferito a persona*: *sogg*) he/she; (: *complemento*) him/her; **essi** *o* **esse** (*sogg*) they; (*complemento*) them; **...o chi per esso** ... or his delegate *o* representative
est [ɛst] SM **1** east; **a est (di)** east (of); **a est di Palermo** east of Palermo; **si trova a est della città** it's east of the city; **il sole sorge a est** the sun rises in the east; **verso est** eastward(s); **il vento dell'est** the east wind **2** (*Pol*): **l'Est** the East; **l'Europa dell'Est** Eastern Europe; **i paesi dell'Est** the Eastern bloc *sg*
■ AGG INV (*gen*) east; (*regione*) eastern; **è partito in direzione est** he set off eastwards *o* in an eastward direction
estasi ['ɛstazi] SF INV (*Rel, fig*) ecstasy; **andare in estasi (per)** (*fig*) to go into ecstasies *o* raptures (over); **mandare in estasi** to send into ecstasies *o* raptures
estasiare [esta'zjare] VT to send into raptures
► **estasiarsi** VIP: **estasiarsi (a, davanti a)** to go into ecstasies *o* raptures (over)
estate [es'tate] SF summer; **d'estate** *o* **in estate** in (the) summer; **un giorno d'estate** one summer's day,

one day in summer; **passa l'estate al mare** she spends the summer by the sea

LO SAPEVI...?
estate non si traduce mai con la parola inglese *estate*

estaticamente [estatika'mente] AVV ecstatically
estatico, a, ci, che [es'tatiko] AGG ecstatic
estemporaneamente [estemporanea'mente] AVV in an improvised way, in an impromptu manner
estemporaneo, a [estempo'raneo] AGG (*discorso*) extempore, impromptu; (*brano musicale*) impromptu
estendere [es'tɛndere] VB IRREG
■ VT (*gen*) to extend
▶ **estendersi** VIP **1** (*diffondersi: epidemia, rivolta*) to spread; (*allargarsi: città*) to spread, expand; (*: attività commerciale*) to increase, expand **2** (*foresta*) to stretch, extend; **la pianura si estendeva a perdita d'occhio** the plain stretched (away) as far as the eye could see
estensibile [esten'sibile] AGG **1** (*materiale*) stretch *attr* **2** **una norma estensibile a tutti i cittadini** a law which applies to all citizens
estensione [esten'sjone] SF **1** (*ampliamento: di diritto, significato, contratto*) extension; (*: di commercio, dominio*) expansion; **per estensione** by extension, in a wider sense; **in tutta l'estensione del termine** in the widest sense of the word **2** (*ampiezza: di fenomeno, territorio*) extent; (*superficie*) expanse **3** (*Mus*) range, compass **4** (*Inform*) extension
estensivamente [estensiva'mente] AVV extensively
estensivo, a [esten'sivo] AGG extensive; **agricoltura estensiva** extensive agriculture
estensore [esten'sore] SM **1** (*Anat: anche:* **muscolo estensore**) extensor (muscle) **2** (*compilatore*) writer, compiler **2** (*attrezzo*) chest expander
estenuante [estenu'ante] AGG wearing, tiring
estenuare [estenu'are] VT (*stancare*) to wear out, tire out
estenuato, a [estenu'ato] AGG worn out, exhausted
estere ['ɛstere] SM (*Chim*) ester
esteriore [este'rjore] AGG (*esterno: aspetto, segni, manifestazioni*) outward *attr*; **il mondo esteriore** the external world; **la sua sicurezza è solo esteriore** he seems confident, but he isn't really
esteriorità [esterjori'ta] SF INV outward appearance
esteriorizzare [esterjorid'dzare] VT (*gioia, sentimenti*) to show
esteriormente [esterjor'mente] AVV outwardly
esternalizzare [esternalid'dzare] VT (*Econ*) to outsource
esternalizzazione [esternaliddzat'tjone] SF (*Econ*) outsourcing
esternamente [esterna'mente] AVV (*fuori*) on the outside
esternare [ester'nare] VT to express; **esternare un sospetto** to voice a suspicion
esternazione [esternat'tsjone] SF expression of one's own opinion
esterno, a [es'tɛrno] AGG **1** (*muro, superficie*) outer, exterior; (*scala, gabinetto*) outside *attr*; (*rivestimento*) exterior; **aspetto esterno** (*di persona*) outward appearance; **l'aspetto esterno della casa** the outside of the house; **il muro esterno** the outside wall; **per uso esterno** (*Med*) for external use only **2** (*fig: influenze, mondo*) external, outside *attr*; (*: interessi*) outside *attr*; (*: realtà*) external **3** (*Geom*): **angolo esterno** exterior angle **4** (*allievo*) day *attr*; (*candidato*) external; **commissione esterna** external examiners *pl*
■ SM (*di edificio*) outside, exterior; (*di scatola*) outside; **all'esterno** on the outside; **dall'esterno** from outside; **l'esterno del palazzo** the outside of the building; **gli esterni sono stati girati a Glasgow** (*Cine*) the location shots were taken in Glasgow
■ SM/F (*allievo*) day pupil; (*candidato*) external candidate
estero, a ['ɛstero] AGG foreign; **vendono giornali esteri?** do they sell foreign newspapers?
■ SM: **andare all'estero** *o* **partire per l'estero** to go abroad; **vivere all'estero** to live abroad *o* in a foreign country; **vorrei andare all'estero** I'd like to go abroad; **non è mai stato all'estero** he's never been abroad; **commercio con l'estero** foreign trade; **ministero degli Esteri** *o* **gli Esteri** Ministry for Foreign Affairs; ≈ Foreign Office (*Brit*), ≈ State Department (*Am*)
esterofilia [esterofi'lia] SF passion for foreign things
esterrefatto, a [esterre'fatto] AGG (*costernato*) horrified; (*sbalordito*) astounded
estesamente [estesa'mente] AVV extensively
estesi *ecc* [e'stesi] VB *vedi* **estendere**
esteso, a [es'teso] PP *di* **estendere**
■ AGG (*gen*) extensive, large; (*territorio*) vast; (*cultura, ricerca*) wide-ranging; **un'area molto estesa** a very large area; **(scrivere) per esteso** (to write) in full
esteta, i, e [es'tɛta] SM/F aesthete
estetica [es'tɛtika] SF (*disciplina*) aesthetics *sg*; (*bellezza*) attractiveness; **tiene molto all'estetica** he's very concerned about his appearance; **gli manca completamente il senso dell'estetica** he has absolutely no taste
esteticamente [estetika'mente] AVV aesthetically; **esteticamente non è il massimo, però funziona bene** it isn't much to look at, but it works fine
estetico, a, ci, che [es'tɛtiko] AGG aesthetic; **chirurgia estetica** plastic surgery, cosmetic surgery; **cura estetica** beauty treatment
estetista, i, e [este'tista] SM/F beautician; **fa l'estetista** she's a beautician
estimo ['ɛstimo] SM (*stima*) valuation; (*disciplina*) surveying
estinguere [es'tingwere] VB IRREG
■ VT **1** (*spegnere*) to put out, extinguish **2** (*Comm: debito*) to pay off; (*: conto in banca*) to close
▶ **estinguersi** VIP (*fuoco*) to go out, die out; (*fama*) to fade away; (*stirpe*) to die out; (*specie*) to become extinct
estinsi *ecc* [es'tinsi] VB *vedi* **estinguere**
estinto, a [es'tinto] PP *di* **estinguere**
■ AGG **1** (*specie, stirpe*) extinct **2** (*Comm: debito*) paid off; (*: conto*) closed
■ SM/F: **il caro estinto** the dear departed
estintore [estin'tore] SM (fire) extinguisher
estinzione [estin'tsjone] SF (*gen, di specie*) extinction; (*di debito*) payment; (*di conto*) closing; (*di incendio*) putting out; **una specie in via di estinzione** a species on the verge of extinction
estirpare [estir'pare] VT (*pianta*) to uproot, pull up; (*dente*) to extract; (*tumore*) to remove; (*fig: vizio*) to eradicate
estivo, a [es'tivo] AGG summer *attr*; **nei mesi estivi** in the summer months; **le vacanze estive** the summer holidays; **una giornata estiva** a summer's day
estone ['ɛstone] AGG, SM/F Estonian
■ SM (*lingua*) Estonian
Estonia [es'tɔnja] SF Estonia
estorcere [es'tɔrtʃere] VT IRREG: **estorcere qc (a qn)** to extort sth (from sb)

Ee

estorsione [estor'sjone] SF extortion; **il denaro frutto delle estorsioni** money acquired by extortion
estorto, a [es'tɔrto] PP *di* **estorcere**
estradare [estra'dare] VT (*Dir*) to extradite
estradizione [estradit'tsjone] SF (*Dir*) extradition
estraggo [es'traggo], **estrai** *ecc* [es'trai] VB *vedi* **estrarre**
estraibile [estra'ibile] AGG (*autoradio*) removable
estraneità [estranei'ta] SF INV (*non implicazione*): **ha tentato di dimostrare la propria estraneità alla faccenda** he tried to prove that he had nothing to do with it, he tried to prove that he was not involved in the matter
estraneo, a [es'traneo] AGG (*gen*) extraneous; **corpo estraneo** foreign body; **estraneo a** (*tema, argomento*) unrelated to; **sentirsi estraneo a** (*famiglia, società*) to feel alienated from; **mantenersi** *o* **rimanere estraneo a** (*litigio, complotto*) to take no part in
■ SM/F stranger; **ingresso vietato agli estranei** no admittance to unauthorized personnel; **è difficile parlare di sé con un estraneo** it's difficult to talk about yourself to a stranger
estraniarsi [estra'njarsi] VR: **estraniarsi (da)** to cut o.s. off (from)
estrapolare [estrapo'lare] VT to extrapolate
estrapolazione [estrapolat'tsjone] SF extrapolation
estrarre [es'trarre] VT IRREG **1** (*gen, Med, Mat*) to extract; (*carbone*) to mine; (*marmo*) to quarry **2** (*sorteggiare*) to draw; **estrarre a sorte** to draw lots
estrassi *ecc* [es'trassi] VB *vedi* **estrarre**
estratto, a [es'tratto] PP *di* **estrarre**
■ SM **1** (*alimentare*) extract; (*per profumeria*) essence; **estratto di carne** meat extract **2** (*sommario: di discorso, documento*) resumé; (*brano: di libro*) extract, excerpt; **estratto conto** (*Banca*) (bank) statement; **estratto di nascita** (*Amm*) birth certificate
estrazione [estrat'tsjone] SF **1** (*vedi vb*) extraction; mining; quarrying; drawing **2** (*sorteggio*) draw **3** (*fig: origine*): **essere di estrazione borghese** to come from a middle-class family
estremamente [estrema'mente] AVV extremely; **è stato estremamente gentile** he was extremely kind
estremismo [estre'mizmo] SM extremism
estremista, i, e [estre'mista] SM/F extremist
estremistico, a, ci, che [estre'mistiko] AGG extremist
estremità [estremi'ta] SF INV **1** (*gen*) end, extremity; (*di ago, matita*) point; (*di villaggio, lago, isola*) far end; **da un'estremità all'altra** from one end to the other; **c'è una scala alle due estremità del corridoio** there are stairs at both ends of the corridor **2** (*Anat*): **estremità** SFPL extremities
estremizzare [estremid'dzare] VT: **estremizzare qc** to take sth to extremes
estremo, a [es'tremo] AGG (*gen*) extreme; (*ultimo: ora, tentativo*) final, last; (*misure*) drastic, extreme; **estrema destra/sinistra** (*Pol*) extreme right/left; **l'Estrema Unzione** (*Rel*) Extreme Unction; **l'Estremo Oriente** the Far East; **sport estremo** extreme sport
■ SM **1** (*gen*) extreme; (*limite: di pazienza, forze*) limit, end; **all'estremo della disperazione** in the depths of despair; **passare da un estremo all'altro** to go from one extreme to the other; **passa da un estremo all'altro** she goes from one extreme to the other; **è pignolo (fino) all'estremo** he is extremely *o* exceedingly fussy; **spingere le cose agli estremi** to go too far **2** **estremi** SMPL (*Amm: dati essenziali*) details, particulars; (*Dir*) essential elements; **gli estremi del caso** the details of the case
estrinsecare [estrinse'kare] VT to express, show
▶ **estrinsecarsi** VIP to express o.s.
estrinseco, a, ci, che [es'trinseko] AGG extrinsic
estro ['ɛstro] SM (*ispirazione*) inspiration; (*talento*) gift, bent; (*capriccio*) whim, fancy; **gli è venuto l'estro di scrivere** he has taken it into his head to become a writer
estrogeno, a [es'trɔdʒeno] AGG, SM oestrogen
estromesso, a [estro'messo] PP *di* **estromettere**
estromettere [estro'mettere] VT IRREG: **estromettere (da)** (*partito, club*) to expel (from); (*discussione*) to exclude (from)
estromissione [estromis'sjone] SF (*vedi vb*) expulsion; exclusion
estrosamente [estrosa'mente] AVV (*con estro*) imaginatively; (*in modo imprevedibile*) unpredictably
estroso, a [es'troso] AGG (*capriccioso*) fanciful; (*creativo*) talented, creative
estroverso, a [estro'vɛrso] AGG extrovert(ed), outgoing; **Claudia è molto estroversa** Claudia's very outgoing
■ SM/F extrovert
estuario, ri [estu'arjo] SM estuary
estubare [estu'bare] VT (*Med*) to extubate
estubazione [estubat'tsjone] SF (*Med*) extubation
esuberante [ezube'rante] AGG exuberant
esuberanza [ezube'rantsa] SF (*vitalità*) exuberance; **esuberanza di personale** (*eccedenza*) surplus staff
esubero [e'zubero] SM: **esubero di personale** surplus staff; **in esubero** (*personale*) due to be laid off
esulare [ezu'lare] VI (*aus* **avere**) **esulare da** (*competenza*) to be beyond; (*compiti*) not to be part of; **esula dalle mie possibilità aiutarti** it is not within my power to help you
esule ['ɛzule] SM/F exile
esultante [ezul'tante] AGG exultant
esultanza [ezul'tantsa] SF exultation
esultare [ezul'tare] VI (*aus* **avere**) **esultare di gioia** to be full of joy; **esultare per la vittoria** to rejoice at one's victory
esumare [ezu'mare] VT (*salma*) to exhume, disinter; (*fig*) to unearth
esumazione [ezumat'tsjone] SF exhumation, disinterment
età [e'ta] SF INV (*gen*) age; **all'età di 8 anni** at the age of 8, at 8 years of age, at (age) 8; **avere l'età per fare qc** to be old enough to do sth; **non ho più l'età per fare queste cose** I'm too old to do this sort of thing; **di mezza età** middle-aged; **con l'età è migliorato** he has improved with age; **in età avanzata** of advanced years; **gente della nostra età** people our age; **Sandra ha la mia età** Sandra's the same age as me; **una ragazza della tua età** a girl your age; **raggiungere la maggior età** to come of age; **essere in età minore** to be under age; **è giunto ad una bella età** he has reached a good age; **limite di età** age limit; **l'età della ragione** the age of reason; **l'età della pietra** the Stone Age; **lei ha la mia età** she is the same age as me *o* as I am
etano [e'tano] SM (*Chim*) ethane
etanolo [eta'nɔlo] SM ethanol
etc. ABBR etc.
etere ['ɛtere] SM (*Chim, letter*) ether; **via etere** on the airwaves
etereo, a [e'tɛreo] AGG ethereal

eternamente [eterna'mente] AVV (*gen*) eternally; **è eternamente al verde** he's always broke
eternare [eter'nare] VT to immortalize
eternità [eterni'ta] SF INV (*anche fig*) eternity; **impiegare** *o* **mettere un'eternità a fare qc** to take ages to do sth; **ti aspetto da un'eternità** I've been waiting for you for ages; **è durato pochi minuti ma mi è sembrato un'eternità** it only lasted a few minutes but it seemed like an eternity
eterno, a [e'tɛrno] AGG (*Rel, Filosofia*) eternal; (*senza fine*) eternal, everlasting; (*duraturo*) perpetual; (*interminabile: lamenti, attesa*) never-ending; **in eterno** for ever, eternally
■ SM eternity; **l'Eterno** (*Dio*) the Eternal (being)
etero ['ɛtero] AGG INV (*fam: eterosessuale*) straight
eterodossia [eterodos'sia] SF heterodoxy
eterodosso, a [etero'dɔsso] AGG heterodox
■ SM/F heterodox person
eterogeneità [eterodʒenei'ta] SF INV heterogeneity, heterogeneousness
eterogeneo, a [etero'dʒɛneo] AGG heterogeneous, mixed, varied
eterologo, a, gi, ghe [ele'rɔlogo] AGG: **inseminazione artificiale eterologa AID**
eterosessuale [eterosessu'ale] AGG, SM/F heterosexual
eterozigote [eteroddzi'gɔte] SM heterozygote
etica ['ɛtika] SF ethics *sg*; **etica professionale** professional ethics
eticamente [etika'mente] AVV ethically
etichetta [eti'ketta] SF label; **si è staccata l'etichetta** the label's come off; **l'etichetta** (*cerimoniale*) etiquette
etichettare [etiket'tare] VT to label
etichettatrice [etiketta'tritʃe] SF (*macchina*) labelling machine, labeller
etico, a, ci, che ['ɛtiko] AGG (*anche banca, conto*) ethical
etilene [eti'lɛne] SM (*Chim*) ethene, ethylene
etilico, a, ci, che [e'tiliko] AGG: **alcol etilico** ethyl alcohol
etilismo [eti'lizmo] SM (*Med*) alcoholism
etilista, i, e [eti'lista] SM/F (*Med*) alcoholic
etilometro [eti'lɔmetro] SM Breathalyzer® (*Brit*), drunkometer (*Am*)
etimologia [etimolo'dʒia] SF etymology
etimologicamente [etimolodʒika'mente] AVV etymologically
etimologico, a, ci, che [etimo'lɔdʒiko] AGG etymological
etiope [e'tiope] AGG, SM/F Ethiopian
Etiopia [eti'ɔpja] SF Ethiopia
etiopico, a, ci, che [eti'ɔpiko] AGG Ethiopian
■ SM (*lingua*) Amharic
Etna ['ɛtna] SM Etna
etnicamente [etnika'mente] AVV ethnically
etnico, a, ci, che ['ɛtniko] AGG ethnic
etnografia [etnogra'fia] SF ethnography
etnologia [etnolo'dʒia] SF ethnology
etnologico, a, ci, che [etno'lɔdʒiko] AGG ethnological
etrusco, a, schi, sche [e'trusko] AGG, SM/F Etruscan
ettaro ['ɛttaro] SM hectare (= *10,000 m²*)
etto ['ɛtto] PREF: **etto...** hecto...
■ ABBR SM *di* **ettogrammo**
ettogrammo [etto'grammo] SM hectogram(me) (= *100 grams*)
ettolitro [et'tɔlitro] SM hectolitre (*Brit*), hectoliter (*Am*)
ettometro [et'tɔmetro] SM hectometre
Ettore ['ɛttore] SM Hector
EU ABBR (= **Europa**) E
eucalipto [euka'lipto] SM eucalyptus
eucaristia [eukaris'tia] SF: **l'eucaristia** the Eucharist
Euclide [eu'klide] SM Euclid
eufemismo [eufe'mizmo] SM euphemism
eufemisticamente [eufemistika'mente] AVV euphemistically
eufemistico, a, ci, che [eufe'mistiko] AGG euphemistic
euforia [eufo'ria] SF euphoria
euforicamente [euforika'mente] AVV euphorically
euforico, a, ci, che [eu'fɔriko] AGG euphoric
eugenetica [eudʒe'nɛtika] SF eugenics
eugenetico, a, ci, che [eudʒe'nɛtiko] AGG eugenic
eunuco, chi [eu'nuko] SM eunuch
Eurasia [eu'razja] SF Eurasia
eurasiatico, a, ci, che [eura'zjatiko] AGG, SM/F Eurasian
EURATOM ['euratom] SIGLA F (= **Comunità Europea dell'Energia Atomica**) Euratom (= *European Atomic Energy Community*)
Euridice [euri'ditʃe] SF Eurydice
Euripide [eu'ripide] SM Euripides
euro ['ɛuro] SM INV euro; **cinque euro** five euros; **una banconota da 100 euro** a 100 euro note
eurocity [euro'siti] SM INV (*Ferr*) *fast train connecting European cities*
eurocorpo [euro'kɔrpo] SM European force
eurodeputato, a [eurodepu'tato] SM/F Euro MP
eurodivisa [eurodi'viza] SF Eurocurrency
eurodollaro [euro'dɔllaro] SM Eurodollar
Eurolandia [euro'landja] SF Euroland
euromercato [euromer'kato] SM Euromarket
euromissile [euro'missile] SM Euro-missile
Europa [eu'rɔpa] SF Europe
europarlamentare [europarlamen'tare] SM/F Member of the European Parliament, MEP
europeismo [europe'izmo] SM (*Pol*) Europeanism
europeizzare [europeid'dzare] VT to europeanize
europeo, a [euro'pɛo] AGG, SM/F European; **l'Unione Europea** the European Union
euroscettico, a, ci, che [euroʃʃettiko] SM/F Eurosceptic
Eurostar [euro'star] SM INV (*treno*) *fast train on which booking is sometimes obligatory*
eurovisione [eurovi'zjone] SF eurovision
eutanasia [eutana'zia] SF euthanasia
EV ABBR = *Eccellenza Vostra*
Eva ['ɛva] SF Eve
evacuamento [evakua'mento] SM evacuation
evacuare [evaku'are] VT, VI (*aus* **avere**) (*gen, Med*) to evacuate
evacuazione [evakuat'tsjone] SF evacuation
evadere [e'vadere] VB IRREG
■ VT **1** (*tasse, imposte*) to evade; **evadere il fisco** to evade (income) tax **2** (*Amm: pratica*) to deal with, dispatch; (*: corrispondenza*) to deal with, clear; (*: ordine*) to deal with
■ VI (*aus* **essere**) **evadere (da)** (*prigione*) to escape (from); **sono evasi dal carcere** they escaped from prison; **far evadere qn** to help sb to escape; **evadere dalla realtà quotidiana** to get away from the realities of daily life
evanescente [evaneʃʃɛnte] AGG evanescent
evanescenza [evaneʃʃɛntsa] SF evanescence

Ee

evangelico, a, ci, che [evan'dʒɛliko] AGG, SM/F evangelical
evangelista, i [evandʒe'lista] SM Evangelist
evangelizzare [evandʒelid'dzare] VT to evangelize
evaporare [evapo'rare] VT, VI (*aus* essere *nel senso di 'trasformarsi in vapore'*; avere *nel senso di 'ridursi per evaporazione'*) to evaporate
evaporazione [evaporat'tsjone] SF evaporation
evasi *ecc* [e'vazi] VB *vedi* **evadere**
evasione [eva'zjone] SF **1** (*da prigione, anche fig*) escape; **letteratura d'evasione** escapist literature **2** (*Amm: disbrigo: di ordine*) carrying out, fulfilment; **occuparsi dell'evasione della corrispondenza** to deal with the correspondence **3** (*Fisco*) evasion; **evasione fiscale** tax evasion
evasivamente [evaziva'mente] AVV evasively
evasivo, a [eva'zivo] AGG evasive
evaso, a [e'vazo] PP *di* **evadere**
■ SM/F escaped prisoner
evasore [eva'zore] SM: **evasore (fiscale)** tax evader
evenienza [eve'njɛntsa] SF: **nell'evenienza che ciò succeda** should that happen; **essere pronto ad ogni evenienza** to be ready for any eventuality; **in ogni evenienza puoi metterti in contatto con me** you can get in touch with me should the need arise
evento [e'vɛnto] SM (*anche Inform*) event
eventuale [eventu'ale] AGG: **contro eventuali danni** against any possible damage; **siamo assicurati contro eventuali danni** we're insured against any damage; **per scongiurare il pericolo di eventuali complicazioni** to avoid the risk of possible complications; **gli eventuali guadagni saranno devoluti in beneficenza** any profit will be given to charity; **per eventuali reclami rivolgersi a...** (any) claims should be addressed to ...; **per eventuali domande rivolgersi a...** if you have any queries contact..
■ SFPL: **varie ed eventuali** any other business

> **LO SAPEVI...?**
> **eventuale** non si traduce mai con la parola inglese *eventual*

eventualità [eventuali'ta] SF INV eventuality, possibility; **tenersi pronto a ogni eventualità** *o* **a tutte le eventualità** to be prepared for any eventuality *o* for all eventualities; **nell'eventualità di** in the event of; **nell'eventualità che non dovesse tornare...** should he not return ...
eventualmente [eventual'mente] AVV if need be, if necessary; **eventualmente ci fossero difficoltà...** should there be any problems ...; **se eventualmente cambiassi idea, sai dove trovarci** if by any chance you change your mind, you know where to find; **eventualmente potremmo andare in treno** we could always go by train

> **LO SAPEVI...?**
> **eventualmente** non si traduce mai con la parola inglese *eventually*

Everest ['ɛverest] SM: **l'Everest, il monte Everest** (Mount) Everest
eversione [ever'sjone] SF subversion
eversivo, a [ever'sivo] AGG subversive
evidente [evi'dɛnte] AGG obvious, evident; **è una prova evidente di...** it's clear proof of ...; **è evidente che** it is obvious *o* evident that; **era evidente che non voleva venire** it was obvious he didn't want to come; **è evidente!** obviously!
evidentemente [evidente'mente] AVV (*palesemente*) obviously, clearly, evidently; **era evidentemente seccato** he was obviously annoyed; **evidentemente avevo capito male** I obviously misunderstood
evidenza [evi'dɛntsa] SF: **l'evidenza dei fatti è schiacciante** the facts are incontrovertible; **arrendersi (di fronte) all'evidenza** to yield to the evidence; **negare l'evidenza** to deny the facts *o* the obvious; **mettere in evidenza** (*problemi*) to highlight, bring to the fore
evidenziare [eviden'tsjare] VT (*sottolineare*) to emphasize, highlight; (*con evidenziatore*) to highlight
evidenziatore [evidentsja'tore] SM (*penna*) highlighter
evirare [evi'rare] VT to castrate
evirazione [evirat'tsjone] SF castration
evitabile [evi'tabile] AGG avoidable
evitare [evi'tare] VT (*gen*) to avoid; (*colpo*) to dodge; (*sguardo*) to evade; **evitare di fare qc** to avoid doing sth; **evita di uscire da solo la notte** avoid going out alone at night; **evita di fare rumore** try not to make any noise; **evitare che qc accada** to prevent sth (from) happening; **evitare qc a qn** to spare sb sth; **ciò gli ha evitato il fastidio di tornare indietro** that saved him the bother of going back; **passiamo di qui per evitare il traffico** we're going this way to avoid the traffic
evo ['ɛvo] SM: **l'evo moderno/antico** modern/ancient times
evocare [evo'kare] VT (*gen*) to evoke; (*ricordo*) to recall, evoke
evocativo, a [evoka'tivo] AGG evocative
evocazione [evokat'tsjone] SF evocation
evocherò *ecc* [evoke'rɔ] VB *vedi* **evocare**
evolutivo, a [evolu'tivo] AGG (*gen, Bio*) evolutionary; (*Med*) progressive
evoluto, a [evo'luto] PP *di* **evolversi**
■ AGG (*popolo, civiltà*) (highly) developed, advanced; (*persona: emancipato*) independent; (*: senza pregiudizi*) broad-minded
evoluzione [evolut'tsjone] SF **1** (*gen*) evolution; (*progresso*) progress, development; **teoria dell'evoluzione** theory of evolution **2** (*movimento*) movement; (*Mil*) manoeuvre
evoluzionismo [evoluttsjo'nizmo] SM evolutionism
evoluzionista, i, e [evoluttsjo'nista] SM/F evolutionist
evoluzionistico, a, ci, che [evoluttsjo'nistiko] AGG evolutionist
evolversi [e'vɔlversi] VIP IRREG to develop, evolve
■ SM: **con l'evolversi della situazione** as the situation developed *o* develops
evvai! [ev'vai] ESCL (*di gioia*) Yes!; (*di incoraggiamento*) Come on!
evviva [ev'viva] ESCL hurrah!; **evviva il re!** long live the King!
■ SM INV applause *no pl*
ex [ɛks] PREF ex, ex-, former; **l'ex Primo ministro** the former Prime Minister
■ SM/F INV: **il mio ex** my ex
ex aequo [ɛg'z ɛkwo] AVV: **classificarsi primo ex aequo** to come joint first, come first equal
excursus [eks'kursus] SM INV digression
exit poll [eksit'pol] SMPL exit poll
ex novo [ɛks 'nɔvo] AVV (*daccapo*) from the beginning
expertise [ɛkspɛr'tiz] SF INV (*di opera d'arte*) authentication
exploit [ɛks'plwa] SM INV feat, achievement
extra ['ɛkstra] AGG INV, SM INV extra; **una spesa extra**

an extra expense; **nel conto c'erano molti extra** there were a lot of extras on the bill

extracomunitario, ria, ri, rie [ekstracomuni'tarjo] AGG non-EU; **i paesi extracomunitari** countries outside the European Union
■ SM/F non-EU national (*often referring to non-European immigrant*)

extraconiugale [ekstrakonju'gale] AGG extramarital

extraeuropeo, a [ekstraeuro'pɛo] AGG non-European

extramoenia [extra'menja] AGG INV = **extramurale**

extramurale [ekstramu'rale] AGG: **attività extramurale** (*di medico*) private practice (*carried on outside hospital*)

extraparlamentare [ekstraparlamen'tare] AGG, SM/F extraparliamentary

extrasensoriale [ekstrasenso'rjale] AGG extrasensory; **percezione extrasensoriale** extrasensory perception

extrasistole [ekstra'sistole] SF (*Med*) extrasystole

extraterrestre [ekstrater'rɛstre] AGG, SM/F extraterrestrial

extraterritoriale [ekstraterrito'rjale] AGG extraterritorial

extraurbano, a [ekstraur'bano] AGG suburban

extrauterino, a [ekstraute'rino] AGG (*Med*): **gravidanza extrauterina** ectopic pregnancy

ex voto [eks'vɔto] SM INV ex voto

Ezechiele [edze'kjɛle] SM Ezekiel

Ee

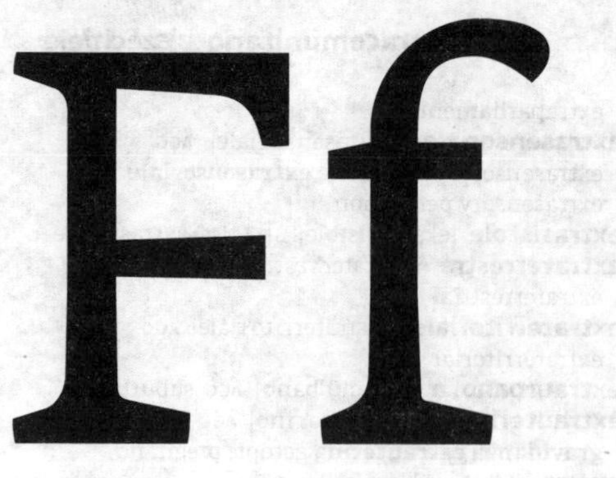

F, f ['effe] SF O M INV (*lettera*) F, f; **F come Firenze** ≈ F for Frederick (*Brit*), ≈ F for Fox (*Am*)

F ABBR (= **Fahrenheit**) F

F. ABBR (= **fiume**) R

fa[1] [fa] 3A PERS SG DEL PRESENTE *di* **fare**
■ AVV: **10 anni fa** 10 years ago; **quanto tempo fa?** how long ago?; **l'ho incontrata due ore fa** I met her two hours ago

fa[2] [fa] SM INV (*Mus*) F; (: *solfeggiando*) fa

fabbisogno [fabbi'zoɲɲo] SM needs *pl*, requirements *pl*; **il fabbisogno nazionale di petrolio** the country's oil requirements; **il fabbisogno del settore pubblico** public sector borrowing requirement (*Brit*), government debt borrowing (*Am*)

fabbrica, che ['fabbrika] SF factory; **fabbrica di mattoni** brickyard; **una fabbrica di automobili** a car factory

> **LO SAPEVI...?**
> **fabbrica** non si traduce mai con la parola inglese ***fabric***

fabbricabile [fabbri'kabile] AGG **1** (*terreno, area*) that can be built on **2** (*prodotto industriale*) manufacturable

fabbricante [fabbri'kante] SM/F manufacturer, maker

fabbricare [fabbri'kare] VT (*produrre*: *gen*) to make, manufacture; (: *a livello industriale*) to manufacture; (*costruire*: *edificio*) to build, put up; (*fig*: *inventare*: *alibi, accuse*) to fabricate; **è fabbricato in Cina** it's made in China

fabbricato [fabbri'kato] SM building

fabbricazione [fabbrikat'tsjone] SF (*vedi vb*) making; manufacture, manufacturing; building; fabrication; **di fabbricazione italiana** made in Italy, Italian made; **difetto di fabbricazione** manufacturing defect

fabbro ['fabbro] SM smith; **fabbro ferraio** (black)smith

faccenda [fat'tʃɛnda] SF (*affare*) business, affair, matter; **una brutta faccenda** a nasty business; **è una faccenda complicata** it's a complicated matter; **devo sbrigare alcune faccende** I've got a few things to see to; **le faccende domestiche** the housework *sg*

faccendiere [fattʃen'djɛre] SM wheeler-dealer, (shady) operator

faccetta [fat'tʃetta] SF (*di pietra preziosa*) facet

faccettatura [fattʃetta'tura] SF (*operazione*) facetting

facchinaggio, gi [fakki'naddʒo] SM porterage

facchino [fak'kino] SM (*gen*) porter; **lavoro da facchino** (*fig*) hard graft

faccia, ce ['fattʃa] SF **1** (*viso, espressione*) face; **una faccia amica** a friendly face; **avere la faccia stanca** to look tired; **fare la faccia imbronciata** to sulk; **dovevi vedere la sua faccia quando...** you should have seen his face when ...; **avere il sole in faccia** to have the sun in one's eyes; **gliel'ho detto in faccia** I told him to his face; **ridere in faccia a qn** to laugh in sb's face; **leggere qc in faccia a qn** to see sth written all over sb's face; **cosa ti sei messa in faccia?** what have you got on your face?; **perdere/salvare la faccia** to lose/save (one's) face; **avere la faccia (tosta) di dire/fare qc** to have the cheek *o* nerve to say/do sth; **hai una bella faccia tosta!** you've got a real cheek! **2** (*lato*: *gen*) side; (: *Geom*) face, side; (: *della terra*) face; (: *fig*: *di problema, questione*) side, aspect; **vorrei cancellarlo dalla faccia della terra** I'd like to wipe him off the face of the earth **3** (*fraseologia*): **(a) faccia a faccia** face to face; **a faccia in su/giù** face up(wards)/down(wards); **fare qc alla faccia di qn** to do sth to spite sb; **di faccia a** opposite, facing; **visto di faccia** seen from the front

faccia a faccia [fattʃa a 'fattʃa] SM INV face to face meeting

facciale [fat'tʃale] AGG facial

facciata [fat'tʃata] SF **1** (*Archit*) façade; (*fig*: *apparenza esterna*) appearances *pl*; **non giudicare dalla facciata** don't judge by appearances **2** (*di pagina*) side; **una lettera di 4 facciate** a 4-page letter; **scrivi su entrambe le facciate** write on both sides

faccio *ecc* ['fattʃo] VB *vedi* **fare**

facente [fa'tʃɛnte] **facente funzione** SM/F (*Amm*) deputy

facessi *ecc* [fa'tʃessi] VB *vedi* **fare**

faceto, a [fa'tʃeto] AGG humorous

facevo *ecc* [fa'tʃevo] VB *vedi* **fare**

facezia [fa'tʃɛttsja] SF witticism, witty remark
fachiro [fa'kiro] SM fakir
facile ['fatʃile] AGG **1** (*gen*) easy; **è più facile a dirsi che a farsi** it's easier said than done; **è l'esercizio più facile del libro** it's the easiest exercise in the book; **è meno facile di quanto sembri** it's harder than it looks, it's not as easy as it looks; **non era facile come pensavo** it wasn't as easy as I thought; **far tutto facile** to make light *o* little of everything; **avere la pistola facile** to be trigger-happy; **avere la lacrima facile** to be easily moved to tears; **è facile all'ira/alla malinconia** he's apt to lose his temper/to get depressed; **avere un carattere facile** to be an easy-going person; **donna di facili costumi** woman of easy virtue, loose woman **2** (*probabile*): **è facile che piova** it's probably going to rain; **è facile che venga** he may well come, he'll probably come
facilità [fatʃili'ta] SF INV **1** (*di lavoro, compito*) easiness; (*di vittoria*) ease; **studia con facilità** he has no problem studying; **arrabbiarsi con facilità** to be apt to lose one's temper **2** (*disposizione, dono*) ability, aptitude; **ha facilità a fare amicizia** he makes friends easily
facilitare [fatʃili'tare] VT to facilitate (*frm*), make easier; **non faciliterà la situazione** it's not going to make matters any easier
facilitazione [fatʃilitat'tsjone] SF: **facilitazioni di pagamento** easy terms, credit facilities
facilmente [fatʃil'mente] AVV (*gen*) easily; (*probabilmente*) probably
facilone, a [fatʃi'lone] SM/F (*pegg*) laid-back type
faciloneria [fatʃilone'ria] SF slapdash attitude
facinoroso, a [fatʃino'roso] AGG violent
■ SM/F thug
facocero [fako'tʃɛro] SM (*Zool*) warthog
facoltà [fakol'ta] SF INV **1** (*capacità mentale*) faculty; (*Chim*) property; **nel pieno possesso delle proprie facoltà mentali** in full possession of one's faculties **2** (*autorità*) power; **dare facoltà a qn di fare qc** to give sb the power *o* authority to do sth; **esula dalle mie facoltà** it's not within my power **3** (*Univ*) department, faculty; **è iscritta alla facoltà di legge** she's a student in the law department
facoltativo, a [fakolta'tivo] AGG optional; **fermata facoltativa** request stop; **un corso facoltativo** an optional course
facoltoso, a [fakol'toso] AGG wealthy
façon [fa'sõ] SF INV: **una pelliccia façon visone** an imitation mink (coat)
facsimile [fak'simile] SM INV facsimile; (*fig: cosa simile*) copy
factotum [fak'tɔtum] SM/F INV: **è il factotum della ditta** he's the one who does most of the work in the firm; **sarebbe una semplice segretaria ma in pratica è la factotum** she's supposed to be a secretary but in reality she does a bit of everything
faggio, gi ['faddʒo] SM (*albero, legno*) beech; **mobili di** *o* **in faggio** beech(wood) furniture
fagiano [fa'dʒano] SM pheasant; **fagiano di monte** black grouse
fagiolino [fadʒo'lino] SM French (*Brit*) *o* string bean
fagiolo [fa'dʒɔlo] SM bean; **capitare a fagiolo** to come at the right time
faglia ['faʎʎa] SF (*Geol*) fault
fagliatura [faʎʎa'tura] SF (*Geol*): **fagliatura a blocchi** block faulting
fagocitare [fagotʃi'tare] VT (*Bio*) to perform phagocytosis on; (*fig: industria*) to absorb, swallow up
fagocitosi [fagotʃi'tɔzi] SF (*Bio*) phagocytosis
fagotto¹ [fa'gɔtto] SM bundle; **fare fagotto** to pack up and go
fagotto² [fa'gɔtto] SM (*Mus*) bassoon
Fahrenheit ['fa:rənhait] SM INV Fahrenheit
fai ['fai] VB *vedi* **fare**
faida ['faida] SF feud
fai da te [faida'te] SM INV DIY, do-it-yourself
faina [fa'ina] SF (*Zool*) stone marten
falange [fa'landʒe] SF (*Anat, Mil*) phalanx
falcata [fal'kata] SF stride
falce ['faltʃe] SF scythe; **una falce di luna** a crescent moon; **falce e martello** (*Pol*) hammer and sickle
falcetto [fal'tʃetto] SM sickle
falchetta [fal'ketta] SF (*Naut*) gunwale
falciare [fal'tʃare] VT **1** (*grano*) to reap; (*erba*) to mow, cut; (*con la falce*) to scythe **2** (*fig: uccidere*): **furono falciati da una raffica di mitra** they were mown down by a hail of machine-gun fire; **migliaia di vite falciate dall'epidemia** thousands of lives wiped out by the epidemic **3** (*Calcio*) to bring down
falciatrice [faltʃa'tritʃe] SF (*per grano*) reaping machine; (*per erba*) mowing machine
falciatura [faltʃa'tura] SF (*vedi vb*) reaping; mowing
falcidia [fal'tʃidja] SF (*fig: strage*) extermination; **all'esame di anatomia hanno fatto una falcidia** they were failing students en masse at the Anatomy exam
falco, chi ['falko] SM (*Zool, fig Pol*) hawk; **occhio di falco!** you're sharp-eyed!; (*Zool*) **falco migratore** *o* **pellegrino** peregrine falcon; **falco di palude** marsh harrier; **falco pescatore** osprey
falcone [fal'kone] SM falcon
falconeria [falkone'ria] SF falconry
falda ['falda] SF (*Geol*) layer, stratum; (*di cappello*) brim; (*di cappotto*) tails *pl*; (*di monte*) lower slope; (*di tetto*) pitch; (*di neve*) flake
falegname [faleɲ'ɲame] SM carpenter, joiner (*Brit*); **mio padre fa il falegname** my father's a carpenter
falegnameria [faleɲɲame'ria] SF **1** (*mestiere*) carpentry **2** (*locale*) carpenter's shop
falena [fa'lɛna] SF (*Zool*) moth
falesia [fa'lɛzja] SF cliff
Falkland ['fɔ:lklənd] SFPL: **le (isole) Falkland** the Falkland Islands
falla ['falla] SF leak
fallace [fal'latʃe] AGG deceptive
fallacia, cie [fal'latʃa] SF fallacy
fallico, a, ci, che ['falliko] AGG phallic
fallimentare [fallimen'tare] AGG (*Comm*) bankruptcy *attr*; **bilancio fallimentare** negative balance, deficit; **diritto fallimentare** bankruptcy law; **"tutto a prezzi fallimentari"** "everything at drastically reduced prices"; **il bilancio della sua vita era fallimentare** his life was a total failure; **fu un'esperienza fallimentare** it was a failure
fallimento [falli'mento] SM **1** (*fiasco*) failure, flop; **è stato un fallimento totale** it was a total failure **2** (*Comm, Dir*) bankruptcy; **molte aziende rischiavano il fallimento** many firms were facing bankruptcy; **essere/andare in fallimento** to be/go bankrupt
fallire [fal'lire] VT (*colpo, bersaglio*) to miss; **Federer ha fallito il colpo** Federer missed the ball
■ VI (*aus* **essere**) **1** **fallire (in)** (*non riuscire*) to fail (in), be unsuccessful (in); **il nostro piano è destinato a fallire** our plan is bound to fail **2** (*Comm, Dir*) to go

Ff

bankrupt; **la ditta è fallita** the firm has gone bankrupt

fallito, a [fal'lito] AGG (*commerciante*) bankrupt; (*tentativo*) unsuccessful
■ SM/F (*Comm*) bankrupt; (*fig*) failure

fallo[1] ['fallo] SM **1** (*errore*) fault; **essere in fallo** to be at fault *o* in error; **mettere il piede in fallo** to slip; **ha messo il piede in fallo ed è caduto** he lost his footing and fell; **cogliere qn in fallo** to catch sb out; **mi ha colto in fallo** he caught me out; **senza fallo** without fail **2** (*difetto*) fault, defect, flaw **3** (*Sport*) fault, foul; (*Tennis*) fault; **fallo di piede** (*Tennis*) foot fault; **fare un fallo di mano** (*Calcio*) to handle the ball; **è stato espulso per un fallo sul portiere** he was sent off for a foul on the goalkeeper

fallo[2] ['fallo] SM (*Anat*) phallus; **fallo di mano** (*Calcio*) handball

fallocrate [fal'lɔkrate] SM (*pegg*) male chauvinist

fallosamente [fallosa'mente] AVV (*Sport*): **giocare fallosamente** to commit fouls, play a dirty game

falloso, a [fal'loso] AGG (*Sport*): **gioco falloso** foul play, unfair play

falò [fa'lɔ] SM INV bonfire

falsamente [falsa'mente] AVV (*gen*) falsely; (*rispondere, dichiarare*) untruthfully

falsare [fal'sare] VT (*notizia, realtà*) to distort

falsariga, ghe [falsa'riga] SF lined page, ruled page; **sulla falsariga di...** (*fig*) along the lines of ...

falsario, ri [fal'sarjo] SM (*di documenti, quadri*) forger; (*di monete*) counterfeiter

falsetto [fal'setto] SM (*Mus*) falsetto; **cantare in falsetto** to sing falsetto

falsificare [falsifi'kare] VT (*firma, documento*) to forge; (*conti*) to falsify; (*monete*) to forge, counterfeit

falsificazione [falsifikat'tsjone] SF forging; **di difficile falsificazione** difficult to forge

falsità [falsi'ta] SF INV (*di persona, notizia*) falseness; (*bugia*) lie

falso, a ['falso] AGG (*denaro, documenti*) forged, fake, counterfeit; (*oro, gioielli*) imitation *attr*; (*pudore, promessa*) false; **fare un passo falso** to stumble; (*fig*) to slip up; **sotto falsa luce** in a false light; **essere un falso magro** to be heavier than one looks; **un nome falso** a false name; **aveva un passaporto falso** he had a forged passport; **un diamante falso** a fake diamond; **falsa partenza** (*anche fig*) false start; **falso allarme** false alarm
■ SM **1** falsehood; **dire il falso** to lie, not to tell the truth; **giurare il falso** (*Dir*) to commit perjury **2** (*Dir*) forgery; **falso in atto pubblico** forgery (of a legal document) **3** (*opera d'arte*) fake; **il quadro era un falso** the painting was a fake **4** **falso in bilancio** false accounting

falsopiano [falso'pjano] SM (*pl* **falsipiani**) slight slope

fama ['fama] SF **1** (*celebrità*) fame, renown; **raggiungere la fama** to become famous; **di fama mondiale** world famous; **un attore di fama mondiale** a world-famous actor; **voglio fama e successo** I want fame and success **2** (*reputazione*) reputation, name; **conoscere qn di** *o* **per fama** to know sb by reputation; **ha (la) fama di essere un dongiovanni** he has a reputation as a Don Juan; **ha una cattiva fama** he's got a bad reputation

fame ['fame] SF hunger; **aver fame** to be hungry; **hai fame?** are you hungry?; **ho una fame da lupo** I'm famished *o* starving, I could eat a horse; **aver fame di** (*fig*: *giustizia*) to hunger *o* long for; **fare la fame** (*fig*) to starve, scrape a living; **morire di fame** to be starving; **il problema della fame nel terzo mondo** the problem of hunger in the Third World

famelico, a, ci, che [fa'mɛliko] AGG ravenous

famigerato, a [famidʒe'rato] AGG notorious

famiglia [fa'miʎʎa] SF (*gen*) (*Zool, Bot*) family; **essere di buona famiglia** to come from a good family; **metter su famiglia** to start a family; **amico/festa di famiglia** family friend/celebration; **in famiglia** (*matrimonio*) quiet; (*funerale*) private; **passare il Natale in famiglia** to spend Christmas with one's family; **è uno della famiglia** (*fig*) he's (quite) one of the family; **viene da una famiglia numerosa** he comes from a large family; **la Sacra Famiglia** the Holy Family

familiare [fami'ljare] AGG **1** (*di famiglia*) family *attr*; **vita familiare** family life; **un'azienda familiare** a family business; **cucina familiare** home cooking; **una FIAT familiare** a FIAT estate (*Brit*) *o* station wagon (*Am*) **2** (*noto*) familiar; **questo nome mi è familiare** I've heard this name before, I know the name; **un viso familiare** a familiar face **3** (*intimo*: *rapporti, atmosfera*) friendly; (: *tono*) informal; (*lessico*: *colloquiale*) informal, colloquial
■ SM/F relative, relation; **va in vacanza con dei familiari** he's going on holiday with relatives; **i miei familiari** my relations *o* family *sg*

familiarità [familjari'ta] SF (*dimestichezza*) familiarity; (*confidenza*) informality; **trattare qn con familiarità** to treat sb in a friendly way; **aver familiarità con qc** to be familiar with sth

familiarizzare [familjarid'dzare] VI (*aus* **avere**) **familiarizzare con qn** to get to know sb; **abbiamo familiarizzato subito** we got on well together from the start; **familiarizzare** *o* **familiarizzarsi con l'ambiente** to familiarize o.s. with one's surroundings

famoso, a [fa'moso] AGG famous, well-known

fanale [fa'nale] SM (*Aut*) light; (*luce stradale*) lamp; (*Naut*) light; (*di faro*) beacon; **fanale di poppa** (*Naut*) stern light

fanalino [fana'lino] SM light; **fanalino di coda** (*Aut, Aer*) rear *o* tail light; (*fig*) tail end; **fanalino di posizione** (*Aut*) sidelight

fanaticamente [fanatika'mente] AVV fanatically

fanatico, a, ci, che [fa'natiko] AGG fanatical; **fanatico di** *o* **per** (*teatro, calcio*) wild *o* mad *o* crazy about; **essere fanatico di** to be mad about; **è fanatico di calcio** he's mad about football
■ SM/F fanatic; (*tifoso*) fan; **è un fanatico del golf/di Fellini** he is a golf/Fellini fanatic

fanatismo [fana'tizmo] SM fanaticism

fanatizzare [fanatid'dzare] VT to rouse to fanaticism

fanciullesco, a, schi, sche [fantʃul'lesko] AGG childlike; (*pegg*) childish

fanciullezza [fantʃul'lettsa] SF childhood

fanciullo, a [fan'tʃullo] SM/F child

fandonia [fan'dɔnja] SF (tall) story, whopper; **fandonie!** nonsense! *sg*, rubbish! *sg*

fanello [fa'nɛllo] SM linnet

fanfara [fan'fara] SF (*banda*) brass band; (*musica*) fanfare

fanfarone [fanfa'rone] SM braggart

fanghiglia [fan'giʎʎa] SF mire, mud

fango, ghi ['fango] SM mud; **ero coperto di fango** I was covered with mud; **gettare fango addosso a qn** (*fig*) to sling mud at sb; **fare i fanghi** (*Med*) to take a course of mud baths

fangosità [fangosi'ta] SF INV muddiness
fangoso, a [fan'goso] AGG muddy
fanno ['fanno] VB *vedi* **fare**
fannullone, a [fannul'lone] SM/F layabout
fantapolitica [fantapo'litika] SF political fiction
fantascientifico, a, ci, che [fantaʃʃen'tifiko] AGG science fiction *attr*
fantascienza [fantaʃʃɛntsa] SF science fiction, sci-fi; **un film di fantascienza** a science fiction film
fantasia [fanta'zia] SF **1** (*facoltà*) imagination, fancy; **avere fantasia** to have imagination; **non ha fantasia** he hasn't got any imagination; **lavori troppo di fantasia** your imagination is running away with you; **sono fantasie le tue!** it's just your imagination!; **nel mondo della fantasia** in the realm(s) of fantasy *o* fancy **2** (*capriccio*) whim, caprice; **fantasia passeggera** passing fancy; **era solo una mia fantasia** it was just a fantasy of mine **3** (*decorazione*) pattern; **lo vuole tinta unita o fantasia?** would you like it plain or patterned?; **non mi piace questa fantasia** I don't like this pattern; **camicia fantasia** patterned shirt **4** (*Mus*) fantasia
fantasiosamente [fantazjosa'mente] AVV imaginatively
fantasioso, a [fanta'zjoso] AGG (*dotato di fantasia*) imaginative; (*bizzarro*) fanciful, strange
fantasista, i, e [fanta'zista] SM/F variety artist
fantasma, i [fan'tazma] SM (*spettro*) ghost, spectre (*letter*), phantom (*letter*)
■AGG: **governo fantasma** shadow cabinet; **città/scrittore fantasma** ghost town/writer
fantasmagoria [fantazmago'ria] SF phantasmagoria
fantasmagorico, a, ci, che [fantazma'gɔriko] AGG phantasmagoric(al)
fantasticamente [fantastika'mente] AVV (*in modo meraviglioso*) fantastically; (*con fantasia*) imaginatively
fantasticare [fantasti'kare] VI (*aus* **avere**) to daydream
fantasticheria [fantastike'ria] SF daydream
fantastico, a, ci, che [fan'tastiko] AGG (*gen*) fantastic; (*potenza, ingegno*) imaginative; **un mondo fantastico** a world of fantasy, a fantasy world; **è una festa fantastica** it's a fantastic party; **fantastico!** fantastic!, terrific!
fante ['fante] SM **1** (*Mil*) infantryman **2** (*Carte*) jack
fanteria [fante'ria] SF (*Mil*) infantry
fantino [fan'tino] SM jockey
fantoccio, ci [fan'tɔttʃo] SM (*manichino*) dummy; (*bambola*) doll; (*fig: persona*) puppet; **fantoccio di pezza** rag doll
■AGG INV: **governo fantoccio** puppet government
fantomatico, a, ci, che [fanto'matiko] AGG (*personaggio*) mythical
FAO ['fao] SIGLA F (= *Food and Agriculture Organization*) FAO
farabutto [fara'butto] SM crook
faraglione [faraʎ'ʎone] SM (*Geog*) stack
faraona [fara'ona] SF (*anche:* **gallina faraona**) guinea fowl
faraone [fara'one] SM **1** (*Storia*) Pharaoh **2** (*Carte*) faro
faraonico, a, ci, che [fara'ɔniko] AGG of the Pharaohs; (*fig*) enormous, huge
farcire [far'tʃire] VT (*carni, peperoni, pomodori*) to stuff; (*torte*) to fill; **farcito di errori** (*fig*) riddled with mistakes
fard [far] SM INV blusher
fardello [far'dello] SM bundle; (*fig*) burden

fare ['fare] VB IRREG **PAROLA CHIAVE**
■VT
1 (*fabbricare: gen*) to make; (: *casa*) to build; (*quadro*) to paint; (*disegno*) to draw; (*pasto*) to cook; (*pane, dolci*) to bake; (*assegno*) to make out; **fanno la stessa classe** they are in the same year; **fare un corso** (*tenere*) to give a series of lessons, teach a course; (*seguire*) to do a course; **che cosa ne hai fatto di quei pantaloni?** what have you done with those trousers?; **fare un errore** to make a mistake; **ha fatto la mia felicità** he made me so happy; **fare una festa** to have *o* hold a party; **ha fatto un figlio** she's had a baby; **quest'albero non fa frutti** this tree doesn't bear fruit; **hai fatto il letto?** have you made the bed?; **lo hanno fatto presidente** they made him president; **fare una promessa** to make a promise; **hai fatto la stanza?** have you cleaned the room?
2 (*attività: gen*) to do; (*vacanza, sogno*) to have; **a scuola facciamo chimica** at school we do chemistry; **fare i compiti** to do one's homework; **cosa fai?** (*adesso*) what are you doing?; (*nella vita*) what do you do?, what is your job?; **non posso farci nulla** I can't do anything about it; **fare la spesa** to do the shopping; **fare del tennis** to play tennis
3 (*funzione*) to be; (*Teatro*) to play, be, act; **fare l'avvocato** to be a lawyer; **fare finta di essere stanco** to pretend to be tired; **fare l'innocente** to act the innocent; **fare il malato** to pretend to be ill; **fare il medico** to be a doctor; **fare il morto** (*in acqua*) to float; **nel film fa il padre** in the film he plays the father
4 (*percorrere*) to do; **fare i 100 metri** (*competere*) to go in for *o* run in the 100 metres; **fa i 100 metri in 10,5** he does the 100 metres in 10.5; **abbiamo fatto 5 chilometri** we've done 5 kilometres; **fare una passeggiata** to go for *o* take a walk; **fare un viaggio** to go on a trip, make a journey
5 (*suscitare: sentimenti*): **fa niente** it doesn't matter; **mi fa orrore** it horrifies me; **fare paura a** to frighten; **mi fa rabbia** it makes me angry
6 (*considerare*): **ti facevo più intelligente** I thought you had more sense; **ti facevo al mare** I thought you were at the seaside; **lo facevo più vecchio** I thought he was older
7 (*ammontare*): **due più due fa quattro** two plus two make(s) *o* equal(s) four; **la città non fa più di 2 milioni di abitanti** the city hasn't more than 2 million inhabitants; **che differenza fa?** what difference does it make?; **fa 50 euro, signora** that'll be 50 euros, madam; **glielo faccio 100 euro** I'll give it to you *o* I'll let you have it for 100 euros; **che ora fa il tuo orologio?** what time is it by your watch?
8 (*+ infinito*): **le faremo avere la merce** we'll get the goods to you; **l'hanno fatto entrare in macchina** (*costringere*) they forced him into the car, they made him get into the car; (*lasciare*) they let him get into the car; **lo farò fare a lei** I'll get her to do it, I'll have her do it; **farsi fregare** to be taken for a ride; **far piangere qn** to make sb cry; **far riparare la macchina** to have one's car repaired; **far scongelare** to defrost, thaw out; **far soffrire qn** to make sb suffer; **mi son fatto tagliare i capelli** I've had my hair cut; **fammi vedere** let me see; **fare venire qn** to send for sb
9 **farsi** *or* **farsi la barba** to have a shave; **farsi la barca** to get a boat; **farsi una gonna** to make o.s. a skirt;

Ff

farsi la macchina to get a car; **si fa da mangiare da solo** he does his own cooking; **si è fatto mia moglie** (*fam*) he's had it off with my wife; **farsi un nome** to make a name for o.s.
10 (*fraseologia*): **farla a qn** to get the better of sb; **me l'hanno fatta!** (*imbrogliare*) I've been done!; (*derubare*) I've been robbed!; (*lasciare nei guai*) I've been lumbered!; **farcela** to succeed, manage; **ne ha fatta una delle sue** he's done it again; **non ce la faccio più** (*a camminare*) I can't go on; (*a sopportare*) I can't take any more; **ce la facciamo?** do you think we'll make it?; **farla finita con qc** to have done with sth; **fare del proprio meglio** to do one's best; **non c'è niente da fare** it's no use; **ormai è stato deciso e non c'è niente da fare** it's been decided and there's nothing we can do about it; **ha fatto di sì con la testa** he nodded
■ VI (*aus* **avere**)
1 (*agire*) to do; **fare presto** to be quick; **faccia pure!** go ahead!; **saperci fare con** (*situazioni, persone*) to know how to deal with; **ci sa fare coi bambini/con le macchine** he's good with children/cars; **ci sa fare con le donne** he's a smooth operator with women; **ci sa fare** he's quite good; **fate come volete** do as you please
2 (*dire*): **"davvero?" fece** "really?" he said
3 **questo non si fa** it's not done, you (just) can't do that; **si fa così!** you do it like this, this is the way it's done; **non si fa così** (*rimprovero*) that's no way to behave!; **questa festa non si farà!** this party won't take place!
4 (*fraseologia*): **fa proprio al caso nostro** it's just what we need; **avere a che fare con qn** to have sth to do with sb; **non so che farmene di lui** I don't know what to do with him; **fare da** (*funzioni*) to act as; **fare da padre a qn** to be like a father to sb; **la cucina fa anche da sala da pranzo** the kitchen also serves as *o* is also used as a dining room; **fai in modo che non ti vedano** make sure they don't see you; **fare per** (*essere adatto*) to be suitable for; (*essere sul punto di*) to be about to; **fece per uscire e poi si fermò** he made as if to go out and then stopped; **non fa per me** it isn't (suitable) for me; **fare a pugni** to come to blows; (*fig*) to clash; **fare in tempo a...** to be in time to ...; **il grigio fa vecchio** grey makes you *o* one look older
■ VB IMPERS: **fa caldo** it's hot; **fa freddo** it's cold; **fa notte** it's getting dark;
▶ **farsi** VR
1 (*rendersi*): **farsi amico di qn** to make friends with sb; **è andata a farsi bella** she's gone to make herself beautiful; **farsi notare** to get o.s. noticed; **farsi prete** to become a priest
2 (*spostarsi*): **farsi avanti** to move forward; (*fig*) to come forward; **fatti più in là!** move along a bit!
3 (*gergo: drogarsi*) to do drugs
▶ **farsi** VIP (*divenire*) to become; **farsi bello** to grow beautiful; **farsi grande** to grow tall; **si fa notte** it's getting dark; **farsi vecchio** to grow old
■ SM: **con fare distratto** absent-mindedly; **ha un fare simpatico** he has a pleasant manner; **sul far del giorno/della notte** at daybreak/nightfall

faretra [fa'rɛtra] SF (*per frecce*) quiver
faretto [fa'retto] SM spot lamp
farfalla [far'falla] SF **1** (*Zool*) butterfly **2** (*cravatta*) bow tie **3** (*Nuoto*) butterfly (stroke); **nuotare a farfalla** to do the butterfly (stroke); **i cento metri farfalla** the hundred metres butterfly **4** (*pasta*) bow **5** (*Aut*): **valvola a farfalla** butterfly valve **6** (*Naut*): **navigare a farfalla** to goosewing
farfallino [farfal'lino] SM (*cravattino*) bow tie
farfallone [farfal'lone] SM (*fig*) philanderer
farfara ['farfara] SF (*Bot*) coltsfoot
farfugliare [farfuʎ'ʎare] VT, VI (*aus* **avere**) to mumble, mutter
farina [fa'rina] SF flour; **questa non è farina del tuo sacco** (*fig*) this isn't your own idea (*o* work); **farina di castagne** chestnut flour; **farina di grano saraceno** buckwheat; **farina di granoturco** *o* **di mais** *o* **gialla** maize (*Brit*) *o* corn (*Am*) flour; **farina integrale** wholemeal (*Brit*) *o* whole-wheat (*Am*) flour; **farina di riso** ground rice; **farina di soia** soya flour; **farine animali** *animal feeds made from recycled livestock*
farinaceo, a [fari'natʃeo] AGG farinaceous
■ **farinacei** SMPL starches, starchy foods
faringe [fa'rindʒe] SF (*Anat*) pharynx
faringeo, a [farin'dʒɛo] AGG (*Anat*) pharyngeal
faringite [farin'dʒite] SF (*Med*) pharyngitis
farinoso, a [fari'noso] AGG (*patate*) floury; (*mela*) woolly; (*neve*) powdery
farisaico, a, ci, che [fari'zaiko] AGG (*Storia*) Pharisaic; (*fig*) pharisaic
fariseo [fari'zɛo] SM (*Storia*) Pharisee; (*fig*) pharisee
farmaceutica [farma'tʃɛutika] SF pharmaceutics *sg*
▷ www.farmindustria.it/
farmaceutico, a, ci, che [farma'tʃɛutiko] AGG pharmaceutical
farmacia, cie [farma'tʃia] SF **1** (*negozio*) chemist's (shop) *o* chemist (*Brit*), pharmacy; **sto andando in farmacia** I'm going to the chemist's; **farmacia di turno** duty chemist **2** (*professione*) pharmacy
farmacista, i, e [farma'tʃista] SM/F (dispensing) chemist (*Brit*), pharmacist
farmaco, ci ['farmako] SM drug, medicine
farmacologia [farmakolo'dʒia] SF pharmacology
farmacologicamente [farmakolodʒika'mente] AVV pharmacologically
farmacologico, a, ci, che [farmako'lɔdʒiko] AGG pharmacological
farmacopea [farmako'pɛa] SF (*catalogo*) pharmacopoeia
farneticare [farneti'kare] VI (*aus* **avere**) (*anche fig*) to be delirious; **stai farneticando!** you're talking nonsense!
farnia ['farnja] SF (*Bot*) English oak
faro ['faro] SM **1** (*Naut*) lighthouse; (*Aer*) beacon; **faro d'atterraggio** landing light **2** (*Aut*) headlight, headlamp (*Brit*); **accendi i fari** switch on your headlights; **fari abbaglianti** headlights on full beam; **fari anabbaglianti** dipped headlights; **fari antinebbia** fog lights *o* lamps
Faroar [fa'roar] SFPL (*anche:* **le isole Faroar**) the Faroes, the Faroe Islands
farragine [far'radʒine] SF (*di libri*) jumble; (*di opinioni, citazioni*) mishmash
farraginoso, a [farradʒi'noso] AGG (*stile*) muddled, confused
farsa ['farsa] SF (*anche fig*) farce
farsesco, a, schi, sche [far'sesko] AGG farcical
fasc. ABBR = fascicolo
fascetta [faʃ'ʃetta] SF (*gen*) narrow band, narrow strip; (*di medaglia*) ribbon; (*Med*) bandage; (*di giornale*) wrapper
fascia, sce ['faʃʃa] SF **1** (*di tessuto, carta, anche fig*) strip, band; (*Med*) bandage; (*di sindaco, ufficiale*) sash; **fascia del cappello** hatband; **fascia elastica** elastic bandage;

essere in fasce (*anche fig*) to be in one's infancy; **ti conosco da quando eri ancora in fasce** I've known you since you were a baby; **fascia di contribuenti** tax group *o* band; **fascia d'età** age group; **fascia blu** *city centre area wholly or partially closed to traffic*; **fascia oraria** (*Radio, TV*) slot; (*Telec*) time band **2** (*Geog*) strip, belt; **fascia equatoriale** equatorial belt **3** (*Tecn*) **fascia elastica** piston ring

fasciame [faʃʃame] SM (*Naut: di legno*) planking; (*: di metallo*) plating

fasciante [faʃʃante] AGG (*aderente*) tight(-fitting)

fasciare [faʃʃare] VT (*gen*) to bind; (*Med*) to bandage; **fasciare un bambino** to put on a baby's nappy (*Brit*) *o* diaper (*Am*); **fasciati il piede** bandage your foot; **gli hanno fasciato il ginocchio** they bandaged his knee; **quel vestito le fasciava i fianchi** the dress clung to her hips

fasciato, a [faʃʃato] AGG bandaged

fasciatoio [faʃʃa'tɔjo] SM changing table

fasciatura [faʃʃa'tura] SF (*azione*) bandaging; (*fascia*) bandage

fascicolo [faʃʃikolo] SM (*opuscolo*) booklet, pamphlet; (*Amm*) file, dossier; (*di pubblicazione*) instalment; (*di rivista*) issue, number

fascina [faʃʃina] SF faggot

fascino ['faʃʃino] SM charm, fascination; **avere fascino** (*persona*) to be fascinating; **subire il fascino di qn** to succumb to sb's charm; **una donna di gran fascino** a woman of great charm

fascio, sci ['faʃʃo] SM **1** (*di legna*) bundle; (*di fieno, frecce*) sheaf; (*di fiori*) bunch; (*di luce*) beam **2** (*Storia*) fasces *pl* **3** (*Pol*): **il Fascio** the Fascist Party

fascismo [faʃʃizmo] SM fascism

fascista, i, e [faʃʃista] AGG, SM/F fascist; **è fascista** he's a fascist

fase ['faze] SF **1** (*gen, Chim, Astron*) phase; **in fase avanzata** at an advanced stage; **essere in fase di miglioramento** to be getting better, be improving; **in fase preliminare** in the preliminary stages; **in fase di espansione** in a period of expansion **2** (*Tecn*) stroke; **essere fuori fase** (*motore*) to be rough (*Brit*), run roughly; (*fig*) to feel rough (*Brit*) *o* rotten; **mettere il motore in fase** to tune the engine

fastello [fas'tɛllo] SM bundle

fastidio, di [fas'tidjo] SM (*disturbo*) trouble, bother; **che fastidio!** what a nuisance!; **dare fastidio a qn** to bother *o* annoy sb; **smettila! mi dai fastidio!** stop it! you're getting on my nerves!; **il rumore mi dava fastidio** the noise was annoying me; **mi dà fastidio il suo modo di fare** his whole attitude gets on my nerves; **le dà fastidio se fumo?** do you mind if I smoke?; **la caviglia mi dà ancora fastidio** my ankle is still bothering me; **sento un po' di fastidio** it hurts a bit; **ha avuto dei fastidi con la polizia** he has had some trouble *o* bother with the police

fastidiosamente [fastidjosa'mente] AVV (*vedi agg*) annoyingly; irritably

fastidioso, a [fasti'djoso] AGG **1** (*gen*) annoying; (*persona*) tiresome, annoying; **un dolore fastidioso** a nagging pain; **è un bambino fastidioso** he's an annoying child **2** (*irritabile*) irritable

LO SAPEVI...?
fastidioso non si traduce mai con la parola inglese *fastidious*

fasto ['fasto] SM pomp, splendour (*Brit*), splendor (*Am*); **i fasti dell'antica Roma** the splendour(s) of ancient Rome

fastosità [fastosi'ta] SF INV pomp, splendour

fastoso, a [fas'toso] AGG sumptuous, lavish

fasullo, a [fa'zullo] AGG (*gen*) fake; (*dichiarazione, persona*) false; (*pretesto*) bogus

fata ['fata] SF fairy; **fata morgana** (*miraggio*) Fata Morgana

fatale [fa'tale] AGG **1** (*inevitabile*) inevitable; **era fatale che succedesse** it was bound to happen **2** (*mortale: incidente, malattia*) fatal; (*: colpo*) fatal, mortal; **errore fatale** fatal error; **essere fatale a qn** to be *o* prove fatal to sb **3** (*irresistibile: sguardo*) irresistible; **donna fatale** femme fatale

fatalismo [fata'lizmo] SM fatalism

fatalista, i, e [fata'lista] SM/F fatalist

fatalisticamente [fatalistika'mente] AVV fatalistically

fatalistico, a, ci, che [fata'listiko] AGG fatalistic

fatalità [fatali'ta] SF INV (*fato*) fate, destiny; (*inevitabilità*) inevitability; (*disgrazia*) misfortune

fatalmente [fatal'mente] AVV **1** (*inevitabilmente*) inevitably; **doveva fatalmente accadere** it was bound to happen **2** (*con gravi conseguenze*) with fatal consequences

fatato, a [fa'tato] AGG (*spada, chiave*) magic; (*castello*) enchanted

fatica, che [fa'tika] SF **1** (*sforzo fisico*) hard work, toil; **animale da fatica** beast of burden; **divisa di fatica** (*Mil*) fatigues *pl*; **uomo di fatica** odd-job man; **fare fatica a fare qc** to have a job doing sth, find it difficult to do sth; **faccio fatica a crederlo** I find that hard to believe; **faccio fatica a capire la matematica** I find it difficult to understand maths; **il paziente deve evitare ogni fatica** the patient must avoid any kind of physical exertion; **accusare** *o* **sentire fatica** to feel tired; **non si è preso nemmeno la fatica di dirmelo** he didn't even take the trouble to tell me; **risparmiarsi la fatica di fare qc** to save o.s. the bother *o* effort of doing sth; **ci vuole tempo e fatica** it takes time and effort; **che fatica!** it's hard work!; **le fatiche di Ercole** the labours of Hercules **2** (*difficoltà*): **a fatica** with difficulty; **respirare a fatica** to have difficulty (in) breathing; **riusciva a fatica a tenere la testa dritta** he could hardly keep his head up; **l'ho convinto a fatica** I had a hard job convincing him **3** (*di metalli*) fatigue

faticaccia, ce [fati'kattʃa] SF (*fam*): **fu una faticaccia** it was a hell of a job

faticare [fati'kare] VI (*aus* **avere**) to work hard, toil; **faticare per fare qc** to struggle to do sth; **faticare a fare qc** to have difficulty in doing sth, have difficulty doing sth

faticata [fati'kata] SF hard work

fatichi *ecc* [fa'tiki] VB *vedi* **faticare**

faticosamente [fatikosa'mente] AVV with effort, laboriously

faticoso, a [fati'koso] AGG (*viaggio, camminata*) tiring, exhausting; (*lavoro*) laborious

fatidicamente [fatidika'mente] AVV as fate would have it

fatidico, a, ci, che [fa'tidiko] AGG fateful

fatiscente [fatiʃʃente] AGG tumbledown

fato ['fato] SM fate, destiny

fatt. ABBR (= **fattura**) inv

fatta ['fatta] SF (*genere, tipo*) kind

fattaccio, ci [fat'tattʃo] SM foul deed

fatterello [fatte'rɛllo] SM insignificant event

fattezze [fat'tettse] SFPL (*del viso*) features

Ff

fattibile [fat'tibile] AGG feasible, possible

fattispecie [fattis'pɛtʃe] SF: **nella** *o* **in fattispecie** in this case *o* instance

fatto[1], a ['fatto] PP *di* **fare**

■ AGG **1** *(prodotto)* made; **fatto a macchina/a mano** machine-/hand-made; **fatto in casa** home-made; **abiti fatti** ready-made *o* off-the-peg clothes **2** *(fraseologia)*: **sono fatto così** that's how I am, I'm like that; **è ben fatta** she has a nice figure; **essere fatto per qc** to be made *o* meant for sth; **è fatto per l'archeologia** he's got what it takes to be an archeologist; **è un uomo fatto** he's a grown man; **a giorno fatto** in broad daylight; **è fatta!** that's it!, I've (*o* you've *ecc*) done it!; **è completamente fatto** *(fam: drogato, ubriaco)* he's (completely) stoned

fatto[2] ['fatto] SM **1** *(accaduto)* fact; **i fatti parlano chiaro** the facts speak for themselves; **questo è un altro fatto** that's another matter; **di fatto** in fact; **il fatto sta** *o* **è che** the fact remains *o* is that; **il fatto è che ha ragione lui** the fact is that he's right; **in fatto di macchine è un genio** when it comes to cars he's a genius **2** *(azione)* deed, act; **cogliere qn sul fatto** to catch sb red-handed *o* in the act; **li hanno colti sul fatto** they caught them red-handed; **porre qn di fronte al fatto compiuto** to present sb with a fait accompli; **c'è stato un nuovo fatto di sangue** there has been further bloodshed; **fatto d'arme** *(frm)* feat of arms; **è uno che sa il fatto suo** he knows what he's about; **gli ho detto il fatto suo** I told him what I thought of him; **fare i fatti propri** to mind one's own business; **pensa ai fatti tuoi!** mind your own business!; **immischiarsi nei fatti altrui** to stick one's nose into other people's business **3** *(avvenimento)* event, occurrence; *(di romanzo, film)* action, story; **fatto di cronaca** news item; **fatto nuovo** new development; **è successo un fatto strano** a strange thing happened; **la mia versione dei fatti** my version of events

fattore [fat'tore] SM **1** *(elemento, Mat)* factor; **fattore di protezione** *(di crema solare)* (protection) factor; **fattore di protezione solare 6** (protection) factor 6 **2** *(Agr)* farm manager

fattoria [fatto'ria] SF *(gen)* farm; *(casa)* farmhouse

LO SAPEVI...?
fattoria non si traduce mai con la parola inglese *factory*

fattorino [fatto'rino] SM *(gen)* errand boy; *(di ufficio)* office junior, office boy; *(d'albergo)* porter

fattrice [fat'tritʃe] SF *(cavalla)* brood mare; *(mucca)* brood cow

fattucchiera [fattuk'kjɛra] SF witch

fattura [fat'tura] SF **1** *(Comm)* invoice **2** *(confezione: di abito)* tailoring **3** *(stregoneria)* spell; **fare una fattura a qn** to cast a spell on sb

fatturare [fattu'rare] VT **1** *(Comm)* to invoice **2** *(adulterare)* to adulterate

fatturato [fattu'rato] SM *(Comm)* turnover

fatturatrice [fattura'tritʃe] SF invoicing machine

fatturazione [fatturat'tsjone] SF invoicing, billing

fatturista, i, e [fattu'rista] SM/F invoice clerk

fatuamente [fatua'mente] AVV fatuously

fatuità [fatui'ta] SF INV fatuousness

fatuo, a ['fatuo] AGG fatuous, vain; **fuoco fatuo** *(anche fig)* will-o'-the-wisp

fauci ['fautʃi] SFPL *(di leone)* jaws; *(di vulcano)* mouth *sg*; **cadere nelle fauci di qn** *(fig)* to fall prey to sb

fauna ['fauna] SF *(Zool)* fauna

fauno ['fauno] SM *(Mitol)* faun

fausto, a ['fausto] AGG *(frm)* happy, propitious; **un fausto evento** a happy event; **un fausto presagio** a good omen

fautore, trice [fau'tore] SM/F advocate, supporter

fava ['fava] SF broad bean

favella [fa'vɛlla] SF speech; **perdere il dono della favella** to be struck dumb

favilla [fa'villa] SF spark; *(fig: di speranza)* glimmer; **fare faville** *(fig: cantante)* to give a sparkling performance

favo ['favo] SM *(di api)* honeycomb

favola ['favola] SF *(fiaba)* fairy tale; *(d'intento morale)* fable; *(fig: fandonia)* tall tale, yarn; **essere la favola del paese** *(oggetto di chiacchiere)* to be the talk of the town; *(zimbello)* to be a laughing stock in the town; **la casa è una favola** the house is a dream

favoleggiare [favoled'dʒare] VI *(aus* **avere***)* to tell stories

favolistica [favo'listika] SF folk tales *pl*

favolosamente [favolosa'mente] AVV fabulously; **è stato favolosamente bravo** he was exceptionally good

favoloso, a [favo'loso] AGG *(gen)* fabulous; *(incredibile)* incredible; **prezzi favolosi** incredible prices; **una casa favolosa** a fabulous house

favore [fa'vore] SM favour *(Brit)*, favor *(Am)*; **chiedere/fare un favore a qn** to ask/do sb a favour; **posso chiederti un favore?** can I ask you a favour?; **mi faresti un favore?** would you do me a favour?; **per favore** please; **godere del favore del pubblico** to enjoy public favour; **prezzo/trattamento di favore** preferential price/treatment; **condizioni di favore** *(Comm)* favourable terms; **biglietto di favore** complimentary ticket; **a favore di** *(votare)* in favour of; *(testimoniare, raccogliere aiuti)* on behalf of; **essere a favore di** to be in favour of; **col favore delle tenebre** under cover of darkness

favoreggiamento [favoreddʒa'mento] SM *(Dir)* aiding and abetting; **favoreggiamento bellico** collaboration (with the enemy)

favoreggiare [favored'dʒare] VT **1** to favour *(Brit)*, favor *(Am)* **2** *(Dir)* to aid and abet

favorevole [favo'revole] AGG: **favorevole (a)** *(situazione, vento)* favourable *(Brit) o*, favorable *(Am)* (to); *(persona)* in favour (of), favourable (to); **essere favorevole a** to be in favour of; **hanno avuto 70 voti favorevoli** they got 70 votes in favour; **aspettare il momento favorevole** to wait for the right moment

favorevolmente [favorevol'mente] AVV favourably *(Brit)*, favorably *(Am)*; **la proposta è stata accolta favorevolmente** the proposal was greeted favourably

favorire [favo'rire] VT **1** *(gen)* to favour *(Brit)*, favor *(Am)*; *(commercio, industria, arti)* to promote, encourage; *(partito, opinione)* to support **2** *(in espressioni di cortesia)*: **favorisca da questa parte** please come this way; **vuole favorire?** won't you help yourself?; **mi favorisca i documenti** please may I see your papers?; **favorisca alla cassa** please pay at the cash-desk

favoritismo [favori'tizmo] SM favouritism *(Brit)*, favoritism *(Am)*

favorito, a [favo'rito] AGG, SM/F favourite *(Brit)*, favorite *(Am)*

fax [faks] SM INV *(anche:* **telefax***)* fax; **mandare qc via fax** to fax sth; **gli ho mandato un fax** I sent him a fax

faxare [fak'sare] VT to fax

fazione [fat'tsjone] SF faction

faziosamente [fattsjosa'mente] AVV in a partisan manner
faziosità [fattsjosi'ta] SF INV bias
fazioso, a [fat'tsjoso] AGG partisan
fazzoletto [fattso'letto] SM *(da naso)* handkerchief; (*: di carta*) (paper) tissue *(Brit)*, Kleenex® *(Am)*; *(da collo)* neckerchief; **un fazzoletto di terra** a patch of land
FBI [efbi'ai] SIGLA F FBI (= *Federal Bureau of Investigation*)
FC ABBR *vedi* **fuoricorso**
f.co ABBR = **franco' AVV**
FE SIGLA = *Ferrara*
febbraio [feb'brajo] SM February; *per fraseologia vedi* **luglio**
febbre ['fɛbbre] SF **1** fever; **avere la febbre** to have a (high) temperature; **hai la febbre?** have you got a temperature?; **misurare la febbre a qn** to take sb's temperature; **misurarsi la febbre** to take one's temperature; **febbre da fieno** hay fever; **febbre gialla** yellow fever; **febbre reumatica** rheumatic fever **2** *(herpes)* cold sore **3** *(fig)*: **la febbre dell'oro** gold fever
febbricitante [febbritʃi'tante] AGG feverish
febbrile [feb'brile] AGG *(anche fig)* feverish
febbrilmente [febbril'mente] AVV feverishly
febbrone [feb'brone] SM high temperature
Febo ['fɛbo] SM Phoebus
fecale [fe'kale] AGG faecal *(Brit)*, fecal *(Am)*
feccia, ce ['fɛttʃa] SF *(anche fig)* dregs *pl*
feci ['fɛtʃi] SFPL faeces *(Brit)*, feces *(Am)*, excrement *sg*
feci *ecc* ['fetʃi] VB *vedi* **fare**
fecola ['fɛkola] SF starch; **fecola di patate** ≈ cornflour
fecondamente [fekonda'mente] AVV fruitfully
fecondare [fekon'dare] VT to fertilize
fecondativo, a [fekonda'tivo] AGG: **un farmaco fecondativo** a fertility drug
fecondazione [fekondat'tsjone] SF fertilization; **fecondazione artificiale** artificial insemination; **fecondazione assistita** assisted conception
fecondità [fekondi'ta] SF INV *(Bio, di terreno, fig: ingegno)* fertility, productiveness; *(di scrittore)* prolificness
fecondo, a [fe'kondo] AGG *(terreno, donna, fig: ingegno)* fertile; *(albero, fig: pensiero, lavoro)* fruitful; (*: scrittore*) prolific
fede ['fede] SF **1** *(credenza)* faith, belief; *(Rel)* faith **2** *(fiducia)* faith, trust; *(fedeltà)* loyalty; **aver fede in** to have faith in; **degno di fede** trustworthy, reliable; **tener fede a** *(ideale)* to remain loyal to; *(giuramento, promessa)* to keep; **in buona fede** in good faith; **ho agito in buona fede** I acted in good faith; **essere in buona/cattiva fede** to act in good/bad faith; **in fede mia!** on my word! **3** *(anello nuziale)* wedding ring **4** *(attestato)* certificate; **in fede di** in proof of *o* as evidence of; **far fede di** to be proof *o* evidence of; **"in fede"** *(Dir)* "in witness whereof"
fedele [fe'dele] AGG **1** *(leale)*: **fedele (a)** faithful (to); **essere fedele a** to be faithful to; **gli è sempre stata fedele** she's always been faithful to him; **essere fedele alla parola data** to keep one's word; **un marito fedele** a faithful husband; **suddito fedele** loyal subject **2** *(veritiero)* true, accurate
■ SM/F *(Rel)* believer; *(seguace)* follower; **i fedeli** *(Rel)* the faithful *pl*
fedelmente [fedel'mente] AVV *(servire, amare)* faithfully
fedeltà [fedel'ta] SF INV **1** *(devozione)* loyalty, faithfulness; *(coniugale)* fidelity; **fedeltà verso** *o* **a qn** loyalty to sb **2** *(esattezza: di copia, traduzione)* accuracy **3** *(Radio ecc)*: **alta fedeltà** high fidelity; **un impianto ad alta fedeltà** a hi-fi system
federa ['fɛdera] SF pillowslip, pillowcase
federale [fede'rale] AGG federal
federalismo [federa'lizmo] SM federalism
federalista, i, e [federa'lista] AGG, SM/F federalist
federarsi [fede'rarsi] VIP to form a federation
federativo, a [federa'tivo] AGG federative
federazione [federat'tsjone] SF federation
FEDERCACCIA [feder'kattʃa] ABBR F (= **Federazione italiana della caccia**) *Italian hunting federation*
FEDERCALCIO [feder'kaltʃo] ABBR F (= **Federazione italiana gioco calcio**) *Italian football association*
FEDERCONSORZI [federkon'sɔrtsi] ABBR F (= **Federazione sindacale dei consorzi agrari**) *Italian federation of farmers' agricultural businesses*
fedifrago, a, ghi, ghe [fe'difrago] AGG faithless, perfidious
fedina [fe'dina] SF *(Dir: fedina penale)* record; **avere la fedina (penale) pulita** to have a clean record; **avere la fedina (penale) sporca** to have a police record
Fedra ['fɛdra] SF Phaedra
fegatino [fega'tino] SM *(di pollame)* liver; **fegatino di pollo** chicken liver
fegato ['fegato] SM **1** *(Anat, Culin)* liver; **fegato di vitello** calf's liver; **mangiarsi** *o* **rodersi il fegato** to be consumed with rage; **fegato ingrossato** *(Med)* enlarged liver; **non mi piace il fegato** I don't like liver **2** *(fig: coraggio)* guts *pl*, nerve; **ha fegato!** he's got guts!
felce ['feltʃe] SF fern
feldmaresciallo [feldmareʃʃallo] SM *(Mil)* field marshal
felice [fe'litʃe] AGG **1** *(contento)* happy; **sono felice di fare la sua conoscenza** pleased to meet you; **adesso sono più felice** I'm happier now; **è stato il giorno più felice della mia vita** it was the happiest day of my life; **felice come una pasqua** as happy as a sandboy **2** *(fortunato)* lucky; (*: scelta*) fortunate, happy; (*: vento*) favourable; **avere la mano felice** to have nimble fingers; **non ho scelto il momento più felice per venire** I don't seem to have chosen the best moment to come
felicemente [felitʃe'mente] AVV *(in modo felice)* happily; *(bene)* successfully, happily; **l'esperimento si è concluso felicemente** the experiment was successful
felicità [felitʃi'ta] SF INV happiness
felicitarsi [felitʃi'tarsi] VIP: **felicitarsi con qn (per qc)** *(congratularsi)* to congratulate sb (on sth)
felicitazioni [felitʃitat'tsjoni] SFPL congratulations
felino, a [fe'lino] AGG *(Zool)* feline; *(fig)* feline, catlike
■ SM feline
felpa ['felpa] SF *(maglia)* sweatshirt
felpato, a [fel'pato] AGG *(tessuto)* brushed; *(passo)* stealthy; **con passo felpato** stealthily
■ SM brushed cotton (*o* nylon *ecc*)
feltrino [fel'trino] SM felt pad *(placed under furniture to protect the floor)*
feltro ['feltro] SM felt; **cappello di feltro** felt hat
feluca, che [fe'luka] SF **1** *(Naut)* felucca **2** *(cappello)* cocked hat
femmina ['femmina] SF *(Zool, Tecn)* female; **ho due figli, un maschio e una femmina** I've got two children, a boy and a girl; **una femmina di panda** *or* **un panda femmina** a female panda
femmineo, a [fem'mineo] AGG *(effeminato)* effeminate
femminile [femmi'nile] AGG *(gen, Gramm)* feminine;

(*sesso*) female; **moda femminile** women's fashion; **una rivista femminile** a women's magazine; **è molto femminile** she's very feminine

femminilità [femminili'ta] SF INV femininity; **un tocco di femminilità** a feminine touch

femminismo [femmi'nizmo] SM feminism

femminista, i, e [femmi'nista] SM/F, AGG feminist; **è femminista** she's a feminist

femminuccia, ce [femmi'nuttʃa] SF (*bambina*) baby girl; (*pegg*) sissy

femore ['femore] SM (*Anat*) thighbone, femur

fendente [fen'dɛnte] SM (*con sciabola*) cut; (*Calcio*) powerful shot; **con un fendente mandò il pallone in rete** he slammed the ball into the back of the net

fendere ['fɛndere] VT IRREG (*fig: aria, flutti, onde*) to cut through, slice (through); **i fari fendevano la nebbia** the headlights pierced the fog; **fendere la folla** to push through the crowd

fendinebbia [fendi'nebbja] SM INV (*Aut*) fog lamp

fenditura [fendi'tura] SF (*gen*) crack; (*di roccia*) cleft, crack

feng-shui ['fɛng 'ʃwei] SM feng shui

fenice [fe'nitʃe] SF (*anche:* **araba fenice**) phoenix

fenicottero [feni'kɔttero] SM flamingo

fenolftaleina [fenolftale'ina] SF (*Chim*) phenolphthalein

fenolo [fe'nɔlo] SM (*Chim*) phenol

fenomenale [fenome'nale] AGG phenomenal

fenomenico, a, ci, che [feno'mɛniko] AGG phenomenal; **mondo fenomenico** external world

fenomeno [fe'nɔmeno] SM (*gen*) phenomenon; (*persona: eccezionale*) character; (*: anormale*) freak; **un fenomeno inspiegabile** an inexplicable phenomenon

fenotipo [feno'tipo] SM (*Bio*) phenotype

feretro ['fɛretro] SM coffin; **il feretro si avviava verso il cimitero** the funeral procession wound its way to the cemetery

feriale [fe'rjale] AGG: **giorno feriale** working day, weekday

ferie ['fɛrje] SFPL holidays (*Brit*), vacation *sg* (*Am*); **ferie retribuite** paid holiday, holiday with pay; **andare in ferie** to go on holiday *o* vacation; **dove vai in ferie?** where are you going on holiday?; **ho fatto le ferie al mare** I spent my holidays at the seaside; **ho 2 settimane di ferie** I have 2 weeks' holidays; **un giorno di ferie** a day off; **prendere un giorno di ferie** to take a day off; **ho preso un giorno di ferie** I took a day off

ferimento [feri'mento] SM wounding; **nella sparatoria si è avuto il ferimento di 3 persone** 3 people were hurt *o* wounded in the shooting

ferire [fe'rire] VT **1** (*gen*) to injure; (*Mil*) to wound; **fu ferito a morte** he was fatally wounded; **nell'incidente sono state ferite 4 persone** 4 people were injured in the accident; **la bomba ha ferito tre persone** the bomb injured three people; **il soldato è stato ferito ad una gamba** the soldier was wounded in the leg **2** (*fig*) to hurt, wound; **ferire qn nell'orgoglio** to hurt *o* wound *o* injure sb's pride; **le sue parole la ferirono** she was wounded *o* hurt by what he said

▶ **ferirse** VR to hurt o.s., injure o.s.; **ferirsi con un coltello** to cut o.s. with a knife; **mi sono ferito ad una mano** I've injured my hand

ferita [fe'rita] SF (*vedi vb*) injury; wound; **riportò gravi ferite** he was seriously wounded; **le sue ferite non erano gravi** his injuries were not serious

ferito, a [fe'rito] SM/F casualty; **hanno portato i feriti all'ospedale** the casualties were taken to hospital; **nell'incidente ci sono stati due feriti** two people were injured in the accident; **un ferito grave** a seriously injured person

feritoia [feri'toja] SF slit

ferma ['ferma] SF **1** (*Mil*) (period of) service **2** (*Caccia*): **cane da ferma** pointer

fermacapelli [fermaka'pelli] SM INV hair slide

fermacarte [ferma'karte] SM INV paperweight

fermacravatta [fermakra'vatta] SM INV tiepin (*Brit*), tie tack (*Am*)

fermaglio, gli [fer'maʎʎo] SM (*gen*) clasp; (*per documenti*) clip

fermamente [ferma'mente] AVV firmly

fermaporta [ferma'porta] SM INV doorstop

fermare [fer'mare] VT **1** (*gen*) to stop, halt; **non cercare di fermarmi** don't try and stop me; **lo fermò con un gesto della mano** (*far cenno*) he gestured to him to stop; (*bloccare*) he put his hand out to stop him **2** (*fissare: bottone*) to make secure; (*: porta*) to stop **3** (*prenotare: stanza, albergo*) to book **4** (*Polizia*) to detain, hold

■ VI (*aus* **avere**) to stop; **il treno ferma a...** the train calls at ...;

▶ **fermarsi** VIP (*gen*) to stop, halt; **fermarsi a guardare/fare** to stop to look/do; **non posso fermarmi di più** I can't stop *o* stay any longer; **mi sono fermato a salutarla** I stopped to say hello to her; **far segno di fermarsi a qn** to signal to sb to stop; (*ad automobilista*) to wave sb down; **fermati!** stop!; **la sua attenzione si fermò sul dipinto** his attention focused on the painting; **l'orologio si è fermato alle tre e cinque** the clock stopped at five past three

fermata [fer'mata] SF stop; **scendo tra 2 fermate** I get off 2 stops from here; **la corriera fa una fermata a Montelupo** the coach stops *o* makes a stop at Montelupo; **fermata dell'autobus** bus stop; **fermata facoltativa** *o* **a richiesta** request stop

fermentare [fermen'tare] VI (*aus* **avere**) to ferment ■ VT to ferment; (*fig*) to be in ferment

fermentazione [fermentat'tsjone] SF fermentation

fermento [fer'mento] SM **1** (*anche fig*) ferment; **in fermento** in a ferment **2** (*Culin: lievito*) yeast; **fermenti lattici** lactobacillus; probiotics

fermezza [fer'mettsa] SF firmness, steadfastness; **fermezza di mente/d'animo** strength of mind/of character; **fermezza di propositi** steadiness of purpose; **rispondere con fermezza** to answer firmly, give a firm answer

fermo, a ['fermo] AGG **1** (*immobile: persona*) still, motionless; (*: veicolo, traffico*) at a standstill, stationary; (*non in funzione*) not working; **era fermo in piedi** he was standing still; **stare fermo** to keep still; **non sta fermo un attimo** he can't keep still for a minute; **stai fermo!** keep still!; **stai fermo con le mani!** keep your hands still!; (*non toccarmi*) keep your hands to yourself!; **fermo!** don't move!, stay where you are!; **tenere fermo qn** to keep sb still; **c'era una macchina ferma al bordo della strada** there was a car stopped at the side of the road; **il treno era fermo in stazione** the train was standing in the station; **ero fermo al semaforo** I was waiting at the traffic lights; **gli affari sono fermi** business is at a standstill; **l'orologio è fermo** the clock has stopped **2** (*costante, risoluto*) firm; (*non tremante: voce, mano*) steady; **restare fermo sulle proprie posizioni** to stick to one's position; **resta**

fermo che... it is settled that ...; **fermo restando che...** it being understood that ...
■SM 1 *(Dir)*: **fermo di polizia** police custody *(before formal accusation of a crime)* 2 *(di porta: gancio)* catch 3 **fermo immagine** pause (button)

fermo posta ['fermo 'pɔsta] AVV, SM, AGG poste restante *(Brit)*, general delivery *(Am)*

feroce [fe'rotʃe] AGG *(animale)* ferocious, fierce; *(persona)* fierce, cruel; *(critica)* savage; *(fame, dolore)* raging; **le bestie feroci** wild animals

ferocemente [ferotʃe'mente] AVV *(aggredire)* ferociously, fiercely; *(criticare)* savagely

ferocia [fe'rɔtʃa] SF ferocity

ferodo® [fe'rɔdo] SM brake lining

Ferr. ABBR = ferrovia

ferraglia [fer'raʎʎa] SF scrap iron; **rumore di ferraglia** clanking noise

ferragosto [ferra'gosto] SM *(festa)* feast of the Assumption; *(data)* August 15

FERRAGOSTO

Ferragosto, 15 August, is a national holiday. Marking the feast of the Assumption, its origins are religious but in recent years it has simply become the most important public holiday of the summer season. Most people take some extra time off work and head out of town to the holiday resorts. Consequently, most of industry and commerce grind to a standstill.

ferraio, aia, ai, aie [fer'rajo] AGG: **fabbro ferraio** blacksmith

ferramenta [ferra'menta] SFPL ironmongery *sg* *(Brit)*, hardware *sg*
■SF *(anche:* **negozio di ferramenta***)* ironmonger's *(Brit)*, hardware shop *o* store *(Am)*

ferrare [fer'rare] VT *(cavallo)* to shoe; *(botte)* to hoop

ferrarese [ferra'rese] AGG of *o* from Ferrara
■SM/F inhabitant *o* native of Ferrara

ferrato, a [fer'rato] AGG 1 *(Ferr)*: **strada ferrata** railway line *(Brit)*, railroad line *(Am)* 2 *(fig)*: **essere ferrato in** *(materia)* to be well up in

ferratura [ferra'tura] SF *(di cavallo)* shoeing

ferravecchio, chi [ferra'vɛkkjo] SM = **ferrovecchio**

ferreo, a ['fɛrreo] AGG *(anche fig)* iron *attr*; **volontà ferrea** iron will; **salute ferrea** iron constitution

ferretto [fer'retto] SM *(di reggiseno)* wire

ferriera [fer'rjɛra] SF ironworks *sg o pl*

ferrigno, a [fer'riɲɲo] AGG *(che contiene ferro)* ferrous; **grigio ferrigno** iron-grey

ferro ['fɛrro] SM 1 *(metallo)* iron; **ferro battuto** wrought iron; **l'età del ferro** the Iron Age; **di ferro** iron; **una sbarra di ferro** an iron bar; **minerali di ferro** iron ore; **ha una memoria di ferro** he has an excellent memory; **ha una salute di ferro** he has an iron constitution; **avere uno stomaco di ferro** to have a cast-iron stomach; **avere un alibi di ferro** to have a cast-iron alibi; **tocca ferro!** touch wood!; **battere il ferro finché è caldo** to strike while the iron is hot 2 *(strumento: gen)* tool; **i ferri del mestiere** the tools of the trade; **a ferro di cavallo** in the shape of a horseshoe; **i ferri del chirurgo** surgical instruments; **essere sotto i ferri** *(di chirurgo)* to be under the knife; **ai ferri** grilled; **una bistecca ai ferri** a grilled steak; **carne ai ferri** grilled meat; **cucinare** *o* **fare qc ai ferri** to grill sth; **ferri da calza** knitting needles; **ferro di cavallo** horseshoe; **ferro da stiro** iron 3 *(arma)* sword; **ferri** SMPL *(ceppi)* irons, chains; **incrociare i ferri** to cross swords; **mettere a ferro e fuoco** to put to the sword; **essere ai ferri corti** *(fig)* to be at daggers drawn

ferroso, a [fer'roso] AGG ferrous

ferrotranviario, ria, ri, rie [ferrotran'vjarjo] AGG public transport *attr*

ferrotranviere [ferrotran'vjɛre] SM public transport employee

FERROTRANVIERI [ferrotran'vjɛri] ABBR F (= **Federazione Nazionale Lavoratori Autoferrotranvieri e Internavigatori**) *transport workers' union*

ferrovecchio, chi [ferro'vɛkkjo] SM *(commerciante: di oggetti di scarso valore)* junk dealer; (: *di ferro vecchio*) scrap merchant

ferrovia [ferro'via] SF railway *(Brit)*, railroad *(Am)*
▷ www.trenitalia.it/

ferroviario, ria, rie, ri [ferro'vjarjo] AGG railway *attr* *(Brit)*, railroad *attr* *(Am)*; **la stazione ferroviaria** the railway station

ferroviere [ferro'vjɛre] SM railwayman *(Brit)*, railroad man *(Am)*

ferry-boat ['fɛri 'bout] SM INV ferry

fertile ['fɛrtile] AGG *(anche fig)* fertile

fertilità [fertili'ta] SF INV fertility

fertilizzante [fertilid'dzante] AGG fertilizing
■SM fertilizer

fertilizzare [fertilid'dzare] VT to fertilize

fertilizzazione [fertiliddzat'tsjone] SF fertilization

fervente [fer'vɛnte] AGG fervent, ardent

ferventemente [fervente'mente] AVV fervently, ardently

fervere ['fervere] VI DIF: **fervono i preparativi per l'arrivo del presidente** preparations for the president's arrival are in full swing

fervidamente [fervida'mente] AVV fervently, fervidly

fervido, a ['fɛrvido] AGG fervent, fervid, ardent; **fervide preghiere** impassioned pleas; **i miei più fervidi auguri** my very best wishes

fervore [fer'vore] SM fervour *(Brit)*, fervor *(Am)*, ardour *(Brit)*, ardor *(Am)*; **nel fervore di** *(discussione, lotta)* in the heat of

fesa ['feza] SF *(Culin)* rump of veal

fesseria [fesse'ria] SF stupidity; **quel film è una fesseria** that film is rubbish; **dire fesserie** to talk nonsense; **fare una fesseria** to do something stupid

fesso, a ['fesso] PP *di* **fendere**
■SM/F idiot, fool; **fare il fesso** to play the fool; **dare del fesso a qn** to call sb a fool
■AGG 1 *(fam)* stupid, daft 2 *(spaccato)* cracked; **con voce fessa** in a cracked voice

fessura [fes'sura] SF *(gen)* crack, split; *(per gettone, moneta)* slot; *(Alpinismo)* crack

festa ['fɛsta] SF 1 *(religiosa)* feast (day); *(civile)* holiday; **oggi è festa** today's a holiday; **giorno di festa** holiday; **il Natale è la festa dei bambini** Christmas is a time for children 2 *(vacanza)* holidays *pl*, vacation *(Am)*; **cosa fai per le feste?** what are you doing over the holidays?; **la settimana scorsa ho avuto 3 giorni di festa** last week I was on holiday for 3 days, I had 3 days off (work) last week 3 *(ricorrenza: compleanno)* birthday; (: *onomastico*) name day; **quand'è la tua festa?** when is your birthday?; **la festa di San Giovanni** St John's Day, the feast of St John 4 *(sagra)* fair; **la festa del paese** the town festival; **festa della birra** beer festival

5 (*ricevimento*) party, celebration; **dare** *o* **fare una festa** to give *o* have a party; **ha dato una festa per il suo compleanno** he gave a party for his birthday
6 (*fraseologia*): **un'aria di festa** a festive air; **fare festa** (*non lavorare*) to have a holiday; (*far baldoria*) to live it up; **fare le feste a qn** to give sb a warm welcome; **tutta la città era in festa** the whole town was celebrating; **le campane suonavano a festa** the bells were pealing; **essere vestito a festa** to be dressed up to the nines
■ **festa comandata** (*Rel*) holiday *o* holy day of obligation; **la festa della donna** International Women's Day; **la festa della mamma/del papà** Mother's/Father's Day; **festa del lavoro** May Day; **festa nazionale** national *o* public holiday; **la festa della repubblica** *national holiday*

FESTA DELLA REPUBBLICA

The **Festa della Repubblica**, 2 June, celebrates the founding of the Italian Republic after the fall of the monarchy and the subsequent referendum in 1946. It is marked by military parades and political speeches.
▷ www.esercito.difesa.it/root/tradizioni/2giugno_Storia.asp

festaiolo, a [festa'jɔlo] AGG (*atmosfera*) festive; **è un tipo festaiolo** he's a great one for parties
festeggiamenti [festeddʒa'menti] SMPL celebrations
festeggiare [fested'dʒare] VT (*anniversario*) to celebrate; (*persona*) to have a celebration for, fête
festeggiato, a [fested'dʒato] SM/F guest of honour; **sei tu il festeggiato!** it's your party!
festino [fes'tino] SM (*festa*) party; (*con balli*) ball
festival ['fɛstival] SM INV festival; **il festival del cinema italiano** the Italian film festival
festività [festivi'ta] SF INV festivity; **festività civile** public holiday
festivo, a [fes'tivo] AGG (*atmosfera*) festive; **giorno festivo** holiday; **"sabato e festivi"** "Saturdays, Sundays and public holidays"
festone [fes'tone] SM festoon
festosamente [festosa'mente] AVV joyfully; **accogliere festosamente qn** to give sb a warm welcome, greet sb warmly
festoso, a [fes'toso] AGG merry, joyful; **un'accoglienza festosa** a warm welcome
fetale [fe'tale] AGG foetal (*Brit*), fetal (*Am*)
fetente [fe'tɛnte] AGG (*puzzolente*) fetid; (*comportamento*) disgusting
■ SM/F (*fam*) stinker, rotter (*Brit*)
feticcio, ci [fe'tittʃo] SM fetish
feticismo [feti'tʃizmo] SM fetishism
feticista, i, e [feti'tʃista] AGG, SM/F fetishist
fetido, a ['fɛtido] AGG fetid, stinking
feto ['fɛto] SM foetus (*Brit*), fetus (*Am*)
fetore [fe'tore] SM stench, stink
fetta ['fetta] SF (*gen*) slice; (*di terra*) strip; (*fig: porzione*) share; **fare/tagliare a fette** (*pane, prosciutto*) to slice; (*fig: persona*) to make mincemeat of; **può tagliarmelo a fette?** can you slice it for me?; **una fetta di pane** a slice of bread; **una fetta del bottino** a share of the loot; **si vedeva solo una fetta di luna/cielo** you could just glimpse the moon/sky; **fette biscottate** crispbread *sg*
fettuccia, ce [fet'tuttʃa] SF tape, ribbon
fettuccine [fettut'tʃine] SFPL (*Culin*) fettu(c)cine (*ribbon-shaped pasta*)
feudale [feu'dale] AGG feudal
feudalesimo [feuda'lezimo] SM feudalism
feudatario, ri [feuda'tarjo] SM feudal lord
feudo ['fɛudo] SM (*Storia*) fief; **un feudo democristiano** (*fig*) a Christian Democrat stronghold
ff ABBR **1** (*Amm*): = **facente funzioni**) **2** (= **fogli**) pp
FF.AA ABBR = **forze armate**
FF.SS. ABBR (= **Ferrovie dello Stato**) *Italian railways*
FG SIGLA = *Foggia*
FI SIGLA = **Firenze**
■ ABBR = **Forza Italia**
fiaba ['fjaba] SF fairy tale; **paesaggio di fiaba** fairy-tale landscape
fiabesco, a, schi, sche [fja'besko] AGG fairy-tale *attr*
fiacca ['fjakka] SF (*stanchezza*) weariness; (*svogliatezza*) listlessness; **avere la fiacca** to be listless; **battere la fiacca** to shirk
fiaccamente [fjakka'mente] AVV weakly
fiaccare [fjak'kare] VT to weaken; **l'artiglieria ha fiaccato le difese nemiche** the artillery wore down the enemy's defences (*Brit*) *o* defenses (*Am*)
fiaccherò *ecc* [fjakke'rɔ] VB *vedi* **fiaccare**
fiacchezza [fjak'kettsa] SF weariness
fiacco, a, chi, che ['fjakko] AGG (*stanco*) tired, weary; (*svogliato*) listless; (*debole*) weak; (: *discorso*) weak, dull; (*fermo: mercato*) stagnant; **mi sento un po' più fiacco di ieri** I feel a bit wearier than I did yesterday
fiaccola ['fjakkola] SF torch (*with flame*)
fiaccolata [fjakko'lata] SF torchlight procession; (*Sci*) torchlit descent
fiala ['fjala] SF phial
fiamma ['fjamma] SF **1** flame; **andare in fiamme** to go up in flames; **la casa è andata in fiamme** the house went up in flames; **dare alle fiamme** to set on fire, burn; **essere in fiamme** to be ablaze; **morì tra le fiamme** he died in the blaze; **le fiamme dell'inferno** hellfire *sg*; **cucinare alla fiamma** (*Culin*) to flambé
2 (*fig: persona amata*) love, flame; **una vecchia fiamma** an old flame **3** (*Mil, Naut*) pennant
fiammante [fjam'mante] AGG (*colore*) flaming; **rosso fiammante** flame red, bright red; **nuovo fiammante** brand new
fiammata [fjam'mata] SF blaze
fiammato [fjam'mato] SM (*anche:* **tessuto fiammato**) iridescent fabric
fiammeggiante [fjammed'dʒante] AGG flaming, blazing; (*fig: occhi*) flashing
fiammeggiare [fjammed'dʒare] VI (*aus* **avere**) (*anche fig: cielo*) to blaze; (: *occhi*) to flash; (: *spada*) to gleam
■ VT (*Culin: pollo*) to singe
fiammifero [fjam'mifero] SM match; **una scatola di fiammiferi** a box of matches
fiammingo, a, ghi, ghe [fjam'mingo] AGG Flemish
■ SM/F Fleming; **i fiamminghi** the Flemish
■ SM (*lingua*) Flemish
fiancata [fjan'kata] SF (*di nave, auto*) side
fiancheggiare [fjanked'dʒare] VT (*gen*) to border; (*Mil*) to flank; (*fig: sostenere*) to support, back (up)
fiancheggiatore, trice [fjankeddʒa'tore] SM/F supporter
fianco, chi ['fjanko] SM (*gen*) side; (*di persona*) hip; (*di animale, esercito*) flank; (*di montagna*) slope; **di fianco** from the side, sideways; **di fianco a** *o* **a fianco di qn/qc** beside *o* next to sb/sth; **si trova a fianco della chiesa** it's next to the church; **avere un dolore al**

fianco to have a pain in one's side; **stare al fianco di qn** (*anche fig*) to stand by sb, stay by sb's side; **ho sempre avuto qualcuno al mio fianco** I have always had somebody by my side; **starò sempre al tuo fianco** I'll always stand by you; **fianco a fianco** side by side; **stare con le mani sui fianchi** to stand with one's hands on one's hips; **avere fianchi larghi/stretti** (*persona*) to have broad/narrow hips, be broad-/narrow-hipped; **ha i fianchi larghi** she's got wide hips; **dormo sempre su un fianco** I always sleep on my side; **una spina nel fianco** (*fig*) a thorn in one's side; **mostrare il fianco al nemico** (*fig*) to reveal one's weak spot *o* Achilles' heel to one's enemy; **offrire** *o* **prestare il fianco a critiche** to leave o.s. open to criticism; **fianco destr/sinistr!** (*Mil*) right/left turn!

fiandra ['fjandra] SF damask linen

Fiandre ['fjandre] SFPL Flanders *sg*

fiasca, sche ['fjaska] SF (hip) flask

fiaschetteria [fjaskette'ria] SF wine shop

fiasco, schi ['fjasko] SM bottle (*in straw holder*); (*fig: fallimento*) fiasco; **un fiasco di vino** a bottle of wine; **essere un fiasco** to be a fiasco; **la festa è stata un fiasco completo** the party was a complete fiasco; **fare fiasco** (*persona*) to come a cropper; (*spettacolo*) to be a flop, be a fiasco

fiatare [fja'tare] VI (*aus* **avere**) (*fig: parlare*): **senza fiatare** without saying a word; **non osarono fiatare** they didn't dare breathe; **non fiatate!** don't say a word!

fiato ['fjato] SM **1** breath; **fiato cattivo** bad breath; **avere il fiato grosso** to pant, be out of breath; **riprendere fiato** (*anche fig*) to get one's breath back, catch one's breath; **mi sono fermato a riprendere fiato** I stopped to get my breath back; **tirare il fiato** to draw breath; (*fig*) to have a breather; **essere senza fiato** to be out of breath; **sono senza fiato** I'm out of breath; **restare senza fiato** to be breathless; **rimanere senza fiato** to be speechless; **quando l'ho saputo sono rimasto senza fiato** I was speechless when I heard about it; **sono rimasto senza fiato** (*fig*) it took my breath away; **tutto d'un fiato** all in one go; **bere tutto d'un fiato** to drink all in one go *o* gulp; **me l'ha raccontato tutto d'un fiato** he told me the whole story without drawing breath; **è fiato sprecato** (*fig*) it's a waste of breath; **quella scena mi ha mozzato il fiato** that scene took my breath away **2** (*capacità di resistenza*) stamina, staying power; **non ho più molto fiato** I haven't got much stamina these days **3** (*Mus*): **i fiati** wind instruments, the winds; **strumento a fiato** wind instrument

fiatone [fja'tone] SM: **avere il fiatone** to be out of breath

fibbia ['fibbja] SF buckle

fibra ['fibra] SF **1** (*gen*) fibre (*Brit*), fiber (*Am*) **2** (*costituzione*) constitution; **persona di fibra forte** person with a strong constitution

■ **fibra di vetro** fibreglass (*Brit*), fiberglass (*Am*); **fibre grezze** roughage *sg*, (dietary) fibre *sg*; **fibre ottiche** optic fibres; **fibre tessili** textile fibres

fibrillazione [fibrillat'tsjone] SF (*Med*) fibrillation

fibrina [fi'brina] SF (*Bio*) fibrin

fibrinogeno [fibri'nɔdʒeno] SM (*Bio*) fibrinogen

fibroma, i [fi'brɔma] SM (*Med*) fibroma

fibrosità [fibrosi'ta] SF INV (*vedi agg*) fibrousness; stringiness

fibroso, a [fi'broso] AGG fibrous; (*carne*) stringy

fibula ['fibula] SF (*Anat, Archeol*) fibula

ficcanaso [fikka'naso] SM/F (*pl m* **ficcanasi**, *pl f* **ficcanaso**) busybody, nos(e)y parker

ficcare [fik'kare] VT **1** (*infilare: in borsa, cassetto*) to put; (*: con forza*) to thrust, push; (*palo, chiodo*) to drive; **dove lo hai ficcato?** where did you put it?; **ha ficcato tutti i libri in borsa** she crammed all the books into her bag; **mi ha ficcato un dito nell'occhio** he poked his finger in my eye; **ficcalo da qualche parte** (*fam*) stick it somewhere; **ficcare il naso negli affari altrui** (*fig*) to poke *o* stick one's nose into other people's business; **non ficcare il naso nei miei affari** don't stick your nose into my business; **lo hanno ficcato dentro** (*fam: in prigione*) they put him away *o* inside **2** **ficcarsi** *or* **ficcarsi le dita nel naso** to pick one's nose; **ficcarsi il cappello in testa** to put *o* thrust one's hat on one's head; **ficcarsi in testa qc** (*fig*) to get sth into one's head; **ficcarsi in testa di fare qc** (*fig*) to take it into one's head to do sth

▶ **ficcarsi** VR (*andare a finire*) to get to; **dove si sarà ficcato?** where can he (*o* it *ecc*) have got to?; **ficcarsi nei pasticci** *o* **nei guai** to get into hot water *o* a fix; **perché ti devi sempre ficcare in mezzo?** why do you always have to stick your oar in?

ficcherò *ecc* [fikke'rɔ] VB *vedi* **ficcare**

fiche [fiʃ] SF INV (*nei giochi d'azzardo*) chip

fico[1], chi ['fiko] SM (*Bot*) fig; **fico d'India** prickly pear; **fico secco** dried fig; **non vale un fico secco** (*fig*) it's not worth a fig *o* a straw; **non ci capisco un fico secco** I don't understand a thing

fico[2], a, chi, che ['fiko], **figo, a, ghi, ghe** ['figo] (*fam*) AGG cool

■ SM/F: **è proprio un figo!** he's really cool, he's a really cool guy

fiction ['fikʃon] SF INV TV drama

> **LO SAPEVI...?**
> **fiction** non si traduce mai con la parola inglese ***fiction***

ficus ['fikus] SM INV (*Bot*) ficus

fidanzamento [fidantsa'mento] SM engagement; **anello/festa di fidanzamento** engagement ring/party

fidanzare [fidan'tsare] VT: **fidanzare a** to betroth to

▶ **fidanzarsi** VR (*uso reciproco*) to get engaged

fidanzato, a [fidan'tsato] AGG engaged

■ SM/F fiancé/fiancée; **i fidanzati** the engaged couple

fidarsi [fi'darsi] VIP: **fidarsi di** to trust; (*fare affidamento*) to rely on; **non mi fido di uscire con questo tempo** I daren't go out in this weather; **fidarsi è bene non fidarsi è meglio** (*Proverbio*) better safe than sorry

fidatezza [fida'tettsa] SF trustworthiness, reliability

fidato, a [fi'dato] AGG (*degno di fiducia*) trustworthy, reliable; (*leale*) loyal, faithful

fideismo [fide'izmo] SM unquestioning belief

fideistico, a, ci, che [fide'istiko] AGG (*atteggiamento, posizione*) totally uncritical

fideiussione [fidejus'sjone] SF (*Dir*) guarantee

fideiussore [fidejus'sore] SM (*Dir*) guarantor

Fidia ['fidja] SM Phidias

fido[1], a ['fido] AGG faithful, loyal

fido[2] ['fido] SM (*Comm*) credit; **fido bancario** banker's credit

fiducia [fi'dutʃa] SF **1** trust, confidence; **avere fiducia in qn** to have faith in sb, trust sb; **ho fiducia in lui** I trust him; **abbi fiducia in Dio** have faith in

Ff

the Lord; **riporre la propria fiducia in qn/qc** to place one's trust in sb/sth; **fiducia in se stesso** self-confidence; **devi avere più fiducia in te stesso** you should have more confidence in yourself; **una persona di fiducia** a trustworthy *o* reliable person; **un prodotto di fiducia** a reliable product; **è il mio uomo di fiducia** he is my right-hand man; **ha un incarico di fiducia** he holds a responsible position; **ha tradito la nostra fiducia** he has betrayed our trust **2** (*Pol*): **voto di fiducia** vote of confidence; **fiducia del Parlamento al Governo** parliamentary vote of confidence; **porre la questione di fiducia** to ask for a vote of confidence

fiduciario, ria, ri, rie [fidu'tʃarjo] AGG, SM (*Dir, Comm*) fiduciary

fiduciosamente [fidutʃosa'mente] AVV trustingly; **guardare fiduciosamente all'avvenire** to look to the future with confidence

fiducioso, a [fidu'tʃoso] AGG trusting

fiele ['fjɛle] SM (*amarezza*) bitterness, bile (*letter*); **parole piene di fiele** (*fig*) bitter words

fienagione [fjena'dʒone] SF (*operazione*) haymaking; (*stagione*) haymaking season

fienile [fje'nile] SM hayloft

fieno ['fjɛno] SM hay

fiera[1] ['fjɛra] SF (*letter: animale*) wild beast

fiera[2] ['fjɛra] SF fair; **fiera di beneficenza** charity bazaar, (garden) fête *o* fete; **fiera del bianco** linen sale; **fiera campionaria** trade fair

fieramente [fjera'mente] AVV (*vedi agg*) proudly; boldly

fierezza [fje'rettsa] SF pride

fiero, a ['fjɛro] AGG **1** (*orgoglioso*) proud; **essere** *o* **andare fiero di qn/qc** to be proud of sb/sth; **i suoi vanno molto fieri di lui** his parents are very proud of him **2** (*valente*) bold, intrepid

fievole ['fjɛvole] AGG (*luce*) dim; (*suono*) faint

fievolmente [fjevol'mente] AVV (*risuonare*) faintly; (*illuminare*) dimly; (*sussurrare*) softly

FIFA ['fifa] SIGLA F (= **Fédération Internationale des Football Associations**) FIFA

fifa ['fifa] SF (*fam*): **che fifa!** what a fright!; **avere fifa** to have the jitters; **ho fifa** I've got the jitters

fifo ['fifo] SM INV (*Comm:* = **first in first out**) FIFO

fifone, a [fi'fone] SM/F (*fam scherz*) chicken, scaredy cat (*used by children*)

fig. ABBR (= **figura**) fig.

figata [fi'gata] SF (*fam*): **essere una figata** to be cool; **che figata!** cool!

FIGC [fidʒi'tʃi] SIGLA F (= **Federazione Italiana Gioco Calcio**) *Italian football association*

fighetto, a [fi'getto] SM/F (*fam pegg*): **fare il fighetto** to show off

Figi ['fidʒi] SFPL: **le (isole) Figi** Fiji *sg*, the Fiji Islands

figlia ['fiʎʎa] SF **1** daughter; **è figlia unica** she's an only child; **figlia di papà** daddy's girl **2** (*Comm*) counterfoil (*Brit*), stub

figliare [fiʎ'ʎare] VI (*aus* **avere**) (*animali*) to give birth

figliastro, a [fiʎ'ʎastro] SM/F stepchild, stepson/stepdaughter

figlio, gli ['fiʎʎo] SM son; (*senza distinzione di sesso*) child; **hanno 2 figli** they have 2 children; **non vuole avere figli** she doesn't want to have children; **aspetta un figlio** she's expecting a baby; **aspetta il secondo figlio** she's expecting her second child; **suo figlio è all'estero** his son is abroad; **mio figlio ha sette anni** my son is seven; **essere figlio d'arte** to come from a theatrical (*o* artistic *ecc*) family; **il Figlio di Dio/dell'uomo** (*Rel*) the Son of God/of Man; **figlio di papà** daddy's boy, spoilt and wealthy young man; **figlio di puttana** (*fam!*) son of a bitch (*fam!*); **figlio unico** only child; **è figlio unico** he's an only child

figlioccio, cia, ci, ce [fiʎ'ʎɔttʃo] SM/F godchild, godson/goddaughter

figliola [fiʎ'ʎɔla] SF daughter; **una bella figliola** (*ragazza*) a fine figure of a girl

figliolo [fiʎ'ʎɔlo] SM son; **un figliolo ubbidiente** (*ragazzo*) an obedient young boy *o* man

figo, a ['figo] AGG, SM/F = **fico[2]**

figura [fi'gura] SF (*gen, Mat*) figure; (*illustrazione*) illustration, picture; (*Carte*) face card; **ritratto a mezza figura** half-length portrait; **fare bella/brutta figura** to create *o* make a good/bad impression; **ho fatto una brutta figura al colloquio** I made a bad impression at the interview; **far fare una brutta figura a qn** to show sb up, make sb look a fool; **fare la figura dello scemo** to look a fool; **che figura!** how embarrassing!; **fare figura** to look good *o* smart; **questo libro ha molte figure** this book has lots of pictures; **figura retorica** figure of speech

figuraccia, ce [figu'rattʃa] SF: **fare una figuraccia** to create a bad impression

figurante [figu'rante] SM (*Teatro, Cine*) extra

figurare [figu'rare] VT: **non riesco a figurarmelo** I can't picture it; **ti disturbo? — ma no, figurati!** am I disturbing you? — no, not at all!; **figurati che...** would you believe that ...?; **figurarsi se non accettava!** wouldn't you just know it — he accepted it!
■ VI (*aus* **avere**) to appear, figure

figuratamente [figurata'mente] AVV figuratively

figurativo, a [figura'tivo] AGG figurative

figurato, a [figu'rato] AGG **1** (*allegorico*) figurative; **linguaggio figurato** figurative language **2** (*illustrato*) illustrated

figurazione [figurat'tsjone] SF (*rappresentazione*) representation, depiction

figurina [figu'rina] SF **1** (*statuetta*) figurine **2** (*da collezione*) picture card

figurinista, i, e [figuri'nista] SM/F dress designer

figurino [figu'rino] SM fashion sketch; **sembra un figurino** she looks like a fashion plate

figuro [fi'guro] SM: **un losco figuro** a suspicious character

figurona [figu'rona] SF, **figurone** [figu'rone] SM (*fam*): **fare una figurona** *o* **un figurone** (*persona, oggetto*) to look terrific; (*persona: con un discorso*) to make an excellent impression

fila ['fila] SF **1** (*gen*) line, row; (*coda*) queue; (*Mil*) rank; (*Teatro*) row; **una fila di alberi** a line of trees; **in fila** in a row *o* line; **in fila indiana** in single file; **mettetevi in fila per due** line up in twos; **ci hanno messo in fila per due** they lined us up in twos; **fare la fila** to queue; **c'era una lunga fila alla fermata dell'autobus** there was a long queue at the bus stop; **serrare/rompere le file** (*Mil*) to close/break ranks; **ero seduto in seconda fila** I was sitting in the second row **2** (*successione*): **di fila** in succession, one after the other; **è piovuto per due mesi di fila** it rained for two months on the trot *o* non-stop; **una fila di avvenimenti** a series of events; **fuoco di fila** (*di armi da fuoco, anche fig: di domande ecc*) volley

filamento [fila'mento] SM filament

filamentoso, a [filamen'toso] AGG (*verdura, carne*) stringy

filanca® [fi'lanka] SF *stretch material*
filanda [fi'landa] SF spinning mill
filante [fi'lante] AGG: **stella filante** *(stella cadente)* shooting star; *(striscia di carta)* streamer
filantropia [filantro'pia] SF philanthropy
filantropicamente [filantropika'mente] AVV philanthropically
filantropico, a, ci, che [filan'trɔpiko] AGG philanthropic(al)
filantropo [fi'lantropo] SM philanthropist
filare[1] [fi'lare] VT **1** *(lana)* to spin; *(metallo)* to draw; **quando Berta filava** in the good old days **2** *(Naut: gomena)* to pay out; *(: remi)* to trail
■VI *(aus* **essere** *nel significato* **a**, **avere** *negli altri significati)* **1** *(persona)* to dash off, run; **filare via** *or* **filarsela** to run away, make off, make o.s. scarce; **fila (via)!** clear off!; **fila a letto subito** off to bed with you; **far filare qn** *(fig)* to make sb behave; **filare dritto** to behave, toe the line; **la macchina fila che è una bellezza** the car goes like a bomb **2** *(discorso, ragionamento)* to be coherent, hang together **3** *(amoreggiare)*: **filare (con)** to go out (with), go steady (with) *(ant)* **4** *(liquido)* to trickle; *(candela)* to smoke; *(formaggio)* to go stringy
filare[2] [fi'lare] SM *(di alberi)* row, line
filarmonica, che [filar'mɔnika] SF music society
filarmonico, a, ci, che [filar'mɔniko] AGG philharmonic
filastrocca, che [filas'trɔkka] SF nursery rhyme
filatelia [filate'lia] SF philately *(frm)*, stamp collecting
filatelica [fila'tɛlika] SF philately *(frm)*, stamp collecting
filatelico, a, ci, che [fila'tɛliko] AGG philatelic
■SM/F philatelist *(frm)*, stamp collector
filato[1], **a** [fi'lato] AGG **1** **zucchero filato** candy floss **2** *(di seguito)* without a break, straight off; **ha parlato per 4 ore filate** he spoke for 4 hours without stopping
■AVV: **vai dritto filato a casa** go straight home
filato[2] [fi'lato] SM *(di lana)* yarn; *(di altri tessuti)* thread
filatoio, oi [fila'tojo] SM *(macchina)* spinning wheel
filatore, trice [fila'tore] SM/F spinner
filatura [fila'tura] SF **1** *(operazione)* spinning **2** *(fabbrica)* spinning mill
file ['fail] SM INV *(Inform)* file; **nome del file** file name; **file di configurazione** setup file; **file di solo testo** text file
fileggiare [filed'dʒare] VI *(aus* **avere**) *(Naut: vela)* to luff
filettare [filet'tare] VT *(Tecn: vite)* to thread
filettatura [filetta'tura] SF *(di viti)* thread
filetto[1] [fi'letto] SM **1** *(ornamento)* braid, trimming **2** *(Tecn)* thread **3** *(Equitazione)* snaffle (bit)
filetto[2] [fi'letto] SM *(di carne, pesce)* fillet
filiale[1] [fi'ljale] AGG filial
filiale[2] [fi'ljale] SF *(Comm)* branch; *(impresa dipendente)* subsidiary (company)
filibustiere [filibus'tjɛre] SM pirate; *(fig)* adventurer
filiera [fi'ljɛra] SF industry
filiforme [fili'forme] AGG threadlike; *(fig: magrissimo)* spindly
filigrana [fili'grana] SF *(di oro)* filigree; *(di banconota, francobollo)* watermark
filigranato, a [filigra'nato] AGG *(carta)* water-marked
filippica [fi'lippika] SF invective
Filippine [filip'pine] SFPL: **le Filippine** the Philippines
filippino, a [filip'pino] AGG, SM/F Filipino
filisteismo [filiste'izmo] SM stuffy bourgeois attitudes
filisteo, a [filis'tɛo] AGG, SM/F stuffy bourgeois
film [film] SM INV *(Fot)* film; *(Cine)* film, movie *(Am)*
filmare [fil'mare] VT *(persona)* to film; *(scena)* to film, shoot
filmato [fil'mato] SM short film
filmina [fil'mina] SF film strip
filo ['filo] SM **1** *(di cotone)* thread; *(di lana)* yarn; *(di perle, burattini)* string; *(di telefono, lampada)* wire, flex; **maglietta di filo di Scozia** fine cotton T-shirt; **calzettoni di filo di Scozia** lisle socks; **i fili della luce/del telefono** the electricity/telephone wires; **il filo del traguardo** the finishing tape; **in fil di ruota** *(Naut)* on a dead run; **un filo d'erba** a blade of grass; **filo a piombo** plumb line; **un filo d'acqua** a trickle of water; **un filo d'aria** *(fig)* a breath of air; **un filo di luce** *(fig)* a ray of light; **un filo di speranza** *(fig)* a ray *o* glimmer of hope; **con un filo di voce** in a weak *o* feeble voice, in a whisper; **filo elettrico** electric wire; **filo di ferro/spinato** wire/barbed wire; **filo interdentale** dental floss **2** *(di lama, rasoio)* edge; **essere** *o* **camminare** *o* **trovarsi sul filo del rasoio** *(fig)* to be on the razor's edge **3** *(di legno)* grain **4** *(fraseologia)*: **perdere il filo** *(di un discorso)* to lose the thread; **ripetere qc per filo e per segno** to repeat sth word for word; **dare del filo da torcere a qn** to create difficulties for sb, make life difficult for sb; **è appeso a un filo** it's hanging by a thread; **fare il filo a qn** *(corteggiare)* to be after sb, chase sb
■**fila** SFPL: **le fila di un complotto** the threads of a plot
filoamericano, a [filoameri'kano] AGG pro-American
filobus ['filobus] SM INV trolley bus
filocinese [filotʃi'nese] AGG pro-Chinese
filodendro [filo'dɛndro] SM philodendron
filodiffusione [filodiffu'zjone] SF rediffusion
▷ www.radio.rai.it/filodiffusione/
filodrammatico, a, ci, che [filodram'matiko] AGG: **(compagnia) filodrammatica** amateur dramatic society
■SM/F amateur actor/amateur actress
filologia [filolo'dʒia] SF philology
filologicamente [filolodʒika'mente] AVV philologically
filologico, a, ci, che [filo'lɔdʒiko] AGG philological
filologo, gi [fi'lɔlogo] SM philologist
filoncino [filon'tʃino] SM ≈ French stick
filone [fi'lone] SM **1** *(di minerale)* seam, vein; *(fig: culturale)* tradition; **un film che appartiene al filone western** a film in the Western genre **2** *(di pane)* ≈ Vienna loaf
filosofale [filozo'fale] AGG: **pietra filosofale** philosopher's stone
filosofare [filozo'fare] VI *(aus* **avere**) to philosophize
filosofeggiare [filozofed'dʒare] VI *(aus* **avere**) *(pegg)* to philosophize
filosofia [filozo'fia] SF philosophy; **con filosofia** *(fig)* philosophically
filosoficamente [filozofika'mente] AVV philosophically
filosofico, a, ci, che [filo'zɔfiko] AGG philosophical
filosofo, a [fi'lɔzofo] SM/F philosopher
filosovietico, a, ci, che [filoso'vjɛtiko] AGG pro-Soviet
filovia [filo'via] SF *(linea)* trolley line; *(bus)* trolley bus
filtraggio, gi [fil'traddʒo] SM *(gen)* filtering
filtrare [fil'trare] VT to filter; *(fig: selezionare)* to screen
■VI *(aus* **essere**) to filter; **la luce filtrava dalla finestra** the light filtered in through the window

Ff

filtrazione [filtrat'tsjone] SF (*vedi vb*) filtration; screening
filtro[1] ['filtro] SM (*gen, Fot*) filter; **sigaretta con filtro** filter-tipped cigarette, filter tip; **filtro dell'aria** (*Aut*) air filter; **filtro dell'olio** (*Aut*) oil filter
filtro[2] ['filtro] SM (*pozione*) potion
filza ['filtsa] SF (*gen, anche fig*) string; **mi ha raccontato una filza di bugie** he told me a string of lies
FIN [fin] SIGLA F (= **Federazione Italiana Nuoto**) *Italian Swimming Federation*
finale [fi'nale] AGG final; **il giudizio finale** (*Rel*) the Last Judgment; **proposizione finale** (*Gramm*) purpose clause
■ SM (*di libro, film*) ending, end; (*Mus, di spettacolo*) finale; **finale a sorpresa** surprise ending; **non mi è piaciuto il finale** I didn't like the ending
■ SF **1** (*Sport*) final; **entrare in finale** to reach the final(s); **sono entrati in finale** they reached the final; **la finale di Coppa** the Cup Final **2** (*Gramm*) last syllable (*o* letter)
finalismo [fina'lizmo] SM (*Filosofia*) finalism
finalissima [fina'lissima] SF (*Sport*) final(s); (*di concorso di bellezza*) grand final
finalista, i, e [fina'lista] SM/F finalist
finalità [finali'ta] SF INV **1** (*scopo*) aim, purpose; **gioco a finalità educativa** educational game **2** (*Filosofia*) finality
finalizzare [finalid'dzare] VT: **finalizzare a** (*ricerca, iniziativa*) to direct towards, aim at; **l'iniziativa è finalizzata alla salvaguardia dell'ambiente** the aim of this project is to protect the environment
finalmente [final'mente] AVV at (long) last, finally; **finalmente!** at (long) last!; **finalmente sei arrivato!** you're here at last!
finanza [fi'nantsa] SF **1** finance; **alta finanza** high finance; **finanza creativa** creative accounting **2 finanze** SFPL finances; **Ministro delle finanze** Minister of Finance; ≈ Chancellor of the Exchequer (*Brit*), ≈ Secretary of the Treasury (*Am*) **3** (*Amm*): **(Guardia di) finanza** (*di frontiera*) ≈ Customs and Excise (*Brit*), ≈ Customs Service (*Am*); **Intendenza di finanza** ≈ Inland Revenue (*Brit*), ≈ Internal Revenue Service (*Am*)
▷ www.mef.gov.it/
▷ http://www.gdf.it/
finanziamento [finantsja'mento] SM (*azione*) financing; (*denaro fornito*) funds *pl*; **la banca ha concesso un finanziamento alla ditta** the bank has agreed to finance *o* fund the company
finanziare [finan'tsjare] VT to finance, fund
finanziaria [finan'tsjarja] SF (*anche:* **legge finanziaria**) finance act, ≈ budget (*Brit*) (*anche:* **società finanziaria**) investment company
finanziariamente [finantsjarja'mente] AVV financially
finanziario, ria, ri, rie [finan'tsjarjo] AGG financial
finanziatore, trice [finantsja'tore] AGG: **ente finanziatore** financing body
■ SM/F backer
finanziere [finan'tsjɛre] SM **1** (*esperto di finanze*) financier **2** (*guardia*) ≈ customs officer
▷ www.gdf.it/
finché [fin'ke] CONG (*fino a quando*) until; (*per tutto il tempo che*) as long as; **ti amerò finché vivrò** I'll love you as long as I live; **non uscirai finché non avrai finito il lavoro** you won't leave until you have finished your work; **finché vorrai** as long as you like; **rimani finché vuoi** stay as long as you like; **aspetta finché non sia uscito** wait until he goes (*o* comes) out; **aspetta finché non sarò tornato** wait until I come back
fine[1] ['fine] AGG **1** (*sottile: lamina, fetta*) thin; (: *capelli, lineamenti, pioggia*) fine; (: *voce*) thin, frail; **penna a punta fine** fine-point pen **2** (*acuto: vista, udito*) sharp, keen; (: *odorato*) fine; (*fig: ingegno*) shrewd; (: *osservazione, ironia*) subtle **3** (*raffinato: persona*) refined, distinguished; **non è fine mangiare con le mani** it's not polite to eat with your fingers
fine[2] ['fine] SM **1** (*scopo*) aim, end, purpose; (*Filosofia*) end; **avere un secondo fine** to have an ulterior motive; **a fin di bene** with the best of intentions; **l'ho fatto a fin di bene** I did it with good intentions; **il fine giustifica i mezzi** the end justifies the means; **al fine di fare qc** (in order) to do sth **2** (*conclusione*) end; **condurre qc a buon fine** to bring sth to a successful conclusion
fine[3] ['fine] SF (*gen*) end; (*di libro, film*) ending; **alla fine** in the end, finally; **senza fine** endlessly (*avv*), endless (*agg*); **porre fine a** to put an end to; **a fine anno/mese** at the end of the year/month; **alla fine** in the end; **alla fine lo ha perdonato** in the end she forgave him; **alla fine della giornata** at the end of the day; **verso la fine di giugno** in late June; **fine settimana** weekend; **alla fin fine** at the end of the day, in the end; **in fin dei conti** when all is said and done; (*tutto sommato*) after all; **dall'inizio alla fine** from beginning to end; **a lieto fine** with a happy ending; **mi piacciono le storie a lieto fine** I like stories with a happy ending; **volgere alla fine** to draw to an end; **fare una brutta fine** to come to a bad end; **che fine ha fatto?** what became of him?; **essere in fin di vita** to be at death's door; **è la fine del mondo!** (*fig: stupendo*) it's out of this world!; (*pegg*) what's the world coming to?; **buona fine e buon principio!** (*augurio*) happy New Year!; **un quadro fine Ottocento** a late nineteenth-century painting; **articoli di fine serie** oddments; **svendita di fine stagione** end-of-season sale
finemente [fine'mente] AVV (*tagliare*) thinly; (*fig: osservare*) shrewdly; **un ricamo finemente lavorato** a finely worked embroidery
fine settimana ['fine setti'mana] SM INV weekend
finestra [fi'nɛstra] SF (*gen, Inform*) window; **affacciarsi alla finestra** to appear at the window; **buttare il denaro dalla finestra** (*fig*) to throw money down the drain; **periodo finestra** symptom-free period; **finestra a battenti** casement window; **finestra a ghigliottina** sash window
finestrino [fines'trino] SM (*di treno, auto*) window
finezza [fi'nettsa] SF (*vedi fine*[1]) thinness; fineness; sharpness, keenness; shrewdness; subtleness, subtlety; refinement
fingere ['findʒere] VB IRREG
■ VT to feign (*letter*); **fingere di fare qc** to pretend to do sth; **fingiamo di dormire** let's pretend we're asleep; **ha finto di non conoscermi** he pretended he didn't recognize me; **fingere un grande dolore** to pretend to be very upset
■ VI (*aus* **avere**) to dissemble (*letter*); **sa fingere molto bene** he's very good at hiding his feelings;
▶ **fingersi** VR to pretend to be; **si è finto ubriaco** he pretended he was drunk; **fingersi medico** to pretend to be a doctor
finimenti [fini'menti] SMPL (*di cavallo*) harness *sg*

finimondo [fini'mondo] SM pandemonium; **successe un finimondo** all hell broke loose

finire [fi'nire] VI (*aus* **essere**)

1 (*gen*) to finish, end; (*pioggia, neve*) to stop, cease; **il film finisce alle dieci** the film finishes at ten; **l'anno scolastico finisce a giugno** the school year ends in June; **un altro giorno è finito** another day is over *o* has come to an end; **tra noi è tutto finito** it's all over between us; **è finito di piovere/nevicare** it has stopped raining/snowing; **finire bene/male** (*film, libro*) to have a happy/an unhappy ending; **finire male** (*persona*) to come to a bad end; **per fortuna tutto è finito bene** luckily everything turned out well in the end; **finire per** *o* **col fare qc** to end up (by) doing sth; **finirà per crederle** he'll end up believing her; **finì col fare il lavoro lui** he ended up doing the job himself; **andare a finire** to get to; **dov'è andato a finire quel libro?** *or* **dov'è finito quel libro?** where has that book got to?; **dove vuoi andare a finire con questo discorso?** what are you driving *o* getting at?; **com'è andata a finire?** what happened in the end?; **è finita!** (*non c'è rimedio*) it's all over!; **com'è finita la partita?** how did the match end?; **finire in** to end with; **finire in galera** to end up *o* finish up in prison

2 (*esaurirsi*) to be finished; **l'olio è finito** we have run out of oil, there's no oil left

■ VT

1 (*gen*) to finish; (*lavoro, corso*) to finish, complete; (*discorso*) to end; **finire di fare qc** to finish doing sth; **ho finito di leggere il libro** I've finished reading the book; **non ho ancora finito i compiti** I haven't finished my homework yet; **ha finito i propri giorni in prigione** he ended his days in prison; **finisci la minestra** finish *o* eat up your soup; **abbiamo finito il pane** we've run out of bread; **mi ha finito la crema** she's used up all my cream

2 (*smettere*) to stop; **finire di fare qc** to stop doing sth; **non finire più di fare qc** to keep on doing sth; **non finisco di meravigliarmi della sua pazienza** her patience never ceases to amaze me

3 (*dare il colpo di grazia*) to finish off

4 (*rifinire*) to finish off, put the finishing touches to

5 (*fam*): **finirla** to pack in; **è ora di finirla con queste storie!** it's time you stopped this nonsense!; **finiscila!** stop it!; **farla finita con qc** to have done with sth; **devi farla finita con questi capricci** you'll have to stop these tantrums; **l'ho fatta finita con la droga** I'm off drugs now; **ho deciso di farla finita con Maria** I've decided to finish with Maria; **farla finita (con la vita)** to put an end to one's life

■ SM (*fine*) end; **sul finire della festa** towards the end of the party

finissaggio, gi [finis'saddʒo] SM (*Tecn: operazione*) finishing; (*: risultato*) finish

finito, a [fi'nito] AGG 1 (*Gramm, Mat, Filosofia*) finite 2 (*terminato, rifinito*) finished; **è un uomo finito** (*fig: rovinato*) he's finished 3 (*esperto: cuoco*) expert; (*: operaio, artigiano*) skilled

finitrice [fini'tritʃe] SF (*Tecn*) finishing machine

finitura [fini'tura] SF finish; **le ultime finiture** the finishing touches

finlandese [finlan'dese] AGG Finnish

■ SM/F Finn; **i finlandesi** the Finns

■ SM (*lingua*) Finnish; **parli finlandese?** do you speak Finnish?

Finlandia [fin'landja] SF Finland; **ti è piaciuta la Finlandia?** did you like Finland?; **andrò in Finlandia quest'estate** I'm going to Finland this summer

fino¹, a ['fino] AGG 1 = **fine¹** 2 (*oro, argento*) pure; **cervello fino** quick brain; *vedi* **fine¹**

fino² ['fino] (*spesso troncato, davanti a consonante, in* fin) AVV (*pure, anche*) even; **hai detto fin troppo** you have said too much *o* more than enough

■ PREP 1 **fino a** (*tempo*) until, up to, till; (*luogo*) as far as; (+ *infin*) so that; **resto fino a venerdì/al 15 gennaio** I'm staying until Friday/until the 15th of January; **vengo con te fino al cinema** I'll come as far as the cinema with you; **ha lavorato fino ad ammalarsi** he worked so hard that he made himself ill; **fino a quando?** *or* **fin quando?** until when?; **fino a quando puoi rimanere?** how long can you stay?; **fino all'ultimo** until the end, to the end, till the end; **fino all'ultimo ha negato, poi ha ceduto** he denied it up till the last minute, then gave way; **arrivare fino a** (*livello*) to reach; **averne fin sopra i capelli** (*fig*) to be fed up to the back teeth; **andare fino in fondo a qc** to get to the bottom of sth 2 **fin da** since, from; **fin dalla nascita/dall'infanzia** from *o* since birth/infancy; **fin da quando sei arrivato** since you arrived, from the time you arrived; **fin d'ora** as of *o* from now; **fin dall'alba** since daybreak; **fin da domani** from tomorrow onwards; **fin da ieri** since yesterday

finocchio, chi [fi'nɔkkjo] SM 1 (*Bot*) fennel 2 (*offensivo: omosessuale*) queer, poof (*Brit*)

finora [fi'nora] AVV up till now, so far; **finora Marco non si è visto** Marco hasn't turned up yet; **finora abbiamo fatto solo il presente** so far we've only studied the present tense

finsi *ecc* ['finsi] VB *vedi* **fingere**

finta ['finta] SF 1 (*finzione*): **fare finta di fare qc** to pretend to do sth; **fa finta di niente** he pretends not to notice; (*comportarsi normalmente*) he's behaving as if nothing had happened; **facciamo finta di dormire** let's pretend we're asleep; **l'ho detto per finta** I was only pretending; (*per scherzo*) I was only kidding 2 (*Pugilato*) feint; (*Calcio ecc*) dummy; **fare una finta** to feint 3 (*Cucito*) flap

fintantoché [fintanto'ke] AVV (*per tutto il tempo che*) as long as; (*fino al momento in cui*) until

finto, a ['finto] PP *di* **fingere**

■ AGG (*capelli, denti*) false; (*fiori*) artificial; (*cuoio, pelle*) imitation *attr*; (*fig: simulato: pazzia*) feigned, pretended; **una giacca in finta pelle** an imitation leather jacket

finzione [fin'tsjone] SF (*simulazione*) pretence (*Brit*), pretense (*Am*), sham; **la finzione scenica** the stage illusion

fio, fii ['fio] SM (*frm*): **pagare il fio (di)** to pay the penalty (for)

fiocamente [fjoka'mente] AVV (*vedi agg*) dimly; faintly

fioccare [fjok'kare] VI (*aus* **essere**) (*neve*) to fall; (*fig: insulti*) to come thick and fast

■ VB IMPERS to snow

fiocchetto [fjok'ketto] SM (*cravattino*) bow

fiocco¹, chi ['fjɔkko] SM 1 (*di neve, cereali*) flake; **un fiocco di neve** a snowflake; **fiocchi di granturco** cornflakes 2 (*di lana*) flock 3 (*nastro*) bow; **coi fiocchi** (*fig*) first-rate; **un pranzo coi fiocchi** a slap-up meal

fiocco², chi ['fjɔkko] SM (*Naut*) jib

fiocina ['fjɔtʃina] SF (*Naut*) harpoon

fioco, a, chi, che ['fjɔko] AGG (*luce*) dim, weak; (*suono,*

Ff

voce) faint, weak; **la luce era sempre più fioca** the light was getting dimmer and dimmer

fionda ['fjonda] SF *(arma)* sling; *(giocattolo)* catapult

fiondarsi [fjon'darsi] VR *(fam: andare precipitosamente)* to make a dash; **si è fiondato al telefono** he rushed to the phone, he made a dash for the phone

fioraio, aia, ai, aie [fjo'rajo] SM/F *(in negozio)* florist; *(ambulante)* flower seller; **sto andando dal fioraio** I'm going to the florist's

fiorato, a [fjo'rato] AGG floral

fiordaliso [fjorda'lizo] SM *(Bot)* cornflower; *(Araldica)* fleur-de-lis *o* -lys

fiordo ['fjɔrdo] SM fjord

fiore ['fjore] SM **1** *(gen, anche fig)* flower; *(di albero)* blossom; **fiori di campo** wild flowers; **essere in fiore** *(pianta, giardino)* to be in bloom; *(albero)* to be in blossom; *(fig)* to be in full bloom; **fiori d'arancio** orange blossom *sg*; **a fiori** with a flower pattern, flowered; **una gonna a fiori** a skirt with a flower pattern; **disegno a fiori** floral design; **nel fiore degli anni** in one's prime; **oggi sei un fiore** you're looking lovely today; **"non fiori ma opere di bene"** *(negli annunci mortuari)* "no flowers please, but donations to charity"; **fiori di Bach** Bach flower remedies **2** *(Carte)*: **fiori** SMPL clubs **3** **a fior di** *or* **a fior d'acqua** on (the surface of) the water; **a fior di labbra** in a whisper; **ho i nervi a fior di pelle** my nerves are all on edge **4** *(fraseologia)*: **un fior di ragazza** a really lovely girl; **è costato fior di quattrini** it cost a pretty penny; **aver fior di quattrini** to be rolling in money; **il fior fiore della società** the cream of society; **fiore all'occhiello** feather in the cap **5** **fior di latte** cream

fiorente [fjo'rɛnte] AGG *(industria, paese)* flourishing; *(salute)* blooming; *(petto)* ample; **fiorente di** *(boschi, vigneti)* rich in

fiorentina [fjoren'tina] SF *(Culin)* T-bone steak

fiorentino, a [fjoren'tino] AGG of *o* from Florence, Florentine

■SM/F inhabitant *o* native of Florence; **i fiorentini** the people of Florence

fioretto[1] [fjo'retto] SM *(piccola rinuncia)* small sacrifice; *(buona azione)* good deed

fioretto[2] [fjo'retto] SM **1** *(Scherma)* foil **2** *(Tecn)* drilling bit

fioriera [fjo'rjɛra] SF *(per piante)* flowerpot; *(per fiori recisi)* vase

fiorino [fjo'rino] SM florin

fiorire [fjo'rire] VI *(aus* **essere***)* *(fiore)* to flower, bloom; *(albero)* to blossom, flower; *(fig: sentimento)* to blossom; *(: commercio, arte)* to flourish

fiorista, i, e [fjo'rista] SM/F florist

fiorito, a [fjo'rito] AGG *(giardino)* in flower, in bloom; *(pianta)* in bloom; *(ramo)* covered with blossom; *(tessuto)* floral, flowered; *(stile)* flowery; **fiorito di errori** full of errors

fioritura [fjori'tura] SF **1** *(di pianta)* flowering, blooming; *(di albero)* blossoming; *(fig: di commercio, arte)* flourishing **2** *(insieme dei fiori)* flowers *pl*; **il ciliegio ha avuto una fioritura abbondante quest'anno** the cherry tree produced a lot of flowers *o* blossom this year **3** *(Mus)* fioritura

fiotto ['fjɔtto] SM *(di lacrime)* flood; *(di sangue)* gush, spurt; **scorrere a fiotti** to gush out *o* forth

FIP [fip] SIGLA F = *Federazione Italiana Pallacanestro*

FIPE ['fipe] SIGLA F (= **Federazione Italiana Pubblici Esercizi**) Italian Federation of Commercial Concerns

Firenze [fi'rɛntse] SF Florence; **sto andando a Firenze** I'm going to Florence; **vive a Firenze** he lives in Florence

▷ www.comune.firenze.it/

firewall [faiə'wəl] SM *(Inform)* firewall

firma ['firma] SF signature; *(fig)* name; **apporre la propria firma a** to put one's signature to; **la mia firma** my signature; **le grandi firme della moda** the big names in fashion

LO SAPEVI...?
firma non si traduce mai con la parola inglese *firm*

firmamento [firma'mento] SM firmament

firmare [fir'mare] VT to sign; **dove devo firmare?** where shall I sign?; **un maglione firmato da Missoni** a Missoni sweater, a sweater by Missoni

firmatario, ria, ri, rie [firma'tarjo] SM/F signatory

fisarmonica, che [fizar'mɔnika] SF accordion

fiscale [fis'kale] AGG **1** fiscal, tax *attr*; **anno fiscale** tax year; **evasione fiscale** tax evasion; **scontrino fiscale** (shop) receipt; **ricevuta fiscale** official receipt *(for tax purposes)*; **medico fiscale** *doctor employed by Social Security to examine people on sick leave* **2** *(fig pegg: meticoloso)* nitpicking

fiscalista, i, e [fiska'lista] SM/F tax consultant

fiscalità [fiskali'ta] SF INV *(vedi agg)* tax system; punctiliousness

fiscalmente [fiskal'mente] AVV *(vedi agg)* from the tax point of view; over-punctiliously

fischiare [fis'kjare] VT **1** *(canzone, motivo)* to whistle; **sai fischiare?** can you whistle?; **fischiare un rigore** to give a penalty; **l'arbitro ha fischiato un rigore** the referee blew his whistle for a penalty **2** *(in segno di disapprovazione)* to hiss, boo; **il pubblico lo ha fischiato** the audience booed him

■VI *(aus* **avere***)* *(gen, fig)* to whistle; *(serpente)* to hiss; *(uccello)* to sing; **mi fischiano le orecchie** I've got a ringing in my ears; *(fig fam)* my ears are burning; **fischiare al cane** to whistle for one's dog

fischiata [fis'kjata] SF *(azione)* whistling; *(fischio)* whistle; **le fischiate del pubblico** the booing *o* boos of the audience

fischiettare [fiskjet'tare] VI *(aus* **avere***)*

■VT to whistle

fischietto [fis'kjetto] SM *(strumento)* whistle

fischio, chi ['fiskjo] SM *(suono)* whistle; **fare un fischio** to whistle, give a whistle; **prendere fischi per fiaschi** to get hold of the wrong end of the stick; **il fischio dell'arbitro** the referee's whistle

fischione [fis'kjone] SM *(Zool)* wigeon

fisco ['fisko] SM tax authorities *pl*; *(Amm)* ≈ Inland Revenue *(Brit)*, ≈ Internal Revenue (Service) *(Am)* *(fam)*: **il fisco** the taxman

fisica ['fizika] SF physics *sg*

▷ www.fisicamente.it/

fisicamente [fizika'mente] AVV physically; **sono fisicamente impossibilitato a venire** it's physically impossible for me to come

fisico, a, ci, che ['fiziko] AGG *(gen)* physical; **il contatto fisico** physical contact; **educazione fisica** PE; **aspetto fisico** appearance

■SM *(corpo)* physique; **avere un bel fisico** *(donna)* to have a good figure; *(uomo)* to have a good physique; **ha un bel fisico** she has a good figure; **hai il fisico dell'atleta** you have an athletic physique *o* the physique of an athlete

■SM/F *(studioso)* physicist; **un fisico nucleare** a nuclear physicist

fisima ['fizima] SF fixation
fisiologia [fizjolo'dʒia] SF physiology
fisiologicamente [fizjolodʒika'mente] AVV physiologically
fisiologico, a, ci, che [fizjo'lɔdʒiko] AGG physiological
fisiologo, a, gi, ghe [fi'zjɔlogo] SM/F physiologist
fisionomia [fizjono'mia] SF physiognomy; **non ricordo bene la sua fisionomia** I don't remember his face very well
fisionomista, i, e [fizjono'mista] SM/F: **sei un buon fisionomista** you have a good memory for faces
fisioterapia [fizjotera'pia] SF physiotherapy
fisioterapico, a, ci, che [fizjote'rapiko] AGG physiotherapy *attr*
fisioterapista, i, e [fizjotera'pista] SM/F physiotherapist
fissaggio, gi [fis'saddʒo] SM (*Fot*) fixing; **bisogna aspettare 2 ore per il fissaggio di questa vernice** you must wait 2 hours for this paint to dry
fissamente [fissa'mente] AVV: **guardare qn/qc fissamente** to stare at sb/sth
fissante [fis'sante] AGG (*spray, lozione*) holding
fissare [fis'sare] VT **1** (*attaccare*): **fissare (a *o* su)** to fix (to), fasten (to); **fissare (su)** (*sguardo*) to fix (on), fasten (on); **fissare qn/qc** (*guardare*) to stare at sb/sth; **non fissarlo tutto il tempo** don't keep staring at him; **fissare qc in mente** to fix sth firmly in one's mind; **è fissato al muro** it's fixed to the wall **2** (*prezzo, data, condizioni*) to fix, set; (*regola*) to lay down; (*appuntamento*) to arrange, fix; **all'ora fissata** at the agreed time; **è tutto fissato** it's all fixed *o* arranged; **hai fissato la data?** have you fixed the date? **3** (*prenotare*) to book, reserve; **ho fissato una stanza per lunedì** I've booked a room for Monday **4** (*Fot, Chim*) to fix
▶ **fissarsi** VIP **1** **fissarsi di fare qc** (*mettersi in testa di*) to set one's heart on doing sth; (*ostinarsi*) to insist on doing sth; **si è fissato di partire con noi** he has set his heart on coming with us; **si è fissato che vuole vederlo subito** he insists on seeing him at once **2** (*concentrarsi*): **l'attenzione del pubblico si fissò su di lui** everybody was staring at him **3** (*uso reciproco*) to stare at each other
fissativo, a [fissa'tivo] AGG, SM fixative
fissato, a [fis'sato] AGG (*gen*) fixed; (*ora*) set, agreed; (*prezzo*) agreed; **essere fissato con qc** to have a thing about sth
■ SM/F person with an obsession; **ma quello è un fissato!** he is obsessed!
fissatore [fissa'tore] SM (*Chim*) fixative; (*Fot*) fixer; (*per capelli*) setting lotion
fissazione [fissat'tsjone] SF (*Psic*) obsession, fixation
fissione [fis'sjone] SF fission
fissità [fissi'ta] SF INV (*di sguardo*) steadiness; (*di principi*) firmness
fisso, a ['fisso] AGG (*gen*) fixed; (*lavoro, lavoratore*) permanent; (*stipendio*) regular; (*presenza*) constant; (*immagine, elemento*) recurring; **avere un ragazzo fisso** to have a steady boyfriend; **senza fissa dimora** of no fixed abode; **prezzo fisso** fixed price; **un lavoro fisso** a permanent job; **uno stipendio fisso** a regular income; **un ragazzo fisso** a steady boyfriend; **telefono fisso** landline
■ SM (*compenso*) fixed sum
■ AVV: **guardar fisso (qn/qc)** to stare (at sb/sth)
fistola ['fistola] SF (*Med*) fistula
fitotermalismo [fitoterma'lizmo] SM herbal hydrotherapy

fitta ['fitta] SF sharp pain; **una fitta di dolore** a sharp twinge of pain; **a volte ho delle fitte al petto** I sometimes get sharp pains in my chest; **una fitta al cuore** (*fig*) a pang of grief
fittamente [fitta'mente] AVV (*intrecciato, tessuto*) thickly; (*in modo denso*) densely; **parlare fittamente** to be deep in conversation
fittavolo [fit'tavolo] SM tenant
fittiziamente [fittittsja'mente] AVV fictitiously
fittizio, zia, zi, zie [fit'tittsjo] AGG (*nome, personaggio*) fictitious, imaginary
fitto[1], a ['fitto] AGG **1** (*bosco, pelo*) thick; (*nebbia*) thick, dense; (*tessuto*) closely-woven; (*pettine*) fine; (*mistero*) impenetrable; **è buio fitto** it's pitch dark **2** (*intenso: fuoco d'artiglieria, pioggia*) heavy; **una giornata fitta di eventi** an eventful day
■ AVV (*nevicare, piovere*) hard; **parlare fitto fitto** to be deep in conversation; **scritto fitto fitto** closely written
■ SM: **nel fitto del bosco** in the heart *o* depths of the wood

LO SAPEVI...?
fitto non si traduce mai con la parola inglese ***fit***

fitto[2] ['fitto] SM (*affitto*) rent; **blocco dei fitti** rents freeze
fiumana [fju'mana] SF (*fiume in piena*) torrent; (*fig: di gente*) flood, stream
fiumara [fju'mara] SF torrent
fiume ['fjume] SM river; (*fig: di gente, parole*) stream; **scorrere a fiumi** (*vino, sangue*) to flow in torrents; **sgorgare a fiumi (da)** (*acqua, sangue*) to pour out (from); **versare fiumi di inchiostro su qc** to write reams about sth
■ AGG INV: **romanzo fiume** roman-fleuve; **processo fiume** long-drawn-out *o* long-running trial
fiutare [fju'tare] VT **1** (*annusare*) to smell, sniff; (*sogg: cane da caccia*) to scent; **fiutare tabacco** to take snuff; **fiutare cocaina** to snort cocaine **2** (*intuire*): **fiutare un pericolo** to smell danger; **fiutare un buon affare** to sniff out a bargain; **fiutare qc di losco** to smell a rat
fiuto ['fjuto] SM (*odorato*) sense of smell; (*fig: intuito*) nose; **avere fiuto per qc** to have a nose for sth; **avere fiuto nel fare qc** to have a flair for doing sth
flaccido, a ['flattʃido] AGG flabby
flacone [fla'kone] SM (*di profumo ecc*) bottle
flagellare [fladʒel'lare] VT to flog, scourge; (*sogg: onde*) to beat against
▶ **flagellarsi** VR to whip o.s.
flagellazione [fladʒellat'tsjone] SF flogging, scourging
flagello [fla'dʒɛllo] SM **1** (*frusta, fig*) scourge **2** (*Bio*) flagellum
flagrante [fla'grante] AGG: **cogliere qn in flagrante** to catch sb red-handed *o* in the act; **hanno colto il ladro in flagrante** they caught the burglar red-handed; **essere in flagrante contraddizione** (*evidente*) to be in blatant contradiction
flamenco [fla'menko] SM flamenco
flan [flɑ̃] SM INV (*Culin*) mould (*Brit*), mold (*Am*)
flanella [fla'nɛlla] SF flannel
flangia, ge ['flandʒa] SF (*Tecn*) flange
flash [flæʃ] SM INV **1** (*Fot, Elettr*) flash **2** (*Radio, TV*) newsflash
flashback ['flæʃbæk] SM INV (*Cine*): **flashback (su *o* di)** flashback (to)
flatting ['flætiŋ] SM INV clear varnish

Ff

flautista, i, e [flau'tista] SM/F flautist
flauto ['flauto] SM: **flauto (traverso)** flute; **flauto dolce** recorder
flebile ['flɛbile] AGG feeble, faint
flebilmente [flebil'mente] AVV faintly
flebite [fle'bite] SF phlebitis
flebo ['flɛbo] ABBR F INV = **fleboclisi**
fleboclisi [flebo'klisi] SF INV (*Med*) drip
flemma ['flɛmma] SF (*calma*) composure, coolness; **rispose con molta flemma** he answered very coolly
flemmaticamente [flemmatika'mente] AVV phlegmatically
flemmatico, a, ci, che [flem'matiko] AGG cool
flessibile [fles'sibile] AGG (*materiale*) flexible, pliable; (*fig*: *carattere*) flexible, adaptable; **orario flessibile** flexitime
■ SM flex
flessibilità [flessibili'ta] SF INV flexibility; **flessibilità (del lavoro)** flexibility
flessione [fles'sjone] SF **1** (*gen*) bending; (*Ginnastica*: *a terra*) sit-up; (: *in piedi*) forward bend; (: *sulle gambe*) knee-bend; (: *sulle braccia*) press-up; **fare una flessione** to bend **2** (*diminuzione*) slight drop *o* fall, blip; **una flessione economica** a downward trend in the economy **3** (*Ling*) inflection
flesso, a ['flɛsso] PP *di* **flettere**
flessuosamente [flessuosa'mente] AVV gracefully
flessuosità [flessuosi'ta] SF INV (*vedi agg*) suppleness; grace(fulness)
flessuoso, a [flessu'oso] AGG (*elastico*) supple, lithe; (*armonico*: *corpo femminile*) graceful; (: *movimenti*) flowing, graceful
flettere ['flɛttere] VB IRREG
■ VT **1** (*gen*) to bend; **flettere il busto in avanti** to bend forward from the waist **2** (*Ling*) to inflect
▶ **flettersi** VR to bend
flippare [flip'pare] VI (*fam*) to flip
flippato, a [flip'pato] AGG (*fam*) out of it
flipper ['flipper] SM INV pinball machine; **giocare a flipper** to play pinball
flirt [flə:t] SM INV brief romance, flirtation
flirtare [flir'tare] VI (*aus* **avere**) to flirt
F.lli ABBR (= **Fratelli**) Bros
floema, i [flo'ɛma] SM (*Bot*) phloem
flora ['flɔra] SF flora; **flora batterica intestinale** intestinal flora
floreale [flore'ale] AGG floral; **una lampada in stile floreale** an Art Nouveau lamp
floricoltore, trice [florikol'tore] SM/F flower grower
floricoltura [florikol'tura] SF flower-growing, floriculture
Florida [flo'rida] SF Florida
floridamente [florida'mente] AVV flourishingly; (*svilupparsi*) greatly
floridezza [flori'dettsa] SF (*di economia, industria*) flourishing state, prosperity; (*di persona*) glowing health
florido, a ['flɔrido] AGG (*industria*) flourishing, thriving, prosperous; (*aspetto*) healthy, glowing with health; (*salute*) excellent; **un'industria florida** a flourishing industry
flosciamente [flɔʃʃa'mente] AVV (*vedi agg*) floppily; flabbily
floscio, scia, sci, sce ['flɔʃʃo] AGG (*cappello, tessuto*) soft, floppy; (*muscoli, carni*) flabby
flotta ['flɔtta] SF fleet; **flotta aerea** fleet of aircraft
flottante [flot'tante] SM (*Borsa*): **titoli a largo flottante** blue chips
flou [flu] AGG INV **1** (*Fot, Cine*: *sfumato*) blurred **2** (*abito*) flowing, loose(-fitting)
fluente [flu'ɛnte] AGG (*fig*: *chioma, barba*) flowing; (: *discorso*) fluent
fluidificante [fluidifi'kante] AGG **1 sostanza fluidificante** fluidizer **2** (*Calcio*): **terzino fluidificante** attacking fullback
fluidificare [fluidifi'kare] VT to fluidify, fluidize; **fluidificare il traffico** (*fig*) to improve the flow of traffic
fluidità [fluidi'ta] SF INV (*gen*) fluidity; (*fig*: *di stile*) fluency
fluido, a ['fluido] AGG (*gen*) fluid
■ SM fluid; (*forza magica*) mysterious power
fluire [flu'ire] VI (*aus* **essere**) to flow
fluorescente [fluoreʃ'ʃɛnte] AGG fluorescent
fluorescenza [fluoreʃ'ʃɛntsa] SF fluorescence
fluoro [flu'ɔro] SM fluorine; **un dentifricio al fluoro** a fluoride toothpaste
fluoruro [fluo'ruro] SM fluoride
flusso ['flusso] SM (*gen, fig*) flow; (*Fis, Elettr*) flux; **flusso e riflusso** ebb and flow; **flusso di cassa** (*Comm*) cash flow
flutto ['flutto] SM (*letter*: *onda*) billow; **tra i flutti** among the waves
fluttuante [fluttu'ante] AGG (*Econ*: *moneta, prezzi*) fluctuating; **debito fluttuante** floating debt
fluttuare [fluttu'are] VI (*aus* **avere**) **1** (*ondeggiare*: *mare*) to rise and fall; (: *barca*) to toss, rock; (: *bandiera*) to flutter **2** (*Econ*: *moneta*) to fluctuate
fluttuazione [fluttuat'tsjone] SF (*Econ, Fis, fig*) fluctuation
fluviale [flu'vjale] AGG river *attr*; **pesca fluviale** freshwater fishing; **navigazione fluviale** river *o* inland navigation
FM ABBR (= **modulazione di frequenza**) FM (= *frequency modulation*)
FME ['effe'ɛmme'e] SIGLA M (= **Fondo Monetario Europeo**) EMF (= *European Monetary Fund*)
FMI ['effe'ɛmme'i] SIGLA M (= **Fondo Monetario Internazionale**) IMF (= *International Monetary Fund*)
▷ www.esteri.it/ita/4_28_65_65.asp
FO SIGLA = *Forlì*
fobia [fo'bia] SF (*Med*) phobia; **ha la fobia dei ragni** he has a phobia about spiders
foca, che ['fɔka] SF (*Zool*) seal
focaccia, ce [fo'kattʃa] SF (*Culin*) *kind of pizza*; (: *dolce*) bun; **rendere pan per focaccia** to get one's own back, give tit for tat
focaia [fo'kaja] AGG F: **pietra focaia** flint
focale [fo'kale] AGG focal
focalizzare [fokalid'dzare] VT (*Fot*: *immagine*) to get into focus; **focalizzare la situazione** to get the situation into perspective; **focalizzare l'attenzione su** to focus one's attention on
foce ['fotʃe] SF (*Geog*) mouth; **la foce del Po** the mouth of the Po
focena [fo'tʃɛna] SF porpoise
focolaio, ai [foko'lajo] SM (*Med*) centre (*Brit*) *o* center (*Am*) of infection, focus; (*fig*) hotbed, breeding ground; **il focolaio della rivolta** the breeding ground of the rebellion
focolare [foko'lare] SM hearth, fireside; (*Tecn*) furnace; **ritornare al focolare domestico** to return to hearth and home

focomelico, a, ci, che [foko'mɛliko] AGG, SM/F (*Med*) phocomelic
focosamente [fokosa'mente] AVV passionately
focoso, a [fo'koso] AGG fiery; (*cavallo*) mettlesome, fiery
focus group ['foʊkəs 'gru:p] SM INV focus group
fodera ['fɔdera] SF (*interna: di vestito*) lining; (*di libro*) dust jacket; (*di divano, poltrona*) cover
foderare [fode'rare] VT (*vestito*) to line; (*Culin*) to line (with pastry); (*libro*) to cover
fodero ['fɔdero] SM (*di spada*) scabbard; (*di pugnale*) sheath; (*di pistola*) holster
foga ['foga] SF enthusiasm, ardour (*Brit*), ardor (*Am*); **nella foga della passione/discussione** in the heat of passion/the discussion; **lavora con foga** he throws himself into his work (with great enthusiasm); **si precipitò con foga ad aprire** he rushed excitedly to the door
foggia, ge ['fɔddʒa] SF (*forma*) shape, form; (*moda*) style, fashion; **un abito di foggia strana** an odd looking suit/dress; **alla foggia degli anni venti** twenties style
foggiano, a [fod'dʒano] AGG of *o* from Foggia
■ SM/F inhabitant *o* native of Foggia
foggiare [fod'dʒare] VT to fashion; (*carattere*) to form
foglia ['fɔʎʎa] SF (*Bot, di metallo*) leaf; **gli alberi stanno mettendo le foglie** the trees are coming into leaf; **ha mangiato la foglia** (*fig*) he's caught on; **tremare come una foglia** (*fig*) to shake like a leaf; **foglia d'argento/oro** silver/gold leaf; **foglia di fico** fig leaf
fogliame [foʎ'ʎame] SM foliage, leaves *pl*
foglietto [foʎ'ʎetto] SM **1** (*piccolo foglio*) slip *o* piece of paper; (*manifestino*) leaflet, handout **2** (*Anat*): **foglietto pleurico** pleural layer
foglio, gli ['fɔʎʎo] SM **1** (*gen, di metallo*) sheet; (*di libro*) page, leaf; **foglio rigato** *o* **a righe** sheet of lined *o* ruled paper; **foglio a quadretti** sheet of squared paper; **foglio protocollo** foolscap; **foglio volante** leaflet **2** **foglio di calcolo** *o* **elettronico** spreadsheet; **foglio rosa** (*Aut: documento*) ≈ provisional driving licence **foglio di via** (*Dir*) expulsion order **3** (*banconota*) (bank)note **4** (*Tip*): **in foglio** folio *attr*
fogliolina [foʎʎo'lina] SF leaflet
foglioso, a [foʎ'ʎoso] AGG leafy
fogna ['foɲɲa] SF sewer; (*fig: luogo sporco*) pigsty; **topo di fogna** sewer rat; **sei una fogna!** (*fig fam: ghiottone*) you're a greedy pig!
fognatura [foɲɲa'tura] SF sewerage
föhn [fø:n] SM INV hair-dryer
folaga, ghe ['fɔlaga] SF coot
folata [fo'lata] SF gust; **il tuo arrivo ha portato una folata di novità** your arrival was like a breath of fresh air
folclore [fol'klore] SM folklore
folcloristico, a, ci, che [folklo'ristiko] AGG (*spettacolo, canzone*) folk *attr*; (*scherz: bizzarro*) weird, freakish; **costume folcloristico** traditional dress
folgorante [folgo'rante] AGG (*luce*) dazzling; (*fig: sguardo*) withering; (*: passione*) violent; (*: dolore, male*) sudden
folgorare [folgo'rare] VT (*sogg: fulmine*) to strike (down); (*: alta tensione*) to electrocute; **mi folgorò con uno sguardo** (*fig*) he gave me a withering look
■ VI (*aus* **avere**) (*rilucere*) to flash
folgorazione [folgorat'tsjone] SF electrocution; **ebbe una folgorazione** (*fig: idea*) he had a brainwave
folgore ['folgore] SF thunderbolt
folk ['fouk] AGG (*cantante*) folk *attr*; (*abito*) peasant *attr*
■ SM (*Mus*) folk; (*moda*) peasant look
folla ['folla] SF (*di persone*) crowd, throng; (*: pegg*) mob; **una folla di idee** a multitude *o* host of ideas
folle ['fɔlle] AGG **1** (*anche fig: idee, trovata*) mad, insane; **a ritmo** *o* **velocità folle** at breakneck speed **2** (*Tecn: ingranaggio*) idle
■ SM/F madman/madwoman
■ SF (*Aut*): **in folle** in neutral; **assicurati che sia in folle** make sure it's in neutral
folleggiare [folled'dʒare] VI (*aus* **avere**) (*divertirsi*) to paint the town red
follemente [folle'mente] AVV madly
folletto [fol'letto] SM elf
follia [fol'lia] SF (*pazzia*) madness; (*atto*) act of madness *o* folly; **in un momento di follia** in a moment of madness; **fare una follia** (*fig*) to do sth mad *o* crazy; **è una follia!** it's crazy!; **è stata una follia fare ciò che ha fatto** it was madness *o* folly to do what he did; **costare una follia** to cost the earth; **la sua macchina nuova dev'essere costata una follia** his new car must have cost the earth; **amare qn alla follia** to love sb to distraction; **lo amo alla follia** I'm madly in love with him; **che follia!** what folly!, what madness!
follicolo [fol'likolo] SM follicle
folto, a ['folto] AGG (*capelli, pelo, bosco*) thick; (*schiera*) dense
■ SM: **nel folto della mischia** in the thick of the fray
fomentare [fomen'tare] VT to stir up, foment (*frm*)
fomentatore, trice [fomenta'tore] SM/F agitator
fomento [fo'mento] SM **1** (*letter: stimolo*): **dare fomento a** to stir up, foment **2** (*Med*) poultice
fon [fɔn] SM INV = **föhn**
fonda ['fonda] SF (*Naut*): **alla fonda** at anchor
fondale [fon'dale] SM **1** (*del mare*) bottom; **il fondale marino** the sea bed **2** (*Teatro*) backdrop
fondamentale [fondamen'tale] AGG fundamental, basic; **è fondamentale che...** it's of prime importance that ...
fondamentalismo [fondamenta'lizmo] SM (*Rel*) fundamentalism
fondamentalista, i, e [fondamenta'lista] AGG, SM/F (*Rel*) fundamentalist
fondamentalistico, a; , ci; , che [fondamenta'listiko] AGG fundamentalist
fondamentalmente [fondamental'mente] AVV fundamentally, basically
fondamento [fonda'mento] SM **1** foundation, basis; **i fondamenti della matematica** the principles of mathematics
■ **fondamenta** SFPL (*Edil*) foundations; **gettare le fondamenta** (*anche fig*) to lay the foundations
fondant [fɔ̃'dɑ̃] SM fondant
fondare [fon'dare] VT (*istituzione, città*) to found; (*fig: teoria, sospetti*) to base; **fondare qc su** to base sth on
▶ **fondarsi** VIP: **fondarsi (su)** (*teorie*) to be based (on)
fondatamente [fondata'mente] AVV with good reason
fondatezza [fonda'tettsa] SF (*di ragioni*) soundness; (*di dubbio, sospetto*) basis in fact
fondato, a [fon'dato] AGG (*sospetto*) well-founded, valid; (*ragione*) valid, sound
fondatore, trice [fonda'tore] SM/F founder
fondazione [fondat'tsjone] SF foundation
fondello [fon'dɛllo] SM (*fig fam*): **prendere qn per i fondelli** to pull sb's leg
fondente [fon'dɛnte] SM (*Metallurgia*) flux
■ AGG: **cioccolato fondente** plain *o* dark chocolate

Ff

fondere ['fondere] VB IRREG
■ VT **1** (*gen*) to melt; (*metallo*) to fuse, melt; (*fig: colori*) to blend, merge; (*: enti, classi, Inform*) to merge
2 (*statua, campana*) to cast
■ VI (*aus* **avere**) to melt; **mi fonde il cervello** (*fig*) I can't think straight any more, my brain has seized up;
▶ **fondersi** VR (*uso reciproco: unirsi: correnti, enti*) to merge, unite
▶ **fondersi** VIP (*sciogliersi*) to melt

fonderia [fonde'ria] SF foundry

fondiario, ria, ri, rie [fon'djarjo] AGG land *attr*; **possidente fondiario** landowner

fondina [fon'dina] SF **1** (*portapistola*) holster **2** (*piatto fondo*) soup plate

fondista, i, e [fon'dista] SM/F (long-)distance runner; (*sciatore*) cross-country skier, langlauf skier

fondo[1], a ['fondo] AGG deep; **piatto fondo** soup plate; **a notte fonda** at dead of night; **una buca fonda 3 metri** a hole 3 metres deep; **qui l'acqua è fonda** the water is deep here
■ SM
1 (*di recipiente, vallata, pozzo*) bottom; (*dei pantaloni*) seat; (*di mare, fiume*) bottom, bed; **fondo marino** sea floor; **fondo stradale** road surface; **doppio fondo** false bottom; **andare** *o* **colare a fondo** (*nave*) to go to the bottom, sink; **la nave è andata a fondo** the ship sank; **dar fondo (all'ancora)** (*Naut*) to drop anchor; **in fondo a** at the bottom of; **in fondo al mare** at the bottom of the sea; **in fondo alla sala** at the back of the room; **in fondo alla pagina** at the bottom of the page; **in fondo al vicolo** at the end of the alley; **laggiù in fondo** (*lontano*) over there; (*in profondità*) down there; **nel fondo del bosco** in the depths *o* heart of the wood; **nel fondo del suo cuore** deep down, in his (*o* her) heart of hearts; **il fondo del bicchiere** the bottom of the glass
2 **fondi** SMPL (*di vino, aceto*) dregs; (*di vino, birra*) lees; (*di caffè*) grounds; (*di tè*) leaves; **fondi di magazzino** old *o* unsold stock *sg*
3 (*sfondo*) background; (*Araldica*) ground; **bianco su fondo nero** white on a black background
4 (*Sport*): **di fondo** long-distance; **sci di fondo** cross-country *o* langlauf skiing; **linea di fondo** (*Tennis*) baseline; (*Calcio*) bye-line; **prova di fondo** (*Equitazione*) speed and endurance (test)
▷ www.fondoitalia.it/
5 (*Giornalismo*): **articolo di fondo** editorial
6 (*fraseologia*): **conoscere a fondo** (*persona*) to know through and through; (*argomento, materia*) to have a thorough knowledge of, know inside out; **conosco a fondo la materia** I know this subject inside out; **studiare a fondo qc** to study sth thoroughly *o* in depth; **andare in fondo a/fino in fondo** (*fig*) to examine thoroughly; **dar fondo a qc** (*risorse*) to use up, consume; **abbiamo dato fondo alle provviste** we've used up all the food; **senza fondo** (*risorse*) infinite, inexhaustible; (*pozzo*) bottomless; **in fondo** after all, all things considered; **in fondo in fondo** actually; **in fondo in fondo avevi ragione** in fact you were right; **toccare il fondo** (*fig*) to plumb the depths

LO SAPEVI...?
fondo non si traduce mai con la parola inglese *fond*

fondo[2] ['fondo] SM **1** (*riserva*) fund; **a fondo perduto** unsecured, without security; **fondo (comune) d'investimento** investment trust; **fondo (di) cassa** cash in hand; (*per piccole spese*) petty cash; **Fondo Monetario Europeo** European Monetary Fund; **Fondo Monetario Internazionale** International Monetary Fund; **fondo pensione** pension fund; **fondo di previdenza** social insurance fund; **fondo di riserva** reserve fund **2** **fondi** SMPL funds; (*capitale*): **fondi pubblici/segreti** public/secret funds; **fondi d'esercizio** working capital *sg*; **fondi neri** slush fund *sg* **3** (*bene immobile*) land, property, estate; **fondo rustico** country estate; **fondo urbano** town property

fondoschiena [fondos'kjɛna] SM INV backside

fondotinta [fondo'tinta] SM INV (*cosmetico*) foundation

fondovalle [fondo'valle] SM (*pl* **fondivalle**) valley bottom

fonduta [fon'duta] SF (*Culin*) fondue

fonema [fo'nɛma] SM phoneme

fonetica [fo'nɛtika] SF phonetics *sg*

foneticamente [fonetika'mente] AVV phonetically

fonetico, a, ci, che [fo'nɛtiko] AGG phonetic

fonico, a, ci, che ['fɔniko] AGG phonic; **accento fonico** stress
■ SM (*tecnico del suono*) sound technician

fonoassorbente [fonoassor'bɛnte] AGG sound-absorbent

fonografo [fo'nɔgrafo] SM gramophone, phonograph (*Am*)

fonologia [fonolo'dʒia] SF phonology

fonologico, a, ci, che [fono'lɔdʒiko] AGG phonological

fontana [fon'tana] SF fountain; **piangere come una fontana** to weep (great) buckets of tears; **fare la fontana** (*Culin*) to make a well

fontanella [fonta'nɛlla] SF **1** (*fontana*) drinking fountain **2** (*Anat*) fontanelle

fonte ['fonte] SF (*sorgente*) spring; (*fig: di calore, informazioni*) source; **risalire alle fonti** to go back to the origins *o* roots; **una fonte di informazioni** a source of information
■ SM: **fonte battesimale** (*Rel*) font

fontina [fon'tina] SF *full fat, hard, sweet cheese from Valle d'Aosta*

football ['futbol] SM INV **: football americano** (American) football

footing ['futiŋ] SM jogging; **fare footing** to jog

foraggiare [forad'dʒare] VT (*cavalli*) to fodder; (*fig fam: sovvenzionare*) to bankroll; (*: illegalmente*) to bribe

foraggio, gi [fo'raddʒo] SM fodder, forage

foraneo, a [fo'raneo] AGG: **diga foranea** breakwater

forapaglie [fora'paʎʎe] SM INV (*Zool*) sedge warbler

forare [fo'rare] VT (*gen*) to make a hole in, pierce; (*biglietto*) to punch; (*pneumatico*) to puncture; (*pallone*) to burst; **forare una gomma** to burst a tyre (*Brit*) *o* tire (*Am*)
■ VI (*aus* **avere**) (*Aut*) to have a puncture; **abbiamo forato** we've got a puncture;
▶ **forarsi** VIP (*gen*) to develop a hole; (*Aut, pallone, timpano*) to burst

foratura [fora'tura] SF (*vedi vb*) piercing; punching; puncturing, puncture; bursting

forbice ['fɔrbitʃe] SF, SPEC PL scissors *pl*; (*Statistica*) range; **un paio di forbici** a pair of scissors; **dare un colpo di forbici a qc** to snip sth; **forbici da giardiniere** (gardening) shears; **forbici per potare** secateurs

forbicina [forbi'tʃina] SF (*Zool*) earwig

forbitamente [forbita'mente] AVV (*parlare*) in a refined way

forbito, a [for'bito] AGG (*stile, modi*) polished; **parla una lingua forbita** he has an elegant turn of phrase

forca, che ['forka] SF **1** (*Agr*) (pitch)fork **2** (*per impiccagione*) gallows *sg o pl*
forcella [for'tʃɛlla] SF (*gen, Tecn*) fork; (*per capelli*) hairpin; (*di volatile*) wishbone; (*di monte*) pass
forchetta [for'ketta] SF fork; (*Statistica*) range; **essere una buona forchetta** to enjoy one's food, be a big eater
forchettata [forket'tata] AVV (*gen*) forkful; **ne prendo solo una forchettata** I'll just have a little
forchettone [forket'tone] SM (*Culin*) carving fork
forcina [for'tʃina] SF hairpin
forcipe ['fɔrtʃipe] SM forceps *pl*
forcone [for'kone] SM pitchfork
forcuto, a [for'kuto] AGG forked
forense [fo'rɛnse] AGG (*linguaggio*) legal; **avvocato forense** barrister (*Brit*), lawyer
foresta [fo'rɛsta] SF (*anche fig*) forest; **foresta pluviale** rain forest
forestale [fores'tale] AGG forest *attr*; **guardia forestale** forester, (forest) ranger
foresteria [foreste'ria] SF (*di convento, palazzo*) guest rooms *pl*, guest quarters *pl*
forestiero, a [fores'tjɛro] SM/F stranger; (*dall'estero*) foreigner
■ AGG foreign
forfait [for'fɛ] SM INV **1** **(prezzo a) forfait** fixed *o* set price; **le diamo un forfait per il suo lavoro** we'll give you a lump sum for your work; **a forfait** on a lump-sum basis **2** **dichiarare forfait** (*Sport*) to withdraw; (*fig*) to give up
forfetario, ria, ri, rie [forfe'tarjo], **forfettario, ria, ri, rie** [forfet'tarjo] AGG: **prezzo forfetario** fixed *o* set price; **somma forfetaria** lump sum
forfora ['forfora] SF dandruff
forgiare [for'dʒare] VT to forge; (*fig*: *carattere*) to mould, form
foriero, a [fo'rjɛro] AGG (*poet*): **essere foriero di** to herald
forlivese [forli'vese] AGG of *o* from Forlì
■ SM/F inhabitant *o* native of Forlì
forma ['forma] SF **1** (*gen, Gramm, Filosofia*) form; (*contorno*) form, shape; **di forma quadrata** square; **a forma di cuore** heart-shaped; **di che forma è?** what shape is it?; **senza forma** (*oggetto*) shapeless; (*pensiero*) unformed; **prendere forma** (*delinearsi*) to take shape; **prendere una medicina in *o* sotto forma di compresse** to take a medicine in tablet form; **una forma rara di cancro** a rare form of cancer; **in forma ufficiale/privata** officially/privately; **forma mentale *o* mentis** way of thinking; **non c'è alcuna forma di vita sulla luna** there is no form of life on the moon; **forma attiva/passiva** (*Gramm*) active/passive voice **2** (*stampo*) mould (*Brit*), mold (*Am*); (*per scarpe*) last; **una forma di formaggio** a (whole) cheese **3** (*modo di esprimersi*) form; **errori di forma** stylistic errors **4** (*anche*: **forma fisica**) form; **essere/non essere in forma** (*atleta, squadra*) to be on/off form; (*persona*) to be in/out of shape; **era in ottima forma e ha segnato tre gol** he was on great form and scored three goals; **la squadra non era in forma** the team was off form; **tenersi in forma** to keep fit *o* in shape; **mi tengo in forma nuotando tutti i giorni** I keep fit by swimming every day **5** (*apparenze*) appearances *pl*; **tenere alla forma** to care about appearances **6** **forme** SFPL (*del corpo*) figure, shape
formaggiera [formad'dʒɛra] SF cheese bowl (*for grated Parmesan*)
formaggino [formad'dʒino] SM processed cheese; **un formaggino** a portion of processed cheese
formaggio, gi [for'maddʒo] SM cheese; **un panino con il formaggio** a cheese roll

FORMAGGI

Italy produces a wide range of cheeses made from cow's, sheep's, goat's and buffalo milk, with many different regional varieties. Cheeses are classified not only according to the type of milk but also according to age, texture and fat content. Among the best known are Parmesan and mozzarella.

formaldeide [formal'dɛide] SF (*Chim*) formaldehyde
formale [for'male] AGG formal
formalina [forma'lina] SF (*Chim*) formalin
formalismo [forma'lizmo] SM (*Arte, Filosofia*) formalism
formalista, i, e [forma'lista] AGG, SM/F formalist
formalistico, a, ci, che [forma'listiko] AGG formalistic
formalità [formali'ta] SF INV formality; **senza tante formalità** (*pasto*) informal
formalizzare [formalid'dzare] VT to formalize
▶ **formalizzarsi** VIP (*farsi scrupoli sulla forma*) to stand on ceremony; (*scandalizzarsi*) to be easily shocked
formalizzazione [formaliddzat'tsjone] SF formalization
formalmente [formal'mente] AVV formally
formare [for'mare] VT **1** (*gen*) to form, shape, make; (*numero telefonico*) to dial; **questi pezzi formano una croce** these pieces make *o* form a cross; **l'appartamento è formato da 3 stanze** the flat comprises 3 rooms; **abbiamo formato un gruppo** we formed a group; **sollevate il ricevitore prima di formare il numero** lift the receiver before dialling the number; **formare una famiglia** to (get married and) start a family **2** (*educare*: *soldati, attori*) to train; (*carattere*) to form, mould (*Brit*), mold (*Am*)
▶ **formarsi** VIP **1** to form, take shape; **il treno si forma a Milano** the train starts from Milan; **si è formata la fila allo sportello** a queue formed at the counter **2** (*educarsi*) to be educated; **Leopardi si formò sui classici greci** Leopardi had a classical Greek background
formativo, a [forma'tivo] AGG formative
formato, a [for'mato] AGG (*maturo*) fully-developed, fully-grown
■ SM (*dimensioni*) size, format; (*Inform*) format; **foto formato tessera** passport-size photo; **formato famiglia** family size; **formato A4** A4 size; **una confezione formato gigante** a giant-size pack
formattare [format'tare] VT (*Inform*) to format
formattazione [formattat'tsjone] SF (*Inform*) formatting
formazione [format'tsjone] SF **1** (*gen, Mil, Sport*) formation; **la formazione del nuovo governo** the formation of the new government **2** (*educazione*) education; (*addestramento*) training; **formazione continua** continuing education; **formazione permanente** lifelong learning; **formazione professionale** vocational training; **un corso di formazione professionale** a vocational training course
▷ www.coinfo.net/
▷ www.fondosocialeuropeo.it/

Ff

formella [for'mɛlla] SF tile
formica¹, che [for'mika] SF *(Zool)* ant
formica²® ['formika] SF Formica®
formicaio, ai [formi'kajo] SM *(sporgente)* anthill; *(sotterraneo)* ants' nest; **quella spiaggia è un formicaio** *(fig)* that beach is always swarming with people
formichiere [formi'kjɛre] SM anteater
formicolare [formiko'lare] VI *(aus* **avere** *nel significato* **a, essere** *nel significato* **b)** **1** *(anche fig: brulicare)*: **formicolare di** to swarm with, be crawling *o* swarming with **2 mi formicola un braccio** I've got pins and needles in my arm
formicolio, lii [formiko'lio] SM *(brulichio)* swarming; *(prurito)* tingling; **avere un formicolio alla gamba** to have pins and needles in one's leg; **sento un formicolio al braccio** I've got pins and needles in my arm
formidabile [formi'dabile] AGG *(temibile)* formidable; *(meraviglioso)* amazing, tremendous, fantastic; *(straordinario)* remarkable; **ho una fame formidabile** I'm incredibly hungry
formidabilmente [formidabil'mente] AVV terribly, incredibly
formoso, a [for'moso] AGG shapely
formula ['fɔrmula] SF *(gen, Chim, Mat)* formula; **formula di struttura** *(Chim)* structural formula; **formula di cortesia** *(nelle lettere)* set phrase; **formula pubblicitaria** advertising slogan; **formula 1** *(Sport)* formula 1
formulare [formu'lare] VT *(giudizio, pensiero)* to formulate
formulario, ri [formu'larjo] SM *(modulo)* form
formulazione [formulat'tsjone] SF formulation; **è un pensiero di difficile formulazione verbale** it's a difficult concept to put into words
fornace [for'natʃe] SF *(Tecn)* kiln
fornaio, ai [for'najo] SM baker; **dal fornaio** at the baker's
fornello [for'nɛllo] SM **1** *(cuocivivande: a spirito, petrolio)* stove; (: *elettrico*) hotplate; (: *a gas*) ring; **fornello a gas** *(di cucina)* gas ring; *(da campeggio)* camping stove; **fornello elettrico** hotplate **2** *(di pipa)* bowl
fornicare [forni'kare] VI *(aus* **avere***)* to fornicate
fornicazione [fornikat'tsjone] SF fornication
fornire [for'nire] VT **1** *(Comm)*: **fornire qc a qn** to supply sth to sb, supply sb with sth **2** *(procurare: abiti, viveri)*: **fornire qc a qn, fornire qn di qc** to supply *o* provide sb with sth; **ci forniscono le materie prime** they supply us with raw materials; **fornire qn di informazioni** to supply *o* provide sb with information, supply *o* provide information to sb; **ci ha fornito tutte le informazioni necessarie** he gave us all the necessary information
▶ **fornirsi** VR: **fornirsi di** *(procurarsi)* to provide o.s. with; **mi fornisco di pane da quel fornaio** I get my bread from that baker; **dobbiamo fornirci di legna per l'inverno** we'll have to stock up with wood for the winter
fornito, a [for'nito] AGG: **ben fornito** *(negozio)* well-stocked
fornitore, trice [forni'tore] AGG: **ditta fornitrice di...** company supplying ...
■ SM/F supplier
■ SM: **fornitore di accesso/servizi** *(Inform)* access/service provider
fornitura [forni'tura] SF supply; **forniture per ufficio** office supplies; **negozio** *o* **società di forniture navali** ship's chandler

LO SAPEVI...?
fornitura non si traduce mai con la parola inglese *furniture*

forno ['forno] SM *(gen)* oven; *(panetteria)* bakery; *(Industria)* furnace; *(per ceramica)* kiln; **cuocere al forno** *(dolci, patate)* to bake; *(carne, patate)* to roast; **pasta al forno** oven-baked pasta; **pollo al forno** roast chicken; **metti la torta nel forno** put the cake in the oven; **fare i forni** *(Med)* to have heat treatment; **questa stanza è un forno!** this room's like an oven!; **forno crematorio** cremator, cinerator *(Am)*; **forno a microonde** microwave (oven)
foro¹ ['foro] SM *(buco)* hole
foro² ['fɔro] SM **1** *(Storia)* forum **2** *(Dir: tribunale)* (law) court; (: *autorità competente*): **del caso si occuperà il foro di Milano** the case will be dealt with by the Milan judiciary; **gli avvocati del foro** ≈ the Bar
forse ['forse] AVV **1** perhaps, maybe; **forse verrà più tardi** he may *o* might come later; **forse hai ragione** maybe you're right; **forse dovremmo andarcene** maybe we should leave; **verrà? – non so. forse** will he come? – I don't know. maybe **2** *(circa)* about; **ti devo forse 10 euro** I must owe you about 10 euros; **mancheranno forse 500 euro** we're about 500 euros short; **sei forse tu il mio padrone?** so you think you own me, do you?
■ SM: **essere in forse** *(persona)* to be undecided; *(evento)* to be in doubt; **mettere in forse la propria vita** to put one's life in danger
forsennatamente [forsennata'mente] AVV *(gridare)* like a madman
forsennato, a [forsen'nato] SM/F madman/madwoman, lunatic
■ AGG mad, crazy, insane
forte¹ ['fɔrte] AGG **1** *(gen, fig)* strong; *(luce, tinta)* strong, bright; *(nevicata, pioggia)* heavy; *(voce, musica)* loud; *(ceffone, colpo)* hard; *(somma, aumento)* large, big; *(spesa)* considerable; **un vento forte** a strong wind; **è più forte di me** he's stronger than me; **ho un forte mal di testa/raffreddore** I have a bad headache/heavy cold; **questo curry è un po' forte** this curry is rather hot; **un forte fumatore** a heavy smoker; **un forte colpo in testa** a hard knock on the head; **un rumore forte** a loud noise; **taglie forti** *(Abbigliamento)* outsize; **usare le maniere forti** to use strong-arm methods *o* tactics; **piatto forte** *(Culin)* main dish; **pezzo forte** pièce de résistance; **dare man forte a qn** to back sb up, support sb; **essere forte in qc** to be good at sth; **è forte in matematica** he is good at maths; **essere forte di qc** to be confident of sth; **farsi forte di qc** to make use of sth, avail o.s. of sth; **non voglio piangere ma è più forte di me** I don't want to cry but I can't help it
2 *(fam: bello, bravo)* amazing, great; **che forte!** *(fam)* amazing!, fantastic!; **è proprio forte!** he's really good!
■ AVV *(velocemente)* fast; *(a volume alto)* loud(ly); *(violentemente)* hard; **tenersi forte** to hold tight; **tieniti forte!** hold tight!; **giocare forte** to play for high stakes; **andare forte** *(fam: essere bravo)* to be amazing, be fantastic; (: *aver successo*) to be all the rage; **correva forte** he was running fast; **ha picchiato forte la testa** she hit her head hard; **non parlare così forte** don't speak so loud; **potresti parlare più forte?** could you speak louder?
■ SM *(persona)*: **il forte e il debole** the strong and the weak; *(punto forte)* strong point, forte

forte² ['fɔrte] SM (*fortezza*) fort
fortemente [forte'mente] AVV (*insistere, consigliare*) strongly; (*stringere*) hard, tight(ly); **fortemente attratto** strongly attracted; **temo fortemente di essere ammalato** I'm very much afraid I'm ill
fortezza [for'tettsa] SF (*luogo fortificato*) fortress; (*morale*) strength
fortificare [fortifi'kare] VT to strengthen, fortify
fortificazione [fortifikat'tsjone] SF fortification
fortino [for'tino] SM fort
FORTRAN ['fɔ:træn] SIGLA M (*Inform*) Fortran, FORTRAN (= *Formula Translating System*)
fortuitamente [fortuita'mente] AVV by chance, fortuitously
fortuito, a [for'tuito] AGG chance, fortuitous, chance *attr*; **per un caso fortuito** by pure chance
fortuna [for'tuna] SF **1** (*destino*) fortune, destiny; (*: favorevole*) luck; **predire la fortuna a qn** to tell sb's future; **la ruota della fortuna** the wheel of fortune; **è girata la fortuna** my (*o* your *ecc*) luck's changed; **tentare la fortuna** to try one's luck; **portare fortuna** to bring luck; **mi ha sempre portato fortuna** it's always brought me good luck; **colpo di fortuna** stroke of luck; **per fortuna** luckily, fortunately; **(per) fortuna che sei passato** *or* **è una fortuna che tu sia passato** it's lucky that you were passing; **per fortuna sei arrivato in tempo** luckily, you arrived in time; **aver fortuna** to be lucky; **avere la fortuna di fare qc** to be lucky enough to do sth; **è tutta fortuna la sua** he's just lucky; **che fortuna!** what luck!; **buona fortuna!** good luck! **2** (*successo, ricchezza*) fortune; **costa una fortuna** it costs a fortune; **fare fortuna** (*persona*) to make one's fortune; (*libro, film ecc*) to be successful; **cercare fortuna** to seek one's fortune **3** **di fortuna** (*riparazione*) makeshift, emergency *attr*; **atterraggio di fortuna** emergency landing; **albero/timone di fortuna** (*Naut*) jury mast
fortunale [fortu'nale] SM storm
fortunatamente [fortunata'mente] AVV luckily, fortunately
fortunato, a [fortu'nato] AGG lucky, fortunate; (*felice*) happy; (*coronato da successo*) successful; **sei più fortunato di me** you're luckier than me; **è la persona più fortunata che conosca** she's the luckiest person I know; **numero fortunato** lucky number
fortunoso, a [fortu'noso] AGG (*vita*) eventful; (*avvenimenti, vicende*) unlucky
foruncolo [fo'runkolo] SM boil
forviare [forvi'are] VI (*aus* **avere**) to go astray
■ VT (*inseguitori, polizia*) to mislead; (*sospetti*) to allay; (*giovani: traviare*) to lead astray
forza ['fɔrtsa] SF **1** (*vigore*) strength; **è per misurare la forza dei muscoli** it's to test the strength of the muscles; **perdere/riacquistare le forze** to lose/regain one's strength; **avere forza nelle braccia** to be strong in the arm; **ha riacquistato presto le forze** he quickly regained his strength; **ha molta forza** he's very strong; **senza forza** *o* **forze** weak; **bella forza!** (*iro*) how clever of you (*o* him *ecc*)!; **farsi forza** (*coraggio*) to pluck up one's courage; **fatti forza!** chin up!, come on!; **forza!** come on!; **con la forza della disperazione** with the strength born of desperation; **l'unione fa la forza** unity is strength; **forza d'animo** strength of mind; **forza di volontà** willpower **2** (*di vento, tempesta*) force; **vento forza 4** force 4 gale; **la forza del vento** the strength of the wind; **la forza dell'esplosione** the force of the explosion **3** (*violenza*) force; **ricorrere alla/adoperare la forza** to resort to/use violence; **a viva forza** by force; **forza bruta** brute force **4** (*Mil*): **le forze armate** the armed forces; **la forza pubblica** the police *pl*; **forza di pace** peacekeeping force **5** (*Dir*): **in forza** in force; **avere forza di legge** to have force of law **6** (*Fis, Tecn*) force; **forza di gravità** force of gravity; **forza motrice** motive power **7** **a forza, con la forza** by force; **mi ha costretto con la forza** he forced me to do it; **a forza di rimproveri/di lavorare** by dint of scolding/working; **perderai la voce a forza di gridare** you'll lose your voice if you shout so much; **con forza** (*violentemente*) violently; (*fermamente*) firmly; **per forza** (*ovviamente*) of course; (*contro la sua volontà*) against one's will; **lo devi fare per forza?** have you got to do it?; **l'ha fatto per forza** he had no choice but to do it, he was forced to do it; **per causa di forza maggiore** (*Dir*) by reason of force majeure; (*per estensione*) due to circumstances beyond one's control; **per forza di cose** through force of circumstances **8** **forza lavoro** (*Econ*) workforce **9** **Forza Italia** (*Pol*) *centre-right party*
forzare [for'tsare] VT **1** (*costringere*): **forzare qn (a fare qc)** to force sb (to do sth), compel sb (to do sth); **hanno forzato la mia volontà** they forced me to do it **2** (*cassaforte, porta*) to force (open); (*serratura*) to force; **la serratura è stata forzata** the lock has been forced **3** (*sforzare: voce*) to strain; **forzare l'andatura** to force the pace; **forzare il significato** (*di parola, testo*) to stretch the meaning; **non voglio forzare la situazione** I don't want to push things
forzatamente [fortsata'mente] AVV (*con sforzo*): **sorridere/ridere forzatamente** to force a smile/a laugh
forzato, a [for'tsato] AGG forced; (*situazione*) artificial; **la mia è stata un'assenza forzata** my absence was due to circumstances beyond my control; **fare un sorriso forzato** to force a smile
■ SM prisoner sentenced to hard labour (*Brit*) *o* labor (*Am*)
forzatura [fortsa'tura] SF **1** (*di cassaforte*) forcing (open) **2** (*di voce*) straining; (*di significato*) stretching; **è una forzatura usare questo termine in quel modo** you're stretching its meaning if you use the word like that
forziere [for'tsjɛre] SM strongbox; (*di pirati*) treasure chest
forzista, i; , e [for'tsista] (*Pol*) AGG relating to supporters of the political party Forza Italia
■ SM/F member (*o* supporter) of Forza Italia
forzuto, a [for'tsuto] AGG (*scherz*) big and strong
foschia [fos'kia] SF haze, mist; **oggi c'è molta foschia** it's very hazy *o* misty today
fosco, a, schi, sche ['fosko] AGG (*colore*) dark; (*cielo*) dull, overcast; (*fig: futuro, pensiero*) dark, gloomy; **dipingere qc a tinte fosche** (*fig*) to paint a gloomy picture of sth
fosfato [fos'fato] SM (*Chim*) phosphate; **fosfato di sodio** sodium phosphate
fosforescente [fosforeʃʃɛnte] AGG phosphorescent; (*insegna, lancetta dell'orologio*) luminous
fosforescenza [fosforeʃʃɛntsa] SF phosphorescence
fosforico, a, ci, che [fos'fɔriko] AGG (*Chim*) phosphoric
fosforo ['fɔsforo] SM (*Chim*) phosphorus
fossa ['fɔssa] SF **1** pit, hole; (*Oceanografia, Mil*) trench; **fossa biologica** cesspool, cesspit; **fossa tettonica** (*Geol*) rift valley **2** (*tomba*) grave; **essere con un piede nella**

Ff

fossa to have one foot in the grave; **fossa comune** mass grave **3** (*Anat*) fossa
fossato [fos'sato] SM ditch; (*di castello*) moat
fossetta [fos'setta] SF dimple
fossi *ecc* ['fossi] VB *vedi* **essere**
fossile ['fɔssile] AGG, SM (*anche fig*) fossil *attr*
fossilizzare [fossilid'dzare] VT
▶ **fossilizzarsi** VR, VIP (*anche fig*) to fossilize
fossilizzazione [fossiliddzat'tsjone] SF (*anche fig*) fossilization
fosso ['fɔsso] SM ditch; (*di castello*) moat; **saltare il fosso** (*fig*) to take the plunge
foste ['foste] VB *vedi* **essere**
foto... ['fɔto] PREF photo...
foto ['fɔto] SF INV, ABBR *di* **fotografia** photo, snap; **fare una foto** to take a photo *o* a snap; **ha fatto molte foto** he took a lot of photos; **una foto in bianco e nero** a black and white photo; **foto ricordo** souvenir photo; **foto tessera** passport (-type) photo
fotocamera [foto'kamera] SF: **fotocamera digitale** digital camera; **telefonino con fotocamera integrata** camera phone
fotocellula [foto'tʃɛllula] SF photocell, electric eye, photoelectric cell
fotochimica [foto'kimika] SF photochemistry
fotochimico, a, ci, che [foto'kimiko] AGG photochemical
fotocomporre [fotokom'porre] VT IRREG to filmset, photocompose (*Am*)
fotocompositore [fotokompozi'tore] SM filmsetter, photocomposer (*Am*)
fotocomposizione [fotokomposit'tsjone] SF filmsetting, (photo)typesetting, photocomposition (*Am*)
fotocopia [foto'kɔpja] SF photocopy
fotocopiare [fotoko'pjare] VT to photocopy
fotocopiatrice [fotokopja'tritʃe] SF photocopier, photocopying machine
fotocopiatura [fotokopja'tura] SF photocopying
fotocopisteria [fotokopiste'ria] SF photocopy shop
fotocromatico, a, ci, che [fotokro'matiko] AGG (*lente*) light-sensitive
fotoelettricità [fotoelettritʃi'ta] SF INV photoelectricity
fotoelettrico, a, ci, che [fotoe'lɛttriko] AGG photoelectric
fotogenico, a, ci, che [foto'dʒɛniko] AGG photogenic
fotografare [fotogra'fare] VT to photograph
fotografia [fotogra'fia] SF (*arte, procedimento*) photography; (*immagine*) photograph; **un corso di fotografia** a photography course; **fotografia a colori/in bianco e nero** colour/black and white photograph; **fare una fotografia** to take a photograph; **farsi fare una fotografia** to have one's photograph taken
fotograficamente [fotografika'mente] AVV photographically
fotografico, a, ci, che [foto'grafiko] AGG photographic; **macchina fotografica** camera; **servizio** *o* **reportage fotografico** photo feature; **studio fotografico** photographer's studio
fotografo, a [fo'tɔgrafo] SM/F photographer
fotogramma, i [foto'gramma] SM (*Cine*) frame
fotoincisione [fotointʃi'zjone] SF photogravure, photoengraving
fotomodello, a [fotomo'dɛllo] SM/F fashion *o* photographic model
fotomontaggio, gi [fotomon'taddʒo] SM photomontage
fotoreporter [fotore'pɔrter] SM/F INV newspaper (*o* magazine) photographer
fotoromanzo [fotoro'mandzo] SM photo love story
fotosensibile [fotosen'sibile] AGG photosensitive
fotosintesi [foto'sintezi] SF (*Bot*) photosynthesis
fototropismo [fototro'pizmo] SM (*Bot*) phototropism
fottere ['fottere] VT (*fam!*) **1** (*avere rapporti sessuali*) to fuck (*fam!*), screw (*fam!*); **vai a farti fottere!** fuck off! (*fam!*) **2** (*rubare*) to pinch, swipe **3** (*fregare*): **mi hanno fottuto** they did the dirty on me, they played a dirty trick on me, I've been screwed (*fam*)
fottuto, a [fot'tuto] AGG (*fam!*) bloody, fucking *attr* (*fam!*)
foulard [fu'lar] SM INV (head)scarf
foyer [fwa'je] SM INV foyer
FR SIGLA = *Frosinone*
fr. ABBR (*moneta*) (= **franco**) fr.
fra[1] [fra] PREP = **tra**
fra[2] [fra] SM (*dav a nomi propri*) = **frate**
frac [frak] SM INV (*abito maschile*) tails *pl*
fracassare [frakas'sare] VT to smash, shatter
▶ **fracassarsi** VIP to smash, break, shatter; (*veicolo*) to crash; (*fare a piccoli pezzi*) to smash to smithereens, shatter
fracasso [fra'kasso] SM (*baccano, confusione*) din; (*di piatti*) crash; **fare fracasso** to make a din
fradicio, cia, ci, ce ['fraditʃo] AGG soaked, soaking (wet), drenched; **bagnato fradicio** soaking wet; **ubriaco fradicio** blind drunk; **ho la camicia fradicia** my shirt is soaked
fragile ['fradʒile] AGG (*gen, fig*) fragile; (*salute, nervi*) delicate; (*vetro*) brittle; **"fragile"** (*sui pacchi*) "fragile, (handle) with care"
fragilità [fradʒili'ta] SF INV (*vedi agg*) fragility; delicacy; brittleness
fragola ['fragola] SF strawberry
fragore [fra'gore] SM (*di cascate, carro armato*) roar; (*di tuono*) rumble
fragorosamente [fragorosa'mente] AVV (*ridere*) uproariously; (*scoppiare*) deafeningly
fragoroso, a [frago'roso] AGG deafening, ear-splitting; **un fragoroso ceffone** a resounding slap; **una risata fragorosa** an uproarious burst of laughter; **scoppiare in una risata fragorosa** to roar with laughter
fragrante [fra'grante] AGG fragrant
fragranza [fra'grantsa] SF fragrance
fraintendere [frain'tɛndere] VT IRREG to misunderstand; **mi hai frainteso** you misunderstood me
fraintendimento [fraintendi'mento] SM misunderstanding
frainteso, a [frain'teso] PP *di* **fraintendere**
frammentariamente [frammentarja'mente] AVV in a fragmented fashion
frammentarietà [frammentarje'ta] SF INV fragmentary nature
frammentario, ria, ri, rie [frammen'tarjo] AGG sketchy, fragmentary; **le notizie giungono frammentarie** as yet we don't have a complete picture of events
frammento [fram'mento] SM (*di roccia*) fragment, bit; (*di testo*) passage, extract
frammesso, a [fram'messo] PP *di* **frammettere**
frammettere [fram'mettere] VB IRREG
■ VT to interpose

▶ **frammettersi** VR to intervene, interfere
frammezzo [fram'meddzo] AVV in between; **frammezzo a** PREP among
frammischiare [frammis'kjare] VT: **frammischiare (a)** to mix up (with)
frammisto, a [fram'misto] AGG: **frammisto a** interspersed with, mixed with
frana ['frana] SF landslip, landslide; (*fig: persona*): **essere una frana in** to be useless *o* hopeless *o* rubbish at
franamento [frana'mento] SM landslide
franare [fra'nare] VI (*aus* **essere**) (*Geol*) to slip, slide down; (: *roccia*) to fall; (*fig: resistenza*) to collapse
francamente [franka'mente] AVV frankly
francescano, a [frantʃes'kano] AGG, SM Franciscan
francese [fran'tʃeze] AGG French
■ SM/F Frenchman/Frenchwoman; **i francesi** the French
■ SM (*lingua*) French; **parli francese?** do you speak French?
francesismo [frantʃe'zizmo] SM Callicism
franchezza [fran'kettsa] SF frankness, openness
franchigia, gie [fran'kidʒa] SF **1** (*Amm*) exemption; **franchigia doganale** exemption from customs duty; **bagaglio in franchigia** (*Aer*) free baggage allowance **2 franchigia assicurativa** insurance excess franchise **3** (*Naut*) shore leave
Francia ['frantʃa] SF France; **ti piace la Francia?** do you like France?; **andrò in Francia quest'estate** I'm going to France this summer
franco[1], a, chi, che ['franko] AGG **1** (*persona, sguardo: sincero*) frank, candid, open, sincere; **rispondere in modo franco** to answer frankly **2** (*Comm*): **porto franco** free port; **franco bordo** free on board; **franco di dazio** *o* **dogana** duty-free; **franco fabbrica** ex factory, ex works; **prezzo franco fabbrica** ex-works price; **franco magazzino** ex warehouse; **franco di porto** carriage free; **franco vagone** free on rail **3 franco tiratore** (*Mil*) irregular (soldier); (*cecchino*) sniper; (*Pol*) *member of parliament who votes against his own party* **4 farla franca** to get away with it, get off scot-free
■ AVV (*francamente*) frankly
franco[2], a, chi, che ['franko] (*Storia*) AGG Frankish
■ SM Frank
■ PREF: **franco...** Franco...
franco[3], chi ['franko] SM (*moneta*) franc
francobollo [franko'bollo] SM (postage) stamp
franco-canadese [frankokana'dese] AGG, SM/F French Canadian
francofilo, a [fran'kɔfilo] AGG, SM/F Francophile
Francoforte [franko'fɔrte] SF Frankfurt
frangente [fran'dʒɛnte] SM **1** (*onda*) breaker **2** (*scoglio affiorante*) reef **3** (*circostanza*) situation, circumstance
frangia, ge ['frandʒa] SF (*gen*) fringe; **frangia costiera** coastal strip; **le frange estremiste del partito** (*fig*) the extremist fringe of the party
frangiflutti [frandʒi'flutti] SM INV breakwater
frangivento [frandʒi'vento] SM INV windbreak
franoso, a [fra'noso] AGG (*terreno*) unstable, subject to landslides
frantoio, oi [fran'tojo] SM (*Agr*) olive-press; (*Tecn*) crusher
frantumare [frantu'mare] VT to break (up), break into pieces, shatter
▶ **frantumarsi** VIP to break, shatter, break into pieces
frantumazione [frantumat'tsjone] SF breaking, shattering
frantume [fran'tume] SM: **andare in frantumi, mandare in frantumi** to shatter, smash to pieces *o* smithereens
frappé [frap'pe] SM INV (*Culin*) milk shake
frapporre [frap'porre] VB IRREG
■ VT: **frapporre ostacoli (a qn)** to place obstacles in the way (of sb); **senza frapporre indugi** without hesitating;
▶ **frapporsi** VR: **frapporsi tra** (*intromettersi*) to come between
frapposizione [frapposit'tsjone] SF interference
frapposto, a [frap'posto] PP *di* **frapporre**
frasario, ri [fra'zarjo] SM (*gergo*) language
frasca, sche ['fraska] SF bough, (leafy) branch; **saltare di palo in frasca** to jump from one subject to another
frase ['fraze] SF **1** (*proposizione*) sentence; **la frase che ha detto non mi è piaciuta** I didn't like what he said; **traduci questa frase** translate this sentence; **frase fatta** stock *o* set phrase **2** (*Mus*) phrase
fraseggio, gi [fra'zeddʒo] SM (*Mus*) phrasing
fraseologia [frazeolo'dʒia] SF phraseology
fraseologico, a, ci, che [frazeo'lɔdʒiko] AGG phraseological
frassino ['frassino] SM ash (tree)
frastagliare [frastaʎ'ʎare] VT to indent
frastagliato, a [frastaʎ'ʎato] AGG (*costa*) indented, jagged
frastornare [frastor'nare] VT (*intontire*) to daze; (*confondere*) to befuddle, bewilder
frastornato, a [frastor'nato] AGG deafened; (*vedi vt*) dazed; bewildered
frastuono [fras'twɔno] SM noise, din
frate ['frate] SM (*Rel*) brother, friar, monk; **farsi frate** to become a monk
fratellanza [fratel'lantsa] SF (*sentimento*) brotherliness; (*associazione*) brotherhood, fraternity
fratellastro [fratel'lastro] SM stepbrother; (*con genitore in comune*) half brother
fratello [fra'tɛllo] SM **1** (*gen*) brother; **questo è mio fratello** this is my brother; **hai fratelli?** have you any brothers or sisters?; **siamo fratelli, disse la donna** we are brother and sister, said the woman; **fratello d'armi** brother in arms; **fratello gemello** twin (brother); **fratello siamese** Siamese twin **2** (*Rel*) brother; **i fratelli cristiani** the Christian brethren
fraternamente [fraterna'mente] AVV fraternally, in a brotherly way
fraternità [fraterni'ta] SF INV fraternity
fraternizzare [fraternid'dzare] VI (*aus* **avere**) to fraternize
fraterno, a [fra'tɛrno] AGG fraternal, brotherly
fratricida, i, e [fratri'tʃida] AGG fratricidal; **guerra fratricida** civil war
■ SM/F fratricide (*person*)
fratta ['fratta] SF thicket
frattaglie [frat'taʎʎe] SFPL (*Culin: gen*) offal *sg*; (: *di pollo*) giblets
frattanto [frat'tanto] AVV meanwhile, in the meantime
frattempo [frat'tɛmpo] **nel frattempo** AVV in the meantime, meanwhile
fratto, a ['fratto] AGG (*Mat: numero, equazione*) fractional; (: *diviso*): **due fratto cinque** 2 divided by 5
frattura [frat'tura] SF (*Med, Geol*) fracture; (*fig: dissenso*)

Ff

split, break; **una grave frattura** a serious fracture; **ha una frattura alla gamba** he's broken his leg

fratturare [frattu'rare] VT (*Med*) to fracture, break; **fratturarsi un braccio/una gamba** to break one's arm/one's leg
▶ **fratturarsi** VIP (*Med*) to fracture, break; (*partito, gruppo*) to split

fraudolento, a [fraudo'lɛnto] AGG fraudulent

fraudolenza [fraudo'lɛntsa] SF fraudulence

frazionamento [frattsjona'mento] SM division, splitting up

frazionare [frattsjo'nare] VT to divide, split up

frazione [frat'tsjone] SF **1** (*gen, Mat*) fraction; **una frazione di secondo** a fraction of a second **2** (*borgata*) ≈ hamlet

freatico, a, ci, che [fre'atiko] AGG (*Geol*): **acqua freatica** groundwater; **falda freatica** phreatic layer

freccetta [fret'tʃetta] SF (*Sport*) dart; **freccette** SFPL: **giocare a freccette** to play darts
▷ www.figg.org/figf/prima.html

freccia, ce ['frettʃa] SF **1** (*di arco*) arrow; **entrare/uscire come una freccia** to dash *o* shoot in/out **2** (*Aut*) indicator; **mettere la freccia (a destra/sinistra)** to indicate that one is turning (right/left); **ha messo la freccia per voltare a destra** he indicated he was turning right **3** (*segnale stradale*) signpost

frecciata [fret'tʃata] SF: **lanciare una frecciata** to make a cutting remark

freddamente [fredda'mente] AVV coldly, coolly

freddare [fred'dare] VT (*minestra*) to cool; (*fig: entusiasmo*) to put a damper on; (*uccidere*) to kill, shoot dead; **fai freddare la minestra** let the soup cool; **freddare qn con lo sguardo** to silence sb with an icy stare
▶ **freddarsi** VIP to cool, become cold

freddezza [fred'dettsa] SF **1** (*indifferenza*) coldness, coolness; **accogliere qn/qc con freddezza** to greet sb/sth coolly **2** (*autocontrollo*) sang-froid; **la sua freddezza ha evitato il peggio** her cool-headedness prevented anything worse happening

freddo, a ['freddo] AGG (*gen*) cold; (*accoglienza*) cool, cold; **la minestra è fredda** the soup is cold; **a mente fredda capì di avere torto** when he had cooled down he realized that he was wrong; **la macchina è ancora fredda** the engine is still cold
■ SM **1** (*gen*) cold; **aver freddo** to be cold; **hai freddo?** are you cold?; **prendere freddo** to catch cold; **soffrire il freddo** to feel the cold; **sudare freddo** to be in a cold sweat; **fa freddo** it's cold; **c'è stata un'ondata di freddo** there's been a cold spell **2 a freddo** (*lavare*) in cold water; (*fig*) deliberately; **a freddo ha poi negato di averlo detto** when he had cooled down, he denied having said it

freddoloso, a [freddo'loso] AGG: **essere freddoloso** to feel *o* be sensitive to the cold

freddura [fred'dura] SF dry comment, pun

freezer ['fri:zə] SM INV fridge-freezer

fregare [fre'gare] VT **1** (*sfregare*) to rub; (*per pulire*) to polish; **fregarsi le mani/gli occhi** to rub one's hands/one's eyes; **si fregava le mani** he was rubbing his hands **2** (*fig fam*): **fregare qn** (*imbrogliare*) to cheat sb, rip sb off, take sb in; **ha cercato di fregarmi** he tried to cheat me; **mi frega sempre a carte** (*vincere*) he always beats me at cards **3** (*rubare*): **fregare qc a qn** to pinch *o* swipe sth from sb; **mi ha fregato il ragazzo** she pinched my boyfriend; **mi ha fregato il portafoglio** he pinched my wallet **4** (*fig fam*): **fregarsene (di qc/qn)** (*infischiarsene*) not to give a damn (about sth/sb); **non gliene frega niente** he doesn't give a damn; **me ne frego** I don't give a damn; **che ti frega?** none of your business!; **chi se ne frega?** who cares?

fregata[1] [fre'gata] SF **1** (*vedi vb 1*) rub; polish; **dare una fregata a qc** to rub sth, polish sth **2** (*fam*) = fregatura

fregata[2] [fre'gata] SF (*Naut*) frigate

fregatura [frega'tura] SF (*fam: imbroglio*) rip-off, con; **mi hanno tirato una fregatura** they ripped me off; **è stata una fregatura** (*delusione*) it's been a let-down

fregherò *ecc* [frege'rɔ] VB *vedi* **fregare**

fregiare [fre'dʒare] VT (*Archit*) to adorn, embellish
▶ **fregiarsi** VR: **fregiarsi di** (*titolo, onore*) to be the proud holder of

fregio, gi ['fredʒo] SM (*gen*) decoration, ornament; (*Archit*) frieze

frego, ghi ['frego] SM line, mark

fregola ['fregola] SF **1** (*Zool: calore*) heat **2** (*fig: smania*): **avere la fregola di fare qc** to have an itch to do sth

fremente [fre'mɛnte] AGG: **essere fremente di** (*gen*) to be trembling with

fremere ['frɛmere] VI (*aus* **avere**) to shake, tremble; **fremere di** to tremble *o* quiver with; **fremere d'impazienza** to be champing at the bit

fremito ['frɛmito] SM shudder, shiver; (*di passione*) wave; **ebbe un fremito d'ira** he shook with anger

frenaggio, gi [fre'naddʒo] SM (*Sport, Aut: azione*) braking; (*: meccanismi*) braking system

frenare [fre'nare] VT (*veicolo*) to slow down; (*progresso, avanzata*) to hold up; (*gioia, evoluzione*) to check; (*cavallo*) to rein in; **frenare la lingua** to hold one's tongue; **frenare le lacrime** to hold back one's tears; **non riusciva a frenare le lacrime** she couldn't hold back her tears; **misure per frenare l'inflazione** measures to curb inflation
■ VI (*aus* **avere**) (*Aut*) to brake; (*Sci*) to slow down; **ha frenato per evitare un cane** he braked to avoid a dog;
▶ **frenarsi** VR to restrain o.s., stop o.s., control o.s.

frenata [fre'nata] SF braking; **fare una brusca frenata** to brake suddenly, hit the brakes; **ha fatto una brusca frenata** he braked suddenly

frenesia [frene'zia] SF frenzy; **con frenesia** frenziedly

freneticamente [frenetika'mente] AVV frantically

frenetico, a, ci, che [fre'nɛtiko] AGG frenetic

freno ['freno] SM **1** (*Aut*) brake; (*di cavallo*) bit; (*fig*) restraint; **bloccare i freni** *or* **azionare i freni** to apply the brakes; **freno a disco** disc brake; **freno a mano** handbrake, parking brake (*Am*); **tira il freno a mano** put the handbrake on **2** (*fraseologia*): **mettere** *o* **porre un freno a** (*inflazione, tendenza*) to put a brake on, keep in check; **tenere a freno** (*passioni*) to restrain; **tenere a freno la lingua** to hold one's tongue; **agire da freno** to act as a restraint

frenologia [frenolo'dʒia] SF phrenology

frenulo ['frɛnulo] SM (*Anat*) fraenum

freon® ['frɛon] SM INV (*Chim*) Freon®

frequentare [frekwen'tare] VT (*scuola, corso*) to attend; (*persona*) to see (regularly *o* often); (*locale, casa, bar*) to go to, frequent; **frequentare cattive compagnie** to keep bad company; **frequento un corso di inglese** I go to English classes; **non li frequento più** I don't see them any more; **la frequento poco** I don't see much of her; **non mi piace la gente che frequenta** I don't like the people he mixes with; **è un locale mal frequentato**

you get some shady types at that place *o* in that bar
▶ **frequentarsi** VR (*uso reciproco*) to see each other (regularly); **si frequentano da anni** they have been seeing each other for years

frequentato, a [frekwen'tato] AGG (*locale*) busy; **è la pizzeria più frequentata della città** it's the most popular pizzeria in town

frequentatore, trice [frekwenta'tore] SM/F: **frequentatore (di)** frequent visitor (to)

frequente [fre'kwɛnte] AGG frequent; **di frequente** frequently

frequentemente [frekwente'mente] AVV frequently, often

frequenza [fre'kwɛntsa] SF (*gen, Fis, Radio, Elettr*) frequency; (*Scol*) attendance; **frequenza respiratoria** breathing rate; **con sempre maggiore frequenza** with increasing frequency

fresa ['freza] SF (*Tecn*) milling cutter

fresare [fre'zare] VT (*Tecn*) to mill

fresatrice [freza'tritʃe] SF (*Tecn*) milling machine

freschezza [fres'kettsa] SF (*gen*) freshness; (*di serata*) coolness

fresco, a, schi, sche ['fresko] AGG (*gen*) fresh; (*temperatura, clima*) fresh, cool; (*vernice*) wet; (*traccia, notizia, ferita*) recent, new; **frutta fresca** fresh fruit; **"vernice fresca"** "wet paint"; **fresco e riposato** (completely) refreshed; **fresca come una rosa** as fresh as a daisy; **bere qc di fresco** to have a cold drink; **fresco di bucato** freshly laundered, newly washed; **fresco di studi** (*fam*) fresh out of university *o* school; **se continui così stai fresco** (*fig*) if you go on like this you'll be in trouble
■ SM (*temperatura*) cool; **è *o* fa fresco** it is cool; **mettere/tenere al fresco** (*fig: persona: in prigione*) to put/keep inside *o* in the cooler; **mettere in fresco** to put in the fridge; **metti il vino in fresco** put the wine in the fridge; **fatto di fresco** newly done; **godersi il fresco** to enjoy the cool air

frescura [fres'kura] SF cool; **la frescura della sera** the cool of the evening

fresia ['frezja] SF freesia

fretta ['fretta] SF hurry, haste; **in fretta** in a hurry; **fallo in fretta** do it quickly; **fai in fretta!** hurry up!; **in tutta fretta** hurriedly, quickly; **in fretta e furia** in a great *o* tearing hurry, in a mad rush; **avere fretta (di fare qc)** to be in a hurry (to do sth); **scusa ma ho un po' di fretta** I'm sorry but I'm in a bit of a hurry; **aveva fretta di andarsene** he was in a hurry to leave; **fare qc in fretta** (*velocemente*) to do sth quickly, hurry up with sth; (*troppo velocemente*) to do sth in a hurry; **l'ho fatto un po' troppo in fretta** I did it in too much of a hurry; **far fretta a qn** to hurry sb; **non farmi fretta** don't hurry me; **che fretta c'è?** what's the hurry?

frettolosamente [frettolosa'mente] AVV hurriedly, in a rush; **salutò frettolosamente e se ne andò** he said a hurried goodbye and left

frettoloso, a [fretto'loso] AGG (*persona*) in a hurry; (*lavoro*) hurried, rushed; **diede una scorsa frettolosa al libro** he flicked through the book; **è un po' troppo frettoloso in quello che fa** he tends to rush things

friabile [fri'abile] AGG (*roccia, terreno*) friable; (*biscotto*) crumbly

friabilità [friabili'ta] SF INV (*vedi agg*) friability; crumbliness

fricassea [frikas'sɛa] SF (*Culin*) fricassee; **pollo in fricassea** chicken fricassee

fricativo, a [frika'tivo] AGG, SF fricative

fricchettone, a [frikket'tone] SM (*fam*) freak

friggere ['friddʒere] VB IRREG
■ VT to fry; **mandare qn a farsi friggere** to tell sb to get lost; **vai a farti friggere!** (*fam*) get lost!
■ VI (*aus* **avere**) (*grasso, olio*) to sizzle; (*fig*): **friggere dalla rabbia** to seethe with rage; **friggere d'impazienza** to fume with impatience

friggitoria [friddʒito'ria] SF ≈ fish and chip shop

friggitrice [friddʒi'tritʃe] SF deep fryer

frigidaire® [friʒi'dɛr] SM INV refrigerator

frigidità [fridʒidi'ta] SF INV frigidity

frigido, a ['fridʒido] AGG frigid

frignare [friɲ'ɲare] VI (*aus* **avere**) to whine, snivel

frignone, a [friɲ'ɲone] SM/F whiner, sniveller

frigo, ghi ['frigo] SM fridge

frigobar [frigo'bar] SM INV minibar

frigorifero, a [frigo'rifero] AGG refrigerated; **cella frigorifera** cold store
■ SM refrigerator

fringuello [frin'gwello] SM chaffinch

frinire [fri'nire] VI (*aus* **avere**) to chirp

frisbee® ['frisbi:] SM INV Frisbee®

frissi *ecc* ['frissi] VB *vedi* **friggere**

frittata [frit'tata] SF (*Culin*) omelette, omelet (*Am*); **la frittata è fatta!** (*fig*) that's torn it!, the damage is done

frittella [frit'tɛlla] SF (*Culin*) fritter

fritto, a ['fritto] PP *di* **friggere**
■ AGG (*patatine, pesce*) fried; **pollo fritto** fried chicken; **patate fritte** chips (*Br*), (French) fries (*Am*); **ormai siamo fritti!** (*fig fam*) now we've had it!; **è un argomento fritto e rifritto** that's old hat
■ SM fried food; **odore di fritto** smell of frying; **fritto misto** mixed fried fish

frittura [frit'tura] SF (*cibo*) fried food; **frittura di pesce** mixed fried fish

friulano, a [friu'lano] AGG of *o* from Friuli, Friulian; inhabitant *o* native of Friuli

frivolamente [frivola'mente] AVV frivolously

frivolezza [frivo'lettsa] SF frivolity

frivolo, a ['frivolo] AGG frivolous

frizionare [frittsjo'nare] VT to rub, massage; **frizionarsi il braccio** to rub one's arm

frizione [frit'tsjone] SF **1** (*massaggio*) rubbing, massage; **fare delle frizioni con una pomata** to rub in an ointment **2** (*lozione*) lotion **3** (*tensione*) friction **4** (*Aut*) clutch **5** (*Fis*) friction

frizzante [frid'dzante] AGG (*gen*) fizzy, sparkling; (*vino*) sparkling; (*persona*) effervescent, bubbly (*fam*); **acqua minerale frizzante** sparkling mineral water

frizzare [frid'dzare] VI (*aus* **avere**) to sparkle, be fizzy

frizzo ['friddzo] SM witticism

frodare [fro'dare] VT to defraud, cheat; **frodare il fisco** to evade tax

frode ['frɔde] SF (*Dir*) fraud; **frode fiscale** tax evasion

frodo ['frɔdo] SM: **di frodo** illegal, contraband; **pescatore/cacciatore di frodo** poacher; **pescare/cacciare di frodo** to poach

frogia, gie *o* ge ['frɔdʒa] SF (*di cavallo*) nostril

frollare [frol'lare] VI (*aus* **essere**) (*carne*) to become high

frollino [frol'lino] SM (*Culin*) pastry (with candied fruit)

frollo, a ['frɔllo] AGG (*Culin: carne*) high; **pasta frolla** short(crust) pastry; (*fig: persona*) soft

Ff

fronda[1] ['fronda] SF *(Bot)* leafy branch; *(spec al pl)* foliage *sg*
fronda[2] ['fronda] SF *(fig Pol)* rebellion, internal opposition
frondista, i, e [fron'dista] SM/F *(fig Pol)* rebel
frondoso, a [fron'doso] AGG *(albero)* leafy; *(fig: stile)* ornate
frontale [fron'tale] AGG *(Anat, Mil)* frontal; **scontro frontale** *(Aut)* head-on collision; **lezione frontale** *traditional lesson with the teacher teaching the whole class*; **insegnamento frontale** whole class teaching
frontalino [fronta'lino] SM *(di autoradio)* faceplate
frontalmente [frontal'mente] AVV frontally
fronte ['fronte] SF **1** *(Anat)* brow, forehead; **a fronte alta** *(anche fig)* with one's head held high; **col sudore della fronte** by the sweat of one's brow; **gli ha dato un bacio in fronte** she gave him a kiss on the forehead **2** **di fronte** *(dirimpetto)* opposite; **l'edificio di fronte** the building opposite; **abita qui di fronte** he lives in the house opposite; **di fronte a** opposite, facing, in front of; *(a paragone di)* compared with; **si è seduto di fronte a me** he sat down opposite me; **la casa di fronte alla mia** the house opposite mine; **testo a fronte** parallel text; **vista di fronte la casa è più bella** seen from the front the house looks much more attractive
■ SM *(Mil, Pol, Meteor)* front; **partì per il fronte a diciotto anni** he left for the front when he was eighteen; **far fronte a** *(nemico, problema)* to confront; *(responsabilità)* to face up to; *(spese)* to meet
fronteggiare [fronted'dʒare] VT *(affrontare: nemico, problema, avversità)* to face, confront, stand up to; *(sostenere: spese)* to meet
frontespizio, zi [frontes'pittsjo] SM *(di libro)* title page
frontiera [fron'tjɛra] SF frontier, border; *(fig)* frontier; **zona di frontiera** frontier *o* border area; **guardia di frontiera** border guard; **polizia di frontiera** border police
frontone [fron'tone] SM pediment
fronzolo ['frondzolo] SM frill; **senza fronzoli** *(fig)* without (any) frills, plainly
fronzuto, a [fron'dzuto] AGG leafy
frotta ['frɔtta] SF crowd; **in frotta** *or* **a frotte** in their hundreds, in droves
frottola ['frɔttola] SF *(fam: bugia)* lie, fib; **raccontare un sacco di frottole** to tell a pack of lies; **questa è una frottola** that's a lie
fru fru [fruf'fru] AGG INV frilly
frugale [fru'gale] AGG frugal
frugalità [frugali'ta] SF INV frugality
frugalmente [frugal'mente] AVV frugally
frugare [fru'gare] VT to search; **frugarsi le tasche** to search through one's pockets; **ho frugato nelle tasche** I searched my pockets
■ VI *(aus* **avere***)* **frugare in** to search, rummage around in
frugherò *ecc* [fruge'rɔ] VB *vedi* **frugare**
frugoletto [frugo'letto] SM cutie-pie *(fam)*
fruibile [fru'ibile] AGG usable; **è fruibile da tutti** it's available to everybody
fruire [fru'ire] VI *(aus* **avere***)* **fruire di qc** to enjoy the use of sth
fruitore, trice [frui'tore] SM user
fruizione [fruit'tsjone] SF use
frullare [frul'lare] VT *(gen)* to blend; *(frutta)* to blend, liquidize; *(uova)* to whisk
■ VI *(aus* **avere***)* *(uccelli)* to flutter, whirr; **cosa ti frulla in mente?** *(fig)* what is going on in that mind of yours?
frullato [frul'lato] SM *(Culin)* milk shake *(made with fresh fruit, cocoa etc)*
frullatore [frulla'tore] SM blender, liquidizer; **frullatore a immersione** hand-held liquidizer
frullino [frul'lino] SM whisk
frullio, lii [frul'lio] SM *(di ali)* flutter
frumentario, ria, ri, rie [frumen'tarjo] AGG grain *attr*, wheat *attr*
frumento [fru'mento] SM grain, wheat
frusciare [fruʃ'ʃare] VI *(aus* **avere***)* to rustle
fruscio, scii [fruʃ'ʃio] SM rustling, rustle
frusinate [fruzi'nate] AGG of *o* from Frosinone
■ SM/F inhabitant *o* native of Frosinone
frusta ['frusta] SF **1** *(per cavalli)* whip; **colpo di frusta** whiplash **2** *(Culin)* whisk
frustare [frus'tare] VT to whip
frustata [frus'tata] SF lash
frustino [frus'tino] SM riding crop
frusto, a ['frusto] AGG *(logoro: abito)* threadbare; *(: argomento)* trite, hackneyed
frustrare [frus'trare] VT to frustrate
frustrato, a [frus'trato] AGG frustrated
■ SM/F frustrated person
frustrazione [frustrat'tsjone] SF frustration
frutta ['frutta] SF fruit; *(portata)* dessert; **frutta fresca** fresh fruit; **vuoi della frutta?** would you like some fruit?; **mi piace molto la frutta** I love fruit; **torta alla frutta** fruit gateau; **gelato alla frutta** fruit-flavoured ice cream; **essere alla frutta** to be finished *o* done; **frutta candita** candied fruit; **frutta sciroppata** fruit in heavy syrup; **frutta secca** *(fichi ecc)* dried fruit; *(noci, mandorle ecc)* nuts
fruttare [frut'tare] VT: **il mio deposito in banca (mi) frutta il 5%** I get 5% interest on my bank deposits; **quella gara gli fruttò la medaglia d'oro** he won the gold medal in that competition
■ VI *(aus* **avere***)* *(investimenti, deposito)* to bear dividends, give a return; **questo investimento ha fruttato poco** this investment did not give much of a return *o* gave a poor yield
fruttato, a [frut'tato] AGG *(vino)* fruity
frutteto [frut'teto] SM orchard
frutticolo, a [frut'tikolo] AGG fruit *attr*
frutticoltore, trice [fruttikol'tore] SM/F fruit grower
frutticoltura [fruttikol'tura] SF fruit growing
fruttiera [frut'tjɛra] SF fruit dish
fruttifero, a [frut'tifero] AGG **1** *(albero)* fruit-bearing **2** *(fig: che frutta)* fruitful, profitable; **deposito fruttifero** interest-bearing deposit
fruttificare [fruttifi'kare] VI *(aus* **avere***)* to bear fruit
fruttivendolo, a [frutti'vendolo] SM/F fruiterer, greengrocer *(Brit)*, produce dealer *(Am)*; **dal fruttivendolo** at the fruit shop *o* greengrocer's *o* fruiterer's
frutto ['frutto] SM *(anche fig)* fruit; **un frutto tropicale** a tropical fruit; **dare frutti** *(anche fig)* to bear fruit; **raccogliere i frutti di qc** *(fig)* to reap the rewards of sth; **essere frutto di** *(fig)* to be the fruit of; **è frutto della tua immaginazione** it's a figment of your imagination; **il frutto del mio lavoro** *(fig)* the fruits of my labour; **senza alcun frutto** *(fig)* fruitlessly, in vain; **frutti di bosco** berries; **frutti di mare** shellfish *sg o pl*, seafood *sg*
fruttosio [frut'tɔzjo] SM fructose
fruttuosamente [fruttuosa'mente] AVV profitably

fruttuoso, a [fruttu'oso] AGG fruitful, profitable
FS ['effe'ɛsse] SIGLA F (= **Ferrovie dello Stato**) *Italian railways*
f.t. ABBR = **fuori testo**
f.to ABBR (= **firmato**) signed
fu [fu] (*3a pers sg del passato remoto di* essere) AGG INV (*defunto*): **il fu Mario Rossi** the late Mario Rossi
fucilare [futʃi'lare] VT to shoot *o* execute (by firing squad)
fucilata [futʃi'lata] SF (rifle) shot; **fu ucciso da una fucilata alla schiena** it was a bullet in the back which killed him
fucilazione [futʃilat'tsjone] SF execution (by firing squad)
fucile [fu'tʃile] SM rifle, gun; **fucile da caccia** shotgun; **fucile a canne mozze** sawn-off shotgun; **fucile subacqueo** (underwater) spear gun
fucina [fu'tʃina] SF (*Tecn*) forge; (*fig: di ingegni*) breeding ground
fuco, chi ['fuko] SM (*ape*) drone
fucsia ['fuksja] SF (*Bot*) fuchsia
■ SM, AGG (*colore*) fuchsia
fuga, ghe ['fuga] SF **1** escape; (*letter*) flight; **mettere qn in fuga** to put sb to flight; **tentare la fuga** to try to escape **2** (*perdita: di gas, notizie*) leak; **fuga di capitali** flight of capital; **fuga di cervelli** brain drain **3** (*Mus*) fugue **4** (*Sport*) breakaway
fugace [fu'gatʃe] AGG fleeting, transient
fugacemente [fugatʃe'mente] AVV fleetingly
fugare [fu'gare] VT (*dubbi, incertezze*) to dispel, drive out
fuggevole [fud'dʒevole] AGG fleeting
fuggevolmente [fuddʒevol'mente] AVV fleetingly
fuggiasco, a, schi, sche [fud'dʒasko] AGG runaway *attr*
■ SM/F fugitive; (*Mil*) deserter
fuggifuggi [fuddʒi'fuddʒi] SM INV stampede
fuggire [fud'dʒire] VT (*anche fig*) to avoid, shun
■ VI (*aus* **essere**) (*ladro*) to run away, flee (*frm*); (*prigioniero*) to escape; (*fig: vita*) to fly *o* slip by; **è fuggito di prigione** he escaped from jail; **è fuggita di casa** she ran away from home; **il tempo fugge** time flies
fuggitivo, a [fuddʒi'tivo] AGG **1** (*in fuga*) fleeing, escaping **2** (*fugace*) fleeting
■ SM/F fugitive; (*Mil*) deserter
fui *ecc* ['fui] VB *vedi* **essere**
fulcro ['fulkro] SM (*Tecn*) fulcrum; (*fig: di discussione, teoria*) central *o* key point
fulgidamente [fuldʒida'mente] AVV brilliantly
fulgido, a ['fuldʒido] AGG bright, shining; (*fig: esempio*) shining
fulgore [ful'gore] SM brilliance; (*fig*) splendour (*Brit*), splendor (*Am*)
fuliggine [fu'liddʒine] SF soot
fuligginoso, a [fuliddʒi'noso] AGG sooty
fulminante [fulmi'nante] AGG (*sguardo*) blazing; **è morto per una polmonite fulminante** he died after suddenly contracting pneumonia
fulminare [fulmi'nare] VB IMPERS: **fulmina** there is lightning
■ VT **1** **essere fulminato** (*da fulmine*) to be struck (by lightning); (*da elettricità*) to be electrocuted **2** (*fig: uccidere*) to shoot dead; **mi fulminò con uno sguardo** he looked daggers at me;
► **fulminarsi** VIP (*lampadina*) to go, blow
fulminato [fulmi'nato] SM (*Chim*) fulminate
fulmine ['fulmine] SM bolt of lightning; **fulmini** lightning *sg*; **tuoni e fulmini** thunder and lightning; **come un fulmine** like lightning; **fulmine a ciel sereno** bolt from the blue; **un colpo di fulmine** (*fig*) love at first sight; **è stato colpito da un fulmine** he was struck by lightning
fulmineamente [fulminea'mente] AVV like lightning, quick as a flash
fulmineo, a [ful'mineo] AGG (*fig: scatto*) rapid; (*minaccioso: sguardo*) threatening; **una morte fulminea** a sudden death
fulvo, a ['fulvo] AGG tawny
fumaiolo [fuma'jɔlo] SM (*gen*) chimney; (*Naut, Ferr*) funnel
fumante [fu'mante] AGG (*piatto*) steaming
fumare [fu'mare] VT (*sigaretta, pipa*) to smoke
■ VI (*aus* **avere**) (*esalare: fumo*) to smoke; (*: vapore*) to steam; **smettere di fumare** to give up smoking; **ha smesso di fumare** she's given up smoking; **fumare come un turco** to smoke like a chimney; **"vietato fumare"** "no smoking"
fumario, ria, ri, rie [fu'marjo] AGG: **canna fumaria** flue
fumarola [fuma'rɔla] SF fumarole
fumata [fu'mata] SF **1** (*il fumare*): **farsi una fumata** to have a smoke **2** (*emissione di fumo*) cloud of smoke; **fumata bianca/nera** (*in Vaticano*) *signal that a new pope has/has not been elected*
fumatore, trice [fuma'tore] SM/F smoker; **è un forte fumatore** he's a heavy smoker; **uno scompartimento fumatori** a smoking compartment
fumé [fy'me] AGG INV smoky grey
fumeria [fume'ria] SF: **una fumeria d'oppio** opium den
fumettista, i, e [fumet'tista] SM/F cartoonist
fumettistico, a, ci, che [fumet'tistiko] AGG comic *attr*; **un personaggio fumettistico** (*pegg*) a stereotype
fumetto [fu'metto] SM **1** (*nuvoletta con parole*) bubble **2** (*storia a vignette*) cartoon, comic strip; **giornale a fumetti** comic (*Brit*), comic book (*Am*); **le piacciono i fumetti** she likes comics
fummo *ecc* ['fummo] VB *vedi* **essere**
fumo ['fumo] SM **1** (*di fuoco, sigaretta*) smoke; (*vapore*) steam; **fare fumo** (*camino ecc*) to smoke; **i fumi industriali** industrial fumes; **sento odore di fumo** I can smell smoke; **essere in preda ai fumi dell'alcol** (*fig*) to be under the influence of alcohol **2** (*il fumare*) smoking; **il fumo fa male** smoking is bad for you; **fumo passivo** passive smoking **3** (*fam: hascisc*) dope **4** (*fraseologia*): **andare in fumo** to go up in smoke; **è solo fumo** it's worthless; **è tutto fumo e niente arrosto** there's no substance to it; **gettare fumo negli occhi a qn** to pull the wool over sb's eyes; **lo vedo come il fumo negli occhi** I can't stand him; **vendere fumo** to deceive, cheat
■ AGG INV: **grigio fumo** smoky grey
fumogeno, a [fu'mɔdʒeno] AGG (*candelotto*) smoke *attr*; **cortina fumogena** smoke screen
■ SM smoke bomb
fumosamente [fumosa'mente] AVV (*fig*) vaguely
fumoso, a [fu'moso] AGG **1** (*ambiente, stanza*) smoky **2** (*fig: idee*) woolly; (*: progetto*) muddled
funambolo, a [fu'nambolo] SM/F tightrope walker
fune ['fune] SF rope, cord; (*più grossa*) cable; **hanno tirato con forza e la fune si è spezzata** they pulled hard and the rope broke
funebre ['funebre] AGG (*gen, corteo, cerimonia*) funeral *attr*; (*atmosfera*) gloomy, funereal; (*voce, sguardo*) funereal, mournful

Ff

funerale [fune'rale] SM funeral; **una faccia da funerale** a long face
funerario, ria, ri, rie [fune'rarjo] AGG (*urna*) funeral *attr*; (*iscrizione*) tombstone *attr*
funereo, a [fu'nɛreo] AGG (*frm*) funeral *attr*; (*sguardo, aspetto*) funereal, mournful
funesto, a [fu'nɛsto] AGG (*incidente*) fatal; (*errore, decisione*) fatal, disastrous; (*atmosfera*) gloomy, dismal
fungaia [fun'gaja] SF mushroom bed
fungere ['fundʒere] VI IRREG (*aus* **avere**) **fungere da** to act as
fungo, ghi ['fungo] SM **1** (*commestibile*) mushroom; **fungo velenoso** toadstool; **funghi secchi** dried mushrooms; **andare a** *o* **per funghi** to go mushrooming; **crescere come i funghi** (*fig*) to spring up overnight; **fungo atomico** mushroom cloud **2** (*Med*) fungus **3** (*di annaffiatoio*) rose
funicolare [funiko'lare] SF funicular railway
funivia [funi'via] SF cablecar
funsi *ecc* ['funsi] VB *vedi* **fungere**
funto, a ['funto] PP *di* **fungere**
funzionale [funtsjo'nale] AGG functional
funzionalità [funtsjonali'ta] SF INV functionality
funzionamento [funtsjona'mento] SM (*vedi vb* 1) working; functioning
funzionante [funtsjo'nante] AGG working
funzionare [funtsjo'nare] VI (*aus* **avere**) **1** (*gen*) to work, function; (*sistema*) to function; **funziona a benzina** it runs on petrol; **far funzionare** to operate; **come funziona?** how does it work?; **l'ascensore non funziona** the lift isn't working; **il telefono non funziona** the telephone is out of order **2 funzionare da** to act as
funzionario, ria, ri, rie [funtsjo'narjo] SM/F (*Amm*: *dirigente*) official; (: *impiegato*) employee; **funzionario dell'amministrazione comunale** local authority employee; **un funzionario del Parlamento Europeo** an official from the European Parliament; **funzionario statale** civil servant
funzione [fun'tsjone] SF **1** (*gen, Gramm, Mat*) function; **in funzione** (*macchina*) in operation; **essere in funzione** to be on; **non si apre quand'è in funzione** it won't open when it's on; **mettere in funzione** to switch on; **la funzione principale di...** the main function of ...; **vive in funzione dei figli/della carriera** he lives for his children/his job; **participio usato in funzione di aggettivo** participle used as an adjective **2** (*carica*) post, office, position; **cessare dalle funzioni** to leave office; **far funzione di sindaco** to act as mayor; **non il presidente ma il facente funzione** not the president but his deputy; **nell'esercizio delle sue funzioni** in the performance of his duties **3** (*Rel*) service, religious ceremony
fuochista, i [fwo'kista] SM stoker; (*Ferr*) stoker, fireman
fuoco, chi ['fwɔko] SM **1** fire; **vicino al fuoco** by the fire; **prendere fuoco** to catch fire; **la tenda ha preso fuoco subito** the curtain caught fire immediately; **dare fuoco a qc** to set fire to sth; **ha dato fuoco alla casa** he set fire to the house; **al fuoco!** fire!; **scherzare col fuoco** (*fig*) to play with fire; **soffiare sul fuoco** (*fig*) to add fuel to the flames **2** (*Culin*: *fornello*) ring; **mettere qc sul fuoco** to put sth on the stove; **cuocere a fuoco lento/vivo** to cook over a low/high heat **3** (*Mil*: *sparo*) fire; **far fuoco** to fire; **cessare/aprire il fuoco** to cease/open fire; **fuoco incrociato** crossfire; **fuoco amico** (*Mil*) friendly fire **4** (*ardore, vivacità*) fire; **parole di fuoco** heated words **5** (*Mat, Ottica*) focus; **mettere a fuoco** to focus; (*fig*: *problema*) to clarify **6** (*fraseologia*): **fare fuoco e fiamme (per fare)** to do one's utmost (to do); **mettere la mano sul fuoco per qc** to stake one's life on sth; **mettere a ferro e fuoco** to put to fire and the sword
■ AGG INV: **rosso fuoco** flame red
■ **fuoco d'artificio** firework; **fuoco fatuo** will-o'-the-wisp; **fuoco di paglia** flash in the pan; **fuoco sacro** *o* **di Sant'Antonio** (*Med fam*) shingles *pl*
fuorché [fwor'ke] CONG, PREP except, apart from
FUORI ['fwɔri] SIGLA M (= **Fronte Unitario Omosessuale Rivoluzionario Italiano**) *Italian gay liberation movement*
fuori ['fwɔri] AVV
1 (*gen*) outside; (*all'aperto*) outdoors, outside; (*fuori casa*) out; (*all'estero*) abroad; **era lì fuori ad aspettarmi** he was outside waiting for me; **ti aspetto fuori** I'll wait for you outside; **fuori è ancora buio** it's still dark outside; **cosa fai là fuori?** what are you doing out there?; **ceniamo fuori?** (*all'aperto*) shall we eat outside?; (*al ristorante*) shall we go out for a meal?, shall we eat out?; **mandali a giocare fuori** send them out to play; **mio marito è fuori** my husband is out *o* is not at home; **ho vissuto in Italia e fuori** I've lived in Italy and abroad; **tiralo fuori dalla scatola** take it out of the box
2 (*fraseologia*): **fuori (di qui)!** get out (of here)!; **fuori i soldi!** hand over your money!; **essere di fuori** to be a stranger; **essere in fuori** (*sporgere*) to stick out; (*denti, occhi*) to be prominent; **ha i denti in fuori** her teeth stick out; **finalmente ne sono fuori** (*da un vizio*) I've managed to break the habit; **far fuori** (*fam*: *soldi*) to spend; (: *cioccolatini*) to eat up; (: *rubare*) to nick; **far fuori qn** (*fam*) to do sb in; **lasciare/mettere fuori** to leave/put out; **essere tagliato fuori** (*da un gruppo, ambiente*) to be excluded; **mi sento tagliato fuori qui** I feel cut off here; **uscire fuori** to come out; **andare/venire fuori** to go/come out; **giocare fuori** (*Sport*) to play away
■ PREP
1 fuori (di) out of, outside; **è fuori città** he's out of town; **abita fuori Roma** he lives outside Rome; **fuori da** outside; **c'era molta gente fuori dal teatro** there were lots of people outside the theatre
2 (*fraseologia*): **è fuori di sé (dalla gioia/rabbia)** he's beside himself (with joy/anger); **è fuori commercio** it's not for sale; **fuori fase** (*motore*) out of phase; **fuori mano** (*casa, paese*) out of the way, remote; **abitare fuori mano** to live in an out-of-the-way place; **fuori luogo** (*osservazione*) out of place, uncalled for; **fuori orario** outside working hours; **fuori pasto** between meals; **fuori pericolo** out of danger; **fuori dai piedi!** get out of the way!; **fuori programma** unscheduled; **è fuori questione** *o* **discussione** it's out of the question; **fuori servizio** out of order; **fuori stagione** out of season; **la macchina è andata fuori strada** the car left the road; **essere fuori tempo** (*Mus*) to be out of time; **è arrivato fuori tempo massimo** he arrived outside the time limit; **illustrazione fuori testo** plate; **fuori uso** out of use; **essere fuori** (*fam*) to be nuts *o* crazy
■ SM outside; **dal di fuori** from the outside
fuoribordo [fwori'bordo] SM INV (*Naut*: *imbarcazione*) outboard, speedboat (with outboard motor); (: *motore*) outboard motor
fuoribusta [fwori'busta] SM INV unofficial payment

fuoricampo [fwori'kampo] AGG INV (*Cine*) out of the picture

fuoriclasse [fwori'klasse] AGG INV unrivalled, unequalled
■ SM/F INV undisputed champion

fuoricorso [fwori'korso] AGG INV **1** (*moneta*) no longer in circulation **2** (*Univ*): **(studente) fuoricorso** *student who takes longer than normal to complete his o her university course*

fuorigioco [fwori'dʒɔko] SM INV (*Sport*): **in fuorigioco** offside; **quando ha segnato era in fuorigioco** he was offside when he scored; **fischiare un fuorigioco** to blow the whistle for offside

fuorilegge [fwori'leddʒe] SM/F INV outlaw

fuoripista [fwori'pista] SM INV, AVV (*Sci*) off-piste

fuoriprogramma [fworipro'gramma] SM INV (*TV, Radio*) unscheduled programme; (*fig*) change of plan *o* programme

fuoriserie [fwori'sɛrje] AGG INV (*macchina*) specially built; (*fig: eccezionale*) outstanding
■ SF INV custom-built car

fuoristrada [fwori'strada] SM INV (*Aut*) Land Rover®, jeep; **fare del fuoristrada** to drive cross-country

fuoriuscita [fworiuʃʃita], **fuoruscita** [fworuʃʃita] SF (*di gas*) leakage, escape; (*di sangue, linfa*) seepage

fuoriuscito, a [fworiuʃʃito], **fuoruscito, a** [fworuʃʃito] SM/F exile, refugee

fuorviare [fworvi'are] VI = **forviare**

furbacchione, a [furbak'kjone] SM/F cunning *o* crafty old devil

furbamente [furba'mente] AVV (*vedi agg*) cleverly; cunningly

furbata [fur'bata] SF (*fam*) cunning trick

furberia [furbe'ria] SF (*qualità*) cunning, slyness; (*azione*) sly trick

furbescamente [furbeska'mente] AVV cunningly, slyly, craftily

furbesco, a, schi, sche [fur'besko] AGG cunning, sly, crafty; **lingua furbesca** thieves' cant

furbizia [fur'bittsja] SF (*vedi agg*) cleverness; cunning; **una furbizia** a cunning trick

furbo, a ['furbo] AGG clever, smart; (*pegg*) cunning, sly; **un ragazzo furbo** a clever boy
■ SM/F clever person, cunning person; **fare il furbo** to (try to) be clever *o* smart; **vuoi fare il furbo?** are you trying to be clever?; **fatti furbo!** show a bit of sense!

furente [fu'rɛnte] AGG: **furente (contro)** furious (with)

fureria [fure'ria] SF (*Mil*) orderly room

furetto [fu'retto] SM ferret

furfante [fur'fante] SM/F rascal, scoundrel

furfanteria [furfante'ria] SF roguery

furgoncino [furgon'tʃino] SM small van

furgone [fur'gone] SM van

furia ['furja] SF **1** (*ira, furore*) fury, rage; (*velocità*) hurry, haste; **andare** *o* **montare su tutte le furie** to get into a towering rage, fly into a rage *o* frenzy; **la furia del vento** the violence of the wind; **a furia di fare qc** by constantly doing sth; **si è fatto largo nella folla a furia di spinte** he shoved his way through the crowd; **perderai la voce a furia di gridare** you'll lose your voice if you shout so much **2** (*Mitol*): **le Furie** the Furies

furibondo, a [furi'bondo] AGG furious

furiere [fu'rjɛre] SM quartermaster

furiosamente [furjosa'mente] AVV furiously

furioso, a [fu'rjoso] AGG (*gen*) furious; (*vento, assalto*) violent, raging; **è un pazzo furioso** he is a raving lunatic

furono ['furono] VB *vedi* **essere**

furore [fu'rore] SM fury; **nel furore della battaglia** in the heat of the battle; **a furor di popolo** by popular acclaim; **far furore** to be all the rage

> **LO SAPEVI...?**
> **furore** non si traduce mai con la parola inglese *furore*

furoreggiare [furored'dʒare] VI (*aus* **avere**) to be all the rage

furtivamente [furtiva'mente] AVV (*vedi agg*) furtively; stealthily

furtivo, a [fur'tivo] AGG (*sguardo*) furtive; (*passo*) stealthy

furto ['furto] SM theft; **commettere un furto** to commit a robbery; **vorrei denunciare un furto** I'd like to report a theft; **furto con scasso** (*Dir*) burglary

fusa ['fusa] SFPL: **fare le fusa** to purr

fuscello [fuʃʃɛllo] SM twig; **magro come un fuscello** thin as a lath

fusciacca, che [fuʃʃakka] SF sash

fuseaux [fy'zo] SMPL leggings

fusi *ecc* ['fuzi] VB *vedi* **fondere**

fusibile [fu'zibile] SM (*Elettr*) fuse

fusillo [fu'sillo] SM (*Culin*) *pasta spiral*

fusione [fu'zjone] SF **1** (*gen, Fis*) fusion; (*di metalli*) melting; (*fig: di idee*) merging, blending **2** (*Comm*) merger, amalgamation

fuso[1], a ['fuzo] PP *di* **fondere**

fuso[2] ['fuzo] SM **1** (*Tessile*) spindle; **diritto come un fuso** as straight as a ramrod **2** **fuso orario** time zone; **non ho tenuto conto del fuso orario** I forgot about the time difference

fusoliera [fuzo'ljɛra] SF (*Aer*) fusillage

fustagno [fus'taɲɲo] SM fustian, corduroy

fustella [fus'tɛlla] SF (*su scatola di medicinali*) tear-off tab

fustigare [fusti'gare] VT (*frustare*) to flog; (*fig: costumi*) to censure, denounce

fustigatore, trice [fustiga'tore] SM/F (*fig*) critic

fustigazione [fustigat'tsjone] SF flogging, beating

fustino [fus'tino] SM (*di detersivo*) tub

fusto ['fusto] SM **1** (*Anat, Bot: di albero*) trunk; (*: di pianta*) stem; (*colonna*) shaft **2** (*recipiente: di metallo*) drum **3** (*fam*) he-man

futile ['futile] AGG futile, vain

futilità [futili'ta] SF INV futility

futilmente [futil'mente] AVV futilely

futon [fu'ton] SM INV futon

futurismo [futu'rizmo] SM futurism

futurista, i, e [futu'rista] SM/F futurist

futuristico, a, ci, che [futu'ristiko] AGG futuristic

futuro, a [fu'turo] AGG future
■ SM future; **futuro anteriore** future perfect

Ff

Gg

G, g [dʒi] SF O M INV (*lettera*) G, g; **G come Genova** ≈ G for George
g ABBR (= **grammo, grammi**) g
gabardine [gabar'din] SM (*tessuto*) gabardine; (*soprabito*) gabardine raincoat
gabbare [gab'bare] VT to deceive, trick, dupe
gabbia ['gabbja] SF **1** (*gen*) cage; (*da imballaggio*) crate; **la gabbia degli accusati** (*Dir*) the dock; **gabbia di matti** (*fig*) madhouse; **gabbia toracica** (*Anat*) rib cage **2** (*Equitazione: ostacolo*) double
gabbiano [gab'bjano] SM (sea)gull; **gabbiano comune** black-headed gull; **gabbiano reale** herring gull
gabella [ga'bɛlla] SF (*Storia: tassa*) duty
gabinetto [gabi'netto] SM **1** (*WC*) lavatory, toilet; **dov'è il gabinetto?** where's the toilet?; **posso andare al gabinetto?** can I go to the toilet, please? **2** (*di medico*) surgery, consulting room **3** (*Pol: ministero*) ≈ ministry (: *di ministro*) advisers *pl*
Gabon [ga'bon] SM Gabon
gaelico, a, ci, che [ga'ɛliko] AGG, SM Gaelic
gaffe [gaf] SF INV blunder, boob (*fam*); **fare una gaffe** to put one's foot in it (*fam*); **ho fatto una gaffe** I've put my foot in it
gag [gæg] SF INV (*Cine, Teatro*) gag
gagà [ga'ga] SM INV fop, dandy
gaggia, gie [gad'dʒia] SF (*Bot*) locust tree, false acacia
gagliardamente [gaʎʎarda'mente] AVV (*in modo valoroso*) courageously, bravely; (*efficacemente*) vigorously, strongly
gagliardetto [gaʎʎar'detto] SM pennant
gagliardo, a [gaʎ'ʎardo] AGG strong, robust
Gaia ['gaja] SF Gaea
gaiamente [gaja'mente] AVV cheerfully, happily
gaiezza [ga'jettsa] SF (*di persona*) gaiety, cheerfulness; (*di colori*) brightness
gaio, aia, ai, aie ['gajo] AGG (*persona*) cheerful, happy; (*colore*) bright, gay
gala ['gala] SF **1** (*ornamento*) bow **2 serata di gala** gala evening; **uniforme di gran gala** full-dress uniform; **pranzo di gala** banquet
■SM gala, festivity
galante [ga'lante] AGG **1** (*cortese*) gallant, chivalrous **2** (*amoroso*) romantic; **avventura galante** love affair
■SM gallant
galantemente [galante'mente] AVV gallantly
galanteria [galante'ria] SF gallantry
galantuomo [galan'twɔmo] SM (*pl* **-uomini**) gentleman
Galapagos [gala'pagos] SFPL (*anche:* **le isole Galapagos**) the Galápagos Islands
galassia [ga'lassja] SF galaxy
galateo [gala'tɛo] SM etiquette
galattico, a, ci, che [ga'lattiko] AGG galactic
galea [ga'lɛa] SF (*Storia: nave*) galley
galeone [gale'one] SM galleon
galeotto [gale'ɔtto] SM (*Storia*) galley slave; (*carcerato*) convict
galera [ga'lɛra] SF **1** (*fam*) prison, gaol; **ha fatto due anni di galera** he spent two years in prison; **avanzo di galera** criminal type; **vita da galera** (*fig*) dog's life **2** (*Naut*) galley
galla[1] ['galla] **a galla** AVV afloat; **stare a galla** to float; (*fig*) to keep one's head above water; **venire a galla** to surface, come to the surface; (*fig: verità*) to come out, come to light
galla[2] ['galla] SF (*Bot*) gall
galleggiabilità [galleddʒabili'ta] SF buoyancy
galleggiamento [galleddʒa'mento] SM floating; **linea di galleggiamento** (*di nave*) waterline
galleggiante [galled'dʒante] AGG floating
■SM (*Tecn, Aer, Pesca*) float; (*natante*) barge; (*boa*) buoy
galleggiare [galled'dʒare] VI (*aus* **avere**) to float
galleria [galle'ria] SF **1** (*traforo*) tunnel; **la galleria del Monte Bianco** the Mont Blanc tunnel; **galleria del vento** *o* **aerodinamica** (*Aer*) wind tunnel **2** (*Archit, d'arte*) gallery; (*strada coperta con negozi*) arcade; (*Cine*) balcony; (*Teatro*) circle; **due poltrone in galleria** two seats in the circle
Galles ['galles] SM Wales; **mi è piaciuto molto il Galles** I really liked Wales; **andremo in Galles quest'estate** we're going to Wales this summer
gallese [gal'lese] AGG Welsh; **la squadra gallese** the Welsh team

■ SM/F Welshman/Welshwoman; **i gallesi** the Welsh
■ SM (*lingua*) Welsh

galletta [gal'letta] SF cracker

galletto [gal'letto] SM young cock, cockerel; (*fig*) cocky young man; **fare il galletto** to show off (*in front of girls*)

Gallia [gal'lja] SF Gaul

gallicismo [galli'tʃizmo] SM gallicism

gallico, a, ci, che ['galliko] AGG Gallic

gallina [gal'lina] SF hen; **gallina lessa** boiled chicken; **andare a letto con le galline** to go to bed early; **la gallina dalle uova d'oro** the goose that lays the golden eggs; **gallina vecchia fa buon brodo** (*Proverbio*) an old hen makes good broth

gallinacei [galli'natʃei] SMPL gallinaceans

gallinella [galli'nɛlla] SF: **gallinella d'acqua** moorhen

gallismo [gal'lizmo] SM machismo

gallo¹ ['gallo] SM cock; **al canto del gallo** at daybreak, at cockcrow; **fare il gallo** to show off (*in front of girls*); **gallo cedrone** capercaillie; **gallo da combattimento** fighting cock
■ AGG INV (*Pugilato*): **peso gallo** bantamweight

gallo², a ['gallo] SM/F (*Storia*) Gaul

galloccia, ce [gal'lɔttʃa] SF (*Naut*) cleat

gallone¹ [gal'lone] SM **1** (*Mil*) stripe; **guadagnarsi i galloni** to be promoted; **perdere i galloni** to lose one's stripes **2** (*ornamento*) braid, piece of braid

gallone² [gal'lone] SM (*unità di misura*) gallon

galoppante [galop'pante] AGG (*inflazione, tisi*) galloping

galoppare [galop'pare] VI (*aus* **avere**) (*cavallo*) to gallop; (*fig: correre affannosamente*) to rush about; (*: fantasia, immaginazione*) to run wild, run riot; **sua madre lo fa galoppare!** his mother runs him off his feet!

galoppata [galop'pata] SF (*di cavallo*) gallop; **ho fatto una galoppata per arrivare in tempo** (*fig*) I had to dash to get here in time

galoppino [galop'pino] SM **1** errand boy **2** (*Pol*) canvasser

galoppo [ga'lɔppo] SM gallop; **piccolo galoppo** canter; **al galoppo** (*anche fig*) at a gallop; **andare al galoppo** to gallop; **partire al galoppo** to set off at a gallop; (*fig*) to rush off *o* away

galoscia, sce [ga'lɔʃʃa] SF = **caloscia**

galvanizzare [galvanid'dzare] VT (*Med, Tecn, anche fig*) to galvanize

galvanizzazione [galvaniddzat'tsjone] SF (*Med, Tecn*) galvanization

gamba ['gamba] SF (*Anat, di mobile*) leg; (*di lettera, nota musicale*) tail; **mi fa male la gamba** my leg hurts; **le gambe del tavolo** the table legs; **con le proprie gambe** on one's own two feet; **essere di buona gamba** *o* **di gamba lesta** to be a good walker; **scappare a gambe levate** *o* **in spalla** to take to one's heels; **darsela a gambe** to take to one's heels; **gambe!** scatter!; **andare a gambe all'aria** to fall headlong; (*fig: progetto*) to fall through; **prendere qc sotto gamba** to treat sth too lightly; **prendere qn sotto gamba** not to take sb seriously; **in gamba** (*capace, sveglio*) bright, smart, clever; (*sul lavoro*) good; **Gloria è una ragazza in gamba** Gloria's a clever girl; **abbiamo un professore molto in gamba** our teacher's very good

gambale [gam'bale] SM (*of boot*) leg

gambaletto [gamba'letto] SM knee-high sock

gamberetto [gambe'retto] SM shrimp

gambero ['gambero] SM (*di mare*) prawn; (*di fiume*) crayfish; **fare come il gambero** to go backwards; **rosso come un gambero** as red as a beetroot (*o* lobster)

gamberone [gambe'rone] SM Dublin Bay prawn

gambetto [gam'betto] SM (*Scacchi*) gambit

Gambia ['gambja] SM: **il Gambia** the Gambia

gambizzare [gambid'dzare] VT to kneecap

gambizzazione [gambiddzat'tsjone] SF kneecapping

gambo ['gambo] SM (*di fiore, bicchiere*) stem; (*di frutta, fungo*) stalk; **gambo della punteria** (*Aut*) push rod

gamella [ga'mɛlla] SF mess tin

gamete [ga'mɛte] SM (*Bio*) gamete

gamma¹ ['gamma] AGG INV: **raggi gamma** gamma rays

gamma² ['gamma] SF (*Mus*) scale; (*fig*) range; **gamma d'onda** (*Radio*) waveband; **una vasta gamma di articoli sportivi** a wide range of sports goods; **gamma di prodotti** product range

ganascia, sce [ga'naʃʃa] SF (*Zool, Tecn*) jaw; (*Aut: del freno*) brake shoes; **mangiare a quattro ganasce** to eat like a horse

gancio, ci ['gantʃo] SM (*gen, Pugilato*) hook; **le chiavi erano appese ad un gancio** the keys were hanging on a hook

gang [gæŋ] SF INV gang

Gange ['gandʒe] SM: **il Gange** the Ganges

ganghero ['gangero] SM (*di porta*) hinge; **uscire dai gangheri** (*fig*) to lose one's temper, go off at the deep end, fly into a rage; **essere fuori dai gangheri** (*fig*) to be beside o.s. with rage

ganglio, gli ['gangljo] SM (*Anat, Med*) ganglion

gangrena [gan'grɛna] SF = **cancrena**

gangster ['gæŋstə] SM INV gangster; (*fig*) shark, crook **Gg**

Ganimede [gani'mɛde] SM (*Mitol*) Ganymede

gara ['gara] SF **1** (*concorso*) competition, contest; (*di velocità*) race; **gara di canto/nuoto/tiro** singing/swimming/shooting competition; **gare automobilistiche/ciclistiche** car/cycle races; **entrare in gara** to enter a competition (*o* race); **essere in gara** to be competing; **partecipare a una gara** to take part in a competition; **facciamo a gara a chi arriva primo!** I'll race you!; **hanno fatto a gara a chi riusciva meglio** they competed *o* vied with each other to see who could do it best **2** (*Comm, Econ*): **gara d'appalto** call for bids

garage [ga'raʒ] SM INV (*autorimessa*) garage; **hai messo la macchina in garage?** have you put the car in the garage?

garagista, i, e [gara'dʒista] SM/F (*proprietario*) garage owner; (*gestore*) garage manager

garante [ga'rante] AGG: **farsi garante di** *o* **per qc** to vouch for sth, guarantee sth; **farsi garante di** *o* **per qn** to stand surety for sb
■ SM/F guarantor

garantire [garan'tire] VT (*gen*) to guarantee; (*dare per certo*) to assure; **ti garantisco che sarà pronto domani** I guarantee that/assure you that it will be ready tomorrow; **questo televisore è garantito per tre anni** this television is guaranteed for three years; **garantire un debito** to stand surety for a debt
▶ **garantirsi** VIP: **garantirsi da** *o* **contro** to insure o.s. against

garantismo [garan'tizmo] SM protection of civil liberties

garantista, i, e [garan'tista] AGG protecting civil liberties

■SM/F civil libertarian

garantito, a [garan'tito] AGG guaranteed; **il successo sembra ormai garantito** success now seems certain; **è garantito che pioverà** it's bound to rain; **se glielo chiedi dirà di no, garantito!** if you ask him he'll be bound to say no!

garanzia [garan'tsia] SF *(gen, Comm)* guarantee; *(pegno)* security, surety; **in garanzia** under guarantee; **l'orologio è ancora in garanzia** the watch is still under guarantee; **questa persona non dà alcuna garanzia** this person is not to be trusted, this person is unreliable

garbare [gar'bare] VI *(aus* **essere***)* **non mi garba** I don't like it *(o* him *ecc)*

garbatamente [garbata'mente] AVV *(vedi agg)* courteously, politely; kindly

garbato, a [gar'bato] AGG *(cortese)* courteous, polite; *(gentile)* kind

garbo ['garbo] SM **1** *(grazia)* grace; **muoversi con garbo/senza garbo** to move gracefully/awkwardly; **non ha garbo nel vestire** she doesn't dress well **2** *(gentilezza)* politeness, courtesy; **una persona di garbo** a well-mannered person

garbuglio, gli [gar'buʎʎo] SM tangle; *(fig)* muddle, mess

garçonnière [garso'njɛr] SF INV bachelor pad

gardenia [gar'dɛnja] SF gardenia

gareggiare [gared'dʒare] VI *(aus* **avere***)* **gareggiare in qc** to compete in sth; **gareggiare con qn** to compete *o* vie with sb

garganella [garga'nɛlla] SF: **a garganella** from the bottle

gargarismo [garga'rizmo] SM gargle; **fare un gargarismo** *o* **i gargarismi** to gargle

garibaldino, a [garibal'dino] AGG *(Storia)* of *(o* relating to) Garibaldi; **alla garibaldina** impetuously

■SM soldier in Garibaldi's army

garitta [ga'ritta] SF *(di caserma)* sentry box

garofano [ga'rɔfano] SM carnation

garrese [gar'rese] SM withers *pl*

garretto [gar'retto] SM hock

garrire [gar'rire] VI *(aus* **avere***)* *(uccelli)* to chirp

garrotta [gar'rɔtta] SF garrotte

garrottare [garrot'tare] VT to garrotte

garrulo, a ['garrulo] AGG **1** *(uccello)* chirping **2** *(loquace)* garrulous, talkative

garza ['gardza] SF *(tessuto, Med)* gauze; **una garza** *(Med)* a gauze bandage

garzone [gar'dzone] SM *(di negozio)* boy; **il garzone del macellaio** the butcher's boy

gas [gas] SM INV **1** gas; **l'uomo del gas** the gasman; **hai spento il gas?** have you turned off the gas?; **scaldabagno/stufa a gas** gas boiler/heater **2** *(Aut)*: **dare gas** to step on the gas, accelerate; **a tutto gas** *(anche fig)* at full speed; **è partito a tutto gas** he roared off

■**gas asfissiante** poison gas; **gas di città** *o* **illuminante** town gas; **gas esilarante** laughing gas; **gas inerti** *o* **nobili** inert gases; **gas lacrimogeno** tear gas; **gas liquido** liquid gas; **gas naturale** natural gas

gasare [ga'zare] VT = **gassare**

▶**gasarsi** VR *(fam)* to get excited; *(montarsi)* to become too full of o.s.

gasato, a [ga'zato] AGG **1** *(bibita)* = **gassato** **2** *(fam: persona)* excited; (: *montato)* big-headed

■SM/F *(fam: persona)* big-head

gasdotto [gaz'dotto] SM gas pipeline

gasista, i [ga'zista] SM = **gassista**

gasolina [gazo'lina] SF gasoline

gasolio [ga'zɔljo] SM diesel (oil)

gasometro [ga'zɔmetro] SM gasometer

gassa ['gassa] SF *(Naut)*: **gassa d'amante** bowline knot

gassare [gas'sare] VT **1** *(liquido)* to aerate, make fizzy **2** *(uccidere col gas)* to gas

gassato, a [gas'sato] AGG *(bibita)* fizzy; **acqua minerale gassata** sparkling mineral water

gassificare [gassifi'kare] VT to gasify

gassista, i [gas'sista] SM gasman

gassometro [gas'sɔmetro] SM = **gasometro**

gassosa [gas'sosa] SF = **gazzosa**

gassoso, a [gas'soso] AGG gaseous

gastrico, a, ci, che ['gastriko] AGG gastric

gastrite [gas'trite] SF gastritis

gastroenterite [gastroente'rite] SF gastroenteritis

gastronomia [gastrono'mia] SF gastronomy

gastronomico, a, ci, che [gastro'nɔmiko] AGG gastronomic

gastronomo, a [gas'trɔnomo] SM/F gourmet, gastronome

GATT [gat] SIGLA M (= **General Agreement on Tariffs and Trade**) GATT

gatta ['gatta] SF (female) cat, she-cat; **una gatta da pelare** *(fam)* a thankless task; **qui gatta ci cova!** I smell a rat!, there's something fishy going on here!

gattabuia [gatta'buja] SF *(fam scherz: prigione)* clink

gattino, a [gat'tino] SM/F kitten

gatto ['gatto] SM *(gen)* cat; *(maschio)* tomcat; **siamo rimasti in quattro gatti** there were only a few of us left; **quando il gatto non c'è i topi ballano** *(Proverbio)* when the cat's away the mice will play

■**gatto delle nevi** *(Sci)* snowcat; **gatto a nove code** cat-o'-nine-tails; **gatto selvatico** wildcat

gattoni [gat'toni] AVV on all fours

gattopardo [gatto'pardo] SM: **gattopardo africano** serval; **gattopardo americano** ocelot

gattuccio, ci [gat'tuttʃo] SM dogfish

gaudente [gau'dɛnte] SM/F pleasure-seeker; **fare la vita del gaudente** to live like a lord

gaudio, di ['gaudjo] SM joy, happiness

gavetta [ga'vetta] SF *(Mil)* mess tin; **venire dalla gavetta** *(fig)* to rise from the ranks

gavina [ga'vina] SF *(Zool)* common gull

gavitello [gavi'tɛllo] SM *(Naut)* mooring buoy

gavone [ga'vone] SM *(Naut)* locker

gazebo [gə'zi:bou] SM INV summerhouse, gazebo

gazolina [gaddzo'lina] SF = **gasolina**

gazza ['gaddza] SF magpie

gazzarra [gad'dzarra] SF racket, din; **fare gazzarra** to make a din

gazzella [gad'dzɛlla] SF **1** *(Zool)* gazelle **2** *(auto dei Carabinieri)* (high-speed) police car

gazzetta [gad'dzetta] SF gazette; **Gazzetta Ufficiale** *official publication containing the text of new laws*

⊳ www.gazzettaufficiale.it/

⊳ http://europa.eu.int/eur-lex/it/

gazzettino [gaddzet'tino] SM **1** *(di giornale: titolo)* gazette; (: *sezione)* page; **gazzettino teatrale** theatre page; **gazzettino regionale** *(alla radio)* regional news *sg* **2** *(fig: persona pettegola)* gossip

gazzosa [gad'dzosa] SF fizzy drink, ≈ lemonade

Gazz. Uff. ABBR = **Gazzetta Ufficiale**

GB SIGLA (= **Gran Bretagna**) GB

GC ABBR = **genio civile**

G.d.F. ABBR = guardia di finanza

GE SIGLA = Genova

geco, chi ['dʒɛko] SM (*Zool*) gecko

gel [dʒɛl] SM INV gel

gelare [dʒe'lare] VT to freeze; **mi ha gelato il sangue** (*fig*) it made my blood run cold
■ VI (*aus* **essere**) to freeze; **il lago è gelato** the lake has frozen over; **chiudi la porta, si gela!** close the door, it's freezing!
■ VB IMPERS to freeze; **gela** it's freezing

gelata [dʒe'lata] SF frost

gelataio, aia, ai, aie [dʒela'tajo] SM/F (*venditore*) ice-cream seller; (*produttore*) ice-cream maker

gelateria [dʒelate'ria] SF ice-cream shop, ice-cream parlour (*Am*)

gelatiera [dʒela'tjɛra] SF ice-cream machine

gelatina [dʒela'tina] SF (*gen, Culin*) gelatine; **gelatina esplosiva** gelignite; **gelatina di frutta** fruit jelly

gelatinoso, a [dʒelati'noso] AGG gelatinous

gelato, a [dʒe'lato] AGG frozen; **ho le mani gelate** my hands are frozen (stiff)
■ SM ice cream; **gelato di fragola/di crema** strawberry/vanilla ice cream

gelidamente [dʒelida'mente] AVV (*fig*) icily

gelido, a ['dʒɛlido] AGG (*aria, vento*) icy, freezing; (*mani, acqua*) freezing, ice-cold; (*fig: accoglienza, espressione, sguardo*) icy, frosty

gelo ['dʒɛlo] SM (*temperatura*) intense cold; (*brina*) frost; (*fig: inverno*) cold weather; **il gelo invernale** the cold winter weather; **sentirsi il gelo nelle ossa** to feel a chill of fear; **il gelo della morte** the chill hand of death

gelone [dʒe'lone] SM chilblain

gelosamente [dʒelosa'mente] AVV jealously

gelosia[1] [dʒelo'sia] SF (*sentimento*) jealousy; **conservare qc con gelosia** to guard sth jealously

gelosia[2] [dʒelo'sia] SF (*persiana*) shutter

geloso, a [dʒe'loso] AGG jealous; **è geloso del fratellino** he's jealous of his baby brother

gelso ['dʒɛlso] SM mulberry (tree); **gelso nero** black mulberry

gelsomino [dʒelso'mino] SM jasmine

gemellaggio, gi [dʒemel'laddʒo] SM twinning

gemellare [dʒemel'lare] AGG twin *attr*
■ VT (*città*) to twin

gemello, a [dʒe'mɛllo] AGG (*fratelli, letti*) twin *attr*
■ SM/F (*persona, oggetto*) twin; **Rossana ha avuto due gemelli** Rossana had twins
■ **gemelli** SMPL **1** (*di camicia*) cufflinks; **un paio di gemelli d'oro** a pair of gold cufflinks **2** (*Astrol*): **Gemelli** Gemini *sg*; **essere dei Gemelli** to be Gemini

gemere ['dʒɛmere] VI (*aus* **avere**) (*ferito*): **gemere (di)** to groan (with), moan (with); (*cane*) to whine; (*piccione, tortora: tubare*) to coo; (*fig: cigolare*) to creak

gemito ['dʒɛmito] SM groan, moan

gemma ['dʒɛmma] SF **1** (*Bot*) bud **2** (*gioiello*) gem, jewel

gemmazione [dʒemmat'tsjone] SF (*Bot*) budding; (*Bio*) gemmation

gemmologia [dʒemmolo'dʒia] SF gemology

Gen. ABBR (*Mil:* = **generale**) Gen.

gen. ABBR (= **generale, generalmente**) gen.

gendarme [dʒen'darme] SM **1** policeman; **essere un gendarme** (*fig*) to be a martinet **2** (*Alpinismo*) gendarme

gene ['dʒɛne] SM gene

genealogia, gie [dʒenealo'dʒia] SF genealogy

genealogico, a, ci, che [dʒenea'lɔdʒiko] AGG genealogical; **albero genealogico** family tree

generale[1] [dʒene'rale] AGG general; **nell'interesse generale** in the interest of everyone, for the common good; **un quadro generale della situazione** a general *o* overall view of the situation; **l'opinione generale** public opinion; **direttore generale** managing director; **console generale** consul general; **in generale** generally, in general; (*parlare*) in general terms; **in generale sto bene** on the whole I am quite well; **mantenersi** *o* **stare sulle generali** to stick to generalities

generale[2] [dʒene'rale] SM general; **generale di brigata** brigadier

generalesco, a, schi, sche [dʒenera'lesko] AGG (*scherz*) as of a general

generalista, i, e [dʒenera'lista] AGG (*rete televisiva*) general-interest

generalità [dʒenerali'ta] SF INV **1** (*qualità*) generality **2** (*maggioranza*) majority; **nella generalità dei casi** in most cases **3** (*dati anagrafici*): **generalità** SFPL particulars; **fornire le proprie generalità** give one's name and address

generalizzare [dʒeneralid'dzare] VT, VI (*aus* **avere**) to generalize

generalizzazione [dʒeneraliddzat'tsjone] SF generalization

generalmente [dʒeneral'mente] AVV generally, usually

generare [dʒene'rare] VT **1** (*dar vita, anche fig*) to give birth to **2** (*produrre: Tecn*) to generate, produce; (*: Geom*) to generate, form **3** (*causare: sospetti*) to arouse; (*: confusione*) to create

generativo, a [dʒenera'tivo] AGG generative

generatore [dʒenera'tore] SM (*Elettr*) generator

generazionale [dʒenerattsjo'nale] AGG generation *attr*

generazione [dʒenerat'tsjone] SF generation; **la nuova generazione** the new *o* younger generation

genere ['dʒɛnere] SM **1** kind, type, sort; **è il genere di musica che preferisco** it's the kind of music I like best; **oggetti di ogni genere** all kinds of things; **cose del** *o* **di questo genere** such things; **qualcosa del genere** something like that; **non ho mai visto una cosa del genere!** I've never seen anything like it!; **non farmi più uno scherzo del genere!** don't ever play such a trick on me again!; **è bravo nel suo genere** in his own way he is quite good; **questo vaso è bello, nel suo genere** this is a nice vase of its kind; **in genere** generally, usually, as a rule; **in genere mi alzo alle sette** I usually get up at seven; **i documentari non sono il mio genere** documentaries aren't my cup of tea **2** (*prodotti*): **generi** SMPL article, product; **generi alimentari** foodstuffs; **generi di consumo** consumer goods; **generi di prima necessità** basic essentials **3** (*Bio, Zool*) (*Bot*) genus; **il genere umano** mankind, the human race **4** (*Gramm*) gender **5** (*Letteratura, Arte*) genre

genericamente [dʒenerika'mente] AVV generically

genericità [dʒeneritʃi'ta] SF vagueness, generality

generico, a, ci, che [dʒe'nɛriko] AGG **1** generic; (*vago: descrizione, accuse*) vague, imprecise **2** (*non specializzato*): **medico generico** general practitioner; GP
■ SM generality; **i suoi discorsi non escono dal generico** his speeches never get beyond generalities

genero ['dʒɛnero] SM son-in-law

generosamente [dʒenerosa'mente] AVV generously

Gg

generosità [dʒenerosi'ta] SF INV generosity; **è un uomo di grande generosità** he's a very generous man
generoso, a [dʒene'roso] AGG generous; **un'offerta generosa** a generous offer; **non è generoso da parte tua** that's not very nice of you; **un vino generoso** a full-bodied wine
genesi ['dʒɛnezi] SF genesis; (*Bibbia*): **la Genesi** Genesis
genetica [dʒe'nɛtika] SF genetics *sg*
geneticamente [dʒenetika'mente] AVV genetically; **organismo geneticamente modificato** genetically modified organism
genetico, a, ci, che [dʒe'nɛtiko] AGG genetic
gengiva [dʒen'dʒiva] SF gum
gengivale [dʒendʒi'vale] AGG gum *attr*
genia [dʒe'nia] SF (*pegg*) mob, gang
geniale [dʒe'njale] AGG (*persona, artista*) of genius; (*idea, soluzione*) brilliant, inspired; **ho avuto un'idea geniale** I've had a brilliant idea

LO SAPEVI...?
geniale non si traduce mai con la parola inglese *genial*

genialità [dʒenjali'ta] SF (*vedi agg*) genius; brilliance

LO SAPEVI...?
genialità non si traduce mai con la parola inglese *geniality*

genialmente [dʒenjal'mente] AVV brilliantly
genialoide [dʒenja'lɔide] SM/F eccentric genius
geniere [dʒe'njɛre] SM (*Mil*) sapper
genio[1], ni ['dʒɛnjo] SM **1** (*persona*) genius; **sei un genio!** you're a genius!; **essere un genio in matematica** he is a mathematical genius *o* wizard; **essere un genio incompreso** to be a misunderstood genius; **avere un lampo di genio** to have a brainwave **2** (*talento*): **avere il genio degli affari** to have a genius *o* flair for business **3** (*gusto*): **andare a genio a qn** to be to sb's liking; **non mi va a genio** I am not very keen on it (*o* him *ecc*) **4** (*Mitol*: *gen*) spirit; (: *arabo*) genie
genio[2] ['dʒɛnjo] SM **1** (*Mil*): **il genio (militare)** the Engineers **2 genio civile** civil engineers *pl*
genitale [dʒeni'tale] AGG genital
■ **genitali** SMPL genitals
genitivo, a [dʒeni'tivo] AGG, SM genitive
genitore, trice [dʒeni'tore] SM/F parent, father (*o* mother); **genitori** SMPL parents
gennaio [dʒen'najo] SM January; *per fraseologia vedi* luglio
genoa ['dʒɛnoa] SM INV (*Naut*) genoa (jib)
genocidio, di [dʒeno'tʃidjo] SM genocide
genoma, i [dʒe'nɔma] SM (*Bio*) genome; **il genoma umano** the human genome
genomica [dʒe'nɔmika] SF (*Bio*) genomics
genomico, a; , ci; , che [dʒe'nɔmiko] SF (*Bio*) genomic
genotipo [dʒeno'tipo] SM (*Bio*) genotype
Genova ['dʒɛnova] SF Genoa; **domani vado a Genova** I'm going to Genoa tomorrow; **abitiamo a Genova** we live in Genoa
▷ www.comune.genova.it/index.jsp
genovese [dʒeno'vese] AGG, SM/F Genoese *pl inv*
gentaglia [dʒen'taʎʎa] SF (*pegg*) rabble, scum
gente ['dʒɛnte] SF people *pl*; **c'era tanta gente** there were lots of people there; **gente di campagna** country people; **gente di città** townspeople; **gente di mare** seafaring folk; **è brava gente** they are nice people; **aspetto gente** I'm waiting for somebody; **ho gente a cena** I've got people to dinner; **le genti anglosassoni** (*letter*: *popolazioni*) the Anglo-Saxon peoples; **diritto delle genti** law of nations
gentildonna [dʒentil'dɔnna] SF gentlewoman, lady
gentile[1] [dʒen'tile] AGG **1** (*buono*) kind; (*garbato*) courteous, polite; **è molto gentile da parte sua** it's very kind *o* nice of you; **vuoi essere tanto gentile da...?** would you be so kind as to ...?; **i commessi sono sempre così gentili** the shop assistants are always so helpful **2** (*delicato*: *lineamenti*) fine; (: *profumo*) delicate; **il gentil sesso** the fair sex **3** (*nelle lettere*): **Gentile Signore** Dear Sir; (*sulla busta*): **Gentile Signor Fernando Villa** Mr Fernando Villa

LO SAPEVI...?
gentile non si traduce mai con la parola inglese *gentle*

gentile[2] [dʒen'tile] SM (*Rel*) Gentile
gentilezza [dʒenti'lettsa] SF **1** (*bontà*) kindness; (*garbatezza*) courtesy; **gentilezze** SFPL acts of kindness; **fare una gentilezza a qn** to do sb a favour; **fammi la gentilezza di chiudere la porta** be so kind as to close the door; **per gentilezza** (*per favore*) please **2** (*grazia*: *di lineamenti*) delicacy; (: *di movimento*) grace
gentilmente [dʒentil'mente] AVV (*vedi agg* 1) kindly; courteously, politely
gentiluomo [dʒenti'lwɔmo] SM (*pl* **-uomini**) gentleman
genuflessione [dʒenufles'sjone] SF genuflection, genuflexion (*Brit*)
genuflesso, a [dʒenu'flɛsso] PP *di* **genuflettersi**
genuflettersi [dʒenu'flɛttersi] VR IRREG to genuflect, kneel
genuinamente [dʒenuina'mente] AVV genuinely
genuinità [dʒenuini'ta] SF (*di prodotti*) naturalness; (*di sentimento*) sincerity, genuineness
genuino, a [dʒenu'ino] AGG (*prodotto*) natural; (*persona, sentimento*) genuine, sincere; (*risata*) natural, unaffected; **ha una genuina vocazione** he has a true *o* real vocation
genziana [dʒen'tsjana] SF gentian
genzianella [dʒentsja'nɛlla] SF gentianella
geodesia [dʒeode'sia] SF geodesy
geofisica [dʒeo'fizika] SF geophysics *sg*
geografia [dʒeogra'fia] SF geography
geograficamente [dʒeografika'mente] AVV geographically
geografico, a, ci, che [dʒeo'grafiko] AGG geographical; **atlante geografico** atlas; **carta geografica** map
geografo, a [dʒe'ɔgrafo] SM/F geographer
geologia [dʒeolo'dʒia] SF geology
geologicamente [dʒeolodʒika'mente] AVV geologically
geologico, a, ci, che [dʒeo'lɔdʒiko] AGG geological
geometra, i, e [dʒe'ɔmetra] SM/F surveyor
geometria [dʒeome'tria] SF geometry
geometricamente [dʒeometrika'mente] AVV geometrically
geometrico, a, ci, che [dʒeo'mɛtriko] AGG geometric(al)
geopolitica [dʒeopo'litika] SF geopolitics *sg*
geopolitico, a, ci, che [dʒeopo'litiko] AGG geopolitical
Georgia [dʒe'ordʒa] SF (*in USA, Europa*) Georgia
georgiano, a [dʒeor'dʒano] (*in Europa, USA*) AGG, SM/F Georgian
geotermico, a, ci, che [dʒeo'tɛrmiko] AGG geothermal
geotropismo [dʒeotro'pizmo] SM geotropism

geranio, ni [dʒe'ranjo] SM geranium
gerarca, chi [dʒe'rarka] SM (*Storia: nel fascismo*) party official
gerarchia [dʒerar'kia] SF hierarchy; **le più alte gerarchie** the upper echelons
gerarchicamente [dʒerarkika'mente] AVV hierarchically
gerarchico, a, ci, che [dʒe'rarkiko] AGG hierarchical
Geremia [dʒere'mia] SM Jeremiah
gerente [dʒe'rɛnte] SM/F manager/manageress
gerenza [dʒe'rɛntsa] SF management
gergale [dʒer'gale] AGG (*vedi sm*) slang *attr*; jargon *attr*
gergo ['dʒɛrgo] SM (*gen*) slang; (*professionale*) jargon; **gergo della malavita** criminals' slang
geriatria [dʒerja'tria] SF geriatrics *sg*
geriatrico, a, ci, che [dʒe'rjatriko] AGG geriatric
Gerico ['dʒɛriko] SM Jericho
gerla ['dʒɛrla] SF *conical wicker basket*
Germania [dʒer'manja] SF Germany; **mi è piaciuta molto la Germania** I really liked Germany; **andremo in Germania quest'estate** we're going to Germany this summer
germanico, a, ci, che [dʒer'maniko] AGG Germanic
germanismo [dʒerma'nizmo] SM Germanism
germano [dʒer'mano] SM (*Zool*): **germano reale** mallard
germe ['dʒɛrme] SM (*gen*) germ; (*fig*) seed; **germi dell'influenza** flu germs; **i germi della ribellione** the seeds of rebellion; **germi di grano** wheatgerm *sg*
germinale [dʒermi'nale] AGG germinal
germinare [dʒermi'nare] VI (*aus* **essere** *o* **avere**) to germinate
germinazione [dʒerminat'tsjone] SF germination
germogliare [dʒermoʎ'ʎare] VI (*aus* **essere** *o* **avere**) (*germinare*) to germinate; (*emettere germogli*) to sprout
germoglio, gli [dʒer'moʎʎo] SM (*gen*) shoot; (*gemma*) bud
geroglifico, ci [dʒero'glifiko] SM hieroglyphic
gerontologia [dʒerontolo'dʒia] SF gerontology
gerontologo, a, gi, ghe [dʒeron'tologo] SM/F specialist in geriatrics
gerundio, di [dʒe'rundjo] SM gerund
Gerusalemme [dʒeruza'lɛmme] SF Jerusalem
gessato, a [dʒes'sato] AGG: **abito gessato** pinstripe suit
gessetto [dʒes'setto] SM piece of chalk
gesso ['dʒɛsso] SM (*gen*) chalk; (*minerale*) gypsum; (*Scultura, Med, Edil*) plaster; (*statuetta*) plaster figure; **mi hanno tolto il gesso** (*Med*) they've taken off my plaster (cast)
gesta ['dʒɛsta] SFPL (*letter*) deeds, feats
gestante [dʒes'tante] SF expectant mother
gestazione [dʒestat'tsjone] SF gestation; **il progetto è ancora in gestazione** (*fig*) the project is still at the planning stage
gesticolare [dʒestiko'lare] VI (*aus* **avere**) to gesticulate
gestionale [dʒestjo'nale] AGG management *attr*
gestione [dʒes'tjone] SF management; **gestione finanziaria** financial management
gestire [dʒes'tire] VT to manage, run
gesto ['dʒɛsto] SM gesture; **ha fatto un gesto di rabbia** he made an angry gesture; **non ha fatto un gesto per aiutarmi** he didn't lift a finger to help me
gestore [dʒes'tore] SM manager
gestuale [dʒestu'ale] AGG: **linguaggio gestuale** sign language
gestualità [dʒestuali'ta] SF (*Arte*) gestural art; (*insieme di gesti*) gestures *pl*
Gesù [dʒe'zu] SM Jesus; **Gesù Bambino** the Christ Child, baby Jesus (*fam*)
gesuita, i [dʒezu'ita] SM Jesuit
Getsemani [dʒet'sɛmani] SM (*Bibbia*) Gethsemane
gettare [dʒet'tare] VT **1** (*lanciare*) to throw; (*: con forza*) to fling, hurl; (*: in aria*) to toss; **gettare (via)** (*liberarsi di*) to throw away; **gettare qc a qn** to throw sth to sb; **gettare qc addosso a qn** (*sasso*) to throw sth at sb; (*acqua, sabbia*) to throw sth over sb; **ha gettato il libro dalla finestra** he threw the book out of the window; **non gettare il giornale per terra** don't throw the paper on the floor; **si gettò un mantello sulle spalle** he threw a coat round his shoulders; **gettare a terra qn** to throw sb to the ground; **gettare le braccia al collo di qn** to throw *o* fling one's arms round sb's neck; **gettare la colpa addosso a qn** to cast the blame on sb; **gettare qc in faccia a qn** (*anche fig*) to throw sth in sb's face; **gettò un rapido sguardo intorno** he had a quick look round; **gettare l'ancora** (*Naut*) to drop anchor; **gettare le reti** to cast the nets; **gettare a mare** (*fig: persona*) to abandon; **quella notizia l'ha gettato nella disperazione** he was plunged into despair at the news **2** (*metalli, cera*) to cast; (*fondamenta*) to lay; **gettare un ponte su un fiume** to throw a bridge over a river **3** (*emettere: acqua*) to spout; (*: grido*) to utter, give **4** (*fraseologia*): **gettare le armi** (*anche fig*) to throw down one's weapons; **gettare la spugna** to throw in the sponge; **gettare la polvere negli occhi a qn** (*fig*) to throw dust in sb's eyes; **gettare luce su qc** to shed light on sth
■ VI (*aus* **avere**) (*pianta*) to sprout
▶ **gettarsi** VR **1** **gettarsi in un'impresa** to throw o.s. into an enterprise; **gettarsi nella mischia** to hurl o.s. into the fray; **gettarsi in acqua** to jump into the water; **gettarsi contro** *o* **addosso a qn** to hurl o.s. at sb; **gettarsi sulla preda** to pounce on one's prey; **gettarsi ai piedi di qn** to throw o.s. at sb's feet **2** (*fiume*) **gettarsi in** to flow into
gettata [dʒet'tata] SF **1** (*di cemento, bronzo, reti*) cast **2** (*in balistica*) range **3** (*diga*) jetty
gettito ['dʒɛttito] SM (*Econ: rendita, introito*) yield, revenue
getto[1] ['dʒɛtto] SM **1** (*azione*) throwing; (*risultato*) throw, cast **2** (*di acqua*) jet; **di getto** (*scrivere*) in one go, straight off; **a getto continuo** in a continuous stream, uninterruptedly; **scrive novelle a getto continuo** he writes one short story after another, he produces a constant stream of short stories; **a getto d'inchiostro** (*stampante*) ink-jet **3** (*Bot*) shoot **4** (*Metallurgia, Edil*) casting
getto[2] ['dʒɛtto] SM (*Meteor*): **corrente a getto** jet stream
gettonare [dʒetto'nare] VT (*fam: canzone in juke-box*) to play; **una canzone molto gettonata** a very popular song
gettonato, a [dʒetto'nato] AGG: **disco gettonato** smash hit; **cantante gettonato** hit singer
gettone [dʒet'tone] SM (*gen*) token; (*per giochi*) counter; (*: roulette*) chip; **gettone di presenza** attendance fee; **gettone del telefono** telephone token
gettoniera [dʒetto'njɛra] SF token vending machine
geyser ['gaizə] SM INV geyser
Ghana ['gana] SM Ghana
ghenga, ghe ['gɛnga] SF (*fam*) gang, crowd
ghepardo [ge'pardo] SM cheetah
gheppio, pi ['geppjo] SM (*Zool*) kestrel

Gg

gheriglio, gli [ge'riʎʎo] SM kernel
ghermire [ger'mire] VT to grasp, clasp, clutch
ghetta ['getta] SF (*gambale*) gaiter
ghettizzare [gettid'dzare] VT to confine to a ghetto; (*fig: isolare*) to ghettoize
ghettizzazione [gettiddzat'tsjone] SF ghettoization
ghetto ['getto] SM ghetto
ghiacciaia [gjat'tʃaja] SF (*anche fig*) icebox
ghiacciaio, ai [gjat'tʃajo] SM glacier; **ghiacciaio continentale** ice sheet
ghiacciare [gjat'tʃare] VI (*aus* **essere**) to freeze; (*lago, fiume*) to ice over, freeze (over); **mi si è ghiacciato il sangue** my blood ran cold; **questa notte è ghiacciato** there was a frost last night
■ VT to freeze
■ VB IMPERS to freeze
ghiacciato, a [gjat'tʃato] AGG (*gen*) frozen; (*bevanda*) ice-cold; **una birra ghiacciata** an ice-cold beer; **avevo le mani ghiacciate** my hands were frozen
ghiaccio ['gjattʃo] SM ice; **un cubetto di ghiaccio** an ice cube; **hai le mani di ghiaccio** your hands are like ice; **restare di ghiaccio** to be dumbfounded; **rompere il ghiaccio** (*fig*) to break the ice; **quella donna è un pezzo di ghiaccio** that woman is as cold as ice; **ghiaccio secco** dry ice
ghiacciolo [gjat'tʃɔlo] SM **1** (*formazione di ghiaccio*) icicle **2** (*gelato*) ice lolly (*Brit*), popsicle (*Am*); **un ghiacciolo al limone** a lemon ice lolly
ghiaia ['gjaja] SF gravel
ghiaioso, a [gja'joso] AGG gravelly
ghianda ['gjanda] SF (*Bot*) acorn
ghiandaia [gjan'daja] SF (*Zool*) jay
ghiandola ['gjandola] SF (*Anat*) gland; **ghiandole endocrine** *o* **a secrezione interna** endocrine *o* ductless glands; **ghiandole esocrine** *o* **a secrezione esterna** exocrine glands
ghiandolare [gjando'lare] AGG glandular
ghiera ['gjɛra] SF (*Tecn*) ring nut
ghigliottina [giʎʎot'tina] SF guillotine
ghigliottinare [giʎʎotti'nare] VT to guillotine
ghignare [giɲ'ɲare] VI (*aus* **avere**) to sneer, laugh derisively
ghignata [giɲ'ɲata] SF (*fam*) laugh; **fare una ghignata** to have a good laugh
ghigno ['giɲɲo] SM (*espressione*) sneer; (*risata*) mocking laugh
ghingheri ['gingeri] SMPL: **in ghingheri** all dolled up; **mettersi in ghingheri** to dress up to the nines
ghiottamente [gjotta'mente] AVV greedily
ghiotto, a ['gjotto] AGG (*persona*): **ghiotto (di)** greedy (for); (*cibi*) appetizing, delicious; (*fig: notizia*) juicy
ghiottone, a [gjot'tone] SM/F **1** (*persona*) glutton **2** (*Zool*) wolverine
ghiottoneria [gjottone'ria] SF (*di persona*) greed, gluttony; (*cibo*) delicacy
ghiribizzo [giri'biddzo] SM whim; **gli è venuto il ghiribizzo della pittura** he's taken it into his head to paint
ghirigoro [giri'gɔro] SM (*scarabocchio*) doodle, scribble; (*arabesco*) flourish
ghirlanda [gir'landa] SF garland, wreath
ghiro ['giro] SM dormouse; **dormire come un ghiro** to sleep like a log *o* top
ghisa ['giza] SF cast iron
GI ABBR = **giudice istruttore**
già [dʒa] AVV **1** (*gen*) already; **te l'ho già detto** I have already told you; **ho finito — di già?** I've finished — already?; **sei già di ritorno?** are you back already?; **già che ci sei...** while you are at it ...; **è successo già da molto tempo** it happened a long time ago; **ma non ci conosciamo già?** haven't we met before?; **fra qualche anno sarà già un pianista famoso** in just a few years he will be a famous pianist; **già da bambino amava la musica** even as a child he loved music; **già sua madre lo faceva** his mother used to do it too **2** (*ex*) formerly; **lo Zimbabwe, già Rodesia** Zimbabwe, formerly Rhodesia **3** (*naturalmente*) of course, naturally; **già, avrei dovuto saperlo!** of course, I should have known!
giacca, che ['dʒakka] SF jacket; **una giacca sportiva** a sports jacket; **giacca a vento** windcheater (*Brit*), windbreaker (*Am*), anorak
giacché [dʒak'ke] CONG since, as
giacchetta [dʒak'ketta] SF (light) jacket
giaccio *ecc* ['dʒattʃo] VB *vedi* **giacere**
giaccone [dʒak'kone] SM heavy jacket
giacente [dʒa'tʃɛnte] AGG (*merce*) unsold; (*posta*) undelivered; (: *non ritirata*) unclaimed; (*Fin: capitale*) idle, uninvested
giacenza [dʒa'tʃɛntsa] SF **1** (*Comm*): **merce in giacenza** (*non reclamata*) unclaimed goods; (*non recapitata*) undelivered goods; **giacenze di cassa** cash on *o* in hand; **giacenze di magazzino** unsold stock **2** (*Fin*): **capitale in giacenza** uninvested *o* idle capital
giacere [dʒa'tʃere] VI IRREG (*aus* **essere**) (*gen*) to lie; (*Fin: capitale*) to lie idle; **il paese giace ai piedi della montagna** the village lies *o* is situated at the foot of the mountain; **giacere nell'ozio** to live in idleness; **la mia domanda giace ancora negli uffici del consolato** my application is still buried somewhere in the consulate
giaciglio, gli [dʒa'tʃiʎʎo] SM bed, pallet
giacimento [dʒatʃi'mento] SM (*Mineralogia*) deposit; **giacimento petrolifero** oil field
giacinto [dʒa'tʃinto] SM hyacinth
giaciuto, a [dʒa'tʃuto] PP *di* **giacere**
giacqui *ecc* ['dʒakkwi] VB *vedi* **giacere**
giaculatoria [dʒakula'tɔrja] SF short prayer; (*scherz: discorso noioso*) boring words *pl*
giada ['dʒada] SF jade
giaggiolo [dʒad'dʒɔlo] SM iris
giaguaro [dʒa'gwaro] SM jaguar
giallastro, a [dʒal'lastro] AGG yellowish; (*carnagione*) sallow
giallistica [dʒal'listika] SF detective stories *pl*
giallo, a ['dʒallo] AGG **1** (*colore*) yellow; (*carnagione*) sallow; **una sciarpa gialla** a yellow scarf; **le Pagine Gialle** ® the Yellow Pages **2** **film/libro giallo** detective film/novel
■ SM **1** (*colore*) yellow; (*di semaforo*) amber; **non attraversare con il giallo** you mustn't cross on an amber light; **dipingere qc di giallo** to paint sth yellow; **il giallo dell'uovo** (egg) yolk **2** (*romanzo*) detective story; (*film*) thriller
giallognolo, a [dʒal'loɲɲolo] AGG yellowish, dirty yellow
Giamaica [dʒja'maika] SF Jamaica
giamaicano, a [dʒamai'kano] AGG, SM/F Jamaican
giammai [dʒam'mai] AVV never
Giano ['dʒano] SM Janus
Giappone [dʒap'pone] SM Japan; **mi è piaciuto molto il Giappone** I really liked Japan; **andremo in Giappone quest'estate** we're going to Japan this summer

giapponese [dʒappo'nese] AGG, SM/F Japanese *inv*; **i giapponesi** the Japanese
■ SM (*lingua*) Japanese; **parla giapponese** she speaks Japanese

giara ['dʒara] SF earthenware vessel

giardinaggio [dʒardi'naddʒo] SM gardening

giardinetta [dʒardi'netta] SF estate car (*Brit*), station wagon (*Am*)

giardiniera [dʒardi'njɛra] SF (*Culin*) mixed pickles *pl*

giardiniere, a [dʒardi'njɛre] SM/F gardener

giardino [dʒar'dino] SM garden; **sono in giardino** they're in the garden; **giardino d'infanzia** nursery school, kindergarten; **giardino pensile** roof garden; **giardino pubblico** public gardens *pl*, (public) park; **giardino zoologico** zoo

giarrettiera [dʒarret'tjɛra] SF garter; **Ordine della Giarrettiera** Order of the Garter

Giasone [dʒa'zone] SM Jason

Giava ['dʒava] SF Java

giavellotto [dʒavel'lɔtto] SM javelin; **lancio del giavellotto** throwing the javelin

gibbone [dʒib'bone] SM (*Zool*) gibbon

gibbosità [dʒibbosi'ta] SF INV: **le gibbosità del terreno** the bumps in the ground

gibboso, a [dʒib'boso] AGG (*superficie*) bumpy; (*naso*) crooked

giberna [dʒi'bɛrna] SF (*Mil*) cartridge case

Gibilterra [dʒibil'tɛrra] SF Gibraltar

GICO ['dʒiko] SIGLA M (= **Gruppo di Investigazione Criminalità Organizzata**) *section of Guardia di Finanza that investigates organized crime*

giga ['dʒiga] SM INV = **gigabyte**

gigabyte [dʒiga'bait] SM INV (*Inform*) gigabyte

gigante [dʒi'gante] AGG gigantic, giant; **un cavolfiore gigante** a giant cauliflower; **confezione/formato gigante** (*Comm*) giant-size
■ SM giant; **gigante della letteratura** literary giant; **compiere passi da gigante** (*scienza*) to make huge strides

giganteggiare [dʒiganted'dʒare] VI (*aus* **avere**) **giganteggiare su** to tower over

gigantesco, a, schi, sche [dʒigan'tesko] AGG gigantic, huge

gigantismo [dʒigan'tizmo] SM (*Med*) gigantism

gigantografia [dʒigantogra'fia] SF (*Fot*) blow-up

giglio, gli ['dʒiʎʎo] SM lily

gigolo [ʒigɔ'lo] SM INV gigolo

gilè [dʒi'lɛ] SM INV (*panciotto*) waistcoat; (*fatto a maglia*) sleeveless cardigan

gin [dʒin] SM INV gin

gincana [dʒin'kana] SF gymkhana

gineceo [dʒine'tʃɛo] SM (*Archeol*) gynaeceum (*Brit*), gyneceum (*Am*); (*Bot*) gynoecium

ginecologia [dʒinekolo'dʒia] SF gynaecology (*Brit*), gynecology (*Am*)

ginecologicamente [dʒinekolodʒika'mente] AVV gynaecologically (*Brit*), gynecologically (*Am*)

ginecologico, a, ci, che [dʒineko'lɔdʒiko] AGG gynaecological (*Brit*), gynecological (*Am*)

ginecologo, a, gi, ghe [dʒine'kɔlogo] SM/F gynaecologist (*Brit*), gynecologist (*Am*)

ginepraio [dʒine'prajo] SM (*fig*): **cacciarsi in un ginepraio** to get o.s. into a fine mess

ginepro [dʒi'nepro] SM juniper

ginestra [dʒi'nɛstra] SF (*Bot*) broom

ginestrone [dʒines'trone] SM (*Bot*) whin

Ginevra [dʒi'nevra] SF Geneva; **domani vado a Ginevra** I'm going to Geneva tomorrow; **abitano a Ginevra** they live in Geneva; **il lago di Ginevra** Lake Geneva

ginevrino, a [dʒine'vrino] AGG, SM/F Genevan

gingillarsi [dʒindʒil'larsi] VIP **1** (*perdere tempo*) to fritter away one's time **2** (*trastullarsi*): **gingillarsi con** to fiddle with

gingillo [dʒin'dʒillo] SM (*ninnolo*) knick-knack, trinket; (*balocco*) plaything

ginnasio, si [dʒin'nazjo] SM *the first and second year of liceo classico (secondary school specializing in classics)*

ginnasta, i, e [dʒin'nasta] SM/F gymnast

ginnastica [dʒin'nastika] SF (*disciplina*) gymnastics *sg*; (*educazione fisica*) physical education; **fare ginnastica** (*Scol*) to do gym; **dovresti fare un po' di ginnastica** you should take some exercise; **vado a fare ginnastica due volte alla settimana** I go to the gym twice a week; **ginnastica artistica** gymnastics; **ginnastica dolce** low-impact exercise; **ginnastica riabilitativa** physiotherapeutic exercise
▷ www.federginnastica.it/

ginnico, a, ci, che ['dʒinniko] AGG gymnastic

ginocchiata [dʒinok'kjata] SF: **mi ha dato una ginocchiata nello stomaco** he kneed me in the stomach; **ho preso** *o* **battuto una ginocchiata contro il letto** I bumped my knee on the bed

ginocchiera [dʒinok'kjɛra] SF (*Sport*) kneepad; (*Med*) elasticated knee bandage

ginocchio [dʒi'nɔkkjo] (*pl f* **ginocchia**) SM knee; **al ginocchio** (*lunghezza*) knee-length; **in ginocchio** on one's knees, kneeling; **mettersi in ginocchio** to kneel (down); **mettere qn in ginocchio** (*vincere*) to bring sb to his knees; **sedersi sulle ginocchia di qn** to sit on sb's lap

ginocchioni [dʒinok'kjoni] AVV on one's knees; **cadere ginocchioni** to fall to one's knees

Giobbe ['dʒɔbbe] SM Job

giocare [dʒo'kare] VI (*aus* **avere**) **1** (*gen*, *Sport*) to play; **giocare a scacchi/ai soldatini/al pallone** to play (at) chess/soldiers/football; **giocava con l'accendino** (*trastullarsi*) he was toying *o* playing with the lighter; **giocare in Nazionale** (*Calcio*) to play for Italy; **il Milan gioca in casa** Milan is playing at home; **giocare i minuti di ricupero** (*Calcio*) to play injury time
2 (*scommettere, anche*: **giocare d'azzardo**) to gamble; **giocare in Borsa** to speculate *o* gamble on the Stock Exchange; **giocare alla roulette** to play roulette; **giocare ai cavalli** to bet on the horses **3** (*intervenire*: *fattore*) to matter, count, come into play; **ciò ha giocato a suo favore** that worked in his favour; **qui gioca l'elemento sorpresa** this is where the surprise element counts **4** (*muoversi liberamente*: *meccanismo*) to play freely **5** (*fraseologia*): **a che gioco giochiamo?** what are you playing at?; **giocare a carte scoperte** to act openly; **giocare sul sicuro** to play safe; **giocare d'astuzia** to be crafty
■ VT **1** (*partita, carta*) to play; **giocare l'atout** to play trumps; **giocare l'ultima carta** (*fig*) to play one's last card **2** (*scommettere*): **giocare (su)** (*Casinò*) to stake (on), wager (on); (*Corse*) to bet (on); **giocare forte** to gamble heavily; **giocarsi una cena** to play for a meal; **si è giocato anche la camicia** he has gambled away his last penny; **ci giocherei l'anima** I'd stake my life on it; **giocarsi tutto** to risk everything; **si sta giocando la carriera** he's putting his career at risk; **ormai è troppo tardi, ti sei giocato la carriera** it's too late now, your career is ruined **3** (*imbrogliare*) to

Gg

deceive, trick, take in; **ci hanno giocato un brutto tiro** they played a dirty trick on us

giocata [dʒoˈkata] SF **1** (*partita*) game **2** (*scommessa*) wager, bet

giocatore, trice [dʒokaˈtore] SM/F **1** (*gen, Sport*) player; **un giocatore di scacchi** a chess player **2** (*d'azzardo*) gambler

giocattolaio, aia, ai, aie [dʒokattoˈlajo] SM/F (*costruttore*) toy-maker; (*venditore*) toy-seller

giocattolo [dʒoˈkattolo] SM toy

giocherellare [dʒokerelˈlare] VI (*aus* **avere**) **giocherellare con** (*giocattolo*) to play with; (*distrattamente*) to fiddle with

giocherellone [dʒokerelˈlone] SM joker

giocherò *ecc* [dʒokeˈrɔ] VB *vedi* **giocare**

giochetto [dʒoˈketto] SM **1** (*gioco*) game; **è un giochetto** (*cosa molto facile*) it's child's play, it's a piece of cake **2** (*tranello*) trick

gioco, chi [ˈdʒɔko] SM **1** (*gen*) game; **facciamo un gioco** let's play a game; **il gioco degli scacchi/delle bocce** (the game of) chess/bowls *sg*; **gioco d'abilità** game of skill; **gioco d'azzardo** game of chance; **gioco di pazienza** puzzle; **gioco di ruolo** roleplaying game; **gioco di società** parlour game; **gioco da tavolo** board game **2** (*Sport: partita, modo di giocare*) game; **gioco di squadra** team game; **due giochi a uno** (*Tennis*) two games to one; **i giochi olimpici** the Olympic Games **3** (*Carte: mano*) hand; **non avere gioco** to have a poor hand **4** **il gioco** (*Casinò*) gambling; (*Corse*) betting; **avere il vizio del gioco** to be a gambler; **casa/tavolo da gioco** gaming house/table; **fortunato al gioco, sfortunato in amore** lucky at cards, unlucky in love **5** (*Tecn*) play; **lo sterzo ha troppo gioco** there is too much play in the steering wheel **6** **giochi di luce** play of light and shade; **giochi d'acqua** play of water **7** (*fraseologia*): **gioco di parole** play on words, pun; **è un gioco da ragazzi** it's child's play; **ho deciso di fare il suo gioco** I've decided to play his game; **entrano in gioco diversi fattori** various factors come into play; **essere in gioco** to be at stake; **è in gioco la mia reputazione** my reputation is at stake; **stare al gioco di qn** to play along with sb; **scoprire il proprio gioco** to show one's hand; **prendersi gioco di qn** to pull sb's leg; **per gioco** in *o* for fun; **far buon viso a cattivo gioco** to make the best of a bad job; **fare il doppio gioco con qn** to double-cross sb; **gioco al massacro** character assassination **8** (*Proverbi*): **un bel gioco dura poco** never take a joke too far; **gioco di mano, gioco di villano** never use your fists; **il gioco non vale la candela** the game's not worth the candle

giocoforza [dʒokoˈfɔrtsa] SM: **essere giocoforza** to be inevitable

giocoliere [dʒokoˈljɛre] SM juggler

giocondità [dʒokondiˈta] SF cheerfulness

giocondo, a [dʒoˈkondo] AGG cheerful, smiling

giocosamente [dʒokosaˈmente] AVV playfully

giocosità [dʒokosiˈta] SF playfulness

giocoso, a [dʒoˈkoso] AGG playful, jocular

giogaia [dʒoˈgaja] SF (*Geog*) range of mountains

giogo, ghi [ˈdʒogo] SM (*Agr, fig*) yoke; (*di montagna*) range; (*di bilancia*) beam; **sotto il giogo di** under the yoke of

gioia¹ [ˈdʒɔja] SF **1** (*felicità*) joy, delight; **essere pazzo di gioia** to be beside o.s. with joy, be overjoyed; **darsi alla pazza gioia** to live it up; **le gioie della vita** the joys of life **2** (*fig*): **gioia mia!** darling!; **è la nostra gioia** he's the light of our life

gioia² [ˈdʒɔja] SF (*pietra preziosa*) jewel, precious stone

gioielleria [dʒojelleˈria] SF **1** (*negozio*) jeweller's (*Brit*) *o* jeweler's (*Am*) (shop) **2** (*arte*) jeweller's (*Brit*) *o* jeweler's (*Am*) craft

gioielliere [dʒojelˈljɛre] SM/F jeweller (*Brit*), jeweler (*Am*)

gioiello [dʒoˈjɛllo] SM jewel, piece of jewellery (*Brit*) *o* jewelry (*Am*); (*fig*) jewel, treasure; **i gioielli di mia madre** my mother's jewellery

gioiosamente [dʒojosaˈmente] AVV joyfully, cheerfully

gioioso, a [dʒoˈjoso] AGG joyful, cheerful

gioire [dʒoˈire] VT: **gioire di qc** to rejoice in sth, be delighted by sth

Giona [ˈdʒɔna] SM Jonah

Giordania [dʒorˈdanja] SF Jordan

Giordano [dʒorˈdano] SM: **il Giordano** the Jordan

giordano, a [dʒorˈdano] AGG, SM/F Jordanian

giornalaio, aia, ai, aie [dʒornaˈlajo] SM/F newsagent (*Brit*), newsdealer (*Am*)

giornale [dʒorˈnale] SM **1** (news)paper; (*periodico*) journal; **l'ho letto sul giornale** I read it in the newspaper; **lo dicono i giornali** *or* **è sui giornali** it's in the papers; **giornale a fumetti** comic; **giornale murale** wall poster; **il giornale radio** the (radio) news; **giornale di strada** *newspaper o magazine sold on the streets by immigrants* **2** (*diario*) diary, journal; **giornale di bordo** (*Naut*) logbook, ship's log

giornaletto [dʒornaˈletto] SM (*fam*) (children's) comic

giornaliero, a [dʒornaˈljɛro] AGG daily
■ SM **1** (*operaio*) day labourer (*Brit*) *o* laborer (*Am*) **2** (*abbonamento*) day pass, day ticket

giornalino [dʒornaˈlino] SM (*fam*) children's comic

giornalismo [dʒornaˈlizmo] SM journalism

giornalista, i, e [dʒornaˈlista] SM/F journalist; **fa la giornalista** she's a journalist

giornalistico, a, ci, che [dʒornaˈlistiko] AGG (*stile*) journalistic

giornalmente [dʒornalˈmente] AVV daily

giornata [dʒorˈnata] SF **1** day; **bella giornata, vero?** lovely day, isn't it?; **durante la giornata** during the day; **durante la giornata di ieri** yesterday; **in giornata** by the end of the day; **fresco di giornata** (*uovo*) new-laid; **è a una giornata di cammino/macchina** it's a day's walk/drive away; **come stai? — mah, va a giornate** how are you? — well, a bit up and down; **vivere alla giornata** to live one day to the next; **è proprio la mia giornata!** (*iro*) it's not my day today!; **giornata lavorativa** working day **2** (*paga*) day's wages, day's pay; **lavorare/pagare a giornata** to work/pay by the day

giorno [ˈdʒorno] SM **1** (*periodo di luce*) day(light), day(time); **giorno e notte** day and night; **si fa giorno** it's getting light; **è già giorno** it's daylight; **di giorno** by day, during the day(time); **preferisco guidare di giorno** I prefer driving during the day; **in pieno giorno** in full daylight; **ci corre come dal giorno alla notte** there's absolutely no comparison **2** (*periodo di tempo*) day; **giorno feriale** weekday; **giorno festivo** holiday; **giorno di paga** payday; **prendere un giorno di ferie** to take a day off; **che giorno è oggi?** what day is it today?; **tutti i giorni** every day; **tutti i santi giorni** every blessed day; **tutto il santo giorno** all day long; **fra 2 giorni** in 2 days' time; **uno di questi giorni** one of these days; **il giorno prima** the day before, the previous day; **il giorno dopo** the day after, the next day, the following day; **a giorni alterni** every other day; **un giorno sì e uno no** on alternate days; **due giorni fa** two days ago; **fra quindici giorni** in a fortnight, in two weeks' time; **al giorno** a *o* per day, per day; **tre volte al giorno** three times a day; **giorno per giorno** day by day; **a giorni** *o* **da un giorno all'altro** any day now **3** *(periodo indeterminato)*: **al giorno d'oggi** nowadays; **ha i giorni contati** his days are numbered; **mettere fine ai propri giorni** to put an end to one's life; **passare i propri giorni a fare qc** to spend one's time doing sth; **il giorno dei Morti** All Souls' Day *(Nov 2nd: relatives visit the graves of loved ones to lay flowers)*

giostra ['dʒɔstra] SF **1** *(nei luna-park)* merry-go-round **2 le giostre** SFPL the funfair *sg* **3** *(Storia)* joust

giostrare [dʒos'trare] VI *(aus* **avere***)* *(Storia)* to joust, tilt
▶ **giostrarsi** VIP to manage; **giostrarsi fra i creditori** to manage one's creditors

Giosué [dʒo'zwɛ] SM Joshua

giov. ABBR (= giovedì) Thurs.

giovamento [dʒova'mento] SM benefit, help; **trarre giovamento da qc** to benefit from sth; **non ho avuto nessun giovamento dalla cura** the treatment hasn't done me any good

giovane ['dʒovane] AGG *(gen)* young; *(aspetto)* youthful; **non è più tanto giovane** he is not as young as he was; **è più giovane di me** he is younger than me; **è il più giovane della squadra** he's the youngest in the team; **vestirsi giovane** to wear young styles; **è morto in giovane età** he died young; **giovane di spirito** young at heart; **è giovane del mestiere** he's new to the job
■ SM youth, young man; **i giovani** the young, young people; **giovane di bottega** apprentice; **da giovane** when I was young
■ SF girl, young woman

giovanetto, a [dʒova'netto] SM/F young man/woman

giovanile [dʒova'nile] AGG *(aspetto)* youthful; *(scritti)* early; *(errore)* of youth

giovanotto [dʒova'nɔtto] SM young man

giovare [dʒo'vare] VI *(aus* **avere** *o* **essere***)* **giovare a** *(essere utile)* to be useful to; *(far bene)* to be good for; **nascondere la verità non ti gioverà di sicuro** it certainly won't do you any good to conceal the truth; **lavorare fino a tardi non ti giova** working late isn't good for you
■ VB IMPERS *(essere bene, utile)* to be useful; **a che giova prendersela?** what's the point of getting upset?; **giova sapere che...** it's useful to know that ...;
▶ **giovarsi** VIP: **giovarsi di qn/qc** to make use of sb/sth

Giove ['dʒɔve] SM *(Mitol)* Jove; *(Astron)* Jupiter

giovedì [dʒove'di] SM INV Thursday; *per fraseologia vedi* martedì

giovenca, che [dʒo'vɛnka] SF heifer

giovenco, chi [dʒo'vɛnko] SM young ox

gioventù [dʒoven'tu] SF **1** *(gen)* youth; **errori di gioventù** errors of youth; **in gioventù** in one's youth, in one's younger days **2** *(persone)* young (people); **la gioventù del giorno d'oggi** young people today; **libri per la gioventù** books for the young

gioviale [dʒo'vjale] AGG jolly, jovial

giovialità [dʒovjali'ta] SF jollity, joviality

giovialmente [dʒovjal'mente] AVV jovially

giovialone, a [dʒovja'lone] SM/F jovial person

giovinastro [dʒovi'nastro] SM young thug

giovincello [dʒovin'tʃɛllo] SM young lad

giovinezza [dʒovi'nettsa] SF *(gen)* youth; *(di spirito)* youthfulness; **godersi la giovinezza** to enjoy one's youth

GIP, gip [dʒip] ABBR M INV *(Dir)* = **giudice per le indagini preliminari**

girabile [dʒi'rabile] AGG *(cambiale, assegno)* endorsable

giradischi [dʒira'diski] SM INV record player

giraffa [dʒi'raffa] SF *(Zool)* giraffe; *(TV, Cine, Radio)* boom

giramento [dʒira'mento] SM: **giramento di testa** fit of dizziness; **mi è venuto un giramento di testa** I feel dizzy

giramondo [dʒira'mondo] SM/F INV globetrotter

girandola [dʒi'randola] SF *(fuochi artificiali)* Catherine wheel; *(giocattolo)* toy windmill; *(banderuola)* weathervane, weathercock

girante [dʒi'rante] SM/F *(chi gira un assegno)* endorser

girare [dʒi'rare] VT
1 *(ruota, chiave, sguardo)* to turn; *(pagina)* to turn (over); **ha girato la testa dall'altra parte** he looked the other way; **girare l'angolo** to turn the corner; **ha girato la domanda al presidente** he referred the question to the president; **non girare il discorso** don't change the subject; **girala come ti pare** *(fig)* look at it whichever way you like
2 *(museo, città, negozio)* to go round; **ha girato il mondo** he has travelled the world; **ho girato tutta la città** I've been all over town; **ho girato tutta Londra per trovarlo** I searched all over London for it
3 *(cambiale, assegno)* to endorse
4 *(Cine, TV: scena)* to shoot, film; *(: film: fare le riprese)* to shoot; *(: esserne il regista)* to make
■ VI *(aus* **avere** *o* **essere***)*
1 *(gen)* to turn; *(trottola)* to spin; *(ruota)* to revolve; *(tassametro)* to tick away; **girare su se stesso** *(persona)* to turn right round; *(: rapidamente)* to spin round; **la terra gira intorno al proprio asse** the earth turns on its axis; **continuavano a girare intorno allo stesso argomento** they kept on discussing the same topic; **gli gira intorno da mesi** she's been hanging round him for months; **la strada gira intorno al lago** the road goes round the lake
2 *(errare)* to go round, wander round; **girare per i negozi** to go *o* wander round the shops
3 *(voltare)* to turn; **giri subito a destra** take the first turning on the right
4 *(denaro, notizie)* to circulate; **girano troppi drogati** there are too many drug addicts about
5 *(fraseologia)*: **mi gira la testa** I feel dizzy, my head's spinning; **quella ragazza fa girare la testa a tutti** that girl is a real show stopper; **gira al largo!** keep your distance!; **gira e rigira...** after a lot of driving *(o* walking) about ...; *(fig)* whichever way you look at it ...; **cosa ti gira?** *(fam)* what's got into you?; **mi ha fatto girare le scatole** *(fam)* he drove me crazy *o* round the bend;
▶ **girarsi** VR *(voltarsi)* to turn (round); *(: nel letto)* to turn over; **si è girata e mi ha guardato** she turned round and looked at me; **si girava e rigirava nel letto** he tossed and turned in bed; **non so più da che parte girarmi** *(fig)* I don't know which way to turn

girarrosto [dʒirar'rɔsto] SM *(Culin)* spit

girasole [dʒira'sole] SM sunflower

girata [dʒi'rata] SF *(di cambiale, assegno)* endorsement

giratario, ria, ri, rie [dʒira'tarjo] SM/F endorsee

giratubi [dʒira'tubi] SM INV pipe wrench

giravolta [dʒira'vɔlta] SF turn, twirl; *(di strada)* sharp bend; *(fig)* about-face, about-turn

girella [dʒi'rɛlla] SF (*carrucola*) pulley; (*giocattolo*) spinning top

girellare [dʒirel'lare] VI (*aus* **avere**) to wander about, stroll about

girello [dʒi'rɛllo] SM **1** (*di bambino*) Babywalker® (*Brit*), go-cart (*Am*) **2** (*taglio di carne*) topside (*Brit*), top round (*Am*)

giretto [dʒi'retto] SM (*passeggiata*) walk, stroll; (: *in macchina*) drive, spin; (: *in bicicletta*) ride

girevole [dʒi'revole] AGG (*sedia*) swivel *attr*; (*porta, piattaforma*) revolving

girino [dʒi'rino] SM tadpole

giro ['dʒiro] SM

1 (*circuito, cerchio*) circle; (*di manovella, chiave*) turn; (*Tecn*) revolution; **3000 giri al minuto** 3000 revolutions *o* revs per minute; **compiere un intero giro** to go full circle; **un giro di vite** a turn of the screw; **dare un giro di vite** (*fig*) to put the screws on, put pressure on; **essere nel giro** to belong to a circle (of friends); **un giro di parole** (*fig*) a circumlocution; **essere giù di giri** (*fig*) to be depressed; **essere su di giri** (*fig*) to be on top of the world; **giro d'affari** (*Comm*) turnover

2 (*passeggiata*) walk, stroll; (: *in macchina*) drive; (: *in bicicletta, a cavallo*) ride; (*viaggio*) tour, trip; (*percorso intorno a*): **fare il giro di** (*parco, città*) to go round; **abbiamo dovuto fare un giro intorno all'isolato** we had to go round the block; **abbiamo dovuto fare un lungo giro** we had to take the long way round; **fare un giro in centro** to have a look round the city centre; **abbiamo fatto un giro in campagna** we went for a walk (*o* a drive *o* a ride) in the country; **giro turistico della città** sightseeing tour of the city; **fare il giro del mondo** to go round the world; **giro d'ispezione** tour of inspection; **il medico sta facendo il giro dei malati** the doctor is doing his rounds

3 (*Sport*: *di pista*) lap; (*Carte*) hand; **sono al primo giro** they are on the first lap; **giro di Francia** Tour de France; **giro d'onore** lap of honour; **giro di prova** (*Aut*) test lap

4 (*di parte del corpo*) measurement; **giro manica** armhole; **giro vita** waist measurement

5 (*di tempo*): **nel giro di** in the course of; **nel giro di un mese** in a month's time; **a (stretto) giro di posta** by return of post

6 (*cerchia, ambiente*): **non ti preoccupare, è del nostro giro** don't worry, he's one of us; **essere nel** *o* **del giro** to be one of a circle; **entrare in un giro** to become one of a group; **essere fuori dal giro** to be no longer part of a group

7 **in giro** *or* **guardarsi in giro** to look around; **andare in giro** to wander about, go about, walk around; **sono stato in giro tutto il giorno** I've been on the go all day; **non trovo la penna, ma dev'essere in giro** I can't find my pen, but it must be around somewhere; **prendere in giro qn** (*stuzzicare*) to pull sb's leg, make fun of sb; (*imbrogliare*) take sb for a ride; **lo prendono in giro perché è grassottello** they make fun of him because he's chubby; **ma va', mi stai prendendo in giro!** come on, you're pulling my leg!; **lascia sempre tutto in giro** he always leaves everything lying about; **mettere in giro** (*voci, denaro*) to circulate; **c'è parecchio denaro falso in giro** there is a lot of counterfeit money in circulation; **c'è molta droga in giro** there are a lot of drugs around

girocollo [dʒiro'kɔllo] SM: **a girocollo** crewneck *attr*

giroconto [dʒiro'konto] SM (*Fin*) giro credit transfer

girone [dʒi'rone] SM **1** (*dantesco*) circle **2** (*Sport*) series of games; **girone di andata/ritorno** first/second half of the season

gironzolare [dʒirondzo'lare] VI (*aus* **avere**) to wander *o* stroll about; **gironzolare intorno a qn** (*pegg: importunare*) to hang around sb

giroscopio, pi [dʒiros'kɔpjo] SM gyroscope

girotondino, a [dʒiroton'dino] SM/F (*Pol*) *someone belonging to a protest movement that is outside political parties and trade unions*

girotondo [dʒiro'tondo] SM ring-a-ring-o'roses (*Brit*), ring-around-the-rosey (*Am*); (*Pol*) *protest where the protesters join hands in a circle*

girovagare [dʒirova'gare] VI (*aus* **avere**) to wander about

girovago, a, ghi, ghe [dʒi'rɔvago] AGG wandering, strolling; **vita girovaga** itinerant life
■ SM/F (*vagabondo*) tramp; (*venditore*) peddler

GIS [dʒis] SIGLA M (= **Gruppo di Intervento Speciale**) *special section of the Carabinieri*

gita ['dʒita] SF trip, outing; **andare in gita** *or* **fare una gita** to go on an outing, go on a trip; **gita in barca** boat trip; **gita scolastica** school trip

gitano, a [dʒi'tano] AGG, SM/F gipsy

gitante [dʒi'tante] SM/F member of a tour

gittata [dʒit'tata] SF (*di arma*) range

giù [dʒu] AVV **1** (*gen*) down; (*dabbasso*) downstairs; **è sceso giù in giardino** he's gone down to the garden; **scese giù per le scale** he came down the stairs; **è giù in cantina** he's down in the cellar; **scendi giù dal tavolo!** get down off the table!; **mi tiri giù quella scatola?** can you get that box down for me?; **vieni giù un minuto** come down a minute; **è venuto giù il tetto** the roof came down; **veniva giù un'acqua!** it was pouring with rain!; **fagli mettere giù quel libro** make him put that book down; **due isolati più in giù** two blocks further down; **spostalo più in giù** move it further down; **la mia casa è un po' più in giù** my house is a bit further on; **cadere a testa in giù** to fall head first; **vai giù di là** go down that way **2** (*al di sotto di*) below; **bambini dai 6 anni in giù** children aged 6 and under; **ce n'erano 30** *o* **giù di lì** there were about 30, there were 30 or thereabouts **3** (*nelle esclamazioni*): **giù!** down!; **giù le mani!** hands off!; **giù di lì!** get down from there!; **e giù botte!** and the fists flew!
4 (*fraseologia*): **essere giù** (*persona: di morale*) to be depressed; (: *di salute*) to be run down; **oggi sono un po' giù** I'm a bit down today; **quel tipo non mi va giù** I can't stand that bloke (*Brit*) *o* guy; **non riesco a mandarla giù** (*fig*) it really sticks in my throat; **buttare giù** *vedi* **buttare 3**

giubba ['dʒubba] SF jacket

giubbetto [dʒub'betto] SM short jacket; **giubbetto equilibratore** (*Sub*) adjustable buoyancy life jacket, stabilizing jacket

giubbone [dʒub'bone] SM heavy jacket

giubbotto [dʒub'bɔtto] SM jerkin; **giubbotto antiproiettile** bulletproof vest; **giubbotto salvagente** life jacket

giubilare [dʒubi'lare] AGG jubilee *attr*
■ VI (*aus* **avere**) to rejoice

giubileo [dʒubi'lɛo] SM jubilee

giubilo ['dʒubilo] SM rejoicing; **grida di giubilo** shouts of joy

Giuda ['dʒuda] SM INV Judas; (*fig*) Judas, traitor

giudaico, a, ci, che [dʒu'daiko] AGG Jewish

giudaismo [dʒuda'izmo] SM Judaism

Giudea [dʒu'dɛa] SF Judea

giudeo, a [dʒu'dɛo] AGG Jewish
■SM/F Jew
giudicabile [dʒudi'kabile] AGG that can be judged
giudicare [dʒudi'kare] VT **1** (*Dir: causa*) to judge; (*: lite*) to arbitrate in; (*: accusato*): **giudicare (per)** to try (for); **l'hanno giudicato e l'hanno trovato colpevole** they tried him and found him guilty; **l'hanno giudicato colpevole** they found him guilty; **il caso verrà giudicato il prossimo anno** the case will be heard next year **2** (*valutare*) to judge; **non giudicarla con tanta severità** don't judge her so harshly; **giudicare qn abile alla leva/idoneo ad un lavoro** to judge sb fit for military service/suitable for a job **3** (*stimare*): **giudicare qn capace di fare qc** to consider sb capable of doing sth; **anche se mi giudicherai pazzo** even though you think I'm mad; **giudicare qn bene/male** to think well/badly of sb; **giudicare opportuno fare** to consider it advisable to do
■VI (*aus* **avere**) (*dare un giudizio*): **giudicare di** to judge; **se devo giudicare in base alla mia esperienza** judging by my experience; **a giudicare da ciò che dice** judging by what he says; **giudicare dalle apparenze** to judge *o* go by appearances; **sta a voi giudicare** it's up to you to decide *o* judge
giudicato [dʒudi'kato] SM (*Dir*): **passare in giudicato** to pass final judgment
giudicatore, trice [dʒudika'tore] AGG judging; **commissione giudicatrice** examining board
giudice ['dʒuditʃe] SM (*gen*) judge; **farsi giudice** *o* **erigersi a giudice di qc** to set o.s. up as a judge of sth; **giudice collegiale** member of the court; **giudice conciliatore** magistrate, justice of the peace; **giudice di gara** (*Sport*) umpire; **giudice per le indagini preliminari** magistrate in charge of preliminary investigations; **giudice istruttore** examining (*Brit*) *o* committing (*Am*) magistrate; **giudice di linea** (*Tennis*) linesman; **giudice popolare** member of a jury
giudiziale [dʒudit'tsjale] AGG judicial
giudiziario, ria, ri, rie [dʒudit'tsjarjo] AGG legal, judicial
giudizio, zi [dʒu'dittsjo] SM **1** (*opinione*) judgment, opinion; **dare** *o* **esprimere un giudizio su qn/qc** to express an opinion on sb/sth; **non vorrei esprimere un giudizio troppo affrettato** I wouldn't like to pass judgment *o* to judge too hastily; **a giudizio di qn** in sb's opinion; **a mio giudizio** in my opinion; **chiedere il giudizio di qn** to ask sb's opinion **2** (*discernimento*) judgment; **essere privo di giudizio** to lack judgment; **l'età del giudizio** the age of reason; **denti del giudizio** wisdom teeth; **fai giudizio!** be good! **3** (*Dir: processo*) trial; (*: verdetto*) judgment, verdict: *in processi civili, decision*; **essere in attesa di giudizio** to be awaiting trial; **l'imputato è stato rinviato a giudizio** the accused has been committed for trial; **citare in giudizio** to summons **4** (*Rel*) judgment; **il giudizio universale** the Last Judgment
giudiziosamente [dʒudittsjosa'mente] AVV judiciously
giudizioso, a [dʒudit'tsjoso] AGG judicious
giuggiola ['dʒuddʒola] SF: **andare in brodo di giuggiole** (*fam*) to be over the moon
giuggiolone [dʒuddʒo'lone] SM (*fig: fam*) silly-billy
giugno ['dʒuɲɲo] SM June; *per fraseologia vedi* **luglio**
giugulare [dʒugu'lare] AGG (*Anat*) jugular
giulivamente [dʒuliva'mente] AVV (*letter*) merrily
giulivo, a [dʒu'livo] AGG (*letter*) merry
giullare [dʒul'lare] SM (*Storia*) jester

giumenta [dʒu'menta] SF mare
giunca, che ['dʒunka] SF junk (*boat*)
giunchiglia [dʒun'kiʎʎa] SF (*Bot*) jonquil
giunco, chi ['dʒunko] SM (*Bot*) rush
giungere ['dʒundʒere] VB IRREG
■VI (*aus* **essere**) **giungere a** to arrive at, reach; **giungere all'orecchio di qn** to come to sb's attention *o* notice; **giungere nuovo a qn** to come as news to sb; **giungere alla meta** to achieve one's aim; **giungere in porto** to reach harbour; (*fig*) to have a successful outcome
■VT (*unire*) to join
giungla ['dʒungla] SF jungle
Giunone [dʒu'none] SF (*Mitol, Astron*) Juno
giunonico, a, ci, che [dʒu'nɔniko] AGG Junoesque
giunsi *ecc* ['dʒunsi] VB *vedi* **giungere**
giunta¹ ['dʒunta] SF (*aggiunta*) addition; (*punto in cui due cose si uniscono*) join; (*Cine*) splice; **questa gonna è troppo corta, dovrò fare una giunta** this skirt is too short, I'll have to add a piece of material; **per giunta** (*inoltre*) what's more
giunta² ['dʒunta] SF (*Amm*) council, board; (*Mil*) junta
giuntare [dʒun'tare] VT to join; (*Cine*) to splice
giuntatrice [dʒunta'tritʃe] SF (*Cine*) splicer
giunto, a ['dʒunto] PP *di* **giungere**
■SM (*Tecn*) coupling, joint; **giunto cardanico** universal joint; **giunto elastico** flexible joint
giuntura [dʒun'tura] SF **1** (*Cucitura*) seam **2** (*Anat*) joint
giunzione [dʒun'tsjone] SF (*Tecn*) joint; (*Elettr*) junction
giuocare *ecc* [dʒwo'kare] VT, VI = **giocare** *ecc*
giuramento [dʒura'mento] SM oath; **fare** *o* **prestare un giuramento** to take *o* swear an oath; **venir meno a un giuramento** to break an oath
giurare [dʒu'rare] VT to swear; **è vero, te lo giuro!** it's true, I swear!; **giurare di fare qc** to swear to do sth; **giurare fedeltà a qn** to swear *o* pledge loyalty to sb; **giurare il falso** to commit perjury; **ti giuro che non sono stato io** I swear it wasn't me; **ti giuro che non ne posso più** I swear I've had more than I can take; **giurerei di averlo visto prima** I'd swear I have seen him somewhere before; **mi pare che fosse lui, ma non potrei giurarci** I think it was him, but I couldn't swear to it; **io non ci giurerei** I wouldn't swear to it; **gliel'ho giurata** I swore I would get even with him
■VI (*aus* **avere**) to swear, take an oath; **giurare su qc** to swear on sth; **giurare su qn** to swear by sb
giurato, a [dʒu'rato] AGG sworn; **nemico giurato** sworn enemy
■SM/F juror, juryman/jurywoman
giureconsulto [dʒurekon'sulto] SM jurist
giurì [dʒu'ri] SM INV (*letter*) jury
giuria [dʒu'ria] SF (*Dir*) jury; (*di gara, concorso*) (panel of) judges
giuridicamente [dʒuridika'mente] AVV juridically
giuridico, a, ci, che [dʒu'ridiko] AGG legal
giurisdizione [dʒurizdit'tsjone] SF jurisdiction
giurisprudenza [dʒurispru'dɛntsa] SF jurisprudence
giurista, i, e [dʒu'rista] SM/F jurist
giustamente [dʒusta'mente] AVV (*gen*) fairly, justly; (*offendersi, seccarsi*) with good reason; **sembra arrabbiato, e giustamente** he seems angry, and with good reason
giustapporre [dʒustap'porre] VT IRREG to juxtapose
giustapposizione [dʒustappozit'tsjone] SF juxtaposition

Gg

giustapposto, a [dʒustap'posto] PP *di* **giustapporre**
giustezza [dʒus'tettsa] SF **1** (*di calcoli*) accuracy; (*di ragionamento*) soundness; (*di osservazione*) aptness **2** (*Tip*) justification
giustificabile [dʒustifi'kabile] AGG justifiable
giustificare [dʒustifi'kare] VT (*gen*) to justify; (*Amm: spese*) to account for; **il fine giustifica i mezzi** the end justifies the means; **posso giustificarlo** I can understand why he did it; **non lo giustifico, però capisco perché l'ha fatto** I don't excuse him but I understand why he did it; **giustificare il proprio ritardo** to give a reason for one's lateness
▶ **giustificarsi** VR: **giustificarsi per il ritardo** to excuse one's lateness; **si è giustificato dicendo che era stanco** his excuse was that he was tired
giustificativo, a [dʒustifika'tivo] AGG (*Amm*): **nota** *o* **pezza giustificativa** receipt
giustificazione [dʒustifikat'tsjone] SF **1** (*spiegazione*) justification, explanation; (*prova*) proof; (*Scol*) excuse note, (note of) excuse; **non c'è alcuna giustificazione per quello che hai fatto** there's no excuse for what you did **2** (*Tip*) justification
giustizia [dʒus'tittsja] SF **1** (*gen*) justice; **in questo mondo non c'è giustizia!** there's no justice in this world!; **render giustizia a qn** to do sb justice; **farsi giustizia (da sé)** (*vendicarsi*) to take the law into one's own hands; **con giustizia** justly, with justice **2** (*autorità*) law; **ricorrere alla giustizia** to have recourse to the law; **affidarsi alla giustizia** to give o.s. up
giustiziare [dʒustit'tsjare] VT to execute, put to death
giustiziere [dʒustit'tsjɛre] SM executioner
giusto, a ['dʒusto] AGG **1** (*persona, sentenza*) just, fair; **per essere giusto verso di lui** *o* **nei suoi confronti** in fairness to him, to be fair to him; **non mi sembra giusto** it doesn't seem fair to me; **non è giusto! vince sempre lui** it's not fair! he always wins; **il giusto prezzo** the right price; **il giusto mezzo** the happy medium **2** (*calcolo, risposta*) right, correct; (*ragionamento*) sound; (*osservazione*) apt; (*misura, peso, ora*) correct, exact; **dobbiamo aspettare il momento giusto** we'll have to wait for the right moment; **non trovo la parola giusta** I can't find the right word; **tre ore giuste** exactly three hours; **i tuoi stivali mi stanno giusti** your boots fit me perfectly; **queste scarpe mi sono un po' troppo giuste** these shoes are a bit tight on me; **giusto di sale** with enough *o* the right amount of salt; **giusto di cottura** well-cooked
■ SM **1** righteous person; **i giusti** SMPL the just; (*Rel*) the righteous **2** (*il dovuto*): **chiedere/dare il giusto** ask for/give what's right
■ AVV **1** (*proprio*) just, exactly; **arrivare giusto in tempo** to arrive just in time; **sono arrivato giusto in tempo** I arrived just in time; **volevo giusto te** you're just *o* exactly the person I wanted; **saranno state giusto le quattro quando mi sono svegliato** it must have been exactly four o'clock when I woke up; **ho finito giusto adesso** I've only just finished; **è andato via giusto adesso** he's just left; **giusto!** right!, of course!; (*a proposito*) that reminds me!; **giusto a me dovevi dare questo lavoro!** why did you have to give this job to me? **2** (*rispondere, capire*) correctly; (*indovinare*) rightly; **mirare giusto** to aim straight
glabro, a ['glabro] AGG hairless
glaciale [gla'tʃale] AGG icy, freezing; (*fig*) icy, frosty; **periodo glaciale** (*Geol*) glacial period, Ice Age
glacialmente [glatʃal'mente] AVV (*fig*) icily, frostily
glaciazione [glatʃat'tsjone] SF glaciation
gladiatore [gladja'tore] SM gladiator
gladiolo [gla'diolo] SM gladiolus
glande ['glande] SM (*Anat*) glans
glandola ['glandola] SF = **ghiandola**
glassa ['glassa] SF (*Culin*) icing; **glassa alla vaniglia** vanilla icing
glassare [glas'sare] VT (*Culin*) to ice
glaucoma [glau'kɔma] SM glaucoma
gli¹ [ʎi] ART DET MPL *vedi* **il**
gli² [ʎi] PRON PERS **1** (*a lui*) (to) him; (*a esso: riferito ad animale*) (to) it, (to) him; **dagli qualcosa da mangiare** (*persona*) give him something to eat; (*animale*) give it something to eat; **gli ho detto tutto** I told him everything; **scrivigli!** write to him!; **gli sembrava una buona idea** it seemed a good idea to him; **gli ha sorriso** he smiled at him; **dagli una lucidata** give it a polish; **aggiungigli un po' di sale** add a bit of salt to it; **dagli un'occhiata** have a look at it **2** (*in coppia con lo, la, li, le, ne: a lui, a lei, a loro, a esso ecc*): **Gabriele lo sa? – sì, gliel'ho detto** does Gabriele know? – yes, I've told him; **dagliela** give it to him (*o* her *o* them); **glieli hai promessi** you promised them to him (*o* her *o* them); **glielo ha detto** he told him (*o* her *o* them); **gliele ha spedite** he sent them to him (*o* her *o* them); **gliene ho parlato** I spoke to him (*o* her *o* them) about it
glicemia [glitʃe'mia] SF (*Med*) glycaemia
glicerina [glitʃe'rina] SF glycerine
glicine ['glitʃine] SM wistaria
glicogeno [gli'kɔdʒeno] SM (*Bio*) glycogen
glicol ['glikol] SM (*Chim*) glycol
gliela *ecc vedi* **gli²**
glissare [glis'sare] VI (*aus* **avere**) **glissare su** (*argomento*) to skate over
globale [glo'bale] AGG (*gen*) overall, inclusive; (*spesa, reddito*) total; (*visione*) global
globalmente [global'mente] AVV globally; **preso globalmente** taken as a whole
globo ['glɔbo] SM globe; **globo oculare** eyeball; **il globo terrestre** the globe
globulare [globu'lare] AGG (*sferico*) globular; (*Anat*) corpuscular
globulina [globu'lina] SF (*Bio*) globulin
globulo ['glɔbulo] SM globule; (*Anat*) **globulo bianco/rosso** white/red corpuscle, white/red blood cell
glomerulo [glo'mɛrulo] SM (*Anat*) glomerulus; (*Bot*) glomerule
gloria¹ ['glɔrja] SF **1** (*fama*) glory, fame; **coprirsi di gloria** to cover o.s. in glory; **lavorare per la gloria** (*iro*) to work for peanuts **2** (*vanto*) pride; **farsi gloria di qc** to pride o.s. on sth, take pride in sth
gloria² ['glɔrja] SM (*Rel*) Gloria
gloriarsi [glo'rjarsi] VIP: **gloriarsi di qc** to glory in sth
glorificare [glorifi'kare] VT to glorify
glorificazione [glorifikat'tsjone] SF glorification
gloriosamente [glorjosa'mente] AVV gloriously
glorioso, a [glo'rjoso] AGG glorious
glossa ['glɔssa] SF gloss
glossario, ri [glos'sarjo] SM glossary
glottide ['glɔttide] SF (*Anat*) glottis
glottologia [glottolo'dʒia] SF linguistics *sg*
glottologico, a, ci, che [glotto'lɔdʒiko] AGG linguistic
glottologo, a, gi, ghe [glot'tɔlogo] SM/F linguist
glucosio [glu'kɔzjo] SM glucose
glutammato [glutam'mato] SM: **glutammato monosodico** monosodium glutamate

gluteo ['gluteo] SM gluteus (*Anat*); **glutei** SMPL buttocks
GM ABBR = **genio militare**
GN ABBR = **gas naturale**
gnocco, chi ['ɲɔkko] SM **1** (*Culin*) *small dumpling made of potato or semolina* **2** (*fig fam*) dolt, idiot
gnomico, a, ci, che ['ɲɔmiko] AGG gnomic
gnomo ['ɲɔmo] SM gnome
gnorri ['ɲɔrri] SM/F INV: **non fare lo gnorri!** stop acting as if you didn't know anything about it!
gnu [ɲu] SM INV (*Zool*) gnu
GO SIGLA = *Gorizia*
goal ['goul] SM INV = **gol**
gobba ['gɔbba] SF (*Anat, Zool*) hump; (*di terreno, naso*) bump
gobbo, a ['gɔbbo] AGG (*che ha una gobba*) hunchbacked; (*ricurvo*) bent
■ SM/F hunchback
Gobi ['gɔbi] SM: **il Deserto dei Gobi** the Gobi Desert
goccia, ce ['gottʃa] SF (*gen*) drop; (*di sudore*) bead; **goccia a goccia** drop by drop; **goccia di rugiada** dewdrop; **le prime gocce di pioggia** the first drops *o* spots of rain; **gocce per il naso/gli occhi** nose/eyedrops; **una goccia d'olio** a drop of oil; **orecchini a goccia** drop earrings; **somigliarsi come due gocce d'acqua** to be as like as two peas in a pod; **avere la goccia al naso** to have a runny nose; **è la goccia che fa traboccare il vaso!** it's the last straw!
goccio, ci ['gottʃo] SM drop, spot; **vuoi un goccio di vino?** would you like some wine?, would you like a drop of wine?
gocciola ['gottʃola] SF (*di lampadario, gioiello*) drop
gocciolare [gottʃo'lare] VI (*aus* **avere** *o* **essere**) to drip; **mi gocciola il naso** I've got a runny nose, my nose is running; **l'acqua gocciola dal rubinetto** *or* **il rubinetto gocciola** the tap's dripping; **l'acqua gocciola dal soffitto** there's water coming in through the ceiling
■ VB IMPERS to drizzle
gocciolatoio, oi [gottʃola'tojo] SM (*Archit*) dripstone
gocciolio, lii [gottʃo'lio] SM dripping
godere [go'dere] VB IRREG
■ VT (*gustare*: *pace, fresco*) to enjoy; (: *bene, rendita*) to enjoy, benefit from **2** **godersi il sole** to soak up the sun; **godersi la vita** to enjoy life; **godersela** to enjoy o.s., have a good time; **si è goduta sua suocera per due mesi** (*iro*) she had the pleasure of her mother-in-law's company for two months
■ VI (*aus* **avere**) **1** (*essere felice*): **godere di** to enjoy, rejoice at *o* in, be delighted (at); **godere nel fare qc** to enjoy *o* delight in doing sth; **godere delle disgrazie altrui** to take pleasure in other people's misfortunes; **godere della compagnia di qn** to enjoy sb's company; **godere all'idea che…** to rejoice at the thought of … **2** (*possedere*): **godere di** (*buona salute, reputazione*) to enjoy; **gode di buona salute** she enjoys good health; **godere di riduzioni speciali** to benefit from special reductions
godereccio, cia, ci, ce [gode'rettʃo] AGG (*persona*) pleasure-loving
godimento [godi'mento] SM **1** (*piacere*) pleasure, enjoyment **2** (*Dir*) enjoyment, possession
godrò *ecc* [go'drɔ] VB *vedi* **godere**
goduria [go'durja] SF (*scherz*) pleasure; **che goduria starsene sdraiati al sole** what bliss to lie in the sun
goffaggine [gof'faddʒine] SF clumsiness
goffamente [goffa'mente] AVV clumsily, awkwardly
goffo, a ['gɔffo] AGG (*persona, gesto*) clumsy, awkward; (*vestito*) inelegant; **è un po' goffo** he's a bit clumsy; **è la persona più goffa che abbia mai conosciuto** he's the clumsiest person I've ever met
goffrare [gof'frare] VT (*carta*) to emboss
gogna ['goɲɲa] SF pillory; **mettere qn alla gogna** (*anche fig*) to pillory sb
go-kart ['gou ka:t] SM INV go-kart
gol [gɔl] SM INV (*Sport*) goal; **segnare un gol** to score a goal; **il gol del pareggio** the equalizer
gola ['gola] SF **1** (*Anat*) throat; **avere mal di gola** to have a sore throat; **tagliare la gola a qn** to cut sb's throat; **ricacciare il pianto** *o* **le lacrime in gola** to swallow one's tears **2** (*golosità*) gluttony, greed; **fare gola a qn** to tempt sb **3** (*di montagna*) gorge **4** (*di camino*) flue
goldone [gol'done] SM (*fam*: *preservativo*) condom
goleador [golea'dor] SM INV (*Calcio*) goal scorer
goletta [go'letta] SF (*Naut*) schooner
golf[1] [gɔlf] SM (*sport*) golf; **giocare a golf** to play golf; **campo da golf** golf course; **giocatore di golf** golfer
▷ www.federgolf.it/
▷ www.golfing.it/
golf[2] [gɔlf] SM INV jumper; (*con bottoni*) cardigan
golfo ['golfo] SM gulf; **il golfo del Messico** the Gulf of Mexico; **il golfo di Napoli** the Bay of Naples; **il golfo Persico** the Gulf
Golgota ['gɔlgota] SM Golgotha
Golia [go'lia] SM Goliath
goliardico, a, ci, che [go'ljardiko] AGG (*canto, vita*) student *attr*
gollismo [gol'lizmo] SM Gaullism
gollista, i, e [gol'lista] AGG, SM/F Gaullist
golosamente [golosa'mente] AVV greedily
golosità [golosi'ta] SF INV greed; (*peccato*) gluttony; (*leccornia*) delicacy
goloso, a [go'loso] AGG greedy; **è golosa di dolci** she has a sweet tooth
golpe ['golpe] SM INV (*Pol*) coup
golpista, i, e [gol'pista] SM/F (*Pol*) leader of a coup
gomena ['gomena] SF (*Naut*) hawser
gomitata [gomi'tata] SF: **dare una gomitata a qn** to elbow sb; (*per zittire ecc*) to nudge sb; **mi ha dato una gomitata nello stomaco** he elbowed me in the stomach; **farsi avanti a (forza** *o* **furia di) gomitate** to elbow one's way through; **fare a gomitate per qc** to fight to get sth
gomito ['gomito] SM (*Anat*) elbow; (*di tubatura*) bend; **a gomito** (*tubo, giunto*) L-shaped; **curva a gomito** hairpin bend; **gomito a gomito** shoulder to shoulder; **alzare il gomito** (*fig*) to drink too much
gomitolo [go'mitolo] SM (*di lana, filo*) ball
gomma ['gomma] SF **1** (*Bot*) gum; (*caucciù*) rubber; (*per cancellare*) rubber (*Brit*), eraser; **mi presti la gomma?** can I borrow your rubber?; **gomma arabica** gum arabic; **gomma da masticare** chewing gum **2** (*pneumatico*) tyre (*Brit*), tire (*Am*); **avere una gomma a terra** to have a flat tyre; **trasporto su gomma** road transport; **gomma rigenerata** (*Aut*) remould
gommapiuma® [gomma'pjuma] SF foam rubber
gommare [gom'mare] VT to rubberize
gommato, a [gom'mato] AGG (*tela*) rubberized; (*carta*) gummed; **nastro gommato** adhesive tape
gommino [gom'mino] SM (*gen*) rubber tip; (*rondella*) rubber washer

Gg

gommista, i, e [gom'mista] SM/F tyre (*Brit*) *o* tire (*Am*) specialist; (*rivenditore*) tyre *o* tire merchant
gommone [gom'mone] SM rubber dinghy
gommosità [gommosi'ta] SF rubberiness
gommoso, a [gom'moso] AGG rubbery
gonade ['gɔnade] SF (*Anat*) gonad
gondola ['gondola] SF **1** gondola **2** (*Aer*): **gondola del motore** engine pod
gondoliere [gondo'ljɛre] SM gondolier
gonfalone [gonfa'lone] SM (*Storia*) banner
gonfiagomme [gonfia'gomme] AGG INV: **bomboletta gonfiagomme** instant puncture sealant
gonfiare [gon'fjare] VT **1** (*palloncino*) to blow up, inflate; (: *con pompa*) to inflate, pump up; (*le guance*) to puff out, blow out; **devo gonfiare le gomme della bici** I need to pump up the tyres on my bike **2** (*fiume, vele*) to swell; **la birra mi gonfia lo stomaco** beer makes me feel bloated **3** (*fig: notizia, fatto*) to exaggerate
▶ **gonfiarsi** VIP (*gen*) to swell (up); (*fiume*) to rise; **mi si è gonfiata la caviglia** my ankle is swollen
gonfio, fia, fi, fie ['gonfjo] AGG **1** (*occhi, piedi*) swollen; (*fiume*) swollen; (*vela*) full; (*stile*) bombastic, wordy; **gonfio di orgoglio** (*persona*) puffed up (with pride); **aveva il cuore gonfio (di dolore)** her heart was heavy; **aveva gli occhi gonfi per il pianto** her eyes were puffy with crying; **ho il piede gonfio** my foot's swollen; **mi sento gonfio** I feel bloated; **avere il portafoglio gonfio** to have a bulging wallet
2 (*palloncino, gomme*) inflated, blown up; (*con pompa*) inflated, pumped up
gonfiore [gon'fjore] SM swelling
gong [gɔng] SM INV gong
gongolare [gongo'lare] VI (*aus* **avere**) **gongolare (per)** to look pleased with o.s. (about); **gongolare di gioia** to be overjoyed
goniometro [go'njɔmetro] SM protractor
gonna ['gonna] SF skirt; **una gonna lunga** a long skirt; **stare attaccato alle gonne della madre** to cling to one's mother's apron strings; **gonna pantalone** culottes *pl*
gonzo ['gondzo] SM simpleton, dolt, fool
Gore-tex® ['goreteks] SM INV Gore-tex
gorgheggiare [gorged'dʒare] VI (*aus* **avere**) (*cantante*) to trill; (*uccello*) to warble
gorgheggio, gi [gor'geddʒo] SM (*Mus*) trill; (*di uccello*) warbling
gorgo, ghi ['gorgo] SM whirlpool; **essere preso nel gorgo della passione** to be in the grip of passion
gorgogliare [gorgoʎ'ʎare] VI (*aus* **avere**) to gurgle
gorgoglio[1] [gor'goʎʎo] SM gurgle
gorgoglio[2], **glii** [gorgoʎ'ʎio] SM gurgling
Gorgone [gor'gone] SF Gorgon
gorgonzola [gorgon'dzɔla] SM INV gorgonzola
gorilla [go'rilla] SM INV **1** (*Zool*) gorilla **2** (*fig: guardia del corpo*) bodyguard
goriziano, a [gorit'tsjano] AGG of *o* from Gorizia
■ SM/F inhabitant *o* native of Gorizia
gotha ['go:ta] SM (*di cinema, letteratura, industria*) leading figures *pl*
gotico, a, ci, che ['gɔtiko] AGG, SM (*scrittura, architettura*) Gothic
Goto ['gɔto] SM (*Storia*) Goth
gotta ['gotta] SF gout
gottoso, a [got'toso] AGG (*attacco*) of gout, gout *attr*; (*persona*) gouty
governante[1] [gover'nante] SM ruler
governante[2] [gover'nante] SF (*donna di servizio*) housekeeper; (*di bambini*) governess
governare [gover'nare] VT **1** (*stato, nazione*) to govern, rule **2** (*barca, nave*) to steer; (*bestiame*) to look after, tend
governativo, a [governa'tivo] AGG (*politica, decreto*) government *attr*, governmental; (*stampa*) pro-government
governatore, trice [governa'tore] SM/F governor; (*di Regione*) *directly elected leader of an Italian region*
governo [go'vɛrno] SM **1** (*regime*) government; (*gabinetto*) Cabinet, Government; **il governo britannico** the British government; **crisi di governo** Government crisis; **governo ponte** caretaker government; **i partiti al governo** the parties in power *o* in office **2** (*di cavallo*) grooming
▷ www.governo.it/
▷ www.italia.gov.it/
gozzo ['gottso] SM (*di uccello*) crop; (*Med*) goitre; (*fig fam*) throat; **restare sul gozzo** (*fig*) to stick in one's throat; **se hai qualcosa sul gozzo sarà meglio che parli** if something is bothering you, you'd better spit it out
gozzovigliare [gottsoviʎ'ʎare] VI (*aus* **avere**) to make merry, carouse
GPL [dʒipi'ɛlle] SIGLA M (= **Gas di Petrolio Liquefatto**) LPG (= *Liquefied Petroleum Gas*)
gpm ABBR (= **giri per minuto**) rpm
GPS [dʒipi'ɛsse] SIGLA M GPS (= *Global Positioning System*)
GR [dʒi'ɛrre] SIGLA = *Grosseto*
■ SIGLA M INV = **giornale radio**
gracchiare [grak'kjare] VI (*aus* **avere**) (*cornacchia*) to caw, croak; (*telefono, radio*) to crackle; (*persona*) to croak
gracchio, chi ['grakkjo] SM (*il gracchiare*) caw, croak
gracidare [gratʃi'dare] VI (*aus* **avere**) (*rana*) to croak
gracidio, dii [gratʃi'dio] SM croaking
gracile ['gratʃile] AGG (*persona, costituzione*) delicate, frail; (*braccia, gambe*) slender
gracilità [gratʃili'ta] SF delicateness, frailness
gradasso [gra'dasso] SM braggart, boaster; **che gradasso!** what a loudmouth!
gradatamente [gradata'mente] AVV gradually, by degrees
gradazione [gradat'tsjone] SF (*sfumatura*) gradation; **gradazione alcolica** alcoholic content *o* strength
gradevole [gra'devole] AGG agreeable, pleasant
gradevolmente [gradevol'mente] AVV agreeably, pleasantly; **essere gradevolmente sorpreso** to be pleasantly surprised
gradiente [gra'djɛnte] SM gradient
gradimento [gradi'mento] SM pleasure, satisfaction; **non è di mio gradimento** it's not to my taste *o* liking
gradinata [gradi'nata] SF (*scalinata*) (flight of) steps *pl*; (*di stadio*) terraces (*Brit*) *pl*, terracing (*Brit*); (*in anfiteatro*) tiers *pl*; **abbiamo seguito la partita dalla gradinata** we watched the match from the terraces
gradino [gra'dino] SM (*gen*) step; (*Alpinismo*) foothold; **"attenti al gradino"** "mind the step"; **è salito di un gradino nella carriera** he has taken a step forward in his career; **è l'ultimo gradino della scala sociale** it's the bottom rung of the social ladder
gradire [gra'dire] VT **1** (*accogliere, ricevere con piacere*) to accept (with pleasure); **gradire un dono/un invito** to accept a gift/an invitation with pleasure; **ho gradito molto il vostro regalo** I was delighted with your present; **...tanto per gradire** I shouldn't, but ...; **gradisca i miei omaggi** please accept my best wishes;

ho gradito la sua visita I enjoyed your visit **2** (*frm: desiderare*) to like, want, wish; **gradisce un caffè?** would you like a coffee?; **gradirei avere un po' di pace** I should like some peace and quiet

gradito, a [gra'dito] AGG welcome

grado[1] ['grado] SM: **di buon grado** willingly

grado[2] ['grado] SM **1** (*gen*) degree; (*livello*) degree, level; (*Alpinismo*) grade; **per gradi** by degrees; **un cugino di primo/secondo grado** a first/second cousin; **essere in grado di fare qc** to be able to do sth; **presto sarà in grado di camminare di nuovo** he'll soon be able to walk again; **non sono in grado di farlo da solo** I can't do it by myself; **cinque gradi sotto zero** five degrees below zero; **subire il terzo grado** (*anche fig*) to be given the third degree **2** (*Mil, sociale*) rank; **salire di grado** to be promoted; **perdere i gradi** to lose one's stripes

graduale [gradu'ale] AGG gradual

gradualità [graduali'ta] SF INV gradualness

gradualmente [gradual'mente] AVV gradually

graduare [gradu'are] VT (*scala, termometro*) to graduate; (*difficoltà*) to increase by degrees

graduato, a [gradu'ato] AGG (*scala, termometro*) graduated; (*esercizi*) graded
■SM (*Mil*) non-commissioned officer

> LO SAPEVI...?
> **graduato** non si traduce mai con la parola inglese *graduate*

graduatoria [gradua'tɔrja] SF (*di concorso*) list; (*per promozione*) order of seniority

graduazione [graduat'tsjone] SF graduation

graffa ['graffa] SF (*Tip: parentesi*) brace; (*punto metallico*) staple

graffetta [graf'fetta] SF (*fermaglio*) paper clip; (*punto metallico*) staple

graffiante [graf'fjante] AGG (*critica, commento*) caustic, biting

graffiare [graf'fjare] VT to scratch; **il gatto mi ha graffiato la mano** the cat scratched my hand
▶ **graffiarsi** VIP to get scratched; **il CD si è graffiato** the CD got scratched

graffiatura [graffja'tura] SF scratch

graffio, fi ['graffjo] SM scratch

graffiti [graf'fiti] SMPL graffiti *sg*

grafia [gra'fia] SF (*di parola*) spelling; (*scrittura*) handwriting

grafica ['grafika] SF graphic arts *pl*

graficamente [grafika'mente] AVV graphically; **parole graficamente differenti** words which are spelt differently

grafico, a, ci, che ['grafiko] AGG graphic
■SM **1** (*diagramma*) graph; **il grafico illustra il calo nelle vendite** the graph shows the drop in sales
2 (*disegnatore*) commercial artist, graphic designer; **fa il grafico** he's a graphic designer; **grafico industriale** draughtsman (*Brit*), draftsman (*Am*)

grafite [gra'fite] SF (*minerale*) graphite

grafomane [gra'fɔmane] SM/F compulsive scribbler

grafomania [grafoma'nia] SF mania for writing

gramaglie [gra'maʎʎe] SFPL: **in gramaglie** in mourning

gramigna [gra'miɲɲa] SF (*Bot*) couch grass; (*erbaccia*) weed

graminacee [grami'natʃee] SFPL (*Bot*) grasses

grammatica, che [gram'matika] SF grammar; **un errore di grammatica** a grammatical error; **libro di grammatica** grammar book

grammaticale [grammati'kale] AGG grammatical

grammaticamente [grammatika'mente] AVV grammatically

grammatico, ci [gram'matiko] SM (*studioso*) grammarian

grammo ['grammo] SM gram, gramme (*Brit*)

grammofono [gram'mɔfono] SM gramophone

gramo, a ['gramo] AGG (*vita*) wretched

gran [gran] AGG *vedi* **grande**

grana[1] ['grana] SF grain; **di grana grossa** coarse-grained

grana[2] ['grana] SF (*fam: seccatura*) trouble; **avere delle grane** to have problems; **piantare grane** to stir up trouble

grana[3] ['grana] SM INV *cheese similar to Parmesan*
▷ www.granapadano.com/

grana[4] ['grana] SF INV (*fam*) cash; **essere pieno di grana** to be rolling in it, be stinking rich

granaglie [gra'naʎʎe] SFPL corn seed *sg*, corn *sg*

granaio, ai [gra'najo] SM barn, granary

granata[1] [gra'nata] SF (*Mil*) grenade

granata[2] [gra'nata] SF (*Bot*) pomegranate
■AGG (*colore*) garnet(-coloured)

granatiere [grana'tjɛre] SM (*Mil*) grenadier; (*fig*) fine figure of a man

granato [gra'nato] SM (*pietra preziosa*) garnet

Gran Bretagna [granbre'taɲɲa] SF Great Britain

grancassa [gran'kassa] SF (*Mus*) bass drum

grancevola [gran'tʃevola] SF spider crab

granché [gran'ke] PRON = **gran che**; *vedi* **grande**

granchio, chi ['grankjo] SM (*Zool*) crab; (*fig: errore*) blunder; **prendere un granchio** (*fig*) to blunder

grandangolo [gran'dangolo], **grandangolare** [grandango'lare] SM (*Fot*) wide-angle lens *sg*

Gg

grande ['grande] PAROLA CHIAVE

■AGG (*a volte* gran + *consonante,* grand' + *vocale*)
1 (*gen*) big; (*quantità*) large; (*alto*) tall; (*: montagna*) high; (*largo*) wide, broad; (*lungo*) long; (*forte: rumore*) loud; (*: vento*) strong, high; (*: pioggia*) heavy; (*: caldo*) intense; (*: affetto, bisogno*) great; (*: sospiro*) deep; **è grande per la sua età** he's big for his age; **un ragazzo grande e grosso** a big strong boy; **un grande invalido** a seriously disabled person; **la gran maggioranza degli italiani** the great *o* vast majority of Italians; **ha una grande opinione di sé** he has a high opinion of himself; **il gran pubblico** the general public; **una taglia più grande** a larger *o* bigger size
2 (*di età*): **sei abbastanza grande per capire** you're big *o* old enough to understand; **farsi grande** to grow up; **hanno due figli grandi** they have two grown-up children; **mio fratello più grande** my big *o* older brother; **è più grande di me** he's older than me
3 (*importante, rilevante*) great; (*illustre, nobile*) noble, great; **è arrivato il gran giorno** the great day dawned; **un grande musicista** a great musician; **un grande poeta** a great poet; **le grandi potenze** (*Pol*) the major powers; **è un gran signore** he's a real gentleman; **ha fatto grandi spese** he's been spending his money
4 (*rafforzativo: lavoratore*) hard; (*: bevitore*) heavy; (*: amico, bugiardo*) great; **è una gran bella donna** she's a very beautiful woman; **una gran bella vita** a great life; **oggi fa un gran caldo** it's extremely hot today; **di gran classe** (*prodotto*) high-class; **una donna di gran**

classe a woman with class; **la famiglia al gran completo** the entire family; **è un gran cretino** he's an utter fool; **per sua gran fortuna non c'era la polizia** he was really lucky that the police weren't around; **oggi fa un gran freddo** it's extremely cold today; **in gran parte** to a large extent, mainly; **ha fatto una gran risata** he laughed loudly; **con mia gran sorpresa** to my great surprise
5 (*fraseologia*): **ti farà un gran bene** it'll do you good; **non ci ho fatto gran caso** I didn't really notice; **non ne so (un) gran che** I don't know very much about it; **non è** *o* **non vale (un) gran che** it (*o* he *ecc*) is nothing special, it (*o* he *ecc*) is not up to much; **quel quadro non è poi (una) gran cosa** that painting's nothing special
■ SM/F
1 (*persona adulta*) adult, grown-up; **cosa farai da grande?** what will you be *o* do when you grow up?
2 (*persona importante*) great man/woman; **fare il grande** (*strafare*) to act big; **Pietro il Grande** Peter the Great
■ SM: **fare le cose in grande** to do things on a grand scale, do things in style

grandeggiare [granded'dʒare] VI (*aus* **avere**) **1 grandeggiare (su)** to tower (over) **2** (*darsi arie*) to put on airs, give o.s. airs

grandemente [grande'mente] AVV greatly, very much

grandezza [gran'dettsa] SF **1** (*dimensione*) size; (*Astron*) magnitude; (*Mat, Fis*) quantity; **di media grandezza** of average size; **a** *o* **in grandezza naturale** life-size(d) **2** (*fig: qualità*) greatness; **grandezza d'animo** nobility of soul **3** (*fasto*) grandeur; **manie di grandezza** delusions of grandeur

grandinare [grandi'nare] VB IMPERS to hail; **ieri è grandinato** it hailed yesterday
■ VI (*aus* **essere**) (*fig: bombe, proiettili*) to hail down

grandine ['grandine] SF hail; **un chicco di grandine** a hailstone

grandiosamente [grandjosa'mente] AVV magnificently

grandiosità [grandjosi'ta] SF grandeur, magnificence

grandioso, a [gran'djoso] AGG grandiose, magnificent; **dalle idee grandiose** with grandiose ideas; **avere un'idea grandiosa** to have a great idea

granduca, chi [gran'duka] SM grand duke

granducato [grandu'kato] SM grand duchy

granduchessa [grandu'kessa] SF grand duchess

granello [gra'nɛllo] SM (*di sabbia, sale*) grain; (*di polvere*) speck; **un granello di pepe** a peppercorn

granita [gra'nita] SF *kind of water ice*

granitico, a, ci, che [gra'nitiko] AGG (*roccia*) granite *attr*; (*fig: fede*) rock-like

granito [gra'nito] SM (*Geol*) granite

grano ['grano] SM **1** (*Bot*) grain, wheat **2** (*chicco: gen*) grain; (: *di rosario*) bead; **un grano di pepe** a peppercorn; **pepe in grani** peppercorns

granturco [gran'turko] SM (*Bot*) maize (*Brit*), (Indian) corn (*Am*); **pannocchia di granturco** corncob

granulare [granu'lare] AGG granular

granulo ['granulo] SM granule; (*Med*) pellet

granuloma, i [granu'lɔma] SM (*Med*) granuloma

granuloso, a [granu'loso] AGG granular

grappa ['grappa] SF grappa

LO SAPEVI...?
grappa non si traduce mai con la parola inglese *grape*

grappolo ['grappolo] SM bunch, cluster; **un grappolo d'uva** a bunch of grapes

grassaggio, gi [gras'saddʒo] SM greasing

grassetto [gras'setto] SM (*Tip*) bold (type) (*Brit*), bold face

grassezza [gras'settsa] SF fatness, stoutness

grasso, a ['grasso] AGG **1** (*gen*) fat; (*cibo*) fatty; (*pelle, capelli*) greasy; (*terreno*) rich, fertile; **un signore grasso** a fat man; **cucina grassa** oily cooking; **dovresti evitare i cibi grassi** you should avoid fatty food; **formaggio grasso** full-fat cheese; **un'annata grassa** (*Agr*) a good year; **pianta grassa** succulent plant **2** (*volgare*) lewd, coarse; **una grassa risata** a coarse laugh
■ SM (*adipe, Culin*) fat; (*unto*) grease; **una macchia di grasso** a grease stain; **grassi animali e vegetali** animal and vegetable fats; **senza grassi** fat free; **grasso per cucinare** cooking fat; **grasso (per lubrificare)** (lubricating) grease; **grasso di balena** blubber

grassoccio, cia, ci, ce [gras'sɔttʃo] AGG plump, podgy

grassone, a [gras'sone] SM/F (*fam: persona*) dumpling

grata ['grata] SF grating

graticcio, ci [gra'tittʃo] SM (*di vimini ecc*) trellis; (*stuoia*) mat

graticola [gra'tikola] SF (*Culin*) grill

gratifica, che [gra'tifika] SF bonus

gratificare [gratifi'kare] VT (*soddisfare*): **questo lavoro non mi gratifica** *or* **non mi sento gratificato in questo lavoro** I don't find this job rewarding

gratificazione [gratifikat'tsjone] SF (*soddisfazione*) satisfaction, reward

gratin [gra'tɛ̃] SM INV (*Culin*): **al gratin** au gratin

gratinare [grati'nare] VT (*Culin*) to cook au gratin

gratinato, a [grati'nato] AGG (*Culin*) au gratin

gratis ['gratis] AVV (*viaggiare*) free; (*lavorare*) for nothing; **i bambini viaggiano gratis** children travel free; **me l'ha riparato gratis** he repaired it for me for nothing; **biglietto gratis** free ticket; **ingresso gratis** admission free

gratitudine [grati'tudine] SF gratitude

grato, a ['grato] AGG (*riconoscente*) grateful; **ti sono molto grato** I am very grateful to you

grattacapo [gratta'kapo] SM worry, headache (*fig*)

grattacielo [gratta'tʃɛlo] SM skyscraper

gratta e vinci ['gratta e 'vintʃi] SM INV (*biglietto*) scratchcard; (*lotteria*) scratchcard lottery

grattare [grat'tare] VT **1** to scratch; **grattar via** (*vernice*) to scrape off; **grattarsi la testa** to scratch one's head; **si grattava la schiena** he was scratching his back; **grattarsi la pancia** (*fig*) to twiddle one's thumbs; **grattare il violino** (*fam*) to scrape on the violin **2** (*grattugiare*) to grate **3** (*fam: rubare*) to pinch, nick (*Brit*)
■ VI (*aus* **avere**) (*stridere*) to grate; (*Aut: marcia*) to grind
▶ **grattarsi** VR to scratch (o.s.); **smettila di grattarti!** stop scratching!

grattata [grat'tata] SF **1** (*alla testa*) scratch; **darsi una grattata alla testa** to scratch one's head **2** (*Aut fam*): **fare una grattata** to grind the gears

grattugia, gie [grat'tudʒa] SF grater

grattugiare [grattu'dʒare] VT to grate; **pane grattugiato** breadcrumbs *pl*

gratuità [gratui'ta] SF (*anche fig*) gratuitousness

LO SAPEVI...?
gratuità non si traduce mai con la parola inglese *gratuity*

gratuitamente [gratuita'mente] AVV (*senza compenso*) free (of charge), without payment; (*fig*: *senza prove, scopo*) gratuitously

gratuito, a [gra'tuito] AGG **1** (*gratis*) free; **l'ingresso è gratuito** admission is free **2** (*fig*: *critiche, commenti*) gratuitous, uncalled-for

gravame [gra'vame] SM: **gravame fiscale** tax

gravare [gra'vare] VT: **gravare di** (*responsabilità, imposte*) to burden with
■ VI (*aus* **essere**) **gravare su** to weigh on, lie heavy on

grave ['grave] AGG **1** (*pericolo, errore*) grave, serious; (*responsabilità*) heavy, grave; (*contegno*) grave, solemn; **una malattia grave** a serious illness; **un malato grave** a seriously ill patient, a person who is seriously ill; **non è grave** it's not serious; **non è niente di grave** it's nothing serious **2** (*suono, voce*) deep, low-pitched **3** (*Gramm*): **accento grave** grave accent
■ SM (*Fis*) (heavy) body

gravemente [grave'mente] AVV (*in modo solenne*) gravely, solemnly; (*seriamente*) seriously, gravely; **è rimasto gravemente ferito** he was seriously injured

gravidanza [gravi'dantsa] SF pregnancy; **una gravidanza difficile** a difficult pregnancy

gravido, a ['gravido] AGG pregnant; **gravido di minaccia** fraught with *o* full of menace

gravità [gravi'ta] SF INV **1** (*di errore, situazione, malattia*) seriousness, gravity; (*di comportamento, occasione*) solemnity, gravity; (*di punizione*) severity **2** (*Fis*) gravity; **la legge di gravità** the law of gravity; **la forza di gravità** gravity

gravitare [gravi'tare] VI (*aus* **avere**) (*Fis, fig*): **gravitare intorno a** to gravitate round; **gravitare verso** to gravitate towards

gravitazionale [gravitattsjo'nale] AGG (*Fis*) gravitational

gravitazione [gravitat'tsjone] SF (*Fis*) gravitation

gravosamente [gravosa'mente] AVV heavily

gravoso, a [gra'voso] AGG (*tasso, imposta*) heavy, onerous; **un compito gravoso** a hard *o* onerous task

grazia ['grattsja] SF **1** (*di persona*) grace; **la grazia di una ballerina** the grace of a ballerina; **piena di grazia** graceful; **muoversi con grazia** to move gracefully; **di buona/mala grazia** with good/bad grace **2** (*favore, benevolenza*) favour (*Brit*), favor (*Am*); **entrare nelle grazie di qn** to win sb's favo(u)r; **essere nelle grazie di qn** to be in sb's good graces *o* books; **di grazia** (*iro*) if you please; **troppa grazia!** (*iro*) you're too generous! **3** (*misericordia*) mercy; (*Dir*) pardon; **concedere la grazia a qn** to pardon sb; **ottenere la grazia** to be pardoned; **Ministero di Grazia e Giustizia** Ministry of Justice; ≈ Lord Chancellor's Office (*Brit*), ≈ Department of Justice (*Am*) **4** (*Rel*) grace; **quanta grazia di Dio!** what abundance! **5** (*Mitol*): **le tre Grazie** the three Graces **6** (*titolo*): **Sua Grazia** Your Grace

graziare [grat'tsjare] VT (*Dir*) to pardon

grazie ['grattsje] ESCL thank you, thanks; **vuole un caffè? — (sì) grazie/no grazie** would you like some coffee? — yes, please/no, thank you; **hai trovato i libri? — sì grazie** did you find the books? — yes, thanks; **mille** *o* **tante grazie!** many thanks!; **Marco non è mai stanco — grazie al cavolo** *o* **grazie tante, lui non fa mai niente!** Marco is never tired — and neither he should be, since he never does a thing!; **grazie a** PREP thanks to; **grazie a lui** thanks to him; **grazie a Dio!** thank God!
■ SM INV thank you; **non ho avuto neanche un grazie** I did not get a word of thanks; **dille un grazie da parte mia** thank her for me

graziosamente [grattsjosa'mente] AVV (*con grazia*) gracefully; (*cortesemente*) graciously

grazioso, a [grat'tsjoso] AGG (*piacevole*) delightful, charming; (*gentile*) kind, gracious

greca ['grɛka] SF (Greek) fret

Grecia ['gretʃa] SF Greece; **mi piace la Grecia** I like Greece; **andremo in Grecia quest'estate** we're going to Greece this summer

greco, a, ci, che ['grɛko] AGG, SM/F Greek
■ SM (*lingua*) Greek; **greco antico/moderno** Ancient/Modern Greek

gregario, ria, ri, rie [gre'garjo] AGG (*Bot, Zool*) gregarious
■ SM (*Ciclismo*) supporting rider; (*Pol*) follower, supporter

gregge ['greddʒe] (*pl f* **greggi**) SM (*gen, fig*) flock; **un gregge di pecore** a flock of sheep

greggio, gia, gi, ge ['greddʒo] AGG (*materia*) raw, unrefined; (*petrolio*) crude; (*diamante*) rough, uncut; (*cuoio*) untanned, untreated; (*tessuto*) unbleached
■ SM crude oil

gregoriano, a [grego'rjano] AGG Gregorian

grembiule [grem'bjule] SM apron; (*sopravveste*) overall (*Brit*), work coat (*Am*)

grembo ['grɛmbo] SM **1** (*ginocchia*) lap; **tenere qn in grembo** to have sb on one's knee *o* in one's arms **2** (*ventre materno*) womb; **in grembo alla famiglia** in the bosom of one's family

gremire [gre'mire] VT (*affollare*) to crowd, pack

gremito, a [gre'mito] AGG: **gremito di** packed *o* crowded *o* crammed with

Grenada [gre'nada] SF Grenada

greppia ['greppja] SF manger

greto ['greto] SM (exposed) gravel bed of a river

grettamente [gretta'mente] AVV (*vedi agg*) pettily, narrow-mindedly; meanly, stingily

grettezza [gret'tettsa] SF (*vedi agg*) pettiness; meanness, stinginess; **grettezza d'animo** narrow-mindedness

gretto, a ['gretto] AGG **1** (*meschino*) petty, narrow-minded **2** (*avaro*) mean, stingy

greve ['grɛve] AGG heavy

grezzo, a ['greddzo] AGG **1** = **greggio** **2** (*poco raffinato*) coarse, rough

gridare [gri'dare] VI (*aus* **avere**) (*gen*) to shout, cry (out); (*strillare*) to scream, yell; (*animale*) to call; **smettila di gridare!** stop shouting!; **gridare a squarciagola** to yell at the top of one's voice; **gridare di dolore** to cry out *o* scream out in pain
■ VT to shout (out), yell (out); **gridare aiuto** to cry *o* shout for help; **abbiamo sentito qn che gridava aiuto** we heard someone shouting for help; **gridare qc ai quattro venti** to shout *o* cry sth from the rooftops; **gridare vendetta** to cry out for vengeance

grido ['grido] SM **1** (*pl f* **grida**) (*gen*) shout, cry; (*strillo*) scream, yell; **le grida dei bambini** the children's shouts; **un grido di dolore** a cry of pain; **un grido di aiuto** a cry for help; **i soccorritori hanno sentito le sue grida di aiuto** the rescuers heard his cries for help; **lanciare grida di gioia** to shout for joy; **un cantante di grido** a famous singer; **è l'ultimo grido (della moda)** it's the latest fashion; **vestito all'ultimo grido** dressed in the latest style **2** (*pl m* **gridi**) (*di animale*) cry

Gg

LO SAPEVI...?
grido non si traduce mai con la parola inglese ***grid***

griffato, a [grif'fato] AGG: **capi griffati** designer clothes
griffe ['griffe] SF INV (*di capo d'abbigliamento*) designer label
grifone [gri'fone] SM (*cane*) griffon; (*Mitol*) griffin
grigiastro, a [gri'dʒastro] AGG greyish (*Brit*), grayish (*Am*)
grigio, gia, gi, gie ['gridʒo] AGG grey (*Brit*), gray (*Am*); (*fig*) dull, boring; **ha i capelli grigi** she's got grey hair; **materia grigia** (*Anat*) grey matter
■ SM grey (*Brit*), gray (*Am*); **grigio argento** silver grey
grigioverde [gridʒo'verde] AGG grey-green (*Brit*), gray-green (*Am*)
griglia ['griʎʎa] SF **1** (*Culin*) grill (*Brit*), broiler (*Am*); **alla griglia** grilled (*Brit*), broiled (*Am*); **una bistecca alla griglia** a grilled steak **2** (*di stufa, focolare*) grate; (*di apertura*) grating **3** (*Aut*) grille **4** (*Elettr*) grid
grigliante [griʎ'ʎante] AGG: **piatto grigliante** grill (*Brit*) *o* broiler (*Am*) tray
grigliata [griʎ'ʎata] SF (*Culin*) grill; **fare una grigliata sulla spiaggia** to have a beach barbecue; **grigliata mista** mixed grill
grilletto [gril'letto] SM trigger; **premere il grilletto** to pull the trigger
grillo ['grillo] SM **1** (*Zool*) cricket **2** (*fig*) whim; **gli è saltato il grillo di...** he's taken it into his head to ...; **ha dei grilli per la testa** his head is full of nonsense **3** (*Naut*) shackle
grimaldello [grimal'dɛllo] SM picklock
grinfia ['grinfja] SF: **cadere nelle grinfie di qn** to fall into sb's clutches
grinta ['grinta] SF (*di persona*) determination; (*nello Sport*) pluck; **avere molta grinta** to be very determined; **una macchina che ha grinta** a car with aggressive acceleration
grintosamente [grintosa'mente] AVV determinedly
grintoso, a [grin'toso] AGG (*persona*) forceful; (: *nello Sport*) plucky, combative
grinza ['grintsa] SF (*di pelle*) wrinkle; (*di stoffa*) wrinkle, crease; **il tuo ragionamento non fa una grinza** your argument is faultless
grinzoso, a [grin'tsoso] AGG (*vedi sf*) wrinkled; creased
grippare [grip'pare] VI (*aus* **avere**), **gripparsi** VIP (*Tecn*) to seize (up), jam
grisou [gri'zu] SM firedamp
grissino [gris'sino] SM bread-stick
groenlandese [groenlan'dese] SM/F Greenlander
■ AGG Greenland *attr*
Groenlandia [groen'landja] SF Greenland
gronda ['gronda] SF eaves *pl*
grondaia [gron'daja] SF gutter
grondante [gron'dante] AGG dripping; **un impermeabile grondante di pioggia** a soaking wet *o* dripping raincoat; **grondante di sudore** in *o* dripping with sweat
grondare [gron'dare] VI (*aus* **essere**) to pour; **il sudore gli grondava dalla fronte** the sweat was pouring down his face
■ VT to drip with
grongo, ghi ['grongo] SM (*Zool*) conger (eel)
groppa ['grɔppa] SF (*di quadrupede*) back, rump; (*fam: di persona*) back, shoulders *pl*; **salire in groppa a un cavallo** to mount a horse
groppo ['groppo] SM (*groviglio*) tangle; **avere un groppo alla gola** (*fig*) to have a lump in one's throat
groppone [grop'pone] SM (*scherz: di persona*) back, shoulders *pl*; **ha un bel po' di anni sul groppone** she's getting on a bit
gros-grain [gro'grɛ̃] SM (*nastro*) petersham
grossa ['grɔssa] SF (*unità di misura*) gross
grossetano, a [grosse'tano] AGG of *o* from Grosseto
■ SM/F inhabitant *o* native of Grosseto
grossezza [gros'settsa] SF (*dimensione*) size; (*spessore*) thickness
grossista, i, e [gros'sista] SM/F (*Comm*) wholesaler
grosso, a ['grɔsso] AGG **1** (*gen*) big, large; (*spesso*) thick; (*pesante*) heavy; **un grosso macigno** a big rock; **una grossa fune** a thick rope **2** (*fig: errore, rischio*) serious, great; (: *patrimonio*) large; (: *tempo, mare*) rough; **una grossa somma** a large sum; **un pezzo grosso** (*fig*) a big shot; **un grosso industriale** a business magnate **3** (*non raffinato: sale, anche fig*) coarse **4** (*fraseologia*): **avere il fiato grosso** to be short of breath; **fare la voce grossa** to raise one's voice; **farla grossa** to do something very stupid; **questa volta l'hai fatta grossa!** now you've done it!; **dirla** *o* **spararla grossa** to shoot a line, to tell tall stories (*Brit*) *o* tales (*Am*); **sbagliarsi di grosso** to be completely wrong *o* mistaken; **ti sbagli di grosso** you're very much mistaken; **questa è grossa!** that's a good one!; **dormire della grossa** to sleep like a log; **grosso modo** = grossomodo
■ SM: **il grosso del lavoro è fatto** the bulk *o* the main part of the work is over; **il grosso dell'esercito** the main body of the army

LO SAPEVI...?
grosso non si traduce mai con la parola inglese ***gross***

grossolanamente [grossolana'mente] AVV (*gen*) coarsely; **un lavoro fatto grossolanamente** a rough piece of work
grossolanità [grossolani'ta] SF INV coarseness
grossolano, a [grosso'lano] AGG (*gen*) coarse; (*lavoro*) roughly done; (*linguaggio*) coarse, crude; (*errore*) stupid, gross
grossomodo [grosso'mɔdo] AVV roughly
grotta ['grɔtta] SF cave
grottescamente [grotteska'mente] AVV grotesquely
grottesco, a, schi, sche [grot'tesko] AGG grotesque
■ SM: **il suo atteggiamento ha del grottesco** his attitude is somewhat ridiculous
groviera [gro'vjɛra] SF O M INV gruyère (cheese)
groviglio, gli [gro'viʎʎo] SM (*di fili, lana*) tangle; (*fig: di idee*) muddle
gru [gru] SF INV (*Zool, Tecn*) crane
gruccia, ce ['gruttʃa] SF **1** (*stampella*) crutch **2** (*per abiti*) coat hanger
grufolare [grufo'lare] VI (*aus* **avere**) to root about
grugnire [gruɲ'ɲire] VI (*aus* **avere**) (*maiale*) to grunt; (*fig: persona*) to grumble, growl
■ VT to mutter, growl out
grugnito [gruɲ'ɲito] SM grunt
grugno ['gruɲɲo] SM (*di maiale*) snout; (*fam: faccia*) mug; **rompere il grugno a qn** to smash sb's face in
grullaggine [grul'laddʒine] SF stupidity
grullo, a ['grullo] AGG stupid, silly
■ SM/F fool, idiot
grumo ['grumo] SM (*di sangue, latte*) clot; (*di farina*) lump; **c'erano dei grumi nella besciamella** there were lumps in the béchamel sauce

grumoso, a [gru'moso] AGG lumpy
gruppetto [grup'petto] SM small group
gruppo ['gruppo] SM **1** group; **suddividere in gruppi di 10** to divide into groups of 10; **arrivare a gruppi di 3** to arrive in groups of 3 *o* in threes; **un gruppo di turisti** a group *o* party of tourists; **un gruppo letterario** a literary circle *o* group; **gruppo elettrogeno** generating set; **gruppo sanguigno** blood group **2** (*Ciclismo*) pack
gruppuscolo [grup'puskolo] SM (*pegg*) small group
gruviera [gru'vjɛra] SF O M INV = **groviera**
gruzzolo ['gruttsolo] SM (*di denaro*) hoard; **ha messo da parte un bel gruzzolo** he has saved a fair bit
GSM [dʒiɛsse'ɛmme] SIGLA M GSM (= *Global System for Mobile Communication*)
GT ABBR (*Aut:* = **gran turismo**) GT
G.U. ABBR = **Gazzetta Ufficiale**
guadagnare [gwadaɲ'ɲare] VT **1** (*stipendio, percentuale, anche fig*) to earn; **guadagna bene** he earns a lot; **quanto guadagni al mese?** how much do you earn per month?; **guadagnarsi la vita/il pane** to earn one's living/one's bread and butter **2** (*conquistare*) to win; **guadagnare la fiducia/l'affetto di qn** to win sb's confidence/affection **3** (*ottenere*) to gain; **guadagnare tempo** (*temporeggiare*) to gain time; (*risparmiare*) to save time; **l'ha detto per guadagnare tempo** he said it to gain time; **guadagnare terreno** (*Mil, fig*) to gain ground; **e io che cosa ci guadagno?** what's in it for me?; **che cosa ci guadagni a fare così?** what will you gain by doing that?; **in tutti i casi ci guadagni** you can't lose; **tanto di guadagnato!** so much the better! **4** (*raggiungere: riva, porto*) to reach
guadagno [gwa'daɲɲo] SM **1** (*gen*) earnings *pl*; (*Comm*) profit; **guadagno lordo/netto** gross/net earnings *pl*; **fare grossi guadagni** to earn a packet; (*Comm*) to make a large profit **2** (*fig: vantaggio*) advantage, gain
guadare [gwa'dare] VT (*fiume*) to ford
guado ['gwado] SM ford; **passare a guado** to ford
guai ['gwai] ESCL: **guai a te (*o* lui *ecc*)!** woe betide you (*o* him *ecc*)!; **guai a te se lo fai un'altra volta!** don't you dare do that again!; **se non lo fai subito guai!** there will be trouble if you don't do it straight away!
guaina [gwa'ina] SF **1** (*fodero*) sheath **2** (*busto*) girdle
guaio, ai ['gwajo] SM trouble, difficulty; (*inconveniente*) trouble, snag; **essere nei guai** to be in trouble *o* in a mess; **sono in un bel guaio** I'm in a real mess; **mettersi *o* ficcarsi nei guai** (*fam*) to get into trouble, get into a spot of bother; **andare a caccia di guai** (*fam*) to go looking for trouble; **il guaio è che...** the trouble *o* snag is that ...; **il guaio è che sono già partiti** the trouble is that they've already left
guaire [gwa'ire] VI (*aus* **avere**) (*cane*) to yelp, to whine; (*persona*) to whine
guaito [gwa'ito] SM (*di cane*) yelp, whine; (*il guaire*) yelping, whining
gualdrappa [gwal'drappa] SF (*di cavallo*) caparison
guancia, ce ['gwantʃa] SF cheek; **porgere l'altra guancia** to turn the other cheek
guanciale [gwan'tʃale] SM pillow; **dormire fra due guanciali** (*fig*) to sleep easy, have no worries
guano ['gwano] SM guano
guanto ['gwanto] SM glove; **un paio di guanti di lana** a pair of woollen gloves; **trattare qn con i guanti** (*fig*) to handle sb with kid gloves; **gettare/raccogliere il guanto** (*fig*) to throw down/take up the gauntlet; **guanto da forno** oven glove; **guanto di spugna** (*per lavarsi*) wash glove
guantone [gwan'tone] SM boxing glove
guardaboschi [gwarda'bɔski] SM INV forester
guardacaccia [gwarda'kattʃa] SM INV gamekeeper
guardacoste [gwarda'kɔste] SM INV (*persona*) coastguard; (*nave*) coastguard patrol vessel
guardalinee [gwarda'linee] SM INV (*Sport*) linesman
guardamacchine [gwarda'makkine] SM/F INV car-park (*Brit*) *o* parking lot (*Am*) attendant
guardapesca [gwarda'peska] SM INV gamekeeper (*for fish*)
guardare [gwar'dare] VT
1 (*oggetto, paesaggio*) to look at; (*persona, cosa in movimento*) to watch; **guardare la televisione** to watch television; **hai guardato la partita ieri sera?** did you watch the match last night?; **guarda chi c'è *o* chi si vede!** look who's here!; **guarda cos'hai combinato!** look what you've done!; **e guarda caso...** as if by coincidence ...
2 (*rapidamente*) to glance at; (*a lungo*) to gaze at; **guardare di sfuggita** to steal a glance at; **guardare con diffidenza** to look warily at; **guardare di traverso** to scowl *o* frown at; **guardare fisso** to stare at; **guardare qc di buon/mal occhio** to look on *o* view sth favourably (*Brit*) *o* favorably (*Am*)/unfavourably (*Brit*) *o* unfavorably (*Am*); **cos'hai da guardare?** what are you looking at?; **guardare qn dall'alto in basso** to look down on sb; **guardare qn in faccia** to look sb in the face; **non guardare in faccia a nessuno** (*fig*) to have no regard for anybody
3 (*esaminare*) to (have a) look at, check; **guardare una parola sul dizionario** to look sth up *o* check a word in the dictionary
4 (*custodire*) to look after, take care of; (*proteggere*) to guard; **guardare a vista qn** (*prigioniero*) to keep a close watch on sb; **chi guarda i bambini?** who is looking after the children?; **Dio me ne guardi!** God forbid!
■ VI (*aus* **avere**)
1 **guardare di** to try to; **guarda di non arrivare in ritardo** try not to be late
2 (*badare*): **guardare a** to mind, be careful about, pay attention to; **comprare qc senza guardare a spese** to buy sth without worrying about the expense; **per il matrimonio di sua figlia non ha guardato a spese** he spared no expense when his daughter got married
3 (*essere rivolto*): **guardare a** to face; **guardare su** to give *o* look onto
4 (*fraseologia*): **guardare dalla finestra** to look out of the window; **guarda un po' lì** (*cerca*) take a look over there; **ma guarda un po'!** good heavens!;
▶ **guardarsi** VR
1 (*uso reciproco*) to look at each other; **si guardavano negli occhi** they were looking into each other's eyes
2 (*in vetrina, specchio*) to look at o.s.; **guardarsi allo specchio** to look at o.s. in the mirror
3 **guardarsi da** (*astenersi*) to refrain from; (*stare in guardia*) to be wary of, beware of; **guardarsi dal fare qc** to take care *o* be careful not to do sth

LO SAPEVI...?
guardare non si traduce mai con la parola inglese *guard*

guardaroba [gwarda'rɔba] SM INV **1** (*armadio*) wardrobe **2** (*locale*) cloakroom, checkroom (*Am*); **ho lasciato l'impermeabile al guardaroba** I left my raincoat in the cloakroom
guardarobiere, a [gwardaro'bjɛre] SM/F **1** (*in albergo, grande casa*) housekeeper **2** (*in locale pubblico*) cloakroom *o* checkroom (*Am*) attendant

Gg

guardasigilli [gwardasi'dʒilli] SM INV **1** (*Storia*) keeper of the seals **2** (*ministro*) ≈ Lord Chancellor (*Brit*), ≈ Attorney General (*Am*)

guardia ['gwardja] SF **1** (*individuo, corpo*) guard; **il cambio della guardia** the changing of the guard; **essere della vecchia guardia** to be one of the old guard; **giocare a guardie e ladri** to play cops and robbers **2** (*sorveglianza*: *gen, Naut*) watch; (*Mil*: *servizio*) guard duty, sentry duty; **lasciare qn a guardia di qc** to leave sb to look after sth, leave sb to keep an eye on sth, leave sth in sb's care; **fare la guardia** to keep watch; **stavo facendo la guardia** I was keeping watch; **fare la guardia a qn/qc** to guard sb/sth; **essere di guardia** to be on duty; **il medico di guardia** the doctor on call; **al cancello c'era un poliziotto di guardia** there was a policeman on duty at the gate; **il fiume ha raggiunto il livello di guardia** the river has reached the high-water mark; **cane da guardia** guard dog **3** (*Pugilato, Scherma*) guard; (*di spada*) hilt; **in guardia!** on guard!; **stare in guardia** (*fig*) to be on one's guard; **mettersi in guardia** to take one's guard; **mettere qn in guardia contro** (*fig*) to put sb on his guard against
■ **guardia carceraria** (prison) warder (*Brit*) *o* guard (*Am*); **guardia del corpo** bodyguard; **guardia di finanza** (*corpo*) customs *pl*; (*persona*) customs officer
guardia forestale forest ranger; **guardia giurata** security guard; **guardia medica** emergency doctor service; **guardia municipale** town policeman; **guardia notturna** night security guard; **guardia di pubblica sicurezza** policeman

GUARDIA DI FINANZA

The **Guardia di Finanza** is a military body which deals with infringements of the laws governing income tax and monopolies. It reports to the Ministers of Finance, Justice or Agriculture, depending on the function it is performing.
▷ www.gdf.it/

guardiacaccia [gwardja'kattʃa] SM INV = **guardacaccia**

guardiano [gwar'djano] SM (*di carcere*) warder (*Brit*), guard (*Am*); (*di stabilimento, villa*) caretaker; (*di faro, zoo*) keeper; (*di museo*) attendant; (*Rel, anche*: **padre guardiano**) Father Guardian; **guardiano dei porci** swineherd; **un guardiano notturno** a night watchman

guardina [gwar'dina] SF cell

guardingo, a, ghi, ghe [gwar'dingo] AGG wary, cautious

guardiola [gwar'djɔla] SF porter's lodge

guardone [gwar'done] SM (*fam pegg*) voyeur, peeping Tom

guardrail ['ga:dreil] SM INV guardrail

guaribile [gwa'ribile] AGG curable

guarigione [gwari'dʒone] SF recovery; **auguri di pronta guarigione!** best wishes for a speedy recovery!; **essere in via di guarigione** to be on the way *o* road to recovery

guarire [gwa'rire] VT (*anche fig*) to cure; (*ferita*) to heal; **guarire qn da qc** to cure sb of sth; **i medici non sono riusciti a guarirlo** the doctors couldn't cure him
■ VI (*aus* **essere**) (*persona*) to recover; (*ferita*) to heal (up); **spero che tu guarisca presto** I hope you'll be better soon; **non sono ancora completamente guarito** I'm not completely better yet; **la ferita guarirà in dieci giorni** the wound will heal up in ten days; **far guarire qn** to cure sb; **è guarito dal vizio del fumo** he is cured of smoking

guaritore, trice [gwari'tore] SM/F healer

guarnigione [gwarni'dʒone] SF (*Mil*) garrison

guarnire [gwar'nire] VT (*ornare*: *abiti*) to trim; (: *Culin*) to garnish

guarnizione [gwarnit'tsjone] SF **1** (*vedi vb*) trimming; garnish **2** (*di rubinetto*) washer; (*Aut*) gasket; **guarnizione della testata** cylinder head gasket; **guarnizioni dei freni** brake linings; **cambiare le guarnizioni dei freni** to reline the brakes

Guascogna [gwas'koɲɲa] SF Gascony

guastafeste [gwasta'fɛste] SM/F INV spoilsport; **non fare il guastafeste!** don't be such a killjoy!

guastare [gwas'tare] VT (*danneggiare*: *gen*) to spoil, ruin; (: *meccanismo*) to break; (: *cibo*) to spoil
▶ **guastarsi** VIP (*meccanismo*) to break down; (*cibo*) to go bad, go off; (*tempo, persona*) to change for the worse

guasto, a ['gwasto] AGG **1** (*non funzionante*: *gen*) broken; (: *telefono, distributore*) out of order; **il mio televisore è guasto** my television isn't working; **"guasto"** "out of order" **2** (*andato a male*) bad, rotten; (: *dente*) decayed, bad; (*fig*: *corrotto*) depraved; **quella mela è guasta** that apple is bad
■ SM (*rottura completa*) breakdown; (*avaria*) failure; **guasto al motore** engine failure; **l'aereo è precipitato per un guasto al motore** the plane crashed because of engine failure; **il meccanico ha riparato un guasto al motore** the mechanic repaired a fault in the engine

Guatemala [gwate'mala] SM Guatemala

guatemalteco, a, chi, che [gwatemal'tɛko] AGG, SM/F Guatemalan

guazza ['gwattsa] SF heavy dew

guazzabuglio, gli [gwattsa'buʎʎo] SM muddle, confusion

guazzare [gwat'tsare] VI = **sguazzare**

guazzo ['gwattso] SM (*Pittura*) gouache

guercio, cia, ci, ce ['gwertʃo] AGG cross-eyed
■ SM/F cross-eyed person

guereza [gwe'rɛddza] SF (*scimmia*) black colobus

guerra ['gwɛrra] SF (*conflitto*) war; (*tecnica bellica*) warfare; **corrispondente di guerra** war correspondent; **in guerra con** at war with *o* against; **fare la guerra (a)** to wage war (against); **essere sul piede di guerra** to be on a war footing; **la grande guerra** the First World War; **la prima/seconda guerra mondiale** the First/Second World War, World War I/II; **ha fatto la prima guerra mondiale** he fought in World War I; **sembra che abbia fatto la guerra** (*fig*) it looks as if it has been in the wars; **tra di loro ormai è guerra aperta** there is open war between them now
■ **guerra batteriologica** germ warfare; **guerra chimica** chemical warfare; **guerra fredda** cold war; **guerra mondiale** world war; **guerra preventiva** preventive war

guerrafondaio, ai [gwerrafon'dajo] SM warmonger

guerreggiare [gwerred'dʒare] VI (*aus* **avere**) **guerreggiare (contro)** to wage war (on, against)

guerresco, a, schi, sche [gwer'resko] AGG (*di guerra*) war *attr*; (*bellicoso*) warlike

guerriero, a [gwer'rjɛro] AGG warlike
■ SM warrior

guerriglia [gwer'riʎʎa] SF guerrilla warfare

guerrigliero, a [gwerriʎ'ʎɛro] SM/F guerrilla
gufo ['gufo] SM owl; **gufo comune** long-eared owl; **gufo reale** eagle-owl
guglia ['guʎʎa] SF (*Archit*) spire; (*di roccia*) needle
gugliata [guʎ'ʎata] SF length of thread
Guiana [gu'jana] SF: **la Guiana francese** French Guiana
guida ['gwida] SF **1** (*manuale*) guide, manual; **guida telefonica** telephone directory; phone book **2** (*capo*) guide; (*direzione*) guidance, direction; **sotto la guida di qn** with sb's guidance; **essere alla guida di** (*governo*) to head; (*spedizione, paese*) to lead; **far da guida a qn** (*mostrare la strada*) to show sb the way; (*in una città*) to show sb (a)round; **guida alpina** mountain guide; **guida turistica** (*persona*) guide; (*libro*) guide(book) **3** (*Aut*) driving; **ha preso la multa per guida in stato di ebbrezza** he was fined for drink-driving; **avere guida a destra/sinistra** to be a right-/left-hand drive; **lezioni di guida** driving lessons; **patente di guida** driving licence (*Brit*), driver's license (*Am*); **posto di guida** driving seat **4** (*tappeto, cassetto*) runner; (*Tecn*) runner, guide **5** (*scout*) (girl) guide (*Brit*), girl scout
guidare [gwi'dare] VT **1** (*gen*) to guide; (*capeggiare*) to lead; **ha guidato una spedizione in Antartide** he led an expedition to Antarctica; **lasciarsi guidare dal proprio istinto** to let o.s. be guided by one's instincts, follow one's instincts; **guidare qn sulla retta via** (*fig*) to steer sb in the right direction; **guidare una spedizione** to lead an expedition; **guidare la classifica** (*Sport*) to head the table **2** (*auto*) to drive; **guidare bene/male** to drive well/badly; **sa guidare?** can you drive?; **ha guidato tutta la notte** she drove all night; **ha mai guidato in Gran Bretagna?** have you ever driven in Britain?
guidatore, trice [gwida'tore] SM/F (*conducente*) driver
Guinea [gwi'nɛa] SF: **la Guinea Equatoriale** Equatorial Guinea; **la (Repubblica di) Guinea** (Republic of) Guinea
guinzaglio, gli [gwin'tsaʎʎo] SM lead (*Brit*), leash (*Am frm*); **un cane al guinzaglio** a dog on a lead; **tenere qn al guinzaglio** (*fig*) to keep sb on a tight rein
guisa ['gwisa] SF manner, way; **a guisa di** like, in the manner of; **in tal guisa** in such a way
guizzante [gwit'tsante] AGG (*luce, fiamma*) flickering; (*pesce*) darting, flashing
guizzare [gwit'tsare] VI (*aus* **essere**) **1** (*pesce, serpente*) to dart; (*fiamma*) to flicker **2** (*balzare*) to leap, slip; **mi guizzò via dalle mani** it leapt *o* slipped out of my hands; **il ladro riuscì a guizzare via** the thief managed to slip away
guizzo ['gwittso] SM (*di animale*) dart; (*di fulmine*) flash; (*di persona*) spring, leap
gup [gup] SIGLA M INV (= **giudice per le udienze preliminari**) *judge who presides over preliminary hearings*
guru ['guru] SM INV (*Rel, anche fig*) guru
guscio, sci ['guʃʃo] SM shell; **uscire dal proprio guscio** (*fig*) to come out of one's shell; **chiudersi nel proprio guscio** (*fig*) to retreat into one's shell; **guscio di noce** nutshell; (*fig: barca*) cockleshell
gustare [gus'tare] VT **1** (*assaggiare*) to taste **2** to enjoy, savour (*Brit*), savor (*Am*); (*fig: apprezzare*) to relish, enjoy, appreciate
■ VI (*aus* **avere**) **gustare (a qn)** to please (sb); **non mi gusta affatto** I don't like it at all
gustativo, a [gusta'tivo] AGG (*Anat*): **papille gustative** taste buds
gusto ['gusto] SM **1** (*senso*) taste; (*sapore*) taste, flavour (*Brit*), flavor (*Am*); **disponibile in tre nuovi gusti** available in three new flavours; **ha un gusto amaro/di lampone** it tastes bitter/of raspberries, it has a bitter/a raspberry taste; **al gusto di fragola** strawberry-flavo(u)red; **privo di gusto** tasteless, flavo(u)rless **2** (*senso estetico*) taste; **con gusto** tastefully; **veste con gusto** she's got good taste in clothes; **di buon/cattivo gusto** in good/bad taste; **uno scherzo di cattivo gusto** a joke in bad taste; **abbiamo gli stessi gusti** we like the same things, we have the same tastes; **abbiamo gusti diversi in fatto di musica** we have different tastes in music; **non è di mio gusto** it is not my taste; **per i miei gusti tu corri un po' troppo** you drive too fast for my liking **3** (*piacere*): **fare qc di** *o* **con gusto** to do sth with pleasure; **lo fa per il gusto di farlo** he does it for the fun of it; **mangiare/ridere di gusto** to eat/laugh heartily; **prendere gusto a qc/a fare qc** to get a taste for sth/for doing sth, get to like sth/doing sth; **ci ha preso gusto** he's acquired a taste for it, he's got to like it; **non c'è gusto a...** there's no pleasure in ...; **tutti i gusti sono gusti** there is no accounting for taste **4** (*stile*) style; **di gusto barocco** in the baroque style

> **LO SAPEVI...?**
> **gusto** non si traduce mai con la parola inglese *gust*

gustosamente [gustosa'mente] AVV (*saporito, cucinato*) deliciously
gustoso, a [gus'toso] AGG (*piatto*) tasty; (*romanzo, commedia*) enjoyable, agreeable; **la carne è più gustosa cucinata così** meat is tastier when it's cooked like this
gutturale [guttu'rale] AGG guttural
Guyana [gu'jana] SF = **Guiana**

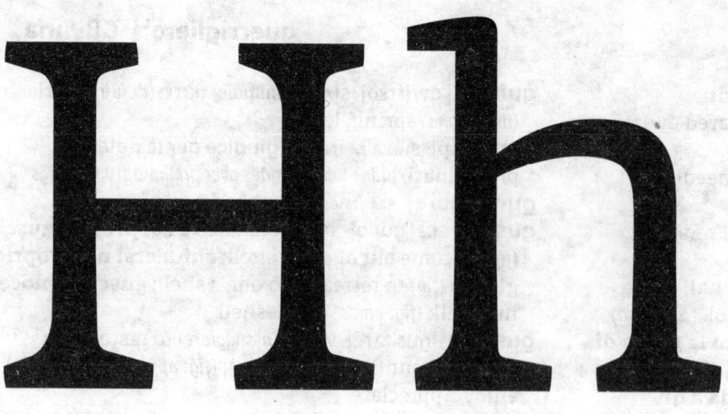

H, h ['akka] SF O M INV (*lettera*) H, h; **H come hotel** ≈ H for Harry (*Brit*), ≈ H for How (*Am*)
■ ABBR **1** = **ora** **2** = **altezza**
ha¹ ABBR (= **ettaro**) ha
ha *ecc²* [a] VB *vedi* **avere**
habitat ['abitat] SM INV (*Bot, Zool*) habitat
habitué [abi'tɥe] SM/F INV (*di locale, ristorante*) regular customer
hacker ['hækəʳ] SM/F INV (*Inform*) hacker
hai *ecc* ['ai] VB *vedi* **avere**
Haiti [a'iti] SF Haiti
haitiano, a [ai'tjano] AGG, SM/F Haitian
hall [hɔ:l] SF INV (*di albergo*) hall, foyer
hamburger [am'burger] SM INV hamburger
hammam [am'mam] SM INV Turkish bath
handicap ['hændikap] SM INV (*Sport, fig*) handicap
handicappato, a [andikap'pato] AGG handicapped
■ SM/F handicapped person, disabled person; **gli handicappati** the handicapped
hangar [ɑ̃'gar] SM INV (*Aer*) hangar
hanno *ecc* ['anno] VB *vedi* **avere**
happening ['hæpəniŋ] SM INV happening
hard [ard] AGG (*pornografico*) hard-core
hard disc [ar'disk] SM INV hard disc
hard discount [ardiks'kaunt] SM INV (*supermercato*) cut-price supermarket
hard rock [ard'rok] SM INV (*Mus*) hard rock
hardware ['ha:dwɛə] SM INV hardware
harem [a'rɛm] SM INV harem
hascisc [aʃʃiʃ] SM INV hashish
haute-couture ['otku'tyr] SF haute couture
hawaiano, a [ava'jano] AGG, SM/F Hawaiian
Hawaii [ə'wa:i:] SFPL Hawaii *sg*
heavy metal [evi'metal] SM INV (*Mus*) heavy metal
help [elp] SM INV: **"Help"** (*Inform*) "Help"
Helsinki ['ɛlsinki] SF Helsinki
henna ['ɛnna] SF henna
herpes ['ɛrpes] SM (*Med*) herpes *sg*; **herpes zoster** shingles *sg*
hezbollah [ezbol'la] SM INV Hezbollah
hg ABBR (= **ettogrammo**) hg
hi-fi ['haifai] SM INV, AGG INV hi-fi
Himalaia [ima'laja] SM: **l'Himalaia** the Himalayas *pl*
hindi ['hindi] AGG INV Hindi
hinterland ['hintərlant] SM INV hinterland
hippy ['hipi] AGG INV, SM/F INV hippy
hitleriano, a [itle'rjano] AGG ATTR Hitler *attr*
■ SM Hitlerite
hit-parade ['hit pə'reid] SF INV hit parade; **è in testa alla hit-parade** it's top of the pops
HIV [akkai'vu] SIGLA M HIV (= *Human Immunodeficiency Virus*)
hl ABBR (= **ettolitro**) hl
ho *ecc* [ɔ] VB *vedi* **avere**
hobby ['hɔbi] SM INV hobby
hockey ['hɔki] SM hockey; **hockey su ghiaccio** ice hockey; **hockey su prato** field hockey, hockey (*Brit*)
▷ www.fihp.org/
▷ www.fisg.it/
holding ['houldiŋ] SF INV holding company
hollywoodiano, a [ollivu'djano] AGG Hollywood *attr*; (*fig*) spectacular
home ['hoʊm] SM INV (*tasto*) Home (key); (*Inform*) home page
home page ['hoʊm pɛidʒ] SF INV (*Inform*) home page
home theatre [hoʊm 'tiatər] SM INV home cinema
Honduras [on'duras] SM Honduras
honduregno, a [ondu'reɲɲo] AGG, SM/F Honduran
Hong Kong [ong'kɔng] SF Hong Kong
Honolulu [ono'lulu] SF Honolulu
honoris causa [o'nɔris 'kauza] AVV honoris causa
hooligan ['uligan] SM/F INV hooligan
host [ost] SM INV, AGG INV (*anche:* **host computer**) host (computer)
hostess ['houstis] SF INV (*assistente di volo*) air hostess (*Brit*), (air) stewardess, flight attendant; (*accompagnatrice*) escort
hot dog ['hɔtdɔg] SM INV **1** (*panino*) hot dog **2** (*Sport: sci acrobatico*) hot-dogging
hotel [o'tɛl] SM INV hotel
hot line [ɔt'lain] SF INV (*erotica*) (sex) chatline
hovercraft ['hɔvəkra:ft] SM INV hovercraft
HTML [akkatiɛlle'ɛmme] SIGLA M HTML (= *Hypertext Markup Language*)

HTTP [akkatiti'pi] SIGLA M HTTP (= *Hypertext Transfer Protocol*)
humour ['hju:mə] SM (sense of) humour
humus ['umus] SM humus
husky ['aski] SM INV (*cane*) husky; (*giaccone*) ® *padded winter jacket*
hutu ['utu] SM/F INV, AGG INV Hutu
Hz ABBR (= **hertz**) Hz

Hh

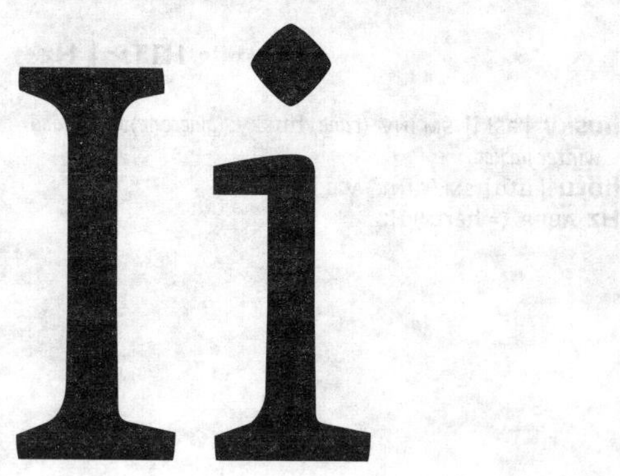

I, i [i] SF O M INV (*lettera*) I, i; **I come Imola** ≈ I for Isaac (*Brit*), ≈ I for Item (*Am*)

i [i] ART DET MPL *vedi* **il**

IACP [iatʃi'pi] SIGLA M (= **Istituto Autonomo per le Case Popolari**) *public housing association*

iato [i'ato] SM hiatus

IBAN ['iban] ABBR (*Banca*) IBAN (= *International Bank Account Number*)

iberico, a, ci, che [i'bɛriko] AGG Iberian; **la penisola iberica** the Iberian Peninsula

ibernare [iber'nare] VI (*aus* **avere**) to hibernate ■ VT (*Med*) to induce hypothermia in

ibernazione [ibernat'tsjone] SF hibernation

ibid. ABBR (= **ibidem**) ib(id).

ibidem [i'bidem] AVV ibid.

ibisco, schi [i'bisko] SM hibiscus

ibrido, a ['ibrido] AGG hybrid; **auto ibrida** hybrid car ■ SM hybrid

IC ABBR = **intercity**

ICE ['itʃe] SIGLA M (= **Istituto nazionale per il Commercio Estero**) *overseas trade board*

iceberg ['aisberg] SM INV iceberg; **la punta dell'iceberg** (*anche fig*) the tip of the iceberg

ICI ['itʃi] SIGLA F (= **Imposta Comunale sugli Immobili**) local property tax

ICIAP ['itʃap] SIGLA F (= **Imposta Comunale per l'esercizio di Imprese, Arti e Professioni**) local business tax

icona [i'kɔna] SF (*Rel, Inform, fig*) icon

iconoclasta, i, e [ikono'klasta] AGG, SM/F iconoclast

iconografia [ikonogra'fia] SF iconography

iconografico, a, ci, che [ikono'grafiko] AGG iconographic(al)

ictus ['iktus] SM INV (*Med, Metrica*) ictus

id. ABBR (= **idem**) do.

Idaho ['aɪdəhəʊ] SM Idaho

Iddio [id'dio] SM God

idea [i'dɛa] SF **1** (*gen*) idea; **non ne ho la minima** *o* **più pallida idea** I haven't the faintest *o* foggiest idea; **farsi un'idea di qc** to get an idea of sth; **non hai idea di quanto sia difficile** you have no idea how difficult it is; **non hai idea del traffico che c'era** you've no idea how much traffic there was; **un'idea geniale** a brilliant *o* clever idea; **chissà che idea gli è saltata in mente adesso?** who knows what idea he may have got into his head now?; **tremo solo all'idea che possa venire** just the thought that he might come is enough to terrify me; **ho idea che...** I have an idea *o* a feeling that ...; **nemmeno neanche** *o* **neppure per idea!** not on your life!, certainly not!, no way!; **pensi di andarci? — neanche per idea!** are you thinking of going? — no way!; **dare l'idea di** to seem, look like; **idea fissa** obsession **2** (*opinione*) opinion, view; **avere le idee chiare** to know one's mind; **cambiare idea** to change one's mind; **ho cambiato idea** I've changed my mind; **essere dell'idea (che)** to be of the opinion (that), think (that) **3** (*intenzione*): **avere una mezza idea di fare qc** to have half a mind to do sth; **la mia idea era di andare al cinema** I had thought of going to the pictures **4** (*ideale*) ideal; **l'idea del bello/della pace** the ideal of beauty/of peace

ideale [ide'ale] AGG ideal; **secondo me è la soluzione ideale** in my opinion it's the ideal solution ■ SM ideal; **l'ideale sarebbe andarsene** the best thing would be to leave; **il mio ideale di casa** my ideal home; **hanno fatto sacrifici per i loro ideali** they have made sacrifices for their ideals

idealismo [idea'lizmo] SM idealism

idealista, i, e [idea'lista] SM/F idealist

idealistico, a, ci, che [idea'listiko] AGG idealistic

idealizzare [idealid'dzare] VT to idealize

idealizzazione [idealiddzat'tsjone] SF idealization

idealmente [ideal'mente] AVV ideally

ideare [ide'are] VT (*escogitare: scherzo*) to think of; (*: piano*) to think out, conceive; (*progettare: congegno*) to invent

ideatore, trice [idea'tore] SM/F (*di piano*) originator; (*di metodo*) inventor

ideazione [ideat'tsjone] SF conception

idem ['idem] AVV idem

identico, a, ci, che [i'dɛntiko] AGG: **identico (a)** identical (to); **è identico al mio** it's exactly the same as mine; **è la stessa identica cosa** it's exactly the same thing

identificabile [identifi'kabile] AGG identifiable
identificare [identifi'kare] VT to identify
▶ **identificarsi** VR: **identificarsi con** to identify o.s. with
identificazione [identifikat'tsjone] SF identification
identikit [identi'kit] SM INV identikit®; **fare l'identikit di** to produce an identikit picture of
identità [identi'ta] SF INV identity; **carta d'identità** identity card
ideogramma, i [ideo'gramma] SM ideogram
ideologia, gie [ideolo'dʒia] SF ideology
ideologico, a, ci, che [ideo'lɔdʒiko] AGG ideological
idilliaco, a, ci, che [idil'liako], **idillico, a, ci, che** [i'dilliko] AGG idyllic
idillicamente [idillika'mente] AVV idyllically
idillio, li [i'dilljo] SM idyll; **tra di loro è nato un idillio** they have fallen in love
idioma, i [i'djɔma] SM language
idiomatico, a, ci, che [idjo'matiko] AGG idiomatic; **frase idiomatica** idiom
idiosincrasia [idjosinkra'zia] SF **1** (*avversione*) dislike; **avere un'idiosincrasia per qc** to dislike sth **2** (*Med*) idiosyncrasy
idiosincratico, a, ci, che [idjosin'kratiko] AGG (*Med*) idiosyncratic
idiota, i, e [i'djɔta] AGG (*Med*) idiotic; (*fig*) idiotic, stupid
■ SM/F idiot
idiotismo [idjo'tizmo] SM (*Med*) idiocy
idiozia [idjot'tsia] SF (*Med*) idiocy; (*fig*) idiocy, stupidity; (: *atto, discorso*) idiotic thing to do (*o* say)
idolatra, i, e [ido'latra] AGG idolatrous
■ SM/F idolater/idolatress
idolatrare [idola'trare] VT (*divinità*) to worship; (*fig*: *persona*) to idolize
idolatria [idola'tria] SF idolatry
idolo ['idolo] SM (*Rel, fig*) idol
idoneità [idonei'ta] SF suitability, fitness; **esame di idoneità** qualifying examination
idoneo, a [i'dɔneo] AGG: **idoneo (a)** suitable (for), fit (for); **idoneo all'insegnamento** qualified to teach; **fare qn idoneo (al servizio militare)** to pass sb as fit (for military service)
idrante [i'drante] SM hydrant
idratante [idra'tante] AGG (*crema*) moisturizing; **crema idratante** moisturizing cream
■ SM moisturizer
idratare [idra'tare] VT (*pelle*) to moisturize
idratazione [idratat'tsjone] SF (*della pelle*) moisturizing
idraulica [i'draulika] SF hydraulics *sg*
idraulico, a, ci, che [i'drauliko] AGG hydraulic
■ SM plumber; **fa l'idraulico** he's a plumber
idrico, a, ci, che ['idriko] AGG water *attr*
idrocarburo [idrokar'buro] SM hydrocarbon
idroelettricità [idroelettritʃi'ta] SF hydroelectricity
idroelettrico, a, ci, che [idroe'lɛttriko] AGG hydroelectric
idrofilo, a [i'drɔfilo] AGG hydrophilic; **cotone idrofilo** cotton wool (*Brit*), absorbent cotton (*Am*)
idrofobia [idrofo'bia] SF (*Med*) rabies *sg*
idrofobo, a [i'drɔfobo] AGG rabid; (*fig*) furious
idrofugo, a, ghi, ghe [i'drɔfugo] AGG (*Chim*) hydrophobic
idrogenazione [idrodʒenat'tsjone] SF hydrogenation
idrogeno [i'drɔdʒeno] SM hydrogen
idrografia [idrogra'fia] SF hydrography
idrografico, a, ci, che [idro'grafiko] AGG hydrographic
idrolipidico, a, ci, che [idroli'pidiko] AGG hydrolipid
idrolisi [i'drɔlizi] SF hydrolysis
idrologico, a, ci, che [idro'lɔdʒiko] AGG hydrological
idromassaggio, gi [idromas'saddʒo] SM water massage; **vasca per idromassaggio** Jacuzzi®
idromele [idro'mɛle] SM mead
idrometro [i'drɔmetro] SM hydrometer
idropisia [idropi'zia] SF (*Med*) dropsy
idrorepellente [idrorepel'lɛnte] AGG water-repellent
■ SM water-repellent substance
idroscalo [idros'kalo] SM (*Aer*) seaplane base
idrosolubile [idroso'lubile] AGG water-soluble
idrovolante [idrovo'lante] SM seaplane
idrovora [i'drɔvora] SF water pump
idruro [i'druro] SM hydride
i.e. ABBR (= id est: *cioè*) i.e.
iella ['jɛlla] SF bad luck; **essere perseguitato dalla iella** to be plagued by bad luck
iellato, a [jel'lato] AGG plagued by bad luck
iena ['jɛna] SF hyena; (*fig*: *persona crudele*) nasty piece of work
ieratico, a, ci, che [je'ratiko] AGG (*Rel*: *scrittura*) hieratic; (*fig*: *atteggiamento*) solemn
ieri ['jɛri] AVV yesterday; **ieri l'altro** *or* **l'altro ieri** *o* **ieri l'altro** the day before yesterday; **ieri mattina** yesterday morning; **ieri sera** yesterday evening, last night; **ieri notte** last night; **sono tornato ieri** I got back yesterday; **non sono nato ieri** I wasn't born yesterday
■ SM yesterday; **il giornale di ieri** yesterday's paper
iettatore, trice [jetta'tore] SM/F jinx; **smettila di fare lo iettatore!** stop trying to put a jinx on things!
iettatura [jetta'tura] SF evil eye; **ho la iettatura addosso!** there must be a jinx on me!
Ifigenia [ifidʒe'nia] SF Iphigenia
igiene [i'dʒɛne] SF hygiene; **igiene del corpo** personal hygiene; **norme d'igiene** sanitary regulations; **igiene mentale** mental health; **igiene pubblica** public health
igienicamente [idʒenika'mente] AVV hygienically
igienico, a, ci, che [i'dʒɛniko] AGG (*gen*) hygienic; (*salubre*: *clima*) healthy; **carta igienica** toilet paper; **impianto igienico** sanitary fittings
igienista, i, e [idʒe'nista] SM/F hygienist
igloo ['iglu] SM INV igloo; (*tenda*) dome tent
IGM [idʒi'ɛmme] SIGLA M = *Istituto Geografico Militare*
ignaro, a [iɲ'ɲaro] AGG: **ignaro (di)** unaware (of), ignorant (of)
ignifugo, a [iɲ'ɲifugo] AGG flame-resistant, fireproof
ignobile [iɲ'ɲɔbile] AGG vile, despicable
ignobilmente [iɲɲobil'mente] AVV vilely, despicably
ignominia [iɲɲo'minja] SF ignominy; **questo monumento è un'ignominia!** (*scherz*) this monument is a disgrace!
ignominioso, a [iɲɲomi'njoso] AGG ignominious
ignorante [iɲɲo'rante] AGG ignorant; **non ho fatto domande per paura di sembrare ignorante** I didn't ask any questions for fear of appearing ignorant; **come sei ignorante!** don't you know anything!
■ SM/F ignoramus; (*villano*) boor
ignoranza [iɲɲo'rantsa] SF ignorance; **è di un'ignoranza spaventosa** he is appallingly ignorant
ignorare [iɲɲo'rare] VT **1** (*non conoscere*) to be ignorant *o* unaware of, not to know; **ignoravo che...** I was unaware that ..., I was ignorant of the fact that ...; **ignoravo che tu fossi qui** I was unaware *o* I didn't

Ii

know that you were here **2** (*fingere di non conoscere*) to ignore; **ha ignorato la mia domanda** he ignored my question; **mi ha ignorato completamente** she completely ignored me

ignoto, a [iɲ'ɲɔto] AGG unknown; **figlio di genitori ignoti** child of unknown parentage; **il Milite Ignoto** the Unknown Soldier
■ SM/F stranger, unknown person
■ SM: **l'ignoto** the unknown

igrometro [i'grɔmetro] SM hygrometer

igroscopico, a, ci, che [igros'kɔpiko] AGG hygroscopic

iguana [i'gwana] SF iguana

ikebana [ike'bana] SF ikebana

il [il] ART DET M (*pl(m)* i; *diventa* **lo** (*pl* **gli**) *dav s impura, gn, pn, ps, x, z; f* **la** (*pl* **le**)) **1** (*determinazione*) the; **il bambino ha la febbre** the baby has a temperature; **le ragazze non sono arrivate** the girls aren't here yet; **i figli dell'architetto** the architect's children; **lo zio di Roberta** Roberta's uncle; **gli studenti del primo anno** first-year students; **l'ora di cena** dinner time
2 (*generalizzazione, astrazione*) *gen non tradotto*; **l'uomo è un animale sociale** man is a social animal; **i cavalli dormono in piedi** horses sleep on their feet; **l'oro è un metallo prezioso** gold is a precious metal; **la leucemia** leukemia; **lo zucchero caria i denti** sugar causes tooth decay; **mi piace la musica classica** I like classical music; **non sopporto il rumore** I can't stand noise; **il bello** the beautiful; **i poveri** the poor
3 (*tempo*) the (*spesso omesso*); **siamo arrivati il lunedì di Pasqua** we arrived on Easter Monday; **la settimana prossima** next week; **l'inverno scorso** last winter; **il venerdì** *ecc* (*abitualmente*) on Fridays *ecc*; (*quel giorno*) on (the) Friday *ecc*; **riceve il venerdì** he sees people on Fridays *o* on a Friday; **la sera** in the evening; **verso le 6** at about 6 o'clock; **è partito il 20 luglio** he left on the 20th of July *o* on July the 20th (*lingua parlata*), he left on July 20th (*lingua scritta*)
4 (*distributivo*) a, an; **costano 2 euro il chilo** they cost 2 euros a *o* per kilo; **li vendono a 70 euro il paio** they are sold at 70 euros a *o* per pair; **120 km l'ora** 120 km an *o* per hour; **ne abbiamo fatto la metà** we have done half of it
5 (*partitivo*) some, any; **hai messo lo zucchero?** have you put sugar in it?; **hai comprato il pane?** did you buy (some *o* any) bread?
6 (*possesso*): **ha aperto gli occhi** he opened his eyes; **mi fa male la gamba** my leg is hurting; **prendo il caffè senza zucchero** I take my coffee without sugar; **avere i capelli neri/il naso rosso** to have dark hair/a red nose
7 (*con nomi propri*): **Plinio il giovane** Pliny the Younger; **il Petrarca** Petrarch; **il Presidente Chirac** President Chirac; **sono arrivati i Martinoni** the Martinonis have arrived; **le sorelle Clari** the Clari sisters; **ma dov'è finito il Cozzi?** whatever happened to the Cozzi boy?
8 (*con nomi geografici*): **il Tevere** the Tiber; **i Pirenei** the Pyrenees; **l'Everest** Everest; **l'Italia** Italy; **il Regno Unito** the United Kingdom

ilare ['ilare] AGG cheerful

ilarità [ilari'ta] SF hilarity, mirth

ileo ['ileo] SM (*Anat*: *intestino*) ileum; (: *osso*) hipbone, ilium

ill. ABBR (= **illustrazione, illustrato**) ill.

illanguidimento [illangwidi'mento] SM languidness, languor

illanguidire [illangwi'dire] VT to weaken
■ VI (*aus* **essere**) to grow weak *o* feeble

illazione [illat'tsjone] SF inference, deduction

illecitamente [illetʃita'mente] AVV illicitly

illecito, a [il'letʃito] AGG illicit

illegale [ille'gale] AGG illegal, unlawful

illegalità [illegali'ta] SF illegality, unlawfulness

illegalmente [illegal'mente] AVV illegally, unlawfully

illeggibile [illed'dʒibile] AGG (*scrittura*) illegible; (*romanzo*) unreadable

illegittimamente [illedʒittima'mente] AVV illegitimately

illegittimità [illedʒittimi'ta] SF illegitimacy

illegittimo, a [ille'dʒittimo] AGG illegitimate

illeso, a [il'lezo] AGG unharmed, unhurt; **è uscito illeso dall'incidente** he escaped unhurt from the accident

illetterato, a [illette'rato] AGG, SM/F illiterate

illibatezza [illiba'tettsa] SF (*verginità*) virginity; (*purezza*) purity

illibato, a [illi'bato] AGG (*vergine*) virgin; (*puro*) pure

illimitatamente [illimitata'mente] AVV (*protrarsi*) indefinitely; (*estendersi*) without limits

illimitato, a [illimi'tato] AGG (*gen*) unlimited, boundless; (*fiducia*) absolute; (*congedo, visto*) indefinite

Illinois [illi'nois] SM Illinois

illividire [illivi'dire] VI (*aus* **essere**) (*volto, mani*) to go blue; (*cielo*) to grow leaden

ill.mo ABBR = **illustrissimo**

illogicamente [illodʒika'mente] AVV illogically

illogicità [illodʒitʃi'ta] SF INV illogicality

illogico, a, ci, che [il'lɔdʒiko] AGG illogical

illudere [il'ludere] VB IRREG
■ VT to deceive, fool, delude; **non voglio illuderti** I don't want to deceive you;
▶ **illudersi** VR to deceive o.s., delude o.s.; **illudersi sul conto di qn** to be mistaken about sb; **si illuse di poter cambiare tutto** he flattered himself that he could change everything; **ti illudi se pensi di riavere i soldi** you're deceiving yourself if you think you'll get the money back; **si illudeva di trovare qn pronto ad aiutarlo** he mistakenly thought he might find sb ready to help (him)

illuminante [illumi'nante] AGG illuminating, enlightening

illuminare [illumi'nare] VT **1** (*strada, stanza*) to light; (*volto*) to illuminate; **la stanza era illuminata da un'unica lampada** the room was lit by a single lamp; **illuminare a giorno** (*con riflettori*) to floodlight; **lo stadio era illuminato a giorno** the stadium was floodlit **2** (*fig*: *informare*) to enlighten
▶ **illuminarsi** VIP (*stanza*) to grow lighter; (*volto*) to light up

illuminato, a [illumi'nato] AGG (*fig*: *sovrano, spirito*) enlightened

illuminazione [illuminat'tsjone] SF **1** (*vedi vb*) lighting, illumination; floodlighting; enlightenment **2** (*lampo di genio*) flash of inspiration

illuminismo [illumi'nizmo] SM (*Storia*): **l'Illuminismo** the Enlightenment

illusi *ecc* [il'luzi] VB *vedi* **illudere**

illusione [illu'zjone] SF illusion; **illusione ottica** optical illusion; **farsi illusioni** to deceive *o* delude o.s.; **non farti illusioni** don't delude yourself, don't kid yourself (*fam*); **ha perso ogni illusione** he has become thoroughly disillusioned

illusionismo [illuzjo'nizmo] SM conjuring
illusionista, i, e [illuzjo'nista] SM/F conjurer
illuso, a [il'luzo] PP *di* **illudere**
■ AGG deluded
■ SM/F: **sei un illuso!** you're fooling yourself!
illusoriamente [illuzorja'mente] AVV illusorily, deceptively
illusorio, ria, ri, rie [illu'zɔrjo] AGG illusory
illustrare [illus'trare] VT to illustrate
illustrativo, a [illustra'tivo] AGG illustrative; **un catalogo illustrativo** a descriptive catalogue
illustrazione [illustrat'tsjone] SF illustration
illustre [il'lustre] AGG eminent, renowned, illustrious
ILOR ['ilor] SIGLA F = **imposta locale sui redditi**
IM SIGLA = *Imperia*
imam [i'mam] SM INV imam
imbacuccare [imbakuk'kare] VT to wrap up
► **imbacuccarsi** VR to wrap (o.s.) up
imbacuccato, a [imbakuk'kato] AGG muffled up, wrapped up
imbaldanzire [imbaldan'tsire] VT to give confidence to
► **imbaldanzirsi** VIP to grow bold, get cocky *(fam)*
imballaggio, gi [imbal'laddʒo] SM **1** *(gen)* packing *no pl*; **cassa da imballaggio** packing case; **carta da imballaggio** brown paper **2** *(costo)* cost of packing
imballare[1] [imbal'lare] VT to pack
imballare[2] [imbal'lare] VT *(Aut: motore)* to race, rev up *(fam)*
► **imballarsi** VIP *(Aut)* to race
imballatore, trice [imballa'tore] SM/F packer
imballo [im'ballo] SM packing
imbalsamare [imbalsa'mare] VT to embalm; *(animale)* to stuff
imbalsamato, a [imbalsa'mato] AGG embalmed
imbalsamatore, trice [imbalsama'tore] SM/F embalmer; *(tassidermista)* taxidermist
imbalsamazione [imbalsamat'tsjone] SF embalming; *(tassidermia)* taxidermy
imbambolato, a [imbambo'lato] AGG *(sguardo, espressione)* vacant, blank
imbandierare [imbandje'rare] VT to deck with flags
imbandire [imban'dire] VT: **imbandire un banchetto** to prepare a lavish feast
imbandito, a [imban'dito] AGG: **tavola imbandita** lavishly *o* sumptuously decked table
imbarazzante [imbarat'tsante] AGG embarrassing, awkward; **una domanda imbarazzante** an awkward question; **una situazione imbarazzante** an embarrassing situation
imbarazzare [imbarat'tsare] VT **1** *(mettere a disagio)* to embarrass **2** *(ostacolare: movimenti)* to hamper; *(ingombrare: stanza)* to clutter up; *(appesantire: stomaco)* to lie heavily on
► **imbarazzarsi** VIP to become embarrassed
imbarazzato, a [imbarat'tsato] AGG *(persona)* embarrassed; **avere lo stomaco imbarazzato** to have an upset stomach; **ero così imbarazzato che non sapevo cosa dire** I was so embarrassed I didn't know what to say
imbarazzo [imba'rattso] SM **1** *(disagio)* embarrassment; **essere** *o* **trovarsi in imbarazzo** to be in an awkward situation *o* predicament; **mettere in imbarazzo** to embarrass; **la sua domanda mi ha messo in imbarazzo** her question embarrassed me; **non è riuscito a mascherare il suo imbarazzo** he couldn't hide his embarrassment **2** *(perplessità)* bewilderment, puzzlement; **avere solo l'imbarazzo della scelta** to be spoilt for choice; **non hai che l'imbarazzo della scelta** you are spoilt for choice **3** *(pesantezza)*: **imbarazzo di stomaco** indigestion
imbarbarimento [imbarbari'mento] SM *(di civiltà, costumi)* barbarization
imbarbarire [imbarba'rire] VT *(costumi)* to make less civilized; *(lingua)* to barbarize
► **imbarbarirsi** VIP *(costumi)* to become less civilized; *(lingua)* to become barbarized
imbarcadero [imbarka'dɛro] SM landing stage
imbarcare [imbar'kare] VT *(passeggeri)* to embark; *(merci)* to load; **imbarcare acqua** *(Naut)* to ship water
► **imbarcarsi** VR **1** **imbarcarsi su** *(nave)* to board, embark on; *(altro veicolo)* to board; **imbarcarsi per l'America** to sail for America **2** *(fig)* **imbarcarsi in** *(affare ecc)* to embark on
imbarcazione [imbarkat'tsjone] SF (small) boat, (small) craft *pl inv*; **imbarcazione da pesca** fishing boat
imbarco [im'barko] SM **1** *(di persone)* embarkation, boarding; *(di merci)* loading; **carta d'imbarco** boarding card; **è già cominciato l'imbarco del mio volo?** has boarding started for my flight yet? **2** *(banchina)* embarkation point, departure point
imbastardire [imbastar'dire] VT to bastardize, debase
► **imbastardirsi** VIP to degenerate, become debased
imbastire [imbas'tire] VT *(Cucito)* to baste, to tack; *(fig: piano)* to sketch out, outline
imbastitura [imbasti'tura] SF *(Cucito)* tacking
imbattersi [im'battersi] VIP: **imbattersi in** to bump *o* run into
imbattibile [imbat'tibile] AGG unbeatable, invincible
imbattuto, a [imbat'tuto] AGG unbeaten
imbavagliare [imbavaʎ'ʎare] VT *(anche fig)* to gag; **l'hanno legato e imbavagliato** they bound and gagged him
imbeccare [imbek'kare] VT *(uccelli)* to feed; *(fig)* to prompt, put words into sb's mouth
imbeccata [imbek'kata] SF *(di uccelli)* beakful of food; *(Teatro)* prompt; **dare l'imbeccata a qn** *(Teatro)* to prompt sb; *(fig)* to give sb their cue
imbecille [imbe'tʃille] AGG *(Psic)* imbecilic; *(fig)* idiotic, stupid
■ SM/F *(Psic)* idiot, imbecile; **fare l'imbecille** to play the fool
imbecillità [imbetʃilli'ta] SF INV *(Med, fig)* imbecility, idiocy; **dire imbecillità** to talk nonsense
imbellettare [imbellet'tare] VT *(viso)* to make up, put make-up on
► **imbellettarsi** VR to make o.s. up, put on one's make-up
imbellettatura [imbelletta'tura] SF *(pegg)* frill
imbellire [imbel'lire] VT to adorn, embellish
■ VI *(aus* **essere**), **imbellirsi** VIP to grow more beautiful
imberbe [im'bɛrbe] AGG beardless; **un giovanotto imberbe** a callow youth
imbestialire [imbestja'lire] VT to infuriate
► **imbestialirsi** VIP to become infuriated, fly into a rage
imbestialito, a [imbestja'lito] AGG furious, enraged
imbevere [im'bevere] VT: **imbevere qc di** to soak sth in
► **imbeversi** VIP *(anche fig)* **imbeversi di** to soak up, absorb
imbevuto, a [imbe'vuto] AGG *(spugna)*: **imbevuto (di)**

Ii

soaked (in); (*fig*: *nozioni*): **imbevuto di** imbued with

imbiancare [imbjan'kare] VT (*gen*) to whiten; (*muro*: *con il bianco di calce*) to whitewash; (: *con qualsiasi pittura*) to paint; **sepolcro imbiancato** (*fig*) whited sepulchre
■ VI (*aus* **essere**), **imbiancarsi** VIP to turn white, go white

imbiancatura [imbjanka'tura] SF (*di muro*: *con bianco di calce*) whitewashing; (: *con altre pitture*) painting

imbianchino [imbjan'kino] SM (house) painter, painter and decorator; **fa l'imbianchino** he's a painter and decorator

imbiondire [imbjon'dire] VT (*capelli*) to lighten; (*Culin*: *cipolla*) to brown
■ VI (*aus* **essere**), **imbiondirsi** VIP (*capelli*) to lighten, bleach; (*messi*) to turn golden, ripen

imbizzarrire [imbiddzar'rire] VI (*aus* **essere**), **imbizzarrirsi** VIP (*cavallo*) to become frisky, get excited

imbizzarrito, a [imbiddzar'rito] AGG (*cavallo*) skittish

imboccare [imbok'kare] VT **1** (*bambino*) to feed **2** (*tromba*) to put to one's mouth **3** (*entrare in*: *strada*) to turn into, enter

imboccatura [imbokka'tura] SF **1** (*di grotta, galleria, fiume*) mouth; (*di strada, porto*) entrance **2** (*Mus*) mouthpiece; (*per cavallo*) bit

imbocco, chi [im'bokko] SM (*di autostrada, galleria*) entrance; (*di valle*) mouth

imbonimento [imboni'mento] SM spiel, patter

imbonitore [imboni'tore] SM (*di spettacolo, circo*) barker

imborghesimento [imborgezi'mento] SM embourgeoisement

imborghesire [imborge'zire] VI (*aus* **essere**), **imborghesirsi** VIP to become bourgeois

imboscare [imbos'kare] VT (*nascondere*) to hide
▶ **imboscarsi** VR (*Mil*) to evade military service, dodge the draft (*Am*); **quei due si sono imboscati di nuovo** (*fig*) those two have disappeared again

imboscata [imbos'kata] SF ambush; **tendere un'imboscata** to lay an ambush; **l'hanno ucciso in un'imboscata** he was killed in an ambush

imboscato [imbos'kato] SM draft dodger (*Am*)

imboschimento [imboski'mento] SM afforestation

imboschire [imbos'kire] VT to afforest
▶ **imboschirsi** VIP to become wooded

imbottigliamento [imbottiʎʎa'mento] SM (*di vino*) bottling; (*di traffico*) congestion

imbottigliare [imbottiʎ'ʎare] VT **1** (*vino*) to bottle **2** (*Mil*: *nemico*) to hem in, bottle up; (: *porto*) to blockade; **siamo rimasti imbottigliati** we got stuck in a traffic jam
▶ **imbottigliarsi** VIP to get *o* be stuck in a traffic jam

imbottigliato, a [imbottiʎ'ʎato] AGG (*vino*) bottled; (*nave, esercito*) hemmed in, bottled up; (*auto*) stuck in a traffic jam

imbottigliatrice [imbottiʎʎa'tritʃe] SF bottling machine

imbottire [imbot'tire] VT (*sedia, cuscino*) to stuff; (*giacca*) to pad; (*panino*) to fill; **gli hanno imbottito la testa di idee strane** they filled his head with silly notions
▶ **imbottirsi** VR (*coprirsi*) to wrap o.s. up; (*rimpinzarsi*) **imbottirsi di** to stuff o.s. with

imbottito, a [imbot'tito] AGG (*sedia*) upholstered; (*giacca*) padded; **panino imbottito** filled roll; **un reggiseno imbottito** a padded bra

imbottitura [imbotti'tura] SF (*vedi vb*) stuffing; padding; filling

imbracare [imbra'kare] VT (*carico, container*) to secure for hoisting; (*cavallo, ferito*) to put into a harness

imbracciare [imbrat'tʃare] VT (*fucile*) to shoulder; (*scudo*) to grasp

imbranato, a [imbra'nato] (*fam*) AGG clumsy, awkward; **con le ragazze è proprio imbranato** he's hopeless with girls
■ SM/F clumsy person; **quell'imbranata non ne combina una giusta!** she's hopeless, she never does anything right!

imbrattacarte [imbratta'karte] SM/F (*pegg*) scribbler

imbrattare [imbrat'tare] VT: **imbrattare (di)** to dirty (with), smear (with), daub (with)
▶ **imbrattarsi** VR: **imbrattarsi (di)** to dirty o.s. (with)

imbrattatele [imbratta'tele] SM/F (*pegg*) dauber

imbrigliare [imbriʎ'ʎare] VT (*cavallo*) to bridle; (*acque*) to dam; (*passioni*) to curb

imbroccare [imbrok'kare] VT (*bersaglio*) to hit; (*fig*: *risposta*) to guess correctly; **non riesco mai ad imbroccarne una!** I never manage to get anything right!

imbrogliare [imbroʎ'ʎare] VT **1** (*ingannare*) to trick, deceive; (*in gioco*) to cheat; **non imbrogliare!** don't cheat! **2** (*confondere*: *documenti*) to muddle up; (: *idee*) to confuse, muddle, mix up; (: *fili*) to tangle up; **e per imbrogliare la faccenda...** and to complicate matters ...; **imbrogliare le carte** to confuse the issue **3** (*Naut*: *vele*) to clew up
▶ **imbrogliarsi** VIP (*vedi vt 2*) to become muddled up; to become confused, become muddled, get mixed up; to get tangled up; **s'imbrogliò nel parlare** his speech became confused

imbroglio, gli [im'brɔʎʎo] SM **1** (*truffa*) swindle, con (*fam*); **niente imbrogli!** no cheating! **2** (*groviglio*) tangle; (*fig*: *situazione confusa*) mess; **cacciarsi in un imbroglio** to get into a mess

imbroglione, a [imbroʎ'ʎone] SM/F cheat, swindler
■ AGG dishonest; **un affarista imbroglione** a dishonest businessman

imbronciarsi [imbron'tʃarsi] VIP (*persona*) to sulk; (*cielo*) to cloud over

imbronciato, a [imbron'tʃato] AGG (*persona*) sulky; (*cielo*) cloudy, threatening

imbrunire [imbru'nire] (*aus* **essere**) VI, VB IMPERS to grow dark
■ SM: **all'imbrunire** at dusk

imbruttire [imbrut'tire] VT to make ugly
■ VI (*aus* **essere**), **imbruttirsi** VIP to grow ugly

imbucare [imbu'kare] VT to post, mail (*Am*)
▶ **imbucarsi** VR (*fam*) to gate-crash

imbufalirsi [imbufa'lirsi] VIP (*fam*) to go up the wall

imbullonare [imbullo'nare] VT to bolt

imburrare [imbur'rare] VT to butter; (*stampo, teglia*) to grease

imbutiforme [imbuti'forme] AGG funnel-shaped

imbuto [im'buto] SM funnel

imene [i'mɛne] SM hymen

imitare [imi'tare] VT (*gen*) to imitate; (*Teatro*) to impersonate, do an impression of; (*gesti*) to mimic; (*firma*) to forge; **un materiale che imita il cuoio** a material which looks like leather

imitativo, a [imita'tivo] AGG imitative

imitatore, trice [imita'tore] SM/F (*gen*) imitator; (*Teatro*) impersonator, impressionist

imitazione [imitat'tsjone] SF (*vedi vb*) imitation, impersonation, impression; mimicry; forgery

immacolato, a [immako'lato] AGG immaculate, spotless; **l'Immacolata Concezione** (*Rel*) the Immaculate Conception

immagazzinaggio, gi [immagaddzi'naddʒo] SM (*di merce, energia*) storing
immagazzinamento [immagaddzina'mento] SM (*di merce, energia*) storing; (*di nozioni, idee*) accumulation
immagazzinare [immagaddzi'nare] VT (*merce, energia*) to store; (*nozioni, idee*) to accumulate
immaginabile [immadʒi'nabile] AGG conceivable, imaginable
immaginare [immadʒi'nare] VT **1** (*credere, supporre*) to imagine, suppose; **immaginare che** to imagine *o* think that; **me lo immaginavo più giovane** I'd thought he was younger; **me lo immaginavo** I thought as much; **me lo immaginavo!** I thought so!; **dovevo immaginarmelo** I should have expected it; **non riesco ad immaginarlo** I can't imagine it; **immagina di essere su un'isola deserta...** imagine you're on a desert island ... **2** (*in espressioni di cortesia*): **s'immagini!** don't mention it!, not at all!; **grazie mille! – S'immagini!** thank you very much! – Don't mention it!
immaginariamente [immadʒinarja'mente] AVV in an imaginary way
immaginario, ria, ri, rie [immadʒi'narjo] AGG imaginary; (*mondo*) make-believe; **un malato immaginario** a hypochondriac
■ SM: **l'immaginario collettivo** the collective imagination
immaginativa [immadʒina'tiva] SF imagination; **mancare d'immaginativa** to lack imagination
immaginativo, a [immadʒina'tivo] AGG imaginative
immaginazione [immadʒinat'tsjone] SF imagination; **è frutto della tua immaginazione** it's a figment of your imagination
immagine [im'madʒine] SF (*gen, Fis*) image; (*rappresentazione, fotografia*) picture; **una bella immagine** a nice picture; **è l'immagine della salute** he's the picture of health; **è l'immagine di suo padre** he's the image of his father; **avere nella mente l'immagine di qn/qc** to have a mental picture of sb/sth; **diritto all'immagine** (*Dir*) right to privacy (*prohibiting unauthorised publication of photographs of a person*); **salvaguardare la propria immagine pubblica** to safeguard one's public image; **immagine dell'azienda** (*Comm*) corporate image *o* identity
immaginoso, a [immadʒi'noso] AGG (*linguaggio, stile*) full of imagery
immalinconire [immalinko'nire] VT to sadden, depress
▶ **immalinconirsi** VIP to become depressed, become melancholy
immancabile [imman'kabile] AGG unfailing; **ecco l'immancabile Giovanna** here comes Giovanna as usual
immancabilmente [immankabil'mente] AVV without fail, unfailingly
immane [im'mane] AGG (*smisurato*) huge; (*spaventoso, inumano*) terrible
immanente [imma'nɛnte] AGG (*Filosofia*) inherent, immanent
immanentismo [immanen'tizmo] SM (*Filosofia*) immanentism
immanenza [imma'nɛntsa] SF (*Filosofia*) immanence
immangiabile [imman'dʒabile] AGG (*non commestibile*) inedible; (*ripugnante*) uneatable, unpalatable; **il cibo era immangiabile** the food was inedible; **è immangiabile** I can't stomach it
immateriale [immate'rjale] AGG incorporeal, immaterial
immatricolare [immatriko'lare] VT (*veicolo*) to register
▶ **immatricolarsi** VR (*Univ*) to matriculate, enrol
immatricolazione [immatrikolat'tsjone] SF (*vedi vb*) registration; matriculation, enrolment
immaturamente [immatura'mente] AVV prematurely
immaturità [immaturi'ta] SF immaturity
immaturo, a [imma'turo] AGG (*frutto*) unripe; (*persona*) immature; (*neonato*) premature; **un ragazzo immaturo** an immature boy
immedesimarsi [immedezi'marsi] VR: **immedesimarsi in** to identify with; **immedesimarsi nella parte** (*Cine, Teatro*) to get into a part, live a part
immedesimazione [immedezimat'tsjone] SF: **immedesimazione (in)** identification (with)
immediatamente [immedjata'mente] AVV (*subito*) immediately, at once; (*direttamente*) immediately; **vai immediatamente dal medico!** go and see the doctor immediately!
immediatezza [immedja'tettsa] SF immediacy
immediato, a [imme'djato] AGG (*gen*) immediate; (*intervento*) prompt
immemorabile [immemo'rabile] AGG immemorial; **da tempo immemorabile** from time immemorial
immemore [im'mɛmore] AGG (*letter*): **immemore di** forgetful of
immensamente [immensa'mente] AVV immensely, infinitely
immensità [immensi'ta] SF immensity
immenso, a [im'mɛnso] AGG (*gen*) immense, huge; (*spazio*) boundless; (*folla*) huge, enormous; (*fig: dolore, tristezza*) immense; **odio immenso** deep hatred; **c'era un giardino immenso** there was a huge garden
immergere [im'mɛrdʒere] VB IRREG, VT (*gen*) to immerse, plunge; **immergere in acqua** (*mani*) to put in water; (*stoffa*) to soak in water; **ha immerso il metallo incandescente nell'acqua** he plunged the red-hot metal into the water; **immerso nello studio** immersed *o* absorbed in one's studies;
▶ **immergersi** VR to plunge; (*sommergibile*) to dive, submerge; **immergersi in** (*fig*) to immerse o.s. in, become absorbed in
immeritatamente [immeritata'mente] AVV (*senza merito*) undeservedly; (*senza colpa*) unjustly
immeritato, a [immeri'tato] AGG (*non meritato*) undeserved, unmerited; (*ingiusto*) unjust
immeritevole [immeri'tevole] AGG undeserving, unworthy
immersione [immer'sjone] SF **1** (*gen*) immersion; (*di sommergibile*) submersion, dive; (*Sport*) diving; (*di palombaro*) dive; **navigare in immersione** to sail underwater; **linea di immersione** (*Naut*) water line **2** (*Geol*) hade
▷ www.fias.it
immerso, a [im'mɛrso] PP *di* immergere
immesso, a [im'messo] PP *di* immettere
immettere [im'mettere] VT IRREG: **immettere (in)** (*gen*) to introduce (into); **immettere aria nei polmoni** to take air into the lungs; **immettere dati in un computer** to feed information into a computer, enter data on a computer
immigrante [immi'grante] AGG, SM/F immigrant
immigrare [immi'grare] VI (*aus* **essere**) to immigrate
immigrato, a [immi'grato] AGG, SM/F immigrant
immigrazione [immigrat'tsjone] SF immigration

imminente [immi'nɛnte] AGG imminent
imminenza [immi'nɛntsa] SF imminence
immischiare [immis'kjare] VT to involve; **immischiare qn in** to involve sb in; **trovarsi immischiato in uno scandalo** to find o.s. mixed up *o* involved in a scandal
▸ **immischiarsi** VIP: **immischiarsi in** to interfere *o* meddle in
immiscibile [immiʃ'ʃibile] AGG (*Chim*) immiscible
immiserimento [immizeri'mento] SM impoverishment
immiserire [immize'rire] VT to impoverish
immissario, ri [immis'sarjo] SM (*Geog*) affluent, tributary
immissione [immis'sjone] SF (*gen*) introduction; (*Tecn, Med*) intake; **immissione di dati** (*Inform*) data entry
immobile [im'mɔbile] AGG motionless, stationary, still; **è rimasto lì, immobile** he stood there, motionless
■ SM item of real estate; **(beni) immobili** real estate *sg*
immobiliare [immobi'ljare] AGG property *attr*; **patrimonio immobiliare** real estate; **agenzia immobiliare** estate agent's (*Brit*), realtor (*Am*); **società immobiliare** property company
■ SF = società immobiliare
immobilismo [immobi'lizmo] SM (*Pol*) opposition to progress
immobilità [immobili'ta] SF immobility; **immobilità politica** political inertia
immobilizzare [immobilid'dzare] VT (*gen*) to immobilize; (*Econ*: *capitali*) to lock up
immobilizzato, a [immobilid'dzato] AGG (*gen*) immobilized; **essere immobilizzato a letto** to be confined to bed
immobilizzazione [immobiliddzat'tsjone] SF (*vedi vb*) immobilization; locking up; **immobilizzazioni tecniche** (*Econ*) fixed assets
immobilizzo [immobi'liddzo] SM: **spese d'immobilizzo** capital expenditure
immodestia [immo'destja] SF immodesty
immodesto, a [immo'dɛsto] AGG immodest, conceited
immolare [immo'lare] VT: **immolare (a)** to sacrifice (to)
▸ **immolarsi** VR: **immolarsi per** to sacrifice o.s. for
immolazione [immolat'tsjone] SF sacrifice
immondezzaio, ai [immondet'tsajo] SM rubbish dump
immondizia [immon'dittsja] SF (*spazzatura*) rubbish *no pl*, refuse *no pl*, trash *no pl* (*Am*)
immondo, a [im'mondo] AGG (*luogo*) filthy, foul; (*azione*) base, vile
immorale [immo'rale] AGG immoral
immoralità [immorali'ta] SF immorality
immoralmente [immoral'mente] AVV immorally
immortalare [immorta'lare] VT to immortalize
▸ **immortalarsi** VIP to win immortality for o.s.
immortale [immor'tale] AGG immortal
immortalità [immortali'ta] SF immortality
immotivato, a [immoti'vato] AGG (*azione*) unmotivated; (*critica*) groundless
immune [im'mune] AGG: **immune da** (*esente*) exempt from; (*Med*) immune to; (*Dir*) immune from
immunità [immuni'ta] SF (*Med, Dir*) immunity; **immunità diplomatica** diplomatic immunity; **immunità parlamentare** ≈ parliamentary privilege
immunizzare [immunid'dzare] VT: **immunizzare contro** to immunize against
▸ **immunizzarsi** VR (*fig*) **immunizzarsi contro** to become immune to
immunizzazione [immuniddzat'tsjone] SF immunization
immunodeficienza [immunodefi'tʃɛntsa] SF: **sindrome da immunodeficienza acquista** acquired immunodeficiency syndrome
immunodepresso, a [immunode'presso] AGG immunodepressed
immunologia [immunolo'dʒia] SF immunology
immunologico, a, ci, che [immuno'lɔdʒiko] AGG immunological
immunostimolante [immunostimo'lante] AGG immunostimulant
immunostimolatore [immunostimola'tore] SM immunostimulant
immunoterapia [immunotera'pia] SF immunotherapy
immusonirsi [immuzo'nirsi] VIP (*fam*) to sulk
immusonito, a [immuzo'nito] AGG sulky
immutabile [immu'tabile] AGG (*gen*) unchanging; (*decreto, decisione*) immutable
immutato, a [immu'tato] AGG unchanged
impaccare [impak'kare] VT to pack
impaccatura [impakka'tura] SF packaging
impacchettare [impakket'tare] VT to wrap up, parcel up; **devo impacchettare il regalo** I've got to wrap up the present
impacciare [impat'tʃare] VT to hamper, hinder; **impacciare qn nei movimenti** to hamper sb's movements
impacciatamente [impattʃata'mente] AVV (*muoversi*) clumsily; (*rispondere*) awkwardly, with embarrassment
impacciato, a [impat'tʃato] AGG **1** (*imbarazzato*) embarrassed; **mi sentivo un po' impacciato** I felt a bit awkward **2** (*goffo*) awkward, clumsy
impaccio, ci [im'pattʃo] SM **1** (*imbarazzo*) embarrassment; (*situazione imbarazzante*) awkward situation; **trarsi d'impaccio** to get out of an awkward situation **2** (*ostacolo*) obstacle; **essere d'impaccio a qn** to be in sb's way
impacco, chi [im'pakko] SM (*Med*) compress; **dovrai fare degli impacchi freddi** you'll have to apply cold compresses
impadronirsi [impadro'nirsi] VIP: **impadronirsi di** (*città, ricchezze*) to seize, take possession of; (*fig*: *lingua*) to master
impagabile [impa'gabile] AGG priceless
impaginare [impadʒi'nare] VT (*Tip*) to make up
impaginazione [impadʒinat'tsjone] SF (*Tip*) make-up
impagliare [impaʎ'ʎare] VT **1** (*animale*: *imbalsamare*) to stuff (with straw) **2** **impagliare una sedia** to cane a chair
impagliatore, trice [impaʎʎa'tore] SM/F (*di animali*) taxidermist; (*di sedie*) chair-mender
impala [im'pala] SM INV (*Zool*) impala
impalare [impa'lare] VT **1** (*persona*) to impale **2** (*viti, piante*) to stake, prop up
▸ **impalarsi** VIP (*fig*: *bloccarsi*) to stand stock-still
impalato, a [impa'lato] AGG (*fig*) stock-still; **non startene lì impalato, fai qualcosa!** don't just stand there, do something!
impalcatura [impalka'tura] SF scaffolding; (*fig*) framework, structure
impallarsi [impal'larsi] VR (*fam*: *computer*) to freeze

impallidire [impalli'dire] VI (*aus* **essere**) to turn pale; (*colore, ricordo*) to fade; **è impallidito per la paura** he went pale with fear

impallinare [impalli'nare] VT to riddle with shot

impalpabile [impal'pabile] AGG impalpable

impalpabilmente [impalpabil'mente] AVV impalpably

impanare [impa'nare] VT **1** (*Culin*) to roll (*o* coat) in breadcrumbs, bread (*Am*) **2** (*Tecn*: *vite*) to thread

impanatura [impana'tura] SF **1** (*vedi vb*) coating in breadcrumbs; threading **2** (*Culin*) breadcrumbs *pl*

impantanarsi [impanta'narsi] VIP to sink into mud; (*fig*) to get bogged down; **la nostra macchina si è impantanata** our car got stuck in the mud

impaperarsi [impape'rarsi] VIP to stumble over a word

impappinarsi [impappi'narsi] VIP to falter, stammer; **si è impappinata per l'emozione** she stammered with emotion

imparabile [impa'rabile] AGG (*Sport*: *tiro, pallone*) unstoppable

imparare [impa'rare] VT to learn; **imparare a fare qc** to learn to do sth; **sto imparando a suonare la chitarra** I'm learning to play the guitar; **imparare qc a memoria** to learn sth (off) by heart; **l'ha imparata a memoria** he's learnt it by heart; **imparare qc a proprie spese** to learn sth to one's cost; **così impari!** that'll teach you!; **sbagliando s'impara** (*Proverbio*) practice makes perfect

imparaticcio, ci [impara'tittʃo] SM half-baked notions *pl*

impareggiabile [impared'dʒabile] AGG incomparable

impareggiabilmente [impareddʒabil'mente] AVV incomparably

imparentare [imparen'tare] VT (*famiglie*) to ally by marriage
▶ **imparentarsi** VIP: **imparentarsi con** to marry into, become related by marriage to

imparentato, a [imparen'tato] AGG: **essere imparentato con** to be related by marriage to

impari ['impari] AGG INV (*disuguale*) unequal

impartire [impar'tire] VT (*ordine*) to give; (*benedizione*) to bestow

imparziale [impar'tsjale] AGG impartial, unbiased

imparzialità [impartsjali'ta] SF impartiality

impasse [ɛ̃'pas] SF INV (*fig*) impasse

impassibile [impas'sibile] AGG impassive

impastare [impas'tare] VT (*pane*) to knead; (*cemento, malta*) to mix

impastato, a [impas'tato] AGG: **impastato di fango** covered in mud; **avere la lingua impastata** to have a furry tongue; **avere gli occhi impastati di sonno** to be half asleep

impasticcarsi [impastik'karsi] VR (*fam*) to pop pills

impasticcato, a [impastik'kato] AGG (*fam*) pill-popping

impasto [im'pasto] SM **1** (*l'impastare*: *di pane*) kneading; (: *cemento*) mixing **2** (*pasta*) dough; (*miscuglio, anche fig*) mixture, blend

impatto [im'patto] SM (*urto, effetto*) impact; **impatto ambientale** impact on the environment

impaurire [impau'rire] VT to frighten, scare; **mi hai impaurito** you frightened me
▶ **impaurirsi** VIP to get *o* grow scared *o* frightened

impavidamente [impavida'mente] AVV fearlessly

impavido, a [im'pavido] AGG intrepid, fearless

impaziente [impat'tsjɛnte] AGG impatient; **impaziente di fare qc** eager to do sth

impazientemente [impattsjente'mente] AVV impatiently

impazienza [impat'tsjɛntsa] SF (*vedi agg*) impatience; eagerness

impazzata [impat'tsata] **all'impazzata** AVV (*correre*) at breakneck speed; (*colpire*) wildly

impazzire [impat'tsire] VI (*aus* **essere**) **1** to go mad; **impazzire per qn/qc** to be mad *o* crazy about sb/sth; **impazzire per lo sport/il gelato** to be mad about sport/ice cream; **impazzire per il dolore** to go mad with grief; **far impazzire qn** to drive sb mad; **questo compito mi fa impazzire** this homework's driving me mad; **impazzisco d'amore per te** I'm mad *o* crazy about you; **ma sei impazzito?** have you gone mad?; **sono impazzito a cercare un taxi** I nearly went crazy trying to find a taxi; **ho un mal di testa da impazzire** I've got a splitting headache; **ho un prurito da impazzire** I've got an itch that's driving me mad **2** (*Culin*: *salsa, maionese*) to curdle

impeccabile [impek'kabile] AGG impeccable; **ha un gusto impeccabile** she's got impeccable taste; **in modo impeccabile** impeccably; **si veste sempre in modo impeccabile** he's always impeccably dressed

impeccabilmente [impekkabil'mente] AVV impeccably

impedenza [impe'dɛntsa] SF (*Fis*) impedance

impedimento [impedi'mento] SM **1** (*ostacolo*) obstacle, hindrance; **essere un impedimento** *o* **d'impedimento a qc/qn** to stand in the way of sth/sb **2** (*Dir*) impediment

impedire [impe'dire] VT **1** (*proibire*): **impedire a qn di fare qc** to prevent *o* stop sb (from) doing sth; **il rumore mi ha impedito di dormire** the noise stopped me sleeping; **l'hanno messo per impedire alle macchine di parcheggiare** they put it there to stop cars parking; **chi ti impedisce di farlo?** who's stopping you? **2** (*ostruire*) to obstruct **3** (*impacciare*) to hamper, hinder; **era impedita dal vestito lungo** she was hampered by her long dress

impegnare [impeɲ'ɲare] VT **1** (*dare in pegno*) to pawn **2** (*vincolare*) to bind **3** (*sogg*: *lavoro*) to keep busy; **quel compito di matematica ha impegnato tutta la classe** the maths exercise kept the whole class busy **4** (*Mil*) to engage; (*Sport*) to put under pressure
▶ **impegnarsi** VR (*vincolarsi*) **impegnarsi a fare qc** to undertake to do sth; **impegnarsi con un contratto** to enter into a contract; **impegnarsi con qn** (*accordarsi*) to come to an agreement with sb; **impegnarsi in qc** (*dedicarsi*) to devote o.s. to sth

impegnativa [impeɲɲa'tiva] SF (*Amm*) ≈ referral (*Health Service authorization for hospital or specialist treatment*)

impegnativo, a [impeɲɲa'tivo] AGG (*lavoro*) demanding; (*promessa*) binding; **un lavoro impegnativo** a demanding job

impegnato, a [impeɲ'ɲato] AGG **1** (*persona*: *occupata*) busy; **sono già impegnato** I have a prior engagement; **oggi sono molto impegnato** I'm very busy today; **mi sembra che sia più impegnato di te** I think he's busier than you; **essere impegnato con** (*lavoro*) to be busy with; (*ditta*) to be involved with **2** (*gioielli*) pawned **3** (*fig*: *romanzo, autore, film*) serious, engagé

impegno [im'peɲɲo] SM **1** (*obbligo*) obligation; (*promessa*) promise, pledge; (*compito, di scrittore*) commitment; **assumere un impegno** to take on a commitment; **penso di venire, ma senza impegno** I'll probably come but I can't promise; **domani non posso, ho un impegno** I can't tomorrow, I've got something on; **ha molti impegni di lavoro** she has a lot of work commitments **2** (*affare, incombenza*) engagement, appointment; **un impegno precedente** a previous engagement **3** (*zelo*) enthusiasm, diligence; **studiare con impegno** to study hard

impegolarsi [impego'larsi], **impelagarsi** [impela'garsi] VR: **impegolarsi in** to get heavily involved in

impellente [impel'lɛnte] AGG pressing, urgent; **un bisogno impellente** an urgent need

impellicciato, a [impellit'tʃato] AGG dressed in furs

impenetrabile [impene'trabile] AGG (*volto*) inscrutable; (*mistero*) complete; (*segreto*) closely-guarded; (*bosco*) impenetrable

impenitente [impeni'tɛnte] AGG impenitent, unrepentant; **scapolo impenitente** confirmed bachelor

impennacchiarsi [impennak'kjarsi] VR (*scherz*) to get all dolled up

impennare [impen'nare] VT (*Aer*): **far impennare l'aereo** to go into a climb
▶ **impennarsi** VIP **1** (*aereo*) to go into a climb; (*cavallo*) to rear (up) **2** (*fig: arrabbiarsi*) to flare up

impennata [impen'nata] SF **1** (*di cavallo*) rearing (up); (*di aereo*) climb, nose-up; (*di motociclo*) wheelie **2** (*fig: scatto d'ira*) burst of anger **3** (*rialzo: di prezzi, valuta*) sharp rise

impensabile [impen'sabile] AGG (*inaccettabile*) unthinkable; (*difficile da concepire*) inconceivable

impensato, a [impen'sato] AGG unexpected, unforeseen

impensierire [impensje'rire] VT to worry
▶ **impensierirsi** VIP: **impensierirsi (per)** to worry (about)

imperante [impe'rante] AGG (*tendenza, moda*) prevailing

imperare [impe'rare] VI (*aus* **avere**) (*anche fig*) to rule, reign

imperativo, a [impera'tivo] AGG (*tono, discorso*) commanding; (*Gramm*) imperative
■ SM (*Gramm*): **l'imperativo** the imperative

imperatore, trice [impera'tore] SM/F emperor/ empress

impercettibile [impertʃet'tibile] AGG imperceptible

impercettibilmente [impertʃettibil'mente] AVV imperceptibly

imperdonabile [imperdo'nabile] AGG unforgivable, unpardonable

imperdonabilmente [imperdonabil'mente] AVV unforgivably, unpardonably

imperfettamente [imperfetta'mente] AVV imperfectly

imperfetto, a [imper'fɛtto] AGG (*gen, Gramm*) imperfect; (*difettoso*) faulty, defective; (*incompleto*) unfinished
■ SM (*Gramm*): **l'imperfetto** the imperfect (tense)

imperfezione [imperfet'tsjone] SF (*gen*) imperfection; (*di gioiello*) flaw; (*della pelle*) blemish, imperfection

imperiale [impe'rjale] AGG imperial

imperialismo [imperja'lizmo] SM imperialism

imperialista, i, e [imperja'lista] AGG, SM/F imperialist

imperialistico, a, ci, che [imperja'listiko] AGG imperialist(ic)

imperiese [impe'rjese] AGG of *o* from Imperia
■ SM/F inhabitant *o* native of Imperia

imperiosamente [imperjosa'mente] AVV imperiously

imperioso, a [impe'rjoso] AGG (*autoritario: persona, tono*) imperious; (*motivo, esigenza*) urgent, pressing

imperituro, a [imperi'turo] AGG (*letter*) everlasting

imperizia [impe'rittsja] SF inexperience, lack of experience

imperlare [imper'lare] VT: **il sudore gli imperlava la fronte** his brow was beaded with perspiration, beads of sweat formed on his forehead
▶ **imperlarsi** VIP: **imperlarsi di sudore** to be (*o* become) beaded with perspiration

impermalire [imperma'lire] VT: **far impermalire qn** to offend sb
▶ **impermalirsi** VIP: **impermalirsi (per)** to take offence *o* umbrage (at)

impermeabile [imperme'abile] AGG (*terreno, roccia*) impermeable; (*tessuto*) waterproof; (*orologio*) water-resistant; **essere impermeabile alle offese** to be thick-skinned, have a thick skin; **tessuto impermeabile** waterproof material
■ SM (*indumento*) raincoat, mac (*Brit*)

impermeabilizzare [impermeabilid'dzare] VT to waterproof

impermeabilizzazione [impermeabiliddzat'tsjone] SF waterproofing

imperniare [imper'njare] VT: **imperniare qc su** to hinge sth on; (*fig: discorso, relazione*) to base sth on; **il mio discorso è imperniato su un unico concetto** my talk hinges on one basic concept
▶ **imperniarsi** VIP (*fig*) **imperniarsi su** to be based on

impero [im'pɛro] SM empire; **l'impero della ragione** (*fig*) the rule of reason; **impero romano** Roman Empire; **impero romano d'oriente** Eastern Roman Empire
■ AGG INV Empire *attr*

imperscrutabile [imperskru'tabile] AGG inscrutable

imperscrutabilità [imperskrutabili'ta] SF inscrutability

impersonale [imperso'nale] AGG impersonal

impersonalità [impersonali'ta] SF impersonality

impersonare [imperso'nare] VT **1** (*qualità, concetto astratto*) to personify **2** (*Teatro*) to play (the part of), act (the part of)
▶ **impersonarsi** VIP (*incarnarsi*) **in lei s'impersona la cupidigia** she is the personification of greed

LO SAPEVI...?
impersonare non si traduce mai con la parola inglese *impersonate*

imperterrito, a [imper'tɛrrito] AGG unperturbed; **continuare imperterrito (a fare qc)** to carry on (doing sth) regardless *o* unperturbed; **è rimasto imperterrito quando gliel'ho detto** he was unperturbed when I told him

impertinente [imperti'nɛnte] AGG impertinent

impertinenza [imperti'nɛntsa] SF impertinence

imperturbabile [imperturbabile] AGG imperturbable

imperturbabilità [imperturbabili'ta] SF imperturbability

imperturbato, a [impertur'bato] AGG unperturbed

imperversare [imperver'sare] VI (*aus* **avere**) (*persona, tempesta, malattia*) to rage; (*scherz: moda, costumi*) to be all the rage

impervio, via, vi, vie [im'pɛrvjo] AGG (*luogo*) inaccessible; (*strada*) impassable

> **LO SAPEVI...?**
> **impervio** non si traduce mai con la parola inglese *impervious*

impetigine [impe'tidʒine] SF (*Med*) impetigo
impeto ['impeto] SM (*moto, forza*) force, impetus; (*assalto*) onslaught; (*fig: d'odio, amore*) surge; **lo uccise in un impeto d'ira** he killed him in a fit of rage; **agire d'impeto** to act on impulse; **con impeto** (*parlare*) forcefully, energetically
impetrare [impe'trare] VT (*letter*) to beg for, beseech
impettinabile [impetti'nabile] AGG (*capelli*) unruly
impettito, a [impet'tito] AGG: **essere tutto impettito** to be as stiff as a ramrod; **camminare impettito** to strut
impetuosamente [impetuosa'mente] AVV (*reagire*) impetuously; (*soffiare: vento*) violently, furiously
impetuosità [impetuosi'ta] SF impetuosity
impetuoso, a [impetu'oso] AGG (*gen*) impetuous; (*vento, corrente*) raging, strong
impiallacciare [impjallat'tʃare] VT (*mobile*) to veneer
impiallacciatura [impjallattʃa'tura] SF (*tecnica*) veneering; (*materiale*) veneer
impiantare [impjan'tare] VT (*installare*) to install; (*avviare: azienda*) to set up, establish
impiantistica [impjan'tistika] SF plant design and installation
impiantito [impjan'tito] SM flooring, floor
impianto [im'pjanto] SM **1** (*installazione*) installation; **spese d'impianto** installation costs **2** (*Anat: di embrione*) implantation **3** (*apparecchiature*) plant; (*sistema*) system; **impianti di risalita** (*Sci*) ski lifts; **impianto elettrico** wiring; **impianto industriale** plant; **impianto di raffreddamento** cooling system; **impianto di riscaldamento** heating system; **impianto sportivo** sports complex; **impianto stereo** stereo system
impiastrare [impjas'trare], **impiastricciare** [impjastrit'tʃare] VT: **impiastrare di** (*fango ecc*) to dirty with; (*pittura, trucco*) to smear with
impiastro [im'pjastro] SM **1** (*Med*) poultice **2** (*fig fam: persona*) nuisance
impiccagione [impikka'dʒone] SF hanging
impiccare [impik'kare] VT to hang; **l'hanno impiccato** he was hanged; **questo colletto m'impicca** (*fig*) this collar's choking me; **non lo farò nemmeno se m'impicchi!** there's no way I'll do that!
▶ **impiccarsi** VR to hang o.s.; **si è impiccato** he hanged himself; **impiccati!** (*fam*) go to hell!
impiccato, a [impik'kato] SM/F hanged man/woman
impicciare [impit'tʃare] VT (*sogg: persona, tavolo*) to be in the way of, get in the way of; (*: abiti*) to hinder, hamper
▶ **impicciarsi** VIP to meddle, interfere; **impicciarsi di** *o* **in qc** to interfere *o* meddle in sth; **impicciati degli affari tuoi!** mind your own business!
impiccio, ci [im'pittʃo] SM **1** (*ostacolo*) hindrance; (*seccatura*) trouble, bother; **essere d'impiccio** to be in the way **2** (*affare imbrogliato*) mess *no pl*; **cavare** *o* **togliere qn dagli impicci** to get sb out of trouble
impiccione, a [impit'tʃone] SM/F busybody; **essere impiccione** to be a busybody
impiccolimento [impikkoli'mento] SM (*di immagine*) reduction
impiccolire [impikko'lire] VT to make smaller, reduce
■ VI (*aus* **essere**), **impiccolirsi** VIP to get smaller
impiegabile [impje'gabile] AVV usable
impiegare [impje'gare] VT **1** (*utilizzare*) to use, employ; (*: tempo*) to spend; (*metterci: tempo*) to take; (*investire: denaro*) to invest; **impiega il tempo libero a dipingere** he spends his free time painting; **impiego un quarto d'ora per andare a casa** it takes me *o* I take a quarter of an hour to get home; **ho impiegato più di due ore a fare i compiti** it took me more than two hours to do my homework; **quanto ci impieghi per arrivare a scuola?** how long does it take you to get to school? **2** (*lavoratore*) to employ
▶ **impiegarsi** VR to get a job, obtain employment
impiegatizio, zia, zi, zie [impjega'tittsjo] AGG clerical, white-collar *attr*; **il ceto impiegatizio** clerical *o* white-collar workers *pl*
impiegato, a [impje'gato] SM/F employee; **impiegato di banca** bank clerk; **impiegato statale** state employee
impiego, ghi [im'pjɛgo] SM **1** (*gen*) use; (*Econ*) investment **2** (*occupazione*) employment; (*posto di lavoro*) post, (regular) job; **un impiego fisso** a permanent job; **pubblico impiego** public sector
impietosire [impjeto'sire] VT to move (to pity)
▶ **impietosirsi** VIP to be moved (to pity)
impietoso, a [impje'toso] AGG pitiless, cruel
impietrire [impje'trire] VT (*anche fig*) to petrify
impigliare [impiʎ'ʎare] VT to catch, entangle
▶ **impigliarsi** VIP: **impigliarsi (in qc)** to get caught *o* entangled (in sth)
impigrire [impi'grire] VT to make lazy
■ VI (*aus* **essere**), **impigrirsi** VIP to get *o* grow lazy
impilare [impi'lare] VT to stack, pile (up)
impinguare [impin'gware] VT (*fig: tasche, casse dello Stato*) to fill; (*maiale*) to fatten
impiombare [impjom'bare] VT **1** (*saldare: tubo ecc*) to seal (with lead); (*sigillare: baule, cassa*) to seal **2** (*dente*) to fill
implacabile [impla'kabile] AGG implacable
implacabilità [implakabili'ta] SF implacability
implacabilmente [implakabil'mente] AVV implacably
implantologia [implantolo'dʒia] SF (*tecnica di trapianto: di capelli*) hair-replacement; (*: di denti*) implantology
implementare [implemen'tare] VT (*Inform*) to implement; (*progetto*) to carry out
implicare [impli'kare] VT **1** (*sottintendere*) to imply; (*comportare*) to entail **2** (*coinvolgere*): **implicare qn (in)** to involve sb (in), implicate sb (in); **essere implicato in un omicidio** to be involved in a murder
▶ **implicarsi** VR: **implicarsi (in)** to get *o* become involved (in)
implicazione [implikat'tsjone] SF implication
implicitamente [implitʃita'mente] AVV implicitly
implicito, a [im'plitʃito] AGG implicit
implorante [implo'rante] AGG imploring, beseeching
implorare [implo'rare] VT to implore, beseech
implorazione [implorat'tsjone] SF plea, entreaty
impluvio, vi [im'pluvjo] SM (*Geol*): **linea di impluvio** watershed
impollinare [impolli'nare] VT to pollinate
impollinazione [impollinat'tsjone] SF pollination
impoltronirsi [impoltro'nirsi] VIP to become lazy
impolverare [impolve'rare] VT to cover with dust
▶ **impolverarsi** VIP to get dusty
impomatare [impoma'tare] VT (*capelli*) to pomade; (*baffi*) to wax; (*pelle*) to put ointment on
▶ **impomatarsi** VR (*fam*) to get spruced up
imponderabile [imponde'rabile] AGG, SM imponderable
impone *ecc* [im'pone] VB *vedi* **imporre**

imponente [impo'nɛnte] AGG (*persona, monumento*) imposing, impressive; **un edificio imponente** an impressive building

impongo *ecc* [im'pongo] VB *vedi* **imporre**

imponibile [impo'nibile] AGG taxable; **reddito imponibile** taxable income
■SM taxable income

impopolare [impopo'lare] AGG unpopular; **un provvedimento impopolare** an unpopular measure

impopolarità [impopolari'ta] SF unpopularity

imporporare [imporpo'rare] VT (*sogg: tramonto*) to redden
▶ **imporporarsi** VIP (*cielo*) to redden; (*persona*) to blush, go red

imporre [im'porre] VB IRREG, VT (*gen*) to impose; (*compito*) to set, impose; (*condizioni*) to impose, lay down; **imporre qc a qn** to impose sth on sb; **imporre a qn di fare qc** to oblige *o* force sb to do sth, make sb do sth; **imporre la propria autorità** to assert one's authority, make one's authority felt; **imporre la propria volontà** to have one's way; **imporsi qc** to impose sth on o.s.; **imporsi di fare qc** to make o.s. do sth, force o.s. to do sth
▶ **imporsi** VR **1** (*farsi valere*) to assert o.s., make o.s. respected; **si è imposto sugli altri per la sua competenza** he commanded the others' respect because of his ability **2** (*aver successo: musicista, attore, sportivo*) to come to the fore, become popular; **imporsi al pubblico** to come into the public eye
▶ **imporsi** VIP **1** (*diventare necessario*) to become necessary; **s'impone una scelta** a choice is called for **2** (*avere successo: moda*) to become established, become popular

importante [impor'tante] AGG (*gen*) important; (*fatti*) important, significant; (*somma*) sizeable; **questo è molto importante** this is very important; **una partita importante** a big match; **poco importante** of little importance *o* significance; **è importante che ci sia anche lui** it is important that he should be there too
■SM: **l'importante è...** the important thing is ..., what is important is ...; **l'importante è arrivare entro domani** the important thing is to get there by tomorrow

importanza [impor'tantsa] SF (*vedi agg*) importance; significance; size; **di una certa importanza** of considerable importance; **della massima importanza** of the utmost importance; **un fatto della massima importanza** a matter of the greatest importance; **avere importanza** to be important; **che importanza ha sapere chi è stato?** what does it matter who it was?; **assumere importanza** to become more important; **dare importanza a qc** to attach importance to sth; **danno molta importanza all'abbigliamento** they think clothes are very important; **dare troppa importanza a qc** to make too much of sth, attach too much importance to sth; **darsi importanza** (*darsi arie*) to give o.s. airs

importare[1] [impor'tare] VT (*introdurre dall'estero*) to import; **la vodka viene importata dalla Russia** vodka is imported from Russia

importare[2] [impor'tare] VI, VB IMPERS (*aus* **essere**) (*essere importante*) to matter, be important; **le tue ragioni non mi importano** your reasons aren't important to me, I don't care about your reasons; **sembra che non gli importi degli esami** he doesn't seem to care about the exams; **ciò che importa di più è...** the most important thing is ...; **non importa!** it doesn't matter!, never mind!; **oggi o domani non importa** today or tomorrow, it doesn't matter; **non preoccuparti, non importa** don't worry, it doesn't matter; **non m'importa niente** I couldn't care less, I don't care; **non m'importa niente di quello che pensano** it doesn't matter to me what they think; **che importa?** what does that matter?; **non importa cosa/quando/dove** it doesn't matter what/when/ where

importatore, trice [importa'tore] AGG importing; **la ditta importatrice di questo prodotto** the firm which imports this product
■SM/F importer

importazione [importat'tsjone] SF (*operazione*) importation; (*merci importate*) imports *pl*; **merci/ prodotti d'importazione** imported goods/products

importo [im'pɔrto] SM (total) amount

importunare [importu'nare] VT **1** (*disturbare*) to bother, disturb; **non vorrei importunarti con le mie richieste** I don't want to bother you with my requests **2** (*molestare*) to pester, annoy; (*: sessualmente*) to harass

importunità [importuni'ta] SF (*di visita*) inopportuneness; (*di persona*) irksomeness, tiresomeness

importuno, a [impor'tuno] AGG (*visita*) inopportune, ill-timed; (*persona*) irksome, annoying
■SM/F troublesome individual

imposi *ecc* [im'posi] VB *vedi* **imporre**

imposizione [impozit'tsjone] SF **1** (*atto*) imposition **2** (*ordine*) order, command; **non accetto imposizioni da nessuno** I don't take orders from anyone **3** (*onere, imposta*) tax

impossessarsi [imposses'sarsi] VIP: **impossessarsi di** (*terreno, beni*) to seize, take possession of; (*segreto*) to get hold of; **si è impossessato della mia stanza** (*fig*) he has taken over my room

impossibile [impos'sibile] AGG impossible; **mi è impossibile farlo** it's impossible for me to do it, I can't (possibly) do it; **ma va', è impossibile!** come off it, it's impossible!; **è impossibile che lo sappia** she can't know about it
■SM: **fare l'impossibile** to do one's utmost, do all one can

impossibilità [impossibili'ta] SF impossibility; **essere** *o* **trovarsi nell'impossibilità di fare qc** to be unable *o* find it impossible to do sth

impossibilitare [impossibili'tare] VT: **impossibilitare qc a qn** to make sth impossible for sb; **impossibilitare qn a fare qc** to prevent sb from doing sth, make it impossible for sb to do sth

impossibilitato, a [impossibili'tato] AGG: **essere impossibilitato a fare qc** to be unable to do sth

imposta[1] [im'pɔsta] SF (*di finestra*) shutter

imposta[2] [im'pɔsta] SF (*tassa*) tax; **imposte dirette/ indirette** direct/indirect taxation *sg*; **ufficio imposte** tax office; **imposta indiretta sui consumi** excise duty *o* tax; **imposta locale sui redditi** tax on unearned income; **imposta patrimoniale** property tax; **imposta sul reddito** income tax; **imposta sul reddito delle persone fisiche** personal income tax; **imposta di successione** capital transfer tax (*Brit*), inheritance tax (*Am*); **imposta sugli utili** tax on profits; **imposta sul valore aggiunto** value added tax (*Brit*), sales tax (*Am*)

impostare[1] [impos'tare] VT **1** (*servizio, organizzazione*) to set up; (*lavoro*) to organize, plan; (*resoconto, rapporto*) to plan; (*questione, problema*) to formulate, set out; (*Tip:*

pagina) to lay out, make up **2** (*Mus*): **impostare la voce** to pitch one's voice

impostare[2] [impos'tare] VT (*lettera*) to post (*Brit*), mail (*Am*)

impostazione[1] [impostat'tsjone] SF (*di problema, questione*) formulation, statement; (*di lavoro*) organization, planning; (*di attività*) setting up; (*Mus: di voce*) pitch

impostazione[2] [impostat'tsjone] SF (*di lettera*) posting (*Brit*), mailing (*Am*)

imposto, a [im'posto] PP *di* **imporre**

impostore, a [impos'tore] SM/F impostor

impostura [impos'tura] SF imposture

impotente [impo'tɛnte] AGG **1** (*persona, governo*) impotent, powerless; **essere impotente di fronte a qc** to be powerless in the face of sth; **sentirsi impotente** to feel helpless **2** (*Med: incapace sessualmente*) impotent

■ SM (*Med*) impotent man

impotenza [impo'tɛntsa] SF (*debolezza*) impotence, powerlessness; (*Med*) impotence

impoverimento [impoveri'mento] SM impoverishment

impoverire [impove'rire] VT to impoverish

■ VI (*aus* **essere**), **impoverirsi** VIP to become poor(er)

impraticabile [imprati'kabile] AGG (*strada*) impassable; (*Sport: campo*) unfit for play, unplayable

impraticabilità [impratikabili'ta] SF: **l'impraticabilità delle strade** the fact that the roads are impassable; **partita sospesa per impraticabilità del campo** (*Sport*) match abandoned due to the pitch being unplayable

impratichirsi [imprati'kirsi] VIP (*fare pratica*) to get practice, gain experience; **impratichirsi in qc** to gain experience in (doing) sth

imprecare [impre'kare] VI (*aus* **avere**) to curse, swear; **imprecare contro** to hurl abuse at

imprecazione [imprekat'tsjone] SF abuse, curse; **lanciare un'imprecazione** to curse

imprecisabile [impretʃi'zabile] AGG indeterminable

imprecisato, a [impretʃi'zato] AGG **1** (*non preciso: quantità, numero*) indeterminate **2** (*non chiaro: dettagli, particolari*) unclear; **per motivi imprecisati** for reasons which are not clear; **ad un'ora imprecisata** at an unspecified time

imprecisione [impretʃi'zjone] SF (*vedi agg*) imprecision; inaccuracy

impreciso, a [impre'tʃizo] AGG (*definizione, descrizione*) imprecise, vague; (*calcolo*) inaccurate; **è impreciso nel suo lavoro** he's a careless worker

impregnare [impreɲ'ɲare] VT: **impregnare (di)** (*imbevere*) to soak *o* impregnate (with); (*riempire: anche fig*) to fill (with)

▶ **impregnarsi** VIP: **impregnarsi di** (*vedi vt*) to become impregnated with; to become filled with

imprenditore [imprendi'tore] SM (*industriale*) entrepreneur; (*appaltatore*) contractor; **piccolo imprenditore** small businessman; **imprenditore edile** building contractor

imprenditoria [imprendito'ria] SF enterprise; (*imprenditori*) entrepreneurs *pl*

imprenditoriale [imprendito'rjale] AGG (*ceto, classe*) entrepreneurial

impreparato, a [imprepa'rato] AGG: **impreparato (a)** (*gen*) unprepared (for); (*lavoratore*) untrained (for); **quel professore di matematica è impreparato** that maths teacher has a poor knowledge of his subject; **cogliere qn impreparato** to catch sb unawares

impreparazione [impreparat'tsjone] SF lack of preparation

impresa [im'presa] SF **1** (*iniziativa*) enterprise, undertaking; **abbandonare un'impresa** to abandon an enterprise *o* an undertaking; **è un'impresa!** that's quite an undertaking!; **sarà un'impresa riuscire a convincerlo!** it'll be hard work persuading him! **2** (*azione gloriosa*) feat, exploit **3** (*ditta, azienda*) firm, concern; **mettere su un'impresa** to set up a business; **lavora nell'impresa del padre** he works in his father's business; **le piccole e medie imprese** small and medium-sized businesses; **un'impresa edile** a building firm; **impresa familiare** family firm; **impresa pubblica** state-owned enterprise

impresario, ria, ri, rie [impre'sarjo] SM/F (*Teatro*) theatre manager; (: *di teatri maggiori, o più teatri*) impresario; **impresario di pompe funebri** funeral director

imprescindibile [impreʃʃin'dibile] AGG (*necessità*) inescapable, unavoidable; (*condizione*) essential; (*obbligo*) binding

impressi *ecc* [im'prɛssi] VB *vedi* **imprimere**

impressionabile [impressjo'nabile] AGG (*persona*) impressionable

impressionabilità [impressjonabili'ta] SF (*di persona*) impressionability

impressionante [impressjo'nante] AGG **1** (*che suscita turbamento*) disturbing, upsetting; **una scena impressionante** a terrible scene **2** (*che suscita sensazione*) impressive; **una velocità impressionante** an amazing speed

impressionare [impressjo'nare] VT **1** (*turbare*) to upset; (*colpire*) to impress; **l'incidente mi ha impressionato moltissimo** the accident upset me a lot; **mi ha impressionato il numero dei partecipanti** I was struck by the number of participants; **mi impressiono alla vista del sangue** I can't stand the sight of blood **2** (*Fot*) to expose

▶ **impressionarsi** VIP (*spaventarsi*) to get *o* be upset; **non impressionarti!** don't get upset!

impressione [impres'sjone] SF **1** (*sensazione*) impression, sensation, feeling; **ho l'impressione che mi nasconda qualcosa** I have the feeling that he's hiding something from me; **ho avuto l'impressione che non si fidasse di me** I had the feeling that she didn't trust me; **far impressione a qn** (*colpire*) to impress sb; (*turbare*) to upset sb, frighten sb; **il sangue mi fa impressione** I can't stand the sight of blood; **fare una buona/cattiva** *o* **brutta impressione a qn** to make a good/bad impression on sb; **che impressione ti ha fatto?** what was your impression of it (*o* him *ecc*)?, what did you make of it (*o* him *ecc*)?; **che impressione!** how awful!, how ghastly! **2** (*Tip: stampa*) printing; (: *ristampa*) impression

impressionismo [impressjo'nizmo] SM impressionism

impresso, a [im'presso] PP *di* **imprimere**

imprestare [impres'tare] VT (*fam*): **imprestare qc a qn** to lend sth to sb

imprevedibile [impreve'dibile] AGG (*destino, futuro*) unforeseeable; (*cambiamento*) unexpected; (*persona, risultato*) unpredictable

imprevedibilmente [imprevedibil'mente] AVV unexpectedly

imprevidente [imprevi'dɛnte] AGG lacking in foresight, improvident

imprevidenza [imprevi'dɛntsa] SF lack of foresight, improvidence
imprevisto, a [impre'visto] AGG (*arrivo, cambiamento*) unexpected; (*circostanza*) unforeseen, unexpected; **una spesa imprevista** an unexpected expense
■ SM unexpected *o* unforeseen event; **salvo imprevisti** unless anything unexpected happens
impreziosire [imprettsjo'sire] VT: **impreziosire con** to embellish with
imprigionamento [impridʒona'mento] SM imprisonment
imprigionare [impridʒo'nare] VT (*chiudere in prigione*) to imprison; (*rinchiudere: in casa ecc*) to shut up, confine; (*fig: intrappolare*) to trap; **la nave era imprigionata nel ghiaccio** the ship was icebound
imprimatur [impri'matur] SM INV imprimatur
imprimé [ɛ̃pri'me] AGG INV (*tessuto*) printed
imprimere [im'primere] VB IRREG, VT **1** (*marchio*) to impress, stamp; **imprimersi qc nella mente** to fix sth firmly in one's mind; **mi è rimasto impresso ciò che hai detto** I have never forgotten what you said **2** (*trasmettere*): **imprimere (un) movimento a** to impart *o* transmit movement to
▶ **imprimersi** VIP (*fig: ricordo*) to stamp itself, imprint itself
improbabile [impro'babile] AGG improbable, unlikely; **è improbabile che venga** he's unlikely to come
improbabilità [improbabili'ta] SF improbability, unlikelihood
improbo, a ['improbo] AGG (*letter: fatica, lavoro*) gruelling (*Brit*), grueling (*Am*), laborious
improduttività [improduttivi'ta] SF unproductiveness
improduttivo, a [improdut'tivo] AGG (*investimento*) unprofitable; (*terreno*) unfruitful; (*fig: sforzo*) fruitless, futile
impronta [im'pronta] SF **1** (*di piede, mano*) print; (*fig: di genio, maestro*) mark, stamp; **lasciare la propria impronta in qc** (*fig*) to leave one's mark on sth; **impronta del piede** footprint; **rilevamento delle impronte genetiche** genetic fingerprinting; **impronte digitali** fingerprints **2** (*di moneta*) impression
improntare [impron'tare] VT (*dare una certa espressione a*): **improntò il suo discorso alla massima semplicità** his speech was couched in terms of the utmost simplicity; **improntò il suo viso al dolore** his face assumed a sad expression
impronunciabile [impronun'tʃabile], **impronunziabile** [impronun'tsjabile] AGG unpronounceable
improperio, ri [impro'pɛrjo] SM (*insulto*) insult; **lanciare un improperio** to swear; **coprire qn d'improperi** to hurl abuse at sb
improponibile [impropo'nibile] AGG (*idea, patto, accordo*) which cannot be proposed *o* suggested
improprietà [improprje'ta] SF INV impropriety; **improprietà (di linguaggio)** incorrect usage
improprio, ria, ri, rie [im'prɔprjo] AGG (*non corretto: uso*) incorrect, improper; (*sconveniente: tono, abbigliamento*) improper, inappropriate; **arma impropria** *something used as a weapon*
improrogabile [improro'gabile] AGG (*termine*) that cannot be extended
improrogabilità [improrogabili'ta] SF (*di termine*) unalterable nature
improvvisamente [improvviza'mente] AVV suddenly, unexpectedly; **improvvisamente si è messo a piovere** it suddenly started to rain; **è arrivato improvvisamente** he arrived unexpectedly
improvvisare [improvvi'zare] VT (*gen*) to improvise; (*cena, piatto*) to knock up, throw together, improvise; **improvvisare una festa** to hold an impromptu party; **abbiamo improvvisato una cenetta alla buona** we put together a simple meal
▶ **improvvisarsi** VR to act as; **si è improvvisato cuoco per l'occasione** he took on the role of chef on that occasion
improvvisata [improvvi'zata] SF (pleasant) surprise; **fare un'improvvisata a qn** to give sb a surprise
improvvisatore, trice [improvviza'tore] SM/F improviser; **è un abile improvvisatore** he's good at improvising
improvvisazione [improvvizat'tsjone] SF improvisation; **spirito d'improvvisazione** spirit of invention; **capacità d'improvvisazione** ability to improvise
improvviso [improv'vizo] AGG (*inaspettato: arrivo ecc*) unexpected; (*subitaneo: simpatia, cambiamento d'umore*) sudden; **all'improvviso** *or* **d'improvviso** (*inaspettatamente*) unexpectedly; (*tutto d'un tratto*) suddenly; **all'improvviso si è spalancata la porta** the door suddenly opened; **è partita all'improvviso** she left suddenly; **un improvviso cambiamento di programma** a sudden change of plan
imprudente [impru'dɛnte] AGG (*gen*) careless, foolish, imprudent; (*osservazione*) unwise; **un guidatore imprudente** a careless driver
■ SM/F imprudent person
imprudentemente [imprudente'mente] AVV imprudently
imprudenza [impru'dɛntsa] SF (*qualità*) carelessness, foolishness, imprudence; (*azione*): **è stata un'imprudenza** that was a rash *o* an imprudent thing to do
impudente [impu'dɛnte] AGG impudent, cheeky
■ SM/F impudent person
impudentemente [impudente'mente] AVV impudently, cheekily
impudenza [impu'dɛntsa] SF impudence, cheek; **avere l'impudenza di fare qc** to have the cheek to do sth
impudicizia [impudi'tʃittsja] SF immodesty
impudico, a, chi, che [impu'diko] AGG immodest
impugnabile [impuɲ'ɲabile] AGG (*Dir*) subject to appeal
impugnare [impuɲ'ɲare] VT **1** (*arma*) to grasp, seize **2** (*Dir: sentenza*) to contest
impugnatura [impuɲɲa'tura] SF (*di coltello, frusta*) handle; (*di spada*) hilt; (*di remo, racchetta*) grip; **impugnatura a due mani** (*Tennis*) two-handed grip *o* grasp
impulsivamente [impulsiva'mente] AVV impulsively
impulsività [impulsivi'ta] SF impulsiveness; **fare qc per impulsività** to do sth impulsively
impulsivo, a [impul'sivo] AGG impulsive; **ha un carattere impulsivo** he's got an impulsive nature
■ SM/F impulsive person
impulso [im'pulso] SM **1** (*Fis, moto istintivo*) impulse; **agire d'impulso** to act on impulse; **ho agito d'impulso** I acted on impulse; **sentì l'impulso di picchiarlo** he was seized with an urge to hit him;

impulso sessuale sex drive **2** (*fig: spinta*) boost; **dare un impulso alle vendite** to boost sales

impunemente [impune'mente] AVV with impunity; **fare qc impunemente** to get away with sth

impunità [impuni'ta] SF impunity

impunito, a [impu'nito] AGG unpunished; **restare impunito** to go unpunished

impuntarsi [impun'tarsi] VIP (*cavallo, asino*) to jib, refuse to budge; (*fig: ostinarsi*) to dig one's heels in, be obstinate

impuntura [impun'tura] SF stitching

impurità [impuri'ta] SF INV impurity

impuro, a [im'puro] AGG impure; **esse impura** (*Fonetica*) "s" impure (*"s" + consonant*)

imputabile [impu'tabile] AGG **1** (*Dir*) chargeable **2** (*attribuibile*): **imputabile a** attributable to

imputare [impu'tare] VT **1** (*Dir*): **imputare qn di** to charge sb with, accuse sb of **2** **imputare qc a** (*attribuire*) to attribute *o* ascribe sth to; (*Contabilità*) to charge sth to

imputato, a [impu'tato] SM/F (*Dir*) defendant, accused

imputazione [imputat'tsjone] SF (*Dir*) charge; **capo d'imputazione** charge, count (of indictment); **imputazione delle spese generali** (*Contabilità*) allocation of overheads

imputridimento [imputridi'mento] SM putrefaction

imputridire [imputri'dire] VT to rot
■ VI (*aus* **essere**) to putrefy, rot

imputridito, a [imputri'dito] AGG putrefied

impuzzolentire [imputtsolen'tire] VT to stink out

in [in] PAROLA CHIAVE
■ PREP (*in + il* = nel, *in + lo* = nello, *in + l'* = nell', *in + la* = nella, *in + i* = nei, *in + gli* = negli, *in + le* = nelle)
1 (*stato in luogo*) in; (*: all'interno*) inside; **sono rimasto in casa** I stayed at home, I stayed indoors; **è nell'editoria/nell'esercito** he is in publishing/in the army; **è in fondo all'armadio** it is at the back of the wardrobe; **è bravo in latino** he's good at Latin; **dottore in legge** doctor of law; **in lei ho trovato una sorella** I found a sister in her; **in lui non c'era più speranza** there was no hope left in him; **nell'opera di Shakespeare** in Shakespeare's works; **vivo in Scozia** I live in Scotland; **aveva le mani in tasca** he had his hands in his pockets; **il pranzo è in tavola** lunch is on the table; **se fossi in te** if I were you; **un giornale diffuso in tutta Italia** a newspaper read all over *o* throughout Italy
2 (*moto a luogo*) to; (*: dentro*) into; **andare in campagna/in montagna** to go into the country/to the mountains; **andrò in Francia** I'm going to France; **entrare in casa** to go into the house; **entrare in macchina** to get into the car; **gettare qc in acqua** to throw sth into the water; **inciampò in una radice** he tripped over a root; **l'ho messo là in alto/basso** I put it up/down there; **spostarsi di città in città** to move from town to town
3 (*moto per luogo*): **il corteo è passato in piazza** the procession passed through the square; **sta facendo un viaggio in Egitto** he's travelling in *o* around Egypt
4 (*tempo*) in; **negli anni ottanta** in the eighties; **nel 1960** in 1960; **è cambiata molto in un anno** she has changed a lot in a year; **in autunno** in autumn; **di giorno in giorno** from day to day; **in gioventù** in one's youth; **in questo istante** at the moment; **in luglio, nel mese di luglio** in July; **lo farò in settimana** I'll do it within the week
5 (*mezzo*) by; **mi piace viaggiare in aereo** I like travelling by plane, I like flying; **pagare in contanti/in dollari** to pay cash/in dollars; **ci andremo in macchina** we'll go there by car, we'll drive there; **siamo andati in treno** we went by train
6 (*modo, maniera*) in; **in abito da sera** in evening dress; **tagliare in due** to cut in two; **in fiamme** on fire, in flames; **in gruppo** in a group; **in guerra** at war; **tradurre in italiano** to translate into Italian; **parlare in italiano** to speak Italian; **nell'oscurità** in the darkness; **in piedi** standing, on one's feet; **in prosa** in prose; **in silenzio** in silence; **scrivere in stampatello** to write in block letters; **in versi** in verse; **Maria Bianchi in Rossi** Maria Rossi née Bianchi
7 (*materia*) made of; **in marmo** made of marble, marble *attr*; **braccialetto in oro** gold bracelet; **lo stesso modello in seta** the same model in silk
8 (*fine, scopo*): **spende tutto in divertimenti** he spends all his money on entertainment; **me lo hanno dato in dono** they gave it to me as a gift; **in favore di** in favour of; **in onore di** in honour of
9 (*misura*) in; **in altezza** in height; **arrivarono in gran numero** they arrived in large numbers; **in lunghezza** in length; **siamo in quattro** there are four of us; **in tutto** in all
10 (*con infinito*): **ha sbagliato nel rispondere male** he was wrong to be rude; **si è fatto male nel salire sull'autobus** he hurt himself as he was getting onto the bus; **nell'udire la notizia** on hearing the news
■ AVV: **essere in** (*di moda, attuale*) to be in
■ AGG INV: **la gente in** the in-crowd

inabbordabile [inabbor'dabile] AGG unapproachable

inabile [i'nabile] AGG (*fisicamente, Mil*): **inabile (a)** unfit (for); (*per infortunio*) disabled; **inabile al servizio militare** unfit for military service

inabilità [inabili'ta] SF (*fisica, Mil*): **inabilità (a)** unfitness (for); (*per infortunio*) disablement

inabissare [inabis'sare] VT (*nave*) to sink
▶ **inabissarsi** VIP to sink, go down

inabitabile [inabi'tabile] AGG uninhabitable

inabitato, a [inabi'tato] AGG uninhabited

inaccessibile [inattʃes'sibile] AGG (*luogo*) inaccessible; (*spesa*) prohibitive; (*persona*) unapproachable; (*mistero*) unfathomable; (*teoria*) incomprehensible

inaccessibilità [inattʃessibili'ta] SF (*di luogo*) inaccessibility; (*di persona*) unapproachableness; (*di teoria ecc*) incomprehensibility; **l'inaccessibilità del prezzo mi ha impedito di comprarlo** the price was so prohibitive that I couldn't buy it

inaccettabile [inattʃet'tabile] AGG unacceptable

inaccettabilità [inattʃettabili'ta] SF unacceptableness

inaccostabile [inakkos'tabile] AGG (*persona*) unapproachable

inacerbire [inatʃer'bire] VT to exacerbate
▶ **inacerbirsi** VIP (*persona*) to become embittered

inacidire [inatʃi'dire] VT (*persona, carattere*) to embitter
■ VI (*aus* **essere**), **inacidirsi** VIP (*latte*) to go sour; (*fig: persona, carattere*) to become sour, become embittered

inadatto, a [ina'datto] AGG: **inadatto (a)** (*persona*) unsuited (to), unfit (for); (*luogo, costruzione, lavoro*) unsuitable (for); (*parole, azione*) inappropriate (to); **le sue scarpe sono inadatte a camminare** her shoes are unsuitable for walking

inadeguatamente [inadegwata'mente] AVV (*vedi agg*) inadequately; unsuitably

Ii

inadeguatezza [inadegwa'tettsa] SF (*vedi agg*) inadequacy; unsuitability
inadeguato, a [inade'gwato] AGG: **inadeguato (a)** (*non sufficiente*) inadequate (for); (*inadatto*) not suitable (for)
inadempiente [inadem'pjɛnte] AGG defaulting ■SM/F defaulter
inadempienza [inadem'pjɛntsa] SF: **inadempienza a un contratto** non-fulfilment of a contract; **dovuto alle inadempienze dei funzionari** due to negligence on the part of the officials
inadempimento [inadempi'mento] SM non-fulfilment
inadempiuto, a [inadem'pjuto] AGG unfulfilled, broken
inafferrabile [inaffer'rabile] AGG (*ladro, criminale*) elusive; (*fig: concetto, significato*) incomprehensible, difficult to grasp
inaffidabile [inaffi'dabile] AGG (*persona*) untrustworthy
inagibile [ina'ʒibile] AGG (*teatro, ospedale*) closed (to the public); (*strada*) closed, impassable; (*terreno da gioco*) unplayable
inagibilità [inaʒibili'ta] SF (*di teatro, ospedale, strada*) closure; **la partita è stata rinviata per inagibilità del campo** the match was called off because the pitch was unplayable
INAIL ['inail] SIGLA M (= **Istituto Nazionale per l'Assicurazione contro gli Infortuni sul Lavoro**) *state body providing sickness benefit to people injured at work*
inalare [ina'lare] VT to inhale
inalatore [inala'tore] SM inhaler
inalazione [inalat'tsjone] SF inhalation
inalberare [inalbe'rare] VT (*bandiera, insegna*) to hoist, run up, raise
▶ **inalberarsi** VIP (*fig: arrabbiarsi*) to flare up, fly off the handle
inalienabile [inalje'nabile] AGG inalienable
inalterabile [inalte'rabile] AGG (*colore*) permanent, fast; (*prezzo, qualità*) stable; (*amicizia*) steadfast; (*affetto*) unchanging, constant; **i termini del contratto sono inalterabili** the terms of the contract cannot be changed
inalterato, a [inalte'rato] AGG (*prezzi*) stable; (*affetto, amicizia, termini di contratto*) unaltered, unchanged
inamidare [inami'dare] VT to starch
inamidato, a [inami'dato] AGG (*colletto, camicia*) starched
inammissibile [inammis'sibile] AGG (*comportamento, reazione*) intolerable; (*Dir: prova*) inadmissible
inamovibile [inamo'vibile] AGG (*Amm: magistrato*) irremovable
inanellato, a [inanel'lato] AGG (*dita, mano*) bejewelled
inanimato, a [inani'mato] AGG (*gen*) inanimate; (*svenuto*) unconscious; (*morto*) lifeless
inappagabile [inappa'gabile] AGG (*desiderio*) insatiable
inappagato, a [inappa'gato] AGG unfulfilled
inappellabile [inappel'labile] AGG (*decisione*) final, irrevocable; (*Dir*) not open to appeal, final
inappellabilità [inappellabili'ta] SF (*di decisione*) finality; **vista l'inappellabilità della sentenza...** (*Dir*) given that no appeal can be made against the sentence ...
inappetenza [inappe'tɛntsa] SF lack of appetite; **soffrire di inappetenza** to have no appetite
inappuntabile [inappun'tabile] AGG (*persona*) irreproachable; (*contegno*) faultless, irreproachable; (*eleganza*) faultless, impeccable
inarcamento [inarka'mento] SM (*vedi vb*) arching; raising; warping
inarcare [inar'kare] VT (*schiena*) to arch; (*sopracciglia*) to raise
▶ **inarcarsi** VIP (*legno*) to warp; (*schiena*) to arch
inaridimento [inaridi'mento] SM (*anche fig*) drying up
inaridire [inari'dire] VT (*terreno*) to parch, dry up; (*fig: vena poetica*) to dry up; (*: persona*) to sour ■VI (*aus* **essere**), **inaridirsi** VIP (*anche fig*) to dry up, become arid; (*persona*) to become soured
inarrestabile [inarres'tabile] AGG **1** (*processo*) irreversible; (*emorragia*) that cannot be staunched **2** (*corsa del tempo*) relentless
inarticolato, a [inartiko'lato] AGG (*suono*) inarticulate
inascoltato, a [inaskol'tato] AGG unheeded, unheard; **rimanere inascoltato** to go unheeded *o* unheard
inaspettatamente [inaspettata'mente] AVV unexpectedly
inaspettato, a [inaspet'tato] AGG unexpected; **una visita inaspettata** an unexpected visit
inasprimento [inaspri'mento] SM (*vedi vt*) tightening up; embitterment; worsening
inasprire [inas'prire] VT (*disciplina*) to tighten up, make harsher; (*persona, carattere*) to embitter, sour; (*rapporti*) to make worse
▶ **inasprirsi** VIP (*vedi vt*) to become harsher; to become bitter; to become worse; **si sono inasprite le ostilità** hostilities have intensified
inattaccabile [inattak'kabile] AGG (*fortezza, castello*) unassailable, impregnable; (*fig: alibi*) cast-iron; (*: posizione*) unassailable; **inattaccabile dagli acidi** proof against acids
inattendibile [inatten'dibile] AGG (*versione dei fatti*) unreliable; (*testimone*) unreliable, untrustworthy
inatteso, a [inat'teso] AGG unexpected
inattivo, a [inat'tivo] AGG (*persona*) idle, inactive; (*vulcano*) inactive, dormant; (*Chim*) inactive
inattuabile [inattu'abile] AGG impracticable
inattuabilità [inattuabili'ta] SF impracticability
inaudito, a [inau'dito] AGG (*crudeltà, ferocia*) unheard-of, unprecedented; (*somma, prezzo*) outrageous; **è inaudito!** it's outrageous!
inaugurale [inaugu'rale] AGG inaugural; **la fase inaugurale** the opening stages
inaugurare [inaugu'rare] VT (*scuola, linea ferroviaria*) to open, inaugurate; (*mostra*) to open; (*monumento*) to unveil; (*era, periodo*) to usher in, inaugurate; (*sistema*) to inaugurate; (*scherz: scarpe, vestito*) to christen; **il nuovo stadio sarà inaugurato domani** the new stadium is being opened tomorrow; **oggi ho inaugurato le scarpe nuove** I wore my new shoes for the first time today
inaugurazione [inaugurat'tsjone] SF (*vedi vt*) opening, inauguration; unveiling; **fare l'inaugurazione di** to inaugurate, open; **l'inaugurazione di una mostra** the opening of an exhibition
inavveduto, a [inavve'duto] AGG (*gesto*) inadvertent, unintentional, careless
inavvertenza [inavver'tɛntsa] SF carelessness, inadvertence
inavvertitamente [inavvertita'mente] AVV inadvertently, unintentionally
inavvicinabile [inavvitʃi'nabile] AGG unapproachable
Inca ['inka] AGG, SM/F INV Inca
incagliarsi [inkaʎ'ʎarsi] VIP (*nave, barca*) to run

aground; (*fig*: *trattative*) to become bogged down, grind to a halt
incaico, a, ci, che [in'kaiko] AGG Inca, Incan
incalcolabile [inkalko'labile] AGG incalculable
incallito, a [inkal'lito] AGG **1** (*mani*) calloused **2** (*fig*: *ladro*) hardened; (: *bugiardo*) inveterate; (: *fumatore, bevitore*) heavy; **è un incallito rubacuori** he's a real heartbreaker
incalzante [inkal'tsante] AGG (*richiesta*) urgent, insistent; (*crisi*) imminent
incalzare [inkal'tsare] VT (*inseguire*) to pursue, follow closely; (*fig*) to press
■ VI (*aus* **essere**) (*urgere*: *tempo*) to be pressing; (*essere imminente*: *pericolo*) to be imminent
incamerare [inkame'rare] VT (*Dir*) to expropriate, confiscate
incamminarsi [inkammi'narsi] VIP to set forth, set out; **incamminarsi verso** to set out for, head for; (*fig*) to head for; **ci siamo incamminati verso la spiaggia** we set off towards the beach
incanalamento [inkanala'mento] SM (*di acque*) canalization
incanalare [inkana'lare] VT (*acque*) to canalize; (*traffico, folla*) to direct, channel
▶ **incanalarsi** VIP: **incanalarsi verso** (*folla*) to converge on
incancrenire [inkankre'nire] VI (*aus* **essere**), **incancrenirsi** VIP to become gangrenous
incandescente [inkandeʃ'ʃɛnte] AGG incandescent, white-hot
incandescenza [inkandeʃ'ʃɛntsa] SF incandescence
incantare [inkan'tare] VT (*per magia, anche fig*: *persona*) to enchant, bewitch; (*serpente*) to charm; **non m'incanti con le tue chiacchiere!** you don't fool me with your fine words!
▶ **incantarsi** VIP (*bloccarsi*: *meccanismo*) to stick, jam; (: *persona*) to be spellbound, be in a daze; **incantarsi nel parlare** to hesitate in one's speech; **incantarsi a guardare qn/qc** to stop and stare at sb/sth
incantato, a [inkan'tato] AGG (*anello, castello*) enchanted; (*fig*: *affascinato*) spellbound, entranced; **rimanere incantato davanti a qc** to stand entranced *o* spellbound before sth
incantatore, trice [inkanta'tore] AGG enchanting, bewitching
■ SM/F enchanter/enchantress; **incantatore di serpenti** snake charmer
incantesimo [inkan'tezimo] SM spell, charm; **rompere l'incantesimo** (*anche fig*) to break the spell
incantevole [inkan'tevole] AGG enchanting, delightful, lovely; **c'era un paesaggio incantevole** the scenery was lovely; **è ancora più incantevole del solito** it's even lovelier than usual
incanto[1] [in'kanto] SM (*incantesimo*) spell, charm, enchantment; **quella ragazza/quel paese è un incanto** that girl/village is enchanting; **sei un incanto stasera** you look enchanting this evening; **l'incanto della montagna** the magic of the mountains; **come per incanto** as if by magic; **l'eczema è scomparso come per incanto** the eczema disappeared as if by magic; **ti sta d'incanto!** (*vestito ecc*) it really suits you!
incanto[2] [in'kanto] SM (*asta*) auction; **vendita all'incanto** sale by auction; **mettere all'incanto** to put up for auction
incanutire [inkanu'tire] VI (*aus* **essere**) to go white
incapace [inka'patʃe] AGG incapable; **essere incapace (di fare qc)** to be incapable (of doing sth); **è incapace di mentire** she's incapable of lying
■ SM/F: **essere un incapace** to be useless, be a dead loss; (*fam*): **solo un incapace poteva...** only an idiot could ...
incapacità [inkapatʃi'ta] SF **1** (*inabilità*) incapability, inability; **incapacità a fare qc** inability to do sth **2** (*Dir*) incapacity; **incapacità d'intendere e di volere** diminished responsibility
incaponirsi [inkapo'nirsi] VIP (*ostinarsi*) to be set on; **incaponirsi a fare qc** to insist on doing sth
incappare [inkap'pare] VI (*aus* **essere**) **incappare in** (*problema, guaio*) to run into, get into; (*persona*) to run into
incappucciare [inkapput'tʃare] VT to put a hood on; **la neve incappuccia le cime dei monti** snow covers the mountain tops
▶ **incappucciarsi** VR (*persona*) to put on a hood
incaprettamento [inkapretta'mento] SM *method of strangulation used by the Mafia whereby a rope is passed around the victim's wrists, ankles and throat*
incapricciarsi [inkaprit'tʃarsi] VIP: **incapricciarsi di** to take a fancy to
incapsulare [inkapsu'lare] VT (*Med*: *dente*) to crown
incarcerare [inkartʃe'rare] VT to imprison, jail
incaricare [inkari'kare] VT: **incaricare qn di fare qc** to give sb the responsibility of doing sth, ask sb to do sth; **mi hanno incaricato di rispondere al telefono** they asked me to answer the phone
▶ **incaricarsi** VIP: **incaricarsi di fare qc** to take it upon o.s. to do sth; **me ne incarico io** I'll see to it
incaricato, a [inkari'kato] AGG: **incaricato (di)** in charge (of), responsible (for); **docente incaricato** (*Univ*) lecturer without tenure
■ SM/F representative; **l'incaricato** the person in charge; **incaricato d'affari** (*Pol*) chargé d'affaires
incarico, chi [in'kariko] SM **1** (*gen, compito*) task, job; **dare un incarico a qn** to give sb a task *o* job to do; **ricevere un incarico** to be given a task *o* job to do; **avere l'incarico di fare qc** to have the job of doing sth; **per incarico di qn** on sb's behalf; **un incarico importante** an important job; **chi aveva l'incarico di comprare i biglietti?** who was supposed to get the tickets? **2** (*Scol, Univ*) *temporary post*
incarnare [inkar'nare] VT (*rappresentare*) to embody
▶ **incarnarsi** VIP (*Rel*) to become incarnate; (*concretarsi*) to be embodied
incarnato[1], a [inkar'nato] AGG (*Rel*) incarnate; **è l'avarizia incarnata** he's avarice personified
incarnato[2] [inkar'nato] SM (*carnagione*) rosy
incarnazione [inkarnat'tsjone] SF (*Rel*) incarnation; (*fig*) embodiment; **è l'incarnazione della virtù** he (*o* she) is the embodiment of virtue; **sembra l'incarnazione di suo nonno** he (*o* she) is the image of his (*o* her) grandfather
incarnire [inkar'nire] VI (*aus* **essere**), **incarnirsi** VIP (*unghia*) to become ingrown
incarnito, a [inkar'nito] AGG (*unghia*) ingrown
incartamento [inkarta'mento] SM dossier, file
incartapecorire [inkartapeko'rire] VI (*aus* **essere**), **incartapecorirsi** VIP to shrivel (up)
incartapecorito, a [inkartapeko'rito] AGG (*pelle*) wizened, shrivelled (*Brit*), shriveled (*Am*)
incartare [inkar'tare] VT to wrap (in paper); **devo ancora incartare i regali** I still have to wrap the presents; **me lo incarta, per favore?** could you wrap it for me please?

Ii

incasellare [inkasel'lare] VT (*posta*) to sort; (*fig: nozioni*) to pigeonhole

incasinare [inkasi'nare] VT (*fam: creare disordine in*) to mess up; (: *creare problemi a*) to screw up; **mio fratello ha incasinato i miei CD** my brother has messed up my CDs

incasinato, a [inkasi'nato] AGG (*fam: gen*) in a mess; (: *mentalmente*) screwed up; **in questo periodo sono proprio incasinata** I'm in a real mess at the moment

incassare [inkas'sare] VT **1** (*Comm: denaro*) to take, receive; (: *assegno, cambiale*) to cash; **puoi incassare l'assegno in qualunque banca** you can cash the cheque at any bank **2** (*Pugilato: colpi*) to take, stand up to; (*fig: offese*) to take **3** (*montare: pietra preziosa*) to set; (: *mobile*) to build in **4** (*imballare: merce*) to pack (in cases)

incassatore, trice [inkassa'tore] SM/F: **è un buon incassatore** (*pugile*) he can take a lot of punishment; (*fig*) he can take it

incasso [in'kasso] SM **1** (*somma incassata*) takings *pl*; (: *per un incontro sportivo*) take; **incasso giornaliero/mensile** daily/monthly takings; **fare un buon incasso** to take a lot of cash *o* money; **i ladri sono fuggiti con l'incasso della giornata** the thieves escaped with the day's takings; **il film ha battuto ogni record d'incasso** the film has been a great box office success **2** (*cavità*): **frigorifero da incasso** fitted refrigerator

incastonare [inkasto'nare] VT to set

incastonatura [inkastona'tura] SF setting

incastrare [inkas'trare] VT **1** (*gen: far combaciare*) to fit in, insert **2** (*intrappolare*) to catch; (: *con false accuse*) to frame; **era ovvio che l'avevano incastrato** it was obvious that he had been framed
▶ **incastrarsi** VIP **1** (*combaciare, pezzi meccanici*) to fit together; **questo pezzo s'incastra qui** this part fits here **2** (*rimanere bloccato*) to get stuck; **la chiave si è incastrata nella serratura** the key got stuck in the lock

incastro [in'kastro] SM (*punto di unione*) joint; (*scanalatura*) slot, groove; **gioco a incastro** interlocking puzzle; **sistema a incastro** interlocking system; **incastro a coda di rondine** dovetail joint

incatenare [inkate'nare] VT: **incatenare qc/qn a qc** to chain sth/sb to sth; **i prigionieri venivano incatenati al muro** the prisoners were chained to the wall
▶ **incatenarsi** VR: **incatenarsi a qc** to chain o.s. to sth

incatramare [inkatra'mare] VT to tar

incattivire [inkatti'vire] VT to make wicked
■ VI (*aus* **essere**), **incattivirsi** VIP to turn nasty

incautamente [inkauta'mente] AVV imprudently, rashly

incauto, a [in'kauto] AGG imprudent, rash

incavare [inka'vare] VT to hollow out

incavato, a [inka'vato] AGG (*gen*) hollow; (*occhi*) sunken

incavo [in'kavo] SM hollow; (*solco*) groove

incavolarsi [inkavo'larsi] VIP (*fam*) to lose one's temper, fly off the handle; **incavolarsi per** *o* **a causa di qc** to get annoyed about sth, lose one's temper over sth; **s'incavola per ogni sciocchezza** she gets angry about the slightest thing; **incavolarsi con qn** to get annoyed *o* lose one's temper with sb; **non t'incavolare con me!** don't get angry with me!

incazzarsi [inkat'tsarsi] VIP (*fam!*) to get pissed off (*fam!*); **mi sono incazzato da morire!** I was really pissed off!

incazzato, a [inkat'tsato] AGG (*fam!*) pissed off (*fam!*); **sono incazzato nero!** I'm really pissed off!

incedere [in'tʃɛdere] VI (*aus* **avere**) to advance solemnly
■ SM solemn gait

incendiare [intʃen'djare] VT (*gen*) to set fire to; (*fig: animi*) to fire; **dei vandali hanno incendiato la scuola** vandals set fire to the school
▶ **incendiarsi** VIP to catch fire, burst into flames

incendiario, ria, ri, rie [intʃen'djarjo] AGG incendiary
■ SM/F arsonist

incendio, di [in'tʃɛndjo] SM fire; **provocare l'incendio di** to set fire to; **i vigili del fuoco hanno domato l'incendio** the firemen have got the fire under control; **incendio doloso** arson

incenerimento [intʃeneri'mento] SM incineration

incenerire [intʃene'rire] VT (*gen*) to incinerate; (*casa, albero*) to burn (down), burn to ashes; **incenerire qn con uno sguardo** to give sb a withering look
▶ **incenerirsi** VIP to be burnt to ashes

inceneritore [intʃeneri'tore] SM incinerator

incensiere [intʃen'sjɛre] SM censer, thurible

incenso [in'tʃɛnso] SM incense; **odore d'incenso** smell of incense; **bastoncini d'incenso** joss sticks

incensurabile [intʃensu'rabile] AGG irreproachable

incensurato, a [intʃensu'rato] AGG (*Dir*): **essere incensurato** to have a clean record

incentivare [intʃenti'vare] VT (*produzione, vendite*) to boost; (*dipendente*) to motivate

incentivazione [intʃentivat'tsjone] SF (*di produzione*) boosting; **incentivazione vendite** sales promotion

incentivo [intʃen'tivo] SM incentive

incentrarsi [intʃen'trarsi] VIP: **incentrarsi su** (*fig*) to centre (*Brit*) *o* center (*Am*) on

inceppare [intʃep'pare] VT (*fig: operazione*) to obstruct, hamper
▶ **incepparsi** VIP (*fucile ecc*) to jam

incerare [intʃe'rare] VT to wax

incerata [intʃe'rata] SF (*impermeabile*) oilskins *pl*; (*tela*) oilcloth, tarpaulin; (: *da letto*) waterproof sheet

incernierato, a [intʃernje'rato] AGG hinged

incerottato, a [intʃerot'tato] AGG: **avere un dito incerottato** to have a plaster (*Brit*) *o* Bandaid® (*Am*) on one's finger

incertamente [intʃerta'mente] AVV (*rispondere*) uncertainly, doubtfully

incertezza [intʃer'tettsa] SF **1** (*di notizie, fonti*) uncertainty, doubtful nature **2** (*esitazione*) uncertainty, hesitation; **un momento d'incertezza** a moment's uncertainty *o* hesitation; **ha avuto un momento d'incertezza nel rispondere** he hesitated for a moment before answering; **rispondere con incertezza** to answer hesitantly **3** (*insicurezza, instabilità*) uncertainty, doubt; **essere nell'incertezza** to be in a state of uncertainty; **tenere qn nell'incertezza** to keep sb in suspense; **vivere nell'incertezza** to live in a state of uncertainty; **un periodo di incertezza politica** a period of political uncertainty

incerto, a [in'tʃɛrto] AGG (*esito, risultato*) uncertain, doubtful; (*tempo*) uncertain; (*persona*) undecided, hesitating; **essere incerto su qc** to be uncertain *o* unsure about sth; **essere incerto sul da farsi** not to know what to do, be uncertain what to do; **camminare con passo incerto** to walk unsteadily; **la situazione è ancora incerta** the situation is still uncertain; **ero incerto se dirglielo o no** I was uncertain whether to tell him or not

■ SM uncertainty; **lasciare il certo per l'incerto** to step out into the unknown, leave certainty behind one; **gli incerti del mestiere** the risks of the job

incespicare [intʃespi'kare] VI (*aus* **avere**) **incespicare (in qc)** to trip (over sth); **incespicare nel parlare** to stumble over one's words

incessante [intʃes'sante] AGG (*gen*) unceasing, incessant; (*serie*) never-ending

incessantemente [intʃessante'mente] AVV incessantly

incesto [in'tʃɛsto] SM incest

incestuoso, a [intʃestu'oso] AGG incestuous

incetta [in'tʃɛtta] SF buying up, hoarding; **fare incetta di** (*prodotti, merce*) to stockpile, buy up; **cercare di fare incetta di voti** to try to get as many votes as possible

inchiesta [in'kjɛsta] SF (*gen, Dir*) inquiry, investigation; (*giornalistica*) report; **fare un'inchiesta su qc** to investigate sth, carry out an investigation *o* inquiry into sth; to report on sth; **è stata aperta un'inchiesta** an inquiry has been opened; **un'inchiesta sui giovani e la droga** a special report on young people and drugs; **inchiesta parlamentare** ≈ parliamentary inquiry (*Brit*), ≈ congressional investigation (*Am*)

inchinare [inki'nare] VT (*schiena*) to bend; (*testa, fronte*) to bow

▶ **inchinarsi** VR to bend down; (*per riverenza*) to bow; (: *donna*) to curts(e)y; **inchinarsi davanti a qn** to bow (*o* curts(e)y) to sb; **m'inchino davanti alla tua bravura** I take off my hat to you

inchino [in'kino] SM (*gen*) bow; (*di donna*) curts(e)y; **fare un inchino** to bow; to curts(e)y

inchiodare [inkjo'dare] VT to nail (down); **inchiodare qc a qc** to nail sth to sth; **ha inchiodato il coperchio alla cassa** he nailed the lid onto the crate; **il lavoro lo inchioda al tavolino** his work keeps him chained to his desk; **sta tutto il giorno inchiodato davanti alla TV** he spends all day glued to the TV; **con queste prove lo hanno inchiodato** they nailed him with this evidence; **inchiodare la macchina** to jam on the brakes

▶ **inchiodarsi** VIP (*fermarsi di colpo*) to stop dead

inchiodatura [inkjoda'tura] SF (*operazione*) nailing down; (*chiodi*) nails *pl*

inchiostro [in'kjostro] SM ink; **una macchia d'inchiostro** an ink blot; **inchiostro di china** Indian ink; **inchiostro simpatico** invisible ink

inciampare [intʃam'pare] VI (*aus* **essere o avere**) to trip, stumble; **inciampare in** (*gradino, pietra*) to trip over; (*fig: persona*) to run into; **sono inciampato nel tappeto** I tripped over the carpet; **far inciampare qn** to trip sb (up)

inciampo [in'tʃampo] SM obstacle; **proseguire senza inciampi** to proceed smoothly

incidentale [intʃiden'tale] AGG **1** (*casuale*) accidental **2** (*secondario*) incidental; **questione incidentale** (*Dir*) interlocutory matter; **proposizione incidentale** (*Gramm*) parenthetical clause

incidentalmente [intʃidental'mente] AVV (*per caso*) by chance; (*per inciso*) incidentally, by the way

incidente [intʃi'dɛnte] SM **1** (*disgrazia*) accident; **incidente aereo** plane crash; **è il terzo incidente aereo in un mese** it's the third plane crash in a month; **incidente d'auto** car crash *o* accident; **sono rimasti feriti in un incidente d'auto** they were injured in a car accident; **incidente ferroviario** train crash; **incidente mortale** fatal accident; **incidente stradale** road accident **2** (*episodio*) incident; **e con questo l'incidente è chiuso** and that is the end of the matter; **incidente diplomatico** diplomatic incident **3** (*Dir*): **incidente probatorio** pre-trial investigation

incidenza [intʃi'dɛntsa] SF **1** (*fig: effetto*): **avere una forte incidenza su qc** to affect sth greatly, have a considerable effect on sth **2** (*Mat*): **angolo di incidenza** angle of incidence

incidere[1] [in'tʃidere] VT IRREG **1** (*tagliare: corteccia, legno*) to cut into, carve; (*scolpire: pietra*) to engrave; **incidere un'iscrizione su** to engrave an inscription on; **incidere ad acquaforte** to etch; **incidere una ferita** (*Med*) to lance a wound **2** (*canzone*) to record; **incidere un disco** to make a record

incidere[2] [in'tʃidere] VI IRREG (*aus* **avere**) (*influire*): **incidere su** to influence, affect, have a bearing upon; **le spese di riscaldamento incidono molto sull'economia domestica** heating costs are an important item of household expenditure

incinta [in'tʃinta] AGG F pregnant; **restare** *o* **rimanere incinta** to become *o* get pregnant; **è rimasta incinta** she got pregnant; **incinta di 5 mesi** 5 months pregnant

incipiente [intʃi'pjɛnte] AGG incipient

incipriare [intʃi'prjare] VT to powder; **andare ad incipriarsi il naso** (*euf*) to go and powder one's nose

▶ **incipriarsi** VR to powder one's face

incirca [in'tʃirka] AVV: **all'incirca** approximately, more or less, very nearly; **è grande all'incirca così** it's about this big; **saranno all'incirca le tre** it must be about three

incisi *ecc* [in'tʃizi] VB *vedi* **incidere**

incisione [intʃi'zjone] SF **1** (*taglio*) cut; (*Med*) incision **2** (*Arte*) engraving; **incisione ad acquaforte** etching; **incisione su legno** woodcut; **incisione su rame** copperplate engraving **3** (*registrazione*) recording; **sala d'incisione** recording studio; **incisione su nastro** tape recording

incisivamente [intʃiziva'mente] AVV (*criticare, scrivere*) incisively

incisività [intʃizivi'ta] SF incisiveness

incisivo, a [intʃi'zivo] AGG **1** (*Anat*): **(dente) incisivo** incisor **2** (*fig: parole, stile*) incisive

inciso, a [in'tʃizo] PP *di* **incidere**

■ SM (*Gramm*) parenthesis; **per inciso** incidentally, by the way

incisore [intʃi'zore] SM (*Arte*) engraver

incitamento [intʃita'mento] SM incitement; **essere d'incitamento per** *o* **a** to be an incitement to

incitare [intʃi'tare] VT: **incitare qn a (fare) qc** to incite sb to (do) sth

inciucio, ci [in'tʃutʃo] SM deal

incivile [intʃi'vile] AGG (*popolazione, costumi*) uncivilized; (*fig: persona, comportamento*) rude, impolite; **una persona incivile** a rude person; **che modi incivili!** what bad manners!

■ SM/F boor

incivilimento [intʃivili'mento] SM civilization

incivilire [intʃivi'lire] VT to civilize

▶ **incivilirsi** VIP to become civilized

incivilmente [intʃivil'mente] AVV (*villanamente*) uncivilly, rudely; (*barbaramente*) in an uncivilized manner

inciviltà [intʃivil'ta] SF **1** (*di popolazione*) barbarism

2 (*fig*: *di trattamento*) barbarity; (: *maleducazione*) incivility, rudeness

incl. ABBR (= incluso) encl.

inclassificabile [inklassifi'kabile] AGG **1** unclassifiable **2** (*fig*: *pessimo*: *compito*) unmarkable; (: *azione, comportamento*) abominable

inclemente [inkle'mɛnte] AGG (*fig*: *clima*) harsh; (: *tempo*) inclement; (*giudice, critica*) severe, harsh

inclemenza [inkle'mɛntsa] SF (*vedi agg*) harshness; inclemency; severity

inclinabile [inkli'nabile] AGG (*schienale*) reclinable

inclinare [inkli'nare] VT (*recipiente*) to tilt, tip; (*schienale*) to tilt (back), recline; **inclinare il busto in avanti** to bend forward, lean forward; **inclina un po' il tavolo** tilt the table a bit
■ VI (*aus* **avere**) **inclinare a qc/a fare** to incline towards sth/doing, tend towards sth/to do
▶ **inclinarsi** VIP (*barca*) to list, heel; (*aereo*) to bank; (*ago magnetico*) to dip

inclinato, a [inkli'nato] AGG (*recipiente*) tilted; (*strada*) sloping; **piano inclinato** (*Mat*) inclined plane

inclinazione [inklinat'tsjone] SF **1** (*pendenza*: *di strada*) gradient; (: *di superficie*) slope; (: *di tetto*) slope, pitch; (: *di retta, piano*) inclination **2** (*fig*: *tendenza*) inclination, bent, tendency; **seguire le proprie inclinazioni** to follow one's inclinations

incline [in'kline] AGG: **essere incline a pensare che...** to be inclined to think that ...; **essere incline alla collera** to be prone to anger, be irascible

includere [in'kludere] VT IRREG: **includere (in)** (*accludere*) to enclose (in); (*comprendere*) to include (in)

inclusione [inklu'zjone] SF inclusion

inclusivo, a [inklu'zivo] AGG: **inclusivo di** inclusive of

incluso, a [in'kluzo] PP *di* **includere**
■ AGG **1** (*accluso*) attached, enclosed **2** (*compreso*) inclusive, included; **fino a giovedì incluso** up to and including Thursday; **leggere da pagina cinque a pagina sette inclusa** read from the beginning of page five to the end of page seven; **incluso mio cugino** including my cousin, my cousin included; **è inclusa la colazione?** is breakfast included?; **spese incluse** inclusive of expenses

incoerente [inkoe'rɛnte] AGG **1** (*terreno, materiali*) loose **2** (*fig*: *confuso*) incoherent; (: *illogico*) inconsistent

incoerentemente [inkoerente'mente] AVV (*vedi agg 2*) incoherently; inconsistently

incoerenza [inkoe'rɛntsa] SF (*vedi agg*) looseness; incoherence; inconsistency

incognita [in'kɔɲɲita] SF (*Mat, fig*: *persona*) unknown quantity; (: *fatto, evento*) matter of uncertainty

incognito, a [in'kɔɲɲito] AGG unknown
■ SM: **mantenere l'incognito** to remain incognito; **in incognito** incognito; **viaggiare in incognito** to travel incognito

incollare [inkol'lare] VT (*gen*) to stick, gum; (*legno, porcellana*) to glue, stick; **incollare un francobollo ad una lettera** to put *o* stick a stamp on a letter; **incollare insieme dei cartoncini** to stick *o* glue pieces of card together; **incollare gli occhi addosso a qn** to fix one's eyes on sb; **ha incollato le sue foto sul diario** she stuck the photos of him into her diary
▶ **incollarsi** VIP (*gen*): **incollarsi (a)** to stick (to); **incollarsi a qn** (*fig*) to stick close to sb; **le pagine si sono incollate** the pages have stuck together; **la camicia bagnata gli si incollò addosso** his wet shirt stuck to him

incollato, a [inkol'lato] AGG (*gen*) stuck; **passa il pomeriggio incollato alla TV** he spends his afternoons glued to the TV

incollatura [inkolla'tura] SF (*Ippica*): **vincere/perdere di un'incollatura** to win/lose by a head

incollerire [inkolle'rire] VI (*aus* **essere**), **incollerirsi** VIP to lose one's temper

incolmabile [inkol'mabile] AGG (*vuoto*) unfillable; (*lacuna*) overwhelming; (*Sport*: *distacco*) irretrievable

incolonnamento [inkolonna'mento] SM (*di cifre*) putting into columns; (*di persone, soldati*) formation (in columns); (*Tip*) printing in columns

incolonnare [inkolon'nare] VT (*cifre*) to put in columns; (*Mil*: *truppe*) to draw up in columns; (*Tip*) to set up in columns; (*con macchina da scrivere*) to tabulate
▶ **incolonnarsi** VIP (*truppe*) to draw up in columns

incolore [inko'lore] AGG (*senza colore*) colourless (*Brit*), colorless (*Am*); (*monotono*) dull

incolpare [inkol'pare] VT (*gen*): **incolpare (di)** to blame (for); **hanno incolpato me** they blamed me; **incolpare qn di aver fatto qc** to accuse sb of having done sth; **mi ha incolpato di avergli rotto il motorino** he accused me of damaging his moped; **incolpare l'inesperienza** to blame one's inexperience

incolto, a [in'kolto] AGG **1** (*terreno*) uncultivated **2** (*trascurato*: *barba*) neglected; (*ignorante*: *persona*) uneducated

incolume [in'kɔlume] AGG unhurt, safe and sound; **è uscito incolume dall'incidente** he escaped from the accident unhurt

incolumità [inkolumi'ta] SF safety; **attentato all'incolumità di qn** attempt on sb's life

incombente [inkom'bɛnte] AGG (*pericolo*) imminent, impending

> **LO SAPEVI...?**
> **incombente** non si traduce mai con la parola inglese *incumbent*

incombenza [inkom'bɛntsa] SF duty, task

incombere [in'kombere] VI DIF: **incombere su** (*sovrastare minacciando*) to hang over, threaten

incombustibile [inkombus'tibile] AGG incombustible

incominciare [inkomin'tʃare] VT to begin, start; **incominciare a fare qc** to begin *o* start doing sth; **ha incominciato a ridere** she started to laugh; **ha incominciato a piangere** she started crying
■ VI (*aus* **essere**) to begin, start; **la partita incomincia alle sette** the match starts at seven; **la prima parola incomincia per F** the first word starts with F

incommensurabile [inkommensu'rabile] AGG (*Mat*) incommensurable; (*fig*: *pregi*) incalculable; (: *distanza*) immeasurable

incommensurabilmente [inkommensurabil'mente] AVV (*vedi agg*) incommensurably; incalculably; immeasurably

incomodare [inkomo'dare] VT to trouble, inconvenience
▶ **incomodarsi** VR to put o.s. out

incomodo [in'kɔmodo] AGG: **fare il terzo incomodo** to play gooseberry
■ SM trouble, inconvenience, bother; **prendersi l'incomodo di fare qc** to take the trouble to do sth; **essere d'incomodo a qn** to be in sb's way; **togliere l'incomodo** (*andarsene*) to take o.s. off

incomparabile [inkompa'rabile] AGG incomparable

incomparabilmente [inkomparabil'mente] AVV incomparably

incompatibile [inkompa'tibile] AGG (*inconciliabile*) incompatible
incompatibilità [inkompatibili'ta] SF incompatibility; **incompatibilità di carattere** (mutual) incompatibility
incompetente [inkompe'tɛnte] AGG (*gen, Dir*) incompetent; **essere incompetente in qc** to be incompetent *o* useless (*fam*) at sth
■ SM/F incompetent person; **è un incompetente** he is incompetent
incompetenza [inkompe'tɛntsa] SF incompetence
incompiuto, a [inkom'pjuto] AGG unfinished, incomplete; **rimanere incompiuto** to be left unfinished; **una sinfonia incompiuta** an unfinished symphony
incompleto, a [inkom'plɛto] AGG incomplete
incomprensibile [inkompren'sibile] AGG (*gen*) incomprehensible
incomprensibilmente [inkomprensibil'mente] AVV incomprehensibly
incomprensione [inkompren'sjone] SF **1** (*mancanza di comprensione*) lack of understanding, incomprehension **2** (*malinteso*) misunderstanding
incompreso, a [inkom'preso] AGG misunderstood, not understood; **sono un genio incompreso** (*scherz*) I'm a misunderstood genius
■ SM/F: **è un incompreso** people don't understand him
incomunicabile [inkomuni'kabile] AGG (*sentimento, sensazione*) incommunicable
inconcepibile [inkontʃe'pibile] AGG (*impensabile*) inconceivable, unthinkable; (*assurdo*) incredible; **è inconcepibile!** it's incredible!
inconciliabile [inkontʃi'ljabile] AGG irreconcilable
inconcludente [inkonklu'dɛnte] AGG (*persona*) ineffectual; (*sforzi*) unavailing; (*discorso: sconclusionato*) disconnected
incondizionatamente [inkondittsjonata'mente] AVV unconditionally
incondizionato, a [inkondittsjo'nato] AGG (*approvazione ecc*) unconditional; (*fiducia*) unquestioning, complete; **resa incondizionata** (*anche fig*) unconditional surrender
inconfessabile [inkonfes'sabile] AGG (*pensiero, peccato*) unmentionable
inconfessato, a [inkonfes'sato] AGG (*desiderio, voglia*) unconfessed, secret
inconfondibile [inkonfon'dibile] AGG unmistakable; **il suo stile è inconfondibile** his style is unmistakable
inconfondibilmente [inkonfondibil'mente] AVV unmistakably
inconfutabile [inkonfu'tabile] AGG irrefutable
incongruente [inkongru'ɛnte] AGG inconsistent
incongruenza [inkongru'ɛntsa] SF inconsistency
incongruo, a [in'kɔngruo] AGG insufficient, inadequate
inconoscibile [inkonoʃ'ʃibile] SM: **l'inconoscibile** (*Filosofia*) the unknowable
inconsapevole [inkonsa'pevole] AGG: **inconsapevole di** unaware of, ignorant of
inconsapevolezza [inkonsapevo'lettsa] SF ignorance, lack of awareness
inconsapevolmente [inkonsapevol'mente] AVV unwittingly
inconsciamente [inkonʃa'mente] AVV unconsciously
inconscio, scia, sci, sce [in'kɔnʃo] AGG (*desiderio, impulso*) unconscious
■ SM: **l'inconscio** (*Psic*) the unconscious
inconsistente [inkonsis'tɛnte] AGG (*dubbio*) unfounded; (*ragionamento, prove*) tenuous, flimsy

> **LO SAPEVI...?**
> **inconsistente** non si traduce mai con la parola inglese *inconsistent*

inconsistenza [inkonsis'tɛntsa] SF (*di dubbio*) lack of foundation; (*di ragionamento, prove*) flimsiness

> **LO SAPEVI...?**
> **inconsistenza** non si traduce mai con la parola inglese *inconsistency*

inconsolabile [inkonso'labile] AGG inconsolable
inconsueto, a [inkonsu'ɛto] AGG unusual
inconsulto, a [inkon'sulto] AGG (*gesto, azione*) rash, impetuous
incontaminato, a [inkontami'nato] AGG uncontaminated
incontenibile [inkonte'nibile] AGG (*rabbia*) uncontrollable; (*entusiasmo*) irrepressible
incontentabile [inkonten'tabile] AGG (*desiderio, avidità*) insatiable; (*persona: capriccioso*) hard to please, very demanding
incontestabile [inkontes'tabile] AGG incontrovertible, indisputable
incontestato, a [inkontes'tato] AGG undisputed
incontinenza [inkonti'nɛntsa] SF (*Med*) incontinence
incontrare [inkon'trare] VT **1** (*gen*) to meet; (*in riunione*) to have a meeting with; (*difficoltà, pericolo*) to meet with, run into, come up against; **incontrare qn per caso** to run *o* bump into sb; **l'ho incontrato ad una festa** I met him at a party; **ho incontrato Maurizio per strada** I bumped into Maurizio in the street; **incontrare il favore del pubblico** (*attore, prodotto ecc*) to find favour with *o* be popular with the public **2** (*Sport: squadra*) to meet, play (against); (*: pugile*) to meet, fight; **l'Inter incontrerà la Juve domenica prossima** Inter Milan are playing Juventus next Sunday
▶ **incontrarsi** VR (*uso reciproco*) **1** (*trovarsi: su appuntamento*) to meet (each other); (*: in riunione*) to have a meeting; **incontriamoci davanti al cinema** let's meet in front of the cinema **2** (*Sport*) to meet
incontrario [inkon'trarjo] **all'incontrario** AVV (*sottosopra*) upside down; (*alla rovescia*) back to front; (*all'indietro*) backwards; (*nel senso contrario*) the other way round
incontrastabile [inkontras'tabile] AGG incontrovertible, indisputable
incontrastato, a [inkontras'tato] AGG (*successo, vittoria, verità*) undisputed
incontro[1] [in'kontro] SM **1** (*gen*) meeting; (*fortuito*) encounter; **un incontro al vertice** a summit (meeting); **un incontro casuale** a chance meeting; **a tarda notte si possono fare brutti incontri** you can have some unpleasant encounters late at night **2** (*Sport*) match; **incontro di calcio** football match (*Brit*), soccer game (*Am*); **incontro di pugilato** boxing match
incontro[2] [in'kontro] **incontro a** PREP (*verso*) towards; **mi è venuto incontro sorridente** he came towards me smiling; **andare incontro a qn** to go to meet sb; (*fig: aiutare*) to meet sb halfway; **andare incontro a** (*brutte sorprese*) to come up against, meet; (*spese*) to incur; **andare incontro alla morte** to go to one's death; **stiamo ormai andando incontro alla primavera** we're moving towards spring now, it'll

Ii

soon be spring; **venire incontro a** (*richieste, esigenze*) to comply with

incontrollabile [inkontrol'labile] AGG uncontrollable

inconveniente [inkonve'njɛnte] SM **1** (*difficoltà*) setback, mishap; **ho avuto degli inconvenienti con la macchina** I had some problems with the car **2** (*svantaggio*) drawback, disadvantage, snag; **ha un unico inconveniente: è troppo piccolo** it's only got one drawback: it's too small

> **LO SAPEVI...?**
> **inconveniente** non si traduce mai con la parola inglese ***inconvenient***

incoraggiamento [inkoraddʒa'mento] SM encouragement; **premio d'incoraggiamento** consolation prize

incoraggiare [inkorad'dʒare] VT (*esortare*) to encourage; **incoraggiare qn a fare qc** to encourage sb to do sth; **i suoi l'hanno incoraggiato a studiare musica** his parents encouraged him to study music; **incoraggiare qn allo studio** to encourage sb to study

incornare [inkor'nare] VT to gore; (*Calcio*) to head

incorniciare [inkorni'tʃare] VT to frame; **ho incorniciato la foto** I've framed the photo; **i lunghi capelli le incorniciavano il volto** her long hair framed her face

incoronare [inkoro'nare] VT (*anche fig*) to crown

Incoronata [inkoro'nata] SF (*Rel*) feast of the Coronation of the Virgin Mary

incoronazione [inkoronat'tsjone] SF coronation

incorporare [inkorpo'rare] VT: **incorporare (in)** (*gen, Comm*) to incorporate (into); (*sostanza*) to mix (in); **"incorporare gli albumi nell'impasto"** (*Culin*) "fold the egg whites into the mixture"

incorporato, a [inkorpo'rato] AGG (*parte di impianto*) built-in

incorporeo, a [inkor'pɔreo] AGG incorporeal; **esseri incorporei** spirits

incorreggibile [inkorred'dʒibile] AGG (*gen*) incorrigible; (*giocatore*) inveterate

incorreggibilmente [inkorreddʒibil'mente] AVV (*gen*) incorrigibly

incorrere [in'korrere] VI IRREG (*aus* **essere**): **incorrere in** (*pericolo, guaio*) to run into, come up against, meet with

incorruttibile [inkorrut'tibile] AGG (*funzionario*) incorruptible; (*fig: fede*) unshakeable; (*: bellezza*) unfading

incorso, a [in'korso] PP *di* **incorrere**

incosciente [inkoʃ'ʃɛnte] AGG **1** (*irresponsabile*) reckless, thoughtless; **un automobilista incosciente** a reckless driver **2** (*privo di sensi*) unconscious; **è rimasto incosciente per alcuni minuti** he was unconscious for several minutes
■ SM/F reckless person, thoughtless person

incoscientemente [inkoʃʃente'mente] AVV recklessly, thoughtlessly

incoscienza [inkoʃ'ʃɛntsa] SF (*vedi agg*) recklessness, thoughtlessness; unconsciousness

incostante [inkos'tante] AGG (*studente, impiegato*) inconsistent; (*carattere*) fickle, inconstant; (*rendimento*) sporadic

incostanza [inkos'tantsa] SF inconstancy, fickleness

incostituzionale [inkostituttsjo'nale] AGG unconstitutional

incostituzionalità [inkostituttsjonali'ta] SF unconstitutionality

incredibile [inkre'dibile] AGG incredible, unbelievable; **è incredibile!** that's incredible!

incredibilmente [inkredibil'mente] AVV incredibly, unbelievably

incredulità [inkreduli'ta] SF incredulity

incredulo, a [in'krɛdulo] AGG incredulous, disbelieving

incrementare [inkremen'tare] VT (*aumentare: vendite, produzione*) to increase; (*dar sviluppo a: commercio*) to promote

incremento [inkre'mento] SM: **incremento (di)** (*aumento numerico*) increase (in), growth (in); (*sviluppo*) development; **un incremento del numero di macchine** an increase in the number of cars; **incremento demografico** population rise *o* growth

incresciosо, a [inkreʃ'ʃoso] AGG (*spiacevole*) unpleasant; **incidente increscioso** regrettable incident

increspare [inkres'pare] VT (*capelli*) to curl; (*stoffa*) to gather; (*superficie: del mare*) to ripple
▶ **incresparsi** VIP (*superficie: di mare, lago*) to ripple

incriminabile [inkrimi'nabile] AGG (*Dir*) chargeable

incriminare [inkrimi'nare] VT (*Dir*): **incriminare qn per qc** to charge sb with sth

incriminato, a [inkrimi'nato] AGG (*Dir*) indicted; **questa è la frase incriminata** (*scherz*) this was the fateful expression

incriminazione [inkriminat'tsjone] SF (*atto d'accusa*) indictment, charge; **non c'erano prove sufficienti per la sua incriminazione** there wasn't sufficient evidence to charge him

incrinare [inkri'nare] VT (*vetro, specchio, vaso*) to crack; (*fig: rapporti, amicizia*) to spoil, create a rift in; **non l'ho rotto, l'ho solo incrinato** I didn't break it, I just cracked it
▶ **incrinarsi** VIP (*vetro, ghiaccio, roccia*) to crack; (*rapporti, amicizia*) to deteriorate

incrinatura [inkrina'tura] SF (*crepa*) crack; (*fig: di rapporti*) rift

incrociare [inkro'tʃare] VT **1** (*gen*) to cross; (*strada, linea*) to cut across; **incrociare le gambe** to cross one's legs; **incrociare le braccia** to fold one's arms; (*fig*) to down tools, refuse to work; **ha incrociato le braccia** he crossed his arms **2** (*autoveicolo, persona*) to meet; **l'ho incrociato per strada** I met him in the street **3** (*animali, piante*) to cross
■ VI (*aus* **avere**) (*Naut, Aer*) to cruise
▶ **incrociarsi** VR (*uso reciproco: strade, rette*) to cross, intersect; (*: persone, veicoli*) to pass each other; (*fig: sguardi*) to meet; (*: battute*) to fly thick and fast; **ci siamo incrociati nel corridoio** we met in the corridor

incrociato, a [inkro'tʃato] AGG: **fuoco incrociato** (*Mil*) crossfire

incrociatore [inkrotʃa'tore] SM (*Naut*) cruiser

incrocio, ci [in'krotʃo] SM **1** (*di strade*) crossroads, junction; (*Ferr*) crossing; **all'incrocio gira a destra** turn right at the junction **2** **l'incrocio dei pali** (*Calcio*) the top corner of the goalposts **3** (*Zool, Bot*) cross; **un incrocio tra un collie e un labrador** a cross between a collie and a labrador

incrollabile [inkrol'labile] AGG (*fede*) unshakeable, firm

incrostare [inkros'tare] VT to encrust
▶ **incrostarsi** VIP: **incrostarsi di** to become encrusted with

incrostato, a [inkros'tato] AGG (*tubi*) furred up; **incrostato (di)** (*fango ecc*) encrusted (with); (*pietre preziose*) studded (with), encrusted (with)

incrostazione [inkrostat'tsjone] SF incrustation,

encrustation; (*di calcare*) scale; (*nelle tubature*) scale, fur (*Brit*)

incruento, a [inkru'ɛnto] AGG (*battaglia*) without bloodshed, bloodless

incubatrice [inkuba'tritʃe] SF incubator

incubazione [inkubat'tsjone] SF incubation

incubo ['inkubo] SM (*anche fig*) nightmare; **stanotte ho avuto un incubo** I had a nightmare last night; **ho l'incubo degli esami** exams are a nightmare for me

incudine [in'kudine] SF anvil; **trovarsi** *o* **essere tra l'incudine e il martello** (*fig*) to be between the devil and the deep blue sea

inculare [inku'lare] VT (*fam: fregare*) to screw

inculata [inku'lata] SF (*fam!: solenne fregatura*): **ho preso una bella inculata** they really screwed me (*fam!*)

inculcare [inkul'kare] VT: **inculcare qc in qn** to inculcate sth into sb, instil sth into sb

incuneare [inkune'are] VT to wedge
▶ **incunearsi** VIP to slot in

incupire [inku'pire] VT (*rendere scuro*) to darken; (*fig: intristire*) to fill with gloom
■ VI (*aus* **essere**), **incupirsi** VIP (*vedi vt*) to darken; to become gloomy

incurabile [inku'rabile] AGG, SM/F incurable; **un male incurabile** an incurable disease

incurabilmente [inkurabil'mente] AVV incurably

incurante [inku'rante] AGG: **incurante (di)** heedless (of), careless (of)

incuria [in'kurja] SF negligence

incuriosire [inkurjo'sire] VT to arouse the curiosity of, make curious
▶ **incuriosirsi** VIP to become curious

incuriosito, a [inkurjo'sito] AGG curious

incursione [inkur'sjone] SF (*Mil, Aer*) incursion, foray, raid; (*di ladri ecc*) raid; **un'incursione aerea** an air raid

incurvare [inkur'vare] VT (*piegare*) to curve, bend; **non incurvare la schiena!** sit *o* stand up straight!; **il lavoro a tavolino gli ha incurvato la schiena** *o* **le spalle** deskwork has made him round-shouldered *o* has given him a stoop
▶ **incurvarsi** VIP (*gen*) to bend; (*legno*) to warp; (*persona*) to develop a stoop, become bent

incurvato, a [inkur'vato] AGG bent

incusso, a [in'kusso] PP *di* **incutere**

incustodito, a [inkusto'dito] AGG (*bagaglio*) unattended, unguarded; **passaggio a livello incustodito** unmanned level crossing; **il parcheggio è incustodito** the car park is unattended; **non lasciare il bagaglio incustodito** don't leave your luggage unattended

incutere [in'kutere] VT IRREG: **incutere rispetto a qn** to command sb's respect; **incutere paura a qn** to strike fear into sb; **incutere soggezione a qn** to cow sb

indaco, chi ['indako] AGG INV, SM indigo

indaffarato, a [indaffa'rato] AGG: **indaffarato (a fare qc)** busy (doing sth); **era indaffarato a riparare la bici** he was busy mending his bike

indagare [inda'gare] VI (*aus* **avere**) **indagare su** to investigate; **la polizia sta indagando sul delitto** the police are investigating the crime; **indagare sul conto di qn** to investigate sb, make enquiries about sb; **è meglio non indagare** it's better not to enquire too closely
■ VT to investigate, look into

indagatore, trice [indaga'tore] AGG (*sguardo, domanda*) searching; (*mente*) inquiring; **rivolgere a qn uno sguardo indagatore** to give sb a searching look

indagine [in'dadʒine] SF **1** (*inchiesta*) investigation, inquiry, enquiry; **fare** *o* **svolgere un'indagine (su)** to carry out an investigation *o* inquiry (into); **le indagini della polizia** police investigations **2** (*ricerca*) research, study; **fare** *o* **svolgere un'indagine su** to carry out *o* do research into, make a study of; **indagine su campione** sample survey; **indagine demoscopica** public opinion poll; **indagine di mercato** market survey

indebitamente [indebita'mente] AVV (*immeritatamente*) undeservedly; (*erroneamente*) wrongfully

indebitamento [indebita'mento] SM debt

indebitare [indebi'tare] VT: **indebitare qn** to get sb into debt
▶ **indebitarsi** VR: **si è indebitato fino al collo** he is up to his eyes in debt; **indebitarsi con qn/con la banca** to owe money to sb/to the bank

indebito, a [in'debito] AGG (*onori, accuse*) undeserved; **appropriazione indebita** embezzlement

indebolimento [indeboli'mento] SM **1** weakening **2** (*debolezza*) weakness

indebolire [indebo'lire] VT to weaken
■ VI (*aus* **essere**), **indebolirsi** VIP (*persona*) to grow weak; (*vista*) to deteriorate

indecente [inde'tʃɛnte] AGG indecent; **in quel ristorante il servizio è indecente** (*inaccettabile*) the service is disgraceful at that restaurant; **quella minigonna è indecente!** that mini skirt is indecent!

indecentemente [indetʃente'mente] AVV (*gen*) indecently; **esprimersi indecentemente** (*oscenamente*) to use obscene language

indecenza [inde'tʃɛntsa] SF indecency; **è un'indecenza!** (*vergogna*) it's scandalous!, it's a disgrace!

indecifrabile [indetʃi'frabile] AGG (*scrittura*) illegible, indecipherable; (*messaggio, testo*) incomprehensible

indecisione [indetʃi'zjone] SF indecision, indecisiveness

indeciso, a [inde'tʃizo] AGG (*persona: titubante*) indecisive; (*: che non ha ancora deciso, questione, risultato*) undecided; (*tempo*) unsettled; (*colore, forma*) indistinct; **sono indeciso tra questi due** I can't decide between these two; **era indeciso su cosa regalarle** he couldn't decide what to give her

indeclinabile [indekli'nabile] AGG (*Gramm*) indeclinable

indecorosamente [indekorosa'mente] AVV indecorously

indecoroso, a [indeko'roso] AGG (*comportamento*) indecorous, unseemly

indefessamente [indefessa'mente] AVV indefatigably, tirelessly

indefesso, a [inde'fɛsso] AGG indefatigable, untiring

indefinibile [indefi'nibile] AGG indefinable

indefinito, a [indefi'nito] AGG (*indeterminato: anche Gramm*) indefinite; (*impreciso*) undefined; (*irrisolto: questione, controversia*) unresolved

indeformabile [indefor'mabile] AGG crushproof

indegnamente [indeɲɲa'mente] AVV (*comportarsi*) shamefully

indegno, a [in'deɲɲo] AGG (*atto*) shameful; (*persona*) unworthy; **è indegno di tanta ammirazione** he doesn't deserve so much admiration

indeiscente [indeiʃʃente] AGG (*Bot*) indehiscent

indelebile [inde'lebile] AGG indelible, permanent

Ii

indelebilmente [indelebil'mente] AVV indelibly

indelicatamente [indelikata'mente] AVV indiscreetly, tactlessly

indelicatezza [indelika'tettsa] SF tactlessness; **è stata un'indelicatezza da parte sua** it was tactless of him

indelicato, a [indeli'kato] AGG *(domanda)* indiscreet, tactless

indemagliabile [indemaʎ'ʎabile] AGG *(calze, tessuto)* run-resist

indemoniato, a [indemo'njato] AGG possessed (by the devil); **quel ragazzino è indemoniato** *(fig)* that boy is a little demon
■SM/F person possessed by the devil; **gridare come un indemoniato** to shout like one possessed

indenne [in'dɛnne] AGG *(illeso)* unscathed, unharmed, unhurt

indennità [indenni'ta] SF INV *(rimborso: di spese)* reimbursement; (: *di perdita*) indemnity, compensation; **indennità di contingenza** cost-of-living allowance; **indennità di fine rapporto** severance payment; **indennità parlamentare** member of parliament's salary; **indennità di trasferta** travel allowance, travel expenses *pl*

indennizzare [indennid'dzare] VT to indemnify, compensate

indennizzo [inden'niddzo] SM *(somma)* indemnity, compensation

inderogabile [indero'gabile] AGG binding

indescrivibile [indeskri'vibile] AGG indescribable

indescrivibilmente [indeskrivibil'mente] AVV indescribably

indesiderabile [indeside'rabile] AGG undesirable; **persona indesiderabile** persona non grata

indesiderato, a [indeside'rato] AGG unwanted

indeterminatezza [indetermina'tettsa] SF vagueness

indeterminativo, a [indetermina'tivo] AGG *(Gramm)* indefinite; **articolo indeterminativo** indefinite article

indeterminato, a [indetermi'nato] AGG *(tempo)* unspecified, indefinite; *(quantità, spazio)* indeterminate; **rimandare qc a tempo indeterminato** to postpone sth indefinitely

indetto, a [in'detto] PP *di* **indire**

India ['indja] SF India; **le Indie occidentali** the West Indies; **mi è piaciuta molto l'India** I really liked India; **andremo in India quest'estate** we're going to India this summer

Indiana [in'djana] SM Indiana

indiano, a [in'djano] AGG Indian; **un ristorante indiano** an Indian restaurant; **l'oceano Indiano** the Indian Ocean
■SM/F *(dell'India)* Indian; *(dell'America)* (American) Indian; **gli indiani** the Indians; **fare l'indiano** *(fig)* to feign ignorance

indiavolato, a [indjavo'lato] AGG *(persona: arrabbiato)* furious; (: *vivace, violento*) wild; *(bambino)* high-spirited; *(chiasso)* terrible, awful; *(danza, ritmo)* frenzied

indicare [indi'kare] VT **1** *(mostrare)* to show, indicate; (: *col dito*) to point to, point out; **indicare qc a qn** to show sb sth; **indicare la strada a qn** to show sb the way; **gli indicherò la strada** I'll show him the way; **indicare qn col dito** to point to *o* at sb; **m'indicò l'uscita** he showed me where the exit was; **la lancetta grande indica i minuti** the big hand shows the minutes; **cosa indica questo segnale?** what does this signal mean?; **le varie tappe erano indicate sulla carta** the various stops were indicated *o* shown *o* marked on the map; **i risultati indicano che...** the results indicate *o* show that ... **2** *(consigliare)* to suggest, recommend; **mi indicò un medico** he recommended a doctor to me

indicativamente [indikativa'mente] AVV as an indication; **qual è il prezzo, indicativamente?** can you give me an idea of the price?

indicativo, a [indika'tivo] AGG *(gen, Gramm)* indicative; *(prezzo)* approximate; **a titolo puramente indicativo** just as an indication
■SM *(Gramm)* indicative (mood)

indicato, a [indi'kato] AGG *(consigliato)* advisable; *(adatto)*: **indicato per** suitable for, appropriate for; **questa cura non è indicata in caso di gravidanza** this treatment is not advisable during pregnancy

indicatore, trice [indika'tore] AGG indicating; **cartello indicatore** sign
■SM *(Tecn)* gauge, indicator; *(Chim)* indicator; **indicatore della benzina** fuel gauge, petrol *(Brit)* *o* gas *(Am)* gauge; **indicatore ecologico** indicator species; **indicatore di radiazioni** radiation detector; **indicatore di velocità** *(Aut)* speedometer; *(Aer)* airspeed indicator; **indicatori di direzione** *(Aut)* indicator lights

indicazione [indikat'tsjone] SF *(gen)* indication; *(istruzione)* instruction, direction; *(informazione)* piece of information; **indicazioni** SFPL *(Med)* directions; **non è stato in grado di fornirmi indicazioni utili** he was unable to give me any useful information; **mi ha dato le indicazioni sbagliate per arrivare lì** he didn't tell me the right way to get there

indice ['inditʃe] SM **1** *(Anat)* index finger, forefinger **2** *(indicatore)* needle, pointer; *(fig: indizio)* sign; **tale comportamento è indice d'ignoranza/di pigrizia** such behaviour is a sign of ignorance/laziness **3** *(di libro)* (table of) contents *pl*; **indice analitico** index **4** *(Rel)*: **l'Indice (dei libri proibiti)** the Index; **mettere all'indice** *(fig)* to blacklist **5** *(Mat, Statistica: rapporto)* index; **indice azionario** *(Borsa)* share index; **indice di gradimento** *(Radio, TV)* popularity rating; **indice dei prezzi al consumo** ≈ retail price index *(Brit)*, ≈ consumer price index *(Am)*; **indice di produzione** production index; **indice di rifrazione costante** *(Fis)* refractive constant
■AGG: **dito indice** index finger, forefinger

indicherò *ecc* [indike'rɔ] VB *vedi* **indicare**

indicibile [indi'tʃibile] AGG inexpressible, unspeakable

indicizzare [inditʃid'dzare] VT *(salari)* to index-link *(Brit)*, index *(Am)*

indicizzato, a [inditʃid'dzato] AGG *(polizza, salario ecc)* index-linked *(Brit)*, indexed *(Am)*

indicizzazione [inditʃiddzat'tsjone] SF indexing

indietreggiare [indjetred'dʒare] VI *(aus* **avere** *o* **essere***)* *(anche fig)* to draw back, retreat; *(Mil)* to retreat

indietro [in'djɛtro] AVV **1** *(stato, tempo)* behind; **essere indietro negli studi** to be behind in one's studies; **rimanere indietro** *(persona: di proposito)* to stay back *o* behind; (: *proprio malgrado*) to drop *o* lag behind, be left behind; **mentre dettava sono rimasto indietro** while he was dictating I got behind, I couldn't keep up with his dictation; **mettere indietro l'orologio** to put one's watch back; **bisogna mettere l'orologio indietro di un'ora** the clock has to be put back an hour; **essere indietro** *(orologio)* to be slow; *(persona: col lavoro)* to be behind; **il mio orologio è indietro** my watch is slow; **essere indietro con i pagamenti** to be behind *o* in arrears with one's payments **2** *(moto)* back, backwards; **tornare indietro** to go back; **torniamo indietro?** shall we turn back?; **mandare** *o* **rimandare qc indietro** to send sth back; **andare avanti e indietro** to walk up and down; **non vado né avanti né indietro** *(fig)* I'm not getting anywhere, I'm getting nowhere; **voltarsi indietro** to look back, look round; **farsi indietro** to move back; **fare un passo indietro** to take a step back *o* backwards; **facciamo un passo indietro negli anni venti** let's go back *o* cast our minds back to the twenties; **ho fatto un passo indietro** I took a step back; **(state) indietro!** get back! **3 dare qc indietro a qn** *(restituire)* to give sth back to sb; **ha voluto indietro i soldi** she wanted her money back **4 all'indietro** backwards; **camminare all'indietro** to walk backwards; **cadere all'indietro** to fall over backwards; **è caduta all'indietro** she fell backwards

indifeso, a [indi'feso] AGG *(città, confine)* undefended; *(persona)* helpless, defenceless *(Brit)*, defenseless *(Am)*; **un povero bambino indifeso** a poor defenceless child

indifferente [indiffe'rɛnte] AGG **1 indifferente (a)** indifferent (to); **lasciare indifferente** to leave cold; **la notizia mi ha lasciato del tutto indifferente** the news left me completely cold; **mi è indifferente** I don't mind, it's all the same to me; **quell'uomo mi è indifferente** that man means nothing to me, I feel quite indifferent towards that man; **a piedi o in auto è indifferente** on foot or by car, it's all the same to me **2 non indifferente** *(notevole: somma, spesa)* sizeable, not inconsiderable
■SM: **fare l'indifferente** to pretend to be indifferent, be *o* act casual; *(fingere di non vedere o sentire)* to pretend not to notice; **cerca di fare l'indifferente, sta venendo da questa parte** try to act casual, she's coming this way; **non fare l'indifferente, sto parlando di te** don't pretend you don't understand, I'm talking about you

indifferentemente [indifferente'mente] AVV without distinction; **bevo indifferentemente tè o caffè** I drink tea or coffee; **prenderei indifferentemente questo o quello** I'd be quite happy with either one, either would do nicely

indifferenza [indiffe'rɛntsa] SF indifference

indifferibile [indiffe'ribile] AGG not deferable

indigeno, a [in'didʒeno] AGG indigenous, native
■SM/F native

indigente [indi'dʒɛnte] AGG destitute, poverty-stricken
■SM/F pauper; **gli indigenti** the poor *o* needy

indigenza [indi'dʒɛntsa] SF extreme poverty, destitution; **vivere nell'indigenza** to live in extreme poverty

indigestione [indidʒes'tjone] SF indigestion; **fare indigestione di qc** to eat too much of sth; *(fig: di romanzi, film)* to have a surfeit of sth, be sick of; **ho fatto un'indigestione di dolci** I've eaten too many cakes

indigesto, a [indi'dʒɛsto] AGG indigestible; *(fig: persona, libro)* unbearable; **il latte mi è indigesto** I find milk indigestible

indignare [indiɲ'ɲare] VT: **indignare qn** to make sb indignant *o* angry, fill sb with indignation; **il suo comportamento mi ha indignato** his behaviour made me angry
▶ **indignarsi** VIP: **indignarsi per** to be (*o* get) indignant about *o* at

indignato, a [indiɲ'ɲato] AGG: **indignato (per)** indignant (about *o* at)

indignazione [indiɲɲat'tsjone] SF indignation; **con sua grande indignazione** much to his indignation

indimenticabile [indimenti'kabile] AGG unforgettable; **una vacanza indimenticabile** an unforgettable holiday

indio, dia, di, die ['indjo] AGG, SM/F (South American) Indian

indipendente [indipen'dɛnte] AGG *(gen, Pol, Gramm)*: **indipendente (da)** independent (of); **è indipendente dalla mia volontà** it is beyond my control; **"affittasi camera con ingresso indipendente"** "room to let with independent access"; **ha un carattere molto indipendente** she's got a very independent nature; **essere economicamente indipendente** to be financially independent; **non sono ancora economicamente indipendente** I'm not yet financially independent
■SM/F *(Pol)* independent

indipendentemente [indipendente'mente] AVV **1** *(in modo libero)* independently **2** *(a prescindere da)*: **verrò indipendentemente dal fatto che lui venga o meno** I'll come anyway, whether he comes or not; **indipendentemente dal fatto che gli piaccia o meno, verrà!** whether he likes it or not, he's coming!, he's coming, whether he likes it or not!

indipendenza [indipen'dɛntsa] SF independence

indire [in'dire] VT IRREG *(concorso)* to announce; *(elezioni)* to call

indirettamente [indiretta'mente] AVV indirectly

indiretto, a [indi'rɛtto] AGG *(gen)* indirect; **per vie indirette** indirectly; **discorso indiretto** indirect speech

indirizzare [indirit'tsare] VT *(lettera, osservazione, richiesta)* to address; **la lettera era indirizzata a me** the letter was addressed to me; **indirizzare la parola a qn** to address sb; **mi hanno indirizzato qui** they sent me here; **un libro indirizzato ai ragazzi** a book intended *o* written for young people; **indirizzare i propri sforzi verso** to direct one's efforts towards; **l'hanno indirizzato alla segretaria del personale** he was referred to the personnel officer
▶ **indirizzarsi** VR *(rivolgersi)*: **indirizzarsi a qn** to speak to sb

indirizzario, ri [indirit'tsarjo] SM mailing list

indirizzo [indi'rittso] SM **1** *(di domicilio)* address; **sbagliare indirizzo** to have the wrong address; **se vieni da me in cerca di aiuto, hai sbagliato indirizzo** if you're looking for help from me, you've come to the wrong person; **mi dai il tuo indirizzo?** can I have your address? **2** *(fig: direzione)* direction, course; (: *tendenza*) trend; **mutare indirizzo** to change course *o* direction; **stanno seguendo l'indirizzo giusto** they're on the right lines, they're going in the right direction; **l'attuale indirizzo politico** the present political trend **3** *(Inform)*: **indirizzo assoluto** absolute address; **indirizzo relativo** relative address

indisciplina [indiʃʃi'plina] SF indiscipline, lack of discipline

indisciplinato, a [indiʃʃipli'nato] AGG undisciplined, unruly

indiscretamente [indiskreta'mente] AVV indiscreetly

indiscreto, a [indis'kreto] AGG indiscreet; **se non sono indiscreto...** if you don't mind my asking ...

indiscrezione [indiskret'tsjone] SF **1** *(qualità)*

Ii

indiscretion **2** (*azione*) indiscretion; (*fuga di notizie*) unconfirmed report
indiscriminatamente [indiskriminata'mente] AVV indiscriminately
indiscriminato, a [indiskrimi'nato] AGG indiscriminate
indiscusso, a [indis'kusso] AGG (*autorità, campione*) undisputed
indiscutibile [indisku'tibile] AGG indisputable, unquestionable
indiscutibilmente [indiskutibil'mente] AVV indisputably, unquestionably
indispensabile [indispen'sabile] AGG (*essenziale*) essential, indispensable; (*necessario*) necessary; **rendersi indispensabile** to make o.s. indispensable; **è uno strumento indispensabile** it's an essential tool; **non è indispensabile che ci sia anche tu** it's not essential for you to be here
■ SM: **porterò con me solo l'indispensabile** I'll take the absolute minimum with me; **ho l'indispensabile per il picnic** I've got everything I need for the picnic
indispettire [indispet'tire] VT to irritate, annoy
■ VI (*aus* **essere**), **indispettirsi** VIP to get *o* grow irritated *o* annoyed
indisponente [indispo'nɛnte] AGG irritating, annoying
indisporre [indis'porre] VT IRREG to antagonize; **il suo modo di fare mi indispone** I find his manner irritating
indisposizione [indispozit'tsjone] SF (slight) indisposition
indisposto, a [indis'posto] PP *di* **indisporre**
■ AGG indisposed (*frm*), unwell; **essere indisposto** to be unwell
indissolubile [indisso'lubile] AGG indissoluble
indissolubilmente [indissolubil'mente] AVV indissolubly
indistintamente [indistinta'mente] AVV **1** (*senza distinzioni*) indiscriminately, without exception **2** (*in modo indefinito*: *vedere, sentire*) vaguely, faintly
indistinto, a [indis'tinto] AGG (*gen*) indistinct; (*colori*) vague
indistruttibile [indistrut'tibile] AGG indestructible
indisturbato, a [indistur'bato] AGG undisturbed
indivia [in'divja] SF endive
individuale [individu'ale] AGG (*gen*) individual; (*libertà*) personal; (*qualità*) distinctive; **libertà individuale** personal freedom; **lezioni individuali** individual tuition
individualismo [individua'lizmo] SM individualism
individualista, i, e [individua'lista] SM/F individualist
individualistico, a, ci, che [individua'listiko] AGG individualistic
individualità [individuali'ta] SF (*unicità*) individuality; (*personalità*) personality
individualizzare [individualid'dzare] VT to individualize
individualizzazione [individualiddzat'tsjone] SF individualization
individualmente [individual'mente] AVV individually
individuare [individu'are] VT **1** (*determinare*) to identify; (: *posizione*) to locate **2** (*riconoscere*) to pick out, single out; **sono riuscito ad individuarlo tra la folla** I managed to pick him out in the crowd; **individuarsi**
▶ **individuarsi** VIP (*assumere forma distinta*) to be characterized
individuazione [individuat'tsjone] SF (*gen*) identification; (*di posizione, relitto ecc*) location
individuo [indi'viduo] SM (*gen*) individual; (*pegg*: *uomo*) character, fellow; **un losco individuo** a shady character
indivisibile [indivi'zibile] AGG (*Mat*) indivisible; **quei due sono indivisibili** those two are inseparable
indivisibilità [indivizibili'ta] SF (*Mat*) indivisibility
indiviso, a [indi'vizo] AGG undivided
indiziare [indit'tsjare] VT: **indiziare qn** to cast suspicion on sb; **essere indiziato di qc** to be suspected of sth
indiziato, a [indit'tsjato] AGG suspected
■ SM/F suspect
indizio, zi [in'dittsjo] SM (*segno*) indication, sign; (*traccia*) clue; (*Dir*) piece of evidence; **la polizia non ha trovato alcun indizio** the police haven't found any clues
Indocina [indo'tʃina] SF Indochina
indoeuropeo, a [indoeuro'pɛo] AGG, SM/F Indo-European
indole ['indole] SF nature, character; **di indole buona** good-natured
indolente [indo'lɛnte] AGG indolent, lazy
indolentemente [indolente'mente] AVV indolently, lazily
indolenza [indo'lɛntsa] SF indolence, laziness
indolenzimento [indolentsi'mento] SM (*vedi vb*) stiffness, ache; numbness
indolenzire [indolen'tsire] VT (*gambe, braccia ecc*) to make stiff, cause to ache; (: *intorpidire*) to numb
■ VI (*aus* **essere**), **indolenzirsi** VIP (*vedi vt*) to become stiff; to go numb
indolenzito, a [indolen'tsito] AGG stiff, aching; (*intorpidito*) numb; **sono tutto indolenzito** I'm aching all over
indolore [indo'lore] AGG (*anche fig*) painless
indomabile [indo'mabile] AGG (*fig*: *volontà*) indomitable; (: *incendio*) uncontrollable; (*animale*) untameable
indomani [indo'mani] SM: **l'indomani** the next day, the following day; **ha detto che sarebbe tornata l'indomani** she said she'd come back the next day
indomito, a [in'dɔmito] AGG (*coraggio*) indomitable
Indonesia [indo'nezja] SF Indonesia
indonesiano, a [indone'zjano] AGG, SM/F, SM Indonesian
indorare [indo'rare] VT (*rivestire in oro*) to gild; (*Culin*) to dip in egg yolk; **indorare la pillola** (*fig*) to sugar the pill
indossare [indos'sare] VT (*mettere indosso*) to put on; (*avere indosso*) to wear, have on
indossatore, trice [indossa'tore] SM/F model; **fare l'indossatore** to be a model; **fa l'indossatrice** she's a model; **indossatrice volante** freelance model
indotto, a [in'dɔtto] PP *di* **indurre**
■ SM (*Econ*) components industry and services connected to a major industry
indottrinamento [indottrina'mento] SM indoctrination
indottrinare [indottri'nare] VT to indoctrinate
indovinare [indovi'nare] VT **1** (*gen*) to guess; (*il futuro*) to predict, foretell; **tirare a indovinare** to hazard a guess, to guess; **non lo sapevo, quindi ho tirato a indovinare** I didn't know, so I had a guess; **indovina chi viene a cena!** guess who's coming to dinner!;

indovina chi ho incontrato ieri! guess who I met yesterday! **2** (*azzeccare*: *risposta*) to get right; **non ne indovini una** you never get anything right; **bravo, hai indovinato!** well done, you've got it right!
indovinato, a [indovi'nato] AGG successful; (*scelta*) inspired; **una festa indovinata** a successful party
indovinello [indovi'nɛllo] SM riddle; **sai risolvere questo indovinello?** do you know the answer to this riddle?
indovino, a [indo'vino] SM/F fortune-teller, soothsayer
indù [in'du] AGG, SM/F Hindu
indubbiamente [indubbja'mente] AVV undoubtedly; **sarai a Parigi per la fine del mese? — indubbiamente** will you be in Paris by the end of the month? — definitely; **è indubbiamente uno dei migliori** it's definitely one of the best
indubbio, bia, bi, bie [in'dubbjo] AGG undoubted, undeniable; **è indubbio che...** there is no doubt that...
indubitabile [indubi'tabile] AGG indubitable
induco *ecc* [in'duko] VB *vedi* **indurre**
indugiare [indu'dʒare] VI (*aus* **avere**) (*attardarsi*) to take one's time, delay; **non ha indugiato ad accettare l'invito** he wasted no time in accepting the invitation
indugio, gi [in'dudʒo] SM (*ritardo*) delay; **senza indugio** without delay, straight away
induismo [indu'izmo] SM Hinduism
indulgente [indul'dʒɛnte] AGG (*gen*) indulgent; (*giudice*) lenient
indulgenza [indul'dʒɛntsa] SF **1** (*vedi agg*) indulgence; leniency **2** (*Rel*) indulgence; **indulgenza plenaria** plenary indulgence
indulgere [in'duldʒere] VI IRREG (*aus* **avere**): **indulgere a qc** (*abbandonarsi*) to indulge in sth; (*accondiscendere*) to comply with sth
indulto [in'dulto] PP *di* **indulgere**
■ SM (*Dir*) pardon
indumento [indu'mento] SM garment, article of clothing; **un indumento pesante** a warm garment; **un negozio di indumenti usati** a secondhand clothes shop; **ha preso alcuni indumenti e se n'è andata** she took some clothes and left; **indumenti intimi** underwear *sg*, underclothing *sg*, underclothes *pl*
indurimento [induri'mento] SM hardening
indurire [indu'rire] VB IRREG
■ VT (*anche fig*: *cuore*) to harden; **viene usato per indurire l'acciaio** it's used to harden steel
■ VI (*aus* **essere**), **indurirsi** VIP to harden, become hard; **il terreno si è indurito** the ground has gone hard
indurre [in'durre] VT IRREG: **indurre qn a fare qc** to induce *o* persuade sb to do sth; **indurre con lusinghe qn a fare qc** to cajole sb into doing sth; **indurre in errore** to mislead, lead astray; **indurre in tentazione** to lead into temptation
indussi *ecc* [in'dussi] VB *vedi* **indurre**
industria [in'dustrja] SF **1** (*attività*) industry; **industria pesante/leggera** heavy/light industry; **la piccola/grande industria** small/big business **2** (*impresa*) factory, industrial concern; **industria di assemblaggio** assembly industry; **industria automobilistica** motor industry; **lavora nell'industria automobilistica** he works in the car industry; **industria tessile** textile industry
⊳ www.minindustria.it/

industriale [indus'trjale] AGG industrial; **una città industriale** an industrial town
■ SM/F industrialist; **è un industriale** he is an industrialist
industrialismo [industrja'lizmo] SM industrialism
industrializzare [industrjalid'dzare] VT to industrialize
industrializzato, a [industrjalid'dzato] AGG industrialized
industrializzazione [industrjaliddzat'tsjone] SF industrialization
industrialmente [industrjal'mente] AVV industrially
industriarsi [indus'trjarsi] VIP to do one's best, try hard
industriosamente [industrjosa'mente] AVV industriously
industrioso, a [indus'trjoso] AGG industrious, hard-working
induttivo, a [indut'tivo] AGG inductive
induttore, trice [indut'tore] AGG (*Elettr*) inductive
■ SM (*Elettr*) inductor
induzione [indut'tsjone] SF induction
inebetire [inebe'tire] VT to stupefy, daze
■ VI (*aus* **essere**), **inebetirsi** VIP to become stupid
inebetito, a [inebe'tito] AGG dazed, stunned
inebriante [inebri'ante] AGG (*alcolico*) intoxicating; (*fig*: *eccitante*) heady, exciting, exhilarating
inebriare [inebri'are] VT (*anche fig*) to intoxicate
▶ **inebriarsi** VIP to become intoxicated; **inebriarsi alla vista di qc** to go into raptures at the sight of sth
inebriato, a [inebri'ato] AGG (*anche fig*) intoxicated, inebriated
ineccepibile [inettʃe'pibile] AGG (*comportamento*) exemplary, unexceptionable
inedia [i'nɛdja] SF starvation; **morire d'inedia** to starve to death
inedito, a [i'nɛdito] AGG (*non pubblicato*) unpublished; **notizia inedita** fresh piece of news
■ SM unpublished work
ineffabile [inef'fabile] AGG ineffable
inefficace [ineffi'katʃe] AGG ineffective
inefficacia [ineffi'katʃa] SF inefficacy, ineffectiveness
inefficiente [ineffi'tʃɛnte] AGG inefficient
inefficienza [ineffi'tʃɛntsa] SF inefficiency
ineguagliabile [inegwaʎ'ʎabile] AGG incomparable, matchless
ineguaglianza [inegwaʎ'ʎantsa] SF (*sociale*) inequality; (*di trattamento*) disparity; (*di superficie, livello*) unevenness
ineguale [ine'gwale] AGG (*non uguale*) unequal; (*irregolare*) uneven
inelegante [inele'gante] AGG (*persona, abito*) inelegant
ineluttabile [inelut'tabile] AGG inescapable
ineluttabilità [ineluttabili'ta] SF inescapability
inenarrabile [inenar'rabile] AGG unutterable
inequivocabile [inekwivo'kabile] AGG unequivocal
inequivocabilmente [inekwivokabil'mente] AVV unequivocally
inerente [ine'rɛnte] AGG: **inerente a** concerning, regarding
inerme [i'nɛrme] AGG unarmed, defenceless (*Brit*), defenseless (*Am*)
inerpicarsi [inerpi'karsi] VIP: **inerpicarsi (su** *o* **per)** (*persona*) to clamber (up); **la strada si inerpicava fino in cima al colle** the road wound steeply up to the top of the hill
inerte [i'nɛrte] AGG **1** (*corpo*) lifeless; (*persona*) inactive;

Ii

peso inerte (*anche fig*) dead weight **2** (*Chim*) inert
inerzia [i'nɛrtsja] SF (*gen, Fis*) inertia; (*inoperosità*) inactivity; **per forza d'inerzia** (*anche fig*) through inertia
inesattezza [inezat'tettsa] SF inaccuracy
inesatto[1], a [ine'zatto] AGG (*impreciso*) inaccurate, inexact; (*erroneo*) incorrect
inesatto[2], a [ine'zatto] AGG (*Amm: non riscosso*) uncollected
inesauribile [inezau'ribile] AGG inexhaustible
inesistente [inezis'tɛnte] AGG non-existent
inesistenza [inezis'tɛntsa] SF non-existence
inesorabile [inezo'rabile] AGG (*destino, nemico, ostilità*) inexorable, relentless; (*giudice*) inflexible
inesorabilità [inezorabili'ta] SF (*vedi agg*) inexorability, relentlessness; inflexibility
inesorabilmente [inezorabil'mente] AVV inexorably, relentlessly
inesperienza [inespe'rjɛntsa] SF inexperience; **un errore dovuto all'inesperienza** a mistake caused by inexperience
inesperto, a [ines'pɛrto] AGG inexperienced; **un giovane medico inesperto** an inexperienced young doctor
inesplicabile [inespli'kabile] AGG inexplicable
inesplicabilità [inesplikabili'ta] SF inexplicableness
inesplicabilmente [inesplikabil'mente] AVV inexplicably
inesplorato, a [inesplo'rato] AGG unexplored
inesploso, a [ines'plɔzo] AGG unexploded
inespressivo, a [inespres'sivo] AGG (*viso*) expressionless, inexpressive
inespresso, a [ines'prɛsso] AGG unexpressed
inesprimibile [inespri'mibile] AGG inexpressible
inespugnabile [inespuɲ'ɲabile] AGG (*fortezza, torre*) impregnable
inespugnato, a [inespuɲ'ɲato] AGG (*fortezza*) unconquered
inestetismo [ineste'tizmo] SM beauty problem, (slight) blemish; **combatte gli inestetismi della cellulite** combats the signs of cellulite
inestimabile [inesti'mabile] AGG (*bene, qualità*) inestimable; (*valore*) incalculable; **un quadro di valore inestimabile** a priceless painting
inestinguibile [inestin'gwibile] AGG inextinguishable
inestirpabile [inestir'pabile] AGG ineradicable
inestricabile [inestri'kabile] AGG (*anche fig*) impenetrable
inestricabilmente [inestrikabil'mente] AVV (*anche fig*) inextricably
inettitudine [inetti'tudine] SF ineptitude
inetto, a [i'nɛtto] AGG (*incapace*) incompetent; (*sciocco*) inept
■ SM/F incompetent
inevaso, a [ine'vazo] AGG (*pratica*) pending; (*corrispondenza*) unanswered
inevitabile [inevi'tabile] AGG (*ostacolo*) unavoidable; (*risultato*) inevitable; **era inevitabile!** it was inevitable!, it was bound to happen!; **era inevitabile che lo scoprisse** he was bound to discover it
■ SM: **l'inevitabile** the inevitable
inevitabilmente [inevitabil'mente] AVV inevitably
in extremis [in eks'trɛmis] AVV in the nick of time
inezia [i'nɛttsja] SF trifle, bagatelle, thing of no importance
infagottare [infagot'tare] VT to bundle up, wrap up; **essere infagottato** to be well wrapped up
▶ **infagottarsi** VR to wrap (o.s.) up
infallibile [infal'libile] AGG infallible; **nessuno è infallibile** nobody is infallible; **un rimedio infallibile contro il raffreddore** an excellent remedy for colds
infallibilità [infallibili'ta] SF infallibility
infamante [infa'mante] AGG (*accusa*) defamatory, slanderous
infamare [infa'mare] VT to defame
infame [in'fame] AGG (*persona*) wicked; (*calunnia*) vile; (*fig: pessimo*) awful, dreadful
infamia [in'famja] SF **1** (*disonore*) infamy **2** (*azione*) infamous deed, vile deed
infangare [infan'gare] VT to cover with mud; (*fig: reputazione, nome*) to sully
▶ **infangarsi** VIP to get covered in mud; (*fig*) to be sullied
infanticida, i, e [infanti'tʃida] SM/F infanticide (*person*)
infanticidio, di [infanti'tʃidjo] SM infanticide
infantile [infan'tile] AGG **1** (*per bambini*) child *attr*; (*malattia*) childhood *attr*; (*di bambino: grazia, ingenuità*) childlike; **asilo infantile** nursery school; **psicologia infantile** child psychology; **letteratura infantile** children's books *pl* **2** (*immaturo: adulto, azione*) childish, infantile; **comportamento infantile** childish behaviour
infantilismo [infanti'lizmo] SM infantilism
infanzia [in'fantsja] SF **1** (*periodo*) childhood; **prima infanzia** infancy, babyhood **2** (*bambini*) children *pl*; **l'infanzia abbandonata** abandoned children
infarcire [infar'tʃire] VT: **infarcire (di)** to fill (with), stuff (with)
infarinare [infari'nare] VT to cover with (*o* sprinkle with *o* dip in) flour; **infarinare di zucchero** to sprinkle with sugar
infarinatura [infarina'tura] SF (*fig: conoscenza superficiale*) smattering; **ho solo un'infarinatura di informatica** I only know a bit about computing
infarto [in'farto] SM (*Med*): **infarto (cardiaco)** heart attack; **ha avuto un infarto** he had a heart attack
infartuato, a [infartu'ato] AGG who has suffered a heart attack
■ SM/F person who has suffered a heart attack, cardiac patient; **reparto infartuati** cardiology (ward), ward for patients treated for heart attack
infastidire [infasti'dire] VT to annoy, irritate
▶ **infastidirsi** VIP to get annoyed *o* irritated
infastidito, a [infasti'dito] AGG annoyed, irritated
infaticabile [infati'kabile] AGG indefatigable, tireless, untiring
infaticabilmente [infatikabil'mente] AVV indefatigably, tirelessly
infatti [in'fatti] CONG as a matter of fact, in fact, actually; **mi aveva promesso un regalo e infatti me l'ha portato** she'd promised me a present and she brought me one; **penso che sia uscito — infatti non risponde nessuno** I think he's out — yes, no one's answering; **ha detto che avrebbe telefonato – sì, infatti...** she said she'd phone – yes, well ...
infatuarsi [infatu'arsi] VIP: **infatuarsi di** to become infatuated with
infatuazione [infatuat'tsjone] SF infatuation; **avere un'infatuazione per qn** to be infatuated with sb
infausto, a [in'fausto] AGG (*infelice*) unhappy, unpropitious, unfavourable (*Brit*), unfavorable (*Am*);

presagio infausto ill omen; **prognosi infausta** (*Med*) fatal prognosis

infecondità [infekondi'ta] SF infertility

infecondo, a [infe'kondo] AGG (*anche fig*) infertile

infedele [infe'dele] AGG unfaithful; **essere infedele a qn** to be unfaithful to sb
■ SM/F (*Storia*) infidel

infedeltà [infedel'ta] SF INV infidelity

infelice [infe'litʃe] AGG **1** (*persona, sguardo, vita*) unhappy; (*incontro, osservazione, posizione*) unfortunate; **una frase infelice** an unfortunate choice of words; **il giorno più infelice della mia vita** the unhappiest day of my life **2** (*mal riuscito: traduzione, lavoro*) bad, poor; **esito infelice** unsuccessful outcome
■ SM/F poor wretch

infelicità [infelitʃi'ta] SF (*gen*) unhappiness; (*inopportunità*) inopportuneness

infeltrire [infel'trire] VI (*aus* **essere**), **infeltrirsi** VIP (*lana*) to become matted

inferenza [infe'rɛntsa] SF inference

inferiore [infe'rjore] AGG (*parte, rango, velocità*) lower; (*quantità, numero*) smaller; (*qualità, intelligenza*) inferior; **il labbro inferiore** the lower lip; **un prodotto di qualità inferiore** a product of inferior quality; **inferiore alla media** below average; **il piano inferiore** the next floor down, the floor below; **inferiore a** (*numero, quantità*) less *o* smaller than, below; (*meno buono*) inferior to; **i bambini di età inferiore ai cinque anni** children under five
■ SM/F inferior

inferiorità [inferjori'ta] SF inferiority; **complesso di inferiorità** inferiority complex

inferire[1] [infe'rire] (*pass rem* **infersi**, *pp* **inferto**) VT IRREG: **inferire un colpo a** to strike

inferire[2] [infe'rire] (*pass rem* **inferii**, *pp* **inferito**) VT IRREG (*dedurre*) to infer, deduce

inferito, a [infe'rito] PP *di* **inferire**[2]

infermeria [inferme'ria] SF (*gen*) infirmary; (*di scuola, nave*) sick bay

infermiera [infer'mjɛra] SF nurse

infermiere [infer'mjɛre] SM male nurse; **fa l'infermiere** he's a nurse

infermità [infermi'ta] SF INV (*stato*) infirmity; (*malattia*) illness; **infermità mentale** mental illness; (*Dir*) insanity

infermo, a [in'fermo] AGG (*fisicamente debole*) infirm; (*malato*) ill; **infermo di mente** mentally ill; (*Dir*) insane
■ SM/F invalid

infernale [infer'nale] AGG (*gen*) infernal; (*complotto, proposito*) diabolical; **fa un caldo infernale** (*fam*) it's roasting; **un tempo infernale** (*fam*) hellish weather

inferno [in'fɛrno] SM hell; **la mia vita è un inferno** my life is hell; **mandare qn all'inferno** to tell sb to go to hell; **soffrire le pene dell'inferno** to go through hell

inferocire [infero'tʃire] VT to make fierce
■ VI (*aus* **essere**), **inferocirsi** VIP to become fierce

inferriata [infer'rjata] SF grating

inferto, a [in'ferto] PP *di* **inferire**[1]

infervorare [infervo'rare] VT to arouse enthusiasm in
▶ **infervorarsi** VIP: **infervorarsi (per qc)** to get excited (about sth), get carried away (by sth); **infervorarsi in una discussione** to get carried away in a discussion

infestare [infes'tare] VT to infest; **infestato dai topi** infested with *o* overrun by mice; **le erbacce infestavano il giardino** the garden was full of *o* overgrown with weeds

infettare [infet'tare] VT (*gen*) to infect; (*acqua, aria*) to pollute, contaminate
▶ **infettarsi** VIP to become infected

infettivo, a [infet'tivo] AGG infectious; **malattia infettiva** infectious disease

infetto, a [in'fɛtto] AGG (*ferita*) infected; (*acque, aria*) polluted, contaminated

infezione [infet'tsjone] SF infection

infiacchire [infjak'kire] VT (*anche fig*) to weaken, exhaust
■ VI (*aus* **essere**), **infiacchirsi** VIP to grow weak

infiammabile [infjam'mabile] AGG, SM inflammable

infiammabilità [infjammabili'ta] SF flammability

infiammare [infjam'mare] VT (*gen*) to set fire to, set alight; (*Med: ferita, organo*) to inflame; **il suo discorso infiammò gli animi dei rivoltosi** his speech inflamed the rebels
▶ **infiammarsi** VIP (*gen*) to catch fire; (*Med*) to become inflamed; **infiammarsi d'amore** to be fired with love

infiammatorio, ria, ri, rie [infjamma'tɔrjo] AGG inflammatory

infiammazione [infjammat'tsjone] SF inflammation

infiascare [infjas'kare] VT (*vino, olio*) to bottle

inficiare [infi'tʃare] VT (*Dir: testimonianza, dichiarazione*) to invalidate

infido, a [in'fido] AGG unreliable, treacherous

infierire [infje'rire] VI (*aus* **avere**) **1** (*comportarsi con ferocia*): **infierire su** (*fisicamente*) to attack furiously; (*verbalmente*) to rage at **2** (*imperversare: epidemia, peste*) to rage *o* sweep through

infiggere [in'fiddʒere] VT IRREG: **infiggere qc in** to thrust *o* drive sth into

infilare [infi'lare] VT **1** (*introdurre: moneta, chiave*) to insert; **infilò le mani in tasca** he put *o* slipped his hands into his pockets; **le infilò un anello al dito** he put *o* slipped a ring on her finger; **infilò la mano nel cassetto** he slid his hand into the drawer; **puoi infilare anche questo nella busta?** can you put this in the same envelope?; **ho infilato la chiave nella serratura** I put the key into the lock; **riesci ad infilarci ancora qualcosa?** (*in borsa, valigia*) can you squeeze anything else in? **2** (*ago, perle*) to thread **3** (*indossare: vestito*) to slip *o* put on; **infilarsi la giacca** to put on one's jacket; **si è infilato la giacca ed è uscito** he put on his jacket and went out **4** (*imboccare: strada*) to turn into, take; **infilò la porta e se ne andò** he slipped through the door and off he went **5** (*far seguire in successione*): **infilare uno sbaglio dopo l'altro** to make one mistake after the other; **infilare sette vittorie consecutive** to win seven matches *o* times on the trot; **abbiamo infilato cinque semafori verdi** we met five green lights in succession
▶ **infilarsi** VR (*introdursi*): **infilarsi in** to slip into; **infilarsi tra la folla** to merge into the crowd; **il gatto si è infilato lì sotto e non riesco a prenderlo** the cat slipped under there and I can't get at it; **infilarsi a letto** to slip into bed; **infilarsi in un taxi** to jump into a taxi

infiltrarsi [infil'trarsi] VIP (*persona*): **infiltrarsi in** to infiltrate; (*fumo, gas, luce*) to penetrate into, filter into; (*umidità, liquido*) to penetrate, seep (into)

infiltrato, a [infil'trato] SM/F infiltrator

infiltrazione [infiltrat'tsjone] SF (*vedi vb*) infiltration; penetration; seepage

infilzare [infil'tsare] VT (*trafiggere*) to run through,

Ii

pierce; (*sullo spiedo*) to skewer; (*infilare*) to string together; **infilzare un pollo sullo spiedo** to spit a chicken

infimo, a ['infimo] AGG (*qualità*) very poor, lowest; **un albergo di infimo ordine** a third-rate hotel; **un impiegato di infimo grado** an employee of the lowest grade

infine [in'fine] AVV (*alla fine*) finally; (*per concludere*) in short; **vorrei dire, infine...** finally I would like to say ...

infingardo, a [infin'gardo] AGG slothful
■ SM/F sluggard

infinità [infini'ta] SF infinity; **un'infinità di** an infinite number of; **ho un'infinità di cose da fare** I have masses of things to do

infinitamente [infinita'mente] AVV (*anche fig*) infinitely; **mi dispiace infinitamente** I'm extremely sorry

infinitesimale [infinitezi'male] AGG infinitesimal

infinitesimo, a [infini'tɛzimo] AGG, SM infinitesimal

infinito, a [infi'nito] AGG (*gen*) infinite; **con infinito rammarico** with deep regret; **con infinita gioia** with great pleasure; **ha una pazienza infinita** she has endless patience; **grazie infinite!** many thanks!
■ SM **1** (*Filosofia*): **l'infinito** the infinite; (*Mat, Fot*) infinity; **all'infinito** (*senza fine*) endlessly; (*Mat*) to infinity; **te l'ho ripetuto all'infinito!** I've told you a thousand times! **2** (*Gramm*) infinitive; **all'infinito** in the infinitive

infinocchiare [infinok'kjare] VT (*fam*) to hoodwink, bamboozle

infiocchettare [infjokket'tare] VT (*pacchetto*) to tie up with ribbons

infiorare [infjo'rare] VT to deck with flowers; **infiorare un discorso di citazioni** to embellish a speech with quotations

infiorescenza [infjoreʃʃɛntsa] SF inflorescence

infirmare [infir'mare] VT (*Dir*) to invalidate

infischiarsi [infis'kjarsi] VIP: **infischiarsi di** not to care about; **me ne infischio!** I couldn't care less!; **mi infischio di quello che pensa** I don't care what he thinks

infisso, a [in'fisso] PP *di* **infiggere**
■ SM (*di porta, finestra*) frame

infittire [infit'tire] VT to thicken
■ VI (*aus* **essere**), **infittirsi** VIP to become thicker, thicken

inflazionare [inflattsjo'nare] VT (*Econ*) to inflate; **inflazionare un'espressione** to overwork an expression; **un titolo di studio inflazionato** an overrated qualification

inflazione [inflat'tsjone] SF **1** (*Econ*) inflation; **il tasso di inflazione** the rate of inflation; **inflazione galoppante** galloping inflation; **inflazione strisciante** creeping inflation **2** (*pegg*: *quantità esagerata*) proliferation; **un'inflazione di telefonini** a proliferation of mobile phones; **un'inflazione di laureati in medicina** an over-abundance of people graduating in medicine

inflazionistico, a, ci, che [inflattsjo'nistiko] AGG (*Econ*) inflationary

inflessibile [infles'sibile] AGG (*gen*) inflexible; (*carattere*) unyielding; (*volontà*) iron *attr*

inflessibilità [inflessibili'ta] SF inflexibility

inflessione [infles'sjone] SF inflexion

infliggere [in'fliddʒere] VT IRREG (*pena, castigo*) to inflict; (*multa*) to impose

inflissi *ecc* [in'flissi] VB *vedi* **infliggere**

inflitto, a [in'flitto] PP *di* **infliggere**

influente [influ'ɛnte] AGG influential

influenza [influ'ɛntsa] SF **1** (*ascendente, peso*) influence; **è una persona che ha influenza** he's an influential person; **avere influenza su qn/qc** to have an influence over sb/sth; **subire l'influenza di qn/qc** to be influenced by sb/sth; **zona** *o* **sfera d'influenza** (*Pol*) sphere of influence **2** (*Med*) influenza, flu; **prendere l'influenza** to catch *o* get (the) flu; **ho l'influenza** I've got flu

influenzabile [influen'tsabile] AGG easily influenced

influenzale [influen'tsale] AGG (*Med*) influenza *attr*

influenzare [influen'tsare] VT to influence, have an influence on; **lasciarsi** *o* **farsi influenzare** to be (easily) influenced; **si lascia influenzare troppo dagli amici** she's too easily influenced by her friends

influenzato, a [influen'tsato] AGG (*ammalato*): **essere influenzato** to have (the) flu; **è a letto influenzato** he's in bed with flu

influire [influ'ire] VI (*aus* **avere**) **influire su** to influence, affect; **non ha influito sulla sua decisione** it didn't influence his decision

influsso [in'flusso] SM influence

> **LO SAPEVI...?**
> **influsso** non si traduce mai con la parola inglese *influx*

INFN [i'ɛnne'effe'ɛnne] SIGLA M = *Istituto Nazionale di Fisica Nucleare*

infocare [info'kare] = **infuocare**

infocato, a [info'kato] AGG = **infuocato**

infognarsi [infoɲ'ɲarsi] VIP (*fam*) to get into a mess; **infognarsi in un mare di debiti** to be up to one's *o* the eyes in debt

in folio [in 'fɔljo] AGG INV: **edizione in folio** folio edition

infoltire [infol'tire] VT to thicken, make thicker
■ VI (*aus* **essere**), **infoltirsi** VIP to become thicker, thicken

infondatezza [infonda'tettsa] SF groundlessness

infondato, a [infon'dato] AGG unfounded, groundless; **un sospetto infondato** an unfounded suspicion

infondere [in'fondere] VT IRREG: **infondere qc in qn** to instil (*Brit*) *o* instill (*Am*) sth in sb; **infondere fiducia in qn** to inspire sb with confidence

inforcare [infor'kare] VT **1** (*prendere con la forca*) to fork (up) **2** (*bicicletta, cavallo*) to mount, get on; (*occhiali*) to put on

informale [infor'male] AGG informal

informare [infor'mare] VT to inform, tell; **informare qn di qc** to inform sb of *o* about sth, tell sb of *o* about sth; **avete informato la polizia?** have you informed the police?
▶ **informarsi** VIP to make inquiries; **informarsi di** *o* **su** to inquire about, ask about, find out about; **mi sono informato sugli orari dei treni** I asked about train times; **un'altra volta informati!** next time make sure you're better informed!

informatica [infor'matika] SF (*scienza*) computer science, computing; (*tecnica*) data processing; **un corso d'informatica** a computing course
▷ www.cnipa.gov.it/site/it-IT/

informatico, a, ci, che [infor'matiko] AGG (*settore*) computer *attr*

informativa [informa'tiva] SF (*Amm*) office circular

informativo, a [informa'tivo] AGG informative; **a titolo informativo** for information only

informatizzare [informatid'dzare] VT to computerize
informatizzazione [informatiddzat'tsjone] SF computerization
informato, a [infor'mato] AGG informed; **tienimi informato** keep me informed; **è sempre informato sulle novità discografiche** he always knows about the latest releases; **tenersi informato** to keep o.s. (well-)informed
informatore, trice [informa'tore] AGG informative ■SM/F (*della polizia*) informer; **informatore medico scientifico** representative (*of pharmaceutical company*)
informazione [informat'tsjone] SF **1** (*ragguaglio*) piece of information; **può darmi un'informazione?** can you give me some information?; **mi ha dato un'informazione utile** he gave me some useful information; **chiedere un'informazione** to ask for (some) information; **ho chiesto un'informazione ad un poliziotto** I asked a policeman for information; **chiedere/prendere informazioni sul conto di qn** to ask for/get information about sb, to make inquiries about sb; **a titolo d'informazione** for information; **per ulteriori informazioni telefonare al numero...** for further information call ...; **ufficio informazioni** information *o* inquiry office; **dov'è l'ufficio informazioni?** where's the information office? **2** (*Inform*) information; **teoria dell'informazione** information theory **3** (*Dir*) **informazione di garanzia** = **avviso di garanzia**; **informazione genetica** (*Bio*) genetic code
informe [in'forme] AGG formless, shapeless
informicolarsi [informiko'larsi], **informicolirsi** [informiko'lirsi] VIP: **mi si è informicolata una gamba** I've got pins and needles in my leg
infornare [infor'nare] VT to put in the oven
infornata [infor'nata] SF (*anche fig*) batch
infortunarsi [infortu'narsi] VIP to injure o.s., have an accident
infortunato, a [infortu'nato] AGG injured, hurt ■SM/F injured person
infortunio, ni [infor'tunjo] SM accident; **infortunio sul lavoro** industrial accident, accident at work; **ha avuto un infortunio sul lavoro** he had an accident at work
infortunistica [infortu'nistika] SF study of (industrial) accidents
infossamento [infossa'mento] SM (*nel terreno*) hollow, depression
infossarsi [infos'sarsi] VIP (*terreno*) to sink; (*guance*) to become hollow
infossato, a [infos'sato] AGG (*guance*) hollow; (*occhi*) deep-set; (: *per malattia*) sunken
infradiciare [infradi'tʃare] VT (*inzuppare*) to soak, drench; (*marcire*) to rot
▶ **infradiciarsi** VIP (*vedi vt*) to get soaked, get drenched; to rot
infradiciato, a [infradi'tʃato] AGG soaked, drenched
infradito [infra'dito] SM INV (*calzatura*) flip flop (*Brit*); thong (*Am*)
infrangere [in'frandʒere] VB IRREG
■VT (*legge, patto*) to violate, break; (*vetro, vaso*) to smash
▶ **infrangersi** VIP (*onde*) to break, smash; **le onde s'infrangevano sugli scogli** the waves were breaking on the rocks
infrangibile [infran'dʒibile] AGG unbreakable
infranto, a [in'franto] PP *di* **infrangere**
■AGG (*anche fig: cuore*) broken
infrarosso, a [infra'rosso] AGG, SM infrared
infrasettimanale [infrasettima'nale] AGG midweek *attr*
infrastruttura [infrastrut'tura] SF infrastructure
infrasuono [infra'swɔno] SM infrasound
infrazione [infrat'tsjone] SF infringement; **infrazione a** violation of; **infrazione al codice della strada** traffic offence
infreddatura [infredda'tura] SF slight cold
infreddolire [infreddo'lire] VI (*aus* **essere**), **infreddolirsi** VIP to get cold
infreddolito, a [infreddo'lito] AGG cold, chilled; **sono tutto infreddolito** I'm chilled to the bone; **sono un po' infreddolito** I'm a bit cold
infrequente [infre'kwɛnte] AGG infrequent, rare
infrequentemente [infrekwente'mente] AVV infrequently, rarely
infrollire [infrol'lire] VI (*aus* **essere**), **infrollirsi** VIP (*selvaggina*) to become high
infruttuoso, a [infruttu'oso] AGG (*anche fig*) unfruitful, fruitless
infuocare [infwo'kare] VT to make red-hot
▶ **infuocarsi** VIP (*metallo*) to become red-hot; (*fig: persona*) to become excited
infuocato, a [infwo'kato] AGG (*metallo*) red-hot; (*sabbia*) burning; (*discorso*) heated, passionate
infuori [in'fwɔri] AVV **1** **infuori** *or* **all'infuori** (*sporgere*) out, outwards; **avere i denti/gli occhi infuori** to have prominent *o* protuberant teeth/eyes; **sporge un po' infuori** it sticks out a bit **2** **all'infuori di** (*eccetto*) except, apart from, with the exception of; **lo sapevano tutti all'infuori di lui** they all knew except him; **non so altro all'infuori di questo** that's all I know
infuriare [infu'rjare] VT to enrage, make furious
■VI (*aus* **avere**) (*tempesta, vento*) to rage
▶ **infuriarsi** VIP to fly into a rage
infuriato, a [infu'rjato] AGG furious
infusione [infu'zjone] SF (*operazione*) infusion; (*infuso*) infusion, herb tea; **lasciare in infusione** to leave to infuse
infuso, a [in'fuzo] PP *di* **infondere**
■AGG: **scienza infusa** (*anche iro*) innate knowledge
■SM infusion, herb tea; **infuso di camomilla** camomile tea
Ing. ABBR = **ingegnere**
ingabbiare [ingab'bjare] VT (*animali*) to (put in a) cage; (*fig: persona*) to cage in
ingaggiare [ingad'dʒare] VT (*assumere: operai*) to take on, hire; (: *Sport: giocatore*) to sign; **essere ingaggiato** to sign; **è stato ingaggiato per la prossima stagione** he's signed for next season; **ingaggiare battaglia** (*Mil*) to engage the enemy
ingaggio, gi [in'gaddʒo] SM (*di operaio*) taking on, hiring; (*Sport*) signing; (: *somma*) signing-on fee
ingagliardire [ingaʎʎar'dire] VT to strengthen, invigorate
■VI (*aus* **essere**), **ingagliardirsi** VIP to grow stronger
ingannare [ingan'nare] VT (*imbrogliare*) to deceive; (*tradire: moglie, marito*) to cheat on, be unfaithful to; **mi hai ingannato!** you deceived me!; **non lasciarti ingannare dalla sua aria innocente** don't be taken in by his air of innocence; **le apparenze spesso ingannano** appearances are often deceptive; **ingannare il tempo** to while away the time; **abbiamo giocato a carte per ingannare l'attesa** while we waited we played cards to kill time
▶ **ingannarsi** VIP to be mistaken, be wrong;

Ii

ingannarsi sul conto di qn to be mistaken *o* wrong about sb
ingannatore, trice [inganna'tore] AGG (*gen*) deceptive; (*persona, sguardo*) deceitful
ingannevole [ingan'nevole] AGG (*gen*) deceptive; (*consiglio*) misleading
inganno [in'ganno] SM (*imbroglio*) deceit, deception; (*menzogna, frode*) con, swindle; (*insidia*) trick; (*illusione*) illusion; **trarre in inganno** to deceive, mislead; **con l'inganno** by a trick; **inganno dei sensi** sensory illusion
ingarbugliare [ingarbuʎ'ʎare] VT (*fili, corde*) to tangle; (*fig: situazione*) to muddle, confuse
▶ **ingarbugliarsi** VIP (*fili, corde, capelli*) to get tangled; (*fig: situazione*) to become confused *o* muddled
ingarbugliato, a [ingarbuʎ'ʎato] AGG (*vedi vb*) tangled; muddled, confused
ingegnarsi [indʒeɲ'ɲarsi] VIP to use one's ingenuity; **non avevamo l'occorrente ma ci siamo ingegnati** we didn't have what we needed but we made do; **ingegnarsi per vivere** to live by one's wits; **basta ingegnarsi un po'** you just need a bit of ingenuity
ingegnere [indʒeɲ'ɲɛre] SM engineer; **fa l'ingegnere** he is an engineer; **ingegnere civile** civil engineer; **ingegnere navale** naval engineer
ingegneria [indʒeɲɲe'ria] SF engineering; **è laureata in ingegneria** she's got a degree in engineering; **ingegneria chimica** chemical engineering; **ingegneria civile** civil engineering; **ingegneria elettrica** electrical engineering; **ingegneria meccanica** mechanical engineering
ingegno [in'dʒeɲɲo] SM **1** (*intelligenza*) intelligence, brains *pl*; (*attitudine, talento*) talent; (*ingegnosità*) ingenuity; **avere dell'ingegno** to have a creative mind; **aguzzare l'ingegno** to sharpen one's wits; **un'alzata d'ingegno** (*anche iro*) a bright idea
2 (*persona*) mind; **è un bell'ingegno** he has a good brain; **i più grandi ingegni del secolo** the greatest minds of the century
ingegnosamente [indʒeɲɲosa'mente] AVV ingeniously
ingegnosità [indʒeɲɲosi'ta] SF ingenuity
ingegnoso, a [indʒeɲ'ɲoso] AGG ingenious, clever
ingelosire [indʒelo'sire] VT to make jealous; **l'ha fatto solo per farlo ingelosire** she just did it to make him jealous
■ VI (*aus* **essere**), **ingelosirsi** VIP to become jealous
ingente [in'dʒɛnte] AGG huge, enormous
ingentilire [indʒenti'lire] VT to refine, civilize
▶ **ingentilirsi** VIP to become more refined *o* civilized
ingenuamente [indʒenua'mente] AVV naïvely, ingenuously
ingenuità [indʒenui'ta] SF naïvety, ingenuousness
ingenuo, a [in'dʒɛnuo] AGG naïve, ingenuous; **è molto ingenua** she's very naïve; **ma come fai ad essere così ingenuo?** how can you be so naïve?
■ SM/F: **è un ingenuo** he is naïve; **fare l'ingenuo** to act the innocent; **non fare l'ingenuo, sai benissimo di cosa parlo** don't act the innocent, you know perfectly well what I'm talking about
ingerenza [indʒe'rɛntsa] SF interference
ingerire [indʒe'rire] VT to ingest
ingessare [indʒes'sare] VT to put in plaster; **gli hanno ingessato il braccio** they put his arm in plaster
ingessatura [indʒessa'tura] SF plaster (cast); **mi hanno tolto l'ingessatura** they took off the plaster
ingestione [indʒes'tjone] SF ingestion

Inghilterra [ingil'tɛrra] SF England; **mi è piaciuta molto l'Inghilterra** I really liked England; **andrò in Inghilterra quest'estate** I'm going to England this summer
inghiottire [ingjot'tire] VT (*anche fig*) to swallow; **la barca fu inghiottita dai flutti** the boat was swallowed up *o* engulfed by the waves; **essere inghiottito dal buio** to be swallowed up by the darkness; **ne ha inghiottite tante nella vita** (*fig: dispiaceri*) he's had so much to put up with in life
inghippo [in'gippo] SM trick
ingiallire [indʒal'lire] VT to turn yellow
■ VI (*aus* **essere**), **ingiallirsi** VIP to (turn *o* go) yellow
ingiallito, a [indʒal'lito] AGG yellowed
ingigantire [indʒigan'tire] VT (*immagine*) to enlarge, magnify; (*fig: problema*) to exaggerate
■ VI (*aus* **essere**), **ingigantirsi** VIP to become gigantic *o* enormous
inginocchiarsi [indʒinok'kjarsi] VIP to kneel (down); **si è inginocchiato accanto al cane** he knelt down beside the dog; **essere inginocchiato** to be kneeling down, be on one's knees
inginocchiatoio, oi [indʒinokkja'tojo] SM prie-dieu
ingioiellare [indʒojel'lare] VT to bejewel, adorn with jewels
▶ **ingioiellarsi** VR to put on one's jewels
ingiù [in'dʒu] AVV down, downwards; **con la testa all'ingiù** head downwards; (*capovolto*) upside down
ingiungere [in'dʒundʒere] VT IRREG: **ingiungere a qn di fare qc** to enjoin *o* order sb to do sth
ingiuntivo, a [indʒun'tivo] AGG (*Dir*): **decreto ingiuntivo** order to pay
ingiunto, a [in'dʒunto] PP *di* **ingiungere**
ingiunzione [indʒun'tsjone] SF injunction, command; **ingiunzione di pagamento** final demand
ingiuria [in'dʒurja] SF (*insulto*) insult; **coprire qn di ingiurie** to heap abuse on sb; **le ingiurie del tempo** the ravages of time

LO SAPEVI...?
ingiuria non si traduce mai con la parola inglese ***injury***

ingiuriare [indʒu'rjare] VT to insult, abuse

LO SAPEVI...?
ingiuriare non si traduce mai con la parola inglese ***injure***

ingiurioso, a [indʒu'rjoso] AGG insulting, abusive
ingiustamente [indʒusta'mente] AVV unjustly
ingiustificabile [indʒustifi'kabile] AGG unjustifiable
ingiustificato, a [indʒustifi'kato] AGG unjustified; **assenza ingiustificata** unexplained absence; (*Scol*) absence without permission; (*Mil*) absence without leave
ingiustizia [indʒus'tittsja] SF injustice; **ha commesso un'ingiustizia** he was unjust, he acted unjustly; **è un'ingiustizia!** that's not fair!
ingiusto, a [in'dʒusto] AGG unjust, unfair; **essere ingiusto con qn** to be unfair *o* unjust to sb; **questo è profondamente ingiusto** this is utterly unfair; **è ingiusto nei miei confronti** it's unfair to me
inglese [in'glese] AGG English; **andarsene** *o* **filarsela all'inglese** to take French leave; **la squadra inglese** the English team
■ SM/F Englishman/Englishwoman; **gli Inglesi** the English, English people
■ SM (*lingua*) English; **parlare (l')inglese** to speak English; **parli inglese?** do you speak English?

inglorioso, a [inglo'rjoso] AGG (*privo di gloria*) inglorious; (*ignominioso*) ignominious
ingobbire [ingob'bire] VI (*aus* **essere**), **ingobbirsi** VIP to become stooped
ingoiare [ingo'jare] VT (*inghiottire*) to swallow; (*: in fretta*) to gulp (down); (*fig*) to swallow (up); **se l'ingoiò in un boccone** he swallowed it in one go; **furono ingoiati dai flutti** they were swallowed up *o* engulfed by the waves; **è stato un boccone amaro da ingoiare** (*fig*) it was a bitter pill to swallow; **ha dovuto ingoiare tante amarezze** he has had to endure so many disappointments; **ha dovuto ingoiare il rospo** he had to accept the situation, whether he liked it or not
ingolfare [ingol'fare] VT (*Aut*) to flood
▶ **ingolfarsi** VIP (*Aut*) to flood; **ingolfarsi nei debiti** to get up to one's *o* the ears in debt
ingollare [ingol'lare] VT (*cibo*) to gulp down
ingolosire [ingolo'sire] VT: **ingolosire qn** to make sb's mouth water; (*fig*) to attract sb
■ VI (*aus* **essere**), **ingolosirsi** VIP to become greedy
ingombrante [ingom'brante] AGG cumbersome; **una valigia ingombrante** a cumbersome case
ingombrare [ingom'brare] VT (*strada*) to block, obstruct; (*stanza, tavolo*) to clutter up; **si prega di non ingombrare il corridoio** please don't block the corridor; **i bagagli ingombravano la stanza** the room was full of luggage
ingombro[1]**, a** [in'gombro] AGG: **ingombro di** (*strada*) blocked by; (*stanza*) cluttered up with
ingombro[2] [in'gombro] SM **1** obstacle; **essere d'ingombro** to be in the way; **per ragioni di ingombro** for reasons of space **2** (*di auto*) overall dimensions *pl*
ingordamente [ingorda'mente] AVV greedily
ingordigia [ingor'didʒa] SF: **ingordigia (di)** (*vedi agg*) greed (for); avidity (for)
ingordo, a [in'gordo] AGG: **ingordo (di)** (*cibo*) greedy (for); (*fig: denaro*) greedy *o* avid (for); **non essere ingordo!** don't be greedy!; **è più ingordo di me** he's greedier than me
■ SM/F glutton
ingorgare [ingor'gare] VT to block
▶ **ingorgarsi** VIP to get blocked
ingorgo, ghi [in'gorgo] SM **1** (*di tubo*) blockage, obstruction **2** (*anche:* **ingorgo stradale**) hold-up; **c'era un ingorgo all'incrocio** there was a hold-up at the junction
ingozzare [ingot'tsare] VT (*animali*) to fatten; **ingozzare (di cibo)** (*persona*) to stuff (with food)
▶ **ingozzarsi** VR: **ingozzarsi (di qc)** to stuff o.s. (with sth)
ingranaggio, gi [ingra'naddʒo] SM (*Tecn*) gear; (*: di orologio*) mechanism; **gli ingranaggi della burocrazia** the bureaucratic machinery; **essere preso nell'ingranaggio** (*fig*) to be caught in the system
ingranare [ingra'nare] VI (*aus* **avere**) (*Tecn*) to engage, mesh; **non riesco ad ingranare nel nuovo lavoro** I can't seem to get into my stride in the new job; **gli affari cominciano ad ingranare** business is beginning to move
■ VT: **ingranare la marcia** (*Aut*) to engage gear, get into gear; **non riesco a ingranare la marcia** I can't get into gear
ingrandimento [ingrandi'mento] SM (*di città, azienda*) development, growth, expansion; (*di casa*) extension; (*di strada*) widening; (*Ottica, Fis*) magnification; (*Fot*) enlargement; **lente d'ingrandimento** magnifying glass; **vorrei un ingrandimento di questa foto** I'd like an enlargement of this photo; **far fare un ingrandimento** to get an enlargement
ingrandire [ingran'dire] VT (*azienda, città*) to develop, expand; (*locale*) to extend; (*strada*) to widen; (*Ottica*) to magnify; (*Fot*) to enlarge; (*fig: storia: esagerare*) to embroider; **ho deciso di ingrandire la casa** I've decided to extend my house
■ VI (*aus* **essere**), **ingrandirsi** VIP (*gen*) to get larger *o* bigger; (*azienda, città*) to grow, expand; (*strada*) to get wider; (*potere*) to grow, increase; (*problema*) to become more serious *o* worse; **la città si sta ingrandendo** the town is getting bigger
ingranditore [ingrandi'tore] SM (*Fot*) enlarger
ingrassaggio, gi [ingras'saddʒo] SM greasing
ingrassare [ingras'sare] VT **1** (*animali*) to fatten (up); (*persone*) to make fat; **ingrassare di** to put on; **sono ingrassato di due chili** I've put on two kilos; **far ingrassare** to be fattening; **i dolci fanno ingrassare** puddings are fattening; **questo vestito ti ingrassa** this dress makes you look fat **2** (*lubrificare*) to grease **3** (*concimare: terreno*) to manure
■ VI (*aus* **essere**), **ingrassarsi** VIP to get fat, put on weight; **sei un po' ingrassata** you've put on a bit of weight; **sei molto ingrassato** you've put on a lot of weight; **ingrassarsi alle spalle altrui** (*fig*) to thrive at the expense of others
ingrassatore [ingrassa'tore] SM (*dispositivo*) lubricator
ingrasso [in'grasso] SM: **mettere all'ingrasso** to forcefeed; **essere all'ingrasso** to be forcefed
ingratitudine [ingrati'tudine] SF ingratitude, ungratefulness
ingrato, a [in'grato] AGG (*persona*) ungrateful; (*lavoro*) thankless, unrewarding
■ SM/F ungrateful person; **sei un ingrato!** you're an ungrateful wretch!
ingraziarsi [ingrat'tsjarsi] VT: **ingraziarsi qn** to ingratiate o.s. with sb
ingrediente [ingre'djɛnte] SM ingredient
ingresso [in'grɛsso] SM **1** (*porta*) entrance, entry; (*atrio*) hall; **non stare qui nell'ingresso, accomodati** don't stand there in the doorway, come in; **ingresso principale** main entrance; **l'ingresso principale è sulla via laterale** the main entrance is in the side street; **ingresso di servizio** tradesmen's entrance **2** (*accesso*) admission; **fare il proprio ingresso** to make one's entrance; **vietato l'ingresso** no admittance; **ingresso libero** admission free; **biglietto d'ingresso** admission ticket, entrance ticket; **prezzo d'ingresso** cost of admission
ingrossamento [ingrossa'mento] SM swelling
ingrossare [ingros'sare] VT (*spessore, patrimonio*) to increase; (*fiume, folla*) to swell; (*muscoli*) to develop; **ingrossare le file** (*Mil, fig*) to swell the ranks; **quest'abito ti ingrossa** this dress makes you look fat
■ VI (*aus* **essere**), **ingrossarsi** VIP (*vedi vt*) to increase; to swell; to develop; (*persona*) to put on weight
ingrosso [in'grɔsso] AVV: **all'ingrosso** (*Comm*) wholesale; (*all'incirca*) roughly, about; **prezzo all'ingrosso** wholesale price; **vendere all'ingrosso** *or* **effettuare vendite all'ingrosso** to sell wholesale
■ SM: **un ingrosso di calzature** a shoe wholesaler
ingrugnato, a [ingruɲ'ɲato] AGG grumpy
inguaiare [ingwa'jare] (*fam*) VT to get (sb) into trouble
▶ **inguaiarsi** VR to get into trouble
inguainare [ingwai'nare] VT to sheathe

Ii

ingualcibile [ingwal'tʃibile] AGG crease-resistant
inguaribile [ingwa'ribile] AGG (*anche fig*) incurable
inguaribilmente [ingwaribil'mente] AVV incurably
inguine ['ingwine] SM (*Anat*) groin; **ho uno strappo all'inguine** I've strained my groin
ingurgitare [ingurdʒi'tare] VT to gulp down
inibire [ini'bire] VT to inhibit
inibito, a [ini'bito] AGG inhibited; **non pensavo che fossi così inibito!** I didn't think you were so inhibited!
■ SM/F inhibited person
inibitorio, ria, ri, rie [inibi'tɔrjo] AGG (*Psic*) inhibitory, inhibitive; (*Dir: provvedimento, misure*) restrictive
inibizione [inibit'tsjone] SF inhibition
iniettare [injet'tare] VT to inject; **iniettare qc a qn** to inject sb with sth; **iniettarsi una sostanza stupefacente** to inject o.s. with a drug; **con gli occhi iniettati di sangue** with bloodshot eyes
▶ **iniettarsi** VIP: **iniettarsi di sangue** (*occhi*) to become bloodshot
iniettore [injet'tore] SM (*Tecn*) injector
iniezione [injet'tsjone] SF **1** (*Med*) injection; **fare** *o* **farsi fare un'iniezione** to get an injection; **fare un'iniezione (a qn)** to give (sb) an injection; **mi hanno fatto un'iniezione di penicillina** they gave me an injection of penicillin; **dare un'iniezione di fiducia a qn** to boost sb's morale *o* confidence
2 (*Aut*): **motore a iniezione** injection engine
inimicare [inimi'kare] VT to alienate, make hostile; **si è inimicato gli amici di un tempo** he has alienated his old friends
▶ **inimicarsi** VIP: **inimicarsi con qn** to fall out with sb
inimicizia [inimi'tʃittsja] SF enmity, animosity
inimitabile [inimi'tabile] AGG inimitable
inimitabilmente [inimitabil'mente] AVV inimitably
inimmaginabile [inimmadʒi'nabile] AGG unimaginable
ininfiammabile [ininfjam'mabile] AGG non-flammable
inintelligibile [inintelli'dʒibile] AGG unintelligible
ininterrottamente [ininterrotta'mente] AVV non-stop, continuously; **è piovuto ininterrottamente per 2 settimane** it rained non-stop *o* continuously for 2 weeks; **ha parlato ininterrottamente per tre ore** he talked non-stop for three hours
ininterrotto, a [ininter'rotto] AGG (*fila*) continuous, unbroken; (*viavai, rumore*) constant
iniquamente [inikwa'mente] AVV iniquitously
iniquità [inikwi'ta] SF INV (*qualità*) iniquity; (*atto*) wicked action
iniquo, a [i'nikwo] AGG iniquitous
iniziale [init'tsjale] AGG initial; **fase iniziale** initial phase; **stipendio iniziale** starting salary
■ SF initial; **firmare con le iniziali** to initial; **un accendino con le sue iniziali** a lighter with his initials
inizializzare [inittsjalid'dzare] VT (*Inform: diskette*) to initialize; (*: computer*) to boot
inizializzazione [inittsjaliddzat'tsjone] SF (*Inform: diskette*) initialization; (*: computer*) start-up
inizialmente [inittsjal'mente] AVV initially, at first
iniziare [init'tsjare] VT **1** (*cominciare*) to begin, start; (*dibattito, ostilità*) to open; **iniziare a fare qc** to start doing sth; **hai iniziato a cucinare?** have you started cooking? **2** (*persona: a un culto*) to initiate into; (*: a un'attività*) to introduce to
■ VI (*aus* **essere**) to begin, start; **il film sta per iniziare** the film is about to start
iniziativa [inittsja'tiva] SF (*gen*) initiative; **di propria iniziativa** on one's own initiative; **è venuta di propria iniziativa** she came on her own initiative; **spirito d'iniziativa** spirit of initiative, drive; **prendere l'iniziativa** to take the initiative; **se vuoi rivederla, devi prendere tu l'iniziativa** if you want to see her again, you'll have to take the; **una serie di iniziative culturali** a series of arts events; **iniziativa privata** (*Comm*) private enterprise
iniziato, a [init'tsjato] AGG (*a un culto*) initiated
■ SM/F initiate; **gli iniziati** the initiated
iniziatore, trice [inittsja'tore] SM/F initiator
iniziazione [inittsjat'tsjone] SF initiation
inizio, zi [i'nittsjo] SM beginning, start; **fin dall'inizio** from the beginning; **all'inizio** at the beginning, at the start; **all'inizio pensavo che scherzasse** at first I thought he was joking; **all'inizio di** at the beginning of; **il pareggio è arrivato all'inizio del secondo tempo** the equalizer came at the beginning of the second half; **essere agli inizi** (*progetto, lavoro ecc*) to be in the initial stages; **dare inizio a qc** to start sth, get sth going; **avere inizio** to begin; **il film ha inizio con una scena d'azione** the film begins with an action scene; **ho riletto l'inizio della lettera dieci volte** I read the beginning of the letter ten times; **l'inizio dei lavori è previsto per la fine del mese** work will begin at the end of the month
in loco [in 'lɔko] AVV (*sul posto*) on the spot
innaffiare *ecc* [innaf'fjare] = **annaffiare** *ecc*
innalzamento [innaltsa'mento] SM (*gen*) raising; **l'innalzamento dell'età pensionabile** the raising of the pension age
innalzare [innal'tsare] VT (*gen: sollevare*) to raise; (*costruire: monumento*) to erect; **innalzare gli occhi al cielo** to raise one's eyes to heaven; **innalzare al trono** to raise to the throne
▶ **innalzarsi** VIP to rise
innamoramento [innamora'mento] SM falling in love
innamorare [innamo'rare] VT to enchant, charm; **un viso che innamora** an enchanting *o* a delightful face
▶ **innamorarsi** VR (*uso reciproco*) to fall in love (with each other)
▶ **innamorarsi** VIP: **innamorarsi (di)** to fall in love (with)
innamorato, a [innamo'rato] AGG: **innamorato (di)** (*anche fig: di lavoro ecc*) in love (with), very fond (of); **essere innamorato di qn** to be in love with someone; **sei innamorato di lei?** are you in love with her?; **è innamorato del suo bambino** he dotes on his child; **è innamorata persa** she's madly in love
■ SM/F boyfriend/girlfriend; (*anche scherz*) sweetheart
innanzi [in'nantsi] AVV **1** (*stato in luogo*) in front, ahead; (*moto a luogo*) forward, on; **stare** *o* **essere innanzi** to be in front *o* ahead; **farsi innanzi** to step forward **2** (*tempo*) before, earlier; **il giorno innanzi** the day before; **d'ora innanzi** from now on
■ PREP **1** (*davanti*): **innanzi a** in front of, before; **lo giuro innanzi a Dio** I swear before God **2** (*prima*) before; **innanzi tempo** ahead of time; **morire innanzi tempo** to die before one's time
innanzitutto [innantsi'tutto] AVV (*soprattutto*) above all; (*per prima cosa*) first of all; **innanzitutto bisogna informarsi degli orari** first of all you need to ask about the times
innato, a [in'nato] AGG innate, inborn

innaturale [innatu'rale] AGG unnatural
innegabile [inne'gabile] AGG undeniable
innegabilmente [innegabil'mente] AVV undeniably
inneggiare [inned'dʒare] VI (*aus* **avere**): **inneggiare a** to sing hymns to; (*fig*) to sing the praises of
innervosire [innervo'sire] VT: **innervosire qn** (*rendere nervoso*) to make sb nervous; (*irritare*) to get on sb's nerves, annoy sb; **il traffico mi innervosisce** the traffic gets on my nerves
▸ **innervosirsi** VIP (*vedi vt*) to become nervous; to get irritated *o* upset; **si è innervosito per il rumore** the noise got on his nerves
innescare [innes'kare] VT **1** (*ordigno esplosivo*) to prime; (*fig: serie di eventi ecc*) to trigger off **2** (*amo*) to bait
innesco, schi [in'nesko] SM primer, fuse
innestare [innes'tare] VT (*Agr, Med*) to graft; (*Tecn*) to engage; (*Elettr: presa*) to put in
innesto [in'nɛsto] SM (*Agr, Med*) graft; (*: azione*) grafting *no pl*; (*Tecn*) clutch; (*Elettr*) connection
innevamento [inneva'mento] SM snowfall; **innevamento artificiale** production of artificial snow
innevato, a [inne'vato] AGG covered in snow; **le discese sono ben innevate quest'anno** the slopes have a good covering of snow this year
inno ['inno] SM (*anche fig*) hymn; **inno nazionale** national anthem
innocente [inno'tʃɛnte] AGG **1** (*gen*) innocent; (*scherzo*) harmless; **uno scherzo innocente** a harmless joke **2** (*Dir*) not guilty; **dichiararsi innocente** to maintain one's innocence; **si è sempre dichiarato innocente** he has always maintained his innocence; **secondo me è innocente** in my opinion he's innocent
■ SM/F innocent person; (*bambino*) innocent
innocentemente [innotʃente'mente] AVV innocently; **l'ha detto innocentemente** he said it in all innocence
innocenza [inno'tʃɛntsa] SF innocence
innocuo, a [in'nɔkuo] AGG innocuous, harmless
innominabile [innomi'nabile] AGG unmentionable
innominato, a [innomi'nato] AGG unnamed
innovare [inno'vare] VT to make changes to
innovativo, a [innova'tivo] AGG innovative
innovatore, trice [innova'tore] AGG innovatory
■ SM/F innovator
innovazione [innovat'tsjone] SF innovation
in nuce [in'nutʃe] AVV (*in embrione*) in embryo; (*in breve*) in a nutshell
innumerevole [innume'revole] AGG innumerable, countless
inoccupato, a [inokku'pato] AGG: **giovane inoccupato** first-time jobseeker
inoculare [inoku'lare] VT (*Med*) to inoculate
inodore [ino'dore], **inodoro, a** [ino'doro] AGG (*gen*) odourless (*Brit*), odorless (*Am*); (*fiore*) scentless; **un gas inodore** an odourless gas
inoffensivo, a [inoffen'sivo] AGG harmless
inoltrare [inol'trare] VT (*Amm: pratica*) to pass on, forward; (*lettera*) to send on, forward
▸ **inoltrarsi** VIP: **inoltrarsi (in)** to advance (into), go forward (into)
inoltrato, a [inol'trato] AGG: **a notte inoltrata** late at night; **a primavera inoltrata** late in the spring
inoltre [i'noltre] AVV besides, moreover
inoltro [i'noltro] SM (*Amm*) forwarding
inondare [inon'dare] VT (*anche fig*) to flood; (*mercato*): **inondare (di)** to flood (with); **la folla inondava la piazza** the crowd flooded into the square; **il sole inondava la stanza** the sun flooded into the room; **le lacrime le inondavano il viso** her face was bathed in tears
inondazione [inondat'tsjone] SF flood, flooding *no pl*
inoperante [inope'rante] AGG (*provvedimento, piano*) inoperative
inoperosità [inoperosi'ta] SF idleness, inactivity
inoperoso, a [inope'roso] AGG idle, inactive
inopinabile [inopi'nabile] AGG (*letter: impensabile*) unimaginable
inopinato, a [inopi'nato] AGG (*letter*) unexpected
inopportunamente [inopportuna'mente] AVV (*arrivare*) inopportunely; **commentare inopportunamente** to make an ill-timed remark
inopportunità [inopportuni'ta] SF (*vedi agg*) inappropriateness; untimeliness
inopportuno, a [inoppor'tuno] AGG (*poco adatto*) inappropriate; (*intempestivo*) untimely, ill-timed; **è arrivato in un momento inopportuno** he arrived at an awkward *o* inopportune moment
inoppugnabile [inoppuɲ'ɲabile] AGG incontrovertible
inorganicità [inorganitʃi'ta] SF (*di sostanza*) inorganic nature; (*di libro, discorso*) lack of structure
inorganico, a, ci, che [inor'ganiko] AGG inorganic
inorgoglire [inorgoʎ'ʎire] VT to make proud
■ VI (*aus* **essere**), **inorgoglirsi** VIP to become proud; **inorgoglirsi per qc** to pride o.s. on sth
inorgoglito, a [inorgoʎ'ʎito] AGG proud
inorridire [inorri'dire] VT to horrify; **far inorridire qn** to horrify sb
■ VI (*aus* **essere**) to be horrified; **ero inorridito** I was horrified
inospitale [inospi'tale] AGG inhospitable
inosservante [inosser'vante] AGG: **essere inosservante di** to fail to comply with
inosservanza [inosser'vantsa] SF non-observance
inosservato, a [inosser'vato] AGG (*non notato*) unobserved, unnoticed; (*non rispettato*) not observed, not kept; **passare inosservato** to go unobserved, escape notice; **l'errore non è passato inosservato** the mistake didn't go unnoticed
inossidabile [inossi'dabile] AGG (*acciaio*) stainless; **acciaio inossidabile** stainless steel
inox ['inoks] AGG INV (*acciaio*) stainless; (*pentole, posate, lavello*) stainless steel
in primis [in'primis] AVV first of all, firstly
INPS ['inps] SIGLA M (= **Istituto Nazionale Previdenza Sociale**) *social security service*
input ['input] SM INV (*Inform*) input; (*fig: avvio*): **dare l'input ad un'iniziativa** to set a project in motion; **un comportamento condizionato da input esterni** behaviour conditioned by external factors
inquadramento [inkwadra'mento] SM (*Amm*) placement; **inquadramento unico** integrated salary scheme
inquadrare [inkwa'drare] VT **1** (*foto, immagine*) to frame; **inquadrare un autore nel suo periodo** to place an author in his historical context; **l'ho inquadrato appena l'ho visto** I recognized his sort as soon as I saw him **2** (*Mil*) to regiment; (*personale*) to organize
▸ **inquadrarsi** VIP (*collocarsi*): **inquadrarsi in** to fit in
inquadratura [inkwadra'tura] SF (*Cine, Fot: atto*) framing; (*: immagine*) shot; (*: sequenza*) sequence
inqualificabile [inkwalifi'kabile] AGG unspeakable
inquietante [inkwje'tante] AGG disturbing, worrying

Ii

inquietare [inkwje'tare] VT *(preoccupare)* to disturb, worry; *(irritare)* to upset
▶ **inquietarsi** VIP *(vedi vt)* to worry, become anxious; to get upset
inquieto, a [in'kwjɛto] AGG *(agitato)* restless; *(preoccupato)* worried, anxious; *(arrabbiato)* upset
inquietudine [inkwje'tudine] SF anxiety, worry
inquilino, a [inkwi'lino] SM/F tenant
inquinamento [inkwina'mento] SM pollution; **inquinamento acustico** noise pollution; **inquinamento luminoso** light pollution; **inquinamento delle prove** *(Dir)* tampering with the evidence
inquinante [inkwi'nante] AGG polluting
inquinare [inkwi'nare] VT to pollute; *(prove)* to contaminate; **le fabbriche hanno inquinato il mare** the factories have polluted the sea
inquinato, a [inkwi'nato] AGG polluted
inquirente [inkwi'rɛnte] AGG *(Dir)*: **magistrato inquirente** examining *(Brit)* *o* committing *(Am)* magistrate; **commissione inquirente** commission of inquiry
inquisire [inkwi'zire] VT, VI *(aus* **avere***)* to investigate
inquisito, a AGG *(persona)* under investigation
■SM person under investigation
inquisitore, trice [inkwizi'tore] AGG *(sguardo)* inquiring
■SM inquisitor
inquisizione [inkwizit'tsjone] SF inquisition
insabbiamento [insabbja'mento] SM *(fig: di pratica)* shelving
insabbiare [insab'bjare] VT *(fig: pratica)* to shelve
▶ **insabbiarsi** VIP *(barca)* to run aground; *(fig: pratica)* to be shelved
insaccare [insak'kare] VT *(grano, farina ecc)* to bag, put into sacks; *(carne)* to put into sausage skins
insaccati [insak'kati] SMPL sausages
insalata [insa'lata] SF *(pianta)* lettuce *(or other green-leaf vegetable)*; *(piatto)* salad; **hai lavato l'insalata?** have you washed the lettuce?; **insalata di mare** seafood salad; **insalata mista** mixed salad; **insalata di pomodori** tomato salad; **insalata russa** Russian salad; **insalata verde** green salad
insalatiera [insala'tjɛra] SF salad bowl
insalubre [insa'lubre] AGG insalubrious *(frm)*, unhealthy
insalubrità [insalubri'ta] SF insalubrity *(frm)*, unhealthiness
insanabile [insa'nabile] AGG *(piaga)* that will not heal; *(fig: situazione)* irremediable; **fra di loro si è creata una rottura insanabile** a rift has developed between them which cannot be healed
insanguinare [insangwi'nare] VT to stain with blood; **arrivò tutto insanguinato** he arrived all covered in blood; **una feroce rivolta insanguinò la Francia** France was plunged into a bloody revolution
▶ **insanguinarsi** VR to get covered in blood
insania [in'sanja] SF *(letter)* insanity
insano, a [in'sano] AGG *(letter: gesto, proposito)* insane
insaponare [insapo'nare] VT to soap; *(con sapone da barba)* to lather; **insaponarsi le mani** to soap one's hands
insaponata [insapo'nata] SF: **dare un'insaponata a qc** to give sth a (quick) soaping
insaponatura [insapona'tura] SF soaping
insapore [insa'pore], **insaporo, a** [insa'poro] AGG tasteless, insipid
insaporire [insapo'rire] VT to flavour *(Brit)* *o* flavor *(Am)*; *(con spezie)* to season
▶ **insaporirsi** VIP to gain flavo(u)r
insaputa [insa'puta] SF: **all'insaputa di qn** without sb's knowledge, unbeknown to sb, without sb knowing; **l'ha comprato all'insaputa dei suoi** she bought it without her parents' knowledge
insaturo, a [in'saturo] AGG *(Chim)* unsaturated
insaziabile [insat'tsjabile] AGG insatiable
insaziabilmente [insattsjabil'mente] AVV insatiably
inscatolare [inskato'lare] VT *(frutta, carne)* to can
inscatolatrice [inskatola'tritʃe] SF canning machine
inscenare [inʃe'nare] VT *(Teatro)* to stage, put on; *(fig: protesta, sciopero)* to stage; **inscenare una commedia** *(fig)* to put on an act
inscindibile [inʃin'dibile] AGG *(fattori)* inseparable; *(legame)* indissoluble
inscritto, a [in'skritto] PP *di* **inscrivere**
inscrivere [in'skrivere] VT IRREG *(Geom)* to inscribe
insecchire [insek'kire] VT *(seccare)* to dry up; (: *piante)* to wither
■VI *(aus* **essere***)*, **insecchirsi** VIP *(vedi vt)* to dry up, become dry; to wither
insediamento [insedja'mento] SM **1** *(Amm: in carica, ufficio)* installation **2** *(villaggio, colonia)* settlement
insediare [inse'djare] VT *(Amm)* to install
▶ **insediarsi** VIP **1** *(Amm)* to take up office **2** *(colonia, profughi ecc)* to settle; *(Mil)* to take up positions
insegna [in'seɲɲa] SF **1** *(stradale, di negozio)* sign; **insegna al neon** neon sign **2** *(bandiera)* flag, banner; *(emblema)* emblem, sign; **insegne** SFPL *(decorazioni)* insignia *pl*; **un'estate all'insegna del maltempo** a summer marked by bad weather
insegnamento [inseɲɲa'mento] SM teaching; **il suo metodo d'insegnamento** her way of teaching; **che ti serva da insegnamento** let this be a lesson to you; **trarre insegnamento da un'esperienza** to learn from an experience
insegnante [inseɲ'ɲante] AGG teaching *attr*
■SM/F teacher; **fare l'insegnante** to be a teacher; **fa l'insegnante** she's a teacher; **insegnante d'inglese** English teacher; **insegnante di storia** History teacher; **insegnante di sostegno** support teacher
insegnare [inseɲ'ɲare] VT to teach; **insegnare alle elementari** to be primary school teacher; **insegnare a qn qc/a fare qc** to teach sb sth/(how) to do sth; **ha insegnato ai bambini i nomi delle piante** she taught the children the names of plants; **mi ha insegnato a suonare la chitarra** he taught me to play the guitar; **vi insegno io a comportarvi bene!** I'll teach you how to behave!; **come lei ben m'insegna...** *(iro)* as you will doubtless be aware ...
inseguimento [insegwi'mento] SM pursuit, chase; **darsi all'inseguimento di qn** to give chase to sb; **(gara di) inseguimento** *(Ciclismo)* pursuit (race)
inseguire [inse'gwire] VT *(anche fig)* to pursue, chase; **la polizia ha inseguito i rapinatori** the police chased the robbers
inseguitore, trice [insegwi'tore] SM/F pursuer; *(Ciclismo)* track rider
insellare [insel'lare] VT *(curvare)* to curve
▶ **insellarsi** VIP *(curvarsi)* to sag
inselvatichire [inselvati'kire] VT *(persona)* to make unsociable
■VI *(aus* **essere***)*, **inselvatichirsi** VIP *(giardino, animale domestico)* to grow wild; *(persona)* to become unsociable
inseminazione [inseminat'tsjone] SF insemination;

inseminazione artificiale artificial insemination; **inseminazione artificiale eterologa** AID; **inseminazione artificiale omologa** AIH
insenatura [insena'tura] SF inlet, creek
insensatamente [insensata'mente] AVV foolishly, stupidly
insensatezza [insensa'tettsa] SF foolishness, stupidity
insensato, a [insen'sato] AGG senseless, stupid
insensibile [insen'sibile] AGG (*anche fig*) insensitive; **è insensibile al freddo** he doesn't feel the cold; **insensibile ai complimenti** indifferent to compliments

LO SAPEVI...?
insensibile non si traduce mai con la parola inglese *insensible*

insensibilità [insensibili'ta] SF insensitivity, insensibility
insensibilmente [insensibil'mente] AVV insensitively
inseparabile [insepa'rabile] AGG inseparable
insepolto, a [inse'polto] AGG unburied
inserimento [inseri'mento] SM (*gen*) insertion; **ha avuto problemi di inserimento nella nuova scuola** he has had problems settling in at his new school
inserire [inse'rire] VT (*introdurre*) to insert; (*Elettr: spina*) to insert, put in; (*allegare*) to enclose; **bisogna inserire la vite nel foro** you need to put the screw in the hole; **inserire la spina della TV** to plug in the TV; **inserire un annuncio sul giornale** to put *o* place an advertisement in the newspaper; **inserire un apparecchio in un circuito elettrico** to connect a machine to an electrical circuit
▶ **inserirsi** VR: **inserirsi in** (*ambiente*) to fit into, become part of
▶ **inserirsi** VIP: **inserirsi in** (*contesto*) to be a part of, be included in; **non si è ancora inserito bene nella nuova scuola** he hasn't settled into his new school yet
inserto [in'sɛrto] SM (*pubblicazione*) insert, supplement; **inserto filmato** (film) clip
inservibile [inser'vibile] AGG useless
inserviente [inser'vjɛnte] SM/F attendant
inserzione [inser'tsjone] SF (*aggiunta*) insertion; (*avviso*) advertisement, ad; **mettere un'inserzione sul giornale** to put *o* place an advertisement in the newspaper; **ho messo un'inserzione sul giornale** I put an advert in the paper
inserzionista, i, e [insertsjo'nista] SM/F advertiser
inserzionistico, a, ci, che [insertsjo'nistiko] AGG: **spazio inserzionistico** advertising space
insetticida, i, e [insetti'tʃida] AGG, SM insecticide; **una bomboletta d'insetticida** a can of insecticide
insettivoro, a [insetti'voro] AGG insectivorous
■ SM insectivore
insetto [in'sɛtto] SM insect; **è un insetto** (*pegg: persona*) he's a louse
insicurezza [insicu'rettsa] SF insecurity
insicuro, a [insi'kuro] AGG insecure
insidia [in'sidja] SF (*pericolo*) hidden danger; (*inganno*) trap, snare; **tendere un'insidia a qn** to lay *o* set a trap for sb
insidiare [insi'djare] VT **1** (*Mil*) to harass **2** **insidiare la vita di qn** to make an attempt on sb's life; **insidiare la virtù di una donna** to make an attempt on a woman's virtue
insidiosamente [insidjosa'mente] AVV insidiously
insidioso, a [insi'djoso] AGG insidious
insieme [in'sjɛme] AVV **1** together; **tutti insieme** all together; **stanno bene insieme** (*persone*) they get on well together; (*colori*) they go well together; **quei due stanno proprio bene insieme** (*coppia*) those two make a nice couple; **da quanto tempo state insieme?** how long have you been together?; **stanno insieme da due anni** they have been (going out) together for two years; **si sono messi insieme due anni fa** they started going out together two years ago; **questo libro non sta più insieme** this book is falling apart
2 (*contemporaneamente*) at the same time; **vuol fare troppe cose insieme** she wants to do too many things at the same time; **abbiamo finito insieme** we finished together *o* at the same time; **l'ha bevuto tutto insieme** (*in una volta*) he drank it at one go *o* in one draught; **forza, spingete tutti insieme!** come on, everyone push together!; **non parlate tutti insieme, per favore** don't all speak at the same time, please
■ **insieme a** PREP (together) with; **ha cenato insieme a noi** he had dinner with us; **bevilo insieme al succo di frutta** take it with a drink of fruit juice; **mettilo insieme al mio** put it along with mine
■ SM **1** (*totalità*) whole; **l'insieme degli elettori** the whole electorate; **l'insieme dei cittadini/degli edifici** all the citizens/buildings; **nell'insieme** on the whole; **nell'insieme mi sembra buono** it seems okay on the whole; **bisogna considerare la cosa nell'insieme** *o* **nel suo insieme** we will have to take an overall view of the matter; **d'insieme** (*sguardo, veduta*) overall, general **2** (*Mat, assortimento*) set; (*Moda*) outfit, ensemble; **nella stanza c'era uno strano insieme di persone/oggetti** there was a strange collection of people/objects in the room
insiemistica [insje'mistika] SF (*Mat*) set theory
insigne [in'siɲɲe] AGG (*persona*) distinguished, eminent; (*città, monumento*) notable
insignificante [insiɲɲifi'kante] AGG (*gen*) insignificant; (*somma*) trifling, insignificant; **un particolare insignificante** an insignificant detail
insignire [insiɲ'ɲire] VT: **insignire qn di** to honour (*Brit*) *o* honor (*Am*) sb with, decorate sb with; **insignire qn del titolo di cavaliere** to knight sb
insilare [insi'lare] VT (*Agr: mangimi*) to ensile
insincero, a [insin'tʃɛro] AGG insincere
insindacabile [insinda'kabile] AGG unquestionable, unchallengeable; **la decisione è insindacabile** (*di giuria*) the decision is final
insinuante [insinu'ante] AGG (*osservazione, sguardo*) insinuating; (*maniere*) ingratiating
insinuare [insinu'are] VT **1** (*introdurre*): **insinuare qc in** to slip *o* slide sth into **2** (*alludere*) to insinuate, imply; **fu lei ad insinuargli il sospetto che...** she was the one who created the suspicion in his mind *o* made him suspect that ...; **cosa vorresti insinuare?** what are you trying to insinuate?
▶ **insinuarsi** VIP (*umidità, acqua*): **insinuarsi (in qc)** to seep in(to sth), penetrate (sth); (*dubbio*) **insinuarsi in** to creep into
▶ **insinuarsi** VR (*persona*): **insinuarsi in** to worm one's way into, insinuate o.s. into
insinuazione [insinuat'tsjone] SF insinuation, innuendo; **fare insinuazioni su qn** to make insinuations about sb
insipido, a [in'sipido] AGG (*anche fig*) insipid
insistente [insis'tɛnte] AGG (*che insiste*) insistent; (: *pioggia, dolore*) persistent

Ii

insistentemente [insistente'mente] AVV repeatedly, persistently
insistenza [insis'tɛntsa] SF *(vedi agg)* insistence; persistence; **chiedere con insistenza** to ask insistently
insistere [in'sistere] VI IRREG *(aus* **avere***)*: **insistere (su qc/a fare qc)** to insist (on sth/on doing sth); **insistere (in qc/a fare qc)** *(perseverare)* to persist in sth/in doing sth; **se proprio insisti, vengo** if you really insist, I'll come; **non insistere, tanto non te lo presto** don't keep on, I'm not going to lend it to you; **è inutile insistere su quell'argomento** there's no point keeping on about this
insistito, a [insis'tito] PP *di* **insistere**
insito, a ['insito] AGG: **insito (in)** inherent (in)
insoddisfacente [insoddisfa'tʃɛnte] AGG unsatisfactory
insoddisfatto, a [insoddis'fatto] AGG *(persona)* dissatisfied; *(desiderio)* unfulfilled, unsatisfied; **essere insoddisfatto di qc** to be dissatisfied with sth
insoddisfazione [insoddisfat'tsjone] SF dissatisfaction
insofferente [insoffe'rɛnte] AGG *(impaziente)* impatient; *(irrequieto)* edgy
insofferenza [insoffe'rɛntsa] SF impatience
insolazione [insolat'tsjone] SF *(Med)* sunstroke; **prendere un'insolazione** to get sunstroke; **ho preso un'insolazione** I got sunstroke
insolente [inso'lɛnte] AGG insolent
■ SM/F insolent person
insolentemente [insolente'mente] AVV insolently
insolentire [insolen'tire] VI *(aus* **essere***)* to grow insolent
■ VT to insult, be rude to
insolenza [inso'lɛntsa] SF *(arroganza)* insolence; *(osservazione)* insolent remark; **è stata un'insolenza da parte sua** *(azione)* that was a piece of insolence on his part
insolito, a [in'sɔlito] AGG unusual, out of the ordinary, strange
insolubile [inso'lubile] AGG **1** *(problema)* insoluble, insolvable **2** *(sostanza)* insoluble
insoluto, a [inso'luto] AGG *(problema)* unsolved; *(debito)* unpaid, outstanding
insolvente [insol'vɛnte] AGG *(Dir)* insolvent
insolvenza [insol'vɛntsa] SF *(Dir)* insolvency
insolvibile [insol'vibile] AGG *(Dir)* insolvent
insomma [in'somma] AVV *(in breve, in conclusione)* in short, all in all; *(dunque)* well; **insomma, sei pronta o no?** well, are you ready or not?; **insomma, cosa ti hanno detto?** well, what did they say to you?; **era sporco, scomodo e caro, insomma un disastro!** it was dirty, uncomfortable and expensive – all in all, a disaster!
■ ESCL: **insomma!** for heaven's sake!; **come stai? — insomma...!** how are you? — not too bad; **insomma, basta!** that's enough!
insondabile [inson'dabile] AGG unfathomable
insonne [in'sɔnne] AGG *(notte)* sleepless
insonnia [in'sɔnnja] SF insomnia, sleeplessness; **soffrire d'insonnia** *(Med)* to suffer from insomnia; **da un po' di tempo soffro d'insonnia** I haven't been able to sleep lately
insonnolito, a [insonno'lito] AGG sleepy, drowsy; **è sempre più insonnolito** he's getting sleepier and sleepier
insonorizzato, a [insonorid'dzato] AGG *(stanza)* soundproofed
insonorizzazione [insonoriddzat'tsjone] SF soundproofing
insopportabile [insoppor'tabile] AGG unbearable; **c'è una puzza insopportabile qui dentro** there's a horrible smell in here; **è una ragazza proprio insopportabile** that girl is a real pain
insopportabilmente [insopportabil'mente] AVV unbearably
insopprimibile [insoppri'mibile] AGG unsuppressible, insuppressible
insorgente [insor'dʒɛnte] AGG: **viste le insorgenti difficoltà...** given the problems which are arising *o* cropping up ...
insorgenza [insor'dʒɛntsa] SF *(di malattia)* onset
insorgere [in'sordʒere] VI IRREG *(aus* **essere***)* **1** *(ribellarsi)*: **insorgere (contro)** to rise up (against), rebel (against) **2** *(manifestarsi improvvisamente)* to arise, come *o* crop up
insormontabile [insormon'tabile] AGG *(ostacolo)* unsurmountable, insurmountable, insuperable
insorsi *ecc* [in'sorsi] VB *vedi* **insorgere**
insorto, a [in'sorto] PP *di* **insorgere**
■ AGG: **il popolo insorto** the rebels, the insurgents
■ SM/F rebel, insurgent
insospettabile [insospet'tabile] AGG **1** *(al di sopra di ogni sospetto)* above suspicion **2** *(inatteso)* unsuspected
insospettato, a [insospet'tato] AGG unsuspected
insospettire [insospet'tire] VT to make suspicious, arouse suspicions in; **il suo atteggiamento mi ha insospettito** her behaviour made me suspicious
■ VI *(aus* essere*)*, **insospettirsi** VIP: **insospettirsi (per/di qc)** to become suspicious (because of/about sth); **si è insospettito e ha chiamato la polizia** he became suspicious and called the police
insostenibile [insoste'nibile] AGG **1** *(posizione, teoria)* untenable **2** *(dolore, situazione)* intolerable, unbearable; **le spese di manutenzione sono insostenibili** the maintenance costs are prohibitive
insostituibile [insostitu'ibile] AGG *(persona)* irreplaceable; *(aiuto, presenza)* invaluable
insozzare [insot'tsare] VT **1** *(pavimento)* to (make) dirty **2** *(fig: reputazione, memoria di qn)* to tarnish, sully
▶ **insozzarsi** VR, VIP to get dirty
insperabile [inspe'rabile] AGG: **la guarigione/ salvezza era insperabile** there was no hope of a cure/ of rescue; **abbiamo ottenuto risultati insperabili** the results we achieved were beyond our expectations
insperato, a [inspe'rato] AGG unhoped-for
inspiegabile [inspje'gabile] AGG inexplicable
inspiegabilmente [inspjegabil'mente] AVV inexplicably
inspirare [inspi'rare] VT to inhale, breathe in
inspirazione [inspirat'tsjone] SF inhaling, breathing in
instabile [in'stabile] AGG *(carico, carattere, situazione)* unstable; *(tempo)* unsettled, changeable; *(umore)* uncertain, changeable; *(equilibrio)* unsteady; **la situazione politica è un po' instabile** the political situation is rather unstable; **il tempo è ancora instabile** the weather is still unsettled; **la sedia è un po' instabile** the chair is a bit unsteady
instabilità [instabili'ta] SF *(gen)* instability; *(del tempo)* changeability; *(di umore)* inconstancy
installabile [instal'labile] AGG: **installabile su** that can be installed on; **un software installabile**

direttamente sul PC a piece of software that can be installed directly on the PC

installare [instal'lare] VT (*impianto, telefono*) to install, put in
▶ **installarsi** VR: **installarsi in** (*sistemarsi*) to set up house, settle in; **si è installata in casa mia** (*scherz*) she has taken up residence at my house

installazione [installat'tsjone] SF **1** (*di telefono ecc*) installation **2** (*impianto*) system; **installazioni di bordo** (*Aer, Naut*) on-board equipment

instancabile [instan'kabile] AGG tireless, untiring

instancabilmente [instankabil'mente] AVV tirelessly

instaurare [instau'rare] VT (*regola, sistema*) to establish, institute; (*moda ecc*) to introduce
▶ **instaurarsi** VIP to be *o* become established

instaurazione [instaurat'tsjone] SF (*vedi vt*) establishment, institution; introduction

instillare [instil'lare] VT to instil

instillazione [instillat'tsjone] SF instillation, instillment (*Brit*), instilment (*Am*)

instradare [instra'dare] VT = **istradare**

insù [in'su] AVV up, upwards; **guardare all'insù** to look up *o* upwards; **nasino all'insù** turned-up nose

insubordinato, a [insubordi'nato] AGG insubordinate

insubordinazione [insubordinat'tsjone] SF insubordination

insuccesso [insut'tʃɛsso] SM failure, flop

insudiciare [insudi'tʃare] VT to dirty, soil; (*fig: reputazione, nome*) to sully, tarnish; **insudiciarsi i vestiti** to get one's clothes dirty, dirty one's clothes
▶ **insudiciarsi** VR, VIP to get dirty

insufficiente [insuffi'tʃɛnte] AGG **1 insufficiente a** *o* **per** (*quantità*) insufficient (for); (*qualità*) inadequate (for); **il cibo è insufficiente** there's not enough food; **200 sterline al mese sono insufficienti per vivere** £200 a month is not enough *o* sufficient to live on **2** (*Scol: voto*) unsatisfactory; (*: compito*) below standard

insufficientemente [insuffitʃente'mente] AVV (*vedi agg 1*) insufficiently; inadequately

insufficienza [insuffi'tʃɛntsa] SF **1** (*di denaro, viveri*) shortage; (*di tempo, spazio*) lack; (*di preparazione*) inadequacy; (*Med*) insufficiency; **insufficienza di prove** (*Dir*) lack of evidence; **l'hanno assolto per insufficienza di prove** he was acquitted because of lack of evidence **2** (*Scol*) fail; **prendere un'insufficienza in** to fail; **ho preso un'insufficienza in chimica** I got a fail in chemistry

insulare [insu'lare] AGG island *attr*

insulina [insu'lina] SF (*Chim*) insulin

insulsaggine [insul'saddʒine] SF (*vedi agg*) dullness, insipidity; inanity; silliness

insulso, a [in'sulso] AGG (*persona*) dull, insipid; (*osservazione*) inane, silly; (*film, romanzo*) crass, silly; **fa discorsi sempre più insulsi** the things he says get sillier and sillier; **è una delle persone più insulse che abbia mai conosciuto** he's one of the dullest people I've ever met

insultare [insul'tare] VT to insult

insulto [in'sulto] SM insult, affront; **coprire qn di insulti** to hurl abuse at sb, heap abuse on sb

insuperabile [insupe'rabile] AGG **1** (*ostacolo, difficoltà*) insuperable, unsurmountable, insurmountable **2** (*eccellente: qualità, prodotto*) unbeatable; (*: persona, interpretazione*) unequalled

insuperato, a [insupe'rato] AGG unsurpassed, unequalled

insuperbire [insuper'bire] VT to make proud, make arrogant; **il successo lo ha insuperbito** success has gone to his head
■ VI (*aus* **essere**), **insuperbirsi** VIP to become arrogant

insurrezionale [insurrettsjo'nale] AGG insurrectionary

insurrezione [insurret'tsjone] SF insurrection, revolt

insussistente [insussis'tɛnte] AGG (*accusa, paura*) unfounded, groundless; (*pericolo*) non-existent

insussistenza [insussis'tɛntsa] SF (*vedi agg*) groundlessness; non-existence

intabarrato, a [intabar'rato] AGG well wrapped up, muffled up

intaccabile [intak'kabile] AGG (*metallo*) subject to corrosion; (*fig: teoria*) open to criticism

intaccare [intak'kare] VT **1** (*sogg: ruggine*) to corrode; (*: acido*) to eat into; **non vorrei intaccare i miei risparmi** I wouldn't want to break into my savings **2** (*fare tacche in*) to cut into, nick **3** (*infettare, fig: reputazione*) to affect, damage

intacco, chi [in'takko] SM notch, nick

intagliare [intaʎ'ʎare] VT (*pietre*) to engrave, carve; (*legno*) to carve

intagliatore, trice [intaʎʎa'tore] SM/F engraver

intaglio, gli [in'taʎʎo] SM intaglio

intangibile [intan'dʒibile] AGG **1** (*eredità, patrimonio*) tied-up **2** (*fig: diritto*) inviolable; (*: differenza*) intangible

intanto [in'tanto] AVV (*nel frattempo*) meanwhile, in the meantime; (*per cominciare*) just to begin with; **intanto che** while; **intanto che aspetti leggiti questo** you can read this while you're waiting; **puoi scusarti quanto vuoi, intanto il male è già stato fatto** it's all very well saying you're sorry, but (the fact remains that) the damage has been done; **intanto prendi questo, poi ti darò il resto** take this for now *o* the time being and I'll give you the rest later; **sì, sì, intanto tocca sempre a me farlo!** yes, yes, but it's always me who has to do it!; **mettiti il cappotto, io intanto chiamo un taxi** put on your coat while I get a taxi

intarsiare [intar'sjare] VT to inlay

intarsio, si [in'tarsjo] SM (*arte, tecnica*) inlaying *no pl*, marquetry *no pl*; (*parte lavorata*) marquetry, inlay; **mobili lavorati a intarsio** inlaid furniture

intasamento [intasa'mento] SM (*ostruzione*) blockage, obstruction; (*Aut: ingorgo*) traffic jam

intasare [inta'sare] VT (*tubo*) to block (up); (*traffico*) to hold up; **ho il naso intasato** I've got a blocked *o* stuffed-up nose
▶ **intasarsi** VIP to become choked *o* blocked

intasato, a [inta'sato] AGG (*lavandino, naso, strada*) blocked

intascare [intas'kare] VT (*denaro, premio*) to pocket

intatto, a [in'tatto] AGG (*gen*) intact; (*puro*) unsullied; **la neve era intatta** there were no footprints in the snow

intavolare [intavo'lare] VT (*discussione, trattative*) to open, start, enter into

integerrimo, a [inte'dʒɛrrimo] AGG honest, upright; **è un uomo integerrimo** he's a man of the utmost integrity

integrale [inte'grale] AGG **1** (*gen*) complete; (*rimborso*) full; (*pane, farina*) wholemeal (*Brit*), wholewheat (*Am*); **pane integrale** wholemeal bread; **abbronzatura integrale** all-over tan; **edizione integrale** unabridged edition; **film in versione integrale** uncut

Ii

version of a film; **auto a trazione integrale** four-wheel drive vehicle **2** (*Mat*) integral
■SM (*Mat*) integral
integralismo [integra'lizmo] SM integralism
integralista, i, e [integra'lista] AGG, SM/F integralist
integralmente [integral'mente] AVV in full, fully
integrante [inte'grante] AGG: **essere parte integrante di** to be an integral part of
integrare [inte'grare] VT **1** (*completare*) to complete; (: *personale*) to bring up to strength; (: *stipendio, dieta ecc*) to supplement; **integra il proprio stipendio dando lezioni private** he supplements his income by giving private lessons **2** (*Sociol, Mat*) to integrate
▶ **integrarsi** VIP (*Sociol*) to become integrated
integrativo, a [integra'tivo] AGG (*assegno*) supplementary; (*Scol*): **esame integrativo** *assessment test sat when changing schools*; **pensione integrativa** personal pension
integrato, a [inte'grato] AGG (*Elettr*) integrated
integratore [integra'tore] SM: **integratori alimentari** nutritional supplements
integrazione [integrat'tsjone] SF integration
integrità [integri'ta] SF **1** (*interezza*: *di patrimonio*) intact state; **tutelare l'integrità fisica dei prigionieri** to guarantee the physical well-being of (the) prisoners **2** (*onestà*) integrity, honesty, uprightness
integro, a ['integro] AGG **1** (*intero*) intact, complete, whole **2** (*onesto*) honest, upright
intelaiatura [intelaja'tura] SF (*Edil*) skeleton, framework, frame; (*fig*: *economica, sociale*) framework, structure
intellegibile [intelle'dʒibile] AGG = **intelligibile**
intellettivo, a [intellet'tivo] AGG (*facoltà*) intellectual
intelletto [intel'lɛtto] SM intellect; **perdere il ben dell'intelletto** (*impazzire*) to go out of one's mind
intellettuale [intellettu'ale] AGG intellectual; **sforzo intellettuale** mental effort
■SM/F intellectual
intellettualizzare [intellettualid'dzare] VT to intellectualize
intellettualmente [intellettual'mente] AVV intellectually
intellettualoide [intellettua'lɔide] (*pegg*) AGG (*atteggiamento*) highbrow, pseudo-intellectual
■SM/F pseudo-intellectual, would-be intellectual
intelligente [intelli'dʒɛnte] AGG (*gen*) intelligent; (*brillante*) clever, bright; (*capace*) clever, able; **missile intelligente** smart missile
intelligentemente [intellidʒente'mente] AVV intelligently
intelligenza [intelli'dʒɛntsa] SF intelligence; **ha un'intelligenza viva** he's got a quick *o* sharp mind; **è una bella intelligenza** he has a fine mind *o* a good brain; **un lavoro fatto con intelligenza** a clever piece of work; **giocato con intelligenza** cleverly played; **intelligenza artificiale** artificial intelligence
intellighenzia [intelli'gɛntsia] SF intelligentsia
intelligibile [intelli'dʒibile] AGG intelligible; **ripetilo in modo chiaro e intelligibile** repeat it loudly and clearly; **un messaggio poco intelligibile** an unclear message; **ha una scrittura chiara e intelligibile** he has clear, legible handwriting
intelligibilità [intellidʒibili'ta] SF intelligibility
intelligibilmente [intellidʒibil'mente] AVV intelligibly
intemerato, a [inteme'rato] (*letter*) AGG (*persona, vita*) blameless, irreproachable; (*coscienza*) clear; (*fama*) unblemished
intemperante [intempe'rante] AGG intemperate, immoderate
intemperanza [intempe'rantsa] SF (*qualità*) intemperance; **intemperanze** SFPL (*eccessi*) excesses
intemperie [intem'pɛrje] SFPL bad weather *sg*; **esposto alle intemperie** exposed to the elements; **resistente alle intemperie** weatherproof
intempestivo, a [intempes'tivo] AGG (*intervento*) untimely, ill-timed
intendente [inten'dɛnte] SM: **intendente di Finanza** inland (*Brit*) *o* internal (*Am*) revenue officer
intendenza [inten'dɛntsa] SF: **intendenza di Finanza** inland (*Brit*) *o* internal (*Am*) revenue office
intendere [in'tɛndere] VB IRREG, VT **1** (*avere intenzione*): **intendere fare qc** to intend *o* mean to do sth, have the intention of doing sth; **non intendo farlo** I have no intention of doing it, I don't intend to do it **2** (*significare*) to mean; **cosa intendevi (dire)?** what did you mean?; **dipende da cosa intendi per "giustizia"** it depends what you mean by "justice". **3** (*capire*) to understand; **mi ha dato a intendere che...** he led me to believe that ...; **ha lasciato intendere che...** he gave (me *o* us) to understand that ...; **ma io non la intendo così** I don't see things that way; **puoi intenderla come vuoi** you can take it how you like; **non riesce a farsi intendere** he cannot make himself understood; **s'intende!** naturally!, of course!; **s'intende che verrai anche tu!** you'll be coming too, of course! **4** (*udire*) to hear; **ho inteso dire che...** I've heard (it said) that ...; **non vuole intendere ragione** he won't listen to reason;
▶ **intendersi** VR (*uso reciproco*: *capirsi*) to understand each other, get on (well); **intendersi con qn su qc** (*accordarsi*) to come to an agreement with sb about sth; **intendiamoci** let's get it quite clear; **ci siamo intesi?** is that clear?, is that understood?; **cominciamo a intenderci** we're beginning to understand each other;
▶ **intendersi** VIP **1** (*conoscere bene*) **intendersi di qc** to know a lot about sth; (: *cibi, vini*) to be a connoisseur of sth; **si intende di fotografia** she knows about photography; **me ne intendo poco** I know very little about it **2** (*avere una relazione amorosa*) **intendersela (con qn)** to have an affair with sb
intendimento [intendi'mento] SM (*proposito*) intention
intenditore, trice [intendi'tore] SM/F expert; (*di vini, cibi*) connoisseur; **a buon intenditor poche parole** (*Proverbio*) a word to the wise ...; **un intenditore di vini** a connoisseur of wine
intenerire [intene'rire] VT (*commuovere*) to touch, move (to pity)
▶ **intenerirsi** VIP to be touched, be moved
intensamente [intensa'mente] AVV intensely
intensificare [intensifi'kare] VT, **intensificarsi** VIP to intensify, increase
intensificazione [intensifikat'tsjone] SF intensification
intensità [intensi'ta] SF INV (*gen, Fis*) intensity; (*del vento*) force, strength
intensivamente [intensiva'mente] AVV intensively
intensivo, a [inten'sivo] AGG intensive
intenso, a [in'tɛnso] AGG (*gen*) intense; (*profumo*) strong; (*luce*) bright; (*colore*) intense, deep; **un calore intenso** intense heat; **una luce intensa** a bright light;

il traffico è più intenso attorno alle otto the traffic is heaviest around eight; **ho avuto un pomeriggio intenso** I had a busy afternoon

intentare [inten'tare] VT (*Dir*): **intentare causa a** *o* **contro qn** to start *o* institute proceedings against sb

intentato, a [inten'tato] AGG: **non lasciare nulla d'intentato** to leave no stone unturned, try everything

intento[1], a [in'tɛnto] AGG intent; **essere intento a qc/a fare qc** to be intent on sth/absorbed in doing sth

intento[2] [in'tɛnto] SM intention, aim, purpose; **fare qc con l'intento di** to do sth with the intention of; **riuscire nell'intento** to achieve one's aim

intenzionale [intentsjo'nale] AGG (*gen*) intentional, deliberate; (*Dir: omicidio*) premeditated; **fallo intenzionale** (*Sport*) deliberate foul

intenzionalmente [intentsjonal'mente] AVV intentionally

intenzionato, a [intentsjo'nato] AGG: **essere intenzionato a fare qc** to intend to do sth, have the intention of doing sth; **ben intenzionato** well-meaning, well-intentioned; **mal intenzionato** ill-intentioned

intenzione [inten'tsjone] SF intention; **avere (l')intenzione di fare qc** to intend to do sth, have the intention of doing sth; **avevo intenzione di andare ma poi ho cambiato idea** I meant to go but then I changed my mind; **non avevo intenzione di offenderti** I didn't mean to offend you; **è mia intenzione farlo** I intend to do it; **non era mia intenzione offenderti** I didn't mean to offend you; **è l'intenzione che conta** it's the thought that counts; **non so quali sono le sue intenzioni** I don't know what her intentions are; **con intenzione** intentionally, deliberately; **senza intenzione** unintentionally; **secondo l'intenzione** *o* **le intenzioni di qn** in accordance with sb's wishes; **animato dalle migliori intenzioni** with the best of intentions

intepidire [intepi'dire] VT = **intiepidire**

interagire [intera'dʒire] VI (*aus* **avere**) to interact

interamente [intera'mente] AVV entirely, completely

interattività [interattivi'ta] SF (*Inform*) interacticity

interattivo, a [interat'tivo] AGG interactive

interazione [interat'tsjone] SF interaction

intercalare [interka'lare] VT: **intercalare a, intercalare in** (*testo, discorso ecc*) to insert into
■ SM pet phrase, stock phrase; **il suo intercalare preferito è "cioè"** one of his favourite expressions is "cioè"

intercambiabile [interkam'bjabile] AGG interchangeable

intercambiabilità [interkambjabili'ta] SF interchangeability

intercapedine [interka'pɛdine] SF gap, cavity

intercedere [inter'tʃɛdere] VI (*aus* **avere**) **intercedere (presso/in favore di)** to intercede (with/on behalf of)

intercessione [intertʃes'sjone] SF intercession

intercettare [intertʃet'tare] VT (*gen, Sport, Telec*) to intercept

intercettazione [intertʃettat'tsjone], **intercettamento** [intertʃetta'mento] SF interception; **intercettazione ambientale** electronic surveillance; **intercettazione telefonica** telephone tapping

intercettore [intertʃet'tore] SM (*Mil*) interceptor

intercity [inter'siti] SM INV (*Ferr*) ≈ intercity (train)

intercomunicante [interkomuni'kante] AGG (inter)communicating

interconfessionale [interkonfessjo'nale] AGG (*Rel*) interdenominational

interconnettere [interkon'nɛttere] VT IRREG to interconnect

intercontinentale [interkontinen'tale] AGG intercontinental

intercorrere [inter'korrere] VI IRREG (*aus* **essere**) **1** (*passare, tempo*) to elapse **2** (*esserci*) to exist; **fra loro intercorrono ottimi rapporti** they are on the very best of terms

intercorso, a [inter'korso] PP *di* **intercorrere**

intercostale [interkos'tale] AGG (*Anat*) intercostal

interdentale [interden'tale] AGG (*Anat*) interdental; **filo interdentale** dental floss

interdetto, a [inter'detto] PP *di* **interdire**
■ AGG (*sconcertato*) dumbfounded; **rimanere interdetto** to be taken aback; **lasciare qn interdetto** to take sb aback, dumbfound
■ SM (*Rel, Dir*) interdict; **gli interdetti per infermità mentale** those who are debarred on the grounds of mental incapacity

interdipendente [interdipen'dɛnte] AGG interdependent

interdipendenza [interdipen'dɛntsa] SF interdependence

interdire [inter'dire] VT IRREG (*gen: vietare*) to forbid, ban, prohibit; (*Rel*) to interdict; (*Dir*) to deprive of civil rights; **interdire qn dai pubblici uffici** to ban *o* debar sb from public office

interdisciplinare [interdiʃʃipli'nare] AGG interdisciplinary

interdizione [interdit'tsjone] SF (*divieto*) prohibition, ban; (*Rel*) interdict; (*Dir*) debarment; **interdizione giudiziale** debarment (*resulting from certification of insanity*); **interdizione legale** deprivation of civil rights

interessamento [interessa'mento] SM (*interesse*) interest; (*intervento*) intervention, good offices *pl*; **grazie al suo interessamento sono riuscito ad avere il lavoro** it was thanks to his good offices that I managed to get the job

interessante [interes'sante] AGG (*gen*) interesting; **essere in stato interessante** (*fam*) to be expecting (a baby)

interessare [interes'sare] VI (*aus* **essere**) **interessare (a qn)** to interest (sb); **forse ti interesserà sapere che...** perhaps you might be interested to know that ...; **se ti interessa ti posso dare il suo indirizzo** if you are interested I can give you his address; **non m'interessa!** I'm not interested!; **a lui non interessano che i suoi libri** he's only interested in his books; **ci interessa che tutto vada bene** what matters to us is that everything should go *o* goes well
■ VT **1** (*suscitare interesse in*) to interest; **interessare qn a qc** to interest sb in sth **2** (*riguardare*) to affect, concern; **la notizia interesserà gli appassionati di cinema** the news will interest cinema fans; **precipitazioni che interessano le regioni settentrionali** rainfall affecting the north; **un provvedimento che interessa gli automobilisti** a regulation affecting *o* concerning motorists **3** (*Comm*): **interessare qn in** (*utili*) to give sb a share *o* an interest in
▶ **interessarsi** VIP **1** (*mostrare curiosità*) **interessarsi (a)** to show interest (in); **si è interessato molto a quel progetto** he showed a lot of interest in the project

Ii

2 (*occuparsi*) **interessarsi di** *o* **a** (*politica, pittura ecc*) to be interested in, take an interest in; **non mi interesso di politica** I'm not interested in politics; **si sono interessati al suo caso** they took up his case; **si è interessato alla mia promozione** he helped me get promotion; **si è interessato di farmi avere quei biglietti** he took the trouble to get me those tickets; **interessati degli affari tuoi!** mind your own business!

interessatamente [interessata'mente] AVV self-interestedly

interessato, a [interes'sato] AGG **1** (*coinvolto*) interested, involved; **le parti interessate** the interested parties; **le regioni interessate dal maltempo** the regions affected by the bad weather **2** (*pegg*): **essere interessato** to act out of self-interest
■ SM/F (*coinvolto*) person concerned; **a tutti gli interessati** to all those concerned, to all interested parties

interesse [inte'rɛsse] SM **1** (*gen*) interest; **ho sempre avuto un certo interesse per...** I've always had a certain interest in ..., I've always been rather interested in ...; **ha ascoltato con grande interesse** she listened with great interest **2** (*affare, attività*): **badare ai propri interessi** to look after one's own interests *o* affairs; **ha degli interessi in quell'azienda** he has a financial interest in that company; **curare gli interessi del proprio cliente** (*avvocato*) to act in the interests of one's client; **interesse privato in atti di ufficio** (*Amm*) abuse of public office **3** (*tornaconto*): **fare qc per interesse** to do sth out of self-interest; **non pensa che a fare il proprio interesse** he only thinks of his own interests; **nell'interesse dell'umanità** in the interests of mankind; **agire nell'interesse comune** to act for the common good *o* in the common interest; **non ho alcun interesse a farlo** *o* **non è nel mio interesse farlo** it is not in my interest to do it; **lo dico nel tuo interesse** I'm saying this for your own good; **l'ha sposata per interesse** he married her for her money; **quando c'è di mezzo l'interesse...** when personal interests are involved ... **4** (*Fin, Comm*) interest; **un interesse del 5%** 5% interest; **interesse composto** compound interest; **interesse maturato** accrued interest; **interesse semplice** simple interest

interessenza [interes'sɛntsa] SF (*Econ*) profit-sharing

interetnico, a, ci, che [inter'ɛtniko] AGG inter-ethnic

interfaccia [inter'fattʃa] SF INV (*Inform*) interface; **interfaccia utente** user interface

interfacciare [interfat'tʃare] VT (*Inform*) to interface

interferenza [interfe'rɛntsa] SF (*gen, Tecn*) interference; **ci sono delle interferenze nella linea** (*Telec*) there is interference on the line

interferire [interfe'rire] VI (*aus* **avere**): **interferire (in)** to interfere (in); **non interferire in questa faccenda!** don't interfere in this!

interfono [inter'fono] SM intercom (*fam*); (*in una casa*) house phone, internal phone

intergalattico, a, ci, che [interga'lattiko] AGG intergalactic

interiezione [interjet'tsjone] SF (*Gramm*) interjection, exclamation

interim ['interim] SM INV **1** (*periodo*) interim, interval; **ministro ad interim** acting *o* interim minister **2** (*incarico*) temporary appointment

interinale [interi'nale] AGG: **lavoro interinale** temporary work (*through an agency*)

interiora [inte'rjora] SFPL entrails *pl*

interiore [inte'rjore] AGG **1** (*interno*) inner *attr*; **parte interiore** inside **2** (*fig: vita, mondo*) inner *attr*

interiorità [interjori'ta] SF inner being

interiorizzare [interjorid'dzare] VT to internalize

interiorizzazione [interjoriddzat'tsjone] SF internalization

interiormente [interjor'mente] AVV (*gen*) internally; (*soffrire*) inwardly, inside

interlinea [inter'linea] SF **1** (*Dattilografia*) line spacing; **interlinea doppia** double spacing **2** (*Tip*) lead, leading

interlineare [interline'are] AGG interlinear
■ VT **1** (*spaziare le righe*) to space (out) **2** (*Tip*) to lead (out)

interlocutore, trice [interloku'tore] SM/F speaker; **il suo interlocutore** the person he was speaking to

interlocutorio, ria, ri, rie [interloku'tɔrjo] AGG interlocutory

interludio, di [inter'ludjo] SM (*Mus, fig*) interlude

intermediario, ria, ri, rie [interme'djarjo] AGG intermediary
■ SM/F intermediary, go-between; (*Comm, Econ*) middleman

intermediazione [intermedjat'tsjone] SF mediation

intermedio, dia, di, die [inter'mɛdjo] AGG intermediate *attr*

intermezzo [inter'mɛddzo] SM (*intervallo*) interval; (*breve spettacolo*) interlude

interminabile [intermi'nabile] AGG interminable, endless, never-ending

interministeriale [interministe'rjale] AGG interministerial

intermittente [intermit'tɛnte] AGG intermittent

intermittentemente [intermittente'mente] AVV intermittently

intermittenza [intermit'tɛntsa] SF: **ad intermittenza** intermittent

internalizzare [internalid'dzare] VT (*Econ*) to internalize

internalizzazione [internaliddzat'tsjone] SF (*Econ*) internalization

internamente [interna'mente] AVV internally

internamento [interna'mento] SM (*vedi vb*) internment; confinement (to a mental hospital)

internare [inter'nare] VT (*Pol*) to intern; (*Med*) to confine to a mental hospital

internato¹, a [inter'nato] (*vedi vb*) AGG interned; confined (to a mental hospital)
■ SM/F internee; inmate (of a mental hospital)

internato² [inter'nato] SM **1** (*collegio*) boarding school **2** (*di medico*) period as a houseman (*Brit*) *o* an intern (*Am*)

internauta, i, e [inter'nauta] SM/F web *o* net surfer

internazionale [internattsjo'nale] AGG international
■ SF: **l'Internazionale** (*Pol: associazione*) the International; (*: inno*) the Internationale

internazionalmente [internattsjonal'mente] AVV internationally

Internet ['internet] SM Internet; **in Internet** on the Internet

internista, i, e [inter'nista] SM/F internist

interno, a [in'tɛrno] AGG (*gen, Med*) internal; (*tasca*) inside *attr*; (*regione, navigazione, mare*) inland *attr*; (*politica, commercio*) domestic; **alunno interno** boarder; **la**

politica interna domestic policy; **commissione interna** (*Scol*) internal examination board; **la tasca interna della giacca** the inside pocket of the jacket; **i confini interni dell'Unione europea** the internal borders of the European Union

■ SM **1** (*di edificio*) inside, interior; (*di scatola*) inside; (*di cappotto*: *fodera*) lining; **dall'interno** from the inside; **le urla provenivano dall'interno della casa** the screams were coming from inside the house; **all'interno (della casa)** inside (the house); **c'erano ancora venti persone all'interno della discoteca** there were still twenty people inside the club; **l'interno della scatola è rosso** the inside of the box is red **2** (*Cine*): **interni** SMPL interior shots; **girare gli interni** to film the indoor shots **3** (*di paese*) interior; **regioni dell'interno** inland areas, areas of the interior; **notizie dall'interno** (*Stampa*) home news; **Ministero degli Interni** Ministry of the Interior, ≈ Home Office (*Brit*), ≈ Department of the Interior (*Am*)

▷ www.interno.it/

4 (*di telefono*) extension; (*di appartamento*) flat (*Brit*) *o* apartment (*Am*) (number); **vorrei l'interno trentadue** can I have extension thirty two, please?; **abita in Via Mangili 6, 2° piano, interno 5** he lives at number 6 Via Mangili, 2nd floor, flat 5

■ SM/F (*Scol*) boarder

intero, a [in'tero] AGG **1** (*gen*) whole, entire; (*quantità*) whole, full; (*Mat*: *numero*) whole; **latte intero** full-cream milk; **ti ho aspettato per un'ora intera** I waited for you for a whole *o* full hour; **ho trascorso l'intera settimana a studiare** I spent the whole week studying; **a prezzo intero** at full price; **pagare il prezzo intero** to pay the full price; **ha ingoiato una prugna tutta intera** he swallowed a plum whole; **ho trascorso l'intera settimana a studiare** I spent the whole *o* entire week studying; **ha girato il mondo intero** he's travelled all over the world, he's been all round the world **2** (*intatto*) intact; **è rimasto intero** it remained intact; **ho 500 euro interi, me li cambi?** I have a 500 euro note, can you give me change for it?

■ SM (*anche Mat*) whole; **scrivere per intero qc** to write sth in full

interparlamentare [interparlamen'tare] AGG interparliamentary

interpellanza [interpel'lantsa] SF (*Pol*: *anche*: **interpellanza parlamentare**) (parliamentary) question; **presentare un'interpellanza** to ask a (parliamentary) question

interpellare [interpel'lare] VT (*consultare*) to consult, ask; (*Pol*) to question

interpellato, a [interpel'lato] SM/F person being questioned

interpersonale [interperso'nale] AGG: **rapporti interpersonali** interpersonal relations

interplanetario, ria, ri, rie [interplane'tarjo] AGG interplanetary

Interpol [inter'pɔl] SF Interpol

interpolare [interpo'lare] VT to interpolate

interpolazione [interpolat'tsjone] SF interpolation

interporre [inter'porre] VB IRREG

■ VT **1** (*ostacoli, difficoltà*): **interporre qc a qc** to put sth in the way of sth; (*influenza*) to use; **ha interposto i suoi buoni uffici per aiutarlo** he used his good offices to help him **2** **interporre appello** (*Dir*) to appeal

► **interporsi** VIP (*intervenire*) to intervene; **interporsi fra** (*mettersi in mezzo*) to come between

interposto, a [inter'posto] PP *di* **interporre**

■ AGG: **per interposta persona** through a third party

interpretare [interpre'tare] VT **1** (*gen*: *spiegare, tradurre, capire*) to interpret; **interpretare male** to misinterpret; **forse hai interpretato male quello che ha detto** perhaps you misunderstood what he said; **non so come interpretare il suo comportamento** I don't know how to interpret his behaviour **2** (*Mus, Teatro*) to perform; (*personaggio, sonata*) to play; (*canzone*) to sing; **ha interpretato il ruolo di Robin Hood** he played the part of Robin Hood

interpretariato [interpreta'rjato] SM interpreting

interpretazione [interpretat'tsjone] SF interpretation

interprete [in'tɛrprete] SM/F **1** (*traduttore*) interpreter; (*portavoce*): **farsi interprete di** to act as a spokesman for; **fa l'interprete** she is an interpreter **2** (*Teatro, Cine*) performer, actor/actress; (*Mus*) performer

interpunzione [interpun'tsjone] SF punctuation; **segni di interpunzione** punctuation marks

interrare [inter'rare] VT **1** (*seme, pianta*) to plant; (*tubature, cavi*) to lay underground; (*Mil*: *pezzo d'artiglieria*) to dig in **2** (*riempire di terra*: *canale*) to fill in

interrato [inter'rato] SM (*anche*: **piano interrato**) basement

interregionale [interredʒo'nale] SM *train that travels between two or more regions of Italy, stopping frequently*

interregno [inter'reɲɲo] SM interregnum

interrogare [interro'gare] VT (*gen*) to question; (*Dir*) to examine; (*Scol*) to examine, test; **essere interrogato** to have an oral test; **sono stato interrogato in storia oggi** I had an oral test in history today; **mi ha interrogato in matematica** he examined me in maths; **l'insegnante di inglese mi ha interrogato sul futuro** the English teacher tested me on the future tense; **la polizia vuole interrogarlo** the police want to question him; **lo interrogarono in merito agli ultimi avvenimenti** they questioned him regarding recent events; **interrogare gli astri** (*Astrol*) to consult the stars

interrogativamente [interrogativa'mente] AVV (*vedi agg*) questioningly, inquiringly; interrogatively

interrogativo, a [interroga'tivo] AGG (*sguardo, espressione*) questioning, inquiring; (*Gramm*) interrogative; **punto interrogativo** (*anche fig*) question mark

■ SM question; (*fig*: *persona, futuro*) mystery; **porsi un interrogativo** to ask o.s. a question

interrogato, a [interro'gato] SM/F person examined (*o* questioned)

interrogatorio, ri [interroga'tɔrjo] SM questioning *no pl*; (*più severo*) interrogation; **subire un interrogatorio** to be questioned; (*anche fig*) to be interrogated

interrogazione [interrogat'tsjone] SF **1** (*Scol*): **interrogazione (di)** (oral) examination (in), oral test (in); **interrogazione ciclica** (*Inform*) polling **2** (*Pol*): **interrogazione (parlamentare)** (parliamentary) question

interrompere [inter'rompere] VB IRREG, VT (*viaggio, studi, trattative*) to interrupt, break off; (*conversazione*) to interrupt; (*gravidanza*) to terminate; (*Elettr*: *circuito*) to break; **interrompere l'erogazione del gas/dell'acqua** to cut off the gas/water supply; **le comunicazioni con il nord sono interrotte** the north is cut off; **scusa se t'interrompo** excuse me for

interrupting; **non interrompere!** don't interrupt!
▶ **interrompersi** VIP (*gen*) to break off, stop; (*corrente, linea telefonica*) to be cut off; (*circuito elettrico*) to be broken; (*trasmissione*) to be interrupted

interrotto, a [inter'rotto] PP *di* **interrompere**

interruttore [interrut'tore] SM switch; **l'interruttore della luce** the light switch

interruzione [interrut'tsjone] SF (*azione*) interruption; (*stato*) break, interruption; **senza interruzione** (*lavorare*) without a break; (*dormire, parlare*) non-stop; **interruzione di gravidanza** termination of pregnancy

interscambio, bi [inter'skambjo] SM import-export trade

intersecare [interse'kare] VT, **intersecarsi** VR (*uso reciproco*) to intersect

intersezione [interset'tsjone] SF intersection

interstizio, zi [inter'stittsjo] SM interstice

interurbano, a [interur'bano] AGG intercity *attr*; (*Telec: telefonata*) long-distance *attr*
■ SF (*Telec*) long-distance call

intervallare [interval'lare] VT to space out

intervallo [inter'vallo] SM **1** (*di tempo: Teatro, Cine, Mus*) interval; (*a scuola*) break; (*in ufficio*) (tea *o* coffee) break; (*Sport: fra due tempi*) half-time; **nell'intervallo** in the interval; at half-time; during break; **fare un intervallo di 10 minuti** to have a 10-minute break; **a intervalli regolari** at regular intervals **2** (*di spazio*) space, gap; **a intervalli di 10 cm** at intervals of 10 cm, every 10 cm

intervenire [interve'nire] VI IRREG (*aus* **essere**) **1 intervenire (in)** (*discussione*) to intervene (in); **è intervenuto nella discussione** he intervened in the discussion; **intervenire a** (*riunione, cerimonia, manifestazione*) to take part in; **tutti possono intervenire alla riunione** everybody can take part in the meeting; **hanno dovuto far intervenire l'esercito** the army had to be brought in; **i vigili del fuoco sono intervenuti immediatamente** the firemen took immediate action **2** (*insorgere: nuovi elementi*) to arise **3** (*Med: operare*) to operate; **intervenire d'urgenza su un paziente** to perform emergency surgery on a patient

interventismo [interven'tizmo] SM (*Pol, Econ*) interventionism

interventista, i, e [interven'tista] AGG, SM/F interventionist

intervento [inter'vento] SM **1** (*gen, Pol, Mil*) intervention; **politica del non intervento** policy of non-intervention; **l'intervento militare americano** the American military intervention; **hanno chiesto l'intervento della polizia** they asked for police assistance, they asked the police to intervene; **un intervento falloso** (*Sport*) a foul **2** (*breve discorso*) speech; (*partecipazione*) participation; **fare un intervento nel corso di** (*dibattito, programma*) to take part in; **un intervento interessante** an interesting speech **3** (*Med*) operation; **subire un intervento** to be operated on, have an operation; **ha subito un intervento delicato** he's had a complicated operation

intervenuto, a [interve'nuto] PP *di* **intervenire gli intervenuti** those present

intervista [inter'vista] SF interview; **fare un'intervista a qn** to interview sb; **non concede interviste** she doesn't give interviews

intervistare [intervis'tare] VT to interview; **è stato intervistato alla TV** he was interviewed on TV

intervistato, a [intervis'tato] SM/F person interviewed

intervistatore, trice [intervista'tore] SM/F interviewer

intesa [in'tesa] SF (*amicizia*) understanding; (*accordo*) agreement; **raggiungere un'intesa** (*comprendersi*) to come to understand each other; (*accordarsi*) to reach an agreement; **uno sguardo d'intesa** a knowing look

inteso, a [in'teso] PP *di* **intendere**
■ AGG **1** (*pattuito*) agreed; (*capito*) understood; **resta inteso che...** it is understood that ...; **non darsi per inteso di qc** to take no notice of sth; **siamo intesi?** ok? **2** (*destinato*): **inteso a fare qc** intended to do sth

intessere [in'tɛssere] VT to weave together; (*fig: trama, storia*) to weave; **intessere lodi a qn** to sing sb's praises

intestardirsi [intestar'dirsi] VIP: **intestardirsi (su qc/ a fare qc)** to insist (on sth/on doing sth)

intestare [intes'tare] VT **1** (*lettera, busta*) to address **2 intestare a** (*casa, proprietà*) to register in the name of; **a chi è intestata la macchina?** whose name is the car registered in ?; **intestare un assegno a qn** to make out a cheque to sb

intestatario, ria, ri, rie [intesta'tarjo] SM/F holder

intestato, a [intes'tato] AGG (*proprietà, casa, conto*) in the name of; (*assegno*) made out to; **carta intestata** headed paper; **la macchina è intestata a lui** the car is registered in his name

intestazione [intestat'tsjone] SF (*gen*) heading; (*su carta da lettere*) letterhead; **qual è l'intestazione dell'assegno?** who is the cheque made out to?

intestinale [intesti'nale] AGG intestinal

intestino, a [intes'tino] AGG internal; **guerra intestina** civil war
■ SM (*Anat*) intestine; **intestino tenue/crasso** small/ large intestine

intiepidire [intjepi'dire] VT (*riscaldare*) to warm (up); (*raffreddare*) to cool (down); (*fig: amicizia ecc*) to cool
▶ **intiepidirsi** VIP (*vedi vt*) to warm (up); to cool (down); to cool

Intifada [inti'fada] SF Intifada

intimamente [intima'mente] AVV intimately; **sono intimamente convinto che...** I'm firmly *o* deeply convinced that ...; **i due fatti sono intimamente connessi** the two events are closely connected

intimare [inti'mare] VT (*ordinare*) to order, command; (*notificare*) to give notice of; **intimare a qn di fare qc** to order sb to do sth; **intimare la resa a qn** (*Mil*) to call upon sb to surrender; **intimare l'alt** to order sb to stop *o* halt; **intimare lo sfratto a qn** (*Dir*) to serve an eviction notice *o* order on sb

> **LO SAPEVI...?**
> **intimare** non si traduce mai con la parola inglese *intimate*

intimazione [intimat'tsjone] SF order, command; **intimazione di sfratto** (*Dir*) eviction notice *o* order

> **LO SAPEVI...?**
> **intimazione** non si traduce mai con la parola inglese *intimation*

intimidatorio, ria, ri, rie [intimida'torjo] AGG threatening; **sparare (in aria) a scopo intimidatorio** to fire warning shots

intimidazione [intimidat'tsjone] SF intimidation; **vittima di intimidazioni** victim of intimidation *o* threats

intimidire [intimi'dire] VT to intimidate
■ VI (*aus* **essere**), **intimidirsi** VIP to become *o* grow shy

intimità [intimi'ta] SF (*vita privata*) privacy; (*familiarità*)

familiarity; (*di rapporto*) intimacy; **nell'intimità della propria casa** in the privacy of one's own home
intimo, a ['intimo] AGG (*amico*) close, intimate; (*affetti, vita*) private; (*gioia, dolore*) deep; (*cerimonia*) quiet; (*atmosfera*) cosy, intimate; (*igiene*) personal; **amico intimo** close friend; **biancheria intima** underwear; **parti intime** (*genitali*) private parts; **rapporti intimi** (*sessuali*) intimate relations; **una cenetta intima** an intimate dinner
■ SM **1** (*persona*) close friend **2** **nell'intimo della sua coscienza** deep down in his conscience; **nell'intimo del suo cuore** in his heart of hearts **3** (*biancheria intima*) underwear; (: *per donna*) lingerie; **saldi del 30% sull'intimo uomo** 30% reductions on men's underwear
intimorire [intimo'rire] VT to frighten, make afraid
▶ **intimorirsi** VIP to become frightened
intimorito, a [intimo'rito] AGG frightened
intingere [in'tindʒere] VT IRREG (*biscotto, pane*) to dunk; (*penna, pennello*) to dip
intingolo [in'tingolo] SM (*sugo*) sauce; (*pietanza*) tasty dish
intinto, a [in'tinto] PP *di* **intingere**
intirizzire [intirid'dzire] VT to numb
■ VI (*aus* **essere**), **intirizzirsi** VIP to grow numb (with cold)
intirizzito, a [intirid'dzito] AGG numb (with cold)
intitolare [intito'lare] VT **1** (*dare un titolo a*) to entitle, give a title to; **come ha intitolato il suo ultimo romanzo?** what title has he given to his latest book?; **ho intitolato questo quadro "Mattina e Sera"** I've called this picture "Morning and Evening"
2 (*dedicare: chiesa, monumento*) to dedicate
▶ **intitolarsi** VIP (*libro, film*) to be called; **come s'intitola il film?** what's the film called?
intoccabile [intok'kabile] AGG, SM/F untouchable
intollerabile [intolle'rabile] AGG intolerable, unbearable
intollerante [intolle'rante] AGG: **intollerante (di)** intolerant (of)
■ SM/F intolerant person
intolleranza [intolle'rantsa] SF intolerance
intonacare [intona'kare] VT to plaster
intonaco, ci [in'tɔnako] SM plaster
intonare [into'nare] VT (*Mus: canzone*) to sing the opening phrases of; (*fig: armonizzare*) to match; **intonare a** *o* **con** to tone in with, match with; **intonare due colori tra di loro** to match two colours
▶ **intonarsi** VIP (*colori*) to go together; **intonarsi a** *o* **con** (*circostanza, carnagione*) to suit; (*abito*) to match, go with
intonato, a [into'nato] AGG (*strumento, voce*) tuneful; (*persona*) able to sing in tune; (*colori*) matching; **essere intonato** to be in tune; **una borsa intonata alle scarpe** a bag which matched her shoes; **portava una cravatta intonata alla camicia** he was wearing a shirt and matching tie
intonazione [intonat'tsjone] SF (*nel cantare*) pitch; (*nel parlare*) intonation
intonso, a [in'tonso] AGG untouched
intontire [inton'tire] VT (*sogg: botta*) to stun, daze; (: *gas, alcolici*) to make dizzy, make woozy (*fam*)
■ VI (*aus* **essere**), **intontirsi** VIP to be stunned *o* dazed
intontito, a [inton'tito] AGG (*persona: da botta*) stunned, dazed; (: *da gas, alcolici*) dizzy, woozy (*fam*); (*sguardo*) glazed; **intontito dal sonno** befuddled with sleep
intoppare [intop'pare] VI (*aus* **essere**), **intopparsi** VIP (*congegno*) to stick; **intoppare in** (*parola difficile, difficoltà*) to stumble over
intoppo [in'tɔppo] SM (*ostacolo*) hitch, stumbling block, obstacle; (*difficoltà*) difficulty
intorbidare [intorbi'dare], **intorbidire** [intorbi'dire] VT (*liquido*) to make turbid; (*mente*) to cloud; **intorbidare le acque** (*fig*) to muddy the waters
■ VI (*aus* **essere**), **intorbidarsi** VIP (*vedi vt*) to become turbid; to cloud, become confused
intorno [in'torno] AVV around, round; **qui/lì intorno** round here/there; **qui intorno non c'è neanche un giornalaio** there's isn't even a paper shop round here; **c'è un castello e tutt'intorno un giardino** there is a castle with a garden surrounding it; **un giardino con una siepe intorno** a garden with a hedge round it
■ **intorno a** PREP **1** (*attorno a, circa*) (a)round about; **smettila di girarmi intorno** stop hanging around me; **erano seduti intorno al tavolo** they were sitting round the table; **successe intorno al 1910** it happened (a)round about 1910 **2** (*riguardo*) about
intorpidimento [intorpidi'mento] SM (*delle membra*) numbness; (*della mente*) torpor, sluggishness
intorpidire [intorpi'dire] VT (*membra*) to numb; (*mente*) to slow down, make sluggish
■ VI (*aus* **essere**), **intorpidirsi** VIP (*membra*) to grow numb; (*mente, persona*) to become sluggish
intossicare [intossi'kare] VT to poison
▶ **intossicarsi** VR: **intossicarsi (con)** to poison o.s. (with)

> **LO SAPEVI...?**
> **intossicare** non si traduce mai con la parola inglese *intoxicate*

intossicazione [intossikat'tsjone] SF poisoning; **intossicazione alimentare** food poisoning
intra... ['intra] PREF intra...
intraducibile [intradu'tʃibile] AGG untranslatable
intraducibilità [intradutʃibili'ta] SF untranslatability
intralciare [intral'tʃare] VT to hamper, hinder, hold up
intralcio, ci [in'traltʃo] SM hitch; **essere d'intralcio** to be in the way
intrallazzare [intrallat'tsare] VI (*aus* **avere**) to intrigue, scheme
intrallazzatore, trice [intrallattsa'tore] SM/F wheeler dealer
intrallazzo [intral'lattso] SM (*Pol*) intrigue, manoeuvre (*Brit*), maneuver (*Am*); (*traffico losco*) racket
intramoenia [intra'menja] AGG INV = **intramurale**
intramontabile [intramon'tabile] AGG timeless
intramurale [intramu'rale] AGG (*attività intramurale*) private practice carried out in a hospital (*paying a fee to the hospital involved*)
intramuscolare [intramusko'lare] AGG intramuscular
intramuscolo [intra'muskolo] AGG INV, SM INV (*anche: iniezione intramuscolo*) intramuscular injection
intransigente [intransi'dʒɛnte] AGG uncompromising, intransigent; **è piuttosto intransigente in fatto di amicizie** he's rather choosy about who he makes friends with
intransigenza [intransi'dʒɛntsa] SF intransigence
intransitivo, a [intransi'tivo] AGG, SM (*Gramm*) intransitive
intrappolare [intrappo'lare] VT to trap; **rimanere intrappolato** to be trapped; **farsi intrappolare** to get caught
intraprendente [intrapren'dɛnte] AGG (*che si dà da*

Ii

fare) enterprising, go-ahead; (*audace*) forward, bold; **un giovane intraprendente** an enterprising young man
intraprendenza [intrapren'dɛntsa] SF (*spirito d'iniziativa*) initiative; (*audacità*) audacity, boldness
intraprendere [intra'prɛndere] VT IRREG (*riforme*) to undertake; (*carriera*) to embark (up)on; **intraprendere una spedizione** to set out on an expedition
intrapreso, a [intra'preso] PP *di* **intraprendere**
intrattabile [intrat'tabile] AGG intractable; **il capo oggi è intrattabile** the boss is impossible today; **oggi sei proprio intrattabile** you're being really awkward today
intrattenere [intratte'nere] VB IRREG, VT **1** (*divertire*) to entertain; (*chiacchierando*) to engage in conversation **2** (*rapporti*) to have, maintain
▶ **intrattenersi** VIP (*fermarsi*: *con ospiti*) to linger; **intrattenersi su** (*argomento, questione*) to dwell on
intrattenimento [intratteni'mento] SM entertainment
intrattenitore, trice [intratteni'tore] SM/F entertainer
intravedere [intrave'dere] VT IRREG **1** (*vedere appena*) to make out, catch a glimpse of; **l'ho intravisto tra la folla** I caught sight of him in the crowd **2** (*presagire*: *difficoltà, pericoli*) to foresee; (: *verità*) to have an inkling of
intravisto, a [intra'visto] PP *di* **intravedere**
intrecciare [intret'tʃare] VT (*gen*) to plait, braid; (*intessere*) to weave, interweave, intertwine; **intrecciare una relazione amorosa** to begin an affair
▶ **intrecciarsi** VIP (*rami, corde*) to become interwoven, intertwine
intreccio, ci [in'trettʃo] SM **1** (*di tessuto*) weave; (*di paglia*) plaiting **2** (*fig*: *trama*) plot, story
intrepido, a [in'trɛpido] AGG intrepid, dauntless, fearless
intricare [intri'kare] VT (*fili*) to tangle; (*fig*: *faccenda*) to complicate
▶ **intricarsi** VIP (*vedi vt*) to become tangled; to become complicated
intricato, a [intri'kato] AGG (*fili ecc*) tangled; (*fig*: *faccenda*) complicated
intrico, chi [in'triko] SM (*anche fig*) tangle
intrigante [intri'gante] AGG (*persona*: *imbroglione*) scheming; (*misterioso*: *sorriso, sguardo*) enigmatic; (: *romanzo*) intriguing
■ SM/F schemer, intriguer
intrigare [intri'gare] VT (*affascinare*) to intrigue
■ VI (*aus* **avere**) to scheme, intrigue, manoeuvre (*Brit*), maneuver (*Am*)
intrigo, ghi [in'trigo] SM (*complotto*) intrigue, scheme, plot; (*situazione complicata*) tricky situation
intrinsecamente [intrinseka'mente] AVV intrinsically
intrinseco, a, ci, che [in'trinseko] AGG intrinsic
intrippato, a [intrip'pato] AGG (*fam*) **1** (*sotto effetto di droghe*) on a trip **2**: **essere intrippato con** (*fissato*) to be mad *o* crazy about
intriso, a [in'trizo] AGG: **intriso di** (*inzuppato*) soaked with; **un film intriso di sentimentalismo** a film dripping with sentimentality
intristire [intris'tire] VI (*aus* **essere**) (*persona*: *diventare triste*) to grow sad; (*pianta*) to wilt
introdotto, a [intro'dotto] PP *di* **introdurre**
■ AGG: **essere bene introdotto** to know all the right people
introdurre [intro'durre] VB IRREG, VT (*gen*) to introduce; (*moneta, chiave*) to insert, put in; (*descrizione, elemento*) to introduce, bring in; (*persona*) to show in; **gli ospiti venivano introdotti in sala** the guests were shown *o* ushered into the room; **introdurre prodotti di contrabbando** to smuggle in goods; **introdurre la moneta nella fessura** put the coin in the slot; **ha introdotto subito l'argomento** he immediately raised the subject
▶ **introdursi** VIP (*penetrare*): **introdursi in** to enter, get into; (: *furtivamente*) to sneak in, slip in; (*moda, tecniche*) to be introduced
introduttivo, a [introdut'tivo] AGG introductory
introduzione [introdut'tsjone] SF introduction; **dobbiamo leggere solo l'introduzione** we only have to read the introduction
introito [in'trɔito] SM (*Comm*: *entrata*) revenue, income
intromesso, a [intro'messo] PP *di* **intromettersi**
intromettersi [intro'mettersi] VR IRREG (*immischiarsi*) to interfere, meddle; (*in conversazione*) to intervene; **s'intromette sempre nei fatti degli altri** she's always interfering in other people's business
intromissione [intromis'sjone] SF (*vedi vb*) interference, meddling; intervention
introspettivo, a [introspet'tivo] AGG introspective
introspezione [introspet'tsjone] SF introspection
introvabile [intro'vabile] AGG (*persona, oggetto*) who (*o* which) cannot be found; (*libro*) unobtainable
introversione [introver'sjone] SF introversion
introverso, a [intro'verso] AGG introverted
■ SM/F introvert
intrufolarsi [intrufo'larsi] VR: **intrufolarsi (in)** (*stanza, casa*) to sneak in(to), slip in(to)
intruglio, gli [in'truʎʎo] SM concoction
intrupparsi [intrup'parsi] VR (*fam*) to band together; **spero che tu non vada ad intrupparti con quei mascalzoni** I hope you aren't going to get involved with that bunch of thugs
intrusione [intru'zjone] SF intrusion, interference; **scusate l'intrusione...** forgive the intrusion ...
intrusivo, a [intru'zivo] AGG intrusive
intruso, a [in'truzo] SM/F (*estraneo*) intruder; (: *ad un ricevimento*) gatecrasher; **mi trattano come un intruso** they treat me as if I had no right to be there
intuibile [intu'ibile] AGG deducible; **è facilmente intuibile che...** one soon realizes that ...
intuire [intu'ire] VT (*presentire, accorgersi*) to realize; (*capire*) to know intuitively; (*indovinare*) to guess; **ha intuito la verità** she realized the truth; **ho intuito subito che c'era qualcosa che non andava** I realized at once that something was wrong
intuitivamente [intuitiva'mente] AVV intuitively
intuitivo, a [intui'tivo] AGG intuitive
intuito [in'tuito] SM (*intuizione*) intuition; (*perspicacia*) perspicacity; **per intuito** intuitively; **capire per intuito** to know intuitively
intuizione [intuit'tsjone] SF intuition
inturgidire [inturdʒi'dire] VI (*aus* **essere**), **inturgidirsi** VIP to swell
inumanamente [inumana'mente] AVV inhumanely
inumanità [inumani'ta] SF inhumanity
inumano, a [inu'mano] AGG inhuman
inumare [inu'mare] VT (*seppellire*) to bury, inter
inumazione [inumat'tsjone] SF burial, interment
inumidire [inumi'dire] VT (*labbra*) to moisten; (*biancheria*) to dampen; **inumidirsi le labbra** to moisten one's lips
▶ **inumidirsi** VIP to get damp *o* wet

inurbamento [inurba'mento] SM urbanization
inusitato, a [inuzi'tato] AGG unusual
inutile [i'nutile] AGG *(che non serve)* useless; *(superfluo)* needless, unnecessary; **un aggeggio inutile** a useless gadget; **mi sento inutile qui** I feel useless here; **è inutile insistere** *o* **che tu insista** it's no use *o* no good insisting, there's no point in insisting; **è stato tutto inutile!** it was all in vain!; **è inutile, tanto non lo convinci** it's pointless, you won't persuade him; **è inutile arrabbiarsi!** there's no point getting angry!
inutilità [inutili'ta] SF *(vedi agg)* uselessness; needlessness
inutilizzabile [inutilid'dzabile] AGG unusable
inutilizzato, a [inutilid'dzato] AGG unused
inutilmente [inutil'mente] AVV *(senza risultato)* fruitlessly; *(senza utilità, scopo)* unnecessarily, needlessly; **l'ho cercato inutilmente** I looked for him in vain; **ti preoccupi inutilmente** you're worrying unnecessarily, there's no need for you to worry
invadente [inva'dɛnte] AGG interfering; **non vorrei essere invadente** I don't want to interfere; **un vicino di casa invadente** an interfering neighbour
■ SM/F interfering person, busybody
invadenza [inva'dɛntsa] SF intrusiveness
invadere [in'vadere] VT IRREG *(gen)* to invade; *(affollare)* to overrun, swarm into; *(sogg: acque)* to flood; **i tifosi hanno invaso il campo** the fans invaded the pitch; **le auto giapponesi hanno invaso il mercato** Japanese cars have flooded the market; **invadere la privacy di qn** to invade sb's privacy
invaghirsi [inva'girsi] VIP: **invaghirsi di** to take a fancy to
invalicabile [invali'kabile] AGG *(montagna)* impassable; *(fig: difficoltà)* insurmountable; **limite invalicabile** *(zona militare)* no unauthorised access
invalidare [invali'dare] VT to invalidate
invalidità [invalidi'ta] SF INV *(vedi agg)* disablement, disability; infirmity; invalidity
invalido, a [in'valido] AGG **1** *(inabile)* disabled; *(malato)* infirm **2** *(Dir: nullo)* invalid
■ SM/F *(inabile)* disabled person; *(malato)* invalid; **invalido di guerra** disabled ex-serviceman; **invalido del lavoro** industrially disabled person
invalso, a [in'valso] AGG *(diffuso)* established
invano [in'vano] AVV in vain
invariabile [inva'rjabile] AGG invariable
invariabilmente [invarjabil'mente] AVV invariably
invariato, a [inva'rjato] AGG unchanged
invasare [inva'zare] VT *(pianta)* to pot
invasato, a [inva'zato] AGG possessed (by the devil)
■ SM/F person possessed by the devil; **urlare come un invasato** to shout like one possessed
invasatura [invaza'tura] SF *(Naut)* slipway, slips *pl*
invasione [inva'zjone] SF invasion
invasivo, a [inva'zivo] AGG *(Med)* invasive
invaso, a [in'vazo] PP *di* **invadere**
invasore [inva'zore] AGG invading
■ SM invader
invecchiamento [invekkja'mento] SM *(di persona)* ageing; **questo whisky ha un invecchiamento di 12 anni** this whisky has been matured for 12 years
invecchiare [invek'kjare] VI *(aus* **essere***)* *(diventare vecchio)* to grow old; *(sembrare più vecchio)* to age; *(vino)* to age; **lo trovo invecchiato** I think he has aged; **molti hanno paura di invecchiare** a lot of people are afraid of getting old
■ VT *(persona)* to make look older, age, put years on; *(vino)* to age
invece [in'vetʃe] AVV *(gen)* instead; *(ma)* but; **credevo di aver ragione e invece no** I thought I was right but I wasn't; **io preferisco i romanzi, Peter invece i gialli** I like novels but Peter prefers detective stories; **invece di qc/di** *o* **che fare qc** instead of sth/of doing sth; **potresti aiutarmi invece di** *o* **che stare lì a guardare la TV** you could help me instead of sitting there watching TV; **preferisco lavorare in Italia invece che all'estero** I prefer to work in Italy rather than abroad; **prendo un tè invece del caffè** I'll have tea instead of coffee
inveire [inve'ire] VI *(aus* **avere***)*: **inveire contro** to rail against
invelenire [invele'nire] VT to embitter
■ VI *(aus* **essere***)*, **invelenirsi** VIP to become bitter
invendibile [inven'dibile] AGG unsaleable
invenduto, a [inven'duto] AGG unsold
■ SM *(Comm)*: **rendere l'invenduto** to return unsold goods
inventare [inven'tare] VT *(gen)* to invent; *(metodo)* to invent, devise; *(gioco, scusa)* to invent, make up, think up; **ho inventato una scusa per uscire prima** I made up an excuse to leave early; **ha inventato un nuovo gioco** he invented a new game; **lui ne inventa di tutti i colori!** what will he think up next!; **se l'è inventata di sana pianta** he made the whole thing up
inventariare [inventa'rjare] VT to make an inventory of, inventory
inventario, ri [inven'tarjo] SM *(gen)* inventory; *(Comm: registro)* stock list; *(: operazione)* stocktaking *no pl*; **inventario fisico** physical stocktaking; **fare l'inventario di** to make an inventory of; **mi ha fatto l'inventario delle sue malattie** *(fig)* he regaled me with his medical history
inventiva [inven'tiva] SF inventiveness
inventivo, a [inven'tivo] AGG inventive
inventore, trice [inven'tore] AGG inventive
■ SM/F inventor
invenzione [inven'tsjone] SF *(gen)* invention; **è tutta un'invenzione** it's pure invention; **una ricetta di mia invenzione** a recipe I made up myself
inverecondia [invere'kondja] SF shamelessness, immodesty
inverecondo, a [invere'kondo] AGG shameless, immodest
invernale [inver'nale] AGG *(gen)* winter *attr*; *(simile all'inverno)* wintry; **una giornata invernale** a winter's day
inverno [in'vɛrno] SM winter; **d'inverno** in (the) winter; **essere in pieno inverno** to be in the depths of winter
inverosimiglianza [inverosimiʎ'ʎantsa] SF improbability, unlikelihood
inverosimile [invero'simile] AGG *(racconto)* unlikely, improbable; *(scusa)* far-fetched
■ SM: **l'inverosimile** the improbable; **ha dell'inverosimile** it's hard to believe, it's incredible
inverosimilmente [inverosimil'mente] AVV unbelievably
inversamente [inversa'mente] AVV inversely; **inversamente proporzionale** in inverse proportion
inversione [inver'sjone] SF inversion; **inversione di tendenza** *(fig)* radical change of direction; *(pegg: spec Pol)* U-turn; **"divieto d'inversione"** *(Aut)* "no U-turns"; **inversione di marcia** *(Aut)* U-turn

inverso, a [in'vɛrso] AGG **1** (*direzione*) opposite; **in ordine inverso** in reverse order; **si è scontrato con una macchina che veniva in senso inverso** he collided with a car coming in the opposite direction **2** (*Mat*) inverse; **in ragione inversa** (*Mat*) in inverse ratio
■ SM: **l'inverso** the opposite, the reverse, the contrary; **capisce tutto all'inverso** he always gets hold of the wrong end of the stick; **fa tutto all'inverso** he does everything the wrong way round
invertebrato, a [inverte'brato] AGG, SM invertebrate
invertire [inver'tire] VT (*gen*) to invert; (*disposizione, posti*) to change; (*ruoli*) to exchange; **invertire la marcia** (*Aut*) to do a U-turn; **invertire la rotta** (*Naut*) to go about; (*fig*) to do a U-turn
invertito, a [inver'tito] AGG (*Chim*): **zucchero invertito** invert sugar
■ SM (*omosessuale*) homosexual
investigare [investi'gare] VT (*indagare*) to investigate; (*analizzare*) to examine
■ VI (*aus* **avere**): **investigare su** to investigate
investigativo, a [investiga'tivo] AGG: **squadra investigativa** detective squad; **agente investigativo** detective
investigatore, trice [investiga'tore] SM/F investigator, detective; **investigatore privato** private detective, private investigator
investigazione [investigat'tsjone] SF investigation, inquiry
investimento [investi'mento] SM **1** (*Econ*) investment; **un buon investimento** a good investment **2** (*di pedone*) running down, knocking down; (*di veicolo*) collision, crash
investire [inves'tire] VT **1** (*Econ*) to invest; **ha investito i suoi risparmi in titoli di stato** he has invested his savings in government bonds **2** (*sogg*: *veicolo*: *pedone*) to run over, knock down; (: *altro veicolo*) to crash into, hit; **è stato investito da un camion** he was run over by a lorry **3** (*apostrofare*) to assail; **investire qn di** *o* **con qc** (*domande*) to besiege sb with sth; (*ingiurie, insulti*) to heap sth on sb **4** (*Dir, Amm*: *incaricare*): **investire qn di** (*poteri*) to invest sb with; (*incarico*) to appoint sb to
▶ **investirsi** VR (*fig*): **investirsi di una parte** to enter thoroughly into a role
investitore, trice [investi'tore] SM/F driver responsible for an accident; (*Econ*) investor; **investitore istituzionale** corporate acquirer
investitura [investi'tura] SF (*Amm, Pol*) appointment, nomination; (*Rel*) investiture
inveterato, a [invete'rato] AGG (*abitudine, vizio*) ingrained; (*giocatore, bugiardo*) inveterate
invetriata [inve'trjata] SF (*vetrata*) picture window
invettiva [invet'tiva] SF invective; **lanciare invettive contro qn/qc** to hurl abuse at sb/sth
inviare [invi'are] VT (*gen*) to send; (*merce*) to dispatch
inviato, a [invi'ato] SM/F (*Pol*) envoy; (*Stampa*) correspondent; **un inviato speciale** a special correspondent
invidia [in'vidja] SF envy; **fare invidia a qn** to make sb envious; **farebbe invidia ai migliori ristoranti** it would be the envy of the best restaurants; **avere** *o* **provare invidia per qn/qc** to be envious of sb/sth; **per invidia** out of envy; **morire d'invidia** to be green with envy; **sta morendo d'invidia** he's green with envy; **degno d'invidia** enviable; **che invidia!** how I envy you!; **è tutta invidia, la tua** you're just jealous
invidiabile [invi'djabile] AGG enviable
invidiabilmente [invidjabil'mente] AVV enviably
invidiare [invi'djare] VT: **invidiare qc a qn** to envy sb sth; **invidiare qn per qc** to envy sb for sth; **l'ha sempre invidiato** he's always envied him; **non aver nulla da invidiare a nessuno** to be as good as the next one
invidioso, a [invi'djoso] AGG envious; **è invidioso perché io ce l'ho e lui no** he's jealous because I've got one and he hasn't

> **LO SAPEVI...?**
> **invidioso** non si traduce mai con la parola inglese *invidious*

invincibile [invin'tʃibile] AGG (*esercito, nemico*) invincible; (*fig*: *antipatia, timidezza*) insurmountable
invio, vii [in'vio] SM **1** (*vedi vb*) sending; dispatching; **chiedere l'invio di qc** to ask for sth to be sent (*o* dispatched) **2** (*insieme di merci*) consignment **3** (*tasto*) Return (key), Enter (key)
inviolabile [invio'labile] AGG inviolable
inviolato, a [invio'lato] AGG **1** (*diritto, segreto*) inviolate **2** (*foresta*) virgin *attr*; (*montagna, vetta*) unscaled
inviperire [invipe'rire] VI (*aus* **essere**), **inviperirsi** VIP to become furious, fly into a temper; **mi ha fatto inviperire** he made me furious
inviperito, a [invipe'rito] AGG furious
invischiare [invis'kjare] VT (*fig*): **invischiare qn in qc** to involve sb in sth, mix sb up in sth
▶ **invischiarsi** VIP: **invischiarsi con qn/in qc** to get mixed up *o* involved with sb/in sth
invisibile [invi'zibile] AGG (*gen, Econ*) invisible; **rendersi invisibile** (*scherz*) to make o.s. scarce
invisibilità [invizibili'ta] SF invisibility
inviso, a [in'vizo] AGG: **inviso a** unpopular with
invitante [invi'tante] AGG (*proposta, odorino*) inviting; (*sorriso*) appealing, attractive
invitare [invi'tare] VT (*gen*) to invite; **invitare qn a fare qc** to invite sb to do sth; **invitare a cena gli amici** to invite *o* ask friends to dinner; **invitare qn a ballare** to ask someone to dance; **mi hanno invitato ad una festa** they've invited me to a party; **furono invitati a entrare** they were invited *o* asked in; **è stato invitato a dimettersi** he was asked to resign; **è una giornata che invita a uscire** it's the sort of day that tempts one to go out
▶ **invitarsi** VR: **si invita sempre da solo** he always invites himself along
invitato, a [invi'tato] SM/F guest
invito [in'vito] SM invitation; **fare un invito a qn** to extend an invitation to sb; **su** *o* **dietro invito di qn** at sb's invitation; **hai ricevuto l'invito?** did you get the invitation?
in vitro [in 'vitro] AVV, AGG INV in vitro
invocare [invo'kare] VT (*aiuto, pietà*) to beg for, cry out for; (*Dio*) to invoke, call upon, appeal to; (*articolo*) to cite, quote
invocazione [invokat'tsjone] SF invocation
invogliare [invoʎ'ʎare] VT (*stimolare*) to encourage; (*invitare*) to tempt, entice; **invogliare qn a fare qc** to tempt sb to do sth, induce sb to do sth; **bisognerebbe invogliarlo a studiare** we should encourage him to study; **la giornata di sole invogliava ad uscire** the sunny weather tempted one out of doors
involarsi [invo'larsi] VR (*Calcio*) to race
involgarire [involga'rire] VT (*sogg*: *abito, trucco*) to make (sb) look vulgar
■ VI (*aus* **essere**), **involgarirsi** VIP to become vulgar

involontariamente [involontarja'mente] AVV (*sorridere*) involuntarily; (*spingere*) unintentionally; **l'incidente di cui fu involontariamente responsabile** the accident of which he was the involuntary cause; **scusami, l'ho fatto involontariamente** I'm sorry, I didn't mean to do it
involontario, ria, ri, rie [involon'tarjo] AGG (*movimento, muscolo*) involuntary; (*offesa, errore*) unintentional
involtino [invol'tino] SM (*Culin*) roulade
involto [in'vɔlto] SM (*fagotto*) bundle; (*pacco*) parcel
involucro [in'vɔlukro] SM (*rivestimento*) covering, cover; (*confezione*) wrapping
involutivo, a [involu'tivo] AGG: **subire un processo involutivo** to regress
involuto, a [invo'luto] AGG (*stile*) convoluted
involuzione [involut'tsjone] SF **1** (*di stile*) convolutedness **2** (*regresso*): **subire un'involuzione** to regress
invulnerabile [invulne'rabile] AGG invulnerable
invulnerabilità [invulnerabili'ta] SF invulnerability
inzaccherare [intsakke'rare] VT to spatter with mud ▶ **inzaccherarsi** VR, VIP to get muddy
inzaccherato, a [intsakke'rato] AGG muddy
inzuppare [intsup'pare] VT (*gen*): **inzuppare qc (di)** to soak sth (in); **inzuppò i biscotti nel latte** he dipped the biscuits in the milk; **abiti inzuppati di pioggia** rain-soaked clothes
▶ **inzupparsi** VIP to get soaked, get drenched
io ['io] PRON PERS I; **sono io** it's me; (*più formale*) it is I; **chi è? — sono io, apri** who's that? — it's me, open the door; **io e te** you and I, you and me (*fam*); **il mio amico ed io ci andremo** my friend and I will go; **io ci vado, tu fai come vuoi** I'm going, you do what you like; **pronto, c'è Paola? — sì, sono io** hello, is Paola there? — yes, speaking; **ho fame — anch'io** I'm hungry — so am I; **vengo anch'io** I'll come too; **non lo sapevo nemmeno io** I didn't even know it myself; **lo farò io** *or* **IO lo farò** I'LL do it; **io stesso(a)** I myself
■ SM INV: **l'io** the self, the ego
iodato, a [jo'dato] AGG iodized
iodio ['jɔdjo] SM iodine
ioduro [jo'duro] SM iodide
ione ['jone] SM ion; **ione idrogeno** hydrogen ion; **ioni complessi** complex ions
ionico[1], a, ci, che ['jɔniko] AGG **1** (*stile, periodo*) Ionic **2** (*Geog*) Ionian
ionico[2], a, ci, che ['jɔniko] AGG (*Chim: legame*) ionic
Ionio ['jɔnjo] SM: **lo Ionio, il mar Ionio** the Ionian (Sea)
ionizzare [jonid'dzare] VT to ionize
ionizzatore [joniddza'tore] SM ionizer
ionizzazione [joniddzat'tsjone] SF ionization
ionosfera [jonos'fɛra] SF ionosphere
iosa ['jɔsa] **a iosa** AVV in abundance, in great quantity; **ce ne sono a iosa** there are thousands of them; **avere matite a iosa** to have pencils galore
Iowa ['aɪəʊə] SM Iowa
IPAB ['ipab] SIGLA FPL (= **Istituzioni Pubbliche di Assistenza e Beneficenza**) *charitable institutions*
iperattivo, a [iperat'tivo] AGG hyperactive
iperbole [i'pɛrbole] SF (*Letteratura*) hyberbole; (*Mat*) hyperbola
iperbolico, a, ci, che [iper'bɔliko] AGG (*Letteratura, Mat*) hyperbolic(al); (*fig: esagerato*) exaggerated
ipercinetico, a; , ci; , che [ipertʃi'nɛtiko] AGG hyperkinetic
ipercritico, a, ci, che [iper'kritiko] AGG hypercritical
iperfocale [iperfo'kale] (*Fot*) AGG hyperfocal
■ SF hyperfocal distance
iperico [i'pɛriko] SM (*Bot*) hypericum, Saint John's wort
ipermercato [ipermer'kato] SM hypermarket
ipermetrope [iper'mɛtrope] AGG (*Med*) long-sighted, hyperopic (*termine tecn*)
ipermetropia [ipermetro'pia] SF (*Med*) long-sightedness, hyperopia (*termine tecn*)
ipersensibile [ipersen'sibile] AGG (*persona*) hypersensitive; (*Fot: lastra, pellicola*) hypersensitized
ipersensibilità [ipersensibili'ta] SF hypersensitivity
ipertecnologico, a, ci, che [ipertekno'lɔdʒiko] AGG hi-tech
ipertensione [iperten'sjone] SF (*Med*) high blood pressure, hypertension (*termine tecn*)
iperteso, a [iper'teso] AGG, SM/F (*Med*) suffering from high blood pressure
ipertesto [iper'tɛsto] SM (*Inform*) hypertext
ipertestuale [ipertes'twale] AGG (*Inform*) hypertext *attr*
iperventilazione [iperventilat'tsjone] SF (*Med, di subacqueo*) hyperventilation
ipnosi [ip'nɔzi] SF INV hypnosis
ipnotico, a, ci, che [ip'nɔtiko] AGG, SM hypnotic
ipnotismo [ipno'tizmo] SM hypnotism
ipnotizzare [ipnotid'dzare] VT to hypnotize; **l'hanno ipnotizzato** he was hypnotized
ipoallergenico, a, ci, che [ipoaller'dʒɛniko], **ipoallergico, a, ci, che** [ipoal'lɛrdʒiko] AGG (*crema, sapone, rossetto*) hypoallergenic
ipocalorico, a, ci, che [ipoka'lɔriko] AGG low-calorie *attr*
ipocentro [ipo'tʃɛntro] SM (*Geol*) focus
ipocondria [ipokon'dria] SF hypochondria
ipocondriaco, a, ci, che [ipokon'driako] AGG, SM/F hypochondriac
ipocrisia [ipokri'zia] SF hypocrisy; **è stata un'ipocrisia da parte sua** that was sheer hypocrisy on his part
ipocrita, i, e [i'pɔkrita] AGG hypocritical
■ SM/F hypocrite
ipocritamente [ipokrita'mente] AVV hypocritically
ipofisi [i'pɔfizi] SF INV hypophysis (*termine tecn*), pituitary gland
iposodico, a, ci, che [ipo'sɔdiko] AGG (*sale*) low sodium *attr*
ipoteca, che [ipo'tɛka] SF mortgage; **fare** *o* **mettere un'ipoteca su qc** to mortgage sth, raise a mortgage on sth; **la squadra ha messo una seria ipoteca sullo scudetto** the team has practically put its name on the cup
ipotecabile [ipote'kabile] AGG mortgageable
ipotecare [ipote'kare] VT (*Dir, fig*) to mortgage
ipotecario, ria, ri, rie [ipote'karjo] AGG mortgage *attr*
ipotensione [ipoten'sjone] SF (*Med*): **ipotensione arteriosa** low blood pressure, hypotension (*termine tecn*)
ipotenusa [ipote'nuza] SF hypotenuse
ipotesi [i'pɔtezi] SF INV hypothesis; **le ipotesi sono due** there are two possibilities; **facciamo l'ipotesi che...** *or* **ammettiamo per ipotesi che...** let's suppose *o* assume that ...; **facciamo l'ipotesi che non venga** supposing he doesn't come; **nella peggiore/migliore delle ipotesi** at worst/best; **nella migliore delle ipotesi lo finirò sabato** at best I'll finish it on

Ii

Saturday; **nell'ipotesi che venga** should he come, if he comes; **se per ipotesi io partissi…** just supposing I were to leave …

ipoteticamente [ipotetika'mente] AVV hypothetically

ipotetico, a, ci, che [ipo'tɛtiko] AGG (*gen*) hypothetical; (*guadagni, profitti*) theoretical, hypothetical; (*mondo*) imaginary; **nel caso ipotetico che tu non arrivi in tempo** should you not arrive in time; **periodo ipotetico** (*Gramm*) conditional clause

ipotizzare [ipotid'dzare] VT: **ipotizzare che** to form the hypothesis that, hypothesize

ippica ['ippika] SF horseracing
▷ www.fise.it/

ippico, a, ci, che ['ippiko] AGG horse *attr*; **un concorso ippico** a horse race

ippocastano [ippokas'tano] SM horse chestnut (tree)

Ippocrate [ip'pɔkrate] SM Hippocrates

ippodromo [ip'pɔdromo] SM racecourse, racetrack

Ippolito [ip'pɔlito] SM Hippolytus

ippopotamo [ippo'pɔtamo] SM hippopotamus

ippoterapia [ippotera'pia] SF riding therapy

ipsilon ['ipsilon] SF O M INV (*lettera*) Y, y; (: *dell'alfabeto greco*) upsilon; **si scrive con la "i" o con la "ipsilon"?** do you spell it with an "i" or with a "y"?

IPSOA [ip'soa] SIGLA M (= **Istituto Postuniversitario per lo Studio dell'Organizzazione Aziendale**) *postgraduate institute of business administration*

IR ABBR (*Ferr*) = **interregionale**

IRA ['ira] SIGLA F (= **Irish Republican Army**) IRA

ira ['ira] SF anger, fury, wrath; **l'ira di Dio** the wrath of God; **ha fatto un'ira di Dio** she made a terrible scene; **costa un'ira di Dio** it costs a king's ransom; **con uno scatto d'ira** in a fit of anger; **farsi prendere dall'ira** to lose one's temper

iracheno, a [ira'kɛno] AGG, SM/F Iraqi

iracondo, a [ira'kondo] AGG irascible, quick-tempered

Irak [i'rak] SM Iraq

Iran ['iran] SM Iran

iraniano, a [ira'njano] AGG, SM/F Iranian

irascibile [iraʃ'ʃibile] AGG irascible, quick-tempered

irascibilità [iraʃʃibili'ta] SF irascibilty

irato, a [i'rato] AGG (*persona, sguardo*) irate, furious

IRCE ['irtʃe] SIGLA M (= **Istituto per le Relazioni Culturali con l'Estero**) ≈ British Council

IRI ['iri] SIGLA M (= **Istituto per la Ricostruzione Industriale**) *state-controlled industrial investment office*

iride ['iride] SF **1** (*Anat*) iris **2** (*arcobaleno*) rainbow

iridescente [irideʃ'ʃɛnte] AGG iridescent

iridescenza [irideʃ'ʃɛntsa] SF iridescence

iridologia [iridolo'dʒia] SF iridology

iridologo, a, gi, ghe [iri'dɔlogo] SM/F iridologist

iris ['iris] SM INV iris

Irlanda [ir'landa] SF Ireland; **il mar d'Irlanda** the Irish Sea; **la Repubblica d'Irlanda** Eire, the Republic of Ireland; **l'Irlanda del Nord** Northern Ireland, Ulster; **mi è piaciuta molto l'Irlanda** I really liked Ireland; **andremo in Irlanda quest'estate** we're going to Ireland this summer

irlandese [irlan'dese] AGG Irish; **la squadra irlandese** the Irish team
■ SM/F Irishman/Irishwoman; **gli Irlandesi** the Irish

ironia [iro'nia] SF irony; **fare dell'ironia su qc** to be sarcastic about sth; **l'ironia della sorte** the irony of fate

ironicamente [ironika'mente] AVV ironically

ironico, a, ci, che [i'rɔniko] AGG ironic(al); **un sorrisetto ironico** an ironic little smile

ironizzare [ironid'dzare] VT, VI (*aus* **avere**) **ironizzare su** to be ironical about

iroso, a [i'roso] AGG (*sguardo, tono*) angry, wrathful; (*persona*) irascible

IRPEF ['irpef] SIGLA F = **imposta sul reddito delle persone fisiche**

irpino, a [ir'pino] AGG of *o* from Irpinia
■ SM/F inhabitant *o* native of Irpinia

irradiare [irra'djare] VT **1** (*illuminare, anche fig*) to light up **2** (*diffondere: calore, energia*) to radiate
■ VI (*aus* **essere**) to radiate
▶ **irradiarsi** VIP: **irradiarsi (da)** (*strade, rette*) to radiate (from)

irradiazione [irradjat'tsjone] SF (*di calore, energia*) radiation

irraggiamento [irraddʒa'mento] SM (*Fis*) radiation

irraggiungibile [irraddʒun'dʒibile] AGG unreachable; (*fig: meta*) unattainable

irragionevole [irradʒo'nevole] AGG (*privo di ragione*) irrational; (*fig: persona, pretese, prezzo*) unreasonable

irrancidire [irrantʃi'dire] VI (*aus* **essere**) to go rancid

irrazionale [irrattsjo'nale] AGG (*gen, Mat*) irrational

irrazionalità [irrattsjonali'ta] SF irrationality

irrazionalmente [irrattsjonal'mente] AVV irrationally

irreale [irre'ale] AGG unreal

irrealizzabile [irrealid'dzabile] AGG (*sogno, desiderio*) unattainable, unrealizable; (*progetto*) unworkable, impracticable

irrealtà [irreal'ta] SF unreality

irrecuperabile [irrekupe'rabile] AGG (*gen*) irretrievable; (*fig: persona*) irredeemable

irrecusabile [irreku'zabile] AGG **1** (*prova*) indisputable, irrefutable **2** (*offerta*) which cannot be refused, not to be refused

irredentismo [irreden'tizmo] SM (*Storia*) irredentism

irredentista, i, e [irreden'tista] AGG, SM/F (*Storia*) Irredentist

irredimibile [irredi'mibile] AGG irredeemable

irrefrenabile [irrefre'nabile] AGG uncontrollable

irrefutabile [irrefu'tabile] AGG irrefutable

irregolare [irrego'lare] AGG (*gen*) irregular; (*terreno*) uneven; (*sonno*) fitful; (*risultati, sviluppo*) erratic; **un verbo irregolare** an irregular verb; **lineamenti irregolari** irregular features
■ SM (*Mil*) irregular

irregolarità [irregolari'ta] SF INV **1** (*vedi agg*) irregularity; unevenness *no pl*; fitfulness; erratic nature **2** (*azione irregolare*) irregularity; (*Sport*) foul

irregolarmente [irregolar'mente] AVV (*vedi agg*) irregularly; unevenly; fitfully; erratically

irreligioso, a [irreli'dʒoso] AGG irreligious

irremovibile [irremo'vibile] AGG (*fig*) unshakable, unyielding; **essere irremovibile in qc** to be adamant about sth

irreparabile [irrepa'rabile] AGG irreparable

irreperibile [irrepe'ribile] AGG who (*o* which) cannot be found, nowhere to be found

irreperibilità [irreperibili'ta] SF: **causa l'irreperibilità dell'imputato…** given that the accused cannot be found …

irreprensibile [irrepren'sibile] AGG irreproachable

irrequietezza [irrekwje'tettsa] SF restlessness

irrequieto, a [irre'kwjɛto] AGG (*agitato*) restless; (*vivace*) lively

irresistibile [irresis'tibile] AGG irresistible
irresistibilmente [irresistibil'mente] AVV irresistibly
irresolubile [irreso'lubile] AGG (*mistero*) insoluble
irresolutezza [irresolu'tettsa] SF irresoluteness, indecisiveness
irresoluto, a [irreso'luto] AGG irresolute, indecisive
irresoluzione [irresolut'tsjone] SF irresolution, indecision
irrespirabile [irrespi'rabile] AGG (*aria*) unbreathable; (: *malsano*) unhealthy; (*fig*: *opprimente*) stifling, oppressive
irresponsabile [irrespon'sabile] AGG irresponsible ■ SM/F irresponsible person
irresponsabilità [irresponsabili'ta] SF irresponsibility
irresponsabilmente [irresponsabil'mente] AVV irresponsibly
irrestringibile [irrestrin'dʒibile] AGG unshrinkable, non-shrink (*Brit*)
irretire [irre'tire] VT to seduce
irreversibile [irrever'sibile] AGG irreversible
irrevocabile [irrevo'kabile] AGG irrevocable
irrevocabilmente [irrevokabil'mente] AVV irrevocably
irriconoscibile [irrikonoʃ'ʃibile] AGG unrecognizable
irriducibile [irridu'tʃibile] AGG (*frazione, cifra*) irreducible; (*fig*: *avversario*) indomitable, unshakable; (: *ostinazione*) unyielding
irriflessivo, a [irrifles'sivo] AGG thoughtless
irrigare [irri'gare] VT (*Agr, Med*) to irrigate
irrigazione [irrigat'tsjone] SF (*Agr, Med*) irrigation
irrigidimento [irridʒidi'mento] SM (*di muscoli*) stiffening; (*fig*: *di disciplina*) tightening; (: *di posizione, atteggiamento*) hardening
irrigidire [irridʒi'dire] VT (*gen*) to stiffen; (*fig*: *disciplina*) to tighten
▶ **irrigidirsi** VIP to stiffen; **irrigidirsi sulle proprie posizioni** to become entrenched in one's position
irriguardoso, a [irrigwar'doso] AGG disrespectful
irriguo, a [ir'riguo] AGG (*terreno*) irrigated; (*acque*) irrigation *attr*
irrilevante [irrile'vante] AGG (*trascurabile*) insignificant
irrimediabile [irrime'djabile] AGG: **un errore irrimediabile** a mistake which cannot be rectified; **danneggiato in modo irrimediabile** irreparably *o* irremediably damaged; **non è irrimediabile!** we can do something about it!
irrimediabilmente [irrimedjabil'mente] AVV irremediably, irreparably
irrinunciabile [irrinun'tʃabile] AGG (*bene, diritto*) that cannot be renounced, which cannot be abandoned
irripetibile [irripe'tibile] AGG unrepeatable
irrisolto, a [irri'sɔlto] AGG (*problema*) unresolved
irrisorio, ria, ri, rie [irri'zɔrjo] AGG ridiculous
irrispettoso, a [irrispet'toso] AGG disrespectful
irritabile [irri'tabile] AGG irritable
irritabilità [irritabili'ta] SF irritability
irritante [irri'tante] AGG (*atteggiamento*) irritating, annoying; (*Med*) irritant
irritare [irri'tare] VT **1** (*infastidire*) to irritate, annoy; **irritare qn** to get on sb's nerves; **il suo modo di ridere mi irrita** his laugh gets on my nerves **2** (*pelle, occhi*) to irritate
▶ **irritarsi** VIP **1**: **irritarsi per qc/con qn** (*infastidirsi*) to get irritated *o* annoyed at sth/with sb; **si irrita moltissimo se qn lo interrompe** he gets very annoyed if anyone interrupts him **2** (*infiammarsi*: *pelle, occhi*) to become irritated
irritato, a [irri'tato] AGG irritated; **aver la gola irritata** to have a sore throat
irritazione [irritat'tsjone] SF (*fastidio*) irritation, annoyance; (*Med*) irritation
irriverente [irrive'rɛnte] AGG irreverent
irriverenza [irrive'rɛntsa] SF (*qualità*) irreverence; (*azione*) irreverent action
irrobustire [irrobus'tire] VT (*persona*) to make stronger, make more robust; (*muscoli*) to strengthen
▶ **irrobustirsi** VIP to become stronger
irrompere [ir'rompere] VI DIF: **irrompere in** to burst into
irrorare [irro'rare] VT (*bagnare*) to bathe; (*Agr*) to spray
irroratrice [irrora'tritʃe] SF (*Agr*) spraying machine
irrorazione [irrorat'tsjone] SF: **irrorazione sanguigna** blood supply
irruente [irru'ɛnte] AGG (*impetuoso*) impetuous; (*chiassoso*) boisterous
irruenza [irru'ɛntsa] SF impetuousness; **con irruenza** impetuously
irruppi *ecc* [ir'ruppi] VB *vedi* **irrompere**
irruvidire [irruvi'dire] VT to roughen ■ VI (*aus* **essere**), **irruvidirsi** VIP to become rough
irruzione [irrut'tsjone] SF: **fare irruzione in** (*sogg*: *polizia*) to raid, burst into; **i tifosi hanno fatto irruzione nel campo** the fans invaded the pitch
irsuto, a [ir'suto] AGG (*petto*) hairy; (*barba*) bristly
irto, a ['irto] AGG (*barba*) bristly; **irto di** (*anche fig*) bristling with
IS SIGLA = *Isernia*
Is. ABBR (= **isola**) I.
Isacco [i'zakko] SM Isaac
Isaia [iza'ia] SM Isaiah
ISBN ABBR (= **International Standard Book Number**) ISBN
iscrissi *ecc* [is'krissi] VB *vedi* **iscrivere**
iscritto[1]**, a** [is'kritto] PP *di* **iscrivere** ■ SM/F registered member (*o* student *o* candidate); **gli iscritti alla gara** the competitors; **gli iscritti al primo anno di università** first year university students
iscritto[2] [is'kritto] **per iscritto** AVV in writing; **mettere per iscritto** to put sth in writing
iscrivere [is'krivere] VB IRREG, VT **1** (*Scol*): **iscrivere (a)** to register (in), enrol (in); (*all'anagrafe*) to register; **iscrivere qn a un club** to enrol sb as a member of a club **2** (*Comm*) to enter; **iscrivere una spesa nel bilancio** to enter an item on the balance sheet;
▶ **iscriversi** VR: **iscriversi a** (*partito, club*) to join; (*gara*) to enter; (*concorso*) to register *o* enter for; (*corso*) to enrol for; (*università*) to register *o* enrol at
iscrizione [iskrit'tsjone] SF **1** (*epigrafe*) inscription **2** (*a scuola, università*) enrolment; (*all'anagrafe*) registration; **chiedere/fare l'iscrizione a un club** to apply for membership of/join a club; **tassa di iscrizione** (*a una gara*) entry fee; (*a un circolo*) membership fee; (*a università*) registration fee **3** (*Comm*) entering
ISDN [iɛssedi'ɛnne] SIGLA M ISDN (= *Integrated Services Digital Network*)
ISEF ['izef] SIGLA M = *Istituto Superiore di Educazione Fisica*
isernino, a [izer'nino] AGG of *o* from Isernia ■ SM/F inhabitant *o* native of Isernia
Islam [iz'lam] SM: **l'Islam** Islam
islamico, a, ci, che [iz'lamiko] AGG Islamic

Ii

islamismo [izla'mizmo] SM Islamism
Islanda [iz'landa] SF Iceland
islandese [izlan'dese] AGG Icelandic
■SM/F Icelander
■SM (*lingua*) Icelandic
isobara [i'zɔbara] SF isobar
isobaro, a [i'zɔbaro] AGG isobaric
isofrequenza [izofre'kwentsa] SF *system that enables drivers to hear traffic news even in tunnels and mountainous areas*
isola ['izola] SF island; **le Isole britanniche** the British Isles; **un'isola deserta** a desert island; **isola pedonale** (*Aut*) pedestrian precinct; **isola spartitraffico** *o* **salvagente** traffic island
isolamento [izola'mento] SM **1** (*gen*) isolation; (*solitudine*) loneliness, solitude; **reparto d'isolamento** (*in ospedale*) isolation ward; **è ricoverata nel reparto d'isolamento** she's been admitted to the isolation ward; **mettere qn in cella di isolamento** to put sb in solitary confinement **2** (*Tecn, Elettr*) insulation; **isolamento acustico** soundproofing; **isolamento termico** thermal insulation
isolano, a [izo'lano] AGG island *attr*
■SM/F islander
isolante [izo'lante] AGG insulating
■SM insulator
isolare [izo'lare] VT **1** (*gen*) to isolate; **la neve ha isolato il paese dal resto del mondo** snow has cut the village off from the rest of the world **2** (*Tecn, Elettr*) to insulate; (: *acusticamente*) to soundproof **3** (*Bio: virus*) to isolate
▶ **isolarsi** VR to isolate o.s., cut o.s. off; **non isolarti, frequenta un po' di gente** don't cut yourself off, go out and meet people
isolato[1], a [izo'lato] AGG (*gen*) isolated; (*luogo*) lonely, remote; **c'è stato un caso isolato di epatite** there was an isolated case of hepatitis; **vivono isolati, in campagna** they live in a remote place in the country; **rimanere isolato** to be cut off; **il paese è rimasto isolato a causa della neve** the village was cut off by the snow
isolato[2] [izo'lato] SM (*gruppo di palazzi*) block; **fare il giro dell'isolato** to walk round the block; **ho fatto il giro dell'isolato** I went round the block; **il cinema è a due isolati da qui** the cinema is two blocks from here
isolatore [izola'tore] SM insulator
isolazionismo [izolattsjo'nizmo] SM isolationism
isolazionista, i, e [izolattsjo'nista] SM/F isolationist
isolotto [izo'lɔtto] SM islet
isomero [i'zɔmero] SM isomer
isometrico, a, ci, che [izo'mɛtriko] AGG isometric
isoscele [i'zɔʃʃele] AGG (*Geom*) isosceles *attr*
isoterma [izo'tɛrma] SF isotherm
isotopo, a [i'zɔtopo] AGG isotopic
■SM isotope
ispanico, a, ci, che [is'paniko] AGG Hispanic
ispessimento [ispessi'mento] SM thickening
ispessire [ispes'sire] VT to thicken
▶ **ispessirsi** VIP to get thicker, thicken
ispettorato [ispetto'rato] SM inspectorate
ispettore, trice [ispet'tore] SM/F (*Amm*) inspector; **ispettore di polizia** police inspector; **ispettore di reparto** shop walker (*Brit*), floor walker (*Am*); **ispettore alle vendite** (*Comm*) supervisor; **ispettore di zona** (*Comm*) area supervisor *o* manager
ispezionare [ispettsjo'nare] VT to inspect
ispezione [ispet'tsjone] SF inspection

ispido, a ['ispido] AGG (*barba*) bristly, shaggy; (*fig: carattere*) prickly, touchy
ispirare [ispi'rare] VT (*gen*) to inspire; **ispirare fiducia a qn** to inspire sb with confidence; **non mi ha ispirato fiducia** he didn't inspire confidence; **è un tipo/un'idea che non mi ispira** *o* **che mi ispira poco** I'm not all that keen on him/the idea; **l'idea m'ispira** the idea appeals to me
▶ **ispirarsi** VIP **1**: **ispirarsi a** (*prendere ispirazione*) to be inspired by, draw one's inspiration from; **per il romanzo si è ispirato a un fatto di cronaca** he got the idea for the novel from a news story
2 (*conformarsi*): **ispirarsi a qc** to be based on sth
ispirato, a [ispi'rato] AGG inspired
ispiratore, trice [ispira'tore] AGG inspiring
■SM/F inspirer
ispirazione [ispirat'tsjone] SF inspiration; **secondo l'ispirazione del momento** according to the mood of the moment; **mi è venuta l'ispirazione di telefonargli** I suddenly thought of phoning him
Israele [izra'ɛle] SM Israel; **andremo in Israele quest'estate** we're going to Israel this summer
israeliano, a [izrae'ljano] AGG, SM/F Israeli
israelita, i, e [izrae'lita] SM/F Jew/Jewess; (*Storia*) Israelite
israelitico, a, ci, che [izrae'litiko] AGG Jewish
issare [is'sare] VT (*bandiera, vela*) to hoist; (*oggetto*) to hoist, haul up; **issare l'ancora** to weigh anchor; **issare qn in spalla** to lift sb onto one's shoulders
Istanbul [istan'bul] SF Istanbul
istantanea [istan'tanea] SF (*Fot*) snapshot
istantaneamente [istantanea'mente] AVV instantaneously
istantaneità [istantanei'ta] SF instantaneousness, immediacy
istantaneo, a [istan'taneo] AGG (*gen*) instantaneous; (*che dura un istante*) momentary
istante [is'tante] SM moment, instant; **all'istante** *or* **sull'istante** at once, immediately, instantly; **in un istante** in a flash; **fra un istante** *or* **tra qualche istante** in a moment *o* minute; **sarò pronta tra un istante** I'll be ready in a moment; **abbiamo saputo proprio in questo istante che...** we have just (this moment) heard that ...; **l'aereo dovrebbe essere atterrato proprio in questo istante** the plane should be landing at this very moment; **in quell'istante** at that very *o* precise moment; **in quell'istante è entrata Paola** at that moment Paola came in
istanza [is'tantsa] SF (*richiesta: Amm, Dir*) request, petition; **fare** *o* **presentare un'istanza a qn** to present a petition to sb; **su istanza di qn** at sb's request; **giudice di prima istanza** (*Dir*) judge of the court of first instance; **giudizio di seconda istanza** judg(e)ment on appeal; **in ultima istanza** (*fig*) finally; **istanza di divorzio** petition for divorce
ISTAT ['istat] SIGLA M = *Istituto Centrale di Statistica*
ISTEL ['istel] SIGLA F = *Indagine sull'ascolto delle televisioni in Italia*
isterectomia [isterekto'mia] SF hysterectomy
isteria [iste'ria] SF hysteria
isterico, a, ci, che [is'tɛriko] AGG hysterical
■SM/F (*Med*) hysteric; (*pegg*) hysterical type
isterilire [isteri'lire] VT (*terreno*) to render infertile; (*fig: fantasia*) to dry up
▶ **isterilirsi** VIP (*vedi vt*) to become infertile; to dry up
isterismo [iste'rizmo] SM hysteria
istigare [isti'gare] VT: **istigare qn a (fare) qc** to incite

sb to (do) sth; **istigare alla prostituzione** (*Dir*) to force into prostitution
istigatore, trice [istiga'tore] SM/F instigator
istigazione [istigat'tsjone] SF incitement, instigation; **su istigazione di qn** (up)on sb's instigation; **istigazione a delinquere** (*Dir*) incitement to crime
istintivamente [istintiva'mente] AVV instinctively
istintivo, a [istin'tivo] AGG instinctive
■ SM/F: **essere un istintivo** to be guided by one's instincts
istinto [is'tinto] SM instinct; **istinto di conservazione** instinct of self-preservation; **per** *o* **d'istinto** instinctively; **ho seguito il mio istinto** I followed my instinct
istituire [istitu'ire] VT (*gen*) to institute; (*borsa di studio*) to found, endow; (*commissione d'inchiesta*) to set up; (*stabilire*: *parallelo*) to establish
istituto [isti'tuto] SM **1** (*gen*) institute; (*Univ*) department; (*Scol*) college, school, institute; **istituto di francese/storia** (*Univ*) French/history department; **capo d'istituto** headteacher **2** (*istituzione*) institution
■ **istituto d'arte** art school; **istituto di bellezza** beauty salon; **istituto di credito** bank, banking institution; **istituto magistrale** teacher training school; **istituto tecnico commerciale** *school specializing in commercial subjects*; **istituto tecnico industriale statale** ≈ technical college
istitutore, trice [istitu'tore] SM/F **1** (*fondatore*) founder **2** (*precettore*) tutor/governess
istituzionale [istituttsjo'nale] AGG institutional
istituzionalizzare [istituttsjonalid'dzare] VT to institutionalize
istituzionalizzato, a [istituttsjonalid'dzato] AGG institutionalized
istituzione [istitut'tsjone] SF **1** (*atto*) institution, founding **2** (*ente, tradizione*) institution; **essere un'istituzione** (*fig*) to be an institution **3** (*stato*): **istituzioni** SFPL state institutions
istmo ['istmo] SM isthmus
istogramma, i [isto'gramma] SM (*Statistica*) histogram
istologia [istolo'dʒia] SF (*Med*) histology
istradare [istra'dare] VT (*fig*: *persona*): **istradare (in** *o* **verso)** to guide sb's steps (in *o* towards); **istradare qn nella via del bene** to set sb on the right path
istriano, a [istri'ano] AGG, SM/F Istrian
istrice ['istritʃe] SM (*Zool*) porcupine; (*fig*: *persona*): **essere un istrice** to be prickly
istrione [istri'one] SM (*Teatro, fig*) ham (actor); **fare l'istrione** to ham
istrionico, a, ci, che [istri'ɔniko] AGG histrionic
istruire [istru'ire] VB IRREG, VT **1** (*dare un'istruzione a*) to educate; (*Mil*) to drill **2** (*dare istruzioni a*): **istruire qn sul da farsi** to instruct *o* tell sb what to do **3** (*Dir*): **istruire una causa** *o* **un processo** to prepare a case
▶ **istruirsi** VR (*informarsi*): **istruirsi su qc** to find out about sth
istruito, a [istru'ito] AGG educated; **una persona molto istruita** a very well-educated person
istruttivo, a [istrut'tivo] AGG (*esempio*) instructive; (*libro, film, discussione*) informative
istruttore, trice [istrut'tore] AGG: **giudice istruttore** (*Dir*) examining (*Brit*) *o* committing (*Am*) magistrate
■ SM/F instructor; **istruttore di nuoto** swimming instructor; **istruttore di scuola guida** driving instructor; **istruttore di volo** flying instructor
istruttoria [istrut'tɔrja] SF (*Dir*) (preliminary) investigation and hearing; **formalizzare un'istruttoria** to proceed to a formal hearing
istruttorio, ria, ri, rie [istrut'tɔrjo] AGG (*Dir*) preliminary; **segreto istruttorio** *obligation to maintain secrecy of disclosures in legal hearings*
istruzione [istrut'tsjone] SF **1** (*gen*) training, instruction; (*Mil*) training; (*Scol*) education; **Ministero della pubblica istruzione** Ministry of Education; **ha avuto una buona istruzione** he had a good education **2** **istruzioni** SFPL (*direttive, avvertenze*) instructions, directions; **siamo in attesa di istruzioni** we're waiting for instructions; **istruzioni per l'uso** instructions (for use) **3** (*Dir*) investigation
▷ www.istruzione.it/
istupidimento [istupidi'mento] SM dazed state
istupidire [istupi'dire] VT (*sogg*: *colpo*) to stun, daze; (: *droga, stanchezza*) to stupefy
■ VI (*aus* **essere**), **istupidirsi** VIP to become stupid
ISVET ['izvet] SIGLA M (= **Istituto per gli studi sullo sviluppo economico e per il progresso tecnico**) *institute for research into economic development and technological progress*
Italia [i'talja] SF Italy; **in Italia** in Italy; **ti è piaciuta l'Italia?** did you like Italy?; **verranno in Italia quest'estate** they're coming to Italy this summer
italianità [italjani'ta] SF Italian character
italianizzare [italjanid'dzare] VT to make Italian, Italianize
▶ **italianizzarsi** VIP to become Italian, be Italianized
italiano, a [ita'ljano] AGG Italian; **all'italiana** in the Italian style
■ SM/F (*abitante*) Italian; **gli Italiani** the Italians
■ SM (*lingua*) Italian; **parlare (l')italiano** to speak Italian; **parli italiano?** do you speak Italian?; **l'insegnante di italiano** the Italian teacher
italico, a, ci, che [i'taliko] AGG (*Storia*) Italic
ITC [iti'tʃi] SIGLA M = **istituto tecnico commerciale**
iter ['iter] SM passage, course; **iter burocratico** bureaucratic process; **iter parlamentare** parliamentary procedure
iterativo, a [itera'tivo] AGG iterative, repetitive
iterazione [iterat'tsjone] SF (*Inform*) loop
itinerante [itine'rante] AGG wandering, itinerant; **spettacolo itinerante** touring show, travelling (*Brit*) *o* traveling (*Am*) show; **mostra itinerante** touring exhibition
itinerario, ria, ri, rie [itine'rarjo] SM (*percorso*) route, itinerary; (*Alpinismo*) route; **itinerario turistico** tourist route
ITIS ['itis] SIGLA M = **istituto tecnico industriale statale**
itterizia [itte'rittsja] SF (*Med*) jaundice
ittico, a, ci, che ['ittiko] AGG fish *attr*; **industria ittica** fishing industry
IUD ['jud] SIGLA M INV IUD (= *intrauterine device*)
Iugoslavia [jugoz'lavja] SF = **Jugoslavia**
iugoslavo, a [jugoz'lavo] = **jugoslavo**
iuta ['juta] SF jute
IVA ['iva] SIGLA F (= **Imposta sul Valore Aggiunto**) VAT (*Brit*)
ivato, a [i'vato] AGG including VAT (*Brit*)
ivi ['ivi] AVV (*letter*) therein; (*nelle citazioni*) ibid.

Ii

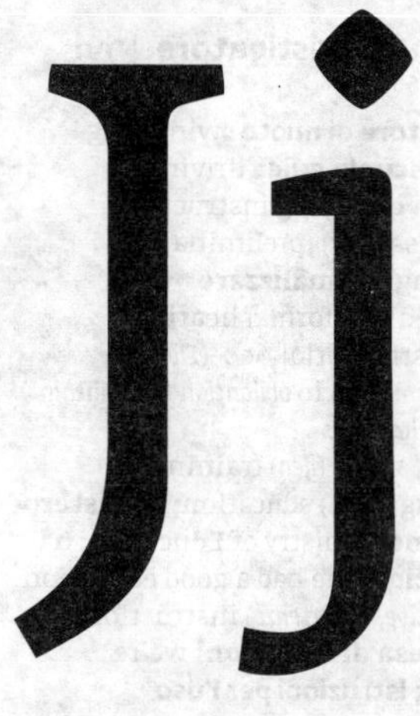

J, j [i'lunga] SM O F INV (*lettera*) J, j; **J come Jersey** ≈ J for Jack (*Brit*), ≈ J for Jig (*Am*)
jabot [ʒa'bo] SM INV (*abbigliamento*) jabot
jack [ʒæk] SM INV (*Carte*) jack, knave (*Brit*); (*Elettr*) jack (plug)
jacquard [ʒa'kar] AGG INV (*tessuto, disegno, maglione*) jacquard *attr*
jais [ʒɛ] SM (*Min*) jet
jam session [dʒem 'seʃʃon] SF INV jam session
jazz [dʒaz] SM INV jazz
■ AGG INV jazz *attr*
▷ www.ijm.it/
▷ www.umbriajazz.com/canale.asp
jazzista, i, e [dʒad'dzista] SM/F jazz player
jeans [dʒinz] SMPL jeans
jeanseria [dʒinse'ria] SF jeans shop
jeep [dʒip] SF INV jeep
jersey ['dʒɛrzi] SM INV jersey (cloth); **jersey di lana/ cotone** jersey wool/cotton
jet lag [dʒet lag] SM INV jet lag
jet set [dʒet set] SM INV jet set
jingle ['dʒiŋgəl] SM INV jingle
jockey ['dʒɔki] SM INV (*fantino*) jockey
jodel ['jodel] SM INV yodel
jogging ['dʒɔgiŋ] SM INV jogging; **fare jogging** to go jogging
joint-venture [dʒɔint'ventʃə] SF INV (*Fin*) joint venture
jojoba [dʒo'dʒɔba] SF jojoba
jolly ['dʒɔli] SM INV joker
■ AGG: **caratteri jolly** wild cards
joystick [dʒois'tik] SM INV joystick
jr. ABBR (= **junior**) Jr., jr.
judo [dʒu'dɔ] SM judo; **fare judo** to do judo
Jugoslavia [jugoz'lavja] SF: **la ex Jugoslavia** the former Yugoslavia
jugoslavo, a [jugoz'lavo] AGG, SM/F Yugoslav(ian)
jujitsu ['zu:zitsu] SM jujitsu
jukebox ['dʒuk'bɔks] SM INV jukebox
julienne [ʒy'ljɛn] SF INV (*zuppa*) julienne; **tagliare le carote alla julienne** to cut carrots into julienne strips
jumbo jet ['dʒumbo 'dʒɛt], **jumbo** ['dʒumbo] SM INV jumbo (jet)
junghiano, a [jun'gjano] AGG, SM/F Jungian
junior ['junjor] AGG INV junior
■ SM (*pl* **juniores**) (*Sport*) under-21; **la Nazionale juniores** the national under-21 team
juta ['juta] SF = **iuta**

Kk

K, k ['kappa] SF O M INV (*lettera*) K, k; **K come Kursaal** ≈ K for King
k ABBR (= **kilo-**) k; (*Inform*) K
Kabul [ka'bul] SF Kabul
kafkiano, a [kaf'kjano] AGG Kafkaesque
Kaiser ['kaizer] SM INV Kaiser
kajal [ka'dʒal] SM INV kohl
kaki ['kaki] AGG INV, SM INV = **cachi**
Kalahari [kala'ari] SM: **il (deserto del) Kalahari** the Kalahari (Desert)
kalashnikov [kalaʃni'kof] SM INV kalashnikov
kamasutra [kama'sutra] SM INV: **il kamasutra** the kamasutra
kamikaze [kami'kaddze] SM INV kamikaze; **una politica economica da kamikaze** (*fig*) a suicidal economic policy
■ AGG INV (*terrorista, commando, missione*) kamikaze *attr*
Kampala [kam'pala] SF Kampala
Kansas ['kansas] SM Kansas
kantiano, a [kan'tjano] AGG Kantian
kapò [ka'po] SM/F INV kapo; *concentration camp guard*
kapoc [ka'pɔk] SM INV kapok
kaputt [ka'put] AGG INV (*fam*) kaput
karakiri [kara'kiri] SM INV hara-kiri; **fare karakiri** to commit hara-kiri
karaoke [kara'oke] SM INV karaoke
karatè [kara'tɛ] SM INV karate; **fare karatè** to do karate
karma ['karma] SM INV karma
kasher [ka'ʃer] AGG INV kosher
Kashmir [kaʃ'mir] SM Kashmir
kasko ['kasko] AGG INV (*assicurazione*) comprehensive
kayak [ka'jak] SM INV kayak
Kazakistan [ka'dzakistan] SM Kazakhstan
kazako, a [ka'dzako] SM/F, AGG Kazakh
kebab [ke'bab] SM INV kebab
kefiah [ke'fija] SF INV keffiyeh
Kelvin ['kɛlvin] SM: **la scala Kelvin** the Kelvin scale
keniota, i, e [ke'njɔta], **keniano, a** [ke'njano] AGG, SM/F Kenyan
Kentucky [ken'taki] SM Kentucky
Kenya ['kɛnja] SM Kenya
képi [ke'pi] SM INV kepi
kermesse [ker'mɛs] SF INV (*nei Paesi Bassi*) kermis; (*fig*) carnival
kerosene [kero'zɛne] SM INV = **cherosene**
ketchup ['ketʃup] SM INV (tomato) ketchup
keyword ['kiword] SF INV (*Inform*) keyword
kg ABBR (= **chilogrammo**) kg
KGB ['kappa'dʒi'bi] SIGLA M: **il KGB** the KGB
Khmer ['kmɛr] AGG INV Khmer
■ SM/F INV Khmer; **i Khmer rossi** the Khmer Rouge *pl*
kibbutz [kib'buts] SM INV kibbutz
kick boxing [kik'bɔksin(g)] SF (*Sport*) kick boxing
Kilimangiaro [kiliman'dʒaro] SM: **il Kilimangiaro** Kilimanjaro
killer ['killer] SM INV killer, hit man/woman (*fam*)
■ AGG (*squalo, cellule ecc*) killer *attr*
kilo *ecc* ['kilo] = **chilo** *ecc*
kilt [kilt] SM INV kilt
kimono [ki'mɔno] SM INV = **chimono**
kinesiterapia [kinezitera'pia] SF = **cinesiterapia**
kirghiso, a [kir'giso] SM/F, AGG Kyrgyz
Kirghizistan [kir'gizistan] SM Kyrgyzstan
kit [kit] SM INV (*gen*) kit; (*Med, Bio*) (testing) kit
kitsch [kitʃ] SM INV, AGG INV kitsch; **arredamento kitsch** (*pegg*) tacky furniture
kiwi ['kiwi] SM INV **1** (*frutto*) kiwi (fruit) **2** (*uccello*) kiwi
kleenex® ['kli:neks] SM INV tissue, Kleenex®
klezmer ['klɛtsmer] AGG INV (*Mus*) klezmer
km ABBR (= **chilometro**) km
km/h ABBR (= **chilometri all'ora**) kmh, kph
kmq ABBR (= **chilometro quadrato**) km²
knock out [nɔk'aut] AGG knocked out
■ AVV: **mettere qn knock out** to knock sb out
■ SM INV (*colpo*) knockout punch; **knock out tecnico** technical knockout
know-how [no'au] SM INV know-how
KO [kappa'o], **k.o.** (= **knockout**) AVV: **mettere qn k.o.** to knock sb out
■ SM INV KO, k.o.; **ha vinto per k.o. tecnico** he won on a technical knockout

koala [ko'ala] SM INV koala (bear)
kosovaro, a [koso'varo] AGG, SM/F Kosovan
Kosovo ['kosovo] SM Kosovo
KR SIGLA = *Crotone*
krapfen ['krapfən] SM INV ≈ doughnut
krypton ['kripton] SM INV (*gas*) krypton
Kuala Lumpur ['kwala 'lumpur] SF Kuala Lumpur
Ku Klux Klan [ku kluks 'klan] SM Ku Klux Klan
Kurdistan ['kurdistan] SM Kurdistan
Kuwait [ku'vait] SM Kuwait
kuwaitiano, a [kuwai'tjano] AGG, SM/F Kuwaiti
kW ABBR (= **kilowatt**) kW
K-way® [kei'wei] SM INV cagoule
kWh ABBR (= **kilowattora**) kW/h

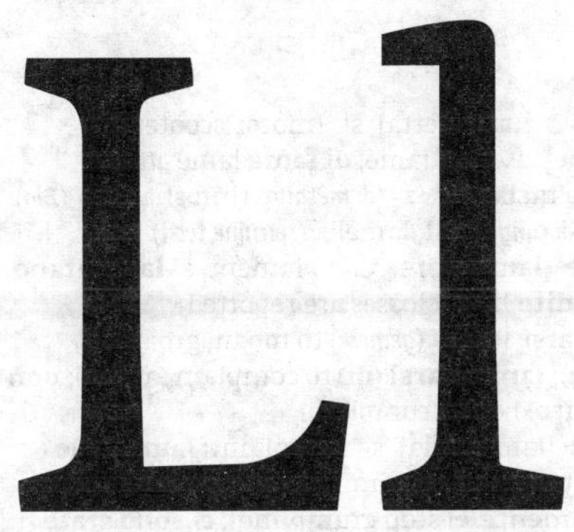

L, l ['ɛlle] SF O M INV (*lettera*) L, l; **L come Livorno** ≈ L for Lucy (*Brit*), ≈ L for Love (*Am*)
L, l ABBR (= **lira**) L, l
L ['ɛlle] SIGLA F (*taglia*) L (= *large*)
l' *vedi* **il, la², lo²**
l ABBR (= **litro**) L, l
la¹ [la] ART DET F *vedi* **il**
la² [la] PRON (*dav vocale* **l'**) **1** (*oggetto: riferito a persona*) her; (*: riferito a cosa*) it; *per fraseologia vedi* **lo** **2** (*oggetto: forma di cortesia, anche:* **La**) you; **in attesa di risentirla** I (*o* we) look forward to hearing from you; **molto lieto di conoscerla** pleased to meet you
la³ [la] SM INV (*Mus*) A; (*: solfeggiando la scala*) lah
là [la] AVV **1** there; **mettilo là** put it there; **eccolo là!** there he (*o* it) is; **resta là dove sei** stay where you are; **là dentro/fuori/sopra/sotto** *ecc* in/out/up (*o* on)/ under there *ecc*; **più in là** (*spazio*) further on; (*tempo*) later on; **la mia casa è un po' più in là** my house is a bit further on; **potresti sederti un po' più in là?** could you move along a bit?; **deciderò più in là** I'll decide later on; **chi va là?** who goes there?; **alto là!** halt! **2**: **di là: di là dal fiume** beyond the river, on the other side of the river; **vieni via di là** come away from there; **mia madre è di là** my mother's in the other room; **al di là di** beyond; **per di là** (*andare, passare*) that way; **se vai per di là allunghi** if you go that way it'll take you longer; **non passo mai per di là** I never go that way; **essere più di là che di qua** to be more dead than alive; **cerca di guardare al di là del fatto in sé** try to look beyond the event itself **3** (*fraseologia*): **là per là** (*sul momento*) there and then; **va' là!** come off it!; **stavolta è andato troppo in là** this time he's gone too far; **essere in là con gli anni** to be getting on (in years)
labbo ['labbo] SM (*uccello*) arctic skua
labbro ['labbro] SM **1** (*Anat*) (*pl f* **labbra**) lip; **leccarsi le labbra** to lick one's lips; **mordersi le labbra** (*fig*) to bite one's tongue; **parlare a fior di labbra** to murmur; **sorridere a fior di labbra** to smile faintly; **pendere dalle labbra di qn** to hang on sb's every word **2** (*pl m* **labbri**) (*di ferita, vaso*) lip
labiale [la'bjale] AGG, SF labial
labile ['labile] AGG fleeting, ephemeral; **avere una memoria labile** to have a poor memory
labirinto [labi'rinto] SM (*Mitol*) labyrinth; (*di stradine*) maze
laboratorio, ri [labora'tɔrjo] SM **1** (*di ricerca*) laboratory; **esperimento di** *o* **da laboratorio** laboratory experiment; **laboratorio linguistico** language laboratory **2** (*per lavori manuali*) workshop; (*stanza*) workroom; **laboratorio fotografico** photo lab
laboriosamente [laborjosa'mente] AVV (*vedi agg*) industriously; laboriously, with difficulty
laboriosità [laborjosi'ta] SF (*industriosità*) industriousness
laborioso, a [labo'rjoso] AGG (*operoso*) industrious, hardworking; (*faticoso*) laborious, difficult
laburismo [labu'rizmo] SM (*Pol*) Labour movement
laburista, i, e [labu'rista] AGG Labour *attr* (*Brit*)
■ SM/F Labour Party member (*Brit*)
lacca, che ['lakka] SF (*per mobili*) varnish, lacquer; (*per capelli*) (hair) lacquer, hair spray; (*per unghie*) nail polish, nail varnish (*Brit*)
laccare [lak'kare] VT (*mobili*) to varnish, lacquer
laccatura [lakka'tura] SF lacquering, varnishing
lacchè [lak'kɛ] SM INV lackey
laccio, ci ['lattʃo] SM lace, string; **lacci delle scarpe** shoelaces; **laccio emostatico** (*Med*) tourniquet
laccolite [lakko'lite] SM O F (*Geol*) laccolith
lacerante [latʃe'rante] AGG (*suono*) piercing, shrill
lacerare [latʃe'rare] VT (*vestiti, stoffa*) to rip, tear; (*: fare a pezzi*) to tear *o* rip to shreds; (*Med, fig*) to lacerate; **un grido lacerò il silenzio** a piercing cry broke the silence; **lacerato dai dubbi/dal rimorso/dal dolore** racked by doubt/remorse/pain
▶ **lacerarsi** VIP to tear, rip
lacerazione [latʃerat'tsjone] SF (*anche Med*) tear
lacero, a ['latʃero] AGG **1** (*abiti*) ripped, torn, tattered; (*persona*) ragged, in rags **2** (*Med*) lacerated; **ferita lacero-contusa** injury with lacerations and bruising
laconicamente [lakonika'mente] AVV laconically
laconico, a, ci, che [la'kɔniko] AGG laconic
lacrima ['lakrima] SF **1** tear; **con le lacrime agli occhi** with tears in one's eyes; **mi ha guardato con le lacrime agli occhi** he looked at me with tears in his

eyes; **essere/scoppiare in lacrime** to be in/burst into tears; **quando ha visto la foto è scoppiata in lacrime** when she saw the photo she burst into tears; **lacrime di coccodrillo** crocodile tears **2** (*goccia*) drop

lacrimale [lakri'male] AGG (*Anat*) tear *attr*; (*ghiandola*) lachrymal (*Med*)

lacrimare [lakri'mare] VI (*aus* **avere**) (*occhi*) to water; (*persona*) to cry, weep

lacrimevole [lakri'mevole] AGG heart-rending, pitiful

lacrimogeno, a [lakri'mɔdʒeno] AGG: **gas lacrimogeno** tear gas

■ SM tear-gas grenade; **hanno lanciato dei lacrimogeni** they fired tear gas

lacrimoso, a [lakri'moso] AGG (*viso, occhi*) tearful; (*commuovente: storia, film*) moving

lacuna [la'kuna] SF (*vuoto*) gap; (*: in un testo*) blank (space); (*: di memoria*) lapse; **colmare una lacuna** to fill a gap; **ho molte lacune in matematica** my knowledge of maths is rather sketchy

lacunoso, a [laku'noso] AGG full of blanks *o* gaps

lacustre [la'kustre] AGG lake *attr*

laddove [lad'dove] CONG whereas

ladro, a ['ladro] AGG thieving; **governo ladro!** (*fam*) damned government!

■ SM/F thief; (*di case*) burglar; **al ladro!** stop thief!; **l'occasione fa l'uomo ladro** (*Proverbio*) opportunity makes the thief

ladrocinio, ni [ladro'tʃinjo] SM theft, robbery

ladroneria [ladrone'ria] SF robbery

ladruncolo, a [la'drunkolo] SM/F petty thief

lager ['la:gər] SM INV lager

laggiù [lad'dʒu] AVV (*in basso*) down there; (*di là*) down *o* over there

lagna ['laɲɲa] SF (*fam: persona, cosa*) drag, bore; **lagne** SFPL whining *sg*, moaning *sg*; **fare la lagna** to whine, moan

lagnanza [laɲ'ɲantsa] SF complaint

lagnarsi [laɲ'ɲarsi] VIP: **lagnarsi (di** *o* **per)** to complain (about), grumble (about)

lagnoso, a [laɲ'ɲoso] AGG (*noioso: film*) boring; **un tipo lagnoso** a moaner

lago, ghi ['lago] SM lake; **il lago di Garda** Lake Garda; **un lago di sangue** a pool of blood; **lago vulcanico** (*Geol*) crater lake

Lagos ['lagos] SF Lagos

lagrima *ecc* ['lagrima] = **lacrima** *ecc*

laguna [la'guna] SF lagoon

lagunare [lagu'nare] AGG lagoon *attr*

■ SM: **i lagunari** SMPL ≈ the marines

laicismo [lai'tʃizmo] SM laicism

laicizzare [laitʃid'dzare] VT to secularize

laico, a, ci, che ['laiko] AGG (*Rel*) lay *attr*; (*stato, potere*) secular; (*scuola*) non-denominational

■ SM/F layman/laywoman

■ SM (*frate converso*) lay brother

laido, a ['laido] AGG filthy, foul; (*osceno*) obscene, filthy

lama¹ ['lama] SF (*di rasoio, spada*) blade; (*spada*) sword; **rasoio a doppia lama** double-edged razor

lama² ['lama] SM INV (*Rel*) lama

lama³ ['lama] SM INV (*animale*) llama

lamantino [laman'tino] SM (*animale*) manatee

lambada [lam'bada] SF (*ballo*) lambada

lambiccare [lambik'kare] VT to distil; **lambiccarsi il cervello** to rack one's brains

lambire [lam'bire] VT (*fig: acqua*) to lap; (*: fiamme*) to lick

lambretta® [lam'bretta] SF (motor)scooter

lamé [la'me] SM INV lamé; **di lamé** lamé *attr*

lamella [la'mɛlla] SF **1** (*di metallo*) thin sheet **2** (*Bio*) lamella; (*di fungo*) gill, lamella (*termine tecn*)

lamentare [lamen'tare] VT to lament; **si lamentano gravi perdite** heavy losses are reported

▶ **lamentarsi** VIP **1** (*gemere*) to moan, groan **2** (*lagnarsi*): **lamentarsi (di)** to complain (about); **non mi lamento!** I can't complain!

lamentela [lamen'tɛla] SF complaint; **lamentele** SFPL complaining *sg*, grumbling *sg*; **smettila con queste lamentele!** stop grumbling!; **ci sono state molte lamentele sul servizio** there have been a lot of complaints about the service

lamentevole [lamen'tevole] AGG (*voce*) plaintive, mournful, complaining; (*stato*) lamentable, pitiful

lamento [la'mento] SM (*gemito*) groan, moan; (*: per la morte di qn*) lament

lamentoso, a [lamen'toso] AGG plaintive, mournful

lametta [la'metta] SF (*da rasoio*) razor blade

lamiera [la'mjɛra] SF (*Tecn*) sheet (metal); **lamiera di ferro/d'acciaio** sheet iron/steel; **lamiera ondulata** corrugated iron

lamina ['lamina] SF (*di metallo*) thin layer *o* sheet *o* plate; (*di sci*) edge; (*Bot, Anat*) lamina; **lamina d'oro** gold leaf *o* foil

laminare¹ [lami'nare] AGG laminar

laminare² [lami'nare] VT to laminate

laminato [lami'nato] SM (*metallico*) rolled section; **laminato plastico** laminated plastic

■ AGG laminated

lampada ['lampada] SF light, lamp; **lampada abbronzante** sun lamp; **lampada alogena** halogen lamp; **lampada a gas** gas lamp; **lampada al neon** neon light; **lampada a petrolio** oil lamp; **lampada da scrivania** reading lamp; **lampada di sicurezza** safety lamp; **lampada a spirito** blowlamp (*Brit*), blowtorch; **lampada a stelo** standard lamp (*Brit*), floor lamp (*Am*); **lampada da tavolo** table lamp

lampadario, ri [lampa'darjo] SM chandelier

lampadina [lampa'dina] SF (*Elettr*) (light) bulb; **una lampadina da 100 watt** a 100 watt bulb; **lampadina tascabile** torch (*Brit*), flashlight (*Am*)

lampante [lam'pante] AGG **1** (*fig: evidente*) blindingly obvious, crystal clear; **prova lampante** clear proof **2** **olio lampante** lamp oil

lampara [lam'para] SF (*lampada*) fishing lamp; (*barca*) *boat for fishing by lamplight in Mediterranean*

lampeggiamento [lampeddʒa'mento] SM flashing

lampeggiare [lamped'dʒare] VI (*aus* **avere**) (*luce, occhi*) to flash; (*Aut*) to flash one's lights

■ VB IMPERS: **lampeggia** it is lightning

lampeggiatore [lampeddʒa'tore] SM (*Aut*) indicator; (*Fot*) flash(gun)

lampione [lam'pjone] SM street light *o* lamp (*Brit*); (*palo*) lamppost

lampo ['lampo] SM (*gen*) flash; (*Meteor*) flash of lightning; **lampi** SMPL (*Meteor*) lightning *sg*; **un lampo di luce** a flash of light; **tuoni e lampi** thunder and lightning; **in un lampo** in a flash; **passare come un lampo** to flash past *o* by; **lampo di speranza** glimmer of hope; **lampo di genio** flash of genius, sudden inspiration; **lampo al magnesio** (*Fot*) magnesium flash

■ AGG INV (*cerimonia, Mil: operazione*) lightning *attr*; **la (cerniera) lampo** zip (fastener) (*Brit*), zipper (*Am*); **guerra lampo** blitzkrieg; **visita lampo** flying visit

lampone [lam'pone] SM (*Bot*) raspberry

lana ['lana] SF wool; **di lana** wool, woollen (*Brit*), woolen (*Am*); **un maglione di lana** a wool sweater; **pura lana vergine** pure new wool; **essere una buona lana** (*fig*) to be a scoundrel *o* rogue; **lana d'acciaio** steel wool; **lana di cammello** camel hair; **lana di vetro** fibreglass (*Brit*); fiberglass (*Am*); glass wool

> LO SAPEVI...?
> **lana** non si traduce mai con la parola inglese ***lane***

lancetta [lan'tʃetta] SF (*di orologio*) hand; (*di barometro*) needle, pointer

lancia[1], **ce** ['lantʃa] SF (*arma*) lance, spear; (*Pesca*) harpoon; (*di pompa antincendio*) nozzle; **spezzare una lancia in favore di qn** to come to sb's defence; **partire lancia in resta** (*fig*) to set off ready for battle

lancia[2], **ce** ['lantʃa] SF (*Naut*) launch; **lancia di salvataggio** lifeboat

lanciabombe [lantʃa'bombe] SM INV (*Mil*) mortar

lanciafiamme [lantʃa'fjamme] SM INV (*Mil*) flame-thrower

lanciamissili [lantʃa'missili] AGG INV missile-launching
■ SM INV missile launcher

lanciapalle [lantʃa'palle] AGG INV: **macchina lanciapalle** (*Tennis*) ball machine

lanciarazzi [lantʃa'raddzi] AGG INV rocket-launching
■ SM INV rocket launcher

lanciare [lan'tʃare] VT **1** (*gen*) to throw; (*con forza*) to hurl, fling; (*bombe*) to drop; (*missili, siluri*) to launch; **lanciare una bomba** to drop a bomb; **lanciare qc a qn** to throw sth to sb; (*per colpirlo*) to throw sth at sb; **lanciare qc in aria** to throw sth into the air; **lanciare una moneta in aria** to toss a coin; **lanciare il peso** (*Sport*) to put the shot; **lanciare il disco** (*Sport*) to throw the discus **2** (*emettere*: *grido*) to give out; (: *invettiva*) to hurl; (: *S.O.S.*) to send out; **mi ha lanciato un'occhiataccia** he flashed me a nasty look; **ha lanciato un urlo** he let out a yell; **ha lanciato un grido di dolore** he let out a cry of pain **3** (*introdurre*: *idea, nave, prodotto, moda*) to launch; **fu quel regista a lanciarla** it was that director who started her on her career; **hanno lanciato una nuova moda** they've started a new fashion **4** (*far andare veloce*: *macchina*) to get up to top speed; **lanciare un cavallo** to set a horse off (at a gallop)
▶ **lanciarsi** VR **1** (*gen*): **lanciarsi in qc** (*anche fig*) to throw o.s. into sth; **lanciarsi contro qn** to hurl *o* fling o.s. at sb; **lanciarsi nella mischia** to throw o.s. into the fray; **lanciarsi all'inseguimento di qn** to set off in pursuit of sb; **lanciarsi col paracadute** to parachute **2** (*fig*: *fare il primo passo*): **lanciarsi in** to launch into; embark upon *o* on; **che aspetti? — lanciati!** what are you waiting for? — off you go!

lanciasiluri [lantʃasi'luri] SM INV torpedo tube

lanciato, a [lan'tʃato] AGG **1** (*affermato*: *attore, prodotto*) well-known, famous **2** (*veicolo*) speeding *o* racing along; **lanciato a tutta velocità** racing along at top speed; **chilometro lanciato** (*Sport*) flying start kilometre

lanciere [lan'tʃɛre] SM (*Mil*) lancer

lancinante [lantʃi'nante] AGG (*dolore*) stabbing, shooting; (*grido*) piercing

lancio, ci ['lantʃo] SM **1** (*vedi vt 1, 2*) throwing *no pl*; hurling *no pl*, flinging *no pl*; dropping *no pl*; launching *no pl* **2** (*Sport*) throw; **lancio di corda** (*Alpinismo*) lassoing; **lancio del disco** the discus; **lancio del giavellotto** the javelin; **lancio del peso** the shot put

landa ['landa] SF (*terreno*) moor

languidamente [langwida'mente] AVV languidly

languido, a ['langwido] AGG (*voce*) languid; (*sguardo, atteggiamento*) languishing

languire [lan'gwire] VI (*aus* **avere**) **1** (*struggersi*) to pine, languish; **languire d'amore** to be languishing with love **2** (*perdere forza*: *persona*) to languish; (: *conversazione*) to flag; (: *affari, commercio*) to be slack; **languire in carcere** to languish in prison

languore [lan'gwore] SM **1** (*debolezza*) weakness, faintness; **sento un languore allo stomaco** I'm feeling a bit peckish **2** (*comportamento*) languor; **mi guardava con languore** he gave me a languishing look

laniero, a [la'njɛro] AGG (*industria, commercio*) wool *attr*, woollen (*Brit*), woolen (*Am*)

lanificio, ci [lani'fitʃo] SM wool mill, woollen (*Brit*) *o* woolen (*Am*) mill

lanolina [lano'lina] SF (*Chim*) lanolin(e)

lanoso, a [la'noso] AGG woolly (*Brit*), wooly (*Am*)

lanterna [lan'tɛrna] SF (*lume, Archit*) lantern; (*faro*) lighthouse; **lanterna magica** (*Cine*) magic lantern

lanternino [lanter'nino] SM: **cercarsele col lanternino** (*fig*) to be asking for trouble

lanugine [la'nudʒine] SF down

lanuginoso, a [lanudʒi'noso] AGG downy

Laocoonte [laoko'onte] SM Laocoon

Laos ['laos] SM Laos

laotiano, a [lao'tiano] AGG, SM/F Laotian

lapalissiano, a [lapalis'sjano] AGG self-evident

laparoscopia [laparosko'pia] SF (*Med*) laparoscopy

La Paz [la'pats] SF La Paz

lapidare [lapi'dare] VT to stone (to death); (*fig*) to tear to pieces

lapidario, ria, ri, rie [lapi'darjo] AGG (*arte*) lapidary; (*fig*: *stile*) succinct, terse

lapide ['lapide] SF (*di sepolcro*) tombstone; (*lastra commemorativa*) memorial stone, plaque

lapin [la'pɛ̃] SM INV rabbit fur, cony

lapis ['lapis] SM INV pencil

lapislazzuli [lapiz'laddzuli] SM INV lapis lazuli

lappone ['lappone] AGG Lappish, Lapp
■ SM/F Laplander, Lapp
■ SM (*lingua*) Lapp, Lappish

Lapponia [lap'ponja] SF Lapland

lapsus ['lapsus] SM INV (*parlando*) slip (of the tongue); (*scrivendo*) slip (of the pen); **lapsus freudiano** Freudian slip

laptop ['læptɔp] SM INV laptop (computer)

lardellare [lardel'lare] VT (*Culin*) to lard

lardo ['lardo] SM (*per cucinare*) lard; (*da affettare*) pork fat (*salted or smoked*)

larga ['larga] SF *vedi* **largo 3**

largamente [larga'mente] AVV (*ampiamente*) widely; (*generosamente*) generously

> LO SAPEVI...?
> **largamente** non si traduce mai con la parola inglese ***largely***

largheggiare [larged'dʒare] VI (*aus* **avere**) to spend freely

larghezza [lar'gettsa] SF **1** (*Mat, misura*) width, breadth; (*di barca*) beam; **larghezza: 20 cm** width: 20 cm; **una stanza della larghezza di 3 metri** a room 3 metres wide **2** (*generosità*) generosity; **larghezza di vedute** (*fig*) broad-mindedness

largire [lar'dʒire] VT (*letter*) to give generously

Ll

largo, a, ghi, ghe ['largo] AGG **1** (*dimensione, misura*) wide, broad; **un cappello a larghe falde** a wide-brimmed hat; **un uomo largo di spalle** *o* **di spalle larghe** a broad-shouldered man; **ha le spalle larghe** he's got broad shoulders; **ha i fianchi larghi** she's got wide hips; **a gambe larghe** with legs wide apart; **un corridoio largo 2 metri** a corridor 2 metres wide
2 (*abiti*) loose; (: *maniche*) wide; **questa gonna mi sta larga** this skirt is loose on me; **questa giacca mi sta larga di spalle** this jacket is too big around the shoulders for me **3** (*ampio: parte, percentuale*) large, big; **in larga misura** to a great *o* large extent; **su larga scala** on a large scale; **di larghe vedute** (*fig: liberale*) broad-minded; **di manica larga** (*fig*) generous, open-handed
■ SM **1 fate largo!** make room *o* way!; **farsi largo tra la folla** to make *o* push one's way through the crowd; **si è fatta largo tra la folla ed è salita sul palco** she pushed her way through the crowd and went up on the stage; **farsi largo a gomitate** to elbow one's way
2 (*piazzetta*) (small) square **3** (*Naut*) open sea; **andare al largo** to sail on the open sea; **non andare al largo** (*nuotando*) don't go too far out; **prendere il largo** to put out to sea; (*fig*) to make off, escape; **al largo di Genova** off (the coast of) Genoa **4** (*Mus*) largo
■ SF: **stare** *o* **tenersi alla larga (da qn/qc)** to keep one's distance (from sb/sth), keep away (from sb/sth); **stai alla larga da casa mia!** keep away from my house!

larice ['laritʃe] SM (*albero*) larch

laringe [la'rindʒe] SF larynx

laringite [larin'dʒite] SF laryngitis

laringoiatra, i, e [laringo'jatra] SM/F (*medico*) throat specialist

larva ['larva] SF (*Zool, Bio*) larva; (*fig pegg: apatico*) zombie; **essere (ridotto a) una larva** (*fig*) to be (all) skin and bone(s)

larvale [lar'vale] AGG (*Zool*) larval; **allo stato larvale** (*fig*) in embryo

larvato, a [lar'vato] AGG (*fig: minacce*) veiled

lasagne [la'zaɲɲe] SFPL lasagna *sg*; **lasagne al forno** baked lasagna *sg*

lascare [las'kare] VT (*Naut*) to slack

lasciapassare [laʃʃapas'sare] SM INV pass, permit

lasciare [laʃ'ʃare] VT **1** (*gen*) to leave; **lasciare qc a qn** to leave sb sth *o* sth to sb; **ha lasciato Roma nel '76** he left Rome in '76; **ho lasciato i soldi a casa** I've left my money at home; **devo lasciare l'università** I have to leave university, I have to give up university; **ha lasciato la scuola a 16 anni** he left school at 16; **lasciare la stanza** to vacate the room; **lasciare la porta aperta** to leave the door open; **lasciare qn solo (a casa)** to leave sb (at home) alone; **ha lasciato la moglie** he's left his wife; **lascia la moglie e due bambini** he leaves a wife and two children; **lasciare qn erede** to make sb one's heir; **lasciare qn perplesso/confuso** to leave sb perplexed/confused
2 (*permettere*): **lasciare qn fare qc** *o* **che qn faccia qc** to let sb do sth, allow sb to do sth; **mio padre non mi lascia uscire fino a tardi** my father doesn't let me stay out late; **lascia fare a me** let me do it; **lascia stare** *o* **correre** *o* **perdere** let it drop, forget it
3 (*deporre: cose*) to leave, deposit; (: *persone*) to leave, drop (off); **ti lascio all'angolo** I'll drop you off at the corner
4 (*dare, concedere*) to give, let have; **mi puoi lasciare la macchina oggi?** can you let me have the car today?; **lasciami il tempo di farlo** give me time to do it
5 (*omettere*) to leave out, forget; **non lasciare tutti i particolari interessanti** don't leave out all the interesting bits
6 (*serbare*) to leave, keep; **lasciami un po' di vino** leave some wine for me
7: **lasciare stare qn** to let sb be, leave sb alone; **lasciare stare qc** to leave sth alone; **lascia stare quel povero gatto!** leave that poor cat alone!; **lascia stare, ci penso io** leave it, I'll see to it; **lascialo stare, non vale la pena di arrabbiarsi** just ignore him, it's not worth getting annoyed; **lascia stare, offro io** it's all right, I'm paying *o* it's on me; **è meglio lasciar stare certi argomenti** it's better not to bring up certain subjects; **volevo insistere ma poi ho lasciato stare** I was going to insist but then I decided to let it go
8: **lasciarsi sfruttare** to let o.s. be exploited; **lasciarsi andare** to let o.s. go
9 (*fraseologia*): **lasciare in bianco** to leave blank; **lasciare (molto) a desiderare** to leave much *o* a lot to be desired; **lasciare detto** *o* **scritto (a qn)** to leave word (for sb); **lasciare qn indifferente** to leave sb unmoved; **non lascia mai niente al caso** he never leaves anything to chance; **lasciami in pace** leave me alone *o* in peace; **lasciare la presa** to lose one's grip; **lasciare il segno (su qc)** to mark (sth); (*fig*) to leave one's *o* a mark (on sth); **ci ha lasciato la vita** it cost him his life
▶ **lasciarsi** VR (*uso reciproco*) to part (from each other); (*coniugi*) to leave each other, split up; **si sono lasciati all'aeroporto** they left each other at the airport, they said goodbye at the airport; **ci siamo lasciati un anno fa** we split up a year ago

lascito ['laʃʃito] SM (*Dir*) legacy, bequest

lascivia [laʃ'ʃivja] SF lust, lasciviousness

lascivo, a [laʃ'ʃivo] AGG lascivious, wanton

lasco ['lasko] SM (*Naut*): **al lasco** on a close reach; **al gran lasco** on a broad reach

laser ['lazer] SM INV, AGG INV: **(raggio) laser** laser (beam); **una stampante laser** a laser printer

lassativo, a [lassa'tivo] AGG, SM laxative

lassismo [las'sizmo] SM laxity

lasso ['lasso] SM: **lasso di tempo** interval, lapse of time

lassù [las'su] AVV (*in alto*) up there; (*in paradiso*) in heaven above

lastra ['lastra] SF **1** (*di marmo, pietra*) slab; (*di vetro, ghiaccio*) sheet; (*di finestra*) pane; (*di metallo*) plate
2 (*Fot*) plate; (*Med*) X-ray; **fare le lastre a qn** (*fam*) to X-ray sb; **ho fatto una lastra alla gamba** I had my leg X-rayed

lastricare [lastri'kare] VT to pave

lastricato [lastri'kato] SM paving(stone)

lastrico, ci o chi ['lastriko] SM paving; **essere sul lastrico** to be penniless; **gettare qn sul lastrico** to leave sb destitute

lastrone [las'trone] SM (*di pietra*) slab; (*Alpinismo*) sheer rock face

lat. ABBR (= **latitudine**) lat. (= *latitude*)

latente [la'tɛnte] AGG latent

laterale [late'rale] AGG (*gen*) side *attr*, lateral; (*uscita, ingresso, linea*) side *attr*; **rimessa laterale** throw-in
■ SM (*Calcio, anche:* **mediano laterale**) halfback

lateralmente [lateral'mente] AVV sideways

laterite [late'rite] SF (*Geol*) laterite

laterizio, zi [late'rittsjo] SM (perforated) brick

latice ['latitʃe] SM = **lattice**

latifondista, i, e [latifon'dista] SM/F large (agricultural) landowner
latifondo [lati'fondo] SM large (agricultural) estate
latinense [lati'nɛnse] AGG of *o* from Latina
■ SM/F inhabitant *o* native of Latina
latinismo [lati'nizmo] SM Latinism
latinista, i, e [lati'nista] SM/F Latin scholar, Latinist
latino, a [la'tino] AGG Latin
■ SM *(lingua)* Latin
latino-americano, a [la'tino ameri'kano] AGG, SM/F Latin-American
latitante [lati'tante] AGG: **essere latitante** *(persona)* to be in hiding *o* on the run; *(fig)* to be an absent force; *(potere, governo)* to be inactive
■ SM/F fugitive (from justice)
latitanza [lati'tantsa] SF *(fig: assenza)* absence; **darsi alla latitanza** *(nascondersi)* to go into hiding
latitudine [lati'tudine] SF latitude
lato[1] ['lato] SM *(gen)* side, part; *(Mat, Geom)* side; *(fig: di problema)* aspect; **l'altro lato della strada** the other side of the street; **da ogni lato** *or* **da tutti i lati** from all sides; **dal lato opposto (di)** from the other *o* opposite side (of); **d'altro lato** *(d'altra parte)* on the other hand; **da un lato… dall'altro lato…** on the one hand … on the other hand …; **l'altro lato della medaglia** *(fig)* the other side of the coin
lato[2] ['lato] AGG: **in senso lato** broadly speaking
latore, trice [la'tore] SM/F *(Comm)* bearer
latrare [la'trare] VI *(aus* **avere***)* to bark
latrato [la'trato] SM howling
latrina [la'trina] SF (public) lavatory *(Brit)*, rest room *(Am)*
latrocinio, ni [latro'tʃinjo] SM = **ladrocinio**
latta ['latta] SF *(sostanza)* tin (plate); *(recipiente)* tin *(Brit)*, can
lattaio, aia, ai, aie [lat'tajo] SM/F *(commerciante)* dairyman/dairywoman; *(distributore)* milkman/ milkwoman; **vado dal lattaio** I'm going to the dairy
lattante [lat'tante] AGG unweaned
■ SM/F unweaned baby
latte ['latte] SM milk; **al latte** milk *attr*; **dare il latte (a un bambino)** *(al seno)* to (breast)feed (a baby); *(con il biberon)* to (bottle-)feed (a baby); **avere ancora il latte alla bocca** *(fig)* to be still wet behind the ears; **tutto latte e miele** *(fig)* all smiles
■ **latte di bellezza** beauty lotion; **latte di cocco** coconut milk; **latte condensato** condensed milk; **latte detergente** cleansing milk *o* lotion; **latte di gallina** eggnog; **latte intero** full-cream milk; **latte a lunga conservazione** long-life milk, UHT milk; **latte magro** *o* **scremato** skimmed milk; **latte materno** mother's milk, breast milk; **latte parzialmente scremato** semi-skimmed milk; **latte in polvere** dried *o* powdered milk
latteo, a ['latteo] AGG *(di latte)* milk *attr*; *(colore)* milky(-white); **la Via Lattea** the Milky Way
latteria [latte'ria] SF dairy
lattice ['lattitʃe] SM latex
latticino [latti'tʃino] SM dairy product
lattico, a, ci, che ['lattiko] AGG lactic
lattiera [lat'tjɛra] SF milk jug
lattiero, a [lat'tjɛro] AGG *(prodotti)* dairy *attr*; **industria lattiero-casearia** dairying
lattiginoso, a [lattidʒi'noso] AGG milky
lattina [lat'tina] SF can; **una lattina di birra** a can of beer
lattosio [lat'tɔzjo] SM *(Chim)* lactose
lattuga, ghe [lat'tuga] SF lettuce

laudano ['laudano] SM laudanum
laurea ['laurea] SF degree *(gained after 4-6 years' study and the presentation of a dissertation)*; **prendere** *o* **conseguire la laurea** to take *o* obtain one's degree, graduate; **ha preso la laurea in legge** he graduated *o* got a degree in law; **laurea breve** *university degree awarded at the end of a two or three year course*

LAUREA

The **Laurea** is awarded to students who successfully complete their degree courses. Traditionally, this takes between four and six years; a major element of the final examinations is the presentation and discussion of a dissertation. A shorter, more vocational course of study, taking from two to three years, is also available; at the end of this time students receive a diploma called the **Laurea breve**.
> www.istruzione.it

laureando, a [laure'ando] AGG final year *attr (Brit)*, senior *(Am)*
■ SM/F final-year student *(Brit)*, senior *(Am)*
laureare [laure'are] VT to confer a degree on
▶ **laurearsi** VIP to graduate; **si è laureato in legge** he graduated in law
laureato, a [laure'ato] AGG graduate *attr*
■ SM/F graduate
lauro ['lauro] SM *(Bot)* laurel; **il lauro della vittoria** the laurels of victory
lauto, a ['lauto] AGG *(pranzo, mancia)* lavish; **lauti guadagni** handsome profits
lava ['lava] SF lava
lavabicchieri [lavabik'kjɛri] SM INV glass-washer *(machine)*
lavabo [la'vabo] SM washbasin *(Brit)*, washbowl *(Am)*
lavabottiglie [lavabot'tiʎʎe] SM INV bottle-washer *(machine)*
lavacristallo [lavakris'tallo] SM *(Aut)* windscreen *(Brit) o* windshield *(Am)* washer
lavaggio, gi [la'vaddʒo] SM *(gen)* washing *no pl*; **lavaggio auto** car wash; **lavaggio del cervello** brainwashing; **gli hanno fatto il lavaggio del cervello** he's been brainwashed; **lavaggio a secco** dry cleaning
lavagna [la'vaɲɲa] SF **1** *(nelle scuole)* blackboard, chalkboard *(Am)*; **scrivere alla lavagna** to write on the blackboard *o* chalkboard; **lavagna luminosa** overhead projector **2** *(minerale)* slate
lavamano [lava'mano] SM INV washstand
lavanda[1] [la'vanda] SF *(gen)* washing; *(Med)* lavage; **fare una lavanda gastrica a qn** to pump sb's stomach
lavanda[2] [la'vanda] SF *(Bot)* lavender
lavandaia [lavan'daja] SF washerwoman; *(fig pegg)* fishwife
lavanderia [lavande'ria] SF *(di ospedale, caserma)* laundry; *(negozio)* laund(e)rette *(Brit)*, laundromat® *(Am)*; *(: lavanderia a secco)* dry-cleaner's
lavandino [lavan'dino] SM *(del bagno)* washbasin *(Brit)*, washbowl *(Am)*; *(della cucina)* sink
lavapiatti [lava'pjatti] SM/F INV *(persona)* dishwasher
■ SF INV *(macchina)* dishwasher, dishwashing machine
lavare [la'vare] VT **1** *(gen)* to wash; **lava la macchina tutte le domeniche** he washes his car every Sunday; **lavare a mano** to wash by hand, handwash; **lavare a secco** to dry-clean; **lavare i piatti** to wash the dishes, do the washing up, wash up; **lavare la testa a qn** to

Ll

wash sb's hair **2** (*fig: purificare*) to cleanse, purify
3: **lavarsi le mani/i capelli** to wash one's hands/hair; **lavarsi i denti** to clean *o* brush one's teeth; **me ne lavo le mani** (*fig*) I wash my hands of it
▶ **lavarsi** VR to wash o.s., have a wash

lavascale [lavas'kale] SM/F INV (*persona*) stair cleaner (*in block of flats*)

lavasecco [lava'sekko] SM INV (*negozio*) dry-cleaner's ■SF INV dry-cleaning machine

lavastoviglie [lavasto'viʎʎe] SF INV dishwasher

lavata [la'vata] SF wash; **dare una lavata a qc** to give sth a wash; **dare una lavata di capo a qn** (*fig*) to give sb a good telling-off

lavativo [lava'tivo] SM (*buono a nulla*) good-for-nothing, idler

lavatoio, oi [lava'tojo] SM (public) washhouse

lavatrice [lava'tritʃe] SF washing machine

lavatura [lava'tura] SF **1** (*atto*) washing *no pl*
2 (*liquido*) dirty water; **lavatura di piatti** dishwater; **questa minestra è lavatura di piatti** this soup is like dishwater

lavavetri [lava'vetri] SM INV (*apparecchio*) window cleaner

lavello [la'vɛllo] SM (kitchen) sink

lavico, a, ci, che ['laviko] AGG lava *attr*

lavina [la'vina] SF snowslide

lavorante [lavo'rante] SM/F worker

lavorare [lavo'rare] VI (*aus* **avere**) **1** (*persona*) to work; **lavoro dalle otto alle cinque** I work from eight to five; **andare a lavorare** to go to work; **vado a lavorare alle sette** I go to work at seven; **va a lavorare!** go and get on with your work!; **lavorare duro** *o* **sodo** to work hard; **lavorare in proprio** to work for o.s., be self-employed; **lavorare a maglia/ad ago** to knit/do needlework; **lavorare a qc** to work on sth; **lavorare di fantasia** (*suggestionarsi*) to imagine things; (*fantasticare*) to let one's imagination run free **2** (*funzionare: macchinari*) to work, run, operate; (*negozi, uffici: far affari*) to do well, do good business; **quel bar non lavora molto** that bar isn't doing very well; **far lavorare il cervello** to use one's brains
■VT (*creta, ferro*) to work; (*legno*) to carve; (*Culin: pane, pasta*) to work, knead; (*: burro*) to beat; (*Agr: terra*) to work, cultivate; **lavorarsi qn** (*fig: convincere*) to work on sb

lavorativo, a [lavora'tivo] AGG (*giorno, capacità*) working *attr*; **attività lavorativa** occupation

lavorato, a [lavo'rato] AGG (*cuoio*) tooled; (*legno, pietra*) carved; (*metallo*) wrought; (*: oro*) worked; (*prodotto*) finished; (*terreno*) cultivated; **lavorato a mano** handmade

lavoratore, trice [lavora'tore] AGG working *attr*; **la classe lavoratrice** the working class
■SM/F worker; **è un gran lavoratore** he's a hard worker; **lavoratore socialmente utile** *person employed by a public body to carry out socially useful work*

lavorazione [lavorat'tsjone] SF **1** (*gen*) working; (*di legno, pietra*) carving; (*di film*) making; (*del terreno*) cultivation; (*di pane, pasta*) working, kneading; (*di prodotto*) manufacture; **lavorazione della carta** paper making; **"lavorazione a mano"** "handmade"; **lavorazione a macchina** machine production; **lavorazione in serie** mass production **2** (*modo di esecuzione*) workmanship

lavorio, rii [lavo'rio] SM intense activity

lavoro [la'voro] SM
1 (*attività*): **il lavoro** work; **lavoro manuale/dei campi** manual/farm work; **avere molto/poco lavoro** to have a lot of/little work to do; **essere al lavoro (su qc)** to be at work (on sth); **mettersi al lavoro** to set to *o* get down to work
2 (*compito*) job, task, work *no pl*; **è un lavoro da specialisti** it's a skilled job, it's a job for a professional; **sta svolgendo un lavoro di ricerca** he is carrying out *o* doing research work; **è un lavoro da niente!** it's no job at all!; **eseguire** *o* **fare (bene/male) un lavoro** to do a job (well/badly)
3 (*posto, impiego*): **il lavoro** work; **un lavoro** a job, an occupation; **avere un buon lavoro** to have a good job; **essere senza lavoro** to be out of work *o* unemployed; **i senza lavoro** the jobless, the unemployed; **è rimasto senza lavoro** he's lost his job; **dar lavoro a** to employ; **l'azienda dà lavoro a 50 dipendenti** the company employs 50 people; **incidente sul lavoro** industrial accident, accident at work; **Ministero del Lavoro e della Previdenza Sociale** ≈ Department of Employment (*Brit*), ≈ Department of Labor (*Am*) **lavoro d'équipe** teamwork; **lavoro interinale** *o* **in affitto** *temporary work*; **lavoro nero** moonlighting (*Brit*), double-dipping (*Am*); **lavoro ripartito** job share; **lavoro straordinario** overtime
4 **lavori** SMPL work *sg*; **lavori scientifici/di ricerca** scientific/research work; **lavori pesanti/leggeri** heavy/light work *o* jobs; **(fare) i lavori di casa** (to do) the housework; **far fare dei lavori in casa** to have some work done in the house; **aprire/chiudere i lavori del parlamento** to open/close the parliamentary session; **il convegno conclude domani i suoi lavori** the conference comes to an end tomorrow; **lavori di scavo** (*Archeol*) excavation works; **Ministero dei Lavori Pubblici** Ministry of Public Works; **"lavori in corso"** "work in progress"; (*segnale stradale*) "roadworks (ahead)"; **questi lavori non si fanno!** you just don't do these things!; **lavori forzati** hard labour *sg*
5 (*opera*) piece of work; (*: artistica*) work
6 (*Econ*) labour (*Brit*), labor (*Am*)
7 (*Fis*) work

laziale [lat'tsjale] AGG of *o* from Lazio
■SM/F inhabitant *o* native of Lazio

lazzaretto [laddza'retto] SM leper hospital

Lazzaro ['laddzaro] SM Lazarus

lazzarone [laddza'rone] SM scoundrel

lazzo ['laddzo] SM jest

LC SIGLA = *Lecco*

LE SIGLA = *Lecce*

le[1] [le] ART DET FPL *vedi* **il**

le[2] [le] PRON PERS **1** (*complemento oggetto*) them; *vedi anche* **lo[2]** **2** (*complemento di termine: a lei*) (to) her; **le ho detto tutto** I told her everything; **le appartiene** it belongs to her; **dalle qualcosa da mangiare** give her something to eat; **le ho già scritto** I've already written to her; **le ho spiegato il motivo** I explained the reason to her; **le ha sorriso** he smiled at her
3 (*forma di cortesia, anche:* **Le**: *complemento di termine*) (to) you; **le posso dire una cosa?** may I tell you something?; **le dispiace attendere?** would you mind waiting?; **le posso offrire qualcosa da bere?** can I get you something to drink?; **le chiedo scusa** I beg your pardon; **le ho prenotato una stanza nello stesso albergo** I've booked you a room at the same hotel

leader ['li:də] SM/F INV leader

leale [le'ale] AGG (*fedele*) loyal, faithful; (*onesto*) fair, honest

lealista, i, e [lea'lista] SM/F loyalist
lealmente [leal'mente] AVV (*vedi agg*) loyally, faithfully; fairly, honestly
lealtà [leal'ta] SF **1** (*fedeltà*) loyalty, faithfulness **2** (*onestà*) fairness, honesty; **comportarsi con lealtà** to behave fairly
leasing ['li:ziŋ] SM INV (*Comm*) leasing
lebbra ['lebbra] SF leprosy
lebbroso, a [leb'broso] AGG leprous
■ SM/F leper
leccaculo [lekka'kulo] SM/F INV (*pegg*) arselicker (*Brit fam!*), arsekisser (*Am fam!*)
lecca lecca ['lekka 'lekka] SM INV lollipop, lolly
leccapiedi [lekka'pjɛdi] SM/F INV (*pegg*) bootlicker
leccarda [lek'karda] SF (*Culin*) dripping pan
leccare [lek'kare] VT to lick; **leccarsi le labbra** *o* **i baffi/le dita** to lick one's lips/fingers; **leccarsi le ferite** (*anche fig*) to lick one's wounds; **leccare (i piedi a) qn** (*fig*) to suck up to sb
▶ **leccarsi** VR (*fig*) to preen o.s.
leccata [lek'kata] SF lick
leccato, a [lek'kato] AGG affected
leccese [let'tʃese] AGG of *o* from Lecce
■ SM/F inhabitant *o* native of Lecce
leccherò *ecc* [lekke'rɔ] VB *vedi* **leccare**
lecchese [lek'kese] AGG of *o* from Lecco
■ SM/F inhabitant *o* native of Lecco
leccio, ci ['lettʃo] SM (*albero*) holm oak, ilex
leccornia [lekkor'nia] SF delicacy, titbit
lecitamente [letʃita'mente] AVV rightly, correctly
lecito, a ['letʃito] AGG (*domanda, comportamento*) permissible; (*Dir*) lawful, legal; **ti par** *o* **sembra lecito che...?** does it seem right to you that ...?; **crede che tutto gli sia lecito** he thinks he can do whatever he likes; **mi sia lecito far presente che...** may I point out that ...?; **se mi è lecito** if I may
■ SM (what is) right
lectio brevis ['lɛktsjo 'brɛvis] SF INV (*Scol*) *shorter school day*
ledere ['lɛdere] VT IRREG to damage; **ledere gli interessi di qn** to prejudice sb's interests
lega¹, ghe ['lega] SF **1** (*Pol, Calcio*) league; **lega doganale** customs union; **far lega (con qn) contro qn/qc** to be in league (with sb) against sb/sth; **la Lega delle Nazioni** the League of Nations; **Lega Nord** (*Pol*) *Italian federalist party* **2** (*Chim*) alloy; **metallo di bassa lega** base metal; **gente di bassa lega** (*fig*) common *o* vulgar people
lega², ghe ['lega] SF (*misura*) league
legaccio, ci [le'gattʃo] SM lace, string
legale [le'gale] AGG (*gen*) legal; **medicina legale** forensic medicine; **studio legale** lawyer's office; **numero legale** quorum; **corso legale delle monete** official exchange rate
■ SM/F lawyer
legalità [legali'ta] SF lawfulness, legality
legalizzare [legalid'dzare] VT **1** (*rendere legale*) to legalize **2** (*autenticare*) to authenticate
legalizzazione [legalid'dzattsjone] SF (*vedi vb*) legalization; authentication
legalmente [legal'mente] AVV legally
legame [le'game] SM **1** (*gen, fig*) tie, bond; **c'è un legame molto forte tra di loro** they're very close; **legame di sangue/di parentela** blood/family tie; **legame di amicizia** bond of friendship; **rompere i legami con qn/qc** to break one's ties with sb/sth **2** (*rapporto logico*) link, connection; **dev'esserci un legame tra i due episodi** there must be a link between the two events **3** (*Chim*) bond
legamento [lega'mento] SM (*Anat*) ligament
legare [le'gare] VT **1** (*gen*) to bind, tie (up); (*Tip: libro*) to bind; **i rapinatori lo hanno legato ad una sedia** the robbers tied him to a chair; **legare le mani a qn** (*anche fig*) to tie sb's hands; **è pazzo da legare** (*fam*) he should be locked up **2** (*persone: unire*) to bind (together), unite; (*vincolare*) to bind; **sono legati da amicizia** they are friends; **siamo legati da questioni di interesse** we have financial interests in common; **questo posto è legato ai ricordi della mia infanzia** this place is bound up with memories of my childhood; **è legata al ricordo di suo marito** she is very attached to her husband's memory; **legarsela al dito** (*fig*) to bear a grudge **3** (*connettere*) to connect, link up; **questi due fatti sono strettamente legati** these two facts are closely linked *o* connected **4** (*Culin: ingredienti, salsa*) to bind; (*: arrosto, pollo*) to truss
■ VI (*aus* **avere**) **1** (*persone*) to get on; **non hanno mai legato** they've never got on; **non ho mai legato con lui** I've never been very friendly with him **2** (*metalli*) to alloy **3** (*Culin*) to bind
▶ **legarsi** VR **1** (*fig*): **legarsi (a qn)** to become attached (to sb) **2** (*Alpinismo*): **legarsi in cordata** to rope up
legatario, ria, ri, rie [lega'tarjo] SM/F (*Dir*) legatee
legato¹, a [le'gato] AGG **1** (*inibito*) awkward; **essere legato nei movimenti** to be stiff in one's movements; **ho le mani legate** (*fig*) my hands are tied **2** (*Mus*): **note legate** notes played legato
■ SM (*Mus*) legato
legato² [le'gato] SM: **legato pontificio** papal legate
legato³ [le'gato] SM (*Dir*) legacy, bequest
legatore, trice [lega'tore] SM/F bookbinder
legatoria [legato'ria] SF (*attività*) bookbinding; (*negozio*) bookbinder's
legatura [lega'tura] SF (*di libri*) binding; (*Tip, Mus*) ligature
legazione [legat'tsjone] SF legation
legenda [le'dʒɛnda] SF *vedi* **leggenda 2**
legge ['leddʒe] SF (*gen*) law; (*Parlamento*) act; **una nuova legge** a new law; **studia legge** he's studying law; **a norma** *o* **termini di legge** according to the law; **per legge** by law; **la legge è uguale per tutti** everybody is equal before the law; **la legge del più forte** the law of survival of the fittest; **ogni suo desiderio è legge** your wish is my command; **la sua parola è legge** his word is law; **le leggi della società** the rules *o* laws of society; **legge marziale** martial law
leggenda [led'dʒɛnda] SF **1** (*mito*) legend; (*diceria*) old wives' tale; **leggenda metropolitana** urban myth **2** (*iscrizione: di moneta*) legend **3** (*chiave di lettura*) key
leggendario, ria, ri, rie [leddʒen'darjo] AGG legendary
leggere ['lɛddʒere] VT IRREG (*gen, Mus*) to read; (*discorso, comunicato*) to read (out); **non ho ancora letto quel libro** I haven't read that book yet; **leggere ad alta voce** to read aloud; **l'ho letto sul giornale** I read (about) it in the newspaper; **leggere nel futuro** (*chiromante*) to read the future; **leggere la mano a qn** to read sb's palm; **leggere qc negli occhi di qn** to see sth in sb's eyes; **leggere nel pensiero a qn** to read sb's mind *o* thoughts; **leggere fra le righe** (*fig*) to read between the lines; **letto e approvato** read and approved
leggerezza [leddʒe'rettsa] SF **1** (*gen*) lightness; (*di*

LI

ballerina) lightness, nimbleness **2** (*sconsideratezza*) thoughtlessness; (*volubilità*) fickleness; **con leggerezza** (*agire*) thoughtlessly

leggermente [leddʒer'mente] AVV (*con leggerezza*) lightly; (*con agilità*) lightly, nimbly; (*un po'*) slightly; **è leggermente cambiato** he has changed a little; **la macchina ha urtato leggermente il muro** the car just grazed the wall

leggero, a [led'dʒɛro] AGG (*gen*) light; (*agile*) light, nimble, agile; (*rumore, dolore*) slight; (*malattia, punizione*) mild, slight; (*cibo, vino*) light; (*caffè, tè*) weak; **un pacco leggero** a light parcel; **un pasto leggero** a light meal; **leggero come una piuma** light as a feather; **avere il sonno leggero** to be a light sleeper; **a passi leggeri** with a light step; **avere un leggero accento straniero** to have a slight foreign accent; **ho un leggero mal di testa** I've got a slight headache; **ha avuto la malattia in forma leggera** she had a mild form of the illness; **fanteria/cavalleria leggera** light infantry/cavalry; **una ragazza leggera** (*fig*) a flirtatious *o* flighty girl; **prendere le cose alla leggera** to take things lightly; **a cuor leggero** light-heartedly

leggiadria [leddʒa'dria] SF loveliness, prettiness; **leggiadria di stile** elegance of style

leggiadro, a [led'dʒadro] AGG (*gen*) lovely, pretty; (*stile, movimenti*) elegant, graceful

leggibile [led'dʒibile] AGG (*calligrafia*) legible; (*libro*) readable

leggio, gii [led'dʒio] SM (*per libri*) bookrest; (*Mus*) music stand; (*in chiesa, Univ*) lectern

legherò *ecc* [lege'rɔ] VB *vedi* **legare**

leghismo [le'gizmo] SM (*Pol*) *in Italy, political movement with federalist tendencies*

leghista, i, e [le'gista] (*Pol*) AGG *of a "lega", especially Lega Nord*

■ SM/F *member o supporter of a "lega", especially Lega Nord*

legiferare [ledʒife'rare] VI (*aus* **avere**) to legislate

legionario, ri [ledʒo'narjo] SM (*volontario*) legionnaire; (*Storia*) legionary

legione [le'dʒone] SF (*Mil*) legion; (*fig*) host, multitude; **la Legione straniera** the Foreign Legion

legislativo, a [ledʒizla'tivo] AGG legislative

legislatore [ledʒizla'tore] SM legislator

legislatura [ledʒizlas'tura] SF legislature

legislazione [ledʒizlat'tsjone] SF legislation

legittima [le'dʒittima] SF (*Dir*) *portion of estate of which a testator cannot dispose freely*

legittimamente [ledʒittima'mente] AVV (*possedere*) legitimately

legittimare [ledʒitti'mare] VT (*figlio*) to legitimize; (*giustificare: comportamento*) to justify

legittimità [ledʒittimi'ta] SF legitimacy

legittimo, a [le'dʒittimo] AGG (*figlio*) legitimate; (*orgoglio*) justifiable; (*dubbio, desiderio*) reasonable; (*fondato: paura, sospetto*) justified; **per legittima difesa** in self-defence (*Brit*), in self-defense (*Am*); **legittimo sospetto** (*Dir*) *transfer of a case to a different court because the impartiality of the judge is in doubt*

legna ['leɲɲa] SF (fire)wood; **legna da ardere** firewood; **stufa a legna** wood stove; **far legna** to gather firewood; **mettere legna al fuoco** (*fig*) to add fuel to the fire

legnaia [leɲ'ɲaja] SF woodshed

legnaiolo [leɲɲa'jɔlo] SM woodcutter

legname [leɲ'ɲame] SM timber, wood

legnata [leɲ'ɲata] SF blow with a stick; **dare a qn un sacco di legnate** to give sb a good hiding

legno ['leɲɲo] SM **1** (*gen*) wood; **di legno** wood *attr*, wooden; **un tavolo di legno** a wooden table; **legno stagionato** seasoned wood; **legno dolce/duro** soft/hardwood; **testa di legno** (*fig*) blockhead **2** (*pezzo di legno*) piece of wood **3** (*fig: nave*) sailing ship **4** (*Mus*): **i legni** SMPL the woodwind *sg o pl*

legnoso, a [leɲ'ɲoso] AGG (*di legno*) woody; (*come legno: movimenti*) stiff, wooden

legume [le'gume] SM pulse; **legumi** SMPL pulses

leguminosa [legumi'nosa] SF leguminous plant

lei[1] ['lɛi] PRON PERS F **1** (*complemento: dopo prep, con valore enfatico*) her; **sono venuto con lei** I came with her; **dimmi qualcosa di lei** tell me something about her; **senza di lei** without her; **se non fosse per lei** if it were not for her; **hanno accusato lei, non me** they accused her, not me; **chiedilo a lei** ask her; **lei qui non la voglio** I don't want her here **2** (*sogg: al posto di 'ella', con valore enfatico*) she; **lei è meglio di te** she is better than you; **prendetela, è lei** catch her, she's the one; **è lei, apri la porta** it's her, open the door; **è stata lei a dirmelo** she told me herself, it was she who told me; **ha ragione lei, non tu** she's right, not you; **viene anche lei?** is she coming too?; **neanche lei ha tutti i torti** even she isn't completely in the wrong; **non lo sapeva nemmeno lei** she didn't even know it herself **3** (*nelle comparazioni*) (*: sogg*) she, her; (*: complemento*) her; **ne so quanto lei** I know as much as she does, I know as much as her

■ SF INV (*scherz*): **la mia lei** my beloved

lei[2] ['lɛi] PRON PERS (*forma di cortesia, anche:* **Lei**) **1** you; **lei per cortesia venga con noi** be so good as to come with us; **senza di lei** without you; **riconosco lei senz'altro** I certainly recognize you; **posso venire con lei?** may I come with you? **2** (*nelle comparazioni*) you; **farò come lei** I'll do the same as you (do)

■ SM: **dare del lei a qn** to address sb as 'lei'

LEI

The third person singular pronoun **lei** is used when speaking to adults with whom you do not have a close relationship as a sign of respect. In some parts of southern Italy, "voi" is still used as a respectful form of address. "Tu" is used when speaking to friends, relatives and children.

leitmotiv ['laitmoti:f] SM INV (*Mus, fig*) leitmotiv

lembo ['lembo] SM (*orlo*) hem; (*striscia: di stoffa, fig: di terra*) strip

LO SAPEVI...?
lembo non si traduce mai con la parola inglese ***limb***

lemma, i ['lɛmma] SM **1** (*di dizionario*) headword; (*di enciclopedia*) (main) entry **2** (*Mat, Filosofia*) lemma

lemmario, ri [lem'marjo] SM word list

lemme lemme ['lɛmme 'lɛmme] AVV (*fam*) (very) very slowly

lemuridi [le'muridi] SMPL (*Zool*) lemurs

lena ['lena] SF: **di buona lena** (*lavorare, camminare*) at a good pace

leninismo [leni'nizmo] SM Leninism

leninista, i, e [leni'nista] AGG, SM/F Leninist

lenire [le'nire] VT to soothe, relieve

lentamente [lenta'mente] AVV slowly

lente ['lɛnte] SF (*Ottica, Fot*) lens; **lente d'ingrandimento** magnifying glass; **lenti (a contatto) morbide** soft lenses; **lenti (a contatto) rigide** hard lenses; **lenti a contatto** contact lenses; **portare le lenti (a contatto)** to wear contacts *o* contact lenses

lentezza [len'tettsa] SF slowness; (*di mente*) slowwittedness; **con lentezza** slowly

lenticchia [len'tikkja] SF (*Bot*) lentil; **per un piatto di lenticchie** (*fig*) for nothing, for peanuts

lenticella [lenti'tʃɛlla] SF (*Bot*) lenticel

lentiggine [len'tiddʒine] SF freckle

lentigginoso, a [lentiddʒi'noso] AGG freckled

lento, a ['lɛnto] AGG **1** (*gen*) slow; **il mio computer è troppo lento** my computer is too slow; **lento a** *o* **nel fare qc** slow in doing sth; **a passi lenti** slowly, with a slow step; **il bambino è un po' lento** (*fig*) the child is a bit slow; **cuocere a fuoco lento** to cook over a low heat **2** (*allentato*) loose; (: *fune*) slack
■ SM (*ballo*) slow dance

lenza ['lɛntsa] SF (fishing) line

lenzuolo [len'tswɔlo] (*pl f* **lenzuola**, *pl m* **lenzuoli**) SM sheet; **lenzuolo (di) sopra/sotto** top/bottom sheet; **lenzuolo funebre** shroud

leoncino [leon'tʃino] SM lion cub

leone [le'one] SM **1** (*Zool*) lion; **fare la parte del leone** (*fig*) to take the lion's share; **leone marino** sea-lion **2** (*Astrol*): **Leone** Leo; **essere del Leone** to be Leo

leonessa [leo'nessa] SF lioness

leonino, a [leo'nino] AGG lion's, leonine

leopardato, a [leopar'dato] AGG (*costume, vestito*) leopard-skin *attr*

leopardo [leo'pardo] SM leopard

leporino, a [lepo'rino] AGG (*Med*): **labbro leporino** harelip

lepre ['lɛpre] SF hare; **lepre delle nevi** mountain *o* blue hare

leprotto [le'prɔtto] SM leveret

leptospirosi [leptospi'rɔzi] SF (*Med*) leptospirosis

lercio, cia, ci, ce ['lɛrtʃo] AGG filthy, foul

lerciume [ler'tʃume] SM filth

lesbica, che ['lɛzbika] SF lesbian

lesbico, a, ci, che ['lɛzbiko] AGG lesbian

lesbismo [lez'bizmo] SM lesbianism

lesinare [lezi'nare] VI (*aus* **avere**) **lesinare (su)** to skimp (on), be stingy (with)
■ VT: **lesinare la lira** to count the pennies

lesione [le'zjone] SF **1** (*danno*) damage; **lesione personale** (*Dir*) personal injury **2** (*Med*) lesion; **lesioni interne** internal injuries **3** (*Edil*) crack

lesivo, a [le'zivo] AGG: **lesivo (di)** detrimental (to), damaging (to)

leso, a ['lezo] PP *di* **ledere**
■ AGG (*Dir*): **parte lesa** injured party; **lesa maestà** lese-majesty

Lesotho [le'sɔto] SM Lesotho

lessare [les'sare] VT (*Culin*) to boil

lessatura [lessa'tura] SF boiling

lessi *ecc* ['lɛssi] VB *vedi* **leggere**

lessicale [lessi'kale] AGG lexical

lessicalmente [lessikal'mente] AVV lexically

lessico, ci ['lɛssiko] SM (*Ling*) lexis, vocabulary; (*dizionario*) lexicon

lessicografia [lessikogra'fia] SF lexicography

lessicografo, a [lessi'kɔgrafo] SM/F lexicographer

lessicologia [lessikolo'dʒia] SF lexicology

lessicologo, a, gi, ghe [lessi'kɔlogo] SM/F lexicologist

lesso, a ['lesso] (*Culin*) AGG boiled
■ SM (*gen*) boiled meat; (*manzo*) boiled beef

lestamente [lesta'mente] AVV quickly

lesto, a ['lɛsto] AGG quick, fast; **lesto di mano** (*fig: per rubare*) light-fingered; (: *per picchiare*) free with one's fists

lestofante [lesto'fante] SM swindler, con man

letale [le'tale] AGG lethal, deadly

letamaio, ai [leta'majo] SM dung *o* manure heap; (*fig*) pigsty

letame [le'tame] SM manure, dung; (*fig*) filth, muck

letargo [le'targo] SM **1** (*di animale*) hibernation; **essere/andare** *o* **cadere in letargo** to be in/go into hibernation **2** (*di persona: Med, anche fig*) lethargy

letizia [le'tittsja] SF joy, happiness

lettera ['lɛttera] SF **1** (*dell'alfabeto*) letter; **scrivere qc con lettere maiuscole/minuscole** to write sth in capitals *o* capital letters/in small letters; **scrivere un numero in lettere** to write out a number in full; **prendere qc alla lettera** to take sth literally; **eseguire qc alla lettera** (*legge, ordine*) to carry out sth to the letter; **restar lettera morta** (*consiglio, invito*) to go unheeded; **diventar lettera morta** (*legge*) to become a dead letter; **lettere maiuscole** capitals *o* capital letters; **lettere minuscole** small letters **2** (*missiva*) letter; **hai ricevuto la mia lettera?** did you get my letter?; **lettera d'affari/d'amore** business/love letter **3** **lettere** SFPL (*letteratura*) literature *sg*; **fa lettere all'università** he is doing an arts degree; **lettere antiche** classics *sg*; **un uomo di lettere** a man of letters
■ **lettera di accompagnamento** covering letter; **lettera assicurata** registered letter; **lettera di cambio** (*Comm*) bill of exchange; **lettera di credito** (*Comm*) letter of credit; **lettera di intenti** (*Comm*) letter of intent; **lettera di presentazione** letter of presentation; **lettera raccomandata** recorded delivery (*Brit*) *o* certified (*Am*) letter

letterale [lette'rale] AGG literal

letteralmente [letteral'mente] AVV literally

letterario, ria, ri, rie [lette'rarjo] AGG literary

letterato, a [lette'rato] AGG cultured
■ SM/F scholar

letteratura [lettera'tura] SF literature

lettiera [let'tjɛra] SF (*per bestiame*) bedding, litter

lettiga, ghe [let'tiga] SF **1** (*barella*) stretcher **2** (*portantina*) litter

lettino [let'tino] SM (*anche:* **lettino solare**) sunbed; (*per bambini*) cot (*Brit*), crib (*Am*)

letto[1], a ['lɛtto] PP *di* **leggere**

letto[2] ['lɛtto] SM (*gen, di fiume, lago*) bed; **(ri)fare il letto** to make the bed; **essere a letto** to be in bed; **andare a letto** *or* **mettersi a letto** to go to bed; **ieri sera sono andato a letto molto tardi** I went to bed very late last night; **andare a letto con qn** to go to bed with sb, sleep with sb; **a letto, bambini!** bedtime, children!; **figlio di primo/secondo letto** child by one's first/second marriage; **sul letto di morte** on one's deathbed; **letti a castello** bunk beds; **letti gemelli** twin beds; **letto matrimoniale** *o* **a due piazze** double bed; **letto a una piazza** single bed

lettone ['lettone] AGG, SM/F Latvian
■ SM (*lingua*) Latvian, Lettish

Lettonia [let'tɔnja] SF Latvia

lettorato [letto'rato] SM **1** (*Univ*) lectorship, assistantship **2** (*Rel*) lectorate, lectorship

lettore, trice [let'tore] SM/F **1** (*gen*) reader; **sono un avido lettore di fantascienza** I'm an avid reader of science fiction; **il pubblico dei lettori** the reading public **2** (*Univ*) lector, assistant

■SM **1** (*Rel*) lector **2** **lettore CD** CD player; **lettore DVD** DVD player; **lettore MP3** MP3 player; **lettore ottico** (*Inform*) optical character reader

lettura [let'tura] SF (*gen*) reading; **un libro di piacevole lettura** a very readable book; **un libro di facile lettura** an easy book to read; **libro di lettura** (*Scol*) reading book; **letture obbligatorie** (*Scol*) set books

LO SAPEVI...?
lettura non si traduce mai con la parola inglese *lecture*

leucemia [leutʃe'mia] SF leukaemia (*Brit*), leukemia (*Am*)

leucocita, i [leuko'tʃita] SM (*Bio*) leucocyte

leva¹ ['lɛva] SF (*anche fig*) lever; **far leva su qc** to lever sth up; (*fig*) to take advantage of sth; **far leva su qn** to work on sb; **leva del freno a mano** handbrake (lever); **avere in mano le leve del comando** (*fig*) to hold the reins; **leva del cambio** gear lever *o* stick (*Brit*), gear shift (*Am*); **leva di comando** control lever

leva² ['lɛva] SF (*Mil*) conscription, call-up (*Brit*), draft (*Am*); **essere di leva** to be due for call-up *o* draft; (*in servizio*) to be a conscript; **le nuove leve** (*fig*) the younger generation

levante [le'vante] SM (*Geog*) east; (*vento*) east wind; (: *nel Mediterraneo*) levanter; **il Levante** the Levant

levapunti [leva'punti] SM INV staple remover

levare [le'vare] VT **1** (*gen*: *togliere*) to remove, take away; (: *coperchio*) to take off; (: *tassa*) to abolish; (: *dente*) to take out; (*Mat*) to subtract, take away; **leva i tuoi libri dal tavolo** take your books off the table; **levare la sete** to quench one's thirst; **levare qn/qc di mezzo** *o* **di torno** to get rid of sb/sth; **levare l'assedio** (*Mil*) to raise the siege; **levare un divieto** to lift a ban; **levare le tende** (*fig*) to pack up and leave **2** (*sollevare*: *occhi, testa*) to lift (up), raise; **levare l'ancora** (*Naut*) to lift *o* weigh anchor; **levare un grido** to let out a cry **3** **levarsi qc** (*vestito*) to take sth off, remove sth; **si è levato le scarpe** he took off his shoes; **levarsi il pensiero** to put one's mind at rest
▶ **levarsi** VR (*persona*: *alzarsi*) to get up; **levati di mezzo** *o* **di lì** *o* **di torno!** get out of the *o* my way!; **puoi levarti dalla luce?** can you get out of my light?;
▶ **levarsi** VIP (*vento, burrasca, sole*) to rise

levata [le'vata] SF **1** (*della posta*) collection; **una levata di scudi** concerted opposition **2** (*Mil*) reveille

levataccia, ce [leva'tattʃa] SF: **fare una levataccia** to get up at an ungodly hour

levatoio, oi [leva'tojo] AGG: **ponte levatoio** drawbridge

levatrice [leva'tritʃe] SF midwife

levatura [leva'tura] SF intellect, intellectual capacity

levigare [levi'gare] VT (*gen*) to smooth; (*marmo*) to polish; (*con carta vetrata*) to sand; (*fig*: *discorso*) polish

levigato, a [levi'gato] AGG (*superficie*) smooth; (*fig*: *stile*) polished; (: *pelle*) flawless

levigatrice [leviga'tritʃe] SF (*Tecn*) polisher

levità [levi'ta] SF (*letter*) lightness

levitare [levi'tare] VI (*aus* **avere** *o* **essere**) to levitate

levitazione [levitat'tsjone] SF levitation

Levitico, a, ci, che [le'vitiko] (*Rel*) SM Leviticus
■AGG Levitical, Levitic

levriere [le'vrjɛre] SM greyhound

lezione [let'tsjone] SF (*Scol*) lesson; (*Univ*) lecture; **ora di lezione** (*Scol*) period; **far lezione (a qn)** to teach (sb), give lessons (to sb); (*Univ*) to give a lecture (to sb); **una lezione di generosità** a lesson in generosity; **servire di lezione a qn** to be a lesson to sb; **lezione privata** private lesson; **do lezioni private** I give private lessons

leziosità [lettsjosi'ta] SF affectation

lezioso, a [let'tsjoso] AGG (*stile*) affected; (*sorriso*) simpering

lezzo ['leddzo] SM stink, stench

LI SIGLA = **Livorno**

li [li] PRON PERS PL them; *vedi anche* **lo²**

lì [li] AVV **1** there; **mettilo lì** put it there; **eccolo lì!** there he (*o* it) is!; **è rimasto lì dov'era** he stayed where he was; **lì dentro/fuori/sopra/sotto** *ecc* in/out/on (*o* up)/under there *ecc*; **di** *o* **da lì** from there; **vieni via di lì** come away from there; **da lì non si entra** you can't come in that way; **per di lì** that way; **di lì a pochi giorni** a few days later; **la discussione è finita lì** the discussion ended there; **fin lì tutto sembrava normale** up until then everything seemed normal; *vedi anche* **quello** **2** (*fraseologia*): **lì per lì** (*sul momento*) there and then, then and there; (*dapprima*) at first; **è arrabbiato, tutto lì** he's angry, that's all; **essere lì (lì) per fare qc** to be on the point of doing sth, be about to do sth; **se non l'ha offeso apertamente siamo lì** he may not have insulted him openly but that's what it amounts to

liana [li'ana] SF liana, liane

libagione [liba'dʒone] SF libation

libanese [liba'nese] AGG, SM/F Lebanese *inv*

Libano ['libano] SM the Lebanon; **andremo in Libano** we're going to Lebanon

libbra ['libbra] SF pound

libeccio, ci [li'bettʃo] SM libeccio, libecchio; *south-west wind*

libellista, i, e [libel'lista] SM/F libeller

libello [li'bɛllo] SM libel

libellula [li'bɛllula] SF dragonfly

liberale [libe'rale] AGG (*gen, Pol*) liberal
■SM/F (*Pol*) Liberal

liberalismo [libera'lizmo] SM liberalism

liberalità [liberali'ta] SF generosity; **con liberalità** generously

liberalizzare [liberalid'dzare] VT to liberalize

liberalizzazione [liberalid'dzattsjone] SF liberalization

liberalmente [liberal'mente] AVV liberally

liberare [libe'rare] VT **1** (*rendere libero*: *prigioniero*) to release; (: *popolo*) to liberate, free; **hanno curato il cigno e poi l'hanno liberato** they treated the swan and then set it free; **liberaci dal male** (*Rel*) deliver us from evil **2** (*sgombrare*: *passaggio*) to clear; (: *stanza*) to vacate; **dobbiamo liberare la stanza entro le undici** we have to vacate the room by eleven **3** (*produrre*: *energia*) to release
▶ **liberarsi** VR to get free; **è riuscito a liberarsi ed è scappato** he managed to get free and escaped; **liberarsi di qn/qc** to get rid of sb/sth; **finalmente mi sono liberata di lui** I finally got rid of him; **liberarsi dagli impegni** to free o.s. from one's commitments; **se riesco a liberarmi per le 5...** if I can manage to be free by 5 o'clock ...;
▶ **liberarsi** VIP (*stanza*) to become vacant; (*telefono, posto*) to become free

liberatore, trice [libera'tore] AGG liberating; **guerra liberatrice** war of liberation
■SM/F liberator

liberatorio, ria, ri, rie [libera'tɔrjo] AGG **1** (*Psic*) liberating **2** (*Fin*): **pagamento liberatorio** payment in full

liberazione [liberat'tsjone] SF **1** (*di prigioniero*) release;

(*di popolo*) liberation; **è stata una liberazione per lui** (*sollievo*) it was a release for him; **che liberazione!** what a relief!; **la liberazione della donna** women's liberation **2 la Liberazione** *national holiday*

LIBERAZIONE

The **Liberazione** is a national holiday which falls on 25 April. It commemorates the liberation of Italy in 1945 from German forces and Mussolini's government and marks the end of the war on Italian soil.

libercolo [li'bɛrkolo] SM (*pegg*) worthless book
Liberia [li'bɛrja] SF Liberia
liberiano, a [libe'rjano] AGG, SM/F Liberian
liberismo [libe'rizmo] SM (*Econ*) laissez-faire
liberista, i, e [libe'rista], **liberistico, a, ci, che** [libe'ristiko] AGG laissez-faire *attr*
libero, a ['libero] AGG **1** (*senza costrizioni*) free; (*persona: non sposata*) unattached; **sei libera domani sera?** are you free tomorrow evening?; **tenersi libero per domani/lunedì** to keep tomorrow/Monday free; **libero da** (*legami, preoccupazioni*) free of *o* from; **essere libero di fare qc** to be free to do sth; **sei libero di rifiutare** you're free *o* at liberty to refuse; **siete liberi di andarvene** you're free to go; **dar libero corso a** to give free rein to; **dar libero sfogo a** to give vent to; **libera discussione** free *o* open discussion; **"ingresso libero"** (*gratuito*) "entrance *o* admission free" **2** (*non occupato: gen*) free; (*: passaggio*) clear; (*: posto*) vacant, free; (*: linea telefonica*) free; **finalmente è libero!** the line is free at last!; **è libero questo posto?** is this seat free?; **avete una camera libera per questa sera?** have you got a room available for tonight?; **non ha mai un momento libero** he never has a free moment; **cosa fai nel tempo libero?** what do you do in your free *o* spare time?; **la strada è libera** the road is clear; **via libera!** all clear!; **avere via libera** to have a free hand; **dare via libera a qn** to give sb the go-ahead
■ SM (*Calcio, anche:* **battitore libero**) sweeper
■ **libera professione** self-employment; **libera uscita** (*Mil*) leave; (*in Marina*) liberty; **libero arbitrio** free will; **libero professionista** self-employed (professional) person; (*che lavora per varie aziende*) freelance, freelancer; **libero scambio** free trade
liberoscambismo [liberoskam'bizmo] SM (*Econ*) free trade
libertà [liber'ta] SF INV **1** (*gen*) freedom, liberty; **combattere per la libertà** to fight for freedom; **il ladro è ancora in libertà** the thief is still at large; **nei momenti di libertà** (*tempo libero*) in one's free time; **le libertà civili** civil liberties; **libertà di espressione** freedom of expression; **libertà di pensiero** freedom of thought; **libertà di scelta** freedom of choice; **libertà di stampa** freedom of the press **2** (*Dir*) freedom, liberty; **concedere la libertà a qn** to release sb; **rimettere qn in libertà** to set sb free, release sb; **essere in libertà provvisoria** to be released on (*o* without) bail; **essere in libertà vigilata** to be on probation **3** (*licenza*) liberty; **prendersi la libertà di** to take the liberty of; **prendersi delle libertà** to take liberties
libertario, ria, ri, rie [liber'tarjo] AGG libertarian
liberticida, i, e [liberti'tʃida] AGG liberticidal
■ SM/F liberticide
libertino, a [liber'tino] AGG, SM/F libertine
liberty ['liberti] AGG INV, SM INV art nouveau
Libia ['libja] SF Libya
libico, a, ci, che ['libiko] AGG, SM/F Libyan
libidine [li'bidine] SF lust, lechery
libidinoso, a [libidi'noso] AGG lustful, lecherous, libidinous
libido [li'bido] SF INV (*Psic*) libido
libraio, ai [li'brajo] SM bookseller
librario, ria, ri, rie [li'brarjo] AGG book *attr*
librarsi [li'brarsi] VR to hover; **librarsi in volo** to soar
libreria [libre'ria] SF **1** (*negozio*) bookshop **2** (*mobile*) bookcase **3** (*Inform*) library
libresco, a, schi, sche [li'bresko] AGG (*pegg: cultura*) bookish
librettista, i, e [libret'tista] SM/F librettist
libretto [li'bretto] SM booklet; (*Mus*) libretto
■ **libretto degli assegni** chequebook (*Brit*), checkbook (*Am*); **libretto di banca** bank book; **libretto di circolazione** (*Aut*) registration document (*Brit*), logbook (*Brit*), registration (*Am*); **libretto d'istruzioni** user's manual, instruction booklet; **libretto di lavoro** *booklet showing a person's current and previous employment*; **libretto di risparmio** bankbook (*Brit*), passbook; **libretto universitario** *booklet showing a university student's academic record*
libro ['libro] SM **1** (*gen*) book; **essere sul libro nero di qn** to be in sb's bad books; **essere un libro aperto** (*fig: persona*) to be an open book; **a libro** (*scala*) folding; **Libro bianco** (*Pol*) white paper (*Brit*); **libro di consultazione** reference book; **libro di cucina** cookery book; **libro elettronico** electronic book; **libro giallo** detective story, thriller; **libro tascabile** paperback; **libro di testo** textbook; **libro usato** second-hand book; **Libro verde** (*Pol*) Green Paper **2** (*registro*) book, register; **tenere i libri** to keep the books; **libri contabili** (account) books; **libri sociali** company records; **libro di cassa** cash book; **libro mastro** ledger; **libro paga** payroll
licantropo [li'kantropo] SM werewolf
liceale [litʃe'ale] AGG secondary school *attr* (*Brit*), high school *attr* (*Am*)
■ SM/F secondary school (*Brit*) *o* high school (*Am*) pupil
licenza [li'tʃɛntsa] SF **1** (*gen, permesso*) permission, leave; **chiedere/dare licenza di fare qc** to ask/give permission to do sth; **prendersi la licenza di fare qc** to take the liberty of doing sth **2** (*autorizzazione*) licence (*Brit*), license (*Am*), permit; **licenza di caccia/di pesca/ matrimoniale** hunting/fishing/marriage licence; **licenza di esportazione/importazione** export/import licence; **licenza di fabbricazione** manufacturer's licence; **su licenza di...** (*Comm*) under licence from ... **3** (*Scol*) school-leaving certificate **4** (*Mil: documento*) pass; **essere/andare in licenza** to be/go on leave **5** (*sfrenatezza*) licence (*Brit*), license (*Am*), licentiousness; **licenza poetica** poetic licence
licenziamento [litʃentsja'mento] SM dismissal; (*per esubero di personale*) redundancy; **licenziamento ingiustificato** unfair dismissal; **licenziamento in massa** mass dismissals *pl o* redundancies *pl*
licenziare [litʃen'tsjare] VT **1** to dismiss, sack (*Brit*), fire (*fam*); (*per esubero di personale*) to make redundant; **ha minacciato di licenziarla** he threatened to sack her; **mio padre è stato licenziato dopo trent'anni di lavoro** my father was made redundant after working there for thirty years **2** (*Scol*) to award a school-leaving certificate to
▶ **licenziarsi** VR **1** (*andare via*) to take one's leave; (*dal lavoro*) to resign, hand in one's notice; give up one's job; **si è licenziata per occuparsi del bambino** she

LI

gave up her job to look after her little boy **2** (*Scol*) to obtain one's school-leaving certificate
licenziosamente [litʃentsjosa'mente] AVV licentiously
licenziosità [litʃentsjosi'ta] SF licentiousness
licenzioso, a [litʃen'tsjoso] AGG licentious
liceo [li'tʃɛo] SM ≈ secondary school (*Brit*), ≈ high school (*Am*); **liceo classico/scientifico** *secondary or high school specializing in classics/scientific subjects*
lichene [li'kɛne] SM (*Bot*) lichen
licitazione [litʃitat'tsjone] SF (*vendita all'asta*) auction; (*offerta di prezzo*) bid; **mettere in licitazione** to put up for auction
licnide ['liknide] SF (*pianta*) campion
lido ['lido] SM (*spiaggia*) beach; (*letter: paese*) shore; **il lido di Venezia** the Venice Lido
Liechtenstein ['liktenʃtain] SM Liechtenstein
lietamente [ljeta'mente] AVV joyfully, gladly
lieto, a ['ljɛto] AGG glad, happy; **a lieto fine** with a happy ending; **lieto evento** happy event; **molto lieto (di fare la sua conoscenza)** pleased to meet you
lieve ['ljɛve] AGG (*tocco, brezza*) soft, light, faint; (*ferita*) slight
lievemente [ljeve'mente] AVV (*vedi agg*) softly, lightly, faintly; slightly
lievità [ljevi'ta] SF = **levità**
lievitare [ljevi'tare] VI (*aus* **essere**) (*pane, pasta, anche fig*) to rise
■ VT to leaven
lievitazione [ljevitat'tsjone] SF rising
lievito ['ljɛvito] SM yeast; **lievito di birra** brewer's yeast; **lievito in polvere** baking powder
lifo ['lifo] SM (*Comm, Fin*) LIFO (= *last in first out*)
lifting ['liftiŋ] SM INV face-lift; **farsi fare il lifting** to have a face-lift
light ['lait] AGG INV (*sigaretta*) low-tar; (*bibita*) light, lite
ligio, a, gi, gie *o* **ge** ['lidʒo] AGG: **ligio (a)** faithful (to), loyal (to); **ligio al dovere** devoted to duty
lignaggio, gi [liɲ'ɲaddʒo] SM descent, lineage
ligneo, a ['liɲɲeo] AGG wooden
lignite [liɲ'ɲite] SF lignite
ligure ['ligure] AGG, SM/F Ligurian; **la Riviera Ligure** the Italian Riviera
Liguria [li'gurja] SF Liguria
ligustro [li'gustro] SM (*arbusto*) privet
Likud ['likud] SM Likud
LILA ['lila] SIGLA F (= **Lega Italiana Lotta all'AIDS**) *organization that combats AIDS*
lilla ['lilla] AGG INV, SM INV (*colore*) lilac
lillà [lil'la] SM INV (*arbusto*) lilac
lillipuziano, a [lilliput'tsjano] AGG, SM/F Lilliputian
Lima ['lima] SF Lima
lima ['lima] SF file; **lima per le unghie** nailfile
limaccioso, a [limat'tʃoso] AGG muddy
limanda [li'manda] SF (*pesce*) dab
limare [li'mare] VT (*superficie, unghie*) to file; (*fig: scritti*) to polish, perfect
limatura [lima'tura] SF (*azione*) filing (down); (*residuo*) filings *pl*
limbo ['limbo] SM (*Rel, fig*) limbo
limetta [li'metta] SF **1** (*per le unghie*) nailfile **2** (*Bot*) lime (*fruit*)
limitare [limi'tare] VT **1** (*circoscrivere*) to bound, mark the bounds of, surround **2** (*contenere*): **limitare (a)** to limit (to), restrict (to); **dobbiamo cercare di limitare le spese** we must try to control our spending
▶ **limitarsi** VR: **limitarsi a qc/a fare qc** to limit *o* confine o.s. to sth/to doing sth; **mi sono limitato a consigliarle di stare attenta** I confined myself to advising her to be careful; **limitarsi nel fumare** to limit one's smoking; **limitarsi nel bere** to drink moderately; **mi limiterò a dire che...** all I'm prepared to say *o* all I'll say is that ...
limitatamente [limitata'mente] AVV to a limited extent; **limitatamente alle mie possibilità** in so far as I am able
limitatezza [limita'tettsa] SF: **limitatezza di idee** narrow-mindedness
limitativo, a [limita'tivo] AGG limiting, restrictive, restricting
limitato, a [limi'tato] AGG (*ristretto*) limited, restricted; (*scarso*) scarce, limited; **persona di idee limitate** narrow-minded person
limitazione [limitat'tsjone] SF (*gen*) limitation, restriction; **limitazione degli armamenti** arms limitation *o* control
limite ['limite] SM (*gen, fig*) limit; (*confine*) boundary, limit, border; **c'è un limite a tutto!** *or* **tutto ha un limite!** there are limits!; **senza limite** *o* **limiti** boundless, limitless; **conoscere i propri limiti** to know one's limitations; **nei limiti del possibile** as far as possible; **ti aiuterò nei limiti del possibile** I'll help you as far as possible; **passare il** *o* **ogni limite** to go too far; **hai passato ogni limite!** you've gone too far!; **entro certi limiti** within certain limits; **al limite** if the worst comes to the worst (*Brit*), if worst comes to worst (*Am*), if necessary; **non portare l'ombrello – al limite te ne presto uno** don't bring your umbrella – if necessary I'll lend you one; **limite d'età** age limit; **limite delle nevi perenni** snow line; **limite di rottura** breaking point; **limite di tempo** time limit; **limite della vegetazione arborea** tree line; **limite di velocità** speed limit
■ AGG INV: **caso limite** extreme case
limitrofo, a [li'mitrofo] AGG neighbouring (*Brit*), neighboring (*Am*)
limo ['limo] SM (*fango*) mud, slime; (*Geog*) silt
limonata [limo'nata] SF lemonade (*Brit*), (lemon) soda (*Am*); (*spremuta*) lemon squash (*Brit*), lemonade (*Am*)
limone [li'mone] SM (*frutto*) lemon; (*albero*) lemon (tree); **l'hanno spremuto come un limone e poi l'hanno licenziato** they worked him to death and then sacked him
limpidamente [limpida'mente] AVV (*esporre*) clearly, lucidly
limpidezza [limpi'dettsa] SF (*di acqua, cielo*) clearness; (*di discorso*) clarity
limpido, a ['limpido] AGG (*acqua*) limpid, clear; (*cielo*) clear; (*fig: discorso*) clear, lucid
lince ['lintʃe] SF lynx; **avere un occhio di lince** to be eagle-eyed
linciaggio, gi [lin'tʃaddʒo] SM lynching
linciare [lin'tʃare] VT to lynch
lindo, a ['lindo] AGG (*casa, stanza*) neat and tidy, spick and span; (*biancheria, abiti*) clean
linea ['linea] SF **1** (*gen, Mat*) line; **a grandi linee** in outline; **in linea di massima** on the whole; **in linea di massima penso che tu abbia ragione** on the whole I think you're right; **in linea d'aria** *or* **il paese dista dieci chilometri da qui in linea d'aria** the village is ten kilometres from here as the crow flies; **avere qualche linea di febbre** to have a slight temperature; **linea di confine** boundary line; **linea continua** solid

line; **linea di cortesia** *a line on the floor in a bank or post office behind which customers are asked to stand until the person at the counter has finished*; **linea punteggiata** dotted line; **linea tratteggiata** broken line **2** (*fig: direzione*) line; **linea d'azione/di condotta** line of action/of conduct; **rimanere in linea col proprio partito** to toe the party line **3** (*figura: di persona*) figure; (*: Moda, Aut*) line; **mantenere la linea** to keep one's figure; **la linea Dior** (*collezione*) the Dior collection; **una giacca di linea classica** a classically styled jacket **4** (*Ferr, Aer*) line; **linea d'autobus** (*percorso*) bus route; (*servizio*) bus service; **aereo di linea** airliner; **volo di linea** scheduled flight; **linea aerea** airline; **nave di linea** (ocean) liner **5** (*Elettr*) line; **linee di alta tensione** high tension cables **6** (*Telec*) line; **la linea è occupata** the line is engaged (*Brit*) *o* busy (*Am*); **è caduta la linea** I (*o* you *ecc*) have been cut off **7** (*Mil*) line; **essere in prima linea** to be in the front line; **linea di mira/tiro** line of sight/fire **8** (*Sport*) line; **linea d'arrivo** finishing line; **linea di fondo** (*Calcio*) goal line; **linea laterale** sideline; **linea di massima pendenza** (*Sci*) fall line; **linea di metà campo** (*Calcio*) halfway line; **linea di pallone morto** (*Rugby*) dead-ball line; **linea di partenza** starting line

lineamenti [linea'menti] SMPL (*di volto*) features; (*fig: elementi essenziali*): **lineamenti di fisica** introduction *sg* to physics

lineare [line'are] AGG (*Mat, disegno*) linear; (*fig*) consistent, coherent, logical

lineetta [line'etta] SF (*trattino*) dash; (*in composti, a fine riga*) hyphen

linfa ['linfa] SF (*Bot*) sap; (*Anat*) lymph; **linfa vitale** (*fig*) lifeblood

linfatico, a, ci, che [lin'fatiko] AGG (*Anat*) lymphatic

linfodrenaggio, gi [linfodre'naddʒo] SM lymphatic drainage

linfonodo [linfo'nɔdo] SM (*Anat*) lymph node

lingottiera [lingot'tjɛra] SF ingot mould

lingotto [lin'gɔtto] SM ingot, bar

lingua ['lingwa] SF **1** (*Anat, Culin, fig*) tongue; **mostrare la lingua a qn** to stick *o* put out one's tongue at sb; **avere qc sulla punta della lingua** (*fig*) to have sth on the tip of one's tongue; **ce l'ho sulla punta della lingua** it's on the tip of my tongue; **avere la lingua sciolta** to have the gift of the gab; **avere una lingua velenosa** (*fig*) to have a nasty tongue; **tenere a freno la lingua** to hold one's tongue; **avere la lingua lunga** (*fig*) to talk too much; **la lingua batte dove il dente duole** (*Proverbio*) it is human nature to dwell on one's misfortunes; **lingua di bue** (*Culin*) ox tongue; **lingue di gatto** (*biscotti*) langues de chat **2** (*linguaggio*) language, tongue; **parla tre lingue** he speaks three languages; **lingua viva/morta** living/dead language; **la lingua italiana** the Italian language; **paesi di lingua inglese** English-speaking countries; **non parliamo la stessa lingua** (*anche fig*) we don't talk the same language; **studiare lingue** to study languages; **studio lingue all'università** I'm studying languages at university; **lingua franca** lingua franca; **lingua madre** mother tongue **3** **lingua di fuoco** tongue of flame; **lingua di terra** spit of land

linguaccia [lin'gwattʃa] SF (*pegg: persona*) spiteful gossip

linguacciuto, a [lingwat'tʃuto] AGG gossipy
■ SM/F gossip

linguaggio, gi [lin'gwaddʒo] SM language; **linguaggio infantile** baby talk; **linguaggio di programmazione** programming language

linguetta [lin'gwetta] SF (*di scarpe*) tongue; (*di busta*) flap; (*di strumento*) reed

linguista, i, e [lin'gwista] SM/F linguist

linguistica [lin'gwistika] SF linguistics *sg*
▷ www.accademiadellacrusca.it/

linguistico, a, ci, che [lin'gwistiko] AGG linguistic
■ SM (*anche:* **liceo linguistico**) *secondary or high school specializing in modern languages*

linimento [lini'mento] SM liniment

link ['link] SM INV (*Inform*) link

lino ['lino] SM (*pianta*) flax; (*tessuto*) linen; **seme di lino** linseed; **una giacca di lino** a linen jacket

linoleum [li'nɔleum] SM INV linoleum, lino (*Brit*)

liofilizzare [liofilid'dzare] VT to freeze-dry

liofilizzato, a [liofilid'dzato] AGG freeze-dried; **caffè liofilizzato** instant coffee
■ SM freeze-dried food

Lione [li'one] SF Lyons

lipasi [li'pazi] SF INV (*Bio*) lipase

lipide [li'pide] SM (*Chim*) lipid

liposoma, i [lipo'sɔma] SM liposome

liposuzione [liposut'tsjone] SF liposuction

LIPU ['lipu] SIGLA F (= **Lega Italiana Protezione Uccelli**) ≈ RSPB (*Brit: = Royal Society for the Protection of Birds*)

liquame [li'kwame] SM liquid sewage

liquefare [likwe'fare] VB IRREG
■ VT (*render liquido*) to liquefy; (*fondere*) to melt
▶ **liquefarsi** VIP to liquefy; (*burro, ghiaccio*) to melt

liquefatto, a [likwe'fatto] PP *di* **liquefare**

liquefazione [likwefat'tsjone] SF liquefaction

liquefeci *ecc* VB *vedi* **liquefare**

liquidare [likwi'dare] VT **1** (*debiti*) to settle, pay off; (*società*) to wind up, liquidate; (*merci*) to sell off, clear; (*pensione*) to pay **2** (*fig: sbarazzarsi di: persona*) to get rid of; (*: uccidere*) to kill, liquidate; **liquidare una questione** to settle a matter once and for all

liquidatore, trice [likwida'tore] SM/F (*Dir, Comm*) liquidator; (*Assicurazione*) claims adjuster

liquidazione [likwidat'tsjone] SF **1** (*pagamento*) settlement, payment; (*di società*) liquidation; (*di merci*) clearance; **vendita/prezzi di liquidazione** clearance sale/prices; **ho comprato questa gonna in liquidazione** I bought this skirt in a sale **2** (*Amm*) severance pay

liquidità [likwidi'ta] SF INV liquidity

liquido, a ['likwido] AGG (*gen, Comm, Fonetica*) liquid; (*Culin*) runny; **un gas liquido** a liquid gas; **denaro liquido** cash, ready money
■ SM **1** (*corpo liquido*) liquid, fluid **2** (*Econ: denaro contante*) ready money *o* cash

liquigas® [likwi'gas] SM INV Calor gas® (*Brit*), butane

liquirizia [likwi'rittsja] SF liquorice

liquore [li'kwore] SM liqueur; **liquori** SMPL (*bevande alcoliche*) spirits

liquoroso, a [likwo'roso] AGG: **vino liquoroso** dessert wine

lira¹ ['lira] SF (*unità monetaria*) lira; **non vale una lira** it's worthless; **non avere una lira** to be penniless; **lira sterlina** pound sterling

lira² ['lira] SF **1** (*Mus*) lyre **2** (*anche:* **uccello lira**) lyrebird

lirica, che ['lirika] SF **1** (*genere di poesia*) lyric poetry; (*poema*) lyric poem **2** (*Mus: anche:* **opera lirica**) opera

liricamente [lirika'mente] AVV lyrically

liricità [liritʃi'ta] SF = **lirismo**

lirico, a, ci, che ['liriko] AGG **1** (*poesia*) lyric; (*impeto,*

LI

descrizione) lyrical **2** (*Mus*) opera *attr*; **musica lirica** opera; **una cantante lirica** an opera singer; **la stagione lirica** the opera season
■ SM lyric poet
lirismo [li'rizmo] SM lyricism
Lisbona [lis'bona] SF Lisbon; **andrò a Lisbona quest'estate** I'm going to Lisbon this summer; **abita a Lisbona** he lives in Lisbon
lisca, sche ['liska] SF (fish)bone
lisciare [liʃ'ʃare] VT (*gen*) to smooth; (*fig: adulare*) to flatter; **lisciarsi i capelli** to smooth (down) one's hair
▶ **lisciarsi** VR (*fig*) to preen o.s.
lisciatura [liʃʃa'tura] SF (*Tecn*) polishing
liscio, scia, sci, sce ['liʃʃo] AGG (*pelo, capelli*) sleek; (*pelle*) smooth; (*affare, faccenda*) simple, straightforward; (*liquore*) neat, straight; **avere i capelli lisci** to have straight hair; **un whisky, per favore — liscio o con ghiaccio?** a whisky, please — straight or with ice?; **è andato tutto liscio** it all went off smoothly *o* without a hitch; **passarla liscia** to get away with it; **non la passerà liscia** he won't get away with it; **com'è andata? — liscia come l'olio** how did it go? — it went like a dream
liscivia [liʃ'ʃivja], **lisciva** [liʃ'ʃiva] SF lye
liseuse [li'zøz] SF INV bed jacket
liso, a ['lizo] AGG worn(-out), threadbare
lisoformio [lizo'fɔrmjo] SM Lysol®
lista ['lista] SF **1** (*gen: elenco*) list; (*menù*) menu; **lista della spesa/degli invitati** shopping/guest list; **fare la lista di qc** to make a list of sth; **mettersi in lista per** to put one's name down for *o* on the list for; **lista elettorale** electoral roll *o* register; **lista nera** (*fig*) blacklist; **lista di nozze** wedding list; **lista delle vivande** menu **2** (*striscia*) strip
listare [lis'tare] VT **1**: **listare (di)** to border (with), edge (with) **2** (*Inform*) to list
listato [lis'tato] SM (*Inform*) list, listing
listello [lis'tɛllo] SM (*Archit*) listel, fillet
listino [lis'tino] SM list; **prezzo di listino** list price; **listino di borsa** (*Fin*) Stock Exchange listing; **listino dei cambi** (*Fin*) (foreign) exchange rate; **listino dei prezzi** price list
litania [lita'nia] SF (*Rel*) litany; (*fig: di nomi, titoli*) string
lite ['lite] SF **1** (*gen*) quarrel, argument; **attaccar lite (con qn)** to pick a fight (with sb) **2** (*Dir*) lawsuit
litigante [liti'gante] SM/F (*gen*) quarreller; (*Dir*) litigant
litigare [liti'gare] VI (*aus* **avere**) (*gen*) to quarrel, argue; (*Dir*) to litigate; **litigo spesso con il mio ragazzo** I often quarrel with my boyfriend; **ho litigato con il mio capo** I had an argument with my boss
litigio, gi [li'tidʒo] SM quarrel, dispute
litigioso, a [liti'dʒoso] AGG (*gen*) quarrelsome; (*Dir*) litigious, contentious
litio ['litjo] SM (*Chim*) lithium
litografia [litogra'fia] SF (*metodo*) lithography; (*stampa*) lithograph; (*stabilimento*) lithographic printing works *sg*
litografico, a, ci, che [lito'grafiko] AGG lithographic
litografo, a [li'tɔgrafo] SM/F lithographer
litorale [lito'rale] SM coast
■ AGG coastal, coast *attr*
litoraneo, a [lito'raneo] AGG coastal
litorina [lito'rina] SF (*mollusco*) periwinkle
litro ['litro] SM litre (*Brit*), liter (*Am*)
littorina [litto'rina] SF (*Ferr*) diesel engine
littorio, ria, ri, rie [lit'tɔrjo] AGG (*Storia romana*) lictorial; **fascio littorio** (*anche Fascismo*) fasces *pl*
Lituania [litu'anja] SF Lithuania
lituano [litu'ano] AGG, SM/F, SM Lithuanian
liturgia, gie [litur'dʒia] SF liturgy
liturgico, a, ci, che [li'turdʒiko] AGG liturgical
liuto [li'uto] SM lute
livella [li'vɛlla] SF (*Tecn*) level; **livella a bolla (d'aria)** spirit level
livellamento [livella'mento] SM levelling
livellare [livel'lare] VT (*anche fig*) to level
▶ **livellarsi** VIP to become level; (*fig*) to level out, balance out
livellatore, trice [livella'tore] AGG levelling
livellatrice [livella'tritʃe] SF steamroller
livello [li'vɛllo] SM **1** (*di olio, acqua*) level; **allo stesso livello** at the same level; **a livello della strada** at street *o* ground level; **livello di guardia** (*anche fig*) danger level; **sotto il/sul livello del mare** (*Geog*) below/above sea level **2** (*grado*) standard; (: *intellettuale, sociale*) level; **un alto livello di vita** a high standard of living; **una conferenza ad alto livello** high-level *o* top-level talks; **contatti ad alto livello** high-level contacts; **allo stesso livello** at the same level; **non è al tuo livello** he is not on the same level as you; **a livello economico/politico** at an economic/a political level; **a livello mondiale** world-wide
■ **livello impiegatizio** employment grading; **livello di magazzino** stock level; **livello occupazionale** level of employment; **livello retributivo** salary grade
livido, a ['livido] AGG (*bluastro*) livid; (*per percosse*) bruised, black and blue; (*plumbeo: cielo*) leaden; **labbra livide dal freddo** lips blue with cold; **livido di collera** *o* **rabbia** livid with rage; **livido di invidia** green with envy
■ SM bruise
livore [li'vore] SM venom
livornese [livor'nese] AGG of *o* from Livorno
■ SM/F inhabitant *o* native of Livorno
Livorno [li'vorno] SF Livorno, Leghorn
livrea [li'vrɛa] SF (*uniforme*) livery; (*di animale*) coat; (*di uccello*) plumage
lizza ['littsa] SF: **entrare** *o* **scendere in lizza** (*anche fig*) to enter the lists; **essere in lizza per** (*fig*) to be competing for, compete for; **rimanere in lizza** (*fig*) to still be in the running
LO SIGLA = *Lodi*
lo[1] [lo] ART DET M *vedi* **il**
lo[2] [lo] PRON (*dav vocale* **l'**) **1** (*riferito a persona*) him; (*riferito ad animale*) it; (: *affettuosamente*) him; (*riferito a cosa*) it; **lo vuoi conoscere?** *o* **vuoi conoscerlo?** would you like to meet him?; **Paolo lo conosco bene, ma Giovanna no** I know Paolo well, but not Giovanna; **lo chiamerò domani mattina** I'll call him tomorrow morning; **lo compro** I'll buy it; **guardalo!** look at him (*o* it)! **2** (*con valore neutro: spesso non tradotto*): **vieni? — non lo so** are you coming? — I don't know; **te lo dicevo io!** I told you so!; **non lo vedi che stai sbagliando?** can't you see you're wrong?; **può sembrare innocuo ma non lo è** he may look harmless but he's not
lobbia ['lɔbbja] SF (*cappello*) homburg
lobbista, i, e [lob'bista] SM/F lobbyist
lobbistico, a, ci, che [lob'bistiko] AGG lobby *attr*
lobby ['lɔbi] SF INV lobby
lobelia [lo'bɛlja] SF (*pianta*) lobelia

lobo ['lɔbo] SM (*Anat, Bot*) lobe; **lobo dell'orecchio** ear lobe
lobotomia [loboto'mia] SF lobotomy
LOC [lok] SIGLA F = *Lega Obiettori di Coscienza*
locale [lo'kale] AGG local; (*treno*) stopping (*Brit*), local (*Am*)
■ SM **1** (*stanza*) room; (*luogo pubblico*) place, premises *pl*; **non si servono alcolici in questo locale** no alcohol is served on the premises; **è un locale molto costoso** it's a very expensive place; **locale caldaie** boiler room; **locale (notturno)** (night)club **2** (*anche:* **treno locale**) stopping train (*Brit*), local train (*Am*)
località [lokali'ta] SF INV locality; **località balneare/ di villeggiatura** seaside/holiday resort
localizzare [lokalid'dzare] VT (*individuare*) to locate, place; (*circoscrivere: epidemia, incendio*) to confine, localize
▶ **localizzarsi** VIP: **localizzarsi in** to become localized in
localizzazione [lokaliddzat'tsjone] SF (*vedi vb*) location; confinement
localmente [lokal'mente] AVV locally
locanda [lo'kanda] SF inn
locandiere, a [lokan'djɛre] SM/F landlord/landlady
locandina [lokan'dina] SF poster
locare [lo'kare] VT (*Dir*) to rent out, let
locatario, ria, ri, rie [loka'tarjo] SM/F (*di casa, appartamento*) tenant; (*di camera*) lodger
locativo, a [loka'tivo] AGG (*Dir*): **valore locativo** rental value
locatore, trice [loka'tore] SM/F landlord/landlady
locazione [lokat'tsjone] SF **1** (*da parte del locatario*) renting; (*da parte del locatore*) renting out, letting; **dare in locazione** to rent out, let **2** (*anche:* **contratto di locazione**) lease; **canone di locazione** rent
locomotiva [lokomo'tiva] SF locomotive, engine
locomotore [lokomo'tore] SM, **locomotrice** [lokomo'tritʃe] SF (electric) locomotive, engine
locomozione [lokomot'tsjone] SF locomotion; **mezzi di locomozione** means of transport
loculo ['lɔkulo] SM burial recess
locusta [lo'kusta] SF locust
locuzione [lokut'tsjone] SF phrase, locution, expression
lodare [lo'dare] VT to praise; **lodare qn per qc/per aver fatto qc** to praise sb for sth/for having done sth; **sia lodato Dio!** God be praised!
lode ['lɔde] SF praise; **degno di lode** praiseworthy; **tessere le lodi di qn** to sing sb's praises; **in lode di** in praise of; **torna a sua lode** it's to his credit; **laurearsi con 110 e lode** (*Univ*) ≈ to graduate with first-class honours *o* a first-class honours degree (*Brit*), ≈ to graduate summa cum laude (*Am*)
loden ['lodən] SM INV (*stoffa*) loden; (*cappotto*) loden overcoat
lodevole [lo'devole] AGG praiseworthy
lodigiano, a [lodi'dʒano] AGG of *o* from Lodi
■ SM/F inhabitant *o* native of Lodi
logaritmo [loga'ritmo] SM (*Mat*) logarithm
loggia, ge ['lɔddʒa] SF (*Archit*) loggia; (*circolo massonico*) lodge
loggione [lod'dʒone] SM (*Teatro*): **il loggione** the gods *sg*
logica ['lɔdʒika] SF logic; **è nella logica delle cose** it is in the nature of things; **a rigor di logica** logically; **privo di logica** illogical
logicamente [lodʒika'mente] AVV naturally, obviously
logicità [lodʒitʃi'ta] SF logicality
logico, a, ci, che ['lɔdʒiko] AGG logical; **quello che dici non è molto logico** what you're saying isn't very logical
■ SM logician
login [lo'gin] SM INV (*Inform*) login
logistica [lo'dʒistika] SF logistics *sg*
logistico, a, ci, che [lo'dʒistiko] AGG logistic
loglio ['lɔʎʎo] SM (*Bot*): **loglio perenne** rye-grass
logo ['lɔgo] SM INV logo
logopedista, i, e [logope'dista] SM/F speech therapist
logorabile [logo'rabile] AGG: **essere logorabile** (*vista, salute*) to be easily ruined
logoramento [logora'mento] SM (*di vestiti*) wear
logorante [logo'rante] AGG exhausting; (*attesa, giornata*) wearing
logorare [logo'rare] VT (*abiti, scarpe*) to wear out; (*scalini, pietra*) to wear away; (*occhi, salute*) to ruin; (*nervi, resistenza*) to wear down; (*persona*) to wear out, exhaust; (*volto*) to line, mark; **logorarsi l'anima** *o* **la vita su qc** to wear o.s. out over sth; **logorarsi la vista** to ruin one's eyesight
▶ **logorarsi** VIP (*abiti, scarpe*) to wear out; (*occhi*) to become ruined; (*nervi*) to go
▶ **logorarsi** VR (*persona*) to wear o.s. out
logorio, rii [logo'rio] SM wear and tear, strain; **il logorio della vita moderna** the stresses and strains *pl* of life today
logoro, a ['logoro] AGG (*scarpe*) worn (out); (*abiti, tappeto*) worn out, threadbare, shabby; (*fig: occhi, vista*) ruined; (*: aspetto*) worn out, exhausted; **indossava un cappotto logoro** he was wearing a shabby overcoat
logorroico, a, ci, che [logor'rɔiko] AGG (*che parla troppo*) loquacious
logout [lo'gaut] SM INV (*Inform*) logout
Loira ['lɔira] SF: **la Loira** the Loire
lombaggine [lom'baddʒine] SF (*Med*) lumbago
Lombardia [lombar'dia] SF Lombardy
▷ www.regione.lombardia.it/
lombardo, a [lom'bardo] AGG, SM/F Lombard
lombare [lom'bare] AGG (*Anat, Med*) lumbar
lombata [lom'bata] SF (*Culin*) loin
lombo ['lombo] SM (*Anat, Culin*) loin
lombrico, chi [lom'briko] SM earthworm
londinese [londi'nese] AGG London *attr*; **il traffico londinese** London traffic; **la vita londinese** life in London
■ SM/F Londoner
Londra ['londra] SF London; **domani vado a Londra** I'm going to London tomorrow; **abita a Londra** he lives in London
long. ABBR (= **longitudine**) long. (= *longitude*)
longanime [lon'ganime] AGG forbearing
longanimità [longanimi'ta] SF forbearance
longevità [londʒevi'ta] SF longevity
longevo, a [lon'dʒɛvo] AGG long-lived
longherone [longe'rone] SM (*Tecn*) metal strut; (*Aer*) longeron
longilineo, a [londʒi'lineo] AGG long-limbed
longitudinale [londʒitudi'nale] AGG longitudinal
longitudinalmente [londʒitudinal'mente] AVV longways, lengthways
longitudine [londʒi'tudine] SF longitude
longobardo, a [longo'bardo] AGG Longobardic
■ SM/F Longobard
long playing ['lɔŋ pleiiŋ] SM INV long-playing record, LP

Ll

lontanamente [lontana'mente] AVV remotely; **non ci pensavo neppure lontanamente** it didn't even occur to me

lontananza [lonta'nantsa] SF (*distanza*) distance; (*assenza*) absence; **in lontananza** in the distance; **vedo una macchina in lontananza** I can see a car in the distance; **la lontananza da casa lo faceva soffrire** being away from home made him unhappy

lontano, a [lon'tano] AGG **1** (*nello spazio, nel tempo*) distant, faraway, far-off; (*di parentela*) distant; **paesi lontani** distant countries; **sento delle voci lontane** I can hear distant voices; **lontano da** far from, a long way from; **essere ben lontano dal pensare che...** to be far from thinking that ...; **tenere qn lontano** to keep sb at a distance; **tenersi lontano da** to keep one's distance from; **lontano dagli occhi lontano dal cuore** (*Proverbio*) out of sight out of mind; **il giorno della sua partenza non era lontano** the day when he was due to leave was not far off *o* away; **amici lontani** absent friends; **siamo parenti alla lontana** we are distantly related; **i nostri ricordi più lontani** our earliest memories; **i tempi lontani dell'università** those far-off days at university; **terre lontane** faraway places **2** (*vago*) vague, slight
■ AVV far; **è lontano** it's a long way; **il mare non è lontano da qui** the sea isn't far from here; **è lontano 10 chilometri** it's 10 kilometres away; **la città è ancora molto lontana** the city is still a long way off; **più lontano** farther, further; **la città più lontana dal mare** the city farthest from the sea; **è più lontano di quanto pensassi** it's farther than I thought; **è meno lontano di quello che pensi** it's not as far as you think; **abita lontano** he lives a long way away, he lives a long way from here; **abiti lontano dalla scuola?** do you live far from school?; **da lontano** from a distance; **da lontano mi sembravi tuo fratello** from a distance you looked like your brother; **vengo da lontano** I've come quite a distance; **lontano nel passato** far back in the past; **lontano nel futuro** in the distant future; **andar lontano** (*anche fig*) to go far; **mirare lontano** (*fig*) to aim high; **vedere lontano** (*fig*) to see far ahead

lontra ['lontra] SF otter

lonza ['lontsa] SF (*Culin*) loin of pork

loquace [lo'kwatʃe] AGG talkative, loquacious; (*fig: occhiata, gesto*) expressive, eloquent

loquacemente [lokwatʃe'mente] AVV (*vedi agg*) loquaciously; eloquently

loquacità [lokwatʃi'ta] SF talkativeness, loquacity

lordo, a ['lordo] AGG **1** (*Comm: peso, stipendio*) gross **2** (*sporco*) dirty, filthy; **lordo di sangue** bloody
■ SM: **al lordo d'imposta** before tax

Lorena [lo'rɛna] SF Lorraine

loro[1] ['loro] PRON PERS PL **1** (*complemento*) them; **chiedi (a) loro** ask them; **disse loro che non sarebbe venuto** he told them he wouldn't be coming; **ho spedito loro una cartolina** I sent them a postcard; **sono venuto con loro** I came with them; **dimmi qualcosa di loro** tell me something about them; **senza di loro** without them; **loro qui non li voglio** I don't want them here **2** (*sogg: al posto di "essi", "esse", con valore enfatico*) they; **loro abitano qui** they live here; **loro sono meglio di te** they are better than you; **vengono anche loro?** are they coming too?; **prendeteli, sono loro** catch them, they're the ones; **sono loro, apri la porta** it's them, open the door; **sono stati loro a dirmelo** they told me themselves, it was they (*frm*) *o* them who told me; **hanno ragione loro, non tu** they are right, not you; **neanche loro hanno tutti i torti** even they aren't completely in the wrong; **non lo sapevano nemmeno loro** they didn't even know it themselves **3** (*nelle comparazioni: sogg*) they, them; (*: complemento*) them; **ne so quanto loro** I know as much as they do, I know as much as them

loro[2] ['loro] PRON PERS PL (*forma di cortesia: anche:* **Loro**) **1** you; **loro capiscono quanto ciò sia penoso** you are aware of how distressing that is; **chiedo lor signori di seguirmi** be so good as to follow me, (if you would) gentlemen **2** (*nelle comparazioni*) you

loro[3] ['loro] AGG POSS INV: **il(la) loro** *or* **i(le) loro** **1** their; **i loro amici** their friends; **un loro amico** a friend of theirs; **verranno con la loro macchina** they'll come in their car; **è colpa loro** it's their fault **2** (*forma di cortesia: anche:* **Loro**) your
■ PRON POSS INV: **il(la) loro** *or* **i(le) loro** **1** theirs; **questi libri sono i loro** those books are theirs; **di chi è questo? – è loro** whose is this? – it's theirs; **la nostra casa è più grande della loro** our house is bigger than theirs **2** (*forma di cortesia: anche:* **Loro**) yours **3** **vivono del loro** they live on what they have; **i loro** (*famiglia*) their family; (*amici*) their own people; **siamo dei loro** *o* **stiamo dalla loro** (*parte*) we're on their side, we're with them; **vogliono sempre dire la loro** they've always got something to say; **ne hanno fatto un'altra delle loro** they've (gone and) done it again

losanga, ghe [lo'zanga] SF lozenge

Los Angeles [los 'andʒeles] SF Los Angeles

Losanna [lo'zanna] SF Lausanne

loscamente [loska'mente] AVV suspiciously

losco, a, schi, sche ['losko] AGG **1** (*occhiata, aspetto*) sullen, surly **2** (*fig: equivoco: persona, affare*) shady, suspicious; **un tipo losco** a shady character
■ SM: **qui c'è del losco** I smell a rat

loto ['lɔto] SM lotus

lotta ['lɔtta] SF (*combattimento*) fight, struggle; (*conflitto*) conflict; (*Sport*) wrestling; **essere in lotta (con)** to be in conflict (with); **fare la lotta (con)** to wrestle (with); **lotta all'ultimo sangue** (*anche fig*) fight to the death; **lotta mortale** mortal combat
■ **lotta armata** armed struggle; **lotta di classe** (*Pol*) class struggle; **lotta contro la droga** war against drugs; **lotta corpo a corpo** hand-to-hand combat; **lotta libera** (*Sport*) all-in wrestling, freestyle; **lotta per la sopravvivenza** struggle *o* fight for survival
▷ www.fijlkam.it/

lottare [lot'tare] VI (*aus* **avere**): **lottare (con *o* contro)** to fight (with *o* against), struggle (with *o* against); (*Sport*) to wrestle; **dobbiamo lottare per i nostri diritti** we must fight for our rights; **ha sempre lottato contro il razzismo** she's always fought against racism; **lottare contro il sonno** to struggle to keep awake; **lottare con la morte** to battle against death

lottatore, trice [lotta'tore] SM/F fighter; (*Sport*) wrestler

lotteria [lotte'ria] SF lottery; (*di gara ippica*) sweepstake; **vincere alla lotteria** to win the lottery; **lotteria istantanea** instant lottery

lottizzare [lottid'dzare] VT (*terreno*) to divide into plots; (*fig*) to share out

lottizzazione [lottiddzat'tsjone] SF (*di terreno*) division into plots; (*fig*) share-out

lotto[1] ['lɔtto] SM (*gen*) lot; (*di terreno*) plot; **lotto fabbricabile *o* edificabile** building lot

lotto[2] ['lɔtto] SM (*gioco*) (state) lottery; **vincere un**

terno al lotto (*anche fig*) to hit the jackpot

LOTTO

The **Lotto** is a lottery authorized and run by the Finance Ministry. It takes the form of a weekly extraction of numbers and can be played by buying a ticket from official outlets called "ricevitorie". Part of the proceeds goes to the Culture Ministry to support cultural activities.
▷ www.giocodellotto.com/

Louisiana [lui'zjana] SF Louisiana
love story [lʌv'stɔ:ri] SF INV affair
lozione [lot'tsjone] SF lotion
LP [ɛlle'pi] SIGLA M (= **long playing**) LP
LSD [ɛlleesse'di] SIGLA M LSD (= *Lysergic Acid Diethylamide*)
L.st. ABBR (= **lire sterline**) £
LSU [ɛlleɛsse'u] SIGLA M INV (= **Lavoratore Socialmente Utile**) *person employed by a public body to carry out socially useful work*
LT SIGLA = *Latina*
LU SIGLA = *Lucca*
lubrificante [lubrifi'kante] AGG lubricating
■SM lubricant
lubrificare [lubrifi'kare] VT to lubricate
lubrificazione [lubrifikat'tsjone] SF lubrication
lucano, a [lu'kano] AGG of *o* from Lucania
■SM/F inhabitant *o* native of Lucania
lucchese [luk'kese] AGG of *o* from Lucca
■SM/F inhabitant *o* native of Lucca
lucchetto [luk'ketto] SM padlock
luccicante [luttʃi'kante] AGG (*vedi vb*) sparkling; twinkling; glittering; glistening
luccicare [luttʃi'kare] VI (*aus* **avere**) (*gen*) to sparkle; (*stella*) to twinkle; (*oro*) to glitter; (*occhi*) to glisten; **non è tutt'oro quel che luccica** (*Proverbio*) all that glitters is not gold
luccichio, chii [luttʃi'kio] SM (*vedi vb*) sparkling; twinkling; glittering; glistening
luccicone [luttʃi'kone] SM: **avere i lucciconi agli occhi** to have tears in one's eyes
luccio, ci ['luttʃo] SM (*pesce*) pike
lucciola ['luttʃola] SF **1** (*Zool*) firefly, glow-worm; **prendere lucciole per lanterne** to get hold of the wrong end of the stick **2** (*euf*: *prostituta*) working girl
luce ['lutʃe] SF **1** (*gen*) light; **alla luce del giorno** in daylight; **luce del sole/della luna** sun/moonlight; **accendere/spegnere la luce** to turn *o* switch the light on/off; **fare luce su qc** (*fig*) to shed *o* throw light on sth; **mettere in luce** (*fig*) to spotlight, highlight; **mettere qn in buona/cattiva luce** (*fig*) to put sb in a good/bad light; **fare qc alla luce del sole** (*fig*) to do sth in the open; **dare alla luce** (*bambino*) to give birth to; **venire alla luce** (*fatto*) to come to light; (*bambino*) to come into the world; **alla luce di questi fatti** in the light of this; **luci della ribalta** (*Teatro*) footlights **2** (*Aut*): **luci di arresto** brake lights; **luci di emergenza** hazard warning lights; **luci di posizione** sidelights (*Brit*), parking lights (*Am*); **luci di retromarcia** reversing lights **3** (*Archit*: *di ponte, arco*) span; (*finestra*) window; **negozio a una luce** shop with one window
lucente [lu'tʃɛnte] AGG shining
lucentezza [lutʃen'tettsa] SF shine
lucerna [lu'tʃɛrna] SF oil lamp
lucernario, ri [lutʃer'narjo] SM skylight
lucertola [lu'tʃɛrtola] SF (*animale*) lizard; (*pellame*) lizardskin
lucertolone [lutʃerto'lone] SM (*iguana*) iguana; (*ramarro*) green lizard
lucherino [luke'rino] SM (*uccello*) siskin
lucidalabbra [lutʃida'labbra] SM INV lip gloss
lucidare [lutʃi'dare] VT **1** (*mobili, scarpe, pavimenti*) to polish **2** (*ricalcare*: *disegno*) to trace
lucidatrice [lutʃida'tritʃe] SF floor polisher
lucidatura [lutʃida'tura] SF polishing
lucidità [lutʃidi'ta] SF lucidity
lucido, a ['lutʃido] AGG **1** shining, bright; **occhi lucidi di pianto/per la febbre** eyes bright with tears/with fever; **una camicia di raso nero lucido** a shiny black satin blouse **2** (*pavimento, argento, scarpe*) polished; **è lucido come uno specchio** you can see your face in it **3** (*mente, discorso*) lucid, clear; (*malato*) lucid; **è ancora lucido** he's still lucid
■SM **1** (*lucentezza*) shine, lustre (*Brit*), luster (*Am*); **perdere il lucido** to lose its shine **2** (*sostanza*) polish; **lucido da scarpe** shoe polish **3** (*disegno, ricalco*) tracing; **carta da lucido** tracing paper
lucignolo [lu'tʃiɲɲolo] SM wick
lucrare [lu'krare] VT to make money (out of)
lucrativo, a [lukra'tivo] AGG lucrative; **organizzazione non lucrativa** non-profit organization
lucro ['lukro] SM profit, gain; **a scopo di lucro** for gain; **organizzazione a scopo di lucro** profit-making organization
lucroso, a [lu'kroso] AGG lucrative, profitable
luculliano, a [lukul'ljano] AGG (*pasto*) sumptuous
ludibrio [lu'dibrjo] SM **1** (*scherno*) mockery, scorn **2** (*zimbello*) laughing stock
ludoteca, che [ludo'tɛka] SF toy library
lue ['lue] SF (*Med*) syphilis
luglio ['luʎʎo] SM July; **nel mese di luglio** in July *o* in the month of July; **il primo luglio** the first of July; **arrivare il 2 luglio** to arrive on the 2nd of July; **all'inizio/alla fine di luglio** at the beginning/at the end of July; **durante il mese di luglio** during July; **a luglio del prossimo anno** in July (of) next year; **ogni anno a luglio** every July; **che fai a luglio?** what are you doing in July?; **è piovuto molto a luglio quest'anno** July was very wet this year
lugubre ['lugubre] AGG gloomy, dismal; **un'atmosfera lugubre** a gloomy atmosphere
lugubremente [lugubre'mente] AVV gloomily, dismally
lui ['lui] PRON PERS M **1** (*complemento*: *dopo prep, con valore enfatico*) him; **sono venuto con lui** I came with him; **dimmi qualcosa di lui** tell me something about him; **senza di lui** without him; **se non fosse per lui** if it were not for him; **hanno accusato lui, non me** they accused him, not me; **chiedilo a lui** ask him; **lui qui non lo voglio** I don't want him here **2** (*sogg*: *al posto di 'egli', con valore enfatico*) he; **lui è meglio di te** he is better than you; **viene anche lui?** is he coming too?; **prendetelo, è lui** catch him, he's the one; **è lui, apri la porta** it's him, open the door; **è stato lui a dirmelo** he told me himself, it was he who told me; **ha ragione lui, non tu** he's right, not you; **neanche lui ha tutti i torti** even he isn't completely in the wrong; **non lo sapeva nemmeno lui** he didn't even know it himself **3** (*nelle comparazioni*: *sogg*) he, him; **ne so quanto lui** I know as much as he does, I know as much as him
■SM INV (*scherz*): **il mio lui** my beloved

luì [lu'i] SM (*uccello*) willow warbler

lumaca, che [lu'maka] SF (*Zool*) slug; (*fam*) (: *chiocciola*) snail; (*fig*) slowcoach (*Brit*), slowpoke (*Am*); **a passo di lumaca** at a snail's pace

lumacone [luma'kone] SM (*Zool*) (large) slug; (*fig*) slowcoach (*Brit*), slowpoke (*Am*)

lume ['lume] SM **1** (*gen*) light; **a lume di candela** by candlelight; **a lume di naso** by rule of thumb; **chiedere lumi a qn** (*fig*) to ask sb for advice; **perdere il lume della ragione** to be blinded by rage **2** (*lampada*) lamp; **lume a olio** oil lamp

lumicino [lumi'tʃino] SM small *o* faint light; **essere (ridotto) al lumicino** to be at death's door

luminaria [lumi'narja] SF (*per feste*) illuminations *pl*

luminescente [lumineʃ'ʃente] AGG luminescent

luminescenza [lumineʃ'ʃentsa] SF luminescence

lumino [lu'mino] SM small light; **lumino da notte** night-light; **lumino per i morti** candle for the dead

luminosamente [luminosa'mente] AVV brightly

luminosità [luminosi'ta] SF brightness; (*fig: di sorriso, volto*) radiance; **c'è una luminosità diffusa sopra la città** there's a hazy glow over the city

luminoso, a [lumi'noso] AGG **1** (*gen*) luminous; (*sorgente*) of light, light *attr*; (*fig: sorriso, volto*) radiant; **insegna luminosa** neon sign **2** (*cielo, occhi, avvenire, idea*) bright; (*sorriso, viso*) bright, radiant; **il soggiorno è molto luminoso** the living room is very bright

lun. ABBR (= lunedì) Mon.

luna ['luna] SF moon; **una notte di luna** a moonlit night; **avere la luna** to be in a bad mood; **svegliarsi con la luna** (*fig*) to get out of bed on the wrong side; **chiedere la luna** to ask for the moon; **luna di miele** honeymoon; **luna nuova** new moon; **luna piena** full moon

luna park ['luna 'park] SM INV amusement park, funfair

lunare [lu'nare] AGG lunar, moon *attr*; **paesaggio lunare** (*fig*) lunar landscape

lunaria [lu'narja] SF (*pietra*) moonstone

lunario, ri [lu'narjo] SM almanac; **sbarcare il lunario** (*fig*) to make ends meet; **riesco a malapena a sbarcare il lunario** I can only just make ends meet

lunatico, a, ci, che [lu'natiko] AGG quirky, temperamental
■ SM/F temperamental person

> **LO SAPEVI...?**
> **lunatico** non si traduce mai con la parola inglese *lunatic*

lunedì [lune'di] SM INV Monday; **lunedì dell'Angelo** Easter Monday; *per fraseologia vedi* **martedì**

lunetta [lu'netta] SF (*Archit*) lunette

lunga ['lunga] SF *vedi* **lungo** SF

lungaggine [lun'gaddʒine] SF slowness; **le lungaggini della burocrazia** red tape *sg*

lungamente [lunga'mente] AVV (*a lungo*) for a long time; (*diffusamente*) at length; **un figlio lungamente atteso** a long-awaited child; **dopo aver lungamente sofferto** after long suffering

lungarno [lun'garno] SM *embankment along the Arno*

lunghezza [lun'gettsa] SF length; **lunghezza: 20 cm** length: 20 cm; **il lungomare si estende per una lunghezza di 5 km** the promenade stretches for 5 km; **nel senso della lunghezza** lengthways, along its length; **vincere per una lunghezza** (*cavallo*) to win by a length; **lunghezza d'onda** wavelength

lungi ['lundʒi] **lungi da** PREP far from; **lungi da me l'idea di offenderti!** far be it from me to offend you!; **lungi dall'essere** far from being

lungimirante [lundʒimi'rante] AGG far-sighted

lungimiranza [lundʒimi'rantsa] SF far-sightedness

lungo, a, ghi, ghe ['lungo] AGG **1** (*gen*) long; (*persona*) tall; (*viaggio*) lengthy; **è lungo quattro metri** it's four metres long; **questa gonna è troppo lunga** this skirt is too long; **hanno fatto una lunga passeggiata** they went for a long walk; **una fila di macchine lunga 2 km** a tailback of cars 2 km long; **amici da lunga data** long-standing *o* old friends; **lo conosco da lungo tempo** I've known him for a long time; **un discorso lungo 2 ore** a 2-hour speech **2** (*lento: persona*) slow; **essere lungo a *o* nel fare qc** to be slow at doing sth, take a long time to do sth; **essere lungo come la fame** to be a slowcoach (*Brit*) *o* slowpoke (*Am*) **3** (*diluito: caffè*) weak, watery; (*brodo*) thin **4** (*fraseologia*): **avere la barba lunga** to be unshaven; **avere le mani lunghe** to be light-fingered; **fare il passo più lungo della gamba** to bite off more than one can chew; **cadere lungo disteso** to measure one's length on the ground; **fare la faccia lunga *o* il muso lungo *o* il viso lungo** to pull a long face; **a lunga gittata** (*Mil*) long-range; **saperla lunga** (*fam*) to know a thing or two, know what's what; **a lunga scadenza** long term; **a lungo andare** in the long run, in the end; **a lungo andare si stuferà** he'll get fed up with it in the end
■ SM length; **per il lungo** along its length, lengthways; **in lungo e in largo** (*girare, cercare*) far and wide, everywhere; **l'ho cercato in lungo e in largo** I looked for it everywhere; **a lungo** (*aspettare*) for a long time; (*spiegare*) in great detail; **abbiamo parlato a lungo** we talked for a long time
■ SF: **di gran lunga** far and away; **è di gran lunga il migliore** it's far and away the best, it's the best by far; **andare per le lunghe** to drag on; **alla lunga** in the long run, in the end; **alla lunga si stuferà** he'll get fed up with it in the end
■ PREP (*spazio*) along, beside; (*tempo*) during; **camminare lungo il fiume** to walk along *o* beside the river; **lungo il corso dei secoli** throughout the centuries, in the course of the centuries; **lungo il viaggio** during the journey

lungodegente [lungode'dʒɛnte] SM/F elderly long-stay patient

lungofiume [lungo'fjume] SM embankment

lungolago [lungo'lago] SM *road round a lake*

lungolinea [lungo'linea] SM INV (*Tennis*) down-the-line shot

lungomare [lungo'mare] SM promenade

lungometraggio, gi [lungome'traddʒo] SM (*Cine*) feature film

lungotevere [lungo'tevere] SM *embankment along the Tiber*

lunotto [lu'nɔtto] SM (*Aut*) rear *o* back window; **lunotto termico** heated rear window

luogo, ghi ['lwɔgo] SM **1** (*gen*) place; **in ogni luogo** everywhere; **in qualsiasi luogo** anywhere; **in qualsiasi luogo vada** wherever you go; **in nessun luogo** nowhere; **sul luogo** on the spot; **fuori luogo** (*fig*) out of place, inopportune; **uno del luogo** a native, a local **2** (*fraseologia*): **aver luogo** to take place; **l'incontro ha avuto luogo a maggio** the meeting took place in May; **far luogo a** to give way to, make room for; **dar luogo a** (*critiche, dubbi*) to give rise to; **in luogo di** in place of, instead of; **in primo/secondo luogo** in the first/second place; **non luogo a procedere** (*Dir*) nonsuit

■ **luogo comune** commonplace, cliché; **luogo del delitto** scene of the crime; **luogo geometrico** locus; **luogo di nascita** (*gen*) birthplace; (*Amm*) place of birth; **luogo di origine** *o* **di provenienza** place of origin; **luogo di pena** penitentiary (*Am*), prison; **luogo pubblico** public place

luogotenente [lwogote'nεnte] SM (*Mil, fig*) lieutenant

lupa ['lupa] SF she-wolf

lupacchiotto [lupak'kjɔtto] SM (*Zool*) (wolf) cub

lupara [lu'para] SF (*fucile*) sawn-off shotgun

luparia [lu'parja] SF (*pianta*) globeflower

lupetto [lu'petto] SM (*Zool*) (wolf) cub; (*negli scouts*) cub (scout)

lupinella [lupi'nεlla] SF (*pianta*) sainfoin

lupino [lu'pino] SM (*pianta*) lupin

lupo ['lupo] SM wolf; **cane lupo** alsatian (*Brit*), German shepherd; **avere una fame da lupi** to be ravenous *o* famished; **gridare al lupo** to cry wolf; **tempo da lupi** filthy weather; **in bocca al lupo!** good luck!; **il lupo perde il pelo ma non il vizio** (*Proverbio*) the leopard cannot change its spots; **lupo mannaro** (*licantropo*) werewolf; **lupo di mare** (*fig*) old salt, sea dog

luppolo ['luppolo] SM (*pianta*) hop

lurido, a ['lurido] AGG (*anche fig*) filthy, foul

> **LO SAPEVI...?**
> **lurido** non si traduce mai con la parola inglese ***lurid***

luridume [luri'dume] SM filth

lusco ['lusko] SM: **tra il lusco e il brusco** at dusk

lusinga, ghe [lu'zinga] SF flattery; **con la lusinga di un lauto stipendio** with the promise of a high salary; **non mi convincerai con le lusinghe** flattery will get you nowhere

lusingare [luzin'gare] VT (*adulare*) to flatter; **si è fatto lusingare dalle promesse di una brillante carriera** he let himself be swayed by promises of a brilliant career; **lusingatissimo!** (*onorato*) I'm honoured!

lusinghiero, a [luzin'gjεro] AGG flattering

lussare [lus'sare] VT (*Med*) to dislocate

lussazione [lussat'tsjone] SF (*Med*) dislocation

lussemburghese [lussembur'gese] AGG of *o* from Luxembourg

■ SM/F native *o* inhabitant of Luxembourg

Lussemburgo [lussem'burgo] SM (*stato*) Luxembourg
■ SF (*città*) Luxembourg

lusso ['lusso] SM luxury; **di lusso** (*macchina, appartamento*) luxury *attr*; (*prodotto*) de luxe *attr*; **vivere nel lusso più sfacciato** to live in unashamed luxury; **non posso permettermi il lusso di una vacanza** I can't afford the luxury of a holiday; **andare di lusso** (*fam*) to go like a dream

lussuosamente [lussuosa'mente] AVV luxuriously

lussuoso, a [lussu'oso] AGG luxurious; **un albergo lussuoso** a luxury hotel

lussureggiante [lussured'dʒante] AGG (*vegetazione, pianta*) luxuriant; (*fig: stile*) profuse, rich

lussureggiare [lussured'dʒare] VI (*aus* **avere**) to be luxuriant

lussuria [lus'surja] SF lust

> **LO SAPEVI...?**
> **lussuria** non si traduce mai con la parola inglese ***luxury***

lussuriosamente [lussurjosa'mente] AVV lasciviously

lussurioso, a [lussu'rjoso] AGG lascivious, lustful

> **LO SAPEVI...?**
> **lussurioso** non si traduce mai con la parola inglese ***luxurious***

lustrare [lus'trare] VT (*mobili, pavimenti*) to polish; (*scarpe*) to polish, shine

lustrascarpe [lustras'karpe] SM/F INV shoeshine

lustrino [lus'trino] SM sequin

lustro, a ['lustro] AGG (*superficie*) shiny; (*capelli, pelo*) glossy; (*occhi*) moist
■ SM **1** shine, gloss **2** (*fig: gloria*) prestige, glory **3** (*quinquennio*) five-year period

luteranesimo [lutera'nezimo] SM Lutheranism

luterano, a [lute'rano] AGG, SM/F Lutheran

Lutero [lu'tero] SM Luther

lutreola [lu'trεola] SF (*Zool*) European mink

lutto ['lutto] SM (*gen*) mourning; (*perdita*) loss, bereavement; **essere in/portare il lutto** to be in/ wear mourning; **un lutto nazionale** an occasion for national mourning; **è stato un grave lutto per il paese** it was a great loss to the country

luttuoso, a [luttu'oso] AGG sad, mournful

Mm

M, m [ˈɛmme] SF O M INV (*lettera*) M, m; **M come Milano** ≈ M for Mary (*Brit*), ≈ M for Mike (*Am*)

M. ABBR = **mare, monte**

M [ˈɛmme] SIGLA F (*taglia*) M (= *medium*)

m [ˈɛmme] ABBR = **metro**

m. ABBR = **mese, miglio**

ma [ma] CONG but; (*tuttavia*) yet, still, but; (*comunque*) however; **mi piacerebbe venire ma non posso** I would love to come but I can't; **non solo non beve più ma ha anche smesso di fumare** he's not just given up drinking, he's stopped smoking too; **hanno fatto quel che potevano ma non sono riusciti a salvarlo** they did what they could, but they couldn't save him; **non se lo merita ma dovremmo cercare di capirlo** even though he doesn't deserve it, we should try to understand him; **ma non se lo merita** he doesn't deserve it though; **incredibile ma vero** incredible but true; **ma si può sapere che cosa vuoi?** just what do you want?; **ma smettila!** give over!, stop it!; **ma va'?** (*dubitativo*) really?; (*esclamazione*) surely not!; **ma davvero?** really?; **ma sì!** (*certo*) yes, of course!; **ma no!** of course not!; **ti dispiace? — ma no!** do you mind? — of course I don't!; **ma insomma!** for goodness sake!; **ma insomma, vuoi smetterla?** stop it, for heaven's sake!

■ SM INV but; **ci sono ancora dei ma** there are still some uncertainties; **non c'è ma che tenga** I'm not going to take no for an answer

ma' [ma] SF (*fam*) mum, mom (*Am*)

macabro, a [ˈmakabro] AGG macabre, gruesome

■ SM: **il gusto del macabro** a taste for the macabre

macaco, chi [maˈkako] SM (*Zool*) macaque; (*fig fam*) clod

macadam [makaˈdam] SM macadam

macadamizzare [makadamidˈdzare] VT to macadamize

macarena [makaˈrɛna] SF Macarena

macché [makˈke] ESCL (*fam*) certainly not!, you must be joking!; **avete finito il lavoro? — macché!, abbiamo appena incominciato!** have you finished the work? — you must be joking, we've hardly started!; **sei innamorata di lui? — macché! è solo un amico** are you in love with him? — of course not! he's just a friend

maccheroni [makkeˈroni] SMPL macaroni *sg*; **sono buoni i maccheroni?** is the macaroni nice?

maccheronico, a, ci, che [makkeˈrɔniko] AGG (*latino, greco*) macaronic; (*pegg*) abysmal

macchia¹ [ˈmakkja] SF **1** (*chiazza*) mark, spot; (*sulla pelle*) blotch, mark; (*sul pelo*) patch; (*di sporco*) stain, mark; **macchie di colore** splashes of colour; **coprirsi di macchie** (*pelle*) to come out in a rash; **a macchie** spotted; **estendersi a macchia d'olio** (*fig: rivolta, epidemia*) to spread rapidly; (*: città*) to grow rapidly; **macchia di caffè** coffee stain; **macchia di grasso** greasy mark, grease stain; **macchia d'inchiostro** ink stain; (*su foglio*) (ink) blot; **macchia di sangue** bloodstain; **macchia di vino** wine stain; **macchie solari** (*Astron*) sunspots **2** (*fig: su reputazione*) blot, stain

macchia² [ˈmakkja] SF (*boscaglia*) scrub; **darsi/vivere alla macchia** (*fig*) to go into/live in hiding

macchiare [makˈkjare] VT **1** (*sporcare: tovaglia, camicia*) to stain; (*con inchiostro: quaderno*) to blot; (*fig: reputazione*) to sully, tarnish; **hai macchiato la tovaglia di caffè** you've got coffee on the tablecloth; **la birra non macchia** beer doesn't stain *o* leave a mark; **mi sono macchiata il vestito** I've got a stain on my dress **2 macchiare il caffè (col latte)** to add a drop of milk to (one's) coffee

▶ **macchiarsi** VIP (*persona*) to get stains *o* marks on one's clothes, get o.s. dirty; (*tessuto*) to get stained *o* marked; **ti sei macchiato tutto!** you've got yourself all dirty!; **macchiarsi di un delitto** to be guilty of a crime

macchiato, a [makˈkjato] AGG **1** (*gen*): **macchiato (di)** stained (with); **caffè macchiato** espresso coffee with a dash of milk; **i suoi vestiti erano macchiati di fango** his clothes were stained with mud **2** (*pelo*) spotted

macchietta [makˈkjetta] SF **1** (*piccola macchia*) spot **2** (*vignetta, Teatro*) caricature; (*fig: persona*) character

macchiettista, i, e [makkjetˈtista] SM/F caricaturist

macchina [ˈmakkina] SF **1** (*automobile*) car; **salire in macchina** to get into the car; **andare/venire in**

macchina to go/come by car; **ci andate in macchina o in treno?** are you going there by car or by train? **2** *(gen, fig)* machine; *(motore, locomotiva)* engine; **sala macchine** *(Naut)* engine room; **la macchina funziona premendo il pulsante** the machine works when you press the button; **la macchina burocratica** the bureaucratic machinery; **scrivere a macchina** to type; **macchina bellica** war machine; **andare in macchina** *(Stampa)* to go to press
■ **macchina per caffè** espresso (machine); **macchina da corsa** racing car; **macchina da cucire** sewing machine; **macchina fotografica** camera; **macchina da presa** cine *o* movie camera; **macchina da scrivere** typewriter; **macchina utensile** machine tool; **macchina a vapore** steam engine

macchinalmente [makkinal'mente] AVV mechanically

macchinare [makki'nare] VT to plot

macchinario, ri [makki'narjo] SM machinery; **macchinari** SMPL machinery *no pl*

macchinata [makki'nata] SF *(fam: carico di lavatrice o lavastoviglie)* load

macchinazione [makkinat'tsjone] SF plot, machination

macchinetta [makki'netta] SF *(fam: caffettiera)* espresso coffee maker; *(: accendino)* lighter; *(: per il taglio dei capelli)* hair clippers; *(: per i denti)* brace; **parlare come una macchinetta** *(fig)* to talk nineteen to the dozen

macchinista, i [makki'nista] SM *(di treno)* engine-driver; *(di nave)* engineer; *(Teatro, Cine, TV)* stagehand

macchinoso, a [makki'noso] AGG complex, complicated

macedone [ma'tʃedone] SM/F, AGG Macedonian

Macedonia [matʃe'dɔnja] SF Macedonia

macedonia [matʃe'dɔnja] SF *(Culin)* fruit salad

macellaio, ai [matʃel'lajo] SM *(anche fig)* butcher

macellare [matʃel'lare] VT *(anche fig)* to slaughter, butcher

macellazione [matʃellat'tsjone] SF slaughtering, butchering

macelleria [matʃelle'ria] SF butcher's (shop); **sono andato in macelleria** I went to the butcher's

macello [ma'tʃɛllo] SM **1** *(mattatoio)* slaughterhouse, abattoir *(Brit)* **2** *(azione, anche fig)* slaughter, massacre; **mandare al macello** *(soldati)* to send to their deaths **3** *(fig fam: disordine)* mess, shambles *sg*; *(: disastro)* disaster; **è un macello!** it's a disaster!

macerare [matʃe'rare] VT *(canapa, carta)* to macerate; *(Culin)* to marinate
▶ **macerarsi** VR *(consumarsi)*: **macerarsi nel rimorso** to be consumed with remorse

maceratese [matʃera'tese] AGG of *o* from Macerata
■ SM/F inhabitant *o* native of Macerata

macerazione [matʃerat'tsjone] SF maceration

macerie [ma'tʃɛrje] SFPL rubble *sg*, debris *sg*

macero ['matʃero] SM *(operazione)* pulping; *(stabilimento)* pulping mill; **carta da macero** paper for pulping

mach [makh] SM INV Mach (number)

machete [ma'tʃete] SM INV machete

machiavellicamente [makjavellika'mente] AVV craftily

machiavellico, a, ci, che [makja'vɛlliko] AGG *(anche fig)* Machiavellian

macho ['matʃo] AGG INV macho
■ SM INV macho type

macigno [ma'tʃiɲɲo] SM *(masso)* rock, boulder; **duro come un macigno** as hard as rock

macilento, a [matʃi'lɛnto] AGG emaciated

macina ['matʃina] SF *(pietra)* millstone; *(macchina)* grinder

macinacaffè [matʃinakaf'fɛ] SM INV coffee grinder, coffee mill

macinapepe [matʃina'pepe] SM INV pepper mill

macinare [matʃi'nare] VT *(grano, caffè)* to grind; *(carne)* to mince *(Brit)*, grind *(Am)*; **caffè macinato** ground coffee; **carne macinata** mince; **macinare i chilometri** to eat up the miles

macinato [matʃi'nato] SM **1** *(cereali, farina)* meal **2** *(carne)* mince, minced *(Brit) o* ground *(Am)* meat

macinatura [matʃina'tura], **macinazione** [matʃinat'tsjone] SF grinding

macinino [matʃi'nino] SM **1** *(per caffè)* mill, coffee grinder; *(per pepe)* mill, pepper mill **2** *(scherz: macchina)* old banger *(Brit)*, clunker *(Am)*

maciste [ma'tʃiste] SM *(scherz)* colossus

maciullare [matʃul'lare] VT *(canapa, lino)* to brake; *(fig: braccio ecc)* to crush

macramè [makra'mɛ] SM macramé

macro... ['makro] PREF macro...

macro ['makro] SF INV *(Inform)* macro; *(Fot)* macro lens

macrobiotica [makrobi'ɔtika] SF macrobiotics *sg*

macrobiotico, a, ci, che [makrobi'ɔtiko] AGG *(dieta, alimenti)* macrobiotic

macroclima, i [makro'klima] SM macroclimate

macrocosmo [makro'kɔzmo] SM macrocosm

macrocriminalità [makrokriminali'ta] SF organized crime

macroeconomia [makroekono'mia] SF macro-economics *sg*

macrofotografia [makrofotogra'fia] SF *(Fot: tecnica)* macrography; *(: singola immagine)* macrograph

macromolecola [makromo'lɛkola] SF macromolecule

macropo ['makropo] SM *(Zool)* red-necked wallaby

macroscopicamente [makroskopika'mente] AVV *(rafforzativo)* glaringly

macroscopico, a, ci, che [makros'kɔpiko] AGG *(dimensione)* macroscopic; *(errore)* glaring

maculato, a [maku'lato] AGG *(pelo)* spotted

madama [ma'dama] SF **1** *(scherz)* madam **2** *(gergo: polizia)* cops *pl*

madamigella [madami'dʒɛlla] SF *(scherz)* young lady

Maddalena [madda'lena] SF *(Rel)* Mary Magdalen(e)

made in Italy SM: **il made in Italy** Italian exports *pl (especially fashion goods)*

Madera [ma'dɛra] SF *(Geog)* Madeira
■ SM INV *(vino)* Madeira

madia ['madja] SF *chest for the making and storage of bread*

madido, a ['madido] AGG *(letter)*: **madido (di)** wet *o* moist (with); **madido di sudore** bathed in sweat

madonna [ma'dɔnna] SF *(Rel)*: **Madonna** Our Lady; *(Arte)* madonna; *(letter, Storia)* my lady, madam; **madonna!** *(fam)* good God!

madonnina [madon'nina] SF *(Arte)* madonna; **con quell'aria da madonnina infilzata** *(iro)* with that look of a demure little madonna

madornale [mador'nale] AGG enormous, huge; **un errore madornale** a huge mistake

madras [ma'dras] SM INV madras cotton

madre ['madre] SF **1** mother; **mia madre** my mother; **la madre dei due bambini** the mother of the two

Mm

children; **la madre di Matteo** Matteo's mother; **senza madre** motherless; **la madre di tutte...** *(fig)* the mother of all ...; **madre adottiva** adoptive mother; **madre coraggio** Mother Courage *(mother who defies the mafia, state etc to defend her child)*; **madre di famiglia** mother; **madre natura** Mother Nature; **madre superiora** *(Rel)* mother superior **2** **madre dell'aceto** mother of vinegar **3** *(matrice di bolletta)* counterfoil
■ AGG INV mother *attr*; **casa madre** *(Rel)* mother house; **ragazza madre** unmarried mother; **regina madre** queen mother; **scena madre** *(Teatro)* principal scene; **ha fatto una scena madre** *(fig)* she made a terrible scene

madrelingua [madre'lingwa] SF mother tongue, native language; **non è di madrelingua inglese** English isn't his mother tongue
■ SM/F INV *(persona)* native speaker; **un madrelingua inglese** an English native speaker

madrepatria [madre'patrja] SF mother country, native land

madreperla [madre'pɛrla] SF mother-of-pearl

madreperlaceo, a [madreper'latʃeo] AGG pearly

madrepora [ma'drɛpora] SF madrepore

Madrid [ma'drid] SF Madrid

madrigale [madri'gale] SM madrigal

madrileno, a [madri'lɛno] AGG of *o* from Madrid
■ SM/F native *o* inhabitant of Madrid

madrina [ma'drina] SF *(di bambino)* godmother; *(di nave)* christener

maestà [maes'ta] SF INV *(gen)* majesty; **Sua Maestà il Re** His Majesty the King; **Sua Maestà la Regina** Her Majesty the Queen

maestosamente [maestosa'mente] AVV majestically

maestosità [maestosi'ta] SF majesty

maestoso, a [maes'toso] AGG majestic

maestra [ma'estra] SF maestra; **maestra di scuola** primary school teacher; **maestra d'asilo** nursery school teacher; **scusi, signora maestra...** miss ...; *vedi anche* **maestro**

maestrale [maes'trale] SM northwest wind, northwesterly
■ AGG northwest *attr*, northwesterly

maestranze [maes'trantse] SFPL workforce *sg*, workers

maestria [maes'tria] SF mastery, skill

maestro, a [ma'ɛstro] SM/F **1** *(anche:* **maestro di scuola** *o* **elementare***)* primary *(Brit) o* grade school *(Am)* teacher; **scusi, signor maestro...** sir ... **2** *(fig: esperto)* expert; **è maestra nella cucina** she's an expert cook; **è stato un colpo da maestro** *(fig)* that was a masterstroke
■ SM **1** *(artigiano)* master; **i Maestri del Rinascimento** the Masters of the Renaissance **2** *(Mus)* maestro **3** *(vento)* northwest wind
■ AGG *(di grande abilità)* masterly, skilful *(Brit)*, skillful *(Am)*; **albero maestro** *(Naut)* main mast; **muro maestro** main wall; **strada maestra** main road
■ **maestra d'asilo** nursery teacher; **maestro di ballo** dancing master; **maestro di cerimonie** master of ceremonies; **maestro d'orchestra** conductor, director *(Am)*; **maestro di piano** piano teacher; **maestro di scherma** fencing master; **maestro di sci** ski *o* skiing instructor

mafia ['mafja] SF Mafia

mafioso, a [ma'fjoso] AGG mafia *attr*
■ SM/F member of the Mafia

maga, ghe ['maga] SF sorceress

magagna [ma'gaɲɲa] SF **1** *(anche fig)* defect, flaw, blemish **2** *(noia, guaio)* problem

magari [ma'gari] ESCL *(esprime desiderio)*: **magari fosse vero!** if only it were true!; **ti piacerebbe andare in Italia? — magari!** would you like to go to Italy? — I certainly would! *o* you bet!; **hai avuto l'aumento? — sì, magari!** did you get the increase? — I should have been so lucky!
■ AVV *(anche)* even; *(forse)* perhaps; **saremo in 5, magari in 6** there will be 5 of us, or maybe 6; **a uscire tutto sudato magari ti prendi un raffreddore** if you go out all sweaty you're likely to *o* you may catch a cold

magazzinaggio, gi [magaddzi'naddʒo] SM storage; **(spese di) magazzinaggio** storage charges *pl*, warehousing charges *pl*

magazziniere [magaddzi'njɛre] SM warehouseman

magazzino [magad'dzino] SM **1** *(deposito)* warehouse; **lo tengono in un magazzino** they keep it in a warehouse; **avere merci in magazzino** to have goods in stock; **fondi di magazzino** unsold stock; **magazzino doganale** bonded warehouse **2** **grande magazzino** department store

maggese [mad'dʒese] SM *(Agr)* fallow field; **lasciare a maggese** to leave fallow

maggio ['maddʒo] SM May; *per fraseologia vedi* **luglio**

maggiolino [maddʒo'lino] SM **1** *(Zool)* cockchafer, May bug **2** *(automobile)* beetle

maggiorana [maddʒo'rana] SF *(Bot)* (sweet) marjoram

maggioranza [maddʒo'rantsa] SF *(gen)* majority; **partito di maggioranza** majority party; **eletto con una maggioranza di** elected by a majority of; **essere in maggioranza** to be in the majority; **nella maggioranza dei casi** in most cases; **la maggioranza di** most; **la maggioranza degli italiani** most Italians, the majority of Italians; **la maggioranza silenziosa** the silent majority; **maggioranza assoluta/relativa** absolute/relative majority; **maggioranza qualificata** qualified majority

maggiorare [maddʒo'rare] VT *(Comm: prezzo, conto)*: **maggiorare (di)** to increase (by)

maggiorazione [maddʒorat'tsjone] SF *(Comm)* rise, increase

maggiordomo [maddʒor'dɔmo] SM butler

maggiore [mad'dʒore] AGG *(comp di* **grande***)* **1** *(più grande)* bigger, larger; *(: di quantità)* greater; **le spese sono state maggiori del previsto** expenses were higher than expected; **con maggiore entusiasmo** with more *o* greater enthusiasm; **ha dimostrato maggior entusiasmo di te** he showed greater enthusiasm than you; **a maggior ragione dovresti parlargli tu** all the more reason for you to speak to him yourself **2** *(più importante)* more important; *(di notevole rilevanza)* major; **opere maggiori** major works **3** *(più anziano: sorella, fratello)* elder, older; **il mio fratello maggiore** my older brother **4** *(di grado)*: **sergente maggiore** sergeant major; **Stato Maggiore** *(Mil)* general staff **5** *(Mus)* major; **do maggiore** C major; **in re maggiore** in D major
■ AGG *(superl di* **grande***)* *(vedi agg comp 1, 2, 3)* biggest, largest; greatest; most important; eldest, oldest; **la maggior parte di** most of; **la maggior parte dei miei amici** most of my friends; **la maggior parte della gente** most people, the majority (of people); **andare per la maggiore** *(cantante, attore ecc)* to be very popular, be "in"; **la maggiore età** majority; **raggiungere la**

maggior età to reach the age of majority; **la maggiore industria automobilistica d'Italia** the biggest car maker in Italy; **il maggiore poeta francese del secolo** the most important French poet of the century
■ SM/F **1** (*grado: Mil*) major; (: *Aer*) squadron leader **2** (*d'età: tra due*) older, elder; (: *tra più di due*) oldest, eldest; **la maggiore delle due sorelle** the older of the two sisters; **il maggiore dei tre fratelli** the oldest of the three brothers

maggiorenne [maddʒo'rɛnne] AGG of age
■ SM/F person who has come of age; **diventare maggiorenne** to come of age, reach one's majority; **adesso sono maggiorenne** now I'm of age; **quando sarai maggiorenne...** when you're eighteen ...

maggiorità [maddʒori'ta] SF (*Mil: di battaglione*) orderly room; (: *di reggimento*) regimental office

maggioritario, ria, ri, rie [maddʒori'tarjo] AGG majority *attr*
■ SM (*Pol*: *anche*: **sistema maggioritario**) first-past-the-post system

maggiormente [maddʒor'mente] AVV more; **impegnandoti maggiormente supereresti l'esame** if you were to work harder you'd pass the exam; **l'artista che lo ha maggiormente influenzato è Rembrandt** the artist who most influenced him was Rembrandt

magia [ma'dʒia] SF magic; **come per magia** as if by magic, like magic; **scomparve come per magia** it disappeared as if by magic

magicamente [madʒika'mente] AVV magically

magico, a, ci, che ['madʒiko] AGG magic; (*fig: serata, incontro*) magical; (: *sorriso*) charming; **pronunciare la formula magica** to say the magic words

magio, gi ['madʒo] SM (*Rel*): **i re Magi** the Magi, the Three Wise Men

magistero [madʒis'tɛro] SM: **Facoltà di Magistero** ≈ teacher(s') training college

magistrale [madʒis'trale] AGG **1** (*Scol*) primary (*Brit*) *o* grade school (*Am*) teachers', primary *o* grade school teaching *attr*; **abilitazione magistrale** *teaching diploma for primary teachers*; **istituto magistrale** *secondary school for the training of primary teachers: attended by students aged 14 – 18* **2** (*abile: colpo, intervento*) masterly, skilful (*Brit*), skillful (*Am*)
■ **magistrali** SFPL = **istituto magistrale**

magistralmente [madʒistral'mente] AVV in a masterly manner, skilfully (*Brit*), skillfully (*Am*)

magistrato [madʒis'trato] SM magistrate

magistratura [madʒistra'tura] SF: **la magistratura** the magistracy, the magistrature

maglia ['maʎʎa] SF **1** (*punto*) stitch; **avviare/calare le maglie** to cast on/off; **maglia dritta** plain; **maglia rovescia** purl; **lavora una maglia dritta, una rovescia** knit one, purl one **2** (*lavoro ai ferri*) knitting *no pl*; **lavorare a maglia** *or* **fare la maglia** to knit; **mi piace lavorare a maglia** I like knitting **3** (*indumento intimo*) vest; (*Sport, maglione, tessuto*) jersey; (*Storia: di armatura*) coat of mail; **indossa la maglia iridata** (*Ciclismo*) he's the world cycling champion **4** (*di catena*) link; (*di armatura*) coat of mail; (*di rete, Tecn*) mesh; **una rete a maglie fitte/grosse** a fine-/wide-mesh net; **passare per le maglie della rete** (*anche fig*) to slip through the net

magliaia [maʎ'ʎaja] SF knitter

maglieria [maʎʎe'ria] SF **1** (*indumenti*) knitwear; **macchina per maglieria** knitting machine **2** (*negozio*) knitwear shop

maglietta [maʎ'ʎetta] SF (*con maniche*) T-shirt; (*canottiera*) vest

maglificio, ci [maʎʎi'fitʃo] SM knitwear factory

maglina [maʎ'ʎina] SF (*tessuto*) jersey

maglio, gli ['maʎʎo] SM (*martello*) mallet; (*Tecn: macchina*) power hammer

maglione [maʎ'ʎone] SM jersey, sweater

magma, i ['magma] SM (*Geol*) magma; **allo stato di magma** (*fig*) inchoate

magnaccia [maɲ'ɲattʃa] SM INV (*pegg*) pimp

Magna Grecia [maɲɲa'gretʃa] SF Magna Graecia

magnanimamente [maɲɲanima'mente] AVV magnanimously

magnanimità [maɲɲanimi'ta] SF magnanimity

magnanimo, a [maɲ'ɲanimo] AGG magnanimous

magnate [maɲ'ɲate] SM tycoon, magnate

magnesia [maɲ'ɲɛzja] SF magnesia

magnesio [maɲ'ɲɛzjo] SM magnesium; **al magnesio** (*lampada, flash*) magnesium *attr*

magnete [maɲ'ɲɛte] SM (*calamita*) magnet; (*Elettr, Aut*) magneto

magneticamente [maɲɲetika'mente] AVV magnetically

magnetico, a, ci, che [maɲ'ɲɛtiko] AGG (*anche fig*) magnetic

magnetismo [maɲɲe'tizmo] SM (*anche fig*) magnetism; **il magnetismo terrestre** the earth's magnetism

magnetizzare [maɲɲetid'dzare] VT (*Fis*) to magnetize; (*fig*) to mesmerize

magnetizzazione [maɲɲetiddzat'tsjone] SF (*Fis*) magnetization

magnetofono® [maɲɲe'tɔfono] SM tape recorder

magnificamente [maɲɲifika'mente] AVV magnificently, extremely well

magnificare [maɲɲifi'kare] VT (*celebrare*) to extol, praise; **magnificare i pregi di qn/qc** to sing the praises of sb/sth

Magnificat [maɲ'ɲifikat] SM INV Magnificat

magnificenza [maɲɲifi'tʃɛntsa] SF magnificence, splendour (*Brit*), splendor (*Am*)

magnifico, a, ci, che [maɲ'ɲifiko] AGG (*gen*) magnificent, splendid; (*serata*) marvellous, wonderful; (*tempo*) gorgeous, superb; **domani si parte — magnifico!** we're setting off tomorrow — terrific!; **uno scenario magnifico** wonderful scenery

magnitudine [maɲɲi'tudine] SF (*Astron, Geol*) magnitude

magno, a ['maɲɲo] AGG: **aula magna** main hall

magnolia [maɲ'ɲɔlja] SF magnolia

magnum ['maɲɲum] SM INV (*bottiglia*) magnum
■ SF INV (*pistola*) magnum

mago, ghi ['mago] SM (*stregone*) magician, wizard; (*illusionista*) magician; (*fam: persona abilissima*) wizard

magone [ma'gone] SM (*fam*): **avere il magone** to have a lump in one's throat

magra ['magra] SF **1** (*di fiume*) low water; **essere in magra** to be very low; **periodo di magra** (*fig*) lean times **2** (*fam: brutta figura*): **fare una magra** to boob (*Brit*), make a boob (*Brit*)

magramente [magra'mente] AVV (*ricompensato*) poorly

magrebino, a; , **maghrebino, a** [magre'bino] SM/F, AGG Maghrebi

magrezza [ma'grettsa] SF (*di persona, corpo*) thinness; (*di risorse*) scarcity

magro, a ['magro] AGG **1** (*persona, corpo*) thin, skinny

Mm

(*pegg*); (*viso*) thin; **è alta e magra** she's tall and thin; **è più magra di me** she's thinner than me **2** (*latte*) skimmed; (*carne*) lean; (*formaggio*) low-fat **3** (*stipendio, guadagno*) poor, meagre (*Brit*), meager (*Am*); (*profitti*) small, slim; (*annata, raccolto*) poor; (*scusa*) poor, lame; (*soddisfazione, consolazione*) scant; (*cena, pasto*) skimpy
■ SM **1** (*carne*) lean meat **2** (*Rel*): **giorno di magro** day of abstinence; **mangiare di magro** not to eat meat
■ SM/F (*persona magra*) slim person; **questi vestiti stanno bene solo alle magre** these clothes only look good on slim women

mah [ma] ESCL (*fam*) well!

mai ['mai] AVV **1** (*negativo*) never, not ...ever; **non esce mai** she never goes out; **non l'ho mai visto** I've never seen it; **non lo aveva mai visto nessuno** nobody had ever seen it; **non sono mai stato in Russia** I've never *o* I haven't ever been to Russia; **non me ne dimenticherò mai** I'll never *o* won't ever forget it; **non avrei mai detto che...** I would never have said that ...; **non le ha mai più telefonato** he never phoned her again, he has never phoned her since; **non si sa mai** you never can tell; **mai e poi mai!** no way!; **mai più** never again; **non lo farò mai più** I'll never do it again; **mai e poi mai** never ever; (*assolutamente no*) no way; **quasi mai** hardly ever, practically never; **non esco quasi mai** I hardly ever go out; **mai, o quasi mai** never, or hardly ever; **ora o mai più** it's now or never; **più che mai** more than ever **2** (*con tempi indefiniti*) ever; **l'hai mai visto prima?** have you ever seen him before?; **il più bello che abbia mai visto** the best I've ever seen; **sei mai in ufficio il sabato?** are you ever in the office on Saturdays?; **se mai ne trovassi uno te lo farei sapere** if I ever found one I would let you know; **i prezzi delle case sono più alti che mai** house prices are higher than ever; **caso mai si mettesse a piovere** in case it starts raining, should it start to rain; **se mai direi che ha sbagliato lui** if anything, I would say that he was in the wrong; **caso mai ti telefono domenica** I might phone you on Sunday; **come mai?** why?, why (*o* how) on earth?; **come mai sei arrivato in ritardo?** why were you late?; **come mai non ci hai avvisato?** why (on earth) didn't you let us know?; **hai fatto molti errori nel tema, come mai?** you made a lot of mistakes in your essay, why was that?; **che dici mai?** what (on earth) are you saying?; **chi/dove/quando mai?** whoever/wherever/whenever?; **quando mai ho detto una cosa simile?** when did I ever say any such thing?

maiale [ma'jale] SM **1** (*Zool, fig pegg*) pig; **mangiare come un maiale** to eat like a pig; **sei proprio un maiale!** you're a real pig! **2** (*Culin*) pork; **una cotoletta di maiale** a pork chop

mail ['meil] SF INV (*messaggio di posta elettronica*) email

mailing ['meiliŋ] SM direct mail

mailing list ['meilin(g) list] SF INV mailing list

Maine ['mein] SM Maine

maiolica [ma'jɔlika] SF majolica

maionese [majo'nese] SF mayonnaise

Maiorca [ma'jɔrka] SF Majorca

mais ['mais] SM (*coltura*) maize (*Brit*), corn (*Am*); (*in scatola*) sweetcorn

maître [mɛtr] SM INV head waiter, maî tre d'hô tel

maiuscola [ma'juskola] SF (*anche:* **lettera maiuscola**) capital (letter)

maiuscoletto [majusko'letto] SM (*Tip*) small capitals *pl*

maiuscolo, a [ma'juskolo] AGG capital; **a lettere maiuscole** in capital letters
■ SM capital letters *pl*; (*Tip*) upper case; **in maiuscolo** in capital letters; **scrivere tutto in maiuscolo** to write everything in capitals *o* in capital letters

maizena [maid'dzɛna] SF cornflour

makò [ma'kɔ] SM (*cotone*) *high quality Egyptian cotton*

mal ['mal] AVV, SM *vedi* **male**

mala ['mala] SF (*gergo*) underworld

malaccorto, a [malak'kɔrto] AGG rash, careless

malachite [mala'kite] SF malachite

malacreanza [malakre'antsa] SF bad manners *pl*

malafede [mala'fede] SF bad faith; **è sicuramente in malafede** he's certainly not sincere; **questo dimostra la tua malafede** this shows you aren't sincere

malaffare [malaf'fare] **di malaffare** AGG (*gente*) shady, dishonest; **donna di malaffare** prostitute

malagevole [mala'dʒevole] AGG difficult, hard

malagrazia [mala'grattsja] SF: **con malagrazia** with bad grace, impolitely

malalingua [mala'lingwa] SF (*pl* **malelingue**) gossip (*person*)

malamente [mala'mente] AVV (*gen*) badly; (*sgarbatamente*) rudely; **finire malamente** (*persona*) to come to a bad end

malandato, a [malan'dato] AGG (*persona: di salute*) in poor health, in a bad way; (: *di condizioni finanziarie*) badly off; (*trascurato: persona*) shabby; (: *cosa*) dilapidated

malandrino, a [malan'drino] AGG (*scherz: occhi, sguardo*) mischievous, roguish
■ SM/F rogue, rascal

malanimo [ma'lanimo] SM ill will, malevolence; **di malanimo** unwillingly, grudgingly

malanno [ma'lanno] SM **1** (*disgrazia*) misfortune **2** (*malattia*) ailment; **prendersi un malanno** to catch something; **mi devo essere preso un malanno** I must have caught something

malaparata [malapa'rata] SF (*fam*) approaching danger; **vista la malaparata...** as things were looking ominous ...

malapena [mala'pena] **a malapena** AVV hardly, scarcely; **ti sento a malapena** I can hardly hear you; **ci vedo a malapena** I can hardly see

malaria [ma'larja] SF malaria

malarico, a, ci, che [ma'lariko] AGG malarial

malasanità [malasanità] SF INV *inefficiency of the Italian health service*

malasorte [mala'sɔrte] SF bad luck, ill luck

malaticcio, cia, ci, ce [mala'tittʃo] AGG sickly

malato, a [ma'lato] AGG (*persona*) ill, sick, unwell; (*organo, pianta*) diseased; **mio nonno è molto malato** my grandfather is very ill; **un bambino malato** a sick child; **ho una gamba malata** I've got a bad leg; **essere malato di cuore** to have heart trouble *o* a bad heart; **malato di mente** mentally ill; **è malato di cancro** he's got cancer; **tu sei malato al cervello!** (*fig*) you're off your head!; **una mente/fantasia malata** a sick mind/morbid imagination; **darsi malato** (*sul lavoro ecc*) to go sick; **essere malato d'amore** to be lovesick
■ SM/F (*infermo*) sick person; (*paziente*) patient; **i malati** the sick; **un malato grave** a person who is seriously ill; **i malati di mente** mentally ill people; **un malato di cancro** a cancer patient

malattia [malat'tia] SF **1** (*Med*) illness, disease; (*di pianta*) disease; (*cattiva salute*) illness, sickness; **è morto dopo una lunga malattia** he died after a long illness; **una malattia infettiva** an infectious disease; **l'AIDS è una terribile malattia** AIDS is a terrible disease;

malattie nervose nervous diseases; **malattie del lavoro** industrial diseases; **mettersi in malattia** to go on sick leave; **fare una malattia di qc** (*fig*: *disperarsi*) to get in a state about sth **2** (*fissazione*) mania; **ha la malattia del gioco** he's addicted to gambling, he's hooked on gambling

malauguratamente [malaugurata'mente] AVV unluckily, unfortunately

malaugurato, a [malaugu'rato] AGG ill-fated, unlucky

malaugurio, ri [malau'gurjo] SM bad *o* ill omen; **uccello del malaugurio** bird of ill omen; (*fig*) jinx, Jonah

malavita [mala'vita] SF underworld; **darsi alla malavita** to turn to crime

malavitoso, a [malavi'toso] SM/F gangster

malavoglia [mala'vɔʎʎa] **di malavoglia** AVV reluctantly, unwillingly; **lo fece di malavoglia** she did it reluctantly

Malawi [ma'lawi] SM Malawi

Malaysia [ma'laizja] SF Malaysia

malaysiano, a [malai'zjano] AGG, SM/F Malaysian

malcapitato, a [malkapi'tato] AGG unlucky, unfortunate
■ SM/F unfortunate person

malcelato [maltʃe'lato] AGG (*evidente*) ill-concealed, unconcealed; **lo guardò con malcelato disprezzo** she looked at him with ill-concealed contempt; **...disse con malcelato orgoglio** ... he said with obvious pride

malconcio, cia, ci, ce [mal'kontʃo] AGG (*abiti, persona*) in a sorry state; **uscire malconcio da qc** (*fig*) to come out of sth badly

malcontento, a [malkon'tɛnto] AGG: **malcontento (di)** dissatisfied (with)
■ SM (*sentimento*) discontent

malcostume [malkos'tume] SM corruption

maldestramente [maldestra'mente] AVV clumsily

maldestro, a [mal'dɛstro] AGG (*goffo*) clumsy, awkward; (*persona*: *inesperto*) inexperienced, inexpert; **è la persona più maldestra che conosca** he's the clumsiest person I know

maldicente [maldi'tʃɛnte] SM/F gossip

maldicenza [maldi'tʃɛntsa] SF malicious gossip; **è solo una maldicenza** *or* **sono solo maldicenze** it's just gossip

maldisposto, a [maldis'posto] AGG: **maldisposto (verso)** ill-disposed (towards)

Maldive [mal'dive] SFPL: **le Maldive** the Maldives, the Maldive Islands

male ['male] AVV **1** (*in modo insoddisfacente*) badly; (*in modo errato*) badly, wrongly; **oggi ho giocato male** I played badly today; **male! non avresti dovuto farlo** that was wrong of you – you shouldn't have done it; **questa porta chiude male** this door doesn't shut properly; **scrivere/comportarsi male** to write/behave badly; **pronunciare male una parola** to pronounce a word wrongly; **rispondere male** (*in modo errato*) to answer wrongly *o* incorrectly; (*in modo sgarbato*) to answer back; **riuscire male** to turn out badly; **qui si mangia molto male** the food is very bad here; **pensi che abbia fatto male ad andare?** do you think it was wrong of him to go?; **parlar male di qn** to speak ill of sb, say bad things about sb; **mi ha parlato male di te** he said bad things about you; **trattar male qn** to ill-treat sb
2 **sentirsi/star male** (*di salute*) to feel/be ill; **mi sono sentita male** I felt ill
3 (*fraseologia*): **gli è andata male di nuovo** he failed again; **per male che vada** however badly things go; **capire male** to misunderstand; **hai capito male** you've misunderstood; **le cose si stanno mettendo male** things are taking a turn for the worse; **ha preso molto male la cosa** he took it very badly; **restare** *o* **rimanere male** (*deluso*) to be disappointed; (*dispiaciuto*) to be sorry; (*offeso*) to be hurt *o* offended; **sta male comportarsi così** that's no way to behave; **quell'abito le sta proprio male** that dress just doesn't suit her, that dress looks terrible on her; **il giallo sta male con il rosa** yellow looks awful with pink; **la vedo male** things look bad (to me), it doesn't look good to me; **bene o male ce la farò** one way or the other I'll manage; **niente male quel ragazzo** that boy's not bad, that boy's a bit of alright (*fam*); **di male in peggio** from bad to worse; **non faresti male a dirglielo** it wouldn't be a bad idea to tell him
■ SM
1 (*ciò che è ingiusto, disonesto*) evil; **il male** evil; **il bene e il male** good and evil; **un male necessario** a necessary evil; **le forze del male** the forces of evil; **il minore dei due mali** the lesser of two evils; **mali sociali** social evils
2 (*danno*) harm; **fare del male a qn** to harm *o* hurt sb; **le sigarette fanno male** cigarettes are bad for you; **che c'è di male?** what's the harm in that?; **che c'è di male se esco con lui?** what harm is there in my going out with him?; **non ho fatto niente di male** I haven't done anything wrong; **non sarebbe (un) male se gliene parlassi** it wouldn't do any harm to talk to him about it; **non farebbe (del) male a una mosca** he wouldn't hurt a fly; **non gli voglio male** I don't bear him ill-will
3 (*dolore*) pain, ache; (*malattia*) illness, disease; **far male** to hurt; **mi fa male una gamba** my leg hurts, I've got a pain in my leg; **mi fa male** it hurts; **farsi male** to hurt o.s.; **fare (del) male a qn** to hurt *o* harm sb; **ahi! mi hai fatto male!** ouch! you've hurt me!; **far male alla salute** to be bad for one's health; **fumare fa male** smoking is bad for you; **avere un brutto male** (*euf*: *cancro*) to have cancer; **i mali della vecchiaia** the infirmities of old age; **mal d'aria** air sickness; **mal d'auto** car sickness; **mal di denti** toothache; **mal di gola** sore throat; **mal di mare** seasickness; **mal di schiena** backache; **mal di stomaco** stomach ache; **mal di testa** headache; **avere mal di testa/di stomaco** to have a headache/stomach ache; **aver mal di denti/d'orecchi/di gola** to have toothache/earache/a sore throat; **avere mal di cuore/di fegato** to have a heart/liver complaint; **avere il mal di mare** to be seasick; **soffrire di mal d'auto** to get car sick
4 (*fraseologia*): **andare a male** (*carne*) to go off *o* bad; (*latte*) to go off; **non avertene a male** *or* **non prendertela a male** don't take it to heart; **come va? — non c'è male** how are you? — not bad *o* O.K. (*fam*); **mal comune mezzo gaudio** (*Proverbio*) a trouble shared is a trouble halved; **a mali estremi, estremi rimedi** (*Proverbio*) desperate circumstances call for desperate remedies; **non tutto il male vien per nuocere** (*Proverbio*) it's an ill wind that blows nobody any good

maledetto, a [male'detto] PP *di* **maledire**
■ AGG **1** (*dannato*) accursed; (*nelle imprecazioni*) cursed, damned **2** (*fig fam*) damned, blasted, confounded; **avere una fame maledetta** to be damned hungry; **spegni quella maledetta radio!** turn off that damn radio!; **ho una paura maledetta dei ragni** I'm scared stiff of spiders; **è stato un giorno maledetto** it's been

Mm

a bloody awful day; **non vedo l'ora di finire questo maledetto lavoro** I can't wait to finish this damn work
maledire [male'dire] VT IRREG to curse
maledizione [maledit'tsjone] SF (*condanna, imprecazione*) curse; **maledizione!** damn!; **devo avere la maledizione addosso!** I must be fated!; **la maledizione del faraone** the curse of the Pharaoh
maleducatamente [maledukata'mente] AVV rudely
maleducato, a [maledu'kato] AGG (*persona*) rude, ill-mannered
■ SM/F ill-mannered person; **fare il maleducato** to be rude
maleducazione [maledukat'tsjone] SF rudeness; **è maleducazione parlare con la bocca piena** it's bad manners to speak with your mouth full
malefatta [male'fatta] SF misdeed
maleficio, ci [male'fitʃo] SM evil spell, witchcraft
malefico, a, ci, che [ma'lɛfiko] AGG (*influsso*) evil; (*clima*) harmful, bad
maleodorante [maleodo'rante] AGG foul-smelling, malodorous
malese [ma'lese] AGG, SM/F Malaysian
■ SM (*lingua*) Malay
Malesia [ma'lesja] SF Malaysia
malessere [ma'lɛssere] SM **1** (*indisposizione*) indisposition, slight illness; **ha avuto un leggero malessere** he didn't feel quite right **2** (*fig: disagio*) disquiet, uneasiness
malevolenza [malevo'lɛntsa] SF malevolence
malevolo, a [ma'lɛvolo] AGG malevolent
malfamato, a [malfa'mato] AGG of ill repute, notorious; **un quartiere malfamato** a rough area
malfatto, a [mal'fatto] AGG (*lavoro*) badly done; (*oggetto*) badly made; (*persona, corpo*) deformed
malfattore, trice [malfat'tore] SM/F wrongdoer; **è una banda di malfattori!** they're a bunch of crooks!
malfermo, a [mal'fermo] AGG (*voce, mano*) shaky; (*passo*) unsteady; (*salute*) poor, delicate; **essere malfermo sulle gambe** to be unsteady on one's legs; **è sempre più malfermo sulle gambe** he's getting increasingly unsteady on his feet
malfidato, a [malfi'dato], **malfidente** [malfi'dɛnte] AGG distrustful, suspicious
malformato, a [malfor'mato] AGG (*Med*) malformed
malformazione [malformat'tsjone] SF (*Med*) malformation
malfunzionamento [malfuntsjona'mento] SM (*Inform*) malfunction
malga, ghe ['malga] SF Alpine hut
malgoverno [malgo'verno] SM (*Pol*) mismanagement, misrule
malgrado [mal'grado] PREP in spite of, despite; **malgrado tutto le sono ancora amico** we are still friends in spite of *o* despite everything; **mio (*o* tuo *ecc*) malgrado** against my (*o* your *ecc*) will; **suo malgrado ha dovuto fare il lavoro** he had to do the work much against his will
■ CONG even though, although; **malgrado fosse tardi...** although it was late ...; **malgrado fossi in ritardo sono riuscito a prendere il treno** even though I was late I managed to get the train
malia [ma'lia] SF (*incantesimo*) spell; (*fig: fascino*) charm
maliarda [mali'arda] SF enchantress
maliardo, a [mali'ardo] AGG (*occhi, sorriso*) bewitching
malignamente [maliɲɲa'mente] AVV maliciously
malignare [maliɲ'ɲare] VI (*aus* **avere**): **malignare su** to malign, speak ill of
malignità [maliɲɲi'ta] SF INV **1** (*qualità*) malice, spite; **con malignità** spitefully, maliciously **2** (*osservazione*) spiteful remark
maligno, a [ma'liɲɲo] AGG **1** (*persona, parole*) malicious; **spirito maligno** evil spirit; **delle insinuazioni maligne** malicious gossip **2** (*Med*) malignant; **un tumore maligno** a malignant tumour
■ SM/F malicious person
malinconia [malinko'nia] SF melancholy, gloom
malinconicamente [malinkonika'mente] AVV melancholically, with a melancholy air
malinconico, a, ci, che [malin'kɔniko] AGG melancholy, sad; **cantava una canzone malinconica** she was singing a sad song; **è sempre più malinconico** he's getting sadder and sadder
malincuore [malin'kwɔre] **a malincuore** AVV reluctantly, unwillingly; **gliel'ho dato a malincuore** I gave it to him reluctantly
malinformato, a [malinfor'mato] AGG misinformed
malintenzionato, a [malintentsjo'nato] AGG ill-intentioned
■ SM/F ill-intentioned person; **è stato aggredito da un malintenzionato** he was attacked by a mugger
malinteso [malin'teso] AGG (*riguardo, senso del dovere*) mistaken, misguided
■ SM misunderstanding
malizia [ma'littsja] SF (*cattiveria*) malice, spite; (*furbizia*) mischievousness; (*astuzia*) clever trick; **con malizia** maliciously, spitefully; mischievously; cleverly
maliziosamente [malittsjosa'mente] AVV (*vedi agg*) maliciously, spitefully; mischievously; cleverly
malizioso, a [malit'tsjoso] AGG (*cattivo*) malicious, spiteful; (*vivace, birichino*) mischievous; (*astuto*) clever
malleabile [malle'abile] AGG malleable
malleolo [mal'lɛolo] SM (*Anat*) malleolus
mallevadore [malleva'dore] SM guarantor
malleveria [malleve'ria] SF guarantee, surety
mallo ['mallo] SM (*Bot*) husk
malloppo [mal'lɔppo] SM (*fam: refurtiva*) loot
malmenare [malme'nare] VT to beat up
malmesso, a [mal'messo] AGG (*persona*) in a difficult situation; (*: vestito male*) poorly dressed, shabby; (*: economicamente*) badly off; (*casa, macchina*) in a poor state of repair
malnutrito, a [malnu'trito] AGG undernourished
malnutrizione [malnutrit'tsjone] SF malnutrition
malo, a ['malo] AGG: **in malo modo** badly; (*sgarbatamente*) rudely; **essere a mal partito** to be in an awkward situation; **mala lingua** = malalingua; **mala sorte** = malasorte; **mala voglia** = malavoglia
malocchio [ma'lɔkkjo] SM evil eye; **guardare di malocchio** to look at with disfavour
malora [ma'lora] SF (*fam*): **andare in malora** to go to the dogs; **alla malora!** hell!; **va in malora!** go to hell!; **è un tirchio della malora!** he's a bloody miser!
malore [ma'lore] SM sudden illness; **venire *o* essere colto da malore** to be suddenly taken ill; **è stato colto da malore** he was suddenly taken ill
malpreparato, a [malprepa'rato] AGG ill-prepared
malridotto, a [malri'dotto] AGG (*abiti, scarpe, persona*) in a sorry state; (*casa*) dilapidated; (*macchina*) in a poor state of repair
malsano, a [mal'sano] AGG unhealthy; **il clima è più malsano qui** the climate is unhealthier here
malsicuro, a [malsi'kuro] AGG (*scala, edificio*) unsafe

Malta ['malta] SF Malta
malta ['malta] SF (*Edil*) mortar
maltagliati [maltaʎ'ʎati] SMPL (*Culin*) *irregularly cut pasta squares*
maltempo [mal'tɛmpo] SM bad weather
maltenuto, a [malte'nuto] AGG badly looked after, badly kept
maltese [mal'tese] AGG, SM/F Maltese
■ SM (*lingua*) Maltese
malto ['malto] SM malt
maltolto [mal'tɔlto] SM: **restituire il maltolto** to give back one's ill-gotten gains
maltosio [mal'tɔzjo] SM maltose
maltrattamento [maltratta'mento] SM ill-treatment; **subire maltrattamenti** to be ill-treated; **maltrattamento di animali** cruelty to animals
maltrattare [maltrat'tare] VT to ill-treat, abuse; **gli ostaggi non sono stati maltrattati** the hostages weren't ill-treated
maluccio [ma'luttʃo] AVV: **stare maluccio** to be poorly; **com'è andato l'esame? — maluccio** how did the exam go? — pretty badly
malumore [malu'more] SM (*irritabilità*) bad temper, ill humour; (*discordia*) ill feeling; **di malumore** in a bad mood; **oggi il capo è di malumore** the boss is in a bad mood today
malva ['malva] SF (*Bot*) mallow
■ SM INV (*colore*) mauve
■ AGG INV mauve
malvagiamente [malvadʒa'mente] AVV wickedly
malvagio, gia, gi, gie [mal'vadʒo] AGG (*uomo, azione*) evil, wicked; **non è malvagio** (*fig*: *vino, cibo*) it's not unpleasant *o* bad; (: *spettacolo, film*) it's not bad
■ SM/F wicked person
malvagità [malvadʒi'ta] SF INV (*qualità*) wickedness; (*azione*) wicked deed
malvasia [malva'zia] SF *Italian dessert wine*
malversazione [malversat'tsjone] SF (*Dir*) embezzlement
malvestito, a [malves'tito] AGG badly dressed, ill-clad
Malvine [mal'vine] SFPL: **le (isole) Malvine** the Falkland Islands, the Falklands
malvisto, a [mal'visto] AGG (*persona, idea, proposta*): **malvisto (da)** unpopular (with)
malvivente [malvi'vɛnte] SM/F criminal
malvolentieri [malvolen'tjɛri] AVV unwillingly, reluctantly
malvolere [malvo'lere] VT DIF: **farsi malvolere (da)** to make o.s. unpopular (with); **essere malvoluto da qn** to be disliked by sb; **prendere qn a malvolere** to take a dislike to sb
mamma ['mamma] SF (*fam*) mum(my) (*Brit*), mom (*Am*); **me l'ha detto la mamma** mum told me that; **la mia mamma** my mum; **come l'ha fatto mamma** in one's birthday suit; **mamma mia!** good heavens!, my goodness!
mammalucco, chi [mamma'lukko] SM dolt, idiot
mammario, ria, ri, rie [mam'marjo] AGG (*Anat*) mammary
mammasantissima [mammasan'tissima] SM INV (*nel crimine organizzato*) boss of bosses
mammella [mam'mɛlla] SF (*di donna*) breast; (*di animale*) udder
mammifero, a [mam'mifero] AGG (*Zool*) mammalian
■ SM (*Zool*) mammal
mammismo [mam'mizmo] SM *excessive attachment to one's mother*
mammografia [mammogra'fia] SF (*Med*) mammography
mammola ['mammola] SF (*Bot*) violet; **è una mammoletta** (*fig scherz*) he's a shrinking violet
mammone, a [mam'mone] SM/F (*fam*) mummy's boy/girl
mammut [mam'mut] SM INV (*Zool*) mammoth
manager ['mænidʒə] SM/F INV manager
manageriale [manadʒe'rjale] AGG managerial
manata [ma'nata] SF (*colpo*) slap; (*quantità*) handful; **a manate** by the handful
manca ['manka] SF left (hand); **a destra e a manca** left, right and centre, on all sides
mancamento [manka'mento] SM (*di forze*) (feeling of) faintness, weakness
mancante [man'kante] AGG (*pagina, tassello, parte ecc*) missing
mancanza [man'kantsa] SF **1**: **mancanza di** (*assenza*) lack of; (*carenza*) shortage of, scarcity of; **mancanza di rispetto** lack of respect; **mancanza di soldi** lack (*o* shortage) of money; **in mancanza di vino berremo acqua** as there is no wine we'll drink water; **in mancanza d'altro/di meglio** for want *o* lack of anything else/better; **per mancanza di tempo** through lack of time; **sentire la mancanza di qn/qc** to miss sb/sth; **sento la tua mancanza** I miss you
2 (*fallo*) fault; (*difetto*) failing, shortcoming; **commettere una mancanza** to commit an error
mancare [man'kare] VI (*aus* **essere**; *nei sensi 4, 5, ed 6* **avere**)
1 (*far difetto*) to be lacking; **mancano i fondi per la ricerca** there aren't the funds to do research; **manca sempre il tempo** there's never enough time; **mi mancano le parole per esprimerti la mia gratitudine** I can't find words to express my gratitude to you; **ci manca il pane** we've run out of bread, we don't have *o* haven't got any bread; **fammi sapere se ti manca qualcosa** let me know if you need anything; **i suoi non gli fanno mancar niente** his family doesn't let him want for anything; **gli sono venuti a mancare i soldi** his money ran out, he ran out of money; **quanto manca all'arrivo del treno?** how long before the train arrives?; **manca un quarto alle 6** it's a quarter to (*Brit*) *o* of (*Am*) 6; **mancano cinque minuti alla fine del film** there's five minutes to go to the end of the film
2 (*non esserci*) to be missing, not to be there; (*persona*: *essere assente*) to be absent; **mancano ancora 10 sterline** we're still £10 short; **quanti pezzi mancano?** how many pieces are missing?; **mancavi solo tu** you were the only one missing, you were the only one who wasn't there; **mi manchi** I miss you; **mancano prove** there's not enough evidence; **mancare da casa** to be away from home; **mancare all'appello** (*persona*) to be absent from roll call; (*cose*) to be missing
3 (*venir meno*: *coraggio, forze*) to fail; (*morire*) to die; **gli è mancato il coraggio** his courage failed him; **gli sono mancate le parole** words failed him; **sentirsi mancare** to feel faint; **gli sono venuti a mancare i genitori** he lost his parents; **è mancata la luce** the electricity went off
4 (*essere in errore*) to be wrong, make a mistake; **mi dispiace se ho mancato** I'm sorry if I was wrong
5: **mancare di** (*coraggio, giudizio*) to lack, be lacking in; (*risorse, soldi*) to be short of, lack; **mancare di rispetto a qn** to be lacking in respect towards sb, be disrespectful towards sb; **mancare di parola** not to keep one's

Mm

word, go back on one's word; **non mancherò di salutarlo da parte tua** of course I'll give him your regards; **non mancherò** I won't forget, I'll make sure I do

6: **mancare a** (*doveri*) to neglect; (*promessa*) to fail to keep; (*appuntamento*) to miss; **mancare alla parola data** to break one's promise

7 (*fraseologia*): **ci mancherebbe altro!** of course I (*o* you *ecc*) will!; **ci mancava solo questa!** *or* **ci mancava anche questo!** that's all we need!; **c'è mancato poco** it was a near thing; **c'è mancato poco** *o* **poco è mancato che si facesse male** he very nearly hurt himself; **gli manca una rotella** (*fig*) he's got a screw loose; **a questo cane manca solo la parola** that dog is almost human

■ VT (*bersaglio*) to miss; **ha mancato la presa ed è caduto** he lost his grip and fell

mancato, a [man'kato] AGG (*tentativo*) abortive, unsuccessful; (*appuntamento*) missed; (*occasione*) lost, wasted; (*artista*) failed; **è un dottore mancato** (*fallito*) he's a failure as a doctor; (*non realizzato*) he should have been a doctor; **mancato pagamento** non-payment; **mancato arrivo** failure to arrive

manche [mɑ̃ʃ] SF INV (*Sport*) heat

mancherò *ecc* [manke'rɔ] VB *vedi* **mancare**

manchevole [man'kevole] AGG (*insufficiente*) inadequate, insufficient

manchevolezza [mankevo'lettsa] SF (*scorrettezza*) fault, shortcoming; **è stata una manchevolezza non invitarlo** it was remiss of us not to invite him

mancia, ce ['mantʃa] SF tip; **dare una mancia a qn** to tip sb, give sb a tip; **ha dato la mancia al cameriere** he tipped the waiter; **mancia competente** reward

manciata [man'tʃata] SF handful; **a manciate** by the handful

mancina [man'tʃina] SF (*mano*) left hand; (*parte*) left, left-hand side

mancinismo [mantʃi'nizmo] SM left-handedness

mancino, a [man'tʃino] AGG (*persona*) left-handed; (*calciatore*) left-footed; (*pugile*) southpaw *attr*; (*fig*): **tiro mancino** dirty trick

■ SM/F left-handed person, left-hander

manco ['manko] AVV (*fam: nemmeno*) not even; **manco per sogno!** *or* **manco per idea!** not on your life!, (I) wouldn't dream of it!

mandante [man'dante] SM/F (*Dir*) principal; (*istigatore*) instigator

mandarancio, ci [manda'rantʃo] SM clementine

mandare [man'dare] VT **1** (*gen*) to send; **mandare qc a qn** to send sb sth; **manderò una cartolina a Loredana** I'll send Loredana a postcard; **mi puoi mandare un po' di denaro?** can you send me some money?; **glielo manderò** I'll send it to him; **mando sempre una cartolina a tutti i miei amici** I always send postcards to all my friends; **mandare qc per posta/per via aerea** to send sth through the *o* by post/by air; **mandare a chiamare qn** to send for sb; **mandare a dire (a qn)** to send word (to sb); **mandare due righe a qn** to drop sb a line; **mandare qn in prigione** to send sb to prison; **mandare un bacio a qn** to blow sb a kiss; **mandare in pezzi** (*vaso, vetro*) to shatter; **mandare in rovina** to ruin; **che Dio ce la mandi buona!** God help us! **2**: **mandare avanti** (*persona*) to send ahead; (*fig: famiglia*) to provide for; (*: ditta, azienda, attività*) to keep going, run; (*: pratica*) to attend to; **mandare giù** (*persona*) to send down; (*cibo, fig*) to swallow; **mandare via** (*persona*) to send away; (*: licenziare*) to sack, fire **3** (*emettere: segnali*) to send out; (*: grido*) to give, utter, let out; **mandare in onda** (*Radio, TV*) to broadcast

mandarino[1] [manda'rino] SM (*Bot*) mandarin (orange)

mandarino[2] [manda'rino] SM (*in Cina*) mandarin

mandata [man'data] SF **1** (*di chiave*) turn; **chiudere a doppia mandata** to double-lock **2** (*quantità*) consignment, lot, batch

mandatario, ri [manda'tarjo] SM (*Dir*) representative, agent

mandato [man'dato] SM **1** (*incarico: di deputato*) mandate; (*durata dell'incarico*) term of office; **su mandato di** by order of **2** (*Dir: penale*) warrant; **mandato d'arresto** *o* **di cattura** warrant for arrest; **mandato di comparizione** summons *sg*; **mandato di perquisizione** search warrant **3** (*Dir: civile*) mandate **4** **mandato di pagamento** postal *o* money order

mandibola [man'dibola] SF (*Anat*) jaw, mandible

mandolino [mando'lino] SM (*Mus*) mandolin(e)

mandorla ['mandorla] SF (*frutto*) almond; **occhi a mandorla** almond(-shaped) eyes

mandorlato [mandor'lato] SM nut brittle

mandorlo ['mandorlo] SM almond tree

mandragola [man'dragola] SF (*Bot*) mandrake

mandria ['mandrja] SF herd

mandriano [mandri'ano] SM cowherd, herdsman

mandrillo [man'drillo] SM (*Zool*) mandrill; (*fig scherz*) lecher

mandrino [man'drino] SM (*Tecn*) mandrel

maneggevole [maned'dʒevole] AGG easy to handle; **poco maneggevole** difficult to handle

maneggiare [maned'dʒare] VT (*utensili, arnesi*) to handle, use; (*cera, creta*) to work; (*fig: persone, denaro*) to handle, deal with; **"maneggiare con cura"** "handle with care"

maneggio, gi [ma'neddʒo] SM **1** (*Equitazione: scuola*) riding school; (*: pista*) ring; **maneggio coperto/all'aperto** indoor/outdoor school **2** (*di denaro, affari*) management, handling **3** (*fig: manovra, intrigo*) scheme, ploy

manesco, a, schi, sche [ma'nesko] AGG ready with one's fists; **una mamma manesca** a mother who smacks a lot

manetta [ma'netta] SF (*di gas, aria*) lever; **andare a manetta** (*Aut fam*) to drive flat out

manette [ma'nette] SFPL handcuffs; **mettere le manette a qn** to handcuff sb

manforte [man'fɔrte] SF INV: **dare manforte a qn** to support sb

manganellare [manganel'lare] VT to club

manganellata [manganel'lata] SF blow with a club *o* cudgel

manganello [manga'nɛllo] SM club, cudgel; (*della polizia*) truncheon, night stick (*Am*)

manganese [manga'nese] SM manganese

mangano ['mangano] SM mangle

mangereccio, cia, ci, ce [mandʒe'rettʃo] AGG edible

mangeria [mandʒe'ria] SF (*fam*) embezzlement of public money

mangiabile [man'dʒabile] AGG edible, eatable

mangiadischi® [mandʒa'diski] SM INV portable record player

mangia-e-bevi ['mandʒa e b'bevi] SM INV (*gelato*) ice-cream sundae

mangiafumo [mandʒa'fumo] AGG INV: **candela mangiafumo** *candle which acts as an air purifier*

mangianastri® [mandʒa'nastri] SM INV cassette-recorder
mangiapane [mandʒa'pane] SM/F: **mangiapane a tradimento** scrounger
mangiapreti [mandʒa'prɛti] SM/F INV hater of priests
mangiare [man'dʒare] VT **1** (*gen*) to eat; **non mangio carne** I don't eat meat; **vuoi mangiare qualcosa?** would you like something to eat?; **mangiare di tutto** to eat anything *o* everything; **qui si mangia bene/male** the food is good/bad here; **non avere da mangiare** not to have enough to eat; **dare da mangiare a qn** to give sb something to eat; **fare da mangiare** to cook; **la mamma sta facendo da mangiare** mum is cooking; **farsi qc da mangiare** to make o.s. sth to eat; **mangiare fuori** to eat out, have a meal out; **resta a mangiare un boccone con noi** stay and have a bite with us; **allora, si mangia?** is it ready then?; **si mangiano questi funghi?** are these mushrooms edible?; **mangiare per due/quattro** (*fig*) to eat enough for two/like a horse; **mangiare come un uccellino** (*fig*) to eat like a bird; **mangiare alle spalle di qn** (*fig*) to live off sb; **sembrava volesse mangiarmi** (*fig*) I thought he was going to kill me; **mangiarsi qn con gli occhi** to devour sb with one's eyes; **mangiarsi qn di baci** to smother sb with kisses; **mangiarsi il patrimonio** to squander one's inheritance; **mangiarsi il fegato** (*fig*) to be consumed with rage; **mi sarei mangiato le mani** I could have kicked myself; **mangiarsi le parole** to mumble; **mangiarsi le unghie** to bite one's nails; **questo mobile è mangiato dai tarli** this piece of furniture has woodworm; **esser mangiato vivo dalle zanzare** to be eaten alive by mosquitoes **2** (*Carte, Scacchi*) to take
■ SM (*cibo*) food; **essere difficile nel mangiare** to be a fussy eater; **il mangiare è pronto** lunch/breakfast/dinner is ready
mangiasoldi [mandʒa'sɔldi] AGG INV (*fam*): **macchinetta mangiasoldi** one-armed bandit
mangiata [man'dʒata] SF: **fare una mangiata di** to stuff o.s. with; **che mangiata!** what a huge meal!; **una mangiata coi fiocchi** a slap-up meal
mangiatoia [mandʒa'toja] SF (feeding-)trough
mangiatore, trice [mandʒa'tore] SM/F eater; **mangiatore di fuoco** fire-eater; **mangiatore di spade** sword swallower; **mangiatrice di uomini** (*scherz*) man-eater
mangiaufo [mandʒa'ufo] SM/F INV (*scroccone*) scrounger; (*poltrone*) idler
mangime [man'dʒime] SM (*foraggio*) fodder; (*becchime*) birdseed
mangione, a [man'dʒone] SM/F (*fam*) glutton
mangiucchiare [mandʒuk'kjare] VT to nibble
mango, ghi ['mango] SM (*frutto*) mango; (*albero*) mango tree
mangrovia [man'grɔvja] SF mangrove
mangusta [man'gusta] SF mongoose
mania [ma'nia] SF (*Psic*) mania; (*fissazione*) obsession; (*abitudine*) odd *o* strange habit; **gli è presa la mania dei francobolli** his latest craze is stamp collecting; **una delle sue manie** one of his funny habits; **ha la mania della puntualità/della pulizia** he's obsessively punctual/clean; **avere la mania di fare qc** to have a habit of doing sth; **mania di grandezza** delusions *pl* of grandeur; **mania di persecuzione** persecution complex *o* mania
maniacale [mania'kale] AGG (*Psic*) maniacal; (*fanatico*) fanatical; **è un igienista maniacale** (*fig*) he's fanatical about hygiene
maniaco, a, ci, che [ma'niako] AGG (*Med: stato*) maniac; (*: persona*) suffering from a mania; **essere maniaco dell'ordine** (*fig*) to be obsessively tidy
■ SM/F (*Med*) maniac; (*fanatico*) fanatic; **un maniaco sessuale** (*anche scherz*) sex maniac; **è un maniaco del calcio** he's football mad *o* crazy
maniaco-depressivo, a [ma'niakodepres'sivo] AGG, SM/F manic-depressive
manica, che ['manika] SF **1** sleeve; **le maniche sono troppo corte** the sleeves are too short; **con le maniche lunghe** long-sleeved; **una maglia con le maniche lunghe** a long-sleeved sweater; **senza maniche** sleeveless; **una maglia senza maniche** a sleeveless sweater; **essere in maniche di camicia** to be in (one's) shirt sleeves; **manica (a) kimono** bat sleeve; **essere di manica larga** (*prodigo*) to be free with one's money; (*indulgente*) to be easy-going; **essere di manica stretta** (*tirchio*) to be stingy, be tight (*fam*); (*rigoroso*) to be strict **2** (*fig: banda*) gang; **una manica di delinquenti** a bunch of criminals; **una manica di ladri** a pack of thieves **3** (*Geog*): **la Manica** *or* **il Canale della Manica** the (English) Channel **4**: **manica a vento** (*Aer*) wind sock; (*Naut*) ventilator
manicaretto [manika'retto] SM delicious dish
manicheismo [manike'izmo] SM **1** (*Rel*) Manich(a)eism **2** **non mi piace il suo manicheismo** I don't like the way he sees everything as black or white
manichetta [mani'ketta] SF (*Tecn*) hose
manichino [mani'kino] SM (*di sarto, vetrina*) dummy
manico, ci *o* **chi** ['maniko] SM (*gen*) handle; (*di strumento musicale*) neck; **manico di scopa** broomstick
manicomio, mi [mani'kɔmjo] SM lunatic asylum, mental hospital; (*fig*) madhouse; **è roba da manicomio!** this is complete lunacy!
manicotto [mani'kɔtto] SM (*di pelliccia*) muff; (*Tecn*) sleeve, coupling; (*Aut*) hose
manicure [mani'kure] SM O F INV manicure; **farsi il** *o* **la manicure** to do one's nails, give o.s. a manicure
■ SF INV (*persona*) manicurist
maniera [ma'njɛra] SF **1** (*modo*) way, manner; **maniera di vivere/di parlare** way of life/of speaking; **in maniera strana** in an odd way; **fare qc alla propria maniera** to do sth one's own way; **in una maniera o nell'altra** one way or another; **in qualche maniera** somehow or other; **in maniera che** so that; **in maniera da** so as to; **fa' in maniera che sia tutto pronto per domani** see to it that everything's ready for tomorrow; **dobbiamo fare in maniera da non ripetere gli stessi errori** we must see that we don't make the same mistakes again; **in tutte le maniere** (*a tutti i costi*) at all costs; **usare le maniere forti** to take tough action; **in nessuna maniera** in no way **2** (*Arte: stile*) style, manner; **alla maniera di** in *o* after the style of; **è un Picasso prima maniera** it's an early Picasso **3** (*comportamento*): **maniere** SFPL manners; **usare buone maniere con qn** to be polite to sb; **non conosce le buone maniere** her manners are awful; **non mi piacciono le sue maniere** I don't like the way he behaves
manierato, a [manje'rato] AGG (*affettato*) affected; (*Arte*) mannered
manierismo [manje'rizmo] SM (*Arte*) mannerism
manieristico, a, ci, che [manje'ristiko] AGG (*Arte*) manneristic

Mm

maniero [ma'njɛro] SM manor
manifattura [manifat'tura] SF (*stabilimento*) factory; (*lavorazione*) manufacture
manifatturiero, a [manifattu'rjɛro] AGG manufacturing *attr*
manifestamente [manifesta'mente] AVV manifestly
manifestante [manifes'tante] SM/F demonstrator
manifestare [manifes'tare] VT (*gen*) to show, display; (*opinioni, intenzioni*) to reveal, disclose; **manifestare il desiderio di fare qc** to express a desire to do sth, indicate one's wish to do sth
■ VI (*aus* **avere**): **manifestare contro/a favore di** to demonstrate against/in favour of
▶ **manifestarsi** VR: **si è manifestato per quello che è** he has shown his true colours; **manifestarsi contrario a un progetto** to reveal one's opposition to a plan; **manifestarsi amico/nemico** to prove to be a friend/an enemy;
▶ **manifestarsi** VIP (*sintomi, malattia*) to appear
manifestazione [manifestat'tsjone] SF **1** (*di opinione, sentimento*) expression; (*di affetto*) demonstration; (*di malattia: comparsa*) manifestation; (*: sintomo*) sign, symptom **2** (*spettacolo*) event, show, display; (*Pol*) demonstration; **manifestazione sportiva** sporting event; **una manifestazione contro il governo** a demonstration against the government
manifestino [manifes'tino] SM leaflet
manifesto, a [mani'fɛsto] AGG (*errore, verità*) obvious, manifest; (*fatto*) well-known; **i giornali hanno reso manifesto il suo rapporto con la mafia** the newspapers have uncovered his links with the Mafia
■ SM **1** (*Letteratura, Arte, Pol*) manifesto **2** (*cartellone*) poster, bill; **manifesto pubblicitario** advertising poster
maniglia [ma'niʎʎa] SF (*di porta, cassetta*) handle; (*sostegno: in autobus*) strap; (*fig fam: appoggio influente*) help from a highly-placed friend; (*Naut*) shackle; **maniglie dell'amore** (*fig*) love handles, spare tyre *sg*
manigoldo [mani'goldo] SM (*anche scherz*) rogue
Manila [ma'nila] SF Manila
manipolare [manipo'lare] VT **1** (*gen*) to manipulate, handle; (*creta, cera*) to work, fashion **2** (*alterare: elezione*) to rig; (*: conti*) to falsify, doctor, fiddle (*fam: notizia, informazioni*), to manipulate; (*: vino*) to adulterate
manipolatore, trice [manipola'tore] SM/F (*di elezioni, imbrogli*) fixer
■ SM (*Tecn*) key
manipolazione [manipolat'tsjone] SF (*gen, Med*) manipulation; (*di conti*) falsification, fiddling (*fam*)
manipolo [ma'nipolo] SM **1** (*drappello*) handful **2** (*Storia, Rel*) maniple
maniscalco, chi [manis'kalko] SM blacksmith, farrier (*Brit*)
manna ['manna] SF (*Rel*) manna; **è una manna dal cielo!** (*fig*) it is a godsend!
mannaia [man'naja] SF (*del boia*) (executioner's) axe *o* ax (*Am*); (*per carni*) cleaver
mannaro [man'naro] AGG: **lupo mannaro** werewolf
mannequin [manə'kɛ̃] SF INV model
mano, i ['mano] SF **1** hand; **dare la mano a qn** to give sb one's hand; (*camminando*) to hold sb's hand; (*per salutare*) to shake hands with sb; **darsi** *o* **stringersi la mano** to hold hands; (*per salutarsi*) to shake hands; **i due ministri si strinsero la mano** the two ministers shook hands; **tenersi per mano** to hold hands; **si tenevano per mano** they were holding hands; **mano nella mano** hand in hand; **battere le mani** to clap (one's hands); **mani in alto!** hands up!; **mi sono scottato la mano** I've burnt my hand; **cadere nelle mani di qn** (*fig*) to fall into sb's hands; **mani pulite** *the judicial operation which brought to trial politicians and industrialists implicated in corruption scandals*
2 (*locuzioni*): **di seconda mano** second-hand; **ha comprato una macchina di seconda mano** she bought a second-hand car; **di prima mano** (*notizia*) first-hand; **a portata di mano** within reach; **tienilo sempre a portata di mano** always keep it within reach; **sotto mano** (*vicino*) to hand; (*furtivamente*) secretly; **ce l'hai sotto mano?** have you got it to hand?; **fuori mano** out of the way; **in mani fidate** in safe hands; **in buone mani** in good hands; **a mani vuote** empty-handed; **rapina a mano armata** armed robbery; **recapitato a mano** (*lettera, pacco*) (delivered) by hand; **fatto a mano** handmade; **cucito a mano** hand-sewn; **bagaglio a mano** hand luggage; **alla mano** (*persona*) easy-going; **con i soldi alla mano** cash in hand; **con i fatti alla mano** with his (*o* her *ecc*) facts at the ready; **a mano a mano che** *or* **man mano che** (*mentre*) as; **man mano** (*gradualmente*) little by little, gradually
3 (*locuzioni verbali*): **andare contro mano** (*Aut*) to go against the (flow of) traffic; **ho le mani legate** (*fig*) my hands are tied; **restare a mani vuote** to be left empty-handed; **avere le mani bucate** to spend money like water; **avere mani di fata** to have a light touch; **aver le mani in pasta** to have a finger in the pie; **avere qc per le mani** (*progetto, lavoro*) to have sth in hand; **alzare le mani su qn** to raise one's hand to sb; **dare una mano a qn** to lend sb a hand, to give sb a hand; **dammi una mano, per favore** give me a hand, please; **gli dai una mano e si prende il braccio** give him an inch and he'll take a mile; **fare man bassa di qc** to run off with sth; **forzare la mano** to go too far; **sai com'è, una mano lava l'altra...** you know how it is – you scratch my back and I'll scratch yours ...; **mettere la mano sul fuoco per qc** (*fig*) to stake one's life on sth; **mettere le mani su qc** to lay one's hands on sth; **mettere mano a qc** to have a hand in sth; **mettere le mani avanti** to safeguard o.s.; **mettere le mani addosso a qn** to lay hands on sb; (*molestare*) to touch sb up; **mettersi una mano sulla coscienza** to examine one's conscience; **ci ho preso la mano** I've got the hang of it; **starsene con le mani in mano** to twiddle one's thumbs; **venire alle mani** to come to blows
4 (*strato*) coat; **dare una mano di vernice a qc** to give sth a coat of paint
5 (*Carte*) hand; **facciamo ancora una mano** let's play one more hand
manodopera [mano'dɔpera] SF manpower, labour (*Brit*), labor (*Am*)
manomesso, a [mano'messo] PP *di* **manomettere**
manometro [ma'nɔmetro] SM manometer
manomettere [mano'mettere] VT IRREG (*alterare: documento, prove*) to tamper with; (*aprire indebitamente: lettera*) to open (without permission); (*: serratura*) to force; (*: cassaforte*) to break open; **la serratura sembrava manomessa** the lock looked as though it had been tampered with
manomissione [manomis'sjone] SF (*di prove*) tampering; (*di lettera*) (unauthorized) opening
manomorta [mano'mɔrta] SF (*Dir*) mortmain
manopola [ma'nɔpola] SF **1** (*di televisore, radio*) knob; (*impugnatura*) hand-grip; (*sostegno: su autobus, vetture*) strap; **girò la manopola per cercare il canale** he

turned the knob to find the station **2** (*di armatura*) gauntlet; (*guanto*) mitten, mitt; (*: di spugna*) wash mitt

manoscritto, a [manos'kritto] AGG handwritten ■ SM manuscript

manovalanza [manova'lantsa] SF (*lavoratori*) unskilled workers *pl*; **la manovalanza mafiosa** (*criminali*) mafia henchmen *pl*, *small-time Mafiosi who do the dirty work*

manovale [mano'vale] SM unskilled worker, labourer (*Brit*), laborer (*Am*)

manovella [mano'vɛlla] SF (*gen*) handle; (*Tecn*) crank; **manovella alzacristalli** (window) winder; **manovella d'avviamento** starting handle; **dare il primo giro di manovella** (*Cine*) to begin filming

manovra [ma'nɔvra] SF **1** (*Mil, fig*) manoeuvre (*Brit*), maneuver (*Am*); (*Pol, Econ*) measures *pl*; **la nuova manovra fiscale** the new tax(ation) measures; **manovra di accerchiamento** encircling movement; **grandi manovre** army manoeuvres *o* exercises; **manovre di corridoio** lobbying **2** (*Ferr*) shunting; **fare manovra** (*Aut*) to manoeuvre; **fare manovra di parcheggio** to park; **mentre faceva manovra di parcheggio** while parking; **manovra di atterraggio** landing **3**: **manovre** SFPL (*Naut*) rigging *sg*; **manovre fisse/correnti** standing/running rigging

manovrabile [mano'vrabile] AGG (*anche fig*) easy to manipulate

manovrare [mano'vrare] VT (*veicolo*) to manoeuvre (*Brit*), maneuver (*Am*); (*macchinario*) to operate, work; (*fig: persona*) to manipulate ■ VI (*aus* avere): **manovrare per parcheggiare l'auto** to pull (*o* back) into a parking space; **mentre manovrava per entrare nel parcheggio** while parking

manovrato, a [mano'vrato] AGG (*Calcio*): **fare un gioco manovrato** to play a well-organized attacking game

manovratore, trice [manovra'tore] SM/F (*di tram*) driver; (*di treno*) shunter

manrovescio, sci [manro'vɛʃʃo] SM slap, back hander

mansalva [man'salva] **a mansalva** AVV freely

mansarda [man'sarda] SF attic

mansione [man'sjone] SF duty, job, task; **non rientra nelle mie mansioni** it's not part of my job; **quali sono le sue mansioni?** what are his duties?; **svolgere** *o* **esplicare le proprie mansioni** to carry out one's duties

> **LO SAPEVI...?**
> **mansione** non si traduce mai con la parola inglese ***mansion***

mansuetamente [mansueta'mente] AVV (*vedi agg*) tamely; docilely

mansueto, a [mansu'ɛto] AGG (*animale*) tame; (*persona*) gentle, docile

mansuetudine [mansue'tudine] SF (*vedi agg*) tameness; gentleness, docility

manta ['manta] SF (*Zool*) manta (ray)

mantecare [mante'kare] VT (*Culin*) to cook until creamy

mantecato, a [mante'kato] (*Culin*) AGG (*risotto*) creamy ■ SM soft ice cream

mantella [man'tɛlla] SF cloak

mantellina [mantel'lina] SF cape

mantello [man'tɛllo] SM **1** (*cappotto*) cloak; (*Zool*) coat; (*fig: di neve*) blanket, mantle **2** (*Tecn: rivestimento*) casing, shell **3** (*Geol*) mantle

mantenere [mante'nere] VB IRREG ■ VT **1** (*gen*) to keep; (*decisione*) to stand by, abide by; (*promessa*) to keep, maintain; (*tradizione*) to maintain, uphold; (*edificio*) to maintain; **mantenere l'equilibrio/la linea** to keep one's balance/one's figure; **mantenere qn in vita** to keep sb alive; **mantenere i prezzi bassi** to hold prices down; **mantenere i contatti con qn** to keep in touch with sb; **mantenere l'ordine** (*Polizia*) to maintain law and order; (*in assemblea ecc*) to keep order; **pensi che manterrà la promessa?** do you think she'll keep her promise?; **cerca di mantenere la calma** try to keep calm **2** (*famiglia*) to maintain, support; **ha una famiglia da mantenere** he's got a family to support ▶ **mantenersi** VR **1** (*conservarsi*): **mantenersi calmo/giovane** to stay *o* keep *o* remain calm/young; **mantenersi bene** to look good for one's age **2** (*sostentarsi*) to keep o.s.; **si mantiene da anni** he has supported himself financially for years; **lavora per mantenersi** he works for a living; **si mantiene facendo la cameriera** (*studentessa*) she supports herself by waitressing ▶ **mantenersi** VIP (*cibi*) to keep; **il tempo si mantiene bello** the weather is holding

mantenimento [manteni'mento] SM (*gen*) maintenance; **provvedere al mantenimento della famiglia** to provide for one's family; **dieta/ginnastica di mantenimento** maintenance diet/gymnastics

mantenuta [mante'nuta] SF (*pegg*) kept woman

mantenuto [mante'nuto] SM (*pegg*) gigolo

mantice [man'titʃe] SM bellows *pl*; **sbuffare** *o* **soffiare come un mantice** to puff like a grampus

mantide ['mantide] SF: **mantide religiosa** praying mantis

mantiglia [man'tiʎʎa] SF mantilla

manto ['manto] SM (*cappotto*) cloak; (*Zool*) coat; (*fig: di neve*) blanket, mantle; **manto stradale** road surface

Mantova ['mantova] SF Mantua; **abito a Mantova** I live in Mantua

mantovana [manto'vana] SF (*di tenda*) pelmet

mantovano, a [manto'vano] AGG of *o* from Mantua ■ SM/F native *o* inhabitant of Mantua

manuale [manu'ale] AGG (*lavoro*) manual ■ SM (*libro*) manual, handbook; **il manuale di istruzioni** the instruction manual; **manuale di fotografia** Teach Yourself Photography; **un caso da manuale** (*fig*) a textbook example

manualistico, a, ci, che [manua'listiko] AGG: **cultura manualistica** (*pegg*) superficial knowledge

manualmente [manual'mente] AVV manually, by hand

manubrio, ri [ma'nubrjo] SM (*gen*) handle; (*di bicicletta*) handlebars *pl*; (*attrezzo da ginnastica*) dumbbell

manufatto [manu'fatto] SM manufactured article; **manufatti** SMPL manufactured goods

manutenzione [manuten'tsjone] SF (*gen*) maintenance; (*di edifici, locali*) upkeep; (*d'impianti*) maintenance, servicing

manzo ['mandzo] SM (*animale*) steer, bullock; (*carne*) beef; **uno spezzatino di manzo** a beef stew

maoista, i, e [mao'ista] AGG, SM/F Maoist

Maometto [mao'metto] SM Mohammed

maori [ma'ɔri] AGG, SM/F Maori ■ SM (*lingua*) Maori

mappa ['mappa] SF map

mappamondo [mappa'mondo] SM (*globo*) globe; (*carta*) map of the world

mappazza [map'pattsa] SF (*fam*) *heavy indigestible food*

Mm

maquillage [maki'jaʒ] SM INV make-up; **fare il maquillage** (*al centro storico*) to smarten up
marabù [mara'bu] SM INV (*Zool*) marabou
marachella [mara'kɛlla] SF mischievous trick
maragià [mara'dʒa] SM INV maharaja(h)
marameo [mara'mɛo] SM: **fare marameo a** to thumb one's nose at
marasca [ma'raska] SF marasca cherry
maraschino [maras'kino] SM maraschino
marasco [ma'rasko] SM marasca
marasma, i [ma'razma] SM (*fig*) decline, decay; **un marasma generale** (*fig: disordine*) chaos
maratona [mara'tona] SF (*Sport, fig*) marathon; **maratona TV** telethon
maratoneta, i, e [marato'nɛta] SM/F (*Sport*) marathon runner
marca, che ['marka] SF **1** (*Comm: di sigarette, caffè*) brand; (*: di scarpe, vestito*) make; (*: marchio di fabbrica*) trademark; **di che marca è il tuo stereo?** what make is your stereo?; **capi di marca** designer clothes; **prodotti di (gran) marca** high-class products **2** (*bollo*) stamp; **marca da bollo** official stamp **3** (*contrassegno, scontrino*) ticket, check

> **LO SAPEVI...?**
> **marca** non si traduce mai con la parola inglese ***mark***

marcamento [marka'mento] SM (*Sport*) marking
marcare [mar'kare] VT **1** (*segnare*) to mark; (*a fuoco: animale*) to brand; (*biancheria*) to mark; **marcare visita** (*Mil*) to report sick **2** (*accentuare*) to stress **3** (*Sport: gol*) to score; (*: avversario*) to mark; **devi marcare il numero otto** mark number eight; **la squadra ha marcato all'ultimo minuto** the team scored in the final minute
marcatamente [markata'mente] AVV markedly
marcato, a [mar'kato] AGG (*lineamenti, accento*) pronounced
marcatore [marka'tore] SM **1** (*Calcio: chi segna i gol*) scorer; (*: chi marca l'avversario*) marker **2** (*penna*) marker (pen)
Marche ['marke] SFPL: **le Marche** the Marches (*region of central Italy*)
marcherò *ecc* [marke'rɔ] VB *vedi* **marcare**
marchesa [mar'keza] SF marchioness
marchese [mar'keze] SM marquis, marquess
marchetta [mar'ketta] SF **1** (*Amm*) ≈ National Insurance Stamp **2**: **fare marchette** (*prostituirsi*) to be on the game
marchiano, a [mar'kjano] AGG (*errore*) glaring, gross
marchiare [mar'kjare] VT (*bestiame*) to mark; **marchiare a fuoco** to brand; **marchiare a vita** (*fig*) to brand for life
marchigiano, a [marki'dʒano] AGG of *o* from the Marches
■ SM/F inhabitant *o* native of the Marches
marchingegno [markin'dʒeɲɲo] SM contraption
marchio, chi ['markjo] SM **1** (*Comm*) mark; **marchio depositato** registered trademark; **marchio di fabbrica** trademark; **marchio registrato** registered trademark **2** (*per bestiame: segno*) brand; (*: strumento*) branding iron; **ha il marchio di bugiardo** he has been branded a liar
marcia, ce ['martʃa] SF **1** (*gen, Mil, Mus*) march; **marcia forzata** forced march; **marcia funebre** funeral march **2**: **mettersi in marcia** to get moving *o* going; **mettiamoci in marcia** let's get going; **mettere in marcia** (*veicolo*) to start (up); (*apparecchio*) to set going, start; **essere in marcia verso** to be marching towards **3** (*Aut*) gear; **cambiare marcia** to change gear; **fare marcia indietro** to reverse; (*fig*) to back-pedal, backtrack **4** (*Sport*) walking
marcialonga, ghe [martʃa'longa] SF (*sci di fondo*) cross-country skiing race; (*a piedi*) long-distance race
marciapiede [martʃa'pjɛde] SM (*di strada*) pavement (*Brit*), sidewalk (*Am*); (*Ferr*) platform
marciare [mar'tʃare] VI (*aus* **avere**) **1** (*Mil*) to march; (*Sport*) to walk; **far marciare dritto qn** (*fig*) to make sb toe the line **2** (*veicolo*) to go, travel; (*fig: funzionare*) to run, work; **il treno marcia a 70 km/h** the train goes *o* travels at 70 km/h; **la ditta marcia bene** the firm is running smoothly
marciatore, trice [martʃa'tore] SM/F (*Sport*) walker
marcio, cia, ci ce ['martʃo] AGG (*uovo, legno*) rotten; (*foglie*) rotting; (*frutta*) rotten, bad; (*ferita, piaga*) festering; (*fig: corrotto*) corrupt, rotten; **avere torto marcio** to be utterly wrong
■ SM (*di frutto ecc*) rotten *o* bad part; **c'è del marcio in questa storia** there's something fishy about this business
marcire [mar'tʃire] VI (*aus* **essere**) (*cibi, frutta*) to go rotten *o* bad; (*cadaveri, legno, foglie*) to rot; (*ferita*) to fester; **marcire in prigione** (*fig*) to rot in prison
■ VT to rot
marcita [mar'tʃita] SF water meadow
marciume [mar'tʃume] SM **1** (*parte guasta: di cibi*) rotten part, bad part **2** (*di radice, pianta*) rot; (*fig: corruzione*) rottenness, corruption
marco, chi ['marko] SM (*moneta*) mark
marconista, i [marko'nista] SM radiotelegraphist
marconiterapia [markonitera'pia] SF (*Med*) diathermy
mare ['mare] SM **1** (*gen*) sea; **mare interno** inland sea; **mare calmo/mosso/grosso** calm/rough/heavy sea; **per mare** by sea; **sul mare** (*barca*) on the sea; (*villaggio, località*) by *o* beside the sea; **in mare** at sea; **è morto in mare** he died at sea; **una casa al mare** a house at the seaside; **una vacanza al mare** a holiday beside *o* by the sea, a seaside holiday; **andare al mare** (*in vacanza*) to go to the seaside; **mettersi in mare** to put out to sea; **c'è un po' di mare oggi** there's a bit of a swell today; **uomo in mare!** man overboard!; **di mare** (*brezza, acqua, uccelli, pesce*) sea *attr*; **essere in alto mare** (*fig*) to have a long way to go; **è una goccia nel mare** (*fig*) it's a drop in the ocean **2** (*gran quantità di: lettere, lamentele*) flood; (*: gente, problemi, difficoltà*) host; (*: lavoro*) pile; **ho un mare di cose da fare** I've got stacks of things to do; **essere in un mare di guai** to be surrounded by problems; **essere in un mare di lacrime** to be in floods of tears; **promettere mari e monti a qn** to promise sb the earth
■ **il Mar Adriatico** the Adriatic; **il mar Caspio** the Caspian Sea; **il mare del Nord** the North Sea; **il mar Morto** the Dead Sea; **il mar Nero** the Black Sea; **il mar Rosso** the Red Sea; **il mar dei Sargassi** the Sargasso Sea; **i mari del Sud** the South Seas; **il mare della Tranquillità** (*sulla luna*) the Sea of Tranquillity; **il mar Mediterraneo** the Mediterranean Sea

> **LO SAPEVI...?**
> **mare** non si traduce mai con la parola inglese ***mare***

marea [ma'rɛa] SF **1** tide; **alta/bassa marea** high/low tide; **c'era bassa marea** it was low tide; **marea calante/montante** ebb/flood *o* rising tide **2** (*fig*) flood; **una marea di gente** hordes of people; **una**

marea di gente affollava la piazza there were hordes of people in the square
mareggiata [mared'dʒata] SF rough seas (*inshore*)
maremma [ma'remma] SF (*Geog*) maremma, swampy coastal area
maremmano, a [marem'mano] AGG **1** (*zona, macchia*) swampy **2** (*della Maremma*) of *o* from the Maremma ■SM/F inhabitant *o* native of the Maremma
maremoto [mare'mɔto] SM seaquake
maresciallo [mareʃ'ʃallo] SM (*Mil*) marshal; (: *sottufficiale*) warrant officer
maretta [ma'retta] SF **1** (*movimento di mare*) choppiness **2** (*tensione, disaccordo*) tension
marezzato, a [mared'dzato] AGG (*seta*) watered, moiré; (*legno*) veined; (*carta*) marbled
margarina [marga'rina] SF margarine
margherita [marge'rita] SF **1** (*Bot*) oxeye daisy, marguerite **2** (*di stampante*) daisy wheel
2: **la Margherita** (*Pol*) the Daisy (*centre-left political grouping*)
margheritina [margeri'tina] SF (*Bot*) daisy
marginale [mardʒi'nale] AGG marginal ■SM/F socially excluded person
marginalità [mardʒinali'ta] SF INV (*di problema, questione*) marginality
marginalmente [mardʒinal'mente] AVV marginally; **l'argomento è stato trattato marginalmente** this point was not the main focus of the discussion
marginare [mardʒi'nare] VT (*foglio, pagina*) to set the margins for
marginatore [mardʒina'tore] SM (*di macchina da scrivere*) margin stop
marginazione [mardʒinat'tsjone] SF margin setting
margine ['mardʒine] SM (*gen*) margin; (*di bosco, via*) edge; **al margine di** on the edge of; **ai margini della società** on the fringes of society; **note in** *o* **a margine** notes in the margin; **avere un buon margine di tempo/denaro** to have plenty of time/money (to spare)
■**margine di errore** margin of error; **margine di guadagno** *o* **di utile** profit margin; **margine operativo** operating margin; **margine sul prezzo** mark-up; **margine di sicurezza** safety margin
margotta [mar'gɔtta] SF (*pianta*) layer
mariano, a [mari'ano] AGG (*Rel*) Marian; **mese mariano** month of Mary
marijuana [mæri'wa:nə] SF marijuana
marina [ma'rina] SF **1** (*costa*) coast; (*quadro*) seascape **2** (*Mil*) navy; **marina mercantile** merchant navy (*Brit*) *o* marine (*Am*); **marina militare** ≈ Royal Navy (*Brit*), ≈ United States Navy (*Am*)
marinaio, ai [mari'najo] SM sailor; **marinaio di acqua dolce** (*pegg*) landlubber
marinare [mari'nare] VT **1** (*Culin*) to marinate; **aringhe marinate** soused *o* pickled herring **2** (*disertare*): **marinare la scuola** to play truant, play hooky (*spec Am*)
marinaresco, a, schi, sche [marina'resko] AGG sailor's *attr*
marinaro, a [mari'naro] AGG (*tradizione, popolo*) seafaring; **borgo marinaro** fishing village/town; **alla marinara** (*vestito, cappello*) sailor *attr*; (*Culin*) with seafood
marinata [mari'nata] SF (*Culin*) marinade
marinato, a [mari'nato] AGG (*Culin*) marinated
marinatura [marina'tura] SF marinading
marine [mə'ri:n] SM INV (*Mil*) marine
marino, a [ma'rino] AGG (*aria, fondali*) sea *attr*; (*fauna*) marine; (*città, colonia*) seaside *attr*
mariolo [mari'ɔlo] SM (*scherz*) rascal
marionetta [marjo'netta] SF puppet, marionette; (*fig: persona debole*) puppet; **teatrino/spettacolo di marionette** puppet theatre/show
▷ www.buma.it/
maritare [mari'tare] VT to marry, give in marriage
▶ **maritarsi** VR: **maritarsi (a *o* con qn)** to get married (to sb), marry (sb)
maritato, a [mari'tato] AGG married
marito [ma'rito] SM husband; **suo marito** her husband; **il marito di mia sorella** my sister's husband; **prendere marito** to get married
maritozzo [mari'tɔttso] SM *type of currant bun*
marittimo, a [ma'rittimo] AGG (*gen*) maritime, sea *attr*; (*città*) coastal; **linee marittime** shipping lines ■SM seaman
marmaglia [mar'maʎʎa] SF (*gente ignobile*) riff-raff, mob; (*ragazzacci*) gang of kids
marmellata [marmel'lata] SF jam; (*di agrumi*) marmalade; **marmellata di fragole** strawberry jam
marmista, i [mar'mista] SM (*operaio*) marble-cutter; (*artigiano*) marble worker
marmitta [mar'mitta] SF **1** (*Aut*) silencer; **marmitta catalitica** catalytic converter **2** (*recipiente*) cauldron **3** (*Geol*) pothole
marmittone [marmit'tone] SM (*scherz: recluta*) raw recruit, rookie (*Am*)
marmo ['marmo] SM marble; **di marmo** marble *attr*, made of marble; **una statua di marmo** a marble statue; **avere un cuore duro come il marmo** to have a heart of stone
marmocchio, chi [mar'mɔkkjo] SM (*fam*) (tiny) tot, (little) kid
marmoreo, a [mar'mɔreo] AGG (*di marmo*) marble *attr*
marmorizzato, a [marmorid'dzato] AGG marbled
marmotta [mar'mɔtta] SF (*Zool*) marmot; (*fig: persona lenta*) slowcoach
marna ['marna] SF (*Geol*) marl
marocchino, a [marok'kino] AGG, SM/F Moroccan ■SM (*cuoio*) morocco (leather)
Marocco [ma'rɔkko] SM Morocco; **mi è piaciuto molto il Marocco** I really liked Morocco; **andremo in Marocco quest'estate** we're going to Morocco this summer
maroso [ma'roso] SM breaker
marpione [mar'pjone] SM (*fam*) slimeball
marra ['marra] SF (*Agr*) hoe; (*Naut*) fluke
Marrakesh [marra'kɛʃ] SF Marrakesh
marrano [mar'rano] SM (*scherz*) boor
marrone [mar'rone] AGG INV brown ■SM **1** (*colore*) brown **2** (*Bot*) chestnut

LO SAPEVI...?
marrone non si traduce mai con la parola inglese ***maroon***

marron glacé [ma'rɔ̃gla'se] SM INV marron glacé
marsala [mar'sala] SM INV (*vino*) Marsala
marsc' [marʃ] ESCL: **(avanti) marsc'!** quick march!
Marsiglia [mar'siʎʎa] SF Marseilles
marsigliese [marsiʎ'ʎese] AGG of *o* from Marseilles ■SM/F inhabitant *o* native of Marseilles
marsina [mar'sina] SF tails *pl*, tail coat
marsupiale [marsu'pjale] SM marsupial
marsupio, pi [mar'supjo] SM **1** (*Zool*) pouch, marsupium (*termine tecn*) **2** (*per neonati*) sling; (*per denaro*) bum-bag

Mm

mart. ABBR (= **martedì**) Tues.
Marte ['marte] SM (*Astron, Mitol*) Mars
martedì [marte'di] SM INV Tuesday; **oggi è martedì 3 aprile** (the date) today is Tuesday 3rd April; **martedì stavo male** I wasn't well on Tuesday; **l'ho vista martedì** I saw her on Tuesday; **ogni martedì** *or* **tutti i martedì** every Tuesday, on Tuesdays; **di** *o* **il martedì** on Tuesdays; **vado in piscina di martedì** I go swimming on Tuesdays; **un martedì sì un martedì no** every other Tuesday; **martedì scorso/prossimo** last/next Tuesday; **il martedì successivo** *or* **il martedì dopo** the following Tuesday; **2 settimane fa, di martedì** a fortnight ago on Tuesday; **martedì fra una settimana/quindici giorni** a week/fortnight on Tuesday, Tuesday week/fortnight; **martedì mattina/pomeriggio/sera** Tuesday morning/afternoon/evening; **il film del martedì** the Tuesday film; **il giornale di martedì** Tuesday's newspaper; **martedì grasso** Shrove Tuesday
martellamento [martella'mento] SM hammering, pounding; **mi fu difficile far fronte al martellamento delle sue domande** I found it hard to stand up to his constant questioning
martellante [martel'lante] AGG (*fig: dolore*) throbbing; **una martellante campagna elettorale** a high-pressure electoral campaign
martellare [martel'lare] VT (*gen*) to hammer; **martellare qn di domande** to fire questions at sb
■ VI (*aus* **avere**) (*pulsare: tempie*) to throb; (*: cuore*) to thump
martellata [martel'lata] SF hammer blow; **dare una martellata a qn/qc** to hit sb/sth with a hammer
martelletto [martel'letto] SM (*di pianoforte*) hammer; (*di macchina da scrivere*) typebar; (*di giudice, nelle vendite all'asta*) gavel; (*Med*) percussion hammer
martellio, lii [martel'lio] SM hammering
martello [mar'tɛllo] SM (*gen, Sport, Anat*) hammer; **battere col martello** to hit with a hammer, hammer; **piantare un chiodo col martello** to hammer in a nail; **lancio del martello** (*Sport*) hammer throw; **suonare a martello** (*fig: campane*) to sound the tocsin; **martello pneumatico** pneumatic drill
martinetto [marti'netto] SM (*Tecn*) jack
martingala [martin'gala] SF (*di giacca*) half-belt; (*di cavallo*) martingale
martin pescatore [mar'tin peska'tore] SM kingfisher
martire ['martire] SM/F (*anche fig*) martyr; **fare il** *o* **atteggiarsi a martire** to play the martyr
martirio, ri [mar'tirjo] SM martyrdom; (*fig*) agony, torture; **vivere con quell'uomo è un martirio** living with that man is hell
martirizzare [martirid'dzare] VT (*Rel*) to martyr; (*persona, animali*) to torture
martora ['martora] SF marten
martoriare [marto'rjare] VT to torment, torture
marxismo [mark'sizmo] SM Marxism
marxista, i, e [mark'sista] AGG, SM/F Marxist
Maryland ['meriland] SM Maryland
marzapane [martsa'pane] SM marzipan
marziale [mar'tsjale] AGG martial
marziano, a [mar'tsjano] AGG Martian
■ SM/F (*di Marte*) Martian; (*extraterrestre*) Martian, little green man; **mi guardavano come se fossi un marziano** (*fam*) they looked at me as if I had two heads
marzo ['martso] SM March; *per fraseologia vedi* **luglio**
marzolino, a [martso'lino] AGG March *attr*

mas [mas] SM INV motor torpedo boat
mascalzonata [maskaltso'nata] SF dirty trick
mascalzone [maskal'tsone] SM (*anche scherz*) rascal, scoundrel
mascara [mas'kara] SM INV mascara
mascarpone [maskar'pone] SM *soft cream cheese often used in desserts*
mascella [maʃʃɛlla] SF (*Anat*) jaw
mascellare [maʃʃel'lare] AGG jaw *attr*
maschera ['maskera] SF **1** (*gen*) mask; (*costume*) fancy dress; **in maschera** (*mascherato*) masked; **una maschera di carnevale** a carnival mask; **mettersi** *o* **vestirsi in maschera** to put on *o* wear fancy-dress; **ballo in maschera** fancy-dress ball; **gettare la maschera** (*fig*) to reveal o.s.; **giù la maschera!** (*fig*) stop acting! **2** (*Cine*) usher/usherette **3** (*Teatro*) stock character **4** (*per nuotare*) mask; **ho comprato la maschera e le pinne** I bought a mask and flippers
■ **maschera antigas** gas mask; **maschera di bellezza** face pack; **maschera ad ossigeno** oxygen mask; **maschera subacquea** diving mask
mascherare [maske'rare] VT (*viso*) to mask; (*entrata, fig: sentimenti, intenzioni*) to hide, conceal; (*Mil*) to camouflage; **mascherare i bambini per una festa** to get the children into fancy dress for a party
▶ **mascherarsi** VR: **mascherarsi (da)** (*travestirsi*) to disguise o.s. (as); (*per un ballo*) to dress up (as)
mascherata [maske'rata] SF (*anche fig*) masquerade
mascherato, a [maske'rato] AGG (*ladro*) masked; (*bambino*) dressed up; (*ballo*) masked; (*fig: nascosto*) concealed
mascherina [maske'rina] SF **1** (*bambino in maschera*) child in fancy dress; (*piccola maschera*) mask; (*di animale*) patch; (*di scarpe*) toe-cap **2** (*Aut*) radiator grille
mascherone [maske'rone] SM (grotesque) mask
maschiaccio, ci [mas'kjattʃo] SM (*scherz: ragazza*) tomboy
maschietto [mas'kjetto] SM little boy
maschile [mas'kile] AGG (*gen, Gramm*) masculine; (*sesso, popolazione*) male *attr*; (*abiti*) men's; (*per ragazzi: scuola*) boys'; **un nome maschile** a masculine noun; **sesso: maschile** sex: male; **una voce maschile** a male voice
■ SM (*Gramm*): **il maschile** the masculine
maschilismo [maski'lizmo] SM (male) chauvinism, sexism
maschilista, i, e [maski'lista] AGG, SM/F (*uomo*) (male) chauvinist, sexist; (*donna*) sexist
maschio, chia, chi, chie ['maskjo] AGG (*figlio*) male; (*comportamento, atteggiamento*) male, masculine; (*volto, voce*) masculine
■ AGG INV (*animale*) male; **una tigre maschio** a male tiger; **i miei colleghi maschi** my male colleagues
■ SM (*gen, Tecn, Bio, Zool*) male; (*uomo*) man; (*ragazzo*) boy; (*figlio*) son; **hanno un maschio e una femmina** they've got a boy and a girl; **un maschio bianco** a white male; **i maschi** the men; **il maschio della tigre** the male tiger; **maschio della vite** screw tap
mascolinità [maskolini'ta] SF masculinity
mascolino, a [masko'lino] AGG masculine
mascotte [mas'kɔt] SF INV mascot
masnada [maz'nada] SF (*pegg: gruppo*) gang, band
masnadiere [mazna'djɛre] SM (*furfante*) ruffian, scoundrel
masochismo [mazo'kizmo] SM masochism
masochista, i, e [mazo'kista] AGG masochistic
■ SM/F masochist
massa ['massa] SF **1** (*volume, Fis*) mass; **massa critica**

(*Fis*) critical mass; **massa d'acqua** body of water; **massa atomica** atomic mass; **massa cerebrale** brain, cerebral mass **2** (*Sociol*): **la massa** *or* **le masse** the masses *pl*; **la massa dei cittadini** the majority of the townspeople; **di massa** mass; **manifestazione/ cultura di massa** mass demonstration/culture; **turismo di massa** mass tourism **3** **una massa di** (*oggetti*) heaps of, loads of; (*errori*) masses of; (*persone*) crowds of, masses of; **siete una massa di idioti!** (*fam*) you're a bunch of idiots! **4** **produzione in massa** mass production; **produrre in massa** to mass-produce; **vendere in massa** (*Comm*) to sell in bulk; **esecuzioni in massa** mass executions; **arrivare in massa** to arrive en masse **5** (*Elettr*) earth; **collegare** *o* **mettere a massa** to earth

Massachusetts [massa'tʃussets] SM Massachusetts

massacrante [massa'krante] AGG exhausting, gruelling

massacrare [massa'krare] VT (*uccidere*) to massacre, slaughter; (: *animali*) to slaughter; (*fig: avversario*) to make mincemeat of; (: *brano musicale*) to murder

massacro [mas'sakro] SM massacre, slaughter; (*fig*) disaster, mess; **fare un massacro** to carry out a massacre; **all'esame i professori hanno fatto un massacro** the lecturers were failing exam candidates left, right and centre

massaggiare [massad'dʒare] VT to massage; **farsi massaggiare** to have a massage

massaggiatore, trice [massaddʒa'tore] SM/F masseur/masseuse
■ SM (*apparecchio*) massager

massaggio, gi [mas'saddʒo] SM massage; **massaggio cardiaco** heart massage

massaia [mas'saja] SF housewife

massaio, ai [mas'sajo] SM (*di podere*) estate manager

massello [mas'sɛllo] SM **1** (*di oro ecc*) ingot **2** **mobili in massello di noce** furniture *sg* made of solid walnut

masseria [masse'ria] SF large farm

masserizie [masse'rittsje] SFPL (household) furnishings

massese [mas'sese] AGG of *o* from Massa
■ SM/F inhabitant *o* native of Massa

massicciamente [massittʃa'mente] AVV (*intervenire*) on a massive scale; **hanno dovuto intervenire massicciamente sul testo** the text had to be heavily edited

massicciata [massit'tʃata] SF (*di strada, ferrovia*) ballast

massiccio, cia, ci, ce [mas'sittʃo] AGG **1** (*mobile, edificio*) massive, solid; (*corporatura*) stout **2** **oro/legno massiccio** solid gold/wood **3** (*fig: attacco*) massive; (: *dose*) heavy, massive
■ SM (*Geog*) massif

massificare [massifi'kare] VT (*individui*) to depersonalize

massificazione [massifikat'tsjone] SF: **la massificazione della cultura** the homogenization of culture

massima ['massima] SF **1** (*motto*) maxim **2** (*Meteor*) maximum temperature **3** **in linea di massima** generally speaking

massimale [massi'male] SM (*Assicurazione*) maximum sum payable by insurers

massimalismo [massima'lizmo] SM (*Pol*) maximalism; (*fig*) radical ideology

massimo, a ['massimo] AGG (*superl di* **grande**) (*gen*) greatest; (*temperatura, livello, prezzo*) maximum, highest; (*importanza, cura*) utmost, greatest; **è una questione della massima importanza** it's a question of the greatest importance; **è della massima importanza che tu ci sia** it is of the utmost importance *o* it is vital that you be *o* are there; **è il massimo poeta del secolo** he is the greatest poet of the century; **erano presenti le massime autorità** all the most important dignitaries were there; **al massimo grado** to the highest degree; **stupido al massimo grado** stupid beyond belief; **ha la mia massima stima/il mio massimo rispetto** I have the highest regard/greatest respect for him; **ottenere il massimo effetto con la minima spesa** to get the best results at the least cost; **in massima parte** for the most part, mainly; **arrivare entro il tempo massimo** to arrive within the time limit; **il tempo massimo concesso** the maximum time allowed; **la velocità massima che questa macchina può raggiungere è...** the top *o* maximum speed of this car is ...; **la velocità massima permessa nei centri abitati** the speed limit in built-up areas
■ SM (*gen*) maximum; **è il massimo che io possa fare** it's the most I can do; **è il massimo della stupidità** (*persona*) you can't get much more stupid than him; (*gesto*) it's the height of stupidity; **è il massimo!** (*colmo*) that's the limit *o* end!; **può portare al massimo cinque persone** it can take five people at the most; **cerca di impegnarti al massimo** try to do your best; **costerà al massimo 5 sterline** it'll cost 5 pounds at (the) most; **lavorare al massimo** to work flat out; **sfruttare qc al massimo** to make full use of sth; **al massimo finiamo lunedì** we'll finish on Monday at the outside; **arriverò al massimo alle 5** I'll arrive at 5 at the latest; **ottenere il massimo dei voti** (*Scol*) to get full marks; (*in votazione*) to be accepted unanimously; **il massimo della pena** (*Dir*) the maximum penalty

massivo, a [mas'sivo] AGG (*intervento*) en masse; (*emigrazione*) mass; (*emorragia*) massive

masso ['masso] SM rock, boulder; **caduta (di) massi** (*cartello*) (beware!) falling rocks; **dormire come un masso** to sleep like a log; **masso erratico** (*Geol*) erratic

massone [mas'sone] SM freemason

massoneria [massone'ria] SF freemasonry

massonico, a, ci, che [mas'sɔniko] AGG masonic

massoterapia [massotera'pia] SF (*Med*) deep massage

mastectomia [mastekto'mia] SF (*Med*) mastectomy

mastello [mas'tɛllo] SM tub

masterizzare [masterid'dzare] VT (CD, DVD) to burn

masterizzatore [masteriddza'tore] SM CD burner *o* writer

masterizzazione [masteriddzat'tsjone] SF (*di CD, DVD*) burning

masticabile [masti'kabile] AGG which can be chewed, chewable

masticare [masti'kare] VT to chew, masticate (*frm*); (*tabacco, gomma*) to chew; **gomma da masticare** chewing gum; **mastico un po' di inglese** I have a smattering of English

mastice ['mastitʃe] SM (*resina*) mastic; (*per vetri*) putty

mastino [mas'tino] SM mastiff

mastodonte [masto'donte] SM mastodon; **è un mastodonte** (*fig*) he's a hulking great brute

mastodontico, a, ci, che [masto'dɔntiko] AGG (*fig*) gigantic, colossal

mastoide [mas'tɔide] SF mastoid

mastoideo, a [mastoi'dɛo] AGG mastoid *attr*

mastro ['mastro] SM **1** (*persona*): **mastro falegname** master carpenter **2** (*Comm*): **(libro) mastro** ledger

Mm

masturbare [mastur'bare] VT, **masturbarsi** VR to masturbate

masturbazione [masturbat'tsjone] SF masturbation; **masturbazione intellettuale** *o* **mentale** *(fig)* intellectual masturbation

matassa [ma'tassa] SF *(gen)* skein, hank; **venire a capo della matassa** *(fig)* to unravel the problem; **ingarbugliare** *o* **imbrogliare la matassa** *(fig)* to confuse the issue

matematica [mate'matika] SF mathematics *sg*; (*(frm)* maths *sg (Brit)*, math *sg (Am)*; **è brava in matematica** she's good at maths

matematicamente [matematika'mente] AVV mathematically; **sono matematicamente sicuro di quello che dico** I am absolutely sure of what I'm saying

matematico, a, ci, che [mate'matiko] AGG mathematical; **avere la certezza matematica che** to be absolutely certain that
■ SM/F mathematician

materano, a [mate'rano] AGG of *o* from Matera
■ SM/F inhabitant *o* native of Matera

materassino [materas'sino] SM mat; **materassino gonfiabile** air bed

materasso [mate'rasso] SM mattress; **materasso ad acqua** water bed; **materasso di gommapiuma** foam mattress; **materasso a molle** spring *o* interior-sprung mattress

materia [ma'tɛrja] SF *(gen, Filosofia, Fis)* matter; *(Scol: argomento)* subject matter, material; *(disciplina)* subject; *(sostanza: Tecn, Comm)* material, substance; **è una materia difficile** it's a difficult subject; **prima di entrare in materia...** before discussing the matter in hand ...; **un esperto in materia (di musica** *ecc***)** an expert on the subject (of music *ecc*); **sono ignorante in materia** I know nothing about it
■ **materia cerebrale** cerebral matter; **materia grassa** fat; **materia grigia** *(anche fig)* grey matter; **materie plastiche** plastics; **materie prime** raw materials

materiale [mate'rjale] AGG *(interessi, necessità, danni)* material; *(persona: materialista)* materialistic; **non ho avuto il tempo materiale di farlo** I simply haven't had the time to do it; **non ha avuto la possibilità materiale di evitarlo** he just couldn't avoid it
■ SM *(gen)* material; *(insieme di strumenti)* equipment *no pl*; **di che materiale è fatto?** what is it made of?; **sto raccogliendo materiale per il mio progetto** I'm collecting material for my project; **hai il materiale per scrivere?** have you got pen and paper?
■ **materiale bellico** war materiel *o* matériel; **materiale da costruzione** building materials *pl*; **materiale rotabile** rolling stock; **materiale di scarto** waste material

materialismo [materja'lizmo] SM materialism

materialista, i, e [materja'lista] AGG materialistic
■ SM/F materialist

materialistico, a, ci, che [materja'listiko] AGG materialistic

materializzarsi [materjalid'dzarsi] VIP to materialize

materialmente [materjal'mente] AVV: **è materialmente impossibile farlo** it's a physical impossibility

maternamente [materna'mente] AVV maternally, like a mother

maternità [materni'ta] SF INV **1** *(condizione)* motherhood; **essere in (congedo di) maternità** to be on maternity leave; **maternità surrogata** *o* **sostitutiva** surrogate motherhood, surrogacy **2** *(clinica)* maternity hospital; **reparto maternità** maternity ward

materno, a [ma'tɛrno] AGG *(gen)* maternal; *(amore, cura)* motherly, maternal; *(nonno)* maternal; *(lingua, terra)* mother *attr*; **scuola materna** nursery school *(attended by children aged 3)*; **l'istinto materno** the maternal instinct; **i miei nonni materni** my mother's parents, my maternal grandparents; **la mia lingua materna** my mother tongue

matinée [mati'ne] SF INV *(Cine, Teatro)* matinée, afternoon performance

matita [ma'tita] SF pencil; **scrivere a matita** to write in pencil; **scrivi le note a matita** write your notes in pencil; **disegno a matita** pencil drawing
■ **matita emostatica** styptic pencil; **matita per (gli) occhi** eyeliner (pencil); **matita per (le) labbra** lip liner; **matite colorate** coloured pencils

matriarca [matri'arka] SF matriarch

matriarcale [matriar'kale] AGG matriarchal

matriarcato [matriar'kato] SM matriarchy

matrice [ma'tritʃe] SF **1** *(Bio, Mat, Tip, Tecn)* matrix; *(per duplicatore)* stencil **2** *(Comm)* counterfoil; *(di assegno)* (cheque) stub **3** *(fig: origine)* background; **l'attentato è di chiara matrice fascista** the fascists are undoubtedly behind this bombing

matricida, i, e [matri'tʃida] AGG matricidal
■ SM/F matricide *(person)*

matricidio, di [matri'tʃidjo] SM matricide *(act)*

matricola [ma'trikola] SF **1** *(registro)* register **2** *(anche:* **numero di matricola***)* registration number; (: *Mil*) regimental number; (: *Tecn*) part number **3** *(studente: nell'università)* freshman, fresher *(Brit fam)*

matricolato, a [matriko'lato] AGG *(ladro, bugiardo)* downright *attr*, out-and-out *attr*

matrigna [ma'triɲɲa] SF stepmother

matrimoniale [matrimo'njale] AGG *(gen)* matrimonial, marriage *attr*; *(rapporto)* marital; *(vita)* married; *(anello)* wedding *attr*; **camera/letto matrimoniale** double room/bed

matrimonio, ni [matri'mɔnjo] SM *(unione)* marriage; *(cerimonia)* wedding; *(durata)* marriage, married life; **dopo 5 anni di matrimonio** after 5 years of marriage; **pubblicazioni di matrimonio** (marriage) banns; **non mi hanno invitato al matrimonio** they didn't invite me to the wedding; **matrimonio religioso/civile** religious/civil wedding; **matrimonio d'amore** love match; **matrimonio di convenienza** marriage of convenience

matrona [ma'trɔna] SF *(fig)* matronly woman

matronale [matro'nale] AGG matronly

matta ['matta] SF *(Carte)* joker

mattacchione, a [mattak'kjone] SM/F joker

mattanza [mat'tantsa] SF *(pesca dei tonni)* tuna fishing; *(fig: serie di uccisioni)* killings *pl*

mattatoio, oi [matta'tojo] SM slaughterhouse, abattoir *(Brit)*

mattatore [matta'tore] SM *(di spettacolo)* star performer

matterello [matte'rɛllo] SM rolling pin

mattina [mat'tina] SF morning; **la** *o* **alla** *o* **di mattina** in the morning; **alle sette di mattina** at seven in the morning; **di prima mattina** *or* **la mattina presto** early in the morning; **domani mattina** tomorrow morning; **ogni mattina** every morning; **la mattina**

prima/dopo the previous/following morning; **la mattina prima di...** the morning before ...; **dalla mattina alla sera** (*continuamente*) from morning to night; (*improvvisamente: cambiare*) overnight; **alle due di mattina** at 2 a.m.

mattinata [matti'nata] SF **1** morning; **in mattinata** in the course of the morning; **sarà pronto in mattinata** it will be ready before noon; **nella mattinata** in the morning; **nella tarda mattinata** at the end of the morning; **nella tarda mattinata di sabato** late on Saturday morning **2** (*spettacolo*) matinée, afternoon performance

mattiniero, a [matti'njɛro] AGG: **essere mattiniero** to be an early riser

mattino [mat'tino] SM morning; **di buon mattino** early in the morning; **sul far del mattino** at daybreak; **il mattino ha l'oro in bocca** (*Proverbio*) the early bird catches the worm

matto, a ['matto] AGG **1** (*gen, fig*) mad, crazy; (*Med*) insane; **sei matto!** you're mad!; **sempre più matto** madder and madder; **diventare matto** to go mad; **sto diventando matta!** I'm going mad!; **far diventare matto qn** to drive sb mad *o* crazy; **mi ha fatto diventar matto** he drove me mad; **andare matto per qc** to be crazy *o* mad about sth; **va matto per il calcio** he's mad about football; **quella testa matta ne ha combinato un'altra** that lunatic has done it again; **matto da legare** as mad as a hatter; **fossi matto!** (*neanche per sogno*) not on your life!; **avere una voglia matta di** (*cibo, cioccolato*) to have a craving for; **ho una voglia matta di incontrarlo** I'm dying to meet him, I can't wait to meet him **2** (*falso*): **oro matto** imitation gold **3** (*opaco*) matt
■ SM/F madman/madwoman, lunatic; **ridere come un matto** to laugh hysterically; **fare il matto** to act the fool; **mi piace da matti la tua giacca** I just love your jacket; **roba da matti!** it's unbelievable!; **una gabbia di matti** (*fig*) a madhouse

mattoide [mat'tɔide] (*fam*) AGG nutty, screwy
■ SM/F nutcase, screwball (*spec Am*)

mattone [mat'tone] SM **1** brick; **una casa di mattoni** a brick house; **un muro di mattoni** a brick wall; **color mattone** *or* **rosso mattone** brick red **2** (*fig*): **questo libro/film è un mattone** this book/film is really heavy going; **ho un mattone sullo stomaco** I feel as though I've got a lead weight in my stomach

mattonella [matto'nɛlla] SF **1** (*piastrella*) tile; **a mattonelle** tiled **2** (*di carbone*) briquette **3** (*del biliardo*) cushion

mattutino, a [mattu'tino] AGG morning *attr*; **il sole mattutino** the morning sun

maturando, a [matu'rando] SM/F ≈ G.C.E. A-level candidate (*Brit*), graduating high-school senior (*Am*)

maturare [matu'rare] VT (*frutta*) to ripen; (*fig: persona*) to (make) mature; **maturare una decisione** to come to a decision
■ VI (*aus* **essere**), **maturarsi** VIP (*frutta, grano*) to ripen; (*ascesso*) to come to a head; (*fig: persona, idea, Econ: interessi*) to mature

maturazione [maturat'tsjone] SF (*di frutta*) ripening; (*di formaggio*) maturing; (*di interessi*) maturity

maturità [maturi'ta] SF **1** maturity; **se avessi un minimo di maturità** if you were a responsible adult **2** (*Scol: anche*: **esame di maturità**) school-leaving examination, ≈ G.C.E. A levels (*Brit*), ≈ (high-school) graduation (*Am*)

MATURITÀ

The diploma of **maturità** is awarded to young people who have passed the exam of the same name at the end of secondary school, at the age of 18-19. Holders of the diploma have the right to attend university.

maturo, a [ma'turo] AGG **1** (*frutto*) ripe, mature; **troppo maturo** overripe; **una pesca matura** a ripe peach **2** (*persona*) mature; **è molto matura per la sua età** she's very mature for her age; **è un uomo maturo** he's middle-aged; **i tempi sono maturi per agire** the time is ripe for action **3** (*Scol: studente*) student who has gained A levels (*Brit*), ≈ high-school graduate (*Am*)

matusa [ma'tuza] SM/F INV (*scherz*) old fogey

Mauritania [mauri'tanja] SF Mauritania

Maurizio [mau'rittsjo] SF: **(l'isola di) Maurizio** Mauritius

mausoleo [mauzo'lɛo] SM mausoleum

max. ABBR (= **massimo**) max.

maxi... ['maksi] PREF maxi...

maxiprocesso [maksipro'tʃɛsso] SM *trial involving a large number of accused*

MAXIPROCESSO

A **maxiprocesso** is a criminal trial which is characterized by the large number of co-defendants. These people are usually members of terrorist or criminal organizations. The trials are often lengthy and many witnesses may be called to give evidence.

Mm

maxischermo [maksis'kermo] SM giant screen

mazurca [mad'dzurka] SF mazurka

mazza ['mattsa] SF (*bastone*) club; (*Mil*) baton; (*nelle cerimonie*) mace; (*martello*) sledgehammer; (*Sport: da golf*) (golf) club; (*: da baseball, cricket*) bat

mazzata [mat'tsata] SF (*anche fig*) heavy blow

mazzetta [mat'tsetta] SF (*di banconote*) bundle; (*fig*) rake-off; (*: tangente*) bribe

mazziere [mat'tsjɛre] SM **1** (*in processioni*) macebearer **2** (*Carte*) dealer

mazzo ['mattso] SM **1** (*di fiori, chiavi*) bunch **2** (*di carte da gioco*) pack; **tenere il mazzo** to be dealer; **fare il mazzo** (*mescolare*) to shuffle the cards **3** (*fam!: culo*): **farsi un** *o* **il mazzo** (*faticare molto*) to work bloody hard, work one's guts out

MC SIGLA = *Macerata*

mcm ABBR (= **minimo comune multiplo**) lcm

ME SIGLA = **Messina**

me [me] PRON PERS **1** (*forma tonica*) me; **parlavate di me?** were you talking about me?; **vieni con me?** are you coming with me?; **dietro di me** behind me; **senza di me** without me; **lo ha dato a me, non a te** he gave it to me *o* ME, not to you *o* YOU; **dopo di me tocca a te** it's your turn after me; **vieni da me?** are you coming to my place?; **l'ho fatto da me** I did it (all) by myself; **il dolce l'ho fatto da me** I made the cake myself; **pensavo tra me e me che...** I was thinking to myself that ...; **se fossi in me cosa faresti?** what would you do if you were me? *o* if you were in my position? **2** (*nelle comparazioni*) I, me; (*in espressioni esclamative*) me; **è alta come me** she's as tall as I am *o* as me; **fai come me** do the same as me, do as I do; **sei bravo quanto me** you are as clever as I (am) *o* as me; **è più giovane di**

me he's younger than I (am) *o* than me; **povero me!** poor me! **3** *vedi* **mi'**

mea culpa ['mɛa'kulpa] SM INV mea culpa; **recitare il mea culpa** (*fig*) to admit one is to blame

meandro [me'andro] SM (*di fiume*) meander; **si è perso nei meandri del palazzo** he lost his way in the building's maze of corridors; **i meandri del pensiero** the mind's meanderings

MEC [mɛk] SIGLA M = Mercato Comune Europeo

mecca ['mɛkka] SF (*Geog*): **la Mecca** Mecca; **la mecca del cinema** (*fig*) the mecca of the film world

meccanica [mek'kanika] SF **1** (*scienza*) mechanics *sg*; (*attività tecnologica*) mechanical engineering; **meccanica agraria** agricultural technology **2** (*meccanismo: di orologio, congegno*) mechanism; **c'è qualcosa che non va nella meccanica di questa macchina** there's something mechanically wrong with this car; **spiegami la meccanica dei fatti** *o* **dell'accaduto** tell me how it happened; **ricostruire la meccanica di un delitto/incidente** to reconstruct all the factors involved in a crime/accident

meccanicamente [mekkanika'mente] AVV mechanically

meccanicistico, a, ci, che [mekkani'tʃistiko] AGG mechanistic

meccanico, a, ci, che [mek'kaniko] AGG (*anche fig*) mechanical; **officina meccanica** garage
■ SM mechanic; **fa il meccanico** he's a mechanic; **devo portare la macchina dal meccanico** I've got to take my car to the garage

meccanismo [mekka'nizmo] SM mechanism

meccanizzare [mekkanid'dzare] VT to mechanize

meccanizzazione [mekkaniddzat'tsjone] SF mechanization

meccanografia [mekkanogra'fia] SF (mechanical) data processing

meccanografico, a, ci, che [mekkano'grafiko] AGG: **centro meccanografico** data processing department

mecenate [metʃe'nate] SM/F patron

mecenatismo [metʃena'tizmo] SM patronage (of the arts)

mèche [mɛʃ] SF INV streak; **farsi le mèche** to have one's hair streaked

medaglia [me'daʎʎa] SF (*gen*) medal; (*distintivo*) badge; **il rovescio della medaglia** (*fig*) the other side of the coin; **medaglia d'oro** (*oggetto*) gold medal; (*atleta*) gold medallist (*Brit*) *o* medalist (*Am*); **ha vinto una medaglia d'oro** he won a gold medal

medagliere [medaʎ'ʎɛre] SM **1** (*raccolta*) medal collection; **il medagliere dell'Italia alle Olimpiadi** (*Sport*) the (total number of) Olympic medals won by Italy **2** (*mobile*) medal cabinet

medaglietta [medaʎ'ʎetta] SF (small) medal; (*per cani*) name tag

medaglione [medaʎ'ʎone] SM **1** (*Arte*) medallion; (*Culin*) médaillon **2** (*gioiello*) locket

Medea [me'dɛa] SF Medea

medesimo, a [me'dezimo] AGG **1** (*identico, uguale*) same; **mi ha detto le medesime cose** he said the same things to me; **sono della medesima taglia** they are the same size **2** (*enfatizzato*) very; **arrivò il medesimo giorno in cui io dovevo partire** he arrived the very day I was due to leave; **è la stessa medesima cosa** it's the very same thing; **le regole medesime del gioco impongono ciò** the very rules of the game require this **3** (*in persona*): **io medesimo/tu medesimo** I myself/you yourself; **il presidente medesimo** the president himself
■ PRON: **il (la) medesimo(a)** the same one

media ['mɛdja] SF **1** (*valore intermedio*) average; **al di sopra/sotto della media** above/below average; **in media** on average; **questa macchina fa in media i 120 km/h** this car has an average speed of 120 km/h; **abbiamo fatto in media settanta chilometri all'ora** we did an average of seventy kilometres an hour; **viaggiare ad una media di ...** to travel at an average speed of ...; **riceve in media 1000 euro al mese** he earns 1000 euros per month on average, he has an average income of 1000 euros per month **2** (*Scol: voto*) end-of-term average; **fu promosso con la media del 7** he passed with an average of 7 out of 10; **ha avuto una media molto bassa** his average marks were very low, he had a very low average mark **3** **medie** SFPL = scuola media; *vedi* **medio** **4** (*Mat*) mean; **media aritmetica/geometrica** arithmetic/geometric mean

mediale [me'djale] AGG media *attr*

mediamente [medja'mente] AVV on average

medianico, a, ci, che [me'djaniko] AGG (*poteri*) extrasensory

mediano, a [me'djano] AGG (*Geom*) median
■ SM (*Calcio*) half-back; **mediano sinistro/destro** left/right half; **mediano di mischia** (*Rugby*) scrum half
■ SF (*Geom*) median

mediante [me'djante] PREP (*per mezzo di*) by (means of)

mediare [me'djare] VT (*fare da mediatore*) to act as mediator in, mediate

mediatico, a, ci, che [me'djatiko] AGG media *attr*

mediato, a [me'djato] AGG indirect

mediatore, trice [medja'tore] SM/F (*gen, Pol*) mediator; (*Comm*) middleman, agent; **fare da mediatore tra** to mediate between; **mediatore d'affari** business agent; **mediatore culturale** *person who helps immigrants with integration into society*

mediazione [medjat'tsjone] SF (*gen, Pol*) mediation; (*Industria*) arbitration; (*Comm: azione, compenso*) brokerage

medicamento [medika'mento] SM medicament

medicamentoso, a [medikamen'toso] AGG medicinal

medicare [medi'kare] VT (*paziente*) to treat; (*ferita*) to dress; **la medicò e la rimandò a casa** he treated her and sent her home; **medicarsi un piede ferito** to dress one's injured foot; **gli medicò la ferita** she dressed his wound

medicato, a [medi'kato] AGG (*garza, shampoo*) medicated

medicazione [medikat'tsjone] SF (*di ferita*) dressing; **fare una medicazione a qn** to dress sb's wounds; **togliere/cambiare la medicazione** to remove/change the dressings

medicina [medi'tʃina] SF **1** (*scienza, preparato medicinale*) medicine; **una medicina contro la tosse** a cough medicine; **il tempo è la miglior medicina** (*fig*) time is a great healer; **medicina legale** forensic medicine **2** (*Univ: anche*: **facoltà di medicina**) medical faculty/school; **studente in medicina** medical student; **laurea in medicina** degree in medicine; **voglio studiare medicina** I want to study medicine
▷ www.ministerosalute.it/
▷ http://cercasalute.it/

medicinale [meditʃi'nale] AGG medicinal
■ SM medicine, drug

medico, a, ci, che ['mɛdiko] AGG (*gen*) medical; (*sostanza, erba*) medicinal; **ricetta medica** prescription; **cure mediche** medical treatment; **visita medica**

medical (examination); **fare una visita medica** to have a medical examination
■SM (*gen*) doctor; **chi è il tuo medico curante?** who's your doctor *o* GP?; (*in ospedale*) which doctor is in charge of your case?; **medico di bordo** ship's doctor; **medico chirurgo** surgeon; **medico di famiglia** family doctor; **medico fiscale** *doctor who checks that the sick leave given to patients by GPs is reasonable*; **medico generico** *o* **di base** general practitioner; **medico legale** forensic scientist

medievale [medje'vale] AGG (*anche fig*) medi(a)eval

medievalistica [medjeva'listika] SF medieval studies *pl*

medio, dia, di, die ['mɛdjo] AGG (*gen*) average; (*misura, corporatura*) average, medium; (*peso, ceto*) middle; **persona di statura media** person of average *o* medium height; **(dito) medio** middle finger; **scuola media** *school for pupils aged 11 – 14: education beyond this level is not compulsory*; **licenza media** *leaving certificate at the end of 3 years of secondary education*; **il Medio Oriente** the Middle East
■SM (*dito*) middle finger

mediocre [me'djɔkre] AGG (*gen*) mediocre; (*qualità, stipendio*) poor; (*persona, impiego*) mediocre, second-rate; **il suo ultimo disco è mediocre** his latest record is mediocre; **un prodotto di qualità mediocre** a poor quality product

mediocremente [medjokre'mente] AVV (*suonare, cantare*) indifferently; **quell'impiegato/quella fabbrica rende mediocremente** that employee/ factory isn't very efficient; **lo pagano mediocremente** he's poorly paid

mediocrità [medjokri'ta] SF (*vedi agg*) mediocrity; poorness

Medioevo [medjo'ɛvo] SM: **il Medioevo** the Middle Ages *pl*

medioleggero [medjoled'dʒɛro] SM welterweight

mediomassimo [medjo'massimo] SM light heavyweight

meditabondo, a [medita'bondo] AGG meditative, thoughtful

meditare [medi'tare] VT to ponder over, meditate on; (*progettare*) to plan, think out; **meditare di fare qc** to contemplate doing sth; (*pianificare*) to plan to do sth
■VI (*aus* **avere**): **meditare (su)** to meditate (on/upon), think (about)

meditativo, a [medita'tivo] AGG meditative, thoughtful

meditato, a [medi'tato] AGG (*gen*) meditated; (*parole*) carefully-weighed; (*vendetta*) premeditated; **ben meditato** (*piano*) well worked-out, neat

meditazione [meditat'tsjone] SF meditation; **dopo lunga meditazione si risolse a partire** after much thought he decided to leave

mediterraneo, a [mediter'raneo] AGG Mediterranean
■SM: **il (mare) Mediterraneo** the Mediterranean (Sea)

medium ['mɛdjum] SM/F INV medium

Medusa [me'duza] SF (*Mitol*) Medusa

medusa [me'duza] SF (*Zool*) jellyfish

mefitico, a, ci, che [me'fitiko] AGG putrid, foul-smelling

mega... ['mɛga] PREF mega...

mega ['mega] SM INV (*Inform*) = **megabyte**

megabyte [mega'bait] SM INV (*Inform*) megabyte

megaciclo [mega'tʃiklo] SM (*Radio*) megacycle

megaconcerto [megakon'tʃɛrto] SM *festival*

megafono [me'gafono] SM megaphone

megagalattico, a, ci, che [megaga'lattiko] AGG (*scherz: grandissimo*) gigantic, massive, mega-; (: *importantissimo*) mega-important

megahertz [mega'ɛrts] SM INV megahertz

megalite [mega'lite] SM megalith

megalomane [mega'lɔmane] AGG, SM/F megalomaniac

megalomania [megaloma'nia] SF megalomania

megalopoli [mega'lɔpoli] SF INV megalopolis

megaparcheggio [megapar'keddʒo] SM *very large car park*

megaton ['mɛgaton] SM INV (*Fis*) megaton

megera [me'dʒɛra] SF (*pegg: donna*) shrew

meglio ['mɛʎʎo] (*comp, superl di* **bene**) AVV **1** better; **sto meglio** I feel better; **gioca meglio di lui** she plays better than he does; **è cambiato in meglio** he has changed for the better, he has improved; **meglio non passare per quella strada** it's better not to take that road **2** (*con senso superlativo*) best; **i meglio allenati** the best trained; **sono le ragazze meglio vestite della scuola** they are the best dressed girls in the school **3 meglio che mai** better than ever; **meglio tardi che mai** better late than never; **meglio poco che niente** half a loaf is better than no bread; **faresti meglio ad andartene** you had better leave; **andare di bene in meglio** *or* **andare sempre meglio** to get better and better
■AGG INV **1** better; **questa casa è meglio dell'altra** this house is better than the other one; **è meglio che tu te ne vada** you'd better leave, it would be better for you to go; **è meglio non raccontargli niente** it would be better not to tell him anything *o* if you didn't tell him anything; **è molto meglio così** it's much better like this; **ha trovato di meglio da fare** he's found something better to do **2 alla meglio** as best one can; **alla bell'e meglio** somehow or other
■SM best; **al meglio delle proprie possibilità** as best one can, to the best of one's ability; **è il meglio che io possa fare** it's the best I can do; **fare del proprio meglio** to do one's best; **le cose si sono messe per il meglio** things turned out for the best; **essere al meglio della forma** to be in top form
■SF: **avere la meglio** to come off best; **aver la meglio su qn** to get the better of sb

mela ['mela] SF apple; **torta di mele** apple tart; **mele cotte** stewed apples; **mela cotogna** quince; **mela selvatica** crab apple

melagrana [mela'grana] SF pomegranate

melammina [melam'mina] SF (*Chim*) melamine

melanconia *ecc* [melanko'nia] = **malinconia** *ecc*

mélange [me'lɑ̃ʒ] SM INV mixture

melanina [mela'nina] SF melanin

melanzana [melan'dzana] SF aubergine (*Brit*), eggplant (*Am*)

melassa [me'lassa] SF (*Culin*) treacle, molasses *sg* (*Am*)

melatonina [melato'nina] SF melatonin

melenso, a [me'lɛnso] AGG dull, stupid

melina [me'lina] SF (*Calcio*): **fare melina** to keep possession of the ball so the opposition cannot score

melissa [me'lissa] SF (lemon) balm

mellifluamente [melliflua'mente] AVV (*pegg: rispondere, sorridere*) with sugary sweetness

mellifluo, a [mel'lifluo] AGG (*pegg*) sugary, honeyed

melma ['melma] SF slime

melmosità [melmosi'ta] SF sliminess

melmoso, a [mel'moso] AGG slimy

melo ['melo] SM apple tree

melodia [melo'dia] SF (*Mus*) melody; (*aria*) melody, tune; **cantare una melodia** to hum a tune
melodico, a, ci, che [me'lɔdiko] AGG melodic
melodiosamente [melodjosa'mente] AVV melodiously, tunefully
melodioso, a [melo'djoso] AGG melodious, tuneful
melodramma, i [melo'dramma] SM (*Teatro, pegg*) melodrama
melodrammaticamente [melodrammatika'mente] AVV melodramatically
melodrammatico, a, ci, che [melodram'matiko] AGG (*Teatro, pegg*) melodramatic
melograno [melo'grano] SM pomegranate tree
melone [me'lone] SM (musk) melon
membrana [mem'brana] SF membrane
membro ['mɛmbro] SM **1** (*pl m* **membri**) (*persona, Mat, Gramm*) member; **diventare membro di** to become a member of; **diventò membro del partito socialista** he became a member of the Socialist Party **2** (*pl f* **membra**) (*Anat*) limb; **riposare le stanche membra** to rest one's weary limbs **3** (*pl m* **membri**): **membro (virile)** male sexual organ
memo ['memo] SM INV reminder, note

LO SAPEVI...?
memo non si traduce mai con la parola inglese *memo*

memorabile [memo'rabile] AGG memorable
memorandum [memo'randum] SM INV memorandum
memore ['mɛmore] AGG (*letter*): **memore di** (*ricordando*) mindful of; (*riconoscente*) grateful for
memoria [me'mɔrja] SF **1** (*gen, Inform*) memory; **avere molta memoria** to have a good memory; **non avere memoria** to have a bad memory; **non ho molta memoria** I haven't got a good memory; **avere una memoria fotografica** to have a photographic memory; **ho una buona memoria** I've got a good memory; **imparare/sapere qc a memoria** to learn/know sth by heart; **ha imparato a memoria la poesia** she learnt the poem by heart; **frugare nella memoria** to search one's memory; **mi è rimasto impresso nella memoria** it was imprinted in my memory; **se la memoria non m'inganna** if I remember correctly **2** (*ricordo*) recollection, memory; **non resta memoria di quel fatto** no one remembers that event; **fatto degno di memoria** memorable deed; **a memoria d'uomo** within living memory; (*da tempo immemorabile*) from time immemorial; **in** *o* **alla memoria di** in (loving) memory of; **medaglia alla memoria** commemorative medal **3**: **memorie** SFPL (*opera autobiografica*) memoirs **4** (*Inform*) memory; **il mio computer non ha abbastanza memoria** my computer hasn't got enough memory; **memoria di cache** (*Inform*) cache memory; **memoria permanente** nonvolatile memory; **memoria di sola lettura** read-only memory; **memoria tampone** buffer; **memoria volatile** volatile memory
memoriale [memo'rjale] SM (*raccolta di memorie*) memoirs *pl*
memorizzare [memorid'dzare] VT (*gen*) to memorize; (*Inform*) to store
memorizzazione [memoriddzat'tsjone] SF (*vedi vb*) memorization; storage; **memorizzazione transitoria** (*Inform*) buffering
menadito [mena'dito] **a menadito** AVV perfectly, thoroughly; **sapere** *o* **conoscere qc a menadito** to know sth inside out
ménage [me'naʒ] SM INV: **un ménage tranquillo** a happy relationship; **ménage a tre** ménage à trois
menagramo [mena'gramo] SM/F INV jinx, Jonah
menare [me'nare] VT **1** (*letter*: *condurre*) to take, lead; **qual buon vento ti mena?** what brings you here?; **menare qn per il naso** (*fig*) to lead sb by the nose; **menare il can per l'aia** (*fig*) to beat about (*Brit*) *o* around (*Am*) the bush; **menare qc per le lunghe** to drag sth out; **menar vanto di qc** to boast about sth **2** (*picchiare*): **menare qn** to hit *o* beat sb; **menare le mani** (*essere manesco*) to be free with one's fists; (*picchiarsi*) to come to blows; **menare calci** to kick; **menare colpi** to deal blows **3** **menarla a qc** (*fam*: *infastidire*) to bore sb, drone on to sb
▶ **menarsi** VR (*uso reciproco*) to come to blows
menata [me'nata] SF **1** (*bastonata*) beating, hiding **2** (*fam*: *lamentela*) moaning; (: *cosa noiosa*) bore
mendace [men'datʃe] AGG (*letter*) lying, mendacious
mendicante [mendi'kante] SM/F beggar
mendicare [mendi'kare] VT (*anche fig*) to beg for; **mendicare qc da qn** to beg sb for sth, beg sth from sb ■VI (*anche fig*) to beg
menefreghismo [menefre'gizmo] SM (*fam*) couldn't-care-less attitude; **il suo è menefreghismo bello e buono!** he simply doesn't give a damn!
menefreghista, i, e [menefre'gista] AGG couldn't-care-less *attr*
■SM/F person who couldn't care less; **quella donna è una menefreghista** that woman couldn't care less about anything *o* doesn't give a damn about anything
Menelao [mene'lao] SM Menelaus
menestrello [menes'trello] SM minstrel
menhir [me'nir] SM INV menhir
meninge [me'nindʒe] SF (*Anat*) meninx; **spremersi le meningi** to rack one's brains
meningite [menin'dʒite] SF (*Med*) meningitis
menisco [me'nisko] SM (*Anat, Mat, Fis*) meniscus

meno ['meno] PAROLA CHIAVE
■AVV **1** less; **meno caro** less expensive, cheaper; **è meno alto di suo fratello/di quel che pensavo** he is not as tall as his brother/as I thought, he is less tall than his brother/than I thought; **ha due anni meno di me** he's two years younger than me; **dovresti mangiare meno** you should eat less, you shouldn't eat so much; **meno ne discutiamo, meglio è** the less we talk about it, the better; **deve avere non meno di trent'anni** he must be at least thirty; **meno fumo più mangio** the less I smoke the more I eat; **andare all'università diventa sempre meno facile** it's getting less and less easy to go to university; **ho speso (di) meno** I spent less; **arrivo tra meno di un'ora** I'll be there in less than *o* in under an hour
2 (*con senso superlativo*) least; **è il meno dotato dei miei studenti** he's the least gifted of my pupils; **è quello che leggo meno spesso** it's the one I read least often
3 (*sottrazione*: *Mat*) minus, less; **5 meno 2** 5 minus 2, 5 take away 2; **sono le otto meno un quarto** it's a quarter to eight (*Brit*) *o* of eight (*Am*); **mi hai dato due carte di meno** you gave me two cards too few; **eh, se avessi dieci anni di meno!** oh, if only I were ten years younger!; **ho una sterlina in meno** I am one pound short; **ci sono meno 25°** it's minus 25°, it is 25° below (zero); **ha preso sette meno** ≈ he got (a) B minus
4 (*fraseologia*): **non è da meno di lui** she is (every bit) as good as he is; **non voglio essere da meno di lui** I don't want to be outdone by him; **fare a meno di** to do

o manage without; **se non c'è zucchero ne faremo a meno** if there isn't any sugar we'll do without; **potresti fare a meno di fumare in macchina?** would you mind not smoking in the car?; **non ho potuto fare a meno di ridere** I couldn't help laughing; **in men che non si dica** in less than no time, quick as a flash; **meno male!** good!, thank goodness!, just as well!; **meno male che sei arrivato** it's a good job that you have come; **men che meno gli inglesi** least of all the English; **fammi sapere se verrai o meno** let me know if you are coming or not; **quanto meno poteva avvertire** he could at least have let us know; **non mi piace come scrive e tanto meno come parla** I don't like the way he writes let alone the way he talks
■ AGG INV (*acqua, lavoro, soldi*) less; (*persone, libri, errori*) fewer; **meno bambini ci sono, meglio è** the fewer children there are the better; **meno storie!** stop messing around!; **meno tempo** less time; **meno turisti** fewer tourists
■ SM INV **1** (*la minor cosa*): **il meno** the least; **era il meno che ti potesse capitare** (*rimprovero*) you were asking for it; **parlare del più e del meno** to talk about this and that; **per lo meno** = **perlomeno**; **i meno** (*la minoranza*) the minority
2 (*Mat*) minus (sign)
■ PREP (*fuorché, eccetto che*) except (for); **a meno che non faccia caldo** unless it is hot; **a meno di prendere un giorno di ferie** unless I (*o* you *ecc*) take a day off; **ci siamo tutti meno lui** we are all here except (for) him; **tutti meno uno** all but one

menomare [meno'mare] VT to maim, disable
menomato, a [meno'mato] AGG (*persona*) disabled
■ SM/F disabled person
menomazione [menomat'tsjone] SF disablement
menopausa [meno'pauza] SF menopause; **essere in menopausa** to be going through the menopause
menorah [meno'ra] SF INV menorah
mensa ['mɛnsa] SF **1** (*locale*) canteen; (: *Mil*) mess; (: *nelle università*) refectory **2** (*fig*) table; **i piaceri della mensa** the pleasures of the table
mensile [men'sile] AGG monthly; **un abbonamento mensile** a monthly ticket
■ SM (*periodico*) monthly (magazine); (*stipendio*) monthly salary
mensilità [mensili'ta] SF INV (*stipendio*) monthly salary; **riscuotere due mensilità arretrate** to get two months' back pay; **13/14/15 mensilità** ≈ once-/twice-/thrice-yearly bonus
mensilmente [mensil'mente] AVV (*ogni mese*) every month; (*una volta al mese*) monthly
mensola ['mɛnsola] SF (*supporto*) bracket; (*ripiano*) shelf; (*Archit*) corbel; **mensola del camino** mantelpiece; **mensola portaspezie** spice rack
menta ['menta] SF (*Bot*) mint; (*caramella*) mint, peppermint; (*bibita*) peppermint cordial; **alla menta** *or* **di menta** mint *attr*; **una caramella alla menta** a mint; **menta da giardino** *o* **comune** *o* **verde** spearmint; **menta piperita** peppermint
mentale [men'tale] AGG mental
mentalità [mentali'ta] SF INV mentality; **mentalità aperta/ristretta** open/narrow mind; **ha una mentalità aperta** he's open-minded; **ha una mentalità ristretta** he's narrow-minded
mentalmente [mental'mente] AVV mentally
mente ['mente] SF **1** (*gen, fig*) mind; **mente aperta/lucida** open/clear mind; **mente agile/acuta** quick/sharp mind; **ha una mente logica** he's got a logical mind; **mente malata** sick mind; **malato di mente** mentally ill; **avevo la mente altrove** my mind was elsewhere, I was miles away **2** (*fraseologia*): **a mente fredda** objectively; **rivedere qc a mente fresca** to take another look at sth when one's mind is fresh; **a mente serena** calmly; **avere in mente qc/qn** to have sth/sb in mind; **ha qualcosa in mente** he's got something in mind; **lo ha sempre in mente** she's always thinking of him; **avere in mente di fare qc** to intend to do sth; **lasciami fare mente locale** let me think; **fare venire in mente qc a qn** to remind sb of sth; **mettersi in mente di fare qc** to make up one's mind to do sth; **gli è passato di mente** he forgot about it; **mi è scappato di mente ciò che ti volevo dire** I've forgotten what I was going to say to you; **volevo farlo ma mi è scappato di mente** I meant to do it, but it went out of my head *o* slipped my mind; **ma cosa ti salta in mente?** what are you thinking of?, you must be crazy!; **tenere a mente qc** to bear sth in mind; **toglitelo dalla mente** forget about it, put it out of your mind; **mi è tornato in mente quell'indirizzo** that address has come back to me, I've remembered that address; **mi è venuto in mente che...** it occurred to me that ...; **non mi passa neppure per la mente** I wouldn't even consider it
mentecatto, a [mente'katto] AGG half-witted
■ SM/F half-wit, imbecile
mentina [men'tina] SF peppermint
mentire [men'tire] VI (*aus* **avere**) **mentire (a qn su qc)** to lie (to sb about sth); **mente** he's lying; **non saper mentire** to be a poor liar; **mentire spudoratamente** to lie through *o* in one's teeth
mentito, a [men'tito] AGG: **sotto mentite spoglie** under false pretences (*Brit*) *o* pretenses (*Am*)
mentitore, trice [menti'tore] SM/F liar
mento ['mento] SM chin; **doppio mento** double chin
mentolo [men'tɔlo] SM menthol
mentre ['mentre] CONG **1** (*temporale*) while, as; **è successo mentre ero fuori** it happened while I was out; **l'ho incontrato mentre entravo nel negozio** I met him as I was going into the shop **2** (*avversativo*) whereas, while; **lui è biondo mentre sua sorella è mora** he's blond while his sister is dark
■ SM: **in quel mentre** at that very moment
menu [me'nu] SM INV **1** (*Culin*) (set) menu; **menu turistico** tourists' menu **2** (*Inform*) menu; **menu a tendina** (*Inform*) pull-down menu
menzionare [mentsjo'nare] VT to mention
menzione [men'tsjone] SF mention; **fare menzione di** to mention; **degno di menzione** worthy of note
menzogna [men'tsoɲɲa] SF lie, falsehood; **dire menzogne** to tell lies
menzognero, a [mentsoɲ'ɲero] AGG (*scuse*) false, untrue; (*persona*) lying
meramente [mera'mente] AVV simply, purely
meraviglia [mera'viʎʎa] SF **1** (*stupore*) amazement, wonder; **non ti nascondo la mia meraviglia** you can imagine my surprise; **con mia (grande) meraviglia** to my amazement, to my great surprise; **suscitare gran meraviglia** to cause quite a stir; **mi fa meraviglia che...** I'm amazed that ...; **quest'abito ti sta a meraviglia** you look wonderful in that dress; **tutto va a meraviglia** everything is going perfectly **2** (*persona, cosa*) marvel, wonder; **hai un bimbo che è una meraviglia** isn't your baby gorgeous!; **il panorama è una meraviglia!** it's a wonderful view!; **le sette**

Mm

meraviglie del mondo the seven Wonders of the World

meravigliare [meraviʎ'ʎare] VT to amaze, surprise, astonish; **sono rimasto meravigliato** I was amazed *o* astonished; **mi meraviglierebbe se...** I'd be surprised if ..., it would surprise me if ...
▶ **meravigliarsi** VIP: **meravigliarsi (di *o* per)** (*stupirsi*) to be amazed (at), be astonished (at); **mi meraviglio di te!** I'm surprised at you!; **non c'è da meravigliarsi** it's not surprising

meravigliosamente [meraviʎʎosa'mente] AVV marvellously, wonderfully

meraviglioso, a [meraviʎ'ʎoso] AGG wonderful, marvellous (*Brit*), marvelous (*Am*)

merc. ABBR (= mercoledì) Wed.

mercante [mer'kante] SM dealer, trader; (*ant*) merchant; **mercante d'arte** art dealer; **mercante di cavalli** horse dealer; **mercante di schiavi** slave trader

mercanteggiare [merkanted'dʒare] VI (*aus* **avere**) to bargain, haggle; **mercanteggiare sul prezzo** to haggle over the price
■ VT (*pegg*: *onore, voto*) to sell

mercantile [merkan'tile] AGG (*gen*) mercantile, commercial; (*marina, nave*) merchant *attr*
■ SM (*nave*) merchantman

mercantilismo [merkanti'lizmo] SM mercantilism

mercanzia [merkan'tsia] SF (*pegg*) stuff

mercatino [merka'tino] SM **1** (*rionale*) local street market **2** (*Econ*) unlisted securities market

mercato [mer'kato] SM **1** (*luogo*) market; **giorno di mercato** market day; **mercato ortofrutticolo/del pesce** fruit/fish market; **mercati generali** wholesale market *sg*; **vado al mercato** I'm going to the market; **mercato delle pulci** flea market **2** (*Econ, Fin*) market; **mettere *o* lanciare qc sul mercato** to put sth on the market; **a buon mercato** (*agg*) cheap; (*avv*) cheaply; **di mercato** (*economia, prezzo, ricerche*) market *attr*
■ **mercato dei cambi** exchange market; **mercato dei capitali** capital market; **il Mercato Comune (Europeo)** the (European) Common Market; **mercato interno *o* nazionale** domestic market; **mercato del lavoro** labour market, job market; **mercato libero** free market; **mercato nero** black market; **mercato al rialzo** (*Borsa*) bull market; **mercato al ribasso** (*Borsa*) bear market; **mercato a termine** forward *o* futures market; **mercato dei valori** stock market

merce ['mɛrtʃe] SF goods *pl*, merchandise *no pl*; **merce in conto vendita** sale or return goods; **merce deperibile** perishable goods *pl*

mercé [mer'tʃe] SF mercy; **essere alla mercé di qn** to be at sb's mercy

mercenario, ria, ri, rie [mertʃe'narjo] AGG, SM/F mercenary

merceologia [mertʃeolo'dʒia] SF study *o* knowledge of commodities

merceria [mertʃe'ria] SF (*articoli*) haberdashery (*Brit*), notions *pl* (*Am*); (*bottega*) haberdasher's shop (*Brit*), notions store (*Am*)

mercerizzare [mertʃerid'dzare] VT (*cotone*) to mercerize

merciaio, aia, ai, aie [mer'tʃajo] SM/F haberdasher

mercificare [mertʃifi'kare] VT to commercialize

mercificazione [mertʃifikat'tsjone] SF commercialization

mercoledì [merkole'di] SM INV Wednesday; **mercoledì delle Ceneri** Ash Wednesday; *per fraseologia vedi* **martedì**

MERCOLEDÌ DELLE CENERI

In the Catholic church, **Mercoledì delle Ceneri** signals the beginning of Lent. Churchgoers are marked on the forehead with ash from the burning of an olive branch. Ash Wednesday is traditionally a day of fasting, abstinence and repentance.

Mercurio [mer'kurjo] SM (*Astron, Mitol*) Mercury

mercurio [mer'kurjo] SM mercury

merda ['mɛrda] SF (*fam!*) shit (*fam!*); **che giornata di merda!** what a lousy/shitty day!; **ho fatto una figura di merda** I looked a right git; **a quelle parole sono rimasto di merda** I felt bloody awful when I heard that; **essere nella merda (fino al collo)** (*nei guai*) to be (right) in the shit

merdoso, a [mer'doso] AGG (*fam!*) shitty

merenda [me'renda] SF afternoon snack; **far merenda** to have an afternoon snack; **ragazzi, venite a fare merenda** children, come and have a snack

merendina [meren'dina] SF snack, *prepacked cakes etc sold as snacks for children*

meretrice [mere'tritʃe] SF (*letter*) harlot

meridiana [meri'djana] SF sundial

meridiano, a [meri'djano] AGG (*di mezzogiorno*) midday *attr*, noonday *attr*
■ SM (*Geog, Agopuntura*) meridian; **meridiano terrestre** meridian

meridionale [meridjo'nale] AGG (*gen*) southern; (*dell'Italia*) Southern Italian
■ SM/F (*gen*) southerner; (*dell'Italia*) Southern Italian; **i meridionali** people from Southern Italy

meridione [meri'djone] SM: **il meridione** the South; (*dell'Italia*) the South of Italy, Southern Italy

meringa, ghe [me'ringa] SF meringue

meringata [merin'gata] SF *meringue and ice-cream based dessert*

merino [me'rino] AGG INV, SM merino

meritare [meri'tare] VT **1** (*premio, stima*) to deserve; **(si) merita un premio/un ceffone** he deserves a prize/a smack; **si è meritato la stima di tutti** he earned everybody's respect; **è una persona che merita** he deserves our respect (*o* affection *ecc*); **se l'è proprio meritato!** it serves him right **2** (*richiedere*): **meritare attenzione/considerazione** to require *o* need attention/consideration **3** (*valere*) to be worth; **questo pranzo non merita il prezzo** this meal's not worth the money
■ VB IMPERS (*valere la pena*): **merita andare** it's worth going; **non merita neanche parlarne** it's not worth talking about; **per quel che merita** for what it's worth

meritatamente [meritata'mente] AVV deservedly

meritato, a [meri'tato] AGG (*vacanza, premio, riposo*) well-deserved

meritevole [meri'tevole] AGG: **meritevole (di)** (*di lode, biasimo*) worthy (of); **è più meritevole di te** he's worthier than you

merito ['merito] SM **1** (*gen*) merit; (*valore*) worth; **dare (il) merito a qn di qc/di aver fatto qc** to give sb credit for sth/for doing sth; **è merito mio se hai avuto quel lavoro** it's thanks to me that you got that job; **è merito suo se hanno vinto** it's thanks to him that they won; **Dio ve ne renda merito!** may God reward you!; **finire a pari merito** to finish joint first (*o* second *ecc*); **le due squadre hanno finito a pari merito** the two teams tied; **medaglia al merito** (*Mil*) medal for bravery **2** (*argomento*): **entrare nel merito di una questione** to go into a matter; **non so niente in merito** I don't know anything about it; **in merito a** as regards, with regard to; **in merito a ciò di cui si è parlato** with reference to what was discussed

meritocratico, a, ci, che [merito'kratiko] AGG meritocratic, based on merit

meritocrazia [meritokrat'tsia] SF meritocracy

meritorio, ria, ri, rie [meri'tɔrjo] AGG praiseworthy

merlato, a [mer'lato] AGG (*Archit*) crenellated

merlatura [merla'tura] SF (*Archit*) battlements *pl*

merlettaia [merlet'taja] SF lacemaker

merletto [mer'letto] SM lace

merlo[1] ['mɛrlo] SM **1** (*Zool*) blackbird; **merlo acquaiolo** dipper; **merlo dal petto bianco** ring ouzel **2** (*sciocco*) fool, idiot

merlo[2] ['mɛrlo] SM (*Archit*) battlement

merluzzo [mer'luttso] SM cod

mero, a ['mɛro] AGG mere, sheer; **per mero caso** by mere *o* sheer chance

mescalina [meska'lina] SF mescaline

mescere ['meʃʃere] VT to pour (out)

meschinamente [meskina'mente] AVV (*grettamente*) meanly, pettily

meschinità [meskini'ta] SF INV (*grettezza*) meanness, pettiness, narrow-mindedness; (*spilorceria*) stinginess; **è stata una meschinità** it was a mean *o* petty trick

meschino, a [mes'kino] AGG (*avaro*) mean; (*gretto*) narrow-minded, mean, petty; (*scarso: guadagno*) meagre (*Brit*), meager (*Am*); **fare una figura meschina** to cut a poor figure, look silly
■ SM/F: **non fare il meschino** (*gretto*) don't be so petty

mescita ['meʃʃita] SF wine bar

mesciuto, a [meʃ'ʃuto] PP *di* **mescere**

mescolanza [mesko'lantsa] SF (*gen*) mixture; (*di ingredienti*) blend, mixture; **una mescolanza di gente/di idee** a mix of people/ideas

mescolare [mesko'lare] VT (*gen, Culin*) to mix; (*col cucchiaio*) to stir; (*vini, colori*) to blend; (*mettere in disordine: fogli, schede*) to mix up, muddle up; (*carte*) to shuffle; **mescolate la farina e lo zucchero** mix the flour and sugar
► **mescolarsi** VR: **mescolarsi alla folla** to mingle with the crowd
► **mescolarsi** VIP (*Culin*) to mix; (*vini, colori*) to blend; (*fogli, schede*) to get mixed up

mescolata [mesko'lata] SF: **dare una mescolata a** (*Culin*) to stir; (*Carte*) to shuffle

mese ['mese] SM month; **fra un mese** in a month('s time); **un mese di vacanza** a month's holiday; **un mese di sciopero** a month-long strike; **il mese scorso** last month; **il corrente mese** this month; **alla fine del mese** at the end of the month; **guadagna 2000 euro al mese** she earns 2000 euros a *o* per month; **tre mesi d'affitto** three months' rent; **un bambino di sei mesi** a six-month-old baby; **è al settimo mese (di gravidanza)** she's six months pregnant

mesetto [me'setto] SM: **un mesetto** about a month

messa[1] ['messa] SF (*Rel*) mass; **andare a** *o* **alla messa** to go to mass; **andiamo a messa di domenica** we go to Mass on Sundays; **dire la messa** (*celebrarla*) to say mass; **messa nera** black *o* Satanic mass

> **LO SAPEVI...?**
> **messa** no si traduce mai con la parola inglese *mess*

messa[2] ['messa] SF (*il mettere*): **messa a fuoco** focusing; **messa in moto** starting-up; **messa in opera** installation; **messa in orbita** launching; **messa in piega** set; **messa in posizione** installation; **messa a punto** (*termine tecn*) adjustment; (*Aut*) tuning; (*di progetto*) finalization; **messa in scena** (*Teatro*) production; **messa a terra** earthing

messaggerie [messaddʒe'rie] SFPL (*ditta: di distribuzione*) distributors; (*: di trasporto*) freight company *sg*

messaggero, a [messad'dʒɛro] SM/F messenger

messaggino [messad'dʒino] SM (*di telefonino*) text (message)

messaggio, gi [mes'saddʒo] SM message; **il messaggio augurale del capo dello stato** ≈ the Queen's Christmas message; **vuole lasciare un messaggio?** would you like to leave a message?; **messaggio di errore** (*Inform*) error message; **messaggio di posta elettronica** e-mail

messaggistica [messad'dʒistika] SF: **messaggistica immediata** (*Inform*) instant messaging; **programma di messaggistica immediata** instant messenger

messale [mes'sale] SM (*Rel*) missal

messe ['mɛsse] SF (*letter*) harvest; **fare messe di** (*fig: lodi, consensi*) to win

messia [mes'sia] SM INV messiah; **il Messia** the Messiah

messianico, a, ci, che [messi'aniko] AGG Messianic

messicano, a [messi'kano] AGG, SM/F Mexican

Messico ['mɛssiko] SM Mexico; **Città del Messico** Mexico City; **mi è piaciuto molto il Messico** I really liked Mexico; **quest'estate andremo in Messico** we're going to Mexico this summer

Messina [mes'sina] SF Messina; **lo stretto di Messina** the Strait of Messina

messinese [messi'nese] AGG of *o* from Messina
■ SM/F inhabitant *o* native of Messina

messinscena [messin'ʃɛna] SF INV (*Teatro*) production; (*fig*) performance; **è tutta una messinscena** it's all an act

messo[1] ['messo] SM messenger

messo[2]**, a** ['messo] PP *di* **mettere**
■ AGG: **essere ben/mal messo** (*economicamente*) to be well-/badly-off; (*di salute*) to be in good/bad health

mestamente [mesta'mente] AVV sadly

mestierante [mestje'rante] SM/F (*pegg*) money-grubber; (*: scrittore*) hack

mestiere [mes'tjɛre] SM (*gen: lavoro*) job; (*: manuale*) trade; (*: artigianale*) craft; (*fig: abilità nel lavoro*) skill, technique; **di mestiere** by trade; **un mestiere difficile** a difficult job; **cosa fa tuo padre di mestiere?** what does your father do?; **fa il mestiere di calzolaio** he is a shoemaker; **imparare un mestiere** to learn a trade; **essere del mestiere** to be in the trade; (*fig*) to be an expert; **conoscere i trucchi del mestiere** to know the tricks of the trade; **essere padrone del mestiere** to know one's job

mestizia [mes'tittsja] SF sadness, melancholy

mesto, a ['mɛsto] AGG sad, melancholy

mestola ['mestola] SF (*Culin*) ladle; (*Edil*) trowel

mestolo ['mestolo] SM ladle

mestolone [mesto'lone] SM (*Zool*) shoveler

mestruale [mestru'ale] AGG menstrual

mestruato, a [mestru'ato] AGG menstruating

mestruazione [mestruat'tsjone] SF menstruation; **avere le mestruazioni** to have one's period

mestruo ['mɛstruo] SM menstrual fluid

meta ['mɛta] SF **1** (*destinazione*) destination; (*fig: scopo*) aim, goal; **finalmente giunsero alla meta** they finally reached their destination; **vagare senza meta** to wander aimlessly; **vagava senza meta** he was wandering aimlessly **2** (*Rugby*) try; **segnare una meta** to score a try

metà [me'ta] SF INV **1** half; **dividere qc a metà** to divide sth in half *o* into two halves, halve sth; **fare a metà di qc con qn** to go halves with sb in sth; **facciamo a metà** let's go halves; **dammene la metà** give me half (of it); **ho impiegato la metà del tempo** it only took me half the time; **siamo arrivati a metà del concerto** we arrived halfway through the concert; **dire le cose a metà** to leave some things unsaid; **fare le cose a metà** to leave things half-done; **la mia dolce metà** (*fam scherz*) my better half; **a metà prezzo** at half price, half-price; **a metà strada** halfway **2** (*punto di mezzo*) middle; **tagliare una pagina per metà** to cut a page down the middle; **a metà settimana** mid-week; **verso la metà del mese** halfway through the month, towards the middle of the month

metabolico, a, ci, che [meta'bɔliko] AGG metabolic

metabolismo [metabo'lizmo] SM metabolism; **metabolismo basale** basal metabolism

metabolizzare [metabolid'dzare] VT (*cibo*) to metabolize; (*fig: idea, concetto*) to take in, to absorb

metabolizzazione [metabolidd̄zat'tsjone] SF (*di cibo, fig*) absorption

metacarpo [meta'karpo] SM metacarpus

metadone [meta'done] SM methadone

metafisica [meta'fizika] SF metaphysics *sg*

metafisicamente [metafizika'mente] AVV metaphysically

metafisico, a, ci, che [meta'fiziko] AGG metaphysical

metafora [me'tafora] SF metaphor; **parlare per metafore** to speak metaphorically; **fuor di metafora** without beating about the bush

metaforicamente [metaforika'mente] AVV metaphorically

metaforico, a, ci, che [meta'fɔriko] AGG metaphorical

metallaro, a [metal'laro] SM/F (*fam*) head-banger

metallico, a, ci, che [me'talliko] AGG (*simile al metallo*) metallic; (*di metallo*) metal *attr*

metallizzato, a [metallid'dzato] AGG (*vernice*) metallic

metallo [me'tallo] SM metal; **di metallo** metal *attr*; **un portacenere di metallo** a metal ashtray

metalloide [metal'lɔide] SM metalloid

metallurgia [metallur'dʒia] SF metallurgy

metallurgico, a, ci, che [metal'lurdʒiko] AGG metallurgical; **l'industria metallurgica** the iron and steel industry
■SM/F metal-worker

metalmeccanico, a, ci, che [metalmek'kaniko] AGG engineering *attr*; **l'industria metalmeccanica** the engineering industry
■SM/F engineering worker

metamorfico, a, ci, che [meta'mɔrfiko] AGG metamorphic

metamorfosi [meta'mɔrfozi] SF INV metamorphosis

metano [me'tano] SM methane; **riscaldamento a metano** gas heating

metanodotto [metano'dotto] SM methane pipeline

metanolo [meta'nɔlo] SM methanol

metastasi [me'tastazi] SF INV (*Med*) metastasis

metatarso [meta'tarso] SM metatarsus

metempsicosi [metempsi'kɔzi] SF INV metempsychosis

meteo ['mɛteo] SM INV weather forecast
■AGG INV = **meteorologico**

meteora [me'tɛora] SF meteor; **quell'attore è passato come una meteora** that actor's success was a flash in the pan

meteorico, a, ci, che [mete'ɔriko] AGG meteoric

meteorismo [meteo'rizmo] SM (*Med*) meteorism

meteorite [meteo'rite] SM meteorite

meteorologia [meteorolo'dʒia] SF meteorology
▷ www.meteoam.it/

meteorologico, a, ci, che [meteoro'lɔdʒiko] AGG (*fenomeno*) meteorological; (*previsione, stazione, carta*) weather *attr*; **bollettino meteorologico** weather report; **ufficio meteorologico dell'Aeronautica** Airforce Meteorological Office

meteorologo, a, gi, ghe [meteo'rɔlogo] SM/F meteorologist

meticcio, cia, ci, ce [me'tittʃo] AGG (*persona*) half-caste; (*animale*) crossbreed
■SM/F half-caste, half-breed

meticolosamente [metikolosa'mente] AVV meticulously

meticolosità [metikolosi'ta] SF INV meticulousness

meticoloso, a [metiko'loso] AGG meticulous

metile [me'tile] SM methyl

metilico, a, ci, che [me'tiliko] AGG methyl *attr*; **alcol metilico** methyl alcohol

metodicità [metoditʃi'ta] SF methodicalness

metodico, a, ci, che [me'tɔdiko] AGG methodical

metodismo [meto'dismo] SM (*Rel*) Methodism

metodista, i, e [meto'dista] AGG, SM/F (*Rel*) Methodist

metodo ['mɛtodo] SM (*procedimento*) method; (*manuale*) tutor (*Brit*), manual; **far qc con/senza metodo** to do sth methodically/unmethodically; **aver il proprio metodo per fare qc** to have one's own way *o* method of doing sth

metodologia [metodolo'dʒia] SF methodology

metraggio, gi [me'traddʒo] SM **1** (*Sartoria*) length; **vendere a metraggio** to sell by the metre **2** (*Cine*) footage; **(film a) lungo metraggio** feature film; **(film a) corto metraggio** short (film)

metratura [metra'tura] SF length

metrica ['mɛtrika] SF (*Poesia*) metrics *sg*, prosody

metrico, a, ci, che ['mɛtriko] AGG metric; (*Poesia*) metrical; **il sistema metrico decimale** the metric system

metro ['mɛtro] SM (*gen*) metre (*Brit*), meter (*Am*); (*strumento: a nastro*) tape measure; (*: ad asta*) (metre) rule; (*fig: criterio*) yardstick; **metro cubo/quadrato** cubic/square metre; **i cento metri** (*Sport*) the hundred metres (race)

metrò [me'trɔ] SM INV underground (*Brit*), subway (*Am*)

metronomo [me'trɔnomo] SM INV metronome

metronotte [metro'nɔtte] SM INV night security guard

metropoli [me'trɔpoli] SF INV metropolis

metropolitana [metropoli'tana] SF (*anche:* **ferrovia metropolitana**) underground (*Brit*), subway (*Am*); **ha preso la metropolitana** he took the underground; **metropolitana leggera** metro (*mainly on the surface*)

metropolitano, a [metropoli'tano] AGG metropolitan; **leggende metropolitane** urban myths

mettere ['mettere] VB IRREG
■VT **1** (*porre*) to put; **dove hai messo la mia penna?** where did you put my pen?; **guarda dove metti i piedi** be careful where you step; **gli ha messo una mano sulla spalla** he put *o* laid a hand on his

shoulder; **mettere qc diritto** to put *o* set sth straight; **mettere un bambino a letto** to put a child to bed; **mettere un annuncio sul giornale** to put an advert in the paper; **mettere il lavoro al di sopra di tutto** to put work before all else; **quando si mette una cosa in testa...** when he gets an idea into his head ...; **mettere qn sulla strada giusta** (*fig*) to set sb right
2 (*infondere*): **mettere fame/allegria/malinconia a qn** to make sb (feel) hungry/happy/sad
3 (*anche:* **mettersi**: *abito: indossare*) to put on; (*: portare*) to wear; **mettiti il maglione** put your jumper on; **si mise le scarpe** he put his shoes on; **non metto più quelle scarpe** I've stopped wearing those shoes, I don't wear those shoes any more; **mettersi il cappello** to put on one's hat; **non so cosa mettermi** I don't know what to wear; **ma che cosa ti sei messo?** what on earth have you got on?
4 (*installare: telefono, gas, finestre*) to put in; (*acqua*) to lay on
5 (*sveglia, allarme*) to set; **hai messo la sveglia?** have you set the alarm?; **hai messo la sicura?** (*Aut*) have you locked the door?
6 (*supporre*): **mettiamo che...** let's suppose *o* say that ...
7 **metterci** *or* **metterci molta cura/molto tempo** to take a lot of care/a lot of time; **quanto tempo ci hai messo?** how long did it take you?; **ci ho messo 3 ore per venire** it's taken me 3 hours to get here; **mettercela tutta** to do one's utmost *o* very best
8 (*fraseologia*): **mettere a confronto** to compare; **mettere in conto** (*somma ecc*) to put on account; **mettere qn contro qn** (*fig*) to turn sb against sb; **mettere qn al corrente di qc** to put sb in the picture about sth; **mettere dentro qn** (*fam: imprigionare*) to put sb inside; **mettere in giro** (*pettegolezzi, voci*) to spread; **mettere insieme** (*gen*) to put together; (*organizzare: spettacolo, gruppo*) to organize, get together; (*soldi*) to save; **mettere in luce** (*problemi, errori*) to show up, highlight; **mettere qn a sedere** to sit sb down; **mettere sotto** (*sopraffare*) to get the better of; **mettere su il caffè** (*fam*) to put the coffee on; **mettere su casa** to set up house; **mettere su un negozio** to start a shop; **mettere su pancia** to develop a paunch; **mettere su peso** to put on weight; **mettere a tacere qn/qc** to keep sb/sth quiet; **mettere via** to put away
▶ **mettersi** VR **1** to put o.s.; **non metterti là** (*seduto*) don't sit there; (*in piedi*) don't stand there; **mettiti là e aspetta** wait there; **mettersi a sedere** to sit down; **mettersi a letto** to go to bed; (*malato*) to take to one's bed
2 (*vestirsi*): **mettersi in costume** to put on one's swimming things; **ti dispiace se mi metto in maniche di camicia?** do you mind if I take off my jacket?
3 (*in gruppo*): **mettersi in società** to set up in business; **si sono messi insieme** (*coppia*) they've started going out together (*Brit*) *o* dating (*Am*)
▶ **mettersi** VIP **1** (*incominciare*): **mettersi a fare qc** to start to do sth; **mettersi a piangere/ridere** to start crying/laughing, start *o* begin to cry/laugh; **mettersi a bere** to take to drink; **mettersi al lavoro** to set to work
2 (*prendere un andamento*): **si mette al bello** (*tempo*) the weather's turning fine; **mettersi bene/male** (*faccenda*) to turn out well/badly; **vediamo come si mettono le cose** let's see how things go

mezza ['mɛddza] SF (*mezzogiorno e mezzo*): **è la mezza** it's half-past twelve (in the afternoon); **sono le due e mezza** it's half past two

mezzadria [meddza'dria] SF (*Agr*) sharecropping

mezzadro [med'dzadro] SM (*Agr*) sharecropper

mezzala [med'dzala] SF (*Calcio*) inside forward; **mezzala destra/sinistra** inside right/left

mezzaluna [meddza'luna] SF (*pl* **mezzelune**) half-moon; (*dell'islamismo*) crescent; (*coltello*) (semicircular) chopping knife

mezzamanica [meddza'manika] SF (*pl* **mezzemaniche**) sleeve guard; (*fig: impiegato*) penpusher

mezzanino [meddza'nino] SM mezzanine (floor)

mezzano, a [med'dzano] AGG (*medio*) average, medium; (*figlio*) middle *attr*; (*vela*) mizzen *attr*
■ SM/F (*intermediario*) go-between; (*ruffiano*) procurer
■ SF (*Naut*): **albero di mezzana** mizzen mast

mezzanotte [meddza'nɔtte] SF midnight; **a mezzanotte** at midnight

mezz'asta [med'dzasta] **a mezz'asta** AVV at half-mast; **bandiera a mezz'asta** flag (flying) at half-mast

mezzeria [meddze'ria] SF (*di strada*) centre line

mezzo[1] ['mɛddzo] SM **1** (*strumento*) means *sg*; (*metodo*) means, way; **mezzi di produzione** means of production; **per mezzo di** by means of, through; **per mezzo della nuova tecnologia** by means of new technology; **a mezzo corriere** by carrier; **cercherò di ottenere il posto con qualsiasi mezzo** I'll try to get the job by whatever means; **non c'è mezzo di fermarlo** there's no way of stopping him; **ci siamo arrangiati con mezzi di fortuna** we managed as best we could; **mezzi di comunicazione** media *pl*; **mezzi di comunicazione di massa** mass media *pl* **2** (*veicolo*) vehicle; **mezzi pubblici** public transport *sg*; **mezzi di trasporto** means of transport; **un mezzo di trasporto** a means of transport **3** **mezzi** SMPL (*possibilità economiche*) means; **è una persona che ha molti mezzi** he has a large income, he's very well off; **farcela con i propri mezzi** to manage on one's own; **fare una vita al di sopra dei propri mezzi** to live beyond one's means **4** (*Fis*) medium

Mm

mezzo[2]**, a** ['mɛddzo] AGG **1** half; **mezza bottiglia di vino** half a bottle of wine; **una mezza bottiglia di vino** a half-bottle of wine; **una mezza dozzina di uova** half a dozen eggs; **ha lasciato mezzo panino** he left half of his sandwich; **c'era mezza città al concerto** half the town was at the concert; **mi ha fatto una mezza promessa** he half-promised me; **aver una mezza idea di fare qc** to have half a mind to do sth; **è venuto mezzo mondo** just about everybody was there; **è stato un mezzo scandalo** it almost caused a scandal; **me l'ha detto a mezza voce** he said it to me in an undertone; **non mi piacciono le mezze misure** I don't like half measures; **mezz'ora** = **mezzora** **2** (*medio*): **di mezza età** middle-aged; **un uomo di mezza età** a middle-aged man; **un soprabito di mezza stagione** a spring (*o* autumn) coat
■ AVV half-; **mezzo pieno/vuoto** *ecc* half-full/empty *ecc*; **mezzo morto** half-dead
■ SM **1** (*metà*) half; **un chilo e mezzo** a kilo and a half, one and a half kilos; **è l'una e mezzo** it's half past one; **una volta e mezzo più grande** one and a half times bigger **2** (*parte centrale*) middle; **nel mezzo della piazza** in the middle of the square; **il sedile di mezzo** the middle seat; **la porta di mezzo** the middle door; **in mezzo a** in the middle of; (*folla*) in the midst of; **era in**

mezzo alla strada he was in the middle of the road; **nel bel mezzo (di)** right in the middle (of) **3** (*fraseologia*): **esserci di mezzo** (*ostacolo*) to be in the way; **quando ci sono di mezzo i numeri non ci capisco più niente** when numbers are involved I get completely lost; **non voglio andarci di mezzo** I don't want to suffer for it; **mettersi di mezzo** to interfere; **non mettermi in mezzo!** don't drag me into it!; **è meglio non porre tempo in mezzo** it'd be better not to delay; **togliere di mezzo** (*persona, cosa*) to get rid of; (*fam: uccidere*) to bump off; **levarsi** *o* **togliersi di mezzo** to get out of the way; **il giusto mezzo** the happy medium; **non c'è una via di mezzo** there's no middle course

mezzobusto [meddzo'busto] SM (*pl* **mezzibusti**) **1** (*statua*) bust; **a mezzobusto** (*ritratto, fotografia*) half-length **2** (*scherz: giornalista televisivo*) talking-head

mezzodì [meddzo'di] SM INV midday, noon

mezzofondista, i, e [meddzofon'dista] SM/F middle-distance runner

mezzofondo [meddzo'fondo] SM middle-distance running

mezzogiorno [meddzo'dʒorno] SM **1** (*ora*) midday, noon; **a mezzogiorno** at 12 (o'clock) *o* midday *o* noon; **a mezzogiorno e mezzo** at half past twelve **2** (*Geog*) south; **il Mezzogiorno (d'Italia)** the South of Italy, Southern Italy

MEZZOGIORNO

The term **Mezzogiorno** is used to refer to the South of Italy, the poorest and least industrialized part of the country. Italian economic planning always includes programmes aimed at reducing the economic gap between the **Mezzogiorno** and the rest of Italy.

mezzoguanto [meddzo'gwanto] SM (*pl* **mezziguanti**) fingerless glove

mezzomarinaro [meddzomari'naro] SM (*pl* **mezzimarinari**) (*Naut*) boathook

mezzora, mezz'ora [med'dzora] SF half an hour, half-hour; **ti aspetterò una mezzora** I'll wait for you for half an hour; **la prima mezzora** the first half-hour

mezzosangue [meddzo'sangwe] SM/F INV (*cavallo*) crossbreed

mezzoservizio [meddzoser'vittsjo] SM INV: **lavorare a mezzoservizio** to do part-time cleaning *o* domestic work

mezzosoprano [meddzoso'prano] SM (*pl* **mezzisoprani**) mezzo-soprano

mezzuccio, ci [med'dzuttʃo] SM mean trick

MI SIGLA = Milano

mi[1] [mi] PRON PERS (*dav lo, la, li, le, ne diventa* **me**) **1** (*ogg diretto*) me; **mi aiuti?** will *o* could you help me?; **mi scusi!** excuse me!; **mi chiamava** he was calling to me; **aspettami!** wait for me! **2** (*complemento di termine*) (to) me; **mi dai il libro?** will you give me the book?; **mi compri il libro?** will you buy me the book?, will you buy the book for me?; **puoi prestarmi la penna?** could you lend me your pen?; **me ne ha parlato** he spoke to me about it, he told me about it; **mi sembrava una buona idea** it seemed a good idea to me; **mi ha sorriso** he smiled at me **3** (*riflessivo*) myself; **mi servo da solo** I'll help myself; **mi sono pettinato** I combed my hair; **mi sono lavato i denti** I brushed my teeth; **mi sono divertita** I enjoyed myself; **mi sono fatto male** I've hurt myself; **mi guardai allo specchio** I looked at myself in the mirror

mi[2] [mi] SM INV (*Mus*) E; (: *solfeggiando la scala*) mi

mia ['mia] *vedi* mio

miagolare [mjago'lare] VI (*aus* **avere**) to miaow, mew

miagolio, lii [mjago'lio] SM miaowing, mewing

miao ['mjao] ESCL, SM INV miaow

miasma, i [mi'azma] SM miasma

MIB [mib] SIGLA M, AGG (= **Milano Indice Borsa**) Milan Stock Exchange; **l'indice MIB** the Milan (Stock Exchange) index

MIBTEL [mibtel] SIGLA M: **Milano Indice Borsa Telematico** Milan Stock Exchange Index

mica[1] ['mika] AVV: **non...mica** (*fam*) not ... at all; **non ci credo mica!** I don't believe that for a minute!; **non ci crederai mica!** you won't believe it!; **non sarà mica partito?** he wouldn't have left, would he?; **non sono mica stanco** I'm not at all tired; **mica male!** not bad (at all)!

mica[2] ['mika] SF (*minerale*) mica

miccia, ce ['mittʃa] SF fuse; **accendere la miccia** to light the fuse

Michigan ['mitʃigan] SM Michigan

micidiale [mitʃi'djale] AGG (*letale*) fatal, deadly; (*fig: musica*) excruciating; (: *liquore*) deadly; **fa un caldo micidiale oggi** it's terribly hot today

micio, cia, ci, cie ['mitʃo] SM/F (*fam*) pussy (cat)

micologo, a, gi, ghe [mi'kɔlogo] SM/F: **esperto micologo** mycologist (*employed to check wild mushrooms before they are sold*)

micosi [mi'kɔzi] SF INV mycosis

micro... ['mikro] PREF micro...

microbiologia [mikrobiolo'dʒia] SF microbiology

microbiologo, a, gi, ghe [mikro'bjɔlogo] SM/F microbiologist

microbo ['mikrobo] SM microbe

microchip [mikro'tʃip] SM INV microchip

microchirurgia, gie [mikrokirur'dʒia] SF (*Med*) microsurgery

microcircuito [mikrotʃir'kuito] SM microcircuit

microclima, i [mikro'klima] SM microclimate

microcosmo [mikro'kɔzmo] SM microcosm

microcredito [mikro'kredito] SM (*Fin*) microcredit

microcriminalità [mikrokriminali'ta] SF INV *crime that is not organized crime*

microelettronica [mikroelet'trɔnika] SF microelectronics *sg*

microfibra [mikro'fibra] SF microfibre

microfiche [mikro'fiʃ] SF INV microfiche

microfilm [mikro'film] SM INV microfilm

microfono [mi'krɔfono] SM microphone

microfotografia [mikrofotogra'fia] SF (*Fot: tecnica*) micrography; (: *singola immagine*) micrograph

microimpresa [mikroim'presa] SF small business (*employing one or two people*)

microinformatica [mikroinfor'matika] SF microcomputing

micrometrico, a, ci, che [mikro'mɛtriko] AGG micrometric; **vite micrometrica** micrometer screw

micrometro [mi'krɔmetro] SM micrometer

micron ['mikron] SM INV micron

microonda [mikro'onda] SF microwave; **forno a microonde** microwave (oven)

microorganismo [mikroorga'nizmo] SM microorganism

microprocessore [mikroprotʃes'sore] SM microprocessor
microscopico, a, ci, che [mikros'kɔpiko] AGG microscopic; **un microscopico bikini** (*scherz*) a microscopic bikini
microscopio, pi [mikros'kɔpjo] SM microscope; **microscopio elettronico** electron microscope; **microscopio ottico** light microscope
microsecondo [mikrose'kondo] SM microsecond
microsolco, chi [mikro'solko] SM (*solco*) microgroove; (*disco a 33 giri*) long-playing record, LP
microspia [mikros'pia] SF hidden microphone, bug (*fam*)
Mida ['mida] SM Midas; **il tocco di Mida** the Midas touch
midollo [mi'dollo] SM (*pl f* **midolla**) (*Anat*) marrow; (*Bot*) pith; **bagnarsi fino alle midolla** *o* **al midollo** (*fig*) to get soaking wet *o* drenched; **midollo allungato** medulla oblungata; **midollo osseo** bone marrow; **midollo spinale** spinal cord
mie ['mie] *vedi* **mio**
miei ['mjɛi] *vedi* **mio**
miele ['mjɛle] SM honey; **color miele** honey-coloured
mietere ['mjɛtere] VT (*Agr, fig*) to reap, harvest; **l'epidemia ha mietuto molte vittime** the epidemic has claimed many victims
mietitrebbiatrice [mjetitrebbja'tritʃe] SF combine harvester
mietitrice [mjeti'tritʃe] SF (*macchina*) harvester
mietitura [mjeti'tura] SF (*raccolto*) harvest; (*lavoro*) harvesting; (*tempo*) harvest time
migliaio [miʎ'ʎajo] SM (*pl f* **migliaia**) thousand; **un migliaio (di)** about a thousand, a thousand or so; **un migliaio di persone** about a thousand people; **due migliaia di persone** about two thousand people; **a migliaia** by the thousand, in thousands; **poche migliaia di persone** a few thousand people; **centinaia di migliaia di persone** hundreds of thousands of people; **parecchie migliaia di copie** several thousand copies; **l'ho fatto migliaia di volte** I've done it thousands of times
migliarino [miʎʎa'rino] SM (*Zool*): **migliarino di palude** reed bunting
miglio¹ ['miʎʎo] SM (*pl f* **miglia**) mile; **camminò per miglia e miglia** she walked for miles and miles; **si vede lontano un miglio che è falso** you can see a mile off that it's a fake; **miglio inglese** *o* **terrestre** (*= 1609,33 metri*) mile; **miglio marino** *o* **nautico** (*= 1852,28 metri*) nautical mile
miglio² ['miʎʎo] SM (*Bot*) millet
miglioramento [miʎʎora'mento] SM improvement; **non c'è ancora nessun miglioramento** there hasn't been any improvement yet
migliorare [miʎʎo'rare] VT, VI (*aus* **essere**; *riferito a persone, anche* **avere**) to improve; **partiremo domani, se il tempo migliora** we'll set off tomorrow, if the weather improves; **fa un corso per migliorare il suo inglese** he's doing a course to improve his English
▸ **migliorarsi** VR to improve o.s.
migliore [miʎ'ʎore] (*comp, superl di* **buono**) AGG (*comparativo*) better; (*superlativo*) best; **migliore (di)** better (than); **il libro è migliore del film** the book is better than the film; **molto migliore** much better; **rendere migliore** to make better, improve; **i migliori auguri** best wishes; **la cosa migliore sarebbe partire subito** the best thing would be to leave immediately
■ SM/F: **il/la migliore** (*comparativo*) the better (one); (*superlativo*) the best (one); **il migliore dei due** the better of the two; **il migliore della classe** the best in the class; **questo è il miglior ristorante della città** this is the best restaurant in town; **nella migliore delle ipotesi** at best; **vinca il migliore** let the best man/woman win
miglioria [miʎʎo'ria] SF improvement; **fare** *o* **apportare delle migliorie** to make *o* carry out improvements
migliorista, i, e [miʎʎo'rista] (*Pol*) AGG (*corrente, candidato, posizione*) *connected with the gradualist wing of the PDS (former communist party)*
■ SM/F PDS gradualist
mignatta [miɲ'ɲatta] SF (*Zool*) leech
mignolo ['miɲɲolo] SM (*di mano*) little finger, pinkie (*fam*); (*di piede*) little toe
mignon [mi'ɲɔ̃] AGG INV: **bottiglia mignon** miniature (bottle); **pasticceria mignon** petit fours *pl*
migrare [mi'grare] VI (*aus* **essere**) to migrate
migratore, trice [migra'tore] AGG migratory
■ SM/F migrant
migratorio, ria, ri, rie [migra'tɔrjo] AGG migratory; **movimento migratorio** migration
migrazione [migrat'tsjone] SF migration
mila ['mila] (*in combinazione con* **due, tre** *ecc*) *vedi* **mille**
milanese [mila'nese] AGG Milanese; **cotoletta alla milanese** Wiener schnitzel; **risotto alla milanese** *risotto with saffron*
■ SM/F inhabitant *o* native of Milan; **i milanesi** the Milanese
Milano [mi'lano] SF Milan; **domani vado a Milano** I'm going to Milan tomorrow; **abitiamo a Milano** we live in Milan
▷ www.comune.milano.it
miliardario, ria, ri, rie [miljar'darjo] AGG, SM/F ≈ billionaire; **è miliardario** he's a billionaire
miliardo [mi'ljardo] SM thousand million, billion; **un miliardo di euro** one thousand million euros, a billion euros; **tre miliardi di euro** three thousand million euros, three billion euros; **miliardi di persone** millions of people
miliare [mi'ljare] AGG: **pietra miliare** (*anche fig*) milestone
milieu [mi'ljø] SM INV milieu
milionario, ria, ri, rie [miljo'narjo] AGG, SM/F millionaire
milione [mi'ljone] SM million; **un milione di dollari** one million dollars; **due milioni di sterline** two million pounds; **parecchi milioni di euro** several million euros; **milioni di persone** millions of people
milionesimo, a [miljo'nɛzimo] AGG, SM/F, SM millionth
militante [mili'tante] AGG, SM/F militant
militanza [mili'tantsa] SF militancy
militare¹ [mili'tare] VI (*aus* **avere**): **militare in** (*partito, gruppo*) to be active in; (*marina, aeronautica*) to serve in; **militare in una squadra** (*Sport*) to play for/in a team; **una squadra che milita in serie A** ≈ a team (which plays) in the Premier division
militare² [mili'tare] AGG army *attr*, military; **governo militare** military government; **il servizio militare** military service; **un ufficiale militare** an army officer
■ SM serviceman; **fare il militare** to do one's military service; **non ho fatto il militare** I didn't do military service; **militare di carriera** regular (soldier)

Mm

militaresco, a, schi, sche [milita'resko] AGG (*portamento*) military *attr*, soldierly
militarismo [milita'rizmo] SM militarism
militarista [milita'rista] AGG militaristic
■ SM/F militarist
militarizzare [militarid'dzare] VT to militarize
militarmente [militar'mente] AVV (*invadere*) by force of arms; (*educare*) in a military fashion
militassolto, a [militas'sɔlto] (*in annunci economici*) AGG having done National Service
■ SM person who has done National Service
milite ['milite] SM (*soldato*) soldier; **il Milite ignoto** the Unknown Soldier *o* Warrior
militesente [milite'zɛnte] AGG exempt from National Service
■ SM person who is exempt from National Service
milizia [mi'littsja] SF militia
miliziano [milit'tsjano] SM militiaman
millantare [millan'tare] VT to boast (of), brag (about)
millantato [millan'tato] AGG: **millantato credito** (*Dir*) *fraudulent claim to influence with public officials, made so as to obtain a bribe*
millantatore, trice [millanta'tore] SM/F boaster
millanteria [millante'ria] SF (*qualità*) boastfulness; **queste sono millanterie** that's just boasting
mille ['mille] AGG INV a *o* one thousand; **mille persone** a thousand people; **duemila** two thousand; **tremila** three thousand; **milleuno** a *o* one thousand and one; **mille grazie** thanks a lot, thank you very much; **a mille (a mille)** in their thousands
■ SM INV a *o* one thousand; **nel mille d.C.** in one thousand A.D.
millefoglie [mille'fɔʎʎe] SM INV (*Culin*) millefeuille
millenario, ria, ri, rie [mille'narjo] AGG millennial; (*fig: molto vecchio*) ancient; (*: dominazione*) age-old
■ SM (*anniversario*) thousandth anniversary, millennium
millennio, ni [mil'lɛnnjo] SM millennium
millepiedi [mille'pjɛdi] SM INV millipede
millerighe [mille'rige] AGG INV needlecord
millesimo, a [mil'lɛzimo] AGG, SM thousandth
milleusi [mille'uzi] AGG INV all-purpose
milli... ['milli] PREF milli...
millibar [milli'bar] SM INV millibar
milligrammo [milli'grammo] SM milligram(me)
millilitro [mil'lilitro] SM millilitre (*Brit*), milliliter (*Am*)
millimetro [mil'limetro] SM millimetre (*Brit*), millimeter (*Am*)
milza ['miltsa] SF (*Anat*) spleen
mimare [mi'mare] VT (*Teatro*) to mime; (*fig: imitare*) to mimic, take off
mimetico, a, ci, che [mi'mɛtiko] AGG (*arte*) mimetic; **tuta mimetica** (*Mil*) camouflage
mimetismo [mime'tizmo] SM (*Bio, Mil*) camouflage
mimetizzare [mimetid'dzare] VT to camouflage
▶ **mimetizzarsi** VR to camouflage o.s.
mimica ['mimika] SF **1** (*arte*) mime **2** (*insieme di gesti*) gestures *pl*; **mimica facciale** facial expressions
mimico, a, ci, che ['mimiko] AGG mime *attr*; (*linguaggio*) sign *attr*; **arte mimica** mime
mimo ['mimo] SM **1** (*attore, spettacolo*) mime **2** (*Zool*) mocking bird
mimosa [mi'mosa] SF mimosa
Min. ABBR (= ministero, ministro) Min.
min. ABBR (= minuto, minimo) min.

mina ['mina] SF **1** (*ordigno*) mine; **mina terrestre** landmine; **mina vagante** time bomb **2** (*di matita*) lead
minaccia, ce [mi'nattʃa] SF threat; **è una grave minaccia per la nazione** it is a serious threat to the nation; **una minaccia per l'ambiente** a threat to the environment; **fare delle minacce a qn** to threaten sb; **in segno di minaccia** as a threat; **sotto la minaccia di** under threat of; **avere una minaccia di aborto** to have a threatened miscarriage
minacciare [minat'tʃare] VT to threaten; **minacciare qn di morte** to threaten sb with death, threaten to kill sb; **minacciare qn con una pistola** to threaten sb with a gun; **lo sciopero minaccia di durare** the strike looks set to continue; **ha minacciato di andarsene** he threatened to leave; **minaccia di piovere** it looks like rain; **minaccia tempesta** there's a storm brewing
minacciosamente [minattʃosa'mente] AVV threateningly, menacingly
minaccioso, a [minat'tʃoso] AGG threatening, menacing
minare [mi'nare] VT (*ponte*) to mine; (*fig: salute, reputazione*) to undermine; **questo campo è minato** this field has been mined; **ha la salute minata dall'alcol** his health has been ruined by drink
minareto [mina'reto] SM minaret
minatore [mina'tore] SM miner
minatorio, ria, ri, rie [mina'tɔrjo] AGG threatening
minchione, a [min'kjone] (*fam*) AGG idiotic
■ SM/F idiot
minchioneria [minkjone'ria] SF (*fam: qualità*) stupidity; (*: azione*) foolish thing
minerale [mine'rale] AGG mineral
■ SM mineral; **minerale di ferro** iron ore
■ SF (*anche:* **acqua minerale**) mineral water
mineralogia [mineralo'dʒia] SF mineralogy
mineralogico, a, ci, che [minera'lɔdʒiko] AGG mineralogical
mineralogista, i, e [mineralo'dʒista] SM/F mineralogist
minerario, ria, ri, rie [mine'rarjo] AGG (*delle miniere*) mining *attr*; (*dei minerali*) ore *attr*
Minerva [mi'nɛrva] SF Minerva
minerva® [mi'nɛrva] SMPL safety matches
minestra [mi'nɛstra] SF soup; **"minestre"** (*sul menu*) "first courses"; **è sempre la solita minestra** (*fig*) it's always the same old story; **o mangi questa minestra o salti dalla finestra** (*Proverbio*) take it or leave it; **minestra in brodo** noodle soup; **minestra di verdura** vegetable soup
minestrina [mines'trina] SF broth
minestrone [mines'trone] SM (*Culin*) minestrone (*thick vegetable and pasta soup*); (*fig*) mix-up, confusion
mingherlino, a [minger'lino] AGG skinny
mini ['mini] AGG INV mini
■ SF INV (*Moda*) miniskirt, mini
mini... ['mini] PREF mini...
miniabito [mini'abito] SM mini-dress
miniappartamento [miniapparta'mento] SM studio flat
miniare [mi'njare] VT to paint in miniature
miniatura [minja'tura] SF (*dipinto*) miniature; (*arte, genere*) miniature painting; **in miniatura** in miniature; **una città/un giardino in miniatura** a model town/garden
miniaturista, i, e [minjatu'rista] SM/F (*pittore*) miniaturist
miniaturizzare [minjaturid'dzare] VT to miniaturize

miniaturizzato, a [minjaturid'dzato] AGG *(Elettr)* miniaturized; *(molto piccolo)* minuscule

miniaturizzazione [minjaturiddzat'tsjone] SF miniaturization

minibar [mini'bar] SM INV minibar

minibus ['minibus] SM INV minibus

minidisco, chi [mini'disko] SM minidisc

minielaboratore [minielabora'tore] SM minicomputer

miniera [mi'njɛra] SF mine; **una miniera di informazioni** *(fig)* a mine of information; **miniera di carbone** *(gen)* coal mine; *(impresa)* colliery *(Brit)*, coalmine; **miniera a cielo aperto** open-cast mine; **miniera d'oro** gold mine; **miniera sotterranea** pit, mine

minigolf [mini'gɔlf] SM INV *(gioco)* minigolf; *(campo da gioco)* minigolf course

minigonna [mini'gonna] SF miniskirt

minima ['minima] SF *(Meteor)* minimum temperature; *(Med)* minimum blood-pressure level

minimalismo [minima'lizmo] SM *(Arte, Letteratura)* minimalism

minimalista, i, e [minima'lista] AGG, SM/F *(Arte, Letteratura)* minimalist

minimarket [mini'market] SM INV ≈ corner shop *(Brit)*, ≈ corner store *(Am)*

minimizzare [minimid'dzare] VT to minimize

minimo, a ['minimo] AGG *(il più piccolo)* least, slightest; *(piccolissimo)* very small, slight; *(il più basso)* lowest, minimum; **la temperatura minima** the minimum temperature; **a un costo minimo** at a minimal cost; **non c'è la minima differenza** there isn't the slightest difference; **la differenza è minima** the difference is minimal *o* very small *o* slight, there's hardly any difference; **non c'è stato il minimo cambiamento** there hasn't been the slightest change; **il prezzo minimo è 100 euro** the lowest *o* minimum price is 100 euros; **gli effetti collaterali della medicina sono minimi** the drug's side effects are minimal; **non ne ho la minima idea** I haven't the slightest idea; **ridurre una frazione ai minimi termini** *(Mat)* to reduce a fraction to its lowest terms; **queste scarpe sono ridotte ai minimi termini** *(fig: molto consumate)* these shoes are completely worn out
■ SM **1** minimum; **è il minimo che tu possa fare** it's the least you can do; **non ha un minimo di comprensione** he is totally lacking in understanding; **gli hanno dato il minimo della pena** they gave him the minimum sentence; **come minimo avrebbe potuto dirmelo** he could at least have told me; **il minimo indispensabile** the bare minimum **2** *(Aut)*: **girare al minimo** to idle; **questo motore ha il minimo basso** this engine has a low idling speed

minio ['minjo] SM red lead

ministeriale [ministe'rjale] AGG *(del ministero)* ministerial; *(del governo)* government *attr*

ministero [minis'tɛro] SM **1** *(Pol)* ministry, department *(spec Am)*; **ministero delle Finanze** Ministry of Finance, ≈ Treasury; **ministero degli Interni** Ministry of the Interior, ≈ Home Office *(Brit)*, ≈ Department of the Interior *(Am)*; **ministero della Pubblica Istruzione** ≈ Department of Education and Science *(Brit)* **2** *(Dir)*: **pubblico ministero** State Prosecutor **3** *(Rel)* ministry

ministro [mi'nistro] SM **1** *(Pol)* minister, secretary *(spec Am)*; **il Primo ministro** the Prime Minister; **ministro delle Finanze** Minister of Finance, ≈ Chancellor of the Exchequer *(Brit)*; **ministro degli Interni** Minister of the Interior, ≈ Home Secretary *(Brit)*, ≈ Secretary of the Interior *(Am)* **2** *(Rel)* minister

Minnesota [minne'sota] SM Minnesota

minoranza [mino'rantsa] SF *(gen)* minority; *(gruppo)* minority (group); **essere in minoranza** to be in the minority

minorato, a [mino'rato] AGG handicapped
■ SM/F physically *(o* mentally*)* handicapped person

minorazione [minorat'tsjone] SF handicap

Minorca [mi'nɔrka] SF Minorca

minore [mi'nore] AGG *(comp di* **piccolo***)* **1** less; *(più piccolo)* smaller; *(più breve)* shorter; *(meno grave)* lesser; *(numero)* lower; **con minore entusiasmo** with less enthusiasm; **un numero minore di studenti** a smaller number of students; **le vendite sono state minori del previsto** sales were less *o* lower than expected; **questo è il male minore** this is the lesser evil; **vocabolario in edizione minore** shorter *o* concise edition of a dictionary; **in misura minore** to a lesser extent **2** *(meno importante)* less important; *(inferiore)* lower, inferior; *(di poco rilievo)* minor; **opere minori** minor works; **le opere minori di Shakespeare** Shakespeare's minor works; **di minor pregio** of inferior quality **3** *(più giovane)* younger; **il mio fratello minore** my younger brother **4** *(Mus)* minor; **(in) do minore** (in) C minor
■ AGG *(superl di* **piccolo***)* *(vedi agg comp 1, 2, 3)* least; smallest; shortest; lowest; least important; youngest; **la minore delle due sorelle** the younger of the two sisters; **il minore dei tre fratelli** the youngest of the three brothers
■ SM/F **1** *(d'età: tra due)* younger; *(: tra più di due)* youngest **2** *(minorenne)* minor, person under age; **minore non accompagnato** unaccompanied minor; **spettacolo vietato ai minori** no admittance to persons under the age of 18 *(to film, show ecc)*; **"vietato ai minori di 18 anni"** "18 certificate"

minorenne [mino'rɛnne] AGG under age; **mia sorella è minorenne** my sister is under 18
■ SM/F minor, person under age; **tribunale dei minorenni** *(Dir)* juvenile court

minorile [mino'rile] AGG juvenile; **carcere minorile** young offenders' institution; **delinquenza minorile** juvenile delinquency

minoritario, ria, ri, rie [minori'tarjo] AGG minority *attr*

Minosse [mi'nɔsse] SM Minos

Minotauro [mino'tauro] SM Minotaur

minuetto [minu'etto] SM *(Mus)* minuet

minuscola [mi'nuskola] SF *(anche:* **lettera minuscola***)* small letter

minuscolo, a [mi'nuskolo] AGG **1** *(piccolissimo)* tiny, minuscule, minute; **un appartamento minuscolo** a tiny flat **2** *(lettera)* small; **a lettere minuscole** in small letters
■ SM small letters *pl*; *(Tip)* lower case; **in minuscolo** in small letters; **scrivere tutto (in) minuscolo** to write everything in small letters

minuta [mi'nuta] SF rough copy, draft

minutamente [minuta'mente] AVV *(tritato)* finely; *(intarsiato, decorato)* delicately, finely; *(analizzato, discusso)* in minute detail

minuto[1], a [mi'nuto] AGG tiny, minute; *(pioggia)* fine; *(corporatura)* delicate, fine; *(lavoro, descrizione)* detailed; **spese minute** minor expenses; **al minuto** *(Comm)* retail; **comprare al minuto** to buy at retail prices, buy retail

minuto² [mi'nuto] SM (*gen*) minute; (*momento*) moment, minute; **all'ultimo minuto** at the (very) last minute *o* moment; **a minuti** *or* **da un minuto all'altro** any second *o* minute now; **in un minuto** in one minute; (*fig: rapidamente*) in a flash; **tra pochi minuti** in a few minutes, in a few minutes' time; **avere i minuti contati** to have very little time; **spaccare il minuto** (*fig: persona*) to be (always) on the dot; (: *orologio*) to be accurate to a split second; **minuti di recupero** (*Calcio*) injury time

minuzia [mi'nuttsja] SF (*cura*) meticulousness; (*particolare*) detail; **perdersi in minuzie** to waste one's time with trifling details

minuziosamente [minuttsjosa'mente] AVV (*vedi agg*) meticulously; in minute detail

minuziosità [minuttsjosi'ta] SF meticulousness

minuzioso, a [minut'tsjoso] AGG (*persona*) meticulous; (*descrizione*) detailed; (*esame*) minute

mio, a ['mio] (*pl* **miei, mie**) AGG POSS: **il mio** *or* **la mia** *ecc* my; **il mio cane** my dog; **mia madre** my mother; **i miei libri** my books; **un mio amico** a friend of mine; **è colpa mia** it's my fault; **è casa mia** *or* **è la mia casa** it's my house; **di chi è questo? — è mio** whose is this? — it's mine; **per amor mio** for my sake

■ PRON POSS: **il mio** *or* **la mia** *ecc* mine, my own; **la sua barca è più lunga della mia** his boat is longer than mine; **la tua casa è più grande della mia** your house is bigger than mine; **è questo il mio?** is this mine?; **è questo il tuo cappotto? — no, il mio è nero** is this your coat? — no, mine's black; **il mio è stato solo un errore** it was simply an error on my part

■ PRON POSS M **1 ho speso del mio** I spent my own money; **vivo del mio** I live on my own income **2 i miei** (*genitori*) my parents; (*famiglia*) my family; (*amici*) my side; **vivo con i miei** I live with my parents; **lui è dei miei** he is on my side

■ PRON POSS F: **la mia** (*opinione*) my view; **è dalla mia** she is on my side; **sono riuscita a dire la mia** I managed to say my piece; **anch'io ho avuto le mie** (*disavventure*) I've had my problems too; **ne ho fatta una della mie!** (*sciocchezze*) I've done it again!; **cerco di stare sulle mie** I try to keep myself to myself

miope ['miope] AGG short-sighted, myopic (*frm*); (*fig*) short-sighted

■ SM/F myopic *o* short-sighted person

miopia [mio'pia] SF short-sightedness, myopia (*frm*); (*fig*) short-sightedness

mira ['mira] SF (*anche fig*) aim; **prendere la mira** to take aim; **prendere di mira qn** (*fig*) to pick on sb, target sb; **avere una buona/cattiva mira** to be a good/bad shot

mirabile [mi'rabile] AGG admirable, wonderful

mirabilmente [mirabil'mente] AVV admirably, wonderfully

mirabolante [mirabo'lante] AGG astonishing, amazing

miracolare [mirako'lare] VT to cure *o* heal miraculously

miracolato, a [mirako'lato] SM/F miraculously-cured person

miracolo [mi'rakolo] SM (*anche fig*) miracle; (*persona*) wonder, prodigy; **miracolo economico** economic miracle; **fare miracoli** to perform *o* do miracles; (*fig*) to work wonders; **sapere vita, morte e miracoli di qn** to know everything there is to know about sb; **per miracolo** by a miracle

miracolosamente [mirakolosa'mente] AVV miraculously

miracoloso, a [mirako'loso] AGG miraculous, prodigious; **non c'è niente di miracoloso** here's nothing extraordinary about it

■ SM, SOLO SG **la sua guarigione ha del miracoloso** his recovery is well nigh miraculous

miraggio, gi [mi'raddʒo] SM (*anche fig*) mirage

mirare [mi'rare] VI (*aus* **avere**): **mirare (a)** (*anche fig*) to aim (at); **mirai al bersaglio e sparai** I aimed at the target and fired; **ha sempre mirato a diventare presidente** it has always been his aim to become president; **mirare al potere** to aspire to power

▶ **mirarsi** VR: **mirarsi allo specchio** to look at o.s. in the mirror

miriade [mi'riade] SF myriad, host

mirino [mi'rino] SM (*di arma da fuoco, strumento ottico*) sight; (*Fot*) viewfinder, viewer; **essere nel mirino della Mafia** (*fig*) to be a target of the Mafia

mirra ['mirra] SF myrrh

mirtillo [mir'tillo] SM bilberry (*Brit*), blueberry (*Am*)

mirto ['mirto] SM myrtle

misantropia [mizantro'pia] SF misanthropy

misantropico, a, ci, che [mizan'trɔpiko] AGG misanthropic

misantropo, a [mi'zantropo] AGG misanthropic

■ SM/F misanthrope, misanthropist

miscela [miʃ'ʃɛla] SF (*gen*) mixture; (*di caffè, tè, tabacco*) blend; (*per motorino*) petrol and oil mixture; **miscela pronta** (*per dolci*) cake mix; **miscela carburante** mixture

miscelare [miʃʃe'lare] VT (*gen*) to mix; (*caffè, tè, tabacco*) to blend

miscelatore, trice [miʃʃela'tore] (*vedi vt*) AGG mixing; blending

■ SM (*macchinario, operaio*) mixer; blender; (*dell'acqua*) mixer tap

miscellanea [miʃʃel'lanea] SF miscellany

miscellaneo, a [miʃʃel'laneo] AGG miscellaneous

mischia ['miskja] SF (*rissa, zuffa*) scuffle, brawl; (*Rugby*) scrum, scrummage; **stare al di fuori della mischia** (*fig*) to stay out of the fray; **mischia aperta/chiusa** (*Rugby*) loose/set scrum

mischiare [mis'kjare] VT (*gen*) to mix; (*caffè, tè*) to blend; (*carte*) to shuffle

▶ **mischiarsi** VIP (*liquidi ecc*) to mix, blend

misconoscere [misko'noʃʃere] VT IRREG (*qualità, coraggio ecc*) to fail to appreciate; **non puoi misconoscere l'arte moderna solo perché non ti piace Picasso** you can't ignore modern art just because you don't like Picasso

misconosciuto, a [miskonoʃ'ʃuto] PP *di* **misconoscere**

■ AGG disregarded, ignored

miscredente [miskre'dɛnte] SM/F (*Rel*) heretic; (: *indifferente*) unbeliever

■ AGG (*vedi sm/f*) heretical; unbelieving

miscuglio, gli [mis'kuʎʎo] SM (*gen*) mixture; (*accozzaglia*) jumble, hotchpotch

mise *ecc* VB *vedi* **mettere**

miserabile [mize'rabile] AGG **1** (*pietoso: vita, condizioni*) miserable, wretched, pitiful; (: *persona*) pitiful, wretched **2** (*povero*) poor, destitute, poverty-stricken; **vivere in condizioni miserabili** to live in abject poverty; **una somma miserabile** a miserable *o* paltry

sum of money **3** (*spregevole*: *azione, persona*) mean, wretched
■ SM/F (*persona spregevole*) wretch

miseramente [mizera'mente] AVV (*vivere*) in wretched poverty; (*fallire*) miserably; **essere ridotto miseramente** (*persona, oggetto*) to be in a wretched *o* pitiful state; **è pagato miseramente** he earns a pittance; **una casa miseramente arredata** a poorly furnished house

miserando, a [mize'rando] AGG (*letter*) pitiful

miserevole [mize'revole] AGG pitiful, wretched, miserable

miseria [mi'zɛrja] SF **1** (*povertà*) (extreme) poverty, destitution; **cadere in miseria** to become destitute; **ridursi in miseria** to be reduced to poverty; **vivere nella miseria più nera** to live in dire poverty; **piangere miseria** to plead poverty; **porca miseria!** (*fam*) (bloody) hell! **2** (*somma*): **comprare qc per una miseria** to buy sth for next to nothing *o* for a song; **costare una miseria** to cost next to nothing; **lo pagano una miseria** they pay him a pittance **3 miserie** SFPL (*brutture*) misfortunes, troubles; **le miserie del mondo** the wretchedness of this world **4** (*Bot*) wandering Jew

misericordia [mizeri'kɔrdja] SF mercy, pity; **avere misericordia di qn** to have pity on sb; **misericordia divina** Divine mercy; **invocare la misericordia di qn** to beg sb for mercy; **misericordia!** my goodness!

misericordiosamente [miserikordjosa'mente] AVV mercifully

misericordioso, a [mizerikor'djoso] AGG merciful

misero, a ['mizero] AGG **1** (*pietoso*: *vita, condizioni*) miserable, wretched, pitiful; (: *persona*) pitiful, wretched; **fare una misera figura** to cut a poor figure **2** (*povero*) poor, poverty-stricken; **una misera somma** a miserable *o* paltry sum **3** (*spregevole, meschino*) mean, wretched; **ho preso un misero 22 all'esame** ≈ I didn't get a very good pass in the exam; **è un misero impiegatuccio** he's a miserable pen-pusher; **una misera scusa** a lame excuse

misfatto [mis'fatto] SM (*cattiva azione*) misdeed; (*delitto*) crime

misi *ecc* VB *vedi* **mettere**

misoginia [mizodʒi'nia] SF misogyny

misogino, a [mi'zɔdʒino] AGG misogynous
■ SM misogynist

miss [mis] SF INV (*in concorso di bellezza*) beauty queen; **Miss Mondo** Miss World

missaggio, gi [mis'saddʒo] SM (*Cine, TV, Mus*) mixing

missile ['missile] SM missile; **missile cruise** *o* **da crociera** cruise missile; **missile teleguidato** guided missile; **missile terra-aria** surface-to-air missile

missilistica [missi'listika] SF rocketry

missilistico, a, ci, che [missi'listiko] AGG missile *attr*

missino, a [mis'sino] (*Pol*) AGG of (*o* belonging to) the Movimento Sociale Italiano (*Italian extreme right-wing party*)
■ SM/F member (*o* supporter) of Movimento Sociale Italiano

missionario, ria, ri, rie [missjo'narjo] AGG, SM/F missionary

missione [mis'sjone] SF mission; **essere/partire in missione** to be/leave on a mission; **missione compiuta** mission accomplished

Mississippi [missis'sippi] SM (*fiume, stato*) Mississippi

missiva [mis'siva] SF (*spec scherz*) missive

Missouri [mis'suri] SM Missouri

mister ['mistə] SM INV **1** (*Calcio*) trainer, boss, gaffer (*fam*) **2** (*in concorso di bellezza*): **Mister Universo** Mr Universe; **mister muscolo** Mr Muscle

misteriosamente [misterjosa'mente] AVV mysteriously

misterioso, a [miste'rjoso] AGG mysterious
■ SM/F: **fare il misterioso** to act mysterious

mistero [mis'tɛro] SM mystery; **fare mistero di qc** to make a mystery out of sth; **non se ne fa un mistero** there's no mystery about it; **quanti misteri!** why all the mystery?

mistica ['mistika] SF mysticism

misticismo [misti'tʃizmo] SM mysticism

mistico, a, ci, che ['mistiko] AGG mystic(al)
■ SM mystic

mistificare [mistifi'kare] VT **1** (*dato, fatti*) to falsify **2** (*ingannare*) to fool, take in

mistificatore, trice [mistifika'tore] SM/F: **è un mistificatore** he is distorting the facts

mistificatorio, ria, ri, rie [mistifika'tɔrjo] AGG (*intervento, comportamento*) intentionally misleading

mistificazione [mistifikat'tsjone] SF (*di fatti*) falsification

misto, a ['misto] AGG (*tutti i sensi*) mixed; (*classe*) mixed, coeducational; **un'insalata mista** a mixed salad; **una grigliata mista** a mixed grill; **una scuola mista** a mixed school; **misto a qc** mixed with sth; **un tessuto in misto lino** a linen mix; **cane di razza mista** a mixed breed of dog, crossbreed dog
■ SM mixture

> **LO SAPEVI...?**
> **misto** non si traduce mai con la parola inglese *mist*

mistral [mis'tral] SM mistral

mistura [mis'tura] SF (*miscuglio*) mixture

misura [mi'zura] SF **1** (*Mat*) measure; **unità di misura** unit of measurement; **misura di capacità** unit of capacity; **misura di lunghezza** unit of length **2** (*dimensione*) measurement; (*taglia*) size; **prendere le misure a qn** to take sb's measurements; **può prendermi le misure?** can you take my measurements?, measure sb; **prendere le misure di qc** to measure sth; **di misura grande/piccola** (*scarpe, abito*) in a large/small size; **ha una misura più piccola?** have you got a smaller size?; **(fatto) su misura** made-to-measure; **un completo fatto su misura** a made-to-measure suit; **a misura d'uomo** on a human scale; **l'episodio dà la misura del livello di corruzione raggiunto** the affair gives an indication of the prevailing level of corruption **3** (*proporzione*): **in misura di** in accordance with, according to; **i prezzi aumenteranno in misura del 5%** prices will increase by 5% **4** (*provvedimento*) measure, step; **ho preso le mie misure** I've taken the necessary steps; **mezze misure** (*fig*) half measures; **misure di prevenzione** precautionary measures; **misure di sicurezza** safety measures **5** (*Mus*) time; (: *gruppo di note*) bar **6** (*Poesia*) measure, metre **7** (*fraseologia*): **in ugual misura** equally, in the same way; **non ha il senso della misura** he doesn't know when to stop; **passare la misura** to overstep the mark, go too far; **bere senza misura** to drink to excess; **oltre misura** beyond measure, excessively; **vincere di stretta misura** to win by a narrow margin

misurare [mizu'rare] VT **1** (*gen*) to measure; (*vista, udito*) to test; (*valore*) to estimate; (*capacità*) to judge; (*terreno*) to survey; **misurare a occhio** to measure

Mm

roughly, give a rough estimate; **misura la distanza fra questi due punti** measure the distance between these two points; **misurare a passi una stanza** to pace out a room **2** (*fig: limitare: spese*) to limit; **misurare le parole** to weigh one's words **3** (*provare*): **misurare** *o* **misurarsi qc** (*abito, scarpe, cappotto*) to try sth on
■VI (*aus* **avere**) to measure; **quanto misura questa stanza?** how big is this room?, what are the measurements of this room?;
▶ **misurarsi** VR **1** (*contenersi, regolarsi*) **misurarsi nel bere** to control one's drinking **2** (*provare le proprie forze*) **misurarsi con qn** to compete with sb, pit o.s. against sb

misuratezza [mizura'tettsa] SF moderation

misurato, a [mizu'rato] AGG (*ponderato*) measured; (*prudente*) cautious; (*moderato*) moderate

misuratore [mizura'tore] SM **1** (*strumento*) gauge **2** (*persona: di terreno*) surveyor

misurazione [mizurat'tsjone] SF measuring, measurement; (*di terreno*) surveying

misurino [mizu'rino] SM (*recipiente*) measuring cup

mite ['mite] AGG (*tempo, persona*) mild; (*condanna*) lenient; (*animale*) meek

mitezza [mi'tettsa] SF (*vedi agg*) mildness; leniency; meekness

mitico, a, ci, che ['mitiko] AGG mythical; (*leggendario*) legendary; (*fam*): **Mitico!** Fantastic!, Brilliant!

mitigare [miti'gare] VT (*gen*) to mitigate, lessen; (*dolore*) to soothe, relieve; (*sapore*) to sweeten
▶ **mitigarsi** VIP (*dolore*) to lessen; (*odio*) to subside; (*clima*) to become milder

mitilo [mi'tilo] SM mussel

mitizzare [mitid'dzare] VT: **mitizzare qn/qc** to mythicize sb/sth, turn sb/sth into a myth

mitizzazione [mitiddzat'tsjone] SF mythicization

mito ['mito] SM myth; **far crollare un mito** to explode a myth; **sei un mito!** (*fam*) you're a star!; **quel cantante è un mito!** that singer's fantastic!

mitologia, gie [mitolo'dʒia] SF mythology

mitologico, a, ci, che [mito'lɔdʒiko] AGG mythological

mitomane [mi'tɔmane] SM/F mythomaniac

mitomania [mitoma'nia] SF mythomania

mitosi [mi'tɔzi] SF INV (*Bio*) mitosis

mitra[1] ['mitra] SM INV (*arma*) sub-machine gun

mitra[2] ['mitra] SF (*Rel*) mitre (*Brit*), miter (*Am*)

mitraglia [mi'traʎʎa] SF **1** (*tipo di munizione*) grapeshot **2** (*arma*) machine gun

mitragliare [mitraʎ'ʎare] VT to machine-gun; **mitragliare qn di domande** (*fig*) to fire questions at sb, bombard sb with questions

mitragliatore, trice [mitraʎʎa'tore] AGG: **fucile mitragliatore** sub-machine gun

mitragliatrice [mitraʎʎa'tritʃe] SF machine gun

mitragliere [mitraʎ'ʎɛre] SM machine-gunner

mitrale [mi'trale] AGG (*Anat*): **valvola mitrale** mitral valve

mitralico, a, ci, che [mi'traliko] AGG (*Anat*) mitral

mitteleuropeo, a [mitteleuro'pɛo] AGG Central European

mittente [mit'tɛnte] SM/F sender; **"rispedire al mittente"** "return to sender"

mixer ['mikser] SM INV (*per cocktail, Cine, TV*) mixer; (*frullatore*) blender

ml ABBR (= **millilitro**) ml

MLD SIGLA M = **Movimento per la Liberazione della Donna**

M.M. ABBR (= **marina militare**) ≈ RN (*Brit*) (= *Royal Navy*)

mm ABBR (= **millimetro**) mm

mms SIGLA M INV (*servizio*) MMS (= *Multimedia Messaging Service*); (*messaggio*) MMS message

MN SIGLA = *Mantova*

M/N, **m/n** ABBR (= **motonave**) MV (= *motor vessel*)

mnemonico, a, ci, che [mne'mɔniko] AGG (*gen*) mnemonic; (*pegg: studio, apprendimento*) mechanical

MO SIGLA = *Modena*

MO ABBR = **Medio Oriente**

mo' [mɔ]: **a mo' di** PREP as; **a mo' di esempio** by way of example

mobbing ['mobbin(g)] SM workplace bullying

> **LO SAPEVI...?**
> **mobbing** non si traduce mai con la parola inglese ***mobbing***

mobile ['mɔbile] AGG **1** (*gen*) mobile; (*parte di meccanismo*) moving; (*Rel: festa*) movable; **beni mobili** (*Fin*) movable property **2** (*occhi*) darting
■SM **1** (*per arredamento*) piece of furniture; **mobili** furniture *sg*; **un negozio di mobili** a furniture shop; **mobile componibile**unit **2** (*Fin*): **mobili** SMPL movable property, movables
■SF: **la (squadra) mobile** the flying squad

mobilia [mo'bilja] SF furniture

mobiliare [mobi'ljare] AGG (*credito*) personal; (*beni*) movable

mobiliere [mobi'ljɛre] SM (*fabbricante*) furniture-maker; (*commerciante*) furniture-seller

mobilificio, ci [mobili'fitʃo] SM furniture factory

mobilio [mo'biljo] SM furniture

mobilità [mobili'ta] SF (*gen*) mobility; **mobilità del lavoro** *o* **della manodopera** labour mobility; **lista di mobilità** redeployment list

mobilitare [mobili'tare] VT (*Mil, fig*) to mobilize; **mobilitare l'opinione pubblica** to mobilize public opinion
▶ **mobilitarsi** VR: **mobilitarsi per fare qc** to go into action to do sth

mobilitazione [mobilitat'tsjone] SF mobilization

moca ['mɔka] SM INV (*tipo di caffè*) mocha coffee
■SF INV (*macchina*) mocha coffee pot

mocassino [mokas'sino] SM moccasin

moccio, ci ['mottʃo] SM (*fam: muco*) snot

moccioso, a [mot'tʃoso] SM/F (*bambino piccolo*) little kid; (*pegg*) snotty-nosed kid

moccolo ['mɔkkolo] SM **1** (*di candela*) candle end; **reggere il moccolo** (*fig*) to play gooseberry (*Brit*) **2** (*fam: bestemmia*): **tirare** *o* **mandare un moccolo** to curse, swear **3** (*fam: moccio*) snot

moda ['mɔda] SF (*gen*) fashion; (*pegg*) craze; **l'alta moda** haute couture; **la moda pronta** ready-to-wear (clothes); **essere alla moda** (*persona*) to be fashionable; **seguire la moda** to follow fashion; **essere di moda** *or* **andare di moda** (*abbigliamento, acconciatura ecc*) to be fashionable, be in fashion; **è di moda il nero** black is in fashion; **veste sempre all'ultima moda** she's always dressed in the latest fashion; **è tornata di moda la mini** the mini is back in fashion; **essere fuori moda** to be out of fashion; **non è più di moda** *or* **è fuori moda** it's (gone) out of fashion, it's no longer fashionable; **è diventato una moda** it has become the fashion; **rivista di moda** fashion magazine; **sfilata di moda** fashion show

modale [mo'dale] AGG (*Gramm, Mus*) modal

modalità [modali'ta] SF INV (*procedura*) formality; **secondo le modalità previste dalla legge** in accordance with what is laid down by the law; **modalità di pagamento** method of payment; **modalità d'uso** instructions; **seguire attentamente le modalità d'uso** to follow the instructions carefully

modanare [moda'nare] VT (*Archit, mobili*) to decorate with mouldings

modanatura [modana'tura] SF (*Archit, di mobili*) moulding; (*Aut*) trim

modella [mo'dɛlla] SF model

modellamento [modella'mento] SM modelling, moulding

modellare [model'lare] VT (*creta, statua*) to model, mould; **modellare qc su qc** (*fig*: *opera, stile ecc*) to model sth on sth; **un vestito che modella la figura** a figure-hugging dress
▶ **modellarsi** VR: **modellarsi su qn/qc** to model o.s. on sb/sth, take sb/sth as a model

modellino [model'lino] SM model

modellismo [model'lizmo] SM model-making
▷ www.modellismo.net/

modellista, i, e [model'lista] SM/F (*di cappelli, abiti*) designer

modello [mo'dɛllo] SM **1** (*gen, fig*) model; (*stampo*) mould (*Brit*), mold (*Am*); **un modello in cera** a wax model; **ha comprato l'ultimo modello della FIAT** he's bought the latest Fiat; **prendere a modello** (*fig*) to take as one's model; **modello di serie/in scala** production/scale model **2** (*Sartoria*) model, style; (*: forma*) style; **gli ultimi modelli di Armani** the latest Armani models *o* styles **3** (*Amm*) form
■ AGG INV (*madre, marito, ospedale ecc*) model *attr*

modem ['mɔdem] SM INV modem

modenese [mode'nese] AGG of *o* from Modena
■ SM/F inhabitant *o* native of Modena

moderare [mode'rare] VT (*gen*) to moderate, curb; **moderare la velocità** to reduce speed; **moderare i termini** to weigh one's words
▶ **moderarsi** VR to restrain o.s.; **moderarsi nel mangiare/nelle spese** to control one's eating/one's spending

moderatamente [moderata'mente] AVV in moderation

moderatezza [modera'tettsa] SF moderation

moderato, a [mode'rato] AGG **1** (*gen, Pol*) moderate **2** (*Mus*) moderato
■ SM (*Pol*) moderate

moderatore, trice [modera'tore] SM/F **1** (*in una discussione*) moderator; **fare da moderatore** to act as moderator **2** (*Fis*) moderator

moderazione [moderat'tsjone] SF (*vedi vb*) moderation; restraint; **bere con moderazione** to drink in moderation; **usare moderazione** (*nel bere, nello spendere*) to be moderate

modernamente [moderna'mente] AVV (*in modo moderno*) in a modern style; (*nei tempi moderni*) nowadays

modernariato [moderna'rjato] SM *collecting of 20th century products and objets d'art*

modernità [moderni'ta] SF INV modernity

modernizzare [modernid'dzare] VT to bring up to date, modernize
▶ **modernizzarsi** VR to get up to date

modernizzazione [moderniddzat'tsjone] SF modernization

moderno, a [mo'dɛrno] AGG (*gen*) modern; **una mamma moderna** an up-to-date young mother, a modern mum
■ SM **1** (*stile*) modern style **2** **gli antichi e i moderni** (the) ancient and (the) modern

modestamente [modesta'mente] AVV modestly; **modestamente, io lo faccio meglio** in all modesty, I'm better at it

modestia [mo'dɛstja] SF modesty; **modestia a parte...** in all modesty ..., though I say it myself ...; **certo non pecca di modestia** modesty isn't one of his faults

modesto, a [mo'dɛsto] AGG modest; **di modeste origini** from humble origins; **una casa modesta** a modest house *o* home

modico, a, ci, che ['mɔdiko] AGG (*gen*) modest, moderate; **prezzi modici** low prices

modifica, che [mo'difika] SF (*a motore*) adjustment; (*ad abito*) alteration; (*a piano*) modification; **fare una modifica** to make an adjustment (*o* alteration *o* modification); **subire delle modifiche** (*cambiamenti*) to undergo some modifications; (*miglioramenti*) to be revamped

modificabile [modifi'kabile] AGG modifiable

modificare [modifi'kare] VT to modify, alter
▶ **modificarsi** VIP to alter, change

modificazione [modifikat'tsjone] SF (*vedi modifica*) adjustment; alteration; modification

modista [mo'dista] SF milliner

modisteria [modiste'ria] SF (*laboratorio*) milliner's (shop)

modo ['mɔdo] SM
1 (*maniera*) way, manner; **allo stesso modo** in the same way; **in modo strano** strangely, in a strange way, in an odd way; **in modo eccessivo** excessively; **a** *o* **in questo/quel modo** (in) this/that way; **fallo in questo modo** do it this way; **va fatto in questo modo** it should be done this way *o* like this; **in nessun modo** in no way; **fare a modo proprio** to do as one likes; **lo farò a modo mio** I'll do it my own way; **non è il modo di comportarsi** this is no way to behave; **a suo modo** *o* **a modo suo le vuole bene** he loves her in his own way; **ha un modo tutto suo di giocare a tennis** he has a highly idiosyncratic way of playing tennis; **un modo di dire** a turn of phrase, an expression; **per modo di dire** so to speak, as it were; **l'ha perdonata per modo di dire** he's forgiven her in a manner of speaking; **non mi piace il suo modo di fare** I don't like the way he goes about things; **non c'è modo di convincerlo** there's no way of persuading him; **c'è modo e modo di farlo** there's a right way and a wrong way of doing it; **aver modo di fare qc** to have the opportunity *o* chance of doing sth; **trovare il modo di fare qc** to find a way *o* the means of doing sth; **ad** *o* **in ogni modo** anyway; **ad ogni modo, non ha importanza** anyway, it doesn't matter; **in qualche modo** somehow (or other); **in qualche modo riuscirò a farlo** I'll manage it somehow; **in un certo qual modo** in a way, in some ways; **in tutti i modi** at all costs; (*comunque sia*) anyway; (*in ogni caso*) in any case; **di** *o* **in modo che** so that; **lo sgriderò in modo che capisca che deve studiare** I'll give him a good telling-off, that way he'll understand he's got to study; **dovrò fare in modo che non mi vedano** I'll have to make sure they don't see me; **in modo da** so as to, in such a way as to; **entrai in punta di piedi in modo da non disturbarlo** I went in on tiptoe so as not to disturb him; **fare in modo di** to try to; **fate in modo di**

Mm

tornare per le cinque try and be back for 5 o'clock
2 (*misura, regola*): **oltre modo** extremely; **fare le cose a modo** to do things properly; **una persona a modo** a well-mannered person
3 **modi** SMPL (*maniere*) manners; **che modi!** what bad manners!; **ha dei modi molto brutti** he has dreadful manners
4 (*Gramm*) mood; **modo congiuntivo/indicativo** subjunctive/indicative mood
5 (*Mus, Inform*) mode; **modo conversazionale** (*Inform*) conversation mode

modulare[1] [modu'lare] VT (*voce, Fis*) to modulate

modulare[2] [modu'lare] AGG modular

modulatore [modula'tore] SM (*Fis*) modulator; **modulatore di frequenza/di luce** frequency/light modulator

modulazione [modulat'tsjone] SF modulation; **modulazione di frequenza** frequency modulation

modulo ['mɔdulo] SM **1** (*modello*) form; **riempire un modulo** to fill in a form; **riempite il modulo in stampatello** fill in the form in block letters; **modulo continuo** continuous stationery; **modulo di domanda** application form; **modulo d'iscrizione** enrolment form; **modulo di versamento** deposit slip **2** (*Archit, Aer*) module; **modulo di comando/lunare** command/lunar module **3** (*Mat*) modulus **4** (*Calcio*) plan

modus vivendi ['mɔdus vi'vɛndi] SM INV modus vivendi

moffetta [mof'fetta] SF skunk

Mogadiscio [moga'diʃʃo] SF Mogadishu

mogano ['mɔgano] SM mahogany

mogio, a, gi, ge *o* **gie** ['mɔdʒo] AGG down in the dumps, dejected; **se n'è andato mogio mogio** he went off with his tail between his legs

moglie ['moʎʎe] SF wife; **questa è mia moglie Anna** this is my wife Anna; **prendere moglie** to get married, take a wife; **tra moglie e marito non mettere il dito** (*Proverbio*) never interfere between husband and wife

mohair [mɔ'ɛr] SM mohair

moicano, a [moi'kano] AGG, SM/F (*indiano*) Mohican; (*acconciatura*) mohican

moine [mo'ine] SFPL (*carezze*) endearments; (*lusinghe*) flattery *sg*, cajolery *sg*; (*smancerie*) affectation *sg*; **fare un sacco di moine a qn** to be all over sb; **è una ragazza tutta moine** she's a very affected girl; **non mi convincerai con le tue moine** you're not going to sweet-talk me into it

moka ['mɔka] = moca

mola ['mɔla] SF (*di mulino*) millstone; (*per utensili ecc*) grindstone

molare[1] [mo'lare] AGG, SM (*dente*) molar

molare[2] [mo'lare] VT to grind, polish

molare[3] [mo'lare] AGG (*Chim, Fis*) molar

molarità [molari'ta] SF INV (*Chim, Fis*) molarity

molato, a [mo'lato] AGG: **vetro molato** cut glass

molatrice [mola'tritʃe] SF grinder

Moldavia [mol'davja] SF Moldova

moldavo, a [mol'davo] SM/F, AGG Moldovan, Moldavian

mole ['mɔle] SF (*gen*) massive shape; (*dimensioni*) size; (*Chim*) mole; **una mole di lavoro** masses (*Brit fam*) *o* loads of work; **una mole di lavoro arretrato** a massive backlog of work; **è comparso sulla porta in tutta la sua mole** his massive shape appeared at the door

> **LO SAPEVI...?**
> **mole** non si traduce mai con la parola inglese ***mole***

molecola [mo'lɛkola] SF molecule

molecolare [moleko'lare] AGG molecular

molestare [moles'tare] VT (*infastidire*) to annoy, bother; (*sessualmente*) to harass; **non molestare quel povero cane** don't torment that poor dog

molestatore, trice [molesta'tore] SM/F (*di bambini*) molester

molestia [mo'lɛstja] SF (*noia, fastidio*) annoyance, bother; (*azione molesta*): **molestie** SFPL trouble *sg*, bother *sg*; **molestie sessuali** sexual harassment *sg*

molesto, a [mo'lɛsto] AGG annoying

molisano, a [moli'zano] AGG of *o* from Molise
■ SM/F inhabitant *o* native of Molise

molla ['mɔlla] SF **1** (*Tecn*) spring; (*fig: incentivo*) motivating force; **molla elicoidale** helical spring, coil spring; **molla di orologio** watch spring; **materasso a molle** spring mattress; **a molla** (*giocattolo*) clockwork; **i soldi sono la molla che lo spinge ad agire** money is the driving force as far as he's concerned **2** (*per camino*): **molle** SFPL tongs; **prendere qn con le molle** to treat sb with kid gloves

mollare [mol'lare] VT (*gen*) to let go; (*far cadere*) to drop; **mollare la presa** to let go; **mollare gli ormeggi** (*Naut*) to cast off; **mollare un pugno a qn** (*fig fam*) to punch sb; **mollare uno schiaffo a qn** (*fig fam*) to slap sb, give sb a slap; **ha mollato il lavoro** she's chucked her job; **ha mollato il suo ragazzo** she's ditched *o* dumped her boyfriend; **ha mollato il pacco qua e se n'è andato** he dumped the parcel here and left; **mi ha mollato i soldi per il cine** he let me have the money to go to the cinema
■ VI (*aus* **avere**) (*cedere, arrendersi*) to give in *o* up; (*fig fam: smettere*) stop; **non mollare proprio adesso!** don't give up now!

molle ['mɔlle] AGG **1** (*gen*) soft; (*muscoli*) flabby **2** (*fig: debole*) weak, feeble

molleggiare [molled'dʒare] VT to spring
■ VI (*aus* **avere**) (*letto*) to be springy
▶ **molleggiarsi** VR: **molleggiarsi sulle gambe** (*Ginnastica*) to do knee-bends; (*camminando*) to have a spring in one's step

molleggiato, a [molled'dʒato] AGG (*letto*) sprung; (*auto*) with good suspension; (*passo, camminata*) springy

molleggio, gi [mol'leddʒo] SM **1** (*per veicoli*) suspension; (*per letti*) springs *pl* **2** (*elasticità*) springiness **3** (*Ginnastica*) knee-bends *pl*

mollemente [molle'mente] AVV (*sdraiarsi, muoversi*) languidly

molletta [mol'letta] SF (*per capelli*) hairgrip; (*per panni*) clothes peg (*Brit*) *o* pin (*Am*); **mollette** SFPL (*per zucchero, ghiaccio*) tongs

mollettone [mollet'tone] SM (*per tavolo*) padded table cover; (*per asse da stiro*) ironing-board cover

mollezza [mol'lettsa] SF **1** (*fig: di carattere*) weakness, feebleness **2** **mollezze** SFPL (*agi, comodità*) luxury *sg*; **vivere nelle mollezze** to live in the lap of luxury

mollica, che [mol'lika] SF soft part of loaf; **molliche** SFPL (*briciole*) crumbs

molliccio, cia, ci, ce [mol'littʃo] AGG **1** (*terreno, impasto*) soggy; (*frutta*) soft **2** (*floscio: mano*) limp; (: *muscolo*) flabby

mollusco, schi [mol'lusko] SM (*Zool*) mollusc

molo ['mɔlo] SM jetty, pier; **attraccare al molo** to dock

molotov ['mɔlotov] SF INV (*anche:* **bottiglia molotov**) Molotov cocktail
molteplice [mol'teplitʃe] AGG (*formato di più elementi*) complex; **molteplici** (*svariati: interessi, attività ecc*) numerous, various
molteplicità [molteplitʃi'ta] SF multiplicity; **una molteplicità di interessi** a wide range of interests
moltiplica, che [mol'tiplika] SF (*di bicicletta*) gear ratio
moltiplicare [moltipli'kare] VT (*anche fig*) to multiply; **moltiplicare 5 per 3** to multiply 5 by 3
▶ **moltiplicarsi** VIP (*gen*) to multiply; (*spese, richieste*) to increase
moltiplicatore, trice [moltiplika'tore] SM (*Tecn, Fis, Mat*) multiplier
moltiplicazione [moltiplikat'tsjone] SF multiplication
moltitudine [molti'tudine] SF **1** **una moltitudine di** a vast number *o* a multitude of **2** (*letter: folla*) multitude

molto, a ['molto] PAROLA CHIAVE
■ AVV **1** a lot, (very) much, a great deal; **non legge molto** he doesn't read much *o* a great deal; **ha viaggiato molto** he has travelled a lot *o* a great deal; **ti è piaciuto? — sì, molto** did you like it? — yes, very much; **questo libro è molto meglio dell'altro** this book is a lot *o* much better than the other one; **ci vorranno a dir molto 3 giorni** it will take 3 days at the most
2 (*con aggettivi, avverbi*) very; (*con participio passato*) (very) much; **l'ha fatto molto bene** he did it very well; **molto lodato** highly *o* (very) much praised; **sono molto stanco** I'm very tired
3 (*distanza, tempo*): **c'è ancora molto da camminare** there's still a long way to go; **ci vuole molto?** (*tempo*) will it take long?; **non la vedo da molto** I haven't seen her for quite a while *o* for a long time; **ne hai ancora per molto?** will you be much longer?; **arriverà fra non molto** he'll arrive soon
■ AGG (*quantità*) a great deal of, a lot of, lots of, much (*in domande e con negazioni*); (*numero*) a lot of, lots of, many (*in domande e con negazioni*); **molta gente** a lot of people, many people; **molti libri** a lot of books, many books; **c'è molta neve** there's a great deal of *o* a lot of snow; **non c'è molto pane** there isn't a lot of bread, there isn't (very) much bread; **non ho molto tempo** I don't have *o* haven't got much time; **non c'erano molti turisti** there weren't many tourists
■ PRON much, a lot; **molti** *o* **molte** many, a lot; **c'è pane? — sì, molto** is there any bread? — yes plenty *o* lots (*fam*); **molti pensano che sia giusto** many (people) think it's right; **molti di noi** many of *o* a lot of us

molva ['mɔlva] SF ling (*fish*)
momentaneamente [momentanea'mente] AVV at the moment, at present; **è momentaneamente assente** she's not here at the moment
momentaneo, a [momen'taneo] AGG (*gioia, dolore*) momentary; (*assenza, scarsità*) temporary
momento [mo'mento] SM **1** (*gen*) moment; **in questo momento** at the moment, at present; **in questo momento è al telefono** he's on the phone at the moment; **la situazione non è rosea in questo momento** *o* **al momento** things don't look too rosy at the moment *o* at present; **da un momento all'altro** any moment now, at any moment; (*all'improvviso*) suddenly; **può arrivare da un momento all'altro** he'll be here any moment now; **il tempo è cambiato da un momento all'altro** the weather changed suddenly; **per il momento** for the time being; **sul momento** there and then; **fino a questo momento** up till now, until now; **in qualunque momento** at any time; **un momento prego!** just a moment, please!; **proprio in quel momento** at that very moment, just at that moment; **non sta fermo un momento** he can't keep still; **posso parlarti un momento?** could I have a word with you?; **dal momento che** given that, since **2** (*contingenza*) time; (*occasione*) opportunity; **sono momenti difficili** *or* **è un momento difficile** it's a difficult time *o* moment; **aspettare il momento favorevole** to wait for the right moment; **è successo al momento sbagliato** it came at the wrong time; **momento culminante** climax; **abbiamo passato momenti bellissimi insieme** we had some great times together; **verremo in un altro momento** we'll come another time; **è l'uomo del momento** he's the man of the moment; **non è il momento di scherzare** this is no time to joke; **al momento di pagare...** when it came to paying ...; **al momento di partire mi sono accorto che...** just as I was leaving, I realised ... **3** **a momenti** (*da un momento all'altro*) any time *o* moment now; (*quasi*) nearly; **arriverà a momenti** he should arrive any time now; **a momenti cadevo** I nearly fell **4** (*Fis*) moment
monaca, che ['mɔnaka] SF (*Rel*) nun; **farsi monaca** to become a nun
monacale [mona'kale] AGG monastic
monachesimo [mona'kezimo] SM monasticism
Monaco ['mɔnako] SF: **(Principato di) Monaco** Monaco; **Monaco (di Baviera)** Munich
monaco, ci ['mɔnako] SM monk
monade ['mɔnade] SF (*Filosofia*) monad
monarca, chi [mo'narka] SM monarch
monarchia [monar'kia] SF monarchy
monarchico, a, ci, che [mo'narkiko] AGG (*stato, autorità*) monarchic; (*partito, fede*) monarchist *attr*
■ SM/F monarchist
monastero [monas'tɛro] SM (*di monaci*) monastery; (*di monache*) convent
monastico, a, ci, che [mo'nastiko] AGG monastic
moncherino [monke'rino] SM stump
monco, a, chi, che ['monco] AGG maimed, mutilated; (*fig*) incomplete; **monco di un braccio** one-armed
■ SM/F maimed *o* mutilated person
moncone [mon'kone] SM stump
mondana [mon'dana] SF (*euf*) prostitute
mondanamente [mondana'mente] AVV: **vivere mondanamente** to move in fashionable circles
mondanità [mondani'ta] SF INV **1** (*frivolezza*) worldliness **2** **le mondanità** SFPL (*piaceri*) worldly pleasures
mondano, a [mon'dano] AGG (*Rel: terrestre*) worldly, earthly; (*riunione, cronaca, vita*) society *attr*; (*obblighi*) social
mondare [mon'dare] VT (*piselli*) to shell; (*frutta, patate*) to peel; (*grano*) to winnow; (*fig: anima*) to cleanse
mondezza [mon'dettsa] SF (*fam*) rubbish *no pl*, refuse *no pl*, trash *no pl* (*Am*)
mondezzaio, ai [mondet'tsajo] SM rubbish (*Brit*) *o* garbage (*Am*) dump; (*fig*) tip (*Brit*)
mondiale [mon'djale] AGG (*gen*) world *attr*; (*crisi, successo*) world-wide; **di fama mondiale** world famous;

Mm

la prima guerra mondiale the First World War; **su scala mondiale** on a world-wide scale
■ SM world championship; **i mondiali di calcio** the World Cup

mondina [mon'dina] SF worker in the paddy fields

mondo[1] ['mondo] SM **1** (*gen, fig*) world; **in tutto il mondo** all over the world, throughout the world; **il migliore del mondo** the best in the world; **nessuno al mondo** no-one in the world; **essere solo al mondo** to have no family; **il mondo dell'aldilà** the next life, the after life; **il gran** *o* **bel mondo** high society; **il mondo del teatro** the world of the theatre
2 (*fraseologia*): **ti faccio un mondo di auguri** *or* **ti auguro un mondo di bene** all the best!; **ti voglio un mondo di bene** I really love you!; **gli voglio tutto il bene di questo mondo ma...** I'm very fond of him but ...; **per niente al mondo** *or* **per nessuna cosa al mondo** not for all the world; **da che mondo è mondo** since time *o* the world began; **(sono) cose dell'altro mondo!** it's incredible!; **non è poi la fine del mondo se non vengo** it won't be the end of the world if I can't make it; **una moto che è la fine del mondo** one hell of a motorbike; **mettere/venire al mondo** to bring/come into the world; **com'è piccolo il mondo!** it's a small world!; **è un uomo di mondo** he's a man of the world; **così va il mondo** that's life; **vivere fuori dal mondo** to be out of touch with the real world; **ma in che mondo vivi?** what planet are you living on?; **vive in un mondo tutto suo** he lives in a world of his own; **mandare qn all'altro mondo** to kill sb; **il mondo è bello perché è vario** (*Proverbio*) variety is the spice of life; **mondo cane!** bloody hell!

mondo[2], **a** ['mondo] AGG (*verdura*) cleaned; (*frutta, patate*) peeled

mondovisione [mondovi'zjone] SF: **trasmettere in mondovisione** to show on TV worldwide

monegasco, a, schi, sche [mone'gasko] AGG Monegasque
■ SM/F native *o* inhabitant of Monaco

monelleria [monelle'ria] SF prank, naughty trick; **fare una monelleria** to play a trick *o* prank

monello, a [mo'nɛllo] SM/F (*ragazzo di strada*) (street) urchin; (*ragazzo vivace*) rascal, scamp

moneta [mo'neta] SF **1** (*pezzo*) coin; **una moneta da due euro** a two euro coin; **ripagare qn della stessa moneta** (*fig*) to pay sb back in his own coin **2** (*denaro*) money; (*spiccioli*) (small) change; **non ho moneta** I haven't (got) any change; **moneta cartacea** paper money **3** (*valuta*) currency; **la sterlina è una moneta forte** the pound is a strong currency; **moneta corrente** currency; **moneta debole/forte** weak/strong currency; **moneta estera** foreign currency; **moneta legale** legal tender; **moneta unica (europea)** single (European) currency

monetario, ria, ri, rie [mone'tarjo] AGG monetary

monetarismo [moneta'rizmo] SM monetarism

monetizzabile [monetid'dzabile] AGG convertible (into cash)

monetizzare [mondetid'dzare] VT to convert (into cash)

monetizzazione [monetiddzat'tsjone] SF conversion (into cash)

mongolfiera [mongol'fjɛra] SF hot-air balloon

Mongolia [mon'gɔlja] SF Mongolia

mongolico, a, ci, che [mon'gɔliko] AGG Mongolian

mongolo, a ['mɔngolo] AGG, SM/F Mongolian, Mongol
■ SM (*lingua*) Mongolian, Mongol

monile [mo'nile] SM (*collana*) necklace; (*gioiello*) jewel

monito ['mɔnito] SM warning; **che ti serva di monito!** let this be a lesson to you!

monitor ['mɔnitə] SM INV monitor

monitoraggio, gi [monito'raddʒo] SM monitoring

monitorare [monito'rare] VT to monitor

monoalbero [mono'albero] AGG INV single-camshaft *attr*

monoblocco, chi [mono'blɔkko] SM (*Aut*) cylinder block

monocamera [mono'kamera] SF one-room flat

monocamerale [monokame'rale] AGG (*Pol: sistema*) single chamber *attr*

monocilindrico, a, ci, che [monotʃi'lindriko] AGG single-cylinder *attr*

monocolo [mo'nɔkolo] SM monocle, eyeglass

monocolore [monoko'lore] SM (*Pol: anche*: **governo monocolore**) one-party government

monocorde [mono'kɔrde] AGG (*monotono*) monotonous

monocotiledone [monokoti'lɛdone] AGG monocotyledon

monocromatico, a, ci, che [monokro'matiko] AGG (*pittura*) monochrome; (*Fis*) monochromatic

monocromatismo [monokroma'tizmo] SM (*Med*) monochromatism

monocromo, a [mo'nɔkromo] AGG monochrome

monodose [mono'dɔze] AGG INV single dose

monoelica [mono'ɛlika] AGG INV (*aereo*) single-propellor *attr*

monofase [mono'faze] AGG (*Elettr*) single-phase

monogamia [monoga'mia] SF monogamy

monogamo, a [mo'nɔgamo] AGG monogamous
■ SM/F monogamist

monogenitore [monodʒeni'tore] AGG INV: **famiglia monogenitore** one-parent family

monografia [monogra'fia] SF monograph

monografico, a, ci, che [mono'grafiko] AGG monographic; **corso monografico** (*Univ*) *course on a single author or topic*

monogramma, i [mono'gramma] SM monogram

monokini [mono'kini] SM INV monokini

monolingue [mono'lingwe] AGG monolingual
■ SM (*dizionario*) monolingual dictionary

monolito [mo'nɔlito] SM monolith

monolocale [monolo'kale] SM studio flat

monologo, ghi [mo'nɔlogo] SM monologue; **il monologo di Amleto** Hamlet's soliloquy; **monologo interiore** (*Letteratura*) interior monologue

monomio, mi [mo'nɔmjo] SM (*Mat*) monomial

monomotore [monomo'tore] AGG (*aereo*) single-engined

mononucleare [mononukle'are] AGG (*famiglia*) nuclear

mononucleosi [mononukle'ɔzi] SF INV glandular fever, mononucleosis (*termine tecn*)

monoparentale [monoparen'tale] AGG single-parent

monopartitismo [monoparti'tizmo] SM single-party system

monopattino [mono'pattino] SM scooter

monopetto [mono'pɛtto] AGG INV (*giacca*) single-breasted

monopezzo [mono'pɛttso] AGG INV one-piece *attr*
■ SM INV one-piece

monopoli® [mo'nɔpoli] SM (*gioco*) Monopoly®

monopolio, li [mono'pɔljo] SM (*Econ, fig*) monopoly; **monopolio di stato** state monopoly

monopolizzare [monopolid'dzare] VT (*Comm, fig*) to monopolize
monopolizzatore, trice [monopoliddza'tore] AGG monopolizing *attr*
■ SM/F monopolizer
monopolizzazione [monopoliddzat'tsjone] SF monopolization
monoposto [mono'posto] AGG INV, SM single-seater
monoreddito [mono'rɛddito] AGG INV single-income; **famiglia monoreddito** single-income family
monosaccaride [monosak'karide] SM monosaccharide
monoscì [monoʃ'ʃi] SM INV (*sci d'acqua*) water-ski; (*sci alpino*) monoski
monosillabico, a, ci, che [monosil'labiko] AGG monosyllabic
monosillabo, a [mono'sillabo] AGG monosyllabic
■ SM monosyllable; **rispondere a monosillabi** (*fig*) to answer in monosyllables
monossido [mo'nɔssido] SM monoxide; **monossido di carbonio** carbon monoxide
monostadio [monos'tadjo] AGG INV (*missile*) single-stage
monoteismo [monote'izmo] SM monotheism
monoteistico, a, ci, che [monote'istiko] AGG monotheistic
monotematico, a, ci, che [monote'matiko] AGG (*film, libro*) with only one idea
monotonamente [monotona'mente] AVV monotonously
monotonia [monoto'nia] SF monotony, dullness
monotono, a [mo'nɔtono] AGG (*gen*) monotonous; (*vita*) humdrum; (*lavoro*) dull, monotonous
monouso [mono'uzo] AGG INV (*siringa*) disposable
monovalente [monova'lɛnte] AGG (*Chim*) monovalent
monovolume [monovo'lume] AGG INV, SF INV: **(automobile) monovolume** people carrier, people mover
Mons. ABBR (= Monsignore) Mgr
monsignore [monsiɲ'ɲore] SM **1** (*titolo ecclesiastico*) monsignor **2** (*titolo: parlando a arcivescovo, vescovo*) Your Grace; (: *parlando di terzi*) His Grace
monsone [mon'sone] SM monsoon
monta ['monta] SF (*accoppiamento*) covering; **stazione di monta** stud farm
montacarichi [monta'kariki] SM INV goods lift, service elevator (*Am*)
montaggio, gi [mon'taddʒo] SM **1** (*di macchina, telaio, mobile*) assembly; **scatola/catena di montaggio** assembly kit/line **2** (*Cine*) editing
montagna [mon'taɲɲa] SF **1** (*monte*) mountain; **una montagna di** (*fig: gran quantità*) a mountain *o* pile *o* heap of; **il Ben Nevis è la montagna più alta della Scozia** Ben Nevis is the highest mountain in Scotland; **montagne russe** (*giostra*) roller coaster *sg*, big dipper *sg* (*Brit*) **2** (*zona, regione*): **la montagna** the mountains *pl*; **andare in montagna** to go to the mountains; **andremo in vacanza in montagna** we're going to the mountains for our holiday; **casa di montagna** house in the mountains; **aria/strada di montagna** mountain air/road; **un paesino di montagna** a mountain village; **mi piace la montagna** I like the mountains; **ha una casa in montagna** he's got a house in the mountains
montagnoso, a [montaɲ'ɲoso] AGG mountainous
Montana [mon'tana] SM Montana
montanaro, a [monta'naro] AGG mountain *attr*
■ SM/F (*persona*) mountain dweller
montano, a [mon'tano] AGG mountain *attr*
montante [mon'tante] SM **1** (*di porta*) jamb; (*di finestra*) upright; (*Calcio: palo*) post **2** (*Pugilato*) upper cut **3** (*Comm*) total amount
montare [mon'tare] VI (*aus* **essere**) **1** (*salire*) to go (*o* come) up; **montare in bicicletta/macchina/in treno** to get on a bicycle/into a car/on a train; **montare su una scala** to climb a ladder; **montare in cima a** to climb to the top of; **montare su tutte le furie** (*fig*) to lose one's temper **2** (*cavalcare*): **montare bene/male** to ride well/badly; **montare a cavallo** to mount *o* get on a horse **3** (*aumentare: vento, marea*) to rise
■ VT **1** (*salire*) to go (*o* come) up; **montare le scale** to go upstairs, climb the stairs **2** (*cavallo*) to ride **3** (*Zool*) to cover **4**: **montare la guardia** (*Mil*) to mount guard **5** (*costruire: macchina, mobile ecc*) to assemble; (*tenda*) to pitch; (*film*) to edit; (*gioielli*) to set; (*fotografia*) to mount; (*Aut: gomma*) to put on; **ha montato l'armadio da solo** he assembled the wardrobe himself; **montarono la tenda vicino al lago** they pitched their tent near the lake **6** (*fig: esagerare: notizia*) to blow up, exaggerate **7** (*fig*): **montare la testa a qn** to turn sb's head; **montarsi la testa** to get *o* become big-headed; **si è montato la testa** he's got big-headed **8** (*Culin: panna*) to whip; (: *albume*) to whisk; **montare a neve** to whisk until stiff; **montate a neve gli albumi** whisk the egg whites until stiff
▶ **montarsi** VIP (*insuperbirsi*) to become big-headed
montatura [monta'tura] SF (*di gioiello*) setting; (*di occhiali*) frames *pl*; (*fig: esagerazione*) exaggeration; **una montatura pubblicitaria** (*fig*) a publicity stunt
montavivande [montavi'vande] SM INV dumbwaiter
monte ['monte] SM **1** mountain; **qual è il monte più alto d'Europa?** which is the highest mountain in Europe?; **a monte (di)** (*fiume*) upstream (from); (*vallata*) at the head (of); **un monte di** (*gran quantità*) a mountain *o* pile *o* heap of; **il problema è a monte** (*fig*) the problem goes back to the early stages; **andare a monte** (*fig*) to come to nothing; **mandare a monte** (*fig: piano, progetto*) to put paid to; **fu quel fatto a mandare a monte il matrimonio** that's what caused the wedding to be called off; **il Monte Bianco** Mont Blanc; **il Monte Everest** Mount Everest; **il Monte degli Ulivi** the Mount of Olives **2** **monte di pietà** pawnbroker's, pawnshop; **portare qc al monte di pietà** (*impegnare*) to pawn sth
Montecitorio [montetʃi'torjo] SM *building which houses the Italian Parliament*
▷ www.camera.it/chiosco.asp?content=/montecitoriochiosco
montenegrino, a [montene'grino] SM/F, AGG Montenegrin
Montenegro [monte'negro] SM Montenegro
montepremi [monte'prɛmi] SM INV jackpot
montgomery [mənt'gʌməri] SM INV duffle *o* duffel coat
montone [mon'tone] SM **1** (*Zool*) ram; **carne di montone** mutton **2** (*anche:* **giacca di montone**) sheepskin (jacket)
montuosità [montuosi'ta] SF mountainous nature
montuoso, a [montu'oso] AGG mountainous
monumentale [monumen'tale] AGG monumental
monumentalità [monumentali'ta] SF monumental nature
monumento [monu'mento] SM monument; **visitare i monumenti** to go sightseeing; **un monumento ai**

Mm

caduti a war memorial; **ti farei un monumento!** *(fig)* you deserve a medal!

moplen® [mo'plɛn] SM moulded plastic

moquette [mɔ'kɛt] SF INV fitted carpet

mora[1] ['mɔra] SF *(Bot: di gelso)* mulberry; *(: di rovo)* blackberry

mora[2] ['mɔra] SF *(Dir)* **1** delay **2** *(somma dovuta)* arrears *pl*

morale [mo'rale] AGG *(gen)* moral
■SF **1** *(norme, consuetudini)* morals *pl*, morality; *(Filosofia)* moral philosophy, ethics *sg*; **non hanno morale** they haven't got any morals; **la morale corrente** current moral standards *pl* **2** *(insegnamento)* moral; **la morale della favola** the moral of the story; **così, morale della favola, siamo rimasti a casa** and the result was that we stayed at home
■SM *(stato d'animo)* morale; **essere giù di morale** to be feeling down; **sono giù di morale** I'm feeling down; **su col morale!** cheer up!; **aver il morale alto/a terra** to be in good/low spirits; **bisogna tener alto il morale delle truppe** we must keep the troops' morale high

moraleggiare [moraled'dʒare] VI *(aus* **avere***)* to moralize, sermonize

moralista, i, e [mora'lista] AGG moralistic
■SM/F moralist

moralisticamente [moralistika'mente] AVV *(analizzare)* from a moral point of view; *(parlare, comportarsi)* in a moralizing way

moralistico, a, ci, che [mora'listiko] AGG moralistic

moralità [morali'ta] SF **1** *(norme di vita, morale)* morality, morals *pl*, moral standards *pl*; **una persona di alta moralità** a person of high moral standards **2** *(di comportamento)* morality

moralizzare [moralid'dzare] VT *(costumi, vita pubblica)* to set moral standards for
■VI *(aus* **avere***)* **moralizzare (su)** to moralize (on, about)

moralizzatore, trice [moraliddza'tore] AGG moralizing
■SM/F moralizer

moralizzazione [moraliddzat'tsjone] SF setting of moral standards

moralmente [moral'mente] AVV morally

moratoria [mora'tɔrja] SF *(Dir)* moratorium

morbidamente [morbida'mente] AVV softly

morbidezza [morbi'dettsa] SF *(vedi agg)* softness; tenderness; smoothness

morbido, a ['mɔrbido] AGG *(gen)* soft; *(carne)* tender; *(pelle)* soft, smooth; **ha la pelle morbida** she's got soft skin

> **LO SAPEVI...?**
> **morbido** non si traduce mai con la parola inglese *morbid*

morbillo [mor'billo] SM measles *sg*; **Giorgio ha il morbillo** Giorgio has got measles

morbo ['mɔrbo] SM *(Med)* disease; *(: epidemia)* epidemic

morbosamente [morbosa'mente] AVV morbidly

morbosità [morbosi'ta] SF morbidity

morboso, a [mor'boso] AGG *(Med, fig)* morbid; **una gelosia morbosa** pathological jealousy

morchia ['mɔrkja] SF sludge, oily deposit

mordace [mor'datʃe] AGG *(fig: satira)* biting; *(: persona, parole)* cutting

mordente [mor'dɛnte] SM **1** *(Chim)* mordant **2** *(fig: di satira, critica, stile)* bite; *(: di persona)* drive

mordere ['mɔrdere] VT IRREG *(sogg: persona, cane, insetto)* to bite; *(addentare: mela, panino)* to bite into; **mordere la gamba a qn** to bite sb's leg, bite sb in the leg; **il cane mi ha morso la gamba** the dog bit my leg; **mordersi le labbra/la lingua** *(anche fig)* to bite one's lips/one's tongue; **mordere il freno** *(anche fig)* to champ at the bit; **mordere l'asfalto** *(Aut)* to grip the road; **mi sarei morso le mani** I could have kicked myself; **can che abbaia non morde** *(Proverbio)* his (*o* her *ecc*) bark is worse than his (*o* her *ecc*) bite

mordicchiare [mordik'kjare] VT *(gen)* to chew at; **mordicchiarsi le labbra** to bite one's lips

morello, a [mo'rɛllo] AGG, SM/F: **(cavallo) morello** black horse

morena [mo'rɛna] SF *(Geol)* moraine

morente [mo'rɛnte] AGG dying
■SM/F *(persona)* dying man/woman; **i morenti** the dying

moresco, a, schi, sche [mo'resko] AGG Moorish

more uxorio ['mɔre uk'sɔrjo] AVV as man and wife

morfina [mor'fina] SF morphine

morfinomane [morfi'nɔmane] SM/F morphine addict

morfologia [morfolo'dʒia] SF morphology

morfologicamente [morfolodʒika'mente] AVV morphologically

morfologico, a, ci, che [morfo'lɔdʒiko] AGG morphological

moria [mo'ria] SF *(di bestiame)* disease; *(Bot)* blight

moribondo, a [mori'bondo] AGG *(persona)* dying
■SM/F dying man/woman

morigerato, a [moridʒe'rato] AGG *(persona, vita)* moderate, sober

morire [mo'rire] VI IRREG *(aus* **essere***)* **1** *(gen)* to die; **morì nel 1857** he died in 1857; **morire di malattia** to die after an illness; **morire di morte violenta/naturale** to die a violent/natural death; **morire di stenti** to die from hardship; **morire in guerra** to die in battle; **morire assassinato** to be murdered; **morire di dolore** to die of a broken heart; **morire di fame** to starve to death, die of hunger; *(fig)* to be starving, be famished; **morire di freddo** to freeze to death; *(fig)* to be frozen (stiff); **morire di sete** *(anche fig)* to die of thirst; **muoio di sete** I'm dying of thirst **2** *(fig)*: **morire d'invidia** to be green with envy; **morire di noia** to be bored to death *o* to tears; **morire di paura** to be scared to death; **morire dalle risate** *o* **dal ridere** to kill o.s. laughing, die laughing; **morire di sonno** to be dead *o* dog tired; **morire dalla voglia di fare qc** to be dying to do sth; **moriva dalla voglia di raccontarle tutto** he was dying to tell her everything; **fa un caldo da morire** it's terribly hot; **ho un caldo da morire** I'm terribly hot; **mi fa male da morire questo braccio** my arm is killing me; **bella da morire** stunning; **le muore dietro e lei neanche lo vede** he worships the ground she treads on, and she doesn't even notice he's there; **chi non muore si rivede!** *(scherz)* fancy meeting you! (after all this time) **3** *(luce, giorno)* to fade, die; *(fiamma)* to die down; *(fuoco, tradizione, civiltà)* to die out; **il blu sul nero muore un po'** blue doesn't show up well on a black background

mormone [mor'mone] SM *(Rel)* Mormon

mormorare [mormo'rare] VI *(aus* **avere***)* **1** *(gen)* to murmur; *(sussurrare: persona, vento)* to murmur, whisper; *(brontolare)* to grumble, mutter; **si mormora che ...** it's rumoured *(Brit)* *o* rumored *(Am)* that ... **2** *(parlare male)*: **mormorare sul conto di qn** to speak ill of sb; **la gente mormora** people are talking

■VT (*parole d'amore ecc*) to whisper, murmur
mormorio, rii [mormo'rio] SM (*di persone, vento, acque*) murmur, murmuring; (*di foglie, fronde*) rustling
moro[1], a ['mɔro] AGG **1** (*Storia*) Moorish **2** (*persona: dai capelli scuri*) dark, dark-haired; (*: di carnagione scura*) dark, dark-skinned
■SM/F (*vedi agg*) Moor; dark-haired person; dark-skinned person
■**i Mori** SMPL (*Storia*) the Moors
moro[2] ['mɔro] SM mulberry tree
moroso, a [mo'roso] AGG (*Dir*) defaulting, in arrears
■SM/F (*fam: innamorato*) sweetheart

LO SAPEVI...?
moroso non si traduce mai con la parola inglese *morose*

morra ['mɔrra] SF *betting game: each of two players shows a number of fingers, simultaneously shouting out a guess at the joint total*
morsa ['mɔrsa] SF (*Tecn*) vice (*Brit*), vise (*Am*); (*fig: stretta*) grip; **stretto in una morsa d'acciaio** (*fig*) held in an iron grip
morse [mɔ:s] AGG INV: **alfabeto morse** Morse (code)
morsetto [mor'setto] SM (*Tecn*) clamp; (*Elettr*) terminal; **morsetto della batteria** (*Aut*) battery lead connection
morsicare [morsi'kare] VT to bite
morso, a ['mɔrso] PP *di* **mordere**
■SM **1** (*gen*) bite; (*di insetto*) sting; **dare un morso a qn** to bite sb; **dare un morso a qc** to bite sth; (*mangiare un pezzetto*) to bite into sth; **diede un morso al panino** he bit into his roll; **mi dai un morso di panino?** can I have a bite of your roll?; **i morsi della fame** hunger pangs **2** (*parte della briglia*) bit
mortadella [morta'dɛlla] SF (*Culin*) mortadella (*type of salted pork meat*)
mortaio, ai [mor'tajo] SM mortar
mortale [mor'tale] AGG **1** (*vita, uomo*) mortal **2** (*veleno*) deadly; (*ferita, incidente*) fatal; **un colpo mortale** a deadly *o* fatal blow; **peccato mortale** (*Rel*) mortal sin
■SM/F mortal
mortalità [mortali'ta] SF **1** (*l'essere mortale*) mortality **2** (*Statistica*) mortality, death rate; **mortalità infantile** infant mortality
mortalmente [mortal'mente] AVV (*gen, fig: offendersi*) mortally; **mi sono mortalmente annoiato** I was bored to death
mortaretto [morta'retto] SM firecracker
morte ['mɔrte] SF **1** (*gen*) death; (*fig: fine, rovina*) death, end; **morte clinica** brain death; **alla morte di sua madre** on the death of his mother; **in punto di morte** at death's door; **in punto di morte ha confessato** he confessed on his deathbed; **essere tra la vita e la morte** to be fighting for one's life; **ferito a morte** (*soldato*) mortally wounded; (*in incidente*) fatally injured; **condannare qn a morte** to sentence sb to death; **pena di/condanna a morte** death penalty/sentence **2** (*fraseologia*): **è questione di vita o di morte** it's a matter of life or death; **essere annoiato a morte** to be bored to death *o* to tears; **avercela a morte con qn** to hate sb like poison; **si odiano a morte** they can't stand the sight of each other; **avere la morte nel cuore** to have a heavy heart; **così facendo ha firmato la sua condanna a morte** by doing that he signed his own death warrant
mortificante [mortifi'kante] AVV mortifying
mortificare [mortifi'kare] VT to mortify
▶ **mortificarsi** VR (*Rel*) to mortify o.s.
▶ **mortificarsi** VIP (*vergognarsi, spiacersi*) to feel mortified
mortificato, a [mortifi'kato] AGG: **essere mortificato (per qc)** to be mortified (about sth)
mortificazione [mortifikat'tsjone] SF mortification
morto, a ['mɔrto] PP *di* **morire**
■AGG (*gen, fig*) dead; **il loro fratello morto** their dead brother; **sono morto di freddo** I'm frozen stiff; **sono stanco morto** I'm dead tired, I'm knackered (*fam!*); **sono morto di paura** I'm scared to death; **l'inverno è una stagione morta per noi** winter is our slack season; **morto e sepolto** (*fig*) dead and buried
■SM/F **1** dead man/woman; **i morti** the dead; **il due novembre commemoriamo i morti** we remember the dead on November the second; **ci sono stati tre morti nella sparatoria** three people were killed in the shooting; **fare il morto** (*in acqua*) to float on one's back; **un morto di fame** (*fig pegg*) a down-and-out; **sembri un morto che cammina** you look like death warmed up; **le campane suonavano a morto** the funeral bells were tolling; **giorno dei morti** All Souls' Day; **il regno dei morti** the world beyond the grave **2** (*Carte*) dummy
mortorio, ri [mor'tɔrjo] SM (*fig: cerimonia, festa*): **quella festa è stata un mortorio** that party was more like a funeral *o* wake
mosaico, ci [mo'zaiko] SM **1** (*Arte*) mosaic; **pavimento a mosaico** mosaic floor; **l'ultimo tassello del mosaico** (*fig*) the final piece of the puzzle **2** (*fig: di lingue, popoli*) mixture
▷ www.mosaico.net/indice.htm
Mosca ['moska] SF Moscow; **vado a Mosca** I'm going to Moscow; **abitano a Mosca** they live in Moscow
mosca ['moska] SF (*pl* **mosche**) **1** (*Zool, Pesca*) fly; **mosca della carne** bluebottle, blowfly; **mosca cavallina** horsefly; **mosca tse-tse** tsetse fly **2** (*fraseologia*): **non farebbe male a una mosca** he wouldn't hurt a fly; **morire come mosche** to die like flies; **non si sentiva volare una mosca** you could have heard a pin drop; **gli è saltata la mosca al naso** he lost his temper; **giocare a mosca cieca** to play blind-man's buff; **essere una mosca bianca** to be like hen's teeth; **rimanere *o* restare con un pugno di mosche** (*fig*) to be left empty-handed **3** (*barba*) goatee
■AGG INV (*Pugilato*): **peso mosca** flyweight
moscato, a [mos'kato] AGG (*uva*) muscat
■SM (*uva*) muscat grape; (*vino*) muscatel, muscat
moscerino [moʃʃe'rino] SM midge, gnat
moschea [mos'kɛa] SF mosque
moschettiere [mosket'tjɛre] SM musketeer
moschetto [mos'ketto] SM musket
moschettone [mosket'tone] SM (*gancio*) spring clip; (*Alpinismo*) karabiner, snaplink; (*Naut*) snapshackle
moschicida, i, e [moski'tʃida] SM flykiller
■AGG: **carta moschicida** flypaper
moscio, scia, sci, sce ['moʃʃo] AGG **1** (*cappello*) soft; (*fig: persona*) lifeless, dull **2** **ha la "r" moscia** he can't roll his "r"s
moscone [mos'kone] SM **1** (*insetto*) bluebottle **2** (*pattino*) pedalo; (*: a remi*) pedalo with oars **3** (*corteggiatore*) suitor
moscovita, i, e [mosko'vita] AGG, SM/F Muscovite
Mosè [mo'zɛ] SM Moses
mossa ['mɔssa] SF **1** (*gen: movimento*) movement; **prendere le mosse da qc** to come about as the result of sth; **datti una mossa!** (*fig*) get a move on!

2 (*Scacchi, Dama, fig*) move; **fare una mossa sbagliata** (*anche fig*) to make a bad move; **ha fatto una mossa sbagliata** he made a bad move

mossi *ecc* ['mɔssi] VB *vedi* **muovere**

mosso, a ['mɔsso] PP *di* **muovere**
■ AGG **1** (*mare*) rough; (*capelli*) wavy; (*fotografia*) blurred; **oggi c'è mare mosso** the sea's rough today; **ha i capelli mossi** he's got wavy hair; **la fotografia è un po' mossa** the photo is a bit blurred **2** (*Mus*) mosso

mostarda [mos'tarda] SF (*Culin*) mustard; **mostarda di Cremona** *pickled fruit with mustard*

mosto ['mosto] SM must

mostra ['mostra] SF **1** (*di oggetti*) exhibition; (*di animali, fiori*) show; **fare una mostra** to put on an exhibition *o* a show; **il negozio ha messo in mostra gli ultimi arrivi** the shop has put its latest stock on display; **essere in mostra** to be on show; **mostra d'arte** art exhibition; **mostra canina** dog show **2** (*locale*) exhibition hall **3** (*fraseologia*): **far mostra di sé** to show off; **fare mostra di fare qc** (*fingere*) to pretend to do sth; **mettersi in mostra** to draw attention to o.s.; **mettere qc in bella mostra** to show sth off

mostrare [mos'trare] VT: **mostrare (qc a qn)** to show (sb sth), show (sth to sb); **ho mostrato le foto a Paolo** I showed Paolo the photos; **le ho mostrato il mio vestito nuovo** I showed her my new dress; **mi mostri come si fa?** will you show me how to do it?; **ha mostrato un notevole coraggio** he displayed great courage; **mostrare i denti** (*anche fig*) to bare one's teeth; **mostrare la lingua** to stick out one's tongue; **mi ma mostrato la lingua** he stuck his tongue out at me; **mostrare i pugni a qn** to shake one's fist at sb; **ha mostrato di non conoscermi** he pretended not to know me
▶ **mostrarsi** VR **1** (*dimostrarsi*) to appear; **si è mostrato felice** he appeared *o* looked happy **2** (*comparire*) to appear, show o.s.; **mostrarsi in pubblico** to appear in public

mostrina [mos'trina] SF (*Mil*) flash

mostro ['mostro] SM (*anche fig*) monster; **sei un mostro di bravura!** you're a genius!; **i mostri sacri del cinema italiano** the giants of the Italian cinema

mostruosamente [mostruosa'mente] AVV monstrously

mostruosità [mostruosi'ta] SF monstrosity

mostruoso, a [mostru'oso] AGG (*anche fig*) monstrous; **un delitto mostruoso** a terrible crime; **ha una cultura mostruosa** she knows an awful lot

mota ['mɔta] SF (*letter*) mire

motel [mo'tɛl] SM INV motel

motilità [motili'ta] SF motility

motivare [moti'vare] VT **1** (*giustificare*) to give reasons for **2** (*causare*) to cause **3** (*stimolare*) to motivate

motivato, a [moti'vato] AGG (*azione*) justified, reasoned; (*persona*) motivated

motivazione [motivat'tsjone] SF (*ragione*) justification; (*stimolo*) motivation

motivo [mo'tivo] SM **1** (*causa, ragione*) reason, grounds *pl*, cause; **senza motivo** for no reason; **qual è il motivo del tuo ritardo?** what is the reason for your lateness?; **avere un motivo valido per fare qc** to have a valid reason for doing sth; **ho un motivo valido per andarmene** I've got a good reason for leaving; **per motivi di salute** for health reasons, on health grounds; **motivi personali** personal reasons; **si è dimesso per motivi personali** he resigned for personal reasons; **per quale motivo?** why?, for what reason?; **per questo motivo** for this reason, therefore; **mia madre sta male, motivo per cui non potrò venire** my mother is ill so I won't be able to come **2** (*Mus*) motif; (*di opera letteraria*) (central) theme; (*disegno*) design, pattern

moto[1] ['mɔto] SM **1** (*di mare, macchina, pianeti*) movement; (*Fis, Tecn*) motion; **quantità di moto** (*Fis*) momentum; **moto armonico semplice** (*Fis*) simple harmonic motion; **verbi di moto** verbs of motion; **mettere in moto qc** (*anche fig*) to set sth in motion; (*motore, macchina*) to start sth (up); **mettersi in moto** (*macchina*) to start; (*persona*) to set off **2** (*esercizio fisico*) exercise; **fare del moto** to take some exercise; **devi fare un po' di moto** you should take some exercise **3** (*gesto*) movement; **un moto d'impazienza** an impatient gesture **4** (*rivolta*) rising, revolt

moto[2] ['mɔto] SF INV (*fam*) (motor)bike; **vado a scuola in moto** I go to school on my motorbike; **moto d'acqua** Jet Ski®

motobarca, che [moto'barka] SF motorboat

motocarro [moto'karro] SM three-wheeler van

motocicletta [mototʃi'kletta] SF motorcycle

motociclismo [mototʃi'klizmo] SM motorcycling, motorcycle racing

motociclista, i, e [mototʃi'klista] SM/F motorcyclist

motociclistico, a, ci, che [mototʃi'klistiko] AGG motorcycle *attr*

motociclo [moto'tʃiklo] SM motorcycle, motorbike (*fam*)

motocross [moto'krɔs] SM motocross

motofurgone [motofur'gone] SM three-wheel van

motonautica [moto'nautika] SF speedboat racing

motonautico, a, ci, che [moto'nautiko] AGG motorboat *attr*, speedboat *attr*

motonave [moto'nave] SF motor vessel

motopeschereccio, ci [motopeske'rettʃo] SM trawler

motopompa [moto'pompa] SF (motor) pump

motore, trice [mo'tore] AGG **1** (*Anat: organo*) motor *attr* **2** (*Tecn*) driving; **albero motore** drive shaft; **forza motrice** driving force
■ SM **1** (*Tecn*) engine, motor; (*di macchina, treno, nave*) engine; **a motore** power-driven, motor *attr*; **una barca a motore** a motor boat; **spegni il motore** switch off the engine; **motore a 2/4 tempi** 2-/4-stroke engine; **motore diesel** diesel engine; **motore a iniezione** fuel-injection engine; **motore a reazione** jet engine; **motore a scoppio** internal combustion engine; **motore turbo** turbo(-charged) engine **2** (*Filosofia*) mover; **il primo motore** the Prime Mover **3 motore di ricerca** (*Inform*) search engine

motoretta [moto'retta] SF motor scooter

motorino [moto'rino] SM **1** (*Aut*): **motorino d'avviamento** starter(-motor) **2** (*fam: ciclomotore*) moped; **vado a scuola in motorino** I go to school on my moped

motorio, ria, ri, rie [mo'tɔrjo] AGG (*Anat*) motor *attr*

motoristica [moto'ristika] SF engine design (*of racing cars*)

motorizzare [motorid'dzare] VT (*polizia, soldati*) to motorize
▶ **motorizzarsi** VR (*fam*) to get a car (*o* motorbike)

motorizzato, a [motorid'dzato] AGG: **reparto motorizzato** (*Mil*) motorized division; **sei motorizzato?** have you got transport?

motorizzazione [motoriddzat'tsjone] SF (*ufficio*

tecnico e organizzativo): **(ufficio della) motorizzazione** road traffic office

motorscooter ['moutəsku:tə] SM INV motor scooter

motoscafo [motos'kafo] SM motorboat

motosega, ghe [moto'sega] SF electric saw

motoslitta [motoz'litta] SF motorized sledge

motovedetta [motove'detta] SF (motor) patrol vessel

motrice [mo'tritʃe] SF (*Tecn*) engine, motor

motteggiare [motted'dʒare] VT (*letter*) to jest, banter

motteggio, gi [mot'teddʒo] SM (*letter*) banter

mottetto [mot'tetto] SM (*Poesia*) witty poem

motto ['mɔtto] SM (*detto arguto*) witty remark; (*massima*) motto, maxim; **il mio motto è...** my motto is ...

mountain bike ['mauntin 'baik] SF INV mountain bike

mouse SM INV mouse *m inv*; **mouse incorporato** touchpad

mousse [mus] SF INV (*Culin*) mousse

movente [mo'vɛnte] SM (*Dir*) motive; **avevano un movente per ucciderlo** they had a motive for killing him

movenza [mo'vɛntsa] SF movement; **sciolto nelle movenze** graceful in one's movements

movimentare [movimen'tare] VT to liven up

movimentato, a [movimen'tato] AGG (*festa, partita*) lively; (*riunione*) animated; (*strada, vita*) busy; (*soggiorno*) eventful

movimento [movi'mento] SM (*gen, Pol, Letteratura*) movement; (*Mus: grado di velocità*) tempo; (*: parte*) movement; (*fig: animazione*) activity, hustle and bustle; **un movimento politico** a political movement; **un movimento brusco** a sudden movement; **un movimento di rotazione/rivoluzione** a rotation/ revolution; **essere sempre in movimento** to be always on the go; **è vietato salire sul treno in movimento** do not get on the train while it is in motion; **fare un movimento falso** to make an awkward movement; **fece un movimento all'indietro** he stepped back; **fare un po' di movimento** (*esercizio fisico*) to take some exercise; **c'è molto movimento in città** the town is very busy
■ **movimento di capitali** movement of capital; **movimento di conto** (*Banca*) (bank) account transaction; **movimento passeggeri e merci** passenger and freight traffic; **Movimento per la Liberazione della Donna** women's liberation movement; **movimento di truppe** troop movement

moviola [mo'vjɔla] SF moviola; **rivedere qc alla moviola** to see an action (*Brit*) *o* instant (*Am*) replay of sth

Mozambico [mottsam'biko] SM Mozambique

mozione [mot'tsjone] SF (*Pol*) motion; **mozione d'ordine** point of order

mozzafiato [mottsa'fjato] AGG INV breathtaking

mozzare [mot'tsare] VT (*testa*) to cut off; (*coda*) to dock; **mozzare il fiato** *o* **il respiro a qn** (*fig*) to take sb's breath away

mozzarella [mottsa'rɛlla] SF mozzarella

mozzatura [mottsa'tura] SF **1** (*azione: di coda*) docking **2** (*parte mozzata*) end

mozzicone [mottsi'kone] SM (*di sigaretta*) stub, end, butt; (*di candela*) end; (*di matita*) stub

mozzo¹, a ['mottso] AGG (*testa*) cut off; (*coda*) docked

mozzo² ['mottso] SM **1** (*Naut*) ship's boy **2**: **mozzo di stalla** stable boy

mozzo³ ['mɔttso] SM (*Tecn*) hub

mq ABBR (= **metro quadro**) sq.m.

MS SIGLA = *Massa Carrara*

ms., MS. ABBR (= **manoscritto**) ms

MSI ['ɛmme'esse'i, mis] SIGLA M (= **Movimento Sociale Italiano**) *former right-wing political party*

M.ti ABBR = *monti*

mucca, che ['mukka] SF cow; **(morbo della) mucca pazza** mad cow disease, BSE; **l'emergenza mucca pazza** the mad cow crisis

mucchio, chi ['mukkjo] SM (*gen*) heap, pile; **a mucchi** in piles; **un mucchio di** (*molto*) heaps *pl* of, lots *pl* of, piles *pl* of; **un mucchio di sassi** a heap of stones; **ho un mucchio di cose da fare** I've got loads of things to do; **ha detto un mucchio di sciocchezze** he talked a load of rubbish

mucillagine [mutʃil'ladʒine] SF (*Bot*) mucilage (*termine tecn*), *green slime produced by plants growing in water*

muco ['muko] SM (*Med*) mucus

mucosa [mu'kosa] SF (*Anat*) mucous membrane

muffa ['muffa] SF (*biancastra*) mildew; (*verdognola*) mould (*Brit*), mold (*Am*); **fare la muffa** to go mouldy (*Brit*) *o* moldy (*Am*); **non ho intenzione di restare a casa a fare la muffa** (*fig*) I'm not going to moulder (*Brit*) *o* molder (*Am*) away at home; **avere odore di muffa** to smell mouldy

muffola ['muffola] SF mitten

muflone [mu'flone] SM mouflon

mugghiare [mug'gjare] VI (*aus* **avere**) (*letter fig: mare, tuono*) to roar; (*: vento*) to howl

muggire [mud'dʒire] VI (*aus* **avere**) (*bovini*) to low; (*vacca*) to moo, low; (*toro*) to bellow; (*fig*) to roar

muggito [mud'dʒito] SM (*vedi vb*) lowing; mooing; bellow; roar; **i muggiti del bestiame** the lowing of the cattle

mughetto [mu'getto] SM **1** (*Bot*) lily of the valley **2** (*Med*) thrush

mugnaio, aia, ai, aie [muɲ'ɲajo] SM/F miller

mugolare [mugo'lare] VI (*aus* **avere**) (*cane*) to whimper, whine; **mugolare (di)** (*fig: persona*) to moan (in *o* with)
■ VT (*borbottare*) to mutter

mugolio, lii [mugo'lio] SM (*vedi vb*) whimpering, whining; moaning; muttering

mugugnare [muguɲ'ɲare] VI (*aus* **avere**) (*fam*) to mutter, mumble

mujaheddin [muʒaid'din] SM INV mujaheddin

mulattiera [mulat'tjɛra] SF mule track

mulattiere [mulat'tjɛre] SM mule-driver

mulatto, a [mu'latto] AGG, SM/F mulatto

muleta [mu'leta] SF INV muleta

muliebre [mu'liebre] AGG (*letter*) feminine, womanly

mulinare [muli'nare] VI (*aus* **avere**) to whirl, spin (round and round)

mulinello [muli'nɛllo] SM **1** (*di vento, acqua*) eddy **2** (*di canna da pesca*) reel **3** (*Naut*) windlass

mulino [mu'lino] SM mill; **lottare** *o* **combattere contro i mulini a vento** (*fig*) to tilt at windmills; **mulino ad acqua** water mill; **mulino a vento** windmill

mulo ['mulo] SM mule; **testardo** *o* **ostinato** *o* **cocciuto come un mulo** as stubborn as a mule

multa ['multa] SF fine; **fare** *o* **dare una multa a qn** to fine sb; **il controllore le ha dato la multa** the inspector fined her; **ho preso una multa di 100 euro** I was fined 100 euros, I got a 100 euro fine; **ho preso una multa per divieto di sosta** I got a parking ticket

multare [mul'tare] VT to fine

Mm

multicolore [multiko'lore] AGG multicoloured (*Brit*), multicolored (*Am*)
multidisciplinare [multidiʃʃipli'nare] AGG (*insegnamento, ricerca*) multidisciplinary
multietnicità [multietnitʃi'ta] SF multiethnicity
multietnico, a, ci, che [multi'ɛtniko] AGG multiethnic
multiforme [multi'forme] AGG (*interessi*) varied; (*ingegno*) versatile
multilaterale [multilate'rale] AGG multilateral
multilingue [multi'lingwe] AGG multilingual
multimediale [multime'djale] AGG multimedia *attr*
multimiliardario, ria, ri, rie [multimiljar'darjo] AGG, SM/F ≈ billionaire
multimilionario, ria, ri, rie [multimiljo'narjo] AGG, SM/F multimillionaire
multinazionale [multinattsjo'nale] AGG, SF multinational; **forza multinazionale di pace** multinational peace-keeping force
multiplex ['multipleks] SM INV multiplex
multiplo, a ['multiplo] AGG multiple
■ SM (*Mat*): **multiplo (di)** multiple (of); **minimo comune multiplo** lowest common multiple
multiproprietà [multiproprje'ta] SF INV time-sharing
multirazziale [multirat'tsjale] AGG multiracial
multisala [multi'sala] AGG INV (*cinema*) multi-screen *attr*
multiscafo [multis'kafo] SM INV (*Naut*) multihull
multisettoriale [multisetto'rjale] AGG cross-sector
multiuso [multi'uzo] AGG INV multipurpose
multiutenza [multiu'tɛntsa] SF (*Inform*) time sharing
multivitaminico, a, ci, che [multivita'miniko] AGG: **complesso multivitaminico** multivitamin
mummia ['mummja] SF mummy; (*fig: persona*) old fogey
mummificare [mummifi'kare] VT to mummify
▶ **mummificarsi** VIP to become mummified
mummificazione [mummifikat'tsjone] SF mummification
mungere ['mundʒere] VT IRREG (*anche fig*) to milk
mungitrice [mundʒi'tritʃe] SF (*macchina*) milking machine
mungitura [mundʒi'tura] SF milking
municipale [munitʃi'pale] AGG (*gen*) municipal; **palazzo municipale** town hall; **autorità municipali** local authority *sg* (*Brit*), local government *sg*
municipalità [munitʃipali'ta] SF INV town council
municipio, pi [muni'tʃipjo] SM (*comune*) town council; (*palazzo*) town hall; **sposarsi in municipio** ≈ to get married in a registry office (*Brit*)
munificamente [munifika'mente] AVV munificently, generously
munificenza [munifi'tʃɛntsa] SF munificence, generosity
munifico, a, ci, che [mu'nifiko] AGG munificent, generous
munire [mu'nire] VT: **munire di** (*fortificare: città*) to fortify with; (*equipaggiare: persona, stanza ecc*) to equip with; **munire una nave di uomini** to man a ship; **munire di firma** (*documento*) to sign
▶ **munirsi** VR: **munirsi di** (*gen: denaro, documenti*) to provide o.s. with; (*armi*) to arm o.s. with; **munirsi di coraggio/pazienza** to arm o.s. with courage/patience; **"si pregano i clienti di munirsi di scontrino"** (*in bar*) "customers must pay at the desk and obtain a receipt before being served"; **si è munito di ombrello ed è uscito** arming himself with an umbrella he sallied out
munizioni [munit'tsjoni] SFPL ammunition *sg*
munsi *ecc* ['munsi] VB *vedi* **mungere**
munto, a ['munto] PP *di* **mungere**
muoio *ecc* ['mwɔjo] VB *vedi* **morire**
muovere ['mwɔvere] VB IRREG
■ VT **1** (*gen*) to move; (*macchina, ruota*) to drive; **non riesco a muovere la gamba** I can't move my leg; **il cane muoveva festosamente la coda** the dog was joyfully wagging its tail; **muovere i primi passi** to take one's first steps; (*fig*) to be starting out; **mosse un passo verso di me** he took a step towards me; **non muove un passo senza interpellare la moglie** (*fig*) he never does anything without asking his wife; **non ha mosso un dito per aiutarmi** he didn't lift a finger to help me; **muovere mari e monti** to move heaven and earth **2** (*fig: sollevare*): **muovere un'accusa a** *o* **contro qn** to make an accusation against sb; **muovere causa a qn** (*Dir*) to take legal action against sb; **muovere guerra a** *o* **contro qn** to wage war against sb; **muovere un'obiezione** to raise an objection **3** (*commuovere*): **muovere a compassione** to move to pity; **muovere al pianto** to move to tears **4** (*Scacchi*) to move; **tocca a te muovere** it's your move
■ VI (*aus* **essere** *o* **avere**) **1** (*gen*) to move; **muovere verso** *or* **muovere in direzione di** to move towards **2** (*derivare*): **muovere da** to derive from; **le sue osservazioni muovono da una premessa errata** his comments are based on a mistaken *o* wrong assumption
▶ **muoversi** VR **1** to move; **non si muove** it won't move; **muoversi in aiuto di qn** to go to sb's aid; **non si muove dalle sue posizioni** (*fig*) he won't budge **2** (*sbrigarsi*) to hurry up, get a move on; **muoviti!** hurry up!; **muoviti, o perdiamo il treno!** hurry up, or we'll miss the train!; **muoviti, cammina!** hurry up and get moving!
▶ **muoversi** VIP **3** (*commuoversi*): **muoversi a compassione** *o* **pietà** to be moved to pity **2** (*essere in movimento*) to move; **finalmente qualcosa si è mosso** (*fig*) at last things are moving
mura ['mura] SFPL *di* **muro le mura della città** the city walls
muraglia [mu'raʎʎa] SF (high) wall; **la grande muraglia cinese** the Great Wall of China
muraglione [muraʎ'ʎone] SM massive wall
murale [mu'rale] AGG wall *attr*; (*Arte*) mural *attr*; **carta murale** wall map; **pittura murale** mural
■ SM (*Arte*) mural
murare [mu'rare] VT (*porta, finestra*) to wall up; (*mensola*) to embed into a wall; **murare qn vivo** to wall sb up
▶ **murarsi** VR: **murarsi in casa** (*fig: rinchiudersi*) to shut o.s. away at home
murario, ria, ri, rie [mu'rarjo] AGG (*tecnica*) building *attr*; **arte muraria** masonry; **opera muraria** piece of masonry work
muratore [mura'tore] SM (*che costruisce con pietre*) mason; (*che costruisce con mattoni*) bricklayer; **mio padre fa il muratore** my father is a bricklayer
muratura [mura'tura] SF **1** (*atto del murare*) walling (up) **2** (*lavoro murario: con pietra*) masonry; (*: con mattoni*) bricklaying; **casa in muratura** (*di pietra*) stonebuilt house; (*di mattoni*) brick house
murena [mu'rɛna] SF moray eel
muro ['muro] SM (*anche fig*) wall; **un muro alto** a

high wall; **armadio a muro** built-in cupboard; **il muro di Berlino** the Berlin Wall; **alzare un muro** to build a wall; **attaccare qc al muro** to hang sth on the wall; **chiudere qc con un muro** (*campo, giardino*) to build a wall around sth; **mettere al muro** (*fucilare*) to shoot *o* execute (by firing squad); **è come parlare al muro** it's like talking to a brick wall; **tra noi c'è un muro** (*fig*) there's a barrier between us; **un muro d'incomprensione** a total lack of understanding
■ **mura** SFPL (*di città, castello*) walls; **chiudersi fra quattro mura** (*fig*) to shut o.s. up at home
■ **muro di cinta** surrounding wall; **muro divisorio** dividing wall; **muro di gomma** (*fig: indifferenza*) the wall of indifference; **muro maestro** main wall; **muro di mattoni** brick wall; **muro a secco** dry-stone wall; **muro del suono** (*Fis*) sound barrier

musa ['muza] SF (*Mitol*) Muse; (*fig*) muse, inspiration

muschiato, a [mus'kjato] AGG **1** (*che odora di muschio*) musky **2** (*Zool*): **bue muschiato** musk ox; **topo muschiato** muskrat

muschio[1], chi ['muskjo] SM (*profumo*) musk

muschio[2], chi ['muskjo] SM (*Bot*) moss

muscolare [musko'lare] AGG (*Anat, tessuto, fascio*) muscular, muscle *attr*; **strappo muscolare** torn muscle

muscolatura [muskola'tura] SF musculature; **muscolatura atletica** athletic build

muscolo ['muskolo] SM **1** (*Anat*) muscle; **scaldare i muscoli** to warm up; **è tutto muscoli e niente cervello** (*fig*) he's all brawn and no brains; **muscolo involontario** involuntary muscle; **muscolo volontario** voluntary muscle **2** (*Culin*) lean meat **3** (*Zool*) mussel

muscoloso, a [musko'loso] AGG muscular

muscoso, a [mus'koso] AGG mossy

museo [mu'zɛo] SM museum; **un pezzo da museo** (*fig*) a museum piece

museruola [muze'rwɔla] SF (*per cani*) muzzle; **mettere la museruola a un cane** to muzzle a dog; **mettere la museruola a qn** (*fig*) to muzzle sb, shut sb up; **i cani devono avere la museruola** dogs have to be muzzled

musica ['muzika] SF (*gen, fig*) music; **musica di sottofondo** background music; **un pezzo** *o* **brano di musica** a piece of music; **mi piace la musica classica** I like classical music; **mettere in musica** to set to music; **è sempre la stessa musica** (*fig*) it's always the same old story; **è ora di cambiare musica** (*fig*) it's time you changed your tune; **musica classica** classical music; **musica da ballo** dance music; **musica da camera** chamber music; **musica disco (o) da discoteca** disco music; **musica leggera** light music; **musica pop** pop music; **musica popolare** folk music

musical ['mju:zikəl] SM INV musical

musicale [muzi'kale] AGG musical; **avere orecchio musicale** to have an ear for music

musicalmente [musikal'mente] AVV musically

musicare [muzi'kare] VT to set to music

musicassetta [muzikas'setta] SF (pre-recorded) cassette

musicista, i, e [muzi'tʃista] SM/F musician; **fa il musicista** he's a musician; **uno dei musicisti dell'orchestra** one of the players in the orchestra

musicomane [muzi'kɔmane] SM/F music lover

musivo, a [mu'zivo] AGG mosaic *attr*

musli ['my:sli] SM muesli

muso ['muzo] SM (*di animale*) muzzle; (*fig: di persona*) face; (*: pegg*) mug; (*: di aereo*) nose; (*: di auto, moto*) front (end); **rompere il muso a qn** to smash sb's face in; **gli diede un pugno sul muso** he punched him in the face; **mettere** *o* **fare il muso** to pull a long face; **tenere il muso** to sulk; **tenere il muso a qn** to be in a huff with sb; **ha storto il muso quando gliene ho parlato** he didn't look at all pleased when I mentioned it; **gliel'ho detto sul muso** I told him so to his face

musone, a [mu'zone] SM/F sulky person

mussola ['mussola] SF muslin

mussoliniano, a [mussoli'njano] AGG (*vita, politica*) of Mussolini; (*stile*) Mussolini-like

must [mast] SM INV must; **è un must della moda di quest'estate** this is a must for this summer's fashion

mustacchi [mus'takki] SMPL (*scherz*) mustachio *sg*

musulmano, a [musul'mano], **mussulmano, a** [mussul'mano] AGG, SM/F Muslim, Moslem

muta[1] ['muta] SF **1** (*di animali: gen*) moulting (*Brit*), molting (*Am*); (*: di serpenti*) shedding of skin; **andare in muta** to moult; shed (one's) skin **2** (*di subacqueo*) wet suit; **una muta subacquea** a wet suit

muta[2] ['muta] SF (*gruppo di cani*) pack

mutabile [mu'tabile] AGG changeable

mutabilità [mutabili'ta] SF changeability

mutamento [muta'mento] SM change

mutande [mu'tande] SFPL (*da uomo*) (under)pants; (*da donna*) pants, knickers; **venne ad aprire la porta in mutande** he came to open the door in his underpants

mutandine [mutan'dine] SFPL (*da bambino*) pants; (*da donna*) panties, knickers; **mutandine di plastica** plastic pants

mutandoni [mutan'doni] SMPL long johns (*fam*)

mutante [mu'tante] SM/F (*Bio, in fantascienza*) mutant

mutare [mu'tare] VT **1** (*gen*) to change; (*opinione, carattere*) to change, alter; **mutare qc in** to change sth into **2** (*Zool: sogg: rettili*) to slough; (*: animali*): **mutare il pelo** to moult
■ VI (*aus* **essere**) to change; **mutare di colore** to change colour; **qualcosa è mutato in lui** there's something different about him; **mutare in meglio/in peggio** to change for the better/for the worse;
▸ **mutarsi** VIP: **mutarsi in** to change into, turn into; **il ghiaccio si mutò in acqua** the ice turned to water; **mutarsi d'abito** to change one's clothes

mutazione [mutat'tsjone] SF change, alteration; (*Bio*) mutation

mutevole [mu'tevole] AGG changeable; **umore mutevole** moodiness

mutevolmente [mutevol'mente] AVV (*comportarsi*) unpredictably

mutilare [muti'lare] VT (*gen, fig*) to mutilate; (*persona*) to maim; (*statua*) to deface; **la fresatrice gli ha mutilato la mano** the milling machine chopped off his hand

mutilato, a [muti'lato] AGG (*vedi vb*) mutilated; maimed; defaced
■ SM/F cripple, disabled person (*through loss of limbs*); **mutilato di guerra** disabled ex-serviceman (*Brit*) *o* war veteran (*Am*); **mutilato del lavoro** person disabled at work

mutilazione [mutilat'tsjone] SF (*vedi vb*) mutilation; maiming; defacement

mutismo [mu'tizmo] SM **1** (*Med*) muteness, mutism **2** (*atteggiamento*) (stubborn) silence; **chiudersi in un mutismo ostinato** to maintain a stubborn silence

muto, a ['muto] AGG (*Med*) dumb, speech-impaired; (*Ling*) silent, mute; (*Geog: cartina, atlante*) blank; **in**

classe mia c'è un ragazzo muto there's a speech-impaired boy in my class; **la h è muta** the h is silent; **il cinema muto** the silent cinema; **muto per lo stupore** *ecc* speechless with amazement *ecc*; **ha fatto scena muta** he didn't utter a word; **giuro che sarò muto come un pesce** I swear I won't say a word; **un muto rimprovero** a silent reproach
■ SM/F (*Med*) dumb person, mute

mutua ['mutua] SF: **medico della mutua** ≈ National Health Service doctor (*Brit*); **cassa mutua** health insurance scheme

mutuabile [mutu'abile] AGG (*farmaco*) *prescribable on the NHS*

mutuare [mutu'are] VT (*fig*) to borrow

mutuato, a [mutu'ato] SM/F ≈ NHS patient

mutuo¹, a ['mutuo] AGG (*reciproco*) mutual; **società di mutuo soccorso** friendly society (*Brit*), benefit society (*Am*)

mutuo² ['mutuo] SM (long-term) loan; **mutuo ipotecario** mortgage; **fare un mutuo** to take out a mortgage; **ho dovuto fare un mutuo per comprare la casa** I had to take out a mortgage to buy the house

Nn

N, **n** [ˈɛnne] SF O M INV *(lettera)* N, n; **N come Napoli** ≈ N for Nellie *(Brit)*, ≈ N for Nan *(Am)*

N ABBR (= **Nord**) N

n. ABBR (= **numero**) no.

NA SIGLA = *Napoli*

nababbo [naˈbabbo] SM *(anche fig)* nabob

nabuk [naˈbuk] SM nubuck

nacchere [ˈnakkere] SFPL castanets

nadir [naˈdir] SM *(Astron)* nadir

nafta [ˈnafta] SF *(Chim)* naphtha; *(carburante)* diesel oil; **motore a nafta** diesel engine

naftalina [naftaˈlina] SF *(Chim)* naphthalene; *(tarmicida)* mothballs *pl*

naia [ˈnaja] SF *(Mil fam)* national service *(Brit)*, draft *(Am)*

naiade [ˈnajade] SF *(Bot, Mitol)* naiad

naïf [naˈif] AGG INV naï ve; **un pittore naïf** a primitive painter

nailon [ˈnailon] SM = **nylon**

Nairobi [naiˈrɔbi] SF Nairobi

nandrolone [nandroˈlɔne] SM nandrolone

nanismo [naˈnizmo] SM *(Med)* dwarfism

nanna [ˈnanna] SF *(fam)* bye-byes *(Brit)*, beddy-byes *(Am)*; **andare a nanna** to go bye-byes *o* beddy-byes; **andiamo a nanna** let's go bye-byes; **fare la nanna** to sleep; **fai la nanna, ora** go to sleep now

nano, a [ˈnano] SM/F dwarf
■ AGG dwarf *attr*

nanometro [nanoˈmɛtro] SM nanometre

nanosecondo [nanoseˈkondo] SM nanosecond

nanotecnologia, gie [nanoteknoloˈdʒia] SF nanotechnology

napalm® [ˈnapalm] SM napalm

Napoleone [napoleˈone] SM Napoleon

napoleonico, a, ci, che [napoleˈɔniko] AGG Napoleonic

napoletana [napoleˈtana] SF *(macchinetta da caffè)* Neapolitan coffeepot

napoletano, a [napoleˈtano] AGG, SM/F Neapolitan; **un ragazzo napoletano** a boy from Naples

Napoli [ˈnapoli] SF Naples; **domani vado a Napoli** I'm going to Naples tomorrow; **abitiamo a Napoli** we live in Naples
▷ www.comune.napoli.it/

nappa [ˈnappa] SF **1** *(ornamento per tende)* tassel **2** *(pelle)* nappa, soft leather

narcisismo [nartʃiˈzizmo] SM narcissism

narcisista, i, e [nartʃiˈzista] SM/F narcissist; **essere narcisista** to have a Narcissus complex

Narciso [narˈtʃizo] SM *(Mitol)* Narcissus

narciso [narˈtʃizo] SM *(Bot)* narcissus

narcodollari [narcoˈdɔllari] SMPL drug money *sg*

narcos [ˈnarkos] SM INV *(colombiano)* Colombian drug trafficker

narcosi [narˈkɔzi] SF INV *(Med)* general anaesthesia *(Brit)* *o* anesthesia *(Am)*, narcosis; **essere sotto narcosi** to be under general anaesthetic *(Brit)* *o* anesthetic *(Am)*

narcotico, a, ci, che [narˈkɔtiko] AGG, SM narcotic

narcotizzare [narkotidˈdzare] VT to narcotize

narcotrafficante [narkotraffiˈkante] SM/F drug trafficker

narcotraffico [narkoˈtraffiko] SM drug trade

narghilè [nargiˈlɛ] SM INV hookah, narghile

narice [naˈritʃe] SF nostril

narrare [narˈrare] VT to tell, narrate, recount; **narrare una storia** to tell a story
■ VI *(aus avere)* **narrare di** to tell the story of

narrativa [narraˈtiva] SF *(branca letteraria)* fiction; **è uno dei capolavori della narrativa europea** it's one of the greatest works of European fiction

narrativo, a [narraˈtivo] AGG narrative

narratore, trice [narraˈtore] SM/F narrator

narrazione [narratˈtsjone] SF **1** *(di fatto, avvenimento)* narration, account **2** *(storia, racconto)* story, tale

narvalo [narˈvalo] SM *(pesce)* narwhal

NAS [nas] SIGLA M INV (= **Nucleo Antisofisticazioni Sanità**) *department of the carabinieri responsible for controls of foodstuff, drinks, medicine etc*

NASA [ˈnaza] SIGLA F (= **National Aeronautics and Space Administration**) NASA

nasale [naˈsale] AGG *(Anat, Fonetica)* nasal
■ SF nasal consonant

nascente [naʃʃente] AGG (*sole, luna*) rising

nascere ['naʃʃere] VI IRREG (*aus* **essere**) **1** (*bambino, animale*) to be born; (*pianta*) to come *o* spring up; **è nato nel 1977** he was born in 1977; **sono nata il 28 aprile** I was born on the 28th of April; **l'uomo nasce libero** man is born free; **nascono più femmine che maschi** there are more girls being born than boys; **è appena nato** he's a newborn baby; **nascere da genitori ricchi/poveri** to be born of rich/poor parents; **essere nato per qc/per fare qc** (*fig*) to be destined for sth/to do sth; **non sono nato ieri** I wasn't born yesterday **2** (*fiume*) to rise, have its source; (*sole*) to rise; (*giorno*) to break; (*dente*) to come through; (*idea, speranza*) to be born; (*difficoltà, dubbio*) to arise; (*industria, movimento*) to start up; **il sole nasce ad oriente** the sun rises in the east; **far nascere** (*industria*) to create; (*sospetto, desiderio*) to arouse; **nascere da** (*fig: derivare, conseguire*) to arise from, be born out of; **l'odio che nasce da tali conflitti** the hatred which springs from such conflicts; **nasce spontanea la domanda...** the question which springs to mind is ...; **da cosa nasce cosa** one thing leads to another; **la rivolta è stata stroncata sul nascere** the revolt was nipped in the bud

nascita ['naʃʃita] SF birth; **di nascita** by birth; **dopo la nascita della bambina** after the baby's birth; **nobile di nascita** of noble birth; **dalla nascita** from birth; **è cieco dalla nascita** he has been blind from birth, he was born blind

nascituro, a [naʃʃi'turo] SM/F future child; **come si chiamerà il nascituro?** what's the baby going to be called?

nascondere [nas'kondere] VB IRREG
■ VT (*gen*) to hide, conceal; **dove hai nascosto la lettera?** where have you hidden the letter?; **nascondere il viso tra le mani** to bury one's face in one's hands; **nascondere qc alla vista di qn** to hide sth from sb; **nascondere la verità a qn** to hide *o* keep the truth from sb; **non nascondo che mi farebbe molto piacere** I make no secret of the fact that I would like it;
▶ **nascondersi** VR to hide; **nascondersi alla vista di qn** to hide from sb, keep out of sb's sight; **dove si è nascosto?** where is he hiding?, where has he got to?; **si è nascosto dietro al divano** he hid behind the sofa; **dovresti nasconderti** you had better hide; (*fig*) you should be ashamed of yourself

nascondiglio, gli [naskon'diʎʎo] SM hiding place

nascondino [naskon'dino] SM: **giocare a nascondino** to play hide-and-seek *o* hide-and-go-seek (*Am*)

nascosi *ecc* [nas'kosi] VB *vedi* **nascondere**

nascostamente [naskosta'mente] AVV furtively, secretly

nascosto, a [nas'kosto] PP *di* **nascondere**
■ AGG hidden; **un pericolo nascosto** a hidden danger; **tenere nascosto qc** to keep sth hidden; **gli hanno tenuto nascosta la notizia** they concealed *o* kept the news from him; **di nascosto** secretly; **fare qc di nascosto** to do sth secretly; **andarsene di nascosto** to slip away

nasello [na'sɛllo] SM (*pesce*) hake

naso ['naso] SM nose; **si è soffiato il naso** he blew his nose; **parlare col naso** to talk through one's nose; **torcere** *o* **arricciare il naso (di fronte a qc)** to turn up one's nose (at sth); **avere naso per gli affari** to have a flair for business; **ha naso per gli affari** he has a flair for business; **mettere il naso negli affari altrui** to poke one's nose into other people's business; **son 2 settimane che non metto il naso fuori di casa** it's 2 weeks since I last stuck my nose out of the door; **guarda, ce l'hai sotto il naso** look, it's right under your nose

nassa ['nassa] SF (*per pesci*) fish trap; (*per aragoste*) lobster pot

Nassau [nas'sau] SF Nassau

nastrino [nas'trino] SM ribbon

nastro ['nastro] SM (*gen, di macchina da scrivere*) ribbon; (*Tecn, Sport*) tape; **un nastro di seta** a silk ribbon; **ha fatto tornare indietro il nastro** he rewound the tape; **a nastro** (*fam*) without a break, non-stop; **nastro adesivo** adhesive tape; **nastro isolante** insulating tape; **nastro magnetico** magnetic tape; **nastro trasportatore** conveyor belt

nastroteca, che [nastro'tɛka] SF tape library

nasturzio, zi [nas'turtsjo] SM cress; **nasturzio indiano** nasturtium

Natale [na'tale] SM Christmas; **cosa fai a Natale?** what are you doing at Christmas? *o* at Christmastime?; **Buon Natale!** Merry Christmas!; **albero di Natale** Christmas tree; **Babbo Natale** Santa Claus, Father Christmas (*Brit*)
▷ www.christmas.it/

natale [na'tale] AGG (*paese, città*) native, of one's birth; **la sua città natale** his native city
■ **natali** SMPL: **di illustri/umili natali** of noble/humble birth

natalità [natali'ta] SF birth rate

natalizio, zia, zi, zie [nata'littsjo] AGG (*del Natale*) Christmas *attr*; **gli addobbi natalizi** Christmas decorations

natante [na'tante] SM craft *inv*, boat

natatorio, ria, ri, rie [nata'tɔrjo] AGG (*Zool*): **vescica natatoria** swim bladder

natica, che ['natika] SF (*Anat*) buttock

natio, tia, tii, tie [na'tio] AGG native

Natività [nativi'ta] SF INV (*Rel*) Nativity

nativo, a [na'tivo] AGG, SM/F (*gen*) native

NATO ['nato] SIGLA F NATO (= *North Atlantic Treaty Organization*)

nato, a ['nato] PP *di* **nascere**
■ AGG **1** (*artista ecc*) born; **un attore nato** a born actor **2** (*di donna, prima di sposarsi*): **la sig.ra Rossi, nata Bianchi** Mrs Rossi, née Bianchi
■ SM: **un nuovo nato** a newborn child; **i nati del** *o* **nel 1960** those born in 1960

natura [na'tura] SF **1** (*mondo naturale*): **la natura** nature; **gli amanti della natura** nature lovers; **il mondo della natura** the world of nature; **vivere a contatto con la natura** to live close to nature; **questa sostanza non esiste in natura** this substance does not exist naturally; **contro natura** unnatural **2** (*carattere*) nature; **la natura umana** human nature; **è nella natura delle cose** it's in the nature of things; **è allegro di natura** he's naturally cheerful; **non è nella sua natura fare così** he's not the sort of person who would do that; **i nostri rapporti sono di natura professionale** our relationship is of a professional nature **3** (*tipo*) nature, kind; **scritti di varia natura** writings of various kinds; **pagare in natura** to pay in kind **4** (*Pittura*): **natura morta** still life

naturale [natu'rale] AGG (*gen*) natural; **è naturale che sia così** it's natural that it should be so; **gli viene naturale comportarsi così** it comes naturally to him to behave like that; **(ma) è naturale!** (*in risposte*) of course!; **posso venire anch'io? – naturale!** can I come

with you? – of course!; **a grandezza naturale** life-size; **figlio naturale** natural child; **risorse naturali** natural resources; **acqua minerale naturale** still mineral water; **i suoi capelli sono biondi naturali** her hair is naturally blonde
■ SM: **al naturale** (*alimenti*) served plain; (*ritratto*) life-size; **tonno al naturale** tuna in brine; **pesche/fragole al naturale** peaches/strawberries in fruit juice; **è più bella al naturale** (*senza trucco*) she's prettier without make-up

naturalezza [natura'lettsa] SF naturalness; **con naturalezza** naturally

naturalista, i, e [natura'lista] SM/F naturalist

naturalistico, a, ci, che [natura'listiko] AGG naturalistic

naturalizzare [naturalid'dzare] VT to naturalize
▶ **naturalizzarsi** VIP to become naturalized; **si è naturalizzato italiano** he's become a naturalized Italian

naturalizzazione [naturaliddzat'tsjone] SF naturalization

naturalmente [natural'mente] AVV naturally; **vieni? — naturalmente** are you coming? — of course *o* naturally

naturismo [natu'rizmo] SM naturism, nudism

naturista, i, e [natu'rista] AGG, SM/F naturist, nudist

naturopata, i; , e [natu'rɔpata] SM/F naturopath

naturopatia [naturopa'tia] SF naturopathy

naufragare [naufra'gare] VI (*aus* **essere** *o* **avere**) (*nave*) to be wrecked; (*persona*) to be shipwrecked; (*fig: progetto, disegno*) to fall through; **la nave è naufragata a causa della tempesta** the ship was wrecked in the storm; **naufragarono poco lontano dall'isola** they were shipwrecked not far from the island; **tutte le nostre speranze naufragarono** all our hopes were dashed

naufragio, gi [nau'fradʒo] SM shipwreck; (*fig*) ruin, failure; **fare naufragio** to be shipwrecked; (*fig*) to fail, fall through

naufrago, a, ghi, ghe ['naufrago] SM/F shipwrecked person, shipwreck victim; (*su un'isola*) castaway

nausea ['nauzea] SF (*Med*) nausea; **avere la nausea** to feel sick (*Brit*) *o* sick to one's stomach (*Am*); **avevo un po' di nausea** I felt a bit sick; **mi dai la nausea!** (*fig*) you make me sick!; **fino alla nausea** ad nauseam; **ho bevuto fino alla nausea** I drank till I felt sick (to my stomach)

nauseabondo, a [nauzea'bondo], **nauseante** [nauze'ante] AGG nauseating, sickening

nauseare [nauze'are] VT to nauseate, make (feel) sick (*Brit*) *o* sick to one's stomach (*Am*); **ho mangiato tanti funghi che ora ne sono nauseato** I've eaten so many mushrooms that now I'm sick of them; **il suo comportamento mi ha nauseato** his behaviour sickened me

nautica ['nautika] SF navigation, nautical science; **nautica da diporto** yachting

nautico, a, ci, che ['nautiko] AGG (*gen*) nautical; **carta nautica** chart; **salone nautico** (*mostra*) boat show; **sci nautico** water-skiing

navale [na'vale] AGG (*gen*) naval; **battaglia navale** naval battle; (*gioco*) battleships *sg*; **cantiere navale** shipyard

navata [na'vata] SF: **navata centrale** nave; **navata laterale** aisle

nave ['nave] SF ship, vessel; **nave ammiraglia** flagship; **nave da carico** cargo ship, freighter; **nave cisterna** tanker; **nave da crociera** cruise liner; **nave da guerra** warship; **nave di linea** liner; **nave mercantile** merchant ship; **nave passeggeri** passenger ship; **nave portaerei** aircraft carrier; **nave scuola** training ship; **nave spaziale** spaceship; **nave da trasporto** cargo ship; **nave a vapore** steamship; **nave a vela** sailing ship

> **LO SAPEVI...?**
> **nave** non si traduce mai con la parola inglese *nave*

navetta [na'vetta] SF **1** (*di telaio*) shuttle **2** (*servizio di collegamento*) shuttle (service)

navicella [navi'tʃɛlla] SF **1** (*di pallone, dirigibile*) gondola; **navicella spaziale** spaceship **2** (*per l'incenso*) incense boat

navigabile [navi'gabile] AGG (*canale, fiume*) navigable

navigante [navi'gante] SM sailor, seaman

navigare [navi'gare] VI (*aus* **avere**) to sail; **suo marito naviga** her husband is a sailor; **navigarono per tre mesi prima di raggiungere la costa** they sailed for three months before they reached land; **navigare in cattive acque** (*fig: finanziariamente*) to be hard up; **navigare in Internet** to surf the Net

navigato, a [navi'gato] AGG (*fig: esperto*) experienced

navigatore, trice [naviga'tore] SM/F (*gen*) navigator; (*Inform*) surfer; **navigatore satellitare** satellite navigator; **navigatore solitario** single-handed sailor

navigazione [navigat'tsjone] SF (*Naut, Aer*) navigation; (*Inform*) surfing; **la storia della navigazione** the history of navigation; **navigazione aerea/interna/fluviale** air/inland/river navigation; **compagnia di navigazione** shipping company; **durante la navigazione** during the (sea *o* river) voyage; **dopo una settimana di navigazione** after a week at sea

naviglio, gli [na'viʎʎo] SM **1** (*letter*) (: *imbarcazione*) ship; (*flotta*) fleet, ships *pl*; **naviglio da pesca** fishing fleet **2** (*canale artificiale*) canal; (*canale navigabile*) (navigable) canal

Nazareno [naddza'rɛno] SM: **Gesù Nazareno** Jesus of Nazareth; **il Nazareno** the Nazarene

Nazaret, Nazareth ['nadzaret] SF Nazareth

nazionale [nattsjo'nale] AGG (*gen*) national; (*arrivi, passeggeri, economia*) domestic; **l'inno nazionale** the national anthem; **un parco nazionale** a national park
■ SF (*Sport*) national team; **la nazionale azzurra** the Italian team

nazionalismo [nattsjona'lizmo] SM nationalism

nazionalista, i, e [nattsjona'lista] AGG, SM/F nationalist

nazionalistico, a, ci, che [nattsjona'listiko] AGG nationalist

nazionalità [nattsjonali'ta] SF INV nationality; **nazionalità: italiana** nationality: Italian; **è di nazionalità britannica** she's British

nazionalizzare [nattsjonalid'dzare] VT to nationalize

nazionalizzato, a [nattsjonalid'dzato] AGG nationalized; **industria nazionalizzata** nationalized industry

nazionalizzazione [nattsjonaliddzat'tsjone] SF nationalization

nazionalsocialismo [nattsjonalsotʃa'lizmo] SM National Socialism, Nazism

nazione [nat'tsjone] SF nation

naziskin ['na:tsi skin] SM/F INV skinhead (*belonging to extreme right-wing group*)

nazismo [nat'tsizmo] SM Nazism

Nn

nazista, i, e [nat'tsista] AGG, SM/F Nazi (*inv*)
nazistico, a, ci, che [nat'tsistiko] AGG Nazi *attr*
NB, **n.b.** ABBR (= **nota bene**) N.B.
N.d.A. ABBR (= **nota dell'autore**) author's note
N.d.D. ABBR (= **nota della direzione**) editor's note
N.d.E. ABBR (= **nota dell'editore**) publisher's note
N.d.R. ABBR (= **nota della redazione**) editor's note
'ndrangheta ['ndrangeta] SF *Mafia-like criminal organization in Calabria*
N.d.T. ABBR (= **nota del traduttore**) translator's note
NE ABBR (= **Nord-Est**) NE
ne [ne] PRON **1** (*di lui, lei, loro*) of him (*o* her *o* them); about him (*o* her *o* them); **ne riconosco la voce** I recognize his (*o* her) voice; **non lo vedo da anni, parlamene** I haven't seen him for years, tell me about him **2** (*con valore partitivo*) of it; of them (*spesso omesso*); **ne voglio ancora** I want some more (of it *o* them); **ne voglio ancora un po'** I want a bit more; **dammene un po'** give me some; **dammene uno, per favore** give me one, please; **hai dei libri? — sì, ne ho** have you got any books? — yes I have; **hai del pane? — no, non ne ho** have you got any bread? — no I haven't any; **quanti anni hai? — ne ho 17** how old are you? — I'm 17 **3** (*riguardo*) about it; about them; **non me ne importa niente** I couldn't care less about it; **cosa ne pensi?** what do you think (about it)?; **cosa ne faremo?** what will we do with it (o them)?; **non parliamone più!** let's not talk about it any more! **4** (*da ciò*): **ne deduco che l'avete trovato** I gather you've found it; **ne consegue che...** it follows therefore that ...
■ AVV (*moto da luogo*: *da lì*) from there: *da qui, from here;* **ne vengo ora** I've just come from there; **è meglio che tu te ne vada** you'd better leave; **me ne vado immediatamente** I'm leaving (here) right away; **siamo arrivati al teatro alle 7 e ne siamo venuti via alle 10** we got to the theatre at 7 and left at 10
né [ne] CONG: **né...né...** neither ... nor ...; **non verranno né Chiara né Donatella** neither Chiara nor Donatella are coming; **né mio padre né mia madre parlano l'italiano** neither my father nor my mother speaks Italian; **non parla né l'italiano né il tedesco** he speaks neither Italian nor German, he doesn't speak either Italian or German; **non voglio discutere né con lui né con mio fratello** I don't want to speak to him or to my brother; **non l'ho più vista né sentita** I didn't see or hear from her again; **non voglio né posso accettare** I neither wish to nor can accept; **non piove né nevica** it isn't raining or snowing; **né da una parte né dall'altra** on neither side; **né più né meno** no more no less; **né l'uno né l'altro** neither of them, neither the one nor the other; **né l'uno né l'altro lo vuole** neither of them wants it; **né l'uno né l'altro gioca a tennis** neither of them plays tennis; **non conosco né l'uno né l'altro** I don't know either of them; **non mi fa né caldo né freddo** it makes no odds to me
neanche [ne'anke] AVV not even; **non mi ha neanche pagato** he didn't even pay me; **non ci vado — neanch'io** I'm not going — neither *o* nor am I; **non l'ho visto — neanch'io** I didn't see him — neither did I *o* I didn't either; **non ne ero sicuro. – neanche lei** i wasn't sure. – neither was she; **neanche lui lo farebbe** not even he would do it, even he wouldn't do it; **neanche un bambino ci crederebbe** not even a child would believe it; **non ho neanche un soldo** I haven't got a single penny; **non ci penso neanche!** I wouldn't dream of it!; **neanche per idea** *o* **per sogno!** certainly not!, not on your life!; **se ne è partito senza neanche salutare** he went off without even saying goodbye; **non parlo spagnolo — e lui? — neanche** I don't speak Spanish — what about him? — he doesn't either *o* neither does he; **lui non è inglese e neanche sua moglie** he isn't English and neither is his wife
■ CONG not even; **neanche a pagarlo lo farebbe** he wouldn't do it even if you paid him; **non... neanche** not even...; **non mi ha neanche pagato** she didn't even pay me; **neanche se** even if; **non potrebbe venire neanche se volesse** he couldn't come even if he wanted to; **non lo sposerei neanche se fosse un re** I wouldn't marry him even if he were a king; **neanche se volesse potrebbe venire** he couldn't come even if he wanted to
nebbia ['nebbja] SF (*densa*) fog; (*foschia*) mist; **odio la nebbia** I hate fog; **oggi c'è nebbia** it's foggy today
nebbiolina [nebbjo'lina] SF mist
nebbione [neb'bjone] SM thick fog
nebbiosità [nebbjosi'ta] SF fogginess
nebbioso, a [neb'bjoso] AGG (*vedi sf*) foggy; misty
Nebraska [ne'braska] SM Nebraska
nebulizzatore [nebuliddza'tore] SM atomizer
nebulosa [nebu'losa] SF nebula
nebulosità [nebulosi'ta] SF haziness
nebuloso, a [nebu'loso] AGG (*atmosfera, cielo*) hazy; (*fig*) hazy, vague
nécessaire [nesɛ'sɛr] SM INV: **nécessaire da cucito** sewing kit; **nécessaire da toilette** make-up bag *o* case; **nécessaire da viaggio** overnight case *o* bag
necessariamente [netʃessarja'mente] AVV necessarily
necessario, ria, ri, rie [netʃes'sarjo] AGG (*gen*) necessary; (*persona*) indispensable; **è necessario che tu vada** you will have to go, you must go; **è necessario far presto** we've got to hurry, it is necessary for you to go; **non è necessario che ti fermi** you don't need to stay; **non ho avuto il tempo necessario** I didn't have enough *o* sufficient time; **se necessario** if need be, if necessary; **rendersi necessario** (*persona*) to make o.s. indispensable; **si rende necessario partire** it has become necessary for me (*o* you *ecc*) to leave; **portami i documenti necessari** bring me the necessary documents
■ SM: **fare il necessario** to do what is necessary; **lo stretto necessario** the bare essentials *pl*; **ha messo in valigia lo stretto necessario** she packed the bare essentials; **hanno appena il necessario per vivere** they have barely enough to live on; **non ho con me il necessario** I haven't got what I need with me; **hai tutto il necessario per scrivere?** have you got all your writing materials?; **lavorare/preoccuparsi più del necessario** to work/worry more than is necessary *o* more than one has to
necessità [netʃessi'ta] SF INV (*bisogno*) necessity, need; (*povertà*) poverty; **per necessità** out of need *o* necessity; **l'ho fatto per necessità** I did it because I had to; **di necessità** (*necessariamente*) of necessity; **in caso di necessità** if need be, if necessary; **non è un lusso, è una necessità** it isn't a luxury, it's a necessity; **non vedo la necessità di andare tutti quanti** I don't see any necessity for us all to go; **trovarsi nella necessità di fare qc** to be forced *o* obliged to do sth, have to do sth; **fare di necessità virtù** to make a virtue of necessity
necessitare [netʃessi'tare] VI (*aus* **essere**) (*aiuto, intervento*) to be necessary, be needed, be required;

necessita il vostro aiuto your help is needed *o* necessary *o* required; **necessitare di** *(aver bisogno)* to need; **necessita di un'attenzione maggiore** it requires greater attention *o* care; **prima di essere pronto necessita di molte altre cose** a lot of other things are needed before it will be ready
■ VT to need, require
necrofilia [nekrofi'lia] SF necrophilia
necrofilo, a [ne'krɔfilo] SM/F necrophiliac
necrologio, gi [nekro'lɔdʒo] SM *(annuncio)* obituary notice; *(registro)* register of deaths
necropoli [ne'krɔpoli] SF INV necropolis
necroscopia [nekrosko'pia] SF necroscopy, necropsy
necrosi [ne'krɔzi] SF INV necrosis
nefando, a [ne'fando] AGG vile
nefasto, a [ne'fasto] AGG *(giorno)* fateful, fatal; *(segno, presagio)* inauspicious, ill-omened; *(fam: persona)* full of gloom and doom
nefrite [ne'frite] SF *(Med)* nephritis
nefritico, a, ci, che [ne'fritiko] AGG nephritic
■ SM/F person suffering from nephritis
negabile [ne'gabile] AGG deniable; **non è negabile** it's undeniable
negare [ne'gare] VT *(gen)* to deny; *(rifiutare)* to deny, refuse; **negare qc/di aver fatto qc** to deny sth/having done sth; **non puoi negarlo** you can't deny it; **ha negato di aver preso i soldi** he denied taking the money; **negare qc a qn** to refuse to give sb sth; **mi ha negato il suo appoggio** he refused to give me his support; **negare a qn il permesso (di fare qc)** to refuse sb permission (to do sth); **negare a qn la possibilità di fare qc** to deny sb the possibility of doing sth; **mi hanno negato un aumento** they turned down my request for a rise *(Brit) o* raise; **negare obbedienza a qn** to refuse to obey sb
negativa [nega'tiva] SF *(Gramm, Fot)* negative
negativamente [negativa'mente] AVV negatively; **rispondere negativamente** to give a negative response, reply in the negative
negatività [negativi'ta] SF *(di atteggiamento)* negativeness, negativity; *(Fis)* negativity
negativizzarsi [negativid'dzarsi] VIP *(Med)* to become HIV negative
negativo, a [nega'tivo] AGG negative; **il risultato del test è stato negativo** the result of the test was negative
■ SM *(Fot)* negative
negato, a [ne'gato] AGG *(persona)*: **essere negato per *o* in qc** to be hopeless at sth, be no good at sth; **sono negato per lo sport** I'm no good at sport
negazione [negat'tsjone] SF negation
negherò *ecc* [nege'rɔ] VB *vedi* **negare**
negletto, a [ne'glɛtto] AGG *(trascurato)* neglected
negli ['neʎʎi] PREP + ART *vedi* **in**
négligé [negli'ʒe] SM INV negligee
negligente [negli'dʒɛnte] AGG *(gen)* negligent; *(non diligente)* careless
negligenza [negli'dʒɛntsa] SF *(vedi agg)* negligence; carelessness
negoziabile [negot'tsjabile] AGG negotiable
negoziante [negot'tsjante] SM/F shopkeeper *(Brit)*, storekeeper *(Am)*
negoziare [negot'tsjare] VT to negotiate
■ VI *(aus* **avere)** **negoziare in** to trade *o* deal in
negoziato [negot'tsjato] SM negotiation; **negoziati per la pace** peace talks *o* negotiations
negoziatore, trice [negottsja'tore] SM/F negotiator
negoziazione [negottsjat'tsjone] SF negotiation
negozio, zi [ne'gɔttsjo] SM **1** *(bottega)* shop *(Brit)*, store *(Am)*; **andare per negozi** to go shopping; **negozio di scarpe** shoe shop *o* store **2** *(Dir)*: **negozio giuridico** legal transaction
negriere, a [ne'grjɛre], **negriero, a** [ne'grjɛro] SM *(Storia)* slaver, slave-trader
■ SM/F *(fig pegg)* slave-driver
negro, a ['negro] AGG *(razza, popolo)* black; **un ragazzo negro** a black boy
■ SM/F black person; **lavorare come un negro** *(fig)* to work like a slave
negroide [ne'grɔide] AGG, SM/F negroid
negromante [negro'mante] SM/F necromancer
negromanzia [negroman'tsia] SF necromancy
Negus ['nɛgus] SM INV Negus
nei ['nei] PREP + ART *vedi* **in**
nembo ['nembo] SM *(Meteor)* nimbus
Nemesi ['nɛmezi] SF *(Mitol, fig)* Nemesis
nemico, a, ci, che [ne'miko] SM/F enemy; **ha molti nemici** he's got a lot of enemies
■ AGG *(Mil)* enemy *attr*; *(ostile)* hostile; **farsi nemico qn** to make an enemy of sb; **essere nemico di qc** to be strongly averse *o* opposed to sth; **il gelo è nemico delle piante** frost is harmful to plants; **territorio nemico** enemy territory
nemmeno [nem'meno] AVV, CONG = **neanche**
nenia ['nɛnja] SF *(canto)* dirge; *(motivo monotono)* monotonous tune; *(fig: discorso)* tale of woe
neo ['nɛo] SM *(gen)* mole; *(sul viso)* beauty spot; *(fig: imperfezione)* (slight) flaw; (: *di persona)* slight defect
neo... ['nɛo] PREF neo...
neoclassico, a, ci, che [neo'klassiko] AGG *(stile, epoca, artista)* neoclassical
■ SM *(stile)* neoclassical; *(artista)* neoclassicist
neocolonialismo [neokolonja'lizmo] SM neocolonialism
neofascismo [neofaʃ'ʃizmo] SM neofascism
neofascista, i, e [neofaʃ'ʃista] AGG, SM/F neofascist
neofita, i, e [ne'ɔfita] SM/F *(Rel)* neophyte; *(fig)* novice
neoformazione [neoformat'tsjone] SF *(Med)* neoplasm
neolatino, a [neola'tino] AGG Romance *attr*
neolaureato, a [neolaure'ato] AGG recently graduated
■ SM/F recent graduate
neoliberismo [neolibe'rizmo] SM neo-liberalism
neoliberista, i; , e [neolibe'rista] SM/F, AGG neo-liberal
neologismo [neolo'dʒizmo] SM neologism
neon ['nɛon] SM INV *(Chim)* neon; *(lampadario)* neon lamp; **luce al neon** neon light
neonato, a [neo'nato] AGG newborn
■ SM/F newborn baby
neonazismo [neonat'tsizmo] SM neonazism
neonazista, i, e [neonat'tsista] AGG, SM/F neonazi
neoprene® [neo'prɛne] SM neoprene
neorealismo [neorea'lizmo] SM neorealism
▷ www.cinemaitaliano.net/Percorsi/neorealismo.htm
▷ www.italica.rai.it/cinema/neorealismo/
neozelandese [neoddzelan'dese] AGG New Zealand *attr*; **la squadra neozelandese** the New Zealand team
■ SM/F New Zealander
Nepal ['nepal] SM Nepal
nepotismo [nepo'tizmo] SM nepotism
neppure [nep'pure] AVV, CONG = **neanche**
nerastro, a [ne'rastro] AGG *(gen)* blackish; *(labbra)* purple
nerbata [ner'bata] SF *(colpo)* blow; *(sferzata)* whiplash

Nn

nerbo ['nɛrbo] SM whip, lash; (*fig: di esercito*) backbone
nerboruto, a [nerbo'ruto] AGG brawny, muscular; (*robusto*) robust
nereide [ne'reide] SF (*Mitol*) Nereid
neretto [ne'retto] SM **1** (*Tip*) bold (type) (*Brit*), bold face **2** (*articolo di giornale*) article in bold type *o* face
nero, a ['nero] AGG **1** (*colore*) black; (*scuro*) dark; (*pelle: abbronzata*) tanned; **ha i capelli neri** she's got black hair; **mettere qc nero su bianco** to put sth down in black and white; **nero come il carbone/la pece** as black as coal/pitch; **quel colletto è nero** (*sporco*) that collar is black *o* filthy **2** (*negro: razza*) black; **l'Africa nera** black Africa **3** (*fig: disperazione, futuro*) black; (*: giornata*) awful; **essere (di umore) nero** to be in a filthy mood; **oggi sono di umore nero** I'm in a very bad mood today; **sono in un periodo nero** I'm going through a bad time; **vedere tutto nero** to look on the black side (of things); **vivono nella miseria più nera** they live in utter *o* abject poverty **4** (*illegale*): **lavoro nero** work in the black economy; **mercato nero** black market; **fondi neri** slush fund *sg*
■ SM (*colore*) black; **vestirsi di** *o* **in nero** to dress in black; **è vestita di nero** she's dressed in black; **essere pagato in nero** to be paid in cash (*to evade payment of taxes*); **lavorare in nero** to moonlight (*Brit*) *o* double-dip (*Am*) (*without statutory deductions of payment of taxes*)
■ SM/F (*persona*) black, black man/woman
nerofumo [nero'fumo] SM lampblack
Nerone [ne'rone] SM Nero
nervatura [nerva'tura] SF (*Anat*) nerves *pl*, nervous system; (*Bot*) veining; (*Archit, Tecn*) rib
nervino, a [ner'vino] AGG (*Chim*): **gas nervino** nerve gas
nervo ['nɛrvo] SM **1** (*Anat*) nerve; (*Bot*) vein; **nervo ottico** optic nerve **2** **avere i nervi** to be very irritable; **avere i nervi a fior di pelle** to be on edge, be edgy; **avere i nervi saldi** to be calm; **ho i nervi scossi** my nerves are shattered; **far venire i nervi a qn** *or* **dare sui nervi a qn** to get on sb's nerves; **quando fa così mi dà proprio sui nervi** it really gets on my nerves when he does that; **avere i nervi saldi** to be calm; **che nervi!** damn (it)!
nervosamente [nervosa'mente] AVV nervously
nervosismo [nervo'sizmo] SM (*Psic*) nervousness; (*irritazione*) irritability; **farsi prendere dal nervosismo** to let one's nerves get the better of one
nervoso, a [ner'voso] AGG **1** (*tensione, sistema*) nervous; (*centro*) nerve *attr*; **esaurimento nervoso** nervous breakdown **2** (*agitato*) nervous, tense; (*irritabile*) irritable, touchy; **è sempre nervoso e si arrabbia spesso** he's always irritable and often loses his temper; **sono sempre un po' nervoso prima di un compito in classe** I'm always a bit nervous before a test at school **3** (*gambe, corpo*) sinewy
■ SM: **far venire il nervoso a qn** (*fam*) to get on sb's nerves; **farsi prendere dal nervoso** to let o.s. get irritated
nespola ['nɛspola] SF (*frutto*) medlar; (*fig*) blow, punch
nespolo ['nɛspolo] SM medlar (tree)
nesso ['nɛsso] SM connection, link
nessuno, a [nes'suno] AGG (*dav sm:* nessun + *consonante, vocale,* nessuno + *s impura, gn, pn, ps, x, z,; dav sf:* nessuna + *consonante,* nessun' + *vocale*)
1 (*non uno*) no, not any; (*espressione negativa*) + any; **nessun uomo è immortale** no man is immortal; **nessun altro** no-one else, nobody else; **nessun altro ti crederà** no one else will believe you; **nessun altro voleva andarci** no one else wanted to go; **non ho incontrato nessun altro** I didn't meet anyone else; **non ho nessun dubbio** I have no doubts; **non ha fatto nessun commento** he didn't make any comment; **non c'è nessun bisogno** there's no need, there isn't any need; **in nessun caso** under no circumstances; **in nessun luogo** nowhere; **da nessuna parte** not... anywhere; **non riesco a trovarlo da nessuna parte** I can't find it anywhere; **nessun'altra cosa** nothing else; **per nessuna cosa nel mondo** not for anything in the world
2 (*qualche*) any; **nessuna obiezione?** any objections?
■ PRON
1 (*non uno*) no-one, nobody, *espressione negativa* + anyone; (*: cosa*) none, *espressione negativa* + any; **nessuno di** (*riferito a persone, cose*) none of; **nessuno mi crede** no-one believes me; **nessuno si muova!** nobody move!; **non c'era nessuno** there was no-one there, there wasn't anyone there; **non è venuto nessuno** nobody came; **non dirlo a nessuno** don't tell that to anybody; **nessuno di loro/dei presenti** none of them/of those present; **non è venuto nessuno di loro** none of them came; **non è venuto nessuno dei due** neither of them came; **non mi fido di nessuno dei due** I don't trust either of them; **ha molti libri ma non me ne piace nessuno** he has lots of books but I don't like any of them; **non ne ho letto nessuno** I haven't read any of them, I have read none of them
2 (*qualcuno*) anyone, anybody; **ha telefonato nessuno?** did anyone phone?; **hai visto nessuno?** did you see anyone?
■ SM (*pegg: nullità*) nobody, nonentity; **e io chi sono, nessuno?** and who am I then, nobody?; **con tutte quelle arie resta comunque un nessuno** despite his airs and graces, he's still a nobody
nettamente [netta'mente] AVV (*chiaramente*) clearly; (*decisamente*) decidedly
nettapiedi [netta'pjɛdi] SM INV (*zerbino*) (door)mat
nettapipe [netta'pipe] SM INV pipe cleaner
nettare[1] [net'tare] VT to clean
nettare[2] ['nɛttare] SM nectar
nettezza [net'tettsa] SF **1** (*pulizia*) cleanness, cleanliness; **nettezza urbana** cleansing department (*Brit*), department of sanitation (*Am*) **2** (*chiarezza*) clarity
netto, a ['netto] AGG **1** (*pulito*) clean **2** (*chiaro: contorni, immagine*) clear, sharp, clear-cut; (*deciso: rifiuto, vittoria*) clear, definite; **la squadra ha riportato una netta vittoria** the team won a clear victory; **tagliare qc di netto** to cut sth clean off; **taglio netto** clean cut; **un taglio netto col passato** a clean break with the past **3** (*stipendio, peso*) net; **peso netto** net weight
■ SM: **al netto delle tasse** after tax, net of tax
■ AVV: **chiaro e netto** plainly
Nettuno [net'tuno] SM (*Mitol, Astron*) Neptune
netturbino [nettur'bino] SM dustman (*Brit*), dustbin man (*Brit*), garbage collector (*Am*) *o* man, trash man (*Am*)
neurite [neu'rite] SF = **nevrite**
neuro... ['neuro] PREF neuro...
neuro ['neuro] SIGLA F = **clinica neurologica**; *vedi* **neurologico**
neurochirurgia [neurokirur'dʒia] SF neurosurgery
neurochirurgo, ghi *o* **gi** [neuroki'rurgo] SM neurosurgeon
neurologia [neurolo'dʒia] SF neurology
neurologico, a, ci, che [neuro'lɔdʒiko] AGG

neurological; **clinica neurologica** neurological clinic
neurologo, a, gi, ghe [neu'rɔlogo] SM/F neurologist
neurone [neu'rone] SM neuron, nerve cell
neuropatia [neuropa'tia] SF neuropathy
neuropatico, a, ci, che [neuro'patiko] AGG neuropathic
■ SM/F neuropath
neuropsichiatra, i, e [neuropsi'kjatra] SM/F neuropsychiatrist
neuropsichiatria [neuropsikja'tria] SF neuropsychiatry
neurosi [neu'rɔzi] SF INV = **nevrosi**
neurovegetativo, a [neurovedʒeta'tivo] AGG (*Med*): **sistema neurovegetativo** autonomic nervous system
neutrale [neu'trale] AGG, SM neutral
neutralità [neutrali'ta] SF neutrality
neutralizzare [neutralid'dzare] VT (*gen, Chim*) to neutralize
neutralizzazione [neutraliddzat'tsjone] SF neutralization
neutrino [neu'trino] SM neutrino
neutro, a ['nɛutro] AGG (*gen*) neutral; (*Gramm, Zool*) neuter
■ SM (*Gramm*) neuter
neutrone [neu'trone] SM neutron
Nevada [ne'vada] SM Nevada
nevaio, ai [ne'vajo] SM snowfield
nevato [ne'vato] SM (*Geog*) nevé
neve ['neve] SF snow; **mi piace camminare sulla neve** I like walking in the snow; **è caduta tanta neve ieri** it snowed a lot yesterday; **c'era un tempo da neve** it was snowy; **montare a neve** (*Culin*) to whip up; **neve carbonica** dry ice
nevicare [nevi'kare] VB IMPERS to snow, be snowing; **nevica** it's snowing
nevicata [nevi'kata] SF snowfall
nevischio, chi [ne'viskjo] SM sleet
nevoso, a [ne'voso] AGG (*montagna*) snow-covered; (*tempo, inverno*) snowy; **manto nevoso** blanket of snow
nevralgia [nevral'dʒia] SF neuralgia; **ho una terribile nevralgia** I've got awful neuralgia
nevralgico, a, ci, che [ne'vraldʒiko] AGG: **punto nevralgico** (*Med*) nerve centre (*Brit*) *o* center (*Am*); (*fig*) crucial point; **è un punto nevralgico del traffico** it is one of the main areas of traffic congestion
nevrastenia [nevraste'nia] SF neurasthenia
nevrastenico, a, ci, che [nevras'tɛniko] AGG (*Med*) neurasthenic; (*fig*) hot-tempered
■ SM/F (*vedi agg*) neurasthenic; hot-tempered person
nevrite [ne'vrite] SF neuritis
nevrosi [ne'vrɔzi] SF INV neurosis
nevrotico, a, ci, che [ne'vrɔtiko] AGG, SM/F (*anche fig*) neurotic
new age [nju 'ɛidʒ] AGG INV (*musica*) new age
new economy [nju e'konomi] SF new economy
New England [nju 'ɪnglənd] SM New England
new global [nju 'global] AGG *relating to a more sensitive type of globalization that takes into account the particular social and cultural circumstances of each country*
New Hampshire [nju 'hæmpʃə] SM New Hampshire
New Jersey [nju 'dʒɛrsi] SM New Jersey
New Mexico [nju 'meksiko] SM New Mexico
newsletter [njuz'lɛtter] SF INV newsletter
newyorchese [njujor'kese] AGG of *o* from New York
■ SM/F New Yorker
New York [nju 'jɔrk] SF New York

Niagara [nja'gara] SM: **le cascate del Niagara** the Niagara Falls
nibbio, bi ['nibbjo] SM (*uccello*) kite
Nicaragua [nika'ragwa] SM Nicaragua
nicaraguense [nikara'gwɛnse], **nicaraguese** [nikara'gwese] AGG, SM/F Nicaraguan
nicchia ['nikkja] SF (*gen, fig*) niche; (*naturale*) cavity, hollow; **nicchia ecologica** niche; **nicchia di mercato** (*Comm*) niche market
nicchiare [nik'kjare] VI (*aus* **avere**) to shilly-shally, hesitate
nichel ['nikel] SM nickel
nichelare [nike'lare] VT to nickel-plate
nichelato, a [nike'lato] AGG nickel-plated
nichelatura [nikela'tura] SF nickel-plating
nichelio [ni'kɛljo] SM = **nichel**
nichilismo [niki'lizmo] SM nihilism
nichilista, i, e [niki'lista] AGG nihilistic
■ SM/F nihilist
Nicosia [niko'zia] SF Nicosia
nicotina [niko'tina] SF nicotine
nidiata [ni'djata] SF (*di uccelli, fig: di bambini*) brood; (*di altri animali*) litter
nidificare [nidifi'kare] VI (*aus* **avere**) to nest
nido ['nido] SM (*Zool*) nest; (*fig: casa*) nest, home; **a nido d'ape** (*tessuto, ricamo*) honeycomb *attr*
■ AGG INV: **asilo nido** crèche (*Brit*), day-care center (*Am*)
niente ['njɛnte] PRON (*nessuna cosa*) nothing; (*qualcosa*) anything; **non... niente** nothing, *espressione negativa* + anything; **niente lo fermerà** nothing will stop him; **non ho visto niente** I saw nothing, I didn't see anything; **non è successo niente** nothing happened; **cos'hai comprato? – niente** what did you buy? – nothing; **hai bisogno di** *o* **ti serve niente?** do you need anything?; **cosa c'è? – niente** what's the matter? – nothing; **niente di grave/nuovo** nothing serious/ new; **non gli va bene niente** he's never satisfied; **un uomo da niente** a nobody, a nonentity; **una cosa da niente** a trivial thing; **non fa niente!** it doesn't matter!; **fa niente se non vengo?** does it matter if I don't come?; **non mi sono fatto niente** I haven't hurt myself at all; **la cura non gli ha fatto niente** the treatment hasn't done anything for him; **non ho niente a che fare con lui** I have nothing to do with him; **ha niente in contrario se...?** would you object if ...?; **come se niente fosse** as if nothing had happened; **niente al mondo** nothing on earth *o* in the world; **niente di niente** absolutely nothing; **nessuno fa niente per niente** no one does anything for nothing; **ho parlato per niente** I spoke to no purpose, I wasted my breath; **sono venuto per niente** there was no point in my coming; **si arrabbia per niente** he gets annoyed at the slightest thing; **nient'altro** nothing else; **nient'altro?** (*in negozio*) is that all?, will that be all?; **nient'altro che** nothing but; (*solamente*) just, only; **so poco o niente di lui** I know next to nothing about him; **non so niente di niente** I know nothing at all; **grazie. – di niente** thanks. – you're welcome; **quel brodo non sa di niente** that soup is tasteless; **niente meno** = **nientemeno**
■ AGG: **non ho niente voglia di farlo** I'm not at all keen to do it; **niente paura!** don't worry!; **e niente scuse!** don't try to make excuses!; **niente male!** not bad at all!
■ SM nothing; **si è fatto dal niente** he's a self-made man; **il mondo è stato creato dal niente** the world was created out of nothing; **un bel niente** absolutely

Nn

nothing; **basta un niente per farlo piangere** the slightest thing is enough to make him cry; **si è ridotto al niente** he has lost everything; **si è ridotto a un niente** he's just skin and bone
■ AVV (*in nessuna misura*): **non...niente** not ... at all; **non è niente buono** it's not good at all; **non...per niente** (*affatto*) not ... at all; **non si è visto per niente** he hasn't been seen at all; **non mi sono divertito per niente** I didn't enjoy it at all; **non è per niente vero** it's not true at all; **niente affatto** not at all, not in the least; **le dispiace se fumo? – niente affatto** do you mind if I smoke? – not at all; **poco o niente** next to nothing

nientedimeno [njentedi'meno], **nientemeno** [njente'meno] AVV (*addirittura*) actually, even; **è diventata nientedimeno che amministratore delegato** she has become managing director, no less
■ ESCL really!, you don't say!

nietzschiano, a [nit'tʃano] AGG Nietzschean

Niger ['nidʒer] SM (*stato*) Niger; (*fiume*) the Niger

Nigeria [ni'dʒɛrja] SF Nigeria

nigeriano, a [nidʒe'rjano] AGG, SM/F Nigerian

night [nait], **night-club** ['naitklʌb] SM INV nightclub, club

Nilo ['nilo] SM: **il Nilo** the Nile

nimbo ['nimbo] SM halo

ninfa ['ninfa] SF nymph

ninfea [nin'fea] SF water lily

ninfetta [nin'fetta] SF nymphet

ninfomane [nin'fɔmane] SF nymphomaniac

ninfomania [ninfoma'nia] SF nymphomania

ninnananna [ninna'nanna] SF lullaby

ninnolo ['ninnolo] SM (*gingillo*) knick-knack; (*balocco*) plaything

nipote [ni'pote] SM/F (*di nonni*) grandchild, grandson/granddaughter; (*di zii*) nephew/niece; **nipotini** SMPL (*maschi e femmine*) grandchildren; **il nonno con i nipotini** grandad with his grandchildren; **un regalo della zia Lucia ai nipoti** (*maschi e femmine*) a present from aunt Lucia for her nephews and nieces

nipponico, a, ci, che [nip'pɔniko] AGG Japanese, Nipponese

nirvana [nir'vana] SM nirvana

nisseno, a [nis'seno] AGG of *o* from Caltanissetta
■ SM/F inhabitant *o* native of Caltanissetta

nitidamente [nitida'mente] AVV clearly

nitidezza [niti'dettsa] SF (*gen*) clearness; (*di stile*) clarity; (*Fot, TV: di immagine*) sharpness

nitido, a ['nitido] AGG (*gen*) clear; (*immagine*) sharp, well-defined; **un'immagine nitida** a sharp image

nitrato [ni'trato] SM nitrate

nitrico, a, ci, che ['nitriko] AGG nitric

nitrificazione [nitrifikat'tsjone] SF nitrification

nitrire [ni'trire] VI (*aus* **avere**) to neigh

nitrito[1] [ni'trito] SM (*di cavallo*) neigh; **nitriti** SMPL neighing *no pl*

nitrito[2] [ni'trito] SM (*Chim*) nitrite

nitroglicerina [nitroglitʃe'rina] SF nitroglycerine

nitroso, a [ni'troso] AGG nitrous

niveo, a ['niveo] AGG snow-white, snowy

Nizza ['nittsa] SF Nice

nizzardo, a [nit'tsardo] AGG of *o* from Nice
■ SM/F inhabitant *o* native of Nice

nn ABBR (= **numeri**) nos

NO SIGLA = *Novara*
■ ABBR (= **Nord-Ovest**) NW

no [nɔ] AVV **1** no; **vieni? — no** are you coming? — no (I'm not); **la conosce? — no** does he know her? — no (he doesn't); **lo conosciamo? — tu no ma io sì** do we know him? — you don't but I do; **ti piace? – no** do you like it? – no, I don't; **ne vuoi ancora? – no, grazie** would you like some more? – no thank you; **verrai, no?** you'll come, won't you?; **hai finito, no?** you've finished, haven't you?; **può venire, no?** he can come, can't he?; **vieni anche tu, no?** you're coming too, aren't you? **2** (*con avverbio, congiunzione*) not; **perché no?** why not?; **no di certo!** certainly not!; **vieni? — come no!** are you coming? — of course! *o* certainly!; **come no?** what do you mean, no?; **vieni o no?** are you coming or not?; **simpatico o no lo devo sopportare** (whether he's) nice or not, I'll have to put up with him **3** **credo di no** I think not, I don't think so; **spero di no** I hope not; **sembra di no** apparently not; **direi di no** I don't think so; **ha detto di no** he said no
■ SM no; **da lui un no non me l'aspettavo** I didn't expect him to say no; **ci sono stati molti no** (*voti, pareri contrari*) there were a lot of votes against, there were a lot of noes

nobildonna [nobil'dɔnna] SF noblewoman

nobile ['nɔbile] AGG noble; **nobili sentimenti** noble sentiments; **di animo nobile** noble-hearted; **una famiglia nobile** an aristocratic family
■ SM/F noble, nobleman/noblewoman; **i nobili** the nobility, the aristocracy

nobiliare [nobi'ljare] AGG noble

nobilitare [nobili'tare] VT (*anche fig*) to ennoble
▶ **nobilitarsi** VR (*rendersi insigne*) to distinguish o.s.

nobilmente [nobil'mente] AVV nobly

nobiltà [nobil'ta] SF INV (*condizione, classe sociale*) nobility; (*fig: di azione, animo*) nobleness

nobiluomo [nobi'lwɔmo] SM (*pl* **nobiluomini**) nobleman

nocca, che ['nɔkka] SF (*Anat*) knuckle; (*di cavallo*) fetlock

nocchiere [nok'kjɛre] SM (*letter*) helmsman

noccio *ecc* ['nɔttʃo] VB *vedi* **nuocere**

nocciola [not'tʃɔla] SF hazelnut; **gelato alla nocciola** hazelnut ice cream
■ AGG INV (*anche:* **color nocciola**) hazel, light brown

nocciolina [nottʃo'lina] SF (*anche:* **nocciolina americana**) peanut

nocciolo[1] ['nɔttʃolo] SM (*di frutto*) stone; (*fig*) heart, core; **veniamo al nocciolo!** let's get to the point!; **nocciolo duro** hard core

nocciolo[2] [not'tʃɔlo] SM (*albero*) hazel

noce ['notʃe] SM (*albero*) walnut (tree); (*legno*) walnut
■ SF (*frutto*) walnut; **noce di cocco** coconut; **noce moscata** nutmeg **2** **una noce di burro** (*Culin*) a knob of butter (*Brit*), a dab of butter (*Am*); **noce di manzo/vitello** beef/veal fillet

nocepesca, sche [notʃe'pɛska] SF nectarine

nocevo *ecc* [no'tʃevo] VB *vedi* **nuocere**

nociuto [no'tʃuto] PP *di* **nuocere**

nocivo, a [no'tʃivo] AGG (*gen*) harmful; (*fumi*) noxious; **non contiene sostanze nocive** it doesn't contain any harmful substances; **insetti nocivi** pests

nocqui *ecc* VB *vedi* **nuocere**

NOCS [noks] SIGLA M (= **Nucleo Operativo Corpi Speciali**) *special section of the police*

nodo ['nɔdo] SM **1** (*gen: di cravatta, fune*) knot; (*fig: legame*) bond, tie; (*: punto centrale*) heart, crux; (*Med, Astron, Bot*) node; **fare/sciogliere un nodo** to tie/untie a knot; **avere i capelli pieni di nodi** to have tangles in one's hair; **avere un nodo alla gola** to have a lump in one's throat; **fare un nodo al fazzoletto** (*fig*) to tie a knot in one's handkerchief; **tutti i nodi vengono al pettine** (*Proverbio*) your sins will find you out; **nodo d'amore** love knot; **nodo scorsoio** slipknot **2** (*Aut, Ferr: incrocio*) junction; **nodo ferroviario** railway junction **3** (*Naut: velocità*) knot

nodosità [nodosi'ta] SF **1** (*di corteccia*) knottiness **2** (*Med*) lump

nodoso, a [no'doso] AGG (*tronco, mani*) gnarled

nodulo ['nɔdulo] SM (*Anat, Bot*) nodule

Noè [no'ɛ] SM Noah; **l'arca di Noè** Noah's ark

no-global [no'global] SM/F anti-globalization protester
■AGG (*movimento, manifestante*) anti-globalization

noi ['noi] PRON PERS **1** (*soggetto*) we; **noi andiamo al cinema** we're going to the cinema; **noi stessi(e)** we ourselves; **non lo sapevamo nemmeno noi** we didn't even know it ourselves; **tutti noi pensiamo che sia giusto** we all think it's right, all of us think it's right; **noi italiani** we Italians; **siamo stati noi a dirglielo** it was us who told him, we were the ones to tell him; **noi accettare? non sia mai detto!** us accept that? never! **2** (*oggetto: per dare rilievo, con preposizione*) us; **noi stessi(e)** ourselves; **chi è? – siamo noi** who is it? – it's us; **vuol vedere proprio noi** it's us he wants to see; **dice a noi?** is he talking to us?; **tocca a noi?** is it our turn?; **chi viene con noi?** who's coming with us?; **da noi** (*nel nostro paese*) in our country, where we come from; (*a casa nostra*) at our house **3** (*comparazioni*) we, us; **vanno veloce come noi** they are going as fast as we are, they are going as fast as us; **fate come noi** do as we do, do the same as us; **sono più giovani di noi** they are younger than we are *o* than us

noia ['nɔja] SF (*tedio*) boredom; (*disturbo, impaccio*) bother *no pl*, trouble *no pl*; (*fastidio*) nuisance; **morire di noia** to die of boredom; **stavano morendo di noia** they were dying of boredom; **mi è venuto a noia** I'm tired of it; **dare noia a qn** to bother *o* annoy sb; **finiscila di dar noia a tua sorella** stop bothering your sister; **le dà noia se fumo?** do you mind if I smoke?; **avere qn/qc a noia** not to like sb/sth; **avere (delle) noie con la polizia** to be in trouble with the police; **che noia!** what a bore!; (*fastidio*) what a nuisance!; **che noia, quel film!** the film was so boring!

noialtri, e [no'jaltri] PRON PERS we

noiosità [nojosi'ta] SF (*di libro, discorso*) dullness

noioso, a [no'joso] AGG (*tedioso*) boring; (*fastidioso*) tiresome, annoying

> **LO SAPEVI...?**
> **noioso** non si traduce mai con la parola inglese *noisy*

noleggiare [noled'dʒare] VT (*auto, bicicletta: prendere a noleggio*) to hire (*Brit*), rent; (*: dare a noleggio*) to hire out (*Brit*), rent out; (*aereo, nave*) to charter; **dove possiamo noleggiare una macchina?** where can we hire a car?; **noleggiano biciclette ai turisti** they hire out bikes to tourists

noleggiatore, trice [noleddʒa'tore] SM/F (*vedi vb*) hirer (*Brit*), renter; charterer

noleggio, gi [no'leddʒo] SM (*di auto, bicicletta*) hire (*Brit*), rental; (*di nave, barca*) charter; **prendere/dare a noleggio** to hire/hire (out) *o* rent/rent out; **prenderemo gli sci a noleggio** we're going to hire skis; **contratto di noleggio** (*Naut*) charter party (contract); **c'è un noleggio di biciclette?** is there a place where you can hire *o* rent bikes?

nolente [no'lɛnte] AGG: **volente o nolente** whether one likes it *o* not, willy-nilly

nolo ['nɔlo] SM (*di auto*) hire (charge) (*Brit*), rental (charge); (*di nave*) charter (fee); (*per trasporto merci*) freight (charge); **prendere/dare a nolo qc** to hire/hire out *o* rent/rent out

nomade ['nɔmade] AGG nomadic
■SM/F nomad

nomadismo [noma'dizmo] SM nomadism

nome ['nome] SM (*gen*) name; **che bel nome!** what a nice name!; **un uomo di nome Giovanni** a man by the name of John, a man called John; **a nome di** (*per conto di*) on behalf of; **parlo a nome dei miei colleghi** I'm speaking on behalf of my colleagues; **tanti saluti anche a nome di mia moglie** my wife asked me to give you her regards; **solo di nome** in name only; **in nome della legge** in the name of the law; **in nome del cielo!** in heaven's name!; **sotto il nome di** under the name of; **sotto falso nome** under an assumed name *o* an alias; **chiamare qn per nome** to call sb by name; **posso chiamarla per nome?** can I call you by your first name?; **li conosce tutti per nome** she knows them all by name; **lo conosco solo di nome** I know him only by name; **fare il nome di qn** to name sb; **faccia pure il mio nome** feel free to mention my name; **farsi un buon/cattivo nome** to get a good/bad name; **ormai si è fatto un nome** he has made a name for himself now; **porta** *o* **gli hanno dato il nome di suo nonno** he is named after his grandfather; **senza nome** nameless; **nome d'arte** stage name; **nome astratto** (*Gramm*) abstract noun; **nome di battaglia** nom de guerre; **nome di battesimo** Christian name; **nome comune** (*Gramm*) common noun; **nome depositato** trade name; **nome di dominio** (*Inform*) domain name; **nome di famiglia** surname; **nome del file** (*Inform*) file name; **nome proprio** (*Gramm*) proper noun; **nome da ragazza** maiden name; **nome da sposata** married name; **nome utente** (*Inform*) username

nomea [no'mɛa] SF notoriety

nomenclatura [nomenkla'tura] SF nomenclature

nomenklatura [nomenkla'tura] SF (*di partito, di stato*) nomenclature

nomignolo [no'miɲɲolo] SM nickname

nomina ['nɔmina] SF appointment; **conferire una nomina a qn** to appoint sb; **ottenere la nomina a presidente** to be appointed president

nominale [nomi'nale] AGG (*gen*) nominal; (*Gramm*) noun *attr*; **valore nominale** face *o* nominal value

nominalmente [nominal'mente] AVV nominally, in name only

nominare [nomi'nare] VT (*citare*) to mention; (*: per nome*) to name; (*eleggere*) to appoint; **l'ha nominata nel suo discorso** he mentioned her in his speech; **non l'ho mai sentito nominare** I've never heard of it (*o* him); **l'hanno nominato segretario generale** he has been appointed secretary-general

nominativo, a [nomina'tivo] AGG (*Gramm*) nominative; (*Comm*) registered; **elenco nominativo** list of names
■SM **1** (*Gramm: anche*: **caso nominativo**) nominative (case) **2** (*Comm, Amm: nome*) name

non [non] AVV **1** not; **non sono inglesi** they are not *o* aren't English; **non ne ho** I haven't (got) any; **non avresti dovuto farlo** you shouldn't have done that; **non devi farlo** you must not *o* mustn't do it; **non puoi**

venire you cannot *o* can't come; **non vieni?** aren't you coming?; **non parli francese?** don't you speak French?; **la legge non è stata ancora approvata** the law has not yet been passed; **Mario non c'è** Mario isn't here; **non è venuto nessuno** nobody came; **non andarci!** don't go!; **non ci sono andato** I didn't go; **non l'ho mai visto** I have never seen it; **non lo so** I don't know; **non lo capisco affatto** I do not *o* don't understand him at all; **non più di 5 minuti** no more than 5 minutes; **non oltre il 15 luglio** no later than (the) 15th (of) July; **grazie — non c'è di che** thank you — don't mention it **2** (*con sostantivo, aggettivo, pronome, avverbio*) not; **un guadagno non indifferente** a not inconsiderable gain; **non pochi sono d'accordo** not a few are in agreement, many are in agreement; **non uno dei presenti si è alzato** not one of those present stood up **3** (*con valore rafforzativo*): **non puoi non vederlo** you can't not see him, you'll have to see him; **finché non torno** until I get back; **per poco non cadevo in acqua** I almost fell into the water
■ PREF non-, un...

nona ['nɔna] SF (*Mus: intervallo*) ninth

non abbiente [non ab'bjɛnte] SM/F: **i non abbienti** the have-nots
■ AGG hard-up

non aggressione [non aggres'sjone] SF: **patto di non aggressione** non-aggression pact

non allineato, a [non alline'ato] AGG: **i paesi non allineati** the nonaligned countries

non belligeranza [non bellidʒe'rantsa] SF: **patto di non belligeranza** non-aggression pact

nonché [non'ke] CONG **1** (*tanto più, tanto meno*) let alone **2** (*e inoltre*) as well as; **lo ricorderò a lui, nonché a suo fratello** I'll remind him as well as his brother

nonconformista, i, e [nonkonfor'mista] AGG, SM/F nonconformist

non credente [non kre'dɛnte] SM/F: **i non credenti** non-believers

noncurante [nonku'rante] AGG: **noncurante (di)** indifferent (to), careless (of); **con fare noncurante** with a nonchalant *o* casual air

noncuranza [nonku'rantsa] SF carelessness, indifference; **assumere un'aria di noncuranza** to put on a nonchalant air

nondimeno [nondi'meno] CONG (*tuttavia*) however; (*nonostante*) nevertheless

non insegnante [non insɛɲ'ɲante] AGG: **personale non insegnante** non-teaching staff

non intervento [non inter'vɛnto] SM: **politica di non intervento** non-intervention policy

nonnismo [non'nizmo] SM (*Mil*) *bullying of new recruits by soldiers who are approaching discharge*

nonno, a ['nɔnno] SM/F grandfather/grandmother; (*in senso più familiare*) grandad *o* grandpa/grandma; **nonni** SMPL grandparents

nonnulla [non'nulla] SM INV: **un nonnulla** nothing, a trifle; **se la prende per un nonnulla** he gets annoyed over the slightest thing

nono, a ['nɔno] AGG, SM/F, SM ninth; *per fraseologia vedi* **quinto**

nonostante [nonos'tante] PREP in spite of, notwithstanding; **ci è riuscita nonostante tutto** she succeeded in spite of everything
■ CONG even though, although, in spite of the fact that; **nonostante fosse notte fonda** in spite of the fact that it was late at night; **nonostante piovesse** even though *o* in spite of the fact that it was raining; **ha voluto alzarsi nonostante fosse ancora malato** he wanted to get up even though he was still ill; **ciò nonostante** nevertheless

non plus ultra ['non plus 'ultra] SM INV: **il non plus ultra (di)** the last word (in)

nonsenso [non'sɛnso] SM absurdity

nontiscordardimé [nontiskordardi'me] SM INV (*Bot*) forget-me-not

non udente [non u'dɛnte] SM/F hearing-impaired person
■ AGG hearing-impaired

non vedente [non ve'dɛnte] SM/F visually-impaired person
■ AGG visually-impaired

non violento, a [non vjo'lɛnto] SM/F *person who is opposed to the use of violence*
■ AGG nonviolent

non violenza [non vjo'lɛntsa] SF nonviolence

no-profit [no'prɔfit] AGG not-for-profit

nord [nɔrd] SM north; **piove di più a nord** it rains more in the north; **la sua famiglia è del nord** his family comes from the north; **a nord (di)** north (of); **si trova a nord della città** it's north of the city; **si è diretto a nord** he headed north; **esposto a nord** north-facing; **verso nord** northward(s), north; **il mare del Nord** the North Sea; **l'America del Nord** North America; **l'Italia del nord** northern Italy
■ AGG INV (*gen*) north; (*regione*) northern; **è partito in direzione nord** he set off northwards *o* in a northward direction

Nord Dakota [nord 'da'kota] SM North Dakota

nord-est [nor'dɛst] SM northeast; **vento di nord-est** northeasterly wind

nordico, a, ci, che ['nɔrdiko] AGG Nordic; (*sci*) nordic
■ SM/F Northern European

nordista, i, e [nor'dista] AGG, SM/F Yankee

nord-ovest [nor'dɔvest] SM northwest; **vento di nord-ovest** northwesterly wind

Norimberga [norim'bɛrga] SF Nuremberg, Nuremberg; **il processo di Norimberga** the Nuremberg trials

norma ['nɔrma] SF (*principio*) norm; (*regola*) regulation, rule; (*consuetudine*) custom, rule; **scostarsi dalla norma** to diverge from the norm; **al di sopra della norma** above average, above the norm; **di norma** normally, as a rule; **di norma chiudo a chiave la porta** I lock the door as a rule; **a norma di legge** in accordance with the law, according to the law, as laid down by law; **per tua norma e regola** for your information; **proporsi una norma di vita** to set o.s. rules to live by; **le norme sociali** social norms; **norme per l'uso** instructions for use; **norme di sicurezza** safety regulations

normale [nor'male] AGG normal; (*solito*) usual, normal; **ma tu non sei normale!** there must be something wrong with you!; **è normale che sia così** it is quite normal for it to be like that
■ SM: **più alto del normale** taller than average; **ha un'intelligenza al di sopra del normale** he is of above average intelligence
■ SF (*Mat*) normal

normalità [normali'ta] SF normality

normalizzare [normalid'dzare] VT to bring back to normal, normalize; (*Pol, Mat*) normalize
▶ **normalizzarsi** VIP to return to normal

normalizzazione [normaliddzat'tsjone] SF (*Pol, Mat*)

normalization; **si è avuta una normalizzazione dei rapporti tra Italia e Cina** relations between Italy and China have returned to normal
normalmente [normal'mente] AVV (*in modo normale*) normally; (*abitualmente*) normally, usually, ordinarily
Normandia [norman'dia] SF Normandy
normanno, a [nor'manno] AGG, SM/F Norman
normativa [norma'tiva] SF regulations *pl*
normativo, a [norma'tivo] AGG normative
normografo [nor'mɔgrafo] SM (*Disegno*) stencil
North Carolina [nɔːθ kærə'laɪnə] SM North Carolina
norvegese [norve'dʒese] AGG, SM/F Norwegian; **i norvegesi** the Norwegians
■ SM (*lingua*) Norwegian; **parla norvegese** he speaks Norwegian
Norvegia [nor'vɛdʒa] SF Norway; **ti è piaciuta la Norvegia?** did you like Norway?; **andremo in Norvegia quest'estate** we're going to Norway this summer
nosocomio, mi [nozo'kɔmjo] SM hospital
nostalgia [nostal'dʒia] SF (*di casa, paese*) homesickness; (*del passato*) nostalgia; **soffrire di nostalgia** to be homesick; **aver nostalgia di casa** to be homesick; **ho nostalgia di casa** I'm homesick; **ho nostalgia dei vecchi tempi** I'm nostalgic for the good old days
nostalgicamente [nostaldʒika'mente] AVV nostalgically
nostalgico, a, ci, che [nos'taldʒiko] AGG (*vedi sf*) homesick; nostalgic
■ SM/F (*Pol*) *person who hopes for the return of Fascism*
nostrano, a [nos'trano] AGG (*gen*) local; (*pianta, frutta*) home-grown
nostro, a ['nɔstro] AGG POSS: **il(la) nostro(a)** *ecc* our; **il nostro giardino** our garden; **la nostra macchina** our car; **i nostri libri** our books; **nostra madre** our mother; **un nostro amico** a friend of ours; **è colpa nostra** it's our fault; **a casa nostra** at our house, at home
■ PRON POSS: **il(la) nostro(a)***ecc* ours, our own; **la vostra barca è più lunga della nostra** your boat is longer than ours; **il nostro è stato solo un errore** it was simply an error on our part; **è questa la vostra macchina? – no, la nostra è nera** is this your car? – no, ours is black; **le sue foto sono più belle delle nostre** his pictures are better than ours; **di chi è questo? – è nostro** whose is this? – it's ours
■ PRON POSS M **1 abbiamo speso del nostro** we spent our own money; **viviamo del nostro** we live on our own income **2 i nostri** (*famiglia*) our family; (*amici*) our own people, our side; **è dei nostri** he's one of us
■ PRON POSS F: **la nostra** (*opinione*) our view; **è dalla nostra** (*parte*) he's on our side; **anche noi abbiamo avuto le nostre** (*disavventure*) we've had our problems too; **alla nostra!** (*brindisi*) to us!
nostromo [nos'trɔmo] SM boatswain
nota ['nɔta] SF **1** (*gen, Mus*) note; **leggi la nota a pagina cinquantasei** read the note on page fifty-six; **prendere nota di qc** to note sth, make a note of sth, write sth down; **ho preso nota di tutto quello che ha detto** I made a note of everything she said; (*fig: fare attenzione*) to note sth, take note of sth; **degno di nota** noteworthy, worthy of note; **una nota di tristezza/allegria** a note of sadness/happiness; **nota fondamentale** (*Mus*) tonic; **note caratteristiche** (*di carattere, stile*) distinguishing marks *o* features; **note a piè di pagina** footnotes **2** (*fattura*) bill; (*elenco*) list; **nota di addebito** debit note; **nota della spesa** shopping list; **nota spese** list of expenses
notabile [no'tabile] AGG (*letter: mutamento, avvenimento*) notable; (*persona*) important
■ SM notable
notaio, ai [no'tajo] SM notary (public)
notare [no'tare] VT (*rilevare, osservare*) to notice, note; (*segnare: errori*) to mark; (*registrare*) to note (down), write down; **hai notato com'era strano?** did you notice how strange he was?; **vi faccio notare che…** I would have you note *o* I wish to point out that …; **gli ho fatto notare che l'errore era suo** I pointed out that it was his mistake; **notare qc a margine** to write sth in the margin; **farsi notare** to get o.s. noticed, draw attention to o.s.; **le piace farsi notare** she likes to draw attention to herself
notarile [nota'rile] AGG: **studio notarile** notary's office; **atto notarile** legal document (*authorized by a notary*)
notazione [notat'tsjone] SF (*Mus*) notation
notebook ['noutbuk] SM INV (*Inform*) notebook
notes ['nɔtes] SM INV notepad
notevole [no'tevole] AGG (*talento*) notable, remarkable; (*peso*) considerable; **si tratta di una somma notevole** it's a considerable sum; **quell'anello ha un valore notevole** that ring is very valuable; **una donna di notevole bellezza** a very beautiful woman
notevolmente [notevol'mente] AVV considerably
notifica, che [no'tifika] SF notification
notificare [notifi'kare] VT (*Dir*): **notificare qc a qn** to notify sb of sth, give sb notice of sth
notificazione [notifikat'tskjone] SF notification
notizia [no'tittsja] SF (piece of) news *sg*; (*informazione*) piece of information; **notizie** SFPL news *sg*, information *sg*; **avere una bella/brutta notizia** to have some good/bad news; **ho delle buone notizie per te** I've got some good news for you; **brutte notizie, purtroppo!** bad news, unfortunately!; **aver notizie di qn** to hear from sb; **non abbiamo sue notizie da un anno** it's a year since we had any news of her; **fammi avere tue notizie!** keep in touch!; **è un avvenimento che fa notizia** it's a sensational event; **questa è una notizia interessante** that's interesting news; **ho sentito la notizia della sua morte per radio** I heard the news of his death on the radio; **la notizia è stata uno shock per lui** the news was a shock to him

> **LO SAPEVI...?**
> **notizia** non si traduce mai con la parola inglese *notice*

notiziario, ri [notit'tsjarjo] SM (*Radio, TV, Stampa*) news *sg*; **l'hanno detto al notiziario delle otto** it was on the eight o'clock news
noto, a ['nɔto] AGG (well-)known; **noto a tutti** (well) known to everybody; **rendere noto qc** to make sth known; **un noto politico** a well-known politician; **suo fratello è più noto** his brother is better known
■ SM: **il noto e l'ignoto** the known and the unknown
notoriamente [notorja'mente] AVV: **è notoriamente risaputo che…** it's generally recognized that …, it's well known that …; **è notoriamente disonesto** he's notoriously dishonest
notorietà [notorje'ta] SF fame; (*pegg*) notoriety
notorio, ria, ri, rie [no'tɔrjo] AGG **1** well-known; (*pegg*) notorious **2** (*Dir*): **atto notorio = atto notarile**; *vedi* **notarile**

Nn

nottambulo, a [not'tambulo] SM/F night owl (*fig*), nighthawk (*Am fig*)
nottata [not'tata] SF night; **ho passato la nottata in piedi** I was up all night
notte ['nɔtte] SF night; (*oscurità*) darkness, night; (*periodo*) night, night-time; **buona notte** goodnight; **dare la buona notte** to say goodnight; **di notte** at night; (*durante la notte*) in the night, during the night; **è meglio non uscire di notte** it's better not to go out at night; **è successo di notte** it happened during the night; **la notte è meglio dormire** it's better to sleep at night; **la notte di sabato** *or* **sabato notte** (on) Saturday night; **questa notte** (*quella passata*) last night; (*quella che viene*) tonight; **rientrare prima di notte** to come back home before dark; **col favore della notte** under cover of darkness; **nella notte dei tempi** in the mists of time; **come va? — peggio che andare di notte** how are things? — worse than ever; **camicia da notte** nightgown; **portiere di notte** night porter; **notte bianca** *o* **in bianco** sleepless night
nottetempo [notte'tɛmpo] AVV at night, during the night
nottola ['nɔttola] SF (*pipistrello*) noctule
notturno, a [not'turno] AGG (*locale, servizio, guardiano*) night *attr*; (*Zool, fig*) nocturnal; **non c'è un servizio notturno** there is no night service
■ SM (*Mus*) nocturne
■ SF (*Sport*) evening match *o* fixture (*Brit*); **in notturna** (*partita*) under floodlights
noumeno [no'umeno] SM (*Filosofia*) noumenon
nova ['nɔva] SF (*Astron*) nova
novanta [no'vanta] AGG INV, SM INV ninety; *per fraseologia vedi* **cinquanta**
novantenne [novan'tɛnne] AGG, SM/F ninety-year-old; *per fraseologia vedi* **cinquantenne**
novantesimo, a [novan'tɛzimo] AGG, SM/F, SM ninetieth; *per fraseologia vedi* **quinto**
novantina [novan'tina] SF: **una novantina (di)** about ninety; *per fraseologia vedi* **cinquantina**
novarese [nova'rese] AGG of *o* from Novara
■ SM/F inhabitant *o* native of Novara
nove ['nɔve] AGG INV, SM INV nine; *per fraseologia vedi* **cinque**
novecentesco, a, schi, sche [novetʃen'tesko] AGG twentieth-century
novecento [nove'tʃɛnto] AGG INV nine hundred
■ SM INV nine hundred; (*secolo*): **il Novecento** the twentieth century
novella [no'vɛlla] SF (*Letteratura*) short story

> **LO SAPEVI...?**
> **novella** non si traduce mai con la parola inglese ***novel***

novelliere [novel'ljɛre] SM short-story writer
novellino, a [novel'lino] SM/F beginner, greenhorn
■ AGG (*pivello*) green, inexperienced
novellista, i, e [novel'lista] SM/F short-story writer
novellistica [novel'listika] SF (*arte*) short-story writing; (*insieme di racconti*) short stories *pl*
novello, a [no'vɛllo] AGG (*piante, patate*) new; (*insalata, verdura*) early; (*sposo*) newly-married; **pollo novello** spring chicken
novembre [no'vɛmbre] SM November; *per fraseologia vedi* **luglio**
novembrino, a [novem'brino] AGG November *attr*
novemila [nove'mila] AGG INV, SM INV nine thousand
novena [no'vɛna] SF (*Rel*) novena
novennale [noven'nale] AGG (*che dura 9 anni*) nine-year *attr*; (*ogni 9 anni*) nine-yearly
novero ['nɔvero] SM (*di fortunati, vincitori*) group; **non è nel novero dei miei amici** I don't number him amongst my friends
novilunio, ni [novi'lunjo] SM (*Astron*) new moon
novità [novi'ta] SF INV **1** (*originalità*) novelty; (*innovazione*) innovation; (*cosa originale, insolita*) something new; (*libro*) new publication; **questa è una novità!** that's new!; **le novità della moda francese** the latest French fashions; **l'ultima novità in fatto di lettori CD** the latest thing in CD players **2** (*notizia*) (piece of) news *sg*; **che novità ci sono?** what's the news?; **ci sono novità?** is there any news?
noviziato [novit'tsjato] SM (*Rel*) novitiate; (*tirocinio*) apprenticeship
novizio, zia, zi, zie [no'vittsjo] SM/F (*Rel*) novice; (*tirocinante*) beginner, apprentice
nozione [not'tsjone] SF notion, idea; **nozioni** SFPL (*rudimenti*) basic knowledge *sg*, rudiments; **la nozione del tempo e dello spazio** the notion of time and space; **ho perso la nozione del tempo** I've lost all notion of time; **le prime nozioni di matematica** the first elements of mathematics; **non ha che alcune nozioni di filosofia** he only has a vague notion of philosophy; **"nozioni di algebra"** "algebra for beginners"
nozionismo [nottsjo'nizmo] SM superficial knowledge
nozionistico, a, ci, che [nottsjo'nistiko] AGG superficial
nozze ['nɔttse] SFPL wedding *sg*, marriage *sg*; **regalo di nozze** wedding present; **viaggio di nozze** honeymoon; **dove andrete in viaggio di nozze?** where are you going on your honeymoon?; **offrendomi quel lavoro mi hanno invitato a nozze** (*fig*) when they offered me that job it was just what I wanted; **nozze d'argento** silver wedding *sg*; **nozze d'oro** golden wedding *sg*
ns. ABBR (*Comm*) = **nostro**
NU SIGLA = *Nuoro*
■ ABBR (= **Nazioni Unite**) UN; = **Nettezza Urbana**; *vedi* **nettezza**
nube ['nube] SF (*anche fig*) cloud
nubifragio, gi [nubi'fradʒo] SM cloudburst
nubilato [nubi'lato] SM single status
nubile ['nubile] AGG (*donna*) unmarried, single
■ SF single *o* unmarried woman
nuca, che ['nuka] SF nape (of the neck)
nucleare [nukle'are] AGG nuclear; **l'energia nucleare** nuclear energy
■ SM: **il nucleare** nuclear energy
nucleico, a, ci, che [nu'klɛiko] AGG nucleic
nucleo ['nukleo] SM (*Bio, Fis*) nucleus; (*Geog*) core; (*fig: parte centrale*) core, nucleus; (*gruppo*) unit, group, team; (*Mil, Polizia*) unit, squad; **il nucleo familiare** the family unit; **nucleo antidroga** anti-drugs squad
nucleone [nukle'one] SM nucleon
nudismo [nu'dizmo] SM nudism
nudista, i, e [nu'dista] SM/F nudist
nudità [nudi'ta] SF INV (*di persona*) nudity, nakedness *sg*; (*parti nude del corpo*) nakedness; (*di paesaggio*) bareness *sg*; **le proprie nudità** one's nakedness
nudo, a ['nudo] AGG (*persona, membra*) bare, naked, nude; (*albero, parete, montagna*) bare; (*verità*) plain, naked; **un uomo nudo** a naked man; **era completamente nuda** she was completely naked; **mezzo/tutto nudo**

half-/stark-naked; **a piedi nudi** barefoot; **camminava a piedi nudi in giardino** he was walking barefoot in the garden; **a occhio nudo** to the naked eye; **è invisibile a occhio nudo** it's not visible to the naked eye; **gli ha detto nudo e crudo che...** he said to him bluntly that ...; **questa è la verità nuda e cruda** this is the plain, unvarnished truth; **mettere a nudo** (*cuore, verità*) to lay bare
■SM (*Arte*) nude

nugolo ['nugolo] SM: **un nugolo di** a whole host of

nulla ['nulla] PRON, AVV = **niente**
■SM **1** **il nulla** nothing, nothingness; **Dio creò il mondo dal nulla** God created the world out of nothing; **svanire nel nulla** to vanish into thin air **2** (*minima quantità*): **basta un nulla per farlo arrabbiare** he gets annoyed over the slightest thing; **te lo cedo per (un) nulla** I am giving it to you for a song *o* for next to nothing

nullaosta [nulla'ɔsta] SM INV authorization, permission

nullatenente [nullate'nɛnte] AGG: **essere nullatenente** to own nothing
■SM/F person with no property

nullità [nulli'ta] SF INV **1** (*Dir*) nullity; (*di idea, ragionamento*) invalidity **2** (*persona*) nonentity

nullo, a ['nullo] AGG (*tentativo, sforzo*) vain, pointless; (*Dir*) null (and void); **scheda nulla** (*Pol*) spoiled vote; **incontro nullo** (*Sport*) draw; **colpo nullo** (*Tennis*) let

nume ['nume] SM numen; **santi numi!** good heavens!

numerale [nume'rale] AGG, SM numeral

numerare [nume'rare] VT to number

numeratore [numera'tore] SM **1** (*Mat*) numerator **2** (*macchina*) numbering device

numerazione [numerat'tsjone] SF numbering; **numerazione araba** arabic numerals *pl*; **numerazione romana** roman numerals *pl*

numericamente [numerika'mente] AVV numerically

numerico, a, ci, che [nu'mɛriko] AGG numerical

numero ['numero] SM **1** (*gen*) number; (*arabo, romano*) numeral; **i Numeri** (*Bibbia*) the Book of Numbers; **dodici di numero** twelve in number; **abito al numero 6** I live at number 6; **ha tutti i numeri per riuscire** he's got what it takes to succeed; **dare i numeri** (*farneticare*) to be not all there; **tanto per fare numero invitiamo anche lui** why don't we invite him to make up the numbers?; **che numero tuo fratello!** your brother is a real character!; **numero chiuso** (*Univ*) selective entry system; **numero civico** house number; **numero legale** quorum; **numero di scarpe** shoe size; **che numero di scarpe porti?** what size (of) shoe do you take? **2** (*Telec, anche:* **numero di telefono**) (tele)phone number; **qual è il tuo numero di telefono?** what's your phone number?; **numero verde** (*Telec*) ≈ Freephone *o* Freefone number (*Brit*), ≈ toll-free number (*Am*); **fare un numero** to dial a number **3** (*di giornale, rivista*) issue, number; **numero arretrato** back number; **numero doppio** issue with supplement **4** (*di spettacolo*) act, turn; **il suo numero è stato molto divertente** his act was very entertaining **5** (*Chim, Fis*) number; **numero di massa** mass number

numeroso, a [nume'roso] AGG **1** numerous, many; **ci sono stati numerosi casi di morbillo quest'anno** there have been numerous cases of measles this year; **le personalità sono intervenute numerose** celebrities were present in large numbers **2** (*folla, famiglia*) large; **ha una famiglia numerosa** he's got a large family

numismatica [numiz'matika] SF numismatics *sg*, coin collecting
▷ www.numismatica.unibo.it/

nunzio, zi ['nuntsjo] SM (*Rel*) nuncio

nuoccio *ecc* ['nwɔttʃo] VB *vedi* **nuocere**

nuocere ['nwɔtʃere] VI IRREG (*aus* **avere**) **nuocere a** to harm, damage; be bad for; **il fumo nuoce alla salute** smoking is bad for your health; **tentar non nuoce** (*Proverbio*) there's no harm in trying

nuociuto, a [nwo'tʃuto] PP *di* **nuocere**

nuora ['nwɔra] SF daughter-in-law

nuorese [nuo'rese] AGG of *o* from Nuoro
■SM/F inhabitant *o* native of Nuoro

nuotare [nwo'tare] VI (*aus* **avere**) to swim; (*galleggiare: oggetti*) to float; **sai nuotare?** can you swim?; **nuotare a rana/sul dorso** to do the breaststroke/backstroke; **nuotare nell'oro** to be rolling in money
■VT to swim

nuotata [nwo'tata] SF swim

nuotatore, trice [nwota'tore] SM/F swimmer; **è un bravo nuotatore** he's a good swimmer

nuoto ['nwɔto] SM swimming; **una gara di nuoto** a swimming gala; **attraversare la Manica a nuoto** to swim (across) the Channel; **nuoto pinnato** fin swimming; **nuoto sincronizzato** synchronized swimming
▷ www.federnuoto.it/

nuova ['nwɔva] SF news *sg*; **che nuove ci sono?** is there any news?; **nessuna nuova buona nuova** (*Proverbio*) no news is good news

Nuova Guinea ['nwɔva gwi'nɛa] SF New Guinea

Nuova Inghilterra ['nwɔva ingil'tɛrra] SF New England

nuovamente [nwɔva'mente] AVV again; **si è nuovamente ammalato** he's ill again

Nuova Scozia ['nwɔva 'skɔttsja] SF Nova Scotia

nuovayorchese [nwovajor'kese] AGG, SM/F = **newyorchese**

Nuova York ['nwɔva 'jɔrk] SF New York

Nuova Zelanda ['nwɔva dze'landa] SF New Zealand; **ti è piaciuta la Nuova Zelanda?** did you like New Zealand?; **andremo in Nuova Zelanda** we're going to New Zealand

nuovo, a ['nwɔvo] AGG **1** (*gen*) new; (*originale: idea*) novel, new; (*: metodo*) new, up-to-date; **un vestito nuovo** a new dress; **nuovo fiammante** *or* **nuovo di zecca** brand-new; **ha una macchina nuova di zecca** he's got a brand-new car; **il nuovo presidente** the new *o* newly-elected president; **sono nuovo del mestiere** I am new to this job; **sono nuova di qui/di Glasgow** I am new here/to Glasgow; **il suo volto non mi è nuovo** I know his face; **come nuovo** as good as new; **sembra nuovo** it looks like new **2** (*altro, secondo*) new, fresh; (*diverso*) new, different; **usa un foglio nuovo** take a fresh sheet of paper; **hai letto il suo nuovo libro?** have you read his new *o* latest book?; **fino a nuovo ordine** until further notice; **c'è stata una nuova serie di scosse** there has been a new *o* further series of tremors; **fare un nuovo tentativo** to make another attempt; **anno nuovo, vita nuova!** it's time to turn over a new leaf! **3** **di nuovo** again; **di nuovo tu?** (is that) you again?; **è successo di nuovo** it happened again

Nn

■SM: **che c'è di nuovo?** what's the news?, what's new?; **non c'è niente di nuovo** there's no news *o* nothing new; **rimettere a nuovo** (*cosa, macchina*) to do up like new; **questa cura mi ha rimesso a nuovo** this treatment has given me a new lease of life

nutria ['nutrja] SF (*animale*) coypu; (*pelliccia*) nutria

nutrice [nu'tritʃe] SF wet nurse

nutriente [nutri'ɛnte] AGG nutritious, nourishing; (*balsamo*) nourishing; **crema nutriente** (*Cosmetica*) nourishing cream

nutrimento [nutri'mento] SM nourishment, food

nutrire [nu'trire] VT to feed; (*fig*: *sentimenti*) to harbour (*Brit*), harbor (*Am*); (: *risentimento, rancore*) to nurse, feel; **la madre nutriva i piccoli** the mother was feeding her young; **nutrivo profonda stima per lui** I felt great respect for him

■VI (*aus* **avere**) (*cibo*) to be nourishing

▶ **nutrirsi** VR: **nutrirsi di** to feed on, eat; **i leoni si nutrono esclusivamente di carne** lions only eat meat

nutritivo, a [nutri'tivo] AGG (*proprietà*) nutritional; (*sostanza*) nutritious

nutrito, a [nu'trito] AGG **1 ben/mal nutrito** well/ poorly fed **2** (*numeroso*) large; (*fitto*) heavy

nutrizione [nutrit'tsjone] SF (*atto*) feeding, nutrition; (*dieta*) nutrition; **una scarsa nutrizione** a poor diet

nuvola ['nuvola] SF cloud; **avere la testa fra le nuvole** to have one's head in the clouds; **ha sempre la testa tra le nuvole** he always has his head in the clouds; **cascare dalle nuvole** to be astonished, be taken aback; **quando gliel'ho detto è cascato dalle nuvole** when I told him he was astonished

nuvolo, a ['nuvolo] AGG cloudy

nuvolosità [nuvolosi'ta] SF INV cloudiness; **nuvolosità persistente** persistent cloud cover

nuvoloso, a [nuvo'loso] AGG (*tempo*) cloudy; (*cielo*) cloudy, overcast; **oggi è più nuvoloso di ieri** it's cloudier today than it was yesterday

nuziale [nut'tsjale] AGG wedding *attr*, nuptial; **la cerimonia nuziale** the wedding ceremony

nylon® ['nailən] SM nylon

O

O, **o** [ɔ] SF O M INV (*lettera*) O, o; **O come Otranto** ≈ O for Oliver (*Brit*), ≈ O for Oboe (*Am*)

O ABBR (= **Ovest**) W

o[1] [o] (*dav vocale talvolta* od) CONG **1** (*gen*) or; **o...o...** either ... or ...; **o meglio** or rather; **due o tre volte** two or three times; **oggi o domani** (either) today or tomorrow; **lo farò o oggi o domani** I'll do it either today or tomorrow; **(o) l'uno o l'altro** either (of them); **sono decisa: o lui o nessuno** I've made up my mind: it's him or nobody **2** (*altrimenti*) (or) else; **sbrigati o faremo tardi** hurry up or (else) we'll be late

o[2] **oh** [o] ESCL **1** oh! **2** (*fam: per chiamare*) hey!

oasi ['ɔazi] SF INV (*anche fig*) oasis; **oasi di pace** haven of peace

obbediente *ecc* [obbe'djɛnte] *vedi* **ubbidiente** *ecc*

obbiettare *ecc* *vedi* **obiettare** *ecc*

obbligare [obbli'gare] VT: **obbligare qn a fare qc** (*sogg: circostanze, persona*) to force *o* oblige sb to do sth; make sb do sth; (*legalmente*) to require sb to do sth; (*Dir*) to bind sb to do sth; **mi ha obbligato a fare i compiti** she made me do my homework; **essere obbligato a fare qc** to have to do sth; **sono obbligato (a farlo)** I have to (do it); **non sei obbligato a farlo** you don't have to do it; **e chi ti obbliga?** who's forcing you (to do it)?; **la mia coscienza mi obbligò a tacere** I was bound by conscience to remain silent; **l'influenza lo obbliga a letto** he's confined to bed with flu
▶ **obbligarsi** VR **1** (*Dir*) **obbligarsi per qn** to stand surety for sb, act as guarantor for sb **2** (*impegnarsi*) **obbligarsi a fare qc** to undertake to do sth

obbligatissimo, a [obbliga'tissimo] AGG: **obbligatissimo!** (*ringraziamento*) much obliged!

obbligato, a [obbli'gato] AGG **1** (*riconoscente*): **obbligato verso qn** obliged *o* indebted to sb; **le sono molto obbligato!** I'm much obliged! **2** (*imposto: percorso, tappa*) set, fixed; **passaggio obbligato** (*fig*) essential requirement; **è stata una scelta obbligata** I (*o* you *ecc*) had no choice

obbligatoriamente [obbligatorja'mente] AVV: **dovete seguire obbligatoriamente le lezioni** the classes are compulsory; **non devi obbligatoriamente farlo** you are not obliged to do it

obbligatorio, ria, ri, rie [obbliga'tɔrjo] AGG (*assicurazione, esame*) compulsory; (*clausola*) (legally) binding

obbligazione [obbligat'tsjone] SF **1** (*gen, Dir*) obligation **2** (*Fin*) bond, debenture; **obbligazione al portatore** bearer bond; **obbligazione dello Stato** government bond; **obbligazioni convertibili** convertible loan stock *sg*, convertible debentures

obbligazionista, i, e [obbligattsjo'nista] SM/F bondholder

obbligo, ghi ['ɔbbligo] SM obligation; (*dovere*) obligation, duty; **avere degli obblighi con** *o* **verso qn** to have obligations to sb; (*essere riconoscente*) to be indebted to sb; **ho degli obblighi nei confronti dei miei genitori** I've got obligations to my parents; **sentire/avere l'obbligo di fare qc** to feel/be obliged to do sth, feel/be under an obligation to do sth; **mi sono sentito in obbligo (di farlo)** I felt obliged to (do it); **non ho l'obbligo di timbrare il cartellino al lavoro** I don't have to clock in at work; **i libri vengono dati in prestito con l'obbligo di restituirli entro 15 giorni** books are lent on condition that they are returned within a fortnight; **essere d'obbligo** (*discorso, applauso*) to be called for; **fare una visita d'obbligo** to make a duty call; **le formalità d'obbligo** the necessary formalities; **frasi d'obbligo** civilities; **"è d'obbligo l'abito scuro"** "black tie"; **scuola dell'obbligo** compulsory education; **obblighi militari** compulsory military service *sg*

obb.mo ABBR = **obbligatissimo**

obbrobrio, bri [ob'brɔbrjo] SM **1** (*infamia*) disgrace, shame **2** (*fig: cosa brutta*) mess, eyesore; **quel palazzo è un obbrobrio** that building's an eyesore

obbrobriosamente [obbrobrjosa'mente] AVV (*in modo infame*) disgracefully, shamefully; (*in modo orribile*) atrociously

obbrobrioso, a [obbrobrj'oso] AGG (*infame*) disgraceful, shameful; (*fig*) ghastly

obelisco, schi [obe'lisko] SM obelisk

oberare [obe'rare] VT: **oberare qn di** (*lavoro, responsabilità, impegni*) to overload sb with

oberato, a [obe'rato] AGG: **oberato di** (*lavoro*)

overloaded *o* overburdened with; **oberato di** *o* **da debiti** crippled with debts
obesità [obesi'ta] SF obesity
obeso, a [o'beso] AGG obese
obice ['ɔbitʃe] SM (*Mil*) howitzer
obiettare [objet'tare] VT: **obiettare che...** to object that ...; **non ho nulla da obiettare** I have no objection (to make), I haven't got any objections; **ha obiettato che non aveva tempo** he pleaded lack of time; **obiettare su qc** to object to sth, raise objections concerning sth
obiettivamente [objettiva'mente] AVV objectively
obiettività [objettivi'ta] SF objectivity
obiettivo, a [objet'tivo] AGG objective
■ SM **1** (*scopo*) objective, aim; **il suo obiettivo è quello di vincere la gara** his aim is to win the competition **2** (*Ottica, Fot*) lens *sg*, objective; **obiettivo a fuoco fisso** fixed-focus lens; **obiettivo grandangolare** wide-angle lens
obiettore [objet'tore] SM objector; **obiettore di coscienza** conscientious objector
obiezione [objet'tsjone] SF objection; **fare** *o* **muovere** *o* **sollevare un'obiezione** to make *o* raise an objection, object; **ci sono obiezioni?** any objections?; **obiezione accolta/respinta** (*Dir*) objection sustained/overruled
obitorio, ri [obi'tɔrjo] SM mortuary, morgue

LO SAPEVI...?
obitorio non si traduce mai con la parola inglese *obituary*

oblato, a [o'blato] SM/F oblate
oblazione [oblat'tsjone] SF oblation
oblio, oblii [o'blio] SM oblivion; **cadere nell'oblio** to sink into oblivion
obliquamente [oblikwa'mente] AVV (*in modo inclinato*) on the slant, slantwise
obliquità [oblikwi'ta] SF obliqueness
obliquo, a [o'blikwo] AGG (*gen, Mat*) oblique; (*calligrafia, raggi*) slanting; (*fig*) devious, underhand; **una linea obliqua** an oblique line
obliterare [oblite'rare] VT (*francobollo*) to cancel; (*biglietto: con timbro*) to stamp; (: *con foratura*) to punch
obliteratrice [oblitera'tritʃe] SF (*anche:* **macchina obliteratrice**) (*vedi vb*) cancelling machine; stamping machine; punch
oblò [o'blɔ] SM INV (*Naut*) porthole
oblungo, a, ghi, ghe [o'blungo] AGG oblong
obnubilato, a [obnubi'lato] AGG (*letter fig: mente*) clouded
oboe ['ɔboe] SM oboe
oboista, i, e [obo'ista] SM/F oboist
obolo ['ɔbolo] SM (*elemosina*) (small) offering, mite
obsolescente [obsoleʃ'ʃɛnte] AGG obsolescent
obsolescenza [obsoleʃ'ʃɛntsa] SF (*Econ*) obsolescence
obsoleto, a [obso'lɛto] AGG obsolete
OC ABBR (= **onde corte**) SW (= *short wave*)
oca ['ɔka] SF (*pl* **oche**) (*Zool*) goose; (*fig pegg: un'oca giuliva*) silly goose; **gioco dell'oca** ≈ snakes and ladders **oca maschio** gander
ocaggine [o'kaddʒine] SF silliness, stupidity
ocarina [oka'rina] SF (*Mus*) ocarina
occasionale [okkazjo'nale] AGG (*incontro*) chance *attr*; (*cliente, guadagni*) casual, occasional
occasionalmente [okkazjonal'mente] AVV occasionally, from time to time
occasionare [okkazjo'nare] VT to cause, bring about
occasione [okka'zjone] SF **1** (*opportunità*) opportunity; (*caso favorevole*) chance; **sarebbe l'occasione buona per fare...** it would be an ideal opportunity to do ...; **avere occasione di fare qc** to have the chance *o* opportunity of doing sth; **alla prima occasione** at the first opportunity; **lo farò alla prima occasione** I'll do it at the first opportunity; **all'occasione** should the need arise **2** (*circostanza*) occasion; **in occasione di** on the occasion of; **in occasione del suo compleanno** on the occasion of his birthday; **a seconda delle** *o* **secondo le occasioni** depending on circumstances *o* on the situation **3** (*motivo, pretesto*) occasion, cause; **dare occasione a** to cause, give rise to **4** (*buon affare*) bargain; **compralo! è un'occasione** buy it! it's a bargain; **d'occasione** (*a buon prezzo*) bargain *attr*; (*di seconda mano*) secondhand; **comprare qc d'occasione** to get sth cheap
occhiacci [ok'kjattʃi] SMPL: **fare gli occhiacci a qn** to scowl at sb
occhiaia [ok'kjaja] SF **1** (*orbita*) eye socket **2 occhiaie** SFPL: **avere le occhiaie** to have bags under one's eyes
occhiali [ok'kjali] SMPL (*da vista*) glasses, spectacles; (*di protezione*) goggles; **occhiali da sole** sunglasses; **porto gli occhiali** I wear glasses
occhialuto, a [okkja'luto] AGG (*scherz*): **un signore occhialuto** a bespectacled man
occhiata [ok'kjata] SF look, glance; **dare un'occhiata a** (*guardare*) to have a look at, glance at; (*badare*) to keep an eye on; **vorrei dare un'occhiata a quel libro** I'd like to have a look at that book; **potresti dare un'occhiata alle mie valigie?** could you keep an eye on my cases?; **un'occhiata d'intesa** a knowing look *o* glance
occhieggiare [okkjed'dʒare] VI (*aus* **avere**) (*apparire qua e là*) to appear here and there, peep out
occhiello [ok'kjɛllo] SM **1** (*asola*) buttonhole; (*di scarpe*) eyelet **2** (*Tip*) half-title
occhio, chi ['ɔkkjo] SM
1 (*Anat*) eye; **avere gli occhi azzurri** to have blue eyes; **dagli occhi castani** brown-eyed; **avere occhi buoni** to have good eyesight; **logorarsi gli occhi** to strain one's eyes; **fare un occhio nero a qn** to give sb a black eye; **a occhio nudo** with the naked eye; **visibile a occhio nudo** visible to the naked eye
2 (*sguardo, espressione*) look; **alzò gli occhi dal libro** he looked up from *o* raised his eyes from his book; **cercare qn con gli occhi** to look *o* glance around for sb; **ha l'occhio smorto oggi** he's looking rather bleary-eyed today
3 (*accortezza, capacità di giudicare*): **avere occhio** to have a good eye; **ci vuole occhio per fare questo lavoro** this job requires a good eye; **vedere di buon/mal occhio qn/qc** to view sb/sth favourably/unfavourably, look favourably/unfavourably on sb/sth
4 (*attenzione*): **occhio!** look out!, watch out!, careful!; **occhio alla borsa!** watch your bag!, keep an eye on your bag!; **essere tutt'occhi** to be all eyes
5 (*cosa a forma d'occhio: di ciclone, patata*) eye; **occhio magico** (*su porta*) peephole
6 (*fraseologia*): **a occhio (e croce)** roughly; round about; **a occhio e croce costerà cento euro** it'll cost round about one hundred euros; **tieni gli occhi aperti per...** keep an eye out for ...; **non riuscivo a tener gli occhi aperti** I couldn't keep my eyes open; **non ho chiuso occhio stanotte** I didn't sleep a wink last night; **aprire gli occhi a qn su qc** to open sb's eyes to sth; **chiudere un occhio (su)** (*fig*) to turn a blind eye (to), shut one's eyes (to); **per questa volta chiuderò un**

occhio I'll turn a blind eye this once; **sognare a occhi aperti** to daydream; **a occhi chiusi** (*anche fig*) with one's eyes shut; **costare un occhio della testa** to cost a fortune, cost and arm and a leg; **costa un occhio della testa** it costs an arm and a leg; **darei un occhio per sapere** I'd give my eyeteeth to know; **dare nell'occhio** to attract attention; (*spiccare*) to stand out a mile; (*vestito, colore*) to be loud *o* gaudy; **vestiti in modo da non dare troppo nell'occhio** dress so as not to attract too much attention; **dare all'occhio** *o* **nell'occhio a qn** to catch sb's eye; **tenere d'occhio qn/qc** to keep an eye on sb/sth; **per favore, tieni d'occhio le mie valigie** please could you keep an eye on my cases?; **fare l'occhio a qc** to get used to sth; **fare gli occhi dolci a qn** to make sheep's eyes at sb; **guardare con tanto d'occhi** to gaze wide-eyed at; **lasciare gli occhi su qc** to set one's heart on sth; **mettere gli occhi addosso a qn/su qc** to have got one's eyes on sb/sth; **a quattr'occhi** privately, in private; **vedendo tutti quei bei vestiti mi sono rifatta gli occhi** it was a real pleasure to see so many lovely clothes; **ce l'hai sotto gli occhi** it's right there in front of you; **mi è capitato sott'occhio un articolo interessante** I happened to see an interesting article; **occhio non vede cuore non duole** (*Proverbio*) what the eye doesn't see the heart doesn't grieve over; **occhio per occhio, dente per dente** (*Proverbio*) an eye for an eye, a tooth for a tooth; **lontano dagli occhi lontano dal cuore** (*Proverbio*) out of sight, out of mind

occhiolino [okkjo'lino] SM: **fare l'occhiolino a qn** to wink at sb; **le fece l'occhiolino** he winked at her

occidentale [ottʃiden'tale] AGG (*Geog*) western, west; (: *vento*) westerly; (*cultura, paesi*) Western; **i paesi occidentali** Western countries; **la costa occidentale della Francia** the west coast of France
■SM/F Westerner

occidentalizzare [ottʃidentalid'dzare] VT to westernize
▶ **occidentalizzarsi** VIP to become westernized

occidentalizzazione [ottʃidentaliddzat'tsjone] SF westernization

occidente [ottʃi'dɛnte] SM west; **a occidente** in the west; **a occidente di** (to the) west of; **il sole tramonta a occidente** the sun sets in the west; **l'Occidente** (*Pol*) the West

occipitale [ottʃipi'tale] AGG: **osso occipitale** occipital bone

occipite [ot'tʃipite] SM back of the head, occiput (*Anat*)

occludere [ok'kludere] VT IRREG to block, occlude (*Med*)

occlusione [okklu'zjone] SF blockage, obstruction, occlusion (*Med*)

occlusivo, a [okklu'zivo] (*Ling*) AGG occlusive
■SF occlusive

occluso, a [ok'kluzo] PP *di* **occludere**

occorrente [okkor'rɛnte] AGG necessary
■SM all that is necessary; **porta con te tutto l'occorrente** bring everything you need; **l'occorrente per scrivere/disegnare** writing/drawing materials *pl*

occorrenza [okkor'rɛntsa] SF **1** (*evenienza*) eventuality **2** (*bisogno*) necessity, need; **all'occorrenza** if need be, if necessary, in case of need

> **LO SAPEVI...?**
> **occorrenza** non si traduce mai con la parola inglese *occurrence*

occorrere [ok'korrere] VI IRREG (*aus* **essere**) (*essere necessario*) to be needed, be required; **ti occorre qc?** do you need anything?; **mi occorre del denaro** I need some money; **mi occorrono 2 mila euro** I need 2 thousand euros; **mi occorre un'ora per arrivarci** it takes me *o* I need an hour to get there
■VB IMPERS: **occorre farlo** it must be done; **occorre far presto** we'll (*o* you'll *ecc*) have to hurry; **non occorre che gli scriva subito** there's no need to write to him at once; **non occorre che mi telefoni** you don't need to phone me

> **LO SAPEVI...?**
> **occorrere** non si traduce mai con la parola inglese *occur*

occorso, a [ok'korso] PP *di* **occorrere**

occultamento [okkulta'mento] SM concealment

occultare [okkul'tare] VT to hide, conceal
▶ **occultarsi** VR: **occultarsi (a)** to hide (from), conceal o.s. (from)

occultismo [okkul'tizmo] SM occultism

occulto, a [ok'kulto] AGG (*segreto*) hidden, secret, concealed; (*arcano*) occult; **le scienze occulte** the occult *sg*, the occult sciences
■SM: **l'occulto** the occult

occupante [okku'pante] AGG (*Mil*) occupying
■SM/F (*di casa*) occupier, occupant; **occupante abusivo** squatter

occupare [okku'pare] VT (*gen, Mil*) to occupy; (*spazio, tempo*) to occupy, take up; (*casa*) to live in; (*carica*) to hold; (*manodopera*) to employ; **l'esercito ha occupato il paese** the army has occupied *o* taken over the country; **la città è stata occupata durante la guerra** the city was occupied during the war; **l'armadio occupa tutta la parete** the cupboard takes up the whole wall; **lo sport mi occupa tutto il tempo libero** sport takes up all my spare time; **gli studenti hanno occupato la scuola** the students have occupied the school; **la casa è stata occupata (abusivamente)** the house has been taken over by squatters
▶ **occuparsi** VIP **1 occuparsi di** (*interessarsi*) to be interested in, take an interest in; (*prendersi cura*) to take care of, look after; (*impicciarsi*) to interfere in, meddle in; **potresti occuparti dei bambini?** could you look after the children?; **si occupa di assicurazioni** he's in insurance; **occupati dei fatti tuoi!** mind your own business! **2 occuparsi in** (*impiegarsi*) to get a job in

occupato, a [okku'pato] AGG (*telefono, gabinetto*) engaged; (*posto, sedia*) taken, occupied; (*zona, fabbrica, scuola*) occupied; (*persona*: *affaccendato*) busy; **è occupato quel posto?** is that seat taken?; **la toilette è occupata** the toilet is engaged; **non riesco a telefonargli; è sempre occupato** I can't get through to him; the line's always engaged; **la scuola è ancora occupata** the school is still occupied; **una città occupata** an occupied city; **in questo momento il signor Rossi è molto occupato** Mr Rossi is very busy at the moment; **domani sarò ancora più occupato** I'll be even busier tomorrow; **essere occupato a fare qc** to be busy doing sth
■SM: **gli occupati e i disoccupati** the employed and the unemployed

occupazionale [okkupattsjo'nale] AGG employment *attr*, of employment

occupazione [okkupat'tsjone] SF **1** (*Mil, di fabbrica, scuola*) occupation; (*di casa*) occupancy, occupation; (*interesse, attività*) occupation; **occupazione abusiva** squatting **2** (*gen*) employment; (*impiego, lavoro*) job, occupation; **sto cercando un'occupazione** I'm looking for a job; **occupazione: infermiere**

Oo

occupation: nurse; **la piena occupazione** full employment

Oceania [otʃe'anja] SF Oceania

oceanico, a, ci, che [otʃe'aniko] AGG oceanic, ocean *attr*; (*fig: immenso*) vast, huge

oceano [o'tʃeano] SM ocean

oceanografia [otʃeanogra'fia] SF oceanography

oceanografico, a, ci, che [otʃeano'grafiko] AGG oceanographic(al)

oceanografo, a [otʃea'nɔgrafo] SM/F oceanographer

ocelot [otʃe'lɔt] SM INV = **ozelot**

ocra ['ɔkra] SF, AGG INV ochre

OCSE ['ɔkse] SIGLA F (= **Organizzazione per la Cooperazione e lo Sviluppo Economico**) OECD (= *Organization for Economic Cooperation and Development*)

oculare [oku'lare] AGG (*bulbo, lenti*) ocular, eye *attr*; **testimone oculare** eyewitness

oculatezza [okula'tettsa] SF (*vedi agg*) caution; shrewdness

oculato, a [oku'lato] AGG (*attento*) cautious, prudent; (*accorto*) shrewd

oculista, i, e [oku'lista] SM/F eye specialist, ophthalmologist; **devo andare dall'oculista** I need to go to the eye specialist

oculistica [oku'listika] SF ophthalmology

oculistico, a, ci, che [oku'listiko] AGG (*gen*) ophthalmic; **studio oculistico** eye clinic; **fare una visita oculistica** to have one's eyes tested

od [od] CONG *vedi* **o'**

ode ['ɔde] SF ode

ode *ecc* ['ɔde] VB *vedi* **udire**

odiare [o'djare] VT to hate, detest, loathe; **ti odio!** I hate you!; **odio le persone egoiste** I hate selfish people; **odiare fare qc** to hate doing sth; **odio alzarmi presto al mattino** I hate getting up early in the morning

▶ **odiarsi** VR to hate o.s.; (*uso reciproco*) to hate each other; **Marco e Matteo si odiano** Marco and Matteo hate each other

odierno, a [o'djɛrno] AGG (*di oggi*) today's, of today; (*attuale*) present, current; **in data odierna** (*frm*) today

odio, **odi** ['ɔdjo] SM hatred, hate; **avere in odio qn/qc** to hate *o* detest sb/sth; **prendere in odio qn/qc** to take a strong dislike to sb/sth

odiosamente [odjosa'mente] AVV hatefully, odiously

odioso, a [o'djoso] AGG (*detestabile*) hateful, odious; (*antipatico*) unpleasant, obnoxious; **sei odioso** you're horrible; **rendersi odioso (a)** to make o.s. thoroughly unpopular (with)

odissea [odis'sɛa] SF odyssey

odo *ecc* ['ɔdo] VB *vedi* **udire**

odontoiatra, i, e [odonto'jatra] SM/F dentist, dental surgeon

odontoiatria [odontoja'tria] SF dentistry

odontoiatrico, a, ci, che [odonto'jatriko] AGG dental

odontotecnico, ci [odonto'tɛkniko] SM dental technician

odorare [odo'rare] VT (*anche fig*) to smell; (*profumare*) to perfume, scent

■ VI (*aus* **avere**) (*anche fig*): **odorare (di)** to smell (of); **questi fiori non odorano** these flowers don't have any smell *o* perfume; **odorare di pulito/fresco** to smell clean/fresh; **odorare di muffa/d'aglio** to smell mouldy/of garlic

odorato [odo'rato] SM sense of smell

odore [o'dore] SM **1** (*gen*) smell, odour (*Brit*), odor (*Am*); (*fragranza*) scent, fragrance; **un buon odore** a nice smell; **un cattivo odore** a bad smell; **senza odore** odo(u)rless; **sentire odore di qc** to smell sth; **sento odore di pesce** I can smell fish; **avere buon/cattivo odore** to smell nice/bad, have a nice *o* good/bad smell; **ha un buon/cattivo odore** it smells nice/bad; **odore di cucina** smell of cooking; **morire in odore di santità** (*Rel*) to die in the odo(u)r of sanctity **2** **odori** SMPL (*Culin*) (aromatic) herbs

odoroso, a [odo'roso] AGG sweet-smelling

off [ɔ:f] AGG **1** (*spento*) off **2** (*Cine, Teatro: alternativo, sperimentale*) alternative

offendere [of'fɛndere] VB IRREG

■ VT **1** (*persona, morale pubblica, senso estetico*) to offend; (*ferire*) to hurt; **offendere qn nell'onore** to offend sb's honour (*Brit*) *o* honor (*Am*); **offendere la vista** (*fig*) to offend the eye **2** (*insultare*) to insult, offend; **non avevo intenzione di offenderti** I didn't mean to insult you **3** (*violare: libertà, diritti*) to violate; (*: legge*) to break; **offendere i diritti di qn** to infringe on sb's rights;

▶ **offendersi** VR (*uso reciproco*) to insult each other

▶ **offendersi** VIP (*risentirsi*) **offendersi (per)** to take offence (*Brit*) *o* offense (*Am*) (at), be offended (by); **se non vieni mi offendo** I'll be offended if you don't come; **si è offeso per non essere stato invitato** he took offence because they didn't invite him

offensiva [offen'siva] SF offensive; **passare all'offensiva** to take the offensive

offensivamente [offensiva'mente] AVV (*in modo ingiurioso*) offensively, insultingly

offensivo, a [offen'sivo] AGG (*parole*) offensive, insulting; (*armi*) offensive

offensore [offen'sore] SM (*Mil*) aggressor

offerente [offe'rɛnte] PART PRES *di* **offrire**

■ SM/F (*ad un'asta*) bidder; **vendere al migliore offerente** to sell to the highest bidder

offerta [of'fɛrta] SF **1** (*gen*) offer; (*in gara d'appalto*) tender; (*ad un'asta*) bid; (*Econ*) supply; **fare un'offerta** to make an offer; (*per appalto*) to tender; (*ad un'asta*) to bid; **mi ha fatto un'offerta generosa** he made me a generous offer; **ci sono poche offerte d'impiego** there aren't many jobs advertised; **ho accettato la sua offerta di lavoro** I've accepted his offer of a job; **"offerte d'impiego"** (*Stampa*) "situations vacant" (*Brit*), "help wanted" (*Am*); **offerta pubblica d'acquisto** takeover bid; **offerta pubblica di vendita** public offer for sale; **offerta reale** tender; **offerta speciale**: **(in) offerta speciale** (*Comm*) (on) special offer; **è in offerta speciale** it's on special offer **2** (*donazione, anche Rel*) offering, donation

offerto, a [of'fɛrto] PP *di* **offrire**

offertorio, ri [offer'tɔrjo] SM (*Rel*) offertory

offesa [of'fesa] SF **1** (*insulto*) offence (*Brit*), offense (*Am*), insult, affront; (*Dir*) offence, offense; **fare** *o* **recare offesa a qn** to give offence *o* offense to sb **2** (*Mil*) attack

offeso, a [of'feso] PP *di* **offendere**

■ AGG **1** (*nei sentimenti*) offended, hurt; (*fisicamente*) hurt, injured; **è terribilmente offesa per quello che hai detto** she's terribly offended about what you said; **sei ancora offeso con me?** are you still annoyed with me? **2** (*Dir*): **la parte offesa** the plaintiff

■ SM/F: **fare l'offeso** to go into a huff

office ['ɔfis] SM INV pantry

officiante [offi'tʃante] AGG (*Rel*) officiating

officiare [offi'tʃare] VI (*aus* **avere**) (*Rel*) to officiate

officina [offi'tʃina] SF workshop; **officina meccanica** (*Aut*) garage; **devo portare la macchina in officina** I have to take the car to the garage
offrire [of'frire] VB IRREG
■ VT **1** (*sigaretta, lavoro, merce, aiuto*) to offer; (*preghiere, messa*) to offer (up); (*ad un'asta*) to bid; **offrire qc a qn** to offer sth to sb, offer sb sth; **mi ha offerto un passaggio** he offered me a lift; **le hanno offerto un lavoro** they've offered her a job; **mi offri una sigaretta?** can I have a cigarette?; **ti offro da bere** I'll buy you a drink; **offro io (da bere)** the drinks are on me; **offro io, questa volta!** I'll pay this time!; **lo offre la casa** it's on the house; **ti va una pizza? offro io** do you feel like a pizza? my treat **2** (*regalare*): **offrire a** to give to; **offrire qc in dono a qn** to present sb with sth **3** (*opportunità, vantaggio*) to offer, present; **offrire il fianco alle critiche** to expose o.s. to criticism; **"offresi posto di segretaria"** "secretarial vacancy", "vacancy for secretary";
▶ **offrirsi** VR: **offrirsi volontario** to offer (o.s.), volunteer; **nessuno si è offerto volontario** nobody volunteered; **offrirsi di fare qc** to offer *o* volunteer to do sth; **si è offerto di aiutarci** he offered to help us; **"segretaria offresi"** "secretary seeks post"
▶ **offrirsi** VIP (*presentarsi: occasione*) to present itself, arise; **una vista stupenda si offrì ai loro occhi** a wonderful view lay before them
offset ['ɔ:fset] SM (*Tip*) offset; **realizzato in offset** printed in offset; **stampa in offset** offset printing
offuscare [offus'kare] VT (*cielo*) to darken; (*sole*) to obscure; (*fig: fama*) to obscure, overshadow; (*: mente*) to dim, cloud
▶ **offuscarsi** VIP (*vedi vt*) to darken, grow dark; to become obscured; to grow dim; (*fig: sguardo*) to cloud over
oftalmia [oftal'mia] SF ophthalmia
oftalmico, a, ci, che [of'talmiko] AGG ophthalmic
oftalmoscopio [oftalmos'kɔpjo] SM ophthalmoscope
oggettivamente [oddʒettiva'mente] AVV objectively
oggettivare [oddʒetti'vare] VT to objectify
▶ **oggettivarsi** VIP to become concrete
oggettività [oddʒettivi'ta] SF objectivity
oggettivo, a [oddʒet'tivo] AGG objective; **proposizione oggettiva** (*Gramm*) object clause
oggetto [od'dʒɛtto] SM **1** (*cosa, articolo*) object, thing; **un oggetto rotondo** a round object; **oggetti preziosi** valuables, articles of value; **oggetti smarriti** lost property *sg* (*Brit*), lost-and-found *sg* (*Am*); **dov'è l'ufficio oggetti smarriti?** where's the lost property office? **2** (*di disputa, discorso, studio*) subject; (*di sogni, pensieri*) object; **essere oggetto di** (*critiche, controversia*) to be the subject of; (*odio, pietà*) to be the object of; **essere oggetto di scherno** to be a laughing stock; **essere oggetto di persecuzione** to be subjected to persecution **3** (*di attività, contratto*) object, purpose **4** (*in lettere commerciali*): **oggetto...** re ...; **in oggetto a quanto detto** as regards the (matter mentioned) above **5** (*Gramm, Filosofia*) object
oggi ['ɔddʒi] AVV today; (*al presente, al giorno d'oggi*) today, nowadays, these days; **oggi è venerdì** it's Friday today; **il giornale di oggi** today's paper; **oggi stesso** today, this very day; **lo farò oggi stesso** I'll do it today; **oggi nel pomeriggio** this afternoon; **oggi (a) otto** a week today, today week; **quanti ne abbiamo oggi?** what's the date today?; **oggi come oggi** at present, as things stand; **oggi qui, domani là** (*fig*) here today, gone tomorrow; **oggi o domani** (*fig*) sooner or later; **oggi a me, domani a te** (*fig*) your day will come; **dagli oggi, dagli domani** in the long run, over time
■ SM today; **dall'oggi al domani** from one day to the next; **potrebbe cambiare tutto dall'oggi al domani** everything could change from one day to the next; **a tutt'oggi** up till now, till today; **le spese a tutt'oggi sono...** expenses to date are ...
oggidì [oddʒi'di] AVV nowadays
oggigiorno [oddʒi'dʒorno] AVV nowadays, these days
■ SM today
ogiva [o'dʒiva] SF ogive, pointed arch
OGM [ɔdʒi'ɛmme] SIGLA MPL (= **Organismi Geneticamente Modificati**) GMOs (= *Genetically Modified Organisms*)
ogni ['oɲɲi] AGG **1** (*ciascuno*) every, each; (*tutti*) all; **ogni passeggero** every *o* each passenger; **ogni cosa** everything; **lo vedo ogni giorno** I see him every day; **ogni sorta di articoli** all sorts *pl* of goods **2** (*qualsiasi*) any, all; **ad ogni costo** at any price, at all costs; **gente d'ogni tipo** people of all sorts; **c'era gente di ogni tipo** there were all sorts of people **3** (*con valore distributivo*) every; **ogni due giorni** every two days, every other day; **viene ogni due giorni** he comes every two days; **l'autobus passa ogni 20 minuti** the bus comes past every 20 minutes; **una persona ogni cento** one person in every hundred **4** (*fraseologia*): **in ogni caso** at any rate, in any case; anyway; **penso che dovresti telefonargli in ogni caso** I think you should phone him anyway; **in ogni luogo** everywhere; **da ogni parte** from everywhere; **in** *o* **ad ogni modo** anyway, anyhow; **ogni tanto** every so often, every now and then; **ogni tanto le scrivo** I write to her every so often; **ogni volta che** every time (that), whenever
ogniqualvolta [oɲɲikwal'vɔlta] CONG whenever
Ognissanti [oɲɲis'santi] SM All Saints' Day
ognuno [oɲ'ɲuno] PRON (*tutti*) everybody, everyone; (*ciascuno*) each (one); **ognuno di noi sa quello che vuole** each of us knows what he wants, we all know what we want; **ad ognuno di voi verrà dato un questionario** each of you will be given a questionnaire; **ognuno ha il diritto di dire quello che pensa** everybody has the right to say what they think
oh [ɔ, o] ESCL *vedi* **o**[2]
ohi ['ɔi] ESCL (*esprime disappunto, spesso ripetuto*) oh!; (*esprime dolore*) ow!; **ohi là!** hey there!
ohimè [oi'mɛ] ESCL oh dear!
Ohio [əu'haɪəu] SM Ohio
OIL ['ɔil] SIGLA F (= **Organizzazione Internazionale del Lavoro**) ILO (= *International Labour Organisation*)
▷ www.ilo.org/public/italian/region/eurpro/rome/
okapi [o'kapi] SM INV (*animale*) okapi
okay ['oukei] ESCL O.K.!, okay!
■ SM INV okay; **ricevere l'okay** to get the okay *o* the go-ahead; **dare l'okay a qc** to okay sth; **ti hanno messo l'okay sul biglietto?** have they confirmed your ticket?
Oklahoma [okla'oma] SM Oklahoma
OL ABBR (= **onde lunghe**) LW (= *long wave*)
ola ['ola] SF (*allo stadio*) Mexican wave
Olanda [o'landa] SF Holland; **mi è piaciuta molto l'Olanda** I liked Holland very much; **andrò in Olanda in giugno** I'm going to Holland in June
olandese [olan'dese] AGG Dutch
■ SM/F Dutchman/Dutchwoman; **gli Olandesi** the Dutch

Oo

■SM **1** (*lingua*) Dutch; **parla olandese** he speaks Dutch **2** (*formaggio*) Dutch cheese
oleaginoso, a [oleadʒi'noso] AGG oleaginous
oleandro [ole'andro] SM oleander
oleario, ria, ri, rie [ole'arjo] AGG oil *attr*
oleato, a [ole'ato] AGG: **carta oleata** greaseproof paper (*Brit*), wax paper (*Am*)
oleificio, ci [olei'fitʃo] SM oil mill
oleodotto [oleo'dɔtto] SM oil pipeline
oleografia [oleogra'fia] SF **1** (*tecnica*) oleography **2** (*riproduzione*) oleograph; (*fig pegg*) imitative painting
oleografico, a, ci, che [oleo'grafiko] AGG oleographic; (*fig pegg*) imitative
oleoso, a [ole'oso] AGG oily; (*che contiene olio*) oil *attr*
olezzo [o'leddzo] SM fragrance; (*scherz: puzzo*) aroma
olfatto [ol'fatto] SM sense of smell
oliare [o'ljare] VT (*meccanismo*) to oil, lubricate; (*Culin*) to grease
oliatore [olja'tore] SM (*recipiente*) oilcan; (*dispositivo*) oiler
oliera [o'ljɛra] SF oil and vinegar cruet
oligarchia [oligar'kia] SF oligarchy
oligarchico, a, ci, che [oli'garkiko] AGG oligarchic(al)
Olimpiadi [olim'piadi] SFPL: **le Olimpiadi** the Olympics, the Olympic games
olimpico, a, ci, che [o'limpiko] AGG Olympic
olimpionico, a, ci, che [olim'pjɔniko] AGG Olympic
■SM/F (*concorrente*) competitor in the Olympics; (*campione*) Olympic champion
Olimpo [o'limpo] SM (*Geog, Mitol*): **(monte) Olimpo** (Mount) Olympus
olio, oli ['ɔljo] SM **1** oil; **sott'olio** (*Culin*) in oil; **tonno/funghi sott'olio** tuna/mushrooms in oil; **il mare è un olio** the sea is like a millpond; **gettare olio sul fuoco** (*fig*) to add fuel to the flames; **una lampada ad olio** an oil lamp; **oli essenziali** essential oils; **olio essenziale di timo** thyme essential oil; **olio di fegato di merluzzo** cod-liver oil; **olio dei freni** (*Aut*) brake fluid; **olio di lino** linseed oil; **olio lubrificante** lubricating oil; **olio d'oliva** olive oil
▷ www.guidaolio.com/
olio di semi vegetable oil; **olio solare** suntan oil **2** (*Rel*): **olio santo** holy oil; **dare l'olio santo a qn** to give sb Extreme Unction **3** (*Pittura*): **un (quadro a) olio** an oil painting; **dipingere a olio** to paint in oils
olistica [o'listika] SF holistic medicine
olistico, a, ci, che [o'listiko] AGG holistic
oliva [o'liva] SF olive
■AGG INV (*colore*) olive(-green)
olivastro, a [oli'vastro] AGG (*colore*) olive-greenish, olive(-coloured) (*Brit*), olive(-colored) (*Am*); (*carnagione*) olive
oliveto [oli'veto] SM olive grove
olivicoltore [olivikol'tore] SM olive grower
olivicoltura [olivikol'tura] SF olive growing
olivo [o'livo] SM olive tree
olmaria [ol'marja] SF (*pianta*) meadowsweet
olmo ['ɔlmo] SM elm
olocausto [olo'kausto] SM (*Rel, fig*) sacrifice; (*genocidio*) holocaust
olofitico, a, ci, che [olo'fitiko] AGG (*Bot*) holophytic
olografia [ologra'fia] SF holography
ologramma, i [olo'gramma] SM hologram
oloturia [olo'turja] SF (*echinoderma*) holothurian
oloturoideo [oloturoi'dɛo] SM sea slug
OLP [ɔlp] SIGLA F (= **Organizzazione per la Liberazione della Palestina**) PLO (= *Palestine Liberation Organization*)
oltraggiare [oltrad'dʒare] VT to offend, insult
oltraggio, gi [ol'traddʒo] SM **1** (*insulto*) insult, offence (*Brit*), offense (*Am*); **fare un oltraggio a** to offend, insult; **subire un oltraggio** to suffer an affront **2** (*Dir*): **accusato di oltraggio a pubblico ufficiale** charged with insulting a public official; **oltraggio alla corte** contempt of court; **oltraggio al pudore** indecent exposure
oltraggiosamente [oltraddʒosa'mente] AVV insultingly, offensively
oltraggioso, a [oltrad'dʒoso] AGG (*offensivo*) insulting, offensive
oltralpe [ol'tralpe] AVV on the other side of the Alps, beyond the Alps; **un paese d'oltralpe** a country beyond the Alps
oltranza [ol'trantsa] SF: **a** *o* **ad oltranza** to the (bitter) end; **continueremo ad oltranza** we'll go on to the bitter end; **sciopero ad oltranza** all-out strike
oltranzismo [oltran'tsismo] SM (*Pol*) extremism
oltranzista, i, e [oltran'tsista] SM/F (*Pol*) extremist
oltre ['oltre] AVV **1** (*di luogo: più in là*) farther, further; (: *fig*) further; **andare troppo oltre** (*fig*) to go too far **2** (*di tempo: di più*): **non...oltre** no more, no longer; **non posso aspettare oltre** I can't wait any longer **3** (*di età*) over; **persone di oltre trent'anni** people over thirty (years of age); **gli uomini oltre i cinquant'anni** men over fifty
■PREP **1** (*di luogo: di là da*) on the other side of, beyond, over; **l'ho gettato oltre il muro** I threw it over the wall; **sono passati oltre i confini** they crossed the border **2** (*di tempo, quantità: più di*) more than, over; **sono oltre 3 mesi che non ti vedo** I haven't seen you for more than *o* for over three months; **non oltre il 10 febbraio** not later than 10th February **3** (*in aggiunta a*): **oltre a** *o* **che** besides, as well as; **è anche piccola, oltre ad essere cara** it's small as well as being expensive; **oltre che piovere fa freddo** it's cold as well as wet; **oltre a tutto** on top of all that **4** (*all'infuori di, eccetto*): **oltre a** besides, except, apart from; **oltre a te non voglio vedere nessuno** apart from you, I don't want to see anyone
oltrecortina [oltrekor'tina] AVV behind the Iron Curtain; **paesi d'oltrecortina** Iron Curtain countries
oltremanica [oltre'manika] AVV across the Channel
oltremare [oltre'mare] AVV overseas; **paesi d'oltremare** overseas countries
oltremarino, a [oltrema'rino] AGG (*colore*) ultramarine
oltremodo [oltre'mɔdo] AVV extremely, greatly
oltreoceano [oltreo'tʃɛano] SM: **paesi d'oltreoceano** overseas countries
oltrepassare [oltrepas'sare] VT (*varcare*) to cross, go beyond; (*superare*) to exceed, go over; **oltrepassarono il confine** they crossed the border; **oltrepassare i limiti** *o* **la misura** (*fig*) to go too far; **questa volta hai oltrepassato ogni limite!** this time you've gone too far!
oltretomba [oltre'tomba] SM: **l'oltretomba** the hereafter
OM ABBR **1** (= **onde medie**) MW (= *medium wave*) **2** (*Mil*) = ospedale militare
omaggio, gi [o'maddʒo] SM **1** (*segno di rispetto*) homage, tribute; **rendere omaggio a** to pay homage *o* tribute to **2** (*dono*) gift; (*Comm*): **fare omaggio di un libro** to give a presentation copy of a book; **copia in omaggio** presentation *o* complimentary copy; **biglietto in omaggio** complimentary ticket, free ticket; **è un omaggio della ditta** it's a present from

the firm; **ecco un piccolo omaggio per le signore** here's a little gift for the ladies; **"in omaggio"** "free gift" **3 omaggi** SMPL (*ossequi*) respects, regards; **presentare i propri omaggi a qn** (*frm*) to pay one's respects to sb
■AGG INV free

Oman [o'man] SM Oman

ombelicale [ombeli'kale] AGG umbilical; **cordone ombelicale** umbilical cord

ombelico, chi [ombe'liko] SM navel

ombra ['ombra] SF **1** (*sagoma scura*) shadow; (*zona non assolata*) shade; (*oscurità*) darkness; **l'ombra di un grattacielo** the shadow of a skyscraper; **sedersi all'ombra (di)** to sit in the shade (of); **mi sedetti all'ombra** I sat down in the shade; **dare ombra a qn** (*fig*) to put sb in the shade; **essere l'ombra di se stesso** to be a shadow of one's former self; **aver paura della propria ombra** to be afraid of one's own shadow **2** (*fantasma*) shade (*letter*), ghost **3** (*fig: oscurità*) obscurity; **nell'ombra** (*tramare, agire*) secretly; **restare nell'ombra** (*persona*) to remain in obscurity **4** (*parvenza, traccia*): **non c'è ombra di verità in quello che dice** there isn't a grain of truth in what he says; **senza ombra di dubbio** without a shadow of a doubt; **un'ombra di burro** a hint *o* touch of butter
■AGG INV: **bandiera ombra** flag of convenience; **governo ombra** (*Pol*) shadow cabinet

ombratura [ombra'tura] SF dark patch

ombreggiare [ombred'dʒare] VT to shade

ombreggiatura [ombreddʒa'tura] SF shading

ombrellificio, ci [ombrelli'fitʃo] SM umbrella factory

ombrellino [ombrel'lino] SM (*parasole*) parasol

ombrello [om'brɛllo] SM (*also fig*) umbrella; **ombrello da sole** parasol, sunshade

ombrellone [ombrel'lone] SM (*da spiaggia*) beach umbrella; (*di caffè, bar*) sunshade

ombretto [om'bretto] SM eyeshadow

ombrosità [ombrosi'ta] SF (*vedi agg*) shadiness; skittishness; touchiness

ombroso, a [om'broso] AGG **1** (*bosco, viale*) shady, shaded **2** (*fig: cavallo*) skittish, nervous; (: *persona*) touchy, easily offended

OMC [oɛmme'tʃi] SIGLA F (= **Organizzazione Mondiale del Commercio**) WTO (= *World Trade Organization*)

omelette [ɔmə'lɛt] SF INV omelette (*Brit*), omelet (*Am*); **un'omelette al prosciutto** a ham omelette

omelia [ome'lia] SF (*Rel*) homily, sermon

omeopata [ome'ɔpata] SM/F homoeopath (*Brit*), homeopath (*Am*)

omeopatia [omeopa'tia] SF homoeopathy (*Brit*), homeopathy (*Am*)

omeopatico, a, ci, che [omeo'patiko] AGG homoeopathic (*Brit*), homeopathic (*Am*)

Omero ['ɔmero] SM Homer

omero ['ɔmero] SM (*Anat*) humerus

omertà [omer'ta] SF conspiracy of silence

omesso, a [o'messo] PP *di* **omettere**

omettere [o'mettere] VT IRREG to leave out, omit; **ho omesso un piccolo particolare** I left out one small detail; **omettere di fare qc** to neglect *o* omit *o* fail to do sth

ometto [o'metto] SM (*fig: bambino*) good little fellow

omiciattolo [omi'tʃattolo] SM creep

omicida, i, e [omi'tʃida] AGG (*maniaco, istinto, furia*) homicidal; (*sguardo, intenzione*) murderous
■SM/F murderer/murderess

omicidio, di [omi'tʃidjo] SM murder, homicide (*Am*); **commettere un omicidio** to commit a murder; **omicidio colposo** (*Dir*) manslaughter, second-degree murder (*Am*); **omicidio premeditato** (*Dir*) murder, first-degree murder (*Am*)

ominide [o'minide] SM hominid

omisi *ecc* [o'mizi] VB *vedi* **omettere**

omissione [omis'sjone] SF **1** (*non inclusione*) omission; **nell'elenco c'erano molte omissioni** there were a lot of omissions from the list; **salvo errori e omissioni** errors and omissions excepted **2** (*Dir*): **reato d'omissione** criminal negligence; **omissione di atti d'ufficio** negligence (*by a public employee*); **omissione di denuncia** failure to report a crime; **omissione di soccorso** failure to stop and give assistance

omnibus ['ɔmnibus] SM INV (*Storia*) horse-drawn omnibus

omofobia [omofo'bia] SF homophobia

omofobo, a [o'mɔfobo] AGG homophobic

omogeneamente [omodʒenea'mente] AVV homogeneously

omogeneità [omodʒenei'ta] SF homogeneity

omogeneizzare [omodʒeneid'dzare] VT to homogenize

omogeneizzato, a [omodʒeneid'dzato] AGG homogenized
■SM (*per bambini*) baby food

omogeneo, a [omo'dʒɛneo] AGG (*gen*) homogeneous; (*fig: insieme di colori*) harmonious

omografo, a [o'mɔgrafo] SM homograph
■AGG homographic

omologare [omolo'gare] VT (*Dir*) to approve, sanction; (*ratificare*) to ratify; **macchina omologata per 5 persone** car authorized to carry 5 people

omologazione [omologat'tsjone] SF (*vedi vb*) approval, sanction; ratification

omologo, a, ghi, ghe [o'mɔlogo] AGG homologous, corresponding; (*Chim*) homologous; **inseminazione artificiale omologa** AIH
■SM/F opposite number, counterpart

omonimia [omoni'mia] SF homonymy; **si tratta di un caso di omonimia** it must be somebody else of the same name

omonimo, a [o'mɔnimo] AGG (*persone, cose*) with the same name; **il film Lolita, tratto dall'omonimo romanzo** the film "Lolita", adapted from the book of the same name
■SM/F (*persona*) namesake; **è un mio omonimo** he's got the same name as me
■SM (*Gramm*) homonym

omosessuale [omosessu'ale] AGG, SM/F homosexual

omosessualità [omosessuali'ta] SF homosexuality

omozigote [omoddzi'gɔte] SM homozygote

OMS [o'ɛmme'ɛsse] SIGLA F (= **Organizzazione Mondiale della Sanità**) WHO (= *World Health Organization*)

omuncolo [o'munkolo] SM = **omiciattolo**

On. ABBR (*Pol*) = **onorevole**

onanismo [ona'nizmo] SM onanism

oncia, ce ['ontʃa] SF (*unità di misura*) ounce

oncologia [onkolo'dʒia] SF oncology

oncologico, a, ci, che [onko'lɔdʒiko] AGG oncological

oncologo, a, gi, ghe [on'kɔlogo] SM/F oncologist

onda ['onda] SF **1** (*flutto, fig*) wave; **si è tuffato tra le onde** he dived into the waves; **un'onda di commozione** a wave *o* surge of excitement; **capelli a onde** wavy hair; **onda lunga** roller; **onda verde** (*Aut*) synchronized traffic lights *pl* **2** (*Fis*) wave; **andare in**

onda (*Radio, TV*) to go on the air, be broadcast, be on; **il programma va in onda alle sei** the programme is on at six o'clock; **mettere** *o* **mandare in onda** (*Radio, TV*) to broadcast; **onde corte** short wave *sg*; **onde lunghe** long wave *sg*; **onde medie** medium wave *sg*

ondata [on'data] SF (*flutto*) wave; (*fig*) wave, surge; **a ondate** (*muovere, avanzare*) in waves; **un'ondata di turisti** an influx of tourists; **un'ondata di entusiasmo** a wave *o* surge of enthusiasm; **un'ondata di caldo** a heatwave; **un'ondata di freddo** a cold spell *o* snap

onde ['onde] CONG (*frm: affinché: con l'infinito*) in order to, so as to; (*: con il congiuntivo*) so that, in order that

ondeggiare [onded'dʒare] VI (*aus* **avere**) (*acqua, superficie, grano*) to ripple; (*bandiera*) to flutter; (*muoversi sulle onde: barca*) to rock, roll; (*fig: folla, alberi, edificio*) to sway; (*: persona: essere incerto*) to waver, hesitate

ondoso, a [on'doso] AGG (*moto*) of the waves

ondulare [ondu'lare] VT (*capelli*) to wave

ondulato, a [ondu'lato] AGG (*capelli*) wavy; (*terreno*) undulating; **cartone ondulato** corrugated paper; **lamiera ondulata** sheet of corrugated iron

ondulatorio, ria, ri, rie [ondula'tɔrjo] AGG (*movimento*) undulating; (*Fis*) undulatory, wave *attr*

ondulazione [ondulat'tsjone] SF undulation; (*di capelli*) wave

onerato, a [one'rato] AGG: **onerato di** burdened with, loaded with

onere ['ɔnere] SM (*peso*) burden; (*responsabilità*) responsibility; **onere finanziario** financial burden; **oneri fiscali** taxes

onerosamente [onerosa'mente] AVV heavily

oneroso, a [one'roso] AGG (*compito*) onerous; (*tasse, pena*) heavy; (*condizioni di contratto*) hard

onestà [ones'ta] SF (*vedi agg*) honesty; fairness; virtue; chastity

onestamente [onesta'mente] AVV (*vedi agg*) honestly; fairly; virtuously; (*in verità*) honestly, frankly

onesto, a [o'nɛsto] AGG (*probo, retto*) honest; (*giusto: persona, prezzi*) fair; (*virtuoso, pudico*) virtuous; (*casto*) chaste; **è una persona onesta** he's an honest person; **mi sembra un prezzo onesto** it seems a fair price; **con intenzioni poco oneste** with dubious intentions

ONG [ɔenne'dʒi] SIGLA F INV (= **Organizzazione Non Governativa**) NGO (= *Non-Governmental Organization*)

onice ['ɔnitʃe] SF onyx

onirico, a, ci, che [o'niriko] AGG dreamlike, dream *attr*

onisco, schi [o'nisko] SM woodlouse

onnipotente [onnipo'tɛnte] AGG omnipotent, all-powerful; **Dio onnipotente** Almighty God
■ SM: **l'Onnipotente** (*Rel*) the Almighty

onnipresente [onnipre'zɛnte] AGG (*of God*) omnipresent; (*fig*) ubiquitous

onnisciente [onniʃ'ʃɛnte] AGG omniscient

onniveggente [onnived'dʒɛnte] AGG all-seeing

onnivoro, a [on'nivoro] AGG omnivorous
■ SM omnivore

onomastico, ci [ono'mastiko] SM name day; **oggi è il mio onomastico** today's my name day

onomatopea [onomato'pɛa] SF onomatopoeia

onomatopeico, a, ci, che [onomato'pɛiko] AGG onomatopoeic

onoranze [ono'rantse] SFPL honours (*Brit*), honors (*Am*); **onoranze funebri** funeral hono(u)rs

onorare [ono'rare] VT (*gen*) to honour (*Brit*), honor (*Am*); (*far onore a*) to be a credit to, do credit to; **onorare qn con** *o* **di qc** to hono(u)r sb with sth; **onorare una cambiale** (*Comm*) to hono(u)r a bill
▶ **onorarsi** VR: **onorarsi di qc/di fare qc** to feel hono(u)red by sth/to do sth

onorario, ria, ri, rie [ono'rarjo] AGG honorary
■ SM fee

onoratissimo, a [onora'tissimo] AGG (*in presentazioni*): **onoratissimo!** delighted to meet you!

onorato, a [ono'rato] AGG (*reputazione, famiglia, carriera*) distinguished; **essere onorato di fare qc** to have the honour (*Brit*) *o* honor (*Am*) to do sth *o* of doing sth; **onorato di conoscerla** (it is) a pleasure to meet you

onore [o'nore] SM **1** (*reputazione, integrità*) honour (*Brit*), honor (*Am*); **giuro sul mio onore che...** I swear on my hono(u)r that ... **2** (*omaggio*) hono(u)r; **rendere onore a qn/qc** to hono(u)r sb/sth **3** (*privilegio*) hono(u)r, privilege; **è un onore per me** it's an hono(u)r for me; **aver l'onore di** to have the hono(u)r of; **posto d'onore** place of hono(u)r **4** (*merito*) credit; **fare onore ai genitori** to be a credit to one's parents; **farsi onore** to distinguish oneself; **si è fatto onore agli esami** he distinguished himself in the exams **5** **onori** SMPL (*onorificenze*) hono(u)rs **6** (*Carte*) hono(u)r (card) **7** (*fraseologia*): **in onore di** in hono(u)r of; **a onor del vero** to tell the truth; **fare onore alla tavola** to do justice to the dinner; **fare gli onori di casa** to play host (*o* hostess), act as host; **Paolo ha fatto gli onori di casa** Paolo acted as host

onorevole [ono'revole] AGG honourable (*Brit*), honorable (*Am*); (*Pol: titolo*): **l'Onorevole...** the Honourable ...
■ SM/F (*Pol*): **Onorevole** ≈ Member of Parliament (*Brit*), ≈ Congressman/Congresswoman (*Am*)

onorevolmente [onorevol'mente] AVV honourably (*Brit*), honorably (*Am*)

onorificenza [onorifi'tʃɛntsa] SF honour (*Brit*), honor (*Am*); (*decorazione*) decoration

onorifico, a, ci, che [ono'rifiko] AGG honorary

onta ['onta] SF **1** (*vergogna*) shame, disgrace; (*affronto*) insult, affront **2** **ad onta di** despite, notwithstanding

ontano [on'tano] SM alder

ontologia [ontolo'dʒia] SF ontology

ONU ['ɔnu] SIGLA F (= **Organizzazione delle Nazioni Unite**) UN, UNO (= *United Nations (Organization)*)
▷ www.onuitalia.it/

OO.PP. ABBR = **opere pubbliche**

OPA ABBR = **offerta pubblica d'acquisto**

opacità [opatʃi'ta] SF (*vedi agg*) opaqueness, opacity; matt quality; dullness

opaco, a, chi, che [o'pako] AGG (*vetro, corpo*) opaque; (*carta*) matt; (*metallo, colore, fig: voce, sguardo, mente*) dull

opale [o'pale] SM O F opal

opalescenza [opaleʃ'ʃɛntsa] SF opalescence

opalina [opa'lina] SF (*vetro*) opaline

OPEC ['opek] SIGLA F OPEC (= *Organization of Petroleum Exporting Countries*)

open ['oupən] AGG INV (*torneo, biglietto*) open
■ SM INV (*Sport*) open (tournament)

òpera ['ɔpera] SF **1** (*attività, lavoro*) work; (*azione rilevante*) action, deed, work; **mettersi/essere all'opera** to get down to/be at work; **vedere qn all'opera** to see sb in action; **abbiamo ottenuto quell'aumento per opera sua** it was thanks to him that we got the rise; **fare opera di persuasione presso qn** to try to convince sb; **fare opere buone** *o* **di carità** to do good works *o* works of charity **2** (*lavoro*

materiale) work, piece of work; **opera di scavo** excavation work *sg*; **opere pubbliche** (*Amm*) public works; **opere di restauro** restoration work *sg* **3** (*produzione artistica: nell'insieme*) works *pl*; (*: libro, quadro*) work; **le opere più importanti di Dante** Dante's most important works; **opera d'arte** work of art **4** (*ente*) foundation, institution, organization; **opera pia** religious charity **5** (*Mus*) opus; (*: melodramma*) opera; (*: teatro*) opera (house); **opera buffa** comic opera; **opera lirica** (grand) opera **6** (*Naut*): **opera morta** topsides *pl*; **opera viva** bottom
▷ www.giuseppeverdi.it/
▷ www.puccini.it/portaleit.htm
▷ www.teatroallascala.org/public/LaScala/index.html

operaio, aia, ai, aie [ope'rajo] AGG **1** (*movimento, partito*) workers' *attr*; (*prete*) worker *attr*; **classe operaia** working class; **movimento operaio** labour movement; **quartiere operaio** working-class district **2** (*Zool: ape, formica*) worker *attr*
■SM worker, workman; **operaio di fabbrica** factory worker; **operaio a giornata** day labourer (*Brit*) *o* laborer (*Am*); **operaio non specializzato** semi-skilled worker; **operaio qualificato** *o* **specializzato** skilled worker
■SF female worker

operante [ope'rante] AGG: **divenire operante** (*legge, piano*) to take effect; **essere operante** (*fabbrica*) to be operative

operare [ope'rare] VT **1** (*riforma*) to carry out, make; (*effetto*) to produce; **operare miracoli** to work wonders **2** (*Med*) to operate on; **il chirurgo ha operato Mario di appendicite** the surgeon operated on Mario for appendicitis; **Matteo è stato operato allo stomaco** Matteo had an operation on his stomach; **operare qn d'urgenza** to perform an emergency operation on sb
■VI (*aus* **avere**) **1** (*agire*) to act, work; (*Mil, Comm*) to operate **2** (*Med*) to operate; **hanno dovuto operare d'urgenza** they had to do an emergency operation;
▶ **operarsi** VIP **1** (*verificarsi*) to take place, occur **2** (*Med*) to have an operation; **dovrò operarmi la prossima settimana** I'm going to have an operation next week; **operarsi d'ernia** to have a hernia operation; **operarsi d'appendicite** to have one's appendix out; **si è operato d'appendicite** he had his appendix out

operativamente [operativa'mente] AVV (*mettere in atto, entrare in funzione*) effectively

operativo, a [opera'tivo] AGG operative, operating; **piano operativo** (*Mil*) plan of operations

operato, a [ope'rato] SM (*comportamento*) actions *pl*
■SM/F (*Med*) patient (*who has undergone an operation*)
■AGG (*tessuto*) diapered; (*carta*) embossed; (*cuoio*) tooled

operatore, trice [opera'tore] SM/F **1** (*TV, Cine*) cameraman/camerawoman; (*Inform*) operator; **operatore cinematografico** projectionist; **operatore ecologico** refuse collector; **operatore del suono** sound recordist **2** (*Econ*) agent; **gli operatori economici del settore** those with commercial interests in that sector; **aperto solo agli operatori** (*Comm*) open to the trade only; **operatore di borsa** dealer on the stock exchange; **operatore economico** agent, broker; **operatore turistico** tour operator

operatorio, ria, ri, rie [opera'tɔrjo] AGG (*Med*) operating

operazione [operat'tsjone] SF (*gen, Med, Mil, Mat*) operation; (*Econ*) transaction

opercolo [o'pɛrkolo] SM (*Bot, Zool*) operculum

operetta [ope'retta] SF (*Mus*) operetta, light opera

operettistico, a, ci, che [operet'tistiko] AGG operetta *attr*

operistico, a, ci, che [ope'ristiko] AGG opera *attr*

operosamente [operosa'mente] AVV industriously

operosità [operosi'ta] SF industry, industriousness

operoso, a [ope'roso] AGG (*attivo*) industrious, hard-working

opificio, ci [opi'fitʃo] SM (*ant*) factory, works *pl*

opinabile [opi'nabile] AGG (*discutibile*) debatable, questionable; **è opinabile** it is a matter of opinion

opinione [opi'njone] SF opinion; **vorrei sapere qual è la tua opinione su di lui** I'd like to know your opinion of him; **secondo la mia opinione** in my opinion; **avere il coraggio delle proprie opinioni** to have the courage of one's convictions; **l'opinione pubblica** public opinion

opinionista, i, e [opinjo'nista] SM/F (political) columnist

op là [op'la] ESCL (*per far saltare*) hup!; (*un bimbo che è caduto*) upsy-daisy!

opossum [o'pɔssum] SM INV opossum

oppio ['ɔppjo] SM opium

oppiomane [op'pjɔmane] SM/F opium addict

opponente [oppo'nɛnte] SM/F opponent
■AGG opposing

oppongo *ecc* [op'pongo] VB *vedi* **opporre**

opporre [op'porre] VB IRREG
■VT **1** (*ragioni, argomenti*) to put forward; **opporre resistenza** to put up a struggle; **si sono arresi senza opporre resistenza** they surrendered without putting up a struggle; **opporre un netto rifiuto a** to give a clear-cut refusal to **2** (*obiettare*) to object; **non ho nulla da opporre** I have no objection;
▶ **opporsi** VR (*fare opposizione*) **opporsi (a)** (*nemico*) to oppose; (*proposta*) to object (to); **ci siamo opposti alla proposta** we objected to the proposal; **mi oppongo alla sua idea** I am opposed to *o* against his idea

opportunamente [opportuna'mente] AVV (*intervenire*) opportunely, at the right time; (*decidere*) conveniently

opportunismo [opportu'nizmo] SM opportunism

opportunista, i, e [opportu'nista] SM/F opportunist; **è un opportunista** he's an opportunist

opportunisticamente [opportunistika'mente] AVV opportunistically

opportunistico, a, ci, che [opportu'nistiko] AGG opportunist(ic)

opportunità [opportuni'ta] SF INV **1** (*convenienza*) opportuneness, timeliness; **avere il senso dell'opportunità** to have a sense of timing **2** (*occasione*) opportunity; **una grossa opportunità** a big opportunity; **avere l'opportunità di fare qc** to have the opportunity of *o* for doing *o* to do sth; **non ho avuto l'opportunità di parlargli** I didn't have the opportunity to speak to him; **Commissione per le Pari Opportunità** Equal Opportunities Commission

opportuno, a [oppor'tuno] AGG (*adatto, conveniente*) opportune, timely; (*giusto*) right, appropriate; **non era il momento opportuno per parlarne** it wasn't the right moment to talk about it; **a tempo opportuno** at the right *o* the appropriate time; **ritengo opportuno che tu gli scriva** I think you should write to him, I think it would be advisable for you to write to him

opposi *ecc* [op'posi] VB *vedi* **opporre**

oppositore, trice [oppozi'tore] SM/F opponent, opposer
■AGG opposing

opposizione [oppozit'tsjone] SF **1** (*resistenza*)

Oo

opposition; (*Pol*): **l'Opposizione** the Opposition; **i partiti dell'opposizione** the opposition parties; **fare opposizione a qn/qc** to oppose sb/sth **2** (*contrasto*) opposition; **essere in netta opposizione** (*idee, opinioni*) to clash, be in complete opposition **3** (*Dir*) objection

opposto, a [op'posto] PP *di* **opporre**
■ AGG **1** (*direzione, lato*) opposite; **veniva dalla direzione opposta** she was coming from the opposite direction **2** (*contrario: idee, vedute*) opposite, conflicting; **le sue idee sono opposte alle mie** his ideas conflict with mine, his ideas are the opposite of mine; **hanno opinioni opposte** they have very different ideas
■ SM: **l'opposto** the opposite, the contrary; **all'opposto** on the contrary; **io, all'opposto di te, non li approvo** unlike you, I don't approve of them

oppressione [oppres'sjone] SF (*Pol*) oppression; (*fisica, morale*) feeling of oppression

oppressivo, a [oppres'sivo] AGG oppressive

oppresso, a [op'prɛsso] PP *di* **opprimere**
■ AGG oppressed
■ **gli oppressi** SMPL the oppressed

oppressore [oppres'sore] SM oppressor
■ AGG oppressive

opprimente [oppri'mɛnte] AGG (*caldo, noia*) oppressive; (*persona: deprimente*) depressing; (*fidanzato: soffocante*) possessive

opprimere [op'primere] VT IRREG **1** (*sogg: caldo, afa*) to suffocate, oppress; **cibo che opprime lo stomaco** food that lies heavy on the stomach **2** (*sogg: ansia, lavoro*) to weigh down, weigh heavily on; **il lavoro mi opprime** my work is getting me down; **mi opprime con la sua gelosia** his jealousy is suffocating me **3** (*tiranneggiare: popolo*) to oppress

oppugnare [oppuɲ'ɲare] VT (*letter fig: dottrina*) to refute

oppugnazione [oppuɲɲat'tsjone] SF (*letter fig*) refutation

oppure [op'pure] CONG (*o invece*) or; (*altrimenti*) otherwise, or (else); **possiamo guardare la TV oppure noleggiare un video** we can watch TV or rent a video

optare [op'tare] VI (*aus* **avere**) **optare per** (*scegliere*) to opt for, decide upon; (*Borsa*) to take (out) an option on

optimum ['ɔptimum] SM INV optimum

optional ['ɔpʃənəl] SM INV optional extra

optometria [optome'tria] SF optometry

opulento, a [opu'lɛnto] AGG (*ricco: paese, società*) rich, wealthy, affluent; (: *stile letterario*) opulent

opulenza [opu'lɛntsa] SF (*vedi agg*) richness, wealth, affluence; opulence

opuscolo [o'puskolo] SM (*letterario, scientifico*) booklet, pamphlet; (*pubblicitario*) brochure, leaflet

OPV ABBR = **offerta pubblica di vendita**

opzionale [optsjo'nale] AGG optional

opzione [op'tsjone] SF (*gen, Comm*) option; **diritto di opzione** (*Borsa*) (right of) option

OR SIGLA = *Oristano*

ora ['ora] SF
1 (*unità di tempo, durata*) hour; **tre ore e mezza** three and a half hours; **mezz'ora** half an hour; **durante le ore d'ufficio** during office hours; **è a un'ora di cammino/d'auto dalla stazione** it's an hour's walk/drive from the station; **aspetto da un'ora** I've been waiting for an hour; **pagare a ore** to pay by the hour; **sono pagati a ore** they're paid by the hour; **all'ora** an hour; **lo pagano 30 euro all'ora** they pay him 30 euros an hour; **70 km all'ora** 70 km an hour
2 (*parte della giornata*): **che ora è?, che ore sono?** — **sono le 4** what time is it? — it's 4 (o'clock); **che ora fai?** what time do you make it?; **a che ora ci vediamo?** what time *o* when shall we meet?; **a che ora parti?** what time are you leaving?; **ora legale** summer time (*Brit*), daylight saving time (*Am*); **ora locale** local time
3 (*momento*) time; **domani a quest'ora** this time tomorrow; **l'ora di pranzo** lunchtime; **l'ora dei pasti** mealtimes; **è ora di partire** it's time to go; **era ora!** about time too!; **le notizie dell'ultima ora** the latest news; **ora di punta** (*Aut*) rush hour; **il traffico dell'ora di punta** the rush hour traffic; **l'ora X** zero hour
4 (*fraseologia*): **non vedo l'ora di finire** I'm looking forward to finishing; (*excitement, frustration*) I can't wait to finish; **non vedo l'ora di dirglielo** I can't wait to tell him; **non vedevo l'ora che arrivasse l'estate** I couldn't wait for summer (to come); **fare le ore piccole** to stay up till the early *o* small hours (of the morning); **di buon'ora** early; **alla buon'ora!** at last!; **di ora in ora** hourly, hour by hour
■ AVV
1 (*adesso*) now; **ora sto meglio** I'm better now; **ora non posso uscire** I can't go out (just) now; **ora sono molto occupata** I'm very busy at the moment; **d'ora in avanti** *o* **poi** from now on; **ora come ora** right now, at present; **per ora** for now
2 (*poco fa*): **è uscito (proprio) ora** he's just gone out; **or ora** just now, a moment ago; **10 anni or sono** 10 years ago
3 (*tra poco*) in a moment, presently, in a minute; **ora arrivo** I'm just coming, I'll be right there
4 (*correlativo*): **ora...ora...** now ..., now ...; **ora qui ora lì** now here now there; **ora piange ora ride** one minute he's crying, the next he's laughing
■ CONG now; **ora che** now (that)

oracolo [o'rakolo] SM oracle

orafo, a ['ɔrafo] SM goldsmith
■ AGG (*arte*) goldsmith's *attr*, of a goldsmith

orale [o'rale] AGG, SM oral; **un esame orale** an oral exam

oralmente [oral'mente] AVV orally

oramai [ora'mai] AVV = **ormai**

orango, ghi [o'rango] SM, **orangutan** [orangu'tan] SM INV orang-utan

orario, ria, ri, rie [o'rarjo] AGG (*cambiamento, media*) hourly; (*velocità*) per hour; (*fuso, segnale*) time *attr*; **disco orario** parking disc; **segnale orario** time signal; **tariffa oraria** hourly rate; **in senso orario** clockwise
■ SM **1** (*di ufficio, visite*) hours *pl*, time(s *pl*); **qual è l'orario delle visite?** when's visiting time?; **fare l'orario ridotto** to be on short time; **in orario** on time; **orario di apertura** opening time; **orario di chiusura** closing time; **orario flessibile** (*Industria*) flexitime; **orario di lavoro** working hours *pl*; **orario di sportello** (*Banca*) bank opening hours *pl*; **orario d'ufficio** office hours *pl*, business hours *pl* **2** (*tabella*) timetable, schedule; **orario ferroviario** railway timetable

orata [o'rata] SF (*pesce*) sea bream

oratore, trice [ora'tore] SM/F (public) speaker, orator

oratoriamente [oratorja'mente] AVV oratorically

oratorio, ria, ri, rie [ora'tɔrjo] AGG oratorical
■ SM **1** (*cappella*) oratory **2** (*Mus*) oratorio
■ SF (*arte*) oratory

Orazio [o'rattsjo] SM Horace

orazione [orat'tsjone] SF **1** (*preghiera*) prayer

2 (*discorso*) oration, speech; **orazione funebre** funeral oration
orbene [or'bɛne] CONG (*letter*) well (then), so
orbita ['ɔrbita] SF **1** (*Anat*) (eye-)socket; **aveva gli occhi fuori dalle orbite** (*fig*) his eyes were popping out of his head **2** (*Astron, Fis*) orbit; **mettere in orbita** to put into orbit; **il razzo fu lanciato in orbita** the rocket was launched into orbit **3** (*fig: ambito d'influenza*) sphere of influence
orbitale [orbi'tale] AGG orbital
orbitare [orbi'tare] VI (*aus* **essere**) to orbit
orbo, a ['ɔrbo] AGG (*scherz*) blind; **e giù botte da orbi** and the fists were flying
orca, che ['ɔrka] SF (*Zool*) killer whale
Orcadi ['ɔrkadi] SFPL: **le (isole) Orcadi** the Orkney Islands, the Orkneys
orchestra [or'kɛstra] SF (*complesso di musicisti, strumenti musicali*) orchestra; (: *da ballo, jazz*) band; (*Teatro: spazio*) orchestra pit
orchestrale [orkes'trale] AGG orchestral
■ SM/F member of an orchestra, orchestra player
orchestrare [orkes'trare] VT (*Mus, fig*) to orchestrate
orchestrazione [orkestrat'tsjone] SF orchestration
orchidea [orki'dɛa] SF orchid
orcio, orci ['ortʃo] SM (earthenware) pot
orco, chi ['ɔrko] SM (*in fiabe*) ogre
orda ['ɔrda] SF (*Storia, fig*) horde
ordigno [or'diɲɲo] SM: **ordigno esplosivo** explosive device
ordinale [ordi'nale] AGG ordinal
■ SM ordinal (number)
ordinamento [ordina'mento] SM (*organizzazione*) order, arrangement; (*regolamento*) regulations *pl*, rules *pl*; **ordinamento giuridico** legal system; **ordinamento scolastico** education system
ordinanza [ordi'nantsa] SF **1** (*Dir*) order **2** (*Amm, decreto*) decree; **ordinanza municipale** by(e-)law **3** (*Mil*) order; (: *prescrizione*) regulation; (: *anche*: **soldato d'ordinanza**) batman, orderly; **d'ordinanza** (*pistola, divisa*) regulation *attr*
ordinare [ordi'nare] VT **1** (*mettere in ordine*) to organize, put in order, arrange **2** (*comandare*) to order; (*prescrivere: cura, medicina*) to prescribe; (*merce, pranzo*) to order; **hai già ordinato?** have you already ordered?; **ordinare che...** to order that ...; **ordinare a qn di fare qc** to order sb to do sth; **gli hanno ordinato di andarsene subito** they ordered him to leave immediately; **il medico mi ha ordinato di riposare** the doctor told me to rest **3** (*Rel: sacerdote*) to ordain
▶ **ordinarsi** VR (*disporsi*) **ordinarsi in fila/in colonna** to line up/form a column
ordinariamente [ordinarja'mente] AVV (*di solito*) ordinarily; (*comunemente*) frequently; (*con mezzi e modi usuali*) as usual, according to the usual practice
ordinarietà [ordinarje'ta] SF (*l'essere ordinario*) ordinary nature; (*pegg: qualità scadente*) mediocrity
ordinario, ria, ri, rie [ordi'narjo] AGG **1** (*consueto, normale*) ordinary, usual; (: *tariffa, spedizione, seduta*) ordinary; **spese ordinarie** ordinary expenses; **di statura ordinaria** of average height; **di ordinaria amministrazione** (*fig*) routine *attr* **2** (*rozzo: persona*) common, coarse; (*scadente: materiale, stoffa*) poor-quality; **è una donna ordinaria** she's just an ordinary woman **3** (*professore: Scol*) permanent; (: *Univ*) full
■ SM **1** **l'ordinario** the ordinary; **fuori dall'ordinario** out of the ordinary; **d'ordinario** usually, as a rule **2** (*Scol*) permanent teacher; (*Univ*) (full) professor
ordinata [ordi'nata] SF (*Mat*) ordinate, y-axis
ordinatamente [ordinata'mente] AVV (*gen*) tidily; (*metodicamente*) methodically
ordinativo, a [ordina'tivo] AGG governing, regulating
■ SM (*Comm*) order
ordinato, a [ordi'nato] AGG (*casa, persona*) tidy, orderly; (*vita*) well-ordered; (*impiegato*) methodical; (*corteo*) orderly; **è la persona più ordinata che abbia mai conosciuto** he's the tidiest person I've ever met
ordinazione [ordinat'tsjone] SF **1** (*Comm*) order; **fare un'ordinazione di qc** to put in an order for sth, order sth; **eseguire qc su ordinazione** to make sth to order **2** (*Rel*) ordination
ordine ['ordine] SM
1 (*disposizione, sequenza*) order; **in ordine alfabetico** in alphabetical order; **in ordine di anzianità/importanza** in order of seniority/importance; **in ordine di battaglia** (*Mil*) in battle order; **ritirarsi in buon ordine** (*Mil*) to retreat in good order; (*fig*) to back down gracefully; **ciò è nell'ordine naturale delle cose** it's in the nature of things
2 (*di persona, camera*) tidiness, orderliness; **in ordine** (*documenti*) in order; (*casa*) tidy, orderly; **essere/tenere in ordine** to be/keep in order; **la casa è in ordine** the house is tidy; **mettere in ordine** to tidy (up), put in order; **stavano mettendo in ordine la loro camera** they were tidying up their room; **mettersi in ordine** to tidy (o.s.) up
3 (*categoria: Archit, Bio*) order
4 (*associazione*) association, order; (: *Rel*) order; **l'ordine degli avvocati** ≈ the Bar **l'ordine dei medici** ≈ the British *o* American Medical Association
5 (*carattere*): **questioni di ordine pratico/generale** questions of a practical/general nature; **un affare dell'ordine di 20 milioni** a deal of the order of 20 million; **di prim'ordine** (*albergo, merce*) first-class; **non rientra nel mio ordine di idee** that's not the way I see things
6 (*principio d'organizzazione*) order; **richiamare all'ordine** to call to order; **le forze dell'ordine** the police; **l'ordine pubblico** law and order, public order; **l'ordine costituito** the established order
7 **ordini** SMPL (*Rel*) (Holy) Orders; **ordini minori/maggiori** minor/major orders
8 (*comando*) order, command; **ho l'ordine di non farvi entrare** I've been told not to let you in; **dare (l')ordine di fare qc** to give the order to do sth; **essere agli ordini di qn** (*Mil*) to be under sb's command; (*fig*) to be at sb's beck and call; **per ordine del preside** by order of the headmaster; **fino a nuovo ordine** until further orders
9 (*Comm, Fin*) order; **pagabile all'ordine di** payable to the order of; **ordine d'acquisto** purchase order; **ordine di pagamento** standing order (*Brit*), automatic payment (*Am*); **ordine di prova** trial order
10 **l'ordine del giorno** (*in riunioni*) the agenda; (*Mil*) the order of the day; **essere all'ordine del giorno** (*di riunione*) to be on the agenda; **gli scioperi sono ormai all'ordine del giorno** (*fig*) strikes are now the order of the day, strikes are now an everyday affair
ordire [or'dire] VT (*tessuto*) to warp; (*fig*) to plot, scheme; **ordire una congiura** *o* **una trama** to hatch a plot, plot
ordito [or'dito] SM (*di tessuto*) warp

Oo

orditore, trice [ordi'tore] SM/F (*Industria tessile*) warper; **orditore di trame** (*fig*) conspirator, plotter
orditura [ordi'tura] SF (*di tessuto*) warpage
orecchia [o'rekkja] SF **1** *vedi* **orecchio** **2 orecchie** SFPL: **fare le orecchie a un libro** to dog-ear a book
orecchiabile [orek'kjabile] AGG (*canzone*) catchy
orecchietta [orek'kjetta] SF (*Anat*) auricle
orecchino [orek'kino] SM earring; **un paio di orecchini d'oro** a pair of gold earrings
orecchio, chi [o'rekkjo] SM **1** (*Anat*) (*pl(f)* **orecchie**) ear; **farsi fare i buchi nelle orecchie** to have one's ears pierced; **mi sono fatta fare i buchi nelle orecchie** I've had my ears pierced; **mi fa male un orecchio** I've got earache; **mi fischiano le orecchie** (*lett*) my ears are singing; (*fig*) my ears are burning; **essere tutto orecchi** to be all ears; **venire all'orecchio di qn** to come to sb's attention; **te lo dico in un orecchio** this is for your ears only; **tapparsi** *o* **turarsi le orecchie** to put one's fingers in one's ears; **fare orecchie da mercante (a)** to turn a deaf ear (to); **tirare le orecchie a qn** to tweak sb's ears; (*fig*) to tell sb off, give sb an earful **2** (*udito*) hearing; **essere debole d'orecchio** to be hard of hearing; **avere orecchio** to have a good ear (for music); **ha orecchio** he's got a good ear; **a orecchio** by ear; **cantare/ suonare a orecchio** to sing/play by ear
orecchioni [orek'kjoni] SMPL (*Med*): **gli orecchioni** (the) mumps *sg*
orefice [o'refitʃe] SM/F (*negoziante*) jeweller (*Brit*), jeweler (*Am*); (*artigiano*) goldsmith
oreficeria [orefitʃe'ria] SF (*negozio*) jeweller's (shop) (*Brit*), jewelry store (*Am*); (*arte*) goldsmith's (*o* silversmith's) art *o* craft; (*gioielli*) jewellery (*Brit*), jewelry (*Am*)
Oregon ['oregon] SM Oregon
Oreste [o'rɛste] SM Orestes
orfano, a ['ɔrfano] AGG orphan(ed); **rimanere orfano** to be orphaned; **è rimasto orfano a dieci anni** he was orphaned at the age of ten; **essere orfano di madre/ padre** to be motherless/fatherless, have lost one's mother/father; **è orfano di madre** he has lost his mother
■SM/F orphan
orfanotrofio, fi [orfano'trɔfjo] SM orphanage
Orfeo [or'feo] SM Orpheus
orfico, a, ci, che ['ɔrfiko] AGG Orphic
orfismo [or'fizmo] SM Orphism
organetto [orga'netto] SM (*strumento a manovella*) barrel organ, street organ; (*fam: armonica a bocca*) mouth organ; (*: fisarmonica*) accordion
organicamente [organika'mente] AVV organically
organico, a, ci, che [or'ganiko] AGG (*Chim, Med, Dir*) organic
■SM (*personale*) staff, personnel; (*: Mil*) cadre; **essere nell'organico** to be on the permanent staff
organigramma, i [organi'gramma] SM (*diagramma gerarchico*) organization chart; (*Inform*) computer flow chart
organismo [orga'nizmo] SM (*vegetale, animale*) organism; (*Anat, Amm*) body, organism; **organismi geneticamente modificati** genetically modified organisms
organista, i, e [orga'nista] SM/F organist
organizzare [organid'dzare] VT to organize, arrange; **hanno organizzato un concerto** they organized a concert; **abbiamo organizzato una gita in campagna** we've arranged a trip to the country
▶ **organizzarsi** VR to organize o.s., get (o.s.) organized
organizzativo, a [organiddza'tivo] AGG organizational
organizzatore, trice [organiddza'tore] AGG organizing
■SM/F organizer
organizzazione [organiddzat'tsjone] SF **1** (*azione*) organizing, organization, arranging; (*risultato*) organization, arrangement; **ci occuperemo dell'organizzazione della festa** we'll organize the party **2** (*associazione*) organization; **un'organizzazione studentesca** a student organization
organo ['ɔrgano] SM (*Anat, Mus, pubblicazione*) organ; (*di congegno*) part; (*Amm*) organ, body; **suona l'organo** she plays the organ; **trapianto d'organi** organ transplants; **organi di comando** (*Tecn*) controls; **organi di trasmissione** (*Tecn*) transmission (unit) *sg*
organza [or'gandza] SF (*tessuto*) organza
orgasmo [or'gazmo] SM **1** (*Fisiologia*) orgasm, climax **2** (*fig: agitazione, ansia*) anxiety, agitation; **essere/ mettersi in orgasmo** to be/get in a state
orgia, ge ['ɔrdʒa] SF orgy; **un'orgia di** a profusion *o* riot of; **un'orgia di colori** an orgy of colour (*Brit*) *o* color (*Am*)
orgiastico, a, ci, che [or'dʒastiko] AGG orgiastic
orgoglio [or'goʎʎo] SM pride
orgogliosamente [orgoʎʎosa'mente] AVV proudly
orgoglioso, a [orgoʎ'ʎoso] AGG proud; **sono orgogliosa di te** I'm proud of you
orientabile [orjen'tabile] AGG adjustable
orientale [orjen'tale] AGG (*paese, regione*) eastern; (*civiltà, lingua, tappeto*) oriental; **l'Europa orientale** eastern Europe; **la costa orientale della Gran Bretagna** the east coast of Britain; **un tappeto orientale** an oriental carpet
■SM/F Oriental
orientaleggiante [orjentaled'dʒante] AGG oriental
orientalista, i, e [orjenta'lista] SM/F Orientalist
orientalizzare [orjentalid'dzare] VT to Orientalize
orientalizzazione [orjentaliddzat'tsjone] SF Orientalization
orientamento [orjenta'mento] SM **1** (*azione*) (*vedi vt*) positioning; orientation; directing **2** (*direzione*) direction; **senso di** *o* **dell'orientamento** sense of direction; **perdere l'orientamento** to lose one's bearings; **ho perso l'orientamento** I've lost my bearings **3** (*tendenza: di partito, rivista*) tendencies *pl*, leanings *pl*; (*: di scienze*) trends *pl*; (*: di ricerche*) direction; **orientamento professionale** careers guidance
orientare [orjen'tare] VT **1** (*disporre: antenna, ventilatore*) to position; (*carta, bussola*) to orientate **2** (*fig: dirigere: ricerche, persona*) to direct; **hanno orientato la conversazione su un tema d'attualità** they steered the conversation round to a topical subject
orientarsi VR **1** (*viaggiatore*) to find one's bearings; (*fig: raccapezzarsi*) to find one's way; **in questa faccenda non riesco a orientarmi** I can't make head nor tail of this business **2 orientarsi per** *o* **verso** (*fig: indirizzarsi*) to take up, go in for; (*: propendere*) to lean towards, tend towards; **mi sto orientando verso l'acquisto di una casa** I'm coming round to the idea of buying a house
orientativamente [orjentativa'mente] AVV: **qual è il prezzo, orientativamente?** can you give me a rough idea of the price?
orientativo, a [orjenta'tivo] AGG indicative,

approximate; **a scopo orientativo** for information

orientazione [orjentat'tsjone] SF (*vedi vt 1*) positioning; orientation

oriente [o'rjɛnte] SM (*levante*) east; **l'Oriente** the East, the Orient; **a oriente** in the east; **il Medio/l'Estremo Oriente** the Middle/Far East

orienteering [ə:rɪən'tɪərɪŋ] SM orienteering

orificio, ci [ori'fitʃo], **orifizio, zi** [ori'fittsjo] SM (*apertura*) opening; (: *di tubo*) mouth; (*Anat*) orifice

origami [ori'gami] SM INV origami
▷ www.origami-cdo.it/

origano [o'rigano] SM (*Bot*) oregano

originale [oridʒi'nale] AGG (*gen*) original; (*nuovo*) new, original; (*bizzarro*) eccentric, odd; **un'idea originale** an original idea; **è un tipo originale** he's a bit eccentric
■ SM (*opera, documento*) original; **vuoi una copia o l'originale?** do you want a copy, or the original?; **originale radiofonico** radio play; **originale televisivo** television play
■ SM/F eccentric; **il tuo amico è un bell'originale!** your friend is a real character!

originalità [oridʒinali'ta] SF **1** (*vedi agg*) originality; eccentricity, oddness **2** (*atto da originale*) eccentric behaviour

originalmente [oridʒinal'mente] AVV (*in origine*) originally; (*in modo originale*) in an original way

originare [oridʒi'nare] VT to cause, give rise to, bring about, produce
■ VI (*aus* **essere**) **originare da** to arise *o* spring from

originariamente [oridʒinarja'mente] AVV (*in origine*) originally; (*dapprincipio*) at first, originally

originario, ria, ri, rie [oridʒi'narjo] AGG **1** **essere originario di** (*persona*) to be a native of; be from; (*animale, pianta*) to be indigenous to, be native to; **è originario di Roma** he is a native of Rome, he's from Rome **2** (*primitivo, originale*) original

origine [o'ridʒine] SF (*gen*) origin; (*provenienza: di persona, famiglia*) origin, extraction; (: *di cosa*) origin, provenance; (*di fiume*) source; (*causa*) origin, cause; **luogo/paese d'origine** place/country of origin; **di origine italiana** of Italian extraction *o* origin; **risalire alle origini** *o* **all'origine di qc** to go back to the origins *o* the beginning of sth; **cominciare dalle origini** to start at the beginning; **dare origine a** to give rise to; **avere origine da** to originate from; **all'origine** originally

origliare [oriʎ'ʎare] VI (*aus* **avere**) **stava origliando alla porta** he was listening at the door
■ VT to eavesdrop (on)

orina [o'rina] SF urine

orinale [ori'nale] SM chamberpot

orinare [ori'nare] VI (*aus* **avere**) to pass water, urinate
■ VT: **orinare sangue** to pass blood

orinatoio, oi [orina'tojo] SM (public) urinal

Orione [ori'one] SM Orion

oritteropo [orit'tɛropo] SM (*animale*) aardvark

oriundo, a [o'rjundo] AGG: **essere oriundo di Milano** to be of Milanese extraction *o* origin
■ SM/F person of foreign extraction *o* origin; **negli Stati Uniti ci sono molti oriundi italiani** in the United States there are many people of Italian extraction *o* origin
■ SM (*Sport: in Italia*) foreign player of Italian extraction

orizzontale [oriddzon'tale] AGG horizontal
■ SF (*di cruciverba*) clue (*o* word) across

orizzontalmente [oriddzontal'mente] AVV horizontally

orizzontarsi [oriddzon'tarsi] VR (*viaggiatore*) to get one's bearings; (*fig: raccapezzarsi*) to find one's way

orizzonte [orid'dzonte] SM **1** horizon; **all'orizzonte** (*apparire*) on the horizon; (*sparire*) below the horizon; **improvvisamente comparve un'isola all'orizzonte** suddenly an island appeared on the horizon **2** (*fig: prospettiva*) horizon; **l'orizzonte politico** the political scene; **fare un giro d'orizzonte** (*di situazione*) to examine the main aspects

ORL [ɔrl] SIGLA F (*Med:* = **otorinolaringoiatria**) ENT (= *ear, nose and throat*)

orlare [or'lare] VT (*gen*) to hem; (*con fettucce, nastri*) to edge, trim

orlatura [orla'tura] SF (*orlo*) hem; (*azione*) hemming *no pl*

orlo ['orlo] SM **1** (*di marciapiede*) edge; (*di recipiente*) rim, brim; (*di precipizio*) brink, edge; **la macchina era sull'orlo del precipizio** the car was on the edge of the precipice; **ha riempito il bicchiere fino all'orlo** she filled the glass to the brim; **pieno fino all'orlo** full to the brim, brimful; **sull'orlo della pazzia/della rovina** on the brink *o* verge of madness/ruin **2** (*ripiegatura: di vestiti*) hem; **l'orlo della tovaglia si è scucito** the hem of the tablecloth has come unstitched; **orlo a giorno** hemstitch

orma ['orma] SF (*di persona*) footprint; (*di animale*) track; (*fig: impronta, traccia*) trace, mark; **segui le orme della volpe** follow the fox's tracks; **la polizia ha trovato delle orme in giardino** the police found footprints in the garden; **seguire** *o* **calcare le orme di qn** to follow in sb's footsteps; **ha seguito le orme del padre** he followed in his father's footsteps

ormai [or'mai] AVV **1** (*riferito al presente*) by now, by this time; (: *a questo punto*) now; **ormai è tardi** it's late now; **ormai dovrebbe essere partito** he must have left by now **2** (*allora*) by then **3** (*riferito al futuro: quasi*) almost, nearly; **ormai siamo arrivati** we're nearly *o* almost there

Oo

ormeggiare [ormed'dʒare] VT, **ormeggiarsi** VR to moor

ormeggio, gi [or'meddʒo] SM (*atto*) mooring *no pl*; (*luogo*) moorings *pl*; **ormeggi** SMPL (*cavi e catene*) moorings; **le navi erano all'ormeggio** the ships were at their moorings; **posto d'ormeggio** berth

ormonale [ormo'nale] AGG (*disfunzione*) hormonal, hormone *attr*; (*cura*) hormone *attr*; **terapia ormonale** hormone therapy

ormone [or'mone] SM hormone

ornamentale [ornamen'tale] AGG ornamental, decorative

ornamento [orna'mento] SM (*gen*) ornament, decoration; (*azione*) adornment, decoration; (*Archit, Arte*) embellishment; **privo di ornamenti** (*stile, vestito, stanza*) plain, unadorned

ornare [or'nare] VT **1** (*tavola, vestito*): **ornare (di** *o* **con)** to decorate (with), adorn (with); (*fig: discorso*) to embellish (with) **2** (*sogg: affresco, statua*) to adorn, decorate
▶ **ornarsi** VR: **ornarsi (di)** to deck o.s. (out) (with)

ornato, a [or'nato] AGG **1** (*adorno*): **ornato di** adorned with, decorated with; **un cappello ornato di piume** a hat trimmed with feathers **2** (*stile*) ornate, florid
■ SM (*Archit*) embellishment

ornitologia [ornitolo'dʒia] SF ornithology

ornitologico, a, ci, che [ornito'lɔdʒiko] AGG ornithological

ornitologo, a, gi *o* **ghi, ghe** [orni'tɔlogo] SM/F ornithologist
ornitorinco, chi [ornito'rinko] SM (*animale*) (duck-billed) platypus
oro ['ɔro] SM **1** gold; **bracciale in oro** *o* **d'oro** gold bracelet; **oro nero** (*petrolio*) black gold; **oro zecchino** pure gold **2 ori** SMPL (*oggetti d'oro*) gold *sg*; (*gioielli*) jewellery *sg* (*Brit*), jewelry *sg* (*Am*); (*Carte*) *suit in Neapolitan pack of cards* **3 d'oro** (*oggetto*) gold; (*colore, occasione*) golden; (*persona*) wonderful, marvellous (*Brit*), marvelous (*Am*); **un orologio d'oro** a gold watch; **ha vinto la medaglia d'oro** he won the gold medal; **un'occasione d'oro** a golden opportunity; **un affare d'oro** a real bargain; **fare affari d'oro** to do excellent business; **avere un cuore d'oro** to have a heart of gold **4** (*fraseologia*): **nuotare nell'oro** to be rolling in money; **prendere qc per oro colato** to take sth as gospel (truth); **non lo farei per tutto l'oro del mondo** I wouldn't do it for all the money in the world; **quell'uomo vale tanto oro quanto pesa** that man is worth his weight in gold; **non è tutt'oro quel che luccica** all that glitters is not gold
orogenesi [oro'dʒɛnezi] SF INV (*Geol*) orogeny, orogenis
orogenetico, a, ci, che [orodʒe'nɛtiko] AGG (*Geol*) orogenic, orogenetic
orografia [orogra'fia] SF (*Geog*) orography
orografico, a, ci, che [oro'grafiko] AGG (*Geog*) orographic
orologeria [orolodʒe'ria] SF (*arte, industria*) watchmaking *no pl*; (*negozio*) watchmaker's (shop); clockmaker's (shop); (*meccanismo*) clockwork; **bomba a orologeria** time bomb
orologiaio, ai [orolo'dʒajo] SM watchmaker; clockmaker
orologio, gi [oro'lɔdʒo] SM (*da muro, a pendolo*) clock; (*da tasca, polso*) watch; **il mio orologio va avanti/indietro** my watch is fast/slow; **una mezz'ora di orologio** exactly half an hour; **andare** *o* **funzionare come un orologio** (*meccanismo*) to run like clockwork; **orologio analogico** analogue watch *o* clock; **orologio biologico** biological clock; **orologio digitale** digital watch *o* clock; **orologio da polso** wristwatch; **orologio al quarzo** quartz watch; **orologio solare** sundial
oroscopo [o'rɔskopo] SM horoscope
orrendamente [orrenda'mente] AVV horrifically, horrendously
orrendo, a [or'rɛndo] AGG (*spaventoso*) horrible, horrendous; (*bruttissimo*) hideous; (*cattivo*) awful, terrible, dreadful; (*ripugnante*) revolting
orribile [or'ribile] AGG (*brutto*) horrible; (*pessimo*) awful, dreadful; (*ripugnante*) revolting
orribilmente [orribil'mente] AVV horribly, hideously
orrido, a ['ɔrrido] AGG horrid, dreadful, fearful
orripilante [orripi'lante] AGG horrifying, hair-raising
orrore [or'rore] SM (*gen*) horror; (*ribrezzo*) disgust, loathing; **avere orrore di qc** to loathe *o* detest sth; **avere in orrore qn/qc** to loathe *o* detest sb/sth; **i ragni mi fanno orrore** I have a horror of spiders, I loathe spiders; **gli orrori della guerra** the horrors of war; **che orrore!** how awful *o* dreadful!; **quel quadro è un orrore** that painting is hideous; **film dell'orrore** horror film (*Brit*) *o* movie (*Am*)
orsa ['orsa] SF she-bear; **l'Orsa maggiore/minore** the Great/Little Bear, Ursa Major/Minor (*Astron*)
orsacchiotto [orsak'kjɔtto] SM (*cucciolo*) bear cub; (*giocattolo*) teddy bear
orso ['orso] SM (*Zool, fig*) bear; **orso bianco** polar bear; **orso bruno** brown bear
orsolina [orso'lina] SF Ursuline
orsù [or'su] ESCL (*letter*) come now!
ortaggio, gi [or'taddʒo] SM vegetable
ortensia [or'tɛnsja] SF hydrangea
ortica, che [or'tika] SF (stinging) nettle; **mi sono punto con le ortiche** I stung myself on the nettles; **falsa ortica** dead-nettle
orticaria [orti'karja] SF nettle rash
orticoltura [ortikol'tura] SF horticulture
orto ['ɔrto] SM vegetable garden, kitchen garden; (*Agr*) market garden (*Brit*), truck farm (*Am*); **orto botanico** botanical garden(s *pl*)
ortocentro [orto'tʃɛntro] SM (*Mat*) orthocentre (*Brit*), orthocenter (*Am*)
ortodontia [ortodon'tia] SF orthodontics *sg*, dental orthopaedics (*Brit*) *o* orthopedics (*Am*) *sg*
ortodossia [ortodos'sia] SF orthodoxy
ortodosso, a [orto'dɔsso] AGG, SM/F orthodox
ortofonia [ortofo'nia] SF (*Ling*) correct pronunciation; (*Med*) speech therapy
ortofrutticolo, a [ortofrut'tikolo] AGG fruit and vegetable *attr*
ortofrutticoltore [ortofruttikol'tore], **ortofrutticultore** [ortofruttikul'tore] SM market gardener
ortofrutticoltura [ortofruttikol'tura], **ortofrutticultura** [ortofruttikul'tura] SF market gardening
ortogonale [ortogo'nale] AGG perpendicular, orthogonal
ortografia [ortogra'fia] SF spelling, orthography; **errori di ortografia** spelling mistakes
ortografico, a, ci, che [orto'grafiko] AGG spelling *attr*, orthographical
ortolano, a [orto'lano] SM/F (*negoziante*) greengrocer (*Brit*), produce dealer (*Am*)
ortomercato [ortomer'kato] SM fruit market
ortopedia [ortope'dia] SF orthopaedics *sg* (*Brit*), orthopedics *sg* (*Am*)
ortopedicamente [ortopedika'mente] AVV orthopaedically (*Brit*), orthopedically (*Am*)
ortopedico, a, ci, che [orto'pɛdiko] AGG orthopaedic (*Brit*), orthopedic (*Am*)
■ SM/F orthopaedic specialist (*Brit*), orthopedist (*Am*)
orzaiolo [ordza'jɔlo], **orzaiuolo** [ordza'jwɔlo] SM (*Med*) sty(e)
orzare [or'tsare] VI (*aus* **avere**) (*Naut*) to head up
orzata[1] [or'dzata] SF (*bevanda*) barley water; (*sciroppo*) *almond-based cordial*
orzata[2] [or'dzata] SF (*Naut*): **fare un'orzata** to head up
orzo ['ɔrdzo] SM barley
OSA ['ɔza] SIGLA F (= **Organizzazione degli Stati Americani**) OAS (= *Organization of American States*)
osanna [o'zanna] SM INV hosanna
osannare [ozan'nare] VT (*lodare*) to applaud, acclaim
osare [o'zare] VT **1 osare (fare)** to dare (do) *o* (to do); **non osava domandargli** he didn't dare (to) ask him; **ha osato sfidarlo** she dared to defy him; **non osavo dirlo** I didn't dare to say it; **oserei dire che…** I dare say that …; **come osi?** how dare you? **2** (*tentare*) to attempt; (*arrischiare*) to risk
oscar ['ɔskar] SM INV (*Cine*) Oscar; (*fig: primo premio*): **oscar (di)** prize (for)
OSCE ['ɔʃe] [ɔesseʧi'e] SIGLA F (= **Organizzazione per la**

Sicurezza e la Cooperazione in Europa) OSCE (= *Organization for Security and Cooperation in Europe*)

oscenamente [oʃʃena'mente] AVV (*in modo indecente*) obscenely; (*in modo pessimo*) appallingly, atrociously

oscenità [oʃʃeni'ta] SF INV obscenity

osceno, a [oʃ'ʃɛno] AGG (*indecente*) obscene; (*bruttissimo*) dreadful, awful; (*ripugnante*) ghastly

oscillante [oʃʃil'lante] AGG **1** (*prezzi, valori*) fluctuating **2** (*Elettr: corrente*) oscillating

oscillare [oʃʃil'lare] VI (*aus* **avere**) (*Fis*) to oscillate; (*pendolo*) to swing; (*fiamma*) to flicker; (*dondolare: al vento*) to rock; (*prezzi, temperatura*): **oscillare (fra)** to fluctuate (between); (*persona: essere indeciso*) to waver (between)

oscillatore [oʃʃilla'tore] SM oscillator

oscillatorio, ria, ri, rie [oʃʃilla'tɔrjo] AGG (*Fis: moto*) swinging, oscillatory (*termine tecn*)

oscillazione [oʃʃillat'tsjone] SF (*Fis*) oscillation; (*di prezzi, temperatura*) fluctuation

oscilloscopio, pi [oʃʃillos'kɔpjo] SM oscilloscope

oscuramente [oskura'mente] AVV (*senza chiarezza*) obscurely; **vivere oscuramente** (*senza fama*) to live in obscurity

oscuramento [oskura'mento] SM **1** (*cielo*) darkening; (*sole*) obscuring; (*vista*) dimming **2** (*in tempo di guerra*) blackout

oscurantismo [oskuran'tizmo] SM obscurantism

oscurare [osku'rare] VT **1** (*rendere scuro*) to darken, obscure; (*offuscare: sole, veduta*) to obscure; (*schermare: lampada*) to shade **2** (*fig*) to obscure
▶ **oscurarsi** VIP **1** (*cielo*) to cloud over, darken, get *o* become darker **2** (*vista, mente*) to dim, grow dim; **si oscurò in volto** his face clouded (over)

oscurità [oskuri'ta] SF (*vedi agg*) darkness; obscurity; gloominess; **la stanza piombò nell'oscurità** the room was plunged into darkness; **sono nell'oscurità più completa per quanto riguarda i loro progetti** I am completely in the dark about their plans

oscuro, a [os'kuro] AGG (*scuro*) dark; (*fig: incomprensibile, sconosciuto*) obscure; (*: triste: pensiero*) gloomy, sombre; (*: umile: vita, natali*) humble, obscure; **ci sono alcuni punti oscuri nel suo racconto** there are some unclear points in his account; **è morto in circostanze oscure** he died in mysterious circumstances
■ SM darkness; **all'oscuro** in the dark; **tenere qn/essere all'oscuro di qc** to keep sb/be in the dark about sth; **mi hanno sempre tenuto all'oscuro della faccenda** they've always kept me in the dark about this

Oslo ['ɔslo] SF Oslo

osmio ['ɔzmjo] SM osmium

osmoregolazione [ozmoregolat'tsjone] SF (*Zool*) osmoregulation

osmosi [oz'mɔzi] SF INV osmosis

osmotico, a, ci, che [oz'mɔtiko] AGG osmotic

ospedale [ospe'dale] SM hospital; **essere ricoverato in ospedale** to be admitted to hospital; **essere all'ospedale** to be in hospital; **Luigi è all'ospedale da una settimana** Luigi's been in hospital for a week; **ospedale da campo** field hospital; **ospedale militare** military hospital

ospedaliero, a [ospeda'ljɛro] AGG hospital *attr*; **attrezzatura ospedaliera** hospital facilities *pl*
■ SM/F hospital worker

ospedalizzare [ospedalid'dzare] VT to hospitalize

ospitale [ospi'tale] AGG (*gente*) hospitable; (*casa, paese*) friendly

ospitalità [ospitali'ta] SF hospitality

ospitare [ospi'tare] VT **1** (*dare alloggio*) to put up; (*: sogg: albergo*) to accommodate; **mi hanno ospitato per una settimana** they put me up for a week **2** (*accogliere: mostre, gare, avvenimenti*) to hold; (*: Sport*) to play at home to; **il Milan ospiterà la Juventus domenica prossima** Milan will play at home to Juventus next Sunday

ospite ['ɔspite] SM/F (*persona ospitata*) guest; (*persona che ospita*) host/hostess; **ero l'unico ospite dell'albergo** I was the only guest at the hotel; **la stanza degli ospiti** the guest room
■ AGG: **squadra ospite** (*Calcio*) visiting team

ospizio, zi [os'pittsjo] SM (*istituto di ricovero*) home; (*per anziani*) old people's home; (*per viaggiatori, pellegrini*) hospice

ossa ['ɔssa] SFPL *vedi* **osso**

ossalide [os'salide] SF (*pianta*) oxalis

ossario, ri [os'sarjo] SM war memorial (*with burial place*)

ossatura [ossa'tura] SF (*di corpo*) bone structure, frame, skeletal structure; (*di edificio, ponte, romanzo*) framework; **è di ossatura robusta** he's strongly built

osseo, a ['ɔsseo] AGG (*Anat, Med*) bone *attr*, bony

ossequente [osse'kwɛnte], **ossequiente** [osse'kwjɛnte] AGG: **ossequente alle leggi** law-abiding

ossequio, qui [os'sɛkwjo] SM **1** respect, deference; **in ossequio a** out of respect for **2** **ossequi** SMPL (*saluto*) respects, regards; **ossequi alla signora!** (give my) respects to your wife!; **porgere i propri ossequi a qn** (*frm*) to pay one's respects to sb; **i miei ossequi** (*in una lettera*) sincere regards

ossequiosamente [ossekwjosa'mente] AVV (*vedi agg*) respectfully; obsequiously

ossequioso, a [osse'kwjoso] AGG (*rispettoso*) respectful; (*servile*) obsequious

osservante [osser'vante] AGG (*Rel*) practising

osservanza [osser'vantsa] SF observance

osservare [osser'vare] VT **1** (*guardare*) to observe; (*: attentamente: nemico*) to watch; (*: al microscopio*) to examine; **osservava attentamente quello che stavo facendo** he was carefully watching what I was doing **2** (*notare, rilevare*) to notice, observe; (*far notare*) to point out, remark, observe; **hai osservato che zoppica un po'?** have you noticed that she limps a bit?; **far osservare qc a qn** to point sth out to sb; **vorrei farvi osservare alcune cose** I'd like to point out a few things to you; **ha osservato che...** (*ha detto*) he remarked that ...; (*ha obiettato*) he objected *o* made the objection that ...; **non ho nulla da osservare** I have no objections **3** (*rispettare: legge, regolamento*) to observe, respect; (*mantenere: silenzio*) to keep; **osservare il digiuno** to fast, keep the fast

osservatore, trice [osserva'tore] AGG observant
■ SM/F observer

osservatorio, ri [osserva'tɔrjo] SM (*Astron, Meteor*) observatory; (*Mil*) observation *o* look-out post

osservazione [osservat'tsjone] SF **1** observation; **tenere qn in *o* sotto osservazione** (*Med*) to keep sb under observation; **l'hanno tenuto sotto osservazione per due giorni** he was kept under observation for two days **2** (*considerazione critica*) comment, observation, remark; (*obiezione*) objection; (*rimprovero*) criticism, reproof; **nessuno ha delle osservazioni da fare?** has anyone got any comments?; **questa è un'osservazione molto acuta** that's a very intelligent remark; **fare un'osservazione** (*considerazione*) to make a remark;

Oo

(*obiezione*) to raise an objection; **fare un'osservazione a qn** to criticise sb; **il professore mi ha fatto un'osservazione ingiusta** the teacher criticized me unfairly; **fare osservazione a qn** to reprimand sb

ossessionante [ossessjo'nante] AGG (*vedi vb*) obsessive, haunting; troublesome

ossessionare [ossessjo'nare] VT (*tormentare*: *sogg*: *idea, ricordo*) to obsess, haunt; (: *sogg*: *persona*) to torment, harass; (*infastidire*) to trouble, bother

ossessione [osses'sjone] SF **1** (*fissazione*) obsession; **aveva l'ossessione del denaro** he was obsessed with money **2** (*seccatura*) nuisance

ossessivamente [ossessiva'mente] AVV (*gen*) obsessively; **gli chiedeva ossessivamente la stessa cosa** she kept on and on asking him the same thing

ossessivo, a [osses'sivo] AGG obsessive, haunting; (*ricordo, idea, persona*) troublesome; **ma sei proprio ossessivo!** you really are a pest!

ossesso, a [os'sεsso] AGG (*spiritato*) possessed
■ SM/F person possessed; (*fig*): **urlare come un ossesso** to shout like a maniac

ossia [os'sia] CONG (*cioè*) that is, to be precise; (*o meglio*) or rather

ossiacido [ossi'atʃido] SM acidic oxide

ossibuchi [ossi'buki] SMPL *di* **ossobuco**

ossicino [ossi'tʃino] SM (*Anat*) ossicle

ossidante [ossi'dante] SM oxidizer

ossidare [ossi'dare] VT, **ossidarsi** VIP to oxidize

ossidazione [ossidat'tsjone] SF oxidization, oxidation

ossidiana [ossi'djana] SF obsidian

ossido ['ɔssido] SM oxide; **ossido di carbonio** carbon monoxide

ossidoriduzione [ossidoridut'tsjone] SF redox, oxidation-reduction

ossidrile [ossi'drile] SM hydroxide

ossificare [ossifi'kare] VT
▶ **ossificarsi** VIP to ossify

ossificazione [ossifikat'tsjone] SF ossification

ossigenare [ossidʒe'nare] VT **1** (*Chim*) to oxygenate; (*decolorare*: *capelli*) to bleach; **ossigenare i polmoni** to get some fresh air (into one's lungs) **2** (*fig*) to inject new life into
▶ **ossigenarsi** VR **1** (*decolorarsi*) to bleach one's hair **2** (*ritemprarsi*) to get some fresh air

ossigenato, a [ossidʒe'nato] AGG: **acqua ossigenata** hydrogen peroxide; **bionda ossigenata** peroxide blonde

ossigenazione [ossidʒenat'tsjone] SF (*del sangue*) oxygenation; (*dei capelli*) bleaching

ossigeno [os'sidʒeno] SM oxygen; **dare l'ossigeno a qn** to give sb oxygen; **dare ossigeno a qn/qc** (*fig*) to give sb/sth a new lease of life

osso ['ɔsso] SM (*pl(f)* ossa *nel senso Anat, o talvolta pl(m)* ossi) **1** bone; **le ossa della gamba** the bones of the leg; **d'osso** (*bottone, manico*) bone *attr*, of bone; **carne senza ossa** boneless *o* boned meat; **osso di balena** whalebone; **osso di seppia** cuttlebone **2** (*fam*: *di pesca*) stone **3** (*fraseologia*): **avere le ossa rotte** to be dead *o* dog tired; **bagnato fino all'osso** soaked to the skin; **rompersi l'osso del collo** to break one's neck; **rimetterci l'osso del collo** (*fig*) to ruin o.s., lose everything; **essere ridotto all'osso** (*fig*: *magro*) to be just skin and bone; (: *senza soldi*) to be in dire straits; **farsi le ossa** to gain experience; **un osso duro** (*persona*) a hard *o* tough nut, a tough cookie (*Am*); (*impresa*) a tall order

ossobuco [osso'buko] SM (*pl* **ossibuchi**) (*Culin*) marrowbone; (: *piatto*) ossobuco; *stew made with knuckle of veal in tomato sauce*

ossonio, ni [os'sɔnjo] AGG (*Chim*): **ione ossonio** oxonium ion

ossuto, a [os'suto] AGG (*persona, viso*) angular; (*animale*) scraggy; (*mano*) bony

ostacolare [ostako'lare] VT (*persona, piano*) to hinder; **le gonne strette ostacolano i movimenti** tight skirts hinder one's movements; **Maurizio ha cercato di ostacolare il mio piano** Maurizio tried to spoil my plan; **hanno cercato di ostacolarmi** they tried to make things difficult for me; **ostacolare la giustizia** to obstruct justice

ostacolista, i, e [ostako'lista] SM/F (*atleta*) hurdler
■ SM (*cavallo*) steeplechaser

ostacolo [os'takolo] SM **1** (*anche fig*) obstacle, difficulty; **ha superato molti ostacoli** she has overcome many difficulties; **essere di ostacolo a qn/qc** (*fig*) to stand in the way of sb/sth **2** (*Atletica*) hurdle; (*Equitazione*) jump, fence; **i quattrocento metri a ostacoli** the four hundred meter hurdles

ostaggio, gi [os'taddʒo] SM hostage; **prendere/tenere qn in ostaggio** to take/keep sb hostage; **i dirottatori hanno preso in ostaggio due donne** the hijackers have taken two women hostage

oste, ostessa ['ɔste] SM/F innkeeper, landlord/landlady

osteggiare [osted'dʒare] VT to oppose, be opposed to

ostello [os'tεllo] SM hostel; **ostello della gioventù** youth hostel

ostensorio, ri [osten'sɔrjo] SM (*Rel*) monstrance

ostentare [osten'tare] VT (*ricchezze, bravura*) to show off, flaunt, make a show of; (*distacco, indifferenza*) to feign

ostentatamente [ostentata'mente] AVV ostentatiously

ostentazione [ostentat'tsjone] SF ostentation, show; **con ostentazione** ostentatiously

osteo... ['ɔsteo] PREF osteo...

osteopata, i; , e [oste'ɔpata] SM/F osteopath

osteopatia [osteopa'tia] SF osteopathy

osteoporosi [osteopo'rɔzi] SF osteoporosis

osteria [oste'ria] SF ≈ pub (*Brit*), ≈ bar

ostetricia [oste'tritʃa] SF obstetrics *sg*

ostetrico, a, ci, che [os'tεtriko] AGG obstetric(al); **clinica ostetrica** maternity hospital *o* home
■ SM/F (*medico*) obstetrician
■ SF (*levatrice*) midwife

ostia ['ɔstja] SF (*Rel*) host; (*per medicinali*) wafer

ostico, a, ci, che ['ɔstiko] AGG difficult, tough

ostile [os'tile] AGG: **ostile (a)** hostile (to *o* towards)

ostilità [ostili'ta] SF INV (*stato, atteggiamento*) hostility; (*atto*) act of hostility; (*Mil*): **le ostilità** hostilities

ostilmente [ostil'mente] AVV hostilely, in a hostile way

ostinarsi [osti'narsi] VIP **1** (*impuntarsi*): **ostinarsi su** *o* **in qc** to insist on sth, dig one's heels in about sth; **ostinarsi a voler fare qc** to be determined to do sth **2** (*persistere*): **ostinarsi a fare qc** to persist (obstinately) in doing sth; keep on doing sth; **è inutile che ti ostini a negarlo** it's no use keeping on denying it

ostinatamente [ostinata'mente] AVV obstinately, stubbornly

ostinato, a [osti'nato] AGG (*persona, resistenza*)

obstinate, stubborn; (*tenace*) determined; (*tosse, pioggia*) persistent
■ SM/F obstinate *o* stubborn person

ostinazione [ostinat'tsjone] SF (*di persone*) obstinacy, stubbornness; **ostinazione a fare qc** obstinate *o* stubborn determination to do sth

ostracismo [ostra'tʃizmo] SM ostracism; **dare l'ostracismo a qn** to ostracize sb

ostrica, che ['ɔstrika] SF oyster; **ostrica perlifera** pearl oyster

LO SAPEVI...?
ostrica non si traduce mai con la parola inglese *ostrich*

ostruire [ostru'ire] VT to obstruct, block; **c'è qualcosa che ostruisce il tubo** there's something blocking the pipe
▶ **ostruirsi** VIP to become obstructed *o* blocked

ostruzione [ostrut'tsjone] SF **1** obstruction, blocking **2** (*effetto, cosa che ostruisce*) obstruction, blockage; (*Sport*) obstruction; **fare ostruzione** (*Calcio*) to obstruct

ostruzionismo [ostruttsjo'nizmo] SM (*Pol*) obstructionism; (*Sport*) obstruction; **fare ostruzionismo a** (*progetto, legge*) to obstruct

ostruzionista, i, e [ostruttsjo'nista] AGG, SM/F obstructionist

ostruzionistico, a, ci, che [ostruttsjo'nistiko] AGG obstructionist

otaria [o'tarja] SF eared seal

otite [o'tite] SF ear infection; **ho l'otite** I've got an ear infection

otorinolaringoiatra, i, e [otorinolaringo'jatra] SM/F, **otorino** [oto'rino] SM ear, nose and throat specialist

otre ['otre] SM (*recipiente*) goatskin

ottagonale [ottago'nale] AGG octagonal, eight-sided

ottagono [ot'tagono] SM octagon

ottano [ot'tano] SM octane; **numero di ottani** octane rating *o* number; **benzina ad alto numero di ottani** high-octane petrol (*Brit*) *o* gasoline (*Am*)

ottanta [ot'tanta] AGG INV, SM INV eighty; *per fraseologia vedi* **cinquanta**

ottantenne [ottan'tɛnne] AGG eighty-year-old; *per fraseologia vedi* **cinquantenne**
■ SM/F octogenarian

ottantesimo, a [ottan'tɛzimo] AGG, SM/F, SM eightieth; *per fraseologia vedi* **quinto**

ottantina [ottan'tina] SF: **una ottantina (di)** about eighty; *per fraseologia vedi* **cinquantina**

ottativo [otta'tivo] SM (*Gramm*) optative

ottavino [otta'vino] SM (*Mus: flauto*) piccolo

ottavo, a [ot'tavo] AGG, SM/F eighth; *per fraseologia vedi* **quinto**
■ SM **1** (*frazione*) eighth **2** (*Tip*) octavo; **edizione in ottavo** octavo edition **3** (*Sport*): **entrare negli ottavi di finale** to get into the last sixteen; **superare gli ottavi di finale** to reach the quarterfinals
■ SF (*Poesia, Mus, Rel*) octave

ottemperanza [ottempe'rantsa] SF (*Amm*): **in ottemperanza a** in accordance with, in compliance with

ottemperare [ottempe'rare] VI (*aus* **avere**) **ottemperare a** to comply with, obey

ottenebrare [ottene'brare] VT (*anche fig*) to cloud; (*sole*) to hide, obscure
▶ **ottenebrarsi** VIP to cloud (over), darken

ottenere [otte'nere] VT IRREG **1** (*risposta, laurea, permesso*) to obtain, get; **ha ottenuto il permesso di uscire** she got permission to go out; **ottenere una promozione** to get promotion; **ha ottenuto di parlargli lunedì** he managed to arrange a meeting with him for Monday; **ha ottenuto che il ragazzo venisse ricoverato** he managed to get the boy admitted to hospital **2** (*totale*) to reach, arrive at; (*risultato*) to achieve, obtain; (*premio, approvazione, fiducia*) to gain, win; **ottenere un buon successo** to have great success; **abbiamo ottenuto un buon risultato** we got a good result; **aggiungendo il giallo al blu si ottiene il verde** green is obtained *o* you get green by adding yellow to blue

ottetto [ot'tetto] SM (*Mus*) octet

ottica ['ɔttika] SF (*Fis: scienza*) optics *sg*; (*Fot: lenti, prismi*) optics *pl*; (*fig: punto di vista*) point of view, viewpoint

ottico, a, ci, che ['ɔttiko] AGG (*nervo*) optic; (*fenomeno, strumento*) optical; **un'illusione ottica** an optical illusion
■ SM optician

ottimale [otti'male] AGG optimal, optimum

ottimamente [ottima'mente] AVV very well, excellently

ottimismo [otti'mizmo] SM optimism

ottimista, i, e [otti'mista] AGG optimistic
■ SM/F optimist

ottimisticamente [ottimistika'mente] AVV optimistically

ottimistico, a, ci, che [otti'mistiko] AGG optimistic

ottimizzare [ottimid'dzare] VT (*servizio, produzione*) optimize

ottimizzazione [ottimiddzat'tsjone] SF optimization

ottimo, a ['ɔttimo] AGG (*superl di* **buono**) very good, excellent; **risultati ottimi** excellent results; **la cena è stata ottima** the dinner was delicious
■ SM (*condizione ottimale*) peak; (*Scol*) top marks *pl*

Oo

otto ['ɔtto] AGG INV eight
■ SM INV (*numero, Canottaggio*) eight; (*tracciato*) figure of eight; **oggi (a) otto** in a week's time, today week; **otto volante** switchback; *per fraseologia vedi* **cinque**

ottobre [ot'tobre] SM October; *per fraseologia vedi* **luglio**

ottobrino, a [otto'brino] AGG October *attr*

ottocentesco, a, schi, sche [ottotʃen'tesko] AGG nineteenth-century

ottocentista, i, e [ottotʃen'tista] SM/F **1** (*studioso*) nineteenth-century scholar *o* specialist; (*artista, scrittore*) nineteenth-century artist (*o* writer) **2** (*Sport*) eight hundred metres runner

ottocento [otto'tʃɛnto] AGG INV eight hundred
■ SM INV eight hundred; (*secolo*): **l'Ottocento** the nineteenth century

ottomila [otto'mila] AGG INV, SM INV eight thousand

ottone [ot'tone] SM brass; **di** *o* **in ottone** brass *attr*; **un campanello di ottone** a brass bell; **gli ottoni** (*Mus*) the brass *sg*

ottuagenario, a, ri [ottuadʒe'narjo] AGG, SM/F octogenarian

ottundere [ot'tundere] VT IRREG (*fig: mente*) to dull

otturare [ottu'rare] VT (*chiudere: falla, apertura*) to stop up, close (up), seal; (*bloccare: lavandino*) to block (up); (*riempire: dente*) to fill; **bisogna otturare la falla** we need to seal the leak; **ci dev'essere qualcosa che ottura il lavandino** there must be something blocking the sink; **il dentista mi ha otturato due denti** the dentist has filled two of my teeth
▶ **otturarsi** VIP (*bloccarsi*) to become *o* get blocked (up)

otturatore [ottura'tore] SM (*Fot*) shutter; (*nelle armi*) breechblock; (*Tecn*) valve

otturazione [otturat'tsjone] SF **1** (*vedi vb*) stopping up, closing (up), sealing; blocking; filling **2** (*di dente*) filling; **fare un'otturazione a qn** to give sb a filling

ottusamente [ottuza'mente] AVV obtusely, slow-wittedly

ottusità [ottuzi'ta] SF (*vedi agg*) obtuseness; dullness

ottuso, a [ot'tuzo] PP *di* **ottundere**
■ AGG (*Mat*) obtuse; (*fig*) obtuse, slow-witted; (*suono*) muffled, dull

ouverture [uver'tyr] SF INV (*Mus*) overture

ovaia [o'vaja] SF, **ovaio** [o'vajo] SM (*Anat*) ovary

ovale [o'vale] AGG, SM oval

ovarico, a, ci, che AGG ovarian

ovario, ri [o'varjo] SM (*Bot*) ovary

ovatta [o'vatta] SF (*per medicazione*) cotton wool; (*per imbottiture*) padding, wadding

ovattare [ovat'tare] VT **1** (*imbottire*) to pad; **ambiente ovattato** (*fig*) cocoon-like environment **2** (*fig: smorzare*) to muffle

ovazione [ovat'tsjone] SF ovation

overbooking [ouvəʀ'bukiŋ] SM (*su aereo*) overbooking

overdose ['ouvədous] SF INV overdose

overdrive ['ouvədraiv] SM INV (*Aut*) overdrive

ovest ['ɔvest] SM INV west; **a ovest (di)** west (of); **si è diretto a ovest** he headed west; **il sole tramonta a ovest** the sun sets in the west; **l'Italia confina a ovest con la Francia** Italy has a border to the west with France; **si trova a ovest della città** it's west of the city; **il vento viene da ovest** the wind comes from the west; **verso ovest** westward(s)
■ AGG INV (*gen*) west; (*regione*) western; **è partito in direzione ovest** he set off westwards *o* in a westward direction

Ovidio [o'vidjo] SM Ovid

ovidotto [ovi'dotto] SM (*Anat*) oviduct

ovile [o'vile] SM pen, (sheep)fold; **tornare all'ovile** (*fig*) to return to the fold

ovino, a [o'vino] AGG (*specie*) ovine (*termine tecn*), sheep *attr*; (*mercato, allevamento*) sheep *attr*

oviparo, a [o'viparo] AGG oviparous

ovoviviparo, a [ovovi'viparo] AGG ovoviviparous

ovulazione [ovulat'tsjone] SF ovulation

ovulo ['ɔvulo] SM (*Anat*) ovum; (*Bot*) ovule

ovunque [o'vunkwe] AVV = **dovunque**

ovvero [ov'vero] CONG (*o meglio*) or (rather); (*ossia*) that is, to be precise; (*oppure*) or (else)

ovviamente [ovvja'mente] AVV obviously

ovviare [ovvi'are] VI (*aus* **avere**) **ovviare a** to remedy; get round; **ovviare all'inconveniente (di)** to get round the problem (of)

ovvio, via, vi, vie ['ɔvvjo] AGG obvious; **è ovvio che...** obviously ..., it is obvious *o* clear that ...

ozelot [oddze'lɔt] SM (*animale*) ocelot

oziare [ot'tsjare] VI (*aus* **avere**) to laze around

ozio, ozi ['ɔttsjo] SM **1** (*peccato*) sloth; (*inattività*) idleness; **stare in ozio** to be idle; **se ne sta tutto il giorno in ozio** he sits around doing nothing all day; **l'ozio è il padre dei vizi** (*Proverbio*) the Devil finds work for idle hands (to do) **2** (*riposo*): **ore d'ozio** leisure *o* spare time *sg*

oziosamente [ottsjosa'mente] AVV idly

ozioso, a [ot'tsjoso] AGG **1** (*sfaccendato*) idle; (*inattivo: persona, giornata*) lazy; (*: per malattia*) inactive **2** (*fig: discorsi*) idle; (*: domanda*) pointless
■ SM/F layabout, idler

ozono [od'dzɔno] SM ozone; **il buco nell'ozono** the hole in the ozone layer; **la fascia** *o* **lo strato d'ozono** the ozone layer

ozonosfera [oddzonos'fera] SF ozonosphere, ozone layer

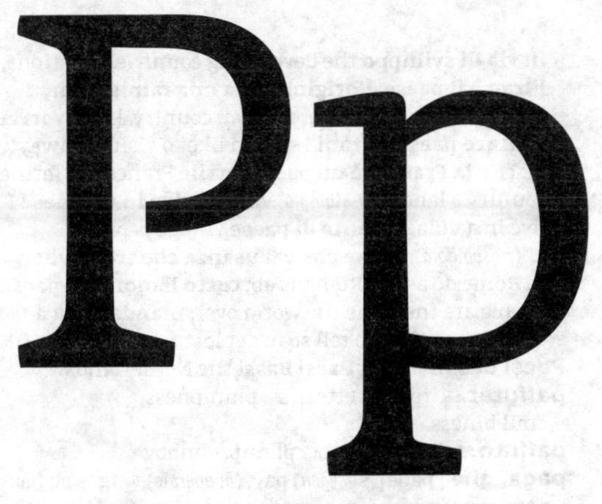

P, p [pi] SF O M INV (*lettera*) P, p; **P come Padova** ≈ P for Peter

P ABBR **1** (= **peso**) wt (= *weight*) **2** (= **parcheggio**) P **3** (*Aut*: = **principiante**) L (= *learner*)

p. ABBR (= **pagina**) p (= *page*)

P2 [pi'due] SIGLA F: **la (loggia) P2** the P2 masonic lodge

PA SIGLA = **Palermo**

■ABBR = **pubblica amministrazione**

pa' [pa] SM (*fam*) dad

PAC [pac] SIGLA M (= **Piano di Accumulo di Capitale**) *savings plan*

■SIGLA F (= **Politica Agricola Comune**) CAP (= *Common Agricultural Policy*)

pacare [pa'kare] VT to calm

▶ **pacarsi** VIP (*tempesta, disordini*) to subside

pacatamente [pakata'mente] AVV (*parlare*) placidly

pacatezza [paka'tettsa] SF (*vedi agg*) placidness; quietness, calmness

pacato, a [pa'kato] AGG (*carattere*) placid; (*voce, tono*) quiet, calm

pacca, che ['pakka] SF slap; **gli ho dato una pacca sulla schiena** I gave him a pat on the back

pacchetto [pak'ketto] SM (*confezione*) parcel; (: *di sigarette*) packet (*Brit*), pack (*Am*); **un pacchetto di sigarette** a packet of cigarettes; **le ho spedito un pacchetto** I sent her a parcel; **pacchetto applicativo** (*Inform*) applications package; **pacchetto azionario** (*Fin*) shareholding; **pacchetto software** (*Inform*) software package; **pacchetto turistico** package holiday (*Brit*) *o* tour

pacchia ['pakkja] SF (*fam*): **è stata una pacchia!** (*divertimento*) we had a great time!; (*di esame: molto facile*) it was a piece of cake!; **che pacchia!** what fun!

pacchiano, a [pak'kjano] AGG (*colori*) garish; (*abiti, arredamento*) vulgar, garish; **ha un gusto veramente pacchiano** she has extremely vulgar taste

pacco, chi ['pakko] SM **1** package, parcel; (*di farina, zucchero*) bag; **un grosso pacco marrone** a large brown parcel; **c'era un grosso pacco per lui sotto l'albero** there was a big parcel for him under the tree; **un pacco di zucchero** a bag of sugar; **carta da pacchi** brown paper; (*da regalo*) wrapping paper; **pacco bomba** parcel bomb; **pacco postale** parcel **2** (*involto*) bundle **3** (*fam!*: *organo genitale maschile*) lunchbox

paccottiglia [pakkot'tiʎʎa] SF trash, junk

pace ['patʃe] SF (*gen*) peace; **trattato di pace** peace treaty; **firmare la pace** to sign a peace treaty; **fare (la) pace con qn** to make (it) up with sb; **ho fatto la pace con Luciana** I've made it up with Luciana; **far fare (la) pace a due persone** to make peace between two people; **non si dà pace per quello che è successo** she can't stop thinking about what happened; **non mi dà un momento di pace** he doesn't give me a moment's peace; **mettersi l'animo in pace** *or* **darsi pace** to resign o.s.; **lasciare qn in pace** to leave sb alone; **lasciami in pace!** leave me alone!; **riposare in pace** to rest in peace; **santa pace!** for heaven's sake!; **pace all'anima sua!** (*anche scherz*) may he rest in peace!; **pace!** (*fa niente*) never mind!

pachiderma, i [paki'derma] SM pachyderm

pachistano, a [pakis'tano] AGG, SM/F Pakistani; **i pachistani** the Pakistanis

paciere, a [pa'tʃere] SM/F peacemaker

pacificamente [patʃifika'mente] AVV (*con intenzioni pacifiche*) peaceably; (*con calma*) peacefully

pacificare [patʃifi'kare] VT (*riconciliare*) to reconcile, make peace between; (*mettere in pace*) to pacify; **riuscì a pacificare gli animi** he managed to pacify *o* mollify everyone

pacificazione [patʃifikat'tsjone] SF (*vedi vb*) reconciliation; pacification

pacifico, a, ci, che [pa'tʃifiko] AGG **1** (*persona, carattere*) peaceable; (*vita, manifestazione*) peaceful **2** (*fig*: *indiscusso*) indisputable; (: *ovvio*) obvious, clear; **è pacifico che resterà in carica** it is obvious *o* it goes without saying that he will stay in office

■SM: **il Pacifico, l'Oceano Pacifico** the Pacific (Ocean)

pacifismo [patʃi'fizmo] SM pacifism

pacifista, i, e [patʃi'fista] AGG pacifist; **è pacifista** he's a pacifist

■SM/F pacifist

padano, a [pa'dano] AGG of the Po; **la pianura padana** the Lombardy plain

padella [pa'dɛlla] SF **1** (*Culin*) frying pan (*Brit*), skillet (*Am*); **cucinare in padella** to fry; **cadere dalla padella nella brace** (*fig*) to jump out of the frying pan into the fire **2** (*per infermi*) bedpan

padiglione [padiʎ'ʎone] SM **1** (*di mostra, ospedale*) pavilion; **padiglione di caccia** hunting lodge **2** (*Anat*): **padiglione auricolare** auricle, pinna

Padova ['padova] SF Padua
▷ www.padovanet.it/

padovano, a [pado'vano] AGG of *o* from Padua
■ SM/F inhabitant *o* native of Padova

padre ['padre] SM **1** father; **mio padre** my father; **il padre di Roberto** Roberto's father; **Rossi padre** Rossi senior; **di padre in figlio** from father to son; **per parte di padre** on my (*o* his *ecc*) father's side; **padre di famiglia** father, family man **2** (*antenati*): **padri** SMPL forefathers, ancestors **3** (*Rel*) father; **Padre mio** Father; **il Santo Padre** (*il Papa*) the Holy Father

Padrenostro [padre'nɔstro] SM: **il Padrenostro** the Lord's prayer, Our Father

Padreterno [padre'tɛrno] SM: **il Padreterno** God the Father; **si crede un padreterno** (*fig*) he thinks he is God Almighty

padrino [pa'drino] SM (*di battesimo*) godfather; (*di cresima*) sponsor; (*di duello*) second

padronale [padro'nale] AGG (*scala, entrata*) main, principal; **casa padronale** country house

padronanza [padro'nantsa] SF (*dominio*) command, mastery; **padronanza di sé** self-control; **avere una buona padronanza dell'inglese** to have a good command of English

padronato [padro'nato] SM: **il padronato** the ruling class

padrone, a [pa'drone] SM/F **1** (*dominatore: anche fig*) master/mistress; (*proprietario*) owner; **chi è il padrone di questo cane?** who's the owner of this dog?; **essere padrone di sé** to be self-possessed; **non era più padrone di sé** he had lost his self-control; **sono padrone di fare ciò che voglio** I am my own master; **si crede padrone del mondo** he thinks he is God Almighty; **essere padrone di una lingua** to have mastered a language; **essere padrone della situazione** to be master of the situation, have the situation in hand; **farla da padrone** to play the lord and master; **non sono più padrone in casa mia** I am no longer master in my own home; **padrona di casa** mistress of the house; (*per gli inquilini*) landlady; **padrone di casa** master of the house; (*per gli inquilini*) landlord **2** (*datore di lavoro*) employer, boss (*fam*); **essere sotto padrone** to be an employee

padroneggiare [padroned'dʒare] VT (*fig: istinti, sentimenti*) to control, master; (*: lingua, materia*) to master, know thoroughly
▶ **padroneggiarsi** VR to control o.s.

paesaggio, gi [pae'zaddʒo] SM (*panorama, Arte*) landscape; (*aspetto di un luogo*) scenery

paesaggista, i, e [paezad'dʒista] SM/F (*pittore*) landscape painter

paesaggistica [paezad'dʒistika] SF (*Pittura*) landscape (painting); (*dipinti*) landscapes *pl*

paesano, a [pae'zano] AGG country *attr*
■ SM/F **1** (*campagnolo*) peasant, rustic; (*abitante di paese*) villager **2** (*concittadino*) fellow countryman/ countrywoman

paese [pa'eze] SM **1** (*nazione*) country, nation; **i paesi in via di sviluppo** the developing countries *o* nations; **l'Iraq è il paese d'origine della mia famiglia** my family comes from Iraq **2** (*terra*) country, land; **vorrei visitare paesi lontani** I should like to visit far away places; **la Francia è un paese fertile** France is a fertile country *o* land **3** (*villaggio*) village; **vivo in un paese** I live in a village; **gente di paese** village people **4** (*fraseologia*): **paese che vai usanze che trovi** when in Rome do as the Romans do; **tutto il mondo è paese** people are the same the world over; **mandare qn a quel paese** (*fam*) to tell sb to get lost

Paesi Bassi SMPL: **i Paesi Bassi** the Netherlands

paffutezza [paffu'tettsa] SF plumpness, chubbiness

paffuto, a [paf'futo] AGG plump, chubby

paga, ghe ['paga] SF (*gen*) pay; (*di operaio*) wages *pl*; (*fig: ricompensa*) reward, recompense; **la paga non è molto alta** the pay's not very good; **dava tutta la paga alla moglie** he gave all his wages to his wife; **giorno di paga** payday

pagabile [pa'gabile] AGG payable; **pagabile alla consegna/a vista** payable on delivery/on demand

pagaia [pa'gaja] SF paddle

pagamento [paga'mento] SM payment; **non lo faccio nemmeno a pagamento** I won't do it even if they pay me; **la TV a pagamento** pay TV; **pagamento anticipato** payment in advance; **pagamento alla consegna** payment on delivery, cash on delivery; **pagamento in contanti** payment in cash; **pagamento all'ordine** cash with order

paganamente [pagana'mente] AVV in a pagan manner

paganesimo [paga'nezimo] SM paganism

pagano, a [pa'gano] AGG, SM/F pagan

pagare [pa'gare] VT **1** (*somma, conto, operaio*) to pay; (*debito*) to pay, settle; **hai pagato il conto?** have you paid the bill?; **pagare una cambiale** to pay a bill, honour (*Brit*) *o* honor (*Am*) a bill; **pagare in contanti** to pay cash; **pagare con carta di credito** to pay by credit card; **posso pagare con la carta di credito?** can I pay by credit card? **2** (*merce, lavoro, fig: colpa*) to pay for; **quanto l'hai pagato?** how much did you pay for it?; **l'ho pagato 10 euro** I paid 10 euros for it; **pagare una macchina 20 mila euro** to pay 20 thousand euros for a car; **me l'ha fatto pagare 35 euro** he charged me 35 euros for it; **l'ho pagato caro/poco** I paid a lot/very little for it; **l'ho pagata cara** (*fig*) I paid dearly for it; **pagare qc salato** *o* **un occhio della testa** to pay through the nose for sth; **te la farò pagare!** (*fig*) I'll make you pay for it!, you'll pay for this!; **ha pagato con la vita** it cost him his life; **pagare di persona** (*fig*) to suffer the consequences; **pagare qc di tasca propria** to pay for sth out of one's own pocket; (*fig*) to learn sth to one's cost; **quanto non pagherei per sapere!** what wouldn't I give to know! **3** (*offrire*): **ti pago da bere** let me buy you a drink; **pago io** this is on me, I'll get it; **pago io questo giro** this is my round **4** (*contraccambiare*) to repay, pay back

pagella [pa'dʒɛlla] SF (*Scol*) school report (*Brit*), report card (*Am*)

paggio, gi ['paddʒo] SM page(boy)

pagherò *ecc*[1] [page'rɔ] VB *vedi* **pagare**

pagherò[2] [page'rɔ] SM INV IOU; **pagherò cambiario** promissory note

pagina ['padʒina] SF page; **a pagina 5** on page 5; **fate l'esercizio 2 a pagina 10** do exercise 2 on page 10; **andate a pagina 5** turn to page 5; **ha scritto un tema**

di tre pagine he wrote a three-page essay; **le più belle pagine del Manzoni** Manzoni's finest passages; **Pagine bianche** phone book, telephone directory; **Pagine gialle** Yellow Pages®

paginare [padʒi'nare] VT (*Inform*) to page

paginazione [padʒinat'tsjone] SF (*Inform*) paging

paglia ['paʎʎa] SF straw; (*fam: sigaretta*) fag; **cappello di paglia** straw hat; **tetto di paglia** thatched roof; **avere la coda di paglia** (*fig*) to have a guilty conscience; **fuoco di paglia** (*fig*) flash in the pan

pagliaccetto [paʎʎat'tʃetto] SM (*per bambini*) rompers *pl*; (*per signora*) camiknickers (*Brit*) *pl*

pagliacciata [paʎʎat'tʃata] SF farce

pagliaccio, ci [paʎ'ʎattʃo] SM clown; **fare il pagliaccio** (*fig*) to play the fool

pagliaio, ai [paʎ'ʎajo] SM haystack

pagliericcio, ci [paʎʎe'rittʃo] SM straw mattress

paglierino, a [paʎʎe'rino] AGG: **giallo paglierino** pale yellow

paglietta [paʎ'ʎetta] SF **1** (*cappello per uomo*) (straw) boater **2** (*per tegami ecc*) steel wool

pagliolato [paʎʎo'lato] SM (*Naut*) floor

pagliuzza [paʎ'ʎuttsa] SF (blade of) straw; (*d'oro ecc*) tiny particle, speck

pagnotta [paɲ'ɲɔtta] SF round loaf

pago, a, ghi, ghe ['pago] AGG: **essere pago di** to be satisfied with

pagoda [pa'gɔda] SF pagoda

paguro [pa'guro] SM hermit crab

paillette [pa'jɛt] SF INV sequin

paio *ecc*[1] ['pajo] VB *vedi* **parere**

paio[2] ['pajo] SM (*pl f* **paia**) (*coppia*) pair; **un paio di** (*guanti, scarpe*) a pair of; (*alcuni*) a couple of; **un paio di occhiali** a pair of glasses; **un paio di giorni** a couple of days; **fra un paio di settimane** in a couple of weeks; **dare un paio di schiaffi a qn** to box sb's ears; **fanno il paio** they are two of a kind; **è un altro paio di maniche** that's another kettle of fish

paiolo [pa'jɔlo], **paiuolo** [pa'jwɔlo] SM (copper) pot

Pakistan [pakis'tan] SM Pakistan

pakistano, a [pakis'tano] AGG, SM/F = **pachistano**

pal. ABBR = **palude**

pala ['pala] SF **1** shovel; (*di remo, ventilatore, elica*) blade; (*di ruota*) paddle **2** (*Rel*): **pala d'altare** altar piece

palacongressi [palakon'grɛssi] SM INV conference centre

paladino [pala'dino] SM (*Storia*) paladin; (*fig: difensore*) champion

palafitta [pala'fitta] SF **1** (*abitazione*) pile-dwelling **2** (*Edil: sostegno*) piles *pl*

palafitticolo, a [palafit'tikolo] AGG pile-dwelling *attr*

palafreniere [palafre'njɛre] SM (*Storia*) groom

palamito [pa'lamito] SM (*Pesca*) trawl line

palanca, che [pa'lanka] SF lifting beam, lever beam

palandrana [palan'drana] SF (*scherz: abito lungo e largo*) tent

palasport [pala'spɔrt] SM INV indoor sports arena

palata [pa'lata] SF (*contenuto*) shovelful; **fa soldi a palate** he is making a mint

palatale [pala'tale] AGG, SF (*Anat, Ling*) palatal

palatino[1], **a** [pala'tino] AGG (*Storia, Rel*) Palatine

palatino[2], **a** [pala'tino] AGG (*Anat: del palato*) palatine

palato [pa'lato] SM (*Anat*) palate; (*gusto*) palate, (sense of) taste; **gradevole al palato** palatable; **avere un palato fine** to have a refined palate

palazzina [palat'tsina] SF (*dimora signorile*) villa

palazzo [pa'lattso] SM (*reggia*) palace; (*edificio*) building; **palazzo dei congressi** conference centre; **palazzo di giustizia** law courts *pl*, courthouse; **palazzo dello sport** indoor sports arena

PALAZZI

Several of the Roman **palazzi** now have political functions. The sixteenth-century **Palazzo Chigi**, in Piazza Colonna, was acquired by the state in 1919 and became the seat of the Ministry of Foreign Affairs; since 1961 it has housed the Prime Minister's office and hosted Cabinet meetings. **Palazzo Madama**, another sixteenth-century building which was originally built for the Medici family, has been the home of the Senate since 1871. **Palazzo di Montecitorio**, completed in 1694, has housed the "Camera dei deputati" since 1870.

▷ www.romaturismo.it/v2/allascopertadiroma/it/palazzidellarepubblica.html

palchetto [pal'ketto] SM shelf

palco, chi ['palko] SM **1** (*tavolato*) platform, stand; (*ripiano*) layer **2** (*Teatro*) box; (*tribuna*) stand

palcoscenico [palkoʃ'ʃɛniko] SM (*Teatro*) stage

paleontologia [paleontolo'dʒia] SF palaeontology

palermitano, a [palermi'tano] AGG of *o* from Palermo ■ SM/F inhabitant *o* native of Palermo

Palermo [pa'lɛrmo] SF Palermo

palesare [pale'zare] VT to reveal, disclose
▶ **palesarsi** VIP (*sentimento*) to reveal *o* show itself

palese [pa'leze] AGG clear, evident; **rendere palesi le proprie intenzioni** to make one's intentions clear

palesemente [paleze'mente] AVV clearly

Palestina [pales'tina] SF Palestine

palestinese [palesti'nese] AGG, SM/F Palestinian

palestra [pa'lɛstra] SF (*luogo*) gymnasium, gym; (*esercizio atletico*) exercise, training; (*fig*) training ground, school; **vado in palestra due volte alla settimana** I go to the gym twice a week; **fare palestra** to work out; **fa palestra un'ora al giorno** he works out for an hour every day; **devo fare un po' di palestra** I must take a bit of exercise; **la scuola è palestra di vita** school is a preparation for life

palestrato, a [pales'trato] AGG (*persona*) toned, buff (*fam*)

paletot [pal'to] SM INV = **paltò**

paletta [pa'letta] SF (*giocattolo*) spade; (*per il focolare*) shovel; (*del capostazione, vigile*) signalling disc; (*Culin: da dolce*) cake slice

paletto [pa'letto] SM (*picchetto*) stake, peg; (*spranga*) bolt; (*Sci*) pole (*marking run*)

palinsesto [palin'sesto] SM (*TV, Radio*) schedule; (*Storia*) palimpsest

palio, li ['paljo] SM (*Storia: drappo*) (prize) banner; **il Palio di Siena** *horse race in which the different districts of Siena compete*; **mettere qc in palio** (*fig*) to offer sth as a prize

PALIO

The **Palio** is a horse race which takes place in a number of Italian towns, the most famous being the "Palio di Siena". The Tuscan race dates back to the thirteenth century; nowadays it is usually held twice a year, on 2 July and 16 August, in the Piazza del Campo. Ten of the 17 city districts or "contrade"

Pp

take part; the winner is the first horse to complete the course, whether or not it still has its rider. The race is preceded by a procession of "contrada" members in historical dress.
▷ www.ilpalio.org/
▷ www.ilpalio.siena.it/

palissandro [palis'sandro] SM rosewood
palizzata [palit'tsata] SF palisade
palla[1] ['palla] SF ball; (*pallottola*) bullet; **giocare a palla** to play (with a) ball; **sei una palla al piede!** you are a drag!; **prendere la palla al balzo** (*fig*) to seize one's opportunity; **rompere le palle a qn** (*fam!*) to be a bloody nuisance to sb; **che palle!** (*fam*) what a pain!; **palla gol** scoring opportunity; **a palla** (*al massimo*: *di volume*) full blast; (: *di velocità*) flat out; **palla da golf** golf ball; **palla di neve** snowball; **palla da tennis** tennis ball
palla[2] ['palla] SF (*Rel*) pall
pallacanestro [pallaka'nɛstro] SF basketball
▷ www.fip.it/
▷ www.legabasket.it/
Pallade ['pallade] SF (*anche:* **Pallade Atena**) Pallas (Athena)
palladiano, a [palla'djano] AGG Palladian
pallamano [palla'mano] SF handball
pallanuoto [palla'nwɔto] SF water polo
▷ www.federnuoto.it/pallanuoto.asp
pallavolo [palla'volo] SF volleyball
▷ www.federvolley.it/
palleggiare [palled'dʒare] VI (*aus* **avere**) (*Calcio*) to practise (*Brit*) *o* practice (*Am*) with the ball; (*Tennis*) to knock up; (*Basket*) to dribble
▶ **palleggiarsi** VR (*uso reciproco*): **si stanno palleggiando le responsabilità** each is trying to shift the responsibility onto the other
palleggio, gi [pal'leddʒo] SM (*gen*) practising (*Brit*) *o* practicing (*Am*) with a ball; (*prima di una partita*) warm-up; (*Tennis*) knock-up; (: *in partita*) rally
palliativo [pallja'tivo] SM (*Med*) palliative; (*fig*) stopgap measure
pallidamente [pallida'mente] AVV palely
pallido, a ['pallido] AGG (*gen*) pale; (*malaticcio*) pallid; (*ricordo*) faint; (*sorriso*) faint, wan; **sei pallida** you're pale; **è diventata pallida** she paled, she turned pale; **non ho la più pallida idea** I haven't the faintest *o* foggiest (idea)
pallina [pal'lina] SF (*bilia*) marble
pallino [pal'lino] SM **1** (*pois*) dot; **bianco a pallini blu** white with blue dots **2** (*Biliardo*) cue ball; (*Bocce*) jack **3** (*proiettile*) pellet **4** (*idea fissa*) craze, obsession; **avere il pallino di** to be crazy about; **ha il pallino della matematica** he has a passion for mathematics
pallonata [pallo'nata] SF blow (from a ball)
palloncino [pallon'tʃino] SM (*giocattolo*) balloon; (*lampioncino*) Chinese lantern
pallone [pal'lone] SM **1** (*palla*) ball; (*Calcio*) football; **giocare a pallone** to play football; **gioco del pallone** football; **essere un pallone gonfiato** (*fig*) to be full of o.s. **2** (*aerostato*) balloon; **pallone sonda** weather balloon **3** (*Chim*) flask
pallonetto [pallo'netto] SM (*Calcio, Tennis*) lob
pallore [pal'lore] SM pallor, paleness
pallottola [pal'lɔttola] SF **1** (*proiettile*) bullet; (: *di fucile da caccia*) pellet **2** (*di carta*) ball; **c'erano delle pallottole di carta nel cestino** there were some bits of screwed-up paper in the wastepaper basket
pallottoliere [pallotto'ljɛre] SM abacus
palma[1] ['palma] SF (*Anat*) palm
palma[2] ['palma] SF (*Bot*) palm; **riportare/vincere la palma** (*fig*) to walk off with/win the prize; **palma da datteri** date palm
palmare [pal'mare] SM INV, AGG INV (*anche:* **computer palmare**) palmtop
palmato, a [pal'mato] AGG (*Zool*: *piede*) webbed; (*Bot*) palmate
palmeto [pal'meto] SM palm grove
palmipede [pal'mipede] AGG web-footed
palmizio, zi [pal'mittsjo] SM (*palma*) palm tree; (*ramo*) palm
palmo ['palmo] SM (*misura*) handbreadth; **palmo a palmo** inch by inch; **hanno ispezionato la stanza palmo a palmo** they searched the room inch by inch; **un palmo di polvere sul tavolo** (*fig*) a layer of dust on the table; **restare con un palmo di naso** (*fig*) to be badly disappointed; **essere alto un palmo** (*fig*) to be tiny
palo ['palo] SM (*legno appuntito*) stake; (*sostegno*) pole; (*Calcio*) goalpost; **fare da** *o* **il palo** (*fig*) to act as look-out; **saltare di palo in frasca** (*fig*) to jump from one topic to another; **palo della luce** lamppost; **palo del telegrafo** telegraph pole
palombaro [palom'baro] SM (deep-sea) diver
palombo [pa'lombo] SM (*pesce*) dogfish; (*colombo*) wood pigeon
palpabile [pal'pabile] AGG (*differenza, errore*) palpable
palpabilmente [palpabil'mente] AVV palpably
palpare [pal'pare] VT (*tastare*) to feel, finger; (*Med*) to palpate
palpebra ['palpebra] SF eyelid
palpitante [palpi'tante] AGG: **palpitante di** (*paura*) trembling with; (*emozione*) quivering with
palpitare [palpi'tare] VI (*aus* **avere**) (*cuore*) to beat; (: *più forte*) to pound, throb; (*fremere*) to quiver; **palpitare di paura** to tremble with fear; **palpitare di gioia** to quiver with delight
palpitazione [palpitat'tsjone] SF (*Med*): **avere le palpitazioni** to have palpitations
palpito ['palpito] SM (*del cuore*) beat; (*fig*: *d'amore*) throb
paltò [pal'tɔ] SM INV overcoat
palude [pa'lude] SF marsh, swamp
paludoso, a [palu'doso] AGG swampy, marshy
palustre [pa'lustre] AGG marsh *attr*, swamp *attr*
pampa ['pampa] SF pampas *sg o pl*
pampino ['pampino] SM vine leaf
Pan ['pan] SM Pan
panacea [pana'tʃɛa] SF panacea
Panama ['panama] SF Panama; **il canale di Panama** the Panama Canal
panama ['panama] SM INV (*cappello*) panama (hat)
panamense [pana'mɛnse] AGG, SM/F Panamanian
panare [pa'nare] VT to dip *o* roll in breadcrumbs
panca, che ['panka] SF bench
pancarré [pankar're] SM INV sliced bread
pancetta [pan'tʃetta] SF **1** (*Culin*) bacon; **pancetta affumicata** smoked streaky bacon **2** (*fam*: *ciccia*) belly; **mio padre ha un po' di pancetta** my dad's got a bit of a belly
panchetto [pan'ketto] SM (*sgabello*) stool
panchina [pan'kina] SF garden seat; (*di giardino pubblico*) (park) bench; (*Sport*) substitutes' bench
pancia, ce ['pantʃa] SF belly, stomach; **aver la pancia** to have a potbelly; **aver la pancia piena** to be full; **aver mal di pancia** to have stomach ache *o* a sore stomach;

mettere su pancia to develop *o* be getting a paunch; **non star lì a grattarti la pancia!** don't sit (*o* stand) there doing nothing!

panciata [pan'tʃata] SF belly flop

panciera [pan'tʃɛra] SF corset

panciolle [pan'tʃɔlle] AVV: **stare in panciolle** to lounge about (*Brit*) *o* around

pancione, a [pan'tʃone] SM (*pancia*) stomach; **quando la mamma aveva il pancione** when mummy was pregnant
■ SM/F (*persona grassa*) potbellied man/fat-bellied woman

panciotto [pan'tʃɔtto] SM waistcoat

panciuto, a [pan'tʃuto] AGG (*persona*) potbellied; (*vaso, bottiglia*) rounded

pancreas ['pankreas] SM INV pancreas

panda ['panda] SM INV panda

pandemia [pande'mia] SF pandemic

pandemico, a, ci, che [pan'dɛmiko] AGG pandemic

pandemonio, ni [pande'mɔnjo] SM pandemonium

Pandora [pan'dɔra] SF Pandora; **il vaso di Pandora** Pandora's box

pandoro [pan'dɔro] SM *type of sponge cake eaten at Christmas*

pane ['pane] SM (*gen*) bread; (*pagnotta*) loaf (of bread); (*di cera*) bar; (*di burro*) block; **il pane quotidiano** one's daily bread; **guadagnarsi il pane** to earn one's living; **mangiare (il) pane a tradimento** to sponge, scrounge; **rendere pan per focaccia** to give tit for tat; **dire pane al pane, vino al vino** to call a spade a spade; **essere buono come il pane** to have a heart of gold; **quella ragazza non è pane per i tuoi denti** that girl's not for you; **per un pezzo di pane** (*comprare, vendere*) for a song
■ **pane a** *o* **in cassetta** sliced bread; **pane bianco** white bread; **pane casereccio** homemade bread; **pane integrale** *o* **nero** wholemeal bread; **pane al latte** milk bread; **pane di segale** rye bread; **pane tostato** toast; **una fetta di pane tostato** a slice of toast; **pan di Spagna** sponge cake; **pan di zucchero** sugar loaf

panegirico, ci [pane'dʒiriko] SM panegyric; **fare un panegirico di qn** to sing sb's praises

panetteria [panette'ria] SF (*forno*) bakery; (*negozio*) baker's (shop), bakery; **la panetteria all'angolo** the bakery on the corner; **vado in panetteria** I'm going to the baker's

panettiere, a [panet'tjɛre] SM/F baker; **fa il panettiere** he's a baker

panetto [pa'netto] SM (*di burro*) block

panettone [panet'tone] SM panettone; *a kind of spiced brioche with sultanas, eaten at Christmas*; (*di cemento*) bollard

panfilo ['panfilo] SM yacht

panforte [pan'fɔrte] SM *Sienese nougat-type delicacy*

pangrattato [pangrat'tato] SM breadcrumbs *pl*

panico, a, ci, che ['paniko] SM panic; **essere in preda al panico** to be panic-stricken; **farsi prendere dal panico** to panic; **si è fatta prendere dal panico** she panicked
■ AGG panic *attr*

paniere [pa'njɛre] SM basket

panificare [panifi'kare] VI (*aus* **avere**) to make bread

panificatore, trice [panifika'tore] SM/F bread-maker, baker

panificio, ci [pani'fitʃo] SM (*forno*) bakery; (*negozio*) baker's (shop), bakery

panino [pa'nino] SM roll; **un panino al prosciutto** a ham roll; **panino imbottito** filled roll

paninoteca, che [panino'tɛka] SF ≈ café

panna[1] ['panna] SF (*Culin*) cream; **panna acida** sour(ed) cream; **panna da cucina** long-life cream used for cooking; **panna montata** whipped cream

panna[2] ['panna] SF (*Naut*): **mettersi in panna** to heave to

panne ['pan] SF INV (*Aut*) breakdown; **la macchina è in panne** the car has broken down; **rimanere in panne** to break down; **siamo rimasti in panne sull'autostrada** we broke down on the motorway

panneggio, gi [pan'neddʒo] SM drapery

pannello [pan'nɛllo] SM panel; **pannello di controllo** control panel; **pannello divisorio** partition; **pannello fonoisolante** acoustic screen; **pannello solare** solar panel

panno ['panno] SM **1** (*tessuto, straccio*) cloth; **un panno umido** a damp cloth **2** (*vestiti*): **panni** SMPL clothes; **panni da lavare** laundry, washing; **mettiti nei miei panni** put yourself in my shoes; **non stava più nei panni dalla gioia** he was beside himself with joy

pannocchia [pan'nɔkkja] SF (*di granturco*) corncob; **non ho mai mangiato le pannocchie** I've never eaten corn on the cob

pannolino [panno'lino] SM (*per bambini*) nappy (*Brit*), diaper (*Am*); (*assorbente*) sanitary towel; **pannolino mutandina** disposable nappy *o* diaper

pannolone [panno'lone] SM (*per adulti*) incontinence pad

panorama, i [pano'rama] SM panorama; **che bel panorama!** what a lovely view!

panoramica, che [pano'ramika] SF **1** (*strada*) scenic route **2** (*Cine*) pan shot; (*Fot*) panorama; **fare una panoramica di qc** (*fig*) to outline sth

panoramicamente [panoramika'mente] AVV panoramically

panoramico, a, ci, che [pano'ramiko] AGG (*gen*) panoramic; **strada panoramica** scenic route; **rassegna panoramica** overall view

panpepato [panpe'pato] SM *type of gingerbread*

pantacollant [pantakol'lan] SM INV leggings *pl*

pantagruelico, a, ci, che [pantagru'ɛliko] AGG (*pranzo, appetito*) gigantic

pantalone [panta'lone] AGG INV: **gonna pantalone** culottes *pl*

pantaloni [panta'loni] SMPL trousers (*Brit*), pants (*Am*); **un paio di pantaloni** a pair of trousers *o* pants

pantano [pan'tano] SM marsh, bog

panteismo [pante'izmo] SM pantheism

panteistico, a, ci, che [pante'istiko] AGG pantheistic

pantera [pan'tɛra] SF **1** (*Zool*) panther **2** (*fam: auto della polizia*) (high-speed) police car

pantheon ['panteon] SM INV pantheon

pantofola [pan'tɔfola] SF slipper

pantografo [pan'tɔgrafo] SM pantograph

pantomima [panto'mima] SF pantomime

panzana [pan'tsana] SF tall story

panzarotto [pantsa'rɔtto] SM *large fried piece of ravioli filled with ham, cheese and tomato*

panzer ['pantsər] SM INV (*Mil*) panzer

paonazzo, a [pao'nattso] AGG purple

papa, i ['papa] SM pope; **ad ogni morte di papa** once in a blue moon; **morto un papa se ne fa un altro** nobody's indispensable; **vivere come un papa** to live like a Lord; **il papa nero** the Black Pope

Pp

PAPA

The Pope is the head of the Roman Catholic Church and resides in Vatican City, a tiny independent state within the city of Rome, whose territory consists mainly of Saint Peter's basilica. The seat of the papacy was transferred to Avignon in France in 1307, returning to Rome in 1377.

▹ www.vatican.va/phome_it.htm

papà [pa'pa] SM INV daddy, dad; **il mio papà** my dad; **il papà di Claudio** Claudio's father; **figlio di papà** spoilt young man
papaia [pa'paja] SF papaya
papale [pa'pale] AGG papal
papalina [papa'lina] SF skullcap
papalino [papa'lino] AGG papal
■ SM (*soldato*) papal guard; (*Pol*) *supporter of the Pope's temporal authority*
papamobile [papa'mɔbile] SF popemobile
paparazzo [papa'rattso] SM paparazzo
papato [pa'pato] SM papacy
papaverina [papave'rina] SF papaverine
papavero [pa'pavero] SM poppy
papera ['papera] SF (*errore*) slip of the tongue; **ha fatto una papera** that was a slip of the tongue on his (o her) part
papero, a ['papero] SM/F (*Zool*) gosling
papilla [pa'pilla] SF (*Anat*): **papilla gustativa** taste bud; **papilla ottica** blind spot
papillon [papi'jɔ̃] SM INV bow tie
papiro [pa'piro] SM papyrus
papirologia [papirolo'dʒia] SF papyrology
pappa ['pappa] SF (*per bambini*) pap; (*pegg: poltiglia*) mush; **hai sempre avuto la pappa pronta** (*fig*) you've never had to stand on your own two feet; **pappa reale** royal jelly
pappagallesco, a, schi, sche [pappagal'lesko] AGG parrot-like
pappagallo [pappa'gallo] SM (*Zool*) parrot; (*fig pegg: uomo*) wolf; **ripetere tutto a pappagallo** to repeat everything parrot-fashion
pappagorgia, ge [pappa'gɔrdʒa] SF double chin
pappardella [pappar'dɛlla] SF (*Culin*) *wide strip of pasta*; (*fig: tiritera*) rigmarole
pappare [pap'pare] VT (*fam: anche: papparsi: mangiare*) to gobble up; (: *appropriarsi di: soldi*) to walk off with
paprica ['paprika] SF paprika
Pap-test ['paptest] SM INV smear test, Pap smear *o* test (*Am*)
par. ABBR (= **paragrafo**) par. (= *paragraph*)
para[1] ['para] SF: **suole di para** crepe soles
para[2] ['para] SF (*fam: paranoia*): **andare in para** to freak out
parà [pa'ra] SM INV para
parabola[1] [pa'rabola] SF (*Mat*) parabola
parabola[2] [pa'rabola] SF (*Rel*) parable
parabolico, a, ci, che [para'bɔliko] AGG parabolic; **antenna parabolica** (satellite) dish
parabordo [para'bordo] SM (*Naut*) fender
parabrezza [para'breddza] SM INV (*Aut*) windscreen (*Brit*), windshield (*Am*)
paracadutare [parakadu'tare] VT
▶ **paracadutarsi** VR to parachute
paracadute [paraka'dute] SM INV parachute
paracadutismo [parakadu'tizmo] SM parachuting
paracadutista, i [parakadu'tista] SM parachutist; (*Mil*) paratrooper
paracarro [para'karro] SM kerbstone (*Brit*), curbstone (*Am*)
paracetamolo [paratʃeta'mɔlo] SM paracetamol
paradenti [para'dɛnti] SM INV (*Pugilato*) gumshield
paradigma, i [para'digma] SM paradigm
paradigmatico, a, ci, che [paradig'matiko] AGG (*Ling*) paradigmatic; (*fig: esemplificante*) exemplary, paradigmatic
paradisiaco, a, ci, che [paradi'ziako] AGG heavenly
paradiso [para'dizo] SM (*anche fig*) paradise, heaven; **sentirsi in paradiso** to be in seventh heaven; **paradisi artificiali** drug-induced fantasies; **paradiso fiscale** tax haven; **il Paradiso terrestre** the Garden of Eden, the Earthly Paradise
paradossale [parados'sale] AGG paradoxical
paradossalmente [paradossal'mente] AVV paradoxically
paradosso [para'dɔsso] SM paradox
parafango, ghi [para'fango] SM (*di auto*) mudflap (*Brit*) *o* splashguard (*Am*); (*di bicicletta*) mudguard (*Brit*) *o* fender (*Am*)
paraffina [paraf'fina] SF paraffin (wax)
parafrasare [parafra'zare] VT to paraphrase
parafrasi [pa'rafrazi] SF INV paraphrase
parafulmine [para'fulmine] SM lightning conductor
paraggi [pa'raddʒi] SMPL: **nei paraggi (di)** in the vicinity (of), near, in the neighbourhood (*Brit*) *o* neighborhood (*Am*) (of); **nei paraggi della stazione** near the station; **dev'essere qui nei paraggi** it's around here somewhere; **in questi paraggi** in this neighbo(u)rhood, somewhere around here
paragonabile [parago'nabile] AGG: **paragonabile (a)** comparable (to)
paragonare [parago'nare] VT to compare; **paragonate le due frasi** compare the two sentences; **paragonare a/con** to compare to/with; **lo paragona sempre al fratello** she's always comparing him with his brother
▶ **paragonarsi** VR: **paragonarsi a/con** to compare o.s. to/with
paragone [para'gone] SM comparison; (*esempio analogo*) analogy, parallel; **fare un paragone tra** to compare; **se facciamo un paragone tra le due macchine...** if we compare the two cars...; **a paragone di** as compared to, in comparison with; **il paragone non regge** the two just can't be compared; **non regge al paragone** it doesn't stand *o* bear comparison; **senza paragone** incomparable, peerless

LO SAPEVI...?
paragone non si traduce mai con la parola inglese *paragon*

paragrafo [pa'ragrafo] SM (*Gramm, fig*) paragraph
paraguaiano, a [paragwa'jano] AGG, SM/F Paraguayan
Paraguay [para'gwai] SM Paraguay
paralisi [pa'ralizi] SF INV (*Med, fig*) paralysis
paralitico, a, ci, che [para'litiko] AGG, SM/F paralytic
paralizzare [paralid'dzare] VT (*Med, fig*) to paralyze
paralizzato, a [paralid'dzato] AGG paralyzed
parallasse [paral'lasse] SF parallax
parallela [paral'lɛla] SF (*Geom*) parallel (line); (*attrezzo ginnico*): **le parallele** SFPL the parallel bars
parallelamente [parallela'mente] AVV: **parallelamente (a)** (*gen*) parallel (to); (*contemporaneamente*) at the same time (as), in parallel (with)

parallelepipedo [parallele'pipedo] SM parallelepiped
parallelismo [paralle'lizmo] SM (*Mat*) parallelism; (*fig: corrispondenza*) similarities *pl*
parallelo, a [paral'lɛlo] AGG (*gen, anche Inform*) parallel; **interfaccia parallela** (*Inform*) parallel interface
■ SM (*Geog, fig*) parallel; **fare un parallelo tra** (*comparazione*) to draw a parallel between
parallelogramma, i [parallelo'gramma] SM parallelogram
paralume [para'lume] SM lampshade
paramedico, a, ci, che [para'mɛdiko] AGG paramedical; **il personale paramedico** the paramedics *pl*
■ SM/F paramedic
paramenti [para'menti] SMPL (*Rel*) vestments
parametro [pa'rametro] SM parameter
paramilitare [paramili'tare] AGG paramilitary
paranco, chi [pa'ranko] SM hoist
paranoia [para'nɔja] SF (*Psicol*) paranoia; **andare/mandare in paranoia** (*fam*) to freak/be freaked out
paranoico, a, ci, che [para'nɔiko] AGG, SM/F paranoid; (*fam*) freaked (out)
paranormale [paranor'male] AGG paranormal
paraocchi [para'ɔkki] SMPL (*anche fig*) blinkers (*Brit*), blinders (*Am*)
paraorecchie [parao'rekkje] SM INV (*di cappello*) earflap
parapendio, dii [parapen'dio] SM (*paracadute*) paraglider; (*sport*) paragliding
parapetto [para'pɛtto] SM parapet
parapiglia [para'piʎʎa] SM INV uproar, commotion
parapioggia [para'pjɔddʒa] SM INV umbrella
paraplegia [paraple'dʒia] SF paraplegia
paraplegico, a, ci, che [para'plɛdʒiko] AGG, SM/F paraplegic
parapsicologia [parapsikolo'dʒia] SF parapsychology
parapsicologico, a, ci, che [parapsiko'lodʒiko] AGG parapsychological
parare [pa'rare] VT **1** (*addobbare*) to adorn, deck (out) **2** (*proteggere: occhi*) to shield, protect **3** (*scansare: colpo: anche fig*) to parry; (*: goal, tiro*) to save; **ha parato il rigore** he saved the penalty
■ VI (*aus* **avere**) **dove vuoi andare a parare?** what are you driving at?
▶ **pararsi** VR (*presentarsi*) to present o.s., appear
parascolastico, a, ci, che [parasko'lastiko] AGG (*attività*) extracurricular
parasole [para'sole] SM INV parasol, sunshade
parassita, i [paras'sita] (*anche fig*) AGG parasitic
■ SM parasite
parassitario, ria, ri, rie [parassi'tarjo] AGG parasitic
parassitismo [parassi'tizmo] SM parasitism
parastatale [parasta'tale] AGG state-controlled
parastato [paras'tato] SM *employees in the state-controlled sector*
parastinchi [paras'tinki] SM INV shin guard
parata¹ [pa'rata] SF (*Sport*) save; **parata in due tempi** (*Calcio*) double save
parata² [pa'rata] SF (*Mil*) review, parade
parati [pa'rati] SMPL hangings; **carta da parati** wallpaper
paratia [para'tia] SF (*Naut*) bulkhead
paraurti [para'urti] SM INV (*Aut*) bumper
paravento [para'vɛnto] SM folding screen; **fare da paravento a qn** (*fig*) to shield sb
parboiled [pa:bɔɪld] AGG INV (*riso*) parboiled
parcella [par'tʃɛlla] SF fee

> **LO SAPEVI...?**
> **parcella** non si traduce mai con la parola inglese *parcel*

Parche ['parke] SFPL: **le Parche** the Fates
parcheggiare [parked'dʒare] VT to park
parcheggiatore, trice [parkeddʒa'tore] SM/F parking attendant
parcheggio, gi [par'keddʒo] SM (*luogo*) car park (*Brit*), parking lot (*Am*); (*azione*) parking *no pl*; (*singolo posto*) parking space; **hanno costruito un nuovo parcheggio** a new car park has been built; **non riesco a trovare parcheggio** I can't find a parking space; **qui c'è divieto di parcheggio** you can't park here; **"divieto di parcheggio"** "no parking"
parchimetro [par'kimetro] SM parking meter
parco¹, chi ['parko] SM **1** (*giardino*) park; **parco dei divertimenti** amusement park, funfair; **parco giochi** (children's) playground; **parco nazionale** national park; **parco a tema** theme park **2** (*insieme di veicoli*) fleet; **parco macchine** car fleet; **parco rotabile** (*Ferr*) rolling stock **3** (*spazio per deposito*) depot
parco², a, chi, che ['parko] AGG: **parco (in)** (*sobrio*) moderate (in); (*avaro*) sparing (with)
parcometro [par'kɔmetro] SM (*Aut*) (Pay and Display) ticket machine
par condicio [par kon'ditʃo] SF (*TV*) *the right to speak for an equal length of time as one's opponents*
parecchio, a, chi [pa'rekkjo] AGG INDEF **1** quite a lot of; **c'è parecchio vino** there is quite a lot of wine; **c'era parecchia gente** there were quite a lot of *o* several people; **ho parecchia fame** I am quite hungry; **parecchio tempo** quite a lot of time, a long time; **non lo vedo da parecchio tempo** I haven't seen him for ages *o* for a long time; **è parecchio tempo che ti aspetto** I have been waiting for you for ages; **parecchio tempo fa** a long time ago, long ago **2** **parecchi(e)** several, quite a lot of; **parecchie persone/volte/cose** several *o* a number of people/times/things; **c'erano parecchie ragazze** there were quite a lot of girls; **ho avuto parecchi guai** I have had quite a lot of trouble
■ PRON INDEF quite a lot, quite a bit; **parecchi(e)** several, quite a lot; **c'è del pane? — parecchio** is there any bread? — yes, quite a lot; **ce n'è parecchio** there's quite a lot; **quanto tempo hai aspettato? — parecchio** how long did you wait? — quite a long time *o* quite a while; **ci ho pensato parecchio** I gave it quite a lot of thought; **parecchi dicono...** several people *o* a number of people say ...; **eravamo in parecchi** there were several of us; **parecchi di noi** several of us, quite a few of us
■ AVV **1** (*seguito da agg*) quite, rather; **è parecchio intelligente** he is quite intelligent **2** (*preceduto da vb*) quite a lot, quite a bit; **mangia parecchio** he eats quite a lot; **è dimagrito parecchio** he has lost quite a lot of weight; **mi è costato parecchio** it cost me quite a lot
pareggiamento [pareddʒa'mento] SM (*di conti, bilancio*) balancing
pareggiare [pared'dʒare] VT (*gen*) to make equal; (*terreno*) to level, make level; (*bilancio, conti*) to balance
■ VI (*aus* **avere**) (*Sport: durante la partita*) to equalize; (*: risultato*) to draw; **hanno pareggiato due a due** they drew two all; **la Juventus ha pareggiato a due minuti dalla fine della partita** Juventus equalized two minutes before the end of the match
pareggio, gi [pa'reddʒo] SM (*Sport*) draw; (*Econ*) balance

Pp

parentado [paren'tado] SM relatives *pl*, relations *pl*; **alla festa c'era tutto il parentado** the whole family was at the party
parentale [paren'tale] AGG (*autorità*) parental; (*malattia*) hereditary
parente [pa'rɛnte] SM/F relative, relation; **è un mio parente** he's a relative of mine

LO SAPEVI...?
parente non si traduce mai con la parola inglese *parent*

parentela [paren'tɛla] SF (*vincolo di sangue, fig*) relationship; (*insieme dei parenti*) relatives *pl*, relations *pl*
parentesi [pa'rɛntezi] SF INV (*segno grafico*) bracket, parenthesis; (*digressione*) digression, parenthesis; **tra parentesi** in brackets; (*fig*) incidentally; **fare una parentesi** (*fig*) to digress; **dopo la parentesi estiva** after the summer break; **parentesi graffe** curly braces; **parentesi quadre** square brackets; **parentesi tonde** round brackets
parentetico, a, ci, che [paren'tɛtiko] AGG parenthetic(al)
parere[1] [pa'rere] SM (*opinione*) opinion; (*consiglio*) advice; **a mio parere** in my opinion
parere[2] [pa'rere] VI IRREG (*aus* **essere**) **1** (*apparire*) to look, seem, appear; **pare onesto** he looks *o* seems *o* appears honest; **pare impossibile ma è così** it doesn't seem possible and yet it's true; **pare di sì/no** it seems/doesn't seem so; **non mi pare vero!** I can scarcely believe it!; **pare che...** it seems *o* appears that ...; apparently; **pare che voglia cambiare squadra** apparently he wants to change teams; **pare che sia stato lui** it seems it was him; **a quanto pare se n'è andato** he seems to have left, he has apparently left **2** (*essere dell'opinione*): **mi pare che...** I think (that) ..., it seems to me (that) ...; **mi pare che sia già arrivato** I think he's already here; **mi pare di sì/no** I think/don't think so; **che te ne pare?** what do you think?; **che te ne pare del mio libro?** what do you think of my book?; **che te ne pare di andare al cinema?** how about going to the cinema?, how do you fancy going to the cinema?; **è ora di andare, non ti pare?** don't you think it's time we left?; **disturbo? — ma le pare!** am I disturbing you? — not at all!; **fai come ti pare!** do what *o* as you like!
paresi ['parezi] SF INV paresis
parete [pa'rete] SF (*muro*) wall; (*di montagna*) face; **fra le pareti domestiche** at home, within one's own four walls; **parete cellulare** (*Bio*) cell wall
pargolo, a ['pargolo] SM/F (*letter o scherz*) child
pari[1] ['pari] AGG INV **1** (*uguale*) equal, (the) same; **hanno pari diritti e doveri** they have equal rights and duties; **essere pari a qn in qc** to be equal to sb in sth; **essere pari di grado** to have the same rank; **essere pari in bellezza/intelligenza** to be equally beautiful/intelligent; **andare di pari passo (con)** to proceed at the same rate (as); **hanno vinto a pari merito** they were joint winners; **pari opportunità** equal opportunities **2** (*piano*) level; **una superficie pari** a level *o* an even surface; **saltare qc a piè pari** (*fig: omettere*) to skip sth **3** (*Mat: numero*) even; **numeri pari** even numbers **4** (*in giochi*) equal, drawn, tied; **la partita è pari** (*Sport*) the match is a draw; **siamo pari, vuoi la rivincita?** it's a draw, do you want a decider?; **siamo pari** (*fig*) we are quits *o* even
■ SM (*numero*) even number; (*parità*): **rimettersi in pari (con)** to catch up (with); **cercherò di rimettermi in pari** I'll try to catch up; **essere intelligente al pari di qn** to be as intelligent as sb; **comportarsi al pari di qn** to behave like sb
■ SM/F peer, equal
■ AVV **1 copiato pari pari dal libro** copied word for word from the book **2 alla pari** on the same level; (*Borsa*) at par; **mettersi alla pari con** to place o.s. on the same level as; **ragazza alla pari** au pair (girl)
pari[2] ['pari] SM INV (*Pol: Brit*) peer; **pari a vita** life peer
paria ['parja] SM INV (*anche fig*) pariah
Paride ['paride] SM (*Mitol*) Paris
parificare [parifi'kare] VT (*scuola*) to recognize officially
parificato, a [parifi'kato] AGG: **scuola parificata** *officially recognized private school*
parificazione [parifikat'tsjone] SF (*di scuola*) official recognition
Parigi [pa'ridʒi] SF Paris; **vado a Parigi quest'estate** I'm going to Paris this summer; **vive a Parigi** he lives in Paris
parigino, a [pari'dʒino] AGG, SM/F Parisian
pariglia [pa'riʎʎa] SF **1** (*tiro di cavalli*) pair **2** (*fig*): **rendere la pariglia** to give tit for tat
parimenti [pari'menti] AVV (*letter: ugualmente*) equally
parità [pari'ta] SF INV parity, equality; **a parità di condizioni** all things being equal; **trattamento di parità** equal treatment; **un risultato di parità** (*Sport*) a draw, a tie; **finire in parità** to end in a draw
paritetico, a, ci, che [pari'tɛtiko] AGG: **rapporto paritetico** equal relationship; **commissione paritetica** joint committee
Parkinson ['parkinson] SM (*anche:* **morbo di Parkinson**) Parkinson's (disease)
parlamentare[1] [parlamen'tare] AGG parliamentary
■ SM/F ≈ Member of Parliament (*Brit*), ≈ Congressman/Congresswoman (*Am*)
parlamentare[2] [parlamen'tare] VI (*aus* **avere**) to negotiate, parley
parlamento [parla'mento] SM parliament; **il Parlamento europeo** the European Parliament
▷ www.europarl.eu.int/home/default_it.htm

PARLAMENTO

The Italian constitution, which came into force on 1 January 1948, states that the **Parlamento** has legislative power. It is made up of two chambers, the "Camera dei deputati" and the "Senato". There are 630 deputies and 315 elected senators, plus life senators who include all former presidents as well as five distinguished members of the public. Parliamentary elections are held every five years.
▷ www.parlamento.it/

parlante [par'lante] AGG (*bambola, pappagallo*) talking; **ritratto parlante** (*fig*) lifelike painting
parlantina [parlan'tina] SF (*fam*) talkativeness; **avere una buona parlantina** to have the gift of the gab
parlare [par'lare] VI (*aus* **avere**)
1 (*facoltà*) to talk; (*modo*) to talk, to speak; **il bambino non sa ancora parlare** the baby can't talk yet; **non parlate tutti insieme** don't all talk at once; **si parlavano a gesti** they were using sign language; **parla piano/più forte** talk *o* speak quietly/louder; **non riusciva a parlare per la gioia** he was speechless with joy; **parla bene!** talk properly!; **parlare tra i denti** to mutter; **parlare come un libro stampato** to

talk like a book; **ha occhi che parlano** he has expressive eyes
2 *(esprimere il proprio pensiero)* to speak; **parlare chiaro** to speak one's mind; **voglio parlare con il direttore!** I want to speak to the manager!; **parlare a caso** *o* **a vanvera** to ramble on; **parlare bene/male di qn/qc** to say nice/nasty things about sb/sth; **fallo** *o* **lascialo parlare** give him a chance to speak, let him have his say; **con rispetto parlando** with respect; **i dati parlano chiaro** the facts speak for themselves
3 *(conversare)* to talk; **abbiamo parlato per ore** we talked for hours; **parlare a/con qn di qc** to talk *o* speak to/with sb about *o* of sth; **lascia che gli parli io** let me talk to him; **gli parlerò di te** I'll talk to him about you; **di che cosa avete parlato?** what did you talk about?; **parlare di lavoro** *o* **d'affari** to talk shop; **non ci parliamo più** we're not on speaking terms; **parlare del più e del meno** to talk about this and that; **è come parlare al vento** *o* **a un muro** it's like talking to a brick wall; **senti, ne parliamo a quattrocchi** look, we'll discuss it *o* talk about it in private; **parliamone** let's talk about it; **non parliamone più** let's just forget about it; **non ne voglio più sentir parlare** let's hear no more about it; **far parlare di sé** to get o.s. talked about; **parlano di matrimonio** they are talking about getting married, they are discussing marriage; **per ora non se ne parla** there's nothing doing for the moment
4 *(Telec)*: **sta parlando al telefono** he's on the phone; **pronto? chi parla?** hello, who's speaking?; **parla Bianchi** Bianchi here *o* speaking; **posso parlare con il Sig. Rossi?** can I speak to Mr Rossi?
5 **parlare di** *(far cenno a)* to mention; *(trattare di: argomento)* to be about, deal with; **per non parlare di...** not to mention ...; **ne ho sentito parlare** I've heard of it (*o* him *o* her ecc); **ne parlano tutti i giornali** it's in all the newspapers; **il libro parla del problema della droga** the book deals with the drug problem; **di cosa parla il suo ultimo romanzo?** what is his latest novel about?
6 *(confessare)* to talk; **far parlare un prigioniero** to make a prisoner talk
■ VT *(una lingua)* to speak; **sai parlare l'inglese?** can you speak English?; **per me parla arabo** *(fig)* it's all Greek to me
■ SM *(dialetto)* dialect

parlata [par'lata] SF *(dialetto)* dialect
parlato[1], a [par'lato] AGG spoken
parlato[2] [par'lato] SM *(Naut: nodo)* clove hitch
parlatore, trice [parla'tore] SM/F *(oratore)* speaker
parlatorio, ri [parla'tɔrjo] SM *(di carcere)* visiting room; *(di collegio, convento)* parlour *(Brit)*, parlor *(Am)*
parlottare [parlot'tare] VI *(aus* **avere***)* to mutter
parlottio, tii [parlot'tio] SM muttering
parmigiano, a [parmi'dʒano] AGG Parma *attr*, of *o* from Parma; **alla parmigiana** *(Culin)* with Parmesan cheese
■ SM/F inhabitant *o* native of Parma
■ SM *(grana)* Parmesan (cheese)
Parnaso [par'nazo] SM *(Geog, Mitol)* Parnassus
parodia [paro'dia] SF parody
parodiare [paro'djare] VT to parody
parola [pa'rɔla] SF 1 *(facoltà)* speech; **ha perso la parola** he's lost the power of speech; **rimanere senza parole** to be speechless; **a quel cane manca solo la parola** that dog is almost human; **avere la parola facile** to have the gift of the gab 2 *(vocabolo)* word; **una parola difficile** a difficult word; **rivolgere la parola a qn** to speak to sb; **mi hai tolto la parola di bocca** you have taken the words right out of my mouth; **mettere una buona parola per qn** to put in a good word for sb; **non è detta l'ultima parola** that's not the end of the matter; **non farne parola a nessuno!** don't breathe a word to anyone!; **è una parola!** it's easier said than done!; **non ho parole per ringraziarti** I don't know how to thank you; **passare dalle parole ai fatti** to get down to business; **in parole povere** in plain English; **parola d'ordine** password; **parole incrociate** crossword (puzzle) *sg*; **sta facendo le parole incrociate** she's doing the crossword 3 **parole** SFPL *(di canzone)* words, lyrics; *(chiacchiere)* talk *sg* 4 *(promessa)* word; **dare la propria parola a qn** to give sb one's word; **gli ho dato la mia parola** I gave him my word; **mantenere la parola** to keep one's word; **ho mantenuto la parola** I've kept my word; **è una persona di parola** he is a man of his word; **rimangiarsi la parola** to go back on one's word, break one's promise; **si è rimangiato la parola** he broke his promise; **parola chiave** keyword; **parola d'onore** word of honour 5 *(in dibattiti)*: **diritto di parola** right to speak; **chiedere la parola** to ask permission to speak; **prendere la parola** to take the floor; **dare la parola a qn** to call on sb to speak
parolaccia, ce [paro'lattʃa] SF bad word, swearword; **dire le parolacce** to swear
parolaio, aia, ai, aie [paro'lajo] SM/F *(pegg)* windbag
paroliere [paro'ljɛre] SM lyricist
parolina [paro'lina] SF: **dire una parolina a qn** *(di rimprovero)* to have a few words with sb; *(d'amore)* to whisper sweet nothings to sb
parolone [paro'lone] SFPL bombast *sg*
parossismo [paros'sizmo] SM *(Med)* paroxysm; *(fig: di amore, odio)* height; **amare/odiare fino al parossismo** to be beside o.s. with love/hate
parossisticamente [parossistika'mente] AVV *(fig)* fiercely
parossistico, a, ci, che [paros'sistiko] AGG *(Med)* paroxysmal, paroxysmic; *(fig)* fierce, violent
parotite [paro'tite] SF *(Med)* parotitis
parquet [par'kɛ] SM INV parquet (flooring)
parricida, i, e [parri'tʃida] SM/F parricide *(person)*
parricidio, di [parri'tʃidjo] SM parricide *(action)*
parrò *ecc* [par'rɔ] VB *vedi* **parere**
parrocchia [par'rɔkkja] SF *(suddivisione)* parish; *(chiesa)* parish church
parrocchiale [parrok'kjale] AGG parish *attr*
parrocchiano, a [parrok'kjano] SM/F parishioner
parroco, ci ['parroko] SM parish priest
parrucca, che [par'rukka] SF wig
parrucchiera [parruk'kjɛra] SF hairdresser
parrucchiere [parruk'kjɛre] SM *(per uomo)* barber; *(per signora)* hairdresser; **fa la parrucchiera** she's a hairdresser; **devo andare dal parrucchiere** I need to go to the hairdresser's
parruccone [parruk'kone] SM *(pegg)* old fogey
parsimonia [parsi'mɔnja] SF parsimony, frugality, thrift
parsimoniosamente [parsimonjosa'mente] AVV parsimoniously
parsimonioso, a [parsimo'njoso] AGG frugal, thrifty
parso, a ['parso] PP *di* **parere**
partaccia, ce [par'tattʃa] SF *(figuraccia)*: **fare una partaccia** to cut a poor figure; *(scenata)*: **fare una partaccia a qn** to give sb a telling-off

Pp

parte ['parte] SF
1 (*gen*) part; (*quota spettante a ciascuno*) share; **la prima parte del libro** the first part of the book; **parte del libro non mi è piaciuta** I didn't like some *o* part of the book; **ognuno ebbe la sua parte** everyone had their share; **una parte di noi** some of us; **gran** *o* **la maggior parte degli spettatori** most of the audience; **in parte** in part, partly; **fare le parti di qc** to divide sth up; **fare la parte del leone** to take the lion's share
2 (*partecipazione*): **fare parte di qc** to belong to sth; **fa parte di un club sportivo** he belongs to a sports club; **prendere parte a** (*dibattito, conversazione*) to take part in, participate in; (*lutto*) to share in; **non ha preso parte alla discussione** he didn't take part in the discussion; **mettere qn a parte di qc** to inform sb of sth, tell sb about sth
3 (*lato: anche fig*) side; (*direzione*) direction; **la parte destra del corpo** the right-hand side of the body; **dall'altra parte della strada** on the other side of the road; **veniva dall'altra parte** he was coming from the opposite direction; **da parte a parte** right through; **essere dalla parte della ragione** to be in the right; **non sapeva da che parte voltarsi** (*fig*) he didn't know which way to turn; **stare dalla parte di qn** to be on sb's side; **prendere le parti di qn** to take sb's side, side with sb; **hanno preso le sue parti** they sided with him; **mettere da parte qc** to save up, put sth aside; **ha messo da parte un bel po' di denaro** he's saved up quite a lot of money
4 (*luogo, regione*): **da qualche parte** somewhere; **da tutte le parti** everywhere; **da questa parte** (*in questa direzione*) this way; **da che parte è andato?** which way did he go?; **da ogni parte** (*stato in luogo*) everywhere, on all sides; (*moto da luogo*) from all sides; **da nessuna parte** nowhere, not... anywhere; **non riesco a trovarlo da nessuna parte** I can't find it anywhere; **da queste parti** (*qui vicino*) around here; **dalle mie parti** where I come from; **abita dalle mie parti** he lives in the same area as I do; **dalle parti di Glasgow Street** in the vicinity of Glasgow Street
5 (*fazione, partito*) group, faction; (*Dir*) party; **la parte avversaria** the opposing party; **uomo di parte** partisan; **la parte lesa** (*Dir*) the injured party; **costituirsi parte civile contro qn** (*Dir*) to associate in an action with the public prosecutor against sb; **le parti in causa** the parties concerned; **parti sociali** *representatives of workers and employers*
6 (*Teatro*) part, role; **avere una parte secondaria** to have a minor role; **fare la parte dello stupido/della vittima** (*fig*) to act the fool/the martyr
7 (*fraseologia*): **a parte** (*con funzione di agg*) separate; (*con funzione di avv*) separately; **fatto a parte** done separately; **pagare qc a parte** to pay for sth separately; **inviare a parte** (*campioni*) to send under separate cover; **scherzi a parte** joking aside, but, seriously; **a parte ciò** apart from that; **da un anno a questa parte** for about a year now; **da parte** (*in disparte*) to one side, aside; **da parte mia** as far as I'm concerned, as for me; **da parte di** (*per conto di*) on behalf of; (*regalo, saluti*) from; **questo è da parte di Giorgio** this is from Giorgio; **da parte di madre** on his (*o* her *ecc*) mother's side; **d'altra parte** on the other hand

partecipante [partetʃi'pante] AGG: **partecipante a** taking part in, participating in
■ SM/F: **partecipante (a)** (*riunione, dibattito*) participant (in); (*gara sportiva*) competitor (in); (*concorso*) entrant (to); **i partecipanti alla cerimonia** those taking part in the ceremony; **tutti i partecipanti alla riunione** everyone who attended the meeting

partecipare [partetʃi'pare] VI (*aus* **avere**) **partecipare a** to take part in, participate in; (*utili*) to share in; (*spese*) to contribute to; (*dolore, successo di qn*) to share (in); **parteciperai alla gara?** are you going to take part in the competition?; **posso partecipare alle spese?** can I help pay?
■ VT: **partecipare le nozze (a)** to announce one's wedding (to)

partecipazione [partetʃipat'tsjone] SF
1 **partecipazione (a)** (*dibattito, cerimonia*) participation (in); (*spettacolo*) appearance (in); (*complotto*) involvement (in); **partecipazione a banda armata** (*Dir*) belonging to an armed gang; **partecipazione di nozze** wedding announcement card 2 (*Econ*) sharing, interest; **ministro delle Partecipazioni statali** *minister responsible for companies in which the state has a financial interest*; **partecipazione di maggioranza** controlling interest; **partecipazione di minoranza** minority interest; **partecipazione agli utili** profit-sharing

partecipe [par'tetʃipe] AGG participating; **essere partecipe del dolore/della gioia di qn** to share in sb's sorrow/joy

parteggiare [parted'dʒare] VI (*aus* **avere**) **parteggiare per** to side with, be on the side of, support

partenariato [partena'rjato] SM partnership

partenza [par'tɛntsa] SF 1 (*gen*) departure; **dopo la mia partenza si deciderà** things will be decided after I leave *o* after my departure; **il tabellone delle partenze** the departure board; **essere in partenza** (*treno, aereo, nave*) to be about to leave; **fa' presto, il treno è in partenza** hurry up, the train is about to leave; **prenderò il primo treno in partenza per Milano** I'll catch the first train for Milan; **"il treno per Roma è in partenza dal binario 15"** "the Rome train is leaving from platform 15"; **passeggeri in partenza per** passengers travelling (*Brit*) *o* traveling (*Am*) to; **siamo tornati al punto di partenza** (*fig*) we are back where we started, we are back to square one
2 (*Sport*) start; **segnale di partenza** start, starting signal; **linea di partenza** start, starting line; **falsa partenza** (*anche fig*) false start

particella [parti'tʃɛlla] SF (*Gramm, Fis*) particle; **particelle alfa/beta** (*Fis*) alpha/beta particles

participio, pi [parti'tʃipjo] SM (*Gramm*) participle; **participio passato** past participle; **participio presente** present participle

particolare [partiko'lare] AGG 1 (*specifico*) particular; (*caratteristico*) distinctive; (*speciale*) special, particular; **in questo caso particolare** in this particular case, in this specific instance; **ha un sapore particolare** it has a distinctive flavour; **in particolare** in particular, particularly 2 (*strano*) peculiar, odd 3 (*insolito*) unusual; **l'ho fatto con cura particolare** I took particular care over it; **amicizie particolari** (*euf*) homosexual relationships 4 (*privato: udienza, ragioni*) private, personal
■ SM detail; **vorrei sapere i particolari** I'd like to know the details; **raccontare un fatto in tutti i particolari** to give all the details *o* particulars of an occurrence; **entrare nei particolari** to go into details

particolareggiato, a [partikolared'dʒato] AGG (extremely) detailed

particolarità [partikolari'ta] SF INV 1 (*carattere*

eccezionale) peculiarity; **data la particolarità del caso** given the peculiarity of the case **2** (*dettaglio*) detail, particularity **3** (*caratteristica specifica*) (distinctive) feature, characteristic

particolarmente [partikolar'mente] AVV particularly, especially; **adoro gli animali, particolarmente i gatti** I adore animals, especially cats; **sono particolarmente contenta oggi** I'm ever so happy today

partigiano, a [parti'dʒano] AGG partisan
■ SM (*Storia*) partisan; (*fautore*) supporter, champion
▷ www.anpi.it/

partire [par'tire] VI (*aus* **essere**) **1** (*gen*) to go, leave; (*lasciare un luogo*) to leave; (*mettersi in cammino*) to set off, set out; (*allontanarsi*) to go away, go off; **partire da/per** to leave from/for; **sono partita da Roma alle 7** I left Rome at 7; **partire in treno/in macchina** to go by train/car; **partire come una freccia** to be off like a shot; **non dargli troppo da bere perché lui parte subito** (*fam*) don't give him too much to drink because it goes straight to his head **2** (*cominciare*: *Sport, fig*): **partire (da)** to start (from); **la corsa parte dal nord della città** the race starts *o* leaves from the north of the town; **la loro è una storia partita male** theirs is a relationship which got off to a bad start **3** (*motore*) to start; (*aereo*) to take off; (*treno*) to leave; **la macchina non parte** the car won't start; **il volo parte da Linate** the flight leaves from Linate; **a che ora parte il treno?** what time does the train leave?; **partire in quarta** to drive off at top speed; (*fig*) to be very enthusiastic; **far partire la macchina** to start (up) the car **4** (*colpo di arma da fuoco, petardo*) to go off; (*tappo*) to pop out, shoot out; **è partito un colpo** the gun went off **5 a partire da** from; **a partire da oggi** from today onwards; **a partire da ora** from now on; **la seconda a partire/partendo da destra** the second from the right; **a partire da 20 euro** from 20 euros

partita [par'tita] SF **1** (*Comm*) lot, consignment **2** (*Contabilità*) entry, item; **partita doppia** double-entry book-keeping; **partita IVA** VAT registration number (*Brit*); **partita semplice** single-entry book-keeping **3** (*gioco, Carte*) game; (*Sport*) match, game; **sono andata alla partita di calcio ieri** I went to the football match yesterday; **una partita a carte** a game of cards; **facciamo una partita a tennis** let's have a game of tennis; **dare partita vinta a qn** to admit defeat (by sb); **partita amichevole** friendly (match) **4** (*escursione*): **partita di caccia** hunting party

partitico, a [par'titiko] AGG (*Pol*): **sistema partitico** party system

partitivo, a [parti'tivo] AGG (*Gramm*) partitive

partito [par'tito] SM **1** (*Pol*) party **2** (*decisione*): **per partito preso** on principle; **non saprei che partito prendere** I wouldn't know what to do; **mettere la testa a partito** to settle down **3** (*persona da sposare*) match; **è un buon partito** (*uomo*) he's a very eligible young man, he's a good match **4** (*condizione*): **essere ridotto a mal partito** to be in desperate straits

partitocratico, a, ci, che [partito'kratiko] AGG party-dominated

partitocrazia [partitokrat'tsia] SF *hijacking of institutions by the party system*

partitura [parti'tura] SF (*Mus*) score

partizione [partit'tsjone] SF (*azione*) division; (*parte*) subdivision

partner ['pa:tnə] SM/F INV partner

parto ['parto] SM (*Med*) labour (*Brit*), labor (*Am*); **durante il parto** during labo(u)r; **i dolori del parto** labo(u)r pains; **sala parto** labo(u)r room; **è stato un parto difficile** it was a difficult birth; **al momento del parto il bambino stava bene** at birth the child was in good health; **morire di parto** to die in childbirth; **parto cesareo** Caesarean (section); **parto naturale** natural childbirth; **parto pilotato** induced labo(u)r; **parto plurigemellare** multiple birth; **parto podalico** breech delivery; **parto prematuro** premature birth *o* delivery

partoriente [parto'rjɛnte] SF woman in labour (*Brit*) *o* labor (*Am*)

partorire [parto'rire] VT to give birth to; (*fig*: *invenzione*) to produce

part time ['pa:t 'taim] AVV, AGG INV part-time

party ['pa:ti] SM INV party

parure [pa'ryr] SF INV (*di biancheria*) (set of) underwear; (*di gioielli*) (set of) jewellery; **parure da letto** matching sheets and pillow slip(s)

parvenu [parvə'ny] SM INV upstart, nouveau riche

parvenza [par'ventsa] SF semblance

parvi *ecc* ['parvi] VB *vedi* **parere**

parziale [par'tsjale] AGG (*limitato*) partial; (*non obiettivo*) biased, partial; **un successo parziale** a partial success

parzialità [partsjali'ta] SF INV **1 parzialità (a favore di qn)** partiality (for sb), bias (towards sb); **parzialità (contro qn)** bias (against sb) **2** (*azione*) unfair action

parzialmente [partsjal'mente] AVV partially; **latte parzialmente scremato** semi-skimmed milk

pascere ['paʃʃere] VB IRREG
■ VI (*aus* **avere**) to graze
■ VT (*brucare*) to graze on
▶ **pascersi** VR: **pascersi di** (*erba, fig*: *illusioni*) to feed on

pascià [paʃʃa] SM INV pasha; **stare come un pascià** (*fig*) to live like a lord

pasciuto, a [paʃʃuto] PP *di* **pascere**
■ AGG: **ben pasciuto** plump

pascolare [pasko'lare] VT, VI (*aus* **avere**) to graze

pascolo ['paskolo] SM (*luogo*) pasture; **diritto di pascolo** grazing rights *pl*

Pasqua ['paskwa] SF **1** Easter; **la domenica di Pasqua** Easter Sunday; **cosa fai per Pasqua?** what are you doing at Easter?; **le vacanze di Pasqua** the Easter holidays; **il lunedì di Pasqua** Easter Monday; **un uovo di Pasqua** an Easter egg; **essere contento come una Pasqua** to be as happy as a sandboy **2 isola di Pasqua** Easter Island

pasquale [pas'kwale] AGG Easter *attr*

pasquetta [pas'kwetta] SF Easter Monday

pass [pas] SM INV (*permesso*) pass

passabile [pas'sabile] AGG fairly good, passable

passabilmente [passabil'mente] AVV fairly *o* reasonably (well)

passaggio, gi [pas'saddʒo] SM **1** (*atto del passare*) passage, passing *no pl*; (*traversata*) crossing *no pl*; **guardare il passaggio degli uccelli** to watch the birds fly past; **essere di passaggio** to be passing through; **sono qui solo di passaggio** I'm just passing through **2** (*trasferimento*: *di poteri, diritti, calciatore*) transfer; **il passaggio dall'infanzia all'adolescenza** the transition from childhood to adolescence; **il passaggio dal giorno alla notte** the change from day to night; **passaggio di proprietà** transfer *o* change of ownership **3** (*luogo*) passage; (*cammino*) way, passage; (*itinerario*) route; **uno stretto passaggio tra le rocce** a narrow passage between the rocks; **impedire il passaggio a qn** to block *o* stand in sb's way; **passaggio**

Pp

a livello level (*Brit*) *o* grade (*Am*) crossing; **passaggio pedonale** pedestrian crossing; **"passaggio di servizio"** "staff only" **4** (*traffico*): **c'è molto passaggio** there's a lot of traffic; **luogo di passaggio** thoroughfare
5 (*Aut*) lift (*Brit*), ride; **dare un passaggio a qn** to give sb a lift; **puoi darmi un passaggio?** can you give me a lift? **6** (*brano*) passage; **un passaggio da "I Promessi Sposi"** a passage from "I Promessi Sposi" **7** (*Sport*) pass; **passaggio in avanti/indietro** forward/back pass; **passaggio in profondità** (*Calcio*) long pass

passamaneria [passamane'ria] SF braid, trimming

passamano [passa'mano] SM braid

passamontagna [passamon'taɲɲa] SM INV balaclava

passante [pas'sante] SM/F passer-by
■ SM (*di cintura*) loop; (*raccordo: stradale*) road link; (: *ferroviario*) (high-speed) rail link

passaparola [passapa'rɔla] SM: **fare il passaparola** (*Mil*) to pass the word; **passaparola!** pass it on!; **giocare a passaparola** to play Chinese whispers (*Brit*), to play telephone (*Am*)

passaporto [passa'pɔrto] SM passport

passare [pas'sare] VI (*aus* **essere**)
1 (*persona, veicolo*) to go by, pass (by); **l'autobus passa davanti a casa nostra** the bus goes past our house; **siamo passati davanti a casa tua** we went past your house, we walked (*o* drove) past your house; **non è passata neanche una macchina** not one car went by; **passare dall'altra parte della strada** to cross (over) to the other side of the street
2 (*fare una breve sosta*) to call in; (: *presso amico*) to call *o* drop in; (*postino*) to come, call; **passa quando vuoi** call in whenever you like; **passare a casa di qn** *o* **da qn** to call *o* drop in on sb; **passo da te dopo cena** I'll call in after dinner; **passare a trovare/salutare qn** to drop by to see sb/say "hello" to sb; **passare a prendere qc/qn** to come and pick sth/sb up; **ti passo a prendere alle otto** I'll come and pick you up at eight o'clock; **passare in banca/ufficio** to call in at the bank/office; **devo passare in banca** I've got to call in at the bank
3 (*filtrare attraverso: aria, sole, luce*) to pass, get through; (: *acqua*) to seep through
4 (*trasferirsi*): **passare da...a** to pass from ... to; **passare di mano in mano** to be passed *o* handed round; **passare di padre in figlio** to be handed *o* passed down *o* from father to son; **passare da un argomento ad un altro** to go from one subject to another; **passare ad altro** to change the subject; (*in una riunione*) to discuss the next item; **passiamo ad altro!** let's go on!; **passare al nemico** to go over to the enemy; **passare alla storia** to pass into history; (*fig*) to become a legend; **passare di moda** to go out of fashion; **passare a miglior vita** (*euf*) to pass away
5 (*trascorrere: giorni, tempo*) to pass, go by; **sono passati molti anni dalla fine della guerra** many years have passed since the end of the war
6 (*allontanarsi: temporale, dolore, voglia*) to pass, go away; **il peggio è passato** the worst is over; **far passare a qn la voglia di qc/di fare qc** to stifle sb's desire for sth/to do sth; **ti è passato il mal di testa?** has your headache gone?; **gli passerà!** he'll get over it!
7 (*essere accettato: proposta di legge*) to be passed; (: *candidato*) to pass; **passare a un esame** to go up (to the next class) after an exam; **passare di grado** to be promoted
8 (*Culin*): **passare di cottura** to be overdone
9 (*Carte*) to pass
10 **30 anni e passa** well over 30 years ago; **c'erano 100 persone e passa** there were well over a 100 people
11 (*esistere*): **ci passa una bella differenza tra i 2 quadri** there's a big difference between the 2 pictures
12 **passare per uno stupido/un genio** to be taken for a fool/a genius; **passare per buono** to be taken as valid, be accepted; **passare inosservato** to go unnoticed; **farsi passare per** to pass o.s. off as, pretend to be
13 **passare attraverso, per** (*anche fig*) to go through; **passare sopra** to pass over *o* above; (*fig: lasciar correre*) to pass over, overlook; **passare sotto** to pass below; **cosa ti passa per la testa?** (*a che pensi?*) what is going through your mind?; (*come puoi pensarlo?*) what are you thinking of!; **per dove si passa per arrivare in centro?** which way do I (*o* we) go to get into town?; **lasciar passare qn/qc** to let sb/sth through; **non mi hanno lasciato passare** they didn't let me through; **far passare qn per** *o* **da** to let sb in (*o* out) by; **far passare avanti qn** to let sb get past *o* by; **questa volta non ci passo sopra** I'm not prepared to overlook it this time
■ VT
1 (*attraversare*) to cross
2 (*esame*) to pass; (*dogana*) to go through, clear; (*visita medica*) to have; **hai passato l'esame?** did you pass the exam?
3 (*approvare*) to pass, approve
4 (*trafiggere*): **passare qn/qc da parte a parte** to pass right through sb/sth
5 (*trascorrere*) to spend, pass; **passare le vacanze in montagna** to spend one's holidays in the mountains; **ho passato due giorni a Parigi** I spent two days in Paris; **non passerà la notte** he (*o* she) won't survive the night; **non passa giorno che non ne combini una delle sue** hardly a day goes by without him getting up to something
6 (*oltrepassare, sorpassare*) to go beyond; (*fig: andare oltre i limiti*) to exceed, go beyond; **ha passato la quarantina** he (*o* she) is over 40
7 (*dare: oggetto*) to pass, give, hand; (*Sport: palla*) to pass; **passare qc a qn** to pass sth to sb, give sb sth; (*trasmettere: messaggio*) to pass sth (on) to sb; **ha passato la palla a Enrico** he passed the ball to Enrico; **potresti passarmi il sale?** could you pass me the salt, please?; **mi hai passato l'influenza** you gave me the flu; **passare indietro qc** to pass *o* give *o* hand sth back; **i miei genitori mi passano 300 euro al mese** my parents give me 300 euros a month; **mi passi Maria?** (*al telefono*) can I speak to Maria?; **le passo il signor Rossi** I'm putting you through to Mr Rossi, here's Mr Rossi
8 (*brodo, verdura*) to strain
9 **passare lo straccio per terra** to give the floor a wipe; **passare l'aspirapolvere** to hoover (*Brit*), vacuum (*Am*); **passare una mano di vernice su qc** to give sth a coat of paint
12 (*fraseologia*): **passarsela bene/male** to get on well/badly; (*economicamente*) to manage well/badly; **come te la passi?** how are you getting on *o* along?; **passarla liscia** to get away with it; **ne ha passate tante** he's been through a lot, he's had some difficult times
■ SM: **col passare del tempo...** with the passing of time ...; **col passare degli anni** (*riferito al presente*) as time goes by; (*riferito al passato*) as time passed *o* went by

passata [pas'sata] SF **1** **dare una passata a qc** (*spolverata*) to dust sth quickly; (*pulita*) to give sth a wipe; (*stirata*) to give sth a quick iron; **dare una**

passata di vernice a qc to give sth a coat of paint **2** (*occhiata*) glance, look; **dare una passata al giornale** to skim through *o* have a glance at the paper

passatempo [passa'tɛmpo] SM pastime, hobby; **per passatempo** as a hobby

passato, a [pas'sato] AGG **1** (*scorso*) last; **l'anno passato** last year; **nel corso degli anni passati** over the past years **2** (*finito: gloria, generazioni*) past; (*usanze*) out of date; (*sfiorito*) faded; **passato di moda** out of fashion; **sono cose ormai passate** that's all over now; **nei tempi passati** in the past; **è acqua passata** it's over and done with, it's water under the bridge **3** (*superato*): **sono le 8 passate** it's past *o* after 8 o'clock; **ha 40 anni passati** he's over 40
■SM **1** past; **ha un passato di droga e furti** he has a history of drugs and theft; **in passato** in the past **2** (*Gramm*) past (tense); **il participio passato** the past participle; **passato prossimo** present perfect; **passato remoto** simple past **3** (*Culin*): **passato di verdura** vegetable purée

passatoia [passa'toja] SF (*di scale*) stair carpet; (*di corridoio*) hall carpet

passaverdura [passaver'dura] SM INV vegetable mill

passavivande [passavi'vande] SM INV serving hatch

passeggero, a [passed'dʒɛro] AGG (*malessere, nuvola, temporale*) passing; (*bellezza, benessere*) transient
■SM/F passenger; **passeggero in arrivo/in partenza/in transito** arriving/departing/transit passenger

passeggiare [passed'dʒare] VI (*aus* **avere**) to stroll, walk; **passeggiava nervosamente nel corridoio** he was pacing nervously up and down the corridor

passeggiata [passed'dʒata] SF **1** (*a piedi*) walk; (*in macchina*) drive; **fare una passeggiata** to go for a walk; (*in veicolo*) to go for a drive **2** (*luogo*) promenade

passeggiatrice [passeddʒa'tritʃe] SF (*euf*) streetwalker

passeggino [passed'dʒino] SM pushchair (*Brit*), stroller (*Am*)

passeggio [pas'seddʒo] SM walk, stroll; (*luogo*) promenade; **andare a passeggio** to go for a walk *o* a stroll; **guardare il passeggio** to watch people out for a stroll

passe-partout ['pas par'tu] SM INV **1** (*chiave*) skeleton *o* master key **2** (*per cornici*) passepartout

passera ['passera] SF (*uccello*) hedge sparrow; (*pesce*) flounder

passerella [passe'rɛlla] SF (*gen, di aereo*) footbridge; (*di nave*) gangway, gangplank; (*pedana: per sfilate*) catwalk

passero ['passero] SM sparrow

passerotto [passe'rɔtto] SM young sparrow

passeur [pa'sœʀ] SM/F INV people trafficker

passibile [pas'sibile] AGG: **passibile di** liable to; **passibile di aumento** liable to go up *o* increase

passino [pas'sino] SM sieve, strainer

passionale [passjo'nale] AGG (*temperamento*) passionate; **delitto passionale** crime of passion

passionalità [passjonali'ta] SF passionate nature

passionalmente [passjonal'mente] AVV (*amare*) passionately; (*agire*) in a fit of passion

passione [pas'sjone] SF passion; **amore e passione** love and passion; **il giardinaggio è la mia più grande passione** gardening is my greatest pleasure; **aver la passione di** *o* **per** to have a passion for; **domenica di Passione** Passion Sunday

passivamente [passiva'mente] AVV passively

passivante [passi'vante] AGG (*Gramm*): **il si passivante** the passive "si"

passività [passivi'ta] SF INV **1** (*qualità*) passivity, passiveness **2** (*Econ*) liability; **passività a breve termine** current liabilities *pl*

passivo, a [pas'sivo] AGG passive; **fumo passivo** passive smoking
■SM **1** (*Gramm*) passive **2** (*Econ*) debit; (*: complesso dei debiti*) liabilities *pl*

passo¹ ['passo] SM **1** (*gen*) step; (*rumore*) (foot)step; (*orma*) footprint; **a due passi da qui** a stone's throw from here; **passo (a) passo** step by step; **seguire qn passo passo** to follow close on sb's heels; **fare i primi passi** (*anche fig*) to take one's first steps; **fare due** *o* **quattro passi** to go for a short walk; **fare un passo avanti/indietro** (*anche fig*) to take a step forward/back; **fai un passo avanti** take a step forward; **mi è sembrato di sentire dei passi** I thought I heard footsteps; **ha fatto passi da gigante in spagnolo** his Spanish has improved by leaps and bounds; **fare il gran passo** to take the plunge; **fare un passo falso** to make a wrong move; **fare i passi necessari** to take the necessary steps; **fare il passo più lungo della gamba** to bite off more than one can chew; **tornare sui propri passi** to retrace one's steps; **non ho intenzione di tornare sui miei passi** (*fig*) I have no intention of starting all over again **2** (*andatura*) pace; (*: Mil, Danza*) step; (*: Equitazione*) walk; **fare il passo dell'oca** to goose-step; **un passo di danza** a dance step; **passo di pattinaggio** (*Sci*) skating turn; **allungare il passo** to quicken one's pace; **avere il passo lento** to walk slowly, be a slow walker; **camminava con passo veloce** he was walking fast; **di buon passo** at a good *o* brisk pace; **marciare al passo** to march; **mettere il cavallo al passo** to walk one's horse; **a passo d'uomo** at walking pace; (*Aut*) dead slow; **le macchine andavano a passo d'uomo** the cars were crawling along; **andare al passo coi tempi** to keep up with the times; **di questo passo** (*fig*) at this rate; **di questo passo non finiremo mai** we'll never finish at this rate **3** (*brano*) passage **4** (*Cine*) gauge

Pp

passo² ['passo] SM **1** (*passaggio*): **cedere il passo a qn** to give way to sb; **sbarrare il passo a qn** to bar sb's way; **uccelli di passo** birds of passage, migratory birds; **"passo carrabile** *o* **carraio"** "vehicle entrance — keep clear" **2** (*valico*) pass

password ['pasword] SF INV (*Inform*) password

pasta ['pasta] SF **1** (*Culin: impasto per pane*) dough; (*: impasto per dolce*) pastry; (*: anche:* **pastasciutta**) pasta; (*pasticcino*) cake, pastry; **lavorare la pasta** to knead the dough; **spianare la pasta** to roll pastry; **pasta in brodo** noodle soup; **pasta fatta in casa** home-made pasta; **pasta frolla** shortcrust pastry; **hai le mani di pasta frolla!** what a butterfingers you are!; **pasta sfoglia** puff pastry; **pasta all'uovo** egg pasta **2** (*sostanza pastosa*) paste; **pasta di acciughe** anchovy paste; **pasta dentifricia** toothpaste; **pasta di mandorle** almond paste **3** (*fig: indole*) nature; **sono tutt'e due della stessa pasta** they're both cast in the same mould (*Brit*) *o* mold (*Am*)

pastasciutta [pastaʃʃutta] SF pasta

pasteggiare [pasted'dʒare] VI (*aus* **avere**) **pasteggiare a vino/champagne** to have wine/champagne with one's meal

pastella [pas'tɛlla] SF batter

pastello [pas'tɛllo] SM pastel
■AGG INV pastel *attr*

pastetta [pas'tetta] SF (*Culin*) = **pastella**
pasticca, che [pas'tikka] SF pastille, lozenge
pasticceria [pastittʃe'ria] SF **1** (*negozio*) cake shop **2** (*pasticcini*) pastries *pl*, cakes *pl* **3** (*arte*) confectionery
pasticciare [pastit'tʃare] VT to mess up, make a mess of
pasticciere, a [pastit'tʃɛre] SM/F pastry-cook; (*gestore di pasticceria*) confectioner
pasticcino [pastit'tʃino] SM petit four
pasticcio, ci [pas'tittʃo] SM **1** (*Culin*) pie; **un pasticcio di carne** a meat pie **2** (*lavoro disordinato, imbroglio*) mess; **è proprio un bel pasticcio** it's a real mess; **cacciarsi nei pasticci** to get into trouble
pasticcione, a [pastit'tʃone] AGG bungling, messy
■ SM/F bungler, messy person
pastiera [pas'tjɛra] SF: **pastiera (napoletana)** *puff pastry filled with cream cheese, barley and candied fruit, traditionally eaten at Easter*
pastificio, ci [pasti'fitʃo] SM pasta factory
pastiglia [pas'tiʎʎa] SF **1** (*Med*) pastille, lozenge; **pastiglie per la gola** throat lozenges *o* pastilles; **pastiglie per la tosse** cough drops *o* pastilles **2** (*Aut*): **pastiglie dei freni** brake lining *sg*
pastina [pas'tina] SF *small pasta shapes used in soup*
pasto ['pasto] SM meal; **saltare i pasti** to skip meals; **da prendersi prima dei pasti** to be taken before meals; **non mangiare fuori pasto** *o* **fuori dei pasti** don't eat between meals; **vino da pasto** table wine; **la notizia fu data in pasto al pubblico** the news was made common knowledge; **lo diedero in pasto ai leoni** (*anche fig*) he was thrown to the lions
pastoia [pas'toja] SF (*fig*): **pastoia burocratica** red tape
pastone [pas'tone] SM (*per animali*) mash; (*pegg: cibo*) overcooked stodge
pastorale [pasto'rale] AGG (*gen*) pastoral
■ SF **1** (*Rel: lettera del vescovo*) pastoral (letter) **2** (*Mus*) pastoral(e)
■ SM (*Rel: bastone*) crook, crosier
pastore [pas'tore] **1** SM (*anche Rel*) shepherd; (*sacerdote*) minister, pastor; **il buon Pastore** (*Rel*) the Good Shepherd **2** (*anche:* **cane (da) pastore**) sheepdog; **pastore scozzese** collie; **pastore tedesco** Alsatian (*Brit*), German shepherd
pastorella [pasto'rɛlla] SF **1** (*persona*) shepherdess **2** (*Poesia*) pastoral
pastorizia [pasto'rittsja] SF sheep-rearing, sheep farming
pastorizzare [pastorid'dzare] VT to pasteurize; **latte pastorizzato** pasteurized milk
pastosità [pastosi'ta] SF (*vedi agg*) doughiness; pastiness; mellowness, softness; mellowness
pastoso, a [pas'toso] AGG **1** (*miscuglio*) doughy; (*: più liquido*) pasty **2** (*fig: colore, voce*) mellow, soft; (*vino*) mellow
pastrano [pas'trano] SM greatcoat
pastura [pas'tura] SF (*atto*) grazing; (*luogo*) pasture; **terreno a pastura** grazing land
patacca, che [pa'takka] SF **1** (*distintivo*) medal, decoration **2** (*fig*) (*: macchia*) grease spot, grease mark; (*: oggetto senza valore*) piece of rubbish; **lì vendono solo patacche** they just sell junk there
patata [pa'tata] SF potato; **che spirito di patata!** (*fam*) some joke that! (*iro*); **patata americana** *o* **dolce** sweet potato, batata, yam (*Am*); **patate arrosto** roast potatoes; **patate fritte** chips (*Brit*), French fries (*Am*)
patatine [pata'tine] SFPL chips (*Brit*), French fries (*Am*); (*confezionate*) (potato) crisps (*Brit*) *o* chips (*Am*)
patatrac [pata'trak] SM INV (*fig: disastro*) disaster; (*: dissesto economico*) crash
pâté [pa'te] SM INV pâté; **pâté di fegato d'oca** pâté de foie gras
patella [pa'tɛlla] SF (*Zool*) limpet
patema, i [pa'tɛma] SM: **patema (d'animo)** anxiety, worry
patentato, a [paten'tato] AGG **1** (*munito di patente*) licensed, certified **2** (*fig scherz: qualificato*) utter, thorough; **un cretino patentato** an utter fool; **un ladro patentato** an out and out thief
patente [pa'tɛnte] SF (*anche:* **patente di guida**) driving licence (*Brit*), driver's license (*Am*); **ho perso la patente** I've lost my driving licence; (*me l'hanno ritirata*) I've had my driving licence taken away; **mio fratello non ha la patente** my brother doesn't drive; **patente a punti** *driving licence with penalty points*

> **LO SAPEVI...?**
> **patente** non si traduce mai con la parola inglese ***patent***

patentino [paten'tino] SM temporary licence (*Brit*) *o* license (*Am*)
paterazzo [pate'rattso] SM (*Naut*) backstay
paternale [pater'nale] SF rebuke, reprimand; **fare una paternale a qn** to rebuke *o* reprimand sb
paternalismo [paterna'lizmo] SM paternalism
paternalista, i, e [paterna'lista] AGG paternalistic
■ SM/F paternalist
paternalistico, a, ci, che [paterna'listiko] AGG paternalistic
paternamente [paterna'mente] AVV like a father, in a fatherly fashion
paternità [paterni'ta] SF INV (*gen*) fatherhood; (*Dir*) paternity; **hanno rivendicato la paternità dell'attentato** (*fig*) they've claimed responsibility for the bombing
paterno, a [pa'tɛrno] AGG (*autorità*) paternal; (*benevolo: affetto, consigli*) fatherly; **lasciare la casa paterna** to leave one's father's house
Paternostro [pater'nɔstro] SM = **Padrenostro**
pateticamente [patetika'mente] AVV pathetically
patetico, a, ci, che [pa'tɛtiko] AGG (*gen, Anat, pegg*) pathetic; (*commovente*) moving, touching; **non essere patetico!** don't be pathetic!
■ SM sentimentalism; **cadere nel patetico** to become (over)sentimental
pathos ['patos] SM INV pathos
patibolo [pa'tibolo] SM scaffold, gallows *sg*; **pare che vada al patibolo!** (*fig*) you'd think his hour had come!
patimento [pati'mento] SM suffering
patina ['patina] SF (*su rame*) patina; (*su medaglie*) coat; (*sulla lingua*) fur, coating
patio ['patjo] SM INV patio
patire [pa'tire] VT (*ingiurie, offese*) to suffer; (*fame, sete*) to suffer (from); (*ingiustizie*) to endure
■ VI (*aus* **avere**) **patire (di)** to suffer (from); **patire di cuore** to have a weak heart; **ha finito di patire** his sufferings are over
patito, a [pa'tito] AGG (*sofferente*) run-down; (*: volto*) wan
■ SM/F: **essere un patito di** (*musica, sport*) to be a fan *o* lover of; **è un patito del calcio** he's a football fan; **un patito di musica classica** a classical music lover
patogeno, a [pa'tɔdʒeno] AGG pathogenic; **agente patogeno** pathogen
patologia [patolo'dʒia] SF (*Med*) pathology

patologico, a, ci, che [pato'lɔdʒiko] AGG (*Med, fig*) pathological
patologo, a, gi, ghe [pa'tɔlogo] SM/F (*Med*) pathologist
patria ['patrja] SF (*paese*) homeland, fatherland; (*fig: città o luogo natale*) birthplace; **Vienna, la patria del walzer** Vienna, the home of the waltz; **tornare in patria** to return to one's own country; **amor di patria** patriotism
patriarca, chi [patri'arka] SM patriarch
patriarcale [patriar'kale] AGG patriarchal
patriarcalmente [patriarkal'mente] AVV patriarchally
patriarcato [patriar'kato] SM (*Antropologia*) patriarchy; (*: sede, territorio, anche Rel*) patriarchate
patrigno [pa'triɲɲo] SM stepfather
patrimoniale [patrimo'njale] AGG patrimonial; **rendita patrimoniale** income from property; **imposta patrimoniale** property tax
■ SF (*imposta*) property tax
patrimonio, ni [patri'mɔnjo] SM **1** estate, property; **mi è costato un patrimonio** (*fig*) it cost me a fortune, I paid a fortune for it; **patrimonio pubblico** public property **2** (*fig: eredità*) heritage; **il nostro patrimonio artistico** our artistic heritage; **patrimonio culturale** cultural heritage; **patrimonio ereditario** hereditary characteristics *pl*; **patrimonio spirituale** spiritual heritage
patrio, ria, rii, rie ['patrjo] AGG **1** (*di patria*) of one's country, native *attr*; **amor patrio** love of one's country **2** (*Dir*): **patria potestà** parental authority
patriota, i, e [patri'ɔta] SM/F patriot
patriotticamente [patriottika'mente] AVV patriotically
patriottico, a, ci, che [patri'ɔttiko] AGG patriotic
patriottismo [patriot'tizmo] SM patriotism
patrocinare [patrotʃi'nare] VT (*Dir*) to defend; (*fig: candidatura: appoggiare*) to support; (*: finanziariamente*) to sponsor
patrocinio, nii [patro'tʃinjo] SM (*vedi vb*) defence (*Brit*), defense (*Am*); support; sponsorship, patronage
patrona [pa'trɔna] SF (*Rel*) patron saint
patronato [patro'nato] SM **1** (*patrocinio*) patronage **2** (*istituzione benefica*) charitable institution *o* society
patronessa [patro'nessa] SF patroness
patronimico, a, ci, che [patro'nimiko] AGG, SM patronymic
patrono [pa'trɔno] SM **1** (*Rel*) patron saint **2** (*benefattore*) patron **3** (*Dir*) counsel
patta¹ ['patta] SF (*di tasca*) flap; (*dei pantaloni*) fly
patta² ['patta] SF (*pareggio*) draw, tie; **essere pari e patta** (*fig*) to be even *o* all square
patteggiamento [patteddʒa'mento] SM (*Dir: anche*: **patteggiamento della pena**) plea bargaining
patteggiare [patted'dʒare] VT (*negoziare: resa, tregua*) to negotiate; (*Dir*): **patteggiare la pena** to plea-bargain
■ VI (*aus* **avere**) **patteggiare con qn** (*scendere a patti*) to negotiate with sb; (*scendere a compromessi*) to come to a compromise with sb
pattinaggio [patti'naddʒo] SM skating; **fare pattinaggio** to go skating; **pattinaggio artistico** figure skating; **pattinaggio sul ghiaccio** ice skating; **pattinaggio a rotelle** roller skating
▷ www.fihp.org/
▷ www.fisg.it/
pattinare [patti'nare] VI (*aus* **avere**) **1** (*Sport*) to skate; **pattinare sul ghiaccio/a rotelle** to ice-/roller-skate **2** (*Aut: scivolare*) to skid
pattinato, a [pattin'nato] AGG: **passo pattinato** (*Sci*) ski skating
pattinatore, trice [pattina'tore] SM/F skater
pattino¹ ['pattino] SM **1** (*Sport*) skate; **pattini da ghiaccio** ice skates; **pattini in linea** Rollerblades®; **pattini a rotelle** roller skates **2** (*Tecn*) sliding block; (*Aer*) skid; (*di slitta*) runner
pattino² [pat'tino] SM (*barca*) *kind of pedalo with oars*
pattista, i, e [pat'tista] AGG (*Pol*) of Patto per l'Italia
■ SM/F (*Pol*) member (*o* supporter) of Patto per l'Italia
patto ['patto] SM **1** (*accordo*) pact, agreement; **fare un patto** to make a pact *o* an agreement; **il Patto di Varsavia** the Warsaw Pact; **patto di non aggressione** non-aggression pact; **il Patto per l'Italia** (*Pol*) *centrist party* **2** (*condizione*) condition, term; **a nessun patto** under no circumstances; **venire** *o* **scendere a patti (con)** to come to an agreement (with), come to terms (with); **a patto che** on condition that
pattuglia [pat'tuʎʎa] SF (*Mil*) patrol; **essere di pattuglia** to be on patrol
pattugliare [pattuʎ'ʎare] VT to patrol
pattuire [pattu'ire] VT to reach an agreement on
pattume [pat'tume] SM rubbish (*Brit*), garbage (*Am*), trash (*Am*)
pattumiera [pattu'mjɛra] SF (dust)bin (*Brit*), garbage can (*Am*), trashcan (*Am*)
paturnie [pa'turnie] SFPL (*fam: malumore*): **avere le paturnie** to be in a bad mood
paura [pa'ura] SF fear; **stava tremando dalla paura** she was trembling with fear; **aver paura di/di fare/che...** to be scared *o* frightened *o* afraid of/of doing/that ...; **avevo molta paura** I was really scared; **ha paura di volare** he's scared of flying; **ho paura di uscire da sola la sera** I'm afraid to go out alone at night; **ho paura dei ragni** I'm scared of spiders; **hai paura del buio?** are you afraid of the dark?; **fare** *o* **mettere paura a qn** to frighten sb; **mi hai fatto paura** you frightened me; **era morto di paura** he was scared to death *o* frightened out of his wits; **che paura!** how scary!; **ho paura di sì/no** I am afraid so/not; **ha paura di ingrassare** she's afraid of *o* worried about putting on weight; **ho paura che non venga** *o* **che non verrà** I'm afraid he won't come; **non aver paura, tutto si risolverà** don't worry, everything will work out in the end; **niente paura, ci penso io** don't worry, I'll see to it; **per paura di/che...** for fear of/that ...; **parlava piano per paura di svegliarlo** she spoke quietly so as not to wake him; **è magro da far paura** he is terribly thin; **ha una faccia da far paura** he looks terrible; **piove da far paura** it's bucketing down
paurosamente [paurosa'mente] AVV **1** (*in modo pauroso*) frighteningly **2** (*con paura*) timidly, fearfully
pauroso, a [pau'roso] AGG **1** (*che incute paura*) frightening; (*fig: straordinario*) awful, dreadful; **un pauroso incidente stradale** an awful road accident **2** (*che ha paura*) timid, fearful, timorous; **essere pauroso** to get scared easily; **è pauroso** he gets scared easily
pausa ['pauza] SF (*sosta*) break; (*nel parlare, Mus*) pause; **fare una pausa di 10 minuti** to have a 10-minute break; **facciamo una pausa** let's have a break; **dopo una pausa** after a pause; **fece una pausa e poi riprese a parlare** he paused then began speaking again
pavé [pa've] SM INV cobbles *pl*

Pp

paventato, a [paven'tato] AGG much-feared
pavese[1] [pa'vese] SM (*Naut*): **gran pavese** bunting
pavese[2] [pa'vese] AGG of *o* from Pavia
■ SM/F inhabitant *o* native of Pavia
pavido, a ['pavido] AGG (*letter*) fearful
pavimentare [pavimen'tare] VT (*stanza*) to floor; (*strada*) to pave
pavimentazione [pavimentat'tsjone] SF (*vedi vb*) flooring; paving
pavimento [pavi'mento] SM floor

LO SAPEVI...?
pavimento non si traduce mai con la parola inglese *pavement*

pavona [pa'vona] SF peahen
pavoncella [pavon'tʃɛlla] SF lapwing
pavone [pa'vone] SM peacock
pavoneggiarsi [pavoned'dʒarsi] VIP to strut about, show off
pazientare [pattsjen'tare] VI (*aus* **avere**) to be patient
paziente [pat'tsjɛnte] AGG patient
■ SM/F (*Med*) patient
pazientemente [pattsjente'mente] AVV patiently
pazienza [pat'tsjɛntsa] SF patience; **aver pazienza** to be patient; **perdere la pazienza** to lose (one's) patience; **alla fine ha perso la pazienza e se n'è andato** finally he lost patience and left; **pazienza!** never mind!; **santa pazienza!** (God) give me patience!
pazzamente [pattsa'mente] AVV madly; **essere pazzamente innamorato** to be madly in love
pazzerellone, a [pattserel'lone] SM/F madcap
pazzescamente [pattseska'mente] AVV (*vedi agg*) crazily; incredibly
pazzesco, a, schi, sche [pat'tsesko] AGG (*assurdo: persona, comportamento*) crazy, daft, mad; (*incredibile: scena*) incredible; **un'idea pazzesca** a crazy idea; **una somma pazzesca** an incredible amount of money; **ad una velocità pazzesca** at breakneck speed; **ha una cultura pazzesca** she's incredibly knowledgeable; **pazzesco!** incredible!
pazzia [pat'tsia] SF (*Med*) madness, lunacy, insanity; (*di azione, decisione*) madness, folly; **dar segni di pazzia** to show signs of madness; **mi sento in vena di far pazzie** I feel like doing something crazy; **ho paura che possa fare una pazzia** I'm afraid he'll do something crazy; **è stata una pazzia!** it was sheer madness!
pazzo, a ['pattso] AGG (*Med*) mad, insane, crazy; (*strano: persona, idea*) wild, mad; **è pazzo!** he's crazy!; **essere pazzo da legare** to be raving mad *o* a raving lunatic; **essere pazzo di** (*gioia, dolore*) to be beside o.s. with, to be mad *o* crazy with; **essere pazzo di gelosia** to be insanely jealous; **essere innamorato pazzo** to be madly in love; **è pazzo di lei** he's crazy about her; **pazzo per qn/qc** mad *o* crazy about sb/sth; **va pazza per il cioccolato** she adores chocolate; **prova un gusto pazzo a prendere in giro la gente** he thoroughly enjoys taking people for a ride; **andava a pazza velocità** he was going at breakneck speed
■ SM/F lunatic, madman/madwoman; **urlava come un pazzo** he was shouting his head off, he was shouting like a lunatic; **guidava come un pazzo** he was driving like a madman; **dovremo lavorare come pazzi per finire in tempo** we'll have to work like mad to finish in time
pazzoide [pat'tsɔide] AGG crazy
■ SM/F (*fam*) nutcase
PC SIGLA = *Piacenza*
■ ABBR (*Comm*) = **polizza di carico**
■ [pi'tʃi] SIGLA M INV (= **personal computer**) PC
p.c. ABBR **1** = *per condoglianze* **2** (= **per conoscenza**) cc
p.c.c. ABBR (= **per copia conforme**) cc
PCI [pi'tʃi] SIGLA M (*Pol:* = **Partito Comunista Italiano**) *former political party*
PCUS [pkus] SIGLA M (*Pol*) = *Partito Comunista dell'Unione Sovietica*
PDCI [piditʃi'i] SIGLA M (= **Partito dei comunisti italiani**) Italian Communist Party
PDS [pidi'ɛsse] SIGLA M (*Pol:* = **Partito Democratico della Sinistra**) *party originating from PCI*
PE SIGLA = *Pescara*
pecan [pɛ'kan] SM INV pecan
pecari ['pɛkari] SM INV (*Zool*) peccary
pecca, che ['pɛkka] SF defect, flaw, fault
peccaminoso, a [pekkami'noso] AGG sinful, wicked
peccare [pek'kare] VI (*aus* **avere**) **1** (*Rel*) to sin; (*fig*) to err; **peccare di superbia** (*anche fig*) to be guilty of pride; **peccare per troppa bontà** to be too kind **2** (*difettare*): **peccare di** to lack, be lacking in; **peccare di modestia** to be lacking in modesty; **quel romanzo pecca nella struttura** that novel lacks structure
peccato [pek'kato] SM (*Rel*) sin; **un peccato di gioventù** (*fig*) a youthful error *o* indiscretion; **che peccato!** what a shame *o* pity!; **è un peccato che sia finita così** it's a shame that it had to end like that; **è un peccato che non sia potuto venire** it's a shame that he couldn't come; **peccato di gola** gluttony; **peccato mortale** mortal sin; **peccato originale** original sin; **peccato veniale** venial sin
peccatore, trice [pekka'tore] SM/F sinner
peccherò *ecc* [pekke'rɔ] VB *vedi* **peccare**
pece ['petʃe] SF pitch
pechinese [peki'nese] AGG, SM/F Pekin(g)ese *inv*
■ SM (*anche:* **cane pechinese**) Pekin(g)ese *inv*, Peke (*fam*)
Pechino [pe'kino] SF Beijing, Peking (*ant*)
pecora ['pɛkora] SF (*gen, fig*) sheep *inv*; (*femmina*) ewe; **c'erano solo due pecore nel campo** there were only two sheep in the field; **latte di pecora** sheep's milk; **pecora nera** (*fig*) black sheep; **la pecora nera della famiglia** the black sheep of the family
pecoraio, ai [peko'rajo] SM shepherd
pecorella [peko'rɛlla] SF lamb; **la pecorella smarrita** the lost sheep; **cielo a pecorelle** (*fig: nuvole*) mackerel sky
pecorino [peko'rino] SM (*anche:* **formaggio pecorino**) pecorino; *cheese made from sheep's milk*
pecorone [peko'rone] SM (*fig pegg*) spineless creature
pectina [pek'tina] SF pectin
peculato [peku'lato] SM (*Dir*) embezzlement
peculiare [peku'ljare] AGG: **peculiare di** peculiar to
peculiarità [pekuljari'ta] SF INV peculiarity
peculiarmente [pekuljar'mente] AVV peculiarly
pecuniario, ria, ri, rie [peku'njarjo] AGG financial, monetary, money *attr*
pedaggio, gi [pe'daddʒo] SM toll
pedagogia [pedago'dʒia] SF pedagogy, pedagogics *sg*, educational methods *pl*
pedagogicamente [pedagodʒika'mente] AVV pedagogically
pedagogico, a, ci, che [peda'gɔdʒiko] AGG pedagogic(al)
pedagogo, a, ghi, ghe [peda'gɔgo] SM/F pedagogue
pedalare [peda'lare] VI (*aus* **avere**) to pedal; (*andare in bicicletta*) to cycle
pedalata [peda'lata] SF push on the pedals

pedale [pe'dale] SM *(gen)* pedal; *(di macchina da cucire)* treadle
pedalò [peda'lɔ] SM INV pedalo
pedana [pe'dana] SF **1** *(gen)* footboard; **pedana della cattedra** platform, dais **2** *(Sport: nel salto)* springboard; *(: nella scherma)* piste; *(: nel lancio del disco)* throwing circle
pedante [pe'dante] AGG pedantic
■SM/F pedant
pedantemente [pedante'mente] AVV pedantically
pedanteria [pedante'ria] SF pedantry
pedata [pe'data] SF *(colpo)* kick; *(impronta)* footprint; **dare una pedata a qn** to kick sb, give sb a kick; **mi ha dato una pedata** he kicked me; **prendere a pedate qn/qc** to kick sb/sth
pedemontano, a [pedemon'tano] AGG *(regione, ghiacciaio)* piedmont *attr*
pederasta, i [pede'rasta] SM pederast
pederastia [pederas'tia] SF pederasty
pedestre [pe'dɛstre] AGG pedestrian
pediatra, i, e [pe'djatra] SM/F paediatrician *(Brit)*, pediatrician *(Am)*; **fa il pediatra** he's a p(a)ediatrician
pediatria [pedja'tria] SF paediatrics *sg (Brit)*, pediatrics *sg (Am)*
pediatrico, a, ci, che [pe'djatriko] AGG paediatric *(Brit)*, pediatric *(Am)*, children's *attr*
pedicello [pedi'tʃɛllo] SM *(Bot)* pedicel
pedicure [pedi'kure] SM/F INV chiropodist *(Brit)*, podiatrist *(Am)*
pediera [pe'djɛra] SF *(del letto)* footboard
pedigree ['pedigri:] SM INV pedigree
pediluvio, vi [pedi'luvjo] SM footbath
pedina [pe'dina] SF *(Dama)* draughtsman *(Brit)*, draftsman *(Am)*; *(Scacchi, fig)* pawn
pedinare [pedi'nare] VT to shadow, tail; **far pedinare qn** to have sb followed, put a tail on sb
pedissequo, a [pe'dissekwo] AGG *(imitatore)* servile; *(traduzione)* literal
pedofilia [pedofi'lia] SF paedophilia *(Brit)*, pedophilia *(Am)*
pedofilo, a [pe'dɔfilo] AGG, SM/F paedophile *(Brit)*, pedophile *(Am)*, paedophiliac *(Brit)*, pedophiliac *(Am)*
pedologico, a, ci, che [pedo'lɔdʒiko] AGG *(Geol)*: **profilo pedologico** soil profile
pedonale [pedo'nale] AGG *(passaggio, isola, traffico ecc)* pedestrian *attr*; **una zona pedonale** a pedestrian precinct
pedone [pe'done] SM **1** *(persona)* pedestrian **2** *(Scacchi)* pawn
pedule [pe'dule] SFPL walking boots
peduncolo [pe'dunkolo] SM peduncle
peeling ['pi:liŋ] SM INV *(Cosmetica)* exfoliation
PEEP [piee'pi] SIGLA M (= **Piano Edilizia Economica Popolare**) *council-house building programme*
Pegaso ['pɛgazo] SM *(Mitol, Astron)* Pegasus
peggio ['pɛddʒo] *(comp, superl di* **male***)* AVV **1** *(con senso comparativo)* worse; **gioca peggio di lui** she plays worse than he does, she's a worse player than he is; **andare peggio** to be worse; **gli affari vanno peggio che mai** business is worse than ever; **Luca è andato peggio di me all'esame** Luca did worse than me in the exam; **cambiare in peggio** to get *o* become worse, change for the worse; **si comporta sempre peggio** his behaviour gets worse and worse; **sta sempre peggio** he's getting worse and worse; **peggio per te!** that's your loss!; **non vuoi venire? peggio per te** you don't want to come? that's your loss; **peggio di così si muore** things couldn't be worse; **è peggio che andar di notte!** it's worse than ever!; **non c'è niente di peggio che...** there's nothing worse than ... **2** *(con senso superlativo)* worst; **i peggio allenati** the worst trained; **la peggio pagata** the worst paid; **sono le ragazze peggio vestite della scuola** they are the worst dressed girls in the school
■AGG INV *(con senso comparativo)* worse; **è peggio di suo fratello** she's worse than her brother
■SM worst; **il peggio è che...** the worst thing *o* the worst of it is that ...
■SF **1 avere la peggio** to come off worse, get the worst of it; **hanno litigato e Gigi ha avuto la peggio** they had an argument and Gigi came off worst **2 alla peggio** if the worst comes to the worst, at worst; **tirare avanti alla meno peggio** to get along as best one can
peggioramento [peddʒora'mento] SM *(gen, di malattia)* worsening; *(di rapporti)* worsening, deterioration; **portare un peggioramento in** *or* **portare ad un peggioramento di** to worsen, lead to a worsening in; **ci sarà un peggioramento** *(Meteor)* the weather will deteriorate *o* become worse
peggiorare [peddʒo'rare] VT to worsen, to make worse
■VI *(aus* **essere***)* to worsen, become *o* grow worse
peggiorativamente [peddʒorativa'mente] AVV pejoratively
peggiorativo, a [peddʒora'tivo] AGG pejorative
peggiore [ped'dʒore] AGG *(comparativo)* worse; *(superlativo)* worst; **peggiore (di)** worse (than); **è peggiore di lui** she's worse than him; **molto peggiore** much worse; **nel peggiore dei casi** if the worst comes to the worst; **le cose non potevano concludersi in modo peggiore** things couldn't have come to a worse end; **ho conosciuto tempi peggiori** I've been through worse
■SM/F: **il/la peggiore** the worst one, the worst (person); **il peggiore dei due** the worse of the two; **il peggiore della classe** the worst in the class
pegno ['peɲɲo] SM **1** *(Dir)* pledge, security; **dare in pegno qc** to pawn sth, leave sth as security; **posso darle in pegno l'orologio** I can leave you my watch as security; **banco dei pegni** pawnshop **2** *(fig: segno)* token, pledge; *(nei giochi di società)* forfeit; **un pegno d'amore** a love token; **in pegno d'amicizia** as a token of friendship
pelame [pe'lame] SM *(di animale)* coat, fur
pelandrone, a [pelan'drone] SM/F loafer, idler
pelapatate [pelapa'tate] SM INV potato peeler
pelare [pe'lare] VT *(spennare)* to pluck; *(spellare)* to skin; *(sbucciare)* to peel; **ti hanno pelato!** *(di capelli)* they've scalped you!; **in quel negozio ti pelano** they make you pay through the nose in that shop
pelata [pe'lata] SF *(calvizie parziale)* bald patch
pelato, a [pe'lato] AGG **1** *(sbucciato)* peeled **2** *(calvo)* bald; **è pelato** he's bald
■**pelati** SMPL *(anche:* **pomodori pelati***)* peeled tomatoes
pellaccia, ce [pel'lattʃa] SF *(fig: persona)*: **essere una pellaccia** to be tough
pellagra [pel'lagra] SF pellagra
pellame [pel'lame] SM *(di animali)* skins *pl*, hides *pl*
pelle ['pɛlle] SF **1** *(gen)* skin; **avere la pelle delicata** to have sensitive skin; **pelle grassa** greasy skin; *(Cosmetica)* oily skin; **pelle mista** combination skin; **pelle secca** dry skin **2** *(di animale)* skin, hide; *(di rettile)* skin; *(conciata)* leather; **borsa/giacca di pelle** leather

handbag/jacket; **pelle di camoscio** suede; **pelle di daino** shammy (leather); **pelli di foca** (*Sci*) skins; **pelle di montone** sheepskin **3** (*buccia*) skin, peel **4** (*fraseologia*): **avere la pelle dura** (*fig*) to be tough; **avere la pelle d'oca** to have goose pimples (*Brit*) *o* goose flesh (*Brit*) *o* goose bumps (*Am*); **mi ha fatto venire la pelle d'oca** (*paura, disgusto*) it made my flesh creep; **avere i nervi a fior di pelle** to be edgy; **essere pelle ed ossa** to be skin and bone; **non stare più nella pelle dalla gioia** to be beside o.s. with delight; **lasciarci la pelle** to lose one's life; **salvare la pelle** to save one's skin; **vendere cara la pelle** to put up a fierce struggle; **amici per la pelle** firm *o* close friends

pellegrinaggio, gi [pellegri'naddʒo] SM pilgrimage; **andare in pellegrinaggio** to go on a pilgrimage

pellegrino, a [pelle'grino] SM/F pilgrim

pellerossa [pelle'rossa] SM/F (*pl* **pellirosse**) redskin, Red Indian

pelletteria [pellette'ria] SF **1** (*negozio*) leather goods shop; **articoli di pelletteria** leather goods **2** (*industria*) leather trade *o* industry

pellettiere [pellet'tjɛre] SM dealer in leather goods

pellicano [pelli'kano] SM pelican

pellicceria [pellittʃe'ria] SF **1** (*negozio*) furrier's (shop) **2** (*pellicce*) furs *pl*

pelliccia, ce [pel'littʃa] SF **1** (*mantello di animale*) fur, coat **2** (*indumento*) fur (coat); **pelliccia ecologica** fake fur; **pelliccia di visone** mink coat

pellicciaio, ciai [pellit'tʃajo] SM furrier

pellicina [pelli'tʃina] SF (*di frutto*) membrane (*del latte*) skin

pellicola [pel'likola] SF **1** (*membrana*) film, layer; **pellicola trasparente** (*Culin*) cling film (*Brit*), plastic wrap (*Am*) **2** (*Fot, Cine*) film

pellirossa [pelli'rossa] SM/F = pellerossa

pelo ['pelo] SM **1** (*gen*) hair; **ho tanti peli sulle gambe** I've got a lot of hair *o* hairs on my legs; **non aver peli sulla lingua** to speak one's mind; **cercare il pelo nell'uovo** to pick holes, split hairs; **per un pelo** nearly; **per un pelo non ho perso il treno** I very nearly missed the train; **l'ha mancato per un pelo** she just missed it; **per un pelo non s'ammazzava** he almost *o* nearly killed himself; **ha perso per un pelo** he lost but only just; **c'è mancato un pelo che affogasse** he narrowly escaped drowning; **è un pelo più grande** (*un po'*) it's a shade bigger **2** (*di animale: pelame*) coat, fur; (: *peli*) hair; (: *pelliccia*) fur; **il gatto ha il pelo morbido** the cat has soft fur *o* a soft coat; **impermeabile con l'interno di pelo** fur-lined raincoat; **pelliccia a pelo lungo** long-haired fur coat; **essere di primo pelo** to be wet behind the ears; **fare il pelo e il contropelo a qn** to give sb a good dressing-down; **il lupo perde il pelo ma non il vizio** (*Proverbio*) the leopard cannot change its spots **3** (*di tappeto*) pile; (*di tessuto*) pile, nap; **tappeto a pelo lungo** thick pile carpet **4** (*superficie: di liquido*) surface; **il pelo dell'acqua** the surface of the water

peloso, a [pe'loso] AGG hairy

pelota [pe'lɔta] SF pelota

peltro ['peltro] SM pewter

peluche [pə'lyʃ] SM (*tessuto*) plush; **giocattoli di peluche** soft *o* cuddly toys; **un cane di peluche** a fluffy dog

peluria [pe'lurja] SF down

pelvi ['pɛlvi] SF INV pelvis

pelvico, a, ci, che ['pɛlviko] AGG pelvic

pena ['pena] SF **1** (*dolore*) sorrow, sadness *no pl*; (*angoscia*) worry, anxiety; **essere** *o* **stare in pena (per qn/qc)** to worry *o* be anxious (about sb/sth); **ero in pena per te** I was worried about you; **le pene dell'inferno** the torments of hell; **ha passato le pene dell'inferno** (*fig*) she went through hell **2** (*pietà*) pity; **far pena** to be pitiful; **mi fa pena** I feel sorry for him; **fa pena vederlo così** it is pitiful to see him like this; **quel cappello fa pena** (*fig*) that hat is a disgrace **3** (*Dir*) sentence; (: *punizione*) penalty, punishment; **fu condannato ad una pena di 5 anni** he was sentenced to 5 years' imprisonment; **scontare una pena** to serve a term of imprisonment; **pena capitale** capital punishment; **pena di morte** death sentence *o* penalty; **sono contrario alla pena di morte** I'm against the death penalty; **è stato condannato alla pena di morte** he was sentenced to death; **pena pecuniaria** fine **4** (*fatica*) trouble *no pl*, effort; (*difficoltà*) difficulty; **prendersi** *o* **darsi la pena di fare qc** to go to the trouble of doing sth, take the trouble to do sth; **valere la pena** to be worth it; **vale la pena farlo** it's worth doing, it's worth it; **non ne vale la pena** it's not worth the effort *o* worth it

penale [pe'nale] AGG (*Dir*) criminal, penal; **codice penale** penal code; **causa penale** criminal trial; **diritto penale** criminal law; **precedenti penali** criminal record
■ SF (*anche:* **clausola penale**) penalty clause; **pagare la penale** to pay the penalty

penalista, i, e [pena'lista] SM/F (*avvocato*) criminal lawyer

penalistico, a, ci, che [pena'listiko] AGG criminal; **fare studi penalistici** to study criminal law

penalità [penali'ta] SF INV penalty

penalizzare [penalid'dzare] VT (*Sport*) to penalize

penalizzazione [penaliddzat'tsjone] SF (*Sport*) penalty

penare [pe'nare] VI (*aus* **avere**) (*patire*) to suffer; (*faticare*) to struggle; **ha finito di penare** his sufferings are over; **penare a fare qc** to have difficulty in doing sth; **lo fecero senza penare troppo** they did it without too much difficulty

penati [pe'nati] SMPL household gods

pencolare [penko'lare] VI (*aus* **avere**) (*dondolare, vacillare*) sway; (*fig: tentennare*) to dither, hesitate

pendaglio, gli [pen'daʎʎo] SM (*ciondolo*) pendant; **pendaglio da forca** (*fig*) gallows bird

pendente [pen'dɛnte] AGG **1** (*appeso*) hanging; (*inclinato*) leaning **2** (*Dir: causa, lite*) pending
■ SM (*pendaglio*) pendant; (*orecchino*) drop earring

pendenza [pen'dɛntsa] SF **1** slope, slant; (*grado d'inclinazione*) gradient; **in pendenza** (*tetto*) sloping; (*strada, terreno*) on a slope; **essere in leggera pendenza** to slope (down) gently; **una strada con una pendenza del 20%** a road with a 1 in 5 gradient **2** (*Dir*) pending suit **3** (*Comm*) outstanding account

pendere ['pɛndere] VI (*aus* **avere**) **1** (*essere appeso*): **pendere (da)** to hang (from); **la lampada che pende dal soffitto** the lamp that hangs from the ceiling; **pendere dalle labbra di qn** to hang on sb's every word **2** (*Dir: causa*) to be pending **3** (*essere inclinato: superficie*) to slope, slant; (: *palo, edificio*) to lean; (: *nave*) to list; **pendere da una parte** to slope to one side; **pendere dalla parte di qn** (*fig*) to be inclined to take sb's part; **la bilancia pende in suo favore** things are in his favour **4** (*fig: incombere*): **pendere su** to hang over

pendice [pen'ditʃe] SF (*di monte*) slope

pendio, dii [pen'dio] SM **1** (*luogo in pendenza*) slope **2** (*pendenza*) slope, slant
pendola ['pɛndola] SF pendulum clock
pendolare [pendo'lare] AGG (*moto*) pendular, pendulum *attr*
■SM/F (*lavoratore*) commuter; **fare il pendolare** to commute
pendolarismo [pendola'rizmo] SM commuting
pendolino [pendo'lino] SM tilting train, pendolino
pendolo ['pɛndolo] SM (*peso*) pendulum; (*anche*: **orologio a pendolo**) pendulum clock
pene ['pɛne] SM (*Anat*) penis
Penelope [pe'nɛlope] SF Penelope
penetrabile [pene'trabile] AGG penetrable
penetrante [pene'trante] AGG (*freddo*) biting, piercing; (*odore*) penetrating; (*sguardo*) penetrating, piercing
penetrare [pene'trare] VI (*aus* **essere**) **1** (*gen*): **penetrare (in qc)** to penetrate (sth), enter (sth); **i ladri sono penetrati in casa di notte** the thieves entered the house at night; **penetrò in casa di nascosto** he entered the house by stealth, he stole into the house **2** (*freddo*) to come *o* get in; (*liquido*) to soak in; **penetrare nella parete** (*chiodo*) to penetrate the wall; (*acqua*) to soak into the wall; **il sole penetrò nella stanza** the sun shone into the room; **il proiettile gli è penetrato nel cuore** the bullet went into his heart; **il freddo mi penetrava nelle ossa** the cold went right through me; **far penetrare** (*aria, luce*) to let in
■VT (*gen, fig*) to penetrate; (*sogg*: *proiettile*) to penetrate; (: *acqua, aria*) to go *o* come into; **penetrare un mistero** to get to the bottom of a mystery
penetrazione [penetrat'tsjone] SF penetration
penicillina [penitʃil'lina] SF penicillin
peninsulare [peninsu'lare] AGG peninsular; **l'Italia peninsulare** mainland Italy
penisola [pe'nizola] SF peninsula; **la penisola italiana** the Italian mainland
penitente [peni'tɛnte] SM/F, AGG penitent
penitenza [peni'tɛntsa] SF **1** (*Rel*: *pentimento*) repentance, penitence; (: *pena*) penance; **far penitenza** to do penance **2** (*nei giochi*) forfeit
penitenziario, ri [peniten'tsjarjo] SM prison, penitentiary (*Am*)
penna ['penna] SF **1** (*di uccello*) feather; **mettere le penne** to grow feathers; **lasciarci** *o* **rimetterci le penne** (*fig*) to get one's fingers burnt; **le penne nere** (*Mil*) *the Italian Alpine troops* **2** (*per scrivere*) pen; **penna biro** biro® (*Brit*), ballpoint (*Am*); **penna luminosa** *o* **ottica** light pen; **penna d'oca** quill; **penna a sfera** ballpoint pen; **penna stilografica** fountain pen **3** (*Culin*): **penne** SFPL quills (*type of pasta*) **4** (*Mus*) pick
pennacchio, chi [pen'nakkjo] SM (*ornamento*) plume; **un pennacchio di fumo** (*fig*) a plume *o* spiral of smoke
pennarello [penna'rɛllo] SM felt(-tip) pen
pennellare [pennel'lare] VI (*aus* **avere**) to paint
pennellata [pennel'lata] SF (*di vernice*) brush stroke; **dare le ultime pennellate a qc** (*anche fig*) to give the finishing touches to sth
pennellessa [pennel'lessa] SF pasting brush
pennello[1] [pen'nɛllo] SM (*gen*) brush; (*di pittore, imbianchino*) (paint)brush; **a pennello** (*perfettamente*) to perfection, perfectly; **quel vestito ti sta a pennello** that dress fits you perfectly; **pennello da barba** shaving brush
pennello[2] [pen'nɛllo] SM (*lungo la costa*) breakwater
Pennini [pen'nini] SMPL: **i Pennini** the Pennines
pennino [pen'nino] SM (pen) nib
pennone [pen'none] SM **1** (*Naut*) yard **2** (*bandiera*) banner, standard
Pennsylvania [pɛnsɪl'vaɪnɪə] SF Pennsylvania
pennuto, a [pen'nuto] AGG feathered
■SM bird
penombra [pe'nombra] SF half-light, dim light; **in penombra** in the half-light; **mi è sembrato di vedere qualcuno nella penombra** I thought I saw someone in the half-light
penosamente [penosa'mente] AVV (*vedi agg*) painfully; anxiously; with difficulty, laboriously; pathetically
penoso, a [pe'noso] AGG (*doloroso*: *esperienza, compito*) painful, distressing; (*angoscioso*: *attesa*) anxious; (*faticoso*: *lavoro, viaggio*) difficult, tiring; (*patetico*: *scena, scusa*) pathetic; **un penoso silenzio** a painful silence
pensante [pen'sante] AGG thinking
■SM/F: **ben pensante** = **benpensante**
pensare [pen'sare] VI (*aus* **avere**)
1 to think; **pensare a** to think of; (*amico, vacanze*) to think of *o* about; (*problema*) to think about; **a chi stai pensando?** who are you thinking about?; **pensava al tempo passato** he was remembering days gone by; **vorrei pensarci su** I would like to think it over *o* give it some thought; **penso di sì** I think so; **penso di no** I don't think so; **a pensarci bene...** on second thoughts (*Brit*) *o* thought (*Am*) ...; **pensare con la propria testa** to think for o.s.; **pensa a come sarebbe bello** think how lovely it would be; **prima di parlare pensa** think before you speak; **se solo ci avessi pensato** if only I had thought about it; **non voglio nemmeno pensarci** I don't even want to think about it; **ciò mi dà da pensare** that gives me something to think about; **pensare bene/male di qn** to think well/badly of sb, have a good/bad opinion of sb; **ma pensa un po'!** just think of that!
2 (*provvedere*): **pensare a qc** to see to sth, take care of sth; **ci penso io** I'll see to *o* take care of it; **ha altro a cui pensare ora** he's got other *o* more important things to think about now; **pensa ai fatti tuoi!** mind your own business!
■VT
1 (*gen*) to think; **che stai pensando?** what are you thinking?; **cosa ne pensi?** what do you think of it?, how do you feel about it?; **penso che sia colpa sua** I think it is his fault *o* that he is to blame; **ciò mi fa pensare che...** that makes me think that ...; **il suo comportamento farebbe pensare che...** his behaviour would lead you to suppose that ..., his behaviour would make you think that ...; **non avrei mai pensato finisse così** I would never have believed it would end like this; **ti pensavo più furbo** I thought you were smarter than that; **chi l'avrebbe mai pensato?** who would have thought it?; **e pensare che...** and to think that ...
2 (*prendere in considerazione*) to realize; **devi pensare che ha appena iniziato** you must realize *o* remember that he's only just started; **non pensa che quello che fa può danneggiare gli altri** he doesn't realize that what he does may harm others
3 (*avere intenzione*): **pensare di fare qc** to think of doing sth; **pensavo di invitare anche lui** I was thinking of inviting him too; **penso di partire in serata** I'm thinking of leaving in the course of the evening
4 (*inventare, escogitare*) to think out; **ne pensa sempre**

Pp

una nuova he's always got something new up his sleeve; **l'ha pensata bella** he had a bright idea; **una ne fa e cento ne pensa** he's always up to something

pensata [pen'sata] SF (*trovata*) idea, thought; **ma che bella pensata!** (*anche iro*) what a good idea!

pensatore, trice [pensa'tore] SM/F thinker

pensée [pɑ̃'se] SF INV (*fiore*) pansy

pensierino [pensje'rino] SM **1** (*pensiero*): **ci farò un pensierino** I'll think about it **2** (*dono*) little gift

pensiero [pen'sjɛro] SM **1** thought; **riandare col pensiero a** to remember, think back to; **leggere il pensiero di qn** to read sb's thoughts *o* mind; **essere assorto nei propri pensieri** to be deep *o* lost in thought; **un pensiero gentile** (*anche fig: dono*) a kind thought; **libertà di pensiero** freedom of thought **2** (*preoccupazione*) worry, care, trouble; **ha tanti pensieri** he has so many worries; **stare in pensiero per qn/qc** to be worried about sb/sth; **darsi pensiero per qc** to worry about sth; **è un tipo senza pensieri** he's a carefree chap **3** (*modo di pensare, dottrina*) thinking *no pl*; **il pensiero di Hegel** Hegelian thinking

pensierosamente [pensjerosa'mente] AVV thoughtfully

pensieroso, a [pensje'roso] AGG pensive, thoughtful

pensile ['pɛnsile] AGG hanging, suspended; **giardino pensile** hanging garden

pensilina [pensi'lina] SF projecting roof; (*di stazione*) platform roof

pensionabile [pensjo'nabile] AGG pensionable; **età pensionabile** retirement age

pensionamento [pensjona'mento] SM retirement; **pensionamento anticipato** early retirement

pensionante [pensjo'nante] SM/F (*presso una famiglia*) lodger; (*in albergo*) resident, guest

pensionato[1] [pensjo'nato] SM (*istituto: per studenti*) hostel; (*: per anziani*) rest home

pensionato[2], a [pensjo'nato] SM/F pensioner

pensione [pen'sjone] SF **1** (*rendita*) pension; **andare in pensione** to retire; **essere in pensione** to be retired; **pensione di anzianità** *occupational pension (paid after a certain number of years of employment)*; **pensione baby** *pension paid to someone who has worked for only a short time, usually 15-20 years*; **pensione di guerra** war pension; **pensione d'invalidità** disability pension; **pensione di reversibilità** spouse's pension; **pensione sociale** *minimum state pension (payable to those on low incomes)*; **pensione di vecchiaia** *old-age pension (payable to those who have made sufficient contributions)* **2** (*albergo*) boarding house; (*vitto e alloggio*) board and lodging; **essere a pensione da qn** to board with sb; **tenere a pensione qn** to have sb as a lodger; **mezza pensione** half board; **pensione completa** full board

pensionistico, a, ci, che [pensjo'nistiko] AGG pension *attr*; **fondo pensionistico** pension fund

pensosamente [pensosa'mente] AVV thoughtfully, pensively

pensoso, a [pen'soso] AGG thoughtful, pensive

pentagonale [pentago'nale] AGG pentagonal

pentagono [pen'tagono] SM **1** (*Geom*) pentagon **2** (*Pol*): **il Pentagono** the Pentagon

pentagramma, i [penta'gramma] SM (*Mus*) staff, stave

pentapartito [pentapar'tito] SM (*Pol*) five-party coalition government

pentathlon ['pɛntatlon] SM INV pentathlon

Pentecoste [pente'kɔste] SF Pentecost, Whit Sunday (*Brit*)

pentimento [penti'mento] SM repentance, contrition; (*rimpianto*) regret

pentirsi [pen'tirsi] VIP (*Rel*) to repent; **pentirsi dei propri peccati** to repent of one's sins; **pentirsi di qc/di aver fatto qc** (*rimpiangere*) to regret sth/doing sth; **mi pento di averglielo detto** I regret telling him; **se segui i miei consigli non te ne pentirai** if you follow my advice you won't regret it; **vieni con noi e non te ne pentirai** if you come with us you won't regret it

pentitismo [penti'tizmo] SM *the phenomenon of criminals or terrorists who decide to collaborate with the police*

PENTITISMO

The practice of **pentitismo** first emerged in Italy during the 1970s, a period marked by major terrorist activity. Once arrested, some members of terrorist groups would collaborate with the authorities by providing information in return for a reduced sentence, or indeed for their own reasons. In recent years it has become common practice for members of Mafia organizations to become "pentiti", and special legislation has had to be introduced to provide for the sentencing and personal protection of these informants.

pentito, a [pen'tito] AGG (*gen: persona, sguardo ecc*) penitent, repentant

■ SM/F (*terrorista, mafioso*) ≈ supergrass (*Brit*) *terrorist/criminal who turns police informer*

pentola ['pentola] SF (*recipiente*) pot; (*contenuto*) pot(ful); **metti la pentola sul fuoco** put the pot on the gas; **qualcosa bolle in pentola** (*fig*) there's something brewing; **pentola a pressione** pressure cooker

pentolino [pento'lino] SM small saucepan; **pentolino del latte** milk pan

penultimo, a [pe'nultimo] AGG penultimate, last but one (*Brit*), next to last; **è arrivato penultimo** he arrived second from last

■ SM/F: **il(la) penultimo(a)** the last but one (*Brit*)

penuria [pe'nurja] SF shortage

LO SAPEVI...?
penuria non si traduce mai con la parola inglese *penury*

penzolare [pendzo'lare] VI (*aus* **avere**) (*pendere*) to hang loosely, dangle

penzoloni [pendzo'loni] AVV (*anche:* **a penzoloni**) hanging down, dangling; **se ne stava con le braccia penzoloni** he stood there with his arms dangling

peonia [pe'ɔnja] SF (*Bot*) peony

pepare [pe'pare] VT to pepper

pepato, a [pe'pato] AGG **1** (*condito con pepe*) peppery, hot **2** (*fig*) (*: pungente*) sharp

pepe ['pepe] SM pepper; **è tutta pepe** (*fig*) she's full of life; **pepe bianco** white pepper; **pepe della Giamaica** allspice; **pepe in grani** whole pepper, peppercorns; **pepe macinato** ground pepper; **pepe nero** black pepper

peperonata [pepero'nata] SF (*Culin*) *stewed peppers, tomatoes and onions*

peperoncino [peperon'tʃino] SM chilli pepper

peperone [pepe'rone] SM capsicum; **rosso come un peperone** as red as a beetroot (*Brit*) *o* beet (*Am*); **peperone rosso** red pepper, capsicum; **peperone verde** green pepper, capsicum; **peperoni ripieni** stuffed peppers

pepiera [pe'pjɛra] SF pepper pot
pepita [pe'pita] SF nugget
pepsina [pep'sina] SF pepsin
peptide [pep'tide] SM peptide

per [per] PREP PAROLA CHIAVE
1 (*direzione*) for, to; **l'autobus per Milano** the Milan bus, the bus for *o* to Milan; **quando parti per Parigi?** when are you leaving for *o* are you off to Paris?; **proseguire per Londra** to go on to London
2 (*verso, nei confronti di*) for, towards; **il suo grande amore per la sorella** his great love for *o* of his sister; **ha una passione per la musica** he is passionately fond of music
3 (*moto attraverso luogo*) through; **l'ho cercata per tutta la casa** I searched the whole house *o* I searched all over the house for it; **ti ho cercato per mari e per monti** I looked everywhere for you; **l'ho incontrato per le scale** I met him on the stairs; **sono passata per Roma** I came through *o* via Rome; **il maestro è passato per i banchi** the teacher went along the rows of desks; **i ladri sono passati per la finestra** the thieves got in (*o* out) through the window
4 (*stato in luogo*): **seduto/sdraiato per terra** sitting/lying on the ground
5 (*tempo*) for; **per anni** for years; **per tutta l'estate** all summer long, all through the summer, throughout the summer; **per tutta la giornata** all day long; **per giorni e giorni** for days on end; **giorno per giorno** day by day; **dobbiamo finirlo per lunedì** we must get it finished by *o* for Monday; **ci rivedremo per Pasqua** we'll see one another again at Easter; **è piovuto per tutta la settimana** it has rained all week long; **per molto tempo** for a long time; **sarò di ritorno per le tre** I'll be back by three o'clock
6 (*mezzo, maniera*) by; **per ferrovia** by rail *o* train; **l'ha fatto per gioco** he did it as a joke; **per lettera** by letter; **l'ha presa per mano** he took her by the hand; **chiamare qn per nome** to call sb by name; **l'ha fatto per scherzo** he did it as a joke; **non mi piace parlare per telefono** I don't like using the phone *o* speaking on the phone; **per via aerea** by air; **per vie legali** through legal channels
7 (*causa*) for, because of, owing to; (*scopo*) for; **per abitudine** out of habit, from habit; **è morto per avvelenamento** he died from poisoning; **le tende per la cucina** the kitchen curtains, the curtains for the kitchen; **per un errore** through *o* by error; **per il freddo** because of the cold; **non stare in pena per lui** don't worry about him; **pastiglie per il mal di gola** throat pastilles *o* lozenges; **chiuso per malattia** closed because of *o* on account of illness; **assentarsi per malattia** to be off because of *o* through *o* owing to illness; **questo lavoro non fa per me** this isn't the right job for me; **per motivi di salute** for health reasons; **condannato per omicidio** convicted of murder; **non l'ha fatto per pigrizia** he didn't do it out of laziness; **processato per rapina a mano armata** tried for armed robbery
8 (*prezzo, misura*) for; **assicurato per un milione** insured for 1 million euros; **l'ho comprato per 500 euro** I bought it for 500 euros; **per miglia e miglia non si vedeva nulla** you couldn't see anything for miles; **il terreno si estende per molti chilometri** the land extends for several kilometres; **lo vendo per poco** I'm selling it for very little, I'm selling it cheap
9 (*limitazione*) for; **è troppo difficile per lui** it's too hard for him; **per me è come una madre** she's like a mother to me; **per quel che mi riguarda** as far as I'm concerned; **per questa volta ci passerò sopra** I'll forget about it this time
10 (*distributivo*): **un interesse del 5 per cento** 5 per cent interest; **dividere 12 per 4** to divide 12 by 4; **2 per 3 fa 6** 2 times 3 equals 6; **in fila per tre!** line up in threes!; **moltiplicare 9 per 3** to multiply 9 by 3; **ce n'è una per parte** there's one on each side; **750 euro per persona** 750 euros per person *o* a head *o* apiece; **vi interrogo uno per uno** I'll question you one by one; **entrate uno per volta** come in one at a time
11 (*in qualità di*) as; (*al posto di*) for; **te lo dico per certo** I tell you it's gospel; **me l'hanno venduto per lana** they sold it to me as (if it were) wool; **lo hanno dato per morto** he was given up for dead; **ha avuto suo padre per professore** he had his father as one of his teachers, he was taught by his father; **prendere qn per uno sciocco** to take sb for a fool; **ti ho preso per tuo fratello** I (mis)took you for your brother
12 (*introduce proposizione finale*) to, in order to; **per fare qc** (so as) to do sth, in order to do sth; **l'ho fatto per aiutarti** I did it to help you; **dicevo così per scherzare** I said it as a joke *o* in fun
13 (*introduce proposizione causale*) for; **per aver fatto qc** for doing sth; **è stato punito per aver picchiato suo fratello** he was punished for hitting his brother; **è morta per aver ingerito troppi barbiturici** she died from *o* of an overdose of barbiturates
14 (*introduce proposizione concessiva*): **per poco che sia** however little it is *o* it may be; little though it is *o* it may be; **per quanto si dia da fare...** however hard he tries ...; **per quanto io sappia** as far as I know

pera ['pera] SF **1** pear; **pere cotte** stewed pears; **cadere come una pera cotta** (*fig: innamorarsi*) to fall head over heels in love **2** **pera di gomma** (*Med: per clistere*) rubber syringe **3** **farsi una pera** (*fig fam*) to shoot up
peraltro [pe'raltro] AVV (*per di più*) moreover, what's more; (*comunque*) however
perbacco [per'bakko] ESCL by Jove!
perbene [per'bene] AGG INV (*ammodo*) respectable, decent; **gente perbene** respectable people
■ AVV (*con cura*) well, properly
perbenismo [perbe'nizmo] SM (so-called) respectability
perbenistico, a, ci, che [perbe'nistiko] AGG supposedly respectable
perborato [perbo'rato] SM perborate
perca, che ['pɛrka] SF perch (*fish*)
percalle [per'kalle] SM percale
percento [per'tʃɛnto] SM INV percentage
■ AVV: **il cinque percento** five percent
percentuale [pertʃentu'ale] AGG percentage *attr*
■ SF percentage; (*provvigione*) commission; **percepisce una percentuale del 20% su ciò che vende** he receives a commission of 20% on what he sells
percepire [pertʃe'pire] VT **1** (*sentire, intuire*) to perceive **2** (*ricevere: somma, compenso*) to receive
percettibile [pertʃet'tibile] AGG perceptible; **un suono appena percettibile** a barely audible sound
percettibilità [pertʃettibili'ta] SF perceptibility
percezione [pertʃet'tsjone] SF perception
perché [per'ke] AVV why; **non so perché** I don't know why; **perché no?** why not?; **perché non vuoi andarci?** why don't you want to go?; **perché l'hai fatto?** why

Pp

did you do it?; **spiegami perché l'hai fatto** tell me why you did it; **vorrei sapere perché non te ne vai** I'd like to know why you don't leave
■ CONG **1** (*causale: poiché*) because; **non posso uscire perché ho molto da fare** I can't go out because *o* as I've a lot to do **2** (*finale: affinché*) so (that), in order that; **te lo do perché tu lo legga** I'm giving it to you so you can read it; **ho telefonato perché non si preoccupassero** I phoned so that they wouldn't worry **3** (*consecutivo: cosicché*): **l'ostacolo era troppo alto perché si potesse scavalcarlo** the obstacle was too high to climb over; **è troppo forte perché si possa vincerlo** he's too strong to be beaten *o* for anyone to beat him
■ SM INV (*motivo*) reason; **non c'è un vero perché** there's no real reason for it; **vorrei sapere il perché di un simile atteggiamento da parte sua** I'd like to know the reason for his attitude; **i perché sono tanti** there are many reasons for it; **voglio sapere il perché e il percome** I want to know the whys and wherefores

perciò [per'tʃɔ] CONG therefore, so, for this (*o* that) reason

percome [per'kome] SM INV: **il perché e il percome** the whys and wherefores

percorrere [per'korrere] VT IRREG (*distanza, circuito, territorio*) to cover; (*strada*) to follow; (*luogo*) to go all over; (*paese*) to travel up and down, go all over; **abbiamo percorso venti chilometri al giorno** we covered twenty kilometres a day; **percorrere un paese in lungo e in largo** to travel all over a country

percorribile [perkor'ribile] AGG (*strada*) which can be followed

percorso, a [per'korso] PP *di* **percorrere**
■ SM (*distanza*) distance; (*tragitto*) journey; (*itinerario*) route; (*Sport*) course; **ho seguito il percorso più breve** I took the shortest route; **lungo il percorso** along the way; **percorso netto** (*Ippica*) clear round; **percorso obbligato** (*Sport*) set course

percossa [per'kɔssa] SF blow

percosso, a [per'kɔsso] PP *di* **percuotere**

percuotere [per'kwɔtere] VT IRREG (*gen*) to beat, hit, strike; **percuotersi il petto** to beat one's breast

percussione [perkus'sjone] SF percussion; **strumenti a percussione** (*Mus*) percussion instruments

percussore [perkus'sore] SM (*in armi*) hammer

perdente [per'dɛnte] AGG losing
■ SM/F loser

perdere ['pɛrdere] VB IRREG
■ VT
1 (*gen*) to lose; (*abitudine*) to get out of; **ho perso il portafoglio** I've lost my wallet; **perdere di vista qn** (*anche fig*) to lose sight of sb; **l'ho perso di vista dopo mezz'ora** I lost sight of him after half an hour; **perdere la speranza/l'appetito/la vista** to lose hope/one's appetite/one's sight; **perdere i capelli** to lose one's hair, go bald; **gli alberi perdono le foglie** the trees are losing *o* shedding their leaves; **perdere al gioco** to lose money gambling; **saper perdere** to be a good loser; **lascia perdere!** (*non insistere*) forget it!, never mind!; **lascialo perdere!** (*non ascoltarlo*) don't listen to him!; **non ho niente da perdere** I've got nothing to lose
2 (*lasciar sfuggire: treno, autobus*) to miss; **ho perso il treno** I've missed the train; **è un'occasione da non perdere** it's a wonderful opportunity; (*affare*) it's a great bargain
3 (*sprecare: tempo, denaro*) to waste; **hai perso tempo e denaro** you've wasted time and money; **ho perso l'intera giornata a cercarlo** I wasted the whole day looking for it; **è fatica persa** it's a waste of effort
4 (*lasciar uscire: sangue*) to lose; **il rubinetto perde** (*acqua*) the tap is leaking; **la stufa perde gas** the gas fire is leaking
5 (*rimetterci*): **hanno alzato i prezzi per non perderci** they put up their prices so as not to make a loss; **non hai perso niente a non vedere quel film** you haven't missed anything by not seeing that film; **ci perdi a non venire** you are missing out by not coming
■ VI (*aus* **avere**) **perdere di** (*diminuire*): **perdere di autorità/importanza** to lose authority/importance; **perdere di valore** to go down in value
▶ **perdersi** VIP
1 (*smarrirsi*) to lose one's way, get lost; **ci siamo persi** we got lost; **perdersi in un bicchiere d'acqua** to be unable to cope with the slightest problem; **perdersi in chiacchiere** to waste time talking; **perdersi dietro a qn** to waste one's time with *o* on sb; **non perderti in queste sciocchezze** don't waste your time with this nonsense
2 (*scomparire: oggetto*) to disappear, vanish; (*: suono*) to fade away; **perdersi alla vista** to disappear from sight
3 (*uso reciproco*): **perdersi di vista** to lose sight of each other; (*fig*) to lose touch; **dopo la scuola si sono persi di vista** they lost touch after leaving school

perdifiato [perdi'fjato] **a perdifiato** AVV (*correre*) at breathtaking speed; (*gridare*) at the top of one's voice

perdigiorno [perdi'dʒorno] SM/F INV idler, loafer, waster

perdimento [perdi'mento] SM (*fig*) perdition, damnation

perdinci [per'dintʃi] ESCL (*euf: con impazienza*) for goodness' sake!; (*: con meraviglia*) golly!, crikey! (*Brit*)

perdio [per'dio] ESCL (*con impazienza*) for God's sake!; (*con meraviglia*) good God!

perdita ['pɛrdita] SF **1** (*gen*) loss; (*di persona: morte*) loss, death; **è una grave perdita** it's a great loss; **a perdita d'occhio** as far as the eye can see; **perdite** casualties **2** (*Econ*) loss, deficit; **siamo in perdita** we are running at a loss **3** (*spreco*) waste; **è una perdita di tempo** it's a waste of time **4** (*spandimento: di rubinetto*) leak; (*: di sangue*) loss; **le perdite bianche** (*Med*) the whites

perditempo [perdi'tɛmpo] SM/F INV waster, idler

perdizione [perdit'tsjone] SF (*Rel*) perdition, damnation; **luogo di perdizione** place of ill repute

perdonabile [perdo'nabile] AGG pardonable, forgivable

perdonare [perdo'nare] VT **1** to forgive, pardon; **perdonare a qn qc/di aver fatto qc** to forgive sb (for) sth/for doing *o* having done sth; **mi perdoni?** will you forgive me?; **le ha comprato dei fiori per farsi perdonare** he bought her flowers as a peace offering; **non gliel'ha mai perdonata** he has never forgiven him for that; **non glielo perdonerò mai** I'll never forgive him for that; **non me lo perdonerò mai** I'll never forgive myself **2** (*scusare*) to excuse, pardon; **perdona la domanda** if you don't mind my asking ...; **vogliate perdonare il (mio) ritardo** my apologies for being late; **perdona la mia ignoranza** forgive my ignorance; **bisogna perdonare la sua giovane età** you must make allowances for his youth
■ VI (*aus* **avere**) to forgive; **un male che non perdona**

an incurable disease; **un uomo che non perdona** an unforgiving man

perdono [per'dono] SM (*gen*) forgiveness; **chiedere perdono a qn (per)** to ask for sb's forgiveness (for); (*scusarsi*) to apologize to sb (for); **l'ho urtata? chiedo perdono** was that you I hit? I do beg your pardon *o* I do apologize; **perdono giudiziale** (*Dir*) pardon

perdurare [perdu'rare] VI (*aus* **avere**; *nel senso di perseverare* **essere**) (*continuare*) to go on, last; (*perseverare*) to persist; **il cattivo tempo perdura** the bad weather continues; **perdurare nei propositi di vendetta** to persist in seeking revenge

perdutamente [perduta'mente] AVV desperately, passionately; **amare perdutamente qn** to be desperately in love with sb

perduto, a [per'duto] PP *di* **perdere**
■ AGG (*gen*) lost; **sentirsi** *o* **vedersi perduto** (*fig*) to realize the hopelessness of one's position; **una donna perduta** (*fig*) a fallen woman

peregrinare [peregri'nare] VI (*aus* **avere**) to wander, roam

peregrinazione [peregrinat'tsjone] SF (*anche fig*) peregrination

perenne [pe'rɛnne] AGG (*Bot*) perennial; (*gloria, ricordo*) everlasting; **nevi perenni** perpetual snow *sg*

perennemente [perenne'mente] AVV perpetually; **un monumento che ricorderà perennemente i caduti** a monument to the eternal memory of those who died in the war

perentoriamente [perentorja'mente] AVV peremptorily

perentorio, ria, ri, rie [peren'tɔrjo] AGG (*tono, ordine*) peremptory; (*definitivo*) final

perequazione [perekwat'tsjone] SF (*Amm*) equal distribution

perestrojka [peres'trɔika] SF (*Pol*) perestroika

perfettamente [perfetta'mente] AVV perfectly; **funziona perfettamente** it works perfectly; **sai perfettamente che...** you know perfectly well that ...

perfettibile [perfet'tibile] AGG perfectible

perfetto, a [per'fetto] AGG (*gen*) perfect; (*silenzio, accordo*) complete, total; **è un perfetto cretino** he's an utter *o* a perfect idiot
■ SM (*Gramm*) perfect (tense)

perfezionamento [perfettsjona'mento] SM (*vedi vb*): **perfezionamento (di)** perfection (of); improvement (in); **un corso di perfezionamento di inglese** a course to improve one's English

perfezionare [perfettsjo'nare] VT (*rendere perfetto*) to perfect; (*migliorare*) to improve
▶ **perfezionarsi** VIP (*tecnica*) to improve; **perfezionarsi in inglese** to improve one's English

perfezione [perfet'tsjone] SF perfection; **alla** *o* **a perfezione** to perfection

perfezionismo [perfettsjo'nizmo] SM perfectionism

perfezionista, i, e [perfettsjo'nista] SM/F perfectionist

perfidamente [perfida'mente] AVV perfidiously

perfidia [per'fidja] SF perfidy

perfido, a ['pɛrfido] AGG perfidious, treacherous

perfino [per'fino] AVV even; **perfino lui si è commosso** even he was moved; **è un peccato perfino pensarlo** you should be ashamed to even think of such a thing

perforare [perfo'rare] VT (*gen*) to pierce; (*banda, schede*) to punch; (*trivellare*) to drill; (*Med*) to perforate; **ulcera perforata** (*Med*) perforated ulcer

perforatore, trice [perfora'tore] SM/F (*Inform: persona*) punch-card operator
■ SM (*macchina*) punch; **perforatore di schede** (*Inform*) card punch
■ SF (*Tecn*) boring *o* drilling machine; (*Inform*) card punch

perforazione [perforat'tsjone] SF **1** (*di sottosuolo*) boring, drilling; (*Inform: atto*) punching; (*: foro*) punch **2** (*Med*) perforation

performante [perfor'mante] AGG high-performance

pergamena [perga'mɛna] SF parchment

pergola ['pɛrgola] SF, **pergolato** [pergo'lato] SM pergola

pericolante [periko'lante] AGG (*muro, edificio*) unsafe; (*fig: economia*) shaky, precarious

pericolo [pe'rikolo] SM danger; **essere/trovarsi in pericolo** to be/find o.s. in danger; **mettere in pericolo** to endanger, put in danger; **essere fuori pericolo** to be out of danger; (*Med*) to be off the danger list; **"pericolo di morte"** (*su centralina elettrica*) ≈ "danger: high voltage"; **è un pericolo pubblico** (*fig: persona*) he's a public menace; **non c'è pericolo che rifiuti** (*iro*) there's no chance of his refusing, there's no fear that he'll refuse

pericolosamente [perikolosa'mente] AVV dangerously

pericolosità [perikolosi'ta] SF (*gen*) danger; **bisogna tener presente la pericolosità di questo criminale** we must bear in mind how dangerous this criminal is

pericoloso, a [periko'loso] AGG (*gen*) dangerous; (*impresa*) hazardous, risky; **zona pericolosa** danger zone

periferia [perife'ria] SF (*anche fig*) periphery; (*di città*) outskirts *pl*, suburbs *pl*; **la periferia di Milano** the outskirts of Milan; **vivere in periferia** to live on the outskirts *o* on the edge of town; **vivo in periferia** I live on the edge of town

periferica [peri'fɛrika] SF (*Inform*) peripheral

perifericamente [periferika'mente] AVV peripherally

periferico, a, ci, che [peri'fɛriko] AGG (*Anat, Inform*) peripheral; (*zona*) outlying

perifrasi [pe'rifrazi] SF INV circumlocution

perimetrale [perime'trale] AGG (*misura*) perimetral; (*muro*) perimeter *attr*

perimetro [pe'rimetro] SM (*gen, Mat*) perimeter

periodicamente [periodika'mente] AVV periodically

periodico, a, ci, che [peri'ɔdiko] AGG periodic(al); (*Mat*) recurring
■ SM (*pubblicazione*) periodical

periodo [pe'riodo] SM (*gen*) period; **un periodo di tre anni** a period of three years; **durante il periodo elettorale** at election time; **durante il periodo estivo** during the summer (period); **periodo contabile** accounting period; **periodo di prova** trial period

peripatetica, che [peripa'tɛtika] SF (*euf: prostituta*) streetwalker

peripezie [peripet'tsie] SFPL vicissitudes, ups and downs

periplo ['periplo] SM circumnavigation

perire [pe'rire] VI (*aus* **essere**) to perish, die

periscopio, pi [peris'kɔpjo] SM periscope

peristalsi [peris'talsi] SF INV peristalsis

perito, a [pe'rito] SM (*esperto*) expert; (*: Edil, Agr, Naut*) surveyor; (*: Assicurazione*) loss adjuster; **è perito chimico/agrario** (*Scol*) he has a qualification *o* diploma in chemistry/agriculture
■ AGG expert, skilled

Pp

peritonite [perito'nite] SF peritonitis

perizia [pe'rittsja] SF **1** (*maestria*) skill, ability; **un lavoro fatto con perizia** a skilful piece of work **2** (*Dir: giudizio tecnico*) expert opinion; (*: scritto*) expert's report; (*stima*) appraisal, valuation; **perizia psichiatrica** psychiatrist's report

perizoma, i [perid'dzɔma] SM (*di popolazioni primitive*) loincloth; (*indumento intimo*) thong; (*di spogliarellista*) G-string

perla ['pɛrla] SF pearl; **una collana di perle** a pearl necklace; **Venezia, la perla dell'Adriatico** Venice, the jewel of the Adriatic; **una perla di marito** a gem of a husband; **perla coltivata** cultured pearl
■ AGG INV (*colore*) pearl *attr*; **grigio perla** pearl grey

perlaceo, a [per'latʃeo] AGG pearly

perlaquale [perla'kwale] (*fam*) AGG INV (*perbene*) respectable; **è un tipo poco perlaquale** he is not to be trusted
■ AVV (*bene*): **oggi non mi sento troppo perlaquale** I don't feel quite right today

perlifero, a [per'lifero] AGG: **ostrica perlifera** pearl oyster

perlina [per'lina] SF bead

perlinato [perli'nato] SM matchboarding

perlomeno [perlo'meno] AVV (*almeno*) at least

perlopiù [perlo'pju] AVV (*quasi sempre*) in most cases, usually

perlustrare [perlus'trare] VT to patrol, reconnoitre

perlustrazione [perlustrat'tsjone] SF patrol, reconnaissance; **andare in perlustrazione** to go on patrol

permalosità [permalosi'ta] SF touchiness

permaloso, a [perma'loso] AGG touchy
■ SM/F touchy person

permanente [perma'nɛnte] AGG (*gen*) permanent; (*esercito, commissione*) standing
■ SF (*acconciatura*) permanent wave, perm; **ha la permanente** she's got a perm; **farsi fare la permanente** to have one's hair permed; **mi sono fatta fare la permanente** I had my hair permed

permanentemente [permanente'mente] AVV permanently

permanenza [perma'nɛntsa] SF **1** (*presenza continua*) permanence **2** (*soggiorno*) stay, sojourn; **buona permanenza!** enjoy your stay!

permanere [perma'nere] VI IRREG (*aus* **essere**) (*rimanere*) to remain; **il cattivo tempo permane sulla Scozia** the bad weather conditions persist over Scotland

permanganato [permanga'nato] SM permanganate; **permanganato di potassio** potassium permanganate

permango *ecc* [per'mango] VB *vedi* **permanere**

permasi *ecc* [per'masi] VB *vedi* **permanere**

permeabile [perme'abile] AGG permeable

permeabilità [permeabili'ta] SF permeability

permeare [perme'are] VT (*anche fig*): **permeare (di)** to permeate (with)

permesso, a [per'messo] PP *di* **permettere**
■ SM **1** (*autorizzazione*) permission; **chiedere il permesso di fare qc** to ask permission to do sth; **ho chiesto il permesso di uscire** I asked permission to leave the room **2** (*Amm, Mil*) leave (of absence); **andare in permesso** to go on leave **3** (*documento*) permit, licence (*Brit*), license (*Am*); (*: Mil*) pass; **permesso di lavoro** work permit; **permesso di soggiorno** residence permit

permettere [per'mettere] VT IRREG **1** (*gen, consentire*) to allow, permit; **permettere a qn di fare qc** (*autorizzare*) to allow *o* permit sb to do sth, let sb do sth; (*dare la possibilità*) to enable sb to do sth; (*dare il diritto*) to entitle sb to do sth; **crede che tutto gli sia permesso** he thinks he can do just as he likes; **i miei impegni non me lo permettono** I'm too busy to be able to do it; **non mi ha permesso di vederla** he didn't allow me to see her; **ci andremo, tempo permettendo** we'll go, weather permitting; **non permetto che mi si tratti così** I will not tolerate being treated in this way **2** **permettersi qc/di fare qc** (*concedersi*) to allow o.s. sth/to do sth; (*avere la possibilità*) to afford sth/to do sth; (*osare*) to dare (to) do sth; **non possono permettersi una casa più grande** they can't afford a bigger house; **non posso permettermi di perdere neanche un minuto** I can't afford to waste a minute; **sai cosa si è permessa di dire?** do you know what she dared to say?; **come ti permetti?** how dare you? **3** (*fraseologia*): **è permesso?** (*posso entrare?*) may I come in?; **scusi, permesso...** (*posso passare?*) excuse me, can I get by *o* past?; **se permetti avrei un'obiezione** if you don't mind I have an objection to raise; **mi sia permesso di sottolineare che...** may I take the liberty of pointing out that ...; **permettete che mi presenti** let me introduce myself, may I introduce myself?

permisi *ecc* [per'mizi] VB *vedi* **permettere**

permissivismo [permissi'vizmo] SM (*atteggiamento*) permissiveness

permissività [permissivi'ta] SF (*qualità*) permissiveness

permissivo, a [permis'sivo] AGG permissive

permuta ['pɛrmuta] SF (*Dir*) transfer; **valore di permuta** (*di macchina*) trade-in value; **accettare qc in permuta** to take sth as a trade-in

permutare [permu'tare] VT to exchange; (*Mat*) to permute

pernacchia [per'nakkja] SF (*fam*) raspberry; **fare una pernacchia** to blow a raspberry

pernice [per'nitʃe] SF partridge; **pernice bianca** ptarmigan

pernicioso, a [perni'tʃoso] AGG pernicious

perno ['pɛrno] SM (*anche fig*) pivot; **fare perno su qc** to pivot on sth

pernottamento [pernotta'mento] SM overnight stay

pernottare [pernot'tare] VI (*aus* **avere**) to spend the night, stay overnight

pero ['pero] SM (*Bot*) pear (tree)

però [pe'rɔ] CONG (*ma*) (and) yet, but (nevertheless); (*tuttavia*) nevertheless, however; **però non è giusto che...** and yet *o* but nevertheless it's not fair that ...; **però avresti potuto dirmelo** you could have told me nevertheless; **mi piace, però è troppo caro** I like it, but it's too expensive; **sono stanco, non tanto però da non poter finire** I'm tired, but not so tired as not to be able to finish

perorare [pero'rare] VT (*Dir, fig*): **perorare la causa di qn** to plead sb's case

perossido [pe'rɔssido] SM peroxide

perpendicolare [perpendiko'lare] AGG perpendicular
■ SF (*Mat*) perpendicular (line)

perpendicolarmente [perpendikolar'mente] AVV perpendicularly

perpendicolo [perpen'dikolo] SM: **a perpendicolo** perpendicularly

perpetrare [perpe'trare] VT to perpetrate, commit

perpetua [per'pɛtua] SF priest's housekeeper

perpetuamente [perpetua'mente] AVV perpetually

perpetuare [perpetu'are] VT to perpetuate
perpetuo, a [per'pɛtuo] AGG (*gen*) perpetual; (*rendita*) life *attr*
perplessamente [perplessa'mente] AVV in *o* with perplexity, with puzzlement
perplessità [perplessi'ta] SF INV perplexity
perplesso, a [per'plɛsso] AGG perplexed, puzzled; **lasciare qn perplesso** to perplex *o* puzzle sb
perquisire [perkwi'zire] VT to search; **all'aeroporto siamo stati perquisiti** we were searched at the airport
perquisizione [perkwizit'tsjone] SF search; **mandato di perquisizione** search warrant; **fare una perquisizione (di)** to carry out a search (of)
persecutore, trice [perseku'tore] SM/F persecutor
persecuzione [persekut'tsjone] SF persecution; **mania di persecuzione** (*Psic*) persecution complex
Persefone [per'sefone] SF Persephone
perseguibile [perse'gwibile] AGG (*reato*) prosecutable
perseguire [perse'gwire] VT **1** (*scopo, intento*) to pursue **2** (*Dir*) to prosecute
perseguitare [persegwi'tare] VT (*anche fig*) to persecute; **essere perseguitato dalla sfortuna** to be dogged by ill luck
perseguitato, a [persegwi'tato] SM/F victim of persecution
Perseo [per'sɛo] SM Perseus
perseverante [perseve'rante] AGG persevering
perseveranza [perseve'rantsa] SF perseverance
perseverare [perseve'rare] VI (*aus* **avere**) to persevere; **perseverare in qc/nel fare qc** to persevere in sth/in doing sth
persi *ecc* ['persi] VB *vedi* **perdere**
Persia ['pɛrsja] SF Persia
persiana [per'sjana] SF shutter; **persiana avvolgibile** roller shutter
persiano, a [per'sjano] AGG, SM/F Persian
■ SM **1** (*lingua*) Persian **2** (*Zool: gatto*) Persian (cat) **3** (*pelliccia*) Persian lamb
persico, a, ci, che ['pɛrsiko] AGG: **il golfo Persico** the Persian Gulf; **pesce persico** perch
persino [per'sino] AVV = **perfino**
persistente [persis'tɛnte] AGG persistent
persistentemente [persistente'mente] AVV persistently
persistenza [persis'tɛntsa] SF persistence
persistere [per'sistere] VI IRREG (*aus* **avere**) to persist; **persistere in qc/a fare qc** to persist in sth/in doing sth; **persiste nella sua opinione** he is sticking to his opinion
persistito, a [persis'tito] PP *di* **persistere**
perso, a ['pɛrso] PP *di* **perdere**
■ AGG (*smarrito: anche fig*) lost; (*sprecato*) wasted; **questo è tempo perso** this is a waste of time; **fare qc a tempo perso** to do sth in one's spare time; **dipinge a tempo perso** she paints in her spare time; **perso per perso** I've (*o* we've *ecc*) got nothing left *o* more to lose; **andare perso** to get lost; **il libro è andato perso** the book got lost; **dare per perso** to give up for lost
persona [per'sona] SF **1** (*essere umano*) person; **una persona intelligente** an intelligent person; **persone** SFPL people *pl*; **c'erano molte persone** there were a lot of people; **tre persone** three people *o* persons (*Am*); **a/per persona** (*a testa*) per head *o* person, a head; **3 euro a persona** three euros a head; **per interposta persona** through a third party *o* an intermediary; **prima persona plurale** (*Gramm*) first person plural; **seconda persona singolare** (*Gramm*) second person singular; **persona giuridica** (*Dir*) legal person; **persona di servizio** domestic servant **2** (*corpo*): **aver cura della propria persona** to look after o.s.; **in persona** *or* **di persona** in person; **ci andrò di persona** I'll go there personally *o* in person; **è l'onestà in persona** he is honesty personified **3** (*Gramm*) person; **alla terza persona singolare** in the third person singular; **vivere qc in prima persona** (*fig*) to experience sth personally **4** (*qualcuno*): **una persona** somebody, someone; **c'era una persona che ti cercava** somebody was looking for you
personaggio, gi [perso'naddʒo] SM **1** (*celebrità*) personage; (*persona ragguardevole*) personality; (*scherz: individuo*) character, individual; **un importante personaggio politico** an important political figure **2** (*di romanzo*) character; (*di quadro*) figure; **i personaggi del romanzo** the characters in the novel
personale [perso'nale] AGG personal
■ SF (*mostra*) one-man (*o* one-woman) exhibition
■ SM **1** (*complesso di dipendenti*) personnel, staff; **il personale dell'azienda** the staff of the company; **ufficio personale** personnel office; **personale di terra** (*Aer*) ground personnel **2** (*corpo, figura*) build; **quella ragazza ha un bel personale** that girl's got a lovely figure
personalità [personali'ta] SF INV (*gen*) personality; **ha una forte personalità** he's got a strong personality; **personalità giuridica** (*Dir*) legal status; **personalità multipla** (*Psic*) multiple personality
personalizzare [personalid'dzare] VT (*arredamento, stile*) to personalize; (*auto, accessorio*) to customize
personalizzato, a [personalid'dzato] AGG (*vedi vb*) personalized; customized
personalmente [personal'mente] AVV personally
personificare [personifi'kare] VT (*rappresentare*) to personify; (*simboleggiare*) to embody
personificazione [personifikat'tsjone] SF (*vedi vb*) personification; embodiment; **essere la personificazione della gentilezza** to be kindness itself
perspicace [perspi'katʃe] AGG discerning, shrewd
perspicacemente [perspikatʃe'mente] AVV perspicaciously, shrewdly
perspicacia [perspi'katʃa] SF perspicacity, shrewdness
persuadere [persua'dere] VB IRREG
■ VT to persuade, convince; **persuadere qn di qc/a fare qc** to persuade *o* convince sb of sth/to do sth; **lasciarsi persuadere** to let o.s. be convinced; **ne sono persuaso** I'm quite sure *o* convinced (of it);
▶ **persuadersi** VR to convince o.s.
persuasione [persua'zjone] SF (*gen*) persuasion; (*credenza*) conviction, belief
persuasivamente [persuaziva'mente] AVV persuasively
persuasivo, a [persua'zivo] AGG persuasive, convincing
persuaso, a [persu'azo] PP *di* **persuadere**
persuasore [persua'zore] SM: **persuasori occulti** hidden persuaders
pertanto [per'tanto] CONG (*quindi*) therefore, so
pertica, che ['pɛrtika] SF (*bastone*) pole, rod; (*Sport*) pole; (*fig: persona alta e magra*) beanpole
pertinace [perti'natʃe] AGG pertinacious
pertinacemente [pertinatʃe'mente] AVV pertinaciously

Pp

pertinacia [perti'natʃa] SF pertinacity
pertinente [perti'nεnte] AGG: **pertinente (a)** pertinent (to), relevant (to); **un'osservazione pertinente** a pertinent remark
pertinenza [perti'nεntsa] SF **1** (*attinenza*) pertinence, relevance **2** (*competenza*): **essere di pertinenza di qn** to be sb's business; **è di pertinenza del tribunale di Napoli** it comes under the jurisdiction of the Naples courts
pertosse [per'tosse] SF (*Med*) whooping cough
pertugio, gi [per'tudʒo] SM opening, hole
perturbare [pertur'bare] VT (*persona*) to upset, disturb, perturb
▶ **perturbarsi** VIP to become *o* get upset
perturbazione [perturbat'tsjone] SF (*Meteor, Astron*) disturbance
Perù [pe'ru] SM Peru
perugino, a [peru'dʒino] AGG of *o* from Perugia
■ SM/F inhabitant *o* native of Perugia
peruviano, a [peru'vjano] AGG, SM/F Peruvian
pervadere [per'vadere] VT IRREG to pervade, permeate
pervaso, a [per'vazo] PP *di* **pervadere**
pervenire [perve'nire] VI IRREG (*aus* **essere**) **1** **pervenire a** to reach, arrive at, come to; **far pervenire qc a qn** to have sth sent to sb; **ci sono pervenute migliaia di lettere** we have received thousands of letters **2** (*venire in possesso*): **gli pervenne una fortuna** he inherited a fortune
pervenuto, a [perve'nuto] PP *di* **pervenire**
perversamente [perversa'mente] AVV in a perverted fashion
perversione [perver'sjone] SF perversion
perversità [perversi'ta] SF INV perversity
perverso, a [per'vεrso] AGG perverted
pervertire [perver'tire] VT to pervert
pervertito, a [perver'tito] AGG perverted
■ SM/F pervert
pervicace [pervi'katʃe] AGG stubborn, obstinate
pervicacia [pervi'katʃa] SF stubbornness, obstinacy
pervinca, che [per'vinka] SF (*Bot*) periwinkle
■ SM INV (*colore*) periwinkle (blue)
p.es. ABBR (= **per esempio**) e.g.
pesa ['pesa] SF (*azione*) weighing *no pl*; (*luogo*) weighhouse; (*apparecchiatura: per merci*) weighing machine; (*: per autoveicoli*) weighbridge; (*: per animali*) cattle-weighing platform
pesalettere [pesa'lεttere] SM INV letter scales *pl*
pesante [pe'sante] AGG (*gen*) heavy; (*cibo*) heavy, rich; (*sonno*) heavy, deep; (*droga*) hard; (*fig: stile*) ponderous; (*: battuta*) crass; (*noioso: conferenza*) dull, boring; (*: persona*) tedious, boring; **quella valigia è troppo pesante** that suitcase is too heavy; **questo libro è pesante** (*fig*) this book is heavy going; **il film era un po' pesante** I found the film rather heavy going; **ho gli occhi pesanti** I can't keep my eyes open; **è andata giù pesante** (*ha esagerato*) she was rather heavy-handed; **avere l'alito pesante** to have bad breath; **atletica pesante** weightlifting and wrestling; **droghe pesanti** hard drugs; **gioco pesante** (*Sport*) physical game; **terreno pesante** (*Sport: per pioggia*) waterlogged pitch
pesantemente [pesante'mente] AVV heavily; **ripercuotersi pesantemente su** (*situazione*) to have grave consequences for; **ha scherzato pesantemente** he went too far with his jokes
pesantezza [pesan'tettsa] SF (*anche fig*) heaviness; **avere pesantezza di stomaco** to feel bloated

pesapersone [pesaper'sone] AGG INV, SF INV: **(bilancia) pesapersone** (weighing) scales *pl*; (*automatica*) weighing machine
pesare [pe'sare] VT to weigh; (*fig: valutare*) to weigh (up); **pesare i pro e i contro** to weigh up the pros and cons; **pesare le parole** to weigh one's words; **pesarsi** to weigh o.s.
■ VI (*aus* **avere**) **1** (*avere un peso*) to weigh; (*essere pesante*) to be heavy; (*fig*) to carry weight; **quanto pesi?** how much do you weigh?; **come pesa!** it weighs a ton!; **l'ho già pesato** I've already weighed it; **pesare sulla coscienza/sullo stomaco** to lie heavy on one's conscience/on one's stomach; **tutta la responsabilità pesa su di lui** all the responsibility rests on his shoulders; **la responsabilità gli pesa** the responsibility weighs heavy on him; **ha sempre pesato sui genitori** he has always been dependent on his parents; **i figli pesano notevolmente sul bilancio familiare** children weigh heavily on the family budget; **è molto gentile ma lo fa pesare** he is very kind but he makes sure it doesn't go unnoticed; **le ha sempre fatto pesare il fatto che viene da una famiglia povera** he has always made her aware of her humble origins **2** (*dispiacere*): **mi pesa partire** I don't want to leave; **mi pesa dirti di no** I regret having to say no to you; **mi pesa sgridarlo** I find it hard to scold him; **è una situazione che mi pesa** it's a difficult situation for me **3** (*contare*) to carry weight, count; **il suo parere pesa molto** his opinion counts for a lot *o* carries a lot of weight
pesarese [peza'rese] AGG of *o* from Pesaro
■ SM/F inhabitant *o* native of Pesaro
pesatura [pesa'tura] SF weighing
pesca[1], sche ['peska] SF (*frutto*) peach
pesca[2] ['peska] SF **1** (*Sport*) fishing; **andare a pesca** to go fishing; **pesca con la lenza** angling; **pesca subacquea** underwater fishing **2** (*pesce pescato*) catch; **avete fatto una buona pesca?** did you get a good catch? **3** (*lotteria*): **pesca di beneficenza** lucky dip
pescaggio, gi [pes'kaddʒo] SM (*Naut*) draught (*Brit*), draft (*Am*)
pescare [pes'kare] VT (*essere pescatore di*) to fish for; (*prendere*) to catch; (*: molluschi*) to gather; (*recuperare qc nell'acqua*) to fish out; (*fig: trovare*) to get hold of, find; **ti insegnerò a pescare** I'll teach you how to fish; **ho pescato un pesce enorme** I caught an enormous fish; **pescare nel torbido** (*fig*) to fish in troubled waters; **ma dove le vai a pescare queste idee?** where on earth do you get hold of such ideas?; **dove hai pescato questo cappello?** where on earth did you get that hat?; **l'hanno pescato con le mani nel sacco** they caught him red-handed
■ VI (*aus* **avere**) (*Naut*) to draw
pescarese [pesca'rese] AGG of *o* from Pescara
■ SM/F inhabitant *o* native of Pescara
pescatore [peska'tore] SM fisherman; (*con lenza*) angler; **un paesino di pescatori** a fishing village
pesce ['peʃʃe] SM **1** fish *gen inv*; **c'erano molti pesci** there were a lot of fish *o* fishes; **ho pescato due pesci** I caught two fish; **ti piace il pesce?** do you like fish? **2** (*Astrol*): **Pesci** SMPL Pisces; **essere dei Pesci** to be Pisces **3** (*Tip*) omission **4** (*fraseologia*): **sano come un pesce** as fit as a fiddle; **buttarsi a pesce su un'offerta** to jump at an offer; **sentirsi un pesce fuor d'acqua** to feel like a fish out of water; **prendere qn a pesci in faccia** to treat sb like dirt; **non saper che pesci prendere** not to know which way to turn;

hanno preso solo i pesci piccoli they only caught the small fry; **chi dorme non piglia pesci** (*Proverbio*) the early bird catches the worm
■ **pesce d'aprile** April Fool; **pesce azzurro** mackerel, sardines and anchovies; **pesce gatto** catfish; **pesce martello** hammerhead; **pesce ragno** weever; **pesce rosso** goldfish; **pesce spada** swordfish

PESCE D'APRILE

Il pesce d'aprile is a sort of April Fool's joke, played on 1 April. Originally it took its name from a paper fish which was secretly attached to a person's back but nowadays all sorts of practical jokes are popular.

pescecane [peʃʃe'kane] SM (*pl* **pescecani** *o* **pescicani**) (*Zool*) shark; (*fig: profittatore*) shark, profiteer
peschereccio, a, ci, ce [peske'rettʃo] SM fishing boat
pescheria [peske'ria] SF fishmonger's (shop) (*Brit*), fish shop
pescherò *ecc* [peske'rɔ] VB *vedi* **pescare**
peschiera [pes'kjɛra] SF fish farm, fishery
pesciera [peʃ'ʃɛra] SF fish kettle
pescivendolo, a [peʃʃi'vendolo] SM/F fishmonger (*Brit*), fish merchant (*Am*); (*negozio*) fishmonger's (shop) (*Brit*), fish shop; Am **andare dal pescivendolo** to go to the fishmonger's
pesco, schi ['pɛsko] SM (*Bot*) peach (tree)
pescoso, a [pes'koso] AGG teeming with fish
peseta [pe'zɛta] SF peseta
pesista, i, e [pe'sista] SM/F (*Sport*) weightlifter
peso ['peso] SM **1** (*gen*) weight; **comprare a peso** to buy by weight; **rubare sul peso** to give short weight; **eccesso di peso** excess weight; **metter su peso** to put on weight; **piegarsi sotto il peso di** (*sogg: trave*) to bend under the weight of; **lo portarono via di peso** they carried him away bodily; **avere due pesi e due misure** (*fig*) to have double standards; **peso lordo** gross weight; **peso morto** dead load *o* weight; **peso netto** net weight; **peso specifico** (*Fis*) specific gravity **2** (*fig: onere*) weight; **il peso degli anni** the weight of years; **avere un peso sullo stomaco** to have something lying heavy on one's stomach; **mi sono liberato di un peso** (*preoccupazione*) that's a load off my mind; **togliersi un peso dalla coscienza** to take a load off one's conscience; **essere di peso a qn** to be a burden to sb; **non voglio essere di peso a nessuno** I don't want to be a burden to anybody; **piegarsi sotto il peso di** (*dispiaceri, problemi*) to be weighed down by **3** (*fig: importanza*) weight, importance; **una questione di un certo peso** a matter of some weight *o* importance; **dar peso a qc** to attach importance to sth; **non ho dato molto peso alle sue parole** I didn't attach much importance to his words **4** (*Sport*) shot; **lancio del peso** putting the shot, the shot put; **sollevamento pesi** weightlifting; **fare pesi** to do weight training; **peso gallo** bantamweight; **peso massimo** heavyweight; **peso medio** middleweight; **peso mosca** flyweight; **peso piuma** featherweight
pessimismo [pessi'mizmo] SM pessimism
pessimista, i, e [pessi'mista] AGG pessimistic
■ SM/F pessimist
pessimisticamente [pessimistika'mente] AVV pessimistically; **vedere le cose pessimisticamente** to look at things pessimistically
pessimistico, a, ci, che [pessi'mistiko] AGG pessimistic
pessimo, a ['pɛssimo] AGG (*superl di* **cattivo**) **1** (*gen*) awful, dreadful, very bad; **abbiamo fatto un pessimo viaggio** we had a dreadful *o* an awful *o* an appalling journey; **c'è un pessimo odore in questa stanza** there's an awful *o* a dreadful smell in this room; **ha fatto un tempo pessimo** the weather has been dreadful; **è un pessimo insegnante** he is a very bad teacher; **di pessima qualità** of very poor quality, very shoddy; **essere di pessimo umore** to be in a foul *o* a terrible mood; **hai un pessimo aspetto** *o* **una pessima cera** you look awful *o* dreadful; **quello scherzo è di pessimo gusto** that joke is in very bad taste **2** (*molto riprovevole*) very wicked, nasty
pestaggio, gi [pes'taddʒo] SM (*rissa*) brawl, punch-up; **è stato vittima di un pestaggio** he was set upon by a gang
pestare [pes'tare] VT **1** (*calpestare*) to tread on, trample on; **pestare un piede a qn** to tread on sb's foot; **pestare i piedi** to stamp one's feet; **pestare i piedi a qn** (*dare fastidio*) to tread on sb's toes; **pestare qn** (*picchiarlo*) to beat sb up **2** (*frantumare: uva, aglio*) to crush; (: *pepe*) to grind
pestata [pes'tata] SF **1 dare una pestata sul piede a qn** to tread on sb's foot **2** (*botte*) beating
peste ['pɛste] SF (*Med*) plague; (*fig: persona*) pest, nuisance; **sei una peste!** you're a pest!; **dire peste e corna di qn** to tear sb to bits
pestello [pes'tɛllo] SM pestle
pesticida, i [pesti'tʃida] SM pesticide
pestifero, a [pes'tifero] AGG (*anche fig*) pestilential, pestiferous; (*odore*) noxious
pestilenza [pesti'lɛntsa] SF (*peste*) plague, pestilence; (*fetore*) stench
pestilenziale [pestilen'tsjale] AGG (*odore*) noxious
pesto, a ['pesto] AGG: **occhio pesto** black eye; **avere gli occhi pesti** (*per la stanchezza*) to have bags under one's eyes; **era buio pesto** it was pitch-black
■ SM (*Culin*) pesto; *sauce made with basil, garlic, cheese and oil*
PET [pet] SIGLA M (= **polietilentereftalato**) PET (= *polyethylene terephthalate*)
petalo ['pɛtalo] SM petal
petardo [pe'tardo] SM firecracker, banger (*Brit*); (*Ferr*) detonator, torpedo (*Am*)
petizione [petit'tsjone] SF (*Dir*) petition; **fare una petizione a** to petition
peto ['peto] SM: **fare un peto** to break wind
Petrarca [pe'trarka] SM Petrarch
petrodollaro [petro'dɔllaro] SM petrodollar
petrografia [petrogra'fia] SF petrography
petrolchimica [petrol'kimika] SF petrochemical industry
petrolchimico, a, ci, che [petrol'kimiko] AGG petrochemical; **prodotto petrolchimico** petrochemical (product)
petroldollaro [petrol'dɔllaro] SM = **petrodollaro**
petroliera [petro'ljɛra] SF (*nave*) (oil) tanker (*ship*)
petroliere [petro'ljɛre] SM **1** (*industriale*) oilman **2** (*tecnico*) worker in the oil industry
petroliero, a [petro'ljɛro] AGG oil *attr*
petrolifero, a [petro'lifero] AGG (*industria, pozzo*) oil *attr*; **l'industria petrolifera** the oil industry
petrolio [pe'trɔljo] SM oil, petroleum; (*per lampada, fornello*) paraffin (*Brit*), kerosene (*Am*); **lume a petrolio** oil *o* paraffin *o* kerosene lamp; **petrolio grezzo** crude oil

LO SAPEVI...?
petrolio non si traduce mai con la parola inglese *petrol*

pettegolare [pettego'lare] VI (*aus* **avere**) to gossip
pettegolezzo [pettego'leddzo] SM gossip *no pl*, piece of gossip; **non mi piacciono i pettegolezzi** I don't like gossip; **sono solo pettegolezzi** it's just gossip; **vuoi sentire un pettegolezzo?** do you want to hear a bit of gossip?; **fare pettegolezzi** to gossip
pettegolo, a [pet'tegolo] AGG gossipy; **è pettegola di carattere** she is given to gossip
■ SM/F gossip; **Lucia è una pettegola** Lucia is a bit of a gossip
pettinare [petti'nare] VT (*capelli*) to comb; (*tessuto*) to comb, tease; **le ho pettinato con cura i capelli** I combed her hair carefully
▸ **pettinarsi** VR to comb one's hair, do one's hair; **ti sei pettinata?** have you combed your hair?
pettinata [petti'nata] SF comb, combing; **darsi una pettinata** to give one's hair a comb
pettinato, a [petti'nato] AGG (*capelli*) combed; (*persona*) with one's hair combed; (*tessuto*) carded, combed
■ SM worsted
pettinatura [pettina'tura] SF **1** (*acconciatura*) hairstyle, hairdo **2** (*di tessuto*) carding, combing
pettine ['pɛttine] SM **1** comb **2** (*Zool*) scallop
pettirosso [petti'rosso] SM robin
petto ['pɛtto] SM **1** (*Anat*) chest; (*: seno*) breast, bust; **ho un dolore al petto** I've got a pain in my chest; **battersi** *o* **picchiarsi il petto** to beat one's breast; **prendere qn/qc di petto** to face up to sb/sth; **giacca a doppio petto** double-breasted jacket **2** (*Culin: di pollo*) breast; **punta di petto** (*carne bovina*) brisket **3** (*Mus*): **voce di petto** chest voice
pettorale [petto'rale] AGG, SM pectoral
pettorina [petto'rina] SF (*di grembiule*) bib
pettoruto, a [petto'ruto] AGG (*uomo*) broad-chested; (*donna*) full-breasted
petulante [petu'lante] AGG insolent
petulanza [petu'lantsa] SF insolence
petunia [pe'tunja] SF petunia
PEX [peks] SIGLA F (*tariffa aerea*) PEX (= *Purchase Excursion*)
pezza ['pɛttsa] SF **1** (*rotolo di tessuto*) bolt of cloth **2** (*toppa*) patch; (*cencio*) rag, cloth; **ha una pezza sui pantaloni** he has a patch on his trousers; **bambola di pezza** rag doll; **mettere una pezza su qc** (*vestito, camera d'aria*) to patch sth; **trattare qn come una pezza da piedi** to treat sb like a doormat **3** (*Amm*): **pezza d'appoggio** *o* **giustificativa** voucher
pezzato, a [pet'tsato] AGG piebald
■ SM (*anche:* **cavallo pezzato**) piebald (horse)
pezzatura [pettsa'tura] SF (*di animale*) piebald marking
pezzente [pet'tsɛnte] SM/F (*accattone*) beggar, wretch; (*fig: tirchio*) miser
pezzo ['pɛttso] SM **1** (*gen*) piece; (*brandello, frammento*) piece, bit; **un pezzo di pane** a piece of bread; **ne vuoi ancora un pezzo?** (*di torta, pane*) would you like a bit more *o* another piece?; **ci ha accompagnato per un bel pezzo di strada** he came quite a long way with us; **andare in pezzi** to shatter; **fare a pezzi qc** to pull sth to pieces; **andare a pezzi** to break into pieces; **essere a pezzi** (*oggetto*) to be in pieces *o* bits; (*fig: persona*) to be shattered; **ho lavorato tutto il giorno e sono a pezzi** I've been working all day and I'm shattered; **ha i nervi a pezzi** his nerves are shattered **2** (*oggetto, negli scacchi*) piece; (*Mil*) gun; **da vendersi al pezzo** to be sold separately *o* individually; **2 euro al pezzo** 2 euros each *o* apiece; **un due pezzi** (*costume*) a bikini; **un servizio da 24 pezzi** (*piatti*) a 24-piece dinner service **3** (*di macchina, arnese*) part; **ha cambiato un pezzo** he's replaced a part; **smontare qc pezzo per pezzo** to dismantle sth piece by piece *o* bit by bit; **pezzo di ricambio** spare part **4** (*brano: Mus*) piece; (*: scritto*) piece, passage; (*: Stampa*) article; **pezzo di cronaca** (*Stampa*) report; **pezzo forte** pièce de résistance
5 (*tempo*): **da un pezzo** for a while; **è qui da un pezzo** he has been here for a while; **resterà per un bel pezzo** he'll stay for quite a long time; **è un pezzo che non lo vedo** I haven't seen him for a while; **aspettare un pezzo** to wait quite a while *o* some time
6 (*fraseologia*): **un pezzo grosso** a big shot, a bigwig; **un (bel) pezzo d'uomo** a fine figure of a man; **essere tutto d'un pezzo** to be a man of integrity; **che pezzo di ragazza!** she's a bit of all right!; **pezzo di cretino** stupid idiot
PG SIGLA = *Perugia*
■ [pi'dʒi] SIGLA M = **procuratore generale**
pH [pi'akka] SIGLA M (*Chim*) pH
PI SIGLA = *Pisa*
■ ABBR = *Pubblica Istruzione*; *vedi* **istruzione**
piaccio *ecc* ['pjattʃo] VB *vedi* **piacere**
piacente [pja'tʃɛnte] AGG attractive
piacentino, a [pjatʃen'tino] AGG of *o* from Piacenza
■ SM/F inhabitant *o* native of Piacenza
piacere[1] [pja'tʃere] SM **1** (*gen*) pleasure; **i piaceri della vita** the pleasures of life; **fare qc per il piacere di farlo** to do sth for the sake of doing it; **ho il piacere di annunciare che...** it gives me great pleasure to tell you that ...; **mi fa piacere per lui** I'm pleased for him; **è un piacere averti qui** it's a pleasure to have you here; **che piacere vederti!** how nice to see you!; **piacere!** *or* **è un piacere conoscerla** pleased to meet you; **mi farebbe piacere rivederlo** I would like to see him again; **se ti fa piacere** if you like; **con piacere** with pleasure, certainly; **fare qc con piacere** to be happy *o* glad to do sth; **ho saputo con piacere che ti sposi** I was delighted to hear you're getting married; **un viaggio di piacere** a pleasure trip; **è un viaggio d'affari o di piacere?** is this trip for business or for pleasure?; **potevi averne a piacere** (*volontà*) you could take as many as you wanted; **tanto piacere!** (*iro*) so what? **2** (*favore*) favour (*Brit*), favor (*Am*); **fare un piacere a qn** to do sb a favo(u)r; **mi faresti un piacere?** would you do me a favo(u)r?; **mi fai il piacere di smetterla?** would you kindly stop that?; **per piacere** please; **per piacere, potresti...?** could you please ...?; **su, mangia la minestra, fammi il piacere** come on, eat your soup like a good boy (*o* girl); **ma fammi il piacere!** for heaven's sake!
piacere[2] [pja'tʃere] VI IRREG (*aus* **essere**) (*persona*): **piacere a qn** to be liked by sb; **mi piace** (*lavoro, film*) I like *o* enjoy it; (*progetto*) it suits me; (*sport, attività*) I enjoy it; **quei ragazzi non mi piacciono** I don't like those boys; **mi piace molto questo quadro** I like this picture very much; **non credo gli piaccia** I don't think he likes it; **mi piace di più così** I like it better this way; **un gusto che piace** a pleasant *o* agreeable flavour; **una ragazza che piace** (*piacevole*) a likeable girl; (*attraente*) an attractive girl; **il suo discorso è piaciuto molto** his speech was well received; **che ti piaccia o no** *or* **ti piaccia o non ti piaccia** whether you like it or not; **che cosa ti piacerebbe fare?** what would you like to

do?, what do you fancy doing?; **gli piacerebbe andare al cinema** he would like to go to the cinema; **mi sarebbe piaciuto andarci** I would have liked to go; **fa' come ti pare e piace** do as you please *o* like; **a Dio piacendo** God willing

piacevole [pja'tʃevole] AGG pleasant, nice, agreeable

piacevolezza [pjatʃevo'lettsa] SF *(di compagnia, persona)* pleasantness

piacevolmente [pjatʃevol'mente] AVV pleasantly

piacimento [pjatʃi'mento] SM: **a piacimento** *(a volontà)* as much as one likes, at will; **lo farà a suo piacimento** he'll do it when it suits him

piaciucchiare [pjatʃuk'kjare] VI *(aus* **essere***)* **lui mi piaciucchia** I quite like him

piaciuto, a [pja'tʃuto] PP *di* **piacere²**

piacqui *ecc* ['pjakkwi] VB *vedi* **piacere²**

piaga, ghe ['pjaga] SF **1** *(Med)* sore; *(ferita: anche fig)* wound; *(fig: flagello)* scourge, curse; **mettere un dito sulla piaga** to touch a sore point; **rigirare il coltello nella piaga** to twist the knife (in the wound); **le piaghe d'Egitto** the plagues of Egypt; **piaghe da decubito** bedsores **2** *(fig pegg: persona)* nuisance, pain in the neck, pest

piagnisteo [pjaɲɲis'tɛo] SM whining, whimpering

piagnucolare [pjaɲɲuko'lare] VI *(aus* **avere***)* to whine, whimper

piagnucolio, lii [pjaɲɲuko'lio] SM whimpering, whining

piagnucolone, a [pjaɲɲuko'lone] SM/F whiner, moaner

piagnucoloso, a [pjaɲɲuko'loso] AGG whiny, whimpering, moaning

pialla ['pjalla] SF *(arnese)* plane

piallare [pjal'lare] VT to plane

piallatore [pjalla'tore] SM *(operaio)* planer

piallatrice [pjalla'tritʃe] SF planing machine

piallatura [pjalla'tura] SF *(lavorazione)* planing

piamente [pia'mente] AVV *(con devozione)* piously, devoutly; *(con misericordia)* charitably

piana ['pjana] SF stretch of level ground; *(più estesa)* plain

pianeggiante [pjaned'dʒante] AGG flat, level

pianella [pja'nɛlla] SF slipper

pianerottolo [pjane'rɔttolo] SM landing

pianeta¹, i [pja'neta] SM *(Astron)* planet

pianeta² [pja'neta] SF *(Rel)* chasuble

piangente [pjan'dʒɛnte] AGG *(espressione, viso)* tearful; *(bambino)* weeping, crying; **salice piangente** weeping willow

piangere ['pjandʒere] VB IRREG

■ VI *(aus* **avere***)* *(gen)* to cry, weep; *(occhi)* to water; **piangere di gioia** to weep for joy; **piangere a calde lacrime** to cry one's heart out; **mi piange il cuore** *(iro)* my heart bleeds; **mi piange il cuore a buttare via tanta roba** I hate having to throw away so much stuff; **è inutile piangere sul latte versato** it's no use crying over spilt milk

■ VT **1** to cry, weep **2** *(lamentare)* to bewail, lament; **piangere la morte di qn** to mourn sb's death; **sta sempre piangendo miseria** he's always claiming he has no money

pianificare [pjanifi'kare] VT to plan

pianificatore, trice [pjanifika'tore] SM/F *(Econ)* planner

pianificazione [pjanifikat'tsjone] SF *(Econ)* planning; **pianificazione aziendale** corporate planning; **pianificazione familiare** family planning

pianista, i, e [pja'nista] SM/F pianist; *(Pol) deputy who votes on behalf of absent colleagues by pressing the voting buttons*

pianistico, a, ci, che [pja'nistiko] AGG *(concerto)* piano *attr*; *(musica)* for the piano

piano¹, a ['pjano] AGG

1 *(piatto)* flat, level; *(senza asperità)* smooth; *(Mat)* plane *attr*; **geometria piana** plane geometry; **corsa piana** *(Sport)* flat race

2 *(facile)* straightforward, simple; *(chiaro)* clear, plain

■ AVV *(lentamente)* slowly; *(con cautela)* carefully, slowly; *(a basso volume o voce)* softly, quietly; **la macchina andava piano** the car was travelling slowly; **vai piano!** *(in macchina)* drive slowly!; **vacci piano!** *(fig: non esagerare: nel bere)* take it easy with that!; *(: nelle minacce)* calm down!; *(: nel lodarsi)* come off it!; **attento, fai piano!** *(fa' meno rumore)* don't make so much noise!; *(sta' attento)* watch out!, be careful!; **parla più piano** *(lentamente)* speak more slowly; *(a bassa voce)* lower your voice, keep your voice down; **pian piano** *(lentamente)* very slowly; *(poco a poco)* little by little; **pian pianino** *o* **pian piano siamo arrivati** slowly but surely we got there; **pian pianino** *o* **pian piano ha acquistato una certa esperienza** he gradually acquired experience

■ SM

1 *(Geom)* plane; *(superficie)* top, surface; *(fig: livello)* level, plane; *(Geog: pianura)* plain; **mettere tutto sullo stesso piano** to lump everything together, give equal importance to everything; **quei due alunni sono sullo stesso piano** those two pupils are at the same level *o* are on a par; **piano inclinato** inclined plane; **piano di lavoro** *(in cucina)* worktop; **piano stradale** road surface

2 *(di edificio)* floor, storey *(Brit)*, story *(Am)*; *(di autobus)* deck; **una casa di 3 piani** a 3-storey *(Brit) o* 3-storied *(Am)* house; **abito al terzo piano** I live on the third floor; **al piano di sopra/di sotto** on the floor above/below; **all'ultimo piano** on the top floor; **al piano terra** on the ground floor *(Brit) o* first floor *(Am)*; **un autobus a due piani** a double-decker (bus)

3 *(Fot, Cine, Arte)*: **primo piano** foreground; **secondo piano** background; **in primo/secondo piano** in the foreground/background; **una figura in primo piano** a figure in the foreground; **fare un primo piano** to take a close-up; **in primissimo piano** right in the foreground; **di primo piano** *(fig)* prominent, high-ranking; **uno scrittore di primo piano** a major author; **mettere qc in secondo piano** to consider sth of secondary importance; **un fattore di secondo piano** a secondary *o* minor factor; **passare in secondo piano** *(questione)* to become less important

piano² ['pjano] SM *(progetto: anche Mil)* plan; *(: industriale)* design; *(programma)* work plan; **un piano di pace** a peace plan; **facciamo un piano** let's draw up a plan; **non era nei nostri piani** we hadn't intended to do it, we hadn't planned on doing so; **tutto va secondo i piani** everything's going according to plan

■ **piano di battaglia** *(Mil)* battle plan; **piano di guerra** *(Mil)* plan of campaign; **piano regolatore** *(Urbanistica)* town-planning scheme; **piano di studi** *(Univ)* study programme *(Brit) o* program *(Am)*, study plan; **piano di volo** *(Aer)* flight plan

piano³ ['pjano] SM *(Mus)* piano

piano-bar [pjano'bar] SM INV piano-bar

pianoforte [pjano'fɔrte] SM piano, pianoforte

pianola [pja'nɔla] SF player piano, Pianola®

pianoterra [pjano'tɛrra] SM INV ground floor *(Brit)*,

first floor (*Am*); **al pianoterra** on the ground *o* first floor

piansi *ecc* ['pjansi] VB *vedi* **piangere**

pianta ['pjanta] SF **1** (*Bot*) plant; **pianta d'appartamento** house plant; **pianta grassa** succulent (plant) **2** (*Anat*: *anche*: **pianta del piede**) sole (of the foot) **3** (*disegno*) plan; (*cartina topografica*) map, plan; **una pianta della città** a map of the city; **pianta stradale** street map *o* plan **4** (*fraseologia*): **l'ha inventato di sana pianta** he made the whole thing up; **in pianta stabile** on the permanent staff; **essere assunto in pianta stabile** to be taken on as a permanent employee; **ormai è qui da noi in pianta stabile** (*fig*) he seems to have taken up residence at our place

piantagione [pjanta'dʒone] SF plantation

piantagrane [pjanta'grane] SM/F INV troublemaker

piantare [pjan'tare] VT **1** (*pianta*) to plant, put in; **ho piantato un albero in giardino** I've planted a tree in the garden **2** **piantare (in)** (*chiodo*) to hammer in(to), knock in(to); (*paletto*) to drive in(to); (*ago*) to stick in(to); **piantare una tenda** to put up a tent, pitch a tent; **piantare grane** to cause trouble **3** (*fig*: *lasciare*: *moglie, figli*) to leave, abandon, desert; **ha piantato il suo ragazzo** she's dumped her boyfriend; **piantare qn in asso** to leave sb in the lurch; **mi ha piantata in asso** he left me in the lurch; **piantala!** stop it!, cut it out!

▶ **piantarsi** VR (*persona*): **mi si piantò davanti** *or* **si piantò davanti a me** he planted himself in front of me

▶ **piantarsi** VIP (*proiettile*): **piantarsi in** to enter; **mi si è piantata una scheggia nel dito** I've got a splinter in my finger

piantato, a [pjan'tato] AGG: **ben piantato** (*persona*) well-built

piantatore [pjanta'tore] SM (*persona*) planter

pianterreno [pjanter'reno] SM ground floor (*Brit*), first floor (*Am*)

pianto, a ['pjanto] PP *di* **piangere**

■ SM crying, weeping, tears *pl*; **scoppiò in un pianto dirotto** she burst into tears; **è uno che ha il pianto facile** he cries easily

piantonare [pjanto'nare] VT to guard, watch over

piantone [pjan'tone] SM **1** (*soldato*) orderly; (*vigilante*) sentry, guard **2** (*Aut*) steering column

pianura [pja'nura] SF (*Geog*) plain

piastra ['pjastra] SF **1** (*di metallo*) sheet, plate; (*di cemento, pietra*) slab; (*Elettr, Fot, di rivestimento*) plate; (*di cucina*) hotplate; **piastra di registrazione** tape deck **2** (*moneta*) piastre

piastrella [pjas'trɛlla] SF tile

piastrellare [pjastrel'lare] VT to tile

piastrina [pjas'trina] SF **1** (*Anat*) platelet **2** **piastrina di riconoscimento** (*Mil*) name tag, identity disc (*Brit*) *o* tag (*Am*)

piattaforma [pjatta'forma] SF (*pl* **piattaforme**) (*gen, fig, Pol*) platform; (*per tuffi*) board; **piattaforma continentale** (*Geog*) continental shelf; **piattaforma girevole** (*Tecn*) turntable; **piattaforma di lancio** (*Mil*) launch(ing) pad; **piattaforma rivendicativa** *document setting out claims of the unions in an industry*

piattamente [pjatta'mente] AVV (*in modo scialbo*) dully

piattello [pjat'tɛllo] SM **1** (*bersaglio*) clay pigeon; **tiro al piattello** clay-pigeon shooting, skeet shooting, trapshooting **2** (*Sci*: *di skilift*) disc

piattina [pjat'tina] SF (*Elettr*) twin lead

piattino [pjat'tino] SM (*di tazza*) saucer

piatto, a ['pjatto] AGG (*gen*) flat; (*fig*: *scialbo*) flat, dreary, dull; **questa zona è più piatta** this area is flatter; **piatto come una tavola** as flat as a pancake

■ SM **1** (*recipiente*) dish, plate; (*quantità*) plate(ful); **metti più piselli nel mio piatto** put more peas on my plate; **lavo io i piatti** I'll wash the dishes; **un piatto di minestra** a plate *o* bowl of soup; **piatto fondo** soup plate *o* dish; **piatto da frutta** side plate; **piatto piano** dinner plate; **piatto di portata** serving dish **2** (*Culin*: *portata*) course; **primo/secondo piatto** first/second course; **un piatto tipico spagnolo** a traditional Spanish dish; **piatto forte** main course; **piatto freddo** cold dish (*meat, cheese, pickles ecc*); **piatto del giorno** dish of the day, plat du jour; **piatti già pronti** ready-cooked dishes **3** (*Tecn*) plate; **piatto della bilancia** scale pan; **piatto del giradischi** turntable **4** (*Mus*): **piatti** SMPL cymbals **5** (*parte piana*) flat (part)

piattola ['pjattola] SF (*pidocchio del pube*) crab louse; (*fig*: *persona noiosa*) pain in the neck

piazza ['pjattsa] SF **1** (*Archit*) square; (*Comm*) market; **piazza San Marco** St Mark's Square; **piazza del mercato** market place; **scendere in piazza** (*dimostrare*) to take to the streets, demonstrate; **gli operai sono scesi in piazza** the workers took to the streets; **vendere sulla pubblica piazza** to sell in the market place; **fare piazza pulita** to make a clean sweep; **mettere in piazza** (*rendere pubblico*) to make public **2** (*Mil*): **piazza d'armi** parade ground **3** (*di letto, lenzuolo*): **a una piazza** single *attr*; **a due piazze** double *attr* **4** **Piazza Affari** *the Italian stock exchange in Milan*

▷ www.piazzaffari.org/

piazzaforte [pjattsa'forte] SF (*pl* **piazzeforti**) (*Mil*) fortified town; (*fig*) stronghold

piazzale [pjat'tsale] SM (*piazza*) (large) square; (*di autostrada, stazione*) service area

piazzamento [pjattsa'mento] SM (*Sport*) place, placing

piazzare [pjat'tsare] VT **1** (*mettere*: *gen*) to place, put; (: *colpo*) to land, place **2** (*Comm*: *vendere*) to place, sell, market

▶ **piazzarsi** VR **1** (*Sport*) be placed; **piazzarsi bene** to finish with the leaders *o* in a good position; **piazzarsi male** to do badly (in a race) **2** (*fig*: *piantarsi*): **si è piazzato di fronte a me** he planted himself in front of me; **si è piazzato a casa mia e non si vuole più muovere** he's moved in at my place and refuses to budge

piazzista, i, e [pjat'tsista] SM/F (*Comm*) travelling salesman/saleswoman

piazzola [pjat'tsɔla] SF **1** (*Aut*) lay-by (*Brit*), (roadside) stopping place **2** (*Mil*) (gun) emplacement **3** (*di tenda*) pitch

picaresco, a, schi, sche [pika'resko] AGG picaresque

picca, che ['pikka] SF (*arma*) pike; (*Carte*): **picche** SFPL spades; **rispondere picche a qn** (*fig*) to give sb a flat refusal

piccante [pik'kante] AGG (*sapore*) spicy, hot; (*fig*: *sconcio*: *barzelletta*) risqué, racy; (: *dettaglio*) titillating, juicy; **è molto piccante?** is it very hot?; **a me piace più piccante** I like it hotter

Piccardia [pik'kardja] SF Picardy

piccarsi [pik'karsi] VIP **1** (*pretendere*): **piccarsi di fare qc** to pride o.s. on one's ability to do sth **2** (*impermalirsi*): **piccarsi per qc** to take offence (*Brit*) *o* offense (*Am*) at sth

piccata [pik'kata] SF (*Culin*) sautéed veal

picchettaggio, gi [pikket'taddʒo] SM picketing
picchettare [pikket'tare] VT **1** (*piantare paletti*) to stake out **2** (*fare picchettaggio*) to picket
picchettatura [pikketta'tura] SF staking (out)
picchetto [pik'ketto] SM **1** (*paletto*) stake, peg **2** (*Mil*) picket; **essere di picchetto** to be on picket duty; **ufficiale di picchetto** orderly officer **3** (*di scioperanti*) picket
picchiare [pik'kjare] VT **1** (*persona: colpire*) to hit, strike; (*: dar botte a*) to beat (up), thrash; **è lui che mi ha picchiato!** it was him who hit me!; **lo picchiarono selvaggiamente** they gave him a savage beating; **picchiare qn a sangue** to beat sb black and blue **2** (*battere*) to beat; (*sbattere*) to bang, knock; **picchiare i pugni sul tavolo** to bang *o* beat one's fists on the table; **ho picchiato la testa contro il muro** I banged my head against *o* on the wall
■ VI (*aus* **avere**) **1** (*bussare*) to knock; (*: con forza*) to bang; **picchiare alla porta di qn** to knock at *o* on sb's door; **qualcuno picchiava alla porta** somebody was knocking at the door **2** (*colpire*) to hit, strike; **ha picchiato sodo** he hit out hard; **il sole picchiava forte** the sun was beating down; **picchiare in testa** (*Aut*) to knock; **picchia e ripicchia** by dint of perseverance
picchiata [pik'kjata] SF **1** (*bussata*) knock; (*: più forte*) bang; (*percosse*) beating, thrashing **2** (*Aer*) (nose-)dive; **scendere in picchiata** to (nose-)dive
picchiettare [pikkjet'tare] VI (*aus* **avere**) (*gen*) to tap; (*pioggia*) to patter
■ VT (*punteggiare*) to spot, dot, fleck; (*colpire*) to tap
picchio, chi ['pikkjo] SM (*Zool*) woodpecker; **picchio muratore** nuthatch
piccino, a [pit'tʃino] AGG little, tiny, (very) small
■ SM/F (*bambino*) small child, little boy/girl; **è uno spettacolo per grandi e piccini** the show is suitable for all ages
picciolo [pit'tʃɔlo] SM (*Bot*) stalk
piccionaia [pittʃo'naja] SF **1** pigeon loft **2** (*soffitta*) loft **3** (*Teatro: loggione*): **la piccionaia** the gods *sg* (*Brit*), the gallery
piccione [pit'tʃone] SM pigeon; **prendere due piccioni con una fava** to kill two birds with one stone; **piccione viaggiatore** carrier pigeon
picco, chi ['pikko] SM (*cima*) peak, summit; (*valore più alto: in diagramma*) peak; **a picco** vertically; **una roccia a picco sul mare** a sheer cliff; **colare a picco** (*Naut, fig*) to sink
piccolezza [pikko'lettsa] SF **1** (*dimensione*) smallness; (*fig: grettezza*) meanness, pettiness **2** (*fig: inezia*) trifle; **è inutile che ti arrabbi per delle piccolezze simili** there's no point in getting annoyed over such trifles
piccolo, a ['pikkolo] AGG **1** (*oggetto, misura*) small; (*vezzeggiativo*) little; **ho una macchina molto piccola** I have a very small car; **me ne dia uno più piccolo** give me a smaller one; **qual è la stanza più piccola della casa?** which is the smallest room in the house?; **una piccola casetta in campagna** a little house in the country; **è piccolo di statura** he is small, he is of small stature; **è più piccolo di me** he is smaller than me; **com'è piccolo il mondo!** it's a small world!
2 (*giovane*) young, small, little; (*vezzeggiativo*) little; **un bambino piccolo** a little boy; **è ancora troppo piccolo** he's still too young; **bambini piccoli** young children; **mio fratello più piccolo** my younger *o* little brother; **Paolo è il più piccolo dei fratelli** Paolo is the youngest of the brothers **3** (*di poco conto: difetto*) slight; (*: regalo*) little; (*: dettaglio*) minor **4** (*breve: viaggio, lettera*) short **5** (*modesto*) small; (*fig pegg: meschino*) petty, mean; **piccolo possidente** smallholder; **la piccola borghesia** the lower middle-classes *pl*; (*pegg*) the petty bourgeoisie; **farsi piccolo** (*umile*) to make o.s. small, to cower
■ SM/F (*bambino*) (small) child, small boy/girl; (*vezzeggiativo*) little one; **da piccolo** as a child; **da piccola ero molto timida** I was very shy as a child
■ SM: **in piccolo** in miniature; **mi sembra il Colosseo in piccolo** it's like a miniature version of the Colosseum; **nel mio piccolo** in my own small way
2 (*di animale*): **piccoli** SMPL young *pl*; **la gatta e i suoi piccoli** the cat and her kittens; **la volpe e i suoi piccoli** the vixen and her young *o* cubs
picconata [pikko'nata] SF blow with a pickaxe (*Brit*) *o* pickax (*Am*)
piccone [pik'kone] SM pick, pickaxe (*Brit*), pickax (*Am*)
piccozza [pik'kɔttsa] SF ice axe (*Brit*), ice ax (*Am*)
pick-up ['pikʌp] SM INV (*di giradischi*) pick-up
picnic [pik'nik] SM INV picnic; **fare un picnic** to have a picnic
pidiessino, a [pidiɛs'sino] AGG (*Pol*) of *o* belonging to the P.D.S (*successor to Italian communist party*)
■ SM/F (*Pol*) member *o* supporter of the P.D.S.
pidocchio, chi [pi'dɔkkjo] SM **1** (*Zool*) louse; **pieno di pidocchi** crawling with lice **2** (*fig: persona gretta*) mean person
pidocchioso, a [pidok'kjoso] AGG **1** (*infestato*) lousy, full of lice **2** (*fig: taccagno*) mean, stingy, tight
piduista, i, e [pidu'ista] AGG P2 *attr* (*masonic lodge*)
■ SM *member of the P2 masonic lodge*
piè [pjɛ] SM INV: **a ogni piè sospinto** (*fig*) at every step; **saltare a piè pari** (*omettere*) to skip; **a piè di pagina** at the foot of the page; **note a piè di pagina** footnotes
pied-à-terre [pjeta'tɛ:r] SM INV pied-à-terre
pied-de-poule ['pjɛdə'pul] SM INV (*tessuto*) hound's-tooth cloth
piede ['pjɛde] SM **1** (*gen*) foot; **mi fanno male i piedi** my feet are sore; **a piedi nudi** barefoot; **avere i piedi piatti** to have flat feet, be flat-footed; **essere** *o* **stare in piedi** to stand, be standing; **stava in piedi in un angolo** he was standing in a corner; **alzarsi in piedi** to get to one's feet, stand up; **andare a piedi** to walk; **ci andrò a piedi** I'll walk; **essere a piedi** to be on foot; **rimanere a piedi** to be without transport; **ai piedi della montagna/del letto** at the foot *o* bottom of the mountains/of the bed; **da capo a piedi** from head to foot, from top to toe **2** (*di mobile*) leg; (*di lampada*) base **3** **piede di porco** (*Tecn*) crowbar; (*per forzare serrature*) jemmy (*Brit*), jimmy (*Am*); (*Culin*) pig's trotter **4** (*Metrica*) foot **5** (*fraseologia*): **avere tutti ai propri piedi** to have the world at one's feet; **essere sul piede di guerra** to be ready for action; **fare qc con i piedi** to do sth badly; **ragionare con i piedi** to reason like a fool; **fuori dai piedi!** get out of the way!; **levarsi** *o* **togliersi dai piedi** to get out from under sb's feet; **tra i piedi** in the way; **è sempre tra i piedi** he's always in the way; **a piede libero** (*Dir*) on bail; **io non ci ho mai messo piede** I've never set foot in there; **mettere i piedi in testa a qn** to walk all over sb; **mettere qn sotto i piedi** to push sb around; **mettere qc in piedi** (*azienda*) to set sth up; **prendere piede** (*teoria, tendenza*) to gain ground, catch on; **puntare i piedi** to dig one's heels in; **sentirsi mancare la terra sotto i piedi** to feel completely lost; **su due piedi** (*rispondere, accettare*) on the spot, at once; **tenere in piedi** (*persona*) to keep

Pp

on his (*o* her) feet; (*fig*: *ditta*) to keep going; **non sta in piedi** (*persona*) he can't stand; (*fig*: *scusa*) it doesn't hold water

piedino [pje'dino] SM: **fare piedino a qn** to play footsie with sb

piedipiatti [pjedi'pjatti] SM/F INV (*fam*: *poliziotto*) cop

piedistallo [pjedis'tallo], **piedestallo** [pjedes'tallo] SM (*anche fig*) pedestal

piega, ghe ['pjɛga] SF **1** (*gen*, *Geol*) fold; (*Cucito*: *di gonna*) pleat; (: *di pantaloni*) crease; (*grinza*) wrinkle, crease; (*della pelle*) (skin) fold; **è tutto pieno di pieghe** (*spiegazzato*) it's all creased; **prendere una brutta** *o* **cattiva piega** (*fig*: *persona*) to get into bad ways; (: *situazione*) to take a turn for the worse; **non fa una piega** (*fig*: *ragionamento*) it's faultless; **non ha fatto una piega** (*fig*: *persona*) he didn't bat an eye(lid) (*Brit*) *o* an eye(lash) (*Am*) **2** (*acconciatura*) set; **farsi (fare) la messa in piega** to have one's hair set

piegaciglia [pjega'tʃiʎʎa] SM INV eyelash curler

piegamento [pjega'mento] SM **1** (*vedi vt*) folding; bending **2** (*Ginnastica*): **piegamento sulle gambe** kneebend

piegare [pje'gare] VT **1** (*ripiegare*: *vestito, tovagliolo, foglio*) to fold (up); (: *sedia, tavola*) to fold up; **piega la cartina e mettila via** fold the map and put it away **2** (*curvare*: *ramo, schiena, braccia*) to bend; **piegare il capo di fronte a qn** (*fig*) to bow to sb; **piegare qn alla propria volontà** to bend sb to one's will

▶ **piegarsi** VR (*curvarsi*: *persona*) to bend (over); (*fig*: *cedere*): **piegarsi (a)** to yield (to), submit (to); **piegarsi in due dalle risate/dal dolore** to double up with laughter/with pain;

▶ **piegarsi** VIP (*asse, superficie*) to sag; (*sedia, tavolo*) to fold (up)

piegata [pje'gata] SF: **dare una piegata a qc** to fold sth (up)

piegatura [pjega'tura] SF (*vedi vt*) **1** folding *no pl*; bending *no pl* **2** (*piega*) fold; bend

piegherò *ecc* [pjege'rɔ] VB *vedi* **piegare**

pieghettare [pjeget'tare] VT to pleat

pieghettato, a [pjeget'tato] AGG pleated

pieghettatura [pjegetta'tura] SF (*azione*) pleating; (*pieghe*) pleats *pl*

pieghevole [pje'gevole] AGG **1** (*ripiegabile*: *porta, sedia*) folding **2** (*flessibile*) pliable, bendable, flexible; (*fig*) pliable, yielding, docile

Piemonte [pje'monte] SM Piedmont
▷ www.regione.piemonte.it/

piemontese [pjemon'tese] AGG, SM/F Piedmontese

piena ['pjɛna] SF **1** (*di corso d'acqua*) flood, spate; **essere in piena** to be in flood *o* in spate; **il fiume è in piena** the river is in flood **2** (*fig*: *calca*) crowd, throng

pienamente [pjena'mente] AVV completely, wholly

pienezza [pje'nettsa] SF fullness

pieno, a ['pjɛno] AGG **1** (*gen*) full; (*giornata, vita*) full, busy; **pieno di** (*gen*) full of; (*idee*) bursting with; (*macchie*) covered in *o* with; **la mia valigia è piena** my suitcase is full; **una borsa piena di libri** a bag full of books; **un bicchiere pieno d'acqua** a glass full of water *o* filled with water; **avere la pancia piena** to be full; **il cinema era pieno zeppo (di gente)** the cinema was packed; **luna piena** full moon **2** (*completo*: *successo, fiducia*) total, complete; **a tempo pieno** full-time; **cerco un lavoro a tempo pieno** I'm looking for a full-time job; **avere pieni poteri** to have full powers; **nel pieno possesso delle sue facoltà** in full possession of his faculties **3** (*muro, mattone*) solid **4** (*fraseologia*): **a piene mani** abundantly; **è una persona che dà a piene mani** he (*o* she) is very generous; **a pieni voti** (*eleggere*) unanimously; **laurearsi a pieni voti** *to graduate with full marks*; **pieno di sé** full of oneself, self-important; **essere pieno di lavoro** to have a lot of work to do; **essere in piena forma** to be in top form; **pieno come un uovo** full to overflowing; **in pieno** (*completamente*: *sbagliare*) completely; (: *colpire, centrare*) bang *o* right in the middle; **in pieno giorno** in broad daylight; **in pieno inverno** in the depths of winter; **in piena notte** in the middle of the night; **in piena stagione** at the height of the season

■ SM **1** **fare il pieno (di benzina)** (*Aut*) to fill up (with petrol (*Brit*) *o* gas (*Am*)); **il pieno, per favore** fill her up, please **2** (*colmo*) height, peak; **arrivò nel pieno della festa** he arrived when the party was in full swing

pienone [pje'none] SM: **c'era un tale pienone a teatro!** the theatre was packed!

pienotto, a [pje'nɔtto] AGG plump, chubby

piercing ['pirsin(g)] SM piercing; **farsi il piercing all'ombelico** to have one's navel pierced

pietà [pje'ta] SF INV (*gen*) pity, compassion; (*Rel*) piety; **non voglio la vostra pietà** I don't want your pity; **sentire** *o* **provare pietà per qn** to pity sb, feel pity for sb; **avere pietà di** (*compassione*) to pity, feel pity for; (*misericordia*) to have pity *o* mercy on; **muovere qn a pietà** to move sb to pity; **senza pietà** (*agire*) ruthlessly; (*persona*) pitiless, ruthless; **far pietà** to arouse pity; (*pegg*) to be terrible *o* awful; **come pianista fa pietà** he's a terrible *o* an awful pianist

pietanza [pje'tantsa] SF course, dish

pietismo [pje'tizmo] SM pietism

pietosamente [pjetosa'mente] AVV (*vedi agg*) compassionately; pitifully

pietoso, a [pje'toso] AGG **1** (*che prova pietà*) compassionate, pitying **2** (*che fa pietà*) pitiful; **uno spettacolo pietoso** a pitiful sight; **essere ridotto in uno stato pietoso** to be reduced to a pitiful *o* sorry state; **ho fatto una figura pietosa** I made an awful fool of myself

pietra ['pjɛtra] SF stone; **di pietra** stone *attr*; **una casa di pietra** a stone house; **avere un cuore di pietra** to be hard-hearted; **porre la prima pietra** (*fondare*) to set up; **scagliare la prima pietra** to cast the first stone; **mettiamoci una pietra sopra** let bygones be bygones

■ **pietra dura** semiprecious stone; **pietra focaia** flint(stone); **pietra di paragone** (*fig*) touchstone; **pietra pomice** pumice stone; **pietra preziosa** precious stone, gem; **pietra dello scandalo** cause of scandal

pietraia [pje'traja] SF (*mucchio*) pile of stones; (*terreno*) stony ground; (*cava*) stone quarry

pietrificare [pjetrifi'kare] VT to petrify; (*fig*) to petrify, transfix, paralyze

▶ **pietrificarsi** VIP (*anche fig*) to be petrified, be turned to stone

pietrina [pje'trina] SF (*per accendino*) flint

pietrisco, schi [pje'trisko] SM crushed stone, road metal

pietroso, a [pje'troso] AGG stony

pieve ['pjeve] SF parish church

piezoelettricità [pjeddzoelettritʃi'ta] SF piezoelectricity

piezoelettrico, a, ci, che [pjeddzoe'lɛttriko] AGG piezoelectric

pifferaio, ai [piffe'rajo] SM piper
piffero ['piffero] SM (*Mus*) pipe, fife
pigiama, i [pi'dʒama] SM pyjamas *pl* (*Brit*), pajamas *pl* (*Am*); **questo pigiama mi è un po' stretto** these pyjamas are a bit tight on me; **essere in pigiama** to be in one's pyjamas; **sei ancora in pigiama?** are you still in your pyjamas?
pigia pigia ['pidʒa 'pidʒa] SM INV throng, crowd, press
pigiare [pi'dʒare] VT (*pulsante*) to press; (*uva*) to tread
pigiatrice [pidʒa'tritʃe] SF (*macchina*) wine press
pigiatura [pidʒa'tura] SF (*di uva*) pressing, treading
pigione [pi'dʒone] SF rent
pigliare [piʎ'ʎare] VT (*fam*) = **prendere**
piglio[1] ['piʎʎo] SM: **dar di piglio a qc** (*fig: incominciare*) to get to grips with sth
piglio[2] ['piʎʎo] SM (*aspetto*) look, countenance, expression
pigmalione [pigma'ljone] SM (*fig*) benefactor
pigmentazione [pigmentat'tsjone] SF pigmentation
pigmento [pig'mento] SM pigment
pigmeo, a [pig'mɛo] AGG, SM/F pigmy
pigna ['piɲɲa] SF (*Bot*) pine cone
pignatta [piɲ'ɲatta] SF pot
pignoleria [piɲɲole'ria] SF fastidiousness, fussiness
pignolo, a [piɲ'ɲɔlo] AGG pernickety, fussy; **è più pignolo di me** he's fussier than me
■ SM/F fussy person
pignone [piɲ'ɲone] SM (*Tecn*) pinion
pignoramento [piɲɲora'mento] SM (*Dir*) distraint
pignorare [piɲɲo'rare] VT (*Dir*) to distrain
pigolare [pigo'lare] VI (*aus* **avere**) to cheep, chirp
pigolio, lii [pigo'lio] SM cheeping *no pl*, chirping *no pl*
pigramente [pigra'mente] AVV lazily
pigrizia [pi'grittsja] SF laziness; **non l'ho fatto per pigrizia** I didn't do it out of laziness
pigro, a ['pigro] AGG (*persona*) lazy, idle; (*fig: mente*) slow, dull; (*andatura*) lazy; (*stomaco*) sluggish; **è il ragazzo più pigro che abbia mai conosciuto** he's the laziest boy I've ever known; **in un pigro pomeriggio d'agosto** on a lazy August afternoon
PIL [pil] SIGLA M (= **Prodotto Interno Lordo**) GDP (= *Gross Domestic Product*)
pila ['pila] SF **1** (*mucchio*) pile **2** (*Elettr*) battery; **una pila di libri** a pile of books; **a pila** *or* **a pile** battery-operated; **funziona a pile** it works on batteries; **pila atomica** nuclear reactor **3** (*fam: torcia*) torch (*Brit*), flashlight (*esp Am*)
pilaf [pi'laf] AGG INV: **riso pilaf** pilaf (rice)
pilastro [pi'lastro] SM (*Archit*) pillar, pilaster; (*Alpinismo*) pillar; (*fig: sostegno*) pillar, mainstay
Pilato [pi'lato] SM: **Ponzio Pilato** Pontius Pilate
pile ['pail] SM INV (*materiale, maglia*) fleece
pillola ['pillola] SF pill; **la pillola (anticoncezionale)** the pill; **prendere la pillola** to be on the pill; **pillola del giorno dopo** morning-after pill
pilone [pi'lone] SM **1** (*di linea elettrica*) pylon; (*di ponte*) pier **2** (*Rugby*) prop
piloro [pi'lɔro] SM (*Anat*) pylorus
pilota, i, e [pi'lɔta] SM/F (*Naut, Aer*) pilot; (*Aut*) driver; **secondo pilota** co-pilot; **pilota automatico** automatic pilot
■ AGG INV pilot *attr*
pilotaggio [pilo'taddʒo] SM: **cabina di pilotaggio** flight deck
pilotare [pilo'tare] VT (*Aer, Naut*) to pilot; (*Aut*) to drive
piluccare [piluk'kare] VT to nibble at; **smettila di piluccare** stop nibbling (at) your food
pimento [pi'mento] SM pimento, allspice
pimpante [pim'pante] AGG lively, full of beans
PIN [pin] SIGLA M PIN (= *Personal Identification Number*)
pinacoteca, che [pinako'tɛka] SF art gallery
pince [pɛ̃s] SF INV (*Sartoria*) dart, tuck
Pinco ['pinko] SM: **Pinco Pallino** so-and-so
pindarico, a, ci, che [pin'dariko] AGG Pindaric; **voli pindarici** flights of fancy
Pindaro ['pindaro] SM Pindar
pineta [pi'neta] SF pinewood, pine forest
ping-pong [ping 'pɔng] SM INV table tennis
▷ www.fitet.org/
pingue ['pingwe] AGG (*grasso*) fat, corpulent; (*fertile*) rich, fertile; (*fig: abbondante: guadagno*) huge
pinguedine [pin'gwɛdine] SF (*adiposità*) fatness, corpulence
pinguino [pin'gwino] SM **1** (*Zool*) penguin **2** (*gelato*) *chocolate-coated ice cream on a stick*
pinna ['pinna] SF **1** (*di pesce*) fin; (*di cetacei*) flipper **2** (*per nuotare*) flipper **3** (*Naut*) stabilizer; (*Aer*) fin **4** (*Anat*): **pinna nasale** ala of the nose
pinnacolo [pin'nakolo] SM pinnacle
pino ['pino] SM (*albero*) pine (tree); (*legno*) pine(wood); **pino silvestre** *o* **di Scozia** Scots pine
pinolo [pi'nɔlo] SM (*seme*) pine kernel
pinta ['pinta] SF pint
pinza ['pintsa] SF **1** (*gen*) pliers *pl*; (*tanaglia*) pincers *pl*; (*molle*) tongs *pl* **2** (*Med*) forceps *pl* **3** (*di granchio*) pincer
pinzatrice [pintsa'tritʃe] SF stapler
pinzette [pin'tsette] SFPL tweezers
pio, pia, pii, pie ['pio] AGG (*devoto*) pious, devout; (*misericordioso: opere, istituzione*) charitable, charity *attr*
pioggerella [pjoddʒe'rɛlla] SF drizzle
pioggia, ge ['pjɔddʒa] SF **1** rain; **sorpreso dalla pioggia** caught in the rain; **sotto la pioggia** in the rain; **pioggia fine** drizzle; **pioggia scrosciante** driving rain; **pioggia acida** acid rain **2** (*fig: di regali, fiori*) shower; (*di insulti*) hail
piolo [pi'ɔlo] SM peg, stake; (*di scala*) rung; **un piolo rotto** a broken rung; **scala a pioli** ladder
piombare[1] [pjom'bare] VI (*aus* **essere**) **1** (*cadere*) to fall heavily; **piombare su** (*sogg: tigre, leone*) to pounce on; (*: rapaci*) to swoop down on; (*: esercito nemico*) to swoop down on, pounce on; **il falco piombò sulla preda** the hawk swooped (down) on its prey; **gli sono piombati addosso** they swooped down on him, they pounced on him; **piombò nella più cupa disperazione** he plunged *o* sank into blackest despair; **piombare a terra** to crash to the ground; **piombare nel vuoto** to fall downwards **2** (*arrivare*) to arrive unexpectedly, turn up; **è piombato qui alle 2 di mattina** he turned up here at 2 in the morning
piombare[2] [pjom'bare] VT (*pacco*) to seal (with lead); (*dente*) to fill
piombatura [pjomba'tura] SF **1** (*vedi* piombare[2]) sealing; filling **2** (*sigillo*) seal; (*di dente*) filling
piombino [pjom'bino] SM (*sigillo*) (lead) seal; (*Pesca*) sinker (weight); (*del filo a piombo*) plummet
piombo ['pjombo] SM **1** (*metallo*) lead; (*Pesca*) sinker; (*Tip*) type; (*sigillo*) (lead) seal; (*proiettile*) (lead) shot; **di piombo** (*tubo*) lead *attr*; (*fig: cielo*) leaden; **soldatino di piombo** tin soldier; **senza piombo** (*benzina*) unleaded, lead-free; **gli anni di piombo** era of terrorist outrages **2** (*fraseologia*): **a piombo** (*muro*) plumb; (*cadere*) straight down; **non essere a piombo** to be out of plumb; **cadere di piombo** to fall suddenly; **andare con i piedi di piombo** to tread carefully; **avere/sentirsi addosso**

Pp

una cappa di piombo to have/feel a great weight on one's shoulders; **riempire qn di piombo** to fill sb with lead
■ AGG INV (*colore*) leaden, lead-coloured; **grigio piombo** lead grey
pioniere, a [pjo'njɛre] SM/F pioneer
pioppo ['pjɔppo] SM poplar; **pioppo bianco** white poplar; **pioppo nero** black poplar; **pioppo tremolo** aspen, trembling poplar
piovanello [pjova'nɛllo] SM (*Zool*): **piovanello alpino** dunlin
piovano, a [pjo'vano] AGG: **acqua piovana** rainwater
piovere ['pjɔvere] VB IMPERS to rain; **piove** it's raining; **piove a dirotto** *o* **a catinelle** it's pouring; **mi piove in casa** the rain comes in through my roof; **su questo non ci piove** (*fig fam*) there's no doubt about it
■ VI IRREG (*aus* **essere**) (*scendere dall'alto*) to rain down; (*fig*: *lettere, regali*) to pour in; (: *persona: arrivare all'improvviso*) to turn up, arrive unexpectedly
piovigginare [pjoviddʒi'nare] VB IMPERS to drizzle
piovigginoso, a [pjoviddʒi'noso] AGG drizzly
piovosità [pjovosi'ta] SF INV (*Meteor*) rainfall
piovoso, a [pjo'voso] AGG rainy, wet
piovra ['pjɔvra] SF octopus
piovve *ecc* [pjɔvve] VB *vedi* **piovere**
pipa ['pipa] SF pipe; (*quantità di tabacco*) pipe(ful); **fumare la pipa** to smoke a pipe
pipetta [pi'petta] SF pipette
pipì [pi'pi] SF INV (*fam*) wee(-wee), pee; **fare (la) pipì** to have a pee, have a wee(-wee)
pipistrello [pipis'trɛllo] SM **1** (*Zool*) bat **2** (*mantello*) cloak
piqué [pi'ke] SM INV (*tessuto*) piqué
piramidale [pirami'dale] AGG pyramidal; **vendite piramidali** pyramid selling
piramide [pi'ramide] SF pyramid; **a piramide** pyramid-shaped
piranha [pi'raɲa] SM INV piranha
pirata, i [pi'rata] SM pirate; (*fig: ladro*) swindler, shark; **pirata dell'aria** hijacker; **pirata informatico** hacker; **pirata della strada** hit-and-run driver
■ AGG INV pirate *attr*; **una cassetta pirata** a pirate tape
pirateria [pirate'ria] SF piracy; (*atto*) act of piracy
pirenaico, a, ci, che [pire'naiko] AGG Pyrenean
Pirenei [pire'nɛi] SMPL: **i Pirenei** the Pyrenees
piretro [pi'rɛtro] SM (*Bot*) pyrethrum
pirex® ['pireks] SM Pyrex®
pirico, a, ci, che ['piriko] AGG: **polvere pirica** gunpowder
pirite [pi'rite] SF pyrite
piro... ['piro] PREF pyro...
piroetta [piro'etta] SF pirouette
piroettare [piroet'tare] VI (*aus* **avere**) to pirouette
pirofila [pi'rɔfila] SF (*tegame*) heat-resistant dish
pirofilo, a [pi'rɔfilo] AGG heat-resistant
piroga, ghe [pi'rɔga] SF dugout (canoe)
pirolisi [piro'lizi] SF INV pyrolysis
piromane [pi'rɔmane] SM/F pyromaniac, arsonist
piromania [piroma'nia] SF pyromania
piro piro ['piro 'piro] SM INV sandpiper
piroscafo [pi'rɔskafo] SM steamship, steamer
pirotecnica [piro'tɛknika] SF pyrotechnics *sg*
pirotecnico, a, ci, che [piro'tɛkniko] AGG pyrotechnical
Pisa ['pisa] SF Pisa
pisano, a [pi'sano] AGG Pisan, of *o* from Pisa
■ SM/F inhabitant *o* native of Pisa
piscia ['piʃʃa] SF (*fam*) piss
pisciare [piʃ'ʃare] VI (*aus* **avere**) (*fam*) to piss
pisciata [piʃ'ʃata] SF (*fam*): **fare una pisciata** to take a leak, have a pee
pisciatoio, toi [piʃʃa'tojo] SM (*fam*) public loo (*Brit*)
piscicoltura [piʃʃikol'tura] SF fish farming
piscina [piʃ'ʃina] SF (swimming) pool; (*pubblica, comunale*) (swimming) baths *pl*; **piscina coperta** indoor swimming pool; **piscina scoperta** open-air *o* outdoor swimming pool
piscio, sci ['piʃʃo] SM (*fam*) piss
pisello [pi'sɛllo] SM (*Bot*) pea; (*fam: pene*) willie (*Brit*), peter (*Am*)
pisolino [pizo'lino] SM nap, snooze; **fare un pisolino** to have a nap
pisside ['pisside] SF (*Rel*) pyx
pista ['pista] SF **1** (*traccia*) track, trail; **siamo su una buona pista** we are on the right track; **la polizia sta seguendo una pista** the police are following a lead; **pista!** get out of the way! **2** (*Radio*) (sound)track; (*Inform*) track; **registrato a doppia pista** double-tracked **3** (*di circo*) ring; (*di stadio*) track; (*Sci*) (ski) run, piste; (*Pattinaggio*) rink; (*Ippica*) course; (*Aer*) runway; **i corridori erano in pista** the runners were on the track
■ **pista artificiale** (*Sci*) dry ski slope; **pista (da ballo)** (dance) floor; **pista ciclabile** cycle track; **pista da fondo** (*Sci*) (cross-country) trail; **pista di lancio** launch(ing) pad; **pista per principianti** (*Sci*) nursery slope; **pista di rullaggio** (*Aer*) taxiway; **pista di volo** (*Aer*) runway
pistacchio, chi [pis'takkjo] SM (*albero*) pistachio (tree); (*seme*) pistachio (nut)
pistard [pis'ta:r] SM INV (*Ciclismo*) track racer, track specialist
pistillo [pis'tillo] SM (*Bot*) pistil
pistoiese [pisto'jese] AGG of *o* from Pistoia
■ SM/F inhabitant *o* native of Pistoia
pistola [pis'tɔla] SF pistol, gun; **sotto la minaccia della pistola** at gunpoint; **pistola ad acqua** water pistol; **pistola automatica** automatic (pistol); **pistola a spruzzo** (*per vernice*) spray gun; **pistola a tamburo** revolver
pistolettata [pistolet'tata] SF pistol shot
pistone [pis'tone] SM (*Tecn*) piston; (*Mus*) valve
Pitagora [pi'tagora] SM Pythagoras
pitagorico, a, ci, che [pita'gɔriko] AGG Pythagorean
pitecantropo [pite'kantropo] SM pithecanthropus
pitoccare [pitok'kare] VT, VI (*aus* **avere**) to beg
pitocco, a, chi, che [pi'tɔkko] AGG mean, stingy
■ SM/F miser, skinflint
pitone [pi'tone] SM python
pittima ['pittima] SF (*fig: persona*) bore
pittore, trice [pit'tore] SM/F **1** (*artista*) painter **2** (*imbianchino*) (house) painter, decorator
pittorescamente [pittoreska'mente] AVV (*vedi agg*) picturesquely; colourfully, vividly
pittoresco, a, schi, sche [pitto'resko] AGG (*veduta, paesaggio*) picturesque; (*modo di parlare*) colourful, vivid
pittorico, a, ci, che [pit'tɔriko] AGG pictorial, painting *attr*, of painting
pittura [pit'tura] SF **1** (*arte*) painting; (*dipinto*) painting, picture; **la pittura astratta** abstract painting; **pittura murale** mural **2** (*vernice*) paint; **pittura fresca** wet paint
pitturare [pittu'rare] VT to paint; **pitturarsi le labbra** to put on lipstick; **pitturarsi le unghie** to paint one's nails

▸ **pitturarsi** VR (*fam: truccarsi*) to make o.s. up, put on make-up

più [pju] PAROLA CHIAVE

■ AVV

1 (*tempo: usato al negativo*): **non…più** no longer, no more, not … any more; **non lavora più** he doesn't work any more, he no longer works; **non ha più detto una parola** he didn't say another word; **non c'è più bisogno che…** there's no longer any need for …; **non riesco più a sopportarla** I can't stand her any more *o* any longer; **non ne posso più!** I can't take any more!; **non ritornerò mai più** I'll never come back; **non è più così giovane** he is not as young as he was

2 (*quantità: usato al negativo*): **non…più** no more; **non abbiamo più vino/soldi** we have no more wine/ money, we haven't got any wine/money (left); **non ce n'è più** there isn't any left; **non ce n'è quasi più** there's hardly any; **non c'è più nessuno** there's no one left; **non c'è più niente da fare** there's nothing else to do, there's nothing more to be done

3 (*uso comparativo*) more, *aggettivo corto* +…er; **più bello** more beautiful; **più elegante** smarter, more elegant; **parla più forte!** speak up!; **e chi più ne ha, più ne metta!** and so on and so forth!; **è più furbo che capace** he's cunning rather than able; **è più che intelligente** he's clever to say the least; **noi lavoriamo più di loro** we work more *o* harder than they do; **mi piace più di ogni altra cosa al mondo** I like it better *o* more than anything else in the world; **non guadagna più di me** he doesn't earn any more than me; **è più intelligente di te** he is more intelligent than you (are); **è più povero di te** he is poorer than you (are); **cammina più veloce di me** she walks more quickly than me *o* than I do; **non ce n'erano più di 15** there were no more than 15; **ha più di 70 anni** she is over 70; **è a più di 10 km da qui** it's more than *o* over 10 km from here; **più di uno gli ha detto che…** several people have told him that …; **si fa sempre più difficile** it is getting more and more difficult; **due volte più grande del mio** twice as big as mine

4 **di più, in più,** more; **ne voglio di più** I want some more; **3 ore/litri di più che** 3 hours/litres more than; **una volta di più** once more; **ci sono 3 persone in più** there are 3 more *o* extra people; **mi ha dato 3 pacchetti in più** he gave me 3 more *o* extra packets; (*troppi*) he gave me 3 packets too many; **e in più fa anche…** and in addition to *o* on top of that he also …

5 (*uso superlativo*) most, *aggettivo corto* +…est; **la più bella del mondo** the most beautiful in the world; **il più bravo di tutta la classe** the best in the class; **il più veloce di tutti** the fastest of all; **è ciò che ho di più caro** it's the thing I hold dearest; **è quello che mi piace di più** it's the one I like the most *o* best; **ciò che mi ha colpito di più** the thing that struck me most; **fare qc il più in fretta possibile** to do sth as quickly as possible; **è il programma che guardo più spesso** it's the programme I watch most often

6 (*Mat*) plus; **2 più 2 fa 4** 2 plus 2 equals 4; **più due** (*gradi*) plus two, two degrees above freezing *o* above zero

7 (*fraseologia*): **a più non posso** as much as possible; **urlava a più non posso** she was shouting at the top of her voice; **al più presto** as soon as possible; **al più tardi** at the latest; **più che altro** above all; **più che mai** more than ever; **chi più chi meno hanno tutti contribuito** everybody made a contribution of some sort; **più o meno** more or less; **avrà più o meno 30 anni** he must be about 30; **sarò lì più o meno alle 4** I'll be there about 4 o'clock; **minuto più minuto meno** give or take a minute; **né più né meno** no more, no less; **né più né meno come sua madre** just like her mother; **e per di più** (*inoltre*) and what's more, moreover; **tanto più che non sai neppure parlare l'inglese** all the more so as you can't even speak English

■ AGG

1 (*comparativo*) more; (*superlativo*) the most; **chi ha più voti di tutti?** who has the most votes?; **più gente viene meglio è** the more the merrier; **ci sono più macchine** there are more cars; **ci vuole più sale** it needs more salt

2 (*molti, parecchi*) several; **abbiamo discusso per più ore** we argued for several hours

■ PREP plus; **i genitori, più i figli** parents plus *o* and their children

■ SM INV

1 (*Mat*) plus (sign)

2 (*la parte maggiore*): **il più** the most; **ottenere il più possibile** to get the best possible; **tutt'al più** *o* **al più possiamo andare al cinema** if the worst comes to the worst we can always go to the cinema; **il più delle volte** more often than not, generally; **il più ormai è fatto** the worst is over, most of it is already done; **parlare del più e del meno** to talk about this and that; **per lo più** = **perlopiù**

3 **i più** the majority; **i più pensano così** most people think so; **la reazione dei più** the reaction of the majority

piuccheperfetto [piukkeper'fɛtto] SM past perfect (tense), pluperfect (tense)

piuma ['pjuma] SF (*di uccello*) feather; (*ornamento*) feather, plume; **piume** SFPL down *sg*; (*piumaggio*) plumage, feathers *pl*; **leggero/morbido come una piuma** light/soft as a feather; **guanciale di piume** feather pillow; **cappello con le piume** plumed hat

piumaggio [pju'maddʒo] SM plumage, feathers *pl*

piumato, a [pju'mato] AGG plumed

piumino [pju'mino] SM (*per letto*) eiderdown; (: *tipo danese*) duvet, continental quilt (*Brit*); (*giacca*) quilted jacket (*with goose-feather padding*); (*per cipria*) powder puff; (*per spolverare*) feather duster

piumone® [pju'mone] SM duvet

piumoso, a [pju'moso] AGG feathery

piuttosto [pjut'tɔsto] AVV **1** (*preferibilmente*) rather; **prenderei piuttosto un'acqua minerale** I'd rather have some mineral water; **piuttosto che** (*anziché*) rather than; **piuttosto che studiare farebbe di tutto** he'd do anything rather than study; **qui piove in primavera piuttosto che in autunno** here it rains in the spring rather than *o* instead of in the autumn; **piuttosto la morte!** I'd rather die! **2** (*alquanto*) quite, rather; **fa piuttosto freddo** it's rather *o* fairly cold; **sono piuttosto stanco** I'm quite *o* rather tired; **siamo piuttosto indietro con il lavoro** we're rather *o* somewhat behind with the work

piva ['piva] SF: **tornarsene con le pive nel sacco** (*fig*) to return empty-handed

pivello, a [pi'vɛllo] SM/F (*fam*) greenhorn

piviale [pi'vjale] SM (*Rel*) cope

piviere [pi'vjɛre] SM (*Zool*) plover

pixel ['piksel] SM INV (*Inform*) pixel

Pp

pizza ['pittsa] SF **1** (*Culin*) pizza; (*fig*: *persona o cosa noiosa*) bore; **che pizza!** what a bore! **2** (*Cine*) reel

pizzaiola [pittsa'jɔla] SF (*Culin*): **alla pizzaiola** *with tomato and oregano sauce*

pizzeria [pittse'ria] SF pizzeria (*place where pizzas are made, sold or eaten*)

pizzicagnolo, a [pittsi'kaɲɲolo] SM/F delicatessen owner

pizzicare [pittsi'kare] VT **1** (*stringere*) to nip; (: *con pinze*) to pinch; (*pungere*: *sogg*: *ape*) to sting; (: *zanzara, pulce*) to bite; (: *sostanza*) to sting; **gli ho pizzicato un braccio** I pinched his arm; **ha un sapore che ti pizzica la gola** the taste makes your mouth tingle; **mi sono pizzicato un dito** I've nipped my finger; **mi sono pizzicato un dito nella porta** I caught my finger in the door **2** (*fig*: *acciuffare*) to nab, pinch; (*fig*: *rubare*) to pinch **3** (*Mus*) to pluck
■ VI (*aus* **avere**) **1** (*prudere*) to itch, be itchy; **mi pizzica il naso** my nose is itching **2** (*essere piccante*) to be spicy, be hot

pizzicata [pittsi'kata] SF pinch; **dare una pizzicata a qn** to give sb a pinch, pinch sb

pizzicato [pittsi'kato] SM (*Mus*) pizzicato

pizzicheria [pittsike'ria] SF (*negozio*) delicatessen

pizzico, chi ['pittsiko] SM (*pizzicotto*) pinch, nip; (*piccola quantità*) pinch, dash; (*puntura*: *di ape, vespa*) sting; (: *di zanzara*) bite; **un pizzico di sale** a pinch of salt; **non ha un pizzico di pudore** he hasn't an ounce of common decency

pizzicore [pittsi'kore] SM (*prurito*) itch

pizzicotto [pittsi'kɔtto] SM pinch, nip

pizzo ['pittso] SM **1** (*merletto*) lace **2** (*barbetta*) goatee (beard) **3** (*cima*) peak **4** (*tangente*) protection money

placare [pla'kare] VT (*persona*) to calm down, pacify; (*desiderio*) to placate, assuage; (*dolore, eccitazione*) to soothe; (*coscienza*) to salve; (*scrupoli*) to allay; **placare la fame** to satisfy one's hunger; **placare la sete** to quench one's thirst; **placare gli animi** to appease the crowd
▸ **placarsi** VIP (*rivolta, tempesta*) to die down; (*persona*) to calm down

placca, che ['plakka] SF **1** (*gen, Elettr*) plate; (*con iscrizione*) plaque **2** (*Med*: *anche*: **placca dentaria**) (dental) plaque **3** (*Culin*): **placca da forno** baking sheet

placcaggio, gi [plak'kaddʒo] SM (*Rugby*) tackle

placcare [plak'kare] VT **1** to plate; **placcato in oro/argento** gold-/silver-plated **2** (*Rugby*) to tackle, bring down

placenta [pla'tʃɛnta] SF placenta

placidamente [platʃida'mente] AVV peacefully

placidità [platʃidi'ta] SF calm, peacefulness

placido, a ['platʃido] AGG (*persona*) placid, calm; (*acque, vento, sera*) calm

plafond [pla'fɔ̃] SM INV (*Fin*) ceiling, upper limit

plafoniera [plafo'njɛra] SF ceiling light

plagiare [pla'dʒare] VT **1** (*copiare*) to plagiarize **2** (*Dir*: *influenzare*) to coerce

plagiario, ria, ri, rie [pla'dʒarjo] SM/F plagiarist

plagio, gi ['pladʒo] SM **1** (*di opera*) plagiarism **2** (*Dir*) duress

plaid [plɛd] SM INV (travelling) rug (*Brit*), lap robe (*Am*)

planare[1] [pla'nare] AGG planar

planare[2] [pla'nare] VI (*aus* **avere**) (*Aer*) to glide; (*Naut*) to skim

plancia, ce ['plantʃa] SF **1** (*Naut*) bridge; (: *passerella*) gangway **2** (*Aut*: *cruscotto*) dashboard

plancton ['plankton] SM INV plankton

planetario, ria, ri, rie [plane'tarjo] AGG planetary
■ SM **1** (*Astron*: *locale*) planetarium **2** (*Aut*) crown wheel

planimetria [planime'tria] SF (*scienza*) planimetry; (*disegno, pianta*) plan

planisfero [planis'fɛro] SM planisphere

plantare [plan'tare] SM orthopaedic (*Brit*) o orthopedic (*Am*) insole, arch support

plasma ['plazma] SM plasma

plasmare [plaz'mare] VT (*anche fig*) shape, to mould (*Brit*), mold (*Am*), shape

plasmatico, a, ci, che [plaz'matiko] AGG plasma *attr*

plasmolisi [plazmo'lizi] SF INV plasmolysis

plastica, che ['plastika] SF **1** (*materiale*) plastic; **di plastica** plastic *attr*; **un piatto di plastica** a plastic plate **2** (*Med*: *anche*: **chirurgia plastica**) plastic surgery; **farsi fare la plastica** to have plastic surgery **3** (*Arte*) plastic art

plasticamente [plastika'mente] AVV plastically

plasticità [plastitʃi'ta] SF (*Arte*) sculptural quality; (*duttilità*) plasticity

plastico, a, ci, che ['plastiko] AGG plastic; **in materiale plastico** plastic
■ SM **1** (*Topografia*) plastic model, relief model **2** (*esplosivo*) plastic explosive; **bomba al plastico** plastic bomb

plastificare [plastifi'kare] VT to coat with plastic

plastilina® [plasti'lina] SF plasticine®

platano ['platano] SM plane tree

platea [pla'tɛa] SF **1** (*Teatro*) stalls *pl* (*Brit*), orchestra (*Am*); (*pubblico*) audience; **un posto in platea** a seat in the stalls; **la platea ha applaudito** the audience applauded **2** (*Geol*) shelf

plateale [plate'ale] AGG (*gesto, atteggiamento*) theatrical

platealmente [plateal'mente] AVV theatrically

plateau [pla'to] SM INV (*Geog*) plateau, tableland

platino ['platino] SM platinum

Platone [pla'tone] SM Plato

platonicamente [platonika'mente] AVV platonically

platonico, a, ci, che [pla'tɔniko] AGG platonic
■ SM Platonist

platonismo [plato'nizmo] SM Platonism

plaudire [plau'dire] VI (*aus* **avere**) (*frm*): **plaudire a** (*progetto, iniziativa*) to applaud

plausibile [plau'zibile] AGG plausible

plausibilità [plauzibili'ta] SF plausibility

plauso ['plauzo] SM (*fig*) approbation, approval

Plauto ['plauto] SM Plautus

playback ['pleibæk] SM INV: **cantare in playback** to mime

playboy ['pleibɔi] SM INV playboy

playmaker ['pleimeikə] SM/F INV (*Sport*) playmaker

play-off ['plei'ɔf] SM INV (*Sport*) play-off

playstation [pleis'taʃon] SF INV Playstation >; ®

plebaglia [ple'baʎʎa] SF (*pegg*) rabble, riffraff *sg o pl*

plebe ['plɛbe] SF common people *pl*; (*pegg*) rabble, riffraff *sg o pl*

plebeo, a [ple'bɛo] AGG plebeian; (*volgare*) coarse, common
■ SM/F plebeian

plebiscito [plebiʃ'ʃito] SM plebiscite

plenariamente [plenarja'mente] AVV plenarily

plenario, ria, ri, rie [ple'narjo] AGG plenary; **in sessione plenaria** in plenary session

plenilunio, ni [pleni'lunjo] SM full moon

plenipotenziario, ria, ri, rie [plenipoten'tsjarjo] AGG, SM plenipotentiary
plenum ['plɛnum] SM INV plenum
pleonasmo [pleo'nazmo] SM pleonasm
pletora ['plɛtora] SF (*Med, fig*) plethora
plettro ['plettro] SM plectrum
pleura ['plɛura] SF (*Anat*) pleura
pleurico, a, ci, che ['plɛuriko] AGG pleural
pleurite [pleu'rite] SF pleurisy
plexiglas® [pleksi'glas] SM Perspex® (*Brit*), Plexiglas® (*Am*)
PLI [pi'ɛlle'i] SIGLA M (*Pol:* = **Partito Liberale Italiano**) *former political party*
plico, chi ['pliko] SM (*pacco*) parcel; **in plico a parte** under separate cover; **plico bomba** letter bomb
Plinio ['plinjo] SM: **Plinio il Giovane/il Vecchio** Pliny the Younger/the Elder
plissé [pli'se] AGG INV, SM INV = **plissettato**
plissettato, a [plisset'tato] AGG: **tessuto plissettato** plissé *attr*
■ SM plissé
plotone [plo'tone] SM (*Mil*) platoon; **plotone d'esecuzione** firing squad
plug-and-play [plagan'plei] AGG (*Inform*) plug-and-play
plug-in [pla'gin] AGG (*Inform*) plug-in
plumbeo, a ['plumbeo] AGG (*colore, cielo*) leaden
plurale [plu'rale] AGG plural
■ SM plural; **mettere al plurale** to put into the plural, pluralize
pluralis maiestatis [plu'ralis maies'tatis] SM: **il pluralis maiestatis** the royal "we"
pluralismo [plura'lizmo] SM pluralism
pluralista, i, e [plura'lista] SM/F pluralist
pluralistico, a, ci, che [plura'listiko] AGG pluralistic
pluralità [plurali'ta] SF plurality; (*maggioranza*) majority
pluricellulare [pluritʃellu'lare] AGG multicellular
pluridecorato, a [plurideko'rato] AGG (*Mil*) much-decorated
plurigemellare [pluridʒemel'lare] AGG: **parto plurigemellare** multiple birth
plurilaureato, a [plurilaure'ato] SM/F person with several degrees
plurimiliardario, ria, ri, rie [plurimiljar'darjo] AGG, SM/F multimillionaire
plurimilionario, ria, ri, rie [plurimiljo'narjo] AGG, SM/F multimillionaire
plurimo, a ['plurimo] AGG multiple
plusvalenza [pluzva'lɛntsa] SF capital gain
plusvalore [plusva'lore] SM (*Econ*) surplus (value)
Plutarco [plu'tarko] SM Plutarch
plutocrate [plu'tɔkrate] SM/F plutocrat
Plutone [plu'tone] SM (*Mitol, Astron*) Pluto
plutonico, a, ci, che [plu'tɔniko] AGG (*Geol*) plutonic
plutonio [plu'tɔnjo] SM plutonium
pluviale [plu'vjale] AGG rain *attr*
pluviometro [plu'vjɔmetro] SM rain gauge
PM [pi'ɛmme] SIGLA M (*Dir*) = *Pubblico Ministero*
■ ABBR (= **Polizia Militare**) MP (= *Military Police*)
pM [pi'ɛmme] ABBR = *peso molecolare*
PMI [piɛmme'i] SIGLA F INV: **Piccola e Media Impresa** SME (= *Small and Medium Enterprise*)
▷ www.confapi.org/
PN SIGLA = *Pordenone*
pneumatico, a, ci, che [pneu'matiko] AGG (*Tecn*) pneumatic; (*gonfiabile*) inflatable
■ SM (*Aut*) tyre (*Brit*), tire (*Am*); **pneumatico chiodato** studded tyre *o* tire; **pneumatico da neve** snow tyre *o* tire; **pneumatico rigenerato** remould
pneumotorace [pneumoto'ratʃe] SM pneumothorax
PNL [pi'ɛnne'ɛlle] SIGLA M (= **Prodotto Nazionale Lordo**) GNP (= *Gross National Product*)
PO SIGLA = *Prato*
■ ABBR = **Posta Ordinaria**
Po [pɔ] SM: **il Po** the Po
po' [pɔ] AVV, SM *vedi* **poco**
pochette [pɔ'ʃɛt] SF INV clutch bag
pochezza [po'kettsa] SF insufficiency, shortage; (*fig: meschinità*) meanness, smallness

poco, a, chi, che ['pɔko] **PAROLA CHIAVE**
■ AVV
1 (*piccola quantità*) little, *negazione* + much; **si accontenta di poco** he's easily satisfied; **c'è poco da ridere** there's nothing to laugh about; **guadagna poco** he doesn't earn much, he earns little; **dorme troppo poco** she doesn't get enough sleep
2 (*con aggettivo, avverbio*) (a) little, *negazione* + very; **sta poco bene** he's not very well; **è poco più alta di lui** she's a little *o* slightly taller than him; **è poco probabile** it's not very likely; **è poco socievole** he's not very sociable
3 (*tempo*): **poco dopo** shortly after(wards); **il film dura poco** the film doesn't last long; **poco fa** a short while *o* time ago; **fra poco** in a little while; **manca poco alla fine** it's almost *o* nearly finished, it's more or less finished; **poco prima** shortly before; **ci vediamo poco** we hardly ever see each other
4 **un po'** a little, a bit; **è un po' corto** it's a little *o* a bit short; **sono un po' stanco** I'm a bit tired; **zoppica un po'** he limps a bit, he has a slight limp; **arriverà fra un po'** he'll arrive shortly *o* in a little while; **un po' prima del solito** a little earlier than usual; **ha dormito un bel po'** he slept for quite a while; **fammi un po' vedere** let me have a look
5 (*fraseologia*): **(a) poco a poco** bit by bit, little by little; **a dir poco** to say the least; **eravamo in 30 a dir poco** there were at least 30 of us; **è una cosa da poco** it's nothing, it's of no importance; **una persona da poco** a worthless individual; **ha vinto di poco** he only just won; **poco male** never mind, it doesn't matter; **per poco non cadevo** I almost *o* nearly fell
■ AGG INDEF
1 (*quantità*) little, *negazione* + (very) much; (*numero*) few, *negazione* + (very) many; **poco denaro** little *o* not much money; **poco vino** little *o* not much wine; **poche persone** few *o* not many people; **poche idee** few *o* not many ideas; **c'era poca gente** there were only a few people; **è un tipo di poche parole** he's a man of few words; **a poco prezzo** at a low price, cheap; **con poca spesa** for a small outlay
2 (*in espressioni ellittiche: tempo*) a short time, a little while; (*: quantità*) (a) little; **ci vediamo fra poco** see you soon *o* shortly; **l'ha comprato per poco** he bought it cheap; **ne abbiamo ancora per poco** we'll only be a little longer; **basta poco per farlo contento** it doesn't take much to make him happy
■ PRON
1 (a) little; **c'è chi ha molto tempo e chi ne ha poco** there are those who have a lot of time and those who have little
2 (*persone*): **pochi, poche** few (people); **pochi la**

Pp

pensano come lui few people think as he does; **pochi di noi** few of us
■SM
1 little; **il poco che guadagno...** what little I earn ...; **vive del poco che ha** she lives on the little she has; *vedi anche* buono
2 **un po'** a little; **un po' di soldi** a little money; **un po' di pane** a little bread; **un po' di zucchero** a little sugar; **un po' di silenzio!** let's have a bit of quiet!; **ha un po' di mal di testa** he has a slight headache; **ha un po' di influenza** she has a touch of flu; **un bel po' di denaro** quite a lot of money, a tidy sum; **facciamo un po' per uno** let's do a bit each
3 **po' po': che po' po' di coraggio!** what courage!; **niente po' po' di meno che il presidente in persona!** no less than the president himself!

podalico, a, ci, che [po'daliko] AGG: **parto podalico** breech delivery
podere [po'dere] SM (*Agr*) farm
poderosamente [poderosa'mente] AVV with great strength
poderoso, a [pode'roso] AGG powerful
podestà [podes'ta] SM INV (*nel fascismo*) mayor, podestà
podio, di ['pɔdjo] SM (*gen*) podium, dais; (*Mus*) platform
podismo [po'dizmo] SM (*Sport: marcia*) walking; (*: corsa*) running
podista, i, e [po'dista] SM/F (*vedi sm*) walker; runner
poema, i [po'ɛma] SM poem; **conciato così sei un poema** (*iro*) you look a pretty sight like that; **è tutto un poema!** (*complicato*) it's a real palaver!
poemetto [poe'metto] SM (short) poem
poesia [poe'zia] SF (*Arte, produzione poetica*) poetry; (*singolo componimento*) poem; (*fig: di incontro*) magic; **una poesia di Foscolo** a poem by Foscolo; **la poesia e la prosa** poetry and prose; **scrivere poesie** to write poetry
poeta, i [po'ɛta] SM poet
poetare [poe'tare] VI (*aus* **avere**) to write poetry, write verse
poetessa [poe'tessa] SF poet(ess)
poetica [po'ɛtika] SF poetics *sg*
poeticamente [poetika'mente] AVV poetically
poeticizzare [poetitʃid'dzare] VT to poeticize
poetico, a, ci, che [po'ɛtiko] AGG poetic(al); **la produzione poetica di Dante** Dante's poetical works
poggiare [pod'dʒare] VT to lean, rest; (*posare*) to lay, place; (*mettere*) to put; **puoi poggiare il pacco sul tavolo** you can put the parcel on the table; **non poggiare i gomiti sulla tavola** don't put your elbows on the table; **poggia la scala al muro** lean the ladder against the wall; **poggiarsi a qc** to lean against sth; **si è dovuto poggiare al muro per sostenersi** he had to lean against the wall for support
■VI (*aus* **avere**) 1 (*anche fig*) to stand, rest 2 (*Naut*) to bear away
poggiatesta [poddʒa'tɛsta] SM INV (*Aut*) headrest
poggio, gi ['pɔddʒo] SM hill, hillock, knoll
poggiolo [pod'dʒɔlo] SM balcony
pogrom [pa'grom] SM INV pogrom
poi ['pɔi] AVV 1 (*gen*) then; (*più tardi*) later (on); (*alla fine*) finally, at last; **e poi cos'è successo?** and then what happened?; **e poi** (*inoltre*) and besides; **non ne ho voglia e poi sono stanco** I don't feel like it and what's more I'm tired; **devi poi sapere che...** you should also know that ...; **prima o poi** sooner or later; **poi te lo dico** I'll tell you later (on); **a poi** till later; **d'ora in poi** from now on; **da domani in poi** from tomorrow onwards 2 (*enfatico*): **lui, poi, non c'entra proprio** he simply doesn't come into it, it's nothing at all to do with him; **questa poi non me l'aspettavo** I just wasn't expecting this at all; **questa poi (è bella)!** (*iro*) that's a good one!
■SM: **il poi** the future; **pensare al poi** to think of the future
poiana [po'jana] SF buzzard
poiché [poi'ke] CONG since, as
pointer ['pɔintə] SM INV pointer (*dog*)
pois [pwa] SM INV (polka) dot; **a pois** spotted, dotted; **bianco a pois rossi** white with red dots
poker ['pɔker] SM INV poker; **un poker d'assi** four aces; **giocare a poker** to play poker
polacchini [polak'kini] SMPL high-laced boots
polacco, a, chi, che [po'lakko] AGG Polish
■SM/F (*persona*) Pole; **i polacchi** the Poles
■SM (*lingua*) Polish; **parli polacco?** do you speak Polish?
polare [po'lare] AGG polar; **la stella polare** the Pole Star
polarità [polari'ta] SF INV polarity
polarizzare [polarid'dzare] VT (*Fis*) to polarize; (*fig: attrarre*) to attract; **polarizzare la propria attenzione su** to focus one's attention on
▶ **polarizzarsi** VIP (*attenzione, sguardo*): **polarizzarsi su** to focus on
polarizzazione [polariddzat'tsjone] SF polarization
polca ['pɔlka] SF = **polka**
polemica, che [po'lɛmika] SF controversy, argument, polemic; **fare polemiche** to be contentious
polemicamente [polemika'mente] AVV contentiously; **perché devi sempre rispondere polemicamente?** why do you always have to argue the point?
polemico, a, ci, che [po'lɛmiko] AGG (*gen*) controversial, polemic(al); (*pegg*) contentious
polemista, i, e [pole'mista] SM/F polemicist; (*pegg*) contentious person
polemizzare [polemid'dzare] VI (*aus* **avere**) **polemizzare (su qc)** to argue (about sth)
polenta [po'lɛnta] SF (*Culin*) polenta; *sort of thick porridge made with maize flour*; (*fig: persona lenta*) slowcoach (*Brit*), slowpoke (*Am*)
polentone, a [polen'tone] SM/F slowcoach (*Brit*), slowpoke (*Am*)
polesano, a [pole'zano] AGG of *o* from Polesine (*area between the Po and the Adige*)
■SM/F inhabitant *o* native of Polesine
POLFER ['polfer] SIGLA F = **polizia ferroviaria**
poli... ['pɔli] PREF poly...
poliambulatorio, ri [poliambula'tɔrjo] SM (*Med*) ≈ health centre (*Brit*)
poliammide [poliam'mide] SF polyamide
poliammidico, a, ci, che [poliam'midiko] AGG polyamide *attr*
policlinico, ci [poli'kliniko] SM (*Med*) general hospital
policromatico, a, ci, che [polikro'matiko] AGG (*Arte, Fis*) polychromatic, polychromous
policromia [polikro'mia] SF polychromy
policromo, a [po'likromo] AGG many-coloured, polychrome
poliedrico, a, ci, che [poli'ɛdriko] AGG (*Mat*) polyhedral; (*fig*) multifaceted
poliedro [poli'ɛdro] SM (*Mat*) polyhedron
poliestere [poli'ɛstere] SM polyester

polietilene [polieti'lɛne] SM polyethylene
polifase [poli'faze] AGG (*Elettr*) multiphase
Polifemo [poli'femo] SM Polyphemus
polifonico, a, ci, che [poli'fɔniko] AGG polyphonic
poligamia [poliga'mia] SF polygamy
poligamo, a [po'ligamo] AGG polygamous
■ SM/F polygamist
poliglotta [poli'glɔtta] AGG, SM/F polyglot
poligonale [poligo'nale] AGG polygonal
poligono [po'ligono] SM **1** (*Mat*) polygon **2 poligono di tiro** rifle range
polimerizzazione [polimeriddzat'tsjone] SF polymerization
polimero [po'limero] SM polymer
Polinesia [poli'nɛzja] SF Polynesia
polinesiano, a [poline'zjano] AGG, SM/F Polynesian
■ SM (*lingua*) Polynesian
polio ['pɔljo] SF polio
poliomielite [poljomie'lite] SF polio(myelitis)
polipo ['pɔlipo] SM (*Zool, Med*) polyp
polipropilene [polipropi'lɛne] SM polypropylene
polisaccaride [polisak'karide] SM polysaccharide
polisemico, a, ci, che [poli'sɛmiko] AGG polysemous
polisillabo, a [poli'sillabo] AGG polysyllabic
■ SM polysyllable
polisportivo, a [polispor'tivo] AGG (*campo, società*) multisports *attr*
polistirolo [polisti'rɔlo] SM polystyrene
politecnico, a, ci, che [poli'tɛkniko] AGG polytechnic
■ SM *university institution providing courses in science, technology and engineering*
▷ www.polimi.it/
▷ www.polito.it/
▷ www.poliba.it/
politeismo [polite'izmo] AGG polytheism
politeistico, a, ci, che [polite'istiko] AGG polytheistic
politica, che [po'litika] SF **1** (*scienza, carriera*) politics *sg*; **si interessa di politica** he's interested in politics; **fare politica** (*militante*) to be a political activist; (*come professione*) to be in politics; **darsi alla politica** to go into politics **2** (*linea di condotta*) policy; (*modo di governare*) policies *pl*; **la politica del governo** the government's policies; **la politica economica del governo** the government's economic policy; **politica aziendale** company policy; **politica estera** foreign policy; **politica dei prezzi** prices policy; **politica dei redditi** incomes policy
politicamente [politika'mente] AVV politically; **politicamente corretto** politically correct
politicante [politi'kante] SM/F (*pegg*) petty politician
politichese [politi'kese] SM (*pegg*) political jargon
politicizzare [polititʃid'dzare] VT to politicize
politico, a, ci, che [po'litiko] AGG political; **la situazione politica** the political situation; **uomo politico** politician; **scienze politiche** political sciences; **elezioni politiche** parliamentary (*Brit*) *o* congressional (*Am*) election(s)
■ SM politician
politologo, gi [poli'tɔlogo] SM political analyst
politonale [polito'nale] AGG (*Mus*) polytonal
politrasfuso, a [politras'fuzo] SM/F *patient who has received more than one blood transfusion*
polittico, ci [po'littiko] SM polyptych
polivalente [poliva'lɛnte] AGG (*Chim*) polyvalent; (*fig*) multi-purpose
polizia [polit'tsia] SF **1** (*Amm*) police (force); (*poliziotti*) police *pl*; **è arrivata la polizia?** have the police arrived?; **chiama la polizia!** call the police!; **agente di polizia** policeman; **polizia ferroviaria** railway (*Brit*) *o* railroad (*Am*) police; **polizia fluviale** river police; **polizia giudiziaria** ≈ Criminal Investigation Department (*Brit*), ≈ Federal Bureau of Investigation (*Am*) **polizia sanitaria** health inspectorate; **polizia stradale** traffic police (*Brit*), state highway patrol (*Am*); **polizia tributaria** tax inspectorate **2** (*commissariato*) police station

POLIZIA DI STATO

The remit of the **polizia di stato** is to maintain public order, to uphold the law, and to prevent and investigate crime. This is a civilian branch of the police force; male and female officers perform similar duties. The **polizia di stato** reports to the Minister of the Interior.
▷ www.poliziadistato.it/pds/

poliziesco, a, schi, sche [polit'tsjesko] AGG (*indagine*) police *attr*; (*film, libro*) detective *attr*; (*pegg*: *modi*) bullying; **un film poliziesco** a detective film
poliziotto [polit'tsjɔtto] SM policeman; **poliziotto di quartiere** community policeman, local police officer
■ AGG INV: **donna poliziotto** policewoman; **cane poliziotto** police dog
polizza ['pɔlittsa] SF **1** (*Assicurazione*) policy; **polizza di assicurazione** insurance policy; **polizza casco** comprehensive insurance policy **2** (*Comm*) bill, voucher; **polizza di carico** bill of lading; **polizza di pegno** pawn ticket
polka ['pɔlka] SF polka
polla ['polla] SF (*sorgente*) spring
pollaio, ai [pol'lajo] SM (*edificio*) henhouse; (*recinto*) chicken run
pollaiolo, a [polla'jɔlo] SM/F poulterer (*Brit*), poultryman/woman
pollame [pol'lame] SM poultry
pollastra [pol'lastra] SF pullet; (*fam*: *ragazza*) chick, bird (*Brit*)
pollastro [pol'lastro] SM (*Zool*) cockerel, young cock; (*fig*: *persona ingenua*) sucker (*fam*)
polleria [polle'ria] SF poulterer's (shop) (*Brit*)
pollice ['pɔllitʃe] SM **1** (*Anat*) thumb; **avere il pollice verde** to have green fingers (*Brit*) *o* a green thumb (*Am*); **girarsi i pollici** to twiddle one's thumbs **2** (*unità di misura*) inch; **uno schermo a 17 pollici** a 17-inch screen
polline ['pɔlline] SM pollen; **sono allergico al polline** I suffer from hay fever
pollivendolo, a [polli'vendolo] SM/F poulterer (*Brit*), poultryman/woman
pollo ['pollo] SM **1** chicken; (*fig*: *persona ingenua*) sucker (*fam*) **2** (*fraseologia*): **conoscere i propri polli** to know who one is dealing with; **far ridere i polli** (*situazione, persona*) to be utterly ridiculous
pollone [pol'lone] SM (*Bot*) sucker
Polluce [pol'lutʃe] SM (*Mitol, Astron*) Pollux
polluzione [pollut'tsjone] SF (*Med*) pollution
polmonare [polmo'nare] AGG lung *attr*, pulmonary
polmone [pol'mone] SM lung; **avere buoni polmoni** to have a good pair of lungs; **gridare a pieni polmoni** to shout at the top of one's voice; **respirare a pieni polmoni** to take deep breaths, breathe deeply; **polmone d'acciaio** iron lung

Pp

polmonite [polmo'nite] SF (*Med*) pneumonia; **polmonite atipica** SARS
Polo ['pɔlo] SM the Pole (*centre right political grouping*)
polo[1] ['pɔlo] SM (*Fis, Mat, Geog*) pole; **abitiamo ai poli opposti della città** we live at opposite ends of the city; **il Polo nord** the North Pole; **il Polo sud** the South Pole
polo[2] ['pɔlo] SM (*Sport*) polo
polo[3] ['pɔlo] SF INV (*maglietta*) polo shirt
Polonia [po'lɔnja] SF Poland; **ti è piaciuta la Polonia?** did you like Poland?; **sei mai stato in Polonia?** have you ever been to Poland?
polpa ['polpa] SF **1** (*di frutto*) pulp, flesh **2** (*di carne*) lean meat
polpaccio, ci [pol'pattʃo] SM (*Anat*) calf
polpastrello [polpas'trɛllo] SM fingertip
polpetta [pol'petta] SF (*in tegame*) meatball; (*fritta*) rissole; **far polpette di qn** to make mincemeat of sb
polpettone [polpet'tone] SM (*Culin*) meatloaf; **questo film/libro è un polpettone** this film/book is far too long and involved
polpo ['polpo] SM octopus
polposo, a [pol'poso] AGG fleshy
polsino [pol'sino] SM cuff
polso ['polso] SM **1** (*Anat*) wrist; (*di camicia*) cuff; (*Med*: *pulsazione*) pulse; **ha un braccialetto al polso** she's got a bracelet on her wrist; **orologio da polso** wristwatch; **con le manette ai polsi** in handcuffs **2** (*fig*: *forza*) drive, vigour (*Brit*), vigor (*Am*); **avere polso** to be strong *o* firm; **un uomo di polso** a strong *o* firm man
POLSTRADA [pols'trada] SIGLA F (= **Polizia Stradale**) traffic police
poltiglia [pol'tiʎʎa] SF (*miscuglio*) paste, mush; (*cibo stracotto*) mush, pulp; (*di fango e neve*) slush; **il riso si era ridotto in poltiglia** the rice had cooked to a mush; **ridurre qn in poltiglia** to make mincemeat of sb
poltrire [pol'trire] VI (*aus* **avere**) (*rimanere a letto*) to have a lie(-in); (*oziare*) to loaf about, laze about, idle
poltrona [pol'trona] SF armchair; (*Teatro*) seat in the front stalls (*Brit*) *o* the orchestra (*Am*); **starsene in poltrona** (*fig*) to laze about; **aspirare alla poltrona di direttore generale** to aspire to the managing directorship; **poltrona letto** put-you-up
poltroncina [poltron'tʃina] SF (*Teatro*) seat in the back stalls (*Brit*) *o* the orchestra (*Am*)
poltrone, a [pol'trone] SM/F loafer, idler
■ AGG lazy, idle
poltronissima [poltro'nissima] SF (*Teatro*) front-row seat
polvere ['polvere] SF (*gen, sostanza ridotta minutissima*) powder, dust; (*pulviscolo*) dust; **c'è uno strato di polvere sul tavolo** there's a layer of dust on the table; **caffè in polvere** instant coffee; **latte in polvere** dried *o* powdered milk; **sapone in polvere** soap powder; **fare polvere** to raise clouds of dust; **ridurre in polvere** to pulverize; **buttare** *o* **gettare la polvere negli occhi a qn** (*fig*) to pull the wool over sb's eyes; **far mangiare la polvere a qn** (*fig*) to leave sb far behind; **polvere di ferro** iron filings *pl*; **polvere d'oro** gold dust; **polvere pirica** *o* **da sparo** gunpowder; **polvere di stelle** stardust; **polveri sottili** particulates
polveriera [polve'rjɛra] SF (*Mil*) (gun)powder magazine; (*fig*: *zona calda*) powder keg
polverificio, ci [polveri'fitʃo] SM explosives factory
polverina [polve'rina] SF (*gen, Med*) powder; (*gergo*: *cocaina*) snow
polverizzare [polverid'dzare] VT (*legno, ferro*) to pulverize; (*liquido*) to atomize; (*fig*: *nemico*) to crush, pulverize; (: *record*) to smash
▶ **polverizzarsi** VIP to turn to dust
polverizzatore [polveriddza'tore] SM (*Tecn*) atomizer
polverone [polve'rone] SM thick cloud of dust; **sollevare un polverone** (*fig*) to raise a stink
polveroso, a [polve'roso] AGG dusty, covered with dust
pomata [po'mata] SF ointment
pomello [po'mɛllo] SM **1** (*impugnatura*) knob **2** (*gota*) cheek
pomeridiano, a [pomeri'djano] AGG afternoon *attr*; **nelle ore pomeridiane** in the afternoon
pomeriggio, gi [pome'riddʒo] SM afternoon; **il** *o* **di pomeriggio** in the afternoon; **nel primo/tardo pomeriggio** in the early/late afternoon; **alle 2 di** *o* **del pomeriggio** at 2 o'clock in the afternoon, at 2 pm; **tutti i pomeriggi** every afternoon; **tutte le domeniche pomeriggio** every Sunday afternoon; **domani/sabato pomeriggio** tomorrow/Saturday afternoon
pomice ['pomitʃe] SF: **(pietra) pomice** pumice (stone)
pomiciare [pomi'tʃare] VI (*aus* **avere**) (*fam*: *sbaciucchiarsi*) to neck
pomiciata [pomi'tʃata] SF (*fam*): **farsi una pomiciata** to neck
pomo ['pomo] SM (*frutto*) apple; (*oggetto sferico*) knob; (*di sella*) pommel; **pomo d'Adamo** (*Anat*) Adam's apple; **pomo della discordia** (*Mitol*) apple of discord; (*fig*) bone of contention
pomodoro [pomo'dɔro] SM (*frutto*) tomato; (*pianta*) tomato plant; **spaghetti al pomodoro** spaghetti with tomato sauce
pompa[1] ['pompa] SF **1** (*fasto*) pomp (and ceremony); **mettersi in pompa magna** to get all dressed up; **accogliere qn in grande pompa** to roll out the red carpet for sb **2** **(impresa di) pompe funebri** undertaker's *sg*, funeral director's *sg* (*Brit*), funeral parlor *o* home (*Am*), mortician's (*Am*)
pompa[2] ['pompa] SF (*Tecn*) pump; **una pompa da bicicletta** a bicycle pump; **pompa antincendio** fire hose; **pompa di benzina** petrol (*Brit*) *o* gas (*Am*) pump; (*distributore*) filling *o* gas (*Am*) station; **pompa idraulica** hydraulic pump; (*Aut*: *dei freni*) master cylinder
pompare [pom'pare] VT to pump; (*estrarre*) to pump out; (*gonfiare d'aria*) to pump up; (*fig*: *esagerare*) to exaggerate, blow up; **devo pompare il materassino** I need to pump up my airbed
pompeiano, a [pompe'jano] AGG of *o* from Pompeii
■ SM/F inhabitant *o* native of Pompeii
pompelmo [pom'pɛlmo] SM (*frutto*) grapefruit; (*albero*) grapefruit (tree)
Pompeo [pom'pɛo] SM: **Pompeo Magno** Pompey the Great
pompiere [pom'pjɛre] SM fireman, firefighter; **fa il pompiere** he's a fireman; **i pompieri** the fire brigade; **chiamare i pompieri** to call the fire brigade (*Brit*) *o* fire department (*Am*)
pompon [pom'pɔn] SM INV pompom, pompon
pomposamente [pomposa'mente] AVV with great pomp
pomposo, a [pom'poso] AGG (*cerimonia*) full of pomp (and circumstance); (*fig*: *discorso, atteggiamento*) pompous
poncho ['pontʃo] SM INV poncho
ponderare [ponde'rare] VT to ponder (over), think over, consider carefully; **ponderare i pro ed i contro**

to weigh up the pros and cons; **fu una decisione ben ponderata** it was a carefully considered decision
ponderazione [ponderat'tsjone] SF thought, consideration
ponderoso, a [ponde'roso] AGG (*anche fig*) weighty
ponente [po'nɛnte] SM (*direzione*) west; (*vento*) west wind
pongo *ecc* ['pongo] VB *vedi* **porre**
poni *ecc* ['poni] VB *vedi* **porre**
ponte ['ponte] SM (*Edil, Med, Mil*) bridge; (*Naut*) deck; (: *anche*: **ponte di comando**) bridge; (*Aut*) axle; (*impalcatura*) scaffold; **è dell'altra parte del ponte** it's across the bridge; **vivere sotto i ponti** to be a tramp; **tagliare** *o* **rompere i ponti con qn** to break off relations with sb; **fare il ponte** to take the extra day off (*between 2 public holidays*); **abbiamo fatto un ponte di 3 giorni** we had 3 days off; **ponte aereo** airlift, air bridge (*Brit*); **ponte di barche** pontoon bridge; **ponte di coperta** (*Naut*) upper deck; **ponte levatoio** drawbridge; **ponte radio** radio link; **ponte (sollevatore)** (*Aut*) hydraulic ramp; **ponte sospeso** suspension bridge
■ AGG INV: **governo ponte** caretaker *o* interim government; **legge ponte** interim law
pontefice [pon'tefitʃe] SM (*Rel*) pontiff
ponticello [ponti'tʃɛllo] SM (*di occhiali, Mus*) bridge
pontificante [pontifi'kante] AGG (*fig*) pontificating
pontificare [pontifi'kare] VI (*aus* **avere**) (*anche fig*) to pontificate
pontificato [pontifi'kato] SM (*Rel*) papacy, pontificate
pontificio, cia, ci, cie [ponti'fitʃo] AGG pontifical, papal; **Stato pontificio** Papal State
pontile [pon'tile] SM jetty
pony ['pɔni] SM INV pony
pool [pu:l] SM INV (*consorzio*) consortium; (*organismo internazionale*) pool; (*di esperti, ricercatori*) team; (*antimafia, antidroga*) working party
pop [pɔp] AGG INV pop *attr*
popcorn ['pɔpkɔ:n] SM INV popcorn
popeline [pɔpə'lin] SF INV poplin
popò [po'pɔ] (*linguaggio infantile*) SM INV (*sedere*) botty
■ SF INV (*cacca*) pooh
popolano, a [popo'lano] AGG of the people, popular; **saggezza popolana** popular lore
■ SM/F man/woman of the people
popolare¹ [popo'lare] VT (*rendere abitato*) to populate
▶ **popolarsi** VIP (*diventare popolato*) to become populated; (*affollarsi*): **popolarsi di** to become crowded with
popolare² [popo'lare] AGG **1** (*gen, fig*) popular; (*quartiere, clientela*) working-class; **un cantante molto popolare** a very popular singer; **canzone popolare** folk song; **case popolari** council houses (*Brit*); **manifestazione popolare** mass demonstration; **repubblica popolare** people's republic **2** (*Pol*) of P.P.I.
■ SM/F (*Pol*) member (*o* supporter) of P.P.I.
popolarità [popolari'ta] SF popularity
popolarmente [popolar'mente] AVV popularly
popolato, a [popo'lato] AGG populated
popolazione [popolat'tsjone] SF population
popolino [popo'lino] SM (*pegg*): **il popolino** the masses *pl*, the common people
popolo ['pɔpolo] SM (*gen*) people; (*classe*): **il popolo** the (common) people; **il popolo italiano** the Italian people, the Italians *pl*; **il popolo della notte** clubbers; **il popolo di Seattle** *the anti-globalization movement*; **a furor di popolo** by popular acclaim
popoloso, a [popo'loso] AGG densely populated, populous
popone [po'pone] SM melon
poppa¹ ['poppa] SF (*Anat*) breast
poppa² ['poppa] SF (*Naut*) stern; **a poppa** aft, astern; **andare a poppa** to go aft; **andare col vento in poppa** to sail before the wind
poppante [pop'pante] SM/F unweaned infant; (*fig: inesperto*) whippersnapper
poppare [pop'pare] VT to suck
poppata [pop'pata] SF (*allattamento*) feed; **l'ora della poppata** feeding time
poppatoio, toi [poppa'tojo] SM (baby's) bottle, feeding bottle (*Brit*), baby bottle (*Am*)
poppiero, a [pop'pjɛro] AGG (*Naut*) after *attr*
populista, i, e [popu'lista] AGG populist
porcaio, ai [por'kajo] SM (*anche fig*) pigsty
porcaro [por'karo] SM swineherd
porcata [por'kata] SF (*libro, film ecc*) load of rubbish; **fare una porcata a qn** to play a dirty trick on sb
porcellana [portʃel'lana] SF porcelain, china; (*oggetto*) piece of porcelain
porcellino [portʃel'lino] SM piglet; **porcellino d'India** guinea pig
porcello, a [por'tʃɛllo] SM (*Zool*) piglet
■ SM/F (*pegg*) pig
porcellone, a [portʃel'lone] SM/F (*pegg*) pig
porcheria [porke'ria] SF (*gen*) dirt, muck, filth; (*azione disonesta*) dirty trick; (*oscenità*) obscenity; (*cosa fatta male*) (load of) rubbish *o* trash; **mangia un sacco di porcherie** he eats a lot of rubbish; **non si fanno queste porcherie!** you shouldn't behave like that!
porchetta [por'ketta] SF (*Culin*) roast sucking pig
porcile [por'tʃile] SM (*anche fig*) pigsty
porcino, a [por'tʃino] AGG of pigs, pork *attr*; **occhi porcini** (*fig*) piggy eyes
■ SM (*anche*: **fungo porcino**) cep
porco, a, ci, che ['pɔrko] SM (*Zool*) pig; (*Culin*) pork; **gettare le perle ai porci** (*fig*) to cast pearls before swine
■ SM/F (*pegg*) pig; **un vecchio porco** a dirty old man
■ AGG (*fam*): **porca miseria!, porco Giuda!** bloody hell! (*Brit*)
porcospino [porkos'pino] SM porcupine; (*fig: persona*): **è chiuso come un porcospino** he doesn't come out of his shell easily
pordenonese [pordeno'nese] AGG of *o* from Pordenone
■ SM/F inhabitant *o* native of Pordenone
porfido ['pɔrfido] SM porphyry
porgere ['pɔrdʒere] VT IRREG to hand, give; (*tendere*) to hold out; **porgere la mano a qn** to hold out one's hand to sb; (*fig*) to give sb a helping hand, lend sb a hand; **porgere l'altra guancia** to turn the other cheek; **porgere orecchio** *o* **ascolto** to pay attention, listen
porno ['pɔrno] (*fam*) AGG INV porno; **film porno** porn film (*Brit*) *o* movie (*Am*)
■ SM INV (*pornografia*) porn
pornodivo, a [porno'divo] SM/F porn star
pornofilm [porno'film] SM INV porn film (*Brit*) *o* movie (*Am*)
pornografia [pornogra'fia] SF pornography
pornograficamente [pornografika'mente] AVV pornographically

Pp

pornografico, a, ci, che [porno'grafiko] AGG pornographic
poro ['pɔro] SM *(Anat)* pore; *(forellino)* hole
poroso, a [po'roso] AGG porous
porpora ['porpora] AGG, SM *(colore)* crimson
■SF *(stoffa, simbolo)* purple
porporino, a [porpo'rino] AGG crimson
porre ['porre] VB IRREG
■VT **1** *(mettere)* to put; *(collocare)* to place; *(posare)* to lay (down), put (down); **porre le fondamenta di** *(edificio)* to lay the foundations of; **porre le basi di** *(fig)* to lay the foundations of, establish; **abbiamo posto le basi per una futura collaborazione** we have laid the foundations for future cooperation; **fu posto al comando del reggimento** he was placed in command of the regiment; **porre la propria fiducia in qn** to place one's trust in sb; **porre fine** *o* **termine a qc** to put an end *o* a stop to sth **2** *(condizioni)* to lay down, set out, state; *(problema)* to pose; *(questione)* to raise; **porre una domanda a qn** to ask sb a question, put a question to sb **3** *(supporre)* to suppose; **poniamo (il caso) che...** let's suppose that ...; **posto che...** supposing that ..., on the assumption that ...;
▶ **porsi** VR: **porsi in cammino** to set out *o* forth; **porsi al lavoro** to get down to work; **porsi a sedere** to sit down; **porsi in salvo** to save o.s.
porro ['pɔrro] SM **1** *(Bot)* leek; **una minestra di porri** leek soup **2** *(Med)* wart
porsi *ecc* ['pɔrsi] VB *vedi* **porgere**
porta ['pɔrta] SF *(gen)* door; *(soglia)* doorstep; *(apertura)* doorway; *(di fortezza, Sci)* gate; *(Calcio, Rugby)* goal; *(Inform)* port; *(di città)* **porte** SFPL gates; **chiudi la porta, per favore** close the door, please; **a tre/cinque porte** *(automobile)* three/five door; **abitare porta a porta con qn** to live right next door to sb; **vendere porta a porta** to sell from door to door; **vendita porta a porta** door-to-door selling; **indicare la porta a qn** *(fig)* to show sb the door; **mettere qn alla porta** *(anche fig)* to throw sb out; **lo hanno messo alla porta** they threw him out; **prendere la porta ed andarsene** to walk out the door; **sbattere** *o* **chiudere la porta in faccia a qn** *(anche fig)* to slam the door in sb's face; **suonare alla porta** to ring the (door)bell; **suonano alla porta** there's somebody at the door; **trovare tutte le porte chiuse** *(fig)* to find the way barred; **a porte chiuse** *(processo)* in camera; **cacciamo questo problema dalla porta e rientra dalla finestra** there's no getting rid of this problem; **esce dalla porta e rientra dalla finestra** there's no getting rid of him; **l'inverno è alle porte** winter is upon us; **tirare in porta** *(Sport)* to take a shot at goal; **porta blindata** reinforced door; **porta parallela** *(Inform)* parallel port; **porta seriale** *(Inform)* serial port; **porta di servizio** tradesman's entrance; **porta di sicurezza** emergency exit; **porta stagna** watertight door; **porta USB** *(Inform)* USB port
portabagagli [portaba'gaʎʎi] SM INV **1** *(facchino)* porter **2** *(Aut)* boot *(Brit)*, trunk *(Am)*; *(: sul tetto)* roof rack; *(in treno, corriera: rete portabagagli)* luggage rack
portabandiera [portaban'djɛra] SM/F INV *(anche fig)* standard bearer
portabiancheria [portabjanke'ria] SM INV *(anche:* **cesto portabiancheria***)* laundry *o* linen basket, hamper *(Am)*
portabicchiere [portabik'kjɛre] SM *(da bagno)* toothmug holder
portabiciclette [portabitʃi'klette] SM INV bicycle rack *(on car)*
portabilità [portabili'ta] SF: **portabilità del numero telefonico** *ability to keep the same (mobile) phone number when changing providers*
portabiti [por'tabiti] SM INV clothes hanger
portaborse [porta'borse] SM/F INV *(pegg)* lackey
portabottiglie [portabot'tiʎʎe] SM INV *(scaffale)* bottle rack; *(per trasporto)* bottle carrier; *(da tavola)* wine cooler
portacarte [porta'karte] SM INV paper holder, paper rack
portacassette [portakas'sette] SM INV cassette holder
porta-CD [portatʃi'di] SM INV CD rack; *(astuccio)* CD holder
portacellulare [portatʃellu'lare] SM mobile (phone) case
portacenere [porta'tʃenere] SM INV ashtray
portachiavi [porta'kjavi] SM INV *(anello)* key ring; *(astuccio)* key case
portacinture [portatʃin'ture] SM INV belt rack
portacipria [porta'tʃipria] SM INV (powder) compact
portacravatte [portakra'vatte] SM INV tie rack
portadocumenti [portadoku'menti] SM INV file, folder
■AGG INV: **valigetta portadocumenti** briefcase
portaerei [porta'ɛrei] SF INV *(anche:* **nave portaerei***)* aircraft carrier
■SM INV *(aereo)* aircraft transporter
portaferiti [portafe'riti] SM INV *(Mil)* stretcher-bearer
portafiammiferi [portafjam'miferi] SM INV match holder
portafinestra [portafi'nɛstra] SF *(pl* **portefinestre***)* French window *o* door *(Am)*
portafiori [porta'fjori] SM INV flower stand
portafoglio, gli [porta'fɔʎʎo] SM **1** *(per soldi)* wallet, billfold *(Am)*; *(cartella)* briefcase; **mettere mano al portafoglio** *(fig)* to put one's hand in one's pocket; **gonna a portafoglio** wrapover skirt **2** *(Fin, Pol)* portfolio; **ministro senza portafoglio** minister without portfolio; **portafoglio titoli** investment portfolio
portafortuna [portafor'tuna] SM INV *(amuleto)* lucky charm; *(persona, animale)* mascot
■AGG INV lucky
portafotografie [portafotogra'fie] SM INV photo(graph) frame
portaghiaccio [porta'gjattʃo] SM INV *(anche:* **secchiello portaghiaccio***)* ice bucket
portagioie [porta'dʒɔje], **portagioielli** [portadʒo'jɛlli] SM INV jewellery *(Brit)* *o* jewelry *(Am)* box
portalampada [porta'lampada] SM INV bulb socket
portale [por'tale] SM *(Archit, Inform)* portal
portalettere [porta'lɛttere] SM/F INV postman/postwoman *(Brit)*, mailman/mailwoman *(Am)*
portamatite [portama'tite] SM INV *(anche:* **astuccio portamatite***)* pencil case
portamento [porta'mento] SM bearing, carriage
portamonete [portamo'nete] SM INV purse *(Brit)*, change purse *(Am)*
portante [por'tante] AGG *(muro)* load-bearing, supporting
portantina [portan'tina] SF **1** *(sedia)* sedan chair **2** *(barella)* stretcher
portaoggetti [portaod'dʒɛtti] AGG INV: **vano portaoggetti** *(Aut)* glove compartment

portaombrelli [portaom'brɛlli] SM INV umbrella stand
portaordini [porta'ordini] SM INV *(Mil)* dispatch rider
portapacchi [porta'pakki] SM INV *(di moto, automobile)* luggage rack
portapenne [porta'penne] SM INV pen holder; *(astuccio)* pencil case
portapillole [porta'pillole] SM INV pillbox
portaposate [portapo'sate] SM INV *(anche:* **vassoio portaposate***)* cutlery *o* flatware *(Am)* tray
portare [por'tare] VT
1 *(sostenere, sorreggere: peso, bambino, pacco)* to carry; **portava il pacco sottobraccio** he was carrying the parcel under his arm; **questa macchina porta 4 persone** this car can carry 4 people; **puoi portarmi la valigia?** can you carry my case for me?; **si porta dietro un sacco di roba** he carries masses of stuff round with him; **portare via** to take away; *(rubare)* to take; **schedare questi documenti porta via molto tempo** filing these documents takes (up) a lot of time; **porta bene i suoi anni** he's wearing well, he doesn't look his age; **ognuno ha la propria croce da portare** we all have our cross to bear
2 *(consegnare, recare)*: **portare qc (a qn)** to take (*o* bring) sth (to sb); **porta il libro in cucina!** *(vicino a chi parla)* bring the book into the kitchen!; *(lontano da chi parla)* take the book into the kitchen!; **portami un bicchiere!** bring me a glass!; **portalo qui** bring it here; **porta questa lettera a Lucia** take this letter to Lucia; **posso portarli a casa?** can I bring (*o* take) them home?; **portare qc alla bocca** to lift *o* put sth to one's lips; **il suo intervento ha portato dei vantaggi** his intervention has brought certain advantages; **portare fortuna/sfortuna a qn** to bring (good) luck/bad luck to sb
3 *(condurre)* to take; *(sogg: strada)* to take, lead; *(fig: indurre)*: **portare qn a (fare) qc** to lead sb to (do) sth; **dove porta questa strada?** where does this road lead?, where does this road take you?; **portare i bambini a spasso** to take the children for a walk; **sta portando i bambini a scuola** she's taking the children to school; **il vento ci sta portando al largo** the wind is carrying us out to sea; **dove ti porterà tutto questo?** where will all this lead you?; **portare qn alla disperazione** to drive sb to despair; **stiamo portando avanti il discorso sul disarmo** we are pursuing the topic of disarmament
4 *(indossare: scarpe, vestito, occhiali)* to wear, have on; **portava un bel vestito** she was wearing a beautiful dress; **non porto più queste scarpe** I don't wear these shoes any more; **porta i capelli lunghi** he wears his hair long, he has long hair
5 *(avere: nome, titolo, firma)* to have, bear; *(fig: sentimenti)* to bear; **porta il nome di suo nonno** he is called after his grandfather; **il documento porta la tua firma** the document has *o* bears your signature; **Firenze porta ancora i segni dell'alluvione** Florence still bears the signs of the flood; **non gli porto rancore** I don't bear him a grudge
▶ **portarsi** VIP *(recarsi)* to go; **la polizia si è portata sul luogo del disastro** the police went to the scene of the disaster; **portarsi al tiro** *(Calcio, Basket) to move into a scoring position*
portaritratti [portari'tratti] SM INV photo(graph) frame
portariviste [portari'viste] SM INV magazine rack
portarotolo [porta'rɔtolo] SM INV *(da bagno)* toilet paper holder; *(da cucina)* kitchen *(Brit)* *o* paper *(Am)* towel holder
portasapone [portasa'pone] SM INV soap dish
portascarpe [portas'karpe] SM INV shoe rack
portascì [portaʃ'ʃi] SM INV *(Aut)* ski rack
portasciugamani [portaʃʃuga'mani] SM INV towel rail
portascopino [portasko'pino] SM INV lavatory brush holder *(Brit)*
portasigarette [portasiga'rette] SM INV cigarette case
portaspazzolino [portaspattso'lino] SM INV toothbrush holder
portaspilli [portas'pilli] SM INV pincushion
portassegni [portas'seɲɲi] SM INV chequebook *(Brit)* *o* checkbook *(Am)* holder
portata [por'tata] SF **1** *(Culin)* course; **un pranzo di 7 portate** a 7-course lunch; **la portata principale** the main course **2** *(di veicolo)* carrying (*o* loading) capacity **3** *(di arma)* range; *(fig: limite)* scope, capability; **a/fuori portata (di)** within/out of reach (of); **a portata di mano** within (arm's) reach; **alla portata di tutti** *(conoscenza)* within everybody's grasp; *(prezzo)* within everybody's means **4** *(fig: importanza)* importance, significance; **di grande portata** of great importance **5** *(volume d'acqua)* (rate of) flow
portatile [por'tatile] AGG portable; **una TV portatile** a portable TV
portato, a [por'tato] AGG *(incline)*: **portato a** inclined *o* apt to; **essere portato per** *(studio, matematica)* to have a bent *o* a gift for; **è portato per le lingue** he has a gift for languages
portatore, trice [porta'tore] SM/F **1** *(di messaggio, assegno)* bearer; **pagabile al portatore** payable to the bearer **2** *(Med)* carrier; **portatore di handicap** disabled person; **portatore sano** (symptomless) carrier **3** *(Alpinismo)* porter
portatovagliolo [portatovaʎ'ʎɔlo] SM *(anello)* napkin ring; *(busta)* napkin holder
portauova [porta'wɔva], **portauovo** [porta'wɔvo] SM INV egg cup; *(scatola)* egg box
portavoce [porta'votʃe] SM/F INV spokesman/ spokeswoman, spokesperson
porte-enfant ['pɔrtɑ̃'fɑ̃] SM INV carrycot *(Brit)*, portacrib® *(Am)*
portello [por'tɛllo] SM *(di portone, aereo)* door; *(Naut)* hatch
portellone [portel'lone] SM *(Aer, Naut)* hold door; *(Aut)* tailgate
portento [por'tɛnto] SM wonder, marvel
portentosamente [portentosa'mente] AVV wonderfully
portentoso, a [porten'toso] AGG wonderful, marvellous *(Brit)*, marvelous *(Am)*
portfolio ['pɔ:tfouljou] SM INV *(Pubblicità)* portfolio
porticato [porti'kato] SM portico
portico ['pɔrtiko] SM *(Archit)* porch, portico; *(riparo)* lean-to; **i portici** the arcades
portiera [por'tjɛra] SF *(Aut)* door
portiere, a [por'tjɛre] SM/F **1** *(portinaio)* concierge, caretaker, janitor *(Am)*; *(di hotel)* porter **2** *(Sport)* goalkeeper
portinaio, naia, nai, naie [porti'najo] SM/F concierge, caretaker, janitor *(Am)*
portineria [portine'ria] SF caretaker's lodge
porto[1] ['pɔrto] SM port, harbour *(Brit)*, harbor *(Am)*; **un porto riparato** a sheltered harbo(u)r; **andare** *o*

Pp

giungere in porto (*fig*) to come to a successful conclusion; **condurre qc in porto** (*fig*) to bring sth to a successful conclusion; **questa casa è un porto di mare** people are always coming and going in this house; **porto fluviale** river port; **porto franco** free port; **porto marittimo** seaport; **porto militare** naval base; **porto di scalo** port of call

porto[2] ['pɔrto] SM **1** (*Comm: spesa di trasporto*) carriage; **franco di porto** carriage free **2 porto d'armi** gun licence (*Brit*) *o* license (*Am*)

porto[3] ['pɔrto] SM INV (*vino*) port (wine)

porto[4], **a** ['pɔrto] PP *di* **porgere**

Portogallo [porto'gallo] SM Portugal; **ti è piaciuto il Portogallo?** did you like Portugal?; **sei mai stato in Portogallo?** have you ever been to Portugal?

portoghese [porto'gese] AGG Portuguese
■ SM/F **1** (*abitante, nativo*) Portuguese *inv*; **i portoghesi** the Portuguese **2** (*spettatore senza biglietto*) gate-crasher
■ SM (*lingua*) Portuguese

portolano [porto'lano] SM (*Naut*) pilot book

portone [por'tone] SM main entrance

portoricano, a [portori'kano] AGG, SM/F Puerto Rican

Portorico [porto'riko] SM Puerto Rico

portuale [portu'ale] AGG port *attr*, dock *attr*, harbour *attr* (*Brit*), harbor *attr* (*Am*); **lavoratori portuali** dockers, dock workers, longshoremen (*Am*)
■ SM docker, dock worker, longshoreman (*Am*)

porzione [por'tsjone] SF (*gen*) portion, share; (*di cibo*) helping, portion; **una porzione abbondante** a big portion

posa ['pɔsa] SF **1** (*atteggiamento, di modello*) pose; (*: affettato*) posing; **teatro di posa** photographic studio; **mettersi in posa** to pose; **assumere pose da grandonna** to act the lady; **è tutta una posa** it's just an act **2** (*Fot*) exposure; **un rullino a 24 pose** a 24 exposure film **3** (*riposo*): **lavorare senza posa** to work without a break **4** (*collocazione*) laying, placing

posacavi [posa'kavi] SF INV (*anche:* **nave posacavi**) cable ship

posacenere [posa'tʃenere] SM INV ashtray

posamine [posa'mine] SM O F INV minelayer

posapiano [posa'pjano] SM/F INV (*scherz*) slowcoach (*Brit*), slowpoke (*Am*)

posare [po'sare] VT (*gen*) to put (down); (*piatto, vassoio*) to lay *o* put (down); (*fondamenta, cavo*) to lay; **ha posato la penna sul tavolo** he put the pen on the table; **posare gli occhi su** to gaze at; (*con mire particolari*) to set one'sights on; **posalo contro il muro** stand *o* put it against the wall
■ VI (*aus* **avere**) **1** (*ponte, edificio, teoria*): **posare su** to rest on **2** (*Fot, Arte*) to pose, sit; (*atteggiarsi*) to pose; **posa a grande scrittore** (*fig*) he poses as a great writer;
▶ **posarsi** VIP (*polvere*) to settle; (*uccello*) to alight; (*ape, mosca*) to land; (*aereo*) to land, touch down; (*sguardo*) to settle, fix

posata [po'sata] SF piece of cutlery *o* flatware (*Am*); **posate** SFPL cutlery *sg*, flatware *sg*

posatamente [posata'mente] AVV composedly

posatezza [posa'tettsa] SF (*di persona*) composure; (*di discorso*) balanced nature

posato, a [po'sato] AGG (*persona*) steady, level-headed; (*comportamento*) steady, sober; (*discorso*) balanced

poscia ['pɔʃʃa] AVV (*letter*) thereafter

poscritto [pos'kritto] SM postscript

posdomani [pozdo'mani] AVV (*letter*) the day after tomorrow

Poseidone [pozei'done] SM Poseidon

posi *ecc* ['posi] VB *vedi* **porre**

positiva [pozi'tiva] SF (*Fot*) (positive) print

positivamente [pozitiva'mente] AVV positively; (*rispondere*) in the affirmative, affirmatively

positivismo [poziti'vizmo] SM positivism

positivo, a [pozi'tivo] AGG, SM positive

posizionare [pozittsjo'nare] VT to position

posizionatore [pozittsjona'tore] SM (*Tecn*) positioning device

posizione [pozit'tsjone] SF (*gen, fig*) position; **una posizione scomoda** an uncomfortable position; **prendere posizione a favore di/contro** to take up a position in favour (*Brit*) *o* favor (*Am*) of/against; **devi prendere una posizione** you must take a stand; **farsi una posizione** to make one's way in the world; **si è fatto una posizione** he's done well; **è arrivato in prima/seconda posizione** (*Sport*) he arrived first/second; **posizione di attesa** (*Tennis*) ready position; **posizione dei piedi** stance; **luci di posizione** (*Aut*) sidelights (*Brit*), parking lights (*Am*)

posologia [pozolo'dʒia] SF dosage, directions *pl* for use

posporre [pos'porre] VT IRREG **1** (*rimandare*) to postpone, defer **2** (*subordinare*) to subordinate, place after

posposto, a [pos'posto] PP *di* **posporre**

posse ['pɔsse] SF INV (*Mus*) *1990s Italian pop groups who based their music on rap*

possedere [posse'dere] VT IRREG (*gen*) to have; (*qualità, virtù, fortuna*) to possess; (*casa, terreno*) to own; (*diploma*) to hold; (*sogg: ira*) to possess; **quasi tutti possiedono una macchina** most people have a car; **possiede una casa in campagna** she owns a house in the country; **era posseduto dal demone** he was possessed by the Devil

possedimento [possedi'mento] SM **1** (*proprietà terriera*) property, estate **2** (*di uno Stato, territorio*) possession

posseditrice [possedi'tritʃe] SF *vedi* **possessore**

possente [pos'sɛnte] AGG strong, powerful

possentemente [possente'mente] AVV powerfully, mightily

possessivo, a [posses'sivo] AGG (*gen, Gramm*) possessive

possesso [pos'sɛsso] SM **1** (*gen, Dir*) possession; **essere in possesso di qc** to be in possession of sth; **prendere possesso di qc** to take possession of sth; **entrare in possesso dell'eredità** to come into one's inheritance **2** (*possedimenti*): **possessi** SMPL property *sg*

possessore [posses'sore] **posseditrice** [possedi'tritʃe] SM/F possessor, owner; (*di carica, diploma*) holder

possibile [pos'sibile] AGG (*gen*) possible; (*fattibile: progetto, piano*) feasible; **non mi sarà possibile farlo** I won't be able to do it; **pensi che sia possibile?** do you think it's possible?; **è possibile che arrivi più tardi** he may *o* might arrive later; **cerca di venir presto, se possibile** try to come early, if possible *o* if you can; **ha trovato tutte le scuse possibili e immaginabili per non venire** he came up with every excuse imaginable for not coming; **il più presto possibile** as soon as possible; **vieni prima possibile** come as soon as possible; **fallo meglio possibile** do it as best you can; **porta meno roba possibile** bring as little as possible; **non è possibile!** (*irrealizzabile*) it's not possible!; (*falso*) that can't be true!; **possibile?** (*sorpresa*) well I never!

■ SM: **fare il possibile** to do everything possible *o* everything in one's power; **nei limiti del possibile** as far as possible

possibilista, i, e [possibi'lista] AGG: **essere possibilista** to keep an open mind

possibilità [possibili'ta] SF INV (*gen*) possibility; **c'è sempre la possibilità che cambi idea** there's always the possibility *o* chance that he'll change his mind; **ci sono varie possibilità** there are various possibilities; **avere la possibilità di fare qc** (*facoltà*) to be in a position to do sth; (*opportunità*) to have the opportunity to do; **non ha avuto la possibilità di andare all'università** he didn't have the opportunity to go to university; **non ha possibilità di salvezza** there's no hope of escape for him; **nella mia posizione non ho avuto la possibilità di aiutarlo** in my position I couldn't assist him *o* I had no means of assisting him **2** (*mezzi*): **possibilità** SFPL means; **vivere secondo le proprie possibilità** (*finanziarie*) to live according to one's means; **nei limiti delle nostre possibilità** in so far as we can

possibilmente [possibil'mente] AVV if possible; **ti telefono possibilmente domani** I'll phone you tomorrow if I can

LO SAPEVI...?
possibilmente non si traduce mai con la parola inglese ***possibly***

possidente [possi'dɛnte] SM/F property owner, landowner

possiedo *ecc* [pos'sjɛdo] VB *vedi* **possedere**

posso *ecc* ['pɔsso] VB *vedi* **potere**

post... [pɔst] PREF post...

posta ['pɔsta] SF **1** (*corrispondenza*) post (*Brit*), mail (*Am*); (*servizio*) postal service, mail service, post; (*ufficio*) post office; **poste** SFPL (*amministrazione*) post office; **c'è posta per me?** are there any letters for me?, is there any post *o* mail for me?; **perché non lo mandi per posta?** why don't you send it by post *o* mail?; **sto andando alla posta** I'm going to the post office; **impiegato delle poste** post office clerk; **piccola posta** (*su giornale*) letters to the editor, letters page; **posta aerea** airmail; **posta elettronica** electronic mail, e-mail; **posta ordinaria** ≈ second-class post *o* mail **posta prioritaria** first class (post); **Poste e Telecomunicazioni** *postal and telecommunications service*; **ministro delle Poste e Telecomunicazioni** Postmaster General **2** (*Giochi: somma in palio*) stake(s); **la posta in gioco è troppo alta** (*fig*) there's too much at stake **3** (*Caccia*) hide (*Brit*), blind (*Am*); **fare la posta a qn** (*fig*) to lie in wait for sb **4** (*apposta*): **a bella posta** on purpose

POSTE

In addition to postal services, the Italian Post Office provides banking, financial and commercial services to private individuals and businesses throughout the country. Post offices are normally open in the morning and afternoon.

▷ www.poste.it/

postacelere [posta'tʃɛlere] SF ≈ special delivery

postagiro [posta'dʒiro] SM post office cheque (*Brit*) *o* check (*Am*), postal giro (*Brit*)

postale [pos'tale] AGG (*servizio, vaglia*) postal *attr* (*Brit*), mail *attr* (*Am*); (*casella, impiegato*) post office *attr*; (*nave, treno*) mail *attr*; **timbro postale** postmark

■ SM (*treno*) mail train; (*nave*) mail boat; (*furgone*) mail van

postazione [postat'tsjone] SF (*Mil*) emplacement

postbellico, a, ci, che [post'bɛlliko] AGG postwar *attr*

postdatare [postda'tare] VT to postdate

posteggiare [posted'dʒare] VT, VI (*aus* **avere**) to park

posteggiatore, trice [posteddʒa'tore] SM/F car-park attendant (*Brit*), parking-lot attendant (*Am*)

posteggio, gi [pos'teddʒo] SM **1** car park (*Brit*), parking lot (*Am*); **un posteggio gratuito** a free car park; **non riesco a trovare posteggio** I can't find a parking space; **posteggio custodito** attended car park *o* parking lot; **posteggio di taxi** taxi rank (*Brit*), taxi stand (*Am*) **2** (*di rivenditore*) pitch

Postel ['pɔstel] SIGLA M (= **servizio pubblico di Posta Elettronica**) *business service of the Italian Post Office that sends out letters and emails on behalf of companies*

postelegrafonico, a, ci, che [postelegra'fɔniko] AGG postal and telecommunications *attr*

poster ['pɔster] SM INV poster

posteri ['pɔsteri] SMPL posterity *sg*; **i nostri posteri** our descendants

posteriore [poste'rjore] AGG **1** (*dietro: parte di oggetto*) back *attr*, rear *attr*; (*zampe*) hind *attr*; **il sedile posteriore** the back seat **2** (*tempo*) later; **questi avvenimenti sono posteriori alla mia partenza** these events occurred after my departure

■ SM (*euf fam: sedere*) behind, bottom

posteriori [poste'rjori] **a posteriori** AGG INV after the event (*dopo sostantivo*)

■ AVV looking back

posteriormente [posterjor'mente] AVV **1** (*nella parte posteriore*) behind, at the back **2** (*in un periodo successivo*) later, subsequently; **posteriormente a** subsequent to

posterità [posteri'ta] SF posterity

posticcio, a, ci, ce [pos'tittʃo] AGG (*capelli, barba*) false

■ SM hairpiece

posticipare [postitʃi'pare] VT to defer, postpone; **posticipare di 3 giorni** to postpone for 3 days; **la riunione è stata posticipata a sabato** the meeting has been postponed until Saturday

posticipo [pos'titʃipo] SM (*Sport*) *deferred match*

postilla [pos'tilla] SF marginal note

postimpressionismo [postimpressjo'nizmo] SM post-impressionism

post-industriale [postindus'trjale] AGG post-industrial

post-industrialismo [postindustrja'lizmo] SM post-industrialism

postino, a [pos'tino] SM/F postman/postwoman (*Brit*), mailman/mailwoman (*Am*)

postmoderno, a [postmo'dɛrno] AGG post-modern

posto¹, a ['posto] PP *di* **porre**

posto² ['pɔsto] SM

1 (*luogo*) place; **è un posto magnifico** it's a beautiful place; **non è un posto adatto ai bambini** it's no place for children; **sul posto** on the spot; **i pompieri sono accorsi sul posto** the firemen rushed to the spot; **lo faremo sul posto** *o* **quando saremo sul posto** we'll do it when we get there; **la gente del posto** the local people; **posto di polizia** police station; **posto telefonico pubblico** public telephone; **posto di villeggiatura** holiday (*Brit*) *o* tourist spot, resort

2 (*spazio libero*) room, space; (*sedile: al teatro, in treno*) seat; (*di parcheggio*) space; **non c'è più posto in macchina** there's no more room in the car; **fate posto!** make way!; **prender posto** to take a seat; **ci sono 20 posti**

Pp

letto in quell'albergo they can sleep 20 in that hotel; **vorrei prenotare due posti** I'd like to book two seats; **vai pure al posto** (*scolaro*) go and sit down; **mi tieni il posto in fila?** will you keep my place in the queue?; **una macchina a 5 posti** a 5-seater car; **posti in piedi** (*Teatro, in autobus*) standing room; **posto a sedere** seat
3 (*impiego*) job, post; **ha un posto di segretaria** she works as *o* has a job as a secretary, she has a secretarial post; **posto di lavoro** job
4 (*posizione in classifica*): **primo/secondo posto** first/ second place; **arrivare al primo posto** to come first; **è arrivato al primo posto** he came first
5 (*Mil*) post; **tutti ai posti di combattimento!** action stations!; **posto di blocco** (*di polizia*) roadblock; (*alla frontiera*) frontier post
6 (*fraseologia*): **al posto di** in place of, instead of; **c'è un film al posto della partita** there's a film in place of the match; **andrò io al suo posto** I'll go instead of him; **l'hanno assunto al posto tuo** they employed him instead of you; **al posto tuo ci andrei** I'd go if I were you; **essere a posto** (*in ordine*: *stanza*) to be tidy; (: *persona*) to be neat and tidy; (*fig*: *questione*) to be settled; (: *persona*) to be OK; **tutto a posto?** is everything OK?; **è gente a posto** they are very respectable (people); **mettere a posto** (*riordinare*) to tidy (up), put in order; (*faccende*: *sistemare*) to straighten out; **metti a posto la tua camera** tidy your room; **rimetti il libro al suo posto** put the book back in its place; **mettere a posto qn** to sort sb out; **sa stare al suo posto** he knows his place; **tenere la lingua a posto** to hold one's tongue; **tieni le mani a posto!** keep your hands to yourself!; **per me non ha la testa tanto a posto!** I don't think he's all there!; **sarebbe ora che mettessi la testa a posto** it's time you got yourself sorted out

postoperatorio, ria, ri, rie [postopera'tɔrjo] AGG (*Med*) postoperative

post partum [post 'partum] SM *period after giving birth* ■ AGG (*dolore, depressione*) postnatal

postribolo [pos'tribolo] SM (*letter*) brothel

postscriptum [post'skriptum] SM INV postscript

postulare [postu'lare] VT (*Filosofia*) to postulate

postulato [postu'lato] SM (*Mat, Filosofia*) postulate

postumo, a ['pɔstumo] AGG posthumous; (*tardivo*) belated
■ **postumi** SMPL (*conseguenze*) consequences, after-effects; **soffrire i postumi della sbornia** to have a hangover

potabile [po'tabile] AGG drinkable; **acqua potabile** drinking water

potare [po'tare] VT (*albero da frutta*) to prune; (*siepe*) to trim

potassio [po'tassjo] SM potassium

potatura [pota'tura] SF pruning

potente [po'tɛnte] AGG (*gen*) powerful; (*nazione*) strong; (*efficace*: *medicina, veleno*) potent, strong; (*argomenti*) potent, forceful; **un motore potente** a powerful engine; **è potente all'interno dell'azienda** he has a lot of influence in the company
■ SMPL: **i potenti** the mighty, the powerful

potentemente [potente'mente] AVV with force

potentino, a [poten'tino] AGG of *o* from Potenza
■ SM/F inhabitant *o* native of Potenza

Potenza [po'tɛntsa] SF Potenza

potenza [po'tɛntsa] SF **1** (*potere, influenza*) power, influence; (*forza*: *fisica, psicologica*) strength; (*efficacia*: *di medicina, veleno*) potency; (*di argomenti, onde, pugni, armi*) force; **la potenza della stampa** the power of the press; **le Grandi Potenze** the Great Powers; **potenza militare** military might *o* strength **2** (*Fis, Mat*) power; **all'ennesima potenza** to the nth degree; **è un idiota all'ennesima potenza** he's a complete and utter idiot

potenziale [poten'tsjale] AGG, SM potential

potenzialmente [potentsjal'mente] AVV potentially; **potenzialmente potrebbe fare molto di più** he has the potential to do far more

potenziamento [potentsja'mento] SM development

potenziare [poten'tsjare] VT to develop

potenziometro [poten'tsjɔmetro] SM potentiometer

potere[1] [po'tere] SM (*gen*) power; **una lotta per il potere** a power struggle; **avere il potere di fare qc** (*capacità*) to have the power *o* ability to do sth; (*autorità*) to have the authority *o* power to do sth; **ha il potere di rovinare sempre tutto** he always manages to ruin everything; **il quarto potere** (*stampa*) the fourth estate; **non ho nessun potere su di lui** I have no power *o* influence over him; **essere al potere** (*Pol*) to be in power *o* in office; **potere d'acquisto** purchasing power; **potere esecutivo** executive power

potere[2] [po'tere] VB IRREG AUS (*nei tempi composti prende l'ausiliare del verbo che accompagna*) **1** (*possibilità, capacità*) can; (*sogg*: *persona*) can, to be able to; **non posso venire** I can't come; **non è potuto venire** he couldn't come, he was unable to come; **potresti aprire la finestra?** could you open the window?; **non potrò venire domani** I won't be able to come tomorrow; **dovresti potercela fare da solo** you should be able to do it by yourself; **non potrà mai farlo da solo** he'll never be able to do it alone; **non ho potuto farlo** I couldn't *o* wasn't able *o* was unable to do it; **come hai potuto fare una cosa simile?** how could you do a thing like that?; **a più non posso** (*correre*) as fast as one can; (*urlare*) as loud as one can **2** (*permesso*) can, may; **posso?** may I?; **posso entrare?** can *o* may I come in?; **potrei parlarti?** could I have a word with you?; **si può sapere dove sei stato?** where on earth have you been?; **si può visitare il castello tutti i giorni dell'anno** you can visit the castle any day of the year
3 (*eventualità*): **può anche esser vero** it may *o* might *o* could even be true; **può aver avuto un incidente** he may have had an accident; **può darsi che non venga** he may not *o* might not come; **può essere che non voglia** he may not *o* might not want to; **può accadere di tutto** anything can happen; **potrebbe avere trent'anni** he must be about thirty; **si può fare** it can be done; **può darsi** perhaps; **pensi di andarci? – può darsi** do you think you'll go? – perhaps **4** (*augurio*): **potessimo trovare un po' di pace!** if only we could get a little peace! **5** (*rimprovero*): **potresti almeno ringraziare!** you could *o* might at least say thank you!; **avresti potuto dirmelo!** you could *o* might have told me!
■ VT IRREG: **puoi molto per me** you can do a lot for me; **non ha potuto niente** he could do nothing; **non ne posso più!** I can't take any more!

potestà [potes'ta] SF INV (*Dir*: *potere*) power, authority

potrò *ecc* [po'trɔ] VB *vedi* **potere**

poveraccio, a, ci, ce [pove'rattʃo] SM/F poor devil

poveramente [povera'mente] AVV (*vestito*) poorly, shabbily; (*arredato*) poorly; **vivere poveramente** to live in poverty

povero, a ['pɔvero] AGG **1** (*gen*) poor; (*stile, scusa*) weak; (*raccolto*) poor, scanty; (*vegetazione*) sparse; (*vestito*) plain; (*stanza*) bare; **sono molto poveri** they're very poor;

povero di lacking in, having little; **minerale povero di ferro** ore with a low iron content; **aria povera di ossigeno** air low in oxygen; **paese povero di risorse** country short of *o* lacking in resources **2** (*fraseologia*): **essere povero in canna** to be as poor as a church mouse; **povero illuso!** poor fool!; **povera piccola!** poor little thing!; **sei un povero stupido!** you're a stupid fool!; **povera me!** poor me!; **in parole povere** in plain language; **povero di spirito** half-wit; **povero te se lo fai!** just you dare!; **il mio povero marito** my poor (late) husband
■ SM/F poor man/woman; **i poveri** the poor

povertà [pover'ta] SF (*vedi agg*) poverty; weakness; scantiness; sparseness

pozione [pot'tsjone] SF potion

pozza ['pottsa] SF (*pozzanghera*) puddle; **una pozza di sangue** a pool of blood

pozzanghera [pot'tsangera] SF puddle

pozzetto [pot'tsetto] SM **1** (*di fognatura*) shaft **2** (*Naut*) well-deck

pozzo ['pottso] SM (*di acqua, petrolio*) well; (*di miniera*) shaft; (*cava: di carbone*) pit; **essere un pozzo di scienza** to be a walking encyclopaedia *o* a mine of information; **essere un pozzo senza fondo** (*ghiottone*) to be a bottomless pit; **pozzo nero** cesspit; **pozzo petrolifero** oil well

p.p. ABBR (= per procura) pp

pp. ABBR (= pagine) pp

PPI [pipi'i] SIGLA M (*Pol:* = **Partito Popolare Italiano**) *party originating from DC*

PP.TT. ABBR = Poste e Telecomunicazioni

PR [pi'erre] SIGLA = *Parma*
■ SIGLA M (*Pol*) = *Partito Radicale*
■ ABBR **1** = piano regolatore **2** = procuratore della Repubblica

PRA [pra] SIGLA M (= **Pubblico Registro Automobilistico**) ≈ DVLA (*Brit:* = *Driver and Vehicle Licensing Agency*

Praga ['praga] SF Prague

pragmatico, a, ci, che [prag'matiko] AGG pragmatic

pralina [pra'lina] SF praline

prammatica [pram'matika] SF custom; **essere di prammatica** to be customary

prammatico, a, ci, che [pram'matiko] AGG pragmatic

pranoterapeuta [pranotera'pɛuta] SM/F faith healer

pranoterapia [pranotera'pia] SF faith healing

pranzare [pran'dzare] VI (*aus* **avere**) to (have) lunch; **abbiamo appena pranzato** we've just had lunch; **pranzare fuori** to go out for lunch; **siamo andati a pranzare fuori** we went out for lunch

pranzetto [pran'dzetto] SM: **un bel pranzetto** a lovely little meal

pranzo ['prandzo] SM (*a mezzogiorno*) lunch; **vieni a pranzo da me?** will you come and have lunch with me?; **pranzo di lavoro** business lunch; **pranzo di nozze** wedding breakfast

prassi ['prassi] SF normal procedure

prataiolo [prata'jɔlo] SM field mushroom

prateria [prate'ria] SF prairie

pratese [pra'tese] AGG of *o* from Prato
■ SM/F inhabitant *o* native of Prato

pratica, che ['pratika] SF **1** (*attività*) practice; **la pratica e la teoria** practice and theory; **in pratica** (*praticamente*) in practice; **mettere in pratica qc** to put sth into practice; **ho messo in pratica i tuoi consigli** I have acted on your advice; **cercate di mettere in pratica questa idea** try to put this idea into practice **2** (*esperienza*) (practical) experience; (*conoscenza*) knowledge, familiarity; (*tirocinio*) training; **far pratica presso un avvocato** to be articled to a solicitor (*Brit*) *o* lawyer (*Am*); **acquistare pratica** to gain experience; **ha fatto pratica presso un altro falegname** he was trained by another carpenter; **devi solo fare un po' di pratica** you only need a bit of practice; **non ho molta pratica di queste cose** I haven't got much experience in these things **3** (*Amm: incartamento*) file, dossier; (: *affare*) matter, case; **può cercarmi quella pratica?** can you get that file for me?; **fare le pratiche per** to do the paperwork for **4** (*usanza*) practice; **pratica restrittiva** restrictive practice; **pratiche illecite** (*abortive*) dishonest practices; **pratiche religiose** religious practices

praticabile [prati'kabile] AGG (*progetto*) practicable, feasible; (*luogo*) passable, practicable

praticamente [pratika'mente] AVV **1** (*quasi*) practically, almost **2** (*in modo pratico*) in a practical way, practically

praticante [prati'kante] AGG practising (*Brit*), practicing (*Am*)
■ SM/F apprentice, trainee; (*Rel*) (regular) churchgoer

praticare [prati'kare] VT **1** (*esercitare: arte, medicina*) to practise (*Brit*), practice (*Am*); (*Sport: calcio, tennis*) to play; (: *nuoto, scherma*) to go in for, do; **pratica molti sport** he does a lot of different sports **2** (*frequentare: persona*) to associate with, mix with; (: *luogo*) to frequent **3** (*eseguire: apertura, incisione*) to make; **praticare uno sconto** to give a discount

praticità [pratitʃi'ta] SF practicality, practicalness; **per praticità** for practicality's sake

pratico, a, ci, che ['pratiko] AGG **1** (*non teorico, realista*) practical; **avere senso pratico** to be practical; **all'atto pratico** in practice **2** (*comodo: gen*) practical; (: *strumento*) handy; **un metodo pratico** a practical method; **un aggeggio molto pratico** a very handy tool; **mi è più pratico venire di pomeriggio** it's more convenient for me to come in the afternoon; **è pratico avere i negozi così vicino** it's handy *o* convenient to have the shops so near **3** **pratico di** (*esperto*) experienced *o* skilled in; (*familiare*) familiar with; **è pratico di motori** he's good with engines; **è pratico del mestiere** he knows his trade; **è pratica del luogo** she knows the place well; **non sono pratica di queste parti** I don't know this area very well

prato ['prato] SM meadow; (*di giardino*) lawn; **prato all'inglese** lawn

preaffrancato, a [preaffran'kato] AGG (*busta*) pre-franked

preallarme [preal'larme] SM warning (signal)

Prealpi [pre'alpi] SFPL: **le Prealpi** (the) Pre-Alps

prealpino, a [preal'pino] AGG of the Pre-Alps

preambolo [pre'ambolo] SM preamble; **senza tanti preamboli** without beating about (*Brit*) *o* around (*Am*) the bush

preannunciare [preannun'tʃare], **preannunziare** [preannun'tsjare] VT to give advance notice of; **le nubi preannunziavano la tempesta** the clouds heralded the storm

preannuncio [prean'nuntʃo], **preannunzio** [prean'nuntsjo] SM advance warning

preavvisare [preavvi'zare] VT to give advance notice of

preavviso [preav'vizo] SM (advance) notice; (*Dir*) notice; **senza preavviso** without notice; **3 giorni di**

Pp

preavviso 3 days' notice; **telefonata con preavviso** personal *o* person-to-person call

prebellico, a, ci, che [pre'bɛlliko] AGG prewar *attr*

precariamente [prekarja'mente] AVV precariously

precariato [preka'rjato] SM temporary employment

precarietà [prekarje'ta] SF precariousness

precario, ria, ri, rie [pre'karjo] AGG **1** precarious; **in precarie condizioni economiche** in a precarious financial state **2** (*Scol*) temporary, without tenure ■SM/F (*Scol*) temporary member of staff

precauzionale [prekauttsjo'nale] AGG precautionary

precauzione [prekaut'tsjone] SF **1** (*cautela*) caution, care **2** (*misura*) precaution; **prendere precauzioni** to take precautions

precedente [pretʃe'dɛnte] AGG previous; **il giorno precedente** the previous day, the day before; **il discorso/film precedente** the previous *o* preceding speech/film ■SM precedent; **senza precedenti** unprecedented; **precedenti penali** (*Dir*) criminal record *sg*

precedentemente [pretʃedente'mente] AVV previously, before

precedenza [pretʃe'dɛntsa] SF **1** (*priorità*) priority, precedence; **dare precedenza assoluta a qc** to give sth top priority **2** (*Aut*): **avere la precedenza** to have right of way; **dare la precedenza** to give way **3** **in precedenza** (*precedentemente*) previously, before

precedere [pre'tʃɛdere] VT to precede, go (*o* come) before

precessione [pretʃes'sjone] SF (*Astron*) precession

precettare [pretʃet'tare] VT (*Mil*) to call up (*Brit*), draft (*Am*); (*scioperanti*) to order back to work (*via an injunction*)

precettazione [pretʃettat'tsjone] SF (*di scioperanti*) labour (*Brit*) *o* labor (*Am*) injunction (*calling off industrial action*)

precetto [pre'tʃɛtto] SM (*gen*) precept; (*Mil*) call-up papers *pl* (*Brit*), draft notice (*Am*)

precettore [pretʃet'tore] SM (private) tutor

precipitare [pretʃipi'tare] VT (*gettare dall'alto in basso*) to hurl down, fling down; (*fig: affrettare*) to hurry, rush; **precipitare una decisione** to make a hasty decision; **non precipitiamo le cose** let's not rush *o* precipitate things ■VI (*aus* **essere**) **1** (*cadere*) fall (headlong); (: *aereo*) to crash; **precipitare da una rupe/in un burrone** to fall off a cliff/down a ravine; **la situazione sta precipitando** the situation is getting out of control **2** (*Chim*) to precipitate
▶ **precipitarsi** VIP (*affrettarsi*) to rush
▶ **precipitarsi** VR (*gettarsi*) **precipitarsi da, in** to hurl *o* fling o.s. from, into

precipitato, a [pretʃipi'tato] AGG hasty ■SM (*Chim*) precipitate

precipitazione [pretʃipitat'tsjone] SF (*Meteor*) precipitation; (*fig*) haste; **con precipitazione** hastily

precipitevolmente [pretʃipitevol'mente], **precipitosamente** [pretʃipitosa'mente] AVV hastily

precipitoso, a [pretʃipi'toso] AGG (*fig: affrettato*) hasty, rushed; (: *avventato*) rash, reckless; **è un po' troppo precipitoso** he's a bit too rash

precipizio, zi [pretʃi'pittsjo] SM precipice; **cadere da un precipizio** to fall over a precipice; **scogli a precipizio sul mare** cliffs rising sheer from the sea; **essere sull'orlo del precipizio** (*fig*) to be on the edge of a precipice; **correre a precipizio** (*fig*) to run headlong

precipuo, a [pre'tʃipuo] AGG main, principal

precisamente [pretʃiza'mente] AVV (*gen*) precisely; (*con esattezza*) exactly; **è precisamente quello che intendevo** that's precisely what I meant

precisare [pretʃi'zare] VT to clarify; (*spiegare*) to explain (in detail); **vi preciseremo la data in seguito** we'll let you know the exact date later; **tengo a precisare che...** I must point out that ...; **vorrei precisare che...** I'd like to point out that ...

precisazione [pretʃizat'tsjone] SF clarification

precisione [pretʃi'zjone] SF (*esattezza*) precision; (*accuratezza*) accuracy; **ci vuole molta precisione** great accuracy is needed; **strumenti di precisione** precision instruments

preciso, a [pre'tʃizo] AGG **1** (*esatto*) precise; (*accurato*) accurate, precise; (*ben determinato: ordine, idee, piano*) precise, definite; **in quel preciso istante** at that precise *o* very moment; **queste sono le sue precise parole** these were his very words; **sono le 4 precise** it's exactly 4 o'clock; **non ho un'idea precisa di come funzioni** I don't know precisely how it works; **è molto preciso nel suo lavoro** he's very careful in his work **2** (*uguale*): **2 vestiti precisi** 2 dresses exactly the same; **il tuo cappello è preciso al mio** your hat is exactly the same as *o* identical to mine

precludere [pre'kludere] VT IRREG to preclude

precluso, a [pre'kluzo] PP *di* **precludere**

precoce [pre'kɔtʃe] AGG (*stagione*) early; (*bambino*) precocious; (*vecchiaia*) premature; (*morte*) untimely; (*decisione*) hasty, premature

precocemente [prekotʃe'mente] AVV (*maturare: bambino*) precociously; (: *frutta*) too early

precocità [prekotʃi'ta] SF (*di morte*) untimeliness; (*di bambino*) precociousness, precocity

precompresso, a [prekom'prɛsso] AGG (*Edil*) prestressed

preconcetto [prekon'tʃɛtto] AGG preconceived ■SM preconceived idea, prejudice

preconfezionare [prekonfettsjo'nare] VT to prepack(age)

preconfezionato, a [prekonfettsjo'nato] AGG prepacked, prepackaged

precorrere [pre'korrere] VT IRREG to anticipate; **precorrere i tempi** to be ahead of one's time

precorritore, trice [prekorri'tore] SM/F precursor, forerunner

precorso, a [pre'korso] PP *di* **precorrere**

precotto, a [pre'kɔtto] AGG precooked

precursore [prekur'sore] SM precursor, forerunner

preda ['prɛda] SF (*animale, fig*) prey; (*bottino*) booty; **uccello da preda** bird of prey; **essere preda di** to fall prey to; **essere in preda a** (*paura, terrore*) to be prey to; **era in preda all'ira** he was beside himself with rage; **era in preda al panico** he was in a panic, he was panicking

predare [pre'dare] VT to plunder

predatore, trice [preda'tore] AGG predatory ■SM/F (*Zool*) predator; (*predone*) plunderer

predecessore, a [predetʃes'sore] SM/F predecessor

predefinito, a [predefi'nito] AGG (*Inform*) preset

predella [pre'dɛlla] SF (*di cattedra*) platform, dais; (*di altare*) predella, altar-step

predellino [predel'lino] SM (*di vettura*) step, footboard

predestinare [predesti'nare] VT to predestine

predestinazione [predestinat'tsjone] SF predestination

predetto, a [pre'detto] PP *di* **predire** ■AGG aforesaid, aforementioned

predica, che ['prɛdika] SF (*Rel*) sermon; (*fig*) lecture, talking-to; **fare una predica** to preach a sermon; **fare una predica a qn** (*fig*) to give sb a lecture *o* a talking-to

predicare [predi'kare] VT to preach
■ VI (*aus* **avere**) (*anche fig*) to preach; **predica bene e razzola male** he doesn't practise what he preaches

predicativo, a [predika'tivo] AGG predicative

predicato [predi'kato] SM (*Gramm*) predicate; **in funzione di predicato** predicatively

predicatore [predika'tore] SM preacher

predicazione [predikat'tsjone] SF preaching

predicozzo [predi'kɔttso] SM (*fam*) lecture, talking-to; **fare un predicozzo a qn** to lecture sb

prediletto, a [predi'lɛtto] PP *di* **prediligere**
■ AGG (*figlio, allievo*) favourite (*Brit*), favorite (*Am*); (*amico*) best, closest
■ SM/F favourite (*Brit*), favorite (*Am*); **il prediletto della mamma** mummy's pet

predilezione [predilet'tsjone] SF partiality, predilection, fondness; **avere una predilezione per qc/qn** to be partial to sth/fond of sb

prediligere [predi'lidʒere] VT IRREG to prefer, have a preference *o* a predilection for; **queste sono le piante che prediligo** these are the plants I like best

predire [pre'dire] VT IRREG to predict, foretell; **aveva predetto che sarebbe successo** he had predicted it would happen; **predire il futuro** to tell *o* predict the future

predisporre [predis'porre] VB IRREG
■ VT to get ready, prepare; **predisporre qn a qc** to prepare sb for sth;
▶ **predisporsi** VR: **predisporsi a qc** to prepare o.s. for sth

predisposizione [predisposit'tsjone] SF (*Med*) predisposition; (*attitudine*) bent, aptitude; **avere predisposizione alla musica** to have a bent *o* gift for music

predisposto, a [predis'posto] PP *di* **predisporre**
■ AGG (*gen*) prepared; **le misure predisposte per prevenire gli incidenti stradali...** the measures which have been drawn up to prevent road accidents ...; **predisposto alle malattie** (*persona*) prone to illness

predizione [predit'tsjone] SF prediction

predominante [predomi'nante] AGG predominant

predominare [predomi'nare] VI (*aus* **avere**) (*prevalere*) to predominate; (*eccellere*) to excel

predominio [predo'minjo] SM (*il prevalere*) predominance; (*supremazia*) supremacy; (*dominio*) domination; (: *fig*) sway; **avere il predominio** (*prevalere*) to be predominant

predone [pre'done] SM marauder, plunderer

preelettorale [peeletto'rale] AGG pre-election

preesistente [preezis'tɛnte] AGG pre-existent

preesistenza [preezis'tɛntsa] SF pre-existence

preesistere [pree'zistere] VI IRREG (*aus* **essere**) to pre-exist

preesistito, a [preezis'tito] PP *di* **preesistere**

prefabbricato, a [prefabbri'kato] AGG (*Edil*) prefabricated
■ SM prefab, prefabricated house

prefazione [prefat'tsjone] SF preface, foreword

preferenza [prefe'rɛntsa] SF preference; **di preferenza** preferably, by preference; **a preferenza di** rather than; **dare la preferenza a qn/qc** to prefer sb/sth; **non ho preferenze** I have no preference either way, I don't mind; **qui non si fanno preferenze** there is no favouritism here

preferenziale [preferen'tsjale] AGG preferential; **corsia preferenziale** (*Aut*) bus and taxi lane; (*fig*) fast track

preferibile [prefe'ribile] AGG: **preferibile (a)** preferable (to), better (than); **sarebbe preferibile andarsene** it would be better if we left

preferibilmente [preferibil'mente] AVV preferably

preferire [prefe'rire] VT to prefer, like better; **preferisco la città alla campagna** I prefer the town to the countryside; **preferisce spendere i suoi soldi in vestiti** he prefers to spend his money on clothes; **preferirei lavorare a casa** I'd rather work at home; **preferisco non parlarne** I'd rather not talk about it; **preferirei non farlo** I'd rather not do it, I'd prefer not to do it; **preferirei morire piuttosto che...** I'd rather die than ...; **cosa preferisci, tè o caffè?** what would you like, tea or coffee?; **preferire il caffè al tè** to prefer coffee to tea, like coffee better than tea; **preferirei un'insalata** I'd rather have a salad

preferito, a [prefe'rito] AGG, SM/F favourite

prefettizio, zia, zi, zie [prefet'tittsjo] AGG prefectorial

prefetto [pre'fɛtto] SM prefect

prefettura [prefet'tura] SF prefecture

prefiggere [pre'fiddʒere] VT IRREG: **prefiggersi qc** (*scopo, meta*) to set o.s. sth

prefigurare [prefigu'rare] VT (*simboleggiare*) to foreshadow; (*prevedere*) to foresee

prefigurazione [prefigurat'tsjone] SF prefiguration

prefissare [prefis'sare] VT to establish in advance

prefisso, a [pre'fisso] PP *di* **prefiggere**
■ SM (*Telec*) dialling (*Brit*) *o* dial (*Am*) code; (*Gramm*) prefix; **qual è il prefisso di Londra?** what's the code for London?

pregare [pre'gare] VT (*Rel*) to pray to; (*supplicare*) to beg; (*chiedere*): **stava pregando** she was praying; **pregare qn di fare qc** to ask sb to do sth; **l'ho pregata di venire** I asked her to come; **i passeggeri sono pregati di...** passengers are requested to ...; **farsi pregare** to need coaxing *o* persuading; **si fa pregare un po' troppo** she plays hard to get; **non si fa pregare due volte** he doesn't wait to be asked twice; **ti prego!** please!; **ti prego, lasciami in pace** please leave me alone; **la prego, stia comodo** please don't get up

pregevole [pre'dʒevole] AGG (*persona, azione*) praiseworthy; (*oggetto, opera*) valuable

pregherò *ecc* [prege'rɔ] VB *vedi* **pregare**

preghiera [pre'gjɛra] SF (*Rel*) prayer; (*richiesta*) request; (*supplica*) plea, entreaty

pregiarsi [pre'dʒarsi] VR (*frm*): **pregiarsi di fare qc** to be honoured to do sth; **mi pregio di farle sapere che...** I am pleased *o* honoured to inform you that ...

pregiatamente [predʒata'mente] AVV (*lavorato, intarsiato*) finely

pregiatissimo, a [predʒa'tissimo] AGG (*in lettere*): **pregiatissimo Signor G. Agelli** G. Agelli, Esq(uire)

pregiato, a [pre'dʒato] AGG (*opera*) valuable; (*tessuto*) fine; (*valuta*) strong; **un tappeto pregiato** a valuable carpet; **vino pregiato** vintage wine

pregio, gi ['prɛdʒo] SM (*valore*) worth, value; (*qualità*) (good) quality, merit; (*frm: stima*) esteem, regard; **avere molti pregi** (*persona*) to have a lot of good qualities; **i pregi artistici di un'opera** the artistic merit of a work; **il pregio di questo sistema è...** the merit of this system is ...; **i pregi e i difetti** the good points and the bad points; **oggetto di pregio** valuable object

Pp

pregiudicare [predʒudi'kare] VT (*compromettere*): **pregiudicare qc** to jeopardize sth, put sth in jeopardy, prejudice sth; **pregiudicare la propria salute** to endanger one's health
pregiudicato, a [predʒudi'kato] SM/F (*Dir*) person with a criminal record
pregiudiziale [predʒudit'tsjale] SF precondition
pregiudizio, zi [predʒu'dittsjo] SM **1** (*opinione errata*) prejudice; (*superstizione*) superstition; **avere dei pregiudizi contro** *o* **nei confronti di qn** to be prejudiced *o* biased against sb; **è un pregiudizio largamente diffuso** it's a widely held superstition; **pregiudizio razziale** racial prejudice **2** (*danno*) harm *no pl*; **essere di pregiudizio a** to be detrimental to; **con pregiudizio della sua salute** to the detriment of his health
Preg.mo ABBR = pregiatissimo
pregnante [preɲ'ɲante] AGG (*fig: frasi, parole*) pregnant, meaningful
pregno, a ['preɲɲo] AGG **1** (*gravido: animale*) pregnant **2** **pregno di** (*odio, passione*) filled with, full of
prego ['prɛgo] ESCL (*a chi ringrazia*) don't mention it!, you're welcome!, not at all!; (*invitando qn ad accomodarsi*) please sit down!; (*invitando qn ad andare prima*) after you!; **prego, si accomodi** (*entri*) please come in; (*si sieda*) please take a seat; **posso prenderlo? — prego!** can I take it? — please do!; **prego?** pardon?, sorry? (*Brit*)
pregustare [pregus'tare] VT to look forward to; **pregustava il piacere della vendetta** he savoured the idea of vengeance
pre-industriale [preindus'trjale] AGG pre-industrial
preistoria [preis'tɔrja] SF prehistory; **fin dalla preistoria** from time immemorial
preistorico, a, ci, che [preis'tɔriko] AGG prehistoric; (*fig: scherz*) antediluvian
prelato [pre'lato] SM prelate
prelavaggio [prela'vaddʒo] SM prewash
prelazione [prelat'tsjone] SF (*Dir*) pre-emption; **avere il diritto di prelazione su qc** to have the first option on sth
prelevamento [preleva'mento] SM (*Banca*) withdrawal; (*di merce*) picking up, collection
prelevare [prele'vare] VT (*Banca*) to withdraw; (*campione di sangue*) to take; (*merce*) to collect, to pick up; (*sogg: polizia*) to arrest; **vorrei prelevare 150 sterline** I'd like to withdraw 150 pounds, please
prelibatamente [prelibata'mente] AVV deliciously
prelibato, a [preli'bato] AGG delicious
prelievo [pre'ljɛvo] SM (*Banca*) withdrawal; (*di merce*) collection; (*di tasse*) levying; **fare un prelievo di sangue** to take a blood sample
preliminare [prelimi'nare] AGG preliminary; **preliminari** SMPL preliminaries; (*in rapporto sessuale*) foreplay *sg*
preludere [pre'ludere] VI IRREG (*aus* **avere**) **preludere a** **1** (*preannunciare: crisi, guerra, temporale*) to herald, be a sign of **2** (*introdurre: dibattito*) to introduce, be a prelude to
preludio, di [pre'ludjo] SM (*Mus, fig*) prelude; (*introduzione*) introduction
preluso, a [pre'luzo] PP *di* **preludere**
pre-maman [pre ma'mã] AGG INV maternity *attr*
■ SM INV maternity dress
prematrimoniale [prematrimo'njale] AGG premarital
prematuramente [prematura'mente] AVV prematurely; **è morto prematuramente** he died before his time
prematuro, a [prema'turo] AGG (*gen*) premature; (*morte*) untimely
■ SM/F premature baby
premeditare [premedi'tare] VT to premeditate, plan; **omicidio premeditato** premeditated murder
premeditatamente [premeditata'mente] AVV with premeditation
premeditazione [premeditat'tsjone] SF (*Dir*) premeditation; **con premeditazione** with intent
premere ['prɛmere] VT (*gen*) to press; **premere il grilletto** to pull the trigger; **premi forte!** press hard!
■ VI (*aus* **avere**) **1** **premere su** (*gen*) to press on; (*pedale*) to press down on; (*fig*) to put pressure on **2** (*fig: stare a cuore*): **è una faccenda che mi preme molto** it's a matter which I am very concerned about; **gli premeva (di) terminare il lavoro** he was anxious to finish the job
premessa [pre'messa] SF (*introduzione*) introduction; (*Filosofia*) premise; **fare una premessa** to make an introductory statement; **mancano le premesse per una buona riuscita** we lack the basis for a successful outcome
premesso, a [pre'messo] PP *di* **premettere**
premestruale [premestru'ale] AGG premenstrual
premettere [pre'mettere] VT IRREG **1** (*dire prima*) to start by saying, state first; **vorrei premettere alcune considerazioni di carattere generale** I should like to begin by making a few general points; **premetto che...** I must say first of all that ...; **premesso che...** given that ...; **ciò premesso...** that (having been) said ... **2** (*porre prima*) to put before; **premettere una prefazione ad un'opera** to preface a work
premiare [pre'mjare] VT (*atleta, studente*) to give a prize to, award a prize to; (*libro, film*) to award a prize to; (*fig: merito, onestà*) to reward; **il preside ha premiato due studenti** the head gave prizes to two students; **il film è stato premiato** the film won a prize; **è stata premiata con una medaglia** she was awarded a medal
premiato, a [pre'mjato] AGG prizewinning
■ SM/F prizewinner
premiazione [premjat'tsjone] SF prize-giving
premier ['prɛmjer] SM INV (*Pol*) premier
première [prə'mjɛr] SF INV (*Teatro, Cine*) première, first performance
preminente [premi'nɛnte] AGG prominent, pre-eminent
preminentemente [preminente'mente] AVV primarily
preminenza [premi'nɛntsa] SF pre-eminence, superiority
premio, mi ['prɛmjo] SM **1** (*gen*) prize; (*ricompensa*) reward; **ho ricevuto un premio** I was given a prize; **in premio per** as a prize (*o* reward) for; **premio di consolazione** consolation prize; **premio Nobel** Nobel prize **2** (*Fin, Assicurazione*) premium **3** (*indennità speciale*) bonus; **premio d'ingaggio** (*Sport*) signing-on fee; **premio di produzione** productivity bonus
■ AGG INV: **vincere una vacanza premio** to win a holiday
premisi *ecc* [pre'mizi] VB *vedi* **premettere**
premonitore, trice [premoni'tore] AGG premonitory
premonizione [premonit'tsjone] SF premonition
premunire [premu'nire] VT: **premunire (contro)** (*nemico, influenza*) to protect (against); **premunire qn**

contro i rischi della droga to make sb aware of the dangers of drugs

▶ **premunirsi** VR: **premunirsi (di** *o* **con)** to arm o.s. (with); **premunirsi (contro)** to protect o.s. (from), guard o.s. (against)

premura [pre'mura] SF **1** *(fretta)* haste, hurry; **aver premura** to be in a hurry; **svelto, che ho premura!** quick, I'm in a hurry!; **far premura a qn** to hurry sb; **mi dispiace farti premura, ma devo andare** I'm sorry to hurry you, but I have to go **2** *(riguardo)* attention, care; **usare ogni premura nei riguardi di qn** *or* **circondare qn di premure** to make a fuss of sb

premurosamente [premurosa'mente] AVV thoughtfully, kindly

premuroso, a [premu'roso] AGG attentive, thoughtful, considerate; **un marito e padre premuroso** a devoted husband and father

prenatale [prena'tale] AGG antenatal, prenatal

prendere ['prɛndere] VB IRREG

■ VT

1 *(gen)* to take; *(portare: cosa)* to get, fetch; *(: persona)* to pick up, fetch; **ha preso il libro dal tavolo** he picked up *o* took the book from the table; **l'ho preso dal cassetto** I took *o* got it out of the drawer; **l'ha preso per mano** she took his hand *o* took him by the hand; **hai preso l'ombrello?** have you taken your umbrella?; **prendi quella borsa** take that bag; **prendere qc in spalla** to shoulder sth; **prendere qc per il manico** to take sth by the handle; **andare a prendere qc** to go and get sth; **vai a prendermi gli occhiali** go and get my glasses; **venire a prendere qn** to come and get sb; **potresti venire a prendermi alla stazione?** could you come and get me from the station?; **abbiamo preso una casa** *(affittare)* we have rented a house; *(comprare)* we have bought a house

2 *(afferrare)* to seize, grab; *(catturare: ladro, pesce)* to catch; *(: fortezza)* to take; **prendere qn per i capelli** to grab sb by the hair; **è stato preso dalla polizia** he was caught by the police; **l'ho preso mentre tentava di scappare** I caught him trying to escape; **ho preso un grosso pesce** I caught a huge fish; **la cintura mi è rimasta presa nella porta** my belt got caught in the door

3 *(direzione, scorciatoia, mezzo pubblico)* to take; **non so che strada prendere** I don't know which road to take; **ha preso il treno** he took the train, he went by train; **ha preso il treno delle 10** he took *o* caught the 10 o'clock train; **preferisco prendere l'aereo anziché il treno** I prefer to go by plane rather than by train; **la nave ha preso il largo** the ship put out to sea

4 *(registrare)* to take (down); **prendere le misure di qn** to take sb's measurements; **prendere le generalità di qn** to take down sb's particulars; **prendere nota di** to take note of

5 *(guadagnare)* to get, earn; *(chiedere: somma, prezzo)* to charge, ask; **quanto prende al mese?** how much does he earn a month?; **prende 2000 euro al mese** he makes *o* earns 2000 euros a month; **quanto prende per un taglio di capelli?** how much do you charge for a haircut?

6 *(ricevere: colpi, schiaffi, sgridata)* to get; *(subire: malattia)* to catch; **le ha prese** he got a good hiding; **ho preso uno spavento** I got such a fright; **ho preso freddo** I've caught a chill; **ho preso l'influenza** I've caught (the) flu; **ho preso un bel voto** I got a good mark; **non so come la prenderà** I don't know how he'll take the news

7 *(ingoiare: pasto, panino, tè)* to have; *(: medicina)* to take; **non prendo nulla fuori pasto** I don't eat between meals; **prendi qualcosa?** *(da bere, da mangiare)* would you like something to eat (*o* drink)?; **prendo un caffè** I'll have a coffee; **prendi pure** help yourself

8 *(assumere: collaboratore, dipendente)* to take on, hire; *(: responsabilità)* to take on, assume; *(: tono, aria)* to put on; *(: colore)* to take on; *(decisione)* to take, make, come to; **prendere un impegno** to take on a commitment; **ha preso uno strano odore** it smells funny; **prendere l'abitudine di** to get into the habit of

9 *(pervadere)*: **essere preso dai rimorsi** to be full of remorse; **essere preso dal panico** to be panic-stricken; **cosa ti prende?** what's got into you?; **quel film mi ha preso** that film caught my imagination

10 *(scambiare)*: **prendere qn/qc per** to mistake sb/sth for; **mi ha preso per mio fratello** he mistook me for my brother; **ha preso le mie parole per** *o* **come un'offesa** he took offence at my words; **per chi mi prendi?** who do you think I am?, what do you take me for?

11 *(trattare: persona)* to handle; **prendere qn per il verso giusto** to handle sb the right way; **prendere qn con le buone/cattive** to handle sb tactfully/rudely; **so come prenderlo** I know how to handle him

12 *(occupare: spazio, tempo)* to take up; **il tavolo prende poco posto** the table doesn't take up much room; **questo lavoro mi sta prendendo troppo tempo** this work is taking up too much of my time

13 *(cominciare)*: **prendere a fare qc** to begin to do sth, start doing sth

14 **prendersela** *(adirarsi)* to get annoyed; *(preoccuparsi)* to get upset, worry; **prendersela a male** to take offence; **prendersela con qn** to get angry with sb; **perché te la prendi sempre con me?** why do you always pick on me?; **prendersela comoda** to take it easy

15 *(fraseologia)*: **prendere da qn** *(assomigliare)* to take after sb; **prendere a calci qn** to kick sb; **prendere qn per fame** to starve sb into submission; **prendere o lasciare** take it or leave it; **prendersi la soddisfazione (di)** to have the satisfaction (of); **prendersi una vacanza** to take a holiday; **prendersi cura di qn/qc** to look after sb/sth; **prendersi gioco di qn** to mock sb; **prendere parte a** to take part in; **prendere fuoco** to catch fire

■ VI *(aus avere)*

1 *(far presa: colla, cemento)* to set; *(: piante)* to take (root); *(: fuoco)* to catch

2 *(andare)*: **prendere a destra** to go *o* turn right; **prendere per i campi** to go across the fields

3 *(fraseologia)*: **mi è preso un colpo** I got such a fright; **mi è preso freddo** I started feeling cold; **mi è presa la voglia di andare al mare** I feel like going to the seaside

▶ **prendersi** VR *(uso reciproco: afferrarsi)* to grab each other, seize each other; **prendersi a pugni** to come to blows, punch each other; **prendersi a calci** to kick each other

prendisole [prendi'sole] SM INV sundress

prenotare [preno'tare] VT *(posto, tavolo)* to book, reserve; *(camera)* to book

▶ **prenotarsi** VR: **prenotarsi per qc** to put one's name down for sth

prenotazione [prenotat'tsjone] SF booking, reservation; **fare una prenotazione** to make a booking *o* reservation

prensile ['prɛnsile] AGG prehensile

Pp

preoccupante [preokku'pante] AGG worrying
preoccupare [preokku'pare] VT (*impensierire*) to worry; **ciò che mi preoccupa è il viaggio** what's worrying *o* bothering me is the journey; **Giovanna mi preoccupa** *or* **sono preoccupato per Giovanna** I am worried about Giovanna; **la sua salute mi preoccupa** I'm concerned *o* anxious about his health
▶ **preoccuparsi** VIP: **preoccuparsi (per qn/qc)** to worry (about sb/sth), be anxious (about sb/sth); **non preoccuparti** don't worry

LO SAPEVI...?
preoccupare non si traduce mai con la parola inglese *preoccupy*

preoccupazione [preokkupat'tsjone] SF (*problema*) worry; (*inquietudine*) anxiety, worry; **è pieno di preoccupazioni** he has lots of worries *o* problems; **la sua unica preoccupazione è vestirsi bene** his only concern *o* preoccupation is to dress well
preordinato, a [preordi'nato] AGG preordained
prepagato, a [prepa'gato] AGG prepaid
preparare [prepa'rare] VT **1** (*gen*) to prepare; (*pranzo*) to make, prepare; (*letto*) to make; (*tavola*) to lay; (*valigia*) to get ready, pack; (*esame, concorso*) to prepare for, study for; **preparare da mangiare** to prepare a meal; **preparare il terreno** (*anche fig*) to prepare the ground; **chissà cosa ci prepara il futuro!** who knows what the future has in store for us! **2 preparare qn a** (*esame*) to prepare *o* coach sb for; (*notizia*) to prepare sb for; **preparare qn per un intervento** to get sb ready for an operation
▶ **prepararsi** VR (*vestirsi*) to get ready; (*atleta: allenarsi*) to train; **prepararsi a qc/a fare qc** to get ready *o* prepare (o.s.) for sth/to do sth; **prepararsi ad un esame** to prepare for *o* study for an exam
preparativi [prepara'tivi] SMPL: **preparativi (per)** preparations (for); **stanno facendo i preparativi per la festa** they're making preparations for the party
preparato, a [prepa'rato] AGG (*gen*) prepared; (*pronto*) ready; **uno studente preparato** a student who has worked hard; **scusi professore ma non sono preparato** sorry, Sir, I haven't done the work
■ SM (*prodotto*) preparation
preparatorio, ria, ri, rie [prepara'tɔrjo] AGG preparatory
preparazione [preparat'tsjone] SF (*gen*) preparation; (*Sport*) training; **preparazione atletica** physical training; **iniziare la preparazione per gli esami** to begin preparation for the exams; **non ha la necessaria preparazione per svolgere questo lavoro** he doesn't have either the knowledge or the experience necessary for the job
prepensionamento [prepensjona'mento] SM early retirement
preponderante [preponde'rante] AGG predominant
preponderanza [preponde'rantsa] SF (*prevalenza*) preponderance; (*superiorità*) superiority
preporre [pre'porre] VT IRREG **1** (*porre innanzi*) to place before; (*fig: preferire*) to prefer, put before **2** (*mettere a capo*): **preporre qn a qc** to put sb in charge of sth; **l'ufficiale preposto al comando del reggimento** the officer in command of the regiment
preposizione [preposit'tsjone] SF (*Gramm*) preposition
preposto, a [pre'posto] PP *di* **preporre**
prepotente [prepo'tɛnte] AGG (*persona*) overbearing, arrogant, domineering; (*fig: desiderio, bisogno*) overwhelming, pressing; **un prepotente desiderio di qc/di fare qc** an overwhelming desire for sth/to do sth; **quel bambino è molto prepotente** that child is a real bully
■ SM/F bully; **è un prepotente** he's a bully
prepotentemente [prepotente'mente] AVV (*vedi agg*) arrogantly; overwhelmingly
prepotenza [prepo'tɛntsa] SF (*arroganza*) arrogance; (*comportamento*) arrogant behaviour (*Brit*) *o* behavior (*Am*); **agire con prepotenza** to behave arrogantly; **è stata una prepotenza da parte tua** it was very high-handed of you
prepuzio, zi [pre'puttsjo] SM (*Anat*) foreskin
prerogativa [preroga'tiva] SF **1** (*privilegio*) prerogative **2** (*peculiarità*) property, quality
presa ['presa] SF **1** (*gen*) grip; (*appiglio*) hold; (*Lotta*) grip, hold; **allentare la presa (di qc)** to loosen one's grip *o* hold (on sth); **ha allentato la presa** he loosened his grip; **avere una presa forte** to have a strong grip; **venire alle prese con qc** (*fig*) to come to grips with sth; **essere alle prese con qc** (*fig*) to be struggling with sth; **di forte presa** (*fig*) with wide appeal; **a presa rapida** (*cemento*) quick-setting; **far presa** (*colla*) to set; **ha fatto presa sul pubblico** (*fig*) it caught the public's imagination; **in presa diretta** direct transmission **2** (*conquista: di città*) taking *no pl*, capture; (*Carte*) trick **3** (*pizzico: di sale, tabacco*) pinch **4** (*Cine*): **macchina da presa** cine camera (*Brit*), movie camera (*Am*)
■ **presa dell'acqua** water (supply) point; **presa d'aria** air inlet *o* intake; **presa di corrente** (*Elettr*) socket; (*: al muro*) point; **presa diretta** (*Aut*) direct drive; **presa del gas** gas (supply) point; **presa in giro** leg-pull (*Brit*), joke; **presa multipla** (*Elettr*) multiple socket; **presa di posizione** stand; **presa di possesso** taking possession; **presa SCART** SCART socket
presagio, gi [pre'zadʒo] SM omen, sign; (*presentimento*) premonition, presentiment
presagire [preza'dʒire] VT (*prevedere*) to predict, foresee; (*presentire*) to have a premonition of
presago, a, ghi, ghe [pre'zago] AGG (*letter*): **essere presago di qc** to have a premonition *o* presentiment of sth
presalario, ri [presa'larjo] SM (*Univ*) grant
presbiopia [prezbio'pia] SF long-sightedness
presbite ['prɛzbite] AGG long-sighted
presbiterianesimo [prezbiterja'nezimo] SM Presbyterianism
presbiteriano, a [prezbite'rjano] AGG, SM/F Presbyterian
presbiterio, ri [prezbi'tɛrjo] SM presbytery
presbitero [prez'bitero] SM presbyter
prescegliere [preʃʃeʎʎere] VT IRREG to select, choose
prescelto, a [preʃʃelto] PP *di* **prescegliere**
prescindere [preʃʃindere] VI IRREG (*aus* **avere**) **prescindere da** to leave aside, leave out of consideration; **prescindendo da** *or* **a prescindere da** leaving aside, apart from
prescisso, a [preʃʃisso] PP *di* **prescindere**
prescolastico, a, ci, che [presko'lastiko] AGG preschool *attr*; **bambini in età prescolastica** children not yet of school age
prescritto, a [pres'kritto] PP *di* **prescrivere**
prescrivere [pres'krivere] VT IRREG (*Med, Dir*) to prescribe; **prescrivere una medicina a qn** to prescribe medicine for sb
prescrizione [preskrit'tsjone] SF (*Med, Dir*) prescription; (*norma*) rule, regulation; **cadere in prescrizione** (*Dir*) to become statute-barred

prese *ecc* ['prese] VB *vedi* **prendere**

preselettore [preselet'tore] SM (*Tecn*) preselector

presentare [prezen'tare] VT **1** (*gen*) to present; (*documento*) to present, show, produce; (*proposta, conti, bilancio*) to present, submit; (*domanda, reclamo*) to put in; **ha presentato domanda di assunzione** he put in a job application **2** (*nuovo modello*) to present; (*spettacolo*) to present, host; (*persona*) to introduce; **presentare qn (a)** to introduce sb (to); **l'ha presentata ai suoi amici** he introduced her to his friends; **presentare qn in società** to introduce sb into society; **presentare qc in un'esposizione** to show *o* display sth at an exhibition; **chi ha presentato lo spettacolo?** who presented the show? **3** (*dono*) to present, give; (*omaggi*) to present, pay; **presentare le armi** (*Mil*) to present arms
▶ **presentarsi** VR **1** (*recarsi, farsi vedere*) to present o.s., appear; **presentarsi davanti al tribunale** to appear before the court; **è così che ti presenti?** is this any way to be seen?; **presentarsi bene/male** to have a good/poor appearance **2** (*farsi conoscere*) to introduce o.s. **3** (*candidato*) to come forward; **presentarsi a** (*elezione*) to stand for (*Brit*), run for (*Am*); (*concorso*) to enter for; (*esame*) to sit, take;
▶ **presentarsi** VIP **1** (*capitare*: *occasione, caso strano*) to occur, arise; **se mi si presenterà una simile occasione** should a similar opportunity occur *o* arise; **presentarsi alla mente** (*idea*) to come *o* spring to mind **2** (*apparire*) to look, seem; **la situazione si presenta difficile** things aren't looking too good, things look a bit tricky

presentatore, trice [prezenta'tore] SM/F (*Radio, TV*) presenter; **presentatore di quiz** quizmaster

presentazione [prezentat'tsjone] SF (*gen*) presentation; (*di persona*) introduction; **fare le presentazioni** to make the introductions

presente[1] [pre'zɛnte] AGG (*gen*) present; (*questo*): **la presente lettera** this letter; **essere presente a una riunione** to be present at *o* attend a meeting; **erano tutti presenti alla lezione** everybody was present at the class; **presente!** here!; **avere presente qn/qc** to know sb/sth; **hai presente la casa rossa vicino alla mia?** you know the red house near mine?; **tener presente qn/qc** to bear sb/sth in mind; **tieni presente che non ho molto tempo libero** bear in mind (that) I don't have much spare time
■ SM/F person present; **i presenti** those present; **esclusi i presenti** present company excepted
■ SM (*Gramm*) present tense; (*tempo attuale*): **il presente** the present; **per il presente** for the present; **al presente** at present
■ SF (*Comm*: *lettera*): **con la presente vi comunico...** this is to inform you that ...

presente[2] [pre'zɛnte] SM (*regalo*) present, gift

presentemente [prezente'mente] AVV at present

> **LO SAPEVI...?**
> **presentemente** non si traduce mai con la parola inglese ***presently***

presentimento [presenti'mento] SM premonition, presentiment; **ho il presentimento che...** I've a feeling that...

presentire [presen'tire] VT to have a presentiment of; **come presentivo non si è fatto più sentire** as I thought *o* foresaw he hasn't called since; **presentivo che sarebbe andata a finire così** I thought *o* had a feeling that it would end like that

presenza [pre'zɛntsa] SF (*gen*) presence; (*Scol*) attendance; **fare atto di presenza** to put in an appearance; **in presenza di** in (the) presence of; **conta 18 presenze in nazionale** (*Sport*) he's won 18 caps, he's played in the national team 18 times; **di bella presenza** of good appearance; **presenza di spirito** presence of mind

presenziare [prezen'tsjare] VI (*aus* **avere**) **presenziare a** to be present at, attend

presepio, pi [pre'zɛpjo], **presepe** [pre'zɛpe] SM nativity scene

preservare [preser'vare] VT to protect; **preservare qn da qc** to protect sb from *o* against sth; **preservare la salute** to protect one's health

preservativo [preserva'tivo] SM (*profilattico*) condom, sheath (*Brit*)

> **LO SAPEVI...?**
> **preservativo** non si traduce mai con la parola inglese ***preservative***

preservazione [preservat'tsjone] SF preservation, protection

presi *ecc* ['presi] VB *vedi* **prendere**

preside ['prɛside] SM/F (*Scol*) headmaster/ headmistress (*Brit*), head (teacher) (*Brit*), principal (*Am*); **preside di facoltà** (*Univ*) dean of faculty

presidente, essa [presi'dɛnte] SM (*di nazione, club*) president; (*di assemblea, riunione, società commerciale*) chairman/chairwoman; (*Dir*) presiding judge *o* magistrate; **Presidente della Camera (dei Deputati)** (*Pol*) ≈ Speaker **Presidente della commissione** (*Scol*) chief examiner; **Presidente del Consiglio (dei Ministri)** (*Pol*) ≈ Prime Minister **Presidente della Repubblica** (*Pol*) President of the Republic

> **PRESIDENTI**
> The **Presidente del Consiglio**, the Italian Prime Minister, is the leader of the Government. He or she submits nominations for ministerial posts to the "Presidente della Repubblica", who then appoints them if approved. The **Presidente del Consiglio** is appointed by the "Presidente della Repubblica", in consultation with the leaders of the parliamentary parties, former heads of state, the "Presidente della Camera" and the "Presidente del Senato". The **Presidente della Repubblica** is the head of state. He or she must be an Italian citizen of at least 50 years of age, and is elected by Parliament and by three delegates from each of the Italian regions. He or she has the power to suspend the implementation of legislation and to dissolve one or both chambers of Parliament, and presides over the magistrates' governing body (the "Consiglio Superiore della Magistratura").
> ▷ www.quirinale.it/
> ▷ www.palazzochigi.it/

presidenza [presi'dɛntsa] SF **1** (*vedi* presidente) presidency, office of president; chairmanship; **essere alla presidenza** to be president; to be chairman/ woman; **assumere la presidenza** to become president; to take the chair; **candidato alla presidenza** presidential candidate; candidate for the chairmanship **2** (*di preside*: *carica*) headship (*Brit*), post of principal (*Am*); (: *ufficio*) headmaster's/ headmistress's office *o* study (*Brit*), principal's office (*Am*)

presidenziale [presiden'tsjale] AGG presidential

presidiare [presi'djare] VT (*Mil*) to garrison; (*casa,*

Pp

fabbrica) to guard
presidio, di [pre'sidjo] SM (*Mil: guarnigione*) garrison; (: *comando territoriale*) command; (: *ufficio*) area recruitment office
presiedere [pre'sjɛdere] VB IRREG
■ VT (*assemblea, riunione*) to preside over, chair; **presiede la Camera dei Deputati** (*Pol*) ≈ he (*o* she) is Speaker of the House of Commons
■ VI (*aus* **avere**) **presiedere a** (*discussione, riunione*) to preside over, chair; (*realizzazione, svolgimento*) direct, be in charge of
presieduto, a [presje'duto] PP *di* **presiedere**
presina [pre'sina] SF (*per le pentole*) pot holder
preso, a ['preso] PP *di* **prendere**
pressa ['prɛssa] SF (*Tecn*) press
pressante [pres'sante] AGG (*bisogno*) urgent, pressing; (*richiesta*) urgent
pressantemente [pressante'mente] AVV urgently
pressappoco [pressap'pɔko] AVV about, roughly, approximately; **sono pressapoco uguali** they are more or less the same; **ha pressappoco quarant'anni** he's about forty
pressare [pres'sare] VT (*Tecn, fig: schiacciare*) to press; **pressare qn con richieste di aiuti** to press sb for assistance
pressione [pres'sjone] SF **1** (*gen, Fis, Med*) pressure; **mettere sotto pressione** (*Tecn*) to pressurize; **la macchina del caffè non è ancora in pressione** there isn't enough steam in the espresso machine yet; **pentola a pressione** pressure cooker; **avere la pressione alta/bassa** (*Med*) to have high/low blood pressure; **pressione atmosferica** atmospheric pressure; **pressione sanguigna** blood pressure; **ha la pressione alta** he's got high blood pressure **2** (*fig: sollecitazione*) pressure; **far pressione su qn** to put pressure on sb; **subire forti pressioni** to be under strong pressure; **essere/mettere qn sotto pressione** to be/put sb under pressure; **gruppo di pressione** pressure group
presso ['prɛsso] AVV **1** (*vicino*) nearby, near, close at hand; **abitava lì presso** he lived nearby *o* near there **2** **di** *o* **da presso** (*incalzare*) closely; **da presso** (*esaminare*) closely; **a un di presso** about, approximately
■ PREP **1** (*vicino a*) close to, near (to); (*accanto a*) beside, next to; **presso a** near (to), by; **stava presso la finestra** she was standing near the window **2** **presso qn** (*in casa di*) at sb's home; **abita presso una zia** he lives with an aunt; **lavora presso di noi** (*alle dipendenze di*) he works for *o* with us; **'presso'** (*su busta, cartolina*) 'care of', 'c/o'; **Lucia Micoli, presso fam. Bianchi** Lucia Micoli, c/o Mr and Mrs Bianchi; **ambasciatore presso la Santa Sede** ambassador to the Holy See **3** (*nell'ambiente di*) among; **diffuso presso le popolazioni primitive** common among primitive peoples; **ha avuto grande successo presso i giovani** it has been a hit with young people
■ SMPL: **nei pressi di** near, in the vicinity of; **nei pressi di Londra** near London
pressoché [presso'ke] AVV nearly, almost
pressurizzare [pressurid'dzare] VT to pressurize
pressurizzato, a [pressurid'dzato] AGG pressurized
pressurizzazione [pressuriddzat'tsjone] SF pressurization
prestabilire [prestabi'lire] VT to arrange beforehand, arrange in advance; **era già tutto prestabilito** everything had already been arranged
prestabilito, a [prestabi'lito] AGG prearranged
prestampato, a [prestam'pato] AGG (*modulo, bollettino*) pre-printed
■ SM pre-printed form
prestanome [presta'nome] SM/F INV (*Dir*) nominee; (*pegg*) front man
prestante [pres'tante] AGG good-looking; **un uomo prestante** a fine figure of a man
prestanza [pres'tantsa] SF (robust) good looks *pl*
prestare [pres'tare] VT to lend; **prestare qc a qn** to lend sb sth, lend sth to sb; **mi ha prestato 25 euro** he lent me 25 euros; **gliel'ho prestato** I lent it to him; **farsi prestare qc da qn** to borrow sth from sb; **mi sono fatto prestare una penna da Luca** I borrowed a pen from Luca; **prestare aiuto a qn** to give sb a helping hand, lend sb a hand; **prestare soccorso a** to give assistance to; **prestare ascolto** *o* **orecchio a** to listen to; **prestare attenzione a** to pay attention to; **prestare fede a** to give credence to; **prestare giuramento** to take an oath
▶ **prestarsi** VR (*offrirsi*) **prestarsi (a fare qc)** to offer (to do sth); **si presta sempre volentieri** he's always willing to lend a hand;
▶ **prestarsi** VIP (*essere adatto*) **prestarsi per** *o* **a** to lend itself to, be suitable for; **la frase si presta a molteplici interpretazioni** the phrase lends itself to numerous interpretations; **quel vestito non si presta all'occasione** that dress isn't suitable for the occasion
prestazione [prestat'tsjone] SF **1** (*Tecn, Sport*) performance **2** (*opera, servizio*): **prestazioni** SFPL services
prestigiatore, trice [prestidʒa'tore] SM/F conjurer
prestigio [pres'tidʒo] SM **1** (*fama, autorità*) prestige; **di prestigio** prestigious; **è una questione di prestigio** it's a matter of prestige **2** (*illusione*): **gioco di prestigio** conjuring trick
prestigiosamente [prestidʒosa'mente] AVV prestigiously
prestigioso, a [presti'dʒoso] AGG prestigious
prestito ['prɛstito] SM loan; **prendere qc in prestito da qn** to borrow sth from sb; **ha preso in prestito 100 euro da sua madre** she borrowed 100 euros from her mother; **dare qc in prestito a qn** to lend sth to sb, lend sb sth; **gli ho dato in prestito la mia bici** I lent him my bike; **mi fai un prestito?** can I borrow some money from you?, will you lend me some money?; **prestito bancario** (*Banca*) bank loan; **prestito linguistico** loan word; **prestito pubblico** (*Fin*) public borrowing
presto ['prɛsto] AVV **1** (*fra poco*) soon; **ci rivedremo presto** we'll see one another soon; **arriverà presto** he'll be here soon; **presto o tardi** sooner or later; **a presto** see you soon; **arrivederci a presto!** goodbye for now!, see you soon!; **il più presto possibile** as soon as possible; **se non la smette, presto avrà dei guai** if he doesn't stop that he'll be for it **2** (*in fretta*) quickly, fast; **fai presto!** hurry up!, be quick (about it)!; **fai presto che è già buio** come on – it's already dark; **più presto che puoi** as quickly *o* fast as you can; **fare presto a fare qc** to hurry up and do sth; (*con facilità*) to have no trouble doing sth; **ha fatto presto a sbrigare quel lavoro** he got through that job quickly; **si fa presto a criticare** it's easy to criticize; **è presto detto** it's easier said than done **3** (*di buon'ora*) early; **mi alzo sempre presto** I always get up early; **mi alzo più presto di te** I get up earlier than you; **sono arrivato troppo presto all'appuntamento** I arrived too early

for the appointment; **è ancora presto per decidere** it's still too early *o* soon to decide

presumere [pre'zumere] VT IRREG **1** (*ritenere, credere*): **presumere che...** to presume *o* imagine that ...; **presumo che venga** I presume *o* imagine he'll come **2** (*pretendere, avere la presunzione di*) to presume, assume; **e tu presumi di potermi criticare?** you have the nerve to think you can criticize me; **presume di sapere più degli altri** he thinks he knows more *o* better than everybody else

presumibile [prezu'mibile] AGG (*dati, risultati*) likely

presumibilmente [prezumibil'mente] AVV presumably

presunsi *ecc* [pre'zunsi] VB *vedi* **presumere**

presunto, a [pre'zunto] PP *di* **presumere**
■ AGG: **il presunto colpevole** the alleged culprit

presuntuosamente [prezuntuosa'mente] AVV presumptuously

presuntuoso, a [prezuntu'oso] AGG presumptuous, conceited
■ SM: **fare il presuntuoso** to be cocksure

presunzione [prezun'tsjone] SF **1** (*congettura*) presumption **2** (*immodestia*) presumptuousness; **peccare di presunzione** to be presumptuous

presupporre [presup'porre] VT IRREG **1** (*immaginare, prevedere*) to assume, suppose **2** (*implicare*) to presuppose

presupposto, a [presup'posto] PP *di* **presupporre**
■ SM (*premessa*) supposition, premise; **partendo dal presupposto che...** assuming that ...; **mancano i presupposti necessari** the necessary conditions are lacking

prêt-à-porter ['prɛt a pɔr'te] SM INV ready-to-wear (clothes)

prete ['prɛte] SM priest; **scherzo da prete** (*fig fam*) nasty trick; **prete operaio** worker-priest

pretendente [preten'dɛnte] SM/F **1** (*aspirante*): **pretendente (a)** pretender (to) **2** (*corteggiatore*) suitor

pretendere [pre'tɛndere] VT IRREG **1** (*esigere*) to demand, require; (*aspettarsi*) to expect; **pretendo un po' di rispetto** I demand some respect; **pretendo la mia parte** I demand *o* claim my share; **pretende di essere pagato in anticipo** he expects to be paid in advance; **pretendi troppo da lui** you expect too much of him **2** (*sostenere, presumere*): **pretendere (che...)** to claim (that ...); **pretende di aver sempre ragione** he thinks he's always right

pretensionatore [pretensjona'tore] SM (*Aut, di cinture di sicurezza*) pre-tensioner

pretenziosamente [pretentsjosa'mente] AVV pretentiously

pretenziosità [pretentsjosi'ta] SF pretentiousness

pretenzioso, a [preten'tsjoso] AGG pretentious

preterintenzionale [preterintentsjo'nale] AGG (*Dir*): **omicidio preterintenzionale** manslaughter

preterito [pre'tɛrito] SM (*Gramm*) preterit(e)

pretesa [pre'tesa] SF **1** (*richiesta, esigenza*) claim, demand; **avanzare una pretesa** to put forward a claim *o* demand; **un uomo di poche pretese** a man who is easily pleased *o* who doesn't ask much in life; **è pieno di pretese** he's difficult to please, he expects too much; **senza pretese** (*persona, casa, arredamento*) unpretentious, modest; (*abito*) simple **2** (*presunzione*) pretension; **hai la pretesa di criticarmi!** you've got the nerve to criticize me!; **non avrai la pretesa di farmelo credere?** you don't really expect me to believe that; **non ho la pretesa di essere bella** I have no pretensions to beauty, I don't pretend to be beautiful

preteso, a [pre'teso] PP *di* **pretendere**

pretesto [pre'tɛsto] SM excuse, pretext; **con il pretesto di** on the pretext of; **mi ha fornito il pretesto per agire** he has provided me with a pretext for taking action

pretestuoso, a [pretestu'oso] AGG (*data, motivo*) used as an excuse

pretore [pre'tore] SM (*Dir*) magistrate

pretrattare [pretrat'tare] VT (*macchia*) to pretreat

prettamente [pretta'mente] AVV (*tipicamente*) decidedly

pretura [pre'tura] SF (*Dir: sede*) magistrate's court (*Brit*), circuit *o* superior court (*Am*); (: *insieme dei pretori*) magistracy

prevalente [preva'lɛnte] AGG prevalent, prevailing

prevalentemente [prevalente'mente] AVV predominantly, mainly, for the most part; **in quella zona si parla prevalentemente il tedesco** German is the main *o* predominant language in that area

prevalenza [preva'lɛntsa] SF predominance; **in prevalenza** predominantly, mainly

prevalere [preva'lere] VI IRREG (*aus* **avere** *o* **essere**) to prevail; **prevalere su tutti per intelligenza** to surpass everyone in intelligence

prevalso, a [pre'valso] PP *di* **prevalere**

prevaricare [prevari'kare] VI (*aus* **avere**) (*abusare del potere*) to abuse one's power

prevaricazione [prevarikat'tsjone] SF (*abuso di potere*) abuse of power

> **LO SAPEVI...?**
> **prevaricazione** non si traduce mai con la parola inglese *prevarication*

Pp

prevedere [preve'dere] VT IRREG **1** (*avvenimento, conseguenza*) to foresee, anticipate; (*tempo*) to forecast; **prevedere il futuro** to foretell the future; **era da prevedere** it was to be expected; **non si sarebbe potuto prevedere** that couldn't have been foreseen; **nulla lasciava prevedere che...** there was nothing to suggest *o* to make one think that ...; **non possiamo prevedere tutto** we can't think of everything; **non possiamo prevedere cosa succederà** we can't foresee what will happen; **come previsto** as expected; **spese previste** anticipated expenditure; **tempo previsto per domani** weather forecast for tomorrow; **è previsto maltempo per il fine settimana** bad weather is forecast for the weekend **2** (*programmare*) to plan; **prevedere di fare qc** to plan to do sth; **avevamo previsto di partire oggi** we had planned to leave today; **all'ora prevista** at the appointed *o* scheduled time; **previsto per martedì** scheduled *o* planned for Tuesday **3** (*sogg: contratto, legge*) to make provision for, provide for; **questo caso non è previsto dalla legge** the law makes no provision for such a case

prevedibile [preve'dibile] AGG predictable; **non era assolutamente prevedibile che...** no one could have foreseen that ...

prevedibilmente [prevedibil'mente] AVV as one would expect *o* have expected

preveggenza [preved'dʒɛntsa] SF foresight

prevendita [pre'vendita] SF (*di biglietti*) advance sale

prevenire [preve'nire] VT IRREG **1** (*anticipare: domanda*) to anticipate; (: *obiezione*) to forestall **2** **prevenire qn (di)** (*preavvertire*) to inform sb in advance (of); (*mettere sull'avviso*) to warn sb (of); **ti hanno prevenuto contro di me** they have already warned you about me

3 (*evitare: malattia, disgrazia*) to prevent; **gli incidenti si possono prevenire** accidents can be prevented

preventivare [preventi'vare] VT (*Comm: spesa*) to estimate; (*: mettere in bilancio*) to budget for; **non avevamo preventivato un figlio** we hadn't reckoned on having a child

preventivo [preven'tivo] AGG (*intervento, cura*) preventive; **carcere preventivo** custody (*pending trial*); **bilancio preventivo** (*Comm*) budget
■ SM (*Comm*) estimate; **fare un preventivo** to give an estimate

prevenuto, a [preve'nuto] PP *di* **prevenire**
■ AGG (*mal disposto*): **prevenuto (contro qn/qc)** prejudiced (against sb/sth)

prevenzione [preven'tsjone] SF **1** prevention; **prevenzione degli infortuni** prevention of accidents **2** (*preconcetto*) prejudice; **avere prevenzioni contro qn/qc** to be prejudiced against sb/sth

previamente [prevja'mente] AVV in advance

previdente [previ'dɛnte] AGG prudent, showing foresight; **essere previdente** to think ahead

previdentemente [previdente'mente] AVV prudently

previdenza [previ'dɛntsa] SF prudence, foresight; **istituto di previdenza** provident institution; **previdenza sociale** social security (*Brit*), welfare (*Am*)

previdenziale [prevident'tsjale] AGG (*sistema, contributi*) social security *attr* (*Brit*), welfare (*Am*)

previdi *ecc* [pre'vidi] VB *vedi* **prevedere**

previo, a, vi ['prɛvjo] AGG (*Comm*): **previo avviso** upon (prior) notice; **previo pagamento** upon payment

previsione [previ'zjone] SF (*gen*) prediction; (*attesa*) expectation; **tutto è andato secondo le previsioni** everything went according to expectation(s); **in previsione di** in anticipation of; **previsioni del tempo** *o* **meteorologiche** weather forecast *sg*

previsto, a [pre'visto] PP *di* **prevedere**
■ SM: **più/meno del previsto** more/less than expected; **prima del previsto** earlier than expected

prevosto [pre'vɔsto] SM (*parroco*) parish priest

preziosamente [prettsjosa'mente] AVV (*ornato*) richly; (*fig: custodire*) jealously

prezioso, a [pret'tsjoso] AGG (*gen*) precious; (*documento*) valuable; (*testimonianza, aiuto, consiglio*) invaluable; **una pietra preziosa** a precious stone; **il loro consiglio mi è stato prezioso** their advice was invaluable to me
■ SM **1** (*gioiello*) jewel; (*oggetto di valore*) valuable; **le hanno rubato tutti i preziosi** they stole all her valuables **2** (*fig: persona*): **fare il prezioso** to play hard to get; **fa il prezioso perché è diventato importante** he puts on airs and graces because he has become important

prezzare [pret'tsare] VT (*articolo*) to price

prezzario, ri [pret'tsarjo] SM price list

prezzemolo [pret'tsemolo] SM (*Bot*) parsley; **essere come il prezzemolo** (*fig*) to turn up everywhere

prezzo ['prɛttso] SM price; **a buon prezzo** cheaply, at a good price; **a prezzo di costo** at cost, at cost price (*Brit*); **a metà prezzo** at half price; **menu a prezzo fisso** set price menu; **il prezzo della benzina** the price of petrol; **il prezzo pattuito è 5000 euro** the agreed price is 5000 euros; **tirare sul prezzo** to bargain, haggle; **ti faccio un prezzo d'amico** *o* **di favore** I'll let you have it at a reduced price; **pagare qc a caro prezzo** (*fig*) to pay dearly for sth; **la libertà non ha prezzo** you can't put a price on freedom; **è una cosa di poco prezzo** it's of little value, it's not worth much
■ **prezzo d'acquisto** purchase price; **prezzo per contanti** cash price; **prezzo di fabbrica** factory price; **prezzo di listino** list price; **prezzo di mercato** market price; **prezzo scontato** reduced price; **prezzo unitario** unit price; **prezzo di vendita** selling price; **prezzo di vendita al dettaglio** retail price

prezzolato, a [prettso'lato] AGG: **soldato prezzolato** mercenary; **giornalista prezzolato** journalist who is in sb's pay; **sicario prezzolato** hired killer

PRG [piɛrre'gi] SIGLA M (= **Piano Regolatore Generale**) *town-planning scheme*

PRI [pi'ɛrre'i] SIGLA M (*Pol:* = **Partito Repubblicano Italiano**) *former political party*

Priamo ['priamo] SM Priam

priapismo [pria'pizmo] SM (*Med*) priapism

prigione [pri'dʒone] SF (*luogo*) prison, jail; (*pena*) imprisonment; **andare/mettere in prigione** to go/send to prison; **scontare un anno di prigione** to spend a year in prison

prigionia [pridʒo'nia] SF imprisonment

prigioniero, a [pridʒo'njɛro] AGG captive; **essere prigioniero** to be a prisoner; **essere prigioniero di un ricordo** to be tormented by a memory
■ SM/F prisoner; **fare/tenere qn prigioniero** to take/hold sb prisoner

prima[1] ['prima] AVV **1** (*in precedenza*) before; (*una volta*) once, formerly; **prima non lo sapevo** I didn't know that before; **due giorni prima** two days before *o* earlier; **ne so quanto prima** I know as much as I did before, I'm none the wiser; **amici come prima!** let's make it up *o* let's be friends again!; **prima non si faceva così** people used not to do that; **usanze di prima** former customs; **non è più la stessa di prima** she's not the same as she was **2** (*in anticipo*) beforehand, in advance; **un'altra volta dimmelo prima** next time let me know in advance *o* beforehand **3** (*più presto*) sooner, earlier; **prima o poi** sooner or later; **prima possibile** as soon as possible; **credevo di fare prima** I thought I'd be finished sooner *o* earlier; **domani devo alzarmi un po' prima** tomorrow I have to get up a bit earlier; **è arrivato prima del previsto** he arrived earlier than expected; **prima lo farai prima sarai libero di uscire** the sooner you do it the sooner you can go out; **chi arriva prima compra i biglietti** whoever arrives first gets the tickets **4** (*innanzi*) before; (*in primo luogo*) first; **prima la famiglia** family first; **prima di tutto** first of all; **prima il dovere e poi il piacere** duty before pleasure
■ **prima di** PREP (*tempo, spazio*) before; **prima del suo arrivo** before his arrival; **sono andati via prima di noi** they left before us; **mi sono alzato prima delle sette** I got up before seven; **prima d'ora** before now; **c'è un cinema prima del semaforo** there's a cinema before the lights
■ **prima di, prima che** CONG before; **prima di fare/che tu faccia** before doing/you do; **pensaci prima che sia troppo tardi** give it some thought before it is too late; **dobbiamo decidere prima che Luca parta** we must decide before Luca leaves

prima[2] ['prima] SF **1** (*gen*) first; (*Teatro*) opening night; (*Cine*) première; (*Ferr*) first class; (*Aut*) first gear; **viaggiare in prima** to travel first class; **ingranare la prima** to engage first gear **2** (*Scol: first year, prima elementare*) ≈ year two (*Brit*), ≈ first grade (*Am*) (*: prima media*) ≈ year seven (*Brit*), ≈ sixth grade (*Am*) (*: prima superiore*) ≈ year ten (*Brit*), ≈ tenth grade (*Am*)

primadonna [prima'dɔnna] SF leading lady; (*di opera*

lirica) prima donna; *(pegg)*: **fare la primadonna** to act the prima donna

primanota [prima'nɔta] SF petty cash book

primariamente [primarja'mente] AVV primarily

primario, ria, ri, rie [pri'marjo] AGG **1** *(funzione, motivo, scopo)* main, chief, primary **2** *(Geol)*: **roccia primaria** primary rock
■ SM *(medico)* head *o* chief physician

primate [pri'mate] SM *(Rel, Zool)* primate

primatista, i, e [prima'tista] SM/F *(Sport)* record holder; **il primatista mondiale del salto in lungo** the world record holder for the long jump

primato [pri'mato] SM **1** *(in campo industriale, artistico)* supremacy; **l'Italia ha il primato nel campo della moda** Italy is the leader *o* holds the lead in the world of fashion **2** *(Sport)* record

primavera [prima'vɛra] SF spring; **in primavera** in spring

primaverile [primave'rile] AGG spring *attr*

primeggiare [primed'dʒare] VI *(aus* **avere***)* **primeggiare (in)** to excel (in), be one of the best (in)

primina [pri'mina] SM *(Scol)* ≈ reception

primipara [pri'mipara] SF *(Med)* primigravida

primitivamente [primitiva'mente] AVV primitively, in a primitive manner

primitivo, a [primi'tivo] AGG *(società, popolazione, usanza)* primitive; *(significato)* original
■ SM/F *(della preistoria, arcaico)* primitive; *(fig: zotico)* uncivilized person

primizia [pri'mittsja] SF **1** *(Agr)*: **primizie** SFPL early fruit and vegetables, early produce *sg* **2** *(notizia inedita)*: **ho una primizia per il tuo giornale** I've got a scoop for your paper

primo, a ['primo] AGG
1 *(gen)* first; *(impressione)* first, initial; *(infanzia)* early; *(Mat: numero)* prime; **le prime 20 pagine** the first 20 pages; **dalla prima all'ultima pagina** from beginning to end; **in prima pagina** *(Stampa)*: **i suoi primi quadri** his early paintings; **questo quadro è un Michelangelo prima maniera** this is an early Michelangelo; **questo film è di Fellini prima maniera** this film is in Fellini's early style; **di prima mattina** early in the morning; **le prime ore del mattino** the early hours of the morning; **posare la prima pietra** to lay the foundation stone; **ai primi freddi** at the first sign of cold weather; **ustioni di primo grado** first-degree burns
2 *(in un ordine)* first; **preferisco il primo pittore al secondo** I prefer the former painter to the latter; **essere primo in classifica** *(squadra)* to be top of the league; *(disco)* to be number one in the charts; **essere in prima posizione** to be in the lead; **sul primo scaffale in alto/in basso** on the top/bottom shelf; **prima classe** first class; **un biglietto di prima classe** a first class ticket; **viaggiare in prima classe** to travel first-class; **di prim'ordine** *o* **prima qualità** first-class, first-rate; **è un attore di prim'ordine** he is a first-rate actor
3 *(prossimo)* first, next; **prendi la prima (strada) a destra** take the first *o* next (street) on the right; **scendo alla prima fermata** I am getting off at the next stop
4 *(principale)* main, principal; **il primo attore** the leading man; **la causa prima** the main reason
5 *(fraseologia)*: **per prima cosa** firstly; **in primo luogo** in the first place, first of all; **in un primo tempo** *o* **momento** at first; **fin dal primo momento** from the very first; **amore a prima vista** love at first sight; **fare i primi passi** to take one's first steps; **fare il primo passo** *(fig)* to make the first move
■ SM/F first (one); **è stata la prima a farlo** she was the first to do it; **fu tra i primi ad arrivare** he was among the first to arrive; **è la prima della classe** she is the top of the class; **non sposerò il primo venuto** I won't marry just anyone
■ SM *(gen)* first; *(piano)* first floor *(Brit)*, second floor *(Am)*; *(Culin)* first course; **il primo luglio** the first of July; **il primo d'Aprile** April Fools' Day; **il primo dell'anno** New Year's Day; **i primi del Novecento** the early twentieth century; **ai primi del mese** at the beginning of the month; **ai primi di maggio** at the beginning of May

primogenito, a [primo'dʒɛnito] SM/F first *o* eldest child, firstborn
■ AGG firstborn

primordi [pri'mɔrdi] SMPL beginnings; **ai primordi della storia** at the dawn of history

primordiale [primor'djale] AGG *(era, scienza)* primordial

primula ['primula] SF primula, primrose; **la primula rossa** *(fig)* the most wanted man

principale [printʃi'pale] AGG *(strada, motivo)* main, principal; *(opera)* major; **è questa la strada principale?** is this the main road?; **proposizione principale** *(Gramm)* main clause; **sede principale** head office
■ SM/F *(fam)* boss; **il principale ti vuole parlare** the boss wants to speak to you

principalmente [printʃipal'mente] AVV mainly, principally

principato [printʃi'pato] SM *(titolo nobiliare)* princedom; *(Stato)* principality

principe ['printʃipe] SM *(titolo nobiliare)* prince; **il principe di Galles** the Prince of Wales; **stare come un principe** *(fig)* to live like a lord; **principe azzurro** *(fig)* prince charming; **principe consorte** prince consort; **principe ereditario** crown prince

principescamente [printʃipeska'mente] AVV in a princely fashion

principesco, a, schi, sche [printʃi'pesko] AGG *(anche fig)* princely

principessa [printʃi'pessa] SF princess

principiante [printʃi'pjante] SM/F beginner; **un lavoro da principianti** *(pegg)* an amateur job

principiare [printʃi'pjare] *(frm)* VT *(discorso, trattative, lavoro)* to start, begin
■ VI *(aus* **(persona) avere; (tempo) essere***)* **principiare a fare qc** to begin *o* start doing *o* to do sth; **a principiare da oggi/domani** starting from today/tomorrow; **a principiare da te/noi** starting with you/us

principio, pi [prin'tʃipjo] SM **1** *(inizio)* beginning, start; **ricominciare dal principio** to start from the beginning again, go back to square one; **fin dal principio** right from the start; **al** *o* **in principio** at first, at the beginning; **dal principio alla fine** from beginning to end, from start to finish **2** *(concetto, norma)* principle; **essere senza principi** to have no principles; **una persona di sani principi morali** a person of sound moral principles; **una questione di principio** a matter of principle; **per principio** on principle; **principio precauzionale** precautionary principle **3** *(Mat)* principle **4** *(Chim)*: **principio attivo** active ingredient

prione [pri'ɔne] SM *(Bio)* prion

Pp

priora [pri'ora] SF (*Rel*) prioress
priorato [prio'rato] SM (*Rel*) priorate; (: *sede*) priory
priore [pri'ore] SM (*Rel, Storia*) prior
priori [pri'ori] **a priori** AGG INV prior, a priori
■ AVV at first glance; (*giudicare, valutare*) initially; (*dedurre, ragionare*) a priori
priorità [priori'ta] SF priority; **avere la priorità (su)** to have priority (over)
prioritario, ria, ri, rie [priori'tarjo] AGG having priority, of utmost importance; **posta prioritaria** first-class mail *o* post
prisma, i ['prizma] SM prism
privacy ['praivəsi] SF INV privacy; **legge sulla privacy** privacy law
privare [pri'vare] VT: **privare qn di qc** to deprive sb of sth; **privare qn della vita** to take sb's life; **non mi ha privato di niente** he didn't deny me anything
▶ **privarsi** VR: **privarsi di qc** to do *o* go without sth; **non privarsi di niente** to deny o.s. nothing
privatista, i, e [priva'tista] SM/F (*studente*) private student; **studiare da** *o* **come privatista** to study privately; **fare un esame da** *o* **come privatista** to be an external candidate at an exam
privativa [priva'tiva] SF (*Econ*) monopoly
privativo, a [priva'tivo] AGG (*Gramm*) privative
privatizzare [privatid'dzare] VT to privatize
privatizzazione [privatiddzat'tsjone] SF privatization
privato, a [pri'vato] AGG (*gen*) private; **diritto privato** (*Dir*) civil law; **proprietà privata** private property; **privato cittadino** private citizen; **ritirarsi a vita privata** to withdraw from public life; **discutere** *o* **parlare in privato** to talk in private
■ SM **1** (*cittadino*) private citizen; (*persona singola*) member of the public; **un'azienda gestita da privati** a privately owned business; **"non vendiamo a privati"** "wholesale only" **2** (*vita privata*) private life
privazione [privat'tsjone] SF **1** (*di diritti, genitori*) loss **2** (*sacrificio*: *spec pl*) hardship, privation
privilegiare [privile'dʒare] VT to favour (*Brit*), favor (*Am*)
privilegiato, a [privile'dʒato] AGG **1** (*individuo, classe*) privileged; (*trattamento*) preferential **2** (*Comm*: *credito*) preferential; **azioni privilegiate** preference shares (*Brit*), preferred stock *sg* (*Am*)
■ SM/F privileged person
privilegio, gi [privi'lɛdʒo] SM privilege; **godere di/concedere un privilegio** to enjoy/grant a privilege; **avere il privilegio di fare** to have the privilege of doing, be privileged to do
privo, a ['privo] AGG: **privo di** (*senza*) without; (*carente in*) lacking in; **privo di scrupoli** without scruples; **è privo di scrupoli** he's got no scruples; **privo di coraggio** lacking in courage; **privo di sensi** unconscious; **parole prive di significato** meaningless words
pro[1] [prɔ] PREP (*in favore di*) for, in favour (*Brit*) *o* favor (*Am*) of, on *o* in (*Am*) behalf of; **pro patria** patriotic; **raccolta pro rifugiati** collection for refugees; **sei pro o contro?** are you for or against?
pro[2] [prɔ] SM, SOLO SG (*vantaggio*) good; (*utilità*) advantage, benefit; **a che pro?** what's the use?; **a che pro l'hai fatto?** why did you do it?; **tutta questa fatica, e a che pro?** all this work, and for what?; **buon pro ti faccia!** much good may it do you!; **i pro e i contro** the pros and cons
probabile [pro'babile] AGG likely, probable; **è probabile che venga** he will probably come, he is likely to come
probabilità [probabili'ta] SF INV **1** probability, likelihood; (*possibilità*) chance; **quali** *o* **che probabilità ci sono?** what chances are there?; **che probabilità hanno di vincere?** what are their chances of winning?; **ha buone probabilità di ottenere il lavoro** he's got a good chance of getting the job; **una probabilità su due** a fifty-fifty chance; **c'è una probabilità su mille** there's a one in a thousand chance; **con molta probabilità** very probably, in all probability **2** (*Mat*) probability
probabilmente [probabil'mente] AVV probably; **probabilmente verrà** he'll probably come
probante [pro'bante] AGG convincing
problema, i [pro'blɛma] SM (*gen, Mat*) problem; (*questione*) issue
problematica [proble'matika] SF problems *pl*
problematicamente [problematika'mente] AVV problematically; **molti adolescenti vivono problematicamente la loro età** many teenagers find adolescence a difficult time
problematico, a, ci, che [proble'matiko] AGG (*situazione*) problematic; (*intesa, esito*) doubtful
proboscide [pro'bɔʃʃide] SF (*di elefante*) trunk; (*di insetto*) proboscis
procacciare [prokat'tʃare] VT to get, obtain; **procacciarsi un lavoro** to get o.s. a job; **procacciarsi il pane** *o* **da vivere** to earn one's living
procacciatore [prokattʃa'tore] SM: **procacciatore d'affari** wheeler-dealer (*fam*)
procace [pro'katʃe] AGG (*donna, aspetto*) provocative
procacemente [prokatʃe'mente] AVV provocatively
pro capite [prɔ'kapite] AVV per capita
procedere [pro'tʃɛdere] VI (*aus* **avere**; *nel senso (a)* **essere**) **1** (*avanzare*) to proceed, advance; (*continuare*) to proceed, go on; **procedere oltre** to go on ahead; **prima di procedere oltre** before going any further; **procedere con lentezza** (*veicolo*) to drive along slowly; (*trattative*) to proceed slowly; **procediamo con ordine** let's do this in an orderly fashion; **gli affari procedono bene** business is going well; **come procede il lavoro?** how's the work going?; **procede nella ricerca scientifica** he is continuing his scientific research **2** (*passare a*): **procedere a** to start, begin; **procediamo alla discussione** let's begin the discussion **3** (*agire*) to proceed; (*comportarsi*) to behave; **non mi piace il suo modo di procedere** I don't like the way he behaves; **bisogna procedere con cautela** we have to proceed cautiously **4** (*Dir*): **procedere contro qc** to start *o* take proceedings against sb; **non luogo a procedere** nonsuit
procedimento [protʃedi'mento] SM **1** (*svolgimento*) course **2** (*metodo*) procedure; (: *Tecn*) process; **il procedimento usato per la fabbricazione** the manufacturing process **3** (*Dir*) proceedings *pl*; **procedimento penale** criminal proceedings *pl*
procedura [protʃe'dura] SF (*gen, Dir*) procedure; **seguire** *o* **osservare la procedura** to follow procedure
procedurale [protʃedu'rale] AGG (*Dir*) procedural
procellaria [protʃel'larja] SF storm petrel
processare [protʃes'sare] VT (*Dir*): **processare qn (per)** to try sb (for)
processione [protʃes'sjone] SF (*gen*) procession
processo [pro'tʃɛsso] SM **1** (*gen, Chim, Med, Tecn*) process; **processo di fabbricazione** manufacturing process; **processo di pace** peace process **2** (*Dir*: *civile*)

(legal) proceedings *pl*, (court) action, lawsuit; (: *penale*) trial; **un processo per omicidio** a murder trial; **essere sotto processo** to be on trial; **mettere sotto processo** (*anche fig*) to put on trial; **fare il processo alle intenzioni di qn** to question sb's motives

processore [protʃes'sore] SM (*Inform*) processor

processuale [protʃessu'ale] AGG (*Dir*): **atti processuali** records of a trial; **spese processuali** legal costs

Proc. Gen. ABBR = procuratore generale

procinto [pro'tʃinto] SM: **in procinto di fare qc** about to do sth, on the point of doing sth; **ero in procinto di partire** I was about to leave *o* on the point of leaving

procione [pro'tʃone] SM (*Zool*) raccoon

proclama, i [pro'klama] SM (*bando, appello*) proclamation

proclamare [prokla'mare] VT (*legge*) to promulgate; (*stato d'assedio, guerra, pace*) to declare; **proclamare qn vincitore** to declare sb the winner; **proclamare la propria innocenza** to proclaim one's innocence

proclamazione [proklamat'tsjone] SF (*dichiarazione*) declaration; (*affermazione*) proclamation

procrastinare [prokrasti'nare] VT (*data*) to postpone; (*pagamento*) to defer

procreare [prokre'are] VT to procreate

procreazione [prokreat'tsjone] SF procreation

procura [pro'kura] SF (*Dir*) **1** proxy, power of attorney; **per procura** by proxy **2** (*ufficio*): **la procura della Repubblica** the Public Prosecutor's office

procurare [proku'rare] VT **1** (*fornire*): **procurare qc a qn** to get *o* obtain sth for sb, provide sb with sth; **procurare danni** to cause damage; **procurare noie a qn** to cause sb trouble; **hai procurato i biglietti?** did you get the tickets? **2** (*fare in modo di*): **procurare di fare qc** to try to do sth

procuratore, trice [prokura'tore] SM/F (*Dir*) ≈ solicitor (*Brit*), ≈ lawyer (*Am*) (*chi è munito di procura*) holder of power of attorney; **procuratore generale** (*in corte d'appello*) public prosecutor; (*in corte di cassazione*) Attorney General; **procuratore legale** ≈ solicitor (*Brit*), ≈ lawyer **procuratore della Repubblica** (*in corte d'assise, tribunale*) public prosecutor

prode ['prɔde] AGG valiant, brave
■ SM brave man

prodezza [pro'dettsa] SF (*qualità*) valour (*Brit*), valor (*Am*), bravery; (*fig*) feat, exploit

prodigalità [prodigali'ta] SF INV prodigality

prodigare [prodi'gare] VT (*lodi, affetto*) to lavish, be lavish with; **gli prodiga tutte le sue cure** she lavishes all her care on him
▶ **prodigarsi** VR: **prodigarsi per qn** to do all one can for sb

prodigio, gi [pro'didʒo] SM (*miracolo*) wonder, marvel; (*fig: persona*) prodigy; **i prodigi della tecnica/scienza** the wonders of technology/science; **fare prodigi** to work wonders
■ AGG INV: **bambino prodigio** child prodigy

prodigiosamente [prodidʒosa'mente] AVV miraculously

prodigioso, a [prodi'dʒoso] AGG wonderful, marvellous (*Brit*), marvelous (*Am*), prodigious; (*fenomenale*) phenomenal

prodigo, a, ghi, ghe ['prɔdigo] AGG: **essere prodigo (di)** (*consigli, attenzioni*) to be lavish (with); (*denaro*) to be extravagant (with); **il figliol prodigo** (*Rel, fig*) the prodigal son

prodotto, a [pro'dotto] PP *di* **produrre**
■ SM (*gen, Mat*) product; (*fig: risultato*) result, fruit, product; **è un buon prodotto** it's a good product; **prodotti agricoli** farm produce *sg*; **prodotti alimentari** foodstuffs; **prodotti di bellezza** cosmetics; **prodotti chimici** chemicals; **prodotto di base** primary product; **prodotto finale** end product; **prodotto interno lordo** (*Econ*) gross domestic product; **prodotto nazionale lordo** (*Econ*) gross national product

prodromo ['prɔdromo] SM (*segno precorritore*) warning sign; (*Med*) prodrome

produco *ecc* [pro'duko] VB *vedi* **produrre**

produrre [pro'durre] VT IRREG **1** (*gen, Cine*) to produce; (*calore*) to generate; (*fabbricare*) to manufacture, make, produce; **produrre in serie** to mass-produce **2** (*causare: angoscia, timori*) to cause, give rise to

produssi *ecc* [pro'dussi] VB *vedi* **produrre**

produttività [produttivi'ta] SF productivity

produttivo, a [produt'tivo] AGG (*lavoro, investimento*) productive; (*metodo, ciclo*) of production, production *attr*

produttore, trice [produt'tore] SM/F (*gen, Cine, Agr*) producer
■ AGG (*gen, Agr*) producing *attr*; **paese produttore di petrolio** oil-producing country

produzione [produt'tsjone] SF **1** (*gen, Cine, TV*) production; **articolo di produzione italiana** article of Italian manufacture; **produzione in serie** mass production **2** (*quantità prodotta*) production, output; (*Agr*) production, yield

proemio, mi [pro'emjo] SM introduction, preface

Prof. ABBR (= **professore**) Prof.

profanare [profa'nare] VT (*Rel*) to profane, to desecrate; (*tomba*) to violate; (*fig: nome, ricordo*) to defile

profanazione [profanat'tsjone] SF (*vedi vb*) profanation, desecration; violation; defilement

profano, a [pro'fano] AGG (*non sacro*) secular, profane; (*sacrilego*) profane; (*fig: orecchio, occhio*) untrained
■ SM/F (*gen*) layman, lay person
■ SM: **il profano** the profane, the secular

proferire [profe'rire] VT IRREG (*parola, nome*) to utter; (*giudizio, desiderio*) to express

proferito, a [profe'rito] PP *di* **proferire**

professare [profes'sare] VT (*opinione, dottrina*) to profess; (*medicina, avvocatura*) to practise (*Brit*), practice (*Am*)
▶ **professarsi** VR: **professarsi innocente** to declare o.s. innocent

professionale [professjo'nale] AGG (*gen*) professional; (*malattia*) occupational; **istituto professionale** training college

professionalità [professjonali'ta] SF professionalism

professionalmente [professjonal'mente] AVV professionally

professione [profes'sjone] SF (*gen*) occupation, profession; (*manuale*) trade; **la professione medica** the medical profession; **libera professione** profession; **fare qc di professione** to do sth for a living; **di professione** professional, by profession; **professione: infermiera** occupation: nurse; **professione di fede** profession of faith

professionismo [professjo'nizmo] SM professionalism

professionista, i, e [professjo'nista] AGG professional; **un fotografo professionista** a professional photographer
■ SM/F (*gen, Sport*) professional; **libero professionista** (*gen*) self-employed; (*avvocato, medico*) professional man/woman; **i liberi professionisti** the self-employed

Pp

professorale [professo'rale] AGG professorial
professore, essa [profes'sore] SM/F (*Scol*) teacher; (*Univ*) ≈ lecturer (: *titolare di cattedra*) professor; **professore d'orchestra** member of an orchestra
profeta, i [pro'fɛta] SM prophet
profetessa [profe'tessa] SF prophetess
profeticamente [profetika'mente] AVV prophetically
profetico, a, ci, che [pro'fɛtiko] AGG prophetic
profetizzare [profetid'dzare] VT to prophesy
profezia [profet'tsia] SF prophecy
profferta [prof'fɛrta] SF: **fare profferte amorose a qn** to make (amorous) advances to sb
profferto, a [prof'fɛrto] PP *di* **proferire**
proficuamente [profikua'mente] AVV profitably
proficuo, a [pro'fikuo] AGG profitable, useful
profilare [profi'lare] VT **1** (*descrivere in breve*) to outline **2** (*ornare*: *vestito*) to edge **3** (*Tecn*: *barra metallica*) to shape
▶ **profilarsi** VIP (*figura*) to stand out, be outlined, be silhouetted; (*soluzione, problemi*) to emerge; (*minaccia, crisi*) to loom up; **profilarsi all'orizzonte** (*anche fig*) to appear on the horizon
profilassi [profi'lassi] SF INV (*Med*) preventive treatment, prophylaxis
profilato [profi'lato] SM (*Tecn*: *trave*) section
profilattico, a, ci, che [profi'lattiko] (*Med*) AGG prophylactic
■ SM (*anticoncezionale*) condom, sheat (*Brit*)
profilo [pro'filo] SM (*gen, fig*) profile; (*breve descrizione*) sketch, outline; **di profilo** in profile; **mettersi di profilo** to turn sideways (on); **considerare qc sotto il profilo giuridico** to consider the legal aspects of sth; **una figura di scarso profilo** an insignificant character
profittare [profit'tare] VI (*aus* **avere**) **profittare di** (*situazione*) to profit by *o* from; (*pegg*: *persona*) to take advantage of
profitto [pro'fitto] SM (*gen, Econ*) profit; (*fig*: *progresso*) progress; **ricavare un profitto da** to make a profit from *o* out of; **un profitto di 8000 euro** an 8000 euro profit; **vendere con profitto** to sell at a profit; **conto profitti e perdite** profit and loss account; **trarre profitto da** (*lezione, esperienza*) to learn from; (*problemi altrui*) to take advantage of; (*invenzione*) to turn to good account; (*tempo libero*) to make the most of
profondamente [profonda'mente] AVV (*conficcare, piantare*) deep; (*fig*: *amare, addolorare, essere radicato*) deeply; (*dormire*) deeply, soundly; **dormiva profondamente** he was sleeping soundly *o* deeply; **era profondamente addormentato** he was fast *o* sound asleep; **sentirsi profondamente legato a qn** to feel very attached to sb; **sono profondamente legata a lui** I am deeply attached to him; **siamo profondamente addolorati per la perdita del caro Giovanni** we are really sorry about Giovanni's death
profondere [pro'fondere] VB IRREG
■ VT (*lodi*) to lavish; (*denaro*) to squander
▶ **profondersi** VIP: **profondersi in** (*scuse, ringraziamenti*) to be profuse in
profondimetro [profon'dimetro] SM (*nuoto subacqueo*) depth gauge
profondità [profondi'ta] SF INV **1** depth; **scavare in profondità** to dig deep; **avere 10 metri di profondità** *or* **avere una profondità di 10 metri** to be 10 metres deep *o* in depth; **il fiume qui ha una profondità di 5 metri** the river here is 5 metres deep; **le profondità del mare** the depths of the sea **2** (*di persona, osservazione*) profundity; (*di sentimento, rispetto*) depth **3** (*Cine, Fot*): **profondità di campo** depth of field
profondo, a [pro'fondo] AGG **1** (*gen*) deep; **poco profondo** shallow; **profondo 5 metri** 5 metres deep **2** (*fig*: *notte, colore, voce*) deep; (: *sospiro*) deep, heavy; (: *sonno*) deep, sound; (: *silenzio, mistero*) total, profound; (: *interesse, sentimento, meditazione*) profound; (: *inchino*) deep, low; (: *causa, significato*) underlying, deeper; (: *tendenza*) deep-seated, underlying
■ SM depth, depths *pl*, bottom; **nel profondo del mare** in the depths of the sea, at the bottom of the sea; **dal profondo del cuore** from the bottom of one's heart; **nel profondo del cuore** *o* **dell'animo** in one's heart of hearts
proforma [pro'forma] AGG routine *attr*
■ AVV: **fare qc proforma** to do sth as a formality
■ SM INV formality
Prof.ssa ABBR (= **professoressa**) Prof.
profugo, a, ghi, ghe ['prɔfugo] SM/F refugee
profumare [profu'mare] VI (*aus* **avere**) to smell good, be fragrant; **profumare di pulito/fresco** to smell clean/fresh
■ VT **1** (*sogg*: *fiori*) to perfume, scent; (*fazzoletto*) to put perfume *o* scent on; **l'aroma del caffè profumava l'aria** the smell of coffee filled the air **2** **profumarsi** (*pelle, capelli*) to put perfume *o* scent on
▶ **profumarsi** VR to put on perfume *o* scent
profumatamente [profumata'mente] AVV: **pagare qc profumatamente** to pay through the nose for sth; **pagare qn profumatamente** to pay sb handsomely
profumato, a [profu'mato] AGG (*fiore, aria*) fragrant; (*fazzoletto, saponetta*) scented; (*pelle*) sweet-smelling; (*persona*) with perfume on
profumazione [profumat'tsjone] SF (*di prodotto*) perfume
profumeria [profume'ria] SF perfumery
profumo [pro'fumo] SM (*sostanza*) perfume, scent; (*fragranza*) scent, fragrance; (*di caffè*) aroma; **mettersi il profumo** to put perfume on; **avere un buon profumo** to smell nice; **questi fiori hanno un buon profumo** these flowers smell lovely; **senti che profumo!** what a lovely smell!; **questa saponetta ha profumo di limone** this soap smells of lemon
profusione [profu'zjone] SF profusion; **a profusione** in plenty
profuso, a [pro'fuzo] PP *di* **profondere**
progenie [pro'dʒɛnje] SF INV (*pegg*: *razza, discendenza*) progeny
progenitore, trice [prodʒeni'tore] SM/F ancestor
progesterone [prodʒeste'rone] SM progesterone
progettare [prodʒet'tare] VT (*ponte, casa*) to plan, design; (*vacanza, fuga, rapina*) to plan; **progettare di fare qc** to plan to do sth
progettazione [prodʒettat'tsjone] SF planning; **in corso di progettazione** at the planning stage
progettista, i, e [prodʒet'tista] SM/F designer
progetto [pro'dʒɛtto] SM **1** (*Archit*) plan; (*idea*) plan, project; **il progetto della casa** the plan of the house; **fare il progetto di una casa** to design a house; **i miei progetti per il futuro** my plans for the future; **fare progetti per il futuro** to make plans for the future; **avere in progetto di fare qc** to be planning to do sth **2** (*Pol*): **progetto di legge** bill
prognosi ['prɔɲɲozi] SF INV (*Med*) prognosis; **essere in prognosi riservata** to be on the danger list; **sciogliere la prognosi su qn** to take sb off the danger list
programma, i [pro'gramma] SM **1** (*Pol, Econ, TV, Radio*)

programme (*Brit*), program (*Am*); (*Inform*) program; **programma applicativo** (*Inform*) application program **2** (*progetto*) plan; **fare programmi** to plan; **avere in programma di fare qc** to be planning to do sth; **hai qualcosa in programma per la serata?** have you anything planned for this evening?; **a causa dello sciopero vi trasmettiamo fuori programma un documentario** because of the strike we are now broadcasting a documentary instead of the scheduled program(me) **3** (*Scol*) syllabus, curriculum; **libri in programma**

programmare [program'mare] VT (*gen*) to plan; (*Inform*) to program; (*Cine: presentare*) to screen; (*TV, Radio*) to put on; **programmare di fare qc** to plan to do sth

programmatore, trice [programma'tore] SM/F (*Inform*) (computer) programmer (*Brit*) *o* programer (*Am*)

programmazione [programmat'tsjone] SF (*Econ*) planning; (*Inform*) programming (*Brit*), programing (*Am*); **in programmazione all'Odeon** (*film*) now showing at the Odeon; **linguaggio di programmazione** (*Inform*) progra(m)ming language

progredire [progre'dire] VI (*aus* ***(persona)*** **essere**; ***(cosa)*** **avere**) (*migliorare*) to progress, make progress; **progredire in qc** to make progress in sth

progredito, a [progre'dito] AGG (*paese, popolo*) advanced

progressione [progres'sjone] SF progression; **progressione aritmetica** (*Mat*) arithmetic progression; **progressione geometrica** geometric progression

progressista, i, e [progres'sista] AGG, SM/F progressive

progressivamente [progressiva'mente] AVV progressively

progressivo, a [progres'sivo] AGG progressive

progresso [pro'grɛsso] SM (*gen*) progress *no pl*; **i progressi della scienza** scientific progress; **fare progressi** to make progress; **sta facendo progressi in matematica** she's making progress in maths

proibire [proi'bire] VT **1** (*vietare*) to forbid, prohibit; (*per legge, regola*) to prohibit; **proibire a qn di fare qc** to forbid sb to do sth; **mi ha proibito di uscire** she has forbidden me to go out; **gli fu proibito di entrare** he was refused admission **2** (*impedire*): **proibire a qn di fare qc** to prevent sb from doing sth

proibitivo, a [proibi'tivo] AGG (*prezzo*) prohibitive; (*condizioni del tempo*) adverse

proibito, a [proi'bito] AGG forbidden; **"è proibito l'accesso"** "no admittance"; **"è proibito fumare"** "no smoking"; **sogni proibiti** impossible dreams; **frutto proibito** (*Rel, fig*) forbidden fruit

proibizione [proibit'tsjone] SF prohibition

proibizionismo [proibittsjo'nizmo] SM prohibition

proiettare [projet'tare] VT **1** (*gen, Geom*) to project; (*Cine: riprodurre su schermo*) to project; (*ombra, luce*) to cast, throw, project **2** (*gettare*) to throw (out); **furono proiettati fuori dalla vettura** they were thrown out of the car **3** (*protendere*): **proiettare le proprie speranze nel futuro** to pin one's hopes on the future

proiettile [pro'jettile] SM (*pallottola*) bullet (*o* shell); (*corpo lanciato in aria*) projectile; **a prova di proiettile** bulletproof

proiettore [projet'tore] SM **1** (*Cine, Fot*) projector **2** (*in stadio*) floodlight; (*Aut*) headlight, headlamp; (*Mil*) searchlight

proiezione [projet'tsjone] SF (*gen, Geom, Cine*) projection; **cabina di proiezione** (*Cine*) projection room

prole ['prɔle] SF children *pl*, offspring; **senza prole** childless

proletariato [proleta'rjato] SM proletariat

proletario, ria, ri, rie [prole'tarjo] AGG, SM/F proletarian

proliferare [prolife'rare] VI (*aus* **avere**) (*anche fig*) to proliferate

prolifico, a, ci, che [pro'lifiko] AGG prolific

prolissamente [prolissa'mente] AVV verbosely

prolissità [prolissi'ta] SF verbosity

prolisso, a [pro'lisso] AGG verbose

prologo, ghi ['prɔlogo] SM prologue

prolunga, ghe [pro'lunga] SF (*di cavo elettrico, telefono*) extension

prolungamento [prolunga'mento] SM (*gen*) extension; (*di strada*) continuation

prolungare [prolun'gare] VT (*discorso, attesa*) to prolong; (*linea, termine*) to extend; (*strada, muro*) to extend, continue; (*vacanza*) to prolong, extend
▶ **prolungarsi** VIP (*film, discussione*) to go on; (*effetto*) to last; **la vacanza si è prolungata di alcuni giorni** we (*o* they *ecc*) extended our (*o* their *ecc*) holiday (*Brit*) *o* vacation (*Am*) by a few days

promemoria [prome'mɔrja] SM INV memorandum, memo

promessa [pro'messa] SF promise; **fare/mantenere una promessa** to make/keep a promise; **gli ha fatto la promessa di tornare** she promised him that she would come back; **è una giovane promessa del teatro** he (*o* she) is a promising young actor (*o* actress); **ogni promessa è debito!** I'll hold you to that!

promesso, a [pro'messo] PP *di* **promettere**
■ AGG: **la terra promessa** the promised land; **sposi promessi** betrothed couple *sg*
■ SM/F (*fidanzato*) betrothed

Prometeo [pro'mɛteo] SM Prometheus

promettente [promet'tɛnte] AGG promising

promettere [pro'mettere] VT IRREG to promise; **te lo prometto** I promise (you); **promettere a qn di fare qc** to promise sb that one will do sth; **ha promesso di venire** *o* **che sarebbe venuto** he promised to come *o* that he would come; **promettimi che scriverai** promise me that you'll write; **promettere mari e monti a qn** to promise sb the earth; **promettere bene** (*tempo*) to be *o* look promising; (*studente, attore*) to show promise, be very promising; **il tempo promette male** *o* **non promette niente di buono** the weather doesn't look very promising

prominente [promi'nɛnte] AGG prominent

prominenza [promi'nɛntsa] SF prominence

promiscuamente [promiskua'mente] AVV (*pegg*) promiscuously

promiscuità [promiskui'ta] SF promiscuity, promiscuousness

promiscuo, a [pro'miskuo] AGG **1** **matrimonio promiscuo** mixed marriage **2** (*Gramm*): **nome promiscuo** common-gender noun

promisi *ecc* [pro'mizi] VB *vedi* **promettere**

promontorio, ri [promon'tɔrjo] SM (*Geog*) promontory, headland

promosso, a [pro'mɔsso] PP *di* **promuovere**

promotore, trice [promo'tore] SM/F (*di iniziativa, campagna*) promoter, organizer
■ AGG: **comitato promotore** organizing committee

Pp

promozionale [promottsjo'nale] AGG promotional; **"vendita promozionale"** "special offer"
promozione [promot'tsjone] SF (*gen, Comm, Sport*) promotion; **avere la promozione a** to be promoted to; **promozione delle vendite** sales promotion
promulgare [promul'gare] VT to promulgate
promulgazione [promulgat'tsjone] SF promulgation
promuovere [pro'mwɔvere] VT IRREG (*gen*) to promote; **promuovere qn (a)** to promote sb (to); **è stata promossa a vicedirettrice** she was promoted to assistant manager; **essere promosso agli esami** to pass one's exams; **lo studente è stato promosso** the student passed (his exams)
pronipote [proni'pote] SM/F (*di nonni*) great-grandchild, great-grandson/granddaughter; (*di zii*) great-nephew/niece; (*discendenti*): **pronipoti** SMPL descendants
pronome [pro'nome] SM pronoun
pronominale [pronomi'nale] AGG pronominal
pronosticare [pronosti'kare] VT to predict, forecast, foretell
pronostico, ci [pro'nɔstiko] SM forecast
prontamente [pronta'mente] AVV promptly, quickly
prontezza [pron'tettsa] SF (*vedi agg*) readiness; quickness, promptness; **prontezza di mente** readiness of mind; **prontezza di riflessi** quick reflexes *pl*; **prontezza di spirito** readiness of wit
pronto, a ['pronto] AGG **1** (*gen*) ready; **è pronto il pranzo?** is lunch ready?; **essere pronto a tutto** to be ready for anything; **essere pronto a fare qc** to be ready to do sth; **tienti pronto a partire** be ready to leave; **pronto all'ira** quick-tempered **2** (*intervento: rapido*) quick, prompt, fast; **ha sempre la risposta pronta** she's always got an answer; **a pronta cassa** (*Comm*) cash (*Brit*) *o* collect (*Am*) on delivery; **pronta consegna** (*Comm*) prompt delivery; **pronti contro termine** (*Fin*) repurchase agreement; **pronto soccorso** (*trattamento*) first aid; (*reparto*) A&E (*Brit*), ER (*Am*)
■ ESCL (*al telefono*) hello; (*in gara, gioco*): **pronti! via!** ready! steady! go!

LO SAPEVI...?
la parole **pronto** è usata in inglese ma con il significato di "subito", "immediatamente"

prontuario, ri [prontu'arjo] SM manual, handbook
pronuncia [pro'nuntʃa] SF (*articolazione di suono*) pronunciation; (*Dir*) judgment; **difetto di pronuncia** speech defect
pronunciabile [pronun'tʃabile] AGG pronounceable
pronunciare [pronun'tʃare] VT (*parola*) to pronounce; (*nome*) to utter; (*discorso*) to deliver; **pronunciare male qc** to mispronounce sth; **pronunciare una sentenza** (*Dir*) to pass sentence
▶ **pronunciarsi** VIP: **pronunciarsi (su qc)** (*dare un'opinione*) to give one's opinion (on sth), comment (on sth); **pronunciarsi a favore/contro** to pronounce o.s. in favour (*Brit*) *o* favor (*Am*) of/against; **non mi pronuncio** I don't want to comment
pronunciato, a [pronun'tʃato] AGG **1** (*accento, tendenza*) pronounced, marked **2** (*lineamenti*) prominent; (*mento*) protruding
pronunzia *ecc* [pro'nuntsja] = **pronuncia** *ecc*
propaganda [propa'ganda] SF propaganda; **fare propaganda per qn/qc** to push sb/sth
propagandare [propagan'dare] VT (*idea*) to propagandize; (*prodotto, invenzione*) to push
propagandista, i, e [propagan'dista] SM/F (*politico*) propagandist; (*Comm*) sales promoter
propagandistico, a, ci, che [propagan'distiko] AGG propaganda *attr*
propagare [propa'gare] VT (*Fis, Bio*) to propagate; (*notizia, idea, contagio*) to spread
▶ **propagarsi** VIP (*gen*) to spread; (*Fis: onde*) to be propagated; (*Bio*) (*: specie*) to propagate
propagatore, trice [propaga'tore] SM/F propagator
propagazione [propagat'tsjone] SF (*vedi vb*) propagation; spreading
propaggine [pro'paddʒine] SF (*Bot*) layer; (*fig: diramazione*) offshoot
propano [pro'pano] SM propane
propedeutica [prope'dɛutika] SF propaedeutics *pl* (*Brit*), propedeutics *pl* (*Am*)
propedeutico, a, ci, che [prope'dɛutiko] AGG (*corso, trattato*) introductory
propellente [propel'lɛnte] AGG, SM propellent
propendere [pro'pɛndere] VI IRREG (*aus* **avere**) **propendere per** to favour (*Brit*), favor (*Am*), lean towards; **propendere a fare qc** to be inclined to do sth; **propendere per il sì** to be in favo(u)r; **propendere per il no** not to be in favo(u)r
propensione [propen'sjone] SF **1** inclination; **avere propensione a credere che...** to be inclined to think that ... **2** (*disposizione*) bent; **avere propensione per la matematica** to have a bent for mathematics
propenso, a [pro'pɛnso] PP *di* **propendere**
■ AGG: **essere propenso a qc** to be in favour (*Brit*) *o* favor (*Am*) of sth; **essere propenso a fare qc** to be inclined to do sth
propinare [propi'nare] VT (*scherz: pietanza*) to serve up; (*: storia, discorso*) to inflict, foist; **propinare veleno a qn** to slip poison to sb; **ci ha propinato tutte le foto di famiglia** he dragged out all the family photographs for us
propiziare [propit'tsjare] VT: **propiziare qn, propiziarsi qn** to gain sb's favour; **propiziarsi gli dei** to propitiate the gods
propiziatorio, ria, ri, rie [propittsja'tɔrjo] AGG propitiatory
propiziazione [propittsjat'tsjone] SF propitiation
propizio, zia, zi, zie [pro'pittsjo] AGG: **propizio (per)** (*gen*) favourable (*Brit*) *o* favorable (*Am*) (to); (*momento*) opportune (for)
proponimento [proponi'mento] SM resolution; **fare il proponimento di fare qc** to resolve to do sth; **nonostante i miei proponimenti** in spite of my good intentions
proporre [pro'porre] VB IRREG
■ VT **1** (*suggerire*) to suggest, propose; (*soluzione, candidato*) to put forward; (*legge, brindisi*) to propose; **proporre qc a qn** to suggest *o* propose sth to sb; **proporre di fare qc** to suggest *o* propose doing sth; **gli ho proposto di venire** I suggested that he should come; **ho proposto di andare al cinema** I suggested going to the cinema **2** (*offrire: aiuto, prezzo*) to offer; **proporre qc a qn** to offer sth to sb, offer sb sth; **proporre di fare qc** to offer to do sth **3** **proporsi qc** (*obiettivo, meta*) to set o.s. sth; **proporsi di fare qc** to propose *o* intend to do sth;
▶ **proporsi** VR: **proporsi come candidato** to put o.s. forward as a candidate
proporzionale [proportsjo'nale] AGG proportional; **proporzionale a** proportional to, proportionate to; **sistema proporzionale** (*Pol*) proportional representation system

proporzionalmente [proportsjonal'mente], **proporzionatamente** [proportsjonata'mente] AVV proportionally, proportionately
proporzionato, a [proportsjo'nato] AGG: **proporzionato a** proportionate to, proportional to; **ben proporzionato** well-proportioned
proporzione [propor'tsjone] SF (*gen, Mat*) proportion; **in proporzione (a)** in proportion (to); **in proporzione diretta/inversa** in direct/inverse proportion *o* ratio; **mancare di proporzione** to be out of proportion; **un movimento di grandi proporzioni** (*fig*) an important movement
proposito [pro'pɔzito] SM **1** (*intenzione*) intention, aim; **avere il proposito di fare qc** to intend to do sth; **fare qc di proposito** to do sth deliberately *o* on purpose; **l'ha fatto di proposito** he did it on purpose; **essere pieno di buoni propositi** to be full of good intentions **2** (*argomento*): **a questo proposito** on this subject; **a quale proposito voleva vedermi?** what did he want to see me about?; **a proposito della tua ragazza...** speaking of your girlfriend ...; **a proposito di** (*in lettera*) regarding, with regard to; **le scrivo a proposito dell'inserzione** I am writing to you with reference to the advertisement; **a proposito, come sta tua madre?** by the way, how's your mother?; **a proposito, sai dirmi...** by the way, can you tell me ...; **capitare** *o* **arrivare a proposito** (*cosa, persona*) to turn up at the right time
proposizione [propozit'tsjone] SF **1** (*Gramm*) clause; (: *periodo*) sentence; **proposizione principale** main clause; **proposizione secondaria** subordinate clause **2** (*Mat*) proposition
proposta [pro'posta] SF (*gen*) proposal; (*suggerimento*) suggestion; **fare una proposta** to put forward a proposal; to make a suggestion; **ha fatto una proposta** he made a suggestion; **proposta di matrimonio** proposal of marriage; **fare una proposta di matrimonio a qn** to propose to sb; **proposta di legge** (*Pol*) bill
proposto, a [pro'posto] PP *di* **proporre**
propriamente [proprja'mente] AVV (*correttamente*) properly, correctly; (*in modo specifico*) specifically; **propriamente detto** in the strict sense of the word; **subito dopo l'ingresso propriamente detto** immediately beyond the hall itself
proprietà [proprje'ta] SF INV **1** (*caratteristica, qualità*) property **2** (*possedimento: casa*) property; (: *terreno*) property, land; (: *beni mobili e immobili*) property *gen no pl*, estate; **avere delle proprietà** to own property; **essere di proprietà di qn** to belong to sb; **proprietà privata** private property **3** (*correttezza: nel parlare, nello scrivere*) correctness; **proprietà di linguaggio** correct use of language
proprietario, ria, ri, rie [proprje'tarjo] SM/F (*gen*) owner; (*di pensione*) landlord/landlady; (*di albergo*) proprietor/proprietress, owner; **piccolo proprietario** (*Agr*) smallholder; **proprietario terriero** landowner
proprio, pria, pri, prie ['prɔprjo] AGG **1** (*possessivo*) own; (: *impersonale*) one's; **l'ha visto con i (suoi) propri occhi** he saw it with his own eyes; **ognuno è arrivato con la propria macchina** everybody arrived in their own car; **ognuno è tornato a casa propria** everybody went back home; **per motivi miei propri** for my own *o* for personal reasons; **fare qc per conto proprio** to do sth for oneself **2** (*tipico, caratteristico*): **proprio di** peculiar to, characteristic of; **è proprio dei mammiferi** it's peculiar to *o* characteristic of mammals; **è un atteggiamento proprio di quel tipo di persona** it's an attitude characteristic *o* typical of that kind of person **3** (*esatto*) proper, exact, correct; **senso proprio di un termine** exact *o* proper meaning of a term; **è stata una vera e propria sciocchezza** it was pure foolishness **4** (*Gramm*): **nome proprio**
■ PRON one's own; **ognuno si prenda il proprio** everybody take their own
■ SM: **mettersi in proprio** (*Comm*) to set up one's own business, set up on one's own; **si è messo in proprio** he set up his own business; **perderci del proprio** to be out of pocket
■ AVV **1** (*precisamente*) exactly, just; **proprio così!** exactly!; **le cose sono andate proprio così** that's just how things went **2** (*veramente*) really; **oggi mi sento proprio bene** I feel really fit today; **sono proprio stanco** I'm really tired; **ma sei proprio certo?** are you really sure?, are you a hundred per cent certain? **3** (*affatto*): **non... proprio** not ... at all; **non mi piace proprio** I don't like it at all; **quel tipo non mi piace proprio** I really can't stand that man; **non voleva proprio farlo** he really didn't want to do it, he didn't want to do it at all
propugnare [propuɲ'ɲare] VT to support
propulsione [propul'sjone] SF (*Tecn, Aer, Naut*) propulsion; **a propulsione atomica** atomic-powered
propulsore [propul'sore] SM (*Tecn*) propeller
prora ['prɔra] SF (*Naut: prua*) bow, bows *pl*, prow; **vento di prora** headwind
proroga, ghe ['prɔroga] SF (*vedi vb*) extension; deferment, postponement
prorogare [proro'gare] VT (*durata*) to extend; (*scadenza, termine*) to defer, postpone
prorompente [prorom'pɛnte] AGG (*fiume, torrente*) gushing; **il suo entusiasmo era prorompente** he was overflowing with enthusiasm
prorompere [pro'rompere] VI IRREG (*aus* **avere**) (*fiume, torrente*): **prorompere dagli argini** to burst its banks; **prorompere in pianto/in una risata** to burst into tears/out laughing
prorotto, a [pro'rotto] PP *di* **prorompere**
proruppi *ecc* [pro'ruppi] VB *vedi* **prorompere**
prosa ['prɔza] SF **1** (*Letteratura*) prose; **la prosa e la poesia** prose and poetry; **scrivere in prosa** to write in prose; **opera in prosa** prose work **2** (*Teatro*): **la stagione della prosa** the theatre season; **attore di prosa** theatre actor; **compagnia di prosa** theatrical company
prosaicamente [prozaika'mente] AVV prosaically
prosaico, a, ci, che [pro'zaiko] AGG prosaic, mundane
prosatore, trice [proza'tore] SM/F prose writer
prosciogliere [proʃ'ʃɔʎʎere] VT IRREG: **prosciogliere qn (da)** (*obbligo, giuramento*) to release sb (from); (*Dir: da accusa*) to acquit sb (of)
proscioglimento [proʃʃoʎʎi'mento] SM (*vedi vb*): **proscioglimento (da)** release (from); acquittal (of)
prosciolto, a [proʃ'ʃɔlto] PP *di* **prosciogliere**
prosciugamento [proʃʃuga'mento] SM (*naturale*) drying up; (*artificiale*) draining; (*bonifica*) reclamation
prosciugare [proʃʃu'gare] VT (*asciugare: naturalmente*) to dry up; (: *artificialmente*) to drain; (*bonificare*) reclaim
▶ **prosciugarsi** VIP to dry up
prosciutto [proʃ'ʃutto] SM ham; **prosciutto affumicato** smoked ham; **prosciutto cotto** cooked *o* boiled ham; **prosciutto crudo** cured ham; **prosciutto di Parma** Parma ham
proscritto, a [pros'kritto] PP *di* **proscrivere**

Pp

■SM/F (*fuorilegge*) outlaw; (*esule*) exile
proscrivere [pros'krivere] VT IRREG (*Storia*) to proscribe; (*esiliare*) to exile, banish; (*fig: abolire*) to ban
proscrizione [proskrit'tsjone] SF (*vedi vb*) proscription; banishment; banning
prosecuzione [prosekut'tsjone] SF continuation
proseguimento [prosegwi'mento] SM (*gen*) continuation; **buon proseguimento!** (*a chi viaggia*) enjoy the rest of your journey!; (*a chi festeggia*) enjoy the rest of the party!; (*a chi cena*) enjoy the rest of your meal!
proseguire [prose'gwire] VT (*studi, viaggio*) to continue, carry on with; (*lavoro*) to continue with; **proseguire il cammino** to continue on one's way; **proseguì dicendo che...** he went on to say that ...; **proseguì la lettura del libro** he carried on reading the book; **decise di proseguire il viaggio** he decided to continue his journey
■VI (*aus* **avere**) (*sogg: persona*) to carry on, go on; (: *lavoro, viaggio*) to continue, go on; **proseguire negli studi** to continue *o* pursue one's studies; **come prosegue?** (*lavoro*) how is it coming along?; **la polizia prosegue nelle ricerche** the police are pursuing their inquiries
proselito, a [pro'zɛlito] SM/F (*Rel, Pol*) convert
prosodia [prozo'dia] SF prosody
prosopopea [prozopo'pɛa] SF pomposity
prosperamente [prospera'mente] AVV (*gen*) prosperously; **vivere prosperamente** to live in affluence
prosperare [prospe'rare] VI (*aus* **avere**) (*commercio, salute*) to flourish; (*finanze*) to thrive; (*paese, commerciante*) to prosper
prosperità [prosperi'ta] SF prosperity
prospero, a ['prɔspero] AGG (*commercio, salute*) flourishing; (*finanze*) thriving; (*paese, commerciante*) prosperous, affluent
prosperosamente [prosperosa'mente] AVV prosperously
prosperoso, a [prospe'roso] AGG (*commercio, salute*) flourishing; (*regione*) prosperous, affluent; **una ragazza prosperosa** (*formosa*) a buxom girl
prospettare [prospet'tare] VT (*possibilità*) to indicate; (*affare*) to outline; (*ipotesi*) to advance
▶ **prospettarsi** VIP (*possibilità*) to present itself; (*situazione, futuro*) to look, seem; **la vacanza si prospetta bene** it looks like being an enjoyable holiday
prospettiva [prospet'tiva] SF **1** (*Disegno*) perspective; (*veduta*) view; **in prospettiva** in perspective **2** (*fig: previsione, possibilità*) prospect; **che prospettive hai?** what are your prospects?; **non ci sono molte prospettive di lavoro** there aren't many job prospects
prospetto [pros'pɛtto] SM **1** (*Disegno*) elevation; (*veduta*) view, prospect; **guardare qc di prospetto** to get a front view of sth **2** (*facciata*) front, façade **3** (*tabella*) table, schedule; (*sommario*) summary; **prospetto delle lezioni** timetable; **prospetto dei verbi** verb table
prospiciente [prospi'tʃɛnte] AGG: **prospiciente qc** (*casa*) facing sth; (*terrazza*) overlooking sth
prossimamente [prossima'mente] AVV soon; **"prossimamente su questi schermi"** (*Cine*) "coming shortly to your screens"
prossimità [prossimi'ta] SF proximity, nearness; **in prossimità di** near (to), close to; **in prossimità delle feste natalizie** as Christmas approaches
prossimo, a ['prɔssimo] AGG **1** (*successivo: in tempo, spazio*) next; **nei prossimi giorni** in the next few days; **scendo alla prossima fermata** I get off at the next stop; **la prossima volta stai attento!** next time be careful!; **venerdì prossimo** next Friday; **venerdì prossimo venturo** (*frm: Amm*) next Friday **2** (*vicino: gen*) near; (: *parente*) close; **in un prossimo futuro** in the near future; **prossimo a** near (to), close to; **essere prossimo alla laurea** *o* **a laurearsi** to be about to graduate; **è prossimo alla fine** (*fig: morte*) he is close to death **3** (*Gramm*): **passato prossimo** present perfect; **trapassato prossimo** past perfect
■SM **1** (*Rel*) neighbour (*Brit*), neighbor (*Am*), fellow man **2** **avanti il prossimo!** (*a sportello ecc*) next please!
prostata ['prɔstata] SF (*Anat*) prostate (gland)
prostituire [prostitu'ire] VT to prostitute
▶ **prostituirsi** VR to prostitute o.s.
prostituta [prosti'tuta] SF prostitute
prostituto [prosti'tuto] SM male prostitute
prostituzione [prostitut'tsjone] SF prostitution
prostrare [pros'trare] VT (*sogg: malattia*) to debilitate seriously; (*fig: nel morale*) to exhaust, wear out; **prostrato dal dolore** overcome *o* prostrate with grief
▶ **prostrarsi** VR to prostrate o.s.; (*fig*) to humble o.s.; **prostrarsi ai piedi di qn/davanti a qn** to bow down at sb's feet/before sb
prostrazione [prostrat'tsjone] SF prostration
protagonista, i, e [protago'nista] SM/F protagonist
proteggere [pro'tɛddʒere] VB IRREG
■VT (*gen*) to protect; (*moralmente*) to guard, shield; (*fig: artista, arte*) to be a patron of
▶ **proteggersi** VR to protect o.s.
proteggi-slip [pro'teddʒi'zlip] SM INV pantyliner
proteico, a, ci, che [pro'tɛiko] AGG protein *attr*; **altamente proteico** high in protein
proteina [prote'ina] SF protein
protendere [pro'tɛndere] VB IRREG
■VT to stretch out
▶ **protendersi** VR to stretch forward; **protendersi dalla finestra** to lean out of the window
protervia [pro'tɛrvja] SF arrogance, haughtiness
protesi ['prɔtezi] SF INV (*Med*) prosthesis; **protesi dentaria** dentures *pl*
proteso, a [pro'teso] PP *di* **protendere**
protesta [pro'tɛsta] SF protest; **fare una protesta contro** to protest against; **di protesta** (*marcia, sciopero*) protest *attr*
protestante [protes'tante] AGG, SM/F Protestant
protestantesimo [protestan'tezimo] SM Protestantism
protestare [protes'tare] VT to protest; **protestare la propria innocenza** to protest one's innocence
■VI (*aus* **avere**) to protest
▶ **protestarsi** VR: **protestarsi innocente** to protest one's innocence
protesto [pro'tɛsto] SM (*Dir*) protest; **mandare una cambiale in protesto** to dishonour (*Brit*) *o* dishonor (*Am*) a bill
protettivo, a [protet'tivo] AGG protective
protetto, a [pro'tɛtto] PP *di* **proteggere**
■AGG (*porto, baia*) sheltered; **una specie protetta** a protected species
■SM/F protégé(e); (*fig: favorito*) favourite (*Brit*), favorite (*Am*)
protettorato [protetto'rato] SM (*Pol*) protectorate
protettore, trice [protet'tore] SM/F (*difensore*) protector, guardian; (*di artista, arte*) patron

■ SM (*di prostituta*) pimp
■ AGG **1** (*Rel*): **santo protettore** patron saint **2 società protettrice degli animali** animal protection society

protezione [protet'tsjone] SF (*difesa*) protection; (*di arte, artista*) patronage; **misure di protezione** protective measures; **prendere qn sotto la propria protezione** to give sb one's patronage; **protezione civile** civil defence (*Brit*) *o* defense (*Am*)

protezionismo [protettsjo'nizmo] SM protectionism

protezionista, i, e [protettsjo'nista] AGG, SM/F protectionist

protezionistico, a, ci, che [protettsjo'nistiko] AGG protectionist

protocollare [protokol'lare] VT (*Amm*) to register
■ AGG of protocol

protocollo [proto'kɔllo] SM **1** (*registro*) register of documents; **numero di protocollo** reference number **2** (*accordo internazionale, cerimoniale*) protocol
■ AGG INV: **foglio protocollo** foolscap

protone [pro'tone] SM proton

protoplasma, i [proto'plazma] SM protoplasm

prototipo [pro'tɔtipo] SM prototype; **il prototipo dell'americano** your typical American

protozoo [protod'dzɔo] SM protozoan

protrarre [pro'trarre] VB IRREG
■ VT (*prolungare*) to prolong; **ha deciso di protrarre il suo soggiorno di un mese** he decided to stay on a month longer;
▶ **protrarsi** VIP to go on, continue

protratto, a [pro'tratto] PP *di* **protrarre**

protuberanza [protube'rantsa] SF (*gen*) bulge, protuberance; (*Anat*) swelling

Prov. ABBR (= **provincia**) Prov.

prova ['prɔva] SF **1** (*esperimento*) test, trial; **essere in prova** (*persona: per lavoro*) to be on probation; **assumere in prova** (*per lavoro*) to employ on a trial basis; **mettere alla prova** to put to the test; **sta mettendo a dura prova la mia pazienza** he is trying my patience severely; **sottoporre ad una prova** to test; **a prova di bomba** bombproof; (*fig*) indestructible; **a prova di proiettile** bulletproof; **la prova del fuoco** (*fig*) the acid test; **circuito/volo di prova** test track/flight; **giro di prova** (*Sport*) test *o* trial run; **prova su pista** (*Ciclismo*) track race **2** (*dimostrazione, anche Mat*) proof *no pl*; (*Dir*) proof *no pl*, evidence *no pl*; **dare prova di** to give proof of; **hai le prove di ciò che dici?** can you prove what you're saying?; **ho la prova che è stato lui** I've got proof that it was him; **avevo ragione e tutto ciò ne è la prova** I was right and this all goes to prove it; **fino a prova contraria** until (it's) proved otherwise; **fino a prova contraria questa è casa mia!** until I hear differently this is my house!; **una prova** (*Dir*) a piece of evidence; **non ci sono abbastanza prove per incriminarlo** there isn't enough evidence to charge him; **assolto per insufficienza di prove** (*Dir*) acquitted because of lack of evidence; **prova a carico** (*Dir*) evidence for the prosecution; **prova a discarico** (*Dir*) evidence for the defence; **prova documentale** (*Dir*) documentary evidence; **prova del nove** (*Mat*) casting out nines; (*fig*) acid test; **prova testimoniale** (*Dir*) testimonial evidence **3** (*tentativo*) attempt, try; **fare una prova** to make an attempt, have a try; **facciamo una prova** let's try it **4** (*Scol*) exam, test; **prova orale/scritta** oral/written exam *o* test **5** (*Teatro, Mus*) rehearsal; **fare le prove** to rehearse; **prova generale** dress rehearsal **6** (*di abito*) fitting

provare [pro'vare] VT **1** (*tentare*) to try, attempt; (*nuova medicina, macchina, freni*) to try out, test; (*scarpe, abito*) to try on; (*assaggiare*) to try, taste; **ho provato una nuova crema** I've tried a new cream; **prova questo gelato, ti piacerà** try this ice cream, you'll like it; **ho provato il suo motorino** I tried out his moped; **provare a fare qc** to try *o* attempt to do sth; **prova tu se ci riesci!** you try and see if you can do it!; **perché non provi a parlargli?** why don't you try talking to him?; **provaci e vedrai!** just you try it!; **ci ha provato con tutte in ufficio** (*fam*) he's tried it on with all the women in the office; **provarsi una gonna** to try on a skirt; **provati questo maglione** try this jumper on **2** (*dimostrare: verità, teoria, Dir*) to prove **3** (*mettere alla prova: coraggio ecc*) to put to the test; **posso provare che ero a casa** I can prove I was at home; **è molto provato da quell'esperienza** the experience has left its mark on him **4** (*sentimento*) to feel; (*sensazione*) to experience; **ho provato rabbia quando l'ho saputo** I felt angry when I found out **5** (*Teatro, Mus*) to rehearse
▶ **provarsi** VIP: **provarsi a fare qc** to try *o* attempt to do sth

provenienza [prove'njɛntsa] SF (*origine*) origin; (*fonte*) source; **luogo di provenienza** place of origin; **controlla la provenienza della notizia** check the source of the news

provenire [prove'nire] VI IRREG (*aus* **essere**) **provenire da** (*per nascita*) to come from; (*essere causato*) to be due to, be the result of

proventi [pro'vɛnti] SMPL revenue *sg*, proceeds

provenuto, a [prove'nuto] PP *di* **provenire**

Provenza [pro'vɛntsa] SF Provence

provenzale [proven'tsale] AGG, SM Provençal

proverbiale [prover'bjale] AGG proverbial

proverbialmente [proverbjal'mente] AVV proverbially

proverbio, bi [pro'vɛrbjo] SM proverb; **come dice il proverbio** as the proverb says, as the saying goes

provetta [pro'vetta] SF (*Chim*) test tube; **bambino in provetta** test-tube baby

provetto, a [pro'vɛtto] AGG skilled, experienced

provider [pro'vaider] SM INV (*Inform*) service provider

provincia, ce *o* **cie** [pro'vintʃa] SF province; **gente/vita di provincia** provincial people/life; **venire dalla provincia** to come from the provinces

PROVINCIA

A **Provincia** is the autonomous political and administrative unit which is on a level between a "Comune" and a "Regione"; there are 103 in the whole of Italy. The **Provincia** is responsible for public health and sanitation, for the maintenance of major roads and public buildings such as schools, and for agriculture and fisheries. Situated in the "capoluogo", or chief town, each **Provincia** is run by a "Giunta provinciale", which is elected by the "Consiglio Provinciale"; both of these bodies are presided over by a "Presidente".

provinciale [provin'tʃale] AGG (*anche pegg*) provincial
■ SM/F (*anche pegg*) provincial
■ SF (*anche:* **strada provinciale**) main road (*Brit*), highway (*Am*)

provincialismo [provintʃa'lizmo] SM (*pegg*) provincialism

provino [pro'vino] SM (*Cine*) screen test; (: *anteprima*)

Pp

trailer; (*campione*) specimen; **fare un provino** (*Cine*) to do a screen test; **ha fatto un provino** she did a screen test
provocante [provo'kante] AGG (*attraente*) provocative
provocare [provo'kare] VT (*incidente, rivolta, risata*) to cause, bring about; (*persona*) to provoke; (*collera, curiosità*) to arouse; **la nebbia ha provocato molti incidenti** the fog caused a lot of accidents; **non provocarmi!** don't provoke me!
provocatore, trice [provoka'tore] SM/F (*di rivolta*) agitator
■ AGG: **agente provocatore** agent provocateur
provocatoriamente [provokatorja'mente] AVV provocatively
provocatorio, ria, ri, rie [provoka'tɔrjo] AGG provocative
provocazione [provokat'tsjone] SF provocation
provvedere [provve'dere] VB IRREG
■ VI (*aus* avere) **1 provvedere a** (*famiglia*) to provide for **2** (*prendere provvedimenti*) to take steps, act; **hanno provveduto a mandare rinforzi** they arranged for reinforcements to be sent **3 provvedere a** (*occuparsi di*) to look after, take charge of; **provvedere alla spesa/a fare la spesa** to do the shopping; **l'azienda che provvede alla raccolta dei rifiuti urbani** the company responsible for refuse collection
■ VT: **provvedere qn di qc** to provide *o* supply sb with sth
▶ **provvedersi** VR: **provvedersi di** to provide o.s. with
provvedimento [provvedi'mento] SM measure, step; (*di previdenza*) precaution; **provvedimento disciplinare** disciplinary measure
provveditorato [provvedito'rato] SM (*Amm*): **provveditorato agli studi** education offices *pl*
provveditore [provvedi'tore] SM (*Amm*): **provveditore agli studi** director (*Brit*) *o* commissioner (*Am*) of education
provvidenza [provvi'dɛntsa] SF: **la provvidenza** providence; **un dono della provvidenza** a godsend; **ti ha mandato la provvidenza!** you're a godsend!
provvidenziale [provviden'tsjale] AGG (*arrivo, pioggia*) providential; **il tuo arrivo è stato provvidenziale!** your coming here was a godsend!
provvidenzialmente [provvidentsjal'mente] AVV providentially
provvido, a ['prɔvvido] AGG (*letter*) prudent
provvigione [provvi'dʒone] SF (*Comm*) commission; **lavoro/stipendio a provvigione** job/salary on a commission basis
provvisorietà [provvizorje'ta] SF (*vedi agg*) temporary nature; provisional nature
provvisorio, ria, ri, rie [provvi'zɔrjo] AGG (*riparo, lavoro*) temporary; (*governo*) provisional, interim; **orario provvisorio** provisional timetable; **un governo provvisorio** a provisional government
provvista [prov'vista] SF supply, stock; **fare provvista di** to stock up with; **fare provviste** to take in supplies; **provviste alimentari** provisions
provvisto, a [prov'visto] PP *di* **provvedere**
prozia [prot'tsia] SF great-aunt
prozio [prot'tsio] SM great-uncle
prua ['prua] SF (*Naut*) bow, bows *pl*, prow
prudente [pru'dɛnte] AGG (*attento*) cautious, prudent; (*assennato*) wise, sensible; **un automobilista prudente** a careful driver; **sarebbe prudente che tu lo facessi** you would be well advised to do it; **non è prudente guidare quando si è stanchi** it's not a good idea to drive when you're tired; **è più prudente aspettare qui** it would be better to wait here; **sii prudente!** be careful!, take care!
prudentemente [prudente'mente] AVV (*gen*) prudently; (*guidare*) carefully
prudenza [pru'dɛntsa] SF (*vedi agg*) caution, prudence; wisdom; **guida con prudenza!** drive carefully!; **per prudenza** as a precaution, to be on the safe side; **ha avuto la prudenza di non dire niente** he had the good sense *o* he was wise enough to keep quiet
prudere ['prudere] VI DIF to be itchy, itch; **mi prude un orecchio** my ear is itchy *o* itching
prugna ['pruɲɲa] SF (*Bot*) plum; **prugna secca** prune
pruno ['pruno] SM (*Bot: cespuglio*) blackthorn; (*: spina*) thorn
pruriginoso, a [prurid͡ʒi'noso] AGG itchy
prurito [pru'rito] SM (*anche fig*) itch, itchiness *no pl*; **ho prurito alla mano** my hand is itchy *o* itching
Prussia ['prussja] SF Prussia
prussiano, a [prus'sjano] AGG, SM/F Prussian
PS SIGLA = *Pesaro* [pi'ɛsse] SIGLA F = **Pubblica Sicurezza**
■ ABBR [pi'ɛsse] **1** (= **Postscriptum**) P.S.
2 (*Contabilità*) = **partita semplice**
PSDI [pi'ɛsse'di'i] SIGLA M (*Pol:* = **Partito Socialista Democratico Italiano**) *former political party*
pseudo... ['psɛudo] PREF pseudo...
pseudobiografico, a, ci, che [pseudobio'grafiko] AGG pseudobiographic(al)
pseudointellettuale [pseudointellettu'ale] AGG, SM/F pseudo-intellectual
pseudonimo [pseu'dɔnimo] SM (*gen*) assumed name; (*di scrittore*) pen name, pseudonym; (*di attore*) stage name
pseudoscientifico, a, ci, che [pseudoʃen'tifiko] AGG pseudoscientific
pseudoscienza [pseudo'ʃɛntsa] SF pseudoscience
PSI [pi'ɛsse'i] SIGLA M (*Pol*) = *Partito Socialista Italiano*
psicanalisi [psika'nalizi] SF INV psychoanalysis
psicanalista, i, e [psikana'lista] SM/F psychoanalyst
psicanalitico, a, ci, che [psikana'litiko] AGG psychoanalytic(al)
psicanalizzare [psikanalid'dzare] VT to psychoanalyse (*Brit*) *o* psycoanalyze (*Am*)
psiche ['psike] SF psyche
psichedelico, a, ci, che [psike'dɛliko] AGG (*Psic, luci*) psychedelic
psichiatra, i, e [psi'kjatra] SM/F psychiatrist
psichiatria [psikja'tria] SF psychiatry
psichiatrico, a, ci, che [psi'kjatriko] AGG (*caso*) psychiatric; (*reparto, ospedale*) psychiatric, mental
psichico, a, ci, che ['psikiko] AGG psychological
psicoattitudinale [psikoattitudi'nale] AGG: **test psicoattitudinale** psychometric test
psicofarmaco, ci [psiko'farmako] SM (*Med*) *drug used in treatment of mental conditions*
psicofisica [psiko'fisika] SF psychophysics *sg*
psicofisico, a, ci, che [psiko'fisiko] AGG psychophysical
psicologia [psikolo'dʒia] SF psychology
psicologicamente [psikolodʒika'mente] AVV psychologically
psicologico, a, ci, che [psiko'lɔdʒiko] AGG psychological
psicologo, a, gi, ghe [psi'kɔlogo] SM/F psychologist
psicopatico, a, ci, che [psiko'patiko] AGG psychopathic
■ SM/F psychopath

psicosi [psi'kɔzi] SF INV (*Med*) psychosis; (*fig*) obsessive fear
psicosomatico, a, ci, che [psikoso'matiko] AGG psychosomatic
psicoterapeuta, i, e [psikotera'pɛuta], **psicoterapista, i, e** [psikotera'pista] SM/F psychotherapist
psicoterapia [psikotera'pia] SF psychotherapy
psoriasi [pso'riazi] SF INV psoriasis
PT SIGLA = *Pistoia*
■ABBR **1** (= **Poste e Telecomunicazioni**) ≈ PO (= *post office*) **2** (*Fisco*) = **polizia tributaria**
p.t. ABBR (= **primo tempo**: *Calcio*) first half
Pt.a ABBR (*Geog*: = **Punta**) Pt.
pterodattilo [ptero'dattilo] SM pterodactyl
pubblicamente [pubblika'mente] AVV publicly
pubblicare [pubbli'kare] VT to publish
pubblicazione [pubblikat'tsjone] SF **1** (*gen*) publication; **pubblicazione periodica** periodical **2** (*di matrimonio*): **pubblicazioni** SFPL (marriage) banns; **fare le pubblicazioni** to publish the (marriage) banns
pubblicista, i, e [pubbli'tʃista] SM/F **1** (*giornalista*) freelance journalist **2** (*Dir*) expert in public law
pubblicistica, che [pubbli'tʃistika] SF current affairs journalism
pubblicità [pubblitʃi'ta] SF INV **1** (*Comm*: *professione*) advertising; **fare pubblicità a qc** to advertise sth; **fa pubblicità ad uno shampoo** she advertises a shampoo; **si occupa di pubblicità** he's in advertising **2** (*annunci in giornali, TV*) advertisements *pl*, ads *pl*, adverts *pl*; **c'è troppa pubblicità in TV** there are too many ads on TV; **ho visto la pubblicità sul giornale** I saw the advert in the paper **3** (*diffusione*) publicity; **fare molta pubblicità a qc** to give sth a lot of publicity
pubblicitario, ria, ri, rie [pubblitʃi'tarjo] AGG (*campagna, agenzia*) advertising *attr*; (*film, trovata*) publicity *attr*; **cartello pubblicitario** advertising poster; **annuncio** *o* **avviso pubblicitario** advertisement
■SM/F advertising agent
pubblicizzare [pubblitʃid'dzare] VT to publicize
pubblico, a, ci, che ['pubbliko] AGG (*gen*) public; (*statale*: *scuola*) state *attr*; **la scuola pubblica** state school; **funzionario pubblico** civil servant; **la pubblica amministrazione** public administration; **un pubblico esercizio** a catering (*o* hotel *o* entertainment) business; **pubbliche relazioni** public relations; **ministero della Pubblica Istruzione** ≈ Department for Education (*Brit*), ≈ Department of Health, Education and Welfare (*Am*); **la Pubblica Sicurezza** the police; **Pubblico Ministero** Public Prosecutor's Office
■SM (*gen*) public; (*spettatori*: *Cine, Teatro*) audience, public; (: *di partita*) spectators *pl*; **è aperto al pubblico di domenica** it's open to the public on Sundays; **il pubblico dei lettori** the reading public; **un libro destinato al grande pubblico** a book written for the general public; **in pubblico** in public
pube ['pube] SM (*Anat*) pubis
pubertà [puber'ta] SF puberty
pudicamente [pudika'mente] AVV modestly
pudicizia [pudi'tʃittsja] SF modesty
pudico, a, ci, che [pu'diko] AGG modest
pudore [pu'dore] SM (sense of) modesty; (*vergogna*) shame; (*riservatezza*) discretion; **falso pudore** false modesty; **oltraggio al pudore** (*Dir*) indecent behaviour
puericultrice [puerikul'tritʃe] SF paediatric (*Brit*) *o* pediatric (*Am*) nurse
puericultura [puerikul'tura] SF paedology (*Brit*), pedology (*Am*), infant care
puerile [pue'rile] AGG (*anche pegg*) childish, puerile
puerilità [puerili'ta] SF childishness, puerility
puerilmente [pueril'mente] AVV (*pegg*) childishly, puerilely
puerpera [pu'ɛrpera] SF *woman who has just given birth*
pugilato [pudʒi'lato] SM boxing; **un incontro di pugilato** a boxing match
▷ www.fpi.it/
pugile ['pudʒile] SM boxer
pugliese [puʎ'ʎese] AGG of *o* from Puglia
■SM/F inhabitant *o* native of Puglia
pugnalare [puɲɲa'lare] VT to stab; **pugnalare qn alle spalle** (*anche fig*) to stab sb in the back
pugnalata [puɲɲa'lata] SF (*ferita*) stab wound; (*fig*: *colpo*) severe blow; **dare una pugnalata a qn** to stab sb; **una pugnalata alle spalle** (*anche fig*) a stab in the back
pugnale [puɲ'ɲale] SM dagger; **colpo di pugnale** stab; **uccidere con un pugnale** to stab to death
pugno ['puɲɲo] SM **1** (*mano*) fist; **a pugni stretti** with clenched fists; **con la pistola in pugno** with one's gun in one's hand; **scrivere qc di proprio pugno** to write sth in one's own hand; **mostrare i pugni a qn** to shake one's fist at sb; **ormai ha la vittoria in pugno** he now has victory within his grasp; **tenere la situazione in pugno** to have control of the situation; **avere qn in pugno** to have sb in the palm of one's hand; **ormai lo abbiamo in pugno** (*con ricatto, minacce*) we've got him in our power now; (*criminale*) we've got him now **2** (*colpo*) punch; **dare un pugno a qn** to punch sb; **gli ha dato un pugno in un occhio** he punched him in the eye; **fare a pugni** to fight; (*fig*: *colori*) to clash; **essere un pugno in un occhio** (*fig*) to be an eyesore; **pugno di ferro** (*tirapugni*) knuckleduster (*Brit*), brass knuckles *pl* (*Am*) **3** (*manciata*): **un pugno di** a handful of; **due pugni di riso** two handfuls of rice; **un pugno di uomini** a handful of men; **rimanere con un pugno di mosche** to be left empty-handed
pula ['pula] SF chaff
pulce ['pultʃe] SF flea; **mercato delle pulci** flea market; **il gioco delle pulci** tiddlywinks *sg*; **mi hai messo una pulce nell'orecchio** (*fig*: *insospettire*) you've aroused my suspicions; **pulce di mare** sand hopper
pulcinella [pultʃi'nɛlla] SM: **Pulcinella** (*maschera*) Punch; **il segreto di pulcinella** (*fig*) an open secret
pulcino [pul'tʃino] SM (*Zool*) chick; (*vezzeggiativo*) pet; **timido come un pulcino** as shy as a mouse; **bagnato come un pulcino** soaked to the skin
pulcioso, a [pul'tʃoso] AGG flea-bitten
puledra [pu'ledra] SF filly
puledro [pu'ledro] SM colt
puleggia, ge [pu'leddʒa] SF (*Tecn*) pulley
pulire [pu'lire] VT **1** (*gen*) to clean; (*giardino*) to clear; (*cassetto*) to clear out; (*lucidare*) to polish; **stava pulendo l'interno della macchina** she was cleaning the inside of the car; **pulire a secco** to dry-clean; **far pulire qc** to have sth cleaned; **ho fatto pulire la macchina** I had my car cleaned; **pulire il piatto** (*fig*) to clear one's plate **2** **pulirsi** (*mani*) to clean; (*naso, bocca*) to wipe;

Pp

pulirsi i denti to brush *o* clean one's teeth; **pulisciti i piedi** wipe your feet
▶ **pulirsi** VR to clean o.s. (up)

pulita [pu'lita] SF quick clean; **dare una pulita a qc** to give sth a quick clean

pulito, a [pu'lito] AGG (*gen*) clean; (*ordinato*) neat, tidy; (*fig: lavoro, persona*) honest; **un pavimento pulito** a clean floor; **una ragazza dalla faccia pulita** (*fig*) an innocent-looking girl; **avere la coscienza pulita** to have a clear conscience

pulitore, trice [puli'tore] SM/F cleaner

pulitura [puli'tura] SF cleaning; **pulitura a secco** dry cleaning

pulizia [pulit'tsia] SF (*condizione*) cleanliness, cleanness; (*atto*) cleaning; **fare le pulizie** (*gen*) to do the cleaning, do the housework; **fare le pulizie di primavera** to spring-clean; **far pulizia** (*fig: portarsi via tutto*) to make a clean sweep; **pulizia etnica** ethnic cleansing

> **LO SAPEVI...?**
> **pulizia** non si traduce mai con la parola inglese ***polish***

pullman ['pulman] SM INV (*per escursioni*) coach (*Brit*), bus (*Am*)

pullover [pul'lɔver] SM INV pullover, sweater, jumper (*Brit*)

pullulare [pullu'lare] VI (*aus* **avere**) (*pesci*) to teem; (*insetti*) to swarm; **il fiume pullula di pesci** the river is teeming with fish; **la piazza pullulava di turisti** the square was swarming with tourists; **in questa zona i ristoranti cinesi pullulano** there are lots of Chinese restaurants in this area

pulmino [pul'mino] SM minibus

pulpito ['pulpito] SM pulpit; **senti da che pulpito viene la predica!** look who's talking!

pulsante [pul'sante] AGG pulsating
■ SM (push) button; **premi il pulsante** press the button

pulsar ['pulsar] SM/F INV pulsar

pulsare [pul'sare] VI (*aus* **avere**) (*cuore*) to beat, pulsate; (*vena*) to throb

pulsazione [pulsat'tsjone] SF (*di cuore*) beat; (*di vena*) throbbing; (*Fis*) pulsation; **(numero di) pulsazioni** (*Med*) pulse rate

pulsione [pul'sjone] SF (*Psic*) drive

pulviscolo [pul'viskolo] SM fine dust; **pulviscolo atmosferico** specks *pl* of dust

puma ['puma] SM INV puma

pungente [pun'dʒente] AGG (*frutto, arbusto, spina*) prickly; (*odore*) pungent; (*fig: freddo, vento*) biting; (*: ironia, critica*) biting, pungent

pungere ['pundʒere] VB IRREG
■ VT **1** (*sogg: spina, ago*) to prick; (*: insetto, ortica*) to sting; (*: freddo*) to bite; **l'ha punto una vespa** a wasp stung him; **pungere qn sul vivo** to cut sb to the quick; **essere punto dal rimorso** to be stricken with remorse **2** **pungersi un dito/una mano** to prick one's finger/one's hand
▶ **pungersi** VR (*con ago, spina*) to prick o.s.

pungiglione [pundʒiʎ'ʎone] SM sting

pungitopo [pundʒi'tɔpo] SM (*Bot*) butcher's-broom

pungolare [pungo'lare] VT (*anche fig: spingere*) goad; **pungolare qn a fare qc** to goad sb into doing sth

pungolo ['pungolo] SM (*per animali*) goad; (*fig: stimolo*) spur; **il pungolo dell'ambizione** the spur of ambition

punibile [pu'nibile] AGG punishable

punire [pu'nire] VT to punish

punitivo, a [puni'tivo] AGG punitive

punizione [punit'tsjone] SF punishment; (*Sport*) penalty; **una punizione severa** a harsh punishment; **calcio di punizione** free kick; **dare una punizione a qn** to punish sb; **dare una punizione esemplare a qn** to make an example of sb; **per punizione** as a punishment

punk [pʌŋk] AGG INV punk *attr*
■ SM/F INV punk

punsi *ecc* ['punsi] VB *vedi* **pungere**

punta[1] ['punta] SF **1** (*di matita, ago, coltello*) point; (*di trapano*) drill; (*di perforatrice*) bit; (*di parte del corpo*) tip; (*di capelli, coda*) tip, end; (*di campanile, albero*) top; (*di monte*) top, peak; **fare la punta a una matita** to sharpen a pencil; **le punte degli alberi** the treetops; **punta della freccia** arrowhead; **in punta di piedi** on tiptoe; **camminare in punta di piedi** to walk on tiptoe, tiptoe; **ballare sulle punte** (*Danza*) to dance on points; **a punta** pointed; **un paio di scarpe a punta** a pair of pointed shoes; **doppie punte** (*di capelli*) split ends; **avere qc sulla punta delle dita** (*fig*) to have sth at one's fingertips; **avere qc sulla punta della lingua** (*fig*) to have sth on the tip of one's tongue; **prendere qc di punta** (*fig*) to meet sth head on; **uomo di punta** (*Sport, Pol*) front-rank *o* leading man **2** (*fig: pizzico: di zucchero, farina*) touch; (*: di sale*) pinch; (*: d'invidia, rancore*) touch, hint; (*traccia*) trace; **c'è una punta d'acido nel latte** the milk tastes slightly sour; **una punta di invidia** a touch of envy **3** (*Geog*) promontory **4** (*massima frequenza o intensità*) peak; **ore di punta** peak hours; **il traffico delle ore di punta** rush-hour traffic; **punta massima/minima** highest/lowest level **5** (*Calcio*) centre forward

punta[2] ['punta] SF: **cane da punta** pointer

puntale [pun'tale] SM (*di ombrello*) tip; (*Sci: di bastoncino*) point, tip; (*: di attacco*) toe-piece

puntapiedi [punta'pjɛdi] SM INV (*Ciclismo*) toe-clip

puntare [pun'tare] VT **1** (*arma*) to point, aim; (*cannocchiale, dito*) to point; **puntare un fucile contro qn** to point a gun at sb; **le ha puntato un fucile contro** he pointed a gun at her; **puntare il dito verso qn/qc** to point (one's finger) at sb/sth; **puntare l'attenzione su qn/qc** to turn one's attention to sb/sth; **puntare gli occhi su qn** to fix one's eyes on sb **2** (*piantare: gomiti, piedi*) to plant; **puntare i piedi** (*fig*) to dig one's heels in **3** (*nei giochi*): **puntare su** to bet on; **ha puntato su quel cavallo** he bet on that horse **4** (*sogg: cane*) to point to
■ VI (*aus* **avere**) **1** **puntare su, puntare verso** (*aereo, nave*) to make for, head for; **puntare a qc/a fare qc** (*mirare*) to aim for sth/to do sth **2** (*contare*): **puntare su qn/qc** to rely on sb/sth, count on sb/sth

puntaspilli [puntas'pilli] SM INV = **portaspilli**

puntata[1] [pun'tata] SF **1** (*in scommessa, gioco*) bet; **fare una puntata** to place a bet **2** (*fig: breve visita*) short trip; **fare una puntata a casa** to pop home; **farò una puntatina a Parigi** I'll pay a flying visit to Paris

puntata[2] [pun'tata] SF (*di romanzo*) instalment (*Brit*), installment (*Am*); (*di sceneggiato*) episode; **hai visto la prima puntata?** did you see the first episode?; **romanzo a puntate** serial; **pubblicare a puntate** to serialize

puntatore [punta'tɔre] SM (*Inform*) pointer

punteggiare [punted'dʒare] VT to punctuate

punteggiatura [punteddʒa'tura] SF punctuation

punteggio, gi [pun'teddʒo] SM (*in gara*) score; (*in esame*) mark; **qual è il punteggio?** what's the score?; **sistema**

di punteggio scoring system; **totalizzare il punteggio massimo** to score maximum points
puntellare [puntel'lare] VT (*ponte, muro*) to shore (up); (*porta, finestra*) to prop up; (*fig: ipotesi*) to back up, support
puntello [pun'tɛllo] SM prop, support
punteria [punte'ria] SF (*Aut*) tappet
punteruolo [punte'rwɔlo] SM (*Tecn*) punch; (: *per stoffa*) bodkin
puntiglio [pun'tiʎʎo] SM (*ostinazione*) obstinacy, stubbornness; **fare qc per puntiglio** to do sth out of sheer obstinacy
puntigliosamente [puntiʎʎosa'mente] AVV punctiliously
puntigliosità [puntiʎʎosi'ta] SF punctiliousness
puntiglioso, a [punti'ʎʎoso] AGG punctilious
puntina [pun'tina] SF **1** (*da disegno*) drawing pin (*Brit*), thumb tack (*Am*) **2** (*del giradischi*) stylus **3** (*Aut*): **puntine** SFPL points
puntino [pun'tino] SM (*di punteggiatura*) dot; **mettere i puntini sulle "i"** (*fig*) to dot the i's and cross the "t"s; **fare le cose a puntino** to do things perfectly; **cotto a puntino** cooked to a turn *o* to perfection; **arrivare a puntino** to arrive at just the right moment; **puntini di sospensione** suspension points
punto[1], a ['punto] PP *di* **pungere**
punto[2] ['punto] SM
1 (*gen*) point; (*luogo*) spot, point, place; (*grado*) point, stage; **ha segnato tre punti** he scored three points; **la casa è in un bel punto** the house is in a nice spot; **a questo punto** *or* **al punto in cui siamo** at this stage; **a che punto sei?** (*con lavoro*) where have you got to?; (*nel prepararsi*) how are you getting on?; **ad un certo punto** at a certain point; **ad un certo punto uno si chiede...** there comes a time when one asks oneself ...; **fino ad un certo punto** to a certain extent; **non si può essere ingenui fino a questo** *o* **tal punto** one cannot be as naï ve as that; **era arrabbiato a tal punto che...** he was so angry that ...; **lo odia al punto tale che...** she hates him so much that ...; **passiamo al prossimo punto** (*in discorso*) let's move on to the next item *o* point; **punto per punto** point by point; **su questo punto siamo d'accordo** we agree on this point; **siamo sempre allo stesso punto** we're still at the same stage; **essere a buon punto** to have reached a satisfactory stage, be getting on well; **aver raggiunto il punto in cui...** to have reached the stage where ...; **venire al punto** to come *o* get to the point; **cotto al punto giusto** cooked to a turn; **di punto in bianco** (*improvvisamente*) all of a sudden; (*inaspettatamente*) out of the blue; **sono le 5 in punto** it's exactly 5 o'clock; **alle 6 in punto** at 6 o'clock sharp *o* on the dot; **vestito di tutto punto** all dressed up; **sul punto di fare qc** (just) about to do sth
2 (*Aer, Naut: posizione*) position; **fare il punto** to take a bearing; **fare il punto della situazione** (*analisi*) to take stock of the situation; (*riassunto*) to sum up the situation
3 (*in alfabeto, in morse, su 'i'*) dot; (*punteggiatura*) full stop (*Brit*), period (*Am*); (*di indirizzo e-mail*) dot; **punto e basta!** that's it!, that's enough!; **due punti** colon; **punto e a capo** new paragraph; **punti di sospensione** suspension points; **punto esclamativo** exclamation mark (*Brit*) *o* point (*Am*); **punto interrogativo** *o* **di domanda** question mark; **punto e virgola** semicolon
4 (*Cucito, Maglia, Med*) stitch
5 (*Tecn*): **mettere a punto** (*gen*) to adjust; (*motore*) to tune; (*cannocchiale*) to focus; (*Inform*) to debug; (*fig: questione*) to define, settle; (: *progetto*) to finalize
■ **punto d'appoggio** (*Alpinismo*) point of contact; **punto d'arrivo** arrival point; **punto caldo** (*Mil*) trouble spot; (*d'attualità*) major issue; **punto cardinale** cardinal point, point of the compass; **punto critico** (*anche fig*) critical point; **punto debole** weak spot, weak point; **punto (di) vendita** retail outlet; **punto di ebollizione** boiling point; **punto d'incontro** meeting place, meeting point; **punto d'intersezione** (*Geom*) point of intersection; **punto morto** standstill; **punto nero** (*comedone*) blackhead; **punto nevralgico** (*anche fig*) nerve centre (*Brit*) *o* center (*Am*); **punto d'onore** point of honour (*Brit*) *o* honor (*Am*); **punto di partenza** (*anche fig*) starting point; **punto di riferimento** landmark; (*fig*) point of reference; **punto di vista** (*fig*) point of view
■ AVV: **non...punto** not ... at all
puntuale [puntu'ale] AGG punctual; **essere puntuale** to be punctual, be on time; **è sempre puntuale** he's always punctual; **arrivare puntuale** to arrive on time; **essere puntuale nei pagamenti** to pay on time
puntualità [puntuali'ta] SF punctuality
puntualizzare [puntualid'dzare] VT to make clear
puntualizzazione [puntualiddzat'tsjone] SF clarification; **vorrei fare delle puntualizzazioni** I'd like to make some things clear, I'd like to clarify some points
puntualmente [puntual'mente] AVV (*gen*) on time; (*iro: al solito*) as usual
puntura [pun'tura] SF **1** (*di insetto*) sting; (*di zanzara, ragno*) bite; (*di spillo*) prick; (*dolore*) sharp pain **2** (*Med: iniezione*) injection; **fare una puntura a qn** to give sb an injection; **gli ha fatto una puntura sul braccio** she gave him an injection in his arm; **puntura lombare** lumbar puncture
punzecchiare [puntsek'kjare] VT to prick; (*fig: molestare*) to tease
▶ **punzecchiarsi** VR (*uso reciproco*) to tease each other
punzonare [puntso'nare] VT (*Tecn*) to stamp
punzone [pun'tsone] SM (*per metalli*) stamp, die
può [pwɔ], **puoi** [pwɔi] VB *vedi* **potere**
pupa ['pupa] SF **1** (*bambola, fam: ragazza*) doll **2** (*Zool*) pupa
pupazzo [pu'pattso] SM puppet; **pupazzo di neve** snowman
pupilla [pu'pilla] SF (*Anat*) pupil
pupillo, a [pu'pillo] SM/F (*prediletto*) pet, favourite (*Brit*), favorite (*Am*); (*Dir*) ward
puramente [pura'mente] AVV (*semplicemente*) purely, simply; (*unicamente*) only, solely
purché [pur'ke] CONG (*a patto che*) as long as, provided that, on condition that; **verrò con te purché non ci sia molto da aspettare** I'll come with you as long as we don't have to wait long; **verrò con te purché non piova** I'll come with you as long as it doesn't rain; **purché sia vero!** if only it were true!
pure ['pure] AVV **1** (*anche*) too, as well, also; (*in proposizioni negative*) either; **viene suo fratello e pure sua sorella** his brother is coming as is his sister, his brother is coming and his sister is too *o* as well; **siamo stati a Zurigo e pure a Lucerna** we went to Zurich and to Lucerne as well; **è venuto pure lui** he came too; **pure lei non lo sa fare** she can't do it either **2** (*con valore concessivo*): **faccia pure!** please do!, by all means!, go ahead!; **te l'avevo pur detto di non andarci** I did tell you not to go
■ CONG **1** (*tuttavia, nondimeno*) but, and yet,

nevertheless; **non è facile, pure bisogna riuscirci** it's not easy and yet we have to succeed; **è giovane, pure ha buon senso** he's young but he's sensible **2** (*anche se, sebbene*) even though; **pur non volendolo, ho dovuto farlo** I had to do it even though I didn't want to; **pur essendo fuori mano** even though it is out of the way **3** (*con valore finale*): **pur di vederlo contento farebbe di tutto** she would do anything to make him happy

purè [pu'rɛ] SM INV, **purea** [pu'rɛa] SF (*Culin*) purée; **purè di patate** mashed potatoes *pl*

purezza [pu'rɛttsa] SF (*gen*) purity; (*di colore*) clarity

purga, ghe ['purga] SF (*Med*) purging *no pl*, purge; (*Pol*) purge

purgante [pur'gante] SM (*Med*) purge, purgative
■ AGG (*Med*) purgative

purgare [pur'gare] VT (*Med: malato*) to purge, give a purgative to; (: *sangue, aria*) to purify; (*fig: testo, discorso*) to expurgate
▶ **purgarsi** VR (*fig*) **purgarsi dei peccati** to purge o.s. of one's sins

purgativo, a [purga'tivo] AGG (*Med*) purgative

purgatorio [purga'tɔrjo] SM (*Rel, fig*) purgatory

purificare [purifi'kare] VT (*gen*) to purify, cleanse; (*metalli*) to refine
▶ **purificarsi** VIP to cleanse o.s.

purificatoio, toi [purifika'tojo] SM (*Rel*) purificator

purificatore [purifika'tore] SM purifier

purificatorio, ria, ri, rie [purifika'tɔrjo] AGG purificatory, purifying, cleansing

purificazione [purifikat'tsjone] SF (*vedi vb*) purification, cleansing; refinement

puritanesimo [purita'nezimo] SM Puritanism

puritano, a [puri'tano] AGG (*Rel*) Puritan; (*fig*) puritanical
■ SM/F (*Rel*) Puritan; (*fig*) puritan

puro, a ['puro] AGG (*gen*) pure; (*acqua*) clear, limpid; (*vino*) undiluted; (*aria*) pure, clean; (*fig: ragazza*) chaste, pure; **di razza pura** thoroughbred; **è pazzia pura** it's sheer madness; **è la pura verità** that's the simple truth; **per pura curiosità** out of sheer curiosity; **per puro caso** by sheer chance, purely by chance; **pura lana vergine** pure new wool

purosangue [puro'sangwe] AGG INV (*cavallo*) thoroughbred; **un inglese purosangue** a full-blooded Englishman
■ SM/F INV (*cavallo*) thoroughbred

purtroppo [pur'trɔppo] AVV unfortunately

purulento, a [puru'lɛnto] AGG (*Med*) purulent, festering

pus [pus] SM (*Med*) pus; **fare pus** to ooze pus

push-up [puʃʃap] AGG INV (*reggiseno*) push-up

pusillanime [puzil'lanime] AGG cowardly
■ SM/F coward

pustola ['pustola] SF (*Med*) pustule; (*foruncolo*) pimple

putacaso [puta'kazo] AVV just supposing, suppose; **metti, putacaso, che arrivi anche lui** just supposing *o* suppose he comes too

putativo, a [puta'tivo] AGG putative

putiferio [puti'fɛrjo] SM row, rumpus; **fare/ scatenare un putiferio** to kick up a row

putrefare [putre'fare] VB IRREG, VI (*aus* **essere**), **putrefarsi** VIP to putrefy, rot

putrefatto, a [putre'fatto] PP *di* **putrefare**
■ AGG (*carne, legno*) rotten; (*cadavere*) putrid, decayed

putrefazione [putrefat'tsjone] SF putrefaction

putrescente [putreʃ'ʃɛnte] AGG putrefying, decaying

putrido, a ['putrido] AGG (*acqua*) putrid; (*carne*) rotten

puttana [put'tana] SF (*fam!*) whore (*fam!*); **figlio di puttana** (*fig*) son of a bitch

puttanata [putta'nata] SF (*fam: azione, osservazione*) bloody (*Brit*) *o* goddamn (*Am*) stupid thing to do (*o* say); (: *film, libro*) bullshit (*fam*); **dire delle puttanate** to talk bullshit

puttanella [putta'nɛlla] SF (*fam*) tart

puttanesco, a, schi, sche [putta'nesko] AGG (*Culin*): **spaghetti alla puttanesca** *spaghetti in a sauce made from anchovies, black olives, capers and tomatoes*

putto ['putto] SM cupid

puzza ['puttsa] SF = **puzzo**

puzzare [put'tsare] VI (*aus* **avere**) **puzzare (di)** to smell (of), stink (of); **puzza di fumo** it stinks of smoke; **gli puzza l'alito** his breath stinks, he's got very bad breath; **la faccenda puzza (d'imbroglio)** there's something fishy about the whole thing, the whole business stinks; **mi puzza!** it smells fishy to me!

puzzle [pʌzl] SM INV jigsaw puzzle

puzzo ['puttso] SM stink, foul smell; **puzzo di bruciato** smell of burning; **puzzo di fritto** stink of fried food; **sento puzzo** there's a horrible smell; **c'è puzzo d'imbroglio** it smells fishy

puzzola ['puttsola] SF (*Zool*) polecat

puzzolente [puttso'lɛnte] AGG smelly, stinking

PV SIGLA = *Pavia*

p.v., p/v ABBR (*Amm*) = *prossimo venturo*

PVC [pivi'tʃi] SIGLA M (= **polivinilcloruro**) PVC

PZ SIGLA = **Potenza**

p.zza ABBR = **piazza**

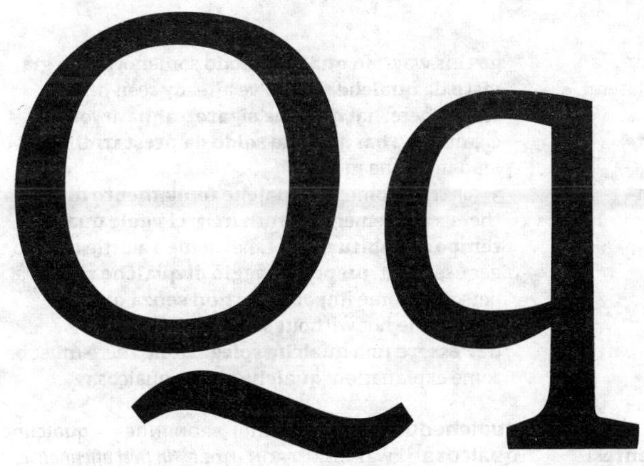

Q, q [ku] SF O M INV (*lettera*) Q, q; **Q come Quarto** ≈ Q for Queen

q ABBR (= **quintale**) q

Qatar ['katar] SM Qatar

qb ABBR (*Culin:* = **quanto basta**) as required; **zucchero qb** sugar to taste

QG ABBR = **quartier generale**

QI ['ku'i] SIGLA M (= **quoziente d'intelligenza**) IQ

qua [kwa] AVV **1** here; **vieni qua** come here; **eccomi qua!** here I am!; **qua dentro/sotto** in/under here; **le penne e le matite sono qua dentro** the pens and pencils are in here; **qua sotto c'è la tua camicia** your shirt is under here; **abita qua sotto** she lives (in the flat) downstairs; **da** *o* **di qua non mi muovo!** I'm not budging from here!; **da** *o* **di qua la vista è stupenda** the view is fantastic from here; **(al) di qua del fiume** on this side of the river; **passavo (per) di qua** I was just passing; **(per) di qua non si passa** you can't get through here *o* this way; **vieni più in qua** come closer **2** (*temporale*): **da un anno in qua** since last year, for a year now; **da quando in qua?** since when?; **da quando in qua ti interessi di musica classica?** since when have you been interested in classical music? **3** (*fraseologia*): **ecco qua cosa succede a non fare attenzione!** just look what happens when you don't pay attention!; **prendi qua questi soldi** here, take this money; **(dammi) qua, ci penso io!** just give it to me, I'll see to it!; **dammi qua, è mio** give it here, it's mine; **guarda qua che confusione!** just look at this mess!; **qua la mano** let's shake on it; **che diavolo vuole questo qua?** what on earth does he want?

quacchero, a ['kwakkero] SM/F Quaker

quaderno [kwa'dɛrno] SM (*per scuola*) exercise book; **quaderno a quadretti** arithmetic exercise book; **quaderno a righe** lined exercise book

quadrangolare [kwadrango'lare] AGG (*Geom*) quadrangular; (*Sport*): **incontro quadrangolare** four-sided tournament

quadrangolo [kwa'drangolo] SM (*Geom*) quadrangle

quadrante [kwa'drante] SM **1** (*dell'orologio*) face **2** (*Naut, Geom*) quadrant

quadrare [kwa'drare] VT **1** (*Geom*) to square **2** (*Contabilità*) to balance, tally; **quadrare il bilancio** to balance the books
■ VI (*aus* **avere** *o* **essere**) (*Contabilità: conti, bilancio*) to tally, balance; (*fig: corrispondere*): **quadrare (con)** to correspond (with); **qui c'è qualcosa che non quadra** there's something here that doesn't add up, there's something wrong here; **quel tipo non mi quadra** (*fam*) there's something fishy *o* I don't like about that guy

quadrato, a [kwa'drato] AGG **1** (*Mat, tavolo, tovaglia*) square; **metro/chilometro quadrato** square metre/ kilometre; **radice quadrata** (*Mat*) square root **2** (*equilibrato*) sensible, level-headed
■ SM **1** (*gen, Mat*) square; **un quadrato rosso** a red square; **elevare al quadrato** (*Mat*) to square; **6 al quadrato** 6 squared **2** (*Pugilato*) ring **3** (*Naut*) officers' mess

quadratura [kwadra'tura] SF **1** (*Mat*) squaring; **la quadratura del cerchio** the squaring of the circle **2** (*Contabilità*) balancing

quadrello [kwa'drɛllo] SM **1** (*mattonella*) square tile **2** (*di guanto*) gusset **3** (*Culin*) loin

quadrettare [kwadret'tare] VT to divide into squares

quadrettato, a [kwadret'tato] AGG (*foglio*) squared; (*tessuto*) checked

quadretto [kwa'dretto] SM **1** (*fig: scena, spettacolo*) picture; **siete un bel quadretto!** you make a lovely picture! **2 a quadretti** (*stoffa*) checked; (*foglio*) squared

quadriennale [kwadrien'nale] AGG (*che dura 4 anni*) four-year *attr*; (*che avviene ogni 4 anni*) four-yearly

quadriennio [kwadri'ɛnnjo] SM quadrennium, four-year period

quadrifoglio, gli [kwadri'fɔʎʎo] SM **1** (*Bot*) four-leaf clover **2 raccordo a quadrifoglio** (*Aut*) cloverleaf

quadrifonia [kwadrifo'nia] SF quadrophonics *sg*; **in quadrifonia** in quadrophonic sound

quadrifonico, a, ci, che [kwadri'fɔniko] AGG quadrophonic

quadrigemino, a [kwadri'dʒɛmino] AGG: **avere un parto quadrigemino** to have quadruplets

quadrigetto [kwadri'dʒɛtto] SM (*Aer*) four-engined jet

Qq

quadriglia [kwa'driʎʎa] SF *(danza)* quadrille
quadrilatero, a [kwadri'latero] AGG, SM quadrilateral
quadrimestrale [kwadrimes'trale] AGG **1** *(carica, durata)* four-month *attr*, of four months **2** *(rivista, esame)* four-monthly
quadrimestre [kwadri'mɛstre] SM *(periodo)* four-month period; *(Scol)* term
quadrimotore [kwadrimo'tore] SM *(Aer)* four-engined plane
quadrinomio, mi [kwadri'nɔmjo] SM *(Mat)* quadrinomial
quadripartito, a [kwadripar'tito] SM *(Pol)* four-party government
■AGG *(Pol: governo)* four-party *attr*; (: *alleanza*) four-power *attr*
quadro[1]**, a** ['kwadro] AGG *(quadrato)* square; **parentesi quadra** square bracket; **essere una testa quadra** *(fig pegg: ostinato)* to be pig-headed; *(tonto)* to be a blockhead
quadro[2] ['kwadro] SM **1** *(Arte)* picture, painting; **un quadro di Van Gogh** a painting by Van Gogh; **dipingere un quadro** to paint a picture, to do a painting; **quadro a olio** oil painting **2** *(quadrato)* square; **a quadri** *(disegno)* checked; **una giacca a quadri** a checked jacket **3** *(fig: descrizione)* outline, description; *(scena)* sight; **fare un quadro della situazione** to outline the situation; **questo ci fornisce un quadro completo della situazione** this gives us a complete picture of the situation; **quadro clinico** *(Med)* case history **4** *(Tecn)* panel, board; **quadro di comando** control panel; **quadro di distribuzione** *(Elettr)* switchboard; **quadro degli strumenti** instrument panel **5** *(fig: tabella di dati)* table, chart **6** *(Teatro)* scene; **quadro!** *(Cine)* focus! **7 quadri** SMPL *(Mil, di partito, organizzazione)* upper echelons, cadres; *(Comm)* managerial staff *sg o pl*, (senior) management *sg o pl*; **quadri intermedi** *(Comm)* middle management *sg o pl* **8 quadri** SMPL *(Carte)* diamonds
quadrumane [kwa'drumane] *(Zool)* AGG quadrumanous
■SM quadrumanous monkey
quadrupede [kwa'drupede] *(Zool)* SM quadruped
■AGG *(animale)* four-footed
quadruplicare [kwadrupli'kare] VT, VI *(aus* **essere**), **quadruplicarsi** VIP to quadruple, increase fourfold
quadruplice [kwa'druplitʃe] AGG quadruple; **un contratto in quadruplice copia** four copies *pl* of a contract
quadruplo, a ['kwadruplo] AGG quadruple; **il lavoro è quadruplo rispetto a quello iniziale** the workload is four times what it was originally
■SM *(Mat)* quadruple; **vorrei il quadruplo del denaro che ho ora** I would like four times as much money as I have now
quaggiù [kwad'dʒu] AVV *(gen)* down here; *(al sud)* here in the south; *(sulla terra)* in this life
quaglia ['kwaʎʎa] SF quail

qualche ['kwalke] AGG INDEF **PAROLA CHIAVE**
1 *(alcuni, non molti)* a few; **per qualche giorno** for a few days; **ho comprato qualche libro** I've bought some *o* a few books; **fra qualche mese** in a few months; **qualche volta** sometimes; **l'ho incontrato qualche volta** I've met him a few times *o* once or twice
2 *(con valore indeterminato: in frasi affermative)* some; (: *in frasi negative e domande)* any; **sai se passa qualche autobus da questa parte?** do you know if any buses go this way?; **in qualche modo** somehow; **l'ho già visto da qualche parte** I've already seen him somewhere; **hai qualche sigaretta?** have you any cigarettes?; **hai qualche soldo da prestarmi?** can you lend me some money?
3 *(un certo)* some; **c'è qualche fondamento di verità** there's an element of truth in it; **ci vuole qualche tempo per abituarsi** it takes some *o* a little time to get used to it; **un personaggio di qualche rilievo** a person of some importance; **non senza qualche esitazione** not without some hesitation; **ci dev'essere una qualche spiegazione** there must be some explanation; **qualche cosa** = qualcosa

qualcheduno [kwalke'duno] PRON INDEF = qualcuno
qualcosa [kwal'kɔsa] PRON INDEF *(in frasi affermative)* something; *(in domande)* anything; **ci dev'essere qualcosa che non va** there must be something wrong *o* the matter; **è già qualcosa** that's something; **ho qualcosa da parte** *(soldi)* I've got a little something put aside; **qualcosa mi dice che...** something tells me that ...; **è medico, o qualcosa di simile** *o* **del genere** he's a doctor or something like that; **bevi qualcosa?** would you like something to drink?; **posso fare qualcosa per te?** can I do anything for you?; **c'è qualcos'altro che desideri?** do you want anything else?; **fammi sapere se hai bisogno di qualcosa** let me know if you need anything; **posso chiederti qualcos'altro?** can I ask you something else?; **voglio fare qualcos'altro** I'd like to do something else; **c'è qualcosa che non va?** is there something *o* anything wrong?; **vedi qc?** can you see anything?; **qualcosa da dichiarare?** anything to declare?; **qualcosa di meglio/di nuovo** something better/new; **hai visto qc di bello?** did you see anything nice?; **la serata fu qualcosa di grande** it was a really great evening
qualcuno [kwal'kuno] PRON INDEF **1** *(in frasi affermative)* somebody, someone; *(in domande, in proposizioni condizionali e dubitative)* anybody, anyone; **ho visto qualcuno là fuori** I saw somebody out there; **ha telefonato qualcuno per te** somebody phoned for you; **qualcuno ha perso la borsa** somebody has lost their bag; **c'è qualcuno alla porta** there's someone at the door; **qualcuno ha visto il mio ombrello?** has anyone seen my umbrella?; **aspetti qualcuno?** are you waiting for somebody?; **c'è qualcuno in casa?** is (there) anybody at home? **2** *(con valore partitivo: affermazioni)* some; (: *domande)* any; **qualcuno di noi** some of us; **qualcuno di voi vuol venire?** do any of you want to come?; **se ti piacciono, prendine qualcuna in più** if you like them, take some *o* a few more; **hai visto i suoi film? – ne ho visto qualcuno** have you seen his films? – I've seen some of them; **qualcun altro** somebody *o* someone else; **chiedilo a qualcun altro** ask somebody else; **ne avresti qualcun altro da prestarmi?** have you got any more you could lend me?; **viene qualcun altro?** is anybody else coming?; **ce n'è rimasto qualcuno?** are there any left? **3** *(persona importante, di prestigio)* somebody; **diventerà qualcuno nella vita** he'll become somebody, he'll make something of his life

quale ['kwale] **PAROLA CHIAVE**
■AGG
1 *(interrogativo)* what; **a quale conclusione è giunta?** what conclusion did she reach?; **per quale data conti di finire?** when do you hope to finish by?; **in quale**

giorno vi siete incontrati? when did you meet?; **quali sono i tuoi programmi?** what are your plans?; **per quale ragione?** why?
2 (*scegliendo tra due o più cose o persone*) which; **quale stanza preferisci?** which room do you prefer?
3 (*esclamazioni*) what; **quale onore!** what an honour!
4 **è tale e quale suo padre** he's just *o* exactly like his father; **è tale quale l'avevo lasciato** it's just *o* exactly as I left it
5 (*con valore relativo*: *qualunque*): **quale che** whatever; **accetterò quali che siano le condizioni** I'll accept whatever the conditions
6 (*fraseologia*): **per la qual cosa** for which reason; **in un certo qual modo** in some way or other, somehow or other
■ PRON INTERROG (*scegliendo tra due o più cose o persone*) which; **quale dei due scegli?** which of the two do you want?
■ PRON REL
1 (*soggetto*: *persona*) who; (: *cosa*) which, that; **a tutti coloro i quali fossero interessati...** to whom it may concern ...; **suo padre, il quale è avvocato** his father, who is a lawyer
2 (*con preposizioni*): **l'albergo al quale ci siamo fermati** the hotel where we stayed *o* which we stayed at; **il signore con il quale parlavi** the gentleman to whom you were talking; **la collina della quale si vede la cima** the hill whose summit you can see; **la ragione per la quale sono qui** the reason why I am here
3 (*in elenchi*) such as, like; **piante quali l'edera e le rose** plants like *o* such as ivy and roses; **pittori quali Raffaello e Leonardo** painters like *o* such as Raphael and Leonardo
4 **per la quale** (*fam*): **non mi sembra una persona troppo per la quale** he doesn't inspire me with confidence; **è stata una cena proprio per la quale** it was everything a dinner party should be
■ AVV (*in veste di, in qualità di*) as; **quale legale della signora** as the lady's lawyer; **lo hanno assunto quale direttore** they employed him as manager

qualifica, che [kwa'lifika] SF qualification; **ha la qualifica di insegnante** he has a teaching qualification, he is a qualified teacher; **sono stato assunto con la qualifica di meccanico** I was taken on as a mechanic

qualificabile [kwalifi'kabile] AGG: **qualificabile (come)** which can be described (as)

qualificare [kwalifi'kare] VT 1 (*giudicare*: *persona, lavoro*) to judge 2 (*definire*) to define, describe; **qualificare qn/qc come** to describe sb/sth as; **il suo gesto lo qualifica per quello che è** by doing that he shows the kind of person he is
▶ **qualificarsi** VR 1 (*presentarsi*): **qualificarsi come** to describe o.s. as 2 (*ottenere una qualifica*) to qualify; **qualificarsi a un concorso** to pass an exam (*to obtain a post*); **qualificarsi per le semifinali** (*Sport*) to qualify for the semifinals

qualificativo, a [kwalifika'tivo] AGG (*Gramm*): **aggettivo qualificativo** qualifying adjective

qualificato, a [kwalifi'kato] AGG (*dotato di qualifica*) qualified; (*esperto, abile*) skilled; **operaio qualificato** skilled worker; **è un medico molto qualificato** he is a very distinguished doctor; **non mi ritengo qualificato per quel lavoro** I don't think I'm qualified for that job

qualificazione [kwalifikat'tsjone] SF 1 (*qualifica*) qualification; **corso di qualificazione professionale** vocational training course 2 (*Sport*: *anche*: **gara di qualificazione**) qualifying event; **lottare per la qualificazione** to fight to qualify

qualità [kwali'ta] SF INV 1 (*gen*) quality; (*di suolo, clima*) nature; **di ottima** *o* **prima qualità** top quality; **è una stoffa di ottima qualità** it's top-quality fabric; **prodotto di qualità** quality product; **un vino di pessima qualità** a very poor wine; **controllo (di) qualità** quality control; **ci interessa la qualità non la quantità** we are interested in quality not quantity; **la qualità della vita** the quality of life 2 (*dote, pregio*) quality; **ha molte qualità** she has many good qualities 3 (*genere, tipo*) kind, type; **fiori di varie qualità** flowers of various kinds; **abbiamo sigarette di ogni qualità** we have cigarettes of every kind; **articoli di ogni qualità** all sorts of goods 4 (*veste, carica*): **in qualità di** in one's capacity as; **in qualità di avvocato** in my (*o your ecc*) capacity as a lawyer; **in qualità di amica** as a friend

qualitativamente [kwalitativa'mente] AVV qualitatively

qualitativo, a [kwalita'tivo] AGG qualitative

qualora [kwa'lora] CONG in case, if; **qualora cambiassi idea** should you (happen to) change your mind

qualsiasi [kwal'siasi] AGG INDEF 1 (*tra molti*) any; **mettiti un vestito qualsiasi** wear anything you like; **in qualsiasi momento** at any time; **qualsiasi cosa** anything; **per lui farei qualsiasi cosa** I'd do anything for him; **a qualsiasi costo** at any cost, whatever the cost, no matter what; **ci riuscirò a qualsiasi costo** I'll manage it no matter what 2 (*tra due*) either; **prendine uno qualsiasi** take either of them 3 (*pegg*) ordinary, indifferent; **non è uno qualsiasi** he's not just anybody; **non voglio un vino qualsiasi** I don't want any old wine; **quale vuoi? — uno qualsiasi** which do you want? — any old one *o* whichever 4 (*rel*) whatever; **qualsiasi cosa accada** whatever happens; **qualsiasi cosa dica** whatever he says; **qualsiasi favore tu mi chieda** whatever you ask of me

qualsivoglia [kwalsi'vɔʎʎa] AGG INDEF (*frm*) = qualsiasi 1

qualunque [kwa'lunkwe] AGG INDEF 1 (*tra molti*) any; **in qualunque momento** at any time *o* moment; **qualunque persona** anybody, anyone; **qualunque cosa** anything; **per lui farei qualunque cosa** I'd do anything for him; **a qualunque costo** at any cost, whatever the cost 2 (*tra due*) either; **prendine uno qualunque** take either of them 3 (*pegg*) ordinary, indifferent; **non è uno qualunque** he's not just anybody; **non voglio un vino qualunque** I don't want any old wine; **quale vuoi? — uno qualunque** which do you want? — any old one *o* whichever; **l'uomo qualunque** the man in the street 4 (*rel*) whatever; **qualunque cosa dica** whatever he says; **qualunque cosa accada** whatever happens; **qualunque favore tu mi chieda** whatever you ask of me

qualunquismo [kwalun'kwizmo] SM (*pegg*) *political apathy*

qualunquista, i, e [kwalun'kwista] SM/F (*pegg*) *politically apathetic person*

qualunquistico, a, ci, che [kwalun'kwistiko] AGG (*pegg*) *(politically) apathetic*

quando ['kwando] AVV when; **quando arriverà?** when is he arriving?, when will he arrive?; **quando vai in vacanza?** when are you going on holiday?;

Qq

passerò a trovarti, ma non so quando I'll come and see you, but I don't know when; **non so quando abbia telefonato** I don't know when he phoned; **da quando** since; **da quando sei qui?** how long have you been here?; **di quando è quel giornale?** which day's paper is that?; **fino a quando continuerà così?** how long will it go on *o* continue like this?; **quando mai avrei detto una cosa del genere?** whenever did I say anything of the kind?; **di quando in quando** from time to time; **ci penso di quando in quando** I think about it from time to time; **a quando i confetti?** when are we going to be hearing wedding bells?
■ CONG when; **ti raggiungo quando ho finito** I'll join you when I've finished; **da quando sono arrivato** (ever) since I arrived; **abita lì da quando era piccola** she has lived there since she was a child; **piange sempre quando parto** she always cries when I leave, she cries whenever I leave; **chiamami quando vuoi** call me whenever you like; **quando fa così non lo sopporto** I can't stand him when he does that; **quand'anche tu volessi parlargli...** even if you wanted to speak to him ...; **si lamenta lui quando ne avrei molto più diritto io** he's the one that's complaining, when in fact I've got much more reason to; **quando te lo dico devi credermi** when I tell you something you should believe me; **ci raccontava di quando era bambino** he told us about when he was a child; **vorrei trovare tutto pronto per quando torno** I'd like to find everything ready for when I come back; **quando si dice la sfortuna...!** talk about bad luck ...!

quantificabile [kwantifi'kabile] AGG quantifiable

quantificare [kwantifi'kare] VT to quantify

quantificazione [kwantifikat'tsjone] SF quantification

quantità [kwanti'ta] SF INV **1** (*entità misurabile*) quantity, amount; **preferisco la qualità alla quantità** I prefer quality to quantity **2** (*gran numero*): **una quantità di** (*denaro, acqua*) a great deal of, a lot of; (*gente, cose*) a great many, a lot of; lots of; a great number of; **hanno invitato una quantità di gente** they invited lots of people; **ho una quantità di cose da fare** I have a lot of things to do; **in grande quantità** in large quantities; **c'è frutta in quantità** there is plenty of fruit **3** (*Mat, di vocale*) quantity

quantitativamente [kwantitativa'mente] AVV quantitatively

quantitativo, a [kwantita'tivo] AGG quantitative
■ SM (*Comm: di merce*) amount, quantity

quanto[1], a ['kwanto] PAROLA CHIAVE
■ AGG
1 (*interrogativo: quantità*) how much; (: *numero*) how many; **quanti anni hai?** how old are you?; **quanti metri desidera?** how many metres would you like?; **quanti soldi ti hanno chiesto?** how much did they ask you (for it)?; **quanta stoffa ti serve?** how much material do you need?; **quanto tempo?** how long?, how much time?; **quanto tempo ci metti da qui all'ufficio?** how long does it take you from here to the office?; **quante volte?** how often?, how many times?
2 (*esclamativo*): **quante storie!** what a fuss!; **quanto tempo sprecato!** what a waste of time!
3 (*relativo: quantità*) as much as; (: *numero*) as many as; **ti darò quanto denaro ti serve** I'll give you as much money as you need; **prendi quanti libri vuoi** take as many books as you want; **fermati quanto tempo vuoi** stay as long as you want
■ PRON
1 (*interrogativo: quantità*) how much; (: *numero*) how many; **quanto costa?** how much does it cost?; **quanto credi costerà?** how much do you think it will cost?; **quanto è da qui al negozio?** how far is it from here to the shop?; **quanti di loro?** how many of them?; **quanto ci hai messo a farlo?** how long did it take you to do it?; **quanti ne desidera?** how many do you want?; **quanti ne abbiamo oggi?** what's the date today?; **quanto stai via?** how long will you be away?; **so che devo prendere del pane, ma non so quanto** I know I must get some bread, but I don't know how much; **quant'è?** how much is it?
2 (*esclamativo*): **vedi quanti hanno accettato!** see how many have accepted!; **quante me ne ha dette!** (*insulti*) the way he insulted me!; (*bugie*) the number of lies he told me!
3 (*relativo: quantità*) as much as; (: *numero*) as many as; **gli darò quanto chiede** I'll give him what *o* as much as he asks for; **è quanto di meglio potessi trovare** it's the best you could find; **a quanto dice lui** according to him; **in risposta a quanto esposto nella sua lettera...** in answer to the points raised in your letter ...; **saranno scelti quanti hanno fatto domanda in tempo** all (those) whose applications arrived in time will be selected; **per quanto ne so** as far as I know; **faremo quanto potremo per aiutarti** we'll do all we can *o* as much as we can to help you; **era tanto felice quanto non lo era mai stato** he was happier than he had ever been; **spende tanto denaro quanto ne guadagna** he spends all that *o* every penny he earns, he spends as much as he earns; **fanne venire quanti vuoi** get as many as you like to come

quanto[2] ['kwanto] AVV PAROLA CHIAVE
1 (*quantità*) how much; (*numero*) how many; **sapessi quanto abbiamo camminato!** if you knew how far we have walked!; **quanto fumi al giorno?** how many (cigarettes) do you smoke a day?; **Dio solo sa quanto mi sono arrabbiato!** God only knows how angry I was!; **quanto pesi?** how much do you weigh?; **quanto sono felice!** how happy I am!
2 (*nella misura o quantità che*) as much as; **aggiungere brodo quanto basta** add sufficient *o* enough stock, add as much stock as is necessary; **dovrai aspettare quanto è necessario** you'll have to wait as long as is necessary; **strillava quanto poteva** she was shouting at the top of her voice *o* as loud as she could
3 (*come*): **siamo ricchi quanto loro** we are as rich as they are; **mi sono riposato quanto mai in questi ultimi tempi** I've had more rest than ever recently; **è una ragazza quanto mai spontanea** she's a very natural girl; **è famoso non tanto per i romanzi quanto per le poesie** he's famous not so much for his novels as for his poetry; **è tanto sciocco quanto cafone** he is as stupid as he is rude, he is both stupid and rude; **quanto è vero Iddio...!** I swear to God ...!
4 **in quanto** (*in qualità di*) as; (*perché, per il fatto che*) as, since; **in quanto insegnante** as a teacher; **non ho suonato in quanto temevo di svegliarti** I didn't ring as *o* since I was afraid I would wake you; **in quanto a** (*per ciò che riguarda*) as for; **in quanto ai soldi che mi devi...** as for the money you owe me ..., as far as the money you owe me is concerned ...
5 **per quanto** (*nonostante, anche se*) however; (*tuttavia*) although; **per quanto si sforzi, non riesce** however hard he tries he can't do it; **per quanto sembri**

complicato however complicated it may seem; **cercherò di fare qualcosa per lui, per quanto non se lo meriti** I'll try and do something for him although *o* even though he doesn't deserve it
6 quanto meno the less; **quanto meno uno insiste tanto più gli viene offerto** the less one demands the more one is offered; **quanto più mi sforzo di ricordare tanto meno ci riesco** the harder *o* the more I try to remember the less I succeed; **quanto più** the more; **quanto più presto potrò** as soon as I can; **verrò quanto prima** I'll come as soon *o* as early as possible

quanto[3] SM (*Fis*) quantum; **teoria dei quanti** quantum theory
quantunque [kwan'tunkwe] CONG (*sebbene*) although, even though; **quantunque mi piaccia non ci vivrei mai** even though I like the place I'd never live there; **accetto quantunque non convinto del tutto** I accept although *o* even though I'm not totally convinced
quaranta [kwa'ranta] AGG INV, SM INV forty; *per fraseologia vedi* **cinquanta**
quarantena [kwaran'tɛna] SF quarantine; **essere in quarantena** to be in quarantine; **mettere in quarantena** to quarantine
quarantenne [kwaran'tɛnne] AGG, SM/F forty-year-old; *per fraseologia vedi* **cinquantenne**
quarantennio, ni [kwaran'tɛnnjo] SM (period of) forty years
quarantesimo, a [kwaran'tɛzimo] AGG, SM/F, SM fortieth; *per fraseologia vedi* **quinto**
quarantina [kwaran'tina] SF: **una quarantina (di)** about forty; *per fraseologia vedi* **cinquantina**
quarantotto [kwaran'tɔtto] AGG INV forty-eight
■ SM INV forty-eight; **fare un quarantotto** (*fam*) to raise hell
Quaresima [kwa'rezima] SF (*Rel*): **la Quaresima** Lent; **osservare** *o* **fare la Quaresima** to keep Lent
Quaresimale [qwarezi'male] AGG (*Rel*) Lenten
quarta ['kwarta] SF (*gen*) fourth; (*Aut*) fourth gear; (*Scol*) fourth year; (*quarta elementare*) ≈ year five (*Brit*), ≈ fourth grade (*Am*); (*quarta superiore*) ≈ upper sixth (*Brit*), ≈ twelfth grade (*Am*); **mettere la quarta** to go into fourth (gear); **partire in quarta** (*fig*) to take off at top speed
quartettista, i, e [kwartet'tista] SM/F (*Mus*) member of a quartet; (*compositore*) composer of quartets
quartetto [kwar'tetto] SM (*Mus*) quartet(te); **che bel quartetto!** just look at the four of them!
quartiere [kwar'tjɛre] SM **1** (*di città*) district, area; **la gente del quartiere** the local people; **lo conoscono tutti nel quartiere** everybody in the neighbourhood knows him; **un quartiere malfamato** a rough area *o* neighbourhood; **quartiere dormitorio** commuter area; **quartiere residenziale** residential area *o* district; **i quartieri alti** the smart *o* exclusive areas; **i quartieri bassi** the poor areas **2** (*Mil*) quarters *pl*; **quartier generale** headquarters *pl* **3 lotta senza quartiere** (*fig*) unrelenting struggle
quartina [kwar'tina] SF (*Poesia*) quatrain
quartino [kwar'tino] SM **1** (*di vino*) quarter litre (*Brit*) *o* liter (*Am*) **2** (*Mus: strumento*) small clarinet
quarto, a ['kwarto] AGG, SM/F fourth; **quarta malattia** fourth disease; **quarto potere** fourth estate; **quarto uomo** (*Calcio*) fourth official; *per fraseologia vedi* **quinto**
■ SM **1** (*frazione*) quarter; **un quarto di vino** a quarter-litre (*Brit*) *o* quarter-liter (*Am*) bottle of wine; **un quarto di pollo** a quarter chicken; **primo/ultimo quarto** (*della luna*) first/last quarter; **un chilo e un quarto** a kilo and a quarter **2** (*ora*): **un quarto d'ora** a quarter of an hour; **tre quarti d'ora** three quarters of an hour; **tre ore e un quarto** three and a quarter hours; **le sei e un quarto** (a) quarter past six; **le otto e tre quarti** *or* **le nove meno un quarto** (a) quarter to (*Brit*) *o* of (*Am*) nine; **passare un brutto quarto d'ora** (*fig*) to have a bad *o* nasty time of it **3 quarti di finale** (*Sport*) quarterfinals **4** (*Naut*) watch; **il primo quarto** the first watch **5** (*Tip*) quarto
quartogenito, a [kwarto'dʒɛnito] SM/F fourth child
quartultimo, a [kwar'tultimo] AGG, SM/F last but three, fourth from last
quarzo ['kwartso] SM quartz; **orologio al quarzo** quartz watch; **quarzo rosa** rose quartz
quasar ['kwazar] SF INV quasar
quasi ['kwazi] AVV (*gen*) almost, nearly; (*restrittivo*) hardly, scarcely; **ha quasi 30 anni** he's almost *o* nearly 30 (years old); **quasi niente** hardly *o* scarcely anything; **non sento quasi niente** I can hardly hear anything; **non è venuto quasi nessuno** hardly anybody came; **quasi mai** hardly ever; **non lo vedo quasi mai** I hardly ever see him; **quasi cadevo** I almost *o* nearly fell; **è quasi un fratello per me** he's like a brother to me; **oserei quasi dire che…** I'd almost say that …; **quasi quasi me ne vado** I've half a mind to leave; **quasi quasi è meglio così** it may even be better this way
■ CONG (*come se*) as if; **urla quasi fosse lui il padrone** he shouts as if he were the boss; **non si è fatto vivo, quasi sospettasse qualcosa** he hasn't been in touch, as if he suspected something
quassù [kwas'su] AVV up here
quaterna [kwa'tɛrna] SF (*Lotto, Tombola*) *set of four winning numbers*; **vincere una quaterna** (*Lotto*) to draw four winning numbers; **fare quaterna** (*Tombola*) to cover four numbers in a row
quaternario, ria, ri, rie [qwater'narjo] (*Geol*) AGG: **l'era quaternaria** the Quaternary period
■ SM: **il quaternario** the Quaternary (period)
quattamente [kwatta'mente] AVV stealthily
quatto, a ['kwatto] AGG: **stare quatto quatto** to keep as quiet as a mouse; **entrare quatto quatto in una stanza** to creep stealthily into a room; **uscire quatto quatto** to slip away
quattordicenne [kwattordi'tʃɛnne] AGG, SM/F fourteen-year-old; *per fraseologia vedi* **cinquantenne**
quattordicesimo, a [kwattordi'tʃɛzimo] AGG, SM/F fourteenth; **la quattordicesima** (*di stipendio*) *annual Christmas bonus equivalent to 1 month's pay*; *per fraseologia vedi* **quinto**
quattordici [kwat'torditʃi] AGG, SM INV fourteen; *per fraseologia vedi* **cinque**
quattrino [kwat'trino] SM **1 non avere un quattrino** *o* **il becco di un quattrino** (*fam*) to be penniless *o* broke **2 quattrini** SMPL money *sg*, cash *sg*; **fare quattrini** to make money; **essere pieno di quattrini** to be rolling in money; **quattrini a palate** piles of money; **costare fior di quattrini** to cost a fortune
quattro ['kwattro] AGG INV **1** four; **c'erano quattro persone** there were four people there **2** (*fig: pochi*): **fare quattro passi** to take a stroll; go for a little walk; **facciamo quattro passi** let's go for a little walk; **c'erano quattro gatti allo spettacolo** there was only a handful of people at the show; **fare quattro salti** to go dancing; **fare quattro chiacchiere** to have a chat;

Qq

lo pagano quattro soldi they pay him peanuts *o* a pittance; **a quattr'occhi** (*tra 2 persone*) face to face; (*privatamente*) in private; **a quattro a quattro** four at a time; **a quattro zampe** on all fours
■ SM INV four; **dirne quattro a qn** to give sb a piece of one's mind; **farsi in quattro per qn** to go out of one's way for sb, put o.s. out for sb; **fare il diavolo a quattro** to kick up a rumpus; **in quattro e quattr'otto** in less than no time, in no time at all; *per fraseologia vedi* **cinque**

quattrocchi [kwat'trɔkki] SM INV (*fig fam: persona con occhiali*) four-eyes

quattrocentesco, a, schi, sche [kwattrotʃen'tesko] AGG fifteenth-century *attr*

quattrocento [kwattro'tʃɛnto] AGG INV four hundred
■ SM INV four hundred; (*secolo*): **il Quattrocento** the fifteenth century

quattromila [kwattro'mila] AGG INV, SM INV four thousand

Quebec [kwe'bɛk] SM il Quebec

quello, a ['kwello] PAROLA CHIAVE
(*davanti a sm* quel + *consonante*, quell'+ *vocale*, quello + *s impura, gn, pn, ps, x, z; pl* quei + *consonante*, quegli + *vocale o s impura, gn, pn, ps, x, z; davanti a sf* quella + *consonante*, quell' + *vocale; pl* quelle)
■ AGG DIMOSTR
1 that, those *pl*; **mi passi quel libro?** could you pass me that book?; **voglio quella camicia lì** *o* **là** I want that shirt there; **dove hai comprato quei quadri?** where did you buy those paintings?; **dove metto quello scatolone?** where shall I put that box?; **chi sono quegli uomini?** who are those men?
2 (*seguito da proposizione relativa*): **con quel poco che abbiamo** with what *o* the little we have; **dov'è quel maglione che mi dicevi?** where's the *o* that jumper you were telling me about?
3 (*enfatico*): **ho una di quelle paure!** I'm scared stiff!; **ne ha fatte di quelle!** (*sciocchezze*) he did some really stupid things!; **una di quelle** (*euf: prostituta*) a working girl; **in quello stesso istante** at that very moment
■ PRON DIMOSTR
1 that (one), those (ones) *pl*; **quale vuoi? — quello bianco** which do you want? — the white one; **il tuo nome e quello di Roberta** your name and Roberta's; **quello di Giovanna è il voto migliore** Giovanna's is the best mark, Giovanna has the best mark; **prendiamo quello là** we'll take that one there; **chi è quello lì?** who is that (person)?; **e quello cos'è?** and what is that?; **quelle sono le mie scarpe** those are my shoes; **ho incontrato quelli della festa** I met the people from the party; **a che ora viene quello del latte?** when does the milkman come?
2 (*egli*) he; (*ella*) she; (*essi, esse*) they; **sarebbe un'occasione d'oro e quelli non vogliono accettare** it's a golden opportunity but they don't want to accept
3 (*in proposizione relativa*): **quello(a) che** (*persona*) the one (who); (*cosa*) the one (which) *o* (that); **quelli(e) che** (*persone*) those who; (*cose*) those which *o* that; **quello che hai comprato tu è più bello** the one (which) you bought is nicer; **quello che hai visto è il padre** the person *o* the one you saw is the father; **quella che hai incontrato è la seconda moglie** the one *o* woman you met is his second wife; **chiedi a quelli che l'hanno conosciuto** ask those who knew him
4 (*ciò*): **quello che** what; (*tutto*) all (that), everything; **ho detto quello che sapevo** I've told you all I know; **ho fatto quello che potevo** I did what I could; **nega, e quel che è peggio, ci scherza sopra** he denies it, and what is worse, jokes about it; **da quello che ho sentito** from what I've heard
5 (*fraseologia*): **in quel di Milano** in the Milan area *o* region; **in quel mentre** at that very moment

quercia, ce ['kwertʃa] SF **1** (*albero*) oak (tree); (*legno*) oak; **quercia rossa** red oak; **forte come una quercia** as strong as an ox **2 la Quercia** (*Pol*) *symbol of P.D.S.*

querela [kwe'rɛla] SF (*Dir*) (legal) action; **sporgere querela contro qn** to bring an action against sb; **querela per diffamazione** libel action

querelante [kwere'lante] SM/F (*Dir*) plaintiff

querelare [kwere'lare] VT (*Dir*) to bring an action against

querelato, a [kwere'lato] SM/F (*Dir*) defendant

querulo, a ['kwɛrulo] AGG (*letter*) querulous

quesito [kwe'sito] SM question, query; **porre un quesito (a)** to put a question (to)

questi ['kwesti] PRON DIMOSTR (*letter*) this person

questionare [kwestjo'nare] VI (*aus* **avere**) (*litigare*) to quarrel, argue; **questionare di** to discuss

questionario, ri [kwestjo'narjo] SM questionnaire

questione [kwes'tjone] SF **1** (*problema, faccenda*) question, matter, problem; (*controversia*) issue; **si tratta di una questione delicata/personale** it's a delicate/personal matter; **è una questione politica** it's a political question *o* matter; **è una questione di vita o di morte** it's a question *o* matter of life and death; **il nocciolo della questione** the heart of the matter; **non conosco i termini della questione** I don't know the details of the matter; **ne ha fatto una questione** he made an issue out of it; **è sorta una questione in merito** they made an issue out of it; **comporre una questione** (*Dir*) to settle an issue; **il caso in questione** the matter at hand; **la persona in questione** the person involved; **non voglio essere chiamato in questione** I don't want to be involved; **è questione di tempo** it's a matter *o* question of time; **non faccio questioni di soldi** it's not a question of money; **litigare per questioni di eredità** *or* **essere in questione per l'eredità** to be in dispute over the inheritance; **la questione meridionale** the Southern Question (*the social/political situation in Southern Italy*)
2 (*dubbio*): **mettere qc in questione** to question sth; **è fuori questione** it's out of the question

questo, a ['kwesto] PAROLA CHIAVE
■ AGG DIMOSTR
1 this, these *pl*; **in questi ultimi giorni** these last few days; **questo libro qui o qua** this book (here); **questo lunedì** this Monday; **ti piace questo maglione?** do you like this jumper?; **quest'oggi** nowadays, today; **questa sera** this evening; **di questi tempi** in times like these
2 (*enfatico*): **con questo caldo** in this heat; **non fatemi più prendere queste paure** don't give me such a fright again
■ PRON DIMOSTR
1 this (one), these (ones) *pl*; **prendo questo qui** *o* **qua** I'll take this one; **questo è il tuo posto** this is your place; **questo cosa significa?** what does this mean?; **questo è troppo!** this is too much *o* the limit!; **questo mi fa piacere** I am pleased about that
2 (*egli*) he; (*ella*) she; (*essi, esse*) they; **e questo mi guarda e ride!** and this guy just looks at me and

laughs!; **una tale occasione, e questi che fanno? – rifiutano** such a great opportunity, and what do they do? – they refuse
3 **questo… quello…** (*il primo… il secondo…*) the former … the latter …; (*l'uno… l'altro…*) the one … the other …; **questi … quelli** some … others; **questi gridavano, quelli ridevano** some were shouting, others were laughing; **preferisci questo o quello?** do you prefer this one or that one?
4 (*fraseologia*): **e con questo?** so what?; **e con questo se n'è andato** and with that he left; **con tutto questo** in spite of this, despite all this; **è per questo che sono venuto** this is why I came; **questa poi!** I don't believe it!; **questo è quanto** that's all; **questo sì che è il colmo!** this is the limit!; **questa non me la dovevi fare** you shouldn't have done this to me

questore [kwes'tore] SM (*Polizia*) *public official in charge of the police in the provincial capital, reporting to the prefetto*; ≈ chief constable (*Brit*), ≈ police commissioner (*Am*)
questua ['kwɛstua] SF collection (of alms)
questura [kwes'tura] SF (*organo*) police force; (*edificio*) police headquarters *pl*
questurino [kwestu'rino] SM (*fam: poliziotto*) cop
qui [kwi] AVV **1** here; **vieni qui** come here; **eccomi qui!** here I am!; **qui dentro/sopra/sotto/vicino** in/up/under/near here; **non c'è molto spazio qui dentro** there's not much room in here; **qui sotto c'è la tua camicia** your shirt's under here; **abita qui sotto** she lives (in the flat) downstairs; **da** *o* **di qui** from here; **da** *o* **di qui non mi muovo!** I'm not budging from here!; **da qui la vista è stupenda** the view is fantastic from here; **di qui non si passa** you can't get through here *o* this way **2** (*temporale*): **da qui in avanti** from now on; **di qui a poco/una settimana** in a little while/a week's time **3** (*fraseologia*): **(dammi) qui, ci penso io!** just give it to me, I'll see to it!; **fin qui tutto bene** so far so good; **ah, qui ti voglio!** that's the problem!; **non è di qui** he's not from around here; **che diavolo vuole questo qui?** what on earth does he want?
quiescente [kwjeʃ'ʃɛnte] AGG dormant
quiescenza [kwjeʃ'ʃɛntsa] SF **1** (*di vulcano*) dormancy **2** (*Amm*): **trattamento di quiescenza** retirement package; **porre qn in quiescenza** to retire sb
quietamente [kwjeta'mente] AVV quietly
quietanza [kwje'tantsa] SF (*Comm*) receipt
quietare [kwje'tare] VT to soothe, calm
▸ **quietarsi** VIP (*mare*) to become calm; (*vento*) to die down; (*bambino*) to calm down
quiete ['kwjɛte] SF **1** (*silenzio*) quiet, stillness, quietness; (*tranquillità*) peace, calmness; **la quiete che precede la tempesta** the calm before the storm; **aver bisogno di quiete** (*riposo*) to need peace and quiet; **la quiete della campagna** the tranquillity *o* peace of the countryside; **turbare la quiete pubblica** (*Dir*) to disturb the peace **2** (*Fis*): **stato di quiete** state of rest
quieto, a ['kwjeto] AGG (*gen*) quiet; (*notte*) quiet, still; (*mare*) calm; **l'ho fatto per il quieto vivere** I did it for a quiet life
quindi ['kwindi] CONG (*perciò*) therefore, so; **avevo freddo e quindi mi sono messo il maglione** I was cold, so I put on a sweater
■ AVV (*in seguito*) then; **devi continuare diritto, quindi girare a destra** you should carry straight on, then turn right; **ho cenato e quindi sono andato al cinema** I had dinner and then went to the cinema

quindicennale [kwinditʃen'nale] AGG (*che dura 15 anni*) fifteen-year *attr*; (*che ricorre ogni 15 anni*) every fifteen years, fifteen-yearly
■ SM (*ricorrenza*) fifteenth anniversary
quindicenne [kwindi'tʃɛnne] AGG, SM/F fifteen-year-old; *per fraseologia vedi* **cinquantenne**
quindicennio, ni [kwindi'tʃɛnnjo] SM (period of) fifteen years
quindicesimo, a [kwindi'tʃɛzimo] AGG, SM/F fifteenth; *per fraseologia vedi* **quinto**
quindici ['kwinditʃi] AGG INV fifteen; **quindici giorni** two weeks, a fortnight (*Brit*); **oggi a quindici** two weeks *o* a fortnight (*Brit*) today; **tra quindici giorni** in two weeks *o* a fortnight (*Brit*)
■ SM INV fifteen; *per fraseologia vedi* **cinque**
quindicina [kwindi'tʃina] SF: **una quindicina (di)** about fifteen; **(fra) una quindicina di giorni** (in) two weeks *o* a fortnight (*Brit*); **la seconda quindicina di marzo** the second half of March; *per fraseologia vedi* **cinquantina**
quindicinale [kwinditʃi'nale] AGG fortnightly (*Brit*), semimonthly (*Am*)
■ SM (*rivista*) fortnightly magazine (*Brit*), semimonthly (*Am*)
quinquennale [kwinkwen'nale] AGG (*che dura 5 anni*) five-year *attr*; (*che avviene ogni 5 anni*) five-yearly
quinquennio, ni [kwin'kwɛnnjo] SM (period of) five years, quinquennial
quinta ['kwinta] SF **1** (*gen*) fifth; (*Aut*) fifth gear; (*Scol*) fifth year; (*quinta elementare*) ≈ year six (*Brit*), ≈ fifth grade (*Am*); (*quinta superiore*) ≈ first year (at college) (*Brit*), ≈ freshman year (at college) (*Am*) **2** **le quinte** (*Teatro*) the wings; **tra** *o* **dietro le quinte** (*fig*) behind the scenes

Qq

quintale [kwin'tale] SM quintal (*= 100 kg*); **pesa un quintale** (*fig*) it weighs a ton
quintessenza [kwintes'sɛntsa] SF quintessence
quintetto [kwin'tetto] SM (*Mus*) quintet(te)
quinto, a ['kwinto] AGG fifth; **la quinta parte di** a fifth of; **la quinta volta** the fifth time; **al quinto piano** on the fifth (*Brit*) *o* sixth (*Am*) floor; **è arrivato quinto nella gara** he came fifth in the competition; **essere al quinto posto in classifica** to be fifth in the championship; **in quinta pagina** on the fifth page, on page five; **quinta colonna** (*fig*) fifth column; **quinta malattia** fifth disease; **quinto potere** fifth estate; (*Am*) *television, seen as a source of influence and propaganda*
■ SM/F fifth; **sei la quinta a cui faccio la domanda** you are the fifth person I have asked; **il quinto da destra** the fifth from the right; **il quinto arrivato vincerà una macchina fotografica** whoever comes fifth will win a camera
■ SM (*frazione*) fifth; **un quinto della popolazione** a fifth of the population; **tre quinti** three fifths
quintultimo, a [kwin'tultimo] AGG, SM/F last but four, fifth from last
quintuplicare [kwintupli'kare] VT, **quintuplicarsi** VIP to increase fivefold
qui pro quo ['kwiprɔ'kwɔ] SM INV misunderstanding
Quirinale [kwiri'nale] SM *one of the seven hills of Rome*

QUIRINALE

The **Quirinale** is the highest of the Seven Hills of Rome and was a place of human settlement from the seventh and sixth centuries BC. It is the site of

- the **Piazza del Quirinale** and the **Palazzo** of the
- same name which is the official residence of the
- "Presidente della Repubblica". The term
- "Quirinale" is often used to refer to the President
- himself.

  ▹ www.quirinale.it/
  ▹ www.romasegreta.it/trevi/quirinale.htm

quisquilia [kwis'kwilja] SF (*inezia, stupidaggine*) trifle

quiz [kwidz] SM INV **1** (*domanda*) question; **risolvere un quiz** to answer a question **2** (*anche:* **gioco a quiz**) quiz game; **quiz televisivo** television quiz

quorum ['kwɔrum] SM INV quorum

quota ['kwɔta] SF **1** (*parte*) quota, share; **la sua quota di azioni** his quota of shares; **le quote del totalizzatore** (*Ippica*) the odds; **quota fissa** fixed amount *o* sum; **quota imponibile** (*Fisco*) taxable income; **quota d'iscrizione** (*Univ*) enrolment fee; (*a gara*) entry fee; (*a club*) membership fee; **quota di mercato** market share; **quota non imponibile** (*Fisco*) personal allowance; **quote latte** milk quotas **2** (*altitudine*) altitude, height; **l'aereo volava a bassa quota** the plane was flying low; **di alta quota** high-altitude *attr*; **a quota zero** at sea level; **a quota 750 metri** 750 metres above sea level; **prendere/perdere quota** (*Aer*) to gain/lose height *o* altitude

quotare [kwo'tare] VT **1** (*Fin, Borsa*) to quote; **la sterlina è quotata a 1 euro e 50** the pound is quoted at 1,50 euros; **queste azioni sono quotate in Borsa** these shares are quoted on the Stock Exchange **2** (*valutare: anche fig*) to value; **questo quadro è stato quotato 15 mila euro** this painting was valued at 15 thousand euros; **è un pittore molto quotato** he is rated highly as a painter, he is a highly rated painter

quotazione [kwotat'tsjone] SF (*Fin*) quotation; (*fig: di artista*) rating

quotidianamente [kwotidjana'mente] AVV daily, every day

quotidiano, a [kwoti'djano] AGG (*di ogni giorno*) daily; (*normale*) everyday; **la vita quotidiana** daily life ■ SM (*giornale*) daily (paper)

quoto ['kwɔto] SM (*Mat*) quotient

quoziente [kwot'tsjɛnte] SM **1** (*Mat*) quotient **2** (*tasso*) rate; **quoziente di crescita zero** zero growth rate; **quoziente d'intelligenza** intelligence quotient; IQ

R, **r** ['ɛrre] SF O M INV (*lettera*) R, r; **R come Roma** ≈ R for Robert (*Brit*) R for Roger (*Am*)
R ABBR **1** (*Posta*) = **raccomandata** **2** (*Ferr*) = **regionale**
RA SIGLA = *Ravenna*
rabarbaro [ra'barbaro] SM (*Bot*) rhubarb; (*liquore*) rhubarb liqueur
Rabat [ra'bat] SF Rabat
rabberciare [rabber'tʃare] VT (*anche fig*) to patch up
rabberciatura [rabbertʃa'tura] SF (*anche fig*) patch job
rabbia ['rabbja] SF **1** (*ira*) anger, rage; (*fig: di onde, vento*) fury; **essere fuori di sé dalla rabbia** to be beside o.s. with rage; **farsi prendere dalla rabbia** to fly into a rage; **fare qc con rabbia** to do sth angrily; **mi fai una rabbia!** you make me so angry!; (*scherz: invidia*) you make me so jealous!; **che rabbia!** what a damned nuisance! **2** (*Med: idrofobia*) rabies *sg*
rabbico, a, ci, che ['rabbiko] AGG (*Med*): **virus rabbico** rabies virus
rabbino [rab'bino] SM rabbi
rabbiosamente [rabbjosa'mente] AVV furiously, angrily
rabbioso, a [rab'bjoso] AGG **1** (*discorso, tono, sguardo*) furious, angry; (*fig: vento, odio*) raging, furious **2** (*Med*) rabid, mad
rabboccare [rabbok'kare] VT (*bottiglia*) to top up
rabbonire [rabbo'nire] VT, **rabbonirsi** VIP to calm down; **l'ha rabbonita** he calmed her down
rabbrividire [rabbrivi'dire] VI (*aus* **essere**) (*per il freddo*) to shiver, shudder; (*fig: per paura*) to shudder; **rabbrividire al solo pensiero di qc/di fare qc** to shudder at the mere thought of sth/of doing sth
rabbuffo [rab'buffo] SM reprimand
rabbuiare [rabbu'jare] VI (*aus* **essere**), **rabbuiarsi** VIP to grow dark, darken; **si rabbuiò in viso** his (*o* her) face darkened
rabdomante [rabdo'mante] SM water diviner
rabdomanzia [rabdoman'tsia] SF rhabdomancy, water divining
racc. ABBR (*Posta*) = **raccomandata**
raccapezzarsi [rakkapet'tsarsi] VIP: **non raccapezzarsi** to be at a loss; **c'è tanta confusione che non mi raccapezzo più** things are in such a mess that I can't make head nor tail of anything
raccapricciante [rakkaprit'tʃante] AGG horrifying; **una scena raccapricciante** a horrifying scene
raccapriccio [rakka'prittʃo] SM horror
raccattapalle [rakkatta'palle] SM INV (*spec Tennis*) ballboy
raccattare [rakkat'tare] VT (*raccogliere, fig: voti*) to pick up
racchetta [rak'ketta] SF (*da tennis*) racket; (*da ping-pong*) bat; **racchetta da neve** snowshoe; **racchetta da sci** ski stick
racchio, chia, chi, chie ['rakkjo] AGG (*fam*) ugly
racchiudere [rak'kjudere] VT IRREG to contain
racchiuso, a [rak'kjuso] PP *di* **racchiudere**
raccogliere [rak'kɔʎʎere] VB IRREG
■VT **1** (*raccattare*) to pick up; **puoi raccogliere i tuoi giocattoli?** can you pick up your toys?; **mi ero chinato a raccogliere la penna** I had bent down to pick up the pen; **l'istituto raccoglie molti bambini abbandonati** the institution takes in many abandoned children; **non ha raccolto il guanto** (*fig*) he didn't take up the gauntlet; **non ha raccolto** (*allusione*) he didn't take the hint; (*frecciata*) he took no notice of it **2** (*frutta, fiori*) to pick, pluck; (*Agr*) to harvest; (*fig: onori, successo*) to reap; (*: approvazione, voti*) to win; **abbiamo raccolto un mazzetto di fiori** we picked a bunch of flowers; **raccogliere il grano** to harvest the wheat; **raccogliere l'uva** to pick grapes; **raccogliere i frutti del proprio lavoro** (*fig*) to reap the benefits of one's work **3** (*radunare: persone*) to assemble; (*notizie, denaro, firme*) to gather, collect; **stiamo raccogliendo libri usati per la biblioteca** we're collecting second-hand books for the library; **raccogliere fondi** to raise funds; **ho raccolto le mie cose e me ne sono andata** I took my things and went; **raccogliere le idee** (*fig*) to gather *o* collect one's thoughts **4** (*collezionare: francobolli, monete, cartoline*) to collect **5** (*ripiegare: ali*) to fold; (*: gambe*) to draw up; (*: vele*) to furl; (*: capelli*) to put up
► **raccogliersi** VIP (*radunarsi*) to gather

raccoglimento [rakkoʎʎi'mento] SM meditation; **un minuto di raccoglimento** a minute's silence
raccoglitore [rakkoʎʎi'tore] SM *(cartella)* folder, binder; (: *per francobolli*) album; **raccoglitore a fogli mobili** loose-leaf binder
raccoglitrice [rakkoʎʎi'tritʃe] SF *(Agr: macchina)* harvester
raccolta [rak'kɔlta] SF **1** *(gen)* collection, collecting *no pl*; **la mia raccolta di CD** my CD collection; **fare (la) raccolta di qc** to collect sth; **faccio raccolta di cartoline** I collect postcards; **raccolta dei rifiuti** refuse *o* rubbish *(Brit) o* garbage *(Am)* collection; **raccolta differenziata** *(dei rifiuti) separate collection of different kinds of household waste* **2** *(Agr)* harvesting *no pl*, gathering *no pl*; **fare la raccolta della frutta** to pick fruit **3** *(di persone)* gathering; **chiamare a raccolta** to gather together **4** **raccolta di fondi** fund-raising
raccolto, a [rak'kɔlto] PP *di* raccogliere
■ AGG **1** *(persona: assorto)* thoughtful; **raccolto in preghiera** absorbed in prayer **2** *(luogo: appartato)* secluded, quiet **3** *(gambe)* drawn up; **raccolto su se stesso** curled up
■ SM *(Agr)* crop, harvest; (: *periodo*) harvest time
raccomandabile [rakkoman'dabile] AGG (highly) commendable; **è un tipo poco raccomandabile** he is not to be trusted
raccomandare [rakkoman'dare] VT **1** *(consigliare)* to recommend; **l'albergo è raccomandato dalla guida** the hotel is recommended by the guide; **te lo raccomando, quello!** *(iro)* watch out for that one!; **raccomandare a qn di fare qc** to recommend that sb does sth; **ti raccomando questo libro/di leggere questo libro** I recommend this book to you/that you read this book; **raccomandare a qn di non fare qc** *(esortare)* to tell *o* warn sb not to do sth; **ti raccomando di non fare tardi** now remember, don't come in late **2** *(affidare)* to entrust; **raccomandare qn a qn/alle cure di qn** to entrust sb to sb/to sb's care **3** *(appoggiare)* to recommend; **raccomandare qn per un lavoro** to recommend sb for a job
▶ **raccomandarsi** VR: **raccomandarsi a qn** to implore sb's help; **raccomandarsi alla pietà di qn** to implore sb's pity; **mi raccomando!** don't forget!; **mi raccomando, scrivimi!** please write to me!; **mi raccomando! non perderlo** please don't lose it!; **mi raccomando! studia bene** be sure and study hard!
raccomandata [rakkoman'data] SF *(anche:* **lettera raccomandata**) recorded-delivery *(Brit) o* certified *(Am)* letter; **spediscilo per raccomandata** send it by recorded delivery; **raccomandata con ricevuta di ritorno** *recorded-delivery letter with advice of receipt*
raccomandatizio, zia, zi, zie [rakkomanda'tittsjo] AGG: **lettera raccomandatizia** letter of introduction
raccomandato, a [rakkoman'dato] AGG **1** *(lettera, pacco)* recorded-delivery *(Brit)*, certified *(Am)* **2** *(candidato)* recommended
■ SM/F: **essere un raccomandato di ferro** to have friends in high places
raccomandazione [rakkomandat'tsjone] SF **1** *(appoggio)* recommendation; **lettera di raccomandazione** letter of introduction; **qui ci vuole la raccomandazione di qualcuno** we need somebody to pull a few strings here **2** *(esortazione)* piece of advice; **mi ha fatto mille raccomandazioni** he gave me lots of advice
raccomodare [rakkomo'dare] VT *(riparare)* to repair, mend
raccontare [rakkon'tare] VT *(storia, bugie)* to tell; *(avventure)* to tell about; **raccontare qc a qn** to tell sb sth; **mi ha raccontato una barzelletta molto divertente** he told me a very funny joke; **non raccontarlo a nessuno** don't tell anyone about it; **raccontano che sia fuggito** they say that he escaped; **nel libro racconta delle sue avventure** in the book he speaks of his adventures; **dai, raccontami tutto** come on, tell me all about it; **a me non la racconti** don't try and kid me; **raccontala a qualcun altro!** try and pull the wool over somebody else's eyes!; **a me lo vieni a raccontare!** don't tell me!; **se ne raccontano delle belle su di lui** I've heard a few stories about him; **cosa mi racconti di nuovo?** what's new?
racconto [rak'konto] SM **1** *(narrazione)* account, telling *no pl*, relating *no pl*; *(fatto raccontato)* story, tale; **il suo racconto dell'avventura** his account of the adventure **2** *(genere letterario)* short story; **racconti per bambini** children's stories
raccorciare [rakkor'tʃare] VT to shorten
▶ **raccorciarsi** VIP to become shorter; **le giornate si stanno raccorciando** the days are drawing in
raccordare [rakkor'dare] VT *(collegare)* to link up, join (up)
raccordo [rak'kɔrdo] SM *(Tecn: giunzione)* joint, connection; *(di autostrada)* slip road *(Brit)*, entrance (*o* exit) ramp *(Am)*; *(Ferr)* siding; **raccordo anulare** *(Aut)* ring road *(Brit)*, beltway *(Am)*
rachitico, a, ci, che [ra'kitiko] AGG *(Med)* suffering from rickets; *(fig: pianta)* spindly; (: *persona*) scrawny
■ SM/F person who suffers from rickets
rachitismo [raki'tizmo] SM *(Med)* rickets *sg*
racimolare [ratʃimo'lare] VT *(denaro)* to scrape together; *(fig: notizie)* to glean
racket ['rækit] SM INV racket
rada ['rada] SF (natural) harbour *(Brit) o* harbor *(Am)*
radar ['radar] SM INV radar
■ AGG INV *(segnale, avvistamento)* radar *attr*; **uomini radar** air traffic controllers
raddensare [radden'sare] VT *(crema, minestra)* to thicken
▶ **raddensarsi** VIP *(marmellata)* to set; *(minestra)* to thicken
raddolcimento [raddoltʃi'mento] SM *(Ling)* palatalization
raddolcire [raddol'tʃire] VT *(persona, carattere)* to soften
▶ **raddolcirsi** VIP *(tempo)* to grow milder; *(persona)* to soften, mellow
raddoppiamento [raddoppja'mento] SM *(gen)* doubling
raddoppiare [raddop'pjare] VI *(aus* **essere**; *nel signif. sportivo* **avere**) to double; *(Calcio)* to score a second goal; **il prezzo del biglietto è raddoppiato** the price of the ticket has doubled
■ VT to double
raddoppio, pi [rad'doppjo] SM *(gen)* doubling; *(Biliardo)* double; *(Calcio)* second goal; *(Equitazione)* gallop
raddrizzabile [raddrit'tsabile] AGG *(gen)* which can be straightened; *(Elettr)* rectifiable
raddrizzamento [raddrittsa'mento] SM straightening
raddrizzare [raddrit'tsare] VT **1** *(mettere dritto)* to straighten; *(fig: correggere)* to put straight, correct **2** *(Elettr)* to rectify
▶ **raddrizzarsi** VR *(persona)* to straighten (o.s.) up
raddrizzatore [raddrittsa'tore] SM *(Elettr)* rectifier
radente [ra'dɛnte] AGG: **tiro radente** *(Mil)* grazing

fire; **attrito radente** (*Fis*) sliding friction

radere ['radere] VB IRREG
■VT **1** (*barba*) to shave off; (*mento*) to shave; **radere i capelli a zero** to shave one's hair off; **s'è fatto radere i capelli a zero** he's had his head shaved **2** (*fig: sfiorare*) to graze, skim **3** (*abbattere*): **radere al suolo** to raze to the ground
▶ **radersi** VR to shave (o.s.); **si rade ogni mattina** he shaves every morning

radiale [ra'djale] AGG, SM (*Anat, Geom, Aut*) radial

radiante [ra'djante] AGG (*superficie, pannello*) radiant
■SM (*Mat*) radian

radiare [ra'djare] VT (*da scuola, partito*) to expel; (*dall'esercito*) to dismiss; (*da albo professionale: medico*) to strike off; (*: avvocato*) to disbar

radiatore [radja'tore] SM radiator

radiazione [radjat'tsjone] SF **1** (*Fis*) radiation; **radiazione nucleare** nuclear radiation
2 (*cancellazione*) striking off; (*espulsione*) expulsion

radica ['radika] SF (*per pipe*) briar, briarwood; **pipa in radica** briar-pipe; **radica di noce** walnut (wood)

radicale [radi'kale] AGG (*gen, Pol*) radical; (*Ling*) root *attr*; **un cambiamento radicale** a radical change
■SM/F (*Pol*) radical
■SM (*Mat, Chim*) radical; (*Ling*) root; **radicali liberi** free radicals

radicalismo [radika'lizmo] SM radicalism

radicalmente [radikal'mente] AVV (*dalla radice*) radically, fundamentally; (*completamente*) thoroughly, completely

radicando [radi'kando] SM (*Mat*) radicand

radicare [radi'kare] VI (*aus* **essere**) (*Bot*) to take root
▶ **radicarsi** VIP (*fig*) to take root

radicato, a [radi'kato] AGG (*pregiudizio, credenza*) deep-seated, deeply-rooted

radicchio [ra'dikkjo] SM radicchio; *variety of chicory*

radice [ra'ditʃe] SF (*gen, Mat, Anat, Ling, fig*) root; **segno di radice** (*Mat*) radical sign; **colpire alla radice** (*fig*) to strike at the root; **mettere radici** (*idee, odio*) to take root; (*persona*) to put down roots; **radice quadrata** (*Mat*) square root

radi e getta ['radi e 'dʒetta] AGG INV: **rasoio radi e getta** disposable *o* throwaway razor

radio[1] ['radjo] SF INV **1** (*apparecchio*) radio (set); **radio portatile** portable radio; **radio ricevente** receiver; **radio a transistor** transistor (radio); **radio trasmittente** transmitter **2** (*radiodiffusione*): **la radio** (the) radio; **l'ho sentito alla radio** I heard it on the radio; **trasmettere via radio a qn** (*messaggio*) to radio to sb; **trasmettere per radio** to broadcast
■AGG INV radio *attr*; **stazione /ponte radio** radio station/link

radio[2]**, di** ['radjo] SM (*Anat*) radius

radio[3] ['radjo] SM (*Chim*) radium

radioabbonato, a [radjoabbo'nato] SM/F radio subscriber

radioamatore, trice [radjoama'tore] SM/F amateur radio operator

radioascoltatore, trice [radjoaskolta'tore] SM/F (radio) listener

radioascolto [radjoas'kolto] SM radio listening

radioassistito, a [radjoassis'tito] AGG: **navigazione radioassistita** radio navigation

radioattività [radjoattivi'ta] SF radioactivity

radioattivo, a [radjoat'tivo] AGG radioactive; **scorie radioattive** radioactive waste

radiobiologia [radjobiolo'dʒia] SF radiobiology

radiobussola [radjo'bussola] SF (*Naut*) radio compass

radiocarbonio [radjokar'bɔnjo] SM radiocarbon

radiocollegamento [radjokollega'mento] SM radio link

radiocomandare [radjokoman'dare] VT to operate by remote control

radiocomandato, a [radjokoman'dato] AGG remote-controlled

radiocomando [radjoko'mando] SM remote control

radiocomunicazione [radjokomunikat'tsjone] SF radio message

radiocronaca, che [radjo'krɔnaka] SF radio commentary; **la radiocronaca della partita** the radio commentary on the match

radiocronista, i, e [radjokro'nista] SM/F radio commentator

radiodiffusione [radjodiffu'zjone] SF (radio) broadcasting

radioelettricità [radjoelettritʃi'ta] SF radioelectricity

radiofaro [radjo'faro] SM radio beacon

radiofonico, a, ci, che [radjo'fɔniko] AGG radio *attr*

radiofrequenza [radjofre'kwɛntsa] SF (radio) frequency

radiogoniometro [radjogo'njɔmetro] SM (*Naut, Aer*) direction finder, radiogoniometer

radiografare [radjogra'fare] VT to X-ray

radiografia [radjogra'fia] SF (*procedimento*) radiography; (*foto*) X-ray (photograph)

radiografico, a, ci, che [radjo'grafiko] AGG X-ray *attr*

radioisotopo [radjoi'zɔtopo] SM radioisotope, radioactive isotope

radiolina [radjo'lina] SF portable radio, transistor (radio)

radiolocalizzare [radjolokalid'dzare] VT to locate by radar

radiologia [radjolo'dʒia] SF radiology

radiologo, a, gi, ghe [ra'djɔlogo] SM/F (*medico*) radiologist; (*tecnico*) radiographer

radioonda [radjo'onda] SF radio wave

radioregistratore [radjoredʒistra'tore] SM radio cassette recorder

radioricevente [radjoritʃe'vɛnte] SF (*anche: apparecchio radioricevente*) receiver

radioscopia [radjosko'pia] SF (*Med*) radioscopy

radioscopico, a, ci, che [radjo'skɔpiko] AGG radioscopic

radiosità [radjosi'ta] SF (*anche fig*) radiance

radioso, a [ra'djoso] AGG (*anche fig*) radiant

radiospia [radjos'pia] SF bug

radiostazione [radjostat'tsjone] SF radio station

radiosveglia [radjoz'veʎʎa] SF radio alarm

radiotaxi [radjo'taksi], **radiotassì** [radjotas'si] SM INV radio taxi

radiotecnica [radjo'tɛknika] SF radio engineering

radiotecnico, a, ci, che [radjo'tɛkniko] AGG radio engineering *attr*
■SM radio engineer

radiotelefono [radjote'lɛfono] SM radiotelephone

radiotelegrafia [radjotelegra'fia] SF radiotelegraphy

radiotelegrafista, i, e [radjotelegra'fista] SM/F radiotelegrapher

radiotelescopio, pi [radjoteles'kɔpjo] SM radio telescope

radioterapia [radjotera'pia] SF radiotherapy

radiotrasmesso, a [radjotraz'messo] PP *di* radiotrasmettere

Rr

radiotrasmettere [radjotraz'mettere] VT IRREG to broadcast (*by radio*)
radiotrasmettitore [radjotrazmetti'tore] SM radio transmitter
radiotrasmittente [radjotrazmit'tɛnte] AGG (radio) broadcasting *attr*
■ SF (radio) broadcasting station
rado, a ['rado] AGG (*capelli*) sparse, thin; (*visite*) infrequent; **di rado** rarely; **vanno di rado al ristorante** they rarely go to a restaurant; **non di rado** not uncommonly
radunare [radu'nare] VT (*persone*) to gather, assemble; (*Mil: truppe*) to rally; (*cose*) to collect, gather together
▶ **radunarsi** VIP to gather, assemble
radunata [radu'nata] SF (*Mil*) muster; (*Dir*): **radunata sediziosa** seditious assembly (*o* gathering)
raduno [ra'duno] SM gathering, meeting
radura [ra'dura] SF clearing
rafano ['rafano] SM (*Bot*) horseradish
Raffaello [raffa'ɛllo] SM: **Raffaello (Sanzio)** Raphael
raffazzonare [raffattso'nare] VT (*riparare*) to patch up; (*mettere insieme alla meglio*) to throw together
raffazzonato, a [raffattso'nato] AGG patched up
raffermo, a [raf'fermo] AGG stale
raffica, che ['raffika] SF (*Meteor*) gust (of wind); **raffica di mitra** burst of machine-gun fire; **il vento soffiava a raffiche** the wind was very blustery; **raffica di insulti** (*fig*) avalanche of insults; **raffica di domande** (*fig*) barrage of questions
raffigurare [raffigu'rare] VT (*rappresentare*) to depict, to represent; (*simboleggiare*) to represent, symbolize; **il quadro raffigura la presa della Bastiglia** the picture shows the storming of the Bastille; **non riesco a raffigurarmelo** I can't picture it
raffigurazione [raffigurat'tsjone] SF depiction, representation
raffinare [raffi'nare] VT (*zucchero, petrolio, fig*) to refine
▶ **raffinarsi** VIP (*fig*) to become refined
raffinatamente [raffinata'mente] AVV (*vestito, arredato*) elegantly, tastefully
raffinatezza [raffina'tettsa] SF refinement; **arredato con raffinatezza** tastefully furnished
raffinato, a [raffi'nato] AGG (*zucchero, sale*) refined; (*persona*) cultivated, polished, refined; (*modi*) polished, sophisticated; (*crudeltà, astuzia*) refined, subtle; (*pranzo*) formal; **una donna raffinata** a sophisticated woman; **cibi raffinati** delicacies
■ SM/F refined person
raffinatore [raffina'tore] SM refiner
raffinazione [raffinat'tsjone] SF (*di sostanza*) refining; **raffinazione del petrolio** oil refining
raffineria [raffine'ria] SF refinery
rafforzamento [raffortsa'mento] SM (*di costruzione*) reinforcement; (*di muscoli, carattere*) strengthening
rafforzare [raffor'tsare] VT (*gen, Mil*) to reinforce
▶ **rafforzarsi** VIP to strengthen, grow stronger; **i miei dubbi su di lui si sono rafforzati** my doubts about him have grown
rafforzativo, a [raffortsa'tivo] (*Gramm*) AGG intensifying
■ SM intensifier
raffreddamento [raffredda'mento] SM (*anche fig*) cooling; **c'è stato un raffreddamento nei loro rapporti** (*fig*) their relationship has cooled; **raffreddamento ad acqua** (*Aut*) water-cooling; **raffreddamento ad aria** (*Aut*) air-cooling
raffreddare [raffred'dare] VT to cool (down); (*fig: entusiasmo*) to have a cooling effect on, dampen; **lascia raffreddare la minestra** leave the soup to cool (down)
▶ **raffreddarsi** VIP **1** (*caffè, minestra ecc*) to cool down; (*aria*) to become cooler, become colder; (*fig: entusiasmo, relazione*) to cool (off); **non lasciare che la minestra si raffreddi** don't let the soup get cold; **aspetta che si raffreddi** wait till it cools down **2** (*prendere un raffreddore*) to catch a cold
raffreddato, a [raffred'dato] AGG (*Med*): **essere raffreddato** to have a cold; **sono raffreddata** I've got a cold
raffreddore [raffred'dore] SM (*Med*) cold; **prendere/avere il raffreddore** to catch/have a cold; **raffreddore da fieno** hay fever
raffrontare [raffron'tare] VT to compare
raffronto [raf'fronto] SM comparison
rafia ['rafja] SF (*fibra*) raffia
rafting ['raftin(g)] SM (*Sport*) rafting
raganella [raga'nɛlla] SF (*Zool*) tree frog
ragazza [ra'gattsa] SF (*gen*) girl; (*giovane donna*) young woman; (*fidanzata*) girlfriend; **una ragazza alta e bionda** a tall blonde girl; **è la mia ragazza** she's my girlfriend; **brava ragazza** nice girl, good sort; **nome da ragazza** maiden name; **da ragazza faceva la commessa** when she was younger she worked as a shop (*Brit*) *o* sales (*Am*) assistant; **ragazza copertina** cover girl; **ragazza madre** unmarried mother; **ragazza alla pari** au-pair girl; **ragazza squillo** call girl
ragazzata [ragat'tsata] SF childish action; **è stata solo una ragazzata** it was just a boyish prank
ragazzo [ra'gattso] SM **1** (*gen*) boy; (*giovanotto*) young man; (*fidanzato*) boyfriend; (*garzone*) boy; **ha litigato con il suo ragazzo** she's quarrelled with her boyfriend; **fin da quando era ragazzo** since he was a boy; **da ragazzo faceva il commesso** when he was younger he worked as a shop (*Brit*) *o* sales (*Am*) assistant; **ragazzo padre** unmarried father; **ragazzo di strada** street urchin; **ragazzo di vita** rent boy (*Brit*), hustler (*Am*) **2 ragazzi** SMPL (*bambini, figli*) children; (*amici*) folks (*fam*), guys (*Am*); **è in vacanza con sua moglie e i ragazzi** he's on holiday with his wife and children; **andiamo ragazzi!** let's go guys (*o* people)!; **film/libro per ragazzi** children's film (*Brit*) *o* movie (*Am*) /book
raggelare [raddʒe'lare] VI (*aus* **essere**), **raggelarsi** VIP to freeze; **si sentì raggelare all'idea** his blood froze *o* ran cold at the idea
■ VT to freeze; **raggelare una conversazione** to stop a conversation dead
raggiante [rad'dʒante] AGG (*sorriso, espressione*) beaming, radiant; **raggiante di gioia** beaming *o* radiant with joy
raggiare [rad'dʒare] VI (*aus* **avere**) **1 raggiare di gioia** to be radiant with joy **2** (*Fis*) to radiate
raggiera [rad'dʒera] SF (*di ruota*) spokes *pl*; **a raggiera** with a sunburst pattern
raggio, gi ['raddʒo] SM **1** (*gen, Fis, fig*) ray, beam; **un raggio di sole** (*anche fig*) a ray of sunshine; **raggio di luna** moonbeam; **raggio di speranza** (*fig*) ray *o* gleam of hope; **raggio laser** laser beam; **raggi X** X-rays **2** (*di ruota*) spoke **3** (*Mat, fig*) radius; **nel raggio di 20 km** within a radius of 20 km *o* a 20-km radius; **a largo raggio** (*esplorazione, incursione*) wide-ranging, extensive in scope; **raggio d'azione** (*di proiettile*) range; (*fig*) range, scope

LO SAPEVI...?
raggio non si traduce mai con la parola inglese *rage*

raggirare [raddʒi'rare] VT to deceive, take in, trick; **si è lasciato raggirare dai suoi discorsi** he was taken in by his arguments

raggiro [rad'dʒiro] SM trick, swindle; **non farti invischiare nei suoi raggiri** don't let yourself get mixed up in his schemes

raggiungere [rad'dʒundʒere] VT IRREG **1** (*persona*): **raggiungere qn** to catch sb up, catch up with sb; (: *telefonicamente*) to get in touch with sb, reach sb; **li abbiamo raggiunti per strada/alla stazione** we caught up with them on the way/at the station; **vi raggiungo più tardi** I'll catch up with you later, I'll join you later; **nella ricerca nucleare l'Italia non ha ancora raggiunto la Francia** *o* **il livello della Francia** Italy still hasn't caught up with France in nuclear research **2** (*luogo, oggetto posto in alto*) to reach; (*obiettivo*) to reach, achieve; **la temperatura ha raggiunto i trenta gradi** the temperature has reached thirty degrees; **la criminalità sta raggiungendo livelli preoccupanti** crime is reaching worrying levels; **raggiungere il proprio scopo** to reach one's goal, achieve one's aim; **raggiungere un accordo** to come to *o* reach an agreement

raggiungibile [raddʒun'dʒibile] AGG (*scopo*) attainable, within reach

raggiungimento [raddʒundʒi'mento] SM (*di scopo*) attainment, achievement

raggiunto, a [rad'dʒunto] PP *di* **raggiungere**

raggomitolare [raggomito'lare] VT (*avvolgere*) to wind up
▶ **raggomitolarsi** VR (*fig*: *rannicchiarsi*) to curl up

raggranellare [raggranel'lare] VT (*soldi*) to scrape together

raggrinzire [raggrin'tsire], **raggrinzare** [raggrin'tsare] VT to crease
■ VI (*aus* **essere**), **raggrinzarsi** VIP (*stoffa*) to wrinkle (up); (*viso, pelle*) to become wrinkled

raggrumare [raggru'mare] VT, **raggrumarsi** VIP (*sangue, latte*) to clot

raggruppamento [raggruppa'mento] SM **1** (*azione*) grouping **2** (*gruppo*) group; (: *Mil*) unit

raggruppare [raggrup'pare] VT (*in un unico gruppo*) to group (together); (*in molti gruppi*) to organize into groups
▶ **raggrupparsi** VR (*in un unico gruppo*) to group (together); (*in molti gruppi*) to form into groups; **raggrupparsi intorno a qn** to gather around sb

ragguagliare [raggwaʎ'ʎare] VT **1** (*informare*): **ragguagliare (su)** to inform (about) **2** (*confrontare*): **ragguagliare qc a qc** to compare sth with sth

ragguaglio, gli [rag'gwaʎʎo] SM **1** (*informazione*) piece of information; **fornire ragguagli su qc** to provide information about sth **2** (*paragone*) comparison

ragguardevole [raggwar'devole] AGG (*persona*) notable, distinguished; (*somma*) considerable, sizeable; (*successo*) remarkable

ragia ['radʒa] SF: **acqua ragia** = **acquaragia**

ragià [ra'dʒa] SM INV rajah

ragionamento [radʒona'mento] SM (*facoltà*) reasoning *no pl*; (*argomentazione*) argument, reasoning; **un ragionamento sbagliato** faulty reasoning; **ci sono arrivato con il ragionamento** I got there through reasoning, I reasoned it out; **è un ragionamento logico** it's a logical argument; **il tuo ragionamento fila** your argument makes sense; **è inutile perdersi in futili ragionamenti** it's pointless getting involved in futile arguments

ragionare [radʒo'nare] VI (*aus* **avere**) **1** (*pensare*) to reason, think; **ragionaci su!** think about it!, think it over!; **cerca di ragionare** try and be reasonable; **non c'è modo di farla ragionare** you can't make her think clearly (*o* use her head); **quando ho fame non ragiono più** I can't think straight when I'm hungry **2** (*discutere*): **ragionare di** to discuss, talk over

ragionato, a [radʒo'nato] AGG (*discorso*) reasoned; (*bibliografia*) annotated

ragione [ra'dʒone] SF **1** (*facoltà*) reason; **perdere il lume della ragione** to lose one's reason, take leave of one's senses **2** (*motivo*) reason, cause, motive; (*argomentazione*) argument; (*diritto*) right; **avrà le sue buone ragioni per dire di no** he must have his reasons for refusing; **non è una buona ragione!** that's no excuse *o* reason!; **ragione di più per fare così** all the more reason for doing so; **... ragion per cui sarebbe meglio partire** ...that's why it would be better to leave; **a maggior ragione dovresti fare qualcosa** all the more reason why you should do something; **a** *o* **con ragione** with good reason, rightly, justly; **senza ragione** for no reason; **a torto o a ragione** rightly or wrongly; **per ragioni di famiglia** for family reasons; **a ragion veduta** after due consideration; (*intenzionalmente*) deliberately; **far valere le proprie ragioni** to assert one's rights **3** (*Mat*) proportion, ratio; **in ragione di 2 euro per articolo** at the rate of 2 euros per item **4** (*fraseologia*): **aver ragione (a fare)** to be right (in doing *o* to do); **sì, hai perfettamente ragione** yes, you're quite right; **aver ragione di qn/qc** to get the better of sb/sth; **avere ragione da vendere** to be absolutely right, be dead right (*fam*); **dare ragione a qn** (*sogg*: *persona*) to side with sb; (: *fatto*) to prove sb right; **farsi una ragione di qc** to accept sth, come to terms with sth; **non sentire ragioni** to refuse to listen to reason; **picchiare qn di santa ragione** to give sb a good hiding
■ **ragione di scambio** (*Econ*) terms *pl* of trade; **ragione sociale** (*Comm*) corporate name; **ragion d'essere** raison d'être; **ragion di stato** reason of State

ragioneria [radʒone'ria] SF (*scienza*) accountancy; (*ufficio*) accounts department; (*scuola*) commercial school, institute of commerce

ragionevole [radʒo'nevole] AGG **1** (*sensato*: *persona*) reasonable, sensible; (: *consiglio*) sensible, sound; **sii ragionevole!** be sensible! **2** (*giusto*: *prezzo*) reasonable, fair; **il prezzo mi sembra ragionevole** the price seems reasonable **3** (*fondato*: *timore, sospetto*) well-founded

ragionevolezza [radʒonevo'lettsa] SF (*sensatezza*) reasonableness

ragionevolmente [radʒonevol'mente] AVV (*sensatamente*) sensibly, reasonably; (*giustamente*) reasonably

ragioniere, a [radʒo'njɛre] SM/F accountant; **fa il ragioniere** he is an accountant

raglan [ra'glan] AGG INV (*manica*) raglan

ragliare [raʎ'ʎare] VI (*aus* **avere**) to bray

raglio, gli ['raʎʎo] SM bray

ragnatela [raɲɲa'tela] SF (spider's) web, cobweb; **la casa era piena di ragnatele** the house was full of cobwebs; **una ragnatela d'intrighi** (*fig*) a web of intrigue

Rr

ragno ['raɲɲo] SM spider; **non cavare un ragno dal buco** (*fig*) to draw a blank, get nowhere
ragù [ra'gu] SM INV (*Culin*) meat sauce; **spaghetti al ragù** spaghetti with meat sauce
ragusano, a [ragu'sano] AGG of *o* from Ragusa
■SM/F inhabitant *o* native of Ragusa
raï [rai] AGG INV: **musica raï** rai
RAI-TV ['raiti'vu] SIGLA F (= **Radio televisione italiana**) *Public Italian Broadcasting Company*
▷ www.rai.it/
ralenti [ralɑ̃'ti] SM INV: **al ralenti** in slow motion
rallegramenti [rallegra'menti] SMPL congratulations
rallegrare [ralle'grare] VT (*persona*) to cheer up; (*stanza, atmosfera*) to brighten up; **la notizia ha rallegrato tutti** the news cheered everyone up; **quel bel tappeto giallo rallegra la stanza** that lovely yellow carpet brightens up the room
▶ **rallegrarsi** VIP **1** (*diventare allegro*) to cheer up; (*provare allegrezza*) to rejoice; **si rallegrò solo a vederlo** he was glad just to see him **2** (*congratularsi*): **rallegrarsi con qn per qc** to congratulate sb on sth
rallentamento [rallenta'mento] SM (*di produzione*) slowing down, slackening; (*del traffico*) slowing down; **subire un rallentamento** to slow down, slacken
rallentando [rallen'tando] SM INV (*Mus*) rallentando
rallentare [rallen'tare] VT (*gen*) to slow down; **rallentare il ritmo** to slow down; **rallentare il passo** to slacken one's pace
■VI (*aus* **essere**) to slow down

LO SAPEVI...?
rallentare non si traduce mai con la parola inglese *relent*

rallentatore [rallenta'tore] SM (*Cine*) slow-motion camera; **al rallentatore** (*anche fig*) in slow motion
rally ['ræli] SM INV (car) rally; **il rally di Montecarlo** the Monte Carlo rally
RAM [ram] SIGLA F RAM (= *random access memory*)
Ramadan [rama'dan] SM INV (*Rel*): **il Ramadan** Ramadan
ramaiolo [rama'jolo] SM ladle
ramanzina [raman'dzina] SF lecture, telling-off; **fare una bella ramanzina a qn** to give sb a lecture, give sb a good talking-to
ramare [ra'mare] VT **1** (*superficie*) to copper, coat with copper **2** (*Agr: vite*) to spray with copper sulphate
ramarro [ra'marro] SM green lizard
ramato, a [ra'mato] AGG (*oggetto: rivestito di rame*) copper-coated, coppered; (*capelli, barba*) coppery, copper-coloured (*Brit*), copper-colored (*Am*)
ramatura [rama'tura] SF (*vedi vb*) coppering; spraying with copper sulphate
ramazza [ra'mattsa] SF (*scopa*) besom
ramazzare [ramat'tsare] VT to sweep
rame ['rame] SM copper; **di rame** copper *attr*; **incisione su rame** copperplate
ramificare [ramifi'kare] VI (*aus* **avere**) (*Bot*) to put out branches
▶ **ramificarsi** VIP (*diramarsi, fig*) to branch out; (*Med: tumore, vene*) to ramify; **ramificarsi in** (*biforcarsi*) to branch into
ramificato, a [ramifi'kato] AGG (*albero, corna*) branched; (*tumore*) ramified; **il tunnel sotterraneo è ramificato in 4 gallerie** the underground tunnel branches into 4 passages
ramificazione [ramifikat'tsjone] SF ramification
ramingo, a, ghi, ghe [ra'mingo] AGG (*letter*): **andare ramingo** to go wandering, wander
ramino [ra'mino] SM (*Carte*) rummy
rammagliare [rammaʎ'ʎare] VT (*calze*) to mend a ladder in
rammaricare [rammari'kare] VT to grieve
▶ **rammaricarsi** VIP: **rammaricarsi di** *o* **per qc** (*dispiacersi*) to regret sth, be sorry about sth; (*lamentarsi*) to complain about sth; **è inutile rammaricarsi** there is no point in feeling sorry
rammarico, chi [ram'mariko] SM regret
rammendare [rammen'dare] VT to mend, darn
rammendo [ram'mɛndo] SM (*azione*) darning *no pl*, mending *no pl*; (*risultato*) darn, mend; **fare un rammendo** to darn, mend
rammentare [rammen'tare] VT to remember, recall; **rammentare qc a qn** to remind sb of sth
▶ **rammentarsi** VIP: **rammentarsi (di qc)** to remember (sth)
rammollimento [rammolli'mento] SM softening
rammollire [rammol'lire] VT to soften
■VI (*aus* **essere**), **rammollirsi** VIP to soften, grow *o* go soft
rammollito, a [rammol'lito] AGG weak
■SM/F weakling
ramo ['ramo] SM (*gen, fig*) branch; (*branca: di una scienza*) branch; (*: di commercio*) field; **non è il mio ramo** it's not my field *o* line; **i due rami del parlamento** the two chambers of parliament

LO SAPEVI...?
ramo non si traduce mai con la parola inglese *ram*

ramoscello [ramoʃ'ʃɛllo] SM twig
rampa ['rampa] SF **1** (*anche:* **rampa di scale**) flight (of stairs) **2** (*breve salita*) slope; **rampa d'accesso** (*in autostrada*) slip road (*Brit*), entrance (*o* exit) ramp (*Am*); (*in marciapiede*) ramp; **rampa di lancio** (*Aer*) launching pad
rampante [ram'pante] AGG (*Araldica*) rampant; (*pegg: arrivista*) aggressively ambitious
■SM/F (*arrivista*): **un giovane rampante** a yuppie
rampicante [rampi'kante] (*Bot*) AGG climbing
■SM creeper, climber
rampichino [rampi'kino] SM (*Zool*): **rampichino alpestre** tree creeper
rampino [ram'pino] SM (*gancio*) hook; (*Naut*) grapnel
rampollo [ram'pollo] SM (*discendente*) descendant; (*scherz: figlio*): **è tutto orgoglioso del suo rampollo** he's very proud of his son and heir
rampone [ram'pone] SM (*fiocina*) harpoon; (*Alpinismo*) crampon
rana ['rana] SF frog; **nuoto a rana** breaststroke; **nuotare a rana** to do the breaststroke; **uomo rana** frogman; **rana pescatrice** angler fish
rancido, a ['rantʃido] AGG rancid
■SM: **odore di rancido** rank odour; **ha odore di rancido** it smells rancid; **sa di rancido** it tastes rancid
rancio, ci ['rantʃo] SM (*Mil*) mess; **ora del rancio** mess time
rancore [ran'kore] SM resentment, rancour (*Brit*), rancor (*Am*); **senza rancore?** no hard feelings?; **dimentichiamo i vecchi rancori** let bygones be bygones; **serbare rancore a qn** *or* **nutrire rancore contro** *o* **verso qn** to bear sb a grudge
randa ['randa] SF (*Naut*) mainsail
randagio, a, gi, gie *o* **ge** [ran'dadʒo] AGG (*gatto, cane*) stray *attr*
randellare [randel'lare] VT to cudgel
randellata [randel'lata] SF blow with a cudgel;

prendere qn a randellate to set about sb with a cudgel
randello [ran'dɛllo] SM cudgel, club
randomizzare [randomid'dzare] VT (*Inform*) to randomize
rango, ghi ['rango] SM **1** (*grado*) rank; (*condizione sociale*) station, social standing; **avere il rango di** to hold the rank of; **gli alti ranghi** the upper ranks; **persone di rango inferiore** people of lower standing **2** (*Mil: schiera*) rank; (*: fila*) line; **rientrare nei ranghi** to fall in; (*fig*) to fall into line; **uscire dai ranghi** to fall out; (*fig*) to step out of line
Rangoon [ran'gun] SF Rangoon
ranista, i, e [ra'nista] SM/F (*Nuoto*) breast-stroke swimmer
rannicchiare [rannik'kjare] VT (*gambe*) to tuck up
▶ **rannicchiarsi** VR to crouch, huddle; **rannicchiarsi sotto le coperte** to curl up under the blankets
rannuvolamento [rannuvola'mento] SM clouding over
rannuvolare [rannuvo'lare] VT to darken
▶ **rannuvolarsi** VIP (*cielo*) to cloud over, become overcast; (*fig: viso*) to darken
ranocchio, chi [ra'nɔkkjo] SM (edible) frog
rantolare [ranto'lare] VI (*aus* **avere**) (*respirare affannosamente*) to wheeze; **si sentiva il moribondo rantolare** you could hear the man's death rattle
rantolio, lii [ranto'lio] SM (*il respirare affannoso*) wheezing; (*: di agonizzante*) death rattle
rantolo ['rantolo] SM (*respiro affannoso*) wheeze; (*: di agonizzante*) death rattle
ranuncolo [ra'nunkolo] SM (*Bot*) buttercup
rap [rɛp] SM, AGG INV (*Mus*) rap
rapa ['rapa] SF turnip; **cime di rapa** turnip tops; **testa di rapa** (*fig*) fathead, idiot; ***è come voler cavar sangue da una rapa*** it's like trying to get blood out of a stone

> **LO SAPEVI...?**
> **rapa** non si traduce mai con la parola inglese *rape*

rapace [ra'patʃe] AGG (*animale*) predatory; (*fig: avido*) rapacious, grasping
■ SM bird of prey
rapacemente [rapatʃe'mente] AVV rapaciously
rapacità [rapatʃi'ta] SF (*anche fig*) rapaciousness, rapacity
rapare [ra'pare] VT (*capelli*) to crop, cut very short; **ti hanno rapato (i capelli) a zero** they have scalped you; **raparsi (i capelli) a zero** to get scalped
▶ **raparsi** VR to have one's head shaved (*o* cropped)
rapidamente [rapida'mente] AVV quickly, rapidly, fast; **l'incendio si è esteso rapidamente** the fire spread quickly
rapide ['rapide] SFPL (*di fiume*) rapids
rapidità [rapidi'ta] SF speed, rapidity; **ha colpito con rapidità** he was quick to strike
rapido, a ['rapido] AGG (*gen*) fast; (*esame, occhiata*) quick, rapid; **gli ho dato solo una rapida occhiata** I just had a quick look at it; **è rapido nell'agire** he is quick to act
■ SM (*Ferr*) express (train) (*on which supplement must be paid*)
rapimento [rapi'mento] SM **1** (*di persona*) kidnapping, abduction; **il rapimento è avvenuto in pieno giorno** the kidnapping happened in broad daylight **2** (*Rel*) ecstasy; (*fig*) rapture; **fu preso da rapimento** he went into ecstasies *o* raptures; **con rapimento** rapturously, ecstatically
rapina [ra'pina] SF robbery; **rapina in banca** bank robbery; **rapina a mano armata** armed robbery
rapinare [rapi'nare] VT to rob; **quella banca è stata rapinata tre volte in un mese** that bank has been robbed three times in a month
rapinatore, trice [rapina'tore] SM/F robber; **i rapinatori sono fuggiti a piedi** the robbers ran away
rapire [ra'pire] VT **1** (*persona*) to kidnap, abduct; **l'hanno rapito due mesi fa** he was kidnapped two months ago **2** (*fig: mandare in estasi*) to enrapture, delight

> **LO SAPEVI...?**
> **rapire** non si traduce mai con la parola inglese *rape*

rapito, a [ra'pito] AGG **1** (*persona*) kidnapped **2** (*fig: in estasi*): **ascoltare rapito qn** to be captivated by sb's words; **guardava rapito il quadro** he gazed at the painting, entranced
■ SM/F kidnapped person
rapitore, trice [rapi'tore] SM/F kidnapper; **i rapitori hanno minacciato di uccidere l'ostaggio** the kidnappers threatened to kill the hostage
rappacificare [rappatʃifi'kare] VT (*riconciliare*) to reconcile
▶ **rappacificarsi** VR (*uso reciproco*) to become reconciled, make it up
rappacificazione [rappatʃifikat'tsjone] SF reconciliation
rappezzare [rappet'tsare] VT to patch; **rappezzare un discorso** (*fig*) to cobble together a speech
rapportare [rappor'tare] VT **1 rapportare qc a qc** (*confrontare*) to compare sth with sth **2** (*riprodurre disegno*): **rapportare su scala più grande** to reproduce on a larger scale
▶ **rapportarsi** VIP: **rapportarsi a** to be related to
rapporto [rap'pɔrto] SM **1** (*legame*) connection, relationship, link; **non avere alcun rapporto con qc** to have nothing to do with sth, be unrelated to sth; **in rapporto a quanto è successo** with regard to *o* in relation to what happened **2** (*relazione*) relationship; **abbiamo un ottimo rapporto** we have a very good relationship; **i rapporti tra loro sono piuttosto tesi** relations between them are rather strained; **essere in buoni/cattivi rapporti con qn** to be on good/bad terms with sb; **rapporti diplomatici** diplomatic relations; **rapporti prematrimoniali** sex *sg* before marriage, premarital sex; **rapporto d'affari** business relations *pl*; **rapporto coniugale** marital relationship; **rapporto intimo** sexual intercourse; **rapporto di lavoro** employer-employee relationship; **indennità di fine rapporto (di lavoro)** severance pay; **rapporto sessuale** (sexual) intercourse *sg*; **avere rapporti sessuali** to have intercourse **3** (*resoconto*) report; **scrivi un rapporto sulla situazione** write a report on the situation; **fare rapporto a qn su qc** to report sth to sb; **chiamare qn a rapporto** (*Mil*) to summon sb; **andare a rapporto da qn** to report to sb **4** (*Mat, Tecn*) ratio; (*di bicicletta*) gear; **in rapporto di 1 a 10** in a ratio of 1 to 10; **rapporto di compressione** (*Tecn*) pressure ratio; **rapporto di distanza** (*Fis*) distance ratio; **rapporto di trasmissione** (*Tecn*) gear
rapprendersi [rap'prɛndersi] VIP IRREG (*sangue*) to coagulate, clot; (*latte*) to curdle
rappresaglia [rappre'saʎʎa] SF reprisal, retaliation; **per rappresaglia** in reprisal *o* retaliation
rappresentante [rapprezen'tante] SM/F (*gen, Pol, Comm*) representative; **il rappresentante di classe** the

Rr

class representative; **rappresentante di commercio** sales representative, sales rep (*fam*); **rappresentante sindacale** union delegate *o* representative

rappresentanza [rapprezen'tantsa] SF **1** (*gen, Pol*) representation; (*gruppo*) delegation, deputation; **in rappresentanza di qn** on behalf of sb; **spese di rappresentanza** entertainment expenses; **macchina di rappresentanza** official car **2** (*Comm*) agency; **avere la rappresentanza di** to be the agent for; **rappresentanza esclusiva** sole agency; **avere la rappresentanza esclusiva** to be sole agent

rappresentare [rapprezen'tare] VT **1** (*sogg: pittore, romanziere, quadro*) to depict, portray; (: *fotografia*) to show; **il quadro rappresenta una scena rurale** the painting depicts a rural scene **2** (*simboleggiare, significare*) to represent; **ciò rappresenta un grave pericolo per la nazione** this represents a serious threat to the nation; **quella ragazza non rappresenta più niente per me** that girl means nothing to me any more **3** (*Teatro: recitare*) to perform, play; (: *mettere in scena*) to perform, put on; **hanno intenzione di rappresentare la Carmen** they intend to stage *o* put on Carmen **4** (*agire per conto di*) to represent; **farsi rappresentare dal proprio legale** to be represented by one's lawyer

rappresentativa [rapprezenta'tiva] SF (*di partito, sindacale*) representative group; (*Sport*): **la rappresentativa italiana** the Italian team

rappresentatività [rapprezentativi'ta] SF representativeness

rappresentativo, a [rapprezenta'tivo] AGG (*gen*) representative; (*tipico*) typical

rappresentazione [rapprezentat'tsjone] SF **1** (*raffigurazione*) representation; (: *di società, paesaggio*) portrayal **2** (*spettacolo*) performance; **prima rappresentazione assoluta** world première; **sacra rappresentazione** religious play

rappreso, a [rap'preso] PP *di* **rapprendersi**
■ AGG (*sangue*) coagulated, clotted; (*latte*) curdled

rapsodia [rapso'dia] SF rhapsody

raptus ['raptus] SM INV: **raptus di follia** fit of madness

raramente [rara'mente] AVV seldom, rarely; **ci vediamo raramente** we rarely see each other

rarefare [rare'fare] VB IRREG, VT, **rarefarsi** VIP to rarefy

rarefatto, a [rare'fatto] AGG rarefied

rarefazione [rarefat'tsjone] SF rarefaction

rarità [rari'ta] SF INV **1** (*scarsezza: di oggetto, malattia*) rarity; (: *di visite*) infrequency **2** (*oggetto*) rarity; (*avvenimento*) rare occurrence, unusual occurrence

raro, a ['raro] AGG **1** (*poco comune*) rare; **è un caso molto raro** it's a very unusual *o* rare case; **è una bestia rara** (*fig*) he's a rare breed **2** (*poco numeroso*) few, rare; **le rare persone che passavano** the few people that went by; **c'era qualche rara nuvola** there was the odd cloud; **i clienti sono diventati rari** customers have become scarce *o* few and far between

ras [ras] SM INV (*titolo etiopico*) ras; (*fig: capetto*) tyrant

rasare [ra'sare] VT (*barba, capelli*) to shave off; (*siepi, erba*) to trim, cut
▶ **rasarsi** VR to shave (o.s.)

rasato, a [ra'sato] AGG (*erba*) trimmed, cut; (*tessuto*) smooth; **avere la barba rasata** *or* **essere ben rasato** to be clean-shaven

rasatura [rasa'tura] SF (*atto*) shaving; (*effetto*) shave

raschiamento [raskja'mento] SM (*Med*) curettage; **raschiamento uterino** D and C

raschiare [ras'kjare] VT to scrape; **raschiare (via) qc** to scrape sth off; **raschiarsi la gola** to clear one's throat

raschiata [ras'kjata] SF: **dare una raschiata a qc** to give sth a scrape, scrape sth

raschietto [ras'kjetto] SM scraper

raschio, chi ['raskjo] SM (*in gola*) irritation

rasentare [razen'tare] VT (*muro*) to hug, keep close to; (*terra*) to skim along (*o* over); (*fig: sfiorare*) to border on; **questo rasenta la pazzia!** this is bordering on insanity!; **rasentare la cinquantina** to be getting on for fifty (years of age)

rasente [ra'zente] PREP: **rasente (a)** close to, very near; **camminare rasente il** *o* **al muro** to hug the wall

raso, a ['raso] PP *di* **radere**
■ AGG **1** (*liscio*): **a pelo raso** (*pelliccia*) short-haired; (*tessuto*) smooth **2** (*con misure di capacità*) level *attr*; (*pieno: bicchiere*) full to the brim; **un cucchiaio raso** a level spoonful
■ PREP: **raso terra** close to the ground; **volare raso terra** to hedgehop
■ SM (*tessuto*) satin

rasoio, oi [ra'sojo] SM razor; **rasoio elettrico** electric shaver *o* razor; **rasoio a lama** cut-throat *o* straight razor; **rasoio radi e getta** disposable *o* throwaway razor

raspa ['raspa] SF (*lima*) rasp

raspare [ras'pare] VT **1** (*levigare*) to rasp **2** (*grattare: sogg: gallina, cane*) to scratch; (: *cavallo*) to paw
■ VI (*aus* **avere**) to scrape, scratch

raspo ['raspo] SM (*di uva*) grape stalk

rassegna [ras'seɲɲa] SF **1** (*Mil*) inspection, review; **passare in rassegna** (*Mil, fig*) to review **2** (*resoconto*) review, survey; (*rivista*) review; (*mostra*) exhibition, show; **una rassegna del cinema latino-americano** a season of Latin American films

rassegnare [rasseɲ'ɲare] VT: **rassegnare le dimissioni** to resign, hand in one's resignation
▶ **rassegnarsi** VIP: **rassegnarsi (a qc)** to resign o.s. (to sth); **bisogna rassegnarsi all'idea** we (*o* you *ecc*) will have to accept *o* get used to the idea; **mai rassegnarsi!** never give up!

rassegnatamente [rasseɲɲata'mente] AVV resignedly

rassegnato, a [rasseɲ'ɲato] AGG (*aria, sguardo, tono*) resigned; **l'ho visto piuttosto rassegnato** he seemed quite resigned to it when I saw him; **sospirò con fare rassegnato** he sighed resignedly

rassegnazione [rasseɲɲat'tsjone] SF resignation; **accettare qc con rassegnazione** to resign o.s. to sth

rasserenamento [rasserena'mento] SM brightening up

rasserenare [rassere'nare] VT (*Meteor*) to clear up, brighten up
■ VT (*persona*) to cheer up
▶ **rasserenarsi** VIP (*Meteor*) to brighten up, clear up; (*persona*) to cheer up

rassettare [rasset'tare] VT to tidy up, put in order
▶ **rassettarsi** VR to tidy o.s. up

rassicurante [rassiku'rante] AGG reassuring

rassicurare [rassiku'rare] VT to reassure; **ho cercato di rassicurarla, ma non è servito** I tried to reassure her, but with no success
▶ **rassicurarsi** VIP to take heart, recover one's confidence

rassicurazione [rassikurat'tsjone] SF reassurance

rassodamento [rassoda'mento] SM (*di muscoli*) hardening, strengthening; (*di tessuti*) firming
rassodante [rasso'dante] AGG (*crema, ginnastica*) toning
rassodare [rasso'dare] VT (*muscoli*) to harden, strengthen; (*tessuti*) to firm (up); (*fig*: *amicizia*) to strengthen, consolidate; **il nuoto aiuta a rassodare i muscoli** swimming helps to tone the muscles
▶ **rassodarsi** VIP (*muscoli*) to harden, strengthen; (*tessuti*) to firm (up)
rassomigliante [rassomiʎ'ʎante] AGG: **questa foto è molto rassomigliante** this photo is a good likeness
rassomiglianza [rassomiʎ'ʎantsa] SF resemblance
rassomigliare [rassomiʎ'ʎare] VI (*aus* **essere** *o* **avere**) **rassomigliare a** to resemble, look like; **rassomigli molto a tua madre** you look very like your mother
▶ **rassomigliarsi** VR (*uso reciproco*) to look alike, resemble each other; **vi rassomigliate moltissimo** you look very alike
rasta ['rasta] AGG INV (*treccine ecc*) Rasta
rastrellamento [rastrella'mento] SM (*di erba, fieno*) raking; (*Mil, di polizia*) (thorough) search; **stanno facendo un rastrellamento nella zona** they are combing the area
rastrellare [rastrel'lare] VT (*erba, fieno*) to rake; (*fig*: *perlustrare*) to comb
rastrelliera [rastrel'ljɛra] SF (*per fieno*) hayrack; (*per fucili, biciclette*) rack; (*per piatti*) dish rack
rastrello [ras'trɛllo] SM rake
rata ['rata] SF instalment (*Brit*), installment (*Am*); **pagare a rate** to pay by instal(l)ments *o* on hire purchase (*Brit*); **comprare/vendere a rate** to buy/sell on hire purchase (*Brit*) *o* on the installment plan (*Am*)
rateale [rate'ale] AGG: **pagamento rateale** payment by instal(l)ments; **vendita rateale** hire purchase (*Brit*), installment plan (*Am*)
rateare [rate'are] VT to divide into instal(l)ments
rateazione [rateat'tsjone] SF division into instal(l)ments
rateizzare [rateid'dzare] VT = **rateare**
rateo ['rateo] SM (*Econ*) accrual
ratifica, che [ra'tifika] SF ratification
ratificare [ratifi'kare] VT (*gen*) to approve, ratify; (*Amm, Dir*) to ratify
ratificazione [ratifikat'tsjone] SF = **ratifica**
rat musqué SM INV (*pelliccia*) muskrat, musquash
ratto[1] ['ratto] SM (*Storia, Dir*) abduction; **il ratto delle Sabine** the rape of the Sabine Women
ratto[2] ['ratto] SM (*Zool*) rat; **ratto comune** black rat
rattoppare [rattop'pare] VT to patch
rattoppo [rat'tɔppo] SM (*risultato*) patch; (*azione*) patching *no pl*; **fare un rattoppo a** *o* **su qc** to patch sth
rattrappire [rattrap'pire] VT (*piedi, mani*) to make stiff
▶ **rattrappirsi** VIP to become stiff
rattristare [rattris'tare] VT (*addolorare*) to sadden
▶ **rattristarsi** VIP to grow *o* become sad
rattristato, a [rattris'tato] AGG saddened
raucamente [rauka'mente] AVV hoarsely
raucedine [rau'tʃɛdine] SF hoarseness; **ho un po' di raucedine** I am a little hoarse
rauco, a, chi, che ['rauko] AGG hoarse
ravanare [rava'nare] VI (*aus* **avere**) (*fam*) to rummage
ravanello [rava'nello] SM radish
rave ['rɛɪv] SM INV, AGG INV (*festa*) rave
ravennate [raven'nate] AGG of *o* from Ravenna
■ SM/F inhabitant *o* native of Ravenna
ravioli [ravi'ɔli] SMPL (*Culin*) ravioli *sg*
ravvedersi [ravve'dersi] VIP IRREG to mend one's ways
ravveduto, a [ravve'duto] PP *di* **ravvedersi**
ravviare [ravvi'are] VT (*capelli*) to tidy; **ravviarsi i capelli** to tidy one's hair
ravviata [ravvi'ata] SF tidying up
ravvicinamento [ravvitʃina'mento] SM (*tra persone*) reconciliation; (*Pol*: *tra paesi*) rapprochement
ravvicinare [ravvitʃi'nare] VT (*oggetti*) to bring closer together; (*fig*: *persone*) to reconcile, bring together again
▶ **ravvicinarsi** VR to be reconciled; **si è ravvicinato alla famiglia** he is now reconciled with his family
ravvisare [ravvi'zare] VT to recognize
ravvivare [ravvi'vare] VT (*fuoco, sentimento*) to revive, rekindle; (*fig*: *rallegrare*) to brighten up
▶ **ravvivarsi** VIP (*fuoco, sentimento*) to be rekindled *o* revived; (*persona, ambiente*) to brighten up
ravvolgere [rav'vɔldʒere] VB IRREG
■ VT (*coperta, lenzuolo*) to roll up; **ravvolgere qn in una coperta** to wrap a blanket round sb;
▶ **ravvolgersi** VR (*coprirsi*) **ravvolgersi in qc** to wrap o.s. up in sth
ravvolto, a [rav'vɔlto] PP *di* **ravvolgere**
ravvoltolare [ravvolto'lare] VT: **ravvoltolare qn in qc** to wrap sb up in sth
▶ **ravvoltolarsi** VR: **ravvoltolarsi in qc** to wrap o.s. up in sth
Rawalpindi [rawal'pindi] SF Rawalpindi
rayon ['rajon] SM rayon
raziocinio [rattsjo'tʃinjo] SM (*facoltà di ragionare*) reasoning *no pl*; (*buon senso*) common sense; **essere dotato di raziocinio** to be able to reason, possess the faculty of reason
razionale [rattsjo'nale] AGG (*gen, Mat*) rational; (*funzionale*) functional; **ci dev'essere una spiegazione razionale** there must be a rational explanation; **un razionale sfruttamento dello spazio** an intelligent use of space
■ SM: **il razionale** the rational
razionalismo [rattsjona'lizmo] SM rationalism
razionalista, i, e [rattsjona'lista] AGG, SM/F rationalist
razionalità [rattsjonali'ta] SF rationality; (*buon senso*) common sense; (*funzionalità*) functionality, practicalness; **con razionalità** rationally, intelligently
razionalizzare [rattsjonalid'dzare] VT (*metodo, lavoro, programma*) to rationalize; (*problema, situazione*) to approach rationally
razionalmente [rattsjonal'mente] AVV rationally; (*funzionalmente*) functionally, practically
razionamento [rattsjona'mento] SM rationing; **il razionamento dell'acqua** water rationing
razionare [rattsjo'nare] VT to ration; **stanno razionando l'acqua** water is being rationed
razione [rat'tsjone] SF (*gen*) ration; (*di soldato*) rations *pl*; (*fig*: *porzione*) share
razza ['rattsa] SF **1** (*etnica*) race; (*Zool*) breed; **di razza** (*gen*) pedigree, purebred; (*cavallo*) thoroughbred; **di che razza è il tuo cane?** what breed is your dog?; **razza da latte** (*bovini*) dairy breed; **razza da macello** *o* **da carne** (*bovini*) beef breed; **essere di buona razza** to come of good stock **2** (*specie, tipo*) sort, kind; **che razza di discorso è?** what sort of argument is that?; **che razza di mascalzone!** what a scoundrel!
razzia [rat'tsia] SF raid, foray; **fare razzia in un pollaio** to raid a henhouse; **ha fatto razzia nel frigorifero** he raided the refrigerator

Rr

razziale [rat'tsjale] AGG racial; **pregiudizi razziali** racial prejudice *sg*
razziare [rattsi'are] VT (*bestiame*) to raid; (*città: saccheggiare*) to plunder, ravage
razzismo [rat'tsizmo] SM racism, racialism; (*intolleranza*) prejudice
razzista, i, e [rat'tsista] AGG, SM/F racist, racialist
razzistico, a, ci, che [rat'tsistiko] AGG racist, racialist
razzo ['raddzo] SM rocket; **lanciare un razzo** to send up *o* fire a rocket; **veloce come un razzo** as quick as lightning; **partire come un razzo** to be off like a shot; **razzo di segnalazione** flare; **razzo vettore** vector rocket
razzolare [rattso'lare] VI (*aus* **avere**) (*galline*) to scratch about
RC ['ɛrre'tʃi] SIGLA F **1** = **Responsabilità Civile; RC-auto** (*assicurazione*) car insurance (*minimum liability*) **2** (= **Rifondazione Comunista**) Communist Refoundation (*Italian left-wing political party*)
■ SIGLA = *Reggio Calabria*
RDT ['ɛrre'di'ti] SIGLA F **1** (= **Rappresentanze Sindacali di Base**) *trades union organization* **2** (= **Repubblica Democratica Tedesca**) GDR
RE SIGLA = *Reggio Emilia*
re[1] [re] SM INV (*gen*) king; (*fig: magnate*) tycoon, magnate; **re Artù** king Arthur; **i Re Magi** the Three Wise Men, the Magi; **Cristo re** Christ the King; **fare una vita da re** (*fig*) to live like a king
re[2] [rɛ] SM INV (*Mus*) D; (: *solfeggiando la scala*) re
reagente [rea'dʒɛnte] AGG reacting
■ SM reagent
reagire [rea'dʒire] VI (*aus* **avere**) (*gen, Chim*) to react; **reagire (a/contro)** to react (to/against); **come ha reagito alla notizia?** how did she react to the news?; **il paziente reagisce bene alle cure** the patient is responding well to treatment
reale[1] [re'ale] AGG (*gen, Mat*) real; (*piacere, miglioramento*) real, genuine; (*Fin: valore, salario*) real, actual; **è basato su un fatto reale** it's based on a true story; **nella vita reale** in real life
■ SM: **il reale** reality
reale[2] [re'ale] AGG (*di, da re*) royal; **la famiglia reale** the royal family
■ SMPL: **i Reali** the Royal family *sg o pl*
realismo [rea'lizmo] SM realism; **con realismo** realistically
realista[1]**, i, e** [rea'lista] AGG (*gen*) realistic; (*Arte, Letteratura*) realist
■ SM/F realist
realista[2]**, i, e** [rea'lista] AGG, SM/F (*Pol*) royalist
realisticamente [realistika'mente] AVV realistically
realistico, a, ci, che [rea'listiko] AGG realistic
realizzabile [realid'dzabile] AGG (*fattibile*) feasible; **questo abito è realizzabile in diversi tessuti** this dress can be made in various materials
realizzabilità [realiddzabili'ta] SF (*di progetto*) feasibility; (*di ideale*) attainability
realizzare [realid'dzare] VT **1** (*opera, progetto*) to carry out, realize; (*scopo*) to achieve; (*sogno, desiderio*) to achieve, fulfil (*Brit*), fulfill (*Am*), realize; **ho realizzato il mio sogno di viaggiare** I've achieved my ambition to travel **2** (*fig: capire*) to realize; **quando Luca ha realizzato quello che era successo...** when Luca realized what had happened ... **3** (*Fin: capitale*) to realize; **abbiamo realizzato 2.000 euro dalla vendita della macchina** we made 2,000 euros from the sale of the car **4** (*Sport: goal*) to score
▶ **realizzarsi** VIP (*sogno, speranza*) to come true, be realized
▶ **realizzarsi** VR (*persona*) to fulfil (*Brit*) *o* fulfill (*Am*) o.s.; **non mi sento realizzata nel mio lavoro** I don't feel fulfilled in my job
realizzazione [realiddzat'tsjone] SF **1** (*di libro, opera*) realization; (*di sogno*) fulfil(l)ment; (*di persona*) self-fulfil(l)ment **2** (*opera, creazione*) achievement; (*Cine, Teatro*) production; **realizzazione scenica** stage production **3** (*Fin*) realization
realizzo [rea'liddzo] SM **1** (*conversione in denaro*) conversion into cash **2** (*vendita forzata*) clearance sale
realmente [real'mente] AVV (*in realtà*) really; (*effettivamente*) actually; **è un fatto realmente accaduto?** did it really happen?
realtà [real'ta] SF INV reality; **la realtà era molto diversa** the reality was very different; **la dura realtà** harsh reality; **diventare realtà** to come true; **il suo sogno è diventato realtà** his dream has become (a) reality *o* has come true; **in realtà** (*in effetti*) in fact; (*a dire il vero*) really; **sembra un ragazzino, in realtà ha quasi quarant'anni** he looks very young, but in fact he's nearly forty; **realtà virtuale** virtual reality
reame [re'ame] SM kingdom, realm; (*fig*) realm
reatino, a [rea'tino] AGG of *o* from Rieti
■ SM/F inhabitant *o* native of Rieti
reato [re'ato] SM (*Dir*) crime, offence (*Brit*), offense (*Am*)
reattività [reattivi'ta] SF (*Chim*): **scala di reattività** reactivity series
reattore [reat'tore] SM (*Aer: aereo*) jet; (: *motore*) jet engine; **reattore nucleare** nuclear reactor
reazionario, ria, ri, rie [reattsjo'narjo] AGG, SM/F reactionary
reazione [reat'tsjone] SF **1** (*gen*) reaction; **la sua prima reazione è stata scappare** her immediate reaction was to run away; **motore/aereo a reazione** jet engine/plane; **reazione a catena** (*anche fig*) chain reaction; **reazione fisica** physical change; **reazione chimica** chemical reaction **2** (*Pol*) reaction, repression; **forze della reazione** reactionary forces
rebbio, bi ['rebbjo] SM prong
rebus ['rɛbus] SM INV (*gioco enigmistico*) rebus; (*fig: persona*) enigma; (: *situazione, comportamento*) puzzle
recapitare [rekapi'tare] VT to deliver
recapito [re'kapito] SM **1** (*indirizzo*) address; **puoi lasciarmi il tuo recapito?** can you give me your address?; **recapito telefonico** telephone number; **ha un recapito telefonico?** do you have a telephone number where you can be reached? **2** (*consegna*) delivery; **recapito a domicilio** home delivery (service)
recare [re'kare] VT **1** (*portare*) to bear, carry; (*contenere*) to bear; **le recò in dono un anello** he brought her a ring as a gift; **il telegramma reca la data di ieri** the telegram bears yesterday's date **2** (*causare, arrecare: gioia, piacere*) to give, bring; (: *danno*) to cause, bring; **non voglio recarvi disturbo** I don't want to cause any inconvenience to you, I don't want to disturb you; **recare danno a qn** to harm sb, cause harm to sb
▶ **recarsi** VIP to go; **recarsi in città/a scuola** to go into town/to school
recedere [re'tʃɛdere] VI (*aus* **avere**) (*ritirarsi, Dir*): **recedere (da)** to withdraw (from)
recensione [retʃen'sjone] SF review; **il film ha avuto delle ottime recensioni** the film has had excellent reviews; **fare la recensione di qc** *or* **scrivere una recensione su qc** to review sth
recensire [retʃen'sire] VT to review

recensore [retʃen'sore] SM reviewer
recente [re'tʃɛnte] AGG recent; **una scoperta recente** a recent discovery; **più recente** latest, most recent; **di recente** recently; **questo ristorante è stato aperto di recente** this restaurant opened recently
recentemente [retʃente'mente] AVV recently; **ha cominciato a lavorare lì solo recentemente** she started working there only recently
recentissime [retʃen'tissime] SFPL (*TV, Radio*) latest news *sg*; (*Stampa*) stop press *sg*
recepire [retʃe'pire] VT take in
recessione [retʃes'sjone] SF recession
recessivo, a [retʃes'sivo] AGG (*Bio, Econ*) recessive
recesso [re'tʃɛsso] SM **1** (*Dir*) withdrawal **2** (*luogo*) recess; **i recessi della mente** (*fig*) the recesses of the mind
recettore [retʃet'tore] SM (*Anat*) receptor
recherò *ecc* [reke'rɔ] VB *vedi* **recare**
recidere [re'tʃidere] VT IRREG to cut off, chop off
recidiva [retʃi'diva] SF (*Dir*) recidivism; (*Med*) relapse
recidività [retʃidivi'ta] SF (*Dir*) recidivism; (*Med*) recurring nature
recidivo, a [retʃi'divo] SM/F (*Dir*) recidivist, second (*o* habitual) offender
recintare [retʃin'tare] VT to enclose, fence off; put a fence round; **hanno recintato il giardino** they've put a fence round the garden
recinto [re'tʃinto] SM **1** (*gen*) enclosure; (*per animali*) pen; (*per cavalli*) paddock **2** (*staccionata*) fence; (*in muratura*) surrounding wall **3** **recinto delle grida** (*Borsa*) floor
recinzione [retʃin'tsjone] SF **1** (*azione*) enclosure, fencing-off **2** (*recinto: di legno*) fence; (*: di mattoni*) wall; (*reticolato*) wire fencing; (*a sbarre*) railings *pl*
recipiente [retʃi'pjɛnte] SM container; **i recipienti di plastica sono più pratici** plastic containers are more practical

> **LO SAPEVI...?**
> **recipiente** non si traduce mai con la parola inglese *recipient*

reciprocamente [retʃiproka'mente] AVV each other, one another, mutually; **aiutarsi reciprocamente** to help each other *o* one another
reciprocità [retʃiprotʃi'ta] SF reciprocity
reciproco, a, ci, che [re'tʃiproko] AGG (*gen*) reciprocal; (*sentimento, interesse*) mutual; **è chiaro che la adora, e l'affetto è reciproco** he obviously adores her, and the affection is mutual
■ SM (*Mat*) reciprocal
reciso, a [re'tʃizo] PP *di* **recidere**
■ AGG (*risposta*) sharp, curt
recita ['rɛtʃita] SF (*Teatro*) performance; (*di poesie*) recital
recital [retʃi'tal] SM INV recital
recitare [retʃi'tare] VI (*Teatro, fig*) to act; **non sa recitare** he can't act; **mi piace recitare** I like acting; **recita molto bene** he's a very good actor
■ VT (*dramma*) to perform; (*poesia, lezione*) to recite; (*ruolo*) to play *o* act (the part of); **recitare una parte** to play a part; **ha recitato la parte di Giulietta** she played the part of Juliet
recitazione [retʃitat'tsjone] SF (*di poesia*) recitation; (*modo di recitare: di attore*) acting; **scuola di recitazione** drama school
reclamare [rekla'mare] VI (*aus* **avere**) **reclamare (contro/presso qn)** to complain (about/to sb)
■ VT (*diritto*) to demand; **reclamare giustizia** to demand justice
réclame [re'klam] SF INV (*pubblicità*) advertising *no pl*; (*annuncio*) advertisement; **fare la réclame di qc** *or* **fare réclame a qc** to advertise sth
reclamizzare [reklamid'dzare] VT to advertise
reclamo [re'klamo] SM complaint; **sporgere reclamo presso** to complain to, make a complaint to; **ufficio reclami** complaints department
reclinabile [rekli'nabile] AGG (*sedile*) reclining
reclinare [rekli'nare] VT (*capo*) to bow, lower; (*sedile*) to tilt
reclusione [reklu'zjone] SF (*Dir*) imprisonment; **10 anni di reclusione** 10 years' imprisonment; **l'hanno condannato a un anno di reclusione** he was sentenced to a year in prison
recluso, a [re'kluzo] AGG (*in prigione*) imprisoned
■ SM/F (*prigioniero*) prisoner; **fare vita da recluso** (*fig*) to lead the life of a recluse
recluta ['rɛkluta] SF (*Mil, fig*) recruit
reclutamento [rekluta'mento] SM recruitment; **ufficio (di) reclutamento** recruiting office
reclutare [reklu'tare] VT (*Mil, fig*) to recruit
recondito, a [re'kondito] AGG (*letter: luogo*) hidden, secluded; (*fig: significato*) secret, hidden
record ['rɛkord] SM INV (*Sport, Inform*) record; **a tempo di record** in record time; **detenere il record di** to hold the record for; **record mondiale** world record; **ha battuto il record mondiale del salto in alto** he beat the world record for the high jump
■ AGG INV record *attr*; **in tempo record** in record time
recriminare [rekrimi'nare] VI (*aus* **avere**) **recriminare (su qc)** to complain (about sth)
recriminatorio, ria, ri, rie [rekrimina'tɔrjo] AGG recriminatory
recriminazione [rekriminat'tsjone] SF recrimination
recrudescenza [rekrudeʃ'ʃɛntsa] SF (*di malattia*) fresh outbreak; (*fig: di violenza, scontri*) fresh wave
recuperare [rekupe'rare] VT = **ricuperare**
redarguire [redar'gwire] VT to rebuke, reproach
redassi *ecc* [re'dassi] VB *vedi* **redigere**
redatto, a [re'datto] PP *di* **redigere**
redattore, trice [redat'tore] SM/F (*Stampa: chi cura*) editor; (*: chi scrive: articolo*) writer; (*: dizionario, enciclopedia*) compiler; **redattore capo** chief editor
redazionale [redattsjo'nale] AGG (*ufficio*) editorial; **articolo redazionale** *article signed by the entire staff*
redazione [redat'tsjone] SF **1** (*Stampa: messa a punto*) editing; (*: stesura: di articolo*) writing; (*: di dizionario, enciclopedia*) compilation **2** (*personale*) editorial staff; (*ufficio*) editorial office(s) **2** (*versione di testo*) version
redditività [redditivi'ta] SF profitability
redditizio, zia, zi, zie [reddi'tittsjo] AGG profitable; **un'attività redditizia** a profitable business
reddito ['rɛddito] SM (*privato*) income; (*statale*) revenue; (*di capitale*) yield; **reddito complessivo** gross income; **reddito fisso** fixed income; **reddito imponibile** taxable income; **reddito da lavoro** earned income; **reddito nazionale** national income; **reddito non imponibile** non-taxable income; **reddito pubblico** public revenue
redditometro [reddi'tɔmetro] SM *system for assessing income*
redensi *ecc* [re'densi] VB *vedi* **redimere**
redento, a [re'dɛnto] PP *di* **redimere**
■ SMPL: **i redenti** the redeemed
redentore, trice [reden'tore] AGG redeeming

Rr

■ SM: **il Redentore** the Redeemer
redenzione [reden'tsjone] SF redemption
redigere [re'didʒere] VT IRREG *(lettera, articolo)* to write; *(contratto, verbale)* to draft, draw up; *(dizionario)* to compile
redimere [re'dimere] VB IRREG
■ VT to redeem
▶ **redimersi** VR to redeem o.s.
redimibile [redi'mibile] AGG *(titoli, azioni)* redeemable
redingote [rədɛ̃'gɔt] SF INV tailored coat, fitted coat
redini ['redini] SFPL *(anche fig)* reins; **tenere le redini** to hold the reins; **tiene le redini dell'azienda** he holds the reins of the company
redivivo, a [redi'vivo] AGG: **sembri tua madre rediviva** you're the living image of your mother
reduce ['rɛdutʃe] AGG *(gen, Mil)*: **reduce da** returning from, back from; **essere reduce da** *(esame, colloquio)* to have been through; *(malattia)* to be just over
■ SM/F *(sopravvissuto)* survivor; *(veterano)* veteran
refe ['refe] SM *(filo)* thread; *(: più grosso)* yarn
referendario, ria, ri, rie [referen'darjo] AGG referendary
referendum [refe'rɛndum] SM INV referendum; **fare un referendum** to hold a referendum
referente [refe'rɛnte] SM *(Ling)* referent
referenza [refe'rɛntsa] SF reference; **avere buone referenze** *(impiegato ecc)* to have good references
referenziare [referen'tsjare] VT: **referenziare qn** to give sb a reference
referenziato, a [referen'tsjato] AGG *(in annunci economici)* with references
referto [re'fɛrto] SM: **referto medico** medical report
refettorio, ri [refet'tɔrjo] SM *(in convento)* refectory; *(Scol)* dining hall
refezione [refet'tsjone] SF *(Scol)* school meal
reflex ['rɛfleks] SF INV *(Fot)* reflex camera
refluo, a ['rɛflwo] AGG: **acque reflue** waste water
refrain [rə'frɛ̃] SM INV *(ritornello)* refrain
refrattario, ria, ri, rie [refrat'tarjo] AGG *(materiale, Med)* refractory; *(fig scherz: persona)*: **refrattario (a)** indifferent (to); **essere refrattario alla matematica** to have no aptitude for mathematics
refrigerante [refridʒe'rante] AGG *(Tecn)* cooling, refrigerating
■ SM *(Chim: fluido)* coolant; *(Tecn: apparecchio)* refrigerator
refrigerare [refridʒe'rare] VT to refrigerate
refrigeratore [refridʒera'tore] SM *(Tecn)* refrigerator
refrigerazione [refridzerat'tsjone] SF refrigeration; *(Tecn)* cooling
refrigerio, ri [refri'dʒɛrjo] SM: **trovare refrigerio** to find somewhere cool
refugium peccatorum [re'fudʒum pekka'tɔrum] SM INV *(scherz)* **1** *(persona)*: **è il nostro refugium peccatorum** he's always ready to help us out **2** *(lavoro)* sinecure; **quella facoltà è un refugium peccatorum** that faculty is regarded as a cushy number
refurtiva [refur'tiva] SF stolen goods *pl*
refuso [re'fuzo] SM typographical error, literal *(Brit)*
Reg. ABBR **1** (= reggimento) Regt **2** *(Amm)* = regolamento
regalare [rega'lare] VT: **regalare qc** to give sth (as a present), make a present of sth; *(fig: vendere a poco prezzo)* to give sth away; **cosa gli regali per il compleanno?** what are you giving him for his birthday?; **non so cosa regalare a mia madre per Natale** I don't know what to get my mother for Christmas; **penso che mi regalerò una vacanza** I think I'll treat myself to a holiday

> **LO SAPEVI...?**
> **regalare** non si traduce mai con la parola inglese ***regale***

regale [re'gale] AGG royal; *(fig: portamento)* regal
regalia [rega'lia] SF *(Amm)* gratuity
regalità [regali'ta] SF *(fig: di portamento)* regality
regalmente [regal'mente] AVV regally
regalo [re'galo] SM present, gift; **regali di Natale** Christmas presents; **ho ricevuto un sacco di regali** I got lots of presents; **"articoli da regalo"** "gifts"; **fare un regalo a qn** to give sb a present; **"con bagnoschiuma in regalo"** "with a free gift of bubble bath"
■ AGG INV: **libro regalo** free book; **mi può fare una confezione regalo?** could you gift-wrap it for me?
regata [re'gata] SF regatta
reggente [red'dʒɛnte] AGG **1** *(sovrano)* reigning; **principe reggente** prince regent **2** *(Gramm: proposizione)* main
■ SM/F regent
■ SF *(Gramm)* main clause
reggenza [red'dʒɛntsa] SF regency
reggere ['rɛddʒere] VB IRREG
■ VT **1** *(tenere: persona)* to hold up, support; *(: pacco, valigia, timone)* to hold; **le gambe non lo reggevano più** his legs could carry him no longer; **reggi questa borsa, per favore** hold this bag, please **2** *(sopportare: peso)* to bear, carry; *(: fig: situazione)* to stand, bear; **reggere l'alcol** to hold one's drink; **non lo reggo più** *(fig: persona)* I can't put up with him any more **3** *(Gramm: sogg: proposizione)* to govern, take, be followed by; **reggere il dativo** to take the dative **4** *(essere a capo di: Stato)* to govern, rule; *(: ditta)* to run, manage
■ VI *(aus* **avere***)* **1** *(resistere)* to hold on; **reggere a** *(peso, pressione)* to bear; *(urto)* to stand up to; **reggere alla tentazione** to resist temptation; **non regge al paragone** it *(o* he *ecc)* doesn't stand comparison; **non ha retto a tali minacce** he was unable to hold out against such threats **2** *(durare: bel tempo, situazione)* to last **3** *(fig: stare in piedi: teoria)* to hold up, hold water; **è un discorso che non regge** the argument doesn't hold water;
▶ **reggersi** VR **1** *(stare dritto)* to stand; *(fig: dominarsi)* to control o.s.; *(tenersi)*: **reggersi a** to hold on to; *(fig: ipotesi)*: **reggersi su** to be based on; **reggersi sulle gambe** *o* **in piedi** to stand up; **non si reggeva in piedi** he could barely stand; **non mi reggo più dalla stanchezza** I'm so tired that I can barely stand; **reggiti a me** hold on to me; **reggiti forte** hold on tight **2** *(uso reciproco)*: **reggersi a vicenda** to support each another
reggia, ge ['rɛddʒa] SF royal palace; *(fig)* palace
reggiano, a [red'dʒano] AGG of *o* from Reggio Emilia
■ SM/F inhabitant *o* native of Reggio Emilia
reggicalze [reddʒi'kaltse] SM INV suspender *(Brit) o* garter *(Am)* belt
reggimentale [reddʒimen'tale] AGG regimental
reggimento [reddʒi'mento] SM regiment; *(fig)* horde
reggino, a [red'dʒino] AGG of *o* from Reggio Calabria
■ SM/F inhabitant *o* native of Reggio Calabria
reggipetto [reddʒi'pɛtto], **reggiseno** [reddʒi'seno] SM bra
regia, gie [re'dʒia] SF *(Teatro)* production; *(TV, Cine)* direction; **regia di Fellini** directed by Fellini

regicida, i, e [redʒi'tʃida] SM/F regicide (*person*)
regicidio, di [redʒi'tʃidjo] SM regicide (*crime*)
regime [re'dʒime] SM **1** (*Pol, anche pegg*) regime; **un regime totalitario** a totalitarian regime **2** (*sistema*) system; **regime (monetario) aureo** (*Fin*) gold standard; **regime tributario** tax system **3** (*regola*): **regime dietetico** diet; **essere a regime** to be on a diet; **regime vegetariano** vegetarian diet **4** (*di fiume, torrente*) flow **5** (*Tecn*) (engine) speed; **funzionare a pieno regime** to run at top revs; **regime di giri** (*di motore*) revs *pl* per minute
regina [re'dʒina] SF (*Pol, Scacchi, Carte, fig*) queen; **la regina Elisabetta** Queen Elizabeth; **la regina madre** the Queen Mother; **la regina della festa** the belle of the ball
reginetta [redʒi'netta] SF: **reginetta di bellezza** beauty queen
regio, gia, gi, gie ['rɛdʒo] AGG royal
regionale [redʒo'nale] AGG regional
■ SM (*treno*) slow local train
regionalismo [redʒona'lizmo] SM regionalism
regionalizzare [redʒonalid'dzare] VT to regionalize
regionalmente [redʒonal'mente] AVV regionally
regione [re'dʒone] SF **1** (*gen*) region; (*fig: zona*) area, region **2** (*istituzione*) *administrative unit*

REGIONE

The **Regione** is the biggest administrative unit in Italy. Each of the 20 **Regioni** consists of a variable number of "Province", which in turn are subdivided into "Comuni". Each of the regions has a "capoluogo", its chief province (for example, Florence is the chief province of the region of Tuscany). Five regions have special status and wider powers: Val d'Aosta, Friuli-Venezia Giulia, Trentino-Alto Adige, Sicily and Sardinia. A **Regione** is run by the "Giunta regionale", which is elected by the "Consiglio regionale"; both are presided over by a "Presidente". The "Giunta" has legislative powers within the region over the police, public health, schools, town planning and agriculture.
▷ www.regioni.it/

regista, i, e [re'dʒista] SM/F (*Teatro*) producer; (*TV, Cine*) director
registrare [redʒis'trare] VT **1** (*Amm: nascita, morte, veicolo*) to register; (*Comm: fattura, ordine*) to enter; **registrare i bagagli** (*Aer*) to check in one's luggage **2** (*notare, constatare*) to report, note; (*sogg: termometro, apparecchio*) to record, register; **è stato registrato un aumento della domanda** an increase in demand has been reported **3** (*su nastro*) to (tape-)record; (*su disco*) to record; **voglio registrare questo programma** I want to record this programme **4** (*Tecn: mettere a punto*) to adjust, regulate; **registrare i freni** to adjust the brakes
registratore [redʒistra'tore] SM (*per incidere*) tape recorder; (*per misurare*) register, recorder; **registratore di cassa** (*Comm*) till, cash register; **registratore a cassette** cassette recorder; **registratore di volo** (*Aer*) flight recorder
registrazione [redʒistrat'tsjone] SF (*vedi vb*) registration; entry; check-in; reporting; recording; adjustment
registro [re'dʒistro] SM **1** (*gen*) register; **registro di bordo** log (*Brit*), logbook (*Am*); **registro di classe** class register; **registro (di cassa)** (*Comm*) ledger **2** (*Amm, Dir*) registry; **ufficio del registro** registrar's office; **(pubblico) registro automobilistico** motor registration office; **registro immobiliare** land register **3** (*Tecn: di orologio*) regulator; (*: di treno*) adjuster **4** (*Mus: di voce*) range, register; (*: di strumento*) register **5** (*Ling*) register
regnante [reɲ'ɲante] AGG reigning, ruling
■ SM/F ruler
regnare [reɲ'ɲare] VI (*aus* **avere**) (*anche fig*) to reign; (*predominare*) to rule; **regnava il silenzio** silence reigned
regno ['reɲɲo] SM **1** (*periodo*) reign; **durante il regno di** during the reign of **2** (*luogo*) kingdom; **il regno della fantasia** the realm of fantasy; **il regno animale** the animal kingdom; **il regno vegetale** the vegetable *o* plant kingdom
Regno Unito ['reɲɲo u'nito] SM: **il Regno Unito** the United Kingdom
regola ['rɛgola] SF **1** (*gen*) rule; **di regola** as a rule; **essere in regola** (*dipendente*) to be a registered employee; (*documenti*) to be in order; **proporsi una regola di vita** to set o.s. rules to live by; **le regole del gioco** (*anche fig*) the rules of the game; **a regola d'arte** (*lavoro*) expert, professional; **per tua (norma e) regola** for your information; **avere le carte in regola** (*gen*) to have one's papers in order; (*fig: essere adatto*) to be the right person; **fare le cose in regola** to do things properly; **un'eccezione alla regola** an exception to the rule **2** (*Rel*) rule
regolabile [rego'labile] AGG adjustable
regolamentare [regolamen'tare] AGG (*distanza, velocità*) regulation *attr*; (*disposizione*) statutory; **lunghezza regolamentare** regulation length; **entro il tempo regolamentare** within the time allowed, within the prescribed time
■ VT (*gen*) to control
regolamento [regola'mento] SM **1** (*norme*) regulations *pl*; **regolamento scolastico** school rules *pl*; **è proibito dal regolamento scolastico** it's against the school rules **2** (*atto del regolare: di debito*) settlement; **un regolamento di conti** (*fig*) a settling of scores
regolare[1] [rego'lare] AGG **1** (*senza variazioni: gen, Gramm, Mat*) regular; (*: velocità*) steady; (*: superficie*) even; (*: passo*) steady, even; **a intervalli regolari** at regular intervals **2** (*in regola: documento, permesso*) in order; **presentare regolare domanda** to apply through the proper channels; **esercito regolare** regular army; **è tutto regolare!** everything is in order!; **tutto ciò non è regolare** that's entirely irregular
regolare[2] [rego'lare] VT (*gen*) to regulate, control; (*questione, debito, conto*) to settle; (*apparecchio*) to adjust, regulate; (*orologio*) to set; **non riesco a regolare il volume** I can't adjust the sound; **regolare i conti** (*fig*) to settle old scores
▶ **regolarsi** VR **1** (*moderarsi*) **regolarsi nel bere/nello spendere** to watch *o* control one's drinking/spending **2** (*comportarsi*) to behave, act; **non so come regolarmi** I don't know what to do; (*nell'usare ingredienti*) I don't know what quantities to add; **regolati come meglio credi** do as you think best
regolarità [regolari'ta] SF **1** (*vedi agg 1*) regularity; steadiness; evenness **2** (*nel pagare*) punctuality
regolarizzare [regolarid'dzare] VT (*posizione*) to regularize; (*debito*) to settle
regolarmente [regolar'mente] AVV **1** (*vedi agg 1*)

Rr

regularly; steadily; evenly; **arriva regolarmente in ritardo** he regularly arrives late **2** (*in modo debito, corretto*) duly; **ho presentato regolarmente domanda** I applied through the proper channels

regolata [rego'lata] SF (*fig*): **darsi una regolata** to pull one's socks up, pull o.s. together

regolatezza [regola'tettsa] SF (*ordine*) orderliness; (*moderazione*) moderation

regolato, a [rego'lato] AGG (*ordinato*) orderly; (*moderato*) moderate

regolatore, trice [regola'tore] AGG (*principio*) controlling *attr*; **piano regolatore** (*Amm*) town-planning scheme
■SM (*Tecn*) regulator; **regolatore di frequenza** frequency control; **regolatore di tensione** voltage regulator; **regolatore di volume** volume control

regolo[1] ['rɛgolo] SM ruler; **regolo calcolatore** slide rule

regolo[2] ['rɛgolo] SM (*uccello*) goldcrest

regredire [regre'dire] VI (*aus* **essere**) to regress; **regredire negli studi** to fall behind in one's studies

regressione [regres'sjone] SF regression

regressivo, a [regres'sivo] AGG regressive

regresso [re'grɛsso] SM (*fig*: *declino*) decline

reidratare [reidra'tare] VT rehydrate

reietto, a [re'jɛtto] SM/F outcast

reiki ['rɛiki] SM reiki

reimbarcare [reimbar'kare] VT, **reimbarcarsi** VR to re-embark

reimpiegare [reimpje'gare] VT (*riusare*) to reuse; (*assumere nuovamente*) to re-employ; (*Fin*) to reinvest

reimpiego [reim'pjɛgo] SM (*vedi vt*) reuse; re-employment; reinvestment

reincarnare [reinkar'nare] VT to reincarnate
▶ **reincarnarsi** VIP to be reincarnated

reincarnazione [reinkarnat'tsjone] SF reincarnation

reinserimento [reinseri'mento] SM (*dopo assenza*) readjustment; (*dopo carcere*) rehabilitation, reintegration

reinserire [reinse'rire] VT (*gen*) to reinsert; (*tossicodipendente, ex-detenuto*) to rehabilitate, reintegrate
▶ **reinserirsi** VR (*dopo assenza*) to readjust; (*dopo carcere*) to rehabilitate o.s.

reintegrare [reinte'grare] VT (*produzione*) to restore; (*energie*) to recover; (*dipendente*) to reinstate; **reintegrare qn in una carica** to reinstate sb in a post

reintegrazione [reintegrat'tsjone] SF (*di produzione*) restoration; (*di dipendente*) reinstatement

reinventare [reinven'tare] VT (*gen*) to reinvent; (*Teatro*) to reinterpret

reiterare [reite'rare] VT to reiterate

reiteratamente [reiterata'mente] AVV repeatedly

reiterazione [reiterat'tsjone] SF reiteration

relais [rə'lɛ] SM INV (*Elettr*) relay

relativamente [relativa'mente] AVV relatively; **relativamente a** as regards

relatività [relativi'ta] SF relativity

relativo, a [rela'tivo] AGG (*gen, Gramm, Mat*) relative; (*attinente*) relevant; (*rispettivo*) respective; **relativo a** (*che concerne*) relating to, concerning; (*proporzionato*) in proportion to

relatore, trice [rela'tore] SM/F (*gen*) spokesman/spokeswoman; (*Univ: di tesi*) supervisor

relax [re'laks] SM relaxation

relazione [relat'tsjone] SF **1** (*legame, nesso*) relationship; **non c'è relazione tra le due cose** there's no connection between the two things, the two things are in no way related; **essere in relazione** to be connected; **mettere in relazione** (*fatti, elementi*) to make the connection between; **in relazione a quanto detto prima** with regard to what has already been said **2** (*rapporto con persone*) relationship; **essere in buone relazioni con qn** to be on good terms with sb; **relazione (sentimentale)** (love) affair; **relazione extraconiugale** extramarital affair; **ha scoperto che il marito ha una relazione** she's discovered that her husband is having an affair; **relazioni** SFPL (*conoscenze*) connections; **pubbliche relazioni** public relations; **relazioni sindacali** labour relations **3** (*resoconto*) report, account; **fare una relazione** to make a report, give an account; **devo scrivere una relazione sulla visita al museo** I've got to write a report on our visit to the museum

relè [re'le] SM INV = **relais**

relegare [rele'gare] VT (*allontanare*) to banish; (*fig*) to relegate

religione [reli'dʒone] SF (*gen, fig*) religion; (*fede*) religious faith; **religione di Stato** state religion; **non c'è più religione!** (*fig*) what's the world coming to!

religioso, a [reli'dʒoso] AGG (*gen*) religious; (*arte*) sacred; (*scuola, matrimonio, musica*) church *attr*; **in religioso silenzio** in reverent silence
■SM/F monk/nun

reliquia [re'likwja] SF (*Rel, fig*) relic; **tenere qc come una reliquia** (*fig*) to treasure sth

reliquiario, ri [reli'kwjarjo] SM reliquary

relitto [re'litto] SM (*gen, fig*) wreck; (*persona*) down-and-out

rem [rɛm] SM INV (*Fis*) rem

remainder [ri'meində] SM INV (*libro*) remainder

remake ['ri:'meik] SM INV (*Cine, Teatro*) remake

remare [re'mare] VI (*aus* **avere**) to row; **ora tocca a te remare** it's your turn to row now

rematore, trice [rema'tore] SM/F oarsman/oarswoman

reminiscenza [reminiʃ'ʃɛntsa] SF reminiscence

remissione [remis'sjone] SF **1** (*di peccato, malattia*) remission; **remissione del debito** (*Dir*) remission of debt; **remissione di querela** (*Dir*) withdrawal of an action **2** (*sottomissione*) submissiveness, compliance

remissivamente [remissiva'mente] AVV compliantly, submissively

remissività [remissivi'ta] SF submissiveness

remissivo, a [remis'sivo] AGG submissive, compliant

Remo ['rɛmo] SM Remus

remo ['rɛmo] SM oar; **barca a remi** rowing boat; **tirare i remi in barca** (*anche fig*) to rest on one's oars

remora ['rɛmora] SF (*letter: indugio*) hesitation; **non avere remore!** don't hesitate!

remoto, a [re'mɔto] AGG **1** (*lontano*) remote **2** (*Gramm*): **passato remoto** past definite; **trapassato remoto** pluperfect

remunerare *ecc* [remune'rare] = **rimunerare** *ecc*

rena ['rena] SF sand

renale [re'nale] AGG kidney *attr*

renano, a [re'nano] AGG Rhine *attr*, of the Rhine

rendere ['rɛndere] VB IRREG
■VT **1** (*ridare*) to give back, return; **potresti rendermi la penna?** could you give me back my pen?; **gli sarà resa la libertà quanto prima** he will be released as soon as possible; **rendere la visita** to pay a return visit; **"vuoto a rendere"** (*bottiglia*) "please return empties"; **a buon rendere!** (*anche iro*) my turn next time!; **rendere l'anima a Dio** (*euf*) to breathe one's

last **2** *(dare)*: **rendere grazie a qn** to thank sb; **rendere omaggio a qn** to honour sb; **rendere un servizio a qn** to do sb a service; **rendere una testimonianza** to give evidence; **rendersi conto di qc** to realize sth; **forse non ti rendi conto di quanto sia pericoloso** maybe you don't realize how dangerous it is **3** *(fruttare)* to yield, bring in; *(uso assoluto: sogg: ditta)* to be profitable; (: *investimento, campo)* to yield, be productive; **rendere il 10%** to yield 10%; **una ditta che non rende** an unprofitable firm **4** *(esprimere, tradurre)* to render; **rendere l'idea** to give the idea; **non so se rendo l'idea!** I don't know if I'm making myself clear! **5** *(+ agg: far diventare)* to make; **il suo intervento ha reso possibile l'affare** his intervention made the whole affair possible; **un po' di diplomazia renderebbe tutto più facile** a bit of diplomacy would make everything easier; **l'hai resa felice** you made her happy; **rendere la vita impossibile a qn** to make life impossible for sb;
▶ **rendersi** VR *(+ agg: apparire)* to make o.s. *+ adj*; **rendersi antipatico/ridicolo/utile** to make o.s. unpleasant/ridiculous/useful; **posso rendermi utile?** can I make myself useful?

rendez-vous [rɑ̃'de'vu] SM INV *(appuntamento)* rendezvous; (: *galante)* date

rendiconto [rendi'konto] SM *(resoconto)* report, account; *(Amm, Comm)* statement (of accounts)

rendimento [rendi'mento] SM *(di manodopera, anche Fis)* efficiency; *(di industria: produttività)* productivity; *(di motore, studente)* performance; *(di podere)* yield; **avere un buon rendimento** *(atleta)* to perform well; *(studente)* to do well

rendita ['rɛndita] SF *(di individuo)* private *o* unearned income; *(Comm)* revenue; **vivere di rendita** to have private means; *(fig: studente)* to survive on one's past results; **rendita annua** annuity; **rendita vitalizia** life annuity

rene ['rɛne] SM kidney

renetta [re'netta] SF *(frutto)* pippin

reni ['reni] SFPL *(schiena)* back *sg*; **spezzare le reni a qn** *(fig)* to annihilate sb

renitente [reni'tɛnte] AGG: **renitente (a)** unwilling (to), reluctant (to), loath (to); **renitente ai consigli di qn** unwilling to follow sb's advice; **essere renitente alla leva** *(Mil)* to fail to report for military service

renna ['rɛnna] SF reindeer *inv*; **di renna** suede *attr*; **una giacca di renna** a suede coat

Reno ['reno] SM: **il Reno** the Rhine

rentrée [rɑ̃'tre] SF INV comeback

reo, a ['rɛo] AGG: **reo (di)** guilty (of)
■ SM/F *(Dir)* offender; **reo confesso** confessed criminal

reostato [re'ɔstato] SM rheostat

reparto [re'parto] SM *(di ospedale)* ward; *(di ufficio, negozio)* department, section; *(Mil: di esercito)* unit, detachment; **reparti d'assalto** *(Mil)* assault troops; **reparto acquisti** purchasing office; **reparto d'attacco** *(Sport)* attack; **reparto maternità** maternity ward; **reparto uomo** *(in negozio)* men's department

repellente [repel'lɛnte] AGG **1** *(che ripugna)* repulsive **2** *(Chim: insettifugo)*: **liquido repellente** (liquid) repellent

repentaglio [repen'taʎʎo] SM: **mettere a repentaglio** to put at risk, jeopardize, endanger

repentinamente [repentina'mente] AVV suddenly, unexpectedly

repentino, a [repen'tino] AGG *(gesto, decisione)* sudden, unexpected

reperibile [repe'ribile] AGG *(articolo, prodotto)* available; **non è reperibile** *(persona)* he can't be reached

reperire [repe'rire] VT to find, trace

reperto [re'pɛrto] SM *(Archeol)* find; *(anche:* **reperto giudiziario***)* exhibit; *(Med)* report

repertorio, ri [reper'tɔrjo] SM *(Teatro)* repertoire, repertory; (: *di canzoni, fig)* repertoire; **immagini di repertorio** *(Cine, TV)* archive footage *sg*

replay ['ri:plei] SM INV *(TV)* (action) replay

replica, che ['rɛplika] SF **1** *(risposta: gen, Pol)* reply, answer; (: *obiezione)* objection **2** *(ripetizione: gen)* repetition; (: *TV, Teatro, Cine)* repeat performance; **domani trasmettono la replica dell'ultima puntata** the repeat of the final episode is on tomorrow; **avere molte repliche** to have a long run **3** *(copia)* replica

replicante [repli'kante] SM/F replicant

replicare [repli'kare] VT **1** *(rispondere)* to reply, answer **2** *(Teatro, Cine)* to repeat

reportage [rəpɔr'taʒ] SM INV *(Stampa)* report

reporter [re'pɔrter] SM/F INV reporter

repressione [repres'sjone] SF repression

repressivo, a [repres'sivo] AGG repressive

represso, a [re'prɛsso] PP *di* **reprimere**
■ AGG repressed
■ SM/F *(persona)* repressed person

reprimere [re'primere] VT IRREG *(gen)* to suppress, repress; *(sommossa)* to put down, suppress; *(sentimenti)* to repress, hold back

repubblica, che [re'pubblika] SF republic; **la Prima/Seconda Repubblica** *terms used to refer to Italy before and after the political changes resulting from the 1994 elections*

repubblicano, a [repubbli'kano] AGG, SM/F republican

repulisti [repu'listi] SM INV *(scherz)*: **fare (un) repulisti** to have a clean-out

repulsione [repul'sjone] SF **1** *(Fis)* repulsion **2** *(fig)* = ripulsione

reputare [repu'tare] VT to consider, judge; **reputare qn intelligente** to consider *o* judge sb (to be) intelligent; **reputo che si possa fare** I think it can be done; **se lo reputerai opportuno** if you think it advisable
▶ **reputarsi** VR to consider o.s.

reputazione [reputat'tsjone] SF *(gen)* reputation; *(buon nome)* reputation, good name; **avere una buona/cattiva reputazione** to have a good/bad reputation; **farsi una cattiva reputazione** to get o.s. a bad name; **rovinarsi la reputazione** to ruin one's reputation

requie ['rɛkwje] SF rest; **dare requie a qn** to give sb some peace; **non dare requie a qn** to give sb no quarter; **senza requie** unceasingly

requiem ['rɛkwjem] SM O F INV *(preghiera)* requiem, prayer for the dead
■ SM INV *(Mus)* Requiem; *(fig: ufficio funebre)* requiem; **messa di requiem** Requiem (mass)

requisire [rekwi'zire] VT to requisition

requisito [rekwi'zito] SM *(gen)* requirement; **uno dei requisiti era la conoscenza del tedesco** one of the requirements was a knowledge of German; **non aveva i requisiti necessari per il lavoro** he didn't have the necessary qualifications for the job

requisitoria [rekwizi'tɔrja] SF *(Dir)* closing speech (for the prosecution)

requisizione [rekwizit'tsjone] SF requisition

resa ['resa] SF **1** *(l'arrendersi)* surrender **2** *(rendimento: di podere)* yield; (: *di operaio)* productivity **3** **resa dei conti** rendering of accounts; **è venuto il momento**

Rr

della resa dei conti (*fig*) the day of reckoning has arrived **4** (*Comm: restituzione*) repayment; (*: merce restituita*) unsold goods

rescindere [reʃʃindere] VT IRREG (*Dir*) to rescind, annul

rescissione [reʃʃis'sjone] SF (*Dir*) rescission, annulment

rescisso, a [reʃʃisso] PP *di* **rescindere**

resettare [reset'tare] VT (*Inform: macchina, computer*) to reset

resi *ecc* ['resi] VB *vedi* **rendere**

residence ['rezidəns] SM INV *hotel with suites of rooms complete with kitchen and bathroom rented for fairly long periods*

residente [resi'dɛnte] AGG, SM/F resident; **è residente a Londra** he lives in London; **sono residenti all'estero** they live abroad; **per i residenti dell'Unione europea** for the residents of the European Union

residenza [resi'dɛntsa] SF **1** (*soggiorno*) stay **2** (*indirizzo, sede*) residence; **la residenza del Primo Ministro** the Prime Minister's residence; **cambiare residenza** to change one's address

residenziale [residen'tsjale] AGG residential; **un quartiere residenziale** a residential area

residuale [residu'ale] AGG residual

residuo, a [re'siduo] AGG (*rimanente*) remaining; (*Chim*) residual
■ SM (*gen*) remainder; (*Chim, fig*) residue; **residui industriali** industrial waste *sg*

resina ['rɛzina] SF resin

resinoso, a [rezi'noso] AGG resinous

resistente [resis'tɛnte] AGG (*persona, oggetto*) strong, tough; (*pianta*) hardy; (*tessuto*) strong, hard-wearing; (*colore*) fast; (*metallo*) strong, resistant; **resistente all'acqua** waterproof; **resistente al calore** heat-resistant; **resistente al fuoco** fireproof; **resistente al gelo** frost-resistant

resistenza [resis'tɛntsa] SF **1** (*gen*) resistance; (*fisica*) stamina, endurance; (*mentale*) endurance, resistance; **opporre resistenza (a)** to offer *o* put up resistance (to); (*decisione, scelta*) to show opposition (to); **prova di resistenza** endurance test; **resistenza passiva** passive resistance; **resistenza a pubblico ufficiale** (*Dir*) use of force or threats against a public official **2** (*Elettr, Tecn, Fis*) resistance; (*Elettr: apparecchio*) resistor; **coefficiente di resistenza** drag coefficient; **resistenza di attrito** frictional resistance **3** (*Pol*): **la Resistenza** the Resistance

RESISTENZA

The Italian **Resistenza** fought against both the Nazis and the Fascists during the Second World War. It was particularly active after the fall of the Fascist government on 25 July 1943, throughout the German occupation and during the period of Mussolini's Republic of Salò in northern Italy. Resistance members spanned the whole political spectrum and played a vital role in the Liberation and in the formation of the new democratic government.
▷ www.anpi.it/
▷ www.resistenza.it/

resistere [re'sistere] VI IRREG (*aus* **avere**): **resistere a** (*gen*) to resist; (*fatica, siccità*) to stand up to, withstand; (*peso*) to take; (*dolore*) to stand; (*tentazione*) to resist; (*tortura*) to endure; (*attacco*) to hold out against; **resistere al calore** to be heat-resistant; **resistere al fuoco** to be fireproof; **resistere alla prova del tempo** to stand the test of time; **resistere alla corrente di un fiume** to hold one's own against the current of a river; **colori che resistono al lavaggio** colours which are fast in the wash; **resistere al peso della responsabilità** to cope with the responsibility; **non ho saputo resistere alla tentazione!** I couldn't resist the temptation!; **resisti!** hold on!; **non ho resistito e gliel'ho detto** I couldn't contain myself any longer and I told him; **non resisterà molto in quell'ufficio** he won't last long in that office; **nessuno sa resistergli** no-one can resist him; **nessuno sa resistere al suo fascino** everybody succumbs to his charm

resistito, a [resis'tito] PP *di* **resistere**

reso, a ['reso] PP *di* **rendere**

resoconto [reso'konto] SM (*gen*) account; (*di giornalista*) report, account; (*di seduta, assemblea*) minutes *pl*; **fare il resoconto di** to give an account of; to give a report of; to take the minutes of

respingente [respin'dʒɛnte] SM (*Ferr*) buffer

respingere [res'pindʒere] VT IRREG **1** (*attacco, nemico*) to drive back, repel; **respingere la palla** (*Calcio*) to kick the ball back; (*Pallavolo*) to return the ball **2** (*rifiutare: pacco, lettera*) to return; (*: invito*) to refuse; (*: proposta*) to reject, turn down; (*: persona*) to reject; **la sua domanda è stata respinta** his application was rejected **3** (*Scol: studente*) to fail

respinto, a [res'pinto] PP *di* **respingere**
■ SM/F (*Scol*) failed candidate

respirare [respi'rare] VI (*aus* **avere**) (*gen*) to breathe; (*inspirare*) to breathe in, inhale; (*fig: distendersi*) to get one's breath (back); (*: rassicurarsi*) to breathe again; **non riuscivo a respirare** I couldn't breathe; **non respiri!** (*dal medico*) hold your breath!
■ VT: **respirare un po' d'aria fresca** (*anche fig*) to get a breath of fresh air; **si respira un'aria di rinnovamento** there is a feeling of renewal in the air

respiratore [respira'tore] SM (*Med*) respirator; (*di subacqueo*) breathing apparatus

respiratorio, ria, ri, rie [respira'tɔrjo] AGG respiratory

respirazione [respirat'tsjone] SF breathing; **esercizi di respirazione** breathing exercises; **respirazione artificiale** artificial respiration; **respirazione bocca a bocca** mouth-to-mouth resuscitation, kiss of life (*fam*)

respiro [res'piro] SM breathing *no pl*; (*singolo atto*) breath; (*fig*) respite, rest; **avere il respiro pesante** to breathe heavily; **trattenere il respiro** to hold one's breath; **esalare l'ultimo respiro** to breathe one's last; **godere di un momento di respiro** to enjoy a moment's rest; **lavorare senza respiro** to work non-stop; **dammi un attimo di respiro** give me a break; **di ampio respiro** (*opera, lavoro*) far-reaching

responsabile [respon'sabile] AGG **1** (*gen, fig*): **responsabile (di)** responsible (for); (*danni*) liable (for), responsible (for); **è un tipo molto responsabile** he's a very responsible person; **si sente responsabile dell'accaduto** she feels responsible for what happened; **sentirsi responsabile di fronte a qn** (*moralmente*) to feel responsible to sb, hold o.s. accountable to sb **2** (*incaricato*): **responsabile (di)** responsible (for), in charge (of)
■ SM/F **1 responsabile (di)** (*danni, delitto*) person responsible (for) **2 responsabile (di)** (*sezione, ufficio*) person in charge (of), manager (of); **vorrei parlare**

con il responsabile I'd like to speak to the person in charge

responsabilità [responsabili'ta] SF INV: **responsabilità (di)** (*gen*) responsibility (for); (*Dir*) liability (for); **non voglio responsabilità** I don't want responsibilities; **assumersi la responsabilità di** to take on the responsibility for; **affidare a qn la responsabilità di qc** to make sb responsible for sth; **avere la responsabilità di** to be responsible for, have responsibility for; **fare qc sotto la propria responsabilità** to do sth on one's own responsibility; **responsabilità civile** civil liability; **responsabilità patrimoniale** debt liability; **responsabilità penale** criminal liability

responsabilizzare [responsabilid'dzare] VT: **responsabilizzare qn** to make sb feel responsible
▶ **responsabilizzarsi** VIP to become responsible

responsabilmente [responsabil'mente] AVV responsibly

responso [res'ponso] SM (*risposta*) answer, reply; (*Dir*) verdict

ressa ['rɛssa] SF crowd, throng; **c'è troppa ressa** it's too crowded; **quanta ressa!** what a crush!; **far ressa intorno a qn** to throng round sb

ressi *ecc* ['rɛssi] VB *vedi* **reggere**

resta ['rɛsta] SF (*fig*): **partire con la lancia in resta** to be ready for battle

restante [res'tante] AGG (*rimanente*) remaining
■ SM (*resto*): **il restante** the remainder *no pl*, the rest *no pl*

restare [res'tare] VI (*aus* **essere**) **1** (*in luogo*) to stay, remain; **restare a casa** to stay *o* remain at home; **restare a letto** to stay *o* remain in bed; **restare a cena** to stay for dinner; **restare a guardare la televisione** to stay and watch television; **dai, resta ancora un po'** go on, stay a bit longer; **che resti tra di noi** (*fig: segreto*) this is just between ourselves **2** (*in una condizione*) to stay, remain; **restare zitto** to remain *o* keep *o* stay silent; **restare sorpreso** to be surprised; **restare orfano** to become *o* be left an orphan; **restare cieco** to become blind; **restare in piedi** (*non sedersi*) to remain standing; (*non coricarsi*) to stay up; **restare amici** to remain friends; **restare in buoni rapporti** to remain on good terms; **restare senza parole** to be left speechless **3** (*sussistere*) to be left, remain; **non restano che poche pietre** there are only a few stones left; **è l'unico parente che le resta** he's her only remaining relative; **coi pochi soldi che mi restano** with what little money I have left; **restano da fare 15 km** there are still 15 km to go; **ne resta ancora un po'** there's still some left; **ne restano solo due** there are only two left; **resta ancora molto da fare** there's still a lot to do; **non ti resta altro (da fare) che accettare** all you can do is accept; **mi resti solo tu** you're all I have left; **mi resta ben poco da dire se non...** I've little left to say except ...; **non resta più niente** there's nothing left

> **LO SAPEVI...?**
> **restare** non si traduce mai con la parola inglese *rest*

restaurare [restau'rare] VT to restore; **stanno restaurando il quadro** the painting is being restored

restauratore, trice [restaura'tore] SM/F restorer

restaurazione [restaurat'tsjone] SF (*Pol*) restoration

restauro [res'tauro] SM (*Archit, Arte*) restoration; **in restauro** under repair; **sotto restauro** (*dipinto*) being restored; **chiuso per restauro** closed for repairs

▷ www.icr.beniculturali.it/

restio, tia, tii, tie [res'tio] AGG (*riluttante*): **restio a** reluctant to

restituibile [restitu'ibile] AGG returnable

restituire [restitu'ire] VT: **restituire qc (a)** (*gen*) to return sth (to), give sth back (to); (*colore, forma, forza*) to restore sth (to); **me lo presti? te lo restituisco domani** will you lend it to me? I'll give it back to you tomorrow; **mi ha restituito i soldi oggi** he paid me back today; **restituire un favore** to return a favour

restituzione [restitut'tsjone] SF (*gen*) return; (*di soldi*) repayment

resto ['rɛsto] SM **1** (*gen*) rest; (*di soldi*) change; (*Mat*) remainder; **dove mettiamo il resto della roba?** where shall we put the rest of the stuff?; **tu porta il vino, al resto penso io** you bring the wine, and I'll see to the rest; **tenga pure il resto** keep the change; **"il resto alla prossima puntata"** "to be continued"; **del resto** besides, moreover; **del resto, cos'altro potevo fare?** after all, what else could I do? **2 resti** SMPL (*di cibo*) leftovers; (*di civiltà*) remains; **resti mortali** (mortal) remains

restringere [res'trindʒere] VB IRREG
■ VT (*strada*) to narrow; (*abito, gonna*) to take in
▶ **restringersi** VIP (*contrarsi*) to contract; (*farsi più stretto: strada, fiume*) to narrow; (*: tessuto*) to shrink; **il campo si restringe** (*fig: di ipotesi, possibilità*) the field is narrowing

restrittivamente [restrittiva'mente] AVV restrictively

restrittivo, a [restrit'tivo] AGG restrictive

restrizione [restrit'tsjone] SF restriction

resurrezione [resurret'tsjone] SF = **risurrezione**

resuscitare [resuʃʃi'tare] VT, VI = **risuscitare**

retaggio, gi [re'taddʒo] SM heritage

retata [re'tata] SF **1** (*Pesca*) haul, catch **2** (*Polizia*): **fare una retata (di)** to round up

rete ['rete] SF **1** (*tessuto, Pesca*) net; (*di equilibristi*) safety net; (*per bagagli*) (luggage) rack; (*di recinzione*) wire netting; (*maglia metallica, di plastica*) mesh; **la pallina ha toccato la rete** the ball touched the net; **finire nella rete** (*fig: trappola*) to be caught in the trap; **calze a rete** fishnet tights *o* stockings; **rete del letto** (sprung) bed base; **rete da pesca** fishing net **2** (*sistema*) network; **la Rete** the Web; **collegarsi in Rete** to get connected to the Net; **rete di distribuzione** distribution network; **rete elettrica** (*nazionale*) (electricity) grid; **rete ferroviaria** railway network; **rete di spionaggio** spy network; **rete stradale** road network; **rete (televisiva)** (*sistema*) network; (*canale*) channel **3** (*Sport*) net; **segnare una rete** (*Calcio*) to score a goal; **tirare in rete** (*Calcio*) to take a shot at goal

reticente [reti'tʃɛnte] AGG reticent

reticenza [reti'tʃɛntsa] SF reticence; **parlare senza reticenze** to speak out

reticolato [retiko'lato] SM (*gen*) grid; (*recinto*) wire netting; (*Mil*) barbed wire (fence)

reticolo [re'tikolo] SM network; **reticolo cristallino** (*Chim*) crystal lattice; **reticolo geografico** grid

retina[1] ['rɛtina] SF (*Anat*) retina

retina[2] [re'tina] SF (*per capelli*) hairnet

retino [re'tino] SM **1** (*Tip*) screen **2** (*da pesca*) landing net; (*per farfalle*) butterfly net

retore ['rɛtore] SM rhetorician

retorica [re'tɔrika] SF (*anche fig*) rhetoric

retoricamente [retorika'mente] AVV rhetorically

retorico, a, ci, che [re'tɔriko] AGG rhetorical;

Rr

domanda retorica rhetorical question; **figura retorica** rhetorical device

retrattile [re'trattile] AGG (*Zool: unghie*) retractile; (*Aer: carrello*) retractable

retribuire [retribu'ire] VT (*gen*) to pay; **retribuire il lavoro di qn** to pay sb for his (*o* her) work; **un lavoro mal retribuito** a poorly-paid job

retributivo, a [retribu'tivo] AGG pay *attr*

retribuzione [retribut'tsjone] SF (*stipendio*) pay, remuneration

retrivo, a [re'trivo] AGG, SM/F reactionary

retro[1] ['retro] SM (*gen*) back; (*di auto*) rear, back; **sul retro c'è un giardino** there's a garden at the back
■AVV: **"vedi retro"** "see over(leaf)"

retro[2] [re'tro] AGG INV: **la moda retro** retro fashion

retroattività [retroattivi'ta] SF (*Dir*) retroactivity

retroattivo, a [retroat'tivo] AGG (*Dir: legge*) retroactive

retrobottega, ghe [retrobot'tega] SF back shop

retrocedere [retro'tʃɛdere] VB IRREG
■VT (*Mil*) to demote; (*Sport*) to relegate
■VI (*aus* **essere**) (*gen*) to move back; (*esercito*) to retreat; (*fig: di fronte a minacce*) to back down; **retrocedere in serie B** (*Calcio*) to be relegated to the second division; **la squadra è retrocessa in serie B** the team has been relegated to the second division

retrocessione [retrotʃes'sjone] SF (*Mil, di impiegato*) demotion; (*Sport*) relegation

retrocesso, a [retro'tʃɛsso] PP *di* **retrocedere**

retrodatare [retroda'tare] VT (*Amm*) to backdate

retrodatazione [retrodatat'tsjone] SF backdating

retrofit ['retrofit] SM INV (*Aut: catalizzatore*) catalytic converter (*fitted after manufacture*)

retrogrado, a [re'trɔgrado] AGG **1** (*retrivo: persona, idee*) reactionary, backward-looking **2** (*Astron: moto*) retrograde, backward
■SM/F reactionary

retroguardia [retro'gwardja] SF (*anche fig*) rearguard

retromarcia [retro'martʃa] SF (*Aut*) reverse; (: *dispositivo*) reverse (gear); **mettere la retromarcia** to go into reverse; **ha messo la retromarcia** he went into reverse; **andare in retromarcia** *or* **fare retromarcia** to reverse; **ho sbattuto facendo retromarcia** I bumped the car when I was reversing

retroscena [retroʃʃɛna] SF INV (*Teatro*) backstage
■SM INV (*fig*) behind-the-scenes activity

retrospettivamente [retrospettiva'mente] AVV retrospectively

retrospettivo, a [retrospet'tivo] AGG retrospective
■SF (*Arte*) retrospective (exhibition)

retrostante [retros'tante] AGG: **retrostante (a)** at the back (of)

retroterra [retro'tɛrra] SM INV **1** (*zona*) hinterland **2** (*sfondo*): **retroterra culturale/storico** historical/cultural background

retrovia [retro'via] SF (*Mil*) zone behind the front; **mandare nelle retrovie** to send to the rear

retrovisore [retrovi'zore] SM (*Aut: anche*: **specchietto retrovisore**) rear-view mirror; (: *laterale*) wing (*Brit*) *o* side (*Am*) mirror

retta ['rɛtta] SF **1** (*Geom*) straight line **2** (*di collegio, convitto*) fee, charge for bed and board **3** (*fig: ascolto*): **dare retta a** to pay attention to, listen to; **non dargli retta, quello s'inventa le cose!** don't listen to him, he makes things up!; **dammi retta, non vale la pena** listen to me, it's not worth it

rettamente [retta'mente] AVV (*in modo onesto*) honestly; (*in modo esatto*) strictly

rettangolare [rettango'lare] AGG rectangular

rettangolo, a [ret'tangolo] AGG right-angled
■SM rectangle

rettifica, che [ret'tifika] SF correction, rectification; **pubblicare una rettifica** (*su giornale*) to publish a retraction; **rettifica delle valvole** (*Aut*) valve grinding

rettificare [rettifi'kare] VT **1** (*gen*) to rectify, correct **2** (*Chim, Elettr, Mat*) to rectify

rettificazione [rettifikat'tsjone] SF rectification

rettifilo [retti'filo] SM (*di strada*) straight (stretch)

rettile ['rɛttile] SM reptile

rettilineo, a [retti'lineo] AGG (*gen, Mat*) rectilinear; (*strada*) straight
■SM (*di strada*) straight; **in rettilineo** on the straight; **rettilineo d'arrivo** (*Sport*) home straight

rettitudine [retti'tudine] SF rectitude, uprightness

retto, a ['rɛtto] PP *di* **reggere**
■AGG **1** (*gen, linea*) straight; **angolo retto** right angle **2** (*fig: onesto*) honest, upright; **abbandonare la retta via** (*fig*) to stray from the straight and narrow; **seguire la retta via** (*fig*) to keep to the straight and narrow
■SM (*Anat*) rectum

rettore [ret'tore] SM **1** (*Univ*) ≈ chancellor **2** (*Rel*) rector

reumatico, a, ci, che [reu'matiko] AGG rheumatic

reumatismo [reuma'tizmo] SM rheumatism *sg*; **soffre di reumatismi** she suffers from rheumatism

Rev. ABBR (= **Reverendo**) Rev(d).

revanscismo [revan'ʃizmo] SM revanchism

reverendo [reve'rɛndo] AGG, SM Reverend

reverente [reve'rɛnte] AGG = **riverente**

reverenza [reve'rɛntsa] SF = **riverenza**

reverenziale [reveren'tsjale] AGG (*titolo*) reverential; **timore reverenziale** awe

revers [rə'vɛr] SM INV lapel

reversibile [rever'sibile] AGG (*gen*) reversible; (*Econ*) convertible, negotiable; (*Dir*) revertible

reversibilità [reversibili'ta] SF (*vedi agg*) reversibility; convertibility, negotiability; revertibility

revisionare [revizjo'nare] VT (*Aut*) to service, overhaul; (*Fin: conti*) to audit

revisione [revi'zjone] SF (*di contratto, processo, sentenza*) review; (*di macchina*) servicing *no pl*, overhaul; (*di conti*) auditing *no pl*; (*di testo*) revision; **revisione di bilancio** audit; **revisione di bozze** proofreading; **revisione contabile interna** internal audit; **revisione dello stipendio** salary review

revisionismo [revizjo'nizmo] SM (*Pol*) revisionism

revisionista [revizjo'nista] AGG, SM/F (*Pol*) revisionist

revisore [revi'zore] SM: **revisore di bozze** proofreader; **revisore dei conti** auditor

revival [ri'vaivəl] SM INV revival; **un revival degli anni settanta** a Seventies revival

revivalismo [reviva'lizmo] SM revivalism

revivalista, i, e [reviva'lista] SM/F revivalist

reviviscenza [revivi∫'ʃɛntsa] SF (*Bio, Med*) revivescence

revoca, che ['rɛvoka] SF (*Dir*) repeal, revocation

revocare [revo'kare] VT (*gen*) to revoke, repeal; (*licenza*) to revoke

revocatorio, ria, ri, rie [revoka'tɔrjo] AGG revocatory, revocative

revolver [re'vɔlver] SM INV revolver

revolverata [revolve'rata] SF revolver shot

Reykjavik ['reikjavik] SF Reykjavik

RFT ['ɛrre'effe'ti] SIGLA F (= **Repubblica Federale Tedesca**) FRG

RG SIGLA = *Ragusa*
Rh ['ɛrre'akka] SIGLA M (*Med*): **fattore Rh** rhesus factor; **Rh positivo/negativo** rhesus positive/negative
Rhode Island [rɛʊd 'aɪlənd] SF Rhode Island
RI SIGLA = *Rieti*
riabbassare [riabbas'sare] VT to lower again
► **riabbassarsi** VIP (*marea*) to ebb, recede
riabbia *ecc* [ri'abbja] VB *vedi* **riavere**
riabbottonare [riabbotto'nare] VT to button up again
riabbracciare [riabbrat'tʃare] VT (*abbracciare di nuovo*) to embrace (*o* hug) again; (*rivedere*) to see (*o* meet) again; **spero di riabbracciarvi presto** (*nella corrispondenza*) hope to see you again soon
riabilitare [riabili'tare] VT (*gen*) to rehabilitate; (*fig*) to restore to favour (*Brit*) *o* favor (*Am*); **quel gesto lo ha riabilitato ai miei occhi** his action restored my good opinion of him
► **riabilitarsi** VR to be rehabilitated; **riabilitarsi agli occhi di qn** to redeem o.s. in sb's eyes
riabilitazione [riabilitat'tsjone] SF rehabilitation
riabituare [riabitu'are] VT to reaccustom
► **riabituarsi** VR: **riabituarsi a qc/a fare qc** to reaccustom o.s. to sth/to doing sth
riaccendere [riat'tʃendere] VB IRREG
■ VT (*sigaretta, fuoco, gas*) to light again; (*luce*) to switch on again; (*fig: sentimenti, interesse*) to rekindle, revive
► **riaccendersi** VIP (*fuoco*) to catch again; (*luce, radio, TV*) to come back on again; (*fig: sentimenti, interesse*) to revive, be rekindled
riacceso, a [riat'tʃeso] PP *di* **riaccendere**
riacchiappare [riakkjap'pare] VT (*fam*) to nab again
riacciuffare [riattʃuf'fare] VT = **riacchiappare**
riacquistare [riakkwis'tare] VT (*gen*) to buy again; (*ciò che si era venduto*) to buy back; (*fig: buonumore, sangue freddo, libertà*) to regain; **riacquistare la salute** to recover (one's health); **riacquistare le forze** to regain one's strength
riacutizzarsi [riakutid'dzarsi] VIP (*malattia*) to worsen again
Riad [ri'ad] SF Riyadh
riadattamento [riadatta'mento] SM (*a luogo, ambiente*) readjustment
riadattare [riadat'tare] VT (*abito*) to alter; (*locale*) to convert
► **riadattarsi** VR: **riadattarsi a qc/a fare qc** to readjust to sth/to doing sth
riaddormentare [riaddormen'tare] VT to put to sleep again
► **riaddormentarsi** VIP to fall asleep again
riadoperare [riadope'rare] VT to reuse
riaffacciarsi [riaffat'tʃarsi] VR: **riaffacciarsi (a)** (*finestra*) to appear (at) again
► **riaffacciarsi** VIP: **l'idea gli si riaffacciò alla mente** the idea occurred to him again
riaffondare [riaffon'dare] VI (*aus* **essere**) to sink again; **riaffondare nel fango** to sink back into the mud
riaffrontare [riaffron'tare] VT (*questione*) to deal with again; (*discorso*) to take up again
riagganciare [riaggan'tʃare] VT (*con un gancio*) to rehook; (*vagone*) to re-couple; (*Telec*): **riagganciare (il ricevitore)** to hang up; **non riagganciare, premi il pulsante e rifai il numero** don't hang up, press the button and redial
► **riagganciarsi** VIP (*ricollegarsi*) **riagganciarsi a** (*fig*) to draw on, be connected with
► **riagganciarsi** VR: **per riagganciarmi a quanto hai detto prima...** in connection with what you were saying earlier ...
riallacciare [riallat'tʃare] VT (*cintura, cavo*) to refasten, tie up *o* fasten again; (*cappotto*) to do up again; (*fig: rapporti, amicizia*) to resume, renew; **riallacciarsi il cappotto** to do one's coat up again
► **riallacciarsi** VIP (*fig: ricollegarsi*) **riallacciarsi a** to draw on, have links with
► **riallacciarsi** VR: **mi riallaccio a quello che ha detto il mio collega...** to go back to what my colleague was saying ...
riallargare [riallar'gare] VT (*passaggio, strada*) to widen; (*vestiti*) to let out
► **riallargarsi** VIP (*strada*) to get wider
riallungare [riallun'gare] VT (*gen*) to lengthen again; (*vestiti*) to lengthen
► **riallungarsi** VIP (*giornate*) to grow longer
rialzare [rial'tsare] VT to raise, lift; (*fondo stradale, superficie*) to make higher, raise, heighten; (*prezzi*) to increase, put up, raise
■ VI (*aus* **essere**) (*prezzi, azioni, febbre*) to rise, go up
► **rialzarsi** VR (*persona*) to get up
rialzato, a [rial'tsato] AGG: **piano rialzato** mezzanine
rialzista, i, e [rial'tsista] SM/F (*Borsa*) bull
rialzo [ri'altso] SM **1** (*Econ*): **rialzo (di)** rise (in), increase (in); **essere in rialzo** (*azioni, prezzi*) to be up; **giocare al rialzo** (*Borsa*) to bull; **tendenza al rialzo** (*Borsa*) upward trend, bullish tendency **2** (*rilievo: di terreno*) rise
riamare [ria'mare] VT (*amare a propria volta*) to love in return; **amare senza essere riamati è doloroso** unrequited love is a painful experience
riammalarsi [riamma'larsi] VIP to fall ill again
riammettere [riam'mettere] VT IRREG (*alunno, socio*) to readmit
riandare [rian'dare] VI IRREG (*aus* **essere**) **riandare (in)** *o* **(a)** to go back (to), return (to); **riandare con la memoria a qc** (*fig*) to reminisce about sth, think back to sth
rianimare [riani'mare] VT (*Med*) to resuscitate; (*fig: rallegrare*) to cheer up; (*: dar coraggio*) to give heart to; **rianimare una festa** to liven up a party
► **rianimarsi** VIP (*vedi vt*) to recover consciousness; to cheer up; to take heart; to liven up; **d'estate il paesino si rianima** the village comes to life in the summer
rianimazione [rianimat'tsjone] SF (*Med*) resuscitation; **(centro di) rianimazione** intensive care (unit); **in rianimazione** in intensive care
riannodare [rianno'dare] VT (*lacci*) to retie; (*cravatta*) to reknot; (*fig: amicizia*) to renew
riaperto, a [ria'pɛrto] PP *di* **riaprire**
riapertura [riaper'tura] SF reopening
riapparire [riappa'rire] VI IRREG (*aus* **essere**) to reappear
riapparizione [riapparit'tsjone] SF reappearance
riapparso, a [riap'parso] PP *di* **riapparire**
riappendere [riap'pɛndere] VT IRREG to hang up again, rehang; (*Telec*) to hang up
riappeso, a [riap'peso] PP *di* **riappendere**
riappisolarsi [riappizo'larsi] VIP to doze (*o* nod) off again
riappropriarsi [riappro'prjarsi] VIP: **riappropriarsi di qc** to take sth back
riaprire [ria'prire] VB IRREG, VT, **riaprirsi** VIP to reopen, open again; **quando riaprono le scuole?** when do the schools reopen?; **il cinema ha riaperto dopo l'incendio** the cinema has reopened after the fire

Rr

riarmare [riar'mare] VT, **riarmarsi** VR to rearm
riarmo [ri'armo] SM (*Mil*) rearmament
riarso, a [ri'arso] AGG (*terreno*) arid; (*gola*) parched; (*labbra*) dry
riascoltare [riaskol'tare] VT: **riascoltare qn/qc** to listen to sb/sth again
riassettare [riasset'tare] VT (*stanza*) to rearrange
riassetto [rias'sɛtto] SM (*di sistema*) reorganization
riassicurare [riassiku'rare] VT (*Assicurazioni*) to reinsure
riassicurazione [riassikurat'tsjone] SF (*Assicurazioni*) reinsurance
riassorbimento [riassorbi'mento] SM reabsorption
riassumere [rias'sumere] VT IRREG **1** (*ricapitolare: storia, racconto*) to summarize; **riassumere un articolo** to summarize an article **2** (*operaio, impiegato, domestico*) to re-employ **3** (*riprendere: attività, funzione*) to resume
riassumibile [riassu'mibile] AGG (*conferenza, racconto*): **è riassumibile in poche parole** it can be summed up in a few words
riassuntivo, a [riassun'tivo] AGG summarizing, recapitulatory
riassunto, a [rias'sunto] PP *di* **riassumere**
■SM summary
riattaccare [riattak'kare] VT **1** (*attaccare di nuovo*): **riattaccare (a)** (*manifesto, francobollo*) to stick back (on); (*bottone*) to sew back (on); (*quadro*) to hang back up (on); **riattaccare (il telefono** *o* **il ricevitore)** to hang up (the receiver); **ha riattaccato senza lasciarmi finire** he hung up without letting me finish **2** (*riprendere*): **riattaccare discorso con qn** to begin talking to sb again; **riattaccare a fare qc** to begin doing sth again
riattare [riat'tare] VT (*casa*) to do up, renovate
riattivare [riatti'vare] VT **1** (*strada, linea ferroviaria*) to reopen **2** (*Med*) to stimulate; (*Cosmetica*) to reactivate; **riattivare la circolazione del sangue** to get the circulation going again **3** (*macchina, motore*) to start up again
riattivazione [riattivat'tsjone] SF (*di strada, linea ferroviaria*) reopening; (*Med: della circolazione*) stimulation
riavere [ria'vere] VB IRREG
■VT **1** (*gen*) to have again; **oggi ho riavuto la nausea** I felt sick again today **2** (*recuperare: soldi, libro ecc*) to get back; **far riavere qn** (*da svenimento*) to bring sb round;
▶ **riaversi** VIP (*da svenimento, stordimento*) to come round; **riaversi dallo stupore** to recover from one's surprise
riavuto, a [ria'vuto] PP *di* **riavere**
riavviare [riavvi'are] VT (*motore, computer*) to restart
riavvicinamento [riavvitʃina'mento] SM (*di persone*) reconciliation; (*di paesi*) rapprochement
riavvicinare [riavvitʃi'nare] VT: **riavvicinare qc a qc** to put sth near sth again; **riavvicinò la sedia al tavolo** he drew the chair up to the table again; **riavvicina i due quadri** put the two pictures next to one another again
▶ **riavvicinarsi** VR: **riavvicinarsi a qc** to approach again; **riavvicinarsi a qn** (*riconciliarsi*) to make one's peace with sb, to make it up with sb
riavvio [riav'vio] SM (*di motore, computer*) restarting; **"Riavvio"** (*Inform*) "Restart"
ribadire [riba'dire] VT to reaffirm, confirm
ribalta [ri'balta] SF **1** (*Teatro, proscenio*) front of the stage; (: *apparecchio d'illuminazione*) footlights *pl*; **essere/venire alla ribalta** (*fig*) to be in/come into the limelight; **tornare alla ribalta** (*personaggio*) to make a comeback; (*problema*) to come up again **2** (*piano, sportello*) flap; (*mobile*) bureau (*Brit*)
ribaltabile [ribal'tabile] AGG (*sedile*) tip-up *attr*
ribaltare [ribal'tare] VT (*rovesciare*) to overturn, tip over; (*fig: situazione*) to reverse; (: *questione*) to turn round
■VI (*aus* **essere**), **ribaltarsi** VIP to overturn, tip over
ribaltone [ribal'tɔne] SM (*Pol*) reversal
ribassare [ribas'sare] VT (*prezzi*) to lower, bring down; **hanno ribassato il prezzo dei CD** they've cut the price of CDs
■VI (*aus* **essere**) to fall, come down
ribassista, i, e [ribas'sista] SM/F (*Borsa*) bear
ribasso [ri'basso] SM (*Econ*): **ribasso (di)** fall *o* reduction (in); **essere in ribasso** (*azioni, prezzi*) to be down; (*fig: popolarità*) to be on the decline; **giocare al ribasso** (*Borsa*) to bear; **tendenza al ribasso** (*Borsa*) downtrend, bearish tendency
ribattere [ri'battere] VT **1** (*controbattere a: accuse*) to refute; **ribattere che...** to retort that ... **2** (*battere di nuovo*) to beat again; (*con macchina da scrivere*) to type again; **ribattere (una palla)** to return a ball
ribattezzare [ribatted'dzare] VT to rename
ribellarsi [ribel'larsi] VIP: **ribellarsi (a** *o* **contro)** to rebel (against); **si è ribellato alla decisione del padre** he rebelled against his father's decision
ribelle [ri'bɛlle] AGG (*soldati, truppe*) rebel; (*carattere, ragazzo*) rebellious; (*capelli*) unruly
■SM/F rebel
ribellione [ribel'ljone] SF: **ribellione (a** *o* **contro)** rebellion (against)
ribes ['ribes] SM INV (*Bot*) currant; **ribes nero** blackcurrant; **ribes rosso** redcurrant
riboflavina [ribofla'vina] SF (*Chim*) riboflavin
ribollire [ribol'lire] VI (*aus* **avere**) (*liquido*) to bubble, boil; (*mare*) to seethe; (*vino*) to ferment; **scene che fanno ribollire il sangue** (*fig*) scenes which make one's blood boil
ribrezzo [ri'breddzo] SM disgust, repugnance, loathing; **avere ribrezzo di qc** *or* **provare ribrezzo per qc** to be disgusted at *o* by sth; **far ribrezzo a qn** to disgust sb
ributtante [ribut'tante] AGG disgusting, revolting
ributtare [ribut'tare] VT **1** (*buttare di nuovo*) to throw back **2** (*vomitare*) to bring up
▶ **ributtarsi** VR to throw o.s. back; **ributtarsi a letto** to jump back into bed
ricacciare [rikat'tʃare] VT (*respingere*) to drive back; **ricacciare fuori qn** to throw sb out; **ricacciare un urlo in gola** to smother/stifle a cry
ricadere [rika'dere] VI IRREG (*aus* **essere**) **1** (*cadere di nuovo*) to fall again; (*fig*): **ricadere nel vizio** to fall back into bad habits; **ricadere nell'errore** to lapse into error **2** (*riversarsi: responsabilità, colpa*): **ricadere su** to fall on **3** (*scendere*) to fall, drop; **i capelli le ricadevano sulle spalle** her hair hung down over her shoulders
ricaduta [rika'duta] SF **1** (*Med, fig*) relapse; **avere una ricaduta** to relapse **2** (*Fis*): **ricaduta radioattiva** fallout
ricalcare [rikal'kare] VT (*Disegno*) to trace; (*fig: imitare*) to follow closely *o* faithfully; **ricalcare le orme di qn** (*fig*) to follow in sb's footsteps
ricalcitrante [rikaltʃi'trante] AGG (*mulo*) kicking; (*fig: persona*) recalcitrant, refractory

ricalcitrare [rikaltʃi'trare] VI *(aus* **avere***)* *(cavallo, asino, mulo)* to kick; *(fig: persona)*: **recalcitrare (di fronte a)** to be recalcitrant (to)

ricamare [rika'mare] VT *(anche fig)* to embroider; **ci ha ricamato su** *(fig)* he's exaggerated it

ricambiare [rikam'bjare] VT *(contraccambiare)* to return; **bisogna ricambiare l'invito** we must return the invitation

ricambio, bi [ri'kambjo] SM **1** *(di biancheria, abiti)* change; **una camicia di ricambio** a spare shirt; **pezzi di ricambio** *(Tecn)* spare parts **2** *(Fisiologia)* metabolism **3** **ricambio del lavoro** (labour *(Brit) o* labor *(Am)*) turnover; **ricambio di magazzino** stock turnover

ricamo [ri'kamo] SM embroidery; **da ricamo** embroidery *attr*; **senza ricami** *(fig)* without frills

ricandidare [rikandi'dare] VT *(Pol)* to present as a candidate again
▶ **ricandidarsi** VR to stand for election again

ricapitolare [rikapito'lare] VT to recapitulate, sum up; **ricapitolando...** *or* **per ricapitolare...** to sum up ...

ricapitolazione [rikapitolat'tsjone] SF recapitulation, summary

ricarica [ri'karika] SF *(di fucile)* reloading; *(di orologio)* rewinding; *(di penna)* refilling; *(di batteria)* recharging

ricaricare [rikari'kare] VT *(arma, macchina fotografica)* to reload; *(orologio, giocattolo)* to rewind; *(penna)* to refill; *(batteria)* to recharge

ricarico, chi [ri'kariko] SM *(Comm)* mark-up

ricascare [rikas'kare] VI *(aus* **essere***)* *(fam: in tranello, truffa)* to be had again

ricattare [rikat'tare] VT to blackmail; **lo stavano ricattando** they were blackmailing him

ricattatore, trice [rikatta'tore] SM/F blackmailer

ricattatorio, ria, ri, rie [rikatta'tɔrjo] AGG *(lettera, telefonata)* blackmail *attr*; *(tono)* blackmailing

ricatto [ri'katto] SM blackmail; **ma questo è un ricatto!** this is blackmail!; **fare un ricatto a qn** to blackmail sb; **subire un ricatto** to be blackmailed; **ricatto morale** emotional blackmail

ricavare [rika'vare] VT **1** *(estrarre)*: **ricavare (da)** to extract (from) **2** *(ottenere)*: **ricavare (da)** to get (from), obtain (from); **ricavare una gonna da un taglio di stoffa** to make a skirt out of a piece of material; **ricavare un profitto** to make a profit; **cosa ne ricavo io?** what do I get out of it?; **dalla vendita ha ricavato ben poco** he made very little on the sale

ricavato [rika'vato] SM *(di vendite)* proceeds *pl*

ricavo [ri'kavo] SM *(gen)* proceeds *pl*; *(Contabilità)* revenue

riccamente [rikka'mente] AVV *(gen)* richly, sumptuously; **riccamente illustrato** lavishly illustrated

ricchezza [rik'kettsa] SF **1** *(di persona, paese)* wealth; *(di terreno, colori)* richness; *(fig: abbondanza)* abundance; **con ricchezza di particolari** in great detail; **in questa zona c'è ricchezza di carbone** there's an abundance of coal in this area **2** **ricchezze** SFPL *(averi)* wealth *sg*, riches; *(tesori)* treasures; **ricchezze naturali** natural resources

riccio¹, cia, ci, ce ['rittʃo] AGG *(capelli)* curly; *(persona)* curly-haired, with curly hair
■ SM **1** *(di capelli)* curl; **farsi i ricci** to curl one's hair **2** *(di legno, metallo)* shaving; *(di burro)* curl

riccio², ci ['rittʃo] SM **1** *(Zool)* hedgehog; (: *anche*: riccio di mare) sea urchin **2** *(Bot)* chestnut husk

ricciolo ['rittʃolo] SM curl

ricciuto, a [rit'tʃuto] AGG *(testa)* curly; *(persona)* curly-haired

ricco, a, chi, che ['rikko] AGG **1** *(gen, fig)* rich; *(facoltoso)* rich, wealthy; *(fertile: terra)* rich, fertile; **è di famiglia ricca** he comes from a rich family; **essere ricco sfondato** to be rolling in money; **un piatto molto ricco** a very rich dish; **una ricca mancia** a large tip; **una ricca documentazione** a wealth of documentation **2** **ricco di** *(illustrazioni, idee)* full of; *(fauna, risorse, proteine, calorie)* rich in; **alimento ricco di vitamine** food rich in vitamins; **un ragazzo ricco di fantasia** a boy with a fertile imagination
■ SM/F rich man/woman; **i ricchi** the rich, the wealthy

ricerca, che [ri'tʃerka] SF **1** **ricerca (di)** *(gen)* search (for); *(piacere, gloria)* pursuit (of); *(perfezione)* quest (for); **mettersi alla ricerca di** to go in search of, look *o* search *o* hunt for; **essere alla ricerca di** to be searching (*o* looking) for; **mia sorella è alla ricerca di un lavoro** my sister is looking for a job; **fare delle ricerche** *(inchiesta)* to make inquiries; **hanno abbandonato le ricerche** the search has been abandoned; **dopo anni di ricerche hanno ritrovato il bambino** after years of searching they found the child; **ricerca di mercato** market research; **ricerca operativa** operational research **2** *(Univ)*: **la ricerca** research; **lavoro di ricerca** piece of research; **la ricerca scientifica** scientific research; **fare delle ricerche su un argomento** to carry out *o* do research into a subject
▷ www.cnr.it/

ricercare [ritʃer'kare] VT *(onore, gloria)* to seek; *(successo, piacere)* to pursue; *(motivi, cause)* to look for, try to determine; **è ricercato dalla polizia** he's wanted by the police

ricercatamente [ritʃerkata'mente] AVV *(vestire)* elegantly, in a refined way; *(con affettazione)* affectedly

ricercatezza [ritʃerka'tettsa] SF *(raffinatezza)* refinement; (: *pegg*) affectation

ricercato, a [ritʃer'kato] AGG **1** *(latitante)*: **è ricercato dalla polizia** he's wanted by the police **2** *(molto richiesto)* in great demand, much sought-after **3** *(raffinato: qualità, gusti, stile)* refined; *(pegg: affettato)* affected; (: *stile*) studied
■ SM/F *(criminale)* wanted man/woman

ricercatore, trice [ritʃerka'tore] SM/F *(Univ)* researcher

ricetrasmettitore [ritʃetrazmetti'tore] SM, **ricetrasmittente** [ritʃetrazmit'tɛnte] SF transceiver, two-way radio

ricetta [ri'tʃɛtta] SF **1** *(Med)* prescription; *(fig: antidoto)*: **ricetta contro** remedy *o* cure *o* recipe for; **fare una ricetta a qn** to make out a prescription for sb **2** *(Culin)* recipe; **mi dai la ricetta della torta di mele?** could I have the recipe for apple pie?

ricettacolo [ritʃet'takolo] SM *(luogo di raccolta)*: **un ricettacolo per i microbi** a breeding-ground for germs; *(pegg: luogo malfamato)* den

ricettario, ri [ritʃet'tarjo] SM **1** *(Med)* prescription pad **2** *(Culin)* recipe book

ricettatore, trice [ritʃetta'tore] SM/F *(Dir)* receiver (of stolen goods)

ricettazione [ritʃettat'tsjone] SF *(Dir)* receiving (stolen goods)

ricettività [ritʃettivi'ta] SF receptiveness

ricettivo, a [ritʃet'tivo] AGG receptive

Rr

ricevente [ritʃe'vɛnte] AGG (*Radio, TV*) receiving ■SM/F (*Comm*) receiver

ricevere [ri'tʃevere] VT **1** (*gen*) to receive, get; (*voto*) to get; **cara Denise, ho ricevuto ieri la tua lettera...** dear Denise, I got your letter yesterday ...; **non ha ancora ricevuto lo stipendio** he hasn't got his pay yet; **ricevere uno schiaffo** to get *o* be given a slap; **ricevere un rifiuto** to meet with a refusal; **"confermiamo di aver ricevuto la merce"** (*Comm*) "we acknowledge receipt of the goods" **2** (*accogliere*) to welcome, receive; (*ammettere alla propria presenza*) to see, receive; **ricevere visite** to have visitors; **il dottore riceve il venerdì** the doctor has his surgery on Fridays; **il dottore la riceverà subito** the doctor will see you at once; **mi hanno ricevuto in salotto** they showed me into the living room **3** (*TV, Radio*) to pick up, receive

ricevimento [ritʃevi'mento] SM **1** (*festa*) reception; **ricevimento di nozze** wedding reception; **dare un ricevimento** to hold a reception *o* party **2** (*il ricevere*) receiving *no pl*, receipt; **al ricevimento della merce** on receipt of the goods

ricevitore [ritʃevi'tore] SM **1** (*Telec, Radio, Tecn*) receiver **2** **ricevitore delle imposte** tax collector; **ricevitore del lotto** receiver for the State lottery; **ricevitore del totocalcio** football pools collector (*Brit*)

ricevitoria [ritʃevito'ria] SF: **ricevitoria delle imposte** ≈ Inland Revenue (*Brit*) *o* Internal Revenue (*Am*) Office; **ricevitoria del lotto** state lottery office; **ricevitoria del totocalcio** football pools office (*Brit*)

ricevuta [ritʃe'vuta] SF (*gen, Comm*) receipt; **mi dà la ricevuta, per favore?** could you give me a receipt please?; **accusare ricevuta di qc** to acknowledge receipt of sth; **ricevuta fiscale** official receipt (for tax purposes); **ricevuta di ritorno** (*Posta*) advice of receipt; **ricevuta di versamento** receipt of payment

ricezione [ritʃet'tsjone] SF (*Radio, TV*) reception

richiamare [rikja'mare] VT **1** (*gen, al telefono*) to call back; (*Mil, Inform*) to recall; **richiamare qn indietro** to call sb back; **richiamare le truppe** to withdraw the troops; **richiamare qn alla realtà** to bring sb back to earth; **richiamare qn in vita** to bring sb back to life; **richiamerò tra un quarto d'ora** I'll call back in a quarter of an hour **2** (*attrarre: folla*) to attract, draw; **richiamare l'attenzione di qn** to draw sb's attention; **desidero richiamare la vostra attenzione su...** I should like to draw your attention to ... **3** (*ricordare*): **richiamare qc alla memoria di qn** (*sogg: avvenimento*) to remind sb of sth; **è un colore che richiama il verde** it's a greenish colour **4** (*rimproverare*) to reprimand; **richiamare qn all'ordine** to call sb to order ▶ **richiamarsi** VIP: **richiamarsi a** (*riferirsi a*) to refer to

richiamato [rikja'mato] SM recalled serviceman

richiamo [ri'kjamo] SM **1** (*di truppe*) recall **2** (*voce, segno*) call; **il richiamo della foresta/della natura** the call of the wild/of nature; **uccello da richiamo** decoy; **servire da richiamo** (*fig: attrazione*) to act as a decoy **3** (*ammonimento*) reprimand; **richiamo all'ordine** call to order **4** (*Med: di vaccinazione*) booster **5** (*rimando*) cross-reference

richiedente [rikje'dɛnte] SM/F applicant

richiedere [ri'kjɛdere] VT IRREG **1** (*chiedere: di nuovo*) to ask again; **richiedere qc** (*in restituzione*) to ask for sth back **2** (*chiedere: prestito, aiuto*) to ask for; (*: passaporto, licenza*) to apply for; **ha richiesto il passaporto più d'un mese fa** he applied for a passport more than a month ago; **hanno richiesto il suo intervento** they asked him to intervene; **tutto ciò non è richiesto** all that is not necessary; **il tuo intervento non era richiesto** no-one asked you to intervene; **essere molto richiesto** to be in great demand **3** (*necessitare*) to need, require; **tutto ciò richiede tempo e pazienza** all this requires time and patience; **un lavoro che richiede molta concentrazione** a job that requires a lot of concentration

richiesta [ri'kjɛsta] SF **1** (*gen*): **richiesta (di)** request (for); (*impiego, documenti, congedo*) application (for); (*salario migliore, condizioni migliori*) demand (for); **una richiesta di aiuto** a request for help; **su** *o* **a richiesta** on request; **a richiesta generale** by general request; **a grande richiesta** by popular demand; **programma a richiesta** (*Radio, TV*) request programme (*Brit*) *o* program (*Am*); **fermata a richiesta** request stop **2** (*Comm, Econ*) demand

richiesto, a [ri'kjɛsto] PP *di* **richiedere**

richiudere [ri'kjudere] VB IRREG ■VT (*porta, finestra, cassetto*) to close again, shut again; **aprì gli occhi e li richiuse subito** she opened her eyes and closed them again immediately ▶ **richiudersi** VIP (*porta*) to close again; (*ferita*) to close up, heal

richiudibile [rikju'dibile] AGG (*confezione*) resealable

richiuso, a [ri'kjuso] PP *di* **richiudere**

riciclaggio, gi [ritʃi'kladdʒo] SM (*di carta, vetro*) recycling; **riciclaggio di denaro sporco** money laundering

riciclare [ritʃi'klare] VT (*carta, vetro*) to recycle; (*denaro sporco*) to launder

riciclato, a [ritʃi'klato] AGG (*vetro ecc*) recycled; (*denaro*) laundered; **un politico riciclato** (*pegg*) *an established politician who changes parties*

ricino ['ritʃino] SM (*Bot*) castor-oil plant; **olio di ricino** castor oil

ricognitore [rikoɲɲi'tore] SM (*Aer*) reconnaissance aircraft *pl inv*

ricognizione [rikoɲɲit'tsjone] SF **1** (*Mil*) reconnaissance; **uscire in ricognizione** to reconnoitre **2** (*Dir*) recognition, acknowledgement

ricollegare [rikolle'gare] VT **1** (*collegare nuovamente: gen*) to join *o* link again **2** (*connettere: fatti*): **ricollegare (a, con)** to connect (with), associate (with) ▶ **ricollegarsi** VIP: **ricollegarsi a** (*sogg: fatti: connettersi*) to be connected to, be associated with ▶ **ricollegarsi** VR (*persona: riferirsi*) to refer to

ricolmare [rikol'mare] VT: **ricolmare qn di** (*fig: regali, gentilezze*) to shower sb with

ricolmo, a [ri'kolmo] AGG: **ricolmo (di)** (*bicchiere*) full to the brim (with); (*stanza, armadio*) full (of); **ricolmo di gioia** overflowing with joy

ricominciare [rikomin'tʃare] VT to start again, begin again; **ho dovuto ricominciare tutto da capo** I had to start all over again; **ricominciare a fare qc** to begin doing *o* to do sth again, start doing *o* to do sth again; **ha ricominciato a fumare** he's started smoking again; **ah, si ricomincia!** here we go again!; **ha ricominciato con la mania dei francobolli** he's off on his stamp craze again ■VI (*aus* **essere** *o* **avere**) (*spettacolo*) to start, begin; **è ricominciato l'inverno** winter is here again; **ricomincia a piovere** it's raining again

ricomparire [rikompa'rire] VI IRREG (*aus* **essere**) (*riapparire: persona*) to reappear; (*: sole*) to come out again; (*: sorriso*) to return

ricomparsa [rikom'parsa] SF reappearance

ricomparso, a [rikom'parso] PP *di* **ricomparire**
ricompattare [rikompat'tare] VT (*partito, gruppo*) to reunite
▶ **ricompattarsi** VIP to reunite
ricompensa [rikom'pensa] SF reward
ricompensare [rikompen'sare] VT to reward
ricomporre [rikom'porre] VB IRREG
■ VT **1** (*viso, lineamenti*) to recompose **2** (*Tip*) to reset
▶ **ricomporsi** VR to compose o.s., regain one's composure
ricomposto, a [rikom'posto] PP *di* **ricomporre**
riconciliare [rikontʃi'ljare] VT to reconcile
▶ **riconciliarsi** VR **1** **riconciliarsi con qn** to make it up with sb, make one's peace with sb **2** (*uso reciproco*) to be reconciled; (: *amici*) to make friends again, make it up again, make peace
riconciliazione [rikontʃiliat'tsjone] SF reconciliation
ricondotto, a [rikon'dotto] PP *di* **ricondurre**
ricondurre [rikon'durre] VT IRREG (*gen*) to bring (*o* take) back
riconferma [rikon'ferma] SF reconfirmation
riconfermare [rikonfer'mare] VT to reconfirm
ricongiungere [rikon'dʒundʒere] VB IRREG
■ VT to join together; (*persone*) to reunite
▶ **ricongiungersi** VR **1** **ricongiungersi a** (*famiglia*) to be reunited with **2** (*uso reciproco: eserciti*) to reunite
ricongiunto, a [rikon'dʒunto] PP *di* **ricongiungere**
riconoscente [rikonoʃ'ʃɛnte] AGG grateful
riconoscenza [rikonoʃ'ʃɛntsa] SF gratitude
riconoscere [riko'noʃʃere] VB IRREG
■ VT **1** (*identificare*) to recognize; (: *cadavere, salma*) to identify; **l'ho riconosciuto dalla voce** I recognized him by his voice; **per non farsi riconoscere** so as not to be recognized; **farsi riconoscere** (*esibendo documento*) to provide identification **2** (*ammettere: gen*) to recognize; (: *errore, torto*) to admit, acknowledge; (: *superiorità*) to acknowledge; **devo riconoscere che hai ragione** I must admit you're right; **riconoscere i propri limiti** to recognize one's own limitations; **riconoscere a qn il diritto di fare qc** to acknowledge sb's right to do sth **3** (*Dir*): **riconoscere un figlio** to acknowledge a child; **riconoscere qn colpevole** to find sb guilty;
▶ **riconoscersi** VR **1** (*ammettere*) **riconoscersi colpevole** to admit one's guilt; **si riconobbe sconfitto** he admitted he was beaten **2** (*uso reciproco*) to recognize each other
riconoscibile [rikonoʃ'ʃibile] AGG recognizable
riconoscimento [rikonoʃʃi'mento] SM (*gen, di diritti*) recognition; (*Dir: di figlio*) acknowledgement; (*di cadavere, salma*) identification; **documento di riconoscimento** means *pl* of identification; **a riconoscimento dei servizi resi** in recognition of services rendered; **segno di riconoscimento** distinguishing mark; **riconoscimento di caratteri** (*Inform*) character recognition
riconosciuto, a [rikonoʃ'ʃuto] PP *di* **riconoscere**
■ AGG recognized
riconquista [rikon'kwista] SF (*Mil*) reconquest, recapture; (*di libertà*) recovery
riconquistare [rikonkwis'tare] VT (*Mil*) to reconquer, recapture; (*libertà, stima*) to win back
riconsegna [rikon'seɲɲa] SF (*restituzione*) handing back
riconsegnare [rikonseɲ'ɲare] VT (*restituire*) to hand back, give back
riconsiderare [rikonside'rare] VT to reconsider
riconsiderazione [rikonsiderat'tsjone] SF reconsideration
riconversione [rikonver'sjone] SF (*Econ*) reconversion
riconvertire [rikonver'tire] VT (*Econ*) to reconvert
ricoperto, a [riko'pɛrto] PP *di* **ricoprire**
■ SM (*gelato*): **un ricoperto (al cioccolato)** choc-ice (*Brit*) *o* ice cream bar (*Am*) on a stick
ricopiare [riko'pjare] VT to copy; **ricopiare qc in bella (copia)** to make a fair copy of sth
ricopiatura [rikopja'tura] SF copying
ricopribile [riko'pribile] AGG (*divano, poltrona*) with loose covers
ricoprire [riko'prire] VB IRREG
■ VT **1** (*gen*): **ricoprire (di)** to cover (with); (*divano, poltrona*) to re-cover (with); (*fig: persona: di gentilezze*) to shower (with); **ricoprire un dente** to cap a tooth **2** (*carica*) to hold
▶ **ricoprirsi** VIP: **ricoprirsi di** (*polvere*) to become covered in; **il cielo si è ricoperto di nuvole** the sky clouded over; **il prato si è ricoperto di fiori** the field is covered with flowers
ricordare [rikor'dare] VT **1** (*nome, persona, fatto*) to remember, recall; **il mio numero è facile da ricordare** my number is easy to remember; **ricordare di fare qc** to remember to do sth; **ricordare di aver fatto qc** to remember having done *o* doing sth; **se ben ricordo** if I remember rightly; **ti ricordo con affetto** (*nella corrispondenza*) I often think of you **2** (*far presente ad altri*): **ricordare a qn qc/di fare qc** to remind sb of sth/to do sth; **ricordami di spedire la lettera** remind me to post the letter; **ti ricordo che c'ero prima io** I'd like to remind you that I was here first; **scene che ricordano il passato** scenes which recall the past; **mi ricorda molto suo padre** he reminds me a lot of his father **3** (*menzionare*) to mention **4** (*commemorare*) to commemorate
▶ **ricordarsi** VIP: **ricordarsi (di)** to remember; **non mi ricordo** I can't remember; **ricordarsi di fare qc** to remember to do sth; **ricordarsi di avere fatto qc** to remember having done *o* doing sth; **ti ricordi di me?** do you remember me?; **non si è più ricordato di darmi il libro** he forgot to give me the book; **non si ricorda dal naso alla bocca** (*fig fam*) he would forget his own name

LO SAPEVI...?
ricordare non si traduce mai con la parola inglese *record*

ricordino [rikor'dino] SM souvenir
ricordo [ri'kɔrdo] SM **1** (*memoria*) memory; **ho dei bellissimi ricordi dell'Irlanda** I have very happy memories of Ireland; **non ho che un vago ricordo di quella giornata** I have only a vague recollection of that day, I only remember that day vaguely; **vivere di ricordi** to live in the past **2** (*oggetto*) keepsake; (: *turistico*) souvenir; **prendere/dare qc per** *o* **in ricordo** to take/give sth as a keepsake; **questo è un ricordo del viaggio in Marocco** this is a souvenir of my trip to Morocco; **un ricordo di famiglia** a family heirloom
■ AGG INV (*foto*) souvenir *attr*
ricorreggere [rikor'rɛddʒere] VT (*gen*) to correct again; (*esame*) to mark (*Brit*) *o* grade (*Am*) again
ricorrente [rikor'rɛnte] AGG recurring, recurrent
■ SM/F (*Dir*) plaintiff
ricorrenza [rikor'rɛntsa] SF **1** (*il ricorrere*) recurrence **2** (*anniversario*) anniversary

Rr

ricorrere [ri'korrere] VI IRREG (*aus* **essere**)
1 (*ripetersi periodicamente*) to recur; **oggi ricorre il 5° anniversario di...** today is the 5th anniversary of ...; **è un elemento che ricorre in tutta la sua poesia** it's a recurring element in all his poetry **2** (*far ricorso a*): **ricorrere a** (*persona*) to turn to; (*forza, stratagemma*) to resort to; **ricorrere alle vie legali** to take legal action **3** (*Dir*): **ricorrere contro una sentenza** to appeal against a sentence; **ricorrere in appello** to lodge an appeal

ricorso, a [ri'korso] PP *di* **ricorrere**
■ SM **1** **fare ricorso a** (*persona*) to turn to; (*mezzo, cosa*) to resort to; **dovette far ricorso a tutto il suo coraggio** he had to summon up all his courage **2** (*Dir*) appeal; **fare ricorso (contro)** to appeal (against) **3** (*il ricorrere*) recurrence; **un tipico esempio dei corsi e ricorsi della storia** a typical example of history repeating itself

ricostituente [rikostitu'ɛnte] AGG (*Med*): **cura ricostituente** tonic treatment
■ SM (*Med*) tonic

ricostituire [rikostitu'ire] VT (*società*) to build up again; (*governo, partito*) to re-form
► **ricostituirsi** VIP (*gruppo, partito*) to re-form

ricostruire [rikostru'ire] VT (*edificio*) to rebuild, reconstruct; (*testo, fatti, delitto*) to reconstruct

ricostruzione [rikostrut'tsjone] SF (*di edificio*) reconstruction, rebuilding *no pl*; (*di testo, fatti, delitto*) reconstruction

ricotta [ri'kɔtta] SF ricotta; *soft white unsalted cheese made from sheep's milk*

ricoverare [rikove'rare] VT (*Med*): **ricoverare qn in ospedale** to admit sb to hospital; **far ricoverare qn in ospedale** to have sb admitted to hospital; **è stato ricoverato d'urgenza (in ospedale)** he has been rushed to hospital

> **LO SAPEVI...?**
> **ricoverare** non si traduce mai con la parola inglese *recover*

ricoverato, a [rikove'rato] SM/F patient

ricovero [ri'kovero] SM **1** (*rifugio*) shelter, refuge **2** (*Med*) admission (to hospital); **foglio di ricovero** admission sheet

> **LO SAPEVI...?**
> **ricovero** non si traduce mai con la parola inglese *recovery*

ricreare [rikre'are] VT **1** (*creare di nuovo*) to recreate **2** (*fig*: *svagare*) to cheer, amuse; **ricreare lo spirito** to restore one's spirits
► **ricrearsi** VR (*fig*: *svagarsi, divertirsi*) to enjoy o.s.

ricreativo, a [rikrea'tivo] AGG recreational; **circolo ricreativo** (*per adulti*) social club; (*per giovani*) youth club

ricreazione [rikreat'tsjone] SF **1** (*Scol*) break; (*alle elementari*) break, playtime **2** (*svago*) recreation, entertainment

ricredersi [ri'kredersi] VR: **ricredersi (su qc/qn)** to change one's mind (about sth/sb); **mi sono ricreduto sul suo conto** I've changed my mind about him

ricrescere [ri'kreʃʃere] VI IRREG (*aus* **essere**) **farsi ricrescere la barba** to let one's beard grow again

ricresciuto, a [rikreʃ'ʃuto] PP *di* **ricrescere**

ricucire [riku'tʃire] VT (*vestito, colletto*) to stitch *o* sew again; (*strappo, buco*) to mend; (*Med*: *ferita*) to stitch *o* sew up; (*fam*: *paziente*) to stitch back up

ricuperabile [rikupe'rabile] AGG (*gen*) recoverable; (*che si può usare di nuovo*) re-usable

ricuperare [rikupe'rare] VT **1** (*gen*) to recover; (*soldi*) to get back; (*peso*) to put back on; **parte della refurtiva è stata ricuperata** some of the stolen goods have been recovered; **ricuperare il tempo perduto** to make up for lost time; **ricuperare la salute/le forze** to recover (one's health)/one's strength; **ricuperare lo svantaggio** (*anche Sport*) to close the gap **2** (*da naufragio, incendio*: *persone*) to rescue; (: *salme*) to recover; (: *oggetti, relitto*) to salvage **3** (*disadattato, ex detenuto*) to rehabilitate **4** (*usare di nuovo*: *cascami, rottami*) to re-use **5** (*Sport*): **ricuperare una partita** to play a match which had been postponed

ricupero [ri'kupero] SM (*gen*) recovery; (*di relitto*) salvaging; (*di disadattato, ex detenuto*) rehabilitation; **di ricupero** (*merce, materiali*) salvage *attr*; **capacità di ricupero** resilience; **partita di ricupero** (*Sport*) postponed match; **minuti di ricupero** (*Sport*) injury time; **ricupero (di) crediti** (*Comm*) debt collection

ricurvo, a [ri'kurvo] AGG (*linea*) curved; **avere le spalle ricurve** to be round-shouldered; **stava ricurvo sul proprio lavoro** he was bent over his work

ricusare [riku'zare] VT **1** (*offerta, carica*) to decline, to refuse **2** (*Dir*): **ricusare un giudice** to challenge a judge

ridacchiare [ridak'kjare] VI (*aus* **avere**) to snigger

ridanciano, a [ridan'tʃano] AGG (*persona*) jolly, fun-loving; (*storiella*) funny, amusing

ridare [ri'dare] VT IRREG (*oggetto*) to give back, return; (*salute, felicità*) to restore; **me lo presti? te lo ridò domani** will you lend it to me? I'll give it back to you tomorrow

ridarella [rida'rɛlla] SF giggles *pl*

ridda ['ridda] SF (*di pensieri*) jumble

ridente [ri'dɛnte] AGG (*occhi, volto*) smiling; (*paesaggio*) delightful

ridere ['ridere] VB IRREG
■ VI (*aus* **avere**) (*gen*) to laugh; (*deridere, beffare*): **ridere di** to laugh at, make fun of; **perché ridi?** why are you laughing?; **ridere alle spalle di qn** *or* **ridere dietro a qn** to laugh behind sb's back; **ridere in faccia a qn** to laugh in sb's face; **ridere sotto i baffi** to laugh up one's sleeve; **ridere a denti stretti** to give a forced laugh; **cerchiamo di riderci sopra** let's try and see the funny side of it; **ridendo e scherzando si è fatto tardi** (*fig*) what with one thing and another, it got late; **ridere di cuore** *o* **di gusto** to laugh heartily; **ridere fino alle lacrime** to laugh till one cries; **far ridere qn** to make sb laugh; **ma non farmi ridere!** don't be ridiculous!, don't make me laugh!; **non c'è niente da ridere** *or* **c'è poco da ridere** it's not a laughing matter, it's not funny; **che c'è da ridere?** what's so funny?; **tutti sono scoppiati a ridere** they all burst out laughing; **lo ha detto per ridere** he was only joking, he said it in fun; **si fa così per ridere** we're just joking; **è roba da ridere** (*facile*) it's nothing, it's dead easy (*fam*); **che ridere!** what a laugh!; **c'è da morire dal ridere!** it's hilarious!, it's really funny!; **le ridevano gli occhi** her eyes sparkled; **ride bene chi ride ultimo** (*Proverbio*) he who laughs last laughs longest (*Brit*) *o* (*Am*) best
► **ridersi** VIP: **ridersela (di qc)** to laugh (at sth); **se la rideva** he had a laugh to himself

ridestare [rides'tare] VT (*fig*: *ricordi, passioni*) to reawaken
► **ridestarsi** VIP (*fig*: *odio*) to be roused again; (*amore, speranza*) to be rekindled

ridetto, a [ri'detto] PP *di* **ridire**

ridicolaggine [ridiko'laddʒine] SF *(di situazione)* absurdity; *(cosa detta o fatta)* nonsense *no pl*
ridicolizzare [ridikolid'dzare] VT to ridicule
ridicolizzazione [ridikoliddzat'tsjone] SF ridiculing
ridicolmente [ridikol'mente] AVV ridiculously
ridicolo [ri'dikolo] AGG *(gen)* ridiculous, absurd; **non essere ridicolo! io non c'entro niente!** don't be ridiculous! it's nothing to do with me!; **rendersi ridicolo** to make a fool of o.s.
■SM: **il ridicolo della situazione** the absurdity of the situation; **il ridicolo della storia era che...** the ridiculous *o* absurd thing about it was ...; **cadere nel ridicolo** to become ridiculous; **mettere in ridicolo** to ridicule; **coprirsi di ridicolo** to make a laughing stock of o.s.
ridimensionamento [ridimensjona'mento] SM reorganization; *(di fatto storico)* reappraisal
ridimensionare [ridimensjo'nare] VT *(ditta, industria)* to reorganize; *(fig: problema, autore, fatto storico)* to put in perspective, see in the right perspective
▶ **ridimensionarsi** VIP *(sogni, ambizioni)* to become more realistic
ridipingere [ridi'pindʒere] VT to repaint
ridire [ri'dire] VT IRREG **1** *(ripetere, riferire)* to repeat; **te l'ho detto e ridetto mille volte** I've told you over and over again **2** *(criticare)*: **trovare da ridire (su qc/qn)** to find fault (with sth/sb), criticize (sb/sth); **trova sempre da ridire sui miei amici** she's always criticizing my friends; **che c'è da ridire?** what's your objection?
ridiscendere [ridiʃʃendere] VB IRREG, VI *(aus* **essere**), VT to go *(o* come) down again
ridistribuire [ridistribu'ire] VT to redistribute
ridistribuzione [ridistribut'tsjone] SF redistribution
ridiventare [ridiven'tare] VI *(aus* **essere**): **ridiventare serio** to grow serious again
ridonare [rido'nare] VT *(salute, allegria)* to restore, give back
ridondante [ridon'dante] AGG *(linguaggio, frase)* flowery; *(discorso)* bombastic; **uno stile ridondante** *(gonfio)* a pompous style
ridosso [ri'dɔsso] **a ridosso di** AVV *(dietro)* behind; *(contro)* against; **costruire una casa a ridosso di una montagna** to build a house in the shelter of a mountain
ridotto, a [ri'dotto] PP *di* **ridurre**
■AGG *(misura, formato)* small; *(versione, edizione)* abridged; *(tariffa)* cheap; *(prezzo)* reduced, cut; **marcia ridotta** *(Aut)* low gear ratio
■SM *(Teatro)* foyer
riduco *ecc* [ri'duko] VB *vedi* **ridurre**
ridurre [ri'durre] VB IRREG
■VT **1** *(gen, Mat)* to reduce; *(prezzo)* to reduce, cut, bring down; *(pressione)* to lessen; *(produzione)* to cut (back), lower; *(spese)* to cut down on, cut back on; **hanno ridotto il prezzo da 50 a 35 sterline** the price was cut from 50 pounds to 35; **ho dovuto ridurre il tema a 60 righe** I had to cut the essay to 60 lines **2** *(opera letteraria: per la radio, TV)* to adapt; *(: accorciare)* to abridge; *(brano musicale)* to arrange **3** *(fraseologia)*: **ridurre qc in cenere** to reduce sth to ashes; **ridurre qn in poltiglia** *(fig)* to make mincemeat of sb; **guarda come hai ridotto quei jeans!** look at the state of your jeans!; **è proprio ridotto male** *o* **mal ridotto** *(oggetto)* it's really in bad condition; *(persona)* he's really in a bad way
▶ **ridursi** VIP **1** *(quantità)*: **ridursi (a)** to be reduced (to); *(fig: questione, problema)* to come down (to); **il livello si è ridotto di un decimo** the level dropped by a tenth **2** *(persona)*: **ridursi male** to be in a bad state *o* way; **ridursi pelle e ossa** to be reduced to skin and bone; **ridursi a uno straccio** to be washed out; **si è ridotto a mendicare** he was reduced to begging; **come ti sei ridotto!** what a state you're in!
ridussi *ecc* [ri'dussi] VB *vedi* **ridurre**
riduttivo, a [ridut'tivo] AGG: **è un giudizio riduttivo** it's an oversimplification
riduttore [ridut'tore] SM *(Tecn, Chim, Elettr)* reducer
riduzione [ridut'tsjone] SF **1** *(diminuzione: di salario, personale)*: **riduzione (di)** reduction (in), cut (in) **2** *(sconto)* reduction, discount; **una riduzione del 10%** a 10% reduction *o* discount **3** *(di opera letteraria: adattamento)* adaptation; *(: accorciamento)* abridgement; **riduzione televisiva a cura di...** adapted for television by ... **4** *(Mat, Chim, Med)* reduction
riebbi *ecc* [ri'ɛbbi] VB *vedi* **riavere**
riecheggiare [rieked'dʒare] VI *(aus* **essere**) to re-echo; **in questi versi riecheggiano motivi leopardiani** in these lines we find echoes of Leopardi
riedificare [riedifi'kare] VT to rebuild
riedificazione [riedifikat'tsjone] SF rebuilding
rieducare [riedu'kare] VT *(persona, arto)* to re-educate; *(malato)* to rehabilitate
rieducazione [riedukat'tsjone] SF *(vedi vb)* re-education; rehabilitation; **centro di rieducazione** rehabilitation centre
rieleggere [rie'lɛddʒere] VT IRREG to re-elect
rieletto, a [rie'lɛtto] PP *di* **rieleggere**
rielezione [rielet'tsjone] SF re-election
riemergere [rie'mɛrdʒere] VI IRREG *(aus* **essere**) *(sottomarino)* to re-emerge; *(fig: problema)* to re-emerge, come up again
riemerso, a [rie'mɛrso] PP *di* **riemergere**
riempimento [riempi'mento] SM filling (up); *(Edil)*: **materiali di riempimento** filling *sg*
riempire [riem'pire] VB IRREG
■VT *(gen, fig)*: **riempire (di)** to fill *o* fill up (with); *(Culin: farcire)* to stuff (with); **ho riempito il termos di caffè, va bene?** I've filled the flask with coffee, okay?; **riempire un modulo** to fill in *o* out a form; **riempirsi le tasche di** to fill one's pockets with; **gli hanno riempito la testa di sciocchezze** they filled his head with nonsense;
▶ **riempirsi** VIP *(gen)*: **riempirsi (di)** to fill *o* fill up (with); **quel quadro si è riempito di polvere** that painting is covered in dust;
▶ **riempirsi** VR: **riempirsi di** *(cibo)* to stuff o.s. with
riempitivo [riempi'tivo] AGG filling
■SM *(anche fig)* filler
rientrante [rien'trante] AGG *(Archit)* receding
rientranza [rien'trantsa] SF *(di costruzione)* recess; *(di costa)* indentation
rientrare [rien'trare] VI *(aus* **essere**) **1** *(entrare di nuovo)* to come *(o* go) back in **2** *(ritornare)* to return, get back; **rientrare (a casa)** to get back home; **sono rientrato molto tardi** I got back very late; **no, Daniela non è ancora rientrata** no, Daniela isn't back yet; **rientrare alla base** *(Mil)* to return to base; **rientrare in possesso di qc** to regain possession of sth **3** *(fig: far parte di, essere incluso)*: **rientrare in** to be included among, form part of; **non rientra nei miei doveri** it isn't my duty; **non rientriamo nelle spese** we are not within our budget **4** *(superficie, linea)* to curve inwards, go in; *(costa)* to be indented

Rr

rientro [ri'entro] SM (*gen, ritorno*) return; (*di astronave*) re-entry; **l'ora del rientro** (*dal lavoro*) the evening rush hour; **è cominciato il grande rientro (dalle vacanze)** everyone is coming back from holiday
riepilogare [riepilo'gare] VT (*discorso, fatti*) to summarize; **dunque, riepilogando...** to sum up, then ...
riepilogo, ghi [rie'pilogo] SM recapitulation; **fare un riepilogo di qc** to summarize sth
riesame [rie'zame] SM re-examination
riesaminare [riezami'nare] VT to re-examine
riesco *ecc* [ri'ɛsko] VB *vedi* **riuscire**
riessere [ri'ɛssere] VI (*aus* **essere**): **ci risiamo!** (*fam*) we're back to this again!, here we go again!
riesumare [riezu'mare] VT (*cadavere*) to exhume, disinter
riesumazione [riezumat'tsjone] SF (*di cadavere*) exhumation, disinterment
rievocare [rievo'kare] VT (*passato*) to recall; (*commemorare: figura, meriti*) to commemorate
rievocativo, a [rievoka'tivo] AGG (*mostra, cerimonia*) commemorative, memorial *attr*
rievocazione [rievokat'tsjone] SF (*vedi vb*) recalling; commemoration
rifacimento [rifatʃi'mento] SM (*di film*) remake; (*di opera letteraria*) rehashing
rifare [ri'fare] VB IRREG
■VT (*ricominciare*) to redo, do again; (*ricostruire*) to make again; (*nodo*) to tie again, do up again; **lo devo rifare da capo** I've got to do it all over again; **è tutto da rifare!** it will have to be completely redone!; **stai tranquillo, non lo rifarà** don't worry, she won't do it again; **rifarsi la bocca** (*anche fig*) to take away a bad taste; **rifarsi il naso** to have a nose job; **rifarsi gli occhi** to look at something pleasant for a change; **rifare il letto** to make the bed; **rifarsi il trucco** to touch up one's make-up; **rifarsi una vita** to make a new life for o.s.; **rifarsi una verginità** to try to clear one's name;
▶ **rifarsi** VIP **1 rifarsi vivo** to re-appear, turn up again **2** (*ricuperare*) **rifarsi di** (*perdita, spesa*) to recover from; **rifarsi del tempo perduto** to make up for lost time; **rifarsi di qc su qn** (*vendicarsi*) to get one's own back on sb for sth, get even with sb for sth **3** (*riferirsi*) **rifarsi a** (*periodo, fenomeno storico*) to go back to; (*stile, autore*) to follow
rifatto, a [ri'fatto] PP *di* **rifare**
riferimento [riferi'mento] SM reference; **in** *o* **con riferimento a** *or* **facendo riferimento a** with reference to; **in riferimento alla Vostra del...** with reference to your letter of...; **far riferimento a** to refer to; **nell'articolo si fa riferimento al recente scandalo** there's a reference in the article to the recent scandal; **punto di riferimento** (*anche fig*) reference point; **ho preso la stazione come punto di riferimento** I took the station as my reference point
riferire [rife'rire] VT **1** (*raccontare, riportare*) to report; **andare a riferire qc a qn** to go and tell sb sth; **è andato a riferire tutto al professore** he went and told the teacher everything; **riferirò** I'll pass on the message **2** (*attribuire*): **riferire qc a** to attribute sth to
■VI (*aus* **avere**) **riferire (su qc)** to make *o* do a report (on sth)
▶ **riferirsi** VIP: **riferirsi a** to refer to; **non ho capito a cosa si riferisse** I didn't understand what he was referring to
rifilare [rifi'lare] VT **1** (*fam: affibbiare*): **rifilare qc a qn** to palm sth off on sb; **gli ho rifilato un ceffone** I gave him a slap **2** (*tagliare a filo*) to trim
rifinire [rifi'nire] VT (*lavoro*) to finish off; (*opera d'arte, vestito*) to put the finishing touches to
rifinito, a [rifi'nito] AGG (*mobile, abito*) well-finished; **ben rifinito** well finished
rifinitura [rifini'tura] SF (*gen*) finishing touch; (*di mobile, auto*) finish *no pl*
rifiorire [rifjo'rire] VI (*aus* **essere**) (*anche fig: persona*) to bloom again; (*fig: studi, arti*) to flourish again, thrive again
rifiutare [rifju'tare] VT (*gen*) to refuse; (*invito, offerta*) to turn down, decline; (*pretendente*) to turn down; **rifiutare qc a qn** to deny sb sth; **rifiutare di fare qc** to refuse to do sth; **ha rifiutato di pagare la sua parte** he refused to pay his share
▶ **rifiutarsi** VIP: **rifiutarsi di fare qc** to refuse to do sth
rifiuto [ri'fjuto] SM **1** (*diniego*) refusal; **opporre un secco rifiuto** to flatly refuse **2** (*scarto*) waste; **rifiuti** SMPL (*immondizie*) refuse *sg*, rubbish (*Brit*) *sg*, garbage (*Am*), trash (*Am*); **i rifiuti della società** (*fig*) the dregs of society; **rifiuti solidi urbani** solid urban waste
riflessione [rifles'sjone] SF **1** (*meditazione*) reflection, meditation, thought; (*osservazione*) observation, remark; **dopo matura riflessione** after due consideration; **ha risposto dopo un attimo di riflessione** she replied after a moment's thought; **ha fatto delle interessanti riflessioni** he made some interesting observations **2** (*Fis*) reflection
riflessivo, a [rifles'sivo] AGG **1** (*persona*) thoughtful, reflective **2** (*Gramm*) reflexive
riflesso, a [ri'flesso] PP *di* **riflettere**
■AGG (*immagine*) reflected; (*atto*) reflex *attr*
■SM **1** (*di luce*) reflection; (*di capelli: naturale*) light; (*: artificiale*) highlight; (*fig: ripercussione*) effect, repercussion; **il riflesso della luna sul mare** the reflection of the moon in the sea; **di riflesso** indirectly **2** (*Fisiologia*) reflex; **avere i riflessi pronti** to have quick reflexes; **quando si beve non si hanno i riflessi pronti** your reflexes are slower when you've been drinking; **riflesso condizionato** conditioned reflex
riflessologia [riflessolod'dʒia] SF: **riflessologia (plantare)** reflexology
riflessologo, a, gi, ghe [rifles'sɔlogo] SM/F reflexologist
riflettente [riflet'tɛnte] AGG (*Fis*) reflective
riflettere [ri'flɛttere] VB IRREG
■VI (*aus* **avere**) **riflettere (su qc)** (*meditare*) to reflect (upon sth); (*pensare*) to think (over sth); **se ti fermi a riflettere** if you stop and think; **agire senza riflettere** to act without thinking; **ci ho riflettuto su e ho deciso di accettare** I've thought about it and have decided to accept; **riflettendoci su...** on reflection ...
■VT (*Fis: fig*) to reflect
▶ **riflettersi** VR **1** (*rispecchiarsi, anche fig*) to be reflected **2** (*ripercuotersi*) **riflettersi su** to have repercussions on
riflettore [riflet'tore] SM **1** (*Fis, Elettr*) reflector; (*Teatro, TV*) spotlight; (*proiettore*) floodlight; (*Mil*) searchlight; **essere sotto i riflettori** (*fig*) to be in the limelight **2** (*telescopio*) reflecting telescope
riflettuto, a [riflet'tuto] PP *di* **riflettere** (*vi*)
rifluire [riflu'ire] VI (*aus* **essere**) (*scorrere: nuovamente*) to flow again; (*: indietro*) to flow back; (*marea*) to go out
riflusso [ri'flusso] SM (*gen*) flowing back; (*di sangue*) flow; (*di acqua, marea*) ebb; **flusso e riflusso** ebb and flow; **un'epoca di riflusso** an era of nostalgia

rifocillarsi [rifotʃil'larsi] VR to take refreshment
rifondatore, trice [rifonda'tɔre] (*Pol*) AGG of/belonging to Rifondazione Comunista (*Italian left-wing party*)
■SM/F *member (o supporter) of Rifondazione Comunista*
rifondazione [rifondat'tsjone] SF refounding
Rifondazione [rifondat'tjone] SF (*anche:* **Rifondazione Comunista**) Communist Refoundation (*Italian left-wing political party*)
rifondere [ri'fondere] VT IRREG **1** (*rimborsare*) to refund, reimburse; **rifondere le spese a qn** to refund sb's expenses; **rifondere i danni a qn** to compensate sb for damages **1** (*metalli, cera*) to remelt, melt down again
rifondino, a [rifon'dino] (*Pol*) AGG of/belonging to Rifondazione Comunista (*Italian left-wing party*)
■SM/F *member (o supporter) of Rifondazione Comunista*
riforma [ri'forma] SF **1** (*gen*) reform; (*Rel*): **la Riforma** the Reformation; **la riforma del sistema sanitario** the reform of the health service **2** (*Mil: di recluta*) declaration of unfitness for service; (: *di soldato*) discharge (*on health grounds*)
riformare [rifor'mare] VT **1** (*formare di nuovo*) to form again, re-form **2** (*Rel, Pol*) to reform; (*Mil: recluta*) to declare unfit for military service; (: *soldato*) to discharge, invalid out
▶ **riformarsi** VIP (*formarsi di nuovo*) to form again, re-form
riformato [rifor'mato] SM (*Rel*) Protestant; (*Mil: recluta*) recruit unfit for military service; (: *soldato*) discharged soldier
riformatore, trice [riforma'tore] AGG reforming
■SM/F reformer
riformatorio, ri [riforma'tɔrjo] SM community home (*Brit*), reformatory (*Am*)
riformattare [riformat'tare] VT (*Inform*) to reformat
riformista, i, e [rifor'mista] AGG, SM/F reformist
rifornimento [riforni'mento] SM **1** (*operazione*) supplying, providing; (*di carburante*) refuelling; **fare rifornimento di** (*viveri*) to stock up with; (*benzina*) to fill up with; **stazione di rifornimento** filling *o* petrol (*Brit*) *o* gas (*Am*) station **2** **rifornimenti** SMPL (*scorte*) stocks, supplies, provisions
rifornire [rifor'nire] VT: **rifornire di** to supply *o* provide with
▶ **rifornirsi** VR: **rifornirsi di** (*provviste*) to get in a supply of, stock up with; (*benzina*) to re-fuel (with), fill up (with)
rifrangere [ri'frandʒere] VB IRREG
■VT (*Fis*) to refract
▶ **rifrangersi** VIP to be refracted
rifratto, a [ri'fratto] PP *di* **rifrangere**
rifrazione [rifrat'tsjone] SF (*Fis*) refraction
rifuggire [rifud'dʒire] VI (*aus* **essere**) **rifuggire da qc** to be averse to sth, shun sth
rifugiarsi [rifu'dʒarsi] VIP: **rifugiarsi in** (*gen, fig*) to take refuge in; (*da pioggia, freddo*) to (take) shelter in
rifugiato, a [rifu'dʒato] SM/F refugee
rifugio, gi [ri'fudʒo] SM (*gen*) shelter, refuge; (*in montagna*) shelter; (*fig*) refuge; **cercare rifugio in qc/presso qn** to seek refuge in sth/with sb; **rifugio antiaereo** air-raid shelter; **rifugio antiatomico** fallout shelter
rifulgere [ri'fuldʒere] VI IRREG (*aus* **essere** *o* **avere**) (*anche fig*): **rifulgere (di)** to shine (with), glow (with)
rifulso, a [ri'fulso] PP *di* **rifulgere**
rifusione [rifu'zjone] SF (*Tecn*) remelting

rifuso, a [ri'fuzo] PP *di* **rifondere**
riga, ghe ['riga] SF **1** (*linea*) line; (*striscia*) stripe; **a righe** (*foglio*) lined; (*tessuto*) striped; **giallo a righe rosse** yellow with red stripes **2** (*scritta*) line; **ne ho letto solo poche righe** I just read a few lines; **buttare giù due righe** (*note*) to jot down a few notes; **mandami due righe appena arrivi** drop me a line as soon as you arrive **3** (*Mil, Scol: fila*) line, row; (*Sport*) line; **rompete le righe!** break ranks!; **mettersi in riga** to line up; **mettere qn in riga** (*fig*) to make sb toe the line; **rimettersi in riga** (*fig*) to get back into line; **sopra le righe** (*fig*) over the top **4** (*righello*) ruler **5** (*scriminatura*) parting; **farsi la riga in mezzo/da una parte** to put one's hair in a middle parting/side parting
rigaglie [ri'gaʎʎe] SFPL (*Culin*) giblets
rigagnolo [ri'gaɲɲolo] SM rivulet
rigare [ri'gare] VT (*pagina, foglio*) to rule; (*superficie: sfregiare*) to score; **col volto rigato di lacrime** with a tear-stained face
■VI (*aus* **avere**) (*fig*): **rigare dritto** to toe the line, behave; **ti conviene rigare dritto!** you'd better behave!
rigatoni [riga'toni] SMPL (*Culin*) rigatoni; *short, ridged pasta shapes*
rigattiere [rigat'tjɛre] SM junk dealer, secondhand dealer
rigatura [riga'tura] SF (*di pagina, quaderno*) lining, ruling; (*di fucile*) rifling
rigelo [ri'dʒɛlo] SM regelation
rigenerare [ridʒene'rare] VT (*gen, Tecn*) to regenerate; (*forze*) to restore; (*gomma*) to retread, remould (*Brit*), recap (*Am*); **gomma rigenerata** retread, remould, recap
▶ **rigenerarsi** VIP (*gen*) to regenerate; (*ramo, tumore*) to regenerate, grow again
rigenerativo, a [ridʒenera'tivo] AGG (*processo*) regenerating
rigeneratore, trice [ridʒenera'tore] AGG regenerative; **lozione rigeneratrice** (*per i capelli*) restorer; (*per la pelle*) rejuvenating lotion
rigenerazione [ridʒenerat'tsjone] SF regeneration
rigettare [ridʒet'tare] VT **1** (*gettare: di nuovo*) to throw again; (: *indietro*) to throw back **2** (*respingere: proposta*) to reject, turn down; (: *Bio, Med*) to reject **3** (*vomitare*) to vomit, bring *o* throw up
▶ **rigettarsi** VR: **rigettarsi in acqua** to jump back into the water
rigetto [ri'dʒɛtto] SM (*gen, Med*) rejection; **crisi di rigetto** (*Med*) rejection crisis; (*fig*) total rejection
righello [ri'gɛllo] SM ruler
righerò *ecc* [rige'rɔ] VB *vedi* **rigare**
rigidamente [ridʒida'mente] AVV (*gen*) rigidly; (*giudicare*) severely
rigidezza [ridʒi'dettsa], **rigidità** [rigidi'ta] SF (*gen*) rigidity; (*di membra*) stiffness; (*fig: di clima*) harshness, severity, rigours *pl* (*Brit*), rigors *pl* (*Am*); (: *severità*) strictness, sternness; **rigidità cadaverica** rigor mortis
rigido, a ['ridʒido] AGG (*gen*) rigid; (*membra, berretto, colletto*) stiff; (*fig: clima, inverno*) harsh, severe; (: *disciplina, principi*) strict
rigirare [ridʒi'rare] VT (*gen*) to turn; **rigirare il discorso** to change the subject; **rigirare qc tra le mani** to turn sth over in one's hands
▶ **rigirarsi** VR (*voltarsi: di nuovo*) to turn round; (: *nel letto*) to turn over; **girarsi e rigirarsi nel letto** to toss and turn in bed

Rr

rigo, ghi ['rigo] SM (*linea*) line; (*Mus*) staff, stave
rigoglio, gli [ri'goʎʎo] SM (*di piante*) luxuriance; **essere in pieno rigoglio** (*fig: commercio, svilupo*) to be thriving
rigogliosamente [rigoʎʎosa'mente] AVV luxuriantly
rigoglioso, a [rigoʎ'ʎoso] AGG (*pianta, giardino*) luxuriant; (*fig: commercio, sviluppo*) thriving
rigonfiamento [rigonfja'mento] SM (*gonfiore: su parte del corpo*) swelling; (*: su legno, intonaco*) bulge
rigonfiare [rigon'fjare] VT to blow up (again), reinflate
rigonfio, fia, fi, fie [ri'gonfjo] AGG (*vela*) full; (*grembiule, sporta*): **rigonfio di** bulging with
rigore [ri'gore] SM **1** (*di sentenza, legge*) severity; (*di disciplina*) strictness, severity; (*di clima*) severity, harshness, rigours *pl* (*Brit*), rigors *pl* (*Am*); **punire qn con rigore** to punish sb severely; **mettere qn in cella di rigore** (*Mil*) to put sb in solitary confinement; **essere di rigore** (*d'obbligo*) to be compulsory; **"è di rigore l'abito da sera"** "evening dress"; **a rigor di termini** *o* **di logica** strictly speaking; **i rigori dell'inverno** the rigo(u)rs of winter **2** (*Calcio: anche*: calcio di rigore) penalty; **battere un rigore** to take a penalty; **segnare un rigore** to score from a penalty; **area di rigore** penalty area *o* box; **vincere ai rigori** to win on penalties
rigorosamente [rigorosa'mente] AVV (*vedi agg*) rigorously, exactly; severely, harshly; strictly; **seguì rigorosamente le istruzioni** he followed the instructions to the letter
rigorosità [rigorosi'ta] SF (*precisione: di conclusioni*) rigour (*Brit*), rigor (*Am*); (*severità: di costumi*) strictness
rigoroso, a [rigo'roso] AGG (*definizione, logica*) rigorous, exact; (*punizione*) severe, harsh; (*persona, ordine*) strict
rigovernare [rigover'nare] VT (*piatti, stoviglie*) to wash (up); **non ho ancora rigovernato** I haven't done the washing-up yet
riguadagnare [rigwadaɲ'ɲare] VT (*recuperare: velocità*) to make up, regain; (*: terreno*) to regain; (*: stima, affetto*) to win back; **riguadagnare il tempo perduto** to make up for lost time
riguardare [rigwar'dare] VT **1** (*concernere*) to concern, regard; **per quel che mi riguarda** as far as I'm concerned; **per quel che mi riguarda la faccenda è chiusa** as far as I'm concerned the matter is closed; **è un problema che ci riguarda tutti** it's a problem which concerns us all; **è un libro che riguarda la vita dei contadini** it's a book which deals with *o* looks at the life of country people; **sono affari che non ti riguardano** it's none of your business **3** (*curare, tenere da conto*) to look after, take care of **2** (*guardare di nuovo*) to look at again, take another look at; (*controllare*) to check
▶ **riguardarsi** VR (*aver cura di sé*) to look after o.s., take care of o.s.; **ti devi riguardare dalle correnti d'aria** you should stay out of draughts
riguardo [ri'gwardo] SM **1** (*rispetto*) respect; (*considerazione*) consideration, regard; **non ha alcun riguardo per gli altri** he has no consideration for other people; **per riguardo a** out of respect for; **trattare qn col massimo riguardo** to treat sb with the greatest respect; **mancare di riguardo verso** *o* **a qn** to be disrespectful towards sb; **ospite/persona di riguardo** very important guest/person; **aver riguardo delle cose altrui** to respect other people's property; **agire/parlare senza (tanti) riguardi** to act/speak freely **2** **riguardo a** (*a proposito di*) regarding, concerning, as regards, with regard to; about; **cos'hai deciso di fare riguardo all'offerta di lavoro?** what have you decided to do about the job offer?; **riguardo a me** as far as I'm concerned
riguardosamente [rigwardosa'mente] AVV respectfully
riguardoso, a [rigwar'doso] AGG (*rispettoso*) respectful; (*premuroso*) considerate, thoughtful
rigurgitare [rigurdʒi'tare] VI (*aus* **essere**) **rigurgitare da** to gush out from
■ VT (*vomitare*) to bring up
rigurgito [ri'gurdʒito] SM (*Med*) regurgitation; (*fig: ritorno, risveglio*) revival
rilanciare [rilan'tʃare] VT (*lanciare di nuovo: gen*) to throw again; (*: moda*) to bring back; (*: prodotto*) to re-launch; (*Carte*) to raise; **rilanciare un'offerta** (*asta*) to make a higher bid
rilancio, ci [ri'lantʃo] SM (*di prodotto*) re-launching; (*Carte, di offerta*) raising
rilasciamento [rilaʃʃa'mento] SM (*di muscoli*) relaxation
rilasciare [rilaʃ'ʃare] VT **1** (*Amm: passaporto, certificato*) to issue; (*intervista*) to give; **rilasciare una dichiarazione** to make a statement **2** (*persona, prigioniero*) to release; **gli ostaggi sono stati rilasciati ieri** the hostages were released yesterday **3** (*muscoli, tensione, nervi*) to relax
▶ **rilasciarsi** VIP to relax
rilascio, sci [ri'laʃʃo] SM (*di documento*) issue; (*di prigioniero*) release
rilassamento [rilassa'mento] SM (*gen, Med*) relaxation
rilassare [rilas'sare] VT (*distendere: nervi, muscoli*) to relax; (*: persona*) to help to relax
▶ **rilassarsi** VR (*gen*) to relax
▶ **rilassarsi** VIP (*fig: disciplina*) to become slack
rilassatezza [rilassa'tettsa] SF (*fig: di costumi, disciplina*) laxity
rilassato, a [rilas'sato] AGG (*persona, muscoli*) relaxed; (*disciplina, costumi*) lax
rilegare [rile'gare] VT (*libro, volume*) to bind
rilegato [rile'gato] AGG: **libro rilegato in pelle** leather-bound book
rilegatore, trice [rilega'tore] SM/F bookbinder
rilegatura [rilega'tura] SF binding
rileggere [ri'lɛddʒere] VT IRREG (*leggere di nuovo*) to read again, reread; (*: per correggere*) to read over; **l'ho letto e riletto cento volte** I've read it over and over again
rilento [ri'lɛnto] **a rilento** AVV slowly; **gli affari vanno a rilento** business is slow
riletta [ri'lɛtta] SF reread
riletto, a [ri'lɛtto] PP *di* **rileggere**
rilettura [rilet'tura] SF (*vedi vt*) rereading; reading over; (*nuova interpretazione*) new interpretation
rilevamento [rileva'mento] SM (*topografico, statistico, geologico*) survey; (*Naut*) bearing
rilevante [rile'vante] AGG (*notevole*) remarkable, considerable; (*importante*) important

LO SAPEVI...?
rilevante non si traduce mai con la parola inglese ***relevant***

rilevanza [rile'vantsa] SF importance
rilevare [rile'vare] VT **1** (*notare*) to notice; **dai sintomi non si rileva alcun pericolo immediato** going by the symptoms, there is no immediate danger; **rilevo con soddisfazione che...** I note with satisfaction that ...; **far rilevare a qn che...** to point out to sb that ... **2** (*raccogliere: dati*) to gather, collect; (*Topografia*) to

survey; (*Naut*: *posizione*) to plot; **la polizia non ha potuto rilevare alcun indizio** the police have been unable to find any evidence **3** (*Comm*: *negozio, ditta*) to take over **4** (*Mil*: *sentinella*) to relieve **5** (*levare di nuovo*) to take off again

rilevazione [rilevat'tsjone] SF survey

rilievo [ri'ljɛvo] SM **1** (*gen, Arte, Geog*) relief; **alto/basso rilievo** high/bas-relief; **i rilievi alpini** the Alps; **in rilievo** (*gen*) in relief; (*ricamo*) raised; **carta in rilievo** relief map **2** (*importanza*) importance; **dar rilievo a** *o* **mettere in rilievo qc** (*fig*) to stress *o* highlight sth, bring sth out; **di poco/nessun rilievo** (*fig*) of little/no importance; **un personaggio di rilievo** an important person **3** (*osservazione*) point, remark **4** (*Topografia, Statistica*) survey

riloga, ghe [ri'lɔga] SF curtain pole

rilucente [rilu'tʃɛnte] AGG bright, shining

riluttante [rilut'tante] AGG reluctant; **essere riluttante a fare qc** to be reluctant to do sth

riluttantemente [riluttante'mente] AVV reluctantly

riluttanza [rilut'tantsa] SF (*gen*) reluctance; **con riluttanza** reluctantly

riluttare [rilut'tare] VI (*aus* **avere**) **riluttare a fare qc** to be reluctant to do sth

rima ['rima] SF (*gen*) rhyme; (*verso*) verse; **far rima con** to rhyme with; **"head" fa rima con "red"** "head" rhymes with "red"; **mettere in rima** to put into rhyme; **rispondere a qn per le rime** (*fig*) to give as good as one gets; **rima baciata** rhyming couplet; **rime alternate** alternate rhymes

rimandare [riman'dare] VT **1** (*mandare*: *di nuovo*) to send again; (: *indietro*) to send back, return; **rimandare qn a** (*fig*: *far riferimento*) to refer sb to **2** (*posporre*: *partenza, appuntamento*): **rimandare (a)** to postpone (till), put off (till); **abbiamo dovuto rimandare la gita di qualche giorno** we had to put off the trip for a few days; **non rimandare a domani quel che puoi fare oggi** (*Proverbio*) don't put off till tomorrow what you can do today **3** (*Scol*): **rimandare qn (a settembre)** to make sb resit (in September); **essere rimandato** to have to resit one's exams; **è stato rimandato in matematica** he has a resit in Maths (*Brit*) *o* Math (*Am*)

rimando [ri'mando] SM (*in testo*) cross-reference; **di rimando** (*fig*) in return

rimaneggiare [rimaned'dʒare] VT (*testo*) to reshape, recast; (*ministero*) to reshuffle

rimanente [rima'nɛnte] AGG remaining
■ SM (*resto*): **il rimanente** the rest, the remainder; **i (o le) rimanenti** (*persone*) the rest *pl* (of them), the others

rimanenza [rima'nɛntsa] SF (*gen*) rest, remainder; **rimanenze di magazzino** (*Comm*) left-over stock *sg*, unsold stock *sg*

rimanere [rima'nere] VI IRREG (*aus* **essere**)
1 (*in luogo*) to stay, remain; **mi piacerebbe rimanere qualche altro giorno** I'd like to stay a few more days; **rimanere a casa/a letto** to stay *o* remain at home/in bed; **rimanere a cena** to stay for dinner; **rimanere a guardare la televisione** to stay and watch television; **che rimanga tra noi** (*fig*: *segreto*) this is just between ourselves; **dove eravamo rimasti?** (*fig*) where were we?
2 (*in una condizione*) to stay, remain; **rimanere in piedi** (*non sedersi*) to remain standing; (*non coricarsi*) to stay up; **rimanere senza benzina/pane** to run out of petrol (*Brit*) *o* gas (*Am*)/bread; **rimanere al buio/senz'acqua** to have one's electricity *o* water cut off; **rimanere indietro** to be left behind; **rimanere indietro col lavoro/con l'affitto** (*fig*) to fall behind with one's work/with the rent; **rimaniamo d'accordo così** that's agreed then, that's settled then; **rimanere amici** to remain friends; **rimanere in buoni rapporti** to remain on good terms; **rimanere senza parole** to be (left) speechless; **sono rimasto senza parole** I was speechless; **rimanere** *o* **rimanerci male** to be hurt *o* offended; **c'è rimasta molto male** she was really hurt; **rimanere** *o* **rimanerci secco** (*fam*: *morire*) to drop dead; **rimanere sorpreso** to be surprised
3 (*divenire*): **rimanere orfano** to become *o* be left an orphan; **rimanere vedovo** to be left a widower; **rimanere incinta** to get pregnant; **rimanere ferito** to be injured; **è rimasto ferito in un incidente d'auto** he was injured in a car accident
4 (*sussistere*) to be left, remain; **è l'unico parente che le rimane** he's her only remaining relative; **coi pochi soldi che mi rimangono** with what little money I have left; **rimangono da fare 15 km** there are still 15 km to go; **ne è rimasto solo uno** there's only one left; **ne rimane ancora un po'** there's still some left; **non rimane più niente** there's nothing left; **rimane ancora molto da fare** there's still a lot to do; **non ti rimane altro (da fare) che accettare** all you can do is accept; **mi rimani solo tu** you're all I have left; **mi rimane ben poco da dire se non…** I've little left to say except …; **rimane da vedere se…** it remains to be seen whether …

rimangiare [riman'dʒare] VT to eat again; **rimangiarsi la parola/una promessa** (*fig*) to go back on one's word/one's promise

rimango *ecc* [ri'mango] VB *vedi* **rimanere**

rimarcare [rimar'kare] VT to remark, observe

rimarchevole [rimar'kevole] AGG (*notevole*) remarkable

rimare [ri'mare] VT, VI (*aus* **avere**) to rhyme

rimarginare [rimardʒi'nare] VT, VI (*aus* **essere**), **rimarginarsi** VIP to heal

rimasto, a [ri'masto] PP *di* **rimanere**

rimasuglio, gli [rima'suʎʎo] SM (*di stoffa*) remnant; (*di cibo*): **rimasugli** SMPL leftovers *pl*

rimbalzare [rimbal'tsare] VI (*aus* **essere** *o* **avere**) **rimbalzare (su)** (*pavimento*) to bounce (off); (*muro*) to rebound (off), bounce back; (*sogg*: *proiettile*) to ricochet (off); **far rimbalzare una palla** to bounce a ball

rimbalzo [rim'baltso] SM (*di palla*) bounce; (*di proiettile*) ricochet; **di rimbalzo** on the rebound; (*fig*) indirectly

rimbambire [rimbam'bire] (*pegg*) VI (*aus* **essere**), **rimbambirsi** VIP to become stupid, grow foolish; **rimbambire** *o* **rimbambirsi con l'età** to become senile

rimbambito, a [rimbam'bito] AGG (*pegg*) senile; **un vecchio rimbambito** a senile old man

rimbeccare [rimbek'kare] VT (*persona*) to answer back; (*offesa*) to return
▶ **rimbeccarsi** VR (*uso reciproco*: *litigare*) to bicker

rimbecillire [rimbetʃil'lire] VT, VI, VIP = **rincretinire**

rimbecillito, a [rimbetʃil'lito] AGG (*rimbambito*) foolish, stupid; (*frastornato*) stunned, stupefied

rimboccare [rimbok'kare] VT (*orlo*) to turn up; (*coperta*) to tuck in; (*pantaloni*) to turn *o* roll up; **rimboccarsi le maniche** (*anche fig*) to roll up one's sleeves

rimbombante [rimbom'bante] AGG (*vedi vb*) resounding; roaring, rumbling; thundering; booming

rimbombare [rimbom'bare] VI (*aus* **avere** *o* **essere**)

Rr

(*suono, passi*) to resound; (*tuono*) to roar, rumble; (*cannonata*) to roar, thunder; (*voce*) boom

rimbombo [rim'bombo] SM (*suono*) sound; (*di voce*) boom; (*di tuono*) roar, rumble; (*di cannonata*) roar, thunder

rimborsare [rimbor'sare] VT (*persona*) to pay back, reimburse; (*spese, biglietto*) to refund, reimburse; **rimborsare qc a qn** to reimburse sb for sth; **mi hanno rimborsato il prezzo del biglietto** they refunded the price of the ticket

rimborso [rim'borso] SM repayment, reimbursement; (*di spese, biglietto*) refund; **rimborso d'imposta** tax rebate

rimboschimento [rimboski'mento] SM re(af)forestation

rimboschire [rimbos'kire] VT to re(af)forest

rimbrottare [rimbrot'tare] VT to reproach

rimbrotto [rim'brɔtto] SM reproach; **fare un rimbrotto a qn** to reproach sb

rimediabile [rime'djabile] AGG (*errore*) remediable, which can be remedied

rimediare [rime'djare] VI (*gen*) to remedy; **rimediare a qc** to remedy sth; **e adesso come si rimedia?** what can we do about it now?; **ha cercato di rimediare al male fatto** he tried to make amends for the wrong he had done
■ VT (*fam*: *procurarsi*) to scrape up *o* together

rimedio, di [ri'mɛdjo] SM (*gen*) remedy; (*cura*) remedy, cure; **un ottimo rimedio contro il raffreddore** an excellent cure for a cold; **un rimedio per tutti i mali** a panacea, a cure-all; **porre rimedio a qc** to remedy sth; **occorre porre rimedio alla situazione** we must remedy the situation; **non c'è rimedio** there's no way out, there's nothing to be done about it; **è una situazione senza rimedio** it's a situation which cannot be remedied

rimescolare [rimesko'lare] VT to mix well, stir well; (*carte*) to shuffle; **sentirsi rimescolare il sangue** (*per paura*) to feel one's blood run cold; (*per rabbia*) to feel one's blood boil

rimescolio, lii [rimesko'lio] SM (*turbamento*) shock; (*trambusto*) bustle

rimessa [ri'messa] SF **1** (*per veicoli*) garage; (*per aerei*) hangar **2** (*Comm*: *di merce*) shipment, consignment; (: *di denaro*) remittance **3** (*Tennis*) return **4** (*Sport*): **rimessa in gioco laterale** (*Calcio*) throw-in; (*Rugby*) line-out; **rimessa in gioco dal fondo** (*Calcio*) goal kick; (*Rugby*) drop-out

rimesso, a [ri'messo] PP *di* **rimettere**

rimestare [rimes'tare] VT (*mescolare*) to mix well, stir well; (*fig*: *passato*) to drag up again

rimettere [ri'mettere] VB IRREG
■ VT **1** (*mettere*: *di nuovo*) to put back; (*indossare*) to put back on; **l'ho rimesso subito sul tavolo** I put it back on the table immediately; **rimettere mano a qc** to take up sth again; **rimettere a nuovo** (*casa ecc*) to do up (*Brit*) *o* over (*Am*) **2** (*affidare*: *decisione*): **rimettere a qn** to refer to sb, leave to sb; **rimettere l'anima a Dio** to entrust one's soul to God **3** (*perdonare*: *peccato*) to forgive; (*condonare*: *pena*) to quash; (: *debito*) to remit **4** (*inviare*: *merce*) to deliver; (: *somma*) to remit **5** (*Sport*: *pallone*) to throw in; (*Tennis*) to return **6** (*vomitare*) to bring up **7** (*perdere*): **rimetterci** to lose; **quando l'ho venduto ci ho rimesso un sacco di soldi** when I sold it I lost a lot of money; **rimetterci di tasca propria** to be out of pocket; **rimetterci la salute** to ruin one's health; **rimetterci la pelle** to lose one's life; **cosa ci rimetti?** what have you got to lose?;
▶ **rimettersi** VIP **1** (*mettersi di nuovo*) **rimettersi a fare qc** to start doing sth again; **rimettersi in cammino** to set off again; **dopo una breve sosta ci siamo rimessi in cammino** after a short stop we set off again; **rimettersi al lavoro** to start working again; **rimettersi a dormire** to go back to sleep; **rimettersi con qn** to get back together with sb **2** (*affidarsi*) **rimettersi a** to trust **3** (*riprendersi*) to recover; **non si è ancora rimesso dall'operazione** he hasn't yet recovered from the operation; **rimettersi in forze** to regain *o* recover one's strength; **rimettersi in salute** to get better, recover one's health; **rimettersi da uno shock** to recover from a shock; **il tempo si è rimesso al bello** the weather has cleared up;
▶ **rimettersi** VR (*uso reciproco*) **rimettersi insieme** to get back together

riminese [rimi'nese] AGG of *o* from Rimini
■ SM/F inhabitant *o* native of Rimini

rimirare [rimi'rare] VT to gaze at
▶ **rimirarsi** VR to gaze at o.s., admire o.s.

rimisi *ecc* [ri'mizi] VB *vedi* **rimettere**

rimmel® ['rimmel] SM INV mascara

rimodernamento [rimoderna'mento] SM modernization

rimodernare [rimoder'nare] VT (*gen*) to modernize; (*vestito*) to remodel

rimonta [ri'monta] SF (*Sport, gen*) recovery; **fare una rimonta in classifica** to climb back up the league

rimontare [rimon'tare] VT **1** (*montare di nuovo*: *meccanismo*) to reassemble, put back together again; (: *tenda*) to put up again **2** (*risalire*): **rimontare la corrente** to go upstream
■ VI (*aus* **essere**) **1** **rimontare in** (*macchina, carrozza*) to get back into; **rimontare a cavallo** *or* **rimontare in sella** to remount; **rimontare su una bici** to get back on a bike **2** (*Sport*) to close the gap

rimorchiare [rimor'kjare] VT (*veicolo*) to tow; (*nave*) to tug; **ci può rimorchiare fino all'officina?** could you tow us to the garage?; **rimorchiare qn** (*fig fam*) to pick sb up

rimorchiatore [rimorkja'tore] SM (*Naut*) tug(boat)

rimorchio, chi [ri'mɔrkjo] SM **1** (*operazione*) towing; **cavo da rimorchio** towrope; **andare a rimorchio** to be towed; **prendere a rimorchio** to tow **2** (*veicolo trainato*) trailer; **autocarro con rimorchio** articulated lorry (*Brit*), semi(trailer) (*Am*)

rimordere [ri'mɔrdere] VT IRREG (*fig*): **non ti rimorde la coscienza?** isn't your conscience bothering you?

rimorso, a [ri'mɔrso] PP *di* **rimordere**
■ SM remorse; **non ha dimostrato alcun rimorso** he showed no remorse; **essere preso dai rimorsi** to be stricken with remorse; **avere il rimorso di aver fatto qc** to deeply regret having done sth

rimosso, a [ri'mɔsso] PP *di* **rimuovere**

rimostranza [rimos'trantsa] SF protest, complaint; **fare le proprie rimostranze a qn** to remonstrate with sb

rimovibile [rimo'vibile] AGG removable

rimozione [rimot'tsjone] SF **1** (*gen*) removal; (*di veicolo*) towing away; **"rimozione forzata"** "illegally parked vehicles will be towed away"; **"zona rimozione"** "vehicles will be towed away" **2** (*da incarico*) dismissal **3** (*Psic*) repression

rimpaginare [rimpadʒi'nare] VT (*Tip*) to repaginate, make up again

rimpallo [rim'pallo] SM (*Calcio*) bounce

rimpastare [rimpas'tare] VT **1** (*pasta lievitata*) to knead again; (*cemento*) to mix again **2** (*Pol: governo*) to reshuffle

rimpasto [rim'pasto] SM (*Pol*) reshuffle; **rimpasto ministeriale** cabinet reshuffle

rimpatriare [rimpa'trjare] VT to repatriate; **sono stati rimpatriati** they have been repatriated
■ VI (*aus* **essere**) to return to one's country

rimpatriata [rimpa'trjata] SF (*fam*): **fare una rimpatriata** to have a get-together *o* reunion

rimpatrio, tri [rim'patrio] SM repatriation; **ottenere il rimpatrio** to be repatriated

rimpiangere [rim'pjandʒere] VT IRREG (*gen*) to regret; (*passato, giovinezza*) to look back on with regret; **rimpiangere di (non) aver fatto qc** to regret (not) having done sth; **ora rimpiange di non essere andato all'università** he regrets not having gone to university

rimpianto, a [rim'pjanto] PP *di* **rimpiangere**
■ AGG (*persona, periodo*) sadly missed
■ SM regret; **non aver rimpianti** to have no regrets

rimpiattino [rimpjat'tino] SM (*gioco*) hide-and-seek, hide-and-go-seek (*Am*)

rimpiazzare [rimpjat'tsare] VT to replace

rimpiazzo [rim'pjattso] SM (*persona, cosa*) replacement

rimpicciolire [rimpittʃo'lire] VT to make smaller
■ VI (*aus* **essere**), **rimpicciolirsi** VIP to become smaller

rimpinzare [rimpin'tsare] (*fam*) VT: **rimpinzare (di)** to cram *o* stuff with
▶ **rimpinzarsi** VR: **rimpinzarsi (di)** to stuff o.s. (with)

rimpolpare [rimpol'pare] VT (*ingrassare*) to fatten (up); (*fig: articolo, discorso, finanze*) to pad out, fill out

rimpossessarsi [rimposses'sarsi] VIP: **rimpossessarsi (di) qc** to take sth back

rimproverare [rimprove'rare] VT (*figlio, scolaro*) to scold, tell off, rebuke; (*dipendente*) to reprimand; **l'hanno rimproverato perché era tornato tardi** he was told off for coming home late; **rimproverare qc a qn** to reproach sb with sth; **non ho niente da rimproverarmi** I've nothing to reproach myself with

rimprovero [rim'prɔvero] SM reproach; **fare un rimprovero a qn** to reproach sb; (*bambino*) to tell sb off; **di rimprovero** (*tono, occhiata*) reproachful; (*parole*) of reproach

rimuginare [rimudʒi'nare] VT: **rimuginare qc** to turn sth over in one's mind; **che starà rimuginando?** what can he be brooding over *o* about?

rimunerare [rimune'rare] VT (*retribuire*) to remunerate; **un lavoro ben rimunerato** a well-paid job

rimunerativo, a [rimunera'tivo] AGG (*lavoro, attività*) remunerative, profitable

rimunerazione [rimunerat'tsjone] SF (*retribuzione*) remuneration; (*ricompensa*) reward

rimuovere [ri'mwɔvere] VT IRREG **1** (*gen, Med*) to remove; (*fig: dubbio*) to remove, eliminate; (*: sospetto*) to eliminate; (*: ostacolo*) to get rid of; **rimuovere qn da una carica** to dismiss sb; **rimuovere qn da un proposito** to deter sb from a purpose **2** (*Psic*) to repress

rinascere [ri'naʃʃere] VI IRREG (*aus* **essere**) (*persona*) to be born again; (*pianta*) to sprout again; (*fig: speranza, interesse*) to be revived; **sentirsi rinascere** to feel a new man (*o* woman)

rinascimentale [rinaʃʃimen'tale] AGG Renaissance *attr*, of the Renaissance

Rinascimento [rinaʃʃi'mento] SM: **il Rinascimento** the Renaissance
▷ www.insr.it/

rinascita [ri'naʃʃita] SF (*fig*) rebirth, revival

rinato, a [ri'nato] PP *di* **rinascere**

rincagnato, a [rinkaɲ'ɲato] AGG: **avere il muso rincagnato** to be pug-faced

rincalzare [rinkal'tsare] VT (*coperte, lenzuola*) to tuck in; (*palo, albero*) to prop up, support

rincalzo [rin'kaltso] SM **1** (*sostegno*) prop, support; (*Mil*): **truppe di rincalzo** reserves **2** (*Sport: giocatore*) reserve (player)

rincarare [rinka'rare] VT (*prezzi*) to raise, put up; (*prodotto*) to raise *o* increase the price of; **rincarare la dose** (*fig*) to pile it on
■ VI (*aus* **essere**) (*prezzo*) to go up, rise; (*prodotto*) to go up (in price), become more expensive; **la benzina è rincarata** petrol has gone up

rincaro [rin'karo] SM: **rincaro (di)** (*prezzi, costo della vita*) increase (in); (*prodotto*) increase in the price (of)

rincartare [rinkar'tare] VT to rewrap

rincasare [rinka'sare] VI (*aus* **essere**) to return home, go (*o* come) back home; **è rincasato molto tardi** he got home very late; **no, Maria non è ancora rincasata** no, Maria isn't back yet

rinchiudere [rin'kjudere] VB IRREG
■ VT: **rinchiudere (in)** (*gen*) to shut up (in); (*persona: in prigione*) to shut *o* lock up (in); **far rinchiudere qn in prigione/manicomio** to have sb put away (in prison/ in a madhouse);
▶ **rinchiudersi** VR: **rinchiudersi in** (*stanza*) to shut o.s. up in; (*: a chiave*) to lock o.s. up in; **rinchiudersi in un convento/monastero** to withdraw into a convent/ monastery; **rinchiudersi in se stesso** to withdraw into o.s.; **si è rinchiuso in un mutismo assoluto** he maintained a stubborn silence

rinchiuso, a [rin'kjuso] PP *di* **rinchiudere**

rincitrullire [rintʃitrul'lire] VT, VI, VIP = **rincretinire**

rincivilire [rintʃivi'lire] = **incivilire**

rincoglionire [rinkoʎʎo'nire] (*fam*) VT, VI, VIP = **rincretinire**

rincominciare [rinkomin'tʃare] = **ricominciare**

rincontrare [rinkon'trare] VT to meet again
▶ **rincontrarsi** VR (*uso reciproco*) to meet (each other) again

rincorare [rinko'rare] VT to cheer up
▶ **rincorarsi** VIP to cheer up

rincorrere [rin'korrere] VB IRREG
■ VT to chase, run after; (*fig: sogno, chimere*) to pursue; **l'ho rincorso ma non sono riuscito ad acchiapparlo** I ran after him but I couldn't catch him;
▶ **rincorrersi** VR (*uso reciproco*) to run after each other; **giocare a rincorrersi** to play tag

rincorsa [rin'korsa] SF (*Sport*) run-up; **prendere la rincorsa** (*atleta*) to take one's run-up; **ha preso la rincorsa prima di saltare** she took a run-up before she jumped; **prendi la rincorsa!** take a run at it!

rincorso, a [rin'korso] PP *di* **rincorrere**

rincrescere [rin'kreʃʃere] VB IMPERS IRREG: **mi rincresce che...** I'm sorry that ..., I regret that ...; **mi rincresce che tu non stia bene** I'm sorry you're not well; **mi rincresce di non poterlo fare** I'm sorry I can't do it, I regret being unable to do it; **se non ti rincresce vorrei pensarci su** if you don't mind I'd like to think it over

rincrescimento [rinkreʃʃi'mento] SM regret; **con mio grande rincrescimento** much to my regret

Rr

rincresciuto, a [rinkreʃʃuto] PP *di* **rincrescere**
rincretinire [rinkreti'nire] VT: **rincretinire qn** (*gen*) to make sb stupid; (*sogg*: *età*) to make sb feeble-minded; (: *televisione*) to addle sb's brain; (: *chiacchiere*) to make sb's head spin *o* go round; **tutto questo rumore mi rincretinisce** I can't think straight with all this noise
■ VI (*aus* **essere**), **rincretinirsi** VIP (*gen*) to become stupid; (*per l'età*) to become senile
rinculare [rinku'lare] VI (*aus* **avere**) (*arma*) to recoil
rinculo [rin'kulo] SM (*di arma*) recoil
rinfacciare [rinfat'tʃare] VT: **rinfacciare qc a qn** to cast sth up at sb, throw sth in sb's face
rinfocolare [rinfoko'lare] VT (*fig*: *odio, passioni*) to rekindle; (: *risentimento, rabbia*) to stir up;;
rinforzare [rinfor'tsare] VT (*muro, argomento, gruppo*) to reinforce; (*muscoli, posizione, prestigio*) to strengthen; (*presa, nodo*) to tighten
■ VI (*aus* **essere**), **rinforzarsi** VIP (*persona*) to become *o* grow stronger; (*amicizia, legame*) to strengthen
rinforzo [rin'fɔrtso] SM **1 mettere un rinforzo a** (*gen*) to strengthen; **di rinforzo** (*asse, sbarra*) strengthening; (*esercito*) supporting; (*personale*) extra, additional **2** (*Mil*): **rinforzi** SMPL reinforcements
rinfrancare [rinfran'kare] VT (*persona*) to encourage, reassure; (*spirito*) to cheer
► **rinfrancarsi** VIP to be reassured
rinfrescante [rinfres'kante] AGG (*bibita*) refreshing
rinfrescare [rinfres'kare] VT (*gen*) to cool (down); (*aria*) to cool, freshen; (*fig*: *pareti, soffitto, abiti*) to freshen up; **il temporale ha rinfrescato l'aria** the storm freshened the air; **rinfrescarsi la gola** to quench one's thirst; **rinfrescarsi il viso** to splash one's face; **rinfrescare la memoria a qn** to refresh sb's memory
■ VI (*aus* **essere**) (*tempo*) to grow *o* get cooler
► **rinfrescarsi** VR (*persona*: *con bibita*) to have something to drink; (: *con doccia, ecc.*) to freshen up; **vorrei rinfrescarmi un po'** I'd like to freshen up a bit
rinfresco, schi [rin'fresko] SM **1** (*ricevimento*) reception; (*festa*) party **2 rinfreschi** SMPL (*cibi e bevande*) refreshments
rinfusa [rin'fuza] **alla rinfusa** AVV higgledy-piggledy, in confusion
ringalluzzire [ringallut'tsire] (*scherz*) VT to make cocky
■ VI (*aus* **essere**), **ringalluzzirsi** VIP to get cocky
ringhiare [rin'gjare] VI (*aus* **avere**) to growl, snarl
ringhiera [rin'gjɛra] SF (*di balcone*) railing; (*di scale*) banisters *pl*
ringhio, ghi ['ringjo] SM growl, snarl
ringhioso, a [rin'gjoso] AGG growling, snarling
ringiovanimento [rindʒovani'mento] SM rejuvenation
ringiovanire [rindʒova'nire] VT: **ringiovanire qn** (*sogg*: *vestito, acconciatura*) to make sb look younger; (: *vacanze*) to rejuvenate sb; **quel taglio la ringiovanisce molto** that hair style makes her look much younger
■ VI (*aus* **essere**), **ringiovanirsi** VIP to become (*o* look) younger; **sembra ringiovanita di dieci anni** she looks ten years younger
ringraziamento [ringrattsja'mento] SM thanks *pl*; **gli ho mandato i miei ringraziamenti** I sent him my thanks; **lettera/biglietto di ringraziamento** thank-you letter/card; **bel ringraziamento!** (*iro*) thanks for nothing!; **il giorno del Ringraziamento** (*negli USA*) Thanksgiving (Day)
ringraziare [ringrat'tsjare] VT to thank; **ringraziare qn di qc/per aver fatto qc** to thank sb for sth/for doing sth; **vi ringrazio per avermi ospitato a Edimburgo** thank you for putting me up in Edinburgh; **ti ringrazio** thank you; **non so come ringraziarti** I don't know how to thank you; **se n'è andato senza neppure ringraziare** he left without even saying thank you *o* without as much as a thank you; **sia ringraziato il Cielo!** thank heavens!
rinnegare [rinne'gare] VT (*fede, idee, partito*) to renounce; (*famiglia, figlio, origini*) to disown, repudiate
rinnegato, a [rinne'gato] AGG, SM/F renegade
rinnovabile [rinno'vabile] AGG renewable
rinnovamento [rinnova'mento] SM (*morale, civile*) renewal; (*economico*) revival
rinnovare [rinno'vare] VT (*gen, fig*) to renew; **devo rinnovare l'abbonamento ferroviario** I need to renew my season ticket; **quest'anno non gli hanno rinnovato il contratto** his contract hasn't been renewed this year; **rinnovare l'arredamento** to buy new furnishings; **l'intero personale è stato rinnovato** the entire staff has been replaced
► **rinnovarsi** VIP (*ripetersi*: *fenomeno, occasione*) to be repeated, recur

LO SAPEVI...?
rinnovare non si traduce mai con la parola inglese ***renovate***

rinnovatore, trice [rinnova'tore] AGG renewing
rinnovo [rin'nɔvo] SM (*di contratto*) renewal; **"chiuso per rinnovo (dei) locali"** (*negozio*) "closed for alterations"
rinoceronte [rinotʃe'ronte] SM rhinoceros
rinomato, a [rino'mato] AGG (*specialista, ristorante*) renowned, famous, celebrated; (*marca*) well-known
rinsaldare [rinsal'dare] VT (*fig*: *vincoli, amicizia*) to strengthen
► **rinsaldarsi** VIP to get stronger, be strengthened
rinsanire [rinsa'nire] VI (*aus* **essere**) to become sane again
rinsavire [rinsa'vire] VI (*aus* **essere**) (*anche fig*) to come to one's senses
rinsecchire [rinsek'kire] VI (*aus* **essere**) (*ramo, pianta*) to shrivel up, wither; (*persona*) to grow gaunt, grow thin
rinsecchito, a [rinsek'kito] AGG (*vecchio, albero*) thin, gaunt
rinserrarsi [rinser'rarsi] VR: **rinserrarsi in casa** to lock o.s. up at home
rintanarsi [rinta'narsi] VIP (*animale*) to go into its den; (*persona*: *nascondersi*) to hide; **rintanarsi in casa** to shut o.s. up in the house
rintoccare [rintok'kare] VI (*aus* **avere**) (*campana*) to toll; (*ora, orologio*) to strike
rintocco, chi [rin'tokko] SM toll; **i rintocchi della campana** the tolling of the bell
rintontire [rinton'tire] VT (*sogg*: *botta*) to stun, daze
■ VI (*aus* **essere**), **rintontirsi** VIP to become dazed
rintontito, a [rinton'tito] AGG (*stordito*) dazed, stunned
rintracciare [rintrat'tʃare] VT (*selvaggina, ladro, persona assente*) to track down; (*persona scomparsa, documento*) to trace; **la polizia sta cercando di rintracciare i testimoni** the police are trying to trace the witnesses
rintronare [rintro'nare] VT (*fam*: *cervello*) to stun; (: *orecchi*) to deafen
■ VI (*aus* **essere** *o* **avere**) (*tuono, cannone*) to boom, roar; **la casa rintronava sotto i colpi** the blows echoed round the house
rintronato, a [rintro'nato] AGG dazed

rintuzzare [rintut'tsare] VT (*ribattere*) to refute

rinuncia, ce [ri'nuntʃa] SF (*gen, Rel*) renunciation; **rinuncia a** (*carica*) resignation from; (*eredità*) relinquishment of; **rinuncia agli atti del giudizio** (*Dir*) abandonment of a claim; **una vita di rinunce** a life of sacrifice

rinunciare [rinun'tʃare] VI (*aus* **avere**) **rinunciare a** to give up, renounce; (*incarico*) to turn down; (*trono, eredità*) to renounce; **ho dovuto rinunciare al viaggio in Giappone** I had to give up my trip to Japan; **rinunciare a fare qc** to give up doing sth; **rinunciò a presentarsi come candidato** he decided not to stand as a candidate; **ci rinuncio!** I give up!

rinunciatario, ria, ri, rie [rinuntʃa'tarjo] AGG renunciatory, defeatist

rinunzia *ecc* [ri'nuntsja] SF = **rinuncia** *ecc*

rinvasare [rinva'zare] VT to re-pot

rinvenimento [rinveni'mento] SM **1** (*ritrovamento*) recovery; (*scoperta*) discovery **2** (*dopo svenimento*) coming to, recovery

rinvenire [rinve'nire] VB IRREG

■ VT (*trovare*) to discover, find out; (: *oggetto smarrito*) to recover, find

■ VI (*aus* **essere**) (*persona*) to come round, regain consciousness; (*fiori*) to revive; **far rinvenire** (*funghi secchi*) to reconstitute

rinvenuto, a [rinve'nuto] PP *di* **rinvenire**

rinverdire [rinver'dire] VI (*aus* **essere**) (*bosco, ramo*) to become green again

rinvestire [rinves'tire] VT (*Econ*) to reinvest

rinviare [rinvi'are] VT **1** (*mandare indietro: pacco*) to send back, return; (: *persona*) to send away; (*Sport: pallone*) to return **2** (*differire*): **rinviare (a/di)** (*partenza, manifestazione*) to put off (till/for), postpone (till/for); (*seduta*) to adjourn (till/for); **rinviare una riunione ad altra data** to put off *o* postpone a meeting till a later date **3** (*in testo, regolamento*): **rinviare qn a** to refer sb to **4** (*Dir*): **rinviare a giudizio** to indict

rinvigorire [rinvigo'rire] VT to reinvigorate, strengthen

■ VI (*aus* **essere**), **rinvigorirsi** VIP to regain strength

rinvio, vii [rin'vio] SM **1** (*gen*) postponement; (*restituzione*) return; (*Dir*) adjournment; **rinvio a giudizio** (*Dir*) indictment **2** (*in testo: rimando*) cross-reference **3** (*Sport: di pallone*) clearance

riò *ecc* [ri'ɔ] VB *vedi* **riavere**

rioccupare [riokku'pare] VT to reoccupy

Rio de Janeiro ['rio de dʒa'nɛiro] SF Rio de Janeiro

rionale [rio'nale] AGG (*mercato, cinema*) local, district *attr*

rione [ri'one] SM district, neighbourhood, quarter

riordinamento [riordina'mento] SM (*di ente, azienda*) reorganization

riordinare [riordi'nare] VT (*armadio, casa, scaffali*) to tidy up; (*finanze, amministrazione*) to reorganize; I must tidy my room

riordino [ri'ordino] SM reorganization

riorganizzare [riorganid'dzare] VT to reorganize

▶ **riorganizzarsi** VR to reorganize o.s.

riorganizzazione [riorganiddzat'tsjone] SF reorganization

riottoso, a [riot'toso] AGG (*letter: attaccabrighe*) quarrelsome; (*indocile*) unruly

ripagare [ripa'gare] VT **1** (*ricompensare*) to repay; **ripagare qn di qc** to repay sb for sth; **ripagare qn con la stessa moneta** (*fig*) to pay sb back in his (*o* her) own coin, give sb tit for tat **2** (*pagare di nuovo*) to pay again

riparare [ripa'rare] VT **1** (*aggiustare*) to repair; **me l'ha riparato in un attimo** he repaired it for me in no time; **portare qc a riparare** to take sth to be repaired; **far riparare qc** to have sth repaired; **ho fatto riparare il videoregistratore** I got the video repaired **2** (*proteggere*): **riparare (da)** to protect (from); **ripararsi gli occhi dalla luce** to shield one's eyes from the light **3** (*rimediare*): **riparare (a)** (*offesa, gaffe*) to make up (for); (*errore*) to put right **4** (*Scol*): **riparare (una materia) a settembre** to resit an exam in September

■ VI (*aus* **essere**), **ripararsi** VR (*rifugiarsi*) to take refuge *o* shelter; **ripararsi dalla pioggia** to shelter from the rain

riparato, a [ripa'rato] AGG (*posto*) sheltered; **stare** *o* **tenersi riparato** to shelter

riparatore, trice [ripara'tore] SM/F repairer

riparazione [riparat'tsjone] SF **1** (*di guasto*) repairing *no pl*; (: *risultato*) repair **2** **riparazione (di)** (*di torto, offesa*) reparation (for); (*di danno*) compensation (for) **3** (*Scol*): **esame di riparazione** resit (*Brit*), test retake (*Am*)

riparlare [ripar'lare] VI (*aus* **avere**) **riparlare di qc** to talk about sth again; **ne riparleremo domani** we'll talk about it tomorrow; **ne riparleremo!** (*in litigio*) you haven't heard the last of this!

riparo [ri'paro] SM (*gen*) shelter, protection; **dobbiamo trovare un riparo** we need to find shelter; **al riparo da** (*sole, vento*) sheltered from; **ormai siamo al riparo** (*al sicuro*) we're safe now; **mettersi al riparo** to take shelter; **sparano, mettiti al riparo!** they're shooting, take cover!; **correre ai ripari** (*fig*) to take remedial action

ripartire[1] [ripar'tire] VI (*aus* **essere**) (*partire di nuovo: persona*) to leave again; (: *motore, macchina*) to start again; **quando riparti?** when are you leaving?; **non riesco a far ripartire la macchina** I can't get the car to start

ripartire[2] [ripar'tire] VT (*dividere*): **ripartire (in)** (*somma, lavoro*) to divide up (into); **ripartire (tra)** to share out (among), distribute (among); **ripartire la posta** to sort the mail; **si sono ripartiti il lavoro** they shared out the work

ripartizione [ripartit'tsjone] SF **1** (*vedi vt*) division; sharing out, distribution **2** (*Amm: dipartimento*) department

ripassare [ripas'sare] VT **1** (*lezione*) to revise (*Brit*), review; (*Am*) go over again; **devo ripassare, domani ho l'esame** I've got to revise, I've got the exam tomorrow **2** (*varcare di nuovo: confine*) to cross again **3** (*passare di nuovo: gen*) to pass again; **mi puoi ripassare Francesco?** (*al telefono*) can I speak to Francesco again? **4** (*stirare*): **ripassare qc** to give sth a quick iron

■ VI (*aus* **essere**) (*ritornare*) to call again; **ripasserò da lui più tardi** I'll call on him again later; **pensavo di ripassare in quel negozio** I was thinking of calling in at that shop again; **ripassiamo per Pisa?** are we going back via Pisa?; **può ripassare più tardi?** can you call back later?

ripassata [ripas'sata] SF: **dare una ripassata a** (*pantaloni*) to give a quick iron to; (*lezione*) to have another look through; (*fig: sgridare: persona*) to give a telling-off to

ripasso [ri'passo] SM (*di lezione*) revision (*Brit*), review (*Am*)

ripensamento [ripensa'mento] SM change of mind,

Rr

second thoughts *pl*; **avere un ripensamento** to have second thoughts, change one's mind

ripensare [ripen'sare] VI **1** (*riflettere*): **ripensare a qc** to think sth over; **ripensaci!** think it over!; **a ripensarci...** on thinking it over ... **2** (*ricordare*): **ripensare a** to recall; **quando ci ripenso mi vergogno un po'** when I think about it I feel rather ashamed **3** (*cambiare idea*): **ripensarci** to change one's mind; **ci ho ripensato, non vengo** I've changed my mind, I'm not coming; **però, ripensandoci...** on second thoughts (*Brit*) *o* thought (*Am*), however ...

ripercorrere [riper'korrere] VT IRREG (*itinerario*) to travel over again; (*strada*) to go along again; (*fig: ricordi, passato*) to go back over

ripercorso, a [riper'korso] PP *di* **ripercorrere**

ripercosso, a [riper'kɔsso] PP *di* **ripercuotersi**

ripercuotersi [riper'kwɔtersi] VIP IRREG (*luce*) to be reflected; (*suono*) to reverberate; (*fig: avere effetto*): **ripercuotersi su** to have repercussions on

ripercussione [riperkus'sjone] SF (*di luce*) reflection; (*di suono*) reverberation; (*fig*) repercussions *pl*; **avere una ripercussione** *o* **delle ripercussioni su** to have repercussions on

ripescaggio, gi [ripes'kaddʒo] SM (*Sport*) repechage; (*Pol*) re-proposal

ripescare [ripes'kare] VT **1** (*pesce*) to catch again; (*recuperare: persona, cosa*) to fish out; (*fig*) to dig out; **ripescare qn a fare qc** (*fig: sorprendere*) to catch sb doing sth again **2** (*riproporre: candidato, progetto*) to re-propose

ripetente [ripe'tɛnte] SM/F student repeating the year, repeater (*Am*)

ripetere [ri'pɛtere] VT (*parole, tentativo*) to repeat; **gliel'ho ripetuto cento volte!** I've told him dozens of times!; **non se l'è fatto ripetere due volte** he didn't need to be asked twice; **dopo ripetuti tentativi** after repeated attempts; **scusi, può ripetere?** excuse me, could you repeat that?; **continua a ripetere le stesse cose** he keeps repeating the same things; **ripetere qc a memoria** to recite sth by heart; **ripetere una lezione** (*studiarla*) to go over a lesson; **ripetere l'anno (scolastico)** to repeat the (school) year

▶ **ripetersi** VR (*persona*) to repeat o.s.

▶ **ripetersi** VIP (*avvenimento, fenomeno*) to recur; happen again; **che non si ripeta più!** don't let this happen again!

ripetitore [ripeti'tore] SM (*Radio, TV*) relay

ripetizione [ripetit'tsjone] SF **1** (*gen*) repetition; **fucile a ripetizione** repeating rifle **2** (*Scol: ripasso*) revision (*Brit*), review (*Am*); (*: lezioni private*) private tutoring *o* coaching *sg*; **dare** *o* **fare ripetizioni a qn** to give sb private lessons; **Malcolm dà ripetizioni di inglese** Malcolm gives private English lessons; **andare a ripetizione** to have private lessons; **vado a ripetizione di matematica** I have private maths lessons

ripetutamente [ripetuta'mente] AVV repeatedly, again and again

ripiano [ri'pjano] SM (*di mobile*) shelf; (*di terreno*) terrace; **l'ho messo sull'ultimo ripiano** I put it on the top shelf

ripicca [ri'pikka] SF: **per ripicca** out of spite **l'ha fatto solo per ripicca** she did it just out of spite

ripidamente [ripida'mente] AVV steeply

ripidezza [ripi'dettsa] SF steepness

ripido, a ['ripido] AGG steep; **c'è una salita ripida per andare al castello** it's a steep climb up to the castle

ripiegamento [ripjega'mento] SM (*Mil*) retreat

ripiegare [ripje'gare] VT **1** (*piegare: di nuovo*) to fold (again), refold; (*: più volte*) to fold up **2** (*reclinare: capo*) to lower

■ VI (*aus* **avere**) (*Mil*) to retreat, fall back; **ripiegare su** (*fig*) to make do with, fall back on; **era troppo caro, ho ripiegato su uno più economico** it was too expensive, I made do with a cheaper one;

▶ **ripiegarsi** VIP (*ramo ecc*) to bend

ripiego, ghi [ri'pjɛgo] SM expedient; **una soluzione di ripiego** a makeshift solution

ripieno, a [ri'pjɛno] AGG: **ripieno (di)** full (of); (*panino*) filled (with); (*tacchino, peperoni*) stuffed (with)

■ SM (*Culin*) stuffing

ripigliare [ripiʎ'ʎare] VT (*pigliare: di nuovo*) to take again; (*: indietro*) to take back; (*fig: forza, vigore*) to recover, get back; **ripigliare fiato** to catch one's breath; (*fig*) to have a breather

ripiombare [ripjom'bare] VI (*aus* **essere**) (*cadere*): **ripiombare per terra** to fall heavily to the ground; **ripiombare nella disperazione** (*fig*) to sink back into despair; **se ne è andato e poi è ripiombato qui mezz'ora più tardi** he went away and then turned up here again half an hour later

ripone [ri'pone], **ripongo** *ecc* [ri'pongo] VB *vedi* **riporre**

ripopolare [ripopo'lare] VT (*gen*) to repopulate; **ripopolare un fiume di pesci** to restock a river with fish

▶ **ripopolarsi** VIP (*zona*) to be repopulated

riporre [ri'porre] VT IRREG **1** (*mettere via*) to put away; (*: dov'era prima*) to put back, replace; **riporre qc al suo posto** to put sth where it belongs **2** **riporre qc in qn** (*fiducia, speranza*) to place *o* put sth in sb

riportare [ripor'tare] VT **1** (*portare di nuovo: gen*) to take back; (*: verso chi parla*) to bring back; **tieni, ti ho riportato il CD** here, I've brought you back your CD; **mi ha riportato a casa** he took me back home; **riportalo in cucina** take it back to the kitchen; **la scena lo riportò col pensiero all'infanzia** the scene took him back to his childhood **2** (*ottenere*) to receive, get; (*: vittoria*) to carry off, win; (*: successo*) to have; **ha riportato gravi ferite** he was seriously injured; (*soldato*) he was seriously wounded; **ha riportato una frattura al braccio** he received a fracture to his arm; **la casa ha riportato gravi danni** the house has suffered serious damage, the house has been seriously damaged **3** (*riferire: notizie*) to report; (*citare*) to quote **4** (*Mat*) to carry (forward); **scrivo 5 e riporto 3** put down 5 and carry 3

▶ **riportarsi** VIP: **riportarsi a** (*anche fig*) to go back to; (*riferirsi a*) to refer to

riporto [ri'pɔrto] SM **1** (*Mat*) amount carried over; **col riporto di 1** carry 1 **2** (*Calzoleria, Sartoria*) appliqué; (*fam: di capelli*) comb-over **3** (*Caccia*): **cane da riporto** retriever

riposante [ripo'sante] AGG (*gen*) restful; (*musica, colore*) soothing

riposare [ripo'sare] VT **1** (*dare sollievo a: occhi, membra*) to rest; **per riposare un po' la mente** to give one's mind a rest **1** (*posare di nuovo*) to put down again

■ VI (*aus* **avere**) **1** (*gen*) to rest; (*dormire*) to sleep; **è andato a riposare** he's having a rest; (*a letto*) he has gone to lie down; **avete riposato bene?** did you sleep well?; **riposi in pace** (*defunto*) may he rest in peace; **qui riposa...** (*su tomba*) here lies ... **2** (*Culin: pasta, liquido*) to stand; (*vino*) to settle; (*terra*) to lie fallow

▶ **riposarsi** VIP to rest; (*dormire*) to sleep; **vado a** riposarmi I'm going to have a rest; (*a letto*) I'm going to lie down; **cerca di riposarti un po'** try to rest

riposato, a [ripo'sato] AGG (*viso, aspetto*) rested; (*mente*) fresh

riposi *ecc* [ri'posi] VB *vedi* **riporre**

riposo [ri'pɔso] SM **1** rest; **eterno riposo** (*morte*) eternal rest; **casa di riposo** (*per anziani*) rest-home; **prendersi un giorno/un mese di riposo** (*da lavoro*) to take a day/a month off; **buon riposo!** sleep well!; **cinque minuti di riposo** five minutes' rest; **senza un attimo di riposo** without a moment's rest; **riposo!** (*Mil, Sport*) at ease!; **"oggi riposo"** (*Cine, Teatro*) "no performance today"; (*ristorante*) "closed today" **2** (*pensione*): **andare a riposo** to go into retirement, retire; **generale a riposo** retired general **3** (*Mus*) rest

ripostiglio, gli [ripos'tiʎʎo] SM (*stanzino*) lumber room (*Brit*), storage room (*Am*)

riposto, a [ri'posto] PP *di* **riporre**
■ AGG (*letter: nascosto: senso, significato*) hidden

riprendere [ri'prɛndere] VB IRREG
■ VT **1** (*prendere di nuovo: gen*) to take again; (*: prigioniero*) to recapture; (*: città*) to retake; (*: impiegato*) to take on again, re-employ; (*: raffreddore*) to catch again; (*: velocità*) to pick up again; (*: quota*) to regain; **riprendere moglie/marito** to get married again; **riprendere i sensi** to recover consciousness, come to *o* round; **riprendere sonno** to go back to sleep, get back to sleep; **non sono riuscito a riprendere sonno** I couldn't get back to sleep; **fu ripreso dal desiderio di vederla** again he felt the desire to see her; **fu ripreso dai dubbi** he began to have doubts again **2** (*riavere*) to get back; (*ritirare: oggetto riparato*) to collect; **riprenditi le tue cose** take your things; **passo a riprendere Francesco/l'impermeabile più tardi** I'll call by to pick up Francesco/the raincoat later; **si è ripreso le sue fotografie** he took his photos back; **puoi riprenderlo, non mi serve più** you can have it back, I don't need it any more **3** (*ricominciare: viaggio, lavoro*) to resume, start again; **riprendere a fare qc** to start doing sth again; **riprendere il cammino** to set off again; **riprendere una conversazione** to continue a conversation; **riprendi tutta la storia dall'inizio** start your story all over again; **"dunque", riprese, "dove eravamo?"** "so", he continued, "where were we?" **4** (*Cine, TV*) to shoot; **riprendere un attore in primo piano** to shoot a close-up of an actor; **questa foto li riprende in un atteggiamento affettuoso** this photo shows them in an affectionate pose **5** (*rimproverare*) to reprimand **6** (*restringere: abito*) to take in **7** (*Sport: raggiungere*) to catch up with
▶ **riprendersi** VIP **1** (*riaversi*) to recover; (*: pianta*) to revive; **si è appena ripreso dalla polmonite** he's just recovered from pneumonia; **era emozionato ma si è ripreso** he was nervous but he pulled himself together **2** (*correggersi*) to correct o.s.

ripresa [ri'presa] SF **1** (*di attività, trattative*) resumption; (*di opera teatrale*) revival; **a più riprese** (*a stadi*) in stages; (*più volte*) on several occasions, several times **2** (*Calcio*) second half; (*Pugilato*) round; (*Equitazione*) riding lesson; **ha segnato al 15° della ripresa** he scored in the fifteenth minute of the second half; **un incontro in 10 riprese** a ten-round fight **3** (*Cine, TV, Fot*) shot; (*: azione*) shooting *no pl*; **in ripresa diretta** live; **ho fatto delle belle riprese nel Galles** I got some nice shots in Wales **4** (*ricupero: di persona, paese*) recovery; **essere in ripresa** to be on the road to recovery; **ripresa economica** economic recovery **5** (*Aut*) acceleration; **quest'auto non ha ripresa** this car's got no acceleration

ripresentare [riprezen'tare] VT (*certificato*) to submit again; (*domanda*) to put forward again; (*persona*) to introduce again
▶ **ripresentarsi** VR (*ritornare: persona*) to come back; **ripresentarsi a** (*esame*) to sit (*Brit*) *o* take (*Am*) again; (*concorso*) to enter again; **ripresentarsi come candidato** (*Pol*) to stand (*Brit*) *o* run (*Am*) again (as a candidate)
▶ **ripresentarsi** VIP (*occasione*) to arise again

ripreso, a [ri'preso] PP *di* **riprendere**

ripristinare [ripristi'nare] VT (*gen*) to restore; (*Inform*) to reset; (*tradizione*) to revive, bring back into use; (*legge*) to bring back into force

ripristino [ri'pristino] SM (*gen*) restoration; (*di tradizioni*) revival

riprodotto, a [ripro'dotto] PP *di* **riprodurre**

riprodurre [ripro'durre] VB IRREG
■ VT to reproduce
▶ **riprodursi** VIP (*moltiplicarsi*) to reproduce; (*ripetersi: situazione, fenomeno*) to occur *o* happen again, recur

riproduttivo, a [riprodut'tivo] AGG reproductive

riproduttore, trice [riprodut'tore] AGG (*organo*) reproductive
■ SM: **riproduttore acustico** pick-up

riproduzione [riprodut'tsjone] SF (*gen*) reproduction; **"riproduzione vietata"** "all rights reserved", "copyright"

ripromesso, a [ripro'messo] PP *di* **ripromettersi**

ripromettersi [ripro'mettersi] VIP IRREG: **ripromettersi di fare qc** to intend to do sth

riproporre [ripro'porre] VB IRREG
■ VT (*soluzione*) to put forward again; (*legge*) to propose again; **riproporre di fare qc** to suggest doing sth again;
▶ **riproporsi** VIP **1** (*intendere*) **riproporsi di fare qc** to intend to do sth; **si è riproposto una lunga vacanza** he's thinking of having a long holiday **2** (*ripresentarsi: problema, situazione*) to come up again, arise again
▶ **riproporsi** VR: **riproporsi come candidato** to propose oneself as candidate again

riproposto, a [ripro'posto] PP *di* **riproporre**

riprova [ri'prɔva] SF confirmation; **a riprova di** as confirmation of

riprovare¹ [ripro'vare] VT (*provare di nuovo: gen*) to try again; (*: vestito*) to try on again; (*: sensazione*) to experience again
■ VI (*aus* **avere**) (*tentare*): **riprovare (a fare qc)** to try (to do sth) again; **riproverò più tardi** I'll try again later; **guai a lui se ci riprova!** God help him if he tries that again!

riprovare² [ripro'vare] VT (*biasimare*) to disapprove of

riprovazione [riprovat'tsjone] SF censure, disapproval

riprovevole [ripro'vevole] AGG reprehensible

riprovevolmente [riprovevol'mente] AVV reprehensibly

ripubblicare [ripubbli'kare] VT to republish

ripudiare [ripu'djare] VT (*moglie, marito*) to repudiate; (*famiglia, patria*) to disown; (*principi, idee*) to reject

ripudio, di [ri'pudjo] SM (*vedi vb*) repudiation; disowning; rejection

ripugnante [ripuɲ'ɲante] AGG repulsive, disgusting

ripugnanza [ripuɲ'ɲantsa] SF repugnance, disgust; **provare ripugnanza per qc/qn** to loathe sth/sb; **avere ripugnanza a fare qc** to loathe doing sth

Rr

ripugnare [ripuɲ'ɲare] VI (*aus* **avere**) **ripugnare a qn** to repel *o* disgust sb; **la sola idea mi ripugna** I find the very idea of it disgusting; **non ti ripugna fare una cosa del genere?** don't you loathe doing such a thing?

ripulire [ripu'lire] VT **1** (*pulire: di nuovo*) to clean again; (*: a fondo*) to clean up; **ripulire il giardino dalle foglie secche** to clear the garden of dead leaves; **ha ripulito il frigorifero** (*fig*) he finished off *o* polished off everything in the refrigerator; **gli hanno ripulito le tasche** (*fig*) they cleaned him out **2** (*perfezionare*) to polish, refine
▶ **ripulirsi** VR to clean o.s. up

ripulita [ripu'lita] SF clean-up; **dare una ripulita a qc** to clean sth up; **darsi una ripulita** to tidy o.s. up, spruce o.s. up

ripulsione [ripul'sjone] SF repulsion

riquadro [ri'kwadro] SM (*gen, spazio*) square; (*di parete, soffitto, mobile*) panel

riqualificare [rikwalifi'kare] VT
▶ **riqualificarsi** VR (*operaio*) to retrain

risacca, che [ri'sakka] SF backwash

risaia [ri'saja] SF paddy field

risalire [risa'lire] VT (*salire di nuovo: gen*) to go up again; (*scale*) to climb again; **risalire la corrente** to go upstream
■ VI (*aus* **essere**) **1** (*gen, livello, prezzi*) to go up again, rise again; **risalire a cavallo** to remount; **risalire in macchina** to get back into the car; **risalire al piano di sopra** to go back upstairs; **risalire in cima alla classifica** to climb back (up) to the top of the league **2** **risalire a** (*data, periodo*) to date back to *o* from, go back to; **il palazzo risale al Cinquecento** the palace dates from the sixteenth century **3** (*ritornare*): **risalire a** to go back to; **risalire alle fonti** to go back to source material

risalita [risa'lita] SF: **impianti di risalita** (*Sci*) ski lifts

risaltare [risal'tare] VI (*aus* **avere** *o* **essere**) (*anche fig*): **risaltare (su/fra)** to stand out (against/among); (*colore*) to show up (against/among)

risalto [ri'salto] SM (*rilievo*) prominence; (*enfasi*) emphasis; **dar risalto a qc** to give prominence to sth, lay emphasis on sth; **mettere** *o* **porre in risalto qc** to make sth stand out

risanamento [risana'mento] SM **1** (*economico*) improvement; **risanamento del bilancio** reorganization of the budget **2** (*bonifica*) reclamation; **risanamento edilizio** urban redevelopment

risanare [risa'nare] VT **1** (*economia*) to improve; (*bilancio*) to reorganize **2** (*palude*) to reclaim; (*quartiere*) to redevelop **3** (*guarire*) to heal, cure
■ VI (*aus* **essere**), **risanarsi** VIP (*guarire, anche fig*) to heal

risapere [risa'pere] VT to come to know of; **è risaputo che...** everyone knows that ..., it's common knowledge that ...

risaputo, a [risa'puto] AGG: **sono cose risapute** it's common knowledge

risarcibile [risar'tʃibile] AGG indemnifiable

risarcimento [risartʃi'mento] SM: **risarcimento (di)** compensation (for); **ha ricevuto un risarcimento di 10.000 euro** he got 10,000 euros compensation; **chiedere il risarcimento** to claim compensation; **aver diritto al risarcimento dei danni** to be entitled to damages

risarcire [risar'tʃire] VT (*compensare: cose*) to pay compensation for; (*: persona*): **risarcire qn di qc** to compensate sb for sth; **risarcire i danni a qn** to pay sb damages

risata [ri'sata] SF laugh; **che risate!** what a laugh!, how we laughed!; **farsi una bella risata** to have a good laugh

riscaldamento [riskalda'mento] SM **1** (*di casa, auto*) heating; **il riscaldamento non funziona** the heating isn't working; **riscaldamento autonomo** central heating (*for one home only*); **riscaldamento centrale** central heating (*serving an entire block of flats*); **riscaldamento globale** global warming **2** (*Sport*) warm-up; **prima della partita facciamo riscaldamento** we do a warm-up before a match

riscaldare [riskal'dare] VT **1** (*scaldare: stanza, acqua*) to heat; (*: mani, persona*) to warm; **un caminetto riscaldava la stanza** the room was heated by an open fire; **riscaldarsi le mani/i piedi** to warm one's hands/feet **2** (*scaldare di nuovo*) to heat up, reheat; **il pollo dev'essere solo riscaldato** the chicken just needs warming up
■ VI (*aus* **avere**) (*stufa*) to heat up; **il motore riscalda troppo** the engine overheats;
▶ **riscaldarsi** VIP (*persona*) to get warm, warm o.s. up; (*atleta*) to warm up; (*fig: infervorarsi*) to get worked up, get excited; (*adirarsi*) to get angry

riscaldo [ris'kaldo] SM (*fam*) (slight) inflammation; **ha un po' di riscaldo** (*brufoletti*) he's got a bit of a rash

riscattabile [riskat'tabile] AGG redeemable

riscattare [riskat'tare] VT (*Dir, fig*) to redeem; (*prigioniero*) to ransom, pay a ransom for
▶ **riscattarsi** VR (*fig*) to redeem o.s.

riscatto [ris'katto] SM (*Dir, fig*) redemption; (*di rapimento*) ransom

rischiarare [riskja'rare] VT (*gen*) to light up; (*colore*) to make lighter; **rischiararsi la voce** to clear one's throat
■ VI (*aus* **essere**), **rischiararsi** VIP (*cielo*) to clear; (*fig: volto*) to brighten up; (*liquido*) to become clear; **si rischiarò in volto** his face lit up; **rischiara** *or* **si sta rischiarando** (*tempo, cielo*) it's clearing up

rischiare [ris'kjare] VT to risk; **ha rischiato la vita** he risked his life; **rischiare il tutto per tutto** to risk everything
■ VI (*aus* **avere**) **rischiare di fare qc** to risk doing sth, run the risk of doing sth; **non voglio rischiare di arrivare in ritardo** I don't want to risk arriving late; **ha rischiato di cadere** he nearly fell

rischio, chi ['riskjo] SM risk; **a rischio di fare qc** at the risk of doing sth; **a proprio rischio e pericolo** at one's own risk; **correre il rischio di fare qc** to run the risk of doing sth; **mettere a rischio qc** to put sth at risk; **un rischio calcolato** a calculated risk; **c'è il rischio che questo viaggio non si possa fare** there is a danger that we (*o* you *ecc*) won't be able to make this trip; **soggetto/categoria a rischio** subject/group at risk; **capitale di rischio** (*Fin*) risk *o* venture capital; **rischio del mestiere** occupational hazard

rischiosità [riskjosi'ta] SF riskiness

rischioso, a [ris'kjoso] AGG risky, dangerous, hazardous; **un'impresa rischiosa** a risky enterprise

risciacquare [riʃʃak'kware] VT (*panni, stoviglie*) to rinse; **risciacquarsi la bocca** to rinse one's mouth out

risciacquatura [riʃʃakkwa'tura] SF **1** (*atto*) rinsing **2** (*dei piatti*) dishwater

risciacquo [riʃʃakkwo] SM rinse

risciò [riʃʃɔ] SM INV rickshaw

riscontare [riskon'tare] VT (*Fin*) to rediscount
riscontrare [riskon'trare] VT **1** (*rilevare*) to notice, find; **non ho riscontrato errori** I haven't found *o* noticed any mistakes **2** (*confrontare*) to compare; (*controllare: conti, motore*) to check, inspect; **riscontrare la copia con l'originale** to compare the copy with the original; (*Tip*) to read against copy
riscontro [ris'kontro] SM **1** (*conferma*) confirmation; **le sue osservazioni non trovano riscontro nella realtà** his remarks are not borne out by the facts **2** (*confronto*) comparison; (*controllo*) check; **mettere a riscontro** to compare, check; **fare il riscontro della copia con l'originale** to compare the copy with the original; (*Tip*) to read against copy; **un avvenimento che non ha avuto riscontro in passato** an event which had no parallel in the past **3** (*Comm: risposta per iscritto*) reply; **in attesa di un vostro cortese riscontro** we look forward to your reply
riscoperto, a [risko'perto] PP *di* **riscoprire**
riscoprire [risko'prire] VT IRREG to rediscover
riscossa [ris'kɔssa] SF (*riconquista*) recovery, reconquest
riscossione [riskos'sjone] SF collection
riscosso, a [ris'kɔsso] PP *di* **riscuotere**
riscritto, a [ris'kritto] PP *di* **riscrivere**
riscrivere [ris'krivere] VT IRREG to rewrite; (*uso assoluto: scrivere in risposta*) to write back
riscrivibile [riskri'vibile] AGG: **CD riscrivibile** rewriteable CD, CD-RW
riscuotere [ris'kwɔtere] VB IRREG
■ VT (*stipendio, pensione*) to draw; (*tasse, affitto*) to collect; (*fig: applausi, approvazione, successo*) to win, earn; **riscuotere un assegno** to cash a cheque (*Brit*) *o* check (*Am*)
▶ **riscuotersi** VIP: **riscuotersi (da)** (*fig*) to rouse o.s. (from), shake o.s. (out of)
rise *ecc* ['rise] VB *vedi* **ridere**
risentimento [risenti'mento] SM resentment; **provare** *o* **avere del risentimento verso** *o* **contro qn** to feel resentful towards sb
risentire [risen'tire] VT (*sentire di nuovo*) to hear again; (*disco*) to listen to again
■ VI: **risentire di** (*esperienza, trauma*) to feel the effects of; (*: portarne i segni*) to show the effects of; **risentire dell'influenza di** to show traces of the influence of; **le piante hanno risentito del freddo** the plants have felt the cold;
▶ **risentirsi** VR (*offendersi*) to take offence (*Brit*) *o* offense (*Am*); **risentirsi di** *o* **per qc** to resent sth, take offence *o* offense at sth
risentitamente [risentita'mente] AVV resentfully
risentito, a [risen'tito] AGG resentful
riserbo [ri'sɛrbo] SM reserve; **è una persona di grande riserbo** he's a very reserved person; **senza riserbo** unreservedly; **mantenere un assoluto riserbo (su qc)** to maintain a complete silence (about sth)
riserva [ri'sɛrva] SF **1** (*provvista, scorta*) reserve; **fare riserva di** (*acqua, cibo*) to get in a supply of, stock up on; **tenere di riserva** to keep in reserve; **entrare in riserva** *or* **essere in riserva** (*Aut*) to be nearly out of petrol (*Brit*) *o* gas (*Am*); **di riserva** (*gen*) reserve *attr*; (*aereo, corriera*) back-up *attr*; **riserva aurea** gold reserves *pl* **2** (*Mil, Sport*) reserve; **domenica scorsa ho giocato come riserva** last Sunday I played as reserve; **(giocatore di) riserva** reserve (player); (*Calcio*) substitute; **truppe della riserva** reserves **3** (*limitazione: anche:* **riserva mentale**) reservation; **con le dovute riserve** with certain reservations; **ha accettato con la riserva di potersi ritirare** he accepted with the proviso that he could pull out; **senza riserve** (*incondizionatamente*) unreservedly **4** (*territorio*): **riserva di caccia/pesca** hunting/fishing preserve; **riserva indiana** Indian reservation; **riserva naturale** nature reserve
riservare [riser'vare] VT **1** (*tenere da parte*) to keep aside; (*mettere da parte*) to put aside; **riservare una sorpresa a qn** to have a surprise in store for sb; **cosa ci riserva il destino?** what has destiny in store for us?; **riservarsi di fare qc** to intend to do sth; **riservarsi il diritto di fare qc** to reserve the right to do sth **2** (*prenotare*) to book, reserve; **vorrei riservare un tavolo per stasera** I'd like to book a table for this evening
riservatamente [riservata'mente] AVV (*vedi agg* 1) in confidence, confidentially; reservedly; discreetly
riservatezza [riserva'tettsa] SF (*vedi agg* 1) confidential nature; reserve; discretion
riservato, a [riser'vato] AGG **1** (*lettera, informazione*) confidential; (*persona, carattere*) reserved; (*: discreto*) discreet **2** (*prenotato*) reserved, booked
riservista, i [riser'vista] SM (*Mil*) reservist
risguardo [riz'gwardo] SM (*di libro*) flyleaf
risi *ecc* ['risi] VB *vedi* **ridere**
risibile [ri'sibile] AGG laughable
risicare [rizi'kare] VI: **chi non risica non rosica** (*Proverbio*) nothing ventured nothing gained
risicato, a [rizi'kato] AGG (*maggioranza*) very narrow
risicoltore, trice [risikol'tore] SM/F rice grower
risicoltura [risikol'tura] SF rice growing
risiedere [ri'sjɛdere] VI **1** (*vivere*): **risiedere in** *o* **a** to reside in **2** (*consistere, stare*): **risiedere in** to lie in; **il motivo del suo successo risiede nel suo senso dell'umorismo** the reason for his success is his sense of humour
risma ['rizma] SF **1** (*di carta*) ream **2** (*fig: pegg: tipo*) kind, sort; **essere della stessa risma** to be all of a kind
riso[1] ['riso] PP *di* **ridere**
■ SM (*pl f* **risa**) (*il ridere*) laughter; (*risata*) laugh; **il riso e il pianto** laughter and tears; **uno scoppio di risa** a burst of laughter; **risa allegre** cheerful laughter; **non riusciva a trattenere il riso** he couldn't help laughing; **sbellicarsi** *o* **crepare dalle risa** (*fam*) to split one's sides laughing; **il riso fa buon sangue** laughter is the best medicine
riso[2] ['riso] SM (*Bot*) rice; **riso in brodo** consommé with rice; **riso in bianco** rice with butter; **riso integrale** brown rice; **carta di riso** (*Arte*) rice paper
risolare [riso'lare], **risuolare** [riswo'lare] VT (*scarpe*) to resole
risolino [riso'lino] SM (*di scherno, ironico*) snigger
risollevare [risolle'vare] VT (*sollevare di nuovo: testa*) to raise again, lift up again; (*fig: questione*) to raise again, bring up again; (*: morale*) to raise; **risollevare le sorti di qc** to improve the chances of sth
▶ **risollevarsi** VR (*da terra*) to rise again; (*fig: da malattia*) to recover
risolsi *ecc* [ri'sɔlsi] VB *vedi* **risolvere**
risolto, a [ri'sɔlto] PP *di* **risolvere**
risolubile [riso'lubile] AGG = **risolvibile**
risolutamente [risoluta'mente] AVV resolutely
risolutezza [risolu'tettsa] SF decisiveness, resolution, determination
risolutivo, a [risolu'tivo] AGG (*determinante*) decisive; **arrivare ad una formula risolutiva** (*che risolve*) to come up with a formula to resolve a situation

Rr

risoluto, a [riso'luto] AGG resolute, determined; **essere risoluto a fare qc** to be determined to do sth

risoluzione [risolut'tsjone] SF **1** (*soluzione, Mat*) solution **2** (*decisione*) resolution **3** (*Dir: di contratto*) annulment, cancellation **4** (*Chim*) resolution **5** (*di schermo*) resolution

risolvere [ri'sɔlvere] VB IRREG
■VT **1** (*problema, Mat*) to solve, work out; (*mistero, indovinello*) to solve; (*difficoltà, faccenda, controversia*) to resolve, sort out; **cosa risolvi facendo così?** what do you solve by doing that? **2** (*decidere*) to decide, resolve; **abbiamo risolto di partire al più presto** we've decided to leave as soon as possible **3** (*Dir: contratto*) to annul, cancel **4** (*Chim*) to break down
▶ **risolversi** VIP **1** (*andare a finire*) **risolversi in bene** to end well, turn out well; **risolversi in nulla** to come to nothing; **l'operazione si è risolta in un fiasco** the operation turned out to be a disaster **2** (*decidersi*) **risolversi a fare qc** to make up one's mind to do sth **3** (*malattia*) to clear up

risolvibile [risol'vibile] AGG solvable

risonante [riso'nante] AGG resonant

risonanza [riso'nantsa] SF (*Fis*) resonance; (*fig: eco*) interest; **suscitare una grande risonanza** to arouse great interest; **aver vasta risonanza** (*fatto, vicenda*) to be known far and wide; **risonanza magnetica** magnetic resonance

risonare [riso'nare] VT, VI = **risuonare**

risorgere [ri'sordʒere] VI IRREG (*aus* **essere**) (*Rel, fig*) to rise again; **risorgeva in lui la speranza** his hopes were revived

risorgimentale [risordʒimen'tale] AGG of the Risorgimento

risorgimento [risordʒi'mento] SM (*di arte, cultura*) revival; **il Risorgimento** *movement that led to the unification of Italy*

RISORGIMENTO

The **Risorgimento**, the period stretching from the early nineteenth century to 1861 and the proclamation of the Kingdom of Italy, saw considerable upheaval and change. Political and personal freedom took on new importance with the desire for political and personal freedom being stimulated by the example of the French Revolution. The Risorgimento paved the way for the unification of Italy in 1871.

▷ www.risorgimento.it/risorgimento/default.htm

risorsa [ri'sorsa] SF (*gen*) resource; **è l'ultima risorsa** it's the last resort; **una persona piena di risorse** a resourceful person; **risorse umane** human resources

risorsi *ecc* [ri'sorsi] VB *vedi* **risorgere**

risorto, a [ri'sorto] PP *di* **risorgere**

risotto [ri'sɔtto] SM (*Culin*) risotto

risparmiare [rispar'mjare] VT **1** (*denaro, cibo, tempo*) to save; (*gas, elettricità*) to economize on, save on; **sto risparmiando per comprare un lettore di MP3** I'm saving up to buy an MP3 player; **risparmiare fatica/fiato** to save one's energy/breath; **risparmiati il disturbo** *o* **la fatica** (*anche iro*) save yourself the trouble; **risparmiare qc a qn** (*fig: evitare*) to spare sb sth; **ti risparmio i particolari** I'll spare you the details **2** (*non uccidere, non colpire*) to spare; **risparmiare la vita a qn** to spare sb's life
■VI (*aus* **avere**) **risparmiare su qc** to economize on sth, save on sth
▶ **risparmiarsi** VR to spare oneself

risparmiatore, trice [risparmja'tore] SM/F saver

risparmio, mi [ris'parmjo] SM **1** (*azione*) saving; **un grosso risparmio di tempo** a big saving in time; **ci riuscimmo con un risparmio di tempo e denaro** we succeeded and saved time and money into the bargain; **senza risparmio di forze** sparing no effort **2** **risparmi** SMPL (*denaro risparmiato*) savings *pl*; **ha speso tutti i suoi risparmi** he spent all his savings

rispecchiare [rispek'kjare] VT to reflect
▶ **rispecchiarsi** VR to be reflected; **è così lucido che ti ci puoi rispecchiare** it's so shiny that you can see your face in it

rispedire [rispe'dire] VT to send back; **rispedire qc a qn** to send sth back to sb

rispettabile [rispet'tabile] AGG **1** (*persona*) respectable **2** (*considerevole: somma*) sizeable, considerable

rispettabilità [rispettabili'ta] SF respectability

rispettare [rispet'tare] VT (*persona, idea*) to respect, have respect for; (*legge*) to obey, comply with, abide by; (*promessa*) to keep; **bisogna rispettare le opinioni altrui** you have to respect other people's opinions; **farsi rispettare da qn** to command sb's respect; **far rispettare la legge** to enforce the law; **rispettare l'ordine alfabetico** to maintain alphabetical order; **rispettare i tempi (stabiliti)** to keep to schedule; **rispettare le distanze** to keep one's distance; **ogni medico che si rispetti** every self-respecting doctor
▶ **rispettarsi** VR to respect o.s.

rispettivamente [rispettiva'mente] AVV respectively

rispettivo, a [rispet'tivo] AGG respective

rispetto [ris'pɛtto] SM **1** **rispetto (di** *o* **per)** (*gen*) respect (for); (*norme, leggi*) observance (of), compliance (with); **portare rispetto a qn/qc** to have *o* feel respect for sb/sth; **mancare di rispetto a qn** to be disrespectful to sb; **non ha alcun rispetto per le cose altrui** she has no respect for other people's property; **con rispetto** (*nelle lettere*) respectfully yours; **con rispetto parlando** if you will excuse my saying so, with respect **2** **rispetti** SMPL (*frm: omaggi*): **(porga) i miei rispetti alla signora** my regards to your wife **3** (*riguardo, relazione*): **rispetto a** (*in confronto*) compared to, in comparison with; (*riguardo a*) as regards, with respect to, regarding, as for; **sotto questo rispetto** from this point of view; **sotto ogni rispetto** in every respect

rispettosamente [rispettosa'mente] AVV respectfully

rispettoso, a [rispet'toso] AGG respectful; **essere rispettoso verso qn** to be respectful to sb, show respect to sb; **essere rispettoso di qc** to have respect for sth

risplendente [risplen'dɛnte] AGG (*sole*) bright, shining; (*occhi*) sparkling; **risplendente di gioia** (*viso*) shining with joy

risplendere [ris'plɛndere] VI (*gen*) to shine; (*luccicare*) to sparkle, glitter

rispondente [rispon'dɛnte] AGG: **rispondente a** in accordance with, in keeping *o* conformity with

rispondenza [rispon'dɛntsa] SF correspondence

rispondere [ris'pondere] VB IRREG
■VI (*aus* **avere**) **1** **rispondere a** (*domanda*) to reply to, answer; (*persona*) to answer; (*invito*) to reply to; **ha risposto alla tua lettera?** has he answered your letter?; **rispondere al telefono** to answer the telephone; **ho telefonato ma non ha risposto**

nessuno I phoned, but nobody answered; **rispondere di sì/di no** to say yes/no; **cosa vuoi che ti risponda?** what can I say?; **rispondere bene** to give the right *o* correct answer; **rispondere male** (*sgarbatamente*) to answer back, answer rudely; (*in modo errato*) to give the wrong answer; **rispondere al nome di** to answer to the name of **2** (*rimbeccare*): **rispondere (a qn)** to answer (sb) back; **rispondere per le rime** (*fig*) to give sb as good as one gets **3** (*reagire: veicolo, freni*) to respond **4** (*corrispondere*): **rispondere a** to correspond to; (*: speranze, bisogno*) to answer; **rispondere alle esigenze di** to meet the needs of **5** (*garantire*): **rispondere di qn** to answer for sb, be responsible for sb, vouch for sb; (*essere responsabile*): **rispondere di qc** to be accountable for sth; **rispondere a qn di qc** to be answerable to sb for sth; **non rispondo più di me stesso** *o* **delle mie azioni** I can't answer for my actions **6** (*Carte*) to follow, reply
■ VT **1** **rispondere che...** to answer that ..., reply that ... **2** **rispondere picche** (*fig*) to give a flat refusal, refuse flatly

risposare [rispo'zare] VT to marry again, remarry
▶ **risposarsi** VIP to get married again, remarry

risposta [ris'posta] SF **1** (*a domanda, lettera*) answer, reply; **la risposta esatta** the right answer; **dare una risposta** to give an answer; **in risposta a** in reply to, in answer to; **diamo risposta alla vostra lettera del...** in reply to your letter of ...; **per tutta risposta mi ha sbattuto la porta in faccia** his only answer was to slam the door in my face **2** (*replica*) reply, retort **3** (*Carte*) reply **4** (*Tennis*): **risposta al servizio** return of serve

risposto, a [ris'posto] PP *di* **rispondere**

rispuntare [rispun'tare] VI (*aus* **essere**) (*sole*) to come out again, reappear; (*persona*) to pop up again, reappear

rissa ['rissa] SF fight, brawl; **ieri c'è stata una rissa nel bar** there was a brawl in the bar yesterday

rissoso, a [ris'soso] AGG quarrelsome

rist. ABBR = **ristampa**

ristabilire [ristabi'lire] VT **1** (*gen*) to re-establish; (*servizio*) to put back in operation; (*ordine, istituzione*) to restore **2** (*sogg: riposo ecc*): **ristabilire qn** to restore sb to health
▶ **ristabilirsi** VIP (*persona*) to recover, get better; **ristabilirsi da** to recover from

ristagnare [ristaɲ'ɲare] VI (*aus* **avere**) (*acqua*) to be stagnant; (*sangue*) to cease flowing; (*fig: affari, industria*) to stagnate

ristagno [ris'taɲɲo] SM (*anche fig*) stagnation; **c'è un ristagno delle vendite** business is slack

ristampa [ris'tampa] SF (*il ristampare*) reprinting *no pl*; (*opera ristampata*) reprint

ristampare [ristam'pare] VT to reprint

ristorante [risto'rante] SM restaurant; **abbiamo mangiato al ristorante** we ate in a restaurant; **ristorante della stazione** station buffet
■ AGG INV restaurant *attr*

ristorare [risto'rare] VT to revive, refresh; **ristorare le forze** to restore one's strength
▶ **ristorarsi** VR (*rifocillarsi*) to have something to eat and drink; (*riposarsi*) to rest, have a rest

ristoratore, trice [ristora'tore] AGG refreshing, reviving
■ SM/F restaurateur

ristoro [ris'tɔro] SM (*bevanda, cibo*) refreshment; **posto di ristoro** refreshment bar, buffet, snack bar; **servizio di ristoro** (*Ferr*) refreshments *pl*

ristrettezza [ristret'tettsa] SF **1** (*scarsità*) shortage, lack, scarcity; **ristrettezza di idee** narrow-mindedness **2** **ristrettezze** SFPL poverty *sg*, straitened circumstances

ristretto, a [ris'tretto] PP *di* **restringere**
■ AGG **1** (*limitato*) limited, restricted; (*angusto*) narrow; (*racchiuso*) enclosed, hemmed in; **ristretto a** restricted *o* limited to; **di idee ristrette** (*fig*) narrow-minded **2** (*concentrato: brodo*) thick; (*: caffè*) extra strong

ristrutturante [ristruttu'rante] AGG (*crema, balsamo*) repair *attr*

ristrutturare [ristruttu'rare] VT (*appartamento*) to do up; (*: ridipingere ecc*) to redecorate; (*edificio*) to restore; (*azienda*) to reorganize; (*pelle, capelli*) to repair

ristrutturazione [ristrutturat'tsjone] SF (*vedi vb*) alteration; redecoration; restoration; reorganization; repair

risucchiare [risuk'kjare] VT (*sogg: vortice*) to swallow up

risucchio, chi [ri'sukkjo] SM (*di acqua*) undertow, pull; (*di aria*) suction

risultante [risul'tante] SM (*Mat, Fis*) resultant
■ SF (*fig*) result, effect

risultare [risul'tare] VI (*aus* **essere**) **1** (*rivelarsi*) to prove to be, turn out to be; (*essere accertato*) to be clear, emerge; (*essere noto*) to appear, seem; **la tue previsioni sono risultate errate** your predictions proved to be wrong; **dalle indagini è risultato che...** it emerged from the inquiry that ...; **dalle analisi è risultato affetto da diabete** it is clear from the tests that he is suffering from diabetes; **risulta appartenere ad un determinato gruppo politico** he's known to belong to a specific political group; **è risultato vincitore** he emerged as the winner **2** **mi risulta che...** I understand that ..., as far as I know ...; **(ne) risulta che...** it follows that ...; **non mi risulta** not as far as I know; **ti risulta che sia ancora qui?** do you know whether he's still here?; **non mi risulta che sia partito** I don't think he's left

risultato [risul'tato] SM (*gen, Mat, Sport*) result; **domani sapremo il risultato degli esami** we'll get the exam results tomorrow; **risultati parziali** (*Sport*) half-time results

risuonare [riswo'nare] VI **1** (*gen*) to resound; **un grido risuonò nel silenzio** a scream pierced the silence; **mi risuonano nella mente le sue parole** his words still echo in my mind **2** (*Fis*) to resonate
■ VT (*suonare di nuovo: musica*) to play again; (*: campanello*) to ring again

risurrezione [risurret'tsjone] SF (*Rel*) resurrection

risuscitare [risuʃʃi'tare] VT to resuscitate, restore to life; (*fig*) to revive, bring back; **risuscitare qn dalla morte** to raise sb from the dead; **questo vino farebbe risuscitare un morto** (*fig scherz*) this wine would revive the dead
■ VI (*aus* **essere**) to rise from the dead; (*fig: riprendere vigore*) to revive

risvegliare [rizveʎ'ʎare] VT (*gen*) to wake up, waken; (*fig: dall'inerzia*): **risvegliare qn (da)** to rouse sb (from); (*fig: interesse*) to stir up, arouse; (*: curiosità*) to arouse; **risvegliare l'appetito** to whet one's appetite; **risvegliare i ricordi** to bring back old memories
▶ **risvegliarsi** VIP to wake up, awaken; (*fig: interesse, curiosità*) to be aroused; **il vulcano si è risvegliato** the volcano has become active again

risveglio, gli [riz'veʎʎo] SM (*azione*) awakening, waking up; (*fig: di arte, cultura, interesse*) revival; **il**

Rr

risveglio della coscienza nazionale the awakening of national consciousness; **al risveglio** when he (*o* she *ecc*) woke up

risvolto [riz'vɔlto] SM **1** (*di giacca*) lapel; (*di manica*) cuff; (*di pantaloni*) turn-up (*Brit*), cuff (*Am*); (*di tasca*) flap; (*di libro*) inside flap **2** (*fig: aspetto secondario*) implication

ritagliare [ritaʎ'ʎare] VT (*tagliare via*): **ritagliare (da)** to cut out (of); **ho ritagliato l'articolo dal giornale** I cut the article out of the paper

ritaglio, gli [ri'taʎʎo] SM (*di giornale*) cutting, clipping; (*di stoffa*) remnant, scrap; **nei ritagli di tempo** in one's spare time

ritardante [ritar'dante] AGG (*effetto*) retardant

ritardare [ritar'dare] VT **1** (*differire*) to delay, hold up; **ha ritardato la partenza di un'ora** he delayed the departure by an hour; **ritardare il pagamento** to defer payment **2** (*rallentare: sviluppo, processo*) to slow down

■ VI (*aus con soggetto inanimato* **essere**; *con soggetto animato* **avere**) (*persona, treno*) to be late; (*orologio*) to be slow; **ritardare a fare qc** to be late in doing sth; **ritardare di un quarto d'ora** to be fifteen minutes late

ritardatario, ria, ri, rie [ritarda'tarjo] SM/F latecomer

ritardato, a [ritar'dato] AGG (*Psic*) retarded

ritardo [ri'tardo] SM **1** (*di treno, posta*) delay; (*di persona*) lateness *no pl*; **essere in ritardo** to be late; **un ritardo di 2 ore** a 2-hour delay; **il volo ha avuto un ritardo di due ore** the flight was two hours late; **arrivò con 2 ore di ritardo** it (*o* he *ecc*) arrived 2 hours late; **scusa il ritardo** sorry I'm late **2** (*mentale*) backwardness, retardation; **un ritardo dello sviluppo mentale** a retarded mental development

ritegno [ri'teɲɲo] SM restraint; **abbi un po' di ritegno!** restrain yourself!; **senza ritegno** unrestrained, without restraint

ritemprare [ritem'prare] VT (*forze, spirito*) to restore

ritenere [rite'nere] VB IRREG

■ VT **1** (*considerare*) to think, believe, consider; **lo ritengo un ottimo insegnante** I think he's an excellent teacher; **ritenere opportuno fare qc** to think it opportune to do sth; **ho ritenuto che fosse opportuno fare così** I felt it opportune to do so; **ritengo di sì** I think so; **ritengo di no** I don't think so; **si ritiene che l'uomo sia fuggito in macchina** they think that the man escaped by car **2** (*trattenere: denaro*) to withhold, deduct; (*: nozioni, concetti*) to retain; **gli hanno ritenuto due giorni di paga** they withheld 2 days' pay; **ho una memoria così labile che non riesco a ritenere nulla** my memory is so poor that I can't seem to retain anything **3** (*umidità, liquidi*) to retain

▶ **ritenersi** VR to consider o.s.; **si ritiene un genio** he thinks he's a genius

ritengo [ri'tengo], **ritenni** [ri'tenni] VB *vedi* **ritenere**

ritentare [riten'tare] VT to try again, make another attempt at

ritenuta [rite'nuta] SF deduction; **ritenuta sulla paga** deduction from one's pay; **ritenuta d'acconto** *advance tax deduction*; **ritenuta alla fonte** taxation at source

ritenzione [riten'tsjone] SF (*Med*) retention; **ritenzione idrica** water retention

riterrò *ecc* [riter'rɔ] VB *vedi* **ritenere**

ritirare [riti'rare] VT **1** (*mano, braccio*) to pull back; (*candidatura*) to withdraw; (*soldi*) to withdraw, take out; (*certificato, bagaglio*) to collect, pick up; (*bucato*) to bring in; **ha ritirato dei soldi** he took out some money; **ritirare (lo stipendio)** to get paid; **appena ritiro (lo stipendio) ti restituisco i soldi** as soon as I get paid I'll pay you back; **dove si ritirano i bagagli?** where is the baggage reclaim?; **ritirare il passaporto a qn** to withdraw sb's passport; **gli hanno ritirato la patente** they disqualified him from driving (*Brit*), they took away his licence (*Brit*) *o* license (*Am*); **ritiro quello che ho detto** I take back what I said **2** (*cambiale*) to retire **3** (*tirare di nuovo*) to pull again; (*lanciare di nuovo*) to throw again

▶ **ritirarsi** VR **1** (*Mil*) to retreat, withdraw; (*persona: da un'attività*) to retire; (*: appartarsi*) to withdraw, retire; **si ritirò nella sua stanza** he withdrew *o* retired to his room; **ritirarsi a vita privata** to withdraw from public life;

▶ **ritirarsi** VIP **1** (*retrocedere: acque*) to recede, subside **2** (*tessuto*) to shrink

ritirata [riti'rata] SF **1** (*Mil*) retreat, withdrawal; (*: in caserma*) tattoo; **suonare la ritirata** to sound the retreat (*o* the tattoo); **essere in ritirata** to be in retreat **2** (*latrina*) lavatory (*Brit*), toilet (*Brit*), bathroom (*Am*)

ritirato, a [riti'rato] AGG secluded; **fare vita ritirata** to live in seclusion

ritiro [ri'tiro] SM **1** (*il ritirare: di truppe, candidatura, soldi*) withdrawal; (*: di biglietti, pacchi*) collection; (*: di passaporto*) confiscation; **ritiro bagagli** baggage reclaim; **la ricevuta vi verrà consegnata al momento del ritiro della merce** you will be given the receipt on collection of the goods; **"per il ritiro dei vaglia postali rivolgersi a..."** "postal orders are issued at ..." **2** (*il ritirarsi: Mil*) withdrawal, retreat; (*: di acque*) subsidence; **dopo il suo ritiro dal mondo dello spettacolo** after retiring from show business; **dopo il suo ritiro dalla gara** after withdrawing from the competition **3** (*luogo appartato: anche Rel*) retreat; **in ritiro** in retreat; **fare quindici giorni di ritiro** to go on a fortnight's retreat; **la squadra andrà in ritiro per una settimana** (*Sport*) the team will go away on a training session for a week

ritmare [rit'mare] VT: **ritmare il passo** *or* **ritmare la corsa** to keep the rhythm, keep in rhythm

ritmato, a [rit'mato] AGG rhythmic(al)

ritmica ['ritmika] SF (*Mus*) rhythmics *sg*

ritmicamente [ritmika'mente] AVV rhythmically

ritmico, a, ci, che ['ritmiko] AGG rhythmic(al)

ritmo ['ritmo] SM **1** (*gen*) rhythm; **ballare al ritmo di valzer** to waltz **2** (*fig: velocità*) speed, rate; **al ritmo di** at a speed *o* rate of; **a questo ritmo** at this rate; **il ritmo frenetico della vita moderna** the frantic pace of life today

rito ['rito] SM (*Rel*) rite; (*cerimonia*) ritual; **di rito** customary, usual

ritoccare [ritok'kare] VT (*disegno, foto, trucco*) to touch up; (*testo, prezzi*) to alter

ritocco, chi [ri'tokko] SM (*di disegno, trucco*) touching up *no pl*; (*di testo*) alteration; **dare un ritocco a qc** to touch sth up; alter sth

ritorcere [ri'tɔrtʃere] VB IRREG

■ VT (*filato*) to twist; (*fig: accusa, insulto*) to throw back

▶ **ritorcersi** VIP (*tornare a danno di*) **ritorcersi contro** to turn against

ritornare [ritor'nare] VI (*aus* **essere**) = **tornare**

■ VT (*restituire*): **ritornare qc a qn** to return sth to sb, give sth back to sb

ritornello [ritor'nɛllo] SM (*Mus, Poesia*) refrain; (*fig: storia*) story; **è sempre il solito ritornello** it's always the same old story

ritorno [ri'torno] SM **1** (*gen*) return; **essere di ritorno** to be back; **sarò di ritorno venerdì prossimo** I'll be back next Friday; **far ritorno** to return; **al ritorno** (*tornando*) on the way back; **al ritorno siamo passati per Bristol** we went through Bristol on the way back; **al mio/tuo ritorno** on my/your return; **il viaggio di ritorno** the return journey; **il viaggio di ritorno è stato più breve** the return journey was shorter; **durante il (viaggio di) ritorno** on the return trip, on the way back; **due ore andata e ritorno** two hours there and back; **un biglietto di andata e ritorno** a return ticket; **girone di ritorno** (*Sport*) second half of the season; **avere un ritorno di fiamma** (*Aut*) to backfire; **hanno avuto un ritorno di fiamma** (*fig*) they're back in love again **2** (*in restituzione*): **fammelo avere di ritorno entro la fine del mese** let me have it back by the end of the month

ritorsione [ritor'sjone] SF (*rappresaglia*) retaliation

ritorto, a [ri'tɔrto] PP *di* **ritorcere**
■ AGG (*cotone, corda*) twisted

ritradurre [ritra'durre] VT (*tradurre: di nuovo*) to retranslate; (*: nella lingua originale*) to back-translate

ritrarre [ri'trarre] VB IRREG
■ VT **1** (*Pittura, fig*) to portray, depict **2** (*tirare indietro*) to withdraw
▶ **ritrarsi** VR to move back

ritrasformare [ritrasfor'mare] VT: **ritrasformare qc in** to turn sth back into
▶ **ritrasformarsi** VIP: **ritrasformarsi in** to turn back into

ritrasmettere [ritraz'mettere] VT IRREG to re-broadcast

ritrattabile [ritrat'tabile] AGG (*dichiarazione, accusa*) retractable

ritrattare [ritrat'tare] VT **1** (*dichiarazione*) to retract, withdraw, take back **2** (*trattare nuovamente*) to deal with again, cover again

ritrattazione [ritrattat'tsjone] SF withdrawal

ritrattista, i, e [ritrat'tista] SM/F portrait painter

ritrattistica [ritrat'tistika] SF (*Art*) portraiture

ritratto, a [ri'tratto] PP *di* **ritrarre**
■ SM portrait; **essere il ritratto della salute** to be the picture of health; **è il ritratto di suo padre** he's his father's image

ritrosamente [ritrosa'mente] AVV shyly

ritrosia [ritro'sia] SF (*riluttanza*) reluctance, unwillingness; (*timidezza*) shyness

ritroso, a [ri'troso] AGG **1** (*timido*) shy, bashful **2** (*restio*): **ritroso a fare qc** reluctant to do sth; **a ritroso** AVV (*indietro*) backwards

ritrovamento [ritrova'mento] SM (*di cadavere, oggetto smarrito*) finding; (*oggetto ritrovato*) find

ritrovare [ritro'vare] VT **1** (*ricuperare: oggetto, persona*) to find; (*pace*) to find again; (*forza*) to find again, recover; **ho ritrovato l'agendina** I've found my diary **2** (*rincontrare*) to meet again; (*: per caso*) to run into
▶ **ritrovarsi** VIP **1** (*in una situazione*) to find o.s.; end up; **si ritrovò solo/a fare i lavori più umili** he ended up alone/doing the most menial tasks; **mi sono ritrovato con 5 euro in più** I found myself with 5 euros extra; **ci ritrovammo al punto di partenza** we ended up where we started **2** (*possedere: fam scherz*) **con la fortuna che si ritrova...** with his luck ... **2** (*incontrarsi*) **ritrovarsi con** (*amici*) to meet

ritrovato [ritro'vato] SM discovery

ritrovo [ri'trɔvo] SM (*punto d'incontro*) meeting place; **ritrovo notturno** night club

ritto, a ['ritto] AGG (*in piedi: persona*) upright, on one's feet; **non riusciva a star ritto** he couldn't stand upright; **aveva i capelli ritti** his hair was standing on end

rituale [ritu'ale] AGG (*di rito*) ritual; (*fig: solito*) customary, usual
■ SM (*Rel*) ritual

ritualmente [ritual'mente] AVV ritually

riunificare [riunifi'kare] VT to reunify

riunificazione [riunifikat'tsjone] SF reunification

riunione [riu'njone] SF (*adunanza*) meeting; (*riconciliazione*) reunion; **una riunione familiare** a family gathering; **essere in riunione** to be in a meeting; **il presidente è in riunione** the president is in a meeting

riunire [riu'nire] VT **1** (*mettere insieme: oggetti*) to gather together, collect; (*: persone*) to assemble, get together; (*: fig: riconciliare*) to bring together (again), reunite; **siamo qui riuniti per festeggiare...** we are gathered here to celebrate ... **2** (*ricongiungere*) to put together, join together
▶ **riunirsi** VIP (*radunarsi*) to meet; (*tornare insieme*) to come together again, be reunited

riunito, a [riu'nito] AGG (*Comm*) associated; **cooperative riunite** associated cooperatives

riusare [riu'zare] VT to reuse

riuscire [riuʃ'ʃire] VI IRREG (*aus* **essere**) **1** (*aver successo*): **riuscire (in qc/a fare qc)** to succeed (in sth/in doing sth), be successful (in sth/in doing sth); **il tentativo non è riuscito** the attempt was unsuccessful; **riuscire negli studi** to do well at school (*o* at university) **2** (*essere capace*) to be able, manage; **riuscire a fare qc** to manage *o* be able to do sth; **siamo riusciti a convincerla** we managed to persuade her; **non riesco a farlo** I can't do it, I am unable to do it; **non mi riesce di farlo** I can't (manage to) do it; **non ci riesco** I can't **3** (*essere, risultare*) to be, prove (to be); **ti riuscirà più facile dopo un po' di pratica** it'll be easier *o* you'll find it easier after a bit of practice; **mi riesce antipatico** I don't like him; **mi riesce difficile** I find it difficult; **la festa è riuscita male** the party wasn't a success **4** (*uscire di nuovo*) to go out again, go back out

riuscita [riuʃ'ʃita] SF (*esito*) result, outcome; (*buon esito*) success; **fare** *o* **avere una buona riuscita** to be a success, be successful

riutilizzare [riutilid'dzare] VT to use again, reuse

riutilizzazione [riutiliddzat'tsjone] SF reuse, reutilization

riva ['riva] SF (*di mare, lago*) shore; (*di fiume*) bank; **in riva al mare** on the (sea) shore

rivaccinare [rivattʃi'nare] VT to revaccinate

rivale [ri'vale] AGG rival *attr*; **appartengono a bande rivali** they belong to rival gangs
■ SM/F rival; **non avere rivali** (*anche fig*) to be unrivalled; **come stilista non ha rivali** as a designer he has no rivals

rivaleggiare [rivaled'dʒare] VI (*aus* **avere**) to compete, vie; **rivaleggiare con qn per qc** to vie with sb for sth; **nessuno può rivaleggiare con lui** he is unrivalled

rivalità [rivali'ta] SF INV rivalry

rivalsa [ri'valsa] SF **1** (*risarcimento*) compensation

Rr

2 (*rivincita*) revenge; **prendersi una rivalsa su qn** to take revenge on sb
rivalutare [rivalu'tare] VT (*Econ*) to revalue; (*fig*) to re-evaluate
rivalutazione [rivalutat'tsjone] SF (*Econ*) revaluation; (*fig*) re-evaluation
rivangare [rivan'gare] VT (*ricordi*) to dig up (again)
■ VI (*aus* **avere**) **rivangare nel passato** to dig up the past again
rivedere [rive'dere] VB IRREG
■ VT **1** (*vedere di nuovo*: *film ecc*) to see again; (: *persona*) to see again, meet again; **dalla scorsa estate non li ho più rivisti** I haven't seen them since last summer; **guarda chi si rivede!** look who it is! **2** (*verificare, correggere*) to revise, check; **rivedere le bozze** to proofread;
▶ **rivedersi** VR (*uso reciproco*) to see each other again, meet (again)
rivedibile [rive'dibile] AGG (*Mil*) *temporarily unfit for service*
rivedibilità [rivedibili'ta] SF (*Mil*) *temporary unfitness for service*
rivedrò *ecc* [rive'drɔ] VB *vedi* **rivedere**
rivelare [rive'lare] VT (*svelare*) to reveal; (: *segreto*) to disclose, reveal; (*dimostrare*: *capacità*) to reveal, display, show; **non ha voluto rivelare il nome dell'informatore** she wouldn't reveal the name of her informant; **quella commedia lo rivelò al grande pubblico** that play revealed him to the public at large
▶ **rivelarsi** VIP (*tendenza, talento*) to be revealed, reveal itself
▶ **rivelarsi** VR to prove to be; **rivelarsi onesto** to prove to be honest; **si è rivelato un ottimo portiere** he proved to be an excellent goalkeeper
rivelatore, trice [rivela'tore] AGG revealing
■ SM (*Tecn*) detector; (*Fot*) developer
rivelazione [rivelat'tsjone] SF (*gen*) revelation; (*di segreto, notizia*) disclosure; **come ballerina è stata una rivelazione!** her dancing was a revelation!; **quell'attore è stato la rivelazione dell'anno** that actor was the discovery of the year
rivendere [ri'vendere] VT (*vendere*: *di nuovo*) to resell, sell again; (: *al dettaglio*) to retail, sell retail
rivendicare [rivendi'kare] VT to claim, demand
rivendicazione [rivendikat'tsjone] SF claim; **rivendicazioni salariali** wage claims; **rivendicazioni sindacali** union demands
rivendita [ri'vendita] SF (*negozio*) retailer's (shop); **rivendita di tabacchi** tobacconist's (shop) (*Brit*), tobacco *o* smoke shop (*Am*)
rivenditore, trice [rivendi'tore] SM/F retailer; **rivenditore autorizzato** authorized dealer
riverberare [riverbe'rare] VT (*luce, calore*) to reflect; (*suono*) to reverberate
riverbero [ri'vɛrbero] SM (*vedi vb*) reflection; reverberation
riverente [rive'rɛnte] AGG reverent, respectful
riverentemente [riverente'mente] AVV reverently, respectfully
riverenza [rive'rɛntsa] SF **1** (*rispetto*) reverence, respect **2** (*inchino*) bow; (: *di donna*) curtsey; **fece una profonda riverenza** he bowed low
riverire [rive'rire] VT (*rispettare*) to revere, respect; **la riverisco, professore** (*salutando*) my respects, professor
riversare [river'sare] VT **1** (*versare*) to pour; (: *di nuovo*) to pour again; (*fig*: *amore, affetto*): **riversare su** to shower on, lavish on; **ha riversato tutte le sue energie in quel lavoro** he threw himself into that job **2** (*Inform*) to dump
▶ **riversarsi** VIP to pour (out); **la folla si riversò nelle strade** the crowd poured into the streets

LO SAPEVI...?
riversare non si traduce mai con la parola inglese *reverse*

rivestimento [rivesti'mento] SM (*azione, materiale*) covering; (*strato*: *di vernice*) coating, veneer
rivestire [rives'tire] VT **1** (*ricoprire*: *gen*): **rivestire (di)** to cover (with); (: *con vernice*) to coat (with); **rivestire in stoffa l'interno di una scatola** to line a box with material; **rivestire di piastrelle** to tile **2** (*carica*) to hold; **rivestire un grado elevato** to be high-ranking **3** (*vestire di nuovo*) to dress again
▶ **rivestirsi** VR to get dressed (again)
rivettatrice [rivetta'tritʃe] SF (*Tecn*: *macchina*) riveter
rivetto [ri'vetto] SM (*Tecn*) rivet
rividi *ecc* [ri'vidi] VB *vedi* **rivedere**
riviera [ri'vjɛra] SF **1** coast; **la Riviera Ligure** the Italian Riviera **2** (*Equitazione*: *ostacolo*) water jump
rivincita [ri'vintʃita] SF (*Sport*) return match; (*Carte*) return game; (*fig*) revenge; **prendersi la rivincita (su qn)** to take *o* get one's revenge (on sb)
rivissuto, a [rivis'suto] PP *di* **rivivere**
rivista [ri'vista] SF **1** (*periodica*) magazine; (*letteraria*) review; (*Tecn, Med*) journal; **una rivista di moda** a fashion magazine **2** (*Teatro, TV*) revue, variety show **3** (*Mil*) inspection; **passare in rivista** to review
rivisto, a [ri'visto] PP *di* **rivedere**
rivitalizzante [rivitalid'dzante] AGG (*prodotti cosmetici*) revitalizing
rivitalizzare [rivitalid'dzare] VT to revitalize
rivivere [ri'vivere] VB IRREG
■ VT: **rivivere qc** (*avventura, esperienza*) to live through sth again
■ VI (*aus* **essere**) (*vivere di nuovo*) to live again; (*prendere vigore*) to come to life again; (*tradizioni*) to be revived; **far rivivere** (*resuscitare*) to bring back to life; (*rinvigorire*) to revive, put new life into; (*epoca, moda*) to revive; **sentirsi rivivere** to feel a new man (*o* woman)
rivo ['rivo] SM (*di lava, lacrime*) stream
rivolere [rivo'lere] VT (*volere*: *indietro*) to want back; (: *di nuovo*) to want again
rivolgere [ri'vɔldʒere] VB IRREG
■ VT (*indirizzare*: *attenzione, sguardo, proiettore*) to turn, direct; (: *parole*) to address; **rivolgere un'arma contro qn** to point a weapon at sb; **rivolgere lo sguardo verso qn** to turn *o* direct one's gaze towards sb; **le rivolse uno sguardo di rimprovero** he gave her a disapproving look; **rivolgere un'accusa/una critica a qn** to accuse/criticize sb; **rivolgere la propria attenzione a un problema** to turn one's attention to a problem; **rivolgere la parola a qn** to talk *o* speak to sb, address sb; **sono due giorni che non mi rivolge la parola** she hasn't spoken to me for two days; **non si rivolgono più la parola** they are no longer on speaking terms; **rivolgere un saluto a qn** to greet sb, say hello to sb;
▶ **rivolgersi** VR **1** **rivolgersi a** (*per informazioni*) to go and see, go and speak to; go and ask; **dovrebbe rivolgersi all'impiegato laggiù** you should go and ask the man over there; **rivolgersi all'ufficio competente** to apply to the office concerned; **non mi rivolgevo a te** I wasn't talking to you; **si rivolse a lei**

dicendo... he turned to her and said ... **2 rivolgersi verso** (*girarsi*) to turn to
rivolgimento [rivoldʒi'mento] SM upheaval
rivolo ['rivolo] SM rivulet
rivolsi *ecc* [ri'vɔlsi] VB *vedi* **rivolgere**
rivolta [ri'vɔlta] SF revolt, rebellion; **in rivolta (contro)** in revolt (against)
rivoltante [rivol'tante] AGG revolting, disgusting
rivoltare [rivol'tare] VT **1** (*voltare: di nuovo*) to turn again; (: *pagine, carte*) to turn over again; (: *vestito*) to turn inside out; (: *bistecca, frittata*) to turn (over) **2** (*disgustare*) to revolt, disgust; **una scena che fa rivoltare lo stomaco** a scene which turns one's stomach
▶ **rivoltarsi** VR (*rigirarsi*) to turn; **rivoltarsi nel letto** to toss and turn (in bed);
▶ **rivoltarsi** VIP (*ribellarsi*) **rivoltarsi (a)** to revolt *o* rebel (against)
rivoltella [rivol'tɛlla] SF (*gen*) pistol; (: *a tamburo*) revolver
rivoltellata [rivoltel'lata] SF (*vedi rivoltella*) (pistol) shot; (revolver) shot
rivolto, a [ri'vɔlto] PP *di* **rivolgere**
rivoltoso, a [rivol'toso] AGG rebellious
■ SM/F rebel
rivoluzionare [rivoluttsjo'nare] VT (*anche fig*) to revolutionize; (*fig: mettere sottosopra*) to turn upside down
rivoluzionario, ria, ri, rie [rivoluttsjo'narjo] AGG, SM/F revolutionary
rivoluzione [rivolut'tsjone] SF (*gen, Pol, Mat, Astron*) revolution; (*fig: scompiglio*) mess; **rivoluzione industriale** industrial revolution
rizoma, i [rid'dzɔma] SM rhizome
rizzare [rit'tsare] VT (*palo*) to erect; (*tenda*) to pitch; (*coda*) to raise, lift; (*orecchie*) to prick up; **è roba da far rizzare i capelli** it's enough to make your hair stand on end
▶ **rizzarsi** VR to stand up; **rizzarsi in piedi** to stand up, get to one's feet; **rizzarsi a sedere** to sit up;
▶ **rizzarsi** VIP: **gli si sono rizzati i capelli** his hair stood on end
RN SIGLA = *Rimini*
RNA ['ɛrre'ɛnne'a] SIGLA M RNA (= *ribonucleic acid*)
RO SIGLA = *Rovigo*
roaming ['roumiŋ] SM (*Telec*) roaming
roano, a [ro'ano] AGG, SM (*cavallo*) roan
roba ['rɔba] SF **1** (*gen*) things *pl*, stuff; (*cose proprie*) belongings *pl*, things *pl*, possessions *pl*; **roba da lavare** washing; **posso mettere la mia roba da lavare in lavatrice?** can I put my washing in the machine?; **roba da mangiare** food, things to eat; **c'era un sacco di roba da mangiare** there was lots of food; **roba da stirare** ironing; **roba usata** secondhand goods; **roba di valore** valuables; **ho un sacco di roba da fare** I've got a lot to do, I've got lots of things to do; **ha ancora qui tutta la sua roba?** has he still got all his things here?; **che roba è questa?** what is this?; **cos'è quella roba sul tavolo?** what's that stuff on the table?; **e chiami whisky questa roba?** and you call this stuff whisky? **2** (*faccenda, affare*) affair, matter; **non è roba che ti riguardi** this doesn't concern you
3 (*fraseologia*): **bella roba!** (*iro: che gran cosa!*) so what!; (: *che mascalzonata!*) that's nice, isn't it!; **roba da matti** *o* **pazzi!** it's sheer madness *o* lunacy!, it's just incredible

LO SAPEVI...?
roba non si traduce mai con la parola inglese *robe*

robinia [ro'binja] SF locust tree
robivecchi [robi'vɛkki] SM/F INV junk dealer
robot ['rɔbot] SM INV robot; **robot di** *o* **da cucina** food-processor
robotica [ro'bɔtika] SF robotics *sg*
robustezza [robus'tettsa] SF (*di persona, pianta*) robustness, sturdiness; (*di edificio, ponte*) soundness
robusto, a [ro'busto] AGG (*persona, pianta*) robust, sturdy; (*euf: persona: grasso*) well-built; (*edificio, ponte*) sound, solid; (*corda, catena*) strong; (*appetito*) healthy; (*vino*) full-bodied; (*voce*) powerful
rocambolesco, a, schi, sche [rokambo'lesko] AGG fantastic, incredible
rocca, che ['rɔkka] SF fortress; **la Rocca di Gibilterra** the Rock of Gibraltar
roccaforte [rokka'fɔrte] SF (*pl* **roccheforti**) (*anche fig*) stronghold
rocchetto [rok'ketto] SM **1** (*di filo*) spool **2** (*Cine*) reel **3** (*Elettr*) coil
roccia, ce ['rɔttʃa] SF (*gen, Geol*) rock; (*sport*) rock climbing; **fare roccia** to go rock climbing
rocciatore, trice [rottʃa'tore] SM/F rock climber
roccioso, a [rot'tʃoso] AGG rocky; **le Montagne Rocciose** the Rocky Mountains
rock [rɔk] AGG, SM (*Mus*) rock; **rock acrobatico** (*ballo*) acrobatic rock
roco, a, chi, che ['rɔko] AGG hoarse
rodaggio, gi [ro'daddʒo] SM (*Aut*) running (*Brit*) *o* breaking (*Am*) in; **la macchina è ancora in rodaggio** the car is still being run *o* broken in; **periodo di rodaggio** (*fig*) period of adjustment
Rodano ['rɔdano] SM: **il Rodano** the Rhone
rodare [ro'dare] VT (*Aut, Tecn*) to run (*Brit*) *o* break (*Am*) in
rodeo [ro'deo] SM rodeo
rodere ['rodere] VB IRREG
■ VT (*rosicchiare*) to gnaw (at); (*corrodere*) to corrode; **rodersi il fegato** (*fig*) to torment o.s.;
▶ **rodersi** VR: **rodersi dal rimorso/dall'invidia** to be consumed with remorse/with envy
Rodi ['rɔdi] SF Rhodes *sg*
rodigino, a [rodi'dʒino] AGG of *o* from Rovigo
■ SM/F inhabitant *o* native of Rovigo
roditore [rodi'tore] SM (*Zool*) rodent
rododendro [rodo'dɛndro] SM (*Bot*) rhododendron
rogito ['rɔdʒito] SM (*Dir*) (notary's) deed
rogna ['roɲɲa] SF (*Med*) scabies *sg*; (*di animale*) mange; (*fig: guaio*) trouble, bother, nuisance; **cercar rogne** to be looking for trouble, to be asking for it; **ha avuto rogne con la polizia** he got into trouble with the police
rognone [roɲ'ɲone] SM (*Culin*) kidney
rognoso, a [roɲ'ɲoso] AGG (*persona*) scabby; (*animale*) mangy; (*fig*) troublesome
rogo, ghi ['rɔgo] SM (*funebre*) funeral pyre; (*supplizio*): **il rogo** the stake; **mandare qn al rogo** to condemn sb to be burned at the stake; **la casa era ormai un rogo** the house was now a mass of flames
rollare [rol'lare] VI (*aus* **avere**) (*Naut, Aer*) to roll
■ VT (*fam: sigaretta*) to roll (up)
rollata [rol'lata] SF (*Naut, Aer*) (excessive) roll
roll-bar ['roul ba:] SM INV (*Aut*) roll bar
rollino [rol'lino] SM = **rullino**
rollio, lii [rol'lio] SM (*Naut, Aer*) roll, rolling

ROM [rom] SIGLA F ROM (= *read-only memory*)
Roma ['roma] SF Rome; **domani andremo a Roma** we're going to Rome tomorrow; **abita a Roma** she lives in Rome
▷ www.comune.roma.it/
▷ www.romasegreta.it/trevi/quirinale.htm
romagnolo, a [romaɲ'ɲɔlo] AGG of *o* from Romagna
■ SM/F inhabitant *o* native of Romagna
romanesco, sca, schi, sche [roma'nesko] AGG Roman
■ SM Roman dialect
Romania [roma'nia] SF Rumania, Romania
romanico, a, ci, che [ro'maniko] AGG, SM (*Arte*) Romanesque
romanità [romani'ta] SF (*Storia*): **la Romanità** the Roman world; (*fig: spirito*) the Roman spirit
romano, a [ro'mano] AGG Roman; **la Chiesa romana** the Roman Catholic Church; **fare** *o* **pagare alla romana** to go Dutch
■ SM/F Roman
romanticamente [romantika'mente] AVV romantically
romanticheria [romantike'ria] SF sentimentality
romanticismo [romanti'tʃizmo] SM romanticism
romantico, a, ci, che [ro'mantiko] AGG, SM/F romantic
romanza [ro'mandza] SF (*Mus, Letteratura*) romance
romanzare [roman'dzare] VT to romanticize
romanzato, a [roman'dzato] AGG romanticized
romanzescamente [romandzeska'mente] AVV fantastically, incredibly
romanzesco, a, schi, sche [roman'dzesko] AGG (*stile, personaggi*) fictional; (*fig: amori, vicende*) fantastic, storybook *attr*
■ SM: **avere del romanzesco** to sound like something out of a novel
romanziere, a [roman'dzjɛre] SM/F novelist
romanzo [ro'mandzo] SM (*gen*) novel; **leggo soprattutto romanzi** I mainly read novels; **romanzo d'amore** love story; **romanzo d'appendice** serial novel, serial (story); **romanzo d'avventure** adventure story; **romanzo cavalleresco** tale of chivalry; **romanzo di fantascienza** science-fiction novel *o* story; **romanzo fiume** saga; **romanzo giallo** detective story; **romanzo poliziesco** detective story; **romanzo rosa** romantic novel; **romanzo sceneggiato** novel adapted for television
■ AGG (*lingua*) Romance *attr*
rombare [rom'bare] VI (*aus* **avere**) to roar, rumble, thunder
rombo[1] ['rombo] SM (*rumore*) roar, rumble, thunder
rombo[2] ['rombo] SM (*Geom*) rhombus
rombo[3] ['rombo] SM (*pesce*) turbot
romeno, a [ro'mɛno], **rumeno, a** [ru'mɛno] AGG, SM/F Rumanian, Romanian
■ SM (*lingua*) Rumanian, Romanian
Romolo ['rɔmolo] SM Romulus
rompere ['rompere] VB IRREG
■ VT (*gen, fig*) to break; (*sfasciare*) to smash up; (*scarpe, calzoni*) to split; (*fidanzamento, negoziati*) to break off; **ho rotto un bicchiere!** I've broken a glass!; **rompere qc in testa a qn** to break sth over sb's head; **il fiume ha rotto gli argini** the river burst its banks; **rompere un contratto** to break a contract; **rompere il silenzio/il ghiaccio** to break the silence/the ice; **rompere gli indugi** (*fig*) to take action; **rompere le scatole a qn** (*fam*) to get on sb's nerves; **hai proprio rotto (le scatole)!** (*fam*) knock it off!; **uffa quanto rompi!** (*fam*) what a pain the neck you are!; **rompere (i rapporti) con qn** to break off with sb; **un rumore che rompe i timpani** a deafening noise; **rompersi una gamba/l'osso del collo** to break a leg/one's neck; **rompersi la testa** (*fig*) to rack one's brains; **rompersi la schiena** (*fig*) to work hard
▶ **rompersi** VIP (*gen*) to break

LO SAPEVI...?
rompere non si traduce mai con la parola inglese *romp*

rompiballe [rompi'balle], **rompipalle** [rompi'palle] SM/F INV (*fam!*) pain in the arse (*Brit fam!*) *o* ass (*Am fam!*)
rompicapo [rompi'kapo] SM (*problema*) worry, headache; (*gioco enigmistico*) brain-teaser, puzzle
rompicollo [rompi'kɔllo] SM daredevil
rompighiaccio, ci [rompi'gjattʃo] SM icebreaker
rompimento [rompi'mento] SM (*fig fam*) nuisance, bother, pain
rompiscatole [rompis'katole] SM/F INV (*fam*) nuisance, pain in the neck, pest; **è un vero rompiscatole!** he's a real pain!
roncola ['ronkola] SF (*Agr*) bill hook
ronda ['ronda] SF (*Mil*) rounds *pl*; (*Polizia*) beat, patrol, rounds *pl*; (*pattuglia*) patrol; **fare la ronda** to be on one's rounds (*o* on patrol); **essere di ronda** to be on patrol duty
rondeau [rɔ̃'do], **rondò** [ron'do] SM INV (*Aut*) roundabout (*Brit*), traffic circle (*Am*)
rondella [ron'dɛlla] SF (*Tecn*) washer
rondine ['rondine] SF (*uccello*) swallow; **una rondine non fa primavera** (*Proverbio*) one swallow doesn't make a summer; **rondine di mare** tern
rondone [ron'done] SM (*uccello*) swift
ronfare [ron'fare] VI (*aus* **avere**) (*persona: russare*) to snore; (*gatto: far le fusa*) to purr
ronzare [ron'dzare] VI (*aus* **avere**) to buzz, hum; **ronzare intorno a qn** (*fig*) to hang about sb; **quell'idea continuava a ronzargli in testa** that idea was still buzzing around in his head; **mi ronzano le orecchie** my ears are buzzing
ronzino [ron'dzino] SM (*pegg: cavallo*) nag
ronzio, ii [ron'dzio] SM (*di insetti*) buzzing, humming; (*del motore*) humming; (*di orecchie*) buzzing, ringing; **ronzio auricolare** (*Med*) tinnitus *sg*
ROS [ros] SIGLA M (= **Raggruppamento operativo speciale**) *Special operations squad*
rosa ['rɔza] AGG INV (*colore*) pink; (*sentimentale: letteratura, romanzo*) romantic; **stampa rosa** women's magazines; **vedere tutto rosa** to see everything through rose-coloured spectacles
■ SF **1** (*Bot*) rose; **non sono tutte rose e fiori** (*fig*) it's not all a bed of roses; **se son rose fioriranno** (*fig*) the proof of the pudding is in the eating; **non c'è rosa senza spine** (*Proverbio*) there's no rose without a thorn; **rosa canina** dog rose; **rosa di Natale** Christmas rose
2 (*fig: gruppo*): **rosa dei candidati** list of candidates
3 **rosa dei venti** wind rose
■ SM INV (*colore*) pink
rosaio, ai [ro'zajo] SM (*pianta*) rosebush, rose tree; (*giardino*) rose garden; (*aiuola*) rosebed
rosario, ri [ro'zarjo] SM (*Rel*) rosary; **dire** *o* **recitare il rosario** to say *o* recite the rosary
rosatello [roza'tɛllo] SM rosè (wine)

rosato, a [ro'zato] AGG (*colore*) pinkish, rosy; (*vino*) rosé
■ SM INV (*vino*) rosé (wine)
rosbif ['rɔzbif] SM INV roast beef
rosé [ro'ze] AGG INV, SM INV rosé
roseo, a ['rɔzeo] AGG (*colorito*) pinkish, rosy; (*fig*: *ottimistico*) rosy, bright
roseto [ro'zeto] SM rose garden
rosetta [ro'zetta] SF **1** (*diamante*) rose-cut diamond **2** (*Tecn, rondella*) washer **3** (*pane*) *kind of roll*
rosi *ecc* ['rosi] VB *vedi* **rodere**
rosicchiare [rosik'kjare] VT (*rodere*) to gnaw (at); (*mangiucchiare*) to nibble (at); **rosicchiarsi le unghie** to bite one's nails
rosicoltore, trice [rozikol'tore] SM/F rose grower
rosmarino [rozma'rino] SM (*Bot*) rosemary
roso, a ['roso] PP *di* **rodere**
rosolare [rozo'lare] VT (*Culin*) to brown
rosolatura [rozola'tura] SF (*Culin*) browning
rosolia [rozo'lia] SF (*Med*) German measles *sg*, rubella (*termine tecn*)
rosone [ro'zone] SM (*finestra*: *su chiese*) rose window; **rosone da soffitto** ceiling rose
rospo ['rɔspo] SM (*Zool*) toad; **è un rospo** (*pegg*: *persona*) she (*o* he) is hideous; **ingoiare un** *o* **il rospo** (*fig*) to swallow a bitter pill; **sputa il rospo!** out with it!
rosseggiare [rossed'dʒare] VI (*aus* **essere**) (*letter*) to redden, turn red
rossetto [ros'setto] SM lipstick
rossiccio, cia, ci, ce [ros'sittʃo] AGG reddish
rosso, a ['rosso] AGG **1** (*gen*) red; **ha i capelli rossi** she's got red hair; **diventare rosso (per la vergogna)** to blush *o* go red (with *o* for shame); **rosso come un gambero** *o* **un peperone** (*per la vergogna*) as red as a beetroot (*Brit*) *o* beet (*Am*); (*per il sole*) as red as a lobster; **l'Armata Rossa** the Red Army; **il mar Rosso** the Red Sea
■ SM (*colore*) red; (*di roulette*) rouge, red; (*di semaforo*) red light; (*d'uovo*) yolk; (*vino*) red wine; **rosso di sera bel tempo si spera** (*Proverbio*) red sky at night shepherd's delight; **rosso di mattina maltempo s'avvicina** (*Proverbio*) red sky at dawning shepherd's warning; **essere in rosso** (*Banca*) to be in the red
■ SM/F (*che ha i capelli rossi*) redhead; (*fig Pol*) Red; (*persona di sinistra*) red, left-winger
rossore [ros'sore] SM (*per infiammazione*) redness; (*delle guance*) flush; (: *per vergogna*) blush; **sentirsi salire il rossore alle guance** (*per vergogna, pudore*) to begin to blush, feel one's cheeks go red
rosticceria [rostittʃe'ria] SF *shop selling roast meat and other prepared food*
rostro ['rɔstro] SM (*di rapace*) beak; (*sulle navi*) rostrum
Rota ['rɔta] SF (*Rel*: *anche*; **Sacra Rota**) Rota
rota ['rɔta] SF (*gergale*) cold turkey
rotabile [ro'tabile] AGG: **strada rotabile** carriageway, roadway; **materiale rotabile** (*Ferr*) rolling stock
rotaia [ro'taja] SF (*Ferr*) rail; (*guida metallica*) rut, track
rotante [ro'tante] AGG rotating
rotare [ro'tare] VT, VI (*aus* **avere**) to rotate
rotativa [rota'tiva] SF rotary press
rotativo, a [rota'tivo] AGG rotating, rotation *attr*
rotatoria [rota'tɔrja] SF roundabout (*Brit*), traffic circle (*Am*); **segnale di rotatoria** "roundabout ahead" sign
rotatorio, ria, ri, rie [rota'tɔrjo] AGG rotary
rotazionale [rotattsjo'nale] AGG: **isola rotazionale** (*Aut*) roundabout (*Brit*), traffic circle (*Am*)
rotazione [rotat'tsjone] SF rotation; **rotazione delle colture** (*Agr*) crop rotation
roteare [rote'are] VT (*spada, bastone*) to whirl; (*occhi*) to roll
■ VI (*aus* **essere**) (*uccello rapace*) to circle
rotella [ro'tɛlla] SF (*gen*) small wheel; (*di pattini*) roller; (*di mobili*) castor; (*ingranaggio*) cog wheel; (*Culin*: *per la pasta*) pastry wheel; **una valigia con le rotelle** a case with wheels; **pattini a rotelle** roller skates; **gli manca una rotella** (*fig fam*) he's got a screw loose
rotocalco, chi [roto'kalko] SM (*rivista*) illustrated magazine; (*Tip*) rotogravure
rotolare [roto'lare] VT, VI (*aus* **essere**) to roll; **il pallone è rotolato giù per le scale** the ball rolled down the steps
▶ **rotolarsi** VR to roll (about); **rotolarsi per terra** to roll about on the floor; **rotolarsi nell'erba** to roll (about) on the grass; **rotolarsi (per terra) dalle risate** to roll about laughing
rotolio, lii [roto'lio] SM rolling
rotolo ['rɔtolo] SM (*di carta, stoffa*) roll; (*di corda*) coil; (*di documenti*) scroll; **un rotolo di carta igienica** a roll of toilet paper; **andare a rotoli** (*fig*) to go to rack and ruin; **mandare a rotoli** (*fig*) to ruin
rotolone [roto'lone] SM tumble, fall; **fare un rotolone** to take a tumble; **fare un rotolone dalle scale** to tumble down the stairs
rotoloni [roto'loni] AVV: **cadere rotoloni** to fall head over heels
rotonda [ro'tonda] SF (*Archit*) rotunda; (*terrazza*) round terrace
rotondeggiante [rotonded'dʒante] AGG roundish
rotondità [rotondi'ta] SF INV roundness, rotundity; **le rotondità femminili** (*scherz*) feminine curves
rotondo, a [ro'tondo] AGG (*circolare*) round; (*paffuto*: *viso*) round, full
rotore [ro'tore] SM (*Tecn*) rotor
rotta[1] ['rotta] SF (*Aer, Naut*) route, course; **essere in rotta per** to be en route for; **fare rotta su** *o* **per** *o* **verso** to head for *o* towards; **cambiare rotta** (*anche fig*) to change course; **in rotta di collisione** on a collision course; **ufficiale di rotta** navigator, navigating officer
rotta[2] ['rotta] SF **1** (*fig*: *rottura*): **essere in rotta con qn** (*fig*) to be on bad terms with sb; **a rotta di collo** at breakneck speed **2** (*disfatta*): **mettere in rotta il nemico** to rout the enemy
rottamare [rotta'mare] VT (*auto*) *to scrap an old vehicle in return for incentives*
rottamazione [rottamat'tsjone] SF *the scrapping of old vehicles in return for incentives*
rottame [rot'tame] SM **1** (*pezzo di ferro*) piece of scrap iron; **rottami** SMPL (*di nave, auto, aereo*) wreckage *sg*; **rottami di ferro** scrap iron *sg* **2** (*fig pegg*: *persona, macchina*) wreck
rotto, a ['rotto] PP *di* **rompere**
■ AGG (*gen*) broken; (*braccio, gamba*) broken, fractured; **avere le ossa rotte** (*fig*) to ache all over; **rotto a** (*persona*: *abituato*) accustomed *o* inured to; **è rotto ad ogni esperienza** (*fig*) he's seen it all, he's been through it all
■ SM: **per il rotto della cuffia** by the skin of one's teeth
■ SMPL: **30 euro e rotti** 30 odd euros

LO SAPEVI...?
rotto non si traduce mai con la parola inglese ***rotten***

Rr

rottura [rot'tura] SF (*azione*) breaking *no pl*; (*di rapporti*) breaking off *no pl*; (*fra amici*) split-up, break-up; (*di negoziati*) breakdown; (*di contratto*) breach; **è una tale rottura!** (*fam*: *persona*) he's such a pain (in the neck)!; (: *situazione*) it's such a drag *o* bore!; **rottura delle acque** (*Med*) breaking of the waters
rotula ['rɔtula] SF kneecap
roulette [ru'lɛt] SF INV roulette; **roulette russa** Russian roulette
roulotte [ru'lɔt] SF INV caravan (*Brit*), trailer (*Am*)
round [raund] SM INV (*Sport*) round
routine [ru'tin] SF INV routine; **di routine** routinely, as a routine
rovente [ro'vɛnte] AGG (*ferro, carbone*) red-hot; (*fig*: *sabbia, sole*) burning
rovere ['rovere] SM O F (*albero*) English oak
■SM (*legno*) oak; **una botte di rovere** an oak barrel
rovesciamento [roveʃʃa'mento] SM (*di macchina*) overturning; (*di barca*) capsizing; (*fig*: *di situazione*) reversal
rovesciare [roveʃ'ʃare] VT (*far cadere*: *gen*) to knock over; (: *liquido*: *intenzionalmente*) to pour; (: *accidentalmente*) to spill; (*capovolgere*: *barca*) to capsize, turn upside down; (*fig*: *situazione*) to reverse; (: *governo*) to overthrow; **mi sono alzato di scatto e ho rovesciato la sedia** I got up in a hurry and knocked over the chair; **rovesciare qc addosso a qn** to pour sth over sb; **ha rovesciato tutto il latte per terra** she spilled all the milk on the floor; **rovesciare la testa all'indietro** to throw one's head back
▸ **rovesciarsi** VIP (*sedia, macchina*) to overturn; (*barca*) to capsize; (*liquido*) to spill; (*fig*: *situazione*) to be reversed; **si è rovesciato tutto per terra** everything fell to the floor; (*liquido*) it all spilled on to the floor; **la folla si rovesciò nella piazza** the crowd poured into the square
rovesciata [roveʃ'ʃata] SF (*Calcio*) overhead kick
rovescio, scia, sci, sce [ro'vɛʃʃo] AGG (*Maglia*) purl *attr*
■SM **1** (*lato*: *di stoffa, indumento*) wrong side, other side; (: *di medaglia*) reverse; **stirala dal rovescio** iron it on the wrong side; **il rovescio della medaglia** (*fig*) the other side of the coin **2** (*Meteor*) downpour, heavy shower **3** (*fig*): **rovescio di fortuna** setback **4** (*Maglia*: *punto rovescio*) purl (stitch) **5** (*Tennis*) backhand (stroke); **ha un rovescio potentissimo** she has a very powerful backhand; **a rovescio, alla rovescia** AVV (*con il davanti dietro*) back to front; (*sottosopra*) upside down; (*con l'esterno all'interno*) inside out; **oggi mi va tutto alla rovescia** everything is going wrong (for me) today; **capisce sempre tutto alla rovescia** he always gets things the wrong way round, he always gets the wrong end of the stick
rovina [ro'vina] SF (*gen, fig*) ruin; **in rovina** (*palazzo*) in ruins; **rovina finanziaria** financial ruin; **mandare in rovina** to ruin; **andare in rovina** (*andare a pezzi*) to collapse; (*fig*) to go to rack and ruin; **sull'orlo della rovina** on the brink of ruin; **sarà la sua rovina** it (*o* she *ecc*) will be the ruination of him
rovinare [rovi'nare] VT (*oggetto, persona, anche fig*) to ruin; (*fig*: *atmosfera, festa*) to ruin, spoil; **si è rovinata il vestito** she has ruined her dress
■VI (*aus* **essere**) (*crollare*) to collapse, fall down; (*precipitare*) to fall
▸ **rovinarsi** VR (*persona*) to be ruined, ruin o.s.; **mi voglio rovinare!** (*fig*: *sogg*: *venditore*) I'm giving it away!;
▸ **rovinarsi** VIP (*oggetto*) to get *o* be ruined
rovinato, a [rovi'nato] AGG (*oggetto*) ruined, damaged; (*fig*: *persona*) ruined
rovinosamente [rovinosa'mente] AVV destructively; **è caduto rovinosamente giù dalle scale** he fell head over heels down the stairs
rovinoso, a [rovi'noso] AGG ruinous
rovistare [rovis'tare] VT (*casa*) to ransack; (*tasche*) to rummage in (*o* through), search thoroughly
rovo ['rovo] SM (*Bot*) blackberry bush, bramble bush; (*cespugli spinosi*) briar
royalty ['rɔiəlti] SF INV (*percentuale*) royalty
rozzezza [rod'dzettsa] SF (*vedi agg*) roughness; coarseness
rozzo, a ['roddzo] AGG (*gen*) rough; (*persona, modi*) uncouth, coarse
RP ['ɛrre'pi] SIGLA FPL (= **Relazioni Pubbliche**) PR
RR ABBR (*Posta*) = **ricevuta di ritorno**
Rrr ABBR = **raccomandata con ricevuta di ritorno**
RSVP ABBR (= **répondez s'il vous plaît**) RSVP
ruba ['ruba] SF: **andare a ruba** to sell like hot cakes
rubacchiare [rubak'kjare] VT to pilfer
rubacuori [ruba'kwɔri] SM/F INV heart-breaker, charmer
rubare [ru'bare] VT: **rubare (qc a qn)** (*gen*) to steal (sth from sb); (*fig*: *idea, affetti, posto*) to steal (sth from sb), take (sth from sb); **gli hanno rubato tutto** they robbed him of everything; **a Londra mi hanno rubato la macchina fotografica** my camera was stolen in London; **rubare il mestiere a qn** to do sb out of a job; **posso rubarti un minuto?** can I steal a minute of your time?; **mi hai rubato le parole di bocca** you've taken the words right out of my mouth
ruberia [rube'ria] SF (*fig*) theft; **è una (vera) ruberia** it's daylight robbery
rubicondo, a [rubi'kondo] AGG ruddy
rubinetto [rubi'netto] SM tap (*Brit*), faucet (*Am*)
rubino [ru'bino] SM ruby
rubizzo, a [ru'bittso] AGG lively, sprightly
rublo ['rublo] SM rouble
rubrica, che [ru'brika] SF **1** (*quaderno*) index notebook; (: *per indirizzi e numeri di telefono*) address book **2** (*di giornale*: *colonna*) column; (: *pagina*) page; **rubrica sportiva** sports page **3** (*Radio, TV*: *parte di un programma*) spot, time; **"rubrica sportiva"** "sports time"
rucola ['rukola], **ruchetta** [ru'ketta] SF (*Bot*) rocket
rude ['rude] AGG (*duro, brusco*) tough; (*rozzo*) rough, coarse
rudemente [rude'mente] AVV (*rispondere*) bluntly, brusquely
rudere ['rudere] SM (*rovina*) ruins *pl*; (*fig*: *persona*) wreck
rudimentale [rudimen'tale] AGG rudimentary, basic
rudimenti [rudi'menti] SMPL (*di disciplina*) rudiments; (*di teoria*) (basic) principles
ruffiano, a [ruf'fjano] SM/F pander, pimp; (*fig*: *leccapiedi*) bootlicker

LO SAPEVI...?
ruffiano non si traduce mai con la parola inglese ***ruffian***

ruga, ghe ['ruga] SF wrinkle
rugby ['rugbi] SM INV rugby (football)
▷ www.rugby.it/
ruggente [rud'dʒɛnte] AGG roaring; **gli anni ruggenti** the Roaring Twenties
ruggine ['ruddʒine] SF (*Chim, Bot, colore*) rust; (*fig*: *rancore*): **fra di loro c'è della vecchia ruggine** there's bad blood between them

■AGG INV (*colore*) rust, rust-coloured
rugginoso, a [ruddʒi'noso] AGG rusty
ruggire [rud'dʒire] VI (*aus* **avere**) to roar
ruggito [rud'dʒito] SM roar
rugiada [ru'dʒada] SF dew
rugoso, a [ru'goso] AGG (*pieno di rughe*) wrinkled; (*scabro: superficie*) rough
rullaggio, gi [rul'laddʒo] SM (*Aer*) taxiing
rullare [rul'lare] VT (*spianare con il rullo*) to roll
■VI (*aus* **avere**) **1** (*tamburo*) to roll **2** (*Aer*) to taxi
rullino [rul'lino] SM (*Fot*) roll of film, spool; **un rullino da ventiquattro foto** a twenty-four exposure film
rullio, lii [rul'lio] SM (*di tamburi*) roll
rullo ['rullo] SM **1** (*di tamburo*) roll **2** (*Tecn, Tip*) roller; (*di stampante, macchina da scrivere*) platen; (*Cine*) reel; **rullo compressore** steam-roller
rum [rum] SM INV rum
rumba ['rumba] SF rumba
ruminante [rumi'nante] SM (*Zool*) ruminant
ruminare [rumi'nare] VT (*Zool*) to ruminate; (*fig*) to ruminate on *o* over, chew over
rumore [ru'more] SM (*gen*) noise; (*di treno*) rumble; (*di motore*) sound; (*di piatti, stoviglie*) clatter; **cos'è questo rumore?** what's that noise?; **un rumore sordo** a thud; **un rumore stridente** a shrill noise; **un rumore di passi** the sound of footsteps; **rumore di sottofondo** background noise; **fare rumore** to make a noise; **cerca di non far rumore, dormono tutti** try not to make a noise, everybody's asleep; **senza far rumore** quietly; **non si sentiva alcun rumore** not a sound could be heard; **la notizia ha fatto molto rumore** (*fig*) the news aroused great interest
rumoreggiare [rumored'dʒare] VI (*aus* **avere**) (*tuono*) to rumble; (*fig: folla*) to clamour (*Brit*), clamor (*Am*)
rumorosamente [rumorosa'mente] AVV noisily
rumoroso, a [rumo'roso] AGG (*gen*) noisy; (*voce, risata*) loud, noisy; **una strada rumorosa** a noisy street
ruolino [rwo'lino] SM: **ruolino di marcia** (*Mil*) marching orders *pl*; (*fig*) schedule, timetable
ruolo ['rwɔlo] SM **1** (*gen, Cine, Teatro*) role, part; **recita nel ruolo di Capitan Uncino** he's playing the part of Captain Hook; **avere un ruolo di primo piano in qc** (*anche fig*) to play a leading role *o* part in sth **2** (*elenco*) roll, register, list; **ruolo d'imposta** (*Fisco*) tax-list, tax-roll **3 di ruolo** (*personale, insegnante*) permanent, on the permanent staff; **professore di ruolo** (*Univ*) ≈ lecturer with tenure; **fuori ruolo** (*personale, insegnante*) temporary
ruota ['rwɔta] SF (*gen*) wheel; (*di ingranaggio*) cog (wheel); **fare la ruota** (*Ginnastica*) to do a cartwheel; **gonna a ruota** flared skirt; **a ruote** wheeled; **veicolo a due ruote** two-wheeled vehicle; **auto a 4 ruote motrici** 4-wheel-drive car; **ruote in lega leggera** light alloy wheel; **la ruota della fortuna** the wheel of fortune; **andare a ruota libera** to freewheel; **parlare a ruota libera** (*fig*) to speak freely; **essere l'ultima ruota del carro** (*fig*) to count for nothing; **ruota anteriore** front wheel; **ruota posteriore** back wheel; **ruota di scorta** spare wheel; **ruota di stampa** (*su stampante*) print wheel; **ruota del timone** (*Naut*) (steering) wheel, helm
ruotino [rwo'tino] SM (*anche:* **ruotino di scorta**) spare wheel *o* tyre (for temporary use)
rupe ['rupe] SF cliff, rock
rupestre [ru'pɛstre] AGG rocky
rupia [ru'pia] SF (*moneta*) rupee
ruppi *ecc* ['ruppi] VB *vedi* **rompere**
rurale [ru'rale] AGG rural, country *attr*
ruscello [ruʃ'ʃɛllo] SM stream, brook
ruspa ['ruspa] SF excavator
ruspante [rus'pante] AGG (*pollo*) free-range
russare [rus'sare] VI (*aus* **avere**) to snore
Russia ['russja] SF Russia
russo, a ['russo] AGG, SM/F, SM Russian
rustico, a, ci, che ['rustiko] AGG (*gente*) country *attr*, rural; (*arredamento*) rustic; (*fig: modi*) rough, unrefined
■SM (*Edil*) shell, carcass; (*deposito per attrezzi*) shed; (*alloggio di contadini*) farm labourer's (*Brit*) *o* farmhand's cottage
ruta ['ruta] SF (*Bot*) rue
ruttare [rut'tare] VI (*aus* **avere**) to belch
ruttino [rut'tino] SM: **fare il ruttino** (*lattante*) to burp
rutto ['rutto] SM belch; **fare un rutto** to belch
ruttore [rut'tore] SM (*Elettr*) contact breaker
ruvido, a ['ruvido] AGG (*gen, fig*) rough, coarse
ruzzolare [ruttso'lare] VI (*aus* **essere**) to roll down, tumble down
ruzzolone [ruttso'lone] SM tumble, fall; **un gran ruzzolone** a heavy fall; **ha fatto un ruzzolone per le scale** he tumbled down the stairs
ruzzoloni [ruttso'loni] AVV: **venir giù ruzzoloni** to fall head over heels; **fare le scale ruzzoloni** to tumble down the stairs

S s

S, s ['esse] SF O M INV (*lettera*) S, s; **S come Savona** ≈ S for Sugar
■ SIGLA F (*taglia*) S (= *small*)
S ABBR (= **Sud**) S
S. ABBR (= **san(to)**) St
SA SIGLA = *Salerno*
■ ABBR = *Società Anonima*
sa *ecc* [sa] VB *vedi* **sapere**
sab. ABBR (= **sabato**) Sat.
sabato ['sabato] SM Saturday; (*Rel*) sabbath; **Sabato Santo** (*Rel*) Holy Saturday; *per fraseologia vedi* **martedì**
sabaudo, a [sa'baudo] AGG of (the House of) Savoy
sabba ['sabba] SM witches' sabbath
sabbatico, a, ci, che [sab'batiko] AGG sabbatical; **anno sabbatico** sabbatical (year)
sabbia ['sabbja] SF sand; **sulla sabbia** on the sand; **sabbie mobili** quicksand *sg*, quicksands *pl*
sabbiato, a [sab'bjato] AGG **1** (*superficie*) sandblasted **2** (TV: *immagine*) snowy
sabbiatrice [sabbja'tritʃe] SF (*Tecn*) sandblaster
sabbiatura [sabbja'tura] SF **1** (*Med*) sand bath; **fare le sabbiature** to take sand baths **2** (*Tecn*) sandblasting
sabbioso, a [sab'bjoso] AGG sandy
sabotaggio, gi [sabo'taddʒo] SM (*Mil, Pol, fig*) sabotage; (: *atto*) act of sabotage
sabotare [sabo'tare] VT to sabotage
sabotatore, trice [sabota'tore] SM/F saboteur
sacca, che ['sakka] SF **1** (*borsa*) bag; **sacca portabiancheria** laundry bag; **sacca da viaggio** travelling bag **2** (*di fiume*) inlet **3** (*di pus*) pocket; **sacca d'aria** air pocket
saccarina [sakka'rina] SF saccharin(e)
saccaroide [sakka'rɔide] SM saccharoid
saccarosio [sakka'rɔzjo] SM saccharose
saccente [sat'tʃɛnte] AGG presumptuous, conceited
■ SM/F know-all (*Brit*), know-it-all (*Am*)
saccenteria [sattʃente'ria] SF presumption, conceit
saccheggiare [sakked'dʒare] VT (*Mil*) to sack, plunder; (*fig*) to raid
saccheggiatore [sakkeddʒa'tore] SM plunderer
saccheggio, gi [sak'keddʒo] SM (*Mil*) plundering, sacking; (*fig*) plundering
sacchetto [sak'ketto] SM **1** (*piccolo sacco*) (small) bag; **sacchetto di carta/di plastica** paper/plastic bag **2** (*quantità*) bag(ful)
sacco, chi ['sakko] SM **1** (*contenitore*) sack, bag; (*quantità*) sack(ful); (*fig*) lots of, heaps of; **un sacco di patate** a sack of potatoes; **un sacco di** a lot of; **un sacco di gente** lots of people; **colazione al sacco** packed lunch; **sacco custodia** (*per vestiti*) clothes bag; **sacco da montagna** rucksack; **sacco per i rifiuti** bin bag (*Brit*), garbage bag (*Am*); **sacco postale** mailbag; **cogliere** *o* **prendere qn con le mani nel sacco** to catch sb red-handed; **vuotare il sacco** to confess, spill the beans (*fam*); **mettere qn nel sacco** to cheat sb; **sacco a pelo** sleeping bag **2** (*tessuto*) sacking **3** (*Anat, Bio*) sac **4** (*saccheggio*) plundering, sack(ing)
sacerdotale [satʃerdo'tale] AGG priestly
sacerdote, essa [satʃer'dɔte] SM/F priest/priestess
sacerdozio, zi [satʃer'dɔttsjo] SM priesthood
Sacra Corona Unita ['sakra ko'rona u'nita] SF the Mafia in Puglia
sacrale [sa'krale] AGG holy, sacred
sacralità [sakrali'ta] SF sacredness
sacramentale [sakramen'tale] AGG sacramental
sacramentare [sakramen'tare] VT (*fam*) to blaspheme
sacramento [sakra'mento] SM (*Rel*) sacrament
sacrario, ri [sa'krarjo] SM memorial chapel
sacrestano [sakres'tano] SM = **sagrestano**
sacrestia [sakres'tia] SF = **sagrestia**
sacrificare [sakrifi'kare] VT (*gen*) to sacrifice
▶ **sacrificarsi** VR to sacrifice o.s.
sacrificato, a [sakrifi'kato] AGG (*gen, Rel*) sacrificed; (*fig: sprecato, sciupato*) wasted; **una vita sacrificata** a life of hardship
sacrificio, ci [sakri'fitʃo] SM (*Rel, fig*) sacrifice; **fare un sacrificio** to make a sacrifice
sacrilegio, gi [sakri'lɛdʒo] SM (*Rel, fig*) sacrilege; **fare sacrilegio** *or* **commettere un sacrilegio** to commit sacrilege
sacrilego, a, ghi, ghe [sa'krilego] AGG (*Rel*) sacrilegious

sacrista, i [sa'krista] SM = **sagrestano**
sacro, a ['sakro] AGG **1** (*Rel*) holy, sacred; (: *arte, diritto*) sacred; **il Sacro Cuore (di Gesù)** the Sacred Heart (of Jesus); **musica sacra** church music **2** (*Anat*): **osso sacro** sacrum
■SM the sacred
sacrosanto, a [sakro'santo] AGG sacrosanct
sadico, a, ci, che ['sadiko] AGG sadistic
■SM/F sadist
sadismo [sa'dizmo] SM sadism; **trattare qn con sadismo** to treat sb sadistically
sadomasochismo [sadomazo'kizmo] SM sadomasochism
sadomasochista, i, e [sadomazo'kista] SM/F sadomasochist
sadomasochistico, a, ci, che [sadomazo'kistiko] AGG (*tendenza*) sadomasochistic
saetta [sa'etta] SF (*fulmine*) thunderbolt; **essere (veloce come) una saetta** (*fig*) to be as quick as lightning
safari [sa'fari] SM INV safari
safena [sa'fɛna] SF (*Anat*) saphena
saga, ghe ['saga] SF saga
sagace [sa'gatʃe] AGG sagacious, shrewd
sagacemente [sagatʃe'mente] AVV sagaciously, shrewdly
sagacia [sa'gatʃa] SF sagacity, shrewdness
saggezza [sad'dʒettsa] SF wisdom
saggiamente [saddʒa'mente] AVV wisely
saggiare [sad'dʒare] VT (*metalli preziosi*) to assay; (*fig: mettere alla prova*) to test
saggina [sad'dʒina] SF (*Bot*) sorghum
saggio[1], gia, gi, ge ['saddʒo] AGG wise
■SM wise man; (*Antichità*) sage
saggio[2], gi ['saddʒo] SM **1** (*prova: di abilità, forza*) proof; **dare saggio di** to give proof of; **saggio di ginnastica** gymnastics display; **saggio di musica** recital **2** (*campione*) sample; (*di libro*) sample copy; **in saggio** as a sample **3** (*scritto: letterario*) essay; (: *Scol*) written test **4** (*di metalli preziosi*) assay; **un saggio su Dante** an essay on Dante
saggista, i, e [sad'dʒista] SM/F essayist
saggistica, che [sad'dʒistika] SF (*attività*) essay writing; (*produzione*) essays *pl*
sagittaria [sadʒit'tarja] SF (*pianta*) arrowhead
Sagittario, ri [sadʒit'tarjo] SM Sagittarius; **essere del Sagittario** to be Sagittarius
sagola ['sagola] SF (*Naut*) line
sagoma ['sagoma] SF **1** (*profilo, linea*) outline, profile; (*forma*) shape, form; (*modello in cartone, legno*) template; (*nel tiro al bersaglio*) target; **da lontano si vedeva la sagoma di una nave** in the distance we saw the outline of a ship; **ha una sagoma irregolare** it has an irregular shape **2** (*fig: persona*) character; **è una sagoma!** he's a scream!
sagomare [sago'mare] VT to shape, mould
sagomato, a [sago'mato] AGG shaped, moulded; **ben sagomato** well-shaped
sagra ['sagra] SF festival, feast

SAGRA

A **sagra** is a rural festival held in the open air with folk music, dancing and games. Many **sagre** are based around one or more culinary specialities, which can usually be sampled in the various booths. These festivals normally take place during the summer months.

sagrato [sa'grato] SM churchyard
sagrestano [sagres'tano] SM sexton, sacristan
sagrestia [sagres'tia], **sagristia** [sagris'tia] SF sacristy
Sahara [sa'ara] SM: **il (deserto del) Sahara** the Sahara (Desert)
sahariana [saa'rjana] SF bush jacket
sahariano, a [saa'rjano] AGG Saharan, Sahara *attr*
Sahel [sa'ɛl] SM (*Geog*) Sahel
sai *ecc* ['sai] VB *vedi* **sapere**
Saigon [sai'gɔn] SF Saigon
saio, sai ['sajo] SM (*Rel*) habit; **prendere** *o* **vestire il saio** to take the habit
sala ['sala] SF (*gen*) room; (*molto grande*) hall; (*salotto*) living room; (*Cine: di proiezione*) cinema; **c'era un tavolo rotondo in mezzo alla sala** there was a round table in the middle of the room; **l'enorme sala era piena zeppa** the enormous hall was packed; **il cinema ha tre sale** the cinema has three screens; **sala d'aspetto** *o* **d'attesa** waiting room; **sala da ballo** dance hall; **sala da biliardo** (*pubblica*) billiard hall; (*privata*) billiard room; **sala dei concerti** concert hall; **sala per conferenze** (*Univ*) lecture hall; (*in aziende*) conference room; **sala (dei) comandi** control room; **sala corse** betting shop; **sala giochi** amusement arcade; **sala di lettura** reading room; **sala macchine** (*Naut*) engine room; **sala di montaggio** (*Cine*) cutting room; **sala operatoria** (*Med*) operating theatre (*Brit*) *o* room (*Am*); **sala partenze** departure lounge; **sala da pranzo** dining room; **sala professori** staff room; **sala per ricevimenti** banqueting hall; **sala delle udienze** (*Dir*) courtroom
salace [sa'latʃe] AGG (*spinto, piccante*) salacious, saucy; (*mordace*) cutting, biting
salamandra [sala'mandra] SF (*Zool*) salamander
salame [sa'lame] SM (*cibo*) salami *no pl*, salami sausage; (*fig: persona sciocca*) dope
salamelecchi [salame'lɛkki] SMPL (*pegg*) bowing and scraping *no pl*; **fare salamelecchi** to bow and scrape; **senza tanti salamelecchi** without ceremony
salamoia [sala'mɔja] SF (*Culin, Chim*) brine; **olive in salamoia** olives in brine
salare [sa'lare] VT **1** (*condire*) to salt, add salt to **2** (*mettere sotto sale: senza acqua*) to salt; (: *con acqua*) to brine
salariale [sala'rjale] AGG wage *attr*, pay *attr*; **aumento salariale** wage *o* pay increase (*Brit*) *o* raise (*Am*)
salariato, a [sala'rjato] AGG wage-earning
■SM/F wage-earner
salario, ri [sa'larjo] SM pay, wage, wages *pl*; **un aumento di salario** a pay rise; **salario base** basic wage; **salario minimo garantito** guaranteed minimum wage
salassare [salas'sare] VT (*Med*) to bleed; (*fig*) to bleed dry *o* white
salasso [sa'lasso] SM (*Med*) bleeding, bloodletting; (*fig: forte spesa*) drain
salatino [sala'tino] SM cracker, salted biscuit
salato, a [sa'lato] AGG (*sapore, cibo*) salty; (*acqua*) salt *attr*; (*burro*) salted; (*fig: costoso*) expensive, costly; (: *prezzo*) stiff, steep; (: *mordace: discorso*) sharp, cutting; **è troppo salato** it's too salty; **preferisco le cose salate** I prefer savoury things; **pagare qc salato** (*acquisto*) to pay through the nose for sth; **l'ha pagata salata** (*fig*) he paid dearly for it
saldare [sal'dare] VT **1** (*Tecn, gen*) to join; (*con saldatore*)

Ss

to solder; (*con saldatura autogena*) to weld **2** (*conto*) to settle, pay; (*fattura, debito*) to pay; **devo saldare il conto** I must settle the bill; **saldare un conto (con qn)** to settle an account (with sb); (*fig*) to settle a score (with sb)
▶ **saldarsi** VIP (*ferita*) to heal

saldatore [salda'tore] SM **1** (*operaio*) (*vedi vt*) solderer; welder **2** (*utensile*) soldering iron

saldatrice [salda'tritʃe] SF (*macchina*) welder, welding machine; **saldatrice ad arco** arc welder

saldatura [salda'tura] SF (*vedi vt*) (*azione*) soldering; welding; (: *punto saldato*) soldered joint; weld; **saldatura ad arco** arc welding; **saldatura autogena** welding

saldezza [sal'dettsa] SF firmness, strength

saldo¹, a ['saldo] AGG (*gen*) steady, firm, stable; (*fig: rapporto*) steady; (: *principi*) sound; **non è più molto saldo sulle gambe** he's not very steady on his feet any more

saldo² ['saldo] SM **1** (*pagamento*) settlement, payment; (*somma residua da pagare*) balance; **pagare a saldo** to pay in full; **saldo attivo** credit; **saldo passivo** deficit; **saldo riportato** balance brought forward **2** (*svendita*) sale

sale ['sale] SM **1** (*gen*) salt; **c'è troppo sale** there's too much salt in it; **conservare sotto sale** to salt; **sotto sale** salted; **acciughe sotto sale** salted anchovies; **restare di sale** (*fig*) to be dumbfounded; **avere molto sale in zucca** to have a lot of good sense; **non ha molto sale in zucca** he doesn't have much sense **2 sali** SMPL (*Med: da annusare*) smelling salts
■ **sale da cucina** cooking salt; **sale fino** table salt; **sale grosso** cooking salt; **sale da tavola** table salt; **sali da bagno** bath salts; **sali minerali** mineral salts; **sali e tabacchi** tobacconist's (shop) *sg*

> **LO SAPEVI...?**
> **sale** non si traduce mai con la parola inglese *sale*

salernitano, a [salerni'tano] AGG of *o* from Salerno
■ SM/F inhabitant *o* native of Salerno

salesiano, a [sale'zjano] AGG, SM/F (*Rel*) Salesian

salgemma [sal'dʒɛmma] SM rock salt

salgo *ecc* ['salgo] VB *vedi* **salire**

salice ['salitʃe] SM (*Bot*) willow; **salice bianco** white willow; **salice piangente** weeping willow

saliente [sa'ljɛnte] AGG salient, main

saliera [sa'ljɛra] SF (*Culin*) saltcellar

salina [sa'lina] SF **1** (*serie di vasche*) saltworks *sg* **2** (*deposito naturale*) salt pan **3** (*miniera di salgemma*) salt mine

salino, a [sa'lino] AGG saline

salire [sa'lire] VB IRREG
■ VT (*scale, pendio*) to climb, go (*o* come) up
■ VI (*aus* **essere**) **1** (*gen*) to go (*o* come) up; (*aereo*) to climb, go up; **sali tu o vengo giù io?** are you coming up or shall I come down?; **è appena salito in camera sua** he's just gone up to his room; **saliva le scale** he was going up the stairs; **salimmo a piedi/con la bicicletta fino in cima** we walked/cycled up to the top; **la strada sale per 2 km** the road climbs for 2 km; **salì sull'albero** he climbed the tree; **salire in quota** (*Aer*) to gain altitude **2 salire in macchina** to get into the car; **salire sull'autobus/sul treno** to get on the bus/on the train; **salire a bordo di** to (get on) board; **salire a cavallo** to mount; **salire su una** *o* **in bicicletta** to get on a bicycle; **salire in sella** to get into the saddle **3** (*prezzo, temperatura*) to rise, go up; (*marea*) to come in; (*fumo*) to rise; **i prezzi sono saliti** prices have gone up; **la temperatura sta salendo** the temperature is rising **4** (*fraseologia*): **salire in cielo** *o* **paradiso** to go to heaven; **salire al potere** to rise to power; **salire al trono** to ascend the throne; **salire alle stelle** (*prezzi*) to rocket; **salire nella stima di qn** to rise in sb's estimation

saliscendi [saliʃ'ʃendi] SM INV latch

salita [sa'lita] SF **1** (*azione*) climb, ascent; **salita a spina di pesce** (*Sci*) herringbone climb; **la salita è stata molto faticosa** the climb was very tiring; **abbiamo dovuto fermarci a metà della salita** we had to stop halfway up the hill **2** (*strada*) hill, slope; **strada in salita** road going uphill

saliva [sa'liva] SF saliva

salivare¹ [sali'vare] AGG salivary

salivare² [sali'vare] VI (*aus* **avere**) to salivate

salma ['salma] SF body (*of dead person*)

salmastro, a [sal'mastro] AGG (*acqua*) salt *attr*; (*sapore*) salty
■ SM (*sapore*) salty taste; (*odore*) salty smell

salmerie [salme'rie] SFPL (*Mil*) train *sg*

salmì [sal'mi] SM INV (*Culin*) salmi; **lepre in salmì** salmi of hare

salmista, i [sal'mista] SM (*Rel*) psalmist

salmo ['salmo] SM (*Rel*) psalm

salmodia [salmo'dia] SF psalmody

salmone [sal'mone] SM salmon

salmonella [salmo'nɛlla] SF salmonella

salmonellosi [salmonel'lɔzi] SF INV salmonellosis

salnitro [sal'nitro] SM (*Chim*) saltpetre

Salomone¹ [salo'mone] SM Solomon

Salomone² [salo'mɔne] SFPL: **le (isole) Salomone** the Solomon Islands

salone [sa'lone] SM **1** (*stanza*) living room, sitting room (*Brit*), lounge (*Brit*); (*di ricevimento*) reception room; (*su nave*) lounge, saloon **2** (*mostra*) show, exhibition; **salone dell'automobile** motor show **3** (*negozio: di parrucchiere*) hairdresser's (salon); **salone di bellezza** beauty salon

saloon [sa'lu:n] SM INV saloon

salopette [salɔ'pɛt] SF INV dungarees *pl*; (*Sci*) salopettes *pl*

salottiero, a [salot'tjɛro] AGG mundane

salotto [sa'lɔtto] SM **1** (*stanza*) living room, sitting room (*Brit*), lounge (*Brit*); (*mobilio*) lounge suite **2** (*circolo letterario*) salon; **chiacchiere da salotto** (*fig*) society gossip *sg*

salpancora [sal'pankora] SM INV (*Naut*) windlass, anchor winch

salpare [sal'pare] (*Naut*) VT: **salpare l'ancora** to weigh anchor
■ VI (*aus* **essere**) to set sail

salsa ['salsa] SF sauce; **in tutte le salse** (*fig*) in all kinds of ways; **salsa di pomodoro** tomato sauce; **spaghetti con salsa di pomodoro** spaghetti with tomato sauce; **salsa verde** *savoury sauce made with parsley, anchovies, onion, olive oil and garlic*

salsedine [sal'sɛdine] SF (*del mare, vento*) saltiness; (*incrostazione*) (dried) salt

salsiccia, ce [sal'sittʃa] SF (pork) sausage

salsiera [sal'sjɛra] SF gravy boat, sauceboat (*Brit*)

salso ['salso] SM (*salsedine*) saltiness

saltare [sal'tare] VT (*siepe, ostacolo*) to jump (over), leap (over); (*fig: capitolo, pasto*) to skip, miss (out); **ho saltato una riga** I've skipped a line; **hai saltato il pranzo oggi?** did you skip lunch today?
■ VI (*aus* **essere** *o* **avere**)

1 (*gen*) to jump, leap; (*saltellare*) to skip; (: *su un piede solo*) to hop; **saltare su/sopra qc** to jump on/over sth; **il gatto è saltato sul tavolo** the cat jumped on the table; **saltare giù** to jump down; **saltare giù da qc** to jump off sth, jump down from sth; **è saltato giù dal treno** he jumped off the train; **saltare addosso a qn** (*aggredire*) to attack sb; **saltare con la corda** to skip; **salta su!** (*in macchina*) jump in!; (*su moto, bici*) jump on!; **è saltato su e mi ha detto che...** he jumped up and told me that ...; **saltare a terra** to jump down; **saltare dal letto/dalla finestra** to jump out of bed/out of the window; **saltare al collo di qn** (*in segno di affetto*) to throw one's arms round sb's neck; (*per strangolarlo*) to grab sb by the neck; **saltare da un argomento all'altro** to jump from one subject to another; **saltare dalla gioia** to jump for joy; **salta agli occhi** it's obvious; **ma che ti salta in mente?** what on earth are you thinking of?; **far saltare un bimbo sulle ginocchia** to bounce a child on one's knees **2** (*bottone*) to pop off; (*bomba*) to explode, blow up; (*ponte, ferrovia*) to blow up; (*valvola*) to blow; (*fig: impiegato*) to be fired; (: *corso*) to be cancelled; **saltare in aria** to blow up **3** **far saltare** (*treno, ponte*) to blow up; (*fusibile*) to blow; (*mina*) to explode; (*serratura: forzare*) to break; (: *con esplosivo*) to blow; (*lezione, appuntamento*) to cancel; **i terroristi hanno fatto saltare in aria l'edificio** terrorists blew up the building; **far saltare il banco** (*Gioco*) to break the bank; **farsi saltare le cervella** to blow one's brains out **4** **saltare fuori** (*apparire improvvisamente*) to jump out, leap out; (*venire trovato*) to turn up; **saltare fuori con** (*dire improvvisamente*) to come out with; **dall'auto sono saltati fuori due ladri** two thieves jumped *o* leapt out of the car; **quel libro è finalmente saltato fuori** that book finally turned up; **da dove salta fuori questa camicia?** where has this shirt appeared from?; **da dove salti fuori?** where did you spring from? **5** (*Culin*) to sauté

saltatore, trice [salta'tore] SM/F (*Sport: persona*) jumper; (: *cavallo*) steeplechaser; **saltatore in alto/lungo** (*Sport*) high/long jumper

saltellare [saltel'lare] VI (*aus* **avere**) to skip; (*su un solo piede*) to hop

saltello [sal'tɛllo] SM little jump; (*su un solo piede*) hop

salterio, ri [sal'tɛrjo] SM (*Rel*) psalter

saltimbanco, a, chi, che [saltim'banko] SM/F (*acrobata*) acrobat; (*pegg*) charlatan, fraud

saltimbocca [saltim'bokka] SM INV (*Culin*) *rolled veal and ham*

saltimpalo [saltim'palo] SM (*uccello*) stonechat

salto ['salto] SM **1** (*gen*) jump, leap; **un salto in avanti** a jump forward; **fare un salto** to jump, leap; (*per la paura*) to start; **fare un salto a Milano** to pop over to Milan; **fare un salto da qn** to drop in on sb; **fare un salto da un amico** to drop in on a friend; **faccio un salto da te questo pomeriggio** I'll drop in on you this afternoon; **fare i salti dalla gioia** to jump for joy; **un salto nel buio** (*fig*) a leap in the dark **2** (*Sport*) **salto in alto** high jump; **salto con l'asta** pole vault; **salto in lungo** long jump; **salto mortale** somersault; **ho fatto i salti mortali per arrivare qui in tempo** (*fig*) I almost killed myself trying to get here on time; **salto dal trampolino** (*Sci*) ski jumping; **salto triplo** triple jump **3** (*dislivello, anche Alpinismo*) drop; **un salto di qualità** a difference in quality; (*miglioramento: nel lavoro, in condizioni*) a step up the ladder

saltuariamente [saltuarja'mente] AVV occasionally, from time to time

saltuario, ria, ri, rie [saltu'arjo] AGG occasional; **lavoro saltuario** occasional work

salubre [sa'lubre] AGG healthy, salubrious (*frm*); **l'aria qui è molto più salubre** the air here is much healthier

salubrità [salubri'ta] SF healthiness

salume [sa'lume] SM (*Culin*) cured pork; **salumi** SMPL cured pork meats

salumeria [salume'ria] SF ≈ delicatessen

salumiere, a [salu'mjɛre] SM/F ≈ delicatessen owner

salumificio, ci [salumi'fitʃo] SM cured pork meat factory

salutare¹ [salu'tare] AGG healthy, salutary, beneficial

salutare² [salu'tare] VT **1** (*incontrandosi*) to greet; (*congedandosi*) to say goodbye to; (*trasmettere i saluti*) to give *o* send one's regards to; **non mi saluta mai** he never says hello to me; **è uscito senza salutare nessuno** he left without saying goodbye to anybody; **è andata a salutarlo alla stazione** she went to see him off at the station; **salutare qn con la mano** to wave to sb; **mi saluti sua moglie** please give my regards to your wife; **salutami Giulia** say hello to Giulia for me **2** (*Mil*) to salute; **salutare la bandiera** to salute the flag

▶ **salutarsi** VR (*uso reciproco: incontrandosi*) to greet each other; (: *congedandosi*) to say goodbye (to each other)

salute [sa'lute] SF health; **fumare fa male alla salute** smoking is bad for your health; **per motivi di salute** for health reasons; **godere di buona salute** to be healthy, to be in good health; **avere una salute di ferro** to have an iron constitution; **bere alla salute di qn** to drink (to) sb's health

■ ESCL (*a chi starnutisce*) bless you!; (*nei brindisi*) your health!, cheers!

LO SAPEVI...?
salute non si traduce mai con la parola inglese *salute*

▷ www.ministerosalute.it/

salutista, i, e [salu'tista] SM/F **1** (*maniaco della salute*) health fanatic **2** (*dell'Esercito della Salvezza*) Salvationist

saluto [sa'luto] SM **1** (*incontrandosi*) greeting; (*congedandosi*) goodbye, farewell; **rivolgere il saluto a qn** to greet sb; **gli ha tolto il saluto** he no longer says hello to him; **tanti saluti** *or* **cari saluti** best regards, best wishes; **cordiali saluti** *or* **distinti saluti** yours truly, yours faithfully, yours sincerely **2** (*gesto: del capo*) nod; (: *con la mano*) wave; **mi fece un cenno di saluto** he nodded to me; he waved to me **3** (*Mil*) salute

salva ['salva] SF salvo; **sparare a salva** to fire a salute

salvacondotto [salvakon'dotto] SM (*Mil*) pass, safe-conduct

salvadanaio, ai [salvada'najo] SM moneybox, piggy bank

salvadoregno, a [salvado'reɲɲo] AGG, SM/F Salvadorean

salvagente [salva'dʒɛnte] SM **1** (*Naut: gen*) life buoy; (: *ciambella*) life belt; (: *per bambini*) rubber ring; (: *giubbotto*) lifejacket (*Brit*), life preserver (*Am*); **sai nuotare senza il salvagente?** can you swim without a rubber ring? **2** (*stradale: pl inv*) traffic island

salvagocce [salva'gottʃe] AGG INV: **tappo salvagocce** dripless pour spout

salvaguardare [salvagwar'dare] VT to safeguard, protect

Ss

salvaguardia [salva'gwardja] SF safeguard; **a salvaguardia di** for the safeguard of
salvare [sal'vare] VT (*gen, Inform*) to save; (*portare soccorso*) to rescue; **lo salvarono da morte sicura** they saved him from certain death; **la cintura di sicurezza lo ha salvato** the seat belt saved him; **i pompieri hanno salvato due bambini** the firemen rescued two children; **hanno salvato poche persone dal naufragio** they rescued few people from the shipwreck; **salvare la vita a qn** to save sb's life; **una volta mi ha salvato la vita** he once saved my life; **mi hai salvato!** (*anche fig*) you saved me!; **hanno salvato poche cose dall'incendio** they salvaged very few items from the fire; **salvare la faccia** (*fam*) to save face; **salvare le apparenze** to keep up appearances; **salvare capra e cavoli** to have the best of both worlds; **Dio salvi la regina!** God save the Queen!
▶ **salvarsi** VR (*salvare la propria vita*) to save o.s.; **non si è salvato nessuno nell'incidente** nobody survived the accident; **si salvi chi può** every man for himself; **non si è salvato nulla** everything was destroyed
salvaschermo [salvas'kermo] SM (*Inform*) screen saver
salvaslip® [salva'zlip] SM INV pantyliner
salvataggio, gi [salva'taddʒo] SM rescue; **c'è stato un ferito durante le operazioni di salvataggio** one person was injured during the rescue operation; **cintura di salvataggio** lifebelt; **giubbotto di salvataggio** life jacket; **scialuppa di salvataggio** lifeboat
salvatore, trice [salva'tore] SM/F rescuer, saviour (*Brit*), savior (*Am*); (*Rel*): **il Salvatore** the Saviour
salvavita [salva'vita] SM INV (*Elettr*) circuit breaker; (*anche:* **farmaco salvavita**) life-saving drug
salvazione [salvat'tsjone] SF (*Rel*) salvation
salve[1] ['salve] ESCL (*ciao*) hello!, hi!
salve[2] ['salve] SF (*colpo*) = **salva**
salveregina [salvere'dʒina] SF (*pl* **salveregina** *o* **salveregine**) (*preghiera*) Salve Regina
salvezza [sal'vettsa] SF salvation; **cercare salvezza nella fuga** to seek safety in flight
salvia ['salvja] SF (*Bot*) sage
salvietta [sal'vjetta] SF napkin, serviette (*Brit*); (*di spugna*) hand towel; **salviette umidificate** wet wipes; **salviette umidificate per bambini** baby wipes
salvo[1]**, a** ['salvo] AGG (*persona*) safe, unhurt, unharmed; (: *fuori pericolo*) safe, out of danger; **sono salvo!** I'm safe!; **uscir salvo da qc** to come out of sth safely; **avere salva la vita** to have one's life spared
■ SM: **essere in salvo** (*persona, cosa*) to be safe; **non preoccuparti, ora sei in salvo** don't worry, you're safe now; **mettere qc in salvo** to put sth in a safe place; **mettersi in salvo** to reach safety; **portare qn in salvo** to lead sb to safety
salvo[2] ['salvo] PREP **1** (*eccetto*) except (for); **è aperto tutti i giorni salvo il lunedì** it's open every day with the exception of *o* except Monday; **vennero tutti salvo lui** everybody came except him; **salvo errori, la somma ammonta a...** unless I am (*o* we are *ecc*) mistaken, it amounts to ...; **salvo imprevisti** all being well; **ci vediamo domani, salvo imprevisti** I'll see you tomorrow, all being well; **salvo errori e omissioni** errors and omissions excepted; **salvo contrordini** barring instructions to the contrary **2 salvo che** (*eccetto che*) except (that); (*a meno che*) unless; **sono soddisfatto salvo che per una cosa** I'm quite satisfied except for one thing; **lo farò salvo che tu non voglia farlo** I'll do it unless you would rather do it
Samaria [sa'marja] SF (*Bibbia*) Samaria
samaritano, a [samari'tano] AGG Samaritan
■ SM/F Samaritan; **buon samaritano** (*anche fig*) Good Samaritan
sambuca [sam'buka] SF (*liquore*) sambuca (*type of anisette*)
sambuco, chi [sam'buko] SM (*Bot*) elder (tree)
samurai [samu'rai] SM INV samurai
san [san] AGG *vedi* **santo**
sanamente [sana'mente] AVV (*in modo sano*) healthily; (*rettamente*) correctly, soundly
sanare [sa'nare] VT (*malato*) to heal, cure; (*economia*) to cure, put right, restore
sanatoria [sana'tɔrja] SF (*Dir*) act of indemnity
sanatoriale [sanato'rjale] AGG sanatorium *attr* (*Brit*), sanitarium *attr* (*Am*)
sanatorio, ri [sana'tɔrjo] SM sanatorium (*Brit*), sanitarium (*Am*)
San Bernardo ['sam ber'nardo] SM INV (*cane*) Saint Bernard
sancire [san'tʃire] VT (*sanzionare*) to sanction; (*ratificare*) to ratify
sancta sanctorum ['sankta sank'tɔrum] SM INV (*fig*) holy of holies
Sanctus ['sanktus] SM INV Sanctus
sandalo ['sandalo] SM **1** (*calzatura*) sandal **2** (*Bot*) sandalwood
San Francisco [san fran'sisko] SF San Francisco
sangallo [san'gallo] SM broderie anglaise
sangria [san'gria] SF (*bibita*) sangria
sangue ['sangwe] SM blood; **devo fare le analisi del sangue** I've got to have a blood test; **animale a sangue caldo/freddo** warm-/cold-blooded animal; **uccidere a sangue freddo** to kill in cold blood; **all'ultimo sangue** (*duello, lotta*) to the death; **il sangue gli salì alla testa** the blood rushed to his head; **non corre buon sangue tra di loro** there's bad blood between them; **ha la musica nel sangue** music is in his blood; **sentirsi gelare il sangue nelle vene** to feel one's blood run cold; **farsi cattivo sangue per qc** to get worked up about sth; **buon sangue non mente!** blood will out!; **al sangue** (*Culin*) rare; **una bistecca al sangue** a rare steak; **sangue freddo** (*fig*) sang-froid, calm; **avere sangue freddo** to stay calm
sanguigno, a [san'gwiɲɲo] AGG (*gruppo, pressione, vaso*) blood *attr*; (*fig: collerico*) bad-tempered; (*color rosso intenso*) blood-red; **vasi sanguigni** blood vessels
sanguinaccio, ci [sangwi'nattʃo] SM (*Culin*) black pudding
sanguinante [sangwi'nante] AGG bleeding
sanguinare [sangwi'nare] VI (*aus* **avere**) (*anche fig*) to bleed
sanguinario, ria, ri, rie [sangwi'narjo] AGG bloodthirsty
sanguinolento, a [sangwino'lɛnto] AGG (*che sanguina*) bleeding; (*fig*) bloody
sanguinoso, a [sangwi'noso] AGG bloody
sanguisuga, ghe [sangwi'suga] SF (*Zool*) leech; (*fig*) leech, bloodsucker
sanità [sani'ta] SF **1** (*gen*) health; **Ministero della Sanità** ≈ Department of Health (*Brit*), ≈ Department of Health and Human Services (*Am*) **2** (*Mil*) army medical corps *sg o pl*
sanitario, ria, ri, rie [sani'tarjo] AGG (*servizio, misure*) health *attr*; (*condizioni*) sanitary; **Ufficiale Sanitario**

Health Officer; **(impianti) sanitari** bathroom *o* sanitary fittings
■ SM (*Amm: medico*) doctor
San Marino [san ma'rino] SF: **(la Repubblica di) San Marino** (the Republic of) San Marino
sanno *ecc* ['sanno] VB *vedi* **sapere**
sano, a ['sano] AGG (*persona, fisico, denti*) healthy; (*alimento*) healthy, wholesome; (*frutto*) sound; (*fig: politica, ambiente*) good; **un bambino sano** a healthy child; **un'alimentazione sana** a healthy diet; **sano e salvo** safe and sound; **è tornata a casa sana e salva** she got home safe and sound; **sano di mente** sane; **di sani principi** of sound principles; **una sana educazione** a good education; **essere sano come un pesce** to be (as) fit as a fiddle; **di sana pianta** completely, entirely
Sanremo [san'remo] SM: **festival di Sanremo** *festival of Italian pop music held in San Remo*
sanscrito, a ['sanskrito] AGG, SM Sanskrit
San Silvestro ['san sil'vɛstro] SM (*giorno*) New Year's Eve; **cosa fai per San Silvestro?** what are you doing on New Year's Eve?
santamente [santa'mente] AVV devoutly; **vivere santamente** to lead a holy life
Santiago [santi'ago] SF: **Santiago (del Cile)** Santiago (de Chile)
santificare [santifi'kare] VT (*dichiarare santo*) to sanctify, hallow; (*feste*) to observe
santino [san'tino] SM holy picture
santissimo, a [san'tissimo] AGG **1 il Santissimo Sacramento** the Blessed Sacrament; **il Padre Santissimo** (*papa*) the Holy Father **2** (*fig*): **fammi il santissimo piacere di star zitto!** do me a favour and keep quiet!
■ SM (*Rel*): **il Santissimo** the Blessed Sacrament
santità [santi'ta] SF INV (*Rel*) sanctity, holiness; (*fig*) sanctity; **Sua/Vostra Santità** His/Your Holiness
santo, a ['santo] AGG **1** (*sacro*) holy; **Venerdì Santo** Good Friday; **la Santa Sede** the Holy See; **santo cielo!** good heavens!; **Dio santo!** good God! **2** (*seguito da sm: san + consonante, sant' + vocale, santo + s impura, gn, pn, ps, x, z*) (*seguito da sf: santa + consonante, sant' + vocale*) saint; **San Pietro** (*apostolo*) Saint Peter; (*chiesa*) Saint Peter's **3** (*fig*) saint; **è una santa donna** she's a saint; **quel sant'uomo di tuo nonno** (*defunto*) your sainted grandfather; **parole sante!** very true!; **vuoi farmi il santo piacere di uscire?** would you do me a favour and get out?; **tutto il santo giorno** the whole blessed day, all day long
■ SM/F (*anche fig*) saint; **non sono una santa** I'm no saint; **qualche santo provvederà** something will turn up; **non c'è santo che tenga!** that's no excuse!; **quella santa di sua moglie** his wife, saint that she is
■ **santi** SMPL: **i Santi** (*Ognissanti*) All Saints' Day
santone [san'tone] SM holy man
Santo Stefano ['santo 'stefano] SM (*giorno*) Boxing Day (*Brit*)
santuario, ri [santu'arjo] SM sanctuary
San Valentino [san valen'tino] SM St Valentine's day
sanzionare [santsjo'nare] VT to sanction
sanzione [san'tsjone] SF **1** (*approvazione*) sanction, approval **2** (*punizione*) sanction, penalty; **sanzioni economiche** economic sanctions
sapere [sa'pere] VB IRREG
■ VT
1 (*conoscere: lezione, nome*) to know; (*venire a sapere: notizia*) to hear; **sai dove abita?** do you know where he lives?; **sai se torna?** do you know if *o* whether he is coming back?; **lo so** I know; **lo so, non è colpa tua** I know, it's not your fault; **non ne so nulla** I don't know anything about it; **sa quattro lingue** he knows *o* can speak four languages; **non sa l'inglese** he doesn't speak English; **non ne vuole più sapere di lei** he doesn't want to have anything more to do with her; **come l'ha saputo?** how did he find out *o* hear about it?; **ho saputo che ti sei sposato** I hear you got married; **vuoi sapere la verità?** do you want to know *o* hear the truth?; **far sapere qc a qn** to let sb know (about) sth, inform sb about sth; **fagli sapere che lo sto cercando** let him know I'm looking for him; **venire a sapere qc (da qn)** to find out *o* hear about sth (from sb)
2 (*essere capace di*) to know how to; **non sa far niente** he can't do anything; **sai nuotare?** do you know how to swim?, can you swim?; **è utile saper guidare** it's useful to be able to drive; **non so guidare** I can't drive; **non sapeva andare in bicicletta** he couldn't ride a bike; **sa (come) cavarsela** he can manage
3 (*rendersi conto*) to know; **non sa cosa dice** he doesn't know *o* realize what he's saying; **sa quello che fa** he knows what he's doing; **so com'è difficile parlargli** I know how difficult it is to talk to him; **senza saperlo** without realizing it, unwittingly
4 (*fraseologia*): **è difficile, e io ne so qualcosa** it's difficult and don't I know it; **e chi lo sa?** who knows?; **si sa che...** it's well known that ..., everybody knows that ...; **non si sa mai** you never know; **non saprei** I don't *o* wouldn't know; **non saprei dire** I couldn't say; **mi dispiace, non so che farci** I'm sorry, I don't see what I can do about it; **averlo saputo!** had I (*o* we *ecc*) known!, if only I (*o* we *ecc*) had known!; **ci sa fare con le donne/macchine** he has a way with women/cars; **lui sì che ci sa fare** he's very good at it
■ VI (*aus* **avere**)
1 sapere di (*aver sapore*) to taste of; (*aver odore*) to smell of; (*fig*) to smack of, resemble; **sa di fragola** it tastes of strawberries; **sa di pesce** it smells of fish; **è un film che non sa di niente** it's a very dull film
2 mi sa che... (*credo*) I think (that) ...; **mi sa che non viene** I don't think he's coming
■ SM knowledge
sapiente [sa'pjɛnte] AGG (*dotto*) learned; (*che rivela abilità*) masterly; **con mano sapiente** with a skilful hand
■ SM/F scholar
sapientemente [sapjente'mente] AVV (*con sapienza*) wisely; (*con capacità*) skilfully
sapientone, a [sapjen'tone] SM/F (*pegg*) know-all (*Brit*), know-it-all (*Am*)
sapienza [sa'pjɛntsa] SF (*saggezza*) wisdom; (*conoscenza*) knowledge, learning
saponaria [sapo'narja] SF (*Bot*) soapwort
saponata [sapo'nata] SF (*acqua*) soapy water; (*schiuma*) (soap)suds *pl*
sapone [sa'pone] SM soap; **sapone da barba** shaving soap; **sapone da bucato** washing soap; **sapone liquido** liquid soap; **sapone in scaglie** soapflakes *pl*
saponetta [sapo'netta] SF bar *o* cake of soap
saponificazione [saponifikat'tsjone] SF saponification
sapore [sa'pore] SM (*anche fig*) flavour (*Brit*), flavor (*Am*); **avere un buon sapore** to taste good; **non ha alcun sapore** it doesn't taste of anything, it doesn't have any flavo(u)r; **è ciò che dà sapore alla vita** this is what

Ss

makes life worth living; **parole di sapore amaro** words with a bitter ring to them
saporitamente [saporita'mente] AVV (*condito*) tastily; **dormire saporitamente** (*fig*) to sleep soundly
saporito, a [sapo'rito] AGG (*cibo*) tasty; (*fig: battuta*) witty; **un piatto saporito** a tasty dish; **è più saporito cucinato così** it's tastier when it's cooked like this; **poco saporito** tasteless; **farsi una dormita saporita** (*fig*) to sleep soundly
saporoso, a [sapo'roso] AGG tasty
sappiamo *ecc* [sap'pjamo] VB *vedi* **sapere**
saprò *ecc* [sa'prɔ] VB *vedi* **sapere**
saprofita, i [sa'prɔfita] SM (*Bot*) saprophyte
saputello, a [sapu'tɛllo] SM/F know-all (*Brit*), know-it-all (*Am*)
sarà *ecc* [sa'ra] VB *vedi* **essere**
sarabanda [sara'banda] SF (*fig*) uproar
saracinesca, sche [saratʃi'neska] SF rolling shutter
sarcasmo [sar'kazmo] SM (*ironia*) sarcasm; (*commento*) sarcastic remark; **fare del sarcasmo** to be sarcastic, make sarcastic remarks
sarcasticamente [sarkastika'mente] AVV sarcastically
sarcastico, a, ci, che [sar'kastiko] AGG sarcastic
sarchiare [sar'kjare] VT (*Agr*) to hoe
sarchiatrice [sarkja'tritʃe] SF (*Agr*) hoeing machine
sarcofago, gi *o* **ghi** [sar'kɔfago] SM sarcophagus
sarda ['sarda] SF (*pesce*) = **sardina**
Sardegna [sar'deɲɲa] SF Sardinia; **mi è piaciuta molto la Sardegna** I really liked Sardinia; **andrò in Sardegna quest'estate** I'm going to Sardinia this summer
▷ www.sardegna.net/
sardina [sar'dina] SF sardine; **pigiati come sardine** (*fig*) packed like sardines
sardo, a ['sardo] AGG, SM/F Sardinian
sardonicamente [sardonika'mente] AVV sardonically
sardonico, a, ci, che [sar'dɔniko] AGG sardonic
sarei *ecc* [sa'rɛi] VB *vedi* **essere**
sargasso [sar'gasso] SM sargasso, gulfweed; **il mar dei Sargassi** the Sargasso Sea
sari ['sari] SM INV sari
Sarin® ['sarin] SM sarin
sarmento [sar'mento] SM (*Bot*) runner; (*di vite, edera*) shoot
SARS [sars] SIGLA F (*Med*) SARS (= *Severe Acute Respiratory Syndrome*)
sarta ['sarta] SF dressmaker
sartia ['sartja] SF (*Naut*) stay
sartiame [sar'tjame] SM (*Naut*) stays *pl*
sarto ['sarto] SM tailor; (*d'alta moda*) couturier; **sarto da donna** ladies' tailor
sartoria [sarto'ria] SF **1** (*attività: di sarto*) tailoring; (*: di sarta*) dressmaking; **sartoria d'alta moda** haute couture **2** (*laboratorio: di sarto*) tailor's (shop); (*: di sarta*) dressmaker's (shop); (*: d'alta moda*) couturier's, fashion house
sassaia [sas'saja] SF (*terreno*) stony ground; (*lungo argini*) (stone) dyke
sassaiola [sassa'jɔla] SF hail of stones
sassarese [sassa'rese] AGG of *o* from Sassari
■SM/F inhabitant *o* native of Sassari
sassata [sas'sata] SF blow with a stone; **infranse il vetro con una sassata** he broke the pane with a stone; **tirare una sassata contro** *o* **a qn/qc** to throw a stone at sb/sth
sassifraga, ghe [sas'sifraga] SF (*pianta*) saxifrage
sasso ['sasso] SM (*pietra*) stone; (*ciottolo*) pebble; (*roccia*) rock; **restare** *o* **rimanere di sasso** (*fig*) to be dumbfounded; **è una cosa che fa piangere i sassi** (*fig: penoso*) it's pitiful
sassofonista, i, e [sassofo'nista] SM/F saxophonist
sassofono [sas'sɔfono] SM saxophone
sassola ['sassola] SF (*Naut*) bailer
sassone ['sassone] AGG, SM/F Saxon
sassoso, a [sas'soso] AGG (*vedi sm*) stony; pebbly; rocky
Satana ['satana] SM Satan
satanasso [sata'nasso] SM (*fig fam: persona*) devil
satanico, a, ci, che [sa'taniko] AGG satanic; (*fig*) diabolical, devilish, fiendish
satellitare [satelli'tare] AGG satellite *attr*; **antenna satellitare** satellite aerial; **televisione satellitare** satellite television
satellite [sa'tɛllite] SM, AGG INV (*anche fig*) satellite; **la TV via satellite** satellite TV
satin [sa'tɛ̃] SM satin
satinato, a [sati'nato] AGG with a satin finish
satira ['satira] SF satire; **fare la satira di qn/qc** to satirize sb/sth
satireggiare [satired'dʒare] VT to satirize
■VI (*aus* **avere**) (*fare della satira*) to be satirical; (*scrivere satire*) to write satires
satiricamente [satirika'mente] AVV satirically
satirico, a, ci, che [sa'tiriko] AGG satiric(al)
satirione [sati'rjone] SM (*fungo*) stinkhorn
satiro ['satiro] SM (*Mitol*) satyr; (*fig*) lecher, satyr
satollarsi [satol'larsi] VIP to eat one's fill
satollo, a [sa'tollo] AGG full, replete
saturare [satu'rare] VT (*Fis, Chim*) to saturate; (*fig: riempire*) to fill, stuff
▶ **saturarsi** VIP (*Fis, Chim*) to become saturated; (*fig: riempire*) to fill, stuff
saturazione [saturat'tsjone] SF (*Fis, Chim*) saturation; **aver raggiunto il punto di saturazione** to have reached saturation point; (*fig*) to have had more than enough *o* as much as one can take
satureia [satu'rɛja] SF (*Bot*) savory
Saturno [sa'turno] SM (*Mitol, Astron*) Saturn; **gli anelli di Saturno** (*Astron*) the rings of Saturn
saturo, a ['saturo] AGG (*gen*) saturated; **saturo (di)** (*fig*) full (of); **saturo d'acqua** (*terreno*) waterlogged
saudita, i, e [sau'dita] AGG: **Arabia Saudita** Saudi Arabia
■SM/F Saudi (Arabian)
sauna ['sauna] SF sauna; **fare la sauna** to have *o* take a sauna; **abbiamo fatto la sauna** we had a sauna
sauro, a ['sauro] AGG, SM/F (*cavallo*) sorrel
savana [sa'vana] SF savannah
savio, via, vi, vie ['savjo] AGG wise, sensible
■SM wise man
Savoia [sa'vɔja] SF Savoy
savoiardo, a [savo'jardo] AGG of Savoy, Savoyard
■SM (*Culin*) sponge finger
savoir-faire [sa'vwar'fɛr] SM INV savoir-faire
savonese [savo'nese] AGG of *o* from Savona
■SM/F inhabitant *o* native of Savona
sax [saks] SM INV (*sassofono*) sax
saziare [sat'tsjare] VT (*anche*) (*: fig*) to satisfy, satiate
▶ **saziarsi** VIP: **saziarsi (di)** to eat one's fill (of); **non si sazia di guardarla** (*fig*) he never tires of looking at her
sazietà [sattsje'ta] SF satiety, satiation; **mangiare a sazietà** to eat one's fill; **ce ne sono a sazietà** there are more than enough

sazio, zia, zi, zie ['sattsjo] AGG: **sazio (di)** sated (with), full (of); **no, grazie, sono sazio** no thanks, I've had enough; **sono sazio di questi discorsi** (*fig*) I'm fed up with this talk

sbaciucchiare [zbatʃuk'kjare] VT, **sbaciucchiarsi** VR (*uso reciproco*) to kiss and cuddle

sbadataggine [zbada'taddʒine] SF (*sventatezza*) carelessness; (*azione*) oversight

sbadatamente [zbadata'mente] AVV carelessly

sbadato, a [zba'dato] AGG careless, inattentive

sbadigliare [zbadiʎ'ʎare] VI (*aus* **avere**) to yawn

sbadiglio, gli [zba'diʎʎo] SM yawn; **fare uno sbadiglio** to yawn

sbafare [zba'fare] VT (*mangiare*) to devour, wolf (down); (*fig: scroccare*) to sponge, scrounge

sbafo ['zbafo] SM: **a sbafo** at somebody else's expense

sbagliare [zbaʎ'ʎare] VT (*gen*) to make a mistake in, get wrong; (*bersaglio*) to miss; **ha sbagliato tutto** he got everything wrong; **ha sbagliato tutto (nella vita)** he has made a mess of his life; **sbagliare la mira** to miss one's aim; **sbagliare strada** to take the wrong road; **sbagliare treno** to get *o* take the wrong train; **scusi, ho sbagliato numero** (*al telefono*) sorry, I've got the wrong number; **per me ha sbagliato mestiere** in my opinion he is in the wrong job; **sbagliò porta** he opened the wrong door; **sbagli tattica** you're going the wrong way about it; **sbagliare una mossa** (*al gioco*) to make a wrong move

■ VI (*aus* **avere**) to make a mistake; **mi dispiace, ho sbagliato** I'm sorry, I've made a mistake; **hai sbagliato a dirle tutto** it was a mistake to tell her everything; **ha sbagliato nel ricopiare il numero** he made a mistake in *o* when copying down the number; **potrei sbagliare ma...** I might be mistaken but ...; **ha sbagliato nei suoi confronti** he behaved badly towards her; **ho sbagliato di pochi centimetri** I miscalculated by a few centimetres, I was a few centimetres out (in my calculations); **sbagliando s'impara** you learn by your mistakes;

▶ **sbagliarsi** VIP (*fare errori*) to make a mistake (*o* mistakes); (*ingannarsi*) to be wrong, be mistaken; **pensavo fosse lei, ma mi sono sbagliato** I thought it was her, but I was wrong; **si è sbagliato nel ricopiare** he made a mistake in *o* when copying; **non c'è da sbagliarsi** there can be no mistake

sbagliato, a [zbaʎ'ʎato] AGG (*gen*) wrong; (*compito*) full of mistakes; (*conclusione*) erroneous

sbaglio, gli ['zbaʎʎo] SM mistake, error; **fare uno sbaglio** to make a mistake; **è stato uno sbaglio** it was a mistake; **ci deve essere uno sbaglio** there must be some mistake; **ha pagato per lo sbaglio commesso** he's paid for his mistake

sbalestrare [zbales'trare] VT (*scagliare*) to fling, hurl

sbalestrato, a [zbales'trato] AGG (*persona: scombussolato*) unsettled

sballare [zbal'lare] VT (*merce*) to unpack

■ VI (*aus* **essere**) **1** (*nel fare un conto*) to overestimate **2** (*Carte*) to go out **2** (*fam*) to be high (on drugs)

sballato, a [zbal'lato] AGG (*calcolo*) wrong; (*fam: ragionamento, persona*) screwy

■ SM/F (*fam: spostato*) misfit; (*: drogato*) junkie

sballo ['zballo] SM (*fam*) **1** (*droga*) trip **2** **che sballo di macchina!** what a totally amazing car!; **un film da sballo** a knockout film

sballottare [zballot'tare] VT to toss (about), throw (about)

sbalordire [zbalor'dire] VT to stun, amaze, astound; **la notizia mi ha sbalordito** I was stunned by the news

■ VI (*aus* **avere**) to be stunned, be amazed, be astounded

sbalorditivamente [zbalorditiva'mente] AVV incredibly

sbalorditivo, a [zbalordi'tivo] AGG (*abilità, memoria*) amazing, astounding; (*prezzo, affitto*) incredible, absurd

sbalzare¹ [zbal'tsare] VT **1** (*scaraventare*) to throw, hurl; **è stato sbalzato fuori dall'auto** he was thrown out of the car; **è stato sbalzato a 10 metri di distanza** he was thrown 10 metres **2** (*rimuovere: da una carica, sede*) to remove, dismiss

■ VI (*aus* **essere**) (*temperatura: alzarsi bruscamente*) to jump, rise; (*: abbassarsi bruscamente*) to fall, plummet

sbalzare² [zbal'tsare] VT (*Arte*) to emboss

sbalzo¹ ['zbaltso] SM (*sussulto*) start; **a sbalzi** jerkily; (*fig*) in fits and starts; **procedere a sbalzi** (*macchina*) to jolt along; **uno sbalzo di temperatura** a sudden change in temperature

sbalzo² ['zbaltso] SM (*Arte*): **lavorare a sbalzo** to emboss

sbancare¹ [zban'kare] VT (*nei giochi*) to break the bank at (*o* of); (*fig*) to ruin, bankrupt

sbancare² [zban'kare] VT (*Edil*) to excavate

sbandamento [zbanda'mento] SM (*di veicolo*) skid; (*Naut*) list; (*fig: di persona*) confusion; **ha avuto un periodo di sbandamento** he went off the rails for a bit

sbandare [zban'dare] VI (*aus* **avere**) (*Aut*) to skid; (*Naut*) to list

▶ **sbandarsi** VIP (*folla*) to disperse; (*truppe*) to scatter; (*fig: famiglia*) to break up

sbandata [zban'data] SF (*Aut*) skid; (*Naut*) list; **prendere** *o* **prendersi una sbandata per qn** (*fig*) to fall for sb

sbandato, a [zban'dato] SM/F mixed-up person

sbandierare [zbandje'rare] VT (*bandiere*) to wave; (*fig: ostentare*) to show off, flaunt, parade

sbando ['zbando] SM: **essere allo sbando** (*fig*) to drift

sbaraccare [zbarak'kare] VT (*fam: libri, piatti*) to clear (up); **sarà meglio sbaraccare** it's time we cleared out

sbaragliare [zbaraʎ'ʎare] VT (*Mil*) to rout; (*in gare sportive*) to beat, defeat

sbaraglio [zba'raʎʎo] SM: **andare** *o* **buttarsi allo sbaraglio** (*soldato*) to throw o.s. into the fray; (*fig: rischiare*) to risk everything

sbarazzare [zbarat'tsare] VT to clear

▶ **sbarazzarsi** VR: **sbarazzarsi di qn/qc** to get rid of sb/sth, rid o.s. of sb/sth

sbarazzino, a [zbarat'tsino] AGG impish, cheeky

■ SM scamp, imp

sbarbare [zbar'bare] VT

▶ **sbarbarsi** VR to shave

sbarbatello [zbarba'tɛllo] SM novice, greenhorn

sbarcare [zbar'kare] VT (*merci*) to unload; (*passeggeri: da nave, aereo*) to disembark, land; (*: da autobus, macchina*) to put down; **sbarcare il lunario** (*fig*) to make ends meet

■ VI (*aus* **essere**) **sbarcare da** (*aereo, nave*) to get off, disembark; **i passeggeri stavano sbarcando** the passengers were disembarking; **sbarcare (da un treno)** to get off (a train), alight (from a train)

sbarco, chi ['zbarko] SM **1** (*vedi vb*) unloading; disembarkation, landing; putting down; **allo sbarco** on disembarking **2** (*Mil*): **forza da sbarco** landing party; **testa di sbarco** beachhead

sbarra ['zbarra] SF **1** (*gen, Sport*) bar; (*di passaggio a*

Ss

livello) barrier; *(di timone)* tiller; **dietro le sbarre** *(fig: in prigione)* behind bars; **presentarsi alla sbarra** *(Dir: in tribunale)* to appear in court; **mettere alla sbarra** *(fig)* to put on trial **2** *(lineetta)* stroke

sbarramento [zbarra'mento] SM *(di strada, passaggio)* barrier; *(diga)* dam, barrage; *(Mil)* barrage; *(Pol)* cut-off point *(level of support below which a political party is excluded from representation in Parliament)*

sbarrare [zbar'rare] VT **1** *(bloccare)* to block, bar; **sbarrare la strada a qn** *(anche fig)* to block *o* bar sb's way; **una macchina della polizia gli ha sbarrato la strada** a police car blocked his way **2** *(spalancare)*: **sbarrare gli occhi** to open one's eyes wide **3** *(cancellare)* to cross out, strike out; **sbarrare un assegno** to cross a cheque *(Brit)*, to endorse a check "for deposit only" *(Am)*

sbarrato, a [zbar'rato] AGG **1** *(porta)* barred; *(passaggio)* blocked, barred; *(strada)* blocked, obstructed **2** *(occhi)* staring **3** *(assegno)* crossed *(Brit)*, endorsed "for deposit only" *(Am)*

sbatacchiare [zbatak'kjare] VT *(porta)* to slam, bang; *(ali)* to flap
■ VI *(aus* **avere***)* to bang

sbattere ['zbattere] VT **1** *(gen)* to beat; *(uova)* to beat, whisk; *(panna)* to whip; *(ali)* to beat, flap; *(porta)* to slam, bang; **sbattere un ginocchio contro qc** to bang one's knee on sth; **ho sbattuto il ginocchio** I banged my knee; **sbattere un pugno sul tavolo** to thump the table; **sbattere la porta in faccia a qn** *(anche fig)* to slam the door in sb's face; **se n'è andato sbattendo la porta** he went out slamming the door; **non sapevo dove sbattere la testa** *(fig)* I didn't know which way to turn; **sbattere la testa contro un muro** *(fig)* to bang one's head against a brick wall; **finché non ci sbatte la testa contro non capirà** he'll find out the hard way **2** *(buttare)* to throw; **sbattere qc per terra** to throw sth to the ground; **sbattere qn fuori/in galera** to throw sb out/into prison; **sbattere via** to throw away *o* out; **sbattilo pure lì** just throw it over there; **sbattere una notizia in prima pagina** to splash a piece of news across the front page **3** *(fam!: possedere sessualmente)* to fuck *(fam!)*
■ VI *(aus* **avere***)* **1** *(porta, finestra)* to bang; *(vele, ali)* to flap; **la finestra sbatte per il vento** the window is banging in the wind; **sbattere contro qc** to knock against sth **2** *(fam)*: **sbattersene** not to give a damn; **me ne sbatto!** I don't give a damn!

sbattitore [zbatti'tore] SM *(Culin)* electric whisk

sbattuto, a [zbat'tuto] AGG **1** *(uovo)* beaten **2** *(fig: persona)* worn out, dejected; *(: pallido)* peaky; **avere un'aria sbattuta** to look worn out

sbavare [zba'vare] VI *(aus* **avere***)* **1** *(gen)* to dribble **2** *(colore)* to run; *(rossetto, inchiostro)* to smudge, smear
■ VT: **sbavare qc** to dribble over sth
▶ **sbavarsi** VR to dribble down o.s.

sbavatura [zbava'tura] SF *(di persone)* dribbling; *(di lumache)* slime; *(di rossetto, vernice)* smear

sbeccare [zbek'kare] VT to chip

sbellicarsi [zbelli'karsi] VIP: **sbellicarsi dalle risa** to split one's sides laughing

sbendare [zben'dare] VT *(togliere le bende)* to remove the bandage(s) from

sberla ['zbɛrla] SF slap; **dare una sberla a qn** to slap *o* hit sb

sberleffo [zber'lɛffo] SM: **fare uno sberleffo a qn** to make a face at sb; **fare gli sberleffi** to pull faces, grimace

sbevazzare [zbevat'tsare] VI *(aus* **avere***)* *(pegg)* to booze

sbiadire [zbja'dire] VI *(aus* **essere***)* to fade; **ricordi che sbiadiscono col tempo** memories which fade with time
■ VT to (cause to) fade

sbiadito, a [zbja'dito] AGG *(scolorito)* faded; *(fig: stile)* colourless *(Brit)*, colorless *(Am)*, dull

sbiancare [zbjan'kare] VI *(aus* **essere***)*, **sbiancarsi** VIP *(persona)*: **sbiancare** *o* **sbiancarsi in viso** to pale, blanch, grow pale *o* white
■ VT to whiten

sbieco, chi ['zbjɛko] AGG *(muro)* at an angle; *(pavimento)* sloping, slanting; **tagliare una stoffa di sbieco** to cut material on the bias; **guardare qn di sbieco** *(fig)* to look askance at sb
■ SM *(Cucito)* bias

sbigottimento [zbigotti'mento] SM dismay, consternation

sbigottire [zbigot'tire] VT to dismay, dumbfound
■ VI *(aus* **essere***)*, **sbigottirsi** VIP to be dismayed, be dumbfounded

sbilanciamento [zbilantʃa'mento] SM *(di carico)* displacement

sbilanciare [zbilan'tʃare] VT to throw off balance
▶ **sbilanciarsi** VIP *(perdere l'equilibrio)* to lose one's balance, overbalance; *(fig: compromettersi)* to compromise o.s.

sbilancio, ci [zbi'lantʃo] SM *(Econ)* deficit

sbilenco, a, chi, che [zbi'lɛnko] AGG *(sedia, tavolino)* rickety; *(persona)* crooked, misshapen; *(fig: idea, ragionamento)* twisted

sbirciare [zbir'tʃare] VT to peep at, cast sidelong glances at, eye

sbirciata [zbir'tʃata] SF: **dare una sbirciata a qc** to glance at sth, have a look at sth

sbirro ['zbirro] SM *(pegg)* cop

sbizzarrirsi [zbiddzar'rirsi] VIP *(sfogare i propri desideri)* to indulge one's whims; *(fare pazzie)* to go wild; **sbizzarrirsi a fare qc** to indulge o.s. in doing sth

sbloccare [zblok'kare] VT *(gen)* to unblock, free; *(passaggio, strada)* to clear, unblock; *(affitti)* to free from controls; *(freno)* to release; **sbloccare la situazione** to get things moving again
▶ **sbloccarsi** VIP *(gen)* to become unblocked; *(passaggio, strada)* to clear, become unblocked; *(Psic: persona)* to free o.s. from a psychological block; **la situazione si è sbloccata** things are moving again

sblocco, chi ['zblɔkko] SM *(vedi vt)* unblocking; clearing; **dopo lo sblocco degli affitti** after the lifting of rent controls

sbobba ['zbɔbba] SF *(fam pegg)* dishwater

sboccare [zbok'kare] VI *(aus* **essere***)* **sboccare in** *(fiume)* to flow into; *(strada)* to lead (in)to; *(valle)* to open into; *(persona)* to emerge into, come (out) into; *(fig: concludersi)* to end (up) in
■ VT *(rompere: vaso, brocca)* to chip

sboccatamente [zbokkata'mente] AVV: **esprimersi sboccatamente** to use foul language

sboccato, a [zbok'kato] AGG *(fig: persona)* foul-mouthed; *(: linguaggio)* coarse, foul

sbocciare [zbot'tʃare] VI *(aus* **essere***)* *(fiori)* to bloom, flower, open (out); *(fig: nascere)* to blossom

sbocco, chi ['zbokko] SM **1** *(di fiume)* mouth; *(di tubazione)* outlet; *(di strada)* end; **una strada senza sbocco** a dead end; **siamo in una situazione senza sbocco** *o* **sbocchi** there's no way out of this for us

2 (*Comm*) outlet
sbocconcellare [zbokkontʃel'lare] VT: **sbocconcellare (qc)** to nibble (at sth)
sbollentare [zbollen'tare] VT (*Culin*) to parboil
sbollire [zbol'lire] VI (*aus* **essere**) (*fig: calmarsi*) to cool down
sbolognare [zboloɲ'ɲare] VT (*fam*): **sbolognare qc/qn** to get rid of sth/sb
sbornia ['zbɔrnja] SF (*fam*): **prendersi una sbornia** to get plastered; **smaltire la sbornia** to sober up
sborsare [zbor'sare] VT to fork out, shell out
sbottare [zbot'tare] VI (*aus* **essere**) **sbottare in una risata** to burst out laughing; **alla fine sono sbottato** in the end I couldn't keep quiet any longer
sbottonare [zbotto'nare] VT to unbutton, undo; **si è sbottonato la camicia** he unbuttoned his shirt
▶ **sbottonarsi** VR to undo one's buttons; (*fig fam: confidarsi*) to unburden o.s.
sbottonato, a [zbotto'nato] AGG undone, unbuttoned
sbozzare [zbot'tsare] VT (*gen*) to sketch out; (*scultura*) to rough-hew; (*fig: progetto*) to draft
sbracato, a [zbra'kato] AGG (*fam: sciatto*) dishevelled, slovenly
sbracciarsi [zbrat'tʃarsi] VIP to wave (one's arms about)
sbracciato, a [zbrat'tʃato] AGG (*persona*) with bare arms, bare-armed; (*indumento: senza maniche*) sleeveless; (: *a maniche corte*) short-sleeved
sbraitare [zbrai'tare] VI (*aus* **avere**) to shout, yell, bawl
sbranare [zbra'nare] VT to tear to pieces
▶ **sbranarsi** VR (*uso reciproco, anche fig*) to tear each other to pieces
sbriciolare [zbritʃo'lare] VT
▶ **sbriciolarsi** VIP to crumble; **la pietra mi si è sbriciolata in mano** the stone crumbled in my hand; **la torta s'è tutta sbriciolata** the cake got all broken
sbriciolato, a [zbritʃo'lato] AGG crumbling
sbrigare [zbri'gare] VT (*lavoro, pratiche*) to deal with, get through; (*clienti*) to attend to, see to, deal with; **ho ancora alcune faccende da sbrigare** I've still got a few things to do; **sbrigare le faccende domestiche** to do the housework; **se la sa sbrigare da solo** he can manage *o* do it by himself
▶ **sbrigarsi** VIP (*fare in fretta*) to hurry (up), get a move on; **devi sbrigarti se non vuoi perdere il treno** you'll have to hurry if you don't want to miss the train; **sbrigatevi!** hurry up!
sbrigativo, a [zbriga'tivo] AGG (*persona, modi*) quick, expeditious; (: *pegg*) abrupt, brusque; (*giudizio*) hasty; **è un piatto sbrigativo** it's a quick dish
sbrigliare [zbriʎ'ʎare] VT (*fig: fantasia*) to give free rein to
sbrinamento [zbrina'mento] SM defrosting
sbrinare [zbri'nare] VT to defrost
sbrinatore [zbrina'tore] SM defroster
sbrindellato, a [zbrindel'lato] AGG tattered, in tatters
sbrodolare [zbrodo'lare] VT to stain, dirty
▶ **sbrodolarsi** VR to stain o.s., dirty o.s.; **ti sei tutto sbrodolato** you've spilt food all down yourself
sbrodolato, a [zbrodo'lato] AGG stained
sbrogliare [zbroʎ'ʎare] VT (*filo, matassa*) to unravel; (*vele*) to unfurl; (*fig: problema*) to solve, find a solution to; **è riuscito a sbrogliarsela** he has managed to sort things out
▶ **sbrogliarsi** VR (*fig: persona*) to disentangle o.s., free o.s.

sbronza ['zbrontsa] SF (*fam*) = **sbornia**
sbronzarsi [zbron'tsarsi] VR (*fam*) to get plastered
sbronzo, a ['zbrontso] AGG (*fam*) plastered
sbruffone, a [zbruf'fone] SM/F boaster, braggart
sbucare [zbu'kare] VI (*aus* **essere**) **sbucare da** to pop out of *o* from; **sbucare fuori** to appear (from nowhere); **un ragazzino è sbucato fuori all'improvviso** a little boy suddenly appeared from nowhere; **da dove è sbucato quel libro?** where did that book spring from?
sbucciapatate [zbuttʃapa'tate] SM INV potato peeler
sbucciare [zbut'tʃare] VT (*gen*) to peel; (*piselli*) to shell; **sbucciarsi un ginocchio** to graze one's knee; **mi sono sbucciato un ginocchio** I grazed my knee
sbucciatura [zbuttʃa'tura] SF graze
sbucherò *ecc* [zbuke'rɔ] VB *vedi* **sbucare**
sbudellare [zbudel'lare] VT to disembowel
▶ **sbudellarsi** VR: **sbudellarsi dalle risate** (*fig*) to split one's sides laughing
sbuffare [zbuf'fare] VI (*aus* **avere**) (*gen*) to puff, pant; (: *con impazienza*) to snort, fume; (*cavallo*) to snort; (*treno*) to puff; **saliva le scale sbuffando per la fatica** he was panting with the effort of climbing the stairs; **sbuffa sempre quando deve lavare i piatti** he always grumbles when he has to wash the dishes
sbuffo ['zbuffo] SM 1 (*di vento*) gust; (*di aria, fumo, vapore*) puff 2 **maniche a sbuffo** puff(ed) sleeves
sbullonare [zbullo'nare] VT to unbolt
SC ABBR 1 = **stato civile** 2 = *Suprema Corte (di Cassazione)*
sc. ABBR (*Teatro*: = **scena**) sc.
scabbia ['skabbja] SF (*Med*) scabies *sg*
scabiosa [ska'bjosa] SF (*Bot*) field scabious
scabro, a ['skabro] AGG (*superficie*) rough; (*fig: stile*) concise, terse
scabrosamente [skabrosa'mente] AVV (*indecentemente*) indecently
scabrosità [skabrosi'ta] SF (*vedi agg*) thorniness; embarrassing nature; indecency
scabroso, a [ska'broso] AGG (*fig: difficile*) difficult, thorny; (: *imbarazzante*) embarrassing; (: *sconcio*) indecent
scacchiera [skak'kjɛra] SF (*Scacchi*) chessboard; (*Dama*) draughtboard (*Brit*), checkerboard (*Am*)
scacchiere [skak'kjɛre] SM 1 (*Mil*) sector 2 (*Pol: in Gran Bretagna*): **Cancelliere dello Scacchiere** Chancellor of the Exchequer
scacchista, i, e [skak'kista] SM/F chessplayer
scacciacani [skattʃa'kani] SM O F INV pistol with blanks
scacciapensieri [skattʃapen'sjɛri] SM INV (*Mus*) jew's-harp
scacciare [skat'tʃare] VT (*mandar via*) to chase away *o* out, drive away *o* out; (*buttar fuori*) to throw out, turn out; (*fig: malinconia, noia*) to overcome; (: *sospetto, dubbio*) to dispel; **scacciare qn di casa** to turn sb out of the house
scacco, chi ['skakko] SM 1 (*pezzo del gioco*) chess piece, chessman; (*riquadro*) square; **scacchi** SMPL chess *sg*; **giocare a scacchi** to play chess; **dare scacco al re** to check the king; **subire uno scacco** (*fig: sconfitta*) to suffer a setback; **scacco matto** checkmate; **dare scacco matto a qn** (*anche fig*) to checkmate sb 2 (*quadretto*) square, check; **tessuto a scacchi** check(ed) material
▷ www.federscacchi.it/
scaccolarsi [skakko'larsi] VR (*fam*) to pick one's nose
scaddi *ecc* ['skaddi] VB *vedi* **scadere**

Ss

scadente [ska'dɛnte] AGG (*qualità*) poor, shoddy; (*voto*) unsatisfactory; (*prodotto*) poor-quality *attr*; (*film, libro*) poor

scadenza [ska'dɛntsa] SF (*di documento*) expiry; (*su prodotto*) sell-by date; (*di cambiale, contratto*) maturity; **data di scadenza** expiry date; (*su prodotto*) sell-by date; **con scadenza il 24 maggio** (*pagamento*) (which falls) due on the 24th of May; (*documento*) expiring on the 24th of May; **a breve/lunga scadenza** (*progetto, piano*) short-/long-term

scadere [ska'dere] VI IRREG (*aus* **essere**) **1** (*perdere valore, stima*) to decline, go down; **scadere agli occhi di qn** *or* **scadere nella stima di qn** to go down in sb's estimation **2** (*perdere validità: documento, contratto*) to expire; (*: cambiale, termine di pagamento*) to fall due

scadimento [skadi'mento] SM decline

scaduto, a [ska'duto] AGG (*passaporto*) out of date; **il biglietto è scaduto** the ticket is no longer valid; **il mio passaporto è scaduto** my passport has expired; **il latte è scaduto** the milk is past its sell-by date

scafandro [ska'fandro] SM (*di palombaro*) diving suit; (*di astronauta*) spacesuit

scaffalatura [skaffala'tura] SF shelving, shelves *pl*

scaffale [skaf'fale] SM (*ripiano*) shelf; (*mobile*) set of shelves

scafista, i [ska'fista] SM (*di immigrati*) people smuggler (*by boat*)

scafo ['skafo] SM (*Naut*) hull

scagionare [skadʒo'nare] VT to exonerate, free from blame
▶ **scagionarsi** VR to exonerate o.s., free o.s. from blame

scaglia ['skaʎʎa] SF (*squama*) scale; (*di metallo, pietra*) splinter, chip; (*di sapone*) flake

scagliare [skaʎ'ʎare] VT (*anche fig*) to throw, hurl, fling
▶ **scagliarsi** VR: **scagliarsi contro qn** *or* **scagliarsi addosso a qn** to fling o.s. at sb, hurl o.s. at sb; (*fig: inveire*) to rail at sb

scaglionamento [skaʎʎona'mento] SM (*Mil*) arrangement in echelons

scaglionare [skaʎʎo'nare] VT (*truppe*) to echelon; (*pagamenti*) to space out, spread out

scaglione [skaʎ'ʎone] SM (*Mil*) echelon; (*Geol*) terrace; **a scaglioni** (*fig*) in groups

scagnozzo [skaɲ'ɲɔttso] SM (*pegg*) lackey, hanger-on

scala ['skala] SF **1** (*in edificio*) stairs *pl*, staircase; (*all'esterno*) steps *pl*; **salire/scendere le scale** to go upstairs/downstairs, go up/down the stairs; **fece le scale in fretta** he hurried up (*o* down) the stairs; **una scala di corda** a rope ladder; **una scala di marmo** a marble staircase; **scala a chiocciola** spiral staircase; **scala a libretto** stepladder; **scala mobile** escalator, moving staircase; **scala a pioli** ladder; **scala di servizio** backstairs *pl*; **scala di sicurezza** (*antincendio*) fire escape **2** (*Econ, Fis, Mat, Geog*) scale; **riproduzione in scala** reproduction to scale; **in scala di 1 a 100.000** on a scale of 1 cm to 1 km; **su larga/piccola scala** on a large/small scale; **su scala nazionale/mondiale** on a national/worldwide scale; **scala Celsius/Fahrenheit** Celsius/Fahrenheit scale; **scala cromatica** (*Mus*) chromatic scale; **scala di misure** system of weights and measures; **scala mobile (dei salari)** index-linked pay scale; **scala termometrica** scale of temperatures **4** (*Mus*) scale; **scala maggiore/minore** major/minor scale **5** (*Carte*) straight; **scala reale** straight flush

Scala ['skala] SF: **la Scala** *theatre in Milan*

LA SCALA

Milan's **la Scala** first opened its doors in 1778 with a performance of Salieri's opera, "L'Europa riconosciuta". Built on the site of the church of Santa Maria della Scala, the theatre suffered serious damage in the bombing campaigns of 1943 but reopened in 1946 with a concert conducted by Toscanini. Enjoying world-wide renown for its opera, **la Scala** also has a famous school of classical dance.

▷ www.teatroallascala.org/

scalare[1] [ska'lare] VT **1** (*Alpinismo, muro*) to climb, scale **2** (*ridurre*): **scalare un debito** to pay off a debt in instalments; **questa somma vi viene scalata dal prezzo originale** this sum is deducted from the original price **3** (*capelli*) to layer

scalare[2] [ska'lare] AGG (*Mat, Fis*) scalar

scalata [ska'lata] SF **1** (*azione*) scaling, climbing **2** (*arrampicata, fig*) climb; (*Alpinismo*) climb, ascent; **scalata al potere** climb to power

scalatore, trice [skala'tore] SM/F climber

scalcagnato, a [skalkaɲ'ɲato] AGG (*logoro*) worn; (*persona*) shabby

scalciare [skal'tʃare] VI (*aus* **avere**) to kick

scalcinato, a [skaltʃi'nato] AGG (*fig pegg*) shabby

scaldaacqua [skalda'akkwa] SM INV (*per casa, Industria*) water heater

scaldabagno [skalda'baɲɲo] SM (*per casa*) water heater

scaldaletto [skalda'lɛtto] SM warming pan, bedwarmer

scaldamuscoli [skalda'muskoli] SM INV legwarmer

scaldare [skal'dare] VT **1** (*latte, stanza*) to heat (up); **scalda un po' di latte** heat some milk; **scaldare i muscoli** to warm up, do warming-up exercises; **scaldare il motore** to warm up the engine; **scaldare la sedia** (*fig*) to twiddle one's thumbs **2** **scaldarsi le mani/i piedi** to warm one's hands/feet
▶ **scaldarsi** VR to warm up; **scaldarsi al fuoco** to warm o.s. by the fire;
▶ **scaldarsi** VIP (*stanza*) to heat up; (*fig: arrabbiarsi*) to get excited, get worked up

LO SAPEVI...?
scaldare non si traduce mai con la parola inglese *scald*

scaldavivande [skaldavi'vande] SM INV dish warmer

scaldino [skal'dino] SM (*per mani*) hand-warmer; (*per piedi*) foot-warmer; (*per letto*) bedwarmer

scaletta [ska'letta] SF **1** (*gen*) short flight of steps; (*portatile*) small stepladder **2** (*di conferenza*) outline; (*Radio, TV*) summary **3** (*Sci*): **salita a scaletta** sidestepping

scalfire [skal'fire] VT (*superficie*) to scratch; (*fig: sicurezza*) to undermine

scalfittura [skalfit'tura] SF scratch

scalinata [skali'nata] SF (*interna*) staircase, (flight of) stairs *pl*; (*esterna*) (flight of) steps *pl*

scalino [ska'lino] SM (*gen, fig*) step; (*di scala a pioli*) rung

scalmana [skal'mana] SF (hot) flush

scalmanarsi [skalma'narsi] VIP (*affaticarsi*) to rush about, rush around; (*agitarsi, darsi da fare*) to get all hot and bothered; (*arrabbiarsi*) to get excited, get steamed up; **non scalmanarti a cercarlo** don't wear yourself out trying to find him

scalmanato, a [skalma'nato] SM/F hothead

scalmiera [skal'mjɛra] SF (*Naut*) rowlock (*Brit*), oarlock (*Am*)
scalo ['skalo] SM **1** (*per varo*) slipway, slips *pl* **2** (*fermata: Naut, Aer*) stop; **fare scalo (a)** (*Naut*) to call (at), put in (at); (*Aer*) to make a stopover (at), land (at); **scalo tecnico** (*Aer*) technical stop *o* landing; **volo senza scalo** non-stop flight **3** (*luogo: Naut*) port of call; (: *Aer*) stopover **4** (*Ferr*): **scalo merci** goods (*Brit*) *o* freight (*Am*) yard
scalogna [ska'loɲɲa] SF (*fam*) bad luck
scalognato, a [skaloɲ'ɲato] AGG (*fam*) unlucky
scalogno [ska'loɲɲo] SM (*Bot*) shallot
scaloppina [skalop'pina] SF (*Culin*) escalope; **una scaloppina di vitello** a veal escalope
scalpellare [skalpel'lare] VT to chisel
scalpellino [skalpel'lino] SM stone-cutter
scalpello [skal'pɛllo] SM (*gen*) chisel; (*Med*) scalpel; (*per pozzi petroliferi*) drill
scalpiccio, cii [skalpit'tʃio] SM (*rumore*) shuffling (noise)
scalpitante [skalpi'tante] AGG (*cavallo*) pawing the ground; (*fig: persona*) champing at the bit
scalpitare [skalpi'tare] VI (*aus* **avere**) (*cavallo*) to paw the ground; (*fig: persona*) to champ at the bit
scalpitio, tii [skalpi'tio] SM (*di cavallo*) pawing of the ground
scalpo ['skalpo] SM scalp
scalpore [skal'pore] SM sensation; **fare** *o* **suscitare scalpore** to cause a sensation *o* a stir
scaltramente [skaltra'mente] AVV (*vedi agg*) shrewdly, astutely; slyly, cunningly
scaltrezza [skal'trettsa] SF (*vedi agg*) shrewdness, astuteness; slyness, cunning
scaltrire [skal'trire] VT: **scaltrire qn** to sharpen sb's wits
▶ **scaltrirsi** VIP to become shrewder
scaltro, a ['skaltro] AGG shrewd, astute; (*pegg*) sly, cunning
scalzacane [skaltsa'kane] SM/F (*incompetente*) bungler, blunderer
scalzare [skal'tsare] VT (*pianta*) to bare the roots of; (*muro, fig*) to undermine
scalzo, a ['skaltso] AGG barefoot(ed); **era scalzo** he was barefoot
scambiare [skam'bjare] VT **1** (*confondere*): **scambiare qn/qc per** to take *o* mistake sb/sth for; **l'ho scambiato per suo fratello** I mistook him for his brother; **scusa, l'ho scambiato per il mio** sorry, I thought it was mine **2** (*barattare*): **scambiare qc per** to exchange sth for; **ho scambiato un CD con due cassette** I exchanged a CD for two cassettes **3** (*conversare*): **scambiare due parole** to exchange a few words
▶ **scambiarsi** VR (*uso reciproco*) to exchange; **scambiarsi gli auguri di Natale** to wish each other a Happy Christmas; **si scambiarono un'occhiata** they exchanged looks
scambievole [skam'bjevole] AGG mutual, reciprocal
scambievolmente [skambjevol'mente] AVV mutually, reciprocally; **aiutarsi scambievolmente** to help one another *o* each other
scambio, bi ['skambjo] SM **1** (*di persone, cose*) exchange; **uno scambio di prigionieri** an exchange of prisoners; **scambi culturali** cultural exchanges; **uno scambio di opinioni** an exchange of views; **fare (uno) scambio** to swap; **facciamo uno scambio?** shall we swap? **2** (*Comm*) trade; **libero scambio** free trade; **scambi con l'estero** foreign trade **3** (*Ferr*) points *pl* (*Brit*), switches (*Am*) **4** (*Calcio*) pass; (*Tennis*) shot and return **5** (*Chim*): **scambio ionico** ion exchange
scambista, i [skam'bista] SM (*Ferr*) pointsman (*Brit*), switchman (*Am*); (*Comm*) trader; (*di coppie*) swinger
scamiciato, a [skami'tʃato] AGG in one's shirt sleeves
■ SM pinafore (dress)
scamosciato, a [skamoʃ'ʃato] AGG suede
scampagnata [skampaɲ'ɲata] SF trip to the country, outing to the country; **fare una scampagnata** to go for a day out in the country
scampanare [skampa'nare] VI (*aus* **avere**) to peal
■ VT (*gonna*) to flare
scampanato, a [skampa'nato] AGG flared
scampanellare [skampanel'lare] VI (*aus* **avere**) to ring loudly
scampanellata [skampanel'lata] SF loud ringing
scampanio, nii [skampa'nio] SM peal
scampare [skam'pare] VT (*pericolo*) to escape; **scampare la morte** to escape death; **scamparla bella** to have a lucky *o* narrow escape; **Dio ci scampi e liberi!** God forbid!
■ VI (*aus* **essere**) **scampare (a qc)** (*pericolo, morte*) to survive (sth), escape (sth); **pochi scamparono alla strage** few escaped (from) the massacre; **pochi scamparono al disastro** few people were untouched *o* unaffected by the disaster
scampo[1] ['skampo] SM (*salvezza*) escape, way out; **non c'è (via di) scampo** there's no way out; **cercare scampo nella fuga** to seek safety in flight
scampo[2] ['skampo] SM (*Zool*) (Dublin Bay) prawn
scampolo ['skampolo] SM remnant
scanalatura [skanala'tura] SF (*azione*) grooving; (*incavo*) groove, channel; (*Archit*) fluting
scandagliare [skandaʎ'ʎare] VT (*mare*) to sound, fathom; (*fig: indagare*) to sound out; (: *anima, sentimenti, intenzioni*) to probe
scandaglio, gli [skan'daʎʎo] SM (*Naut: azione*) sounding, fathoming; (: *strumento*) sounding line
scandalistico, a, ci, che [skanda'listiko] AGG (*settimanale*) sensational, sensationalist *attr*
scandalizzare [skandalid'dzare] VT to scandalize, to shock
▶ **scandalizzarsi** VIP to be scandalized, be shocked; **si scandalizza per un nonnulla** she's easily shocked
scandalizzato, a [skandalid'dzato] AGG scandalized, shocked
scandalo ['skandalo] SM scandal; **il loro comportamento è motivo di scandalo** their behaviour is scandalous; **dare scandalo** to cause a scandal
scandalosamente [skandalosa'mente] AVV scandalously, shockingly, outrageously
scandaloso, a [skanda'loso] AGG scandalous, shocking, outrageous
Scandinavia [skandi'navja] SF Scandinavia
scandinavo, a [skandi'navo] AGG, SM/F Scandinavian
scandire [skan'dire] VT (*versi*) to scan; (*parole*) to articulate, pronounce clearly *o* distinctly; **scandire il tempo** (*Mus*) to beat time
scannare [skan'nare] VT (*animale*) to butcher, slaughter; (*persona*) to cut *o* slit the throat of
scannatoio, oi [skanna'tojo] SM (*fig, fam*) bachelor pad
scanner ['skanner] SM INV (*Inform*) scanner

Ss

scannerare [skanne'rare] VT, **scannerizzare** [skannerid'dzare] VT (*Inform*) to scan
scannerizzatore [skanneriddza'tɔre] SM = scanner
scanno ['skanno] SM seat, bench
scansafatiche [skansafa'tike] SM/F INV idler, loafer
scansare [skan'sare] VT **1** (*spostare*) to move (aside), shift **2** (*evitare*: *colpo*) to dodge; (: *pericolo*) to avoid
▶ **scansarsi** VR (*spostarsi*) to get out of the way, move out of the way; (: *per evitare un colpo*) to dodge
scansia [skan'sia] SF (*ripiano*) shelf; (*mobile*) bookcase, shelves *pl*
scansionare [skansjo'nare] VT (*Inform*) to scan
scansione [skan'sjone] SF **1** (*Poesia*) scansion **2** (*Tecn*, *Med*) scanning
scanso ['skanso] SM: **a scanso di** in order to avoid, as a precaution against; **a scanso di equivoci** to avoid (any) misunderstanding
scantinato [skanti'nato] SM basement
scantonare [skanto'nare] VI (*aus* **avere**) **1** (*per non essere visto*) to duck round the corner **2** (*fig*) to become irrelevant
scanzonato, a [skantso'nato] AGG easy-going
scapaccione [skapat'tʃone] SM clout, slap; **dare uno scapaccione a qn** to clout sb; **prendere qn a scapaccioni** to slap sb about
scapestrato, a [skapes'trato] AGG loose-living, dissolute
■ SM/F dissolute person
scapigliare [skapiʎ'ʎare] VT: **scapigliare qn** to dishevel sb's hair
scapigliato, a [skapiʎ'ʎato] AGG (*spettinato*) dishevelled; (*fig*: *scapestrato*) dissolute
scapito ['skapito] SM: **a scapito di** to the detriment of
scapola ['skapola] SF (*Anat*) shoulder blade
scapolo ['skapolo] SM bachelor
scappamento [skappa'mento] SM (*Aut*) exhaust; **tubo di scappamento** exhaust pipe
scappare [skap'pare] VI (*aus* **essere**) **1** (*gen*): **scappare (da)** (*città, stato, stanza*) to escape (from); **i ladri sono scappati** the thieves got away; **scappare di prigione** to escape from prison; **scappare di casa** to run away from home; **far scappare qn** (*mettere in fuga*) to scare sb away; (*aiutare a fuggire*) to help sb to escape; **scappar via** to run away, escape; **scappare all'estero** to flee the country; **scusa, devo scappare** I'm sorry, but I must dash; **scappare a gambe levate** to take to one's heels **2** (*sfuggire*): **mi è scappato di mano** it slipped out of my hands; **mi è scappato di mente** it slipped my mind; **mi è scappato da ridere** I burst out laughing; **mi scappa la pipì** I'm bursting **3 lasciarsi scappare** (*occasione, affare*) to miss, let go by; (*dettaglio*) to overlook; (*parola*) to let slip; (*prigioniero*) to let escape; **non lasciarti scappare l'occasione** don't miss this opportunity
scappata [skap'pata] SF (*breve visita*): **fare una scappata da qn** to call *o* drop *o* in on sb; **farò una scappata a Parigi/a casa tua** I'll pop over to Paris/to your place; **faccio una scappata in centro** I'm just going to pop into town
scappatella [skappa'tɛlla] SF escapade
scappatoia [skappa'toja] SF (*gen*) way out; (*nella burocrazia*) loophole
scappellotto [skappel'lɔtto] SM clout, slap; **dare uno scappellotto a qn** to clout sb
scarabeo [skara'bɛo] SM (*Zool*) scarab (beetle); (*gioco*) Scrabble®
scarabocchiare [skarabok'kjare] VT (*fare scarabocchi*) to scribble, doodle, scrawl; (*scrivere svogliatamente*) to scribble off
scarabocchio, chi [skara'bɔkkjo] SM (*sgorbio*) scribble, scrawl; (*disegno*) doodle; (*fig pegg*: *quadro*) daub; (*macchia d'inchiostro*) blot
scarafaggio, gi [skara'faddʒo] SM (*Zool*) cockroach
scaramanzia [skaraman'tsia] SF: **per scaramanzia** for luck; **incrocia le dita per scaramanzia** cross your fingers for luck; **non gliel'ho ancora detto per scaramanzia** I haven't told him yet, just in case
scaramuccia, ce [skara'muttʃa] SF skirmish
scaraventare [skaraven'tare] VT to fling, hurl
▶ **scaraventarsi** VR: **scaraventarsi contro qn/qc** to fling o.s. at sb/sth
scarcerare [skartʃe'rare] VT to release (from prison)
scarcerazione [skartʃerat'tsjone] SF release (from prison)
scardinare [skardi'nare] VT to take off its hinges
scarica, che ['skarika] SF **1** (*di arma*) shot; (*fig*: *di insulti*) flood; (: *di sassi, pugni*) hail, shower; **una scarica di mitra** a burst of machine-gun fire **2** (*Elettr*): **scarica (elettrica)** discharge (of electricity)
scaricabarili [skarikaba'rili] SM: **fare a scaricabarili** (*fig*) to blame each other
scaricare [skari'kare] VT (*merce, veicolo*) to unload; (*passeggeri*) to set down; (*Inform*) to download; (*batteria*) to cause to run down, cause to go flat (*Brit*) *o* dead (*Am*); (*fig*: *coscienza*) to unburden, relieve; (: *fam*: *fidanzata, amico*) to drop; **stanno scaricando il camion** they're unloading the lorry; **ci vuole un'ora per scaricare il file** it takes an hour to download the file; **scaricare qc in** (*sogg*: *fabbrica*) to discharge sth into; (: *corso d'acqua*) to empty sth into, pour sth into; **il canale scarica i rifiuti in mare** the canal deposits the rubbish in the sea; **scaricare un'arma** (*togliendo la carica*) to unload a gun; (*sparando*) to discharge a gun; **scaricare le proprie responsabilità su qn** to off-load one's responsibilities onto sb; **scaricare la colpa addosso a qn** to blame sb else; **scaricare la tensione** (*fig*) (: *rilassarsi*) to unwind; (: *sfogarsi*) to let off steam
▶ **scaricarsi** VIP (*molla, orologio*) to run *o* wind down, stop; (*batteria*) to go flat (*Brit*) *o* dead (*Am*); **la batteria si è scaricata** the battery is flat; **il fulmine si scaricò su un albero** the lightning struck a tree;
▶ **scaricarsi** VR (*fig*: *persona*) to unwind; (: *sfogarsi*) to let off steam; **scaricarsi di ogni responsabilità** to relieve o.s. of all responsibilities; **piangendo si è scaricata** she had a good cry and felt better for it
scaricatore [skarika'tore] SM: **scaricatore di porto** docker
scarico[1], a, chi, che ['skariko] AGG (*fucile*) unloaded, empty; (*orologio*) wound down; (*batteria*) run down, flat (*Brit*), dead (*Am*)
scarico[2], chi ['skariko] SM (*di merci, materiali*) unloading; (*di immondizie*) dumping, tipping (*Brit*); (: *luogo*) refuse *o* rubbish (*Brit*) *o* garbage (*Am*) dump; (*Tecn*: *deflusso*) draining; (: *dispositivo*) drain; (*Aut*) exhaust; **scarico del lavandino** waste outlet
scarlattina [skarlat'tina] SF scarlet fever
scarlatto, a [skar'latto] AGG, SM scarlet
scarmigliare [skarmiʎ'ʎare] VT to dishevel
▶ **scarmigliarsi** VR to be dishevelled
scarnificare [skarnifi'kare] VT to strip the flesh from
scarno, a ['skarno] AGG (*persona*) lean, bony; (*volto*) gaunt; (*mano*) thin, bony; (*fig*: *insufficiente*) meagre (*Brit*), meager (*Am*); (: *spoglio*) (: *stile*) bare
scarpa ['skarpa] SF shoe; **un paio di scarpe** a pair of

shoes; **mettiti le scarpe** put on your shoes; **fare le scarpe a qn** (*fig*) to double-cross sb; **essere una scarpa** (*fig fam*) to be useless; **scarpe coi tacchi (alti)** high-heeled shoes; **scarpe col tacco basso** low-heeled shoes; **scarpe da ginnastica** gym shoes, plimsolls; **scarpe senza tacco** flat shoes; **scarpe sportive** trainers; **scarpe da tennis** tennis shoes

scarpata [skar'pata] SF escarpment

scarpiera [skar'pjɛra] SF shoe rack

scarpinata [skarpi'nata] SF (*fam*) trek; **abbiamo fatto una scarpinata** it was some trek

scarpone [skar'pone] SM boot; **scarponi da montagna** climbing boots; **scarponi da sci** ski boots

scarrocciare [skarrot'tʃare] VI (*aus* **avere**) (*Naut*) to drift leeward

scarroccio [skar'rɔttʃo] SM (*Naut*) leeway

scarrozzare [skarrot'tsare] VT to drive around

scarrucolare [skarruko'lare] VI (*aus* **avere**) to slip off a pulley

scarsamente [skarsa'mente] AVV (*preparato, organizzato*) poorly

LO SAPEVI...?
scarsamente non si traduce mai con la parola inglese ***scarcely***

scarseggiare [skarsed'dʒare] VI (*aus* **avere**) (*viveri, risorse*) to be scarce, be lacking; **i viveri scarseggiavano** food was in short supply; **cominciano a scarseggiare i medicinali** supplies of medicine are starting to run low; **scarseggiare di qc** to lack sth, be short of sth

scarsezza [skar'settsa] SF shortage, lack, scarcity

scarsità [skarsi'ta] SF shortage

scarso, a ['skarso] AGG (*raccolto*) poor, lean; (*risorse*) meagre (*Brit*), meager (*Am*); (*qualità*) poor; (*alunno, voto*) mediocre; **è un chilo/metro scarso** it's just under the kilo/metre; **le porzioni erano scarse** the portions were rather small; **di scarso interesse** of little interest; **hanno scarse risorse a disposizione** they have few resources at their disposal; **scarsa visibilità** poor visibility; **ha dimostrato scarsa maturità/intelligenza** he showed little maturity/intelligence; **scarso di** lacking in

scartabellare [skartabel'lare] VT to skim through, glance through

scartafaccio, ci [skarta'fattʃo] SM notebook

scartamento [skarta'mento] SM (*Ferr*) gauge; **a scartamento ridotto** narrow-gauge

scartare[1] [skar'tare] VT (*regalo, caramella*) to unwrap; **hai scartato i regali?** have you unwrapped your presents?

scartare[2] [skar'tare] VT **1** (*Carte*) to discard **2** (*fig: possibilità, idea*) to reject; **hanno scartato tutte le mie proposte** they rejected all my suggestions **3** (*concorrente*) to reject, eliminate; (*Mil*) to declare unfit for military service

scartare[3] [skar'tare] VI (*aus* **avere**) (*deviare*) to swerve; **scartare a sinistra** to swerve to the left ■VT (*Calcio*) to dodge (past); (*Equitazione*): **scartare (l'ostacolo)** to run out

scarto[1] ['skarto] SM **1** (*prodotto, oggetto scartato*) reject **2** (*Carte*) discard

scarto[2] ['skarto] SM **1** (*movimento brusco*) swerve; (*Equitazione*) run-out; **fare uno scarto** to swerve; to run out **2** (*differenza*) gap, difference; **scarto salariale** wage differential

scartocciare [skartot'tʃare] VT (*gen*) to unwrap; (*mais*) to husk

scartoffie [skar'tɔffje] SFPL (*pegg*) papers

scassare [skas'sare] VT **1** (*fam: rompere*) to wreck, smash **2** (*dissodare*) to plough up ▶ **scassarsi** VIP (*rompersi*) to be wrecked

scassinare [skassi'nare] VT to force, break open

scassinatore, trice [skassina'tore] SM/F (*di case*) housebreaker, burglar; (*di banche*) bank robber; (*di casseforti*) safe-cracker

scasso ['skasso] SM (*Dir*) breaking and entering; **furto con scasso** burglary

scatenare [skate'nare] VT (*reazione, rabbia*) to provoke; (*rivolta*) to spark off; (*guai*) to stir up ▶ **scatenarsi** VIP (*temporale*) to break; (*rivolta*) to break out; (*persona*): **scatenarsi contro qn** to rage at sb

scatenato, a [skate'nato] AGG wild

scatola ['skatola] SF (*gen*) box; (*di latta*) tin (*Brit*), can (*Am*); **cibo in scatola** tinned (*Brit*) *o* canned (*Am*) foods; **una scatola di sardine** a tin *o* can of sardines; **una scatola di cioccolatini** a box of chocolates; **comprare qc a scatola chiusa** to buy sth sight unseen; **accettare qc a scatola chiusa** (*fig*) to accept sth blindly; **avere le scatole piene (di qn/qc)** (*fam*) to be fed up to the back teeth (with sb/sth); **rompere le scatole a qn** (*fam*) to get on sb's nerves; **levati** *o* **togliti dalle scatole!** get out of the way!
■ **scatola di cartone** cardboard box; **scatola cranica** cranium; **scatola del differenziale** (*Aut*) differential housing; **scatola di fiammiferi** (*vuota*) matchbox; (*piena*) box of matches; **scatola dei fusibili** fuse box; **scatola nera** (*Aer*) black box

scatolame [skato'lame] SM tinned (*Brit*) *o* canned (*Am*) food; (*insieme di scatole*) tins *pl* (*Brit*), cans *pl* (*Am*)

scatoletta [skato'letta] SF (*gen*) (small) box; (*di latta*) (small) tin (*Brit*), (small) can (*Am*)

scatolone [skato'lone] SM cardboard box

Ss

scattante [skat'tante] AGG (*svelto*) quick off the mark; (*agile*) agile

scattare [skat'tare] VI (*aus* **essere**) (*molla*) to be released; (*grilletto, interruttore*) to spring back; (*serratura: aprirsi*) to click open; (*: chiudersi*) to click shut; (*iniziare: legge, provvedimento*) to come into effect; (*Sport*) to put on a spurt; **è scattato l'allarme** the alarm went off; **far scattare** to release; **ha fatto scattare l'allarme** he set the alarm off; **scattare in piedi** to spring *o* leap to one's feet; **sono scattati in piedi** they sprang to their feet; **scattare sull'attenti** to spring *o* leap to attention; **scatta per niente** (*si arrabbia*) he flies off the handle at the slightest provocation; **domani scatta l'ora legale** tomorrow the clocks go forward (*o* back) ■VT (*Fot*): **scattare una foto** to take a photograph *o* a photo *o* a picture

scattista, i, e [skat'tista] SM/F (*Sport*) sprinter

scatto ['skatto] SM **1** (*congegno*) release; (*: di arma da fuoco*) trigger mechanism; (*rumore*) click; **serratura a scatto** spring lock; **ho sentito lo scatto della serratura** I heard the lock click, I heard the click of the lock; **scatto automatico** automatic release; (*Fot*) (automatic) timer **2** (*Telec*) unit **3** (*Sport*) spurt; **ha sorpassato gli altri corridori con uno scatto** he put on a spurt and overtook the other runners **4** (*di persona*) jump, start; **muoversi a scatti** to move jerkily; **ha avuto uno scatto (d'ira)** he flew off the handle; **di scatto** suddenly; **si alzò di scatto** he sprang *o* leapt to his feet **5** (*aumento*): **scatto d'anzianità** long service bonus; **scatto di stipendio** increment

scaturire [skatu'rire] VI (*aus* **essere**) (*liquido*): **scaturire (da)** to spurt (from), gush (from); (*fig: avere origine*) to derive (from)

scavalcare [skaval'kare] VT (*ostacolo, anche fig*) to pass (*o* climb) over; (*fig: concorrenti*) to overtake, get ahead of; (: *collega*) to be promoted over (the head of); **abbiamo scavalcato il muretto** we climbed over the wall
scavare [ska'vare] VT (*gen, terreno*) to dig; (*trincea, Archeol*) to dig, excavate; (*pozzo, galleria*) to bore; (*tronco, pietra: renderlo cavo*) to hollow (out); **scavarsi la fossa** (*fig*) to dig one's own grave; **un volto scavato dalla stanchezza** a haggard face; **scavare nell'animo di qn** to search sb's soul; **scavare nel passato di qn** to dig into sb's past
scavatore [skava'tore] SM (*macchina, persona*) digger
scavatrice [skava'tritʃe] SF (*macchina*) excavator
scavezzacollo, a [skavettsa'kɔllo] SM/F daredevil
scavo ['skavo] SM (*luogo*) excavation; (*azione*) excavating *no pl*; **fare degli scavi in una zona** to excavate an area
scazzarsi [skat'tsarsi] VIP (*fam!*) to be pissed off (*fam!*)
scazzato, a [skat'tsato] AGG (*fam!: stufo, annoiato*) pissed off (*fam!*)
scazzo ['skattso] SM (*fam!*): **hanno avuto uno scazzo ieri sera** they were knocking the shit out of each other last night (*fam!*)
scazzottare [skattsot'tare] (*fam*) VT to beat up, give a thrashing to
▶ **scazzottarsi** VR (*uso reciproco*) to beat each other up
scazzottata [skattsot'tata] SF (*fam*) fight, punch-up
scegliere ['ʃeʎʎere] VT IRREG (*gen*) to choose; (*prodotto, candidato*) to select, choose; **hai scelto il suo regalo?** have you chosen her present?; **scegliere di fare qc** to choose to do sth; **scegliere il campo** (*Sport*) to toss for ends
sceiccato [ʃeik'kato] SM (*titolo*) title of sheik; (*territorio*) sheikdom
sceicco, chi [ʃe'ikko] SM sheik
scekerare *ecc* [ʃeke'rare] VT = **shakerare**
scelgo *ecc* ['ʃelgo] VB *vedi* **scegliere**
scellerataggine [ʃellera'taddʒine], **scelleratezza** [ʃellera'tettsa] SF (*qualità*) wickedness; (*azione*) wicked deed, crime
scellerato, a [ʃelle'rato] AGG wicked, evil
■ SM/F villain
scellino [ʃel'lino] SM (*inglese, austriaco*) schilling
scelta ['ʃelta] SF (*gen*) choice; (*selezione*) selection, choice; **fare una scelta** to make a choice, choose; **hai fatto la scelta giusta** you made the right choice; **non avere scelta** to have no choice *o* option; **non ho scelta, devo accettare** I've got no choice, I have to agree; **potete avere frutta o formaggio a scelta** you have the choice of fruit or cheese; **di prima scelta** top grade *o* quality; **verdura di prima scelta** top quality vegetables; **c'è un'ampia scelta di prodotti** there's a wide selection *o* choice of products
scelto, a ['ʃelto] PP *di* **scegliere**
■ AGG (*gruppo*) carefully selected; (*frutta, verdura*) top-quality, choice; **brani scelti** selected passages; **una compagnia scelta** a distinguished company; **pubblico scelto** select audience; **tiratore scelto** crack shot, highly skilled marksman
scemare [ʃe'mare] VI (*aus* **essere**) (*rumore, applausi, interesse*) to lessen; (*forze*) to decline; (*vento*) to drop, abate
scemata [ʃe'mata] SF: **fare/dire una scemata** to do/say something foolish *o* silly; **il film era una scemata** it was a very stupid film
scemenza [ʃe'mɛntsa] SF stupidity *no pl*; **dire scemenze** to talk nonsense *o* rubbish; **ha fatto una scemenza** he behaved foolishly *o* stupidly; **è stata una scemenza** it was sheer stupidity
scemo, a ['ʃemo] AGG stupid, foolish, silly
■ SM/F idiot, fool; **fare lo scemo** to play the fool
scempiaggine [ʃem'pjaddʒine] SF (*qualità*) foolishness; (*atto, discorso*): **fare/dire una scempiaggine** to do/say something foolish *o* silly
scempio, pi ['ʃempjo] SM (*strage*) massacre, slaughter; (*deturpazione*) destruction; **fare scempio di qc** (*fig*) to destroy sth, wreak havoc with sth, ruin sth; **lo scempio dei centri storici** the destruction of historic town centres; **quel viadotto è uno scempio** that viaduct is an eyesore
scena ['ʃɛna] SF **1** (*gen, Teatro, Cine*) scene; **nella prima scena** in the first scene, in scene one; **la scena si svolge a Parigi** the action takes place in Paris, the scene is set in Paris; **cambiamento di scena** scene change; **una scena di caccia** a hunting scene; **sulla scena internazionale** on the international scene; **ho assistito a tutta la scena** I was present at *o* during the whole scene; **fare una scena** (*fig*) to make a scene; **fu una scena orribile** it was a horrible sight; **ha fatto scena muta** (*fig*) he didn't open his mouth
2 (*palcoscenico*) stage; **entrare in scena** to come on stage; (*fig*) to come on the scene; **uscire di scena** to leave the stage; (*fig*) to leave the scene; **mettere in scena** (*personaggio*) to present on the stage; (*commedia*) to stage, direct
scenario, ri [ʃe'narjo] SM (*Teatro*) scenery, set; (*fig: sfondo*) backdrop
scenata [ʃe'nata] SF row, scene; **fare una scenata (a qn)** to make a scene; **Sandra ha fatto una scenata al ristorante** Sandra made a scene at the restaurant
scendere ['ʃendere] VB IRREG
■ VT (*scale, sentiero*) to go (*o* come) down, descend
■ VI (*aus* **essere**) **1** (*gen*) to go (*o* come) down, descend; (*fiume, torrente*) to flow down; (*strada*) to slope down, descend; (*aereo*) to come down, descend; **scendere con l'ascensore** to go (*o* come) down in the lift (*Brit*) *o* elevator (*Am*); **scendere in città** to go into town; **scendere in strada** to go down into the street; **scendere in piazza** (*folla, manifestanti*) to take to the streets; **scendere in sciopero** to come out on strike; **scendere a piedi/correndo** to walk/run down; **scendo ad aprirgli il portone** I'll go down and open the door for him; **sali tu o scendo io?** are you coming up or shall I come down?; **scendo subito!** I'm just coming!; **siamo scesi in mezz'ora** (*da collina*) we got down in half an hour; **quando i Longobardi scesero in Italia** when the Longobards descended on Italy; **i capelli le scendevano sulle spalle** her hair fell to her shoulders; **scendere a terra** (*sbarcare*) to go ashore; **scendere ad un albergo** to put up *o* stay at a hotel
2 **scendere da** (*macchina, treno*) to get out of; (*nave*) to disembark from, get off; (*aereo, autobus, bici*) to get off; **scendere da cavallo** to dismount, get off one's horse; **scendere dal letto** to get out of bed; **scendere dalle scale** to go (*o* come) down the stairs; **scendo alla prossima fermata** I'm getting off at the next stop; **scendi da quell'albero!** come down from that tree!
3 (*prezzi, temperatura*) to fall, drop; (*livello*) to fall, drop, go down; (*marea*) to go out; (*notte, oscurità*) to fall; (*sole, strada*) to go down; (*nebbia*) to come down; **la temperatura è scesa di due gradi** the temperature fell by two degrees
scendiletto [ʃendi'lɛtto] SM INV bedside rug
sceneggiare [ʃened'dʒare] VT to dramatize

sceneggiato [ʃened'dʒato] SM (TV) television drama
sceneggiatore, trice [ʃeneddʒa'tore] SM/F scriptwriter
sceneggiatura [ʃeneddʒa'tura] SF (*Teatro*) scenario; (*Cine*) screenplay, scenario
scenico, a, ci, che ['ʃɛniko] AGG stage *attr*
scenografia [ʃenogra'fia] SF (*Teatro*) stage design; (*Cine*) set design; (*elementi scenici*) scenery
scenografico, a, ci, che [ʃeno'grafiko] AGG stage *attr*, set *attr*
scenografo, a [ʃe'nɔgrafo] SM/F set designer
sceriffo [ʃe'riffo] SM sheriff
scervellarsi [ʃervel'larsi] VIP: **scervellarsi (su qc)** to rack one's brains (over sth)
scervellato, a [ʃervel'lato] SM/F half-wit, idiot ■ AGG feather-brained, scatterbrained
sceso, a ['ʃeso] PP *di* **scendere**
scetticamente [ʃettika'mente] AVV sceptically (*Brit*), skeptically (*Am*)
scetticismo [ʃetti'tʃizmo] SM scepticism (*Brit*), skepticism (*Am*)
scettico, a, ci, che ['ʃɛttiko] AGG sceptical (*Brit*), skeptical (*Am*) ■ SM/F sceptic (*Brit*), skeptic (*Am*)
scettro ['ʃɛttro] SM sceptre (*Brit*), scepter (*Am*)
scevro, a ['ʃevro] AGG (*letter*): **scevro di** free from, devoid of
scheda ['skɛda] SF (*di schedario*) (index) card; (*di elezioni*) ballot paper; (*in libro*) inset; (*servizio televisivo*) brief report; **scheda audio** (*Inform*) sound card; **scheda bianca/nulla** (*Pol*) unmarked/spoiled ballot paper; **scheda madre** (*Inform*) motherboard; **scheda perforata** punch card; **scheda ricaricabile** (*Tel*) top-up card; **scheda telefonica** phonecard; **scheda video** (*Inform*) video card
schedare [ske'dare] VT (*dati*) to file; (*registrare su scheda*) to card-index; (*: libri*) to catalogue; (*: della polizia*) to put on record
schedario, ri [ske'darjo] SM card index, file; (*mobile*) filing cabinet
schedato, a [ske'dato] AGG with a (police) record ■ SM/F person with a (police) record
schedina [ske'dina] SF ≈ pools coupon (*Brit*); **giocare la schedina** to do the football pools
scheggia, ge ['skeddʒa] SF (*gen*) splinter; (*di vetro*) splinter, sliver; (*di porcellana*) chip; **scheggia impazzita** (*fig*) loose cannon
scheggiare [sked'dʒare] VT, **scheggiarsi** (*gen*) VIP (*gen*) to splinter, chip; (*porcellana*) to chip
scheggiatura [skeddʒa'tura] SF **1** (*azione: vedi vb*) splintering; chipping **2** (*punto scheggiato*) chip
scheletrico, a, ci, che [ske'lɛtriko] AGG (*anche Anat*) skeletal; (*fig: essenziale*) skeleton *attr*
scheletrito, a [skele'trito] AGG (*persona*) skeleton-like, all skin and bone; (*ramo, stile*) bare
scheletro ['skɛletro] SM (*Anat*) skeleton; (*fig: struttura*) frame, framework; (*: di trama*) outline; **essere ridotto a uno scheletro** to be all skin and bone; **avere uno scheletro nell'armadio** (*fig*) to have a skeleton in the closet *o* cupboard (*Brit*)
schema, i ['skɛma] SM **1** (*gen*) outline; (*diagramma*) diagram, sketch; **ha disegnato lo schema alla lavagna** he drew the diagram on the board; **schema riassuntivo** outline of the main points; **schema di legge** bill **2** (*fig: modello*): **ribellarsi agli schemi** to rebel against traditional values; **secondo gli schemi tradizionali** in accordance with traditional values
schematico, a, ci, che [ske'matiko] AGG schematic
schematismo [skema'tizmo] SM (*di discorso, testo*) sketchiness
schematizzare [skematid'dzare] VT to schematize
scherma ['skerma] SF (*Sport*) fencing; **faccio scherma** I do fencing; **tirare di scherma** to fence
▷ www.federscherma.it/
schermaglia [sker'maʎʎa] SF (*fig*) skirmish
schermare [sker'mare] VT to screen
schermata [sker'mata] SF (*Inform*) screenful
schermire [sker'mire] VT to protect, shield ▶ **schermirsi** VR to defend o.s., protect o.s.
schermitore, trice [skermi'tore] SM/F (*Sport*) fencer
schermo ['skermo] SM **1** (*gen*) screen; **farsi schermo con la mano** (*per proteggersi dalla luce*) to shield one's eyes with one's hand **2** (*TV, Cine*): **il piccolo/grande schermo** the small/big screen; **divo dello schermo** screen star; **a schermo panoramico** (*TV*) widescreen
schermografia [skermogra'fia] SF X-rays *pl*
schermografico, a, ci, che [skermo'grafiko] AGG X-ray *attr*
schernire [sker'nire] VT to mock, sneer at
scherno ['skerno] SM scorn; **farsi scherno di** to sneer at; **essere oggetto di scherno** to be a laughing stock; **di scherno** (*parole*) scornful, sneering; (*gesto*) scornful; **grida di scherno** jeers
scherzare [sker'tsare] VI (*aus* **avere**) (*gen*) to joke; **stavo scherzando** I was only joking *o* kidding; **è meglio non scherzare su queste cose** it's better not to joke about these things; **quello è un tipo che non scherza** he is not a man to be trifled with; **c'è poco da scherzare!** it's no laughing matter!, it's no joke!; **scherzare con i sentimenti altrui** to trifle with other people's feelings; **non scherzare col fuoco!** (*fig*) you shouldn't play with fire!
scherzo ['skertso] SM **1** (*gen*) joke; (*burla*) (practical) joke, prank; **fare uno scherzo a qn** to play a (practical) joke *o* prank *o* trick on sb; **facciamo uno scherzo a Daniele!** let's play a trick on Daniele!; **per scherzo** as *o* for a joke, for a laugh, for fun; **fare un brutto scherzo a qn** to play a nasty trick on sb; **neppure per scherzo** not even in fun; **non sa stare allo scherzo** he can't take a joke; **scherzi a parte** seriously, joking apart; **scherzi a parte, penso che sia una ragazza intelligente** seriously, I think she's a clever girl; **...e niente scherzi!** ... and no funny business!; **uno scherzo da prete** a dirty trick; **è uno scherzo!** (*facile*) it's child's play!, it's easy!; **scherzi d'acqua** waterworks; **scherzi di luce** effects of the light **2** (*Mus*) scherzo
scherzosamente [skertsosa'mente] AVV jokingly
scherzoso, a [sker'tsoso] AGG (*tono, gesto*) playful; (*osservazione*) facetious; **è un tipo scherzoso** he likes *o* is fond of a joke
schettinare [sketti'nare] VI (*aus* **avere**) to (roller) skate
schettino ['skɛttino] SM (roller) skate
schiaccianoci [skjattʃa'notʃi] SM INV nutcracker
schiacciante [skjat'tʃante] AGG overwhelming
schiacciapatate [skjattʃapa'tate] SM INV potato masher
schiacciare [skjat'tʃare] VT **1** (*gen*) to squash, crush; (*patate*) to mash; (*aglio*) to crush; (*noce*) to crack; (*mozzicone*) to stub out; **la macchina gli ha schiacciato un piede** the car crushed his foot; **schiacciare la palla** (*Tennis, Pallavolo*) to smash the ball; **schiacciare un sonnellino** to take *o* have a nap; **schiacciarsi un dito**

Ss

nella porta to shut one's finger in the door **2** (*pulsante*) to press; (*pedale*) to press down **3** (*fig: opposizione, nemico*) to crush; (*: squadra avversaria*) to hammer; **era schiacciato da un senso di colpa** he was weighed down by feelings of guilt
▶ **schiacciarsi** VIP to get squashed, get crushed

schiacciasassi [skjattʃa'sassi] SM INV steamroller

schiacciata [skjat'tʃata] SF (*Tennis, Pallavolo*) smash

schiacciato, a [skjat'tʃato] AGG (*naso*) flat; **ha una forma schiacciata** it's flat

schiaffare [skjaf'fare] VT to throw, chuck; **lo hanno schiaffato dentro** (*fam: in prigione*) they threw him in the cooler, they put him away
▶ **schiaffarsi** VIP to throw o.s.

schiaffeggiare [skjaffed'dʒare] VT to smack, slap

schiaffo ['skjaffo] SM slap (in the face); **dare uno schiaffo a qn** to slap sb; **prendere qn a schiaffi** to slap sb about *o* around; **uno schiaffo morale** a slap in the face, a rebuff; **avere una faccia da schiaffi** to look impudent

schiamazzare [skjamat'tsare] VI (*aus* **avere**) (*galline, oche*) to squawk, cackle; (*fig: persone*) to make a din, make a racket

schiamazzatore, trice [skjamattsa'tore] SM/F rowdy

schiamazzo [skja'mattso] SM (*fig: chiasso*) din, racket

schiantare [skjan'tare] VT (*spezzare*) to break, tear apart; **il fulmine ha schiantato l'albero** the lightning split the tree
▶ **schiantarsi** VIP (*macchina*): **schiantarsi contro** to crash into; (*aereo*): **schiantarsi al suolo** to crash (to the ground)

schianto ['skjanto] SM (*rumore*) crash; **di schianto** (*improvvisamente*) all of a sudden; **quella macchina è uno schianto!** (*fam*) that car's great; **quella ragazza è uno schianto!** that girl's terrific!

schiappa ['skjappa] SF (*fig*): **essere una schiappa in qc** to be a washout at sth

schiarimento [skjari'mento] SM (*del cielo*) clearing up, brightening; (*fig: delucidazione*) clarification, explanation

schiarire [skja'rire] VT (*gen*) to lighten, make lighter; (*Fot*) to make brighter; (*tende, tessuto: far sbiadire*) to fade; **schiarirsi la gola** *o* **la voce** to clear one's throat; **schiarirsi i capelli** to dye one's hair blonde; **si è schiarita i capelli** she's dyed her hair blonde; **schiarire le idee a qn** (*fig*) to put sb straight
■ VI (*aus* **essere**), **schiarirsi** VIP (*cielo, tempo*) to clear up; (*colore*) to become lighter; (*: sbiadire*) to fade

schiarita [skja'rita] SF (*Meteor*) bright spell; (*fig*) improvement, turn for the better

schiatta ['skjatta] SF (*poet*) lineage, descent

schiattare [skjat'tare] VI (*aus* **essere**) (*fig: scoppiare*) to burst; **schiattare d'invidia** to be green with envy; **schiattare di rabbia** to be beside o.s. with rage

schiavismo [skja'vizmo] SM slavery; (*Pol*) support of slavery, anti-abolitionism

schiavista, i, e [skja'vista] AGG slave *attr*
■ SM/F (*trafficante*) slave trader, slaver; (*Pol*) supporter of slavery, anti-abolitionist; **il nostro capo è uno schiavista** (*fig*) our boss is a slave driver

schiavistico, a, ci, che [skja'vistiko] AGG (*economia*) slave *attr*

schiavitù [skjavi'tu] SF slavery; **ridurre in schiavitù** to subject, subjugate

schiavizzare [skjavid'dzare] VT (*anche fig*) to reduce to slavery, enslave; (*dipendenti, figli*) to tyrannize over

schiavo, a ['skjavo] AGG enslaved; **essere schiavo delle proprie abitudini** to be a slave to habit
■ SM/F slave

schiena ['skjɛna] SF back; **soffrire di mal di schiena** to have a bad back; **avere mal di schiena** *or* **avere la schiena a pezzi** to have backache, have a pain in one's back; **ho mal di schiena** I've got backache; **avere la schiena curva** (*con le spalle curve*) to be round-shouldered; (*con la spina dorsale curva*) to have a stoop; **voltare la schiena a qn** (*fig*) to turn one's back on sb; **mi ha voltato la schiena proprio quando avevo bisogno di lui** he turned his back on me just when I needed him; **rompersi la schiena** to break one's back; (*fig: lavorare sodo*) to work one's fingers to the bone; **visto di schiena** seen from behind *o* from the back; **a schiena di mulo** (*ponte*) humpback; (*strada*) steeply cambered

schienale [skje'nale] SM **1** (*di poltrona, sedia*) back **2** (*di animale macellato*) saddle

schiera ['skjɛra] SF (*Mil: linea*) rank; **le schiere dei nemici** the enemy forces; **una schiera di persone** a crowd of people; **arrivarono a schiere** they arrived in their hundreds; **villetta a schiera** ≈ terraced house

schieramento [skjera'mento] SM (*Mil*) (rank) formation; (*Sport*) formation; (*fig*) alliance

schierare [skje'rare] VT (*Mil*) to draw up, line up, marshal
▶ **schierarsi** VR (*Mil*) to draw up; (*fig*): **schierarsi con** *o* **dalla parte di/contro qn** to side with/oppose sb

schiettamente [skjetta'mente] AVV frankly

schiettezza [skjet'tettsa] SF frankness, straightforwardness

schietto, a ['skjɛtto] AGG frank, straightforward

schifare [ski'fare] VT to disgust
▶ **schifarsi** VIP to be disgusted

schifezza [ski'fettsa] SF: **essere una schifezza** (*cibo, bibita*) to be disgusting; (*film, libro*) to be dreadful; **mangia un sacco di schifezze** he eats a lot of rubbish

schifiltosamente [skifiltosa'mente] AVV fussily

schifiltoso, a [skifil'toso] AGG fussy, difficult; **fare lo schifiltoso** to be fussy

schifo ['skifo] SM (*sensazione*) disgust; **è uno schifo!** it's disgusting!; **fare schifo** (*cibo, insetto*) to be disgusting; (*libro, film*) to be dreadful *o* awful; **mi fai schifo** you make me sick; **la nostra squadra ha fatto schifo** our team was useless

schifosamente [skifosa'mente] AVV (*vedi agg*) disgustingly, revolvingly; dreadfully, awfully; **sei schifosamente fortunato!** you're terribly lucky!

schifoso, a [ski'foso] AGG (*che fa ribrezzo*) disgusting, revolting; (*pessimo*) dreadful, awful; **hai avuto una fortuna schifosa** (*fam*) you've been terribly lucky

schioccare [skjok'kare] VT (*frusta*) to crack; (*dita*) to snap, click; (*lingua*) to click; (*labbra*) to smack; **le schioccò un bacio** he gave her a smacker (*fam*)

schiocco, chi ['skjɔkko] SM (*di frusta*) crack; (*di dita*) snap, click; (*di lingua*) click; (*di labbra*) smack

schiodare [skjo'dare] VT to unnail; **non riesco a schiodarlo dal computer** (*fig fam*) I can't get him away from the computer

schioppettata [skjoppet'tata] SF gunshot

schioppo ['skjɔppo] SM rifle, gun; **essere a un tiro di schioppo da** to be a stone's throw from

schiudere ['skjudere] VB IRREG
■ VT to open
▶ **schiudersi** VIP (*fiore*) to open, come out

schiuma ['skjuma] SF (*gen*) foam; (*di bevande*) froth; (*di sapone*) lather; **avere la schiuma alla bocca** (*fig:*

arrabbiato) to be foaming at the mouth; **schiuma da barba** shaving foam

schiumaiola [skjuma'jɔla] SF (*Culin*) skimmer

schiumare [skju'mare] VT (*brodo*) to skim
■ VI (*aus* **avere**) to foam; **schiumare di rabbia** to foam at the mouth

schiumoso, a [skju'moso] AGG foamy, frothy

schiuso, a ['skjuso] PP *di* **schiudere**

schivare [ski'vare] VT (*colpo, proiettile*) to dodge, avoid; (*persona, pericolo*) to avoid; (*domanda*) to evade

schivo, a ['skivo] AGG (*ritroso*) reserved; (*timido*) shy

schizofrenia [skiddzofre'nia] SF schizophrenia

schizofrenico, a, ci, che [skiddzo'frɛniko] AGG, SM/F schizophrenic

schizoide [skid'dzɔide] AGG, SM/F schizoid

schizzare [skit'tsare] VT **1** (*gen*) to squirt; (*inzuppare*) to splash; (*macchiare*) to spatter; **mi ha schizzato d'acqua** he splashed water over me, he splashed me with water; **finiscila di schizzarmi** stop splashing me; **ha schizzato inchiostro sulla tovaglia** he spattered ink on the tablecloth, he spattered the tablecloth with ink; **ti sei schizzato la giacca di vino** you've got wine on your jacket **2** (*disegnare*) to sketch
■ VI (*aus* **essere**) (*liquido*) to squirt; (: *con violenza*) to gush, spurt; **schizzare via** (*animale, persona*) to dart away; (*macchina, moto*) to speed off; **schizzare fuori** (*persona*) to dash out; **schizzare fuori dal letto** to leap *o* jump out of bed; **gli occhi gli schizzarono dalle orbite** (*fig*) his eyes nearly popped out of his head

schizzato, a [skit'tsato] AGG (*fam: fuori di testa*) wired

schizzinosamente [skittsinosa'mente] AVV fussily

schizzinoso, a [skittsi'noso] AGG fussy, difficult, finicky; **è più schizzinosa di me** she's fussier than me
■ SM/F fussy person, difficult person; **non fare lo schizzinoso!** don't be so fussy!

schizzo ['skittso] SM **1** (*di liquido*) squirt, splash; (*macchia*) stain, spot; **uno schizzo d'acqua** a splash of water **2** (*abbozzo*) sketch

schnauzer ['ʃnautsər] SM INV (*cane*) schnauzer

schuss [ʃus] SM INV (*Sci*) schuss

sci [ʃi] SM INV (*Sport: attività*) skiing; (: *attrezzo*) ski; **sci a monte** uphill ski; **un paio di sci** a pair of skis; **una gara di sci** a ski race; **lo sci mi piace molto** I love skiing; **fare dello sci** to ski; **sci acrobatico** hot-dogging, free-styling; **sci alpinismo** *o* **d'alta quota** ski mountaineering; **sci alpino** alpine skiing; **sci di fondo** cross-country skiing, ski touring (*Am*); **sci nautico** water-skiing; **sci nordico** Nordic skiing

scia ['ʃia] SF (*di imbarcazione*) wake; (*fig: di fumo, profumo*) trail

scià [ʃa] SM INV shah

sciabola ['ʃabola] SF sabre (*Brit*), saber (*Am*)

sciabolata [ʃabo'lata] SF sabre (*Brit*) *o* saber (*Am*) cut

sciabordio, dii [ʃabor'dio] SM lapping

sciacallo [ʃa'kallo] SM (*Zool*) jackal; (*fig pegg: profittatore*) shark, profiteer; (: *ladro*) looter

sciacquadita [ʃakkwa'dita] SM INV fingerbowl

sciacquare [ʃak'kware] VT (*mani, capelli*) to rinse; (*panni*) to rinse (out); **sciacquarsi la bocca** to rinse one's mouth

sciacquata [ʃak'kwata] SF rinse; **dare una sciacquata a qc** to rinse sth, give sth a rinse

sciacquatura [ʃakkwa'tura] SF (*azione*) rinsing; (*acqua*) rinsing water; (: *di piatti*) dishwater

sciacquio, quii [ʃak'kwio] SM (*rumore*) swish

sciacquo ['ʃakkwo] SM (*azione*) rinsing of the mouth; (*prodotto*) mouthwash; **fare degli sciacqui** to rinse one's mouth (with mouthwash)

sciacquone [ʃak'kwone] SM (*del water*) flush

sciagura [ʃa'gura] SF disaster, calamity; **una sciagura aerea** an air disaster

sciaguratamente [ʃagurata'mente] AVV (*malvagiamente*) wickedly; (*disgraziatamente*) unfortunately

sciagurato, a [ʃagu'rato] AGG (*disgraziato*) wretched, unfortunate; (*malvagio*) wicked
■ SM/F wretch

scialacquare [ʃalak'kware] VT to squander

scialacquatore, trice [ʃalakkwa'tore] SM/F squanderer

scialare [ʃa'lare] VI (*aus* **avere**) throw one's money around; **c'è poco da scialare** there's little money to spare

scialbo, a ['ʃalbo] AGG (*colore*) pale, dull; (*fig: persona*) dull, colourless (*Brit*), colorless (*Am*)

scialle ['ʃalle] SM shawl

scialo ['ʃalo] SM squandering, waste; **fare scialo di qc** to squander sth (away)

scialuppa [ʃa'luppa] SF (*Naut*) sloop; **scialuppa di salvataggio** lifeboat

sciamannato, a [ʃaman'nato] AGG, SM/F (*fig fam: disgraziato*) good-for-nothing

sciamano [ʃa'mano] SM shaman

sciamare [ʃa'mare] VI (*aus* **avere** *o* **essere**) to swarm

sciame ['ʃame] SM swarm; (*fig: di persone*) crowd, swarm

sciancato, a [ʃan'kato] AGG (*persona*) crippled, lame; (*fig: mobile*) rickety

sciancrato, a [ʃan'krato] AGG (*abito*) waisted

sciangai [ʃan'gai] SM (*gioco*) pick-up-sticks *sg*

sciantosa [ʃan'tosa] SF cabaret singer

sciantung ['ʃantung] SM shantung

sciarada [ʃa'rada] SF charades *pl*

sciare [ʃi'are] VI (*aus* **avere**) to ski; **sai sciare?** can you ski?; **andare a sciare** to go skiing

sciarpa ['ʃarpa] SF scarf

sciatica ['ʃatika] SF (*Med*) sciatica

sciatico, a, ci, che ['ʃatiko] AGG (*Med*) sciatic

sciatore, trice [ʃia'tore] SM/F skier

sciattamente [ʃatta'mente] AVV in a slovenly manner

sciattezza [ʃat'tettsa] SF slovenliness

sciatto, a ['ʃatto] AGG (*persona*) slovenly, unkempt; (*lavoro*) sloppy, careless

sciattone, a [ʃat'tone] SM/F sloven

scibile ['ʃibile] SM knowledge

sciccheria [ʃikke'ria] SF stylishness, chic; **che sciccheria!** how chic!; **questo vestito è una sciccheria** this dress is very chic

sciccoso, a [ʃik'koso] AGG (*fam, elegante*) chic

SCICO ['ʃiko] SIGLA M (= **Servizio Centrale Investigativo Criminalità Organizzata**) *section of Guardia di Finanza that investigates organized crime*

scientificamente [ʃentifika'mente] AVV scientifically

scientifico, a, ci, che [ʃen'tifiko] AGG (*gen*) scientific; (*materia, insegnamento*) science *attr*; **la ricerca scientifica** scientific research; **una materia scientifica** a science subject; **ha scelto il ramo scientifico** he chose science; **la (polizia) scientifica** the forensic department

scienza ['ʃɛntsa] SF **1** (*gen*) science; **scienze** SFPL (*Scol*) science *sg*; **la scienza e la tecnologia** science and technology; **scienze della comunicazione** (*Univ*)

Ss

media studies; **scienze motorie** (*Univ*) sports science; **scienze naturali** natural sciences; **scienze occulte** occult sciences; **scienze politiche** political science *pl*; **scienze sociali** (*Univ*) social sciences **2** (*conoscenza*) knowledge, learning

scienziato, a [ʃen'tsjato] SM/F scientist

sciistico, a, ci, che [ʃi'istiko] AGG skiing *attr*

sciita, i; , e ['ʃita] SM/F Shiite

Scilla ['ʃilla] SF Scylla

Scilly ['ʃilli] SFPL: **le (isole) Scilly** the Scilly Isles

scimmia ['ʃimmja] SF (*Zool*) monkey; (: *più grande*) ape; (*fig*: *persona brutta*) horror; **avere la scimmia** (*fam: dipendenza da droga*) to have a monkey on one's back (*Am*)

scimmiesco, a, schi, sche [ʃim'mjesko] AGG monkey-like, ape-like

scimmiottare [ʃimmjot'tare] VT (*beffeggiare*) to mock, make fun of; (*imitare*) to mimic, ape

scimpanzé [ʃimpan'tse] SM INV chimpanzee

scimunito, a [ʃimu'nito] AGG idiotic, stupid, silly
■SM/F fool, idiot

scindere ['ʃindere] VB IRREG
■VT to split (up), divide
▶ **scindersi** VIP to split (up), break up; **scindersi in** to split into

scintilla [ʃin'tilla] SF (*anche fig*) spark; **fare scintille** to give off sparks, spark

scintillante [ʃintil'lante] AGG (*occhi, diamante, acque*) sparkling; (*stelle*) twinkling; (*capelli*) shining, gleaming

scintillare [ʃintil'lare] VI (*aus* **avere**) to give off sparks, spark; (*acqua, occhi*) to sparkle, glitter; **gli occhi le scintillavano di gioia** her eyes were sparkling with joy

scintillio, lii [ʃintil'lio] SM sparkling, glittering

scioccamente [ʃokka'mente] AVV foolishly

scioccare [ʃok'kare] VT to shock

sciocchezza [ʃok'kettsa] SF **1** (*qualità*) foolishness *no pl*, silliness *no pl*, stupidity *no pl*; **fare una sciocchezza** to do something silly; **mi raccomando, non fare sciocchezze!** make sure you don't do anything silly!; **è stata una sciocchezza** it was really foolish; **per me ha fatto una sciocchezza** I think it was very foolish *o* silly of him to do that; **dire sciocchezze** to talk nonsense; **ha detto un sacco di sciocchezze** he talked a load of nonsense; **sciocchezze!** nonsense! **2 l'ho pagato una sciocchezza** I hardly paid anything for it; **è solo una sciocchezza** (*regalo*) it's only a trifle

sciocco, a, chi, che ['ʃɔkko] AGG silly, foolish, stupid; **è l'idea più sciocca che abbia mai sentito** it's the silliest idea I've ever heard
■SM/F fool

sciogliere ['ʃɔʎʎere] VB IRREG
■VT **1** (*liquefare*) to melt; (*nell'acqua: zucchero*) to dissolve; (*neve*) to melt, thaw; **il sole ha sciolto la neve** the sun has melted the snow; **sciogliere il ghiaccio** (*fig*) to break the ice **2** (*disfare: nodo*) to undo, untie; (: *capelli*) to loosen **3** (*slegare: persona, animale*) to set free, release, untie; (*fig: persona: da obbligo*) to absolve, release; (: *contratto*) to cancel, annul; (: *parlamento, matrimonio*) to dissolve; (: *riunione*) to break up, bring to an end; (: *società*) to dissolve, wind up; **sciogliere le vele** (*Naut*) to set sail; **sciogliere i muscoli** to limber up; **esercizi per sciogliere i muscoli** warm-up exercises; **(far) sciogliere la lingua a qn** to loosen sb's tongue; **sciogliere un mistero** to solve *o* unravel a mystery;
▶ **sciogliersi** VIP **1** (*vedi vt* 1) to melt; to dissolve; to thaw; **questa carne si scioglie in bocca** this meat melts in the mouth; **sciogliersi in lacrime** to burst into tears **2** (*assemblea, corteo, duo*) to break up
▶ **sciogliersi** VR (*liberarsi*) to free o.s., release o.s.; **sciogliersi dai legami** (*fig*) to free o.s. from all ties

scioglilingua [ʃoʎʎi'lingwa] SM INV tongue-twister

sciolgo *ecc* ['ʃɔlgo] VB *vedi* **sciogliere**

sciolina [ʃio'lina] SF (ski) wax

sciolinare [ʃioli'nare] VT to wax

sciolinatura [ʃiolina'tura] SF waxing (of skis)

scioltezza [ʃol'tettsa] SF (*agilità*) agility, nimbleness, suppleness; (*disinvoltura*) ease, smoothness; (: *nel parlare*) fluency, ease

sciolto, a ['ʃɔlto] PP *di* **sciogliere**
■AGG **1** (*persona: agile*) agile, nimble; (: *disinvolto*) easy-going, free and easy; **essere sciolto nei movimenti** to be supple; **avere la lingua sciolta** to have the gift of the gab **2** (*Comm: sfuso*) loose **3** (*in poesia*): **versi sciolti** blank verse

scioperante [ʃope'rante] AGG on strike
■SM/F striker

scioperare [ʃope'rare] VI (*aus* **avere**) (*fare sciopero*) to strike, go on strike; (*entrare in sciopero*) to go on strike

scioperato, a [ʃope'rato] AGG idle, lazy
■SM/F idler, loafer

sciopero ['ʃɔpero] SM strike; **essere in sciopero** *or* **fare sciopero** to be on strike; **entrare in sciopero** to go on *o* come out on strike; **sciopero bianco** work-to-rule (*Brit*), slowdown (*Am*); **sciopero della fame** hunger strike; **sta facendo lo sciopero della fame** he is on hunger strike; **sciopero selvaggio** wildcat strike; **sciopero a singhiozzo** on-off strike; **sciopero di solidarietà** sympathy strike

sciorinare [ʃori'nare] VT **1** (*ostentare*) to show off, display **2** (*dire con disinvoltura: consigli, citazioni*) to rattle off; **sciorinare bugie** to tell one lie after another **3** (*bucato*) to hang out

sciovia [ʃio'via] SF ski tow

sciovinismo [ʃovi'nizmo] SM chauvinism

sciovinista, i, e [ʃovi'nista] SM/F chauvinist

sciovinistico, a, ci, che [ʃovi'nistiko] AGG chauvinistic

scipito, a [ʃi'pito] AGG insipid

scippare [ʃip'pare] VT: **scippare qn** to snatch sb's bag; **mi hanno scippato** my bag was snatched

scippatore [ʃippa'tore] SM bag-snatcher

scippo ['ʃippo] SM bag-snatching; **ci sono stati troppi scippi ultimamente** there's been a lot of bag-snatching lately

sciroccato, a [ʃirok'kato] AGG (*fam: stravagante*) loony, nutty

scirocco [ʃi'rɔkko] SM sirocco

sciroppare [ʃirop'pare] VT (*frutta*) to put in syrup; **sciropparsi qn/qc** (*fig fam*) to put up with sb/sth

sciroppato, a [ʃirop'pato] AGG in syrup

sciroppo [ʃi'rɔppo] SM syrup; **sciroppo per la tosse** cough syrup, cough mixture

sciropposo, a [ʃirop'poso] AGG syrupy

scisma, i ['ʃizma] SM (*Rel, Pol*) schism

scismatico, a, ci, che [ʃiz'matiko] AGG, SM schismatic

scissione [ʃis'sjone] SF (*Fis, Bio*) fission; (*di gruppo, partito*) splitting (up), division, split; **ha causato una scissione nel partito** it caused a split in the party

scisso, a ['ʃisso] PP *di* **scindere**

sciupare [ʃu'pare] VT **1** (*rovinare*) to ruin, spoil **2** (*sprecare: tempo, denaro*) to waste, throw away; (: *occasione*) to miss

▶ **sciuparsi** VIP *(rovinarsi)* to get spoiled *o* ruined; **le scarpe nuove si sono sciupate** my new shoes were ruined; **l'ho vista molto sciupata** she looked very run down when I saw her

scivolamento [ʃivola'mento] SM *(gen)* slipping; *(Sci)* glide

scivolare [ʃivo'lare] VI *(aus* **essere***)* *(cadere)* to slip; **scivolare sul ghiaccio** *(persona)* to slip on the ice; (: *per gioco)* to slide on the ice; *(macchina)* to skid on the ice; **è scivolato giù dalle scale** he slipped and fell down the stairs; **attento, si scivola** be careful, it's slippery; **il vaso gli scivolò dalle mani** the vase slipped out of his hands; **scivolò via non visto** he slipped away unseen; **l'uomo scivolò silenziosamente nella stanza** the man slipped silently into the room; **gli fece scivolare il biglietto in tasca** he slipped the note into his pocket; **scivolare su una buccia di banana** *(anche fig)* to slip on a banana skin

scivolata [ʃivo'lata] SF *(anche Aer)* slip; *(Sci)* glide; **fare una scivolata** to slip

scivolo ['ʃivolo] SM *(gioco)* slide; *(Tecn)* chute

scivolone [ʃivo'lone] SM tumble, fall; **fare uno scivolone** to take a tumble

scivoloso, a [ʃivo'loso] AGG slippery

sclera ['sklɛra] SF *(Anat)* sclerotic, sclera

sclerosi [skle'rɔzi] SF INV *(Med)* sclerosis; **sclerosi multipla** multiple sclerosis

sclerotico, a, ci, che [skle'rɔtiko] AGG sclerotic
■ SM/F sclerosis sufferer

sclerotizzare [sklerotid'dzare] VT *(fig)* to make inflexible
▶ **sclerotizzarsi** VIP *(Med)* to become sclerotic; *(fig)* to become inflexible

scocca, che ['skɔkka] SF *(Aut)* body

scoccare [skok'kare] VT **1** *(freccia)* to shoot **2** *(ore)* to strike; **l'orologio scoccò le 8** the clock struck 8 **3 scoccare un bacio a qn** to give sb a smacker
■ VI *(aus* **essere***)* **1** *(freccia)* to shoot out; *(scintilla)* to fly up **2** *(ore)* to strike; **scoccavano le 11** it was striking 11

scoccherò *ecc* [skokke'rɔ] VB *vedi* **scoccare**

scocciare [skot'tʃare] VT to annoy, bother; **le sue continue lamentele mi hanno scocciato** his constant complaints have annoyed me; **mi hai scocciato** *(stufato)* I'm fed up with you; *(seccato)* I'm annoyed with you; **se non ti scoccia** if it doesn't bother you, if you don't mind; **ti scoccia se...?** do you mind if ...?; **e ancora faceva lo scocciato** and he still wasn't happy
▶ **scocciarsi** VIP *(stufarsi)* to get fed up; *(seccarsi)* to get annoyed; **si è un po' scocciato** he was rather annoyed

scocciato, a [skot'tʃato] AGG *(seccato)* annoyed; *(stufato)* fed up

scocciatore, trice [skottʃa'tore] SM/F nuisance, pest *(fam)*

scocciatura [skottʃa'tura] SF nuisance, bore; **che scocciatura!** what a nuisance!

scodella [sko'dɛlla] SF *(ciotola)* bowl; *(piatto fondo)* soup plate

scodellare [skodel'lare] VT to dish out, dish up

scodinzolare [skodintso'lare] VI *(aus* **avere***)* *(cane)* to wag its tail; **il cane scodinzola** the dog is wagging its tail

scogliera [skoʎ'ʎɛra] SF *(scogli)* rocks *pl*, reef; *(rupe)* cliff; **le bianche scogliere di Dover** the white cliffs of Dover; **la nave è finita sulla scogliera** the ship went onto the rocks

scoglio, gli ['skɔʎʎo] SM rock; *(fig: ostacolo)* difficulty, stumbling block

scoglioso, a [skoʎ'ʎoso] AGG rocky

scoiattolo [sko'jattolo] SM *(Zool)* squirrel; **agile come uno scoiattolo** *(fig)* agile as a monkey

scolapasta [skola'pasta] SM INV colander

scolapiatti [skola'pjatti] SM INV *(del lavandino)* draining board; *(rastrelliera)* plate rack

scolaposate [skolapo'sate] SM INV cutlery drainer

scolare[1] [sko'lare] VT to drain; **puoi scolare la pasta per favore?** can you drain the pasta, please?; **si è scolato una bottiglia!** he's drained *o* downed a bottle!
■ VI *(aus* **essere***)* to drip

scolare[2] [sko'lare] AGG: **in età scolare** school-age *attr*

scolaresca, sche [skola'reska] SF schoolchildren *pl*, pupils *pl*

scolaro, a [sko'laro] SM/F pupil, schoolboy/schoolgirl; *(discepolo)* disciple, follower

LO SAPEVI...?
scolaro non si traduce mai con la parola inglese *scholar*

scolasticamente [skolastika'mente] AVV scholastically

scolastico, a, ci, che [sko'lastiko] AGG *(gen)* scholastic; *(libro, anno, divisa)* school *attr*; *(pegg: cultura)* superficial; *(francese, inglese, ecc)* basic; **l'anno scolastico** the school year

scoliosi [sko'ljɔzi] SF INV *(Med)* scoliosis

scollacciato, a [skolliat'tʃato] AGG *(vestito)* low-cut, with a low neckline; *(donna)* in a low-necked dress *(o blouse ecc)*

scollare [skol'lare] VT to unstick, unglue
▶ **scollarsi** VIP to come unstuck, come off *o* away

scollato, a [skol'lato] AGG *(vestito)* low-cut, low-necked; *(donna)* wearing a low-cut dress *(o blouse ecc)*

scollatura [skolla'tura] SF, **scollo** ['skɔllo] SM neckline, neck; **scollo a barchetta** boat neck

scolo ['skolo] SM **1** *(condotto)* drainage; *(sbocco)* drain; **canale di scolo** drain; **tubo di scolo** drainpipe **2** *(acqua)* waste water

scolorare [skolo'rare], **scolorire** [skolo'rire] VT to discolour *(Brit)*, discolor *(Am)*; *(sbiadire)* to fade
▶ **scolorarsi, scolorirsi** VIP *(vedi vt)* to become discolo(u)red; to fade, become faded; *(impallidire)* to turn pale

scolorato, a [skolo'rato], **scolorito, a** [skolo'rito] AGG faded

scolpare [skol'pare] VT to free from blame, exonerate
▶ **scolparsi** VR to free o.s. from blame, exonerate o.s.

scolpire [skol'pire] VT *(pietra)* to sculpt, sculpture; *(legno)* to carve; *(metallo)* to engrave; **quelle parole rimasero scolpite nella sua memoria** *(fig)* those words were engraved on his memory

scombinare [skombi'nare] VT *(scomporre)* to mess up, ruin, upset; *(mandare a monte)* to break off, cancel

scombinato, a [skombi'nato] AGG confused, muddled

scombussolare [skombusso'lare] VT *(persona)* to upset, disturb; *(piani)* to upset, mess up

scommessa [skom'messa] SF *(azione)* bet; *(somma)* bet, stake; **Sergio ha mangiato 50 uova per scommessa** Sergio ate 50 eggs for a bet; **fare una scommessa** to bet, to make a bet; **ho fatto una scommessa con Martina** I made a bet with Martina

scommesso, a [skom'messo] PP *di* **scommettere**

scommettere [skom'mettere] VT IRREG to bet; **scommettere 20 euro** to bet *o* wager 20 euros; **scommettere su un cavallo** to bet on a horse; **scommettiamo?** do you want to (take a) bet on it?;

Ss

non ci scommetterei I wouldn't bet on it; **ci avrei scommesso!** I would have put money on it!; **puoi scommetterci** you can count on it; **quanto scommmettiamo che...?** what's the betting that ...?
scomodamente [skomoda'mente] AVV uncomfortably
scomodare [skomo'dare] VT to disturb, bother, trouble; (*fig: nome famoso*) to involve, drag in
▶ **scomodarsi** VR to bother, trouble (o.s.), put o.s. out; **scomodarsi a fare qc** to go to the bother of doing sth
scomodità [skomodi'ta] SF INV (*di sedia, letto*) discomfort; (*di orario, sistemazione*) inconvenience
scomodo, a ['skɔmodo] AGG (*sedia, letto, posizione*) uncomfortable; (*orario, turno, sistemazione, posto*) inconvenient, awkward; **stare scomodo** to be uncomfortable; **mi è scomodo venire la sera** it's inconvenient for me to come in the evening; **l'orario della banca mi è scomodo** the opening hours of the bank are inconvenient for me; **è scomodo da portare** it's difficult to carry, it's cumbersome
scompaginare [skompadʒi'nare] VT to upset, throw into disorder
▶ **scompaginarsi** VIP to be thrown into disorder
scompagnato, a [skompaɲ'ɲato] AGG (*scarpe, calzini*) odd
scomparire [skompa'rire] VI IRREG (*aus* **essere**) (*sparire*) to disappear, vanish; (*fig: non risaltare*) to look (*o* be) insignificant; **la nave è scomparsa all'orizzonte** the ship disappeared over the horizon; **dov'eri scomparso?** where did you get to?
scomparsa [skom'parsa] SF (*sparizione*) disappearance; (*euf*) passing away
scomparso, a [skom'parso] PP *di* **scomparire**
scompartimento [skomparti'mento] SM **1** (*sezione*) division **2** (*Ferr*) compartment
scomparto [skom'parto] SM division, compartment
scompenso [skom'pɛnso] SM imbalance, lack of balance; (*Med*) decompensation
scompigliare [skompiʎ'ʎare] VT to mess up, muddle up; (*capelli*) to mess up, ruffle; (*fig: piani*) to upset; (*: idee*) to mess up, confuse
scompigliato, a [skompiʎ'ʎato] AGG dishevelled
scompiglio, gli [skom'piʎʎo] SM confusion, chaos; **portare lo scompiglio in** to cause confusion in
scomporre [skom'porre] VB IRREG
■ VT (*parola, numero*) to break up; (*Chim*) to decompose
▶ **scomporsi** VIP **1** (*Chim*) to decompose **2** (*fig: turbarsi*) to lose one's composure, get upset; **senza scomporsi** unperturbed
scompostezza [skompos'tettsa] SF unseemliness
scomposto, a [skom'posto] PP *di* **scomporre**
■ AGG **1** (*parola, numero*) broken up **2** (*persona: sguaiato*) unseemly **3** (*capelli, vestiti: in disordine*) dishevelled, in a mess
scomunica, che [sko'munika] SF (*Rel*) excommunication
scomunicare [skomuni'kare] VT (*Rel*) to excommunicate
scomunicato, a [skomuni'kato] SM/F excommunicate
sconcertante [skontʃer'tante] AGG disconcerting
sconcertare [skontʃer'tare] VT to disconcert, bewilder
▶ **sconcertarsi** VIP to be disconcerted
sconcertato, a [skontʃer'tato] AGG disconcerted
sconcezza [skon'tʃettsa] SF obscenity, indecency; **è una sconcezza!** it's a disgrace!
sconciamente [skontʃa'mente] AVV obscenely, indecently
sconcio, cia, ci, ce ['skontʃo] AGG (*osceno*) obscene, indecent; (*: parole*) rude, dirty; **una barzelletta sconcia** a dirty joke
■ SM (*cosa mal fatta*) disgrace
sconclusionato, a [skonkluzjo'nato] AGG incoherent, illogical
scondito, a [skon'dito] AGG (*minestra*) unseasoned; (*insalata*) without dressing
sconfessare [skonfes'sare] VT (*ritrattare*) to renounce, retract; (*smentire*) to repudiate
sconfiggere [skon'fiddʒere] VT IRREG (*gen, Pol, Sport*) to defeat, overcome
sconfinamento [skonfina'mento] SM (*di frontiera*) border violation; (*di proprietà*) trespassing
sconfinare [skonfi'nare] VI to cross the border; (*da proprietà*) to trespass; (*: involontariamente*) to stray; (*fig: uscire dai limiti fissati*): **sconfinare da** (*verità, sentiero*) to stray from; (*tema, argomento*) to digress from, stray from
sconfinatamente [skonfinata'mente] AVV (*estendersi*) infinitely
sconfinato, a [skonfi'nato] AGG (*spazio*) limitless, boundless; (*fig: conoscenza, pazienza*) unlimited
sconfitta [skon'fitta] SF (*gen, Pol, Sport*) defeat; **subire** *o* **riportare una sconfitta** to be defeated
sconfitto, a [skon'fitto] PP *di* **sconfiggere**
sconfortante [skonfor'tante] AGG discouraging, disheartening
sconfortare [skonfor'tare] VT to discourage, dishearten
▶ **sconfortarsi** VIP to become discouraged, become disheartened, lose heart
sconfortato, a [skonfor'tato] AGG dejected
sconforto [skon'fɔrto] SM dejection, despondency; **essere in preda allo sconforto** to be dejected
scongelare [skondʒe'lare] VT to defrost
scongiurare [skondʒu'rare] VT **1** (*supplicare*) to beg, implore, beseech; **ti scongiuro, aiutami** I beg you, help me **2** (*allontanare*) to avert, ward off; **il pericolo è scongiurato** we're out of danger
scongiuro [skon'dʒuro] SM (*esorcismo*) exorcism; (*formula*) spell, charm; **fare gli scongiuri** to touch wood (*Brit*), knock on wood (*Am*)
sconnesso, a [skon'nɛsso] AGG (*staccato*) disconnected; (*fig: sconclusionato*) incoherent, disconnected, rambling
sconosciuto, a [skonoʃ'ʃuto] AGG unknown; **un attore sconosciuto** an unknown actor; **è una zona sconosciuta** it's a little-known area; **una gioia sconosciuta** a strange joy; **il suo viso mi è sconosciuto** his face is new to me
■ SM/F unknown person, stranger; **non parlare agli sconosciuti** don't talk to strangers
sconquassare [skonkwas'sare] VT to shatter, smash
sconquasso [skon'kwasso] SM (*danno*) damage; (*fig*) confusion
sconsacrare [skonsa'krare] VT (*Rel*) to deconsecrate
sconsacrato, a [skonsa'krato] AGG deconsecrated
sconsideratezza [skonsidera'tettsa] SF lack of consideration, thoughtlessness
sconsiderato, a [skonside'rato] AGG thoughtless, inconsiderate, rash
■ SM/F thoughtless person, inconsiderate person
sconsigliare [skonsiʎ'ʎare] VT: **sconsigliare qc a qn** to advise sb against sth; **sconsigliare a qn di fare qc** to advise sb not to do sth; **ti avevo sconsigliato di telefonarle** I advised you not to phone her; **ti**

sconsiglio di provarci I advise you against trying; **quel ristorante? te lo sconsiglio!** that restaurant? I wouldn't recommend it!; **volevo andare ma mi hanno sconsigliato** I wanted to go but they advised me not to

sconsolatamente [skonsolata'mente] AVV disconsolately

sconsolato, a [skonso'lato] AGG disconsolate

scontare [skon'tare] VT **1** (*Comm: detrarre*) to deduct, discount; **scontare una cambiale** to discount a bill of exchange; **scontare un debito** to pay off a debt in instalments **2** (*peccato, colpa*) to pay for, suffer for; (*Dir: pena*) to serve; **scontare 5 anni di prigione** to serve 5 years in prison

scontato, a [skon'tato] AGG **1** (*prezzo, merce*) discounted, at a discount; **tutto a prezzi scontati** everything at reduced prices **2** (*previsto*) foreseen, taken for granted; **il finale del film era scontato** the ending of the film was predictable; **era scontato che finisse così** it was bound to end that way; **dare qc per scontato** to take sth for granted

scontentare [skonten'tare] VT to displease, dissatisfy

scontentezza [skonten'tettsa] SF displeasure, dissatisfaction

scontento, a [skon'tɛnto] AGG dissatisfied, displeased; **è sempre scontento** he's always unhappy; **essere scontento di qc** to be displeased *o* dissatisfied with sth
■ SM discontent, dissatisfaction

sconto ['skonto] SM (*Comm*) discount; **fare** *o* **concedere uno sconto** to give a discount; **mi ha fatto uno sconto** he gave me a discount; **uno sconto del 10%** a 10% discount; **sconto (sulla) quantità** quantity *o* volume discount

scontrarsi [skon'trarsi] VR **1** (*veicolo, persona*): **scontrarsi con** to collide with; **la macchina si è scontrata con un autobus** the car crashed into a bus **2** (*uso reciproco: veicoli, persone*) to collide, to crash; (*Mil, fig: opinioni*) to clash

scontrino [skon'trino] SM (*biglietto*) ticket (*Brit*), check (*Am*); (*di cassa*) receipt

scontro ['skontro] SM (*di veicoli*) collision, crash; (*Mil*) clash, engagement; (*fig: litigio*) disagreement; **è rimasto ferito nello scontro** he was injured in the crash; **uno scontro frontale** a head-on collision; **ci sono stati scontri tra polizia e dimostranti** there were clashes between police and demonstrators, police and demonstrators clashed; **scontro a fuoco** shoot-out

scontrosità [skontrosi'ta] SF surliness

scontroso, a [skon'troso] AGG (*poco socievole*) surly, sullen; (*permaloso*) touchy

sconveniente [skonve'njɛnte] AGG **1** (*comportamento, modi*) unseemly; (*osservazione, proposta*) improper **2** (*prezzo, affare*) disadvantageous, unattractive

sconvenientemente [skonvenjente'mente] AVV (*vedi agg*) in an unseemly manner; improperly; disadvantageously

sconvenienza [skonve'njɛntsa] SF (*vedi agg*) unseemliness; impropriety; unattractiveness

sconvolgente [skonvol'dʒɛnte] AGG (*notizia, brutta esperienza*) upsetting, disturbing; (*bellezza*) amazing; (*passione*) overwhelming

sconvolgere [skon'vɔldʒere] VB IRREG
■ VT (*persona*) to upset, disturb; (*piani*) to upset; **la notizia mi ha sconvolto** the news upset me; **sconvolgere l'opinione pubblica** to shock *o* shake public opinion; **la notizia ha sconvolto il mondo intero** the news shook the whole world; **la zona sconvolta dal terremoto** the area hit *o* affected by the earthquake; **le campagne sconvolte dall'alluvione** the flooded countryside, the countryside devastated by the floods
▶ **sconvolgersi** VIP to become upset

sconvolgimento [skonvoldʒi'mento] SM (*scompiglio*) confusion; (*devastazione*) devastation

sconvolto, a [skon'vɔlto] PP *di* **sconvolgere**
■ AGG (*persona*) distraught, very upset; (*mente*) disturbed, deranged; **era sconvolto per la morte dell'amico** he was devastated by the death of his friend; **una faccia sconvolta** a ravaged face; **sconvolto dal dolore** beside o.s. with grief

scooter ['skuter] SM INV scooter

scopa[1] ['skopa] SF broom; **sembra un manico di scopa** (*fig*) he's as thin as a rake

scopa[2] ['skopa] SF *Italian card game*

scopare [sko'pare] VT **1** (*spazzare*) to sweep **2** (*fam*) to bonk (*Brit*)
■ VI (*aus* **avere**) (*fam*) to bonk (*Brit*)

scopata [sko'pata] SF **1** sweep; **dare una scopata a qc** to give sth a sweep, sweep sth out; **dare una scopata a qn** to hit sb with a broom **2** (*fam*) bonk (*Brit fam*)

scoperchiare [skoper'kjare] VT (*pentola, vaso*) to take the lid off, uncover; (*casa*) to take the roof off

scoperta [sko'pɛrta] SF discovery; **bella scoperta!** (*iro*) what a revelation!

scopertamente [skoperta'mente] AVV openly

scoperto, a [sko'pɛrto] PP *di* **scoprire**
■ AGG **1** (*pentola*) uncovered, with the lid off; (*macchina*) open; (*spalle, braccia*) bare, uncovered; (*Mil*) exposed, without cover; **a capo scoperto** bare-headed; **dormire scoperto** to sleep uncovered; **giocare a carte scoperte** (*anche fig*) to put one's cards on the table **2** (*Banca*): **assegno scoperto** dud cheque (*Brit*), rubber check (*Am*); **conto scoperto** overdrawn account; **avere un conto scoperto** to be overdrawn
■ SM **1** **allo scoperto** (*dormire*) out in the open; **è uscito allo scoperto** (*fig*) he came out into the open **2** (*Banca*): **scoperto di conto** bank overdraft

scopiazzare [skopjat'tsare] VT (*pegg*) to copy

scopino [sko'pino] SM **1** (*spazzino*) roadsweeper (*Brit*), streetsweeper (*Am*) **2** (*del gabinetto*) lavatory brush (*Brit*)

scopo ['skɔpo] SM aim, purpose; **lo scopo di questo studio** the aim of this research; **allo scopo di fare qc** in order to do sth; **cercare uno scopo nella vita** to look for an aim *o* a purpose in life; **senza scopo** (*fare, cercare*) pointlessly; **la sua vita è senza scopo** his life is pointless; **a scopo di lucro** for gain *o* money; **adatto allo scopo** fit for its purpose; **a che scopo?** what for?; **a che scopo lavori tanto?** what are you working so hard for?

> **LO SAPEVI...?**
> **scopo** non si traduce mai con la parola inglese *scope*

scopone [sko'pone] SM *Italian card game*

scoppiare [skop'pjare] VI (*aus* **essere**) **1** (*bomba, serbatoio*) to explode; (*pneumatico, palloncino*) to burst; (*fig: rivolta, guerra, epidemia*) to break out; **la bomba è scoppiata alle 11 precise** the bomb went off at exactly 11 o'clock; **la guerra è scoppiata nel 1939** war broke out in 1939; **mi è scoppiata una gomma sull'autostrada** my tyre burst on the motorway; **la**

Ss

notizia fece scoppiare uno scandalo the news caused a scandal **2** (*fraseologia*): **scoppiare dal caldo** to be boiling; **scoppiare dall'invidia** to be dying of envy; **scoppiare a piangere** *o* **in lacrime** to burst into tears; **scoppiare a ridere** to burst out laughing; **scoppiare di salute** to be the picture of health; **scoppiare dalla voglia di fare qc** to be dying *o* longing to do sth; **a quel punto sono scoppiato** (*dalla rabbia, dal ridere*) at that point I couldn't contain myself any longer

scoppiato, a [skop'pjato] AGG (*fig: pugile*) played out; (*: drogato*) strung out

scoppiettante [skoppjet'tante] AGG (*fuoco*) crackling

scoppiettare [skoppjet'tare] VI (*aus* **avere**) (*fuoco*) to crackle; (*motore*) to chug

scoppiettio, tii [skoppjet'tio] SM crackling

scoppio, pi ['skɔppjo] SM (*esplosione*) explosion; (*di pneumatico*) bang; (*di tuono, arma*) crash; (*fig: di rivolta, guerra, epidemia*) outbreak; **bomba a scoppio ritardato** delayed-action bomb; **reazione a scoppio ritardato** delayed *o* slow reaction; **uno scoppio di risa** a burst of laughter; **uno scoppio di collera** an explosion of anger

scoprire [sko'prire] VB IRREG

■VT **1** (*trovare*) to discover; (*causa, verità*) to discover, find out; **ha scoperto la verità** he's found out the truth; **scoprire che.../come ...** to find out *o* discover that .../how ...; **ha scoperto di avere uno zio in India** he found out *o* discovered he has an uncle in India; **chi ha scoperto l'America?** who discovered America?; **hai scoperto l'America!** (*iro*) you mean you've only just found out about it! **2** (*pentola*) to take the lid off; (*statua*) to unveil; (*rovine, cadaveri*) to uncover; (*spalle, braccia*) to bare, uncover; **una camicetta che scopre la schiena** a blouse with a low-cut back; **scoprirsi il capo** to take off one's hat, bare one's head; **scoprirsi il fianco** (*fig*) to leave one's flank exposed;

▶ **scoprirsi** VR (*esporsi: Sport, fig*) to expose o.s.; (*fig: rivelare le proprie idee*) to betray o.s., give o.s. away; **non scoprirti che fa freddo** keep well wrapped up because it's cold; **il bambino si è scoperto durante la notte** the child threw off the bedclothes during the night

scopritore, trice [skopri'tore] SM/F discoverer

scoraggiamento [skoraddʒa'mento] SM discouragement, dejection

scoraggiante [skorad'dʒante] AGG discouraging

scoraggiare [skorad'dʒare] VT to discourage

▶ **scoraggiarsi** VIP to become discouraged, become disheartened, lose heart

scorbutico, a, ci, che [skor'butiko] AGG (*fig*) peevish, cantankerous

scorbuto [skor'buto] SM (*Med*) scurvy

scorciare [skor'tʃare] VT = **accorciare**

scorciatoia [skortʃa'toja] SF (*anche fig*) short cut; **ho preso una scorciatoia** I took a short cut

scorcio, ci ['skortʃo] SM **1** (*Arte*) foreshortening **2** (*di paesaggio*) glimpse; (*fig: di secolo, periodo*) end, close

scordare¹ [skor'dare] VT (*gen*) to forget; (*appuntamento, preoccupazione*) to forget (about); **ho scordato il suo numero di telefono** I've forgotten his phone number; **ho scordato a casa l'ombrello** I left my umbrella at home; **scordare di fare qc** to forget to do sth; **scordavo di avertelo già chiesto** I forgot that I had already asked you

▶ **scordarsi** VIP: **scordarsi di qc/di fare qc** to forget sth/to do sth; **mi sono scordato di telefonargli** I forgot to phone him; **scordarsi di qn** to forget about sb

scordare² [skor'dare] VT (*Mus*) to put out of tune

▶ **scordarsi** VIP to go out of tune

scoreggia, ge [sko'reddʒa], **scorreggia, ge** [skor'reddʒa] SF (*fam*) fart (*fam!*)

scoreggiare [skored'dʒare], **scorreggiare** [skorred'dʒare] VI (*aus* **avere**) (*fam*) to fart (*fam!*)

scorfano ['skɔrfano] SM (*Zool*) scorpion fish; (*fig: persona brutta*) fright

scorgere ['skɔrdʒere] VT IRREG to see, catch sight of; (*fig: accorgersi di*) to become aware of, realize; **senza farsi scorgere** unnoticed, without being seen

scoria ['skɔrja] SF (*di metalli*) slag; (*vulcanica*) scoria; **scorie radioattive** (*Fis*) radioactive waste *sg*

scornare [skor'nare] VT (*fig*) to humiliate

scornato, a [skor'nato] AGG (*fig*) humiliated

scorno ['skɔrno] SM humiliation, ignominy, disgrace

scorpacciata [skorpat'tʃata] SF big feed; **farsi una scorpacciata (di qc)** to stuff o.s. (with sth)

scorpione [skor'pjone] SM **1** (*Zool*) scorpion **2** (*Astrol*): **Scorpione** Scorpio; **essere dello Scorpione** to be Scorpio

scorporo [skɔrporo] SM (*Pol*) *transfer of votes aimed at increasing the chances of representation for minority parties*

scorrazzare [skorrat'tsare] VI (*aus* **avere**) to run about, romp about

scorrere ['skorrere] VB IRREG

■VI (*aus* **essere**) (*liquido, fiume*) to run, flow; (*fune*) to run; (*cassetto, porta*) to slide easily; (*tempo*) to pass (by); (*traffico*) to flow; **lascia scorrere l'acqua** let the water run, leave the water running; **il tempo scorre lento** time passes slowly; **ha uno stile che scorre** he (*o* it *ecc*) has a flowing style

■VT (*leggere*) to glance through, run one's eye over

scorreria [skorre'ria] SF raid, incursion

scorrettamente [skorretta'mente] AVV (*vedi agg*) incorrectly; impolitely; unfairly

scorrettezza [skorret'tettsa] SF (*vedi agg*) incorrectness; lack of politeness, rudeness; unfairness; **scorrettezza nel gioco** foul play *no pl*; **con scorrettezza** (*sgarbatamente*) rudely, impolitely; **è stata una scorrettezza da parte sua** it was rude of him, it was bad manners on his part; **commettere una scorrettezza** (*essere sleale*) to be unfair

scorretto, a [skor'rɛtto] AGG (*traduzione, uso*) incorrect; (*persona: sgarbato*) impolite, rude; (*: sleale*) unfair; (*gioco*) foul; **un uso scorretto** an incorrect use; **è stato scorretto da parte tua** it was unfair of you

scorrevole [skor'revole] AGG (*porta*) sliding; (*nastro*) moving; (*fig: stile*) flowing, fluent

scorrevolezza [skorrevo'lettsa] SF (*fig: di stile*) fluency

scorribanda [skorri'banda] SF (*Mil*) raid, incursion; (*escursione*) trip, excursion

scorsa ['skorsa] SF glance, quick look; **dare una scorsa a qc** to glance over *o* through sth

scorsi *ecc* ['skɔrsi] VB *vedi* **scorgere**

scorso, a ['skorso] PP *di* **scorrere**

■AGG last; **lo scorso mese** last month

scorsoio, oia, oi, oie [skor'sojo] AGG: **nodo scorsoio** slipknot, noose

scorta ['skɔrta] SF **1** (*gen, di personalità, convoglio, Mil*) escort; **il ministro è arrivato con la scorta** the minister arrived with a police escort; **fare la scorta a qn** to escort sb; **sotto la scorta di due agenti** escorted by two policemen **2** (*provvista*) supply, stock; **fare**

scorta di to stock up with, get in a supply of; **di scorta** (*materiali*) spare; **ruota di scorta** spare wheel

scortare [skor'tare] VT to escort

scortese [skor'tese] AGG impolite, discourteous, rude; **in modo scortese** rudely

scortesemente [skortese'mente] AVV impolitely, discourteously, rudely

scortesia [skorte'zia] SF (*qualità*) impoliteness, discourtesy, rudeness; (*azione*) discourtesy

scorticare [skorti'kare] VT (*animali*) to skin, flay; **scorticarsi un gomito** to skin *o* graze one's elbow

scorto, a ['skɔrto] PP *di* **scorgere**

scorza ['skɔrdza] SF (*di albero*) bark; (*di agrumi*) peel, skin; **avere la scorza dura** (*fig: persona*) to be thick-skinned; **sotto la scorza c'è un animo gentile** he's kind-hearted beneath his crusty exterior

scosceso, a [skoʃʃeso] AGG steep; **sempre più scosceso** steeper and steeper

scossa ['skɔssa] SF (*sobbalzo*) jolt, jerk; (*elettrica*) shock; **procedere a scosse** to jolt *o* jerk along; **dare una scossa a qn** (*fig*) to shake sb; **prendere la scossa** to get an electric shock; **ho preso la scossa accendendo la lampada** I got an electric shock when I switched on the lamp; **scossa di terremoto** earth tremor

scosso, a ['skɔsso] PP *di* **scuotere**
■ AGG (*persona*) shaken, upset; **sono ancora scosso** I'm still shaken; **ho i nervi scossi** my nerves are shattered

scossone [skos'sone] SM: **dare uno scossone a qn** to give sb a shake; **procedere a scossoni** (*auto*) to jolt *o* jerk along

scostante [skos'tante] AGG (*persona, modi*) unpleasant, off-putting

scostare [skos'tare] VT to push aside, move aside; **far scostare qn** to push sb aside; **scosta la poltrona dal muro** move the armchair away from the wall
▶ **scostarsi** VR to move aside; **scostati dal muro** move away from the wall

scostumatamente [skostumata'mente] AVV (*vedi agg*) immorally, dissolutely; boorishly

scostumato, a [skostu'mato] AGG (*immorale*) immoral, dissolute; (*maleducato*) bad-mannered, boorish
■ SM (*vedi agg*) dissolute person; boor

scotch[1] [skɔtʃ] SM INV (*whisky*) Scotch

scotch[2]® [skɔtʃ] SM INV (*nastro adesivo*) Sellotape® (*Brit*), Scotch tape® (*Am*)

scotennare [skoten'nare] VT (*animale*) to skin; (*persona*) to scalp

scotta ['skɔtta] SF (*Naut*) sheet

scottante [skot'tante] AGG (*urgente*) pressing; (*delicato*) delicate

scottare [skot'tare] VT (*gen*) to burn; (*con liquido, vapore*) to scald, burn; (*Culin: in acqua*) to scald; (*: friggendo*) to sear; **scottarsi una mano** to burn one's hand; **sono già stato scottato una volta** (*fig*) I've already burnt my fingers once
■ VI (*aus* **avere**) (*gen*) to be very hot; (*sole, sabbia*) to be burning, be scorching; **attento che scotta** be careful, it's hot; **il sole scotta in agosto** the sun is hot in August; **è roba che scotta** (*fig: refurtiva*) it's hot; **sono argomenti che scottano** (*fig: delicati*) these are delicate issues; **gli scotta la terra sotto ai piedi** (*fig*) he's itching to be off;
▶ **scottarsi** VR (*gen*) to burn o.s.; (*con liquido, vapore*) to scald o.s., burn o.s.; (*al sole*) to get burnt

scottata [skot'tata] SF (*Culin*): **dare una scottata a qc** (*in acqua*) to scald sth; (*friggendo*) to sear sth

scottatura [skotta'tura] SF (*gen*) burn; (*con liquido, vapore*) scald, burn

scotto[1], **a** ['skɔtto] AGG (*Culin*) overcooked, overdone

scotto[2] ['skɔtto] SM (*fig: punizione*): **pagare lo scotto** to pay the consequences

scovare [sko'vare] VT (*Caccia*) to drive out, flush out, put up; (*fig*) to unearth, find, discover

Scozia ['skɔttsja] SF Scotland; **mi è piaciuta molto la Scozia** I really liked Scotland; **andremo in Scozia quest'estate** we're going to Scotland this summer

scozzese [skot'tsese] AGG (*gen*) Scottish; (*whisky*) Scotch; **tessuto scozzese** tartan; **gonna scozzese** kilt; **le isole scozzesi** the Scottish islands
■ SM/F Scot, Scotsman/Scotswoman; **gli scozzesi** the Scots

screanzatamente [skreantsata'mente] AVV rudely, boorishly

screanzato, a [skrean'tsato] AGG ill-mannered
■ SM/F boor

screditare [skredi'tare] VT to discredit
▶ **screditarsi** VIP to be discredited

screen saver ['skriːnseɪvər] SM INV (*Inform*) screen saver

scremare [skre'mare] VT to skim

scremato, a [skre'mato] AGG skimmed; **parzialmente scremato** semi-skimmed

scrematrice [skrema'trice] SF skimmer

screpolare [skrepo'lare] VT (*pelle, labbra*) to chap, crack; (*mani*) to chap; (*intonaco*) to crack
▶ **screpolarsi** VIP (*vedi vt*) to chap; to crack

screpolato, a [skrepo'lato] AGG (*vedi vt*) chapped; cracked

screpolatura [skrepola'tura] SF (*su pelle, labbra, mani*) chap; (*su intonaco*) crack, cracking *no pl*

screziato, a [skret'tsjato] AGG (*striato*) streaked

screzio, zi ['skrɛttsjo] SM friction, disagreement; **hanno avuto degli screzi** there was some friction between them

scribacchiare [skribak'kjare] VT to scribble

scribacchino [skribak'kino] SM (*pegg: impiegato*) penpusher; (*: scrittore*) hack

scricchiolare [skrikkjo'lare] VI (*aus* **avere**) to creak, squeak

scricchiolio, lii [skrikkjo'lio] SM creaking

scricciolo ['skrittʃolo] SM (*uccello*) wren; **è uno scricciolo** (*fig: persona gracile*) she's like a little bird

scrigno ['skriɲɲo] SM casket

scriminatura [skrimina'tura] SF (*di capelli*) parting

scripo ['skripo] SM (*Bot*) deer grass

scrissi *ecc* ['skrissi] VB *vedi* **scrivere**

scriteriato, a [skrite'rjato] AGG scatterbrained
■ SM/F scatterbrain

scritta ['skritta] SF (*iscrizione*) inscription; (*avviso*) notice; **cosa dice la scritta sul cartello?** what does the (writing on the) sign say?

scritto, a ['skritto] PP *di* **scrivere**
■ AGG (*lingua, esame*) written
■ SM **1** (*lettera*) letter, note; **per** *o* **in scritto** in writing **2** (*opera*) work; **gli scritti di** the works *o* the writings of

scrittoio, oi [skrit'tojo] SM (writing-)desk

scrittore, trice [skrit'tore] SM/F writer, author

scrittura [skrit'tura] SF **1** (*calligrafia*) (hand)writing; **non riesco a leggere la sua scrittura** I can't read his writing; **avere una bella/brutta scrittura** to have good/bad handwriting **2** (*Rel*): **la Sacra Scrittura**

Ss

the Scriptures *pl* **3** (*Cine, Teatro, TV: contratto*) contract **4** (*Dir*) document; **scrittura privata** parol, contract **5** (*Comm*): **scritture** SFPL accounts, books; **scritture contabili** (account) books

scritturare [skrittu'rare] VT **1** (*Cine, Teatro, TV*) to engage, sign on *o* up **2** (*Comm*) to enter

scrivania [skriva'nia] SF (writing-)desk

scrivano [skri'vano] SM (*amanuense*) scribe; (*impiegato*) clerk

scrivente [skri'vɛnte] SM/F writer

scrivere ['skrivere] VT IRREG (*gen*) to write; **scrivere qc a qn** to write sth to sb; **ho scritto una lettera a Luca** I wrote Luca a letter; **scrivo sempre cartoline a tutti i miei amici** I always write postcards to all my friends; **scrivimi presto** write to me soon; **scrivere qc a macchina** to type sth; **scrivere a penna/matita** to write in pen/pencil; **scrivere qc maiuscolo/minuscolo** to write sth in capital/small letters; **scrivere alla lavagna** to write on the blackboard; **come si scrive questa parola?** how do you write *o* spell this word?; **si scrive con la K** it's spelt with a K; **era scritto che dovesse succedere** (*fig*) it was fated *o* bound to happen

scroccare [skrok'kare] VT (*fam*) to scrounge, cadge

scrocco¹ ['skrokko] SM: **vivere a scrocco** (*fam*) to be a sponger

scrocco², chi ['skrokko] SM **1** (*rumore*) click **2 coltello a scrocco** jack-knife

scroccone, a [skrok'kone] SM/F (*fam*) scrounger, sponger

scrofa ['skrɔfa] SF (*Zool*) sow

scrollare [skrol'lare] VT **1** (*scuotere*) to shake; **scrollare la testa** to shake one's head; **ha scrollato la testa** he shook his head; **scrollare le spalle** to shrug one's shoulders **2 scrollarsi qc di dosso** to shake sth off; (*fig: malinconia, stanchezza*) to shrug sth off

▶ **scrollarsi** VIP to shake o.s.; (*fig*) to stir o.s., give o.s. a shake

scrollata [skrol'lata] SF shake; **dare una scrollata a qc** to give sth a shake; **scrollata di spalle** shrug (of one's shoulders)

scrosciante [skroʃ'ʃante] AGG (*pioggia*) pouring; (*fig: applausi*) thunderous

scrosciare [skroʃ'ʃare] VI (*aus* **avere** *o* **essere**) (*pioggia*) to pelt down, pour down; (*torrente*) to thunder, roar; **gli applausi scrosciavano** there was thunderous applause

scroscio, sci ['skrɔʃʃo] SM (*di torrente, cascata*) roar; (*di applausi*) thunder; **sentivamo lo scroscio della pioggia** we could hear the rain pelting down

scrostare [skros'tare] VT (*vernice, intonaco*) to scrape off, strip (off); (*tubo*) to descale; **scrostare una ferita** to remove the scab (from a wound)

▶ **scrostarsi** VIP (*vernice, intonaco*) to peel off, flake off

scroto ['skrɔto] SM (*Anat*) scrotum

scrupolo ['skrupolo] SM (*morale*) scruple; (*diligenza*) care, conscientiousness; **scrupolo morale** *or* **scrupolo di coscienza** scruple; **essere senza scrupoli** to be unscrupulous; **non farti tanti scrupoli con lui** I wouldn't have any scruples about him if I were you; **non mi farei degli scrupoli a chiederglielo** I wouldn't have any scruples about asking him; **lavoro fatto con scrupolo** a conscientious piece of work; **è onesto fino allo scrupolo** he's scrupulously honest

scrupolosamente [skrupolosa'mente] AVV scrupulously

scrupolosità [skrupolosi'ta] SF (*vedi agg*) scrupulousness; conscientiousness

scrupoloso, a [skrupo'loso] AGG (*onesto*) scrupulous; (*diligente*) conscientious

scrutare [skru'tare] VT (*orizzonte, vallata*) to scan; (*cielo, volto*) to search; (*persona*) to scrutinize; (*intenzioni, causa*) to examine, scrutinize

scrutatore, trice [skruta'tore] AGG (*sguardo*) searching ■SM/F (*di votazione*) scrutineer

scrutinare [skruti'nare] VT (*voti*) to scrutinize, count

scrutinatore, trice [skrutina'tore] SM/F scrutineer

scrutinio, ni [skru'tinjo] SM **1** (*votazione*) ballot; (*insieme delle operazioni*) poll; **scrutinio segreto** secret ballot **2** (*Scol*) (*meeting for*) *assignment of marks at end of a term or year*

scucire [sku'tʃire] VT (*abito, tasca*) to unstitch, unpick, undo; (*fam: soldi*) to fork out

▶ **scucirsi** VIP to come unstitched

scucito, a [sku'tʃito] AGG unstitched

scuderia [skude'ria] SF (*stalla*) stable; (*Aut*) team

scudetto [sku'detto] SM (*Sport*) (championship) shield; **vincere lo scudetto** to win the championship; **il Milan ha vinto lo scudetto** Milan has won the championship

scudiero [sku'djɛro] SM squire

scudiscio, sci [sku'diʃʃo] SM (riding) crop, (riding) whip

scudo ['skudo] SM (*gen*) shield; **farsi scudo di** *o* **con qc** to shield o.s. with sth; **scudo aereo** air defence (*Brit*) *o* defense (*Am*); **scudo missilistico** missile defence (*Brit*) *o* defense (*Am*); **scudo termico** heat shield

scuffiare [skuf'fjare] VI (*aus* **avere**) (*barca*) to capsize

scugnizzo [skuɲ'ɲittso] SM street urchin

sculacciare [skulat'tʃare] VT to spank

sculacciata [skulat'tʃata] SF, **sculaccione** [skulat'tʃone] SM spanking; **dare una sculacciata a qn** to spank sb, give sb a spanking

sculettare [skulet'tare] VI (*aus* **avere**) to sway one's hips, wiggle one's hips

scultore, trice [skul'tore] SM/F (*di pietra*) sculptor/sculptress; (*di legno*) woodcarver

scultoreo, a [skul'tɔreo] AGG of sculpture, sculptural; **arte scultorea** sculpture

scultura [skul'tura] SF (*di pietra*) sculpture; (*di legno*) woodcarving

scuola ['skwɔla] SF **1** (*istituzione, edificio*) school; **andare a scuola** to go to school; **non c'è scuola domani** there's no school tomorrow; **ci vediamo dopo la scuola** see you after school; **scuola guida** driving school; **scuola dell'infanzia** nursery school; **scuola dell'obbligo** compulsory education; **scuola primaria** primary (*Brit*) *o* grade (*Am*) school; **scuola privata** private school; **scuola secondaria di primo grado** *lower secondary school*; **scuola pubblica** state school (*Brit*), public school (*Am*); **scuola secondaria di secondo grado** secondary school; **scuola serale** night school **2** (*Arte*) school; **un artista che ha fatto scuola** an artist who has developed a following

■AGG INV: **nave scuola** training ship

SCUOLA

Following the passage of the law on educational reform in 2003, Italian children go to "scuola dell'infanzia" for three years (age 3-6), after which they attend "scuola primaria" for five years (age 6-11). The first stage of education is then completed by

three years of "scuola secondaria di primo grado" (age 11-14). For the second stage of their education, students can choose between various types of school and can specialize in various subjects.
▷ www.istruzione.it/

scuolabus ['skwɔlabus] SM INV school bus
scuotere ['skwɔtere] VB IRREG
■ VT **1** (*anche fig*) to shake; **scuotere la testa** to shake one's head; **ha scosso la testa** he shook his head; **scuotere le spalle** to shrug one's shoulders; **cercò di scuoterlo dalla sua apatia** he tried to shake him out of *o* rouse him from his apathy **2 scuotersi di dosso qc** to shake sth off; (*fig: malinconia, stanchezza*) to shrug sth off
▶ **scuotersi** VIP to shake o.s.; (*fig*) to stir o.s.; **scuotersi dall'apatia** to rouse o.s. from one's apathy
scure ['skure] SF axe (*Brit*), ax (*Am*)
scurire [sku'rire] VT to darken, make darker
■ VI (*aus* **essere**), **scurirsi** VIP to darken, become dark, grow dark
scuro¹, a ['skuro] AGG (*colore, vestito, capelli*) dark; **una gonna verde scuro** a dark green skirt; **avere una faccia scura** to have a grim expression on one's face
■ SM (*colore*) dark colour (*Brit*) *o* color (*Am*); **vestire di scuro** to wear dark colo(u)rs
scuro² ['skuro] SM (*di finestra*) (window) shutter
scurrile [skur'rile] AGG scurrilous
scurrilità [skurrili'ta] SF INV (*qualità*) scurrility; (*parola*) obscenity
scusa ['skuza] SF **1** (*gen*) apology; **vi prego di accettare le mie scuse** please accept my apologies; **chiedere scusa a qn per qc** to apologize to sb for sth; **devi chiedere scusa all'insegnante** you must apologize to the teacher; **chiedo** *o* **domando scusa** I apologize, I beg your pardon; **fare/presentare le proprie scuse** to make/give one's apologies; **una lettera di scuse** a letter of apology **2** (*pretesto*) excuse; **era solo una scusa per andarsene** it was just an excuse to leave; **cercare una scusa/delle scuse** to look for an excuse/excuses; **questa è una scusa bella e buona!** that's some excuse!; **non c'è scusa che tenga!** there's no possible excuse!
scusare [sku'zare] VT (*gen*) to excuse; (*perdonare*) to forgive; **scusare qn di** *o* **per qc** to forgive sb for sth; **scusami** *or* **scusa** *or* **mi scusi** (I'm) sorry; (*più formale*) I beg your pardon; **scusa il ritardo** I'm sorry I'm late; **tutto questo non ti scusa** this is no excuse; **scusi, sa dirmi dove...?** excuse me, can you tell me where ...?; **scusate un attimo, torno subito** excuse me, I'll be back in a minute
▶ **scusarsi** VR to apologize; **scusarsi con qn di** *o* **per qc** to apologize to sb for sth; **ti sei scusato con lui?** did you apologize to him?; **si è scusato del ritardo** he apologized for being late; **potresti almeno scusarti** you could at least say you're sorry; **non so come scusarmi** I don't know how to apologize; **non cercare di scusarti!** don't look for excuses!
SCV SIGLA = *Stato della Città del Vaticano*
sdaziare [zdat'tsjare] VT to pay customs duties on
sdebitarsi [zdebi'tarsi] VR: **sdebitarsi (con qn di** *o* **per qc)** (*anche fig*) to repay (sb for sth)
sdegnare [zdeɲ'ɲare] VT (*disprezzare*) to scorn, despise
▶ **sdegnarsi** VIP (*arrabbiarsi*) **sdegnarsi (con)** to get angry (with)
sdegnato, a [zdeɲ'ɲato] AGG indignant, angry
sdegno ['zdeɲɲo] SM (*disprezzo*) scorn, disdain; (*indignazione*) indignation
sdegnosamente [zdeɲɲosa'mente] AVV scornfully, contemptuously, disdainfully
sdegnosità [zdeɲɲosi'ta] SF scorn, disdain
sdegnoso, a [zdeɲ'ɲoso] AGG scornful, contemptuous, disdainful
sdentare [zden'tare] VT (*sega*) to break the teeth of
▶ **sdentarsi** VIP to lose one's teeth
sdentato, a [zden'tato] AGG (*senza denti: persona*) toothless; (: *sega*) without teeth
sdilinquirsi [zdilin'kwirsi] VIP (*illanguidirsi*) to become sentimental
sdoganamento [zdogana'mento] SM (customs) clearance
sdoganare [zdoga'nare] VT (*Comm*) to clear through customs
sdolcinatamente [zdoltʃinata'mente] AVV (*comportarsi, parlare*) in an affected way
sdolcinato, a [zdoltʃi'nato] AGG (*persona*) gushing; (*parole*) sugary; (*modi*) affected; (*film, libro*) oversentimental, mawkish
sdoppiamento [zdoppja'mento] SM (*Chim: di composto*) splitting; (*Psic*): **sdoppiamento della personalità** split personality
sdoppiare [zdop'pjare] VT
▶ **sdoppiarsi** VIP to divide *o* split in two
sdoppiato, a [zdop'pjato] AGG split; **sedile posteriore sdoppiato** split rear seat
sdraiare [zdra'jare] VT to lay down; **sdraiare qn a terra/sul letto** to lay sb down on the ground/on the bed
▶ **sdraiarsi** VR to lie down; **sdraiarsi a terra/sul letto** to lie down on the ground/on the bed; **sdraiarsi al sole** to stretch out in the sun
sdraiato, a [zdra'jato] AGG lying down; **mettersi sdraiato** to lie down
sdraio, ai ['zdrajo] SM (*anche: sedia a sdraio*) deckchair
sdrammatizzare [zdrammatid'dzare] VT to play down, minimize
sdrucciolare [zdruttʃo'lare] VI (*aus* **avere** *o* **essere**) (*persona*) to slip, slide
sdrucciolevole [zdruttʃo'levole] AGG slippery
sdrucciolo, a ['zdruttʃolo] AGG (*Ling*) proparoxytone
■ SM trisyllabic verse
sdrucito, a [zdru'tʃito] AGG (*strappato*) torn; (*logoro*) threadbare
SE ABBR **1** (= Sud-Est) SE **2** (= Sua Eccellenza) HE

se¹ [se] PAROLA CHIAVE
■ CONG
1 (*condizionale, concessiva*) if; **se fosse più furbo verrebbe** if he were smarter he would come; **se fosse stato interessato sarebbe venuto** if he had been interested he would have come; **se fossi in te** if I were you; **deve essere così se lo dice lui** it must be so if he says so; **se nevica non vengo** *or* **non verrò** I won't come if it snows; **se invece preferisci questo...** should you *o* if you prefer this one ...
2 (*dubitativa, in domande indirette*) whether, if; **mi chiedevo se avesse capito** I wondered whether he had understood; **guarda lì se c'è** look and see whether *o* if it's there; **non so se scrivere o telefonare** I don't known whether *o* if I should write or phone; **lo so io se mi manca** I know how much I miss him
3 (*ottativa*) if only; **se (solo) me l'avesse detto prima!**

Ss

if only he had told me earlier!; **se ci fosse ancora lui!** if only he were still here!
4 (*fraseologia*): **come se** as if; **come se non lo sapesse!** as if he didn't know!; **e se andassimo in montagna?** how about going to the mountains?; **ma se l'ho visto io!** but I saw it myself!; **se mai passassi per di qua** should you ever *o* if ever you pass this way; **lascialo nell'atrio se mai** leave it in the hall if necessary; **siamo noi se mai che le siamo grati** it is we who should be grateful to you; **se no** (*altrimenti*) or (else), otherwise; **non fiatare, se no vedi!** don't breathe a word or else!; **mangia, se no non reggi fino a stasera** eat up, otherwise *o* or else you'll be starving by this evening; **scappo se no perdo l'autobus** I must dash or I'll miss the bus; **se non** (*anzi*) if not; (*tranne*) except; **costa lo stesso, se non meno** it costs the same, if not less; **non lo darò a nessuno se non a lui** I won't give it to anybody except *o* other than *o* but him; **se non altro** if nothing else, at least; **se non altro non disturba** at least he's no trouble; **se poi decidesse di restare** should he decide *o* were he to decide to stay; **e se poi se ne accorge?** and what if he notices?; **se pure** = **seppure**
■ SM if; **c'è solo un grosso se** there's just one big if

se² [se] *vedi* **si'**
sé [se] PRON RIFLESSIVO (*gen*) oneself; (*maschile*) himself; (*femminile*) herself; (*neutro*) itself; (*pl*) themselves; **l'ha fatto da sé** he did it (all) by himself; **lo portò con sé** he took it with him; **pensa solo a sé** *o* **se stesso** he thinks only of himself; **è piena di sé** she's full of herself; **hanno tenuto la notizia per sé** they kept the news to themselves; **di per sé non è un problema** it's no problem in itself; **parlare tra sé e sé** to talk to oneself; **tornare in sé** to come to (one's senses); **va da sé che...** it goes without saying that ..., it's obvious that ..., it stands to reason that ...; **è un caso a sé (stante)** it's a special case; **si chiude da sé** (*porta*) it closes automatically; **un uomo che s'è fatto da sé** a self-made man; **chi fa da sé fa per tre** (*Proverbio*) if you want something done well *o* properly do it yourself
SEATO [se'ato] SIGLA F SEATO (= *Southeast Asia Treaty Organization*)
sebaceo, a [se'batʃeo] AGG sebaceous
sebbene [seb'bɛne] CONG (even) though, although; **sebbene non sia colpa sua...** although *o* (even) though it is not his fault ...; **lo farò, sebbene mi pesi molto** I'll do it, even though I'm not very happy about it
sebo ['sɛbo] SM sebum
sec ABBR (= secolo) c. (= *century*)
SECAM ['sɛkam] SIGLA M (= **séquentiel couleur à mémoire**) SECAM
secante [se'kante] SF (*Mat*) secant
secca, che ['sekka] SF (*Naut*) bank, shallows *pl*; **andare in secca** to run aground
seccamente [sekka'mente] AVV (*rispondere, rifiutare*) sharply, curtly
seccante [sek'kante] AGG tiresome, annoying
seccare [sek'kare] VT **1** (*gen*) to dry; (*prosciugare*) to dry (up); (*fiori: far appassire*) to wither; **il vento secca la pelle** wind dries the skin **2** (*infastidire*) to annoy, bother; **smettila di seccarmi!** stop bothering me!; **questa volta mi hai proprio seccato** I've had enough of you this time; **ti secca se aspetto qui?** do you mind if I wait here?; **se ti secca chiederglielo lo faccio io** if you don't like to ask him I'll do it; **mi secca fare tutta questa fila** it annoys me having to queue like this
■ VI (*aus* **essere**) to dry (up)
▶ **seccarsi** VIP **1** (*diventar secco: gen*) to dry (up); (*pelle*) to become dry; (*fiori*) to wither **2** (*infastidirsi*) to become annoyed, grow annoyed, get annoyed; **si è seccato molto** he got very annoyed
seccato, a [sek'kato] AGG (*fig: infastidito*) bothered, annoyed; (: *stufo*) fed up
seccatore, trice [sekka'tore] SM/F nuisance, bother
seccatura [sekka'tura] SF nuisance, bother *no pl*, trouble *no pl*; **che seccatura!** what a nuisance!; **non voglio seccature!** I don't want any bother!
seccherò *ecc* [sekke'rɔ] VB *vedi* **seccare**
secchia ['sekkja] SF bucket, pail
secchiata [sek'kjata] SF bucket(ful)
secchiello [sek'kjɛllo] SM (*per bambini*) bucket, pail; **secchiello del ghiaccio** ice bucket
secchio, chi ['sekkjo] SM bucket, pail; **un secchio d'acqua** a bucket of water; **secchio della spazzatura** *o* **delle immondizie** dustbin (*Brit*), garbage can (*Am*), trash can (*Am*)
secchione, a [sek'kjone] SM/F (*fam pegg*) swot (*Brit*), grind (*Am*)
secco, a, chi, che ['sekko] AGG **1** (*gen*) dry; (*terreno*) arid, dry; (*uva, fichi, pesce*) dried; (*foglie, ramo*) withered; (*fig: risposta*) sharp; **ho la pelle molto secca** I've got very dry skin; **avere la gola secca** to feel dry, be parched; **potrei avere qualcosa da bere? ho la gola secca** could I have something to drink please? I'm parched; **un no secco** a curt no; **un colpo secco** a sharp blow; **frutta secca** (*noci, mandorle ecc*) nuts; (*fichi, datteri ecc*) dried fruit **2** (*persona: magro*) thin, skinny; **secco come un chiodo** as thin as a rake **3** (*fraseologia*): **fare secco qn** (*assassinare*) to knock sb off; **ci è rimasto secco** (*fig: morto*) it killed him
■ SM **1** (*di clima*) dryness; (*siccità*) drought
2 (*fraseologia*): **lavare a secco** to dry-clean; **devo far lavare a secco la giacca** I need to get my jacket dry-cleaned; **tirare a secco** (*barca*) to beach; **essere a secco (di soldi)** to be broke; **rimanere a secco di benzina** to run out of petrol (*Brit*) *o* gas (*Am*)
secentesco, a, schi, sche [setʃen'tesko] AGG seventeenth-century
secernere [se'tʃɛrnere] VT to secrete
secessione [setʃes'sjone] SF (*Pol*) secession
secolare [seko'lare] AGG **1** (*antico*) centuries-old, age-old **2** (*laico*) secular, lay *attr*; **clero secolare** lay clergy
secolarizzare [sekolarit'tsare] VT to secularize
secolo ['sɛkolo] SM **1** century; (*epoca*) century, age; **nel terzo secolo a.C.** in the third century B.C.; **nel nostro secolo** this century; **l'avvenimento del secolo** the event of the century; **il secolo della Ragione** the Age of Reason; **per tutti i secoli dei secoli** (*Rel*) forever and ever; **Giovanni Paolo II, al secolo Carol Wojtyla** John Paul II, whose original name was Carol Wojtyla **2** (*fig*): **è un secolo che non ti vedo** I haven't seen you in ages; **è un secolo che aspetto** I've been waiting for ages
seconda [se'konda] SF **1** (*Aut*) second (gear); **mettere in seconda** to go into second gear **2** (*Scol*) second year; (: *seconda elementare*) ≈ year three (*Brit*), ≈ second grade (*Am*) (: *seconda media*) ≈ year eight (*Brit*), ≈ seventh grade (*Am*) (*seconda superiore*) ≈ year eleven (*Brit*), ≈ tenth grade (*Am*) **3** (*Ferr*) second class; **viaggiare in seconda** to travel second class; **un biglietto di seconda** a second-class ticket **4** **comandante in seconda** second-in-command **5** **a seconda di** PREP according

to, in accordance with; **le tariffe cambiano a seconda dell'ora** charges vary according to the time of day

secondariamente [sekondarja'mente] AVV secondly

secondario, ria, ri, rie [sekon'darjo] AGG secondary, minor; **di secondaria importanza** of secondary *o* minor importance; **scuola/istruzione secondaria** secondary school/education

secondino [sekon'dino] SM prison officer, warder (*Brit*), prison guard (*Am*)

secondo[1], a [se'kondo] AGG (*gen*) second; **in seconda fila** in the second row; **in secondo luogo** in the second place; **prendi la seconda strada a destra** take the second street on the right; **si è classificato al secondo posto** he came second; **il suo disco è secondo in classifica** his record is number two in the charts; **figlio di seconde nozze** son by a second marriage; **passare a seconde nozze** to remarry, marry for a second time; **elevare alla seconda (potenza)** (*Mat*) to raise to the power of two; **Carlo secondo** Charles the Second; **è un secondo Picasso** he's another *o* a second Picasso; **un albergo di second'ordine** a second-class hotel; **un biglietto di seconda classe** a second class ticket; **viaggiare in seconda classe** to travel second-class; **di seconda mano** (*oggetto, informazione*) second-hand; **una moto di seconda mano** a second-hand motorbike; **avere un secondo fine** to have an ulterior motive
■ SM **1** (*tempo*) second; **un minuto e dieci secondi** one minute and ten seconds; **aspetta un secondo!** wait a moment!; **un secondo, arrivo subito!** I won't be a minute! **2** (*anche:* **secondo piatto**) main course, second course; **come secondo vorrei del salmone alla griglia** I'd like grilled salmon for my main course
■ SM/F second (person); **sei il secondo che me lo dice** you're the second person to tell me that; *per fraseologia vedi* **quinto**

secondo[2] [se'kondo] PREP **1** (*in base a, nell'opinione di*) according to; (*nel modo prescritto da, stando a*) in accordance with; **secondo lui** according to him, in his opinion; **secondo me** in my opinion; **secondo me dovresti scrivergli** in my opinion you should write to him; **secondo il giornale quel film è da non perdere** according to the paper that film shouldn't be missed; **secondo le mie possibilità** according to my means; **tutto sta andando secondo i piani** everything's going according to plan; **il Vangelo secondo Matteo** the Gospel according to St Matthew; **secondo la legge/quanto si era deciso** in accordance with the law/the decision taken; **agire secondo coscienza** to follow one's conscience **2** (*in direzione di: vento, corrente*) with; (*: linea*) along

secondogenito, a [sekondo'dʒɛnito] SM/F second-born

secrétaire [səkre'tɛr] SM INV secretaire, writing desk

secretare [sekre'tare] VT (*Dir, documento, verbale*) to mark as confidential *o* secret

secrezione [sekret'tsjone] SF (*Bio*) secretion

sedano ['sɛdano] SM celery; **sedano rapa** celeriac

sedare [se'dare] VT **1** (*dolore*) to soothe **2** (*rivolta*) to put down, suppress

sedativo, a [seda'tivo] AGG, SM (*Med*) sedative

sede ['sɛde] SF **1** (*luogo di residenza*) (place of) residence; **prendere sede** to take up residence; **cambiare sede** to change one's residence **2** (*di società: principale*) head office; (*: secondaria*) branch (office); (*di partito*) headquarters *pl*; (*di governo, parlamento*) seat; (*Rel*) see; **la Santa Sede** the Holy See; **un'azienda con diverse sedi in città** a firm with several branches in the city; **il presidente è fuori sede** the chairman is not in the office; **sede sociale** registered office **3** (*località*) site; **Londra sarà sede di un'importante mostra** London will be the site of an important exhibition **4** **in sede di** (*in occasione di*) during; **in sede d'esame** during the exam; **in sede di discussione** during the discussion; **in sede legislativa** in legislative sitting; **in altra sede** on another occasion

sedentario, ria, ri, rie [seden'tarjo] AGG sedentary

sedere[1] [se'dere] VB IRREG
■ VI (*aus* **essere**) **1** (*essere seduto*) to be sitting, be seated; **sedeva a tavola** he was sitting at table; **era seduta accanto a me** she was sitting beside me; **posto a sedere** seat; **siede in Parlamento** he has a seat in Parliament **2** (*mettersi seduto*) to sit (down); **siedi qui** sit here; **mettiti a sedere** sit down, take a seat; **sieda per cortesia** please sit down, please take a seat; **mettersi seduto** (*da posizione orizzontale*) to sit up;
▶ **sedersi** VIP to sit (down); **sono così stanca che non vedo l'ora di sedermi!** I'm so tired I can't wait to sit down!; **siediti qui** sit down (here); **sedersi per terra** (*in casa*) to sit on the floor; (*all'esterno*) to sit on the ground

sedere[2] [se'dere] SM (*deretano*) bottom; **lo ha spedito fuori a calci nel sedere** he kicked him out

sedia ['sɛdja] SF chair; **sedia elettrica** electric chair; **sedia pieghevole** folding chair; **sedia a rotelle** wheelchair

sedicenne [sedi'tʃɛnne] AGG, SM/F sixteen-year-old; *per fraseologia vedi* **cinquantenne**

sedicente [sedi'tʃɛnte] AGG self-styled

sedicesimo, a [sedi'tʃɛzimo] AGG, SM/F, SM **1** sixteenth **2** (*Tip*): **in sedicesimo** sexto decimo; *per fraseologia vedi* **quinto**

sedici ['seditʃi] AGG INV, SM INV sixteen; *per fraseologia vedi* **cinque**

sedile [se'dile] SM (*in automezzi*) seat

sedimentare [sedimen'tare] VI (*aus* **essere** *o* **avere**) to leave *o* deposit a sediment

sedimentario, ria, ri, rie [sedimen'tarjo] AGG sedimentary

sedimento [sedi'mento] SM sediment

sedizione [sedit'tsjone] SF uprising, insurrection

sediziosamente [sedittsjosa'mente] AVV seditiously

sedizioso, a [sedit'tsjoso] AGG seditious
■ SM/F insurrectionist

sedotto, a [se'dotto] PP *di* **sedurre**

seducente [sedu'tʃɛnte] AGG (*donna*) seductive; (*proposta*) very attractive

sedurre [se'durre] VT IRREG **1** (*abusare di*) to seduce **2** (*affascinare*) to charm, captivate; (*: sogg: idea*) to appeal to

seduta [se'duta] SF (*gen*) session, sitting; **una seduta del parlamento** a parliamentary sitting; **essere in seduta** to be in session, be sitting; **seduta stante** (*fig: immediatamente*) straight away, immediately; **seduta spiritica** seance

seduttore, trice [sedut'tore] SM/F seducer/seductress

seduzione [sedut'tsjone] SF (*vedi vb*) seduction; charm; appeal

S.E.eO. ABBR (= **salvo errori e omissioni**) E and OE

sega, ghe ['sega] SF **1** (*Tecn*) saw; **sega circolare** circular saw; **sega a mano** handsaw **2** **farsi una sega** (*fam!: masturbarsi*) to have a wank (*Brit fam!*), to jerk off (*Am fam!*); **non capire una sega** (*fam*) to understand damn all

Ss

segala ['segala], **segale** ['segale] SF (*Bot*) rye
segare [se'gare] VT to saw; (*in più parti*) to saw up; (*fam: bocciare*) to flunk; **segare via** to saw off; **segare in due** to saw in two; **le corde le segavano i polsi** the ropes were cutting into her wrists
segatrice [sega'tritʃe] SF: **segatrice a disco** circular saw; **segatrice a nastro** band saw
segatura [sega'tura] SF sawdust
seggio, gi ['sɛddʒo] SM **1** (*gen*) seat **2 seggio elettorale** polling station

LO SAPEVI...?
seggio non si traduce mai con la parola inglese *siege*

seggiola ['sɛddʒola] SF chair
seggiolino [seddʒo'lino] SM seat; (*per bambini*) child's chair; **seggiolino di sicurezza** (*su auto*) child safety seat
seggiolone [seddʒo'lone] SM (*per bambini*) highchair
seggiovia [seddʒo'via] SF chair lift
segheria [sege'ria] SF sawmill
segherò *ecc* [sege'rɔ] VB *vedi* **segare**
seghettare [seget'tare] VT to serrate
seghettato, a [seget'tato] AGG serrated
seghettatura [segetta'tura] SF serration
seghetto [se'getto] SM hacksaw
segmentare [segmen'tare] VT to segment
segmentazione [segmentat'tsjone] SF segmentation
segmento [seg'mento] SM segment
segnalamento [seɲɲala'mento] SM signalling
segnalare [seɲɲa'lare] VT (*essere segno di*) to indicate, be a sign of; (*avvertire*) to signal; (*menzionare*) to indicate; (: *fatto, risultato, aumento, guasto*) to report; (: *errore, dettaglio*) to point out; **ho segnalato il fatto alla polizia** I reported the incident to the police; **segnalare una svolta a sinistra** (*Aut*) to indicate *o* signal a left turn; **segnalare la posizione di una nave** to signal the position of a ship; **niente da segnalare** nothing to report; **potresti segnalarci un buon albergo?** could you recommend a good hotel?; **l'insegnante ha segnalato alcuni nomi per la borsa di studio** the teacher suggested a few names for the scholarship; **segnalare qn a qn** (*per lavoro*) to bring sb to sb's attention
▶ **segnalarsi** VR (*distinguersi*) to distinguish o.s.
segnalazione [seɲɲalat'tsjone] SF **1** (*azione*) signalling; (*segnale*) signal; **segnalazioni acustiche** acoustic *o* sound signals; **segnalazioni stradali** road signs **2** (*annuncio*) report; (*raccomandazione*) recommendation
segnale [seɲ'ɲale] SM (*gen*) signal; **al mio segnale spegnete la luce** when I give the signal switch the light off; **segnale acustico** acoustic *o* sound signal; (*di segreteria telefonica*) tone; **lasciate un messaggio dopo il segnale acustico** please leave a message after the tone; **segnale d'allarme** alarm; (*sui treni*) communication cord (*Brit*); **segnale di linea libera** (*Telec*) dialling (*Brit*) *o* dial (*Am*) tone; **segnale luminoso** light signal; **segnale di occupato** (*Telec*) engaged tone (*Brit*), busy signal (*Am*); **segnale orario** (*Radio, TV*) time signal; **segnale stradale** road sign
segnaletica [seɲɲa'lɛtika] SF: **segnaletica (stradale)** road signs *pl*, traffic signs *pl*
segnalibro [seɲɲa'libro] SM (*anche Inform*) bookmark
segnaposto [seɲɲa'posto] SM INV place card
segnaprezzo [seɲɲa'prɛttso] SM INV (*anche*: **cartellino segnaprezzo**) price tag
segnapunti [seɲɲa'punti] SM/F INV scorer, scorekeeper
■ SM INV scorecard
segnare [seɲ'ɲare] VT **1** (*fare un segno: gen*) to mark; (*scalfire*) to score, mark, cut into; (*graffiare*) to scratch; **segnare il passo** (*Mil, anche fig*) to mark time; **è molto segnato da quell'esperienza** that experience has left its mark on him; **aveva il volto segnato dalla stanchezza** his face was drawn and tired **2** (*annotare*) to make a note of, jot down, note; **segna quanto ti devo** make a note of what I owe you **3** (*indicare*) to show, indicate, mark; **non segna la velocità giusta** it's not showing the right speed; **quella lancetta serve a segnare le ore** that hand shows *o* indicates the hours; **il mio orologio segna le 5** my watch says 5 o'clock; **gli errori sono segnati in rosso** the mistakes are marked in red; **segnare a dito** to point at; **essere segnato a dito** (*fig*) to be talked about **4** (*Sport*) to score; **segnare di testa** (*Calcio*) to score with a header; **segnare un rigore** to score a penalty; **segnare su rigore** to score with a penalty; **ha segnato nella ripresa** he scored in the second half
▶ **segnarsi** VR (*Rel*) to cross o.s., make the sign of the cross
segnatura [seɲɲa'tura] SF (*in archivio, biblioteca*) shelf mark, pressmark (*Brit*)
segno ['seɲɲo] SM **1** (*gen*) sign; (*traccia*) mark, sign; (*graffio*) scratch; (*indizio*) sign, indication; **aveva dei segni rossi sul viso** she had red marks on her face; **lasciare un segno** (*anche fig*) to leave a mark; **non c'era segno di vita** there was no sign of life; **non ha dato segni di vita** he gave no sign of life; **è brutto segno** it's a bad sign; **in** *o* **come segno d'amicizia** as a mark *o* token of friendship; **diede segno di voler andare** he indicated that he wanted to leave; **perdere il segno** (*leggendo*) to lose one's place; **il segno dei suoi passi** his footprints *pl*; **fare segno di sì** to nod; **fare segno di no** to shake one's head; **fare segno con la mano** to make a sign with one's hand; **mi fece segno di spostarmi/avvicinarmi/fermarmi** he made a sign to me to move/come nearer/stop; **di che segno sei?** what sign are you?; **essere del segno dell'Acquario** *ecc* to be an Aquarian *ecc* **2** (*bersaglio*) target; **tiro a segno** target shooting; **cogliere** *o* **colpire nel segno** to hit the target *o* mark; (*fig*) to hit the bullseye, hit the nail on the head
■ **"segni particolari"** (*su documento*) "distinguishing marks"; **il segno della croce** (*Rel*) the sign of the cross; **segno meno** (*Mat*) minus sign; **segno più** plus sign; **segno zodiacale** sign of the zodiac
segregare [segre'gare] VT (*gen*) to segregate; (*pazzo*) to confine
▶ **segregarsi** VIP (*fig: isolarsi*): **segregarsi in casa** to shut o.s. up in the house
segregazione [segregat'tsjone] SF segregation
segregazionismo [segregattsjo'nizmo] SM segregationism
segregazionista, i, e [segregattsjo'nista] AGG, SM/F segregationist
segreta [se'greta] SF dungeon
segretamente [segreta'mente] AVV secretly; **riunirsi segretamente** to meet secretly *o* in secret
segretariato [segreta'rjato] SM secretariat
segretario, ria, ri, rie [segre'tarjo] SM/F (*gen*) secretary; **segretaria di direzione** personal assistant; **segretario comunale** town clerk; **segretario del partito** party leader
segreteria [segrete'ria] SF **1** (*ufficio*) secretary's office; (*in enti*) secretarial offices *pl* **2** (*Pol: carica*)

secretaryship, office of Secretary; (: *segretariato*) secretariat **3** **segreteria telefonica** answering machine

segretezza [segre'tettsa] SF secrecy; **notizie della massima segretezza** highly confidential information *sg*; **in tutta segretezza** in secret; (*confidenzialmente*) in confidence

segreto, a [se'greto] AGG (*gen*) secret; (*documenti*) confidential, secret; **tenere segreto qc** to keep sth secret; **passaggio segreto** secret passage
■ SM (*gen*) secret; **in segreto** in secret, secretly; (*in confidenza*) in confidence; **mantenere** *o* **tenere un segreto** to keep a secret; **sai mantenere un segreto?** can you keep a secret?; **il segreto professionale** professional secrecy; **un segreto professionale** a professional secret; **il segreto di Pulcinella** an open secret; **il segreto del successo** the secret of *o* key to success; **nel segreto dell'animo** in the depths of one's soul, deep down

seguace [se'gwatʃe] SM/F (*Rel, gen*) disciple, follower

seguente [se'gwɛnte] AGG following, next; **il giorno seguente** the next *o* following day; **i seguenti candidati sono pregati di farsi avanti** would the following candidates please come forward; **nel modo seguente** as follows, in the following way

segugio, gi [se'gudʒo] SM **1** (*Zool*) hound, hunting dog **2** (*fig*) private eye, sleuth

seguire [se'gwire] VT **1** (*gen*) to follow; **seguire qn come un'ombra** to follow sb about like a shadow; **segui quella macchina!** follow that car!; **mi ha seguita fino a casa** he followed me home; **ha fatto seguire la moglie** he had his wife followed; **mi segua, la prego** this way *o* follow me, please; **segui la statale per 15 km** follow *o* keep to the main road for 15 km; **seguire una cura** to follow a course of treatment; **seguire i consigli di qn** to follow *o* take sb's advice; **perché non segui i miei consigli?** why don't you take my advice?; **seguire una dieta** to be on a diet; **far seguire una dieta a qn** to put sb on a diet; **le cose seguono il loro corso** things are taking *o* running their course; **seguire un programma alla TV** to watch a programme on TV; **seguire un alunno** (*fig*) to follow the progress of a pupil; **seguire gli avvenimenti di attualità** to follow *o* keep up with current events **2** (*capire: persona, argomento*) to follow; **scusa, non ti seguo** I'm sorry, I don't follow (you) *o* I'm not with you; **mi segui o vado troppo veloce?** are you following me or am I going too fast? **3** (*corso, lezione: gen*) to follow, take; (: *essere presente a*) to attend, go to; **seguire un corso per corrispondenza** to follow *o* take a correspondence course; **non è obbligatorio seguire le lezioni** attendance at lessons is not compulsory
■ VI (*aus* **essere**) **1** (*venir dopo, fig: derivare*) to follow; **come segue** as follows; **a Pio XI seguì Pio XII** Pius XI was succeeded by Pius XII; **a ciò seguì un aumento dei prezzi** this was followed by a rise in prices **2** (*continuare*) to continue; **"segue"** "to be continued"

seguitare [segwi'tare] VT to continue, carry on with; **seguitare a fare qc** to continue doing sth
■ VI (*aus* **avere** *o* **essere**) to continue, carry on

seguito ['segwito] SM **1** (*di persone*) retinue, suite; (*discepoli, ammiratori*) followers *pl*; **essere al seguito di qn** to be among sb's suite, be one of sb's retinue **2** (*continuazione: di film*) sequel; (: *nuovo episodio*) continuation; (*resto*) remainder, rest; **il seguito la settimana prossima** to be continued next week; **manca il seguito** the rest is missing **3** (*conseguenze*): **non aver seguito** to have no repercussions **4** **in seguito** then, later on; **ora leggete; in seguito vi farò delle domande** now read it, then I'll ask you some questions; **in seguito a** *or* **a seguito di** following; **facciamo seguito alla lettera del...** further to *o* in answer to your letter of ...; **di seguito** at a stretch, on end; **è piovuto per tre settimane di seguito** it rained non-stop for three weeks; **tre volte di seguito** three times in a row

sei[1] ['sɛi] AGG INV, SM INV six; *per fraseologia vedi* **cinque**

sei[2] ['sɛi] VB *vedi* **essere**

Seicelle [sei'tʃɛlle] SFPL: **le (isole) Seicelle** the Seychelles

seicentesco, a, schi, sche [seitʃen'tesko] AGG seventeenth-century

seicento [sei'tʃɛnto] AGG INV six hundred
■ SM INV six hundred; (*secolo*): **il Seicento** the seventeenth century

seimila [sei'mila] AGG INV, SM INV six thousand

selce ['seltʃe] SF flint, flintstone

selciato [sel'tʃato] SM cobbled surface; **si sentirono i suoi passi sul selciato** you could hear his footsteps on the cobbles

selettività [selettivi'ta] SF selectivity

selettivo, a [selet'tivo] AGG selective

selettore [selet'tore] SM (*Tecn*) selector; **selettore dei canali** (*TV*) channel selector

selezionare [selettsjo'nare] VT to select, choose

selezionatore [selettsjona'tore] SM (*Sport*) selector

selezione [selet'tsjone] SF selection, choice; **fare una selezione** to make a selection *o* choice; **selezione naturale** (*Bio*) natural selection

sella ['sɛlla] SF saddle; **montare in sella** to mount, get into the saddle

sellaio, ai [sel'lajo] SM saddler

sellare [sel'lare] VT to saddle, put a saddle on

selleria [selle'ria] SF **1** (*equipaggiamento, negozio*) saddlery; (*di scuderia*) tack room **2** (*Aut*) (interior) trim

sellino [sel'lino] SM saddle

seltz [sɛlts] SM INV soda (water)

selva ['selva] SF (*letter: bosco*) wood; (: *foresta*) forest; (*fig: di gente, capelli*) mass

selvaggina [selvad'dʒina] SF game

selvaggio, gia, gi, ge [sel'vaddʒo] AGG (*gen*) wild; (*incontrollato: fenomeno, aumento*) uncontrolled; (*tribù*) savage, primitive, uncivilized; (*pegg: omicidio*) savage, ferocious; (: *torture*) brutal, cruel; **sciopero selvaggio** wildcat strike; **inflazione selvaggia** runaway inflation
■ SM/F savage

selvatico, a, ci, che [sel'vatiko] AGG (*animali, fiori*) wild; (*fig: persona, timido*) unsociable
■ SM (*di selvaggina*): **sapere di selvatico** to taste gamy; **puzzare di selvatico** to smell high *o* gamy

selvicoltura [selvikol'tura] SF forestry
▷ www.selvicoltura.org/
▷ www.ricercaforestale.it/index/index.htm

S.Em. ABBR (= **Sua Eminenza**) HE

semaforo [se'maforo] SM (*Aut*) traffic lights *pl*; (*Ferr*) signal; **attento! il semaforo è rosso** watch out! the traffic lights are red

semantica [se'mantika] SF semantics *sg*

semantico, a, ci, che [se'mantiko] AGG semantic

semantista, i, e [seman'tista] SM/F semanticist

sembiante [sem'bjante] SM (*poet: aspetto*) appearance; (: *volto*) countenance

sembianza [sem'bjantsa] SF (*poet*) **1** (*aspetto*)

Ss

appearance **2** **sembianze** SFPL (*lineamenti*) features; (*fig: falsa apparenza*) semblance *sg*

sembrare [sem'brare] (*aus* **essere**) VI (*gen*) to seem; **sembra simpatico** he seems *o* appears (to be) nice; **sembrava più giovane** he seemed *o* looked younger; **sembra una ragazzina** she looks like a young girl; **sembra suo padre** he looks like his father; **sembra caffè** it tastes like coffee; **al tocco sembrava seta** it felt like silk; **sembra odore di bruciato** it smells as if something is burning

■ VB IMPERS: **sembra che** it seems that; **mi sembra che...** (*ho l'impressione*) it seems to me that ..., it looks to me as though ...; (*penso*) I think (that) ..., I have a feeling that ...; **non è facile come sembra** it's not as easy as it seems; **ti sembra giusto?** do you think it's fair?; **non gli sembrava onesto farlo** he didn't think it was honest to do it; **le sembra di sapere tutto** she thinks she knows everything; **fai come ti sembra** do as you please *o* as you see fit; **non mi sembra vero!** I can't believe it!

seme ['seme] SM **1** (*gen*) seed; (*di agrumi, mela, pera*) pip; (*di ciliegia, pesca*) stone; **gettare il seme della discordia** to sow the seeds of discord; **olio di semi** vegetable oil **2** (*Anat: sperma*) semen **3** (*Carte*) suit

semeiotica [seme'jɔtika] SF semiotics *sg*

semente [se'mente] SF seed

semestrale [semes'trale] AGG (*che dura 6 mesi*) six-month *attr*; (*che avviene ogni 6 mesi*) six-monthly

semestre [se'mɛstre] SM (*gen*) six months *pl*, six-month period, half-year; (*Scol*) semester; **nel primo semestre dell'anno** in the first half of the year

semi... ['sɛmi] PREF semi...

semiaperto, a [semia'pɛrto] AGG half-open

semiasse [semi'asse] SM (*Aut*) drive shaft

semiautomatico, a, ci, che [semiauto'matiko] AGG semiautomatic

semibreve [semi'brɛve] SF (*Mus*) semibreve (*Brit*), whole note (*Am*)

semicerchio, chi [semi'tʃerkjo] SM semicircle

semichiuso, a [semi'kjuso] AGG half shut; **lasciare la porta semichiusa** to leave the door ajar

semicircolare [semitʃirko'lare] AGG semicircular

semiconduttore [semikondut'tore] SM semiconductor

semicroma [semi'krɔma] SF (*Mus*) semiquaver (*Brit*), sixteenth note (*Am*)

semidetenzione [semideten'tsjone] SF *custodial sentence of a minimum 10 hours per day in prison*

semidistrutto, a [semidis'trutto] AGG partly destroyed

semifinale [semifi'nale] SF (*Sport*) semifinal

semifinalista, i, e [semifina'lista] SM/F semifinalist

semifreddo [semi'freddo] SM (*Culin*) *chilled dessert made with ice cream*

semilavorato, a [semilavo'rato] AGG semifinished

semilibertà [semiliber'ta] SF *custodial sentence allowing part-time study or work outside prison*

semiminima [semi'minima] SF (*Mus*) crotchet (*Brit*), quarter note (*Am*)

semina ['semina] SF (*Agr*) sowing; **periodo della semina** sowing time

seminale [semi'nale] AGG (*Anat*) seminal, sperm *attr*

seminare [semi'nare] VT **1** (*Agr*) to sow; (*fig: vestiti, libri*) to scatter, leave lying around; **chi non semina non raccoglie** (*Proverbio*) as you sow, so shall you reap **2** (*inseguitore*) to lose, shake off

seminario, ri [semi'narjo] SM **1** (*Rel*) seminary **2** (*Scol*) seminar; **ho seguito un seminario di storia** I attended a history seminar

seminativo, a [semina'tivo] AGG (*terreno*) arable

seminato [semi'nato] SM: **uscire dal seminato** (*fig*) to wander off the point

seminatore [semina'tore] SM sower

seminatrice [semina'tritʃe] SF (*macchina*) seeder

seminfermità [seminfermi'ta] SF (*Med*) partial infirmity

seminterrato [seminter'rato] SM (*piano*) basement; (*appartamento*) basement flat (*Brit*) *o* apartment (*Am*)

seminudo, a [semi'nudo] AGG half-naked

semiologia [semjolo'dʒia] SF semiology

semiologico, a, ci, che [semio'lɔdʒiko] AGG semiological

semiologo, a, gi, ghe [se'mjɔlogo] SM/F semiologist

semioscurità [semioskuri'ta] SF half-light, semi-darkness

semiotica [se'mjɔtika] SF semiotics *sg*

semipermeabile [semiperme'abile] AGG (*terreno*) selectively permeable

semipresidenziale [semipresident'tsjale] AGG (*Pol, repubblica*) dual executive *attr*

semipresidenzialismo [semipresidentsja'lizmo] SM (*Pol*) dual executive

semipresidenzialista, i, e [semipresidentsja'lista] AGG (*Pol*) dual executive *attr*

semireazione [semireat'tsjone] SF (*Chim*) half-reaction

semisecco, a [semi'sekko] AGG (*vino*) medium-dry

semiserio, ria, ri, rie [semi'sɛrjo] AGG half-serious

semitico, a, ci, che [se'mitiko] AGG Semitic

semitono [semi'tɔno] SM (*Mus*) semitone (*Brit*), half step (*Am*)

semivuoto, a [semi'vwɔto] AGG half empty

semmai [sem'mai] = **se mai**; *vedi* **se'**

semola ['semola] SF bran; **semola di grano duro** durum wheat

semolato [semo'lato] AGG: **zucchero semolato** caster sugar

semolino [semo'lino] SM semolina

semovente [semo'vɛnte] AGG self-propelled

semplice ['semplitʃe] AGG **1** (*gen: non complicato*) simple; (*persona, modi: non affettato*) simple, unaffected; (*: ingenuo*) simple, ingenuous; **l'esercizio è molto semplice** the exercise is very simple; **conduce una vita semplice** he lives a simple life; **è semplice da capire** it's easy *o* simple to understand; **una visione della vita un po' semplice** a simplistic view of life; **è una semplice formalità** it's a mere formality; **è una semplice questione d'orgoglio** it's simply a matter of pride; **è pazzia pura e semplice** it's sheer madness; **acqua semplice** tap water **2** (*Gramm*) simple **3** (*Mil*): **marinaio semplice** ordinary seaman; **soldato semplice** private

semplicemente [semplitʃe'mente] AVV **1** (*in maniera semplice*) simply, in a simple way; **parla semplicemente e lentamente** speak slowly and simply **2** (*solamente*) only, merely, simply; **desidero semplicemente la verità** I merely want the truth; **è semplicemente ridicolo** it's simply ridiculous **3** (*con modestia*) simply, modestly; **vive molto semplicemente** he lives very simply

semplicione [sempli'tʃone] SM (*fam*) simpleton

semplicistico, a, ci, che [sempli'tʃistiko] AGG simplistic

semplicità [semplitʃi'ta] SF simplicity, simpleness

semplificare [semplifi'kare] VT to simplify

semplificativo, a [semplifika'tivo] AGG simplifying

semplificazione [semplifikat'tsjone] SF simplification; **fare una semplificazione di** to simplify

sempre ['sɛmpre] AVV **1** (*continuità*) always; (*eternamente*) always, forever; **viene sempre alle 5** he always comes at 5 o'clock; **crede di aver sempre ragione** she thinks she's always right; **è sempre in ritardo** he's always late; **ti amerò sempre** I'll always love you, I'll love you for ever; **come sempre** as usual; **è la persona di sempre** he's the same as ever, he's his usual self; **sei il cretino di sempre** *or* **sei sempre il solito cretino** you're as stupid as ever; **per sempre** forever; **la situazione non durerà per sempre** the situation won't last for ever; **da sempre** always; **lo so da sempre** I've always known it; **una volta per sempre** once and for all; **arriva sempre a disturbarmi** he's always *o* forever coming to disturb me; **è sempre nevicato** it snowed all the time; **è un abito che puoi indossare sempre** it's a dress you can wear any time *o* on any occasion; **è rimasto sempre lì fermo** he stayed there, immobile **2** (*ancora, comunque*) still; **esci sempre con lui?** are you still going out with him?; **c'è sempre la possibilità che...** there's still a chance that ..., there's always the possibility that ...; **ha una certa età ma è sempre bella** she is getting on but is still very attractive; **è (pur) sempre tuo fratello** he is still your brother (however); **è sempre meglio che niente** it's better than nothing; **posso sempre tentare** I can always *o* still try **3 sempre che** as long as, provided (that); **sempre che non piova** as long as *o* provided that it doesn't rain, unless it rains; **sempre che tu non cambi idea** as long as you don't change your mind, unless you change your mind **4** (*rafforzativo*): **sempre più** more and more; **diventa sempre più difficile** it's getting more and more difficult; **sempre meno** less and less; **l'attività è sempre meno redditizia** the business is getting less and less profitable; **va sempre meglio** things are getting better and better; **diventa sempre più raro** it's getting rarer and rarer; **è sempre più giovane** she gets younger and younger

sempreverde [sempre'verde] AGG, SM O F (*Bot*) evergreen

sen. ABBR (= **senatore**) Sen.

senape ['sɛnape] SF (*Bot, Culin*) mustard ■AGG INV (*colore*) mustard-coloured, mustard *attr*

senapismo [sena'pizmo] SM mustard plaster

senato [se'nato] SM **1** (*Storia*) senate **2 il Senato** *upper chamber of the Italian parliament*

SENATO

The **Senato** is the upper house of the Italian parliament, with similar functions to the "Camera dei deputati". Candidates must be at least 40 years of age and electors must be 25 or over. Elections are held every five years. Former heads of state become senators for life, as do five distinguished members of the public who are chosen by the head of state for their scientific, social, artistic or literary achievements. The chamber is presided over by the "Presidente del Senato", who is elected by the senators.

▷www.senato.it/

senatore, trice [sena'tore] SM/F senator

senatoriale [senato'rjale] AGG senatorial

Seneca ['sɛneka] SM Seneca

Senegal ['sɛnegal] SM Senegal

senegalese [senega'lese] AGG, SM/F Senegalese *inv*

senese [se'nese] AGG Sienese, of *o* from Siena ■SM/F inhabitant *o* native of Siena

senile [se'nile] AGG senile

senilismo [seni'lizmo] SM premature old age

senilità [senili'ta] SF senility

Senna ['senna] SF: **la Senna** the Seine

senno ['senno] SM judgment, good sense, (common) sense; **uscire di senno** to lose one's mind *o* wits, go mad; **col senno di poi** with hindsight; **del senno di poi son piene le fosse** (*Proverbio*) it's easy to be wise after the event

sennò [sen'nɔ] AVV = **se no**; *vedi* **se'**

seno[1] ['seno] SM **1** (*Anat*) bosom; (: *mammella*) breast; (*grembo*) womb; **portare un figlio in seno** to carry a child (in one's womb); **in seno alla famiglia** in the bosom of the family; **in seno al partito/all'organizzazione** within the party/the organization **2** (*Anat, Zool: cavità*) sinus **3** (*Geog*) inlet, creek

seno[2] ['seno] SM (*Mat*) sine

Senofonte [seno'fonte] SM Xenophon

sensale [sen'sale] SM (*Comm*) agent

sensatamente [sensata'mente] AVV sensibly

sensatezza [sensa'tettsa] SF good sense, good judgment

sensato, a [sen'sato] AGG sensible

sensazionale [sensattsjo'nale] AGG sensational, exciting

sensazione [sensat'tsjone] SF feeling, sensation; **ho la sensazione di averlo già incontrato** I have a feeling I've met him before; **fare sensazione** (*interesse, stupore*) to cause a sensation, create a stir; **essere a caccia di nuove sensazioni** to be after new thrills *o* experiences

sensibile [sen'sibile] AGG **1** (*gen*) sensitive; (*obiettivo, Mil*) high-risk; *vedi anche* **dato è un ragazzo sensibile** he's a sensitive boy; **ha un animo sensibile** he's tender-hearted; **essere sensibile a** (*freddo, caldo*) to be sensitive to; (*complimenti, adulazioni, fascino*) to be susceptible to **2** (*notevole: progresso, differenze*) appreciable, noticeable; **c'è stato un sensibile aumento della temperatura** there's been a considerable rise in the temperature **3** (*Fot: pellicola*) sensitive

LO SAPEVI...?

sensibile non si traduce mai con la parola inglese *sensible*

sensibilità [sensibili'ta] SF sensitivity, sensitiveness

sensibilizzare [sensibilid'dzare] VT (*fig*) to make aware, awaken; **sensibilizzare l'opinione pubblica su qc** to raise public awareness of sth

sensibilmente [sensibil'mente] AVV (*notevolmente*) appreciably

sensitività [sensitivi'ta] SF (*Med*) sensitivitity

sensitivo, a [sensi'tivo] AGG **1** (*Anat*) sensory, sensorial; **percezioni sensitive** sensory perception *sg* **2** (*persona*) sensitive, susceptible ■SM/F sensitive person; (*medium*) medium

senso ['sɛnso] SM **1** (*istinto, coscienza*) sense; **i 5 sensi** the 5 senses; **perdere/riprendere i sensi** to lose/regain consciousness; **senso d'orientamento** sense of direction; **avere senso pratico** to be practical; **ha**

Ss

molto senso pratico she's very practical; **senso del dovere/dell'umorismo** sense of duty/humour; **avere un sesto senso** to have a sixth sense; **i piaceri dei sensi** (*della sensualità*) sensual pleasures, the pleasures of the senses **2** (*sensazione*) feeling, sense, sensation; **un senso di angoscia** a feeling *o* sense of anxiety; **provare un senso di inquietudine** to feel anxious; **fare senso (a qn)** (*ribrezzo*) to disgust (sb), repel (sb); **mi fa senso** it disgusts me; **senso di colpa** sense of guilt **3** (*significato*) meaning, sense; **nel senso letterale/figurato** in the literal/figurative sense; **senza** *o* **privo di senso** meaningless; **un discorso senza senso** a meaningless speech; **in un certo senso ha ragione lui** in a way *o* sense he's right; **nel senso che...** in the sense that ...; **avere senso** to make sense; **che senso ha?** where's the sense in that?; **(per me) non ha senso** it doesn't make (any) sense (to me); **nel vero senso della parola** in the true sense of the word **4** (*direzione*) direction; **in senso opposto** in the opposite direction; **nel senso della lunghezza** lengthwise, lengthways; **nel senso della larghezza** widthwise; **io venivo in senso contrario** I was coming from the opposite direction; **in senso orario** clockwise; **in senso antiorario** anticlockwise (*Brit*), counterclockwise (*Am*); **ho dato disposizioni in quel senso** I've given instructions to that end *o* effect **5** (*Aut*): **a senso unico** (*strada*) one-way; **una via a senso unico** a one-way street; **"senso vietato"** "no entry" **6** (*Dir*): **ai sensi di legge** in compliance with the law

sensoriale [senso'rjale] AGG sensory *attr*

sensuale [sensu'ale] AGG (*persona, sguardo*) sensual; (*voce*) sensuous

sensualità [sensuali'ta] SF (*vedi agg*) sensuality; sensuousness

sensualmente [sensual'mente] AVV sensually

sentenza [sen'tɛntsa] SF **1** (*Dir*) sentence; **pronunciare una sentenza di morte contro qn** to sentence sb to death **2** (*massima*) maxim; **sputar sentenze** (*fig*) to moralize

sentenziare [senten'tsjare] (*Dir*) VT: **sentenziare che...** to rule that ...; **sentenziare la pena di morte** to pass the death sentence
■ VI (*aus* **avere**) to pass judgment

sentenzioso, a [senten'tsjoso] AGG sententious

sentiero [sen'tjɛro] SM path

sentimentale [sentimen'tale] AGG (*gen*) sentimental; (*pegg*) soppy; **vita sentimentale** love life
■ SM/F sentimentalist

sentimentalmente [sentimental'mente] AVV (*vedi agg*) sentimentally; soppily

sentimento [senti'mento] SM (*gen*) feeling; **aveva sempre nascosto i suoi sentimenti per lei** he had always hidden his feelings for her; **una persona di nobili sentimenti** a person of noble sentiments; **urtare i sentimenti di qn** to hurt sb's feelings

sentina [sen'tina] SF (*Naut*) bilge

sentinella [senti'nɛlla] SF (*Mil*) sentry, guard; **essere di sentinella** to be on guard *o* sentry duty

sentire [sen'tire] VT
1 (*percepire: gen, al tatto*) to feel; **sentire freddo/caldo** to feel cold/hot; **sentire dolore** to feel pain; **sento un gran male qui** I've got a terrible pain here; **senti quanto pesa** feel how heavy it is; **non sento niente** I can't feel a thing; **il caldo si fa sentire** the heat is oppressive; **la sua assenza si fa sentire** his absence is noticeable
2 (*emozione*) to feel; **sentire un profondo affetto per qn** to feel deep affection for sb; **non sento niente per lui** I don't feel anything for him; **sentire la mancanza di qn** to miss sb; **sento che succederà qualcosa** I've got a feeling that something is going to happen; **sento che mente** I can sense that he is lying; **sento che mi vuole lasciare** I can sense that he wants to leave me; **dice sempre quello che sente** he always says what he feels
3 (*al gusto*) to taste; (*all'olfatto*) to smell; **senti se ti piace questa salsa** taste this sauce to see if you like it; **senti se ti piace questo profumo** smell this perfume to see if you like it; **sento odore di pesce** I can smell fish; **ho il raffreddore e non sento gli odori/i sapori** I've got a cold and I can't smell/taste anything
4 (*udire*) to hear; (*ascoltare*) to listen to; **mi sentite?** can you hear me?; **sento dei passi** I can hear footsteps; **mi piace sentire la musica** I like listening to music; **stare a sentire** to listen; **hai sentito l'ultima?** have you heard the latest?; **senti, mi presti quel disco?** listen, will you lend me that record?; **ho sentito dire che...** I have heard that ...; **stammi a sentire!** listen to me!; **stammi bene a sentire!** just you listen to me!; **a sentir lui...** to hear him talk ...; **farsi sentire** to make o.s. heard; **fatti sentire** keep in touch; **non ci sente** (*sordo*) he's deaf, he can't hear; **non ci sente da quell'orecchio** (*fig*) he always turns a deaf ear to things like that; **senti quello che ti dice l'avvocato** go and ask your lawyer for advice; **intendo sentire il mio legale/il parere di un medico** I'm going to consult my lawyer/a doctor; **senti cosa vuole** see what he wants; **ma senti un po'!** just fancy that!; **senti questa!** just listen to this!; **si sente che è straniero** you can tell he's a foreigner; **per sentito dire** by hearsay
▶ **sentirsi** VR
1 (*gen*) to feel; **sentirsi bene/male** to feel well/unwell *o* ill; **come ti senti?** how are you?, how do you feel?; **sentirsi svenire** to feel faint
2 (*essere disposto*): **sentirsi di fare qc** to feel like doing sth; **non me la sento** I don't feel like it; **proprio non se la sente di continuare** he doesn't feel like carrying on
3 (*uso reciproco*) to hear from each other, be in touch; **ci sentiamo spesso** (*al telefono*) we often talk on the phone; **si sono sentiti di recente** they were in touch (with each other) recently

sentitamente [sentita'mente] AVV sincerely; **ringraziare sentitamente** to thank sincerely

sentito, a [sen'tito] AGG (*ringraziamenti, condoglianze*) sincere, deep; **le mie più sentite scuse** my most sincere apologies

sentore [sen'tore] SM talk, rumour (*Brit*), rumor (*Am*); **aver sentore di qc** to hear about sth

senza ['sɛntsa] PREP without; **uscì senza ombrello** he went out without an *o* his umbrella; **non so cosa farei senza il suo aiuto** I don't know what I'd do without his help; **non senza alcune riserve** not without some reservations; **senza di te** without you; **non posso stare senza di te** I can't live without you; **siamo rimasti senza zucchero/tè** we've run out of sugar/tea, we have no sugar/tea left; **forza, senza tante chiacchiere** come on, stop the talking and let's get on with it; **senza casa** homeless; **senza padre** fatherless; **senza amici** friendless; **senza preoccupazioni** carefree; **senza scrupoli** unscrupulous; **senza impegno** without obligation; **un dettato senza errori** an error-free dictation; **un discorso senza**

senso a meaningless speech; **i senza lavoro** the jobless, the unemployed; **senz'altro** of course, certainly; **mi scriverai? – senz'altro!** will you write to me? – of course!; **lo farò senz'altro domani** I'll do it tomorrow without fail; **senza dubbio** no doubt
■ CONG without; **senza batter ciglio** without batting an eyelid; **ho trascorso tutta la notte senza chiudere occhio** I didn't sleep a wink all night, I didn't get a wink of sleep all night; **senza dire niente** without saying a thing; **è andato via senza dire niente** he left without saying anything; **parlò senza riflettere** he spoke without thinking; **senza che tu lo sapessi** without your knowing about it; **senza dire che...** not to mention (the fact) that ...; **senza contare che...** without considering that ...

senzatetto [sentsa'tetto] SM/F INV homeless person; **i senzatetto** the homeless
■ AGG INV homeless

sepalo ['sɛpalo] SM (*Bot*) sepal

separare [sepa'rare] VT (*gen*) to separate; (*litiganti*) to pull apart, part; (*aspetti, problemi*) to distinguish between; **le Alpi separano la Svizzera dall'Italia** the Alps divide *o* separate Italy from Switzerland; **separare il bene dal male** to distinguish between good and evil; **solo pochi chilometri lo separavano da casa** only a few kilometres separated him from home *o* stood between him and home
▶ **separarsi** VR **1** (*lasciare*): **separarsi da** (*persona*) to leave; (*oggetto*) to part with; **gli dispiaceva separarsi dai propri cari/da quegli oggetti cari** he didn't want to leave his loved ones/to part with those dear objects; **si è separata dal marito** she has left her husband **2** (*staccarsi*): **separarsi da** to split off from, separate off from **3** (*uso reciproco*: *gen*) to part; (: *coniugi, soci*) to part, split up, separate; **dopo 2 ore di cammino si separarono** after 2 hours' walk they parted (company); **i miei genitori si sono separati quando ero piccolo** my parents split up when I was little

separatamente [separata'mente] AVV separately

separatismo [separa'tizmo] SM separatism

separatista, i, e [separa'tista] AGG, SM/F separatist

separato, a [sepa'rato] AGG (*gen*) separate; **abbiamo chiesto conti separati** we asked for separate bills; **i miei genitori sono separati** my parents are separated; **vivono separati** (*coniugi*) they have separated; **in separata sede** (*privatamente*) in private

separazione [separat'tsjone] SF (*gen, Dir*) separation; **dopo la separazione** (*di coniugi*) after they parted; **separazione dei beni** (*Dir*) division of property

séparé [sepa're] SM INV screen

sepolcrale [sepol'krale] AGG sepulchral

sepolcro [se'polkro] SM sepulchre (*Brit*), sepulcher (*Am*); **il Santo Sepolcro** the Holy Sepulchre *o* Sepulcher

sepolto, a [se'polto] PP *di* **seppellire**
■ AGG (*gen, fig*) buried; **morto e sepolto** (*anche fig*) dead and buried; **sepolto nel profondo del cuore** buried deep in one's heart

sepoltura [sepol'tura] SF burial; **dare sepoltura a qn** to bury sb

seppellimento [seppelli'mento] SM burial

seppellire [seppel'lire] VB IRREG
■ VT (*gen*) to bury; (*fig*: *passato, ricordi*) to bury, forget; **il villaggio era sepolto dalla neve** the village was buried under the snow; **seppellire antichi rancori** to bury the hatchet, let bygones be bygones;
▶ **seppellirsi** VR (*fig*: *isolarsi*) to shut o.s. off, cut o.s. off; **seppellirsi tra i libri** to bury o.s. in one's books

seppi *ecc* ['sɛppi] VB *vedi* **sapere**

seppia ['seppja] SF (*Zool*) cuttlefish; **nero di seppia** sepia

seppure [sep'pure] CONG even if

sequela [se'kwela] SF (*di avvenimenti*) series *inv*, sequence; (*di offese, ingiurie*) string

sequenza [se'kwɛntsa] SF sequence

sequenziale [sekwen'tsjale] AGG sequential

sequestrare [sekwes'trare] VT **1** (*gen*) to confiscate; (*Dir, beni*) to sequestrate; (*film, libri*) to impound **2** (*rapire*) to kidnap

sequestro [se'kwɛstro] SM **1** (*gen*) confiscation, seizure; (*Dir*) sequestration, impounding **2** (*anche*: **sequestro di persona**) kidnapping

sequoia [se'kwɔja] SF sequoia; **sequoia gigante** giant sequoia; **sequoia sempreverde** redwood

sera ['sera] SF evening; **si fa sera** it's getting dark, night is falling; **di sera** in the evening; **alle 6 di sera** at 6 o'clock in the evening, at 6 p.m.; **alle 11 di sera** at 11 o'clock at night, at 11 p.m.; **domani sera** tomorrow evening; **questa sera** this evening, tonight; **dalla mattina alla sera** from morning to night

seracco [se'rakko] SM (*Alpinismo*) sérac

serafico, a, ci, che [se'rafiko] AGG seraphic

serafino [sera'fino] SM seraph

serale [se'rale] AGG evening *attr*; **scuola serale** evening classes *pl*, night school

serata [se'rata] SF **1** (*sera*) evening; **grazie per la bella serata** thanks for the lovely evening **2** (*ricevimento*) soirée, party; **serata danzante** dance **3** (*Teatro*) evening performance; **serata di gala/d'addio** gala/farewell performance

serbare [ser'bare] VT (*tenere*) to keep; (*mettere da parte*) to put aside, keep; **serbare rancore a qn** to bear *o* harbour a grudge against sb

serbatoio, oi [serba'tojo] SM (*gen*) tank; (*cisterna*) cistern; **serbatoio (della benzina)** (*Aut*) (petrol) (*Brit*) *o* (gas) (*Am*) tank

serbo[1] ['sɛrbo] SM: **in serbo** (*sorpresa*) in store; **te lo tengo in serbo** I'll put it aside for you

serbo[2], **a** ['sɛrbo] AGG Serbian
■ SM/F Serbian, Serb *attr*
■ SM (*lingua*) Serbian

serbocroato, a [serbokro'ato] AGG, SM/F Serbo-Croat

serenamente [serena'mente] AVV (*guardare*) serenely, calmly; (*giudicare*) dispassionately; (*vivere*) quietly

serenata [sere'nata] SF serenade; **fare la serenata a qn** to serenade sb, sing sb a serenade, sing a serenade to sb

serenità [sereni'ta] SF peace, tranquillity, serenity; **serenità d'animo** peace of mind

sereno, a [se'reno] AGG (*tempo, cielo*) clear, serene; (*volto, persona*) calm, serene; (*giudizio*) dispassionate; (*vita*) quiet; **un fulmine a ciel sereno** (*fig*) a bolt from the blue
■ SM (*tempo*) good weather

serg. ABBR (= **sergente**) Sgt.

sergente [ser'dʒɛnte] SM (*Mil*) sergeant; **sergente maggiore** sergeant major

seriale [se'rjale] AGG (*Inform*) serial

seriamente [serja'mente] AVV (*gen*) **1** (*con serietà*) seriously, earnestly; **sto parlando seriamente!** I'm serious!; **lavorare seriamente** to take one's job seriously **2** (*gravemente*) seriously, gravely; **è seriamente malato** he's seriously ill

sericoltura [serikol'tura] SF sericulture

serie ['sɛrje] SF INV **1** (*gen*) series *inv*; (*di numeri*) series, sequence; (*di chiavi*) set; **tutta una serie di problemi** a whole string *o* series of problems; **una serie di furti** a series of robberies **2** (*Sport*) division; **serie A/B** ≈ first/second division; (*Calcio*) ≈ Premier League (*England*), ≈ Premier Division (*Scotland*); (*fig*) first/second class **3** (*Comm*): **produzione in serie** mass production; **produrre in serie** to mass-produce; **modello di serie/fuori serie** (*Aut*) standard/custom-built model

serietà [serje'ta] SF (*vedi agg*) seriousness; earnestness; reliability

serigrafia [serigra'fia] SF (*metodo*) serigraphy; (*stampa*) serigraph

serio, ria, ri, rie ['sɛrjo] AGG (*gen*) serious; (*persona, conversazione*) serious, earnest; (*persona, ditta: affidabile*) reliable, responsible, dependable; **è una ditta seria** it's a reliable firm; **è una faccenda seria** it's a serious matter; **restare serio** to keep a straight face; **sii serio!** be serious!; **aveva una faccia seria** he looked serious; **è una ragazza seria** (*per bene*) she's a respectable girl ■ SM: **sul serio** seriously, in earnest; **sul serio ti ha invitato?** did he really invite you?; **sul serio vuoi andarci?** do you really want to go?; **non facevo sul serio** *or* **non dicevo sul serio** I wasn't being serious; **faccio sul serio** I mean it; **prendere qn/qc sul serio** to take sb/sth seriously; **prende lo studio molto sul serio** he takes his schoolwork very seriously

serioso, a [se'rjoso] AGG (*persona, modi*): **un po' serioso** a bit too serious

sermone [ser'mone] SM (*Rel*) sermon; (*fig*) lecture, sermon; **fare un sermone a qn** (*fig*) to give sb a lecture *o* sermon

serotonina [seroto'nina] SF serotonin

serpe ['sɛrpe] SF snake; (*fig pegg*) viper; **scaldare** *o* **allevare una serpe in seno** to nurse a viper in one's bosom

serpeggiante [serped'dʒante] AGG winding, twisting

serpeggiare [serped'dʒare] VI (*aus* **avere**) (*strada, fiume*) to wind, snake, twist; (*fig: malcontento, rivolta*) to spread (insidiously)

serpente [ser'pɛnte] SM **1** (*Zool*) snake, serpent; **serpente a sonagli** rattlesnake **2** (*pelle*) snakeskin **3** (*Fin*): **il serpente monetario** the (currency) snake

serpentina [serpen'tina] SF **1** **a serpentina** (*strada*) winding **2** (*Equitazione*) serpentine **3** (*Sci*) welden; **fare la serpentina** to welden

serra[1] ['sɛrra] SF (*Agr*) greenhouse; (: *riscaldata*) hothouse; **l'effetto serra** the greenhouse effect

serra[2] ['sɛrra] SF (*Geog*) sierra

serraglio, gli [ser'raʎʎo] SM **1** (*di animali*) menagerie **2** (*di sultano*) harem

serramanico [serra'maniko] SM: **coltello a serramanico** flick-knife, clasp knife

serranda [ser'randa] SF (rolling *o* roller) shutter

serrare [ser'rare] VT (*chiudere*) to close, shut; (*stringere*) to shut tightly; **serrare i pugni/i denti** to clench one's fists/teeth; **serrare le file** (*anche fig*) to close ranks; **serrare il nemico** to close in on the enemy

serrata [ser'rata] SF (*Industria*) lockout

serrato, a [ser'rato] AGG **1** (*porta, finestra*) closed, shut; (*pugni, denti*) clenched; (*occhi*) tightly closed **2** (*stringato*) logical, coherent **3** (*veloce*): **a ritmo serrato** quickly, fast

> **LO SAPEVI...?**
> **serrato** non si traduce mai con la parola inglese *serrated*

serratura [serra'tura] SF lock

Serse ['sɛrse] SM Xerxes

SERT [sert] SIGLA M (= **Servizio Tossicodipendenze**) *public body that helps drug addicts*

serva ['sɛrva] SF *vedi* **servo**

servalo [ser'valo] SM (*animale*) serval

server ['sɛrver] SM INV (*Inform*) server

servigio, gi [ser'vidʒo] SM favour (*Brit*), favor (*Am*), service

servile [ser'vile] AGG **1** (*gen, fig*) servile **2** (*Gramm: verbo*) modal

servilismo [servi'lizmo] SM servility

servilmente [servil'mente] AVV servilely

servire [ser'vire] VT **1** (*essere al servizio di*) to serve; **servire qn** (*in negozio*) to attend to *o* serve sb; (*al ristorante*) to wait on *o* serve sb; **gli piace farsi servire** he likes to be waited on; **in cosa posso servirla?** (*negozio*) can I help you?; **adesso ti servo io!** (*iro*) now I'll show you!; **servire la Messa/la Patria** to serve Mass/one's country **2** (*piatto*) to serve; **servire qc a qn** to serve sb with sth, help sb to sth; **"servire ghiacciato"** "serve chilled"; **servire a tavola** to wait on table; **servire da bere a qn** to serve a drink to sb; **il pranzo è servito** dinner is served; **dopo la cena ha servito il caffè** after dinner she served coffee **3** (*Carte*) to deal **4** (*Calcio: giocatore*) to pass the ball to ■ VI **1** (*aus* **essere**) **servire a (fare) qc** (*essere utile*) to be used for (doing) sth, be for sth; **servire a qn** to be of use to sb; **a che cosa serve?** what's it for?; **a cosa serve questo aggeggio?** what is this gadget (used) for?; **serve a tagliare la frutta** it's for cutting fruit; **questa stanza serve da studio** this room is used as a study; **che ti serva da lezione** let that be a lesson to you; **ha insistito ma non è servito (a niente)** he insisted but to no purpose; **mi serve un paio di forbici** I need a pair of scissors; **non mi serve più** I don't need it any more; **te lo presto, se ti serve** I'll lend it to you, if you need it; **non serve a niente** it's not of any use; **piangere non serve a niente** it's no use crying, crying doesn't help; **a che serve lamentarsi?** what would be the point of complaining? **2** (*Tennis*) to serve ▶ **servirsi** VIP **1** (*fare uso*) **servirsi di** to make use of, use **2** (*a tavola*) to help o.s.; **serviti pure!** help yourself! **3** **servirsi da** (*negoziante*) to shop at, be a regular customer at, go to

servitore, trice [servi'tore] SM/F servant

servitù [servi'tu] SF INV **1** (*condizione*) slavery, bondage, servitude; **servitù della gleba** (*Storia*) serfdom **2** (*domestici*) servants *pl*, domestic staff *sg o pl* **3** (*Dir*): **servitù di passaggio** right of way

servizievole [servit'tsjevole] AGG obliging, helpful, willing to help

servizio, zi [ser'vittsjo] SM
1 (*lavoro*) duty; **essere di** *o* **in servizio** to be on duty; **non bevo in servizio** I don't drink on duty; **prendere servizio** to come on duty; **avere 20 anni di servizio** to have done *o* completed 20 years' service
2 (*come domestico*) (domestic) service; **andare/essere a servizio** to go into/be in service; **entrata di servizio** service *o* tradesman's (*Brit*) entrance
3 **servizio civile** community service (*chosen instead of military service, especially by conscientious objectors*); **il servizio militare** military service; **prestare servizio militare** to do one's military *o* national service; **servizio d'ordine** (*Polizia*) police patrol; (*di manifestanti*) team of stewards (*for crowd control*); **servizio segreto** secret service; **servizi di sicurezza** security forces

4 (*istituzioni pubbliche*) service; **servizio postale/telefonico** postal/telephone service; **servizio sanitario nazionale** ≈ National Health Service (*Brit*), ≈ Medicaid/Medicare (*Am*)
5 (*funzionamento*) service; **fuori servizio** out of order; **rimettere in servizio** to put *o* bring back into service
6 (*favore*) service, favour (*Brit*), favor (*Am*); (*prestazioni*): **servizi** services; **offrire i propri servizi a qn** to offer sb one's services, offer one's services to sb; **bel servizio mi hai fatto!** (*iro*) you've been a real help!; **sono al suo servizio** I am at your service
7 (*al ristorante*) service; (*sul conto*) service (charge); **servizio a bordo** (*Aer*) in-flight service; **servizio compreso/escluso** service included/not included; **il servizio è compreso?** is service included?
8 (*TV, Radio, Stampa*) report; **un servizio sul terremoto in Afghanistan** a report on the earthquake in Afghanistan; **servizio in diretta** live coverage; **servizio fotografico** (*Stampa*) photo feature
9 (*Rel*) service
10 (*Tennis*) service; **ha un servizio potentissimo** she has a very powerful serve; **al servizio Sampras** Sampras to serve; **servizio vincente** ace
11 (*insieme di oggetti*): **servizio all'americana** tablemat and napkin set; **servizio da tè** tea set; **servizio di cristallo** set of crystal glassware; **servizio di posate** set of cutlery
12 **i servizi** SMPL (*di casa*) kitchen and bathroom; **casa con doppi servizi** house with two bathrooms
13 (*Econ*): **servizi** SMPL services

servo, a ['sɛrvo] SM/F servant, manservant/maidservant
servoassistito, a [servoassis'tito] AGG: **freno servoassistito** servo brake; **sterzo servoassistito** power steering
servofreno [servo'freno] SM (*Aut*) servo brake
servomeccanismo [servomekka'nizmo] SM servomechanism
servomotore [servomo'tore] SM servomotor
servosterzo [servos'tertso] SM (*Aut*) power steering
sesamo ['sɛzamo] SM (*Bot*) sesame; **apriti sesamo!** open sesame!
sessanta [ses'santa] AGG INV, SM INV sixty; *per fraseologia vedi* **cinquanta**
sessantenne [sessan'tɛnne] AGG, SM/F sixty-year-old; *per fraseologia vedi* **cinquantenne**
sessantesimo, a [sessan'tɛzimo] AGG, SM/F, SM sixtieth; *per fraseologia vedi* **quinto**
sessantina [sessan'tina] SF: **una sessantina (di)** about sixty; *per fraseologia vedi* **cinquantina**
sessantottino, a [sessantot'tino] SM/F (*fam*) *a person who took part in the events of 1968 (sessantotto)*
sessantotto SM [sessan'tɔtto] (*fam*): **il sessantotto** *student protest movement of 1968*

SESSANTOTTO

Sessantotto refers to 1968, the year of student protests. Originating in France, unrest soon spread to other industrialized countries including Italy. What began as a purely student concern gradually came to include other parts of society and led to major political and social change. Among the changes that resulted from the protests were reform of schools and universities and the referendum on divorce.

sessile ['sɛssile] AGG (*Bot, Bio*) sessile
sessione [ses'sjone] SF session
sesso ['sɛsso] SM sex; **il sesso debole/forte** the weaker/stronger sex; **fare sesso** to have sex; **sesso sicuro** safe sex
sessuale [sessu'ale] AGG (*gen*) sexual; (*vita, organo, educazione*) sex *attr*, sexual
sessualità [sessuali'ta] SF sexuality
sessualmente [sessual'mente] AVV sexually
sessuologia [sessuolo'dʒia] SF sexology
sessuologo, a, gi, ghe [sessu'ɔlogo] SM/F sexologist, sex specialist
sestante [ses'tante] SM (*Naut*) sextant
sestetto [ses'tetto] SM (*Mus*) sextet(te)
sestina [ses'tina] SF (*Poesia: di sonetto*) sestet; (: *di canzone*) sestina, sextain
sesto[1], a ['sɛsto] AGG, SM/F, SM (*numerale*) sixth; **sesta malattia** sixth disease; **sesto senso** sixth sense; *vedi anche* **quinto**
sesto[2] ['sɛsto] SM (*Archit*): **arco a sesto acuto** pointed arch; **arco a tutto sesto** rounded arch
sesto[3] ['sɛsto] SM: **rimettere in sesto** (*aggiustare*) to put back in order; (*fig: persona*) to put back on his (*o* her) feet; **rimettersi in sesto** (*riprendersi*) to recover, get well; (*riassettarsi*) to tidy o.s. up
sestultimo, a [ses'tultimo] AGG, SM/F last but five, sixth from last
set [set] SM INV set
seta ['seta] SF silk; **una camicia di seta** a silk shirt
setacciare [setat'tʃare] VT (*farina*) to sift, sieve; (*fig: zona*) to search, comb
setaccio, ci [se'tattʃo] SM sieve; **passare al setaccio** (*fig*) to search, comb
sete ['sete] SF (*anche fig*) thirst; **avere sete** to be thirsty; **soffrire la sete** to suffer from thirst; **morire di sete** to die of thirst; **muoio di sete** I'm dying of thirst; **sete di potere** thirst for power
setificato, a [setifi'kato] AGG (*collant, calza*) shiny
setificio, ci [seti'fitʃo] SM silk factory
setola ['setola] SF bristle
setoloso, a [seto'loso] AGG bristly
setta ['sɛtta] SF (*Rel*) sect
settanta [set'tanta] AGG INV, SM INV seventy; *per fraseologia vedi* **cinquanta**
settantenne [settan'tɛnne] AGG, SM/F seventy-year-old; *per fraseologia vedi* **cinquantenne**
settantesimo, a [settan'tɛzimo] AGG, SM/F, SM seventieth; *per fraseologia vedi* **quinto**
settantina [settan'tina] SF: **una settantina (di)** about seventy; *per fraseologia vedi* **cinquantina**
settare [set'tare] VT to set
settario, ria, ri, rie [set'tarjo] AGG, SM sectarian
settarismo [setta'rizmo] SM sectarianism
sette ['sɛtte] AGG INV, SM INV seven; *per fraseologia vedi* **cinque**
settecentesco, a, schi, sche [settetʃen'tesko] AGG eighteenth-century
settecento [sette'tʃɛnto] AGG INV seven hundred
■ SM INV seven hundred; **il Settecento** (*secolo*) the eighteenth century
settembre [set'tɛmbre] SM September; *per fraseologia vedi* **luglio**
settentrionale [settentrjo'nale] AGG northern; **Italia settentrionale** Northern Italy; **vento settentrionale** north *o* northerly wind
■ SM/F northerner, person from the north
settentrione [setten'trjone] SM north; **del**

Ss

settentrione north(ern), of the north; (*vento*) north(erly)
setter ['sɛtter] SM INV (*cane*) setter
setticemia [settitʃe'mia] SF blood poisoning, septicaemia (*Brit*), septicemia (*Am*)
settico, a, ci, che ['sɛttiko] AGG septic
settimana [setti'mana] SF **1** week; **una volta/due volte alla settimana** once/twice a week; **questa settimana** this week; **la settimana scorsa/prossima** last/next week; **a metà settimana** in the middle of the week; **2 settimane fa** 2 weeks ago; **fra 2 settimane** in 2 weeks' time, in 2 weeks; **prendere 3 settimane di ferie** to take 3 weeks' holiday; **settimana dopo settimana** week after week, week in, week out; **una settimana sì, una no** every other week; **settimana lavorativa** working week; **settimana bianca** winter-sports holiday; **settimana santa** Holy Week **2** (*paga*) week's pay, wages *pl*; (*per bambini*) pocket money (*Brit*), allowance (*Am*)
settimanale [settima'nale] AGG weekly
■SM (*rivista*) weekly (publication)
settimino, a [setti'mino] SM/F (*neonato*) *baby born two months premature*
settimo, a ['sɛttimo] AGG, SM/F, SM seventh; **essere al settimo cielo** (*fig*) to be in seventh heaven; *per fraseologia vedi* **quinto**
setto ['sɛtto] SM (*Anat*) septum
settore [set'tore] SM (*Econ, Geom, Mil*) sector; (*fig*) area; **settore primario/secondario/terziario** primary/secondary/tertiary sector; **settore privato/pubblico** private/public sector
settoriale [setto'rjale] AGG sector-based
Seul [se'ul] SF Seoul
severamente [severa'mente] AVV (*vedi agg*) severely; strictly
severità [severi'ta] SF (*vedi agg*) severity; strictness
severo, a [se'vɛro] AGG (*gen*) severe; (*padre, insegnante, giudice*) strict
seviziare [sevit'tsjare] VT (*torturare*) to torture; (*picchiare*) to beat up
sevizie [se'vittsje] SFPL torture *sg*
sexy ['seksi] AGG INV sexy
sez. ABBR = **sezione**
sezionare [settsjo'nare] VT (*gen*) to divide up, cut up, divide into sections; (*Med*) to dissect
sezione [set'tsjone] SF (*gen, Geom, Archit, Tecn*) section; (*di ufficio*) department; (*a scuola*) ≈ class (*Med*) dissection
sfaccendato, a [sfattʃen'dato] AGG lazy, idle
■SM/F idler, loafer
sfaccettare [sfattʃet'tare] VT (*pietre preziose*) to cut, facet
sfaccettatura [sfattʃetta'tura] SF (*azione*) faceting; (*parte sfaccettata, fig*) facet
sfacchinare [sfakki'nare] VI (*aus* **avere**) (*fam*) to toil, drudge
sfacchinata [sfakki'nata] SF (*fam*) toil *no pl*, chore, drudgery *no pl*; **è stata una bella sfacchinata!** it was really exhausting!
sfacciataggine [sfattʃa'taddʒine] SF insolence, cheek; **ma che sfacciataggine!** what a cheek *o* nerve!; **avere la sfacciataggine di fare qc** to have the nerve *o* cheek to do sth
sfacciatamente [sfattʃata'mente] AVV insolently, cheekily
sfacciato, a [sfat'tʃato] AGG insolent, cheeky, impudent; **è la ragazza più sfacciata della classe** she's the cheekiest girl in the class
sfacelo [sfa'tʃɛlo] SM (*fig: di famiglia, organizzazione*) break-up; **andare in sfacelo** (*costruzione*) to fall to pieces; (*piani*) to be ruined
sfaldarsi [sfal'darsi] VIP (*rocce*) to exfoliate
sfalsare [sfal'sare] VT to stagger
sfamare [sfa'mare] VT (*nutrire*) to feed; (*soddisfare la fame*): **sfamare qn** to satisfy sb's hunger
▶ **sfamarsi** VR to satisfy one's hunger, fill o.s. up
sfare ['sfare] VB IRREG
■VT = **disfare**
▶ **sfarsi** VIP (*neve*) to melt
sfarfallare [sfarfal'lare] VI (*aus* **avere**) **1** (*fig: persona*) to flutter about **2** (*Cine, TV*) to flicker
sfarfallio, lii [sfarfal'lio] SM (*Cine, TV*) flickering
sfarzo ['sfartso] SM pomp, splendour (*Brit*), splendor (*Am*), magnificence
sfarzosamente [sfartsosa'mente] AVV splendidly, magnificently
sfarzoso, a [sfar'tsoso] AGG splendid, magnificent
sfasamento [sfaza'mento] SM (*Elettr*) phase displacement; (*fig*) confusion, bewilderment
sfasato, a [sfa'zato] AGG (*Elettr, motore*) out of phase; (*fig: persona*) confused, bewildered
sfasciare[1] [sfaʃ'ʃare] VT (*togliere una fascia*) to unbandage
sfasciare[2] [sfaʃ'ʃare] VT (*macchina*) to smash, wreck; (*vaso*) to smash, shatter; (*letto, sedia*) to wreck, break
▶ **sfasciarsi** VIP (*macchina*) to be smashed, be wrecked; (*vaso*) to shatter, smash; (*letto, sedia*) to fall to pieces
sfatare [sfa'tare] VT (*leggenda, mito*) to explode
sfaticato, a [sfati'kato] AGG lazy, idle
■SM/F idler, loafer
sfatto, a ['sfatto] PP *di* **sfare**
■AGG (*letto*) unmade; (*orlo*) undone; (*gelato, neve*) melted; (*frutta*) overripe; (*riso, pasta*) overdone, overcooked; (*fam: persona, corpo*) flabby
sfavillante [sfavil'lante] AGG (*vedi vb*) sparkling; flickering
sfavillare [sfavil'lare] VI (*aus* **avere**) (*diamante, occhi*) to sparkle; (*fiamma*) to flicker, spark, send out sparks
sfavillio, lii [sfavil'lio] SM (*vedi vb*) sparkling; flickering
sfavore [sfa'vore] SM disfavour (*Brit*), disfavor (*Am*), disapproval
sfavorevole [sfavo'revole] AGG unfavourable (*Brit*), unfavorable (*Am*)
sfavorevolmente [sfavorevol'mente] AVV unfavourably (*Brit*), unfavorably (*Am*)
sfebbrare [sfeb'brare] VI (*aus* **essere**) **entro qualche giorno sfebbrerà** his temperature will go down in a few days
sfegatato, a [sfega'tato] AGG (*anche pegg*) fanatical
sfera ['sfɛra] SF **1** (*anche fig*) sphere; **sfera di cristallo** crystal ball; **penna a sfera** ballpoint pen; **sfera d'influenza** sphere of influence **2** (*di macchina da scrivere*) golf ball
sferico, a, ci, che ['sfɛriko] AGG spherical
sferragliare [sferraʎ'ʎare] VI (*aus* **avere**) to rattle, clatter
sferrare [sfer'rare] VT (*fig: attacco*) to launch; **sferrare un colpo a qn** to hit out at sb, lash out at sb (with one's fist); **sferrare un calcio a qn** to kick out at sb, lash out at sb (with one's foot)
▶ **sferrarsi** VIP: **sferrarsi contro qn** (*lanciarsi*) to hurl *o* fling o.s. at sb
sferruzzare [sferrut'tsare] VI (*aus* **avere**) to knit away
sferza ['sfɛrtsa] SF whip, lash

sferzante [sfer'tsante] AGG (*critiche, parole*) stinging
sferzare [sfer'tsare] VT (*gen*) to whip; (*sogg: vento*) to lash; (*: onde*) to lash against, break on; (*fig*) to lash out at
sferzata [sfer'tsata] SF (*frustata*) whipping; (*fig*) lashing
sfiancare [sfjan'kare] VT to wear out, exhaust
▶ **sfiancarsi** VIP to exhaust o.s., wear o.s. out
sfiancato, a [sfjan'kato] AGG (*animale*) hollow-flanked; (*fig: persona*) exhausted, worn out
sfiatare [sfja'tare] VI (*aus* **avere**) to allow air *o* gas to escape
sfiatatoio, oi [sfjata'tojo] SM **1** (*Tecn*) vent **2** (*Zool*) blowhole
sfibbiare [sfib'bjare] VT to undo, unbuckle
sfibrante [sfi'brante] AGG exhausting, energy-sapping
sfibrare [sfi'brare] VT (*indebolire*) to exhaust, enervate
sfibrato, a [sfi'brato] AGG exhausted, worn out
sfida ['sfida] SF challenge; **lanciare una sfida a qn** to challenge sb; **uno sguardo di sfida** (*fig*) a defiant look
sfidante [sfi'dante] AGG challenging
■ SM/F challenger
sfidare [sfi'dare] VT **1** (*avversario*) to challenge; **l'ho sfidato a scacchi** I challenged him to a game of chess; **sfidare qn a duello** to challenge sb to a duel; **sfidare qn a fare qc** to challenge sb to do sth **2** (*fig: affrontare*) to defy, brave; **sfidare la morte** to defy death; **sfidare un pericolo** to brave a danger **3** (*fraseologia*): **sfido io!** naturally!, of course!, no wonder!; **non si sente bene – sfido io, è tutto il giorno che mangia patatine** he's not feeling well – no wonder, he's been eating crisps all day
▶ **sfidarsi** VR (*uso reciproco*) to challenge each other
sfiducia [sfi'dutʃa] SF distrust, mistrust; **avere sfiducia in qn/qc** to distrust sb/sth; **voto di sfiducia** (*Pol*) vote of no confidence
sfiduciato, a [sfidu'tʃato] AGG discouraged, disheartened
sfigato, a [sfi'gato] (*fam*) AGG (*sfortunato*) unlucky; **una ragazza sfigata** (*pegg fam*) a dog, a minger
■ SM/F (*fallito, sfortunato*) loser; (*fuori moda ecc*) dork
sfigurare [sfigu'rare] VT (*persona*) to disfigure; (*quadro, statua*) to deface; **ha sfigurato il quadro** he defaced the picture; **l'incidente lo ha sfigurato** the accident left him disfigured
■ VI (*aus* **avere**) to make a bad impression, cut a poor figure; **non vorrei sfigurare** I don't want to make a bad impression
sfilacciare [sfilat'tʃare] VT, VI (*aus* **essere**), **sfilacciarsi** VIP to fray
sfilacciato, a [sfilat'tʃato] AGG (*tessuto*) frayed
sfilare¹ [sfi'lare] VT **1** (*orlo, tessuto*) to pull the threads out of; (*perle*) to unstring; (*ago*) to unthread **2** (*togliere: stivali, scarpe*) to take off, slip off; **gli sfilò il portafoglio** he pinched *o* lifted his wallet; **sfilarsi il vestito/le scarpe** to take one's dress/shoes off; **gli ho sfilato le scarpe** I took his shoes off
▶ **sfilarsi** VIP (*orlo, tessuto*) to fray; (*calza*) to ladder, run; (*perle*) to come unstrung
sfilare² [sfi'lare] VI (*aus* **avere** *o* **essere**) (*truppe*) to parade, march past; (*manifestanti*) to march; (*modelle*) to parade
sfilata [sfi'lata] SF (*Mil*) parade; (*di manifestanti*) march; **sfilata (di moda)** fashion show
sfilettare [sfilet'tare] VT (*Culin*) to fillet
sfilza ['sfiltsa] SF (*di case*) row; (*di errori*) series *inv*
sfinge ['sfindʒe] SF sphinx
sfinimento [sfini'mento] SM exhaustion
sfinire [sfi'nire] VT to exhaust, wear out
▶ **sfinirsi** VIP to wear o.s. out, exhaust o.s.
sfinito, a [sfi'nito] AGG exhausted, worn out
sfintere [sfin'tɛre] SM (*Anat*) sphincter
sfiorare [sfjo'rare] VT (*acqua, cime di alberi*) to skim (over); (*volto, guancia*) to brush (against); **qualcosa mi ha sfiorato la gamba** something brushed against my leg; **il proiettile l'ha solo sfiorato** the bullet only grazed him; **sfiorare un argomento** to touch on *o* upon a subject; **non ha neppure sfiorato l'argomento** he didn't even touch on the subject; **è un'idea che non mi sfiora nemmeno** it's an idea which hasn't even crossed my mind; **non ti ha mai sfiorato il dubbio che possa rifiutare?** has it never occurred to you *o* has it never crossed your mind that he might refuse?; **sfiorare la velocità di 150 km/h** to touch 150 km/h
sfiorire [sfjo'rire] VI (*aus* **essere**) (*fiore, pianta*) to wither, fade; (*fig: bellezza*) to fade
sfiorito, a [sfjo'rito] AGG (*fiore, bellezza*) faded
sfitto, a ['sfitto] AGG vacant, empty
sfizio, zi ['sfittsjo] SM whim, fancy; **togliersi lo sfizio di fare qc** to satisfy one's whim to do sth
sfocare [sfo'kare] VT (*Fot*) to blur
sfocato, a [sfo'kato] AGG (*Fot*) blurred, out of focus; (*fig: ricordo, immagine*) vague, dim
sfociare [sfo'tʃare] VI (*aus* **essere**) (*fiume*): **sfociare in** to flow into; **il malcontento sfociò in una rivolta** (*fig*) the discontent developed into open rebellion
sfoderare [sfode'rare] VT **1** (*spada, pugnale*) to draw, unsheathe; (*pistola*) to draw; (*fig: ostentare: cultura*) to display, parade, show off; **sfoderare un sorriso** to give a smile **2** (*togliere la fodera a*) to remove the lining from
sfoderato, a [sfode'rato] AGG (*vestito*) unlined
sfogare [sfo'gare] VT (*gioia, tristezza*) to give vent to; (*energia*) to work off; **sfogare la propria rabbia su qn** to vent one's anger on sb
■ VI (*aus* **essere**) (*liquido*) to flow out; (*gas*) to escape; (*malattia, febbre*) to run its course
▶ **sfogarsi** VR (*persona*) to give vent to one's feelings; (*: liberarsi di un peso*) to get a load off one's chest; **sfogarsi con qn** (*confidarsi*) to unburden o.s. *o* open one's heart to sb, pour out one's feelings to sb; **pianse e finalmente si sfogò** she had a good cry and finally let it all out; **non sfogarti su di me!** don't take it out on me!
sfoggiare [sfod'dʒare] VT to show off; **voglio sfoggiare il mio vestito nuovo** I want to show off my new dress
sfoggio, gi ['sfɔddʒo] SM show, display; **fare sfoggio di** to show off, display
sfogherò *ecc* [sfoge'rɔ] VB *vedi* **sfogare**
sfoglia ['sfɔʎʎa] SF (*gen*) thin layer; (*Culin*) sheet of pasta dough; **pasta sfoglia** puff pastry
sfogliare¹ [sfoʎ'ʎare] VT (*fiore*) to pluck the petals off
sfogliare² [sfoʎ'ʎare] VT (*libro, rivista*) to leaf through; **stava sfogliando una rivista** she was leafing through a magazine
sfogliata¹ [sfoʎ'ʎata] SF (*scorsa*) glance, look; **dare una sfogliata a** to leaf through
sfogliata² [sfoʎ'ʎata] SF (*Culin*) puff
sfogo, ghi ['sfogo] SM **1** (*di liquido, gas*) outlet; (*di aria*) vent; (*fig: di rabbia*) outburst; **dare sfogo a** (*fig*) to give vent to **2** (*eruzione cutanea*) rash

Ss

sfolgorante [sfolgo'rante] AGG (*luce*) blazing; (*fig*: *vittoria*) brilliant
sfolgorare [sfolgo'rare] VI (*aus* **avere**) to blaze
sfolgorio, rii [sfolgo'rio] SM blaze, glare
sfollagente [sfolla'dʒɛnte] SM INV truncheon (*Brit*), nightstick (*Am*), billy club (*Am*)
sfollamento [sfolla'mento] SM (*vedi vt*) clearing, emptying; evacuation
sfollare [sfol'lare] VT (*piazza, strada*) to clear, empty; (*edificio*) to evacuate, empty
■ VI (*aus* **essere**) (*gente, dimostranti*) to disperse; **sfollare da una città** to evacuate a town
sfollato, a [sfol'lato] AGG evacuated
■ SM/F evacuee
sfoltire [sfol'tire] VT, **sfoltirsi** VIP to thin (out)
sfoltita [sfol'tita] SF thinning; **dare una sfoltita a qc** to thin sth
sfondamento [sfonda'mento] SM (*di porta*) breaking down; (*di parete*) knocking down; (*Mil*) breaking through, breach
sfondare [sfon'dare] VT (*porta*) to break down; (*parete*) to break down, knock down; (*pavimento*) to break through; (*scarpe*) to wear through, wear a hole in; (*sedia, barca*) to knock the bottom out of; (*scatola*) to burst, knock the bottom out of; **ha sfondato la porta** he broke down the door; **sfondare le linee nemiche** (*Mil*) to break through the enemy lines; **sfondare il tetto di** (*fig*) to go beyond the limit of
■ VI (*aus* **avere**) (*fig*: *attore, scrittore*: *avere successo*) to make a name for o.s.; **è difficile sfondare nel cinema** it's difficult to be successful in the film world;
▶ **sfondarsi** VIP (*porta, sedia, pavimento*) to give way; (*parete*) to fall down; (*scarpe*) to wear out; (*scatola*) to burst
sfondato, a [sfon'dato] AGG (*scarpe*) worn out; (*scatola*) burst; (*sedia*) broken, damaged; **essere ricco sfondato** to be rolling in it
sfondo ['sfondo] SM (*gen, Pittura, Fot*) background; (*di film, libro*) background, setting; **sullo sfondo** in the background; **bianco su sfondo rosso** white on a red background
sforare [sfo'rare] VI (*aus* **avere**) (*TV, Radio*) to overrun
sforbiciata [sforbi'tʃata] SF **1** (*taglio*) snip, cut **2** (*Sport*) scissor kick
sformare [sfor'mare] VT **1** to put out of shape, knock out of shape **2** (*dolce, budino*) to turn out
▶ **sformarsi** VIP to lose shape, get out of shape
sformato[1], a [sfor'mato] AGG (*che ha perso forma*) shapeless
sformato[2] [sfor'mato] SM (*Culin*) *type of soufflé*
sfornare [sfor'nare] VT (*Culin*) to take out of the oven; (*fig*: *libri, film*) to churn out
sfornito, a [sfor'nito] AGG: **sfornito di** lacking in, without; (*negozio*) out of
sfortuna [sfor'tuna] SF misfortune, bad *o* ill luck *no pl*; **avere sfortuna** to be unlucky; **ho avuto sfortuna ieri sera, non ho vinto niente** I was unlucky last night, I didn't win anything; **che sfortuna!** what bad luck!; **portare sfortuna** to be unlucky; **passare sotto una scala porta sfortuna** it's unlucky to walk under a ladder; **per sfortuna** unfortunately
sfortunatamente [sfortunata'mente] AVV unfortunately, unluckily
sfortunato, a [sfortu'nato] AGG (*persona, numero*) unlucky; (*impresa, film*) unsuccessful
sforzare [sfor'tsare] VT (*gen*) to force; (*voce, occhi*) to strain; **sforzare qn a fare qc** to force sb to do sth
▶ **sforzarsi** VIP: **sforzarsi (a fare qc)** (*costringersi*) to force o.s. (to do sth); (*fare uno sforzo*) to make an effort (to do sth); **sforzarsi di fare qc** to try to do sth; **sforzati di ricordare!** try to remember!
sforzo ['sfɔrtso] SM (*gen*) effort; (*Tecn*) stress, strain; **fare uno sforzo** to make an effort; **essere sotto sforzo** (*motore, macchina, fig*: *persona*) to be under stress; **che** *o* **bello sforzo!** (*iro*) that didn't take much effort!
sfottere ['sfottere] VT (*fam*) to tease
sfracellare [sfratʃel'lare] VT to smash
▶ **sfracellarsi** VIP to smash; **sfracellarsi al suolo** to crash to the ground
sfrangiato, a [sfran'dʒato] AGG (*tessuto, orlo*) fringed
sfrattare [sfrat'tare] VT to evict
sfrattato, a [sfrat'tato] AGG evicted
■ SM/F evicted person
sfratto ['sfratto] SM eviction; **dare lo sfratto a qn** to give sb notice to quit; **ci hanno dato lo sfratto** we've been given notice to quit
sfrecciare [sfret'tʃare] VI (*aus* **essere**) to shoot *o* flash past
sfregamento [sfrega'mento] SM (*vedi vb*) rubbing; scratching
sfregare [sfre'gare] VT (*strofinare*) to rub; (*graffiare*) to scratch; **sfregare un fiammifero** to strike a match; **sfregarsi le mani** to rub one's hands; **si sfregava gli occhi** he was rubbing his eyes
sfregiare [sfre'dʒare] VT to slash, gash; (*volto*) to disfigure, slash; (*quadro*) to deface, slash
▶ **sfregiarsi** VIP to be disfigured
sfregio, gi ['sfredʒo] SM **1** (*cicatrice*) scar; (*ferita*) gash; (*graffio*) scratch **2** (*fig*: *offesa*) affront, insult
sfrenatamente [sfrenata'mente] AVV unrestrainedly; **vivere sfrenatamente** to lead a dissolute life
sfrenato, a [sfre'nato] AGG (*persona*) wild, uncontrolled; (: *dissoluto*) dissolute; (*passioni*) unbridled, unrestrained; (*bambino*) unruly; **essere sfrenato nel bere/nel mangiare** to drink/eat excessively; **vivere in un lusso sfrenato** to live in unrestrained luxury
sfrigolare [sfrigo'lare] VI (*aus* **avere**) (*olio*) to sizzle; (*legno*) to crackle
sfrondare [sfron'dare] VT (*albero*) to prune, thin out; (*fig*: *discorso, scritto*) to prune (down)
sfrontatamente [sfrontata'mente] AVV impudently, cheekily
sfrontatezza [sfronta'tettsa] SF impudence, cheek; **avere la sfrontatezza di fare qc** to have the cheek to do sth
sfrontato, a [sfron'tato] AGG impudent, cheeky; **è sempre più sfrontato** he's getting cheekier and cheekier
sfruttamento [sfrutta'mento] SM exploitation
sfruttare [sfrut'tare] VT (*terreno*) to overwork, exhaust; (*miniera*) to exploit, work; (*operaio*) to exploit; (*occasione, momento*) to make the most of, take advantage of; **dobbiamo sfruttare lo spazio che abbiamo** we have to make the most of the space we have
sfruttato, a [sfrut'tato] AGG (*persona*) exploited; (*idea*) overworked
sfruttatore, trice [sfrutta'tore] SM/F exploiter
sfuggente [sfud'dʒɛnte] AGG (*fig*: *sguardo*) elusive; (*mento, fronte*) receding
sfuggire [sfud'dʒire] VI (*aus* **essere**) (*gen*) to escape; **sfuggire alla polizia** to escape from the police; **sfuggire alla morte/alla cattura** to escape death/capture; **il sapone mi è sfuggito di mano** the soap slipped out of my hands; **mi sfugge il nome** his name

escapes me; **mi è sfuggito di mente** it slipped my mind; **si è lasciato sfuggire il nome** he let slip the name; **non ti sfugge niente** nothing escapes you, you don't miss a thing; **lasciarsi sfuggire un'occasione** to let an opportunity go by, miss an opportunity; **non lasciarti sfuggire l'occasione** don't miss this opportunity; **sfuggire al controllo** (*macchina*) to go out of control; (*situazione*) to get out of control

sfuggita [sfud'dʒita] SF: **di sfuggita** (*notare, salutare*) in passing; **vedere di sfuggita** to catch a glimpse of

sfumare [sfu'mare] VT (*colore: schiarire*) to soften, shade off; (*suono*) to fade out; (*capelli*) to taper
■ VI (*aus* **essere**) (*colore*): **sfumare in** to fade into, shade off into; (*fig: speranza*) to vanish, disappear, come to nothing

sfumato, a [sfu'mato] AGG (*colore*) soft, mellow

sfumatura [sfuma'tura] SF **1** (*azione: vedi vt*) softening, shading off; fading out; tapering **2** (*di colore*) shade, tone; **diverse sfumature di significato** different shades of meaning, different nuances; **una sfumatura d'ironia** a hint of irony

sfuocato, a [sfwo'kato] AGG = **sfocato**

sfuriata [sfu'rjata] SF outburst of rage, fit of rage *o* anger; **fare una sfuriata a qn** to give sb a good telling off

sfuso, a ['sfuso] AGG (*caramelle*) loose, unpacked; (*vino*) unbottled; (*birra*) draught (*Brit*), draft (*Am*)

S.G. ABBR = *Sua Grazia*

sg. ABBR = **seguente**

sgabello [zga'bɛllo] SM stool

sgabuzzino [zgabud'dzino] SM lumber room (*Brit*), storage room (*Am*)

sgamare [zga'mare] VT (*fam: scoprire: persona*) to rumble; (*: situazione*) to suss out; **farsi sgamare** to be rumbled

sgambettare [zgambet'tare] VI (*aus* **avere**) to kick (one's legs) about; (*bambino*) to toddle

sgambetto [zgam'betto] SM: **fare lo sgambetto a qn** to trip sb up; (*fig*) to oust sb

sganasciarsi [zganaʃ'ʃarsi] VIP: **sganasciarsi dalle risate** *o* **dal ridere** to roar with laughter

sganciamento [zgantʃa'mento] SM (*gen*) unhooking; (*treno*) uncoupling; (*di bombe*) dropping

sganciare [zgan'tʃare] VT (*gen*) to unhook; (*chiusura*) to unfasten, undo; (*treno*) to uncouple; (*bombe*) to drop, release; (*fig fam: soldi*) to fork out
▸ **sganciarsi** VIP (*gen*) to come unhooked; (*chiusura*) to come unfastened, come undone; (*treno*) to come uncoupled; **sganciarsi da** (*fig: persona*) to get away from

sgangherare [zgange'rare] VT (*porta*) to unhinge; (*cassa, baule: sfasciare*) to smash
▸ **sgangherarsi** VIP: **sgangherarsi dalle risate** to split one's sides laughing

sgangherato, a [zgange'rato] AGG (*porta*) unhinged, off its hinges; (*auto*) ramshackle, rickety; (*risata*) wild, boisterous

sgarbatamente [zgarbata'mente] AVV rudely, impolitely

sgarbatezza [zgarba'tettsa] SF (*qualità*) rudeness, impoliteness, bad manners *pl*; **è stata una sgarbatezza arrivare tardi** it was rude to arrive late

sgarbato, a [zgar'bato] AGG rude, ill-mannered, impolite

sgarbo ['zgarbo] SM: **fare uno sgarbo a qn** to be rude to sb

sgargiante [zgar'dʒante] AGG gaudy, showy

sgarrare [zgar'rare] VI (*aus* **avere**) (*persona*) to step out of line; (*orologio: essere avanti*) to gain; (*: essere indietro*) to lose; **e guarda di non sgarrare!** watch your step!; **l'orologio sgarra di 2 minuti** the clock is 2 minutes fast (*o* slow)

sgarro ['zgarro] SM (*mancanza di correttezza*) mistake, inaccuracy; **non ammetto sgarri** I won't allow anyone to step out of line

sgasare [zga'zare] VT (*bibita*) to make flat

sgattaiolare [zgattajo'lare] VI (*aus* **essere**) **sgattaiolare fuori** to slip out, sneak out; **sgattaiolare via** to sneak away *o* off

sgelare [zdʒe'lare] VT, VI (*aus* **essere**), **sgelarsi** VIP to melt, thaw

sghembo, a ['zgembo] AGG (*storto*) crooked; **di sghembo** (*storto*) crookedly; (*obliquamente*) on the slant

sghignazzare [zgiɲɲat'tsare] VI (*aus* **avere**) to laugh scornfully, sneer

sghignazzata [zgiɲɲat'tsata] SF scornful laugh, sneer

sghimbescio [zgim'bɛʃʃo] SM: **a** *o* **di sghimbescio** (*storto*) crookedly; (*obliquamente*) on the slant

sghiribizzo [zgiri'biddzo] SM (*fam: capriccio*) whim, fancy; **avere lo sghiribizzo di (fare) qc** to fancy (doing) sth

sgobbare [zgob'bare] VI (*aus* **avere**) (*fam: lavorare*) to slog, slave; (*: a scuola*) to swot (*Brit*), cram (*Am*); **sgobbare sui libri** to slog away at one's books

sgobbata [zgob'bata] SF (*fam: lavoro*) slog, grind

sgobbone [zgob'bone] SM (*fam*) slogger; (*: secchione*) swot (*Brit*), grind (*Am*)

sgocciolare [zgottʃo'lare] VT (*acqua*) to drip; (*cosa immersa in un liquido*) to drain
■ VI (*aus* **essere**) to drip

sgocciolatura [zgottʃola'tura] SF **1** (*azione*) dripping **2** (*gocce*) drops *pl*; (*di pittura*) runs *pl*, streaks *pl*

sgoccioli ['zgottʃoli] SMPL: **essere agli sgoccioli** (*lavoro, provviste*) to be nearly finished; (*periodo*) to be nearly over; **siamo agli sgoccioli** we've nearly finished, the end is in sight

sgolarsi [zgo'larsi] VIP to become hoarse, talk (*o* shout *o* sing) o.s. hoarse; (*fig: parlare inutilmente*) to waste one's breath

sgomberare [zgombe'rare] VT (*stanza, aula, strada*) to clear; (*alloggio*) to move out of, vacate; (*zona: evacuare*) to evacuate; **stanno sgomberando la stanza** they're clearing the room
■ VI (*aus* **avere**) (*traslocare*) to move; **dobbiamo sgomberare entro lunedì** we have to move out by Monday

sgombero ['zgombero] SM (*di strada, stanze*) clearing; (*di città*) evacuation; (*trasloco*) moving

sgombrare [zgom'brare] VT = **sgomberare**

sgombro¹, a ['zgombro] AGG (*gen*) clear, empty
■ SM = **sgombero**

sgombro² ['zgombro] SM (*pesce*) mackerel

sgomentare [zgomen'tare] VT to dismay, alarm
▸ **sgomentarsi** VIP to be dismayed, be alarmed

sgomento, a [zgo'mento] AGG dismayed, alarmed
■ SM dismay, alarm; **farsi prendere dallo sgomento** to be filled with dismay, be alarmed

sgominare [zgomi'nare] VT (*nemico*) to rout; (*avversario*) to defeat; (*fig: epidemia*) to overcome

sgonfiare [zgon'fjare] VT (*gen*) to deflate, let the air out of, let down; (*fig: persona*) to bring down a peg or two; **sgonfia il materassino** let down the airbed
▸ **sgonfiarsi** VIP **1** (*gen*) to deflate; (*pneumatico*) to go

Ss

flat; (*fig: persona*) to be deflated **2** (*Med*) to go down; **la caviglia si è sgonfiata** my ankle is no longer swollen
sgonfio, fia, fi, fie ['zgonfjo] AGG **1** (*pneumatico, pallone*) flat; **hai una gomma sgonfia** you've got a flat tyre **2** (*Med*) no longer inflamed *o* swollen
sgorbio, bi ['zgɔrbjo] SM (*macchia*) blot; (*scarabocchio*) scrawl, scribble; (*pegg: quadro*) daub; (*fam: persona brutta*) fright
sgorgare [zgor'gare] VI (*aus* **essere**) (*gen*) to gush (out), spurt (out); (*lacrime*) to pour, flow; **il sangue sgorgava dalla ferita** the blood gushed *o* spurted from the wound
sgottare [zgot'tare] VT (*barca, acqua*) to bale out
sgozzare [zgot'tsare] VT to cut the throat of; (*macellare: anche fig*) to slaughter
sgradevole [zgra'devole] AGG unpleasant; (*voce, odore*) unpleasant, disagreeable
sgradevolmente [zgradevol'mente] AVV unpleasantly
sgradito, a [zgra'dito] AGG unwelcome
sgraffignare [zgraffiɲ'ɲare] VT (*fam*) to pinch, swipe
sgrammaticato, a [zgrammati'kato] AGG ungrammatical
sgranare [zgra'nare] VT (*fagioli*) to shell; (*pannocchia*) to remove the corn from; **sgranare gli occhi** (*fig*) to open one's eyes wide
sgranchire [zgran'kire] VT to stretch; **sgranchirsi le gambe** to stretch one's legs
sgranocchiare [zgranok'kjare] VT to munch, crunch
sgrassare [zgras'sare] VT to remove the grease from
sgravare [zgra'vare] VT: **sgravare qn/qc (di)** (*peso, anche fig*) to relieve sb/sth (of)
▶ **sgravarsi** VR (*partorire*) to give birth
sgravio, vi ['zgravjo] SM: **sgravio fiscale** *o* **contributivo** tax relief
sgraziato, a [zgrat'tsjato] AGG ungraceful, awkward, clumsy, ungainly
sgretolamento [zgretola'mento] SM (*vedi vb*) splitting; flaking off; crumbling
sgretolare [zgreto'lare] VT (*roccia*) to split; (*intonaco*) to cause to flake off
▶ **sgretolarsi** VIP (*muro, creta, gesso*) to crumble; (*roccia*) to split
sgretolato, a [zgreto'lato] AGG (*intonaco*) flaking, chipped; (*roccia, muro*) crumbling
sgridare [zgri'dare] VT: **sgridare qn** to tell sb off, scold sb; **perché mi sgridi?** why are you telling me off?
sgridata [zgri'data] SF telling off, scolding
sgroppare [zgrop'pare] VI (*aus* **avere**) (*cavallo*) to buck
sgroppata [zgrop'pata] SF (*di cavallo*) buck
sgroppino [zgrop'pino] SM *sorbet made with vodka, sparkling wine etc.*
sgrossare [zgros'sare] VT (*marmo, legno*) to rough-hew; (*fig: modi*) to polish, refine
sguaiataggine [zgwaja'taddʒine] SF coarseness
sguaiato, a [zgwa'jato] AGG coarse, vulgar; **una risata sguaiata** a guffaw
sguainare [zgwai'nare] VT to draw, unsheathe
sgualcire [zgwal'tʃire] VT to crumple (up), crease; **attenta a non sgualcire il vestito** mind you don't crease your dress
▶ **sgualcirsi** VIP to become *o* get crumpled, become *o* get creased
sgualcito, a [zgwal'tʃito] AGG crumpled, creased
sgualdrina [zgwal'drina] SF trollop
sguardo ['zgwardo] SM **1** (*occhiata*) glance, look; **dare uno sguardo a qc** to glance at sth, cast a glance *o* an eye over sth; **lanciare uno sguardo di rimprovero a qn** to give sb a reproachful look; **mi ha lanciato uno sguardo d'intesa** he gave me a knowing look **2** (*espressione*) expression, look (in one's eye); **avere lo sguardo fisso** to have a fixed expression; **ha uno sguardo intelligente** he has an intelligent expression; **aveva lo sguardo triste** he looked sad **3** (*occhi*): **alzare** *o* **sollevare lo sguardo** to raise one's eyes, look up; **abbassare lo sguardo** to lower one's eyes, look down; **cercare qn/qc con lo sguardo** to look (a)round for sb/sth; **distogliere lo sguardo da qn/qc** to take one's eyes off sb/sth; **fissare lo sguardo su qn/qc** to stare at sb/sth; **soffermarsi con lo sguardo su qn/qc** to let one's eyes rest on sb/sth; **volgere lo sguardo altrove** to look elsewhere; **attirare gli sguardi** (*fig: attenzione*) to attract (people's) attention
sguarnire [zgwar'nire] VT **1** (*togliere la guarnizione*) to take the trimming off **2** (*Mil: lasciare indifeso*) to leave undefended
sguarnito, a [zgwar'nito] AGG (*vedi vb*) untrimmed; undefended
sguattero, a ['zgwattero] SM scullery boy/maid
sguazzare [zgwat'tsare] VI (*aus* **avere**) (*in acqua*) to splash (about); (*nel fango*) to wallow; (*fig: trovarsi a proprio agio*) to be in one's element; **sguazzare nell'oro** to be rolling in money
sguinzagliare [zgwintsaʎ'ʎare] VT (*cane*) to let off the leash; (*fig: persona*): **sguinzagliare qn dietro a qn** to set sb on sb
sgusciare[1] [zguʃ'ʃare] VT (*uovo, piselli*) to shell
sgusciare[2] [zguʃ'ʃare] VI (*aus* **essere**) to slip; **sgusciare di mano** to slip out of one's hand; **sgusciare via** (*scappare*) to escape, slip *o* slink away
shaker ['ʃeikə] SM INV (cocktail) shaker
shakerare [ʃeke'rare] VT (*cocktail*) to shake
shakerato, a [ʃeke'rato] AGG (*mescolato*) shaken
shampoo ['ʃampo] SM INV shampoo
share [ʃer] SM INV *number of people who watch a particular programme*

LO SAPEVI...?
share non si traduce mai con la parola inglese ***share***

sherpa ['ʃɛrpa] SM INV sherpa
sherry ['ʃeri] SM INV sherry
shiatsu, **shiatzu** [ʃi'attsu] SM, AGG INV shiatsu
shoccare [ʃok'kare] VT = **scioccare**
shock [ʃɔk] SM INV (*gen, Med*) shock; **sotto shock** in a state of shock
shockare [ʃok'kare] VT = **scioccare**
shorts [ʃɔ:ts] SMPL shorts
SI SIGLA = *Siena*

si[1] [si] **PAROLA CHIAVE**
PRON (*davanti* la, li, le, ne *diventa* se)
1 (*in verbi riflessivi: impersonale*) oneself; (: *maschile*) himself; (: *femminile*) herself; (: *plurale*) themselves; (*in verbi intransitivi pronominali*) itself; **si crede importante** he (*o* she) thinks a lot of himself (*o* herself); **se ne è dimenticata** she forgot about it; **si è dimenticato di me** he has forgotten me; **l'orologio si è fermato** the clock has stopped; **si guardava allo specchio** he was looking at himself in the mirror; **lavarsi** to wash (oneself); **si nascosero** they hid; **pettinarsi** to comb one's hair; **si è rotto** it has broken; **digli di sbrigarsi**

tell him to hurry up; **sporcarsi** to get dirty; **si è tagliato** he's cut himself
2 (*con complemento oggetto*): **si è tolto il cappello** he took off his hat; **lavarsi le mani** to wash one's hands; **si è sporcato i pantaloni** he got his trousers (*Brit*) *o* pants (*Am*) dirty; **se l'è ricordato** he remembered it; **si godette la vacanza** he (*o* she) enjoyed his (*o* her) holiday
3 (*uso reciproco*) each other, one another; **si baciarono** they kissed; **si incontrarono alle 5** they met at 5 o'clock; **si odiano** they hate each other *o* one another
4 (*passivo*): **dove si parla russo** where Russian is spoken, where they speak Russian; **si ripara facilmente** it can easily be repaired; **si vende al chilo** it is sold by the kilo
5 (*impersonale*): **si dice che...** it is said that ..., people say that ...; **mi si dice che...** I am told that ...; **non si risponde così!** that's no way to answer somebody!; **non si sa mai** you never can tell, you never know; **si vede che è nuovo** one (*o* you) can tell it's new

si² [si] SM INV (*Mus*) B; (: *solfeggiando la scala*) ti
sì¹ [si] AVV **1** yes; **hai finito? — sì** have you finished? — yes (I have); **sei sicuro? — sì, certo** are you sure? — yes, of course (I am); **vuoi un caffè? – sì, grazie** would you like a coffee? – yes, please; **siete andati al cinema ieri? – sì** did you go to the cinema yesterday? – yes, we did; **ma sì!** yes, of course!, I should say so!; **sì e no** yes and no; **avrà sì e no 10 anni** he must be about 10 years old; **saranno stati sì e no in 20** there must have been about 20 of them; **uno sì e uno no** every other one; **un giorno sì e uno no** every other day; **sì, domani!** *or* **sì, proprio!** (*iro*) you'll be lucky!, fat chance of that!
2 (*rafforzativo*): **allora vieni, sì o no?** are you coming or not?; **questa sì che è bella!** that's a good one! **3** **dire di sì** to say yes; **spero/penso di sì** I hope/think so; **forse (che) sì, forse (che) no** maybe, maybe not; **fece di sì col capo** he nodded (his head); **vieni? se sì ci vediamo dopo** are you coming? if so I'll see you later; **e sì che...** and to think that ...
■ SM yes; **non mi aspettavo un sì** I didn't expect him (*o* her *ecc*) to say yes; **sono tra il sì e il no** I'm uncertain, I can't make up my mind; **per me è sì** I should think so, I expect so
sì² [si] AVV = **così**
sia¹ ['sia] CONG **1** **sia...sia..., sia...che...** (*tanto... quanto...*) both ... and ...; **sia Franco sia Mario hanno accettato** *or* **sia Franco che Mario hanno accettato** both Franco and Mario have accepted **2** **sia che...sia che...** (*o... o...*) whether ... or ...; **sia che accetti sia che non accetti** whether he accepts or not
sia² ['sia] VB *vedi* **essere**
SIAE [si'ae] SIGLA F = *Società Italiana Autori ed Editori*
sial ['sial] SM INV (*Geol*) sial
Siam ['siam] SM Siam
siamese [sia'mese] AGG Siamese; **gatto siamese** Siamese (cat); **fratelli siamesi** Siamese twins
■ SM/F Siamese *inv*
■ SM (*lingua*) Siamese
siamo ['sjamo] VB *vedi* **essere**
Siberia [si'bɛrja] SF Siberia
siberiano, a [sibe'rjano] AGG, SM/F Siberian
sibilante [sibi'lante] AGG (*suono*) hissing; (*Fonetica*) sibilant
■ SF (*Fonetica*) sibilant
sibilare [sibi'lare] VI (*aus* **avere**) (*serpente*) to hiss; (*vento*) to whistle
sibilla [si'billa] SF (*Mitol*) sibyl
sibillino, a [sibil'lino] AGG (*anche fig*) sibylline; **parole sibilline** enigmatic words
sibilo ['sibilo] SM (*di serpente*) hiss(ing); (*di vento*) whistling, whistle
sicario, ri [si'karjo] SM hired assassin *o* killer
sicché [sik'ke] CONG (*così che*) so (that), therefore; (*allora*) (and) so
siccità [sittʃi'ta] SF drought
siccome [sik'kome] CONG since, as; **siccome era tardi ho deciso di tornare a casa** since it was late I decided to go home
Sicilia [si'tʃilja] SF Sicily; **mi è piaciuta molto la Sicilia** I really liked Sicily; **vado in Sicilia quest'estate** I'm going to Sicily this summer
▷ www.regione.sicilia.it/
siciliano, a [sitʃi'ljano] AGG, SM/F Sicilian
sicomoro [siko'mɔro] SM sycamore
siculo, a ['sikulo] AGG, SM/F Sicilian
sicura [si'kura] SF (*di arma, di spilla*) safety catch; (*di portiera*) safety lock
sicuramente [sikura'mente] AVV (*con sicurezza, comportarsi, dichiarare*) confidently; (*certamente*) undoubtedly, certainly
sicurezza [siku'rettsa] SF **1** (*immunità*) safety; **una campagna per la sicurezza stradale** a road safety campaign; **di sicurezza** (*dispositivo, margine*) safety *attr*; **cintura di sicurezza** seat belt **2** (*salvaguardia di diritti*) security; **per la sicurezza nazionale** for national security; **(forze di) Pubblica Sicurezza** police (force) **3** (*certezza*) certainty; **avere la sicurezza di qc** to be sure *o* certain of sth; **lo so con sicurezza** I am quite certain **4** (*fiducia, tranquillità*) confidence; **sicurezza (di sé)** self-confidence, self-assurance; **ha risposto con molta sicurezza** he answered very confidently; **per sicurezza** just in case; **per sicurezza portati l'ombrello** take your umbrella, just in case
sicuro, a [si'kuro] AGG **1** (*senza pericolo*) safe; (*ben difeso*) safe, secure; **non è sicuro qui** it isn't safe here; **sentirsi sicuro** to feel safe *o* secure; **non mi sento sicuro qui** I don't feel safe here **2** (*certo*) certain, sure; **la vittoria è sicura** victory is assured; **essere sicuro di qc/che...** to be sure of sth/that ...; **sono sicuro che ce la farai** I'm sure you'll manage it; **ne ero sicuro!** I knew it!; **ne sei proprio sicuro?** are you sure *o* certain? **3** (*fiducioso, tranquillo*) (self-)confident, sure of o.s.; **essere sicuro di sé** to be self-confident, be sure of o.s.; **è molto sicuro di sé** he's very self-confident **4** (*attendibile*) reliable, sure; (: *rimedio*) sure, safe; (*esperto*) skilled; **da fonte sicura** from a reliable source; **l'ho saputo da fonte sicura** I heard about it from a reliable source **5** (*saldo*) firm, steady; **con mano sicura** with a steady hand
■ AVV of course, certainly; **verrai? – sicuro!** will you come? – of course I will!; **di sicuro** (*senz'altro*) certainly; (*con certezza*) for sure; **non sappiamo di sicuro cosa sia successo** we don't know for sure what happened
■ SM **1** (*cosa certa*): **dare qc per sicuro** to be sure about sth; **dare per sicuro che...** to be sure that ... **2** (*luogo sicuro*): **essere al sicuro** to be safe, be in a safe place; **non preoccuparti, qui siamo al sicuro** don't worry, we're safe here; **mettersi al sicuro** to take cover; **mettere qc al sicuro** to put sth away (in a safe place); **ho messo il tuo anello al sicuro** I've put your ring in a safe place **3** (*non rischiare*): **andare sul sicuro** to play safe
siderurgia [siderur'dʒia] SF iron and steel industry

Ss

siderurgico, a, ci, che [side'rurdʒiko] AGG iron and steel *attr*
sidro ['sidro] SM cider
siedo *ecc* ['sjɛdo] VB *vedi* **sedere**
siepe ['sjɛpe] SF hedge; (*Sport*) hedge, hurdle
siero ['sjɛro] SM serum; **siero antivipera** snake bite serum; **siero del latte** whey; **siero della verità** truth serum *o* drug
sieronegatività [sjeronegativi'ta] SF HIV-negative status
sieronegativo, a [sjeronega'tivo] AGG HIV-negative ■ SM/F HIV-negative (person)
sieropositività [sjeropozitivi'ta] SF HIV-positive status
sieropositivo, a [sjeropozi'tivo] AGG HIV positive ■ SM/F HIV-positive (person)
sieroterapia [sjerotera'pia] SF serotherapy
sierra ['sjɛrra] SF (*Geog*) sierra
Sierra Leone ['sjɛrra le'one] SF Sierra Leone
siesta ['sjɛsta] SF siesta, (afternoon) nap; **fare la siesta** to have a nap *o* siesta
siete ['sjɛte] VB *vedi* **essere**
sifilide [si'filide] SF syphilis
sifilitico, a, ci, che [sifi'litiko] AGG, SM/F syphilitic
sifone [si'fone] SM (*Tecn*) siphon; (*per seltz*) (soda) siphon (*Brit*), soda-water siphon (*Am*)
Sig. ABBR (= **signore**) Mr
sigaretta [siga'retta] SF cigarette
sigaro ['sigaro] SM cigar
Sigg. ABBR (= **signori**) Messrs
sigillare [sidʒil'lare] VT to seal
sigillo [si'dʒillo] SM seal; **mettere** *o* **porre i sigilli a qc** to seal sth, put seals on sth; **anello con sigillo** signet ring
sigla ['sigla] SF **1** (*abbreviazione*) acronym, abbreviation; (*iniziali*) initials *pl*; (*monogramma*) monogram; **sigla automobilistica** *abbreviation of province on vehicle number plate* **2** **sigla musicale** signature tune
siglare [si'glare] VT to initial
Sig.na ABBR (= **signorina**) Miss, Ms
significare [siɲɲifi'kare] VT **1** (*aver senso*) to mean; **cosa significa?** what does this mean?; **cosa significa questa parola?** what does this word mean? **2** (*avere importanza*) to mean, matter; **tu significhi molto per me** you mean a lot to me
significativamente [siɲɲifikativa'mente] AVV (*in modo significativo*) significantly; (*efficacemente*) effectively
significativo, a [siɲɲifika'tivo] AGG significant
significato [siɲɲifi'kato] SM meaning, sense; (*valore, importanza*) importance; **senza significato** meaningless; **non ha alcun significato per me** it doesn't mean anything to me
signora [siɲ'ɲora] SF **1** (*donna*) lady; (*moglie*) wife; **ti cercava una signora** there was a lady looking for you; **è una signora molto simpatica** she's a very nice lady; **è una vera signora** she's a real lady; **vive da signora** she leads a life of luxury; **le presento la mia signora** may I introduce my wife?; **il signor Rossi e signora** Mr Rossi and his wife; **Signore e Signori!** Ladies and Gentlemen!; **Nostra Signora** (*Rel*) Our Lady
2 (*rivolgendosi a qualcuno*): **buon giorno signora** good morning; (*deferente*) good morning Madam; (*quando si conosce il nome*) good morning Mrs (*o* Ms) X; **signora maestra!** please Mrs (*o* Ms) X!, please Miss!
3 (*parlando di qualcuno*): **la signora Rossi sta male** Mrs (*o* Ms) Rossi is ill; **lo dirò alla signora** I'll let Mrs (*o* Ms) X know **4** (*in lettere*): **Gentile Signora** Dear Madam; **Gentile (*o* Cara) Signora Rossi** Dear Mrs (*o* Ms) Rossi; **Gentile Signora Anna Rossi** (*sulle buste*) Mrs (*o* Ms) Anna Rossi
signore [siɲ'ɲore] SM **1** (*uomo*) gentleman; **c'è un signore che ti cerca** there's a gentleman looking for you; **è un signore molto simpatico** h's a very nice man; **è un vero signore** he's a real gentleman; **fa una vita da (gran) signore** he lives like a lord; **fanno una vita da signori** they lead a life of luxury; **il Signore** (*Rel*) the Lord; **oh Signore!** oh Lord!, oh God!
2 (*rivolgendosi a qualcuno*): **buon giorno signore** good morning; (*deferente*) good morning Sir; (*quando si conosce il nome*) good morning Mr X; **signor maestro!** please Mr X!, please Sir!; **signor Presidente** Mr Chairman
3 (*parlando di qualcuno*): **il signor Rossi sta male** Mr Rossi is ill; **lo dirò al signore** I'll let Mr X know; **i signori Bianchi** (*coniugi*) Mr and Mrs Bianchi **4** (*in lettere*): **Gentile Signore** Dear Sir; **Gentile (*o* Caro) Signor Rossi** Dear Mr Rossi; **Gentile Signor Paolo Rossi** (*sulle buste*) Mr Paolo Rossi
signoria [siɲɲo'ria] SF (*Storia*) seignory, signoria
signorile [siɲɲo'rile] AGG (*distinto*) refined, distinguished; (*: quartiere*) exclusive; (*da signore*) gentlemanly, gentlemanlike; (*da signora*) ladylike
signorilità [siɲɲorili'ta] SF (*raffinatezza*) refinement; (*eleganza*) elegance
signorilmente [siɲɲoril'mente] AVV (*comportarsi*) in a gentlemanly (*o* ladylike) manner
signorina [siɲɲo'rina] SF **1** (*giovane donna*) young woman; **è la signorina che abita al piano di sotto** she's the young woman who lives downstairs; **ormai sei una signorina!** (*complimento*) how grown up you are!; (*rimprovero*) you're not a child any more!; **rimanere signorina** to remain a spinster
2 (*rivolgendosi a qualcuno*): **buon giorno signorina** good morning; (*deferente*) good morning Madam; (*quando si conosce il nome*) good morning Miss (*o* Ms) X **3** (*parlando di qualcuno*): **la signorina Rossi sta male** Miss (*o* Ms) Rossi is ill **4** (*in lettere*): **Gentile signorina** Dear Madam; **Gentile (*o* Cara) Signorina Rossi** Dear Miss (*o* Ms) Rossi; **Gentile Signorina Anna Rossi** (*sulle buste*) Miss (*o* Ms) Anna Rossi
signorino [siɲɲo'rino] SM young master
signorsì [siɲɲor'si] AVV (*anche scherz*) yes sir, aye aye sir
Sig.ra ABBR (= **signora**) Mrs, Ms
silenziatore [silentsja'tore] SM (*di arma, Tecn*) silencer
silenzio, zi [si'lɛntsjo] SM **1** (*gen*) silence; **fare silenzio** to be quiet, stop talking; **fate silenzio!** be quiet!; **restare in silenzio** to keep quiet; **in silenzio** in silence; **ascoltavano in silenzio** they listened in silence; **far passare qc sotto silenzio** to keep quiet about sth, hush sth up; **silenzio assenso** *mechanism by which an official request is considered to have been granted if no answer is received within a certain period*; **silenzio stampa** press blackout **2** (*calma, pace*) silence, still(ness), quiet; **nel silenzio della notte** in the still of the night **3** (*Mil*) lights out
silenziosamente [silentsjosa'mente] AVV silently, quietly
silenzioso, a [silen'tsjoso] AGG (*gen*) silent, quiet; (*motore*) quiet; **è un ragazzino silenzioso** he's a quiet boy
silhouette [si'lwɛt] SF INV (*sagoma*) outline,

silhouette; (*figura*) figure
silice ['silitʃe] SF silica
silicio [si'litʃo] SM silicon
silicone [sili'kone] SM silicone
silicosi [sili'kɔzi] SF INV (*Med*) silicosis
sillaba ['sillaba] SF syllable; **dividere in sillabe** to divide into syllables; **non ho capito una sillaba di quello che hai detto** I haven't understood a single word of what you've said; **senza cambiare una sillaba** word for word
sillabare [silla'bare] VT to divide into syllables
sillabario, ri [silla'barjo] SM spelling book
sillabico, a, ci, che [sil'labiko] AGG syllabic
sillogismo [sillo'dʒizmo] SM syllogism
silo ['silo] SM silo
silografia [silogra'fia] SF wood engraving, xylography
siluramento [silura'mento] SM (*Mil*) torpedoing; (*fig*: *progetto*) wrecking; (: *persona*) ousting, dismissal
silurare [silu'rare] VT (*Mil*, *fig*: *legge*) to torpedo; (: *progetto*) wreck; (: *persona di comando*) to remove from power, dismiss
siluro [si'luro] SM (*Mil*) torpedo
silvestre [sil'vɛstre] AGG woodland *attr*
SIM [sim] SIGLA F INV **1** = Società di Intermediazione Mobiliare brokerage company **2 SIM card** SIM card
simbiosi [simbi'ɔzi] SF INV (*Bio*, *fig*) symbiosis
simboleggiare [simboled'dʒare] VT to symbolize, represent
simbolicamente [simbolika'mente] AVV symbolically
simbolico, a, ci, che [sim'bɔliko] AGG symbolic(al)
simbolismo [simbo'lizmo] SM symbolism
simbolista, i, e [simbo'lista] AGG symbolist *attr* ■ SM/F symbolist
simbolo ['simbolo] SM (*gen*, *Mat*, *Chim*) symbol; **simbolo di successo** status symbol
similare [simi'lare] AGG similar
simile ['simile] AGG **1** (*gen*, *analogo*) similar; **simile a** like, similar to; **hai la gonna simile alla mia** you've got a skirt like mine; **avevo un vestito simile una volta** I had a dress like that once; **abbiamo gusti simili** we have similar tastes **2** (*pegg*: *tale*) such; **una cosa simile** such a thing; **un uomo simile** such a man, a man like this **3 di simile** *or* **non ho mai visto niente di simile** I've never seen anything of the sort *o* like that; **è insegnante o qualcosa di simile** he's a teacher or something like that
■ SM/F **1** (*spec al pl*: *persona*) fellow being; **i suoi simili** one's fellow men; (*pari*) one's peers **2** (*oggetti*): **vendono vasi e simili** they sell vases and things like that
similitudine [simili'tudine] SF **1** (*Retorica*) simile **2** (*Mat*) similarity
similmente [simil'mente] AVV similarly
similpelle [simil'pɛlle] SF Leatherette®
simmetria [simme'tria] SF symmetry
simmetrico, a, ci, che [sim'mɛtriko] AGG symmetric(al)
simpatia [simpa'tia] SF (*qualità*) pleasantness; (*inclinazione*) liking; **è di una simpatia!** she's extremely nice *o* pleasant!; **con simpatia** (*su lettera*) with much affection; **avere** *o* **provare simpatia per qn** to like sb, have a liking for sb; **prendere qn in simpatia** to take (a liking) to sb; **guadagnarsi la simpatia di qn** to gain sb's affection; **avere una simpatia per qn** (*esserne attratto*) to feel attracted to sb

LO SAPEVI...?
simpatia non si traduce mai con la parola inglese ***sympathy***

simpaticamente [simpatika'mente] AVV (*sorridere*, *scherzare*) pleasantly, in a friendly fashion
simpatico[1], a, ci, che [sim'patiko] AGG **1** (*persona*) nice, pleasant, likeable; (*appartamento*, *albergo*) nice, pleasant; **è una ragazza simpatica** she's a nice girl; **mi è molto simpatico** I like him very much, I really like him; **non è simpatico quando succedono queste cose** it's not very nice when these things happen; **un modo di fare simpatico** a friendly manner **2 inchiostro simpatico** invisible ink

LO SAPEVI...?
simpatico non si traduce mai con la parola inglese ***sympathetic***

simpatico[2], a, ci che [sim'patiko] AGG (*nervo*, *sistema nervoso*) sympathetic; (*Anat*) sympathetic nervous system
simpatizzante [simpatid'dzante] SM/F sympathizer
simpatizzare [simpatid'dzare] VI (*aus* **avere**) **simpatizzare con** to take a liking to

LO SAPEVI...?
simpatizzare non si traduce mai con la parola inglese ***sympathize***

simposio, si [sim'pɔzjo] SM symposium
simulacro [simu'lakro] SM (*statua*, *immagine*) image, simulacrum; (*fig*: *traccia*, *parvenza*) semblance
simulare [simu'lare] VT (*gen*, *Tecn*) to simulate; (*sentimento*) to fake, feign; **simulare uno svenimento** to pretend to faint; **simulare una malattia** to pretend to be ill, feign *o* fake illness
simulatore [simula'tore] SM (*Tecn*) simulator; **simulatore di volo** (*Aer*) flight simulator
simulazione [simulat'tsjone] SF (*vedi vb*) simulation; faking, feigning; **fu tutta una simulazione** it was all a pretence
simultaneamente [simultanea'mente] AVV simultaneously, at the same time
simultaneità [simultanei'ta] SF simultaneity
simultaneo, a [simul'taneo] AGG simultaneous
sin. ABBR (= sinistra) L
sinagoga [sina'gɔga] SF synagogue
sinapsi [si'napsi] SF INV (*Bio*) synapse
sinceramente [sintʃera'mente] AVV (*gen*) sincerely; (*francamente*) honestly, sincerely; **lo credo sinceramente** I honestly believe this; **sinceramente non riesco a capirti** I really don't understand you
sincerarsi [sintʃe'rarsi] VIP: **sincerarsi (di qc)** to make sure (of sth)
sincerità [sintʃeri'ta] SF (*vedi agg*) sincerity; genuineness; **con tutta sincerità** in all sincerity, honestly
sincero, a [sin'tʃɛro] AGG **1** (*onesto*) sincere, honest; **essere sincero con qn** to be honest with sb; **sii sincero con me** be honest with me; **per essere sincero** to be honest, honestly **2** (*genuino*) real, genuine, true; **un amico sincero** a real friend
sinclinale [sinkli'nale] SF, AGG (*Geol*) syncline
sincopato, a [sinko'pato] AGG (*Mus*) syncopated
sincope ['sinkope] SF (*Ling*) syncope; (*Med*) fainting fit, blackout; (*Mus*) syncopation
sincronia [sinkro'nia] SF (*di movimento*) synchronism
sincronico, a, ci, che [sin'krɔniko] AGG synchronic
sincronizzare [sinkronid'dzare] VT to synchronize
sincronizzato, a [sinkronid'dzato] AGG synchronized; **marce sincronizzate** (*Aut*) syncromesh (gears)

Ss

sincronizzatore [sinkroniddza'tore] SM synchronizer
sincronizzazione [sinkroniddzat'tsjone] SF synchronization
sindacale [sinda'kale] AGG (*legge, lotta, riunione*) (trade) union *attr*; (*dottrina*) unionist; **una riunione sindacale** a trade-union meeting
sindacalismo [sindaka'lizmo] SM (trade) unionism
sindacalista, i, e [sindaka'lista] SM/F trade unionist
sindacare [sinda'kare] VT **1** (*controllare*) to inspect **2** (*fig: criticare*) to criticize
sindacato [sinda'kato] SM (*di lavoratori*) (trade) union; (*di datori di lavoro*) association
▷ www.cgil.it/
▷ www.cisl.it/
▷ www.uil.it/
▷ www.ugl.it/ugl/default.asp
sindaco, ci ['sindako] SM mayor
sindone ['sindone] SF (*Rel*): **la Sacra Sindone** the Holy Shroud
sindrome ['sindrome] SF (*Med*) syndrome; **sindrome da affaticamento cronico** chronic fatigue syndrome, ME; **sindrome da immunodeficienza acquisita** acquired immune deficiency syndrome, AIDS; **sindrome di Peter Pan** Peter Pan syndrome; **sindrome di Stoccolma** Stockholm syndrome
sinedrio, ri [si'nɛdrjo] SM (*tribunale ebraico*) Sanhedrin
sinergia, gie [siner'dʒia] SF (*anche: fig*) synergy
sinergico, a, ci, che [si'nɛrdʒiko] AGG synergistic
sinfonia [sinfo'nia] SF symphony
sinfonico, a, ci, che [sin'fɔniko] AGG symphonic; (*orchestra*) symphony *attr*
singalese AGG [singa'lese] SM/F Sin(g)halese *inv*
Singapore [singa'pore] SF Singapore
singhiozzante [singjot'tsante] AGG sobbing
singhiozzare [singjot'tsare] VI (*aus* **avere**) **1** (*piangere*) to sob **2** (*avere il singhiozzo*) to hiccup
singhiozzo [sin'gjottso] SM **1** (*Med*) hiccup; **avere il singhiozzo** to have (the) hiccups; **a singhiozzo** *o* **singhiozzi** (*fig*) by fits and starts; **sciopero a singhiozzo** on-off strike; **la macchina andava a singhiozzi** the car jolted *o* jerked along **2** (*di pianto*) sob; **scoppiare in singhiozzi** to burst into tears; **addormentarsi tra i singhiozzi** to sob o.s. to sleep
single ['siŋgol] SM/F INV, AGG INV single
singolare [singo'lare] AGG **1** (*Gramm*) singular; **1 persona singolare** 1st person singular **2** (*insolito, particolare*) remarkable, singular; (*strano*) strange, peculiar, odd
■ SM **1** (*Gramm*) singular; **al singolare** in the singular **2** (*Tennis*): **un singolare** a singles (match)
singolarmente [singolar'mente] AVV **1** (*separatamente*) individually, one at a time **2** (*in modo strano*) strangely, peculiarly, oddly
singolo, a ['singolo] AGG (*gen*) single, individual; **ogni singolo caso** every single case, each case; **ogni singolo individuo** each individual; **camera singola** single room
■ SM **1** (*individuo*) individual **2** (*Tennis*): **un singolo** a singles (match); **il singolo maschile** the men's singles
sinistra [si'nistra] SF **1** (*mano*) left hand; **scrive con la sinistra** he writes with his left hand **2** (*parte*) left, left-hand side; **a sinistra** (*stato in luogo*) on the left; (*moto a luogo*) to the left; **a sinistra di** to the left of; **corsia di sinistra** left-hand lane; **guida a sinistra** left-hand drive; **tenere la sinistra** to keep to the left; **voltare a sinistra** to turn left **3** (*Pol*): **la sinistra** the left; **ha vinto la sinistra** the left won the election; **di sinistra** left-wing; **un partito di sinistra** a left-wing party
sinistramente [sinistra'mente] AVV sinisterly, in a sinister way
sinistrato, a [sinis'trato] AGG damaged; **zona sinistrata** disaster area
■ SM/F (*vittima di catastrofe*) disaster victim
sinistro, a [si'nistro] AGG **1** (*mano, piede*) left; (*parte, lato*) left(-hand) **2** (*bieco*) sinister
■ SM **1** (*incidente*) accident **2** (*Pugilato*) left; (*Calcio*): **tirare di sinistro** to kick with one's left foot
sinistroide [sinis'trɔide] AGG, SM/F (*pegg*) leftist
sino ['sino] PREP = **fino**
sino... ['sino] PREF sino...
sinodo ['sinodo] SM (*Rel*) synod
sinonimo [si'nɔnimo] SM synonym
■ AGG synonymous; **un nome che è sinonimo di qualità** a name which is synonymous with good quality
sinoviale [sino'vjale] AGG (*Anat*) synovial
sintagma, i [sin'tagma] SM syntagm
sintassi [sin'tassi] SF INV syntax
sintatticamente [sintattika'mente] AVV syntactically
sintattico, a, ci, che [sin'tattiko] AGG syntactic
sintesi ['sintezi] SF INV **1** (*Chim, Filosofia*) synthesis **2** (*riassunto*) summary, résumé; **fare la sintesi di qc** to make a summary of sth; **in sintesi** in brief, in short
sinteticamente [sintetika'mente] AVV (*vedi agg*) briefly, concisely; synthetically
sintetico, a, ci, che [sin'tɛtiko] AGG **1** (*conciso*) brief, concise **2** (*fibre, materiale*) synthetic
sintetizzare [sintetid'dzare] VT (*Bio, Chim*) to synthesize; (*riassumere: testo*) to summarize
sintetizzatore [sintetiddza'tore] SM (*Mus*) synthesizer
sintomatico, a, ci, che [sinto'matiko] AGG (*Med, fig*) symptomatic
sintomo ['sintomo] SM (*Med, fig*) symptom; **presentare i sintomi di** to show symptoms of
sintonia [sinto'nia] SF (*Radio*) tuning; **essere in sintonia con qn** (*fig*) to be on the same wavelength as sb
sintonizzare [sintonid'dzare] VT to tune (in)
▶ **sintonizzarsi** VIP: **sintonizzarsi su** to tune in to
sintonizzatore [sintoniddza'tore] SM tuner
sintonizzazione [sintoniddzat'tsjone] SF tuning
sinuosamente [sinuosa'mente] AVV (*gen*) sinuously
sinuosità [sinuosi'ta] SF INV (*di strada, fiume*) winding; (*di corpo*) curve
sinuoso, a [sinu'oso] AGG (*gen*) sinuous; (*fiume, strada*) winding, sinuous
sinusite [sinu'zite] SF (*Med*) sinusitis
sinusoidale [sinuzoi'dale] AGG (*Mat*) sinusoidal
sinusoide [sinu'zɔide] SF (*Mat*) sine curve, sinusoid
sionismo [sio'nizmo] SM Zionism
sionista, i, e [sio'nista] AGG, SM/F Zionist
SIP [sip] SIGLA F (= **società italiana per l'esercizio delle telecomunicazioni**) *formerly, Italian telephone company*
sipario, ri [si'parjo] SM (*Teatro*) curtain; **calare il sipario su qc** (*fig: concluderla*) to bring the curtain down over sth
Siracusa [sira'kusa] SF Syracuse
siracusano, a [siraku'zano] AGG of *o* from Syracuse
■ SM/F inhabitant *o* native of Syracuse
sire ['sire] SM (*al re*): **Sire** Sire

sirena¹ [si'rɛna] SF (*Mitol, fig*) mermaid, siren
sirena² [si'rɛna] SF (*segnale: di polizia, ambulanza, pompieri*) siren; (: *di fabbrica*) hooter; **sirena d'allarme** (*per incendio*) fire alarm; (*per furto*) burglar alarm
Siria ['sirja] SF Syria
siriano, a [si'rjano] AGG, SM/F Syrian
siringa, ghe [si'ringa] SF **1** (*Med*) syringe **2** (*Culin*) ≈ piping *o* forcing bag
siringare [sirin'gare] VT (*Med*) to syringe
SISDE ['sizde] SIGLA M (= **Servizio per l'informazione e la sicurezza democratica**) *security service*
Sisifo ['sizifo] SM Sisyphus
sisma, i ['sizma] SM earthquake
SISMI ['sizmi] SIGLA M (= **Servizio per l'informazione e la sicurezza militari**) *military security service*
sismico, a, ci, che ['sizmiko] AGG (*gen*) seismic; (*zona*) earthquake *attr*
sismografo [siz'mɔgrafo] SM seismograph
sismologia [sizmolo'dʒia] SF seismology
sismologo, a, gi, ghe [siz'mɔlogo] SM/F seismologist
sissignore [sissiɲ'ɲore] AVV (*a un superiore*) yes, sir; (*enfatico*) yes indeed, of course
sistema, i [sis'tɛma] SM **1** (*Anat, Mat, Filosofia*) system; **sistema decimale/nervoso/solare** decimal/nervous/solar system; **sistema operativo** operating system; **sistema di sicurezza** security system; **sistema operativo** (*Inform*) operating system **2** (*metodo*) method, way; (*procedimento*) process; **è meglio seguire questo sistema** it's better to follow this method; **è un nuovo sistema per imparare le lingue** it's a new way to learn languages; **il suo sistema di vita** his way of life; **trovare il sistema per fare qc** to find a way to do sth; **non è questo il sistema di lavorare!** this is no way to work!; **ti suggerisco di cambiare sistema** I suggest you go about things in a different way; **bel sistema di trovare la soluzione!** (*iro*) that's some solution! **3** (*Totocalcio*) system
sistemare [siste'mare] VT **1** (*mettere a posto: stanza*) to tidy (up), put in order; (: *arredamento*) to arrange; **mi piace come hai sistemato la casa** I like the way you've got the house; **ha sistemato tutti i libri sullo scaffale** he arranged all the books on the shelf; **sistemarsi i capelli** to tidy one's hair; **sistemarsi i vestiti** to straighten one's clothes **2** **sistemare qn** (*trovargli lavoro*) to fix sb up with a job; (*trovargli marito o moglie*) to marry sb off; (*fare i conti con*) to fix sb; **sistemare qn in un albergo** to fix sb up with a hotel; **l'abbiamo sistemato da noi** we put him up; **sistemare qn per le feste** to beat sb up; **ti sistemo io!** I'll soon sort you out! **3** (*questione, faccenda*) to settle, sort out; **sistemo tutto io** I'll see to everything; **abbiamo ancora una questione da sistemare** we've still got one question to settle
▶ **sistemarsi** VR (*persona: trovare alloggio*) to find accommodation (*Brit*) *o* accommodations (*Am*); (: *trovarsi un lavoro*) to find a job, to get fixed up with a job; (: *sposarsi*) to get married; **è ora che ti sistemi** it's time you settled down; **si è sistemato in un albergo** he found a room in a hotel, he fixed himself up with a hotel; **si sistemò sul divano** he slept on the sofa;
▶ **sistemarsi** VIP (*problema, questione*) to be settled; **vedrai, tutto si sistemerà** you'll see, everything will work out
sistematicamente [sistematika'mente] AVV systematically
sistematico, a, ci, che [siste'matiko] AGG systematic, methodical
sistemazione [sistemat'tsjone] SF **1** (*di stanza, casa: assetto*) tidying up; (: *disposizione*) arrangement, layout, order **2** **cercare una sistemazione** (*alloggio*) to look for accommodation (*Brit*) *o* accommodations (*Am*); (*lavoro*) to look for work *o* employment; **è solo una sistemazione provvisoria** it's only temporary accommodation **3** (*di problema, questione*) settlement
sistemista, i, e [siste'mista] (*Inform*) SM/F systems engineer; (*analista*) systems analyst
sistemone [siste'mone] SM *a complicated system for betting on the football pools*
sistole ['sistole] SF systole
sito, a ['sito] AGG (*Amm*) situated
■ SM **1** (*archeologico, su Internet*) site; **un sito Internet** a web site **2** (*letter*) place
situare [situ'are] VT (*casa*) to site, situate, locate; (*film, romanzo*) to set; **la casa è situata su una collina/in riva al mare** the house is situated on a hill/on the coast
situazione [situat'tsjone] SF situation; **vista la tua situazione familiare** given your family situation *o* circumstances; **nella tua situazione** in your position *o* situation; **mi trovo in una situazione critica** I'm in a very difficult situation *o* position
siviera [si'vjɛra] SF (*Metallurgia*) ladle
skai® ['skai] SM Leatherette®
skating ['skeɪtɪŋ] SM (*Sci*) ski skating
sketch [sketʃ] SM INV (*Teatro*) sketch
ski-bob ['ski:bɔb] SM INV ski-bob
ski-lift ['ski:lift] SM INV ski tow
skinhead ['skin hed] SM/F skinhead
skipass ['ski:pa:s] SM INV ski pass
ski stopper ['ski:stɔpəʳ] SM INV ski stopper
slabbrare [zlab'brare] VT (*ferita*), **slabbrarsi** VIP to open
slabbrato, a [zlab'brato] AGG (*ferita*) open
slacciare [zlat'tʃare] VT (*nodo*) to untie, undo, unfasten; (*scarpa*) to unlace; (*bottoni*) to unfasten; (*abito, cravatta, cappotto*) to undo
▶ **slacciarsi** VIP (*vedi vt*) to come untied, come undone; to come unlaced; to come unfastened
slalom ['zlalom] SM INV (*Sci*) slalom; **fare lo slalom** to slalom; **slalom gigante** giant slalom; **slalom speciale** (special) slalom
slalomista, i, e [zlalo'mista] SM/F slalom specialist, slalom racer
slanciare [zlan'tʃare] VT to hurl, fling, throw
▶ **slanciarsi** VR to throw o.s., hurl o.s.; **slanciarsi contro qn** to throw o.s. on sb; **slanciarsi nella mischia** to throw o.s. into the fray
slanciato, a [zlan'tʃato] AGG (*persona*) slender, slim; (*colonna*) slender
slancio, ci ['zlantʃo] SM dash, leap; (*fig*) surge; **darsi** *o* **prendere lo slancio** (*da fermo*) to spring up; (*correndo*) to bound forward; **in uno slancio d'affetto** in a burst *o* rush of affection; **abbracciare qn con slancio** to hug sb enthusiastically; **agire di slancio** to act impetuously; **uno slancio di generosità** a fit of generosity
slargo, ghi ['zlargo] SM widening
slavato, a [zla'vato] AGG (*colore*) washed out, faded; (*persona*) mousy; (*viso*) pale, colourless (*Brit*), colorless (*Am*)
slavina [zla'vina] SF snowslide

slavo, a ['zlavo] AGG Slav(onic); **lingue slave** slavonic languages
■SM/F Slav
■SM (*lingua*) Slavonic
sleale [zle'ale] AGG (*persona: non leale*) disloyal; (*concorrenza*) unfair; **essere sleale con** to be disloyal towards; **gioco sleale** (*Sport*) foul play; **essere sleale al gioco** to cheat
slealmente [zleal'mente] AVV (*senza lealtà*) disloyally; (*senza correttezza*) unfairly
slealtà [zleal'ta] SF (*vedi agg*) disloyalty; unfairness
slegare [zle'gare] VT (*gen*) to untie; (*liberare*) to free, release
► **slegarsi** VR (*vedi vt*) to untie o.s.; to free o.s.
slegato, a [zle'gato] AGG (*animale*) loose; (*fig: discorso, stile*) disconnected
slip [zlip] SM INV (*mutandine*) briefs *pl*; (*da bagno: per uomo*) (swimming) trunks *pl*; (*: per donna*) bikini briefs *pl*
slitta ['zlitta] SF (*gen*) sledge; (*trainata*) sleigh
slittamento [zlitta'mento] SM (*vedi vb*) slipping; skidding; sliding; fall; postponement; **slittamento salariale** wage drift
slittare [zlit'tare] VI (*gen*) to slip, slide; (*automobile*) to skid; (*fig: partito*) to slide; (*: valuta*) to fall; (*: incontro, conferenza*) to be put off, be postponed
slittino [zlit'tino] SM toboggan; **andare in slittino** to toboggan
s.l.m. ABBR (= **sul livello del mare**) a.s.l. (= *above sea level*)
slogan ['zlɔgan] SM INV slogan
slogare [zlo'gare] VT (*Med: caviglia, polso*) to sprain; (*: spalla*) to dislocate; **mi si è slogata la caviglia** I've sprained my ankle
slogatura [zloga'tura] SF (*di spalla*) dislocation; (*di caviglia, polso*) sprain
sloggiare [zlod'dʒare] VT: **sloggiare (da)** (*nemico*) to dislodge (from), drive out (of); (*inquilino*) to turn out (of)
■VI (*aus* **avere**) **sloggiare (da)** to move out (of); **sloggia!** (*fam*) shove off!, clear off!
slot machine ['slɔt mə'ʃi:n] SF INV one-armed bandit, fruit machine (*Brit*), slot machine (*Am*)
Slovacchia [zlo'vakkja] SF Slovakia
slovacco, a, ci, che [zlo'vakko] AGG, SM/F Slovak, Slovakian; **la Repubblica Slovacca** the Slovak Republic
Slovenia [zlo'vɛnja] SF Slovenia
sloveno, a [zlo'vɛno] AGG, SM/F Slovene, Slovenian
■SM (*lingua*) Slovene
SM ABBR **1** (*Mil*) = **Stato Maggiore** **2** (= **Sua Maestà**) HM
smaccato, a [zmak'kato] AGG (*fig*) excessive
smacchiare [zmak'kjare] VT to remove stains from
smacchiatore [zmakkja'tore] SM stain remover
smacco, chi ['zmakko] SM humiliating defeat; **subire uno smacco** to be humiliated
smagliante [zmaʎ'ʎante] AGG (*anche fig*) dazzling, brilliant; **un sorriso smagliante** a dazzling smile
smagliare [zmaʎ'ʎare] VT (*catena, rete*) to break; (*calze*) to ladder (*Brit*), get a run in (*Am*)
► **smagliarsi** VIP (*calze*) to ladder (*Brit*), run (*Am*)
smagliatura [zmaʎʎa'tura] SF **1** (*su calza*) ladder (*Brit*), run (*Am*) **2** (*sulla pelle*) stretch mark
smagrire [zma'grire] VT to make thin
■VI (*aus* **essere**), **smagrirsi** VIP to get *o* grow thin, lose weight
smagrito, a [zma'grito] AGG: **essere smagrito** to have lost a lot of weight
smaliziare [zmalit'tsjare] VT: **smaliziare qn** to teach sb a thing or two
► **smaliziarsi** VIP to learn a thing or two
smaliziato, a [zmalit'tsjato] AGG shrewd, cunning
smaltare [zmal'tare] VT to enamel; (*ceramica*) to glaze; **smaltarsi le unghie** to put on nail polish *o* varnish (*Brit*)
smaltato, a [zmal'tato] AGG (*vedi vb*) enamelled; glazed; **aveva le unghie smaltate** she was wearing nail polish *o* varnish (*Brit*)
smaltimento [zmalti'mento] SM (*vedi vt*) digestion; loss; selling off; draining away *o* off; disposal; **smaltimento dei rifiuti** waste disposal
smaltire [zmal'tire] VT **1** (*cibo*) to digest; (*fig: peso*) to lose; (*: rabbia*) to get over; **smaltire la sbornia** to get over one's hangover, sober up; (*dormendo*) to sleep it off **2** (*merce*) to sell off **3** (*acque di scarico*) to drain away *o* off **4** (*rifiuti*) to dispose of
smalto ['zmalto] SM **1** (*per metalli*) enamel; (*per ceramica*) glaze; **smalto per le unghie** nail polish, nail varnish (*Brit*); **mettersi lo smalto** to put on nail polish *o* varnish (*Brit*); **mi sto mettendo lo smalto** I'm putting my nail polish on **2** (*Anat: di denti*) enamel
smammare [zmam'mare] VI (*fam*) to shove off, clear off
smancerie [zmantʃe'rie] SFPL mawkishness *sg*
smanettare [zmanet'tare] VI (*aus* **avere**) (*in moto*) to go flat out; (*con il computer*) to fiddle (around) with
smangiato, a [zman'dʒato] AGG (*corroso, consumato*) eaten away, corroded
smania ['zmanja] SF (*agitazione*) agitation, restlessness; (*fig: di potere, ricchezze*): **smania di** craving for, thirst for; **ha una gran smania di andarsene** he's desperate to leave; **avere la smania addosso** to have the fidgets
smaniare [zma'njare] VI (*aus* **avere**) to be agitated, be restless; **smaniare di fare qc** (*fig*) to long *o* yearn to do sth
smanioso, a [zma'njoso] AGG eager; **essere smanioso di fare qc** to long *o* yearn to do sth; **sono smanioso di rivederla** I'm dying *o* longing to see her again
smantellamento [zmantella'mento] SM (*anche fig*) dismantling
smantellare [zmantel'lare] VT (*gen*) to dismantle; (*anche fig: demolire*) to demolish
smarcante [zmar'kante] AGG (*Sport: passaggio*) well-placed
smarcare [zmar'kare] (*Sport*) VT: **smarcare qn** to help sb to get away from his (*o* her) marker
► **smarcarsi** VIP (*Sport*) to escape one's marker
smargiasso [zmar'dʒasso] SM show-off; **fare lo smargiasso** to show off
smarrimento [zmarri'mento] SM **1** (*perdita*) loss **2** (*fig: turbamento*) confusion, bewilderment; (*: sgomento*) dismay; **avere un attimo di smarrimento** to be momentarily nonplussed *o* bewildered
smarrire [zmar'rire] VT (*perdere*) to lose, mislay; **ho smarrito il portafoglio** I've lost my wallet; **smarrire la strada** to lose one's way
► **smarrirsi** VIP to get lost, lose one's way; **si sono smarriti nel bosco** they got lost in the woods
smarrito, a [zmar'rito] AGG **1** (*oggetto*) lost; **ufficio oggetti smarriti** lost property office (*Brit*), lost and found (*Am*) **2** (*fig: confuso: persona*) bewildered, nonplussed; (*: sguardo*) bewildered
smart card [zmart card] SF INV (*Inform*) smart card

smascherare [zmaske'rare] VT *(colpevole)* to unmask; *(intrigo, complotto)* to uncover
▶ **smascherarsi** VR to give o.s. away
smaterializzarsi [zmaterjalid'dzarsi] VIP to dematerialize
smazzata [zmat'tsata] SF *(Carte: mano)* hand
SME [zmɛ] ABBR = *Stato Maggiore Esercito*
■ SIGLA M (= **Sistema Monetario Europeo**) EMS (= *European Monetary System*)
smembrare [zmem'brare] VT *(gruppo, partito)* to split
▶ **smembrarsi** VIP to split up
smemorataggine [zmemora'taddʒine] SF absent-mindedness
smemorato, a [zmemo'rato] AGG forgetful, absent-minded
■ SM/F forgetful person, absent-minded person
smentire [zmen'tire] VT *(notizie)* to deny; *(testimonianza)* to refute; **il ministro ha smentito le voci** the minister denied the rumours; **smentisco quello che afferma il testimone** I refute what the witness is saying; **i fatti smentiscono le sue parole** the facts belie his words; **ha smentito la sua fama di dongiovanni** it gave the lie to his reputation of being a Don Juan
▶ **smentirsi** VR to be inconsistent; **non ti smentisci mai** you're always the same; **ancora una volta non si è smentita** once again she was true to herself
smentita [zmen'tita] SF *(di notizie)* denial; *(di testimonianza)* refutation
smeraldo [zme'raldo] SM, AGG INV emerald; **un anello con smeraldo** an emerald ring
smerciare [zmer'tʃare] VT *(gen)* to sell; *(rimanenze)* to sell off
smercio, ci ['zmertʃo] SM sale; **avere poco/molto smercio** to have poor/good sales
smergo, ghi ['zmergo] SM *(anatra)* merganser; **smergo maggiore** goosander; **smergo minore** red-breasted merganser
smerigliato, a [zmeriʎ'ʎato] AGG: **carta smerigliata** emery paper; **vetro smerigliato** frosted glass
smerigliatrice [zmeriʎʎa'tritʃe] SF *(Tecn)* sander
smeriglio, gli [zme'riʎʎo] SM emery
smerlare [zmer'lare] VT to scallop
smerlo ['zmɛrlo] SM: **punto (a) smerlo** scallop stitch
smesso, a ['zmesso] PP *di* **smettere**
■ AGG: **abiti smessi** cast-offs
smettere ['zmettere] VB IRREG
■ VT *(gen)* to stop; *(studi)* to give up; *(vestiti)* to stop wearing; **smettila!** stop it!; **smettila di urlare!** stop shouting!
■ VI *(aus* **avere***)* *(interrompersi)* to stop, cease; **smettere di fare qc** to stop doing sth; **quando sono entrato hanno smesso di parlare** when I came in they stopped talking; **smettere di fumare** to stop *o* give up smoking; **sta cercando di smettere di fumare** he's trying to stop smoking; **smise di piovere** it stopped raining; **a che ora smetti (di lavorare) stasera?** when do you finish (work) this evening?
smidollato, a [zmidol'lato] AGG *(fig: persona)* spineless
■ SM/F spineless person
smilitarizzare [zmilitarid'dzare] VT to demilitarize
smilitarizzazione [zmilitariddzat'tsjone] SF demilitarization
smilzo, a ['zmiltso] AGG thin, lean
sminuire [zminu'ire] VT *(diminuire)* to diminish, lessen; *(fig)* to belittle, make light of, minimize; **sminuire l'importanza di qc** to play sth down
▶ **sminuirsi** VR *(fig)* to run o.s. down, belittle o.s.
sminuzzare [zminut'tsare] VT *(gen)* to break into small pieces; *(pane)* to crumble; *(carta)* to tear into small pieces
smisi *ecc* ['zmizi] VB *vedi* **smettere**
smistamento [zmista'mento] SM *(di posta)* sorting; *(Ferr)* shunting
smistare [zmis'tare] VT *(posta)* to sort; *(Ferr)* to shunt; **hanno smistato gli alunni in varie classi** they sorted the pupils into different classes
smisuratamente [zmizurata'mente] AVV *(crescere, allargarsi)* disproportionately, inordinately; *(mangiare)* excessively
smisurato, a [zmizu'rato] AGG enormous, immense; *(eccessivo)* excessive; *(senza limiti)* boundless, immeasurable
smitizzare [zmitid'dzare] VT to debunk
smobilitare [zmobili'tare] VT to demobilize
smobilitazione [zmobilitat'tsjone] SF demobilization
smobilizzo [zmobi'liddzo] SM *(Comm)* disinvestment
smoccolare [zmokko'lare] VI *(aus* **avere***)* *(fam)* to swear
smodato, a [zmo'dato] AGG excessive, unrestrained
smoderatamente [zmoderata'mente] AVV immoderately
smoderato, a [zmode'rato] AGG *(gen)* immoderate; **smoderato nel bere** intemperate
smog [zmɔg] SM INV smog
smoking ['smoukiŋ] SM INV dinner jacket *(Brit)*, tuxedo *(Am)*

LO SAPEVI...?
smoking non si traduce mai con la parola inglese *smoking*

smontabile [zmon'tabile] AGG *(gen)* which can be dismantled
smontare [zmon'tare] VT *(gen)* to take to pieces; *(macchina, mobile)* to dismantle, take to pieces; *(motore)* to strip (down); *(fig: persona: scoraggiare)* to discourage, dishearten
■ VI *(aus* **essere***)* **smontare (da)** *(bicicletta, treno)* to get off; *(sedia)* to get down (from); *(macchina)* to get out (of); **smontare da cavallo** to dismount; **a che ora smonti?** *(fig: da lavoro)* when do you knock off?, when do you finish (work)?;
▶ **smontarsi** VIP *(fig: persona: scoraggiarsi)* to lose heart, lose one's enthusiasm
smorfia ['zmɔrfja] SF *(gen)* **1** grimace; **una smorfia di dolore** a grimace of pain; **fare una smorfia di dolore** to grimace with pain; **fare smorfie** *(boccacce)* to make faces **2** *(atteggiamento lezioso)* simpering
smorfioso, a [zmor'fjoso] AGG simpering
■ SM/F: **non fare lo smorfioso** stop simpering; **fare la smorfiosa con qn** *(ragazza: civettare)* to flirt with sb
smorto, a ['zmɔrto] AGG *(viso)* pale, wan; *(colore, stile)* dull; *(voce, faccia)* expressionless, lifeless; **ci vuole un colore un po' più smorto** we need a colour that's not quite so bright
smorzare [zmor'tsare] VT *(suoni)* to muffle, deaden; *(colori)* to tone down; *(luce)* to dim; *(sete)* to quench; *(entusiasmo)* to dampen
▶ **smorzarsi** VIP *(suoni)* to die down, fade; *(luce)* to fade; *(entusiasmo)* to dampen
smorzata [zmor'tsata] SF *(Tennis)* drop shot
smosso, a ['zmɔsso] PP *di* **smuovere**
smottamento [zmotta'mento] SM landslide
smottare [zmot'tare] VI *(aus* **essere***)* to slide

Ss

sms [ɛsseɛmme'ɛsse] SIGLA M INV (*messaggino*: = **short message service**) text (message)
smunto, a ['zmunto] AGG haggard, pinched
smuovere ['zmwɔvere] VB IRREG
■ VT (*oggetto*) to move, shift; (*fig*: *persona*: *scuotere*) to rouse, stir; (: *dissuadere*): **smuovere qn da qc** to dissuade *o* deter sb from sth
▶ **smuoversi** VIP (*fig*: *persona*: *scuotersi*) to rouse o.s.; (: *dissuadersi*): **smuoversi da qc** to change one's mind about sth
smussare [zmus'sare] VT (*angolo*) to round off, smooth down; (*lama*) to blunt; (*fig*: *carattere*) to soften
▶ **smussarsi** VIP (*lama*) to become blunt; (*fig*: *carattere*) to soften
s.n. ABBR = *senza numero*
snaturare [znatu'rare] VT (*intenzioni, idee*) to distort, misrepresent
snaturato, a [znatu'rato] AGG cruel, heartless, inhuman; **una madre snaturata** a heartless mother
snazionalizzare [znattsjonalid'dzare] VT to denationalize
s.n.c. [ɛsseɛnne'tʃi] SIGLA F = **società in nome collettivo**
snellimento [znelli'mento] SM (*di traffico*) speeding up; (*di procedura*) streamlining
snellire [znel'lire] VT (*persona*) to make slim; (*traffico*) to speed up; (*procedura*) to streamline
▶ **snellirsi** VIP (*persona*) to (get) slim; (*traffico*) to speed up
snello, a ['znɛllo] AGG (*slanciato*) slim, slender; (*fig*: *stile*) easy, flowing
snervante [zner'vante] AGG (*attesa, lavoro*) exhausting; **l'attesa è stata snervante** it was a strain having to wait
snervare [zner'vare] VT to wear out, enervate
snervato, a [zner'vato] AGG worn out
snidare [zni'dare] VT (*selvaggina, anche fig*) to drive out, flush out; (*uccelli*) to flush (out)
sniffare [znif'fare] VT (*fam*: *cocaina*) to snort
snob [znɔb] AGG snobbish *inv*
■ SM/F INV snob
snobbare [znob'bare] VT to snub
snobismo [zno'bizmo] SM snobbery
snocciolare [znottʃo'lare] VT (*frutta*) to stone; (*fig*: *bugie, lamentele*) to rattle off; (: *verità*) to blab; (: *fam*: *soldi*) to shell out
snocciolatoio, oi [znottʃola'tojo] SM stoner
snodabile [zno'dabile] AGG (*lampada*) adjustable; (*tubo, braccio*) hinged; **rasoio con testina snodabile** swivel-head razor
snodare [zno'dare] VT (*nodo*) to untie, undo; (*membra*) to loosen (up), limber up
▶ **snodarsi** VIP (*tubatura*) to be hinged; (*fig*: *strada, fiume*) to wind
snowboard [snoʊbo:d] SM INV snowboard
SO SIGLA = *Sondrio*
■ ABBR (= **Sud-Ovest**) SW
so [sɔ] VB *vedi* **sapere**
soave [so'ave] AGG (*voce, maniere*) gentle; (*volto*) delicate, sweet; (*musica*) soft, sweet; (*profumo*) delicate

> **LO SAPEVI...?**
> **soave** non si traduce mai con la parola inglese *suave*

soavemente [soave'mente] AVV (*parlare*) gently; (*cantare*) sweetly; (*profumato*) delicately
soavità [soavi'ta] SF (*vedi agg*) gentleness; delicacy; sweetness; softness
sobbalzare [sobbal'tsare] VI (*aus* **avere**) (*veicolo*) to bump, jolt, jerk; (*persona*: *trasalire*) to jump, start
sobbalzo [sob'baltso] SM (*vedi vb*) bump, jolt, jerk; jump, start
sobbarcarsi [sobbar'karsi] VR: **sobbarcarsi a** to undertake, take on
sobborgo, ghi [sob'borgo] SM suburb
sobillare [sobil'lare] VT to stir up, incite
sobillatore, trice [sobilla'tore] SM/F instigator
sobriamente [sobrja'mente] AVV (*gen*) soberly; **vivere sobriamente** to lead a simple life
sobrietà [sobrje'ta] SF INV (*gen*) sobriety; (*nel mangiare, bere*) moderation; (*di colore, stile*) simplicity
sobrio, ria, ri, rie ['sɔbrjo] AGG (*persona*) sober, moderate; (: *non ubriaco*) sober; (*colore, stile*) sober, simple; (*vita*) moderate, simple; **vestire in modo sobrio** to dress soberly
Soc. ABBR (= **Società**) Soc.
socchiudere [sok'kjudere] VT IRREG (*occhi*) to half-close; (*porta, finestra*) to leave ajar; **ha socchiuso la porta** he left the door ajar; **ho socchiuso gli occhi** I half-closed my eyes
socchiuso, a [sok'kjuso] PP *di* **socchiudere**
■ AGG (*porta, finestra*) ajar; (*occhi*) half-closed; **lascia la porta socchiusa** leave the door ajar; **aveva gli occhi socchiusi** his eyes were half-closed
soccida ['sɔttʃida] SF (*Dir*): **contratto di soccida** agistment contract
soccombere [sok'kombere] VI DIF to succumb, give way
soccorrere [sok'korrere] VT IRREG to help, assist
soccorritore, trice [sokkorri'tore] SM/F rescuer
soccorso, a [sok'korso] PP *di* **soccorrere**
■ SM (*gen*) help, assistance, aid; (*di vittime di terremoto ecc*) rescue; **organizzare soccorsi per i terremotati** to organize relief *o* aid for the earthquake victims; **prestare soccorso a qn** to help *o* assist sb; **nessuno si è fermato a prestare soccorso** nobody stopped to help; **venire in soccorso di qn** to help sb, come to sb's aid; **operazioni di soccorso** rescue operations; **omissione di soccorso** failure to offer assistance; **pronto soccorso** (*assistenza*) first aid; (*reparto*) casualty; **soccorso stradale** breakdown service
socialdemocratico, a, ci, che [sotʃaldemo'kratiko] AGG Social Democratic
■ SM/F Social Democrat
socialdemocrazia [sotʃaldemokrat'tsia] SF Social Democracy
sociale [so'tʃale] AGG **1** (*gen*) social; **la realtà sociale** the reality of life **2** (*di ditta, società*) company *attr* **3** (*di associazione*) club *attr*, association *attr*
socialismo [sotʃa'lizmo] SM socialism
socialista, i, e [sotʃa'lista] AGG, SM/F socialist
socializzare [sotʃalid'dzare] VI (*aus* **avere**) to socialize
socializzazione [sotʃaliddzat'tsjone] SF socialization
socialmente [sotʃal'mente] AVV socially
società [sotʃe'ta] SF INV **1** (*comunità*) society; **vivere in società** to live in society; **l'alta società** high society; **la buona società** polite society; **la società dei consumi** the consumer society; **giochi di società** parlour games **2** (*associazione*) association, club, society; **una società segreta** a secret society; **società sportiva** sports club **3** (*Comm*) company, firm; **in società con qn** in partnership with sb; **mettersi in società con qn** to go into business with sb; **si è messo in società con suo fratello** he went into business with his brother; **società per azioni** joint-stock

company; **società finanziaria** holding company; **società di intermediazione mobiliare** brokerage company; **società in nome collettivo** unlimited company; **società a responsabilità limitata** *type of limited liability company*

socievole [so'tʃevole] AGG sociable

socievolezza [sotʃevo'lettsa] SF sociability, sociableness

socio, ci ['sɔtʃo] SM **1** (*Comm*) partner, associate (*Am*); **socio non attivo** silent partner; **"Bianchi e Soci"** "Bianchi & Co" **2** (*membro*) member; (*di società scientifiche*) fellow; **farsi socio di un circolo** to become a member of a club

socioeconomico, a, ci, che [sotʃoeko'nɔmiko] AGG socioeconomic

sociologia [sotʃolo'dʒia] SF sociology

sociologico, a, ci, che [sotʃo'lɔdʒiko] AGG sociological

sociologo, a, gi, ghe [so'tʃɔlogo] SM/F sociologist

sociopolitico, a, ci, che [sotʃopo'litiko] AGG sociopolitical

Socrate ['sɔkrate] SM Socrates

soda ['sɔda] SF **1** (*Chim*) soda; **soda caustica** caustic soda **2** (*per bevande*) soda (water)

sodalizio, zi [soda'littsjo] SM association, society

soddisfacente [soddisfa'tʃɛnte] AGG satisfactory

soddisfacentemente [soddisfatʃente'mente] AVV satisfactorily

soddisfare [soddis'fare] VB IRREG, VT, VI (*aus* **avere**) **soddisfare (a)** (*gen*) to satisfy; (*impegno*) to fulfil; (*richiesta*) to comply with, meet; **il mio lavoro non mi soddisfa** my job doesn't satisfy me

soddisfatto, a [soddis'fatto] PP *di* **soddisfare**
■ AGG satisfied, pleased; **essere soddisfatto di** to be satisfied *o* pleased with; **sono soddisfatto del risultato** I'm pleased with the result; **mostrarsi soddisfatto** to show one's satisfaction

soddisfazione [soddisfat'tsjone] SF (*gen, di offesa*) satisfaction; **avere la soddisfazione di** to have the satisfaction of; **dare la soddisfazione a qn di** to give sb the satisfaction of; **la vita mi ha dato tante soddisfazioni!** life has given me so much satisfaction!

sodio ['sɔdjo] SM (*Chim*) sodium

sodo, a ['sɔdo] AGG (*terreno*) hard, firm; (*corpo*) firm; **uova sode** hard-boiled eggs
■ SM: **venire al sodo** to come to the point; **vieni al sodo!** come to the point!
■ AVV: **picchiare sodo** to hit hard; **dormire sodo** to sleep soundly; **lavorare sodo** to work hard

sodomia [sodo'mia] SF sodomy

sodomita, i [sodo'mita] SM sodomite

sofà [so'fa] SM INV sofa

sofferente [soffe'rɛnte] AGG suffering

sofferenza [soffe'rɛntsa] SF **1** (*gen*) suffering; **dopo anni di sofferenze** (*povertà, stenti*) after years of hardship **2** (*Comm*): **in sofferenza** unpaid

soffermare [soffer'mare] VT: **soffermò lo sguardo su...** his eyes lingered on ...
▶ **soffermarsi** VIP: **soffermarsi su** (*argomento, punto*) to dwell on

sofferto, a [sof'fɛrto] PP *di* **soffrire**
■ AGG (*vittoria*) hard-fought, hard-won; (*distacco*) painful; **una decisione sofferta** a painful decision; **ha un viso sofferto** she has the face of someone who has suffered

soffiare [sof'fjare] VT **1** (*gen*) to blow; **soffiarsi il naso** to blow one's nose; **si è soffiata il naso rumorosamente** she blew her nose loudly; **soffiare il vetro** to blow glass **2** (*fig fam: rubare*): **soffiare qn/qc a qn** to pinch *o* steal sb/sth from sb
■ VI (*aus* **avere**) (*gen*) to blow; (*sbuffare*) to puff (and blow); **soffiava un forte vento** a strong wind was blowing; **soffiare sul fuoco** (*fig*) to fan the flames

soffiata [sof'fjata] SF (*fam*) tip-off; **fare una soffiata alla polizia** to tip off the police

soffice ['sɔffitʃe] AGG soft

sofficemente [soffitʃe'mente] AVV softly

soffietto [sof'fjetto] SM **1** (*Mus, per fuoco*) bellows *pl* **2** **porta a soffietto** folding door

soffio, fi ['soffjo] SM **1** (*di aria, vento*) breath; **non c'era neanche un soffio di vento** there wasn't a breath of wind; **in un soffio** (*fig*) in a flash; **per un soffio** (*fig*) by a hair's breadth **2** (*Med*) murmur; **soffio cardiaco** heart murmur

soffione[1] [sof'fjone] SM (*Geol*): **soffione boracifero** fumarole

soffione[2] [sof'fjone] SM (*pianta*) dandelion

soffitta [sof'fitta] SF (*solaio*) attic, loft; (*appartamento*) attic flat (*Brit*) *o* apartment (*Am*)

soffitto [sof'fitto] SM ceiling

soffocamento [soffoka'mento] SM suffocation; **è morto per soffocamento** he died of suffocation

soffocante [soffo'kante] AGG (*caldo, atmosfera*) suffocating, stifling; (*fig: persona*): **ma sei proprio soffocante!** you're stifling me!

soffocare [soffo'kare] VT (*gen*) to suffocate; (*fiamme*) to smother, put out; (*fig: sommossa*) to suppress; (*sentimento*) to stifle, repress; (*sbadiglio*) to stifle; **ho rischiato di soffocare** I nearly suffocated; **qui dentro si soffoca** it's stifling in here; **soffocare qn di baci/d'affetto** to smother sb with kisses/with affection

Ss

soffocato, a [soffo'kato] AGG (*gemito, grido*) stifled; **è morto soffocato** he was suffocated

soffocazione [soffokat'tsjone] SF (*gen*) suffocation; (*di sommossa*) suppression

soffriggere [sof'friddʒere] VB IRREG, VT, VI (*aus* **avere**) to fry lightly

soffrire [sof'frire] VB IRREG
■ VT **1** (*patire*) to suffer; **soffrire la fame/sete** to suffer (from) hunger/thirst; **soffrire le pene dell'inferno** (*fig*) to go through *o* suffer hell **2** (*sopportare*) to stand, bear; **non lo posso soffrire** I can't stand him
■ VI (*aus* **avere**) **1** to suffer, be in pain; **sta soffrendo molto** he's suffering a lot; **la tua vita privata ne soffrirà** your private life will suffer **2** (*Med*): **soffrire di qc** to suffer from sth; **soffre di frequenti mal di testa** he suffers from frequent headaches

soffritto, a [sof'fritto] PP *di* **soffriggere**
■ SM (*Culin*) *fried mixture of herbs, bacon and onions*

soffuso, a [sof'fuzo] AGG (*luce*) suffused, diffused

sofisticare [sofisti'kare] VT (*vino*) to adulterate

sofisticato, a [sofisti'kato] AGG **1** (*vino*) adulterated **2** (*macchina, persona*) sophisticated

sofisticazione [sofistikat'tsjone] SF (*di vino*) adulteration

Sofocle ['sɔfokle] SM Sophocles

soft [sɔft] AGG INV (*atmosfera, ambiente*) relaxed; (*luce, illuminazione*) soft; (*approccio, atteggiamento, tattica*) softly-softly

software [sɔft'wɛə] SM INV: **software applicativo** applications package

soggettista, i, e [soddʒet'tista] SM/F (*Cine, TV*) scriptwriter

soggettivamente [soddʒettiva'mente] AVV subjectively
soggettività [soddʒettivi'ta] SF subjectivity
soggettivo, a [soddʒet'tivo] AGG subjective
soggetto[1], a [sod'dʒɛtto] AGG: **soggetto a** (*a variazioni, danni*) subject *o* liable to; **soggetto a tassa** taxable; **andare** *o* **essere soggetto a frequenti mal di testa** to be prone to frequent headaches
soggetto[2] [sod'dʒɛtto] SM **1** (*argomento*) subject, topic; **recitare a soggetto** (*Teatro*) to improvise **2** (*Gramm*) subject **3** (*persona: Med*) subject; (*: pegg*) sort; **è un cattivo soggetto** (*pegg*) he's a bad sort
soggezione [soddʒet'tsjone] SF **1** (*imbarazzo, disagio*) uneasiness; **incutere soggezione a qn** *or* **mettere qn in soggezione** to make sb feel uneasy; **avere soggezione di qn** to feel uneasy with sb, be ill at ease in sb's presence, be in awe of sb; **aveva soggezione del fratello maggiore** he was in awe of his older brother **2** (*sottomissione*) subjection
sogghignare [soggiɲ'ɲare] VI (*aus* **avere**) to sneer
sogghigno [sog'giɲɲo] SM sneer
soggiacere [soddʒa'tʃere] VI IRREG (*aus* **essere**) **soggiacere a** (*leggi*) to be subject to; (*essere sottomesso a*) to be subjected to, submit to
soggiogare [soddʒo'gare] VT to subdue, subjugate
soggiornare [soddʒor'nare] VI (*aus* **avere**) to stay
soggiorno [sod'dʒorno] SM **1** (*permanenza*) stay; **un soggiorno di due settimane a Londra** a two-week stay in London; **luogo di soggiorno** holiday (*Brit*) *o* vacation (*Am*) resort **2** (*stanza*) living room, sitting room (*Brit*), lounge (*Brit*) **3** (*mobili*) living-room suite
soggiungere [sod'dʒundʒere] VT IRREG to add
soggiunto, a [sod'dʒunto] PP *di* **soggiungere**
soggolo [sog'golo] SM (*Rel*) wimple
soglia ['sɔʎʎa] SF **1** (*di porta*) doorstep; (*fig*) threshold; **varcare la soglia** to cross the threshold; **essere sulla soglia della vecchiaia** to be on the threshold of old age **2** (*Geol*) sill
sogliola ['sɔʎʎola] SF (*pesce*) sole
sognante [soɲ'ɲante] AGG dreamy
sognare [soɲ'ɲare] VT **1** **sognare qc** to dream of *o* about sth; **ho sognato di essere sulla luna** I dreamt I was on the moon; **stanotte ti ho sognato** I dreamt about you last night; **ha sempre sognato una casa così/di avere una casa così** he has always dreamt of a house like that/of having a house like that **2** (*fig fam*): **non me lo sogno nemmeno!** I wouldn't dream of it!; **te lo puoi sognare!** you can forget it!, in your dreams!; **non me lo sono mica sognato!** I didn't dream it up!
■VI (*aus* **avere**) to dream; **sognare a occhi aperti** to daydream;
▶ **sognarsi** VIP: **sognarsi di qn/qc** to dream of sb/sth
sognatore, trice [soɲɲa'tore] SM/F dreamer
sogno ['soɲɲo] SM dream; **un brutto sogno** a bad dream; **fare un sogno** to have a dream; **ho fatto uno strano sogno** I had a strange dream; **un sogno ad occhi aperti** a daydream; **la donna dei suoi sogni** the woman of his dreams; **quella ragazza è un sogno** that girl is gorgeous; **una crociera/casa di sogno** a dream cruise/house; **nemmeno** *o* **neanche per sogno!** not on your life!, no way!
soia ['sɔja] SF (*Bot*) soya
sol [sɔl] SM INV (*Mus*) G; (*: solfeggiando la scala*) so(h)
solaio, ai [so'lajo] SM (*soffitta*) attic, loft
solamente [sola'mente] AVV only, just
solanum [so'lanum] SM (*Bot*) solanum
solare [so'lare] AGG **1** (*Astron*) solar; (*crema*) sun *attr*; **crema solare** sun cream; **energia solare** solar power; **luce solare** sunlight; **pannelli solari** solar panels; **plesso solare** (*Anat*) solar plexus **2** (*fig: ragionamento*) clear; **una persona solare** a sunny-natured person
solarium [so'larjum] SM INV solarium
solcare [sol'kare] VT (*terreno, fig: mari*) to plough (*Brit*), plow (*Am*)
solco, chi ['solko] SM (*di aratro*) furrow; (*di ruota*) track, rut; (*di nave*) wake; (*su disco*) groove; (*sulla fronte*) wrinkle, furrow
solcometro [sol'kɔmetro] SM (*Naut*) log (*device*)
soldatesca [solda'teska] SF (*pegg*) soldiers *pl*, troops *pl*
soldatesco, a [solda'tesko] AGG (*pegg*) soldierlike, rough
soldatino [solda'tino] SM toy soldier
soldato [sol'dato] SM soldier; **fare il soldato** to serve in the army; **andare (a fare il) soldato** to enlist (in the army); **soldato di leva** conscript; **soldato semplice** private
soldo ['sɔldo] SM **1** (*quattrino, moneta*) penny, cent (*Am*); **non ho un soldo** I haven't got a penny; **non vale un soldo bucato** it isn't worth a penny; **per quattro soldi** for next to nothing; **è roba da pochi soldi** it's cheap stuff **2** **soldi** SMPL (*denaro*) money *sg*; **fare soldi** to make money; **essere pieno di soldi** to have lots of money; **buttare via i soldi** to throw one's money away; **avere un sacco di soldi** to be loaded, to be rolling in money
sole ['sole] SM (*astro*) sun; (*luce*) sun(light); (*calore*) sun(shine); **preferirei stare al sole** I'd rather stay in the sun; **c'è il sole** the sun is shining; **una giornata di sole** a sunny day; **prendere il sole** to sunbathe; **al calar del sole** at sunset; **il Sole che ride** (*Pol*) *symbol of the Italian Green Party*

> **LO SAPEVI...?**
> **sole** non si traduce mai con la parola inglese *sole*

soleggiato, a [soled'dʒato] AGG sunny; **il mio appartamento è più soleggiato del suo** my flat is sunnier than hers
solenne [so'lɛnne] AGG (*giuramento, voto*) solemn; (*scherz: ceffone*) almighty, sound
solennemente [solenne'mente] AVV solemnly
solennità [solenni'ta] SF **1** (*di cerimonia*) solemnity **2** (*festività*) holiday, feast day
solenoide [sole'nɔide] SM (*Elettr*) solenoid
solere [so'lere] VB DIF
■VT: **solere fare qc** to be in the habit of doing sth; **soleva raccontare lunghe storie della guerra** he used to tell long stories about the war
■VB IMPERS (*aus* **essere**) **come suole accadere** as is usually the case, as usually happens; **come si suol dire** as they say
solerte [so'lɛrte] AGG diligent
solertemente [solerte'mente] AVV diligently
solerzia [so'lɛrtsja] SF diligence
soletta [so'letta] SF **1** (*per scarpe*) insole **2** (*di sci*) running surface **3** (*Edil*) slab
solfa ['sɔlfa] SF: **è sempre la solita solfa** it's always the same old story
solfatara [solfa'tara] SF (*Geol*) solfatara
solfato [sol'fato] SM (*Chim*) sulphate (*Brit*), sulfate (*Am*); **solfato ferroso** iron sulphate *o* sulfate; **solfato di rame** copper sulphate *o* sulfate
solfeggio, gi [sol'feddʒo] SM (*Mus*) solfeggio
solfito [sol'fito] SM (*Chim*) sulphite

solforico, a, ci, che [sol'fɔriko] AGG (*Chim*) sulphuric (*Brit*), sulfuric (*Am*); **acido solforico** sulphuric *o* sulfuric acid
solfuro [sol'furo] SM (*Chim*) sulphur (*Brit*), sulfur (*Am*)
solidale [soli'dale] AGG in agreement; **essere solidale con qn** (*essere d'accordo*) to be in agreement with sb; (*appoggiare*) to be behind sb
solidamente [solida'mente] AVV solidly
solidarietà [solidarje'ta] SF solidarity
solidarizzare [solidarid'dzare] VI (*aus* **avere**) **solidarizzare con** to express one's solidarity with
solidificare [solidifi'kare] VT, VI (*aus* **essere**), **solidificarsi** VIP to solidify
solidificazione [solidifikat'tsjone] SF solidification
solidità [solidi'ta] SF (*vedi agg*) solidity; firmness; strength; soundness; reliability
solido, a ['sɔlido] AGG **1** (*non liquido*) solid **2** (*robusto: oggetto, muscoli, fede*) firm, strong; (*gambe, muri*) sturdy, sound; (*nervi, salute*) sound, strong; (*amicizia, matrimonio*) sound, solid; (*società*) reliable, sound
■ SM (*Mat*) solid
soliloquio, qui [soli'lɔkwjo] SM (*Teatro*) soliloquy; (*discorso tra sé e sé*) monologue
solipsismo [solip'sizmo] SM (*Filosofia*) solipsism
solista, i, e [so'lista] AGG solo
■ SM/F soloist
solitamente [solita'mente] AVV usually, generally, as a rule
solitaria [soli'tarja] SF (*Naut*): **in solitaria** single-handed
solitariamente [solitarja'mente] AVV alone
solitario, ria, ri, rie [soli'tarjo] AGG (*gen*) solitary; (*passante, navigatore*) lone, solitary; (*luogo, strada*) lonely, deserted, secluded; (*vita*) lonely, secluded; **una strada buia e solitaria** a dark, lonely road; **è un tipo solitario** he is a loner
■ SM/F (*persona*) solitary person, loner
■ SM **1** (*brillante*) solitaire **2** (*Carte*) patience; **sto facendo un solitario** I'm playing patience
solito, a ['sɔlito] AGG usual; **essere solito fare qc** to be in the habit of doing sth; **è solito mangiare alle otto** he usually eats at eight o'clock, he is in the habit of eating at eight o'clock; **era solito passeggiare di notte** he used to go for walks during the night; **è sempre la solita storia!** it's always the same old story!; **siamo alle solite!** (*fam*) here we go again!
■ SM: **di solito** usually, generally, as a rule; **di solito mi alzo alle sette** I usually get up at seven o'clock; **(come) al solito** as usual; **più tardi del solito** later than usual
solitudine [soli'tudine] SF **1** (*tranquillità*) solitude; (*l'essere solo*) loneliness; (*di posto*) loneliness **2** (*luogo solitario*) solitude
sollazzare [sollat'tsare] VT to entertain
▶ **sollazzarsi** VIP to amuse o.s.
sollazzo [sol'lattso] SM amusement
sollecitamente [solletʃita'mente] AVV promptly, quickly
sollecitare [solletʃi'tare] VT **1** (*affrettare: pratica, lavoro, telefonata*) to speed up; (*: persona*) to urge on; (*chiedere con insistenza*) to press for, request urgently; **sollecitare qn perché faccia qc** to urge sb to do sth **2** (*stimolare: fantasia*) to stimulate, rouse **3** (*Tecn*) to stress
sollecitazione [solletʃitat'tsjone] SF **1** (*richiesta*) request, entreaty; (*fig: stimolo*) stimulus, incentive; **lettera di sollecitazione** (*Comm*) reminder **2** (*Tecn*) stress
sollecito, a [sol'letʃito] AGG prompt, quick; **essere sollecito nel fare qc** to be prompt in doing sth
■ SM (*Comm*) reminder; **sollecito di pagamento** payment reminder
sollecitudine [solletʃi'tudine] SF promptness, speed
solleone [solle'one] SM (*periodo estivo*) dog days *pl*; (*gran caldo*) summer heat
solleticare [solleti'kare] VT (*gen*) to tickle; (*fig: curiosità*) to arouse; (*: fantasia*) to excite; (*: appetito*) to whet
solletico [sol'letiko] SM tickling; **fare il solletico a qn** to tickle sb; **mi ha fatto il solletico** he tickled me; **soffrire il solletico** to be ticklish; **soffro molto il solletico** I'm very ticklish
sollevamento [solleva'mento] SM **1** (*gen*) raising, lifting; **c'è stato un sollevamento del terreno** (*Geol*) the ground has risen; **sollevamento pesi** (*Sport*) weightlifting
▷ www.fipcf.org/
2 (*rivolta*) revolt, rebellion
sollevare [solle'vare] VT **1** (*peso, occhi, testa*) to lift, raise; (*polvere, sabbia*) to raise; (*con argani*) to hoist; **non riesco a sollevare la valigia** I can't lift the suitcase; **ha sollevato gli occhi dal libro** she raised her eyes from the book; **sollevare da terra** to lift up, lift off the ground; **il motoscafo sollevò delle onde** the motorboat made waves; **sollevare un'obiezione** (*fig*) to raise an objection **2** (*fig: dar conforto*) to comfort, cheer up; **sollevare il morale a qn** to raise sb's morale **3** (*rendere libero*): **sollevare qn da** (*incarico*) to dismiss sb from; (*fatica*) to relieve sb of; **sollevare qn da un peso** (*fig*) to take a load off sb's mind **4** (*fig: folla*) to rouse, stir up, stir (to revolt)
▶ **sollevarsi** VIP **1** (*persona*) to get up; **sollevati un po'** (*dal letto*) sit up a little; (*da una sedia*) stand up a minute; **sollevarsi da terra** (*persona*) to get up from the ground; (*aereo*) to take off **2** (*vento, polvere*) to rise; (*nebbia*) to lift, clear; **si sollevarono onde enormi** the sea became very rough **3** (*fig: riprendersi*) to feel better, recover; **sollevarsi da qc** (*malattia, spavento*) to get over sth; **sentirsi sollevato** to feel relieved **4** (*fig: truppe, popolo*) to rise up, rebel
sollievo [sol'ljɛvo] SM relief; (*conforto*) comfort; **con mio grande sollievo** to my great relief; **un sospiro di sollievo** a sigh of relief; **ho tirato un sospiro di sollievo** I heaved a sigh of relief
sollucchero [sol'lukkero] SM: **andare in sollucchero** (*fig*) to go into ecstasy
solo, a ['solo] AGG **1** (*senza compagnia*) alone, on one's (*o* its *ecc*) own, by oneself (*o* itself *ecc*); (*isolato*) lonely; **da solo** (*senza aiuti*) by oneself (*o* himself *ecc*); **entra pure, sono solo** please come in, I'm alone *o* there's no-one with me; **vive (da) solo** he lives on his own; **è tanto solo** he's very lonely; **ci vado da sola** I'll go on my own; **riesci a farlo da solo?** can you do it by yourself?; **parlare da solo** to talk to oneself **2** (*senza altri*): **finalmente soli!** alone at last!; **vogliono stare sole** they want to be alone; **possiamo vederci da soli?** can I see you in private? **3** (*seguito da sostantivo*) only; **il solo motivo** the only *o* sole reason; **c'è un solo libro** there is only one book; **ha un solo figlio maschio** she has only one son; **è il solo proprietario** he's the sole proprietor; **essi sono una persona sola** they are as one; **non si vive di solo pane** man does not live by bread alone; **l'incontrò due sole volte** he only met him twice; **la sola idea mi fa tremare** the very *o* mere thought of it is enough to make me tremble; **la mia**

Ss

sola speranza è che... my only hope is that ...; **non un solo istante ho creduto che...** I didn't believe for a single moment that ... **4** (*con agg numerale*): **veniamo noi tre soli** just *o* only the three of us are coming
■AVV (*soltanto*) only, just; **resto solo un giorno** I'm only staying one day; **l'ho incontrato solo due volte** I've only met him twice; **mancavi solo tu** you were the only one missing, you were the only one who wasn't there; **non solo ha negato, ma...** not only did he deny it, but ...; **solo che**
■CONG but; **l'ho visto, solo che non son riuscito a parlargli** I saw him, but I didn't get a chance to speak to him
■SM/F: **sono il solo a poter giudicare** I'm the only one who can judge; **è la sola che ha chiesto notizie** she was the only one to ask for news
■SM: **a solo** (*Mus*) = **assolo**

solstizio, zi [sol'stittsjo] SM solstice

soltanto [sol'tanto] AVV (*gen*) only; **c'era soltanto lui** there was only him; **restano qui soltanto 2 giorni** they are only staying 2 days; **sono arrivato soltanto ieri** I only arrived yesterday; **chiedo soltanto questo!** that's all I ask!
■CONG but, only; **vorrei, soltanto (che) non posso** I would like to, but I can't; **ha la macchina, soltanto temo che non funzioni** he has a car, only *o* but I don't think it's working

solubile [so'lubile] AGG soluble; **caffè solubile** instant coffee

solubilità [solubili'ta] SF (*Chim*) solubility

soluto [so'luto] SM (*Chim*) solute

soluzione [solut'tsjone] SF (*gen, Mat, Chim*) solution; (*di indovinello*) answer; **non riesco a trovare una soluzione** I can't find a solution; **non c'è altra soluzione!** there's no alternative!; **senza soluzione di continuità** uninterruptedly

solvente [sol'vεnte] AGG (*Chim*) solvent
■SM (*Chim*) solvent; **solvente per unghie** nail polish *o* nail varnish (*Brit*) remover; **solvente per vernici** paint remover *o* stripper

solvenza [sol'vεntsa] SF (*Comm*) solvency

soma ['sɔma] SF burden, load; **bestia da soma** pack animal, beast of burden

Somalia [so'malja] SF Somalia

somalo, a ['sɔmalo] AGG, SM/F Somali, Somalian
■SM (*lingua*) Somali

somaro [so'maro] SM (*Zool*) donkey, ass; (*fig*) dunce; **sei un somaro!** you're an idiot!

somatico, a, ci, che [so'matiko] AGG (*Bio*) somatic

somatizzare [somatid'dzare] VT (*Psic*): **somatizzare le proprie ansie** to make o.s. physically ill with worry

somatizzazione [somatiddzat'tsjone] SF psychosomatic reaction

somatostatina [somatosta'tina] SF (*Med*) somatostatin

sombrero [som'brεro] SM INV sombrero

somigliante [somiʎ'ʎante] AGG similar; **essere somigliante a qc** to be similar to *o* like sth; **essere somigliante a qn** to look like sb; **sono molto somiglianti** they are very alike; **è un ritratto molto somigliante** it's a very good likeness

somiglianza [somiʎ'ʎantsa] SF (*tra cose*) similarity; (*tra persone*) resemblance

somigliare [somiʎ'ʎare] VI (*aus* **avere**) **somigliare a** to resemble, look like, be like; **somiglia a sua sorella** she looks like *o* resembles her sister; **somiglio moltissimo a mia madre** I look very like my mother; **somiglia al mio** it looks like mine
▶ **somigliarsi** VR (*uso reciproco*) to be alike, look alike, resemble each other; **non si somigliano affatto** they don't look at all like each other

somma ['somma] SF **1** (*Mat*) addition; (*: risultato*) sum; (*fig: sostanza*) conclusion; **sai fare le somme?** can you add up?; **tirare le somme** (*fig*) to sum up; **tirate le somme** (*fig*) all things considered **2** (*di denaro*) amount, sum (of money); **una grossa somma di denaro** a large sum of money

sommamente [somma'mente] AVV extremely, immensely

sommare [som'mare] VT (*Mat*) to add up, add together; (*aggiungere*) to add; **somma i due numeri** add the two numbers together; **tutto sommato** (*fig*) all things considered, all in all; **tutto sommato sono contento di essere venuto** all in all I'm glad I came
■VI (*aus* **avere** *o* **essere**) (*ammontare*): **sommare a** to add up, amount to

sommariamente [sommarja'mente] AVV (*analizzare, discutere*) in brief; **l'hanno giudicato sommariamente** (*Dir*) he was given a summary trial

sommario, ria, ri, rie [som'marjo] AGG **1** (*esame*) brief; (*lavoro*) rough; **racconto sommario** brief summary **2** (*Dir*) summary
■SM (*breve riassunto*) summary; (*compendio*) compendium; **sommario del telegiornale** (TV) news headlines *pl*

sommelier [sɔmə'lje] SM INV wine waiter

sommergere [som'mεrdʒere] VT IRREG (*barca*) to submerge; **le onde hanno sommerso la barca** the waves swamped the boat; **sommergere qn di** (*doni, gentilezze*) to overwhelm sb with; (*baci*) to smother sb with

sommergibile [sommer'dʒibile] AGG submersible
■SM (*Naut*) submarine

sommergibilista, i [sommerdʒibi'lista] SM submariner

sommerso, a [som'mεrso] PP *di* **sommergere**
■AGG (*tesori, città*) sunken; **l'economia sommersa** the black economy
■SM: **il sommerso** (*economia*) the black economy

sommesso, a [som'messo] AGG soft, low, subdued

somministrare [somminis'trare] VT to give, administer

somministrazione [somministrat'tsjone] SF giving, administration

sommità [sommi'ta] SF INV summit, top; (*fig*) peak, height

sommo, a ['sommo] AGG (*grado, livello*) highest; (*rispetto*) highest, greatest; (*poeta, artista*) great, outstanding; **il Sommo Pontefice** the Supreme Pontiff; **per sommi capi** in short, in brief
■SM (*fig*) peak, height

sommossa [som'mɔssa] SF uprising, revolt

sommozzatore [sommottsa'tore] SM (deep-sea) diver; (*Mil*) frogman

sonagliera [sonaʎ'ʎεra] SF bell-collar

sonaglio, gli [so'naʎʎo] SM (*di mucche*) bell; (*per bambini*) rattle

sonante [so'nante] AGG: **denaro** *o* **moneta sonante** (ready) cash

sonar ['sɔnar] SM INV (*Naut*) sonar, echo sounder

sonare *ecc* [so'nare] = **suonare** *ecc*

sonata [so'nata] SF (*Mus*) sonata

sonda ['sonda] SF (*Med, Meteor, Aer*) probe; (*Mineralogia*) drill

■ AGG INV: **pallone sonda** weather balloon
sondaggio, gi [son'daddʒo] SM (*vedi vb*) sounding; drilling, boring; probing; survey; **sondaggio d'opinioni** opinion poll
sondare [son'dare] VT (*Naut*) to sound; (*Mineralogia*) to drill, to bore; (*Meteor, Med*) to probe; (*fig: opinione*) to survey, poll
sondriese [son'drjese] AGG of *o* from Sondrio
■ SM/F inhabitant *o* native of Sondrio
sonetto [so'netto] SM sonnet
sonnacchiosamente [sonnakkjosa'mente] AVV sleepily
sonnacchioso, a [sonnak'kjoso] AGG sleepy
sonnambulismo [sonnambu'lizmo] SM somnambulism, sleepwalking
sonnambulo, a [son'nambulo] SM/F somnambulist, sleepwalker
sonnecchiare [sonnek'kjare] VI (*aus* **avere**) to doze, drowse, nod
sonnellino [sonnel'lino] SM nap; **fare un sonnellino** to have a nap
sonnifero [son'nifero] SM (*pillola*) sleeping pill *o* drug; (*gocce*) sleeping draught (*Brit*) *o* draft (*Am*)
sonno ['sonno] SM **1** (*il dormire*) sleep; **avere il sonno pesante/leggero** to be a heavy/light sleeper; **parli durante il sonno** you talk in your sleep; **prendere sonno** to fall asleep; **ho perso 4 ore di sonno** I lost 4 hours' sleep; **il sonno eterno** (*euf*) eternal rest
2 (*bisogno di dormire*) sleepiness, sleep; **avere sonno** to be sleepy; **cascare dal sonno** to be asleep on one's feet; **far venire sonno a qn** (*fig*) to send sb to sleep
sonnolento, a [sonno'lɛnto] AGG (*persona*) sleepy, drowsy; (*movimenti*) sluggish
sonnolenza [sonno'lɛntsa] SF sleepiness, drowsiness
sono ['sono] VB *vedi* **essere**
sonometro [so'nɔmetro] SM (*Fis*) sonometer
sonoramente [sonora'mente] AVV: **schiaffeggiare qn sonoramente** to give sb a resounding slap
sonorità [sonori'ta] SF sonority, resonance
sonorizzare [sonorid'dzare] VT (*Ling*) to voice; (*Cine*) to add a soundtrack to
sonorizzazione [sonoriddzat'tsjone] SF (*Cine*) addition of a soundtrack
sonoro, a [so'nɔro] AGG **1** (*ambiente*) resonant; (*voce*) sonorous; (*schiaffo, risata*) loud; (*fig: parole*) high-flown, high-sounding; **una risata sonora** a loud laugh
2 (*Cine*) sound *attr*; **colonna sonora di un film** soundtrack of a film; **il cinema sonoro** the talkies *pl*
3 (*Ling*) voiced
■ SM: **il sonoro** (*cinema*) the talkies *pl*; (*parte sonora*) soundtrack
sontuosamente [sontuosa'mente] AVV sumptuously
sontuosità [sontuosi'ta] SF INV sumptuousness
sontuoso, a [sontu'oso] AGG sumptuous
soperchieria [soperkje'ria] SF = **soverchieria**
sopire [so'pire] VT (*dolore, tensione*) to soothe
sopore [so'pore] SM drowsiness
soporifero, a [sopo'rifero] AGG (*sostanza*) soporific; (*fig: discorso*) tedious, soporific
soppalco, chi [sop'palko] SM mezzanine
sopperire [soppe'rire] VI (*aus* **avere**) **sopperire a** to provide for; **sopperire alla mancanza di qc** to make up for the lack of sth
soppesare [soppe'sare] VT to weigh in one's hand(s), feel the weight of; **soppesare i pro e i contro** to weigh up the pros and cons
soppiantare [soppjan'tare] VT to supplant
soppiatto [sop'pjatto] AVV: **di soppiatto** secretly, furtively; **se n'è andato di soppiatto** he stole off *o* away
sopportabile [soppor'tabile] AGG tolerable, bearable
sopportabilità [sopportabili'ta] SF: **è al limite della sopportabilità** it is scarcely tolerable
sopportare [soppor'tare] VT **1** (*peso*) to support, bear
2 (*subire: perdita, spese*) to bear, sustain; (: *conseguenze, disagi*) to bear, suffer **3** (*tollerare: persona, comportamento*) to stand, put up with, bear, tolerate, endure; (: *temperatura, sforzo*) to take, stand, withstand; **non sopporto il pesce/il giallo** I can't stand fish/yellow; **non sopporto le persone disoneste!** I can't stand dishonest people!; **non lo sopporto** I can't stand him
sopportazione [sopportat'tsjone] SF patience; **avere spirito** *o* **capacità di sopportazione** to be long-suffering; **la mia sopportazione ha un limite** there is a limit to my patience; **ho raggiunto il limite della sopportazione** I am at the end of my tether
soppressione [soppres'sjone] SF **1** (*di legge*) abolition; (*di linea ferroviaria*) closure; (*di servizio*) withdrawal
2 (*uccisione*) elimination, liquidation
soppresso, a [sop'prɛsso] PP *di* **sopprimere**
sopprimere [sop'primere] VT IRREG **1** (*privilegi, carica*) to do away with, abolish; (*servizio*) to withdraw; (*giornale*) to suppress; (*clausola, parola, frase*) to cut out, delete; **il servizio navetta è stato soppresso** the shuttle service has been withdrawn **2** (*uccidere*) to eliminate, liquidate
sopra ['sopra] PREP
1 (*gen*) over; **c'era un lampadario sopra il tavolo** there was a chandelier over the table; **indossava un golf sopra la camicetta** she was wearing a sweater over her blouse; **mettiti il cappotto sopra le spalle** put your coat over your shoulders; **costruirono un ponte sopra il fiume** they built a bridge over the river; **guadagna sopra i 2000 euro al mese** he earns over 2,000 euros a month; **pesa sopra il chilo** it weighs over *o* more than a kilo; **persone sopra i 30 anni** people over 30 (years of age); **passar sopra a qc** (*anche fig*) to pass over sth; **sopra pensiero** = **soprappensiero**
2 (*più in su di*) above; **l'aereo volava sopra le nuvole** the plane was flying above the clouds; **100 metri sopra il livello del mare** 100 metres above sea level; **5 gradi sopra lo zero** 5 degrees above zero; **sopra l'orizzonte** above the horizon; **sopra l'equatore** north of *o* above the equator; **un paesino sopra Napoli** a village north of Naples; **abitano sopra di noi** they live above us; **ha un appartamento sopra il negozio** he has a flat (*Brit*) *o* apartment (*Am*) over the shop; **essere al di sopra di ogni sospetto** to be above suspicion; **amare qn sopra ogni cosa** to love sb above all else
3 (*a contatto con*) on; (*moto*) on(to); (*in cima a*) on (top of); **il libro è sopra il tavolo** the book is on the table; **il dizionario è sopra quella pila di libri** the dictionary is on top of that pile of books; **il gatto è salito sopra il tavolo** the cat climbed onto the table; **mettilo sopra l'armadio** put it on top of the wardrobe (*Brit*) *o* closet (*Am*); **si buttò sopra di lui** he threw himself on him
4 (*intorno a, riguardo a*) about, on; **un dibattito sopra la riforma carceraria** a debate about *o* on prison reform; **chiedere un parere sopra qc** to ask for an opinion about *o* on sth
■ AVV
1 (*su*) up; (*in superficie*) on top; **là sopra** up there; **metti**

Ss

tutto lì *o* **là sopra** put everything up there; **qua sopra** up here; **sopra è un po' rovinato** (*libro, borsa*) it's a bit damaged on top; **una torta con sopra la panna** a cake topped with cream; **un disegno con sopra la firma** a signed drawing
2 (al piano) di sopra upstairs; **abitano di sopra** they live upstairs; **vado di sopra a chiudere le finestre** I'm just going upstairs to close the windows; **la tua è la stanza di sopra** yours is the upstairs room
3 (*prima*) above; **per i motivi sopra illustrati** for the above-mentioned reasons, for the reasons shown above; **vedi/come sopra** see/as above; **mettilo nel cassetto sopra** put it in the drawer above
4 pensaci sopra think it over; **dormirci sopra** (*fig*) to sleep on it
■SM top; **il sopra del tavolo è in mogano** the top of the table is mahogany; **il di sopra** the top, the upper part

soprabito [so'prabito] SM overcoat
sopraccennato, a [soprattʃen'nato] AGG above-mentioned
sopracciglio [soprat'tʃiʎʎo] SM (*pl m* **sopraccigli**, *pl f* **sopracciglia**) eyebrow
sopracciliare [soprattʃi'ljare] AGG eyebrow *attr*
sopraccoperta [soprakko'pɛrta] SF (*di letto*) bedspread; (*di libro*) jacket
■AVV (*Naut*) on deck
sopraddetto, a [soprad'detto] AGG aforesaid
sopraffare [sopraf'fare] VT IRREG to overwhelm, overpower, overcome
sopraffascia [sopraf'faʃʃa] SM INV (*Equitazione*) roller
sopraffatto, a [sopraf'fatto] PP *di* **sopraffare**
sopraffazione [sopraffat'tsjone] SF overwhelming, overpowering
sopraffino, a [sopraf'fino] AGG (*olio*) extra fine; (*burro*) best-quality *attr*; (*pranzo, gusto*) excellent; (*fig: astuzia, mente*) masterly
sopraggitto [soprad'dʒitto] SM (*Cucito*) whipstitch
sopraggiungere [soprad'dʒundʒere] VI IRREG (*aus* **essere**) (*persone, rinforzi*) to arrive (unexpectedly); (*fig: difficoltà, complicazioni*) to arise *o* occur (unexpectedly)
sopraggiunto, a [soprad'dʒunto] PP *di* **sopraggiungere**
sopralluogo, ghi [sopral'lwɔgo] SM (*di esperti*) inspection; (*di polizia*) on-the-spot investigation
soprammobile [sopram'mɔbile] SM ornament
soprannaturale [soprannatu'rale] AGG, SM supernatural
soprannome [sopran'nome] SM nickname
soprannominare [sopprannomi'nare] VT to nickname
soprannumero [sopran'numero] AVV: **in soprannumero** in excess; **in questa classe siamo in soprannumero** there are too many in this class
soprano [so'prano] SM/F (*pl m* **soprani**, *pl f* **soprano**) (*Mus*) soprano
soprappensiero [soprappen'sjɛro] AVV lost in thought
soprappiù [soprap'pju] SM surplus, extra; **in soprappiù** (*in eccesso*) extra, surplus; (*per giunta*) besides, in addition; **l'offerta è in soprappiù rispetto alla domanda** there is more supply than demand
soprassalto [sopras'salto] SM: **di soprassalto** with a jump, with a start; **mi sono svegliata di soprassalto** I woke up with a start
soprassaturo, a [sopras'saturo] AGG supersaturated
soprassedere [soprasse'dere] VI IRREG (*aus* **avere**) **soprassedere a** to put off, postpone, delay
soprattassa [soprat'tassa] SF (*Fin*) surtax
soprattutto [soprat'tutto] AVV **1** (*anzitutto*) above all; **dipende soprattutto da lui** it depends mainly on him **2** (*specialmente*) especially, particularly; **Firenze è piena di turisti, soprattutto d'estate** Florence is full of tourists, especially in the summer
sopravvalutare [sopravvalu'tare] VT (*persona, capacità*) to overestimate, overrate
sopravvalutazione [sopravvalutat'tsjone] SF over-estimation, overevaluation
sopravvenire [sopravve'nire] VI IRREG (*aus* **essere**) (*persone, macchine, rinforzi*) to arrive suddenly; (*difficoltà, complicazioni*) to arise, occur
sopravvento [soprav'vɛnto] SM: **avere/prendere il sopravvento su qn** to have/get the upper hand over sb
■AVV windward; **essere/mettersi sopravvento** to be/get on the windward side
sopravvenuto, a [sopravve'nuto] PP *di* **sopravvenire**
sopravvissuto, a [sopravvis'suto] PP *di* **sopravvivere**
■SM/F survivor
sopravvivenza [sopravvi'vɛntsa] SF survival
sopravvivere [soprav'vivere] VI IRREG (*aus* **essere**) to survive; **riuscirà a sopravvivere?** will he survive?; **sopravvivere a** (*incidente, guerra*) to survive; (*persona*) to outlive, survive; **è sopravvissuto all'incidente** he survived the accident
soprelencato, a [soprelen'kato] AGG above-listed *attr*, listed above
soprelevata [soprele'vata] SF (*di strada, ferrovia*) elevated section
soprelevato, a [soprele'vato] AGG elevated, raised
soprelevazione [soprelevat'tsjone] SF (*Edil*) raising; (*parte soprelevata*) raised part
soprintendente [soprinten'dɛnte] SM/F (*gen*) superintendent, supervisor; (*funzionario: di museo*) director, head
soprintendenza [soprinten'dɛntsa] SF **1** (*gen*) superintendence, supervision **2** (*ente statale*): **Soprintendenza ai beni ambientali e architettonici** *government department responsible for the environment and historical buildings*; **Soprintendenza ai beni artistici e storici** *government department responsible for monuments and other treasures*
soprintendere [soprin'tɛndere] VI IRREG: **soprintendere a** to superintend, supervise
soprinteso, a [soprin'teso] PP *di* **soprintendere**
sopruso [so'pruzo] SM abuse (of power); **subire un sopruso** to be abused; **questo è un sopruso!** this is an outrage!
soqquadro [sok'kwadro] SM: **mettere a soqquadro** to turn upside-down
sorbettiera [sorbet'tjɛra] SF ice-cream churn
sorbetto [sor'betto] SM sorbet, water ice (*Brit*)
sorbire [sor'bire] VT to sip; **sorbirsi qn/qc** (*fig*) to put up with sb/sth
sorbo ['sɔrbo] SM (*Bot*) service tree, sorb
sorcio, ci ['sortʃo] SM mouse; **far vedere i sorci verdi a qn** (*fig*) to give sb a rough time
sordidamente [sordida'mente] AVV (*vedi agg*) sordidly; meanly
sordidezza [sordi'dettsa] SF (*vedi agg*) sordidness, squalor; meanness
sordido, a ['sɔrdido] AGG (*locale, appartamento*) sordid, squalid; (*fig: affare, storia*) sordid; (*: gretto*) mean, stingy
sordina [sor'dina] SF (*Mus*) mute; **mettere la sordina**

a qc to mute sth; **in sordina** softly; **cantare in sordina** to hum softly; **andarsene in sordina** (*fig*) to sneak off

sordità [sordi'ta] SF deafness

sordo, a ['sordo] AGG **1** (*persona*) deaf; **essere sordo da un orecchio** to be deaf in one ear; **essere sordo come una campana** to be as deaf as a post; **sordo ai consigli** deaf to advice **2** (*rumore, colpo*) muffled; (*dolore*) dull; (*odio, rancore*) veiled; (*lotta*) silent, hidden; **un rumore sordo** a dull sound **3** (*Fonetica*) voiceless
■ SM/F deaf person; **i sordi** the deaf; **non fare il sordo!** don't pretend you didn't hear me!

sordomuto, a [sordo'muto] AGG deaf-and-dumb
■ SM/F deaf-mute

sorella [so'rɛlla] SF (*gen, Rel*) sister; **mia sorella** my sister; **la sorella di Nadia** Nadia's sister; **è come una sorella per me** she's like a sister to me
■ AGG (*organizzazione, nave*) sister *attr*

sorellanza [sorel'lantsa] SF sisterhood

sorellastra [sorel'lastra] SF stepsister; (*con genitore in comune*) half sister

sorgente [sor'dʒɛnte] SF (*fonte*) spring; (*di fiume, fig, Fis*) source; **acqua di sorgente** spring water; **sorgente di calore** source of heat; **sorgente luminosa** source of light, light source; **sorgente termale** thermal spring

sorgere ['sordʒere] VB IRREG
■ VI (*aus* **essere**) (*gen*) to rise; (*fig: difficoltà*) to arise; **mi sorge il dubbio che...** I am beginning to suspect that ...; **mi sorge un dubbio, forse ho lasciato il gas acceso** I wonder, did I leave the gas on?
■ SM: **al sorgere del sole** at sunrise

sorgo ['sorgo] SM (*Bot*) sorghum

soriano, a [so'rjano] AGG, SM/F tabby

sormontare [sormon'tare] VT (*fig: ostacoli, difficoltà*) to overcome, surmount

sornione, a [sor'njone] AGG sly, crafty
■ SM/F sly one

sorpassare [sorpas'sare] VT (*oltrepassare*) to go past; (*auto*) to overtake; (*fig*) to surpass; (*rivali*) to surpass, outdo; **sorpassare qn in intelligenza** to be more intelligent *o* brighter than sb; **l'ha sorpassato in altezza** she has grown taller than him

sorpassato, a [sorpas'sato] AGG (*metodo, moda*) outmoded, old-fashioned; (*macchina*) obsolete

sorpasso [sor'passo] SM overtaking; **fare un sorpasso** to overtake

sorprendente [sorpren'dɛnte] AGG surprising; (*eccezionale, inaspettato*) astonishing, amazing

sorprendentemente [sorprendente'mente] AVV surprisingly

sorprendere [sor'prɛndere] VB IRREG
■ VT **1** (*cogliere di sorpresa*) to catch; (*: ladro*) to surprise, catch in the act; **l'ha sorpreso a fumare** she caught him smoking; **furono sorpresi dalla bufera** they were caught in the storm **2** (*fig: stupire*) to surprise; **mi ha sorpreso molto la sua risposta** his answer really surprised me; **non mi sorprenderebbe affatto!** I wouldn't be at all surprised!;
▶ **sorprendersi** VIP **1** (*meravigliarsi*): **sorprendersi di qc** to be surprised about *o* at sth **2** (*trovarsi*): **sorprendersi a pensare a qn** to catch *o* find o.s. thinking of sb

sorpresa [sor'presa] SF (*gen*) surprise; **fare una sorpresa a qn** to give sb a surprise; **voglio fargli una sorpresa per il suo compleanno** I want to give him a surprise for his birthday; **attaccare di sorpresa** to make a surprise attack on; **prendere qn di sorpresa** to take sb by surprise *o* unawares; **risultato a sorpresa** surprise result

sorpreso, a [sor'preso] PP *di* **sorprendere**

sorreggere [sor'rɛddʒere] VT IRREG (*malato, bambino*) to support, hold up; (*fig: sogg: fede, speranza*) to sustain

sorretto, a [sor'rɛtto] PP *di* **sorreggere**

sorridere [sor'ridere] VI IRREG (*aus* **avere**) to smile; **sorridere a qn** to smile at sb, give sb a smile; **mi sorrideva** she was smiling at me; **la vita ti sorride** life smiles on you; **mi sorride l'idea di rivederlo** the idea of seeing him again appeals to me

sorriso [sor'riso] PP *di* **sorridere**
■ SM smile; **mi ha fatto un sorriso** he gave me a smile, he smiled at me; **un accenno di sorriso** a faint smile

sorsata [sor'sata] SF gulp; **bere a sorsate** to gulp

sorseggiare [sorsed'dʒare] VT to sip

sorsi *ecc* ['sorsi] VB *vedi* **sorgere**

sorso ['sorso] SM sip; **vuoi un sorso?** do you want a sip?; **ne ho bevuto solo un sorso** I only had a sip; **d'un sorso** *or* **in un sorso solo** at one gulp; **l'ho bevuto tutto d'un sorso** I drank it all in one gulp

sorta ['sɔrta] SF sort, kind; **ogni sorta di** all sorts *pl* of; **di ogni sorta** of every kind, of all sorts; **non voglio regali di sorta** I want no presents whatsoever *o* of any kind *o* at all

sorte ['sɔrte] SF (*fato*) fate, destiny; (*caso*) chance; **decidere della sorte di qn** to decide sb's fate; **tentare la sorte** to try one's luck; **tirare a sorte** to draw lots; **hanno tirato a sorte per decidere chi doveva andare per primo** they drew lots to decide who should go first; **non sappiamo quale sarà la sua sorte** we don't know what his fate will be; **la sua sorte è segnata** his fate is sealed

sorteggiare [sorted'dʒare] VT to draw for

sorteggio, gi [sor'teddʒo] SM draw

sortilegio, gi [sorti'lɛdʒo] SM spell, witchcraft *no pl*; **fare un sortilegio a qn** to cast *o* put a spell on sb

sortire [sor'tire] VT (*ottenere*) to produce; **sortire l'effetto contrario** to have the opposite effect

sortita [sor'tita] SF (*Mil*) sortie; (*fig: battuta*) witty remark

sorto, a ['sorto] PP *di* **sorgere**

sorvegliante [sorveʎ'ʎante] SM/F (*di carcere*) warder (*Brit*), guard (*Am*); (*di fabbrica*) supervisor; (*notturno*) night watchman

sorveglianza [sorveʎ'ʎantsa] SF (*controllo*) supervision, watch; (*: Polizia, Mil*) surveillance; **fare sorveglianza agli esami** to invigilate (at) the exams

sorvegliare [sorveʎ'ʎare] VT (*detenuto, bambino, bagaglio*) to watch, keep an eye on; (*casa*) to watch, keep watch on; (*operai, lavori*) to supervise, oversee; **la polizia sorveglia la casa notte e giorno** the police are watching the house night and day

sorvolare [sorvo'lare] VT, VI (*aus* **avere**) **sorvolare su** (*territorio*) to fly over; (*fig: argomento, dettagli*) to pass over, skim over, say nothing about; **sorvoliamo!** let's skip it!

SOS ['ɛsse 'o 'ɛsse] SIGLA M INV SOS, mayday; **lanciare un SOS** to send (out) an SOS

sosia ['sɔzja] SM/F INV double; **è un tuo sosia!** he's your double!

sospendere [sos'pɛndere] VT IRREG **1** (*appendere*) to hang (up); **sospendere un lampadario al soffitto** to hang a chandelier from the ceiling **2** (*interrompere: gen*) to suspend; (*: vacanze, trasmissione*) to interrupt; (*seduta*) to adjourn; **la partita è stata sospesa** the

Ss

match was suspended **3** (*funzionario, alunno*) to suspend; **sospendere qn dal suo incarico** to suspend sb from office

sospensione [sospen'sjone] SF (*gen, Aut, Chim*) suspension; (*rinvio: di processo*) adjournment; (*: di partita*) postponement

sospeso, a [sos'peso] PP *di* **sospendere**
■ AGG (*mano, braccio*) raised; (*vallata*) hanging; (*treno, autobus*) cancelled; **ponte sospeso** suspension bridge; **col fiato sospeso** with bated breath; **tenere qn col fiato sospeso** to keep sb in suspense; **in sospeso** (*pratica*) pending; (*discorso*) unfinished; (*conto*) outstanding

sospettabile [sospet'tabile] AGG suspect

sospettare [sospet'tare] VT to suspect; **nessuno sospettava niente** nobody suspected anything; **sospettare qn di qc** (*furto, omicidio*) to suspect sb of sth; **sospettare che...** to suspect (that) ...; **lo sospettavo!** I suspected as much!
■ VI (*aus* **avere**) **sospettare (di qn)** to suspect (sb); (*diffidare*) to be suspicious (of sb); **la polizia sospettava di loro** the police suspected them; **non sospetta di niente** he doesn't suspect a thing

sospetto[1]**, a** [sos'pɛtto] AGG (*individuo*) suspicious; (*affermazione*) suspect

sospetto[2] [sos'pɛtto] SM suspicion; **destare i sospetti di qn** to arouse sb's suspicions; **destare sospetti** to give rise to suspicion, arouse suspicion; **avere dei sospetti** to have one's suspicions; **avevo dei sospetti su di lui** I had my suspicions about him; **ho il sospetto che...** I suspect (that) ...; **guardare qn con sospetto** to look suspiciously at sb

sospettosamente [sospettosa'mente] AVV suspiciously

sospettoso, a [sospet'toso] AGG suspicious

sospingere [sos'pindʒere] VT IRREG to push, to drive; (*fig: incitare*) to urge, impel; **il vento li sospinse al largo** the wind drove them out to sea

sospinto, a [sos'pinto] PP *di* **sospingere**

sospirare [sospi'rare] VI (*aus* **avere**) to sigh
■ VT to yearn for, long for; **fare sospirare qc a qn** to keep sb waiting *o* hanging around for sth

sospiro [sos'piro] SM sigh; **sospiro di sollievo** sigh of relief; **fare** *o* **trarre un sospiro** to sigh, heave a sigh; **ho tirato un sospiro di sollievo** I heaved a sigh of relief

sosta ['sɔsta] SF (*fermata*) stop, halt; (*pausa, interruzione*) pause, break; **fare una sosta** to stop; **abbiamo fatto una sosta a Torino** we stopped in Turin; **"divieto di sosta"** (*Aut*) "no parking"; **senza sosta** without a break, non-stop; **abbiamo lavorato senza sosta tutto il pomeriggio** we worked non-stop all afternoon; **avere un attimo di sosta** to have a moment's rest; **non dar sosta a qn** to give sb no peace, allow sb no respite

sostantivare [sostanti'vare] VT (*Gramm*) to use as a noun

sostantivato, a [sostanti'vato] AGG (*Gramm*): **aggettivo sostantivato** adjective used as a noun

sostantivo [sostan'tivo] SM (*Gramm*) noun, substantive; **sostantivo in funzione di aggettivo** noun used as an adjective

sostanza [sos'tantsa] SF **1** substance; **badare alla sostanza delle cose** to pay attention to essentials; **la sostanza del discorso** the essence of the speech; **in sostanza** in short, to sum up **2 sostanze** SFPL (*ricchezze*) wealth *sg*; (*beni*) property *sg*, possessions

sostanziale [sostan'tsjale] AGG substantial

sostanzialmente [sostantsjal'mente] AVV essentially, substantially

sostanzioso, a [sostan'tsjoso] AGG (*cibo, pasto*) nourishing, substantial; (*fig: patrimonio, resoconto*) substantial; **un libro sostanzioso** a book of substance

sostare [sos'tare] VI (*aus* **avere**) (*fermarsi*) to stop; (*: macchina*) to stop, park; (*fare una pausa*) to take a break; (*pernottare: in albergo*) to stay, stop (for a while); (*: in città*) to stop over; **sostare in preghiera/raccoglimento** to pause in prayer/in thought

sostegno [sos'teɲɲo] SM support; **a sostegno di** in support of; **muro di sostegno** supporting wall

sostenere [soste'nere] VB IRREG
■ VT **1** (*gen: tenere su*) to support, hold up; (*con medicina*) to sustain; **sostenere il peso di** (*anche fig*) to bear the weight of; **l'albero è sostenuto da una sbarra di ferro** the tree is supported by an iron bar **2** (*candidato, partito*) to support, back; (*famiglia*) to support; **il partito è sostenuto dall'industria** the party is supported by industry; **sostenere qn** (*moralmente*) to be a support to sb; (*difendere*) to stand up for sb, take sb's part **3** (*attacco, shock*) to stand up to, withstand; (*sguardo*) to bear, stand; (*sforzo*) to keep up, sustain; (*esame*) to take; **sostenere gli esami** to sit one's exams; **ho sostenuto gli esami in giugno** I sat my exams in June; **sostenere il confronto** to bear *o* stand comparison; **sostenere delle spese** to meet *o* incur expenses; **sostenere un'ingente spesa** to have a large outlay **4** (*teoria*) to maintain, uphold; (*diritti*) to assert; (*innocenza*) to maintain; **la tesi da lui sostenuta è che...** he maintains that ...; **ha sempre sostenuto la propria innocenza** he's always maintained his innocence **5** (*Teatro, Cine*): **sostenere una parte** to play a role; **sostenere la parte di** to play the part of;
▶ **sostenersi** VR **1** (*tenersi su*) to hold o.s. up, support o.s.; (*con medicine*) to keep o.s. going, keep one's strength up; **sostenersi al muro** (*appoggiarsi*) to hold on to the wall, lean on the wall **2** (*uso reciproco*) to hold each other up; (*fig: moralmente*) to stand by each other, support each other

sostenibile [soste'nibile] AGG (*tesi*) tenable; (*spese*) bearable; (*sviluppo, turismo*) sustainable

sostenitore, trice [sosteni'tore] SM/F (*di partito, candidato*) supporter, backer; (*di tesi*) upholder, supporter

sostentamento [sostenta'mento] SM sustenance, maintenance, support; **mezzi di sostentamento** means of support

sostenuto, a [soste'nuto] AGG (*stile*) elevated; (*prezzo, velocità*) high; **lavora a ritmo sostenuto** she works very fast
■ SM/F: **fare il sostenuto** to be standoffish, keep one's distance

sostituibile [sostitu'ibile] AGG replaceable

sostituire [sostitu'ire] VT **1 sostituire (a/con)** to substitute (for/with); **sostituire il rosso col verde** to replace red with green; **sostituire un pezzo difettoso** to replace a faulty part; **devo sostituire la cartuccia** I need to change the cartridge **2** (*prendere il posto di: persona*) to replace, take the place of; (*: temporaneamente*) to stand in for; (*: cosa*) to take the place of; **era stanco e il suo collega l'ha sostituito** he was tired and his colleague took his place
▶ **sostituirsi** VR: **sostituirsi a qn** to replace sb, take the place of sb

sostitutivo, a [sostitu'tivo] AGG (*Amm: documento, certificato*) equivalent
sostituto, a [sosti'tuto] SM/F substitute, deputy; **sostituto procuratore della Repubblica** (*Dir*) ≈ deputy public prosecutor (*Brit*), assistant district attorney (*Am*)
sostituzione [sostitut'tsjone] SF substitution; **ha fatto una sostituzione all'ultimo minuto della partita** he made a substitution in the last minute of the game; **in sostituzione di** in place of, as a substitute for
sostrato [sos'trato] SM (*Geol*) substratum; (*fig: essenza, fondamento*) basis, foundation
sottaceto, sott'aceto [sotta'tʃeto] (*Culin*) SM (*spec al pl*): **i sottaceti** pickles
■ AGG INV (*cetriolini, cipolline*) pickled
■ AVV: **mettere sottaceto** to pickle
sottana [sot'tana] SF (*gonna*) skirt; (*Rel*) cassock, soutane; **correre dietro alle sottane** (*fig*) to run after women; **stare sempre attaccato alla sottane della mamma** (*fig*) to be tied to one's mother's apron-strings
sottecchi [sot'tekki] AVV: **guardare di sottecchi** to steal a glance at
sotterfugio, gi [sotter'fudʒo] SM subterfuge
sotterramento [sotterra'mento] SM burial, interment
sotterranea [sotter'ranea] SF (*anche:* **ferrovia sotterranea**) underground, tube (*Brit*), subway (*Am*)
sotterraneo, a [sotter'raneo] AGG underground; **un fiume sotterraneo** an underground river
■ SM (*spec al pl*) vault, cellar
sotterrare [sotter'rare] VT (*oggetto*) to bury; (*morto*) to bury, inter; **mi sarei sotterrato per la vergogna!** (*fig fam*) I wished the ground would open up and swallow me!
sottigliezza [sottiʎ'ʎettsa] SF **1** (*di spessore*) thinness; (*fig: acutezza*) subtlety **2 sottigliezze** SFPL: **perdersi in sottigliezze** to get bogged down in details; **non bado a certe sottigliezze** I don't care about such niceties
sottile [sot'tile] AGG **1** (*fetta, corda, viso*) thin; (*figura, caviglia*) slim, slender; (*capelli*) fine; (*profumo*) delicate **2** (*fig: vista*) sharp, keen; (*: ragionamento, significato, ironia*) subtle; (*: mente*) subtle, shrewd; (*differenza*) slight
■ SM: **non andare troppo per il sottile** not to mince matters
sottilizzare [sottilid'dzare] VI (*aus* **avere**) to split hairs
sottilmente [sottil'mente] AVV (*tagliare*) finely; (*criticare*) subtly
sottintendere [sottin'tendere] VT IRREG (*implicare*) to imply; **è sottinteso che...** it is understood that ..., it goes without saying that ...; **lasciare sottintendere che...** to let it be understood that ...; **il soggetto è sottinteso** (*Gramm*) the subject is understood
sottinteso, a [sottin'teso] PP *di* **sottintendere**
■ SM insinuation, allusion; **smetti di parlare per sottintesi** *or* **parla senza sottintesi** speak plainly, speak your mind
sotto ['sotto] PREP
1 (*posizione*) under, beneath, underneath; **dov'era? — sotto il giornale** where was it? — under *o* beneath *o* underneath the newspaper; **la cartina è sotto quel libro** the map is under that book; **si riparò sotto un albero** he sheltered under *o* beneath *o* underneath a tree; **sotto la superficie** under *o* beneath the surface; **si nascose sotto il letto** he hid under *o* underneath the bed; **sotto il soprabito indossava un vestito verde** she was wearing a green dress under her coat; **portare qc sotto il braccio** to carry sth under one's arm; **vieni sotto l'ombrello** come under the umbrella; **dormire sotto la tenda** to sleep under canvas *o* in a tent; **sotto la pioggia** in the rain; **camminare sotto la pioggia** to walk in the rain; **sotto il sole** in the sun; **finire sotto un treno** to get run over by a train; **infilarsi sotto le lenzuola** to get in between the sheets; **c'incontriamo sotto casa** we'll meet outside my house; **sotto le mura** (*di città*) beneath the walls
2 (*più in basso di*) below; (*a sud di*) south of, below; **sotto il livello del mare** below sea level; **sotto zero** below zero; **tutti quelli sotto i 18 anni** all those under 18 (years of age) (*Brit*) *o* under age 18 (*Am*); **questo giocattolo non è adatto ai bambini sotto i 3 anni** this toy is not suitable for children under 3; **quest'anno le gonne si portano sotto il ginocchio** this year skirts are being worn below the knee; **Palermo è sotto Napoli** Palermo is south of *o* below Naples; **sotto il chilo** under *o* less than a kilo; **abita sotto di noi** he lives below us
3 (*durante il governo di*) under; **l'Italia sotto Vittorio Emanuele** Italy under Victor Emmanuel; **sotto il regno di** during the reign of
4 (*soggetto a*) under; **ha 5 impiegati sotto di sé** he has 5 clerks under him; **sotto l'effetto dell'alcol** under the influence of alcohol; **sotto anestesia** under anaesthetic; **tenere qn sotto la propria protezione** to keep sb under one's wing; **tenere qn/qc sott'occhio** to keep an eye on sb/sth; **sotto l'alto patronato di** under the patronage of
5 (*tempo: in prossimità di*) near; **siamo sotto Natale/Pasqua** it's nearly Christmas/Easter
6 (*da*): **analizzare qc sotto un altro aspetto** to examine sth from another point of view; **sotto un certo punto di vista** in a sense
7 (*fraseologia*): **sotto forma di** in the form of; **sotto falso nome** under a false name; **non c'è niente di nuovo sotto il sole** there is nothing new under the sun; **avere qc sotto il naso/gli occhi** to have sth under one's nose/before one's eyes
■ AVV
1 (*giù*) down; (*nella parte inferiore*) underneath, beneath; **qua/là sotto** down here/there; **qui/lì sotto** down here/there; **sotto c'è uno strato di cioccolato** there's a layer of chocolate underneath; **sotto, la scatola è rossa** underneath, the box is red; **sei sotto tu!** (*nei giochi*) you're it!
2 (al piano) di sotto downstairs; **ti aspetto (di) sotto** I'll wait for you downstairs; **quelli di sotto** the people who live downstairs
3 (*oltre*) below; **vedi sotto** see below; **la riga sotto** the line below
4 (*addosso*) underneath; **cos'hai sotto?** what have you got on underneath?
■ SM INV bottom; **il sotto della pentola** the bottom of the pan
sottoalimentato, a [sottoalimen'tato] AGG
1 (*denutrito*) undernourished, underfed **2** (*Elettr, Tecn*): **il circuito è sottoalimentato** not enough electricity is flowing through the circuit; **il motore è sottoalimentato** not enough fuel is reaching the engine
sottoalimentazione [sottoalimentat'tsjone] SF undernourishment
sottobanco [sotto'banko] AVV (*di nascosto: vendere,*

Ss

comprare) under the counter; (*agire*) in an underhand way; **passare una notizia sottobanco** to hush up a piece of news

sottobicchiere [sottobik'kjɛre] SM mat, coaster

sottobosco, schi [sotto'bɔsko] SM undergrowth *no pl*

sottobottiglia [sottobot'tiʎʎa] SM INV coaster

sottobraccio [sotto'brattʃo] AVV by the arm; **prendere qn sottobraccio** to take sb by the arm; **camminare sottobraccio a qn** to walk arm in arm with sb

sottocchio [sot'tɔkkjo] AVV in front of one, to hand; **non l'ho sottocchio** (*articolo, documento*) I haven't got it in front of me *o* to hand

sottoccupazione [sottokkupat'tsjone] SF underemployment

sottochiave [sotto'kjave] AVV under lock and key

sottocoperta [sottoko'pɛrta] AVV (*Naut*) below deck

sottocosto [sotto'kɔsto] AVV below cost (price)

sottocutaneo, a [sottoku'taneo] AGG subcutaneous

sottodimensionato, a [sottodimensjo'nato] AGG (*personale*) below strength, reduced; (*programma*) inadequate

sottoelencato, a [sottoelen'kato] AGG listed below, under-mentioned *attr*

sottoesporre [sottoes'porre] VT IRREG (*Fot*) to underexpose

sottoesposizione [sottoespozit'tsjone] SF (*Fot*) underexposure

sottoesposto, a [sottoes'posto] PP *di* **sottoesporre**
■ AGG (*fotografia, pellicola*) underexposed

sottofondo [sotto'fondo] SM background; **sottofondo musicale** background music

sottogamba [sotto'gamba] AVV: **prendere qn/qc sottogamba** (*con leggerezza*) not to take sb/sth seriously; (*sottovalutare*) to underestimate sb/sth

sottogonna [sotto'gonna] SF underskirt

sottogoverno [sottogo'vɛrno] SM political patronage

sottogruppo [sotto'gruppo] SM subgroup

sottolineare [sottoline'are] VT to underline; (*fig*) to underline, emphasize, stress; **hai sottolineato le parole che non conosci?** have you underlined the words you don't know?; **vorrei sottolineare l'importanza di quello che ha detto** I'd like to stress the importance of what he said

sottolineatura [sottolinea'tura] SF underlining

sottolio, li; sott'olio [sot'tɔljo] SM: **sottoli** SMPL vegetables pickled in oil
■ AGG INV (*funghetti, melanzane, tonno*) in oil
■ AVV: **conservare sottolio** to bottle in oil

sottomano [sotto'mano] AVV **1** (*a portata di mano*) within reach, to *o* on *o* at hand **2** (*di nascosto*) secretly

sottomarino, a [sottoma'rino] AGG (*flora, paesaggio*) submarine; (*cavo, galleria, navigazione*) underwater *attr*
■ SM (*Naut*) submarine

sottomesso, a [sotto'messo] PP *di* **sottomettere**
■ AGG submissive

sottomettere [sotto'mettere] VB IRREG
■ VT (*gen*) to subject; (*popolo, nemico*) to subjugate, subdue; **sottomettere qn alla propria volontà** to impose one's will on sb;
▶ **sottomettersi** VR to submit; **sottomettersi alla volontà di qn** to bow to sb's will

sottomissione [sottomis'sjone] SF submission

sottopancia [sotto'pantʃa] SM INV (*Equitazione*) girth

sottopassaggio, gi [sottopas'saddʒo] SM (*per auto*) underpass; (*pedonale*) subway (*Brit*), underpass (*Am*)

sottopentola [sotto'pentola] SM INV heat-resistant mat

sottopeso [sotto'peso] AVV underweight

sottopiatto [sotto'pjatto] SM INV plate (*placed under another*)

sottoporre [sotto'porre] VB IRREG
■ VT **1** (*costringere*): **sottoporre qn/qc a** to subject sb/sth to; **sottoporre ad un esame** to subject to an examination **2** (*fig: presentare*): **sottoporre qc a qn** *o* **all'attenzione di qn** to submit sth to sb, put sth to sb; **gli ho sottoposto la mia richiesta** I submitted my request to him;
▶ **sottoporsi** VR: **sottoporsi a** (*volontà*) to submit to; (*operazione*) to undergo

sottoposto, a [sotto'posto] PP *di* **sottoporre**

sottoprodotto [sottopro'dotto] SM by-product

sottoproduzione [sottoprodut'tsjone] SF underproduction

sottoprogramma, i [sottopro'gramma] SM (*Inform*) subroutine

sottoproletariato [sottoproleta'rjato] SM: **il sottoproletariato** the underclasses *pl*, the underprivileged classes *pl*

sottoproletario, ria, ri, rie [sottoprole'tarjo] SM/F: **i sottoproletari** the underprivileged

sottordine [sot'tordine] **in sottordine** AVV: **passare in sottordine** to become of minor importance
■ SM (*Bot, Zool*) sub-order

sottoscala [sottos'kala] SM INV (*ripostiglio*) cupboard (*Brit*) *o* closet (*Am*) under the stairs; (*stanza*) room under the stairs

sottoscritto, a [sottos'kritto] PP *di* **sottoscrivere**
■ SM/F: **il(la) sottoscritto(a)** the undersigned

sottoscrivere [sottos'krivere] VB IRREG
■ VT (*firmare: atto, petizione*) to sign; (*titoli, azioni*) to underwrite; **sottoscrivere per 10 euro** (*contribuire*) to contribute 10 euros
■ VI (*aus* **avere**) **sottoscrivere a** (*programma*) to subscribe to

sottoscrizione [sottoskrit'tsjone] SF **1** (*firma*) signing **2** (*raccolta di adesioni*) subscription; **è iniziata la sottoscrizione per il referendum** signatures in favour of a referendum are now being collected

sottosegretario, ria, ri, rie [sottosegre'tarjo] SM/F (*Pol*) undersecretary; **sottosegretario di stato** under-secretary of state (*Brit*), assistant secretary of state (*Am*)

sottosopra [sotto'sopra] AVV (*capovolto*) upside down, topsy-turvy; **mettere tutto sottosopra** to turn everything upside down; **hanno messo la casa sottosopra** they turned the house upside down; **sentirsi sottosopra** *or* **avere lo stomaco sottosopra** to feel queasy; **sentirsi sottosopra** (*turbato*) to be in a whirl

sottospecie [sottos'pɛtʃe] SF INV (*Bot, Zool*) subspecies *inv*; **è una sottospecie di musica** (*pegg*) it's hardly what you would call music

sottostante [sottos'tante] AGG (*piani*) lower; (*zona*) underlying; **la valle sottostante** the valley below

sottostare [sottos'tare] VI IRREG (*aus* **essere**) **sottostare a** (*assoggettarsi a*) to submit to; (*: richieste*) to give in to; (*subire: prova*) to undergo

sottosterzante [sottoster'tsante] AGG (*Aut*): **essere sottosterzante** to understeer

sottosuolo [sotto'swɔlo] SM subsoil

sottosviluppato, a [sottozvilup'pato] AGG underdeveloped

sottosviluppo [sottozvi'luppo] SM underdevelopment
sottotenente [sottote'nɛnte] SM *(Mil)* second lieutenant
sottoterra [sotto'tɛrra] AVV underground
sottotetto [sotto'tetto] SM attic
sottotitolare [sottotito'lare] VT *(TV)* to subtitle
sottotitolo [sotto'titolo] SM subtitle
sottovalutare [sottovalu'tare] VT *(persona, prova)* to underestimate, underrate; *(Econ)* to undervalue
▶ **sottovalutarsi** VR to underrate o.s.
sottovalutazione [sottovalutat'tsjone] SF *(gen)* underestimation; *(Econ)* undervaluing
sottovaso [sotto'vazo] SM flowerpot saucer
sottovento [sotto'vɛnto] *(Naut)* AVV leeward(s)
■ AGG INV *(lato)* leeward
sottoveste [sotto'vɛste] SF petticoat, slip
sottovoce [sotto'votʃe] AVV in a low voice, softly
sottovuoto [sotto'vwɔto] AVV: **confezionare sottovuoto** to vacuum-pack
■ AGG INV: **confezione sottovuoto** vacuum pack
sottrarre [sot'trarre] VB IRREG
■ VT **1** *(Mat)* to subtract, take away; *(dedurre)* to deduct; **sottratte le spese** once expenses have been deducted **2** *(portar via)*: **sottrarre a** to take away from; *(liberare)*: **sottrarre a** *o* **da** to save from, rescue from; *(rubare)*: **sottrarre da** to remove from, steal from; **gli hanno sottratto il portafoglio** they stole his wallet; **sottrarre qn/qc alla vista di qn** to remove sb/sth from sb's sight;
▶ **sottrarsi** VR: **sottrarsi a** *(sfuggire)* to escape; *(evitare)* to avoid; **sottrarsi alle proprie responsabilità** to avoid one's responsibilities; **cerca di sottrarsi alle sue responsabilità** he's trying to avoid his responsibilities
sottratto, a [sot'tratto] PP *di* **sottrarre**
sottrazione [sottrat'tsjone] SF *(Mat)* subtraction; *(furto)* removal
sottufficiale [sottuffi'tʃale] SM *(Mil)* non-commissioned officer; *(Naut)* petty officer
soubrette [su'brɛt] SF INV showgirl
soufflé [su'fle] SM INV *(Culin)* soufflé
souvenir [suvə'nir] SM INV souvenir
sovente [so'vɛnte] AVV *(letter)* frequently
soverchiare [sover'kjare] VT to overpower, overwhelm
soverchieria [soverkje'ria] SF *(prepotenza)* abuse (of power)
soverchio, chia, chi, chie [so'vɛrkjo] AGG *(letter)* excessive, immoderate
soviet [so'vjɛt] SM INV soviet
sovietico, a, ci, che [so'vjɛtiko] AGG Soviet
■ SM/F Soviet citizen
sovrabbondante [sovrabbon'dante] AGG overabundant
sovrabbondanza [sovrabbon'dantsa] SF overabundance; **in sovrabbondanza** in excess
sovraccaricare [sovrakkari'kare] VT to overload; **sovraccaricare qn di lavoro** to overload sb with work
sovraccarico, a, chi, che [sovrak'kariko] AGG: **sovraccarico (di)** overloaded (with); **sovraccarico di lavoro** overworked
■ SM excess load; **sovraccarico di lavoro** extra work
sovradimensionato, a [sovradimensjo'nato] AGG oversized
sovraesporre [sovraes'porre] VT IRREG *(Fot)* to overexpose
sovraesposizione [sovraespozit'tsjone] SF *(Fot)* overexposure
sovraesposto, a [sovraes'posto] PP *di* **sovraesporre**
sovraffollato, a [sovraffol'lato] AGG overcrowded
sovralimentato, a [sovralimen'tato] AGG **1** *(bambino)* overfed **2** *(Tecn: motore)* supercharged; **circuito sovralimentato** *(Elettr)* overloaded circuit
sovranità [sovrani'ta] SF *(potere)* sovereignty; *(fig: superiorità)* supremacy
sovrannaturale AGG [sovrannatu'rale] = **soprannaturale**
sovrano, a [so'vrano] AGG *(gen)* sovereign *attr*; *(fig: sommo)* supreme
■ SM/F sovereign
sovraoccupazione [sovraokkupat'tsjone] SF overemployment
sovrappeso [sovrap'peso] AVV overweight
sovrappopolare [sovrappopo'lare] VT to overpopulate
sovrapporre [sovrap'porre] VB IRREG
■ VT *(gen)* to place on top of, put on top of; *(Fot, Geom)* to superimpose; **sovrapponili** place *o* put them one on top of the other
▶ **sovrapporsi** VIP *(Fot)* to be superimposed; *(fig: aggiungersi)* **sovrapporsi a** to arise in addition to
sovrapposizione [sovrappozit'tsjone] SF superimposition
sovrapposto, a [sovrap'posto] PP *di* **sovrapporre**
sovrapproduzione [sovrapprodut'tsjone] SF overproduction
sovrascrivere [sovras'krivere] VT *(Inform)* to overwrite
sovrastante [sovras'tante] AGG *(montagna)* dominating; *(pericolo)* impending
sovrastare [sovras'tare] VT IRREG **1** *(sogg: montagna, fortezza)* to dominate; *(: nube)* to hang over; **è così alto che sovrasta gli altri** he's so tall that he towers over the others; **il pericolo di un'epidemia sovrasta la città** the danger of an epidemic threatens the city **2** *(fig: superare)* to surpass
sovrasterzante [sovraster'tsante] AGG *(Aut)*: **essere sovrasterzante** to oversteer
sovrastruttura [sovrastrut'tura] SF superstructure
sovratensione [sovraten'sjone] SF *(Elettr)* overvoltage
sovreccitabile [sovrettʃi'tabile] AGG overexcitable
sovreccitabilità [sovrettʃitabili'ta] SF overexcitability
sovreccitare [sovrettʃi'tare] VT to overexcite
sovreccitazione [sovrettʃitat'tsjone] SF overexcitement
sovrimpressione [sovrimpres'sjone] SF *(Fot, Cine)* superimposition; *(: per errore)* double exposure; **immagini in sovrimpressione** superimposed images; **il numero in sovrimpressione** *(TV)* the number appearing on the screen
sovrintendente *ecc* [sovrinten'dɛnte] = **soprintendente** *ecc*
sovrumano, a [sovru'mano] AGG superhuman
sovvenire [sovve'nire] VI IRREG *(aus* **essere***)* *(letter: venire in mente)*: **sovvenire a** to occur to; **mi sovvenne che...** it occurred to me that ...
sovvenzionare [sovventsjo'nare] VT to subsidize; **sovvenzionato dallo Stato** state-subsidized
sovvenzione [sovven'tsjone] SF subsidy, grant
sovversione [sovver'sjone] SF subversion
sovversivo, a [sovver'sivo] SM/F, AGG subversive

sovvertimento [sovverti'mento] SM subverting, undermining
sovvertire [sovver'tire] VT (*Pol: ordine, stato*) to subvert, undermine
sovvertitore, trice [sovverti'tore] SM/F subverter
sozzamente [sottsa'mente] AVV filthily
sozzo, a ['sottso] AGG filthy, dirty
sozzume [sot'tsume] SM filth
sozzura [sot'tsura] SF filth
SP SIGLA = *La Spezia*
S.P. ABBR = **strada provinciale**; *vedi* **provinciale**
S.p.A. ['ɛssepi'a] SIGLA F = **società per azioni**
spaccalegna [spakka'leɲɲa] SM INV woodcutter
spaccare [spak'kare] VT (*rompere*) to break, split; (*legna*) to chop; (*partito, maggioranza*) to split; **ti spacco il muso!** I'll smash your face in!; **è caduto e si è spaccato la testa** he fell and cut his head open; **o la va o la spacca** it's all or nothing; **quest'orologio spacca il minuto** this watch keeps perfect time; **c'è un sole che spacca le pietre** it's hot enough to fry an egg; **una questione che ha spaccato l'opinione pubblica** an issue which has split public opinion
► **spaccarsi** VIP (*rompersi*) to break, split; (*fig: scindersi: partito*) to split
spaccata [spak'kata] SF (*Ginnastica*): **fare una spaccata** to do the splits
spaccato, a [spak'kato] AGG **1** (*terreno, labbra*) cracked **2** (*fig*): **è sordo spaccato** he is as deaf as a post; **sei tuo padre spaccato** you're the spitting image of your father
■ SM (*Archit*) vertical section; (*fig: descrizione*) outline
spaccatura [spakka'tura] SF (*gen, fig*) split; (*in un muro*) crack; (*nel terreno*) crack, fissure
spaccherò *ecc* [spakke'rɔ] VB *vedi* **spaccare**
spacciare [spat'tʃare] VT (*merce rubata*) to traffic in; (*droga*) to sell, push; (*denaro falso*) to pass; **spacciare per** (*far passare per*) to pass off as; **l'ha spacciata per sua moglie** he passed her off as his wife
► **spacciarsi** VR (*farsi credere*) **spacciarsi per** to pass o.s. off as, pretend to be; **si è spacciata per tua cugina** she pretended to be your cousin
spacciato, a [spat'tʃato] AGG (*fam: malato, fuggiasco*): **essere spacciato** to be done for
spacciatore, trice [spattʃa'tore] SM/F (*di droga*) pusher; (*di denaro falso*) dealer
spaccio, ci ['spattʃo] SM **1** **spaccio (di)** (*merce rubata*) trafficking (in); (*denaro falso*) passing (of); **spaccio di droga** drug dealing **2** (*negozio*) shop
spacco, chi ['spakko] SM **1** (*incrinatura*) crack, split; (*strappo*) tear **2** (*di gonna*) slit; (*di giacca*) vent
spacconata [spakko'nata] SF: **non dire spacconate!** stop boasting!; **non fare spacconate!** stop showing off!
spaccone, a [spak'kone] SM/F (*fam*) boaster, braggart
spada ['spada] SF **1** sword **2** (*Carte*): **spade** SFPL *suit in Neapolitan pack of cards*
spadaccino, a [spadat'tʃino] SM/F swordsman/woman
spadino [spa'dino] SM dress sword
spadroneggiare [spadroned'dʒare] VI (*aus* **avere**) to swagger; **pensa di poter spadroneggiare** he thinks he can boss everyone about; **non ti permetto di spadroneggiare in casa mia** I won't allow you to lord it in my house
spaesato, a [spae'zato] AGG lost, disorientated; **si sentiva spaesato nella grande città** he felt lost in the big city; **mi sentivo spaesato tra di loro** I felt lost *o* out of my depth in their company
spaghettata [spaget'tata] SF spaghetti meal
spaghetteria [spagette'ria] SF spaghetti restaurant
spaghetti [spa'getti] SMPL (*Culin*) spaghetti *sg*; **sono buoni gli spaghetti?** is the spaghetti nice?
Spagna ['spaɲɲa] SF Spain; **mi è piaciuta molto la Spagna** I really liked Spain; **andrò in Spagna quest'estate** I'm going to Spain this summer
spagnoletta [spaɲɲo'letta] SF spool
spagnolo, a [spaɲ'ɲɔlo] AGG Spanish
■ SM/F (*abitante*) Spaniard; **gli spagnoli** the Spanish
■ SM (*lingua*) Spanish; **parli spagnolo?** do you speak Spanish?; **un insegnante di spagnolo** a Spanish teacher
spago, ghi ['spago] SM string, twine; **un rotolo di spago** a ball of string; **dare spago a qn** (*fig*) to let sb have his (*o* her) way
spaiato, a [spa'jato] AGG (*calza, guanto*) odd
spalancare [spalan'kare] VT to open wide; **spalancò la porta** he flung the door open
► **spalancarsi** VIP to open wide
spalancato, a [spalan'kato] AGG (*porta, bocca*) wide open; **con gli occhi spalancati** with eyes wide open; **accogliere qn a braccia spalancate** to welcome sb with open arms
spalare [spa'lare] VT (*terra, neve*) to shovel
spalatore [spala'tore] SM (*lavoratore*) shoveller
spalatrice [spala'tritʃe] SF mechanical shovel
spalla ['spalla] SF **1** (*Anat, Geog, Alpinismo*) shoulder; **mi fa male una spalla** one of my shoulders hurts; **questa giacca mi sta grande di spalle** this jacket is too big across the shoulders; **avere le spalle curve** to have round shoulders, be round-shouldered; **avere le spalle larghe** (*anche fig*) to have broad shoulders; **portare qn/qc in** *o* **a spalle** to carry sb/sth on one's shoulders; **alzare le spalle** to shrug one's shoulders; **avere la famiglia sulle spalle** to have a family to support; **vivere alle spalle di qn** to live off sb, live at sb's expense **2** (*schiena*): **spalle** SFPL back; **di spalle** from behind; **seduto alle mie spalle** sitting behind me; **voltare le spalle a qn/qc** (*fig*) to turn one's back on sb/sth; **mi ha voltato le spalle proprio quando avevo bisogno di lui** he turned his back on me just when I needed him; **ridere alle spalle di qn** (*fig*) to laugh behind sb's back; **prendere/colpire qn alle spalle** to take/hit sb from behind; **mettere qn con le spalle al muro** (*fig*) to get sb with his (*o* her) back to the wall **3** (*Teatro*) stooge; **fare da spalla a qn** to act as sb's stooge
spallata [spal'lata] SF push (*o* shove) with the shoulder; **dare una spallata a qc** to give sth a push (*o* a shove) with one's shoulder
spalleggiare [spalled'dʒare] VT to support, back up
spalletta [spal'letta] SF parapet
spalliera [spal'ljɛra] SF (*di sedia, poltrona*) back; (*di letto: alla testa*) head(board); (*: ai piedi*) foot(board); (*Ginnastica*) wall bars *pl*; (*Agr*) espalier
spallina [spal'lina] SF **1** (*di sottoveste, maglietta*) strap; **senza spalline** strapless **2** (*anche:* **spallina imbottita**) shoulder pad **3** (*Mil*) epaulette
spalluccia, ce [spal'luttʃa] SF: **fare spallucce** to shrug
spalmare [spal'mare] VT to spread; **spalmare il burro sul pane** *or* **spalmare il pane di burro** to butter one's bread, spread butter on one's bread; **spalmare una crema sulla pelle** to rub a cream into one's skin; **stava spalmandosi la crema sulle gambe** she was rubbing cream on her legs

▶ **spalmarsi** VR: **spalmarsi di** to cover o.s. with
spalti ['spalti] SMPL (*di stadio*) terraces (*Brit*), ≈ bleachers (*Am*)
spamming ['spammin(g)] SM (*Inform*) spamming
spanare [spa'nare] VT (*vite*) to strip
spanato, a [spa'nato] AGG (*vite*) stripped
spanciarsi [span'tʃarsi] VIP (*fig fam*): **spanciarsi dalle risate** *o* **dal ridere** to split one's sides laughing
spanciata [span'tʃata] SF belly flop
spandere ['spandere] VB IRREG
■ VT **1** (*stendere: cera, crema*) to spread **2** (*spargere: liquido*) to pour (out); (: *polvere*) to scatter; (: *calore, profumo*) to give off; (: *fig: notizie*) to spread; **spandere lacrime** to shed tears;
▶ **spandersi** VIP to spread
spanna ['spanna] SF (*lunghezza della mano*) span; **a spanne** (*approssimativamente*) at a rough guess; **è più alto di me di una spanna** he's about half a head taller than me; **essere alto una spanna** (*fig: persona*) to be pint-sized
spanto, a ['spanto] PP *di* **spandere**
spappolare [spappo'lare] VT (*ossa, gamba*) to crush; (*fegato, milza*) to rupture; **non far spappolare le patate** (*cuocere troppo*) don't reduce the potatoes to mush
▶ **spappolarsi** VIP (*ossa, gamba*) to be crushed; (*fegato, milza*) to rupture; (*patate*) to become mushy
sparare [spa'rare] VT (*arma, colpo*) to fire; **sparare a bruciapelo** to shoot at point-blank range; **sparare un colpo** to fire a shot; **si è sparato un colpo alla tempia** he shot himself in the head; **sparare fandonie** to talk nonsense; **sparare grosse** to exaggerate; **ha sparato un prezzo assurdo** he came out with a ridiculous price; **sparare calci** to kick out
■ VI (*aus* **avere**) (*arma*) to fire; (*soldato, persona*) to shoot, fire; **sparare a qn/qc** (*colpire*) to shoot sb/sth; (*mirare*) to fire at sb/sth; **sparare a zero contro qn** (*fig*) to be ruthless with sb, to show sb no pity
sparata [spa'rata] SF (*fig*) tall story (*Brit*) *o* tale (*Am*)
sparato [spa'rato] SM (*di camicia*) dicky
sparatore, trice [spara'tore] SM/F gunman/gunwoman
sparatoria [spara'tɔrja] SF (*tra polizia e malviventi*) exchange of shots; (*tra malviventi*) shoot-out
sparecchiare [sparek'kjare] VT: **sparecchiare (la tavola)** to clear the table; **ti aiuto a sparecchiare?** shall I help you clear the table?
spareggio, gi [spa'reddʒo] SM (*Sport*) play-off
spargere ['spardʒere] VB IRREG
■ VT **1** (*sparpagliare*) to scatter; **i miei fogli erano sparsi sulla scrivania** my papers were scattered over the desk **2** (*versare: vino*) to spill; (: *sangue, lacrime*) to shed **3** (*diffondere: notizia*) to spread; (: *luce*) to give off (*o* out)
▶ **spargersi** VIP (*persone*) to scatter; (*voce, notizia*) to spread; **si è sparsa una voce sul suo conto** there is a rumour going round about him
spargimento [spardʒi'mento] SM: **spargimento di sangue** bloodshed
sparire [spa'rire] VI IRREG (*aus* **essere**) to disappear, vanish; **la nave sparì all'orizzonte** the ship disappeared over the horizon; **sparire dalla circolazione** (*fig fam*) to lie low, keep a low profile; **far sparire** (*fig: rubare*) to steal, pinch; (: *mangiare*) to go through, put away; **far sparire qn** (*uccidere*) to kill sb, bump sb off (*fam*); **dov'è sparita la mia penna?** where has my pen gone?; **chissà dove è sparito il mio passaporto!** I wonder where my passport has got to!; **sparisci!** (*fig fam*) scram!, beat it!
sparizione [sparit'tsjone] SF disappearance
sparlare [spar'lare] VI (*aus* **avere**) **sparlare di qn/qc** to run sb/sth down, bad-mouth sb/sth (*fam*); **sparla sempre di lei con i suoi amici** he's always saying nasty things about her to his friends
sparo ['sparo] SM shot
sparpagliare [sparpaʎ'ʎare] VT, **sparpagliarsi** VIP to scatter
sparpagliato, a [sparpaʎ'ʎato] AGG scattered; **i giocattoli erano sparpagliati sul pavimento** the toys were scattered over the floor
sparso, a ['sparso] PP *di* **spargere**
■ AGG (*fogli*) scattered; (*capelli*) loose; **in ordine sparso** (*Mil*) in open order
Sparta ['sparta] SF Sparta
spartano, a [spar'tano] AGG (*Storia*) Spartan; (*fig*) spartan
■ SM/F Spartan
spartiacque [sparti'akkwe] SM INV (*Geog*) watershed; (*fig: divergenza*) basic difference
spartineve [sparti'neve] SM INV snowplough (*Brit*), snowplow (*Am*)
spartire [spar'tire] VT **1** (*denaro, eredità*) to share out; **non ho nulla da spartire con lui** (*fig*) I have nothing in common with him; **ci siamo spartiti il bottino** we split up the loot **2** (*separare: avversari*) to separate
spartito [spar'tito] SM (*Mus*) score
spartitraffico [sparti'traffiko] SM INV (*Aut: banchina: in città*) traffic island
■ AGG INV: **aiuola spartitraffico** traffic island
spartizione [spartit'tsjone] SF division; **la spartizione dell'eredità** the dividing up of the inheritance
sparuto, a [spa'ruto] AGG (*scarno: viso*) gaunt, haggard; (*esiguo: gruppo*) small, thin
sparviero [spar'vjɛro] SM (*Zool*) sparrowhawk
spasimante [spazi'mante] SM (*corteggiatore*) suitor; (*scherz: innamorato*) sweetheart, lover
spasimare [spazi'mare] VI (*aus* **avere**) to be in agony; **spasimare di fare** (*fig*) to long to do sth, be dying to do sth, yearn to do sth; **spasimare per qn** to be madly in love with sb
spasimo ['spazimo] SM pang; **morire tra atroci spasimi** to die in agony
spasmo ['spazmo] SM (*Med*) spasm
spasmodicamente [spazmodika'mente] AVV spasmodically
spasmodico, a, ci, che [spaz'mɔdiko] AGG **1** (*affannoso: attesa, ricerca*) agonizing **2** (*Med*) spasmodic
spassarsi [spas'sarsi] VIP (*aus* **essere**) **spassarsela** to enjoy o.s., have a good time
spassionatamente [spassjonata'mente] AVV dispassionately
spassionato, a [spassjo'nato] AGG (*parere, consiglio*) impartial, dispassionate
spasso ['spasso] SM **1** (*divertimento*) amusement, enjoyment; **per spasso** for amusement; **che spasso!** what a laugh!; **sei uno spasso!** you're a scream! **2** (*passeggiata*): **andare a spasso** to go for a walk; **portare qn a spasso** to take sb for a walk; **portare a spasso il cane** to take the dog for a walk; **essere a spasso** (*fig*) to be unemployed *o* out of work; **mandare qn a spasso** (*fig fam: licenziare*) to give sb the sack
spassoso, a [spas'soso] AGG amusing, entertaining
spastico, a, ci, che ['spastiko] AGG, SM/F spastic

Ss

spatola ['spatola] SF **1** (*Med*) spatula (*Brit*), tongue depressor (*Am*); (*di muratore*) trowel; (*di decoratore*) putty knife; (*di sci*) tip; (*Culin: di legno*) spatula; (*: di metallo*) palette knife **2** (*uccello*) spoonbill
spauracchio, chi [spau'rakkjo] SM (*spaventapasseri*) scarecrow; (*fig*) bogey, bugbear
spaurire [spau'rire] VT to frighten, terrify
spaurito, a [spau'rito] AGG frightened, terrified
spavaldamente [spavalda'mente] AVV cockily
spavalderia [spavalde'ria] SF cockiness
spavaldo, a [spa'valdo] AGG cocky; **ora è più spavaldo che mai** now he's cockier than ever
spaventapasseri [spaventa'passeri] SM INV scarecrow
spaventare [spaven'tare] VT to frighten, scare; **l'idea mi spaventa un po'** the idea scares me a bit
▶ **spaventarsi** VIP to become frightened, become scared, be scared; **si è spaventato molto vedendo la pistola** he was very scared when he saw the gun
spavento [spa'vento] SM fear, fright; **fare** *o* **mettere spavento a qn** to frighten *o* scare sb, give sb a fright; **morire di spavento** (*fig*) to be scared to death; **è uno spavento** *or* **è brutto da far spavento** he is terribly ugly
spaventosamente [spaventosa'mente] AVV (*in modo spaventoso*) frighteningly; (*fig fam: eccessivamente*) terribly, incredibly
spaventoso, a [spaven'toso] AGG (*sogno, avventura*) frightening; (*incidente, delitto*) horrifying, terrible; (*fig fam: incredibile*) incredible; (*: tempesta*) terrible; (*: prezzi*) appalling; **ho una fame spaventosa** I'm ravenous; **ho fatto una figura spaventosa** I made an awful fool of myself
spaziale [spat'tsjale] AGG **1** (*volo, nave, tuta*) space *attr* **2** (*Archit, Geom*) spatial
spaziare [spat'tsjare] VI (*aus* avere) **spaziare in** *or* **spaziare per** to range over; **spaziare col pensiero** to let one's thoughts wander
■ VT (*Tip: parole, lettere*) to space (out)
spaziatura [spattsja'tura] SF (*Tip*) spacing
spazientirsi [spattsjen'tirsi] VIP to lose one's patience; **si è spazientito e se n'è andato** he lost patience and left
spazio, zi ['spattsjo] SM (*gen, Fis, Mus, Tip*) space; (*posto*) room, space; **occupa molto spazio** it takes up a lot of room; **non c'è più spazio nell'armadio** there's no more room in the wardrobe; **fare spazio per qn/qc** to make room for sb/sth; **dare spazio a** (*fig*) to make room for; **ci manca lo spazio** we are short of room *o* space; **lo spazio tra le file** the space *o* gap between the rows; **grandi spazi aperti** wide open spaces; **è riuscita a parcheggiare in uno spazio piccolissimo** she managed to park in a tiny space; **nello spazio di un'ora** within an hour, in the space of an hour; **hanno lanciato un satellite nello spazio** they've launched a satellite into space; **spazio aereo** airspace; **spazio su disco** (*Inform*) disk space; **spazio vitale** living space
spazioso, a [spat'tsjoso] AGG (*casa, macchina*) spacious, roomy; (*strada*) wide
spazzacamino [spattsaka'mino] SM chimney sweep
spazzaneve [spattsa'neve] SM INV (*spartineve, Sci*) snowplough (*Brit*), snowplow (*Am*)
spazzare [spat'tsare] VT (*pavimento, strada*) to sweep; (*foglie, polvere*) to sweep up; **spazzare via** to sweep away; (*fig: cibo*) to put away
spazzatura [spattsa'tura] SF (*immondizia*) rubbish (*Brit*), garbage (*Am*), trash (*Am*); **puoi portare fuori la spazzatura?** can you take the rubbish out?; **camion della spazzatura** dustcart (*Brit*); garbage truck (*Am*)
■ AGG INV (*giornale, romanzo*) trashy; **posta-spazzatura** junk mail *sg*
spazzino, a [spat'tsino] SM/F roadsweeper (*Brit*), street sweeper (*Am*)
spazzola ['spattsola] SF brush; **capelli a spazzola** crew cut *sg*; **spazzola per abiti** clothes brush; **spazzola da bagno** back scrubber; **spazzola per capelli** hairbrush; **spazzola di ferro** wire brush; **spazzola per le scarpe** shoebrush; **spazzola rotante** (*Aut*) rotor arm
spazzolare [spattso'lare] VT to brush
spazzolata [spattso'lata] SF brush, brushing
spazzolino [spattso'lino] SM (small) brush; **spazzolino da denti** toothbrush; **spazzolino per unghie** nailbrush
spazzolone [spattso'lone] SM (*per pulire*) scrubbing brush; (*per lucidare*) floor polisher
speaker ['spi:kə] SM/F INV announcer
specchiarsi [spek'kjarsi] VR to look at o.s. in a mirror; **si specchia in tutte le vetrine** she looks at herself in all the shop windows; **il pavimento è così pulito che ti ci puoi specchiare** the floor is so clean you can see your face in it
■ VIP: **le montagne si specchiano nel lago** the mountains are reflected in the lake
specchiera [spek'kjɛra] SF **1** (*specchio*) large mirror **2** (*mobile*) dressing table
specchietto[1] [spek'kjetto] SM (small) mirror; **specchietto per le allodole** (*Caccia*) lure; (*fig*) bait; **specchietto da borsetta** pocket mirror; **specchietto di cortesia** (*Aut*) vanity mirror; **specchietto laterale** wing mirror; **specchietto retrovisore** (*Aut*) rear-view mirror
specchietto[2] [spek'kjetto] SM (*tabella*) table, chart
specchio, chi ['spekkjo] SM mirror; **mi sono guardata allo specchio** I looked at myself in the mirror; **la sua casa è uno specchio** her house is spotlessly clean; **il mare è uno specchio** the sea is as calm as a millpond; **uno specchio d'acqua** a sheet of water
special ['spɛtʃal] SM INV (*TV*) special feature
speciale [spe'tʃale] AGG (*gen*) special; (*specifico*) particular; (*singolare*) peculiar, singular; **hai qualche motivo speciale per sospettare di lui?** do you have any particular reason to suspect him?; **ha un modo tutto speciale di parlare** he has a highly individual way of speaking; **questo arrosto è speciale** this roast is delicious; **in special modo** especially; **inviato speciale** (*Radio, TV, Stampa*) special correspondent; **offerta speciale** special offer; **treno speciale** special *o* extra train; **poteri/leggi speciali** (*Pol*) emergency powers/legislation *sg*
specialista, i, e [spetʃa'lista] SM/F (*gen*) expert, specialist; (*Med*) specialist
specialistico, a, ci, che [spetʃa'listiko] AGG (*conoscenza, preparazione*) specialized; **devo fare una visita specialista** (*Med*) I have to see a specialist
specialità [spetʃali'ta] SF INV **1** (*prodotto tipico*) speciality (*Brit*), specialty (*Am*) **2** (*branca di studio*) specialism
specializzando, a [spetʃalid'dzando] SM/F *person who is specializing*
specializzare [spetʃalid'dzare] VT (*industria*) to make more specialized
▶ **specializzarsi** VR: **specializzarsi (in)** (*studio,*

professione) to specialize (in); **mi sono specializzato nel fare torte** I'm a dab hand at baking cakes

specializzato, a [spetʃalid'dzato] AGG (*manodopera*) skilled; (*elaboratore*) dedicated; **operaio non specializzato** unskilled worker; **essere specializzato in** to be a specialist in

specializzazione [spetʃaliddzat'tsjone] SF specialization; **prendere la specializzazione in** to specialize in

specialmente [spetʃal'mente] AVV especially, particularly

specie ['spɛtʃe] SF INV **1** (*Bio, Bot, Zool*) species *inv*; **una specie in via di estinzione** an endangered species; **alcune specie rare di piante** some rare species of plants; **la specie umana** mankind **2** (*tipo*) sort, kind, variety; **una specie di** a kind of; **è una specie di piatto con grandi manici** it's a sort of dish with big handles; **gente di ogni specie** all kinds of people; **mi fa specie** it surprises me

■ AVV especially, particularly

specifica, che [spe'tʃifika] SF specification

specificamente [spetʃifika'mente] AVV specifically

specificare [spetʃifi'kare] VT to specify, state (clearly)

specificatamente [spetʃifikata'mente] AVV in detail

specificazione [spetʃifikat'tsjone] SF **1** (*gen*) specification **2** (*Gramm*): **complemento di specificazione** genitive case

specificità [spetʃifitʃi'ta] SF specificity

specifico, a, ci, che [spe'tʃifiko] AGG (*gen, Med*) specific; **mi ha rivolto accuse specifiche** his accusations were very specific; **nel caso specifico** in this particular case

specioso, a [spe'tʃoso] AGG (*letter*) specious

speck [ʃpɛk] SM INV *kind of smoked ham*

speculare[1] [speku'lare] VI (*aus* **avere**) **1** (*Comm*) to speculate; (*fig: approfittare*): **speculare su** to take advantage of; **speculare in Borsa** to speculate on the Stock Exchange **2** (*Filosofia*): **speculare (su)** to speculate (on *o* about)

speculare[2] [speku'lare] AGG (*immagine, scrittura*) mirror *attr*

speculativo, a [spekula'tivo] AGG (*Filosofia, Comm*) speculative

speculatore, trice [spekula'tore] SM/F (*Comm*) speculator

speculazione [spekulat'tsjone] SF speculation

spedire [spe'dire] VT (*gen*) to send, dispatch; (*Comm*) to dispatch, forward; **non ho ancora spedito la lettera** I haven't sent the letter yet; **spedire qc a qn** to send sb sth; **gli ho spedito una cartolina** I sent him a postcard; **gliel'ho già spedito** I've already sent it to him; **spedire per posta** to post (*Brit*), mail (*Am*); **spedire per mare** to ship; **spedire qn all'altro mondo** to send sb to meet his (*o* her) maker

> **LO SAPEVI...?**
> **spedire** non si traduce mai con la parola inglese *expedite*

speditamente [spedita'mente] AVV (*lavorare*) quickly; (*parlare: veloce*) quickly; (: *con sicurezza*) fluently; **camminare speditamente** to walk at a brisk pace

spedito, a [spe'dito] AGG (*gen*) quick; **con passo spedito** at a brisk pace; **ha una pronuncia spedita** he has a fluent manner of speaking

■ AVV = **speditamente**

spedizione [spedit'tsjone] SF **1** (*atto*) sending, posting; (*Comm: gen*) forwarding; (: *via mare*) shipping; (*collo, merce*) consignment; (: *via mare*) shipment; **agenzia di spedizione** forwarding agency; **spese di spedizione** (*gen*) postal (*Brit*) *o* mail (*Am*) charges; (*Comm*) forwarding charges; **fare una spedizione** to send a consignment **2** (*scientifica, Mil, Alpinismo*) expedition; **una spedizione punitiva** a punitive raid

spedizioniere [spedittsjo'njɛre] SM forwarding agent, shipping agent

spegnere ['spɛɲɲere] VB IRREG

■ VT (*fuoco, sigaretta*) to put out, extinguish; (*apparecchio elettrico*) to switch *o* turn off; (*luce*) to switch *o* turn off; (*gas*) to turn off; (*fig: suoni, passioni*) to stifle; (: *debito*) to extinguish

▶ **spegnersi** VIP **1** (*fuoco, sigaretta*) to go out; (*apparecchio elettrico, luce*) to go off; (*motore*) to stall; (*fig: passioni, suoni*) to die down; (: *ricordo*) to fade; **la luce si è spenta all'improvviso** the light went off suddenly; **mi si è spenta la macchina al semaforo** the car stalled at the traffic lights **2** (*euf: morire*) to pass away

spegnimento [speɲɲi'mento] SM (*di debito*) extinguishing; (*di luce, apparecchio elettrico*) switching off; (*di incendio*) putting out

spelacchiato, a [spelak'kjato] AGG (*gatto, cane*) mangy; (*coperta, tappeto*) threadbare, worn-out; (*pelliccia, animale di pezza*) shabby

spelare [spe'lare] VT (*Elettr: fili*) to strip

▶ **spelarsi** VIP (*animali*) to moult; (*pelliccia*) to lose hair

speleologia [speleolo'dʒia] SF (*scienza*) speleology; (*pratica*) potholing (*Brit*), spelunking (*Am*)

speleologo, a, gi, ghe [spele'ɔlogo] SM/F (*vedi sf*) speleologist; potholer (*Brit*), spelunker (*Am*)

spellare [spel'lare] VT **1** (*coniglio*) to skin; (*fam: scorticare*) to graze; **mi sono spellato il ginocchio** I grazed my knee **2** (*fig: cliente*) to fleece

▶ **spellarsi** VIP (*persona: per il troppo sole*) to peel; (: *scorticarsi*) to graze o.s.; (*rettile*) to shed its skin

spelonca, che [spe'lonka] SF (*caverna*) cave, cavern; (*fig: casa squallida*) hovel

spendaccione, a [spendat'tʃone] SM/F spendthrift

spendere ['spɛndere] VT IRREG (*denaro, tempo*) to spend; **quanto ti hanno fatto spendere?** how much did they charge you?; **quanto hai speso?** how much did you spend?; **quanto hai speso per quel vestito?** how much did you spend on *o* pay for that dress?; **si mangia bene e si spende poco** the food's good and it doesn't cost much; **spendere un occhio della testa** to spend a fortune; **spendere una buona parola per qn** to put in a good word for sb; **spendere e spandere** to squander one's money; **spendere la vita sui libri** to spend one's life studying

spengo *ecc* ['spɛngo] VB *vedi* **spegnere**

spennacchiare [spennak'kjare] VT (*gallina*) to pluck

▶ **spennacchiarsi** VIP to moult, lose its feathers

spennacchiato, a [spennak'kjato] AGG (*con poche penne*) moulting

spennare [spen'nare] VT (*gallina*) to pluck; (*fig: cliente*) to fleece

▶ **spennarsi** VIP to moult, lose its feathers

spennellare [spennel'lare] VI (*aus* **avere**) to paint

■ VT (*Med*): **spennellare una ferita con la tintura di iodio** to dab a wound with iodine; (*Culin*): **spennellare un dolce con l'uovo** to brush the cake with beaten egg

spennellata [spennel'lata] SF brush-stroke

spensi *ecc* ['spɛnsi] VB *vedi* **spegnere**

spensieratamente [spensjerata'mente] AVV in a carefree manner, lightheartedly

Ss

spensieratezza [spensjera'tettsa] SF carefreeness, lightheartedness
spensierato, a [spensje'rato] AGG carefree, lighthearted
spento, a ['spɛnto] PP *di* **spegnere**
■ AGG (*luce, fuoco, sigaretta*) out; (*colore*) dull, faded; (*vulcano, civiltà*) extinct; (*persona, sguardo, festa*) lifeless; (*suono*) muffled
speranza [spe'rantsa] SF hope; **nella speranza di rivederti** (*in lettera*) hoping to see *o* in the hope of seeing you again; **avere la speranza che...** to be hopeful that ...; **avere la speranza di qc/di fare qc** to be hopeful of sth/of doing sth; **hai qualche speranza di vincere?** have you any hope *o* chance of winning?; **hai qualche speranza di rivederlo?** do you have any hope of seeing him again?; **pieno di speranze** hopeful; **senza speranza** (*situazione*) hopeless; (*amare*) without hope; **quel giovane è una speranza dell'atletica** that boy is a promising athlete; **speranza di vita** life expectancy
speranzoso, a [speran'tsoso] AGG hopeful
sperare [spe'rare] VT: **sperare qc/di fare qc** to hope for sth/to do sth; **spero che Luca arrivi in tempo** I hope Luca arrives in time; **spero di trovare un lavoro presto** I hope to find a job soon; **spero di sì** I hope so; **spero di no** I hope not; **speriamo bene!** let's hope so!; **lo spero** I hope so; **non speravo più di vederti** I'd given up hope of seeing you
■ VI (*aus* **avere**) **sperare in** (*successo*) to hope for; **spero in Dio** to trust in God; **spero in te per risolvere la situazione** I'm counting on you to sort things out; **tutto fa sperare per il meglio** everything leads one to hope for the best
sperduto, a [sper'duto] AGG (*isolato: casa, villaggio*) out-of-the-way; (*persona: smarrito*) lost; (*: a disagio*) ill at ease
spergiurare [sperdʒu'rare] VI (*aus* **avere**) to commit perjury, perjure o.s.; **giurare e spergiurare** to swear blind
spergiuro, a [sper'dʒuro] AGG perjured
■ SM/F perjurer
■ SM perjury
spericolato, a [speriko'lato] AGG (*gen*) fearless, daring; (*guidatore*) reckless
■ SM/F daredevil
sperimentale [sperimen'tale] AGG experimental; **scuola sperimentale** pilot school; **fare qc in via sperimentale** to try sth out
sperimentalmente [sperimental'mente] AVV experimentally
sperimentare [sperimen'tare] VT **1** (*nuovo farmaco*) to experiment with, test; (*metodo*) to try out, test out; **sperimentare qc sugli animali** to test sth on animals **2** (*fig: tentare*) to try; (*: mettere alla prova*) to test, put to the test
sperimentatore, trice [sperimenta'tore] SM/F experimenter
sperimentazione [sperimentat'tsjone] SF experimentation; **sperimentazione sugli animali** animal testing
sperma ['spɛrma] SM sperm, semen
spermatozoo, i [spermatod'dzɔo] SM spermatozoon
spermicida, i, e [spermi'tʃida] AGG (*pomata, schiuma*) spermicidal
■ SM spermicide
speronamento [sperona'mento] SM ramming
speronare [spero'nare] VT (*nave, auto*) to ram
sperone [spe'rone] SM (*di stivali, Geog*) spur; (*Naut: rostro*) ram; (*Archit*) buttress; (*Zool*) dew claw
sperperare [sperpe'rare] VT (*denaro*) to squander
sperpero ['spɛrpero] SM (*di denaro*) squandering, waste; (*di cibo, materiali*) waste
sperso, a ['spɛrso] AGG (*persona: smarrito*) lost; (*: a disagio*) ill at ease
spersonalizzare [spersonalid'dzare] VT (*persona*) to deprive of individuality; (*stile, narrazione*) to depersonalize
▶ **spersonalizzarsi** VIP (*persona*) to lose one's individuality
spersonalizzazione [spersonaliddzat'tsjone] SF depersonalization
spesa ['spesa] SF **1** (*soldi spesi*) expense; (*uscita*) outlay, expenditure; (*costo*) cost; **una grossa spesa** a big expense; **la spesa è di 200 euro** it will cost 200 euros; **con la modica spesa di 1000 euro** for the modest sum *o* outlay of 1,000 euros; **ridurre le spese** (*gen*) to cut down (on spending); (*Comm*) to reduce expenditure; **a spese della ditta** at the firm's expense; **sono andata a Parigi a spese della ditta** I went to Paris at the company's expense; **le spese ti verranno rimborsate** your expenses will be reimbursed; **a mie spese** (*fig*) at my expense; **fare le spese di qc** (*fig*) to pay the price for sth **2** (*acquisto*) buy, purchase; (*fam: compere*) shopping *no pl*; **fare la spesa** to do the shopping; **fare (delle) spese** to go shopping; **adoro fare spese** I love shopping
■ **spesa pubblica** public expenditure; **spese in conto capitale** (*Comm*) capital expenditure *sg*; **spese fisse** (*di azienda*) fixed costs; **spese generali** (*Comm*) overheads; **spese di gestione** operating expenses; **spese d'impianto** (*Comm*) initial outlay *sg*; **spese legali** legal costs; **spese di manutenzione** maintenance costs; **spese postali** postage *o* postal (*Brit*) *o* mail (*Am*) charges; **spese di trasporto** handling charges; **spese straordinarie** extraordinary expenses; **spese di viaggio** travelling (*Brit*) *o* traveling (*Am*) expenses
spesare [spe'sare] VT: **sono spesato dalla società** the company pays my expenses; **un viaggio tutto spesato** an all-expenses-paid trip
speso, a ['speso] PP *di* **spendere**
spessimetro [spes'simetro] SM thickness gauge, feeler gauge
spesso[1] ['spesso] AVV often; **andiamo spesso al cinema** we often go to the cinema; **anche troppo spesso** all too often; **spesso e volentieri** very often
spesso[2]**, a** ['spesso] AGG (*nebbia, fumo*) thick, dense; (*stoffa*) heavy, heavyweight; (*carta*) thick, heavy; **spesso 40 mm** 40 mm thick
spessore [spes'sore] SM **1** thickness; (*fig: importanza: di ricerca*) significance; (*: di personaggio*) stature; **ha uno spessore di 20 cm** it is 20 cm thick **2** (*Tecn*) gauge
Spett. ABBR = **spettabile**
spettabile [spet'tabile] AGG (*Comm*): **spettabile ditta X** (*sulla busta*) Messrs X and Co; (*inizio lettera*) Dear Sirs, ...; **avvertiamo la spettabile clientela...** we inform our customers ...
spettacolare [spettako'lare] AGG spectacular
spettacolarità [spettakolari'ta] SF spectacular nature
spettacolo [spet'takolo] SM **1** (*Cine, TV, Teatro*) show, performance; **uno spettacolo televisivo** a TV show; **mettere su uno spettacolo** to put on a show; **gli spettacoli iniziano alle 20** performances begin at 8 pm; **primo/secondo spettacolo** (*Cine*) first/second showing; **andremo al primo spettacolo** we'll go to the first showing **2** (*vista, scena*) sight; **dare**

spettacolo di sé to make an exhibition *o* a spectacle of o.s.

spettacoloso, a [spettako'loso] AGG (*vista*) spectacular; (*fig*) amazing, incredible

spettanza [spet'tantsa] SF (*frm*) **1** (*competenza*) concern; **non è di mia spettanza** it's no concern of mine **2** (*somma dovuta*): **spettanze** SFPL amount due; **non ho ancora avuto le mie spettanze** I haven't yet received what is owing to me

spettare [spet'tare] VI (*aus* **essere**) **spettare a** (*decisione*) to be up to; (*stipendio*) to be due to; **spetta a te decidere** it's up to you to decide; **mi spetta una parte degli incassi** I'm due a share of the takings; **voglio solo quello che mi spetta** I only want what's due to me

spettatore, trice [spetta'tore] SM/F (*Cine, Teatro*) member of the audience; (*TV*) viewer; (*Sport*) spectator; (*di avvenimento*) witness; **è stato spettatore di un incidente** he witnessed an accident

spettegolare [spettego'lare] VI (*aus* **avere**) to gossip

spettinare [spetti'nare] VT: **spettinare qn** to ruffle sb's hair
▸ **spettinarsi** VR to get one's hair in a mess

spettinato, a [spetti'nato] AGG dishevelled; **sono tutta spettinata** my hair's in a mess

spettrale [spet'trale] AGG (*gen*) spectral, ghostly

spettro ['spettro] SM **1** (*fantasma*) spectre (*Brit*), specter (*Am*), ghost **2** (*Fis*) spectrum

spezie ['spettsje] SFPL (*Culin*) spices

spezzare [spet'tsare] VT (*rompere*) to break, snap; (*fig: interrompere*) to break up; **basta, mi spezzi il braccio!** stop it! you're breaking my arm!; **spezzare il cuore a qn** to break sb's heart; **spezzare il viaggio** to break one's journey; **mi spezza la giornata** it breaks up my day
▸ **spezzarsi** VIP to break, snap; **la fune si è spezzata** the rope broke

spezzatino [spettsa'tino] SM (*Culin*) stew

spezzato, a [spet'tsato] AGG (*unghia, ramo, braccio*) broken; **fare orario spezzato** to work a split shift
■ SM (*abito maschile*) (coordinated) jacket and trousers (*Brit*) *o* pants (*Am*)

spezzettamento [spettsetta'mento] SM breaking up

spezzettare [spettset'tare] VT to break up (*o* chop) into small pieces; **spezzettare il pane** to crumble bread

spezzino, a [spet'tsino] AGG of *o* from La Spezia
■ SM/F inhabitant *o* native of La Spezia

spezzone [spet'tsone] SM (*Cine*) clip

spia ['spia] SF **1** (*gen*) spy; (*confidente della polizia*) informer; **non fare la spia** (*gen*) don't give me (*o* us *ecc*) away; (*di bambini*) don't be a telltale *o* a sneak **2** (*Elettr*: *anche*: **spia luminosa**) warning light, indicating light; (*di porta*) spyhole, peephole; (*fig: sintomo*) sign, indication; **spia dell'olio** (*Aut*) oil warning light

spiaccicare [spjattʃi'kare] VT (*fam: schiacciare*) to squash, crush; **ti spiaccico al muro** I'll flatten you

spiacente [spja'tʃɛnte] AGG sorry; **siamo spiacenti di non poter accettare** we regret being unable to accept, we are sorry we cannot accept; **siamo spiacenti di quanto è successo** we regret what happened, we are sorry about what happened; **siamo spiacenti di dovervi annunciare che...** we regret to inform you that ...; **sono molto spiacente ma...** I am extremely sorry, but ...

spiacere [spja'tʃere] = **dispiacere** VB

spiacevole [spja'tʃevole] AGG (*compito*) unpleasant; (*incidente, equivoco*) regrettable

spiacevolmente [spjatʃevol'mente] AVV unpleasantly, disagreeably

spiaggia, ge ['spjaddʒa] SF beach; **una spiaggia sabbiosa** a sandy beach

spianare [spja'nare] VT (*terreno*) to level, make level; (*palazzo, città*) to raze to the ground; (*pasta*) to roll out; **spianare il fucile** to level one's gun; **spianare la strada** (*fig*) to prepare *o* clear the ground

spianata [spja'nata] SF (*radura*) clearing

spianatoia [spjana'toja] SF (*Culin*) pastry board

spiano ['spjano] **a tutto spiano** AVV (*lavorare*) flat out; (*spendere*) lavishly

spiantato, a [spjan'tato] AGG penniless
■ SM penniless person

spiare [spi'are] VT to spy on; **spiare le mosse di qn** to spy on sb's movements; **spiare l'occasione propizia** to wait for the right moment; **ci stava spiando da dietro la porta** he was spying on us from behind the door; **spiare attraverso il buco della serratura** to spy through the keyhole

spiata [spi'ata] SF tip-off

spiattellare [spjattel'lare] VT (*fam: verità, segreto*) to blurt out; **spiattellare tutto** to spill the beans

spiazzo ['spjattso] SM (*gen*) open space; (*radura*) clearing; **giocano in uno spiazzo davanti alla casa** they play on a piece of ground in front of the house; **si fermarono in uno spiazzo nel bosco** they stopped in a clearing in the forest

spiccare [spik'kare] VT **1** **spiccare un balzo** to jump, leap; **spiccare il volo** (*uccello*) to take wing; (*fig*) to spread one's wings **2** (*Dir, Comm: mandato, assegno*) to issue
■ VI (*aus* **avere**) (*risaltare*) to stand out

spiccatamente [spikkata'mente] AVV (*nettamente*) distinctly; **parla con un accento spiccatamente tedesco** he speaks with a strong German accent

spiccato, a [spik'kato] AGG (*senso del dovere, dell'umorismo*) marked, strong; (*gusto*) definite, marked; (*accento*) broad; **ha una spiccata simpatia per lui** she is very fond of him

spiccherò *ecc* [spikke'rɔ] VB *vedi* **spiccare**

spicchio, chi ['spikkjo] SM (*di agrumi*) segment; (*di aglio*) clove; (*di formaggio*) piece; **fare** *o* **tagliare a spicchi** to divide into segments

spicciare [spit'tʃare] VT (*lavoro, faccenda*) to finish off; (*cliente*) to attend to
▸ **spicciarsi** VIP to hurry up, get a move on

spicciativo, a [spittʃa'tivo] AGG quick

spiccicare [spittʃi'kare] VT (*adesivo, francobollo*) to unstick, detach; **non ha spiccicato parola** he didn't utter a word
▸ **spiccicarsi** VIP (*francobollo*) to come unstuck, come off

spiccio, cia, ci, ce ['spittʃo] AGG **1** (*faccenda*) quick; **andare per le spicce** not to waste time on niceties **2** **denaro spiccio** (small) change
■ SMPL (*moneta*): **spicci** (small) change *sg*

spicciolata [spittʃo'lata] AVV: **alla spicciolata** in dribs and drabs, a few at a time

spicciolo, a ['spittʃolo] AGG: **denaro spicciolo** *or* **moneta spicciola** (small) change
■ SM: **non ho uno spicciolo** I'm penniless; **hai degli spiccioli?** have you got any (small) change?

spicco ['spikko] SM: **fare spicco** to stand out; **di spicco** (*personaggio*) prominent; (*tema*) main, principal

Ss

spider ['spaidə] SM O F INV (*Aut*) two-seater convertible sports car
spidocchiare [spidok'kjare] VT to delouse
▶ **spidocchiarsi** VR to delouse o.s.
spiedino [spje'dino] SM **1** (*utensile*) skewer **2** (*Culin: di carne, pesce*) kebab
spiedo ['spjɛdo] SM (*Culin*) spit; **allo spiedo** on a spit; **pollo allo spiedo** spit-roasted chicken
spiegamento [spjega'mento] SM (*Mil*): **spiegamento di forze** deployment of forces
spiegare [spje'gare] VT **1** (*significato, mistero*) to explain; **spiegare qc a qn** to explain sth to sb; **potresti spiegarci il motivo?** could you explain the reason to us?; **gli ho spiegato la situazione** I explained the situation to him; **farsi spiegare qc** to get *o* have sth explained **2** (*tovaglia*) to unfold; (*vele*) to unfurl; **a voce spiegata** at the top of one's voice; **a sirene spiegate** with sirens wailing **3** (*Mil*) to deploy
▶ **spiegarsi** VR (*farsi capire*) to explain o.s., make o.s. clear; (*capire*) to understand; **era così agitato che non riusciva a spiegarsi** he was so upset that he couldn't make himself understood; **mi spiego?** do I make myself clear?, do you understand?; **non so se mi spiego!** need I say more!; **spieghiamoci una volta per tutte!** let's get things straight once and for all!; **non mi spiego come...** I can't understand how ...; **non mi spiego come sia potuto accadere** I can't understand how it could have happened; **ora si spiega tutto!** now everything is clear!
spiegazione [spjegat'tsjone] SF explanation; **avere una spiegazione con qn** to have it out with sb
spiegazzare [spjegat'tsare] VT to crease, crumple
spiegazzato, a [spjegat'tsato] AGG creased, crumpled
spiegherò *ecc* [spjege'rɔ] VB *vedi* **spiegare**
spietatamente [spjetata'mente] AVV ruthlessly, without pity
spietatezza [spjeta'tettsa] SF ruthlessness
spietato, a [spje'tato] AGG (*persona*) ruthless, pitiless; (*guerra*) cruel, bitter; (*fig: concorrenza*) fierce; **fare una corte spietata a qn** to chase (after) sb
spifferare [spiffe'rare] VT (*fam*) to blurt out, blab
spiffero ['spiffero] SM (*fam: corrente d'aria*) draught (*Brit*), draft (*Am*); **questa stanza è piena di spifferi** this room is full of draughts
spiga, ghe ['spiga] SF (*Bot: di grano*) ear
spigato, a [spi'gato] AGG (*tessuto*) herringbone
spigliatamente [spiʎʎata'mente] AVV confidently, with ease
spigliatezza [spiʎʎa'tettsa] SF ease, self-confidence
spigliato, a [spiʎ'ʎato] AGG (*persona*) self-confident, self-possessed; (*modi*) (free and) easy
spignattare [spiɲɲat'tare] VI (*aus* **avere**) (*fam*) to slave over a hot stove
spigola ['spigola] SF (*Zool*) bass
spigolare [spigo'lare] VT (*anche fig*) to glean
spigolatura [spigola'tura] SF (*anche fig*) gleaning
spigolo ['spigolo] SM (*di mobile, muro*) corner, edge; (*Geom*) edge; **smussare gli spigoli** (*fig*) to knock off the rough edges
spigoloso, a [spigo'loso] AGG (*mobile*) angular; (*persona, carattere*) difficult
spilla ['spilla] SF (*gen*) brooch; (*da cravatta, cappello*) pin; **spilla di sicurezza** *o* **da balia** safety pin
spillare [spil'lare] VT **1** (*botte, vino, fig*) to tap; **spillare denaro/notizie a qn** to tap sb for money/information **2** (*fogli*) to clip together
spillo ['spillo] SM (*gen*) pin; (*da cappello*) hatpin; (*da cravatta*) tiepin; **tacco a spillo** stiletto heel (*Brit*), spike heel (*Am*); **valvola a spillo** needle valve
spillone [spil'lone] SM (*per cappello*) hatpin
spilluzzicare [spilluttsi'kare] VT (*cibo*) to nibble, peck at
spilorceria [spilortʃe'ria] SF meanness, stinginess; **questa è una spilorceria!** that's really mean *o* stingy!
spilorciamente [spilortʃa'mente] AVV meanly, stingily
spilorcio, cia, ci, ce [spi'lortʃo] AGG mean, stingy, tight-fisted
■ SM/F miser, stingy person
spilungone, a [spilun'gone] SM/F beanpole
spina ['spina] SF **1** (*Bot: di rosa*) thorn; **avere una spina nel cuore** to have a thorn in one's flesh *o* side; **stare sulle spine** (*fig*) to be on tenterhooks; **spina nel fianco** thorn in sb's side **2** (*Zool: di riccio, istrice*) spine, prickle; (*: di pesce*) bone; **a spina di pesce** (*tessuto*) herringbone; **spina dorsale** (*Anat*) backbone **3** (*Elettr*) plug; **staccare la spina** (*Elettr*) to pull out the plug; (*di malato terminale*) to turn off the life support; (*fig: interrompere un'attività*) to knock off **4** (*di botte*) bunghole; **birra alla spina** draught (*Brit*) *o* draft (*Am*) beer
spinacio, ci [spi'natʃo] SM (*Bot*) spinach; (*Culin*): **spinaci** SMPL spinach *sg*
spinale [spi'nale] AGG (*Anat*) spinal
spinare [spi'nare] VT (*pesce*) to bone
spinato, a [spi'nato] AGG **1** **filo spinato** barbed wire **2** (*tessuto*) herringbone *attr*
spinello [spi'nɛllo] SM (*Droga*) joint
spinetta [spi'netta] SF (*Mus*) spinet
spingere ['spindʒere] VB IRREG
■ VT **1** (*gen*) to push; (*premere*) to press, push; **non spingete** don't push *o* shove; **"spingere"** "push"; **mi spingi?** (*sull'altalena*) can you give me a push?; **le onde ci hanno spinto contro gli scogli** the waves drove us onto the rocks; **spingere le cose all'eccesso** to take *o* carry things too far *o* to extremes; **spingere lo sguardo lontano** to look into the distance **2** (*fig: stimolare*): **spingere qn a fare qc** to urge *o* press sb to do sth; **spingere qn al delitto/suicidio** to drive sb to crime/suicide; **spinto dalla fame/disperazione** driven by hunger/despair; **è stato spinto dalla gelosia** he was driven by jealousy; **che cosa ti spinge a continuare?** what drives you on?
■ VI (*aus* **avere**) to push
▶ **spingersi** VIP: **spingersi troppo lontano** (*anche fig*) to go too far; **ci siamo spinti fino al faro** we ventured as far as the lighthouse
spingidisco, schi [spindʒi'disko] SM (*Aut*) (clutch) pressure plate
spinnaker ['spinəkə] SM INV (*Naut*) spinnaker
spinning ['spinnin(g)] SM (*Sport*) Spinning®
spino ['spino] SM (*Bot*) thorn bush
spinone [spi'none] SM (*cane*) griffon
spinoso, a [spi'noso] AGG (*anche fig*) thorny, prickly
spinsi *ecc* ['spinsi] VB *vedi* **spingere**
spinta ['spinta] SF **1** (*gen*) push; (*urto*) push, shove; (*Fis*) thrust; **mi aiuta a dare una spinta alla macchina?** could you help me give the car a push?; **spinta verso l'alto** upthrust **2** (*fig: stimolo*) incentive, spur; (*: raccomandazione*): **ho bisogno di una spinta** I need someone to pull some strings for me
spintarella [spinta'rɛlla] SF (*fig: raccomandazione*): **gli hanno dato una spintarella** someone pulled strings for him

spinterogeno [spinte'rɔdʒeno] SM (*Aut*) ignition coil
spinto, a ['spinto] PP *di* **spingere**
■ AGG (*film, barzelletta*) risqué
spintonare [spinto'nare] VT (*spingere*) to shove, push
spintone [spin'tone] SM shove, push
spionaggio [spio'naddʒo] SM espionage, spying; **è stato accusato di spionaggio** he was accused of spying; **un film di spionaggio** a spy film
spioncino [spion'tʃino] SM peephole, spyhole
spione, a [spi'one] SM/F (*fam*) telltale, sneak
spionistico, a, ci, che [spio'nistiko] AGG (*organizzazione*) spy *attr*; **rete spionistica** spy ring
spiovente [spjo'vɛnte] AGG (*tetto*) sloping; **palla** *o* **tiro spiovente** (*Calcio*) arcing shot
■ SM (*Calcio*) arcing shot
spiovere[1] ['spjɔvere] VB IMPERS (*Meteor*) (*aus* **essere** *o* **avere**) to stop raining
spiovere[2] ['spjɔvere] VI IRREG (*aus* **essere**) (*scorrere*) to flow down; (*ricadere: capelli*) to hang down, fall
spira ['spira] SF (*gen*) coil; (*di fumo*) curl
spiraglio, gli [spi'raʎʎo] SM (*fessura*) chink, narrow opening; (*raggio di luce, anche fig*) glimmer, gleam; **uno spiraglio di speranza** a glimmer of hope, a faint hope
spirale [spi'rale] SF **1** spiral; **a spirale** spiral(-shaped); **molla a spirale** (*di orologio*) hairspring; **spirale inflazionistica** inflationary spiral **2** (*contraccettivo*) coil
spirare[1] [spi'rare] VI (*aus* **avere**) (*vento*) to blow; (*odore: emanare*): **spirare da** to come from; **spira aria di burrasca** (*fig*) there's trouble brewing
spirare[2] [spi'rare] VI (*aus* **essere**) (*morire*) to expire, pass away; (*scadere*) to expire
spiritato, a [spiri'tato] AGG (*occhi, espressione*) wild
■ SM/F person possessed by a devil; **come uno spiritato** like one possessed

LO SAPEVI...?
spiritato non si traduce mai con la parola inglese *spirited*

spiritico, a, ci, che [spi'ritiko] AGG spiritualist; **seduta spiritica** séance
spiritismo [spiri'tizmo] SM spiritualism
spiritista, i, e [spiri'tista] SM/F spiritualist
spirito ['spirito] SM **1** (*gen*) spirit; (*fantasma*) spirit, ghost; **lo Spirito Santo** the Holy Spirit *o* Ghost; **valori dello spirito** spiritual values; **aver paura degli spiriti** to be afraid of ghosts **2** (*intelletto*) mind; **uno dei più grandi spiriti della storia** one of the greatest minds in history **3** (*disposizione d'animo*) spirit, disposition; (*significato: di legge, epoca, testo*) spirit; **ha preso lo scherzo con lo spirito giusto** he took the joke in the right spirit; **per sollevarti lo spirito** to raise your spirits; **in buone condizioni di spirito** in the right frame of mind; **non ha spirito di parte** he never takes sides; **spirito di squadra** team spirit; **ha detto di no per spirito di contraddizione** he said no just to be awkward **4** (*arguzia*) wit; (*umorismo*) humour (*Brit*), humor (*Am*), wit; **battuta di spirito** joke; **è una persona di spirito** he has a sense of humo(u)r; **non fare dello spirito** don't try to be witty **5** (*Chim*) spirit, alcohol; **sotto spirito** preserved in alcohol
spiritosaggine [spirito'saddʒine] SF (*qualità*) wittiness; (*battuta*) witticism
spiritosamente [spiritosa'mente] AVV wittily
spiritoso, a [spiri'toso] AGG witty; **è il più spiritoso del gruppo** he's the wittiest in the group
■ SM/F wit, witty person; **non fare lo spiritoso!** don't try and be funny!
spirituale [spiritu'ale] AGG (*gen, Filosofia, Rel*) spiritual
spiritualità [spirituali'ta] SF spirituality
spiritualizzare [spiritualid'dzare] VT to spiritualize
spiritualmente [spiritual'mente] AVV spiritually
spizzicare [spittsi'kare] VT to nibble, peck at
splendente [splen'dɛnte] AGG (*giornata*) bright, sunny; (*occhi*) shining; (*pavimento*) shining, gleaming
splendere ['splɛndere] VI DIF to shine; **il sole splende** the sun is shining
splendidamente [splendida'mente] AVV (*gen*) splendidly, magnificently; **l'esame è andato splendidamente** the exam went extremely well
splendido, a ['splɛndido] AGG (*gen*) magnificent, splendid; (*carriera*) brilliant; **una giornata splendida** a glorious day
splendore [splen'dore] SM splendour (*Brit*), splendor (*Am*); (*luce intensa*) brilliance, brightness; **gli splendori dell'antica Roma** the splendo(u)r of ancient Rome; **che splendore di ragazza!** what a beautiful girl!
spodestare [spodes'tare] VT (*sovrano*) to depose, dethrone; **spodestare da** to oust from
spoetizzare [spoetid'dzare] VT (*momento, fatto*) to take the beauty out of
spoglia ['spɔʎʎa] SF **1** (*di rettile*) slough; **sotto mentite spoglie** (*fig*) in disguise **2** (*letter: salma*) remains *pl*
spogliare [spoʎ'ʎare] VT **1** (*svestire*) to undress; (*: con la forza*) to strip; (*fig: privare: di autorità*) to divest, strip; (*: di tesori*) to strip; **spogliare qn di qc** (*derubare*) to strip *o* rob sb of sth **2** (*fare lo spoglio: di schede elettorali*) to count
▶ **spogliarsi** VR (*persona*) to undress, get undressed, strip; (*serpente*) to slough (off) *o* shed its skin
▶ **spogliarsi** VIP (*albero*) to shed its leaves; (*persona*): **spogliarsi di** (*fig: ricchezze*) to strip o.s. of; (*: pregiudizi*) to get rid of, rid o.s. of
spogliarellista, i, e [spoʎʎarel'lista] SM/F striptease artist, stripper
spogliarello [spoʎʎa'rɛllo] SM striptease
spogliatoio, oi [spoʎʎa'tojo] SM changing room
spoglio[1], glia, gli, glie ['spɔʎʎo] AGG (*stanza*) empty, bare; (*terreno, albero*) bare; (*stile*) simple
spoglio[2], gli ['spɔʎʎo] SM: **spoglio dei voti** counting of the votes
spoiler ['spɔilə] SM INV (*Aut*) spoiler
spola ['spɔla] SF (*Cucito: bobina*) spool; (*: navetta*) shuttle; **fare la spola (fra)** (*sogg: autobus, persona*) to go to and fro *o* shuttle (between)
spoletta [spo'letta] SF (*Cucito: bobina*) spool; (*di bomba*) fuse
spoliticizzare [spolititʃid'dzare] VT to make nonpolitical
▶ **spoliticizzarsi** VIP to become nonpolitical
spoliticizzazione [spolititʃiddzat'tsjone] SF making nonpolitical
spolmonarsi [spolmo'narsi] VIP to shout o.s. hoarse
spolpare [spol'pare] VT (*pollo*) to strip the flesh off; (*fig fam: spennare*) to skin, fleece; **ci hanno spolpato con queste tasse** they have bled us white with these taxes
spolverare[1] [spolve'rare] VT (*mobile*) to dust; (*fig: mangiare*) to polish off
■ VI (*aus* **avere**) to dust
spolverare[2] [spolve'rare] VT (*Culin*): **spolverare (di)** to sprinkle (with), dust (with)
spolverata[1] [spolve'rata] SF (quick) dust(ing)
spolverata[2] [spolve'rata] SF (*di neve*) light fall; **dare**

Ss

una spolverata di zucchero a qc to sprinkle sth with sugar

spolverino [spolve'rino] SM (*soprabito*) dust coat, duster (*Am*)

spolverizzare [spolverid'dzare] VT (*Culin*): **spolverizzare qc di** to dust *o* sprinkle sth with

spompato, a [spom'pato] AGG (*fam: sfinito*) worn out

sponda ['sponda] SF **1** (*di fiume*) bank; (*di mare, lago*) shore **2** (*bordo: di letto, carro*) side, edge

sponsor ['spɔnsə] SM/F INV sponsor

sponsorizzare [sponsorid'dzare] VT to sponsor

sponsorizzato, a [sponsorid'dzato] AGG sponsored

sponsorizzazione [sponsoriddzat'tsjone] SF sponsorship

spontaneamente [spontanea'mente] AVV (*agire*) naturally, spontaneously; (*reagire*) instinctively, spontaneously; (*pianta: crescere*) wild; **offrirsi spontaneamente di fare qc** to volunteer to do sth

spontaneità [spontanei'ta] SF spontaneity

spontaneo, a [spon'taneo] AGG (*gen*) spontaneous; (*affetto, persona*) natural, unaffected; (*vegetazione*) wild; **è stato un gesto spontaneo da parte sua** it was a spontaneous gesture on his part; **di sua spontanea volontà** of his own free will; **viene spontanea la domanda...** the question springs to mind ...; **i bambini sono sempre spontanei** children always act naturally; **sii spontanea quando ti fanno una foto!** try to be natural when you're having your photo taken!

spopolamento [spopola'mento] SM depopulation

spopolare [spopo'lare] VT to depopulate
■VI (*aus* **avere**) (*fam: aver successo: cantante, attore*) to draw the crowds
▶ **spopolarsi** VIP to become depopulated

spora ['spɔra] SF spore

sporadicamente [sporadika'mente] AVV sporadically

sporadicità [sporaditʃi'ta] SF sporadic nature

sporadico, a, ci, che [spo'radiko] AGG sporadic

sporcaccione, a [sporkat'tʃone] AGG filthy, disgusting; (*sessualmente*): **un vecchio sporcaccione** a dirty old man
■SM/F filthy person; (*sessualmente*) filthy beast, pig

sporcare [spor'kare] VT (*gen*) to dirty, make dirty; (*macchiare*) to stain; (*fig: reputazione*) to sully, soil; **attento a non sporcare il divano** mind you don't dirty the sofa; **mi sono sporcato la camicia riparando la moto** I got my shirt dirty when I was fixing the motorbike; **si è sporcato la camicia di sugo** he's got sauce on his shirt; **sporcarsi le mani** (*anche fig*) to dirty one's hands; **sporcarsi la reputazione** to sully one's reputation; **sporcarsi la fedina penale** to get a police record
▶ **sporcarsi** VR to get dirty; **deve essersi sporcato in giardino** he must have got dirty in the garden

sporcizia [spor'tʃittsja] SF (*sudiciume*) filth, dirt; **c'era tanta di quella sporcizia per le strade** the streets were really filthy *o* dirty; **vivere nella sporcizia** to live in squalor

sporco, a, chi, che ['spɔrko] AGG (*gen*) dirty, filthy; (*macchiato*) stained; (*fig: immorale*) dirty; (*: losco: politica, faccenda*) shady; (*: denaro*) dirty; **il fazzoletto è sporco** the handkerchief is dirty; **il fazzoletto è sporco di inchiostro/sangue** there is ink/blood on the handkerchief; **hai le scarpe sporche di fango** there is mud on your shoes, your shoes are muddy; **avere la coscienza sporca** to have a guilty conscience; **avere la fedina penale sporca** to have a police record; **sporco bastardo!** dirty bastard!; **farla sporca a qn** (*fig fam*) to do the dirty on sb
■SM dirt, filth

sporgente [spor'dʒɛnte] AGG (*occhi*) protuberant, bulging; (*denti*) prominent, protruding; (*mento*) prominent; **ha le ossa sporgenti** his bones stick out

sporgenza [spor'dʒɛntsa] SF (*su scogli, rocce*) projection; (*su parete*) bulge

sporgere ['spɔrdʒere] VB IRREG
■VT **1** (*braccio, testa*): **sporgere da** to put out of, stretch out of **2** (*Dir*): **sporgere querela contro qn** to sue sb, take legal action against sb
■VI (*aus* **essere**) (*venire in fuori*) to stick out; (*protendersi: massi*) to jut out; **sporge un po' troppo** it sticks out a bit too much;
▶ **sporgersi** VR: **sporgersi da** to lean out of (*Brit*); **non sporgerti dal finestrino** don't lean out of the window

sporsi *ecc* ['spɔrsi] VB *vedi* **sporgere**

sport [spɔrt] SM INV sport; **fare dello sport** to do sport; **che sport fai?** what sports do you play?; **fa diversi sport** he does various sports; **fare qc per sport** to do sth for fun; **sport estremi** extreme sports

sporta ['spɔrta] SF (*borsa*) shopping bag; **dirne un sacco e una sporta a qn** (*insultare*) to give sb a mouthful

sportello [spor'tɛllo] SM **1** (*di veicolo, mobile*) door **2** (*di banca, ufficio*) counter, window; **sportello automatico** (*di banca*) cash dispenser (*Brit*), automated teller machine (*Am*)

sportivamente [sportiva'mente] AVV sportingly

sportività [sportivi'ta] SF sportsmanship

sportivo, a [spor'tivo] AGG (*gara, giornale, auto*) sports *attr*; (*persona, spirito, atteggiamento*) sporting; (*abito*) casual; **la pagina sportiva** the sports page; **è molto sportiva** she's very sporty; **abbigliamento sportivo** casual clothes; **giacca sportiva** sports (*Brit*) *o* sport (*Am*) jacket; **un atteggiamento molto poco sportivo** a very unsporting attitude; **campo sportivo** playing field
■SM/F sportsman/sportswoman

sporto, a ['spɔrto] PP *di* **sporgere**

sposa ['spɔza] SF (*nel giorno delle nozze*) bride; (*moglie*) wife; **abito** *o* **vestito da sposa** wedding dress; **dare qn in sposa a** to give sb in marriage to

sposalizio, zi [spoza'littsjo] SM wedding (ceremony)

sposare [spo'zare] VT (*gen*) to marry; (*sogg: genitori*) to marry off; (*fig: idea, fede, causa*) to embrace, espouse; **le ha chiesto di sposarlo** he asked her to marry him
▶ **sposarsi** VR (*uso reciproco*) to get married, marry; **si sono sposati a giugno** they got married in June; **sposarsi con qn** to marry sb, get married to sb; **si è sposato con Paola** he married Paola

sposato, a [spo'zato] AGG married

sposo ['spɔzo] SM (*nel giorno delle nozze*) (bride)groom; (*marito*) husband; **gli sposi** the newlyweds; **viva gli sposi!** to the bride and groom!

spossante [spos'sante] AGG exhausting

spossare [spos'sare] VT to exhaust, wear out

spossatezza [spossa'tettsa] SF exhaustion

spossato, a [spos'sato] AGG exhausted, worn-out

spostamento [sposta'mento] SM movement, change of position; **il mio lavoro mi costringe a continui spostamenti** I have to travel constantly for my work; **spostamento d'aria** blast

spostare [spos'tare] VT **1** (*gen*) to move; (*mobile*) to move, shift; **mi aiuti a spostare il tavolo?** can you

help me move the table? **2** (*cambiare: orario, data*) to change; **hanno spostato la data** they've changed the date; **hanno spostato la partenza di qualche giorno** they postponed *o* put off their departure for a few days
▶ **spostarsi** VR to move; **potresti spostarti più in là?** could you move along a bit?
spostato, a [spos'tato] SM/F misfit
spot [spɔt] SM INV **1** (*faretto*) spotlight, spot **2** (TV): **spot pubblicitario** advertisement, commercial
spranga, ghe ['spranga] SF (*barra*) bar; (*catenaccio*) bolt
sprangare [spran'gare] VT (*con barra*) to bar; (*con catenaccio*) to bolt
spray ['sprai] SM INV (*dispositivo, sostanza*) spray
■ AGG INV (*bombola, confezione*) spray *attr*
sprazzo ['sprattso] SM (*di luce, sole*) flash; (*fig: di gioia*) burst; (*: di intelligenza*) flash
sprecare [spre'kare] VT (*gen, fig*) to waste; (*denaro*) to waste, squander; **è fatica sprecata!** it's a waste of effort!; **è fiato sprecato!** it's a waste of breath!; **stai sprecando tempo** you're wasting time; **sei sprecato qui!** your talents are wasted here!
▶ **sprecarsi** VIP (*persona*) to waste one's energy; **non sprecarti!** (*iro: non affaticarti*) don't strain yourself!; **si sono sprecati!** (*iro*) they certainly didn't break the bank!
spreco, chi ['sprɛko] SM waste; **che spreco!** what a waste!
sprecone, a [spre'kone] SM/F waster
spregevole [spre'dʒevole] AGG contemptible, despicable
spregevolmente [spredʒevol'mente] AVV contemptibly, despicably
spregiare [spre'dʒare] VT (*letter*) to despise, be contemptuous of
spregiativo, a [spredʒa'tivo] AGG pejorative, derogatory
■ SM (*Gramm*) pejorative
spregio, gi ['sprɛdʒo] SM (*disprezzo*) contempt, scorn, disdain
spregiudicatezza [spredʒudika'tettsa] SF lack of scruples
spregiudicato, a [spredʒudi'kato] AGG (*senza pregiudizi*) unprejudiced, unbiased; (*senza scrupoli*) unscrupulous
spremere ['sprɛmere] VT (*agrumi*) to squeeze; (*olive*) to press; **spremere denaro a** *o* **da qn** to squeeze money out of sb; **spremersi le meningi** to rack one's brains
spremiaglio, gli [spremi'aʎʎo] SM (*Culin*) garlic press
spremiagrumi [spremia'grumi], **spremilimoni** [spremili'moni] SM INV lemon squeezer
spremuta [spre'muta] SF freshly squeezed fruit juice; **spremuta d'arancia** freshly-squeezed orange juice
spretarsi [spre'tarsi] VIP to abandon the priesthood
sprezzante [spret'tsante] AGG (*sguardo, modi, parole*) contemptuous, scornful, disdainful
sprezzantemente [sprettsante'mente] AVV contemptuously, scornfully, disdainfully
sprezzo ['sprɛttso] SM contempt, scorn, disdain; **con sprezzo del pericolo** without heeding the danger
sprigionare [spridʒo'nare] VT (*calore, odore*) to give off, emit; (*gas tossici*) to release; (*fig: energia*) to unleash
▶ **sprigionarsi** VIP: **sprigionarsi da** (*sogg: calore*) to emanate from, be given off by; (*: con impeto: gas*) to burst (out) from; (*: petrolio, acqua*) to gush out from
sprimacciare [sprimat'tʃare] VT (*cuscino*) to plump up
sprint [sprint] SM INV (*scatto*) sprint
sprizzare [sprit'tsare] VI (*aus* **essere**) to spurt
■ VT (*scaturire*) to spurt; (*fig: gioia, vitalità*) to be bursting with; **sprizza salute da tutti i pori** he's bursting with health
sprofondare [sprofon'dare] VI (*aus* **essere**) (*casa, tetto*) to collapse; (*pavimento, terreno*) to subside, give way; (*nave*) to sink; **i suoi piedi sprofondavano nella neve** his feet sank into the snow; **sprofondò nel dolore** he was overcome with grief
▶ **sprofondarsi** VR: **sprofondarsi in** (*poltrona*) to sink into; (*fig: studio, lavoro*) to become engrossed in
sproloquiare [sprolo'kwjare] VI (*aus* **avere**) to ramble on
sproloquio, qui [spro'lɔkwjo] SM rambling speech
spronare [spro'nare] VT (*cavallo*) to spur (on); (*fig: persona*) to spur on, encourage; **spronare qn a fare qc** to encourage sb to do sth
sprone ['sprone] SM (*sperone*) spur; (*fig*) spur, incentive; **fuggire a spron battuto** to take to one's heels
sproporzionatamente [sproportsjonata'mente] AVV disproportionately
sproporzionato, a [sproportsjo'nato] AGG (*gen*) disproportionate, out of all proportion; (*prezzo*) exorbitant; (*condanna*) excessive; **sproporzionato (rispetto) a** out of proportion to; **il suo peso è sproporzionato all'altezza** his weight is out of proportion to his height
sproporzione [spropor'tsjone] SF disproportion
spropositatamente [spropozitata'mente] AVV excessively
spropositato, a [spropozi'tato] AGG (*costo*) excessive; (*lettera, discorso*) full of mistakes
sproposito [spro'pɔzito] SM (*azione sconsiderata*) blunder; **ho fatto uno sproposito** (*pazzia*) I did something silly; **per quella donna farei uno sproposito** I'd do anything for that woman; **non dire spropositi** don't talk nonsense *o* rubbish (*Brit*); **non farmi dire uno sproposito** don't make me say something I'll regret; **costa uno sproposito!** it costs a fortune!; **arrivare a sproposito** to arrive at the wrong time; **parlare a sproposito** to talk out of turn
sprovveduto, a [sprovve'duto] AGG inexperienced, naïve
sprovvisto, a [sprov'visto] AGG **1 sprovvisto di** lacking in, without; **passeggeri sprovvisti di passaporto** passengers without a passport; **siamo sprovvisti di bicchieri** we haven't enough glasses; **ne siamo sprovvisti** (*negozio*) we are out of it (*o* them) **2 prendere qn alla sprovvista** to catch sb unawares
spruzzare [sprut'tsare] VT (*nebulizzare*) to spray; (*aspergere*) to sprinkle; (*inzaccherare*) to splash
spruzzata [sprut'tsata] SF (*di acqua*) splash; (*di profumo*) spray; (*di neve*) light fall; **dare una spruzzata di zucchero a qc** to sprinkle sth with sugar
spruzzatore [spruttsa'tore] SM (*per profumi*) spray, atomizer; (*per biancheria*) spray
spruzzo ['spruttso] SM splash; **verniciatura a spruzzo** spray painting
spudoratamente [spudorata'mente] AVV shamelessly
spudoratezza [spudora'tettsa] SF shamelessness
spudorato, a [spudo'rato] AGG shameless; **è stato così spudorato da venire a chiedermi aiuto** he had the cheek to come and ask me for help
spugna ['spuɲɲa] SF (*Zool*) sponge; (*tessuto*) (terry) towelling, terrycloth; **una spugna insaponata** a soapy sponge; **di spugna** towelling; **un accappatoio di spugna** a towelling bathrobe; **bere come una**

Ss

spugna to drink like a fish; **gettare la spugna** (*Pugilato, fig*) to throw in the sponge *o* towel
spugnatura [spuɲɲa'tura] SF sponging, sponge down
spugnoso, a [spuɲ'ɲoso] AGG spongy
spulciare [spul'tʃare] VT (*animali*) to rid of fleas; (*fig: testo, compito*) to examine thoroughly
spuma ['spuma] SF (*schiuma*) foam; (*bibita*) fizzy drink; (*Culin*) mousse
spumante [spu'mante] SM sparkling wine
spumeggiante [spumed'dʒante] AGG (*vino, fig*) sparkling; (*mare*) foaming
spumeggiare [spumed'dʒare] VI (*aus* **avere**) (*vino*) to sparkle; (*mare*) to foam
spumone [spu'mone] SM (*dolce*) *light, frothy dessert made with egg whites and cream*; (*gelato*) *soft ice cream made with whipped cream*
spuntare[1] [spun'tare] VT (*lapis, coltello*) to break the point of; (*capelli, baffi*) to trim; **spuntarla** (*fig: vincere*) to succeed, win (through); (*: averla vinta*) to get one's own way
■VI (*aus* **essere**) (*nascere: germogli*) to sprout; (*: capelli*) to begin to grow; (*: dente*) to come through; (*apparire: sole*) to rise; (*: giorno*) to dawn; **gli è spuntato un dente** he has cut a tooth; **è spuntato da chissà dove** (*fig*) he turned up from out of the blue;
▶ **spuntarsi** VIP to lose its point, become blunt
■SM: **allo spuntare del sole** at sunrise; **allo spuntare del giorno** at daybreak
spuntare[2] [spun'tare] VT (*elenco*) to tick off (*Brit*), check off (*Am*)
spuntino [spun'tino] SM snack; **fare uno spuntino** to have a snack
spunto ['spunto] SM (*Mus, Teatro*) cue; (*fig: base*) starting point; (*: idea*) idea; **dare** *o* **fornire lo spunto a qc** (*polemiche*) to give rise to sth; **ciò mi ha dato lo spunto per iniziare a dipingere** it started me painting; **prendere spunto da qc** to take sth as one's starting point, take inspiration from sth; **il regista ha preso spunto da un fatto realmente accaduto** the director took his inspiration from a real life story
spuntone [spun'tone] SM (*Alpinismo*) (rocky) spike
spupazzare [spupat'tsare] VT (*fam: portare in giro*) to cart around
spurgare [spur'gare] VT (*fogna, canale*) to clear, clean; (*bronchi*) to clean; (*Aut: freni*) to bleed
spurgo, ghi ['spurgo] SM (*di fogna, canale*) clearing, cleaning; (*di bronchi: azione*) cleaning; (*: materia espulsa*) discharge; (*di freni*) bleeding; **valvola di spurgo** bleeder
spurio, ria, ri, rie ['spurjo] AGG (*non autentico: opera*) spurious, false
sputacchiare [sputak'kjare] VI (*aus* **avere**) to spit
sputacchiera [sputak'kjɛra] SF spittoon
sputare [spu'tare] VT to spit (out); **mi ha fatto sputar sangue** (*fig*) he made me sweat blood; **sputare veleno** (*fig*) to talk spitefully; **sputa fuori!** (*anche fig*) spit it out!; **sputa l'osso!** (*fig*) out with it!; **è suo padre sputato** (*fam*) he's the spitting image of his father
■VI (*aus* **avere**) to spit; **sputare in faccia a qn** (*fig*) to spit in sb's face; **sputare addosso a qn** (*fig*) to despise sb; **non ci sputerei sopra** (*fig*) I wouldn't turn my nose up at it; **non sputare nel piatto in cui mangi** don't bite the hand that feeds you
sputasentenze [sputasen'tɛntse] SM/F INV know-all
sputo ['sputo] SM spittle *no pl*, spit *no pl*; **questo libro deve essere appiccicato con lo sputo** this book just comes apart in your hands
sputtanare [sputta'nare] (*fam*) VT (*sparlare*) to bad-mouth; (*sperperare*) to piss away (*fam!*)
▶ **sputtanarsi** VIP to make an arse of o.s. (*Brit fam!*)
sputtanato, a [sputta'nato] AGG (*fam*): **essere sputtanato** to be fucked (*fam!*)
squadra[1] ['skwadra] SF (*strumento*) (set) square; **a squadra** at right angles; **essere fuori squadra** (*gen*) to be crooked; (*fig: persona*) to be out of sorts
squadra[2] ['skwadra] SF (*gruppo*) team, squad; (*di operai*) gang, squad; (*Sport*) team; (*Mil*) squad; (*: Aer, Naut*) squadron; **lavoro a squadre** teamwork; **squadra del buon costume** (*Polizia*) vice squad; **squadra mobile** flying squad (*Brit*); **squadra di soccorso** rescue party
squadrare [skwa'drare] VT to square, make square; **squadrare qn da capo a piedi** to look sb up and down
squadriglia [skwa'driʎʎa] SF (*Aer*) flight; (*Naut*) squadron
squadrone [skwa'drone] SM (*Mil*) squadron
squagliare [skwaʎ'ʎare] VT to melt
▶ **squagliarsi** VIP to melt; **squagliarsi** *or* **squagliarsela** (*fig fam*) to sneak off
squalifica, che [skwa'lifika] SF disqualification
squalificare [skwalifi'kare] VT (*gen, Sport*) to disqualify; (*fig: screditare*) to bring discredit on
▶ **squalificarsi** VR to bring discredit on o.s.
squalificato, a [skwalifi'kato] AGG disqualified
squallido, a ['skwallido] AGG (*luogo*) wretched, bleak; (*vita*) miserable; (*vicenda*) squalid, sordid; **una squallida stanza d'albergo** a dingy hotel room
squallore [skwal'lore] SM (*vedi agg*) wretchedness, bleakness; misery; squalor
squalo ['skwalo] SM shark
squama ['skwama] SF (*scaglia*) scale
squamare [skwa'mare] VT to scale
▶ **squamarsi** VIP (*pelle: gen*) to flake *o* peel (off); (*: per malattia*) to desquamate
squarciagola [skwartʃa'gola] **a squarciagola** AVV at the top of one's voice; **gridava a squarciagola** he was shouting at the top of his voice
squarciare [skwar'tʃare] VT (*corpo*) to rip open; (*tessuto*) to rip; (*fig: tenebre, silenzio*) to split; (*: nuvole*) to pierce
▶ **squarciarsi** VIP (*vedi vt*) to rip open; to rip; (*nuvole*) to part
squarcio, ci ['skwartʃo] SM **1** (*ferita*) gash; (*in lenzuolo, abito*) rip; (*in nave*) hole; **uno squarcio di sole** a burst of sunlight **2** (*brano*) passage, excerpt
squartare [skwar'tare] VT (*animale macellato*) to quarter, cut up; (*persona*) to dismember
squattrinato, a [skwattri'nato] AGG penniless
■SM/F (*gen*) penniless person
squilibrare [skwili'brare] VT to unbalance; (*psicologicamente*) to derange, unbalance; **squilibrare qn finanziariamente** to upset sb's bank balance
squilibrato, a [skwili'brato] AGG (*alimentazione*) unbalanced; (*mente*) deranged, unbalanced; **una dieta squilibrata** an unbalanced diet
■SM/F (*anche:* **squilibrato mentale**) deranged person
squilibrio, ri [skwi'librjo] SM **1** (*Psic: anche:* **squilibrio mentale**) derangement **2** (*Econ: differenza*) imbalance
squillante [skwil'lante] AGG (*suono*) shrill, sharp; (*voce*) shrill; (*fig: colore*) loud
squillare [skwil'lare] VI (*aus* **avere** *o* **essere**) (*campanello, telefono*) to ring (out); (*tromba*) to blare
squillo ['skwillo] SM (*di campanello*) ring, ringing *no pl*; (*di tromba*) blast, blare; **ti avverto con tre squilli di telefono** I'll let the phone ring three times to warn you

■ SF INV (*anche:* **ragazza squillo**) call girl
squinternato, a [skwinter'nato] AGG crazy
■ SM/F lunatic
squisitamente [skwizita'mente] AVV exquisitely
squisitezza [skwizi'tettsa] SF (*di sentimenti, gusto*) refinement; (*di modi*) considerateness; **questo pollo è una squisitezza** this chicken is delicious
squisito, a [skwi'zito] AGG (*gen*) lovely, exquisite; (*gusto, gioiello*) exquisite; (*persona*) delightful; (*modi*) considerate; (*cibo*) delicious
squittire [skwit'tire] VI (*aus* **avere**) (*uccello*) to squawk; (*topo*) to squeak
SR SIGLA = **Siracusa**
sradicare [zradi'kare] VT (*albero*) to uproot; (*erba*) to root out; (*fig: vizio*) to eradicate; **sentirsi sradicato** to feel uprooted
sragionare [zradʒo'nare] VI (*aus* **avere**) (*vaneggiare*) to rave; (*fare discorsi sconnessi*) to talk nonsense
sregolatezza [zregola'tettsa] SF (*nel mangiare, bere*) lack of moderation; (*di vita*) dissoluteness, dissipation; **le sue sgregolatezze gli costeranno care** his excesses will cost him dear
sregolato, a [zrego'lato] AGG (*vita: senza ordine*) disorderly; (*: dissoluta*) dissolute; **è sregolato nel mangiare** he has irregular eating habits
Sri Lanka [sri'lanka] SM Sri Lanka
srilankese, i [srilan'kese] AGG, SM/F Sri Lankan
S.r.l. ['ɛsse 'ɛrre 'ɛlle] SIGLA F = **società a responsabilità limitata**
srotolare [zroto'lare] VT, **srotolarsi** VIP to unroll
SS SIGLA = *Sassari*
S.S. ABBR **1** (*Rel*) = *Sua Santità* **2** (*Rel*) = **Santa Sede** **3** (*Rel*) = **Santi, Santissimo** **4** (*Aut*) = **strada statale**; *vedi* **statale**
SSIS [sis] SIGLA F (= **scuola di specializzazione per l'insegnamento**) *teacher training college (for postgraduates)*
SSN ABBR (= **Servizio Sanitario Nazionale**) ≈ NHS (*Brit*), ≈ Medicaid (*Am*), ≈ Medicare (*Am*)
s.t. ABBR (= **secondo tempo** *Calcio*) second half
sta *ecc* [sta] VB *vedi* **stare**
stabbio, bi ['stabbjo] SM **1** (*recinto*) pen, fold; (*: di maiali*) pigsty **2** (*letame*) manure
stabile ['stabile] AGG (*gen*) stable, steady; (*fondamenta*) solid; (*impiego*) steady, permanent; (*tempo*) settled; **un'occupazione stabile** a steady job; **la scala non è stabile** the ladder is shaky; **il ponte non è stabile** the bridge is unstable; **essere stabile nei propri propositi** to stick to one's decisions, keep to one's plans; **compagnia stabile** (*Teatro*) resident company; **teatro stabile** civic theatre
■ SM (*edificio*) building
stabilimento [stabili'mento] SM (*fabbrica*) plant, factory; **stabilimento balneare** bathing establishment; **stabilimento carcerario** prison; **stabilimento tessile** textile mill
stabilire [stabi'lire] VT (*gen*) to establish; (*fissare: prezzi, data*) to fix; (*decidere*) to decide; **hanno stabilito la chiusura di tutte le scuole** they decided to close all the schools; **stabilire un aumento dei prezzi** to decide on a price increase; **stabilire un collegamento** to establish contact; **resta stabilito che...** it is agreed that ...
▶ **stabilirsi** VR (*prendere dimora*) to settle; **si sono stabiliti qui tre anni fa** they settled here three years ago
stabilità [stabili'ta] SF stability
stabilizzare [stabilid'dzare] VT to stabilize
▶ **stabilizzarsi** VIP (*situazione economica, malato*) to become stable; (*tempo*) to become settled
stabilizzatore, trice [stabiliddza'tore] AGG stabilizing
■ SM (*Aer, Naut, Chim*) stabilizer; (*Elettr*): **stabilizzatore di tensione** voltage regulator
stabilizzazione [stabiliddzat'tsjone] SF stabilization
stabilmente [stabil'mente] AVV permanently; **l'hanno assunto stabilmente** they have employed him on a permanent basis
stacanovista, i, e [stakano'vista] SM/F (*scherz*) eager beaver
staccare [stak'kare] VT **1** (*togliere*): **staccare (da)** to remove (from), take (from); (*quadro*) to take down (from); (*foglio, pagina*) to tear out (of), remove (from); **ha staccato una pagina dal quaderno** he tore a page out of the exercise book; **hai staccato l'etichetta dal dischetto?** did you remove the label from the disk?; **stacca la sedia dal muro** pull the chair away from the wall; **staccare la televisione/il telefono** to disconnect the television/the phone; **se non paghi ti staccheranno il telefono** if you don't pay they'll disconnect your phone; **ho staccato il telefono perché la bambina dormiva** I unplugged the phone because the baby was sleeping; **staccare un assegno** to write a cheque; **non riusciva a staccare gli occhi da quella scena** he could not take his eyes off the scene before him **2** (*separare: anche fig*) to separate, divide; (*: buoi*) to unyoke; (*: cavalli*) to unharness; **staccare la locomotiva dal treno** to uncouple the locomotive from the train; **staccare le parole** to pronounce one's words clearly; **staccare le note** (*Mus*) to play staccato **3** (*Sport: distanziare*) to leave behind
■ VI (*aus* **avere**) **1** (*risaltare*) to stand out **2** (*fam: finire di lavorare*) to knock off
▶ **staccarsi** VIP **1** (*venir via: bottone*) to come off; (*: foglio*) to come out; (*sganciarsi*) to break loose; **mi si è staccato un bottone della camicia** a button has come off my shirt **2** (*persona*): **staccarsi da** (*allontanarsi*) to move away from; (*: dalla famiglia*) to leave; **non si stacca mai dalla televisione** he's always glued to the television
staccato, a [stak'kato] AGG (*foglio*) loose; (*fascicolo*) separate
■ SM (*Mus*) staccato
staccionata [stattʃo'nata] SF fence
stacco, chi ['stakko] SM **1** (*intervallo*) gap; (*: tra due scene*) break; (*differenza*) difference; **fare uno stacco tra una parola e l'altra** to articulate one's words; **c'è troppo stacco tra i due colori** there's too much of a difference between the two colours; **fare stacco su** to stand out against **2** (*Sport: nel salto*) takeoff
stadera [sta'dɛra] SF lever scales *pl*
stadio, di ['stadjo] SM **1** (*Sport*) stadium **2** (*periodo, fase*) stage, phase; **durante l'ultimo stadio della malattia** during the final stage of the illness; **a due/tre stadi** two-/three-stage *attr*
staffa ['staffa] SF **1** (*gen, Tecn, Edil*) stirrup; (*Alpinismo*) étrier (*Brit*), stirrup (*Am*); **perdere le staffe** (*fig*) to fly off the handle; **tenere il piede in due staffe** (*fig*) to run with the hare and hunt with the hounds **2** (*Anat*) stirrup bone
staffetta [staf'fetta] SF **1** (*messo*) courier, dispatch rider **2** (*Sport*) relay race
staffile [staf'file] SM (*Equitazione*) stirrup leather; (*: sferza*) whip
stafilococco, chi [stafilo'kɔkko] SM (*Bio*) staphylococcus

stage [staʒ] SM INV work experience, internship

> **LO SAPEVI...?**
> **stage** non si traduce mai con la parola inglese *stage*

stagflazione [stagflat'tsjone] SF (*Econ*) stagflation

stagionale [stadʒo'nale] AGG seasonal; **"apertura stagionale"** "open during the tourist season"
■SM/F seasonal worker

stagionare [stadʒo'nare] VT, VI (*aus* **essere**), **stagionarsi** VIP (*legno*) to season; (*formaggi*) to mature

stagionato, a [stadʒo'nato] AGG (*vedi vb*) seasoned; matured; (*scherz*: *attempato*) getting on in years

stagionatura [stadʒona'tura] SF (*vedi vb*) seasoning; maturing

stagione [sta'dʒone] SF season; **la bella stagione** the summer months; **la stagione delle piogge** the rainy season; **in questa stagione** at this time of year; **frutta di stagione** seasonal fruit; **saldi di fine stagione** end-of-season sales; **vestiti di mezza stagione** clothes for spring and autumn; **alta/bassa stagione** (*Turismo*) high/low *o* off-season

stagista, i, e [sta'dʒista] SM/F trainee (*Brit*), intern (*Am*)

stagliarsi [staʎ'ʎarsi] VIP: **stagliarsi contro** *o* **su** to stand out against, be silhouetted against

stagnante [staɲ'ɲante] AGG (*anche fig*) stagnant

stagnare[1] [staɲ'ɲare] VT **1** (*ricoprire di stagno*) to tin-plate; (*saldare*) to solder **2** (*rendere ermetico*) to make watertight

stagnare[2] [staɲ'ɲare] VI (*aus* **avere**) (*acqua*, *Econ*) to stagnate; **l'aria stagnava nella stanza** the air in the room was stale
■VT (*sangue*) to stop

stagnatura [staɲɲa'tura] SF tinning, tin-plating

stagnino [staɲ'ɲino] SM tinsmith

stagno[1] ['staɲɲo] SM (*Chim*) tin; (*per saldare*) solder

stagno[2] ['staɲɲo] SM (*acquitrino*) pond

stagno[3]**, a** ['staɲɲo] AGG (*a tenuta d'acqua*) watertight; (*a tenuta d'aria*) airtight

stagnola [staɲ'ɲɔla] SF (*anche*: **carta stagnola**) tinfoil, aluminium foil (*Am*)

stalagmite [stalag'mite] SF stalagmite

stalattite [stalat'tite] SF stalactite

stalinismo [stali'nizmo] SM (*Pol*) Stalinism

stalinista, i, e [stali'nista] AGG, SM/F Stalinist

stalla ['stalla] SF (*per bovini*) cowshed; (*per cavalli*) stable; (*fig*: *casa sporca*) pigsty; **passare dalle stelle alle stalle** (*fig*) to come down in the world

stallia [stal'lia] SF (*Comm*) lay days *pl*

stalliere [stal'ljɛre] SM groom, stableboy

stallo ['stallo] SM **1** stall, seat **2** (*Scacchi*) stalemate; (*Aer*) stall; **situazione di stallo** (*fig*) stalemate

stallone [stal'lone] SM stallion

stamani [sta'mani], **stamattina** [stamat'tina] AVV this morning

stambecco, chi [stam'bekko] SM (*Zool*) ibex

stamberga, ghe [stam'bɛrga] SF hovel

stame ['stame] SM (*Bot*) stamen

staminale [stami'nale] AGG (*Bio*): **cellula staminale** stem cell

stampa ['stampa] SF **1** (*Tip*, *Fot*: *tecnica*) printing; (: *riproduzione*, *copia*) print; (*insieme dei quotidiani*, *giornalisti*): **la stampa** the press; **stampa a diffusione nazionale** national press; **andare in stampa** to go to press; **mandare in stampa** to pass for press; **il libro è in stampa** the book is being printed; **fuori stampa** out of print; **dare alle stampe un'opera** to have a work published; **errore di stampa** printing error; **prova di stampa** print sample; **libertà di stampa** freedom of the press; **"stampe"** "printed matter" *sg* **2** (*Tecn*: *di plastica*) moulding (*Brit*), molding (*Am*: *di metallo*), pressing: *di tessuto, printing*

stampabile [stam'pabile] AGG printable

stampaggio, gi [stam'paddʒo] SM (*di plastica*) moulding (*Brit*), molding (*Am*); (*di metalli*) pressing

stampante [stam'pante] SF (*Inform*) printer; **stampante ad aghi** dot matrix printer; **stampante a getto d'inchiostro** ink jet printer; **stampante laser** laser printer; **stampante di linea** line printer; **stampante a margherita** daisy wheel printer

stampare [stam'pare] VT **1** (*gen*, *Tip*, *Fot*) to print; (*denaro*) to strike, coin; (*pubblicare*) to publish; **ce l'ho stampato nella memoria** it's engraved in my memory; **stampatelo bene in testa!** get it into your head!; **gli ha stampato un bacio in fronte** she planted a kiss on his forehead; **non li stampo mica i soldi** I am not made of money **2** (*Tecn*: *plastica*) to mould (*Brit*), to mold (*Am*); (: *metalli*) to press; (: *tessuti*) to print
▶ **stamparsi** VIP: **stamparsi nella mente** *o* **nella memoria** to be imprinted in one's memory

stampatello [stampa'tɛllo] SM block capitals *pl*, block letters *pl*; **scrivere in** *o* **a stampatello** to write in block capitals *o* letters; **devo scrivere il mio nome in stampatello?** shall I write my name in block letters?

stampato, a [stam'pato] AGG printed
■SM (*opuscolo*) leaflet; (*modulo*) form; (*Inform*) hard copy

stampatore, trice [stampa'tore] SM/F printer
■SF (*Cine*, *Fot*) printing machine

stampella [stam'pɛlla] SF (*apparecchio ortopedico*) crutch

stamperia [stampe'ria] SF (*di libri*) printing works *inv*, printing house; (*di tessuti*) printworks *inv*

stampigliare [stampiʎ'ʎare] VT to stamp

stampigliatura [stampiʎʎa'tura] SF (*atto*) stamping; (*marchio*) stamp

stampinare [stampi'nare] VT (*disegno*) to stencil

stampino [stam'pino] SM (*normografo*) stencil; (*punteruolo*) punch; **stampino per biscotti** (*Culin*) pastry cutter

stampo ['stampo] SM (*gen*, *Culin*) mould (*Brit*), mold (*Am*); (*Tecn*) mo(u)ld, die; (*fig*: *indole*) type, kind, sort; **di stampo antico** old-fashioned; **essere fatto con lo stampo** (*fig*) to be all the same; **stampo a cerniera** (*Culin*) spring-release tin; **stampo per plum-cake** (*Culin*) loaf tin

> **LO SAPEVI...?**
> **stampo** non si traduce mai con la parola inglese *stamp*

stanare [sta'nare] VT to drive out

stanca ['stanka] SF (*negli affari*): **periodo di stanca** slack period

stancamente [stanka'mente] AVV tiredly, wearily

stancare [stan'kare] VT (*spossare*) to tire, make tired; (*annoiare*) to bore; (*infastidire*) to annoy; **non stancare i bambini con troppi giochi** don't tire the children with too many games; **il viaggio lo ha stancato molto** the journey tired him out; **mi hai stancato con le tue lamentele** I'm fed up of your complaining
▶ **stancarsi** VIP to get tired, tire o.s. out; **non stancarti troppo** don't get too tired; **stancarsi (di)** (*stufarsi*) to grow tired (of), get fed up (with), grow weary (of); **mi sono stancato di aspettare** I got tired of waiting

stanchezza [stan'kettsa] SF (*fisica*) fatigue, tiredness;

(*mentale*) tiredness, weariness; (*fig*: *noia*) weariness, boredom; **dare segni di stanchezza** to show signs of tiredness; **che stanchezza!** *or* **ho una stanchezza addosso!** I'm dead beat!

stanco, a, chi, che ['stanko] AGG tired; **sei stanco?** are you tired?; **stanco morto** dead tired; **con una voce stanca disse...** he said wearily ...; **stanco di** (*stufo*) tired of, fed up with; **sono stanco di ripetere la stessa cosa** I'm tired of repeating the same thing; **stanco di vivere** tired of life; **nato stanco** (*scherz*) bone idle

stand [stænd] SM INV (*in fiera*) stand

standard ['standard] AGG INV standard

■ SM INV standard; **standard di vita** standard of living

standardizzare [standardid'dzare] VT to standardize

standardizzato, a [standardid'dzato] AGG (*gen*) standardized; (*fig*: *teoria, idea*) unoriginal

standardizzazione [standardiddzat'tsjone] SF standardization

standing ovation ['stɛnding(g) o'veʃʃon] SF INV standing ovation

standista, i, e [stan'dista] SM/F (*in una fiera*) person responsible for a stand

stanga, ghe ['stanga] SM (*gen*) bar; (*di carro*) shaft; (*fig fam*: *persona alta*) beanpole

stangare [stan'gare] VT (*colpire*) to beat, thrash; (*fig*: *far pagare troppo*) to sting; (: *bocciare*) to fail

stangata [stan'gata] SF (*gen, fig*) blow; (*Calcio*) shot; **prendere una stangata** (*fam*: *pagare troppo*) to get stung; (: *agli esami*) to fail miserably; **stangata fiscale** tax hike

stanghetta [stan'getta] SF **1** (*di occhiali*) leg **2** (*Mus, di scrittura*) bar-line

stanno ['stanno] VB *vedi* **stare**

stanotte [sta'nɔtte] AVV (*nella notte in corso o che sta per venire*) tonight; (*nella notte appena passata*) last night; **stanotte ci saranno i fuochi d'artificio** there are going to be fireworks tonight; **stanotte non ho dormito bene** I didn't sleep well last night

stante ['stante] AGG: **a sé stante** (*appartamento, casa*) independent, separate; **seduta stante** (*fig*: *subito*) on the spot

■ PREP owing to, because of

stantio, tia, tii, tie [stan'tio] AGG (*anche fig*) stale; (*burro*) rancid; **sapere di stantio** to taste stale (*o* rancid); **idee stantie** old-fashioned ideas

stantuffo [stan'tuffo] SM piston

stanza ['stantsa] SF **1** (*vano*) room; **stanza da bagno** bathroom; **stanza dei bottoni** (*fig*) control room; **stanza da letto** bedroom **2** (*Poesia*) stanza **3** **essere di stanza a** (*Mil*) to be stationed in

LO SAPEVI...?
stanza non si traduce mai con la parola inglese *stance*

stanziabile [stan'tsjabile] AGG allocatable

stanziamento [stantsja'mento] SM allocation

stanziare [stan'tsjare] VT to allocate

▶ **stanziarsi** VIP (*gen*) to settle; (*Mil*) to be stationed

stanzino [stan'tsino] SM (*ripostiglio*) storeroom; (*spogliatoio*) changing room (*Brit*), locker room (*Am*)

stappare [stap'pare] VT (*bottiglia*: *con tappo di sughero*) to uncork; (: *con tappo a corona*) to uncap

star [star] SF INV (*attore, attrice*) star

stare ['stare] VI IRREG (*aus* **essere**)

1 (*rimanere*) to stay, be, remain; **stare in piedi** to stand; **stare fermo** to keep *o* stay still; **stare seduto** to sit, be sitting; **stare disteso** to lie; **stare zitto** to keep *o* be quiet; **stai dove sei!** stay where you are!; **stai ancora un po'!** stay a bit longer!; **starò a Roma per qualche giorno** I'll stay *o* be in Rome for a few days; **stare a casa** to be *o* stay at home; **è stato su tutta la notte** he stayed up *o* was up all night; **stare in equilibrio** to keep one's balance

2 (*abitare*: *temporaneamente*) to stay; (: *permanentemente*) to live; **sta con i suoi** he lives with his parents; **sta da solo** he lives on his own; **dove stai di casa?** where do you live?; **sta in via Rossetti 5** he lives at No. 5 via Rossetti; **al momento sta con degli amici** he's staying with friends at the moment

3 (*essere, trovarsi*) to be, be situated; **la casa sta in cima al colle** the house is at the top of the hill; **stando così le cose** given the situation; **le cose stanno così** this is the situation; **non voglio stare da solo** I don't want to be on my own; **sei mai stato in Francia?** have you ever been to France?; **sono stato dal dentista** I've been to the dentist; **come stai?** how are you?; **sto bene, grazie** I'm fine, thanks; **sta bene!** (*d'accordo così*) that's fine!; **non sta bene ridacchiare mentre l'insegnante spiega** you really ought not to laugh when the teacher is explaining something; **come mi sta?** how does it look?; **quel vestito ti sta bene/male** that dress suits/doesn't suit you; **queste scarpe mi stanno strette** these shoes are too tight for me; **questa giacca non mi sta** this jacket doesn't fit me; **gli sta bene!** (*così impara*) it serves him right!; **stai sicuro che non la passerà liscia!** rest assured he won't get away with it!; **stare al banco** (*cameriere*) to serve at the bar; **stare alla cassa** to work at the till; **stare a dieta** to be on a diet

4 (*seguito da gerundio*): **stavo andando a casa** I was going home; **cosa stai facendo?** what are you doing?; **sta studiando** he's studying; **stava piovendo** it was raining

5 **stare per fare qc** to be about to do sth, be on the point of doing sth; **stavo per uscire quando ha squillato il telefono** I was about to go out when the phone rang; **stavi per rovinare tutto** you nearly spoiled *o* ruined everything

6 **stare a sentire** to listen; **sta' a sentire** listen a minute; **stare ad insistere** to insist; **è inutile che stai a dirmi tutte queste cose** there's no good *o* use telling me all this; **sta a te decidere** it's up to you to decide; **stando a ciò che dice lui** according to him *o* to his version; **stando ai fatti, sembrerebbe che...** the facts would seem to indicate that ...; **staremo a vedere** let's wait and see; **stiamo a vedere cosa succede** let's wait and see (what happens); **stai a vedere che aveva ragione lei!** she would have to be right!

7 **starci** (*essere contenuto*): **ci sta ancora qualcosa lì dentro?** is there room for anything else?; **nel bagagliaio non ci sta più niente** there's no room for anything more in the boot; **non credo ci stia tutta quella pasta** I don't think there's room for all that pasta; **non ci stanno più di 4 persone in quella macchina** there is only room for 4 in that car; **il 5 nel 25 ci sta 5 volte** 5 goes into 25 5 times

8 **starci** (*essere d'accordo*): **ci stai se andiamo** *o* **ad andare fuori a cena?** do you want to go out for a meal?; **ha detto che non ci sta** he said he didn't agree, he said he was against the idea; **OK, ci sto** OK, that's fine

9 **starsene** *or* **se ne stava lì in un angolo** he was over in the corner; **se n'è stato zitto** he never opened his

Ss

mouth; **non startene lì seduto, fa' qualcosa** don't just sit there, do something; **stasera me ne sto a casa** I'll be staying in tonight

LO SAPEVI...?
stare non si traduce mai con la parola inglese *stare*

starna ['starna] SF (*Zool*) partridge

starnazzare [starnat'tsare] VI (*aus* **avere**) to squawk; (*fig: far chiasso*) to make a din

starnutire [starnu'tire] VI (*aus* **avere**) to sneeze

starnuto [star'nuto] SM sneeze; **fare uno starnuto** to sneeze

starter ['starter] SM INV (*Aut, Sport*) starter

stasare [sta'sare] VT (*lavandino, condotto*) to unblock

stasera [sta'sera] AVV this evening, tonight

stasi ['stazi] SF (*Med, fig*) stasis

statale [sta'tale] AGG government *attr*, state *attr*; **bilancio statale** national budget; **impiegato statale** state employee, civil servant; **un'industria statale** a state-owned industry; **strada statale** ≈ main *o* trunk (*Brit*) road
■ SM/F (*impiegato*) state employee, ≈ civil servant
■ SF (*strada*) ≈ main *o* trunk (*Brit*) road

statalizzare [statalid'dzare] VT to nationalize, put under state control

statalizzazione [stataliddzat'tsjone] SF nationalization

statica ['statika] SF statics *sg*

staticità [statitʃi'ta] SF (*di situazione*) static nature

statico, a, ci, che ['statiko] AGG (*Elettr, fig*) static

statino [sta'tino] SM (*Univ*) *statement of examination results*

station wagon [stɛʃʃon 'wɛgon] SF INV estate (car) (*Brit*), station wagon (*Am*)

statista, i [sta'tista] SM statesman

statistica [sta'tistika] SF (*scienza*) statistics *sg*; (*raccolta di dati*) statistic; **la statistica è una materia obbligatoria** statistics is a compulsory subject; **le statistiche dimostrano che...** statistics show that ...; **fare una statistica** to carry out a statistical examination
▷ www.istat.it/

statisticamente [statistika'mente] AVV statistically

statistico, a, ci, che [sta'tistiko] AGG statistical

stato¹, a ['stato] PP *di* **essere, stare**

stato² ['stato] SM **1** (*condizione, gen*) state; (*di paziente*) condition; **la macchina è in buono stato** the car is in good condition; **stato d'animo** state of mind; **stato (di salute)** state of health; **guarda in che stato si è ridotto!** look at the state it (*o* he) is in!; **vivere allo stato selvaggio** to live in the wild **2** (*fraseologia*): **essere in stato d'accusa** (*Dir*) to have been charged with an offence (*Brit*) *o* offense (*Am*), be committed for trial; **essere in stato d'arresto** (*Dir*) to be under arrest; **essere in stato d'assedio** to be under siege; **essere in stato d'emergenza** to be in a state of emergency; **essere in stato interessante** to be pregnant; **allo stato liquido/gassoso** in the liquid/gaseous state
■ **stato civile** (*Amm*) marital status; **stato di famiglia** (*Amm*) *certificate giving details of a household and its dependents*; **Stato Maggiore** (*Mil*) general staff *sg o pl*; **stato patrimoniale** statement of assets and liabilities

stato³ ['stato] SM (*Pol*) state; **di stato** state *attr*; **uno stato totalitario** a totalitarian state; **un capo di stato** a head of state
■ **stato assistenziale** (*pegg*) welfare state; **stato di diritto** legally constituted state; **stato sociale** welfare state; **gli Stati Uniti (d'America)** the United States (of America)

statua ['statua] SF statue

statuario, ria, ri, rie [statu'arjo] AGG (*fig: bellezza, posa*) statuesque

statunitense [statuni'tɛnse] AGG United States *attr*, of the United States; **il governo statunitense** the government of the United States
■ SM/F American citizen, citizen of the United States

statura [sta'tura] SF (*gen*) height; (*fig*) stature; **essere alto/basso di statura** to be tall/short; **un uomo politico della sua statura** (*fig*) a politician of his stature

status ['status] SM INV status

statutario, ria, ri, rie [statu'tarjo] AGG statutory

statuto [sta'tuto] SM statute; **regione a statuto speciale** *Italian region with political autonomy in certain matters*; **statuto della società** (*Comm*) articles *pl* of association

stavolta [sta'vɔlta] AVV this time

stazionamento [stattsjona'mento] SM (*Aut*) parking; (*: sosta*) waiting; **freno di stazionamento** handbrake

stazionare [stattsjo'nare] VI (*aus* **avere**) (*veicolo*) to be parked

stazionarietà [stattsjonarje'ta] SF: **stazionarietà (di)** lack of change (in)

stazionario, ria, ri, rie [stattsjo'narjo] AGG (*temperatura, condizioni di salute*) stable, unchanged

stazione [stat'tsjone] SF **1** (*gen, Radio*) station; **stazione degli autobus** bus *o* coach (*Brit*) station; **stazione ferroviaria** railway (*Brit*) *o* railroad (*Am*) station; **stazione di lavoro** (*Inform*) work station; **stazione meteorologica** weather station; **stazione radio** radio station; **stazione di servizio** filling *o* petrol (*Brit*) *o* gas (*Am*) station; **stazione trasmittente** (*Radio, TV*) transmitting station **2** (*località*): **stazione balneare** seaside resort; **stazione climatica** health resort; **stazione invernale** winter sports resort; **stazione sciistica** ski resort; **stazione termale** (thermal) spa **3** (*Rel*): **stazione della Via Crucis** Station of the Cross

stazza ['stattsa] SF (*gen*) tonnage; (*di regata*) rating

st. civ. ABBR = **stato civile**

stearina [stea'rina] SF (*Chim*) stearin(e)

stecca, che ['stekka] SF (*gen*) stick; (*di ombrello*) rib; (*da biliardo*) cue; (*Med*) splint; (*di sigarette*) carton; **prendere una stecca** (*fig: stonatura: cantando*) to sing a wrong note; (*: suonando*) to play a wrong note

steccare [stek'kare] VT (*Med*) to splint

steccato [stek'kato] SM fence

stecchetto [stek'ketto] SM (*fam*): **tenere qn a stecchetto** to keep sb on short rations

stecchino [stek'kino] SM toothpick

stecchire [stek'kire] VT (*fam: ammazzare*) to kill (stone dead)

stecchito, a [stek'kito] AGG (*ramo*) dried up; (*persona*) skinny; **morto stecchito** stone dead; **lasciare qn stecchito** (*fig: sorpreso*) to leave sb flabbergasted

stecco, chi ['stekko] SM (*ramo*) twig; (*bastoncino*) stick; (*fig: persona magra*) beanpole

stechiometria [stekjome'tria] SF (*Chim*) stoichiometry

stele ['stɛle] SF INV stele

stella ['stella] SF star; **stanotte si vedono le stelle** you can see the stars tonight; **senza stelle** starless; **alla luce delle stelle** by starlight; **dormire sotto le**

stelle to sleep out under the stars; **vedere le stelle** (*per il dolore*) to see stars; **ringrazia la tua buona stella** thank your lucky stars; **nascere sotto una buona/cattiva stella** to be born under a lucky/an unlucky star; **i prezzi sono andati** *o* **saliti alle stelle** prices have gone sky-high; **portare alle stelle qn** to lavish praise on sb; **una stella del cinema** a film star; **la sua stella sta tramontando** his star is waning; **stella alpina** (*Bot*) edelweiss; **stella cadente** shooting star; **stella di mare** (*Zool*) starfish; **stella di Natale** (*Bot*) poinsettia; **stella polare** pole *o* north star; **stelle filanti** (*per carnevale*) streamers

stellare [stel'lare] AGG stellar; **luce stellare** starlight

stellato, a [stel'lato] AGG (*cielo, notte*) starry

stelletta [stel'letta] SF **1** (*Mil*) star; **guadagnarsi/rimetterci le stellette** to be promoted/demoted **2** (*Tip*) asterisk

stelo ['stɛlo] SM (*Bot*) stem; (*asta*) rod; **lampada a stelo** standard lamp (*Brit*), floor lamp (*Am*)

stemma, i ['stemma] SM coat of arms

> **LO SAPEVI...?**
> **stemma** non si traduce mai con la parola inglese ***stem***

stemmo *ecc* ['stemmo] VB *vedi* **stare**

stemperare [stempe'rare] VT (*calce, colore*) to dissolve

stempiarsi [stem'pjarsi] VIP to develop a receding hairline

stempiato, a [stem'pjato] AGG with a receding hairline; **essere stempiato** to have a receding hairline

stempiatura [stempja'tura] SF receding hairline

stendardo [sten'dardo] SM standard

stendere ['stɛndere] VB IRREG

■ VT **1** (*braccia, gambe*) to stretch (out); (*tovaglia*) to spread (out); (*bucato*) to hang out; (*spalmare*) to spread; (*pasta*) to roll out **2** (*persona: far giacere*) to lay (down); (: *gettare a terra, fig: vincere*) to floor; (: *uccidere*) to kill; **far stendere qn** to lay sb down **3** (*lettera, verbale*) to draw up

▶ **stendersi** VR (*persona*) to lie down; **stendersi a terra/sul letto** to lie down on the ground/on the bed; **si è steso sul letto** he lay down on the bed;

▶ **stendersi** VIP (*pianura, vallata*) to extend, stretch

stendibiancheria [stendibjanke'ria] SM INV clotheshorse

stendino [sten'dino] SM = **stendibiancheria**

stenditoio, oi [stendi'tojo] SM (*locale*) drying room; (*stendibiancheria*) clotheshorse

stenodattilografia [stenodattilogra'fia] SF shorthand typing (*Brit*), stenography (*Am*)

stenodattilografo, a [stenodatti'lɔgrafo] SM/F shorthand typist (*Brit*), stenographer (*Am*)

stenografare [stenogra'fare] VT to take down in shorthand

stenografia [stenogra'fia] SF shorthand, stenography (*Am*)

stenografico, a, ci, che [steno'grafiko] AGG shorthand *attr*, stenographic (*Am*)

stenografo, a [ste'nɔgrafo] SM/F shorthand typist (*Brit*), stenographer (*Am*)

stenosi [ste'nɔzi] SF (*Med*) stenosis

stenotipia [stenoti'pia] SF stenotype

stentare [sten'tare] VI (*aus* **avere**) **stentare a fare qc** to have difficulty in doing sth, find it hard to do sth; **stento a crederci** I find it hard to believe

stentatamente [stentata'mente] AVV with difficulty

stentato, a [sten'tato] AGG (*compito, stile*) laboured (*Brit*), labored (*Am*); (*sorriso*) forced

stento ['stɛnto] SM **1 stenti** SMPL (*privazioni*) hardship *sg*, privation *sg*; **una vita di stenti** a life of hardship *o* privation; **vivere tra gli stenti** to live a life of hardship *o* privation **2 a stento** AVV with difficulty, barely; **capire qc a stento** to understand sth with difficulty; **riesco a stento a pagare l'affitto** I only just manage to pay the rent

stentoreo, a [sten'tɔreo] AGG stentorian

step [step] SM (*ginnastica*) step

steppa ['steppa] SF steppe

sterco ['stɛrko] SM dung

stereo ['stɛreo] AGG INV, SM INV stereo

stereofonia [stereofo'nia] SF stereophony

stereofonico, a, ci, che [stereo'fɔniko] AGG stereo(phonic)

stereoscopico, a, ci, che [stereos'kɔpiko] AGG stereoscopic

stereoscopio, pi [stereos'kɔpjo] SM stereoscope

stereotipato, a [stereoti'pato] AGG (*anche fig*) stereotyped

stereotipia [stereoti'pia] SF (*Tecn, Psic*) stereotypy; (*Tip*) stereotype print

stereotipo [stere'ɔtipo] SM stereotype; **pensare per stereotipi** to think in clichés

sterile ['stɛrile] AGG (*terreno*) arid, barren; (*persona*) sterile; (*fig: polemica*) fruitless, futile

sterilità [sterili'ta] SF (*vedi agg*) barrenness; sterility; fruitlessness

sterilizzare [sterilid'dzare] VT to sterilize

sterilizzazione [steriliddzat'tsjone] SF sterilization

sterlina [ster'lina] SF pound (sterling)

sterminare [stermi'nare] VT to exterminate, wipe out

sterminato, a [stermi'nato] AGG immense, endless

sterminio, ni [ster'minjo] SM extermination, destruction; **campo di sterminio** death camp

sterna ['stɛrna] SF (*Zool*) tern

sterno ['stɛrno] SM (*Anat*) breastbone, sternum (*termine tecn*)

steroide [ste'rɔide] SM steroid

sterpaglia [ster'paʎʎa] SF brushwood

sterpo ['stɛrpo] SM dry twig

sterrare [ster'rare] VT to excavate

sterratore [sterra'tore] SM labourer (*Brit*), laborer (*Am*), navvy (*Brit*)

sterzare [ster'tsare] VT, VI (*aus* **avere**) (*Aut*) to steer; (: *bruscamente*) to swerve; (*Pol*): **sterzare a destra/a sinistra** to veer to the right/the left

sterzata [ster'tsata] SF (*Aut*) turn of the wheel; (: *brusca*) swerve; (*fig*) sudden shift; **fare** *o* **dare una sterzata** to steer; (*bruscamente*) to swerve

sterzo ['stɛrtso] SM (*volante*) steering wheel

steso, a ['steso] PP *di* **stendere**

stessi *ecc* ['stessi] VB *vedi* **stare**

stesso, a ['stesso] AGG **1** (*medesimo, identico*) same; **aveva lo stesso vestito** she had the same dress; **abbiamo gli stessi gusti** we have the same tastes; **al tempo stesso** at the same time; **è sempre la stessa storia** it's always the same old thing **2** (*esatto, preciso*) very; **in quello stesso istante** at that very moment; **quello stesso giorno** the very same day; **oggi stesso** today **3** (*rafforzativo: dopo sostantivo*): **il medico stesso lo sconsiglia** even the doctor *o* the doctor himself advises against it; **è venuto il ministro stesso ad inaugurarlo** the minister himself came to inaugurate

Ss

it **4** (*rafforzativo: dopo pron pers sogg*): **l'ho visto io stesso** I saw him myself; **voi stessi sapete bene che...** you (yourselves) know very well that ...; **lei stessa è venuta a dirmelo** she came and told me herself, she herself came and told me **5** (*rafforzativo: dopo pron rifl*): **me stesso** myself; **te stesso** yourself; **se stesso** himself; (*neutro*) itself; (*indef*) oneself; **se stessa** herself; **noi stessi** ourselves; **voi stessi** yourselves; **loro stessi** themselves; **ama solo se stesso** he only loves himself; **di per sé stesso non ha un gran valore** it's not worth a lot in itself **6** (*proprio*) own; **l'ho visto con i miei stessi occhi** I saw it with my own eyes; **l'ho sentito con le mie stesse orecchie** I heard it with my own ears; **l'ha fatto con le sue stesse mani** he did it with his own hands
■ PRON DIMOSTR: **lo(la) stesso(a)** the same (one); **sei la stessa di sempre** you're the same as ever; **chi canta? — lo stesso di prima** who's singing? — the same singer as before; **per me fa lo stesso** it's all the same to me; **per me è lo stesso** it doesn't matter to me
■ **lo stesso** AVV (*comunque*) all the same, even so; **parto lo stesso** I'm going all the same

stesura [ste'sura] SF (*azione*) drafting *no pl*, drawing up *no pl*; (*documento*) draft

stetoscopio, pi [stetos'kɔpjo] SM stethoscope

stetti *ecc* ['stetti] VB *vedi* **stare**

stia[1] *ecc* ['stia] VB *vedi* **stare**

stia[2] ['stia] SF (chicken) coop

Stige ['stidʒe] SM: **lo Stige** the Styx

stigma, i ['stigma] SM (*Bot, Zool, anche fig*) stigma

stigmate ['stigmate] SFPL (*Rel*) stigmata *pl*

stigmatizzare [stigmatid'dzare] VT to stigmatize

stilare [sti'lare] VT to draw up, draft

stile ['stile] SM (*gen*) style; (*classe*) style, class; (*Nuoto*): **gli stili architettonici** architectural styles; **bisogna ammettere che ha stile!** you have to admit he's got style!; **stile libero** freestyle, crawl; **sai nuotare a stile libero?** can you do the crawl?; **i cento metri stile libero** the hundred metres freestyle; **mobili in stile** period furniture; **in grande stile** in great style; **è proprio nel suo stile** (*fig*) it's just like him; **non è nel suo stile** (*fig*) it's not like him

stilettata [stilet'tata] SF (*pugnalata*) stab with a stiletto; (*fig: dolore*): **quelle parole furono una stilettata al cuore** those words cut him (*o her ecc*) to the quick; **fu ucciso con una stilettata** he was stabbed to death

stiletto [sti'letto] SM stiletto

stilista, i, e [sti'lista] SM/F (*Moda*) designer

stilisticamente [stilistika'mente] AVV stylistically

stilistico, a, ci, che [sti'listiko] AGG stylistic

stilizzare [stilid'dzare] VT to stylize

stilizzato, a [stilid'dzato] AGG stylized

stillare [stil'lare] VT, VI (*aus* **essere**) (*gocciolare*) to drip; (*trasudare*) to ooze

stillicidio, di [stilli'tʃidjo] SM (*fig*): **uno stillicidio di rivelazioni** a steady stream of revelations

stilo ['stilo] SM (*Bot*) style

stilografica, che [stilo'grafika] SF (*anche:* **penna stilografica**) fountain pen

Stim. ABBR = stimato

stima ['stima] SF **1** (*buona opinione*) respect, esteem; **avere stima di qn** to have respect for sb; **ho molta stima di lui** I have great respect for him; **godere della stima di qn** to enjoy sb's respect **2** (*Econ, Fin*) estimate, valuation, assessment; **fare la stima di qc** to estimate the value of sth; **la stima dei danni** estimate of the damage; **stima approssimativa** guesstimate (*fam*)

stimabile [sti'mabile] AGG **1** (*rispettabile*) respectable, worthy of respect **2** (*valutabile*) assessable

stimare [sti'mare] VT **1** (*persona*) to respect, esteem, hold in high regard; **la stimo molto** I really respect her **2** (*Econ, Fin*) to assess the value of, estimate the value of, value

stimato, a [sti'mato] AGG: **Stimata Ditta** Dear Sirs

stimma, i ['stimma] SM = **stigma**

stimolante [stimo'lante] AGG stimulating
■ SM stimulant

stimolare [stimo'lare] VT (*gen*) to stimulate; **stimolare qn a fare qc** (*incitare*) to spur sb on to do sth

stimolazione [stimolat'tsjone] SF stimulation

stimolo ['stimolo] SM (*anche fig*) stimulus

stinco, chi ['stinko] SM (*Anat: persona*) shinbone, shin; (: *di animale*) shank; **non essere uno stinco di santo** to be no saint

stingere ['stindʒere] VB IRREG, VT, VI (*aus* **essere**), **stingersi** VIP to fade

stinto, a ['stinto] PP *di* **stingere**
■ AGG faded

stipare [sti'pare] VT to cram, pack
▶ **stiparsi** VIP (*accalcarsi*) **stiparsi in** to crowd into, throng

stipato, a [sti'pato] AGG (*merce, gente*) packed, crammed

stipendiare [stipen'djare] VT (*pagare*) to pay (a salary to)

stipendiato, a [stipen'djato] AGG salaried
■ SM/F salaried worker

stipendio, di [sti'pendjo] SM salary

stipetto [sti'petto] SM (*armadietto*) locker

stipite ['stipite] SM (*di porta, finestra*) jamb

stipulare [stipu'lare] VT (*accordo, contratto*) to draw up

> **LO SAPEVI...?**
> **stipulare** non si traduce mai con la parola inglese ***stipulate***

stipulazione [stipulat'tsjone] SF (*di contratto, stesura*) drafting; (: *firma*) signing

stiracalzoni [stirakal'tsoni] SM INV trouser press

stiracchiare [stirak'kjare] VT (*fig: significato di una parola*) to stretch, force
▶ **stiracchiarsi** VR (*persona*) to stretch

stiracchiato, a [stirak'kjato] AGG (*sforzato*) forced

stiramaniche [stira'manike] SM INV sleeve board

stiramento [stira'mento] SM (*Med*) sprain

stirare [sti'rare] VT **1** (*con ferro da stiro*) to iron **2** (*distendere*) to stretch; (*Med*): **stirarsi un legamento** to pull a ligament
▶ **stirarsi** VR to stretch (o.s.)

stiratoio, oi [stira'tojo] SM (*Tecn*) drawing frame

stiratrice [stira'tritʃe] SF (*donna*) laundry worker; (*macchina*) laundry press

stiratura [stira'tura] SF **1** (*con ferro da stiro*) ironing **2** (*Med*) sprain

stiro ['stiro] SM: **ferro da stiro** iron; **asse** *o* **tavolo da stiro** ironing board

stirpe ['stirpe] SF **1** (*schiatta*) birth, stock; **di nobile stirpe** of noble descent **2** (*discendenti*) descendants *pl*

stitichezza [stiti'kettsa] SF constipation

stitico, a, ci, che ['stitiko] AGG constipated

stiva ['stiva] SF (*di nave, aereo*) hold

stivale [sti'vale] SM boot; **quel medico dei miei stivali!** (*pegg*) that apology for a doctor!; **stivale da birra** boot-shaped beer glass; **stivali di gomma** wellingtons

stivaletto [stiva'letto] SM ankle boot
stivare [sti'vare] VT to stow, load
stizza ['stittsa] SF anger, vexation
stizzire [stit'tsire] VT to irritate
▶ **stizzirsi** VIP to become irritated, become vexed
stizzosamente [stittsosa'mente] AVV angrily
stizzoso, a [stit'tsoso] AGG (*persona*) irascible, quick-tempered; (*risposta*) angry
stoccafisso [stokka'fisso] SM stockfish, dried cod
stoccaggio [stok'kaddʒo] SM (*Comm*) warehousing
Stoccarda [stok'karda] SF Stuttgart
stoccata [stok'kata] SF (*Scherma*) thrust, stab; (*Calcio*) shot; (*fig: allusione*) gibe, cutting remark
Stoccolma [stok'kolma] SF Stockholm
stock [stɔk] SM INV (*Comm*) stock
stock house [sto'kaus] SF INV discount shop (for clothes)
stoffa ['stɔffa] SF material, fabric; **avere della stoffa** (*fig*) to have what it takes; **avere la stoffa per diventare qc** to have the makings of sth
stoicamente [stoika'mente] AVV stoically
stoicismo [stoi'tʃizmo] SM stoicism
stoico, a, ci, che ['stɔiko] AGG, SM/F (*anche fig*) stoic(al)
stoino [sto'ino] SM doormat
stola ['stɔla] SF (*gen, Rel*) stole
stolidità [stolidi'ta] SF INV stolidity
stolido, a ['stɔlido] AGG stolid
stolone [sto'lone] SM (*Bot*) stolon
stoltezza [stol'tettsa] SF (*qualità*) stupidity; (*azione*) foolish action
stolto, a ['stolto] AGG stupid, foolish
■ SM/F fool
stoma, i ['stɔma] SM (*Bot*) stoma
stomacare [stoma'kare] VT (*nauseare*) to nauseate
▶ **stomacarsi** VIP: **stomacarsi di qc** to become nauseated by sth
stomachevole [stoma'kevole] AGG disgusting
stomaco, chi ['stɔmako] SM stomach; **ho mal di stomaco** I've got stomach ache; **dare di stomaco** to be sick; **avere qc sullo stomaco** to have sth lying on one's stomach; **quel tipo mi sta sullo stomaco** I can't stand that guy; **mi fa rivoltare lo stomaco** (*anche fig*) it makes me sick; **bisogna avere dello stomaco per fare quel lavoro** you need a strong stomach to do that kind of work
stomatite [stoma'tite] SF (*Med*) stomatitis
stomatologico, a, ci, che [stomato'lɔdʒiko] AGG (*Med*) stomatological; **reparto stomatologico** department of oral medicine
stonare [sto'nare] VT (*cantando*) to sing out of tune; (*suonando*) to play out of tune
■ VI (*aus* **avere**) to be out of tune, sing *o* play out of tune; (*fig: colori*) to clash
stonato, a [sto'nato] AGG (*persona, strumento*) off-key, out of tune; **c'era una nota stonata** (*fig*) something didn't ring true
stonatura [stona'tura] SF (*suono*) false note
stop [stɔp] SM INV **1** (*Aut: fanalino*) brake-light; (*: segnale stradale*) stop sign **2** (*Telegrafia*) stop
stoppa ['stoppa] SF tow; **come stoppa** (*capelli*) tow-coloured (*Brit*), tow-colored (*Am*); **essere come un pulcino nella stoppa** to look lost and helpless
stoppare [stop'pare] VT (*Calcio*) to stop; **stoppare la palla** to trap the ball; **stoppare qn** (*Basket*) to block sb's shot
stoppata [stop'pata] SF (*Calcio*) action of stopping the ball; (*Basket*) blocked shot
stoppia ['stoppja] SF stubble
stoppino [stop'pino] SM (*di candela*) wick; (*miccia*) fuse
stoppione [stop'pjone] SM (*Bot*) thistle
stopposo, a [stop'poso] AGG tow-coloured (*Brit*), tow-colored (*Am*)
storcere ['stɔrtʃere] VB IRREG
■ VT (*gen*) to twist; **storcere il naso** (*fig*) to turn up one's nose; **storcersi la caviglia** to twist one's ankle;
▶ **storcersi** VIP to writhe, twist
stordimento [stordi'mento] SM (*gen*) daze; (*da droga*) stupefaction
stordire [stor'dire] VT (*sogg: colpo, notizia, droga*) to stun, daze
▶ **stordirsi** VR (*fig*) **stordirsi col bere** to dull one's senses with drink, drink o.s. stupid
stordito, a [stor'dito] AGG (*intontito*) dazed, stunned; (*sventato*) scatterbrained, heedless
storia ['stɔrja] SF **1** (*scienza, materia, opera*) history; **l'insegnante di storia** the history teacher; **libro di storia** history book; **passare alla storia** to go down in history; **storia dell'arte** history of art **2** (*racconto, bugia*) story; (*pretesto*) excuse, pretext; **una storia d'amore** a love story; **è sempre la stessa storia** it's the same old story; **mi racconti una storia?** will you tell me a story?; **mi ha raccontato un sacco di storie** he told me a lot of nonsense *o* rubbish (*Brit*); **sono tutte storie!** it's all lies! **3** (*faccenda*) business; **non voglio saperne più di questa storia** I don't want to hear any more about this business; **è sempre la solita storia** it's always the same old story **4** **storie** SFPL (*capricci*) fuss *sg*; **non ha fatto storie** he didn't make a fuss; **senza tante storie!** don't make such a fuss! **5** (*relazione amorosa*) affair
storicamente [storika'mente] AVV historically
storicità [storitʃi'ta] SF historical authenticity
storico, a, ci, che ['stɔriko] AGG (*gen*) historical; (*memorabile*) historic; **un personaggio storico** a historical figure; **è stato un momento storico** it was a historic moment
■ SM/F historian
storiella [sto'rjɛlla] SF (*storia divertente*) funny story; (*frottola*) story
storiografia [storjogra'fia] SF historiography
storiografo, a [sto'rjɔgrafo] SM/F historiographer
storione [sto'rjone] SM (*Zool*) sturgeon
stormire [stor'mire] VI (*aus* **avere**) to rustle
stormo ['stormo] SM (*di uccelli*) flock
stornare [stor'nare] VT **1** (*Comm*) to transfer **2** (*fig: evitare: pericolo*) to avert
stornello [stor'nɛllo] SM *kind of folk song*
storno ['storno] SM **1** (*Zool*) starling **2** (*Comm*) transfer
storpiare [stor'pjare] VT (*persona*) to cripple, maim; (*fig: parole*) to mangle
▶ **storpiarsi** VIP to become crippled
storpiatura [storpja'tura] SF (*fig: di significato*) mangling
storpio, pia, pi, pie ['stɔrpjo] AGG crippled, maimed
■ SM/F cripple
storsi *ecc* ['stɔrsi] VB *vedi* **storcere**
storta[1] ['stɔrta] SF (*distorsione*) sprain, twist; **prendere una storta al piede** to sprain one's foot
storta[2] ['stɔrta] SF (*alambicco*) retort
storto, a ['stɔrto] PP *di* **storcere**
■ AGG (*tubo, chiodo*) twisted, bent; (*ruota*) buckled, warped; (*manubrio, quadro*) crooked; (*fig: ragionamento*)

Ss

false, wrong; **avere le gambe storte** to have crooked legs; **avere gli occhi storti** to have a squint, be cross-eyed; **mi va tutto storto** *or* **mi vanno tutte storte** (*fam*) everything's going wrong
■ AVV: **guardare storto qn** (*fig*) to look askance at sb

stoviglie [sto'viʎʎe] SFPL dishes

Str. ABBR (*Geog*) = **stretto**

strabico, a, ci, che ['strabiko] AGG (*occhi*) squint; (*persona*): **essere strabico** to have a squint

strabiliante [strabi'ljante] AGG astonishing, amazing

strabiliare [strabi'ljare] VI (*aus* **avere**) to astonish, amaze

strabismo [stra'bizmo] SM squinting

strabuzzare [strabud'dzare] VT: **strabuzzare gli occhi** to open one's eyes wide

stracarico, a, chi, che [stra'kariko] AGG overloaded

straccare [strak'kare] VT (*sfinire*) to tire out

stracchino [strak'kino] SM *type of soft cheese*

stracciare [strat'tʃare] VT to tear up, rip up; **ho stracciato la lettera** I tore up the letter; **stracciare gli avversari** to wipe the floor with one's opponents
▶ **stracciarsi** VIP to tear, rip

stracciatella [strattʃa'tɛlla] SF (*minestra*) *broth made with beaten eggs, semolina and parmesan cheese*; (*gelato*) *vanilla-flavoured ice-cream with chocolate chips*

straccio, cia, ci, ce ['strattʃo] AGG: **carta straccia** wastepaper
■ SM (*gen*) rag; (*per pulire*) cloth, duster; (*fig*: *persona*) wretch; **non ho uno straccio di vestito** I haven't got a thing to wear; **non trova uno straccio di marito** she can't find a husband of any description

straccione, a [strat'tʃone] SM/F ragamuffin

straccivendolo [strattʃi'vendolo] SM ragman

stracco, a, chi, che ['strakko] AGG: **stracco (morto)** exhausted, dead tired

stracotto, a [stra'kɔtto] PP *di* **stracuocere**
■ AGG overcooked
■ SM (*Culin*) beef stew

stracuocere [stra'kwɔtʃere] VT IRREG to overdo, overcook

strada ['strada] SF **1** (*gen*) road; (*di città*) street; **andare fuori strada** (*Aut*) to go off the road; **attraversare la strada** to cross the road; **tagliare la strada a qn** to cut across in front of sb; **l'uomo della strada** (*fig*) the man in the street; **donna di strada** (*fig pegg*) streetwalker; **ragazzo di strada** (*fig pegg*) street urchin; **strada ferrata** railway (*Brit*), railroad (*Am*); **strada principale** main road; **strada a senso unico** one-way street; **strada senza uscita** dead end, cul-de-sac **2** (*percorso*) way; **qual è la strada per andare al cinema?** which is the way to the cinema?, how does one get to the cinema?; **mostrare la strada a qn** to show sb the way; **c'è tanta strada da fare?** is it a long way?; **tre ore di strada (a piedi)/(in macchina)** three hours' walk/drive; **non è sulla mia strada** it's not on my way; **facciamo la strada insieme?** shall we go along together?; **strada facendo** on the way **3** (*fig*) path, way, road; **essere sulla buona strada** (*nella vita*) to be on the right road *o* path; (*Polizia, ricerca*) to be on the right track; **essere fuori strada** (*Polizia*) to be on the wrong track; **portare qn sulla cattiva strada** to lead sb astray **4** (*fraseologia*): **fare** *o* **farsi strada** (*fig*: *persona*) to get on in life; **farsi strada tra la folla** to make one's way through the crowd; **trovarsi in mezzo ad una strada** to find o.s. out on the streets; **fare strada a qn** to show sb the way; **ti faccio strada** I'll show you the way

STRADE

Italy has a good network of roads and motorways. Main roads are indicated by blue signs, while the motorways have green signs. Italian motorways are numbered A1, A2, A3 and so on, and almost all are toll roads. The speed limit in Italy is 50 kmh in built-up areas, 90 kmh on main roads and 130 kmh on motorways, unless a different limit is indicated.

stradale [stra'dale] AGG (*gen*) road *attr*; (*polizia, regolamento*) traffic *attr*; **un cartello stradale** a road sign
■ SF (*polizia*) traffic police

stradario, ri [stra'darjo] SM street guide

stradino [stra'dino] SM road worker

stradista, i [stra'dista] SM (*Ciclismo*) road rider, road racer

stradivario, ri [stradi'varjo] SM Stradivarius

stradone [stra'done] SM wide road

strafalcione [strafal'tʃone] SM (*errore*) howler, blunder

strafare [stra'fare] VI IRREG (*aus* **avere**) to overdo it

strafatto, a [stra'fatto] PP *di* **strafare**

straforo [stra'foro] **di straforo** AVV (*di nascosto*) on the sly

strafottente [strafot'tɛnte] AGG arrogant
■ SM/F arrogant person

strafottenza [strafot'tɛntsa] SF arrogance

strage ['stradʒe] SF massacre, slaughter; **fare una strage** to carry out a massacre *o* slaughter; **fare strage di** (*animali*) to slaughter; **fare strage di cuori** to be a heartbreaker

stragismo [stra'dʒizmo] SM campaign of violence

stragista [stra'dʒista] SM/F terrorist killer

stragrande [stra'grande] AGG: **la stragrande maggioranza** the overwhelming majority

stralciare [stral'tʃare] VT to remove

stralcio, ci ['straltʃo] SM (*Comm*): **vendere a stralcio** to sell off (at bargain prices), clear
■ AGG INV: **legge stralcio** *abridged version of an act*

strale ['strale] SM (*fig letter*: *freccia*) arrow, dart

strallo ['strallo] SM (*Naut*): **strallo di prua** forestay; **strallo di poppa** backstay

stralunato, a [stralu'nato] AGG (*occhi*) staring; (*persona*) dazed, thunderstruck

stramaledetto, a [stramale'detto] PP *di* **stramaledire**
■ AGG (*fam*) damned

stramaledire [stramale'dire] VT IRREG (*fam*) to curse

stramazzare [stramat'tsare] VI (*aus* **essere**) to collapse, fall heavily; **stramazzare al suolo** to crash to the floor

strambamente [stramba'mente] AVV oddly, strangely

strambare [stram'bare] VI (*aus* **avere**) (*Naut*) to gybe

stramberia [strambe'ria] SF eccentricity

strambo, a ['strambo] AGG strange, queer; **un tipo strambo** an odd person

strame ['strame] SM hay, straw

strampalato, a [strampa'lato] AGG odd, eccentric

stranamente [strana'mente] AVV (*comportarsi, vestirsi*) oddly, strangely; **e lui, stranamente, ha accettato** and, surprisingly, he agreed

stranezza [stra'nettsa] SF (*qualità*) strangeness; (*atto*): **le sue stranezze mi preoccupano** his strange behaviour (*Brit*) *o* behavior (*Am*) worries me

strangolamento [strangola'mento] SM (*atto*) strangling; (*effetto*) strangulation

strangolare [strango'lare] VT to strangle
■ VIP to choke

straniero, a [stra'njɛro] AGG (*gen*) foreign; (*Amm*) alien; **un paese straniero** a foreign country
■ SM/F (*gen*) foreigner; (*Amm*) alien; **cacciare lo straniero** to drive out foreigners

LO SAPEVI...?
straniero non si traduce mai con la parola inglese *stranger*

stranito, a [stra'nito] AGG (*sguardo, aria*) dazed

strano, a ['strano] AGG (*gen*) strange; (*bizzarro*) strange, odd, queer; **è strano che...** it is odd that ...; **e cosa strana...** strangely enough ...

straordinariamente [straordinarja'mente] AVV extraordinarily

straordinario, ria, ri, rie [straordi'narjo] AGG (*gen*) extraordinary; (*treno, imposta*) special; (*impiegato*) temporary; **lavoro straordinario** overtime
■ SM (*impiegato*) temporary employee; (*lavoro*) overtime; **ho fatto tre ore di straordinario** I did three hours' overtime

straorzare [straor'tsare] VI (*aus* **avere**) (*Naut*) to broach

strapagare [strapa'gare] VT (*persona*) to overpay; (*merce*) to pay too much for

strapazzare [strapat'tsare] VT (*maltrattare: persona, oggetto*) to handle roughly, ill-treat; (*affaticare*) to tire out
► **strapazzarsi** VR to tire o.s. out, overdo things

strapazzata [strapat'tsata] SF **1** (*gran fatica*) strain **2** (*rimprovero*) telling-off; **dare una strapazzata a qn** to give sb a telling-off, tear sb off a strip (*Brit*)

strapazzato, a [strapat'tsato] AGG (*persona: affaticato*) worn out; **uova strapazzate** scrambled eggs

strapazzo [stra'pattso] SM **1** strain, fatigue **2 da strapazzo** (*fig pegg: persona*) third-rate

strapieno, a [stra'pjɛno] AGG overflowing, full to overflowing; **essere** *o* **sentirsi strapieno** to be *o* feel full up

strapiombo [stra'pjombo] SM (*roccia*) overhanging rock; **a strapiombo** overhanging

strapotere [strapo'tere] SM excessive power

strappalacrime [strappa'lakrime] AGG INV (*fam*): **romanzo (o film) strappalacrime** tear-jerker

strappare [strap'pare] VT (*gen*) to tear, rip; (*pagina*) to tear off, tear out; (*erbacce*) to pull up; (*bottone*) to pull off; **ha strappato la lettera** she tore up the letter; **strappare qc di mano a qn** to snatch sth out of sb's hand; **mi ha strappato la borsa** he snatched the bag from me; **si strappò la gonna** she tore *o* ripped her skirt; **strapparsi i vestiti di dosso** to rip one's clothes off; **strapparsi i capelli** to tear one's hair; **strapparsi un muscolo** to tear a muscle; **strappare una promessa a qn** to extract a promise from sb; **strappare un segreto a qn** to wring a secret from sb; **strappare gli applausi del pubblico** to win the audience's applause; **strappare qn dal suo ambiente** to take sb away from his (*o* her) own environment; **una scena che strappa il cuore** a heart-rending scene
► **strapparsi** VIP (*lacerarsi*) to tear, rip; **la camicia si è strappata sulla manica** the sleeve of the shirt is torn

strappato, a [strap'pato] AGG (*lacerato*) torn, ripped

strappo ['strappo] SM **1** (*lacerazione*) tear, rip; **c'è uno strappo nella camicia** there's a tear in the shirt; **strappo muscolare** (*Med*) strain, tear, torn muscle **2** (*strattone*) tug, pull; **dare uno strappo a qc** to give sth a tug; **fare uno strappo alla regola** to make an exception to the rule **3** (*fig fam: passaggio*) lift (*Brit*), ride (*Am*); **puoi darmi uno strappo (fino) in centro?** can you give me a lift *o* ride into town?

strapuntino [strapun'tino] SM (*sedile*) foldaway seat, jump seat

straricco, a, chi, che [stra'rikko] AGG extremely rich

straripamento [straripa'mento] SM overflowing

straripare [strari'pare] VI (*aus* **essere** *o* **avere**) (*fiume*) to overflow, burst its banks

Strasburgo [straz'burgo] SF Strasbourg

strascicare [straʃʃi'kare] VT (*trascinare*): **strascicare qc per terra** to drag sth along the ground, trail sth along the ground; **strascicare i piedi** to drag one's feet; **strascicare le parole** to drawl; **strascicare un lavoro** to drag out *o* draw out a piece of work; **strascicare una malattia** to be unable to shake off an illness
■ VI (*aus* **avere**) to trail
► **strascicarsi** VR (*trascinarsi*) to drag o.s. (along)

strascico, chi ['straʃʃiko] SM **1** (*di abito*) train; **reggere lo strascico a qn** to carry sb's train; (*fig*) to lick sb's boots **2 rete a strascico** trawl (net); **pesca a strascico** trawling **3** (*fig: conseguenza*) after-effect

strascinare [straʃʃi'nare] VT to drag
► **strascinarsi** VIP to drag o.s. (along); (*fig: lavoro*) to drag on

strass [stras] SM INV paste, strass

stratagemma, i [strata'dʒɛmma] SM (*Mil, fig*) stratagem

stratega, ghi [stra'tɛga] SM strategist

strategia, gie [strate'dʒia] SF (*Mil, fig*) strategy

strategicamente [stratedʒika'mente] AVV (*gen*) strategically; (*astutamente*) cunningly

strategico, a, ci, che [stra'tɛdʒiko] AGG (*Mil, fig*) strategic

stratificare [stratifi'kare] VT to stratify
► **stratificarsi** VIP to become stratified

stratificato, a [stratifi'kato] AGG (*roccia*) stratified; (*parabrezza, vetro*) laminated

stratificazione [stratifikat'tsjone] SF stratification

stratiforme [strati'forme] AGG stratiform

strato ['strato] SM (*gen*) layer; (*di vernice*) coat, coating; (*Meteor*) stratus; (*Geol*) stratum; **uno strato di polvere** a layer of dust; **i vari strati della società** the various strata of society; **strato sociale** social stratum

stratosfera [stratos'fɛra] SF stratosphere

strattone [strat'tone] SM tug, jerk; **dare uno strattone a qc** to tug *o* jerk sth, give sth a tug *o* jerk

stravaccarsi [stravak'karsi] VR: **stravaccarsi su** to flop down on, sprawl out on

stravaccato, a [stravak'kato] AGG sprawling

stravagante [strava'gante] AGG eccentric, odd

stravaganza [strava'gantsa] SF eccentricity

stravecchio, chia, chi, chie [stra'vɛkkjo] AGG (*gen*) very old; (*vino*) mellow; (*formaggio*) very mature

stravedere [strave'dere] VI IRREG (*aus* **avere**) **stravedere per qn** to dote on sb

stravincere [stra'vintʃere] VT IRREG to win easily; **stravincere qn** to beat sb hollow

stravinto, a [stra'vinto] PP *di* **stravincere**

stravisto, a [stra'visto] PP *di* **stravedere**

stravizio, zi [stra'vittsjo] SM excess; **darsi agli stravizi** to lead a dissolute life

stravolgere [stra'vɔldʒere] VT IRREG (*persona*) to upset; (*volto*) to contort; (*organizzazione, sistema*) to shake, rock; (*significato*) to twist, distort

stravolto, a [stra'vɔlto] PP *di* **stravolgere**
■ AGG (*persona: per stanchezza*) in a terrible state; (: *per*

Ss

sofferenza) distraught; **era stravolto dalla stanchezza** he was shattered; **aveva la faccia stravolta** he looked terrible

straziante [strat'tsjante] AGG (*scena*) harrowing; (*urlo*) bloodcurdling; (*dolore*) excruciating

straziare [strat'tsjare] VT (*carni, corpo*) to torment, torture; **straziare il cuore a qn** to break sb's heart; **una musica che strazia le orecchie** an excruciating piece of music

strazio, zi ['strattsjo] SM (*di torture*) torment; **fare strazio di** (*corpo, vittima*) to mutilate; **la scena era uno strazio** it was a harrowing scene; **questo libro è uno strazio!** this book is appalling!; **che strazio!** (*compito*) what a mess!; (*spettacolo*) what a disaster!

strega, ghe ['strega] SF (*anche fig*: *donna malvagia*) witch; (*pegg*: *donna brutta*) old hag, old witch

stregare [stre'gare] VT (*anche fig*) to bewitch

stregato, a [stre'gato] AGG (*castello, anello*) enchanted; (*persona*) bewitched

stregone [stre'gone] SM (*in tribù*) witch doctor; (*mago*) sorcerer, wizard

stregoneria [stregone'ria] SF (*pratica*) witchcraft; (*incantesimo*) spell; **fare una stregoneria** to cast a spell

stregua ['stregwa] SF: **alla (stessa) stregua di** on a par with; **trattare tutti alla stessa stregua** to treat everybody in the same manner

stremare [stre'mare] VT to exhaust

stremato, a [stre'mato] AGG exhausted, worn out

stremo ['strɛmo] SM: **essere allo stremo (delle forze)** to be at the end of one's tether

strenna ['strɛnna] SF: **strenna natalizia** (*regalo*) Christmas present; (*libro*) *book published for the Christmas market*

strenuo, a ['strɛnuo] AGG (*valoroso*) brave, courageous; (*infaticabile*) tireless

strepitare [strepi'tare] VI (*aus* **avere**) to yell and shout

strepito ['strɛpito] SM (*di voci, folla*) clamour (*Brit*), clamor (*Am*); (*di catene*) clanking, rattling; **fare strepito** (*notizia, scandalo*) to cause an uproar

strepitosamente [strepitosa'mente] AVV: **vincere strepitosamente** to win a resounding victory

strepitoso, a [strepi'toso] AGG (*successo*) resounding; (*applauso*) clamorous, deafening

streptococco, chi [strepto'kɔkko] SM streptococcus

stress [strɛs] SM INV stress

stressante [stres'sante] AGG stressful; **fa un lavoro stressante** he has a stressful job

stressare [stres'sare] VT to put under stress

stressato, a [stres'sato] AGG under stress; **è un po' stressato ultimamente** he's been rather stressed lately

stretch [stretʃ] AGG INV stretch

stretching [strɛtʃin(g)] SM (*Sport*) stretching

stretta ['stretta] SF (*gen*) grip, firm hold; **una stretta di mano** a handshake; **dare una stretta di mano a qn** to shake hands with sb, shake sb's hand; **una stretta di spalle** a shrug (of one's shoulders); **una stretta al cuore** a sudden sadness; **essere alle strette** to be in a tight corner, have one's back to the wall; **mettere qn alle strette** to put sb in a tight corner, get sb with his (*o* her) back to the wall; **stretta creditizia** (*Econ*) credit squeeze

strettamente [stretta'mente] AVV **1** (*in modo stretto*) tightly **2** (*fig*: *rigorosamente*) strictly, closely; **attenersi strettamente alle regole** to keep strictly to the rules, stick closely to the rules

strettezza [stret'tettsa] SF **1** (*gen*) narrowness **2 strettezze** SFPL poverty *sg*, straitened circumstances

stretto, a ['stretto] PP *di* **stringere**

■ AGG **1** (*corridoio, stanza, limiti*) narrow; (*gonna, scarpe, nodo*) tight; (*curva*) tight, sharp; **la strada diventa stretta in quel punto** the road gets narrow there; **questa gonna mi è stretta** this skirt is tight on me; **stavamo stretti in macchina** we were packed tight in the car; **tienti stretto!** hold on tight!; **tenere stretto qn/qc** to hold sb/sth tight; **a denti stretti** with clenched teeth **2** (*parente, amico*) close; **un parente stretto** a close relative **3** (*preciso, esatto*: *significato*) strict, exact; (*rigoroso*: *osservanza, rigoroso*) strict **4** (*soltanto*): **lo stretto necessario** the bare minimum

■ SM (*di mare*) strait

strettoia [stret'toja] SF (*di strada*) bottleneck; (*fig*) tricky situation

stria ['stria] SF streak

striare [stri'are] VT to streak

striato, a [stri'ato] AGG streaked

striatura [stria'tura] SF (*atto*) streaking; (*effetto*) streaks *pl*

stricnina [strik'nina] SF strychnine

stridente [stri'dɛnte] AGG (*rumore*) strident; (*colori*) clashing

stridere ['stridere] VI DIF (*porta*) to squeak; (*animale*) to screech, shriek; (*colori*) to clash

stridio, dii [stri'dio] SM screeching

strido ['strido] SM (*fpl* **strida**) (*di animale*) screech, shriek; (*urlo*) scream

stridore [stri'dore] SM screeching, shrieking

stridulo, a ['stridulo] AGG (*voce*) shrill

striglia ['striʎʎa] SF currycomb

strigliare [striʎ'ʎare] VT (*cavallo*) to curry

strigliata [striʎ'ʎata] SF (*di cavallo*) currying; (*fig*): **dare una strigliata a qn** to give sb a dressing-down

strillare [stril'lare] VI (*aus* **avere**) (*gridare*) to scream, shriek; **non strillare!** (*parla piano*) don't shout!

■ VT: **strillare aiuto** to cry for help; **strillò arrivederci** he shouted goodbye

strillo ['strillo] SM scream, shriek; **fare uno strillo** to let out a scream

strillone [stril'lone] SM news vendor, newspaper seller

striminzito, a [strimin'tsito] AGG (*misero*) shabby; (*molto magro*) skinny

strimpellare [strimpel'lare] VT (*chitarra*) to strum away on; (*pianoforte*) to plonk away on

stringa, ghe ['stringa] SF (*cordoncino*) lace; (*Inform, Ling*) string

stringare [strin'gare] VT (*fig*: *discorso*) to condense

stringatamente [stringata'mente] AVV concisely

stringatezza [stringa'tettsa] SF concision, terseness

stringato, a [strin'gato] AGG (*fig*) concise

stringere ['strindʒere] VB IRREG

■ VT **1** (*con la mano*) to grip, hold tight; **stringere il braccio di qn** to clasp sb's arm; **stringere la mano a qn** (*afferrarla*) to squeeze *o* press sb's hand; (*salutando*) to shake sb's hand, shake hands with sb; **si strinsero la mano** they shook hands; **stringere qn alla gola** to grab sb by the throat **2** (*pugno, mascella*) to clench; (*labbra*) to compress; **una scena che stringe il cuore** a scene which brings a lump to one's throat; **stringere i denti** to clench one's teeth; (*fig*) to grit one's teeth **3** (*gonna, vestito*) to take in **4** (*vite*) to tighten;

(*rubinetto*) to turn tight; (*cintura, nodo*) to tighten, pull tight **5** (*avvicinare: oggetti*) to close up, put close together; (*: persone*) squeeze together; **se vi stringete un po' posso sedermi anch'io** if you squeeze up a bit I'll be able to sit down **6** (*fraseologia*): **stringere qn tra le braccia** to clasp sb in one's arms; **stringere amicizia con qn** to make friends with sb; **stringere un patto** to conclude a treaty; **stringere un'alleanza** to form an alliance; **stringi stringi** in conclusion; **stringi!** get to the point!; **stringere qn in curva** (*Aut*) to cut in on sb on a bend

■ VI (*aus* **avere**) (*essere stretto*) to be tight; (*scarpe*) to pinch, be tight; (*fig: arrivare al dunque*) to come to the point; **queste scarpe mi stringono** these shoes are tight on me; **il tempo stringe** time is short;

▶ **stringersi** VR (*persona*) **stringersi a** (*muro, parete*) to press o.s. up against; **si strinse a lui** she drew close to him

strinsi *ecc* ['strinsi] VB *vedi* **stringere**

striptease ['strip ti:z] SM INV striptease; **fare lo striptease** to do a striptease

striscia, sce ['striʃʃa] SF (*di tessuto, carta, fumetto*) strip; (*riga*) stripe; **a strisce** striped; **una maglia a strisce blu e bianche** a blue and white striped jumper; **la striscia di Gaza** the Gaza strip; **strisce pedonali** zebra crossing *sg* (*Brit*), crosswalk *sg* (*Am*)

strisciante [striʃʃante] AGG **1** (*fig pegg*) unctuous **2** (*Econ: inflazione*) creeping

strisciare [striʃʃare] VT (*piedi*) to drag; (*muro, macchina*) to scrape, graze

■ VI (*aus* **avere**) (*gen*) to crawl, creep; **stava strisciando sul pavimento** he was crawling on the floor; **strisciare contro un muro** to sidle along a wall; **strisciare con la macchina contro il muro** to scrape one's car against the wall; **lo farò strisciare ai miei piedi** I'll make him crawl at my feet

strisciata [striʃʃata] SF (*segno*) scratch

striscio, sci ['striʃʃo] SM **1** (*segno*) scratch; **colpire di striscio** to graze **2** (*Med: esame*) smear (test), pap smear (*Am*)

striscione [striʃʃone] SM banner

stritolamento [stritola'mento] SM crushing

stritolare [strito'lare] VT (*anche fig*) to crush, grind

strizzacervelli [strittsatʃer'vɛlli] SM/F INV (*scherz*) shrink

strizzare [strit'tsare] VT (*panni*) to wring (out); **strizzare l'occhio (a qn)** to wink (at sb); **mi ha strizzato l'occhio** she winked at me

strizzata [strit'tsata] SF: **dare una strizzata a qc** to give sth a wring; **una strizzata d'occhio** a wink

strofa ['strɔfa] SF, **strofe** ['strɔfe] SF INV strophe

strofinaccio, ci [strofi'nattʃo] SM (*gen*) duster, cloth; (*per piatti*) dishcloth; (*per pavimenti*) floorcloth

strofinare [strofi'nare] VT (*gen*) to rub; (*lucidare*) to polish; (*pavimento*) to wipe; **strofinarsi gli occhi/le mani** to rub one's eyes/one's hands

▶ **strofinarsi** VR: **strofinarsi (contro)** to rub o.s. (against)

strofinio, nii [strofi'nio] SM (continual) rubbing

strombazzare [strombat'tsare] VT (*divulgare*) to proclaim; **strombazzare i propri meriti** to blow one's own trumpet; **strombazzare qc ai quattro venti** to proclaim sth to the four winds

■ VI (*aus* **avere**) (*fam: suonare il clacson*) to hoot

strombettare [strombet'tare] VI (*aus* **avere**) (*con tromba*) to blare away; (*con clacson*) to hoot

stroncare [stron'kare] VT (*ramo*) to break off; (*fig: rivolta*) to put down, suppress; (*: libro, film*) to pan, tear to pieces; **fu stroncato da un infarto** he was carried off by a heart attack

stronzata [stron'tsata] SF (*fam!*) damned stupid thing to do (*o* say); **non puoi credere a queste stronzate!** surely you don't believe such bullshit! (*fam!*) *o* crap (*fam!*); **come si possono fare certe stronzate?** how can people do such damned stupid things?

stronzio ['strɔntsjo] SM (*Chim*) strontium

stronzo ['strontso] SM (*fig fam!: persona*) shit (*fam!*), turd (*fam!*); (*sterco*) turd

stropicciare [stropit'tʃare] VT **1** (*strofinare*) to rub; **stropicciarsi gli occhi** to rub one's eyes **2** (*spiegazzare*) to crease

strozzare [strot'tsare] VT (*persona*) to choke, strangle; (*sogg: cibo*) to choke; (*conduttura*) to narrow

▶ **strozzarsi** VIP to choke

strozzascotte [strottsa'skɔtte] SM INV (*Naut*) clam cleat

strozzatura [strottsa'tura] SF (*di conduttura*) narrowing; (*di strada, fig*) bottleneck

strozzinaggio, gi [strottsi'naddʒo] SM usury

strozzino, a [strot'tsino] SM/F (*usuraio*) usurer; (*fig*) shark

struccare [struk'kare] VT to remove make-up from

▶ **struccarsi** VR to remove one's make-up

struccatore [strukka'tore] SM make-up remover

strudel ['strudel] SM INV (*Culin*) strudel

struggere ['struddʒere] VB IRREG (*letter*)

■ VT (*sogg: amore*) to consume

▶ **struggersi** VIP: **struggersi d'amore per qn** to be consumed with love for sb; **struggersi dal dolore** to be consumed with grief

struggimento [struddʒi'mento] SM (*desiderio*) yearning

strumentale [strumen'tale] AGG (*gen, Mus*) instrumental; (*Aer: volo*) instrument *attr*; **fare uso strumentale di qc** to make (instrumental) use of sth

strumentalizzare [strumentalid'dzare] VT to exploit, use for one's own ends

strumentalizzazione [strumentaliddzat'tsjone] SF exploitation, use for one's own ends

strumentare [strumen'tare] VT (*Mus*) to orchestrate

strumentazione [strumentat'tsjone] SF **1** (*Mus*) orchestration **2** (*Tecn*) instrumentation

strumentista, i, e [strumen'tista] SM/F (*Mus*) instrumentalist

strumento [stru'mento] SM **1** (*arnese*) tool; **essere lo strumento di qn** (*fig: persona*) to be sb's tool; **strumenti di bordo** (*Aer*) flight instruments; (*Naut*) ship instruments; **strumenti di precisione** precision instruments **2** (*Mus*) instrument; **strumento ad arco** string(ed) instrument; **strumento a corda** string(ed) instrument; **strumento a fiato** wind instrument

strusciare [struʃʃare] VT (*piedi*) to shuffle; (*gomiti*) to rub

▶ **strusciarsi** VR: **strusciarsi contro qc** to rub o.s. against sth; **gli si strusciava addosso** she was all over him

strussi *ecc* ['strussi] VB *vedi* **struggere**

strutto[1], a ['strutto] PP *di* **struggere**

strutto[2] ['strutto] SM (*Culin*) lard

struttura [strut'tura] SF (*tutti i sensi*) structure; **struttura portante** (*Edil*) supporting structure; **struttura sociale** social structure

strutturale [struttu'rale] AGG (*gen, Gramm*) structural

strutturalismo [struttura'lizmo] SM structuralism

Ss

strutturalista, i, e [struttura'lista] SM/F structuralist
strutturalistico, a, ci, che [struttura'listiko] AGG structuralist
strutturalmente [struttural'mente] AVV structurally
strutturare [struttu'rare] VT to structure
struzzo ['struttso] SM (*Zool*) ostrich; **piume di struzzo** ostrich feathers; **fare lo struzzo** *or* **fare la politica dello struzzo** to bury one's head in the sand; **avere uno stomaco di struzzo** to have a cast-iron stomach
stuccare [stuk'kare] VT (*muro*) to plaster; (*vetro*) to putty; (*decorare con stucchi*) to stucco
stuccatore, trice [stukka'tore] SM/F (*operaio*) plasterer; (*artista*) stucco worker
stuccatura [stukka'tura] SF (*vedi vb*) plastering; puttying; stuccoing
stucchevole [stuk'kevole] AGG (*cibo*) nauseating; (*scena, spettacolo*) tedious, boring
stucco, chi ['stukko] SM (*per muro*) plaster; (*per vetri*) putty; (*ornamentale*) stucco; **una stanza piena di stucchi** a room full of stucco work; **rimanere di stucco** to be dumbfounded, be left speechless
studente, essa [stu'dɛnte] SM/F (*gen*) student; (*scolaro*) pupil, schoolboy/schoolgirl; (*Univ*) student, undergraduate; **uno studente di medicina** a medical student
studentesco, a, schi, sche [studen'tesko] AGG student *attr*
studiacchiare [studjak'kjare] VT, VI (*aus* **avere**) to study halfheartedly
studiare [stu'djare] VT (*gen*) to study; (*lezione*) to learn; **studiare un sistema per fare qc** to try to find a way of doing sth; **una persona che studia i gesti/le parole** a person of studied manners/speech
■ VI (*aus* **avere**) to study
▶ **studiarsi** VR **1** (*osservarsi*) to examine o.s. **2** (*uso reciproco*) to eye *o* weigh one another up
studiato, a [stu'djato] AGG (*modi, sorriso*) affected
studio, di ['studjo] SM **1** (*gen: azione*) studying, study; **una giornata di studio** a day's studying; **ha interrotto gli studi per un anno** he took a break from his studies for a year; **mantenersi agli studi** to pay one's way through college (*o* university); **fare studi letterari/scientifici** to study arts/science; **alla fine degli studi** at the end of one's course (of studies) **2** (*lavoro, ricerca, disegno*) study; **fare uno studio** *o* **degli studi su qn/qc** to do research on sb/sth, make a study of sb/sth; **secondo recenti studi, appare che...** recent research indicates that ...; **ho letto uno studio recente sull'inquinamento** I read a recent piece of research on pollution; **uno studio critico** a critical study; **uno studio dal vero** a life study; **studio di settore** *system for calculating the presumed income of particular categories of taxpayers, used by the tax authorities to combat tax evasion* **3** (*progettazione*) project; **la proposta è allo studio** the proposal is under consideration **4** (*stanza*) study; (*di professionista*) office; (*di medico*) surgery (*Brit*), office (*Am*); **il nonno legge nello studio** grandpa's reading in the study; **studio fotografico** photographer's studio; **studio legale** lawyer's office **5** (*TV, Cine*) studio; **trasmettiamo dagli studi di Roma** we are broadcasting from our Rome studios
studiosamente [studjosa'mente] AVV (*con diligenza*) diligently; (*a bella posta*) carefully
studioso, a [stu'djoso] AGG studious, hardworking
■ SM/F scholar
stufa ['stufa] SF (*gen*) stove; (*elettrica*) electric fire *o* heater; **stufa a legna/carbone** wood-burning/coal stove; **stufa a gas** gas heater
stufare [stu'fare] VT **1** (*Culin*) to stew **2** (*fig fam*) to bore, weary; **mi avete proprio stufato con le vostre lamentele** I am really fed up with your moaning; **mi hai proprio stufato** I am really fed up with you
▶ **stufarsi** VIP: **stufarsi (di)** to grow weary (of); **mi sono stufato di loro** I got fed up with them; **si è stufato di ascoltarlo** he got fed up listening to him
stufato [stu'fato] SM (*Culin*) stew
stufo, a ['stufo] AGG (*fam*): **essere stufo (di)** to be fed up (with), be sick and tired (of); **sei già stufa?** are you fed up already?; **sono stufo di studiare** I'm fed up of studying
stuoia ['stwɔja] SF (*tappeto*) mat; (*tessuto*) rush matting
stuolo ['stwɔlo] SM crowd, host
stupefacente [stupefa'tʃɛnte] AGG amazing, astounding; **sostanze stupefacenti** drugs
■ SM drug, narcotic
stupefare [stupe'fare] VT IRREG to stun, astound
stupefatto, a [stupe'fatto] PP *di* **stupefare**
stupefazione [stupefat'tsjone] SF astonishment
stupendo, a [stu'pɛndo] AGG marvellous, wonderful
stupidaggine [stupi'daddʒine] SF (*qualità*) stupidity, foolishness; (*atto, discorso*): **dire una stupidaggine** to say something stupid; **dire stupidaggini** to talk nonsense; **non dire stupidaggini!** don't talk nonsense!; **fare una stupidaggine** to do something stupid; **ho fatto una stupidaggine** I did something stupid; **ti ho preso una stupidaggine** (*regalino*) I bought you a little something
stupidamente [stupida'mente] AVV stupidly; **ho sbagliato stupidamente** I made a stupid mistake
stupidità [stupidi'ta] SF (*qualità*) stupidity
stupido, a ['stupido] AGG stupid
■ SM/F fool, idiot; **fare lo stupido** to fool around
stupire [stu'pire] VT to amaze, stun; **la sua risposta mi ha stupito molto** his answer really amazed me
■ VI (*aus* **essere**), **stupirsi** VIP to be amazed (at), be stunned (by); **mi sono stupito del suo coraggio** I was amazed at his courage; **non c'è da stupirsi** it's not surprising
stupito, a [stu'pito] AGG amazed
stupore [stu'pore] SM amazement, astonishment; **con mio grande stupore ho scoperto che...** much to my amazement I discovered that ...

LO SAPEVI...?
stupore non si traduce mai con la parola inglese *stupor*

stuprare [stu'prare] VT to rape
stupratore [stupra'tore] SM rapist
stupro ['stupro] SM rape
sturare [stu'rare] VT (*lavandino*) to unblock; (*bottiglia*) to uncork; **sturati le orecchie!** (*fig*) clean your ears out!
stuzzicadenti [stuttsika'dɛnti] SM INV toothpick; (*fig: persona magra*) beanpole
stuzzicante [stuttsi'kante] AGG (*gen*) stimulating; (*appetitoso*) appetizing; **che idea stuzzicante** what a nice idea
stuzzicare [stuttsi'kare] VT (*ferita*) to poke (at), prod (at); (*fig: persona*) to tease; (*: appetito*) to whet; (*: curiosità*) to stimulate; **smettila di stuzzicarlo** stop teasing him; **stuzzicarsi i denti** to pick one's teeth
stuzzichino [stuttsi'kino] SM (*Culin*) appetizer

su [su] **PAROLA CHIAVE**
■ PREP (*su* + *il*=sul, *su* + *lo*=sullo, *su* + *l'*=sull', *su* + *la*=sulla, *su* + *i*=sui, *su* + *gli*=sugli, *su* + *le*=sulle)

1 (*gen*) on; (*moto*) on(to); (*in cima a*) on (top of); **non è mai stato su un aereo** he's never been in a plane; **puntare una somma su un cavallo** to bet a sum on a horse; **è sulla destra** it's on the right; **conto su di te** I'm counting on you; **fa errori su errori** he makes one mistake after another; **fece fuoco sulla folla** he fired on the crowd; **la finestra dà sul giardino** the window looks onto the garden; **l'ho visto sul giornale** I saw it in the paper; **fecero rotta su Palermo** they set out towards Palermo; **gettarsi sulla preda** to throw o.s. on one's prey; **la marcia su Roma** the march on Rome; **mettilo sulla scrivania** put it on the desk; **ricamo su seta** embroidery on silk; **procedi sulla sinistra** keep on *o* to the left; **sta sulle sue** he keeps to himself; **il libro è sul tavolo** the book is on the table; **è salito sul tavolo** he got up on(to) the table; **olio su tela** oil on canvas; **basare un argomento su** to base an argument on

2 (*addosso*) over; **buttati uno scialle sulle spalle** throw a shawl over *o* round your shoulders; **sul vestito indossava un golf rosso** she was wearing a red sweater over her dress

3 (*da una parte all'altra*) over; **un ponte sul fiume** a bridge over the river; **un aereo passò sulle nostre teste** an aeroplane flew over our heads

4 (*autorità, dominio*) over; **non ha alcun potere su di lui** he has no power over him

5 (*più in alto di*) above; **100 metri sul livello del mare** 100 metres above sea level

6 (*argomento*) about, on; **discutere su un argomento** to discuss a subject; **un articolo sulla prima guerra mondiale** an article on *o* about the First World War; **una conferenza sulla pace nel mondo** a conference on *o* about world peace

7 (*circa*) about, around; **è costato sui due milioni** it cost about two million euros; **c'erano sulle 100 persone** there were about 100 people; **sarà sulla sessantina** he must be about sixty

8 (*proporzione*) out of, in; **50 su 100 hanno votato contro** 50 out of 100 voted against (it); **2 giorni su 3** 2 days out of 3, 2 days in 3; **uno su tre** one in three; **5 su 10** (*voto*) 5 out of 10

9 (*modo*): **scarpe su misura** handmade shoes; **spedire qc su richiesta** to send sth on request

■ AVV

1 (*in alto, verso l'alto*) up; (*al piano superiore*) upstairs; **guarda su** look up; **lì su** up there; **su le mani!** hands up!; **qui su** up here; **era su che ci aspettava** he was waiting for us upstairs

2 (*in poi*) onwards; **dal numero 39 in su** from number 39 onwards; **dai 20 anni in su** from the age of 20 onwards; **prezzi dalle 50 euro in su** prices from 50 euros (upwards)

3 (*addosso*) on; **cos'hai su?** what have you got on?; **aveva su una strana tunica** she had a strange tunic on; **posso metterlo su?** can I put it on?

4 (*fraseologia*): **su coraggio!** come on, cheer up!; **andare su e giù** to go up and down; **andava su e giù per il corridoio** he paced up and down the corridor; **su per giù** = **suppergiù**; **su smettila!** come on, that's enough of that!; **su su non fare così!** now, now, don't behave like that!; **su svelto!** come on, hurry up!; **venir su dal niente** to rise from nothing

sua ['sua] *vedi* **suo**
suadente [sua'dɛnte] AGG persuasive
sub [sub] SM/F INV skin-diver
■ SM (*sport*) skin diving
subacqueo, a [su'bakkweo] AGG underwater *attr*; **esplorazione subacquea** underwater exploration; **una muta subacquea** a wetsuit
■ SM skin-diver
subaffittare [subaffit'tare] VT to sublet
subaffitto [subaf'fitto] SM (*contratto*) sublet
subalterno, a [subal'tɛrno] AGG, SM (*gen*) subordinate; (*Mil*) subaltern
subappaltare [subappal'tare] VT to subcontract
subappalto [subap'palto] SM subcontract
subatomico, a, ci, che [suba'tɔmiko] AGG subatomic
subbuglio [sub'buʎʎo] SM confusion, turmoil; **essere/mettere in subbuglio** to be in/throw into a turmoil
subconscio, scia, sci, scie [sub'kɔnʃo], **subcosciente** [subkoʃʃɛnte] AGG, SM subconscious
subdolamente [subdola'mente] AVV in an underhand manner
subdolo, a ['subdolo] AGG sneaky, underhand
subentrare [suben'trare] VI (*aus* **essere**) **è subentrato al padre nella direzione della ditta** he took over the management of the firm from his father; **alla sorpresa subentrò la paura** surprise gave way to fear; **sono subentrati altri problemi** other problems have arisen
subequatoriale [subekwato'rjale] AGG subequatorial
subire [su'bire] VT (*gen*) to suffer, endure; (*operazione*) to undergo; **subire un interrogatorio** to undergo an interrogation, be interrogated; **subire una tortura** to be tortured; **ha subito un torto** he suffered an injustice; **dovrai subirne le conseguenze** you'll have to suffer the consequences; **ha dovuto subire e tacere** he had to suffer in silence; **hanno dovuto subire molte umiliazioni** they had to put up with a lot of humiliation; **per quanto ancora dobbiamo subire questo despota?** for how long must we put up with this despot?; **il progetto ha subito alcune modifiche** the project has undergone some modifications
subissare [subis'sare] VT: **subissare qn di** (*domande, richieste*) to overwhelm with; (*doni, lodi*) to shower sb with
subitamente [subita'mente] AVV suddenly
subitaneo, a [subi'taneo] AGG sudden
subito ['subito] AVV immediately, at once, straight away; **è arrivato subito dopo di te** he arrived immediately after you; **fallo subito!** do it immediately!; **torno subito** I'll be right back; **è subito fatto** it's easily done
sublimare [subli'mare] VT (*Rel, fig*) to exalt; (*Psic*) to sublimate; (*Chim*) to sublime
sublimazione [sublimat'tsjone] SF (*Rel, fig*) exaltation; (*Psic, Chim*) sublimation
sublime [su'blime] AGG, SM sublime
sublimemente [sublime'mente] AVV sublimely
sublocare [sublo'kare] VT to sublease
sublocazione [sublokat'tsjone] SF sublease
subnormale [subnor'male] AGG subnormal
■ SM/F mentally handicapped person
subodorare [subodo'rare] VT (*insidia*) to smell, suspect
subordinare [subordi'nare] VT to subordinate
subordinata [subordi'nata] SF (*Gramm*) subordinate clause
subordinato, a [subordi'nato] AGG (*gen, Gramm*) subordinate; (*dipendente*): **proposizione subordinata** subordinate clause; **subordinato a** dependent on, subject to

Ss

subordinazione [subordinat'tsjone] SF subordination
subordine [su'bordine] SM: **in subordine** secondarily
subsonico, a, ci, che [sub'sɔniko] AGG subsonic
substrato [sub'strato] SM (*gen*) substrate, substratum; (*Bio, Chim: di enzima*) substrate
subtotale [subto'tale] SM subtotal
subtropicale [subtropi'kale] AGG subtropical
suburbano, a [subur'bano] AGG suburban
succedaneo, a [suttʃe'daneo] AGG substitute *attr*
■SM substitute
succedere [sut'tʃɛdere] VB IRREG
■VI (*aus* essere) **1** (*accadere*) to happen; **sapessi cosa mi è successo!** wait till you hear what happened to me!; **cosa ti succede?** what's the matter with you?; **cos'è successo?** what happened?; **dev'essergli successo qualcosa** something must have happened to him; **sono cose che succedono** these things happen **2** **succedere a** (*seguire: persona*) to succeed; (*venire dopo*) to follow; **succedere al trono** to succeed to the throne;
▶ **succedersi** VIP to follow each other; **i mesi si succedevano lenti** the months dragged on
successione [suttʃes'sjone] SF succession; **imposta di successione** death duty (*Brit*), inheritance tax (*Am*)
successivamente [suttʃessiva'mente] AVV (*in seguito*) later, subsequently
successivo, a [suttʃes'sivo] AGG (*continuo*) successive; (*che segue*) following; **il giorno successivo** the following *o* next day; **in un momento successivo** subsequently
successo, a [sut'tʃɛsso] PP *di* **succedere**
■SM (*gen*) success; (*disco*) hit; (*libro*) bestseller; (*film*) box-office success, hit; **è stato un successo!** it was a success!; **arrivare al successo** to become a success; **avere successo** (*persona*) to be successful; (*idea*) to be well received; **non ho avuto successo** I was unsuccessful; **ho provato, ma senza successo** I tried, but without success, I tried in vain; **di successo** (*attore, cantante*) successful; **un film di successo** a successful film; **canzone di successo** hit (song)
successore [suttʃes'sore] AGG successive
■SM successor
succhiare [suk'kjare] VT (*gen*) to suck (up); **succhiare il sangue a qn** (*fig*) to bleed sb dry
succhiello [suk'kjɛllo] SM gimlet
succhiotto [suk'kjɔtto] SM (*tettarella*) dummy (*Brit*), pacifier (*Am*), comforter (*Am*); (*fam: segno sul collo*) lovebite, hickey (*Am*)
succintamente [suttʃinta'mente] AVV (*parlare*) succinctly; (*vestito*) scantily
succinto, a [sut'tʃinto] AGG (*discorso*) succinct; (*abito*) scanty
succo, chi ['sukko] SM (*Anat, di frutto*) juice; (*fig: della conferenza*) gist; **il succo del discorso** (*fig*) the essence of the speech; **succo di frutta** fruit juice; **succo di pomodoro** tomato juice
succosità [sukkosi'ta] SF juiciness; (*fig*) pithiness
succoso, a [suk'koso] AGG juicy; (*fig*) pithy
succube ['sukkube] SM/F victim; **essere succube di qn** to be dominated by sb, be under sb's thumb
succulento, a [sukku'lɛnto] AGG (*sugoso*) succulent; (*gustoso: pranzo, cibo*) tasty
succulenza [sukku'lɛntsa] SF (*vedi agg*) succulence; tastiness
succursale [sukkur'sale] SF branch (office)
sud [sud] SM south; **la sua famiglia è del sud** his family is from the south; **a sud (di)** south (of); **si trova a sud della città** it's south of the city; **la Svizzera confina a sud con l'Italia** to the south Switzerland has a border with Italy; **il vento viene da sud** the wind comes from the south; **esposto a sud** facing south; **verso sud** south, southwards; **si è diretto a sud** he headed south; **i mari del Sud** the South Seas; **l'Italia del Sud** Southern Italy; **l'America del Sud** South America
■AGG INV (*gen*) south; (*regione*) southern; **partirono in direzione sud** they set off southwards *o* in a southerly direction, they headed south
Sudafrica [su'dafrika] SM South Africa
sudafricano, a [sudafri'kano] AGG, SM/F South African
Sudamerica [suda'merika] SM South America
sudamericano, a [sudameri'kano] AGG, SM/F South American
Sudan [su'dan] SM: **(il) Sudan** (the) Sudan
sudanese [suda'nese] AGG, SM/F Sudanese *inv*
sudare [su'dare] VI (*aus* **avere**) to perspire, sweat; **ho dovuto sudare per finire quella traduzione** (*fig*) I had to work hard to finish that translation; **mi ha fatto sudare** (*fig*) he made me work hard; **sudare freddo** (*anche fig*) to come out in a cold sweat
■VT to work hard for; **sudarsi il pane** to earn one's bread by the sweat of one's brow
sudario, ri [su'darjo] SM shroud
sudata [su'data] SF (*anche fig*) sweat; **ho fatto una bella sudata per finire in tempo** (*fig*) it was a real sweat to finish in time
sudaticcio, cia, ci, ce [suda'tittʃo] AGG sweaty, damp
sudato, a [su'dato] AGG (*persona, mani*) sweaty; (*fig: denaro*) hard-earned; **una vittoria sudata** a hard-won victory
Sud Carolina [sud kærə'laınə] SM South Carolina
Sud Dakota [sud da'kota] SF South Dakota
suddetto, a [sud'detto] AGG above-mentioned *attr*
suddiaconato [suddiako'nato] SM subdiaconate
suddiacono [suddi'akono] SM subdeacon
sudditanza [suddi'tantsa] SF subjection
suddito, a ['suddito] SM/F subject
suddividere [suddi'videre] VT IRREG to subdivide
suddivisione [suddivi'zjone] SF subdivision
suddiviso, a [suddi'vizo] PP *di* **suddividere**
sud-est [su'dest] SM south-east; **vento di sud-est** south-easterly wind; **il sud-est asiatico** South-East Asia
sudiceria [suditʃe'ria] SF (*qualità*) filthiness, dirtiness; (*cosa sporca*) dirty thing; **libro pieno di sudicerie** filthy *o* obscene book
sudicio, cia, ci, ce ['suditʃo] AGG dirty, filthy; (*fig: indecente*) dirty, filthy, indecent; (*: disonesto*) dirty
■SM (*anche fig*) dirt, filth
sudicione, a [sudi'tʃone] SM/F (*anche fig*) filthy person, pig (*fam*)
sudiciume [sudi'tʃume] SM (*anche fig*) dirt, filth
sudore [su'dore] SM perspiration, sweat; **si è asciugato il sudore dalla fronte** he wiped the sweat off his forehead; **essere in un bagno di sudore** to be bathed in sweat; **col sudore della propria fronte** (*fig*) with the sweat of one's brow
sudoriparo, a [sudo'riparo] AGG: **ghiandola sudoripara** sweat gland
sud-ovest SM [su'dɔvest] south-west; **vento di sud-ovest** south-westerly wind
sue ['sue] *vedi* **suo**

Suez ['suez] SF: **il canale di Suez** the Suez Canal
sufficiente [suffi'tʃɛnte] AGG **1** (*adeguato*) sufficient, enough; (*abbastanza*) enough; (*voto*) satisfactory; **questo fu sufficiente a farlo tacere** that was enough to shut him up; **non c'è spazio sufficiente per tutti** there is not enough room for everyone; **pensi che il pane sia sufficiente?** do you think there's enough bread?; **credi sia sufficiente?** do you think that will do?; **è più che sufficiente** it is more than enough **2** (*borioso*) self-important
■ SM: **avere il sufficiente per vivere** to have enough to live on
sufficientemente [suffitʃente'mente] AVV (*guadagnare, darsi da fare*) enough; **sufficientemente bene** well enough, sufficiently well
sufficienza [suffi'tʃɛntsa] SF **1 a sufficienza** enough; **ne hai a sufficienza?** have you got enough?; **ne ho a sufficienza** I have got plenty; **ne ho avuto a sufficienza!** (*sono stufo*) I've had enough of this!; **ce ne sono a sufficienza** there are enough **2 con un'aria di sufficienza** (*fig*) with a condescending air **3** (*Scol*) pass mark; **sono riuscito a prendere la sufficienza** I managed to get a pass mark
suffisso [suf'fisso] SM (*Gramm*) suffix
suffragare [suffra'gare] VT (*fig: affermazioni*) to support
suffragetta [suffra'dʒetta] SF suffragette
suffragio, gi [suf'fradʒo] SM **1** (*Pol: voto*) vote; **suffragio universale** universal suffrage **2** (*Rel*) intercession; **messa di suffragio** mass for somebody's soul
suggellare [suddʒel'lare] VT (*anche fig*) to seal
suggello [sud'dʒɛllo] SM (*anche fig*) seal
suggerimento [suddʒeri'mento] SM suggestion, hint; **qualcuno ha altri suggerimenti?** has anyone got any other suggestions?; **dietro suo suggerimento** on his advice
suggerire [suddʒe'rire] VT (*gen*) to suggest; (*soluzione*) to suggest, put forward; (*Teatro*) to prompt; **cosa suggerisci?** what do you suggest?; **suggerirei di trovarci lì** I'd suggest that we meet there, I'd suggest meeting there; **suggerire a qn di fare qc** to suggest to sb that he (*o* she) do (*o* should do) sth; **gli ho suggerito di dire tutto ai suoi genitori** I suggested he told his parents everything; **mi ha suggerito un periodo di riposo** he advised me to take some time off; **non suggerire!** (*in classe*) don't help!
suggeritore, trice [suddʒeri'tore] SM/F (*Teatro*) prompter
suggestionare [suddʒestjo'nare] VT to influence; **non lasciarti suggestionare da quello che dice** don't let yourself be influenced by what he says
▶ **suggestionarsi** VIP to be influenced
suggestione [suddʒes'tjone] SF (*Psic*) suggestion; (*fascino*) fascination
suggestivamente [suddʒestiva'mente] AVV evocatively
suggestivo, a [suddʒes'tivo] AGG (*paesaggio*) evocative; (*veduta*) enchanting; (*teoria*) interesting, attractive
sughero ['sugero] SM (*gen*) cork; (*albero*) cork oak; **tappo di sughero** cork
sugli ['suʎʎi] PREP + ART *vedi* **su**
sugna ['suɲɲa] SF lard
sugo, ghi ['sugo] SM (*succo*) juice; (*di carne*) gravy; (*per pastasciutta*) sauce; (*fig: del discorso*) essence; **senza sugo** (*fig: persona*) insipid, wishy-washy; (*discorso*) pointless, senseless
sugoso, a [su'goso] AGG (*frutto*) juicy; (*fig: articolo*) pithy
sui ['sui] PREP + ART *vedi* **su**
suicida, i, e [sui'tʃida] AGG suicidal
■ SM/F suicide (*person*)
suicidarsi [suitʃi'darsi] VR to commit suicide
suicidio, di [sui'tʃidjo] SM suicide (*action*)
suino, a [su'ino] AGG: **carne suina** pork
■ SM pig; **i suini** swine *pl*
sul [sul] PREP + ART *vedi* **su**
sulfamidico, a, ci, che [sulfa'midiko] AGG, SM sulphonamide *attr*
sulfureo, a [sul'fureo] AGG sulphur *attr* (*Brit*), sulfur *attr* (*Am*)
sulky ['sʌlki] SM INV (*Ippica*) sulky
sull' [sull], **sulla** ['sulla], **sulle** ['sulle], **sullo** ['sullo] PREP + ART *vedi* **su**
sultanina [sulta'nina] SF: **(uva) sultanina** sultana
sultano, a [sul'tano] SM/F sultan/sultana
Sumatra [su'matra] SF Sumatra
summa ['summa] SF (*Rel, Filosofia*) summa
summit ['summit] SM INV summit
SUNIA [su'nia] SIGLA M (= **Sindacato Unitario Nazionale Inquilini e Assegnatari**) *national association of tenants*
sunnita, i, e [sun'nita] SM/F Sunni
sunnominato, a [sunnomi'nato] AGG aforesaid *attr*
sunto ['sunto] SM summary; **fare il sunto di qc** to summarize sth
suo[1], a ['suo] (*pl* **suoi, sue**) AGG POSS: **il(la) suo(a)** (*maschile*) his; (*femminile*) her; (*neutro*) its; **il cane dorme nella sua cuccia** the dog is sleeping in its kennel; **il suo giardino** his (*o* her) garden; **sua madre** his (*o* her) mother; **suo padre** his (*o* her) father; **un suo amico** a friend of his (*o* hers); **Luciana e le sue amiche** Luciana and her friends; **è colpa sua** it's his (*o* her) fault; **è casa sua** *or* **è la sua casa** it's his (*o* her) house; **per amor suo** for love of him (*o* her); **Sua Altezza** His (*o* Her) Highness
■ PRON POSS: **il(la) suo(a)** (*maschile*) his, his own; (*femminile*) hers, her own; (*neutro*) its, its own; **la mia barca è più lunga della sua** my boat is longer than his (*o* hers); **è di Roberta questa macchina? – sì, è sua** is this Roberta's car? – yes, it's hers; **il suo è stato solo un errore** it was simply an error on his (*o* her) part
■ SM **1 ha speso del suo** he (*o* she) spent his (*o* her) own money; **vive del suo** he (*o* she) lives on his (*o* her) own income **2 i suoi** SMPL (*genitori*) his (*o* her) parents; (*famiglia*) his (*o* her) family; (*amici, alleati*) his (*o* her) own people, his (*o* her) side; **lui è dei suoi** he is on his (*o* her) side
■ SF: **la sua** (*opinione*) his (*o* her) view; **è dalla sua** (*parte*) he's on his (*o* her) side; **anche lui ha avuto le sue** (*disavventure*) he's had his problems too; **sta sulle sue** he keeps himself to himself
suo[2], a ['suo] (*pl* **suoi, sue**) (*forma di cortesia: Suo*) AGG POSS: **il(la) suo(a)** your; **il suo ombrello, signore!** your umbrella, sir!; **Sua Altezza** Your Highness; **suo devotissimo** (*in lettere*) your devoted servant
■ PRON POSS: **il(la) suo(a)** yours, your own; **scusi signore, è suo questo?** excuse me sir, is this yours?; **la sua è pura scortesia** that's sheer discourtesy on your part
■ PRON POSS M: **ha speso del suo?** did you spend your own money?
■ PRON POSS F: **la sua** (*opinione*) your view; **è dalla sua** he's on your side; **alla sua!** your very good health!

Ss

suocera ['swɔtʃera] SF mother-in-law
suocero ['swɔtʃero] SM father-in-law; **i suoceri** father- and mother-in-law; **i miei suoceri** my in-laws
suoi ['swɔi] *vedi* suo
suola ['swɔla] SF (*di scarpa*) sole; **rifare le suole alle scarpe** to have one's shoes resoled
suolo ['swɔlo] SM (*terreno*) ground; (*terra*) soil; **studia gli effetti dell'inquinamento sul suolo** she's studying the effects of pollution on the soil; **cadde al suolo** he fell to the ground; **in suolo italiano** on Italian soil
suonare [swo'nare] VT (*strumento, pezzo musicale*) to play; (*campana, campanello*) to ring; (*clacson, allarme, ritirata*) to sound; **sai suonare la chitarra?** can you play the guitar?; **l'orologio ha suonato le cinque** the clock struck five; **suonare il clacson** to hoot, sound the horn; **gliele ho suonate** (*fam*) I gave him a thrashing
■ VI (*aus* **avere**) (*musicista*) to play; (*campane, campanello, telefono*) to ring; (*ore*) to strike; (*fig*) (: *discorso*) to sound, ring; **sta suonando il telefono** the phone is ringing; **le campane suonano a morto** the bells are sounding a death knell; **mi suona strano** (*fig*) it sounds strange to me
suonato, a [swo'nato] AGG **1** (*compiuto*): **ha cinquant'anni suonati** he is well over fifty **2** (*Pugilato*) punch-drunk; (*fig fam*: *rimbambito*) soft in the head
suonatore, trice [swona'tore] SM/F player; **suonatore ambulante** street musician
suoneria [swone'ria] SF alarm; (*di telefono*) ring tone
suono ['swɔno] SM (*gen*) sound; (*di campane*) sound, ringing; **ballare al suono di un'orchestra** to dance to the music of an orchestra; **lo accolsero a suon di fischi** they booed and jeered him as he arrived
suora ['swɔra] SF (*Rel*) nun; **vuole farsi suora** she wants to become a nun; **Suor Maria** Sister Maria
super ['super] AGG INV: **(benzina) super** four-star (petrol) (*Brit*), premium (*Am*)
■ PREF super..., over...
superaccessoriato, a [superattʃesso'rjato] AGG (*auto*) fully accessorized
superaffollamento [superaffolla'mento] SM overcrowding
superaffollato, a [superaffol'lato] AGG overcrowded
superalcolico, a, ci, che [superal'kɔliko] AGG alcoholic (*of drink made with distilled alcohol*)
■ SM: **i superalcolici** spirits, liquors
superalimentazione [superalimentat'tsjone] SF overfeeding
superamento [supera'mento] SM (*di ostacolo*) overcoming; (*di montagna*) crossing; **arrivare al superamento di** (*idee, dottrine*) to move on from
superare [supe'rare] VT (*limite, aspettative*) to exceed; (*traguardo, montagne*) to cross; (*esame*) to pass; (*muro*) to get over; (*fig*: *ostacolo, malattia, paura*) to overcome; (: *rivale*) to beat, surpass, outdo; (*Aut*: *sorpassare*) to overtake; **il risultato ha superato le aspettative** the result exceeded expectations; **sono certo che riusciremo a superare queste difficoltà** I'm sure we can overcome these difficulties; **ha superato l'esame di guida** he's passed his driving test; **superare i limiti di velocità** to exceed *o* break the speed limit; **ha superato il limite di velocità** he broke the speed limit; **superare qn in altezza/peso** to be taller/heavier than sb; **ha superato la cinquantina** he's over fifty (years of age); **stavolta ha superato se stesso** this time he has surpassed himself
superato, a [supe'rato] AGG outmoded
superattico, ci [supe'rattiko] SM penthouse
superbamente [superba'mente] AVV **1** (*vantarsi*) proudly; (*comportarsi, rispondere*) haughtily **2** (*magnificamente*) superbly, magnificently
superbia [su'pɛrbja] SF pride
superbo, a [su'pɛrbo] AGG **1** (*persona*) proud, haughty **2** (*fig*: *grandioso, splendido*) superb, magnificent
■ SM/F haughty person
supercarcere [super'kartʃere] SM maximum security prison
superconduttività [superkonduttivi'ta] SF superconductivity
superconduttore [superkondut'tore] SM superconductor
superdonna [super'dɔnna] SF (*iro*) superwoman
superdotato, a [superdo'tato] AGG highly gifted
■ SM/F highly gifted person
Super-Ego [super 'ɛgo] SM INV (*Psic*) superego
superenalotto® [superena'lɔtto] SM ≈ National Lottery
superficiale [superfi'tʃale] AGG (*gen*) superficial; **fortunatamente è solo una ferita superficiale** fortunately, it's only a superficial wound; **è un po' superficiale** she's a bit superficial; **acque superficiali** surface water *sg*
■ SM/F superficial person
superficialità [superfitʃali'ta] SF superficiality
superficialmente [superfitʃal'mente] AVV superficially
superficie [super'fitʃe] SF **1** (*di muro, specchio*) surface; **superficie terrestre** surface of the earth; **tornare in superficie** (*a galla*) to return to the surface; (*fig*: *problemi*) to resurface; **non va mai oltre la superficie delle cose** he has a superficial approach **2** (*area*) surface area; **superficie alare** (*Aer*) wing area; **superficie velica** (*Naut*) sail area
superfluità [superflui'ta] SF INV (*vedi agg*) superfluity; unnecessariness; **le superfluità** the extras
superfluo, a [su'pɛrfluo] AGG (*gen*) superfluous; (*spese*) unnecessary; **peli superflui** unwanted hair *sg*
■ SM surplus
supergigante [superdʒi'gante] SM (*Sci*) supergiant
Super-Io [super 'io] SM INV (*Psic*) superego
superiora [supe'rjora] SF (*Rel*: *anche*: **madre superiora**) mother superior
superiore [supe'rjore] AGG **1** (*intelligenza, qualità*) superior; (*numero*) greater; (*quantità, somma*) larger; **intelligenza superiore alla media** above-average intelligence; **la temperatura è superiore alla media** the temperature is above average; **è superiore alle mie forze** it's beyond me; **sono superiore a queste cose** I'm above such things **2** (*che sta più in alto*: *rami, classe*) upper; (*livello*) higher; **la parte superiore del corpo** the upper part of the body; **il corso superiore di un fiume** the upper reaches *pl* of a river; **al piano superiore** on the upper floor; (*di edificio a più piani*) on the floor above; **scuola superiore** *or* **scuole superiori** ≈ secondary school (*Brit*), senior high (school) (*Am*); **istruzione superiore** higher education; **per ordine superiore** on orders from above
■ SM superior; **è il mio superiore** he's my superior
■ SFPL (*Scol*): **le superiori** ≈ secondary school (*Brit*), ≈ senior high (school) (*Am*)
superiorità [superjori'ta] SF INV superiority; **ha dimostrato una netta superiorità sull'avversario**

he was clearly superior to his opponent; **aria di superiorità** air of superiority
superiormente [superjor'mente] AVV on the upper part
superlativo, a [superla'tivo] AGG, SM (*gen, Gramm*) superlative
superlavoro [superla'voro] SM overwork
supermercato [supermer'kato] SM, **supermarket** [super'market] SM INV supermarket
supernova, ae [super'nɔva] SF (*Astron*) supernova
superpotenza [superpo'tentsa] SF (*Pol*) superpower
superprocuratore [superprokura'tɔre] SM (*Dir*) special prosecutor; who deals with organized crime
supersonico, a, ci, che [super'sɔniko] AGG supersonic
superstite [su'pɛrstite] AGG surviving
■ SM/F survivor
superstizione [superstit'tsjone] SF superstition
superstizioso, a [superstit'tsjoso] AGG superstitious
■ SM/F superstitious person
superstrada [super'strada] SF ≈ motorway (*Brit*), ≈ expressway (*Am*)
supertestimone [supertesti'mɔne] SM/F star witness
superuomo [supe'rwɔmo] SM (*pl* **-uomini**) superman
supervisione [supervi'zjone] SF supervision
supervisore [supervi'zore] SM supervisor
supino, a [su'pino] AGG supine; **dormire supino** to sleep on one's back; **accettazione supina** (*fig*) blind acceptance
suppellettile [suppel'lɛttile] SF (*gen*) ornaments *pl*; (*arredo*) furnishings *pl*; (*Archeol*) grave goods
suppergiù [supper'dʒu] AVV roughly, more or less, approximately
suppl. ABBR (= **supplemento**) supp(l)
supplementare [supplemen'tare] AGG **1** (*gen*) extra; (*entrate*) additional; (*treno*) relief *attr*; **tempi supplementari** (*Sport*) extra time *sg*; **hanno segnato nei tempi supplementari** they scored in extra time **2** (*Geom*) supplementary
supplemento [supple'mento] SM supplement
supplente [sup'plɛnte] AGG (*insegnante*) supply *attr* (*Brit*), substitute *attr* (*Am*)
■ SM/F supply *o* substitute teacher
supplenza [sup'plɛntsa] SF (*Scol*): **fare supplenza** to do supply (*Brit*) *o* substitute (*Am*) teaching; **ha avuto una supplenza di un anno** he's been asked to do a year's supply *o* substitute teaching
suppletivo, a [supple'tivo] AGG (*gen*) supplementary; (*sessione d'esami*) extra
supplì [sup'pli] SM INV (*Culin*) rice croquette
supplica, che ['supplika] SF (*Rel, fig*) supplication, plea; **con un tono di supplica** in an imploring voice
supplicare [suppli'kare] VT to implore, beseech; **ti supplico, non andartene** don't go, I beg you
supplichevole [suppli'kevole] AGG imploring
supplichevolmente [supplikevol'mente] AVV imploringly
supplire [sup'plire] VT to stand in for, replace temporarily
■ VI (*aus* **avere**) **supplire a** (*difetto, mancanza*) to make up for, compensate for
supplizio, zi [sup'plittsjo] SM (*tortura*) torture; (*fig*) torment; **fu condotto al supplizio** (*a morte*) he was led to execution
suppongo [sup'pongo], **supponi** *ecc* [sup'poni] VB *vedi* supporre
supporre [sup'porre] VT IRREG (*gen*) to suppose; **supponiamo che...** let's *o* just suppose that ...; **suppongo che sia lo stesso** I imagine it's the same; **suppongo di sì/di no** I suppose so/not
supporto [sup'pɔrto] SM (*sostegno*) support; (*struttura*) stand, holder
supposizione [suppozit'tsjone] SF supposition; **le mie sono solo supposizioni** I'm only guessing; **è una supposizione infondata** it's a groundless assumption
supposta [sup'posta] SF (*Med*) suppository
supposto [sup'posto] PP *di* **supporre**; **supposto che...** CONG supposing that ...
suppurare [suppu'rare] VI (*aus* **avere**) to suppurate
suppurazione [suppurat'tsjone] SF suppuration
supremazia [supremat'tsia] SF supremacy
supremo, a [su'prɛmo] AGG (*gen*) supreme; **con supremo disprezzo** with the utmost contempt; **l'ora suprema** (*fig*) one's last hour; **il giudizio supremo** (*Rel*) the Last Judgement
surclassare [surklas'sare] VT to outclass
surgelamento [surdʒela'mento] SM (deep-)freezing
surgelare [surdʒe'lare] VT to (deep-)freeze
surgelato, a [surdʒe'lato] AGG (deep-)frozen; **cibo surgelato** frozen food
■ SMPL: **i surgelati** frozen food *sg*
surmenage [syrmə'naʒ] SM INV (*fisico*) overwork; (*mentale*) mental strain; (*Sport*) overtraining
surplus [syr'ply] SM INV (*Econ*) surplus; **surplus di manodopera** overmanning
surreale [surre'ale] AGG surrealistic
surrealismo [surrea'lizmo] SM surrealism
surrenale [surre'nale] SF (*Anat*: *anche*: **ghiandola surrenale**) adrenal gland
surriscaldamento [surriskalda'mento] SM (*gen, Tecn*) overheating
surriscaldare [surriskal'dare] VT, **surriscaldarsi** VIP (*gen, Tecn*) to overheat
surriscaldato, a [surriskal'dato] AGG overheated
surrogato, a [surro'gato] AGG, SM substitute *attr*
suscettibile [suʃʃet'tibile] AGG **1** (*permaloso*) touchy, sensitive; **è molto suscettibile** she's very touchy **2** **suscettibile di** (*cambiamento*) subject to; **suscettibile di miglioramento** open to improvement
suscettibilità [suʃʃettibili'ta] SF touchiness; **urtare la suscettibilità di qn** to hurt sb's feelings
suscitare [suʃʃi'tare] VT (*provocare*) to cause, provoke; (*destare*: *ira*) to arouse; **suscitare uno scroscio di applausi** to provoke thunderous applause
sushi ['suʃʃi] SM, AGG INV sushi
susina [su'sina] SF plum
susino [su'sino] SM plum (tree)
suspense [səs'pens] SF INV suspense
susseguire [susse'gwire] VT, VI (*aus* **essere**) to follow; **da ciò sussegue che...** it follows that ...
▶ **susseguirsi** VR (*uso reciproco*) to succeed each other, follow each other; **le sorprese continuavano a susseguirsi** there was a continual succession of surprises
sussidiario, ria, ri, rie [sussi'djarjo] AGG (*gen*) subsidiary; (*fermata*) extra; (*nave*) supply *attr*
sussidio, di [sus'sidjo] SM **1** (*aiuto*) aid; **sussidi audiovisivi** audiovisual aids; **sussidi didattici** teaching aids **2** (*sovvenzione*) subsidy; **sussidio di disoccupazione** unemployment benefit (*Brit*) *o* benefits *pl* (*Am*); **sussidio per malattia** sickness benefit

Ss

sussiego [sus'sjɛgo] SM haughtiness; **con aria di sussiego** haughtily
sussistenza [sussis'tɛntsa] SF **1** (*esistenza*) existence **2** (*sostentamento*) subsistence; **mezzi di sussistenza** means of subsistence **3** (*Mil*) provisioning
sussistere [sus'sistere] VI (*aus* **essere**) (*esistere*) to exist; (*essere fondato: motivi*) to be valid *o* sound
sussultare [sussul'tare] VI (*aus* **avere**) (*per spavento*) to start
sussulto [sus'sulto] SM start; **dare** *o* **avere un sussulto** to give a start, start
sussurrare [sussur'rare] VT to whisper; **gli sussurrò qualcosa all'orecchio** he whispered something in his ear; **si sussurra che...** it's rumoured (*Brit*) *o* rumored (*Am*) that ...
■ VI (*aus* **avere**) (*fronde*) to rustle; (*acque*) to murmur
sussurro [sus'surro] SM (*vedi vb*) whisper; rustle; murmur
sutura [su'tura] SF (*Med*) suture
suturare [sutu'rare] VT (*Med*) to stitch up, suture
suvvia [suv'via] ESCL come on!
suzione [sut'tsjone] SF sucking
SV SIGLA = *Savona*
■ ABBR = **Signoria Vostra**
svagare [zva'gare] VT (*divertire*) to amuse; (*distrarre*): **svagare qn** to take sb's mind off things
▶ **svagarsi** VR (*divertirsi*) to amuse o.s.; (*distrarsi*) to take one's mind off things
svagato, a [zva'gato] AGG (*persona*) absent-minded; (*scolaro*) inattentive
svago, ghi ['zvago] SM (*riposo*) relaxation; (*passatempo*) pastime, amusement; **l'ho fatto per svago** I did it just to pass the time
svaligiare [zvali'dʒare] VT (*banca*) to rob; (*casa*) burgle (*Brit*), burglarize (*Am*)
svaligiatore, trice [zvalidʒa'tore] SM/F (*di banca*) robber; (*di casa*) burglar
svalutare [zvalu'tare] VT (*Econ*) to devalue; (*fig*) to belittle
▶ **svalutarsi** VIP (*Econ*) to be devalued
svalutazione [zvalutat'tsjone] SF (*Econ*) devaluation
svampito, a [zvam'pito] AGG absent-minded
■ SM/F absent-minded person
svanire [zva'nire] VI (*aus* **essere**) (*anche fig*) to disappear, vanish; (*rumore*) to fade; **svanire nel nulla** to disappear *o* vanish completely
svanito, a [zva'nito] AGG (*fig: persona*) absent-minded
■ SM/F absent-minded person
svantaggiato, a [zvantad'dʒato] AGG at a disadvantage; **i bambini svantaggiati** disadvantaged children
svantaggio, gi [zvan'taddʒo] SM disadvantage; (*inconveniente*) drawback, disadvantage; **i vantaggi e gli svantaggi della situazione** the advantages and disadvantages of the situation; **tornerà a suo svantaggio** it will work against you; **sono in svantaggio rispetto a te** you have an advantage over me; **essere in svantaggio di due gol** (*Calcio*) to be two goals down; **essere in svantaggio di due minuti** (*Sport*) to be two minutes behind
svantaggiosamente [zvantaddʒosa'mente] AVV disadvantageously
svantaggioso, a [zvantad'dʒoso] AGG disadvantageous; **è un'offerta svantaggiosa per me** it is not in my interest to accept this offer; **è un prezzo svantaggioso** it is not an attractive price
svaporare [zvapo'rare] VI (*aus* **essere**) to evaporate
svaporato, a [zvapo'rato] AGG (*bibita*) flat
svariatamente [zvarjata'mente] AVV: **un tessuto svariatamente colorato** a multicoloured fabric
svariato, a [zva'rjato] AGG (*numeroso*) various; (*vario, diverso*) varied; **di questa macchina esistono svariati modelli** this car comes in a variety of models
svasare [zva'zare] VT **1** (*pianta*) to repot **2** (*Cucito: gonna*) to flare
svasato, a [zva'zato] AGG (*gonna*) flared
svastica, che ['zvastika] SF swastika
svedese [zve'dese] AGG **1** (*della Svezia*) Swedish; **il governo svedese** the Swedish government **2 (fiammiferi) svedesi** safety matches
■ SM/F Swede; **gli svedesi** the Swedes
■ SM (*lingua*) Swedish; **parla svedese** he speaks Swedish
sveglia ['zveʎʎa] SF **1** (*azione*) waking up; (*Mil*) reveille; **la sveglia è alle 7** we have to get up at 7; **mi può dare la sveglia alle 9?** would you wake me up at 9?; **suonare la sveglia** (*Mil*) to sound the reveille **2** (*orologio*) alarm (clock); **hai puntato la sveglia?** have you set the alarm clock?; **non ho sentito la sveglia stamattina** I didn't hear the alarm clock this morning; **sveglia telefonica** alarm call
svegliare [zveʎ'ʎare] VT (*persona*) to wake (up), waken; (*fig: sentimenti*) to awaken, arouse; **svegliami alle 7** wake me up at 7; **la camminata ha svegliato il suo appetito** the walk gave him an appetite
▶ **svegliarsi** VR to wake up; (*fig*) to waken o.s. up; **mi sveglio sempre presto** I always wake up early
sveglio, glia, gli, glie ['zveʎʎo] AGG (*gen*) awake; (*fig: attento, pronto*) quick-witted, alert; (*: furbo*) smart; **sei sveglio?** are you awake?; **ero sveglio quando ha telefonato** I was awake when he phoned; **un ragazzo sveglio** a bright boy; **non è molto sveglio** he's not very bright
svelare [zve'lare] VT (*segreto*) to reveal; (*mistero*) to uncover
▶ **svelarsi** VR to show o.s.; **con quell'azione si è svelato per quello che è** that action has shown him up for what he is
svellere ['zvellere] VT to uproot
sveltamente [zvelta'mente] AVV (*vedi agg*) quickly; briskly; quick-wittedly
sveltezza [zvel'tettsa] SF (*gen*) speed; (*mentale*) quick-wittedness
sveltire [zvel'tire] VT (*gen*) to speed up; (*procedura*) to streamline; **sveltire il traffico** to speed up the flow of traffic; **sveltire il passo** to quicken one's pace
▶ **sveltirsi** VR (*fig: persona*) to waken o.s. up
svelto, a ['zvɛlto] AGG (*gen*) quick; (*passo*) brisk; (*fig: persona: sveglio*) quick-witted, alert; (*linea*) slim, slender; **essere svelto di mano** (*rubare*) to be light-fingered; (*picchiare*) to be free with one's hands *o* fists; **alla svelta** quickly; **facciamo alla svelta** let's get a move on; **svelto, vieni qua!** quick, come here!
svenare [zve'nare] VT to slash the veins of; (*fig: privare di tutto*) to bleed dry
▶ **svenarsi** VR to slash one's wrists; (*fig*) to reduce o.s. to poverty
svendere ['zvendere] VT to sell off, clear
svendita ['zvendita] SF (*Comm*) (clearance) sale; **una svendita di fine stagione** an end-of-season sale; **in svendita** in a sale; **ho comprato questo cappotto in svendita** I bought this coat in a sale
svenevole [zve'nevole] AGG mawkish
svengo *ecc* ['zvɛngo] VB *vedi* **svenire**

svenimento [zveni'mento] SM fainting fit, faint; **avere uno svenimento** to faint
svenire [zve'nire] VI IRREG (*aus* **essere**) to faint, pass out
sventare [zven'tare] VT to foil, thwart
sventatezza [zventa'tettsa] SF (*qualità: distrazione*) absent-mindedness; (*: mancanza di prudenza*) rashness; **è stata una sventatezza da parte sua accettare...** it was rash of him to accept ...
sventato, a [zven'tato] AGG (*distratto*) scatterbrained; (*imprudente*) rash
■ SM/F scatterbrain
sventola ['zvɛntola] SF **1** (*fig: sberla*) slap; **mollare una sventola a qn** to slap sb **2 orecchie a sventola** sticking-out ears
sventolare [zvento'lare] VT (*bandiera*) to wave
■ VI (*aus* **avere**) to flutter; **sulla torre del castello sventolavano delle bandiere** flags were waving on the castle tower
sventrare [zven'trare] VT (*animale*) to disembowel; (*persona*) to rip open; **hanno completamente sventrato il centro medievale** they have demolished the medieval town centre
sventura [zven'tura] SF (*sorte avversa*) misfortune; (*disgrazia*) mishap; **per colmo di sventura** to crown it all; **è stata una sventura** it was a piece of bad luck; **compagno di sventura** (*scherz*) fellow sufferer
sventuratamente [zventurata'mente] AVV unluckily, unfortunately
sventurato, a [zventu'rato] AGG unlucky, unfortunate
■ SM/F (*sfortunato*) unlucky person; (*scherz*) poor unfortunate
svenuto, a [sve'nuto] PP *di* **svenire**
sverginare [zverdʒi'nare] VT to deflower
svergognare [zvergoɲ'ɲare] VT to shame
svergognatamente [zvergoɲɲata'mente] AVV shamelessly
svergognato, a [zvergoɲ'ɲato] AGG (*privo di: pudore*) shameless, brazen; (*: ritegno*) impudent
■ SM/F (*vedi agg*) shameless person; impudent person
svernare [zver'nare] VI (*aus* **avere**) to winter, spend the winter
sverniciatore [zvernitʃa'tore] SM (*Tecn*) paint stripper
sverrò *ecc* [zver'rɔ] VB *vedi* **svenire**
svestire [zves'tire] VT to undress
▶ **svestirsi** VR to get undressed
svettare [zvet'tare] VI (*aus* **avere**) (*montagna*): **svettare nel cielo** to stand out against the sky
Svezia ['zvɛtsja] SF Sweden; **ti è piaciuta la Svezia?** did you like Sweden?; **andrò in Svezia quest'estate** I'm going to Sweden this summer
svezzamento [zvettsa'mento] SM (*anche fig*) weaning
svezzare [zvet'tsare] VT to wean
sviare [zvi'are] VT (*sospetti*) to divert; (*attenzione*) to distract; (*colpo*) to ward off; (*traviare*) to lead astray; **sviare le indagini della polizia** to put the police off the track; **sviare il discorso** to change the subject
svicolare [zviko'lare] VI (*aus* **essere** *o* **avere**) (*scantonare*) to slip down an alley; (*fig*) to sneak off
svignarsela [zviɲ'ɲarsela] VIP to slip away, sneak off
svilimento [zvili'mento] SM debasement
svilire [zvi'lire] VT to debase
sviluppare [zvilup'pare] VT (*gen, Fot, Mat*) to develop; (*commercio*) to expand; (*incendio*) to cause; (*gas*) to emit; **hai già fatto sviluppare le foto?** have you had the photos developed yet?
▶ **svilupparsi** VIP (*gen*) to develop; (*città*) to expand, grow; (*commercio*) to develop, expand; **si sviluppano dei gas** there is a build-up of gas
sviluppatrice [zviluppa'tritʃe] SF (*Fot, Chim*) developer
sviluppo [zvi'luppo] SM (*gen, Fot, Mat,Econ*) development; (*di città*) development, growth; (*di concetto, tema*) development, treatment; (*di industria*) expansion; **gli sviluppi della situazione** the developments in the situation; **in via di sviluppo** in the process of development; **paesi in via di sviluppo** developing countries; **sviluppo economico** economic growth; **sviluppo sostenibile** sustainable development
svincolare [zvinko'lare] VT (*da vincolo*) to free, release; (*Comm: merce*) to clear
▶ **svincolarsi** VR to free o.s.
svincolo ['zvinkolo] SM **1** (*Aut*) motorway (*Brit*) *o* expressway (*Am*) intersection **2** (*Comm*) clearance
sviolinata [zvioli'nata] SF (*fam*) fawning
svisare [zvi'zare] VT (*fig: fatti*) to twist
sviscerare [zviʃʃe'rare] VT (*fig: argomento*) to examine *o* analyse in depth
svisceratamente [zviʃʃerata'mente] AVV passionately
sviscerato, a [zviʃʃe'rato] AGG (*amore, odio*) passionate
svista ['zvista] SF oversight, slip
svitare [zvi'tare] VT to unscrew
svitato, a [zvi'tato] (*fam*) AGG (*persona*) unhinged, nutty
■ SM/F screwball
Svizzera ['zvittsera] SF Switzerland; **ti è piaciuta la Svizzera?** did you like Switzerland?; **andrò in Svizzera quest'inverno** I'm going to Switzerland this winter
svizzero, a ['zvittsero] AGG, SM/F Swiss *inv*; **il formaggio svizzero** Swiss cheese; **gli svizzeri** the Swiss
svogliatamente [zvoʎʎata'mente] AVV (*vedi agg*) listlessly; indolently
svogliatezza [zvoʎʎa'tettsa] SF (*vedi agg*) listlessness; indolence
svogliato, a [zvoʎ'ʎato] AGG (*senza entusiasmo*) listless; (*pigro*) lazy, indolent
■ SM/F lazybones *sg*
svolazzare [zvolat'tsare] VI (*aus* **avere**) to flutter (about)
svolazzo [zvo'lattso] SM (*fig: di calligrafia*) flourish
svolgere ['zvɔldʒere] VB IRREG
■ VT (*rotolo*) to unroll; (*gomitolo*) to unwind; (*fig: argomento, tema*) to discuss, develop; (*: piano, programma*) to carry out; **svolgere un tema** to write an essay; **che attività svolge?** what does she do?; **quale professione svolge?** what is your occupation?;
▶ **svolgersi** VIP (*filo*) to unwind; (*rotolo*) to unroll; (*fig: vita, eventi: procedere*) to go on; (*: aver luogo: scena, film*) to be set, take place; **come si sono svolti veramente i fatti?** how did it actually happen?; **ecco come si sono svolti i fatti** this was the sequence of events; **tutto si è svolto secondo i piani** everything went according to plan
svolgimento [zvoldʒi'mento] SM (*di tema*) discussion; (*di programma*) carrying out; **lo svolgimento dei fatti** the sequence of events
svolsi *ecc* ['zvɔlsi] VB *vedi* **svolgere**
svolta ['zvɔlta] SF (*curva*) turn, bend; (*fig: mutamento*) turning point; **divieto di svolta a sinistra** no left turn; **prendi la prima svolta a destra** take the first turning on your right; **svolta a destra/a sinistra** (*Pol*) swing to the right/to the left; **essere ad una svolta nella propria vita** to be at a crossroads in one's life

Ss

svoltare [zvol'tare] VI (*aus* avere) to turn; **all'incrocio svolta a destra** turn right at the junction
svolto, a ['zvɔlto] PP *di* **svolgere**
SVP [ɛssevu'pi] SIGLA M (= **Sudtiroler Volkspartei**) South Tyrol People's Party; *party that seeks autonomy for the Alto Adige*
svuotamento [zvwota'mento] SM emptying
svuotare [zvwo'tare] VT (*vuotare*) to empty (out); (: *fig*): **svuotare di** to deprive of; **ho dovuto svuotare tutti i cassetti per trovarlo** I had to empty all the drawers to find it
Swaziland ['swadziland] SM Swaziland
Sydney ['sidnei] SF Sydney

T, t [ti] SF O M INV (*lettera*) T, t; **T come Taranto** ≈ T for Tommy
T [ti] ABBR = **tabaccheria**
t [ti] ABBR **1** = **tara 2** = **tonnellata**
TA SIGLA = *Taranto*
tab. ABBR (= **tabella**) tab. (= *table*)
tabaccaio, aia, ai, aie [tabak'kajo] SM/F tobacconist (*Brit*), tobacco dealer (*Am*)
tabaccheria [tabakke'ria] SF tobacconist's (shop) (*Brit*), tobacco *o* smoke shop (*Am*)

TABACCHERIA

Cigarettes and tobacco can be purchased at **tabaccherie**, which have a sign outside with a white T on a black background. All tobacconists sell postage stamps, stamps for official documents and bus tickets, and some also sell newspapers.

tabacchiera [tabak'kjɛra] SF snuffbox
tabacco, chi [ta'bakko] SM tobacco
tabagismo [tabe'dʒizmo] SM nicotine *o* smoking addiction
tabagista [taba'dʒista] SM/F (*Med*) nicotine addict; (*fumatore incallito*) heavy smoker
tabella [ta'bɛlla] SF (*prospetto*) table, list; (*cartellone*) board; (*Inform*) array; **tabella di marcia** schedule; **tabella dei prezzi** price list
tabellina [tabel'lina] SF (*Scol*) (multiplication) table; **studiare la tabellina del 3** to learn one's 3 times table
tabellone [tabel'lone] SM (*per pubblicità*) billboard; (*per informazioni*) notice board (*Brit*), bulletin board (*Am*); (: *in stazione*) timetable board
tabernacolo [taber'nakolo] SM tabernacle
tabù [ta'bu] AGG INV, SM INV taboo; **un argomento tabù** a taboo subject
tabula rasa ['tabula 'raza] SF tabula rasa; **fare tabula rasa** (*fig*) to make a clean sweep; **ha fatto tabula rasa di tutti i dolci** he polished off all the cakes
tabulare [tabu'lare] VT (*compilare una tabella*) to tabulate
tabulato [tabu'lato] SM (*Inform*) printout
tabulatore [tabula'tore] SM (*anche*: **tasto tabulatore**) tabulator
tabulatrice [tabula'tritʃe] SF (*Inform*) printer
tabulazione [tabulat'tsjone] SF tabulation
TAC [tak] SIGLA F INV (*Med*) = **Tomografia Assiale Computerizzata 1** (*esame*) CT *o* CAT scan **2** (*apparecchiatura*) CT *o* CAT scanner
tacca, che ['takka] SF (*gen*) notch; (*meno profondo*) nick; **di mezza tacca** (*fig pegg*) mediocre
taccagneria [takkaɲɲe'ria] SF meanness, stinginess
taccagno, a [tak'kaɲɲo] AGG mean, stingy
■SM/F miser, mean *o* stingy person
taccheggiare [takked'dʒare] VT to shoplift
taccheggiatore, trice [takkeddʒa'tore] SM/F shoplifter
taccheggio, gi [tak'keddʒo] SM (*furto*) shoplifting
tacchetto [tak'ketto] SM (*di scarpa*) low heel; (: *Sport*) stud
tacchino [tak'kino] SM turkey
taccia, ce ['tattʃa] SF bad reputation
tacciare [tat'tʃare] VT: **tacciare qn di** (*vigliaccheria ecc*) to accuse sb of
taccio *ecc* ['tattʃo] VB *vedi* **tacere**
tacco, chi ['takko] SM **1** (*di scarpe*) heel; **scarpe senza tacco** flat shoes; **coi tacchi bassi/alti** low-/high-heeled; **tacco a spillo** stiletto (heel) (*Brit*), spike heel (*Am*) **2** (*cuneo per fermare le ruote*) chock
taccuino [takku'ino] SM notebook
tacere [ta'tʃere] VB IRREG
■VI (*aus* **avere**) (*stare in silenzio*) to be silent *o* quiet; (*smettere di parlare*) to fall silent; **continuava a tacere** he remained silent; **taci!** be quiet!; **fatelo tacere** make him be quiet; **tutto taceva** all was silent *o* quiet; **i cannoni tacquero** the cannons fell silent; **mettere a tacere qn** to silence sb; **mettere a tacere qc** to hush sth up
■VT (*particolare, accaduto*) to keep silent about, keep to oneself, say nothing about; **tacere la verità** to hold back the truth
tachicardia [takikar'dia] SF (*Med*) tachycardia
tachimetro [ta'kimetro] SM speedometer

Tt

tacitamente [tatʃita'mente] AVV (*vedi agg*) tacitly; silently
tacitare [tatʃi'tare] VT (*creditore*) to pay off; (*scandalo*) to hush up
Tacito ['tatʃito] SM Tacitus
tacito, a ['tatʃito] AGG (*sottinteso*) tacit, unspoken; (*silenzioso*) silent
taciturno, a [tatʃi'turno] AGG taciturn
taciuto, a [ta'tʃuto] PP *di* **tacere**
tacqui *ecc* ['takkwi] VB *vedi* **tacere**
tactel® ['taktel] SM Tactel®
tafano [ta'fano] SM horsefly
tafferuglio, gli [taffe'ruʎʎo] SM brawl, scuffle
taffettà [taffet'ta] SM INV taffeta
taglia ['taʎʎa] SF **1** (*misura: di abito*) size; **che taglia porti?** what size do you wear *o* take?; **taglia forte** outsize; **taglia unica** one size; **taglie forti** extra large sizes **2** (*misura: di animali*) size **3** (*su criminale*) reward; **c'è una taglia sulla sua testa** there is a price on his head
tagliaboschi [taʎʎa'bɔski] SM INV woodcutter
tagliacarte [taʎʎa'karte] SM INV paperknife
tagliaerba [taʎʎa'ɛrba] SM INV lawn-mower
taglialegna [taʎʎa'leɲɲa] SM INV woodcutter, lumberjack (*Am*)
tagliando [taʎ'ʎando] SM **1** (*cedola*) coupon, voucher; **tagliando controllo bagaglio** (*Aer*) luggage (*Brit*) *o* baggage (*Am*) identification tag **2** (*Aut*): **fare il tagliando** to have one's car serviced
tagliapietre [taʎʎa'pjɛtre] SM INV stonecutter
tagliare [taʎ'ʎare] VT **1** (*gen*) to cut; (*torta, salame*) to cut, slice; (*arrosto*) to carve; (*siepe*) to trim; (*fieno, prato*) to mow; (*grano*) to reap; (*albero*) to fell, cut down; **tagliare qc in due/in più parti** to cut sth in two/into several pieces; **tagliare la gola a qn** to cut *o* slit sb's throat; **tagliare il capo** *o* **la testa a qn** to behead sb, cut sb's head off; **mi tagli una fetta di torta?** would you cut me a slice of cake?; **tagliarsi** to cut oneself; **mi sono tagliato** I've cut myself; **mi sono tagliato un dito** I've cut my finger; **tagliarsi i capelli** to have one's hair cut; **devo tagliarmi i capelli** I need to get my hair cut; **ti sei tagliato i capelli?** have you had your hair cut?; **tagliarsi le unghie** to cut one's nails; **una lama che taglia** a sharp blade; **taglia e incolla** (*Inform*) cut and paste **2** (*articolo, scritto, scena*) to cut; (*acqua, telefono, gas*) to cut off; **mio padre mi ha tagliato i viveri** my father is refusing to support me any more **3** (*intersecare: sogg: strada*) to cut across; **tagliare la strada a qn** (*in macchina*) to cut in on sb; (*a piedi*) to cut across in front of sb **4** (*curva*) to cut; (*traguardo*) to cross; (*palla*) to put a spin on **5** (*carte*) to cut **6** (*vini*) to blend; (*droga*) to cut **7** (*fraseologia*): **tagliare la corda** to sneak off; **tagliare la testa al toro** to settle things once and for all; **tagliare corto** to cut short; **tagliare le gambe a qn** (*fig*) to make it impossible for sb to act, tie sb's hands; **un vino che taglia le gambe** a very strong wine; **tagliare i panni addosso a qn** (*sparlare*) to tear sb to pieces
■ VI (*aus* **avere**) (*prendere una scorciatoia*) to take a short cut; **tagliare per i campi** to cut across the fields; **tagliamo per di là** let's cut across that way
tagliata [taʎ'ʎata] SF *grilled beef sliced and served with olive oil and spices*
tagliatelle [taʎʎa'tɛlle] SFPL tagliatelle *sg*
tagliato, a [taʎ'ʎato] AGG: **essere tagliato per qc** (*fig*) to be cut out for sth
tagliatrice [taʎʎa'tritʃe] SF (*Tecn*) cutter
tagliaunghie [taʎʎa'ungje] SM INV nail clippers *pl*
taglieggiare [taʎʎed'dʒare] VT to extort money from; (*Storia*) to exact a tribute from
taglieggiatore, trice [taʎʎeddʒa'tore] SM/F extortionist
tagliente [taʎ'ʎɛnte] AGG (*lama*) sharp; (*fig: tono, parole*) cutting, sharp
tagliere [taʎ'ʎɛre] SM (*gen*) chopping board; (*per il pane*) bread board
taglierina [taʎʎe'rina] SF (*Tecn: per metalli, tessuti*) cutter; (: *per carta*) guillotine; (: *per fotografie*) trimmer
taglierini [taʎʎe'rini] SMPL (*Culin*) thin soup noodles
taglio, gli ['taʎʎo] SM **1** (*gen: atto*) cutting, cut; (*di capelli*) (hair)cut; (*di fieno, erba*) mowing; (*di vini*) blending; **vino da taglio** blending wine; **dare un taglio netto a qc** (*fig*) to make a clean break with sth; **taglio cesareo** (*Med*) Caesarean section **2** (*effetto*) cut; **farsi un taglio al dito** to cut one's finger; **ha un taglio sulla fronte** he's got a cut on his forehead; **taglio netto** clean cut; **c'erano dei tagli nel film/nel libro** cuts were made in the film (*Brit*) *o* movie (*Am*)/in the book; **un taglio alla spesa pubblica** a cut in public spending **3** (*pezzo: di carne*) piece; (: *di stoffa*) length; **pizza al taglio** pizza by the slice; **banconote di piccolo/grosso taglio** small-/large-denomination notes **4** (*stile: di abito*) cut, style; (: *di capelli*) (hair)style; (: *di pietra preziosa*) cut; **questo taglio di capelli ti dona moltissimo** that hairstyle really suits you; **di taglio classico** with a classic cut; **scuola di taglio** dressmaking school **5** (*di lama*) cutting edge, edge; **colpire qc di taglio** to hit sth on edge *o* edgeways **6** (*Sport*) spin; **dare il taglio alla palla** to put a spin on the ball
tagliola [taʎ'ʎɔla] SF trap, snare
taglione [taʎ'ʎone] SM: **la legge del taglione** the concept of an eye for an eye (and a tooth for a tooth)
tagliuzzare [taʎʎut'tsare] VT to cut into small pieces
Tahiti [ta'iti] SF Tahiti
tailandese [tailan'dese] AGG, SM/F Thai
■ SM (*lingua*) Thai
Tailandia [tai'landja] SF Thailand
tailleur [ta'jœr] SM INV (lady's) suit
talamo ['talamo] SM (*letter*) bridal bed
talare [ta'lare] AGG: **abito** *o* **veste talare** priest's cassock; **indossare l'abito talare** to become a priest
talassemia [talasse'mia] SF (*Med*) thalassaemia (*Brit*), thalassemia (*Am*)
talco, chi ['talko] SM talcum powder

tale ['tale] PAROLA CHIAVE
■ AGG DIMOSTR
1 (*simile, così grande*) such (a); **è di una tale arroganza** he is so arrogant; **tale articolo è in vendita presso tutte le nostre filiali** the above-mentioned article is on sale at all our branches; **tali discorsi sono inaccettabili** such talk is not acceptable; **non avevo mai visto un tale disordine** I had never seen such a mess; **e con tali scuse è riuscito ad evitare la punizione** and with excuses like those he managed to escape punishment; **cosa ti fa credere che nutra tali sentimenti?** what makes you think he feels like that?
2 (*nelle similitudini*): **tale...tale...** like ... like ...; **tale padre tale figlio** like father like son; **è tale quale suo nonno** he's the spitting image of *o* exactly like his grandfather; **il tuo vestito è tale quale il mio** your dress is just *o* exactly like mine; **hanno riportato una vittoria tale, quale non avevano sperato** they won

an even greater victory than they had expected

■ AGG INDEF

1 (*certo*): **quella tale persona desidera parlarti** that man (*o* woman) wants to see you; **ti cercava una tale Giovanna** somebody called Giovanna was looking for you; **ha detto che vedeva un amico, un tal Rossi** he said he was meeting a friend, a certain Rossi

2 (*persona o cosa indeterminata*) such-and-such; **il tale giorno alla tale ora** on such and such a day at such and such a time

■ PRON INDEF

1 **un(una) tale** (*una certa persona*) someone; (*quella persona già menzionata*) the one, the person, that person, that man/woman; **è fidanzata con un tale dell'ufficio contabilità** she's engaged to someone in accounts; **hai più visto quel tale di cui mi dicevi?** did you ever see that person *o* man you were telling me about again?; **ha telefonato di nuovo quella tale** that woman phoned again

2 **il tal dei tali** whatshisname; **la tal dei tali** whatshername; **diciamo che l'ho saputo dal tal dei tali** let's just say I had *o* heard it from you know who

talea [ta'lɛa] SF (*Giardinaggio*) cutting

talebano [tale'bano] SM Taliban

taleggio [ta'leddʒo] SM *type of soft cheese*

talento [ta'lɛnto] SM (*capacità*) talent; (*persona*) talented person; **avere talento per qc** to have a talent for sth; **essere privo/pieno di talento** to be untalented/very talented

Talete [ta'lɛte] SM Thales

talismano [taliz'mano] SM talisman

talk-show ['tɔːkʃou] SM INV chat (*Brit*) *o* talk (*Am*) show

tallonaggio, gi [tallo'naddʒo] SM (*Rugby*) close marking

tallonamento [tallona'mento] SM (*di giocatore*) close marking

tallonare [tallo'nare] VT (*inseguire*) to follow (hot) on the heels of, pursue; (*Sport*) to pursue; **tallonare il pallone** (*Rugby*) to heel the ball; (*Calcio*) to back-heel the ball

tallonata [tallo'nata] SF (*Rugby*) heel; (*Calcio*) back-heel

talloncino [tallon'tʃino] SM stub, counterfoil (*Brit*); **talloncino del prezzo** (*di medicinali*) tear-off tag

tallone [tal'lone] SM heel; **tallone di Achille** Achilles' heel

LO SAPEVI...?
tallone non si traduce mai con la parola inglese *talon*

talmente [tal'mente] AVV (*così tanto*) so; **sono talmente contento!** I'm so happy!; **ero talmente emozionato che...** I was so excited that ...; **l'Irlanda mi è talmente piaciuta che ci tornerei domani** I liked Ireland so much that I'd go back there tomorrow; **è stato talmente ingenuo da cascarci** he was naïve enough to fall for it

Talmud [tal'mud] SM: **il Talmud** the Talmud

talora [ta'lora] AVV = **talvolta**

talpa ['talpa] SF (*Zool, fig*) mole; **cieco come una talpa** as blind as a bat

talvolta [tal'vɔlta] AVV sometimes, at times

tamarindo [tama'rindo] SM tamarind

tamburellare [tamburel'lare] VI (*aus* **avere**) (*pioggia*) to drum; **tamburellare con le dita** to drum one's fingers

tamburello [tambu'rɛllo] SM (*Mus*) tambourine; (*gioco*) *ball game played with tambourine-shaped bats*

tamburino [tambu'rino] SM drummer boy

tamburo [tam'buro] SM 1 (*Mus: strumento*) drum; (*: suonatore*) drummer; **a tamburo battente** (*fig*) immediately, at once 2 (*Tecn, Aut*) drum; (*di armi*) cylinder; (*di orologio*) barrel; **freni a tamburo** drum brakes; **pistola a tamburo** revolver

tamerice [tame'ritʃe] SF tamarisk

tamia ['tamja] SM INV: **tamia striato** chipmunk

Tamigi [ta'midʒi] SM: **il Tamigi** the Thames

tamil [ta'mil] SM/F INV Tamil

tampinare [tamp'nare] VT (*fam*) to bug

tamponamento [tampona'mento] SM (*Aut*) collision; **tamponamento a catena** pile-up

tamponare [tampo'nare] VT 1 (*urtare: macchina*) to go into the back of; **abbiamo tamponato un furgone** we went into the back of a van 2 (*otturare*) to plug

tampone [tam'pone] SM 1 (*assorbente interno*) tampon 2 (*Med: gen*) plug; (*: di cotone*) wad; (*: per pulire una ferita*) swab; (*: per stendere un liquido*) pad 3 (*cuscinetto: per timbri*) ink-pad; (*: di carta assorbente*) blotter

■ AGG INV: **provvedimento tampone** stopgap measure

tamtam, tam-tam [tam'tam] SM INV (*Mus*) tomtom; (*fig*): **il tamtam dei carcerati** the prison grapevine

tana ['tana] SF (*gen*) lair, den; (*di coniglio*) burrow; (*fig: nascondiglio*) den, hideout

tandem ['tandem] SM INV (*bicicletta*) tandem; (*fig: coppia*) duo

tanfo ['tanfo] SM stench

tanga ['tanga] SM INV tanga

tangente [tan'dʒɛnte] AGG (*Geom*): **tangente (a)** tangential (to)

■ SF 1 (*Geom*) tangent; **filare per la tangente** (*fig: svignarsela*) to make one's getaway; **partire per la tangente** (*fig: divagare*) to go off at a tangent 2 (*pizzo*) protection money *sg*; (*bustarella*) kickback; **lo scandalo delle tangenti** the kickback scandal

tangentizio, zia, zi, zie [tandʒen'tittsjo] AGG (*relativo alle tangenti*) corrupt

tangentopoli [tandʒen'tɔpoli] SF *corruption scandal involving government ministers, industrialists and businessmen: it began in 1992, in Milan, which was consequently dubbed Tangentopoli (Bribesville)*

tangenza [tan'dʒɛntsa] SF (*Geom*) tangency; (*Aer*) ceiling

tangenziale [tandʒen'tsjale] AGG (*Geom*) tangential; **retta tangenziale** tangent

■ SF (*anche:* **strada tangenziale**) bypass

Tangeri ['tandʒeri] SF Tangier(s)

tanghero ['tangero] SM (*pegg*) bumpkin

tangibile [tan'dʒibile] AGG tangible

tangibilità [tandʒibili'ta] SF tangibleness

tangibilmente [tandʒibil'mente] AVV tangibly

tango, ghi ['tango] SM tango

tanica, che ['tanika] SF (*contenitore*) jerry can; (*Naut: serbatoio*) tank

tannino [tan'nino] SM tannin

tantino [tan'tino] **un tantino** AVV (*un po'*) a little, a bit; (*alquanto*) rather

■ SM: **un tantino di** a little bit of

tanto, a ['tanto] PAROLA CHIAVE

■ AGG INDEF

1 (*molto: quantità*) a lot of, much; (*: numero*) a lot of, many; (*così tanto: quantità*) so much, such a lot of;

Tt

(: *numero*) so many, such a lot of; **ogni tanti chilometri/giorni** every so many kilometres/days; **tante persone, tante opinioni diverse** there are as many different opinions as there are people; **c'è ancora tanta strada da fare!** there's still a long way to go!; **tante volte** so many times, so often
2 (*rafforzativo*) such; **l'ha detto con tanta gentilezza** he said it with such kindness *o* so kindly; **ho aspettato per tanto tempo** I waited so long *o* for such a long time
3 **tanto… quanto…** (*quantità*) as much … as …; (*numero*) as many … as …; **ho tanta pazienza quanta ne hai tu** I am as patient as you are, I have as much patience as you (have); **ha tanti amici quanti nemici** he has as many friends as he has enemies; **ho tanti libri quanti ne ha lui** I have as many books as him *o* as he has
■ PRON INDEF
1 (*molto*) much, a lot; (*così tanto*) so much, such a lot; (*plurale*): **tanti(e)** (*molti*) many, a lot; (*così tanti*) so many, such a lot; **è una ragazza come tante** she's like any other girl; **è solo uno dei tanti che…** he's just one of the many who …; **credevo ce ne fosse tanto** I thought there was (such) a lot, I thought there was plenty; **se cerchi un bicchiere, lassù ce ne sono tanti** if you are looking for a glass there are a lot *o* lots up there; **tanti credono sia semplice farlo** many people believe it is easy to do
2 (*altrettanto*): **tanto quanto** as much as; (*plurale*): **tanti quanti** as many as; **tempo? ne ho tanto quanto basta** time? I have as much as I need
3 (*con valore indeterminato*): **riceve un tanto al mese** he receives so much a month; **costa un tanto al metro** it costs so much per *o* a metre; **della somma che ho a disposizione tanto andrà per il vitto, tanto per l'alloggio** of the money I've got so much will go on food and so much on accommodation; **nell'anno millecinquecento e tanti** in the year fifteen hundred and something
4 (*fraseologia*): **me ne ha dette tante!** he gave me a real mouthful!; **di tanto in tanto** every so often, (every) now and again; **è rimasto con tanto di naso** he was left feeling disappointed; **tanto di guadagnato!** so much the better!; **tanto meglio così!** so much the better!; **se tanto mi dà tanto** oh well, if that's the case …; **guardare qc con tanto d'occhi** to gaze wide-eyed at sth; **ogni tanto** every so often, (every) now and then; **ascoltava con tanto d'orecchi** he was all ears; **tanto vale che…** you may *o* might as well …
■ AVV
1 (*così, in questo modo: con verbo*) so much, such a lot; (: *con avverbio, aggettivo*) so; (*così a lungo*) so long; **tanto… che…** so … (that) …; **è tanto bello che sembra finto** it's so beautiful (that) it seems unreal; **tanto… da…** so … as …; **saresti tanto gentile da prendermi una tazza?** would you be so kind as to get me a cup?; **è stato tanto idiota da crederci** he was stupid enough to believe it; **non lavorare tanto!** don't work so hard!; **perché piangeva tanto?** why was she crying so (much)?; **stanno tanto bene insieme!** they go so well together!
2 (*nei comparativi*): **tanto… quanto…** as … as …; **è tanto gentile quanto discreto** he is as kind as he is discreet; **non è poi tanto difficile quanto sembra** it is not as difficult as it seems after all; **mi piace non tanto per l'aspetto quanto per il suo carattere** I like her not so much for her looks as for her personality; **conosco tanto Carlo quanto suo padre** I know both Carlo and his father
3 (*molto*) very; **un'ora a dir tanto** an hour at the most; **non ci vuole tanto a capirlo** it doesn't take much to understand it; **non è poi tanto giovane** he is not all that young after all; **l'ho visto tanto giù** he seemed *o* looked very down to me; **scusami tanto** I'm very sorry, do excuse me; **sono tanto tanto contento di vederti** I'm so very happy to see you; **vengo tanto volentieri** I'd love to come
4 (*a lungo*) (for) long; **starai via tanto?** will you be away (for) long?; **non stare fuori tanto** don't stay out for long
5 (*solamente*) just; **tanto per cambiare** (*anche iro*) just for a change; **parla tanto per parlare** he talks just for the sake of talking; **tanto per ridere** just for a laugh; **una volta tanto** just for once
6 (*con valore moltiplicativo*): **due volte tanto** twice as much; **tre volte tanto** three times as much
7 **tanto più insisti tanto più non mollerà** the more you insist the more stubborn he'll be; **tanto più lo vedo tanto meno mi piace** the more I see him the less I like him
■ CONG after all; **lo farò, tanto non mi costa niente** I'll do it, after all it won't cost me anything; **fanne a meno, tanto a me non importa** do without then, I don't care; **tanto è inutile** in any case it's useless

Tanzania [tan'dzanja] SF Tanzania
tapioca [ta'pjɔka] SF tapioca
tapiro [ta'piro] SM tapir
tapis roulant [ta'pi ru'lã] SM INV travolator (*Brit*), moving sidewalk (*Am*)
tappa ['tappa] SF **1** (*luogo di sosta, fermata*) stop, halt; **la prima tappa del nostro viaggio sarà Pisa** the first stop on our journey will be Pisa; **fare tappa** to stop off; **abbiamo fatto tappa a Bath** we stopped off in Bath
2 (*Sport: parte di percorso*) stage, leg; (*fig: stadio*) stage; **a tappe** in stages; **bruciare le tappe** (*fig*) to get there fast

LO SAPEVI...?
tappa non si traduce mai con la parola inglese ***tap***

tappabuchi [tappa'buki] SM/F INV stopgap; **fare da tappabuchi** to act as a stopgap
tappare [tap'pare] VT (*otturare*) to plug, stop up; (: *bottiglia*) to cork; **potresti tappare la bottiglia?** could you put the cork in the bottle, please?; **tapparsi il naso** to hold one's nose; **mi si è tappato il naso** my nose is blocked; **tapparsi le orecchie** to cover one's ears; **tappare un buco** (*fig*) to provide a short-term remedy; **tappare la bocca a qn** (*fig*) to shut sb up; **tapparsi le orecchie/gli occhi** (*fig*) to turn a deaf ear/a blind eye
▶ **tapparsi** VR: **tapparsi in casa** to shut o.s. up at home
tapparella [tappa'rɛlla] SF rolling shutter
tappatrice [tappa'tritʃe] SF (bottle-)corking machine
tappetino [tappe'tino] SM (*per auto*) car mat; **tappetino antiscivolo** (*da bagno*) non-slip mat; **tappetino del mouse** mouse pad
tappeto [tap'peto] SM (*gen*) carpet; (*piccolo*) rug; (*stuoia*) mat; (*per tavolo*) cloth; **un tappeto persiano** a Persian rug; **bombardamento a tappeto** carpet bombing; **andare al tappeto** (*Pugilato*) to go down for the count; (*fig*) to be floored; **mandare qn al tappeto** (*fig*) to floor sb; **mettere sul tappeto** (*fig: questione*) to table; **tappeto erboso** lawn; **tappeto verde** (*panno*) green

baize (cloth); (*tavolo da gioco*) gaming table
tappezzare [tappet'tsare] VT (*pareti*) to paper; (*divano, sedia*) to cover; **tappezzare una stanza di manifesti** to cover a room with posters
tappezzeria [tappettse'ria] SF (*arredamento*) soft furnishings *pl*; (*carta da parati*) wallpaper; (*tessuto*) wall covering; (*di automobile*) upholstery; **in camera da letto c'era la tappezzeria rosa** there was pink wallpaper in the bedroom; **fare da tappezzeria** (*fig*) to be a wallflower
tappezziere, a [tappet'tsjɛre] SM/F upholsterer
tappo ['tappo] SM (*di bottiglia: in sughero*) cork; (*: in vetro, plastica*) stopper; (*di barattolo, serbatoio, radiatore*) cap; (*di penna*) top; (*di vasca, lavandino*) plug; (*scherz: persona bassa*) shorty; **tappi per le orecchie** earplugs; **tappo a corona** bottle top; **tappo salvagocce** dripless pour spout; **tappo di scarico della coppa** (*Aut*) drain plug; **tappo con serratura** (*Aut*) locking petrol cap; **tappo a vite** screw top
TAR [tar] SIGLA M = *Tribunale Amministrativo Regionale*
tara ['tara] SF **1** (*peso*) tare **2** (*Med*) hereditary defect; (*difetto*) flaw
tarantella [taran'tɛlla] SF (*danza*) tarantella
tarantino, a [taran'tino] AGG of *o* from Taranto
■SM/F inhabitant *o* native of Taranto
tarantola [ta'rantola] SF tarantula
tarare [ta'rare] VT (*Comm*) to tare; (*Tecn*) to calibrate
tarato, a [ta'rato] AGG **1** (*Comm*) tared; (*Tecn*) calibrated **2** (*Med*) with a hereditary defect; **ma tu sei tarato** (*scherz*) you're nuts
taratura [tara'tura] SF (*Comm*) taring; (*Tecn*) calibration
tarchiato, a [tar'kjato] AGG stocky, thickset
tardare [tar'dare] VI (*aus* **avere**) to be late; **ha tardato molto** he was very late; **come mai hai tardato tanto?** how come you're so late?; **tardare a fare qc** (*involontariamente*) to be late in doing sth; (*apposta*) to delay doing sth; **scusa se ho tardato a rispondere alla tua lettera, ma...** I'm sorry I've taken so long to reply to your letter, but ...
■VT (*consegna*) to delay
tardi ['tardi] AVV late; **ormai è troppo tardi** it's too late now; **alzarsi tardi** to get up late; **svegliarsi tardi** to wake up late, oversleep; **arrivare tardi** to arrive late; **lavorare fino a tardi** to work late; **fare tardi** (*essere in ritardo*) to be late; (*restare alzato*) to stay up late; **scusa se ho fatto tardi, ho perso l'autobus** I'm sorry I'm late, I missed the bus; **non devo fare tardi stasera, domani ho l'esame** I mustn't stay up late tonight, I've got an exam tomorrow; **meglio tardi che mai** better late than never; **più tardi** later (on); **vi raggiungo più tardi** I'll join you later; **a più tardi!** see you later!; **al più tardi** at the latest; **presto o tardi** sooner or later; **presto o tardi se ne pentirà** sooner or later he'll be sorry; **si è fatto tardi** it is late; **sul tardi** (*verso sera*) late in the day; **ci siamo incontrati sul tardi** we met quite late
tardivamente [tardiva'mente] AVV late
tardivo, a [tar'divo] AGG (*primavera, fioritura, sviluppo*) late; (*rimedio, pentimento*) belated
tardo, a ['tardo] AGG (*lento, ottuso*) slow; (*avanzato: mattinata, primavera*) late; (*tardivo: pentimento*) belated; **nel tardo pomeriggio** late in the afternoon
tardona [tar'dona] SF (*pegg*): **essere una tardona** to be mutton dressed as lamb (*Brit*)
targa, ghe ['targa] SF (*gen*) plate; (*su una porta*) nameplate; (*Aut*) numberplate (*Brit*), license plate (*Am*); (*placca*) plaque; **non sono riuscito a leggere la targa** I couldn't read the number plate; **circolazione a targhe alterne** (*Aut*) *anti-pollution measure whereby, on days with an even date, only cars whose numberplate ends in an even number may be on the road, while on days with an odd date, only cars whose numberplate ends in an odd number may be on the road*
targare [tar'gare] VT (*Aut*) to register
targato, a [tar'gato] AGG (*Aut*): **una macchina targata BO** a car with a Bologna numberplate (*Brit*) *o* license plate (*Am*); (*fig*): **una vacanza targata Soletur** a Soletur holiday; **un attentato targato IRA** a bombing bearing all the hallmarks of the IRA
targhetta [tar'getta] SF (*con nome*) nameplate (*on door*); (*su bagaglio*) name tag
tariffa [ta'riffa] SF (*gen*) rate, tariff; (*di trasporti*) fare; **la tariffa in vigore** the going rate; **tariffa inserzioni per pagina** (*Stampa*) page rate; **tariffa normale** (*gen*) standard rate; (*su mezzi di trasporto*) full fare; **tariffa professionale** fee; **tariffa ridotta** (*gen*) reduced rate; (*su mezzi di trasporto*) reduced *o* concessionary fare; **c'è una tariffa ridotta per i bambini** there are reduced fares for children; **tariffa salariale** wage rate; **tariffa unica** flat rate; **tariffe doganali** customs rates *o* tariff *sg*; **tariffe ferroviarie** train fares; **tariffe postali** postal charges; **tariffe telefoniche** telephone charges
tariffare [tarif'fare] VT (*beni, servizi pubblici*) to fix the charges *o* rates for
tariffario, ria, ri, rie [tarif'farjo] AGG: **aumento tariffario** increase in charges *o* rates
■SM tariff, table of charges
tarlare [tar'lare] VI (*aus* **essere**), **tarlarsi** VIP (*legno*) to have woodworm; (*tessuto*) to be moth-eaten
tarlato, a [tar'lato] AGG (*legno*) worm-eaten; (*tessuto*) moth-eaten
tarlo ['tarlo] SM **1** (*insetto*) woodworm **2 il tarlo della gelosia** the pangs *pl* of jealousy; **il tarlo del dubbio lo assillava** doubts ate away at him
tarma ['tarma] SF moth
tarmare [tar'mare] VI (*aus* **essere**), **tarmarsi** VIP to be moth-eaten
tarmicida, i [tarmi'tʃida] AGG, SM moth-killer
tarocco, chi [ta'rɔkko] SM tarot card; **il gioco dei tarocchi** tarot
tarpare [tar'pare] VT (*fig*): **tarpare le ali a qn** to clip sb's wings
tarso ['tarso] SM (*Anat*) tarsus
TARSU ['tarsu] SIGLA F (= **Tassa Rifiuti Solidi Urbani**) *tax on household refuse*
tartagliare [tartaʎ'ʎare] VI (*aus* **avere**) to stutter, stammer
■VT to mutter
tartan[1] ['tartan] SM INV (*tessuto*) tartan
tartan[2]® ['tartan] SM INV Tartan®
tartaro, a ['tartaro] AGG (*Storia*) Tartar; (*Culin*) tartar(e); **bistecca alla tartara** steak tartare
■SM/F Tartar
tartaruga, ghe [tarta'ruga] SF (*testuggine*) tortoise; (*: di mare*) turtle; (*materiale*) tortoiseshell; **zuppa di tartaruga** turtle soup; **essere lento come una tartaruga** to be a slowcoach (*Brit*) *o* slowpoke (*Am*)
tartassare [tartas'sare] VT (*fam*): **tartassare qn** to give sb the works; **tartassare qn a un esame** to give sb a grilling at an exam; **smettila di tartassare quel piano!** stop thumping on that piano!; **essere tartassato dal fisco** to be hard hit by the taxman
tartina [tar'tina] SF canapé

Tt

tartufo [tar'tufo] SM **1** (*fungo*) truffle; (*semifreddo*) *individual filled chocolate ice-cream cake* **2** **tartufo di mare** (*Zool*) Venus clam **3** (*naso di cane*) nose

tasca, sche ['taska] SF (*gen*) pocket; (*scomparto*: *di valigia*) compartment; (*Zool, Anat*) pouch; **l'ho messo nella tasca della giacca** I put it in my jacket pocket; **tasca dei pantaloni** trouser (*Brit*) *o* pants (*Am*) pocket; **da tasca** pocket *attr*; **non ho un soldo in tasca** (*al momento*) I haven't any money *o* a penny on me; (*essere al verde*) I'm broke; **riempirsi le tasche di qc** to fill one's pockets with sth; **non startene con le mani in tasca** (*fig*) don't just stand there with your hands in your pockets; **non me ne viene niente in tasca** I get nothing out of it; **che cosa me ne viene in tasca?** what's in it for me?; **fare i conti in tasca a qn** to meddle in sb's affairs; **conosco Roma come le mie tasche** I know Rome like the back of my hand; **averne le tasche piene di** to be fed up with; **tasca da pasticciere** piping bag

tascabile [tas'kabile] AGG (*libro*) pocket *attr*; **una calcolatrice tascabile** a pocket calculator; **un'edizione tascabile** a pocket edition
■ SM ≈ paperback

tascapane [taska'pane] SM haversack

taschina [tas'kina] SF (*Filatelia*) stamp envelope

taschino [tas'kino] SM breast pocket

Tasmania [taz'manja] SF Tasmania

tassa ['tassa] SF (*imposta*) tax; (*doganale*) duty; (*Scol, Univ*) fee; **non aveva pagato le tasse** he hadn't paid his taxes; **soggetto a tasse** taxable; **tassa di circolazione** road tax (*Brit*); **tassa di soggiorno** tourist tax; **tasse scolastiche** school fees

tassabile [tas'sabile] AGG taxable

tassametro [tas'sametro] SM taximeter

tassare [tas'sare] VT (*gen*) to tax; (*sogg*: *dogana*) to levy a duty on
► **tassarsi** VR: **tassarsi per** to chip in, contribute

tassativamente [tassativa'mente] AVV (*dire, ordinare*) peremptorily; **è tassativamente vietato** it is strictly forbidden

tassativo, a [tassa'tivo] AGG peremptory

tassazione [tassat'tsjone] SF taxation; **soggetto a tassazione** taxable

tassello [tas'sɛllo] SM **1** (*anche*: **tassello a espansione**) Rawlplug® **2** (*pezzetto*: *di legno, pietra*) plug; (*per vestiti*) gusset; (*assaggio*: *di formaggio, cocomero*) wedge

tassì [tas'si] SM INV = **taxi**

tassidermia [tassider'mia] SF taxidermy

tassidermista, i, e [tassider'mista] SM/F taxidermist

tassista, i, e [tas'sista] SM/F taxi driver, cab driver; **fa il tassista** he's a taxi driver

tasso[1] ['tasso] SM (*di natalità, mortalità*) rate; **tasso agevolato** (*Banca*) special rate; **tasso di cambio** rate of exchange; **tasso di crescita** growth rate; **tasso glicemico** (*Med*) blood sugar level; **tasso d'inquinamento** pollution level; **tasso di interesse** rate of interest; **tasso ufficiale di sconto** (*Econ*) official discount rate

tasso[2] ['tasso] SM (*Bot*) yew

tasso[3] ['tasso] SM (*Zool*) badger

tassonomia [tassono'mia] SF taxonomy

tastare [tas'tare] VT to feel; **tastare il polso a qn** to feel sb's pulse; **tastare il terreno** to test the ground; (*fig*) to see how the land lies

tastiera [tas'tjera] SF (*gen, Mus, Inform*) keyboard; (*di strumenti a corda*) fingerboard; **apparecchio (telefonico) a tastiera** push-button phone

tastierino [tastje'rino] SM: **tastierino numerico** numeric keypad

tastierista [tastje'rista] SM/F (*gen*) keyboard operator, keyboarder; (*Mus*) keyboard(s) player, keyboardist

tasto ['tasto] SM (*gen, Tecn, Mus*) key; (*tatto*) touch, feel; (*fig*: *argomento*) topic, subject; **toccare un tasto delicato** to touch on a delicate subject; **toccare il tasto giusto** (*fig*) to strike the right note; **tasto di controllo** (*Inform*) control key; **tasto funzione** (*Inform*) function key; **tasto delle maiuscole** (*su macchina da scrivere*) shift key; **tasto di ritorno a margine** (*Inform*) return key; **tasto di scelta rapida** (*Inform*) hot key; **tasto tabulatore** (*su macchina da scrivere*) tab (key)

LO SAPEVI...?
tasto non si traduce mai con la parola inglese *taste*

tastoni [tas'toni] AVV: **procedere (a) tastoni** to grope one's way forward

tata ['tata] SF (*linguaggio infantile*) nanny

tattica ['tattika] SF tactics *pl*

tatticamente [tattika'mente] AVV tactically

tatticismo [tatti'tʃizmo] SM use of tactics

tattico, a, ci, che ['tattiko] AGG tactical
■ SM (*Mil, fig*) tactician

tattile ['tattile] AGG tactile

tatto ['tatto] SM **1** (*senso*) touch; **duro al tatto** hard to the touch **2** (*diplomazia*) tact; **aver tatto** to be tactful, have tact; **essere privo di tatto** *or* **non avere tatto** to be tactless

tatuaggio, gi [tatu'addʒo] SM (*operazione*) tattooing; (*disegno*) tattoo; **ha un tatuaggio sul braccio** he's got a tattoo on his arm

tatuare [tatu'are] VT to tattoo
► **tatuarsi** VR to have o.s. tattooed

taumaturgico, a, ci, che [tauma'turdʒiko] AGG (*fig*) miraculous

taumaturgo, ghi [tauma'turgo] SM miracle worker

taurino, a [tau'rino] AGG bull-like; **ha un collo taurino** he is bull-necked

tauromachia [tauroma'kia] SF (*arte*) bullfighting, tauromachy (*termine tecn*); (*corrida*) bullfight

tautologia, gie [tautolo'dʒia] SF tautology

taverna [ta'vɛrna] SF (*osteria*) tavern

tavola ['tavola] SF **1** (*mobile*) table; **a tavola!** come and eat!, dinner's ready!; **essere a tavola** to be having a meal; **preparare la tavola** to lay *o* set the table; **sedersi a tavola** to sit down to eat, sit down at the table; **ama i piaceri della tavola** he enjoys his food; **la buona tavola** good food **2** (*asse*) plank, board; **il mare è una tavola** the sea is like a millpond **3** (*tabella*) table; (*illustrazione*) plate; (*quadro su legno*) panel (painting)
■ **tavola calda** snack bar; **tavola periodica degli elementi** (*Chim*) periodic table; **tavola pitagorica** multiplication table; **tavola reale** (*gioco*) backgammon; **tavola rotonda** (*anche fig*) round table; **tavola a vela** sailboard

tavolata [tavo'lata] SF (*commensali*) table

tavolato [tavo'lato] SM **1** (*gen*) planking, boarding; (*di palco*) boards *pl* **2** (*Geog*) plateau

tavoletta [tavo'letta] SF (*di cioccolata*) bar; **andare a tavoletta** (*Aut*) to go flat out; **tavoletta grafica** (*Inform*) graphics tablet

tavoliere [tavo'ljɛre] SM (*Geog*) tableland, plateau

tavolino [tavo'lino] SM (*gen*) small table; (*scrittoio, banco*) desk; **un bar con i tavolini all'aperto** a café with tables outside; **mettersi a tavolino** to get down to work; **decidere qc a tavolino** (*fig*) to decide sth on a theoretical level *o* in theory; **il risultato della partita è stato deciso a tavolino** the result of the match was decided by the referee; **tavolino da gioco** card table; **tavolino da tè** coffee table

tavolo ['tavolo] SM (*gen*) table; (*scrittoio*) desk; **vieni a sedere al nostro tavolo** come and sit at our table; **da tavolo** table *attr*; **tavolo anatomico** mortuary slab; **tavolo da disegno** drawing board; **tavolo da lavoro** (*gen*) desk; (*Tecn*) workbench; **tavolo dei negoziati** negotiating table; **tavolo operatorio** operating table; **tavolo pieghevole** folding table; **tavolo da ping-pong** table-tennis table; **tavolo a ribalta** drop-leaf table

tavolozza [tavo'lɔttsa] SF (*Arte*) palette

taxi ['taksi] SM INV taxi

tazza ['tattsa] SF (*recipiente*) cup; (*contenuto*) cupful; (*fam: di gabinetto*) bowl, pan (*Brit*); **una tazza di caffè/tè** a cup of coffee/tea; **tazza da caffè** coffee cup; **tazza da tè** teacup

tazzina [tat'tsina] SF coffee cup

TBC [tibi'tʃi] SIGLA F (= **tubercolosi**) TB

TCI [titʃi'i] SIGLA M = *Touring Club Italiano*

TE SIGLA = *Teramo*

te [te] PRON PERS **1** (*dopo prep, accentato*) you; **lo ha dato a te, non a me** he gave it to you, not to me; **parlavamo di te** we were talking about you; **vengo con te** I'm coming with you; **dietro di te** behind you; **verrò da te** I'll come round to your place, I'll drop in and see you; **fallo da te** do it yourself; **se fossi in te** if I were you; **povero te!** poor you! **2** (*nelle comparazioni*) you; **è alto come te** he's as tall as you (are); **parla come te** she speaks like you (do); **è più giovane di te** he's younger than you (are) **3** *vedi* **ti**

tè [te] SM INV (*bevanda*) tea; (*pianta*) tea plant; (*trattenimento*) tea party; **da tè** tea *attr*; **vuoi un tè?** would you like a cup of tea?

teatino, a [tea'tino] AGG of *o* from Chieti ■ SM/F inhabitant *o* native of Chieti

teatrale [tea'trale] AGG (*spettacolo*) theatrical, stage *attr*; (*stagione, compagnia, attore*) theatre *attr* (*Brit*), theater *attr* (*Am*); (*fig: gesto, atteggiamento*) theatrical; **siamo andati a vedere uno spettacolo teatrale** we went to the theatre *o* theater

teatralità [teatrali'ta] SF (*anche fig*) theatricality

teatralmente [teatral'mente] AVV (*rappresentare*) on (the) stage; (*fig: comportarsi*) theatrically

teatro [te'atro] SM **1** (*edificio*) theatre (*Brit*), theater (*Am*); (*pubblico*) house, audience; (*fig: luogo*) scene; **andare a teatro** to go to the theatre *o* theater; **qualche volta vanno a teatro** they sometimes go to the theatre; **il teatro era pieno** there was a full house; **il teatro delle operazioni** (*Mil*) the theatre *o* theater of operations; **la sua casa è stata teatro di un orrendo delitto** his house was the scene of a hideous crime; **teatro all'aperto** open-air theatre *o* theater; **teatro di posa** film studio; **teatro tenda** marquee (*used for pop concerts ecc*) **2** (*genere*) theatre (*Brit*), theater (*Am*); (*professione*) theatre (*Brit*), theater (*Am*), stage; **il teatro classico** classical theatre *o* theater *o* drama; **il teatro di Pirandello** Pirandello's plays *o* dramatic works, the theatre *o* theater of Pirandello; **interessarsi di teatro** to be interested in drama *o* the theatre *o* theater; **è un uomo di teatro** he's in the theatre *o* theater; **teatro comico** comedy; **teatro lirico** opera; **teatro di strada** street theatre

Tebe ['tebe] SF Thebes *sg*

teca, che ['tɛka] SF (*Rel*) reliquary

technicolor® [tekni'kɔlor] SM Technicolor®

techno ['tekno] AGG INV (*musica*) techno

tecnica, che ['tɛknika] SF (*scienza*) technology; (*metodo*) technique

tecnicamente [teknika'mente] AVV technically

tecnicismo [tekni'tʃizmo] SM **1** (*predominio dell'aspetto tecnico*) excessive attention to technical details **2** (*termine tecnico*) technical term

tecnico, a, ci, che ['tɛkniko] AGG technical; **fa l'istituto tecnico** he goes to the technical college ■ SM/F (*gen*) technician; (*esperto*) expert; **è venuto il tecnico per riparare la TV** the repair man's come to fix the TV; **tecnico del suono** sound engineer; **tecnico della televisione** television engineer

tecnigrafo [tek'nigrafo] SM (*squadra*) draughtsman's (*Brit*) *o* draftsman's rule; (*Am*) (*tavolo*) drawing table

tecnocrate [tek'nɔkrate] SM/F technocrat

tecnocrazia [teknokrat'tsia] SF technocracy

tecnologia, gie [teknolo'dʒia] SF (*scienza*) technology; (*tecnica*) technique; **alta tecnologia** high technology, hi-tech; **nuove tecnologie** new technology *sg*

tecnologico, a, ci, che [tekno'lɔdʒiko] AGG technological

tecnologo, a, gi, ghe [tek'nɔlogo] SM/F technologist

tedesco, a, schi, sche [te'desko] AGG, SM/F German; **è tedesca** she's German; **i tedeschi** the Germans ■ SM (*lingua*) German; **parli tedesco?** do you speak German?

tediare [te'djare] VT (*infastidire*) to bother, annoy; (*annoiare*) to bore

tedio ['tɛdjo] SM tedium, boredom

tediosità [tedjosi'ta] SF tediousness

tedioso, a [te'djoso] AGG tedious, boring

Teflon® ['tɛflon] SM Teflon®

tegame [te'game] SM (*Culin*) (frying) pan, skillet (*Am*); (*contenuto*) panful; **al tegame** fried

teglia ['teʎʎa] SF (*Culin: per dolci*) (baking) tin (*Brit*), cake pan (*Am*); (*: per arrosti*) (roasting) tin *o* pan

tegola ['tegola] SF (roofing) tile

tegumento [tegu'mento] SM (*Bio*) integument

Teheran [te'ran] SF Teh(e)ran

teiera [te'jɛra] SF teapot

teina [te'ina] SF (*Chim*) theine

tek ['tɛk] SM INV teak

tel. [tel] ABBR (= **telefono**) tel.

tela ['tela] SF **1** (*tessuto*) cloth; **una pezza di tela** a piece of cloth; **di tela** (*lenzuolo*) linen; (*pantaloni*) (heavy) cotton *attr*; (*scarpe, borsa*) canvas *attr*; **rilegato in tela** clothbound **2** (*Pittura: supporto*) canvas; (*: dipinto*) canvas, painting ■ **tela cerata** oilcloth; **tela (da) vela** sailcloth; **tela di ragno** spider's web, cobweb; **tela di sacco** sackcloth, sacking

telaio, ai [te'lajo] SM (*per tessere*) loom; (*struttura*) frame; (*Aut*) chassis; **telaio da ricamo** embroidery frame

Tel Aviv [tela'viv] SF Tel Aviv

tele ['tɛle] SF INV (*fam*) telly (*Brit*), TV (*Am*)

tele... ['tɛle] PREF tele...

teleabbonato, a [teleabbo'nato] SM/F television *o* TV licence holder (*Brit*)

telecabina [teleka'bina] SF (*Sci*) cablecar

telecamera [tele'kamera] SF television *o* TV camera

telecomandare [telekoman'dare] VT to operate by remote control

telecomandato, a [telekoman'dato] AGG operated by remote control

Tt

telecomando [teleko'mando] SM remote control
telecomunicazioni [telekomunikat'tsjoni] SFPL telecommunications
▷ www.comunicazioni.it/it/
teleconferenza [telekonfe'rɛntsa] SF teleconference
telecronaca, che [tele'krɔnaka] SF television *o* TV report; **telecronaca differita** (pre-)recorded (TV) report; **telecronaca diretta** live (TV) report
telecronista, i, e [telekro'nista] SM/F (television) commentator
teledipendente [teledipen'dɛnte] SM/F telly addict ■ AGG: **un pigrone teledipendente** a couch potato
teledipendenza [teledipen'dɛntsa] SF addiction to TV
telefax ['tɛlefaks] SM INV fax
teleferica, che [tele'fɛrika] SF cableway
telefilm [tele'film] SM INV television *o* TV film (*Brit*) *o* movie (*Am*)
telefonare [telefo'nare] VI (*aus* **avere**) (*gen*) to (tele)phone, ring; (*fare una chiamata*) to make a phone call; **stamattina ha telefonato tua madre** your mother phoned this morning; **telefonare a qn** to telephone sb, phone *o* ring *o* call sb (up); **ieri ho telefonato a Richard** I phoned Richard yesterday; **sta telefonando** he is on the phone
■ VT to (tele)phone
telefonata [telefo'nata] SF (telephone) *o* (phone) call; **posso fare una telefonata?** can I make a phone call?; **telefonata a carico del destinatario** reverse charge (*Brit*) *o* collect (*Am*) call; **telefonata interurbana** long-distance call; **telefonata in teleselezione** STD (*Brit*) *o*, direct-dialing (*Am*) call; **telefonata urbana** local call
telefonia [telefo'nia] SF telephony; **telefonia fissa/mobile** landline/mobile telephony
telefonicamente [telefonika'mente] AVV by (tele)phone
telefonico, a, ci, che [tele'fɔniko] AGG (tele)phone *attr*; **cabina telefonica** phone box; **elenco telefonico** phone book; **scheda telefonica** phone card
telefonino [telefo'nino] SM mobile phone
telefonista, i, e [telefo'nista] SM/F (*gen*) telephonist; (*di centralino*) switchboard operator
telefono [te'lɛfono] SM (*sistema*) telephone; (*apparecchio*) (tele)phone; **avere il telefono** to be on the (tele)phone; **è al telefono** she's on the phone; **un colpo di telefono** a call, a ring; **ti do un colpo di telefono più tardi** I'll give you a ring later; **numero di telefono** phone number; **telefono amico** ≈ the Samaritans *pl* **telefono azzurro** ≈ Childline **telefono a disco** dial (tele)phone; **telefono fisso** landline; **telefono interno** internal phone; **telefono mobile** mobile (phone) (*Brit*), cellphone (*Am*); **telefono a monete** pay phone; **telefono pubblico** public (tele)phone; **telefono rosa** rape crisis line; **telefono satellitare** satellite phone; **telefono a scheda (magnetica)** cardphone (*Brit*); **telefono a tastiera** push-button phone
telegenico, a, ci, che [tele'dʒɛniko] AGG telegenic
telegiornale [teledʒor'nale] SM (*notiziario*) (television) news *sg*; **l'hanno detto al telegiornale** it was on the news; **il telegiornale è alle otto** the news is at eight
telegrafare [telegra'fare] VT, VI (*aus* **avere**) to telegraph, cable
telegrafia [telegra'fia] SF telegraphy
telegraficamente [telegrafika'mente] AVV (*anche fig*) telegraphically; (*trasmettere*) by telegraph
telegrafico, a, ci, che [tele'grafiko] AGG telegraph *attr*; (*fig: stile*) telegraphic
telegrafista, i, e [telegra'fista] SM/F telegraphist, telegraph operator
telegrafo [te'lɛgrafo] SM (*apparecchio*) telegraph; (*ufficio*) telegraph office
telegramma, i [tele'gramma] SM telegram
teleguidare [telegwi'dare] VT (*telecomandare*) to radio-control, operate by remote control
telelavoratore, trice [telelavora'tore] SM/F teleworker
telelavoro [telela'voro] SM teleworking
telelibera [tele'libera] SF (local) independent television station
Telemaco [te'lɛmako] SM Telemachus
telematica [tele'matika] SF (*servizio*) data transmission; (*disciplina*) telematics *sg*
telematico, a, ci, che [tele'matiko] AGG telematic
telemetro [te'lɛmetro] SM telemeter
telenovela [teleno'vɛla] SF soap opera
teleobiettivo [teleobjet'tivo] SM telephoto lens *sg*
teleologia [teleolo'dʒia] SF teleology
telepass® [tele'pas] SM INV (*Aut*) electronic pass (for motorways)
telepatia [telepa'tia] SF telepathy
telepatico, a, ci, che [tele'patiko] AGG telepathic
telepromozione [telepromot'tjone] SF TV advertising
telequiz [tele'kwits] SM INV (TV) game show
teleromanzo [telero'mandzo] SM television *o* TV serial
teleschermo [teles'kermo] SM television *o* TV screen
telescopico, a, ci, che [teles'kɔpiko] AGG telescopic
telescopio, pi [teles'kɔpjo] SM telescope; **a telescopio** telescopic
telescrivente [teleskri'vɛnte] AGG teleprinting
■ SF teleprinter (*Brit*), teletypewriter (*Am*)
teleselettivo, a [teleselet'tivo] AGG: **prefisso teleselettivo** STD code (*Brit*), dialling code (*Brit*), dial code (*Am*)
teleselezione [teleselet'tsjone] SF ≈ subscriber trunk dialling (*Brit*), ≈ direct dialing (*Am*); **telefonata in teleselezione** STD (*Brit*) *o* direct-dialing (*Am*) call
telespettatore, trice [telespetta'tore] SM/F (television) viewer
teletext [tele'tɛkst] SM INV Teletext®
teletrasmesso, a [teletraz'messo] PP *di* teletrasmettere
teletrasmettere [teletraz'mettere] VT IRREG to televise
teleutente [teleu'tɛnte] SM/F television subscriber
televendita [tele'vendita] SF teleshopping
televenditore, trice [televendi'tore] SM/F *presenter on a TV home-shopping channel*
televideo [tele'video] SM ≈ Teletext®
▷ www.televideo.rai.it/
televisione [televi'zjone] SF (*gen*) television; (*televisore*) television (set); **alla televisione** on television; **l'ho visto alla televisione** I saw it on television

TELEVISIONE

Three state-owned channels, RAI 1, 2 and 3, and a large number of private companies broadcast television programmes in Italy. Some of the latter function at purely local level, while others are

- national; some form part of a network, while others remain independent. The main private network is Mediaset, which includes Italia 1, Canale 5 and Rete 4. As a public corporation, RAI reports to the Post and Telecommunications Ministry. Both RAI and the private-sector channels compete for advertising revenues.
  - ▷ www.rai.it/
  - ▷ www.mediaset.it/
  - ▷ www.auditel.it

televisivo, a [televi'zivo] AGG television *attr*
televisore [televi'zore] SM television (set); **un televisore nuovo** a new television
telex ['tɛleks] AGG INV telex *attr*
■ SM INV telex
tellurico, a, ci, che [tel'luriko] AGG (*Geol*) telluric
telo ['telo] SM length of cloth; **telo da bagno** bath towel; **telo cerato** (*per materasso*) rubber sheet; **telo da spiaggia** beach towel
telone [te'lone] SM **1** (*per copertura*) tarpaulin **2** (*sipario*) drop curtain
tema, i ['tɛma] SM **1** (*argomento*) theme; (*: di conversazione*) subject, topic; (*Mus*) theme, motif; (*Scol*) essay, composition; **ho consegnato il tema senza rileggerlo** I handed in my essay without reading it through; **il tema della lezione di oggi** the subject of today's lecture; **tema libero** (*Scol*) free composition; **andare fuori tema** to go off the subject **2** (*Ling*) theme, stem
tematica [te'matika] SF basic themes *pl*
tematico, a, ci, che [te'matiko] AGG (*tutti i sensi*) thematic
temerariamente [temerarja'mente] AVV recklessly, rashly
temerarietà [temerarje'ta] SF recklessness, rashness
temerario, ria, ri, rie [teme'rarjo] AGG reckless, rash
■ SM/F reckless person
temere [te'mere] VT to be afraid of, fear; **temo il pericolo** I am afraid of danger; **non temo la sua reazione** I'm not afraid of his reaction; **temo che non venga** I am afraid he won't come; **temo che se ne sia andato** I'm afraid he's gone; **temo di non farcela** I am afraid I won't make it; **temere il peggio** to fear the worst; **temere una brutta sorpresa** to expect a nasty surprise; **mi hai fatto temere che...** you had me worried that ...; **temo di sì/no** I'm afraid so/not; **temere il freddo** (*pianta*) to be sensitive to cold
■ VI (*aus* **avere**) to be afraid; **temere per** (*preoccuparsi*) to worry about; **non temere!** (*non aver paura*) don't be afraid!; (*non preoccuparti*) don't worry!
tempaccio [tem'pattʃo] SM bad weather
tempera ['tɛmpera] SF **1** (*Arte: colore, tecnica*) tempera; (*: dipinto*) painting in tempera; **colori a tempera** tempera *sg*; **dipingere a tempera** to paint in tempera **2** (*Tecn*) = tempra
temperalapis [tempera'lapis], **temperamatite** [temperama'tite] SM INV pencil sharpener
temperamento [tempera'mento] SM (*carattere*) temperament, character; **è nervoso di temperamento** he has a nervous temperament *o* disposition *o* character; **avere del temperamento** to have a strong personality; **manca di temperamento** he's weak-willed
temperante [tempe'rante] AGG moderate
temperare [tempe'rare] VT **1** (*matita*) to sharpen **2** (*metalli*) to temper
temperato, a [tempe'rato] AGG **1** (*moderato*) moderate, temperate; (*clima*) temperate **2** (*acciaio*) tempered
temperatura [tempera'tura] SF temperature; **temperatura ambiente** room temperature
temperino [tempe'rino] SM penknife
tempesta [tem'pɛsta] SF **1** (*Meteor*) storm; **il mare era in tempesta** the sea was stormy; **una tempesta in un bicchier d'acqua** a storm in a teacup (*Brit*), a tempest in a teapot (*Am*); **c'è aria di tempesta** (*fig*) there is a storm brewing; **tempesta magnetica** magnetic storm; **tempesta di neve** snowstorm; **tempesta di sabbia** sandstorm **2** (*fitta serie*): **una tempesta di pugni** a hail of blows; **una tempesta di domande** a barrage of questions
tempestare [tempes'tare] VT **1** **tempestare qn di colpi** to rain blows on sb; **tempestare qn di domande/telefonate** to bombard sb with questions/(phone)calls **2** (*ornare*) to stud
tempestivamente [tempestiva'mente] AVV opportunely, at the right time
tempestività [tempestivi'ta] SF timeliness
tempestivo, a [tempes'tivo] AGG timely, well-timed
tempestoso, a [tempes'toso] AGG stormy
tempia ['tɛmpja] SF (*Anat*) temple
tempio, pi ['tɛmpjo] SM (*Rel, anche fig*) temple
tempismo [tem'pizmo] SM sense of timing
tempista, i, e [tem'pista] SM/F person with a good sense of timing
templare [tem'plare] SM (*Rel, Storia*) (Knight) Templar
tempo ['tɛmpo] SM
1 (*gen*) time; **il tempo e lo spazio** time and space; **il tempo vola!** time flies!; **il tempo stringe** time is short; **ci vuole tempo** it takes time; **abbiamo tempo 3 giorni** we have 3 days; **scusa, adesso non ho tempo** sorry, I haven't got time at the moment; **c'è** *o* **abbiamo tempo** there is plenty of time; **rilassati, abbiamo ancora tempo!** relax, we've still got time!; **c'è sempre tempo** there is still time; **non c'è tempo da perdere** there is no time to lose; **perdere tempo** (*sprecare tempo*) to waste time; (*far tardi*) to lose time; **trovare il tempo di fare qc** to find the time to do sth; **col tempo** with time; **con l'andare del tempo** with the passing of time; **a tempo di record** in record time; **a tempo pieno** full time; **lavoro a tempo pieno** I work full time; **un lavoratore a tempo pieno** a full-time worker; **un impiego a tempo pieno** a full-time job; **nei ritagli di tempo** *or* **a tempo perso** in one's spare moments; **tempo libero** free *o* spare time
2 (*periodo*) time; **da tempo** for a long time now; **aspetto da tempo** I've been waiting for a long time; **da quanto tempo?** since when?; **tempo fa** some time ago; **poco tempo dopo** not long after; **per qualche tempo** for a while; **un po' di tempo** a while; **non lo vedo da un po' di tempo** I haven't seen him for a while; **era qui un po' di tempo fa** she was here a while ago; **dove sei stato tutto questo tempo?** where have you been all this time?; **a tempo e luogo** at the right time and place; **a suo tempo** in due course, at the appropriate time; **ogni cosa a suo tempo** we'll (*o* you'll *ecc*) deal with it in due course; **in tempo utile** in due time *o* course; **al tempo stesso** *or* **a un tempo** at the same time; **fare in tempo a fare qc** to manage to do sth; **farai in tempo a prendere il treno?** will you be in time for the train?; **arrivare/essere in tempo** to arrive/be in time; **per tempo** in good time, early; **un tempo** once
3 (*durata di un'operazione*) time; (*fase*) stage; **rispettare i**

Tt

tempi to keep to the schedule *o* timetable; **stringere i tempi** to speed things up; **tempi di esecuzione** (*Comm*) time scale *sg*; **tempi di lavorazione** (*Industria*) throughput time *sg*; **tempi morti** (*Comm*) downtime *sg*, idle time *sg*; **tempo di accesso** (*Inform*) access time; **tempo di cottura** cooking time; **tempo reale** (*Inform, Comm*) real time
4 (*stagione*) season; **quando arriva il tempo delle ciliege** when the cherries ripen
5 (*epoca*) time, times *pl*; **al tempo della Rivoluzione Culturale** at the time of *o* in the days of the Cultural Revolution; **tempi duri** hard times; **altri tempi!** those were the days!; **con i tempi che corrono** these days; **andare al passo con i tempi** to keep pace *o* keep up with the times; **nella notte dei tempi** in the dim and distant past; **in tempo di pace** in peace time; **in questi ultimi tempi** of late; **ai miei tempi** in my day; **aver fatto il proprio tempo** to have had its (*o* his *ecc*) day
6 (*Meteor*) weather; **che tempo fa?** what's the weather like?; **fa bel/brutto tempo** the weather's fine/bad; **con questo tempo!** in this weather!; **tempo da lupi** *o* **da cani** foul weather; **condizioni del tempo** weather conditions; **previsioni del tempo** weather forecast *sg*
7 (*Mus*) time; (: *battuta*) beat; (: *grado di velocità*) tempo; (: *movimento*) movement; **andare a tempo** to keep time; **essere fuori tempo** to be out of time; **battere** *o* **segnare il tempo** to mark time; **in tre tempi** in triple time
8 (*Gramm*) tense; **tempo presente** present tense
9 **primo/secondo tempo** (*Teatro, Cine*) first/second part; (*Sport*) first/second half; **il primo tempo era un po' noioso** the first part was a bit boring; **ha segnato nel secondo tempo** he scored in the second half; **tempi supplementari** (*Sport*) extra time *sg*
10 (*di motore a scoppio*) stroke; **motore a due tempi** two-stroke engine
11 (*fraseologia*): **dare tempo al tempo** to let matters take their course; **chi ha tempo non aspetti tempo** there's no time like the present; **fare il bello e il cattivo tempo** to rule the roost; **il tempo è denaro** time is money; **è un provvedimento che lascia il tempo che trova** it's a measure that doesn't really change anything; **cerchiamo di guadagnare tempo** (*indugiare*) let's play for time; (*finire in anticipo*) let's try to gain some time; **senza tempo** timeless
▷ www.meteoam.it/

temporale[1] [tempo'rale] SM (*Meteor*) (thunder)storm
temporale[2] [tempo'rale] AGG (*gen*) temporal; **avverbi temporali** adverbs of time
■ SF (*Gramm*) temporal *o* time clause
temporalesco, a, schi, sche [tempora'lesko] AGG stormy
temporaneamente [temporanea'mente] AVV temporarily
temporaneità [temporanei'ta] SF temporariness, provisional nature
temporaneo, a [tempo'raneo] AGG temporary; **una sistemazione temporanea** temporary accommodation; (*lavoro, lavoratore*) temporary
temporeggiamento [temporeddʒa'mento] SM playing for time, temporizing
temporeggiare [tempored'dʒare] VI (*aus* **avere**) to play for time, temporize
temporeggiatore, trice [temporeddʒa'tore] SM/F temporizer
temporizzatore [temporiddza'tore] SM (*Elettr*) timer
tempra ['tɛmpra] SF **1** (*Tecn*: *atto*) tempering, hardening; (: *effetto*) temper **2** (*fig*: *costituzione fisica*) constitution; (: *intellettuale*) temperament
temprare [tem'prare] VT (*gen, Tecn*) to temper; (*fig*) to strengthen, toughen
▶ **temprarsi** VR, VIP (*anche fig*) to become stronger *o* tougher
tenace [te'natʃe] AGG (*odio*) lasting; (*volontà*) strong, firm; (*persona*) tenacious
tenacemente [tenatʃe'mente] AVV tenaciously
tenacia [te'natʃa] SF tenacity
tenacità [tenatʃi'ta] SF (*di metallo*) toughness
tenaglie [te'naʎʎe] SFPL (*arnese, chele*) pincers *pl*; (*del dentista*) forceps *pl*
tenda ['tɛnda] SF **1** (*di finestra*) curtain; (*riparo*: *di negozio, terrazza*) awning; **tirare le tende** to draw the curtains *o* drapes (*Am*); **tenda per doccia** shower curtain **2** (*Mil, da campeggio*) tent; **piantare le tende** to pitch one's tent; (*fig*) to settle down; **è ora di levar le tende** (*fig*) it's time to hit the trail *o* pack up and go **3** **tenda a ossigeno** oxygen tent
tendaggio [ten'daddʒo] SM curtaining, curtains *pl*, drapes *pl* (*Am*)
tendalino [tenda'lino] SM (*di imbarcazione*) canopy
tendenza [ten'dɛntsa] SF (*gen*) tendency; (*inclinazione*) inclination; (*orientamento*: *Pol, Econ*) trend; **avere la tendenza a** to tend to; **ha tendenza a ingrassare** he tends to put on weight; **avere tendenza a** *o* **per qc** to have a bent for sth; **con tendenza al bello** (*Meteor*) tending to fair; **tendenza al rialzo** (*Borsa*) upward trend; **tendenza al ribasso** (*Borsa*) downward trend
tendenzialmente [tendentsjal'mente] AVV: **è tendenzialmente sincero** he tends to be frank with people
tendenziosamente [tendentsjosa'mente] AVV tendentiously
tendenziosità [tendentsjosi'ta] SF tendentiousness
tendenzioso, a [tenden'tsjoso] AGG tendentious, bias(s)ed
tendere ['tɛndere] VB IRREG
■ VT **1** (*mettere in tensione*: *corda*) to tighten, pull tight; (: *elastico, muscoli*) to stretch; (: *tessuto*) to stretch, pull *o* draw tight; **hanno teso una corda tra due alberi** they stretched a rope between two trees; **tendere una trappola a qn** to set a trap for sb **2** (*sporgere*: *collo*) to crane; (: *mano*) to hold out; (: *braccio*) to stretch out; **tendere la mano** to hold out one's hand; (*fig*: *chiedere l'elemosina*) to beg; (: *aiutare*) to lend a helping hand; **tendere gli orecchi** (*fig*) to prick up one's ears
■ VI (*aus* **avere**) **tendere a qc/a fare qc** (*aver la tendenza*) to tend towards sth/to do sth; (*mirare a*) to aim at sth/to do sth; **tende ad ingrassare** she tends to put on weight; **tutti i nostri sforzi sono tesi a...** all our efforts are geared towards ...; **tende al pessimismo** he tends to be pessimistic; **tendere a sinistra** (*Pol*) to have left-wing tendencies; **la situazione tende a migliorare** the situation is improving; **il tempo tende al bello** the weather is improving; **un blu che tende al verde** a greenish blue
tendina [ten'dina] SF curtain
tendine ['tɛndine] SM tendon, sinew
tendiracchetta [tendirak'ketta] SM INV racket press
tendiscarpe [tendis'karpe] SM INV shoetree
tendone [ten'done] SM (*da circo*) big top

LO SAPEVI...?
tendone non si traduce mai con la parola inglese *tendon*

tendopoli [ten'dɔpoli] SF INV (large) camp
tenebre ['tɛnebre] SFPL darkness *sg*, gloom *sg*
tenebrosamente [tenebrosa'mente] AVV (*misteriosamente*) mysteriously
tenebroso, a [tene'broso] AGG (*gen*) dark, gloomy; (*fig*) mysterious
■ SM/F: **un bel tenebroso** a tall, dark and handsome man
tenente [te'nɛnte] SM lieutenant

> **LO SAPEVI...?**
> **tenente** non si traduce mai con la parola inglese ***tenant***

teneramente [tenera'mente] AVV tenderly
tenere [te'nere] VB IRREG
■ VT
1 (*reggere: in mano*) to hold; (*: in posizione*) to hold, keep; (*: in una condizione*) to keep; **tieni!** here!; **tieni, usa il mio** here, use mine; **tieni, questo è per te** here, this is for you; **non mi serve, puoi tenerlo** I don't need it, you can keep it; **tenere qn per mano** to hold sb by the hand; **tenere in braccio un bambino** to hold a baby; **tenere una pentola per il manico** to hold a pan by the handle; **tiene la racchetta con la sinistra** he holds the racket with his left hand; **tieni la porta aperta** hold the door open; **tengono sempre la porta aperta** they always keep their door open; **tiene sempre la camicia sbottonata** he always has his shirt unbuttoned; **tenere le mani in tasca** to keep one's hands in one's pockets; **tieni gli occhi chiusi** keep your eyes shut *o* closed; **un cappotto che tiene caldo** a warm coat; **tiene la casa molto bene** her house is always tidy; **tenere presente qc** to bear sth in mind; **tenere la rotta** (*Naut*) to keep *o* stay on course; **il nemico teneva la città** the enemy had the city under its control *o* held the city; **tenere la destra/la sinistra** (*Aut*) to keep to the right/the left
2 (*dare: conferenza, lezione*) to give; (*organizzare: riunione, assemblea*) to hold
3 (*occupare: spazio*) to take up, occupy; **tenere il posto a qn** to keep sb's seat; **mi tieni il posto? torno subito** will you keep my seat for me? I'll be right back
4 (*contenere: sogg: recipiente*) to hold
5 (*resistere a*): **tenere il mare** (*Naut*) to be seaworthy; **tenere la strada** (*Aut*) to hold the road
6 (*considerare*): **tenere conto di qn/qc** to take sb/sth into account *o* consideration; **tenere in gran conto** *o* **considerazione qn** to have a high regard for sb, think highly of sb
■ VI (*aus* **avere**)
1 (*resistere*) to hold out, last; (*: chiusura, nodo*) to hold; **tiene quella scatola?** is that box strong enough?; **questa vite non tiene** this screw is loose; **non ci sono scuse che tengano** I'll take no excuses; **tenere duro** (*resistere*) to stand firm, hold out
2 (*parteggiare*): **tenere per qn/qc** to support sb/sth; **io tengo per lui** I am on his side
3 **tenere a** (*reputazione, persona, vestiario*) to attach great importance to; **tiene molto all'educazione** he is a great believer in education
4 (*dare importanza*): **tenere a, tenerci a** to care about, attach great importance to; **tenere a fare** to want to do, be keen to do; **ci tengo ad ottenere la presidenza** it's important for me to become chairman; **ci tenevo ad andare** I was keen on going, I was keen to go; **ci tiene che lo sappia** he wants him to know; **non ci tengo** I don't care about it, it's not that important to me; **se ci tieni proprio!** if you really want!
▶ **tenersi** VR
1 (*reggersi*) **tenersi a qn/qc** to hold onto sb/sth; **tieniti al corrimano** hold onto the rail; **tieniti forte!** hold on tight!; **tenersi per mano** (*uso reciproco*) to hold hands; **si tenevano per mano** they were holding hands; **tenersi in piedi** to stay on one's feet; **non si teneva più dal ridere** (*fig*) he couldn't help laughing, he couldn't keep from laughing
2 (*mantenersi*) to keep, be; **tenersi pronto (a fare qc)** to be ready (to do sth); **tieniti pronta per le cinque** be ready by five; **tenersi vicino al/lontano dal muro** to keep close to/away from the wall; **tenersi sulla corsia di destra** to stay in the right-hand lane; **tenersi a destra/sinistra** to keep right/left
3 (*attenersi*) **tenersi a** to comply with, stick to
tenerezza [tene'rettsa] SF tenderness; **che tenerezza che mi fa questo piccolino!** what a lovely little baby!; **non sono abituato a tutte queste tenerezze** I am not used to all this attention
tenero, a ['tɛnero] AGG 1 (*carne, verdura*) tender; (*pietra, cera, colore*) soft; **grano tenero** soft wheat; **erba tenera** young grass; **è morto in tenera età** he died young; **alla sua tenera età** (*scherz*) at his tender age
2 (*indulgente*) soft, tender; (*che esprime tenerezza*) tender, loving; **un tenero padre** a loving father; **avere il cuore tenero** to be tender-hearted; **che tenero!** how lovely!
■ SM 1 (*parte tenera*) tender part 2 (*affetto*): **tra quei due c'è del tenero** there's a romance budding between those two
tengo *ecc* ['tɛngo] VB *vedi* **tenere**
tenia ['tɛnja] SF tapeworm
Tennessee [tɛnɪs'iː] SM Tennessee
tenni *ecc* ['tenni] VB *vedi* **tenere**
tennis ['tɛnnis] SM INV tennis; **giocare a tennis** to play tennis; **giochi a tennis?** do you play tennis?; **da tennis** tennis *attr*; **tennis da tavolo** table tennis
▷ www.federtennis.it/
▷ www.fitet.org/
tennista, i, e [ten'nista] SM/F tennis player
tennistico, a, ci, che [ten'nistiko] AGG tennis *attr*
tenore [te'nore] SM 1 (*tono*) tone; **il tenore della sua lettera** the tone of his letter; **tenore di vita** (*modo di vivere*) way of life; (*livello*) standard of living 2 (*Mus*) tenor
tensiometro [ten'sjɔmetro] SM (*Tecn*) tensiometer
tensione [ten'sjone] SF (*gen*) tension; (*Elettr*) tension, voltage; **ad alta tensione** (*Elettr*) high-voltage *attr*, high-tension *attr*; **c'è un po' di tensione** (*fig*) things are a bit tense
tensivo, a [ten'sivo] AGG: **cefalea tensiva** tension headache
tentabile [ten'tabile] AGG worth attempting, worth a try; **è una strada tentabile per risolvere il problema** it's a possible way of solving the problem
■ SM: **tentare il tentabile** to try everything possible
tentacolare [tentako'lare] AGG (*appendice, protuberanza*) tentacular; (*fig: città*) magnet-like
tentacolo [ten'takolo] SM (*anche fig*) tentacle
tentare [ten'tare] VT 1 (*provare*): **tentare qc/di fare qc** to attempt *o* try sth/to do sth; **ho tentato l'esame, ma non l'ho passato** I attempted the exam but I didn't pass it; **tenterà di battere il record mondiale** she's going to try to beat the world record; **tentare il suicidio** to attempt suicide, try to commit suicide; **tentato suicidio** attempted suicide; **tentare un nuovo metodo** (*sperimentare*) to try out a new method;

le ho tentate tutte per convincerli I tried everything to persuade them; **tentare la sorte** to try one's luck; **tentar non nuoce** there's no harm in trying **2** (*cercare di corrompere, allettare*) to tempt; (*mettere alla prova*) to test; **non lo tentare** don't tempt him

tentativo [tenta'tivo] SM attempt; **fa' ancora un tentativo** try again

tentatore, trice [tenta'tore] AGG tempting ■ SM/F tempter/temptress

tentazione [tentat'tsjone] SF temptation; **non ho saputo resistere alla tentazione!** I couldn't resist the temptation!; **aver la tentazione di fare qc** to be tempted to do sth

tentennamento [tentenna'mento] SM (*fig*) hesitation, wavering; **dopo molti tentennamenti** after much hesitation

tentennare [tenten'nare] VI (*aus* **avere**) (*persona*) to totter, stagger; (*fig*) to hesitate, waver; **gli tentenna un dente** he's got a wobbly *o* loose tooth; **il vecchio uscì tentennando** the old man staggered out ■ VT: **tentennare il capo** to shake one's head

tentoni [ten'toni] AVV (*anche fig*): **a tentoni** gropingly; **andare (a) tentoni** to grope one's way

tenue ['tɛnue] AGG **1** (*colore*) soft; (*voce*) feeble; (*luce*) faint; (*fig: speranza*) slender, slight **2** (*Anat*): **intestino tenue** small intestine

tenuemente [tenue'mente] AVV (*colorato*) softly; (*illuminato*) dimly

tenuta [te'nuta] SF **1** (*capacità*) capacity; **a tenuta d'aria** airtight; **tenuta di strada** (*Aut*) roadholding **2** (*divisa*) uniform; **in tenuta da lavoro** in one's work(ing) clothes; **in tenuta da sci** in a skiing outfit; **in tenuta da calciatore** in a football strip (*Brit*) **3** (*podere*) estate

tenutario, ria, ri, rie [tenu'tarjo] SM/F brothel-keeper

tenzone [ten'tsone] SF (*letter: combattimento*) strife; (*: disputa letteraria*) literary dispute

teocentrico, a, ci, che [teo'tʃɛntriko] AGG theocentric

teologale [teolo'gale] AGG theological; **virtù teologali** theological virtues

teologia [teolo'dʒia] SF theology; **la teologia della liberazione** the liberation theology

teologico, a, ci, che [teo'lɔdʒiko] AGG theological

teologo, a, gi, ghe [te'ɔlogo] SM/F theologian

teorema, i [teo'rɛma] SM (*Mat*) theorem

teoreticamente [teoretika'mente] AVV theoretically

teoretico, a, ci, che [teo'rɛtiko] AGG theoretical

teoria [teo'ria] SF theory; **in teoria** in theory, theoretically

teoricamente [teorika'mente] AVV in theory

teorico, a, ci, che [te'ɔriko] AGG theoretic(al); **a livello teorico** *or* **in linea teorica** theoretically, in theory ■ SM/F theorist, theoretician

teorizzare [teorid'dzare] VT to theorize

tepido, a ['tepido] AGG = **tiepido**

tepore [te'pore] SM warmth

teppa ['teppa] SF mob, hooligans *pl*

teppaglia [tep'paʎʎa] SF hooligans *pl*

teppismo [tep'pizmo] SM hooliganism

teppista, i, e [tep'pista] SM/F hooligan

tequila [te'kila] SF INV tequila

terapeuta, i, e [tera'pɛuta] SM/F therapist

terapeutica [tera'pɛutika] SF therapeutics *sg*

terapeutico, a, ci, che [tera'pɛutiko] AGG therapeutic

terapia [tera'pia] SF (*Med*) therapeutics *sg*, therapy; (*: cura*) therapy, treatment; **terapia di gruppo** group therapy; **terapia intensiva** intensive care; **terapia d'urto** massive-dose treatment; (*fig*) shock treatment *o* therapy

terapista, i, e [tera'pista] SM/F therapist

tergere ['tɛrdʒere] VT IRREG (*sudore, pianto*) to wipe

tergicristallo [terdʒikris'tallo] SM windscreen (*Brit*) *o* windshield (*Am*) wiper; **tergicristallo (a funzionamento) intermittente** intermittent wiper

tergifari [terdʒi'fari] SM INV (*Aut*) headlight wiper

tergilunotto [terdʒilu'nɔtto] SM (*Aut*) rear wiper

tergiversare [terdʒiver'sare] VI (*aus* **avere**) to beat about the bush, shilly-shally

tergo, ghi ['tɛrgo] SM back; (*di moneta*) reverse; **a tergo** behind; **vedi a tergo** please turn over, see overleaf

terital® ['tɛrital] SM INV Terylene®

termale [ter'male] AGG thermal; **sorgente termale** hot spring; **stazione termale** spa resort

terme ['tɛrme] SFPL (thermal) baths

termico, a, ci, che ['tɛrmiko] AGG (*Fis*) thermic, thermal; **borsa termica** cool bag *o* box (*Brit*); cooler (*Am*); **centrale termica** thermal power station

terminal ['tə:minl] SM INV (*gen*) terminal; (*Aer*) air terminal

terminale [termi'nale] AGG (*fase, parte*) final; (*Med*) terminal; **i malati terminali** the terminally ill *pl*; **tratto terminale** (*di fiume*) lower reaches *pl* ■ SM terminal

terminalista, i, e [termina'lista] SM/F computer operator, VDU operator

terminare [termi'nare] VT (*gen*) to end; (*lavoro*) to finish; **dopo aver terminato l'università** after finishing university ■ VI (*aus* **essere**) to end; **a che ora termina il film?** what time does the film finish?; **terminare a punta** to end in a point; **terminare in consonante** to end in *o* with a consonant; **dove termina la valle c'è un lago** there is a lake at the end of the valley

terminazione [terminat'tsjone] SF (*fine*) end; (*Gramm*) ending; **terminazioni nervose** (*Anat*) nerve endings

termine ['tɛrmine] SM **1** (*confine*) boundary, limit; (*punto estremo*) end; **al termine della strada** at the end of the road; **porre termine a qc** to put an end to sth; **avere termine** to end; **portare a termine qc** to bring sth to a conclusion **2** (*spazio di tempo*) stipulated period; (*scadenza*) deadline; **entro un termine di tre ore** within three hours; **fissare un termine** to set a deadline; **entro il termine convenuto** within the stipulated period; **qual è il termine per la presentazione delle domande?** what is the deadline for applications?; **a breve/lungo termine** short-/long-term; **contratto a termine** (*Dir*) fixed-term contract; (*Comm*) forward contract **3** **termini** (*condizioni*) terms; (*limiti*) limits; **ai termini di legge** by law; **questo contratto non è valido ai termini di legge** this contract is not valid under law; **fissare i termini della questione** to define the problem; **la questione sta in questi termini** this is how the matter stands; **essere in buoni/cattivi termini con qn** to be on good/bad terms with sb **4** (*Gramm, Mat*) term; **un termine tecnico/scientifico** a technical/scientific term; **ridurre ai minimi termini** (*Mat*) to reduce to the lowest terms; **termini di paragone** terms of comparison; **in altri termini** in other words; **modera i termini!** moderate your language!; **parlare senza mezzi termini** not to mince one's words

terminologia [terminolo'dʒia] SF terminology

termitano, a [termi'tano] AGG of *o* from Teramo
■ SM/F inhabitant *o* native of Teramo
termite ['tɛrmite] SF termite
termo... ['tɛrmo] PREF thermo...
termoconvettore [termokonvet'tore] SM convector heater
termocoperta [termoko'pɛrta] SF electric blanket
termodinamica [termodi'namika] SF thermodynamics *sg*
termodinamico, a, ci, che [termodi'namiko] AGG thermodynamic
termoelettrico, a, ci, che [termoe'lɛttriko] AGG thermoelectric(al)
termoindurente [termoindu'rɛnte] AGG thermosetting
termometro [ter'mɔmetro] SM (*anche fig*) thermometer
termonucleare [termonukle'are] AGG thermonuclear
termoplastico, a, ci, che [termo'plastiko] AGG thermoplastic
termoregolazione [termoregolat'tsjone] SF thermostatic temperature control
termos ['tɛrmos] SM INV = **thermos**
termosaldare [termosal'dare] VT (*materie plastiche*) to heat-seal
termosifone [termosi'fone] SM (*radiatore*) radiator; (*sistema di riscaldamento*) central heating
termostato [ter'mɔstato] SM thermostat
termoterapia [termotera'pia] SF heat treatment
terna ['tɛrna] SF (*gen*) set of three; (*lista di tre nomi*) list of three candidates; **terna arbitrale** (*Calcio*) referee and linesmen
ternano, a [ter'nano] AGG of *o* from Terni
■ SM/F inhabitant *o* native of Terni
ternario, ria, ri, rie [ter'narjo] AGG (*Poesia*: *verso*) three-syllable *attr*; (*Chim*) ternary
terno ['tɛrno] SM (*al lotto*) (set of) three winning numbers; **vincere un terno al lotto** (*fig*) to hit the jackpot
terra ['tɛrra] SF **1 la Terra** (*pianeta*) the earth; (*fig*: *mondo*) the world; **sulla faccia della terra** on the face of the earth; **i piaceri di questa terra** the pleasures of this world **2** (*terreno, suolo*) ground; (*sostanza*) soil, earth; (*argilla*) clay; **la terra è bagnata** the ground's wet; **la pioggia laverà via la terra** the rain will wash away the soil; **per terra** (*appoggiare, sedersi*) on the ground; (*cadere*) to the ground; **il tesoro è sotto terra** the treasure is buried; **il fiume passa sotto terra** the stream runs underground; **strada in terra battuta** dirt track **3** (*distesa, campagna*) land *no pl*; **un pezzo di terra** (*gen*) a piece of land; (*fabbricabile, per orto*) a plot of land; **una lingua di terra** a strip of land; **le sue terre** (*possedimento*) his estate **4** (*terraferma*) land *no pl*; **scendere a terra** to go ashore; **via terra** (*viaggiare*) by land, overland **5** (*paese, regione*) land, country; **in terra straniera** in foreign parts; **la mia terra** my native land; **è della mia terra** he is a fellow countryman; **tattica della terra bruciata** (*Mil*) scorched earth policy **6** (*Elettr*) earth (*Brit*), ground (*Am*); **mettere a terra** to earth *o* ground **7** (*fraseologia*): **avere una gomma a terra** to have a flat tyre; **essere a terra** (*fig*: *depresso*) to be at rock bottom; **terra terra** (*fig*: *persona, argomento*) prosaic, pedestrian; **cercare qn/qc per mare e per terra** to look high and low for sb/sth; **non sta né in cielo né in terra** it is quite unheard of; **stare con i piedi per terra** (*fig*) to have both feet on the ground
■ **terra di nessuno** no-man's-land; **la terra promessa** the Promised Land; **la Terra Santa** the Holy Land; **terra di Siena** sienna
terra-aria ['tɛrra 'arja] AGG INV (*Mil*) ground-to-air, surface-to-air
terracotta [terra'kɔtta] SF (*pl* **terrecotte**) terracotta *no pl*; **di terracotta** terracotta *attr*; **vasellame di terracotta** earthenware; **terracotta smaltata** glazed earthenware
terracqueo, a [ter'rakkweo] AGG: **il globo terracqueo** the globe
terraferma [terra'ferma] SF (*terra emersa*) dry land, terra firma; (*continente*) mainland; **avvistare la terraferma** to sight land
terraglia [ter'raʎʎa] SF **1** pottery *sg* **2 terraglie** SFPL (*oggetti*) crockery *sg*, earthenware *sg*
Terranova [terra'nɔva] SF Newfoundland
terrapieno [terra'pjɛno] SM embankment, bank
terra-terra ['tɛrra 'tɛrra] AGG INV (*Mil*) ground-to-ground, surface-to-surface
terrazza [ter'rattsa] SF (*gen, Agr*) terrace; **erano seduti in terrazza** they were sitting on the terrace
terrazzamento [terrattsa'mento] SM (*Agr*) terracing
terrazzare [terrat'tsare] VT (*gen, Agr*) to terrace
terrazzato, a [terrat'tsato] AGG (*gen, Agr*) terraced
terrazzino [terrat'tsino] SM (small) balcony
terrazzo [ter'rattso] SM (*gen, Agr, Geog*) terrace; (*balcone*) balcony
terremotato, a [terremo'tato] AGG (*zona*) devastated by an earthquake
■ SM/F earthquake victim
terremoto [terre'mɔto] SM earthquake; (*fig scherz*: *bambino*) terror; (: *sconvolgimento*) havoc
terreno, a [ter'reno] SM **1** (*gen*) ground; (*suolo*) soil, ground; **il terreno è bagnato** the ground's wet; **un terreno montuoso** a mountainous terrain; **dissodare il terreno** to till the soil; **preparare il terreno** (*fig*) to prepare the ground; **tastare il terreno** (*fig*) to see how the land lies; **terreno alluvionale** (*Geol*) alluvial soil **2** (*area coltivabile, edificabile*) land *no pl*, plot (of land); **hanno dei terreni in Toscana** they've got land in Tuscany; **ho comprato un terreno** I bought a piece *o* a plot of land; **una casa con 500 ettari di terreno** a house with 500 hectares of land **3** (*Mil*: *teatro di operazioni*) field; (: *guadagnato, perduto*) ground; **perdere terreno** (*anche fig*) to lose ground **4** (*Sport*): **terreno di gioco** field; **una partita sospesa a causa del terreno pesante** a match postponed because of ground waterlogged
■ AGG **1** (*vita, beni*) earthly **2** (*a livello della strada*): **piano terreno** ground floor (*Brit*), first floor (*Am*)
terreo, a ['tɛrreo] AGG (*viso, colorito*) wan
terrestre [ter'rɛstre] AGG (*della terra*: *superficie*) of the earth, earth's *attr*; (: *magnetismo*) terrestrial; (*di terra*: *battaglia, animale*) land *attr*; **un animale terrestre** a land animal; **il globo terrestre** the globe
■ SM/F earthling
terribile [ter'ribile] AGG (*orribile*) terrible, dreadful; (: *nemico*) terrible; (: *visione*) fearful; (: *forza*) tremendous; (*fam*: *formidabile*) terrific, tremendous; **ho una fame terribile** I am terribly hungry
terribilmente [terribil'mente] AVV terribly
terriccio, ci [ter'rittʃo] SM soil
terrier [tɛ'rje] SM INV (*cane*) terrier

Tt

terriero, a [ter'rjɛro] AGG: **proprietà terriera** landed property; **proprietario terriero** landowner

terrificante [terrifi'kante] AGG terrifying

> **LO SAPEVI...?**
> **terrificante** non si traduce mai con la parola inglese *terrific*

terrina [ter'rina] SF *(zuppiera)* tureen; *(ciotola)* terracotta bowl; *(per paté)* terrine

territoriale [territo'rjale] AGG territorial

territorialistico, a, ci, che [territorja'listiko] AGG territorial

territorio, ri [terri'tɔrjo] SM *(gen)* territory; *(di comune)* precinct; *(di giudice)* jurisdiction; **i Territori occupati** the Occupied Territories

terrone, a [ter'rone] SM/F *derogatory term used by Northern Italians to describe Southern Italians*

terrore [ter'rore] SM *(anche fig)* terror; **il Terrore** *(Storia)* the Reign of Terror; **incutere terrore a qn** to strike terror into sb's heart; **avere (il) terrore di qc/di fare qc** to be terrified of sth/of doing sth; **Anna ha il terrore dei ragni/di volare** Anna's terrified of spiders/of flying; **con terrore** in terror; **del terrore** *(film, racconto)* horror *attr*; **un film del terrore** a horror film

terrorismo [terro'rizmo] SM terrorism

terrorista, i, e [terro'rista] SM/F terrorist

terroristico, a, ci, che [terro'ristiko] AGG terrorist *attr*

terrorizzare [terrorid'dzare] VT *(gen)* to terrify; *(popolazione)* to terrorize; **l'idea mi terrorizza** the idea terrifies me; **l'idea di viaggiare in aereo lo terrorizza** he is terrified of flying

terroso, a [ter'roso] AGG *(acqua)* muddy; *(sporco di terra)* covered with earth; *(Chim: metallo)* earth *attr*

terso, a ['tɛrso] PP *di* **tergere**
■AGG clear

terza ['tɛrtsa] SF *(gen)* third; *(Aut)* third gear; *(Scol: terza elementare)* ≈ year four *(Brit)*, ≈ third grade *(Am)* (: *terza media)* ≈ year nine *(Brit)*, ≈ eighth grade *(Am)* (: *terza superiore)* ≈ lower sixth *(Brit)*, ≈ eleventh grade *(Am)*

terzetto [ter'tsetto] SM *(Mus)* trio, terzetto; *(di persone)* trio

terziario, ria, ri, rie [ter'tsjarjo] AGG *(Geol, Econ)* tertiary
■SM **1** *(Geol)* tertiary period **2** *(Econ)* tertiary *o* service sector; **terziario avanzato** high-tech service sector
■SM/F *(Rel)* tertiary

terzina [ter'tsina] SF *(Letteratura)* tercet; *(Mus)* triplet

terzino [ter'tsino] SM *(Calcio)* fullback, back; **terzino destro/sinistro** right/left back; **gioca da terzino destro** he plays right back

terzo, a ['tɛrtso] AGG third; **abito al terzo piano** I live on the third floor; **terzo** *or* **in terzo luogo** thirdly, in the third place; **di terz'ordine** third-rate; **il terzo mondo** the Third World; **la terza pagina** *(Stampa)* the Arts page; **la terza età** old age
■SM/F third
■**terzi** SMPL *(altri)* others, other people *pl*; *(Dir)* third party *sg*; **agire per conto terzi** to act on behalf of a third party; **assicurazione contro terzi** third-party insurance *(Brit)*, liability insurance *(Am)*
■SM *(frazione)* third; *per fraseologia vedi* **quinto**

terzogenito, a [tertso'dʒɛnito] AGG, SM/F third-born, third eldest

terzultimo, a [ter'tsultimo] AGG, SM/F third from last, last but two

tesa ['tesa] SF *(di cappello)* brim; **a larghe tese** wide-brimmed

teschio, chi ['tɛskjo] SM skull

Teseo [te'zeo] SM Theseus

tesi ['tɛsi] SF INV *(gen)* thesis; *(Univ: anche:* **tesi di laurea**) (degree) thesis, dissertation; **presenterà una tesi su Jane Austen** she's going to do a dissertation on Jane Austen; **sostenere una tesi** to uphold a theory

tesi *ecc* ['tesi] VB *vedi* **tendere**

tesista, i, e [te'zista] SM/F *person who is writing a thesis*

teso, a ['teso] PP *di* **tendere**
■AGG *(corda)* taut, tight; *(nervi, volto)* tense; *(rapporti)* strained; *(braccia)* outstretched; **è molto teso in questi giorni** he's very tense these days; **con la mano tesa** with outstretched hand; **stava lì con le orecchie tese** he was all ears; **essere teso come una corda di violino** to be very tense

tesoreria [tezore'ria] SF treasury

tesoriere, a [tezo'rjɛre] SM/F treasurer

tesoro [te'zɔro] SM **1** *(gen, fig)* treasure; **far tesoro dei consigli di qn** to take sb's advice to heart; **sei un tesoro!** how nice of you!; **che tesoro di ragazza** what a nice girl; **grazie tesoro!** thank you darling!; **caccia al tesoro** treasure hunt **2** *(Fin)*: **il Tesoro** the Exchequer *(Brit)*; **il ministero del Tesoro** the Treasury; **buono del Tesoro** Treasury Bond
▷ www.tesoro.it/welcome.asp

tessera ['tɛssera] SF **1** *(di socio)* (membership) card; *(di abbonato)* season ticket; *(di giornalista)* pass, press card; **ho la tessera del Milan** I've got a season ticket for AC-Milan; **ha la tessera del partito** he's a party member; **tessera magnetica** swipe card; **tessera dell'autobus** bus pass; **tessera di riduzione ferroviaria** ≈ Railcard *(Brit)* **2** *(di mosaico)* tessera

tesseramento [tessera'mento] SM: **campagna di tesseramento (di un partito)** (party) membership drive

tesserare [tesse'rare] VT *(iscrivere)* to give a membership card to
▶ **tesserarsi** VIP to get one's membership card

tesserato, a [tesse'rato] SM/F *(di società sportiva)* (fully paid-up) member; *(Pol)* (card-carrying) member

tessere ['tɛssere] VT *(gen)* to weave; *(fig: inganni, tradimenti)* to plan, plot; **tessere le lodi di qn** to sing sb's praises

tessile ['tɛssile] AGG textile
■SM/F textile worker

tessitore, trice [tessi'tore] SM/F weaver

tessitura [tessi'tura] SF *(operazione)* weaving; *(impianto)* weaving mill *o* factory

tessuto [tes'suto] SM **1** material, fabric; *(di lana)* cloth, material; **tessuti** SMPL textiles **2** *(Bio)* tissue

test ['test] SM INV test

testa ['tɛsta] SF
1 *(gen, Anat)* head; **ho battuto la testa contro il pensile** I banged my head on the cupboard; **a testa alta** with one's head held high; **a testa bassa** *(correre)* headlong; *(con aria dimessa)* with head bowed; **gettarsi in qc a testa bassa** to rush headlong into sth; **cadere a testa in giù** to fall head first; **dalla testa ai piedi** from head to foot; **a testa** a head; **15 euro a testa** 15 euros apiece *o* a head *o* per person; **vincere di mezza testa** *(Ippica)* to win by half a head; **testa della racchetta** *(Tennis)* racket head; **una testa d'aglio** a bulb of garlic
2 *(fig: cervello)* head, brain(s); **testa di rapa** blockhead; **che testa di cavolo!** what a moron!; **essere una testa**

calda to be hot headed; **avere la testa dura** to be stubborn; **avere la testa vuota** to be empty-headed; **avere la testa tra le nuvole** to have one's head in the clouds; **non avere testa** to be scatterbrained; **usare la testa** to use one's head *o* brains; **ma dove hai la testa?** what on earth are you thinking of?; **ha poca testa per la matematica** he hasn't got much of a head for maths (*Brit*) *o* math (*Am*); **fare di testa propria** to do as one pleases; **far entrare qc in testa a qn** to din sth into sb's head; **mettersi in testa di fare qc** to take it into one's head to do sth; **che cosa gli hai messo in testa?** what ideas have you been putting into his head?; **non so che cosa gli sia passato per la testa** I don't know what's come over him

3 (*parte anteriore: di treno, processione*) front, head; (*: di colonna militare*) head; (*: di pagina, lista*) top, head; **le carrozze di testa** (*Ferr*) the front of the train; **essere in testa** (*pilota, ciclista*) to be in the lead, be the leader; **essere in testa alla classifica** (*pilota, ciclista*) to be number one; (*squadra*) to be top of the league; (*disco*) to be top of the charts, be number one; **essere alla testa di qc** (*società*) to be the head of; (*esercito*) to be at the head of; **testa di serie** (*Sport: giocatore*) seed, seeded player; (*: squadra*) top of the league

4 (*fraseologia*): **avere la testa sulle spalle** to have one's head screwed on; **dare alla testa** to go to one's head; **montarsi la testa** to become big-headed; **mettere la testa a posto** *o* **a partito** to settle down; **essere fuori** *o* **via di testa** to be off one's head; **perdere la testa per qn** to lose one's head over sb; **perdere la testa** (*per ira*) to lose one's head; **ci scommetterei la testa** I'd bet my boots; **tener testa a qn** (*nemico, avversario*) to stand up to sb; **lavata di testa** telling-off, ticking-off (*Brit*); **testa o croce?** heads or tails?; **fare a testa o croce** to toss (for sth); **facciamo a testa o croce?** shall we toss for it?

testa-coda ['tεsta 'kɔda] SM INV (*Aut*) spin

testamentario, ria, ri, rie [testamen'tarjo] AGG (*Dir*) testamentary; **le sue disposizioni testamentarie** the provisions of his will

testamento [testa'mento] SM **1** (*Dir*) will, testament; **fare testamento** to make one's will; **ha deciso di fare testamento** he decided to make his will; **testamento spirituale** (*fig*) spiritual testament; **testamento biologico** living will **2** (*Rel*): **l'Antico/il Nuovo Testamento** the Old/New Testament

testardaggine [testar'daddʒine] SF stubbornness, obstinacy

testardamente [testarda'mente] AVV obstinately, stubbornly

testardo, a [tes'tardo] AGG stubborn, obstinate
■ SM/F stubborn *o* obstinate person

testare [tes'tare] VT to test

testata [tes'tata] SF **1** (*di letto*) headboard **2** (*di giornale*) heading; (*il giornale stesso*) paper; **concentrazione delle testate** concentration of press ownership **3** (*Aut*) (cylinder) head; (*Aer: di missile*) head; **missile a testata nucleare** nuclear missile; **missile a testata convenzionale** missile with a conventional warhead **4** (*colpo: accidentale*) bang on the head; (*: intenzionale*) head butt; **dare una testata contro qc** to bang one's head on sth; **dare una testata a qn** to head-butt sb

teste ['tεste] SM/F (*Dir*) witness

testicolo [tes'tikolo] SM testicle

testiera [tes'tjεra] SF **1** (*del letto*) headboard **2** (*di cavallo*) headpiece

testimone [testi'mɔne] SM/F witness; **non c'erano testimoni** there weren't any witnesses; **fare da testimone alle nozze di qn** to be a witness at sb's wedding; **queste rovine sono testimoni della grandezza di Roma** these ruins bear witness to the former greatness of Rome; **testimone di Geova** (*Rel*) Jehovah's Witness; **testimone oculare** eye witness
■ SM (*Sport*) baton

testimonial [testi'mounjəl] SM/F INV *celebrity who advertises a particular product*

testimoniale [testimo'njale] AGG: **prova testimoniale** testimonial evidence

testimonianza [testimo'njantsa] SF (*atto*) deposition; (*effetto*) evidence; (*fig: prova*) proof; **accusare qn di falsa testimonianza** to accuse sb of perjury; **rilasciare una testimonianza** to give evidence; **ne fanno testimonianza altri autori contemporanei** (*fig*) other contemporary authors testify to it; **ha dato testimonianza di grande fedeltà** he proved his great loyalty

testimoniare [testimo'njare] VT: **testimoniare che...** to testify that ..., give evidence that ...; **testimoniare il vero** to tell the truth; **testimoniare il falso** to perjure o.s.; **le impronte testimoniano la sua colpevolezza** the fingerprints are proof of his guilt; **testimoniare a favore di/contro qn** to testify for/against sb, give evidence for/against sb; **era disposta a testimoniare contro di lui** she was ready to give evidence against him; **è stato chiamato a testimoniare** he was called upon to give evidence
■ VI (*aus* **avere**) to testify, give evidence; **non ha voluto testimoniare sull'accaduto** he didn't want to give evidence on *o* about what happened

testina [tes'tina] SF (*di registratore, rasoio*) head; **testina rotante** (*di macchina da scrivere*) golf ball; **testina di stampa** (*Inform*) print head

testo ['tεsto] SM (*gen*) text; (*originale di traduzione*) original text; **un testo difficile** a difficult text; **libro di testo** (*Scol*) textbook; **fare testo** (*autore*) to be authoritative; (*opera*) be a standard work; **questo libro non fa testo** this book is not essential reading; **le sue parole fanno testo** his words carry weight

testone, a [tes'tone] SM/F (*ostinato*) pig-headed person; (*stupido*) blockhead, dunderhead

testosterone [testoste'rone] SM testosterone

testuale [testu'ale] AGG textual; **le sue testuali parole furono...** his (*o* her) actual *o* exact words were ...

testuggine [tes'tuddʒine] SF (*Zool*) tortoise; (*: marina*) turtle

tetano ['tεtano] SM (*Med*) tetanus

tête-à-tête ['tεta'tεt] SM INV tête-à-tête

tetramente [tetra'mente] AVV gloomily

tetravalente [tetrava'lεnte] AGG tetravalent

tetro, a ['tεtro] AGG (*anche fig*) gloomy; **era di umore tetro** he was gloomy *o* glum

tetta ['tetta] SF (*fam*) boob, tit

tettarella [tetta'rεlla] SF teat

tetto ['tetto] SM **1** (*gen*) roof; (*di veicolo*) roof, top; (*fig*) house, home; **restare senza tetto** to be homeless *o* without a roof over one's head; **abbandonare il tetto coniugale** to desert one's family; **tetto apribile** (*Aut*) sun roof; **tetto a cupola** dome; **tetto a terrazza** roof terrace **2** (*limite massimo: Econ*) (maximum) limit, ceiling; **porre un tetto alla spesa pubblica** to impose a limit on public spending

tettoia [tet'toja] SF (*gen*) canopy; (*di stazione*) roof

Tt

tettonica [tet'tɔnika] SF tectonics *sg*
teutonico, a, ci, che [teu'tɔniko] AGG Teutonic
Tevere ['tevere] SM: **il Tevere** the Tiber
Texas ['teksas] SM Texas
TFR [tiɛffe'ɛrre] SIGLA M (= **Trattamento di Fine Rapporto**) lump sum (payable on retirement)
TG, Tg [ti'dʒi] SIGLA M INV (= **telegiornale**) TV news *sg*
thai chi [tai'cʃi] SM t'ai chi
thermos® ['tɛrmos] SM INV Thermos® (flask)
thriller ['θrilə] SM INV (*libro, film*) thriller
ti [ti] PRON PERS (*dav* lo, la, li, le, ne *diventa* te) **1** (*ogg diretto*) you; **non ti ascolta mai** he never listens to you; **non ti ho visto stamattina** I didn't see you this morning **2** (*complemento di termine*) (to) you; **ti dirò tutto** I'll tell you everything; **te lo ha dato?** did he give it to you?; **ti ha sorriso** he smiled at you; **ti piace?** do you like it? **3** (*riflessivo e medio*) yourself; **ti sei lavata?** have you washed (yourself)?; **ti sei pettinato?** have you combed your hair?; **ti sei divertito?** did you enjoy yourself?; **quando ti prendi una vacanza?** when are you going to have yourself a holiday?; **ti ricordi?** do you remember?
tiara ['tjara] SF tiara
Tibet ['tibet] SM Tibet
tibetano, a [tibe'tano] AGG, SM/F Tibetan
tibia ['tibja] SF (*Anat*) tibia, shinbone
tiburio, ri [ti'burjo] SM (*Archit*) lantern
tic [tik] SM INV **1** (*gen*) click; (*di orologio*) tick **2** (*Med*: *anche*: **tic nervoso**) tic; (*fig*) mannerism
ticchettio, tii [tikket'tio] SM (*di macchina da scrivere*) clatter; (*di orologio*) ticking; (*di pioggia*) pattering, patter
ticchio, chi ['tikkjo] SM (*tic*) tic; (*fig*: *capriccio*) whim; **mi è preso il ticchio di andare in Africa** I've taken a notion to visit Africa
ticket ['tikit] SM INV (*sui farmaci*) prescription charge (*Brit*); (*per prestazioni mediche*) medical charge

TICKET

The **ticket** is the amount you have to pay for some medical services, including emergency treatment, and for the purchase of medicines on prescription.

tictac [tik'tak] SM INV tick-tock
tiene *ecc* ['tjɛne] VB *vedi* **tenere**
tiepidamente [tjepida'mente] AVV (*fig*) in a lukewarm way, half-heartedly; **accogliere qn/qc tiepidamente** to give sb/sth a lukewarm reception
tiepidezza [tjepi'dettsa] SF (*di clima*) warmth; (*di accoglienza*) lukewarmness
tiepido, a ['tjɛpido] AGG (*gen*) lukewarm, tepid; (*fig*: *accoglienza*) lukewarm; (: *entusiasmo*) half-hearted; **acqua tiepida** lukewarm water
tifare [ti'fare] VI (*aus* **avere**) **tifare per** (*squadra*) to be a fan of, support; (*parteggiare*) to side with
tifo ['tifo] SM **1** (*Med*) typhus **2** (*Sport*): **fare il tifo per** to be a fan of, support; **faccio il tifo per la Juventus** I support Juventus
tifone [ti'fone] SM (*Meteor*) typhoon
tifoseria [tifose'ria] SF fans *pl*, supporters *pl*
tifoso, a [ti'foso] AGG: **essere tifoso di** to be a fan of; **sono tifoso del Milan** I'm a Milan supporter
■ SM/F (*Sport*) supporter, fan; **i tifosi del Liverpool** the Liverpool supporters
tight ['tait] SM INV morning suit
tigì [tid'dʒi] SM INV TV news
tiglio, gli ['tiʎʎo] SM lime (tree), linden (tree)
tigna ['tiɲɲa] SF (*Med*) ringworm
tignola [tiɲ'ɲɔla] SF (*Zool*) moth
tignosa [tiɲ'ɲosa] SF (*Bot*) amanita (*mushroom*)
tigrato, a [ti'grato] AGG striped
tigre ['tigre] SF tiger; (*femmina*) tigress; **cavalcare la tigre** (*fig*) to have a tiger by the tail; **occhio di tigre** (*Mineralogia*) tiger's eye, tigereye; **tigre di carta** (*fig*) paper tiger
tigrotto [ti'grɔtto] SM tiger cub
tilde ['tilde] SM O F tilde
tilt [tilt] SM INV: **andare** *o* **essere in tilt** (*macchina*) to go/be on the blink; (*fig*) to go/be haywire
timballo [tim'ballo] SM (*Culin*) timbale
timbrare [tim'brare] VT (*gen*) to stamp; (*annullare*: *francobolli*) to postmark; **hai timbrato il biglietto?** have you stamped your ticket?; **timbrare il cartellino** to clock in
timbratura [timbra'tura] SF (*vedi vb*) stamping; postmarking
timbro ['timbro] SM **1** (*strumento*) (rubber) stamp; (*su documento*) stamp; (*su francobollo*) postmark; **mettere il timbro su qc** to stamp sth; **gli hanno messo il timbro sul passaporto** they stamped his passport **2** (*Mus*) tone, timbre
timidamente [timida'mente] AVV (*vedi agg*) shyly, timidly; bashfully
timidezza [timi'dettsa] SF shyness, timidity
timido, a ['timido] AGG (*persona, animale*) shy, timid; (*tentativo*) bashful
■ SM/F shy person
timo[1] ['timo] SM (*Bot*) thyme
timo[2] ['timo] SM (*Anat*) thymus
timone [ti'mone] SM (*Naut*) helm; (: *parte sommersa*) rudder; (*Aer*) rudder; (*di carro*) shaft; **barra del timone** (*Naut*) tiller; **ruota del timone** (*Naut*) wheel; **essere al timone** (*anche fig*) to be at the helm; **prendere il timone** (*anche fig*) to take the helm; **timone di direzione** (*Aer*) rudder; **timone di profondità** (*Aer*) tail flap
timoneria [timone'ria] SF (*Naut*: *apparecchiature*) steering gear
timoniera [timo'njɛra] SF pilot house, wheelhouse
timoniere [timo'njɛre] SM (*Naut*) helmsman; (*Canottaggio*) cox
timorato, a [timo'rato] AGG conscientious; **timorato di Dio** God-fearing
timore [ti'more] SM (*paura*) fear, dread; (*preoccupazione*) fear; (*rispetto*) awe; **avere timore di qn/qc** (*paura*) to be afraid of sb/sth; **ho il timore che non ci arriveremo** I fear we won't make it; **i miei timori si sono rivelati infondati** my fears proved to be unfounded; **ha un timore reverenziale di suo padre** he stands in awe of his father
timorese [timo'rese] SM Timorese
Timor est ['timor est] SM East Timor
timorosamente [timorosa'mente] AVV fearfully
timoroso, a [timo'roso] AGG (*diffidente*) timid, timorous; (*pauroso*) frightened, afraid; (*preoccupato*) worried, afraid
timpano ['timpano] SM **1** (*Anat*) tympanum, eardrum; **rompere i timpani a qn** to burst sb's eardrums **2** (*Mus*) kettledrum; **i timpani** the timpani
tinca, che ['tinka] SF tench
tinello [ti'nɛllo] SM small dining room
tingere ['tindʒere] VB IRREG
■ VT (*stoffa, capelli*) to dye; **il tramonto tingeva il cielo**

di rosso the sunset was reddening the sky *o* was turning the sky red
▶ **tingersi** VIP: **il cielo si è tinto di rosso** the sky turned red

tino ['tino] SM vat

tinozza [ti'nɔttsa] SF tub

tinsi *ecc* ['tinsi] VB *vedi* **tingere**

tinta ['tinta] SF **1** (*colore*) shade, colour (*Brit*), color (*Am*); **una tinta vivace** a bright colour; **una stoffa di tinta scura** a dark material; **una borsetta in tinta con le scarpe** a bag and matching shoes; **un vestito (in *o* a) tinta unita** a plain suit; **un vestito giallo in tinta unita** a plain yellow dress **2** (*per muri*) paint; (*per capelli*) dye; **un barattolo di tinta** a tin of paint; **dare una mano di tinta a qc** to give sth a coat of paint; **dipingere qc a tinte fosche** (*fig*) to paint a gloomy picture of sth; **un racconto a forti tinte** a dramatic story

tintarella [tinta'rɛlla] SF (*fam*) (sun)tan; **prendere la tintarella** to get a tan

tinteggiare [tinted'dʒare] VT to paint

tintinnare [tintin'nare] VI (*aus* **avere**) (*campanelle*) to tinkle; (*bicchieri*) to clink, tinkle

tintinnio, nii [tintin'nio] SM tinkling

tinto, a ['tinto] PP *di* **tingere**

tintore [tin'tore] SM (*di tessuti*) dyer

tintoria [tinto'ria] SF (*lavasecco*) dry cleaner's (shop); (*officina*) dyeworks *inv*; **devo portare il cappotto in tintoria** I need to take my coat to the dry cleaner's

tintura [tin'tura] SF **1** (*operazione*) dyeing; (*soluzione colorante*) dye; **tintura per capelli** hair dye **2** (*Med*) tincture; **tintura di iodio** tincture of iodine

tipicamente [tipika'mente] AVV typically

tipicità [tipitʃi'ta] SF typicalness

tipico, a, ci, che ['tipiko] AGG typical; **un esempio tipico** a typical example; **un tipico pub inglese** a traditional English pub; **un tipico piatto scozzese** a traditional Scottish dish

tipo, a ['tipo] SM **1** (*genere*) kind, sort, type; **vestiti di tutti i tipi** all kinds of clothes; **piante di tutti i tipi** all sorts of plants; **che tipo di bici hai?** what sort of bike have you got?; **sul tipo di questo** of this sort; **non è il mio tipo** he's not my type; **non è bella ma è un tipo** she might not be beautiful but she's got something **2** (*modello*) type, model
■ SM/F (*fam: individuo*) character; **sei un bel tipo!** you're a fine one!; **chi era quel tipo?** who was that guy?; **mi sembra un tipo simpatico** he seems nice; **è una tipa molto sicura di sé** she's very self-confident
■ AGG INV average, typical

tipografia [tipogra'fia] SF typography

tipografico, a, ci, che [tipo'grafiko] AGG typographic(al)

tipografo, a [ti'pɔgrafo] SM/F typographer

tipologia [tipolo'dʒia] SF typology

tip tap [tip tap] SM INV tap dancing

TIR [tir] SIGLA M INV (= **Transports Internationaux Routiers**) International Heavy Goods Vehicle

tira e molla [tirae'mɔlla] SM INV = **tiremmolla**

tiraggio, gi [ti'raddʒo] SM (*di camino*) draught (*Brit*), draft (*Am*)

tiralinee [tira'linee] SM INV drawing pen

tiramisù [tirami'su] SM INV tiramisu; *dessert with a sponge base soaked in coffee and topped with a cream cheese dredged with chocolate*

Tirana [ti'rana] SF Tirana

tiranneggiare [tiranned'dʒare] VT to tyrannize

tirannia [tiran'nia] SF tyranny

tirannicamente [tirannika'mente] AVV tyrannically

tirannico, a, ci, che [ti'ranniko] AGG tyrannical

tirannide [ti'rannide] SF tyranny

tiranno, a [ti'ranno] SM tyrant
■ AGG tyrannical

tirannosauro [tiranno'sauro] SM tyrannosaurus

tirante [ti'rante] SM (*Naut, di tenda*) guy; (*Edil*) brace

tirapiedi [tira'pjɛdi] SM/F INV hanger-on

tirapugni [tira'puɲɲi] SM INV knuckle-duster (*Brit*), brass knuckles *pl* (*Am*)

tirare [ti'rare] VT
1 (*gen*) to pull; (*slitta*) to pull, drag; (*rimorchio*) to tow; (*Culin: pasta*) to stretch; **tira!** pull!; **tirare qn per la manica** to tug at sb's sleeve; **tirare qn da parte** to take *o* draw sb aside; **tirare gli orecchi a qn** to tweak sb's ears; **mi ha tirato i capelli** she pulled my hair; **tirare qn per i capelli** to pull sb's hair; (*fig*) to force sb; **tirare qc per le lunghe** to drag sth out; **tirare le somme** (*fig*) to draw a conclusion; **tirare un sospiro di sollievo** to heave a sigh of relief; **una cosa tira l'altra** one thing leads to another; **tirare fuori** to pull out, take out; **il vigile mi fece tirare fuori i documenti** the policeman made me produce my identification papers; **alla fine ha tirato fuori tutta la verità** in the end he came out with the whole truth; **tirare giù** to pull down; **tirare su qn/qc** to pull sb/sth up; **tirare su qn** (*fig: rallegrare*) to cheer sb up; (*: allevare*) to bring sb up; **tirarsi dietro qn** to bring *o* drag sb along; **tirarsi su i capelli** to put one's hair up; **tirarsi addosso qc** to pull sth down on top of o.s.; (*fig*) to bring sth upon o.s.
2 (*chiudere: tende*) to draw, close, pull; **tirare la porta** to close the door, pull the door to
3 (*tracciare, disegnare*) to draw, trace; (*stampare*) to print
4 (*lanciare: sasso, palla*) to throw, fling; (*: colpo, freccia*) to fire; (*: fig: bestemmie, imprecazioni*) to hurl, let fly; **ha tirato un sasso e poi si è nascosto** he threw a stone and then hid; **tirami la palla!** throw me the ball!; **tirare un pugno a qn** to punch sb; **gli ho tirato un pugno** I punched him; **tirare uno schiaffo a qn** to slap sb; **gli ho tirato uno schiaffo** I slapped him; **tirare un calcio** to kick; **tirare calci** to kick; **tirare il pallone** (*Calcio*) to kick the ball
■ VI (*aus* **avere**) (*sogg: pipa, camino*) to draw; (*: vestito, indumento*) to be tight; **tirare avanti** (*fig: vivere*) to get by; (*: proseguire*) to struggle on; **tirare diritto** to keep right on going; **tirare tardi/mattina** to stay up late/ till the early hours *o* dawn; **tirare col fucile/con l'arco** to shoot with a rifle/with a bow and arrow; **tirava un forte vento** a strong wind was blowing; **che aria tira?** (*fig*) what are things like?, what's the situation like?; **tirare a campare** to keep going as best one can; **tirare a indovinare** to take a guess; **tirare sul prezzo** to bargain; **tirare di scherma** to fence; **tirare in porta** (*Calcio*) to shoot (at goal); **la fantascienza è un genere che tira molto** science fiction is very popular; **il mercato/l'economia tira** the market/the economy is thriving
▶ **tirarsi** VR: **tirarsi indietro** to draw *o* move back; (*fig*) to back out; **aveva promesso di aiutarmi ma poi si è tirato indietro** he promised to help me and then backed out; **tirarsi su** to pull o.s. up; (*fig*) to cheer o.s. up

tirata [ti'rata] SF **1** (*strattone*) pull, tug; **tirata d'orecchi** (*fig*) telling-off, ticking-off (*Brit*) **2** (*di sigaretta*) drag, puff **3** (*svolgimento ininterrotto*): **abbiamo fatto tutta una tirata** we did it all in one go; **l'ho**

letto in una tirata I read it at one go **4** (*discorso polemico*) tirade

tirato, a [ti'rato] AGG (*teso*) taut; (*stanco: viso, espressione*) drawn; (*avaro: persona*) stingy

tiratore, trice [tira'tore] SM/F shot; **un buon tiratore** a good shot; **franco tiratore** (*Mil*) irregular; (: *cecchino*) sniper; (*Pol*) ≈ rebel (*who votes against his/her own party in a secret ballot*) **tiratore scelto** marksman

tiratura [tira'tura] SF (*di giornali*) circulation; (*di libri*) printing, (print) run

tirchieria [tirkje'ria] SF meanness, stinginess

tirchio, chia, chi, chie ['tirkjo] AGG mean, stingy; **quant'è tirchio!** he's so mean!

■ SM/F miser

tiremmolla [tirem'mɔlla] SM INV hesitation, shilly-shallying *no pl*

tiritera [tiri'tɛra] SF (*fam*) drivel, hot air

tiro ['tiro] SM **1** (*di cavalli, buoi*) team; **tiro a quattro** coach and four; **cavallo da tiro** carthorse **2** (*di pistola, freccia, Calcio*) shooting *no pl*; (: *colpo*) shot; **è stato un buon tiro** that was a good shot; **essere a tiro** to be in range; (*fig*) to be within reach; **se mi capita** *o* **viene a tiro!** if I get my hands on him (*o* her)!; **a un tiro di schioppo** a stone's throw away **3** (*lancio*) throwing *no pl*; (: *effetto*) throw **4** (*fig*): **giocare un brutto tiro** *o* **un tiro mancino a qn** to play a dirty trick on sb **4** **mettersi in tiro** (*fam: vestirsi elegante*) to get dolled up

■ **tiro al bersaglio** target shooting; **tiro alla fune** tug-of-war; **tiro con l'arco** archery

▷ www.fitarco.it/

tiro al piattello clay pigeon shooting, skeet shooting (*Am*); **tiro al piccione** pigeon shooting; **tiro a segno** (*esercitazione*) target shooting; (*luogo*) shooting range

tirocinante [tirotʃi'nante] AGG apprentice *attr*, trainee *attr*

■ SM/F apprentice, trainee

tirocinio, ni [tiro'tʃinjo] SM: **tirocinio (in)** (*di mestiere*) apprenticeship (in); (*di professione*) training (in); **fare il proprio tirocinio** to serve one's apprenticeship; to do one's training

tiroide [ti'rɔide] SF (*Anat*) thyroid (gland)

tirolese [tiro'lese] AGG, SM/F Tyrolean, Tyrolese *inv*

Tirolo [ti'rɔlo] SM: **il Tirolo** the Tyrol

tirrenico, a, ci, che [tir'rɛniko] AGG Tyrrhenian

Tirreno [tir'rɛno] SM: **il (mar) Tirreno** the Tyrrhenian Sea

tirso ['tirso] SM (*Mitol*) thyrsus

tisana [ti'zana] SF herb tea, tisane

tisi ['tizi] SF (*Med*) consumption

tisico, a, ci, che ['tiziko] AGG (*Med*) consumptive; (*fig: gracile*) frail

■ SM/F (*Med*) consumptive (person)

tisiologo, gi [ti'zjɔlogo] SM phthisiologist

titanico, a, ci, che [ti'taniko] AGG gigantic, enormous; **un'impresa titanica** an operation of titanic proportions

titanio [ti'tanjo] SM (*Chim*) titanium

titano [ti'tano] SM (*Mitol, fig*) titan

titillare [titil'lare] VT (*solleticare*) to tickle; (*fig*) to titillate

titolare [tito'lare] AGG (*gen*) appointed; (*Univ*) with a full-time appointment; (*sovrano, vescovo*) titular

■ SM/F (*gen*) holder, incumbent; (*proprietario*) owner, proprietor; (*Sport: in squadra*) regular first-team player; (: *a livello nazionale*) regular member of the national team; **titolare di cattedra** (*Univ*) full professor

titolato, a [tito'lato] AGG (*persona*) titled

titolazione [titolat'tsjone] SF (*Chim*) titration

Tito Livio ['tito 'livjo] SM (Titus) Livy

titolo ['titolo] SM **1** (*di libro*) title; (*di giornale*) headline; **qual è il titolo di quella canzone?** what's the title of that song?; **titoli di coda** (*Cine, TV*) closing credits; **titoli di testa** (*Cine, TV*) opening credits **2** (*Fin: gen*) security; (: *azione*) share, stock; **titoli esteri** foreign securities; **titoli di stato** government securities *o* bonds; **titolo di credito** document of credit; **titolo obbligazionario** bond, share certificate; **titolo al portatore** bearer bond; **titolo di proprietà** title deed; **titolo spazzatura** junk bond **3** (*qualifica: nobiliare, Sport*) title; (: *di studio*) qualification; **titolo mondiale** (*Sport*) world title; **ha conservato il titolo mondiale** he retained the world title **4** (*fig: motivo*): **a che titolo sei venuto?** why *o* for what reason have you come?; **a titolo di amicizia** for *o* out of friendship; **a titolo di curiosità** out of curiosity; **a titolo di prestito/favore** as a loan/favour (*Brit*) *o* favor (*Am*); **a titolo di cronaca** for your information

titubante [titu'bante] AGG hesitant, undecided, irresolute; **è titubante per natura** he is a born ditherer

titubanza [titu'bantsa] SF hesitation, indecision

titubare [titu'bare] VI (*aus* **avere**) to hesitate; **titubare nel fare qc** to hesitate to do sth

tivù [ti'vu] SF INV (*fam*) TV, telly (*Brit*); **cosa c'è in tivù stasera?** what's on TV tonight?

tizio, zia, zi, zie ['tittsjo] SM/F character, individual; **chi era quel tizio?** who was that guy?; **chi era quella tizia?** who was that girl?; **Tizio, Caio e Sempronio** Tom, Dick and Harry

tizzone [tit'tsone] SM (*di legno*) (fire)brand; (*di carbone*) live coal

TMG ['ti'ɛmme'dʒi] SIGLA M (= **Tempo Medio di Greenwich**) GMT

TN SIGLA = *Trento*

TNT [tienne'ti] SIGLA M (*Chim*: = **trinitrotoluene**) TNT

TO SIGLA = **Torino**

to' [tɔ] ESCL **1** (*dando qualcosa*) here you are!; **to', tieni!** here, take this! **2** (*guarda un po'*): **to'! chi si vede** look who's here!; **to'! questa è bella** (*iro*) well, that's very nice!

toast ['toust] SM INV toasted sandwich

> **LO SAPEVI...?**
> **toast** non si traduce mai con la parola inglese *toast*

toccante [tok'kante] AGG (*commovente*) touching, moving

toccare [tok'kare] VT **1** (*gen*) to touch; (*tastare*) to feel; (*fig: sfiorare: argomento, tema*) to touch on; **non toccare!** don't touch it!; **non toccare la mia roba** don't touch my things; **non ha toccato cibo** he hasn't touched his food; **non voglio toccare i miei risparmi** I don't want to touch my savings; **toccare un tasto delicato** to touch a sore point; **hai toccato il mio punto debole** you have hit on my weak point; **toccare con mano** (*fig*) to find out for o.s. **2** (*raggiungere*) to touch, reach; **si tocca?** (*in acqua*) can you touch the bottom?; **toccare il fondo** to touch the bottom; (*fig*) to touch rock bottom; **toccare terra** (*Naut*) to reach land; (*Aer*) to touch down; **abbiamo toccato diverse città** we stopped at a number of towns; **abbiamo toccato diversi porti** we put in at various ports; **ha appena toccato la cinquantina** he has just turned fifty **3** (*commuovere*) to touch, move; (*ferire*) to hurt, wound;

le tue allusioni non mi toccano your remarks don't bother me; **toccare qn sul vivo** to cut sb to the quick; **la vicenda ci tocca da vicino** the matter concerns *o* affects us closely

■ VI (*aus* essere) **1** (*capitare*): **mi è toccata una bella fortuna** I've had great good fortune; **perché toccano sempre a me queste cose?** why is it always me who has to do these things?; **a chi tocca, tocca** that's life **2** (*essere costretto*): **mi tocca andare** I have to go; **che cosa mi tocca sentire!** what's this I hear?; **sai che cosa mi è toccato fare?** do you know what I had to do?; **mi è toccato pagare per tutti** I had to pay for everybody; **perché tocca sempre a me farlo?** why do I always have to do it? **3** (*spettare*): **toccare a** to be the turn of; **a chi tocca?** whose turn *o* go is it?; **tocca a me** it's my turn *o* go; **non tocca a me giudicare** it is not for me to judge; **tocca a te difenderci** it's up to you to defend us;

▶ **toccarsi** VR **1** (*masturbarsi*) to play with o.s. **2** (*uso reciproco*): **gli estremi si toccano** (*anche fig*) extremes meet

toccasana [tokka'sana] SM INV miracle cure

toccata [tok'kata] SF (*gen*) touch; (*Mus*) toccata

toccato, a [tok'kato] AGG **1** (*come escl*: *Scherma, anche fig*) touché **2** (*svitato*) mad, touched

toccherò *ecc* [tokke'rɔ] VB *vedi* **toccare**

tocco[1], a, chi, che ['tokko] AGG mad, touched

tocco[2], chi ['tokko] SM **1** (*gen, Mus*) touch; **gli ultimi tocchi** the finishing touches **2** (*colpo*: *di campana, orologio, pennello*) stroke

tocco[3], chi ['tɔkko] SM (*di pane, formaggio*) piece, chunk

toc toc [tɔk tɔk] ESCL knock knock

toeletta [toe'lɛtta] SF = **toilette**

tofu ['tɔfu] SM INV tofu

toga, ghe ['tɔga] SF (*di magistrato*) gown, robe; (*Storia*) toga

togato, a [to'gato] AGG: **giudice togato** magistrate

togliere ['tɔʎʎere] VB IRREG

■ VT **1** (*gen*) to remove, take away *o* off; **togli il quadro dal muro** take the picture off the wall; **ho tolto il poster dalla parete** I took the poster off the wall; **mi hanno tolto due denti** I had two teeth taken out; **togliere le mani di tasca** to take one's hands out of one's pockets; **togliere qn di mezzo** (*allontanare*) to get rid of sb; (*uccidere*) to bump sb off; **togliere qc a qn** to take sth (away) from sb; **togliere la parola a qn** to interrupt sb; **togliere la parola di bocca a qn** to take the words out of sb's mouth; **togliere il saluto a qn** to ignore sb, snub sb; **mi hai tolto un peso** you've taken a weight off my mind; **volevo togliermi un peso (dalla coscienza)** I wanted to get it off my chest; **togliersi la vita** to take one's (own) life; **togliersi i guanti/il vestito/il trucco** to take off one's gloves/suit/make-up; **togliti il cappotto** take off your coat; **togliersi una voglia** to satisfy an urge *o* a whim; **togliersi la soddisfazione di** to have the satisfaction of; **ciò non toglie che...** that doesn't alter the fact that ..., nevertheless ..., be that as it may ... **2** (*Mat*) to take away, subtract; **togliere 3 da 7** to take 3 away from 7;

▶ **togliersi** VR: **togliersi di mezzo** to get out of the way; **togliti dai piedi!** get out of the way!

Togo ['tɔgo] SM Togo

toilette [twa'lɛt] SF INV, **toletta** [to'letta] SF **1** (*gabinetto*) toilet (*Brit*), bathroom (*Am*); **dov'è la toilette?** where's the toilet? **2** (*abbigliamento*) gown, dress **3** (*mobile*) dressing table **4** **fare toilette** to make o.s. beautiful

Tokyo ['tɔkjo] SF Tokyo

tolgo *ecc* ['tɔlgo] VB *vedi* **togliere**

tollerante [tolle'rante] AGG tolerant

tolleranza [tolle'rantsa] SF (*gen*) tolerance; (*Rel*) toleration; **non ha un minimo di tolleranza** he is completely intolerant; **casa di tolleranza** brothel

tollerare [tolle'rare] VT **1** (*sopportare*: *ingiustizia, offese*) to tolerate, put up with; (: *alcolici*) to take; (: *persona*) to put up with, bear, stand; **tollerare il freddo/caldo** to stand *o* take the cold/the heat **2** (*ammettere*) to tolerate, allow; **non tollero repliche** I won't stand for objections; **non sono tollerati ritardi** lateness will not be tolerated

Tolosa [to'loza] SF Toulouse

tolsi *ecc* ['tɔlsi] VB *vedi* **togliere**

tolto, a ['tɔlto] PP *di* **togliere**

■ PREP (*eccetto*) except for

■ SM: **mal tolto** = **maltolto**

tomaia [to'maja] SF (*di scarpa*) upper

tomba ['tomba] SF (*gen*) grave; (*cappella sotterranea*) tomb; **è una tomba** (*fig*: *persona*) he won't give anything away; **non temere, sarò una tomba** don't worry, my lips are sealed; **nelle strade c'era un silenzio di tomba** it was as silent as the grave in the streets; **lo accolsero con un silenzio di tomba** he was greeted with a deathly hush; **avere un piede nella tomba** to have one foot in the grave

tombale [tom'bale] AGG: **pietra tombale** tombstone, gravestone

tombarolo [tomba'rɔlo] SM (*fam*) grave robber

tombino [tom'bino] SM (*pozzetto*) manhole; (*coperchio*) manhole cover

tombola[1] ['tombola] SF (*gioco*) tombola, bingo; **giocare a tombola** to play bingo

tombola[2] ['tombola] SF (*fam*: *caduta*) tumble; **tombola!** upsy-daisy!

tombolo ['tombolo] SM **1** (*per ricamo*) lace pillow; **merletto a tombolo** bobbin lace **2** (*fam scherz*: *persona grassoccia*) podge

tomo ['tɔmo] SM **1** (*volume*) volume, tome **2** (*persona*) queer fish

tomografia [tomogra'fia] SF (*Med*) tomography; **tomografia assiale computerizzata** computerised axial tomography

tonaca, che ['tɔnaka] SF (*Rel*) habit; **indossare la tonaca** (*frate*) to take the habit; (*monaca*) to take the veil

tonale [to'nale] AGG (*Mus*) tonal, tone *attr*; (*Pittura*) tonal

tonalità [tonali'ta] SF INV **1** (*di colore*) shade **2** (*Mus*) tonality

tonante [to'nante] AGG (*voce*) loud, booming

tonare [to'nare] VI = **tuonare**

tondeggiante [tonded'dʒante] AGG roundish

tondino [ton'dino] SM (*Edil*) reinforcing rod

tondo, a ['tondo] AGG (*circolare*) round; **un cuscino tondo** a round cushion; **fare cifra tonda** to round up (*o* down); **tre mesi tondi** exactly three months; **gli ho detto chiaro e tondo** I told him very clearly *o* bluntly; **parentesi tonde** round brackets

■ SM (*cerchio*) circle; **scultura a tutto tondo** full-relief sculpture

tonfo ['tonfo] SM (*rumore sordo*) thud, thump; (*nell'acqua*) plop; **fare un tonfo** (*cadere*) to take a tumble

Tonga ['tɔnga] SM Tonga

Tt

tonico, a, ci, che ['tɔniko] AGG tonic
■SM **1** *(cosmetico)* toner **2** *(Med)* tonic
tonificante [tonifi'kante] AGG invigorating, bracing
tonificare [tonifi'kare] VT *(gen)* to invigorate; *(muscoli, pelle)* to tone up
tonnara [ton'nara] SF tuna-fishing nets *pl*
tonnato, a [ton'nato] AGG *(Culin)*: **salsa tonnata** tuna fish sauce; **vitello tonnato** veal with tuna fish sauce
tonneau [tɔ'no] SM INV *(Aer)* (acrobatic) roll
tonnellaggio [tonnel'laddʒo] SM *(Naut)* tonnage
tonnellata [tonnel'lata] SF ton; **questa valigia pesa una tonnellata!** this suitcase weighs a ton!
tonno ['tonno] SM tuna (fish); **un tramezzino al tonno** a tuna sandwich
tono ['tɔno] SM *(gen, Mus)* tone; *(di colore)* tone, shade; **parlare con tono minaccioso** to speak in a threatening tone *o* threateningly; **abbassa il tono (della voce)!** don't take that tone (of voice) with me!; **il tono della lettera/del discorso** the tone of the letter/speech; **dal tono si capiva che era seccata** you could tell she was annoyed by her tone of voice; **se la metti su questo tono...** if that's the way you want to put it ...; **rispondere a tono** *(a proposito)* to answer to the point; *(nello stesso modo)* to answer in kind; *(per le rime)* to answer back; **essere giù di tono** to be unwell *o* off-colour *(Brit)*; **cercava di darsi un tono** she tried to act in a more refined way
tonsilla [ton'silla] SF *(Med)* tonsil; **farsi togliere le tonsille** to have one's tonsils out; **operarsi di tonsille** to have one's tonsils out
tonsillare [tonsil'lare] AGG tonsillar, of the tonsils
tonsillectomia [tonsillekto'mia] SF tonsillectomy
tonsillite [tonsil'lite] SF *(Med)* tonsillitis
tonsura [ton'sura] SF tonsure
tonto, a ['tonto] AGG stupid, silly, dumb; **è un po' tonto** he's a bit thick
■SM/F blockhead, dunce; **fare il finto tonto** to play dumb
top [tɔp] SM INV *(vertice, Abbigliamento)* top
topaia [to'paja] SF *(casa)* hovel, dump; *(tana: di topo)* mousehole; *(: di ratto)* rat's nest
topazio, zi [to'pattsjo] SM topaz
topicida, i [topi'tʃida] SM rat poison
topinambur [topinam'bur] SM INV Jerusalem artichoke
topino [to'pino] SM *(uccello)* sand martin
topless ['tɔplis] SM INV topless bathing costume
top model SF INV supermodel
topo ['tɔpo] SM **1** *(Zool)* mouse; *(ratto)* rat; **veleno per topi** rat poison; **color grigio topo** mousey grey; **topo campagnolo comune** fieldmouse; **topo delle chiaviche** brown rat; **topo domestico** house mouse; **topo muschiato** muskrat **2** *(persona)*: **topo d'albergo** hotel thief; **topo d'auto** car thief; **topo di biblioteca** bookworm
topografia [topogra'fia] SF topography
topografico, a, ci, che [topo'grafiko] AGG topographic(al)
topografo [to'pɔgrafo] SM topographer
topolino [topo'lino] SM *(piccolo topo)* baby mouse; *(scherz: bambino)* scamp; **topolino delle risaie** harvest mouse
toponimo [to'pɔnimo] SM place name
toponomastica [topono'mastika] SF toponymy
toporagno [topo'raɲɲo] SM shrewmouse
toppa ['tɔppa] SF **1** *(di stoffa)* patch; **mettere una toppa** *(fig)* to find a stopgap *o* short term solution **2** *(serratura)* keyhole
torà [to'ra] SM INV Torah
torace [to'ratʃe] SM *(Anat)* thorax, chest; *(Zool)* thorax
toracico, a, ci, che [to'ratʃiko] AGG thoracic, chest *attr*; **gabbia** *o* **cassa toracica** rib cage
torba ['torba] SF peat
torbidamente [torbida'mente] AVV *(fig)* sinisterly
torbidezza [torbi'dettsa] SF *(vedi agg)* cloudiness; muddiness; darkness
torbido, a ['torbido] AGG *(liquido)* cloudy; *(: fiume)* muddy; *(fig: pensieri)* dark, sinister
■SM: **qui c'è del torbido** there is something fishy going on here; **pescare nel torbido** to fish in troubled waters
torbiera [tor'bjɛra] SF peat bog
torcere ['tɔrtʃere] VB IRREG
■VT **1** *(gen)* to twist; *(biancheria)* to wring (out); **torcere un braccio a qn** to twist sb's arm; **torcere il naso** *(per disgusto)* to wrinkle (up) one's nose; **avrei voluto torcergli il collo** I felt like wringing his neck; **non torcere un capello a qn** not to hurt a hair of sb's head; **dare del filo da torcere a qn** to make life *o* things difficult for sb **2** *(piegare)* to bend
▸ **torcersi** VR: **torcersi dal dolore** to writhe in pain; **torcersi dalle risa** to double up laughing
torchiare [tor'kjare] VT *(olive)* to press; *(fig fam: persona)* to grill
torchiatura [torkja'tura] SF *(di olive)* pressing
torchio, chi ['tɔrkjo] SM press; **mettere** *o* **tenere qn sotto il torchio** *(fig fam: interrogare)* to grill sb
torcia, ce ['tɔrtʃa] SF *(fiaccola)* torch; **torcia elettrica** torch *(Brit)*, flashlight *(Am)*; **torcia umana** *(fig)* human torch
torcicollo [tortʃi'kɔllo] SM: **avere il torcicollo** to have a stiff neck; **ho il torcicollo** I've got a stiff neck
tordo ['tordo] SM thrush; **grasso come un tordo** fat as a pig; **tordo comune** song thrush
torero [to'rɛro] SM bullfighter, toreador
torinese [tori'nese] AGG of *o* from Turin
■SM/F inhabitant *o* native of Turin
Torino [to'rino] SF Turin; **domani andremo a Torino** we're going to Turin tomorrow; **abita a Torino** she lives in Turin
▹ www.comune.torino.it/
torma ['torma] SF crowd, throng
tormalina [torma'lina] SF tourmaline
tormenta [tor'menta] SF snowstorm, blizzard
tormentare [tormen'tare] VT *(gen)* to torment; *(fig: infastidire)* to bother, pester; **smettila di tormentare quel povero cane** stop tormenting that poor dog
▸ **tormentarsi** VR to worry, torture o.s., fret
tormentato, a [tormen'tato] AGG *(gen)* tormented; **tormentato dal dolore/dal rimorso** racked by pain/remorse; **un'anima tormentata** a tormented soul
tormento [tor'mento] SM **1** *(dolore fisico, morale)* torment, agony; **morire fra atroci tormenti** to die in terrible agony **2** *(fastidio: di zanzare, caldo)* torment; *(: fam: persona)* pest
tormentosamente [tormentosa'mente] AVV tormentingly
tormentoso, a [tormen'toso] AGG *(angoscia)* tormenting; *(dubbio, pena)* tormenting, nagging; *(esistenza)* tormented
tornaconto [torna'konto] SM advantage, benefit; **pensa solo al proprio tornaconto** he thinks only of his own interest

tornado [tor'nado] SM tornado
tornante [tor'nante] SM hairpin bend (*Brit*) *o* curve (*Am*)
tornare [tor'nare] VI (*aus* **essere**) **1** to return, go (*o* come) back; **quando sei tornato?** when did you get back?; **sono tornato domenica mattina** I got back on Sunday morning; **non sono ancora tornati dalle vacanze** they're not back from their holidays yet; **tornare a casa** to go (*o* come) home; **tornare da scuola** to come home from school; **a che ora torni da scuola?** what time do you get home from school?; **torno tra un attimo** I'll be back in a minute; **un'occasione così non torna più** such an opportunity won't repeat itself, you won't get another chance like this; **non torniamo più sull'argomento** let's drop the subject; **continua a tornare sull'argomento** he harps on about it; **è tornato alla carica con la sua idea di...** he's gone back to the old idea of ...; **è tornato a dire/a fare...** he's back to saying/doing ...; **mi è tornato alla mente** I've just remembered; **tornare al punto di partenza** to start again; **siamo tornati al punto di partenza** we are back where we started; **tornare in sé** (*dopo svenimento*) to regain consciousness, come to one's senses, come round; (*rinsavire*) to be back to one's old self; **tornare su** to come up; **la cipolla mi torna su** onions repeat on me **2** (*ridiventare*) to become again; **tornare di moda** to become *o* be fashionable again, be back in fashion (again); **il cielo è tornato sereno** it's cleared up again **3** (*quadrare*) to be right, be correct; **i conti tornano** the accounts balance; (*fig*) it all falls into place; **qualcosa non torna in questa storia** there's something not quite right about this business **4** (*essere, risultare*) to turn out (to be), prove (to be); **tornare utile** to prove *o* turn out (to be) useful; **tornerà a tuo danno** it will come home to roost; **tornare a onore di qn** to be a credit to sb, do sb credit
■ VT (*fam*): **tornare qc a qn** to return sth to sb, give sth back to sb
tornasole [torna'sole] SM INV litmus
tornata [tor'nata] SF: **tornata elettorale** election
torneo [tor'nεo] SM (*Sport*) tournament, competition; (*Storia*) tournament; **un torneo di tennis** a tennis tournament
tornio, ni ['tornjo] SM lathe; **tornio da vasaio** potter's wheel
tornire [tor'nire] VT (*Tecn*) to turn (on a lathe); (*fig*) to shape, polish
tornito, a [tor'nito] AGG: **ben tornito** (*gambe, braccia*) well-shaped
tornitore, trice [torni'tore] SM/F (*Tecn*) (lathe-)turner
tornitura [torni'tura] SF **1** (*Tecn*) turning; (*di legno*) wood turning **2** (*trucioli: di legno,metallo*) shavings *pl*
torno ['torno] SM: **levarsi** *o* **togliersi qn di torno** to get rid of sb; **levati di torno!** clear off!
toro ['tɔro] SM **1** (*Zool, fig*) bull; **essere forte come un toro** to be as strong as an ox; **prendere il toro per le corna** (*fig*) to take the bull by the horns **2** (*Astron, Astrol*): **Toro** Taurus; **essere del Toro** to be Taurus **3** (*Borsa*) bull
torpedine [tor'pεdine] SF **1** (*Zool*) stingray **2** (*Mil: mina*) torpedo
torpediniera [torpedi'njεra] SF (*Naut*) torpedo boat
torpedo [tor'pεdo] SF INV (*Aut*) tourer (*Brit*), touring car (*Am*)
torpedone [torpe'done] SM (tourist) coach (*Brit*) *o* bus (*Am*)
torpidamente [torpida'mente] AVV sluggishly
torpido, a ['tɔrpido] AGG torpid
torpore [tor'pore] SM torpor
torre ['torre] SF **1** (*di città, castello*) tower; (*di computer*) tower; **la torre pendente di Pisa** the Leaning Tower of Pisa; **torre d'avorio** (*fig*) ivory tower; **torre di controllo** (*Aer*) control tower; **torre di osservazione** lookout tower **2** (*Scacchi*) rook, castle
torrefare [torre'fare] VT IRREG (*caffè*) to roast
torrefatto, a [torre'fatto] PP *di* **torrefare**
torrefazione [torrefat'tsjone] SF (*del caffè*) roasting
torreggiare [torred'dʒare] VI (*aus* **avere**) **torreggiare (su)** to tower (over)
torrente [tor'rεnte] SM torrent; (*fig*) flood, stream
torrentizio, zia, zi, zie [torren'tittsjo] AGG (*di torrente*) torrential
torrenziale [torren'tsjale] AGG (*pioggia*) torrential
torretta [tor'retta] SF (*gen, Mil*) turret; (*Naut*) tower; **torretta di comando** (*Naut*) conning tower
torrido, a ['tɔrrido] AGG scorching, torrid; **zona torrida** (*Geog*) Torrid Zone
torrione [tor'rjone] SM (*torre*) keep, tower; (*Naut*) conning tower
torrone [tor'rone] SM (*Culin*) *kind of nougat*
torsi *ecc* ['tɔrsi] VB *vedi* **torcere**
torsione [tor'sjone] SF (*gen*) twisting; (*Tecn*) torsion; (*Ginnastica*) twist
torso ['torso] SM (*Anat, Arte*) torso; (*di frutta*) core; **a torso nudo** bare-chested
torsolo ['torsolo] SM (*di cavolo*) stump; (*di mela*) core; **un torsolo di mela** an apple core
torta ['torta] SF (*Culin*) cake; **una fetta di torta** a slice of cake; **spartirsi la torta** (*fig*) to split the loot; **torta di mele** apple pie; (*tipo crostata*) apple tart (*Brit*) *o* pie (*Am*); **torta salata** savoury flan
tortellino [tortel'lino] SM (*Culin*) tortellino (*single piece of pasta*); **tortellini** SMPL (*piatto*) tortellini
tortelloni [tortel'loni] SMPL (*Culin*): **tortelloni di magro** *ravioli-like pasta filled with cheese, eggs and spinach*
tortiera [tor'tjεra] SF cake tin (*Brit*), cake pan (*Am*)
tortino [tor'tino] SM (*Culin*) savoury pie
torto[1], a ['tɔrto] PP *di* **torcere**
torto[2] ['tɔrto] SM (*ingiustizia*) wrong; (*colpa*) fault; **fare un torto a qn** to wrong sb; **ricevere un torto** to be wronged; **avere torto** to be wrong; **mi dispiace ma hai torto** I'm sorry, but you're wrong; **hai torto marcio** you're dead wrong; **a torto** wrongly, unjustly; **a torto o a ragione** rightly or wrongly; **ho avuto l'unico torto di dissentire da lui** the only thing I did wrong was to disagree with him; **quest'azione ti fa torto** this action is unworthy of you; **gli ho dato torto** I said he was wrong; **tutti hanno dato torto a Marina** everybody said Marina was wrong; **i fatti gli hanno dato torto** the facts proved him wrong; **passare/essere dalla parte del torto** to put o.s./be in the wrong; **non ha tutti i torti** there's something in what he says
tortora ['tortora] SF (*Zool*) turtledove
■ AGG INV: **grigio tortora** dove-grey
tortuosamente [tortuosa'mente] AVV (*esprimersi, pensare*) in a convoluted way
tortuosità [tortuosi'ta] SF INV (*qualità: di strada*) winding nature; (: *di ragionamento*) convoluted nature; (*curva*): **le tortuosità del fiume** the twists and turns of the river
tortuoso, a [tortu'oso] AGG (*strada*) winding; (*fig: discorso, ragionamento*) convoluted; (: *politica*) tortuous;

Tt

esprimersi in modo tortuoso to express o.s. in a convoluted way

tortura [tor'tura] SF (*sevizia*) torture; (*fig*) torment, torture; **sottoporre qn alla tortura** to torture sb

torturare [tortu'rare] VT to torture; (*fig*) to torment, torture; **smetti di torturare quel povero gatto!** stop tormenting that poor cat!; **torturarsi il cervello** to rack one's brains
▶ **torturarsi** VR to torment o.s.

torvamente [torva'mente] AVV: **guardare qn torvamente** to give sb a surly look

torvo, a ['torvo] AGG (*occhi, sguardo*) surly, menacing, grim; **era torvo in viso** he looked grim; **guardare qn con occhi torvi** to give sb a surly look

tosaerba [toza'ɛrba] SM INV (lawn)mower

tosare [to'zare] VT (*pecore*) to shear; (*cani*) to clip; (*siepi*) to trim, clip; **ti hanno tosato** (*scherz*) you've been scalped

tosasiepi [toza'sjɛpi] SM INV hedge clippers *pl*

tosatrice [toza'tritʃe] SF (*per pecore*) electric shears *pl*; (*per capelli*) clippers *pl*

tosatura [toza'tura] SF (*di pecore*) shearing; (*di cani*) clipping; (*di siepi*) trimming, clipping

Toscana [tos'kana] SF Tuscany; **andrò in Toscana quest'estate** I'm going to Tuscany this summer; **ti è piaciuta la Toscana?** did you like Tuscany?
▷ www.regione.toscana.it/

toscano, a [tos'kano] AGG, SM/F Tuscan
■ SM (*anche*: **sigaro toscano**) *strong Italian cigar*

tosse ['tosse] SF cough; **colpo di tosse** fit of coughing; **avere la tosse** to have a cough; **ho la tosse** I've got a cough; **tosse asinina** *o* **canina** whooping cough

tossicchiare [tossik'kjare] VI (*aus* **avere**) to cough

tossicità [tossitʃi'ta] SF toxicity

tossico, a, ci, che ['tɔssiko] AGG toxic
■ SM/F (*fam*: *drogato*) junkie, druggie

tossicodipendente [tossikodipen'dɛnte] SM/F drug addict

tossicodipendenza [tossikodipen'dɛntsa] SF drug addiction

tossicologia [tossikolo'dʒia] SF toxicology

tossicologo, a, gi, ghe [tossi'kɔlogo] SM/F toxicologist

tossicomane [tossi'kɔmane] SM/F drug addict

tossicomania [tossikoma'nia] SF drug addiction

tossiemia [tossie'mia] SF toxaemia (*Brit*), toxemia (*Am*)

tossina [tos'sina] SF toxin

tossire [tos'sire] VI (*aus* **avere**) to cough

tostapane [tosta'pane] SM INV toaster

tostare [tos'tare] VT (*pane*) to toast; (*caffè, mandorle*) to roast

tostatura [tosta'tura] SF (*di pane*) toasting; (*di caffè*) roasting

tosto[1] ['tɔsto] AVV (*letter*) forthwith, immediately; **tosto che** as soon as

tosto[2]**, a** ['tɔsto] AGG **1 che faccia tosta!** what cheek!; **hai una bella faccia tosta!** you've got a real cheek! **2** (*fam*: *eccezionale*) ace; **una tipa tosta** a cool girl

tot [tɔt] AGG INDEF so many, X; **il giorno tot all'ora tot** on such and such a day at such and such a time; **diciamo che costa tot milioni** let's say it costs so many *o* X million
■ SM: **un tot** so much; **mi dà un tot al mese** he gives me so much a month

totale [to'tale] AGG (*gen*) total; **la festa è stata un fallimento totale** the party was a total failure; **anestesia totale** general anaesthetic (*Brit*) *o* anesthetic (*Am*)
■ SM total; **il totale è di sessanta sterline** the total is sixty pounds

totalità [totali'ta] SF totality, entirety; **nella totalità dei casi** in all cases; **la totalità dei presenti** all of those present

totalitario, ria, ri, rie [totali'tarjo] AGG (*Pol*) totalitarian

totalitarismo [totalita'rizmo] SM (*Pol*) totalitarianism

totalizzare [totalid'dzare] VT to total, make a total of; (*Sport*: *punti*) to score

totalizzatore [totaliddza'tore] SM (*Tecn*) totalizator; (*Ippica*) totalizator, tote

totalmente [total'mente] AVV (*gen*) totally, completely

totem ['tɔtem] SM INV totem (pole)

totip [to'tip] SM *gambling pool based on horse racing*

totocalcio [toto'kaltʃo] SM ≈ (football) pools *pl* (*Brit*); **giocare al totocalcio** to do the pools; **gioco al totocalcio ogni settimana** I do the pools every week

TOTOCALCIO

Totocalcio, the system for betting on the results of Italian football matches, was set up in 1946. It is extremely popular. In 2003 the game was altered to allow for betting on 14 matches rather than the original 13.

touche [tuʃ] SF INV (*Rugby*) line-out

toupet [tu'pɛ] SM INV toupee

tour [tur] SM INV (*giro*) tour; (*Ciclismo*: *anche*: **tour de France**) tour de France

tourbillon [turbi'jø] SM INV (*di luci, colori*) whirl; (*di notizie*) flurry

tour de force [turdɛ'fɔrs] SM INV (*Sport, anche fig*) tremendous effort

tournée [tur'ne] SF INV tour; **essere in tournée** to be on tour; **sono in tournée in Italia** they're on tour in Italy

tout court [tu'kur] AVV (*rispondere, domandare*) bluntly

tovaglia [to'vaʎʎa] SF tablecloth

tovaglietta [tovaʎ'ʎetta] SF: **tovaglietta all'americana** place mat

tovagliolo [tovaʎ'ʎɔlo] SM napkin, serviette (*Brit*); **tovagliolo di carta** paper napkin

tozzo[1]**, a** ['tɔttso] AGG (*persona*) stocky, thickset; (*cosa*) squat

tozzo[2] ['tɔttso] SM piece, morsel; **tozzo di pane** crust of bread; **per un tozzo di pane** (*fig*) for a song

TP SIGLA = *Trapani*

TR SIGLA = *Terni*

Tr ABBR (*Comm*) = **tratta**

tra [tra] PREP **1** (*fra due*) between; (*fra più di due*) among(st); **c'è un giardino tra le due case** there's a garden between the two houses; **era seduto tra il padre e lo zio** he was sitting between his father and his uncle; **era tra gente sconosciuta** he was among strangers; **tra i presenti c'era anche il sindaco** the mayor was also among those present; **tra i feriti c'era anche il pilota dell'aereo** the pilot of the plane was among the injured; **esitare tra il sì e il no** to hesitate between yes and no; **avrà tra i 15 e i 20 anni** he must be between 15 and 20 years old; **costerà tra i 20 e i 25**

euro it'll cost between 20 and 25 euros; **(sia) detto tra noi...** between you and me ...; **detto tra noi, non piace neanche a me** between you and me, I don't like it either; **mi raccomando, che resti tra noi** remember, that's between you and me; **tra sé e sé** (*parlare, riflettere*) to oneself; **scomparire tra la folla/gli alberi** to disappear into the crowd/among the trees; **tra una cosa e l'altra** what with one thing and another; **tra vitto e alloggio fanno 450 euro** food and accommodation together come to 450 euros; **tra casa mia e casa loro ci sono 10 minuti di strada** it's 10 minutes from my house to theirs **2** (*attraverso*) through; **il sole filtrava tra le persiane** the sun filtered through the shutters; **una strada tra i campi** a road through the fields; **farsi strada tra la folla** to make one's way through the crowd **3** (*in*) in; **prendere qn tra le braccia** to take sb in one's arms; **tra venti chilometri c'è un'area di servizio** it's twenty kilometres to the next service area **4** (*tempo*) in, within; **torno tra un'ora** I'll be back in an hour; **tra qualche giorno** in a few days; **tra 5 giorni** in 5 days' time; **tra poco** soon; **sarà qui tra poco** he'll be here soon *o* shortly; **tra breve** soon, shortly **5 tra l'altro** (*inoltre*) besides which, what is more; **tra tutti non saranno più di venti** there won't be more than twenty in all

traballante [trabal'lante] AGG (*mobile*) shaky

traballare [trabal'lare] VI (*aus* **avere**) (*persona*) to stagger, totter; (*mobile, fig: governo*) to be shaky

trabeazione [trabeat'tsjone] SF (*Archit*) trabeation

trabiccolo [tra'bikkolo] SM (*scherz: vecchia auto*) jalopy, old banger (*Brit*)

traboccare [trabok'kare] VI **1** (*aus* **essere**) (*liquido*): **traboccare (da)** to overflow (from) **2** (*aus* **avere**) (*contenitore*): **traboccare (di)** to overflow (with); **il teatro traboccava di gente** the theatre was full to bursting; **il suo cuore traboccava di felicità** his heart was bursting with happiness

trabocchetto [trabok'ketto] SM (*botola*) trap door; (*fig*) trap; **non cadere nel trabocchetto** don't fall into the trap; **tendere un trabocchetto a qn** to set a trap for sb
■ AGG INV trap *attr*; **domanda trabocchetto** trick question

tracagnotto, a [trakaɲ'ɲɔtto] AGG dumpy
■ SM/F dumpy person

tracannare [trakan'nare] VT to down, gulp down

traccia, ce ['trattʃa] SF **1** (*gen, fig: segno*) mark; (*di lumaca*) trace; (*di ruota*) track, trail; (*di animale*) tracks *pl*; (*di persona*) footprints *pl*; **sul bicchiere c'erano tracce di rossetto** there were traces of lipstick on the glass; **essere sulle tracce di qn** to be on sb's trail; **perdere le tracce di qn** to lose track of *o* lose the trail of sb; **seguire le tracce di qn** to follow sb's footprints *o* tracks; (*fig*) to follow in sb's footsteps; **la polizia sta chiaramente seguendo una falsa traccia** the police are clearly on the wrong track; **è sparito senza lasciare tracce** he vanished without trace **2** (*residuo, vestigia di civiltà*) trace; (*indizio*) sign; **nella sua voce non c'è traccia di accento straniero** he speaks without a trace of a foreign accent; **hanno fatto sparire ogni traccia della loro presenza** they removed all sign of their presence **3** (*schema*) outline

tracciabilità [trattʃabili'ta] SF (*di prodotto*) traceability

tracciare [trat'tʃare] VT **1** (*percorso, strada*) to mark out, trace; (*confini*) to map out; (*rotta*) to plot **2** (*disegnare*) to sketch, draw; **tracciare una linea** to draw a line; **tracciare un arco** to describe a curve **3** (*fig*) to sketch out, outline; **tracciare un quadro della situazione** to outline the situation

tracciato [trat'tʃato] SM (*grafico*) layout, plan; **strada dal tracciato irregolare** winding road; **tracciato di gara** (*Sport*) (race) route

tracciatore [trattʃa'tore] SM (*Inform*): **tracciatore di grafici** plotter

trachea [tra'kɛa] SF windpipe, trachea

tracheale [trake'ale] AGG tracheal

tracheite [trake'ite] SF tracheitis

tracimare [tratʃi'mare] VI (*aus* **avere**) (*fiume*) to burst its banks, overflow

tracimazione [tratʃimat'tsjone] SF (*di fiume*) overflowing

tracolla [tra'kɔlla] SF shoulder strap; **portare qc a tracolla** to carry sth over one's shoulder; **borsa a tracolla** shoulder bag

tracollo [tra'kɔllo] SM (*fig*) collapse, ruin; **avere un tracollo** (*Med*) to have a setback; (*Fin*) to slip, fall; (*Comm*) to collapse; **tracollo finanziario** crash

tracotante [trako'tante] AGG arrogant, overbearing
■ SM/F arrogant person

tracotanza [trako'tantsa] SF arrogance

trad. ABBR = **traduzione**

tradimento [tradi'mento] SM (*gen*) betrayal; (*Dir, Mil*) treason; **lo considero un tradimento da parte sua** I consider it a betrayal on his part; **alto tradimento** high treason; **a tradimento** by surprise; **mangiare (il) pane a tradimento** to live off other people

tradire [tra'dire] VT **1** (*gen*) to betray; (*coniuge*) to cheat on, be unfaithful to; **ha tradito suo marito** she was unfaithful to her husband; **tradire la fiducia di qn** to betray sb's trust; **hai tradito la mia fiducia** you betrayed my trust; **ha tradito le attese di tutti** he let everyone down; **se la memoria non mi tradisce** if my memory serves me well **2** (*rivelare: segreto*) to reveal, let out, give away
▶ **tradirsi** VR to give o.s. away

traditore, trice [tradi'tore] SM/F traitor
■ AGG treacherous

tradizionale [tradittsjo'nale] AGG traditional

tradizionalismo [tradittsjona'lizmo] SM traditionalism

tradizionalista [tradittsjona'lista] SM/F traditionalist, conservative

tradizionalistico, a, ci, che [tradittsjona'listiko] AGG traditionalist

tradizionalmente [tradittsjonal'mente] AVV traditionally

tradizione [tradit'tsjone] SF tradition; **secondo la tradizione** traditionally, according to tradition

tradotta [tra'dotta] SF (*Mil*) troop train

tradotto, a [tra'dotto] PP *di* **tradurre**

tradurre [tra'durre] VT IRREG **1** (*testo: scritto, orale*) to translate; **tradurre dall'inglese in italiano** to translate from English into Italian; **tradurre alla lettera** to translate literally; **tradurre parola per parola** to translate word for word **2** (*esprimere*) to render, convey; **tradurre in parole povere** to explain simply; **tradurre in cifre** to put into figures; **tradurre in atto** (*fig*) to put into effect **3** (*Dir*): **tradurre qn in carcere/tribunale** to take sb to prison/court; **tradurre qn davanti al giudice** to bring sb before the court

traduttore, trice [tradut'tore] SM/F translator; **traduttore elettronico** hand-held electronic translator; **traduttore simultaneo** simultaneous interpreter

traduzione [tradut'tsjone] SF **1** (*di lingue*) translation; **traduzione assistita** computer-assisted translation; **traduzione simultanea** simultaneous interpreting **2** (*Dir*) transfer

trae ['trae] VB *vedi* **trarre**

traente [tra'ɛnte] SM/F (*di assegno*) drawer

trafelato, a [trafe'lato] AGG breathless, out of breath

trafficante [traffi'kante] SM/F (*di droga*) trafficker

trafficare [traffi'kare] VI (*aus* **avere**) **1** (*commerciare*): **trafficare (in)** to traffic (in), deal *o* trade illicitly (in) **2** (*affaccendarsi*) to busy o.s.

■ VT (*droga*) to traffic in

trafficato, a [traffi'kato] AGG (*strada, zona*) busy

traffico ['traffiko] SM **1** (*stradale*) traffic; **c'è un traffico pazzesco** the traffic's terrible; **regolare il traffico** to control *o* regulate the traffic; **chiudere una strada al traffico** to close a road to traffic **2** (*movimento*) traffic; **traffico aereo** air traffic; **traffico ferroviario** rail traffic **3** (*commercio illecito*) traffic; **traffico di droga** drug trafficking

trafficone, a [traffi'kone] SM/F wheeler-dealer

trafiggere [tra'fiddʒere] VT IRREG (*ferire*) to run through, stab; (: *fig*) to pierce

trafila [tra'fila] SF procedure; **bisognerà seguire la solita trafila** we'll have to go through the usual routine *o* rigmarole

trafiletto [trafi'letto] SM (*di giornale*) short article

trafitto, a [tra'fitto] PP *di* **trafiggere**

traforare [trafo'rare] VT (*gen*) to pierce; (*montagna*) to tunnel through, make a tunnel through; (*legno, metallo*) to drill, bore; **il proiettile gli ha traforato il cuore** the bullet pierced his heart

traforato, a [trafo'rato] AGG (*calze, orlo*) openwork

traforo [tra'foro] SM **1** (*operazione*: *vedi vb*) piercing; tunnelling; drilling, boring **2** (*galleria*) tunnel **3** **lavoro di traforo** (*su metallo, legno*) fretwork

trafugamento [trafuga'mento] SM purloining; **trafugamento di opere d'arte** purloining of works of art; **trafugamento di salme** body snatching

trafugare [trafu'gare] VT to purloin

tragedia [tra'dʒɛdja] SF (*Teatro, fig*: *disastro*) tragedy; **tragedia greca/latina** Greek/Roman tragedy; **non farne una tragedia** don't make a fuss about it; **non è il caso di farne una tragedia!** there's no need to make such a fuss about it!

traggo *ecc* ['traggo] VB *vedi* **trarre**

traghettare [traget'tare] VT (*persone*) to ferry; (*fiume*) to cross by ferry

traghettatore, trice [tragetta'tore] SM/F ferryman/ ferrywoman

traghetto [tra'getto] SM (*trasporto*) ferrying, crossing; (*luogo*) ferry; (*mezzo*) ferry(boat); **siamo andati in Irlanda col traghetto** we went to Ireland by ferry

■ AGG INV ferry *attr*

tragicamente [tradʒika'mente] AVV tragically

tragicità [tradʒitʃi'ta] SF tragedy

tragico, a, ci, che ['tradʒiko] AGG tragic

■ SM/F (*tragediografo*) tragedian; **non fare il tragico** (*fig*) don't make a song and dance over it

■ SM: **il tragico della faccenda è che...** the worst thing about it is ...

tragicomico, a, ci, che [tradʒi'kɔmiko] AGG tragicomic

tragicommedia [tradʒikom'mɛdja] SF tragicomedy

tragitto [tra'dʒitto] SM **1** (*viaggio*) journey; **un breve tragitto** a short journey; **durante il tragitto** on the journey **2** (*tratto di strada*) way; **durante il tragitto** on the way

traguardo [tra'gwardo] SM (*Sport*) finish, finishing post; (: *linea*) finishing line; (*fig*) aim, goal; **tagliare il traguardo** to cross the (finishing) line; **è stato il primo a tagliare il traguardo** he was the first to cross the finishing line; **raggiungere il traguardo** (*in gara*) to reach the finish; (*fig*) to reach one's goal

trai *ecc* ['trai] VB *vedi* **trarre**

traiettoria [trajet'tɔrja] SF trajectory

trainante [trai'nante] AGG (*cavo, fune*) towing; (*Econ*: *settore*) driving; (: *paese*) leading

trainare [trai'nare] VT (*carro*) to draw, pull, drag, haul; (*auto*) to tow; **il carro attrezzi ha trainato la macchina fino alla città più vicina** the breakdown van towed the car to the nearest town; **farsi trainare** (*fig*) to follow blindly

training ['treinin] SM INV (*di personale*) training

traino ['traino] SM **1** (*operazione*) drawing, pulling; (: *di auto*) towing; **al traino** on tow; **fare da traino** (*Econ*) to be a driving force **2** (*cosa trainata*) trailer load

trait d'union ['trɛ dy'njɔ̃] SM INV: **fare da trait d'union** to liaise

tralasciare [tralaʃ'ʃare] VT **1** (*omettere*: *dettagli*) to leave out, omit; **tralasciamo i particolari** let's skip the details **2** (*trascurare*: *studi*) to neglect

tralcio, ci ['traltʃo] SM shoot (*of a plant*)

traliccio, ci [tra'littʃo] SM (*pilone*) pylon; (*struttura*) trellis

tralice [tra'litʃe] **in tralice** AVV: **guardare qn in tralice** to look askance at sb

trallallà [trallal'la] ESCL tra-la-la!

tram [tram] SM INV tram (*Brit*), streetcar (*Am*)

trama ['trama] SF **1** (*filo*) weft **2** (*di opera*) plot; (*inganno*) plot, conspiracy; **la trama del film è un po' complicata** the plot of the film is rather complicated; **ordire una trama ai danni di qn** to hatch a plot against sb

tramandare [traman'dare] VT to hand down, pass on

tramare [tra'mare] VT to plot, scheme; **tramare un complotto** to plot

trambusto [tram'busto] SM (*rumore*) racket; (*disordine*) turmoil

tramestio, tii [trames'tio] SM bustle, bustling

tramezzare [tramed'dzare] VT (*Edil*) to partition (off)

tramezzino [tramed'dzino] SM sandwich; **un tramezzino al prosciutto** a ham sandwich

tramezzo [tra'mɛddzo] SM partition, dividing wall

tramite ['tramite] SM means *pl*; **agire/fare da tramite** to act as/be a go-between

■ PREP (*per mezzo di*: *cosa*) by means of; (: *persona*) through

tramontana [tramon'tana] SF (*Meteor*) north wind; **perdere la tramontana** (*fig*) to lose one's bearings

tramontare [tramon'tare] VI (*aus* **essere**) (*astri*) to go down, set; (*fig*: *bellezza, gloria*) to fade

tramonto [tra'monto] SM (*del sole*) sunset; (*di astri*) setting; **è sul viale del tramonto** (*attore*) he has passed his peak

tramortire [tramor'tire] VT to knock out, knock unconscious, stun

■ VI (*aus* **essere**) to pass out, faint, lose consciousness

trampolino [trampo'lino] SM (*Sport*: *per tuffi*) springboard; (: *in muratura*) diving board; (: *per lo sci*) ski jump; **servire da trampolino** (*fig*) to serve as a springboard

trampolo ['trampolo] SM stilt
tramutare [tramu'tare] VT: **tramutare in** to change *o* turn into
▶ **tramutarsi** VR: **tramutarsi in** to change *o* turn into
trance ['tra:ns] SF INV trance; **in (stato di) trance** in a (state of) trance; **cadere in trance** to fall into a trance
tranche de vie [trɑ̃ʃ də vi] SF INV slice of life
trancia, ce ['trantʃa] SF **1** (*Tecn*) shears *pl*, shearing machine **2** (*fetta*) slice; **trancia di salmone** (*Culin*) salmon steak; **a trance** in slices
tranciare [tran'tʃare] VT (*Tecn*) to shear
trancio, ci ['trantʃo] SM = **trancia 2**
tranello [tra'nɛllo] SM trap; **tendere un tranello a qn** to set a trap for sb; **cadere in un tranello** to fall into a trap
trangugiare [trangu'dʒare] VT to gulp down; (*fig*: *amarezze*) to swallow
tranne ['tranne] PREP (*eccetto*) except (for), but (for); **c'erano tutti tranne lui** they were all there except *o* but him; **tutti i giorni tranne il venerdì** every day except *o* with the exception of Friday; **ha invitato tutti tranne me** he invited everybody except me; **va d'accordo con tutti tranne che con me** he gets on with everybody except *o* but me; **tranne che** CONG unless
tranquillamente [trankwilla'mente] AVV (*vivere, dormire*) peacefully; (*rispondere, spiegare*) calmly
tranquillante [trankwil'lante] SM (*Med*) tranquillizer
tranquillità [trankwilli'ta] SF (*stabilità*) tranquillity; (*immobilità*) calm, stillness; (*calma*) quietness; (*di animo*) peace of mind; **la tranquillità della campagna** the peace of the countryside; **è ritornata la tranquillità** the situation has returned to normal; **per mia tranquillità** to set my mind at ease; **con tranquillità** calmly; **gli ha risposto con molta tranquillità** she replied to him very calmly
tranquillizzare [trankwillid'dzare] VT to reassure; **l'ho detto per tranquillizzarla** I said it to reassure her
▶ **tranquillizzarsi** VIP to calm down
tranquillo, a [tran'kwillo] AGG **1** (*luogo*) calm, peaceful, quiet; **il mare è tranquillo** the sea is calm; **cerchiamo un angolo tranquillo** let's find a quiet corner **2** (*persona*) calm; (: *sicuro*) sure, confident; **dormire sonni tranquilli** to sleep easy *o* peacefully; **avere la coscienza tranquilla** to have a clear conscience; **stai tranquillo che ce la fa!** don't worry – he'll do it all right!
transalpino, a [transal'pino] AGG transalpine
transatlantico, a, ci, che [transat'lantiko] AGG transatlantic
■ SM **1** (*Naut*) transatlantic liner **2** (*Pol*) *room in the Palazzo di Montecitorio*

TRANSATLANTICO

The **transatlantico** is a room in the Palazzo di Montecitorio which is used by "deputati" between parliamentary sessions for relaxation and conversation. It is also used for media interviews and press conferences.

transatto, a [tran'satto] PP *di* **transigere**
transazione [transat'tsjone] SF (*Dir*) settlement; (*Comm*) transaction, deal
transcodificazione [transkodifikat'tsjone] SF (*Inform*) data conversion
transenna [tran'senna] SF (*cavalletto*) barrier
transessuale [transessu'ale] SM/F transsexual
transetto [tran'sɛtto] SM (*Archit*) transept
transeuropeo, a [transeuro'pɛo] AGG trans-European
transfert ['transfert] SM INV (*Psic*) transference
transfrontaliero, a [transfronta'ljɛro] AGG (*commercio, traffico*) cross-border
transgenico, a, ci, che [trans'dʒɛniko] AGG genetically modified
transiberiano, a [transibe'rjano] AGG trans-Siberian
transigere [tran'sidʒere] VI IRREG (*aus* **avere**) to compromise; **su queste cose non transigo** I don't compromise on these things; **è uno che non transige** he is intransigent; **in fatto di sincerità io non transigo** I won't put up with insincerity
transistor [tran'sistor] SM INV (*Elettr*) transistor; (*Radio*) transistor (radio)
transitabile [transi'tabile] AGG passable; **"strada transitabile solo con catene"** "road passable only with snow chains"
transitabilità [transitabili'ta] SF INV: **transitabilità delle strade** road *o* driving conditions *pl*
transitare [transi'tare] VI (*aus* **essere**) to pass
transitivo, a [transi'tivo] AGG transitive
transito ['transito] SM transit; **"divieto di transito"** "no entry"; **"transito interrotto"** "road closed"; **stazione di transito** transit station
transitorio, ria, ri, rie [transi'tɔrjo] AGG (*temporaneo*: *provvedimenti, disposizioni*) temporary, provisional; (: *gloria*) transitory, fleeting, transient
transizione [transit'tsjone] SF transition; **età/periodo di transizione** age/period of transition
transoceanico, a, ci, che [transotʃe'aniko] AGG transoceanic
transumanza [transu'mantsa] SF transhumance
transustanziarsi [transustan'tsjarsi] VR (*Rel*) to transubstantiate
transustanziazione [transustantsjat'tsjone] SF (*Rel*) transubstantiation
tran tran [tran 'tran] SM INV routine; **il solito tran tran** the same old routine
tranvia [tran'via] SF tramway (*Brit*), streetcar line (*Am*)
tranviario, ria, ri, rie [tran'vjarjo] AGG tram *attr* (*Brit*), streetcar *attr* (*Am*); **linea tranviaria** tramline, streetcar line
tranviere [tran'vjɛre] SM (*conducente*) tram driver (*Brit*), streetcar driver (*Am*); (*bigliettaio*) tram *o* streetcar conductor
trapanare [trapa'nare] VT to drill
trapanazione [trapanat'tsjone] SF drilling; **trapanazione del cranio** trepanation, trephination
trapanese [trapa'nese] AGG of *o* from Trapani
■ SM/F inhabitant *o* native of Trapani
trapano ['trapano] SM drill; **trapano da dentista** dentist's drill; **trapano elettrico** electric drill; **trapano a mano** hand drill
trapassare [trapas'sare] VT to go through, pierce
■ VI (*aus* **essere**) (*fig letter*: *morire*) to pass away
trapassato, a [trapas'sato] SM (*Gramm*) past perfect
trapasso [tra'passo] SM **1** (*Dir*: *passaggio*): **trapasso di proprietà** (*di case*) conveyancing; (*di auto*) legal transfer **2** **l'ora del trapasso** (*letter*) one's final hour
trapelare [trape'lare] VI (*aus* **essere**) (*luce*) to filter through; (*fig*: *segreto, indiscrezione*) to leak (out); **dal suo viso trapelava tutta la sua gioia** his face shone with joy

Tt

trapezio, zi [tra'pettsjo] SM **1** (*Mat*) trapezium **2** (*Sport*) trapeze **3** (*Anat*) trapezius
trapezista, i, e [trapet'tsista] SM/F trapeze artist
trapiantare [trapjan'tare] VT (*Bot, Med*) to transplant; (*fig: moda, usanza*) to introduce
▶ **trapiantarsi** VIP to move; **ormai si sono trapiantati in Kenia** they have now settled in Kenya
trapianto [tra'pjanto] SM (*Med*) transplant; (*Bot*) transplanting
trappista, i [trap'pista] SM Trappist (monk)
trappola ['trappola] SF **1** (*anche fig*) trap; **prendere qn/qc in trappola** (*anche fig*) to catch sb/sth in a trap; **cadere in trappola** (*anche fig*) to fall into a trap; **sono caduti nella trappola della polizia** they fell into the police trap; **tendere una trappola a qn** to set a trap for sb **2** (*pegg: auto*) old wreck
trapunta [tra'punta] SF quilt
trarre ['trarre] VB IRREG
■ VT **1** to draw, pull; **trarre in inganno** to be misleading; **la sua aria innocente trae in inganno** his innocent appearance is misleading *o* deceptive; **sono stato tratto in inganno dal suo modo di fare** I was misled *o* deceived by his manner; **trarre qn d'impaccio** to get sb out of an awkward situation; **trarre in salvo** to rescue; **sono stati tratti in salvo dai vigili del fuoco** they were rescued by the fire brigade **2** (*estrarre*) to pull out, draw **3** (*derivare*) to obtain, get; **trarre guadagno** to make a profit; **trarre beneficio** *o* **profitto da qc** to benefit from sth; **trarre origine da qc** to have its origins *o* originate in sth; **trarre esempio da qn** to follow sb's example; **trarre un film da un libro** to make a film (*Brit*) *o* movie (*Am*) from a book; **un film tratto da un romanzo di A. Christie** a film based on a novel by A. Christie; **trarre le conclusioni** to draw one's own conclusions; **sta a te trarre le conclusioni** you can draw your own conclusions
▶ **trarsi** VR: **trarsi da** to get (o.s.) out of; **stai tranquillo che sa trarsi d'impaccio da solo** don't worry, he knows how to look after himself
trasalire [trasa'lire] VI (*aus* **avere** *o* **essere**) to jump, (give a) start; **fare trasalire qn** to make sb jump *o* start
trasandato, a [trazan'dato] AGG (*persona, abito*) scruffy, shabby; **è trasandato nel vestire** he wears scruffy clothes
trasbordare [trazbor'dare] VT (*gen*) to transfer; (*Naut*) to tran(s)ship
■ VI (*aus* **avere**) (*Naut*) to change ship; (*Aer*) to change plane; (*Ferr*) to change trains
trasbordo [traz'bordo] SM transfer
trascendentale [traʃʃenden'tale] AGG (*Filosofia*) transcendental; (*fig*): **non è niente di trascendentale** it (*o* he *ecc*) is nothing exceptional
trascendentalità [traʃʃendentali'ta] SF transcendental nature
trascendente [traʃʃen'dɛnte] AGG (*Filosofia*) transcendent(al); (*Mat*) transcendental
trascendere [traʃʃendere] VT IRREG (*Filosofia, Rel*) to transcend; (*fig: superare*) to surpass, go beyond
trasceso, a [traʃʃeso] PP *di* **trascendere**
trascinante [traʃʃi'nante] AGG (*musica, spettacolo*) enthralling
trascinare [traʃʃi'nare] VT (*gen*) to drag; **trascinare i piedi** to drag one's feet; **trascina una gamba** he has a stiff leg; **trascinare qn in tribunale** to take sb to court; **sa trascinare la folla** he knows how to carry the crowd; **la sua musica ti trascina** his music is enthralling; **trascinare qn sulla via del male** to lead sb astray
▶ **trascinarsi** VR (*strisciare*) to drag o.s. (along)
▶ **trascinarsi** VIP (*controversia*) to drag on
trascinatore [traʃʃina'tore] SM: **trascinatore fogli a modulo continuo** paper feed
trascolorare [traskolo'rare] VI (*aus* **essere**) **trascolorò in volto** his face changed colour
trascorrere [tras'korrere] VB IRREG
■ VT (*vacanze, giorni*) to spend, pass; **trascorrono sempre le vacanze al mare** they always spend their holidays at the seaside
■ VI (*aus* **essere**) (*passare: ore, mesi, giorni*) to pass; **le ore trascorrevano lente** the hours dragged by; **sono trascorsi sei giorni da allora** six days have passed since then; **hai lasciato trascorrere troppo tempo** you've allowed too much time to pass
trascorso, a [tras'korso] PP *di* **trascorrere**
■ AGG past
■ SM mistake; **non voglio conoscere i suoi trascorsi** I don't want to know about his past
trascritto, a [tras'kritto] PP *di* **trascrivere**
trascrivere [tras'krivere] VT IRREG **1** (*citazioni, frasi, idee*) to write down, copy down **2** (*traslitterare*) to transliterate; (*: sistema fonetico e delle note musicali*) to transcribe
trascrizione [traskrit'tsjone] SF (*gen*) writing down, copying down; (*di discorso*) transcript; (*traslitterazione*) transliteration; (*: nel sistema fonetico e delle note musicali*) transcription
trascurabile [trasku'rabile] AGG negligible
trascurare [trasku'rare] VT **1** (*studio, lavoro, famiglia*) to neglect **2** (*omettere*) to omit, skip, leave out **3** (*non tener conto di*) to ignore, overlook; (*non considerare*) to disregard
▶ **trascurarsi** VR to neglect o.s.
trascuratamente [traskurata'mente] AVV carelessly
trascuratezza [traskura'tettsa] SF (*negligenza*) carelessness, negligence; (*disordine*) untidiness
trascurato, a [trasku'rato] AGG **1** (*sciatto*) slovenly **2** (*negligente*) careless, negligent **3** (*non curato*) neglected; **sentirsi trascurato** to feel neglected; **un'influenza trascurata può portare alla polmonite** if you neglect a bout of flu it can develop into pneumonia
trasduttore [trazdut'tore] SM (*Fis*) transducer
trasecolare [traseko'lare] VI (*aus* **avere** *o* **essere**) to be dumbfounded
trasecolato, a [traseko'lato] AGG astounded, amazed, dumbfounded
trasferibile [trasfe'ribile] AGG transferable; **"non trasferibile"** (*su assegno*) "account payee only"; **caratteri trasferibili** transfers
trasferimento [trasferi'mento] SM **1** (*cambiamento di sede*) transfer; **ha chiesto il trasferimento** he's asked for a transfer **2** (*Dir: di titoli*) transfer; (*: di proprietà*) conveyancing **3** **trasferimento di chiamata** call diversion
trasferire [trasfe'rire] VT **1** (*sede, potere*) to transfer; **è stato trasferito a Milano** he's been transferred to Milan **2** (*Dir: titoli*) to transfer; (*: proprietà*) to transfer, convey
▶ **trasferirsi** VIP to move; **il mese prossimo ci trasferiamo a Firenze** we're moving to Florence next month
trasferta [tras'fɛrta] SF **1** (*di funzionario*) temporary transfer; **essere in trasferta** to be on temporary

transfer **2** (*anche:* **indennità di trasferta**) travel allowance, travel expenses *pl* **3** (*Sport*) away game; **giocare in trasferta** to play away (from home); **la prossima settimana giochiamo in trasferta** we're playing away from home next week
trasfigurare [trasfigu'rare] VT to transfigure
▶ **trasfigurarsi** VIP to be transfigured
trasfigurazione [trasfigurat'tsjone] SF transfiguration
trasfondere [tras'fondere] VT IRREG (*fig*) to instil
trasformabile [trasfor'mabile] AGG (*divano*) convertible
trasformare [trasfor'mare] VT **1** (*gen*) to change, alter; (*radicalmente*) to transform; **hanno trasformato la stalla in un ristorante** they converted the stable into a restaurant; **la strega trasformò il principe in un albero** the witch turned the prince into a tree; **quel vestito ti trasforma** that dress completely transforms you; **il soggiorno in America l'ha trasformato** his stay in America has transformed him **2** (*Rugby*) to convert; **trasformare un rigore** (*Calcio*) to score from a penalty
▶ **trasformarsi** VIP (*embrione, larva*) to be transformed, transform itself; (*energia*) to be converted; (*persona, paese*) to change, alter; (: *radicalmente*) to be transformed; **un tavolo che si trasforma in asse da stiro** a table that converts into an ironing board
trasformatore [trasforma'tore] SM (*Elettr*) transformer
trasformazionale [trasformattsjo'nale] AGG transformational
trasformazione [trasformat'tsjone] SF (*vedi vb*) change, alteration; transformation; conversion
trasformismo [trasfor'mizmo] SM (*Pol*) *system whereby a government attempts to hold on to power by forming coalitions to prevent the formation of any credible opposition*
trasformista, i, e [trasfor'mista] SM/F **1** (*Pol*) transformist (*politician who attempts to hold on to power by forming coalitions to prevent the formation of any credible opposition*); (*fig*) opportunist; (*pegg*) timeserver **2** (*artista*) quick-change artist
trasfusione [trasfu'zjone] SF (*Med*) transfusion
trasgredire [trazgre'dire] VT, VI (*aus* **avere**) **trasgredire a** (*legge, regola*) to break, infringe; (*ordini*) to disobey
trasgressione [trazgres'sjone] SF **1** (*vedi vb*) breaking, infringement; disobeying **2** (*anticonformismo*) transgression, rule-breaking
trasgressivo, a [trazgres'sivo] AGG (*personaggio, atteggiamento*) rule-breaking *attr*
trasgressore [trazgres'sore], **trasgreditrice** [trazgredi'tritʃe] SM/F (*Dir*) transgressor
traslare [traz'lare] VT (*salma*) to transfer
traslato, a [traz'lato] AGG metaphorical, figurative
■ SM metaphor
traslazione [trazlat'tsjone] SF **1** (*gen, Fin*) transfer **2** (*Fis*) translation
traslitterare [trazlitte'rare] VT to transliterate
traslitterazione [trazlitterat'tsjone] SF transliteration
traslocare [trazlo'kare] VT, VI (*aus* **avere**) to move
trasloco, chi [traz'lɔko] SM removal; **una ditta di traslochi** a removal firm; **fare un trasloco** to move house; **li ho aiutati a fare il trasloco** I helped them to move house
traslucido, a [traz'lutʃido] AGG translucent
trasmesso, a [traz'messo] PP *di* **trasmettere**
trasmettere [traz'mettere] VB IRREG
■ VT **1** (*Telec*) to transmit; (*Radio, TV*) to broadcast; **trasmettere in diretta** to broadcast live; **trasmettere una partita in diretta** to broadcast a match live; **il concerto sarà trasmesso in diretta** the concert will be broadcast live; **trasmettono un western** (*TV*) they're showing a western **2** (*usanza, diritto, titolo*) to pass on; (*lettera, telegramma, notizia*) to send; **trasmettere una malattia a qn** to pass a disease on to sb;
▶ **trasmettersi** VIP (*usanza*) to be passed on; (*Med*) to be spread, be transmitted
trasmettitore, trice [trazmetti'tore] AGG transmitting
■ SM transmitter
trasmigrazione [trazmigrat'tsjone] SF (*di anime*) transmigration
trasmissione [trazmis'sjone] SF **1** (*gen*) transmission; (*di titolo, eredità*) passing on, handing down; **albero di trasmissione** (*Aut*) transmission shaft; **trasmissione (dei) dati** (*Inform*) data transmission; **trasmissione del pensiero** thought transference **2** (*Radio, TV: programma*) transmission, broadcast, programme (*Brit*), program (*Am*); **una trasmissione radiofonica** a radio programme; **le trasmissioni riprenderanno domani** program(me)s will resume tomorrow
trasmittente [trazmit'tɛnte] AGG transmitting
■ SF transmitter, transmitting *o* broadcasting station
trasognato, a [trasoɲ'ɲato] AGG dreamy
trasparente [traspa'rɛnte] AGG (*anche fig*) transparent; (*sottile*) wafer-thin
■ SM transparency
trasparenza [traspa'rɛntsa] SF (*anche fig*) transparency; **guardare qc in trasparenza** to look at sth against the light
trasparire [traspa'rire] VI IRREG (*aus* **essere**) **1** to shine through; **lasciare trasparire la luce** to let the light shine through **2** (*vedersi*) to be visible, show (through); **sotto il vestito traspare la sottoveste** her slip shows *o* can be seen through her dress; **dal suo volto traspariva la gioia** his face shone with joy; **la sua espressione non lasciava trasparire nulla** his face gave nothing away
trasparso, a [tras'parso] PP *di* **trasparire**
traspirare [traspi'rare] VI (*aus* **essere**) (*sudare*) to perspire; (*fig: trapelare*) to leak out
traspirazione [traspirat'tsjone] SF (*sudorazione*) perspiration; (*Bot*) transpiration
trasporre [tras'porre] VT IRREG to transpose
trasportare [traspor'tare] VT **1** (*gen, fig*) to carry; (*con veicolo*) to carry, transport, convey; **il camion trasportava un carico di arance** the lorry was carrying a load of oranges; **lo hanno trasportato d'urgenza in ospedale** they rushed him to hospital; **questo libro ci trasporta al Rinascimento** this book takes us back to the Renaissance **2** **lasciarsi trasportare (da qc)** (*gioia, entusiasmo*) to let o.s. be carried away (by sth); **lasciarsi trasportare dall'ira** to lose one's temper **3** (*trascinare*) to carry off; **l'hanno trasportato in questura** they took him off to the police station
trasportatore, trice [trasporta'tore] AGG transport *attr*
■ SM/F (*persona*) transporter, carrier; (: *per strada*) haulier (*Brit*), hauler (*Am*)
■ SM (*macchina*) conveyor

Tt

trasporto [tras'pɔrto] SM **1** (*gen*) transport; **danneggiato durante il trasporto** damaged in transit; **mezzi di trasporto** means of transport; **nave/aereo da trasporto** transport ship/aircraft *inv*; **compagnia di trasporto** carrier; (*per strada*) hauliers *pl* (*Brit*), haulers *pl* (*Am*); **i trasporti** transport *sg*; **un sistema di trasporti efficiente** an efficient transport system; **il ministero dei trasporti** ≈ the Department of Transport (*Brit*), ≈ the Department of Transportation (*Am*) **trasporti pubblici** public transport *sg*; **qui i trasporti pubblici funzionano molto bene** public transport is very efficient here; **trasporto aereo** air transport; **trasporto marittimo** sea transport; **trasporto stradale** (road) haulage **2** (*fig*) rapture, passion; **con trasporto** passionately; **un trasporto d'ira** a fit of anger

trasposizione [traspozit'tsjone] SF (*Ling*) transposition

trasposto, a [tras'posto] PP *di* **trasporre**

trassato [tras'sato] SM (*di assegno*) drawee

trassi *ecc* ['trassi] VB *vedi* **trarre**

trastullare [trastul'lare] VT (*bambino*) to play with, amuse
▸ **trastullarsi** VR (*divertirsi*) **trastullarsi con qc** to amuse o.s. with sth; (*gingillarsi*) to fritter away one's time

trastullo [tras'tullo] SM game

trasudare [trasu'dare] VT to ooze with
■ VI (*aus* **essere**) to ooze (out)

trasversale [trazver'sale] AGG (*taglio, sbarra*) cross *attr*; (*retta*) transverse; **via trasversale** side street; **motore trasversale** (*Aut*) transverse engine; **una camicia a righe trasversali** a shirt with horizontal stripes; **partito trasversale** (*fig*) *unofficial grouping of diverse political interests*

trasversalmente [trazversal'mente] AVV (*di traverso*) horizontally; (*indirettamente*) indirectly

trasvolare [trazvo'lare] VT to fly across *o* over

trasvolata [trazvo'lata] SF non-stop long-haul flight

tratta ['tratta] SF **1** (*traffico*): **la tratta degli schiavi** the slave trade; **la tratta delle bianche** the white slave trade **2** (*Comm*) draft; **tratta documentaria** documentary bill of exchange

trattamento [tratta'mento] SM **1** (*gen*) treatment; (*servizio in ristorante*) service; **trattamento di riguardo** special treatment; **ricevere un buon trattamento** (*cliente*) to get good service; **fare un trattamento di favore** to give special treatment **2** (*Tecn, Med*) treatment; **trattamento di bellezza** beauty treatment **3** (*Econ*) payment; **trattamento di fine rapporto** severance pay **4** (*Inform*): **trattamento testi** word processing

trattare [trat'tare] VT **1** (*discutere: tema, argomento*) to deal with, discuss; (*negoziare: pace, resa*) to negotiate; **trattare un affare** to negotiate a deal **2** (*comportarsi con*) to treat; **trattare bene/male qn** to treat sb well/badly; **trattare qn con i guanti** to handle *o* treat sb with kid gloves; **lo tratta come una pezza da piedi** she treats him like dirt **3** (*Comm: vendere*) to deal in, handle **4** (*Tecn, Med*) to treat
■ VI (*aus* **avere**) **1** (*libro, film*): **trattare di** to deal with, be about; **di cosa tratta il libro?** what's the book about? **2** (*avere relazioni*): **trattare con** to deal with; **con lui non si può trattare** he's impossible to deal with; **ho trattato direttamente con il proprietario** I dealt directly with the owner **3** (*forma impers*): **si tratta di sua moglie** it's about his wife; **si tratta di pochi minuti** it will only take a few minutes; **si tratterebbe solo di poche ore** it would just be a matter of a few hours; **di che si tratta?** what's it about?; **ti ha detto di cosa si tratta?** did he tell you what it's about?; **si tratta di vita o di morte** it's a matter of life or death;
▸ **trattarsi** VR: **trattarsi bene** to look after o.s. (well)

trattativa [tratta'tiva] SF negotiation; **trattative** SFPL (*tra Stati, governi*) talks; **essere in trattativa con qn** to be in negotiation with sb

trattato, a [trat'tato] SM **1** (*accordo*) treaty; **firmare/ratificare un trattato** to sign/ratify a treaty; **trattato commerciale** trade agreement; **trattato di pace** peace treaty **2** (*opera*) treatise
■ AGG: **non trattato** (*prodotto, alimento*) untreated (with pesticides)

trattazione [trattat'tsjone] SF treatment

tratteggiare [tratted'dʒare] VT (*ombreggiare*) to hatch; (*abbozzare*) to sketch; (*fig: descrivere*) to outline; **linea tratteggiata** dotted line

tratteggio, gi [trat'teddʒo] SM (*Disegno*) hatching

trattenere [tratte'nere] VB IRREG
■ VT **1** (*fermare*) to keep back; (*: in ospedale*) to keep; (*: in carcere*) to detain; **trattenere qn dal fare qc** to restrain sb *o* hold sb back from doing sth; **trattenere in osservazione** (*in ospedale*) to keep in for observation; **ho cercato di trattenerlo** I tried to hold him back; **se non l'avessimo trattenuto l'avrebbe picchiato** if we hadn't held him back he would have hit him; **non ti tratterrò a lungo** I won't keep you long; **sono stato trattenuto in ufficio** I was delayed at the office; **mi hanno trattenuto a pranzo** they had me stay for lunch **2** (*lacrime, riso*) to hold back, keep back, restrain; (*respiro*) to hold; **prova a trattenere il respiro** try to hold your breath **3** (*detrarre*) to withhold, keep back, deduct
▸ **trattenersi** VIP (*fermarsi*) to stay, remain; **quanto ti trattieni?** how long are you staying?; **mi sono trattenuto in ufficio** I stayed on at the office; **mi sono trattenuto a cena** I stayed for dinner;
▸ **trattenersi** VR (*astenersi*) to restrain o.s., stop o.s.; **trattenersi dal fare qc** to keep *o* stop o.s. from doing sth; **non sono più riuscito a trattenermi** I just couldn't stop myself

trattenimento [tratteni'mento] SM (*festa*) party; **trattenimento danzante** dance

trattenuta [tratte'nuta] SF (*anche:* **trattenuta sullo stipendio**) deduction

trattino [trat'tino] SM (*nelle parole composte*) hyphen; (*per iniziare il discorso diretto*) dash; **si scrive con il trattino** it's spelt with a hyphen

tratto[1]**, a** ['tratto] PP *di* **trarre**

tratto[2] ['tratto] SM **1** (*di penna, matita*) stroke; **disegnare a grandi tratti** to sketch; **descrivere qc a grandi tratti** to give an outline of sth **2 tratti** SMPL (*caratteristiche*) features; **ha i tratti molto marcati** he has very prominent features; **i tratti essenziali del periodo/del suo carattere** the essential features of the period/his character **3** (*segmento*) part, section; (*: di mare*) stretch, expanse; (*: di strada*) stretch; **è un tratto di strada molto pericoloso** it's a very dangerous stretch of road; **dobbiamo fare ancora un bel tratto a piedi** we still have quite a long way to walk; **c'è ancora un bel tratto da fare** we've still got a long way to go; **alcuni tratti del suo romanzo** some parts of his novel **4** (*spazio di tempo*) time, period (of time); **a tratti** at times; **(tutto) ad un tratto** *or* **d'un**

tratto (*all'improvviso*) suddenly; **tutt'a un tratto ha cominciato a piovere** it suddenly started to rain

trattore [trat'tore] SM tractor

trattoria [tratto'ria] SF trattoria, small restaurant

trauma, i ['trauma] SM (*Med*: *anche*: **trauma psichico**) trauma; **la morte del padre è stata un trauma per lui** his father's death was a traumatic experience for him; **trauma cranico** concussion

traumatico, a, ci, che [trau'matiko] AGG traumatic

traumatizzante [traumatid'dzante] AGG traumatizing, traumatic

traumatizzare [traumatid'dzare] VT (*Med*) to traumatize; (*fig*: *impressionare*) to shock; **è rimasto traumatizzato da quell'esperienza** he was traumatized by the experience; **le scene di violenza possono traumatizzare i bambini** scenes of violence can be traumatic for children

traumatizzato, a [traumatid'dzato] AGG (*vedi vb*) traumatized; shocked

traumatologia [traumatolo'dʒia] SF traumatology

traumatologico, a, ci, che [traumato'lɔdʒiko] AGG traumatological; **centro traumatologico** accident and emergency unit *o* hospital

traumatologo, a, gi, ghe [trauma'tɔlogo] SM/F trauma specialist, accident and emergency specialist

travagliare [travaʎ'ʎare] VT (*affliggere*) to trouble, afflict; (*fig*: *tormentare*) to torment; **ha avuto un'esistenza travagliata** he has had a difficult life
■ VI (*aus* **avere**) (*letter*) to suffer

travaglio, gli [tra'vaʎʎo] SM **1** (*sofferenza*: *mentale*) anguish, distress; (: *fisica*) pain, suffering **2** (*Med*: *anche*: **travaglio di parto**) labour (*Brit*) *o* labor (*Am*) pains *pl*

travasare [trava'zare] VT (*liquidi*) to pour; (: *vino*) to decant

travaso [tra'vazo] SM (*vedi vb*) pouring; decanting

travatura [trava'tura] SF beams *pl*

trave ['trave] SF beam

traveggole [tra'veggole] SFPL: **avere le traveggole** to be seeing things

traversa [tra'vɛrsa] SF **1** (*trave trasversale*) crossbeam, crosspiece; (*Ferr*) sleeper (*Brit*), (railroad) tie (*Am*); (*Calcio, Rugby*) crossbar; **la palla ha colpito la traversa** the ball hit the crossbar **2** (*lenzuolo*) draw-sheet **3** (*via*) sideroad, sidestreet; **prendi la seconda traversa a destra** take the second right; **abita in una traversa di via Roma** she lives in a sidestreet off via Roma; **via Giotto è una traversa di via Rossetti** via Giotto is off Via Rossetti

traversare [traver'sare] VT (*attraversare*) to cross; **traversare un fiume a nuoto** to swim across a river

traversata [traver'sata] SF (*gen, Naut*) crossing; (*Aer*) flight, trip; **la traversata dell'Atlantico** the crossing of the Atlantic

traversie [traver'sie] SFPL hardships

traversina [traver'sina] SF (*Ferr*) sleeper (*Brit*), (railroad) tie (*Am*)

traverso, a [tra'vɛrso] AGG cross *attr*, transverse; **flauto traverso** (transverse) flute; **via traversa** sideroad; **ottenere qc per vie traverse** to obtain sth in an underhand way
■ **di traverso** AVV sideways; **camminare di traverso** to walk sideways (on); **mettilo di traverso** put it sideways; **andare di traverso** (*cibo*) to go down the wrong way; **il latte mi è andato di traverso** the milk went down the wrong way; **guardare qn di traverso** to give sb a nasty look; **avere la luna di traverso** to be in a bad mood; **messo di traverso** sideways on

traversone [traver'sone] SM (*Calcio*) cross

travertino [traver'tino] SM travertine

travestimento [travesti'mento] SM (*gen*) disguise; (*per carnevale*) costume

travestire [traves'tire] VT (*camuffare*) to disguise; (*in costume*) to dress up
▶ **travestirsi** VR (*vedi vt*) to disguise o.s.; to dress up; **travestirsi da donna** to dress up as a woman

travestitismo [travesti'tizmo] SM transvestism, cross-dressing

travestito [traves'tito] SM transvestite, cross-dresser

traviare [travi'are] VT to lead astray
▶ **traviarsi** VIP to go off the straight and narrow

traviato, a [travi'ato] AGG corrupt

travisare [travi'zare] VT to distort, misrepresent

travolgente [travol'dʒɛnte] AGG (*entusiasmo*) overwhelming; (*bellezza, fascino*) captivating; (*comicità, umorismo*) side-splitting; (*passione*) uncontrollable; (*amore*) passionate

travolgere [tra'vɔldʒere] VT IRREG (*sogg*: *piena, valanga*) to sweep away; (*fig*) to overwhelm; **è stato travolto da un'auto** he was run over by a car; **si è lasciato travolgere dalla passione** he was overwhelmed by passion

travolto, a [tra'vɔlto] PP *di* **travolgere**

trazione [trat'tsjone] SF (*Med, Tecn*) traction; (*Aut*) drive; **a trazione integrale** (*Aut*) four wheel drive; **trazione anteriore** (*Aut*) front-wheel drive; **trazione posteriore** (*Aut*) rear-wheel drive

tre [tre] AGG INV three; **tre volte** three times
■ SM INV three; **non c'è due senza tre** it never rains but it pours; *per fraseologia vedi* **cinque**

trealberi [tre'alberi] SM INV (*Naut*) three-master

trebbia ['trebbja] SF (*Agr*: *operazione*) threshing; (: *stagione*) threshing season

trebbiare [treb'bjare] VT (*Agr*) to thresh

trebbiatrice [trebbja'tritʃe] SF (*Agr*) threshing machine

trebbiatura [trebbja'tura] SF threshing

trebisonda [trebi'zonda] SF: **perdere la trebisonda** to lose one's head

treccia, ce ['trettʃa] SF (*di capelli*) plait, braid; (*di tessuti, fili*) braid; **Anita ha le trecce** Anita has plaits; **lavorato a trecce** (*pullover*) cable-knit

trecentesco, a, schi, sche [tretʃen'tesko] AGG fourteenth-century

trecento [tre'tʃɛnto] AGG INV three hundred
■ SM INV three hundred; (*secolo*): **il Trecento** the fourteenth century

tredicenne [tredi'tʃenne] AGG, SM/F thirteen-year-old; *per fraseologia vedi* **cinquantenne**

tredicesima [tredi'tʃɛzima] SF *Christmas bonus of a month's pay*

tredicesimo, a [tredi'tʃɛzimo] AGG, SM/F, SM thirteenth; *per fraseologia vedi* **quinto**

tredici ['treditʃi] AGG INV thirteen
■ SM INV thirteen; **fare tredici** (*Totocalcio*) to win the pools (*Brit*); *per fraseologia vedi* **cinque**

tregenda [tre'dʒɛnda] SF: **notte di tregenda** stormy night

tregua ['tregwa] SF (*Mil, Pol*) truce; (*fig*) rest, respite; **il dolore non gli dà tregua** the pain gives him no peace, he is in constant pain; **senza tregua** non-stop, without stopping, uninterruptedly

tremante [tre'mante] AGG trembling, shaking

tremare [tre'mare] VI (*aus* **avere**) **1** (*gen*) to tremble, shake; (*fig: temere*) to be afraid; **tremare di** (*freddo*) to shiver *o* tremble with; (*paura, rabbia*) to shake *o* tremble with; **tremava di freddo** she was shivering with cold; **tremavo di paura** I was shaking with fear; **tremare come una foglia** to shake like a leaf; **mi tremano le gambe** my legs are shaking; **tremare per la sorte di qn** to fear for sb; **faceva tremare gli studenti** he made the students tremble with fear **2** (*oscillare: vetri*) to vibrate; (: *terra*) to shake; (: *voce*) to shake, tremble; (: *luce, candela*) to flicker; **mi trema la vista** I can't see straight

tremarella [trema'rɛlla] SF shivers *pl*; **ho la tremarella** I have got the shivers; **mi ha fatto venire la tremarella** it gave me the shivers

tremendamente [tremenda'mente] AVV (*divertente, imbarazzato*) terribly, awfully

tremendo, a [tre'mɛndo] AGG (*in tutti i sensi*) terrible, awful, dreadful; **avere una fame tremenda** to be awfully *o* terribly hungry, be famished; **faceva un caldo tremendo** it was dreadfully *o* terribly hot; **aveva un mal di testa tremendo** he had a terrible headache

trementina [tremen'tina] SF turpentine

tremila [tre'mila] AGG INV, SM INV three thousand

tremito ['trɛmito] SM trembling *no pl*; **mi è venuto un tremito** I started to tremble

tremolante [tremo'lante] AGG (*vedi vb*) trembling, shaking; flickering; twinkling; quivering

tremolare [tremo'lare] VI (*aus* **avere**) (*gen*) to tremble, shake; (*luci, candele*) to flicker; (*stelle*) to twinkle; (*foglie*) to quiver

tremolio, lii [tremo'lio] SM (*gen*) trembling, shaking; (*di luci*) flickering

tremolo ['trɛmolo] SM (*Mus*) tremolo

tremore [tre'more] SM tremor

tremulo, a ['trɛmulo] AGG **1** (*gen*) trembling, shaking; (*stelle*) twinkling; (*luci*) flickering **2** (*Bot*): **pioppo tremulo** trembling poplar

trend [trend] SM INV (*Econ*) trend

trenette [tre'nette] SFPL (*Culin*) *long, flat noodles*

trenino [tre'nino] SM (*giocattolo*) toy train

Trenitalia [treni'talja] SF *Italian national railway*
▷ www.trenitalia.it/

treno ['trɛno] SM **1** (*Ferr*) train; **prendere/perdere il treno** to catch/miss the train; **ho perso il treno** I missed the train; **salire in/scendere dal treno** to get on/get off the train; **andare/viaggiare in treno** to go/travel by train; **siamo andati in treno** we went by train; **treno espresso** express train; **treno interregionale** long-distance train; **treno locale** stopping (*Brit*) *o* local (*Am*) train; **treno merci** goods (*Brit*) *o* freight (*Am*) train; **treno rapido** express (train); **treno regionale** stopping *o* local train; **treno straordinario** special train; **treno viaggiatori** passenger train **2** (*Aut*): **treno di gomme** set of tyres (*Brit*) *o* tires (*Am*)

TRENI

There are various types of train in Italy. For short journeys there are the "Regionali" (R) which generally operate within a particular region and stop at almost every station, and the "Interregionali" (IR), which operate beyond regional boundaries in order to connect with more distant locations, especially tourist centres. Medium and long distance passenger journeys are carried out by Intercity (I) and Eurocity (EC) trains, while the Eurostar service (ES) offers fast connections between the major Italian cities. Night services are operated by Intercity Notte (ICN), Euronight (EN) and by "Espressi" (EXP). These trains consist of seating carriages, sleepers and couchettes. The high-speed "pendolino", which offers both first- and second-class travel, runs between the major cities.
▷ www.trenitalia.it/

trenta ['trenta] AGG INV thirty
■SM INV **1** thirty **2** (*Univ*): **trenta su trenta** full marks; **trenta e lode** full marks plus distinction *o* cum laude; *per fraseologia vedi* **cinquanta**

trentenne [tren'tɛnne] AGG, SM/F thirty-year-old; *per fraseologia vedi* **cinquantenne**

trentennio, ni [tren'tɛnnjo] SM period of thirty years

trentesimo, a [tren'tɛzimo] AGG, SM/F, SM thirtieth; *per fraseologia vedi* **quinto**

trentina [tren'tina] SF about thirty, thirty or so; *per fraseologia vedi* **cinquantina**

trentino, a [tren'tino] AGG of *o* from Trento
■SM/F inhabitant *o* native of Trento

trepidante [trepi'dante] AGG anxious

trepidare [trepi'dare] VI (*aus* **avere**) to be anxious; **trepidare per qn** to be anxious about sb; **trepidava nell'attesa** she waited in trepidation

trepido, a ['trɛpido] AGG (*letter*) anxious

treppiede [trep'pjede] SM (*per fotografia*) tripod; (*per cucina*) trivet

trequarti [tre'kwarti] SM INV **1** (*indumento*) three-quarter-length coat **2** (*Rugby*) three-quarter

tresca, sche ['treska] SF (*relazione amorosa*) affair; (*intrigo*) intrigue, plot

trespolo ['trespolo] SM (*sostegno*) trestle; (: *per uccelli*) perch

trevigiano, a [trevi'dʒano], **trevisano, a** [trevi'sano] AGG of *o* from Treviso
■SM/F inhabitant *o* native of Treviso

triade ['triade] SF (*gen, Mus*) triad

triangolare [triango'lare] AGG triangular

triangolo [tri'angolo] SM (*gen, fig, Mat, Mus*) triangle; (*Aut*) warning triangle; **il solito** *o* **classico triangolo** (*fig*) the eternal triangle; **triangolo ottusangolo** obtuse-angled triangle; **triangolo rettangolo** right-angled triangle

tribalismo [triba'lizmo] SM tribalism

tribolare [tribo'lare] VI (*aus* **avere**) (*patire*) to suffer; (*fare fatica*) to have a lot of trouble; **ha finito di tribolare** (*euf: è morto*) death has put an end to his suffering; **ha tribolato parecchio per ottenerlo** he went to a lot of trouble to get it

tribolazione [tribolat'tsjone] SF tribulation, suffering; **quel figlio è la mia tribolazione** that son of mine brings me nothing but suffering; **una vita di tribolazioni** a life of trials and tribulations

tribordo [tri'bordo] SM (*Naut*) starboard

tribù [tri'bu] SF INV tribe

tribuna [tri'buna] SF **1** (*per oratore*) platform **2** (*per il pubblico*) gallery; (: *di stadio*) stand; (: *di ippodromo*) grandstand; **tribuna della stampa/riservata al pubblico** press/public gallery **3** (*TV, Radio*): **tribuna politica** ≈ party political broadcast (*Brit*), ≈ paid political broadcast (*Am*)

tribunale [tribu'nale] SM (*Dir*) court; **chiamare in tribunale** to take to court; **presentarsi** *o* **comparire**

in tribunale to appear in court; **tribunale amministrativo regionale** *regional administrative court*; **tribunale militare** military tribunal; **Tribunale penale internazionale** International Criminal Tribunal; **tribunale del riesame** *provincial court that re-examines cases of those who have been imprisoned and can order their release*
tribuno [tri'buno] SM (*Storia*) tribune
tributare [tribu'tare] VT to bestow; **tributare gli onori dovuti a qn** to pay tribute to sb
tributario, ria, ri, rie [tribu'tarjo] AGG **1** (*Fisco*) tax *attr*, fiscal **2** (*Geog*): **fiume tributario** tributary
tributo [tri'buto] SM (*imposta*) tax; (*Storia*: *fig*) tribute
tricheco, chi [tri'kɛko] SM walrus
triciclo [tri'tʃiklo] SM tricycle
triclinio, ni [tri'klinjo] SM (*Storia*) triclinium
tricolore [triko'lore] AGG three-coloured (*Brit*), three-colored (*Am*)
■ SM (*bandiera*) tricolo(u)r; **il tricolore** the Italian flag
tridente [tri'dɛnte] SM (*gen*) trident; (*per fieno*) pitchfork
tridimensionale [tridimensjo'nale] AGG three-dimensional
triennale [trien'nale] AGG (*che dura 3 anni*) three-year *attr*; (*che avviene ogni 3 anni*) three-yearly
triennio, ni [tri'ɛnnjo] SM (period of) three years
triestino, a [tries'tino] AGG of *o* from Trieste
■ SM/F inhabitant *o* native of Trieste
trifase [tri'faze] AGG INV (*Elettr*) three-phase
trifoglio, gli [tri'fɔʎʎo] SM clover; **trifoglio bianco** white clover; **trifoglio pratense** *o* **rosso** red clover
trifolato, a [trifo'lato] AGG (*Culin*) *cooked in oil, garlic and parsley*
trigemino, a [tri'dʒɛmino] AGG **1** (*Med*): **avere un parto trigemino** to give birth to triplets **2** (*Anat*) trigeminal
■ SM (*Anat*) trigeminal (nerve)
triglia ['triʎʎa] SF mullet; **fare gli occhi di triglia a qn** to make sheep's eyes at sb; **triglia di scoglio** red mullet
trigonometria [trigonome'tria] SF trigonometry
trigonometrico, a, ci, che [trigono'mɛtriko] AGG trigonometric
trilaterale [trilate'rale] AGG (*accordo, patto, alleanza*) trilateral
trilione [tri'ljone] SM trillion
trillare [tril'lare] VI (*aus* **avere**) (*Mus*) to trill; (*campanello*) to ring
trillo ['trillo] SM (*Mus*) trill; (*di campanello*) ring
trimarano [trima'rano] SM trimaran
trimestrale [trimes'trale] AGG (*periodo, abbonamento*) three-month *attr*; (*scadenza, pubblicazione*) quarterly
trimestralmente [trimestral'mente] AVV every three months, quarterly
trimestre [tri'mɛstre] SM **1** (*periodo*) three months, period of three months, quarter; (: *Scol*) term, quarter (*Am*) **2** (*rata*) quarterly payment
trimotore [trimo'tore] SM (*Aer*) three-engined plane
trina ['trina] SF lace
trincare [trin'kare] VT (*fam*: *bere alcolici*) to knock back; **trinca come una spugna** he drinks like a fish
trincea [trin'tʃɛa] SF (*Mil*) trench; **guerra di trincea** trench warfare
trinceramento [trintʃera'mento] SM (*Mil*) entrenchment
trincerare [trintʃe'rare] VT (*Mil*) to entrench
▸ **trincerarsi** VIP (*Mil*) to entrench o.s.; **trincerarsi nel silenzio più assoluto** to take refuge in silence; **trincerarsi dietro un pretesto** to hide behind an excuse
trincetto [trin'tʃetto] SM cobbler's knife
trinchetto [trin'ketto] SM (*Naut*: *albero*) foremast; (: *vela*) foresail
trinciapollo [trintʃa'pollo] SM INV poultry shears *pl*
trinciare [trin'tʃare] VT **1** to cut up **2** (*fig*): **trinciare giudizi (su qn/qc)** to make rash judgments (about sb/sth)
Trinidad ['trinidad] SM: **Trinidad e Tobago** Trinidad and Tobago
trinità [trini'ta] SF trinity; **la (santissima) Trinità** the (Holy) Trinity
trinomio, mi [tri'nɔmjo] SM (*Mat*) trinomial
trio, trii ['trio] SM (*Mus, fig*) trio
trionfale [trion'fale] AGG (*arco, entrata*) triumphal; (*successo*) triumphant
trionfalismo [trionfa'lizmo] SM triumphalism
trionfalista [trionfa'lista] SM/F triumphant winner
trionfalistico, a [trionfa'listiko] AGG triumphalist
trionfalmente [trionfal'mente] AVV triumphantly
trionfante [trion'fante] AGG triumphant
trionfare [trion'fare] VI (*aus* **avere**) **1** (*gen, Mil*) to triumph; (*commedia, film*) to be a great success; **la verità alla fine trionfa sempre** truth will out; **trionfare su** to triumph over, overcome; **trionfare sui nemici** to triumph over one's enemies **2** (*esultare*) to rejoice; **trionfare per qc** to rejoice at *o* over sth
trionfatore, trice [trionfa'tore] AGG (*truppe*) triumphant, victorious
■ SM/F victor
trionfo [tri'onfo] SM (*gen*) triumph; (*morale*) (moral) victory; **il trionfo della nazionale italiana** the triumph of the Italian team; **in trionfo** in triumph
tripartitico, a, ci, che [tripar'titiko], **tripartito** [tripar'tito] AGG (*Pol*) tripartite, three-party *attr*
tripletta [tri'pletta] SF (*Calcio*) hat trick (*Brit*); **realizzare una tripletta** to score a hat trick
triplicare [tripli'kare] VT, VI (*aus* **essere**), **triplicarsi** VIP to treble, triple
triplice ['triplitʃe] AGG triple; **in triplice copia** in triplicate; **la Triplice Alleanza** the Triple Alliance
triplo, a ['triplo] AGG triple, treble; **salto triplo** (*Sport*) triple jump; **la spesa è tripla** it costs three times as much
■ SM: **il triplo (di)** three times as much (as); **guadagna il triplo di lei** he earns three times as much as her; **mi occorre il triplo** I need three times as much; **lavorare il triplo** to work three times as hard
tripode ['tripode] SM tripod
tripolare [tripo'lare] AGG (*Elettr*) triple-pole *attr*
Tripoli ['tripoli] SF Tripoli
trippa ['trippa] SF (*Culin*) tripe; (*fig*: *pancia*) paunch
tripsina [trip'sina] SF (*Bio*) trypsin
tripudiare [tripu'djare] VI (*aus* **avere**) to exult, rejoice
tripudio, di [tri'pudjo] SM (*esultanza*) triumph, jubilation; (*fig*: *di colori*) galaxy
trireattore [trireat'tore] SM (*Aer*) three-engine jet
tris [tris] SM INV (*Carte*): **tris d'assi/di re** three aces/kings *pl*
trisavolo, a [tri'zavolo] SM/F great-great-grandfather/grandmother; (*antenato*) forebear, ancestor
trisillabo, a [tri'sillabo] AGG trisyllabic
■ SM trisyllable
triste ['triste] AGG (*gen*) sad; (*persona, destino*) unhappy, sad; (*sguardo*) sorrowful, sad; (*spettacolo, condizioni*)

Tt

miserable; (*luogo*) gloomy, dismal, dreary; (*esperienza*) painful; **aveva un'aria molto triste** he looked very sad; **una stanzetta triste** a gloomy little room

tristemente [triste'mente] AVV (*gen*) sadly; **finire tristemente** to come to a sorry end; **tristemente famoso per** notorious for

tristezza [tris'tettsa] SF (*gen*) sadness; (*dolore*) sorrow; (*di paesaggio*) bleakness, dreariness; **che tristezza!** how sad!

tristo, a ['tristo] AGG (*letter*: *cattivo*) wicked, evil; (: *meschino*) poor, mean, sorry

tritacarne [trita'karne] SM INV mincer, grinder (*Am*)

tritaghiaccio [trita'gjattʃo] SM INV ice crusher

tritaprezzemolo [tritapret'tsemolo] SM INV parsley chopper

tritare [tri'tare] VT (*carne*) to mince, grind (*Am*); (*verdura, cipolla*) to chop

tritarifiuti [tritari'fjuti] SM INV waste (*Brit*) *o* garbage (*Am*) disposal unit

tritatutto [trita'tutto] SM INV mincer, grinder (*Am*)

trito, a ['trito] AGG (*carne*) minced, ground (*Am*); **trito e ritrito** (*idee, argomenti, frasi*) trite, hackneyed
■ SM: **fare un trito di cipolla** to chop an onion finely

tritolo [tri'tɔlo] SM trinitrotoluene

tritone [tri'tone] SM **1** (*Zool*) newt **2** (*Mitol*): **Tritone** Triton

trittico, ci ['trittiko] SM triptych

trittongo, ghi [trit'tɔngo] SM triphthong

triturare [tritu'rare] VT to grind

triunvirato [triunvi'rato] SM triumvirate

trivella [tri'vɛlla] SF (*Falegnameria*) auger; (*per miniera, pozzi*) drill

trivellare [trivel'lare] VT to drill

trivellazione [trivellat'tsjone] SF drilling; **torre di trivellazione** derrick

triviale [tri'vjale] AGG (*volgare*) coarse, crude, vulgar

> **LO SAPEVI...?**
> **triviale** non si traduce mai con la parola inglese ***trivial***

trivialità [trivjali'ta] SF INV (*volgarità*) coarseness, crudeness; (: *osservazione*) coarse *o* crude remark

> **LO SAPEVI...?**
> **trivialità** non si traduce mai con la parola inglese ***triviality***

trivialmente [trivjal'mente] AVV coarsely, crudely

trofeo [tro'fɛo] SM trophy

troglodita, i, e [troglo'dita] SM/F troglodyte, cave dweller; (*fig*) barbarian

trogolo ['trɔgolo] SM trough

Troia ['trɔja] SF Troy

troia ['trɔja] SF (*fam*: *scrofa*) sow; (*fam! pegg*) whore

troiaio, ai [tro'jajo] SM (*fam*: *luogo sporco*) pigsty

troiano, a [tro'jano] AGG, SM/F Trojan

troika ['trɔika] SF INV (*anche fig*) troika

tromba ['tromba] SF **1** (*Mus*) trumpet; (*Aut*) horn; (*Mil*) bugle; **suono la tromba** I play the trumpet; **partire in tromba** (*fig*) to be off like a shot
2 (*suonatore*) trumpeter; (: *Mil*) bugler
■ **tromba d'aria** (*Meteor*) whirlwind; **tromba d'Eustachio** (*Anat*) Eustachian tube; **tromba di Falloppio** (*Anat*) Fallopian tube; **tromba marina** (*Meteor*) waterspout; **tromba delle scale** (*Archit*) stairwell

trombare [trom'bare] VT **1** (*fam!*: *avere rapporti sessuali*) to fuck (*fam!*), screw (*fam!*) **2** (*fig*: *bocciare*: *candidato*) to reject

trombetta [trom'betta] SF toy trumpet

trombettiere [trombet'tjɛre] SM (*Mil*) bugler

trombettista, i, e [trombet'tista] SM/F trumpeter, trumpet (player)

trombone [trom'bone] SM **1** (*Mus*: *strumento*) trombone; (: *suonatore*) trombonist, trombone (player) **2** (*fig*: *persona*) windbag **3** (*Bot*) daffodil

trombosi [trom'bɔzi] SF INV thrombosis

troncamento [tronka'mento] SM (*Ling*) apocope

troncare [tron'kare] VT **1** (*spezzare*) to break off; (*con cesoie, ascia*) to cut off **2** (*Ling*) to apocopate **3** (*amicizia, relazione*) to break off; (*carriera*) to ruin, cut short; **una salita che tronca le gambe** a tiring climb

tronchese [tron'kese] SM O F clippers *pl*

tronchesina [tronke'sina] SM (*per unghie*) nail clippers *pl*

tronchetto [tron'kɛtto] SM: **tronchetto della felicità** (*Bot*) dracaena, dragon tree

tronco[1], a, chi, che ['tronko] AGG (*colonna, parola*) truncated; **licenziare qn in tronco** to fire sb on the spot

tronco[2], chi ['tronko] SM (*Bot, Anat*) trunk; (*d'albero tagliato*) log; (*fig*: *tratto*: *di strada, ferrovia*) section; **tronco di cono** (*Geom*) truncated cone

troneggiare [troned'dʒare] VI (*aus* **avere**)
1 (*sovrastare*): **troneggiare su qn/qc** to tower over *o* dominate sb/sth **2** (*imporsi all'attenzione*): **troneggiare in mezzo a qc** to dominate sth; **un grosso brillante troneggiava al centro della vetrina** a large diamond dominated the window display

tronfio, fia, fi, fie ['tronfjo] AGG conceited, pompous

trono ['trɔno] SM throne; **salire** *o* **ascendere al trono** to come to *o* ascend the throne

tropicale [tropi'kale] AGG tropical

tropico, ci ['trɔpiko] SM tropic; **i tropici** the tropics; **tropico del Cancro** Tropic of Cancer; **tropico del Capricorno** Tropic of Capricorn

tropismo [tro'pizmo] SM (*Bot, Bio*) tropism

troppo, a ['trɔppo] **PAROLA CHIAVE**
■ AGG INDEF (*quantità*: *tempo, acqua*) too much; (*numero*: *persone, promesse*) too many; **non vorrei causarvi troppo disturbo** I wouldn't like to put you to too much trouble; **c'era troppa gente** there were too many people
■ PRON INDEF (*quantità eccessiva*) too much; (*numero eccessivo*) too many; **ha detto anche troppo** he's said far too much *o* quite enough; **non ne prendo più, ne ho fin troppi** I won't take any more, I've got far too many; **eravamo in troppi** there were too many of us; **ne vorrei ancora un po', ma non troppo** I'd like a little more, but not too much though; **troppi la pensano come lui** too many (people) think like him
■ AVV
1 (*con aggettivo, avverbio*) too; (*con verbo*: *gen*) too much; (: *aspettare, durare*) too long; **ho aspettato troppo** I've waited too long; **è troppo bello per essere vero** it's too good to be true; **fa troppo caldo** it's too hot; **fidarsi troppo di qn** to trust sb too much; **è fin troppo furbo!** he's too clever by half!; **troppo poco** too little; **sei arrivato troppo tardi** you arrived too late
2 (*rafforzativo*) too, so (very); **troppo buono da parte tua!** (*anche iro*) you're too kind!; **non ci sarebbe troppo da stupirsi se rifiutasse** I wouldn't be surprised if he refused; **non esserne troppo sicuro!** don't be too *o* so sure of that!; **non troppo volentieri** none too willingly

3 **di troppo** too much; **100 euro di troppo** 100 euros too much; **essere di troppo** to be in the way; **ha bevuto qualche bicchiere di troppo** he's had a few too many

trota ['trɔta] SF trout; **trota arcobaleno** *o* **iridea** rainbow trout; **trota di mare** sea trout; **trota salmonata** salmon trout

trottare [trot'tare] VI (*aus* **avere**) (*cavallo, cavaliere*) to trot; (*bambino, cucciolo*) to trot along

trottata [trot'tata] SF trot

trottatore, trice [trotta'tore] SM/F (*cavallo*) trotter

trotterellare [trotterel'lare] VI (*aus* **avere**) (*cavallo*) to jog along; (*cucciolo*) to trot along; (*bambino*) to trot along, toddle

trotto ['trɔtto] SM trot; **andare al trotto** to trot; **corse al trotto** trotting races

trottola ['trɔttola] SF (spinning) top

troupe [trup] SF INV troupe, company

trousse [trus] SF INV (*di cosmetici*) make-up set; (*borsetta da sera*) evening bag

trovare [tro'vare] VT
1 (*gen*) to find; (*per caso*) to find, come upon *o* across; (*difficoltà*) to come up against, meet with; **trovare lavoro/casa** to find work *o* a job/a house; **ha trovato lavoro** she's found a job; **far trovare qc a qn** to help sb find sth; **non trovo le scarpe** I can't find my shoes; **non riesco a trovare le chiavi** I can't find my keys; **andare/venire a trovare qn** to go/come and see sb; **ieri sono andato a trovare Chris** I went to see Chris yesterday; **trovare la morte** to meet one's death
2 **trovare da ridire (su tutto)** to find sth to criticize (in everything); **trovare da dormire** to find somewhere to sleep
3 (*giudicare*): **trovare che...** to find *o* think that ...; **lo trovo un po' invecchiato** I think he has aged a bit; **l'ho trovato molto cambiato** I thought he'd changed a lot; **ti trovo dimagrito** you look thinner; **trovi?** do you think so?; **fa caldo, non trovi?** it's hot, don't you think?; **trovo giusto/sbagliato che...** I think/don't think it's right that ...; **lo trovo bello** *o* **buono** I like it; **trovare qn colpevole** to find sb guilty
4 (*cogliere*) to find, catch; **la notizia ci trovò impreparati** the news caught us unawares
▶ **trovarsi** VIP
1 (*essere situato*) to be; **dove si trova la stazione?** where is the station?; **l'albergo si trova proprio al centro** the hotel's right in the town centre; **in quel periodo mi trovavo a Londra** at that time I was in London
2 (*capitare*) to find o.s.; **ci siamo trovati a Napoli** we found ourselves in Naples
3 (*essere*) to be; **trovarsi bene/male** to get on well/badly; **mi sono trovata benissimo con i suoi** I got on very well with his parents; **trovarsi in pericolo/smarrito** to be in danger/lost; **trovarsi nell'impossibilità di rispondere** to be unable to answer; **trovarsi d'accordo con qn** to be in agreement with sb; **trovarsi a disagio** to feel ill at ease; **trovarsi solo** to find o.s. alone; **trovarsi nei pasticci** to find o.s. in trouble; **trovarsi con un pugno di mosche in mano** to be left empty-handed
▶ **trovarsi** VR (*uso reciproco: incontrarsi*) to meet; **troviamoci alle cinque davanti al cinema** let's meet at five in front of the cinema; **si sono trovati in piazza** they met (each other) in the square

trovata [tro'vata] SF (*idea*) brainwave, stroke of genius; **trovata pubblicitaria** publicity stunt, (advertising) gimmick

trovatello, a [trova'tɛllo] SM/F foundling

truccare [truk'kare] VT 1 (*Sport: partita, incontro*) to fix, rig; (*carte da gioco*) to mark; (*dadi*) to load; (*Aut: motore*) to soup up 2 (*attore, viso, occhi*) to make up; **truccarsi il viso** to make up one's face; **truccarsi gli occhi** to put on eye make-up
▶ **truccarsi** VR (*gen, Teatro, Cine*) to make o.s. up; **truccarsi da** to make o.s. up as

truccato, a [truk'kato] AGG 1 (*partita, incontro*) rigged; (*carte*) marked; (*dadi*) loaded; (*motore*) souped-up
2 (*occhi, viso*) made up; **non ti ho mai vista truccata** I've never seen you with make-up on

truccatore, trice [trukka'tore] SM/F make-up artist

trucco, chi ['trukko] SM 1 (*cosmesi*) make-up; **aveva un trucco pesante** she was wearing heavy make-up
2 (*artificio*) trick; (*Cine*) effect, trick; **ti mostro un trucco che riesce sempre** I'll show you a trick that always works; **i trucchi del mestiere** the tricks of the trade

truce ['trutʃe] AGG (*viso, sguardo*) grim, cruel; (*tiranno*) cruel

> **LO SAPEVI...?**
> **truce** non si traduce mai con la parola inglese *truce*

trucidare [trutʃi'dare] VT to slay, massacre, slaughter

truciolato [trutʃo'lato] SM chipboard

truciolo ['trutʃolo] SM (*di legno, metallo*) shaving; **trucioli di paglia/carta** straw/paper packing material *sg*

truculento, a [truku'lɛnto] AGG (*persona, espressione*) truculent, grim; (*film, romanzo*) gory

truffa ['truffa] SF (*Dir*) fraud; (*imbroglio*) swindle

truffare [truf'fare] VT to swindle, cheat; **sono stato truffato** I've been swindled

truffatore, trice [truffa'tore] SM/F swindler, cheat

trullo ['trullo] SM (*nelle Puglie*) *cylindrical house with conical roof*

truppa ['truppa] SF 1 (*Mil*) troop; (*soldati semplici*) troops *pl*; **truppe d'assalto** assault troops, shock troops 2 (*fig: di amici*) group, band, troop

trust [trʌst] SM INV (*Econ*) trust; **trust di cervelli** brains trust

TS SIGLA = *Trieste*

tse-tse [tsɛt'tsɛ] AGG INV: **mosca tse-tse** tsetse fly

tsunami [tsu'nami] SM INV tsunami

tu [tu] PRON PERS you; **tu faresti meglio a tacere!** you'd do better to keep quiet!; **questo lo dici tu!** that's what you say!; **proprio tu lo dici!** you're a right one to talk!; **sei tu quello che fa sempre storie** you're the one who always causes a fuss
■ SM: **dare del tu a qn** to address sb as "tu", ≈ be on first-name terms with sb; **trovarsi a tu per tu con qn** to find o.s. face to face with sb; **perché non gli parli a tu per tu?** why don't you have a word with him in private?

tua ['tua] *vedi* **tuo**

tuba ['tuba] SF 1 (*Mus*) tuba 2 (*Anat*) tube
3 (*cappello*) top hat

tubare [tu'bare] VI (*aus* **avere**) (*colombi*) to coo; (*fig: innamorati*) to bill and coo

tubatura [tuba'tura], **tubazione** [tubat'tsjone] SF pipes *pl*, piping *no pl*

tubercolare [tuberko'lare] AGG tubercular

tubercolina [tuberko'lina] SF tuberculin

tubercolo [tu'bɛrkolo] SM tubercle

Tt

tubercolosi [tuberko'lɔzi] SF tuberculosis
tubero ['tubero] SM (*Bot*) tuber
tuberosa [tube'rosa] SF tuberose
tubetto [tu'betto] SM (*di dentifricio*) tube
tubino [tu'bino] SM **1** (*abito da donna*) sheath dress **2** (*cappello*) bowler (hat) (*Brit*), derby (*Am*)
tubo ['tubo] SM (*gen*) tube; (*per condutture*) pipe; **un tubo di cartone** a cardboard tube; **i tubi dell'acqua** the pipes; **non capisce/non sa un tubo** (*fam*) he doesn't understand/know a thing; **non me ne importa un tubo** (*fam*) I couldn't care less, I don't give a damn
■ **tubo catodico** *o* **a raggi catodici** (*Fis*) cathode-ray tube; **tubo digerente** (*Anat*) digestive tract, alimentary canal; **tubo elettronico** (*Tecn*) electron tube; **tubo di scappamento** (*Aut*) exhaust (pipe); **tubo di scarico** waste pipe
tubolare [tubo'lare] AGG tubular; **elastico tubolare** elastic thread
■ SM tubeless tyre (*Brit*) *o* tire (*Am*)
tucano [tu'kano] SM toucan
Tucidide [tu'tʃidide] SM Thucydides
tue ['tue] *vedi* **tuo**
tuffare [tuf'fare] VT (*immergere*) to plunge; (*intingere*) to dip
▶ **tuffarsi** VR (*gen*) to dive; **tuffarsi in mare** to dive *o* plunge into the sea; **tuffarsi nella mischia** to rush *o* dive into the fray; **tuffarsi nello studio** to bury *o* immerse o.s. in one's studies; **tuffarsi a capofitto in qc** to throw o.s. into sth
tuffatore, trice [tuffa'tore] SM/F (*Sport*) diver
tuffo ['tuffo] SM (*gen*) dive; (*breve bagno*) dip; (*Calcio*) dive; (*Sport*): **tuffi** diving *no pl*; **fare un tuffo** to dive; **fare un tuffo nel passato** to jump back into the past; **ho provato un tuffo al cuore** my heart skipped *o* missed a beat
▷ www.federnuoto.it/tuffi.asp
tufo ['tufo] SM tuff
tuga ['tuga] SF (*Naut*) deckhouse
tugurio, ri [tu'gurjo] SM hovel
tulipano [tuli'pano] SM tulip
tulle ['tulle] SM INV (*tessuto*) tulle
tumefare [tume'fare] VB IRREG
■ VT to cause to swell
▶ **tumefarsi** VIP to swell
tumefatto, a [tume'fatto] PP *di* **tumefare**
■ AGG swollen
tumefazione [tumefat'tsjone] SF swelling
tumido, a ['tumido] AGG (*gonfio*) swollen; (*carnoso: labbra*) thick
tumore [tu'more] SM tumour (*Brit*), tumor (*Am*); **tumore benigno** benignant tumo(u)r; **tumore maligno** malignant tumo(u)r
tumulazione [tumulat'tsjone] SF burial
tumulo ['tumulo] SM (*Archeol*) tumulus
tumulto [tu'multo] SM **1** (*di folla: rumore*) commotion, uproar; (: *agitazione*) turmoil, tumult; (*sommossa*) riot **2** (*fig: di pensieri, desideri*) turmoil; **avere l'animo in tumulto** to be in a turmoil
tumultuosamente [tumultuosa'mente] AVV turbulently
tumultuoso, a [tumultu'oso] AGG (*folla*) turbulent, rowdy, unruly; (*assemblea*) stormy, turbulent; (*fiume*) turbulent; (*passione*) tumultuous, turbulent
tundra ['tundra] SF tundra
tungsteno [tung'stɛno] SM tungsten
tunica, che ['tunika] SF tunic
Tunisi ['tunizi] SF Tunis
Tunisia [tuni'zia] SF Tunisia; **viene dalla Tunisia** he comes from Tunisia
tunisino, a [tuni'zino] AGG, SM/F Tunisian
tunnel ['tunnel] SM INV tunnel
tuo, a ['tuo] (*pl f* **tue**, *pl m* **tuoi**) AGG POSS: **il(la) tuo(a)** *ecc* your; **il tuo cane** your dog; **tuo padre** your father; **una tua amica** a friend of yours; **è colpa tua** it's your fault; **è casa tua** *or* **è la tua casa** it's your house; **per amor tuo** for love of you
■ PRON POSS: **il(la) tuo(a)** *ecc* yours, your own; **la nostra barca è più lunga della tua** our boat is longer than yours; **la tua è più bella della mia** yours is nicer than mine; **è questo il tuo?** is this (one) yours?; **il tuo è stato solo un errore** it was simply an error on your part
■ SM **1 hai speso del tuo?** did you spend your own money?; **vivi del tuo?** do you live on your own income? **2 i tuoi** (*genitori*) your parents; (*famiglia*) your family; (*amici*) your (own) people, your side; **cosa hanno detto i tuoi?** what did your parents say?; **è dei tuoi** he is on your side
■ SF: **la tua** (*opinione*) your view; **è dalla tua** he is on your side; **ne hai fatta una delle tue!** (*sciocchezze*) you've done it again!; **anche tu hai avuto le tue** (*disavventure*) you've had your problems too; **alla tua!** (*brindisi*) your health!
tuoi ['twɔi] *vedi* **tuo**
tuonare [two'nare] VI (*aus* **avere**) (*fig: armi, voce*) to thunder, boom; **tuonare contro qn/qc** (*inveire*) to rage against sb/sth
■ VB IMPERS (*aus* **avere** *o* **essere**) **sta tuonando** there is thunder, it is thundering
tuono ['twɔno] SM (*anche fig*) thunder
tuorlo ['twɔrlo] SM yolk
turacciolo [tu'rattʃolo] SM (*tappo*) stopper; (*di sughero*) cork
turare [tu'rare] VT (*buco, falla*) to stop, plug; (*bottiglia*) to cork; **turarsi il naso** to hold one's nose; **ho il naso turato** my nose is blocked; **turarsi le orecchie** to stop one's ears
turba ['turba] SF **1** (*folla*) crowd, throng; (: *pegg*) mob **2** (*Med*) disorder; **soffrire di turbe psichiche** to suffer from a mental disorder
turbamento [turba'mento] SM (*di animo*) anxiety, agitation; (*della pace, quiete*) disturbance; **provò un profondo turbamento** he was extremely upset
turbante [tur'bante] SM turban
turbare [tur'bare] VT to disturb, trouble; **le sue parole mi hanno turbato** her words upset me; **turbare la quiete pubblica** (*Dir*) to disturb the peace; **turbare l'opinione pubblica** to upset public opinion
▶ **turbarsi** VIP to get upset
turbato, a [tur'bato] AGG upset; (*preoccupato, ansioso*) anxious
turbina [tur'bina] SF turbine
turbinare [turbi'nare] VI (*aus* **avere**) (*anche fig*) to whirl
turbine ['turbine] SM whirlwind; **il turbine della danza** the whirl of the dance; **il turbine della passione** the turmoil of passion; **turbine di neve** gust *o* swirl of snow; **turbine di polvere** dust storm; **turbine di sabbia** sandstorm
turbinosamente [turbinosa'mente] AVV: **volteggiare turbinosamente** to whirl round and round
turbinoso, a [turbi'noso] AGG (*vento, danza*) whirling
turbo... ['turbo] PREF turbo...
turbodiesel [turbo'dizel] SM turbo diesel

turboelica, che [turbo'ɛlika] SF (*motore*) turbojet (engine)
■ SM INV (*velivolo*) turbojet
turbolento, a [turbo'lɛnto] AGG (*ragazzo*) boisterous, unruly; (*tempi, anni*) turbulent
turbolenza [turbo'lɛntsa] SF (*vedi agg*) boisterousness; turbulence
turboreattore [turboreat'tore] SM turbojet engine
turchese [tur'kese] AGG, SM (*colore*) turquoise
■ SF (*minerale*) turquoise
Turchia [tur'kia] SF Turkey; **andremo in Turchia quest'estate** we're going to Turkey this summer; **mi è piaciuta molto la Turchia** I really liked Turkey
turchino, a [tur'kino] AGG, SM deep blue
turco, a, chi, che ['turko] AGG Turkish; **è turca** she's Turkish; **bagno turco** Turkish bath; **ho fatto un bagno turco** (*fig*) I sweated like a pig (*fam*); **caffè alla turca** Turkish coffee
■ SM/F (*persona*) Turk; **i turchi** the Turks; **fumare come un turco** (*fig*) to smoke like a chimney; **bestemmiare come un turco** (*fig*) to swear like a trooper
■ SM (*lingua*) Turkish; **parla turco?** does he speak Turkish?; **parlare turco** (*fig*) to talk double Dutch
turgido, a ['turdʒido] AGG swollen
turgore [tur'gore] SM swelling
turibolo [tu'ribolo] SM (*Rel*) thurible, censer
turismo [tu'rizmo] SM tourism; **turismo del sesso** sex tourism
turista, i, e [tu'rista] SM/F tourist; **turista del sesso** sex tourist
turisticamente [turistika'mente] AVV: **una zona turisticamente rinomata** a well-known tourist area; **turisticamente parlando** from the tourist point of view
turisticizzare [turistitʃid'dzare] VT to open to tourism
turistico, a, ci, che [tu'ristiko] AGG tourist *attr*; **una località turistica** a tourist resort
turlupinare [turlupi'nare] VT to cheat
turnista, i, e [tur'nista] SM/F shift worker
turno ['turno] SM (*volta*) turn; (*di lavoro*) shift; **è il tuo turno** it's your turn; **essere di turno** (*soldato, medico, custode*) to be on duty; **qual è la farmacia di turno domenica?** which chemist (*Brit*) *o* drugstore (*Am*) will be open on Sunday?; **rispondere a turno** to answer in turn; **aspettare il proprio turno** to await one's turn; **fare a turno a fare qc** to take (it in) turns to do sth; **abbiamo fatto a turno a guidare** we took turns to drive; **un turno di sei ore** a six-hour shift; **turni articolati** split shifts; **turno di guardia** (*Mil*) sentry *o* guard duty; **turno di notte** night shift
turpe ['turpe] AGG (*voglia*) filthy; (*accusa*) foul, vile; (*persona*) vile, repugnant
turpemente [turpe'mente] AVV (*comportarsi*) vilely
turpiloquio, qui [turpi'lɔkwjo] SM obscene *o* foul language
turrito, a [tur'rito] AGG turreted
TUS SIGLA M (*Econ*) = **Tasso Ufficiale di Sconto**
TUT SIGLA F (*Telec:* = **Tariffa Urbana a Tempo**) local rate
tuta ['tuta] SF overalls *pl*; (*Sport*) tracksuit; (*Sci*) ski suit; **tuta mimetica** (*Mil*) camouflage clothing; **tuta spaziale** spacesuit; **tuta subacquea** wetsuit; **le tute blu** (*gli operai*) blue collar workers
tutela [tu'tɛla] SF **1** (*Dir*) guardianship; **essere sotto la tutela di qn** to be sb's ward; **tutela di un minore** guardianship of a minor **2** (*protezione*) protection; **fare qc a tutela dei propri interessi** to do sth to protect one's interests; **tutela dell'ambiente** environmental protection; **tutela del consumatore** consumer protection
tutelare[1] [tute'lare] VT to protect, defend
▶ **tutelarsi** VR to protect o.s.
tutelare[2] [tute'lare] AGG (*Dir*): **giudice tutelare** *judge with responsibility for guardianship cases*
tutina [tu'tina] SF (*per neonato*) Babygro®; (*per ginnastica*) leotard
tutore, trice [tu'tore] SM/F (*Dir*) guardian; (*protettore*) protector, defender; **i tutori dell'ordine pubblico** the police *pl*
tutsi ['tutsi] SM/F INV, AGG INV Tutsi
tuttavia [tutta'via] CONG nevertheless, yet; **il compito era difficile, tuttavia ce l'ho fatta** the test was difficult, but I managed to do it

tutto, a ['tutto] PAROLA CHIAVE
■ AGG
1 (*intero*) all (of), the whole (of); **ha letto tutto Dante** he has read all of Dante; **tutta l'Europa** the whole of *o* all Europe; **ho tutta la sua fiducia** I have his complete confidence; **ha studiato tutto il giorno** he studied the whole day *o* all day long; **famoso in tutto il mondo** world-famous, famous the world over; **rimanere sveglio tutta la notte** to stay awake all night (long); **a tutt'oggi** so far, up till now; **si diffuse in tutto il paese** it spread through the whole country; **sarò qui tutta la settimana** I'll be here all week *o* the whole week; **tutta una bottiglia** a whole bottle; **tutta la verità** the whole truth
2 (*proprio*): **è tutt'altra cosa** *or* **cosa** (*è ben diverso*) that's quite another thing; **viaggiare in aereo è tutt'altra cosa** (*è meglio*) travelling by plane is altogether different; **è tutta sua madre** she's just *o* exactly like her mother; **è tutto l'opposto di...** it's the exact opposite of ...
3 (*completamente*): **era tutta contenta** she was overjoyed; **è tutta gambe e braccia** she's all arms and legs; **è tutto naso** he's got a big nose; **essere tutt'occhi** to be all eyes; **essere tutt'orecchi** to be all ears; **è tutta presa dal suo lavoro** she's completely *o* entirely taken up by her work; **era tutta sorrisi e sorrisetti** she was all smiles; **tremava tutto** he was trembling all over; **era tutta vestita di nero** she was dressed all in black
4 (*plurale, collettivo*) all; **tutti gli animali** all animals; **tutte queste cose** all these things; **in tutte le direzioni** in all directions, in every direction; **tutti e cinque** all five of us (*o* them); **tutti e due** both *o* each of us (*o* them); **con tutti i pensieri che ho** worried as I am, with all my worries; **tutti i posti erano occupati** all the seats were *o* every seat was occupied; **tutti i ragazzi** all the boys; **tutti gli uomini** all men; **una volta per tutte** once and for all
5 (*qualsiasi*) all; **a tutti i costi** at all costs; **in tutti i modi** (*a qualsiasi costo*) at all costs; (*comunque*) anyway; **telefona a tutte le ore** she phones at all hours
6 (*ogni*): **tutti gli anni** every year; **tutti i santi giorni** every blessed day; **tutti i venerdì** every Friday; **tutte le volte che** every time (that)
7 (*fraseologia*): **con tutta l'anima** wholeheartedly; **con tutto il cuore** wholeheartedly; **la sua fedeltà è a tutta prova** his loyalty is unshakeable *o* will stand any test; **per me è tutt'uno** it's all one and the same

to me; **a tutta velocità** at full *o* top speed; **con tutta la mia buona volontà, non posso aiutarti** however much I may want to, I can't help you

■ PRON

1 (*ogni cosa*) everything, all; (*qualunque cosa*) anything; **ha fatto (un po') di tutto** he's done (a bit of) everything; **essere capace di tutto** to be capable of anything; **mangia di tutto** he eats anything; **farebbe di tutto per ferirti** he would do anything to hurt you; **dimmi tutto** tell me everything; **tutto dipende da lui** everything *o* it all depends on him; **tutto è in ordine** everything's in order; **questo è tutto quello che ho** this is all I have; **tutto sta a vedere se...** it all depends on whether or not ...; **tutto sta nel cominciare** the essential *o* important thing is to get started

2 (*fraseologia*): **tutto compreso** inclusive, all-in (*Brit*); **questo è tutto** that's all (I have to say); **con tutto che** (*malgrado*) although; **tutto considerato** all things considered; **...che è tutto dire** ... and that's saying a lot; **ecco tutto** that's all (I have to say); **in tutto** (*complessivamente*) in all; **in tutto sono 180 euro** that's 180 euros in all; **in tutto e per tutto** (*completamente*) entirely, completely; **dipende in tutto e per tutto dai suoi** he is entirely *o* completely dependent on his parents; **innanzi tutto** first of all; **e non è tutto** and that's not all; **prima di tutto** first of all; **tutto sommato** all things considered

■ **tutti(e)** SM/FPL (*tutte le persone*) all (of them); (*ognuno*) everybody; **erano tutti presenti** everybody was *o* they were all present; **vengono tutti** they are all coming, everybody's coming; **tutti quanti** all and sundry

■ AVV

1 (*completamente*) entirely, quite, completely; **è tutto il contrario** it's quite *o* exactly the opposite; **è tutto il contrario di ciò che credi** it's not what you think at all; **fa tutto il contrario di quello che gli dico** he does the exact opposite of what I tell him to do; **del tutto** completely; **non sono del tutto convinto/sicuro** I'm not entirely convinced/sure; **è tutto l'opposto** it's quite *o* exactly the opposite

2 (*fraseologia*): **saranno stati tutt'al più una cinquantina** there were about fifty of them at (the very) most; **tutt'al più possiamo prendere un treno** if the worst comes to the worst we can catch a train; **tutt'altro** (*al contrario*) on the contrary; (*affatto*) not at all; **tutt'altro che felice** anything but happy; **tutt'intorno** all around; **tutto a un tratto** all of a sudden, suddenly

■ SM (*l'insieme*): **il tutto** the whole lot, all of it; **il tutto costa 550 euro** the whole thing *o* lot costs 550 euros; **vi manderemo il tutto nel corso della settimana** we'll send you the (whole) lot during the course of the week; **il tutto si è risolto in bene** everything turned out for the best; **rischiare il tutto per tutto** to risk everything

tuttofare [tutto'fare] AGG INV: **domestica tuttofare** general maid; **ragazzo tuttofare** office boy
■ SM/F INV handyman/woman

tuttologia [tuttolo'dʒia] SF *belief that one knows everything*

tuttologo, a, gi, ghe [tut'tɔlogo] SM/F know-it-all, know-all

tuttora [tut'tora] AVV still

tutù [tu'tu] SM INV tutu

TV [ti'vu] SF INV TV; **l'hanno detto alla TV** it was on TV; **TV digitale** digital TV; **TV al plasma** plasma screen TV; **TV verità** reality TV
■ SIGLA = **Treviso**

TVBN ABBR (*Tel:* = **ti voglio bene**) ILY, ILU

twin set [twin set] SM INV twin set

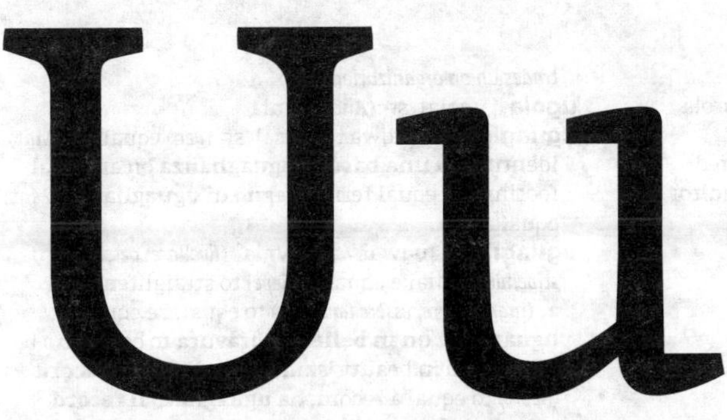

U, u [u] SF O M INV (*lettera*) U, u; **U come Udine** ≈ U for Uncle; **inversione ad U** U-turn
uadi ['wadi] SM INV wadi
ubbia [ub'bia] SF (*letter*) irrational fear
ubbidiente [ubbi'djɛnte] AGG obedient
ubbidientemente [ubbidjente'mente] AVV obediently
ubbidienza [ubbi'djɛntsa] SF obedience
ubbidire [ubbi'dire] VI (*aus* **avere**) **ubbidire a** to obey; (*sogg*: *veicolo, macchina*) to respond to; **ubbidire a qn** to obey sb; **farsi ubbidire** to enforce *o* compel obedience
ubertoso, a [uber'toso] AGG (*letter*) fertile
ubicato, a [ubi'kato] AGG situated, located
ubicazione [ubikat'tsjone] SF site, location
ubiquità [ubikwi'ta] SF ubiquity; **non ho il dono dell'ubiquità!** I can't be everywhere at once!
ubriacare [ubria'kare] VT: **ubriacare qn** (*sogg*: *persona*) to get sb drunk; (: *bevanda*) to make sb drunk, intoxicate sb; (*con discorsi, promesse*) to intoxicate sb, make sb's head spin *o* reel
▶ **ubriacarsi** VIP to get drunk
ubriacatura [ubriaka'tura] SF: **prendersi una solenne ubriacatura** to get blind *o* roaring drunk (*fam*)
ubriachezza [ubria'kettsa] SF drunkenness; **essere arrestato per ubriachezza molesta** to be arrested for being drunk and disorderly; **guidare in stato di ubriachezza** to drive under the influence of alcohol
ubriaco, a, chi, che [ubri'ako] AGG drunk; **era un po' ubriaco** he was a bit drunk; **essere ubriaco fradicio** to be blind *o* roaring drunk (*fam*); **ubriaco di stanchezza** reeling from tiredness; **ubriaco di gelosia** beside o.s. with jealousy
■ SM/F drunkard, drunk; **un ubriaco cantava a squarciagola** a drunk was singing at the top of his voice
ubriacone, a [ubria'kone] SM/F drunkard
uccellagione [uttʃella'dʒone] SF bird catching
uccellatore, trice [uttʃella'tore] SM/F bird catcher
uccelliera [uttʃel'ljɛra] SF aviary
uccellino [uttʃel'lino] SM baby bird, chick
uccello [ut'tʃello] SM **1** (*Zool*) bird; **uccello del malaugurio** (*fig*) bird of ill omen; **essere uccel di bosco** (*latitante*) to be nowhere to be found, have flown the coop **2** (*fam!*: *pene*) dick (*fam!*)
uccidere [ut'tʃidere] VB IRREG
■ VT (*gen*) to kill; (*assassinare*) to murder, kill; (*sogg*: *malattia*) to carry off, kill; **uccidere a colpi d'arma da fuoco** to shoot dead; **uccidere a coltellate** to stab to death; **è rimasto ucciso in un incidente** he was killed in an accident; **il fumo uccide** smoking kills; **uccidere un uomo morto** (*fig*) to kick a man when he's down;
▶ **uccidersi** VR **1** (*uso reciproco*) to kill each other **2** (*suicidarsi*) to kill o.s.; **si è ucciso** he killed himself; **uccidersi col gas** to gas o.s.;
▶ **uccidersi** VIP (*perdere la vita*) to be killed
uccisione [uttʃi'zjone] SF (*gen*) killing; (*assassinio*) murder
ucciso, a [ut'tʃizo] PP *di* **uccidere**
■ SM/F person killed, victim; **gli uccisi** the dead
uccisore [uttʃi'zore] SM killer
Ucraina [u'kraina] SF Ukraine
ucraino, a [u'kraino] AGG, SM/F Ukranian
UD SIGLA = *Udine*
UDC [udi'tʃi] SIGLA F (= **Unione dei Democratici Cristiani e Democratici di Centro**) Union of Christian Democrats and Centrists
udente [u'dɛnte] SM/F: **i non udenti** the hard of hearing
UDI ['udi] SIGLA F (= **Unione Donne Italiane**) *Italian feminist organization*
udibile [u'dibile] AGG audible
udienza [u'djɛntsa] SF (*gen*) audience; (*Dir*) hearing; **dare udienza a** to grant an audience to; **udienza a porte chiuse** hearing in camera
udinese [udi'nese] AGG of *o* from Udine
■ SM/F inhabitant *o* native of Udine
udire [u'dire] VT IRREG (*gen*) to hear; **l'abbiamo udita piangere** we heard her crying
uditivo, a [udi'tivo] AGG auditory
udito [u'dito] SM (sense of) hearing

> **LO SAPEVI...?**
> **udito** non si traduce mai con la parola inglese ***audit***

uditore, trice [udi'tore] SM/F (*Univ*) unregistered student (*who is allowed to attend lectures (Brit)*), auditor (*Am*); **uditore giudiziario** (*Dir*) auditor

uditorio, ri [udi'tɔrjo] SM audience

UE [u'e] SIGLA F (= **Unione Europea**) EU
■ABBR = **uso esterno**
▷ http://europa.eu.int/index_it.htm

UEFA [u'efa] SIGLA F UEFA (= *Union of European Football Associations*)

UEM [wem] SIGLA F (= **Unione Economica e Monetaria**) EMU (= *Economic and Monetary Union*)

uf [uf], **uff** [uff], **uffa** ['uffa] ESCL (*con insofferenza*) oh; **uffa! sono stanco!** oh, I'm tired!; **uf(f)! che caldo!** phew! it's hot!

ufficiale [uffi'tʃale] AGG (*gen*) official; **è in visita ufficiale in Italia** he's on an official visit to Italy
■SM **1** (*Mil, Naut*) officer; **un ufficiale di Marina** a naval officer; **primo ufficiale** (*Naut*) first mate; **ufficiale di marina** naval officer **2** (*Amm*) official, officer; **pubblico ufficiale** public official; **ufficiale giudiziario** (*Dir*) clerk of the court; **ufficiale sanitario** health inspector; **ufficiale di stato civile** registrar

ufficializzare [uffitʃalid'dzare] VT to make official

ufficialmente [uffitʃal'mente] AVV officially

ufficio, ci [uf'fitʃo] SM **1** (*luogo: gen*) office; (*organo*) office, bureau, agency; (*reparto*) department; **andare in ufficio** to go to the office; **oggi non è andata in ufficio** she didn't go to the office today; **ufficio brevetti** patent office; **ufficio di collocamento** employment office; **ufficio informazioni** information desk; **ufficio oggetti smarriti** lost property office (*Brit*), lost and found (*Am*); **ufficio del personale** personnel department; **ufficio postale** post office; **ufficio vendite** sales department **2** (*incarico*) office; (*dovere*) duty; (*mansione*) function, task, job; **l'ufficio di direttore generale** the office *o* position of general manager; **coprire/accettare un ufficio** to hold/accept a position; **provvedere d'ufficio** to act officially **3** (*Dir*): **difensore** *o* **avvocato d'ufficio** court-appointed counsel for the defence (*Brit*) *o* defense (*Am*); **convocare d'ufficio** to summons **4** (*intervento*): **grazie ai suoi buoni uffici** thanks to his good offices **5** (*Rel*) office, service

ufficiosamente [uffitʃosa'mente] AVV unofficially, off the record

ufficioso, a [uffi'tʃoso] AGG unofficial

> **LO SAPEVI...?**
> **ufficioso** non si traduce mai con la parola inglese ***officious***

UFO, ufo ['ufo] SM INV UFO (= *unidentified flying object*)

ufo ['ufo] **a ufo** AVV free, for nothing; **mangiare a ufo** to sponge a meal

ufologia [ufolo'dʒia] SF ufology

Uganda [u'ganda] SF Uganda

ugandese [ugan'dese] AGG, SM/F Ugandan

ugello [u'dʒɛllo] SM nozzle

uggia, ge ['uddʒa] SF (*noia*) boredom; (*fastidio*) bore; **avere/prendere qn in uggia** to dislike/take a dislike to sb

uggiolare [uddʒo'lare] VI (*aus* **avere**) to whine

uggiolio, lii [uddʒo'lio] SM whine

uggioso, a [ud'dʒoso] AGG (*gen*) tiresome; (*tempo*) dull, dreary

UGL [udʒi'ɛlle] SIGLA F (= **Unione Generale del Lavoro**) *trades union organization*

ugola ['ugola] SF (*Anat*) uvula

uguaglianza [ugwaʎ'ʎantsa] SF (*gen*) equality; (*Mat*) identity; **su una base di uguaglianza** on an equal footing, on equal terms; **segno di uguaglianza** (*Mat*) equals sign

uguagliare [ugwaʎ'ʎare] VT **1** (*livellare: persone, stipendi*) to make equal; (*: siepe*) to straighten **2** (*raggiungere, essere uguale a*) to equal, be equal to; **uguagliare qn in bellezza/bravura** to equal sb *o* be equal to sb in beauty/skill; **uguagliare un record** (*Sport*) to equal a record; **ha uguagliato il record mondiale** he equalled the world record; **in lui l'intelligenza uguaglia la bontà** he is as intelligent as he is good
▶ **uguagliarsi** VR (*paragonarsi*): **uguagliarsi a** *o* **con qn** to compare o.s. to sb
▶ **uguagliarsi** VIP to be equal

uguale [u'gwale] AGG **1** (*avente il medesimo valore*) equal; (*identico*) identical, the same; **sono esattamente uguali** they're exactly the same; **di peso/valore uguale** of equal weight/value; **a uguale distanza da** equidistant from; **abbiamo stipendi uguali** our salaries are the same; **uguale a** the same as; **il tuo maglione è uguale al mio** your sweater is the same as mine; **due più due è uguale a quattro** two and two equals four; **per me è uguale** (*lo stesso*) it's all the same to me; **che venga oppure no, per me è uguale** it's all the same to me whether he comes or not; **decidi tu, per me è uguale** you decide, I don't mind **2** (*uniforme: superficie*) even, level; (*: andatura*) even; (*: voce*) steady
■AVV: **costano uguale** they cost the same; **siamo alti uguale** we are the same height; **sono bravi uguale** they're equally good
■SM/F equal; **non ha uguali per ostinazione** when it comes to stubbornness there's no-one like him
■SM (*Mat*) equals sign

ugualmente [ugwal'mente] AVV **1** (*allo stesso modo*) equally; **sono ugualmente testardi** both of them are equally stubborn **2** (*lo stesso*) all the same, just the same; **ci siamo divertiti ugualmente** we enjoyed ourselves all the same; **lo farò ugualmente** I'm going to do it anyway

UI ABBR = *uso interno*

UIL [wil] SIGLA F (= **Unione Italiana del Lavoro**) *trade union federation*

UISP [wisp] SIGLA F = *Unione Italiana Sport Popolare*

ulcera ['ultʃera] SF ulcer; **avere l'ulcera** to have an ulcer

ulcerazione [ultʃerat'tsjone] SF ulceration

Ulisse [u'lisse] SM Ulysses

uliva *ecc* [u'liva] = **oliva** *ecc*

Ulivo [u'livo] SM the Olive Tree (*centre-left Italian political grouping*)

ulivo [u'livo] SM = **olivo**

ulna ['ulna] SF ulna

ulteriore [ulte'rjore] AGG further

> **LO SAPEVI...?**
> **ulteriore** non si traduce mai con la parola inglese ***ulterior***

ulteriormente [ulterjor'mente] AVV further

ultimamente [ultima'mente] AVV lately, of late; **non hanno giocato bene ultimamente** they haven't been playing well lately

> **LO SAPEVI...?**
> **ultimamente** non si traduce mai con la parola inglese ***ultimately***

ultimare [ulti'mare] VT to finish, complete
ultimatum [ulti'matum] SM INV ultimatum
ultimissime [ulti'missime] SFPL latest news *sg*; (*in corso di stampa*) stop press *sg*
ultimo, a ['ultimo] AGG
1 (*di serie: gen*) last; (*: piano*) top; (*: fila*) back; (*: mano di vernice*) last, final; **l'ultimo scalino** (*in basso*) the bottom step; (*in alto*) the top step; **l'ultimo piano** the top floor; **abitare all'ultimo piano** to live on the top floor; **le ultime 20 pagine** the last 20 pages; **in ultima pagina** (*di giornale*) on the back page; **per ultimo** (*entrare, arrivare*) last; **arrivare per ultimo** to arrive last; **Marco è arrivato per ultimo alla festa** Marco arrived last at the party; **arrivare ultimo** to come last; **Chiara è arrivata ultima nella gara** Chiara came last in the competition
2 (*tempo: gen*) last; (*: più recente*) latest; (*: finale*) final; **negli ultimi tempi** recently; **gli ultimi giorni prima di partire** the last days before leaving; **l'ultima volta che l'ho visto** the last time I saw him; **quella è stata l'ultima volta che l'ho vista** that was the last time I saw her; **all'ultimo momento** at the last minute; **ha cambiato idea all'ultimo momento** he changed his mind at the last minute; **hai visto l'ultimo film di Spielberg?** have you seen Spielberg's latest film?; **il loro ultimo album è in testa alla classifica** their latest album is at the top of the charts; **ci vediamo poco, negli ultimi tempi** we haven't seen each other much recently; **l'ultimo anno** the final year; **fa l'ultimo anno dell'università** she is in her final year at university; **il termine ultimo** the deadline; **le ultime notizie** the latest news; **all'ultima moda** in the latest fashion; **...la vostra lettera del 7 aprile ultimo scorso** ... your letter of April 7th last
3 (*estremo: speranza, risorsa*) last, final; (*: più lontano*) farthest, utmost; **l'ultimo lembo di terra italiana** the farthest tip of Italy; **spendere fino all'ultimo centesimo** to spend every last penny; **dare un'ultima occhiata a qc** to have one last look at sth
4 (*per importanza*) last; **è l'ultimo film che vorrei andare a vedere** that's the last film I would want to go and see; **qual è l'ultimo prezzo (che mi può fare)?** what's the lowest you'll go?
5 (*Filosofia*) ultimate
6 (*fraseologia*): **in ultima analisi** in the final *o* last analysis; **in ultimo luogo** finally; **avere** *o* **dire l'ultima parola** to have the last word; **le ultime parole famose!** famous last words!; **esalare** *o* **rendere l'ultimo respiro** to breathe one's last
■ SM/F last (one); **questi sono gli ultimi** these are the last ones; **l'ultimo nato** the youngest (child); **l'ultimo ad entrare** the last (person) to come in; **gli ultimi arrivati** the last ones to arrive; **lei è stata l'ultima ad arrivare** she was the last one to arrive; **è l'ultima della classe** she's (at the) bottom of the class; **questa è l'ultima delle mie preoccupazioni** that's the least of my worries; **è l'ultimo degli ultimi** he's the lowest of the low; **quest'ultimo** (*tra due*) the latter; (*tra più di due*) this last, the last-mentioned
■ SM: **l'ultimo del mese/dell'anno** the last day of the month/year; **l'ultimo dell'anno** New Year's Eve; **all'ultimo ho deciso di restare** in the end I decided to stay; **fino all'ultimo** to the last, till the end, until the end; **in ultimo** *or* **da ultimo** in the end, finally; **essere all'ultimo** *o* **agli ultimi** to be at death's door
■ SF (*notizia, barzelletta*): **hai sentito l'ultima?** have you heard the latest?; **questa è l'ultima (che mi combini)** that's the last time you'll play that trick on me
ultimogenito, a [ultimo'dʒɛnito] AGG (*figlio*) last-born
■ SM/F last-born child, youngest child
ultrà, ultra [ul'tra] SM/F INV (*Pol*) extremist; (*Sport*): **gli ultrà della Juve** fanatical Juventus supporters
ultramoderno, a [ultramo'dɛrno] AGG ultramodern
ultranazionalismo [ultranattsjona'listiko] SM extreme nationalism
ultranazionalista, i, e [ultranattsjona'lista] AGG, SM/F extreme nationalist
ultrapiatto, a [ultra'pjatto] AGG (*orologio*) ultra-thin
ultrarapido, a [ultra'rapido] AGG (*Fot*) high-speed
ultrasensibile [ultrasen'sibile] AGG ultrasensitive
ultrasonico, a, ci, che [ultra'sɔniko] AGG ultrasonic
ultrasuono [ultra'swɔno] SM ultrasound
ultraterreno, a [ultrater'reno] AGG: **la vita ultraterrena** the afterlife
ultravioletto, a [ultravio'letto] AGG, SM ultraviolet
ululare [ulu'lare] VI (*aus* **avere**) to howl
ululato [ulu'lato] SM (*urlo*) howl; (*l'ululare*) howling *no pl*
umanamente [umana'mente] AVV (*con umanità*) humanely; (*nei limiti delle capacità umane*) humanly; **è umanamente impossibile** it's not humanly possible
umanesimo [uma'nezimo] SM humanism
umanistico, a, ci, che [uma'nistiko] AGG: **studi umanistici** humanities; **materia umanistica** arts subject
umanità [umani'ta] SF (*gen*) humanity; **l'umanità** humanity, mankind
umanitario, ria, ri, rie [umani'tarjo] AGG humanitarian; **aiuti umanitari** humanitarian aid *sg*
umanitarismo [umanita'rizmo] SM humanitarianism
umanizzare [umanid'dzare] VT to humanize
umano, a [u'mano] AGG (*gen*) human; (*comprensivo*) humane; **essere** *o* **mostrarsi umano (con qn)** to show humanity (towards sb), act humanely (towards sb); **errare è umano** to err is human; **un essere umano** a human being; **il corpo umano** the human body; **il genere umano** mankind; **è umano comportarsi così** it's quite normal to behave like that
■ SM human
umbro, a ['umbro] AGG, SM/F Umbrian
umettare [umet'tare] VT (*labbra*) to moisten
umidiccio, cia, ci, ce [umi'dittʃo] AGG (*terreno*) damp; (*mano*) moist, clammy
umidificare [umidifi'kare] VT to humidify
umidificatore [umidifika'tore] SM humidifier
umidità [umidi'ta] SF (*vedi agg*) dampness; moistness, clamminess; humidity; **proteggere qc dall'umidità** to protect sth from damp; **"teme l'umidità"** (*su etichetta*) "to be kept dry"; **nella casa c'era molta umidità** the house was very damp
umido, a ['umido] AGG (*gen*) damp; (*mano*) moist, clammy; (*clima: caldo*) humid; (*: freddo*) damp; **un clima caldo e umido** a hot, damp climate; **l'erba è un po' umida** the grass is a bit wet; **aveva gli occhi umidi di pianto** her eyes were moist with tears
■ SM **1** (*umidità*) dampness, damp **2** (*Culin*): **carne in umido** stew
umile ['umile] AGG (*gen*) humble; **di umili origini** of humble origin(s); **i lavori più umili** the most menial tasks
umiliante [umi'ljante] AGG humiliating

Uu

umiliare [umi'ljare] VT (*gen*) to humiliate; **umiliare la carne** to mortify the flesh
▶ **umiliarsi** VR: **umiliarsi (davanti a)** to humiliate *o* humble o.s. (before)
umiliazione [umiljat'tsjone] SF humiliation
umilmente [umil'mente] AVV (*con umiltà*) humbly; (*in modo modesto*) unpretentiously
umiltà [umil'ta] SF humility, humbleness; **con umiltà** humbly
umore [u'more] SM **1** (*indole*) temper, temperament; (*disposizione d'animo*) mood, humour (*Brit*), humor (*Am*); **un vecchio d'umore irascibile** an irascible *o* bad-tempered old man; **di che umore è, oggi?** what mood is he in today?; **essere di buon umore** to be in a good mood; **essere di cattivo umore** to be in a bad mood; **di buon/cattivo umore** in a good/bad mood *o* humo(u)r **2** (*Bio*) humo(u)r
umorismo [umo'rizmo] SM humour (*Brit*), humor (*Am*); **senso dell'umorismo** sense of humo(u)r; **avere il senso dell'umorismo** to have a sense of humour; **ti sembra il momento di fare dell'umorismo?** this is no time to be funny!
umorista, i, e [umo'rista] SM/F humorist
umoristicamente [umoristika'mente] AVV humorously
umoristico, a, ci, che [umo'ristiko] AGG (*battuta, racconto*) humorous, funny; **un racconto più umoristico** a funnier story
UMTS [uɛmmeti'ɛsse] SIGLA M (*Tel*) UMTS (= *Universal Mobile Telecommunications System*)
un [un], **un'** [un], **una** ['una] *vedi* **uno**
unanimemente [unanima'mente] AVV unanimously
unanime [u'nanime] AGG unanimous; **è stata una decisione unanime** it was a unanimous decision
unanimità [unanimi'ta] SF unanimity; **all'unanimità** unanimously
una tantum ['una 'tantum] AGG one-off *attr*
■ SF INV (*imposta*) one-off tax
uncinare [untʃi'nare] VT to hook
uncinato, a [untʃi'nato] AGG (*amo*) barbed; (*ferro*) hooked; **croce uncinata** swastika
uncinetto [untʃi'netto] SM crochet hook; **lavorare all'uncinetto** to crochet; **lavoro all'uncinetto** crochet work
uncino [un'tʃino] SM hook
undicenne [undi'tʃɛnne] AGG, SM/F eleven-year-old; *per fraseologia vedi* **cinquantenne**
undicesimo, a [undi'tʃɛzimo] AGG, SM/F, SM eleventh; *per fraseologia vedi* **quinto**
undici ['unditʃi] AGG INV, SM INV eleven; *per fraseologia vedi* **cinque**
UNESCO [u'nɛsko] SIGLA F UNESCO (= *United Nations Educational, Scientific and Cultural Organization*)
ungere ['undʒere] VB IRREG
■ VT (*macchina*) to oil, lubricate; (*teglia*) to grease; (*Rel*) to anoint; (*fig*) to flatter; **ungere le ruote a qn** (*fig: corrompere*) to grease sb's palm; **devo ungere la catena della bici** I need to oil the chain of my bike; **ungi bene la teglia** grease the tin well;
▶ **ungersi** VR: **ungersi con la crema** to put cream on
▶ **ungersi** VIP (*macchiarsi*) to get covered in grease
ungherese [unge'rese] AGG, SM/F Hungarian
■ SM (*lingua*) Hungarian
Ungheria [unge'ria] SF Hungary; **ti è piaciuta l'Ungheria?** did you like Hungary?; **andrò in Ungheria quest'estate** I'm going to Hungary this summer
unghia ['ungja] SF **1** (*Anat*) nail; (*di animale*) claw; (*di rapace*) talon; (*di cavallo, bue*) hoof; **le unghie delle mani** the fingernails; **Marina si mangia le unghie** Marina bites her nails; **le unghie dei piedi** the toenails; **difendersi con le unghie e con i denti** to defend o.s. tooth and nail; **tirar fuori le unghie** (*anche fig*) to show one's claws; **pagare sull'unghia** to pay on the nail; **unghia incarnita** ingrown nail **2** (*di temperino*) groove **3** (*quantità*): **ce ne vuole un'unghia di più/di meno** a fraction more/less is needed
unghiata [un'gjata] SF (*graffio*) scratch
unguento [un'gwɛnto] SM ointment
unicamente [unika'mente] AVV only
unicamerale [unikame'rale] AGG (*Pol*) unicameral
UNICEF ['unitʃef] SIGLA M UNICEF (= *United Nations International Children's Emergency Fund*)
unicellulare [unitʃellu'lare] AGG unicellular
unicità [unitʃi'ta] SF uniqueness
unico, a, ci, che ['uniko] AGG **1** (*solo*) only; (*esclusivo*) sole; **è la mia unica speranza** it's my only hope; **la mia unica speranza è che...** my one *o* only hope is that ...; **è stata l'unica volta che l'ho visto** it was the only time I saw him; **è figlio unico** he's an only child; **è l'unico esemplare in Italia** it's the only one of its kind in Italy; **due aspetti di un unico problema** two aspects of one and the same problem; **atto unico** (*Teatro*) one-act play; **agente unico** (*Comm*) sole agent; **binario unico** (*Ferr*) single track; **numero unico** (*di giornale*) special issue; **senso unico** (*Aut*) one way **2** (*eccezionale*) unique; **unico nel suo genere** unique of its kind; **unico al mondo** absolutely unique, the only one of its kind in the world; **sei unico!** you're priceless!; **è un tipo più unico che raro** he's one of a kind
■ SM/F the only one; **fu l'unico a capire** he was the only one who understood *o* to understand
■ SF only thing to do; **l'unica è aspettare** the only thing to do is to wait, all we can do is wait
unicorno [uni'kɔrno] SM unicorn
unidimensionale [unidimensjo'nale] AGG one-dimensional
unidirezionale [unidirettsjo'nale] AGG unidirectional
unifamiliare [unifami'ljare] AGG (*villetta*) one-family *attr*
unificare [unifi'kare] VT (*stato, leggi*) to unify, unite; (*standardizzare: prodotti*) to standardize
unificazione [unifikat'tsjone] SF (*vedi vb*) unification; standardization; **dopo l'unificazione della Germania** after the unification of Germany
uniformare [unifor'mare] VT (*terreno, superficie*) to level; **uniformare qc a** to adjust *o* relate sth to
▶ **uniformarsi** VR: **uniformarsi a** to conform to
uniforme[1] [uni'forme] AGG (*gen*) uniform; (*superficie*) even
uniforme[2] [uni'forme] SF (*divisa*) uniform; **in uniforme** in uniform; **alta uniforme** dress uniform; **indossava l'uniforme della Marina** he was wearing naval uniform
uniformemente [uniforme'mente] AVV (*vedi agg*) uniformly; evenly
uniformità [uniformi'ta] SF (*vedi agg*) uniformity; evenness
unigenito [uni'dʒɛnito] AGG (*Rel*): **figlio unigenito di Dio** God's only-begotten son
unilaterale [unilate'rale] AGG (*Dir, Pol*) unilateral; (*fig*) one-sided

unilateralità [unilaterali'ta] SF (*arbitrarietà*) one-sidedness
unilateralmente [unilateral'mente] AVV (*vedi agg*) unilaterally; one-sidedly
uninominale [uninomi'nale] AGG (*Pol*): **collegio uninominale** single-member constituency
unione [u'njone] SF (*alleanza, matrimonio*) union; (*di colori*) combination, blending; (*di elementi*) cohesion; (*fig: concordia*) unity, harmony; **l'unione fa la forza** strength through unity; **l'Unione Europea** the European Union; **l'(ex) Unione Sovietica** the (former) Soviet Union; **unione sindacale** trade union (*Brit*), labor union (*Am*)
unionista, i, e [unjo'nista] SM/F unionist
unire [u'nire] VT **1** (*associare*): **unire (a)** to unite (with); **unire in matrimonio** to unite *o* join in matrimony; **il sentimento che li unisce** the feeling which binds them together *o* unites them **2** (*congiungere: città, linee*) to join, link, connect; (*mescolare: ingredienti*) to mix; **abbiamo deciso di unire i nostri sforzi** we decided to join forces; **se uniamo i due tavoli ci stiamo tutti** if we put the two tables together there'll be room for all of us **3** (*colori, suoni*) to combine
▶ **unirsi** VR: **unirsi contro/a** to unite against/with; **unirsi in matrimonio** to be joined (together) in marriage;
▶ **unirsi** VIP: **unirsi a** to join; **unirsi a un gruppo** to join a group; **due ragazzi svizzeri si sono uniti a noi** two Swiss boys joined us
unisex ['uniseks] AGG INV unisex
unisono [u'nisono] **all'unisono** AVV (*Mus, fig*) in unison
unità [uni'ta] SF INV **1** (*unione*) unity; **un passo avanti verso l'unità europea** a step towards European unity **2** (*Mat, Comm, elemento*) unit; (*didattica*) unit; **unità di misura** unit of measurement; **unità monetaria** monetary unit **3** (*Mil*) unit; (*Naut*) (war)ship; (*Aer*) aeroplane **4** (*Inform*): **unità centrale (di elaborazione)** central processing unit; **unità disco** disk drive; **unità periferica** peripheral unit; **unità video** visual display unit
unitamente [unita'mente] AVV (*d'accordo*) unitedly, together; (*insieme*): **unitamente a** *o* **con** (together) with
unitariamente [unitarja'mente] AVV (*lavorare, votare, decidere*) together, as a unit
unitario, ria, ri, rie [uni'tarjo] AGG (*gen*) unitary; (*Pol, Rel*) unitarian; **prezzo** *o* **costo unitario** unit price, price per unit
unito, a [u'nito] AGG **1** (*gen*) united; (*amici, coppia*) close; (*famiglia*) close(-knit), united; **la mia è una famiglia molto unita** my family's very close **2** (*colore*) plain; **in tinta unita** plain, self-coloured (*Brit*), self-colored (*Am*); **una cravatta in tinta unita** a plain tie
universale [univer'sale] AGG (*gen*) universal; (*plauso, consenso*) general; (*mente, genio*) wide-ranging; **il giudizio universale** (*Rel*) the Last Judgment; **suffragio universale** (*Pol*) universal suffrage; **erede universale** sole heir; **donatore universale** universal donor
universalità [universali'ta] SF universality
universalizzare [universalid'dzare] VT to make universal
universalmente [universal'mente] AVV universally
università [universi'ta] SF INV university; **l'ho visto uscire dall'università** I saw him coming out of the university; **fa l'università** she's at university; **andrai all'università?** are you going to go to university?
▷ www.istruzione.it/
universitario, ria, ri, rie [universi'tarjo] AGG (*gen*) university *attr*; (*studi*) university, academic; **uno studente universitario** a university student
■ SM/F (*studente*) university student; (*docente*) academic, university lecturer
universo [uni'verso] SM universe
univoco, a, ci, che [u'nivoko] AGG unambiguous
Unno ['unno] SM Hun

uno, a ['uno] PAROLA CHIAVE
(*davanti a sm* un + *consonante, vocale*, uno + *s impura, gn, pn, ps, x, z; davanti a sf* un' + *vocale*, una + *consonante*)
■ AGG one; **non ha una lira** he hasn't a penny, he's penniless; **ho comprato una mela e due pere** I bought one apple and two pears; **ho passato un mese in Italia** I spent one month in Italy; **una camera solo per una notte** a room for one night only
■ ART INDET
1 a, an (+ *vocale*); **era una giornata splendida** it was a beautiful day; **un mio amico** a friend of mine; **è un artista** he's an artist; **un programma interessante** an interesting programme; **un giorno gli ho telefonato** one day I called him; **uno gnomo** a gnome; **dammene un po'** give me some; **è uno sciocco** he's a fool; **ho visto un uomo** I saw a man; **uno zingaro** a gypsy
2 (*intensivo*): **una noia!** such a bore!; **ho una paura!** I'm terrified!; **ma questo è un porcile!** it's an absolute pigsty in here!
3 (*circa*): **disterà un 10 km** it's round about 10 km away; **costerà un 300 euro** it'll cost round about 300 euros
■ PRON
1 one; **me ne dai uno?** will you give me one (of them)?; **ne ho comprato uno stamattina** I bought one this morning; **ce n'è uno a testa** there's one each; **a uno a uno** one by one; **è uno dei più veloci** it's one of the fastest; **uno dei tanti** one of the many; **uno di noi** one of us; **facciamo metà per uno** let's go halves
2 (*un tale*) somebody, someone; **ho incontrato uno che ti conosce** I met someone who knows you; **c'era una al telefono** there was a woman on the phone; **è una del mio paese** she's from the same village as I am
3 (*in costruzione impersonale*) one, you; **se uno vuole** if one wants, if you want; **se uno ha i soldi** if one has the money
4 (*con articolo determinativo*): **l'uno** one; **non confondere gli uni con gli altri** don't confuse one lot with the other; **abbiamo visto l'uno e l'altro** we've seen both of them; **sono entrati l'uno dopo l'altro** they came in one after the other; **si amano l'un l'altro** they love each other; **o l'uno o l'altro** either of them; **o l'uno o l'altro per me va bene** either of them will be fine; **né l'uno né l'altro** neither of them; **quale prendi? – Né l'uno né l'altro** which one are you going to take? – Neither of them; **non prendo né l'uno né l'altro** I'm not going to take either of them
5 **ne ha detta una!** you should have heard what he said!; **ne hai combinata una delle tue!** you've done it again, haven't you!; **ne vuoi sentire una?** do you want to hear a good one?; **non me ne va mai bene una** nothing ever goes right for me
■ SM one; **uno più uno fa due** one plus one equals two
■ SF (*ora*) one o'clock; **che ore sono? – è l'una** what time is it? – it's one (o'clock)

unsi *ecc* ['unsi] VB *vedi* **ungere**
unto, a ['unto] PP *di* **ungere**
■AGG greasy, oily; **unto e bisunto** filthy dirty
■SM grease
untuosità [untuosi'ta] SF greasiness; (*fig: servilismo*) unctuousness
untuoso, a [untu'oso] AGG (*pelle*) greasy, oily; (*cibo*) oily; (*fig: persona*) unctuous, smooth
unzione [un'tsjone] SF: **l'Estrema Unzione** (*Rel*) Extreme Unction
uomo ['wɔmo] (*pl* **uomini**) SM (*gen*) man; (*specie umana*): **l'uomo** mankind, humanity; **da** *o* **per uomo** (*abito, scarpe*) men's, for men; **scarpe da uomo** men's shoes; **parlare da uomo a uomo** to have a man-to-man talk, talk man to man; **a memoria d'uomo** since the world began; **a passo d'uomo** at walking pace; **è un uomo finito** he's finished; **l'uomo della strada** the man in the street; **uomo avvisato mezzo salvato** (*Proverbio*) forewarned is forearmed; **un uomo di mezz'età** a middle-aged man; **c'erano due uomini nell'ufficio** there were two men in the office
■**uomo d'affari** businessman; **uomo d'azione** man of action; **uomo delle caverne** caveman; **uomo d'equipaggio**: **una nave con 30 uomini d'equipaggio** a ship with a crew of 30 men; **uomo di fatica** workhand; **uomo di fiducia** right-hand man; **uomo del gas** gasman; **uomo di mondo** man of the world; **uomo di paglia** stooge; **uomo rana** frogman
uopo ['wɔpo] SM: **all'uopo** if necessary, in case of need; **è d'uopo far così** it is necessary to do this
uovo ['wɔvo] SM (*pl f* **uova**) **1** egg; **uovo fresco** new-laid *o* fresh egg; **uova strapazzate** scrambled eggs; **uovo affogato** *o* **in camicia** poached egg; **uovo bazzotto** soft-boiled egg; **uovo in cocotte** baked egg; **uovo alla coque** (soft-)boiled egg; **uovo all'ostrica** prairie oyster; **uovo di Pasqua** Easter egg; **uovo sodo** hard-boiled egg; **uovo al tegame** *o* **all'occhio di bue** *o* **fritto** fried egg **2** (*fraseologia*): **è l'uovo di Colombo!** it's as plain as the nose on your face!; **essere pieno come un uovo** to be full (up); **cercare il pelo nell'uovo** to split hairs; **rompere le uova nel paniere a qn** to upset sb's plans; **meglio un uovo oggi che una gallina domani** (*Proverbio*) a bird in the hand is worth two in the bush
upupa ['upupa] SF hoopoe
uragano [ura'gano] SM hurricane; (*fig: di applausi, proteste*) storm
Urali [u'rali] SMPL: **gli Urali** the Urals; **i monti Urali** the Ural Mountains
uranio [u'ranjo] SM uranium; **uranio impoverito** depleted uranium
Urano [u'rano] SM (*Mitol, Astron*) Uranus
urbanamente [urbana'mente] AVV courteously, politely
urbanesimo [urba'nezimo] SM urbanization
urbanista, i, e [urba'nista] SM/F town planner
urbanistica [urba'nistika] SF town planning
urbanistico, a, ci, che [urba'nistiko] AGG urban, town *attr*
urbanità [urbani'ta] SF urbanity
urbanizzare [urbanid'dzare] VT to urbanize
urbanizzazione [urbaniddzat'tsjone] SF urbanization
urbano, a [ur'bano] AGG **1** (*gen: sviluppo ecc*) urban, city *attr*, town *attr*; (*telefonata*) local **2** (*cortese: modi, risposta*) urbane
urdu ['urdu] SM INV, AGG INV Urdu
urea [u'rɛa] SF urea
uretere [ure'tere] SM ureter
uretra [u'rɛtra] SF urethra
urgente [ur'dʒɛnte] AGG urgent; **ha detto che era urgente** he said it was urgent
urgentemente [urdʒente'mente] AVV urgently
urgenza [ur'dʒɛntsa] SF (*di decisione, situazione*) urgency; **non c'è urgenza** there's no hurry; **fare qc d'urgenza** to do sth as a matter of urgency; **trasportare qn d'urgenza all'ospedale** to rush sb to hospital; **essere ricoverato d'urgenza** to be rushed into hospital; **il direttore l'ha convocato d'urgenza** the director requested to see him urgently *o* immediately; **questo lavoro va fatto con urgenza** this work is urgent; **questo lavoro va fatto con molta urgenza** this work is very urgent; **chiamata/provvedimento d'urgenza** emergency call/measure; **diritto d'urgenza** (*Amm*) surtax paid for faster handling
urgere ['urdʒere] VI DIF: **urge aiuto** help is needed urgently; **urge provvedere** something needs to be done urgently
uria ['urja] SF (*Zool*) guillemot
urina [u'rina] SF urine
urinare [uri'nare] VI (*aus* **avere**) to urinate
URL [url] SIGLA M URL (= *Uniform Resource Locator*)
urlante [ur'lante] AGG (*vedi vb*) screaming, yelling; howling
urlare [ur'lare] VI (*aus* **avere**) (*persona*) to scream, yell; (*animale, vento*) to howl; **non urlare, ti sento benissimo** there's no need to shout, I can hear you perfectly well; **ho dovuto urlare per farmi sentire** I had to shout to make myself heard; **urlare di dolore** to scream with pain
■VT: **urlare qc (a qn)** to scream *o* yell sth (at sb); **urlare a qn di fare qc** to scream at sb to do sth; **gliene ho urlate dietro di tutti i colori** I hurled abuse at him
urlatore, trice [urla'tore] AGG howling, shrieking
urlo ['urlo] SM (*pl m* **urli**, *pl f* **urla**) (*di persona*) scream, yell; **urla di terrore** screams of terror; (*di animale, vento*) howl; (*di sirena*) wail; **lanciare un urlo (di)** to scream (with); **quando l'ha visto ha lanciato un urlo** she screamed when she saw him
urna ['urna] SF **1** (*vaso*) urn **2** (*Pol*): **urna (elettorale)** ballot box; **andare alle urne** to vote, go to the polls
urogenitale [urodʒeni'tale] AGG urogenital
urrà [ur'ra] ESCL hurrah!
URSS [urs] SIGLA F = *Unione delle Repubbliche Socialiste Sovietiche*; **l'(ex) URSS** the (former) USSR
urtante [ur'tante] AGG (*comportamento*) irritating, annoying
urtare [ur'tare] VT **1** (*persona, ostacolo*) to bump into, knock against; (*gomito, testa*) to knock, bump; **l'ha urtata e l'ha fatta cadere** he bumped into her and knocked her down **2** (*irritare*) to annoy, irritate; **urtare i nervi a qn** to get on sb's nerves
■VI (*aus* **avere**) **urtare contro** (*auto, barca*) to bump into; (*persona*) to bump into, knock against
► **urtarsi** VR (*uso reciproco: scontrarsi*) to collide; (*: fig*) to clash
► **urtarsi** VIP (*irritarsi*) to get annoyed, get irritated

LO SAPEVI...?
urtare non si traduce mai con la parola inglese *hurt*

urto ['urto] SM (*collisione*) crash, collision; (*colpo*) knock, bump; (*fig: contrasto*) clash; (*Mil*) attack; **nell'urto si è rotto il vetro** the impact of the crash broke the glass; **essere in urto con qn per qc** (*fig*) to clash with sb over sth; **terapia d'urto** (*Med*) massive-dose treatment; (*fig*) shock treatment *o* therapy; **dose d'urto** (*Med*) massive dose; **contingente d'urto** (*Mil*) shock troops *pl*

uruguaiano, a [urugwa'jano] AGG, SM/F Uruguayan

Uruguay [uru'gwai] SM Uruguay

u.s. ABBR = ultimo scorso

USA, U.S.A. ['uza] SIGLA MPL: **gli USA** the USA

usa e getta [uzae'dʒɛtta] AGG INV (*rasoio, siringa*) disposable, throwaway

usanza [u'zantsa] SF (*costume*) custom; **è l'usanza** it's the custom; **è un'usanza del posto** it's a local custom, it's what's done; **secondo l'usanza** according to custom, as is customary

usare [u'zare] VT **1** (*adoperare*) to use; **posso usare la tua macchina?** may I use your car?; **me lo fai usare?** will you let me use it?; **non mi lascia usare il suo computer** he doesn't let me use his computer; **grazie per il tavolo, l'ho usato molto** thank you for the table, I got a lot of use out of it; **come si usa questo coso?** how do you use this thing?; **sai usare** *o* **come si usa la lavatrice?** do you know how to use the washing machine?; **non usare tutta l'acqua** (*consumare*) don't use (up) all the water; **cerca di usare il cervello!** try to use your head!; **usa gli occhi/le orecchie!** use your eyes/ears!; **usare la forza** to use force; **usare violenza a qn** (*violentare*) to rape sb; **usare le mani** (*picchiare*) to use one's fists; **usare la massima cura nel fare qc** to exercise great care when doing sth; **dovresti usare un po' di comprensione** you should show a little understanding; **potresti usarmi la cortesia di spegnere la radio?** would you be so kind as to switch off the radio? **2** (*aver l'abitudine*): **usare fare qc** to be in the habit of doing sth, be accustomed to doing sth; **a casa nostra si usa fare così** this is how we do things at home

■ VI (*aus* **avere**) **1** (*essere di moda*) to be fashionable, to be in fashion; **si usano di nuovo i tacchi alti** high heels are fashionable again *o* are back in fashion; **quest'anno si usano le gonne lunghe** this year long skirts are in fashion **2** **usare di** (*servirsi di*) to use; (: *diritto*) to exercise

■ VB IMPERS to be customary; **da queste parti usa così** it's the custom round here, this is customary round here

usato, a [u'zato] AGG **1** (*logoro*) worn (out) **2** (*di seconda mano*) used, second-hand; **ha comprato una macchina usata** he bought a second-hand car

■ SM (*gen*) second-hand goods *pl*; **il mercato dell'usato** the second-hand market

USB [uesse'bi] ABBR (*Inform*) = *Universal Serial Bus*; **porta USB** USB port

uscente [uʃ'ʃɛnte] AGG (*Amm*) outgoing

usciere [uʃ'ʃɛre] SM usher

uscio, sci ['uʃʃo] SM door; **sull'uscio** on the doorstep

uscire [uʃ'ʃire] VI IRREG (*aus* **essere**)

1 (*persona: andare fuori*) to go out, leave; (: *venire fuori*) to come out, leave; (: *a piedi*) to walk out; (: *a spasso, la sera*) to go out; **uscire in automobile** to go out in the car, go for a drive; **ieri sono uscita con degli amici** I went out with friends yesterday; **è uscito senza dire una parola** he went out without saying a word; **uscire a prendere il giornale** to go for the paper; **è uscita a comprare il giornale** she's gone for the paper; **lasciatemi** *o* **fatemi uscire!** let me out!; **uscite!** get out!; **uscire da** (*posto*) to go (*o* come) out of, leave; (: *carcere*) to get out of; **uscire da** *o* **di casa** to go out; **uscirà dall'ospedale domani** he's coming out of hospital tomorrow; **l'ho incontrata che usciva dalla farmacia** I met her coming out of the chemist's; **è uscito dalla porta di servizio/per la finestra** he left by the tradesman's entrance/got out through the window; **da dove sei uscito?** where did you spring from?; **uscire dall'acqua/dal letto** to get out of the water/of bed

2 (*oggetto: gen*) to come out; **la merce che esce dal paese dev'essere dichiarata** goods leaving *o* going out of the country must be declared

3 (*giornale, libro*) to come out; (*disco, film*) to be released; (*numero alla lotteria*) to come up; **la rivista esce di lunedì** the magazine comes out on Mondays; **è appena uscito il loro ultimo album** their latest album has just come out

4 (*andar fuori, sconfinare*): **uscire dagli argini** (*fiume*) to overflow its banks; **uscire dai binari** (*treno*) to leave the rails; **uscire di strada** (*auto*) to go off *o* leave the road; **la macchina è uscita di strada** the car left the road; **l'acqua sta uscendo dalla vasca** the bath is overflowing; **uscire dall'ordinario** to be out of the ordinary

5 (*passare da una condizione a un'altra*): **uscire dall'adolescenza** to leave adolescence behind; **uscire da una brutta malattia** to recover from *o* get over a bad illness; **è uscito bene da quella storia** he came out of that business well; **è uscito illeso dall'incidente** he emerged from the accident unscathed

6 (*fraseologia*): **chissà cosa uscirà da tutta questa storia?** who knows what will come of all this?; **se ne uscì con una delle sue** he came out with one of his typical remarks; **uscire dai gangheri** to fly off the handle; **uscire di senno** *o* **di sé** to fly into a rage; **mi è uscito di mente** it slipped my mind; **uscire da un programma** (*Comput*) to quit a program

uscita [uʃ'ʃita] SF **1** (*azione: di persona*) leaving, exit; **è l'ora dell'uscita degli scolari** school's over for the day, the children are coming out of school; **mia zia ha incontrato Claudia all'uscita di scuola** my aunt met Claudia as she was coming out of school; **un'uscita veloce** a quick exit; **sono in libera uscita** (*Mil*) I'm off duty **2** (*porta, passaggio*) exit, way out; (*Aer*) gate; **dov'è l'uscita?** where's the exit?; **"vietata l'uscita"** "no exit"; **uscita di sicurezza** emergency exit

3 (*passeggiata*) outing; (*Mil*) foray; **è la sua prima uscita dopo la malattia** it's his first day out since his illness **4** (*fig: battuta*) witty remark; **ha di quelle uscite** he comes out with some odd remarks

5 (*Comm*) outlay; **entrate ed uscite** income and expenditure *sg* **6** (*Elettr*) output

usignolo [uziɲ'ɲɔlo] SM nightingale

uso[1] ['uzo] SM **1** (*gen*) use; (*di parola*) usage; (*Dir*) exercise; **a uso di** for (the use of); **l'uso corretto di quell'espressione** the correct usage of that expression; **testo a uso delle elementari** book for use in primary (*Brit*) *o* elementary (*Am*) schools; **per uso esterno** (*Med*) for external use only; **per uso personale** for personal use; **fare buon/cattivo uso di qc** to make good/bad use of sth; **istruzioni per l'uso** instructions; **fuori uso** out of use; **fare uso di qc** to use sth; **perdere l'uso della ragione** to go out of one's mind **2** (*esercizio*) practice; **con l'uso** with practice

3 (*abitudine*) usage, custom; **d'uso** (*corrente*) in use; **essere in uso** to be in common *o* current use; **gli usi e i**

Uu

costumi degli antichi romani the customs of the ancient Romans
uso[2], a ['uzo] AGG (*letter*): **uso a qc/a fare qc** accustomed to sth/to doing sth
ustionare [ustjo'nare] VT to burn
▶ **ustionarsi** VR to burn o.s.
ustionato, a [ustjo'nato] AGG burnt
■ SM/F: **centro (grandi) ustionati** burns unit
ustione [us'tjone] SF burn; **ustioni di terzo grado** third-degree burns; **aveva ustioni di terzo grado** he had third-degree burns
ustorio, ria, ri, rie [us'tɔrjo] AGG: **specchio ustorio** burning glass
usuale [uzu'ale] AGG (*frase*) everyday *attr*; (*oggetto*) everyday, ordinary, common
usualmente [uzual'mente] AVV usually, as a rule
usucapione [uzuka'pjone] SF (*Dir*) usucaption
usufruire [uzufru'ire] VI (*aus* **avere**) **usufruire di** (*valersi di*) to take advantage of, make use of
usufrutto [uzu'frutto] SM (*Dir*) usufruct
usufruttuario, ri [uzufruttu'arjo] SM (*Dir*) usufructuary
usura[1] [u'zura] SF usury; **prestare a usura** to lend at exorbitant interest
usura[2] [u'zura] SF (*logoramento*) wear (and tear); **usura dei freni** wear on the brakes
usuraio, aia, ai, aie [uzu'rajo] SM/F usurer
usurante [uzu'rante] AGG: **lavoro usurante** *work in heavy industries (such as coal mining, steelmaking)*
usurpare [uzur'pare] VT (*trono, potere*) to usurp
usurpatore, trice [uzurpa'tore] SM/F usurper
usurpazione [uzurpat'tsjone] SF usurpation
Utah ['uta] SM Utah
utensile [uten'sile] AGG: **macchina utensile** machine tool
■ SM tool, implement; **utensili da cucina** kitchen utensils
utensileria [utensile'ria] SF **1** (*utensili*) tools *pl* **2** (*reparto*) tool room
utente [u'tɛnte] SM/F (*gen*) user; (*di gas*) consumer; (*del telefono*) subscriber; **utente finale** end user; **utente della strada** road user
utenza [u'tɛntsa] SF **1** (*uso*) use **2** (*utenti*) users *pl*; (: *di gas*) consumers *pl*; (*del telefono*) subscribers *pl*
uterino, a [ute'rino] AGG uterine
utero ['utero] SM uterus, womb; **utero in affitto** host womb
utile ['utile] AGG (*gen*) useful; (*consiglio, persona*) helpful; **mi è stato molto utile** (*oggetto*) it came in very handy, it was very useful; **grazie per la guida, mi è stata molto utile** thanks for the guide book, it was very useful; **questo ti sarà utile** this will be of use to you; **posso esserle utile?** can I help you?, can I be of help?; **posso esserti utile?** can I do anything for you?; **in tempo utile per** in time for; **rendersi utile** to make o.s. useful; **posso rendermi utile?** can I make myself useful?
■ SM **1 badare solo all'utile** to think only of what is useful; **unire l'utile al dilettevole** to combine business with pleasure **2** (*vantaggio*) advantage, benefit; (*Econ*) profit; **partecipare agli utili** to share in the profits; **non ha saputo trarne alcun utile** (*fig*) he couldn't get anything out of it
utilità [utili'ta] SF usefulness; (*vantaggio*) benefit; **senza utilità pratica** without practical application, of no real use; **essere di grande utilità** to be very useful
utilitaria [utili'tarja] SF (*Aut*) runabout, economy car
utilitario, ria, ri, rie [utili'tarjo] AGG utilitarian
utilitarista, i, e [utilita'rista] SM/F utilitarian
utilitaristico, a, ci, che [utilita'ristiko] AGG utilitarian
utilizzare [utilid'dzare] VT to use, make use of, utilize; **l'ho fatto utilizzando ritagli di stoffa** I made it using scraps of material
utilizzazione [utiliddzat'tsjone] SF use, utilization
utilizzo [uti'liddzo] SM (*Amm*) utilization; (*Banca*: *di credito*) availment
utilmente [util'mente] AVV usefully, profitably
utopia [uto'pia] SF utopia; **è pura utopia** that's sheer utopianism
utopistico, a, ci, che [uto'pistiko] AGG utopian
UVA [uvi'a] SIGLA M = *ultravioletto prossimo*; **gli UVA** UVA
■ AGG INV (*raggi*) UVA
uva ['uva] SF grapes *pl*; **un grappolo d'uva** a bunch of grapes; **uva passa** raisins *pl*; **uva spina** gooseberry; **uva sultanina** sultanas *pl*
UVB [uvi'bi] SIGLA M = *ultravioletto lontano*; **gli UVB** UVB
■ AGG INV (*raggi*) UVB
uvetta [u'vetta] SF raisins *pl*
uxoricida, i, e [uksori'tʃida] SM/F: **essere uxoricida** to have killed one's own husband (*o* wife)
Uzbechistan [udz'bekistan] SM Uzbekistan
uzbeco, a, chi, che [udz'bɛko] AGG, SM/F Uzbek

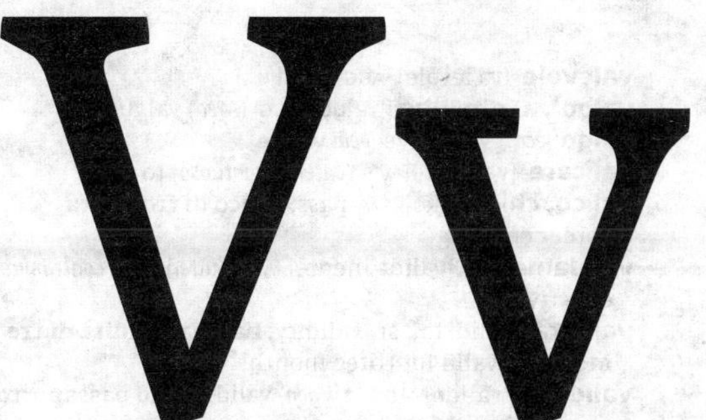

V, v [vu, vi] SF O M INV (*lettera*) V, v; **V come Venezia** ≈ V for Victor
V ABBR (= **volt**) V
v. ABBR **1** (= **vedi**) v. (= *vide: see*) **2** (= **verso**) v. (= *verse*)
VA SIGLA = *Varese*
val. ABBR = **valuta**
va, va' [va] VB *vedi* **andare**
vacante [va'kante] AGG vacant
vacanza [va'kantsa] SF **1** (*riposo, ferie*) holiday(s *pl*) (*Brit*), vacation (*Am*); (*giorno di permesso*) day off; **essere/andare in vacanza** to be/go on holiday *o* vacation; **dove andrai in vacanza quest'anno?** where are you going on holiday this year?; **prendersi una vacanza** to take a holiday *o* vacation; **un giorno/mese di vacanza** a day's/month's holiday *o* vacation; **far vacanza** to have a holiday *o* vacation; **ho fatto una lunga vacanza** I had a long holiday; **trascorriamo sempre le vacanze al mare** we always spend our holidays at the seaside; **vacanze** SFPL (*periodo di ferie*) holidays, vacation *sg*; **le vacanze di Pasqua** the Easter holidays; **le vacanze scolastiche** the school holidays; **vacanze estive** summer holiday(s) *o* vacation **2** (*l'essere vacante: di lavoro, cattedra ecc*) vacancy
vacanziere [vakan'tsjɛre] SM holiday-maker (*Brit*), vacationer (*Am*), vacationist (*Am*)
vacanziero, a [vakan'tsjɛro] AGG (*folla*) holiday (*Brit*) *attr*, vacationing (*Am*) *attr*
vacca, che ['vakka] SF **1** (*mucca*) cow; **tempo delle vacche grasse/magre** fat/lean years **2** (*pegg: sgualdrina*) slut
vaccinare [vattʃi'nare] VT (*Med*): **vaccinare qn contro qc** to vaccinate sb against sth; **farsi vaccinare** to have a vaccination, get vaccinated; **si è fatto vaccinare contro l'influenza** he got vaccinated against flu; **ormai sono vaccinato contro le delusioni amorose** I am immune to disappointments in love now; **essere grande e vaccinato (per fare qc)** to be big enough and ugly enough (to do sth)
vaccinazione [vattʃinat'tsjone] SF vaccination
vaccino, a [vat'tʃino] AGG: **latte vaccino** cow's milk ■ SM vaccine; **fare un vaccino** to have a vaccination; **fare un vaccino a qn** to vaccinate sb
vacillante [vatʃil'lante] AGG (*edificio, vecchio*) shaky, unsteady; (*salute, memoria*) shaky, failing; (*fiamma*) flickering; **camminava con passo vacillante** he was walking shakily *o* unsteadily
vacillare [vatʃil'lare] VI (*aus* **avere**) **1** (*edificio, muro, ubriaco*) to sway (to and fro); **camminare vacillando** (*vecchio*) to totter along; (*ubriaco, persona stanca*) to stagger along; **il pugno lo fece vacillare** the punch made him reel **2** (*salute, memoria*) to be shaky, be failing; (*fiamma*) to flicker; (*trono, governo*) to be unstable; (*fede*) to waver, be shaky; (*coraggio*) to falter, waver, be failing
vacuità [vakui'ta] SF vacuity, vacuousness
vacuo, a ['vakuo] AGG vacuous, empty
vacuometro [vaku'ɔmetro] SM vacuum gauge
vademecum [vade'mɛkum] SM INV vademecum
vado *ecc* ['vado] VB *vedi* **andare**
va e vieni [va e 'vjɛni] SM INV (*di persone*) coming and going
vaffanculo [vaffan'kulo] ESCL (*fam!*) fuck off! (*fam!*)
vagabondaggio, gi [vagabon'daddʒo] SM wandering, roaming; (*Dir*) vagrancy
vagabondare [vagabon'dare] VI (*aus* **avere**) to roam, wander; **vagabondare per le strade** to roam *o* wander (about) the streets
vagabondo, a [vaga'bondo] AGG (*gente, vita*) wandering *attr*; (*fig: fannullone*) idle ■ SM/F (*gen*) vagrant, tramp, vagabond; (*fig: fannullone*) layabout, loafer, idler
vagamente [vaga'mente] AVV vaguely
vagante [va'gante] AGG (*gen*) wandering; **"animali vaganti"** (*segnale stradale*) *wandering o stray animals*; **proiettile vagante** stray bullet; **mina vagante** (*fig: pericolo*) time bomb
vagare [va'gare] VI (*aus* **avere**) **vagare per** (*persona*) to wander around, roam around; (*animale*) to roam; **vagava senza meta per la città** he was wandering aimlessly around the town; **vagare con la mente** to let one's mind wander; **vagare con la fantasia** to give free rein to one's imagination, let one's imagination run away with one

vagheggiare [vaged'dʒare] VT (*letter: desiderare*) to long for, yearn for
vagherò *ecc* [vage'rɔ] VB *vedi* **vagare**
vaghezza [va'gettsa] SF vagueness
vagina [va'dʒina] SF vagina
vaginale [vadʒi'nale] AGG vaginal
vagire [va'dʒire] VI (*aus* **avere**) (*neonato*) to cry, wail
vagito [va'dʒito] SM (*di neonato*) crying, wailing
vaglia ['vaʎʎa] SM INV (*Comm*) money order; **vaglia bancario** bank draft; **vaglia cambiario** promissory note; **vaglia postale** postal order
vagliare [vaʎ'ʎare] VT (*sabbia*) to riddle, sift; (*grano*) to sift; (*fig: proposta, problema*) to weigh up
vaglio, gli ['vaʎʎo] SM sieve; **passare al vaglio** (*fig*) to examine closely
vago, a, ghi, ghe ['vago] AGG (*gen*) vague
■SM **1** vagueness; **tenersi nel vago** to keep it all rather vague, stick to generalities **2** (*Anat*) vagus (nerve)
vagone [va'gone] SM (*Ferr: per merci*) truck (*Brit*), wagon (*Brit*), freight car (*Am*); (*: per passeggeri*) carriage (*Brit*), car (*Am*); **vagone letto** sleeping car, sleeper; **vagone ristorante** restaurant *o* dining car
vai *ecc* ['vai] VB *vedi* **andare**
vaiolo [va'jɔlo] SM smallpox
valanga, ghe [va'langa] SF avalanche; (*fig: grande quantità: di lettere, regali*) flood; **arrivare/riversarsi a valanghe** (*fig: turisti*) to flood in/pour out
valchiria [val'kirja] SF (*Mitol*) Valkyrie
valdese [val'dese] AGG, SM/F (*Rel*) Waldensian
valente [va'lɛnte] AGG able, talented
valenza [va'lɛntsa] SF (*fig: significato*) content; (*Chim*) valency (*Brit*), valence (*Am*)
valere [va'lere] VB IRREG
■VI (*aus* **essere**) **1** (*persona: contare*) to be worth; **come medico non vale molto** he's not much of a doctor; **vale tanto oro quanto pesa** she's worth her weight in gold; **far valere le proprie ragioni** to make o.s. heard; **far valere la propria autorità** to assert one's authority; **farsi valere** to make o.s. appreciated *o* respected **2** (*avere efficacia: documento*) to be valid; (*avere vigore*) to hold, apply; **questo vale anche per te** this applies to you, too **3** (*essere regolamentare: partita*) to be valid, count; **così non vale!** that's not fair! **4** (*giovare*) to be of use; **i suoi sforzi non sono valsi a niente** his efforts came to nought; **i tuoi consigli sono valsi a fargli cambiare idea** your advice convinced him to change his mind; **prima o poi lo verrà a sapere, tanto vale dirglielo subito** he'll find out sooner or later, so we (*o* you *ecc*) might as well tell him now; **tanto vale che te lo dica** I might as well tell you **5** (*equivalere*) to be equal to; (*essere comparabile a*) to be worth; (*significare*) to amount to; **l'uno vale l'altro** the one is as good as the other, they amount to the same thing; **valere la pena** to be worth the effort *o* worth it; **non ne vale la pena** it's not worth it; **non vale la pena arrabbiarsi tanto** it's not worth getting so angry; **vale a dire** that is to say **6** (*cosa: avere pregio*) to be worth; **l'auto vale tremila euro** the car is worth three thousand euros; **non valere niente** to be worthless; **non vale niente** it's worthless
■VT (*procurare*): **gli ha valso il primo premio** it earned him first prize; **ciò gli ha valso un esaurimento** that was what brought on *o* caused his nervous breakdown
▶ **valersi** VIP: **valersi di** to take advantage of; **valersi dei consigli di qn** to take *o* act upon sb's advice
valeriana [vale'rjana] SF (*Bot, Med*) valerian
valevole [va'levole] AGG valid
valgo¹, a, ghi, ghe ['valgo] AGG (*Med*) valgus
valgo² *ecc* ['valgo] VB *vedi* **valere**
valicare [vali'kare] VT (*catena montuosa*) to cross
valico, chi ['valiko] SM pass; **valico di frontiera** border crossing
validamente [valida'mente] AVV (*intervenire, contribuire*) effectively
validità [validi'ta] SF validity; **ha una validità di tre mesi** it is valid for three months
valido, a ['valido] AGG **1** (*gen*) valid; **il suo passaporto non è più valido** your passport is no longer valid; **l'incontro non è valido per la finale** the match doesn't count for the final; **non è valido!** (*in giochi*) that doesn't count! **2** (*efficace: resistenza, rimedio*) effective; (*: aiuto*) real; (*: contributo*) substantial; (*: scusa, argomento*) valid; **essere di valido aiuto a qn** to be a great help to sb **3** (*persona: bravo*) worthy; (*: vigoroso*) healthy, strong; **uno dei registi più validi degli ultimi anni** one of the best directors of recent years
valigeria [validʒe'ria] SF (*assortimento*) leather goods *pl*; (*negozio*) leather goods shop; (*fabbrica*) leather goods factory
valigetta [validʒɛtta] SF: **valigetta ventiquattrore** attaché case
valigia, gie *o* **ge** [va'lidʒa] SF (suit)case; **fare le valigie** to pack (one's bags); (*fig*) to pack (up); **disfare le valigie** to unpack (one's bags); **valigia diplomatica** (*Pol*) diplomatic bag
vallata [val'lata] SF valley
valle ['valle] SF **1** valley; **a valle** (*di fiume*) downstream; **scendere a valle** to go downhill **2 valli** SFPL (*tipo di laguna*) marshes
valletta [val'letta] SF (*TV*) assistant
valletto [val'letto] SM **1** (*domestico*) valet **2** (*TV*) assistant
valligiano, a [valli'dʒano] SM/F inhabitant of a valley
vallo ['vallo] SM (*fortificazione*) wall; **il vallo Adriano** Hadrian's Wall
vallone¹ [val'lone] SM **1** (*valle: grande*) deep valley; (*: stretto*) narrow valley; (*burrone*) ravine **2** (*canale marino*) deep inlet
vallone², a [val'lone] AGG, SM/F Walloon
valore [va'lore] SM **1** (*pregio: di merce*) value, worth; (*Fin: di moneta, titolo*) value, price; **il valore della merce** the value of the goods; **il valore di un anello** the value of a ring; **crescere/diminuire di valore** to go up/down in value, gain/lose in value; **è di gran valore** it's worth a lot, it's very valuable; **è un anello di gran valore** it's a very valuable ring; **senza valore** worthless **2 valori** SMPL (*titoli*) securities; (*oggetti preziosi*) valuables; **Borsa Valori** Stock Exchange **3** (*di persona*) worth, merit; (*di opera*) merit, value; (*di vita, amicizia*) value; **artista di valore** artist of considerable merit; **valori morali/estetici** moral/aesthetic values; **scala dei valori** scale of values; **per te l'amicizia non ha alcun valore** friendship means nothing to you **4** (*significato*) meaning; (*funzione*) value; **le sue parole hanno (il) valore di una promessa** what he said amounts to *o* is tantamount to a promise; **il valore di un vocabolo** the exact meaning of a word; **qui il participio ha valore di aggettivo** the participle acts as *o* is used as an adjective here **5** (*coraggio*) courage, valour (*Brit*), valor (*Am*); **difendersi/combattere con gran valore** to defend o.s./fight with great courage; **medaglia al valor militare** medal for gallantry; **atti di valore** acts of bravery *o* gallantry **6** (*Dir: validità*):

questo documento non ha valore legale this document has no legal validity; **valore aggiunto** (*lit, fig*) added value; **valore contabile** book value; **valore effettivo** real value; **valore facciale** nominal value; **valore di mercato** market value; **valore nominale** nominal value; **valore di realizzo** break-up value; **valore di riscatto** surrender value; **valori bollati** (revenue) stamps; **valori mobiliari** transferable securities

valorizzare [valorid'dzare] VT **1** (*prodotto*) to enhance the value of **2** (*mettere in risalto*) to set off, make the most of; **quel trucco valorizza i suoi occhi** that make-up makes the most of her eyes *o* accentuates her eyes

valorizzazione [valoriddzat'tsjone] SF increase in value

valorosamente [valorosa'mente] AVV courageously, bravely

valoroso, a [valo'roso] AGG courageous, valorous

valso, a ['valso] PP *di* **valere**

valuta [va'luta] SF **1** (*Fin: moneta*) currency, money; **valuta estera** foreign currency **2** (*Banca*): **con valuta 15 gennaio** interest to run from January 15th

valutare [valu'tare] VT **1** (*Econ: stimare: casa, gioiello*) to value; (*: danni, costo*) to assess, evaluate; (*: approssimativamente*) to estimate; (*fig: capacità*) to appreciate; **la casa è stata valutata centomila euro** the house has been valued at a hundred thousand euros; **i danni sono valutati attorno a cinquecentomila euro** the damage has been assessed at about five hundred thousand **2** (*vagliare*) to weigh (up); **valutare i pro e i contro** to weigh up the pros and cons; **bisogna valutare i pro e i contro** we need to weigh up the pros and cons

valutario, ria, ri, rie [valu'tarjo] AGG (*Fin: norme*) currency *attr*

valutativo, a [valuta'tivo] AGG (*criterio*) assessment *attr*

valutazione [valutat'tsjone] SF (*vedi vb 1*) valuation; assessment, evaluation; estimate; **stando alle prime valutazioni,...** going by initial estimates, ...; **valutazione di impatto ambientale** environmental impact assessment; **valutazione di rischio** risk assessment

valva ['valva] SF (*Zool, Bot*) valve

valvola ['valvola] SF (*gen, Anat*) valve; (*Elettr: fusibile*) fuse; **valvola a farfalla** (*Aut*) throttle; **valvola di sicurezza** (*anche fig*) safety valve; **valvola in testa** (*Aut*) overhead valve

valzer ['valtser] SM INV waltz; **sai ballare il valzer?** can you do the waltz?

vamp [vamp] SF INV vamp

vampa ['vampa] SF (*del sole*) burning heat; (*fiamma*) flame; (*fig: rossore: per calore, ira*) flush; (*: per vergogna*) blush

vampata [vam'pata] SF (*fiammata*) blaze; (*di calore*) blast; (*fig: al viso*) flush

vampiro [vam'piro] SM (*gen*) vampire; (*Zool*) vampire bat

vanadio [va'nadjo] SM vanadium

vanagloria [vana'glɔrja] SF boastfulness

vanaglorioso, a [vanaglo'rjoso] AGG boastful

vanamente [vana'mente] AVV (*inutilmente*) in vain, pointlessly; (*con vanità*) vainly, conceitedly

vandalicamente [vandalika'mente] AVV (*comportarsi*) like a vandal

vandalico, a, ci, che [van'daliko] AGG vandal *attr*; **atto vandalico** act of vandalism

vandalismo [vanda'lizmo] SM vandalism; **un atto di vandalismo** an act of vandalism

vandalo, a ['vandalo] SM/F vandal

vaneggiamento [vaneddʒa'mento] SM raving, delirium

vaneggiare [vaned'dʒare] VI (*aus* **avere**) to rave, be delirious; **ma tu vaneggi!** you must be mad!

vanesio, sia, si, sie [va'nɛzjo] AGG vain, conceited

vanga, ghe ['vanga] SF spade

vangare [van'gare] VT to dig

vangata [van'gata] SF (*colpo*) blow with a spade; (*quantità di terra*) spadeful

vangelo [van'dʒɛlo] SM (*Rel, fig*) gospel; **per me è vangelo** (*fig*) it's gospel as far as I'm concerned

vanificare [vanifi'kare] VT to nullify

vaniglia [va'niʎʎa] SF vanilla; **un gelato alla vaniglia** a vanilla ice cream

vanigliato, a [vaniʎ'ʎato] AGG: **zucchero vanigliato** (*Culin*) vanilla sugar

vanillina [vanil'lina] SF vanillin

vaniloquio, qui [vani'lɔkwjo] SM (*discorso futile*) nonsense

vanità [vani'ta] SF **1** (*vanagloria*) vanity, pride, conceit; **l'ha fatto per vanità** he did it out of vanity **2** (*futilità: di promessa*) emptiness, vanity; (*: di sforzo*) futility, fruitlessness

vanitosamente [vanitosa'mente] AVV vainly

vanitoso, a [vani'toso] AGG vain, conceited
■ SM/F vain person

vanno ['vanno] VB *vedi* **andare**

vano, a ['vano] AGG **1** (*illusione, promessa*) vain, empty; (*fatiche*) vain, futile, fruitless; (*proteste, minacce*) idle; **vane speranze** vain hopes; **riuscire vano** to come to nothing; **tutti i nostri sforzi sono stati vani** all our efforts were useless **2** (*vanitoso*) vain, conceited
■ SM **1** (*spazio vuoto*) space; **il vano della porta** the doorway; **vano portabagagli** (*Aut*) boot (*Brit*), trunk (*Am*); **vano portaoggetti** (*Aut*) glove compartment **2** (*stanza*) room; **un appartamento di quattro vani** a four-roomed flat (*Brit*) *o* apartment (*Am*)

vantaggio, gi [van'taddʒo] SM **1** (*gen*) advantage; **avere il vantaggio (di)** to have the advantage (of); **i vantaggi e gli svantaggi di vivere in città** the advantages and disadvantages of living in a city **2** (*profitto*) benefit, advantage; **tornerà a tuo vantaggio** it will be to your advantage; **sei in una posizione di vantaggio** you're at an advantage; **trarre vantaggio da qc** to benefit from sth; **non trarre alcun vantaggio da qc** to get nothing out of sth **3** (*distacco*) start; (*: Sport*) lead; (*: Tennis*) advantage; **hanno un vantaggio di 3 ore su di noi** they have a 3-hour start on us; (*Sport*) they have a 3-hour lead over us; **essere/portarsi in vantaggio** (*Sport*) to be in/take the lead; **siamo in vantaggio** we're in the lead; **sono in vantaggio di due punti sugli avversari** they have a two-point lead over their opponents

vantaggiosamente [vantaddʒosa'mente] AVV advantageously, favourably (*Brit*), favorably (*Am*)

vantaggioso, a [vantad'dʒoso] AGG advantageous, favourable (*Brit*), favorable (*Am*); **mi ha fatto un'offerta molto vantaggiosa** he made me a very good offer; **un prezzo vantaggioso** a good price

vantare [van'tare] VT **1** (*lodare: persona, cosa, prodotto*) to speak highly of, praise; (*avere: qualità*) to boast, have **2** (*andare fiero di*) to boast of *o* about, vaunt
▶ **vantarsi** VR: **vantarsi di qc/di aver fatto qc** to boast *o* brag about sth/about having done sth; **non**

Vv

faccio per vantarmi without false modesty, without wishing to boast *o* brag

vanteria [vante'ria] SF (*qualità*) boasting; (*atto, detto*) boast

vanto ['vanto] SM **1** **menar vanto di** to boast *o* brag about **2** (*merito*) merit, virtue **3** (*orgoglio*) pride; **è il vanto di sua madre** he's his mother's pride and joy

vanvera ['vanvera] **a vanvera** AVV haphazardly; **parlare a vanvera** to talk nonsense

vapore [va'pore] SM **1** (*Chim, Fis*) vapour (*Brit*), vapor (*Am*); **vapori** SMPL fumes; **vapore acqueo** steam, (water) vapour; **a vapore** (*ferro, locomotiva, turbina*) steam *attr*; **un ferro a vapore** a steam iron; **al vapore** (*Culin*) steamed; **verdure al vapore** steamed vegetables; **andare a tutto vapore** (*fig: persona, macchina*) to go at full speed **2** (*nave*) steamer

vaporetto [vapo'retto] SM steamer

vaporiera [vapo'rjɛra] SF steam engine

vaporizzare [vaporid'dzare] VT to vaporize; (*Cosmetica*) to steam

vaporizzatore [vaporiddza'tore] SM spray

vaporizzazione [vaporiddzat'tsjone] SF vaporization

vaporosità [vaporosi'ta] SF (*vedi agg*) filminess; fullness

vaporoso, a [vapo'roso] AGG (*tessuto*) filmy; (*capelli*) soft and full

varano [va'rano] SM (*Zool*) monitor

varare [va'rare] VT (*Naut, fig*) to launch; (*legge*) to pass; **varare una nave** to launch a ship; **varare una legge** to pass a law

varcare [var'kare] VT to cross; **varcare i limiti** to overstep *o* exceed the limits; **ha varcato l'ottantina** he's just over eighty

varco, chi ['varko] SM passage; **aprirsi un varco tra la folla** to push one's way through the crowd; **aspettare qn al varco** (*fig*) to lie in wait for sb

varechina [vare'kina] SF bleach

varesino, a [vare'sino] AGG of *o* from Varese
■ SM/F inhabitant *o* native of Varese

variabile [va'rjabile] AGG (*gen*) variable; (*tempo*) changeable, unsettled, variable; (*umore*) changeable; **la qualità del prodotto è molto variabile** the quality of the product is very variable; **il tempo si manterrà variabile** the weather will continue unsettled
■ SF (*Mat, Econ*) variable

variabilità [varjabili'ta] SF INV (*gen, Bio*) variability; (*di tempo, umore*) changeableness

variamente [varja'mente] AVV (*distribuiti, colorati*) variously

variante [va'rjante] SF (*gen*) variation, change; (*di percorso*) alternative route; (*di piano, progetto*) modification; (*Ling*) variant

variare [va'rjare] VT to vary
■ VI (*aus sogg: persona* **essere**; *sogg: cosa* **avere**) (*sogg: persona, cosa*) to vary; (*prezzi*) to range

variato, a [va'rjato] AGG varied

variazione [varjat'tsjone] SF (*gen*) variation, change; (*Mat, Mus*) variation; **le variazioni della temperatura** variations in the temperature; **una variazione di programma** a change of plan; **variazioni sul tema** (*Mus, fig*) variations on a theme

varice [va'ritʃe] SF varicose vein

varicella [vari'tʃɛlla] SF chickenpox

varicoso, a [vari'koso] AGG: **vena varicosa** varicose vein

variegato, a [varje'gato] AGG variegated

varietà [varje'ta] SF (*gen*) variety; **hanno una grande varietà di piatti** they have a great variety of dishes
■ SM INV: **(spettacolo di) varietà** variety show

vario, ria, ri, rie ['varjo] AGG **1** (*diversificato: stile, paesaggio*) varied; **il paesaggio è molto vario** the landscape is very varied **2** **vari(e)** (*parecchi: oggetti, argomenti*) various; **avere varie cose da fare** to have quite a few things to do; **devo vedere varie persone oggi** I've got to see various people today; **varie volte** several times **3** (*instabile: tempo*) unsettled; (*: umore*) changeable, uncertain
■ PRON PL: **vari** several people
■ SFPL: **varie ed eventuali** (*nell'ordine del giorno*) any other business

variopinto, a [varjo'pinto] AGG multicoloured (*Brit*), multicolored (*Am*)

varo ['varo] SM (*Naut, fig*) launch, launching; (*di leggi*) passing

varrò *ecc* [var'rɔ] VB *vedi* **valere**

Varsavia [var'savja] SF Warsaw

vasaio, aia, ai, aie [va'zajo] SM/F potter

vasca, sche ['vaska] SF **1** (*gen*) tub; (*per pesci*) tank; (*cisterna*) water butt; (*da bucato*) basin; (*anche:* **vasca da bagno**) bath(tub); **vasca dei pesci** fish tank **2** (*piscina*) (swimming) pool; (*: lunghezza della vasca*) length; **fare una vasca** to swim a length

vascello [vaʃ'ʃɛllo] SM (*Naut*) vessel, ship; **capitano di vascello** captain; **tenente di vascello** lieutenant

vaschetta [vas'ketta] SF (*per gelato*) tub; (*per sviluppare fotografie*) basin, dish; **una vaschetta di gelato** a tub of ice cream; **vaschetta per il ghiaccio** ice tray

vascolare [vasko'lare] AGG vascular

vasectomia [vazekto'mia] SF vasectomy

vasectomizzare [vazektomid'dzare] VT to give a vasectomy to; **farsi vasectomizzare** to have a vasectomy

vaselina® [vaze'lina] SF Vaseline®, petroleum jelly

vasellame [vazel'lame] SM (*stoviglie*) crockery; (*: di porcellana*) china; (*: d'oro, argento*) plate

vaso ['vazo] SM **1** (*recipiente: per fiori*) vase; (*: per piante*) flowerpot; (*: ornamentale*) vase, pot; (*: per conserve*) jar, pot; **vaso da notte** chamber pot; **vaso di Pandora** (*also fig*) Pandora's box **2** (*Anat, Bot, Fis*) vessel; **vasi comunicanti** (*Fis*) communicating vessels; **vasi sanguigni** (*Anat*) blood vessels

vasocostrittore, trice [vazokostrit'tore] AGG, SM vasoconstrictor

vasodilatatore, trice [vazodilata'tore] AGG, SM vasodilator

vassallo [vas'sallo] SM vassal

vassoio, oi [vas'sojo] SM tray

vastamente [vasta'mente] AVV vastly

vastità [vasti'ta] SF vastness

vasto, a ['vasto] AGG (*gen*) vast, huge, immense; **una vasta area** a vast area; **di vasta cultura** widely read; **di vaste proporzioni** (*incendio*) huge; (*fenomeno, rivolta*) widespread; **su vasta scala** on a vast *o* huge scale

vaticano, a [vati'kano] AGG Vatican *attr*
■ SM: **il Vaticano** the Vatican; **la Città del Vaticano** the Vatican City
▷ www.vatican.va/phome_it.htm

vaticinare [vatitʃi'nare] VT (*letter*) to foretell, prophesy

vaticinio, ni [vati'tʃinjo] SM (*profezia*) prophecy

vattelappesca [vattelap'peska] ESCL (*fam*): **come si chiama? — vattelappesca!** what's his name? — who knows?

VB SIGLA = *Verbano-Cusio-Ossola*

VC SIGLA = *Vercelli*

VE SIGLA = **Venezia**
■ABBR = *Vostra Eccellenza*
ve [ve] PRON, AVV *vedi* **vi**
vecchiaia [vek'kjaja] SF old age; **sarai il bastone della mia vecchiaia** you'll support me in my old age
vecchio, chia, chi, chie ['vekkjo] AGG **1** (*gen*) old; **è più vecchio di me** he is older than me; **la casa più vecchia della via** the oldest house in the street; **è un mio vecchio amico** he's an old friend of mine; **ho una macchina vecchia** I've got an old car; **è una vecchia storia** it's an old story; **è un uomo vecchio stile** *o* **stampo** he's an old-fashioned man; **è vecchio del mestiere** he's an old hand at the job; **vecchia volpe** (*fig*) cunning *o* wily old fox; **vecchio come il mondo** as old as the hills **2** (*precedente*) old, former; **il vecchio sindaco** the old *o* former mayor; **la sua macchina vecchia** his old car **3** (*stagionato*: *vino, formaggio*) mature; (: *legno*) weathered; (*stantio*: *pane*) stale
■SM old; **il contrasto tra il vecchio e il nuovo** the contrast between old and new
■SM/F (*persona*) old man/woman; **i vecchi** SMPL the old *o* aged, old *o* elderly people, old folk; **come stanno i tuoi vecchi?** (*fam*: *genitori*) how are your folks?; **il mio vecchio** (*padre*) the *o* my old man; **la mia vecchia** (*madre*) the *o* my old woman; **vecchio mio!** old man!, old chap!
vecchiume [vek'kjume] SM (*pegg*: *cose*) old junk, old rubbish (*Brit*); **il vecchiume delle sue idee** his old-fashioned ideas
veccia, ce ['vettʃa] SF (*Bot*) vetch
vece ['vetʃe] SF (*funzione*) place, stead; **firma del padre o di chi ne fa le veci** signature of the father or guardian; **in vece mia/tua** in my/your place *o* stead
vedente [ve'dɛnte] SM/F: **non vedente** visually handicapped
vedere [ve'dere] VB IRREG
■VT
1 to see; **senza occhiali, non ci vedo** I can't see without my glasses; **non si vede niente** *or* **non (ci) si vede** (*è buio*) you can't see a thing; **non si vede** (*non è visibile*) it doesn't show, you can't see it; **vedere qn fare qc** to see sb do sth; **è una partita da vedere** it'll be a match worth seeing; **l'ho visto nascere** (*fig*) I've known him since he was born; **ho visto costruire questa casa** I saw this house being built
2 (*raffigurarsi*) to see; **vedere tutto nero** to take a bleak view of things; **non vedo una via d'uscita** I can see no way out; **modo di vedere** outlook, view of things; **vorrei vedere te al posto suo!** I would like to see you in his place!; **lo vedo male questo progetto** I can't see this project working
3 (*esaminare*: *libro, prodotto*) to see, look at; (: *conti*) to go over, check; **vedi pagina 8** see page 8; **mi fai vedere il vestito nuovo?** let me see *o* have a look at the new dress; **fammi vedere il tuo tema** let me see your essay
4 (*scoprire*) to see, find out; **vai a vedere cos'è successo** go and see *o* find out what has happened; **voglio vedere come vanno le cose/che possibilità ci sono** I want to see *o* find out how things are going/what opportunities there are; **vediamo se funziona** let's see if it works; **è da vedere se...** it remains to be seen whether ...
5 (*incontrare*) to see, meet; **non lo vedo da molto tempo** I haven't seen him for a long time; **guarda chi si vede!** look who it is!; **farsi vedere** to show one's face; **da quella volta non si è fatto più vedere** he hasn't shown his face since; **fatti vedere ogni tanto** come and see us (*o* me *ecc*) from time to time; **non farsi più vedere in giro** to disappear from the scene; **non la posso proprio vedere** (*fig*) I can't stand her
6 (*visitare*: *museo, mostra*) to visit; (*consultare*: *medico, avvocato*) to see, consult; **farsi vedere da un medico** to go and see a doctor
7 (*capire*) to see, grasp; **ho visto subito che...** I immediately realized that ...; **si vede!** that's obvious!; **si vede che sono stanchi** you can tell they are tired; **non vedo la ragione di farlo** I can't see any reason to do it *o* for doing it; **è triste ma non lo dà a vedere** he is sad but he isn't letting it show *o* he is hiding it; **ci vedo poco chiaro in questa faccenda** I can't quite understand this business
8 (*fare in modo*): **vedere di fare qc** to see (to it) that sth is done, make sure that sth is done; **vedi di non arrivare in ritardo** see *o* make sure you don't arrive late; **vedi tu se ci riesci** see if you can do it; **vedi tu** (*decidi tu*) it's up to you
9 (*fraseologia*): **vedetevela voi** you see to it; **se l'è vista brutta** he thought his last hour had come; **essere ben/mal visto da qn** to be/not to be well thought of by sb; **visto che...** seeing that ...; **non vedere qn di buon occhio** to disapprove of sb; **non avere niente a che vedere con qn/qc** to have nothing to do with sb/sth; **vedere la luce** (*nascere*) to come into being, see the light of the day; **vedere le stelle** (*dal dolore*) to see stars; **vederci doppio** to see double; **vedere lontano** (*fig*) to be farsighted; **non vedere più lontano del proprio naso** to be unable to see beyond the end of one's nose; **chi s'è visto s'è visto!** and that's that!; **non vederci più dalla rabbia** to be beside o.s. with rage; **non vederci più dalla fame** to be ravenous *o* starving; **non vedere l'ora di fare qc** to look forward to doing sth; **non vedo l'ora che arrivino** I can't wait for them to arrive; **non vedo l'ora di conoscerlo** I can't wait to meet him; **a vederlo si direbbe che...** by the look of him you'd think that ...; **in vita mia ne ho viste di tutti i colori** I've been through a lot in my time; **ti faccio vedere io!** I'll show you!
▶ **vedersi** VR
1 (*specchiarsi, raffigurarsi*) to see o.s.
2 **si vide perduto** he realized (that) he was lost; **si vide negare l'ingresso** he was refused admission; **si vide costretto a...** he found himself forced to ...
3 (*uso reciproco*) to see each other, meet; **ci vedremo da mio cugino** I'll see you at my cousin's; **ci vediamo domani!** see you tomorrow!
vedetta [ve'detta] SF **1** (*Mil*: *luogo, guardia*) lookout; **essere** *o* **stare di vedetta** to be on lookout duty **2** (*Naut*) patrol ship *o* boat
vedette [və'det] SF INV (*attore, attrice*) star
vedova ['vedova] SF widow; **mia madre è vedova** my mother is a widow; **rimanere vedova** to be widowed; **vedova nera** (*Zool*) black widow spider
vedovanza [vedo'vantsa] SF widowhood
vedovo, a ['vedovo] AGG widowed; **mio padre è vedovo** my father is a widower; **rimanere vedovo** to be widowed
■SM widower
vedrò *ecc* [ve'drɔ] VB *vedi* **vedere**
veduta [ve'duta] SF **1** (*panorama, rappresentazione di paesaggio*) view; **da quassù si ha una stupenda veduta sul mare** you get a wonderful view of the sea from up here **2** **vedute** SFPL (*fig*) views, opinions; **di larghe** *o* **ampie vedute** broad-minded; **di vedute ristrette** *o*

limitate narrow-minded; **i miei sono di larghe vedute** my parents are broad-minded

veemente [vee'mɛnte] AGG (*discorso, azione*) vehement; (*assalto*) vigorous; (*passione, desiderio*) overwhelming

veementemente [veemente'mente] AVV vehemently

veemenza [vee'mɛntsa] SF vehemence; **con veemenza** vehemently; **la veemenza dell'attacco** the force of the attack

vegano, a [ve'gano] SM/F vegan

vegetale [vedʒe'tale] AGG (*gen*) vegetable *attr*; (*organismo*) plant *attr*; **regno vegetale** plant *o* vegetable kingdom
■ SM plant

vegetaliano, a [vedʒeta'ljano] AGG, SM/F vegan

vegetare [vedʒe'tare] VI (*aus* **avere**) **1** (*piante*) to grow **2** (*fig*: *persona*) to vegetate

vegetarianismo [vedʒetarja'nizmo] SM vegetarianism

vegetariano, a [vedʒeta'rjano] AGG, SM/F vegetarian

vegetativo, a [vedʒeta'tivo] AGG vegetative

vegetazione [vedʒetat'tsjone] SF vegetation

vegeto, a ['vɛdʒeto] AGG (*pianta*) thriving; (*persona*) strong, robust, vigorous; **vivo e vegeto** (*persona*) alive and kicking

veggente [ved'dʒɛnte] SM/F (*indovino*) clairvoyant

veglia ['veʎʎa] SF **1** (*atto*) vigil, watch; **fare la veglia a un malato** to sit with a sick person; **veglia funebre** wake **2** **ha passato ore di veglia sui libri** he stayed up late working away at his books; **tra la veglia e il sonno** half awake

vegliardo, a [veʎ'ʎardo] SM/F venerable old man/ woman, elder

vegliare [veʎ'ʎare] VT (*malato, morto*) to watch over, sit up with
■ VI (*aus* **avere**) **1** (*stare sveglio*) to stay up, sit up; **vegliare al capezzale di qn** to sit up with sb, watch by sb's bedside; **vegliare pregando** to pass the night in prayer **2** (*prendersi cura*): **vegliare su qn** to watch over sb

veglione [veʎ'ʎone] SM ball, dance; **veglione di Capodanno** New Year's Eve party; **veglione danzante** all-night dance

veicolare¹ [veiko'lare] AGG vehicular, of vehicles; **traffico veicolare** vehicular traffic

veicolare² [veiko'lare] VT (*malattia*) to carry

veicolo [ve'ikolo] SM **1** (*Tecn*) vehicle; **veicolo industriale** industrial vehicle; **veicolo a motore** motor vehicle; **veicolo spaziale** spacecraft *inv* **2** (*mezzo di diffusione*: *di idee, suoni*) vehicle, medium; (: *di malattia*) carrier; **veicolo pubblicitario** advertising medium

vela ['vela] SF **1** (*Naut*) sail; **una barca a vela** a sailing boat; **issare/spiegare/ammainare le vele** to hoist/ unfurl/strike the sails; **far vela per** (*salpare*) to set sail for; **tutto va a gonfie vele** (*fig*) everything is going perfectly **2** (*Sport*) sailing; **andare a vela** to go sailing
▷ http://domino.federvela.it/

velare¹ [ve'lare] VT (*anche fig*) to veil, cover; **velarsi il volto** to cover one's face (with a veil); **le lacrime gli velarono gli occhi** his eyes were clouded with tears
► **velarsi** VIP (*occhi, luna*) to mist over; (*voce*) to become husky; **gli occhi le si velarono di pianto** *o* **lacrime** her eyes clouded with tears; **lo sguardo le si velò** her eyes grew dim; **l'acqua si velò di ghiaccio** ice formed on the water

velare² [ve'lare] AGG (*Ling*) velar

velatamente [velata'mente] AVV (*alludere, accennare*) covertly

velato, a [ve'lato] AGG (*anche fig*: *accenno*) veiled; **occhi velati di lacrime** eyes clouded with tears; **sorriso velato di tristezza** smile tinged with sadness; **con la voce velata per l'emozione** in a voice thick with emotion; **calze velate** sheer stockings

velatura [vela'tura] SF (*Naut*) sails *pl*

velcro® ['vɛlkro] SM INV Velcro®

veleggiare [veled'dʒare] VI (*aus* **avere**) **1** (*Naut*) to sail **2** (*aliante, deltaplano*) to soar, glide

veleggiatore [veleddʒa'tore] SM (*Aer*) sailplane

veleno [ve'leno] SM (*sostanza tossica*) poison; (*di serpente*) venom; **gli alcolici sono un veleno per il fegato** alcohol poisons your liver; **parole piene di veleno** venomous words; **sputa sempre veleno su tutti** he is always making spiteful remarks about everybody

velenosamente [velenosa'mente] AVV maliciously, venomously

velenoso, a [vele'noso] AGG (*sostanza, fungo, animale*) poisonous; (*persona, lingua, risposta*) venomous

veleria [vele'ria] SF sailmaker's (shop)

veletta [ve'letta] SF (*di cappello*) veil

velico, a, ci, che ['veliko] AGG (*regata*) sailing *attr*; **superficie velica** sail area

veliero [ve'ljɛro] SM (*Naut*) sailing ship

velina [ve'lina] SF (*anche*: **carta velina**: *per impacchettare*) tissue paper; (: *per copie*) flimsy paper; (: *copia*) carbon (copy)

velista, i, e [ve'lista] SM/F yachtsman/yachtswoman

velivolo [ve'livolo] SM aircraft

velleità [vellei'ta] SF INV vain ambition, vain desire

velleitario, ria, ri, rie [vellei'tarjo] AGG (*aspirazione*) fanciful, unrealistic; (*politica, tentativo*) unrealistic

vello ['vɛllo] SM (*di pecora, montone*) fleece

vellutato, a [vellu'tato] AGG (*stoffa, petalo, pesca, colore*) velvety; (*voce*) mellow

velluto [vel'luto] SM (*stoffa*) velvet; **velluto di cotone/ seta** cotton/silk velvet; **di velluto** (*fig*: *pelle, guance*) velvety; **un paio di pantaloni di velluto** a pair of cords *o* corduroy trousers; **velluto a coste** corduroy, cord

velo ['velo] SM **1** (*gen*) veil; (*strato sottile*) film, layer; (: *di nebbia*) layer, veil; **prendere il velo** (*Rel*) to take the veil; **un velo di ghiaccio** a film of ice; **nel suo sorriso c'era un velo di tristezza** there was a hint *o* touch of sadness in his smile; **senza veli** (*nudo*) without a stitch on; (*fig*: *esplicito*) explicit; **stendere un velo (pietoso) su qc** (*fig*) to draw a veil over sth; **velo nuziale** *o* **da sposa** bridal veil **2** (*tessuto*) voile **3** (*Anat*): **velo palatino** soft palate

veloce [ve'lotʃe] AGG (*gen*) quick, rapid; (*veicolo, cavallo, corridore*) fast; **è una macchina veloce** it's a fast car; **la mia moto è più veloce della tua** my motorbike is faster than yours; **è uno dei corridori più veloci del mondo** he's one of the fastest drivers in the world; **su, veloce, corri a casa!** quick, go home!; **il veloce scorrere del tempo** the swift passage of time; **veloce come un lampo** as quick as lightning; **più veloce della luce** (*fig*) as quick as a flash
■ AVV fast, quickly; **guidi troppo veloce** you drive too fast

velocemente [velotʃe'mente] AVV quickly

velocipede [velo'tʃipede] SM velocipede

velocista, i, e [velo'tʃista] SM/F (*Sport*) sprinter

velocità [velotʃi'ta] SF INV **1** (*gen, Fis*) speed, velocity; **la sua velocità nel reagire** the swiftness of his reaction; **a grande velocità** very quickly *o* fast; **a forte velocità** at high speed; **a tutta velocità** at full speed;

guidava a tutta velocità he was driving at full speed; **aumentare la velocità** to accelerate; **diminuire** *o* **ridurre la velocità** to reduce speed; **prendere velocità** to gain speed; **viaggiava alla velocità di 130 chilometri all'ora** it (*o* he) was travelling at a speed of 130 kilometres an hour; **a una velocità costante di 90 km/h** at a constant 90 kilometres per hour; **l'Europa a due velocità** two-speed Europe; **alta velocità** (*Ferr: servizio ferroviario*) high-speed rail service; **velocità di crociera** cruising speed; **velocità di fuga** (*Fis*) escape velocity; **velocità di reazione** (*Chim*) rate of reaction **2** (*Sport*): **gara** *o* **corsa di velocità** sprint, dash

velocizzare [velotʃid'dzare] VT to speed up, make faster
▶ **velocizzarsi** VIP to speed up

velodromo [ve'lɔdromo] SM velodrome

ven. ABBR (= venerdì) Fri.

vena ['vena] SF **1** (*Anat*) vein; (*aurifera, di piombo*) vein, lode; (*di carbone*) seam; (*d'acqua*) spring; (*venatura: di marmo*) vein, streak; (*: di legno*) grain; **le vene e le arterie** veins and arteries; **tagliarsi le vene** to slash one's wrists; **una vena di tristezza** (*fig*) a hint of sadness **2** (*estro*) inspiration; (*disposizione*) mood; **essere/sentirsi in vena di fare qc** to be/feel in the mood to do sth; **oggi non sono in vena** I'm not in the mood today; **non sono in vena di scherzi** I'm not in the mood for jokes, I'm not in a joking mood

venale [ve'nale] AGG **1** (*Comm: valore*) market *attr*; (*: prezzo*) selling, market *attr*; **cose venali** (*fig*) material things **2** (*fig: persona*) venal; **ma come sei venale!** how mercenary you are!

venalità [venali'ta] SF venality

venalmente [venal'mente] AVV venally

venato, a [ve'nato] AGG (*marmo*) veined, streaked; (*legno*) grained

venatorio, ria, ri, rie [vena'tɔrjo] AGG hunting *attr*; **la stagione venatoria** the hunting season

venatura [vena'tura] SF (*di marmo*) vein, streak; (*di legno*) grain *no pl*; **le venature del legno** the grain of the wood

vendemmia [ven'demmja] SF (*attività*) grape harvest, vintage; (*quantità d'uva*) grape crop, grapes *pl*; **fare la vendemmia** to pick *o* harvest the grapes

vendemmiare [vendem'mjare] VI (*aus* **avere**) to pick *o* harvest the grapes
■ VT (*uva*) to pick, harvest

vendemmiatore, trice [vendemmja'tore] SM/F grape-picker

vendere ['vɛndere] VT (*anche fig*) to sell; **vendere qc a qn** to sell sb sth, sell sth to sb; **vendere qc a** *o* **per 20 sterline** to sell sth for £20; **l'ho venduto per tremila euro** i sold it for three thousand euros; **vendere all'ingrosso/al dettaglio** *o* **minuto** to sell wholesale/ retail; **vendere a rate** to sell on hire purchase (*Brit*) *o* the instalment plan (*Am*); **una pubblicità che fa vendere** an advertisement which increases sales; **"vendesi"** "for sale"; **vendere all'asta** to auction, sell by auction; **vendere a buon mercato** to sell cheaply *o* at a good price; **questi articoli si vendono bene/ male** these articles sell well/don't sell well; **vendere cara la pelle** (*fig*) to sell one's life dearly; **vendere l'anima al diavolo** to sell one's soul to the devil; **vendere il proprio corpo** (*prostituirsi*) to sell one's body; **vendere fumo** to talk hot air; **averne da vendere** (*fig*) to have enough and to spare; **vendere la pelle dell'orso prima di averlo ucciso** to count one's chickens before they're hatched
▶ **vendersi** VR **1** (*tradire*): **vendersi al nemico** to sell out to the enemy **2** (*prostituirsi*) to prostitute o.s., sell o.s.

vendetta [ven'detta] SF revenge, vengeance; **prendersi una vendetta** to take one's revenge, wreak vengeance; **farsi vendetta** to take one's revenge; **ha deciso di farsi vendetta da solo** he decided to take his revenge; **essere assetato di vendetta** to thirst for revenge; **vendetta trasversale** (*della mafia*) *revenge against somebody by attacking his family or friends*

vendicare [vendi'kare] VT to avenge, revenge
▶ **vendicarsi** VR: **vendicarsi (di qc)** to avenge *o* revenge o.s. (for sth); (*per rancore*) to take one's revenge (for sth); **vendicarsi su qn** to avenge *o* revenge o.s. on sb

> **LO SAPEVI...?**
> **vendicare** non si traduce mai con la parola inglese *vindicate*

vendicativamente [vendikativa'mente] AVV vindictively

vendicativo, a [vendika'tivo] AGG (*persona, carattere*) vindictive

vendicatore, trice [vendika'tore] AGG (*furia*) avenging
■ SM/F avenger

vendita ['vendita] SF sale; **la vendita** (*attività*) selling; (*smercio*) sales *pl*; **contratto di vendita** sales agreement; **reparto vendite** sales department; **mettere in vendita** to put on sale; **hanno messo in vendita la casa** they have put their house up for sale; **in vendita presso** on sale at; **i biglietti saranno in vendita da venerdì** tickets will be on sale from Friday; **punto (di) vendita** retail outlet; **vendita all'asta** auction (sale), sale by auction; **vendita per corrispondenza** mail order; **vendita al dettaglio** retail; **vendita a domicilio** door-to-door selling; **vendita all'ingrosso** wholesale; **vendita al minuto** retail; **vendita porta a porta** door-to-door selling

venditore, trice [vendi'tore] SM/F seller, vendor, salesman/saleswoman; **venditore ambulante** hawker, pedlar; **venditore al dettaglio** retailer; **venditore all'ingrosso** wholesaler; **venditore al minuto** retailer

venduto, a [ven'duto] AGG (*merce*) sold; (*fig: corrotto*) corrupt
■ SM (*Comm*) goods *pl* sold

venefico, a, ci, che [ve'nɛfiko] AGG poisonous; (*fig: insinuazione*) poisonous, venomous

venerabile [vene'rabile], **venerando, a** [vene'rando] AGG venerable

venerare [vene'rare] VT to venerate, revere

venerazione [venerat'tsjone] SF veneration, reverence

venerdì [vener'di] SM INV Friday; **venerdì santo** Good Friday; **gli manca qualche venerdì** (*fig*) he's got a screw loose; *per fraseologia vedi* **martedì**

Venere ['vɛnere] SF (*Astron, Mitol*) Venus; **monte di Venere** (*Anat*) mons veneris

venereo, a [ve'nɛreo] AGG venereal; **malattia venerea** venereal disease

veneto, a ['vɛneto] AGG of *o* from the Veneto
■ SM/F inhabitant *o* native of the Veneto

Venezia [ve'nettsja] SF Venice; **abito a Venezia** I live in Venice; **domani vado a Venezia** I'm going to Venice tomorrow
▷ www.comune.venezia.it/

veneziana [venet'tsjana] SF (*tenda*) venetian blind

veneziano, a [venet'tsjano] AGG, SM/F Venetian

Vv

Venezuela [venet'tswεla] SM Venezuela
venezuelano, a [venettsue'lano] AGG, SM/F Venezuelan
vengo *ecc* ['vεngo] VB *vedi* **venire**
venia ['vεnja] SF: **chiedere venia** to beg pardon, apologize
veniale [ve'njale] AGG (*Rel*: *peccato*) venial
venire [ve'nire] VB IRREG
■VI (*aus* **essere**)
1 to come; **verremo a salutarti** we'll come and say goodbye; **vieni a trovarci** come and see us; **è venuto in macchina/treno** he came by car/train; **sono venuto a piedi** I came on foot; **vieni di corsa** come quickly; **vengo!** I'm coming!, just coming!; **da dove vieni?** where do you come from?
2 (*giungere*) to come, arrive; **non è ancora venuto** he hasn't come *o* arrived yet; **prendere le cose come vengono** to take things as they come; **fallo come viene viene** do it any old how; **venire al mondo** *o* **alla luce** to come into the world; **venire a patti/alle mani** to come to an agreement/to blows; **venire a capo di qc** to unravel sth, sort sth out; **venire a sapere qc** to learn sth; **venire al dunque** *o* **nocciolo** *o* **fatto** *o* **sodo** to come to the point; **questo lavoro/quel tipo mi è venuto a noia** I'm fed up with this work/with that guy; **è venuto il momento di...** the time has come to ...; **è venuto il momento di dire la verità** the time has come to tell the truth; **negli anni a venire** in the years to come, in future; **sono cose di là da venire** these things are still a long way off; **mi è venuta un'idea** I've had an idea; **ma che ti viene in mente?** whatever are you thinking of?; **gli era venuto il dubbio** *o* **sospetto che...** he began to suspect that ...; **mi è venuto un dubbio** I began to have doubts; **mi è venuto il raffreddore** I've got a cold; **gli è venuto il mal di testa** he's got a headache; **mi viene da vomitare** I feel sick; **mi viene da piangere/ridere** I feel like crying/laughing; **ti venisse un colpo/accidente!** (*fam*) drop dead!
3 (*provenire*): **venire da** to come from
4 (*riuscire*: *lavoro*) to turn out; **venire bene/male** to turn out well/badly; **il dolce è venuto bene** the cake turned out well; **il maglione viene troppo lungo/stretto** the sweater is going to end up too long/tight; **non mi viene** (*problema, operazione, calcolo*) I can't get it to come out right
5 (*fam*: *raggiungere l'orgasmo*) to come
6 (*costare*) to cost; **quanto viene?** how much is it *o* does it cost?
7 (*essere sorteggiato*) to come up
8 (*con avv*): **venire fuori** to come out; **venire fuori con** (*battuta*) to come out with; **venire giù** to come down; **venire meno** (*svenire*) to faint; **venire meno a** (*promessa*) to break; (*impegno, dovere*) not to fulfil (*Brit*) *o* fulfill (*Am*); **venire su** (*crescere*: *persona*) to grow (up); (: *pianta*) to come up; **il bambino sta venendo su molto robusto** the baby's growing very strong; **venire via** to come away *o* off; (*macchia*) to come out
9 **far venire** (*medico*) to call, send for; **far venire qn** to call sb; **mi hai fatto venire per niente** you got me to come *o* you made me come for nothing; **mi fa venire il vomito** (*anche fig*) it (*o* he *ecc*) makes me sick; **mi fa venire i brividi** (*anche fig*) it (*o* he *ecc*) gives me creeps
12 (*come ausiliare*: *essere*): **viene ammirato da tutti** he is admired by everyone; **venire stimato da tutti** to be respected by everybody; **viene venduto al chilo** it's sold by the kilo; **verrà giudicato in base al suo punteggio** he will be judged on his marks (*Brit*) *o* grades (*Am*)
▶ **venirsene** VIP: **venirsene via** to come away; **venirsene verso casa** to come home
■SM: **tutto quell'andare e venire mi rendeva nervoso** all that coming and going made me irritable
venni *ecc* ['venni] VB *vedi* **venire**
venoso, a [ve'noso] AGG venous
ventaglio, gli [ven'taʎʎo] SM fan; **a ventaglio** fan-shaped; **disporsi a ventaglio** to fan out
ventata [ven'tata] SF (*folata*) gust (of wind); **come una ventata d'aria fresca** (*fig*) like a breath of fresh air; **una ventata di nazionalismo** a wave of nationalism
ventennale [venten'nale] AGG (*che dura 20 anni*) twenty-year *attr*; (*che ricorre ogni 20 anni*) which takes place every twenty years
ventenne [ven'tεnne] AGG, SM/F twenty-year-old; *per fraseologia vedi* **cinquantenne**
ventennio, ni [ven'tεnnjo] SM period of twenty years; **il ventennio fascista** the Fascist period
ventesimo, a [ven'tεzimo] AGG, SM/F, SM twentieth; **il ventesimo secolo** the twentieth century; *per fraseologia vedi* **quinto**
venti ['venti] AGG INV, SM INV twenty; *per fraseologia vedi* **cinquanta**
ventilare [venti'lare] VT **1** (*stanza*) to air, ventilate; (*fig*: *idea, proposta*) to air **2** (*Agr*) to winnow
ventilato, a [venti'lato] AGG (*camera, zona*) airy; **poco ventilato** airless; **una zona troppo ventilata** a windy area
ventilatore [ventila'tore] SM (*per ambienti*) fan; (*Med*) ventilator
ventilazione [ventilat'tsjone] SF ventilation
ventina [ven'tina] SF: **una ventina (di)** around twenty, twenty or so, about twenty; *per fraseologia vedi* **cinquantina**
ventiquattro [venti'kwattro] AGG INV twenty-four; **ventiquattr'ore su ventiquattro** around the clock, 24 hours a day
■SM INV twenty-four; *per fraseologia vedi* **cinque**
ventiquattr'ore [ventikwat'trore] SFPL (*periodo*) twenty-four hours
■SF INV **1** (*valigetta*) overnight case **2** (*Sport*) twenty-four-hour race
ventisette [venti'sεtte] AGG INV twenty-seven
■SM INV: **il ventisette** (*giorno di paga*) ≈ (monthly) pay day *per fraseologia vedi* **cinque**
ventitré [venti'tre] AGG INV, SM INV twenty-three; *per fraseologia vedi* **cinque**
■SFPL: **portava il cappello sulle ventitré** he wore his hat at a jaunty angle
vento ['vεnto] SM wind; **un vento caldo** a warm wind; **c'è vento** it's windy; **un colpo di vento** a gust of wind; **a prova di vento** windproof; **contro vento** against the wind; **c'è una barca sopra/sotto vento** (*Naut*) there is a boat to windward/leeward of us; **con i capelli al vento** with windswept hair; **fatica buttata al vento** wasted effort; **parlare al vento** to waste one's breath; **non andare a dirlo ai quattro venti** don't go spreading it around; **un vento di rivolta** a wind of revolt; **qual buon vento ti porta?** to what do I (*o* we) owe the pleasure of seeing you?; **vento contrario** (*Naut*) headwind

LO SAPEVI...?
vento non si traduce mai con la parola inglese *vent*

ventola ['vεntola] SF (*Aut, Tecn*) fan

ventosa [ven'tosa] SF *(di gomma)* suction cap *o* pad; *(Zool)* sucker; **funziona a ventosa** it works by suction
ventoso, a [ven'toso] AGG windy; **questa zona è più ventosa** this area is windier
ventotto [ven'tɔtto] AGG INV, SM INV twenty-eight; *per fraseologia vedi* **cinque**
ventrale [ven'trale] AGG *(gen)* abdominal; *(pinna, diaframma)* ventral
ventre ['vɛntre] SM *(addome)* stomach; *(grembo)* womb; **avere dolori al ventre** to have (a) stomach ache; **sdraiato sul ventre** lying on one's stomach *o* front; **il ventre della terra** *(fig)* the depths of the earth; **il basso ventre** lower abdomen; **colpire qn al basso ventre** to hit sb in the groin
ventricolare [ventriko'lare] AGG *(Anat)* ventricular
ventricolo [ven'trikolo] SM ventricle
ventriglio, gli [ven'triʎʎo] SM *(Zool)* gizzard
ventriloquo, a [ven'trilokwo] SM/F ventriloquist
ventuno [ven'tuno] AGG INV, SM INV twenty-one; *per fraseologia vedi* **cinque**
ventura [ven'tura] SF fortune, chance; **andare alla ventura** to trust to luck; **soldato di ventura** mercenary; **compagnia di ventura** company of mercenaries
venturo, a [ven'turo] AGG next, coming
venuta [ve'nuta] SF coming, arrival; **per la venuta della regina hanno organizzato un ricevimento** they have organized a reception for the queen's visit
venuto, a [ve'nuto] PP *di* **venire**
■SM/F: **il primo venuto, la prima venuta** the first person who comes along
vera ['vera] SF wedding ring
verace [ve'ratʃe] AGG *(testimone)* truthful; *(testimonianza)* accurate, veracious; *(cibi)* real, genuine
veracità [veratʃi'ta] SF *(vedi agg)* truthfulness; accuracy, veracity; genuineness
veramente [vera'mente] AVV *(realmente)* really; **veramente?** really?; **è veramente bella** she's really beautiful; **è veramente cretino** he's a real idiot; **io, veramente, al posto tuo...** frankly, in your place, I ...; **veramente, non ne sapevo niente** actually, I didn't know anything about it
veranda [ve'randa] SF veranda(h)
verbale [ver'bale] AGG **1** *(orale)* verbal, spoken; **un accordo verbale** a verbal agreement **2** *(Gramm)* verbal
■SM *(di riunione)* minutes *pl*; *(Dir)* record; **le faccio il verbale** *(Polizia)* I'll have to report this; **mettere a verbale** to place in the minutes *o* on record
verbalmente [verbal'mente] AVV verbally
verbena [ver'bɛna] SF *(Bot)* vervain, verbena
verbo ['verbo] SM **1** *(Gramm)* verb; **un verbo transitivo** a transitive verb **2** *(parola)* word; **il Verbo** *(Rel)* the Word
verbosamente [verbosa'mente] AVV verbosely
verbosità [verbosi'ta] SF wordiness, verbosity
verboso, a [ver'boso] AGG wordy, verbose
vercellese [vertʃel'lese] AGG of *o* from Vercelli
■SM/F inhabitant *o* native of Vercelli
verdastro, a [ver'dastro] AGG greenish
verdazzurro, a [verdad'dzurro] AGG bluish green
verde ['verde] AGG **1** *(colore)* green; **verde dalla bile** livid *o* white with rage; **verde d'invidia** green with envy **2** *(acerbo: frutta)* green, unripe; *(legna)* green; **gli anni verdi** youth **3** *(Telec)*: **numero verde** freefone (line) **4** *(ecologista: associazione, gruppo)* green; *(ecologico)* ecological, green; **benzina verde** lead-free *o* unleaded petrol
■SM **1** *(colore)* green; **essere al verde** to be broke; **una camicia verde scuro** a dark green shirt; **verde bottiglia** bottle green; **verde oliva** olive green; **verde pisello** pea green **2** *(vegetazione)* greenery; **c'è molto verde in questa città** this city is very green; **una casa immersa nel verde** a house surrounded by greenery; **ho bisogno di un po' di verde** I feel in need of country air **3** *(semaforo)* green (light); **i Verdi** SMPL *(Pol)* the Greens
verdeggiante [verded'dʒante] AGG green, verdant
verdeggiare [verded'dʒare] VI *(aus* **avere***)* **una distesa di prati verdeggiava davanti a noi** green fields spread out before us; **qualcosa verdeggiava in lontananza** there was something green in the distance
verdemare [verde'mare] AGG INV, SM INV sea-green
verderame [verde'rame] SM *(Chim)* verdigris
verdetto [ver'detto] SM *(Dir, gen)* verdict
verdognolo, a [ver'doɲɲolo] AGG greenish
verdone [ver'done] SM *(Zool)* greenfinch
verdura [ver'dura] SF *(Culin)* vegetables *pl*; **non mi piace la verdura** I don't like vegetables; **minestra di verdura** vegetable soup; **negozio di frutta e verdura** fruit and vegetable shop, greengrocer's *(Brit)*
verecondia [vere'kondja] SF modesty
verecondo, a [vere'kondo] AGG modest
verga, ghe ['verga] SF *(bastone)* cane, rod; *(di pastore)* crook; **percuotere qn con la verga** to cane sb; **verga d'oro** *(lingotto)* gold bar; *(pianta)* goldenrod
vergare [ver'gare] VT **1** *(scrivere)* to write **2** *(percuotere)* to cane, beat
vergatina [verga'tina] SF *(anche:* **carta vergatina***: per macchina da scrivere)* flimsy
vergato, a [ver'gato] AGG: **carta vergata** laid paper
verginale [verdʒi'nale] AGG virginal, virgin *attr*
vergine ['verdʒine] SF **1** *(gen)* virgin; **la Vergine** the Virgin Mary *o* Mother **2** *(Astrol)*: **Vergine** Virgo; **essere della Vergine** to be Virgo
■AGG *(persona, terra)* virgin *attr*; **essere vergine** to be a virgin; **foresta vergine** virgin forest; **pura lana vergine** pure new wool; **olio vergine d'oliva** virgin olive oil; **cassetta vergine** blank cassette
verginità [verdʒini'ta] SF virginity; **rifarsi una verginità** *(fig)* to regain one's reputation, clear one's name
vergogna [ver'goɲɲa] SF **1** *(gen)* shame; *(timidezza)* shyness; *(imbarazzo)* embarrassment; **è arrossito per la vergogna** he went red with embarrassment; **provava vergogna per ciò che era successo** he felt ashamed about what had happened; **provo vergogna davanti a lui** he makes me feel shy; **vincere la propria vergogna** to overcome one's shyness; **non avere vergogna di nessuno** to be shameless; **sprofondare per la vergogna** to be overcome by embarrassment **2** *(onta, disonore)* disgrace; **è una vergogna!** it's a disgrace!; **è la vergogna della famiglia** he is a disgrace to his family
vergognarsi [vergoɲ'ɲarsi] VIP *(vedi sf 1)*: **vergognarsi (di)** to be *o* feel ashamed (of); to be *o* feel shy (about); be *o* feel embarrassed (about); **non ti vergogni di aver copiato all'esame?** aren't you ashamed that you copied in the exam?; **dai, suonaci qualcosa – no, mi vergogno** come on, play something – no, I'm embarrassed; **vergognati!** you should be ashamed of yourself!, shame on you!

Vv

vergognosamente [vergoɲɲosa'mente] AVV (*vedi agg*) timidly, shyly; shamefully; disgracefully
vergognoso, a [vergoɲ'ɲoso] AGG (*timido*) timid, shy; (*pieno di vergogna*) ashamed, embarrassed; (*che causa vergogna*) shameful; (*che causa disonore*) disgraceful; **è vergognoso che debbano ancora succedere cose simili!** it's outrageous that such things still happen!
veridicità [veriditʃi'ta] SF truthfulness; **nessuno mette in dubbio la veridicità delle sue parole** nobody doubts the truth of what he said
veridico, a, ci, che [ve'ridiko] AGG truthful
verifica, che [ve'rifika] SF **1** checking *no pl*; **fare una verifica di** (*freni, testimonianza, firma*) to check; **questo lavoro è una continua verifica delle proprie capacità** (*fig*) this work is a continual test of one's abilities **2** (*Fin*): **verifica contabile** audit
verificabile [verifi'kabile] AGG verifiable
verificabilità [verifikabili'ta] SF verifiability
verificare [verifi'kare] VT **1** (*controllare*: *verità*) to check, verify **2** (*Fin*) to audit **3** (*Mat*: *teoria, postulato*) to prove
▶ **verificarsi** VIP (*accadere*) to happen, occur, take place; (*avverarsi*) to prove (to be)
verità [veri'ta] SF INV **1** (*gen*) truth; **hai detto la verità?** did you tell the truth?; **la pura verità** the absolute truth; **la verità nuda e cruda** the plain unvarnished truth; **è una verità sacrosanta** it's gospel; **travisare la verità** to distort the truth; **a dire la verità** *or* **per la verità** to tell the truth, actually; **macchina della verità** lie-detector; **siero della verità** truth serum **2** (*assioma*) truth; **le verità scientifiche** scientific truths
veritiero, a [veri'tjɛro] AGG (*conforme a verità*) true, accurate; (*che dice la verità*) truthful
verme ['vɛrme] SM (*gen, fig*) worm; (*di frutto, formaggio*) maggot; **nudo come un verme** stark naked; **mi sento un verme!** (*fig*) I could die!, I feel awful!; **verme solitario** tapeworm
vermicelli [vermi'tʃɛlli] SMPL (*pasta*) vermicelli *sg*
vermifugo, a [ver'mifugo] AGG, SM vermifuge
vermiglio, glia, gli, glie [ver'miʎʎo] AGG, SM vermilion, scarlet
Vermont [ver'mont] SM Vermont
vermouth, vermut ['vɛrmut] SM INV vermouth
vernacolo, a [ver'nakolo] AGG, SM vernacular
vernice [ver'nitʃe] SF **1** (*trasparente*) varnish; (*pittura*: *lucida*) gloss (paint); (: *opaca*) matt (paint); **"vernice fresca"** "wet paint" **2** (*pelle*) patent leather; **scarpe/borsa di vernice** patent leather shoes/bag
verniciare [verni'tʃare] VT (*con vernice trasparente*) to varnish; (*pitturare*) to paint
verniciatore [vernitʃa'tore] SM **1** (*operaio*) varnisher **2** (*dispositivo*): **verniciatore a spruzzo** spray gun
verniciatura [vernitʃa'tura] SF (*con vernice trasparente*) varnishing; (*con vernice colorata*) painting
verniero [ver'njɛro] SM (*calibro*) vernier
vernissage [vɛrni'saʒ] SM INV (*Arte*) preview
vero, a ['vero] AGG (*gen*) true; (*reale*) real; (*autentico*) genuine; **vero o falso?** true or false?; **questa è una storia vera** this is a true story; **incredibile ma vero** incredible but true; **vero e proprio** real; **questo è un vero e proprio affare** this is a real bargain; **un vero e proprio delinquente** a real criminal, an out and out criminal; **il suo vero nome è Giovanni** his real *o* true name is Giovanni; **ma è vero questo Modigliani?** is this a genuine *o* real Modigliani?; **perle vere** genuine pearls; **quei fiori sembrano veri** those flowers look real; **il vero problema è...** the real problem is ...; **fosse vero!** if only it were true!; **nulla di più vero!** you've said it!, how true!; **non mi pare vero!** it doesn't seem possible!; **come è vero Dio** I swear to God; **tant'è vero che...** so much so that ...; **vero?** isn't that right?; **hai tu il mio libro, vero?** you've got my book, haven't you?; **sei italiano, vero?** you're Italian, aren't you?; **questa è la tua macchina, vero?** this is your car, isn't it?; **è andata stamattina, vero?** she went this morning, didn't she?; **vorresti andare, vero?** you'd like to go, wouldn't you?; **ti piace la cioccolata, vero?** you like chocolate, don't you?
■ SM (*verità*) truth; **c'è del vero in ciò che dice** there is some truth in what he says; **sto dicendo il vero** I am telling the truth; **a onor del vero** *or* **a dire il vero** to tell the truth; **è una copia dal vero** (*disegno*) it's a copy from life
Verona [ve'rɔna] SF Verona
veronese [vero'nese] AGG, SM/F Veronese *inv*
veronica¹ [ve'rɔnika] SF (*Bot*) veronica
veronica² [ve'rɔnika] SF (*in corrida*) veronica
verosimiglianza [verosimiʎ'ʎantsa] SF (*vedi agg*) likelihood, probability; plausibility
verosimile [vero'simile] AGG (*racconto, ipotesi*) likely, probable; (*trama*) plausible, convincing; **poco verosimile** (*racconto*) improbable, unlikely; (*trama*) implausible
verosimilmente [verosimil'mente] AVV realistically
verro ['vɛrro] SM (*Zool*) boar
verrò *ecc* [ver'rɔ] VB *vedi* **venire**
verruca, che [ver'ruka] SF (*Med, Bot*) verruca, wart
vers. ABBR = **versamento**
versaccio, ci [ver'sattʃo] SM: **fare i versacci (a qn)** (*smorfie*) to make faces (at sb); (*grida di scherno*) to jeer (at sb)
versamento [versa'mento] SM **1** (*gen*) payment; (*deposito in banca*) deposit; **modulo** *o* **distinta di versamento** (*Banca*) pay-in slip **2** (*Med*) effusion
versante [ver'sante] SM (*Geog*) side, slopes *pl*; **sul versante del lavoro non ci sono novità** there's no news on the work front
versare¹ [ver'sare] VT **1** (*liquido, polvere*) to pour; (*servire*: *caffè*) to pour (out); **versare da bere a qn** to pour sb a drink; **mi versi un po' d'acqua?** can you pour me some water?; **versare la minestra** to serve (up) the soup; **versare a filo** (*olio*) to drizzle **2** (*spargere*: *liquidi, polvere*) to spill; (: *lacrime, sangue*) to shed; **mi sono versato il caffè addosso** I've spilt coffee over myself; **ho versato un po' di vino sulla tovaglia** I spilt some wine on the tablecloth; **versare acqua sul fuoco** (*fig*) to pour oil on troubled waters **3** **il Po versa le proprie acque nell'Adriatico** the Po flows into the Adriatic **4** (*Econ*: *pagare*) to pay; (: *depositare*) to deposit, pay in; **ho versato la somma sul mio conto** I paid the sum into my account, I deposited the sum in my account; **vorrei versare duecentocinquanta euro sul mio conto corrente** I'd like to pay two hundred and fifty euros into my current account; **versare una cauzione** to pay a deposit
▶ **versarsi** VIP **1** (*rovesciarsi*) to spill; **il latte si è versato sul fuoco** the milk has boiled over **2** **versarsi in** (*sogg*: *fiume*) to flow into; (: *folla*) to pour into
versare² [ver'sare] VI (*aus* **avere**) **versare in fin di vita** to be dying; **versare in gravi difficoltà** to find o.s. with serious problems

versatile [ver'satile] AGG versatile
versatilità [versatili'ta] SF versatility
versato, a [ver'sato] AGG: **essere versato in** to be (well-)versed in
verseggiare [versed'dʒare] VT to put into verse
■ VI (*aus* **avere**) to write verse, write poetry
■ SM verse, poetry
versetto [ver'setto] SM (*di poesia*) line; (*Rel*) verse
versione [ver'sjone] SF **1** (*gen*) version; **vorrei sentire la sua versione dell'accaduto** I'd like to hear her version of what happened; **una versione più aggiornata della guida** a more up-to-date edition of the guide; **in versione originale** (*libro*) in the original (version); (*film*) in the original language *o* version; **la versione cinematografica del suo ultimo libro** the film of his latest book; **versione lusso** (*Aut*) luxury model; **versione 4 porte** (*Aut*) 4-door model **2** (*traduzione*) translation
verso[1] ['vɛrso] SM INV (*di pagina*) verso; (*di moneta*) reverse
verso[2] ['vɛrso] SM **1** (*di animale, uccello*) call, cry; **qual è il verso del gatto?** what noise *o* sound does a cat make?; **che verso fa il maiale?** what noise does a pig make?; **verso di richiamo** call; **ha fatto un verso di dolore** she cried out in pain *o* gave a cry of pain; **smettila di fare tutti quei versi** stop making those noises; **fare il verso a qn** (*imitare*) to take sb off, mimic sb; **faceva il verso al professore** he mimicked the teacher **2** (*riga: di poesia*) line, verse; **versi** SMPL (*poesia*) verse *sg*; **in versi** in verse; **versi sciolti** blank verse *sg* **3** (*direzione, Mat*) direction; (*di legno, stoffa*) grain; **prendere qn/qc per il verso giusto** to approach sb/sth the right way; **non c'è verso di convincerlo** it is impossible to persuade him, there's no way of persuading him, he can't be persuaded; **non c'è verso di fargli cambiare idea** there's no way of making him change his mind; **per un verso o per l'altro** one way or another; **per un verso sono d'accordo, per l'altro...** on the one hand I agree (with you), but on the other ...; **chi per un verso, chi per un altro tutti decisero di partire** for one reason or another they all decided to leave
verso[3] ['vɛrso] PREP **1** (*in direzione di*) toward(s), to; **andando verso la stazione** going towards the station; **stavo camminando verso la stazione quando l'ho visto** I was walking towards the station when I saw him; **è tardi, faremmo bene ad avviarci verso casa** it's late, we'd better head for home; **veniva verso di me** he was coming towards me; **verso l'alto** upwards; **verso il basso** downwards; **tirare l'anello verso il basso** pull the ring downwards; **guardare verso il cielo** to look heavenwards *o* skywards; **navigare verso sud** to sail south(wards) **2** (*nei pressi di*) near, around (about); **abito verso il centro** I live near the centre (*Brit*) *o* center (*Am*) **3** (*in senso temporale*) about, around; **arrivi verso che ora?** around *o* about what time will you arrive?; **arriverò verso le sette** I'll be there at around seven; **verso sera** towards evening; **verso la fine dell'anno** towards the end of the year; **ci rivediamo verso la fine di novembre** I'll see you around the end of November **4** (*nei confronti di*) for, towards; **dimostrare rispetto verso gli anziani** to show respect for *o* towards the elderly
vertebra ['vɛrtebra] SF vertebra
vertebrale [verte'brale] AGG vertebral; **colonna vertebrale** spinal column, spine
vertebrato, a [verte'brato] AGG, SM vertebrate
vertenza [ver'tɛntsa] SF (*lite*) lawsuit, case; (*sindacale*) dispute
vertere ['vɛrtere] VI DIF: **vertere su** to deal with, be about
verticale [verti'kale] AGG vertical; **in posizione verticale** in an upright position
■ SF **1** (*linea*) vertical **2** (*Ginnastica: sulle mani*) handstand; (*: sulla testa*) headstand; **fare la verticale** to do a handstand (*o* headstand) **3** (*nei cruciverba*) clue (*o* word) down
verticalmente [vertikal'mente] AVV vertically
vertice ['vɛrtitʃe] SM **1** (*Geom*) vertex **2** (*vetta*) summit, peak, top; (*fig: punto più alto*) peak, height; **il vertice della carriera** the peak of one's career **3** (*Pol*) summit; **incontro/conferenza al vertice** summit meeting/conference
vertigine [ver'tidʒine] SF giddiness *no pl*, dizziness *no pl*, dizzy spell; (*Med*) vertigo; **soffrire di vertigini** to be afraid of heights, have vertigo (*termine tecn*); **mi fa venire le vertigini** it makes my head spin; **avere le vertigini** to feel dizzy
vertiginosamente [vertidʒinosa'mente] AVV (*girare*) dizzily; **aumentare/diminuire vertiginosamente** (*prezzi*) to rise/fall steeply
vertiginoso, a [vertidʒi'noso] AGG (*altezza*) dizzy; (*velocità*) breakneck *attr*; (*danza*) breathless; (*cifra*) exorbitant; (*scollatura*) plunging; **il ritmo vertiginoso della vita moderna** the frenetic pace of modern life
verve [vɛrv] SF INV verve
verza ['verdza] SF Savoy cabbage
vescia, sce ['veʃʃa] SF (*fungo*) puffball
vescica, che [veʃ'ʃika] SF **1** (*Anat*) bladder **2** (*Med: bolla*) blister; **ho una vescica sul piede** I've got a blister on my foot
vescovado [vesko'vado] SM (*Rel: diocesi*) bishopric; (*: sede*) bishop's palace
vescovile [vesko'vile] AGG episcopal
vescovo ['veskovo] SM bishop
vespa[1] ['vɛspa] SF (*Zool*) wasp; **ha un vitino di vespa** she's wasp-waisted
vespa[2]® ['vɛspa] SF (motor) scooter, Vespa®
vespaio, ai [ves'pajo] SM wasps' nest; **suscitare un vespaio** (*fig*) to stir up a hornets' nest
Vespasiano [vespa'zjano] SM (*Storia*) Vespasian
vespasiano [vespa'zjano] SM urinal
vespro ['vɛspro] SM (*letter: sera*) evening; (*Rel*) vespers *pl*
vessare [ves'sare] VT (*letter*) to oppress
vessazione [vessat'tsjone] SF (*letter*) oppression
vessillo [ves'sillo] SM (*Mil*) standard; (*bandiera*) flag; (*fig*) banner, ensign; **il vessillo della libertà** the banner of freedom
vestaglia [ves'taʎʎa] SF dressing gown (*Brit*), bathrobe (*Am*)
vestale [ves'tale] SF vestal virgin
veste ['vɛste] SF **1** (*gen*) garment; (*da donna*) dress; (*di monaco, suora*) habit; **vesti** SFPL clothes, clothing *sg*; **veste da camera** dressing gown (*Brit*), bathrobe (*Am*) **2** (*fig: di libro*): **veste editoriale** layout **3** (*funzione*) capacity; (*fig: apparenza*) appearance; **in veste di** (in one's capacity) as; **in veste ufficiale** in an official capacity; **si è presentato in veste di amico** he passed himself off as a friend

LO SAPEVI...?
veste non si traduce mai con la parola inglese *vest*

vestiario, ri [ves'tjarjo] SM wardrobe, clothes *pl*; **capo di vestiario** article of clothing, garment

Vv

vestibolo [ves'tibolo] SM **1** (*ingresso*) (entrance) hall; (*Archeol*) vestibule **2** (*Anat*) vestibule
vestigia [ves'tidʒa] SFPL **1** (*tracce*) vestiges, traces **2** (*rovine*) ruins, remains
vestire [ves'tire] VT **1** (*gen*): **vestire (di)** to dress (in); (*mascherare*): **vestire da** to dress up as **2** (*provvedere degli indumenti necessari*) to clothe; **Valentino veste le attrici più famose** Valentino makes *o* designs clothes for all the most famous actresses **3** (*indossare*: *stato*) to wear, have on; (: *atto*) to put on
■ VI (*aus* **essere**) (*indossare*) to wear; (*abbigliarsi*) to dress; **vestire di bianco/a lutto** to wear white/mourning; **vestire con eleganza** to dress smartly; **questa giacca veste bene** this is a well-cut jacket;
▶ **vestirsi** VR (*gen*) to dress, get dressed; (*abbigliarsi*) to dress; **vestirsi da** (*negozio*) to buy *o* get one's clothes at; (*sarto*) to have one's clothes made at; **vestirsi da pirata/Peter Pan** to dress up as a pirate/Peter Pan; **si è vestito da donna** he dressed up as a woman; **vestirsi a festa** to wear one's Sunday best *o* one's best clothes; **vestirsi a lutto** to wear mourning; **vestirsi bene/con gusto** to dress well/tastefully; **si veste bene** she dresses well; **vestiti, che usciamo** get dressed, we're going out; **si è vestito in fretta ed è uscito** he got dressed quickly and went out; **come mi devo vestire stasera?** what should I wear this evening?
vestito[1], a [ves'tito] AGG dressed; **vestito di bianco** dressed in white; **vestito da** (*in maschera*) dressed up as; **vestito di tutto punto** all dressed up; **dormire vestito** to sleep in one's clothes
vestito[2] [ves'tito] SM (*gen*) garment; (*abito*: *da donna*) dress; (: *da uomo*) suit; **vestiti** SMPL clothes; **ho messo alcuni vestiti in valigia** I put some clothes in a suitcase; **cambiare vestiti** to change one's clothes; **farsi fare un vestito** to have a dress (*o* suit) made
Vesuvio [ve'zuvjo] SM Vesuvius
veterano, a [vete'rano] SM (*Mil*) veteran
■ SM/F (*fig*) veteran, old hand
veterinaria [veteri'narja] SF veterinary medicine
veterinario, ria, ri, rie [veteri'narjo] AGG veterinary
■ SM vet (*Brit*), veterinary surgeon (*Brit*), veterinarian (*Am*)
veto ['vɛto] SM (*Dir, fig*) veto; **diritto di veto** right of veto; **porre il veto a qc** to veto sth
vetraio, ai [ve'trajo] SM (*gen*) glazier, glass-worker; (*chi soffia il vetro*) glass-blower, glassmaker
vetrata [ve'trata] SF glass door (*o* window); (*di chiesa*) stained-glass window
vetrato, a [ve'trato] AGG glass *attr*; (*porta, finestra*) glazed; **carta vetrata** sandpaper
vetreria [vetre'ria] SF (*fabbrica*) glassworks *inv*; (*oggetti di vetro*) glassware *no pl*
vetrificante [vetrifi'kante] AGG vitrescent
vetrificare [vetrifi'kare] VT to vitrify; (*ceramica*) to glaze
▶ **vetrificarsi** VIP to vitrify
vetrificazione [vetrifikat'tsjone] SF vitrification
vetrina [ve'trina] SF **1** (*di negozio*) (shop) window; **in vetrina** in the window; **c'è una gonna che mi piace in vetrina** there's a skirt I like in the window; **allestire una vetrina** to dress a window; **andare a guardare le vetrine** to go window-shopping; **mettersi in vetrina** (*fig*) to show off **2** (*rassegna*) showcase **3** (*mobile*: *di museo*) showcase, display cabinet; (: *di negozio*) display cabinet
vetrinista, i, e [vetri'nista] SM/F window dresser; **fa la vetrinista** she's a window dresser
vetrinistica [vetri'nistika] SF window dressing
vetrino [ve'trino] SM (*di microscopio*) slide
vetriolo [vetri'ɔlo] SM vitriol; **al vetriolo** (*fig*: *critica, risposta*) vitriolic
vetro ['vetro] SM **1** (*materiale*) glass; (*frammento*) piece of glass; (*scheggia*) splinter of glass; **un vaso di vetro** a glass vase; **lana di vetro** glass fibre (*Brit*) *o* fiber (*Am*); **fibra di vetro** fibreglass (*Brit*) *o* fiberglass (*Am*); **mettere qc sotto vetro** to put sth under glass **2** (*di finestra, porta*) (window) pane; (*di orologio*) watch glass; **devo pulire i vetri** I have to clean the windows; **porta a vetri** glass door **3** (*oggetto*): **i vetri di Murano** Murano glassware *sg*
■ **vetro blindato** bulletproof glass; **vetro infrangibile** shatterproof glass; **vetro di sicurezza** safety glass; **vetro smerigliato** frosted glass
▷ www.vetrodimurano.org/
vetroresina [vetro'rɛzina] SF fibreglass (*Brit*) *o* fiberglass (*Am*)
vetroso, a [ve'troso] AGG vitreous
vetta ['vetta] SF (*di montagna*) top, summit, peak; (*di albero*) top; **abbiamo raggiunto la vetta in quattro ore** we reached the summit in four hours; **toccare le più alte vette del successo** to reach the top of the ladder; **essere in vetta alla classifica** (*squadra*) to be at the top of the league; (*canzone*) to be at the top of the charts
vettore [vet'tore] SM **1** (*Mat, Fis*) vector **2** (*trasportatore*) carrier
■ AGG: **razzo vettore** booster rocket
vettoriale [vetto'rjale] AGG (*Mat*) vectorial; **calcolo vettoriale** vector analysis
vettovagliamento [vettovaʎʎa'mento] SM provisioning
vettovagliare [vettovaʎ'ʎare] VT to supply with provisions, provision
vettovaglie [vetto'vaʎʎe] SFPL provisions, supplies
vettura [vet'tura] SF **1** (*carrozza*) coach, carriage; **vettura di piazza** hackney carriage **2** (*Ferr*) coach, carriage (*Brit*), car (*Am*); **in vettura!** all aboard! **3** (*auto*) car, automobile (*Am*); **vettura da noleggio senza autista** car for self-drive hire (*Brit*) *o* rent (*Am*)
vetturino [vettu'rino] SM coach driver, coachman
vezzeggiamento [vettseddʒa'mento] SM caressing
vezzeggiare [vettsed'dʒare] VT to make a fuss of
vezzeggiativo, a [vettseddʒa'tivo] AGG of endearment
■ SM term of endearment
vezzo ['vettso] SM **1** (*abitudine*) (affected) habit; **avere il vezzo di fare qc** to have the habit of doing sth **2** (*gesto affettuoso*) caress **3** **vezzi** SMPL (*moine*) affected ways; (*grazia*) charm *sg*, charms
vezzosamente [vettsosa'mente] AVV (*vedi agg*) charmingly; affectedly
vezzosità [vettsosi'ta] SF INV (*grazia*) charm; (*leziosità*) affected ways *pl*, affectation
vezzoso, a [vet'tsoso] AGG **1** (*grazioso*) pretty, charming **2** (*lezioso*) affected
■ SM/F: **fare il(la) vezzoso(a)** to turn on the charm
VF ABBR = **vigili del fuoco**
V.G. ABBR = *Vostra Grazia*
VI SIGLA = *Vicenza*
vi [vi] (*dav* lo, la, li, le, ne *diventa* ve) PRON PERS **1** (*ogg diretto*) you; **vi stavo cercando** I was looking for you; **vorrei aiutarvi** I'd like to help you **2** (*complemento di termine*) (to) you; **ve l'hanno dato** they gave it to you; **vi darò un consiglio** I'll give you some advice; **vi**

scriverò I'll write to you; **vi ha salutato?** did he say hello to you?; **ve lo do subito** I'll give it to you in a moment; **vi ha sorriso** he smiled at you **3** (*riflessivo*) yourselves; (*reciproco*) each other; **vestitevi** get dressed; **pettinatevi** comb your hair; **divertitevi** enjoy yourselves; **vi siete divertiti?** did you enjoy yourselves?; **vi siete fatti male?** did you hurt yourselves?; **ve ne pentirete** you'll regret it; **vi conoscete?** do you know each other?

■ PRON DIMOSTR = **ci**

■ AVV (*in questo luogo*) here; (*in quel luogo*) there; **vi sono stato parecchie volte** I've been there several times; **non vi erano che pochi turisti** there were only a few tourists there; **vi sono molti modi di farlo** there are many ways of doing it

VIA ['via] SIGLA F (= **Valutazione d'Impatto Ambientale**) environmental (impact) study

via[1] ['via] SF **1** (*strada*) road; (: *di città*) street, road; (*cammino*) way; (*percorso*) route; (*sentiero, pista*) path, track; **abito in una via molto stretta** i live in a very narrow street; **abito in via Manzoni 5** i live at number 5, Via Manzoni; **la via dell'oppio** the opium trail; **vie di comunicazione** communication routes; **che via fai di solito?** what route do you usually take?; **sulla via di casa** on one's way home; **hai via libera** (*a un incrocio*) the road is clear; **dare via libera a qc** (*fig*) to give the green light *o* the go-ahead; **allontanarsi dalla retta via** (*fig*) to stray from the straight and narrow; **in via di guarigione** on the road to recovery; **paese in via di sviluppo** developing country; **la sua laurea gli apre molte vie** his degree offers him many possibilities **2** (*mezzo*) way, means; (*procedimento*) channels *pl*; (*fig: modo*) way; **tentare tutte le vie** to try everything possible; **per vie traverse** by underhand means; **non avevo altra via** I had no alternative; **non c'è via di scampo** *o* **d'uscita** there's no way out; **via di mezzo** halfway; **è una via di mezzo tra...** it's halfway between...; **non c'è via di mezzo** there's no middle ground; **scegliere la via di mezzo** to compromise; **te lo dico in via privata** *o* **confidenziale** I'm telling you in confidence; (*ufficiosamente*) I'm telling you unofficially; **in via eccezionale** as an exception; **in via provvisoria** provisionally; **in via amichevole** in a friendly manner; **comporre una disputa in via amichevole** (*Dir*) to settle a dispute out of court; **adire le vie legali** to take legal proceedings; **le vie del Signore** the ways of the Lord; **passare alle vie di fatto** to resort to violence; **per via aerea** by air; **spedire per via aerea** to send by airmail; **via satellite** by satellite; **via Dover** via Dover; **per via di** because of, on account of **3** (*Anat*) tract; **le vie respiratorie** the respiratory tracts; **per via orale** (*Med*) orally **4** (*Astron*): **la Via Lattea** the Milky Way

via[2] ['via] AVV **1** (*allontanamento*) away; (: *temporaneo*) out; **buttare** *o* **gettare via qc** to throw sth away; **l'ho buttato via** i threw it away; **tagliare via** to cut off *o* away; **dare via qc** to give sth away; **è andato via** (*per poco tempo*) he has gone out; (*per molto tempo*) he has gone away; **sono stato via per 3 settimane** I was away for three weeks; **vai via!** go away!, clear off! (*fam*); **questa macchia non va via** this mark won't come out **2** (*eccetera*): **e così via** and so on; **e via dicendo** *or* **e via di questo passo** and so on (and so forth) **3** **via via** (*pian piano*) gradually; **via via che** (*man mano*) as

■ **via da** PREP away from; **non andare via da me** don't leave me

■ ESCL (*suvvia*) come on!; (*allontanati*) go away!; (: *a un animale*) shoo!; **pronti, via!** ready, steady, go!

■ SM (*Sport*) (signal to) start, starting signal; **dare il via** to start the race, give the starting signal; **quando darai il via?** when are you going to give the starting signal?; **dare il via a un progetto** to give the green light to a project; **hanno dato il via ai lavori** they've begun *o* started work

viabilità [viabili'ta] SF (*percorribilità*) practicability; (*rete stradale*) roads *pl*, road network; **la viabilità è interrotta a causa di una frana** the road is blocked because of a landslide; **un piano per migliorare la viabilità del centro** a plan to improve traffic circulation in the centre (*Brit*) *o* center (*Am*)

Viacard® [via'kard] SF INV *credit card used to pay motorway tolls*

via crucis [via'krutʃis] SF (*Rel*): **la Via Crucis** the Way of the Cross; **la sua vita da emigrato è stata una via crucis** his life as an emigrant has been purgatory *o* a real trial

viado [vi'ado] SM INV *Brazilian transsexual prostitute*

viadotto [via'dotto] SM viaduct

viaggiare [viad'dʒare] VI (*aus* **avere**) **1** (*gen*) to travel; **mi piace viaggiare** I like travelling (*Brit*) *o* traveling (*Am*); **viaggi spesso per lavoro?** do you travel much for your job?; **viaggiare in treno/aereo** to travel by train/plane; **è uno che ha viaggiato molto** he's well-travel(l)ed, he has travel(l)ed a lot; **la macchina viaggiava a 50 chilometri all'ora** the car was travel(l)ing at (a speed of) 50 kilometres per hour; **il treno viaggia con 50 minuti di ritardo** the train is running 50 minutes late; **le merci viaggiano via mare** the goods go *o* are sent by sea **2** (*fare il commesso viaggiatore*): **viaggiare per una ditta** to be a travel(l)ing salesman *o* a sales representative for a company; **viaggio in tessuti** I travel in textiles

viaggiatore, trice [viaddʒa'tore] AGG travelling (*Brit*), traveling (*Am*); **piccione viaggiatore** carrier pigeon; **commesso viaggiatore** travel(l)ing salesman

■ SM/F (*gen*) traveller (*Brit*), traveler (*Am*); (*passeggero*) passenger

viaggio, gi [vi'addʒo] SM (*gen*) travel, travelling (*Brit*), traveling (*Am*); (*tragitto*) journey, trip; (*in aereo*) flight; (*via mare*) voyage; **buon viaggio!** have a good trip!; **avete fatto buon viaggio?** did you have a good journey?; **è stato un viaggio molto faticoso** it was a very tiring journey; **vorrei fare un viaggio in Cina** I'd like to visit China; **è in viaggio** he's away; **agenzia di viaggi** travel agency; **spese di viaggio** travel(l)ing expenses; **ho dovuto fare due viaggi per portar su i libri** I had to make two trips to bring the books up; **fare un viaggio a vuoto** to make a wasted journey; **mi hanno rimborsato il viaggio** they gave me my travel(l)ing expenses; **buon viaggio!** have a good trip!; **viaggio d'affari** business trip; **papà è in viaggio d'affari** Dad's on a business trip; **viaggio di nozze** honeymoon; **dove andranno in viaggio di nozze?** where are they going on their honeymoon?; **viaggio organizzato** package tour *o* holiday; **sono andato a Praga con un viaggio organizzato** I went to Prague on a package tour; **viaggio di piacere** pleasure trip

Viagra ['vjagra] SM Viagra®

viale [vi'ale] SM **1** (*in città*) avenue **2** (*in parco*) path, walk **3** **è sul viale del tramonto** his star is on the wane

viandante [vian'dante] SM/F wayfarer

viario, ria, ri, rie [vi'arjo] AGG (*Aut*): **rete viaria** road network; (*in città*) street network

viatico, ci [vi'atiko] SM (*Rel*) viaticum
viavai [via'vai] SM INV coming and going, bustle; **c'era un gran viavai** there was a lot of coming and going
vibonese, a [vibo'nese] AGG of *o* from Vibo Valentia ■SM/F inhabitant *o* native of Vibo Valentia
vibrafono [vi'brafono] SM vibraphone
vibrante [vi'brante] AGG (*membrana*) vibrating; (*voce, suono*) vibrant, resonant; **vibrante di** vibrant with
vibrare [vi'brare] VT (*dare con forza*): **vibrare un colpo a qn** to strike sb; **vibrare una coltellata a qn** to stab sb ■VI (*aus* **avere**) **1** (*gen, Fis*) to vibrate; **vibrare (di)** (*voce*) to quiver (with), be vibrant (with); **il suo cuore vibrava di emozione** her heart throbbed with emotion **2** (*risuonare*) to resound, ring
vibrato [vi'brato] SM (*Mus*) vibrato
vibratore, trice [vibra'tore] AGG vibrating ■SM vibrator
vibratorio, ria, ri, rie [vibra'tɔrjo] AGG vibratory
vibrazione [vibrat'tsjone] SF vibration
vibrissa [vi'brissa] SF (*Zool*) vibrissa
vibromassaggiatore [vibromassaddʒa'tore] SM: **vibromassaggiatore (elettrico)** vibrator
viburno [vi'burno] SM (*Bot*) viburnum
vicario, ri [vi'karjo] SM (*Rel*) vicar
vice ['vitʃe] SM/F deputy
vice- ['vitʃe] PREF vice-; **viceammiraglio** vice-admiral
viceconsole [vitʃe'kɔnsole] SM vice-consul
vicedirettore, trice [vitʃediret'tore] SM/F (*gen*) deputy manager/manageress, assistant manager/manageress; (*di giornale*) deputy editor; (*di scuola*) deputy headmaster/headmistress (*Brit*), vice-principal (*Am*)
vicenda [vi'tʃɛnda] SF **1** (*episodio*) event; **il libro parla delle vicende che hanno portato alla guerra** the book discusses the events that led up to the war; **è una vicenda estremamente complicata** it's an extremely complicated story **2 vicende** SFPL (*sorte*) fortunes; **con alterne vicende** with mixed fortunes; **a vicenda** ■AVV **1** (*reciprocamente*) each other, one another; **ci siamo aiutati a vicenda** we helped each other **2** (*alternativamente*) in turn(s)
vicendevole [vitʃen'devole] AGG mutual, reciprocal
vicendevolmente [vitʃendevol'mente] AVV each other, one another, mutually; **si rimproverano vicendevolmente** they blame each other
vicentino, a [vitʃen'tino] AGG of *o* from Vicenza ■SM/F inhabitant *o* native of Vicenza
vicepreside [vitʃe'preside] SM/F deputy headmaster/headmistress (*Brit*), vice-principal (*Am*)
vicepresidente [vitʃepresi'dɛnte] SM (*di stato*) vice-president; (*di società*) vice-chairman
vicepresidenza [vitʃepresi'dɛntsa] SF (*di stato*) vice-presidency; (*di società*) vice-chairmanship
viceré [vitʃe're] SM INV viceroy
vicesegretario, ri [vitʃesegre'tarjo] SM vice-secretary, deputy secretary
viceversa [vitʃe'vɛrsa] AVV vice versa; **da Roma a Pisa e viceversa** from Rome to Pisa and back
vichingo, a, ghi, ghe [vi'kingo] AGG, SM/F Viking
vicinanza [vitʃi'nantsa] SF **1** (*prossimità*) proximity, closeness, nearness **2 vicinanze** SFPL (*paraggi*) vicinity *sg*; **nelle vicinanze ci sono due panettieri** there are two bakers in the vicinity *o* in the area
vicinato [vitʃi'nato] SM (*zona*) neighbourhood (*Brit*), neighborhood (*Am*); (*vicini*) neighbo(u)rs *pl*; **avere rapporti di buon vicinato** to get on well with one's neighbo(u)rs
vicino, a [vi'tʃino] AGG **1** (*a poca distanza*) near, nearby; (*: paese*) neighbouring (*Brit*), neighboring (*Am*), nearby; **vicino a** near, close to; **un paese vicino** a nearby village; **l'interruttore della luce è vicino alla porta** the light switch is near the door; **la stazione è vicina** the station is near, the station is close (by); **dov'è il ristorante più vicino?** where is the nearest restaurant?; **quei quadri sono troppo vicini** those pictures are too close (together *o* to each other); **mi sono stati molto vicini** (*fig*) they were very supportive towards me **2** (*accanto*) next; **la mia stanza è vicina alla tua** my room is next to yours **3** (*nel tempo*) near, close at hand; **la fine è vicina** the end is near *o* imminent; **siamo vicini alla fine** we've almost *o* nearly finished; **le vacanze sono vicine** the holidays are (*Brit*) *o* the vacation is (*Am*) approaching; **è vicina ai trent'anni** she's almost thirty ■AVV **1** (*a poca distanza*) near, nearby, close (by); (*: nel tempo*) near, close; **vieni più vicino** come closer; **abitiamo qui vicino** we live near here; **stai vicino!** stay close to me! **2 da vicino** close to; (*esaminare, seguire*) closely; (*sparare*) at close quarters; **guardare qc da vicino** to take a close look at sth; **guardalo da vicino!** take a close look at it!; **da vicino è più bella** she's much prettier when you see her close up; **fai la fotografia da vicino** take the photograph close up **3 vicino a** close to, near (to); (*accanto a*) beside, next to; **vivono vicino al mare** they live close to *o* near the sea; **era seduto vicino a me** he was sitting near me; (*accanto a*) he was sitting next to *o* beside me; **state vicino a vostro padre** (*anche fig*) stay close to your father; **ci sono andato vicino** (*fig: quasi indovinato*) I almost got it ■SM/F neighbour (*Brit*), neighbor (*Am*); **i nostri vicini di casa** our next-door neighbo(u)rs; **il mio vicino di banco** the person at the desk next to mine, my neighbo(u)r
vicissitudini [vitʃissi'tudini] SFPL trials and tribulations; **le vicissitudini della vita** the ups and downs of life
vicolo ['vikolo] SM alley; **vicolo cieco** blind alley
videata [vide'ata] SF (*Inform*) screenful
video ['video] SM INV **1** (*TV: schermo*) screen; **ci sono dei disturbi al video** the picture is not very good **2** (*Inform: schermo*) screen; (*: videoterminale*) visual display unit **3** (*video musicale*) video
videocamera [video'kamera] SF camcorder
videocassetta [videokas'setta] SF videocassette; **abbiamo noleggiato una videocassetta** we rented a video
videocitofono [videotʃi'tɔfono] SM video entryphone
videoclip [video'klip] SF INV video clip
videocomunicare [videokomuni'kare] VI (*aus* **avere**) to communicate via videophone
videocomunicazione [videokomunikat'tsjone] SF video communication
videoconferenza [videokonfe'rɛnza] SF videoconference
videodipendente [videodipen'dɛnte] SM/F telly addict ■AGG: **un pigrone videodipendente** a couch potato
videodipendenza [videodipen'dɛntsa] SF addiction to TV
videofonino [videofo'nino] SM video mobile
videogioco, chi [video'dʒɔko] SM video game

videoleso, a [video'lezo] AGG, SM/F visually handicapped
videonoleggio [videonoled'dʒo] SM video rental
videoregistratore [videoredʒistra'tore] SM video (recorder)
videoscrittura [videoskrit'tura] SF computer printing
videoteca, che [video'tɛka] SF video shop
videotel® [video'tɛl] SM INV ≈ Videotex®
videotelefono [videote'lɛfono] SM videophone
videoterminale [videotermi'nale] SM visual display unit
vidi *ecc* ['vidi] VB *vedi* **vedere**
vidimare [vidi'mare] VT *(Amm)* to authenticate
vidimazione [vidimat'tsjone] SF *(Amm)* authentication
Vienna ['vjenna] SF Vienna
viennese [vjen'nese] AGG, SM/F Viennese *inv*
vietare [vje'tare] VT *(proibire)* to forbid; *(Amm: importazione, sosta)* to prohibit, ban; *(: sciopero, manifestazione)* to ban, prohibit; **vietare a qn di fare qc** to forbid sb to do sth, prohibit sb from doing sth; **il dottore gli ha vietato di fumare** the doctor has forbidden him to smoke; **hanno vietato il passaggio dei camion in centro** lorries have been banned from *o* prohibited in the centre; **nulla ti vieta di farlo** there is nothing to prevent *o* stop you doing it; **nulla vieta che io lo faccia** there is nothing to stop me; **e chi te lo vieta?** who's stopping you?
vietato, a [vje'tato] AGG *(vedi vb)* forbidden; prohibited; banned; **"vietato calpestare le aiuole"** "keep off the grass"; **"vietato fumare"** "no smoking"; **qui è vietato fumare** smoking is not allowed here; **"vietato sporgersi dal finestrino"** "do not lean out of the window"; **"senso vietato"** *(Aut)* "no entry"; **"sosta vietata"** *(Aut)* "no parking"; **"vietata l'affissione"** "post *o* stick no bills", "bill stickers will be prosecuted"; **"vietato ai minori di 14/18 anni"** "prohibited to children under 14/18"; **è un film vietato ai minori di 18 anni** you have to be eighteen to see that film
Vietnam [vjet'nam] SM Vietnam
vietnamita, i, e [vjetna'mita] AGG, SM/F, SM Vietnamese *inv*
vieto, a ['vjɛto] AGG *(antiquato)* antiquated
vigente [vi'dʒɛnte] AGG *(Dir: legge)* in force; *(fig)* current, in use
vigere ['vidʒere] VI DIF *(si usa solo alla terza persona)* to be in force; **in Italia vige ancora l'obbligo del servizio militare** in Italy national service is still compulsory; **in casa mia vige l'abitudine di...** at home we are in the habit of ...
vigilante [vidʒi'lante] AGG vigilant, watchful
■SM/F security guard
vigilanza [vidʒi'lantsa] SF *(sorveglianza: di operai, alunni)* supervision; *(: di sospetti, criminali)* surveillance; **chiamate la vigilanza!** call security!; **occorre aumentare la vigilanza** we need to be more vigilant; **vigilanza notturna** night-watchman service
vigilare [vidʒi'lare] VT *(sorvegliare: bambini)* to watch over, keep an eye on; *(: operai, studenti, lavori)* to supervise; *(: sospetti, criminali)* to keep under surveillance
■VI *(aus* **avere***)* *(provvedere a)*: **vigilare che...** to make sure that ..., see to it that ...
vigilato, a [vidʒi'lato] AGG *(Dir)*: **essere in libertà vigilata** to be on probation
■SM/F *(Dir)* person under police surveillance
vigilatrice [vidʒila'tritʃe] SF: **vigilatrice d'infanzia** nursery assistant, nursery nurse *(Brit)*
vigile ['vidʒile] AGG *(persona, occhio)* vigilant, watchful; *(cura)* vigilant
■SM/F *(anche:* **vigile urbano***)* (traffic) policeman/policewoman; **i vigili urbani** *municipal police*; **vigile di quartiere** local police officer
■SM: **vigile del fuoco** fireman; firefighter; **i vigili del fuoco** the fire brigade; **chiamare i vigili del fuoco** to call the fire brigade *(Brit) o* department *(Am)*

VIGILI URBANI

The **vigili urbani** are a municipal police force attached to the "Comune". Their duties involve everyday aspects of life such as traffic, public works and services, and commerce.
▷ www.ivigiliurbani.it/

vigilia [vi'dʒilja] SF **1** *(giorno antecedente)* eve; **alla vigilia di** on the eve of; **alla vigilia degli esami** on the eve of the exams; **vigilia di Capodanno** New Year's Eve; **vigilia di Natale** Christmas Eve **2** *(Rel: digiuno)* fast **3** *(letter: veglia)* vigil
vigliaccamente [viʎʎakka'mente] AVV in a cowardly way
vigliaccheria [viʎʎakke'ria] SF *(qualità)* cowardice; *(azione)* act of cowardice, cowardly action; **è stata una vigliaccheria da parte sua** it was contemptible of him
vigliacco, a, chi, che [viʎ'ʎakko] AGG *(persona, azione)* cowardly; *(: spregevole)* contemptible
■SM/F **1** *(codardo)* coward **2** *(profittatore)* rogue, scoundrel
vigna ['viɲɲa] SF vineyard
vigneto [viɲ'ɲeto] SM (large) vineyard
vignetta [viɲ'ɲetta] SF *(disegno)* illustration; *(umoristica)* cartoon; *(bollino autostradale)* motorway pass *(used in countries such as Austria and Switzerland)*
vignettista, i, e [viɲɲet'tista] SM/F illustrator; *(di vignette umoristiche)* cartoonist
vigogna [vi'goɲɲa] SF vicuña
vigore [vi'gore] SM **1** *(gen)* vigour *(Brit)*, vigor *(Am)*, strength; *(fig: forza)* vigo(u)r, force; **nel suo pieno vigore** in his prime, in the prime of life; **perdere vigore** *(persona)* to lose strength; *(campagna elettorale)* to lose impetus; *(discorso, stile)* to become less vigorous *o* energetic; **riacquistare vigore** *(persona)* to regain one's strength **2** *(Dir)*: **essere in vigore** to be in force; **entrare in vigore** to come into force *o* effect; **non è più in vigore** it is no longer in force, it no longer applies
vigoria [vigo'ria] SF vigour *(Brit)*, vigor *(Am)*, strength
vigorosamente [vigorosa'mente] AVV *(opporsi, protestare)* strongly; *(remare)* vigorously
vigoroso, a [vigo'roso] AGG *(gen)* vigorous; *(membra)* strong, powerful; *(stile)* vigorous, energetic; *(resistenza)* vigorous, strenuous; **una vigorosa stretta di mano** a firm handshake
vile ['vile] AGG *(vigliacco)* cowardly; *(spregevole)* contemptible, base, low, mean; **una vile menzogna** a wicked lie; **il vile denaro** filthy lucre
■SM/F coward
vilipendere [vili'pɛndere] VT IRREG to despise, scorn
vilipendio, di [vili'pɛndjo] SM *(Dir)* contempt, scorn;

vilipendio alla bandiera contempt for the national flag
vilipeso, a [vili'peso] PP *di* **vilipendere**
villa ['villa] SF (*in città*) detached house; (*in campagna*) country house; (*al mare*) villa
villaggio, gi [vil'laddʒo] SM village; **un villaggio africano** an african village; **villaggio globale** global village; **villaggio olimpico** Olympic village; **villaggio residenziale** commuter town; **villaggio turistico** holiday village (*Brit*)
villanamente [villana'mente] AVV rudely
villanata [villa'nata] SF (*azione*) rude act, impolite act; (*parola*) piece of rudeness
villania [villa'nia] SF (*sgarbataggine*) rudeness, bad manners *pl*, lack of manners; **è stata una villania da parte sua** it was very rude of him; **fare (*o* dire) una villania a qn** to be rude to sb
villano, a [vil'lano] AGG rude, ill-mannered; **modi villani** bad manners
■SM/F **1** (*maleducato*) lout, boor **2** (*letter*: *contadino*) peasant; **un villano rifatto** (*pegg*) a nouveau riche, an upstart

> **LO SAPEVI...?**
> **villano** non si traduce mai con la parola inglese ***villain***

villanzone, a [villan'tsone] SM/F ill-bred person, boor
villeggiante [villed'dʒante] SM/F holiday-maker (*Brit*), vacationer (*Am*), vacationist (*Am*)
villeggiare [villed'dʒare] VI (*aus* **avere**) to holiday (*Brit*), spend one's holidays (*Brit*), vacation (*Am*)
villeggiatura [villeddʒa'tura] SF holiday(s *pl*) (*Brit*), vacation (*Am*); **andare/essere in villeggiatura** to go/ be on holiday *o* vacation; **luogo di villeggiatura** (holiday *o* vacation) resort
villetta [vil'letta] SF, **villino** [vil'lino] SM (*in città*) small (detached) house (*with a garden*); (*in campagna*) cottage; **villette a schiera** terraced houses
villocentesi [villo'tʃɛntezi] SF (*Med*) chorionic villus sampling
villoso, a [vil'loso] AGG hairy
vilmente [vil'mente] AVV (*vigliaccamente*) like a coward, in a cowardly way; (*spregevolmente*) contemptibly
viltà [vil'ta] SF INV cowardice *no pl*; **atto di viltà** act of cowardice, cowardly act
viluppo [vi'luppo] SM tangle
Viminale [vimi'nale] SM *one of the Seven Hills of Rome*

> **VIMINALE**
> The **Viminale**, which takes its name from one of the famous Seven Hills of Rome on which it stands, is home to the Ministry of the Interior.
> ▷ www.interno.it/
> ▷ www.romasegreta.it/monti/viminale.htm

vimine ['vimine] SM (*Bot*) osier; **di vimini** (*sedia*) wicker *attr*, wickerwork *attr*
vinaio, ai [vi'najo] SM wine merchant
vincente [vin'tʃɛnte] AGG winning; **carta vincente** winning card; (*fig*) trump card
vincenzina [vintʃen'tsina] SF Sister of Charity
vincere ['vintʃere] VB IRREG
■VT **1** (*gen*) to win; **vincere una causa** (*Dir*) to win a case *o* suit; **vincere un premio** to win a prize; **ieri abbiamo vinto la partita** we won the match yesterday **2** (*sconfiggere*: *nemico*) to defeat, vanquish; (: *avversario*) to beat; **vincere qn a tennis** to beat sb at tennis **3** (*superare*: *sentimenti*) to overcome; (*avere ragione di*) to get the better of, outdo; **ho vinto la paura** I got over my fear; **fu vinto dalla stanchezza** tiredness overcame him; **lasciarsi vincere dalla tentazione** to succumb *o* yield to temptation; **vincere qn in** (*abilità*) to outdo *o* surpass sb in; (*bellezza*) to surpass sb in; **vuole sempre averla vinta** he always wants to have the upper hand
■VI (*aus* **avere**) **1** (*in gioco, battaglia*) to win; **vinca il migliore** may the best man win **2** (*prevalere*) to win, prevail
▶ **vincersi** VR to control o.s.
vincita ['vintʃita] SF (*il vincere*) win, victory; (*cosa vinta*) winnings *pl*
vincitore, trice [vintʃi'tore] AGG winning, victorious
■SM/F (*in gara*) winner; (*in battaglia*) victor, winner
vincolante [vinko'lante] AGG binding
vincolare [vinko'lare] VT **1** (*Dir*) to bind; (*fig*: *sogg*: *famiglia, lavoro*) to tie down **2** (*Fin*): **vincolare una somma in banca** to place a sum on fixed deposit
vincolato, a [vinko'lato] AGG (*vedi vt*) bound; tied; **deposito vincolato** fixed deposit
vincolo ['vinkolo] SM (*gen*) bond, tie; (*di sangue*) tie; (*Dir*) encumbrance, obligation; **libero da ogni vincolo** free from all ties; (*Dir*) unencumbered
vinicolo, a [vi'nikolo] AGG wine *attr*; **regione vinicola** wine-producing area
vinificatore [vinifika'tore] SM wine-maker, wine-producer
vinificazione [vinifikat'tsjone] SF wine-making
vinile [vi'nile] SM vinyl
vinilpelle® [vinil'pɛlle] SF Leatherette®
vino ['vino] SM wine; **lista *o* carta dei vini** wine list; **vino bianco/rosso/rosato** white/red/rosé wine; **buon vino fa buon sangue** (*Proverbio*) good wine makes good cheer; **vin brûlé** mulled wine

> **LO SAPEVI...?**
> **vino** non si traduce mai con la parola inglese ***vine***

> **VINO**
> Italy, along with France, is the world's major wine producer. There are many different types of wine whose production is often connected with a particular geographical area. Quality wines usually have D.O.C. (denominazione d'origine controllata) or D.O.C.G. (denominazione d'origine controllata e garantita) stamped on the label.

vinsanto [vin'santo] SM *type of sweet white wine*
vinsi *ecc* ['vinsi] VB *vedi* **vincere**
vinto, a ['vinto] PP *di* **vincere**
■AGG **1** (*sconfitto*) defeated, beaten **2** (*oggetto*): **i soldi vinti al gioco** money won gambling; **darla vinta a qn** to let sb have his (*o* her) way; **darsi per vinto** to give up, give in; **vuol sempre avere partita vinta** he always wants to have the upper hand
■SM/F (*gen*) loser
■SMPL (*Mil*): **i vinti** the defeated (side), the vanquished
viola[1] [vi'ɔla] SF (*Bot*) violet; **viola del pensiero** pansy
■SM INV (*colore*) violet, purple
viola[2] [vi'ɔla] SF (*Mus*) viola
violacciocca, che [violat'tʃɔkka] SF (*Bot*) stock
violaceo, a [vio'latʃeo] AGG mauvish
violare [vio'lare] VT (*gen*) to violate; (*legge*) to violate,

infringe, break; (*promessa*) to break; (*domicilio*) to break into; (*tempio*) to desecrate; (*donna*) to rape; **violare la privacy di qn** to invade sb's privacy

violazione [violat'tsjone] SF (*vedi vb*) violation; infringement, breach; breaking; breaking into; desecration; **violazione di domicilio** (*Dir*) unlawful entry

violentare [violen'tare] VT to use violence on; (*sessualmente*) to rape; (*fig: coscienza*) to outrage; **in questo modo violenti la sua volontà** you are forcing him to do it against his will

violentemente [violente'mente] AVV violently

violento, a [vio'lɛnto] AGG (*gen*) violent; (*suono*) loud; (*luce*) blinding; (*colore*) loud, garish; (*incendio*) raging; **usare un tono violento** to express o.s. with violence; **usare modi violenti** to use violence; **morire di morte violenta** to die a violent death
■ SM/F violent person

violenza [vio'lɛntsa] SF (*gen*) violence; (*di vento, temporale*) violence, force; **ricorrere alla/far uso della violenza** to resort to/use violence; **ottenere qc con la violenza** to obtain sth by violent means *o* by the use of violence; **violenza carnale** (*Dir*) rape

violetta [vio'letta] SF (*Bot*) violet

violetto, a [vio'letto] AGG, SM (*colore*) violet

violinista, i, e [violi'nista] SM/F violinist

violino [vio'lino] SM violin; **essere teso come una corda di violino** (*fig*) to be very tense; **primo violino** first violin; **chiave di violino** treble clef

violoncellista, i, e [violontʃel'lista] SM/F cellist, cello player

violoncello [violon'tʃɛllo] SM violoncello, cello

viottolo [vi'ɔttolo] SM path, track

VIP [vip] SM/F INV (= **Very Important Person**) VIP

vipera ['vipera] SF (*Zool*) viper, adder; (*fig*) catty person; **ha una lingua di vipera** she has a vicious tongue

viperino, a [vipe'rino] AGG (*Zool*) viper *attr*, viper's *attr*; (*fig*) venomous

viraggio, gi [vi'raddʒo] SM **1** (*Naut*) coming about; (*Aer*) turn **2** (*Fot*) toning

virago [vi'rago] SF virago

virale [vi'rale] AGG viral

virare [vi'rare] VI (*aus* **avere**) **1** (*Naut*) to come about; (*Aer*) to turn; **virare di bordo** to change course **2** (*Fot*) to tone

virata [vi'rata] SF (*vedi vb 1*) coming about; turning; change of course; (*Sport: nuoto*) turn; **la virata del governo in materia fiscale** the government's U-turn on fiscal policy

Virgilio [vir'dʒiljo] SM Virgil

Virginia [vir'dʒinja] SF Virginia

virgola ['virgola] SF (*nella punteggiatura*) comma; (*Mat*) (decimal) point; **non c'è una virgola fuori posto** (*fig: in uno scritto*) it's an excellent piece of work; **non cambiare una virgola** (*fig*) don't change a thing; **punto e virgola** semicolon

virgolette [virgo'lette] SFPL quotation marks, inverted commas (*Brit*); **tra virgolette** in quotation marks *o* inverted commas; **una parola scritta tra virgolette** a word written in inverted commas

virgulto [vir'gulto] SM (*Bot*) shoot; (*letter fig: discendente*) scion

virile [vi'rile] AGG (*aspetto, voce*) masculine; (*atteggiamento, lineamenti*) manly, virile; (*bellezza*) male *attr*; (*stile*) vigorous, virile; (*linguaggio*) firm; **età virile** manhood

virilità [virili'ta] SF (*vedi agg*) masculinity; manliness; virility; vigour (*Brit*), vigor (*Am*); firmness

virilmente [viril'mente] AVV in a manly way

virologia [virolo'dʒia] SF virology

virtù [vir'tu] SF INV **1** (*Rel*) virtue; (*pregio, qualità*) virtue, quality; (*virtuosità, castità*) virtuousness; **un modello di virtù** a paragon of virtue; **fare di necessità virtù** to make a virtue of necessity
2 (*capacità: di persona*) ability; (*proprietà: di erbe, sostanze*) property; **in virtù di questa legge** by virtue of this law; **in virtù della nostra amicizia** for friendship's sake

virtuale [virtu'ale] AGG (*gen*) potential; (*Fis*) virtual; **realtà virtuale** virtual reality

virtualmente [virtual'mente] AVV potentially

> **LO SAPEVI...?**
> **virtualmente** non si traduce mai con la parola inglese ***virtually***

virtuosamente [virtuosa'mente] AVV virtuously

virtuosismo [virtuo'sizmo] SM (*abilità*) virtuosity; **esibirsi in inutili virtuosismi** to show off

virtuoso, a [virtu'oso] AGG virtuous
■ SM/F (*del violino, pennello*) virtuoso, master/mistress

virulento, a [viru'lɛnto] AGG virulent

virulenza [viru'lɛntsa] SF virulence

virus ['virus] SM INV (*Med, Inform*) virus

visagista, i, e [viza'dʒista] SM/F beautician

vis-à-vis [viz a 'vi] AVV: **eravamo seduti vis-à-vis** we were sitting opposite each other

viscerale [viʃʃe'rale] AGG (*Med*) visceral; (*fig*) profound, deep-rooted

viscere ['viʃʃere] SM (*Anat*) internal organ
■ SFPL (*di animale*) entrails *pl*; (*fig*) depths *pl*, bowels *pl*; **nelle viscere della terra** in the bowels of the earth

Vv

vischio ['viskjo] SM **1** (*Bot*) mistletoe **2** (*pania*) birdlime

vischiosità [viskjosi'ta] SF (*collosità*) stickiness; (*Fis, Chim*) viscosity

vischioso, a [vis'kjoso] AGG (*colloso*) sticky; (*viscoso*) viscous

viscidamente [viʃʃida'mente] AVV (*vedi agg*) slimily; smarmily

viscidità [viʃʃidi'ta] SF (*vedi agg*) sliminess; smarminess

viscido, a ['viʃʃido] AGG (*lumaca, pelle*) slimy; (*fig: persona*) smarmy

visciola ['viʃʃola] SF sour cherry

visconte, essa [vis'konte] SM/F viscount/viscountess

viscosa [vis'kosa] SF viscose

viscosità [viskosi'ta] SF viscosity

viscoso, a [vis'koso] AGG viscous

visibile [vi'zibile] AGG (*gen*) visible; (*imbarazzo*) obvious, evident, visible; (*progresso*) clear, perceptible

visibilio [vizi'biljo] SM: **andare in visibilio (per qc)** to go into ecstasies *o* raptures (over sth)

visibilità [vizibili'ta] SF visibility

visibilmente [vizibil'mente] AVV visibly

visiera [vi'zjɛra] SF (*di cappello*) peak; (*di elmo, casco*) visor

Visigoto [vizi'gɔto] SM Visigoth

visionare [vizjo'nare] VT (*gen*) to look at, examine; (*Cine*) to screen

visionario, ria, ri, rie [vizjo'narjo] AGG, SM/F visionary

visione [vi'zjone] SF **1** (*gen, Rel*) vision; (*scena*) sight; (*idea, concetto*) view; **hanno avuto una visione della Madonna** they had a vision of the Virgin Mary; **ma tu**

hai le visioni! you must be seeing things!; **la mia visione della realtà** my view of reality; **avere una visione limitata della realtà** to have a narrow view of reality **2** (*atto del vedere*) vision, sight; **prendere visione di qc** to have a look at sth, examine sth, look sth over; **mandare qc in visione** (*Comm*) to send sth on approval; **prima/seconda visione** (*Cine*) first/second showing, first run/rerun; **trasmettiamo in prima visione il film...** we're showing the first screening of the film ...; **film in prima visione** newly released film; **cinema di prima visione** *cinema where films are shown on first release*

visir [vi'zir] SM INV (*Storia*) vizier

visita ['vizita] SF **1** (*gen*) visit; (*di amico, rappresentante*) visit, call; **far visita a qn** *or* **andare in visita da qn** to visit sb, pay sb a visit; **andiamo a fargli visita** let's go and visit him; **in visita ufficiale in Italia** on an official visit to Italy; **biglietto da visita** (visiting) card; **abbiamo visite** we have visitors *o* guests; **c'è una visita per te** you've got a visitor **2** (*turistica*: *di città*) tour; (: *di museo*) tour, visit; **la visita del castello dura 2 ore** the tour of the castle takes 2 hours, it takes 2 hours to go round the castle; **visita guidata** guided tour; **quanto costa la visita guidata della città?** how much is a guided tour of the city? **3** (*Med*: *esame*) examination; **il medico sta facendo il giro delle visite** the doctor is doing his rounds; **orario di visite** (*ospedale*) visiting hours; (*ambulatorio*) consulting *o* surgery (*Brit*) hours; **marcare visita** (*Mil*) to report sick; **visita di controllo** checkup; **ho fatto una visita di controllo** i had a check-up; **visita domiciliare** house call; **visita fiscale** *house call made on state employee by doctor to verify condition of patient*; **visita di leva** (*Mil*) medical (*Brit*) *o* physical (*Am*) examination

visitare [vizi'tare] VT **1** (*andare in visita*) to visit, call on, go and see; (*rappresentante*) to call on; **andare a visitare qn** to go and see *o* visit sb **2** (*museo*) to visit, go round; **ci ha fatto visitare la casa/il castello** he showed us round the house/castle; **hai già visitato la National Gallery?** have you visited the National Gallery?; **visitate il nostro sito Internet** visit our web site **3** (*Med*) to examine; **siamo rimasti con lei finché il dottore l'ha visitata** we stayed with her until the doctor examined her; **visitare i pazienti a casa** to see patients at home; **il medico sta visitando** the doctor is seeing *o* receiving patients now; **il medico visita solo il giovedì** the doctor only sees patients on Thursdays; **bisogna che mi faccia visitare** I must go and have a medical examination *o* a checkup

visitatore, trice [vizita'tore] SM/F **1** (*ospite*) visitor, guest **2** (*turista*) visitor, tourist

visivamente [viziva'mente] AVV visually

visivo, a [vi'zivo] AGG visual; **memoria visiva** visual memory; **gli organi visivi** the eyes

viso ['vizo] SM face; **si è spalmata la crema sul viso** she rubbed the cream into her face; **crema per il viso** face cream; **guardare in viso qn** to look sb in the face, look straight at sb; **fare buon viso a cattivo gioco** to make the best of things; **a viso aperto** openly; **viso pallido** (*uomo bianco*) paleface

visone [vi'zone] SM (*Zool*) mink; (*pelliccia*) mink (coat); **una pelliccia di visone** a mink coat

visore [vi'zore] SM (*Fot*) viewer

vispo, a ['vispo] AGG (*bambino*) lively; (*vecchietto*) sprightly; (*occhi*) bright

vissi *ecc* ['vissi] VB *vedi* **vivere**

vissuto, a [vis'suto] PP *di* **vivere**

■ AGG **1** **storia di vita vissuta** story from real life **2** (*persona*) experienced, who has had many experiences

vista ['vista] SF **1** (*gen*) sight; (*capacità visiva*) eyesight, sight; **avere la vista buona** to have good eyesight; **avere la vista corta/lunga** to be short-/long-sighted; (*fig*) to be short-/far-sighted; **ho avuto un improvviso abbassamento della vista** my eyesight suddenly got worse; **la vista mi si sta indebolendo** my sight is deteriorating; **difetti della vista** eye problems; **esame della vista** eye test; **occhiali da vista** glasses; **sottrarsi alla vista di qn** to disappear from sb's sight; **mettersi in vista** to draw attention to o.s.; (*pegg*) to show off; **essere in vista** (*persona*) to be in the public eye; **terra in vista!** land ahoy!; **è in vista una ripresa economica** economic recovery is in sight; **a prima vista** at first sight; **è stato amore a prima vista** it was love at first sight; **conoscere qn di vista** to know sb by sight; **lo conosco solo di vista** I only know him by sight; **in vista di qc** in view of sth; **sparare a vista** to shoot on sight; **pagabile a vista** payable on demand; **avere in vista qc** to have sth in view; **a vista d'occhio** as far as the eye can see; (*fig*) before one's very eyes; **perdere qn di vista** (*anche fig*) to lose sight of sb; **correva così veloce che l'ho perso di vista** he was running so fast that I lost sight of him; **dopo aver finito l'università si sono persi di vista** they lost touch after they left university **2** (*veduta*) view; **una camera con vista sul lago** a room with a view of the lake

vistare [vis'tare] VT to approve; (*Amm*: *passaporto*) to visa

visto, a ['visto] PP *di* **vedere**

■ SM **1** (*segno*) tick (*Brit*), check (*Am*); (*Amm*: *approvazione*) approval **2** (*Amm*) visa; **visto d'ingresso** entry visa; **visto permanente** permanent visa; **visto di soggiorno visto di transito** transit visa

vistosamente [vistosa'mente] AVV (*vestirsi*) gaudily, showily, garishly

vistosità [vistosi'ta] SF gaudiness, showiness, garishness

vistoso, a [vis'toso] AGG (*colore*) garish; (*bellezza*) flashy; (*scritta, insegna*) showy; (*aumento*) enormous, huge

visuale [vizu'ale] AGG visual

■ SF (*gen*) view; (*Ottica*) line of vision; (*nel tiro*) line of sight; **togliere la visuale a qn** to block sb's view

visualizzare [vizualid'dzare] VT to visualize

visualizzatore [vizualiddza'tore] SM (*Inform*) display, visual display unit, VDU; **visualizzatore a cristalli liquidi** liquid crystal display

visualizzazione [vizualiddzat'tsjone] SF (*Inform*) display

vita[1] ['vita] SF

1 (*gen*) life; **essere in vita** to be alive; **quando sono arrivati era ancora in vita** when they got there he was still alive; **perdere la vita** to lose one's life; **far ritornare in vita qn** to bring sb back to life; **dare la vita per qn/qc** to give one's life for sb/sth; **ha rischiato la vita per aiutarla** he risked his life to help her; **pieno di vita** full of life; **ha dato un po' di vita alla festa** he livened up the party a bit

2 (*modo di vivere*) life, lifestyle; **nella vita quotidiana** *o* **di ogni giorno** in everyday life; **la vita da studente** life as a student; **la vita in Scozia** life in Scotland; **la vita degli animali** animal life; **condurre una vita attiva** to lead an active life; **avere una doppia vita** to lead a double life; **cambiare vita** to change one's way

of life *o* one's lifestyle; **vita notturna** nightlife
3 (*mezzi di sussistenza*) living; **guadagnarsi la vita** to earn one's living; **il costo della vita** the cost of living; **la vita è cara a Parigi** it's expensive to live in Paris
4 (*durata*) life, lifetime; **ti amerò per tutta la vita** I'll love you for ever *o* all my life; **ho lavorato per tutta la vita** I've worked all my life; **una volta nella vita** once in a lifetime; **capita una volta sola nella vita** it only happens once in a lifetime; **mai...in vita mia** never; **non l'ho mai fatto in vita mia** I've never done it; **membro a vita** life member; **carcere a vita** life imprisonment; **avere sette vite** to have nine lives; **non basterebbe una vita per spiegartelo** it would take a lifetime to explain it to you; **vita media** average life expectancy
5 (*biografia*) life (story); **mi ha raccontato tutta la sua vita** she told me her life story *o* the story of her life
6 (*fraseologia*): **l'altra vita** the hereafter; **o la borsa o la vita!** your money or your life!; **ci metti una vita!** you are taking ages!; **da una vita** for a long time; **non lo vedo da una vita** I haven't seen him for a long time; **è la vita!** that's life!; **che vita da cani!** what a dog's life!; **su con la vita!** cheer up; **fare la vita** (*euf*) to be on the game (*Brit*); **fare la bella vita** to live the good life; **finché c'è vita c'è speranza** while there's life there's hope; **pena la vita** on pain of death; **rendere la vita difficile a qn** to make life difficult for sb; **sapere vita, morte e miracoli di qn** to know all the ins and outs of sb's life, know all there is to know about sb

vita[2] ['vita] SF (*Anat*) waist; **abito a vita alta/bassa** dress with a high/low waist; **mi è un po' largo in vita** it's a bit loose round the waist; **punto (di) vita** (*Sartoria*) waist

vitale [vi'tale] AGG **1** (*gen*) vital; (*vivace: persona*) lively, vital; **spazio vitale** living space **2** (*che può vivere*) viable

vitalità [vitali'ta] SF vitality, vigour (*Brit*), vigor (*Am*)

vitalizio, zia, zi, zie [vita'littsjo] AGG life *attr*
■ SM (*Dir*) life annuity

vitamina [vita'mina] SF vitamin

vitaminico, a, ci, che [vita'miniko] AGG vitamin *attr*

vitaminizzare [vitaminid'dzare] VT to enrich with vitamins

vitaminizzato, a [vitaminid'dzato] AGG with added vitamins, vitamin-enriched

vite[1] ['vite] SF (*Bot*) (grape)vine; **vite del Canada** Virginia creeper

vite[2] ['vite] SF **1** (*Tecn*) screw; **giro di vite** (*anche fig*) turn of the screw; **tappo a vite** screw(-on) cap *o* top; **vite senza fine** endless screw **2** (*Aer*) (tail)spin

vitella [vi'tɛlla] SF **1** (*Zool*) calf **2** (*Culin*) veal

vitello [vi'tɛllo] SM **1** (*Zool*) calf **2** (*Culin*) veal; **una scaloppina di vitello** a veal escalope; **vitello tonnato** veal in tuna fish sauce **3** (*pelle*) calf(skin)

vitellone [vitel'lone] SM **1** (*Zool*) bullock **2** (*Culin*) tender young beef **3** (*fig*) loafer

viterbese [viter'bese] AGG of *o* from Viterbo
■ SM/F inhabitant *o* native of Viterbo

viticcio, ci [vi'tittʃo] SM (*Bot*) tendril

viticoltore [vitikol'tore] SM vine grower

viticoltura [vitikol'tura] SF vine growing

vitreo, a ['vitreo] AGG (*sostanza*) vitreous; (*occhio, sguardo*) glassy

vittima ['vittima] SF (*gen*) victim; (*di incidente*) casualty, victim; **fare la vittima** to play the martyr

vittimismo [vitti'mizmo] SM self-pity

vittimista, i, e [vitti'mista] SM/F self-pitying person

vittimistico, a, ci, che [vitti'mistiko] AGG self-pitying

vitto ['vitto] SM (*cibo*) food; (*in pensioni*) board; **vitto e alloggio** room and board, board and lodging

vittoria [vit'tɔrja] SF victory; **cantar vittoria** to crow (over one's victory)

vittoriano, a [vitto'rjano] AGG, SM/F Victorian

vittoriosamente [vittorjosa'mente] AVV victoriously, triumphantly

vittorioso, a [vitto'rjoso] AGG victorious, triumphant

vituperare [vitupe'rare] VT (*letter*) to berate, rail at *o* against

vituperio, ri [vitu'pɛrjo] (*letter*) SM insult

viuzza [vi'uttsa] SF (*in città*) alley

viva ['viva] ESCL long live; **viva il re!** long live the king!; **viva il Milan!** three cheers for Milan!; **viva gli sposi!** to the bride and groom!; **viva l'Italia!** hooray for Italy!

vivacchiare [vivak'kjare] VI (*aus* **avere**) to scrape a living

vivace [vi'vatʃe] AGG **1** (*gen*) lively; (*intelligenza*) lively, keen; (*colore*) vivid, brilliant, bright; **una ragazza vivace** a lively girl; **è più vivace della sorella** she's livelier than her sister; **un colore vivace** a bright colour **2** (*Mus*) vivace

vivacemente [vivatʃe'mente] AVV (*discutere, giocare*) in a lively way; (*contrastare: colori*) vividly

vivacità [vivatʃi'ta] SF (*vedi agg*) liveliness; keenness; vividness, brilliance, brightness

vivacizzare [vivatʃid'dzare] VT to liven up

vivaio, ai [vi'vajo] SM (*di piante*) nursery; (*di pesci*) fish farm, hatchery; (*fig*) breeding ground

vivamente [viva'mente] AVV (*commuoversi*) deeply, profoundly; (*ringraziare*) sincerely, warmly

vivanda [vi'vanda] SF (*cibo*) food *no pl*; (*piatto*) dish

vivavoce [viva'votʃe] SM INV (*dispositivo*) loudspeaker; **mettere in vivavoce** to switch on the loudspeakerAGG INV: **telefono vivavoce** speakerphone

vivente [vi'vɛnte] AGG living, alive; **è il ritratto vivente del nonno** he is the spitting image of his grandfather; **l'autore è ancora vivente** the author is still alive; **è il massimo poeta vivente** he is the greatest living poet
■ SMPL: **i viventi** the living

vivere ['vivere] VB IRREG
■ VI (*aus* **essere**) **1** (*gen*) to live; (*essere vivo*) to live, be alive; **vivere fino a 100 anni** to live to be 100; **non gli resta molto da vivere** he hasn't long to live; **ha cessato di vivere** he is dead; **finché vivrò** as long as I live; **chi vivrà vedrà** only time will tell; **vivi e lascia vivere** live and let live; **vivere fuori dalla realtà** to live in another world, be out of touch with reality
2 (*abitare*) to live; **mi piacerebbe vivere in Scozia** I'd like to live in Scotland; **vivo in campagna** I live in the country; **viviamo insieme** we live together
3 (*sostentarsi*): **vivere (di)** to live (on); (*cibarsi*): **vivere di** to live on, feed on; **io vivo di poco o niente** I live on little or nothing; **ho giusto di che vivere** I have just enough to live on; **guadagnarsi da vivere** to earn one's living; **si guadagna da vivere dando lezioni di piano** she earns her living by giving piano lessons; **vivere d'aria e d'amore** to live on love alone; **vivere alla giornata** to live from day to day; **vivere nell'indigenza** to live in utter poverty; **vivere da signore** to live like a lord; **vivere nel lusso** to live a life of luxury; **vivere alle spalle di qn** to live off sb
4 (*comportarsi*) to live; **devi ancora imparare a vivere**

Vv

you've still got a lot to learn about life; **modo di vivere** way of life **5** (*Tip*): **vive** stet
■VT (*vita*) to live; (*avvenimento, esperienza*) to live through, go through; **vivere una vita tranquilla** to lead a quiet life; **vivere giorni di dolore** to live through a sad period; **ha vissuto la scuola come una punizione** he hated his school days
■SM life; **lo faccio per il quieto vivere!** anything for a quiet life!

viveri ['viveri] SMPL food *sg*, provisions, supplies

viveur [vi'vœr] SM INV pleasure-seeker

vivido, a ['vivido] AGG (*ricordo*) vivid, very clear; (*luce*) bright, brilliant; (*colore*) bright, vivid; **di vivido ingegno** quick-witted, bright

vivificare [vivifi'kare] VT (*materia*) to give life to, enliven; (*ravvivare: piante*) to revive, refresh; (*fig: racconto*) to bring to life

viviparo, a [vi'viparo] AGG viviparous

vivisezionare [vivisettsjo'nare] VT to vivisect

vivisezione [viviset'tsjone] SF vivisection

vivo, a ['vivo] AGG **1** (*in vita*) alive, living; (*in uso: espressione, tradizione*) living; **è ancora vivo** he is still alive *o* living; **il pesce era ancora vivo** the fish was still alive; **esperimenti su animali vivi** experiments on live *o* living animals; **lingua viva** living language; **non c'era anima viva** there wasn't a (living) soul there; **me lo mangerei vivo!** (*fig*) I could eat him alive!, I could murder him!; **vivo o morto** dead or alive; **essere più morto che vivo** to be more dead than alive **2** (*intenso: ricordo*) vivid, very clear; (: *emozione*) intense; (: *luce*) brilliant, bright; (: *colore*) bright, vivid; **sguardo vivo** bright eyes; **viva commozione** intense emotion; **con vivo rammarico** with deep regret; **congratulazioni vivissime** sincerest *o* heartiest congratulations; **con i più vivi ringraziamenti** with deepest *o* warmest thanks; **cuocere a fuoco vivo** to cook on a high flame *o* heat **3** (*vivace: persona*) lively, vivacious; (: *città, strada, discussione*) lively, animated; **ha un'intelligenza molto viva** he has a very lively mind **4** (*fraseologia*): **farsi vivo** to keep in touch; **fatti vivo!** keep in touch!; **è tanto che non si fa vivo** he hasn't been in touch for ages; **spese vive** immediate *o* out-of-pocket expenses; **spigolo vivo** sharp edge; **l'ho sentito dalla sua viva voce** I heard it from the horse's mouth *o* from his own lips
■SM **1** (*essere*) living being; **i vivi** SMPL the living **2** **entrare nel vivo di una questione** to get to the heart of a matter; **registrazione dal vivo** live recording; **un programma dal vivo** a live program; **ritrarre dal vivo** to paint from life; **pungere** *o* **colpire qn nel vivo** to cut sb to the quick

vivrò *ecc* [viv'rɔ] VB *vedi* **vivere**

viziare [vit'tsjare] VT **1** (*persona*) to spoil **2** (*Dir*) to invalidate; (*rovinare: rapporti, ragionamento*) to ruin, spoil

viziato, a [vit'tsjato] AGG **1** (*persona*) spoilt; **un bambino viziato** a spoilt child **2** (*Dir*) invalid, invalidated; (*rapporti, ragionamento*) ruined, spoiled **3** (*aria*) stale, foul; **aria viziata** stale air

vizio, zi ['vittsjo] SM **1** (*morale*) vice; (*cattiva abitudine*) bad habit; **vivere nel vizio** to live a life of vice; **i vizi e le virtù** vices and virtues; **ha il vizio del gioco** he's addicted to gambling; **il mio unico vizio è quello di mangiarmi le unghie** biting my nails is my only bad habit **2** (*Dir*) flaw, defect; **vizio di forma** legal flaw *o* irregularity; **vizio procedurale** procedural error **3** (*Med*): **vizio cardiaco** heart defect

viziosamente [vittsjosa'mente] AVV (*vivere*) in a depraved way

vizioso, a [vit'tsjoso] AGG **1** (*corrotto*) depraved; **vita viziosa** life of vice **2** (*difettoso*) incorrect, wrong; **circolo vizioso** vicious circle
■SM/F depraved person

vizzo, a ['vittso] AGG (*Bot*) withered; (*fig: pelle, guance*) withered, wrinkled

V.le ABBR (= Viale) Ave. (= *Avenue*)

v.o. ABBR (*Cine:* = **versione originale**) original version

vocabolario, ri [vokabo'larjo] SM (*dizionario*) dictionary; (*lessico personale*) vocabulary; **un vocabolario di italiano** an Italian dictionary; **il suo vocabolario è limitato** his vocabulary is limited

vocabolo [vo'kabolo] SM word

vocale[1] [vo'kale] AGG (*Anat, Mus*) vocal

vocale[2] [vo'kale] SF vowel

vocalico, a, ci, che [vo'kaliko] AGG vowel *attr*, vocalic

vocalizzare [vokalid'dzare] VI, VT to vocalize

vocativo, a [voka'tivo] AGG, SM vocative

vocazione [vokat'tsjone] SF (*anche Rel*) vocation; (*inclinazione naturale*) (natural) bent; **non ho vocazione per la matematica** I'm not cut out to study Maths (*Brit*) *o* Math (*Am*), I have no gift for Math(s)

voce ['votʃe] SF **1** (*gen*) voice; **ho perso la voce** I've lost my voice; **la voce della coscienza** the voice of conscience; **parlare a alta/bassa voce** to speak loudly/quietly; **leggi il brano ad alta voce** read the passage aloud; **con un fil di voce** in a weak voice; **dar voce a qc** to voice *o* give voice to sth; **dare una voce a qn** to call sb, give sb a call; **fare la voce grossa** to raise one's voice; **a gran voce** in a loud voice, loudly; **l'hanno acclamato a gran voce** they greeted him with thunderous applause; **me l'ha detto a voce** he told me himself *o* in person; **te lo dico a voce** I'll tell you when I see you; **a una voce** unanimously **2** (*opinione*) opinion; (*diceria*) rumour (*Brit*), rumor (*Am*); **aver voce in capitolo** to have a say in the matter; **circolano delle voci secondo cui il governo si dimetterà** it is rumo(u)red *o* rumo(u)r has it that the government will resign; **voci di corridoio** rumo(u)rs; **sono solo voci di corridoio** they're only rumo(u)rs **3** (*Mus*) voice; **cantare a due voci** to sing in two parts **4** (*Gramm*) voice **5** (*vocabolo*) word; (*di elenco, bilancio*) item; (*di dizionario*) entry; **è una voce antiquata** it is an obsolete term *o* word

vociare [vo'tʃare] VI (*aus* **avere**) to shout, yell
■SM shouting

vociferare [votʃife'rare] VI (*aus* **avere**) **si vocifera che...** it's rumoured (*Brit*) *o* rumored (*Am*) that ...

vocio [vo'tʃio] SM shouting

vodka ['vɔdka] SF INV vodka

voga[1] ['voga] SF (*Naut*) rowing

voga[2] ['voga] SF: **essere in voga** (*abito*) to be fashionable, be in fashion *o* in vogue; (*canzone*) to be popular

vogare [vo'gare] VI (*aus* **avere**) to row

vogata [vo'gata] SF (*colpo di remi*) stroke; **fare una vogata** to go for a row, go rowing

vogatore, trice [voga'tore] SM/F oarsman/oarswoman
■SM rowing machine

vogherò *ecc* [voge'rɔ] VB *vedi* **vogare**

voglia ['vɔʎʎa] SF **1** (*desiderio*) wish, desire; (*di donna incinta*) craving; **aver voglia di qc/di fare qc** to feel like sth/like doing sth; (*più forte*) to want sth/to do sth; **morire dalla voglia di fare qc/di qc** to be dying *o* longing to do sth/for sth; **muoio dalla voglia di**

vederlo I'm dying to see him; **adesso non ho voglia di mangiare** I don't feel like eating just now; **e chi ne ha voglia?** I don't feel like it at the moment; **hai voglia di gridare, tanto non ti sente!** (*fam*) he can't hear you however much you shout **2** (*disposizione*) will; **di buona voglia** willingly; **contro voglia** *or* **di mala voglia** unwillingly **3** (*desiderio sessuale*) desire, lust **4** (*macchia della pelle*) birthmark

voglio *ecc* ['vɔʎʎo] VB *vedi* **volere**

vogliosamente [voʎʎosa'mente] AVV longingly, yearningly

voglioso, a [voʎ'ʎoso] AGG (*sguardo*) longing; (*sessualmente*) full of desire

voi ['voi] PRON PERS **1** (*soggetto*) you; **voi tutti lo sapete** all of you know, you all know; **voi che ne dite?** what do you think?; **io ci vado, voi fate come volete** I'm going, you do what you like; **venite anche voi?** are you coming too?; **voi italiani** you Italians; **voi stessi(e)** you yourselves; **siete stati voi a dirglielo** it was you who told him, you were the ones to tell him; **non lo sapevate nemmeno voi** you didn't even know it yourselves **2** (*oggetto*: *per dare rilievo, con preposizione*) you; **vuol vedere proprio voi** it's you he wants to see; **parlo a voi, non a lui** I'm talking to YOU, not to him; **tocca a voi** it's your turn; **da voi** (*nel vostro paese*) where you come from, in your country; (*a casa vostra*) at your house **3** (*comparazioni*) you; **sono alti come voi** they are as tall as you (are); **faremo come voi** we'll do as you do, we'll do the same as you; **sono più giovani di voi** they are younger than you

voialtri, e ['vojaltri] PRON PERS you

voilà [vwa'la] ESCL: **e voilà!** hey presto!

voile [vwal] SM INV voile

vol. ABBR (= **volume**) vol.

volano [vo'lano] SM **1** (*palla*) shuttlecock; (*gioco*) badminton **2** (*Tecn*) flywheel

volant [vɔ'lɑ̃] SM INV frill

volante[1] [vo'lante] AGG (*gen*) flying; (*foglio*) loose; (*indossatrice*) freelance
■ SF (*Polizia*: *anche*: **squadra volante**) flying squad

volante[2] [vo'lante] SM (*Aut*) (steering) wheel; **essere al volante** to drive, be at the wheel; **un asso del volante** ace driver

volantinaggio [volanti'naddʒo] SM leafleting

volantinare [volanti'nare] VI (*aus* **avere**) to leaflet

volantino [volan'tino] SM (*foglietto*) leaflet, pamphlet

volare [vo'lare] VI (*aus* **avere** *o* **essere**) **1** (*aereo, uccello, passeggero*) to fly; **far volare un aquilone** to fly a kite **2** (*fig*: *tempo*) to fly, go by very quickly; (: *notizie*) to spread quickly; (: *pugni, insulti*) to fly; **quando ho sentito la notizia sono volato da lei** when I heard the news I rushed round to her place; **il pallone è volato fuori dal campo** the ball flew off the pitch; **volare in cielo** *o* **paradiso** (*euf*: *morire*) to go to heaven **3** (*allontanarsi*): **volare via** (*cappello, fogli*) to blow away, fly away *o* off; (*fig*: *tempo*) to fly; (*cadere*): **volare giù** (*vaso, persona*) to fall

volata [vo'lata] SF **1** (*fig*: *corsa*) rush; **faccio una volata a casa** I am just going to pop home; **passare di volata da qn** to drop in on sb briefly **2** (*Ciclismo*) final sprint; **vincere in volata** to sprint home to win **3 volata di uccelli** (*stormo*) flock *o* flight of birds

volatile [vo'latile] AGG (*Chim*) volatile
■ SM (*uccello*) bird, winged creature

volatilizzare [volatilid'dzare] VT (*Chim*) to volatilize
▶ **volatilizzarsi** VIP (*Chim*) to volatilize; (*fig*) to vanish, disappear

vol-au-vent ['vɔlovɑ̃] SM INV (*Culin*) vol-au-vent

volée [vɔle] SF INV (*Tennis*) volley; **volée smorzata** drop volley

volente [vo'lɛnte] AGG: **verrai volente o nolente** you'll come whether you like it or not

volenterosamente [volenterosa'mente] AVV willingly

volenteroso, a [volente'roso] AGG willing, keen; **un alunno volenteroso** a willing pupil

volentieri [volen'tjɛri] AVV willingly, gladly; **l'ho fatto volentieri** I did it willingly; **spesso e volentieri** frequently, very often; **volentieri!** certainly!, of course!; **mi aiuti? – volentieri!** will you help me? – certainly!; **verresti a cena da noi stasera? – grazie, volentieri!** would you like to come to dinner with us this evening? – yes, I'd love to!

volere [vo'lere] VB IRREG **PAROLA CHIAVE**

■ VT (*nei tempi composti prende l'ausiliare del verbo che accompagna*)

1 (*gen*) to want; **voglio una risposta da voi** I want an answer from you; **voglio che ti lavi le mani** I want you to wash your hands; **che tu lo voglia o no** whether you like it or not; **vuol venire a tutti i costi** he wants to come at all costs; **quanto vuole per quel quadro?** how much does he want for that painting?; **voglio comprare una macchina nuova** I want to buy a new car; **che cosa vuoi che faccia?** what do you want me to do?

2 (*desiderare*): **vorrei del pane** I would like some bread; **vorrei farlo/che tu lo facessi** I would like to do it/you to do it; **mi vorrebbero vedere sposato** they would like to see me married, they would like me to marry; **se volete, possiamo partire subito** if you like *o* want, we can leave right away; **come vuoi** as you like; **devo pagare subito o posso pagare domani? – come vuole** do I have to pay now or can I pay tomorrow? – as you prefer; **volevo parlartene** I meant to talk to you about it; **se volesse potrebbe farcela** he could do it if he wanted to; **vuole un po' di caffè?** would you like some coffee?; **adesso vorrei andarmene** i'd like to go now; **vorrebbe andare in America** she'd like to go to America

3 (*con funzione di richiesta o offerta*): **vuole** *o* **vorrebbe essere così gentile da...?** would you be so kind as to ...?; **vuoi chiudere la finestra?** would you mind closing the window?; **non vuole accomodarsi?** won't you sit down?; **vogliamo sederci?** shall we sit down?; **prendine quanto vuoi** help yourself, take as many (*o* much) as you like; **ne vuoi ancora?** would you like some more?; **vuoi che io faccia qualcosa?** would you like me to do something?, shall I do something?; **ma vuoi star zitto!** oh, do be quiet!

4 (*consentire*): **se la padrona di casa vuole, ti posso ospitare** if my landlady agrees I can put you up; **ho chiesto di parlargli, ma non ha voluto ricevermi** I asked to have a word with him but he wouldn't see me; **la macchina non vuole partire** the car won't start; **parla bene l'inglese quando vuole** he can speak English well when he has a mind to *o* when he feels like it

5 (*aspettarsi*) to want, expect; (*richiedere*) to want, require, demand; **che cosa vuoi da me?** what do you want from me?, what do you expect of me?; **la tradizione vuole che...** custom requires that ...; **vuole troppo dai suoi studenti** he expects too much of his students; **il verbo transitivo vuole il**

complemento oggetto transitive verbs require a direct object
6 volerne a qn to have sth against sb, have a grudge against sb, bear sb a grudge; **me ne vuole ancora per quello che gli ho fatto** he still bears me a grudge for what I did to him; **non me ne volere** don't hold it against me
7 voler dire (che)... (*significare*) to mean (that) ...; **cosa vuol dire questa parola?** what does this word mean?; **se non puoi oggi vorrà dire che ci vediamo domani** if you can't make it today, I'll see you tomorrow; **vuoi dire che non parti più?** do you mean that you're not leaving after all?; **voglio dire...** (*per correggersi*) I mean ...; **volevo ben dire!** I thought as much!
8 (*ritenere*) to think; **la leggenda vuole che...** legend has it that ...; **si vuole che anche lui sia coinvolto nella faccenda** he is also thought to be involved in the matter
9 volerci (*essere necessario: materiale, attenzione*) to need; (*: tempo*) to take; **ci vuol ben altro per farmi arrabbiare** it'll take a lot more than that to make me angry; **quanto ci vuole per andare da Roma a Firenze?** to how long does it take to go from Rome to Florence?; **quanta farina ci vuole per questa torta?** how much flour do you need to make this cake?; **ci vorrebbe un bel caffè** a nice cup of coffee is just what's needed; **è quel che ci vuole** it's just what is needed; **ce ne vuole per fargliela entrare nella zucca** it's not easy to get it into his thick skull; **per una giacca ci vogliono quattro metri di stoffa** you need four metres of material to make a jacket; **ci vuole il pane** we need bread
10 (*fraseologia*): **voler bene a qn** (*amore*) to love sb; (*affetto*) to be fond of sb, like sb very much; **volesse il cielo che...** God grant that ...; **se Dio vuole** God willing; **voler male a qn** to dislike sb; **sembra che voglia piovere** it looks like rain; **sembra che voglia mettersi al bello** the weather seems to be clearing up; **volere è potere** where there's a will there's a way; **qui ti voglio** that's the problem; **non vorrei sbagliarmi, ma...** I may be wrong, but ...; **senza volere** unwittingly, without meaning to, unintentionally; **l'ho spinto senza volere** I accidentally pushed him; **chi troppo vuole nulla stringe** (*Proverbio*) don't ask for too much or you may come away empty-handed; **te la sei voluta** you asked for it; **voglio vedere se rifiuta** I bet she doesn't refuse; **vorrei proprio vedere!** I'm not at all surprised!, that doesn't surprise me in the slightest!; **vuoi...vuoi...** either ... or ...
▶ **volersi** VR (*uso reciproco*) **volersi bene** (*amore*) to love each other; (*affetto*) to be fond of *o* like each other
■ SM will, wish(es); **contro il volere di** against the wishes of; **per volere del padre** in obedience to his father's will *o* wishes

volgare [vol'gare] AGG **1** (*grossolano*) vulgar, coarse **2** (*comune*) common, popular
■ SM vernacular
volgarità [volgari'ta] SF INV vulgarity
volgarizzare [volgarid'dzare] VT **1** (*divulgare*) to popularize **2** (*tradurre*) to translate into the vernacular
volgarmente [volgar'mente] AVV **1** (*in modo volgare*) vulgarly, coarsely **2** (*comunemente*) commonly, popularly

volgere ['vɔldʒere] VB IRREG
■ VI (*aus* **avere**) **1 volgere a** (*piegare verso*) to turn to *o* towards, bend round to *o* towards; **la strada volge a destra** the road bends round to the right **2** (*avvicinarsi a*): **volgere al peggio** to take a turn for the worse; **volgere al termine** to draw to an end; **le vacanze volgono al termine** the holidays are coming to an end; **il giorno volge al termine** the day is drawing to its close; **il tempo volge al brutto/al bello** the weather is breaking/is setting fair; **la situazione volge al peggio** the situation is deteriorating; **un rosso che volge al viola** a red verging on purple
■ VT **1** (*voltare*) to turn; **volgere le spalle a qn** (*anche fig*) to turn one's back on sb **2** (*trasformare*) to turn; **volge sempre tutto in tragedia** he always turns everything into a tragedy;
▶ **volgersi** VR to turn; **si volse e mi guardò** he turned round and looked at me; **si volse verso di lui** he turned to *o* towards him; **la sua ira si volse contro di noi** he turned his anger on us
volgo, ghi ['volgo] SM (*anche pegg*) common people *pl*
voliera [vo'ljɛra] SF aviary
volitivo, a [voli'tivo] AGG wilful (*Brit*), willful (*Am*); (*persona*) wil(l)ful, strong-willed
■ SM/F strong-willed person
volli *ecc* ['vɔlli] VB *vedi* **volere**
volo ['volo] SM **1** (*gen*) flight; **il tuo volo è alle tre** your flight leaves at three o'clock; **ci sono due ore di volo da Londra a Milano** it's a two-hour flight from London to Milan; **velocità/condizioni di volo** flying speed/conditions; **essere in volo** (*uccello*) to be in flight; (*Aer*) to be flying; **colpire un uccello in volo** to shoot a bird on the wing *o* in flight; **"volo cancellato"** "flight cancelled"; **"volo in chiusura"** "flight closing"; **volo di addestramento** training flight; **volo di andata** outward flight; **volo charter** charter flight; **volo di linea** scheduled flight; **volo di ritorno** return flight; **volo a vela** gliding **2** (*fraseologia*): **capire al volo** to understand straight away *o* straight away; **ha capito al volo la situazione** he understood the situation immediately; **prendere al volo** (*autobus, treno*) to only just catch; (*palla*) to catch as it flies past; (*fig: occasione*) to seize; **ho preso il treno al volo** I only just caught the train; **prendere il volo** (*aereo*) to take off; (*uccello*) to fly away; (*fig: giovane*) to leave home; (*: cosa: sparire*) to vanish; **fare un volo** (*cadere*) to go flying; **ha fatto un volo dalle scale** he went flying down the stairs; **veduta a volo d'uccello** bird's-eye view
volontà [volon'ta] SF INV **1** (*capacità di volere*) will; **ha molta volontà** he has a very strong will; **non ha volontà** he is weak-willed; **contro la sua volontà** against his will; **di sua spontanea volontà** of his own free will; **l'ha fatto di sua spontanea volontà** he did it of his own free will; **riuscire a forza di volontà** to succeed through sheer willpower *o* determination
2 (*disposizione*): **manifestare la volontà di fare qc** to show one's desire to do sth; **buona/cattiva volontà** goodwill/lack of goodwill; **ci ho messo tutta la mia buona volontà** I did it to the best of my ability; **a volontà** (*mangiare, bere*) as much as one likes; **ce ne sono a volontà** there are more than enough of them; **prendine a volontà** help yourself, take as much (*o* many) as you like; **"zuccherare a volontà"** "sugar to taste" **3 le sue ultime volontà** (*testamento*) his last will and testament *sg*; **quali sono le sue ultime volontà?** what are his last wishes?

volontariamente [volontarja'mente] AVV voluntarily
volontariato [volonta'rjato] SM **1** (*Mil*) voluntary service **2** (*attività gratuita*) voluntary work
volontario, ria, ri, rie [volon'tarjo] AGG (*gen*) voluntary; (*Mil*) volunteer *attr*; **esilio volontario** voluntary exile
■ SM/F (*gen, Mil*) volunteer; (*di organizzazione*) voluntary worker; **c'è qualche volontario?** are there any volunteers?; **lavoro come volontario** I'm a voluntary worker
volpe ['volpe] SF (*Zool*) fox; (: *femmina*) vixen; (*pelliccia*) fox; (*fig*) sly fox, crafty person; (: *ironico*) clever person, bright spark; **volpe della sabbia** *o* **del deserto** fennec
volpino, a [vol'pino] AGG (*pelo, coda*) fox's *attr*; (*aspetto, astuzia*) fox-like
■ SM (*cane*) Pomeranian
volpoca, che [vol'pɔka] SF (*Zool*) shelduck; (*maschio*) sheldrake
volpone, a [vol'pone] SM/F (*fig*): **un vecchio volpone** a crafty old fox
volsi *ecc* ['vɔlsi] VB *vedi* **volgere**
volt [vɔlt] SM INV (*Elettr*) volt
volta[1] ['vɔlta] SF
1 (*gen*) time; **una volta** once; **una volta alla settimana** once a week; **due volte** twice; **gli ho telefonato due volte** I phoned him twice; **tre volte** three times; **una volta ogni due settimane** once every two weeks; **9 volte su 10** 9 times out of 10; **la prima/l'ultima volta che l'ho visto** the first/last time I saw him; **per questa volta passi** I'll let you off this time; **ci ho pensato due volte prima di decidere** I thought twice about it before making a decision; **tutto in una volta** all at once; **una volta per tutte** *o* **una buona volta** once and for all; **deciditi una volta per tutte** make up your mind once and for all; **una volta tanto** just for once; **una volta tanto potresti pagare tu** you could pay, just for once; **una volta ogni tanto** from time to time; **una volta sola** only once; **le ho scritto una volta sola** I wrote to her only once; **di volta in volta** as we go; **decideremo di volta in volta cosa fare** we'll decide what to do as we go; **delle** *o* **alle** *o* **certe volte** *or* **a volte** sometimes, at times; **certe volte sono un po' triste** I feel a bit down sometimes; **una volta o l'altra** one of these days; **una volta o l'altra glielo dirò** I'll tell him one of these days; **una cosa per volta** one thing at a time; **facciamo una cosa per volta** let's do one thing at a time; **te le darò volta per volta** (*istruzioni*) I'll give them to you a few at a time
2 (*tempo, occasione*): **c'era una volta...** once upon a time there was ...; **una volta** (*un tempo*) once, in the past; **una volta si camminava di più** people used to walk more in the past; **le cose di una volta** the things of the past; **una volta che sei partito** once *o* when you have left; **ti ricordi quella volta che...** do you remember (the time) when ...; **pensa a tutte le volte che...** think of all the occasions on which ...; **lo facciamo un'altra volta** we'll do it another time *o* some other time; **gli telefonerò un'altra volta, adesso non ne ho voglia** I'll phone him some other time, I don't feel like it now
3 (*Mat*): **3 volte 2** 3 times 2; **3 volte 4 fa 12** 3 times 4 makes 12; **4 volte di più** 4 times as much
4 (*fraseologia*): **a sua volta** (*turno*) in (his *o* her *ecc*) turn; **partire alla volta di** to set off for; **ti ha dato di volta il cervello?** have you gone out of your mind?

volta[2] ['vɔlta] SF (*Archit, Anat*) vault; **la volta celeste** the vault of heaven
voltafaccia [volta'fattʃa] SM INV about-turn, volte-face
voltagabbana [voltagab'bana] SM/F INV turncoat
voltaggio [vol'taddʒo] SM voltage
voltare [vol'tare] VT (*girare*) to turn; (: *moneta*) to turn over; (*rigirare*) to turn round; **voltate pagina** turn the page; **voltare pagina** (*fig*) to turn over a new leaf; **voltare le spalle a qn** (*anche fig*) to turn one's back on sb
■ VI (*aus* **avere**) to turn; **voltare a destra/sinistra** to turn (to the) left/right; **volta a sinistra e poi va' dritto** turn left and then go straight on;
▶ **voltarsi** VR to turn; **voltarsi da un lato** to turn to one side; **voltarsi indietro** to turn back; **si è allontanato senza voltarsi indietro** he went off without looking back; **voltarsi dall'altra parte** to turn the other way; **non sapere da che parte voltarsi** (*fig*) not to know which way to turn
voltastomaco [voltas'tɔmako] SM nausea; **dare il voltastomaco a qn** to make sb sick; **la sua ipocrisia mi dà il voltastomaco** his hypocrisy makes me sick
volteggiare [volted'dʒare] VI **1** (*volare girando: uccello, piuma*) to circle; **la ballerina volteggiava sul palco** the dancer twirled *o* spun across the stage **2** (*Ginnastica*) to vault; (*sul cavallo*) to do trick riding
voltmetro ['vɔltmetro] SM voltmeter
volto[1], **a** ['vɔlto] PP *di* **volgere**
■ AGG: **volto a 1** (*rivolto verso: casa*) facing **2** (*inteso a*): **il mio discorso è volto a spiegare...** in my speech I intend to explain ...; **il corso è volto a introdurre gli studenti all'analisi matematica** the course is intended to introduce students to calculus
volto[2] ['volto] SM (*faccia*) face; (*fig*) face, nature
voltolarsi [volto'larsi] VR: **voltolarsi in** to wallow in, roll about in
voltura [vol'tura] SF (*Dir: trascrizione*) registration; **voltura di contratto** (*di telefono, gas*) transfer of contract
volubile [vo'lubile] AGG (*persona*) changeable, fickle; (*tempo*) changeable, variable

> **LO SAPEVI...?**
> **volubile** non si traduce mai con la parola inglese ***voluble***

volubilità [volubili'ta] SF (*di persona*) fickleness, inconstancy; (*di tempo*) variability
volubilmente [volubil'mente] AVV (*comportarsi*) in a fickle way
volume [vo'lume] SM (*gen*) volume; **potresti abbassare il volume?** could you turn down the volume, please?; **fa volume** (*oggetto*) it takes up a lot of space, it is very bulky; **volume delle vendite** (*Comm*) sales volume
volumetrico, a, ci, che [volu'mɛtriko] AGG volumetric
voluminoso, a [volumi'noso] AGG bulky, voluminous
voluta [vo'luta] SF (*gen*) spiral; (*Archit*) volute
volutamente [voluta'mente] AVV deliberately, intentionally
voluto, a [vo'luto] AGG **1** (*intenzionale*) deliberate, intentional; **era voluto** it was intentional; **un errore voluto** a deliberate mistake **2** (*desiderato: bambino*) wanted; (: *somma*) desired
voluttà [volut'ta] SF INV sensual pleasure *o* delight
voluttuario, ria, ri, rie [voluttu'arjo] AGG (*spese*) unnecessary, non-essential

Vv

voluttuosamente [voluttuosa'mente] AVV voluptuously
voluttuosità [voluttuosi'ta] SF INV voluptuousness
voluttuoso, a [voluttu'oso] AGG voluptuous, sensual
volvente [vol'vɛnte] AGG (*Fis*): **attrito volvente** rolling friction
vombato [vom'bato] SM (*Zool*) wombat
vomere ['vɔmere] SM (*Agr*) ploughshare (*Brit*), plowshare (*Am*)
vomico, a, ci, che ['vɔmiko] AGG: **noce vomica** nux vomica
vomitare [vomi'tare] VT to vomit, throw up; **vomitare ingiurie** (*fig*) to spew out insults; **questo quadro mi fa vomitare** this painting makes me sick
■ VI (*aus* **avere**) to be sick, vomit, throw up
vomitevole [vomi'tevole] AGG (*anche fig*) nauseating
vomito ['vɔmito] SM vomit; **ho il vomito** I feel sick; **mi fa venire il vomito** (*anche fig*) it makes me sick
vongola ['vongola] SF (*Zool*) clam
vorace [vo'ratʃe] AGG (*appetito*) voracious, greedy; **essere vorace** to have a huge appetite; **è un bambino vorace** this child has a voracious appetite
voracemente [voratʃe'mente] AVV voraciously
voracità [voratʃi'ta] SF voracity, voraciousness
voragine [vo'radʒine] SF chasm, abyss
vorrò *ecc* [vor'rɔ] VB *vedi* **volere**
vorticare [vorti'kare] VI (*aus* **avere**) to whirl, swirl
vortice ['vɔrtitʃe] SM whirl, vortex; (*fig*) vortex; **un vortice di vento** a whirlwind
vorticosamente [vortikosa'mente] AVV: **ruotare** *o* **girare vorticosamente** to whirl round and round
vorticoso, a [vorti'koso] AGG whirling
vostro, a ['vɔstro] AGG POSS: **il(la) vostro(a)** your; **il vostro cane** your dog; **i vostri libri** your books; **un vostro conoscente** an acquaintance of yours; **un vostro amico** a friend of yours; **vostra zia** your aunt; **è colpa vostra** it's your fault; **a casa vostra** at your house
■ PRON POSS: **il(la) vostro(a)** yours, your own; **la nostra casa è più grande della vostra** our house is bigger than yours; **la vostra è stata una brutta storia** your story is an unpleasant one; **di chi è questo? – è vostro** whose is this? – it's yours
■ SM **1 avete speso del vostro?** did you spend your own money?; **ci potreste rimettere del vostro in quell'affare** you could well lose money in that business **2 i vostri** SMPL (*famiglia*) your family; **è dei vostri** he's on your side
■ SF: **la vostra** (*opinione*) your view; **l'ultima vostra** (*Comm: lettera*) your most recent letter; **alla vostra!** (*brindisi*) here's to you!, your health!; **è dalla vostra** he's on your side
votante [vo'tante] SM/F voter
votare [vo'tare] VI (*aus* **avere**) to vote
■ VT **1** (*gen*) to vote for; (*sottoporre a votazione*) to take a vote on; (*approvare*) to pass; **ho votato per loro** I voted for them **2 votare a** (*vita*) to devote to, dedicate to
▶ **votarsi** VR: **votarsi a** to devote o.s. to
votazione [votat'tsjone] SF **1** (*gen, Pol: atto*) voting, vote; **alle votazioni** at the elections **2** (*Scol*) mark (*Brit*), grade (*Am*); **votazione finale** results *pl*
votivo, a [vo'tivo] AGG votive
voto ['voto] SM **1** (*Scol*) mark (*Brit*), grade (*Am*); **ho preso un bel voto in matematica** i got a good mark in maths; **laurearsi a pieni voti** ≈ to graduate with a first class degree (*Brit*) *o* summa cum laude (*Am*) **2** (*Pol*) vote; **hanno vinto per pochi voti** they won by a few votes; **mettere ai voti** to put to the vote; **voto di fiducia** vote of confidence; **voto di scambio** vote-buying **3** (*Rel*) vow; (*: offerta*) votive offering; **prendere i voti** to take one's vows
voyeur [vwa'jœr] SM INV voyeur
voyeurismo [voje'rizmo] SM voyeurism
VP ABBR (= **Vicepresidente**) VP
VQPRD ABBR (= **Vino di Qualità Prodotto in Regioni Determinate**) *mark guaranteeing the quality of a wine from a particular region*
VR SIGLA = **Verona**
v.r. ABBR (= **vedi retro**) PTO (= *please turn over*)
V.S. ABBR **1** = **Vostra Santità** **2** = *Vostra Signoria*
v.s. ABBR = *vedi sopra*
vs. ABBR (= **vostro**) yr (= *your*)
VT SIGLA = *Viterbo*
VU ABBR = **vigile urbano**
vu cumprà [vukum'pra] SM/F INV *street pedlar, usually of African origin*
vudù [vu'du] SM INV, AGG INV voodoo *attr*
vuduismo [vudu'izmo] SM voodooism
vulcanico, a, ci, che [vul'kaniko] AGG volcanic; **ha una fantasia vulcanica** he has a fertile imagination
vulcanismo [vulka'nizmo] SM volcanism
vulcanizzare [vulkanid'dzare] VT (*Tecn*) to vulcanize
vulcanizzazione [vulkaniddzat'tsjone] SF (*Tecn*) vulcanization
Vulcano [vul'kano] SM (*Mitol*) Vulcan
vulcano [vul'kano] SM volcano; **quel ragazzo è un vulcano di idee** that boy is bursting with ideas
vulnerabile [vulne'rabile] AGG vulnerable
vulnerabilità [vulnerabili'ta] SF vulnerability
vulva ['vulva] SF (*Anat*) vulva
vuoi ['vwɔi], **vuole** ['vwɔle] VB *vedi* **volere**
vuotare [vwo'tare] VT (*bicchiere, stanza*) to empty; (*vasca, piscina*) to drain, empty; **vuotare il sacco** (*fig*) to confess, spill the beans (*fam*); **i ladri mi hanno vuotato la casa** the burglars cleaned out my house
▶ **vuotarsi** VIP to empty
vuoto, a ['vwɔto] AGG **1** (*gen*) empty; **a stomaco vuoto** on an empty stomach; **a mani vuote** empty-handed; **è arrivato a mani vuote** he arrived empty-handed **2** (*non occupato: posto*) vacant, free; (*: spazio*) empty; **un appartamento vuoto** an empty flat **3** (*fig: discorso, persona*) shallow, superficial; **è una testa vuota** he's an empty headed person; **mi sento la testa vuota** my mind feels a complete blank
■ SM **1** (*spazio*) void, empty space, gap; (*: in bianco*) blank; (*fig: mancanza*) gap, void; (*Fis*) vacuum; **è rimasto sospeso nel vuoto** (*alpinista*) he was left hanging in mid-air; **aver paura del vuoto** to be afraid of heights; **guardare nel vuoto** to gaze into space; **fare il vuoto intorno a sé** to alienate o.s. from everybody; **ha lasciato un vuoto fra di noi** he has left a real gap; **ho un vuoto allo stomaco** my stomach feels empty; **sotto vuoto** = sottovuoto; **vuoto d'aria** (*Aer*) air pocket **2** (*bottiglia*) empty; **"vuoto a perdere"** "no deposit"; **"vuoto a rendere"** "returnable (bottle)"; **a vuoto** AVV (*inutilmente*) vainly, in vain; (*senza effetto*) to no purpose; **parlare a vuoto** to waste one's breath; **ho fatto un viaggio a vuoto** I have had a wasted journey; **andare a vuoto** to come to nothing, fail; **assegno a vuoto** dud cheque (*Brit*), bad check (*Am*); **girare a vuoto** (*Aut*) to idle
VV SIGLA = *Vibo Valentia*
v.v. ABBR (= **viceversa**) vv (= *vice versa*)

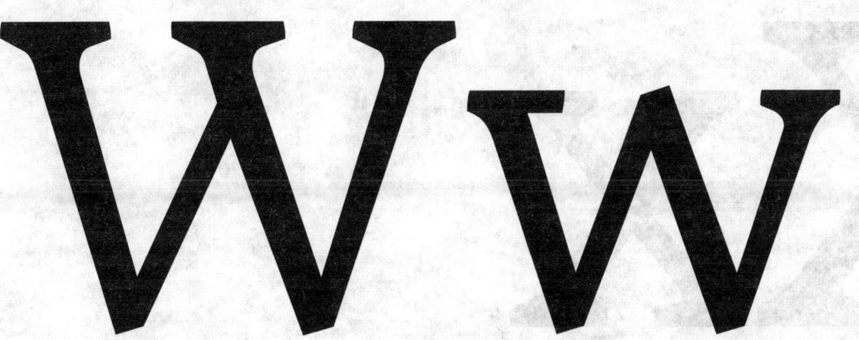

W, w ['dɔppjo vu] SF O M INV (*lettera*) W, w; **W come Washington** ≈ W for William
W ['dɔppjo vu] ABBR = **evviva**
wafer ['vafer] SM INV (*Culin, Elettr*) wafer
wagon-lit [vagɔ̃'li] SM INV (*Ferr*) sleeping car
walkie-talkie ['wɔ:ki'tɔ:ki] SM INV walkie-talkie
walkman® ['wɔ:kmən] SM INV Walkman®, personal stereo
Washington ['wɔʃiŋtən] SF Washington
wassermann ['vasərman] SF INV (*Med*) Wassermann test, Wassermann reaction
water ['vater] SM INV toilet (bowl); **l'ho gettato nel water** I threw it in the toilet
water closet ['wɔ:tə 'klɔzit] SM INV toilet (*Brit*), lavatory (*Brit*), bathroom (*Am*)
watt [vat] SM INV (*Elettr*) watt
wattora [vat'tora] SM INV (*Elettr*) watt-hour
WC [vi'tʃi] SM INV WC (*Brit*), bathroom (*Am*)
web [web] SM: **il web** the Web; **cercare nel web** to search the Web
■ AGG: **pagina web** webpage
webcam [web'kam] SF INV webcam
weekend [wi'kɛnd] SM INV weekend
Wellington ['wɛllinŋtən] SF (*Geog*) Wellington
western ['wɛstern] AGG (*Cine*) cowboy *attr*
■ SM INV (*Cine*) western, cowboy film (*Brit*) *o* movie (*Am*); **western all'italiana** spaghetti western
West Virginia [west vir'dʒinja] SM West Virginia
whisky ['wiski] SM INV whisky
windsurf [wind'sɛrf] SM INV (*tavola*) windsurfer, windsurfing board, sailboard; (*sport*) windsurfing; **fare windsurf** to go windsurfing
Wisconsin SM [wɪs'kɒnsɪn] Wisconsin
wok [wɔk] SM INV wok
würstel ['vyrstəl] SM INV frankfurter; **vorrei un würstel con la senape** I'd like a frankfurter with mustard
Wyoming [waɪ'əumiŋ] SM Wyoming

X, x [iks] SF O M INV (*lettera*) X, x; **X come Xeres** ≈ X for Xmas
xeno ['ksɛno] SM (*Chim*) xenon
xenofobia [ksenofo'bia] SF xenophobia
xenofobo, a [kse'nɔfobo] AGG xenophobic ■SM/F xenophobe
xeres ['ksɛres] SM INV sherry
xerocopia [ksero'kɔpja] SF photocopy, xerox®
xerocopiare [kseroko'pjare] VT to photocopy, xerox®
xerografia [kserogra'fia] SF xerography
xilema, i [ksi'lɛma] SM (*Bot*) xylem
xilofono [ksi'lɔfono] SM xylophone
XL [iks'ɛlle] SIGLA F (*taglia*) XL (= *extra large*)
XS [iks'ɛsse] SIGLA F (*taglia*) XS (= *extra small*)

Yy

Y, **y** ['ipsilon] SF O M INV (*lettera*) Y, y; **Y come Yacht** ≈ Y for Yellow (*Brit*), ≈ Y for Yoke (*Am*)
yacht [jɔt] SM INV yacht
yak [jak] SM INV (*animale*) yak
yankee ['jæŋki] SM/F INV Yank, Yankee
YCI ['itʃi] SIGLA M = *Yacht Club d'Italia*
Yemen ['jɛmen] SM: **lo Yemen** Yemen
yemenita, i, e [jeme'nita] AGG, SM/F Yemeni
yen [jen] SM INV (*moneta*) yen
yiddish ['jidiʃ] AGG INV, SM INV Yiddish
yoga ['jɔga] AGG INV, SM INV yoga (*attr*); **fare yoga** to do yoga
yogurt ['jɔgurt] SM INV yog(h)urt; **uno yogurt alla fragola** a strawberry yoghurt
yogurtiera [jogur'tjɛra] SF yog(h)urt-maker
yuppie ['jʌppi] SM/F yuppie

Zz

Z, z ['dzɛta] SF O M INV (*lettera*) Z, z; **Z come Zara** ≈ Z for Zebra
zabaione [dzaba'jone], **zabaglione** [dzabaʎ'ʎone] SM zabaglione; *dessert made of egg yolks, sugar and marsala*
zaffata [tsaf'fata] SF (*di odore*) stench, stink
zafferano [dzaffe'rano] SM saffron
zaffiro [dzaf'firo] SM sapphire
zagara ['dzagara] SF orange blossom
zainetto [dzai'netto] SM (small) rucksack
zaino ['dzaino] SM rucksack (*Brit*), backpack (*Am*)
Zaire [dza'ire] SM Zaire
zairese [dzai'rese] AGG, SM/F Zairian
Zambia ['dzambja] SM Zambia
zambiano, a [dzam'bjano] AGG, SM/F Zambian
zampa ['tsampa] SF (*di animale*) leg; (: *con artigli*) paw; (*di elefante, uccello*) foot; **pantaloni a zampa d'elefante** bell-bottom trousers, bell-bottoms; (*più larghi*) flares; **camminare a quattro zampe** to go on all fours; **giù le zampe!** (*fam*) paws off!; **zampe di gallina** (*rughe*) crow's feet; (*calligrafia*) scrawl *sg*
zampata [tsam'pata] SF (*di cane, gatto*) blow with a paw
zampettare [tsampet'tare] VI (*aus* **avere**) to scamper
zampillante [tsampil'lante] AGG gushing, spurting
zampillare [tsampil'lare] VI (*aus* **avere**) to gush, spurt
zampillo [tsam'pillo] SM gush, spurt
zampino [tsam'pino] SM paw; **ci ha messo lo zampino lui** (*fig*) he's had a hand in this; **zampino di coniglio** (*portafortuna*) lucky rabbit's foot
zampirone [dzampi'rone] SM mosquito repellent
zampogna [tsam'poɲɲa] SF Italian bagpipes *pl*
zampognaro [tsampoɲ'ɲaro] SM Italian bagpipes player
zampone [tsam'pone] SM (*Culin*) *stuffed pig's trotter*
zangola ['tsangola] SF churn
zanna ['tsanna] SF (*di elefante, cinghiale*) tusk; (*di cane, lupo*) fang
zanzara [dzan'dzara] SF mosquito; **zanzara tigre** *type of striped mosquito*
zanzariera [dzandza'rjɛra] SF mosquito net
zapatista, i, e [dzapa'tista] SM/F follower of Emiliano Zapata
zappa ['tsappa] SF (*Agr*) hoe; **darsi la zappa sui piedi** (*fig*) to shoot o.s. in the foot
zappare [tsap'pare] VT (*Agr*) to hoe
zappatore [tsappa'tore] SM (*Agr*) hoer; (*Mil*) sapper (*Brit*)
zappatrice [tsappa'tritʃe] SF (*Agr: macchina*) mechanical hoe
zappatura [tsappa'tura] SF (*Agr*) hoeing
zapping ['dzappin(g)] SM (*TV*) channel hopping
zar [tsar] SM INV tsar
zarina [tsa'rina] SF tsarina
zattera ['tsattera] SF raft; **zattera di salvataggio** life raft
zavorra [dza'vɔrra] SF (*Naut, Aer*) ballast; (*fig*) junk; **gettare la zavorra** to dump ballast
zazzera ['tsattsera] SF shock of hair, mop
zebra ['dzɛbra] SF **1** (*Zool*) zebra **2 le zebre** SFPL (*Aut*) zebra crossing *sg* (*Brit*), crosswalk *sg* (*Am*)
zebrato, a [dze'brato] AGG with black and white stripes; **passaggio** *o* **attraversamento zebrato** (*Aut*) zebra crossing (*Brit*), crosswalk (*Am*)
zebù [dze'bu] SM INV (*animale*) zebu
zecca¹, che ['tsekka] SF (*insetto*) tick
zecca² ['tsekka] SF (*di monete*) mint; **nuovo di zecca** brand-new
zecchino [tsek'kino] SM gold coin; **oro zecchino** pure gold
zefiro ['dzɛfiro] SM (*vento*) zephyr
zelante [dze'lante] AGG zealous
zelantemente [dzelante'mente] AVV zealously
zelo ['dzɛlo] SM zeal; **mostrare troppo zelo** to be overzealous
zenit ['dzɛnit] SM (*Astron*) zenith
zenzero ['dzendzero] SM ginger
zeppa ['tseppa] SF (*di mobili*) wedge; (*di scarpe*) platform
zeppelin ['tsɛpəli:n] SM INV zeppelin, airship
zeppo, a ['tseppo] AGG: **zeppo** *o* **pieno zeppo (di)** jam-packed (with), crammed (with); **era zeppo di gente** it was crammed with people
zerbino [dzer'bino] SM (door)mat
zerbinotto [dzerbi'nɔtto] SM dandy, fop
zero ['dzɛro] SM **1** (*gen, Scol, Mat*) zero, nought (*Brit*); (*in*

un numero di telefono) O; **zero virgola cinque** (zero *o* nought) point five; **2 gradi sopra zero** 2 degrees above freezing point *o* above zero; **3 gradi sotto zero** 3 degrees below zero; **zero in condotta** (*Scol*) bad marks for behaviour (*Brit*); **ridursi a zero** (*fig*) to have nothing left, be at rock-bottom; **capelli tagliati a zero** close-cropped hair; **sparare a zero su qn/qc** (*fig*) to lay into sb/sth; **ricominciare da zero** to go back to square one; **partire da zero** to start from scratch **2** (*Calcio*) nil (*Brit*); (*Tennis*) love; **vincere per tre a zero** to win three-nil; **trenta a zero** thirty love
■ AGG INV zero *attr*; **l'ora zero** zero hour; **a emissioni zero** zero-emission; **tolleranza zero** zero tolerance

zeta ['dzɛta] SM O F (*pl f inv* **zeta**, *pl f* **zete**, *pl m inv* **zeta**) (*lettera*) zed (*Brit*), zee (*Am*), (the letter) z

Zeus ['dzɛus] SM Zeus

zia ['tsia] SF aunt

zibaldone [dzibal'done] SM (*Letteratura*) author's notebook

zibellino [dzibel'lino] SM (*animale, pelliccia*) sable

zibetto [dzi'betto] SM (*animale*) zibet; (*sostanza*) civet

zibibbo [dzi'bibbo] SM *kind of muscat grape*

zigano, a [tsi'gano] AGG, SM/F gypsy

zigolo ['dzigolo] SM (*Zool*) bunting

zigomo ['dzigomo] SM cheekbone; **zigomi sporgenti** high cheekbones

zigote [dzi'gɔte] SM (*Bio*) zygote

zigrinare [dzigri'nare] VT (*gen*) to knurl; (*pellame*) to grain; (*monete*) to mill

zig zag [dzig'dzag] SM INV zigzag; **camminare/andare a zig zag** to zigzag

zigzagare [dzigdza'gare] VI (*aus* **avere**) to zigzag

Zimbabwe [dzim'babwe] SM Zimbabwe

zimbello [tsim'bɛllo] SM (*Caccia*) decoy (bird); (*fig*) laughing stock

zincare [tsin'kare] VT to galvanize, coat with zinc

zinco ['tsinko] SM zinc

zingaresco, a, schi, sche [tsinga'resko] AGG gypsy *attr*

zingaro, a ['tsingaro] AGG, SM/F gypsy

zio, zii ['tsio] SM uncle; **i miei zii** (*zio e zia*) my uncle and aunt; **zio d'America** (*fig*) rich uncle

zipolo ['tsipolo] SM (*di botte*) bung

zippare [dzip'pare] VT (*file*) to zip

zircone [dzir'kone] SM zircon

zitella [tsi'tɛlla] SF (*pegg*) spinster, old maid

zitellone [tsitel'lone] SM (elderly) bachelor

zittire [tsit'tire] VT to silence, hush *o* shut up
■ VI (*aus* **avere**) to hiss

zitto, a ['tsitto] AGG quiet, silent; **zitto!** be quiet!, shut up! (*fam*); **stare zitto** to keep quiet, shut up (*fam*); **zitto zitto** (*di nascosto*) on the quiet

zizzania [dzid'dzanja] SF (*pianta*) darnel; (*fig*) discord; **seminare zizzania** to sow discord

zoccolo ['tsɔkkolo] SM **1** (*di cavallo*) hoof **2** (*calzatura*) clog **3** (*Archit*) plinth; (*di parete*) skirting (board) (*Brit*), baseboard (*Am*); (*di armadio*) base (support)

zodiacale [dzodia'kale] AGG of the zodiac, zodiac *attr*; **segno zodiacale** sign of the zodiac

zodiaco [dzo'diako] SM zodiac

zolfanello [tsolfa'nɛllo] SM (sulphur (*Brit*) *o* sulfur (*Am*)) match

zolfatara [tsolfa'tara] SF sulphur (*Brit*) *o* sulfur (*Am*) mine

zolfo ['tsolfo] SM sulphur (*Brit*), sulfur (*Am*)

zolla ['dzolla] SF (*di terra*) clod (of earth)

zolletta [dzol'letta] SF (*di zucchero*) (sugar) lump *o* cube

zona ['dzɔna] SF (*gen*) area, zone; (*regione*) area, region; (*di città*) district; **una zona malfamata** a rough area; **zona di depressione** (*Meteor*) trough of low pressure; **zona disco** (*Aut*) ≈ meter zone; **zona erogena** erogenous zone; **zona giorno** (*di casa*) living area; **zona di guerra** war zone; **zona industriale** industrial estate; **zona di interdizione del traffico aereo** no-fly zone; **zona notte** (*di casa*) sleeping area; **zona pedonale** pedestrian precinct (*Brit*) *o* mall (*Am*); **zona a traffico limitato** controlled traffic zone; **zona verde** (*Aut*) restricted parking zone *o* area; (*Urbanistica*) green area

zonale [dzo'nale] AGG district *attr*, area *attr*

zonizzare [dzonid'dzare] VT to zone

zonizzazione [dzoniddzat'tsjone] SF zoning

zonzo ['dzondzo] **a zonzo** AVV: **andare a zonzo** to wander about, stroll about

zoo ['dzɔo] SM INV zoo

zoologia [dzoolo'dʒia] SF zoology

zoologico, a, ci, che [dzoo'lɔdʒiko] AGG zoological; **giardino zoologico** zoological garden(s), zoo

zoologo, a, gi, ghe [dzo'ɔlogo] SM/F zoologist

zoom [zu:m] SM INV (*Fot*) zoom (lens)

zoosafari [dzoosa'fari] SM INV safari park

zootecnia [dzootek'nia] SF zootechnics *sg*

zootecnico, a, ci, che [dzoo'tɛkniko] AGG zootechnical; **il patrimonio zootecnico di un paese** a country's livestock resources

zoppia [tsop'pia] SF (*di cavallo*) lameness

zoppicante [tsoppi'kante] AGG (*persona*) limping; (*fig*) shaky, weak

zoppicare [tsoppi'kare] VI (*aus* **avere**) (*persona*) to have a limp, walk with a limp, limp; (: *essere zoppo*) to be lame; (*fig: mobile*) to be shaky; **zoppica in matematica** (*fig*) he's weak in maths (*Brit*) *o* math (*Am*), math(s) isn't his strong point

Zz

zoppo, a ['tsɔppo] AGG (*persona*) lame; (*mobile*) wobbly, shaky
■ SM/F lame person

zoster ['dzɔster] AGG INV = **herpes zoster**

zotico, a ['dzɔtiko] SM/F lout, boor

ZTL [dzetati'ɛlle] SIGLA F (= **Zona a Traffico Limitato**) *controlled traffic zone*

zuava [dzu'ava] SF: **pantaloni alla zuava** knickerbockers

zucca ['tsukka] SF (*Bot*) pumpkin; (: *di forma allungata*) marrow (*Brit*), vegetable marrow; (*scherz*) head; **avere sale in zucca** to be sensible, have sense; **non gli entra in zucca** it won't enter his thick skull

zuccherare [tsukke'rare] VT to sugar, put sugar in, add sugar to

zuccherato, a [tsukke'rato] AGG sweet, sweetened; **non zuccherato** unsweetened

zuccheriera [tsukke'rjɛra] SF sugar bowl

zuccherificio, ci [tsukkeri'fitʃo] SM sugar refinery

zuccherino, a [tsukke'rino] AGG sweet, sugary
■ SM piece of sugar, lump of sugar

zucchero ['tsukkero] SM sugar; **zucchero di canna** cane sugar; **zucchero caramellato** caramel; **zucchero filato** candy floss (*Brit*), cotton candy (*Am*); **zucchero in grani** crushed sugar lumps; **zucchero in polvere** caster sugar; **zucchero semolato** granulated sugar; **zucchero a velo** icing sugar (*Brit*), confectioner's sugar (*Am*)

zuccheroso, a [tsukke'roso] AGG sweet, sugary

zucchetto [tsuk'ketto] SM skullcap

zucchina [tsuk'kina] SF, **zucchino** [tsuk'kino] SM courgette (*Brit*), zucchini (*Am*)

zuccone, a [tsuk'kone] AGG dull, dense, slow(-witted)

■ SM/F dunce, blockhead

zuccotto [tsuk'kɔtto] SM (*Culin*) *dome-shaped dessert made of sponge, cream, chocolate and candied fruit*

zuffa ['tsuffa] SF fight, brawl

zufolare [tsufo'lare] VT, VI (*aus* **avere**) to whistle

zufolio, lii [tsufo'lio] SM whistling

zufolo ['tsufolo] SM (*Mus*) flageolet

zumare [dzu'mare] VI (*aus* **avere**)

■ VT (*Cine, Fot*) to zoom in; **zumare qn** to zoom in on sb

zuppa ['tsuppa] SF soup; **una zuppa di verdura** a vegetable soup; **se non è zuppa è pan bagnato** (*fig*) it's six of one and half a dozen of the other; **zuppa inglese** (*Culin*) *liqueur-soaked sponge with a filling of cream and chocolate*

zuppiera [tsup'pjɛra] SF (soup) tureen

zuppo, a ['tsuppo] AGG: **zuppo (di)** soaked (with), drenched (with); **sono zuppo** I'm soaked

Zurigo [dzu'rigo] SF Zurich